S0-BME-266

POLITICAL HANDBOOK

OF THE

WORLD

2016–2017

Edited by Tom Lansford

Associate Editors
John Callahan
Jack Covarrubias
David Harms Holt
Wayne F. Lesperance Jr.
Robert Redding

Volume 2

ARCTIC OCEAN
Greenland
Beaufort Sea
Baffin Bay
Chukchi Sea
Bering Strait
ALASKA
Davis Strait
Denmark Strait
ICELAND
Norwegian Sea
Faroe Islands
Hudson Bay
Gulf of Alaska
CANADA
Northern Ireland
UNITED KINGDOM
IRELAND
Aleutian Islands
Newfoundland
LUXEMBOURG
NORTH ATLANTIC OCEAN
UNITED STATES
ANDORRA
PORTUGAL
SPAIN
Bermuda
MOROCCO
Canary Islands
ALGERIA
Gulf of Mexico
BAHAMAS
Turks and Caicos Island
Andros Islands
ANTIGUA and BARBUDA
Western Sahara
Hawaiian Islands
MEXICO
WEST INDIES
CUBA
HAITI
DOMINICAN REPUBLIC
Montserrat
Guadeloupe
DOMINICA
Martinique
MAURITANIA
JAMAICA
Virgin Islands
Puerto Rico
ST. KITTS and NEVIS
ST. LUCIA
BARBADOS
ST. VINCENT and THE GRENADINES
MALI
CAPE VERDE ISLANDS
SENEGAL
GAMBIA
GUINEA-BISSAU
BELIZE
HONDURAS
GUATEMALA
EL SALVADOR
Caribbean Sea
Netherlands Antilles
Aruba
NICARAGUA
GRENADA
BURKINA FASO
GUINEA
COSTA RICA
TRINIDAD and TOBAGO
CÔTE D'IVOIRE
SIERRA LEONE
LIBERIA
PANAMA
VENEZUELA
GUYANA
SURINAME
French Guiana
GHANA
TOGO
POLYNESIA
Kiritimati
Line Islands
Galapagos Islands
COLOMBIA
EQUATORIAL G
Phoenix Islands
KIRIBATI
ECUADOR
AND PRINCIPE
PERU
BRAZIL
Tokelau
SAMOA
American Samoa
Cook Islands
Niue
French Polynesia
Tahiti
SOUTH ATLANTIC OCEAN
BOLIVIA
PARAGUAY
CHILE
PACIFIC OCEAN
URUGUAY
ARGENTINA
Falkland/Malvinas Islands
South Georgia

ARCTIC OCEAN
Svalbard
Barents Sea
Kara Sea
Laptev Sea
East Siberian Sea
ARCTIC OCEAN
RUSSIA
SWEDEN
FINLAND
ESTONIA
LATVIA
LITHUANIA
Baltic Sea
BELARUS
POLAND
UKRAINE
SLOVAKIA
MOLDOVA
HUNGARY
BOSNIA and HERZ.
ROMANIA
SERBIA
MONTENEGRO
KOSOVO
BULGARIA
MACEDONIA
ALBANIA
GREECE
MALTA
Black Sea
GEORGIA
ARMENIA
AZERBAIJAN
TURKEY
CYPRUS
SYRIA
LEBANON
ISRAEL
JORDAN
IRAQ
IRAN
KUWAIT
BAHRAIN
QATAR
SAUDI ARABIA
UNITED ARAB EMIRATES
OMAN
YEMEN
Persian Gulf
Red Sea
Caspian Sea
Aral Sea
KAZAKHSTAN
UZBEKISTAN
TURKMENISTAN
KYRGYZSTAN
TAJIKISTAN
AFGHANISTAN
PAKISTAN
MONGOLIA
PEOPLE'S REPUBLIC OF CHINA
DEMOCRATIC PEOPLE'S REPUBLIC OF KOREA
REPUBLIC OF KOREA
JAPAN
Sea of Japan
Yellow Sea
East China Sea
Sea of Okhotsk
Bering Sea
Aleutian Islands
NEPAL
BHUTAN
BANGLADESH
INDIA
TAIWAN
Hong Kong
Macau
MYANMAR (BURMA)
LAOS
VIETNAM
THAILAND
CAMBODIA
South China Sea
PHILIPPINES
Spratly Islands
Philippine Sea
Northern Marianas
Guam
PALAU
FEDERATED STATES OF MICRONESIA
Caroline Islands
MARSHALL ISLANDS
PACIFIC OCEAN
Arabian Sea
Bay of Bengal
SRI LANKA
MALDIVES
BRUNEI
MALAYSIA
SINGAPORE
Celebes Sea
INDONESIA
EAST TIMOR
TIMOR-LESTE
PAPUA NEW GUINEA
MELANESIA
NAURU
Gilbert Islands
KIRIBATI
Phoenix Islands
SOLOMON ISLANDS
TUVALU
Wallis & Futuna
VANUATU
FIJI
Coral Sea
New Caledonia
TONGA
Great Barrier Reef
Norfolk Island
AUSTRALIA
Tasman Sea
North Islands
Chatham Islands
NEW ZEALAND
South Islands
LIBYA
EGYPT
CHAD
SUDAN
ERITREA
DJIBOUTI
Somaliland
ETHIOPIA
CENTRAL AFRICAN REPUBLIC
SOUTH SUDAN
SOMALIA
DEMOCRATIC REPUBLIC OF THE CONGO
REPUBLIC OF THE CONGO
UGANDA
KENYA
RWANDA
BURUNDI
TANZANIA
SEYCHELLES
INDIAN OCEAN
ANGOLA
ZAMBIA
MALAWI
COMORO ISLANDS
MOZAMBIQUE
MADAGASCAR
MAURITIUS
Réunion
NAMIBIA
ZIMBABWE
BOTSWANA
SWAZILAND
LESOTHO
SOUTH AFRICA
ANTARCTICA

FOR INFORMATION:

CQ Press
SAGE Publications, Inc.
2455 Teller Road
Thousand Oaks, California 91320
E-mail: order@sagepub.com

SAGE Publications Ltd.
1 Oliver's Yard
55 City Road
London EC1Y 1SP
United Kingdom

SAGE Publications India Pvt. Ltd.
B 1/I 1 Mohan Cooperative Industrial Area
Mathura Road, New Delhi 110 044
India

SAGE Publications Asia-Pacific Pte. Ltd.
3 Church Street
#10-04 Samsung Hub
Singapore 049483

Editor, Reference Publishing: Laura Notton
Editorial Assistant to Tom Lansford: Jordan Roberts
Production Editor: Tracy Buyan
Copy Editors: Terri Lee Paulsen, Pam Schroeder
Typesetter: C&M Digitals (P) Ltd.
Proofreader: Laura Webb
Cover Designer: Michael Dubowe
Marketing Manager: Kate Brummitt

Printed in the United States of America.

Print ISBN: 978-1-5063-2718-1
ISSN: 0193-175X

Publishing history continues on page 1941 (volume 2), which is to be considered an extension of the copyright page.

17 18 19 20 21 10 9 8 7 6 5 4 3 2 1

CONTENTS

Intergovernmental Organization Abbreviations ix

GOVERNMENTS

Volume 1

Afghanistan 3
Albania 16
Algeria 26
Andorra 38
Angola 43
Antarctica 54
Antigua and Barbuda 57
Argentina 60
Contested Territory 70
Armenia 71
Australia 81
Related Territories 88
Austria 90
Azerbaijan 98
Bahamas 108
Bahrain 110
Bangladesh 117
Barbados 127
Belarus 130
Belgium 138
Belize 146
Benin 150
Bhutan 156
Bolivia 160
Bosnia and Herzegovina 169
Botswana 185
Brazil 189
Brunei 196
Bulgaria 198
Burkina Faso 209
Burundi 218
Cambodia 229
Cameroon 236
Canada 246
Cape Verde 256
Central African Republic 260
Chad 270
Chile 283
China 290
People's Republic of China 292
Taiwan 301
Colombia 308
Comoros 318
Democratic Republic of the Congo 328
Republic of the Congo 342
Costa Rica 352
Côte d'Ivoire 356
Croatia 365
Cuba 375
Cyprus 381
Turkish Sector 388
Czech Republic 395
Denmark 409
Related Territories 415
Djibouti 417
Dominica 424
Dominican Republic 427
Ecuador 435
Egypt 444
El Salvador 457
Equatorial Guinea 465
Eritrea 473
Estonia 478
Ethiopia 485
Fiji 499
Finland 505
Related Territory 511
France 511
Related Territories 520
Gabon 527
Gambia 536
Georgia 541
Germany 553
Ghana 566
Greece 574
Grenada 585
Guatemala 588
Guinea 597
Guinea-Bissau 606
Guyana 615
Haiti 623
Honduras 634

Hungary....642
Iceland....653
India....658
Indonesia....678
Annexed Territory....688
Iran....688
Iraq....705
Ireland....721
Israel....730
Italy....746
Jamaica....759
Japan....763
Jordan....772
Kazakhstan....783
Kenya....790
Kiribati....808
Korea....811
Democratic People's Republic of Korea....814
Republic of Korea....820
Kosovo....828
Kuwait....835
Kyrgyzstan....842
Laos....851
Latvia....854
Lebanon....862
Lesotho....869
Liberia....877
Libya....888
Liechtenstein....895
Lithuania....899
Luxembourg....906

Volume 2

Macedonia....911
Madagascar....920
Malawi....930
Malaysia....937
Maldives....946
Mali....951
Malta....960
Marshall Islands....964
Mauritania....967
Mauritius....979
Mexico....986
Micronesia, Federated States of....996
Moldova....998
Monaco....1007
Mongolia....1010
Montenegro....1016
Morocco....1024
Disputed Territory....1032
Mozambique....1035
Myanmar (Burma)....1043
Namibia....1055
Nauru....1065
Nepal....1068
Netherlands....1079
Aruba....1087
Curaçao....1089
St. Maarten....1092
New Zealand....1095
Related Territories....1102
Nicaragua....1104
Niger....1113
Nigeria....1125
Norway....1136
Related Territories....1142
Oman....1143
Pakistan....1147
Related Territories....1161
Palau....1163
Panama....1165
Panama Canal Zone....1173
Papua New Guinea....1174
Paraguay....1181
Peru....1187
Philippines....1199
Poland....1211
Portugal....1224
Related Territories....1231
Qatar....1233
Romania....1237
Russia....1250
Rwanda....1265
St. Kitts and Nevis....1275
St. Lucia....1278
St. Vincent and the Grenadines....1281
Samoa....1283
San Marino....1287
São Tomé and Príncipe....1292
Saudi Arabia....1298
Senegal....1303
Serbia....1314
Seychelles....1329
Sierra Leone....1334
Singapore....1344
Slovakia....1349
Slovenia....1358
Solomon Islands....1366
Somalia....1371
Somaliland....1380
South Africa....1385
South Sudan....1400
Spain....1403
Related Territories....1420
Sri Lanka....1421
Sudan....1436
Suriname....1449
Swaziland....1456
Sweden....1460
Switzerland....1467
Syria....1474
Tajikistan....1482
Tanzania....1489
Thailand....1498
Timor-Leste (East Timor)....1508
Togo....1515
Tonga....1525
Trinidad and Tobago....1528
Tunisia....1533

Turkey 1541
Turkmenistan 1554
Tuvalu 1558
Uganda 1562
Ukraine 1572
United Arab Emirates 1591
United Kingdom 1595
Related Territories 1610
United Kingdom: Northern Ireland 1620
United States 1634
Related Territories 1649
Uruguay 1654
Uzbekistan 1661
Vanuatu 1668
Vatican City State 1674
Venezuela 1678
Vietnam 1686
Yemen 1692
Zambia 1700
Zimbabwe 1709
Palestinian Authority/Palestine Liberation Organization 1719

INTERGOVERNMENTAL ORGANIZATIONS

African Union (AU) 1738
Arab League 1740
Asia-Pacific Economic Cooperation (APEC) 1742
Association of Southeast Asian Nations (ASEAN) 1744
Caribbean Community and Common Market (Caricom) 1747
Common Market for Eastern and Southern Africa (Comesa) 1749
The Commonwealth 1751
Commonwealth of Independent States (CIS) 1754
Council of Europe 1757
Economic Community of West African States (ECOWAS) 1759
European Free Trade Association (EFTA) 1761
European Union (EU) 1763
European Atomic Energy Community (Euratom) 1778
Group of Eight 1779
Group of Twenty 1781
International Criminal Court (ICC) 1783
International Energy Agency (IEA) 1785
International Organization for Migration (IOM) 1786
Non-aligned Movement 1788
North Atlantic Treaty Organization (NATO) 1790
Organization for Economic Cooperation and Development (OECD) 1797
Organization of Eastern Caribbean States (OECS) 1799
Organization for Security and Cooperation in Europe (OSCE) 1801
Organization of American States (OAS) 1805
Organization of Islamic Cooperation (OIC) 1808
Organization of the Petroleum Exporting Countries (OPEC) 1810
Pacific Islands Forum (PIF) 1813
Regional Development Banks 1815
African Development Bank (AfDB/BAD) 1815
Asian Development Bank (ADB) 1817
European Bank for Reconstruction and Development (EBRD/BERD) 1818
European Investment Bank (EIB) 1820
Inter-American Development Bank (IADB/BID) 1821
Shanghai Cooperation Organization (SCO) 1823
South Asian Association for Regional Cooperation (SAARC) 1824
Southern African Development Community (SADC) 1826
Southern Cone Common Market (Mercosur/Mercosul) 1829
United Nations (UN) 1831
General Assembly 1833
General Assembly: Special Bodies 1839
United Nations Children's Fund 1839
United Nations Conference on Trade and Development 1840
United Nations Development Program 1841
United Nations Environment Program 1842
United Nations Institute for Training and Research 1844
United Nations Office of High Commissioner for Refugees 1845
United Nations Population Fund 1846
United Nations Relief and Works Agency for Palestine Refugees in the Near East 1847
United Nations Research Institute for Social Development 1848
United Nations University 1849
Security Council 1850
Security Council: Peacekeeping Forces and Missions 1856
United Nations/African Union Hybrid Operation in Darfur (UNAMID) 1856
United Nations Disengagement Observer Force (UNDOF) 1856
United Nations Force in Cyprus (UNFICYP) 1856
United Nations Interim Administration Mission in Kosovo (UNMIK) 1857
United Nations Interim Force in Lebanon (UNIFIL) ... 1857
United Nations Military Observer Group in India and Pakistan (UNMOGIP) 1857
United Nations Mission for the Referendum in Western Sahara 1857
United Nations Mission in Liberia (UNMIL) 1857
United Nations Mission in the Republic of South Sudan (UNMISS) 1857
United Nations Operation in Côte d'Ivoire 1858
United Nations Organization Stabilization Mission in the Democratic Republic of the Congo 1858
United Nations Stabilization Mission in Haiti 1858

United Nations Truce Supervision Organization (UNTSO) 1858
United Nations Interim Security Force for Abyei (UNISFA) 1858
United Nations Multidimensional Integrated Stabilization Mission in Mali 1859
United Nations Multidimensional Integrated Stabilization Mission in the Central African Republic 1859
Security Council: International Criminal Tribunals 1859
International Criminal Tribunal for the Former Yugoslavia (ICTY) 1860
International Criminal Tribunal for Rwanda (ICTR) 1860
Economic and Social Council (ECOSOC) 1860
Economic and Social Council: Functional Commissions 1861
Commission on Crime Prevention and Criminal Justice 1861
Commission on Narcotic Drugs 1862
Commission on Population and Development 1862
Commission on Science and Technology for Development 1862
Commission for Social Development 1862
Commission on the Status of Women 1862
Statistical Commission 1862
Economic and Social Council: Regional Commissions 1862
Economic Commission for Africa (ECA) 1862
Economic Commission for Europe (ECE) 1863
Economic Commission for Latin America and the Caribbean (ECLAC) 1864
Economic and Social Commission for Asia and the Pacific (ESCAP) 1865
Economic and Social Commission for Western Asia (ESCWA) 1866
Trusteeship Council 1867
International Court of Justice (ICJ) 1868
Secretariat 1871
United Nations: Specialized Agencies 1875
Food and Agriculture Organization of the United Nations (FAO) 1875
International Civil Aviation Organization (ICAO) 1878
International Fund for Agricultural Development (IFAD) 1879
International Labour Organization (ILO) 1881
International Maritime Organization (IMO) 1883
International Monetary Fund (IMF) 1885
International Telecommunication Union (ITU) 1890
United Nations Educational, Scientific and Cultural Organization (UNESCO) 1892
United Nations Industrial Development Organization (UNIDO) 1895
World Bank 1896
International Bank for Reconstruction and Development (IBRD) 1897
International Development Association (IDA) 1899
International Finance Corporation (IFC) 1900
World Health Organization (WHO) 1902
World Intellectual Property Organization (WIPO) 1905
United Nations: Related Organizations 1906
International Atomic Energy Agency (IAEA) 1906
World Trade Organization (WTO) 1910

APPENDIXES

Appendix A: Chronology of Major International Political Events: 1945–2016 1916
Appendix B: Chronology of Major International Conferences Sponsored by the United Nations: 1946–2016 1930
Appendix C: Membership of the United Nations and Its Specialized and Related Agencies 1936
Appendix D: Serials List 1940

INTERGOVERNMENTAL ORGANIZATION ABBREVIATIONS

Country membership in an intergovernmental organization is given in one of two locations: Appendix C lists membership of the United Nations and its specialized and related agencies; non-UN memberships are listed at the end of each country section, under Intergovernmental Representation, using the abbreviations below. An asterisk indicates a nonofficial abbreviation. In the individual country sections, associate memberships are in italics.

ADB	Asian Development Bank
*AfDB	African Development Bank
APEC	Asia-Pacific Economic Cooperation
ASEAN	Association of Southeast Asian Nations
AU	African Union
Caricom	Caribbean Community and Common Market
*CEUR	Council of Europe
CIS	Commonwealth of Independent States
Comesa	Common Market for Eastern and Southern Africa
*CWTH	Commonwealth
EBRD	European Bank for Reconstruction and Development
ECOWAS	Economic Community of West African States
EFTA	European Free Trade Association
EIB	European Investment Bank
EU	European Union
GCC	Gulf Cooperation Council
G-7	Group of Seven
G-8	Group of Eight
G-20	Group of Twenty
*IADB	Inter-American Development Bank
ICC	International Criminal Court
IEA	International Energy Agency
IOM	International Organization for Migration
LAS	League of Arab States (Arab League)
Mercosur	Southern Cone Common Market
*NAM	Nonaligned Movement
NATO	North Atlantic Treaty Organization
OAS	Organization of American States
OECD	Organization for Economic Cooperation and Development
*OIC	Organization of the Islamic Conference
OPEC	Organization of the Petroleum Exporting Countries
OSCE	Organization for Security and Cooperation in Europe
PIF	Pacific Islands Forum
SAARC	South Asian Association for Regional Cooperation
SADC	Southern African Development Community
SCO	Shanghai Cooperation Organization
WEU	Western European Union
WTO	World Trade Organization

MACEDONIA

Republic of Macedonia
Republika Makedonija

Note: The country was admitted to the United Nations in April 1993 as "The former Yugoslav Republic of Macedonia," although international usage of this title (particularly in regard to capitalization) has varied, with the abbreviation FYROM sometimes being invoked. As of 2014 no resolution had been achieved in the dispute with Greece over use of "Macedonia" in the country's official name.

Political Status: Former constituent republic of the Socialist Federal Republic of Yugoslavia; independence proclaimed under constitution of November 17, 1991, on the basis of a referendum conducted September 8.

Area: 9,928 sq. mi. (25,713 sq. km).

Population: 2,081,000 (2016E—UN); 2,100,025 (2016E—U.S. Census).

Major Urban Center (2015E—UN): SKOPJE (503,000).

Official Languages: Macedonian, Albanian. Macedonian, with a Cyrillic alphabet, is further designated as the official language for international relations. Albanian, with a Latin alphabet, became an official language under a 2001 constitutional revision that authorized that status for any language spoken by at least 20 percent of the population. Moreover, in local jurisdictions other languages used by at least 20 percent of the citizens are considered official. (Local authorities may also permit additional languages to be used in public interactions with the government.)

Monetary Unit: New Macedonian Denar (market rate October 1, 2016: 54.69 denars = $1US).

President: Gjorge IVANOV (Internal Macedonian Revolutionary Organization–Democratic Party for Macedonian National Unity); directly elected in second-round balloting on April 5, 2009, and sworn in for a five-year term on May 12, succeeding Branko CRVENKOVSKI (Social Democratic Union of Macedonia); reelected on April 27, 2014.

Chair of the Council of Ministers (Prime Minister): Emil DIMITRIEV (Internal Macedonian Revolutionary Organization–Democratic Party for Macedonian National Unity); nominated on an interim basis under the 2015 crisis agreement (see Government and Politics, below) on January 15, 2015, following the planned resignation of Nikola GRUEVSKI (Internal Macedonian Revolutionary Organization–Democratic Party for Macedonian National Unity); assumed office on January 18, 2015.

THE COUNTRY

The former Yugoslavian component of historical Macedonia is a landlocked country bordered on the east by Bulgaria, on the north by Serbia and Montenegro, on the west by Albania, and on the south by Greece. According to the 2002 census, 64.2 percent of the population is ethnic Macedonian and 25.2 percent ethnic Albanian, with Turks, Roma, Serbs, Bosniaks, Vlachs, and others forming smaller groups. Most of the Macedonian majority supports the Macedonian Orthodox (Christian) Church; the Albanians are predominantly Muslim. Demography contributes to the ethnic tensions within the country. The higher birthrate among the ethnic Albanian, Turkish, and Roma communities is frequently cited by ethnic Macedonian nationalist politicians as eroding the nature of the state as the homeland of the "Macedonian people." Equally important is the depopulation of the countryside; two-thirds of Macedonian towns and villages continue to see long-term population decline because of internal migration, primarily to Skopje. The perception that rural areas are underfunded has contributed, in part, to past ethnic conflict.

Agriculture accounted for about 10 percent of GDP and roughly 19 percent of employment in 2013, the principal crops being fruits, vegetables, grains, and tobacco. The industrial sector, contributing about 28 percent of GDP and 28 percent of employment, principally exports iron and steel, footwear and clothing, nonferrous metals, tobacco products, and beverages (especially wine). Women constitute 40 percent of the labor force. Extractable resources include lignite, copper, lead, and zinc. Germany, Greece, Serbia, the United Kingdom, and Italy are Macedonia's leading trading partners.

The poorest of the former Yugoslav republics, Macedonia was economically distressed in the post-independence period by regional conflict and the disruption of established trading links with neighboring countries. Industrial and agricultural production declined sharply, yielding GDP contraction of about one-third in 1990–1993, during which inflation averaged 600 percent per year and unemployment rose to 40 percent. Beginning in 1994 the government initiated a structural reform program suggested by the International Monetary Fund (IMF) and World Bank; initiatives included liberalization of trade regulations, modernization of customs procedures, privatization of state-run enterprises, and reform of the financial sector. Macedonia gained membership in the World Trade Organization (WTO) in 2003 and the Central European Free Trade Association (CEFTA) in 2006.

Severe difficulties have continued since independence, however, including a dearth of foreign investment, continued high unemployment, and increasing poverty (30 percent of the population lived below the poverty line in 2011). The ethnic Albanian Muslim minority has been disproportionally affected by economic problems, generating additional resentment in a segment of the population already embittered over perceived "second class" treatment.

The European Union (EU) formally declared Macedonia as a candidate for EU membership in December 2005, but among other things, EU accession appeared dependent on a resolution of the name dispute with Greece (see Current issues, below). The effects of the global economic crisis produced GDP contraction of 2.4 percent in 2009 and an average annual growth of less than 1.8 percent over 2010–2012. In addition, corruption remained a problem, while official unemployment in mid-2013 surpassed 30 percent, one of the highest rates in Europe. (The rate was almost 54 percent for those under 25 years of age.) In 2014 unemployment dropped to 28 percent, and then to 27 percent in 2015, before rising to 28 percent in 2016. GDP growth reached 3.1 percent in 2013, and 3.5 percent in 2014. The IMF estimated 3.6 percent growth in both 2015 and 2016. Inflation grew by 1.3 percent in 2016, while GDP per capita was $5,185.

GOVERNMENT AND POLITICS

Political background. Greater geographic Macedonia was contested between rival Balkan empires until its incorporation into the Ottoman Empire. Ottoman rule lasted five centuries prior to the Second

Balkan War and the Treaty of Bucharest of 1913, which divided most of the territory between Greece and Serbia, the respective portions being known as Aegean (or Greek) Macedonia and Vardar Macedonia. A much smaller portion (Pirin Macedonia) was awarded to Bulgaria. After World War I Vardar Macedonia became part of the Kingdom of the Serbs, Croats, and Slovenes, later renamed Yugoslavia in October 1929. In 1944 it was accorded the status of a constituent republic of the communist-ruled federal Yugoslavia.

Following Belgrade's endorsement of a multiparty system in early 1990, Vladimir MITKOV of the newly styled League of Communists of Macedonia–Party of Democratic Change (*Sojuz na Komunistite na Makedonija–Partija za Demokratska Preobrazba*—SKM-PDP) was named president of the republic's State Presidency, pending a general election. The balloting for a 120-member Assembly, conducted in three stages on November 11 and 25 and December 9, was marked by ethnic tension between the Macedonian and Albanian communities and yielded an inconclusive outcome: the opposition Internal Macedonian Revolutionary Organization–Democratic Party for Macedonian National Unity (*Vnatrešno Makedonska Revolucionerna Organizacija–Demokratska Partija za Makedonsko Nacionalno Edinstvo*—VMRO-DPMNE) won a plurality of 37 seats, compared with 31 for the second-place SKM-PDP, and a total of 25 for two Albanian groups. As a result of the stand-off, Kiro GLIGOROV of the SKM-PDP (subsequently the Social Democratic Union of Macedonia [*Socijaldemokratski Sojuz na Makedonija*—SDSM]) was named to succeed Mitkov as president.

On January 25, 1991, the Assembly unanimously adopted a declaration of sovereignty that asserted a right of self-determination, including secession from Yugoslavia. On September 8, 75 percent of the republic's registered voters (with most Albanians abstaining) participated in a referendum that endorsed independence by an overwhelming margin. On November 17 the Assembly approved a new constitution, and on December 24 Macedonia joined Bosnia and Herzegovina, Croatia, and Slovenia in seeking recognition from the European Community (EC, subsequently the EU). The ethnic Albanians reacted in January 1992 with a 99.9 percent vote in favor of territorial and political autonomy for the Albanian-majority regions in western Macedonia. While Belgrade tacitly recognized Macedonian autonomy by withdrawing its own military forces from the republic, most foreign governments withheld recognition because of Greek protests over the country's name (see Foreign relations, below).

A mid-1992 cabinet crisis resulted in the formation of a new coalition headed by Branko CRVENKOVSKI of the SDSM and including the Party for Democratic Prosperity (*Partija za Demokratski Prosperite/Partia për Prosperitet Demokratik*—PDP/PPD), a primarily ethnic Albanian party. The new government introduced short-term emergency economic measures, including devaluations of the denar in October and December. Meanwhile, in light of an influx of some 60,000 refugees from the war in Bosnia and Herzegovina, the Assembly in October approved a 15-year residency requirement for Macedonian citizenship, which was modified to eight years in 2003.

The prime importance attached by the government to securing full international recognition helped to ensure the survival of the disparate ruling coalition, which had been mandated to cement national unity. Nevertheless, underlying tensions between the ethnic Macedonian and ethnic Albanian communities surfaced in 1993 amid accusations of Albanian separatism, and in early 1994 the PDP/PPD split into moderate and nationalist factions, the latter joining the opposition.

In the October 1994 presidential election Gligorov secured easy reelection as the candidate of an SDSM-led alliance, winning 78.4 percent of the valid votes cast (52.4 percent of the total electorate), against 21.6 percent for the nominee of the VMRO-DPMNE, Ljubčo GEORGIEVSKI. In the two-stage legislative election the SDSM-led alliance won 95 of the 120 seats and then opted to maintain the coalition with the PDP/PPD. The opposition parties claimed that both the presidential and legislative elections had been riddled with fraud, a view that received some support from international observers.

On October 3, 1995, President Gligorov suffered serious injuries in a bomb attack on his car in Skopje that resulted in two fatalities. (For details, see the 2012 *Handbook.*)

In a major cabinet reshuffle in February 1996, Prime Minister Crvenkovski dropped the LPM from the ruling coalition. An LPM attempt in April to force an early election was easily rebuffed, given the government's comfortable parliamentary majority, the SDSM's position being reinforced when it won a plurality of council seats as well as mayoralties in the municipal elections in late 1996.

In February 1997 an estimated 3,000 ethnic Macedonian students protested against a law permitting the Albanian language to be used in teaching at Skopje University's teacher college, reflecting nationalistic sentiment that the government should not yield to perceived separatism on the part of ethnic Albanians. In March the EU formally expressed concern over rising ethnic tensions. Rioting, resulting in 3 deaths, 100 wounded, and 500 arrests, erupted in July in Gostivar over the right to fly the Albanian flag at municipal buildings in ethnic Albanian areas.

The problems of ethnic Albanians in Kosovo subsequently spilled over into Macedonia, including a series of car bomb explosions in January and February 1998 that were disputably claimed by the Kosovo Liberation Army—KLA (*Ushtria Çlirimtare e Kosovës*). The leaders of several ethnic Albanian parties were charged in mid-March with violating (during a pro-Kosovo rally) Macedonian laws limiting the display of Albanian nationalist symbols. In addition, the mayors of Tetovo and Gostivar were imprisoned for flying the Albanian flag over municipal buildings. In response, the PDP and the Democratic Party of Albanians (*Demokratska Partija na Albancite/Partia Demokratike Shqiptare*—DPA/PDSh), under the leadership of longtime Albanian nationalist Arben XHAFERI, threatened to withdraw from governmental institutions.

The legislative election in October–November 1998 gave a majority of 62 seats to the VMRO-DPMNE and its electoral partner, the Democratic Alternative (*Demokratska Alternativa*—DA). A governmental crisis was averted after the election, when Prime Minister-Designate Georgievski negotiated a coalition agreement that included the DPA/PDSh. Georgievski's new VMRO-DPMNE-DA-DPA/PDSh government pledged to further integrate Albanians into Macedonian institutions and society as a whole. Pardons were granted for several Albanian figures charged with political crimes, including the mayors of Tetovo and Gostivar.

In presidential balloting to replace the retiring Gligorov, the VMRO-DPMNE candidate, Boris TRAJKOVSKI, captured 52.9 percent of the second-round vote in November 1999, outdistancing the SDSM's Tito PETKOVSKI, who had finished first in the initial round. Trajkovski's victory came with the support of the DA and the DPA/PDSh, both of which had fielded their own candidates in the first round. Official confirmation of Trajkovski's victory was delayed, however, when the Supreme Court ordered that a revote be held in selected precincts because of ballot stuffing and other irregularities. The results of the reballoting proved nearly identical to the previous totals, and Trajkovski was inaugurated on December 15.

In February 2001 fighting erupted in Tanuševci (Tanusevçi), on the border with Kosovo, precipitated by members of the Albanian National Liberation Army—NLA (*Ushtrisë Çlirimtare Kombëtare*—UÇK) led by Ali AHMETI. By mid-March fighting had spread to the Tetovo area, leading the UN Security Council to pass a unanimous resolution condemning "extremist violence" as "a threat to the security and stability of the wider region." In April the DPA and PDP, both having condemned the NLA, began discussions with the government on possible constitutional changes that would address the status of ethnic Albanians. In May the Assembly, by a vote of 104–1, approved formation of a national unity government that, in addition to the three parties in the previous Georgievski administration, included the SDSM, the PDP, the Internal Macedonian Revolutionary Organization–True Macedonian Reform Option (*Vnatrešno Makedonska Revolucionerna Organizacija–Vistinska Makedonska Reformska Opcija*—VMRO-VMRO), and the Liberal-Democratic Party (*Liberalno-Demokratska Partija*—LDP), which incorporated elements of the LPM. Fighting nevertheless escalated in succeeding weeks, and as of June some 65,000 ethnic Albanians had fled to Kosovo to escape the conflict.

A Western-brokered peace agreement (the Ohrid Framework Agreement) was achieved on August 13, 2001. Two weeks later NLA members began surrendering their arms to a 3,500-member NATO force, "Operation Essential Harvest," which had entered the country at the request of President Trajkovski and which transitioned to "Operation Amber Fox" in September to oversee the implementation of the Ohrid Agreement. On September 6 the Assembly formally approved the peace accords. The pact called in part for constitutional revisions that would excise the privileged status accorded the Macedonian majority and grant official status to other languages with a native-speaking population of at least 20 percent, effectively making Albanian a second official language. An amnesty bill regarding the 2001 conflict passed in March 2002, and a series of language laws won approval in June, the Assembly finally enacting a package of related constitutional amendments on November 16. Five days later, declaring that the national unity government had achieved its aim of restoring domestic stability, the SDSM and LDP resigned from the administration, which was quickly joined by the New Democracy Party (*Nova Demokratija*—ND).

In the parliamentary election of September 15, 2002, former prime minister Branko Crvenkovski's SDSM led a ten-party alliance, the Coalition for Macedonia Together (*Koalicija za Makedonija Zaedno—Koalicija*—ZMZ), to a near-majority of 60 seats in the 120-seat *Sobranje.* Prime Minister Georgievski's VMRO-DPMNE and its principal ally, the LPM, managed to win only 33 seats. The Democratic Union for Integration (*Demokratska Unija za Integracija/Bashkimit Demokratik për Integrim*—DUI/BDI), chaired by former Albanian National Liberation Army leader Ali Ahmeti, won 16 seats and joined a new Crvenkovski coalition government, which took office on November 1.

On February 26, 2004, President Trajkovski and six of his staff members were killed in a plane crash near Mostar in Bosnia and Herzegovina. In the first round of elections to choose Trajkovski's successor on April 14, Prime Minister Crvenkovski of the SDSM and Sasko KEDEV of the VMRO-DPMNE advanced, leaving behind two ethnic Albanian candidates. Crvenkovski won the April 28 runoff with 62.7 percent of the vote and was sworn in as president on May 12, Assembly Speaker Ljubčo JORDANOVSKI having served in the interim as acting president. Interior Minister Hari KOSTOV succeeded Crvenkovski as prime minister and was sworn in on June 2. On November 15, however, Kostov resigned in protest against corruption and nepotism within the coalition. He was replaced by Vlado BUČKOVSKI, who also took over as SDSM chair. On December 17 the Assembly approved Bučkovski's coalition government, which included the DUI/BDI.

Parliamentary elections were held on July 5 and July 19, 2006, in balloting judged generally free and fair, although the process was marred by outbreaks of violence and allegations of electoral irregularities. The VMRO-DPMNE, leading a broad coalition, won 45 seats, defeating rival coalitions led by the SDSM and DUI/BDI. Negotiations between the VMRO-DPMNE's Nikola GRUEVSKI, the prospective prime minister, quickly brought the New Social Democratic Party (*Nova Socijal Demokratska Partija*—NSDP), the SPM, and the LPM into government. However, the search to find a partner from the country's three ethnic Albanian parties proved more protracted. Following unsuccessful negotiations with the DUI/BDI and PDP/PPD, an agreement was made with the DPA/PDSh. The cabinet was inaugurated on August 26.

Prime Minister Gruevski's inclusion of the DPA/PDSh in the ensuing government deepened rifts among the political parties representing ethnic Albanians. Outbreaks of ethnic and political violence were subsequently reported, including a rocket-powered grenade attack on the central building of the government in August 2007. The key provisions of the Ohrid accords continued to be implemented, but only slowly and with some opposition among ethnic Macedonians. Among other things, certain elements within the Albanian community expressed a preference for union with Kosovo, and former members of the NLA called for a referendum to allow the village of Tanuševci (one of the flash points of the 2001 war) to accede to Kosovo. Subsequent police raids seized small but significant caches of weapons reportedly held by NLA splinter groups.

In 2007 both the SDSM and DUI/BDI coalitions broke apart, leading to broader support for the government with the PDP/PDD and several smaller parties joining the ruling coalition. Nevertheless, the government was unable to secure sufficient legislative support to enact economic reforms and proposals regarding the ethnic Albanian minority. The government faced an additional setback in April 2008 when Greece vetoed the expected offer of NATO membership for Macedonia, citing the continued name dispute. The VMRO-DPMNE and allied parties consequently voted for an early election in 2008, hoping for a "mandate" to enact change.

The June 2, 2008, Assembly elections were tarnished by outbreaks of violence and voting irregularities. Much of the conflict was between supporters of the DPA/PDSh and DUI/BDI (see the 2012 *Handbook*). Irregularities at some stations led to the State Electoral Commission invalidating the results in several districts, where revotes were held on June 15. Following new problems in that round, a third round was held in some districts on June 29. The VMRO-DPMNE secured a decisive victory, with its coalition winning an outright majority with 63 seats. Prime Minister Gruevski subsequently formed a new government with the DUI/BDI that was also supported by the Party for a European Future (*Partija za Evropska Idnina*—PEI). As a result, the government was backed by 82 legislators, more than the two-thirds necessary to enact constitutional reforms.

Gjorge IVANOV of the VMRO-DPMNE finished first among seven candidates in the first round of presidential balloting on March 22, 2009, with 35.0 percent of the vote, followed by the SDSM's Ljubomir FRČKOSKI with 20.5 percent. Ivanov won the runoff with Frčkoski on April 5 with 63.1 percent of the vote. The EU had indicated that open, free, and peaceful presidential elections in 2009 would be a precondition for progress regarding EU membership for Macedonia. Those conditions were largely met, although turnout declined from over 1 million voters in the first round to 750,000 in the second round, largely reflecting a boycott by ethnic Albanian voters.

In January 2011 the SDSM, its coalition allies, and the ND boycotted parliament in protest against what, according to them, were measures to put the "media under the direct control of the democracy." Gruevski responded in February 2011 by calling for new elections. Following negotiations in March over changes to the electoral law (which included the inclusion of three new seats for Macedonians living abroad), parliament was dissolved on April 14.

The June 5, 2011, election was judged generally free, fair, and without incident. The coalition led by the VMRO-DPMNE won 56 seats, defeating rival coalitions led by the SDSM and DUI/BDI, although the SDSM significantly increased its position in parliament. Negotiations to retain the DUI/BDI proceeded smoothly, and a restructured cabinet was approved by the *Sobranje* on July 28.

Disagreement between the ruling VMRO-DPMNE and BUI/BDI over whether to offer a joint presidential candidate in 2014 led to the BUI/BDI calling in February for early legislative elections. Parliament was accordingly dissolved on March 5.

Ivanov finished first of four candidates in the first round of presidential balloting on April 13, 2014, winning 51.7 percent of the vote, followed by the SDSM's Stevo PENDAROVSKI's with 37.5 percent of the vote. Ivanov secured reelection in the second round on April 27 with 55.3 percent of the vote. The BUI/BDI discouraged Albanian voters from participating in the presidential election, likely contributing to the low turnout rate of 48.9 percent of registered voters in the first round (compared to 56.9 percent in the first round in 2009).

In the legislative election, the coalition led by the VMRO-DPMNE won 61 seats, defeating the rival coalition led by the SDSM. Election monitors noted some shortcomings in the process, including a failure to "separate party from state activities" and "biased media coverage." An agreement with the DUI/BDI to extend the ruling government was completed by May 10, and a slightly restructured cabinet was approved by the *Sobranje* on June 30. The SDSM led an opposition coalition that boycotted parliament.

In February 2015 the SDSM released more than 670,000 illegally recorded conversations from more than 20,000 phone numbers, reportedly collected at the behest of Gruevski by Macedonian security services. The revelations prompted widespread protests across the country in May, calling for the prime minister to resign. Mediation by the United States and the EU resulted in the June 2 Pržino Agreement, which called for new elections by April 2016. A protocol to the accord required the SDSM to end its boycott of parliament by September 2015 and to join the government by October, after which Gruevski would resign and an interim government would be put in place to oversee the April balloting.

Gruevski resigned on January 15, 2016, and was replaced by Emil DIMITRIEV (VMRO-DPMNE) three days later. International election monitors determined that balloting in April was logistically impossible and the legislature voted to postpone the polling until June. After the SDSM withdrew from the unity government, a second U.S.–EU mediation effort in July resulted in a further postponement of the elections until December.

Meanwhile, Deputy Prime Minister and Finance Minister Zoran STAVRESKI (VRMO-DPMNE) resigned on June 14, 2016, for health reasons. The finance portfolio was given to Kiril MINOSKI (ind.). On September 2 two SDSM ministers returned to the government.

Constitution and government. The constitution proclaimed in November 1991 defines Macedonia as a state based on citizenship, not ethnicity, and specifically rules out any territorial claims on neighboring countries. The Albanian minority, however, asserted that the preamble and dozens of provisions of the basic law accorded privileged status to the ethnic and religious Macedonian majority. This perception contributed to the violent events of 2001 and led to enactment of a series of corrective amendments later that year. The principal changes were a revised preamble referring to nonethnic Macedonian communities as citizens; a requirement that certain legislation obtain minority group approval as well as passage by the full legislature (a "double majority"); provision for additional official languages in areas where native speakers constitute 20 percent of the population; and proportional representation of ethnic Albanians in the Constitutional Court, public administration, and security forces.

The constitution provides for a directly elected president serving a five-year term as head of state and a cabinet, headed by a prime minister, owing responsibility to a unicameral national Assembly (*Sobranje*). The Assembly is elected for a four-year term by a combination of majority and proportional voting. Ultimate judicial authority is vested in a Supreme Court, with a Constitutional Court adjudicating constitutional issues.

In 2002 the Assembly approved legislation providing for the devolution of greater authority to local government, effectively granting a measure of self-rule to ethnic Albanian regions. In other measures to integrate ethnic Albanians into national life, legislators passed a controversial law granting status as a state university to the underground Albanian-language university in Tetovo. A new citizenship law passed in 2003 enabled foreign nationals to qualify for citizenship after 8 rather than 15 years of legal residence.

In 2004 the Assembly passed a redistricting law cutting the number of administrative districts from 123 to 84, in 16 of which Albanians claimed a majority. The law, which was in accordance with the 2001 Ohrid peace accords, gave local authorities greater powers in regional planning, finance, and health care. The measure was opposed by many ethnic Macedonians, who feared that redistricting could lead to partition of the country along ethnic lines, but a November referendum to annul the legislation was boycotted by many parties and groups and therefore failed by nearly half to obtain the necessary 50 percent participation rate. Three seats for émigré Macedonian citizens in North America, Europe, and Asia/Australia were added in 2011, a significant overrepresentation of their numbers.

Freedom of the press is protected by the constitution. In 2016 Reporters Without Borders ranked the Macedonian government's respect for freedom of the press in 118th place out of 180 countries. Since 2014 Macedonia has risen five places.

Foreign relations. Recognition of Macedonia by the EC/EU was stalled by the insistence of Greece that recognition be conditioned on Macedonia's changing its name. Greece based its position on historical considerations, including the fact that its own northernmost province is also named Macedonia. Thus, the EC/EU foreign ministers declared at a meeting in May 1992 that the community was "willing to recognize Macedonia as a sovereign and independent state within its existing borders and under a name that can be accepted by all parties concerned."

On December 11, 1992, the UN Security Council authorized the dispatch of some 700 UN peacekeeping troops and military observers to the Macedonia–Serbia/Kosovo border in an effort to prevent the fighting in Bosnia and Herzegovina from spreading to the south; the United States committed an eventual 500-strong U.S. contingent to join the UN Preventive Deployment Force (UNPREDEP) in Macedonia. The force's mandate was renewed at six-month intervals thereafter, with its size increasing to 1,150 by November 1996.

Disagreements with Greece, including the nomenclature dispute, continued throughout the 1990s. After the Skopje government formally applied for UN membership on January 7, 1993, a partial Greek concession permitted the new state to join the UN in April as "The former Yugoslav Republic of Macedonia." Under the compromise, a definitive name as well as a related dispute over the use of Alexander the Great's Star of Vergina symbol on the Macedonian flag would have to be negotiated.

Strains with Greece were aggravated by the return to power of a socialist government in Athens in October 1993. Greek Prime Minister Andreas Papandreou was incensed by the decision of the leading EU states in December to recognize Macedonia, and on February 16, 1994, after Washington had extended recognition, Athens imposed a partial trade embargo on Macedonia, cutting the landlocked republic off from the northern Greek port of Salonika (Thessaloniki), its main import-export channel, for all goods except food and medicine.

UN and U.S. mediation brought Macedonia's dispute with Greece to partial resolution on September 13, 1995, when the respective foreign ministers initialed an agreement in New York covering border definition, revision of the Macedonian constitution to exclude any hint of territorial claims, and a new Macedonian flag. Following ratification by the Macedonian Assembly, the accord was formally signed in Skopje on October 15, whereupon Greece lifted its trade embargo. In light of the accommodation with Greece, Macedonia was admitted to full membership in the Organization for Security and Cooperation in Europe (OSCE) on October 12, 1995, and to the Council of Europe a week later. Despite the 1995 agreement, the Greek government has continued to strongly oppose the name "Republic of Macedonia."

Moves by the Skopje government to counter a developing Belgrade-Athens axis on Balkan matters included the cultivation of relations with Bulgaria, which had recognized Macedonia in January 1992, and with Turkey. Relations with Bulgaria were complicated by the widespread view in Bulgaria that Macedonians are really Bulgarians (and their language a variant of Bulgarian); while Bulgaria had recognized Macedonia, it had not recognized Macedonian nationality. Although several bilateral accords have been signed, extending to Bulgaria's provision of military aid for the Macedonian army, the Bulgarian government continues to deny aspects of ethnic Macedonian identity, language, and history. (See the 2013 *Handbook* for details.) This was underscored on July 24, 2006, when Bulgarian Minister of Foreign Affairs Ivailo Kalfin noted that "aggression towards the Bulgarian nation or history on behalf of the Macedonian authorities" might limit Bulgaria's support for Macedonian membership in the EU following its own accession on January 1, 2007.

The Belgrade–Athens axis and Serb claims on Macedonian territory militated against a natural alignment between the Macedonians and the Serbs, despite widespread sympathy within Macedonia for Serbia in the Yugoslav conflicts. The NATO bombing campaign launched against Yugoslavia in March–June 1999 precipitated the temporary flight of more than 250,000 ethnic Albanians into Macedonia from Kosovo. Most ethnic Macedonians, concerned over the broader regional implications of greater autonomy for the Albanian Kosovars, reportedly opposed the NATO action, while ethnic Albanians in Macedonia called upon the government to provide their confreres with massive assistance. In addition, some ethnic Albanians in Macedonia indicated they might join the KLA in combating Serbian forces, raising the specter of a spillover of the conflict into Macedonia. However, the DPA/PDSh's Xhaferi successfully appealed for calm among ethnic Albanians in Macedonia, while the government dutifully accepted the temporary deployment of some 12,000 NATO forces in Macedonia as part of the peacekeeping force proposed for Kosovo.

In view of the Kosovo conflict, most UN members had wanted UNPREDEP to continue to function, but China vetoed a further extension of the mission beyond February 28, 1999. The decision appeared directly related, despite Beijing's denials, to Skopje's establishment of relations with Taiwan in January, seeking to facilitate foreign investment and aid from the latter. The action caused China to sever ties to Macedonia. Skopje renewed diplomatic ties with Beijing on June 18, 2001, as a consequence of which Taiwan immediately broke relations with Macedonia.

In early 2001 Macedonia indicated that it would no longer pursue new diplomatic ties to countries that refused to recognize the country's designation as the "Republic of Macedonia." (The United States officially recognized Macedonia by its constitutional name, the Republic of Macedonia, in 2004.) Meanwhile, negotiations with Athens over the name issue continued, even while economic ties between the neighbors moved forward. In November 1999, for example, Greece and Macedonia concluded an agreement on construction of a $90 million oil pipeline between Thessaloniki and Skopje, while in April 2000 the National Bank of Greece was one of three foreign investors to purchase Macedonia's largest bank from the government. In May 2002 the Greek and Macedonian defense ministers concluded a military cooperation agreement. (Military ties with the West were subsequently further strengthened by Macedonia's contribution of 40 soldiers to the U.S.-led force in Iraq and 140 troops to the NATO mission in Afghanistan.)

Macedonia formally submitted its application for EU membership in 2004. EU concern was raised when the OSCE criticized the conduct of the March 2005 local elections, but the European Commission deemed Macedonia a "worthy candidate" in November, and the EU summit granted official candidate status in December. However, substantive negotiations for admission were delayed due to the dispute between Greece and Macedonia over the latter's name. In December 2006 the name dispute was exacerbated when Skopje airport was named "Aleksandar Makedonski Airport," resulting in protests from the Greek government and a rebuke from the EU.

During 2000–2007 more than 75,000 Macedonian citizens applied for Bulgarian passports (including former prime minister Ljubčo Georgievski, who was granted Bulgarian citizenship). As a result, accusations arose in Macedonia that the Bulgarian government was attempting an assimilation policy that would lead to Macedonia's "suicide."

The unilateral declaration of independence by Kosovo in February 2008 and subsequent recognition by the United States and majority of EU members were met with caution in Macedonia, but on October 9, 2008, Macedonia formally recognized Kosovo's independence.

The name dispute with Greece took center stage once more in April 2008, when Macedonia's bid to join NATO was formally vetoed by Greece pending the resolution of the issue. The Greek government warned that it would similarly oppose any EU application by Macedonia while the question remained open. The resulting public anger among ethnic Macedonians was widely credited by domestic media as one factor in the VMRO-DPMNE's electoral victory in 2008. (Prime Minister Gruevski had promised not to "trade off" changing the state's name for NATO and EU admission.)

In November 2008 Macedonia filed a complaint with the International Court of Justice arguing that Greek actions to block Macedonian membership in the EU and NATO were contrary to the 1995 interim agreement between the two countries (the court found in Macedonia's favor in December 2011, but did not impose penalties). Tensions were increased further by the Gruevski government's decision to name the country's north-south highway after Alexander the Great and to name the main soccer stadium in Skopje after Phillip II of Macedonia.

The domestic media and Albanian political leaders reported rising ethnic tensions in 2009, in part stemming from divisions along ethnic lines regarding the continuing dispute with Greece, which was seen as hindering Macedonia's chances to join the EU and NATO. On October 14, 2009, the European Commission recommended that membership negotiations be opened with Macedonia, while urging Gruevski's government to resolve the name issue with Greece.

Negotiations between Macedonia and Greece continued in 2010 over the potential compromise name of "Republic of Northern Macedonia." On February 27, 2011, Foreign Minister Antonio MILOSOSKI announced that Macedonia would be willing to open negotiations that the name be resolved as "Republic of Macedonia (Skopje)," as suggested by UN mediators, but only if approved by a general referendum.

While resolving the naming issue would aid Macedonia's accession to the EU, the European Commission warned that reforms in the judiciary and public administration, greater media freedom, and anticorruption efforts all require additional progress.

In April 2012 NATO reiterated that Macedonian membership could only come with a solution to the name issue.

Little progress was reported on resolving the dispute, and actions by both sides continued to keep tensions high. In May 2012 the Macedonian government unveiled a 42-foot (13-meter) statue of Philip II, father of Alexander the Great, in Skopje; in June Greek customs officials placed FYROM stickers on the license plates of Macedonian- registered cars crossing the border, obscuring the abbreviation MK (for Macedonia).

Macedonia closed its border with Greece in January 2016 in an effort to staunch the flow of migrants into the EU. The EU provided 80 police officers to help secure the border. By the end of February, Macedonia reported that it has prevented more than 83,000 refugees from entering the EU.

In July 2016 Macedonia signed a bilateral extradition agreement with Italy. At the time, Macedonia was pursuing extradition accords with ten other countries.

Current issues. The name conflict was complicated by the unveiling in February 2010 of the controversial "Skopje 2014" town plan, which called for rebuilding the city center. Ethnic Albanian leaders protested the proposed incorporation of an Orthodox cathedral but not a mosque in the project; opposition leaders criticized the estimated cost (200 million euros); and the Greek government objected to the proposed centerpiece, a statue of Alexander the Great that would stand roughly 72 feet (22 meters) tall.

In April 2010 Greece suggested its most recent compromise name, "Northern Macedonia," which Gruevski rejected. Meanwhile, the Greek government continued to insist it would approve Macedonia's accession to the EU and NATO only after the name dispute is resolved.

A series of scandals emerged in September 2010 concerning the lustration process, intended to provide information on secret agents and informers of the Yugoslav-era security services. Among other things, leaders of the opposition charged the VMRO-DPMNE with using the Lustration Commission as a means of harassing political rivals.

Criticism was raised in 2011 by domestic journalists and by international groups that the Gruevski government had acted to restrict or silence critical media outlets. In January 2011 the government acted to freeze the accounts of several media outlets due to claims of overdue taxes, including A1 television, the largest private broadcaster in the country. On July 3 three daily newspapers were closed on similar allegations of overdue taxes.

In 2012 tensions were raised by ethnic clashes following the killing of two ethnic Albanians by an off-duty police officer in February and the shooting of five ethnic Macedonian fishermen in April. In September the DUI/BDI blocked a bill providing benefits for families of deceased soldiers and veterans of the 2001 conflict unless these were extended to the NLA. As the year drew to a close, politicians were struggling to agree on a budget for 2013, leading to street protests and the ejection from the Assembly of SDSM members for brawling in the chamber. In response, the SDSM boycotted the Assembly into March 2013 and threatened to also boycott upcoming local elections. The boycott, among other issues, was cited by the EU enlargement commissioner as a factor in the decision to postpone negotiations over Macedonia's candidacy. The February appointment of Talat XHAFERI, an ethnic Albanian commander in the NLA during the 2001 fighting, as minister of defense triggered a series of ethnic riot. On July 1, 2013, former prime minister Bučkovski was sentenced to three years in jail for corruption, stemming from a 2001 case involving the procurement of spare parts for tanks during his tenure as minister of defense. Leaders of the VMRO-DPMNE and DUI/BDI publicly clashed in July 2013 over the continued failure to obtain a start date for accession negotiations with the EU. Lack of progress on the name dispute was reportedly linked to Macedonia's failure to advance its EU accession status, leading Gruevski to suggest bilateral talks with Greece in July.

Following the April 2014 election, parties within the SDSM coalition rejected the results and accused the VMRO-DPMNE of fraud. On May 28 all but one of the 33 elected parliamentarians from the SDSM coalition tendered their resignations and boycotted parliament. In June SDSM president Zoran ZAEV set demands for the government to meet before the opposition would return, including the formation of a caretaker government and a series of electoral reforms. The SDSM and VMRO-DPMNE had begun talks to resolve the issue in June.

In June 2014 six ethnic Albanians, accused of "terrorism" and the April 2012 killings of ethnic Macedonian fishermen, were found guilty and sentenced to life imprisonment. The sentencing was met with protests by ethnic Albanians in several towns, including violent protests in Skopje and Tetovo in early July.

In April 2016 President Ivanov pardoned 56 individuals involved in the previous year's wiretapping scandal. This decision sparked protests across the country. The demonstrations were led by the civil movement "I Protest" (*Protestiram*), and targeted government facilities. Protests continued into June and sparked parallel demonstrations by the SDSM.

POLITICAL PARTIES

For four and a half decades after World War II, the only authorized political party in Yugoslavia was the Communist Party, which was redesignated in 1952 as the **League of Communists of Yugoslavia** (in Serbo-Croatian, *Savez Kumunista Jugoslavija*—SKJ). In 1989 non-Communist groups began to emerge in the republics, and in early 1990 the SKJ approved the introduction of a multiparty system, thereby triggering its own demise. In Macedonia the party's local branch, the **League of Communists of Macedonia** (*Sojuz na Komunistite na Makedonija*—SKM), had been succeeded by the SKM-PDP in 1989 (see SDSM, below).

Nearly three dozen parties offered candidates in each legislative election from 1998 to 2014, on their own, in coalitions, or both.

Government and Government-Supportive Parties:

Coalition Internal Macedonian Revolutionary Organization–Democratic Party for Macedonian National Unity (*Koalicija Vnatrešno Makedonska Revolucionerna Organizacija–Demokratska Partija za Makedonsko Nacionalno Edinstvo—Koalicija* VMRO-DPMNE). A continuation of the 2011 coalition of the same name, which was in turn a continuation of the **Coalition for a Better Macedonia** (*Koalicija za Podobra Makedonija*—KzPM), a 19-party electoral list by that name established for the 2008 legislative election. The KzPM was, in turn, the continuation of the 2006 VMRO-DPMNE–led "National Unity" coalition.

The 2014 coalition included a number of small ethnic parties, many of which had been part of the 2008 and 2011 coalitions but previously had supported the opposition in 2006. Their joining the KzPM in 2008 reflected Prime Minister Gruevski's interest in reforming the parliament by adding dedicated seats for ethnic minorities.

The coalition-won 61 seats with almost 43 percent of the vote in the April 2014 legislative elections.

Smaller coalition members in 2014 that were allocated one seat each in parliament included the **Democratic Party of Turks in Macedonia** (*Partija za Dviženje na Turcite vo Makedonija*—PDTM), the **Democratic Party of Serbs in Macedonia** (*Demokratska Partija na Srbite vo Makedonija*—DPSM), the **Union of Roma in Macedonia** (*Sojuz na Romite na Makedonija*—SRM), and the **Party for Democratic Action of Macedonia** (*Stranka na Demokratska Akcija na Makedonija*—SDA). Coalition members that did not receive representation included the **United Party for Emancipation** (*Obedineta Partija za Emancipacija*—OPE), the **Party of Justice** (*Partija na Pravata*), the **Party for Integration of the Roma** (*Partija za Integracija na Romite*—PIR), the **Democratic Party of the Bosniaks** (*Bošnjačka Demokratska Partija*—BDP), the **People's Movement of Macedonia** (*Narodno Dviženje za Makedonija*—NDM), the **New Liberal Party** (*Nova Liberalna Partija*—NLP), the **Party of Vlachs in Macedonia** (*Partija na Vlasite od Makedonija*—PVM), the **Democratic Forces of the Roma** (*Demokratski Sili na Romite*—DSR), the **Permanent Macedonian Radical Unification** (*Trajno Makedonsko Radikalno Obedinuvanje*—TMRO), the **Internal Macedonian Revolutionary Organization–Democratic Party** (*Vnatrešno Makedonska Revolucionerna Organizacija–Demokratska Partija*—VMRO-DP), the **Internal Macedonian Revolutionary Organization–United** (*Vnatrešno Makedonska Revolucionerna Organizacija–Demokratska Partija–Obedinena*—VMRO-Ob), the **Macedonian Alliance** (*Makedonska Alijansa*—MA), the **Internal Macedonian Revolutionary Organization–Macedonian** (*Vnatrešno Makedonska Revolucionerna Organizacija-Macedonska*—VMRO-*Makedonska*), and the **Homeland Macedonian Organization for Radical Reconstruction–Vardar–Egej–Pirin** (*Tatkovinska Makedonska Organizacija na Radikalna Obnova–Vardar–Egej–Pirin*—TMORO-VEP).

Internal Macedonian Revolutionary Organization–Democratic Party for Macedonian National Unity (*Vnatrešno Makedonska Revolucionerna Organizacija–Demokratska Partija za Makedonsko Nacionalno Edinstvo*—VMRO-DPMNE). The VMRO is named after a historic group (founded in 1893) that fought for independence from the Ottoman Empire.

The VMRO-DPMNE, with significant support within the ethnic Macedonian population, strongly endorsed a revival of Macedonian cultural identity, its nationalistic stance being broadly perceived as anti-Albanian and right-wing, despite the group's description of itself as representing the "democratic center." The party won a plurality of 39 seats in the 1990 Assembly, subsequently serving as the main opposition to the Communist-led government. The VMRO-DPMNE's presidential candidate in 1994, Ljubčo Georgievski, gained 21.6 percent of the vote against the SDSM's Kiro Gligorov. However, the VMRO-DPMNE boycotted the second round of the 1994 legislative balloting, alleging fraud in the first round, in which it had been credited with no seats.

The VMRO-DPMNE competed for many of the single-member district seats in the 1998 legislative balloting in an alliance with the DA called "For Changes." It emerged from that balloting with 49 seats, having led all parties in the proportional contest with 28.1 percent of the vote. By that time, the VMRO-DPMNE appeared to have substantially moderated its platform, presenting itself as dedicated to "reconciliation and progress." Nevertheless, it was still a surprise when Georgievski invited the DPA, a hard-line ethnic Albanian grouping, to join his new government.

The VMRO-DPMNE presidential candidate, Boris Trajkovski, won the 1999 election over the SDSM candidate, taking 52.9 percent of the vote in second-round balloting on November 14. In the September–October 2000 local elections, a VMRO-DPMNE/DA alliance won the majority of mayoralties.

The government's legislative majority was briefly threatened in November 2000 when the DA left the governing coalition, but Georgievski quickly announced the inclusion of the LPM, which, with added independent support, permitted the administration to remain in power.

The party did poorly in the 2002 legislative elections, winning less than 25 percent of the vote. The poor showing, and the rise of Nikola Gruevski to leadership of the party, resulted in July 2004 in supporters of Georgievski leaving the VMRO-DPMNE to form the VMRO-NP (below) and others to form the short-lived **Democratic Republican Union for Macedonia** (*Demokratski Republički Sojuz za Makedonija*—DRUM).

The split by much of the party's conservative wing effectively moved the VMRO-DPMNE closer to the political center. The VMRO-DPMNE led a coalition with some 13 other (mostly smaller) parties for the 2006 Assembly balloting, winning 38 seats (out of a total of 45 for the coalition). Success has allowed the VMRO-DPMNE to subsequently absorb eight smaller political parties, including the **League for Democracy** (*Liga za Demokratija*), the **Internal Macedonian Revolutionary Organization–True Macedonian Reform Option** (*Vnatrešno-Makedonska Revolucionerna Organizacija–Vistinska Makedonska Reformska Opcija*—VMRO-VMRO), the DRUM, and the **Agricultural People's Party of Macedonia** (*Zemjodelska Narodna Partija na Makedonia*—ZNPM).

Following the 2006 elections, the VMRO-DPMNE's reform agenda was stymied by opposition in parliament. As a result, in April 2008 it led government parties in calling for early elections.

Following the 2011 election, VMRO-DPMNE received 47 seats from the coalition's total and continued to lead the ruling government. In early elections in April 2014, the VMRO-DPMNE strengthened its position, having received 52 seats as part of a coalition and forming a slightly reshuffled government with the DUI/BDI.

In January 2016 Emil DIMITRIEV was appointed acting prime minister.

Leaders: Nikola GRUEVSKI (President of the Party), Gjorge IVANOV (President of the Republic), Emil DIMITRIEV (Acting Prime Minister and General Secretary), Trajko SLAVESKI, Gordana JANKULOVSKA.

Socialist Party of Macedonia (*Socijalistička Partija na Makedonija*—SPM). Formerly called the **Socialist League–Socialist Party of Macedonia** (*Socijalistički Sojuz–Socijalistička Partija na Makedonija*—SS-SPM), the SPM is the successor to the local branch of the former **Socialist League of the Working People of Yugoslavia** (in Serbo-Croatian, *Socijalistički Savez Radnog Narodna Jugoslavija*—SSRNJ).

In the wake of the collapse of the SM in 1996, the SPM contested the proportional seats and some of the single-member district seats in the 1998 Assembly balloting in coalition with the **Party for the Total Emancipation of Roma in Macedonia** (*Partija za Celosna Emancipacija na Romite vo Makedonija*—PCERM) and the **Democratic Progressive Party of the Roma in Macedonia** (*Demokratska Progresivna Partija na Romite od Makedonija*—DPPRM) as well as some ethnic parties. The SPM won one constituency seat, but the coalition, the Movement for Cultural Tolerance and Civic Cooperation, won only 4.7 percent of the proportional vote and therefore no proportional seats.

The SPM retained its single seat in the 2002 Assembly poll. Subsequently, in December 2003, it announced the formation of a coalition called the Third Way that also included the DA and the Democratic Union (below). The SPM joined the VMRO-DPMNE's electoral bloc in 2006, winning three seats in parliament and entering the coalition government. It retained these seats in 2011 and 2014. The SPM retained one portfolio in the 2015 and 2016 unity governments.

Leaders: Ljubisav IVANOV-DZINGO (President), Ljupčo DIMOVSKI (General Secretary).

Democratic Union (*Demokratski Sojuz*—DS). The DS was founded on March 25, 2000, by former minister of the interior Pavle Trajanov. Its program emphasizes the rule of law, the territorial integrity of Macedonia, and an "effective campaign against organized crime, corruption, and drugs." It entered into a coalition with the Socialist Party of Macedonia in 2005 and then joined the SPM in coalition with the VMRO-DPMNE. In the 2011 elections it took one seat in parliament as part of the coalition, and retained this seat in 2014.

Leader: Pavle TRAJANOV (President).

Democratic Renewal of Macedonia (*Demokratcka Obnova na Makedonija*—DOM). The DOM was founded in November 2005 by former LDP member Liljana Popovska. The DOM's platform calls for "sustainable development" and the promotion of tourism and environmental protection, and the party self-identifies as a Green party. In the 2011 elections it took one seat in parliament as part of the coalition, and retained this seat in 2014.

Leader: Liljana POPOVSKA (President).

Democratic Union for Integration (*Demokratska Unija za Integracija/Bashkimit Demokratik për Integrim*—DUI/BDI). The DUI/BDI was formed in June 2002 by Ali Ahmeti, the former head of the Albanian National Liberation Army—NLA (*Ushtrisë Çlirimtare Kombëtare*—UÇK), which had been dissolved in late September 2001 as a consequence of the August peace accord with the government. The principal focus of the DUI/BDI, according to its chair, was the full implementation of the provisions of the Ohrid accords.

In 2003 the BUI/BDI merged with the **National Democratic Party** (*Nacionala Demokratska Partija/Partisë Demokratike Kombëtar*—NDP/PDK), another Albanian party led by Kastriot HAXHIREXHA and comprising former members of the NLA. However, some NDP/PDK members denounced Haxhirexha for having abandoned the "pursuit of federalism." Claiming "no common interest" with the DUI/BDI, the rump NDP/PDK elected new leaders, including Basri HALITI as chair, with the split reportedly persisting until at least 2006. (See the entry in the 2011 *Handbook* for details.)

In the 2006 parliamentary elections the DUI/BDI led an electoral bloc that included the PDP/PPD and the **Democratic League of Bosnians** (*Demokratska Liga na Bošnjacite/Demokratski Savez Bošnjaka*—DLB/DSB). The DUI/BDI won 14 seats, establishing it as the strongest ethnic Albanian party in parliament. Although the VMRO-DPMNE initially approached it with regards to joining the government, it ultimately chose DPA/PDSh as a partner. The DUI/BDI responded with protests, roadblocks, and mass rallies.

Claiming that the government was failing to uphold the Ohrid accords, the DUI/BDI boycotted parliament from January 26 through August 2007, precipitating a political crisis. In May 2007 Menduh Thaçi threatened to remove the DPA/PDSh from the government coalition if the VMRO-DPMNE reached a political agreement with the DUI/BDI, reflecting continued rivalry and conflict between ethnic Albanian political parties. In July 2007 Fazli VELIU, a member of the DUI parliamentary group and one of the founders of the National Liberation Army, suggested that renewed military struggle was a possibility if Kosovo failed to receive independence and ethnic Albanians failed to receive equality within Macedonia. The DUI/BDI leadership subsequently criticized Veliu's statement that "thousands" of ethnic Albanians in Macedonia were ready to take up arms to defend Kosovo.

In the 2008 Assembly election the party took 18 parliamentary seats, strengthening its position as the leading ethnic Albanian party. After negotiations with both the DPA/PDSh and DUI/BDI, the VMRO-DPMNE (which possessed sufficient legislative strength to rule alone) brought the latter into the ruling coalition government, even though previous disagreements between the two parties (particularly over the recognition of Kosovo) remained unresolved. In response to reports of rising ethnic Albanian frustration in 2009, the DUI/BDI urged its coalition partners in the ruling government to find a compromise with Greece over the name dispute by the end of the year. The DUI/BDI still defended the Ohrid Agreement as resolving key minority demands, though the party suggested that implementation might be hastened.

The DUI/BDI's Agron Buxhaku won 7.5 percent of the vote in the first round of the 2009 presidential poll.

In October 2010 allegations were made based on files reportedly leaked from the Lustration Commission that several leading DUI/BDI members had served as informers or agents for the Yugoslav-era security services.

In the June 2011 election the DUI/BDI led a coalition with the DLB/DSB. The coalition won 10.2 percent of the vote and 15 seats, of which the DUI/BDI received 14 and the DLB/DSB received 1.

The DUI/BDI precipitated early elections in 2014 after it failed to reach an accord with the VMRO-DPMNE for a joint presidential candidate. In the April 2014 legislative balloting the DUI/BDI won 13.7 percent of the vote and 19 seats. Despite the recent disputes with the VMRO-DPMNE and the DUI/BDI's encouragement of ethnic Albanians to boycott the 2014 presidential elections, the two parties agreed to a reformed coalition government. The DUI/BDI retained two deputy prime minister positions along with five other portfolios in the January coalition government.

Leaders: Ali AHMETI (Chair), Agron BUXHAKU (2009 presidential candidate), Abdilaqim ADEMI (Secretary General).

Other Parliamentary Parties:

Social Democratic Union of Macedonia Coalition (*Socijaldemokratski Sojuz na Makedonija Koalicija*—SDSM *Koalicija*). A continuation of the 2011 alliance of the same name, which in turn had been a continuation of the 2008 **Sun–Coalition for Europe** (*Sonce–Koalicija za Evropa*) and the 2002 and 2006 **Coalition for Macedonia Together** (*Koalicija Za Makedonija Zaedno*—*Koalicija* ZMZ). The 2014 formation, however, saw the departure of the STLS, PSD, and SNSM, all of which joined the Coalition GROM (see below). The LDP returned to the coalition after having run independently in 2011. It had been an integral part of the coalition in the 2002, 2006, and 2008 elections.

In addition to the parties below, the SDSM coalition included one smaller party that gained one seat after the coalition's seats were distributed: the **Party for Movement of the Turks in Macedonia** (*Partija za Dvizhenje na Turtsite vo Makedonija*—PDTM). Smaller parties that did not gain representation included the **Party for the Total Emancipation of Roma in Macedonia** (*Partija za Celosna Emancipacija na Romite vo Makedonija*—PCERM), the **Democratic Union of Vlachs from Macedonia** (*Demokratski Sojuz na Vlasite ot Makedonija*—DSVM), **the Serbian Party in Macedonia** (*Srubska partija v Makedonija*—SPvM), and the **Sandzak League** (*Sanjačka Liga*—SL).

The coalition won 25.3 percent of the popular vote and 34 seats in the 2014 Assembly balloting, a decline from the 2011 election.

Social Democratic Union of Macedonia (*Socijaldemokratski Sojuz na Makedonija*—SDSM). The SDSM was the name adopted in 1991 by the League of Communists of Macedonia–Party of Democratic Change (*Sojuz na Komunistite na Makedonija–Partija za Demokratska Preobrazba*—SKM-PDP), which had been launched in 1989 as successor to the SKM. Although the SKM-PDP had run second to the VMRO-DPMNE in the 1990 legislative poll, its nominee, Kiro Gligorov, was subsequently designated president of the republican presidency.

The SDSM was the largest component of the Union of Macedonia (*Sojuz na Makedonija*—SM), an electoral alliance formed for the 1994 presidential and legislative balloting by the SDSM, SPM, and LPM, the three non-Albanian parties of the post-1992 government. The SM supported the SDSM's Gligorov in his successful bid for a second presidential term in 1994, and the SM secured 95 seats (58 for the SDSM) in the controversial concurrent legislative poll, with the SDSM's Branko CRVENKOVSKI remaining as prime minister of the subsequent SM-led government. However, friction developed within the SM, leading to the departure of the LPM from the government in a February 1996 reshuffle. The SM was subsequently described as having collapsed, and minimal cooperation between the SDSM and the SPM was reported in the 1998 legislative elections, from which the SDSM emerged with only 27 seats. (One of the seats credited to the SDSM was won in coalition with the Social Democratic Party of Macedonia [SDPM], which had won a seat in 1994.)

In the 1999 presidential contest the SDSM candidate, former Assembly speaker Tito Petkovski, finished first in the first round, with 32.7 percent of the vote, but lost in the November runoff to the governing coalition's candidate. In May 2000 the SDSM and the LDP concluded a cooperation agreement for the upcoming local elections and the next general election, soon joined by the League for Democracy. An SDSM-led rally in Skopje in mid-May attracted 40,000 people, who heard Crvenkovski charge the government with corruption, failure to raise the standard of living, and an inability to fulfill its election promises.

In 2004 Crvenkovski was elected president of the republic as the candidate of the *Koalicija* ZMZ. The coalition was renewed for the 2006 Assembly election, at which the SDSM won 23 of the coalition's 32 seats. The defeat resulted in an internal shake-up within the party, with party leader Vlado Bučkovski being removed after losing a no-confidence vote and with Crvenkovski sidelined within the party. In the November 2006 party elections Radmila Sekerinska became the first female leader of a major Macedonian political party since independence.

Following the announcement in April 2008 of early elections, the SDSM organized the *Sonce* coalition, pledging to achieve NATO membership and begin the first steps in EU accession talks by the end of the year. *Sonce*'s poor performance in the June 2008 elections led Sekerinska (and other senior party members) to announce their resignations from their posts in July. Although a temporary party leadership was appointed, Crvenkovski's role was strengthened and he resumed leadership of the party after finishing his presidential term in May 2009.

In the June 2011 election, the SDSM received 29 seats from the coalition's total.

Despite an electoral alliance with the NSDP, VMRO-NP, OM, and LDP in the 2013 local elections, SDSM won only 4 of 80 municipal mayoral races. Crvenkovski resigned as party president, with Zoran ZAEV elected at a party congress on June 2, 2013.

For the April 2014 early elections the SDSM campaigned that "new people with new ideas" were needed to realize Macedonia's accession to EU and NATO.

The SDSM received 27 seats from the coalition's total. Despite the defeat, a post-election party congress in May reconfirmed Zaev as party president. The SDSM launched a political crisis in 2015 by boycotting parliament and then releasing transcripts of illicit wire-tapping. After international mediation, the SDSM agreed to join the unity government, although its two ministers did not take office until September 2016.

Leaders: Zoran ZAEV (President), Branko CRVENKOVSKI (Former President of the Republic), Radmila ŠEKERINSKA (Deputy President), Stevo PENDAROVSKI (2014 presidential candidate), Oliver SPASOVSKI (General Secretary).

New Social Democratic Party (*Nova Socijal Demokratsčka Partija*—NSDP). The NSDP was formed in November 2005 by former members of the SDSM who sought a more centrist social democratic party. Its party platform is broadly pro-Western and technocratic, stressing Macedonian membership in the EU, improved relations with the United States, investment in "information and communication technology," and the need for economic development. In the 2006 legislative elections the party won seven seats and was subsequently invited to join the government, assuming the ministries of both defense and the economy. In 2008 the party joined the opposition prior to the elections, taking three seats in parliament. In the 2011 Assembly election, the party received four seats from the coalition's total; in 2014 the party received three.

Leader: Tito PETKOVSKI (President).

Liberal-Democratic Party (*Liberalno-Demokratska Partija*—LDP). The centrist LDP was formed in January 1997 by what proved to be a temporary merger of the LPM (below) and the **Democratic Party of Macedonia** (*Demokratska Partija Makedonija*—DPM). The DPM had been registered in July 1993 under the leadership of a Communist-era prime minister but unexpectedly failed to have much impact in the 1994 balloting. When the DPM and LPM merged as the LDP, the DPM's Petar Gošev became leader of the new formation.

The LDP won only four seats in the 1998 legislative poll, securing 7 percent in the proportional balloting; Gošev resigned as chair in January 1999 in view of that poor electoral performance. In 2000 the LPM was reestablished as a separate party, taking with it three of the four LDP parliamentary deputies. In May 2000 the LDP joined the SDSM in an electoral alliance for the September local elections and the 2002 Assembly election.

The LDP's participation in the *Koalicija* ZKM contributed to the coalition's success in the 2004 presidential election. In 2006 the party won five seats in parliament. The coalition's poor showing led, in 2007, to party leader Risto PENOV's resignation, the election of Jovan MANASIEVSKI as party president, and a decision for the party to leave the *Koalicija* ZKM, positioning the party for an independent bid in the expected 2010 elections. The 2008 early elections, however, saw the party remain in coalition with its previous partners. It received four seats in parliament.

The LDP's Nano Ruzin won 4.1 percent of the vote in the first round of the 2009 presidential balloting.

After the party failed to secure any seats in the 2011 elections, Manasievski resigned as party leader.

Following the April 2014 election, the LDP received three of the coalition's seats.

Leaders: Goran MILEVSKI (President), Petar GOŠEV.

United for Macedonia (*Obedineti za Makedonija*—OM). The conservative OM was founded in May 2009 by Ljube BOŠKOSKI. A former VMRO-DPMNE figure and interior minister, Boškoski was tried by the International Criminal Tribunal for the former Yugoslavia for possible involvement as minister in the attacks on ethnic Albanians during the 2001 conflict. He was acquitted on all charges and returned to found the OM in May 2009.

In June 2011, one day after the Assembly election, Boškoski was arrested, allegedly for improper campaign financing. OM has charged that the accused the allegations were politically motivated by a ruling government seeking to silence a conservative rival. In November 2011 Boškoski was sentenced to seven years in prison, the sentence later reduced on appeal to five years.

Leader: Ljube BOŠKOSKI.

Democratic Party of Albanians (*Demokratska Partija na Albancite/Partia Demokratike Shqiptare*—DPA/PDSh). The DPA/PDSh was formed in mid-1997 by the merger of the Party for **Democratic Prosperity of Albanians in Macedonia** (*Partija za Demokratski Prosperitet na Albancite vo Makedonija*—PDPA) and the **People's Democratic Party** (*Narodna Demokratska Partija*—NDP). The NDP was an ethnic Albanian grouping that resulted from a split between the moderate majority of the ethnic Albanian Party for Democratic Prosperity and an antigovernment minority, led by Ilijaz HALIMI, at a congress of the parent party in February 1994. The PDPA had been launched in April 1995 as another breakaway from the PDP by a group opposed to the parent party's participation in the government coalition. Its leader was Arben Xhaferi, a spokesperson for the militant Albanian population who had spent many years in the separatist movement in Kosovo before establishing a base in Tetovo in western Macedonia and being elected as an independent to the Macedonian legislature. Officially referenced as the PDPA/NDP in the 1998 legislative election (where the party entered a partial alliance with the PDP and won 11 legislative seats), the DPA/PDSh title gained official sanction after the party joined the VMRO-DPMNE-led coalition government. However, the DPA/PDSh was not officially registered under that name until July 2002.

Following its entrance into the government, the DPA/PDSh appeared to moderate its course, although Deputy Chair Menduh Thaçi remained one of the more hard-line advocates for Albanian rights. In the 1999 presidential election the party's candidate, Muharem NEXHIPI, finished fourth, with 14.8 percent of the vote; in the second round, the DPA/PDSh threw its support to the successful VMRO-DPMNE candidate. The DPA/PDSh won 7 seats in the 2002 Assembly poll, but from April 2005 through January 2006 the delegates boycotted parliamentary sessions in protest of "manipulated results" in the 2005 local elections. In the 2006 parliamentary elections the DPA/PDSh ran independently, winning 11 seats. After failing to reach an agreement with the DUI/BDI, the VMRO-DPMNE negotiated for the DPA/PDSh's entrance into the government.

There were reports during the 2008 Assembly election of violence between members of the DPA/PDSh and the DUI/BDI and of serious electoral irregularities in several districts with a majority of ethnic Albanians. The DPA/PDSh rejected the results of the second round of voting on June 15 but accepted the third round, while accusing the DUI/BDI of fostering division and violence within the Albanian community. Meanwhile, merger discussions with the PDP/PPD proved unsuccessful, although PDP/PPD leader Abduljhadi Vejseli and a significant faction of the PDP/PPD joined the DPA/PDSh (see PDP/PPD below for details).

The DPA/PDSh's Mirushe HOXHA won 3.1 percent of the vote in the first round of presidential balloting in 2009.

In the 2011 Assembly election, the DPA/PDSh won 5.9 percent of the popular vote and eight seats.

The DPA/PDSh's Ilijaz Halimi won 4.5 percent of the vote in the first round of presidential balloting in 2014 as the only ethnic Albanian candidate in the race.

In the 2014 Assembly election, the DPA/PDSh won 5.9 percent of the popular vote, securing seven seats.

Leaders: Menduh THAÇI (Chair); Ernad FEJZULLAHU, Miat SADIKU (Vice Presidents); Ilijaz HALIMI (2014 presidential candidate); Metin IZETI.

Coalition Citizen Option for Macedonia (*Koalicija Grajanska Opcija za Makedonija*—*Koaliciaja* GROM). Formed for the 2014 election, in addition to the parties below, the coalition included three small parties that had previously supported SDSM coalitions: the **Union of Tito's Left Forces** (*Sojuz na Titovi Levi Sili*—STLS), the **Party of Free Democrats** (*Partija na Slobodni Demokrati*—PSD), and the **Serbian Progressive Party in Macedonia** (*Srpska Napredna Stranka vo Makedonija*—SNSM). The coalition won 2.8 percent of the vote and a single seat in parliament, allocated to GROM.

Citizen Option for Macedonia (*Grajanska Opcija za Makedonija*—GROM). The acronym GROM forms the Macedonian word for "thunder." The party was founded in September 2013 by Stevce JAKIMOVSKI, a former vice president of the SDSM who had broken with the party over its initial decision to boycott the 2013 local elections. GROM's party platform calls for a consolidated and functional democracy, a strong middle class, and embracing the multi-ethnic character of the country. The GROM's Zoran POPOVSKI won 3.6 percent of the vote in the first round of presidential balloting in 2014, placing fourth.

Leaders: Stevce JAKIMOVSKI (Chair), Zoran POPOVSKI (2014 presidential candidate).

Liberal Party of Macedonia (*Liberalna Partija na Makedonija*—LPM). The LPM was organized initially as the **Alliance of Reform Forces of Macedonia** (*Sojuz na Reformskite Sili na Makedonija*—SRSM), an affiliate of the federal **Alliance of Yugoslav Reform Forces** (in Serbo-Croatian, *Savez Reformskih Snaga Jugoslavije*—SRSJ). In the 1990 balloting it was allied in some areas with the **Young Democratic and Progressive Party** (in Serbo-Croatian, *Mlas Demokratska Progresivna Partija*—MDPS), which it later absorbed, adopting the name **Reform Forces of Macedonia–Liberal Party** (*Reformskite Sili na Makedonija–Liberalna Partija*—RSM-LP) in 1992. Using the shorter LPM rubric, the party won 29 seats in the 1994 election as part of the Union of Macedonia (see under SDSM, above) and continued to be a component of the ruling coalition. However, growing friction with the dominant SDSM culminated in ejection of the LPM from the coalition in February 1996, whereupon party leader Stojan Andov resigned as speaker of the legislature and committed the LPM to vigorous opposition. A 1997 merger with the Democratic Party of Macedonia (DPM) to form the Liberal-Democratic Party (LDP) ended in 2000, when the LPM reemerged as a separate organization. In November 2000 the revived party joined the governing coalition led by the VMRO-DPMNE. The LPM participated in the electoral bloc led by the VMRO-DPMNE for the 2006 Assembly poll, winning two seats in parliament and subsequently participating in government. In 2008 it moved to join the opposition, stating dissatisfaction with the government's progress in obtaining NATO and EU membership. In the 2011 election, it received a single seat as part of the coalition.

Leader: Ivon VELIČKOVSKI (President).

National Democratic Renewal (*Nacionalna Demokratska Prerodba/Rilindja Demokratike Kombëtare*—NDP/RDK). The NDP/RDK was founded in March 2011 on a platform of Albanian minority rights. Its founder, Rufi OSMANI, had previously served a prison term for his role in the 1997 dispute over the flying of the Albanian flag in front of municipal buildings in the town of Gostivar.

In the June 2011 election, the NDR/RDK won 2.7 percent of the popular vote and two seats in parliament. In the April 2014 election, the party won 1.6 percent of the vote and secured one seat in parliament.

Leader: Rufi OSMANI (Chair).

Other Parties That Contested the 2014 Legislative Elections:

Internal Macedonian Revolutionary Organization–People's Party (*Vnatrešno Makedonska Revolucionerna Organizacija–Narodna Partija*—VMRO-NP). The VMRO-NP, a conservative party whose platform closely resembles the VMRO-DPMNE, was formed in Skopje in July 2004 by supporters of former VMRO-DPMNE chair and prime minister Ljubčo GEORGIEVSKI. In the 2006 parliamentary elections it won six seats, but three members of parliament subsequently left the party. Georgievski took Bulgarian citizenship in 2006, resigned as party president in 2007 (though retaining an honorary position as "party leader"), and subsequently entered Bulgarian politics as a mayoral candidate for Blagoevgrad. In May 2008 the state election commission revoked the party's candidate list, citing that the group missed submission deadlines. In the 2011 election, the party took 2.5 percent of the popular vote but failed to pass the threshold to gain representation.

In February 2012 party president Marjan DODEVSKI resigned and led a faction that joined the VMRO-DPMNE, with Georgievski taking over active leadership.

In the April 2014 election the party won 1.5 percent of the vote and again failed to pass the threshold to gain representation.

Leader: Ljubčo GEORGIEVSKI (President).

Party for a European Future (*Partija za Evropska Idnina*—PEI). The PEI, formed in March 2006 by Fijat CANOSKI, is a centrist party that advocates deeper integration with NATO and the EU. In 2006 and 2008 it won a single seat in parliament. Although it did not receive a cabinet position following the 2008 balloting, the PEI pledged legislative support for the government. It moved to the opposition prior to the 2011 election and received three seats, in mid-June forming its own independent opposition bloc.

In the 2014 election, the party won less than 1 percent of the vote and failed to pass the threshold to gain representation. In response to the poor showing, Canoski resigned as party leader on May 13.

Leader: Fijat CANOSKI.

The **Coalition for Positive Macedonia** (*Koalicija za Pozitvna Makeonija*—KPM). Formed by the **Alliance for Positive Macedonia** (*Alijansa za Pozitivna Makedonija*—APM), a party founded in March 2014 and led by Ljupčo Zikov. The coalition includes the **Party of Pensioners of the Republic of Macedonia** (*Partija na Penzionerite na Republika Makedonija*—PPRM) and the **Citizens of the Republic of Macedonia** (*Grajanite na Republika Makedonija*—GRM). The KPM won less than 1 percent of the popular vote, failing to pass the threshold and secure representation.

Leader: Ljupčo ZIKOV.

Party for Democratic Prosperity (*Partija za Demokratski Prosperite/Partia për Prosperitet Demokratik*—PDP/PPD). The PDP/PPD was one of the principal vehicles for supporting ethnic Albanian interests in Macedonia after its May 1990 launch. Subsequent to the 1990 election (in which it won 25 seats), it absorbed a smaller party with the same abbreviation, the **Popular Democratic Party of Ilijaz Halimi**.

The PDP/PPD was riven by splits between the progovernment moderates and antigovernment nationalists in February 1994 and April 1995 and the respective breakaway of the NDP and the PDPA (for both, see DPA, above). Having lost ground in the October–November 1994 Assembly balloting, the PDP/PPD continued as a government party.

The PDP/PPD contested the 1998 legislative balloting in partial coalition with the DPA/PDSh (PDPA/NDP), securing 14 seats. However, the PDP/PPD subsequently moved into opposition, while the DPA/PDSH joined the new VMRO-DPMNE–led cabinet. Following the poor showing of the party's 1999 presidential candidate, Muhamed HALILI, who finished sixth with 4.2 percent of the vote, the party leadership was replaced virtually en masse in April 2000, President Abdurahman HALITI giving way to Imer IMERI (Ymer YMERI). Although the party competed in the first round of the local elections in 2000, it pulled out of the second round, alleging major irregularities.

With the departure of the DA from the government in November 2000, the PDP/PPD entered unsuccessful talks with the DPA/PDSh and the VMRO-DPMNE to join the ruling government. (For more details, see the 2014 *Handbook.*) Early in 2001 speculation rose that the PDP/PPD and the DPA/PDSh might merge, but that was before the outbreak of hostilities between militant Albanians and the government. International pressure reportedly led the PDP/PPD to join the May 2001 national unity administration.

In May 2002 Haliti returned to the party presidency following Imeri's resignation for health reasons. The PDP/PPD won two seats in the 2002 Assembly poll.

In the 2006 legislative elections the party ran in an electoral bloc with the DUI/BDI, winning three seats. The DUI/BDI's conflict with the VMRO-DPMNE resulted in a boycott of parliament in 2007 by both the DUI/BDI and PDP/PPD. Fears that the PDP/PPD was becoming marginalized prompted it to break its coalition in May 2007. On June 12 the PDP/PPD formally entered the government, where it attempted to moderate relations between the VMRO-DPMNE and the DUI/BDI.

The PDP/PPD performed poorly in the June 2, 2008, legislative elections, taking less than 1 percent of the vote and no seats. Party leader Abduljhadi Vejseli consequently proposed a full merger with the DPA/PDSh, and PDP/PPD members were encouraged to vote for the DPA/PDSh in the revotes held on June 15 and June 29. However, the merger proposal provoked a backlash within the PDP/PPD that prompted Vejseli to leave the party and join the DPA/PDSh.

Sefedin HARUNI was appointed president of the PDP/PPD in August 2008 and confirmed at a party congress in December. In June 2009 Haruni joined other Albanian political figures (including Hisni SHAQIRI, a former prominent parliamentarian and current leader of the NDU/BDK, below) in calling for extensive constitutional changes to Macedonia beyond those laid out in the Ohrid Framework. Among other things, they proposed the creation of a "bi-national" state under a federal structure.

In the June 2011 election the erosion of support for the PDP/PDD continued, polling in 17th place out of 18 parties and coalitions. In 2012 Sefedin Haruni reportedly stepped down as chair of the party after the Lustration Commission had reported him to be an informer for the Yugoslav secret police before 1989.

In January 2014 the PDP/PDD was reestablished. For the April 2014 election the PDP submitted a candidate list for only one locality; the party won less than a tenth of a percent of the popular vote.

Leader: Abudladi VEJSELI.

Minor parties participating in the 2014 election include the political party **Dignity** (*Dostoinostvo*), led by Stojance ANGELOV; the **Party for Economic Changes 21** (*Partija za Ekonomski Promeni 21*—PEP 21), led by Biljana JOVANOVSKA; the **Social Democratic Party of Macedonia** (*Socijaldemokratska Partija na Makedonija*—SDPM), led by Branko JANVESKI; and the **Popular Movement for Macedonia** (*Narodno Dvizhenje na Makedonija*—NDM), led by Janko BACEV. None of these parties obtained even 1 percent of the total vote.

Other Parties That Contested the 2011 Legislative Elections:

New Democracy (*Nova Demokratija/Demokracia e Re*—ND/DR). The ND/DR was formed in September 2008 as a new party representing Albanian interests by Imer SELMANI, former vice president of the DPA/PDSh, and other DPA/PDSh members (including a number of legislators) who cited policy differences with the DPA/PDSh leadership for their defection. Selmani won 15 percent of the vote in the first round of the 2009 presidential election, finishing ahead of the candidates from rival ethnic Albanian parties. The ND/DR was subsequently reported to have five legislators within its membership. In the 2011 election the party took 1.8 percent of the vote, failing to pass the threshold to gain representation. Selmani subsequently resigned as party leader in June 2011 and was replaced by Kastriot Haxhirexha, a former leader of the NDP/PDK. In 2014 the ND/DR was reported to support the DUI/BDI's candidates, although the parties were not formally registered in a coalition.

Leader: Kastriot HAXHIREXHA.

Minor parties participating in the 2011 election include the **Democratic Union of Albanians** (*Demokratska Unija na Albancite/Bashkimi Demokratik Shqiptar*—DUA/BDSh), the **Party of United Democrats of Macedonia** (*Partija na Obedineti Demokrati na Makedonija*—PODEM), the **Social Democratic Union** (*Socialdemokratska Unija*—SDU), the **Democratic Right** (*Demokratska Desnica*—DD), the **National Democratic Union** (*Nacionalna Demokratska Unija/Bashkimi Demokratik Kombëtar*—NDU/BDK), and the **European Party of Macedonia** (*Evropska Partija na Makedonija*—EPM). None of these parties was able to obtain even 1 percent of the total vote.

LEGISLATURE

The present Macedonian **Assembly** (*Sobranje*) is a directly elected unicameral body of 123 members, elected for a four-year term through proportional representation from six electoral districts, each with 20 seats. In 2011, 3 seats were added to represent Macedonian citizens resident in Europe, North America, and Asia/Australia. Prior to 2002, 85 of the legislators were directly elected in two-round (if necessary) majoritarian balloting in single-member districts; the other 35 were elected on a nationwide proportional basis, with seats distributed to parties winning at least 5 percent of the national vote.

Following the early election of April 27, 2014, the seat distribution was as follows: Coalition VMRO-DPMNE, 61 (Internal Macedonian Revolutionary Organization–Democratic Party for Macedonian National Unity, 52; Socialist Party of Macedonia, 3; Democratic Union, 1; Democratic Party of Serbs in Macedonia, 1; Democratic Renewal of Macedonia, 1; Democratic Party of Turks in Macedonia, 1; Party of Democratic Action of Macedonia, 1; Union of Roma in Macedonia, 1); Coalition SDSM, 34 (Social Democratic Union of Macedonia, 27; New Social Democratic Party, 3; Liberal Democratic Party, 3; Movement of National Unity of Turks in Macedonia, 1); Democratic Union for Integration, 19; Democratic Party of Albanians, 7; Coalition Citizen Option for Macedonia, 1; and National Democratic Revival, 1.

Speaker: Trajko VELJANOSKI.

CABINET

[as of October 1, 2016]

Prime Minister	Emil Dimitriev (Acting) (VMRO-DPMNE)
Deputy Prime Minister (Economy)	Vladimir Peshevski (VMRO-DPMNE)
Deputy Prime Minister (European Affairs)	Fatmir Besimi (DUI/BDI)
Deputy Prime Minister (Ohrid Agreement Implementation)	Musa Xhaferri (DUI/BDI)

Ministers

Agriculture, Forestry, and Water Supply	Mihail Cvetkov (SPM)
Culture	Elizabeta Kančevska Milevska (VMRO-DPMNE) [f]
Defense	Zoran Jolevski (DUI/BDI)
Economy	Bekim Neziri (DUI/BDI)
Education and Science	Abdilaqim Ademi (DUI/BDI)
Environment and Physical Planning	Nurhan Izairi (DUI/BDI)
Finance	Kiril Minoski (ind.)
Foreign Affairs	Nikola Popovski VMRO-DPMNE)
Health	Nikola Todorov (VMRO-DPMNE)
Information Society	Marta Arsovska-Tomovska (VMRO-DPMNE) [f]
Internal Affairs	Oliver Spasovski (SDSM)
Justice	Adnan Jashari (DUI/BDI)
Labor and Social Policy	Frosina Remenski (SDSM) [f]
Local Self-Government	Lirim Shabani (DUI/BDI)
Transport and Communications	Vlado Misajlovski (VMRO-DPMNE)
Without Portfolio	Neždet Mustafa (OPE)
Without Portfolio	Vele Samak (ind.)
Without Portfolio	Bill Pavleski (ind.)
Without Portfolio	Jerry Naumoff (ind.)
Without Portfolio	Furkan Çako (ind.)
Without Portfolio	Visar Fida (DUI/BDI)
Without Portfolio	Goran Mickovski (ind.)

[f] = female

INTERGOVERNMENTAL REPRESENTATION

Ambassador to the U.S.: Vasko NAUMOVSKI.

U.S. Ambassador to Macedonia: Jess BAILEY.

Permanent Representative to the UN: Vasile ANDONOSKI.

IGO Memberships (Non-UN): CEUR, EBRD, ICC, OSCE, WTO.

For Further Reference:

Cowan, Jane, ed. *Macedonia: The Politics of Identity and Difference.* London: Pluto Press, 2000.

De Munck, Victor C., and Ljupcho Risteski. *Macedonia: The Political, Social Economic, and Cultural Foundations.* London: I. B. Taurus, 2013.

Shea, John. *Macedonia and Greece: The Struggle to Define a New Balkan Nation.* Jefferson, NC: McFarland, 1997; Reprint, 2008.

MADAGASCAR

Republic of Madagascar
Repoblikan'i Madagasikara (Malagasy)
République de Madagascar (French)

Political Status: Established as the Malagasy Republic within the French Community in 1958; became independent June 26, 1960; military regime established May 18, 1972; name of Democratic Republic of Madagascar and single-party system adopted in new constitution and Socialist Revolutionary Charter approved by national referendum on December 21, 1975; present name adopted in the new constitution of the Third Republic (codifying multiparty activity first authorized by presidential decree of March 1990) that was approved by national referendum on August 19, 1992, but was subsequently the subject of extensive political conflict; federal system established by constitutional amendments approved by national referendum on March 15, 1998, and promulgated on April 8; federal system restructured by constitutional amendments passed by referendum on April 4, 2007, and promulgated April 28; transitional government following a coup on March 17, 2009; new constitution approved by referendum on November 17, 2010.

Area: 226,657 sq. mi. (587,041 sq. km).

Population: 24,916,825 (2016E—UN); 24,430,325 (2016E—U.S. Census).

Major Urban Center (2016E—UN): ANTANANARIVO (2,739,000, urban area).

Official Languages: Malagasy, French, English.

Monetary Unit: Ariary (official rate October 1, 2016: 3,128.00 ariarys = $1US). The ariary replaced the Madagasy Franc in mid-2003.

President: Hery Martial RAJAONARIMAMPIANINA Rakotoarimanana (A New Force for Madagascar); elected in runoff balloting on December 20, 2013, and inaugurated on January 25, succeeding Andry RAJOELINA (Young Malagasies Determined).

Prime Minister: Olivier Mahafaly SOLONANDRASANA (ind.); assumed office on April 13, 2016; succeeding Jean RAVELONARIVO (ind.).

THE COUNTRY

The Republic of Madagascar, consisting of the large island of Madagascar and five small island dependencies, is situated in the Indian Ocean off the southeast coast of Africa. The island is renowned for its biodiversity and its treasure trove of unique plant and animal species. Although the population includes some 18 distinct ethnic groups, the main division is between the Asian Mérina people (the largest ethnic group [26 percent of the population]) of the central plateau and the sub-Saharan peoples of the coastal regions (*côtiers*). The Malagasy language is of Malayo-Polynesian origin, yet reflects African, Arabic, and European influences. The nonindigenous population includes some 30,000 Comorans and smaller groups of French, Indians, Pakistanis, and Chinese. Women constitute more than 49 percent of the labor force in 2012, according to the World Bank. However, due largely to matriarchal elements in precolonial Malagasy culture, females are significantly better represented in government and urban managerial occupations than their mainland counterparts. In 2016 the Inter-Parliamentary Union ranked Madagascar at 84th of 180 countries in terms of women's representation in parliament. Madagascar currently has 31 women (20.5 percent) in the 151-member lower house (National Assembly), and 12 (19 percent) in the upper house (Senate). There are four women in the current cabinet.

Agriculture, forestry, and fishing account for more than one-fourth of Madagascar's gross domestic product (GDP) but employ more than four-fifths of the labor force, the majority at a subsistence level. Leading export crops are coffee, cloves, and vanilla, while industry is concentrated in food processing (notably seafood) and textiles. Mineral resources include deposits of graphite, nickel, chromium, and gemstones (particularly sapphires), in addition to undeveloped reserves of bauxite, iron, titanium, and petroleum.

In the 1970s much of the country's economic base, formerly dominated by foreign businesses, was nationalized by a strongly socialist regime. However, in the face of mounting external debt, worsening trade deficits, and capital flight, the administration in 1980 abandoned its formal commitment to socialism and called for assistance from the International Monetary Fund (IMF), the World Bank, and U.S. and European donors. In addition, budget austerity, currency devaluations, and measures to reduce food imports by boosting agricultural production were introduced. Although foreign creditors applauded such actions, no measurable economic progress was subsequently achieved, with economic reforms aggravating the decline of living standards in urban areas.

In the early 1990s a series of economic reforms, including deregulation and the privatization of some state-run industries, was instituted following suspension from the IMF and a series of austerity measures placed upon the country. These measures led to a period of sustained growth in the late 1990s, but the country suffered a series of economic shocks in the early 2000s. The country's accession in May 2006 to the Southern African Development Community (SADC) was expected to expand regional trade opportunities. Beginning in 2007, the nation's mining sector began expanding due to the discovery of nickel, copper, and platinum deposits and the development of chromite and ilmenite mines.

Madagascar's protracted political crisis of 2009–2010 resulted in a significant drop in foreign investment, development aid, and revenue from tourism. Meanwhile a severe drought in the south, several major cyclones, and the steep increase in food prices contributed to a humanitarian emergency in 2009. The additional impact of the global financial crisis resulted in GDP contraction of 4.1 percent in 2009, according to the IMF. The agrarian sector subsequently rebounded with above-average rice harvests, but the tourism industry remained in decline and international development aid, accounting for roughly 40 percent of government expenditures, remained frozen. GDP grew by 0.4 percent in 2010, and growth slowly continued into the new decade, with GDP gaining 1.8 percent in 2011, 1.9 percent in 2012, and 2.4 percent in 2013.

Madagascar remains one of the world's poorest countries, however, ranking sixth in the world for malnutrition. Worsening conditions prompted the World Bank to award $167 million in emergency assistance in December 2012, though warning the package did not indicate the "normalization" of relations. The United Nations (UN) ranked Madagascar 151st out of 185 countries in its 2013 Human Development Index. The IMF restored relations with Madagascar in March 2014, following the democratic election of President Hery RAJAONARIMAMPIANINA. In June the IMF approved a rapid credit facility of $47.1 million to help the government improve the battered economy. GDP growth was 3 percent in 2014, 5 percent in 2015, and an estimated 5 percent in 2016. Inflation in 2016 was 6.9 percent. GDP per capita that year was $461.

GOVERNMENT AND POLITICS

Political background. During the 18th century and most of the 19th century, Madagascar was dominated by the Mérina people of the plateau. However, after a brief period of British influence, the French gained control and by 1896 had destroyed the Mérina monarchy. Renamed the Malagasy Republic, it became an autonomous state within the French Community in 1958 and gained full independence on June 26, 1960, under the presidency of Philibert TSIRANANA, a *côtier* who governed with the support of the Social Democratic Party (*Parti Social Démocrate*—PSD).

Tsiranana's coastal-dominated government ultimately proved unable to deal with a variety of problems, including ethnic conflict stemming from Mérina opposition to the government's pro-French policies. In addition, economic reverses led to a revolt in 1971 by peasants in Tulear Province, while students, dissatisfied with their job prospects in a stagnating economy, mounted a rebellion in early 1972. Having acknowledged his growing inability to rule in May, Tsiranana abdicated his duties as head of state and chief of government in favor of Maj. Gen. Gabriel RAMANANTSOA, a Mérina, who was confirmed for a five-year term by a referendum held October 8.

An attempted coup by dissident *côtier* officers led to Ramanantsoa's resignation on February 5, 1975; his successor, Col. Richard RATSIMANDRAVA, a Mérina, was assassinated six days later, with Brig. Gen. Gilles ANDRIAMAHAZO assuming the leadership of a Military Directorate. Cdr. Didier RATSIRAKA in turn succeeded Andriamahazo on June 15. Subsequently, on December 21, 1975, voters approved a Socialist Revolutionary Charter and a new constitution that called for the establishment of a National Front for the Defense of the Malagasy Socialist Revolution (*Front National pour la Défense de la Révolution Socialiste Malgache*—FNDR) as an overarching political formation. The voters also designated Ratsiraka, a *côtier*, for a seven-year term as president of the newly styled Democratic Republic of Madagascar; thereby he continued his role as chair of a Supreme Revolutionary Council (*Conseil Suprême de la Revolution*—CSR) that had been established in 1972.

The new Ratsiraka government formed on January 11, 1976, was designed to reflect a regional balance of both military and civilian elements. The government was reconstituted on August 20 following the accidental death of Prime Minister Joël RAKOTOMALALA on July 30 and his replacement by Justin RAKOTONIAINA on August 12. Local elections, the first since the constitutional revision, began in March 1977 and were dominated by the Vanguard of the Malagasy Revolution (*Antoky'ny Revolosiona Malagasy*—Arema), established by Ratsiraka a year earlier as the main FNDR component. Arema members also filled 112 of the 137 positions on the FNDR's single list of National Assembly candidates, which was approved by a reported 90 percent of voters on June 30. Ratsiraka subsequently appointed a new cabinet, headed by Prime Minister Lt. Col. Désiré RAKOTOARIJAONA.

President Ratsiraka was popularly reelected to a seven-year term on November 7, 1982, by a four-to-one margin over Monja JAONA of the National Movement for the Independence of Madagascar (*Mouvement National pour l'Indépendqnce de Madagascar*—Monima). Assembly elections scheduled for 1982 were postponed until August 23, 1983, at which time more than 500 candidates from FNDR-affiliated groups were allowed on the ballot. Arema secured 117 seats on the basis of a 65 percent vote share.

On February 12, 1988, Lt. Col. Victor RAMAHATRA (theretofore minister of public works) was named to succeed Colonel Rakotoarijaona as prime minister. With the FNDR increasingly unable to maintain control of its constituent groups, the scheduled 1988 assembly elections were postponed, ostensibly to permit their being held simultaneously with presidential balloting in November 1989. However, under powers granted by a constitutional amendment approved by the assembly in December 1988, Ratsiraka moved the presidential election up to March 12, 1989. Aided by disunity within the opposition, which fielded three candidates, Ratsiraka was reelected to another term, albeit with a reduced majority (63 percent) and with waning support in Antananarivo and other urban areas. Arema had little trouble maintaining its large majority in assembly balloting on May 28.

After the government thwarted a coup attempt in Antananarivo in July 1989, party leaders became increasingly critical of the administration's policies. In early 1990 President Ratsiraka issued a decree that abolished mandatory participation in the FNDR as of March 1. A number of new parties immediately emerged, six of which joined with the Christian Council of Churches of Madagascar (*Fikambanan'ny Fiangonana Kristiana Malagasy*—FFKM) in sponsoring a National Meeting for a New Constitution on May 23. Ten days earlier, three people had been killed and some two-dozen injured in a coup attempt by the Republican Committee for Public Safety (*Comité Républican pour le Salut Publique*). Thereafter, highly publicized FFKM-opposition party conferences held August 16–19 and December 5–9 demanded abolition of the CSR, the formation of an all-party transitional government, and the convening of a constituent assembly to define the institutions of a Third Republic. Ratsiraka announced in January 1991 that he had asked the government to present a series of proposals to the assembly to bring the constitution into closer conformity with the "national and international context."

On July 28, 1991, following seven weeks of strikes and demonstrations in Antananarivo by the opposition Living Forces (*Forces Vives/Hery Velona*) group, Ratsiraka dissolved the government and announced that he would call for constitutional reform by the end of the year. On August 8 he appointed as prime minister the mayor of Antananarivo, Guy Willy RAZANAMASY, who, after being granted extensive executive powers, proclaimed a desire to lead his country "down the tortuous and difficult road to democracy." However, an interim government announced by Razanamasy on August 26 included no representatives from the FFKM or *Hery Velona,* which was composed of 16 political parties. As a result, the opposition launched a general strike and organized a protest rally in the capital of some 300,000 persons, bringing economic life to a sudden halt. In the wake of Ratsiraka's loss of control, Dr. Albert ZAFY, the leader of *Hery Velona*, set up a shadow government, proclaiming himself as the prime minister and the *Haute Autorité*, a political body composed of the parties in the *Hery Velona*, as the national assembly.

In the wake of continued unrest, Ratsiraka and Razanamasy agreed on October 29, 1991, to the formation of a new unity government that would include representatives of opposition formations, religious groups, and the armed forces. In addition, both the CSR and the assembly transferred their functions to the transitional High State Authority (*Haute Autorité d'État*—HAE) and a Committee for Economic and Social Recovery (*Comité pour le Redressement Économique et Social*—CRES). On October 31 Ratsiraka and the *Hery Velona* signed the Panorama Convention, which established a transitional government. The terms of the convention left Ratsiraka as president but transferred most of his powers to the HAE and CRES, promising a new constitution, which would be submitted to a popular referendum by the end of the year. Zafy was named HAE president on November 23, and Rakotonirina and Andriamanjato became cochairs of the CRES. The result was a quadripartite distribution of power involving the prime minister, the HAE president, the CRES chairs, and the increasingly marginalized president of the republic. A 1,400-member National Forum met March 22–29, 1992, to draw up the new constitution, which was approved by referendum on August 19.

Zafy received 45.2 percent of the vote against seven other candidates in first-round presidential balloting on November 25, 1992. In a runoff against Ratsiraka on February 10, 1993, Zafy defeated the incumbent president by a two-to-one margin. Subsequent legislative balloting on June 16, 1993, gave Zafy supporters a majority of 75 of 138 seats on a 55 percent vote share. The new assembly approved Francisque RAVONY as prime minister on August 9.

By mid-1995 the president and prime minister were at odds, with Zafy accusing Ravony of having impoverished the country through maladministration of its structural adjustment program. However, Zafy was unable to mount sufficient legislative support to secure Ravony's removal from office. As a result of the impasse, the two leaders arrived at an unusual compromise whereby Ravony would receive long-sought authorization to name a new cabinet (implemented on August 18, with the exclusion of Zafy supporters), while a constitutional referendum would be held to give the president opportunity to appoint a new prime minister.

Despite complaints of a return to authoritarianism, Zafy won a 63 percent "yes" vote in the referendum of September 17, 1995, and on October 30 he appointed Emmanuel RAKOTOVAHINY to succeed Ravony, who had resigned on October 13. Rakotovahiny's cabinet, appointed on November 10, was dominated by members of Zafy's UNDD. The ongoing controversy over economic policy came to a head in early May 1996 when IMF director Michel Camdessus, during a visit to Antananarivo, announced that the government as constituted was not suitable to negotiate new agreements with the IMF and World Bank. Consequently, on May 17, the assembly passed a motion of no-confidence in the government by a vote of 109–15. Although Rakotovahiny challenged the constitutionality of the vote, he submitted his resignation on May 20, and on May 28 Zafy appointed Norbert RATSIRAHONANA, chief judge of the High Constitutional Court, as the new prime minister. The cabinet announced by Ratsirahonana on June 5 was again comprised primarily of UNDD members.

The executive/legislative conflict culminated on July 26, 1996, in a 99–39 assembly vote to remove Zafy from office on grounds that he had violated his oath of office by taking numerous actions contrary to the constitution and the "interests of the entire Malagasy people." Zafy challenged the legality of the decision, charging that the assembly was attempting a "constitutional coup." However, on September 5 the High Constitutional Court upheld the assembly's action and appointed Prime Minister Ratsirahonana interim president. In September Ratsirahonana presented the government's revised economic policy to IMF officials.

Fifteen candidates contested the presidential balloting on November 3, 1996. The front-runner was former president Ratsiraka (who had returned in late September from 18 months of self-imposed exile in Paris), with 36.6 percent of the vote. He was followed by Zafy, 23.4 percent; Herizo RAZAFIMAHALEO (head of the Leader–*Fanilo* party), 15 percent; Ratsirahonana, 10 percent; and National Assembly Speaker Rev. Richard ANDRIAMANJATO, 5 percent. Runoff balloting between Ratsiraka and Zafy took place on December 29, Razafimahaleo having thrown his support to the former. Preliminary results showed Ratsiraka ahead by about 30,000 votes, but Zafy alleged fraud during vote tabulation. However, on January 30, 1997, Ratsiraka was proclaimed president by virtue of a 51 percent share of the second-round polling. On February 21 Ratsiraka named Pascal RAKOTOMAVO, a business executive and Arema official, as prime minister. One week later Rakotomavo formed a new multiparty government.

Relations between the president and his opponents plummeted when he announced plans to organize a constitutional referendum on his proposal to return Madagascar to its pre-1995 provincial system. On February 4, 1998, opposition legislators failed in their effort to impeach Ratsiraka over the matter, and on March 15 the referendum was approved by a narrow margin (51 percent). The constitution of the Third Republic entered into force on April 8, providing for a federal system comprising six provincial governments. At the same time, opponents of Ratsiraka accused him of attempting to consolidate power in a "presidential regime." (Under the new constitution the president could name the prime minister and other members of government without reference to the assembly and could dissolve the assembly without any provision for an automatic subsequent election. Whereas previously representative groups nominated 30 senators for appointment by the president, the president could appoint the senators without them having to be nominated by groups. The amendments also left largely to presidential interpretation the relationship between the central and provincial governments.)

In legislative balloting on May 17, 1998, Arema captured 63 seats. The next largest bloc of seats, 32, went to a group of independent, but predominantly propresidential, candidates. On July 6 a power struggle between Prime Minister Rakotomavo and Deputy Prime Minister Rajaonarivelo culminated in the resignation from the government of the latter along with 17 other ministers. Unable to govern and constitutionally obligated to resign following assembly elections, Rakotomavo left office on July 22. The following day the president appointed Tantely René Gabrio ANDRIANARIVO, an Arema stalwart and former deputy prime minister, to replace Rakotomavo. On July 31 a new government was named in which Arema controlled all the key portfolios, underscoring the extent to which President Ratsiraka and Arema had secured political control. On the other hand, the administration's economic recovery program continued to falter, with its halting privatization efforts and apparent unwillingness to adhere to international reform prescriptions undermining its chances of securing much needed financial aid.

The opposition remained disorganized, as evidenced by Arema's successes in the first provincial government elections on December 3, 2000, in which Arema won a majority in all provinces except Antananarivo, and in the first Senate election on March 18, 2001, in which Arema secured 49 of the 60 elected seats. However, a number of smaller parties subsequently endorsed the presidential candidacy of Marc RAVALOMANANA, the supermarket magnate and mayor of Antananarivo who had gained strong support among the middle class with his promises to spur economic growth.

There were six candidates in the presidential election on December 16, 2001, and balloting produced highly controversial and destabilizing results. The government reported that no candidate had secured 50 percent of the votes and that a runoff was required between President Ratsiraka (officially credited with 41 percent of the first-round votes) and Ravalomanana, who had been credited with a front-running 46 percent. However, Ravalomanana, supported by the I Love Madagascar (*Tiako I Madagasikara*—TIM) party, claimed he had in fact won nearly 52 percent of first-round votes, setting the stage for massive political turmoil in early 2002. Ravalomanana's supporters poured into the streets of the capital in late January to protest the government's ruling that a second round of balloting was required. International observers concluded that massive tampering had occurred in the initial official tabulations.

As demonstrations continued, Ravalomanana declared himself president on February 22, 2002, and began installation of his own cabinet under the leadership of Jacques SYLLA. Ratsiraka responded by declaring a national state of emergency on the same day and martial law on February 28. Ravalomanana ignored the declaration of martial law, forming a government without resistance from the army or the security forces. On March 4 the pro-Ratsiraka governors of the five provinces declared that they were autonomous from Antananarivo and established their "capital" in Ratsiraka's home town of Toamasina with the support of five of the six provinces' governors. The army then split its support between the rival candidates. Conditions deteriorated in March as groups loyal to the two parallel governments clashed violently in Antananarivo, control of which was ultimately gained by Ravalomanana's forces, while many of his supporters were arrested, tortured, or killed in the provinces. Negotiations in Senegal in April pointed toward a compromise settlement. However, on April 16 the administrative chamber of the Supreme Court declared the initial published results of the December 16 voting void and ordered a recount, which, as reported by the High Constitutional Court, showed that Ravalomanana had won a first-round majority of 51.5 percent. Ravalomanana was formally inaugurated on May 6, becoming the first elected Mérina president. He subsequently sent the army to regain control of the provinces, replacing provincial governors with special presidential delegates. Ratsiraka refused to accept the legitimacy of that situation and continued to fight it. However, the United States officially recognized Ravalomanana as president of Madagascar on June 26, and similar action by France on July 3 sealed the fate of Ratsiraka, who left the country on July 5 for eventual exile in France.

On June 18, 2002, President Ravalomanana reappointed Sylla as prime minister. Hopes for reconciliation were dashed when the new cabinet excluded Ratsiraka's supporters, with the exception of one Arema minister. In the next month, President Ravalomanana used his power to appoint 30 senators, but Arema retained a majority in the Senate. Early legislative elections, observed for the first time by foreign monitors, were held on December 15, 2002, with Ravalomanana's TIM party winning a majority of 103 seats in the 160-seat assembly. The Patriot Front, an electoral alliance supporting Ravalomanana, gained an additional 22 seats, while Arema's representation declined to 3 seats. Significantly, 23 deputies were elected as independents. Sylla was reappointed prime minister on January 12, 2003.

In August 2003 Ratsiraka and two former Central Bank officials were tried and sentenced in absentia to ten years hard labor for allegedly embezzling $8.25 million from the bank during the crisis. The former Arema prime minister and the secretary-general of the party also received sentences in 2003.

In early 2004 there was a major cabinet reshuffle to incorporate leaders of other parties, and Ravalomanana released some prisoners convicted of crimes committed during the political crisis of 2002. Ravalomanana managed to neutralize the challenges to his reelection. Pierrot RAJAONARIVELO, the exiled Arema leader, was twice barred from entering the country to register his candidacy before the official deadline. The president was easily reelected on December 3, 2006 and subsequently appointed Gen. Charles RABEMANANJARA as prime minister, marking the first time in Madagascar's post-independence history that Mérina highlanders filled both the presidential and prime ministerial offices.

The TIM then expanded its majority in the assembly to 106 out of 127 seats in balloting on September 23, 2007. The national opposition parties managed to capture only 1 seat in the lower house, with the remainder going to independents. Since the former ruling party Arema remained in disarray, Madagascar's opposition parties had become small, fragmented, and driven by personalities. The only significant electoral setback for the TIM during this period came when Andry RAJOELINA defeated the TIM candidate to become mayor of Antananarivo on December 12, 2007. The opposition fared badly in the Senate balloting of April 20, 2008, when TIM swept every seat.

By 2008 President Ravalomanana came under increasing criticism for corruption and authoritarianism. The president, a wealthy businessman, appeared to use the authority of the office to enhance the interests of his Tiko company. His most unpopular initiative was to lease 3 million acres (1.3 million hectares) of arable land to the South Korean company Daewoo, which planned to practice export-oriented agriculture, an agreement questioned by critics at a time of economic crisis and widespread food insecurity.

The mayor of Antananarivo, Andry RAJOELINA, capitalized on the president's floundering popularity. The former disc jockey and owner of the Vivo radio and television stations galvanized popular discontent, just as Ravalomanana himself had as mayor of the capital. In December Vivo TV aired an interview with Didier Ratsiraka, in which the exiled former leader called for open revolt against the government. Ravalomanana reacted by shutting down the TV station on December 13. For the next three months, protests took place in the capital almost daily. More than 40 people were killed on January 26, 2009, as security forces opened fire on rioting crowds. With his opposition movement, Young Malagasies Determined (*Tanora malaGasy Vonona*—TGV), demonstrating relentlessly against the Ravalomanana regime, Rajoelina demanded the president's resignation on January 31, and proclaimed that he would henceforth lead the nation. Ravalomanana in turn used his prerogative to sack the mayor on February 3.

Undaunted, Rajoelina announced on February 7 that he had asked Monja ROINDEFO of the Monima party to become prime minister of a transitional government. That day the presidential guard killed more than 20 protesters.

As the showdown continued, the army grew unwilling to put down the ongoing demonstrations. In March 2009 mutinying soldiers ousted the defense minister and army chief of staff, and a coup appeared imminent. Rajoelina demanded the president's arrest on March 14. Soldiers loyal to the opposition occupied a presidential palace and the central bank building on March 16. The following day, Ravalomanana announced that he was stepping down, dissolving the government, and transferring power to a self-chosen group of four senior military officials. The officers, however, declined to become a ruling directorate and instead invited Rajoelina to form a transitional government. The High Constitutional Court approved the transfer of power on March 18. On March 19 Rajoelina announced he was nullifying the government's land agreement with Daewoo. Rajoelina was sworn in as head of state on March 21, in a ceremony notable for the absence of invited foreign dignitaries. The new leader committed to elections within two years. On March 31 he named 44 members to the High Authority of the Transition (HAT), with himself as its president. The transitional body was made up of representatives of numerous political parties and most of the country's geographical regions; its precise function remained ambiguous.

On June 3 a court sentenced Ravalomanana in absentia to four years in jail, on corruption charges stemming from the president's 2008 purchase of a $60 million presidential jet. On August 9 negotiations hosted by Mozambican president Joaquim Chissano between Rajoelina, Ravalomanana, Ratsiraka, and Zafy resulted in an agreement that called for elections within 15 months, a general amnesty, and the creation of government of national unity led by an agreed-upon prime minister and three deputy prime ministers. After further negotiations, on November 13 Eugene Mangalaza was inaugurated as the new "consensus" prime minister, and two "co-presidents" (representing the Ravalomanana and Zafy camps) were appointed later in the month. On December 18 Rajoelina declared the power-sharing agreement void, dismissed the two co-presidents, and unilaterally appointed Col. Vital Albert Camille as prime minister, prompting widespread international criticism.

In May 2010 Rajoelina unilaterally announced a timetable for elections and declared that he would not stand for election as president. On August 8 former president Ravalomanana was sentenced in absentia to life imprisonment with hard labor for ordering the presidential guard to fire on demonstrators in the capital on February 7, 2009.

In Antananarivo on August 13, 2010, Rajoelina announced that he had entered into an agreement with 99 political parties and civic associations to lead the nation out of its political impasse, boasting that the pact was reached without international mediation, though Ravalomanana, Zafy, and Ratsiraka spurned the agreement. The agreement, signed in Ivato, called for the convening of a national conference, to be followed by a referendum on a proposed constitution on November 17, 2010. The new constitution was approved with 70.5 percent of the vote, as the minimum age to be president was lowered to 35, thereby legalizing Rajoelina's tenure as chief executive.

On March 26, 2011, a new unity government was announced by the HAT. Vital was reappointed prime minister. However, the major opposition parties boycotted the new cabinet, prompting new negotiations to end the political stalemate.

Legislative and presidential elections were scheduled for March 16 and May 4, 2011, respectively. Rajoelina vowed not to participate in the presidential balloting, but until the assumption of office by the new president, Rajoelina continued to serve as president of the transition, and a prime minister of his choosing would lead the government. He named the members of a bicameral transition parliament.

Negotiations under the auspices of the SADC resulted in a road map agreement on September 17, 2011, to resolve the crisis. Rajoelina and former presidents Ravalomanana and Zafy, along with the leaders of six other parties, signed the agreement, which called for the creation of a bicameral transitional legislature, future elections, and the appointment of representatives of the former presidents as co-presidents. Ex-president Didier Ratsiraka opposed the accord. Prime Minister Vital and his entire government resigned on October 28, and he was replaced by Omer BERIZIKY in accordance with the agreement. Beriziky appointed a new cabinet composed of supporters of both the current and former governments.

The first presidential balloting since the 2009 political crisis was held on October 25, 2013. Hery RAJAONARIMAMPIANINA and Richard Jean-Louis ROBINSON proceeded to the runoff election on December 20, concurrent with legislative balloting. Rajaonarimampianina won with 53.5 percent of the vote. (For more on the 2013 elections, see Current issues, below.) Roger KOLO (ind.) was named prime minister and sworn in on April 16, 2014. Kolo named a broad, multiparty cabinet on April 18.

On January 12, 2015, Kolo and his cabinet resigned under popular pressure from protests over electrical blackouts and pervasive poverty. Rajaonarimampianina appointed Air Com. Jean RAVELONARIVO as prime minister on January 17, and Ravelonarivo unveiled a new cabinet on January 25.

Relations between Rajaonarimampianina and the assembly worsened steadily during the first half of 2015 as lawmakers criticized the president for failing to improve the economy and for not working more closely with the legislature. On May 26, 2015, the assembly impeached president Rajaonarimampianina on a vote of 121–4. The president appealed the vote to the constitutional court, which ruled in favor of Rajaonarimampianina, citing discrepancies between the vote total and the number of legislators present during the vote.

In indirect balloting for the Senate, the newly formed pro-presidential New Forces for Madagascar (*Hery Vaovao ho an'i Madagasikara*—HVM), won 34 seats, followed by I Love Madagascar (*Tiako I Madagasikara*—TIM) with 3, and With President Andry Rajoelina (*miaraka amin'ny Prezida Andry Rajoelina*—MAPAR), 2.

Rajaonarimampianina claimed Ravelonarivo resigned on April 8, 2016, although the prime minister disputed the claim. The president appointed Olivier Mahafaly SOLONANDRASANA (ind.) prime minister on April 10, and he was sworn in on April 13. The new prime minister named a 32-member unity government on April 15.

Constitution and government. Under the 2010 constitution, the president is directly elected for a five-year term, renewable twice, by runoff between the two leading contenders if such is needed to secure a majority. Cabinet leadership is assigned to a prime minister, responsible to the legislature but now appointed by the president (from a legislative list) and subject to dismissal by the president. The bicameral Parliament consists of a Senate of both indirectly elected and presidential appointees and a National Assembly of deputies directly elected by proportional representation. While the president can dissolve the assembly, it retains the power to pass a motion of censure requiring the prime minister and the cabinet to step down.

In 1995 Madagascar's former six provinces were replaced by 28 regions. The former 111 prefectures (*fivondronana*) were replaced by 148 departments and the former 1,252 subprefectures (*firaisana*) by 1,400 communes, of which 45 were urban.

The constitutional amendments of 1998 reversed the changes incorporated in 1995, restoring a federal system with six semiautonomous provinces. The amended document also included provisions for the establishment of regional and communal districts; however, as of mid-2010 no further progress toward their creation had been reported. Authority over regional representatives and budget allocations was centralized in the national government under President Ravalomanana.

A package of constitutional amendments was approved by referendum on April 4, 2007. These revisions again abolished the six provinces, replacing them with 22 regions. In addition, the constitution recognized English as an official language, alongside Malagasy and French; allowed the president to legislate by decree in national emergencies; and upheld President Ravalomanana's economic policy, the Madagascar Action Plan (MAP).

Under Madagascar's constitution at the time, the president must be no less than 40 years of age, and thus Rajoelina was not legally entitled to hold the office until 2014. After some delays, a new constitution, containing mostly minor revisions from the 2007 text, was approved on November 17, 2010. The major change was a reduction in the minimum age to be president.

Media censorship in Madagascar was formally lifted in March 1989. Madagascar's Communication Code of 1990 provided further liberalization but made defamation and insult punishable by up to six months in prison. In its 2016 annual index of press freedom, Reporters Without Borders ranked Madagascar 56th out of 180 countries. The organization had ranked the country at 134 after the 2009 coup. A cybercrime law adopted in August 2014 drew international criticism for criminalizing online defamation. Many press agencies were censored or even closed prior to the election of 2013 to "respect the rule of law" and to "overhaul the media landscape," according to Reporters Without Borders.

Foreign relations. During the Tsiranana administration, Madagascar retained close economic, defense, and cultural ties with France. In 1973, however, the Ramanantsoa government renegotiated all cooperation agreements with the former colonial power, withdrew from the Franc Zone, and terminated its membership in the francophone Common African and Malagasy Organization.

Subsequently, there was a drift toward the West. Ambassadorial links with Washington were restored in November 1980 after a lapse of more than four years. Aid agreements were negotiated with the United States, France, Japan, and a number of Scandinavian countries, although ties were also maintained with the Soviet Union and China.

In a dramatic policy reversal in mid-1990, economic and air links were established with South Africa as President Ratsiraka, heralding President F.W. de Klerk's "courageous" efforts to reverse apartheid laws, sought Pretoria's aid in developing Madagascar's mineral and tourism industries. In September 1998 Ratsiraka attended an international conference in Durban, thus becoming the first Malagasy head of state to visit South Africa. Subsequent regional negotiations focused on Madagascar candidacy for SADC membership (achieved in 2005).

Following the disputed presidential election of 2001, several countries terminated diplomatic relations with Madagascar and the country was suspended from meetings of the African Union (AU) for over a year. In June 2002 the Ravalomanana government was recognized by the United States; France and Senegal followed suit one month later, and the administration gradually established substantial international support. During a January 2007 visit, a high European Union (EU) official confirmed the union's support for Madagascar. The introduction of English as an official language underscored the nation's closer relations with English-speaking countries, especially the United States.

In June 2008 the president met with foreign donors, including China and India, to showcase the nation's economic growth and secure aid for poverty reduction efforts, indicative of the increasing economic influence of Asian countries in Madagascar.

The international community roundly condemned the unconstitutional transfer of power to Andry Rajeolina. The AU suspended Madagascar on March 20, and foreign diplomats boycotted Rajeolina's inauguration as head of the transition authority the following day. No state recognized the new regime. Several nations suspended nonhumanitarian foreign aid, which constituted more than 40 percent of the government's budget, and the United States halted development funding through the Millennium Challenge Corporation. Mediated negotiations between four political groupings, led by the UN, AU, and SADC, broke down in May. In June the SADC appointed Joaquim Chissano, former president of Mozambique, to mediate a new round of talks, which yielded a tentative agreement on August 9. The transitional government's failure to implement this agreement, however, meant that development aid continued to be withheld in 2010. The nation's duty-free trade status with the United States, provided by the African Growth and Opportunity Act, was suspended in January 2010, leading to the reported loss of 50,000 jobs in textiles, formerly Madagascar's leading export industry.

Ahead of presidential elections initially slated for July 24, 2013, three controversial candidates, including Rajoelina, drew calls for withdrawal from international observers and prompted the EU to suspend funding for printing the presidential ballots. A June meeting of the International Contact Group on Madagascar (ICG-M), which includes representatives from the AU, UN, SADC, and others, produced a seven-point electoral reform plan (see Current issues, below). On August 6, the EU threatened sanctions if the plan was not implemented within two weeks.

Following the election of Hery Rajaonarimampianina, foreign relations began to improve. The installation of the democratically elected president paved way for restoration of relations with the IMF in March 2014, marked by the IMF's approval of emergency funds for Madagascar in June. Meanwhile, in May the EU also restored aid. In December 2015 the World Bank announced a $55 million grant to improve public finance transparency and reduce government inefficiencies.

In an effort to attract foreign investment, on July 10, 2016, Madagascar announced it would join the 13-member African Trade Insurance Agency (ATI) by the end of September.

Current issues. Under immense pressure from foreign governments, President Rajoelina met with exiled, former president Marc Ravalomanana in late July 2012 to come up with an agreement for how to resolve the crisis and hold free elections. Over several meetings, they resolved few of their differences, but through mediation of the SADC, a timetable was reached to allow the return of Ravalomanana to Madagascar by mid-October. In January 2013 both Rajoelina and Ravolomanana agreed not to contest the presidential election.

In April 2013 former first lady Lalao Ravalomanana received the presidential nomination of the former president's party Ravalomanana Movement (*Mouvance Ravalomanana*), leading Rajoelina to rescind his previous nonparticipation pledge and throw his hat in. Lalao Ravalomanana, Rajoelina, and former president Didier Ratsiraka were all included on the 41-candidate list approved by CENIT on May 3, drawing sharp criticism from abroad (see Foreign relations, above). In June the polls were postponed from the original date of July 24 to August 23.

In order to comply with an internationally recommended seven-point plan, CENIT was restructured in August. Eight presidential candidates, including Lalao Ravalomanana, Rajoelina, and Ratsiraka, were disqualified, and on August 22, polling was further postponed until October 25. Subsequently the Ravalomanana Movement backed Jean-Louis Robinson of the Avana Party. Rajoelina threw his support behind Hery Rajaonarimampianina. Observers from the EU and SADC hailed October 25 balloting, in which 33 candidates contested, as free and fair. Robinson, with 21.1 percent of the vote, and Rajaonarimampianina, with 15.9 percent, proceeded to the runoff on December 20, concurrent with legislative balloting.

On January 3, 2014, Rajaonarimampianina was declared the winner with 53.5 percent of the vote, defeating Robinson, who filed complaints with the electoral court. On January 17, after dismissing allegations of vote rigging, the court finalized Rajaonarimampianina's victory. He was inaugurated on January 25. In the legislature, which convened on February 18, 2014, after the results were confirmed, a stalemate between Rajoelina's party, MAPAR, and Ravalomanana's TIM, delayed the appointment of a new prime minister until April 11, when, with the backing of more than a dozen parties, Rajaonarimampianina appointed independent Roger Kolo.

On October 13, 2014, Ravalomanana was arrested upon his return to Madagascar from South Africa. Ravalomanana was living in exile in South Africa after he fled the country just after he was removed from office. He was placed under house arrest, but his life sentence was commuted in May 2015.

In November 2014 the World Health Organization reported that 40 had died since August of an outbreak of the Bubonic plague; the last outbreak was in December of 2013. On January 21, 2015, Tropical Storm Chedza made landfall north of Monondava, killing 49 and forcing 42,000 from their homes, swelling concerns about another Bubonic plague outbreak. In March 2015 a severe drought impacted the food security of more than 200,000 people, according to the UN World Food Programme.

POLITICAL PARTIES AND GROUPS

While Madagascar has long featured multiple parties, they were required under the 1975 constitution to function as components of a national front (see Arema, below). The requirement was rescinded under a decree that became effective on March 1, 1990, restoring a multiparty system. For details on the principal electoral alliances formed before 2009, see the entry in the 2009 *Handbook*. Thirty-one political parties won representation in the December 2013 legislative elections. The elections were marked by a trend toward candidates contesting as independents, with many pre-2009 groupings dissolving, and 25 independents securing seats.

Government Parties:

New Force for Madagascar (*Hery Vaovao ho an'i Madagasikara*—HVM). The New Force was formed in 2013 as a pro-presidential grouping for Hery RAJAONARIMAMPIANINA. "New Force" is a play on the name Hery, which means "force," and *vaovao*, which means "new." The HVM won 34 of the 42 seats in the December 2015 Senate.
Leader: Hery RAJAONARIMAMPIANINA.

With President Andry Rajoelina (*miaraka amin'ny Prezida Andry Rajoelina*—MAPAR). This TGV-led coalition organized ahead of the 2013 presidential and legislative elections. After Rajoelina was barred from participating in the 2013 election, he threw the support of his party behind Rajaonarimampianina, who had launched his own party **New Force for Madagascar** (*Hery Vavao ho an'i Madagasikara*) (see above) in 2012 to support his candidacy. MAPAR won 49 seats in the legislative balloting, making it the largest legislative bloc. MAPAR won two seats in the December 29, 2015, Senate election.

Young Malagasies Determined (*Tanora malaGasy Vonona*—TGV). This group began in 2007 as a vehicle for Andry Rajoelina's campaign for mayor of Antananarivo. His party's acronym, TGV—which also alludes to the French high-speed train—was soon applied as a moniker for Rajoelina himself. Rajoelina defeated an experienced TIM politician for the mayoralty of the capital, and mounted a challenge to Ravalomanana. The president temporarily shut down Rajoelina's Vivo TV station in December 2008, after it aired an incendiary interview with the exiled former president Didier Ratsiraka. The incident raised Rajoelina's profile and catalyzed the street protest movement that ultimately defeated Ravalomanana. The TGV demonstrations attracted a large number of young supporters for Rajoelina, significant as roughly half of Madagascar's population was under age 21.

The TGV political association was relatively slow to develop the trappings and formal infrastructure of a traditional party. The ministers Rajoelina selected for his provisional government mostly belonged to other parties or were independents. Rajoelina vowed not to compete in the presidential elections that would inaugurate Madagascar's Fourth Republic. The TGV backed Edgar RAZAFINDRAVAHY, however Radoelina reentered the 2013 presidential race in April. Following his disqualification in August (see Current issues, above), Rajoelina backed former finance minister Hery Rajaonarimampianina, who placed second in the October 2013 election, proceeding to win the December 20 runoff. MAPAR, Raloelina's parliamentary bloc, secured 49 seats in concurrent legislative balloting. After nearly four months of deadlock between MAPAR and TIM, Rajaonarimampianina appointed Roger Kolo prime minister, against Rajoelina's ambitions, prompting MAPAR to assert that the president was acting unconstitutionally. Nonetheless, because of Rajoelina's power in parliament, Rajaonarimampianina relied heavily on the support of the former coup leader.

Leaders: Andry RAJOELINA (President of the Party and Former President of the High Authority of the Transition), Lanto RAKOTOMAVO (National Secretary).

Union of Democrats and Republicans for Change (*Union des Democrates et Republicains pour le Changement*—UDR-C). The UDR-C is a coalition party formed in 2010, following the Ivato Agreement, by a group of supporters for transition president Andry Rajoelina. While the UDR-C organizations were signatories of the Ivato Agreement, the UDR-C is an opposing party of Escopol, but it retained its seats in the government by virtue of backing Rajoelina. The UDR-C was awarded 25 of 90 seats in the CST and 29 of 256 seats in the CT. Following the declaration of UDR-C president Jean LAHINIRIKO that he would contest the 2013 presidential election with the PSDUM (below), the party backed Andry Rajoelina. Following Rajoelina's disqualification in August 2013, the UDR-C backed Rajaonarimampianina. In April 2014, following the appointment of Roger Kolo as prime minister, the UDR-C diverged from MAPAR leadership in pledging total support to Rajaonarimampianina.

Leader: Julien REBOZA (President).

Other Legislative Parties and Groups:

Rainbow Party (AVANA). The Rainbow Party was formed by Dr. Jean-Louis Robinson just four months before the 2013 election with Robinson initially being a proxy candidate for the deposed president, Marc Ravalomanana. Ravalomanana was deemed ineligible to run for election because he had been exiled in 2009 and therefore was not in Madagascar for the six months leading up to the election. The Rainbow Party was the de facto opposition party before the election but has fallen from power with many party members declaring themselves independent.

Leader: Jean-Louis ROBINSON.

I Love Madagascar (*Tiako I Madagasikara*—TIM). A "political association," TIM was formed to support the presidential campaign of Marc Ravalomanana, the businessman who had been elected mayor of Antananarivo in 1999 as an independent, and who had the endorsement of parties including the AVI, RPSD, PMDM/MFM, and *Grad-Iloafo.* TIM became a formal party in mid-2002 and became the majority party in the assembly following the 2002 legislative elections, when it received 34.3 percent of the vote and 103 seats.

After an internal power struggle within the TIM, Prime Minister Jacques Sylla failed to be reelected as the party's secretary general at a congress in January 2005. A rift between Ravalomanana and then assembly speaker Jean Lahiniriko, who had become increasingly critical of the government, resulted in his dismissal in May 2006, having faced criticism for praising Iran's nuclear program. Lahiniriko was also ejected from the TIM and launched his own party in February 2007 (see below).

By 2008 the party controlled the national legislature and local politics. However, rising protests against President Ravalomanana unraveled the party's control, and after the incidents of January 26 and February 7, 2009, in which security forces killed scores of demonstrators, the momentum decisively shifted to Andry Rajoelina and his TGV movement. Shortly after attaining power in March, Rajoelina dissolved the legislature and took over the office of the prime minister, effectively wiping out what remained of the TIM's power base in the national government.

Representatives of the TIM, now referred to in the press as "the Ravalomanana faction," participated in the internationally mediated four-party negotiations throughout 2009. The goal of restoring the former president to power—the objective of his "legalist" supporters in the TIM—grew more remote after Ravalomanana was sentenced in absentia on corruption charges in June, and three former officials in the TIM government were accused of responsibility for a bomb attack in the capital in July. In August 2010 the former president was given a life sentence on murder charges for his role in the killings of February 7, 2009.

The August 2010 Ivato accord (see Current issues, above) widened a split within the TIM as Ravalomanana and the top TIM leaders denounced these initiatives as unilateralist, but a former TIM deputy, Raharinaivo Andrianantoandro, endorsed the agreement. In October Andrianantoandro was elected president of the Congress of the Transition. Officials close to Ravalomanana disputed Andrianantoandro's claim that a majority of regional TIM leaders supported his nomination as deputy president of the party. Former first lady Neny Lalao Ravalomanana returned from exile in March 2013 and won the presidential nomination of the party, under the banner **Ravalomanana Movement** (*Mouvance Ravalomanana*). Following her disqualification in August, the TIM backed Jean-Louis Robinson, who won the first round of presidential balloting in October 2013, but placed second in the December 20 runoff. The group won 20 seats in concurrent legislative balloting. In May 2015 Ravalomanana was again elected president of the party. TIM won 3 seats in December 29, 2015, election for Senate.

Leaders: Marc RAVALOMANANA (Former President of the Republic and President of the Party), Ivohasina RAZAFIMAHEFA (Secretary General).

Vondrona Politika Miara-Dia–Malagy Miara-Miainga (VPM-MMM). Former Deputy Prime Minister Hajo ANDRIANAINARIVELO declared his candidacy in the October 2013 presidential elections in April of that year, launching from a new grouping, the VPN-MMM. Though Andrianainarivelo was knocked out in the first round of balloting, coming in third with 10.5 percent of the vote, his party went on to be the third largest bloc in the legislature following the December elections. The VPM-MMM did not officially support either presidential runoff candidate, but the VPM-MMM was among the coalition of parties that supported Roger Kolo for prime minister in April 2014.

Leader: Hajo ANDRIANAINARIVELO (2013 presidential candidate).

We'll All Be Together (*Hiaraka Isika*). *Hiaraka Isika* launched in September 2013 to support the presidential bid of former prime minister of HAT Camille Vital after Vital did not receive the backing of his former party, the TGV, for the 2013 presidential election. Vital campaigned on a platform of increased security, but did not qualify for the runoff election, placing fifth in October balloting. However, *Hiaraka Isika* won five seats in the legislative balloting in December. Although the party did not back the nomination of Roger Kolo for prime minister, Vital said in late April that he supported the prime minister and that *Hiaraka Isika* "will not be in the opposition."

Leader: Albert Camille VITAL (Party Leader, Former Prime Minister, and 2013 presidential candidate).

Leader–*Fanilo*. Launched in 1993 by a group of self-styled "nonpoliticians," Leader–*Fanilo* opposed President Zafy in the September 1995 referendum and expelled Trade and Tourism Minister Henri RAKOTONIRAINY for accepting cabinet reappointment two months later.

Party leader Herizo Razafimahaleo finished third in the first round of the 1996 presidential balloting with 15 percent of the vote and fourth in 2001 with 4.2 percent. (Three Leader–*Fanilo* cabinet members resigned from the government in early October 2001 after Razafimahaleo announced his intention to campaign for the presidency.) Razafimahaleo finished fourth in the 2006 presidential balloting with 9 percent of the vote.

Leader–*Fanilo* was the only nationally organized party, apart from the TIM, to win an assembly seat in the 2007 balloting. On July 25, 2008, the opposition party suffered a significant loss Razafimahaleo's death. He was succeeded as president by party Secretary General Manassé Esoavelomandroso. Rajoelina named Prezaly to the High Authority of the Transition in March 2009. Leader–*Fanilo* opposed the efforts of SADC to isolate Madagascar's transitional government and strongly supported the multiparty agreement of August 2010. Omer BERIZIKY of Leader–*Fanilo* became prime minister in 2011.

Ahead of the 2013 election, Leader–*Fanilo* initially backed Camille Vital, though reportedly switched to support Hery Rajaonarimampianina in September. The party won five seats in the December 20 legislative elections. It also won one seat in the 2015 Senate balloting.

Leaders: Jean Max RAKOTOMAMONJY (President), Omer BERIZIKY (Transitional Prime Minister).

Pillar of Madagascar (AIM). AIM was formally the **National Association for Rural and Industrial Development Madagascar** (*Association Nationale pour le Développement Rural et Industriel de Madagascar—ANDRIN'I Madagasikara*). *ANDRIN'I Madagasikara* is organized on the platform of promotion of rural and agricultural regions of the country. Andry Rakotovao, party founder and veteran of the rice industry, asserted during the campaign that Madagascar has the capability to become a major exporter of rice. The new party won two seats in December 2013 balloting.

Leader: Andry RAKOTOVAO.

Madagascar Green Party (*Parti Vert Hasin'i Madagasikara/ Antoko Maitso*—AMHM). Launched in 2009, AMHM was represented by Saraha Georget Rabeharisoa in the October 2013 presidential elections. In the December legislative elections, the party secured two seats, and supported the nomination of Roger Kolo for prime minister.

Leader: Saraha Georget RABEHARISOA.

Noah's Ark (*Sambo Fiaran'i Noe*). The party, consisting largely of young people, endorsed Edgard Razafindravahy for the presidential election of October 2013, even as the TGV withdrew their support in April. The party won two sets in the December legislative balloting.

Leader: Andriambolanarivo PARISOA.

***Trano Kasaka*.** The Sambava-based party won two seats in the December 20, 2013, election.

Leader: Norbert MAMANGY.

Rally for Socialism and Democracy (*Rassemblement pour le Socialisme et la Démocratie*—RPSD). The RPSD is the current incarnation of the **Social Democratic Party** (*Parti Social Démocrate*—PSD) that was legalized in March 1990 as a revival of the party originally formed in 1957 by Philibert Tsiranana. (The group is still frequently referenced under the PSD rubric.) Although initially sympathetic to the Ratsiraka government, in the second half of 1990 the party moved into opposition. The RPSD supported Albert Zafy in the second presidential round (after a bid by Marson had failed in the first) and went into opposition after the June 1993 assembly poll. Jean Eugène Voninahitsy, RPSD secretary general and vice president of the National Assembly, received 2.79 percent of the vote in the first round of the 1996 presidential election.

The RPSD won 11 assembly seats in May 1998, and reportedly joined Arema's legislative alliance. In late 2000, however, relations between Arema and the RPSD were strained when Voninahitsy was arrested on charges of insulting the head of state and "putting out false information." The RPSD left Arema's legislative faction and supported opposition candidate Marc Ravalomanana in the 2001 presidential campaign. Disaffected members left the RPSD to join the Patriotic Front (FP) prior to the 2002 assembly elections. The RPSD allied itself with the TIM in the election and secured five seats in the polling.

In 2003 RPSD dissidents led by former secretary general Voninahitsy left the party to form a new group, the New RPSD or **RPSD-Nouveau** (RPSD-*Vaovao*), which was active in the anti-Ravalomanana protests of October 2005. Voninahitsy was subsequently convicted of corruption and sentenced to two years in jail in December 2005. He was expected to run in the 2006 presidential race but was arrested on additional charges in February 2006 and received a four-year jail sentence, which was upheld by an appeals court in June 2008. The RPSD did not field a candidate in the 2006 presidential election, but a former RPSD leader, Philippe TSIRANANA, son of former president Philibert Tsiranana, stood as an independent. Marson was appointed to the High Authority of the Transition on March 31, 2009, as was Pelops Ariane VONINAHITSY, the wife of Jean Eugène Voninahitsy. Husband and wife both became members of the Parliament of the Transition in October 2010. Jean Eugène Voninahitsy contested the October 2013 presidential election as the head of a grouping called **Les AS** (*Les Autres Sensibilités*). The new banner secured one seat in the December 2013 legislative election.

Leaders: Evariste MARSON (President), Jean Eugène VONINAHITSY (2013 presidential candidate).

Militant Party for the Development of Madagascar (*Parti Militant pour le Développement de Madagascar*—MDM/MFM). The MDM/MFM is a successor name for the **Movement for Proletarian Power** (*Mouvement pour le Pouvoir Prolétarien/Mpitolona ho'amin'ny Fanjakan'ny Madinika*—MFM) formed in 1972 by student radicals who helped to overthrow President Tsiranana. The party adopted its current name at a 1990 party congress.

The MFM initially opposed the Ratsiraka government and remained outside the FNDR framework until 1977. The group won three assembly seats in 1983 and seven in 1989. Party leader Manandafy Rakotonirina placed second in the 1989 presidential balloting with 19 percent of the vote. As an opposition party, the MFM was part of the movement that forced Ratsiraka from power in 1991. The party completed a conversion from Marxism to liberalism in the 1990s.

MFM leader Rakotonirina, who stood as a first-round presidential contender in 1992, supported Albert Zafy in the second round. Following the legislative poll of June 1993, the MFM went into opposition. It supported prime minister and interim president Norbert Ratsirahonana in the 1996 presidential balloting but reportedly swung back over to the government camp following the May 1998 legislative elections. The MFM supported opposition candidate Marc Ravalomanana in the 2001 presidential campaign. In the 2002 elections the MFM won two seats in the National Assembly.

Despite its initial closeness to Ravalomanana, the MFM subsequently shifted to the opposition, joining the SPDUN (from which it withdrew in March 2006) and. The party declared unconstitutional Ravalomanana's decision to move the presidential election date to December 2006. As an independent candidate, Rakotonirina won 0.3 percent of the vote. The MFM won no seats in the 2007 legislative voting.

On April 20, 2009, while in exile in Johannesburg, Ravalomanana declared MFM's Rakotonirina his nominee to be Madagascar's next prime minister. Rakotonirina released a partial list of ministers for a prospective legalist government on April 28, but was arrested at an Antananarivo hotel by a militia loyal to Rajoelina. The 70-year-old Rakotonirina was incarcerated at Mantasoa but later released to allow him to participate in August's four-party talks in Maputo. He received a two-year suspended sentence. The MFM won one seat in the 2013 legislative election.

Leaders: Razafimahatratra PAULÉON, Ramarosonarivo JEANSON, Manandafy RAKOTONIRINA.

In addition to the above, the following parties each secured one seat in the 2013 legislative elections: ***La Parti Travailliste de Madagascar*** (PATRAM); ***Fifampiofanana Fanabeazan Fikolokoloana*** (FFF); ***303 Ihany Ny Antsika***; **Action for Humanist Development** (*Action pour le Développement Humaniste*); **Association of Young Entrepreneurs** (*Association des Jeunes Entrep*); ***Parti Bainga***; ***Association Toliara Miaranga***; **Fanamby 88 Association** (*Association Fanamby 88*); ***Fanasina Ho Fampandrosoana***; ***Firaisam-Pirenena Ho An Ny Fandrosoana Sy Ny Fahaf***; ***Fitarikandro***; **Gedeon for Overcoming Poverty in Madagascar** (*Gédéon pour Vaincre la Pauvreté à Madagascar/ Giedeona Fandresena ny Fahantrana eto Madagasikara*—GFFM); ***Parti HARENA***; the Malagasy **Tonga Saina** (MTS); ***Mampiray Antsika***; ***Mpirahalahy Mian/Ala***; **Papasolo**; **PSD**; and **Union** (*Tambatra*).

Other Parties and Groups:

Judged By One's Works (*Asa Vita no Ifampitsanara*—AVI). In May 1998 the AVI won 14 assembly seats as a moderate opposition party under the leadership of former prime minister and interim president Norbert Ratsirahonana. Subsequently, however, the AVI joined the Arema-led propresidential legislative alliance. In the 2001 presidential campaign, Ratsirahonana withdrew his candidacy in late October and endorsed Marc Ravalomanana. In 2002 the AVI joined Ravalomanana's first government as part of the now-defunct pro-Ravalomanana Patriot Front (*Firaisankinam-Pirenenai*—FP) formed in conjunction with former RPSD members. The FP secured 20 of the coalition's 22 seats in that year's legislative elections. In late 2003 the AVI began to distance itself from the president and joined the opposition group the **Parliamentary Solidarity for Democracy and National Union** (*Solidarité des Parlementaires pour la Défense de la Démocratie et de l'Unité National*—SPDUN), which it left in March 2006. Ratsirahonana formally split from the president in October 2006, claiming Ravalomanana had become a dictator, and entered that year's presidential election as the AVI candidate, winning 4.2 percent of the vote. The poor showing weakened the party's position among the opposition. Ratsirahonana was a major supporter of Andry Rajoelina's struggle to unseat Ravalomanana, standing by the new leader's side as he assumed power on March 17, 2009, and arguing his claim before the High Constitutional Court. He was subsequently named to the High Authority of the Transition and was perceived as one of Rajoelina's most influential counselors.

Leader: Norbert RATSIRAHONANA (Secretary General).

National Reconciliation Committee (*Comité pour la Réconciliation Nationale*—CRN). The CRN was launched in 2002 by former president Albert Zafy and other prominent former officials in an attempt to foster a solution to the "post-election crisis," pitting the supporters of former president Ratsiraka against the supporters of President Ravalomanana.

Zafy had led the **National Union for Development and Democracy** (*Union Nationale pour le Développement et la Démocratie*—UNDD), a party originally organized in 1955 and revived by Zafy in 1998. The UNDD stridently denounced "corruption" under the Ratsiraka regime. (For more on the CRN in the early 1990s, see the 2014 *Handbook*.)

In legislative balloting in May 1998, what remained of the pro-Zafy grouping competed under the banner of the recently established **Action, Truth, Development, and Harmony** (*Asa Fahamarianana Fampandrosoana Arinda*—AFFA). Six AFFA candidates, including Zafy, were elected. The AFFA supported Zafy in the 2001 presidential election but failed to gain any seats for itself in the 2002 legislative balloting.

Zafy and the CRN never formally recognized the legitimacy of Marc Ravalomanana's presidency. At the national conference in June 2005, the CRN advocated creating a "parallel government." In December 2006 Zafy's property was raided by the police as part of the government's investigation of General Fidy's alleged November coup attempt; the police sought to locate and arrest Zafy. Despite Ravalomanana's reelection, the CRN continued to press for a national reconciliation.

Zafy took part in the negotiations mediated by the UN and the AU after the March 2009 coup. The former president advocated for an inclusive, consensual basis for a democratic transition, calling for a truth and reconciliation commission based on the South African model. He rebuked Rajoelina in December for reneging on agreements the transition leader had made with the three former presidents. The CRN was not among the 99 parties to endorse the election timetable outlined in Ivato in August 2010.

Leaders: Dr. Albert ZAFY (Former President of the Republic), Tabera RANDRIAMANANTSOA (CRN Leader).

National Movement for the Independence of Madagascar/Madagascar for the Malagasy Party (*Mouvement National pour l'Indépendance de Madagascar/Madagasikara Otronin'ny Malagasy*—Monima). A left-wing nationalist party based in the south, Monima (also called *Monima Ka Miviombio*—Monima K) withdrew from the National Front FNDR in 1977. Its longtime leader, Monja JAONA, was under house arrest from November 1980 to March 1982, at which time he brought the group back into the FNDR and was appointed to the Supreme Revolutionary Council (CSR). He joined the 1982 presidential election as Commander Ratsiraka's only competitor, winning almost 20 percent of the vote. That December he was again placed under house arrest for activities "likely to bring about the fall of the country." He was released in mid-August 1983 and returned to the legislature as one of Monima's two representatives. Jaona won 3 percent in the 1989 presidential balloting and became Monima's sole assembly representative. Monima's deputy general secretary, René RANAIVOSOA, resigned from the party in June 1990, following a dispute with Jaona, and established the **Democratic Party for Madagascar Development** (*Parti Démocratique pour le Développement de Madagascar*—PDDM/ADFM).

The party reportedly endorsed President Ratsiraka's reelection bid and did not support Ravalomanana in the 2002 crisis. In the 2002 and 2007 assembly balloting, Monima won no seats. Jaona's son, Monja ROINDEFO Zafitsimilavo, stood as an independent in the 2006 presidential election and came in last.

Andry Rajeolina announced that Roindefo would serve as prime minister of his transitional administration on February 7, 2009. Roindefo's position became official in March, after Rajeolina was installed as leader. In June the party spoke out against the involvement of the SADC in mediation efforts, and opposed extending amnesty to either Ravalomanana or Ratsiraka. Rajoelina sacked Roindefo on October 9 following an internationally mediated power sharing agreement with three former presidents. Roindefo refused to accept his replacement by Eugene Mangalaza and continued to refer to himself as the nation's legal prime minister a year later, even in the absence of political support.

Roindefo contested the October 2013 presidential election, winning 1.5 percent of the vote.

Leaders: Monja ROINDEFO (Chair and 2013 presidential candidate), Gabriel RABEARIMANANA (Secretary General).

Socialist and Democratic Party for the Union of Madagascar (*Parti Socialiste et Démocratique pour l'Union à Madagascar*—PSDUM). This party was launched on February 3, 2007, by Jean LAHINIRIKO, speaker of the National Assembly from 2003 to 2006. During a visit to Iran in April 2006, Lahiniriko congratulated the Tehran government on the success of its nuclear program. His comment was not meant to represent official state policy; nevertheless, some of his fellow legislators accused him of treason. Lahiniriko was removed from office and expelled from the ruling TIM party. Running as an independent, he finished second with 11.65 percent in the December 2006 vote. As he launched his new party, he warned that "a programmed return of dictatorship" was threatening Madagascar. He ran and was defeated as a PSDUM candidate for assembly in September 2007.

Lahiniriko declared his support for Rajoelina just before the demonstrations of January 26, 2009. Lahiniriko and another party leader, former government minister Julien Reboza, were named to the High Authority of the Transition on March 31. Lahiniriko contested the October 2013 presidential elections and won less than 1 percent of the vote. The party won one legislative seat in December 2013.

Leader: Jean LAHINIRIKO (2013 presidential candidate and Former Speaker of the Assembly).

Vanguard of the Malagasy Revolution (*Avant-Garde de la Révolution Malgache/Antoky'ny Revolosiona Malagasy*—Arema). Arema was organized by Didier Ratsiraka in 1976 and subsequently served as the nucleus of the National Front for the Defense of the Malagasy Socialist Revolution (*Front National pour la Défense de la Révolution Socialiste Malgache*—FNDR), which was renamed the Militant Movement for Malagasy Socialism (*Mouvement Militant pour le Socialisme Malgache*—MMSM) in mid-1990. The 1975 constitution provided for organization of the FNDR as the country's overarching political entity, with a variety of "revolutionary associations" permitted to participate in elections as FNDR components. However, three FNDR members (the MFM, Vonjy, and Monima) initiated joint antigovernment activity, beginning in early 1987, and contested the 1989 presidential and legislative elections as the equivalent of opposition formations, thus dissolving the FNDR's political monopoly.

After losing the 1992 presidential election, Ratsiraka eventually moved to Paris, France. He remained a force in Malagasy politics, regularly criticizing the Zafy administration and what he described as the nation's political "chaos." In 1993 he formed the **Vanguard for Economic and Social Recovery** (*Avant-Garde pour le Redressement Économique et Social*—ARES) as a successor to Arema; however, his supporters and media groups continue to use the Arema acronym and earlier title.

Ratsiraka regained the presidency in February 1997. On November 29 of that year, at Arema's first party congress since taking power, Deputy

Prime Minister Pierrot Rajaonarivelo was elected to the secretary general's post vacated by Ratsiraka. The party also reportedly adopted the Malagasy title, *Andry sy Riana Enti-Manavotra an'i Madagasikara,* or Supporting Pillar and Structure for the Salvation of Madagascar.

In legislative balloting in May 1998 Arema and its allies secured an overwhelming mandate. On July 6 Rajaonarivelo and 17 of his ministerial allies withdrew from the cabinet, thereby paralyzing the Rakotomavo government and effectively destroying Rakotomavo's chances for reappointment.

Following the violence surrounding the 2001 presidential election, Ratsiraka and other senior Arema figures, including Secretary General Pierrot Rajaonarivelo, went into exile in France. In the legislative balloting in 2002, Arema secured only three seats, and it boycotted local elections in 2003. In 2003 Rajaonarivelo was sentenced in absentia to five years in prison on several charges involving his alleged abuse of office while deputy prime minister. His sentence was reduced to three years in 2005.

Arema was significantly weakened in 2006 by internal divisions over whether to support Pierrot Rajaonarivelo's presidential candidacy and whether to advocate the revision of the electoral code. Reports subsequently indicated a growing split in the party, with one faction loyal to the exiled leadership and a second group (led by Assistant Secretary General Pierre RAHARIJOANA) eager to distance itself from the exiles.

In 2006 Rajaonarivelo called upon the government to issue an amnesty to potential candidates, such as himself, whose sentences would otherwise preclude them from participating in the upcoming presidential poll. Rajaonarivelo, considered Ravalomanana's main opponent, officially announced his candidacy for the presidential election in May. However, he was convicted in absentia of embezzlement of public funds in August and sentenced to 15 years of hard labor and barred from holding office. Rajaonarivelo twice attempted and failed to return to Madagascar to register his candidacy. Arema then announced that it would boycott the election. In 2007 Arema was divided, with factions supporting each of the two exiled leaders, Ratsiraka and Rajaonarivelo. The pro-Ratsiraka contingent challenged the standing of the interim national secretary, Pierre Houlder Ramaholimasy. Arema won no seats in the 2007 legislative election.

Ratsiraka's televised interview calling for insurrection against the government led to the shutdown of Rajoelina's Viva television network in December 2008, sparking the overthrow of Ravalomanana. Rajoelina, who had received early financial backing from Rajaonarivelo for his business enterprises, was perceived by numerous analysts as a front for the exiled Arema leaders. Arema initially supported the coup, but Ratsiraka later condemned it. Rajoelina named Ramaholimasy to the High Authority of the Transition. Rajaonarivelo returned from exile in April 2009, stating that he hoped to foster national reconciliation. But Ratsiraka himself, still exiled and in frail health, led the Arema delegation in the UN-mediated four-party talks on the crisis. The admiral clearly signaled his intention to resume command of the party, pushing Rajaonarivelo aside. The negotiations led to two failed provisional power-sharing agreements in 2009.

Ratsiraka, returning from exile in April 2013, stood for president but was disqualified in August. The party holds no legislative seats because it was barred from participating in the December 2013 elections.

Leaders: Adm. Didier RATSIRAKA (Former President of the Republic), Pierre Houlder RAMAHOLIMASY (Acting National Secretary).

Space for Concerted Political Action (*Escopol Espace Politique*—Escopol). Escopol was founded in 2010 as a coalition of the signatories of the August 2010 Ivato Agreement (see Current issues, above). Under the formation of the transitional parliament, Escopol was awarded 18 of 90 seats in the upper house, the High Council of Transition (CST), and 62 of 256 seats in the lower house, the Transitional Congress (CT). Escopol is the largest party in the CT. In August 2011 the members of Escopol signed its Republican Pact, solidifying its ideological commitment to resolving the Madagascar crisis.

Leader: Benjamina Ramanantsoa RAMARCEL (Coordinator General).

For more on the parties that contested the 2006 election, see the 2014 *Handbook.* For more information on the **Congress Party for Madagascar Independence–Renewal** (*Parti du Congès de l'Indépendance de Madagascar–Renouveau*—AKFM-*Fanavaozana*), see the 2008 *Handbook.*

LEGISLATURE

The 1992 constitution provides for a bicameral **Parliament** (*Parlement*) consisting of a Senate and a National Assembly. Both houses were suspended immediately following the coup of March 17, 2009. A transitional legislature was convened on October 13, 2011, to remain in place until new elections for the Senate and National Assembly were conducted in 2013. The upper chamber, the Higher Transition Council (*Conseil Supérieur de la Transition*—CST), had 90 appointed members. The lower chamber, the Congress of Transition (*Congrès de la Transition*—CT), included 256 members. Rasolosoa DOLIN was elected president of the CST and Raharinaivo Andrianantoandro, president of the CT.

Senate (*Sénat*). Prior to the constitutional amendments of April 2008, the Senate had 60 elected members (10 representing each of the six provinces) and 30 appointed members. Arema won 49 of the 60 elected seats in the balloting of March 18, 2001, and President Ratsiraka made appointments the following month. After taking power in 2002, President Ravalomanana used his constitutional power to replace the appointed senators, mostly with members of his new I Love Madagascar party.

Madagascar's upper house has 63 members: 42 (seven from each province) are elected by electoral colleges composed of regional and municipal officials, and 21 are appointed by the president. The term of office is five years. In legislative elections held on April 20, 2008, I Love Madagascar received all the elective seats. The Senate was dissolved by Andry Rajoelina on March 19, 2009. No new members were named until the December 29, 2015, balloting, which resulted in the following distribution of indirectly elected seats: New Force for Madagascar, 34; I Love Madagascar, 3; With President Andry Rajoelina, 2; Leader—*Fanilo*, 1; and independents, 2.

President: Honoré RAKOTOMANANA.

National Assembly (*Assemblée Nationale*). The lower house encompasses 151 members, who are directly elected by proportional representation for five-year terms. The results of the balloting on December 20, 2013, which convened for the first time on February 18, 2014, were as follows: With President Andry Rajoelina, 49; I Love Madagascar, 20; *Vondrona Politika Miara-Dia—Malagy Miara-Miainga*, 13; We'll All Be Together, 5; Leader—*Fanilo*, 5; National Association for Rural and Industrial Development Madagascar, 2; Madagascar Green Party, 2; Noah's Ark, 2; *Trano Kasaka*, 2; independents, 25. The following parties won one seat each: *La Parti Travailliste de Madagascar*, *Fifampiofanana Fanabeazan Fikolokoloana*, *303 Ihany Ny Antsika*, Action for Humanist Development, Association of Young Entrepreneurs, *Parti Bainga*, Toliara Miranga Association, Fanamby 88 Association, *Fanasina Ho Fampandrosoana*, *Firaisam-Pirenena Ho An Ny Fandrosoana Sy Ny Fahaf*, *Fitarikandro*, Gedeon for Overcoming Poverty in Madagascar, HARENA Party, the Malagasy Tonga Saina, *Mampiray Antsika*, *Mpirahalahy Mian/Ala*, Papasolo, PSD, and Union.

CABINET

[as of June 24, 2016]

Prime Minister	Olivier Mahafaly Solonandrasana (ind.)
Ministers	
Employment, Technical Education, and Professional Training	Marie Lydie Toto Raharimalala [f]
Energy and Hydrocarbons	Rodolphe Ramanantsoa
Finance and Budget	François Marie Maurice Gervais Rakotoarimanana
Fishery Resources and Fishing	François Gilbert
Foreign Affairs	Béatrice Attalah [f]
Higher Education and Scientific Research	Marie Monique Rasoazananera (ind.) [f]
Industry and Private Sector Development	Chabani Nourdine
Justice, Keeper of The Seals	Charles Andriamiseza
National Defense	Béni Xavier Rasolofonirina
National Education	Andrianiaina Paul Rabary (ind.)

Population, Social Protection, and the Promotion of Women	Onitiana Voahariniaina Realy [f]
Posts, Telecommunications, and Digital Development	André Neypatraiky Rakotomamonjy
Public Health	Mamy Lalatiana Andriamanarivo
Public Security	Norbert Anandra
Public Works	Eric Razafimandimby
Tourism	Iarovana Roland Ratsiraka
Transport and Meteorology	Ramarcel Benjamine Ramanantsoa (ind.)
Water, Sanitation, and Hygiene	Roland Ravatomanga
Youth and Sports	Jean Anicet Andriamosarisoa (ind.)
Secretary of State	
Fishery Resources and Fishing, responsible for The Sea	Léonide Ylénia Randrianarisoa [f]
National Defence, in Charge of the Gendarmerie	Didier Gérard Paza (ind.)

[f] = female

INTERGOVERNMENTAL REPRESENTATION

Ambassador to the U.S.: Jocelyn Bertin RADIFERA.

U.S. Ambassador to Madagascar: Robert T. YAMATE.

Permanent Representative to the UN: Zina ANDRIANARIVELO RAZAFY.

IGO Memberships (Non-UN): AfDB, AU, Comesa, ICC, IOM, NAM, SADC, WTO.

For Further Reference:

Dewar, Bob, Simon Massey, and Bruce Baker. *Madagascar: Time to Make a Fresh Start*. London: Chatham House, 2013.

Doorenspleet, Renske, and Lia Nijzink, eds. *One-Party Dominance in African Democracies*. Boulder, CO: Lynne Rienner, 2013.

Scales, Ivan R., ed. *Conservation and Environmental Management in Madagascar*. New York: Routledge, 2014.

Thomson, Alex. *An Introduction to African Politics*. New York: Routledge, 2016.

MALAWI

Republic of Malawi

Political Status: Independent member of the Commonwealth since 1964; republic under one-party presidential rule established July 6, 1966; constitution amended on June 22, 1993, to provide for multiparty activity following national referendum of June 15; new constitution enacted provisionally as of May 16, 1994, and adopted permanently (as amended) on May 18, 1995.

Area: 45,747 sq. mi. (118,484 sq. km).

Population: 17,750,000 (2016E—UN); 18,570,321 (2016E—U.S. Census).

Major Urban Centers (2015E—UN): LILONGWE (905,000), Blantyre-Limbe (808,000).

Official Language: English. (Chichewa is classified as a national language.)

Monetary Unit: Kwacha (market rate October 1, 2016: 721.07 kwacha = $1US).

President: Peter MUTHARIKA (Democratic Progressive Party); popularly elected on May 20, 2014, and sworn in on May 31 to succeed Joyce BANDA (People's Party).

Vice President: Saulos CHILIMA (Democratic Progressive Party); popularly elected along with the president on May 20, 2014, and sworn in on May 31 to succeed Khumbo Hastings KACHALI (People's Party).

THE COUNTRY

Malawi, the former British protectorate of Nyasaland, is a landlocked southeastern African nation bordering the western side of 360-mile-long Lake Malawi (formerly Lake Nyasa). The country's name is a contemporary spelling of "Maravi," which historically referenced the interrelated Bantu peoples who inhabit the area. The main tribal groups are the Chewas, the Nyanja, and the Tumbuka. It is estimated that 83 percent of the population is Christian and 13 percent Muslim, with the remainder, except for a very small Hindu population, adhering to traditional African beliefs. A small non-African segment of the population includes Europeans and Asians. Three-quarters of adult females are subsistence agricultural workers, while the number of households headed by women has increased in recent years as men have relocated to pursue cash-crop labor. Following the 2014 elections, women held 32 of 192 seats (16.7 percent) in parliament, a decline from the previous balloting in 2009 when women secured 43 seats (23.3 percent). In 2013 women held 9 of 26 cabinet ministries, one of the highest proportions in the region. Following the 2014 balloting, that number declined to 3 of 18.

About 90 percent of the population is engaged in agriculture, the most important cash crops being tobacco, tea, peanuts, sugar, and cotton. Agriculture accounts for 31 percent of the nation's gross domestic product (GDP) and 80 percent of export revenues. Development efforts have focused on integrated rural production, diversification in light industry (particularly agriprocessing and import substitution), and improved transportation facilities.

In 2000 Malawi was approved for $1 billion in debt reduction under the World Bank's Heavily Indebted Poor Countries (HIPC) initiative, and the International Monetary Fund (IMF) provided a $65 million loan for poverty reduction. (For an overview of the economy prior to 2000, see the 2011 *Handbook*.) However, excessive government spending, corruption, and the slow pace of economic reforms led international donors, including the World Bank, IMF, United States, and European Union (EU), to suspend some economic aid during 2001–2002, although humanitarian assistance continued in light of Malawi's worsening food crisis (caused by drought in some areas and severe flooding in others). Meanwhile, the EU resumed full economic and development aid, including support for ports, hydroelectric facilities, and direct financial contributions to limit the government's deficit. In April 2006 the IMF reported that the new government had made progress in regard to economic reforms and approved a three-year, $59 million aid program (contingent on continued reform and the meeting of certain economic benchmarks). The World Bank also approved aid to develop rural infrastructure.

In 2006 Malawi qualified for additional debt relief under the HIPC. (More than 90 percent of the country's external debt, or $3.1 billion, has been forgiven.) In 2007 the IMF provided $18 million as part of the country's Poverty Reduction and Growth Facility agreement. Between 1997 and 2007, child mortality rates fell from 221 per 1,000 to 120 per 1,000.

The EU pledged to provide Malawi $677 million in economic assistance over a six-year period beginning in 2008. In response to rising fuel prices, the IMF agreed to a $77.1 million loan in December 2008. In 2010 Malawi's GDP growth was 6.6 percent. In 2010 the IMF announced an $80.1 million loan to promote economic development. Disputes with the UK and other foreign donors led to the suspension of some international aid in 2011, although some assistance was restored in 2012 (see Foreign relations, below). GDP grew by 4.3 percent in 2011, 1.9 percent in 2012, and 5 percent the next year. In 2012 inflation increased dramatically to 21.3 percent before rising further to 28.3 percent in 2013. At least 60 percent of the population was reported to live below the poverty level, and unofficial estimates put the unemployment rate at 45.5 percent. GDP grew by 5.7 percent in 2014, 5.5 percent in 2015, and 5.7 percent in 2016. Inflation decreased significantly, falling to 17.3 percent in 2015, and then 10 percent in 2016. GDP per capita in 2016 was $306.

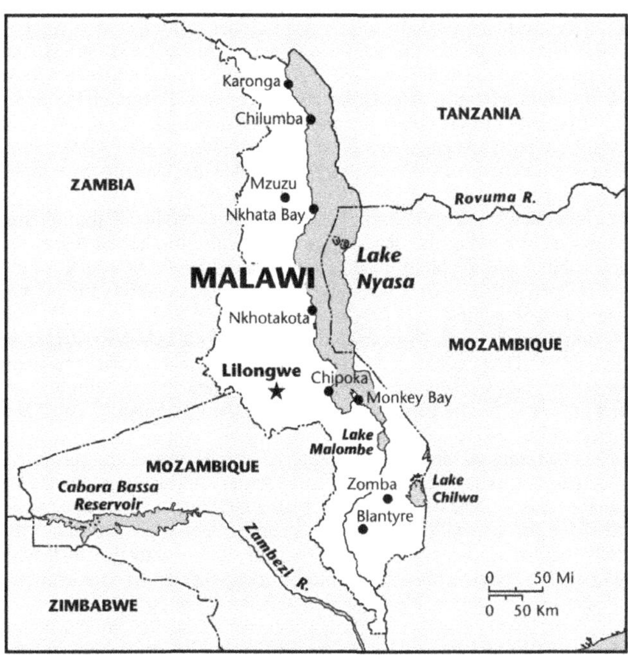

GOVERNMENT AND POLITICS

Political background. Under British rule since 1891, the Nyasaland protectorate was joined with Northern and Southern Rhodesia in 1953 to form the Federation of Rhodesia and Nyasaland. Internal opposition to the federation proved so vigorous that a state of emergency was declared, with nationalist leaders H. B. M. CHIPEMBERE, Kanyama CHIUME, and Hastings Kamuzu BANDA being imprisoned. They were released upon the attainment of internal self-government on February 1, 1963, and dissolution of the federation at the end of that year. Nyasaland became a fully independent member of the Commonwealth under the name of Malawi on July 6, 1964, and a republic two years later, with Prime Minister Banda being installed as the country's president.

The early years of the Banda presidency were marked by conservative policies, including the retention of white civil service personnel and the maintenance of good relations with South Africa. Younger, more radical leaders soon became disenchanted, and in 1965 a minor insurrection was led by Chipembere, while a second, led by Yatuta CHISIZA, took place in 1967. Both were easily contained, however, and Banda became entrenched as the nation's political leader.

In March 1983 Dr. Attati MPAKATI of the Socialist League of Malawi (one of the two principal exile groups) was assassinated in Zimbabwe. In May Orton CHIRWA, the former leader of the other main exile organization (the Malawi Freedom Movement—Mafremo) was found guilty of treason and was sentenced to death. (Chirwa had been jailed, along with his wife and son, since December 1981.) Subsequent appeals in December 1983 and February 1984 were denied, and Chirwa, who claimed that he and his family had been abducted from Zambia to permit their arrest, became an object of international human rights attention. Bowing to the pressure, Banda commuted the sentence to life imprisonment in June 1984. (Chirwa died in 1992 under unclear circumstances.)

In an apparent response to pressure from international aid donors, President Banda instructed the National Assembly in December 1991 to "make a final decision" on unipartyism, albeit prefacing his call for debate by commending the "successes" of his Malawi Congress Party (MCP), which had voted for a continuation of the existing system only three months before. Thus, despite the country's first mass protests against MCP rule in May 1992, no opposition groups were permitted to present candidates in legislative balloting on June 26–27. Somewhat unexpectedly, given another MCP vote against pluralism on October 2, President Banda on October 18 announced plans for a national referendum to decide Malawi's future political structure. On June 15, 1993, 63.5 percent of those participating voted in favor of a multiparty system.

On October 13, 1993, 11 days after Banda underwent emergency brain surgery, the office of the president announced the formation of a three-member Presidential Council, thus rejecting the opposition's call for a "neutral" president to rule in Banda's absence. The council was comprised of the MCP's recently appointed secretary general, Stephen Gwandanguluwe CHAKUAMBA Phiri, as well as MCP stalwarts John TEMBO and Robson CHIRWA. Nevertheless, preparations for the May 1994 multiparty balloting continued, with the assembly approving constitutional amendments reforming the electoral process and presidency (see Constitution and government, below) and authorizing the formation of two transitional bodies: the National Consultative Council (NCC) and the National Executive Council (NEC), charged with electoral preparation and oversight.

In early December 1993 the Presidential Council ordered the disarmament of the Malawi Young Pioneers (MYP), an MCP-affiliated paramilitary group whose recent killing of two regular army soldiers had exacerbated tensions between the two armed forces. The ensuing crackdown, resulting in 32 deaths and the reported flight of 1,000 pioneers to Mozambique, was denounced by the NCC, which accused the Presidential Council of having "lost control." Consequently, on December 7 a still visibly ailing Banda dissolved the Presidential Council and reassumed presidential powers. Shortly thereafter, Banda appointed a new defense minister, Maj. Gen. Wilfred John MPONERA, who, on January 7, 1994, announced the completion of MYP disarmament.

In the country's first multiparty election on May 17, 1994, voters decisively rejected bids by Banda and two other presidential candidates in favor of Bakili MULUZI of the United Democratic Front (UDF). In simultaneous legislative balloting, the UDF also led the field, although it fell short of a majority by five seats. Four days after his inauguration on May 21, President Muluzi announced a coalition government in which two minor parties—the Malawi National Democratic Party (MNDP) and the United Front for Multiparty Democracy (UFMD)—were allocated one portfolio each.

On July 21, 1994, the MCP and the Alliance for Democracy (Aford) announced the formation of a shadow government that included Banda's former second in command, John Tembo, as finance minister. However, the MCP-Aford pact was effectively terminated when Aford president Chakufwa CHIHANA accepted an appointment by Muluzi as second vice president designate and three other Aford members joined an expanded cabinet on September 24. Constitutional revision was required to accommodate Chihana's appointment (see Constitution and government, below).

In response to domestic and international criticism of the size of his cabinet, Muluzi reshuffled it and reduced its size from 35 to 32 members on July 16, 1995. A more significant change occurred on July 27, when the UDF and Aford announced that they had signed an agreement to form a coalition government. However, in December relations between the two groups cooled when Aford leader Chihana accused the government of "lacking transparency" and failing to combat corruption.

On December 23, 1995, former president Banda and his five codefendants were acquitted of all charges relating to the murder of "reformist" politicians in 1983 (see MCP in Political Parties and Groups, below). Shortly thereafter, Banda apologized for the "pain and suffering" that had occurred while he was in office. However, he continued to deny personal responsibility, instead blaming "selfish individuals" in his government. Meanwhile, the new UDF-led government continued to press inquiries into a wide range of abuses that were alleged to have taken place under Banda's rule. Ultimately, although official scrutiny remained leveled at some of Banda's former confidants, investigative fervor in general dissipated substantially upon Banda's death on November 25.

On May 2, 1996, Chihana resigned from the government, saying that he wanted to concentrate on his party responsibilities. Six Aford cabinet ministers refused to comply with Chihana's demand that they resign from the government as well, and they declared themselves "independents." In response, Aford and the MCP suspended their participation in the assembly, accusing the UDF of attempting to secure a legislative majority by "poaching" their representatives as cabinet ministers. Assembly activity subsequently remained blocked (the UDF proving unable to muster a quorum) until April 1997, when Aford and the MCP ended their boycott after President Muluzi agreed to pursue constitutional amendments that would "prevent political horse trading and chicanery." However, the matter was not resolved on July 24, when Muluzi appointed a new cabinet that still included Aford representatives against the wishes of Aford leaders.

On June 15, 1999, President Muluzi was reelected to a second five-year term with 51.4 percent of the vote, compared to 44.3 percent for runner-up Chakuamba, the joint MCP-Aford candidate. (Aford's Chihana had served as Chakuamba's vice presidential running mate.) In concurrent legislative polling the UDF secured a plurality of 93 of 193 seats. The opposition accused the government of numerous irregularities, including manipulation of the media and the voter registration process as well as vote rigging. The losing candidates also argued that a runoff should have been held because Muluzi's vote total had not surpassed the level of 50 percent of the registered voters. Although the international community generally accepted the balloting as free and fair and the courts in Malawi upheld the results, Chakufwa Chihana of Aford, the MCP-Aford vice presidential candidate, called for a campaign of civil disobedience to protest the government's actions. Muluzi's critics also challenged the cabinet he appointed on July 1 for containing too many ministers (21 of 36) from the southern part of the country, the UDF stronghold.

Corruption charges prompted the appointment of new cabinets in March and November 2000. Meanwhile severe intraparty infighting continued to hamper both the MCP and Aford, as evidenced by their poor showing in the November 2000 local elections, which were dominated by the UDF, albeit in the context of a low voter turnout. Muluzi's second term was marked by a bitter dispute over proposed constitutional changes to allow a president to seek a third term. The initial proposal failed to gain the needed two-thirds majority in the assembly in 2002, and a second effort in the legislature was rebuffed in 2003. The UDF attempted to have the measure brought to the public in a national referendum. However, it became clear that the constitutional amendment would fail because of widespread opposition, and the referendum request was withdrawn. Muluzi subsequently announced that he would not seek a third term. Instead he handpicked his successor, economist Bingu wa MUTHARIKA, who had run as a presidential candidate in 1999 for the defunct United Party (UP).

Presidential polling in 2004 was delayed by two days as a result of complaints by opposition parties that some 1 million voters, including many of their supporters, had been purged from the list of eligible voters. However, the High Court accepted the government's explanation that only double registrations and ineligible voters had been eliminated from the rolls.

In January 2004 a coalition of seven small parties, calling itself *Mgwirizano* (Unity), was launched to present Chakuamba as a joint presidential candidate. However, President Mutharika was reelected in balloting on May 20 with 35.9 percent of the vote, compared to 27.1 percent for Tembo (the MCP candidate) and 25.7 percent for Chakuamba. In concurrent legislative balloting, the MCP secured 60 seats, followed by the UDF with 49. Opposition parties and candidates challenged the legitimacy of the polling. However, Chakuamba withdrew his objections and accepted the post of minister of agriculture in the new Mutharika government, which also included the UDF, the National Democratic Alliance, the *Mgwirizano* coalition, and independents. Many independent legislators agreed to support the UDF in the assembly, some 23 of them subsequently joining the UDF. Additional realignments occurred after a dispute within the UDF prompted Mutharika to form a new party (see Current issues, below). As part of his anti-corruption campaign, the president dismissed 35 senior government officials between 2004 and 2006.

Mutharika announced a new economic plan in 2007 designed to enhance the country's agricultural sector through new investments in technology and infrastructure. Tensions between the president and individual government ministers led to four cabinet reshuffles in the period 2004–2008, with Mutharika assuming the portfolios of minister of agriculture and food security, and of education, science, and technology.

On May 16, 2009, the president dissolved the cabinet ahead of national elections. In the presidential elections on May 19, Mutharika was reelected with 66.4 percent of the vote. Tembo placed second with 30.3 percent. Five other minor party candidates received less than 1 percent each in polling that was criticized by some domestic and foreign monitors (see Current issues, below). In legislative balloting held on the same day, the Democratic Progressive Party (DPP) won an outright majority in the assembly with 113 seats. A new cabinet was appointed on June 15. Only eight ministers were retained from the previous cabinet. Mutharika's brother Peter was appointed minister of justice and constitutional affairs and the president retained the portfolio of agriculture and food security. Islamic groups protested the new cabinet because it included only two Muslims, as opposed to the seven in the previous government.

The president carried out a major cabinet reshuffle on August 9, 2010. He relinquished the portfolio of agriculture and food safety, and his brother moved to the ministry of education, science, and technology. As part of the reshuffle, Mutharika named his wife Callista CHIMOMBO as "first lady" in charge of the ministry of maternal, infant and child health. Reports indicated that Mutharika's replacement of some ministers was part of an effort to reflect greater tribal and clan diversity in the government.

In January 2011 Mutharika assumed the portfolio of the defense minister. Following the deadly protests in July, Mutharika dismissed the cabinet and declared that the government would be run from the president's office (see Current issues, below). A new cabinet was named on September 7.

On April 5, 2012, Mutharika died of a heart attack. Vice President Joyce BANDA (People's Party—PP) was sworn in as interim president on April 7 (see Current issues, below). She named a new coalition cabinet on April 26. The cabinet was reshuffled on December 6, 2012, and again in July 2013.

In balloting on May 20, 2014, Peter Mutharika was elected president (see Current issues, below). He was sworn in on May 31 and named a smaller cabinet that was dominated by the DPP but included one minister from the opposition UDF. In concurrent legislative balloting, the DPP secured a small plurality, with 50 seats, followed by the MCP, with 48, and the People's Party (PP) with 26. Independents won the majority of seats, 52, reflecting dissatisfaction with the major parties.

There were a series of minor cabinet reshuffles in April and August 2015 and then again in April 2016. Reports indicated that the August reshuffle was part of an effort to reduce corruption in the affected ministries.

Constitution and government. The constitution of July 6, 1966, established a one-party system under which the MCP was accorded a political monopoly and its leader extensive powers as head of state, head of government, and commander in chief. Originally elected to a five-year presidential term by the National Assembly in 1966, Hastings Banda was designated president for life in 1971.

Following approval of a multiparty system in a national referendum on June 15, 1993, the assembly on June 22 amended the basic law to permit the registration of parties beyond the MCP. In November further revision abolished the life presidency and repealed the requirement that presidential candidates be MCP members. Following the return of ailing President Banda to active status in early December, an additional amendment was enacted to provide for an acting president in case of the president's incapacitation.

A new constitution (proposed by a National Constitutional Conference) was approved by the assembly on May 16, 1994, and entered into effect provisionally for one year on May 18. The new basic law incorporated the 1993 amendments, while also providing for a new Constitutional Committee and a Human Rights Commission. It also authorized the eventual creation of a second legislative body (the Senate) no sooner than 1999. However, in January 2001, much to the consternation of opposition parties and some civic organizations, the assembly revised the basic law to eliminate reference to the proposed Senate. The government argued that the creation of the Senate would have burdened the country's fragile economy, but opponents claimed that the administration was in reality primarily concerned that the new body would have had the power to impeach the president. Following review and refinement by the Constitutional Conference, the new constitution was once again approved by the assembly and promulgated as a permanent document on May 18, 1995. One of the amendments approved by the assembly in November 1994 provided for a presidentially appointed second vice president. The first vice president is elected as a running mate to the president and assumes the presidency if that office becomes vacant. The president is not required to designate a second vice president, but any such appointment must be made outside the president's political party.

The 1995 constitution provided for a Western-style judicial system, including a Supreme Court of Appeal, a High Court, and magistrates' courts. No mention is made of the so-called traditional courts (headed by local chiefs), which had been restored in 1970. For administrative purposes Malawi is divided into 3 regions, and 28 districts, which are headed by regional ministers and district commissioners, respectively.

Most newspapers are privately owned and operated. Constitutional amendments in the 1990s eased press restrictions but censorship remains a problem; two journalists were arrested in 2005 after publishing a story in which they suggested that the president was afraid of ghosts and had moved out of the presidential mansion because he believed it to be haunted. In the 2007 budget, opposition members of parliament managed to reduce funding of the state broadcasting companies to a symbolic one kwacha because of claims that the media had become organs of the government. The Malawi Electoral Commission criticized the state radio and television station for failing to provide equal access to all parties during the 2009 balloting. In January 2011 Mutharika approved a highly restrictive press law that gave the information minister the authority to censor any content judged "contrary to the public interest." In its 2012 ratings of global press freedom, Reporters Without Borders ranked Malawi 75th out of 179 countries, a rise from 146th the previous year. The dramatic increase was attributed to the removal of a range of press restrictions by the Banda government. The group ranked Malawi 66th out of 180 countries in 2016, reflecting the continuing expansion of press freedoms.

Foreign relations. Malawi under President Banda's leadership sought to combine African nationalism with multiracialism at home and a strongly pro-Western and anticommunist position in world affairs. Citing economic necessity, Malawi was one of the few black African states to maintain uninterrupted relations with white-ruled South Africa. A consequence of the linkage was a September 1986 meeting in Blantyre, during which the leaders of Mozambique, Zambia, and Zimbabwe reportedly warned Banda to change his policies, particularly concerning alleged Malawian support for Renamo rebels in Mozambique. Banda, while denying the allegations, nevertheless quickly concluded a joint defense and security pact with Mozambique. The government also reaffirmed its commitment to an effort by the Southern African Development Coordination Conference (SADCC, subsequently the Southern African Development Community—SADC) to reduce dependence on South African trade routes. To that end, Malawi in 1987 agreed to increase shipments through Tanzania, with which it had established diplomatic ties in 1985 despite long-standing complaints of Tanzanian aid to Banda's opponents. Relations with Zambia had also been strained by Malawi's claim to Zambian territory in the vicinity of their common border.

In 1994 the new Muluzi administration moved quickly to strengthen regional ties, the president traveling to Zimbabwe, Zambia, and Botswana. In addition, Malawi and Mozambique created a joint commission to locate and repatriate former rebels located in the opposite state. Malawi also endeavored to improve relations and security ties with the United States. In June 2003 five suspected al-Qaida terrorists were turned over to U.S. custody.

President Mutharika's anticorruption campaign won international praise from European states, the United States, and international organizations such as the IMF and the World Bank. As a result, donors increased aid and assistance to the government, Malawi receiving about $60 million annually in U.S. economic aid in 2005 and 2006. Concurrently, Malawi's exports to the United States increased dramatically through the African Growth and Opportunity Act (AGOA), which eliminated U.S. tariffs on more than two-thirds of Malawian exports.

Following record maize harvests in 2006 and 2007, the government purchased excess crops from farmers to donate to Swaziland and Lesotho following a widespread drought. Malawi also increased sales of maize to Zimbabwe to record levels—400,000 tons per year. The two countries signed an economic cooperation agreement in May 2006, despite international criticism that closer ties undermined efforts to democratize Zimbabwe.

Relations between Malawi and China were strained in 2006 after Malawi refused an invitation to participate in a 2006 conference called by China in an effort to convince a group of African countries to break off diplomatic and economic relations with Taiwan. Instead of accepting the Chinese overtures, Malawi, Burkina Faso, Gambia, São Tomé and Principe, and Swaziland signed a joint declaration of support in 2007 for Taiwan. Among other things, Taiwan since 2002 has provided financial and technical support to Malawi for a number of programs designed to improve education and health care, including an initiative to combat the spread of HIV/AIDS.

However, in January 2008 Malawi announced the suspension of diplomatic relations with Taiwan and the initiation of new ties with China. China subsequently pledged $287 million in new economic aid for Malawi. Chinese officials also promised new infrastructure assistance. The new relationship was expected to be especially beneficial to Malawi's tobacco sector, the largest in Africa, because China accounted for one-third of worldwide tobacco. In May Malawi and Zambia agreed on a joint electrification program whereby Malawi would provide power to remote areas along the border of the two countries. Malawi agreed to deploy 50 police officers to the Darfur region of Sudan as part of the UN–African Union (AU) peacekeeping force and pledged an additional 800 troops. In September Malawi withdrew recognition of the Polisario Front government in the Western Sahara and instead called for a negotiated settlement over the disputed region.

In 2009 foreign minister Yang Jiechi became the first senior Chinese official to visit Malawi and he announced a $90 million loan for economic development during the trip.

In January 2010 Malawi and India signed four new bilateral trade agreements. Trade between India and Malawi has increased 100 percent since 2003. In February Mutharika was elected as the new leader of the AU. A number of foreign governments protested the trial and conviction of two Malawians for homosexuality (see Current issues, below).

The Millennium Challenge Corporation (MCC) announced in January 2011 that it would provide $350 million to Malawi for infrastructure projects. However, after countries such as Germany announced the reduction of aid because of the newly enacted press restrictions (see Current issues, below) and the criminalization of homosexuality, the MCC first delayed signing the agreement until April and then froze payments in July. Meanwhile, in April a diplomatic cable written by the British high commissioner to Malawi, Fergus Cochrane-Dyet, was printed by the Malawian newspaper the *Weekend Nation.* The note was critical of Mutharika and led to the expulsion of Cochrane-Dyet. The British retaliated and expelled the Malawian representative to London, Flossie Gomile CHIDYAONGA. The UK subsequently froze $122.8 million in aid for Malawi in July following reports of human rights violations by the government (see Current issues, below).

In September 2012 Malawi and the UK reestablished diplomatic ties. Meanwhile, after the inauguration of Banda in April, donors, including the UK, the United States, and the World Bank restored most aid to the country. In October Banda requested that the AU arbitrate Malawi's maritime border dispute with Tanzania over Lake Malawi (Lake Nyasa). Subsequent bilateral negotiations launched in November failed and were superseded in March 2013 by talks under the auspices of the Forum for Former African Heads of State and Government. Also in October 2012 the United States announced it would provide $105 million to Malawi for economic and social development, including funds to upgrade health care facilities and services.

Malawi agreed in March 2013 to contribute troops to a UN peacekeeping force in the Democratic Republic of the Congo (see entry on the DRC). In November, revelations of a massive government corruption scandal (see Current issues, below) led foreign donors to withhold more than $150 million in aid. However, in January 2014, the IMF disbursed $20 million in assistance. The IMF released an additional $18.1 million in March 2015 in response to new anticorruption efforts by the government.

Fighting in Mozambique (see entry on Mozambique) prompted a wave of refugees to flee to Malawi. From July 2015 to January 2016, an estimated 4,000 Mozambicans crossed into Malawi, taxing the country's fragile social systems.

China announced in August 2016 that it would donate 6,000 tons of rice, worth $9.4 million, in response to a widespread draught in Malawi (see Current issues, below). Also, the AfDB provided $7 million in emergency funds.

Current issues. Following the 2004 elections, new president Mutharika launched a broad anticorruption campaign that earned praise (and additional aid) from donors such as the EU and the United States. However, the initiative generated a rift between Mutharika and former president Muluzi, some of whose close allies (including several UDF leaders) were arrested on corruption charges. (Critics of Mutharika accused him of using the new anticorruption bureau as a personal political tool.) Consequently, supporters in the assembly of Muluzi (who remained leader of the UDF after leaving the presidency) began to block legislation presented by the Mutharika administration. The conflict culminated in the president's decision in February 2005 to quit the UDF and form a new DPP, which attracted a number of Mutharika's supporters within the UDF and other parties and prompted significant legislative realignment.

In March 2005 the UDF and MCP attempted without success to impeach Mutharika for inappropriate use of government funds. Opposition parties (led by the UDF) again attempted to start impeachment proceedings against the president in June. The assembly formally approved the start of impeachment proceedings in mid-October 2005, but the High Court ordered them stopped after pro-Mutharika demonstrations deteriorated into "riots" in which opposition legislators were reportedly attacked. In any event, it had been widely expected that the impeachment motion would not have garnered the two-thirds assembly vote required for success. In addition, analysts suggested that much of the population considered the impeachment initiative a waste of time and resources, particularly in view of the nation's severe food crisis.

The government conducted another string of arrests in November 2005 as part of its anticorruption campaign. Among those charged were two legislators who had led the recent impeachment drive and Vice President Cassim CHILUMPHA (UDF). However, the High Court ruled that Chilumpha could not be brought up on criminal charges while serving as vice president. In February 2006 Mutharika attempted to dismiss Chilumpha for "undermining the government," but the High Court declared the president lacked the constitutional authority for such a move. At the end of April, Chilumpha and some 12 others (including senior members of the UDF) were arrested on treason charges, the administration accusing them of having plotted the assassination of Mutharika. The charges against most of those arrested were quickly dropped, but Chilumpha remained under house arrest along with two codefendants. Meanwhile, former president Muluzi was arrested on corruption charges in July, but he was released the following day after all charges were dismissed.

The restrictions on Vice President Chilumpha's house arrest were gradually relaxed as his trial began in January 2007. Meanwhile, the crackdown on the UDF continued, as three party officials were arrested on charges of treason in January.

In June 2007 the Supreme Court upheld the article in the constitution that declared that any member of parliament who switched parties could be expelled and forced to stand for office in a by-election. Opposition members of parliament initially blocked debate on the government's proposed budget in an effort to force the by-elections. A compromise was finally reached in September that allowed passage of the budget in return for subsequent legislative debate on the management of new polling for by-elections.

In February 2008 opposition parties boycotted the opening of the assembly and insisted that debate over by-elections be the first priority of the parliament. Only 6 of the 105 opposition deputies attended the opening of the legislature. In May the government arrested a number of opposition figures, including former president Muluzi, on charges that they were plotting a coup. Also charged were former senior military leaders and the secretary general of the UDF, Kennedy MAKWANGWALA. Opposition leaders decried the arrests as part of an intimidation campaign ahead of presidential and legislative elections scheduled for 2009. All were subsequently released on bail. Also in May, Mutharika initiated the parliamentary budgetary session despite the ongoing opposition boycott. Meanwhile, the government announced a 17 percent increase in pay for civil servants in an effort to prevent a general strike.

In the presidential and legislative balloting, concerns were raised over potential fraud. Protests were also lodged to the electoral commission over the use of state media to support the ruling Mutharika and the ruling DPP. However, most domestic and foreign observers asserted that the balloting was generally free and fair. The polling marked the first time in Malawi that a woman, Loveness Gondwe of the New Rainbow Coalition (see Political Parties and Groups, below), ran for the presidency. Although Gondwe did not win, Joyce Banda of the DPP became the country's first female vice president.

The construction of a new presidential palace for Mutharika in the midst of economic uncertainties prompted protest and threats of parliamentary investigations. In May two Malawians were convicted of homosexuality and sentenced to 14 years in prison. The United States and a number of other countries protested the sentences. In addition, some foreign donors reportedly threatened to suspend aid payments unless the case was reexamined. In September a corruption trial began for former president Muluzi on charges from 2005.

Security forces brutally suppressed protests against rising fuel and energy costs on July 20, 2011. At least 19 people were killed and more than 250 arrested. Two days after the demonstrations, Mutharika replaced the head of the Malawian army in an effort to ease tensions. Additional protests scheduled for August 17 were cancelled following an agreement between opposition leaders and the government to launch a national dialogue. On August 19 Mutharika dismissed the cabinet, ostensibly in response to the government's crackdown on the demonstrators. Opposition groups and critics charged that the action was designed to consolidate the president's power. Meanwhile, Banda formed a new political grouping, the People's Party (PP) (see Political Parties and Groups, below).

Mutharika died on April 5, and DPP loyalists sought to conceal his death, even reportedly flying the president's body to South Africa and asserting that he was undergoing medical treatment, in an effort to prevent Banda from assuming the presidency. However, Banda secured the support of the military and was sworn on April 7. She subsequently named a new cabinet that was purged of Mutharika loyalists, including the former president's brother and wife. Following Banda's inauguration, up to 45 members of the parliament attempted to switch parties and join the PP. However, as Malawian law requires a member of parliament to resign and stand in a by-election when changing parties, the majority remained formally in their original groupings but supported the government.

In March 2013 ten current and former government officials were arrested on suspicion of plotting a coup in the aftermath of Mutharika's death by keeping Banda from taking office. Among those arrested where Peter Mutharika, the dead president's brother, and a former foreign minister. The trials of those accused were postponed by the High Court in April. Strong harvests in the summer of 2013 increased government revenues and allowed an increase in farm aid to the poor. In June Anastasia MSOSA became the first woman chief justice of Malawi's judiciary. In November former justice minister Ralph KASAMBARA was arrested for attempted murder in a corruption scandal that tainted a number of past and present government officials. Dubbed "Cashgate", the scandal involved the embezzlement of more than $100 million in state funds and subsequent efforts to cover up the crimes.

Hurt by the Cashgate scandal and her refusal to participate in two preelection debates, Banda placed third in presidential balloting on May 20, 2014, with 20.2 percent of the vote. Peter Mutharika placed first among 12 candidates with 36.4 percent, followed by Lazarus CHAKWERA (MCP), with 27.8 percent. Banda alleged widespread fraud and attempted to nullify the vote on May 24, when only about one-third of the votes were counted. On May 30 the High Court ruled that the results should be released, confirming Mutharika's victory. In concurrent legislative polling, no party secured a majority, reflecting the contemporary fractured nature of Malawi's politics.

Massive flooding caused by record rainfall in January 2015 left more than 200 dead and 200,000 homeless. The flooding also destroyed a significant portion of the nation's crops, affecting more than 2.8 Malawians and prompting a call by the World Food Program for $81 million in emergency aid.

On September 4, 2015, Oswald LUTEPO was sentenced to 11 years in prison for defrauding the government and for money laundering as part of the Cashgate scandal. Lupeto worked with government officials to divert funds into shell companies for goods and services that were never delivered, personally earning some $8.5 million. In October Mutharika announced a new series of anticorruption measures, including a ban on foreign travel. The following month, 63 civil workers in the health ministry were suspended for corruption.

Former justice minister Kasambara was convicted of conspiracy to commit murder on July 21, 2016. Meanwhile, the government announced that 6.5 million faced food shortages in 2016 as the result of a drought that followed the 2015 torrential rains. Mutharika declared a state of emergency over the food shortages.

POLITICAL PARTIES AND GROUPS

For nearly three decades prior to the 1993 national referendum, the Malawi Congress Party (MCP) was the only authorized political group, and it exercised complete control of the government. On June 29, 1993, the constitution was amended to allow for multiparty activity, and on August 17 the government announced that the first groups had been authorized to function as legal parties.

Legislative Parties:

Democratic Progressive Party (DPP). The DPP was launched in February 2005 by President Bingu wa Mutharika and other UDF dissidents who opposed UDF president Muluzi. Disaffected members of other parties and a number of independents also joined the DDP, which as of mid-2006 was credited with controlling some 74 assembly seats. DPP Vice President Gwanda Chakuamba was dismissed from the cabinet and expelled from the party in September 2005 after he strongly criticized President Mutharika. Ralph KASAMBARA was dismissed as attorney general in 2006 and left the party to form the **Congress for Democrats** (CODE). Chakuamba's successor as party vice president, Uladi MUSSA, was also dismissed in January 2007 on charges that he was attempting to launch a new political party. Mussa was replaced by the party's Secretary General Heatherwick Ntaba.

Mutharika was reelected president of the republic in May 2009 during elections in which the DPP secured 113 seats and an outright majority in the assembly. Reports indicated that factions emerged within the party over a possible successor to Mutharika, who was constitutionally prevented from seeking another term as president in 2014. After Vice President Joyce BANDA refused to support Mutharika's brother and hand-picked successor, Peter Mutharika's bid to be the DPP candidate in 2014, she and a number of her supporters were dismissed from the DPP. Banda went on to form a new entity, the People's Party (see below).

The government's suppression of protests in July 2011 created divisions within the party and led to the expulsion of several prominent party leaders, including Henry Dama PHOYA, who was reported to be organizing a new political grouping to challenge the DPP. Peter Mutharika succeeded his brother as party leader after the latter's death on April 5, 2012. In October DPP Secretary General Elias Wakuda KAANGA defected to the PP.

In April 2012 Mutharika defeated Parliamentary Speaker Henry CHIMUNTHU to be reelected party president. Mutharika was elected president of Malawi in May 2014, while the DPP won 50 seats in concurrent legislative balloting, and 165 local government seats. Reports in January 2016 claimed that Mutharika was in ill health and might be forced to resign, claims that were vigorously rejected by the DPP.

Leaders: Peter MUTHARIKA (President of the Republic and President of the Party), Saulos CHILIMA (Vice President of the Republic), Goodall Edward GONDWE (First Vice President of the Party and Minister for Finance and Economic Development), Jean KALILANI (Secretary General).

United Democratic Front (UDF). The UDF was founded in April 1992 by former MCP officials who operated clandestinely until October, when they announced their intention to campaign for a multiparty democracy. A party congress on December 30, 1993, chose UDF chair Bakili Muluzi to be the UDF's presidential candidate. Meanwhile, the UDF leaders were embarrassed by allegations, attributed to the MCP, that they had engaged in anti-opposition activities while MCP members.

Muluzi defeated incumbent president Banda and two other candidates in March 1994 with a 47.3 percent plurality of the vote. In the legislative balloting the UDF won a plurality of 84 of 177 seats. Muluzi was reelected with 51.4 percent of the vote in 1999, while the UDF increased its legislative plurality to 93 out of 193 seats in 1999.

Beginning in 2000, the party suffered serious internal divisions, leading to the formation of the anti-Muluzi NDA (below). In 2003 dissident members of the UDF left the party to form a new entity, the People's Progressive Movement (PPM), led by former UDF party vice president Aleke Banda. In the 2004 legislative elections the UDF lost its plurality and became the second-largest party (49 seats) in the assembly behind the MCP.

Following the 2004 presidential election, a leadership struggle emerged between Muluzi, who remained party president, and his hand-picked successor as Malawi's president, Bingu wa Mutharika. Among other things, Muluzi's supporters objected to elements of the broad anticorruption efforts by Mutharika, who in February 2005 left the UDF to form the DPP (above).

The UDF led the subsequent effort to impeach President Mutharika, although its legislative representation had reportedly fallen to 30 by mid-2006 due to defections to the DPP. In addition, many UDF leaders faced corruption charges pressed by the Mutharika administration (see Current issues, above). Muluzi announced in March 2007 that he intended to be the UDF candidate for the presidency in 2009, and he won the party's nomination at a convention in April 2008. The subsequent ruling by the constitutional court that Muluzi was ineligible to run led many UDF supporters to back MCP candidate John Tembo (see below). In the legislative balloting the UDF secured 17 seats. Many party members blamed the UDF's poor performance on Muluzi's failed presidential effort. In December 2009 Muluzi announced his retirement from politics. Friday JUMBE was chosen as interim leader of the MCP to replace Muluzi. In September 2010 a dissident faction of the UDF, calling itself the UDF Task Force for Change, attempted unsuccessfully to force Jumbe to resign. Muluzi's son Atupele MULUZI was appointed minister of Development Planning and Cooperation in 2012. In October the younger Muluzi was elected party president. He subsequently lost his cabinet post in a cabinet reshuffle. Jumbe subsequently joined the **Labor Party** and was that grouping's candidate in the 2014 presidential balloting, receiving 0.2 percent of the vote.

Muluzi was the party's candidate in the 2014 presidential elections. He placed fourth with 13.7 percent of the vote. The UDF secured 14 seats in parliament in concurrent balloting along with 57 seats on local councils. Muluzi was given a post in the subsequent DPP government. Reports in December 2015 indicated that the party had expelled UDF first vice president Iqbar OMAR for misconduct.

Leaders: Atupele MULUZI (President and Minister of Lands, Housing, and Urban Development), Gerald MPONDA (Secretary General).

Malawi Congress Party (MCP). The MCP is a continuation of the Nyasaland African Congress (NAC), which was formed in 1959 under the leadership of President H. Kamuzu Banda. Overtly pro-Western and dedicated to multiracialism and internal development, the party was frequently criticized for being excessively conservative. It held all legislative seats prior to the multiparty poll of May 1994, when it ran second in both the presidential and legislative races.

On August 25, 1994, Banda retired from politics although he retained the title of MCP president for life. The 1994 vice presidential candidate, Stephen Chakuamba, assumed leadership of the party. Thereafter, in early 1995, the party was shaken by the arrests of Banda, John Tembo (longtime Banda associate and MCP leader), and others for alleged involvement in the killing 12 years earlier of Dick MATENJE and several other MCP cabinet ministers. At the time of his death, Matenje had headed an increasingly popular reform wing within the party that had clashed with Tembo and his supporters. Banda, Tembo, and their codefendants in the murder trial were acquitted on all charges in December. Related charges against Cecilia KADZAMIRA, Banda's longtime companion who had been the country's "official hostess" during the latter part of the Banda regime, had been dismissed prior to trial on technical grounds. However, the government continued to press the case by appealing the verdict to the High Court, which ultimately upheld the acquittal. Meanwhile, Tembo and Kadzamira were arrested in September 1996 on charges of conspiracy to commit murder in connection with an alleged plot to assassinate cabinet members in 1995. They were quickly released on bail, and it was subsequently unclear if the case would be pursued. Similar ambiguity existed regarding fraud charges against Tembo and Kadzamira stemming from alleged malfeasance during the accumulation of the vast Banda "economic empire." Banda himself had been the focus of a corruption investigation in early 1997, but the case was dropped later in the year when it became apparent that the former president had little time to live.

Conflict between Banda's supporters and MCP "reformists" continued through 1997, with the latter clearly gaining the ascendancy at the party convention in July. In a surprisingly decisive vote of 406–109, Tembo was defeated in the race for MCP president by Chakuamba, who immediately declared his intention to run for president of the republic in 1999, insisting that the MCP should merge with Aford (below) to present the strongest possible challenge to the UDF. However, the proposed merger was shelved in the wake of objections from MCP veterans, including Tembo, who had been elected unopposed as MCP vice president.

In intraparty polling in January 1999, Chakuamba defeated Tembo in a contest to decide who would be the MCP's standard-bearer in mid-year presidential balloting. Subsequently, Chakuamba rejected suggestions that he choose Tembo as his running mate and named Aford's Chakufwa Chihana to his campaign ticket. On February 8 an electoral alliance for the presidential race between the two parties was officially inaugurated. Meanwhile, pro-Tembo activists staged demonstrations to protest what they (and reportedly Tembo) considered an affront. The MCP/Aford ticket finished second (with 44.3 percent of the vote) in the June presidential ballot, while the MCP secured 66 seats (on 33.82 percent of the vote) in the legislative poll. Meanwhile, tension between Chakuamba and Tembo continued, and in late May Tembo called upon Chakuamba to step down as party leader. In early June, Chakuamba called for an MCP boycott of the opening session of parliament, but his request was ignored and he was given a one-year suspension from the house (later voided by the High Court). On June 24 Speaker Sam Mpasu endorsed Tembo as new leader of the opposition in parliament, a decision that was subsequently challenged by Chakuamba.

The MCP infighting continued unabated into 2000, and the rival factions held separate conventions in August at which Chakuamba and Tembo were each declared party chair. However, the following summer the High Court nullified the parallel conventions. Meanwhile, the Chakuamba faction, which announced it had expelled Tembo and his supporters from the party, pursued ties with the NDA, the newly formed antigovernment grouping, while the Tembo faction was perceived as cooperating more and more with the administration. Chakuamba subsequently joined the Republican Party (below) in December 2003. The MCP became the largest party in the assembly after the 2004 elections, but Tembo lost his presidential bid. MCP Secretary General Kate KAINGA-KALULUMA joined the new Mutharika government and subsequently left the MCP to join the DPP. Subsequently, the MCP cooperated with the UDF's attempt to impeach President Mutharika, although internal MCP dissension was reported regarding that and other issues. (A dissident faction led by Respicius DZANJALIMODZI reportedly challenged Tembo's supporters for party supremacy.)

In 2007 Tembo rejected a proposal from the UDF to rally behind a single candidate in the 2009 presidential elections. Under the proposal, Tembo would have run as the vice presidential candidate with Muluzi as the presidential contender. Dissatisfied with Tembo's leadership, former party vice president Nicholas DAUSI and at least 60 MCP members and elected officials left the party in 2008 to join the DPP.

During the 2009 elections the MCP campaigned on a pledge to implement a universal subsidy for all farmers. Tembo placed second in the presidential balloting and the MCP became the second largest party in the legislature with 27 seats, although it lost more than half its former seats. After the balloting many MCP officials who criticized Tembo, including party spokesperson Ishmael Chafukira, who had called for the presidential candidate's resignation, were removed from their positions. In November Ephraim Adele KAYEMBE of the MCP was elected leader of the opposition in parliament after a rule change that allowed the entire legislature to vote for the opposition leader (Kayembe won because of votes from the DPP). However, Tembo successfully challenged the election in court on the grounds that only opposition parties should be allowed to participate in selecting the opposition leader. Tembo subsequently replaced Kayembe in June. Following protests in July 21, the government accused the MCP of inciting violence. The MCP continued to be the largest opposition party after Banda became president in April 2012.

In August 2013 Lazarus CHAKWERA was elected MCP president, while Chriss DAZA was elected secretary general. Chakwera, a former religious leader, was second in the 2014 presidential elections, while the MCP secured 48 seats in parliament and 131 seats on local councils in concurrent polling.

MCP spokesperson and member of parliament, Jessie KABWILA, was arrested on February 22, 2016, for an online post that the government claimed advocated the overthrow of President Mutharika,

Leaders: Lazarus CHAKWERA (President), Chriss DAZA (General Secretary).

Alliance for Democracy (Aford). Aford was launched in Lilongwe on September 21, 1992, by trade union leader and prodemocracy advocate Chakufwa Chihana, who at the time of the group's founding was awaiting trial on sedition charges. The grouping was led by a 13-member interim committee that included civil servants, academics, and businesspeople. Although Aford described itself as "not a party but a pressure group," the government on November 7 declared membership in the group illegal. In late December many of its members were arrested during demonstrations ignited by the sentencing of Chihana to three years imprisonment.

In March 1993 a spokesperson for the Zimbabwean-based Malawi Freedom Movement (Mafremo) announced that the group had dissolved and had merged with Aford. (Mafremo, in the wake of the 1981 arrest and imprisonment of its leader, Orton CHIRWA, had been relatively inactive until an early 1987 attack on a police station near the Tanzanian border that was attributed to the group's military wing, the Malawi National Liberation Army. Although initially based in Dares Salaam, Mafremo had subsequently been reported to have secured Zimbabwean support through the efforts of a new leader, Dr. Edward YAPWANTHA, who was expelled from Zimbabwe in mid-1990, apparently as a result of improved Malawian–Zimbabwean relations.)

In mid-1994 Chihana, who had been granted a sentence reduction and released two days before the multiparty referendum, pressed President Banda to resign in favor of an MCP-UDF-Aford transitional government. In August Aford turned back a merger bid from another opposition party—the Congress for the Second Republic (CSR)—asserting an interest in the CSR's then exiled leader, Kanyama CHUIME, but not the party.

Following its third-place showing in the 1994 assembly balloting, Aford declined an invitation to participate in a government coalition with the UDF, which was five seats short of a legislative majority. On June 20 Aford signed a memorandum of understanding with the MCP, in which the two groups committed themselves to preservation of "the endangered national unity and security of the country." However, in September Chihana joined the Muluzi government as second vice president designate, while three other Aford members accepted cabinet posts. Although Chihana rejected reports that the party was defecting to the UDF, in January 1995 Aford announced the dissolution of its alliance with the MCP.

Relations between the UDF and Aford deteriorated over the next year, and on May 2, 1996, Chihana, who had criticized the UDF on several points in December 1995, resigned from the second vice presidency, ostensibly to devote more time to party affairs. In June it was reported that an Aford national congress had voted to withdraw from the government coalition and had ordered its members in the cabinet to resign their posts. However, most of the ministers refused to leave the government, and it was reported that at least six members of the Aford executive council rejected the decision to separate from the coalition with the UDF. In response, Chihana called for the ouster of the "renegade" members. The issue remained clouded throughout 1997 as the new cabinet announced in July included not only the previous Aford ministers but also several other Aford members. Meanwhile, at the party's annual congress in December, Aford delegates voted against a merger with the MCP that had been advocated by many within the Chihana camp.

In June 1998 two Aford legislators, Joseph MSEKAWANTHU and Edward MUSYANI, declared their independence from the party, charging that the party's dictatorial" leadership policies had marginalized them. In October Aford officially acknowledged having decided to compete for the presidency on a joint ticket with the MCP, and in February 1999 Chihana agreed to campaign for the vice presidency on a ticket led by MCP leader Chakuamba. Aford was credited with 10.5 percent of the vote and 29 seats in the June 1999 assembly balloting.

Intraparty fighting continued in 2000–2001 over issues such as the future of the alliance with the MCP and whether the party should cooperate with the government. The Chihana faction was reportedly in favor of continuing an antigovernment stance, another wing pressed to form a national unity government with the UDF. Aford won only six seats in the 2004 elections and supported the subsequent Mutharika government after Chihana was appointed minister of agriculture and food security, a post he left in February 2005. Four of Aford's legislators reportedly defected to the DPP in 2005. In June 2006 Chihana died in South Africa; he was succeeded as party leader by Chipimpha Mughogho. At a party conference in December, Aford officials voted to expel members who did not support Mughogho as Aford leader. In October 2007 Dindi Gowa NYASULU was elected president of Aford at a congress that was marred by the death of 26 Aford delegates who perished in a bus accident on the way to the convention.

Nyasulu was the Aford presidential candidate in the 2009 balloting. He placed last among the six contenders with less than 1 percent of the vote. In the concurrent assembly polling, Aford secured only one seat. Aford received one cabinet post in the Banda government appointed in April 2012. Godfrey SHAWA became Aford's president following the resignation of Nyasulu in November 2012. (Nyasulu died of natural causes on December 11.) Aford won one seat in the 2014 parliamentary balloting and supported Banda of the PP in the concurrent presidential election.

Leaders: Godfrey SHAWA (President), Khwauli MSISKA (Secretary General).

People's Party (PP). Formed by then vice president Joyce Banda in September 2011, the PP attracted dissidents from a range of parties, including former vice president Cassim Chilumpha of the UDF. Following the death of president Mutharika in April 2012, Banda became president of Malawi and named a coalition cabinet that included members of the PP and other legislative parties. In August Banda was reelected party chair, as was General Secretary Henry CHIBWANA. Chilumpha was elected second vice president. Banda was defeated in the 2014 presidential election, while the PP won 26 seats in parliament and 65 seats on local councils. Following allegations of involvement in the Cashgate scandal, Banda fled into self-imposed exile in South Africa.

Leaders: Joyce BANDA (Former President of the Republic and Party Chair), Khumbo Hastings KACHALI (Former Vice President of the Republic), Henry CHIBWANA (Secretary General).

The small **Chipani Cha Pfuko** (CCP) won one seat in the 2014 parliamentary elections, while its leader Davis KATSONGA received 0.1 percent of the vote in the presidential balloting.

Other Parties That Contested Recent Legislative Election:

Republican Party (RP). The RP was formed in 2004 by Gwanda Chakuamba, Stanley Masauli, and other opponents of John Tembo from the MCP. Using the RP as the nucleus of the anti-Muluzi coalition *Mgwirizano,* Chakuamba placed third in the 2004 presidential balloting with 25.7 percent of the vote. He subsequently joined the government as minister of agriculture and food security. In the legislative elections, the RP became the third largest party with 15 seats.

In March 2005 Chakuamba resigned from the RP, along with a number of RP members, to join the new DPP. Chakuamba initially announced the dissolution of the RP, but the RP's executive council rejected the proposed "merger" with the DPP. Following his dismissal from the government and the DPP in September, Chakuamba attempted to reassert control over the RP. However, he was formally expelled from the RP in October, and he subsequently announced the formation of the **New Republican Party** (NRP). The NRP supported Muluzi of the UDF in the 2009 presidential elections but was subsequently described as defunct.

In the 2009 elections Stanley Masauli was the RP presidential candidate, but he received less than 1 percent of the vote. The RP failed to secure any seats in the concurrent assembly elections.

Leaders: Anastansia MSOSA (Chair), Stanley MASAULI (2009 presidential candidate).

People's Progressive Movement (PPM). Formed in 2003 by former UDF vice president Aleke Banda and other UDF members opposed to their party's Muluzi faction, the PPM joined the *Mgwirizano* coalition for the 2004 elections, gaining six seats in the assembly. Party member and former vice president of the republic John MALEWEZI ran as a presidential candidate for the PPM in 2004, placing fifth with just 2.5 percent of the vote. In 2005 a number of PPM members joined the DPP, although the PPM retained its status as an independent party. The party endorsed Mutharika in the 2009 presidential balloting. Party founder Banda died on April 9, 2010. The PPM was active in the protests and demonstrations in July 2011. Mark KATSONGA was the PPM candidate in the 2014 presidential elections, receiving 0.3 percent of the vote.

Leader: Mark KATSONGA.

Other parties that contested the 2009 or 2014 elections included the **People's Transformation Party** (Petra), which gained one seat in the 2004 balloting, but failed to gain any representation in 2009 and whose presidential candidate Kamuzu CHIBAMBO placed third; the **National Unity Party** (NUP), formed in 2005 and led by Harry CHIUME; the **Pamodzi Freedom Party** (PFP), established in 2002 and led by Rainsford NDIWO; **Congress for Democracy** (CODE), led by Ralph KASAMBARA; the **Congress for National Unity** (CONU), led by Bishop Daniel NKHUMBWE; the **United Democratic Party** (UDP), formed in 2005 by Kenedy Solomon KALAMBO; the **Malawi Forum for Unity and Development** (MAFUNDE), led by George MNESA and which secured one seat in the 2009 elections; the **National Salvation Front** (NSF), led by James NYONDO); the **United Independent Party** (UIP); the **Umodzi Alliance**; the **People's Transformation Party** (PTP); and the **Tisinthe Alliance**.

For information on the **National Democratic Alliance** (NDA), see the 2009 *Handbook.* For information on the **Movement for Genuine Democratic Change** (MGODE), **Malawi Democratic Party** (MDP), **New Congress for Democracy** (NCD), and **New Republican Party** (NRP), see the 2010 *Handbook.* For information on the **New Rainbow Coalition** (NARC) and the **Mgwirizano** (Unity) coalition, see the 2013 *Handbook.* For information on the **Maravi People's Party** (MPP), see the 2014 *Handbook.*

LEGISLATURE

Members of the unicameral **National Assembly** normally sit for five-year terms. From 1978 through 1992 candidates had to be approved by the MCP. The first multiparty balloting was held on May 17, 1994, for an enlarged body of 177 members. The number of legislators was increased to 193 for the balloting of July 15, 1999. In legislative balloting on May 20, 2014, the Democratic Progressive Party secured 50 seats; the Malawi Congress Party, 48; the People's Party, 26; the United Democratic Front, 14; Alliance for Democracy, 1; Chipani Cha Pfuko, 1; and independents, 52. One seat was not filled during the balloting.

Speaker: Richard MSOWOYA (MCP).

CABINET

[as of September 1, 2016]

President	Peter Mutharika
Vice President	Saulos Chilima
Ministers	
Agriculture and Irrigation	George Chaponda
Civil Service Administration, Disaster Management, Public Events, and Statutory Corporations	Saulos Chilima
Defense	Peter Mutharika
Education, Science, and Technology	Emmanuel Fabiano
Finance and Economic Development	Goodall Gondwe
Foreign Affairs and International Cooperation	Francis Kasaila
Gender, Children, and Social Welfare	Jean Kalilani [f]
Health	Peter Kumpalume
Home Affairs	Jappie Mhango
Industry, Trade, and Tourism	Joseph Mwanamveka
Information and Civic Education	Patricia Kaliati [f]
Justice and Constitutional Affairs	Samuel Tembenu
Labor, Youth, and Manpower Development	Henry Mussa
Lands, Housing, and Urban Development	Atupele Muluzi (UDF)
Local Government and Rural Development	Kondwani Nankhumwa
Natural Resources, Energy and Mining	Bright Msaka
Sports and Culture	Grace Obama Chiumia [f]
Transport and Public Works	Malison Ndau

[f] = female

Note: Except where noted, all cabinet members belong to the DPP.

INTERGOVERNMENTAL REPRESENTATION

Ambassador to the U.S.: Edward SAWERENGERA.

U.S. Ambassador to Malawi: Virginia PALMER.

Permanent Representative to the UN: Necton D. MHURA.

IGO Memberships (Non-UN): AfDB, AU, Comesa, CWTH, ICC, NAM, SADC, WTO.

For Further Reference:

Banik, Dan, and Blessings Chinsinga. *Political Transition and Inclusive Development in Malawi.* New York: Routledge, 2016.

Currey, James. *A History of Malawi: 1869–1966.* Woodbridge, Suffolk: Boydell & Brewer, 2012.

Power, Joey. *Political Culture and Nationalism in Malawi: Building Kwacha.* Rochester, NY: University of Rochester Press, 2010.

MALAYSIA

Political Status: Independent Federation of Malaya within the Commonwealth established August 31, 1957; Malaysia established September 16, 1963, with the addition of Sarawak, Sabah, and Singapore (which withdrew in August 1965).

Area: 127,316 sq. mi. (329,749 sq. km), encompassing Peninsular Malaysia, 50,806 sq. mi. (131,588 sq. km); Sarawak, 48,050 sq. mi. (124,450 sq. km); Sabah, 28,460 sq. mi. (73,711 sq. km).

Population: 30,752,000 (2016E—UN); 30,949,962 (2016E—U.S. Census).

Major Urban Centers (urban area, 2015—UN): KUALA LUMPUR (6,837,000), Johor Bahru (912,000), Ipoh (737,000), Kuching (560,000). The new administrative capital, Putrajaya (88,300), is 25 miles south of Kuala Lumpur.

Official Language: Bahasa Malaysia.

Monetary Unit: Malaysian ringgit (market rate October 1, 2016: 4.14 ringgit = $1US).

Paramount Ruler: Sultan ABDUL HALIM al-Muadzam Shah (Sovereign of Kedah); elected for a five-year term on October 30, 2011, by the Conference of Rulers; sworn in on December 13 and formally installed on April 11, 2012, succeeding Sultan MIZAN Zainal Abidin ibni al-Marhum Sultan Mahmud al-Muftaki Billah Shah (Sovereign of Terengganu).

Deputy Paramount Ruler: Sultan MUHAMMAD V (Sovereign of Kelantan); elected on October 30, 2011, and sworn in on December 13 for a term concurrent with that of the paramount ruler, succeeding Sultan ABDUL HALIM al-Muadzam Shah (Sovereign of Kedah).

Prime Minister: Mohamad NAJIB Abdul Razak (United Malays National Organization); appointed on April 3, 2009, and sworn in the same day to succeed ABDULLAH bin Ahmad Badawi (United Malays National Organization), who had resigned on April 2; formed new government on April 9; sworn in for second term on May 6, 2013; and formed a new government on May 15.

THE COUNTRY

Situated partly on the Malay Peninsula and partly on the island of Borneo, Malaysia consists of 11 states of the former Federation of Malaya (Peninsular or West Malaysia) plus the states of Sarawak and Sabah (East Malaysia). Thailand and Singapore are the mainland's northern and southern neighbors, respectively, while Sarawak and Sabah share a common border with the Indonesian province of Kalimantan. The multiracial population is comprised predominantly of Malays (50 percent), followed by Chinese (24 percent), non-Malay tribals (11 percent), and Indians and Pakistanis (7 percent). Although the Malay-based Bahasa Malaysia is the official language, English, Tamil, and several Chinese dialects are widely spoken. Islam is the state religion, but the freedom to profess other faiths is constitutionally guaranteed. Minority religious groups include Buddhists (19 percent), Christians (9 percent), and Hindus (6 percent). The status of women is largely determined by ethnic group and location, urban Malay women being better educated than their rural counterparts. Overall, women comprise 36 percent of the active workforce, concentrated in services and manufacturing. Following the May 2013 balloting, women held 22 of 222 seats (10.4 percent) in the House of Representatives and 15 of 70 seats in the Senate (29.4 percent).

Malaysia continues to be the world's principal supplier of palm oil and a significant source of its other traditional exports, rubber and tin, but these and other commodity exports, including petroleum, liquefied natural gas, and timber, have been superseded in importance by manufactures—chiefly semiconductors and electrical equipment and appliances, which together account for about 50 percent of export earnings. Agriculture and fishing contribute only 11.2 percent of GDP and employ 11.1 percent of the labor force, while industry accounts for 40.6 percent of GDP and 36 percent of jobs.

GDP growth in 2002–2008 averaged 5.7 percent annually, but in 2009 GDP growth contracted by 2 percent, owing in large part to a sharp decline in exports as a result of the global economic crisis. (For more on the Malaysian economy prior to 2002, see the 2012 *Handbook.*) Restrictions on foreign participation in the economy were loosened in 2009, as were percentage requirements for Malays in most public employment. The economy rebounded in 2010 with a 10-year-high growth of 7 percent and 5 percent in 2011. Annual GDP growth averaged 5.4 percent between 2012 and 2015. In 2016 the IMF estimated that GDP grew by 4.9 percent. That year, inflation was 3 percent and GDP per capita was $11,646. In 2016 the World Bank ranked Malaysia 18th out of 189 countries, between Ireland and Iceland, in its annual ease of conducting business report.

GOVERNMENT AND POLITICS

Political background. Malaysia came into existence as a member of the Commonwealth on September 16, 1963, through merger of the already independent Federation of Malaya with the self-governing state of Singapore and the British Crown Colonies of Sarawak and Sabah. The Malay states, organized by the British in the 19th century, had achieved sovereign status in 1957, following the suppression of a long-standing communist insurgency. Tunku ABDUL RAHMAN, head of the United Malays National Organization (UMNO) and subsequently of the Alliance Party, became Malaya's first prime minister and continued in that capacity after the formation of Malaysia. Singapore, with its predominantly Chinese population, had been ruled as a separate British colony that became internally self-governing in 1959 under the leadership of LEE Kuan Yew of the People's Action Party (PAP). Its inclusion in Malaysia was terminated in August 1965, primarily because the PAP's attempt to extend its influence beyond the confines of Singapore was viewed as a threat to Malay dominance of the federation.

In May 1969 racial riots in Kuala Lumpur led to a declaration of national emergency. A nine-member National Operations Council was given full powers to quell the disturbances. Parliamentary government was not fully restored until February 1971. Meanwhile, communist guerrillas, relatively quiescent since 1960, had begun returning from sanctuaries across the Malaysian-Thai border, and by early 1974 they were once again posing a serious threat to domestic security. In the context of a vigorous campaign against the insurgents, an August election resulted in an impressive victory for Prime Minister ABDUL RAZAK bin Hussein's newly styled National Front (*Barisan Nasional*—BN) coalition of ethnic and regional parties.

In January 1976 Abdul Razak died and was succeeded by the deputy prime minister, HUSSEIN bin Onn, who was also designated chair of the BN. Under Hussein's leadership the front retained overwhelming control of the federal House of Representatives in an early election in July 1978. In May 1981 Hussein announced that for health reasons he would not stand for reelection as UMNO president, and he was succeeded in June by the party's deputy president, MAHATHIR bin Mohamad, who formed a new government following his designation as prime minister in July.

In early elections in 1982 and 1986 the BN continued to win easy victories. In early 1987, however, a major crisis surfaced within UMNO as it prepared for a triennial leadership poll in April. Accusing Mahathir of tolerating corruption, mismanagement, and extravagant spending, Deputy Prime Minister MUSA bin Hital joined with a number of other prominent UMNO figures in supporting the candidacy of Trade and Industry Minister Tengku RAZALEIGH Hamzah for the party presidency. After an intensely fought campaign, Mahathir narrowly defeated Razaleigh, with Abdul GHAFFAR bin Baba outpacing Musa by an even closer margin for the deputy presidency. The party thereupon divided into two factions, a "Team A" headed by the prime minister and a dissident "Team B."

In February 1988 Peninsular Malaysia's High Court ruled that UMNO was an illegal entity under the country's Societies Act because members of 30 unregistered branches had participated in the April 1987 balloting. Former prime ministers Abdul Rahman and Hussein bin Onn, on behalf of the Team B dissidents, thereupon filed for recognition of a new party (UMNO-Malaysia) but were rebuffed by the Registrar of Societies on the grounds that the High Court order had not yet become effective. Mahathir, applying on February 13 (the date of deregistration), was granted permission to begin the process of legalizing a government-supportive "new" UMNO (UMNO-*Baru*). Subsequently, the government secured legislation authorizing the transfer of UMNO assets to UMNO-*Baru* and also saw enacted a series of constitutional amendments rescinding the right of the High Court to interpret acts of Parliament.

The prime minister subsequently invited Razaleigh and Musa to join UMNO-*Baru.* While both dissidents initially rejected the offer, their somewhat uneasy alliance collapsed in January 1989, when Musa rejoined the government formation. Razaleigh subsequently announced that the successor to Team B, *Semangat '46* (Spirit of '46, after the year of UMNO's founding), had formed a coalition with the opposition *Parti Islam* (Pas) that, with the addition of two smaller formations, was registered in May as the Muslim Unity Movement (*Angkatan Perpaduan Ummah*—APU). Although the APU secured only 53 of 180 seats in the federal parliamentary election of October 1990, at the state level the opposition won control in Kelantan and ousted UMNO's chief minister in Penang.

In November 1993 Finance Minister ANWAR Ibrahim emerged as Prime Minister Mahathir's most likely successor by replacing Ghaffar bin Baba as UMNO deputy president. In December Mahathir followed tradition by naming Anwar deputy prime minister.

In parliamentary elections in April 1995 the BN scored a landslide victory, capturing 162 of 192 seats. In addition, front parties won overwhelming majorities in 10 of the 11 contested state assemblies. A year later the governing alliance in Kelantan between Pas and *Semangat '46* collapsed, Razaleigh Hamzah having announced in May his intention to return to UMNO. Shortly thereafter the fundamentalist Pas, which still held a legislative majority in Kelantan, was forced by the federal government to suspend a plan to introduce a harsh Islamic criminal code similar to the one imposed by the Taliban in Afghanistan.

In the second half of 1997, differences between Mahathir and his deputy began to surface in their approaches to the regional financial crisis that was drawing Malaysia into its grasp. Mahathir, an economic nationalist, attributed the crisis to foreign-currency traders and speculators, who were abetting international institutions and foreign powers that wanted to "recolonize" the country. In contrast, Anwar, a proponent of the global marketplace, responded to the crisis by introducing a series of austerity and financial reform measures, including a relaxation of racial quota laws to allow the country's Chinese and Indian minorities greater participation in Malay-dominated companies. In September 1998 Mahathir dismissed Anwar from the cabinet, and later he removed him as deputy president of UMNO. Anwar quickly opened a campaign against Mahathir under the banner of *reformasi,* the call for political reform that had accompanied President Suharto's resignation in Indonesia earlier in the year. Mahathir then stated that he had removed Anwar because of "moral misconduct," alluding to widely circulated rumors that Anwar had engaged in both homosexual and heterosexual liaisons.

On September 20, 1998, addressing a crowd variously estimated at between 30,000 and 50,000—the country's largest opposition rally in three decades—Anwar called for Mahathir to resign. Later that day he was arrested under the Internal Security Act (ISA). (For subsequent information on the ISA, see Current issues, below.) By late October 1998 Anwar faced five counts of sodomy as well as five of corruption for using his office to interfere with official investigations into his activities. In April 1999 Anwar was convicted of corruption and sentenced to six years (later reduced to four years) in prison. The verdict sparked renewed rioting by Anwar's supporters. In August 2000 the High Court in Kuala Lumpur convicted Anwar of sodomy and pronounced an additional nine-year prison sentence.

In June 1999 the principal opposition parties had announced that they would join forces. The resultant Alternative Front (*Barisan Alternatif*—BA) included Pas, the Democratic Action Party (DAP), the small Malaysian People's Party (*Parti Rakyat Malaysia*—PRM), and the new National Justice Party (*Parti Keadilan Nasional*—PKN), which had been formed in early April by Anwar's wife, Wan AZIZAH Wan Ismail, an eye surgeon and political novice.

In late November 1999 the BN won more than enough seats to maintain its two-thirds majority in the House of Representatives. Mahathir took the oath of office for his fifth term in December, after which he named Deputy Prime Minister ABDULLAH bin Ahmad Badawi as his preferred successor to head UMNO upon his eventual retirement.

On October 31, 2003, Prime Minister Mahathir handed the prime ministership over to Abdullah Badawi, who took a cautious approach to ministerial changes until confirming his support at the polls in an early election held March 21, 2004. The BN captured 198 of 219 seats in an expanded House of Representatives, while Pas saw its numbers diminish to 7.

In September 2004 with his sodomy conviction having been overturned on final appeal, Anwar Ibrahim was released from prison. Under the terms of his 1999 corruption sentence, he remained barred from holding public office until 2008. As an adviser to the People's Justice Party (*Parti Keadilan Rakyat*—PKR), of which his wife Wan Azizah was president, Anwar helped unify the opposition ahead of the 2008 general election. In voting on March 8, the opposition People's Front (later changed to People's Alliance [*Pakatan Rakyat*—PR]) claimed 82 seats in the House of Representatives, depriving the governing BN of a two-thirds majority for the first time since 1969, and won control of five state governments (although defections later returned one to the BN).

Under increasing pressure by the governing party to leave office early, Abdullah resigned as prime minister on April 2, 2009. The BN's Mohamad NAJIB Abdul Razak was designated prime minister on April 3 and six days later named a reshuffled cabinet.

Razak announced the New Economic Model in March 2010 designed to move affirmative action from being ethnically based to need based (see 2014 *Handbook*), and the cabinet was reshuffled on June 1, 2010. Opposition leader Anwar Ibrahim was again brought to trial in 2011 on sex abuse charges stemming from an alleged incident in 2008. He adamantly proclaimed his innocence in court, declaring that the accusations were motivated by the prime minister's desire to send him into "political oblivion." Prime Minister Najib, for his part, said the trial was not politically motivated. Anwar Ibrahim was acquitted on January 9, 2012.

Sultan ABDUL HALIM al-Muadzam Shah, sovereign of Kedah and former deputy paramount ruler, was elected for a five-year term as paramount ruler on October 30, 2011, becoming the first person to hold the post twice and, at 83, the oldest person to hold the office. He was sworn in on December 13.

In legislative balloting on May 5, 2013, the BN coalition maintained its majority, and Najib was reappointed prime minister (see Current issues, below). He formed a new coalition government on May 15.

The cabinet was reshuffled on July 28, 2015, and the deputy prime minister replaced. A further reshuffle was conducted on June 27, 2016.

Constitution and government. The constitution of Malaysia is based on that of the former Federation of Malaya, as amended to accommodate the special interests of Sarawak and Sabah, which joined in 1963. It established a federal system of government under an elective constitutional monarchy. The administration of the 13 states (11 in the west, 2 in the east) is carried out by rulers or governors acting on the advice of State Executive Councils. Each state has its own constitution and a unicameral State Assembly that shares legislative powers with the federal Parliament. The supreme head of the federation is the paramount ruler (*Yang di-Pertuan Agong*), who exercises the powers of a constitutional monarch in a parliamentary democracy. He and the deputy paramount ruler (*Timbalan Yang di-Pertuan Agong*) are chosen for five-year terms by and from among the nine hereditary rulers of the Malay states, who, along with the heads of state of Malacca, Penang, Sabah, and Sarawak, constitute the Conference of Rulers (*Majlis Raja Raja*). In 1993, with the reluctant agreement of the rulers, constitutional amendments were enacted that curbed royal legal immunities; a further restriction in 1994 ended the paramount ruler's authority to block legislation.

Executive power is vested in a prime minister and cabinet responsible to a bicameral legislature consisting of a partially appointed Senate with few real powers and a directly elected House of Representatives. Ultimate judicial authority is vested in a Federal Court (formerly called the Supreme Court); Peninsular and East Malaysia have separate high courts. An intermediary Court of Appeal was established by constitutional amendment in 1994. The pattern of local government varies to some extent from state to state.

The federal government has authority over such matters as external affairs, defense, internal security, justice (except Islamic and native law), federal citizenship, finance, commerce, industry, communications, and transportation. Sarawak and Sabah, however, enjoy guarantees of autonomy with regard to immigration, civil service, and customs matters.

Journalists are subject to arrest under the Official Secrets Act, and Sedition Act, and the home minister is empowered "at any time by notification in writing" to alter a newspaper license. Self-censorship as well as official censorship is common. Party newspapers of the PKR and Pas were banned two weeks before legislative by-elections in March 2009, but Prime Minister Najib lifted the bans on April 3, his first day in office. Malaysia suspended weekly magazine *The Heat* in December 2013. In 2016 Reporters Without Borders ranked Malaysia 146th in freedom of the press out of 180 countries.

Foreign relations. From the early 1960s, Malaysia was a staunch advocate of regional cooperation among the non-Communist states of Southeast Asia, and it has been an active member of the Association of Southeast Asian Nations (ASEAN) since the organization's inception in 1967. Although threatened by leftist insurgency in the first two decades of independence, Malaysia committed itself to a nonaligned posture. At the same time, it maintained links with Western powers, Britain, Australia, and New Zealand all pledging to defend the nation's sovereignty and assisting Malaysia against Indonesia's armed "confrontation" policy of 1963–1966. Britain, Australia, New Zealand, Malaysia, and Singapore are further linked through the Five Power Defense Arrangement. (For more on Malaysia's foreign affairs prior to the 1980s, see the 2013 *Handbook.*)

In February 1982 Malaysia became the first neighboring state to recognize Indonesia's archipelagic method of defining territorial seas by means of lines drawn between the outermost extensions of outlying islands. In return, Indonesia agreed to respect Malaysian maritime rights between its peninsular and Borneo territories, and in 1984 the two countries concluded a joint security agreement that strengthened a 1972 accord. In January 1994 talks between Malaysia and Indonesia ended without resolution of conflicting claims to two islands, Sipadan and Ligitan, off the east coast of Borneo, although the two sides agreed to settle the dispute in accordance with principles of international law. In December 2002 the International Court of Justice (ICJ) awarded both islands to Malaysia, but since then access to surrounding waters in the Sulawesi Sea has become a persistent irritant.

In January 1998 Jakarta received assurances that Indonesians holding valid temporary work permits in Malaysia would be exempt from a recently announced "Operation Go Away," the expulsion of tens of thousands of mainly illegal foreign workers who had been welcomed during Malaysia's economic boom. A large percentage of illegal workers were Indonesian, however, and the Mahathir government moved quickly to begin deporting them. The most violent incident occurred on March 26 at the Seminyeh repatriation camp, where rioting claimed nine lives. Subsequently, several dozen members of Indonesia's Acehnese minority, fearing reprisals related to a decades-old separatist conflict in Aceh district, sought asylum by breaking into a handful of foreign missions in Kuala Lumpur. Although Brunei, French, and Swiss officials quickly permitted Malaysian authorities to remove the Acehnese, in August some 20 who had sought refuge at the U.S. embassy and the offices of the UN High Commissioner for Refugees were granted asylum by Denmark and Norway. In 2004–2005 Malaysia's threatened expulsion of up to 1.5 million illegal immigrant workers, most of them Indonesian, again drew protests from Jakarta. In late May 2005 Malaysia, faced with an unexpected labor shortage, reversed the policy. In 2009, however, Indonesia placed a temporary ban on the hiring of Indonesians for domestic work in Malaysia. The announcement came in the wake of reported abuses by Malaysian employers.

Relations with Singapore, which were cool following Singapore's withdrawal from the Federation of Malaya in August 1965, improved in subsequent years. In April 1998 the two states agreed to submit to the ICJ competing claims to the islet of Pulau Batu Putih (Pedra Branca) off the coast of Johor. In September 2001 Malaysia and Singapore agreed to settle differences over such matters as water supplies to Singapore and the use of Malaysian airspace by Singapore's aircraft. Little additional progress was achieved through 2003, however, because Singapore sought to resolve open issues as a package. In December 2004 the two countries launched new talks, which also focused on releasing Malaysian workers' pension funds held by Singapore and on building a bridge to replace the outdated causeway that connects Singapore to the mainland. In April 2006, however, Malaysia scrapped plans for the bridge, construction of which Singapore continued to link to restoration of full airspace rights as well as to a 20-year commitment from Malaysia for 1 billion cubic meters of sand for reclamation. On May 23, 2008, the ICJ found that sovereignty over Pulau Batu Putih had passed to Singapore.

Relations with China have been particularly strong in recent years, despite competing claims to the Spratly Islands. Both sides have endorsed a code of conduct for all claimants. Regionally, Malaysia under Mahathir advanced the idea of a broad East Asian Economic Community, to include the ASEAN countries plus China, Japan, and South Korea, and in 2005 hosted the first East Asian summit.

Following Prime Minister Najib's appointment in 2009, relations with the United States warmed, and in May U.S. secretary of state Hillary Clinton declared that relations between the two countries were excellent, with cooperation in security matters as well as trade and investment. Najib's April 2010 visit to the United States included discussions with President Barack Obama.

In July 2011 the Malaysian government and the Vatican agreed to establish diplomatic ties following a meeting between Pope Benedict XVI and the prime minister. Talks leading to the diplomatic agreement had been going on for years, as the Malaysian government aimed to reassure Christians, who have long complained of discrimination or marginalization.

In February 2012 Malaysia deported Saudi journalist Hamza KASHGARI to his home country to face charges of blasphemy. Kashgari fled to Malaysia after posting remarks on social media that were deemed insulting to the prophet Muhammad. The deportation led to both domestic and international protests. Also in February, Malaysian police arrested an Iranian wanted in Thailand for participation in a failed terrorist attack on the Israeli embassy in Bangkok. In May a court in the United Kingdom opened an inquiry into a 1948 massacre in which 24 ethnic Chinese Malaysians were shot by British troops. However in September a British appeals court issued an injunction stopping the inquiry. The incident had long been a source of tension between the two countries. In December Malaysia announced it would recruit up to 100,000 Bangladeshis to work on plantations. Malaysia had previously stopped using Bangladeshi labor in 2009.

In January 2013 Malaysia and South Korea signed an extradition treaty. Also in January the Malaysian–Australian free trade agreement came into effect. In February a group of some 200 Filipino militia fighters, calling itself the Royal Army of the Sulu Sultanate, landed in Sabah. Fighting between the group and Malaysian security forces left 68 dead (see entry on the Philippines). More than 4,000 ethnic Filipinos left the region and returned to the Philippines during the strife. In October 2013 Malaysia was reelected to the International Civil Aviation Organization. In April 2014 Turkey and Malaysia signed a free trade agreement.

On June 19, 2015, Malaysian naval forces captured a hijacked oil tanker that had been seized by Indonesian pirates on June 11. In April 2016 Malaysia and Kuwait finalized a free trade accord.

Current issues. Further government crackdowns came in 2011, most notably during a July 9 rally by some 10,000 demonstrators calling for electoral reform, specifically longer campaign periods and an end to vote buying ahead of upcoming elections. The rally in Kuala Lumpur was broken up by the police, who used tear gas on the demonstrators, 500 of whom were arrested, including Ibrahim. Some 31 activists, including members of the Socialist Party of Malaysia (*Parti Sosialis Malaysia*—PSM), had been arrested ahead of the rally, allegedly for promoting a communist ideology and thus "waging war against the king." In the wake of the protest, the prime minister announced the formation of a new parliamentary committee, comprising government and opposition representatives, to review ways to make the electoral process more democratic. In September Prime Minister Najib called for what was described as the biggest overhaul to national security measures in decades, including plans to abolish the law that allows detention of suspects without a trial. Late in the year the prime minister rejected the proposal to hold a general election in 2011. The next polls are due in 2013.

In April 2012 the ISA was replaced by a new security law. The new measure ended the power of the police to hold suspects indefinitely, but security forces were still allowed to detain individuals for up to 28 days without charging them. In December the high court ruled that 2,036 hectares of land that the government had reserved for ethnic Malays belonged to the indigenous Orang Asli community. The decision was reported as a major victory for indigenous peoples.

The BN won 133 seats in the May 5, 2013, legislative balloting, securing a reduced majority in the House. The opposition PR declared the balloting to be fraudulent, and subsequently launched street protests. The PR also launched a campaign to challenge the results in 25 constituencies. By August the PR had lost a succession of those challenges and been fined $45,788 for each losing challenge.

On March 8, 2014, a Malaysian airliner MH370, carrying 227 passengers and 12 crew members, was lost over the South China Sea, bringing international attention to Malaysia. The missing plane remained in the news for much of 2014, with international resources directed towards the search. The plane has not been located as of September 9, 2016.

Malaysia Airlines experienced another airplane loss on July 17, 2014—131 days after the loss of MH370. MH17, carrying 283 passengers and 15 crew members, was traveling from Amsterdam to Kaula Lumpur. The flight was reportedly shot down in Ukrainian airspace by a Soviet-designed Buk missile system. International outrage centered on the confusing role of Russia and Ukrainian separatists in the incident. Malaysian prime minister Najib negotiated with the separatists in order to retrieve the bodies and black box immediately following the incident in an unprecedented and direct manner; however as of September the crash site remained inaccessible. Malaysia has remained reticent to assign blame prior to the end of the official investigation, which is being conducted by the Netherlands, but asked the UN on September 27 for a peacekeeping force to secure the site.

In what was described as the worst flooding in more than 30 years, monsoon flooding in the eastern peninsula area killed 21 and left more than 200,000 homeless in December 2014.

Reports in July 2015 alleged that Prime Minister Najib received payments of more than $681 million to various bank accounts he controlled during the 2013 legislative campaign. The government blocked Internet access to websites that reported the story, but the following month there were widespread protests both for and against the prime minister in Kuala Lumpur. Najib claimed the payments were donations to his political campaign from the Saudi royal family and that $620 million had been returned. Opposition groups and parties called for Najib to resign, and protests continued over the next several months.

POLITICAL PARTIES

Malaysia's political system has long been dominated by the National Front (*Barisan Nasional*—BN) coalition. Numerous opposition coalitions have formed, but until 2008, none had ever posed a meaningful threat to the UMNO-led alliance.

In September 1998, following the ouster and arrest of Anwar Ibrahim, two loose opposition coalitions emerged: the **Coalition for a People's Democracy** (*Gagasan Demokrasi Rakyat*—Gagasan), chaired by TIAN Chua, and the **People's Justice Movement** (*Gerakan Keadilan Rakyat*—Gerak), chaired by Fadzil NOR of Pas. The two shared overlapping memberships that encompassed various social and reform organizations as well as several political parties. Out of this organizing came the **Alternative Front** (*Barisan Alternatif*—BA), an ideologically incongruous grouping that won 42 seats in the November 1999 election. With the Democratic Action Party (DAP) having withdrawn from the BA in 2001, the coalition won only 7 seats in the March 2004 general election. The People's Alliance (*Pakatan Rakyat*—PR) emerged as the successor to the BA prior to the 2008 balloting.

Government Coalition:

National Front (*Barisan Nasional*—BN). Malaysia's leading formation since its launching in 1973, the BN is a coalition of parties representing the country's leading ethnic groups. The nucleus of an earlier coalition, organized in 1952 as the Alliance Party, was Tunku Abdul Rahman's United Malays National Organization (UMNO). With the establishment of Malaysia, the alliance was augmented by similar coalitions in Sarawak and Sabah. By September 1996 the BN controlled 12 of the country's 13 state assemblies, the sole exception being Kelantan's.

Although the number of member parties has varied somewhat over the years, the BN long held a two-thirds legislative majority until 2008, when a strong showing by the opposition brought it to within 30 seats of controlling the House of Representatives. At the same time, the BN lost control of several state governments, although a subsequent realignment in the Perak legislature enabled the BN to replace the PR government. As of 2013 the BN controlled 10 of 13 states. In the May 2013 balloting, the BN secured 133 seats, with 40.4 percent of the vote. It also won 330 of 576 state assembly seats.

Leaders: Mohamad NAJIB Abdul Razak (Prime Minister), Tengku Adnan MANSOR (Secretary General).

United Malays National Organization—UMNO (*Pertubuhan Kebangsaan Melayu Bersatu*). The leading component of the BN, UMNO has long supported the interests of the numerically predominant Malays while acknowledging the right of all Malaysians, irrespective of racial origins, to participate in the political, social, and economic life of the nation. Party officials are selected by indirect election every three years.

In April 1987 Prime Minister Mahathir bin Mohamad retained the presidency by a paper-thin margin after an unprecedented internal contest. The intraparty struggle culminated in deregistration of the original party in February 1988, in the wake of which the pro-Mahathir faction organized the "new" UMNO (UMNO-*Baru*). The dissidents, led by Tengku Razaleigh Hamzah, were denied an opportunity to regroup as UMNO-Malaysia. In 1989 Mahathir launched a partially successful campaign to woo back the dissidents. The party dropped "*Baru*" and restored its original name in 1997.

In the November 1999 federal election UMNO won 71 seats, 17 fewer than in 1995, which analysts attributed to a loss of support among Malay backers of Anwar Ibrahim, who had been ousted as deputy president in September 1998. In December, having already announced that he was serving his final term as prime minister, Mahathir named Deputy Prime Minister Abdullah Badawi as his successor.

In May 2001 the People's Justice Movement (*Angkatan Keadilan Rakyat*—Akar) overwhelmingly voted to disband and join UMNO. Akar, formed in 1989 by former members of the Sabah United Party (PBS), had participated in the BN since 1991.

With Mahathir having stepped down from party and government posts in October 2003, Abdullah Badawi led UMNO to victory at the polls in March 2004, when the party won 110 lower house seats. Mahathir subsequently denounced the policies of his successor and briefly quit the party in the wake of the BN's setbacks in the 2008 balloting, hoping to create pressure on Abdullah to resign. Abdullah responded in July by announcing that Deputy Prime Minister Najib Razak would succeed him in June 2010. However, facing increasing pressure from party members, Abdullah resigned in 2009. At the party's congress in March, Najib was unanimously elected party president, and a week later, he was sworn in as Malaysia's sixth prime minister. Najib pledged to reform the party, which was widely acknowledged to be in danger of losing its dominance.

In August 2010 the UMNO Supreme Council accepted the **Malaysian Indian Muslim Congress** (*Parti Kongres Indian Muslim Malaysia*—Kimma), led by Syed Ibrahim KADER, as an affiliate, thereby granting Kimma privileges that include observer status at the UMNO annual assembly and access to alliances with other BN parties. Kimma, founded in 1977 as a means of uniting Malaysia's Indian Muslims, had repeatedly sought BN membership.

In July 2011 Tengku Razaleigh Hamzah formed the nonpartisan **Movement for Independence Trust** (*Amanah*) and invited members of the UMNO and the opposition to join, in what observers described as an attempt to position himself as a third force ahead of national elections. In August 2012 the party reportedly launched an effort to reintegrate some splinter parties and groups that had been formed by former UMNO members. The UMNO increased its seats in the House in the 2013 balloting, from 79 to 88, and Najib was reappointed prime minister of a MUNO-dominated coalition cabinet.

Various reports accused Najib of corruption beginning in July 2015 (see Current issues, above). UMNO official Khairuddin Abu HASSAN was arrested on September 18 and charged with sabotage for allegedly providing information to foreign media sources that initiated the investigation into the prime minister.

Leaders: Mohamad NAJIB Abdul Razak (Prime Minister and President of the Party), Ahmad ZAHID Hamidi, HISHAMMUDDIN Hussein (Vice President), Mohammad SHAFIE Apdal (Vice President), Tengku Adnan MANSOR (Secretary General).

Malaysian Chinese Association—MCA (*Persatuan China Malaysia*). The MCA supports the interests of the Chinese community but is committed to "moderation" and the maintenance of interracial goodwill and harmony. More conservative than the Chinese opposition DAP, it has participated in the governing alliance continuously since 1982.

For over a decade the MCA's representation in the lower house of Parliament had been stable at around 30 seats, but it dropped to 15 after the March 2008 election. Taking responsibility for the poor showing, party president ONG Ka Ting declined to seek reelection. At the party congress in October, Transport Minister Ong Tee Keat (no relation) won the party presidency, and NG Yen Yen, the minister of tourism, became the first female vice president of a major BN party. Ong announced a plan to revive grassroots participation in the party and assess the performance of party leaders, but his leadership soon came under attack, culminating in a three-way contest for the presidency in March 2010. Ong Tee Keat and former president Ong Ka Ting were defeated by Deputy President Chua Soi Lek, and in June Ong Tee Keat was dropped from the cabinet.

The party only won seven House seats in the 2013 legislative balloting and received no posts in the subsequent coalition government. However, in a June 26, 2014, reshuffle, Prime Minister Najib appointed LIOW Tiong Lai and Wee Ka Siong as ministers in an attempt to improve popularity with ethnic Chinese. Both retained their posts in the cabinet reshuffles in 2015 and 2016.

Leaders: LIOW Tiong Lai (President), Wee Ka SIONG (Deputy President), Ong Ka CHUAN (Secretary General).

United Traditional Bumiputra Party (*Parti Pesaka Bumiputra Bersatu*—PBB). Founded in 1983, the PBB traces its origins to the **Sarawak Alliance of *Bumiputra*,** a mixed ethnic party; ***Pesaka*,** a Dayak and Malay party; and the **Sarawak Chinese Association**. The PBB won a plurality of 19 seats in the 1983 Sarawak state assembly election and subsequently formed a coalition government with the Sarawak Native People's Party (PBDS; see the PRS, below) and the SUPP (below). This coalition, dominated by the PBB, has controlled Sarawak's government ever since, with PBB president Abdul Taib Mahmud serving continuously as the state's chief minister.

In 2004 the party won 11 seats in the House of Representatives, and in 2008 it added 3 more. In May 2006 the party won all 35 seats it contested in the state assembly elections. The PBB won state balloting in 2012, and Taib was reelected chief minister. In the 2013 House balloting, the PBB won 14 seats and 35 of 71 seats in the Sarawak state assembly. The party was given two portfolios in the subsequent UMNO government.

Leaders: Adenan SATEM (Chief Minister of Sarawak and President of the Party), ABANG Johari Tun Abang Openg (Deputy President), Alfred JABU Anak Numpang (Deputy President), AWANG Tengah Ali Hasan, Douglas UGGAH Embas.

Sarawak People's Party (*Party Rakyat Sarawak*—PRS). Registered in October 2005, the PRS traces its origin to a leadership dispute that split the now-defunct **Sarawak Native People's Party** (*Parti Bansa Dayak Sarawak*—PBDS), which had been organized in 1983 by a number of legislators from the Sarawak National Party (SNAP, below) who wished to affiliate with a purely ethnic Dayak party. The new formation was accepted as a National Front partner in 1984. In the 1999 and 2004 national elections it won six seats, but it was deregistered in October 2004 because of a protracted leadership dispute precipitated by the retirement of longtime party leader and cabinet member Leo MOGGIE anak Irok.

The new PRS was already being organized under SIDI Munan when the PBDS was deregistered. As expected, the PBDS faction loyal to James Masing joined the new party, with Masing being named president shortly thereafter. In June 2005 the PRS was accepted into the BN.

In January 2006 the PRS and another National Front party, the SPDP (below), announced their intention to merge, but discussions were ultimately postponed, first because of the May 2006 state election, in which the PRS won eight of the nine seats it contested, and then because of a leadership dispute within the PRS. Masing was reelected president at a conference in December 2006, while Larry SNG Wei Shien claimed leadership of a faction loyal to former deputy president SNG Chee Hua, his father. Masing expelled Sng from the party in April 2008, a month after the PRS won six lower house seats. The split appeared to have driven many former PRS members into the ranks of the opposition PKR.

The PRS won six House seats in the 2013 national elections and received one post in the subsequent coalition government.

Leaders: James Jemut MASING (President), Wilfred Rata NISSOM (Secretary General).

Sarawak United People's Party—SUPP (*Parti Bersatu Rakyat Sarawak*). The SUPP was organized in 1959 as a left-wing Sarawak party. Although the SUPP began as a Chinese ethnic party, it has since become one of Malaysia's most ethnically diverse parties. In November 1999 it won eight seats in the House of Representatives. That number dropped to six in the 2004 and 2008 national elections.

At the state level, in May 2006 it won 11 legislative seats, unexpectedly losing 8 of those it contested as part of the National Front. In 2011 Peter CHIN Fah Kui was elected PRS leader. In 2013 the SUPP won one House seat and six seats in the Sarawak state assembly. It received one post in the UMNO-led coalition government.

Leader: Sim Kui HIAN (President).

Sarawak Progressive Democratic Party—SPDP (*Parti Demokratik Maju Sarawak*). The SPDP was established in November 2002 following a leadership crisis in the Sarawak National Party (SNAP, below) that led to SNAP's deregistration. Several months before, William MAWAN had been elected president of SNAP, but a competing SNAP faction refused to accept the decision. Within days of SNAP's deregistration, Mawan announced formation of the multiracial SPDP, which was soon accepted into the BN as SNAP's replacement.

In the 2004 and 2008 general elections the SPDP won four seats. In June 2008 the SPDP and PRS agreed to merge, but grassroots opposition to the plan, and Anwar Ibrahim's challenge to the sitting government, slowed the process. In 2009 the party was trying to form new branches outside Sarawak, in West Malaysia, although internal disputes continued to cause difficulties. The SPDP won six seats in the 2011 Sarawak elections. In the 2013 national elections, the SPDP won four House seats.

Leaders: Tiong King SING (President), Anthony NOGEH (Secretary General).

United Pasok Momogun Kadazandusun Murut Organization—UPKO (*Pertubuhan Pasok Momogan Kadazandusun Murut Bersatu*). Reviving the name of a Sabah party from the 1960s, a congress of the **Sabah Democratic Party** (*Parti Demokratik Sabah*—PDS) voted in 1999 to adopt the UPKO designation. The PDS had been organized in 1994 by withdrawal from the PBS of a group of dissidents led by Deputy President Bernard DOMPOK. The original UPKO had been established by the 1964 merger of the ***Pasok Momogun*** party and the **United National Kadazan Organization** (UNKO), but the party dissolved in 1967.

Intended to unite the majority Kadazandusun community and the Murut population of Sabah, the current UPKO subsequently indicated its willingness to discuss mergers not only with other Sabah-based BN parties but also with the PBS. UPKO won four lower house seats at the 2004 and 2008 general elections. The party has been active on immigration and citizenship issues. In 2009 party leader Dompok was appointed minister of agricultural development and commodities. In balloting for the House in 2013, the UPKO secured three seats, and Ewon EBIN was appointed minister of science, technology, and innovation. He was replaced in the July 2015 cabinet reshuffle by UPKO president Wilfred Madius TANGAU.

Leaders: Wilfred Madius TANGAU (President), Siringan GUBAT (Deputy President).

Malaysian Indian Congress—MIC (*Kongresi India Malaysia*). The leading representative of the Indian community in Malaysia, the MIC was founded in 1946 and joined the alliance in 1955. S. Samy VELLU first won the party presidency in 1979. In March 2009 he was reelected to an 11th term, but in September 2010 he announced his retirement and identified his preferred successor as Deputy President G. PALANIVEL.

The MIC won seven House seats in the 1995, 1999, and March 2004 elections, but its parliamentary representation dropped to three in the 2008 vote. The Hindu Rights Action Force (Hindraf; see below), a nongovernment group banned by the home ministry in 2008, has posed a challenge to the MIC's leadership among Malaysia's Indian population. Vellu resigned in January 2011. The MIC secured four seats in the 2013 House elections, and Palanivel was appointed minister of natural resources and environment. He was expelled from the party and replaced in the July 2015 government reshuffle, but new party president S. SUBRAMANIAM was named minister of health at the time.

Leaders: S. SUBRAMANIAM (President); S. K. DEVAMANY (Deputy President); S. VIGNESWARAN, T. MOHAN, Jaspal SINGH (Vice Presidents); T. RAJAGOPALU (Secretary-General).

Sabah United Party (*Parti Bersatu Sabah*—PBS). A predominantly Kadazan party with a Roman Catholic leader, the PBS was founded by defectors from the now-moribund **Sabah People's**

Union (*Bersatu Rakyat Jelata Sabah*—Berjaya) in 1985. Appealing to urban, middle-class voters disaffected with the Berjaya-led government, it won a majority of state assembly seats in April. Having been admitted to the BN in 1986, in 1988 the PBS announced a "loose alliance" with fellow BN member *Gerakan.*

The PBS retained control of the Sabah assembly in a state general election in July 1990, but less than a week before the federal legislative poll of October 1990 it withdrew from the BN and went into opposition. In what some viewed as an act of political retaliation, the party president, Joseph PAIRIN Kitingan, was arrested by federal authorities in early 1991. His conviction on corruption charges resulted in a fine of approximately $4,600.

In 1993 the PBS attracted almost half of the state assembly contingent of the United Sabah National Organization (USNO), immediately prior to that party's long-envisaged merger with UMNO. In an early state election in 1994 the PBS obtained a plurality of seats but because of subsequent defections was obliged to yield to a BN administration. It won only 17 of 48 seats in the 1999 state election and then lost 2 to defections.

The PBS was readmitted to the BN in January 2002, and in the March 2004 election won 4 seats in the federal House of Representatives and 13 in the Sabah legislature. It secured one post in the UMNO-led government.

Leaders: Joseph PAIRIN Kitingan (President), Henrynus AMIN (Secretary General).

Malaysian People's Movement Party (*Parti Gerakan Rakyat Malaysia*). Based in Pulau Pinang (Penang), *Gerakan* is a social democratic party that has attracted many intellectual supporters, especially in the Chinese community. It was organized in 1968 by TAN Chee Khoon, who left the party after the 1969 election to form the now-defunct Social Justice Party (*Parti Keadilan Masyaraka*—Pekemas). The party was weakened by a leadership dispute in 1988 that saw numerous members defect to the MCA and two of its vice presidents resign.

In April 2007 Lim Keng Yaik retired after 26 years of party leadership. Former Penang chief minister KOH Tsu Koon, initially the acting president, was elected president at the party's 2008 congress. Koh called for the party to reinvent itself after its poor showing in the 2008 election, when its lower house membership fell from 10 seats to 2. That year the party also lost control of the state government in Penang, which it had led for nearly four decades.

With the party's power diminishing, several prominent members quit, and some members advocated pulling out of the BN coalition. In the 2013 national elections, the party won one seat in the House. Keong was appointed minister in the prime minister's office on June 25, 2014, as part of a reshuffle of the cabinet and then minister of plantation industries and commodities in June 2016.

Leaders: Mah Siew KEONG (President), Cheah Soon HAI (Deputy President).

United Sabah People's Party (*Parti Bersatu Rakyat Sabah*—PBRS). The PBRS was launched in 1994 by Joseph KURUP, theretofore secretary general of the PBS. In the 1999 national election Kurup came within a few hundred votes of unseating PBS President Joseph Pairin Kitingan. In 2002 a leadership dispute ended with a decision by the Registrar of Societies that Kurup was the legitimate president. His challenger, Jeffrey Kitingan, was then expelled by the party. (He joined the PKR in October 2006.)

In the 2008 election, Kurup won the party's only seat in parliament, running unopposed after an officer rejected the nomination papers of PKR candidate Danny Anthony ANDIPAI. Subsequently, Malaysia's Election Court declared the vote void, but on March 13, 2009, a federal court upheld Kurup's election. In 2013 the PBRS won one House seat. Kurup was appointed as a minister without portfolio in the UMNO-led government.

Leaders: Joseph KURUP (President), Ellron ANGIN (Deputy President).

Liberal Democratic Party—LDP (*Parti Liberal Demokratik*). A Chinese-dominated party based in Sabah, the LDP formed in 1989 and joined the BN in 1991. In 1999, under the leadership of its first president, CHONG Kah Kiat, it captured one seat in the House of Representatives; it lost the seat in 2004, but V. K. LIEW won it back in 2008. Liew was appointed a deputy minister in April 2009. The LDP secured only 0.1 percent of the vote in the 2013 national elections and no seats in the House.

Leader: Teo Chee KANG (President).

People's Progressive Party of Malaysia—PPP (*Parti Kemajuan Rakyat Malaysia*). Centered in Ipoh, where there is a heavy concentration of Chinese, the multiracial, left-wing PPP was organized in 1955. In 1996 the Registrar of Societies approved a new constitution for the party, which thereupon adopted the name *Parti Progressif Penduduk Malaysia (Baru),* or PPP (New). However, a four-year-old dispute over the party leadership continued. In September 1999 the High Court annulled the presidency of M. KAYVEAS, who had been elected in 1993, and threw out the 1996 constitutional changes, at which time the party reverted to its original name. Kayveas quickly obtained a stay from the Court of Appeal, which confirmed him as president in November. Kayveas was reelected president in September 2005.

The PPP won one seat in parliament in the 2004 general election but none in 2008. In May 2009 the party expelled a member of its supreme council for corruption. The party failed to secure any seats in the 2013 balloting.

Leader: M. KAYVEAS (President).

Parliamentary Opposition:

People's Alliance (*Pakatan Rakyat*—PR). The Democratic Action Party (DAP), Pan-Malaysian Islamic Party (Pas), and People's Justice Party (PKR), along with the **Malaysian People's Party** (PRM; see PKR, below), organized the Alternative Front (*Barisan Alternatif*—BA) in 1999. The BA put forth Anwar Ibrahim as a candidate for prime minister in that year's election, although the former Mahathir deputy was incarcerated after his corruption conviction. The DAP withdrew from the BA in September 2001 because of opposition to Pas's Islamic agenda, and in the 2004 national election the BA won only seven seats.

On April 1, 2008, following their successful cooperation in the March elections, the leaders of the DAP, Pas, and PKR announced that they would solidify their relationship under the PR banner. By agreeing not to compete with each other, the three won control of 5 of Malaysia's 13 state assemblies (in Kedah, Kelantan, Penang, Perak, and Selangor) and had ended the BN's two-thirds majority in the House of Representatives. Despite their ideological differences, the three parties agree on the nation's need for transparent and egalitarian governance.

ANWAR Ibrahim reentered Parliament on August 28, 2008, and took over leadership of the PKR and the PR from his wife, Dr. Wan Azizah Wan Ismail. At first, Anwar set out to engineer enough defections from the BN to allow the PR to capture the government. That plan failed, but the coalition demonstrated increasing strength in 2009 by winning two of three by-elections on April 7.

In February 2010 the Federal Court brought an end to a year-long constitutional crisis in Perak, ruling that defections by MPs from the PR had legitimately permitted the BN to take over the state government. Two months later, the Sarawak National Party (SNAP) joined the PR.

In the 2013 national elections, the PR won a majority of the vote, 50.9 percent, but only 89 seats. The coalition also won 244 of 576 state assemblies. The PR subsequently unsuccessfully challenged a number of the election results.

Reports indicated that the PR became defunct on June 8, 2015, after the Pas withdrew from the coalition (see DAP and Pas, below).

Leaders: ANWAR Ibrahim, LIM Kit Siang, Abdul HADI Awang.

Democratic Action Party—DAP (*Parti Tindakan Demokratik*). A predominantly Chinese, democratic socialist party, the DAP is a 1965 offshoot of the ruling People's Action Party (PAP) of Singapore.

In 1987 a number of DAP politicians, including parliamentary opposition leader LIM Kit Siang, were arrested and held without trial for "provoking racial tensions." In 1989 Lim was released from jail and the party agreed to cooperate with the APU in upcoming elections, although refusing to join the coalition because of its Muslim orientation. The DAP went on to win 20 seats in the House of Representatives in 1990 but saw its representation plummet to 9 in 1995.

In August 1998 LIM Guan Eng, deputy secretary general of the party and son of Lim Kit Siang, was sentenced to prison on charges of sedition relating to a political pamphlet he had written. An effort by the elder Lim to mount support for his son led critics to charge the secretary general with nepotism and dictatorial actions. Lim responded by suspending the party's vice chair, treasurer, and publicity secretary, all of whom subsequently helped found the MDP (below).

Lim Guan Eng was released from prison in August 1999. Three months later, as part of the Alternative Front, the DAP won only 10 seats in the national election, although it remained the leading legislative opponent of various BN parties in a majority of states. The elder Lim resigned as party secretary general—a post he had held for three decades—but he was immediately named party chair.

In September 2001 objecting to Pas's call for establishing an Islamic state, the DAP withdrew from the BA. In the March 2004 election, the DAP kept its distance from Pas and went on to win 12 seats, thereby becoming the leading opposition party once again. At a party congress in September Lim Kit Siang stepped down as chair. Lim Guan Eng was elected secretary general.

The DAP returned to cooperating with Pas and the PKR in the 2008 voting, winning 28 lower house seats. In September, Lim Kit Siang called on Prime Minister Abdullah to convene a special session of Parliament to vote on a no-confidence measure. A DAP parliamentarian, Teresa KOK, along with a journalist and a popular blogger, were arrested on September 12 under the ISA. The party called the arrests politically motivated and demanded the abolition of the ISA. In March 2009 DAP national chair Karpal SINGH was charged with sedition; he in turn accused the government of using the sedition laws selectively against political opponents. In 2010 the charges were dismissed, but the dismissal was reversed in 2012. On March 29, 2014, Karpal Singh resigned as party chairman to appeal his conviction under the sedition act, but was killed in a car crash on April 17, 2014.

In the 2013 national elections, the DAP secured 38 seats in the House and is the second largest party represented. Tensions between the DAP and Pas deteriorated through 2014 as the former strenuously opposed the latter's drive to impose Islamic law in the state of Kelantan.

Leaders: TAN Kok Wai (Acting Chair and Deputy Chair), LIM Guan Eng (Secretary General).

Pan-Malaysian Islamic Party (*Parti Islam SeMalaysia*—Pas). An Islamic party with a strong rural base, Pas participated in the governing coalition in 1973–1977 but since then has been in opposition. Pas has governed Kelantan State continuously since 1990. It increased its federal legislative representation from 7 to 27 seats in 1999, rising to lead the opposition and also capturing the state of Terengganu.

Pas membership is open only to Muslims, and the party prohibits women candidates at the state and federal levels. Officially, the party seeks the establishment of an Islamic state, but its leaders have stated that should it win control of the federal government and introduce Islamic law, non-Muslims could be tried in accordance with the country's current secular legal system. In Kelantan, non-Muslims are exempt from some of the strictest aspects of sharia (Islamic) law.

In June 2002 the party's president, the moderate Fadzil Mohamad NOR, died. His immediate successor, Abdul Hadi Awang, a more radical Islamist and longtime supporter of Afghanistan's ousted Taliban regime, announced in July that Islamic law would be strictly enforced in the state of Terengganu, where he served as chief minister until Pas was ousted in the March 2004 state election. Nationally, it saw its lower house representation plummet to six seats. A loss in a state by-election in December 2005 reduced the party's majority in the Kelantan assembly to a single seat.

Party elections held in June 2005 were notable for the success of more moderate politicians. Although Abdul HADI Awang had no challengers, the new deputy president and all three vice presidents were regarded as reformers. The party election of June 2007 reconfirmed the ascendancy of the "young Turks," led by Deputy President Nasaruddin Mat Isa, although the presidency was again uncontested.

In 2008 Pas won control of the state of Kedah, expanded its majority in Kelantan, and joined coalition governments in two other states with its People's Alliance partners. In an effort to broaden the party's base, Pas toned down its rhetoric about imposing Islamic law and pledged to uphold social equality and freedom of religion. Its relative success at attracting Chinese and Indian support with a more moderate image reflected the shifts in the country's racial and political dynamics.

Hadi Awang was reelected to his post, again uncontested, in May 2009. Internal debates reflected a division between party moderates committed to the PR and conservatives open to cooperation with UMNO. The party won 21 House seats in the 2013 balloting.

At a party conference on June 8, 2015, Pas voted to end its alliance with the DAP over the latter's opposition to Islamic law. At the same congress, Awang was reelected party president.

Leaders: Abdul HADI Awang (President), Haron DIN (Spiritual Leader of Pas), Tuan Ibrahim Tuan MAN (Deputy President), Nasruddin HASSAN (Secretary General).

People's Justice Party (*Parti Keadilan Rakyat*—PKR). The PKR resulted from the August 2003 merger of the **National Justice Party** (*Parti Keadilan Nasional*—PKN) and the Malaysian People's Party (*Parti Rakyat Malaysia*—PRM).

Announced in April 1999 by Wan Azizah Wan Ismail as a centrist, multiracial formation, the PKN was organized by supporters of Anwar Ibrahim in an effort to unite anti-Mahathir forces. The party was largely an outgrowth of the nonparty **Movement for Social Justice** (*Pergerakan Keadilan Sosial*—Adil), which had been announced by Wan Azizah the previous December as a vehicle for reform. Anwar indicated from prison that he would not officially join the party. As part of the BA, *Keadilan* won five lower house seats in November 1999. It unexpectedly picked up a sixth, at the BN's expense, in a November 2000 by-election.

Formerly the **Malaysian People's Socialist Party** (*Parti Sosialis Rakyat Malaysia*—PSRM), the PRM was a left-leaning party that never held legislative seats. Its former leader, KASSIM Ahmad, was arrested in 1976 on suspicion of having engaged in communist activities and was not released until 1981. Another leader, Syed Husin Ali, was similarly detained without trial under the country's Internal Security Act from 1974 until 1980. In 1989 the party changed its name back to its pre-1970 title as part of an effort to assume a more moderate position.

In July 2002 the PRM and *Keadilan* signed a memorandum of understanding to merge as the PKR, which was accomplished in August 2003. At the party's fourth congress, held in May 2007, Wan AZIZAH was reelected president. Anwar Ibrahim, concerned that his election might result in the party's deregistration, decided not to run.

Meanwhile, the PKR's representation ballooned to 31 in the March 2008 election, making it the second strongest party in the House of Representatives. Wan Azizah resigned her seat on July 31 to allow her husband to run in a by-election, which he won handily on August 28, 2008. He subsequently took over leadership of the PKR and the PR from his wife.

In May 2009, in what the party termed "an unprecedented move for a political party in Malaysia," the PKR announced the adoption of direct "one-member, one-vote" election of all party officials. Wan Azizah became surrogate party leader while her husband faced trial on sexual abuse charges (see Current issues, above). In 2013 the PKR secured 30 seats in the House elections.

Leaders: Wan AZIZAH Wan Ismail, ANWAR Ibrahim, SYED HUSIN Ali, TIAN Chua, Saifuddin NASUTION Ismail (Secretary General).

Socialist Party of Malaysia (*Parti Sosialis Malaysia*—PSM). The leftist PSM was formed in 1998 but was denied registration by the government, which viewed it as a threat to national security, until after the 2008 election. At that time the PSM claimed a seat in the lower house, its representative having been elected as a PKR candidate. At the party's congress in June 2010, the PSM decided that it would not join the PR but would commit itself to "close cooperation," including campaigning with or participating in an electoral pact with the opposition alliance for the next election. The party failed to secure any seats in the 2013 balloting.

Leaders: NASIR Hashim (Chair), S. ARUTCHELVAN (Secretary General).

Other Parties:

Sabah Progressive Party—SAPP (*Parti Maju Sabah*). Formally registered in 1994, the SAPP is a Chinese formation that was admitted to the BN after splitting from the PBS. It won two seats in the 1999 balloting. In September 2002 one of the seats was vacated when the Election Commission found the party's president guilty of corrupt electoral practices. In March 2008 the SAPP won two seats in the House of Representatives.

Party president YONG Teck Lee threatened in June 2008 to file a no-confidence motion against Prime Minister Abdullah Ahmad Badawi. The motion did not go forward, but on September 17, SAPP withdrew from the BN to become an independent party. Deputy president Raymond TAN, who was also deputy chief minister of Sabah, subsequently quit the party and later joined *Gerakan.* The party failed to win any seats in the 2013 federal parliament balloting.

Leaders: YONG Teck Lee (President), LIEW Teck Chan, Eric Enchin MAJIMBUN (Deputy Presidents), Richard YONG We Kong (Secretary General).

Indian Progressive Front—IPF (*Barisan Kemajuan India SeMalaysia*). The IPF was launched in 1990 by M.G. PANDITHAN, who had been an MIC vice president until ousted by Samy Vellu. The IPF supported the BN for the 1999 and 2004 elections. Although the MIC opposed the party's inclusion in the front, Vellu and Pandithan reconciled in April 2007.

Pandithan died in May 2008, and his wife, Jayashree PANDITHAN, took over as party leader. However, after the Registrar of Societies nullified her election in February 2009, the IPF was riven by factions. Prime Minister Abdullah Badawi attempted to heal the divide, dangling a potential offer to join the BN if the party reconciled. In June 2010 M. SAMBANTHAN was elected president. The party did not win any seats in the 2013 House elections.

Leaders: M. SAMBANTHAN (President), M. GEORGE (Deputy President), K. VELAYUTHAN (Secretary General).

Malaysia Makkal Sakthi Party (MMSP). Established in 2009 under the leadership of R.S. Thanenthiran, formerly the national coordinator of the Hindu Rights Action Force (Hindraf), the MMSP represents a division within the Hindraf movement. The Registrar of Societies approved the new party on May 11, less than two months after it had applied. The Party supports the BN.

In late 2009 the MMSP became embroiled in a leadership dispute that saw competing factions loyal to Thanenthiran and Deputy President A. VATHEMURTHY both claiming control. In September 2010 the dissident group convened what it called an emergency general meeting that named the party's initial secretary general, Kannan RAMASAMY, as president. In October the Thanenthiran forces, with support from the BN, held an annual general meeting at which it continued to claim legitimacy. A possible merger with IDF and PPP was rejected in May 2013.

Leaders: R. S. THANENTHIRAN (President), U. THAMOTHARAN (Deputy President).

Sarawak National Party—SNAP (*Parti Kebangsaan Sarawak*). Long a leading Sarawak party, SNAP ran in the 1974 federal election as an opposition party, capturing nine seats in the lower house. Supported largely by the Iban population of Sarawak, it joined the BN at both the state and federal levels in 1976.

On November 5, 2002, SNAP was formally deregistered because of a leadership dispute in which the party's deputy president, Peter TINGGOM Karmarau, had challenged its longtime president, James WONG Kim Ming. In August an extraordinary party meeting had elected William Mawan Ikom as successor to Wong, who refused to accept what he termed a "coup d'état." Within days of the deregistration, which Wong planned to challenge, Mawan announced formation of the Sarawak Progressive Democratic Party (SPDP).

The deregistration was suspended by the Court of Appeal in April 2003, permitting SNAP to compete in the March 2004 national election. SNAP won only one state seat in 2006, and in 2008 it contested six lower house seats. In April 2010, as part of an effort to revitalize the party, SNAP joined the opposition PR. However it withdrew in May 2012. In January 2013 the party was officially deregistered and subsequently reported as defunct.

Hindu Rights Action Force—Hindraf (*Barisan Bertindak Hak-Hak Hindu*). This union of nongovernmental organizations, formed to advocate for the rights of Malaysia's Indian community, captured the nation's attention in November 2007. The group held a massive rally in Kuala Lumpur, without obtaining a government permit, to protest against social and economic discrimination against Indians and the destruction of Hindu temples. Police arrested more than 200 people, and five leaders were later detained without charges for more than a year. Party leader P. Waytha Moorthy's six-year-old daughter was reportedly among those arrested. The unusual street demonstration galvanized Malaysia's ethnic minorities and played a significant role in the loss of support for the BN in the 2008 polling. The home minister declared Hindraf an illegal organization in October 2008. Prime Minister Najib freed the five detained leaders during his first month in office in 2009.

In 2011 the party held a rally to protest the government's requirement that the school curriculum include a book Hindraf considers to be racist. More than 100 arrests were made at the demonstration, which the authorities declared illegal. In August 2012 Waytha Moorthy returned to Malaysia after a four-year absence. In January 2013 the home ministry lifted the ban on the organization and approved its registration in March of that year. In August 2013 Waytha Moorthy was appointed a deputy minister in the prime minister's office in the UMNO-led government.

Leader: P. Waytha MOORTHY (Chair).

There are numerous other small parties, including The **Malaysian Justice Movement** (*Parti Angkatan Keadilan Insan Malaysia*—AKIM), launched in 1995 by a number of *Semangat '46* and Pas dissidents and led by Hanafi MAMAT; the **Malaysian Punjabi Party** (*Parti Punjabi Malaysia*), led by Sushel KAUR, the only woman to head a Malaysian party; the **State Reform Party**—Star (*Parti Reformasi Negeri*), led by former SNAP vice president, PATAU Rubis; and the **Malaysian Workers' Party** (*Parti Pekerja-Pekerja Malaysia*), which dates from 1978.

Sabah opposition parties include the **Sabah People's Unity Front** (*Parti Barisan Rakyat Sabah*—Bersekutu), led by Barman ANGKAP; the **Sabah People's United Democratic Party** (*Parti Demokratik Setiasehati Kuasa Rakyat Bersatu Sabah*—Setia); and the **United Pasok Nunkragang National Organization** (*Pertubuhan Kebangsaan Pasok Nunkragang Bersatu*—Pasok).

There are numerous parties within the Indian community. They include, in addition to the MIC, the IPF, and the MMSP, the **Malaysian Indian United Party** (MIUP), founded in 2007 and led by S. NALLAKARUPAN, and the **Malaysian Indian Democratic Action Front** (Mindraf), established in 2009 by the former journalist Manuel LOPEZ. The **Parti Cinta Malaysia,** whose leaders include Huan Cheng GUAN and Gabriel Adit DEMONG, was formed in 2009. In 2010 P. UTHAYAKUMAR, a legal adviser to Hindraf (Hindu Rights Action Force, below), established the **Human Rights Party** (HRP). The **Parti Ekonomi Sarawak Bersatu** (PERSB) was formed by a group of plantation owners.

Radical Islamic Group:

Malaysian Mujahideen Group (*Kumpulan Mujahideen Malaysia*—KMM). The shadowy KMM, which advocates Malaysia's conversion to an Islamic state, was apparently organized in 1998 as the Malaysian Militant Group (*Kumpulan Militan Malaysia*). It is regarded as an affiliate of the Indonesian-based terrorist group *Jemaah Islamiah.*

A number of alleged KMM members have been jailed under Malaysia's security law, which permits detention without trial. In many cases the KMM detainees have been Pas members, including NIK ADLI Nik Abdul Aziz Nik Mat, son of the chief minister of Kelantan, who was held from August 2001 until October 2006.

In 2011 KMM leader Zulkifli bin Hir, who allegedly fought alongside Osama bin Laden, was on the most wanted terrorists list of the U.S. Federal Bureau of Investigation for alleged crimes in Indonesia, Malaysia, and the Philippines. Reports in 2012 indicated that Zulkifli was killed in February 2012 by an airstrike; however, as of June 2014, reports have surfaced indicating he is alive.

Leader: ZULKIFLI bin Hir.

LEGISLATURE

The federal **Parliament** (*Parliamen Malaysia*) is a bicameral body consisting of a Senate and a House of Representatives.

Senate (*Dewan Negara*). The upper chamber comprises 70 members: 44 appointed by the paramount ruler (including 2 senators from the Federal Territory of Kuala Lumpur and 1 each from Labuan and Putrajaya) and 2 selected by each of the 13 state legislatures. Members serve once-renewable three-year terms. The Senate is never dissolved, new elections being held by the appropriate state legislative assembly as often as there are vacancies among the elected members. As of May 21, 2013, the National Front held 56 seats (United Malays National Organization, 30; Malaysian Chinese Association, 10; Malaysian Indian Congress, 6; United Traditional Bumiputra Party, 3; Malaysian People's Movement Party, 2; People's Progressive Party, 1; Sarawak United People's Party, 2; United *Pasok Momogun Kadazandusun Murut* Organization, 1; Sarawak Progressive Democratic Party, 1; Sarawak People's Party, 1); People's Alliance, 8 (Pan-Malaysian Islamic Party, 3; People's Justice Movement, 3; Democratic Action Party, 2). There were six vacancies.

President: Abu ZAHAR Ujang (UMNO).

House of Representatives (*Dewan Rakyat*). The lower house currently has 222 elected members. The term of the House is five years, subject to dissolution. Elections are by universal adult suffrage, but the voting is weighted in favor of the predominantly Malay rural areas, with some urban (mainly Chinese) constituencies having three to four times as many voters as their rural counterparts.

In the most recent election of May 5, 2013, the National Front (BN) won 133 seats (United Malays National Organization, 88; United

Traditional Bumiputra Party, 14; Malaysian Chinese Association, 7; Sarawak People's Party, 6; Malaysian Indian Congress, 4; Sabah United Party, 4; Sarawak Progressive Democratic Party, 4; United *Pasok Momogun Kadazandusun Murut* Organization, 3; Malaysian People's Movement Party, 1; Sarawak United People's Party, 1; and United Sabah People's Party, 1). The opposition People's Front won 89 seats, distributed as follows: Democratic Action Party, 38; People's Justice Party, 30; and Pan-Malaysian Islamic Party, 21.

Speaker: PANDIKAR Amin Mulia (UMNO).

CABINET

[as of September 1, 2016]

Prime Minister	Mohamed Najib Abdul Razak (UMNO)
Deputy Prime Minister	Ahmad Zahid bin Hamidi (UMNO)
Ministers	
Agriculture and Agro-Base Industry	Ahmad Shabery bin Cheek (UMNO)
Communication and Multimedia	Salleh bin Tun Said Keruak (UMNO)
Defense	Hishammuddin Hussein (UMNO)
Domestic Trade, Cooperative, and Consumerism	Hamzah bin Zainudin (UMNO)
Education and Higher Education	Mahdzir bin Khalid (UMNO)
Energy, Green Technology, and Water	Maximus Johnity Ongkili (PBS)
Federal Territories	Tengku Adnan Tengku Mansor (UMNO)
Finance	Mohamed Najib Abdul Razak (UMNO)
Finance, Second Ministry	Johari Abdul Ghani (UMNO)
Foreign Affairs	Anifah Aman (UMNO)
Health	S. Subramaniam (MIC)
Higher Education	Idris Jusoh (UMNO)
Home Affairs	Ahmad Zahid bin Hamidi (UMNO)
Human Resources	Richard Riot Anak Jaem (SUPP)
International Trade and Industry	Mustapha Mohamed (UMNO)
Natural Resources and Environment	Wan Junaidi bin Tuanku Jaafar (PBB)
Plantation Industries and Commodities	Mah Siew Keong (Gerakin)
Prime Minister's Office, without Portfolio	Joseph Kurup (PBRS)
Prime Minister's Office, without Portfolio	Maj. Gen. (Ret.) Jamil Khir Baharom (UMNO)
Prime Minister's Office, without Portfolio	Azalina Othman Said (UMNO)
Prime Minister's Office, without Portfolio	Idris Jala (ind.)
Prime Minister's Office, without Portfolio	Joseph Entulu Anak Belaun (ind.)
Prime Minister's Office, without Portfolio	Shahidan bin Kassim (UMNO)
Prime Minister's Office, without Portfolio	Abdul Rahman bin Haji Dahlan (UMNO)
Prime Minister's Office, without Portfolio	Paul Low Seng Kwan (ind.)
Prime Minister's Office, without Portfolio	Wee ka Siong (MCA)
Prime Minister's Office, without Portfolio	Nancy Binti Shukri (PRS) [f]
Rural and Regional Development	Ismail Sabri bin Yaakob (UMNO)
Science, Technology, and Innovation	Wilfred Madius Tangau (UPKO)
Tourism and Culture	Mohamed Nazri bin Abdul Aziz (UMNO)
Transport	Liow Tiong Lai (MCA)
Urban Welfare, Housing, and Local Government	Noh Omar (UMNO)
Women, Family, and Community Development	Rohani Abdul Karim (UMNO) [f]
Works	Fadillah Yusof (UMNO)
Youth and Sports	Khairy Jamaluddin abu Bakar (UMNO)

[f] = female

INTERGOVERNMENTAL REPRESENTATION

Ambassador to the U.S.: Zulhasnan RAFIQUE.

U.S. Ambassador to Malaysia: Kamala Shirin LAKHDHIR.

Permanent Representative to the UN: Ramlan Bin IBRAHIM.

IGO Memberships (Non-UN): ADB, APEC, ASEAN, CWTH, NAM, OIC, WTO.

For Further Reference:

Baker, Marshall. *Crossroads: A Popular History of Malaysia and Singapore.* Singapore: Marshall Cavendish, 2008.

Chin, James, and Joern Dosch, eds. *Malaysia Post-Mahathir: A Decade of Change?* Singapore: Marshall Cavendish, 2015.

Nonini, Donald. *"Getting By": Class and State Formation among Chinese in Malaysia.* Ithaca, NY: Cornell University Press, 2015.

MALDIVES

Republic of Maldives
Dhivehi Jumhuriyah

Note: The Maldives withdrew from the Commonwealth on October 13, 2016, after the organization warned the island nation that it would be suspended if it did not make more progress toward democratization.

Political Status: Former British protectorate; independent since July 26, 1965; sultanate replaced by republican regime November 11, 1968; present constitution promulgated August 7, 2008.

Area: 115 sq. mi. (298 sq. km).

Population: 370,000 (2016E—UN); 392,960 (2016E—U.S. Census).

Major Urban Center (2014E—UN): MALÉ (156,000).

Official Language: Dhivehi.

Monetary Unit: Maldivian Rufiyaa (market rate October 1, 2016: 15.35 rufiyaa = $1US).

President: Abdullah YAMEEN Abdul Gayoom (Progressive Party of the Maldives); sworn in on November 17, 2013 following the runoff election of November 16, succeeding Mohammed WAHEED Hassan Manik (National Unity Party), who assumed office on February 7, 2012.

Vice President: Abdulla JIHAD (Progressive Party of the Maldives); appointed on June 22, 2016, to succeed Ahmed ADEEB (Progressive Party of the Maldives) who was impeached on November 5, 2015.

THE COUNTRY

The Republic of Maldives is a 500-mile-long chain of small, low-lying coral islands in the Indian Ocean, southwest of India's tip. Grouped into 20 atoll clusters, the more than 1,200 islands (only about 200 are inhabited) have vegetation ranging from scrub to dense tropical forest. The population displays mixed Sinhalese, Dravidian, and Arab traits. The official language, Dhivehi, is related to Sinhalese. Islam is the state religion, most of the population belonging to the Sunni sect. Women make up 42 percent of the active labor force, but only 5 were elected to the 85-seat national legislature in 2014. The Inter-Parliamentarian Union ranked the Maldives at 173rd out of 181 countries in women's representation in parliament.

The economy was traditionally dependent on fishing, which continues to lead the islands' exports but agriculture and fishing now account for only 5.6 percent of GDP and 11 percent of employment. In recent years fishing has been surpassed in importance by a booming tourism sector, which accounts for 28 percent of GDP. Manufacturing, which contributes about 16.9 percent of GDP and employs 23 percent of the active labor force, is limited, the most important products being canned fish and garments. Cottage industries and handicraft production are also significant sources of employment and income. The government dominates most economic activity, but private sector participation has been increasingly encouraged.

In the first ten years of the 21st century, the Maldives suffered two serious economic blows: first with the December 2004 Indian Ocean tsunami, which prompted contraction of 8.7 percent the next year; and the impact of the global financial crisis, causing a decline of 3.6 percent in 2009. With considerable IMF loan assistance, GDP grew by 7 percent in 2010 and 2011. In 2013 growth slowed to 3.8 percent. Inflation was 5.8 percent, down from an 11.3 percent peak in 2011. During a February 2014 visit, an IMF delegation praised the "resilience" of the domestic economy, despite high public debt and budget deficits. That year recorded GDP growth of 5 percent, with inflation of 2.5 percent. GDP also grew by 5 percent in 2015, before slowing to an estimated 4 percent in 2016. Inflation in 2016 was estimated to be 2.2 percent. The World Bank ranked the Maldives as 128th out of 189 countries in its 2016 annual ease of doing business survey.

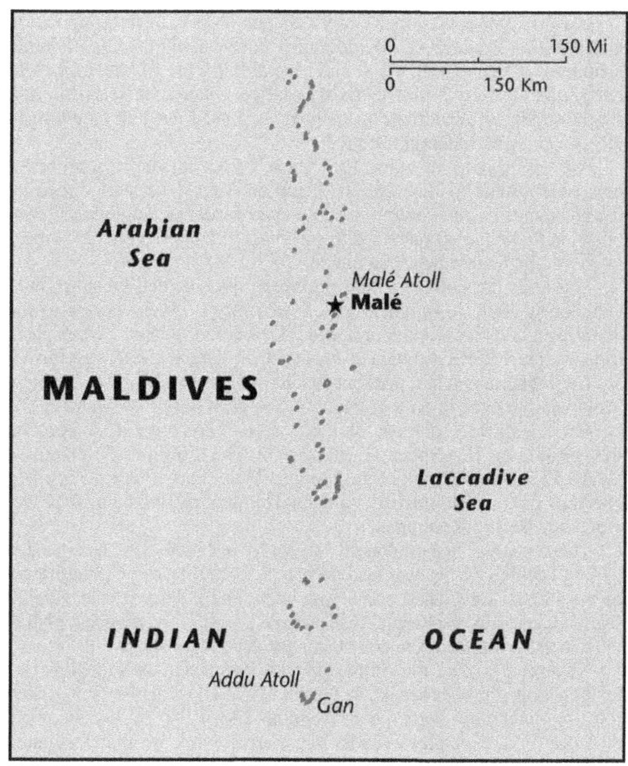

GOVERNMENT AND POLITICS

Political background. Subjected to a brief period of Portuguese domination in the 16th century, the Maldives came under British influence in 1796 and was declared a British protectorate in 1887. Internal self-government was instituted in 1960, and full independence was achieved on July 26, 1965, following negotiations with the United Kingdom covering economic assistance and the retention of a British air facility on southern Gan Island. The centuries-old Maldivian sultanate, which had been temporarily replaced by a republican form of government in 1953–1954, was then reinstated until 1968, when the Maldives again became a republic following a national referendum.

Appointed prime minister in 1972, Ahmed ZAKI was redesignated in February 1975 but was removed from office and placed under arrest in March. President Ibrahim NASIR assumed executive responsibilities, and Zaki was banished. The change in governmental structure was then codified by a constitutional revision.

After 21 years of rule, President Nasir announced in mid-1978 that he would not seek reelection. The Majlis (Citizens' Assembly) thereupon nominated as his successor Transport Minister Maumoon Abdul GAYOOM. Prior to Gayoom's installation in November, outgoing President Nasir pardoned a number of those under house arrest or banished, including former prime minister Zaki, who subsequently served as UN representative. The Majlis renominated President Gayoom for additional terms in 1983 and 1988, with confirmation by referendum.

In November 1988 an attempted coup by more than 400 mercenaries was crushed by India's dispatch of some 1,600 paratroopers. A trial of 73 individuals involved in the affair concluded in August 1989 with 17 sentenced to death (later commuted) and the rest to lengthy prison terms. In 1993 President Gayoom's renomination was unexpectedly challenged by his brother-in-law, Ilyas IBRAHIM. Gayoom reportedly defeated Ibrahim by an informal vote of 28–18 in the Majlis, which then proceeded to unanimously nominate Gayoom. Ibrahim was charged with illegally attempting to influence members of the Majlis and fled the country prior to being sentenced in absentia to 15 years' imprisonment. Gayoom was inaugurated for a fourth term in November, following endorsement by referendum.

Amid growing calls for political reform, in December 1994 contests for the 40 elective seats in the Majlis drew 229 candidates, all standing as independents. Those elected included several leaders of the "proreform" movement, notably former ministers Abdulla KAMALUDHEEN and Ahmed MUJUTABA.

Ilyas Ibrahim returned to house arrest in 1996 but was released in 1997, his case apparently having influenced the way presidential balloting in the legislature was to be conducted under a new constitution that was promulgated on January 1, 1998. Although four others sought the presidential nomination during secret balloting in the legislature in September 1998, President Gayoom received a unanimous endorsement. Following confirmation by referendum, he took the oath of office for a fifth term in November. The new cabinet introduced by President Gayoom included his erstwhile adversary Ilyas Ibrahim as well as Abdulla Kamaludheen.

The People's Majlis election of November 1999 saw a nearly 50 percent turnover in the elected membership. A total of 129 independent candidates contested the election.

In 2003 President Gayoom won unanimous endorsement for a sixth term. He was confirmed by 90.3 percent of the voters on October 17 and sworn in on November 11.

On August 13, 2004, the president declared a state of emergency following demonstrations demanding the release of political prisoners. When the state of emergency was lifted on October 10, 2004, nearly 80 of the 185 who had been arrested in August were still being held.

Legislative elections to the 50-seat People's Majlis, originally scheduled for December 31, 2004, but postponed because of the Indian Ocean tsunami, were held on January 22, 2005. Although all candidates were required to run as independents, reform advocates performed strongly. Those endorsed by the Maldivian Democratic Party (MDP), an opposition party then based in Sri Lanka, captured 18 of the 42 elective seats.

On May 28, 2004, voters cast ballots for a partially elected People's Special Majlis that was assigned the task of drafting another new constitution. On June 2, 2005, at President Gayoom's request, the People's Majlis unanimously passed a reform allowing the registration of political parties. The MDP quickly registered and immediately became the principal opposition to President Gayoom's newly organized *Dhivehi Rayyithunge* Party (DRP).

In August 2005 more than 130 demonstrators were arrested, including the MDP chair, Mohamed NASHEED (familiarly called Anni), who had returned from exile in April. Nasheed faced charges of terrorism and sedition. In October Jennifer LATHEEF, daughter of exiled MDP founder Mohamed LATHEEF, was convicted of inciting a riot in September 2003 and sentenced to ten years in prison. In August 2006, however, Jennifer Latheef was released from house arrest, as was Nasheed in September. The releases came in the context of "Westminster House" talks, chaired by the United Kingdom's high commissioner to the Maldives, between the government and the opposition.

On August 18, 2007, some 62 percent of voters in a national referendum supported maintaining a strong presidency, while the balance favored a parliamentary system.

In May 2008 a National Unity Alliance (NUA) of five opposition groups—the Maldivian Democratic Party (MDP), the Islamic Democratic Party (IDP), the Social Liberal Party (SLP), the *Adhaalath* Party, and the New Maldives (NM)—failed to agree on selection of a single opposition candidate to compete against President Gayoom in the upcoming presidential election.

After four years of work, the People's Special Majlis approved a new constitution on June 26, 2008, and on August 7 it was signed by the president. The day before, Gayoom had pardoned a number of prisoners, including others who had been convicted of terrorism in connection with the September 2003 unrest.

Voting in the country's first multiparty presidential election, held October 8, 2008, Maldivians gave a plurality of 40.3 percent to the incumbent, President Gayoom, and 24.9 percent to the second-place finisher, the MDP's Mohamed Nasheed. Finishing third was former attorney general and independent candidate Hassan SAEED of the New Maldives movement. In the resultant two-way runoff on October 29, Nasheed won 53.7 percent of the vote to Gayoom's 45.3 percent. Inaugurated on November 11, along with Vice President Mohammed WAHEED Hassan Manik of the National Unity Party (NUP), President Nasheed named a multiparty cabinet. The peaceful transfer of power won wide international praise.

The country's first multiparty legislative election, for an expanded 77-seat People's Majlis, was held on May 9, 2009. Eleven of 13 registered parties offered candidates, and 5 won seats. The DRP won a leading 28 seats, while its ally, the People's Alliance (PA), won 7. The president's MDP took 26 seats, with independents claiming most of the balance.

On June 29, 2010, the entire cabinet resigned. On the same day two leading opposition lawmakers, Gasim IBRAHIM of the Republican Party (*Jumhooree* Party) and Abdulla YAMEEN of the People's Alliance (PA), were placed under house arrest while being investigated for allegedly bribing other lawmakers to vote against the government. On July 11 the Supreme Court ordered their release. Four days earlier, Nasheed had reinstated the cabinet, an action that DRP leaders questioned on constitutional grounds.

On December 9, 2010, the Supreme Court ruled that cabinet appointees who had not been confirmed by the opposition-controlled legislature could not remain in office. The ruling arose from a dispute between the executive and legislative branches over President Mohamed Nasheed's decision, five months earlier, to reappoint the members of his cabinet en masse following their June 29 resignations. On December 11 Nasheed announced a reshuffled cabinet in which a number of portfolios were assigned on an acting basis. By August 2011 the parliament had approved replacements for the ministers who had resigned.

Following widespread protests and rioting, on February 7, 2012, President Mohamed Nasheed resigned amid a mutiny by security forces (see Current issues, below). Vice President Waheed was sworn in as interim president on the same day. A new coalition government was named in stages, beginning February 8.

Former president Nasheed secured a clear victory as MDP candidate in the first round of 2013 presidential elections on September 7, the results of which were subsequently annulled by the Supreme Court. Abdulla Yameen of the Progressive Party of the Maldives (PPM) secured the presidency in the second round of a new election in November (see Current issues, below). In balloting on March 22, 2014, the PPM retained control of parliament in alliance with the JP and the MDA. The coalition briefly held a two-thirds majority until the JP departed the coalition on May 28 (see Current issues, below).

On July 21, 2015, Vice President Mohamed JAMEEL Ahmed (PPM) was impeached by Parliament and amid allegations that he was plotting a coup against Yameen. The charges were vehemently denied by Jameel, who fled into exile (see Political Parties, below). On July 22 tourism minister Ahmed ADEEB (PPM) was appointed vice president.

On September 28, 2015, an explosion occurred on a speedboat carrying President Yameen in an apparent assassination attempt. Yameen was uninjured, but his wife and two aides were wounded. On October 8 two military personnel and an immigration officer were arrested as suspects in the assassination plot.

Upon his arrival from a diplomatic trip to China on October 28, 2015, Vice President Adeeb was arrested on charges that he obstructed the investigation into the attempted assassination. He was subsequently expelled from the PPM and impeached on November 5, a day after the president declared a state of emergency in the country (see Current issues, below).

On June 22, 2016, Yameen appointed Abdulla JIHAD (PPM) as vice president and reshuffled the cabinet.

Constitution and government. Following adoption of a republican constitution in 1968, the Maldivian government combined constitutional rule with de facto control by members of a small hereditary elite. The 1998 basic law, which was drafted over a 17-year period by a Citizens' Special Majlis, provided for a unicameral legislature controlled by an elected majority. The legislature nominated the president for a five-year term, with confirmation required by popular referendum. The 1998 constitution also provided for a People's Special Majlis (previously the Citizens' Special Majlis) to draft or amend a constitution. Either the president or the legislature, the People's Majlis, could convene a People's Special Majlis, whose membership included the 50 members of the legislature, an additional 42 elected members, 8 presidential appointees, and the members of the cabinet.

The new constitution approved by the People's Special Majlis in June 2008 and signed by President Gayoom in August retains a strong presidential system but reduces some powers and limits the president to two terms in office. It provides for a two-way runoff should no presidential candidate achieve 50 percent of the vote in a first round. A president must be the child of Maldivian citizens and must practice the Sunni branch of Islam. Cabinet ministers are named by the president but must receive legislative endorsement. The People's Majlis, now wholly elected using a first-past-the-post system, was expanded from 50 to 77 seats.

The 2008 constitution also enumerates a broad range of human rights, including freedom of speech, assembly, and association, and provides for the separation of executive, legislative, and judicial powers. The judicial system encompasses a Supreme Court, a High Court, and trial courts. Independent bodies are to be established for human rights, defense, police, elections, and corruption investigations. The constitution prohibits ministers from having private businesses, one immediate consequence being that four cabinet members tendered their resignations on August 6, 2008.

The current constitution includes no provision for a People's Special Majlis. Constitutional amendments require the assent of three-fourth of the full People's Majlis and the signature of the president, although the legislature may call for a referendum if the president does not assent to a change.

There are 20 atoll-based administrative divisions. The capital constitutes a separate, centrally administered district. In the past, each atoll was governed by a presidentially appointed atoll chief (*verin*), who was advised by an elected committee. Under the 2008 constitution, all divisions are to be "administered decentrally." As authorized by law, the president may create constituencies, posts, and councils, with the members of all councils to be elected democratically. Each council may then elect a president and vice president to serve as administrative officers for the jurisdiction.

Freedom of the press is protected. In 2016 the media group Reporters Without Borders ranked the Maldives 112th in media freedom, a sharp decline from 73rd in 2011, reflecting threats and attacks on journalists from the time of President Nasheed's controversial resignation onward.

Foreign relations. An active participant in the Nonaligned Movement, the Republic of Maldives has long sought to have the Indian Ocean declared a "Zone of Peace," with foreign (particularly nuclear) military forces permanently banned from the area. Thus, despite the adverse impact on an already depressed economy, the government welcomed the withdrawal of the British Royal Air Force from Gan Island in 1976 and rejected a subsequent Soviet bid to establish a base there. The republic became a "special member" of the Commonwealth in July 1982 and a full member in June 1985. It continues to claim some 62,000 square miles (160,000 square kilometers) of the British Indian Ocean Territory.

Maldives is a founding member of the South Asian Association for Regional Cooperation (SAARC). The Gayoom government took an active role addressing global warming. In November 2009 Maldives hosted the first meeting of the 11-member Climate Vulnerable Forum (V-11).

India remains the Maldives's closest international partner and the only country with which Malé has a defense cooperation agreement. In 2010 the two governments negotiated a pact on combating terrorism and subsequently expanded antipiracy cooperation. China and the Maldives signed an economic cooperation agreement in August 2010.

In January 2012 the Maldives and Burkina Faso established diplomatic ties. Following the February coup (see Current issues, below), the Commonwealth suspended the Maldives from its ministerial action group and dispatched a fact finding mission that was critical of the transfer of power. In September Waheed announced that the entire Maldives would become a marine reserve by 2017.

A budget shortfall in July 2013 led the Maldives to seek a $300 million credit facility from Saudi Arabia. The new friendship was formalized with a visit to the Maldives by crown prince Salman bin Abdulaziz in February 2014.

Indian prime minister Narendra Modi cancelled a scheduled visit in March 2015 in protest of the trial of former president Nasheed (see Current issues).

In April 2016 the Maldives parliament ratified the Paris agreement on climate change (see entry on the United Nations). In May the Maldives severed diplomatic ties with Iran over that country's support for terrorism and its interventions in Syria and Yemen.

Current issues. On January 17, 2012, Nasheed ordered the arrest of the chief justice of nation's criminal court, Abdulla MOHAMED, for blocking corruption investigations after the latter released a leading government critic. The arrest prompted widespread protests and criticism by government members and opponents, including Vice President Waheed. On February 7 Nasheed resigned, reportedly at gunpoint, as police and military units mutinied. Pro-Nasheed demonstrators took to the streets in running battles with police that left 50 injured, 90 in jail, and 18 police stations burned. Waheed took office, forming a unity cabinet that included all of the country's main parties except the MDP.

With the ratification of new regulations under the Political Party Act in March 2013, 11 parties were dissolved for failing to have the requisite membership of 10,000, reducing the number of registered parties to 5. In September the Supreme Court reduced the membership requirement to 3,000, enabling more parties to qualify for registration.

Four candidates contested the September 2013 presidential elections. Former president Nasheed, as MDP candidate, was the clear leader with 45.5 percent of the vote. Abdulla Yameen, half brother of former president Gayoom, running for the Progressive Party of the Maldives (PPM), followed with 25.4 percent of the vote. Incumbent Mohamed Waheed placed fourth with just 5.1 percent. On September 23 the Supreme Court suspended runoff balloting until the claims could be investigated and subsequently annulled the results. Mass protests, led by the MDP, broke out, and the election commission criticized the Supreme Court ruling. The Supreme Court's decision elicited concern from the United Nations, the Commonwealth, the United States, and a host of other international observers.

A second election scheduled for October 19 was suspended on the grounds that Gasim and Yameen had failed to approve the voter register. After the candidates came to an agreement in early November, polling was held on November 9, in which Nasheed was the clear leader with 46.9 percent of the vote. As no candidate secured the necessary 50 percent, Nasheed and the runner-up, Yameen, proceeded to runoff balloting on November 16. Yameen won with 51.3 percent of the vote, while Nasheed secured 48.6 percent. Yameen was sworn in the following day.

On March 9, 2014, the Supreme Court sentenced all four election commissioners to six-month prison sentences and three years suspension for "disobeying orders" over the presidential elections. Former president Nasheed called the decision "the saddest day in the history of Maldives' constitutional life."

Parliamentary balloting on March 22, 2014, resulted in a sound victory of 53 seats for a PPM-led coalition, which included the JP and the MDA. The MDP placed second with 26 seats, three of which defected. Two former MDP members joined the PPM, producing a in a two-thirds majority for the coalition. However, the ruling coalition divided on May 28 when the JP's Gasim stood for parliamentary speaker, challenging, unsuccessfully, Abdulla MASEEH Mohamed of the PPM.

Nasheed was arrested on February 22, 2015, and indicted on terrorism and kidnapping charges. He was convicted and sentenced on March 13 to 13 years in prison. Also in March, a new law forbade people serving prison sentences from belonging to political parties in an effort to force Nasheed to surrender the presidency of the MDP. An appeal by the former president was denied by the high court on September 10.

Widespread antigovernment protests in May 2015 prompted changes to the nation's antiterrorism legislation that criminalized "any activity aimed at imposing undue influence on the government" and "creating situations hazardous to health and safety" are acts of terrorism."

Under foreign pressure, Yameen agreed to restart all-party talks in February 2016. Nasheed entered the UK in May 2016 on parole from prison for medical treatment; while there he applied for and was granted asylum. Foreign Minister Dunya MAUMOON (PPM) resigned on July 5 in protest of government plans to reintroduce capital punishment.

POLITICAL PARTIES

Governing Coalition:

Progressive Party of the Maldives (PPM) was formed in September 2011 by former president Gayoom and defectors from the Z-DRP faction of the DRP. The PPM joined the February 2012 unity cabinet and received two portfolios. Abdulla Yameen, Gayoom's half-brother and former leader of the PA, contested the September 2013 elections on the PPM ticket, placing second in the first round with 25.4 percent of the vote. The NUP subsequently endorsed Yameen, who won the second round of presidential balloting in November. Campaigning on a promise to improve the economy, the PPM retained control of the Majlis winning 33 seats in March 2014 elections with the support of coalition partners, the JP (below) and the MDA. Reports in 2016 indicated growing fractionalization within the PPM, with increasing discontent with Yameen's leadership.

Leaders: Abdullah YAMEEN Abdul Gayoom (President of the Republic), Abdulla JIHAD (Vice President of the Republic), Maumoon Abdul GAYOOM (Party Chair and Former President of the Republic).

Maldives Development Alliance (MDA). Organized by tourism tycoon Ahmed Shiyam MOHAMED, the MDA received official status in October 2013, when former independent MP Kurendhoo Ahmed MOOSA joined, bringing the parliamentary presence to three seats. The MDA backed the PPM's Yameen for president in November 2013 balloting. In the March 2014 parliamentary poll, the MDA won five seats with 7.5 percent of the vote as a member of the PPM's ruling coalition.

Leader: Ahmed Shiyam MOHAMED (Leader and Founder).

Parliamentary Opposition:

Maldivian Democratic Party (MDP). Efforts to establish a legal MDP date back to 2001, when the government refused to register it. As a result, the MDP was based in Colombo, Sri Lanka, from 2003 until officially registered in the Maldives in June 2005. The Majlis elected in 1999 reportedly included 7 MDP supporters; 18 representatives elected in January 2005 had run with MDP endorsements. Following legalization of political parties, the center-right MDP assumed leadership of the parliamentary opposition. In May 2006 the party president, Ibrahim ISMAIL, resigned over tactical issues.

In November 2006 officials arrested 100 MDP members and supporters and later charged acting MDP president Ibrahim Hussein ZAKI with treason for voicing support for protesting fishermen. In April 2007 the MDP was fined, not for the first time, for holding illegal gatherings, this time to welcome home Majlis member Mariya Ahmed DIDI, who in March had received an International Woman of Courage Award from the U.S. State Department for her advocacy of women's rights.

In June 2007 former attorney general Mohamed MUNAVVAR was elected chair. In a presidential primary, Mohamed Nasheed (Anni) defeated Munavvar and Moosa "Reeko" Manik. Nasheed secured 24.9 percent of the first-round 2008 presidential vote for second place and defeated the incumbent president with 53.7 percent in the second round.

In the May 2009 legislative election the MDP finished second, with 26 seats, despite claiming a plurality of votes, 30.8 percent. As of September 2010, the MDP held a plurality of 32 seats but was still outnumbered by the combined opposition. In March 2011 former party leader Munavvar established a new party, the Maldives Reform Party (MRP).

In February 2012 Nasheed was forced to resign amid public protests, as well as pressure from security forces. The MDP subsequently rejected an invitation to join a unity government.

Nasheed, with running mate Mustafa LUTFI, contested the September 2013 presidential election, emerging the clear leader in the first round of voting with 45.5 percent but failing to pass the 50 percent mark. Following the JP's call for annulment of the election, the MDP offered a "truce" with *Adhaalath*, which was rejected. Party supporters protested the postponing of the runoff election, and Nasheed was eventually defeated in a second round of balloting in November. In March 2014 parliamentary balloting, the MDP won 26 seats. Moosa Manik subsequently resigned the chairmanship. Despite a government ban on street protests in 2016, the MDP continued to hold antigovernment demonstrations. The MDP and other opposition groups formed an antigovernment coalition, Maldives United Opposition, under the leadership of former vice president Jameel in exile in the United Kingdom.

Leaders: Mohamed NASHEED (Former President of the Republic and President of the Party), Ali WAHEED (Chair), Mohamed SHIFAZ (Vice President), Moosa MANIK (Deputy Speaker of Parliament).

Republican Party (*Jumhooree* Party—JP). The JP was founded in May 2008 by Ahmed Nashid, an associate of former finance minister Gasim Ibrahim, reputedly the country's wealthiest businessman. Ibrahim, who resigned from the cabinet and the DRP in mid-July, joined the JP in August and was quickly named its presidential candidate. By then, the JP had reportedly become the largest opposition party in the People's Majlis, with nine seats.

Ibrahim finished fourth in the 2008 presidential election, winning 15.2 percent of the vote as the candidate of the Republican Coalition, which also included *Adhaalath* and the Maldivian National Congress (MNC, below). Ibrahim and two others joined the cabinet. Ibrahim resigned in December 2008, however, and in May 2009 Fathimath Diyana SAEED was dismissed by President Nasheed for criticizing the government. The JP threatened court action against the MDP for failing to fulfill their coalition agreement.

In the May 2009 People's Majlis election the JP won one seat. On June 29, 2010, Ibrahim, now aligned with the opposition, was arrested as part of a bribery investigation. He was released in July after the Supreme Court determined that his detention was unwarranted. Following the 2012 resignation of president Nasheed, the JP became part of the unity government and received one cabinet post.

Ibrahim contested the September 2013 election, with the support of a coalition of the JP, the Maldives National Party (see DQP, below), and *Adhaalath.* He placed third with 24.1 percent of the vote, on the heels of Yameen of the PPM. Ibrahim challenged the results, accusing the electoral commission of negligence and staging party protests (see Current issues, above). The JP contested the March 2014 parliamentary elections in alliance with the PPM, and won 15 seats, but left the majority coalition in May because of divisions over the parliamentary speaker election.

Leader: Qasim IBRAHIM.

Justice Party (*Adhaalath* Party). The Justice Party, registered in August 2005, is Islamic in orientation, including Muslim clerics and scholars among its membership. Some members have called for adoption of strict sharia law and the death penalty for Muslims who convert to other religions. The party endorsed Gasim Ibrahim of the JP for president in 2008 but in July 2009 signed a coalition agreement with the MDP for the next local council elections. In May the party had won less than 1 percent of the vote and no People's Majlis seats. Sheikh Imran Abdulla was elected party leader in July 2011. *Adhaalath* joined the NUP-led unity government in February 2012. In 2013 *Adhaalath* again backed Ibrahim for president.

In February 2014 *Adhaalath* withdrew support for the PPM, unhappy with the coalition's allotment of constituencies for the March 22 parliamentary elections. Standing independently, *Adhaalath* won one seat with 2.7 percent. *Adhaalath* ended support for the PPM and joined the opposition in February 2015, after organizing a protest against President Yameen. Abdulla was sentenced to 12 years for comments made against the government in February 2016.

Leaders: Sheikh Imran ABDULLA (President), Mohamed MUIZZU, Mohamed Shaheem ALI Saeed.

Other Parties Contesting the 2014 Parliamentary Election:

Maldive People's Party (*Dhivehi Rayyithunge Party*—DRP). Registered shortly after the legalization of parties, the DRP was established by President Gayoom. Its members included the cabinet and the government-supportive members of the People's Majlis and the People's Special Majlis. The party held its first congress April 19–21, 2006, at which time Gayoom was formally elected party chair by a vote of 887–33 over reform activist Ali SHAFEEQ. (For more on the history of the party, see the 2015 *Handbook.*)

Gayoom's January 2010 announcement that he would not seek reelection was seen as a step toward party unification; however, tensions mounted following Thasmeen's election to party chair. The former president created a faction within the party, the Z-DRP, which subsequently formed a parliamentary coalition with the JP, the DQP and the PA (see below) opposition coalition within. In September 2011 Gayoom formed the PPM.

Thasmeen stood as running mate of incumbent President Waheed, of the NUP, in the first round of presidential balloting in September 2013. Following a fourth-place finish, the DRP backed the MDP for the runoff. The DRP contested the 2014 parliamentary election, but failed to secure any seats.

Leaders: Ahmed THASMEEN Ali (Leader and 2013 vice presidential candidate), Ibrahim SHAREEF (Deputy Leader), Abdul RASHEED Nafiz (Secretary General).

Other Parties:

National Unity Party—NUP (*Gaumee Itthihaad*). Former education minister Mohamed Waheed Hassan launched the NUP, sometimes referenced in English as the National Alliance Party (NAP), in mid-2008. Initially the party's presidential candidate, Waheed formed an alliance with the MDP and became Mohamed Nasheed's running mate for the October election. In the May 2009 legislative election the NUP won only 0.3 percent of the vote and no seats. Following the resignation of Nasheed in February 2012, Waheed became president of the Maldives and formed a unity cabinet.

Following controversy over whether the NUP fulfilled the new regulation to have membership of at least 10,000, Waheed contested the September 2013 election as an independent. The incumbent suffered a resounding defeat, placing fourth with just 5.1 percent of the vote. Subsequently, he announced the NUP's support for the PPM.

Leaders: Mohamed WAHEED Hassan Manik (Party President and Former President of the Republic), Ahmed THAUFEEQ (Secretary General).

Maldives National Party (*Dhivehi Qaumee Party*—DQP). The DQP originated in the New Maldives (NM) movement, which was formed by former attorney general Hassan Saeed and former foreign minister Ahmed SHAHEED, both of whom had resigned from the government in August 2007 and had criticized President Gayoom for delaying democratic reforms. Mohamed Latheef, an MDP founder, joined upon returning from exile in January 2007. (For more on the history of the party, see the 2015 *Handbook.*)

In May 2009 the newly registered DQP won 3.5 percent of the national vote and two seats in the People's Majlis. In October it withdrew from the government, charging the MDP with not consulting its coalition partners and with failing to improve governance. In response, Shaheed announced that he was joining the MDP. In 2011 the DQP joined the Z-DRP-led opposition grouping, and in 2012 it joined the NUP-led unity cabinet. Ahead of the 2013 presidential elections, the DQP joined the JP-led coalition fronted by Gasim Ibrahim.

Leaders: Hassan SAEED (Chair and 2008 presidential candidate), Abdulla AMEEN (Secretary General).

Other parties include the following: the **National Alliance** (NA), led by Mohamed WAHEED and formed in 2008; the **Maldivian Labor Party** (MLP), established in 2008 as the Poverty Alleviating Party; and the **Maldivian National Congress** (MNC), chaired by Mohamed NAEEM, which won less than 0.1 percent of the vote in 2009.

For more information on the **Maldivian Social Democratic Party** (MSDP) and the **People's Party** (PP), see the 2011 *Handbook.* For more information on the **Social Liberal Party** (SLP), see the 2012 *Handbook.*

LEGISLATURE

Prior to adoption of the 2008 constitution, the Maldivian **People's Majlis** was a unicameral body of 50 members: 8 appointed by the president and 42 popularly elected as independents. The country's first multiparty election, for a 77-seat People's Majlis, was held May 9, 2009. In the election for the People's Majlis, which had been enlarged to 85 seats to reflect population growth, on March 22, 2014, the results were as follows: Progressive Part of Maldives, 33; Maldives Democratic Party, 26; Republican Party, 15; Maldives Development Alliance, 5; *Adhaalath* Party, 1; independents, 5. Representatives, all of whom are now elected from districts drawn on the basis of population, serve five-year terms.

Speaker: Abdulla MASEEH Mohamed.

CABINET

[as of July 15, 2016]

President	Abdulla Yameen Abdul Gayoom (PPM)
Vice President	Abdulla Jihad

Ministers

Defense and National Security	Adam Shareef
Economic Development	Mohamed Saeed (PPM)
Education	Aishath Shiham (PPM) [f]
Environment and Energy	Thoriq Ibrahim (PPM)
Finance and Treasury	Ahmed Munawwar (ind.)
Fisheries and Agriculture	Mohamed Shainee (PPM)
Foreign Affairs	Mohamed Asim (ind.)
Gender and Family	Aminath Zenysha Shadeed Zaki (ind.)
Health	Abudulla Nazim Ibrahim (ind.)
Home Affairs	Ahmed Zuhoor
Housing and Infrastructure	Mohamed Muizzu (MDA)
Islamic Affairs	Ahmed Ziyad (ind.)
Tourism	Moosa Zameer
Youth and Sports	Iruthisham Adam (ind.) [f]
Attorney General	Mohamed Anil (ind.)

[f] = female

INTERGOVERNMENTAL REPRESENTATION

Ambassador to the U.S. and Permanent Representative to the UN: Ahmed SAREER.

U.S. Ambassador to the Maldives (resident in Sri Lanka): Atul KESHAP.

Permanent Representative to the UN: Ahmed SAREER.

IGO Memberships (Non-UN): ADB, ICC, NAM, OIC, SAARC, WTO.

For Further Reference:

Brassard, Caroline, David W. Giles, and Arnold M. Howitt, eds. *Natural Disaster Management in the Asia-Pacific*. Japan: Springer, 2015.

Musthaq, Fathima. "Tumult in the Maldives." *Journal of Democracy* 25, no. 2 (2014): 164–170.

Robinson, J. J. "The Maldives: What Went Wrong with the Democracy Experiment?" *The Round Table* 105, no. 2 (2016): 223–225.

MALI

Republic of Mali
République du Mali

Political Status: Independent republic proclaimed September 22, 1960; military regime established November 19, 1968; civilian rule reestablished under constitution approved in 1974 and promulgated June 19, 1979; 1974 constitution suspended on March 26, 1991, and replaced by interim Fundamental Act on March 31; multiparty constitution drafted by National Conference in July–August 1991, approved by popular referendum on January 12, 1992, and formally proclaimed on February 14, 1992; military regime briefly established by coup of March 21–22, 2012, followed by installation of a transitional government pending new presidential and legislative elections; permanent government inaugurated in September 2013 following presidential elections.

Area: 478,764 sq. mi. (1,240,000 sq. km).

Population: 18,135,000 (2016E—UN); 17,467,108 (2016E—U.S. Census).

Major Urban Center (2016E—UN): BAMAKO (2,651,000).

Official Language: French. Bambara, Fulfuldé, Songhai, and Tamasaq are also commonly spoken.

Monetary Unit: CFA franc (official rate October 1, 2016: 592.38 CFA francs = $1US). The CFA franc, previously pegged to the French franc, is now permanently pegged to the euro at 655.93 CFA francs = 1 euro.

President: Ibrahim Boubacar KEÏTA (Rally for Mali); elected in second-round balloting on August 11, 2013, and inaugurated on September 4 for a five-year term in succession to Interim President Dioncounda TRAORÉ (Alliance for Democracy in Mali/Party for Liberty, Solidarity, and Justice).

Prime Minister: Modibo KEITA (Alliance for Democracy in Mali); appointed by the president on January 9, 2015, to succeed Moussa MARA (Change), who resigned on January 8.

THE COUNTRY

Of predominantly desert and semidesert terrain, landlocked Mali stretches northward into the Sahara from the upper basin of the Niger and Senegal rivers. The country's lifeline is the Niger River, which flows northeastward past Bamako, Ségou, and Timbuktu in Mali and then southeastward through Niger and Nigeria to the Gulf of Guinea. Mali's overwhelmingly Muslim population falls into several distinct ethnic groups, including the Bambara and other southern peoples, who are mostly farmers. The Peul, or Fulani, as well as the Tuaregs (who are Berbers) pursue a primarily nomadic and pastoral existence on the fringes of the Sahara. Women constitute only about 15 percent of the formal workforce, and female involvement in politics has traditionally been minimal. However, in April 2011 the country's first woman prime minister was appointed, and in 2013 women won 14 seats (9.5 percent of the total) in the national legislature.

Approximately 80 percent of the economically active population is dependent on agriculture and fishing, with cotton, peanuts, and livestock being the leading sources of foreign exchange. Although the country was once dubbed the potential "breadbasket of Africa," Mali's food output has periodically been severely depressed by droughts, locust infestations, and land mismanagement. Industrial activity is concentrated in agroprocessing, some enterprises having been privatized as part of an overall retreat from state dominance of the economy. Extraction of minerals such as uranium, bauxite, ferronickel, phosphates, and gold has attracted international investment, and despite inferior transport and power facilities, gold is the nation's biggest export earner. Although some progress toward economic reconstruction has been registered with assistance from various foreign sources, Mali remains one of the world's poorest countries.

Good harvests helped Mali avoid contagion from the global economic downturn in 2009–2011. (For more on the history of the economy, see the 2015 *Handbook*.) The IMF approved new lending in December 2011, although disbursements were subsequently compromised by a coup in March 2012. Further undercut by a temporary rebel takeover in the north, real GDP fell by 0.4 percent in 2012. Although the return to an elected civilian government in the second half of 2013 appeared to lay the foundation for the resumption of normal economic activity (including aid transfers), GDP grew by only 1.7 percent for 2013 because of poor harvests. Normal growth returned in 2014, when GDP expanded by 6.8 percent, falling slightly to 5.6 percent the following year. In 2016 GDP was estimated to have grown by 5.1 percent, while inflation was 2 percent, and GDP per capita was $699. The World Bank ranked Mali 144th, between Burkina Faso and Papua New Guinea, out of 189 countries in its 2016 ease of doing business survey.

GOVERNMENT AND POLITICS

Political background. Mali, the former French colony of Soudan, takes its name from a medieval African kingdom whose capital was located near the present capital city of Bamako. As a part of French West Africa, Soudan took part in the general process of post–World War II decolonization and became a self-governing member state of the French Community in 1958. Full independence within the community was achieved on June 20, 1960, in association with Senegal, with which Soudan had joined in January 1959 to form a union known as the Federation of Mali. However, Senegal seceded from the federation on August 20, 1960, and on September 22 Mali proclaimed itself an independent republic and withdrew from the French Community.

Mali's government, led by President Modibo KEITA of the Soudanese Union/African Democratic Rally (*Union Soudanaise/Rassemblement Démocratique Africain*—US/RDA), gradually developed into a leftist, one-party dictatorship with a strongly collectivist policy at home and close ties internationally to the Soviet bloc and the People's Republic of China. In late 1968 the Keita regime was ousted

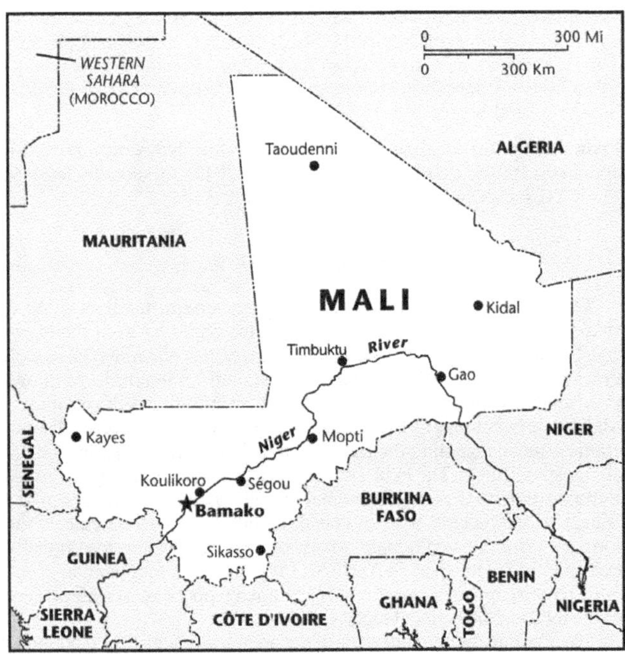

in a bloodless coup d'état led by Lt. Moussa TRAORÉ and Capt. Yoro DIAKITÉ under the auspices of a Military Committee of National Liberation (*Comité Militaire de Libération Nationale*—CMLN).

The new military regime of 1968 began to reverse the economic policies of the Keita government and pledged that civil and political rights would soon be restored. However, further centralization of the military command took place in 1972 following the trial and imprisonment of Captain Diakité and two associates for allegedly plotting another coup. Overthrow attempts were also reported in 1976 and 1978, the latter involving a reputed pro-Soviet faction of the CMLN that opposed a projected return to civilian rule under a constitution approved in 1974.

In March 1979 the Malian People's Democratic Union (*Union Démocratique du Peuple Malien*—UDPM) was formally constituted as the country's sole political party. Civilian government was formally restored on June 19, when General Traoré was elected, unopposed, to a five-year term as president and prime minister. In 1982 the presidential term was increased to six years.

On June 6, 1985, the president carried out a cabinet reshuffle that included the designation of Dr. Mamadou DEMBELE as prime minister. Three days later President Traoré was reelected coincident with pro forma legislative balloting. The prime ministership was abolished on June 6, 1988, in the course of a cabinet shakeup that preceded assembly renewal on June 26.

Widespread opposition to harsh conditions under the Traoré regime erupted into rioting in Bamako and other towns in January–March 1991 amid mounting demands for the introduction of a multiparty system. On March 26 Traoré was ousted by an army group under the leadership of Lt. Col. Amadou Toumani TOURÉ, who formed a 17-member Council of National Reconciliation (*Conseil de la Réconciliation Nationale*—CRN). On March 30 the CRN joined with anti-Traoré political leaders in establishing a Transitional Committee for the Salvation of the People (*Comité de Transition pour le Salut du Peuple*—CTSP), comprised of 10 military and 15 civilian members. On April 2 the CTSP announced the appointment of Soumana SACKO, a highly respected senior official of the UN Development Program, as prime minister. The cabinet that was announced two days later consisted largely of unknown technocrats, although military officers were awarded a number of key portfolios.

On April 5, 1991, the CTSP authorized the formation of political parties and declared its intention to rule for a nine-month period ending with a constitutional referendum and multiparty elections. However, Traoré supporters were subsequently purged from the government and military, and, following a foiled attempt to liberate the imprisoned former president in June, a coup attempt by the then territorial administration minister, Maj. Lamine DIABIRA, failed in mid-July.

At a National Conference on July 29–August 14, 1991, charged by the CTSP with the founding of a "third republic" based on "legality and freedom," 1,000 delegates from 42 parties and 100 associations drafted a new constitution. On January 12, 1992, the new proposed constitution was approved by 98.35 percent of referendum participants. One week later the Alliance for Democracy in Mali (*Alliance pour la Démocratie au Mali*—Adema) won a majority of seats in municipal balloting. Both polls, as well as legislative balloting in February–March, were marred by low voter turnout, coupled with allegations of electoral fraud and inappropriate CTSP support for Adema. In addition, a number of parties protested a reported CTSP decision to assign Tuareg groups in the north uncontested legislative seats as an outgrowth of a National Peace Pact concluded with the long-active rebels on March 25.

Adema leader Alpha Oumar KONARÉ led eight competitors in first-round presidential balloting on April 12, 1992, and went on to defeat Tréoulé Mamadou KONATÉ by a 40 percent margin in the runoff two weeks later. On June 8 Younoussi TOURÉ, a former Central Bank president, was named to succeed Sacko as prime minister.

On May 18, 1993, the Supreme Court upheld death sentences that had been passed on former President Traoré and three associates for causing the "premeditated murder" of 106 persons during prodemocracy riots in the capital in March 1991. Meanwhile, an escalation of student demonstrations, which had commenced seven months earlier, yielded arson attacks on a number of public installations including the National Assembly building. On April 9, in response to the unrest, President Konaré announced the resignation of the Touré government and appointed Defense Minister Abdoulaye Sekou SOW to head a new administration.

Citing austerity concerns, Prime Minister Sow downsized his fledgling cabinet on November 7; however, Adema membership in the reshuffled, technocratic government grew as its members replaced three nonparty ministers. In December the government confirmed reports that an imprisoned former Traoré aide, Lt. Col. Oumar DIALLO, and five others had been charged with plotting to "topple democratic institutions" and "dispose" of anyone opposed to Diallo's release.

On February 2, 1994, Sow became the second consecutive prime minister to resign amid student protests over government spending decisions. Collaterally, Sow, like his predecessor, argued that Adema members had undermined his premiership. Two days later President Konaré named an Adema member, Ibrahim Boubacar KEÏTA, as the new prime minister. On February 6 the cabinet was thrown into disarray when ministers from the National Congress for Democratic Initiative (*Congrès National d'Initiative Démocratique*—CNID) and the Rally for Democracy and Progress (*Rassemblement pour la Démocratie et le Progrès*—RDP) resigned, with CNID leader Mountaga TALL accusing the administration of having "marginalized" non-Adema ministers. Subsequently, the government named by Keïta on February 7 included only 16 members—11 from Adema and 5 from minor parties.

The military conflict between the government and Tuaregs appeared to end in June 1995 when the last active rebel group, the Arab Islamic Front of the Azawad, halted its guerrilla campaign and indicated its interest in peace negotiations. In November the government announced that approximately 20,000 Tuareg refugees had returned from exile in Mauritania, and by February 1996 more than 3,000 former rebels had reportedly been integrated into the armed forces.

The first of two rounds of new assembly balloting was held on April 13, 1997; however, the polling was marred by reported gross irregularities, including a shortage of balloting papers. Consequently, on April 25 the Constitutional Court annulled the first-round results and postponed the second round indefinitely. At the same time, the court ordered that preparations for presidential polling continue, despite opposition threats to boycott such balloting if it preceded the assembly elections.

In presidential balloting on May 11, 1997, President Konaré garnered 95.9 percent of the vote, overwhelming his sole opponent, Mamadou Maribatourou DIABY of the small Unity, Development, and Progress Party (*Parti pour l'Unité, le Développement, et le Progrès*—PUDP). Eight other opposition candidates boycotted the polling, which was marked by a low voter turnout and antigovernment demonstrations. Subsequently, in two rounds of legislative balloting on July 20 and August 3, Adema candidates also easily dominated an electoral field depleted by an opposition boycott. On September 13 Konaré reappointed Prime Minister Keïta, who rejected opposition calls for a "unity" government and named a cabinet on September 16 that was dominated by propresidential parties and moderate opposition groups.

President Konaré made a number of conciliatory gestures to his opponents in the second half of 1997, including releasing opposition members arrested during the violent unrest that surrounded the May–August polling and reducing the death sentences of former president Traoré and his associates to life imprisonment. The president's pledge to convene an all-inclusive national forum gained momentum in mid-April 1998, when a broad range of opposition groups responded positively to a conciliatory proposal brokered by former U.S. president Jimmy Carter. However, on April 20 hard-line opposition groups in the Collective of Opposition Political Parties (*Coordination des Partis Politiques de l'Opposition*—COPPO) refused to attend a government-sponsored summit, asserting that the government representatives lacked legitimacy and vowing to boycott the upcoming local elections and launch a civil disobedience campaign.

In municipal balloting on June 21, 1998, Adema candidates captured an overwhelming number of mayoral and local council posts. In August the government announced that further local polling, then tentatively scheduled for November, would be postponed in the hopes of avoiding an opposition boycott, previous boycotts having undermined the credibility of Mali's democratization and decentralization efforts. In January 1999 the government convened an internationally monitored national forum to garner input from Malian political leaders on the electoral process. However, only four of the parties aligned with the so-called radical opposition attended, and COPPO again urged its supporters not to vote in the May 2 and June 5 balloting, in which Adema secured about 60 percent of the seats on local councils.

Prime Minister Keïta resigned on February 14, 2000, and was succeeded the following day by Mande SIDIBÉ, one of President Konaré's economic advisors. The cabinet announced on February 21 included 15 new ministers. Keïta's resignation was seen in some quarters as designed to permit him to concentrate on an anticipated campaign to succeed Konaré in 2002. (The president had earlier announced he would not attempt to circumvent the two-term limit imposed by the constitution, despite encouragement from his supporters to seek reelection.) At mid-year COPPO leaders announced plans to present a coalition opposition candidate in the campaign. Subsequently, former president Amadou Touré resigned from his army post in September 2001 as required by law to be able to run for the presidency.

Forty parties signed a "pact of good conduct" in January 2001 in preparation for the 2002 balloting. However, late in the year President Konaré suspended plans for a referendum on new electoral laws that had been approved by the assembly in mid-2000 based on recommendations from the 1999 national forum. In February 2002 the assembly adopted new electoral legislation that did not require a referendum, paving the way for first-round presidential balloting in late April and legislative elections in July. Most parties agreed to participate in the polls.

Prime Minister Sidibé resigned on March 18, 2002, to contest the upcoming presidential election. He was succeeded by former president Modibo Keïta. In the first round of balloting on April 28, Amadou Touré, backed by a number of parties, finished first among more than 20 candidates. He was elected president on May 12 by securing about 64 percent of the vote in a runoff against Soumaïla CISSÉ of Adema. Touré appointed Mohamed Ag AMANI (nonparty) as the new prime minister on June 9; on June 15 a new "national unity" cabinet, including members of a number of parties as well as independents, was named. One of President Touré's first acts was to pardon former President Traoré in an attempt to promote national unity and reconciliation. In controversial assembly balloting on July 14 and 28, Hope 2002 (*Espoir 2002*)—an alliance of parties upset over the conduct of the first round of the earlier presidential poll—won 66 seats, followed by the Alliance for the Republic and Democracy (a coalition that included Adema and others), with 51 seats, and Alternation and Change (a coalition of parties that had supported Touré in the presidential balloting), with 10.

In assembly by-elections on October 20, 2002, Adema won all 8 seats being contested and became the largest single party in the assembly with 53 seats. However, Hope 2002 combined with 19 presidential-supportive deputies to create a stable presidential majority within the legislature.

Local elections on May 30, 2003, were relatively free of the problems that had surrounded the 2002 presidential and assembly elections. In part due to a government campaign to encourage voting, turnout was high, and more than 20 parties won seats, with Hope 2002 securing a majority of the mayoral posts.

Prime Minister Amani resigned on April 28, 2004. He was replaced by former transport minister Ousmane Issoufi MAÏGA (nonparty), who formed a new cabinet on May 2.

Tuareg rebels renewed their fight against the government by launching attacks on several cities and military bases in the north in early May 2006, prompting renewed Algerian-mediated negotiations that led to a July accord under which the Tuaregs agreed to cease their militancy and to drop their demand for autonomy. In return the government promised to invest in major development programs in the north. A second pact in February 2007 endorsed Tuareg disarmament and integration of former rebels into the Malian military. However some Tuaregs remained disaffected, and the situation was complicated by the influx into the region of militants from the Algerian-based al-Qaida in the Islamic Maghred (AQIM, see the article on Algeria for additional information).

As the candidate of the new Alliance for Democracy and Progress (*Alliance pour la Démocratie et le Progrès*—ADP), President Touré was reelected to a second term in the first round of balloting on April 29, 2007, with 68 percent of the vote. Former prime minister Ibrahim Keïta of the recently formed Front for Democracy and the Republic (*Front pour la Démocratie et la République*—FDR) finished second with 19 percent. Opposition parties condemned the balloting as fraudulent, but international observers generally described the poll as free and fair. Touré subsequently reappointed Prime Minister Maïga and most of the incumbent cabinet ministers. The ADP also dominated the two-round assembly balloting in July, capturing 113 seats. Maïga resigned from the prime minister's post on September 27 and was replaced the next day by Modibo SIDIBÉ, a nonparty technocrat.

President Touré reshuffled the cabinet on April 9, 2009, reappointing Sidibé and moving several of the prime minister's political allies into key cabinet positions.

In the second half of 2009 the Tuaregs and other ethnic groups in the north who had been involved in sporadic fighting among themselves agreed to establish a permanent intercommunity political structure to resolve their differences peacefully. Under government pressure, the groups also reportedly endorsed a campaign against the AQIM, whose highly publicized kidnappings of Westerners had compromised the region's important tourism sector.

In September 2010 President Touré announced that he did not intend to pursue another term in 2012, which would have required constitutional revision of the current two-term presidential limit. Analysts subsequently described Prime Minister Sidibé as the front-runner for the post, and he resigned on March 30, 2011, in order to campaign for the presidency. Independent political figure Cissé Mariam Kaïdama SIDIBÉ (no relation) was named as the country's first female head of government on April 3.

In late 2011 Tuareg restiveness in the north intensified into an uprising, led by the National Movement for the Liberation of the Azawad (*Mouvement National pour la Libération de l'Azawad*—MNLA), a recently formed rebel group that reportedly included Tuareg fighters returning from Libya, where they had fought alongside Muammar Qadhafi's security forces. In early February 2012 demonstrations were held in Bamako to protest the government's perceived ineffectiveness to quell the revolt and attendant violence. (It was estimated that some 130,000 people had been displaced by that time.)

Components of the Malian military perpetrated an essentially bloodless coup on March 21–22, 2012, under the leadership of Capt. Amadou Hayo SANOGO, who announced the formation of a National Committee for the Recovery of Democracy and the Restoration of the State (*Comité National pour le Redressement pour la Démocratie et la Restauration de l'État*—(CNRDRE) to govern the country (under his leadership) indefinitely pending new elections. The junta took a number of government officials into temporary custody and announced that it would restore civilian rule only after order had been restored in the north. However, ECOWAS immediately closed the borders to Mali and froze Malian assets in ECOWAS member states in an effort to force Captain Sanogo and the CNRDRE to endorse a specific (and short) transitional timetable. The United States and other countries concurrently suspended foreign aid payments. Consequently, the CNRDRE in early April agreed to a specific framework for the beginning of the return to civilian government. Under an agreement negotiated with ECOWAS, Dioncounda TRAORÉ, who as speaker of the assembly was constitutionally authorized to become president if the sitting president became unable to perform the duties of the office, was inaugurated as interim president (as endorsed by the Constitutional Court) on April 8 after President Touré submitted his resignation. (Touré, who had gone into hiding after the putsch, agreed to resign for the sake of his "love for Mali," and all the officials who had been detained in March were released.) It was also reported that Captain Sanogo had announced his resignation as self-appointed head of state, the accord with ECOWAS providing amnesty for all members of the junta. Meanwhile, reports surfaced that the coup had resonated positively with those segments of the population upset by high prices and perceived systemic corruption in the government, although several conflicts were reported between Touré loyalists in the military and the putschists.

On April 17, 2012, President Traoré appointed Cheick Modibo DIARRA, the grandson of former president Moussa Traoré, as interim prime minister. The cabinet named by Diarra on April 24 included three members of the junta, which retained significant de facto authority. Again reportedly reacting to ECOWAS pressure, Sanogo at the end of May agreed to the extension of Interim President Traoré's term for a year (the initial appointment had been for only 40 days). In August interim prime minister Diarra appointed what he described as a national unity government, although military influence remained apparent. Meanwhile Islamist militants had joined and, to some extent, co-opted the rebellion in the north, gaining ascendancy in a number of important towns and attracting intense attention from regional and Western governments concerned over the spread of jihadism.

On December 11, 2012, the military leaders forced Prime Minister Diarra to resign, along with his cabinet. Among other things, Diarra reportedly had urged international intervention in the north, while the military argued that Malian forces could handle the insurgency on their own. Interim president Traoré appointed Django SISSOKO, the former head of the prime minister's office as prime minister the next day, and a reshuffled cabinet was named on December 15.

Following a French-led military ouster of the Islamist militants in the north in early 2013 (see Foreign relations, below) and the subsequent restoration (for the most part) of Malian government control there, the first round of presidential elections was held on July 28, 2013. Former prime minister Ibrahim Keïta, the candidate of his Rally for Mali (*Rassemblement pour le Mali*—RPM), led 27 candidates with 39.8 percent of the vote, and he defeated Soumaïla Cissé of the URD in the August 11 runoff with a vote share of 77.6 percent. Following his inauguration in September, Keïta named Oumar Tatam LY, an economist and former regional bank officer, as the new prime minister.

In the November–December 2013 balloting for the National Assembly, the RPM was credited with winning a plurality of 66 of 147 seats, and RPM allies (including Adema) secured enough additional seats to provide Keïta with a comfortable legislative majority. Prime Minister Ly resigned on April 5, 2014, and was succeeded by Moussa MARA, theretofore the minister for urban affairs.

Mara resigned on January 8, 2015, and was replaced the next day by Modibo KEITA (Adema), who named a reshuffled cabinet. Further cabinet reshuffles took place in September 2015 and January 2016, before a major reorganization of the cabinet was implemented on July 7, 2016.

Constitution and government. The constitution adopted at independence in 1960 was abrogated by the military in November 1968. A new constitution was approved by referendum on June 2, 1974, but did not enter into force until June 19, 1979. The constitution drafted by the National Conference of July 29–August 14, 1991, and approved by referendum on January 12, 1992, replaced the interim *Acte Fondamental* that the CTSP had promulgated in April 1991 following abrogation of the 1974 document. The new basic law includes an extensive bill of individual rights, a charter for political parties, guarantees of trade union and press freedoms, and separation of executive, legislative, and judicial powers. A directly elected president, who may serve no more than two five-year terms, appoints a prime minister and other cabinet members, who are, however, responsible to a popularly elected unicameral National Assembly. The judicial system is headed by a Supreme Court, which is divided into judicial, administrative, and fiscal sections. There is also a nine-member Constitutional Court, while a High Court of Justice is empowered to hear cases of treason.

Mali is administratively divided into eight regions, the eighth being created in May 1991 by the halving of a northern region as a concession to Tuareg separatists. The regions, headed by appointed governors, are subdivided into 46 districts (*cercles*) and 282 counties (*arrondissements*), also administered by appointed officials. Most municipalities have elected councils, which have been given increased authority in connection with recent decentralization program efforts.

The military junta that assumed control in March 2012 immediately announced it was suspending the constitution and "dissolving" all national institutions, but the de facto constitutional effect of the coup ultimately appeared negligible in view of the plan (which included the restoration of the constitution) that was quickly adopted for new presidential and legislative elections in 2013. (Constitutional amendments had been slated for a national referendum in conjunction with the presidential elections that had been scheduled, prior to the coup, for April 2012. The revisions, which had been heavily promoted by President Touré [ousted by the coup], had among other things, called for the formation of an upper house [Senate] in the national legislature and installation of an independent electoral commission. Other provisions appeared designed to strengthen presidential authority. The proposals were subsequently shelved.)

Mali has long been considered an African exemplar of respect for freedom of the press. However, conditions deteriorated temporarily following the March 2012 coup as a number of journalists were attacked in both the south and north. In 2016 the media watchdog group Reporters Without Borders ranked Mali 122nd out of 180 countries in freedom of the press.

Foreign relations. Reflecting a commitment to "dynamic nonalignment," Mali improved its relations with France, Britain, the United States, and other Western nations under General Traoré. It also cultivated links to China and the former Soviet Union.

For two decades Mali was locked in a dispute with Burkina Faso (formerly Upper Volta) over ownership of the 100-mile long, 12-mile wide Agacher strip between the two countries. The controversy triggered a number of military encounters, including a four-day battle in December 1985.

Some 2,500 Malian workers were expelled from Libya in 1985 as part of the Qadhafi regime's drive to reduce its dependence on foreign labor. Subsequently, Mali charged Libya with supporting Tuareg insurgents in northern Mali. (Relations between the two countries had previously cooled due to Libya's involvement in the Chadian civil war.)

The dispute with Burkina Faso was finally settled by a ruling in late 1986 from the International Court of Justice that divided the disputed territory into roughly equal parts, with the border being defined in accordance with traditional patterns of nomadic passage. Border tensions with Mauritania were similarly resolved by a border demarcation agreement in May 1988.

In January 1991 the Algerian government mediated a truce between the Malian government and moderate Tuareg party leaders. International diplomatic efforts were subsequently credited with generating agreements among Algeria, Mali, and Niger in 1992, which resulted in the repatriation of thousands of Tuaregs from Algeria to Mali in August 1993. Negotiations between Mali and Algeria in February 1995 yielded an accord on border security issues.

The growing presence of foreign Islamic extremists, mainly from Pakistan and Afghanistan, prompted the Malian government in 2004 to seek international counterterrorism aid. Consequently, U.S. military advisers initiated an antiterrorism training program for the Malian armed forces. The Malian government also gave permission for U.S. special operations units to undertake antiterrorism missions in the north of the country, where Algerian militants had reportedly established a presence. The United States subsequently announced it would use its Malian base as a headquarters for regional antiterrorism efforts.

Mali signed a broad economic accord with China in 2006. In return for increased exports of cotton from Mali to China, China agreed to expand investment in Mali's agriculture, tourism, and telecommunications sectors.

In September 2009 military leaders from Algeria, Mali, Mauritania, and Niger announced plans for joint initiatives against terrorism and cross-border crime in the region. The antiterrorism plan was primarily aimed at the activities of the AQIM, which had recently expanded its activities to sparsely populated northern Mali. In an apparently related development, the United States in October announced it would give Mali $4.5 in military equipment and provide additional counterterrorism training for Malian security forces. In the first half of 2010 regional neighbors criticized the Malian government for being too lax in regard to the battle with the AQIM, especially when several AQIM hostages were released in Mali after ransoms were apparently paid by European countries for their nationals. Subsequently, President Touré reportedly strengthened his resolve to confront the AQIM, and in September Mali permitted Mauritanian troops to enter Malian territory in pursuit of the Islamic militants. Mali also pledged troops for the regional command headquarters being established in Algeria to combat terrorism. By 2011 it was estimated that there were 200–300 AQIM fighters in Mali.

The international community strongly condemned the March 2012 coup in Mali, having previously promoted the country as one of Africa's strongest and most stable democracies. Regional neighbors aligned in ECOWAS adopted a particularly hard line and pressured the Malian junta into quickly accepting a plan for the full return of civilian government within a year. Subsequently, the world's focus turned to the chaotic conditions in northern Mali where the rapidly rising influence of Islamic militants posed a threat to neighboring countries as well as the broader international community. By midyear Islamic jihadists had surpassed the MNLA in significance in the north, where the harsh imposition of sharia (Islamic religious law) by the Islamists had reportedly appalled some of the Tuareg population. In September the Traoré/Diarra administration called upon the UN Security Council to approve the proposed deployment of an ECOWAS force to combat the northern rebels. However Captain Sanogo opposed international intervention, insisting that the Malian army was up to the task.

Fighters from *Ansar Dine*, one of the recently emergent Islamist groups in the north, unexpectedly began to move toward the south in early January 2013. In response, France, which for many months had advocated military intervention, immediately launched air strikes against rebel positions in the north, following up with a ground assault that had largely routed the militants by mid-February. (Malian and Chadian forces also participated in the offensive, while a number of Western nations contributed indirect support.) At midyear a new UN peacekeeping force began to assume a wide range of responsibilities, while international donors pledged $4.1 billion in reconstruction aid. However, jihadist activity continued in the north (albeit at a reduced level) into mid-2014, prompting several major attacks by French forces on "terrorist" locales. Meanwhile, the United States announced it was forming a special force to counter terrorism in Mali and other countries in the Sahel and North Africa, while France announced that its troops in Mali (1,700) would be merged into a single antiterrorism operation for the entire region.

In December 2014 the IMF and the EU resumed aid to Mali after having suspended assistance following audits of the government's accounts. On December 9 French hostage Serge LAZAREVIC was set free by AQIM in return for the release of four senior AQIM leaders, including Mohamed Aly AG WADOUSSENE.

In April 2015 France announced it would cancel approximately $71 million of Mali's debt. In June the UN Security Council reauthorized MINUSMA through June 2016 and approved the deployment of 40 military personnel to monitor a peace agreement between the government and Taureg rebels (see Current issues, below).

AQIM launched an attack on a MINUSMA convoy near Timbuktu on July 2, 2015, killing six international troops and wounding five others. On July 5 France reported that its forces had killed Ag Wadoussene, who had again emerged as a leader in AQIM after his December 2014 release. In October 2015 France announced it would provide Mali with $408 million in aid in 2016–2017.

In June 2016 the UN Security Council approved the extension and expansion of MINUSMA, increasing its troop strength to 13,289 and its police monitors to 1,920.

Current issues. The July–August 2013 presidential elections were seen as the first step in the "restoration of democracy" and observers characterized the poll as a success in regard to normal electoral standards. The international community broadly welcomed the decisive victory by former prime minister Ibrahim Keïta as well as the subsequent appointment of new prime minister Oumar Ly, a nonpartisan banker who pledged to pursue economic reform and combat corruption. The November–December assembly elections were also described as acceptable by international observers despite turnouts of only 38 percent in each round. Meanwhile, in a sharp reversal of the government's previous conciliatory approach, Amadou Sanogo, the leader of the 2012 coup, was arrested in late 2013 on charges related to alleged kidnappings and murders in the wake of the coup. A number of other members of the former CNRDRE were similarly charged in early 2014.

Prime Minister Ly cited "too much interference" in his reform efforts in announcing his surprise resignation in April 2014. Skeptics about the chances for genuine reform noted that the new prime minister was closely allied with President Keïta and that the legislative opposition remained weak. Attention subsequently focused on continued unsettled conditions in the north, where deadly jihadist activity once again intensified and conflict with the MNLA in May produced a "humiliating defeat" for government forces (see MNLA, below, for details). The administration negotiated a tentative accord with the MNLA and five other Tuareg groups in July.

In February 2015 UN-mediated negotiations in Algiers led to a cease-fire agreement between the government and the six major Tuareg groups. A comprehensive peace agreement, which included devolved powers for the Tuaregs, was finalized in March and signed by rebel groups on May 15 and June 20. Nonetheless, sporadic fighting continued as some rebel elements demanded full autonomy for the region. A new rebel grouping, the Massina Liberation Front (MLF), comprising ethnic Fulanis (Peuls), launched a series of attacks in southern Mali in June. Terrorists seized control of the Byblos Hotel in Sévaré in northeast Mali on August 7. Security forces, backed by French special operations forces, stormed the facility the next day. Seventeen people, including four terrorists and four soldiers, were killed in the incident. By year's end, the UN estimated that continuing strife had displaced more than 100,000 Malians.

On November 20, 2016, two terrorists attacked the luxury Radisson Blu hotel in Bamako, killing 19 civilians and a security guard. The attackers were killed by Malian security forces, supported by French and U.S. special operations forces. An al-Qaida–affiliated terrorist group, The Sentinels (*al-Mourabitoun*), claimed responsibility.

Three French soldiers were killed by a roadside bomb on April 12, 2016. French troops subsequently arrested more than a dozen suspects in Kidal, prompting protests that turned violent. Two demonstrators were killed by UN peacekeeping forces as they endeavored to restore order. Taureg militias then kidnapped three local Red Cross workers, who were later released after the French military let go the majority of those detained. Also in April, Parliament approved the creation of interim governments at the local and regional levels in the area covered by the March 2015 peace agreement.

POLITICAL PARTIES AND GROUPS

The only authorized party from 1982 until the March 1991 coup was the **Malian People's Democratic Union** (*Union Démocratique du Peuple Malien*—UDPM). It was dissolved in the wake of President Traoré's ouster. Public demonstrations that preceded the 1991 coup were orchestrated by a number of groups (including Adema), which were linked in a Coordination Committee of Democratic Associations and Organizations (CCADO), which joined the CRN in forming the CTSP on March 30, after which both the CCADO and the CRN were dissolved. On April 5 the CTSP authorized the formation of political parties, and by late 1991 approximately 50 formations, many with links to pre-1968 political personalities or groups, had applied for legal status, though only 27 parties presented legislative candidates in 1992.

For the 2007 presidential and legislative elections, more than 40 parties came together to form the ADP (below) to support Touré's reelection. (For comprehensive information on a number of opposition coalitions from 1992 to 2002, see the 2012 *Handbook*.)

The following party structure reflects the results of the 2007 legislative elections, successful candidates in that balloting having had their terms of offices extended in June 2012 until new elections were held in the wake of the March 2012 coup. Many electoral pacts were formed for the 2013 assembly elections, with the composition of the alliances often differing significantly from constituency to constituency.

Legislative Parties:

Rally for Mali (*Rassemblement pour le Mali*—RPM). Launched initially in February 2001 as "Alternative 2000," the RPM was a breakaway faction from Adema supportive of former Prime Minister Ibrahim Keïta, who left Adema in October 2000 and placed third in the first round of the 2002 presidential balloting with 21 percent of the vote. The RPM gained 46 seats in the 2002 assembly poll as part of the Hope 2002 alliance (see Political Background, above), and in September Keïta was elected president of the assembly.

Keïta was one of the main leaders (along with Adema member Soumaylou Boubèye Maïga) behind the formation by some 16 parties in advance of the 2007 elections of the **Front for Democracy and the Republic** (*Front pour la Démocratie et la République*—FDR), which opposed the reelection of President Touré. (In addition to the RPM, other members of the FDR included Parena and the CDS.) Meanwhile, Keïta resigned his post of president of the assembly to run again for the presidency of the republic. Four of the FDR members (including the small, newly formed Convergence 2007, led by Maïga) presented their own candidates in the first round of the presidential poll in an unsuccessful effort to force a runoff election. (Keïta was the leading candidate from among the FDR components, placing second overall to Touré with 19 percent of the vote.) The FDR secured 15 seats in the subsequent assembly elections, 11 by the RPM and 4 by Parena.

Several key members of the RPM broke away from the party in January 2008 to form the base of a new Malian political formation, the FDM/MNJ (see below).

In July 2011 the RPM chose Keïta as its candidate for the 2012 presidential balloting, which was precluded by the March 2012 coup. The FDR formally opposed the coup, but Keïta was not subsequently subjected to mistreatment (as other leading anti-coup political figures were). Keïta, supported by some 15 other small political parties, finished first in the first round of the 2013 presidential poll with 39.8 percent of the vote, and won the runoff with 77.6 percent.

Leaders: Ibrahim Boubacar KEÏTA (President of the Republic), Issaka SIDIBÉ (President of the National Assembly), Bocary TRETA (Secretary General).

Alliance for Democracy in Mali/Pan African Party for Liberty, Solidarity, and Justice (*Alliance pour la Démocratie au Mali/Parti Pan-Africain pour la Solidarité et la Justice*—Adema/PASJ). A principal organizer of anti-Traoré demonstrations and subsequently among those groups represented in the CTSP, Adema registered for legal status in April 1991. Its candidates won substantial majorities in the 1992 local and National Assembly elections, and the party also captured the presidency on April 26 with a 70 percent second-round vote share for Alpha Oumar Konaré.

At Adema's July 1993 congress, dissident members released a manifesto calling for the "appointment to positions of responsibility [within the party]...of competent men and women of integrity" and the "destruction of the old state apparatus." Subsequently former prime ministers Younoussi Touré and Abdoulaye Sow cited subversive activities by "radical" elements within Adema as among their reasons for resigning from the party. Observers attributed the intraparty friction to a conflict between members identifying with the former prime ministers and favoring integration of non-Adema political groups into the government and a smaller faction advocating Adema's unilateral rule.

At a party congress on September 25–27, 1994, founding member Mohamed Lamine TRAORÉ lost the party chair in an action spearheaded by Prime Minister Ibrahim Boubacar Keïta, who had hinted at dramatic party changes at his investiture. Subsequently, Traoré, Secretary General Mohamedoun DICKO, and a number of other senior members resigned from the party; two months later the dissidents launched MIRIA (below).

Keïta was reelected as party chair in October 1999. He resigned from all his party duties, however, in October 2000 in reaction to the advances registered by the "reformist" wing. Keïta then launched his own formation, the RPM (above). In March 2002, in a bitterly contested party election, Adema chose Soumaïla Cissé over former Prime Minister Mandé Sidibé to be the party's presidential candidate. Subsequently, Adema's parliamentary majority was reduced from 128 seats to 53 in legislative balloting, although the party remained the largest single group in the assembly. The electoral decline led to infighting within the party, and Cissé led a group of dissident members in the formation of a new rival party, the URD (below).

In 2006 former defense minister Soumaylou Boubèye Maïga announced he intended to seek Adema's nomination for the 2007 presidential election. However, Adema subsequently was instrumental in the formation of the **Alliance for Democracy and Progress** (*Alliance pour la Démocratie et le Progrès*—ADP), a coalition of more than 40 parties supportive of President Touré's reelection. Maïga, ignoring the party's preference, ran in the presidential election as the leader of a small grouping, Convergence 2007, and was endorsed by the "rival" FDR (see RPM, above.) In addition to Adema, other members of the ADP included the URD, UDD, CNID, US/RDA, and MPR. Other minor parties in the ADP included the BDIA (see UM RDA, below); the **Alternation Bloc for Renewal, Integration, and African Cooperation** (*Bloc des Alternances pour la Renaissance, l'Intégration, et la Coopération Afrique*—BARICA); the **Movement for African Independence, Renewal, and Integration** (*Mouvement pour l'Indépendence, la Renaissance, et l'Intégration Africaine*—MIRIA), established by dissident members of Adema, including Mohamed Lamine Traoré; the **National Rally for Democracy** (*Rassemblement National pour la Démocratie*—RND), established in 1997 and led by Abdoulaye Garba TAPO; the **Solidarity and Progress Party** (*Parti de la Solidarité et du Progrès*—PSP); and the liberal **Citizens' Party for Renewal** (*Parti Citoyen pour le Renouveau*—PCR), formed in July 2005.

The ADP was credited with winning 113 seats in the 2007 assembly poll (Adema, 51 seats; URD, 34; MPR, 8; CNID, 7; UDD, 3; BARICA, 2; PSP, 2; MIRIA, 2; BDIA, 1; RND, 1; PCR, 1; and US/RDA, 1). Adema leader Dioncounda Traoré was subsequently elected president of the assembly.

The Adema/PASJ candidates were the top winners in the April 2009 municipal elections, securing a majority in all regions and four out of six communes in Bamako. Party president Traoré was named the Adema/PASJ candidate for the presidential elections that were scheduled for April 2012 but were not held due to the coup in March. (Following his overthrow, President Touré was granted asylum in Senegal.) Adema leader Traoré, a former cabinet minister described as a "consensus builder," was subsequently appointed interim president of the republic because of his position prior to the coup of speaker of the assembly. As a condition for ECOWAS's endorsement of Traoré's appointment, he was declared ineligible to run for president in 2013. Consequently Adema/PASJ nominated Dramane Dembélé, an engineering professor described as one of Traoré's protégées. Dembélé finished third in the first round of balloting with 9.7 percent of the vote.

Adema member Modibo KEITA was appointed prime minister on January 9, 2015.

Leaders: Modibo KEITA (Prime Minister), Dioncounda TRAORÉ (Former Interim President of the Republic and President of the Party), Alpha Oumar KONARÉ (Former President of the Republic), Dramane DEMBÉLÉ (2013 presidential candidate), Abdel Karim KONATÉ (Secretary General of the National Bureau).

Convergence for the Development of Mali (*Convergence pour le Développement du Mali*—CODEM). CODEM was formed in May 2008 by five national legislators, including Housseini Guindo, who finished fifth in the first round of the 2013 presidential poll with 4.75 percent of the vote. He endorsed Ibrahim Keïta in the second round.

Leader: Housseini GUINDO.

National Congress for Democratic Initiative (*Congrès National d'Initiative Démocratique*—CNID). Launched in 1990 as the **National Committee for Democratic Initiative** (*Comité National d'Initiative Démocratique*), the CNID was included in the April 1991 formation of the CTSP in recognition of the CNID's role in the overthrow of the Traoré regime. In 1992 the party, supported by a predominantly youthful constituency, secured 96 municipal and 9 National Assembly seats. Mountaga Tall, the party's 35-year-old presidential candidate, finished third in the first round of the 1992 presidential balloting with 11.4 percent of the vote.

In March 1995, on the eve of the party's first conference, a group of dissidents reacted to the expulsion of ten governing committee members by holding a rival conference of the "true" CNID (see Parena, below). In 1998 the CNID emerged as one of the most prominent of the radical opposition groups, organizing boycotts of the June elections and allegedly attempting to interfere with polling. However, the group's stance toward the government reportedly softened in 2000–2001, and the CNID participated in presidential and legislative balloting in 2002. Tall finished fifth as the CNID's candidate in the first round of the presidential poll with 3.75 percent of the vote. Meanwhile, the CNID joined Hope 2002 for the legislative poll, reportedly securing 13 of that coalition's seats.

The CNID's representation was reduced to seven seats following the 2007 assembly elections, in which it participated in the ADP. The party subsequently suffered from a rift among its senior leadership over party activities in Bamako.

CNID chair Tall was named as the party's candidate for the 2012 presidential poll, although he supported the March 2012 coup that blocked that election. He received 1.5 percent of the vote in the first round of the 2013 presidential balloting, apparently running formally as an independent. Tall was appointed a minister in the new cabinet appointed in July 2016.

Leaders: Mountaga TALL (Chair), Fanta Mantchini DIARRA (Senior Deputy), N'Diaye BAH (Secretary General).

Patriotic Movement for Renewal (*Mouvement Patriotique pour le Renouveau*—MPR). The MPR, which described itself as a descendant of the UDPM, was legalized in January 1995. Because of its ties to former President Traoré, the MPR was reportedly widely denigrated until 1997, when it assumed a prominent role in the opposition camp.

The MPR was described by *Africa Confidential* in 1999 as being "openly aligned" with the imprisoned Traoré but committed to the pursuit of "national reconciliation." Indeed, in 2000 the group decided to participate in presidential and legislative elections in 2002, nominating Choguel Maïga for president. Maïga received 2.71 percent of the vote in the first round, and the MPR joined Hope 2002 for the subsequent legislative balloting. The MPR secured eight of the ADP's seats in the 2007 balloting, and the MPR supported the reelection of President

Touré that year. Maïga finished seventh in the first round of the 2013 presidential election with 2.4 percent of the vote.

Leader: Choguel Kokalla MAÏGA (President and 2002 and 2013 presidential candidate).

Union for Democracy and Development (*Union pour la Démocratie et le Développement*—UDD). Running on a platform calling for "security, good citizenship, and clean streets," the UDD, whose founder, Moussa Balla COULIBALY, was an official in the Traoré government, won 62 seats in the 1992 municipal elections.

In 1999 it was reported that the Socialist Party for Progress and Development had merged into the UDD. In late 2001 Coulibaly was nominated as the UDD's presidential candidate for the 2002 presidential contest. He was eliminated in the first round, and the UDD supported Soumaïla Cissé of Adema in the second round.

The UDD won three assembly seats in 2007 as part of the ADP. Despite his age, the 77-year-old Coulibaly had been expected to be the UDD candidate in the ultimately aborted 2012 presidential balloting. Party official Tiéman Hubert COULIBALY was appointed minister of defense in the July 2016 government.

Leaders: Moussa Balla COULIBALY (Chair and 2002 presidential candidate), Tiéman Hubert COULIBALY.

Democratic Alliance for Peace–Maliba (*Alliance Démocratique pour la Paix–Maliba*—ADP-Maliba). Recently formed under the leadership of gold mine owner Aliou Boubacar Diallo, the ADP-Maliba ("Greater Mali") ultimately supported the RPM's Ibrahim Keïta in the 2013 presidential poll.

Leaders: Aliou Boubacar DIALLO, Amadou THIAM (Secretary General).

Democratic and Social Convention (*Convention Démocratique Sociale*—CDS). The self-styled "centrist" CDS was launched by Mamadou Bakary "Blaise" SANGARÉ in 1996. Unlike its moderate opposition party peers, the CDS chose not to join the government named in September 1997.

Sangaré received 2.21 percent of the vote in the first round of presidential balloting in 2002. The CDS joined the FDR in 2007, and Sangaré ran as one of the four presidential candidates from the coalition, finishing fifth in the first round of balloting. He secured 1.1 percent of the vote in the first round of the 2013 presidential election.

Leader: Mamadou Bakary SANGARÉ (Party President and 2007 presidential candidate).

Malian Union of the African Democratic Rally (*Union Malienne du Rassemblement Démocratique Africain*—UM RDA). The UM RDA was formed in 2010 via the merger of the **Sudanese Union/African Democratic Rally** (*Union Soudanaise/Rassemblement Démocratique Africain*—US/RDA) and the **Democratic Bloc for African Integration** (*Bloc Démocratique pour l'Intégration Africaine*—BDIA).

Supported by a rural constituency, the US/RDA (formed in 1946) came to power with the formation of Modibo Keïta's post-independence government in 1960 but went underground following his ouster in 1968. At a special congress in January 1992, the US/RDA split over the selection of a presidential candidate. Members initially selected Tréoulé Mamadou KONATÉ, the son of an RDA founder and an advocate of purging "Stalinism" from the party, but the party leadership ultimately repudiated the action, nominating instead former UN official Baba Hakib HAIDARA. Subsequently, both stood as candidates, with Konaté finishing second in the first round of balloting but securing only 30 percent of the second-round vote in a contest with Alpha Oumar Konaré. In October 1995 Konaté was killed in a car crash.

The US/RDA supported former president Amadou Touré's presidential campaign in 2002. It reportedly won three seats in the 2002 legislative balloting as part of the **Alliance for Alternation and Change** (*Alliance pour l'Alternance et le Changement*—ACC), a grouping of some 28 parties. In the 2007 balloting the US/RDA secured one of the ADP's seats.

A liberal party formed in 1993 under the leadership of Youssouf TRAORÉ, the BDIA won three seats in the 2002 assembly elections and one seat, as a member of the ADP, in the 2007 balloting.

The UM RDA secured one seat in the 2013 assembly elections and subsequently joined the presidential majority. Party Leader Bocar Moussa DIARRA was named a minister of state in 2014 but was not included in the July 2016 government.

Leader: Bocar Moussa DIARRA.

Other parties that won legislative seats in 2013 in cooperation with the RPM and/or Adema included the **Alliance for Solidarity in Mali–Convergence of Patriotic Forces** (*Alliance pour la Solidarité au Mali–Convergence des Forces Patriotiques*—ASMA-CFP), which had been recently formed by former Adema leader Soumeylou Boubèye MAÏGRA and others (Maïgra was named to the September 2013 cabinet); **Change** (*Yelema*), whose president, Moussa MARA, won 1.5 percent of the vote in the 2013 presidential election and was named to the September 2013 cabinet before being appointed prime minister in April 2014; and MIRIA (see Adema/PASJ, above).

Other Legislative Parties:

Union for the Republic and Democracy (*Union pour la République et la Démocratie*—URD). Launched in 2003 by former members of Adema who supported former presidential candidate Soumaïla CISSÉ, the URD is a centrist party that supports secularism and economic reforms. As part of the ADP, the URD won 34 seats in the 2007 legislative election, and URD candidates won the second largest number of seats in the April 2009 municipal elections.

Cissé, a regional bank official, was scheduled to be the URD candidate for president again in 2012. Following the March 2013 coup, Cissé was a prominent member of the **Rejection Front** (*Front du Refus*), a group of parties strongly opposed to the coup. Cissé finished second in the first round of presidential balloting in July 2013 with 19.7 percent of the vote and only improved to 22.4 percent in the August runoff, despite endorsements from several of the candidates eliminated in the first round. The URD became the largest opposition party with 17 seats in the 2013 assembly balloting.

Leaders: Soumaïla CISSÉ (Founder and 2013 presidential candidate), Younoussi TOURÉ (President), Lassana KONÉ (Secretary General).

Alternative Forces for Renewal and Emergence (*Forces Alternatives pour le Renouveau et l'Émergence*—FARE). The FARE was formed to support the 2013 presidential candidacy of Modibo Sidibé, who had resigned as prime minister in 2011 with the expectation that he would be elected to succeed President Touré. Following the March 2012 coup that overthrew Touré, Sidibé was arrested and briefly held in detention, with his home reportedly being looted. Also supported by the Convergence for a New Political Division (comprising numerous associations and political formations), Sidibé finished fourth in the first round of the 2013 presidential balloting with 5 percent of the vote. He endorsed Soumaïla Cissé of the URD in the second round, following through with a preelection pact among anti-coup parties that they would support the top vote getter from among their ranks. However, some other prominent FARE leaders supported Ibrahim Keïta in the second round.

The FARE became the fourth largest party (with six seats) in the assembly at the 2013 legislative balloting, following which it established a parliamentary faction with the SADI. Internal FARE disputes regarding the level of cooperation with the government appeared for the most part to be resolved at a March 2014 congress that elected Sidibé as the new FARE president. Sidibé announced that the FARE would serve as part of a "strong and constructive opposition" but would not be "obstructionist."

Leaders: Modibo SIDIBÉ (President and 2013 presidential candidate), Alou KEÏTA (Former President), Mahamadou KEÏTA (Secretary General).

African Solidarity for Democracy and Independence (*Solidarité Africaine pour la Démocratie et l'Indépendence*—SADI). Established in 2002 prior to the presidential elections, the SADI presented Oumar Mariko as its presidential candidate. He received less than 1 percent of the vote in the first-round balloting. In the subsequent legislative elections, the SADI won six seats. Mariko was also the party's candidate in 2007; he placed fourth in the first round of balloting with 2.7 percent of the vote. SADI legislative candidates won four seats in the July 2007 elections. The SADI rejected an invitation to join the new government appointed in April 2011, and the party opposed the 2011 constitutional reforms.

The SADI was described as providing political backing for the junta responsible for the March 2012 coup, Mariko having reportedly routinely criticized the Touré administration in the past for co-opting potential opponents through government favors. Mariko finished sixth in the first round of the 2013 presidential elections with 2.6 percent of the vote and endorsed the RPM's Ibrahim Keïta in the second round.

Following the 2013 legislative elections (at which the SADI secured five seats), it formed an opposition faction in the assembly with the FARE (above), having rejected an overture from Prime Minister Ly to join the presidential majority.

Leaders: Cheick Oumar SISSOKO (Chair), Oumar MARIKO (Secretary General and 2002, 2007, and 2013 presidential candidate).

Party for National Renaissance (*Parti pour la Renaissance Nationale*—Parena). Parena was officially launched in September 1995 after its founders, CNID dissidents Capt. Yoro Diakité and Tiéblé Dramé, lost their five-month legal battle for control of the CNID. A number of Parena leaders were former or current Konaré government ministers, a status reflected in the signing of the Parena-Adema cooperation pact in February 1996.

In 2001 Parena distanced itself from Adema, and Dramé became Parena's presidential candidate in 2002, finishing fourth in the first round of balloting with 4 percent of the vote. Parena reportedly won one of the ACC seats in the 2002 legislative poll. Dramé again was the party's candidate in the 2007 presidential poll, in which he placed third with 3 percent of the vote in the first round. Parena was credited with 4 of the 15 assembly seats won by the FDR in 2007. In April 2011 Parena agreed to support the governing coalition.

Dramé, who had helped negotiate the June 2013 tentative peace agreement between the government and northern Tuaregs, initially was presented as Parena's candidate for the July presidential poll. However he withdrew his candidacy in mid-July on the grounds that the balloting was being inappropriately rushed. Parena won three seats in the 2013 assembly elections, subsequently sitting in opposition to the RPM-led government.

Leaders: Tiéblé DRAMÉ (Party President and 2002 and 2007 presidential candidate), Amidou DIABATE (Secretary General).

Party for Economic Development and Solidarity (*Parti pour le Développement Économique et la Solidarité*—PDES). Formed in mid-2010 by a number of cabinet ministers and members of the pro-government **Citizen Movement** (*Mouvement Citoyen*—MC), the PDES was considered a vehicle for extending the influence of President Touré, who was constitutionally precluded from seeking another term in 2012. (The MC had arisen in 2002 as an informal association of Touré supporters from a variety of political parties and civic organizations.) PDES leaders, who included Lobbo Traoré TOURÉ (the president's wife), pledged to support President Touré's recent efforts to promote transparency in governmental affairs.

Following President Touré's overthrow in March 2012, the PDES reportedly fragmented. Party vice president Jeamille BITTAR ran for president of the republic in 2013, securing 1.8 percent of the first-round vote. After the PDES won three seats in the 2013 legislative poll, party leaders in 2014 agreed with other oppositionists that Mali was heading toward a "regime crisis."

Leaders: Ahmadou Abdoulaye DIALLO (Secretary General), Hamed Diané SÉMÉGA.

Other parties that secured seats in 2013 included the **Union of Patriots for Renewal** (*Union des Patriotes Pour le Renouveau*—UPPR), led by Moussa BAMADO; and the **Party for the Restoration of Mali's Values** (*Parti pour la Restauration des Valeurs du Mali*—PRVM), led by Mamadou SIDIBÉ.

Other Parties:

Front for Mali's Development (*Front pour le Développement du Mali/Mali Niéta Jekulu*—FDM/MNJ). Created in January 2008, the FDM/MNJ included a number of former RPM members. The group described itself as a response to poor governance under President Touré, whom party leaders accused of violating the spirit of the 1991 coup d'état that ousted Gen. Traoré from power.

Leader: Harouna SISSOKO (President).

Other parties presenting candidates in the 2013 presidential election included the **Alliance Chato 2013**, whose candidate, Aïchata Alassane HAÏDARA (a former union activist), received 0.8 percent of the first-round vote; the **National Convention for African Solidarity**, whose candidate, former prime minister Soumana Sacko, won 0.9 percent; the **Party for the Civic and Patriotic**, a new party whose candidate, Niankoro Yeah SAMAKE, won 0.6 percent; and the PCR (see Adema, PASJ, above), whose candidate, Ousmane Ben TRAORÉ, won 0.5 percent.

In the 2007 presidential election, Sidibé Aminata DIALLO was the candidate of the **Movement for Environmental Education and Sustainable Development** (*Rassemblement pour l'Éducation Environnementale et le Développement Durableé*—REDD), while Madiassa MAGUIRAGA was the candidate of the **Popular Party for Progress** (*Parti Populaire pour le Progrès*—PPP). Both candidates received less than 1 percent of the vote in the first round of balloting. (Diallo was Mali's first female presidential candidate.)

Mamadou Maribatourou DIABY, the incumbent's sole challenger in the 1997 presidential balloting, was a member of the **Unity, Development, and Progress Party** (*Parti pour l'Unité, le Développement, et le Progrès*—PUDP). (Diaby also ran unsuccessfully for the presidency in 2002.)

In 2011 the **African Convergence for Renewal** was launched under the leadership of Cheick Bougadary TRAORÉ, the son of former president Moussa Traoré. Bougadary Traoré, who had been living in the United States since 1991, returned to Mali in 2012 and won 0.3 percent of the vote in the first round of the 2013 presidential balloting. Another new party formed in 2011 was the **Rally for the Development of Mali** (*Rasemblement pour le Développement du Mali*—RPDM), which nominated Cheick Modibo Diarra, an astrophysicist and president of Microsoft Africa, as its candidate for the 2012 presidential election. After that balloting was postponed by the March 2012 coup, Diarra was named interim prime minister in April. After being forced out of that position in December 2012, Diarra won 2.1 percent of the vote in the first round of the 2013 presidential election.

Following the March 2012 military takeover, coup supporters reportedly coalesced initially as the **Coordination of Patriotic Organizations of Mali** (*Coordination des Organisations Patriotiques du Mali*—Copam), while anti-coup groupings formed the **United Front for the Protection of Democracy and the Republic** (*Front Uni pour la Sauvegarde de la Démocratie et de la République*), led by Adema member Kasssoum TAPO. (In addition to Adema, other parties and groups that objected to the coup reportedly included the URD, MPR, UDD, PSP, and FDR.)

For information on additional minor parties that were active in the 1990s and early 2000s, see the 2012 *Handbook*.

Northern Groups:

National Movement for the Liberation of the Azawad (*Mouvement National pour la Libération de l'Azawad*—MNLA). Launched in the fall of 2011 by Tuareg rebels (many of whom had recently returned from Libya where they had served in the security forces of Muammar Qadhafi), the MNLA subsequently attacked Malian forces in the north at an increasing rate. Although some MNLA leaders advocated independence for northern Mali, other MNLA components called for autonomy rather than full independence. MNLA support included that of the **National Movement for the Azawad** (*Mouvement National pour l'Azawad*—MNA), which had been formed in 2010 by exiled Tuareg activists, and the **National Front for the Liberation of the Azawad** (*Front National pour la Libération de l'Azawad*—FNLA), described as a secular Arab militia. (*Azawad* is derived from a Berber word that has historically referenced a Tuareg-populated region covering parts of Mali and several neighboring countries.)

The MNLA assumed control of a number of northern towns by defeating Malian army units in early 2012, and in April it declared the "independent state of *Azawad*." However, the MNLA's dominance was soon challenged by the Islamist *Ansar Dine* (see below). The two groups surprisingly announced an alliance in May to govern an "Islamic Republic" in northern Mali. However, the alliance quickly collapsed because of the conflicting ideologies and goals of the two groups. (The MNLA, primarily comprising secular, French-speaking Tuaregs, reportedly chafed at *Ansar Dine*'s planned "Arabization" of the region and imposition of sharia.)

After losing the area it had previously controlled to *Ansar Dine* and another Islamist group (MUJAO, see below), the MNLA indicated its interest in being part of any future political settlement in the north. Following the rout of Islamist forces by French-led troops in early 2013, the MNLA reassumed control of the important northern city of Kidal. In June the MNLA signed a cease-fire under which government forces were subsequently permitted to enter Kidel and the UN was authorized to establish a regional peacekeeping force (French troops also remained active in the region). However, relations between the MNLA, which retained control of parts of Kidal and surrounding areas, and the government remained contentious, with negotiations breaking down several times as policy differences were reported between the MNLA's political and military wings.

In November 2013 the MNLA announced an agreement to cooperate regarding peace negotiations with the two other major rebel groups in the north—the **High Council for the Unity of Azawad** (*Haut Conseil pour l'Unité de l'Azawad*—HCUA) and the **Arab Movement of Azawad** (*Mouvement Arabe de l'Azawad*—MAA). The leader of the HCUA at that time was Alghabas AG INTALLAH, the son of the traditional leader of the dominant Tuareg clan. Earlier, in 2013, he had formed the **Islamic Movement of Azawad** (*Mouvement Islamique de l'Azawad*—MIA), which was considered an attempt by former members of *Ansar Dine* to project a non-jihadist stance that would be palatable to the international community. The MIA rejected ties with the AQIM and MUJAO and pledged to pursue a negotiated settlement with the government regarding limited autonomy for the north. The MIA shortly thereafter merged with the similarly minded HCUA.

The MAA rubric was adopted by the FNLA in 2012 as Arabs in the north opposed advances into Timbuktu by the MNLA and *Ansar Dine*. The tentative rapprochement with the MNLA and HCUA in 2013 was seen as an effort to strengthen the secular voice of the MAA in peace negotiations with the Malian government.

In May 2014 clashes broke out between MNLA and government forces when new prime minister Moussa Mara made what the MNLA characterized as a "provocative" visit to Kidal. Some 1,500 government troops subsequently moved on MNLA locations but they were quickly routed by rebel forces before a new cease-fire agreement was reached.

Fighting between the MNLA and the MAA in January 2015 prompted MINUSMA to mediate negotiations between the two groups to prevent an escalation of violence. In June the MNLA signed a peace agreement with the government.

Leaders: Col. Mohamed AG NAJEM (Chief of Staff), Hama AG SID'AHMED (Spokesperson), Bilal AG ACHERIF (Secretary General).

Movement for Oneness and Jihad in West Africa (*Mouvement pour l'Unicité et le Jihad en Afrique de l'Ouest*—MUJAO). The jihadist MUJAO first surfaced in 2011, its forces reportedly augmented in July by militant Islamists from Algeria. The MUJAO appeared to have links with the AQIM, to which some observers attributed the "professionalism" displayed by the MUJAO fighters when they defeated the MNLA for control of the northern city of Gao in July 2012. Most of the MUJAO's membership was considered non-Malian and therefore unlikely to be approached by southern leaders regarding a possible political (rather than military) settlement. The MUJAO/AQIM fighters seized control of several other northern towns in late 2012, but they were pushed out by the French-led campaign in early 2013. Apparently continuing to operate from secluded mountainous regions in Mali and neighboring countries, the MUJAO claimed responsibility for several subsequent attacks through 2016.

Leaders: Ould Mohamed KHEIROU, Sultan Ould BADI, Abu Walid SAHRAOUI.

Ansar Dine (Defenders of the Faith). Launched at the end of 2011, the militant Islamist *Ansar Dine*, comprising both Arabs (the majority) and some Tuaregs, reportedly had ties to the Algeria-based al-Qaida in the Islamic Maghreb. (See Current issues, above, and the entry on Algeria for additional information on the AQIM.) *Ansar Dine* made significant military strides in northern Mali in the first half of 2012, for a brief time in a sketchy alliance with the MNLA (see MNLA, above, for details). Iyad Ag Ghali, a Tuareg described as a "veteran rebel leader" who had recently turned to "radical Islam," said that *Ansar Dine*'s primary goal was the imposition of sharia in northern Mali. However, other components of the group, while likewise committed to sharia, also appeared to favor independence for the region. Its forces having reportedly been augmented by former MNLA fighters, *Ansar Dine* by September controlled large areas of northern Mali, including the important towns of Kidal and Timbuktu. Meanwhile, the precise relationship between *Ansar Dine* and the AQIM (and, for that matter, the MUJAO [the other prominent Islamist group in the region]) remained unclear.

Although *Ansar Dine* in late 2012 reportedly agreed to peace talks with the government, its forces launched an offensive toward the south in January 2013, prompting the French-led campaign that ultimately forced most of the Islamist militants to abandon the territory they had controlled in the north. However, *Ansar Dine* was reported to have "reemerged" in northern Mali by August 2014. *Ansar Dine* commander Ahmad AL-FAQI (Abu Tourab) was detained in Nigeria and turned over to the International Criminal Court in September 2015 to be tried for war crimes for destroying religiously significant sites in Mali.

Leader: Iyad AG GHALI.

Previously, the major Tuareg political organization was the **Alliance for Democracy and Change** (*Alliance pour la Démocratie et le Changement*—ADC), most of whose members endorsed, at least in principle, the Algerian-mediated peace plan of 2006 between Tuaregs and the Malian government. However, some Tuaregs subsequently continued their antigovernment activities. Although the ADC signed a disarmament accord in early 2009, the **Tuareg Alliance of Northern Mali** (*Alliance Tuareg Nord-Mali*—ATNM) led by Ibrahim AG BAHANDA, rejected that agreement. Following a government offensive against his forces in February 2009, Ag Bahanda fled to Algeria, from where he expressed interest in returning to peace negotiations. Although the Malian government declined direct talks with Ag Bahanda, it negotiated a reconciliation agreement in the second half of the year with the Tuareg community and other ethnic groups in northern Mali. However Turaeg leaders subsequently continued to criticize the government for its perceived failure to follow through on its development pledges for the north.

LEGISLATURE

Following the March 1991 coup, the UDPM-dominated legislature was dissolved, with its powers being assigned to the CTSP. The current **National Assembly** (*Assemblée Nationale*) contains 147 members serving (subject to dissolution) five-year terms. Legislators are directly elected in two-round balloting (as necessary) from 125 constituencies, in which candidates are presented in lists representing individual parties, coalitions of parties (which vary widely from constituency to constituency), or independents. (Voters cast a single vote for the list of their choice.) The next election was scheduled for July 1, 2012, but was canceled because of the March coup. In June the assembly voted to extend the term of office of the current members until the completion of the recently negotiated transitional period.

Following the most recent elections on November 24 and December 15, 2013, the Rally for Mali held 66 seats; Union for the Republic and Democracy, 17; Alliance for Democracy in Mali/Pan African Party for Liberty, Solidarity, and Justice, 16; Alternative Forces for Renewal and Emergence, 6; Convergence for the Development of Mali, 5; African Solidarity for Democracy and Independence, 5; National Congress for Democratic Initiative, 4; Party for National Renaissance, 3; Party for Economic Development and Solidarity, 3; Patriotic Movement for Renewal, 3; Alliance for Solidarity in Mali–Convergence of Patriotic Forces, 3; Democratic Alliance for Peace–Maliba, 2; Democratic and Social Convention, 2; Movement for African Independence, Renewal, and Integration, 2; Malian Union of the Democratic African Rally, 2; Change, 1; Union for Democracy and Development, 1; Party for the Restoration of Mali's Values, 1; the Union of Patriots for Renewal, 1; and independents, 4.

President: Issaka SIDIBÉ (RPM).

CABINET

[as of September 1, 2016]

Prime Minister	Modibo Keita (Adema)
Ministers	
Agriculture	Kassoum Denon
Culture	N'Diaye Ramatoulaye Diallo [f]
Decentralization and State Reform	Mohamed Ag Erlaf
Defense and Veterans	Tiéman Hubert Coulibaly (UDD)
Digital Economy, Information, and Communication	Mountaga Tall (CNID)
Economy and Finance	Boubou Cissé
Employment and Professional Training	Mahamane Baby
Energy and Water	Malick Alhousseini
Environment and Sanitation	Keïta Aida M'Bo [f]
Equipment, Transportation, and Access	Traoré Seynabou Diop [f]

Foreign Affairs, African Integration, and International Cooperation	Abdoulaye Diop
Handicrafts and Tourism	Nina Walett Intallou [f]
Health and Public Hygiene	Marie Madeleine Togo [f]
Higher Education and Scientific Research	Assétou Founè Samaké Migan [f]
Housing and Urban Affairs	Ousmane Koné
Interior and Security	Gen. Salif Traoré
Justice, Human Rights, and Keeper of the Seals	Ishmael Mamadou Konaté
Labor, Civil Service, and Relations with Institutions	Diarra Raky Talla [f]
Livestock and Fishing	Nango Dembélé
Malians Abroad	Abdourhamane Sylla (RPM)
Mines	Tiémoko Sangaré
National Education	Kénékouo Barthélémy Togo
National Reconciliation	Mohamed el Moctar
Promotion of Investment and the Private Sector	Konimba Sidibé
Promotion of Women, Children, and the Family	Sangaré Oumou Ba (RPM) [f]
Religious Affairs and Worship	Tierno Amadou Omar Hass Diallo
Solidarity, Humanitarian Action, and Reconstruction of the North	Hamadoun Konaté
Sports	Housseïni Amion Guindo
State Property, Land Affairs, and Heritage	Mohamed Ali Bathily
Territorial Administration	Abdoulaye Idrissa Maïga
Territorial Development and Population	Sambel Bana Diallo
Trade and Industry	Abdel Karim Konaté
Youth and Citizenship	Amadou Koïta

[f] = female

INTERGOVERNMENTAL REPRESENTATION

Ambassador to the U.S.: Tiéna COULIBALY.

U.S. Ambassador to Mali: Paul A. FOLMSBEE.

Permanent Representative to the UN: Issa KONFOUROU.

IGO Memberships (Non-UN): AfDB, AU, ECOWAS, ICC, IOM, NAM, OIC, WTO.

For Further Reference:

Chivas, Christopher. *The French War on Al Qa'ida in Africa.* Cambridge: Cambridge University Press, 2015.

Harmon, Stephen. *Terror and Insurgency in the Sahara-Sahel Region: Corruption, Contraband, Jihad and the Mali War of 2012–2013.* New York: Routledge, 2014.

Wing, Susan. *Constructing Democracy in Transitioning Societies of Africa: Constitutionalism and Deliberation in Mali.* New York: Palgrave Macmillan, 2008.

MALTA

Republic of Malta
Repubblika ta' Malta

Political Status: Became independent within the Commonwealth on September 21, 1964; republic declared by constitutional amendment on December 13, 1974.

Area: 122 sq. mi. (316 sq. km).

Population: 420,000 (2016E—UN); 415,196 (2016E—U.S. Census).

Major Urban Centers (2014E—Government): VALLETTA (5,677), Birkirkara (22,047), Mosta (19,806), Qormi (16,315), Sliema (14,904).

Official Languages: Maltese, English; Italian is also widely spoken.

Monetary Unit: Euro (market rate October 1, 2016: 0.89 euro = $1US). The euro became Malta's official currency on January 1, 2008, at a fixed rate of 1 euro = 0.4293 Maltese lira.

President: Marie-Louise COLEIRO PRECA (Malta Labour Party); elected on April 1, 2014, to a five-year term by the House of Representatives and sworn in on April 4, succeeding George ABELA (Malta Labour Party). (Presidents resign from their parties upon election.)

Prime Minister: Joseph MUSCAT (Malta Labour Party); sworn in on March 11, 2013, to replace Lawrence GONZI (Nationalist Party), following legislative elections on March 9.

THE COUNTRY

Strategically located in the central Mediterranean some 60 miles south of Sicily, Malta comprises the two main islands of Malta and Gozo in addition to the small island of Comino. The population is predominantly of Carthaginian and Phoenician descent and of mixed Arab-Italian cultural traditions. The indigenous language, Maltese, is of Semitic origin. Roman Catholicism is the state religion, but other faiths are permitted.

Malta has few natural resources, and its terrain is not well adapted to agriculture. Wholesale, retail, transportation, and food services comprise 22 percent of GDP, followed by public administration, healthcare, and education (19 percent) and mining, manufacturing, and utilities (13 percent). Historically, the country has been dependent upon British military installations and expenditures, but today it focuses on tourism and shipping. Tourism reached record high levels in 2011, and the country has become a global leader in the online gaming industry. (For details on the Malta economy in the 1970s and 1980s, see the 2012 *Handbook.*)

Malta joined the European Union (EU) in 2004 and adopted the euro at the start of 2008. Compared with other European nations, Malta weathered the global recession well. GDP grew by 2.3 percent in 2010 and 2.1 percent in 2011, 0.8 percent in 2012, 2.7 percent in 2013, and 3.6 percent in 2014. In 2015 GDP grew by 3.2 percent, while inflation rose by 1 percent, and unemployment increased to 6.1 percent. GDP per capita was $22,319.

GOVERNMENT AND POLITICS

Political background. Malta has a long history of conquest and rule by foreign powers. It first came under British control in 1800, possession being formalized by the Treaty of Paris in 1814, and its strategic importance being enhanced by the opening of the Suez Canal in 1869. Ruled by a military governor throughout the 19th century, it experienced an unsuccessful period of internal autonomy immediately following World War I. Autonomy was abolished in 1933, and Malta reverted to its former status as a Crown Colony. A more successful attempt at internal self-government was initiated in 1947, after Malta had been awarded the George Cross by Britain for its resistance to Axis air assaults during World War II. In 1956 the islanders voted three to one in favor of full integration with Britain, as proposed by the ruling Malta Labour Party (MLP), led by Dominic (Dom) MINTOFF. However, British reservations, combined with a change of government in Malta, resulted in the submission in 1962 of a formal request for independence within the Commonwealth by Prime Minister Giorgio BORG OLIVIER of the Nationalist Party (*Partit Nazzjonalista*—PN), who led the islands to full sovereignty on September 21, 1964. The first post-independence change of government came in the 1971 election, which returned the MLP and Mintoff to power. Disenchanted with the British connection, Mintoff led Malta to republican status within the Commonwealth in December 1974.

The MLP retained its legislative majority in the elections of 1976 and 1981. The results of the 1981 poll were challenged by the opposition PN, which had won a slim majority of the popular vote and which, after being rebuffed in an appeal for electoral reform, instituted a boycott of parliamentary proceedings. In a countermove to the boycott, Prime Minister Mintoff declared the 31 Nationalist-held seats vacant in

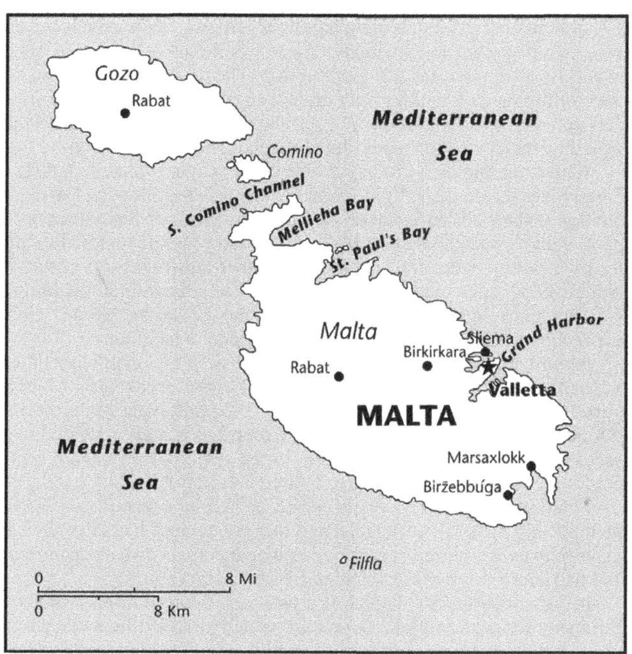

April 1982, with the PN subsequently refusing to make by-election nominations. In March 1983, however, PN leader Edward FENECH ADAMI agreed to resume parliamentary activity on the basis of a commitment from Mintoff to discuss changes in the electoral law.

The interparty talks were suspended in July 1983 in the wake of increasingly violent antigovernment activity and the adoption of a legislative measure that prohibited the charging of fees by private schools and indirectly authorized the confiscation of upwards of 75 percent of the assets of the Maltese Catholic Church. During 1984 the conflict erupted into a major confrontation between church and state, with the Catholic hierarchy ordering the closure of all schools under its jurisdiction—half the island's total—in September. The schools reopened two months later, with Vatican officials agreeing in April 1985 to the introduction of free education over a three-year period in return for government assurances of noninterference in teaching and participation in a joint commission to discuss remaining church-state issues, including those regarding church property.

Meanwhile, in December 1984 Mintoff had stepped down as prime minister in favor of Karmenu MIFSUD BONNICI. The church-state dispute was officially resolved in July 1986, while in January 1987 both the MLP and the PN supported constitutional changes that included modification of the electoral law to ensure that a party winning a majority of the popular vote would have a parliamentary majority.

In the bitterly contested 1987 election, Labour, as in 1981, won 34 of 65 legislative seats, but, after 16 years in office, lost control of the government because the PN had obtained a popular majority and was therefore awarded additional seats. Thus, PN leader Fenech Adami became prime minister. Earlier in the year, at the conclusion of her five-year term, President Agatha BARBARA had yielded her office, on an acting basis, to the Speaker of the House of Representatives, Paul XUEREB. Xuereb retained the position from February 1987 until the House elected the PN's Dr. Vincent TABONE as his successor in April 1989.

In the election of February 1992 the PN won 34 legislative seats with a vote share of 51.8 percent, while the MLP obtained 31 seats with 46.5 percent. Five days later, Fenech Adami formed a new government in which all senior ministers were retained. In 1994 former PN leader Ugo MIFSUD BONNICI was sworn in as Malta's fifth president.

In March 1995 Fenech Adami brought in a younger generation of ministers as part of a strategy to retain power in the next general election. However, the prime minister's decision to call an early election for October 1996 proved a miscalculation. Labour unexpectedly outpolled the PN 50.7 to 47.8 percent in fiercely contested balloting that drew a record turnout of 97 percent. Although the PN won 34 elective seats to Labour's 31, the 1987 constitutional amendment entitled Labour to 4 additional seats, handing it a parliamentary majority. The new Labour government was sworn in under the premiership of Alfred SANT, a Harvard-educated former physicist. Fulfilling one of its major domestic campaign promises, the Sant government in July 1997 abolished the country's 15 percent value-added tax (VAT), which had been introduced in 1995.

The government's single-seat majority evaporated when former prime minister Mintoff, Sant's aging MLP predecessor, deserted the party on two votes relating to a development project in Mintoff's district. Plagued by resignations, bitter attacks from Mintoff, and dissatisfaction within the MLP over Sant's failure to follow traditional patronage policies and his perceived drift to the right, the prime minister called an election for September 1998, three years early. The PN emerged with 35 seats to the MLP's 30, permitting the PN's Fenech Adami to return as prime minister. In March 1999 voting along straight party lines, the House of Representatives elected as president the PN's Guido DE MARCO, until then the deputy prime minister and foreign minister.

Membership in the EU became one of the main priorities of Fenech Adami's government. In response to criticism from the anti-EU MLP, Fenech Adami called a nonbinding referendum on EU membership for March 8, 2003. Although those voting endorsed membership by 53.65 to 46.35 percent, Sant and other MLP leaders argued that the closeness of the vote, when combined with the 9 percent of the eligible voters who did not cast a ballot, meant that the majority of Maltese opposed accession. In response, Fenech Adami called for elections on April 12, 2003, just four days before Malta was to sign the accession treaty, to affirm support for membership. Turnout was 96.2 percent. The PN received 51.8 percent of the vote and 35 seats, while the MLP won 47.5 percent and 30 seats. Malta signed the EU accession treaty on April 16 and formally entered the EU a year later, on May 1, 2004.

Having decided to seek the presidency, Fenech Adami resigned as prime minister on March 23, 2004. He was replaced by Lawrence GONZI (PN), who reshuffled and expanded the cabinet, sworn in on the same day as Fenech Adami's resignation. Fenech Adami, elected president by the House of Representatives on March 29, was sworn into office on April 4.

European parliamentary elections on June 12, 2004, showed that EU membership remained a contentious issue. Each of the major parties ran a full slate of candidates, and there were a number of fringe and independent candidates as well. The MLP, which ran a Euro-skeptic campaign, outpolled the ruling PN, while the small pro-EU green-oriented Democratic Alternative (*Alternattiva Demokratika*—AD) gained no seats but had its highest electoral vote in history at 9.3 percent. The MLP received 48.4 percent of the vote and three seats, and the PN secured 39.8 percent and two seats.

The campaign for the March 8, 2008, legislative elections, was principally between the PN and MLP, despite increased public attention on immigration issues and the emergence of two new political parties (the National Action and Empire Europe) with strong anti-immigrant positions. The PN outpolled the MLP by a slim margin in the national vote, but it won only 31 seats, based on the results within the voting districts. As in 1987, the PN was awarded 4 more seats, giving it a 35–34 majority. President Adami subsequently reappointed Gonzi as prime minister, and Gonzi was sworn in on March 11. His cabinet was approved and sworn in the following day.

After lengthy negotiations, an agreement was announced in July by the PN and MLP to cooperate through a new special committee in the House of Representatives designed to facilitate compromise on outstanding issues. The accord was considered a victory for the MLP, which had long complained of being left out of the decision-making process during the last 20 years of PN rule. Prime Minister Gonzi's government also reached across the aisle and nominated George ABELA of the MLP for president. The House of Representatives unanimously approved Abela on the same day, and he was sworn in on April 4.

The MLP won four seats in the June 2009 balloting for the European Parliament, while the PN won two. Prime Minister Gonzi struggled to hold onto his one-seat parliamentary majority due to party defections in 2011 and 2012. Backbencher Franco DEBONO frequently clashed with Gonzi and threatened to withhold his vote on key legislation.

On December 10, 2012, Debono withdrew his support for the 2013 budget. The defection triggered the dissolution of parliament. In elections held on March 9, 2013, the PN won 43.34 percent of the vote and 30 seats. After 15 years in opposition, the Labour Party returned to power with 54.8 percent of the vote and 39 seats, the largest vote share since 1955. MLP leader Joseph MUSCAT was sworn in as prime minister on March 11.

On March 30, 2014, there was a minor cabinet reshuffle. Marie-Louise COLEIRO PRECA (MLP) was unanimously elected president by parliament on April 1, becoming, at 55-years-old, the youngest head of state in Maltese history and the second woman to hold the office.

The cabinet was reshuffled in April 2016 after allegations emerged that the energy and health minister, Konrad MIZZI, had created a shell corporation in Panama to hide income. Mizzi was forced to resign his portfolio but remained in the cabinet, pending an investigation (see Current issues, below). The charges emerged as part of the leak of the "Panama Papers" (see entry on Panama).

Constitution and government. The 1964 constitution established Malta as an independent parliamentary monarchy within the Commonwealth, with executive power exercised by a prime minister and cabinet, both appointed by the governor general but chosen from and responsible to parliament. By constitutional amendment, the country became a republic on December 13, 1974, with an indirectly elected president of Maltese nationality replacing the British monarch as de jure head of state. The president serves a five-year term, as does the prime minister, subject to the retention of a legislative majority. The parliament consists of a unicameral House of Representatives elected on the basis of proportional representation every five years, assuming no prior dissolution. Under an amendment adopted in February 1987, the party winning a majority of the popular vote is awarded additional House seats, if needed to secure a legislative majority.

The judicial system encompasses a Constitutional Court, a Court of Appeal, a Criminal Court of Appeal, and lower courts. The president appoints the judges for the Constitutional Court and the Court of Appeal. There was little established local government in Malta until 1993, when a Local Councils Act (subsequently amended) was passed. In 2001 provisions for local councils were incorporated into the constitution. At present, there are 68 directly elected local councils, 54 on the island of Malta and 14 on Gozo.

Reporters Without Borders ranked Malta 46th out of 180 countries in its 2016 index of press freedom. Many print and broadcast outlets are owned by political parties, unions, or the Catholic Church.

Foreign relations. After independence, Maltese foreign policy centered primarily on the country's relationship with Great Britain and thus with the North Atlantic Treaty Organization (NATO). A ten-year Mutual Defense and Assistance Agreement, signed in 1964, was abrogated in 1971 by the Mintoff government. Under a new seven-year agreement, concluded in 1972 after months of negotiation, the rental payments for use of military facilities by Britain were tripled. Early in 1973 Mintoff reopened the issue, asking additional payment to compensate for devaluation of the British pound, but he settled for a token adjustment pending British withdrawal from the facilities in March 1979. Rebuffed in an effort to obtain a quadripartite guarantee of Maltese neutrality and a five-year budgetary subsidy from France, Italy, Algeria, and Libya, the Mintoff government turned to Libya. During ceremonies marking the British departure, the Libyan leader, Col. Muammar al-Qadhafi, promised "unlimited" support. In the course of the following year, however, the relationship cooled because of overlapping claims to offshore oil rights, and in September 1980 an agreement was concluded with Italy whereby Rome guaranteed Malta's future neutrality and promised a combination of loans and subsidies totaling $95 million over a five-year period. In 1981 Malta also signed neutrality agreements with Algeria, France, and the Soviet Union.

In December 1984 Prime Minister Mintoff announced that the defense and aid agreement with Italy would be permitted to lapse in favor of a new alignment with Libya, which would undertake to train Maltese forces to withstand "threats or acts of aggression." Six months later the maritime issue was resolved, the International Court of Justice establishing a boundary 18 nautical miles north of a line equidistant between the two countries.

In March 1986 Prime Minister Karmenu Mifsud Bonnici met with Colonel Qadhafi in Tripoli in what was described as an effort to ease the confrontation between Libya and the United States in the Gulf of Sidra. In August the Maltese leader stated that his government had warned Libya of the approach of "unidentified planes" prior to the April attack by U.S. aircraft on Tripoli and Benghazi, although there was no indication that Libyan authorities had acted on the information.

Upon assuming office in May 1987, Prime Minister Fenech Adami indicated that the military clauses of the 1984 agreement with Libya would not be renewed, although all other commitments would be continued. Cooperation between the two countries at the political and economic levels was reaffirmed in 1988, with Libya renewing its $38 million oil supply pact with Malta late in the year.

A member of the United Nations, the Conference on (later Organization for) Security and Cooperation in Europe (CSCE/OSCE), and a number of other international organizations, Malta concluded an association agreement with the European Community (EC) in 1970 and in July 1990 applied for full membership. The government's perseverance in the face of initial reservations in Brussels was rewarded by a decision of the EU summit in Essen in December 1994 that Malta would be included in the next round of enlargement negotiations.

While maintaining its neutrality, Malta also joined NATO's Partnership for Peace (PfP) program in April 1995. Following Labour's victory at the polls in October 1996, Prime Minister Sant suspended participation, contending that Malta could best promote regional stability by a policy of neutrality that was neither anti-European nor anti-American. He also made it clear that Malta would continue to observe UN sanctions imposed on Tripoli over the Lockerbie affair, while expressing the hope that the sanctions would soon be lifted.

Almost immediately following his victory in the snap election of September 1998, Prime Minister Fenech Adami accelerated Malta's pursuit of EU membership. In February 1999, following Malta's reintroduction of the VAT, the European Commission recommended that accession talks with Malta start later in the year. Malta signed the EU accession treaty in 2003 and joined the EU on May 1, 2004.

Following the PN's victory in March 2008, Malta reactivated its PfP membership in April. Officials noted that the country had been unable to participate in training exercises that would help its own armed forces and had been barred from attending EU–NATO meetings.

In July 2009 the EU launched a two-year €2 million pilot project, European Relocation Malta (Eurema), which provided financial assistance for EU member states that would resettle asylum seekers from Malta. (For more on Malta and migration, see the 2015 *Handbook.*)

The Maltese government cut ties with the Qadhafi regime in 2011. Thousands of refugees from Libya sought asylum in Malta—2,000 on April 30, 2011, alone. Malta helped evacuate 12,000 citizens from 89 different countries from Libya in February 2011, and the World Health Organization based its Libyan relief operations in Malta.

Relations with the EU were damaged in 2012 when PN politician John DALLI resigned as EU commissioner for health and consumer policy. An internal investigation by the EU accused Dalli of influence peddling, specifically, telling a Swedish tobacco firm that he could arrange for exemptions from EU laws. Dalli was replaced by Deputy Prime Minister and Foreign Minister Tonio BORG, also of the PN. Dalli later asked the European Court of Justice to annul his resignation and award him compensation, saying he had been forced to resign by EC president José Manuel Barroso.

Prime Minister Joseph Muscat became the first Maltese leader to pay an official visit to Israel in October 2013. In November the Commonwealth announced that Malta would host the heads of government meeting of the organization in 2015.

In January 2014 Malta agreed to revise a plan that would allow non-EU citizens to purchase a Maltese passport for €1.15 million without residing in the country. New guidelines required that the passport seekers live in Malta for a minimum of one year. The United States donated two new patrol boats to the Maltese military in May. In June Malta established diplomatic relations with Somalia.

In June 2016 Malta and Cambodia signed a memorandum of understanding on the adoption of Cambodian children by Maltese parents. Malta became one of the first countries, along with Spain, in Europe to resume the adoption of Cambodian children after that country's government banned foreign adoptions in 2011.

After voters in the United Kingdom endorsed a UK exit ("Brexit") from the EU (see entry on the United Kingdom) in June 2016, Malta announced that it would seek bilateral agreements to replace existing accords between the two countries to cover issues such as health care, taxes, and trade.

Current issues. In July 2011 the Maltese legislature passed a law that made divorce legal under certain conditions, following a nonbinding referendum on the issue in which 53 percent of the voters supported the measure. Also in 2011, the European Commission questioned the optimism of Malta's 2012 budget and asked for spending cuts worth €40 million.

The auditor general released a scathing report in July 2013 regarding the amateurish management of the Enemalta (the national energy company) fuel procurement committee from 2008 through 2010. Executives stood accused of taking kickbacks and price-fixing. Few policy documents existed, and meeting minutes were often "handwritten and undecipherable." Austin GATT, the PN appointee responsible for Enemalta, blithely announced that he was "not interested" in the findings.

The number of migrants intercepted or rescued by Maltese forces increased in mid-2013. A three-day standoff between Malta and Italy ensued in August, when Malta refused entry to a tanker carrying 102 migrants rescued in the waters near Libya. Italy eventually accepted the migrants. On October 3 a ship carrying 500 migrants from Africa capsized near Lampedusa Island, and more than 300 perished. A boat carrying 250 migrants from Syria sank on October 11, prompting Muscat to appeal to the EU to formulate a common immigration strategy. In 2014 Muscat announced that Malta would cease detention of children who sought asylum.

As part of a broad effort to crack down on tax evasion, business owners were being increasingly investigated and prosecuted for not paying value-added tax (VAT). A report in June 2014 found that 15,000 VAT-evasion cases had been heard in the past three years. In July, the government rejected an opposition proposal for state funding of political parties. The proposal was an amendment to a campaign finance reform bill that would cap individual contributions to parties at €50,000 and require any contribution over €10,000 to be reported.

In April 2016 the government of Malta announced plans to sell its 49 percent stake in Air Malta to Alitalia. The proposed sale created worry and uncertainty among airline workers and trade unions over possible changes to compensation and working conditions. Also in April, the government won a confidence vote, 38–31, in the wake of revelations that the minister of energy and health had created secret companies allegedly to avoid taxes. In July the government rejected a proposal to legalize euthanasia for the disabled or elderly.

POLITICAL PARTIES

Government Party:

Malta Labour Party—MLP (*Partit Laburista*). In power from 1971 to 1987, the MLP advocated a socialist and "progressive" policy, including anticolonialism in international affairs, a neutralist foreign policy, and emphasis on Malta's role as "a bridge of peace between Europe and the Arab world." The party has periodically complained of intrusion by the Catholic Church into political and economic affairs. (See the 2015 *Handbook* for information on the history of the party.)

In 1992 the party's vote-share fell to 46.5 percent, prompting former prime minister Karmenu Mifsud Bonnici to announce his retirement as party leader. His successor, Alfred Sant, initiated a modernization of the party's organization and policies while maintaining the MLP's commitment to neutrality and opposition to EU accession. Labour returned to power in 1996, winning 50.7 percent of the popular vote but was ousted when it secured only 47 percent in September 1998. In the 2003 elections the MLP received 47.5 percent of the vote and 30 seats. As a result of the election, Sant resigned as party leader, but he was subsequently reelected to the post. Sant resigned again following the March 2008 legislative poll, in which the MLP had won a majority of seats (34) but finished second (with 48.8 percent of the votes) to the PN as far as the total vote was concerned. Sant was succeeded as MLP leader by Joseph Muscat, a 34-year-old member of the European Parliament, who won the June 6 party leadership election on the second ballot. In January 2009 Prime Minister Gonzi announced his government would nominate MLP member George Abela for the Maltese presidency. Abela officially resigned from the party to pave the way for his accession to the post on April 1.

The MLP scored a resounding victory in the June 2009 balloting in Malta for the European Parliament by securing 55 percent of the vote, compared to 40 percent for the PN and only 2.3 percent for the AD. Most analysts attributed the MLP's surge to dissatisfaction among the populace over rising unemployment and steady increases in the cost of living. The MLP also led in concurrent balloting for one-third of the nation's local councils.

The MLP regained control of parliament in elections held March 9, 2013, taking 39 seats. In EU elections in 2014 the MLP won 53.3 percent of the vote and 3 seats. The MLP was shocked by the revelation of the "Panama Papers," which prompted the resignation of Konrad MIZZI as deputy party leader. In June 2016 Chris CARDONA defeated Owen BONNICI in party elections for Mizzi's MLP post.

Leaders: Joseph MUSCAT (Prime Minister of Malta and Party Leader), Louis GRECH (Deputy Prime Minister of Malta and Deputy Party Leader in the House of Representatives), Chris CARDONA (Deputy Leader).

Opposition Party:

Nationalist Party (*Partit Nazzjonalista*—PN). Advocating the retention of Roman Catholic and European principles, the PN brought Malta to independence. It formerly supported alignment with NATO and membership in the EC, but because of a constitutional pact with Labour, in February 1987 it adopted a neutral foreign policy. The party obtained 50.9 percent of the vote in the 1981 election without, however, winning control of the legislature. In the 1987 balloting it again obtained only a minority of elective seats but under the February constitutional amendment was permitted to form a government because of its popular majority.

The Nationalists retained power in the 1992 election but were unexpectedly defeated in 1996, when their share of the popular vote slipped from 51.8 to 47.8 percent. The PN returned to power in the election of September 1998 with a vote share of 51.8 percent. In the April 2003 elections, the PN won 51.8 percent and 35 seats. In March 2004 Edward Fenech Adami, theretofore the prime minister, was elected president, and PN Vice Chair Lawrence Gonzi became prime minister.

Although the PN finished second in seat totals to the MLP in the 2008 legislative poll, it secured a plurality of the nationwide votes (49.3 percent) and was therefore awarded additional seats to give it a slim parliamentary majority and continued governmental control.

Internal bickering eclipsed policymaking in 2011 and 2012, and on July 12, 2012, the PN executive committee announced that three current members of parliament (MPs), Jeffrey PULLICINO ORLANDO, Franco DEBONO, and Jesmond MUGLIETT, would not be on the PN list for the next parliamentary election because they had "voted with the opposition" twice in June. (For details see the 2013 *Handbook*.) Debono's refusal to support the budget led to the collapse of the Gonzi government in December 2012. The party dropped from 35 seats to 30 following the parliamentary election of March 9, 2013, and lost control of the government after 15 years in power. Gonzi immediately resigned as party chair. Simon BUSUTTIL, a lawyer and member of the European Parliament, was elected deputy party chair when Tonio BORG resigned in late 2012. Busuttil beat three opponents to become party chair in May 2013.

After the election, the PN was discovered to be on the brink of bankruptcy. The party and its affiliated media holdings were at least €8 million in debt. Over half of the staff was laid off, and plans were made to sell off property and real estate belonging to the party. Angry party members accused Gonzi of fiscal mismanagement. In the 2014 EU balloting, the NP secured 40 percent of the vote and three seats.

In April 2016 the PN organized an unsuccessful vote of no confidence in the MLP government in the wake of the "Panama Papers" scandal (see MLP, above).

Leaders: Simon BUSUTTIL (Chair), Lawrence GONZI (Former Prime Minister), Mario DE MARCO (Deputy Chair), Chris SAID (Secretary General).

Other Parties That Contested the 2013 Legislative Election:

Democratic Alternative (*Alternattiva Demokratika*—AD). An ecologically oriented grouping launched in 1989, the AD, also referenced as the Maltese Green Party, ran a distant third in the 1992 balloting, securing no legislative seats on a vote share of 1.7 percent. It was again unsuccessful in 1996, when its vote share slipped to 1.5 percent, and in September 1998, when it won 1.2 percent of the vote. In the 2003 elections the AD received only 0.7 percent of the vote, and, after the AD won only 1.3 percent in 2008, Harry VASSALO resigned as party leader. The AD collected 5,506 votes in 2013 (1.8 percent). Michael BRIGUGLIO subsequently declined to seek another term as party leader and was replaced by Arnold Cassola. The AD won 2.9 percent of the vote in the 2014 EU elections.

Leaders: Arnold CASSOLA (Chair), Carmel CACOPARDO (Deputy Chair), Ralph CASSAR (Secretary General).

Other minor parties include the **Empire of Europe** (*Imperium Europa*), a rightwing grouping led by Norman LOWELL; and the **Liberal Democratic Alliance of Malta** (*Alleanza Liberal-Demokratika Malta*—ALDM).

For information on the defunct **National Action** (*Azzjoni Nazzjonali*—AN) party, see the 2013 *Handbook*.

LEGISLATURE

The **House of Representatives** (*Il-Kamra Tad-Deputati*) consists of 65 elective members returned for a five-year term (subject to dissolution) on the basis of proportional representation applied in

13 electoral districts. The constitution requires that the party obtaining the highest number of votes nationwide must also end up with a legislative majority, assuming only two parties win seats. Consequently, if a party wins the nationwide vote but trails in seats awarded in the district results, it is given enough additional seats to reach a majority.

In the most recent election, held March 9, 2013, the Malta Labour Party (MLP) secured a majority with 39 seats, winning a majority in 23 of 35 electoral districts. The Nationalist Party (PN) won only 26 seats, but it was awarded 4 additional seats because of its share of first-preference votes.

Speaker: Angelo (Anġlu) FARRUGIA (MLP).

CABINET

[as of July 10, 2015]

Prime Minister	Joseph Muscat
Deputy Prime Minister	Louis Grech
Ministers	
Economy, Investment, and Small Business	Christian Cardona
Education and Employment	Evarist Bartolo
Energy	Joseph Muscat
European Affairs and Implementation of the Electoral Manifesto	Louis Grech
Family and Social Solidarity	Michael Farrugia
Finance	Edward Scicluna
Foreign Affairs	George Vella
Gozo Island	Anton Refalo
Health	Chris Fearne
Home Affairs and National Security	Carmelo Abela
Justice, Culture, and Local Government	Owen Bonnici
Social Dialogue, Consumer Affairs, and Civil Liberties	Helena Dalli [f]
Sustainable Development, Environment, and Climate Change	José Herrera
Tourism	Edward Zammit Lewis
Transport and Infrastructure	Joe Mizzi
Without Portfolio	Konrad Mizzi

[f] = female

INTERGOVERNMENTAL REPRESENTATION

Ambassador to the U.S.: Pierre Clive AGIUS.

U.S. Ambassador to Malta: G. Kathleen HILL.

Permanent Representative to the UN: Oscar DE ROJAS.

IGO Memberships (Non-UN): CEUR, CWTH, EBRD, EIB, EU, ICC, IOM, OSCE, WTO.

For Further Reference:

European Commission Economic and Financial Affairs. "Economies of the Member States: Malta." Accessed June 30, 2016. http://ec.europa.eu/economy_finance/eu/countries/malta_en.htm.

Frendo, Henry. *Europe and Empire: Culture, Politics and Identity in Malta and the Mediterranean.* Valletta, Malta: Midsea Books, 2011.

Pace, Roderick. *EU's Enlargement towards the Mediterranean: Cyprus and Malta.* London: Frank Cass, 2004.

MARSHALL ISLANDS

Republic of the Marshall Islands

Political Status: Sovereign state in free association with the United States (which retains authority with regard to defense) since October 21, 1986.

Area: 70 sq. mi. (181 sq. km).

Population: 53,000 (2016E—UN); 73,376 (2016E—U.S. Census). It is estimated that more than 22,000 of the Marshellese citizens reside in the U.S. territory of Guam or elsewhere in the United States.

Major Urban Center (2014E—UN): Majuro (31,000).

Official Languages: Marshallese. English is also widely spoken.

Monetary Unit: U.S. Dollar. (See the entry on United States for principal exchange rates.)

President: Hilda C. HEINE (ind.); elected on January 27, 2016, by the House of Representatives to succeed Casten HEMRA (ind.), who was elected on January 4, 2016, but left office following a vote of no confidence on January 26.

THE COUNTRY

The Republic of the Marshall Islands (RMI) consists of a double chain of coral atolls and islands (comprising 29 atolls, 5 single islands, and more than 850 reefs) within the Pacific region known as Micronesia, some 2,000 miles southwest of Hawaii. The two chains are about 80 miles apart, the eastern (which includes the capital, Majuro) being known as the Rataks ("Sunrise") Chain and the western (which includes Bikini, Eniwetak, and Kwajalein) being known as the Ralik ("Sunset") Chain. More than 90 percent of the inhabitants are indigenous Marshallese. Christianity is the principal religion, with adherents of Roman Catholicism the most numerous. The Inter-Parliamentary Union ranked RMI at 162nd out of 191 countries in women's representation. Only 9.1 percent of parliamentary seats (3 of 33) were held by women in 2016. In 2016 the first woman president of the country was elected.

Copra products have long dominated exports, although a decline in copra oil prices in the early 1980s led to a severe trade imbalance. The sale of fishing licenses and income from fishing-related services (the RMI is currently the Western Pacific's largest tuna transshipment port) now make up a significant portion of external earnings. Financial assistance from the United States (currently at about $80 million annually, approximately 60 percent of the RMI budget) is a crucial component of government revenue for a country whose GDP declined by nearly 25 percent in 1995–2001, with debt servicing equaling about 40 percent of budget outlays and far exceeding export earnings. For a number of years, the unemployment rate has been relatively unchanged at around 30 percent; nearly half of those in the salaried work force are employed by the government.

In late 2007 the Organization for Economic Cooperation and Development (OECD) removed the Marshalls from the watch list of "uncooperative" tax havens after the government pledged to improve the transparency of its accounts. However, it was subsequently placed on an OECD "gray list," members of which must negotiate tax information exchange agreements with a minimum of 12 countries to be moved onto the OECD's "white list." Although the RMI does not license offshore financial activity (a primary focus of OECD attention), it has attracted scrutiny in regard to its large nonresident corporate registry and flag of convenience ship registry, both of which can be used for tax evasion purposes. The RMI was also strongly criticized for poor safety standards affiliated with its ship registry (one of the world's largest) in 2010, when it was learned that the Deepwater Horizon oil rig, which exploded in the Gulf of Mexico in April 2010, was registered in the RMI.

In the wake of a continuing investigation of government employees allegedly involved in fraud in regard to U.S. grants, the United States in March 2012 added the RMI to its "concern list" regarding money laundering. In a possibly related vein, France several months later put the RMI on the French blacklist of uncooperative nations regarding tax matters.

The IMF in late 2012 called upon the RMI government to reduce subsidies to state-owned enterprises (which control nearly all major industries), reform the public employee pension system, and revamp the tax code in the interest of promoting the budgetary self-reliance that will be required when the grant component of the current Compact of Association with the United States expires in 2023.

GDP grew by 3.2 percent in fiscal year 2012 (primarily because of surging fishery output), but growth declined to 0.8 percent in fiscal year 2013 as delays were experienced in Compact-related infrastructure projects. In 2014 the Asian Development Bank announced increased

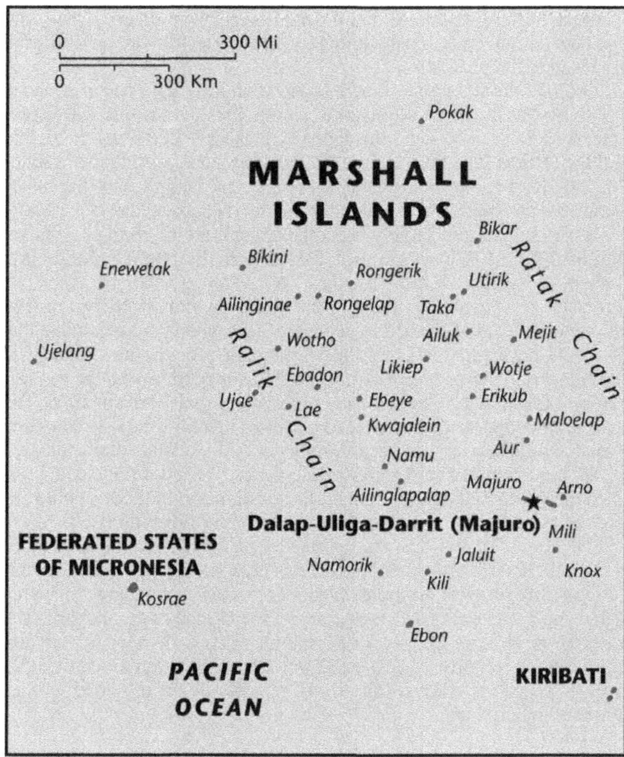

funding for RMI development plans, analysts calling for significantly strengthened emphasis on private sector development, but the GDP growth rate was only 0.5 percent. The GDP growth rate for 2015 improved slightly to 1.6 percent. The World Bank ranked RMI at 140th out of 189 countries for ease in doing business mainly for its failure to protect minority investors, high taxes, and difficulty in securing property rights.

GOVERNMENT AND POLITICS

Political background. Purchased by Germany from Spain in 1899, the Marshalls were seized in 1914 by Japan and retained as part of the mandate awarded by the League of Nations in 1920. The islands were occupied by U.S. forces near the end of World War II and (along with the Caroline and Northern Mariana Islands) became part of the U.S. Trust Territory of the Pacific in 1947. The United States conducted nearly 70 nuclear tests in the Marshalls following the war, leading eventually to massive legal claims regarding radioactive contamination and the dislocation of islanders (see Foreign relations, below).

In 1965 a Congress of Micronesia was established, with the Marshalls electing 4 of the 21 members of the Congress's House of Representatives. Subsequently the Marshall Islands district drafted its own constitution, which came into effect on May 1, 1979. Three years later the RMI concluded a Compact of Free Association with the United States, which was declared to be in effect on October 21, 1986, following ratification by the U.S. Congress and final approval by the RMI government. The RMI became a fully sovereign state under the Compact, save with regard to defense, which was to remain a U.S. responsibility for at least a 15-year period; the RMI was also obligated to "consult" with Washington regarding major foreign policy matters. (See below for information on extension of the Compact.)

The islands' first president was Amata KABUA, who assumed office on May 1, 1979, and was subsequently reelected to four successive four-year terms. He died on December 20, 1996, while undergoing medical treatment in Honolulu. Minister of Transportation Kunio D. LEMARI was named acting president pending legislative designation of a successor. In balloting within the House of Representatives (*Nitijela*) on January 14, 1997, Imata KABUA (a cousin of Amata Kabua and a minister without portfolio in the previous government) was elected to fulfill the remainder of Amata Kabua's term.

In the legislative poll of November 15, 1999, the United Democratic Party (UDP) won a first-ever majority for an opposition group, and on January 3, 2000, the UDP named Kessai H. NOTE, theretofore *Nitijela* speaker, to succeed Imata Kabua as president. (Note was the first commoner to be elected president.)

On November 1, 2002, after several rounds of negotiations, the U.S.'s George W. Bush administration and the Note government initialed a new 20-year Compact of Association. However, the RMI voiced reservations with regard to specific monetary figures pending completion of negotiations governing future use by the United States of the defense facilities on Kwajalein (a major contributor to the RMI economy). That issue was resolved in early 2003 when the United States agreed to a five-year lease renewal for the Kwajalein missile range, which had been renamed the Ronald Reagan Missile Defense Test Site in 2001. Consequently, the new Compact was signed in May, providing for some $960 million in grants through 2023 and an annual U.S. contribution of $7 million toward a trust fund, which was scheduled to provide budgetary support after the conclusion of the grant component. The new Compact also preserved the right of citizens to enter, reside, and work in the United States without visas.

On November 17, 2003, the UDP secured a 20-seat majority in the *Nitijela,* and on January 4, 2004, President Note won reelection by a 20–9 House vote over Justin DeBRUM. Subsequently, in 2005 concern was expressed in 2005 in the RMI that the trust fund established under the Compact of Free Association with the United States might not be sufficient to finance government services following the scheduled cessation of grants in 2023.

The Our Islands (*Ailon Kein Ad*—AKA) grouping and its allies (primarily the United People's Party—UPP) won a majority of seats in the November 19, 2007, balloting for the *Nitijela.* Consequently, Note's bid for a third term was rejected on January 7, 2008, by the *Nitijela,* which elected its speaker, Litokwa TOMEING of the UPP, as Note's successor.

In early 2008 residents of Kwajalein Atoll temporarily rejected extension of a land-use agreement with the U.S. Defense Department for the Reagan test site, insisting that they be given $19 million in annual rent rather than the $15 million offered by the Pentagon. The dispute prompted a split between President Tomeing, who favored conciliatory talks with Washington over the issue, and his influential foreign minister, Tony DeBRUM, who, as a legislator from Kwajalein, called for a confrontational posture. Faced with the potential loss of a confidence vote, Tomeing expelled DeBrum from the cabinet in February 2009 and took the unusual approach of bringing five opposition members into a drastically reshuffled cabinet. As a result of the complicated dispute, Tomeing was ousted by a nonconfidence vote of 17–15 in the House of Representatives on October 21, as several AKA legislators supported his removal. Five days later, the AKA's Jurelang ZEDKAIA was elected president by a two-vote margin over Note. His subsequent cabinet retained many of the previous members.

The Kwajalein dispute was finally resolved in May 2011, when the landowners accepted the initial offer of $15 million per year, bolstered by an escrow account that had grown to an additional $32 million. The agreement provided for 50 more years of U.S. use of the missile range.

President Zedkaia and his supporters (now reportedly aligned as the Our Government [*Kein Eo Am*—KEA] political grouping) were unable to gain a legislative majority in the November 21, 2011, balloting for the House of Representatives. Consequently, with the support of Note's UDP and independents, Christopher J. LOEAK of the rump AKA was elected president by a vote of 21–11 in the *Nitijela* on January 2, 2012.

In legislative balloting on November 16, 2015, 14 new senators were elected, and a new reformist bloc, the "Solid Eight," group of 8 senators held the balance of power in the legislative. On January 4, 2016, the legislature elected Casten NEMRA as president on a vote of 17–16. He was removed from office following a no-confidence vote of 21–12 on January 26. The following day, Hilda HEINE was elected with 24 votes and 6 abstentions. She was the first woman president of the country.

Constitution and government. The 1979 constitution provides for a bicameral parliament whose popularly elected lower house, the *Nitijela,* performs most legislative functions. The 33-member *Nitijela* selects from its own ranks an executive president, who serves for the duration of the four-year parliamentary term, assuming the retention of parliamentary support. The upper house is a council of 12 traditional chiefs who make recommendations with regard to customary law and practice. Municipalities are governed by elected mayors and councils, while villages follow traditional forms of rule.

The judicial system encompasses a Supreme Court (comprising three part-time justices resident in the United States); a High Court, which presides over District and Community Courts; and a Traditional Rights Court, which deals primarily with land and customary title disputes. The latter, inactive for many years, was revived in mid-2010 with a number of new government appointments.

Foreign relations. The effective degree of the RMI's autonomy in foreign affairs is not entirely clear. In early 1987 the *Nitijela* debated whether to endorse the Treaty of Rarotonga, which called for the establishment of a South Pacific Nuclear Free Zone. However, unlike the Federated States of Micronesia (see entry on Federated States of Micronesia), the RMI decided not to take action in the matter after a Washington official had termed adherence to the treaty "inappropriate" given the U.S. obligation under the Compact of Free Association to defend the Marshalls, coupled with the U.S. decision not to sign the document.

In December 1990 the UN Security Council formally abrogated the U.S. Trusteeship in respect to the Marshall Islands, the Federated States of Micronesia, and the Commonwealth of the Northern Marianas, and in September 1991 both the FSM and the Marshalls were admitted to the United Nations. In May 1992 the Marshalls became the 161st member of the IMF and the 157th member of the World Bank. Regionally, the RMI belongs to the Asian Development Bank, the Pacific Community, and the Pacific Islands Forum.

In 1998 the Marshalls established diplomatic relations with Taiwan, hoping thereby to attract both trade and investment. Already linked to the People's Republic of China, the RMI government hoped that a "two-Chinas" policy might be possible; however, China, saying that the Marshalls "must correct their mistake," severed relations three weeks later.

In April 2006 the RMI government supported a lawsuit by residents of Bikini against the United States for nonpayment of approximately $560 million of a 2000 award and $150 million of a 2001 award by the Marshall Islands Nuclear Claims Tribunal (NCT). The NCT had been allocated $150 million by the 1986 Compact to pay for claims associated with the 67 tests of nuclear weapons conducted by the United States from1946–1958. Following the disbursement of the original funds, however, no money was available to cover the new awards. In April 2010 the U.S. Supreme Court rejected a petition from the RMI plaintiffs to review a lower court decision that the 1986 payments were final and that no additional funds were legally required.

In recent years the RMI has joined a number of its low-lying neighbors in warning of the consequences of an anticipated rise in sea levels because of global warming. In the years after the global meeting on climate change in Copenhagen in 2009, the RMI complained that very little of the $45 billion pledged at the meeting had been given to the Marshall Islands and other low-lying countries that needed it.

The new government installed in 2012 argued that the RMI was losing development assistance because of its close alignment with the United States in the UN. Among other things, RMI officials said they had lost aid from Arab states because of the RMI's adherence to the U.S. stance on UN votes concerning Israel. The RMI also continued to press the United States for additional compensation in regard to the Nuclear Claims Tribunal. In that vein, a special UN rapporteur concluded in 2013 that "durable solutions" to the dislocation of the island inhabitants by the U.S. nuclear tests have not yet been found.

In April 2014 the RMI filed a suit against the United States in a U.S. federal court arguing that the United States had failed to negotiate in good faith regarding nuclear disarmament as required by the 1958 Nuclear Non-Proliferation Treaty. Concurrently, the RMI filed a similar suit at the International Court of Justice (ICJ) against the United States and eight other nuclear powers, urging that comprehensive nuclear disarmament tests begin by 2015. The case was later reduced to include only India, Pakistan, and the United Kingdom. In October 2016 the ICJ ruled that it had no jurisdiction in the matter and dismissed the case.

Current issues. The run-up to the November 2011 legislative poll was complicated by an apparent split within the AKA and the emergence of the new pro-Zedkaia KEA. President Zedkaia and his supporters pledged to continue recent government economic initiatives and to protect islanders' access to the United States in the face of proposed new restrictions. (Several members of the U.S. Congress had recently called for limitations to be imposed on the visa-free system because of the increasing expenses being borne by U.S. states in assisting RMI immigrants.) Meanwhile, the rump AKA (at that point the leading opposition group) called for improved educational services and intensified cooperation between the government and the business sector. Following the election of Christopher Loeak, a traditional chief and longtime senator, as the nation's new president in January 2012, Zedkaia initially promised that he and his allies would cooperate with the new administration, which included Tony DeBrum as an influential assistant to the president.

In 2013 the RMI government argued that low-lying countries faced "oblivion" as the result of global warming. President Loeak was subsequently delegated by regional leaders to present a declaration to the UN calling on developed countries to sign a new treaty on carbon emissions by 2015 and to provide greater assistance in dealing with the major problems that have already been created by rising sea levels.

In a strange and largely unexplained initiative, Foreign Minister Phillip MULLER in December 2013 reportedly appointed a former Lebanese security chief as the RMI's ambassador to the UN Educational, Scientific, and Cultural Organization (UNESCO). The appointment was rescinded in February 2014 when it was revealed that it would have provided diplomatic immunity for the new UNESCO ambassador, who had been investigated in connection with the assassination of former Lebanese prime minister Rafiq al-Hariri in 2006. The controversy apparently influenced a cabinet reshuffle in early March in which Muller was named health minister and DeBrum was appointed as the new foreign affairs minister. However, the opposition, led by former president Zedkaia, continued to question the motives behind the star-crossed appointment, arguing that, among other things, it might further fray relations with the United States. The government survived a nonconfidence motion on the matter in mid-March by a vote of 17–13.

A severe drought prompted a national state of emergency in March 2016 and a declaration of emergency by the United States in April. The drought resulted in shortages of drinking water and water for sanitary purposes. In response, the Asian Development Bank provided the RMI with a $200,000 grant, while the U.S. government provided various types of material aid.

POLITICAL GROUPS

Although there are no legal restrictions against the organization of political parties, traditionally there have been no formal parties in the Marshalls. In the 1991 legislative balloting, however, an Our Islands "presidential caucus" chaired by Amata Kabua defeated a **Ralik-Ratak Democratic Party** organized by Tony DeBrum, a former Kabua protégé. Several other groups have also recently emerged, although their structures and formal memberships remain amorphous and fluid.

Our Islands (*Ailon Kein Ad*—AKA). An outgrowth of the earlier Our Islands caucus, the AKA was formally launched in 2002. It contested the November 2007 legislative elections in coalition with the **United People's Party** (UPP), a conservative grouping to which Litokwa Tomeing of the UDP (below) had recently defected. After several successful independent legislative candidates announced their support for the AKA/UPP coalition, Tomeing, a traditional chief, was elected president of the republic in January 2008. However, following a split between Tomeing and influential AKA leader Tony DeBrum in 2008–2009 (see Political background, above), many AKA legislators supported the nonconfidence motion that ousted Tomeing in October 2009. Tomeing's successor, Jurelang Zedkaia, was also referenced as a member of the AKA, but shortly before the 2011 legislative balloting Tomeing and his supporters launched a new grouping (see KEA, below). The rump AKA (for a short time considered an opposition grouping following the formation of the KEA) was credited by some sources with securing approximately 11 legislative seats in the November poll. The AKA subsequently reached an agreement with the UDP that led to the election of the AKA's Christopher Loeak in January 2012 as president of the republic. Loeak left office in January 2016, and the AKA supported the election of Casten NEMRA on January 4. Nemra won a narrow vote and took office on January 11, but was forced to resign after losing a vote of no-confidence on January 26, following the defection of AKA supporters.

Leaders: Christopher LOEAK, Michael KABUA, Tony DeBRUM.

United Democratic Party (UDP). The main opposition grouping prior to the legislative poll of November 1999, the UDP supported the successful presidential candidacy of Kessai Note in 2000 and his reelection in 2004. The UDP was credited with controlling 13–15 seats following the 2007 balloting for the House of Representatives.

In January 2008 Note lost his bid for a third presidential term by a vote of 18–15 in the *Nitijela* to Litokwa Tomeing, a protégé of Note's who had left the UDP to join the UPP (see AKA, above) shortly before the 2007 legislative poll. After Tomeing was deposed by a nonconfidence vote in

October 2009, Note reportedly attempted to secure enough parliamentary support for his own candidacy to return to the presidency. When that effort failed, some of the UDP legislators reportedly endorsed the successful candidacy of the AKA's Jurelang Zedkaia, although Note's relationship with the Zedkaia administration subsequently remained distant.

Note and his UDP supporters reportedly secured control of approximately five seats in the November 2011 legislative poll and subsequently formed an anti-Zedkaia alliance with the rump AKA in support of the successful presidential candidacy of the AKA's Christopher Loeak in January 2012. Consequently, Note allies were appointed to several key positions in the new cabinet.

Leaders: Kessai H. NOTE, Donald F. CAPELLE.

Our Government (*Kien Eo Am*—KEA). The KEA was reportedly formed in October 2011 by supporters of President Zedkaia and other legislators and cabinet members (including Alvin Jacklick, then speaker of the House of Representatives) who had apparently separated from the AKA. Initial reports credited the KEA and its supporters with gaining control of approximately 15 seats (including seats for Zedkaia and Jacklick) in the House of Representatives in the November poll, but Zedkaia earned only 11 (out of 32) votes in his unsuccessful bid to retain the presidency in January 2012. It was subsequently unclear if the KEA would continue to function as a political grouping, although Zedkaia and Jacklick as of mid-2014 remained leaders of the legislative opposition. The KEA backed the election of Hilda HEINE as president in January 2016.

Leaders: Jurelang ZEDKAIA, Alvin JACKLICK, Litowka TOMEING.

LEGISLATURE

Technically, a bicameral system prevails, although only the lower house, the *Nitijela,* engages in normal legislative activity.

Council of Chiefs (Council of *Iroij*). The council is composed of 12 traditional leaders who tender advice on matters affecting customary law and practice.

Chair: Iroij Kotak LOEAK.

House of Representatives (*Nitijela*). The *Nitijela* comprises 33 members (called senators) directly elected on a majoritarian basis for four-year terms from 24 electoral districts (19 single-member, 5 multi-member). Initial reports on the most recent balloting on November 16, 2015, credited Our Islands and its allies with as many as 23 seats. However, a coalition of eight senators, including Our Government supporters and independents, formed a swing bloc that held the balance of power as alliances shifted between Our Government and Our Islands. (Affiliations with political groupings are very loose, and election results should be considered imprecise.)

Speaker: Kenneth KEDI.

CABINET

[as of September 15, 2016]

President	Hilda C. Heine
Ministers	
Assistance to the President	Mattlan Zackhras
Education	Wilbur Heine
Finance	Brenson S. Wase
Foreign Affairs	John M. Silk
Health	Kalani Kaneko
Internal Affairs	Amenta Matthew [f]
Justice	Thomas Heine
Public Works	Tony Muller
Resources and Development	Alfred Alfred Jr.
Transportation and Communication	Mike Halferty

[f] = female

INTERGOVERNMENTAL REPRESENTATION

Ambassador to the U.S.: Gerald ZACKIOS.

U.S. Ambassador to the Marshall Islands: Karen Brevard STEWART.

Permanent Representative to the UN: Amatlain Elizabeth KABUA.

IGO Memberships (Non-UN): ADB, ICC, PIF.

For Further Reference:

Barnett, Jon, and Elissa Waters. "Rethinking the Vulnerability of Small Island States: Climate Change and Development in the Pacific Islands." In *The Palgrave Handbook of International Development*, edited by Jean Grugel and Daniel Hammett. New York: Palgrave Macmillan, 2016.

Crate, Susan A., and Mark Nuttall. *Anthropology and Climate Change: From Actions to Transformations*. New York: Routledge, 2016.

Levine, Stephen, ed. *Pacific Ways: Government and Politics in the Pacific Islands*. Melbourne: Victoria University Press, 2016.

MAURITANIA

Islamic Republic of Mauritania
al-Jumhuriyah al-Islamiyah al-Muritaniyah

Political Status: Independent republic since November 28, 1960; 1961 constitution suspended by the Military Committee for National Recovery on July 20, 1978; present constitution, providing for multiparty civilian government, approved by referendum July 12, 1991; constitution suspended by the High Council of State following bloodless coup on August 6, 2008; multiparty civilian government restored following presidential election on July 18, 2009.

Area: 397,953 sq. mi. (1,030,700 sq. km).

Population: 4,167,000 (2016E—UN); 3,617,000 (2016E—U.S. Census).

Major Urban Center (2015E—UN): NOUAKCHOTT (968,000). In recent years the population of Nouakchott has grown rapidly, as many former nomads have taken up permanent residence in the capital since the 1970s.

Official Language: Arabic. (Three languages of the Black African community—Poular, Soninke, and Wolof—are constitutionally designated as national languages. French, an official language until 1991, is still widely spoken, particularly in the commercial sector. Since 1999 the government has designated French as the "language for science and technical subjects" in Mauritanian schools.)

Monetary Unit: Ouguiya (official rate October 1, 2016: 357.52 ouguiyas = $1US).

President: Gen. Mohamed Ould ABDELAZIZ (Union for the Republic), reelected on June 21, 2014, for a five-year term, elected for a five-year term in multiparty balloting on July 18, 2009, to succeed acting president Ba Mamadou MBARÉ, who had acceded from Senate president on April 15 following Abdelaziz's resignation the same day as chair of the High Council of State; inaugurated on August 5, 2009.

Prime Minister: Yahya Ould HADEMINE appointed on August 21, 2014, to succeed Moulaye Ould Mohamed LAGHDAF, appointed by the chair of the High Council of State on August 14, 2008, to succeed Yahya Ould Ahmed el-WAGHF (National Pact for Development and Democracy), who was ousted in the bloodless coup on August 6; named new government on August 31; reinstated with new transitional government on June 26, 2009; reappointed by the president on August 6, 2009, and formed new government on August 11; reappointed by the president on February 3, 2014.

THE COUNTRY

Situated on the western bulge of Africa, Mauritania is a sparsely populated, predominantly desert country, overwhelmingly Muslim and, except in the south, Arabic in language. The dominant Beydane (Arabic for "white") Moors, descendants of northern Arabs and Berbers, have

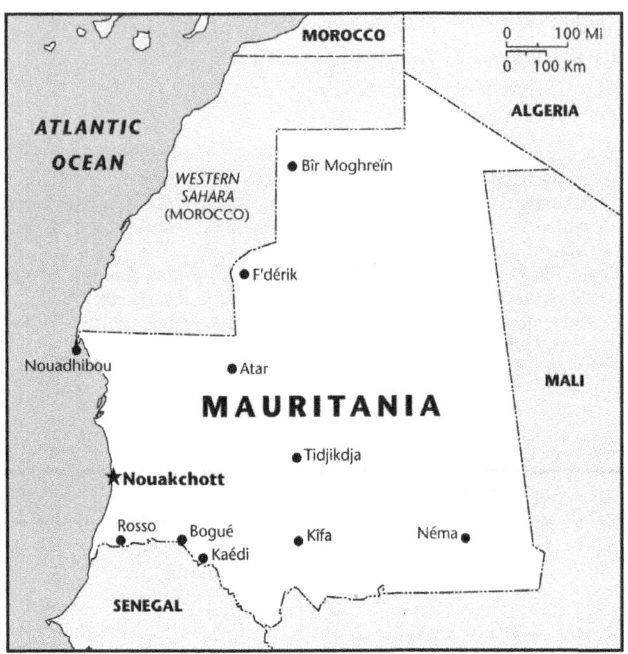

been estimated as constituting one-third of the population, with an equal number of Haratines (mixed-race descendants of black slaves) having adopted Berber customs. Black Africans, the most important tribal groups of which are the Toucouleur, the Fulani, the Sarakole, and the Wolof, are concentrated in the rich alluvial farming lands of the Senegal River valley. They have recently claimed to account for a much larger population share than is officially acknowledged, their case being supported by the government's refusal to release pertinent portions of the last two censuses. Racial tension, exacerbated by government "arabization" efforts, has contributed to internal unrest and conflict with several neighboring nations. Further complicating matters has been the de facto continuation of slavery, officially banned in 1981 but still reportedly encompassing 4 percent of the population, an estimated 100,000–400,000 Haratines and blacks in servitude to Arab masters.

Before 1970 nearly all of the northern population was engaged in nomadic cattle raising, but the proportion had shrunk to less than one-quarter by 1986. Prolonged droughts, desertification, the loss of herds, and a devastating locust attack in 2004 that destroyed about half of the country's crops, have driven more Mauritanians to urban areas, where many depend on foreign relief aid. Many Mauritanians seek their livelihood in other countries.

The country's first deep water port, financed by China, opened near Nouakchott in 1986. Mauritania's coastal waters are among the richest fishing grounds in the world and generate more than half of its foreign exchange, although the region is also routinely fished by foreign trawlers.

To secure aid from international donors, the government initiated numerous economic reforms, including privatization of state-owned enterprises, promotion of free market activity, and currency devaluation. The government also endorsed political liberalization, although genuine progress in that regard has been minimal, while international lenders called for measures to address the unequal distribution of wealth. More than 50 percent of the population lives in poverty, and the social services sector is considered grossly inadequate.

In 2002 the International Monetary Fund (IMF) and the World Bank announced debt relief of $1.1 billion for Mauritania. In 2003 exploratory tests indicated the presence of offshore oil fields, prompting investments from international oil companies. Annual GDP growth remained stable at an average of 5.2 percent in 2003–2005. Further, following the military coup in August 2005 and the transitional government's reforms, there was a significant decline in inflation. The exportation of crude oil began in 2006, with daily production reportedly averaging 54,000 barrels per day, contributing to robust annual growth of about 10 percent. Growth contracted to 3.7 percent in 2008, and then dipped to –1 percent in 2009, owing in large part to a decrease in donor revenue due to a perceived lack of progress in restoring democracy after the August 2008 coup, followed by the global financial crisis, which had a negative impact on food and fuel prices. Additionally, iron and oil prices declined sharply, key investors pulled out of plans to privatize the country's largest mining company, and the government instituted price controls on food and fuel. Following the multiparty presidential election in 2009, the World Bank restored some $14 million to improve infrastructure. GDP growth expanded to 4.6 percent in 2010. On another positive note, the IMF agreed to contribute $118 million through 2012 to support development for the poorest segment of the population, while the government began instituting reforms in the energy sector and efforts to bolster the non-oil sector. Despite robust annual GDP growth averaging 5.6 percent for 2011–2012, the IMF noted that high unemployment and widespread poverty remained "serious challenges." On the heels of a 2011 drought, a rebound in agricultural production and a pickup in the building and public works sector drove strong economic recovery in 2012, as GDP grew by 7 percent. In 2013 GDP expanded by 6.7 percent, and in 2014 by 6.5 percent, slowing to 1.9 percent in 2015, with an estimated 4 percent growth for 2016. Meanwhile, inflation declined to 4.1 percent in 2013 and 3.4 percent in 2014, bottoming out at less than 1 percent in 2015 before rising to an estimated 3.8 percent in 2016. GDP per capita for 2016 rose to $1,577.

The government reported in 2014 that it had produced 6 million barrels of oil in 2015, an improvement over 2.45 million in 2013. Citing improvements in corruption and infrastructure, the World Bank rated Mauritania as 168th out of 189 countries in its 2016 annual report on the ease of doing business index.

GOVERNMENT AND POLITICS

Political background. Under nominal French administration from the turn of the century, Mauritania became a French colony in 1920, but de facto control was not established until 1934. It became an autonomous republic within the French Community in 1958 and an independent "Islamic Republic" on November 28, 1960. President Moktar OULD DADDAH (died October 14, 2003), who led the country to independence, established a one-party regime with predominantly Moorish backing and endorsed a policy of moderate socialism at home combined with nonalignment abroad. Opposition to his 18-year presidency was periodically voiced by northern groups seeking union with Morocco, inhabitants of the predominantly black south who feared Arab domination, and leftist elements in both student and trade union organizations.

Under an agreement concluded in November 1975 by Mauritania, Morocco, and Spain, the Ould Daddah regime assumed control of the southern third of Western (Spanish) Sahara on February 28, 1976, coincident with the withdrawal of Spanish forces and Morocco's occupation of the northern two-thirds (see map and discussion under entry for Morocco). However, an inability to contain Algerian-supported insurgents in the annexed territory contributed to the president's ouster in a bloodless coup on July 10, 1978, and the installation of Lt. Col. Mustapha OULD SALEK as head of state by a newly formed Military Committee for National Recovery (*Comité Militaire de Recouvrement National*—CMRN). Ould Salek, arguing that the struggle against the insurgents had "nearly destroyed" the Mauritanian economy, indicated that his government would be willing to withdraw from Tiris El-Gharbia (the Mauritanian sector of Western Sahara) if a settlement acceptable to Morocco, Algeria, and the insurgents could be found. However, the overture was rejected by Morocco, and in October the Algerian-backed Popular Front for the Liberation of Saguia el Hamra and Rio de Oro (Polisario) announced that the insurgency would cease only if Mauritania were to withdraw from the sector and recognize Polisario's government in exile, the Saharan Arab Democratic Republic (SADR).

In March 1979 Ould Salek reiterated his government's desire to extricate itself from the conflict but dismissed several CMRN members known to favor direct talks with Polisario. Subsequently, on April 6 he dissolved the CMRN in favor of a new Military Committee for National Salvation (*Comité Militaire de Salut National*—CMSN) and relinquished the office of prime minister to Lt. Col. Ahmed OULD BOUCEIF, who was immediately hailed as effective leader of the Nouakchott regime. On May 27, however, Ould Bouceif was killed in an airplane crash and was succeeded (following the interim incumbency of Lt. Col. Ahmed Salem OULD SIDI) by Lt. Col. Mohamed Khouna OULD HAIDALLA on May 31.

President Ould Salek was forced to resign on June 3, and the CMSN named Lt. Col. Mohamed Mahmoud Ould Ahmed LOULY as his replacement. Colonel Louly immediately declared his commitment to a cessation of hostilities and on August 5, after three days of talks in Algiers, concluded a peace agreement with Polisario representatives. While the pact did not entail recognition of the SADR, Mauritania formally renounced all claims to Tiris El-Gharbia and subsequently withdrew its troops from the territory, which was thereupon occupied by Moroccan forces and renamed Oued Eddahab.

On January 4, 1980, President Louly was replaced by Col. Ould Haidalla, who also continued to serve as chief of government. The following December Ould Haidalla announced that, as a first step toward restoration of democratic institutions, his largely military administration would be replaced by a civilian government headed by Sid Ahmad OULD BNEIJARA. Only one army officer was named to the cabinet announced on December 15, while the CMSN published a draft constitution four days later that proposed establishment of a multiparty system.

The move toward civilianization was abruptly halted on March 16, 1981, as the result of an attempted coup by a group of officers (who were allegedly backed by Morocco), and Prime Minister Ould Bneijara was replaced on April 26 by the army chief of staff, Col. Maaouya Ould Sidahmed TAYA. A further coup attempt, involving an effort to abduct President Ould Haidalla at Nouakchott airport on February 6, 1982, resulted in the arrest of Ould Bneijara and former president Ould Salek, both of whom were sentenced to ten-year prison terms by a special tribunal on March 5.

On March 8, 1984, in a major leadership reshuffle, Taya returned to his former military post, and the president reclaimed the prime ministry, to which was added the defense portfolio. The following December Ould Haidalla was ousted in a bloodless coup led by Colonel Taya, who assumed the titles of president, prime minister, and chair of the CMSN.

Amid increasingly vocal black opposition to Moorish domination, Colonel Taya announced plans in mid-1986 for a gradual return to democratic rule (see Constitution and government, below), and local councils were elected in the country's regional capitals in December. However, north-south friction persisted, with 3 Toucouleur officers being executed and some 40 others imprisoned for involvement in an alleged coup attempt in October 1987.

Although the Taya regime was subsequently charged with systematic repression of opponents, particularly southerners, elections were held for councils in the principal townships and rural districts in January 1988 and 1989, respectively. New elections to all the municipal councils, originally planned for late 1989 but postponed because of a violent dispute with Senegal (see Foreign relations, below), were held in December 1990. Meanwhile, racial tension remained high because of reports that security forces had imprisoned thousands of black army officers and government officials, several hundred of whom had allegedly been executed or tortured to death. Although the government claimed that the arrests had been made in connection with a coup plot, opponents charged that the regime was merely intensifying an already virulent antiblack campaign.

On April 15, 1991, Colonel Taya surprised observers by announcing that a referendum would be held soon on a new constitution, followed by multiparty presidential and legislative elections. The draft constitution was released on June 10 by the CMSN, approved by nearly 98 percent of voters in a national referendum on July 12, and formally entered into effect on July 21. Four days later the CMSN adopted legislation on the legalization of political parties, six of which were quickly recognized, including the regime-supportive Democratic and Social Republican Party (*Parti Républicain Démocratique et Social*—PRDS). On June 29 Colonel Taya declared a general amnesty for detainees held on state security charges, thereby somewhat mollifying black hostility.

In presidential balloting on January 24, 1992, Colonel Taya, as the PRDS nominee, was credited with winning 63 percent of the vote; his principal challenger, Ahmed OULD DADDAH, received 33 percent. Ould Daddah, the previously exiled brother of former president Moktar Ould Daddah, was supported by a number of the new political parties, including the influential Union of Democratic Forces (*Union des Forces Démocratiques*—UFD), which challenged the accuracy of the official election results.

On February 10, 1992, five opposition parties requested postponement of National Assembly elections scheduled for March 6 and 13 to avoid a repetition of what they claimed had been massive fraud in the presidential poll. Their appeal rejected, 6 of the 14 opposition groups, including the UFD, boycotted the balloting, in which the PRDS won an overwhelming majority of seats on a turnout of little more than a third of the electorate.

In indirect senatorial balloting on April 3 and 10, 1992, the participants were further reduced to the PRDS and the small Avante-Guard Party (*Parti Avant-Garde*—PAG). The PAG received none of the available seats, as contrasted with 36 for the PRDS and 17 for independents. On April 18, following Colonel Taya's inauguration as president, Taya yielded the office of prime minister to a young technocrat, Sidi Mohamed OULD BOUBACAR, who announced the formation of a new government on April 20.

In 1994 the government party won control of 172 of the 208 municipal councils (as compared to 19 for independents and 17 for the UFD), prompting opposition charges of extensive electoral fraud. The opposition also questioned the results of the April Senate replenishment, in which the PRDS won 16 of 17 seats. In September it was reported that President Taya had dropped his military title in pursuit of a more civilian image. At the same time, the government launched a crackdown on Islamic "agitators," fundamentalists having reportedly gained converts by providing much-needed social services in urban areas.

Taya dismissed Ould Boubacar on January 2, 1996, replacing him with Cheikh el Avia Ould Mohamed KHOUNA. The December 12, 1997, elections won President Taya another six-year term, with an official 90 percent of the vote, and named Mohamed Lemine Ould GUIG, an academician, as prime minister. The UFD and several other opposition parties boycotted the balloting in objection to the regime's failure to establish an independent electoral commission, among other things. Despite growing opposition, President Taya's PRDS maintained a firm grip on power, winning a majority of seats in the 1996 and 2001 National Assembly elections.

The Mauritanian cabinet underwent more than a dozen reshufflings between June 1997 and May 2003, prompting concerns about the stability of the government. On June 7, 2003, those concerns were validated when rebels stormed the presidential palace in a coup attempt that led to two days of fighting in the capital. After regaining power on June 9, President Taya began a crackdown on the Muslim extremists he blamed for the uprising. On July 7, 2003, Taya appointed Sighair OULD MBARECK as prime minister, replacing Khouna. Ould Mbareck was the first former slave to hold the position.

Four months later Taya was elected to his third term. His principal challenger, former president Ould Haidalla, who had assembled a coalition of prominent Islamists, Arab nationals, and reformers, won 18.7 percent of the vote. Ould Haidalla and several of his supporters were arrested and detained on the day before the election, then released, only to be arrested and released again the next day. International monitors were not permitted to observe the elections, which were labeled fraudulent by Taya's opponents.

In August and September 2004 government officials announced discovery of two more coup attempts, allegedly organized by former army officers Saleh OULD HANENA and Mohamed Cheikhna. Officials accused Libya and Burkina Faso of arming and financing the coup, charges the two countries denied.

In February 2005 Ould Haidalla was acquitted on charges relating to the 2003 and 2004 attempted coups. Four soldiers were found guilty and sentenced to life in prison. A bloodless coup was staged on August 3, 2005, when Taya was in Saudi Arabia attending the funeral of King Fahd. A group of security and army officers led by Col. Ely Ould Mohamed VALL established themselves as the ruling Military Council for Justice and Democracy (MCJD) with Vall as head of state. On August 5 the parliament was dissolved. Mbareck resigned as prime minister on August 7 and was immediately replaced by Ould Boubacar, ambassador to France, who resigned from the former ruling PRDS party on August 9. A new cabinet, described as consisting primarily of technocrats, was announced on August 10.

In keeping with their promise of a quick return to a civilian government, the leaders of the junta presented constitutional amendments in a national referendum in June 2006 that provided for new legislative and presidential elections. Balloting for the National Assembly was held on November 19 and December 3, while senate elections were held on January 21 and February 4, 2007. Many of the successful candidates in both houses were technically independents (see Current issues, below, for details), although a coalition of opponents of the Taya regime called the Coalition of Forces of Democratic Change (*Coalition des Forces des Changement Démocratique*—CFCD) secured 38 seats in assembly elections. Women held 18 percent of seats in the assembly and 16 percent of seats in the senate, close to the junta's goal of 20 percent participation by women.

Of the 20 candidates in first-round presidential balloting on March 11, 2007, only 8 ran under the banner of political parties. Sidi Mohamed Ould Cheikh ABDALLAHI ran as an independent, though he was considered by many to be representing the MCJD. However, among his backers was Gen. Mohamed Ould ABDELAZIZ, who had participated in the 2005 military coup that ousted Taya. Abdallahi won with 53 percent of the vote in a runoff election on March 25 (with the support of half of the first-round candidates), defeating Ahmed Ould Daddah of the Rally of Democratic Forces (*Rassemblement des Forces Démocratiques*—RFD), who garnered 47 percent. Abdallahi was sworn in on April 19, and on April 20 he appointed as prime minister Zeine Ould ZEIDANE, the former head of the Central Bank who had finished third in the first round of presidential balloting. The new government formed on April 28 reportedly was made up largely of technocrats and at least four members of the Popular Progressive Alliance (*Alliance Populaire et Progressive*—APP).

In January 2008 independents and supporters of Abdallahi from small political parties formed the National Pact for Development and Democracy (*Pacte National pour le Développment et le Démocratie*—PNDD), which subsequently became the governing party. On May 6, 2008, Abdallahi replaced Zeidance as prime minister, appointing the PNDD's Yahya Ould Ahmed el-WAGHF, and on May 11 el-Waghf reshuffled the cabinet. Though dominated by the PNDD, the cabinet included for the first time a small number of opposition party representatives as well as the National Rally for Reform and Development (*Rassemblement Nationale pour la Réforme* et *le Développement*—RNRD), described as a moderate Islamist party. El-Waghf resigned along with the entire cabinet on July 3 in advance of a proposed no-confidence vote by parliament, but he was immediately reappointed by the president. A new, expanded cabinet, consisting entirely of PNDD members, was named on July 15.

On August 6, 2008, Abdallahi was deposed in a bloodless coup led by Gen. Abdelaziz, the head of the Presidential Guard, who formed an 11-member High Council of State. Abdallahi, el-Waghf, and the minister of the interior were arrested (all of whom were subsequently released). On August 14 Abdelaziz appointed Moulaye Ould Mohamed LAGHDAF, a diplomat, as prime minister. Laghdaf formed a new government on August 31, retaining four ministers from the previous government. On April 15, 2009, Ba Mamadou MBARÉ, the president of the Senate, became interim head of government, following the resignation of Abdelaziz, who stepped down to contest the presidential elections that had been set for June 6. Abdelaziz and his supporters subsequently formed a new party, styled as the Union for the Republic (*Union pour la République*—UPR), comprising pro-junta parliamentarians, including many from the former governing PNDD. Opposition parties threatened to boycott the balloting amid claims that junta leaders had ensured Abdelaziz's election, since all candidates approved by the Constitutional Court were reportedly pro-junta. Mediation by Senegalese officials in mid-July ended a series of street protests by the opposition coalition National Front for the Defense of Democracy (*Avant National pour la Défense de la Démocratie*—FNDD) and averted a boycott, with both sides agreeing on a new election date of July 18, and a provision for the formal resignation of Abdallahi. Abdallahi officially resigned on June 27, one day after naming a transitional unity government with Laghdaf as prime minister. The new government retained 13 ministers and added 13 ministers from the opposition.

In presidential balloting on July 18, 2009, Abdelaziz secured 52.6 percent of the vote to defeat nine other candidates. Speaker of parliament and APP leader Massaoud Ould Boulkheir, running as the candidate of the FNDD, finished a distant second, with 16.3 percent. The RFD's Ahmed Ould Daddah, who had backed Abdallahi in the 2007 election, was third, with 13.7 percent. None of the remaining candidates received more than 4.8 percent of the vote. Though the opposition immediately lodged complaints of vote rigging, international observers declared the elections free and fair. Prime Minister Laghdaf was reappointed on August 6, and his new government, formed on August 11, was comprised chiefly of Abdelaziz loyalists from the new UPR. Notable among cabinet members was Naha Mint MOUKNASS, president of the Union for Democracy and Progress (*Union pour la Démocratie et le Progrès*—UDP). Mouknass, who previously had strong ties to the Taya regime, was tapped as Mauritania's first female foreign minister. In the Senate replenishment on November 8 and 15, the UPR and its allies won 14 of the 18 seats. The RNRD, previously aligned with the FNDD, formed a parliamentary alliance with the UPR after the opposition failed to win the 3 seats required to form its own parliamentary group.

President Abdelaziz reshuffled the cabinet on March 31, 2010, and three ministers were dismissed on December 16.

The cabinet was reshuffled on February 12, 2011, and Foreign Affairs Minister Naha Mint Mouknass resigned on March 23 and was replaced by the minister of defense, with other changes following (see Current issues, below). The cabinet underwent a minor reshuffle in April 2013, and a more significant one in September, ahead of Chamber balloting.

The first round of parliamentary elections were held on November 23, 2013, and a second round on December 21. The elections solidified the position of the ruling UPR, earning them 75 seats in the 146-seat National Assembly. UPR Coalition partners took an additional 34 seats. The opposition largely boycotted the elections; however, the RNRD participated, earning 12 seats in the Assembly.

On February 2, 2014, the prime minister and cabinet resigned, but the president reappointed Laghdaf as the head of a reshuffled cabinet, the next day. In presidential balloting on June 21, Abdelaziz was overwhelmingly reelected. The cabinet was reorganized in January, May, and September 2015. A further reorganization took place on February 9, 2016, when the foreign minister was replaced and the ministries of economic affairs and finance were combined.

Constitution and government. The constitution of May 23, 1961, which had replaced Mauritania's former parliamentary-type government with a one-party presidential system, was formally suspended by the CMRN on July 20, 1978. A Constitutional Charter issued by the Military Committee confirmed the dissolution of the National Assembly and the Mauritanian People's Party (*Parti du Peuple Mauritanien*—PPM) and authorized the installation of the committee's chair as head of state until such time as "new democratic institutions are established."

In December 1980 the CMSN published a constitutional proposal that was to have been submitted to a referendum in 1981. However, no balloting was held prior to the coup of December 1984. Subsequently, Colonel Taya indicated that the military would prepare for a return to democracy through a program called the Structure for the Education of the Masses that would involve the election of councilors at the local level to advise the government on measures to improve literacy, social integration, and labor productivity. In the series of municipal elections conducted in 1986–1990, voters chose from multiple lists of candidates approved by the government, although no formal political party activity was permitted.

The 1991 constitution declared Mauritania to be an "Islamic Arab and African republic," guaranteed "freedom of association, thought, and expression," and conferred strong executive powers on the president, including the authority to appoint the prime minister. Directly elected by universal suffrage in two-round voting, the president was allowed to serve an unlimited number of six-year terms. The new basic law also established a bicameral legislature (comprising a directly elected National Assembly and an indirectly elected Senate), as well as constitutional, economic and social, and Islamic councils.

The legal system traditionally reflected a combination of French and Islamic codes, with the judiciary encompassing a Supreme Court; a High Court of Justice; courts of first instance; and civil, labor, and military courts. In June 1978 a commission was appointed to revise the system according to Islamic precepts, and in March 1980, a month after the replacement of "modern" codes by Islamic law (sharia), the CMSN established an Islamic Court consisting of a Muslim magistrate, two councilors, and two *ulemas* (interpreters of the Koran). Earlier, in October 1978, a special Court of State Security had been created. The 1991 constitution provided for an independent judiciary, with sharia serving as the "single source of law."

The Military Council for Justice and Democracy (MCJD), formed by the leaders of the August 2005 coup, maintained the 1991 constitution, supplementing it with a military council "charter" that stipulated the MCJD held power over the executive and legislative branches, dissolved the parliament, and gave the MCJD advisory power over the Constitutional Council. Constitutional amendments proposed by the transitional government were approved by 97 percent of voters in a June 25, 2006, limiting a president to two terms of five years each and setting a maximum age limit of 75 for a president, among other things.

The constitution was suspended by the military junta's High Council of State following the bloodless coup in August 2008. Constitutional order was restored after multiparty elections on July 18, 2009.

For administrative purposes the country is divided into 12 regions, plus the capital district of Nouakchott, and 32 departments; in addition, 208 urban and rural districts (areas populated by at least 500 inhabitants) were created in October 1988.

Freedom of the press is constitutionally guaranteed. In June 2013 Khira Mint CHEIKHANY became the first woman to head Mauritania's state television. In 2014 the media group Reporters Without Borders ranked Mauritania 60th out of 180 countries. For 2016 that number was upgraded to 48th out of 180 countries following a significant drop in crimes and reprisals against journalists.

Foreign relations. Mauritania has combined nonalignment in world affairs with membership in such groups as the Arab League (since 1973) and, as of 1989, the Arab Maghreb Union (AMU). Following independence, economic and cultural cooperation with France continued on the basis of agreements first negotiated in 1961 and renegotiated in 1973 to exclude special arrangements in monetary and military affairs. As a consequence, French military advisers were recalled and Mauritania withdrew from the Franc Zone, establishing its own currency. In late 1979 a limited number of French troops returned to ensure Mauritania's territorial integrity following Nouakchott's withdrawal from Western Sahara and the annexation of its sector by Morocco.

Mauritania's settlement with the Polisario Front was followed by restoration of diplomatic relations with Algeria, which had been severed upon Algiers' recognition of the Saharan Arab Democratic Republic (SADR) in 1976. During 1980–1982 Nouakchott maintained formal neutrality in Polisario's continuing confrontation with Morocco, withholding formal recognition of the SADR but criticizing Rabat's military efforts to retain control of the entire Western Sahara. In 1983 Colonel Ould Haidalla concluded a Maghreb Fraternity and Cooperation Treaty with Algeria and Tunisia that was implicitly directed against Rabat and Tripoli. On the other hand, declaring that the conflict in the Western Sahara had "poisoned the atmosphere," Colonel Taya subsequently attempted to return Mauritania to its traditional posture of regional neutralism. While still maintaining its "moral support" for the SADR, which it officially recognized in 1984, the Taya regime normalized relations with Morocco and Libya, thereby balancing growing ties with Algeria that included the signing of a border demarcation agreement in April 1986.

Relations with Senegal were tense after an April 1989 incident when violence erupted between villagers along the border, provoking race riots in both nations' capitals that reportedly caused the death of nearly 500 people and injury to more than 1,000. During the ensuing months an estimated 170,000–240,000 Mauritanian expatriates fled Senegal, while Mauritania reportedly expelled 70,000 Senegalese and 40,000 of its own black residents. Mauritania and Senegal severed diplomatic relations in August, with each country accusing the other of instigating further violence. Although the countries restored ties in April 1992 and the border was partially reopened the following November, tension continued as black Mauritanians charged they were being prevented from returning to Mauritania, and Senegal attributed widespread "banditry" along the border to the refugee situation. Despite several flare-ups, relations between the two countries improved after Senegal's president Abdoulaye Wade expressed his support for the Taya regime, following the 2003 coup attempt in Mauritania, and extradited a suspected coup plotter to Mauritania.

Mauritania has also had strained relations with Mali, whose black-dominated Traoré regime accused Nouakchott in the late 1980s of supporting antigovernment activity among its ethnically Berber Tuareg population. Following the resolution of the Tuareg situation in the mid-1990s, relations with Mali warmed.

Mauritania attracted an unusual amount of international attention because of its support for Iraq in the 1990–1991 Gulf crisis, causing Western donors to sharply curtail aid to Nouakchott. However, assistance was subsequently restored, apparently reflecting Western support for the Taya regime's strong antifundamentalist posture. The government distanced itself from Iraq, expelling Baghdad's ambassador in October 1995 amid reports of a coup plot among "pro-Baathist" elements. Among other things, the policy shift contributed to improved relations with Gulf Arab states.

In November 1995 Nouakchott announced plans to open an "interest" office in Tel Aviv as part of what was expected to be eventual restoration of full relations with Israel. The action was condemned by some hard-line Arab states, including Libya, which recalled its ambassador and discontinued all aid to Mauritania. However, Tunisian mediation in early 1997 helped restore relations between Mauritania and Tripoli. In late 1999 the Taya government completed the foreign policy reversal started in mid-decade by severing relations with Iraq and becoming only the third Arab state (after Egypt and Jordan) to establish full diplomatic relations with Israel.

French officials have been critical of Mauritania's human rights record, but relations between the two countries improved after France offered support to the Taya regime following the 2003 coup attempt.

The government has cooperated with the United States in several counterterrorism training programs beginning in 2003. Such programs target al-Qaida-affiliated groups operating in Mauritania and several neighboring countries. In a major decision, Mauritania announced in December that it was withdrawing from the Economic Community of West African States (ECOWAS); analysts suggested that Nouakchott had grown increasingly concerned over the possibility that the non-Francophone countries in ECOWAS would adopt a common currency to the detriment of the ouguiya. Subsequently, the Taya administration declared that it would focus on affairs in northern Africa, particularly through the proposed rejuvenation of the Arab Maghreb Union, rather than on its relations with its southern neighbors. (As a result, Nouakchott was described in 2000 as having informally accepted the premise that the Western Sahara would remain a province of Morocco.)

Regional tensions increased in August and September 2004 after President Taya accused Libya and Burkina Faso of arming renegade soldiers allegedly preparing to topple the Taya regime in two separate coup attempts. Both countries denied the accusations.

Following the August 2005 coup, Colonel Vall pledged to maintain Mauritania's relations with Israel. The African Union (AU) suspended Mauritania's membership the day after the coup but readmitted the country on April 10, 2007, following democratic elections.

In November 2007 Mauritania, Senegal, and the United Nations High Commissioner for Refugees (UNHCR) signed a tripartite agreement to initiate the return of thousands of black Mauritanian refugees.

After the bloodless coup in 2008, Algeria and Nigeria condemned the military takeover, while Libya expressed its support for the junta. Morocco and Senegal were reported to have "shown understanding," while a French minister canceled a planned visit in October after the junta refused to release the deposed president from house arrest. Relations were mended in late 2009, as France renewed cooperation with Mauritania in counterterrorism efforts, and the European Union (EU) restored aid that had been frozen in the aftermath of the coup. Algeria, Mali, Niger, and the United States also provided counterterrorism support in late 2009.

Mauritania and Israel severed ties in 2009 over the issue of Israel's recent retaliatory attacks against Palestinians in the Gaza Strip. Mauritania withdrew its ambassador from Israel, and Israel closed its embassy in Nouakchott on March 6 after the junta asked the ambassador to leave. Iran then stepped in to expand its ties with Mauritania, and in January 2010 President Abdelaziz made an official visit to Tehran.

Relations with Mali were strained in February 2010 when Mauritania withdrew its ambassador in the wake of Mali's agreement to a demand by al-Qaida in the Islamic Maghreb that it release four al-Qaida members in exchange for a French hostage. Meanwhile, France and Spain provided weapons and training for the Mauritanian army to further enhance its counterterrorism operations, and NATO pledged to back Mauritania in its fight against terrorism at its borders.

In August 2012 Mauritania agreed to provide troops to a 45,000-member rapid reaction military force, along with Algeria, Burkina Faso, and Niger, to fight Islamist militants in the region. In September Malian troops killed 16 Islamic clerics, including 9 Mauritanians, prompting denunciations by the Abdelaziz government. Human rights groups protested the election of Mauritania to the vice president's position on the UN Human Rights Council because of the continuation of slavery in the country.

In January 2013 China announced it would provide $260 million for development projects in Mauritania. Mauritania deployed 1,800 troops as part of an AU-led military force in Mali (see entry on Mali) in April. In addition, Mauritania allowed French forces to use the country to support its military operations in Mali. Meanwhile the fighting in Mali was reported to have produced more than 100,000 refugees who fled to Mauritania. Also in April Mauritania and Morocco signed 17 economic, cultural, and educational cooperation agreements. In August Mauritania and Niger finalized a defense cooperation accord.

At the AU Summit in Addis Ababa, Ethiopia, on January 30–31, 2014, Abdelaziz was elected as chair of the organization. Reports in 2014 indicated a growing number of insurgents were crossing the border from Mali and conducting raids into Mauritania. In response, the United States increased security assistance to Mauritania, including donating two surveillance airplanes worth $21 million. In May Mauritania signed the European Convention for Energy and Minerals and became an observer within the treaty regime. The accord was expected to increase cooperation between Mauritania and the EU in energy and mining.

Through 2016 the ongoing conflict in Mali (see the entry on Mali) continued to impact Mauritania. The UN estimated that 50,000 Malian refugees were in Mauritania, taxing local resources.

Clashes with drug smugglers and human traffickers also continued. In March two tons of cocaine were seized by authorities, while over a dozen traffickers from several countries were apprehended. In April President Abdelaziz visited Egypt to expand bilateral relations and add to agreements reached at a similar summit in 2006.

Current issues. Domestic discontent, spurred by rising food prices and allegations of corruption against President Sidi Mohamed Ould Cheikh Abdallahi and his wife, stirred unrest throughout early 2008. Abdallahi, who is Muslim, was criticized for using public money to build a mosque at the presidential compound, for seeking dialogue with Islamists allegedly linked to an al-Qaida affiliate in North Africa, and for releasing some Islamist prisoners. In addition, the administration was criticized for not representing the majority parties in parliament. In May Abdallahi replaced the government, naming Yahya Ould Ahmed el-Waghf, leader of the newly formed governing party PNDD, as prime minister and installing several ministers from the former Taya regime, as well as some opposition parties in the reshuffled cabinet. The RFD refused to participate in a unity government, party leader Ahmed Ould Daddah claiming that the opposition parties had essentially been invited to sign on to the president's political program. Within months, el-Waghf found himself facing the prospect of a no-confidence vote in parliament, initiated by disaffected PNDD members who opposed the new government appointments. El-Waghf resigned in July, along with the entire cabinet, but he was immediately reappointed by the president. The new cabinet, named within two weeks, comprised only members of the PNDD. Disaffection with Abdallahi and his perceived ineptitude in curbing high food prices, coupled with allegations of corruption against him, ultimately led 48 members of the PNDD to resign on August 4. Two days later, Abdallahi fired several members of his elite Presidential Guard, including its head, General Abdelaziz, who had backed Abdallahi in his bid for the presidency. Hours after the security staff were dismissed, Abdelaziz staged a bloodless coup, with soldiers surrounding the palace. Abdallahi, el-Waghf, and the interior minister were immediately placed under arrest. State-run radio and television were shut down, and the country was returned to military rule. Police dispersed, without violence, throngs of citizens outside the palace, and Abdelaziz took over as chair of an 11-member High Council of State. Despite Abdelaziz's pledge that he would hold elections at some unspecified date, the African Union (AU), the EU, the UN, and the United States immediately condemned the coup and called for a return to constitutional rule. Further, the United States announced it was suspending aid, and Mauritania's biggest bilateral donor, the French Agency for Development, suspended all non-emergency funding.

The interior minister and the former prime minister were released on August 11, 2008, but Abdallahi remained in custody. The following day the junta authorized laws granting its members the right to rule until such time as a presidential election could be organized. Mohamed Lemine Ould Guig, a former prime minister in the Taya regime, was named secretary general of the High Council of State. Two days later Abdelaziz named Moulaye Ould Mohamed Laghdaf as prime minister. Observers noted his choice of a former ambassador for prime minister and his anti-Islamist stance, not only in direct opposition to former president Abdallahi's inclinations, but also as elements that would appeal to the West, and the United States in particular. However, Washington refused to recognize the military government.

Laghdaf's new cabinet retained four key ministers—defense, justice, economy, and finance—and all ministers were reported to be from parties that supported the coup, including the RFD and the Islamist RNRD party led by Mohamed Jemil Ould Mansour. Meanwhile, members of the PNDD, APP, and UFP, as well as some civil societies, formed the opposition alliance FNDD in protest of the coup. The coup appeared to have the support of the majority of members of parliament, as more than two-thirds from both chambers signed a declaration praising the junta.

On September 2, 2008, the assembly named a council to try Abdallahi on charges of corruption and obstructing parliament. (An attempt by parliament before the coup to hold a special session to conduct the corruption probe had been blocked by Abdallahi.) The former president's supporters claimed that the allegations were a front that gave the military leaders an excuse to stage the coup. The assembly also launched an investigation of Abdallahi's wife, who was accused of stealing public funds. Meanwhile, it was reported that another former coup leader and associate of Abdelaziz, Col. Vall, had returned to Mauritania on September 1.

Turmoil continued on another front in 2008 as al-Qaida in the Islamic Maghreb denounced the coup and called for a "holy war" in Mauritania, claiming the junta leaders had been acting in concert with the "infidels" of Israel, the United States, and France. On September 15 al-Qaida militants killed 12 Mauritanian soldiers in what news reports said was an attempt by the terrorist group to avenge the coup. That same day the National Assembly voted to hold elections within 12 to 14 months. Meanwhile, General Abdelaziz vowed to crack down on al-Qaida.

In mid-September 2008 General Abdelaziz rejected an ultimatum by the AU that Mauritania restore constitutional order by October 6 and reinstate President Abdallahi or else face sanctions. A "democratic convention" scheduled for December was boycotted by the opposition, the FNDD saying that participation would be the equivalent of recognizing the junta. In January 2009 the junta announced that a presidential election would be held on June 6, Abdelaziz having announced earlier that he would not be a candidate. Meanwhile, Abdallahi, who had been released from custody—reportedly to avert EU sanctions—said he would accept the outcome of a new election only if the army abdicated authority and constitutional order was restored. Mass demonstrations protesting his release were reported, with Abdallahi claiming that the rallies were arranged by the junta, while some observers said public opinion was mixed.

The junta formed an independent electoral commission in March 2009 to supervise the upcoming presidential election. Further, Abdelaziz stepped down on April 15 in order to be eligible to contest the election, though earlier he had said he would not run. The following day Senate president Ba Mamadou MBARÊ moved into the position of interim head of government. Abdelaziz officially announced his presidential candidacy, as did Kane Hamidou Baba, who withdrew as vice president of the RFD in a rift over his support for the junta, and former prime minister Sighair Ould Mbareck, who ran as an independent. Opposition parties, under the umbrella FNDD, threatened to boycott the balloting, claiming that all the candidates were pro-junta. During pro-Abdallahi demonstrations in advance of the election, hundreds of protesters were reportedly beaten by police. The elections, originally scheduled for June, were postponed while efforts were under way to persuade opposition parties to participate. Subsequently, as tensions increased, Senegalese president Abdoulaye Wade helped avert a political crisis by mediating talks in Dakar between junta leaders and the chairs of the FNDD and the RFD. In early June an agreement was reached not only on a new election date of July 18, but also on the formation of a transitional unity government, with Laghdaf retained as prime minister and a cabinet that included equal numbers of opposition and government ministers. On June 27 Abdallahi, in accordance with the agreement reached in Senegal, officially resigned as president. At the end of the month, the AU dropped its sanctions against Mauritania, citing the junta's efforts to restore democracy. Meanwhile, former coup leader Col. Vall announced his candidacy. Vall, a cousin and former ally of Abdelaziz, condemned the most recent coup, saying it was "wrong and there was no reason for it." A month before the election, assembly speaker Massaoud Ould Boulkheir announced his candidacy under the banner of the opposition FNDD; a few days later, Mohamed Jemil Ould Mansour of the RNRD announced his candidacy, reportedly becoming the first Islamist to run for president. Other parties, including new ones formed ahead of the election, subsequently named candidates, bringing the field to ten. Colonel Vall ran as an independent, as did former prime minister Ould Mbareck. General Abdelaziz, for his part, campaigned under the banner of the UPR as "the candidate of the poor," pledging to lower food and fuel prices and provide greater access to health care. Meanwhile, three weeks before the election, al-Qaida of the Islamic Maghreb (AQIM) claimed responsibility for the killing of an American aid worker in Nouakchott, as observers began warning of Mauritania's becoming a "hotbed" for al-Qaida and jihadists. Nevertheless, there was no violence during the election, which General Abdelaziz won handily. Despite accusations of fraud from opposition candidates, and the resignation a few days later of the head of the electoral commission (who cited concerns about the validity of the results but lacked sufficient evidence to pursue them), General Abdelaziz's victory stood. Subsequently, the constitutional court confirmed the outcome. The new government formed by Prime Minister Laghdaf was comprised chiefly of presidential loyalists.

Domestic tensions heightened at the end of December, as thousands of people protested price hikes and the new government's "dictatorial policies." The protesters rallied under the umbrella of a new opposition coalition, the Coordination of Forces of Democratic Opposition (*Coordination des Forces Démocratique*—CFOD [see Political Parties, below]). In January 2010 the CFOD boycotted a government-sponsored political forum to discuss constitutional revisions and other democratic reforms. CFOD member parties claimed they had not been consulted in advance of the conference.

With legislative elections scheduled for October 1, 2011, in January the CFOD began efforts, driven by RFD leader Daddah and UFP president Mohammed Ould MAALOUD, to present a "formidable challenge" to the presidential party. The PNDD, however, agreed to work with the ruling party. Subsequently, civil unrest, which had begun in the Middle East and North Africa, prompted pro-reform demonstrations in Nouakchott against rising prices and security policies. The RNRD had urged government officials to take action to avoid unrest ahead of the protests that included HATEM and the UPSD, among other small parties. Another protest, which took place over two days in February in a town southeast of the capital, was halted by the police, and several people were arrested. A resurgence on the terrorism front occurred in February, when government forces killed AQIM militants linked to a suicide bomb plot, and Mali extradited an AQIM fighter suspected in another failed suicide bomb attack. Domestically, calls for reform increased, particularly among young people, as many formed a movement called February 25 Youth, defined more by social networking than by a political agenda. Their demands included the resignation of the prime minister, establishment of a coalition government of technocrats, and abolition of the Senate, among other things. They also had the support of other civil groups, including trade unions. Meanwhile, as unrest spread throughout North Africa and the Middle East, Mauritania's foreign minister, Naha Mint Mouknass, was dismissed in March, reportedly because of her close ties with Libyan leader Muammar Qadhafi, whose regime was under attack by rebels within the country. Mauritanian authorities subsequently seized land they had sold to Libya to build a hotel and called for a halt to the violence, much of it perpetrated by Qadhafi against the civilian population. Prime Minister Laghdaf, prompted in part by pressure from the RNRD, called on the youth movement to submit their demands and appoint a representative with whom the government could negotiate. Opposition parties scored another concession when elections scheduled for April 24 to renew one-third of the Senate were postponed indefinitely after the CFOD requested it. The coalition claimed that conditions did not exist for holding free and fair elections, alleging bribery of voters by the ruling party and use of state resources for partisan gain.

In May 2011 President Abdelaziz supported an initiative urged by rights groups to find the remains and mark the graves of black Mauritanians who disappeared during civil unrest since independence in 1960. In July, in the run-up to municipal and legislative elections scheduled for October, the government began revising the electoral rolls, though some observers said the lists did not include 200,000 refugees, mainly black Mauritanians, who had returned from Senegal and lacked proper identification. Subsequently, the UFP and the RFD said they would boycott the elections. Meanwhile, the RNRD said it would join the CFOD, but the APP dropped out, claiming too many differences with other member parties. On a positive note, the opposition coalition in July approved the president's national dialogue document, which included a recommendation for review of the electoral process and was aimed at promoting further talks between the president and the opposition.

In March 2012 Abdullah Senussi, chief of Libyan intelligence services under Qadhafi, was arrested at Nouakchott airport after flying in from Morocco with a fake passport and disguised as a Tuareg chieftain. In September authorities bowed to Libyan demands for his extradition in what was seen as a blow to the International Criminal Court, which wanted to try him for crimes against humanity.

On March 6, 2012, the legislature adopted constitutional amendments reinforcing its powers, prohibiting coups, and criminalizing slavery. A new seven-member national electoral authority was created on June 13. The basis for the National Independent Electoral Commission had been established in an October deal the government signed with four opposition parties, but which the CFOD refused to recognize.

On October 13, 2012, Abdelaziz was slightly wounded when troops opened fire on his presidential convoy. Officially the shooting was an accident, but reports indicate that it may have been an abortive coup attempt. On January 11, 2013, former interim president and current Senate President Mbaré died of natural causes in Paris.

In March the government established an agency to aid former slaves in their integration into society and to combat household slavery, reportedly still common throughout the country. The 2013 *Global Slavery Index* ranked Mauritania as the nation with the highest proportion of slaves in the world, with up to 20 percent of the population enslaved. In February 2014 Mauritania agreed to adopt a UN-sponsored plan to eradicate slavery. In 2015 new legislation set up special courts to investigate and prosecute slavery-related crimes. In May 2016 the new courts sentenced two slave traders to five-year prison terms. In a related decision, the national Supreme Court freed antislavery activist Biram Ould Dah Ould ABEID—who was also President Abdelaziz's strongest rival in the presidential elections—from prison after his arrest for unauthorized assembly (participating in an antislavery march) in January 2016.

The UPR won a majority in Chamber balloting in October and December 2013 and Laghdhaf was reappointed prime minister. The major opposition parties boycotted the polling, as they did the subsequent presidential balloting on June 21, 2014. Abdelaziz was reelected with 81.9 percent of the vote. Biram Dah ABEID, a prominent leader in the antislavery movement, placed second with 8.7 percent, followed by three other candidates. Abdelaziz reshuffled the cabinet on August 21 appointing Yahya Ould HADEMINE to replace longtime ally, Laghdaf.

Beginning on September 7, 2015, the government convened a week-long political meeting intended to generate dialogue between the political parties; however, the National Forum for Democracy and Unity (*Forum National pour la Démocratie et l'Unité*—FNDU) boycotted the event.

Senate elections had been planned for March 15, 2016, but were postponed after opposition parties, most notably the FNDU, refused to take part. President Abdelaziz continued to delay new elections for the Senate, threatening to dissolve the body completely. In return, the FNDU and other opposition parties were skeptical that Abdelaziz would actually relinquish power when his current term ends in 2019, particularly as the government has suggested that the constitution be changed to allow for a three-term presidency. Pending the resolution of the Senate issues, the next elections, those for the National Assembly, are scheduled for 2018.

POLITICAL PARTIES

Mauritania became a one-party state in 1964, when the **Mauritanian People's Party** (*Parti du Peuple Mauritanien*—PPM/ *Hizb al-Shah al-Muritani*) was assigned legal supremacy over all governmental organs. The PPM was dissolved following the coup of July 1978. Although partisan activity was not permitted, some candidates in municipal elections in 1986–1990 were linked to various informal groups.

The constitution approved in July 1991 guaranteed "freedom of association," and subsequent legislation established regulations for the legalization of political parties. Groups based on race or region were proscribed, while Islamic organizations were declared ineligible for registration on the ground that Islam belonged to "all the people" and could not be "claimed" by electoral bodies.

In view of the near-total dominance of the Democratic and Social Republican Party (PRDS) in national and municipal elections, legislation was adopted in late 2000 providing for a degree of proportional representation in the 2001 assembly balloting and concurrent local polls. It was also announced that all parties securing at least 1 percent of the votes in the municipal elections would receive government financing (based on their total vote) and that "equal access" to the state-controlled media would be provided to opposition parties. (For a history of party developments between the 2005 and 2008 coups, see the 2012 *Handbook*.)

Following the bloodless coup of 2008, the PNDD, APP, and UFP, as well as some civil societies, formed an alliance under the rubric **National Front for the Defense of Democracy** (*Avant National pour la Défense de la Démocratie*—FNDD) in opposition to the coup. It later included the RNRD, but that party dropped out after its leader was defeated in the 2009 presidential election.

Following a large rally in December 2009 to protest the Abdelaziz government, nine parties formed the **Coordination of Forces of Democratic Opposition** (*Coordination des Forces Démocratique*—CFOD) to promote democratic principles. The coalition, chaired by Massaoud Ould Boulkheir, included the UFP, the Alternative, the APP, the RFD, the PLEJ, and the PNDD, and three minor parties. Another opposition grouping, reportedly open only to parties represented in parliament, was formed about the same time by the RFD's Ahmed Ould Daddah. The CFOD was said by Boulkheir to be open to all parties.

Ahead of presidential balloting in June 2014, a coalition of opposition groups and civil society organizations, the **National Forum for Democracy and Unity** (*Forum National pour la Démocratie et l'Unité*—FNDU) called for a boycott of the balloting.

Governing Party:

Union for the Republic (*Union pour la République*—UPR). General Abdelaziz and members of parliament who supported the 2008 coup and the subsequent ruling High Council of State formed the UPR in April 2009 in the run-up to the presidential election. Many of the parliamentarians were from the former governing PNDD (below). In May 2009 it was widely reported that 83 of 151 legislators had joined the new party. Shortly thereafter, some 50 members of the RFD reportedly defected to the UPR after their party's vice president, Kane Hamidou Baba, announced his support for the junta. Abdelaziz resigned as head of state and as chair of the party in order to contest the presidential election. The party subsequently elected former defense minister Mohamed Mahmoud Ould Mohamed Lemine as chair in August.

In the 2013 Chamber balloting, the party secured 75 seats. Abdelaziz was reelected president of Mauritania on June 21, 2014. In March 2015 the party expelled five officials for violating the UPR's bylaws. Reports indicated that the expulsions were the result of disloyalty to the president.

Leaders: Gen. Mohamed Ould ABDELAZIZ (President of the Republic), Mohamed Mahmoud Ould Mohamed LEMINE (Chair), Mohamed Yhaya Ould HORMA (Vice President), Saleh Ould DEHMACH, Abah Ould SIDATI, Ali Ould Ahmed SALEM (Secretary General).

Other Legislative Parties:

Alliance for Justice and Democracy (*Alliance pour la Justice et la Démocratie*—AJD)—**Movement for Renovation** (*Mouvement pour la Rénové*—MR). The AJD was formed in 2000 by Massoud Ould Boulkheir, former leader of the outlawed Action for Change, and other AC dissidents. The AJD was officially recognized in 2001, primarily representing the Black African minority in southern Mauritania. It opposed the Taya regime on the issue of recognition of Israel, the AJD urging the government to cut all ties with Israel, and it appealed for a fair resolution to the problems of Mauritanian refugees in Senegal. Boulkheir was the AJD's presidential candidate in 2003.

The AJD boycotted the 2006 constitutional referendum, saying the proposed amendments did not adequately address the issue of slavery, among other things.

According to the *Africa Research Bulletin*, a leading figure in FLAM (see below), Ba Mamadou BOCAR, was elected AJD vice president in August 2007. The party was subsequently referenced as having merged with the MR and as having "integrated" FLAM–Renovation (see below). It was unclear what the latter association meant.

Ibrahima Moctar Sarr, a journalist, ran as an independent in the 2007 presidential balloting, receiving just under 8 percent of the vote; he supported Ould Daddah in the second round. In the 2009 presidential election, Sarr received 4.6 percent of the vote. The party won 4 seats in the 2013 balloting. Sarr ran again in the 2014 presidential election, placing fourth with 4.4 percent of the vote. In 2015 the AJD condemned any effort to change the constitution to allow the president a third term.

Leaders: Ibrahima Moctar SARR (President and 2007, 2008, 2009, and 2013 presidential candidate), Kebe ABDOULAYE, Alpha DIALLO, Cisse Amadou CHEIKH (Secretary General).

Republican Democratic Party for Renovation (*Parti Républicain Démocratique et Renouvellement*—PRDR). This party is a successor to the **Democratic and Social Republican Party** (*Parti Républicain Démocratique et Social*—PRDS). The PRDS was launched in support of President Taya by a longtime associate, Cheikh Sid Ahmed Ould BABA, who resigned from the cabinet and military in mid-1991 to concentrate on party politics. As the PRDS nominee, Taya won the January 1992 presidential poll by a substantial margin, and the PRDS assumed essentially unchallenged political control by winning large majorities in the subsequent elections for the National Assembly and the Senate, which were boycotted by most opposition groups. The party also dominated the municipal and senate balloting of early 1994.

In March 1995 the PRDS absorbed the MDI, led by Bechir el-HASSEN, which had left the UFD (above) in June 1994.

The party won 70 of 79 seats in the 1996 legislative balloting on its own right and also had the support of the seven independent legislators (some of whom were former PRDS members) and the RDU representative in the assembly. Taya was reelected as party leader in November 1999. The PRDS won 64 of 81 seats in the assembly in the 2001 balloting and 15 of 18 open seats in the April 2004 partial senate elections. In 2003 President Taya won his third term in office.

Following the August 3, 2005, coup, Colonel Vall named PRDS member Sidi Mohamed Ould Boubacar as prime minister, and Boubacar quit the party on August 9. Support for Taya, widely reported to be a repressive leader who imprisoned dissidents, particularly Islamists, had waned over the years, and his policy of engagement with Israel angered Arab nationalists, observers said. On September 19 the party took the further step of abolishing the chair that Taya had held for 15 years. In October the party held an extraordinary congress and reportedly changed its name to the Republican Democratic Party for Renovation. However, the actions of the congress were canceled in November by a Mauritanian court, which also ordered the party's assets seized pending the outcome of a dispute within the party over whether an audit should have been conducted during the congress. Further turmoil was evidenced when the party's Islamist wing, led by Abdou MAHAM, severed its ties the same month, reportedly to join the Rally for Democracy and Unity (*Rassemblement pour la Démocratie et l'Unité*—RDU). On November 25 the PRDS elected Ethmane Ould Cheikh Abou Ali Maali, Mauritania's ambassador to Kuwait, as president. The party further distanced itself from Taya by announcing its opposition to the diplomatic ties with Israel that the former president had established. In the 2006 parliamentary elections, the party won seven seats.

The party supported the 2008 coup, and Maali was appointed to the transitional unity government in mid-2009. He retained his cabinet post following the 2009 presidential election and the pursuant cabinet reshuffle but was subsequently dismissed from the government. In the 2013 Chamber elections, the party won three seats. In 2016 the party rejected a government initiative to open a dialogue with opposition parties, charging that the regime was seeking to divide its opponents.

Leaders: Ethmane Ould Cheikh Abou Ali MAALI (President and 2007 presidential candidate), Cheikh El Avia Ould Mohamed KHOUNA (Former Prime Minister), Rachid Ould SALEH (Former Speaker of the National Assembly), Sidi Mohamed Ould Mohamed VALL (Secretary General).

National Rally for Reform and Development (*Rassemblement Nationale pour la Réforme* et *le Développement*—RNRD). A moderate Islamist party, the RNRD, also referenced as *Tawassoul*, gained legal status in 2007. Among its leaders is Zainab bint DADEH, a former Baath party member. More recently, the party is described as one that promotes "democratic Islam." In May 2008 the party accepted a cabinet post in the government of Prime Minister Yahya Ould Ahmed el-Waghf. Following the August coup, the party joined the opposition FNDD coalition in 2009. After his defeat in the 2009 presidential election, party leader Mohamed Mansour dropped out of the FNDD, and in the wake of the opposition's failure to win any seats in the Senate replenishment in November (the RNRD blaming corruption), the party joined a legislative alliance with the governing UPR. The party is affiliated with the Muslim Brotherhood.

In mid-2011 the RNRD agreed to join the opposition coalition CFOD. Unlike other major opposition parties, the RNRD campaigned in the 2013 Chamber elections, winning 16 seats. The party boycotted the 2014 presidential election.

Leaders: Mohamed Jemil Ould MANSOUR (Chair and 2009 presidential candidate), Zainab bint DADEH, Ahmed Ould WEDIA.

Due to the opposition boycott of the balloting, a number of minor parties won seats in the 2013 balloting, including the **Party of the Democratic and Social Agreement** (*Parti de l'Entente Démocratique et Sociale*—PEDS), led by Boïdiel Ould HOUMEIT, who placed third in the 2014 presidential balloting (10 seats); ***El Karam***, led by Cheikhna Ould Mohamed Ould HAJBOU (6); **Burst of Youth for the Nation** (*Parti du Sursaut de la Jeunesse pour la Nation*—PSJN), led by Lalla CHERIVA (4); **Virtue** (*El Vadilla*), led by Ethmane Ould Ahmed ABOULMAALY (3); **Party of Unity and Development** (*Parti de l'Unité et du Développement*—PUD), led by Mohamed BARO (3); *Ravah* Party, led by Mohamed Ould VALL (3); the **Democratic Justice Party** (*Parti de la Justice Démocratique*—PJD) (2); the **Party of**

Mauritanian Authenticity (*Parti de l'Authenticité Mauritanienne*—PAM), led by Mohamed Mahmoud EL GHARACHI (1); **Socialist Democratic Unionist Party** (*Parti Unioniste Démocratique et Socialiste*—PUDS), led by Mahfouz Weld AL-AZIZ (1); **The Reform** (*El Islah*), led by Sidna Ould MAHAM (1); the **Party of Democratic People** (*Parti du Peuple Démocratique*—PPD) (1); and the **Dignity and Action Party** (*Parti Dignité et Action*—PDA) (1).

Other Parties That Contested Recent Elections:

National Pact for Development and Democracy (*Pacte National pour le Développment et le Démocratie*—PNDD). The governing party during the term of former president Sidi Mohamed Ould Cheikh Abdallahi, the PNDD was established in January 2008 over the strident objections of the opposition and smaller parties. The PNDD (also referenced as the PNDD-ADIL) named Yahya Ould Ahmed el-Waghf as chair, since the country's constitution prohibits a president from heading a political party. The party was seen as supporting Abdallahi's move to consolidate government authority in the executive and legislative branches (the PNDD was reported to have held a majority of seats in parliament and all of the cabinet posts under Abdallahi's tenure as president). Among its founders were political activists and some members of the RDU who had backed President Abdallahi and his programs. El-Waghf, for his part, served as secretary general of the presidency in the Abdallahi administration. In May 2008 he was appointed prime minister.

In mid-2008, some 40 party dissidents called for a no-confidence vote against Prime Minister el-Waghf, criticizing him for not representing the will of the electorate by including opposition members and others formerly aligned with the Taya regime in the government. Among those who resigned was the party's secretary general, Mohamed Lemine Ould ABOYE. Just prior to the coup in August, some 48 PNDD parliamentarians resigned in the wake of mounting criticism of Adballahi. The disaffected party members objected to the cabinet reshuffle in May, owing to the number of Taya loyalists, and accused the president of corruption. Those who resigned, including one of the party's leaders, Sidi Mohamed Ould MAHAM (who was elected to the Supreme Court a month after the coup), said they intended to form a new political group (subsequently, the UPR, above). As a result, the PNDD lost its legislative majority, though it remained the single largest party in parliament. Shortly after General Abdelaziz seized control as head of state and announced that a presidential election would be held, another 26 pro-coup PNDD members resigned.

However, other PNDD members, led by Boïdiel Ould HOUMEIT, were among the organizers of the FNDD, formed to give voice to those groups that opposed the August 2008 coup. After the junta installed itself, several members of the PNDD were arrested, and el-Waghf was imprisoned for six months. His release in June 2009 was among the conditions set forth by the opposition during negotiations in Senegal in May (see Current issues, above). In December the PNDD was among nine parties that formed the opposition CFOD. In 2011 Houmeit left the party to form a new grouping, the Party of the Democratic and Social Agreement. The party boycotted the 2013 and 2014 elections.

Leaders: Yahya Ould Ahmed el-WAGHF (Chair and Former Prime Minister), Sidi Mohamed Ould Cheikh ABDALLAHI (Former President of the Republic), Yahya Ould ABDELGHAHAR, Mohamed Mahmoud Ould DAHMANE (Deputy Secretary General).

Rally of Democratic Forces (*Rassemblement des Forces Démocratiques*—RFD). The RFD was formed in 2001 by former members of the **Union of Democratic Forces** (*Union des Forces Démocratiques*—UFD), which had been legalized in October 1991 under the leadership of Hadrami Ould KHATTRY and had originally encompassed a number of diverse opposition groups whose desire to oust the Taya regime appeared to be their only common bond. Widely viewed as the strongest opposition formation at that time, the UFD supported Ahmed Ould Daddah, half-brother of former Mauritanian president Moktar Ould Daddah, in the January 1992 presidential election while spearheading the subsequent legislative boycotts. In May 1992 it was announced that the supporters of Ahmed Ould Daddah had been incorporated into the union, which was reported thereupon to have adopted the name of **Union of Democratic Forces–New Era** (*Union des Forces Démocratiques–Ere Nouvelle*—UFD-EN). However, news reports often continued to use the original name when referencing the group.

The party remained highly critical of the government; Ahmed Ould Daddah, who was elected UFD president in June 1992, charged that official harassment was impeding "normal" party activity. After Ould Daddah was reconfirmed as leader in early 1993, several prominent members left the party and formed the UDP. More serious were the announced defections in June 1994 of two of the union's most important components, *El-Hor,* which formed the **Action for Change and the Movement of Independent Democrats** (*Mouvement des Démocrates Indépendants*—MDI), which joined the PRDS.

The UFD was one of only two opposition parties (the UDP being the other) to contest the municipal elections in early 1994, gaining a majority in 17 of the country's 208 local councils. It boycotted the 1992 legislative poll but obtained one senate seat in 1994. The UFD competed unsuccessfully in the first round of 1996 legislative balloting but boycotted the second round, charging that the government had tampered with voting lists to excise supporters of the opposition.

In October 2000 the government banned the UFD-EN, accusing the party of inciting violence in connection with pro-Palestinian street demonstrations. Supporters subsequently launched the RFD, which won three assembly seats in the 2001 legislative balloting and control of four districts in municipal polls. Ahmed Ould Daddah was unanimously elected as president of the RFD in January 2002.

In April 2002 the RFD won one seat in partial Senate elections, the first of Taya's radical opposition ever to do so. A year later, in May 2003, a senior RFD member was arrested in the wake of the U.S.-led attack on Iraq and subsequent crackdown on Mauritanian Islamic groups. That same month the government appointed a close associate of Ahmed Ould Daddah, Abdellahi Ould Souleimana Ould CHEIKH SIDYA, to a cabinet position in an apparent attempt to gain some RFD support.

In 2004 Ahmed Ould Daddah was charged with helping to finance the opposition Knights of Change (see below), a movement in exile that reportedly advocated the armed overthrow of the Taya government. Daddah was later acquitted.

The RFD refused to join the new government of Prime Minister el-Waghf in May 2008, and in July the party further indicated its unhappiness with the current administration by aligning itself with those in parliament who proposed a no-confidence vote against the prime minister, prompting his resignation. (The president reappointed el-Waghf, and the no-confidence vote was never held.)

Though the RFD initially supported the 2008 junta, it later announced that it would boycott the upcoming presidential election, calling it a "masquerade," and the RFD aligned itself with the opposition grouping FNDD. However, the RFD subsequently agreed to participate in the election, following a compromise agreement between junta leaders and political parties. Party vice president Kane Hamidou Baba resigned, along with some 50 other dissidents, after declaring support for the junta. Subsequently, Baba announced his bid for the presidency without the backing of the RFD, which instead endorsed Ould Daddah, now allied with the FNDD. Ould Daddah, with 13.6 percent of the vote, finished a distant third to General Abdelaziz. Baba, who was deputy speaker of parliament, ran as an independent and received just 1.5 percent of the vote.

The RFD joined the opposition coalition CFOD in 2009, pledging to support a challenge to the president and his party in the upcoming elections. In mid-2011 the party announced its plans to boycott municipal and legislative elections scheduled for October. The party boycotted legislative elections in 2013 and presidential balloting in 2014. Reports in 2015 indicated a growing split in the party, with several leading RFD members defecting to other parties.

Leaders: Ahmed OULD DADDAH (President of the Party and 1992, 2003, 2007, and 2009 presidential candidate), Mohamed Ould BOILIL.

Rally for Democracy and Unity (*Rassemblement pour la Démocratie et l'Unité*—RDU). Led by the mayor of Atar who had served as a cabinet minister under Mauritania's first president, the RDU supported President Taya in the January 1992 presidential campaign, but, after winning one seat in the first round of the March assembly election, broke with the government and boycotted the second round, as well as the subsequent senate race. However, as of the 1996 legislative elections, in which it retained its seat, the RDU was once again described as allied with the PRDS, and the RDU leader was named an adviser to the president in the government announced in December 1998. In the 2004 Senate elections, the RDU won one seat.

The RDU, which had been critical of the 2005 coup, soon reversed its position and supported the military junta, saying it hoped the junta could return stability to the country and lead Mauritania to democracy. The RDU boycotted balloting in 2013 and 2014.

Leader: Ahmed Moktar Sidi BABA.

Union for Democracy and Progress (*Union pour la Démocratie et le Progrès*—UDP). The UDP was legalized in June 1993, its ranks including prominent ex-UFD members, some of whom had also served in the administration of Mauritania's first president, Moktar Ould Daddah. UDP leaders pledged to work toward "restoration of national unity," which, in contrast to government policy, appeared to be aimed at conciliation with black Mauritanians. However, despite its professed multiracial stance, the UDP more recently has been described as continuing, for the most part, to represent conservative Moorish interests.

The UDP participated in the 1994 municipal balloting, although it did not gain control of any of the 19 local boards for which it offered candidates, party leaders reportedly having encouraged supporters to vote for whichever opposition candidate had the best chance of defeating the PRDS candidate. Said to be suffering from internal dissension, the UDP won no seats in the 1996 legislative poll. When UDP leader Hamdi OULD MOUKNASS was appointed as a presidential adviser in December 1997, the UDP moved into a position as a government-supportive party. At the same time, some party members had reportedly aligned with the FPO, the recently organized leading opposition coalition.

Hamdi Ould Mouknass died in September 1999 and was succeeded as UDP president in May 2000 by his daughter, Naha Mint Mouknass, who thereby became one of two female party leaders in the Arab world. She was also named a presidential adviser, reaffirming the rump UDP's ties to the government.

In August 2009 Mouknass was named Mauritania's first female foreign minister. In November the party won one seat in the partial Senate elections. The UDP boycotted the 2013 and 2014 balloting.

Leaders: Naha Mint MOUKNASS (President), Sheikh Saad Bouh CAMARA, Ahmed OULD MENAYA (Secretary General).

Union of Progressive Forces (*Union des Forces Progressives*—UFP). Formed by former members of the UFD (above), the UFP, whose leadership includes former Marxists, called for dialogue with the PRDS in order to "improve the political atmosphere." The new party won three seats in the 2001 assembly balloting. In 2003 the UFP supported Ould Haidalla for president and joined other opposition groups in complaining of fraud following the Taya victory. The party considered boycotting the 2004 Senate elections but ultimately participated with two nominees. Both lost, one by a narrow margin, to PRDS candidates. In 2005 the party demanded the return of Mauritanian exiles and an end to slavery in the country, precepts it pushed for in the transitional program following the August coup.

Party chair Mohammed Ould Maaloud received 4.08 percent of the vote in the first round in the 2007 presidential election; he supported Ould Daddah in the second round.

The UFP opposed the August 2008 coup, and Maaloud became a leader of the opposition grouping FNDD.

In 2009 the party joined the opposition grouping styled the CFOD. In July 2011 the UFP said it would boycott elections set to take place in October. The UFP boycott elections in 2013 and 2014. As of 2016, Maaloud was a professor of history in Geneva, Switzerland.

Leaders: Mohammed Ould MAALOUD (Party Chair and 2007 presidential candidate), Kadiata Malick DIALLO (Vice Chair), Mohamed Moustafa Ould BEDREDINE (Secretary General).

Popular Front (*Front Populaire*—FP). The FP, formerly referenced as the **Popular and Democratic Front** (*Front Populaire et Démocratique*—FPD), is led by former minister Mohamed Lemine Chbih Ould Cheikh Malainine, who finished second (with 7 percent of the vote) as an independent candidate in the December 1997 presidential polling. Malainine, a Muslim spiritual leader, was elected chair of the FP at its first congress in April 1998.

In early 2001 Malainine announced that the FPD would participate in the October legislative balloting, eliciting criticism from the UFD-EN. Despite Malainine's apparently conciliatory gesture toward the government, he was arrested in April on charges of conspiring with Libya to commit acts of terrorism and sentenced to five years in prison (he was released after having served two-and-a-half years). Amnesty International described Malainine as a "prisoner of conscience" and charged that his arrest was merely an attempt to "stifle" the opposition. The sentence was also strongly condemned by other opposition parties. In October 2002 the FP formed, with the Cavaliers for Change and RFD, the United Opposition Framework (UOF), which sought dialogue on democratic reform between the government and opposition groups.

In July 2006, in the run-up to legislative elections, FP leader Malainine helped form the CFCD. In the first round of the 2007 presidential election, he ran as an independent, finishing with less than 1 percent of the vote. The party won just 0.4 percent of the vote in the 2013 legislative balloting.

Leaders: Mohamed Lemine Chbih Ould Cheikh MALAININE (Party President and 2007 presidential candidate), Mohamed Fadel SIDIYA (Political Secretary), Badi Ould IBNOU.

Popular Progressive Alliance (*Alliance Populaire et Progressive*—APP). A number of APP members were arrested in early 1997 on "conspiracy" charges emanating from the group's allegedly "pro-Libyan" tendencies. The APP boycotted the 2001 elections. On August 1, 2004, Massaoud Ould Boulkheir, the former leader of the dissolved Action for Change, was elected president of the APP, replacing Mohamed El-Hafedh Ould Ismail. That same month the party won two seats in the partial senate elections. In the first round of the 2007 presidential election, Boulkheir placed fourth with 9.8 percent of the vote and pledged to support the new president (despite his ties with the CFCD, led by Ahmed Ould Daddah).

The party was among several that called on the government in 2007 to sever ties with Israel.

The APP opposed the 2008 bloodless coup, and in 2009 Boulkheir ran for president as the candidate of the FNDD. He agreed to support the RFD's Ould Daddah if a second round of voting was held. That proved not to be the case, as Ould Daddah finished third, and Boulkheir himself finished a distant second with 16.3 percent of the vote. The APP subsequently joined the opposition grouping CFOD. In July 2011 the APP withdrew from the coalition, citing differences with other member parties. The party boycotted the 2013 and 2014 polling. In March 2016 the party signaled its support for the self-determination of the Sahawari people.

Leaders: Massaoud Ould BOULKHEIR (Chair, Speaker of the Assembly, and 2007 and 2009 presidential candidate), El Khalil Ould TEYIB (Vice Chair), Mohamed Lamine Ould el-NATI.

Mauritanian Party of Union and Change (*Parti Mauritanien pour l'Union et le Changement*—HATEM). This party originated in 2003 as a military organization referenced as the **Knights of Change** (*Umat*), led by former army colonel Saleh Ould Hanena. The Knights had staged several failed coup attempts against President Taya, and Hanena was accused of being the mastermind behind the 2003 plot. In February 2005 Hanena was sentenced to life imprisonment, but he was released by the new junta later that year.

The group became a political party in 2006 and changed its name to HATEM. In the first round of the 2007 presidential election, Hanena won 7.7 percent of the vote. He and his Islamist supporters backed Ould Daddah for president in the second round. The party, along with the APP and El Sawab, among others, urged the new government to break diplomatic ties with Israel.

Following the 2008 coup, HATEM was among the first parties to support the junta. Subsequently, in January 2009, some 57 senior party members resigned to form a prodemocracy group, the **Patriotic Sphere of Influence**. The group was reportedly dissatisfied with HATEM's leadership. In the July presidential election, party leader Hanena received 1.3 percent of the vote.

In 2010 the HATEM members of the legislature, lacking the three-seat threshold for a parliamentary group, were seated as independents. In 2011 HATEM joined the CFOD. Following his wounding in October 2012, HATEM called for Abdelaziz to step down, asserting that the president was physically unable to perform his duties.

Leader: Saleh Ould HANENA (2007 and 2009 presidential candidate).

El Sawab ("The Correct," "The Right Track"). El Sawab, formed in May 2004 by politicians close to former head of state Mohamed Khouna Ould Haidalla, said it had an "original" society program. The party, which was officially recognized in July 2004, opposed Taya's regime. It was described in 2008 as a Baathist party that opposed Mauritania's support for Israel and called on the media to "expose the Zionists" in Mauritania. The party campaigned in the 2013 balloting, but failed to secure any seats.

Leaders: Abdelsalam Ould HOURMA (Chair), Mohamed Ould GUELMA.

Party for Democratic Convergence (PCD). Many Mauritanians refer to the PCD as "Haidalla's friends," referring to former president Mohamed Khouna Ould Haidalla, but the Arabic initials, formed in May 2004, reveal another allegiance: they spell El Hamd, literally, "praise to God." The PCD is composed of a wide range of groups that were persecuted under the Taya regime, including many black Mauritanians, Islamic radicals, and those who supported the 2003 coup attempt. The vice president of the group, former Nouakchott mayor Mohamed Jemil Ould MANSOUR, an accused Islamic radical, was arrested in 2003 but escaped from prison during the coup attempt and fled to Belgium. There Mansour helped found the **Mauritanian Forum for Reform and Democracy**, along with other political exiles from the 2003 coup. Upon returning to Mauritania, Mansour was arrested again and then released.

Ould Haidalla, who had challenged Taya in the November 2003 presidential election, was arrested two days after the election, and in December he was convicted of plotting a coup against Taya. Ould Haidalla, who denied the charges, received a suspended sentence. In 2005 he was acquitted on charges relating to attempted coups in 2003 and 2004. Also in 2005 the ruling junta refused to recognize the PCD because it contended the party advocated the monopoly of Islam in politics. Party leaders denied it had Islamist links, despite having religious leaders among its members. In the first round of the 2007 presidential election, party leader Isselmou Ould Moustapha was officially credited with 0.2 percent of the vote. It was unclear why he appeared on the ballot under the PCD banner since the PCD had been banned. In the same election, Ould Haidalla ran as an independent, receiving 1.7 percent of the vote in the first round.

Leaders: Isselmou Ould MOUSTAPHA (2007 presidential candidate), Mohamed Khouna OULD HAIDALLA (2003 presidential candidate).

National Union for Democracy and Development (*Union Nationale pour la Démocratie et le Développement*—UNDD). Formed by Sen. Tidjane Koita after he left the AC in 1997, the UNDD has been described as the "moderate opposition" and a proponent of dialogue between the PRDS and the more strident antiregime groups. None of the UNDD's candidates was successful in the 2001 assembly balloting. Social justice and national unity are listed as key party goals. The party campaigned in the 2013 legislative balloting, but received less than 0.1 percent of the vote.

Leader: Tidjane KOITA.

Mauritanian Renewal Party (*Parti Mauritanien pour le Renouvellement*—PMR). Shortly after legalization of the PMR, also referenced as the **Mauritanian Party for Renewal and Concord** (PMRC), in mid-September 1991, its leaders charged that inappropriate links had been formed between the PRDS and long-standing national and municipal leaders, placing other groups at a disadvantage in forthcoming elections. The PMR, however, won one seat in the 1992 legislative balloting. In the 1997 presidential balloting, PMR leader Moulaye al-Hassan OULD JEYDID finished third with less than 1 percent of the vote.

In April 2001 the government announced the recognition of a new party also named the Mauritanian Renewal Party, led by Atiq OULD ATTIA.

In 2007 leaders Ould Jeydid and Rajel dit Rachit MOUSTAPHA each received less than 1 percent of the vote as presidential candidates representing the PMRC and the PMR, respectively. The relationship between the two parties was unclear. The party failed to win seats in the 2009 partial Senate elections. In the 2013 Chamber elections, the PMRC won 0.8 percent of the vote, while the PMR won 0.7 percent.

Party for Liberty, Equality, and Justice (*Parti pour la Liberté, l'Egalité, et la Justice*—PLEJ). The PLEJ was founded in 1991 by Ba Mamadou Alassane, a former ambassador and cabinet minister who was among the first Black Africans to head a political party in Mauritania. In 1997 party member Kane Amadou Moctar was one of four candidates who challenged Taya in the presidential election.

In the first round of the 2007 presidential election, Alassane received less than 1 percent of the vote; he supported Ould Daddah in the second round. The party opposed the 2008 coup.

Leaders: Ba Mamadou ALASSANE (Chair and 2007 presidential candidate), Daouda MBAGNIGA.

Alternative (*El Badil*). The Alternative was founded in 2006 and chaired by Mohamed Yahdi Ould Moctar HACEN, a former interior minister in the Abdhallahi government. The party was reported to be the main party supporting the 2008 coup. Hacen, secretary general of the former ruling PRDS and formerly a close ally of President Abdallahi, left the government before the coup. In 2009 he was nominated as the Alternative's presidential candidate, but he did not run.

Leaders: Mohamed Yahdi Ould Moctar HACEN (Chair), Mamadou LY (Vice President).

Other parties and groups that participated in recent elections include the **Third Generation** (*Parti de la Troisienne Generation*—PTG), led by Lebat OULD JEH; the **Social Democratic Party**, formed in 2005 by Mohamed Salek Ould DIDAH; the **Rally for Mauritania**, formed in 2005 by Cheikh Ould HORMA; the **Mauritanian Party for the Defense of the Environment** (*Parti Mauritanien pour la Défense de l'Environment*—PMDE), also known as the Green Party, established in 2003 by Mohamed Ould DELLAHI; the **Mauritanian Party of Liberal Democrats** (*Parti Mauritanien des Libéraux Democrates*—PMLD), led by Moustapha Ould LEMRABOTT; the **Socialist and Democratic Popular Union** (*Union Populaire Socialiste et Démocratique*—UPSD); the **Union of the Democratic Center** (*Union du Centre Démocratique*—UCD); the **Party of Labor and National Unity** (*Parti du Travail et de l'Unité Nationale*—PTUN), led by Ali Bouna Ould OUENINA and Mohamed Ould EL BAH; the **Democratic and Social Union** (*Union Démocratique et Sociale*—UDS); the **Mauritanian Hope Party**, led by Tahi bint LAHBIB; the **National Rally for Democracy, Liberty, and Equality;** the **Union of Democratic Youth,** formed by Jeddou Ould AHMAD; and the **Democratic Renovation Party,** led by Moustapha Ould ABEIDERRAHMANE.

Other Parties and Groups:

African Liberation Forces of Mauritania (*Forces de Libération Africaine de Mauritanie*—FLAM). Organized in 1983 in opposition to what were perceived as repressive policies toward blacks, FLAM was believed responsible for an "Oppressed Black" manifesto that in 1986 was widely distributed within Mauritania and at the nonaligned summit in Zimbabwe. Based partly in Dakar, Senegal, the group also condemned reprisals against blacks by the Taya regime following an alleged coup attempt in 1987. Many FLAM supporters were reported to be among those who fled or were expelled to Senegal in 1989. Subsequently engaged in guerrilla activity, FLAM leaders announced in July 1991 that they were suspending "armed struggle" in response to the government's general amnesty and promulgation of a new Mauritanian constitution. FLAM endorsed Ahmed Ould Daddah in the January 1992 presidential election, after which it renewed its antigovernment military campaign near the Senegalese border. Leaders of the group stated in early 1995 that they were neither secessionists nor terrorists, reiterating their support for the establishment of a federal system that would ensure an appropriate level of black representation in government while protecting the rights of blacks throughout Mauritanian society. In early 2001 the FLAM called upon the international community to exert pressure on the Mauritanian government to address the issue of black refugees remaining in Senegal and Mali as the result of the 1989 exodus.

The group, along with the Patriotic Alliance and other anti-Taya organizations, again pledged to give up its armed struggle following the 2005 coup.

In February 2006 a breakaway group formed under the rubric **FLAM–Renovation,** reportedly planning to join in the political process in Mauritania, though it was unclear how it intended to do so (see AJD-MR, above). The breakaway group, issuing a report from Senegal, called on the government to address the refugee issue.

FLAM had called for a boycott of the constitutional referendum in 2006 and criticized the approved amendments on the grounds that they did not adequately address the issue of slavery, among other things. According to FLAM's website, the group has never participated in an election in Mauritania because FLAM's "standard conditions," including issues like human rights, slavery, and refugees, have not been met. In June 2007 a group of Mauritanian expatriates living in New York filed a suit against Taya, alleging torture and other human rights violations. The suit included claims by two black Mauritanians that they were among the victims of "ethnic cleansing" under the Taya regime.

In November 2007 following the signing of a tripartite agreement by Mauritania, Senegal, and the UNHCR to allow for the return of thousands of black Mauritanian refugees, FLAM raised concerns about the country's ability to handle the influx.

Despite the adoption in 2007 of a law making slavery illegal in Mauritania, black Mauritanians were still allegedly being persecuted. In early 2011 it was reported that the antislavery campaigner Biram Dah ABEID remained in custody since December 2010, charged with assaulting two police officers. FLAM and other groups claimed he was being harassed because of his antislavery campaign. FLAM opposed Mauritania's troop deployment to Mali in 2013 and called on all

Mauritanian political parties to work together to end the Israeli invasion of Gaza in 2014.

As of 2016 there has been no resolution either to FLAM's dislocation or FLAM–Renovation's merger with AJD-MR.

Leader: Samba THIAM (President).

In 1994 security forces accused a number of previously unknown extremist organizations, including **Call to Islam** and the **Mauritanian Islamic** Movement (*Hasim*) of conspiring to overthrow the government. As part of its antiterrorism efforts, backed by the United States, the Mauritanian government in October 2004 arrested three leaders of the Mauritanian Islamic Movement—Mohamed El-Hacen Ould DEDOW, Moctar Ould Mohamed MOUSSA, and Mohamed Jemil Ould Mansour—on charges of subversion. Mansour, who was later listed as the leader of the **Centrist Reformers**, described as moderate Islamists, has been named as among the leaders of several parties or groups.

Among 18 new parties licensed by the government in August 2007 were the Work and Equality Party; the Conservative Party; the Alternation and Consultation Party; and the Coalition for Democracy in Mauritania. Also licensed was the Movement for Direct Democracy (MDD), led by Omar Ould RABAH. The MDD was banned in 2005, but its members aligned themselves with the CFCD prior to the 2006 assembly elections. The MDD was described as reformist rather than Islamist, in accordance with the political parties law, although it was reported to be an offshoot of the Muslim Brotherhood (see Mauritanian Islamic Movement, above).

Additional parties include the **Mauritanian Labor Party,** led by Mohamed Hafid OULD DENNA; the **Democratic Alliance,** led by Mohamed Ould Taleb OTHMAN; the **National Renaissance Party** (*Parti de la Renaissance Nationale*—PRN), led by Mohamed Ould Abdellaki Ould EYYE; the **National Pact** (*Pacte National*—PN), led by former PRDS member Mohamed Abdallah OULD KHARCY; the **Popular Initiatives Rally**, which supported the 2008 junta, led by Mohamed SALEM; and the **National Union for Democratic Alternative**. Other parties licensed by the Junta in 2009 were the **Party for Peace and Democratic Progress**; **Mauritanian National Congress**; **Mauritanian Loyalty Party**; **League of Mauritanians for the Homeland**; **Rally of National Youth**; **Democratic Choice**; **Wellbeing Party**; **Union of Social Forces**; and **Mauritanian People's Rally**.

For information on the **Patriotic Alliance** (a.k.a. Democratic Alliance), see the 2014 *Handbook.*

LEGISLATURE

The 1991 constitution provides for a bicameral legislature consisting of an indirectly chosen Senate and a popularly elected National Assembly. The parliament was dissolved by the Military Council for Justice and Democracy following the August 3, 2005, coup. Constitutional amendments approved in a public referendum on June 25, 2006, included provisions for restoring the **Parliament**.

Senate (*Majlis al-Shuyukh*). The Senate is renewed by thirds every two years for six-year terms, with 53 of its 56 members selected by the country's mayors and municipal councilors and three seats representing Mauritanians abroad chosen by the elected senators.

In the election on January 21 and February 4, 2007, the seat distribution was as follows: independents, 34; Rally of Democratic Forces (RFD), 5; Republican Democratic Party for Renovation, 3; Coalition of Forces of Democratic Change, 3; Mauritanian Party of Union and Change (HATEM), 2; Union of Progressive Forces, 1; RFD/UFP, 1; RFD/Independents, 1; HATEM/Independents, 1; Union for Democracy (UDP) and Progress/Independents, 1; and People's Progressive Alliance /Independents, 1.

In partial elections on November 8 and November 15, 2009, for one-third of the members, or 17 seats, the Union for the Republic won a total of 13 seats; independents, 2; National Rally for Reform and Development, 1; and UDP, 1. (Parties that win fewer than 3 seats sit as independents unless they join an alliance.)

President: Mohamed Hassan Ould HAJ.

National Assembly (*Majlis al-Watani*). For the 2013 balloting, the size of the assembly was increased from 95 to 147 seats, 20 of which are elected nationally in proportional balloting on a party basis and 107 of which are elected in regional constituencies. There is a separate national female list through which 20 women are directly elected. The mixed voting system is majoritarian in single-member and 2-seat constituencies, with proportional representation in constituencies of 3 or more seats. All members are elected for five-year terms.

In the balloting on November 23 and December 21, 2013, the seat distribution was as follows: Union for the Republic, 75; National Rally for Reform and Development, 16; Party of the Democratic and Social Agreement, 10; People's Progressive Alliance, 7; Union for Democracy and Progress, 6; *El Karam*, 6; Alliance for Justice and Democracy/Movement for Renovation, 4; Burst of Youth for the Nation, 4; Virtue, 3; Party of Unity and Development, 3; Ravah Party, 3; Republican Democratic Party for Renovation, 3; Democratic Justice Party, 2; Party of Mauritanian Authenticity, 1; Socialist Democratic Unionist Party, 1; Dignity and Action Party, 1; Party of Democratic People, 1; and The Reform, 1.

Speaker: Mohamed Ould BOILIL.

CABINET

[as of September 15, 2016]

Prime Minister	Yahya Ould Hademine
Ministers	
Agriculture	Lemini Mint El Ghotob Ould Moma [f]
Commerce, Industry, and Tourism	Naha Mint Hamdi Ould Mouknass [f]
Communications and Relations with Parliament	Izidbih Ould Mohamed Mahmoud
Culture and Handicrafts	Mohamed Lemine Ould Cheikh
Defense	Diallo Mamadou Bathia
Economic and Finance	Mokhtar Ould Djay
Education	Sidi El Moktar Ould Isselmou Ould Lehbib
Employment, Professional Training and Information, and Communications Technologies	Moktar Dia Malal
Environment and Sustainable Development	Amedi Camara
Equipment and Transport	Ahmed Salem Ould Abderraouf
Fisheries and Maritime Economy	Nani Ould Chrougha
Foreign Affairs and Cooperation	Isselkou Ould Ahmed Izid Bih
Health	Kane Boubacar
Higher Education and Scientific Research	Sidi Ould Salem
Housing, Town Planning, and Spatial Planning	Amal Mint Maouloud [f]
Interior and Decentralization	Ahmedou Ould Abdalla
Islamic Affairs and Religious Education	Ahmed Ould Daoud Ehel
Justice	Brahim Ould Daddah
Livestock	Fatma Vall Mint Soueinae [f]
Petroleum, Energy, and Mines	Mohamed Abdel Vetah
Public Services, Labor, and Administration Modernization	Seyedna Ali Ould Mohamed Khouna
Secretary General of the Government	Zeinabou Mint Ely Salem [f]
Social Affairs, Children, and Families	Fatima Mint Habib [f]
Water Resources and Sanitation	Mohamed Abdellahi Ould Oudaa
Youth and Sports	Coumba Ba [f]
Minister Delegate	
Economic Affairs and Finance	Mohamed Ould Kembou

[f] = female

INTERGOVERNMENTAL REPRESENTATION

Ambassador to the U.S.: Mohamedoun DADDAH.

U.S. Ambassador: Larry Edward ANDRE.

Permanent Representative to the UN: Sidi Mohamed BOUBACAR.

IGO Memberships (Non–UN): ACP, AfDB, AL, AU, IOM, LAS, NAM, OIC, WTO.

For Further Reference:

Foster, Noel. *Mauritania: The Struggle for Democracy.* Boulder, CO: Lynne Rienner, 2010.
Sene, Sidi. *The Ignored Cries of Pain and Injustice from Mauritania.* Bloomington, IN: Trafford Publishing, 2011.
U.S. Department of State. *Mauritania: 2015 Human Rights Guide.* Washington, DC: GPO, 2016.

MAURITIUS

Republic of Mauritius

Political Status: Constitutional monarchy under multiparty parliamentary system established upon independence within the Commonwealth on March 12, 1968; became a republic on March 12, 1992.

Area: 790 sq. mi. (2,045 sq. km).

Population: 1,278,000 (2016E—UN); 1,348,242 (2016E—U.S. Census).

Major Urban Centers (2011E—UN): PORT LOUIS (148,638), Beau Bassin/Rose Hill (110,687), Vacoas-Phoenix (108,186).

Official Language: English (French is also used, while Creole is the lingua franca and Hindi the most widely spoken).

Monetary Unit: Mauritian rupee (official rate October 1, 2016: 35.48 rupees = $1US).

President: Ameenah GURIB-FAKIM (ind.); elected by the National Assembly on June 4, 2015, for a five-year term, to succeed Rajkeswur PURRYAG (Mauritius Labour Party), who resigned on May 29, 2015.

Vice President: Paramasivum Pillay VYAPOORY (Mauritian Socialist Movement); elected by the National Assembly on March 29, 2016, and sworn in on April 4 for a term concurrent with the remainder of that of the president, to succeed Monique Ohsan BELLEPEAU (Mauritius Labour Party).

Prime Minister: Sir Anerood JUGNAUTH (Mauritian Socialist Movement); named prime minister on December 14, 2015, in succession to Navin RAMGOOLAM (Mauritius Labour Party) following legislative election of December 10, 2014, and sworn in on December 17.

THE COUNTRY

The island of Mauritius, once known as Ile de France, is situated 500 miles east of Madagascar, in the southwestern Indian Ocean; Rodrigues Island, the Agalega Islands, and the Cardagos Carajos Shoals (St. Brandon Islands) also are national territory. (Mauritius also claims Diego Garcia and other islands in the Chagos Archipelago, currently controlled by the United Kingdom as part of the British Indian Ocean Territory [see Foreign relations, below].) The diversity of contemporary Mauritian society is a reflection of its history as a colonial sugar plantation. African slave laborers were imported initially, and they were followed by the migration of Indians (who now constitute two-thirds of the population), Chinese, French, and English. Religious affiliations include Hinduism, to which 48 percent of the population adheres; Christianity (predominantly Roman Catholicism), 24 percent; and Islam, 17 percent. Women are significantly engaged in subsistence agriculture, although they comprise only 32 percent of the paid labor force. Eight women were elected to the National Assembly in 2014 (11.6 percent of the total deputies). Women have been elected as both president and vice president of the country.

The overall strong economic performance in the 1990s led some experts to reference a “Mauritian miracle” and to describe the country as a case study in the successful management of a developing country

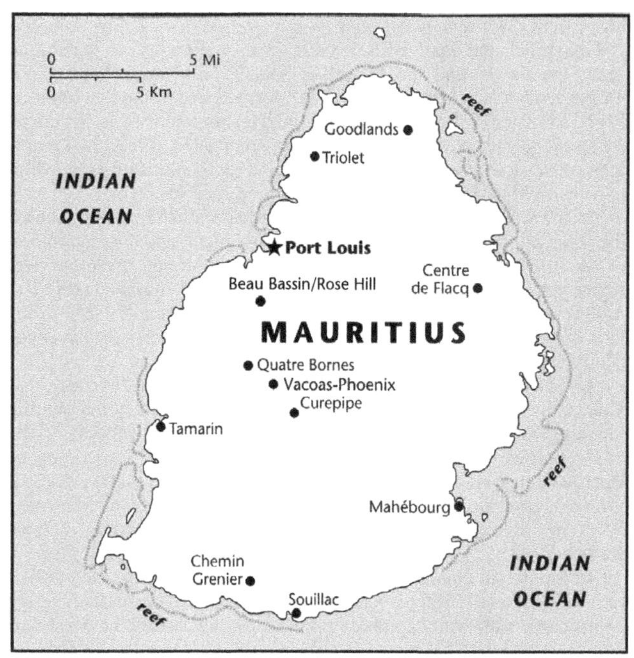

that pursued investor-friendly policies. (For more on the history of the economy, see the 2013 *Handbook.*)

GDP growth averaged 4.2 between 2000 and 2008, while inflation averaged 6.3 percent. Unemployment during this period peaked at 10.2 percent in 2004, before declining to 7.3 percent by 2009. Reforms lowered average tariffs from 19.9 percent in 2001 to just 6.6 percent in 2007, while the financial services sector, valued at $35.86 billion, continued to draw foreign investment. The global economic crisis slowed the economy in late 2008 and early 2009; however, GDP grew by 4 percent in 2010, while inflation remained low at 2.9 percent, and unemployment was 7.5 percent.

Growth for 2011 was estimated at 3.8 percent, while GDP growth slowed to 3.3 percent in 2012 because of a slowdown in sugar production as well as the impact of the European debt crisis on tourism and demand for exports such as textiles. In 2013 and 2014 GDP increased by 3.2 percent before accelerating to 3.5 percent in 2015 and 2016. In 2016 inflation was 3 percent, and unemployment 7.9 percent. The 2016 World Bank report ranked Mauritius 32nd out of 189 countries, and best in Africa, for ease in conducting business. That year, according to the International Monetary Fund (IMF), real per capita income was $11,233—one of the highest levels in Africa.

GOVERNMENT AND POLITICS

Political background. Because of its location, Mauritius had strategic importance during the age of European exploration and expansion, and the Dutch, French, and English successively occupied the island. France ruled Mauritius from 1710 to 1810, when Britain assumed control to protect its shipping during the Napoleonic wars. Political evolution began as early as 1831 under a constitution that provided for a Council of Government, but the franchise was largely restricted until after World War II. The postwar era also witnessed the introduction of political parties and increased participation in local government.

An election under a system of internal parliamentary democracy initiated in 1967 revealed a majority preference for full independence, which was granted by Britain on March 12, 1968, with Sir Seewoosagur RAMGOOLAM of the Independence Party (IP) as prime minister. A state of emergency, occasioned by an outbreak of severe communal strife between Muslims and Creoles, was lifted in 1970, although new disorder brought its reimposition from December 1971 to March 1978.

Under constitutional arrangements agreed upon in 1969, the mandate of the existing Legislative Assembly was extended by four years. In the election of December 20, 1976, the radical Mauritian Militant

Movement (*Mouvement Militant Mauricien*—MMM), led by Anerood JUGNAUTH and Paul BÉRENGER, won a plurality of legislative seats, but the IP and the Mauritian Social Democratic Party (*Parti Mauricien Social-Démocrate*—PMSD) formed a coalition that retained Prime Minister Ramgoolam in office with a slim majority. In the country's second postindependence balloting on June 11, 1982, the incumbent parties lost all of their directly elective seats, Jugnauth proceeding to form an MMM-dominated government on June 15.

In the wake of a government crisis in March 1983, which yielded the resignation of 12 ministers, including Bérenger, and the repudiation of the prime minister by his own party, Jugnauth and his supporters regrouped as the Mauritian Socialist Movement (*Mouvement Socialiste Mauricien*—MSM) and, in alliance with Ramgoolam's Mauritius Labour Party (MLP) wing of the IP and the PMSD, won a decisive legislative majority in a new election held August 21.

In February 1984 Ramgoolam's successor as MLP leader, Sir Satcam BOOLELL, was relieved of his post as minister of economic planning, whereupon the MLP voted to terminate its support of the MSM. However, 11 Labour deputies, under the leadership of Beergoonath GHURBURRUN, refused to follow Boolell into opposition and remained in the government alliance (initially as the Mauritian Workers' Movement—MWM and later as the Mauritian Labour Rally—RTM).

In municipal council balloting on December 8, 1985, the opposition MMM won 57.2 percent of the vote, decisively defeating the coalition parties, who captured only 36.8 percent, while the MLP was a distant third with 5.4 percent. Although insisting that the MMM victory represented a rejection of Jugnauth's policies, Bérenger did not immediately call for the government to resign. However, such an appeal was made in the wake of a major scandal at the end of the month, which stemmed from the arrest on drug charges of four coalition members at Amsterdam's Schipol Airport. Subsequently, the MLP agreed to reconcile with the MSM, and Boolell was awarded three portfolios and the post of second deputy prime minister in a cabinet reorganization August 8, 1986.

At an early election on August 30, 1987, called largely because of favorable economic conditions, a reconstituted Jugnauth coalition consisting of the MSM, the MLP, the RTM (subsequently absorbed by the MSM), the PMSD, and the Rodriguan People's Organization (*Organisation du Peuple Rodriguais*—OPR) retained power by capturing 41 of 62 elective legislative seats. In August 1988, however, the PMSD, whose leader, Sir Gaëtan DUVAL, had frequently been at odds with the coalition mainstream in domestic and foreign policy, withdrew from the government, forcing Jugnauth to form a new cabinet whose assembly support had fallen to a majority of 10. Two months later the largely urban-based coalition suspended participation in municipal balloting to avoid the embarrassment of a major defeat, with the MMM (allied with several small parties) winning all of the seats in a two-way contest with the PMSD.

In an effort to strengthen his parliamentary position, Jugnauth in July 1990 concluded an electoral pact with the opposition MMM. However, the move angered a number of his fellow MSM ministers, as well as MLP leader Boolell. In August, after the government narrowly failed to secure the 75 percent approval necessary to make the country a republic within the Commonwealth, Jugnauth dismissed the dissident ministers and announced that he would continue as head of a minority administration with the parliamentary support of the MMM. A month later the MMM formally joined the government, with its president, Dr. Prem NABABSINGH, named deputy prime minister.

At an early election on September 15, 1991, the governing alliance won 59 of 62 legislative seats, far in excess of the 75 percent required to implement a change to republican status, which was approved by the Legislative Assembly on December 10, with effect from March 12, 1992. By agreement between the coalition's leading parties, Sir Veerasamy RINGADOO, who had been appointed governor general in January 1986, was designated nonexecutive president of the new republic for three months; he was succeeded on June 30 by the MMM's Cassam UTEEM.

In a cabinet reshuffle on August 18, 1993, Bérenger, who had been openly critical of government policies, was ousted as foreign minister. Two months later he was removed as MMM secretary general by the party's Political Bureau, which named Jean-Claude DE L'ESTRAC as his successor. However, the action was reversed on October 23 by the MMM Central Committee, which proceeded to name a new, pro-Bérenger party leadership. On November 16 Bérenger crossed the aisle to sit with the opposition, although he formally rejected the opposition leadership on the grounds that he had no electoral mandate for such a role. A year later Bérenger and De L'Estrac resigned as MPs; only the former regained his seat in by-elections in January 1995.

After the MLP had in January 1995 rebuffed Prime Minister Jugnauth's offer of power sharing, the PMSD agreed in early February to join the coalition, which then encompassed the MSM, MTD, OPR, and the Mauritian Militant Renaissance, despite opposition from a number of leading PMSD members, with a cabinet realignment following on February 13. An early election was then called after Jugnauth had failed to secure passage of a constitutional amendment to introduce a variety of languages (Hindi, Urdu, Tamil, Marathi, Telegu, Chinese, and Arabic) into the educational curriculum. The Creole opposition strongly opposed the amendment, which also provoked the withdrawal not only of the recently appointed PMSD members but also of the OPR representative, thus effectively shrinking the government coalition.

In an outcome not dissimilar to Prime Minister Jugnauth's 1982 electoral victory, an opposition MLP-MMM alliance swept the legislative balloting of December 20, 1995, with the MLP's Dr. Navin RAMGOOLAM, son of former prime minister Sir Seewoosagur Ramgoolam, forming a new government on December 31. It consisted of 13 MLP ministers, 9 MMM ministers (including Bérenger as deputy prime minister and foreign minister), and 1 OPR representative at the junior ministerial level. However, Bérenger was dismissed from the cabinet on June 20, 1997, and most of the other MMM ministers resigned their posts in protest. After reportedly failing to convince the PMSD to participate in the government, Ramgoolam on July 2 formed a new cabinet, which included only MLP ministers except for 1 OPR member and 1 independent (Dr. Ahmed Rashid BEEBEEJAUN, who had recently left the MMM rather than give up his portfolio for land transport, shipping, and public safety). Meanwhile, President Uteem was reappointed to another term, although his relationship with the MMM (which had promoted his initial appointment) remained unclear. Ramgoolam reshuffled his cabinet on October 25, 1998, reportedly to enhance the role of young MLP legislators in the government after an alliance formed between Bérenger's MMM and Jugnauth's MSM. The prime minister also attempted to shore up his control by including the recently formed Xavier Duval Mauritian Party (PMXD) in a cabinet reshuffle on September 26, 1999.

The Ramgoolam administration was buffeted by the resignation of several top officials tainted by scandal in 1999, as well as by drought-induced economic decline. Consequently, in August 2000 the prime minister felt compelled to dissolve the National Assembly and call for new elections in September, four months early. The MSM and MMM quickly concluded an unbeatable electoral alliance, based on an agreement that former prime minister Jugnauth would reassume the reins of government for three years, with Bérenger serving as prime minister the following two years. The new administration appeared to have the support of the private sector, notably the sugar companies and the Catholic Church.

However, in the legislative balloting on September 11, 2000, the MSM-MMM electoral coalition soundly trounced the MLP-PMXD alliance, securing 54 of the 62 elected seats. Consequently, Jugnauth returned as prime minister on September 17 to lead with Bérenger a MSM-MMM coalition government, which required Jugnauth to resign after three years and Bérenger to assume the premiership.

On February 15, 2002, President Uteem resigned after he refused to approve an antiterrorism law recently passed by the National Assembly. (Uteem argued that the new legislation could undermine national sovereignty in the name of U.S. security concerns.) He was replaced by Vice President Angidi Verriah Chettiar, who resigned on February 18 after he also refused to sign the bill into law. In accordance with the constitution, Chief Justice Arriranga PILLAY replaced Chettiar as the interim president on February 18 and subsequently signed the controversial legislation. On February 25 the National Assembly elected Karl Auguste OFFMANN and Raouf BUNDHUN as the president and vice president, respectively.

On September 29, 2002, the OPR won 10 of 18 seats in the new Rodrigues Regional Assembly, while the Rodrigues Movement won the remaining 8 seats.

Although many observers doubted the MSM-MMM "marriage" of 2000 would survive, Bérenger assumed the premiership on October 1, 2003, and Jugnauth took the largely ceremonial presidency on October 7. Bérenger, a Creole, became the nation's first non-Hindu prime minister. The most noteworthy of Bérenger's subsequent cabinet changes was the appointment of Pravind Kumar JUGNAUTH (the son of Anerood Jugnauth) as deputy prime minister and finance minister.

In balloting for 62 elected members of the National Assembly on July 3, 2005, the Social Alliance (led by the MLP) won 38 seats, while the alliance of the MSM and the MMM won 22 and the OPR won 2. Prime Minister Bérenger resigned on July 5 and was succeeded the same day by MLP leader Navin Ramgoolam, who formed a new cabinet comprising (for the most part) the parties that had formed the Social Alliance. The Social Alliance also swept municipal balloting in October, winning 122 of 124 seats in five towns, including all 30 seats in the capital, Port Louis. It also won the majority of mayoral contests.

In regional balloting in December 2006, the Rodriguan Movement (*Mouvement Rodriguais*—MR) gained a majority in the Regional Assembly after two decades of dominance of island politics by the Rodriguan People's Organization (*Organisation du Peuple Rodriguais*—OPR).

Although new presidential balloting was technically due in 2007, the government postponed the election until 2008, arguing that President Jugnauth was entitled to a full five-year term. The MSM appeared comfortable with that decision but strongly objected to the MLP's insistence that new vice-presidential elections should proceed as scheduled in 2007. Nevertheless, Prime Minister Ramgoolam nominated former vice president Chettiar to the post in August 2007, and the appointment was endorsed by the MLP-dominated assembly. In September former prime minister Paul Bérenger of the MMM was appointed opposition leader in the assembly, following the resignation of Nando Bodha of the MSM (see Political Parties, below).

Ramgoolam dismissed the foreign minister in March 2008 after the minister publicly criticized the coalition government. The prime minster then took over the foreign ministry portfolio, but carried out a major cabinet reshuffle on September 13 in which four new ministers were appointed and thirteen ministers had their portfolios altered. The cabinet continued to be dominated by the MLP and the reshuffle was reportedly an effort to improve the government's popularity ahead of the 2010 legislative balloting. On September 19 Jugnauth was unanimously reelected president by the assembly in balloting that had been postponed for a year.

Prior to the assembly elections, Ramgoolan formed a new electoral coalition, the Alliance of the Future (*Alliance de L'Avenir*), that included the MLP, MSM, and the PMSD (see Current issues, below). The coalition secured a comfortable majority with 45 seats. The rival Alliance of the Heart (*Alliance du Coeur*) which included the MMM, the Mauritian Socialist Party (*Parti Socialiste Mauricien*—PSM), and the National Union (*Union Nationale*), received 20. Ramgoolan was reappointed prime minister of a reshuffled cabinet that was sworn into office on May 11. The new cabinet also included 14 members from the MLP, 7 from the MSM, 2 from the PMSD, and 1 from the MR, which had not been part of the electoral coalition.

Monique Ohsan BELLEPEAU (MLP) was elected vice president by the National Assembly on November 11, 2010, to replace Angidi Verriah Chettiar, who died in office on September 15. She was the first female vice president of the country.

Ramgoolan dismissed Health Minister Santi Bai HANOOMANJEE (MSM) on July 26, 2011, following her arrest on corruption charges. That day, all MSM members of the cabinet resigned, and were replaced on August 7 by officials from other parties in the governing coalition.

On June 6, 2014, Vice Prime Minister and Finance Minister Xavier DUVAL, leader of the PMSD, resigned and his party withdrew from the government (see Current issues, below) joining the opposition. Ramgoolan assumed the finance ministry.

In legislative balloting on December 10, 2014, a coalition of the MSM, the PMSD, and the newly formed Muvman Liberater (ML) won a majority in Parliament with 47 elected seats. Party leader and former president Jugnauth (MSM) was sworn in as prime minister, along with a new coalition cabinet, on December 17.

On June 4, 2015, Ameenah GURIB-FAKIM (independent) was elected the first woman president of Mauritius by the assembly.

Constitution and government. The Mauritius Independence Order of 1968, as amended the following year by the Constitution of Mauritius (Amendment) Act, provided for a unicameral system of parliamentary government with executive authority exercised by a prime minister appointed by the governor general (as the representative of the Crown) from among the majority members of the Legislative Assembly. In December 1991 the assembly approved a change to republican status as of March 12, 1992, with an essentially titular president, appointed by the assembly to a five-year term, replacing the queen as head of state. The change also included creation of an indirectly elective vice presidency. The legislature (known under the present basic law as the National Assembly) includes a Speaker, 60 representatives directly elected from three-member districts on the main island, plus 2 from Rodrigues, and the attorney general, if not an elected member. In addition, up to 8 "best loser" seats may be awarded on the basis of party or ethnic underrepresentation as indicated by shares of total vote and total population, respectively. Judicial authority, based on both French and British precedents, is exercised by a Supreme Court, four of whose five judges (excluding the chief justice) preside additionally over Appeal, Intermediate, District, and Industrial court proceedings. There are also inferior courts and a Court of Assizes. In conformity with the practice of a number of other small republican members of the Commonwealth, final appeal continues to be to the Judicial Committee of the Privy Council in London.

Nine districts constitute the principal administrative divisions, with separate administrative structures governing the Mauritian dependencies. The Agalega and Cargados Carajos islands are ruled directly from Port Louis, while Rodrigues Island has a central government under a resident commissioner. On the main island, municipal and town councils are elected in urban areas and district and village councils in rural areas.

In 1991 a Rodrigues Local Council, comprising 21 members appointed by the minister for Rodriguan affairs, was established to exercise a degree of autonomy on Rodrigues. However, its mandate expired in 1996 amid political infighting concerning the issue. Subsequently, in November 2001, the National Assembly authorized creation of an elected Rodrigues Regional Assembly (see Legislature, below). In addition to enjoying the same authority as that of local bodies on the main island, the new Regional Assembly was empowered to propose bills to the National Assembly and to oversee development projects and otherwise administer internal initiatives.

The traditionally free Mauritian press was subject to censorship under the state of emergency imposed in 1971, but restrictions were lifted on May 1, 1976. Radio and television are under the semipublic control of the government-appointed Independent Broadcasting Authority. In its 2016 report, Reporters Without Borders asserted that press freedoms in Mauritius were similar to those in Western, developed countries and ranked Mauritius 61st out of 180 countries in freedom of the press.

Foreign relations. Mauritius maintains diplomatic relations with most major foreign governments. One principal external issue has been the status of Diego Garcia Island, which was considered a Mauritian dependency until 1965, when London transferred administration of the Chagos Archipelago to the British Indian Ocean Territory (BIOT). The following year, Britain concluded an agreement with the United States whereby the latter obtained use of the island for 50 years. Following independence in 1968 Mauritius pressed its claim to Diego Garcia, while international attention was drawn to the issue in 1980 when Washington announced that it intended to make the island the chief U.S. naval and air base in the Indian Ocean. In July the Organization of African Unity unanimously backed Port Louis's claim, but efforts by Prime Minister Ramgoolam to garner support from the UK government were rebuffed.

In July 1982 Britain agreed to pay $4 million in compensation for its 1965–1973 relocation of families from the Chagos islands to Mauritius. In accepting the payment, Port Louis reversed its position in regard to Diego Garcia and insisted that existence of the U.S. base violated a 1967 commitment by the United Kingdom (denied by London) that the island would not be used for military purposes. (For more on the dispute between 1989 and 2000, see the 2012 *Handbook.*) In October 2000 the British High Court ruled that some 2,000 inhabitants of Diego Garcia and other islands of the Chagos Archipelago had been "unlawfully removed" to Mauritius prior to independence, possibly opening the way for the return of Chagossians to all of the islands in question except, notably, Diego Garcia. Suits have been filed for substantial UK and U.S. financial support for the proposed return, while Mauritius has continued to press its claim to sovereignty over the islands. In 2004 lawyers representing the Chagossians petitioned Queen Elizabeth to permit the Chagossians to return to the Chagos Archipelago and to compensate them further for the UK's previous "unlawful actions." The petition also requested that the UK rebuild the infrastructure on the islands to permit the resumption of fishing and agriculture. In 2006 the UK High Court ruled in favor of the return of the Chagossians. The ruling was appealed by the UK Foreign Office, but the Court of Appeal affirmed the original decision. Chagossians were allowed to return to any of some 65 islands in the archipelago, but not Diego Garcia. Since many of the Chagossians had assimilated well in Mauritius, it was expected that only a small number would actually return to the islands, which had been uninhabited for more than 30 years. (For additional information, see the British Indian Ocean Territory section in the entry on the United Kingdom.)

Many years earlier, in June 1980, the Ramgoolam government had announced that it was amending the country's constitution to encompass the French-held island of Tromelin, located some 350 miles to the north of Mauritius, thus reaffirming a claim that Paris had formally rejected in 1976. In December 1989 the Jugnauth administration announced that it would seek a ruling on Tromelin from the General Assembly's Committee on Decolonization. Six months later French President François Mitterrand, during a tour of the Indian Ocean region, agreed to Franco-Mauritian discussions on the future of the island, although its status remained unchanged as of 2010.

Mauritius is a member of the Indian Ocean Commission (IOC). In February 1995 it hosted a ministerial meeting to form a regional economic bloc, the Indian Ocean Rim Association for Regional Cooperation (IOR-ARC), which first met in Mauritius in March 1997. In August 1995 Mauritius became a member of the Southern African Development Community (SADC). It is also a member of the Common Market for Eastern and Southern Africa (Comesa). Mauritius is pushing for trade expansion through the IOR-ARC because it finds the IOC and Comesa ineffective.

In an effort to overcome reductions in EU subsidies for Mauritian exports of sugar and textiles, the Ramgoolam government signed the U.S.–Mauritian Trade and Investment Framework in September 2006. The accord reduced tariffs on trade between the two countries and led to a rise in Mauritian exports to the United States, with total trade between the two countries at $237 million in 2007. Meanwhile, the government signed an interim trade agreement with the EU in December 2007. Also in December, Mauritius and India signed a 30-point antiterrorism agreement, which focused on efforts to curtail financial support for illegal organizations and activities.

In appreciation for continued Chinese investment, in March 2008 business leaders chartered the Mauritian Council for the Promotion of Peaceful Reunification of China to support unification of China and Taiwan. In May Mauritius donated $300,000 for the victims of the earthquake in southwest China. Nonetheless, there were tensions over China's growing influence (see Current issues). In July the two countries signed a series of bilateral economic agreements. In August Mauritius opposed the SADC Gender Protocol which set, among other goals, a requirement that women comprise 50 percent of all government posts and elected offices by 2015. Mauritian delegates argued that the protocol would require the country's constitution to be changed and replace existing equal rights measures with quota systems.

During a February 2009 visit to Mauritius, Chinese president Jintao Hu announced that his country would invest $260 million to expand the country's main airport. The following year, China committed to invest more than $700 million in a special economic zone in Mauritius.

Mauritius and the Seychelles met before the UN in August to defend rival claims for an extended maritime boundary. Both countries indicated they would accept whatever ruling the UN put forth. Mauritius and the Seychelles also agreed to increase naval cooperation to combat piracy and terrorism in the Indian Ocean. In December Mauritius announced that it would challenge British plans to create a marine sanctuary in the disputed Chagos islands. Also in December Mauritius and Bangladesh agreed on a memorandum of understanding to increase the number of Bangladeshi workers in the islands (in 2011 there were an estimated 11,500 Bangladeshi workers in Mauritius). The following year, Mauritius began negotiations to allow as many as 30,000 Ugandans to work in the country.

In 2011 a dispute over a 30-year-old treaty on taxation between Mauritius and India strained relations between the two countries. The agreement allowed Indian companies to avoid some taxes if they routed investments through Mauritius. India sought to renegotiate the accord, through which it lost an estimated $600 million a year. Through eight rounds of talks since 2006, Mauritian officials had refused to substantially alter the arrangement, despite warnings from the IMF that the end of the treaty would significantly erode the Mauritian economy.

In June 2012 a new deal was announced with the UK under which pirates the Royal Navy picked up at sea could be transferred to Mauritius for prosecution.

In January 2013 a tribunal of the UN Convention on the Law of the Sea (UNCLOS) agreed to review a Mauritian challenge to the British transfer of the Chagos Islands to the BIOT. Mauritius and the Maldives announced the formation of a joint economic commission in March, an initiative that was part of the broader effort to increase regional economic collaboration. Also in March Mauritius and India agreed to increase security cooperation, including the expansion of existing training programs. India further agreed to provide aircraft parts and equipment in a subsequent agreement. In November Ramgoolan announced he would not attend the Commonwealth meeting in Sri Lanka in protest of that country's human rights record.

In March 2014 Mauritius protested a visit by the British undersecretary of state for foreign and Commonwealth affairs to the Chagos Archipelago. In May the parliament enacted legislation to ensure that Mauritius was compliant with the World Intellectual Property Organization (WIPO) copyright treaty.

The Permanent Court of Arbitration at The Hague ruled on March 19, 2015, that the United Kingdom's 2010 declaration of a marine sanctuary around the Chagos was illegal and ordered both governments to negotiate the status of the sanctuary. The court declared that it did not have the authority to rule on the Mauritian claim that the transfer of the Chagos to the BIOT was illegal.

Indian prime minister Narendra Modi visited Mauritius in March 2015 and announced a $500 million credit for infrastructure projects in the country.

Current issues. The 2010 assembly campaign highlighted continuing ethnic divisions in Mauritius, with Ramgoolan and the Alliance of the Future drawing support from the majority South Asian community, while Bérenger and the Alliance of the Heart secured the backing of most Creoles and made a concerted effort to gain the votes of the Muslim community. The main issue in the balloting was the economy, and voters rewarded Ramgoolan's pragmatic approach to economic policy that allowed Mauritius to maintain growth, despite the global slowdown. Ramgoolan also brought the MSM into his coalition, further bolstering his appeal. The prime minister's new alliance won the May balloting with an expanded majority.

Health Minister Hanoomanjee (MSM) was arrested in July 2011 on charges that she had illegally awarded a government contract to the son-in-law of President Jugnauth. Ramgoolan dismissed her from the cabinet. Hanoomanjee's supporters claimed that the arrest and removal from office were politically motivated and designed to undermine the MSM and the president. On July 26 all of the MSM members of the cabinet resigned in protest, and the party left the governing coalition. This reduced the coalition's majority in the parliament to three seats (36 to 33).

After several weeks of political crisis in early 2012, Jugnauth resigned his post as president on March 31, ending a standoff triggered by Paul Bérenger's announcement of a new MSM-MMM opposition alliance that would be headed by Jugnauth. Ramgoolan reportedly told Jugnauth to either deny the statement or else to resign. Jugnauth has plans to run for prime minister in the 2015 elections, and the MSSM-MMM alliance, which replicates the one he had previously fronted and won the office of prime minister with in 2000, was said to be working to topple the government. Vice President Monique Ohsan Bellepeau took over as acting president. Rajkeswur PURRYAG, a former president of the National Assembly, was elected the new president at a special parliamentary session on July 21 and sworn in the next day. Razack PEEROO was subsequently elected speaker of the Assembly. In February 2013 Peeroo was elected speaker of the SADC's parliamentary forum.

Local elections in 2012 were the first to be held under a quota system in which one-third of a party's candidates had to be women. In the balloting, the MMM-MSM won majorities on three councils, including Port Louis, while the MLP-PMSD won one council, Vacoas-Phoenix. The final council was divided, with seven councilors each for the MMM-MSM and the MLP-PMSD and one seat for the small Mauritian Social Democratic Movement (*Mouvement Mauricien Sociale Démocrate*—MMSD).

In March 2013 Ramgoolam announced his support for electoral reforms, including the elimination of the system whereby the ethnicity and religion of candidates was listed on ballots. Opposition leaders have also endorsed the reforms. On March 30 severe flooding devastated Port Louis. More than 6 inches of rain fell in less than an hour, killing 11 and causing widespread damage.

Ramgoolam announced support for an electoral reform bill that would reduce the number of constituencies and major political parties in order to reduce the need for coalition governments. Vice Prime Minister Xavier Duval resigned in June 2014, and his party, the PMSD, withdrew from the governing coalition. Duval opposed Ramgoolan's proposals for constitutional and electoral reform, insisting that any potential changes be subject to a referendum. Also in June, the Global fund announced an award of $5.1 million to combat HIV/AIDS in Mauritius.

On February 6, 2015, former prime minister Ramgoolan was arrested after police discovered $3.17 million in cash at his home and charged him with corruption. He was released the following day on bail.

Pravind Jugnauth, son of the prime minister, resigned as minister of technology, communications, and innovation, on July 1, 2015, following a conviction on conflict of interest charges. On May 25, 2016, Jugnauth's conviction was overturned, and he was appointed minister of finance and economic development on May 26.

POLITICAL PARTIES

More than 60 political parties have contested the recent Mauritian elections but because most of the groups are leftist in orientation, ideological differences tend to be blurred, with recurrent cleavages based largely on pragmatic considerations.

Government and Government-Supportive Parties:

Mauritian Social Democratic Party (*Parti Mauricien Social-Démocrate*—PMSD). Composed chiefly of Franco-Mauritian landowners and middle-class Creoles, the PMSD initially opposed independence but subsequently accepted it as a fait accompli. Antisocialist at home and anticommunist in foreign affairs, it has long been distinguished for its Francophile stance. The party was part of the Ramgoolam government coalition until 1973, when it went into opposition.

In January 1994 Sir Gaëtan Duval, the leader of the PMSD, failed in an attempt to persuade Prime Minister Jugnauth to form a common front to block the threatened electoral alliance between the MLP and the MMM. At a party congress on May 22, he turned the leadership over to his son, Xavier Luc Duval, under whom the PMSD moved to the center. The party joined the MSM-led coalition in February 1995, with the younger Duval being given the industry and tourism portfolios; however, the move was opposed by the PMSD Central Committee, which in April called on Duval to resign from the government (a move that he undertook only in October for a quite different reason—his opposition to the proposed language amendment). The episode reflected a growing rift between the two Duvals, with Sir Gaëtan subsequently withdrawing from the PMSD to form the **Gaëtan Duval Party** (*Parti Gaëtan Duval*—PGD). As the PGD candidate, he reentered the assembly on a "best loser" basis after the December elections. Because the PMSD had failed to gain representation, the elder Duval effectively resumed its leadership until his death in May 1996, when his seat in the legislature passed to his brother, Hervé Duval. It was reported that Prime Minister Ramgoolam had approached Hervé Duval with a proposal to join the government in late June 1997 following the split in the MLP-MMM coalition. However, the PMSD leader decided to align instead with the MMM in the short-lived National Alliance opposition grouping (see MMM, below), a decision that apparently exacerbated Duval's differences with Charles Gaëtan Xavier Luc DUVAL, who subsequently formed his own grouping, the **Xavier Duval Mauritian Party** (*Parti Mauricien Xavier Duval*—PMXD). Following his split with his uncle, Xavier Luc Duval was elected to the National Assembly in a by-election on September 19, 1999, on a MLP-PMXD ticket. He was subsequently named minister of industry, commerce, corporate affairs, and financial services in the new MLP-led cabinet announced on September 26, and the party ran in alliance with the MLP in the September 2000 legislative poll, Duval securing one of the "best loser" seats in the assembly following that poll. In the 2000 balloting, the PMSD was described as associated with the coalition led by the MSM and MMM. (Hervé Duval's supporters have also been referenced as the ***Vrai Bleus*** [True Blues].) The party joined the MSM-MMM electoral coalition for the 2005 assembly balloting. When the MLP's Navin Ramgoolam became prime minister in 2005, he named Xavier Luc Duval one of his three deputy prime ministers (a position that was subsequently retitled vice prime minister in 2008).

In September 2006 the PMSD switched its support to the governing MLP-led coalition, reportedly in hopes of gaining a cabinet post. Duval subsequently reintegrated with the PMSD prior to the 2010 balloting, and the PMSD joined the MLP-led electoral coalition for the balloting and in the subsequent MLP-led coalition government. Duval's domestic popularity increased dramatically following his selection in 2012 as African minister of finance by *African Leadership Magazine*. On December 31 the party expelled the Minister for Tourism, Leisure, and External Communications, John Michaël Tzoun Sao Yeung Sik YUEN, over disputes with party leader Duval.

On June 6, 2014, Duval resigned as vice prime minister, and the PMSD withdrew from the governing coalition in a dispute over constitutional reforms. The PMSD was part of the MSM-led electoral alliance that won the 2014 national elections with 51 seats. Duval was subsequently appointed deputy prime minister, and the party was given five posts in the MSM-led coalition government.

Leaders: Charles Gaëtan Xavier Luc DUVAL (Deputy Prime Minister and President of the Party), Clifford EMPEIGNE.

Mauritian Socialist Movement (*Mouvement Socialiste Mauricien*—MSM). The MSM was organized initially on April 8, 1983, as the Militant Socialist Movement (*Mouvement Socialiste Militant*) by Prime Minister Jugnauth following his expulsion, in late March, from the MMM. Prior to the 1983 election, the MSM, with the MLP, the PMSD, and the OPR, formed a coalition that secured a clear majority of legislative seats. In February 1984 the MLP withdrew from the alliance, although a number of its deputies remained loyal to the government.

The MSM secured 26 of the 41 elective seats won in August 1987 by the reconstituted five-party alliance, from which the PMSD withdrew a year later. The MLP again moved into opposition following an electoral agreement between the MSM and MMM in July 1990, with the new MSM-led alliance winning 59 of the 62 elective seats in September 1991. In a disastrous loss in December 1995, all of the MSM deputies, including Jugnauth, lost their seats. However, the MSM formed a coalition with the MMM for the snap legislative elections in September 2000 and secured 54 of the elected seats with 51.7 percent of the vote.

Pravind Kumar Jugnauth succeeded his father as leader of the MSM in April 2003. In 2004 he called for retention of the MSM-MMM electoral alliance in the 2005 assembly balloting, prompting several prominent MSM members to quit the party to form the new MSD (above). Tensions grew within the MSM-MMM coalition in March 2008 over the MSM's demand that should the coalition win the next election, the new prime minister would be the younger Jugnauth, the current MSM party chair. In the 2010 balloting the MSM joined the MLP-led Alliance of the Future. Pravind Jugnauth was subsequently appointed vice prime minister in the MLP-led government. The MSM withdrew from the governing coalition in July 2011 after the dismissal of MSM health minister Santi Bai Hanoomanjee on corruption charges. In 2012 the party was reportedly seeking to change its mainly Hindu image by reaching out to disaffected Creole politicians from the MLP.

After resigning from the presidency on March 31 to return to party politics in an alliance between the MSM and the MMM, Anerood Jugnauth surprised the MMM leadership by announcing on April 2 that he would be merely an observer of negotiations between the parties, leaving his son Pravind in charge. But the MMM leadership insisted that, if the alliance wins the election, Anerood Jugnauth himself would become prime minister for three years, before handing the position over to Bérenger. At a meeting three days later, Pravind Jugnauth reportedly acquiesced.

The MSM and the MMM formed an electoral coalition for the 2012 local balloting. The MSM formed an alliance with the PMSD and the new Muvman Liberater party (ML, see below) for the 2014 elections, winning that balloting with 51 seats. Jugnauth formed a coalition government and was sworn in as prime minister on December 17.

Leaders: Sir Anerood JUGNAUTH (Prime Minister and Former President of the Republic), Pravind Kumar JUGNAUTH (Chair of the Party), Nando BODHA (Secretary General).

Muvman Liberater (ML). The ML was founded as a center-left grouping in 2014 by defectors from the MMM, led by Ivan COLLENDAVELLOO. The renegades opposed the MMM's 2014 electoral alliance with the MLP. The ML joined the MSM-led coalition, which won the 2014 assembly balloting. In the subsequent government, Collendavelloo was named a vice prime minister.

Leader: Ivan COLLENDAVELLOO (Vice Prime Minister and Chair).

Opposition Parties:

Mauritius Labour Party (MLP). A Hindu-based party, the MLP (also referenced as the **Workers' Party** [*Parti des Travailleurs*—PTr]), under the leadership of Seewoosagur Ramgoolam, joined the country's other leading Indian group, the Muslim Action Committee (CAM), in forming the Independence Party (IP) prior to the 1976 election. Collectively, the MLP and the CAM won an overwhelming majority of 47 legislative seats in the 1967 preindependence balloting, whereas the IP retained only 28 in 1976 and lost all but 2 in 1982 (both awarded to the MLP on a "best loser" basis). A condition of the MLP joining the 1983 government alliance was said to be the designation of Ramgoolam as president upon the country's becoming a republic; following failure of a republic bill in December 1983, the longtime MLP leader was named governor general.

In February 1984, after MLP leader Sir Satcam Boolell was relieved of his post as minister of planning and economic development, the party went into opposition. It reentered the government in August 1986, with Boolell as second deputy prime minister. In September 1990 the MLP again moved into opposition, Seewoosagur Ramgoolam's son, Navin, succeeding Boolell as party leader and assuming the post of leader of the opposition. On the basis of a preelectoral accord with the MMM's Paul Bérenger, the younger Ramgoolam became prime minister following the MLP-MMM victory in December 1995. The MLP-MMM coalition dissolved in mid-1997 with Ramgoolam subsequently remaining the head of an all-MLP (with the exception of one OPR minister) cabinet. At that point the MLP was described as holding a majority of 35–37 seats in the assembly. With the MMM aligning with the MSM for the September 2000 assembly balloting, the MLP was left with only the PMXD and several small parties as electoral partners, their coalition securing 36.6 percent of the vote but only 6 of the 62 elected seats.

The **Rally for Reform** (*Rassemblement pour la Réforme*—RPR) joined the MLP prior to the 2005 legislative elections. The RPR was launched in August 1996 by a dissident faction of the MSM led by Rama Sithanen (a former finance minister) and Sheila Bappoo (who had briefly been MSM secretary general). It formed an alliance with the PMSD for the October 1996 municipal elections, the combined list polling some 25 percent of the vote. In the September 2000 assembly balloting, the RPR was aligned with the MLP-PMXD coalition. Its leaders, Rama SITHANEN and Sheila BAPPOO, both subsequently gained cabinet posts in the MLP-led government after the 2005 elections.

The **Social Democratic Movement** (*Movement Social-Démocrate*—MSD) joined the MLP ahead of the 2010 balloting. The MSD was formed in March 2005 by four MSM legislators (including two who had recently resigned from the cabinet) to protest the proposed continuation of the MSM-MMM electoral alliance. The new party joined the Social Alliance for the July legislative balloting and integrated with MLP for the May 2010 balloting. MSD leaders Anil Kumar BAICHOO and Mookhesswur CHOONEE both received cabinet posts in the MLP government.

For the 2005 assembly elections, the MLP led a Social Alliance (*Alliance Sociale*) that included the new MSD, the PMXD, the MR, and the MMSN. In 2006 former vice president Angidi Verriah Chettiar was chosen as the honorary president of the party. He was subsequently appointed vice president of the republic in 2007. Chettiar died in office in 2010.

Ahead of the 2010 assembly elections, the MLP formed the Alliance for the Future, which included the MSM, and the PMSD. The coalition won the election with 49.3 percent of the vote, and Ramgoolan was reappointed prime minister. On November 11, 2011, Monique Ohsan BELLEPEAU was elected vice president of Mauritius. In local balloting in 2012, the MLP formed an electoral coalition with the PMSD. After the PMSD withdrew from the government in June 2014, Ramgoolan began negotiations with the MMM on an electoral alliance ahead of the 2014 balloting. The alliance campaigned on a proposal to directly elect the president and strengthen the powers of the office. The MLP-MMM alliance secured 16 seats in the December 2014 elections.

Leaders: Dr. Navin RAMGOOLAM (Former Prime Minister and Leader of the Party), Monique Ohsan BELLEPEAU (Vice President of the Republic), Ahmed Rashid BEEBEEJAUN (Former Deputy Prime Minister and Deputy Party Leader), Patrick ASSIRVADEN (Chair), Lormus BUNDHOO (Secretary General).

Mauritian Militant Movement (*Mouvement Militant Mauricien*—MMM). The leadership of the MMM was detained during the 1971 disturbances because of its "confrontational politics," which, unlike that of other Mauritian parties, was intended to cut across ethnic-communal lines. Following the 1976 election, the party's leadership strength was only 2 seats short of a majority; in 1982, campaigning in alliance with the Mauritian Socialist Party, it obtained an absolute majority of 42 seats.

In March 1983, 12 members of the MMM government of Anerood Jugnauth, led by Finance Minister Paul Bérenger, resigned in disagreement over economic policy and because they and their supporters believed that Creole should be designated the national language. Immediately thereafter, Jugnauth was expelled and proceeded to form the MSM (above), which, with its allies, achieved a decisive victory in the August 21 election.

Prior to the 1987 balloting, Bérenger, long viewed as a Marxist, characterized himself as a "democratic socialist." However, he was unsuccessful in securing an assembly seat on either a direct or "best loser" basis. The party itself campaigned as the leading component of a Union for the Future alliance, which included two minor groups, the **Democratic Workers' Movement** (*Mouvement des Travaillistes Démocrates*—MTD), then led by Anil Kumar BAICHOO and later by Sanjeet TEELOCK; and the **Socialist Workers' Front** (*Front des Travailleurs Socialistes*—FTS). On July 17, 1990, the MMM concluded an electoral accord with the MSM and MTD and formally entered the Jugnauth government on September 26.

In October 1993 Bérenger was briefly ousted as MMM secretary general, but he was returned to office by the party's Central Committee, which proceeded to expel the anti-Bérenger majority of Political Bureau members, including Prem Nababsingh and Dharmanand Goopt FOKEER, theretofore MMM president and chair, respectively, who remained members of the Jugnauth administration. In April 1994 Bérenger concluded an electoral pact with Navin Ramgoolam of the MLP under which, in the event of a coalition victory, Ramgoolam was to become prime minister and Bérenger his deputy. Two months later Nababsingh and his supporters formally left the MMM to organize the Mauritian Militant Renaissance.

Bérenger resigned his parliamentary seat on November 29, 1994, after having charged the MSM of manipulating the 1991 election, despite having been a government minister at the time. He regained his MP status in a by-election in January 1995 and became deputy prime minister and foreign minister as a result of the MLP-MMM victory in December 1995. However, Bérenger was relieved of his cabinet posts in June 1997, and the MMM moved into opposition when all but one of the party's nine other ministers resigned from the government.

In August 1997 Bérenger spearheaded the organization of a **National Alliance** (*Alliance Nationale*—AN) in an apparent attempt to improve his chances of securing the top governmental post in the next election. In addition to the MMM, the AN comprised the PMSD, the RPR, and the MMSM. However, the grouping did poorly in an April 1998 by-election (the AN candidate finished third with 16 percent of the vote), and a correspondent for the *Indian Ocean Newsletter* described the AN as "having been shot at dawn." Bérenger subsequently joined with Jugnauth in late 1998 to announce a MMM-MSM "federation" that would present joint candidates in the next general election and share governmental responsibility in the event of success. The federation was formally established in January 1999, and, as expected, Bérenger assumed a deputy post in the coalition with the understanding that he would be named to a similar rank in a Jugnauth-headed government. Following the landslide victory of the MSM-MMM coalition in the September 2000 balloting, Bérenger was named deputy prime minister, with the understanding that he would succeed Jugnauth as prime minister in three years. Bérenger also negotiated a similar proposed arrangement with Pravind Jugnauth of the MSM prior to the 2005 balloting.

On April 8, 2006, Bérenger resigned his position as leader of the opposition in the assembly because relations between the MMM and the MSM had deteriorated following the MMM-MSM coalition's defeat in the 2005 elections.

In May 2007 the MMM launched a campaign to attract younger, professional voters after a new Central Committee was elected. The effort was part of a larger initiative to remake the image of the party in advance of upcoming local and national elections. In September Bérenger was appointed leader of the opposition in the assembly. Reports indicated that the MMM and the MSM were unable to form a coalition because of the demand by the MSM's that party leader Pravind Jugnauth be prime minister, if a MMM-MSM coalition won the next election. In November 2008 Bérenger launched an initiative to reform the Mauritian electoral system by adopting a proportional system of representation.

The MMM formed the Alliance of the Heart prior to the 2010 balloting, which included the MMSM and the UN. The coalition was placed second in the balloting, losing to an MLP-led grouping. Bérenger led efforts to force MSM health minister Santi Bai

Hanoomanjee to resign in 2011. The MMM has since formed an alliance with the MSM (see Current issues, above).

In January 2013 MMM party leader Alan GANOO became the official leader of the opposition in the Assembly. The MMM joined the MLP in an electoral coalition that won 16 seats in the 2014 balloting.

Leaders: Paul BÉRENGER (Opposition Leader and Former Prime Minister), Premnath RAMNAH (Former Speaker of the National Assembly), Alan GANOO (Party President), Rajesh BHAGWAN (General Secretary), Jaya Krishna CUTTAREE (Deputy Party Leader).

Rodriguan People's Organization (*Organisation du Peuple Rodriguais*—OPR). The OPR captured the two Rodrigues Island seats in the 1982 and 1983 balloting and, having earlier indicated that it would support the MSM-Labour alliance, was assigned one cabinet post in the Jugnauth government of August 1983; it retained the post after the ensuing two elections. The OPR again won Rodrigues's two elective parliamentary seats in 1995, despite its affiliation with the Jugnauth administration. It joined the resultant MLP-led government, although its customary full ministerial responsibility for Rodrigues affairs was downgraded to junior level under the prime minister. The OPR regained the full cabinet authority for Rodrigues affairs in the new government announced in July 1997. The party again secured the two elective seats from Rodrigues in the 2000 and 2005 legislative polls.

In 2006 two OPR deputies in the Regional Assembly defected to the opposition **Rodriguan Movement** (*Mouvement Rodriguais*—MR), which gave the MR a majority in the assembly and forced Louis Serge Claire to resign as chief commissioner. Clair subsequently became the leader of the opposition in the assembly, and the OPR remained in opposition following regional elections in 2006. The MR secured 8 seats after the February 2012 election, the OPR secured 11, and the **Rodrigues Patriotic Front** (RPF) secured 2 seats.

The OPR won the two seats from Rodrigues in the 2014 legislative balloting.

Leaders: Louis Serge CLAIR (Former Rodrigues Island Minister, Leader of the Opposition in the Regional Assembly and Leader of the Party), Jean Alex NANCY (Secretary).

Other Parties and Groupings:

Rodriguan Movement (*Mouvement Rodriguais*—MR). A regional rival of the OPR favoring U.S.-style federalism rather than separation, the MR was awarded two "best loser" seats following both the 1995 and 2000 legislative polls. Following the defection of two OPR deputies and the loss of that party's majority in the Regional Assembly in 2006, MR member Johnson ROUSSETY was appointed chief commissioner of the island. The MR subsequently won a majority in the 2006 regional elections, and Roussety was reappointed.

In the 2010 legislative balloting the MR secured 2 seats. It subsequently joined the MLP-led government, and was given one ministry in the coalition government. The MR won 8 of 21 seats in the 2012 Rodriguan regional assembly balloting. The party lost its 2 seats in the national assembly in the 2014 elections.

Leaders: Johnson ROUSSETY (Chief Commissioner of Rodrigues), Nicolas VON MALLY (Party Leader).

Mauritian Militant Socialist Movement (MMSM). The MMSM is a radical Hindu group led by former agriculture minister Madun DULLO. It participated in the MLP-PMXD electoral alliance in the September 2000 assembly poll and the MLP-led Social Alliance in 2005. Dullo was dismissed as foreign minister in March 2008, and reports indicated that the MMSM would withdraw its support from the coalition government. The MMSM joined the MMM-led electoral coalition for the 2010 assembly balloting. However, MMSM member of parliament Eric GUIMBEAU left the parliament and became an independent in 2010 before forming the **Mauritian Social Democratic Movement** (*Mouvement Mauricien Sociale Démocrate*—MMSD). The MMSD secured 1 percent of the vote in the 2014 balloting and no assembly seats.

Leader: Madun DULLO.

Mauritian Solidarity Front (*Front Solidarite Mauriciene*—FSM), formed as the **Party of God** (*Hizbullah*), the Islamic party obtained one assembly seat as a "best loser" in the December 1995 election. (Some subsequent reports referenced the seat as belonging to the **Mauritian Liberal Movement** [*Mouvement Libéral Mauricien*—MLM], described as *Hizbullah*'s "ally.") Party leader Cehl MEEAH was held for three years on murder charges before being released in 2003. The party led an effort to replace the "best loser" system with one based on ethnic representation. In 2005 the FSM adopted its current name. The party secured one seat in the 2010 assembly balloting. In 2010 media reports indicated an increasing radicalization of the MSF. The party won 2 percent of the vote in the 2014 balloting but no seats.

Leader: Cehl MEEAH.

Green Party (*Les Verts*). The Green Party was reportedly aligned with the MSM-MMM electoral coalition in the September 2000 legislative balloting, and party leader Sylvio Louis MICHEL was named minister of fisheries in the new cabinet. For the 2005 balloting, the party joined the MLP-led electoral alliance, but failed to gain any seats, nor did it secure representation following the 2010 or 2014 balloting.

Leader: Sylvio Louis MICHEL.

Republican Movement (*Mouvement Républicain*—MR). The MR was founded on the eve of the October 1996 municipal balloting, in which its leader, Rama VALAYDEN, won a local council seat. Valayden had presented himself as an heir to the policies pursued by the late Sir Gaëtan Duval of the PMSD. (For more on the history of the MR, see the 2014 *Handbook*.) In 2006 the MR's Mirella CHAUVIN was elected mayor of Beau Bassin/Rose Hill, the second largest city in Mauritius. The MR negotiated with the MLP on an electoral alliance for the 2010 balloting, but did not join the Alliance of the Future and failed to gain any seats in the balloting. In 2010 Chauvin was appointed ambassador to Australia. In 2011 Valayden led an initiative to publicize the plight of sex workers in Mauritius. In December 2013 Valayden was arrested for allegedly tampering with a witness in a bribery case.

Leaders: Rama VALAYDEN, Sada ETWAROO, Mirella CHAUVIN.

Mauritian Socialist Party (*Parti Socialiste Mauricien*—PSM). The original PSM was formed in 1979 by the withdrawal from the MLP of a group of dissidents led by Harish BOODHOO. It was dissolved in May 1983 by absorption into the MSM, and Boodhoo was named deputy prime minister. In January 1986 Boodhoo resigned his government post in the wake of a disagreement with Prime Minister Jugnauth over drug policy, and he withdrew from the assembly the following November. (For more on the history of the PSM, see the 2014 *Handbook*.) The PSM did not gain any seats in the 2010 assembly balloting or the 2012 local elections.

Leader: Harish BOODHOO.

The small **National Union** (*Union Nationale*) joined the MMM-led **Alliance of the Heart** in the 2010 balloting but did not gain any seats of its own. In addition, there are two far-left organizations that remain active: **The Struggle** (*Lalit*), and the **Socialist Workers' Party** (*Parti Socialiste Ouvriére*—PSO).

Other parties participating in the 2000, 2005, 2010, or 2014 assembly elections were the **Agricultural Planting Movement** (*Mouvement Planteur Agricole*—MPA); **Authentic Mauritian Movement** (*Mouvement Authentique Mauricien*—MAM); **Liberal Action Party** (*Parti Action Libéral*—PAL); **Mauritian Democracy** (*Démocratie Mauricienne*—DM); **Mauritian Democratic Movement** (*Mouvement Démocratique Mauricien*—MDM); **Mauritius Party Rights** (MPR); **National Democratic Movement** (*Mouvement Démocratique National*—MDN); **NouvoLizur,** a grouping that supports "Chagossian rights"; **Party of the Mauritian People** (*Parti du Peuple Mauricien*—PPM); **Socialist Workers Movement** (*Mouvement Travailliste Socialiste*—MTS); **Tamil Council** (TC); **Mauritian Union** (*Union Mauricienne*—UM); **Muslim Action Committee** (*Comité d'Action Musulman*—CAM); **National Mauritian Movement** (*Mouvement National Mauricien*—MNM); and **Resistance and Alternative**.

LEGISLATURE

The Mauritian **National Assembly** is a unicameral body containing 62 elected deputies (3 from each of the 20 constituencies on the main island and 2 from Rodrigues Island), plus up to 8 appointed from the list of unsuccessful candidates under a "best loser" system designed to provide "balanced" ethnic and political representation. The legislative term is five years, subject to dissolution. In the National Assembly elections held on December 10, 2014, the Alliance of the People (*Alliance Lepep*), led by the MSM, won 47 of the 60 elected seats from the main island; 16 went to the MLP-MMM Alliance. The OPR won the 2 elected seats on Rodrigues Island. In the subsequent "best loser" distribution of appointed seats for the assembly, the Alliance of the People was accorded 4 additional seats; and the MLP-MMM Alliance, 3.

Speaker: Maya HANOONMANJEE (MSM).

Rodrigues Regional Assembly. As authorized by a constitutional amendment approved by the National Assembly in November 2001, the Rodrigues Regional Assembly comprises 18 members, 12 elected from six constituencies on a first-past-the-post system and 6 elected on a proportional basis. To comply with formulas governing the proportional allocation of seats, 3 extra seats were given to the RPO after balloting on February 5, 2012. The RPO secured 11 seats, the MR secured 8 seats, and the RPF secured 2 seats.

Chair: Joseph Chenlye LAMVOHEE.

CABINET

[as of September 1, 2016]

Prime Minister	Anerood Jugnauth (MSM)
Deputy Prime Minister	Charles Gaëtan Xavier-Luc Duval (PMSD)
Vice Prime Ministers	Showkutally Soodhun (MSM)
	Ivan Collendavelloo (ML)
Ministers	
Agro-Industries, Food Protection, and Security	Mahen Kumar Seeruttun (MSM)
Art and Culture	Santaram Baboo (PMSD)
Business, Enterprise, and Cooperatives	Soomilduth Bholah (MSM)
Civil Service Affairs and Administrative Reforms	Marie Roland Alain Wong Yen Cheong (PMSD)
Defense	Anerood Jugnauth (MSM)
Education, Human Resources, and Scientific Research	Leela Devi Dookun-Luchoomun (MSM) [f]
Energy and Public Utilities	Ivan Collendavelloo (ML)
Environment and National Development	Marie Roland Alain Wong Yen Cheong (PMSD)
External Communications and Tourism	Charles Gaëtan Xavier-Luc Duval (PMSD)
Finance and Economic Development	Pravind Jugnauth (MSM)
Financial Services, Good Governance, and Institutional Reforms	Sudarshan (Roshi) Bhadain (MSM)
Foreign Affairs, International Trade, and Regional Cooperation	Seetanah Lutchmeenaraidoo (MSM)
Gender Equality, Child Development, and Family Welfare	Aurore Perraud (PMSD) [f]
Health and Quality of Life	Anil Kumarsingh Gayan (ML)
Home Affairs	Anerood Jugnauth (MSM)
Housing and Lands	Showkutally Soodhun (MSM)
Industry, Commerce, and Consumer Protection	Ashit Kumar Gungah (MSM)
Island of Rodrigues	Anerood Jugnauth (MSM)
Justice and Attorney General	Ravi Yerrigadoo (MSM)
Labor, Industrial Relations, and Employment	Soodesh Satkam Callichurn (MSM)
Local Government	Mohammad Anwar Husnoo (ML)
Ocean Economy, Marine Resources, Fisheries, Shipping, and Outer Islands	Premdut Koonjoo (MSM)
Public Infrastructure and Land Transport	Nandcoomar Bodha (MSM)
Social Integration and Economic Empowerment	Prithvirajsing Roopun (MSM)
Social Security, National Solidarity, and Reform Institutions	Fazila Daureeawoo (MSM) [f]
Technology, Communication, and Innovation	Etienne Sinatambou (MSM)
Youth and Sports	Yogida Sawmynaden (MSM)

[f] = female

INTERGOVERNMENTAL REPRESENTATION

Ambassador to the U.S.: Sooroojdev PHOKEER.

U.S. Ambassador to Mauritius: Melanie ZIMMERMAN (Chargé d'Affaires).

Permanent Representative to the UN: Jagdish Dharamchand KOONJUL.

IGO Memberships (Non-UN): AfDB, AU, Comesa, CWTH, ICC, IOM, NAM, SADC, WTO.

For Further Reference:

Bowman, Larry. *Mauritius: Democracy and Development in the Indian Ocean.* Sudbury, MA: Dartmouth Publishing, 1991.

Lange, Matthew. *Lineages of Despotism and Development: British Colonialism and State Power.* Chicago: University of Chicago Press, 2009.

Salverda, Tijo. *The Franco-Mauritian Elite: Power and Anxiety in the Face of Change.* New York: Berghahn Books, 2015.

MEXICO

United Mexican States
Estados Unidos Mexicanos

Political Status: Independence originally proclaimed 1810; present federal constitution adopted February 5, 1917.

Area: 761,600 sq. mi. (1,972,544 sq. km).

Population: 128,632,000 (2016E—UN); 123,167,000 (2016E—U.S. Census).

Major Urban Centers (2016E urban area—UN): MEXICO CITY (Federal District, 21,157,000), Guadalajara (4,920,000), Monterrey (4,589,000), Puebla (3,032,000), Tijuana (2,032,000), León de los Aldamas (1,845,000), Ciudad Juárez (1,401,000), Mexicali (1,053,000).

Official Language: Spanish.

Monetary Unit: New Peso (market rate October 1, 2016: 19.39 pesos = $1US).

President: Enrique PEÑA Nieto (Institutional Revolutionary Party); elected July 1, 2012, and sworn in for a six-year term, along with a new government on December 1, succeeding Felipe CALDERÓN Hinojosa (National Action Party).

THE COUNTRY

Extending southeastward from the U.S. border to the jungles of Yucatán and Guatemala, Mexico ranks third in size and second in population among North American countries and holds comparable rank among the countries of Latin America. Its varied terrain encompasses low-lying coastal jungles, a broad central plateau framed by high mountain ranges, and large tracts of desert territory in the north. The people are mainly of mixed Indian and Spanish (*mestizo*) descent, with minority groups of pure Indians and Caucasians. Despite the predominance of Roman Catholicism, constitutional separation of church and state has prevailed since 1857, with links to the Vatican in abeyance until 1992 (see Foreign relations, below). About one-seventh of the population is still engaged in agriculture, which now contributes less than 5 percent of GDP. In 2000 women constituted 37 percent of the nonagricultural labor force, concentrated mainly in trade, manufacturing, and domestic service; in the export-oriented border factories (*maquiladoras*), the majority of the workforce is female.

Industrialization has been rapid since World War II, but its benefits have been unevenly distributed, and much of the rural population remained substantially unaffected. (For more on the history of the

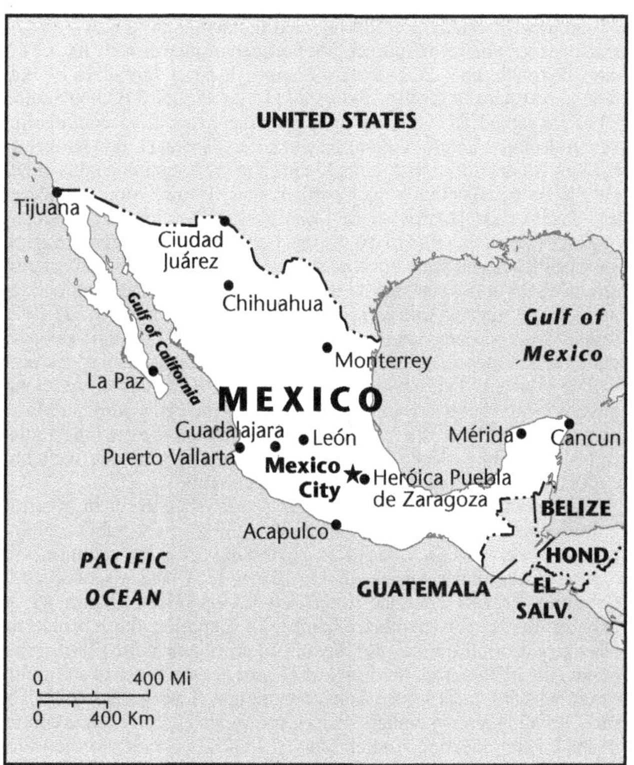

economy, see the 2015 *Handbook.*) Mexico's economy was transformed by passage of the North American Free Trade Agreement (NAFTA), which went into effect on January 1, 1994, severely weakening the agricultural sector and accelerating the growth of the *maquiladoras.* That December the country was engulfed by a fiscal crisis that prompted a $50 billion U.S.-led rescue package in January 1995.

During the global financial crisis beginning in 2008, Mexico's "resiliency was severely tested," according to the IMF, particularly as the currency depreciated—the peso fell 25 percent against the U.S. dollar in 2009. In addition, an outbreak of swine flu hit Mexico in midyear, and manufacturing exports declined. The IMF granted Mexico a flexible credit line of some $47 billion in April.

The economy shrunk nearly 7 percent in 2009, the government reporting it as the worst contraction in 30 years. However, with prompt intervention, growth resumed rapidly by early 2010, rebounding to 5.1 percent; the exchange rate recovered; and economic stability returned. Fund managers granted another $48 billion credit line and commended Mexican authorities for instituting tax reform measures to offset losses from declining oil production. Strong annual growth continued in 2011, with GDP of 4.5 percent, owing in large part to domestic demand, "benign" inflation, and increased foreign investment. GDP grew 4 percent in 2011 and 3.9 percent in 2012, while unemployment dipped from 5.2 percent in 2011 to 4.8 percent in 2012. GDP increased by 1.4 percent in 2013, 2.1 percent in 2014, and 3 percent in 2015. In 2016 GDP grew by an estimated 3.3 percent, and inflation was 3 percent and unemployment was 4 percent. In its 2016 annual report on the ease of doing business index, the World Bank ranked Mexico 38th out of 189 countries, a dramatic improvement from 53rd in 2014, mainly as a result of the decline in drug-related violence.

GOVERNMENT AND POLITICS

Political background. The territory that is now Mexico was conquered by Spain in the 16th century. Mexico proclaimed its independence in 1810 and the establishment of a republic in 1822. The country was ruled by Gen. Antonio López de SANTA ANNA from 1833 to 1855, a period that encompassed the declaration of Texan independence in 1836 and war with the United States from 1846 to 1848. Archduke MAXIMILIAN of Austria, installed as emperor of Mexico by Napoleon III in 1865, was deposed and executed by Benito JUAREZ in 1867. The dominant figure during the latter years of the 19th century was Gen. Porfirio DÍAZ, who served as president from 1877 to 1910.

Modern Mexican history dates from the Revolution of 1910, which shattered an outmoded social and political system and cleared the way for a generally progressive republican regime whose foundations were laid in 1917. From 1928 political life was dominated by a nationwide grouping known since 1946 as the Institutional Revolutionary Party (*Partido Revolucionario Institucional*—PRI), which purported to carry forward the work of the 1917 constitution.

Luis ECHEVERRÍA Alvarez, who assumed the presidency in 1970, sought to overcome inequitable distribution of income, widespread alienation and unrest, scattered urban and rural violence, and a visible erosion in the prestige, if not the power, of the PRI. Echeverría's efforts were opposed both by the right, because of a feeling that the traditional favoritism shown to business interests was waning, and by the left, because of a conviction that the reform was a sham.

In the presidential election of July 4, 1976, Finance Minister José LÓPEZ Portillo, running as the PRI candidate, obtained 94.4 percent of the popular vote against a group of independents, no opposition party having presented an endorsed candidate. Soon after his inauguration on December 1, the new chief executive introduced a far-reaching program of political reform that resulted in three previously unrecognized parties, including the Mexican Communist Party, being conditionally legalized prior to the legislative election of July 1979, after which all three were granted seats in the Chamber of Deputies according to their vote totals.

A left-wing coalition known as the Unified Socialist Party of Mexico (*Partido Socialista Unificado de México*—PSUM) formed in November 1981 by the Communists and four smaller parties, failed to gain ground against the entrenched PRI in the July 1982 balloting. The ruling party captured all but one elective congressional seat and saw its presidential candidate, former minister of programming and budget, Miguel de la MADRID Hurtado, win 74.4 percent of the vote in a field of seven nominees. During the ensuing four years the PRI was buffeted by an unprecedented, if minor, set of electoral losses to the rightist National Action Party (*Partido Acción Nacional*—PAN). In the lower house election of July 1985 PAN won nine elective seats, while in a supplementary distribution under proportional representation the leftist parties gained substantially more seats than in 1982.

At a congress in October 1987 the PRI ratified the selection of former planning and budget minister Carlos SALINAS de Gortari as its 1988 presidential candidate. Although seemingly assured of victory, Salinas was credited with a bare 50.4 percent vote share in the balloting of July 6, 1988. His three competitors, Cuauhtémoc CÁRDENAS Solórzano of the leftist National Democratic Front (*Frente Democrático Nacional*—FDN), PAN's Manuel CLOUTHIER, and Rosario IBARRA de la Piedra of the far-left Revolutionary Workers' Party (*Partido Revolucionario de los Trabajadores*—PRT), immediately brought charges of widespread fraud, which in September were rejected by the Congress sitting as an electoral college to review the results.

In the legislative and gubernatorial elections of August 18, 1991, the PRI won 31 of 32 available Senate seats and 290 of 300 directly contested Chamber seats. It was also declared the winner in all six state governorship contests, although two of the victors were forced to withdraw because of manifest voting irregularities. Subsequent gubernatorial, state, and municipal elections in 1992–1993 showed a pattern of eroding PRI support, occasional opposition successes, frequent violence, and continual opposition charges of fraudulent electoral practice. Following disclosures that the PRI had received large financial donations from the beneficiaries of privatization, party chair Genaro BORREGO Estrada in March 1993 announced a limit on individual contributions; later that month he was removed from office by President Salinas. The president, seeking to respond to domestic and international criticism of Mexican political practice, then initiated other PRI leadership changes and introduced electoral reform measures that were approved by Congress in September (see Constitution and government, below). Meanwhile, the government had come under strong censure for its unconvincing response to the killing on May 25 of the archbishop of Guadalajara, Cardinal Juan Jesús POSADAS Ocambo, who was caught in an apparent shootout between rival drug gangs at the city's airport.

In November 1993 the PRI leadership endorsed Luis Donaldo COLOSIO Murrieta, the social development secretary and a Salinas loyalist, as the party's presidential candidate for the 1994 election. However, a state of crisis generated by the eruption of a major insurgency in the southern state of Chiapas in January 1994 was compounded by the assassination of Colosio in the northern border city of

Tijuana on March 23. The replacement PRI candidate, Ernesto ZEDILLO Ponce de Léon (another Salinas loyalist but regarded as more conservative than Colosio), was duly elected president on August 21, but with the PRI's lowest-ever share of the popular vote, while simultaneous congressional elections yielded significant gains for opposition parties. Even more ominous for the PRI was a near sweep by PAN of executive and legislative races in the state of Jalisco on February 12, 1995, and the party's capture of the Guanajuato governorship on May 28. Meanwhile, the assassination of PRI secretary general José Francisco RUIZ Massieu on September 28, 1994 prompted an ever-widening inquiry into possible linkage with the Colosio killing and speculation as to ties between political figures and drug traffickers. On February 28, 1995, Raúl SALINAS de Gortari, the former president's older brother, was arrested for allegedly masterminding the Ruiz Massieu killing. (For more on the case, see the 2012 *Handbook.*)

In August 1995 the PAN retained control of Baja California (where the PRI in 1988 had experienced its first state-level defeat), its third victory of the year out of four such contests. By mid-November both the PAN and the leftist Democratic Revolutionary Party (*Partido de la Revolución Democrática*—PRD) had substantially increased their local representation, although the PRI succeeded in retaining the governorship of Michoacán, a PRD stronghold. The ruling party was subsequently embarrassed in the state of Guerrero, whose governor, Rubén FIGUEROA Alcocer, was obliged to resign on March 12, 1996, after being accused of attempting to cover up a police massacre of 17 opposition peasants. Meanwhile, PAN had pulled out of electoral reform talks with the PRI, although the PRD, which had earlier withdrawn from the discussion, returned to the negotiating table, paving the way for a tentative agreement on April 15 by parties holding 70 percent of the federal legislative seats.

Meanwhile, the outbreak of insurgent activity in the southernmost state of Chiapas continued under the direction of an indigenous formation styling itself the Zapatista National Liberation Army (*Ejército Zapatista de Liberación Nacional*—EZLN). Led by a charismatic *mestizo* using the alias "Subcomandante Marcos," the group issued a "Declaration of the Lacandona Jungle" that sought redress from "a dictatorship of more than 70 years."

On January 1, 1996, the Zapatistas announced the creation of a Zapatista National Liberation Front (*Frente Zapatista de Liberación Nacional*—FZLN), characterized as "a new political force with its base in the EZLN" that would work for the "transforming of Mexico." A month later the government and the EZLN reached agreement on a draft charter expanding the rights of Indians, thus clearing the way for a peace accord. However, the pact was threatened in late May, when the Zapatistas declared a "red alert" in areas under their control because of alleged military provocations by the government. The rebels again withdrew from the peace process but agreed on June 10 to return following the release of two high-ranking Zapatista leaders who had been captured in February. Meanwhile, an even more radical Popular Revolutionary Army (*Ejército Popular Revolucionario*—EPR) had emerged in the southern state of Guerrero. With no apparent links to the EZLN, EPR guerrillas mounted an attack on police and military installations in four Mexican states on August 28 that left 13 dead and 23 wounded.

By late 1996 the government also faced continued erosion in its political strength in the rest of the country. The PAN and the PRD both made significant inroads against PRI dominance in elections held in the states of Coahuila and México, winning a number of mayoralties. In addition, public opinion polls indicated that the PRI faced a genuine challenge in retaining its legislative majority in the national elections scheduled for mid-1997 and could also lose the concurrent first-ever direct balloting for mayor of Mexico City (considered the second-most influential office in the country). On July 6, 1997, the PRI retained only 238 of 500 lower house seats and yielded the Mexico City mayoralty to the PRD's Cárdenas Solórzano.

Following the election, the PRD, PAN, and two smaller legislative groups, the Labor Party (*Partido del Trabajo*—PT) and the Mexican Green Ecologist Party (*Partido Verde Ecologista de México*—PVEM), formed a working majority to constrain the PRI's theretofore unchallenged domination of the lower house, particularly in regard to the allocation of committee chairs. While the right-wing PAN subsequently insisted that its participation in the alliance was tactical, not strategic, it joined with the other opposition members in a semiformal *Grupo de los Cuatro* in mid-October.

On December 22, 1997, a band of gunmen, reportedly PRI adherents, attacked a small village in Chiapas, killing 45 Indians, including 15 children. President Zedillo branded the attack as "a cruel, absurd, and unacceptable criminal act." Subsequent contacts with the EZLN were distinctly uneven. Despite a number of peace initiatives by both federal and state authorities, talks stalled, and on June 8 Bishop Samuel RUIZ, resigned as the head of Conai, the negotiation commission, which declared its dissolution the same day. However, on October 18 the EZLN announced that it would return to the bargaining table, albeit only to attend talks involving a parliamentary Commission of Concord and Pacification (*Comisión de Concordia y Pacificación*—Cocopa), originally set up parallel to Conai, that had no executive representation.

The PRI closed out 1998 with a record of seven victories in ten governors' races, thus reversing a three-year decline that had cast doubt on its electoral appeal. In a verdict handed down on January 21, 1999, Raúl Salinas was convicted of ordering the 1994 Ruiz Massieu assassination and sentenced to 50 years' imprisonment (subsequently reduced to 27.5 years). In February state elections the PRI held three additional governorships but lost Baja California Sur to the PRD, while in March about 90 percent of the 3 million voters participating in the Indian rights plebiscite voiced support for the Zapatista program, including explicit constitutional recognition of Indian rights.

The election of July 2, 2000, was a watershed event in Mexican political history. Although consistently trailing in the public opinion polls, Vicente FOX Quesada of the right-wing PAN, in a coalition with a number of smaller parties called Alliance for Change, succeeded in defeating the PRI nominee, Francisco LABASTIDA Ochoa, 43–36 percent. In the 500-member Chamber of Deputies, the Alliance for Change won a substantial plurality of 223 seats, and in the 128-member Senate the PRI's former majority of 77 seats was reduced to a plurality of 60, with the Alliance for Change gaining a close second at 51. The PRD, heading a six-member Alliance for Mexico City, retained control of the capital, electing Andrés Manuel LÓPEZ Obrador to the office from which Cárdenas had resigned to run for the presidency.

In late April 2001 the government passed an Indigenous Rights Bill that authorized constitutional changes prohibiting discrimination based on race, religion, or gender. It also permitted election of indigenous officials by standard electoral practices; guaranteed the right to preserve Indian languages and cultures; and offered indigenous peoples preferential use of natural resources. Though Fox had offered concessions to the Zapatistas, including the closure of military bases in Chiapas, the EZLN and its supporters had traveled en masse to Mexico City in March, rallying some 200,000 people from diverse groups to lobby for the EZLN's preconditions. Meanwhile, some Indian groups opposed the bill because of last-minute changes that altered the conditions of autonomy. Ultimately, the EZLN refused to resume peace talks with the government. In late 2003 the group declared political autonomy in 30 of its indigenous municipalities.

The 2003 general congressional balloting yielded significant changes in the political landscape. The PAN representation plummeted, while that of the PRI rose to just short of a majority. The biggest surprise, however, was the success of the PRD in nearly doubling its representation from 52 to 95, enhancing López Obrador's presidential prospects.

Though López Obrador was the front-runner during much of the 2006 presidential campaign, he lost to the PAN's Felipe CALDERÓN Hinojosa by just 0.5 percent of the vote in controversial balloting on July 2. López Obrador demanded a national recount, alleging widespread election irregularities. He and his allies staged massive protests in Mexico City, and though the rallies lost popular support over time, López Obrador continued to dispute the outcome of the election. After a partial recount in August, the Federal Electoral Court certified the results and declared Calderón president-elect on September 5. He was inaugurated along with a new cabinet on December 1 while López Obrador led a massive march along the central avenue of the city. In concurrent parliamentary elections, the PAN won a plurality in both the Senate and the Chamber of Deputies.

In 2009 President Calderón dispatched 45,000 troops and 30,000 federal police to cities hard-hit by drug-related violence. In February drug gangs killed an army general assigned to head the police in Cancún, engaged in a prolonged firefight with the army in Chihuahua, and forced the resignation of the police chief in Ciudad Juárez, where more than 6,000 people were killed in 2008. The troops replaced corrupt, ineffective, or overwhelmed local police. Among the cartels fighting for control of the region were the Arellano FÉLIX or Tijuana organization; *Los Aztecas,* headed by Arturo GALLEGOS Castrellón; the Sinaloa cartel, which included the factions of Joaquín "*El Chapo*" ("Shorty") GUZMÁN and the BELTRÁN LEYVA brothers; the Gulf cartel, also known as *Las Zetas* or *La Compañía;* and the Michoacán-based *La Familia.* Meanwhile, the Sinaloa cartel's Guzmán appeared in *Forbes* magazine's list of the richest people in the world, his fortunes owing to cocaine trafficking. He was also cited for allegedly being responsible for "thousands of murders" (see Current issues, below)

In the July 5, 2009, midterm balloting for the Chamber of Deputies, the PRI secured 237 seats, an increase of 133 compared with 2006. The PAN was second with 143 seats, a loss of 63 seats compared with the previous election.

By September 2009 drug-related killings, reported at nearly 6,000, had surpassed the total for all of 2008. Observers said the government crackdown helped fuel the rise in homicides, as drug cartels were broken up and infighting occurred. Late in the year the government's security woes were compounded by economic issues, as 20,000 demonstrators, led by members of the electrical workers union, rallied in a symbolic "taking of Mexico City" demonstration to protest President Calderón's having seized a large central power plant in October, liquidating its assets, and firing all 45,000 workers. The government's move was meant to dissolve the union, whose members had been a leading force in organizing protests against the president's economic policies, including his effort to privatize the power industry, observers said.

The drug war continued to take its toll in 2010. In March three people connected with the U.S. consulate in Ciudad Juárez were killed. Calderón maintained that the increasing bloodshed demonstrated that the cartels had become desperate. It was reported that the majority of firearms used by the drug gangs were manufactured in or imported from the United States, according to U.S. and Mexican authorities (see Foreign relations, below). Government figures for the year showed that violent crime associated with drug cartels had resulted in 15,273 deaths, an increase of 59 percent compared with 2009.

A minor cabinet reshuffle occurred on March 10, 2010. On July 14, following a dispute between the president and Interior Minister Fernando GÓMEZ MONT, the minister resigned in protest of Calderón's overtures to the PRD to form an alliance against the PRI, and he also quit the PAN. The cabinet, including a new economy minister, comprised members of the PAN, the military, and independents.

In the run-up to the July 4, 2010, gubernatorial elections, several candidates were assassinated, including the front-running PRI candidate for governor of Tamaulipas. President Calderón blamed the drug cartels for the killings. As tensions heightened, the PAN, PRD, PT, and Convergence parties asked the electoral coalition to take the unusual step of monitoring the state elections. Meanwhile, the PRD was losing electoral traction due to infighting. Subsequently, though the PRI made overall gains in the elections, it lost control of the politically important states of Oaxaca, Sinaloa, and Puebla, where it was defeated by the faction known as the anti-PRI alliance. The upsets were the PRI's first gubernatorial defeats in those three states in decades.

The PRI swept presidential and legislative balloting on July 1, 2012. The party secured 212 of 500 seats in the Chamber of Deputies, followed by PAN with 114, the PRD with 114, and the remainder to smaller parties. The PRI won 52 seats in the Senate, with 38 going to PAN, 22 to the PRD, and the rest to minor groupings. An alliance with the PVEM, which won 29 seats in the Chamber and 9 in the Senate, gave the PRI effective majorities in both chambers. PRI candidate Enrique PEÑA Nieto was elected president and sworn in on December 1, returning the PRI to power after 12 years.

In midterm balloting on June 7, 2015, the PRI again won a majority with 203 seats, followed by PAN with 108, and the PRD with 56, among others. In the polling, the newly formed, left-wing National Regeneration Movement (*Movimiento Regeneración Nacional*—MORENA), led by former presidential candidate López Obrador, won 35 seats (see Political Parties, below). Following the elections, the president reshuffled the cabinet on August 24.

Constitution and government. Under its frequently amended constitution of February 5, 1917, Mexico is a federal republic consisting of 31 states (each with its own constitution, elected governor, and legislative chamber) plus a Federal District, whose chief executive (formerly appointed, but elected as of 1997) is advised by 365 elected councilors. The president is directly elected for a single six-year term. Since 2000 only one, rather than both, parents of presidential contenders must be native-born Mexicans. There is no vice president. Mexico has no constitutionally defined line of succession should the president resign or become incapacitated; in that event, the Congress chooses the next president by secret ballot.

The bicameral Congress, consisting of an elected Senate and Chamber of Deputies (both under a mixed direct and proportional system), was long confined by the party system to a secondary role in the determination of national policy; at present, however, with different parties controlling the legislative and executive branches, its influence has drastically increased. The judicial system is headed by a 21-member Supreme Court, which has four divisions: administrative, civil, labor, and penal. The justices of the Supreme Court are appointed for life by the president with the approval of the Senate. Lower courts include collegiate and single-judge circuit courts, district courts, and jury courts. The basis of local government is the municipality (*municipio*).

State and Capital	*Area (sq. mi.)*	*Population (2015E)*
Aguascalientes (Aguascalientes)	2,112	1,312,544
Baja California Norte (Mexicali)	26,997	3,315,766
Baja California Sur (La Paz)	28,369	712,029
Campeche (Campeche)	19,619	899,931
Chiapas (Tuxtla Gutiérrez)	28,653	5,217,908
Chihuahua (Chihuahua)	94,571	3,556,574
Coahuila (Saltillo)	57,908	2,954,915
Colima (Colima)	2,004	711,235
Durango (Durango)	47,560	1,754,754
Guanajuato (Guanajuato)	11,773	5,853,677
Guerrero (Chilpancingo)	24,819	3,533,251
Hidalgo (Pachuca)	8,036	2,858,359
Jalisco (Guadalajara)	30,535	7,844,830
México (Toluca)	8,245	16,187,608
Michoacán (Morelia)	23,138	4,584,471
Morelos (Cuernavaca)	1,911	1,903,811
Nayarit (Tepic)	10,417	1,181,050
Nuevo León (Monterrey)	24,792	5,119,504
Oaxaca (Oaxaca)	36,275	3,967,889
Puebla (Puebla)	13,090	6,168,883
Querétaro (Querétaro)	4,421	2,038,372
Quintana Roo (Chetumal)	19,387	1,501,562
San Luis Potosí (San Luis Potosí)	24,351	2,717,820
Sinaloa (Culiacán)	22,486	2,966,321
Sonora (Hermosillo)	70,291	2,850,330
Tabasco (Villa Hermosa)	9,756	2,395,272
Tamaulipas (Ciudad Victoria)	30,650	3,441,698
Tlaxcala (Tlaxcala)	1,511	1,272,847
Veracruz-Llave (Veracruz)	27,683	8,112,505
Yucatán (Mérida)	14,827	2,097,372
Zacatecas (Zacatecas)	28,283	1,579,209
Federal District		
Ciudad de México	579	8,918,653

Reporters Without Borders described Mexico as "the western hemisphere's deadliest country for the media" and ranked Mexico 148th out of 180 countries in its 2016 Index of Press Freedom.

Foreign relations. A founding member of the United Nations, the Organization of American States (OAS), and related organizations, Mexico has generally adhered to an independent foreign policy based on the principles of nonintervention and self-determination. One of the initiators of the 1967 Treaty for the Prohibition of Nuclear Weapons in Latin America (Treaty of Tlatelolco), it is the only non-South American member of the Latin American Integration Association (ALADI) and the only OAS state to have continually maintained formal relations with Cuba. In return, Mexico was the only major Latin American country for which Castro refused to train guerrillas.

Under President de la Madrid the country continued to exercise a leadership role in the region, despite a diminution of influence because of its economic difficulties. In the 1980s, as a participant in the Contadora Group, which also included Colombia, Panama, and Venezuela as original members, Mexico took the group's agenda for regional peace to both South America and the United States. U.S. military policy in Central America continued to be a major source of strain in the traditionally cordial relationship between Mexico and its northern neighbor.

In 1988–1989 the United States pledged to support Mexico's efforts to enact economic reforms and negotiate a debt reduction agreement.

Meanwhile, U.S.–Mexico commercial relations continued to expand; in November 1989 the leaders of the two nations signed a trade accord, and in September 1990 Mexico, in a dramatic reversal of its traditional posture, formally requested the opening of free trade talks. Thereafter, Canada, which had concluded a free trade agreement with the United States in December 1989, was invited to participate in the discussions, which commenced in mid-1991 and concluded with agreement on the precedent-shattering NAFTA on August 11–12, 1992.

In a historic move, Mexico and the Vatican reestablished diplomatic relations in September 1992—for the first time in well over a century since President Juarez confiscated all church property. The renewal of ties followed President Salinas's unprecedented audience with Pope John Paul II the previous year and revisions in July to sections of the constitution dating to 1917 that had denied legal status to the Roman Catholic Church and to other religious groups.

NAFTA was ratified by the Mexican Congress in December 1993 (coming into effect on January 1, 1994) following agreement months earlier on some contentious labor and environmental subclauses. In late 1993 Mexico joined with Colombia and Venezuela (the so-called Group of Three) in a regional trade pact intended to create an economic market encompassing some 145 million people.

Counternarcotics policy has been a continuing subject of cooperation and contention between the United States and Mexico. In 1997, during a period of increased U.S. assistance in combating the drugs trade, the head of Mexico's antidrug agency, Gen. Jesús GONZÁLEZ Rebollo, was arrested on charges of collusion with traffickers. In the wake of the U.S. action, opposition legislators charged the Zedillo administration with sacrificing Mexican interests to Washington's agenda. Further fueling the controversy was the charge by a high-ranking U.S. Drug Enforcement Agency official in mid-1997 that Colombian drug activities had been "eclipsed" by those of the Mexican cartels.

In December 2000 the Mexican Senate ratified a free trade agreement with Guatemala, Honduras, and El Salvador that had been concluded six months earlier.

Despite a decline in U.S.–Mexico cooperation in countering drug trafficking, President Fox was the first foreign leader President George W. Bush traveled to meet, in February 2001. Fox's subsequent trip to Washington in early September marked the first state visit under President Bush. Following the September 11 terrorist attacks in the United States, however, relations with Mexico became a much lower priority for the Bush administration. Relations with the United States grew more distant after President Fox refused to back U.S. policy in Iraq and opposed as "inadequate" most overtures by President Bush on resolving the status of Mexican nationals in the United States (who were said to account for approximately 60 percent of all illegal immigrants).

Mexico and Venezuela severed diplomatic ties in November 2005 after President Hugo Chavez accused President Fox of being "a puppy" of U.S. president Bush, and Fox demanded an immediate apology. The withdrawal of their respective ambassadors highlighted the two countries' differences over trade relations with the United States.

In 2007, at the conclusion of a five-country tour of Latin America, President Bush pledged to push Congress to approve a comprehensive immigration reform package to increase efforts to stem the demand for illegal drugs in the United States, as well as to restrict supplies from Latin America and combat arms trafficking from the United States to Mexico and Central America.

In July 2007 Argentina's president, Néstor Kirchner, and his wife Cristina Fernández (the president-elect) visited Mexico to sign agreements enhancing trade, and encouraged Mexico to apply for full membership in Mercosur, the South American customs union of which Mexico is an associate member. Mexico also began a dialogue to repair relations with Venezuela and Cuba.

In June 2008 the Mérida Initiative, a framework for U.S. counterdrug assistance worth $1.4 billion over three years benefiting Mexico, the Dominican Republic, Haiti, and the countries of Central America, was signed into law.

An increase in drug-related crime near the U.S.–Mexico border, including an October 11, 2008, grenade and gunfire attack on the U.S. consulate in Monterrey, revived Mexico as a top concern of U.S. policymakers. Numerous U.S. administration officials visited Mexico between October 2008 and August 2009, including a visit by President Barack Obama, to discuss law enforcement and cooperation on security.

U.S.–Mexican security cooperation was enhanced in 2009 when the Mexican Navy participated in its first joint exercise with the United States. The U.S. Congress subsequently approved an additional $420 million for Mexican security in June, well beyond the $66 million the Obama administration had requested.

Relations between Mexico and Honduras were restored in August 2010. Mexico had withdrawn its ambassador from Tegucigalpa following the coup that ousted President Manuel Zelaya in June 2009.

Formal negotiations on a strategic bilateral accord with Brazil began in November 2010.

In April 2010 violence related to drug trafficking in the area of the U.S.–Mexico border had escalated to the point that the U.S. government began issuing travel advisories for northern Mexico. Tensions increased significantly as a result of the fallout from Operation Fast and Furious, a U.S. initiative in 2009–2010 aimed at curbing the flow of arms to drug traffickers and other criminals in Mexico. Following the death by shooting of a U.S. Border Patrol agent in late 2010, reportedly by use of a weapon linked to Fast and Furious, controversy over the program and cross-border tensions heightened, and a U.S. congressional investigation determined that lax management had allowed weapons to fall into the hands of criminals.

In February 2012 Mexico and the United States signed the Transboundary Hydrocarbons Agreement, which facilitated joint exploration of offshore oil and gas reserves in the western Gulf of Mexico.

In October 2013 revelations emerged that in 2010, the United States had hacked into the email accounts of then President Calderón and future President Peña Nieto. The spying was condemned by the Mexican government that summoned the U.S. ambassador. The United States pledged a full investigation into the incident and promised not to repeat the spying.

In January 2014 Mexico and Guatemala announced a $1.2 billion project to construct a 600 km gas pipeline to supply energy to southern Guatemala. The pipeline was projected to be complete in 2016. Over an eight month period ending in June 2014, more than 52,100 unaccompanied minors were caught trying to cross the border into the United States, almost double the number form the previous year. Approximately 40,000 of these were from Central America, the majority from Honduras and Guatemala. The flood of children prompted President Peña Nieto to call for immigration reform in the United States (see entry on the United States).

On October 12, 2015, Mexico joined 11 other nations in signing the Trans-Pacific Partnership free trade agreement (see entry on the United States). The accord generated considerable domestic opposition.

Mexico's leading drug kingpin, Joaquín "El Chapo" GUZMÁN was captured on February 22, 2014. Mexico initially denied U.S. requests to extradite El Chapo. However, after he escaped in July 2015 and was recaptured in January 2016, Mexico agreed to send El Chapo to the United States, although the kingpin's lawyers continued through 2016 to resist the move.

Current issues. As he entered the last year of his presidency, Calderón's tactics against drug-related crime continued to come under fire. The military units he deployed in high crime areas were criticized for excessive force, brutality, and human rights violations by both domestic and international human rights groups. A Supreme Court ruling in July 2011 ordered that soldiers on domestic security duty and accused of human rights violations be tried in civilian, not military, courts. The high court also ruled that all judges in Mexico are required to ensure that rulings meet universal human rights standards in accordance with the Mexican constitution.

On July 1, 2012, Mexico held elections for the president, both chambers of the Union Congress, and governors. Slow economic growth and the bloody drug wars topped the political agenda. Over 50,000 people were murdered in drug-gang violence during Calderón's presidency, including 16,000 in 2011, and the body count grew during in the final days of the campaign. (For more on the drug war through 2012, see the 2014 *Handbook.*)

The PRI swept the elections, winning the presidency and pluralities in both the Senate and the Chamber of Deputies. In alliance with PVEN, the PRI has a majority in the Chamber and was just two votes shy of a majority in the Senate. The party also controlled 21 of Mexico's 32 states. After 12 years of PAN rule, the PRI again dominated the Mexican political scene.

In the presidential race, Enrique Peña Nieto (PRI) received 38.2 percent of the vote, followed by Andrés Manuel López Obrador (PRD) with 31.6 percent. Josefina Vázquez Mota (PAN), the first woman to head the slate of a major party, finished third, with 25.4 percent, followed by Gabriel QUADRI (Panal) with 2.3 percent. Peña Nieto, the 46-year-old former governor of the state of Mexico, campaigned on a platform that presented him as the "new generation" of the PRI. He promised to spur economic growth, cut crime, and open the state oil company *Petroleos Mexicanos* (Pemex) to private investment.

López Obrador finished the 2012 election much as he had the 2006 presidential race: in second place by a very slim margin. At his insistence, the Mexican electoral authority retabulated the results from 50 percent of the polling stations, confirmed their original vote count, and certified Peña Nieto as the winner on August 31.

The recount did not satisfy all voters. Anti-PRI groups joined López Obrador in accusing Peña Nieto of buying votes with store gift cards and biased media coverage. Hackers took over a dozen government websites on September 16, Mexican Independence Day, calling Peña Nieto an "imposed president." The attacks have been linked to "#YoSoy132," a social media-based student movement that criticized media coverage of Peña in the last weeks of the campaign.

The outgoing Congress approved a bipartisan labor reform package on November 2012 that better regulated temporary and part-time workers and offered improved protections to women and child laborers.

Peña Nieto was sworn in on December 1 and announced an ambitious reform agenda consisting of five broad "pillars": reducing violence, combating poverty, boosting economic growth, reforming education, and fostering social responsibility. Peña Nieto plans to pay for new programs, such as social security, by raising the top income tax rate, taxing capital gains, and expanding value-added taxes to food and medications. On December 10 he also announced a 5 percent pay cut for all mid-level and upper-level civil servants. He also opened the telecommunications sector to foreign investment.

Peña Nieto called for opening PEMEX to outside investors, which required a constitutional amendment—and support from two-thirds of Congress. To this end, he announced a Pact for Mexico on December 2 in which the opposition PAN and PRD pledged to support legislation to implement the five pillars. Shortly thereafter, Congress passed legislation that transferred control of the national school system from the National Union of Education Workers (*Sindicato Nacional de Trabajadores de la Educación*—SNTC) to the federal government.

On January 31, 2013, an explosion ripped through the PEMEX office tower in downtown Mexico City, killing 37 people and injuring more than 100. It was later determined to be the result of a gas buildup, not a bomb.

In a major crackdown on corruption, Elba Esther GORDILLO Morales, head of SNTC, was arrested on February 27, 2013, and charged with embezzling $150 million. Gordillo had previously been secretary general of the PRI before launching Panal.

Mexican officials arrested several high-profile drug lords, including a dozen members of *La Familia Michoacana* in January, Jonathan "The Ghost" SALAS of the Sinaloa cartel in February, and Miguel Angel "Z-40" TREVIÑO Morales, the leader of *Las Zetas* drug cartel, in July.

Local elections in 900 municipalities were held on July 7, 2013, and PRI candidates won roughly half of the contested seats. The run-up to the votes was marred by violence; 12 candidates were assassinated, and many more dropped out. On September 13, 2013, a protest in Mexico City against educational reforms turned violent, leading to the arrests of 31 people. Hurricane Manuel struck the southwest coast on September 15, killing more than 130 and displacing more than 59,000. The hurricane, combined with Tropical Strom Ingrid that struck the eastern coast the following day, was estimated to have destroyed more than 613,000 hectares of farmland.

On December 20, 2013, the president signed into law measures that amended Mexico's constitution by ending Pemex's monopoly and allowing private investment in the energy sector. The amendments had been approved by the federal legislature on December 12 and by a majority of state legislatures by December 18.

In January 2014 Congress approved legislation allowing senators and mayors to serve two consecutive terms, and chamber deputies to serve four consecutive terms. Presidents were still limited to a single six-year term.

The government achieved a number of successes against the drug cartels through 2014. Officials reported that drug-related violence had declined by 20 percent since Peña Nieto was inaugurated. For instance, Knights Templar leader Dionisio "*El Tio*" Loya PLANCARTE was caught on January 27, 2014. On February 23 *Sinaloa* cartel leader Guzmán was captured by police in Mazatlán. On March 9 Nazario Moreno GONZALES, a leader of *La Familia,* was killed by federal police. However, spectacular acts of violence continued. For instance, during a two week period in February, two mass graves one with 20 bodies in Tingüindín, the other with 17 in Guadalajara, were discovered, while the severed heads of four men were found together in Zacán.

Meanwhile, some armed citizen groups that had emerged to fight the drug cartels, were given official recognition and status as "rural police forces." The self-defense groups were able to suppress drug crime in some areas, including in the violence-plagued state of Michoácan. However, increasing violence between the vigilante groups and the drug cartels led the government to deploy troops and federal police to Michoácan in January 2014. Federal security forces arrested 38 members of the Knights Templar, including a senior leader of the group, Jesus VASQUEZ Macias. In March Hipolito MORA, the leader of one of the self-defense groups was arrested on suspicion of murdering two rival vigilantes. Four members of another Michoácan self-defense group were also arrested for allegedly murdering the mayor of Tanhuato, an outspoken critic of the vigilantes.

On September 26, 2014, 43 students were abducted from a teachers' college in Iguala, Guerrero, Mexico. The victims were reportedly taken into police custody and then turned over to a drug cartel under the orders of the mayor of Iguala, José Luis ABARCA Velázquez. The students were all believed to have been killed. Abarca and his wife were arrested after they attempted to flee. Various members of the local police also fled or were implicated in the incident, which prompted the resignation of the governor of Guerrero and led to nationwide demonstrations against drug violence in Mexico. In response the federal government introduced a number of criminal justice reforms, including a proposal to replace local police forces with state officers.

Violence associated with the drug cartels was down from 2011 to 2014. However, in 2015 the trend reversed, with an estimated 17,000 homicides, of which 50 percent were reportedly drug related. Nevertheless, the 8.7 percent uptick in drug-related violence did not appear to have had a significant impact on elections.

In December 2015 legislators approved a measure to make the Mexico City federal district the country's 32nd state. In state elections on June 5, 2016, PAN won seven gubernatorial races, while the PRI won five. The PRI had controlled nine of the 12 governorships in contention.

POLITICAL PARTIES

Mexican politics for more than seven decades after the late 1920s featured the dominance of a single party, the Institutional Revolutionary Party (*Partido Revolucionario Institucional*—PRI), which enjoyed virtually unchallenged control of the presidency, the Congress, and state governments. The situation changed dramatically, however, when the PRI lost the election of July 2, 2000. After a dozen years in the opposition, the PRI returned to power in 2012, albeit by a very small margin. Today, three parties dominate Mexico's political landscape: the National Action Party (*Partido Acción Nacional*—PAN), the Democratic Revolution Party (*Partido de la Revolución Democrática*—PRD), and the PRI.

Parties must now capture a mandated minimum of 2 percent of the total vote in a national election to maintain their registrations. Seven parties qualified for the 2012 national elections. In January 2013, 11 groups applied to the Federal Electoral Institute (*Instituto Federal Electoral*—IFE) for new party recognition.

Government Party:

Institutional Revolutionary Party (*Partido Revolucionario Institucional*—PRI). Founded in 1929 as the **National Revolutionary Party** (*Partido Nacional Revolucionario*—PNR) and redesignated in 1938 as the **Mexican Revolutionary Party** (*Partido de la Revolución Mexicana*—PRM), the PRI took its present name in 1946. As a union of local and state groups with roots in the revolutionary period, it was gradually established with a broad popular base and retains a tripartite organization based on three distinct sectors (labor, agrarian, and "popular"), although in 1978 it was officially designated as a "workers' party." While the PRI's general outlook may be characterized as moderately left-wing, its membership includes a variety of factions and outlooks. Since the early 1980s controversies surrounding electoral outcomes have led to internal turmoil, which in late 1986 resulted in the formation of the Democratic Current (*Corriente Democrática*—CD) faction under the leadership of Cuauhtémoc Cárdenas Solórzano and former party president Porfiro MUÑOZ LEDO, which called for more openness in PRI affairs, including the abolition of secrecy (*tapadismo*) in the selection of presidential candidates. In June 1987, five months after a shake-up in which half of the party's 30-member Executive Committee was replaced, the PRI withdrew recognition of the CD and in 1988 Cárdenas accepted the presidential nomination of the National Democratic Front (FDN; see under PRD, below), prior to organizing the PRD.

The precipitous decline of the PRI's presidential vote (94.4 percent in 1976, 71.0 in 1982, 50.4 in 1988), coupled with diminished congressional representation, prompted Carlos Salinas in the wake of the 1988 campaign to pledge thorough reform of the party apparatus, which Secretary General Manuel CAMACHO Solís characterized as being ridden by "bureaucratization, autocracy, [and] corruption." The issue intensified in the wake of charges that the central government had provided upward of $10 million to finance the PRI's unsuccessful Baja California Norte gubernatorial campaign in 1989. Thus, during the party's 14th National Assembly in Mexico City in September 1990, Salinas persuaded the delegates to adopt a series of measures that included direct and secret balloting for most leadership posts and the selection of a presidential candidate by a democratically elected convention rather than by the outgoing chief executive.

In March 1993 controversy over donations to the PRI from newly privatized enterprises led to the appointment as party chair of Fernando ORTIZ Arana, who dismissed six of the seven PRI Executive Committee members. Notwithstanding the 1990 assembly decisions, the PRI's first 1994 presidential candidate, Luis Donaldo Colosio Murrieta, was effectively chosen by Salinas, as was Ernesto ZEDILLO Ponce de León, following Colosio's assassination in March 1994. This continuance of the so-called *destape* ("unveiling") tradition of nomination by the presidential incumbent was condemned by the PRI's Democracy 2000 (*Democracia 2000*) faction but did not prevent Zedillo from being elected in August, albeit with a record low share (48.8 percent) of the popular vote. On September 28 the PRI's newly appointed secretary general, José Francisco Ruiz Massieu, was assassinated in Mexico City. A little over a year later, on October 13, 1995, a disaffected Camacho Solís, who had been passed over as the PRI's 1994 presidential nominee, quit the party to work for "real political change."

In the election of July 6, 1997, the PRI for the first time lost control of the Chamber of Deputies and also failed to capture the newly elective mayoralty of Mexico City. On March 17, 1999, the party's president, Mariano PALACIOS Alcocer, and its secretary general, Carlos ROJAS Gutiérrez, both resigned, ostensibly to reduce the role of the party hierarchy in selecting its 2000 presidential candidate. Earlier, President Zedillo had announced that he would break tradition by not designating his successor, proposing instead an open primary in fall 1999.

Following Vicente Fox's stunning defeat of Francisco LABASTIDA Ochoa on July 2, 2000, Dulce María SAURI Riancho, who had been appointed in November 1999 as party president, submitted her resignation, but she was persuaded to stay on pending the designation of a successor. In the next year the PRI lost several governorships, and by November 2001 it held only 17 of 31. Meanwhile, it was facing an internal leadership struggle pitting its traditionalists (dubbed the *dinosaurios* by opponents and the media) against a reform-oriented wing (the *técnicos*). An open election for the PRI presidency was held in February 2002, with Roberto MADRAZO Pintado, a former Tabasco governor, narrowly defeating Beatriz PAREDES Rangel, then president of the Chamber of Deputies.

A serious intraparty row erupted in late 2003 between Madrazo and the party's secretary general, Elba Esther GORDILLO. As a result of the dispute, Gordillo lost her post as bloc leader in the Chamber of Deputies and subsequently withdrew to launch her own formation, the New Alliance Party (below).

The PRI contested the 2006 election in a coalition with the PVEM (below) styled the Alliance for Mexico (*Alianza por México*). Since Madrazo's third-place finish in that election, the PRI has been a principal beneficiary of the decline in support for President Calderón's PAN, securing a number of governorships. The PRI generally cooperated with the president on major initiatives in 2008. Of particular note was the PRI's support of private company participation in off-shore drilling.

With voters turning away from the PAN, and the PRD riven by infighting, the PRI was the overwhelming winner of the midterm election on July 5, 2009. With 36.7 percent of the vote, the party saw its representation in the Chamber of Deputies more than double, and it also gained a plurality in the Senate.

The party remained resurgent in the July 2010 state elections, winning 9 of 12 gubernatorial races, though it lost three long-held key statehouses to a coalition of the PAN, the PRD, and other left-wing parties in an anti-PRI alliance. In September the PRI gained the presidency of both houses of Congress. Enrique Peña Nieto, the youthful governor of the state of México, as well as former party president Beatriz Paredes Rangel and Senate leader Manlio Fabio Beltrones, were seen as likely contenders to be the party's standard bearer in the 2012 presidential election.

In October 2010 the PRI put forth its own labor reform proposal in direct counterpoint to the measures proposed by the labor secretary, which were viewed as hostile to workers. Party leader Humberto MOREIRA Valdés resigned in December 2011, following controversy over the budget deficit of Coahuila state when he was governor.

The PRI formed an electoral alliances with the PVEM, "Committed to Mexico," for the 2012 elections. Enrique Peña Nieto won the 2012 presidential poll, leading the party to take control of both chambers of the Union Congress, with 52 senators and 212 deputies. In April 2014 the PRI leader of Mexico City, Cuauhtémoc GUTIÉRREZ DE LA TORRE was accused of using public funds to pay for prostitutes in a scandal that badly tarnished the party.

In the 2015 midterm elections, PRI won 203 seats. In July 2016 Enrique OCHOA Reza was elected president of the party.

Leaders: Enrique PEÑA Nieto (President of Mexico), Enrique OCHOA Reza (President), Carolina MONROY del Mazo (Secretary General).

Mexican Green Ecologist Party (*Partido Verde Ecologista de México*—PVEM). An outgrowth of the **National Ecologist Alliance** (*Alianza Ecologista Nacional*), Mexico's Greens initially adopted the name Green Ecologist Party (PVE) upon formally entering the political arena in 1987. Having failed to obtain registration in time for the 1988 election, the PVE participated in the FDN. A dispute over the party name led to its registration as the Ecologist Party of Mexico (PEM) for the 1991 election, but the party narrowly failed to secure the minimum necessary to gain full legal status. It assumed its present name in 1993.

PVEM founder Jorge GONZÁLEZ Torres received 0.9 percent of the vote in the August 1994 presidential poll, and the party failed to win congressional representation. However, it won 6 Chamber seats in 1997, on a vote share of 4 percent. The party went on to secure 5 Senate and 15 Chamber seats as an ally of PAN in 2000, although its leadership had come under fire from like-minded groups for abandoning environmental issues in its pursuit of electoral success. It won 2 additional lower house seats in 2003 but in early 2004 became entangled in a bribery scandal stemming from a tape-recorded solicitation of Jorge Emilio González Martínez, the son of Gonzáles Torres and current party president. In 2008 the party made advocacy of the death penalty, especially for kidnappers, a signature issue, which caused the European Green Party to withdraw its recognition of the PVEM as a "green" party.

The PVEM contested the 2006 election in a coalition with the PRI styled the Alliance for Mexico (*Alianza por México*). The party won 17 seats in the Chamber of Deputies and 4 in the Senate. It maintained this alliance for the 2009 legislative elections, winning 21 seats in the Chamber of Deputies.

In the 2010 gubernatorial elections, the PVEM's alliances with the PRI in seven states helped the PRI gain its overall total of nine governorships.

The PRI and PVEM formed a new coalition for 2012, "Committed to Mexico." PVEM candidates won 9 seats in the Senate and 29 in the Chamber of Deputies. In July 2014 the PVEM led a successful campaign to ban the use of animals in circuses in Mexico City. Circus owners subsequently unsuccessfully challenged the measure in court.

In the 2015 midterm polling, the party secured 47 seats,

Leaders: Arturo ESCOBAR Vega (President of the Party), Jorge Emilio GONZÁLEZ Martínez (1994 presidential candidate), Jorge LEGORRETA Ordorica (Executive Secretary).

Other Legislative Parties:

National Action Party (*Partido Acción Nacional*—PAN). Founded in 1939 and dependent on urban middle-class support, the long-time leading opposition party has an essentially conservative, proclerical, and probusiness orientation, and favors limitations on the government's economic role. It has traditionally been strongest in the north and west of the country. Largely because of fragmentation within the leftist opposition, PAN was, until recently, the main beneficiary of erosion in PRI support. In 1982, despite losing all but 1 of its directly elective Chamber seats, the party's proportional representation rose from 39 to 54, with party spokespeople claiming that they had been denied a number of victories as the result of PRI electoral fraud. Similar claims were made after the 1985 election, in which PAN gained 9 directly elective Chamber seats and a number of mayoralties, and was widely acknowledged to have gained the majority of votes in two gubernatorial races awarded to the PRI. The party ran third in both the presidential and legislative balloting of July 1988.

On July 2, 1989, Ernesto RUFFO Appel, PAN's Baja California Norte gubernatorial candidate, captured the party's first governorship. In November 1990 PAN again accused the PRI of fraud after it had secured landslide victories in state and local balloting.

The party secured its first Senate seat in the August 1991 balloting, despite a drop in Chamber representation from 101 to 99. The most startling development, however, was in the Guanajuato gubernatorial race, in which the official victor, a PRI hard-liner, was induced to defer to the interim incumbency of PAN's Carlos MEDINA Plascencia. The party registered another notable gain by winning the state governorship of Chihuahua in July 1992. However, a number of influential party dissidents insisted that the victories were achieved through a policy of rapprochement with the PRI and vowed to respond to the *"salinista"* drift by formation of a breakaway party.

In the August 1994 presidential balloting the PAN candidate, Diego FERNÁNDEZ de Cevallos, came in second with 25.9 percent of the popular vote, while PAN representation in the Chamber rose to 119 seats and in the enlarged Senate to 25. Far more impressive was the stunning defeat inflicted on the PRI in Jalisco on February 13, 1995, with PAN capturing the governor's office, the Guadalajara mayoralty, and an overwhelming majority of state legislative seats. In mid-March Secretary General Felipe Calderón Hinojosa defeated Ruffo Appel in a contest to succeed Carlos CASTILLO Peraza as party president. Calderón Hinojosa was succeeded on March 6, 1999, by Luis BRAVO Mena.

PAN contested the 2000 election in a coalition with the Mexican Green Ecologist Party (PVEM, below), styled the Alliance for Change (*Alianza por el Cambio*), which won the presidency and a plurality of 223 seats in the Chamber of Deputies. In the following year the party won several additional governorships, a number of which were lost in 2004.

In July 2006 Calderón Hinojosa, a member of the party's conservative wing, defeated the PRD's López Obrador for the presidency by a narrow margin of 35.9–35.4 percent. PAN also became the largest party in both the Senate and the Chamber of Deputies.

Despite the party's electoral success, tension arose between Calderón and party president Manuel ESPINO Barrientos, who pushed for Mexican membership in the Christian Democratic Organization of the Americas (*Organización Demócrata Cristiana de América*), of which he was also president. The poor showing of PAN in the local elections following the 2006 presidential elections prompted Espino to step down. He was replaced on December 9, 2007, by a loyalist, Germán MARTÍNEZ Cázares.

In the July 5, 2009, midterm elections, the party finished second, more than eight points behind the PRI, and its representation in the Chamber of Deputies dropped from 206 to 143 members. The party won only one of six state governorship contests; of the five losses, two were in states that had previously had PAN governors. Martínez quit the party presidency shortly after the elections. On August 11 the party chose President Calderón's former private secretary, César NAVA, as its new president.

The PAN crossed ideological lines in an unusual alliance with the PRD and other left-wing parties against the PRI in the gubernatorial elections on July 4, 2010. The anti-PRI alliance prompted Interior Secretary Fernando Gómez Mont, who had reportedly promised PRI leaders that no such left-right partnership would occur, to quit the party. After the strategy was vindicated by coalition victories in the key states of Oaxaca, Sinaloa, and Puebla, Gómez Mont resigned from the government. In December Senator Gustavo MADERO Muñoz was elected party president. On July 21 electoral regulators ruled that President Calderón had violated the article of the constitution that prohibits presidents and governors from participating in election campaigns. The ruling referred to a televised speech by the president in June in which he voiced support for the anti-PRI alliance.

The party chose Josefina VÁZQUEZ MOTA, leader of the PAN delegation in the Chamber of Deputies, as its 2012 presidential candidate. With a later start than other presidential contenders, she finished in third place with 25.4 percent of the vote. PAN dropped from 52 to 38 Senate seats and 114 deputies, down from 147 in 2009. PAN joined President Piña Nieto's Pact for Mexico alliance in December 2012. Madero was reelected party president in May 2014.

The party secured 108 seats in the 2015 midterm elections. On August 16, 2015, Ricardo ANAYA Cortés was elected PAN president.

Leaders: Ricardo ANAYA Cortés (President), Felipe CALDERÓN Hinojosa (Former President of Mexico), César NAVA, Vicente FOX Quesada (Former President of Mexico), Josefina VÁZQUEZ MOTA.

Democratic Revolutionary Party (*Partido de la Revolución Democrática*—PRD). The PRD was launched in 1988 by Cuauhtémoc Cárdenas Solórzano, who had previously led the dissident Democratic Current (CD) within the PRI and had placed second in the July presidential balloting as standard-bearer of the **National Democratic Front** (*Frente Democrático Nacional*—FDN) coalition. Other participants in the FDN included the PVE (see PVEM, above), the **Authentic Party of the Mexican Revolution** (*Partido Auténtico de la Revolución Mexicana*—PARM), the **Popular Socialist Party** (*Partido Popular Socialista*—PPS, the **Social Democratic Party** (*Partido Social Demócrata*—PSD), the **Movement Toward Socialism** (*Movimiento al Socialismo*—MAS), and the **Mexican Socialist Party** (*Partido Mexicano Socialista*—PMS).

The PMS had been launched in March 1987 by merger of Mexico's two principal leftist groups, the **Unified Socialist Party of Mexico** (*Partido Socialista Unificado de México*—PSUM) and the **Mexican Workers' Party** (*Partido Mexicano de los Trabajadores*—PMT), and three smaller formations. Recognized by the Soviet Union as the country's official Communist Party, the PSUM dated from the November 1981 merger of the **Mexican Communist Party** (*Partido Comunista Mexicano*—PCM) with four smaller groups. (The PCM, formed in 1919, was accorded legal recognition from 1932 to 1942 and was thereafter semi-clandestine until returned, conditionally, to legal status in 1978.)

Following the 1987 launch of the PMS, discussions with the FDN during the latter half of the year failed to yield agreement on a joint candidate for the 1988 presidential election. As a result, the PMS nominated Herberto CASTILLO of the PMT. It was not until early June 1988 that Castillo withdrew in favor of the FDN's Cuauhtémoc Cárdenas, who a month later narrowly lost to the PRI's Carlos Salinas in a widely disputed election. Formation of the PRD as a unified party followed, with a variety of additional political and social organizations joining the CD, PMS, and MAS.

The newly formed PRD's July 1989 loss to the PRI in the Michoacán gubernatorial balloting was widely viewed as the result of fraudulent vote tallying. Subsequently, PRD members occupied municipal buildings and commandeered public roads, leading to clashes with PRI adherents and government forces that continued into 1990. Meanwhile, the party, which had been denied legalization on a national basis in June, sought international assistance in investigating the alleged political assassination of some 60 of its members since 1988.

In November 1990, defying a new law criminalizing false fraud accusations, the PRD claimed that the PRI had employed "all known forms of violating the vote" in capturing elections in México and Hidalgo states. The PRD's México state vote fell from 1.2 million for Cárdenas alone in 1988 to 200,000 for all PRD candidates in 1990. Meanwhile, observers described the January 1991 resignation of a PRD leader, Jorge ALCOCER, who accused Cárdenas of being "authoritarian and intolerant," as symptomatic of the dissension that had wracked the party since the 1988 balloting. In the August 1994 presidential balloting Cárdenas came in third with 16.6 percent of the popular vote, while PRD representation in the Chamber rose to 71 seats and in the enlarged Senate to 8 seats.

In June 1996 the PRD became the first Mexican party not only to place selection of its leadership in the direct vote of its members but also to confer the franchise on all registered voters who opted to join on polling day. Andrés Manuel López Obrador, PRD leader in Tabasco, defeated two other candidates for the party presidency in July.

At the election of July 6, 1997, the PRD placed second in the Chamber of Deputies, with 125 seats, while Cárdenas became the first elected mayor of Mexico City. In February 1999 the PRD claimed its third governorship, winning Baja California Sur from the PRI.

For the 2000 election Cárdenas resigned his mayoralty for a renewed presidential bid, but he ran a distant third as head of the Alliance for Mexico (*Alianza por México*), which included the **Labor Party**, Convergence for Democracy (see Citizens' Movement, below), **Nationalist Society Party**, and **Social Alliance Party**.

The PRD, which had been supportive of the Fox regime, severed its links with the federal government in early 2004 because of its conviction that the administration had been orchestrating charges of corruption in the capital to damage the presidential prospects of its popular incumbent mayor, López Obrador. Following massive demonstrations in support of López Obrador, President Fox in April 2005 suspended charges against the mayor.

For the 2006 campaign, the PRD formed a grouping with the PT and the Convergence Party (below), styled the **Coalition for the Good of All** (*Coalición por el Bien de Todos*). Despite López Obrador's narrow defeat by the PAN's Calderón Hinojosa in the disputed 2006 presidential elections, the PRD became the second largest party in the Chamber of Deputies with 25 percent of the seats. The party subsequently split over how to respond to Calderón's victory, as radicals supported López Obrador's street protests and his creation of a "legitimate" government, while moderates were willing to engage the government. The divisions were evident in the March 16, 2008, elections for PRD president, which pitted Jesús ORTEGA of the moderate **New Left** (*Nueva Izquierda*) against Alejandro ENCINAS, who supported López Obrador. With 70 percent of the ballots counted and accusations of fraud from both sides, the party annulled the election after missing several deadlines for releasing the results. Finally, on November 12, 2008, the national elections tribunal ruled in favor of Ortega.

In December 2008 the PRD's national congress decided not to form alliances with other parties for the 2009 midterm elections, effectively dissolving the Coalition for the Good of All. In party primaries on March 15, New Left candidates generally fared worse than supporters of López Obrador. For his part, López Obrador campaigned against moderate PRD candidates in some districts, openly supporting candidates from the Labor Party and the Convergence Party. On July 5, 2009, the divided party finished a distant third with 12.2 percent of the vote; its representation in the lower house of Congress fell from 126 to 71 seats.

The PRD's unusual alliance with the PAN for the July 2010 local elections succeeded in defeating incumbent PRI governors in Oaxaca and two other key states. PRD leaders disagreed over whether to reprise the strategy in 2011 against Enrique Peña Nieto, governor of the state of México and PRI presidential hopeful. Mexico City mayor Marcelo EBRARD and the moderates supported the left-right coalition, while López Obrador opposed such a move. The conflict revealed the early jockeying among aspirants for the next presidential race. Ultimately, López Obrador, 59, won the bid as the candidate of the left. Ebrard accepted the results, which left him in a position to handpick his successor as mayor, observers said. López Obrador finished second in the presidential race, with 31.6 percent, and publically questioned the validity of the voting process. The PRD picked up 32 deputies, increasing its delegation from 72 to 104, but lost 4 Senate seats, dropping from 26 to 22. On September 9, 2012, López Obrador announced that he was leaving the PRD to form a new political movement (see National Regeneration Movement, below).

PRD joined President Piña Nieto's Pact for Mexico alliance in December 2012. Carlos NAVARRETE Ruiz resigned from his post as Mexico City's secretary of labor in October 2013 in order to seek the presidency of the PRD. In November 2013 the PRD announced it was withdrawing from the Pact for Mexico. On October 5, 2014, Carlos NAVARRETE Ruiz was elected president of the party.

Former PRD president Jésus ZAMBRANO Grijalva became speaker of the lower house on September 1, 2015. On November 7 Agustín BASAVE Benítez was elected PRD president after the resignation of Navarrette, who was criticized for failing to turn the party around after steep losses in the 2015 midterms.

Leaders: Carlos NAVARRETE Ruiz (President), Miguel Angel MANCERA (Mayor of Mexico City), Beatriz MOJICA Morga (Secretary General).

National Regeneration Movement (*Movimiento Regeneración Nacional*—MORENA). MORENA was a left-wing grouping formed in 2014 by former PRD leader and 2012 presidential candidate Andrés Manuel LÓPEZ Obrador. In the 2015 midterm elections, MORENA shocked the political establishment when it secured 35 seats.

Leaders: Andrés Manuel LÓPEZ Obrador (Founder and 2012 presidential candidate), Martí BATRES Guadarrama (President).

Labor Party (*Partido del Trabajo*—PT). A moderate leftist formation founded in 1990 by a number of organizations, the PT won 1.2 percent of the vote in the 1991 congressional poll. In the August 1994 presidential contest Cecilia SOTO González fought a vigorous campaign that drew support away from the more established PRD and gave her 2.7 percent of the national vote. Ten PT candidates were elected to the Chamber of Deputies in 1994, 7 in 1997, 8 in 2000, and 6 in 2003.

In 2006 the PT joined the Convergence Party (below) and the Coalition for the Good of All. Andrés Manuel López Obrador, the PRD's 2006 presidential candidate, campaigned on behalf of some PT candidates, some of whom had been close advisors during his candidacy and his tenure as Mexico City mayor.

In the July 2009 balloting for the Chamber of Deputies, the party won 13 seats. In July 2012 Labor received 5 Senate seats and 15 in the Chamber of Deputies. Labor party member and mayor of Santa Ana Maya, Ygnacio LOPEZ MENDOZA, was killed on November 7, 2013, allegedly by the Knights Templar for publicizing efforts by the cartel to corrupt local politicians. The PT secured 6 seats in the 2015 midterm balloting.

Leader: María Guadalupe RODRÍGUEZ Martínez (National Coordinator).

New Alliance Party (*Partido Nueva Alianza*—Panal). Panal was launched in 2005 by former PRI secretary general Elba Esther Gordillo, leader of the National Education Workers' Syndicate (*Sindicato Nacional de Trabajadores de la Educación*—SNTE), the largest labor union in Latin America and the driving force behind civil disturbances in Oaxaca in 2006.

In 2006 the party won nine seats in the Chamber of Deputies and one Senate seat. Panal retained its nine seats in the Chamber of Deputies in the 2009 elections. Gabriel Quadri represented Panal in the 2012 presidential race, finishing a distant fourth with 2.3 percent of the vote. The party retained its single Senate seat and took ten seats in the Chamber of Deputies.

Party founder Elba Esther Gordillo was arrested for embezzlement in February 2013 (see Current issues, above), triggering a crisis within the party, as her daughter, Mónica T. ARRIOLA Gordillo, had recently become Panal's secretary general. She resigned from that post in September. The party supported President Peña Nieto's energy reform initiatives in 2014. It again won 10 seats in the 2015 elections.

Leader: Luis CASTRO Obregón (President).

Citizens' Movement (*Movimiento Ciudadano*). Established in 1999 as the **Convergence for Democracy** (*Convergencia por la Democracia*—CD), the democratic party was led by former Veracruz governor Dante Delgado and other PRI dissidents. In the 2000 federal election it participated in the Alliance for Mexico, and as a result, secured one Senate seat and two Chamber seats.

In 2002 the party voted to adopt the shortened form of its name, Convergence (*Convergencia*). It won five seats in the Chamber of Deputies in 2003.

In 2006 the party participated in the Coalition for the Good of All with the PT and PRD, fielding the PRD's Andrés López Obrador as its presidential candidate. It won 17 seats in the Chamber of Deputies and 5 in the Senate. Subsequently, the coalition dissolved.

In the 2009 balloting for the Chamber of Deputies, the party won six seats in the Chamber of Deputies on a vote share of 2.4 percent, barely exceeding the 2 percent threshold required to maintain its legal status.

In the 2010 state elections the party allied with the leftist PRD and PT in Oaxaca, where Convergence member Gabino CUÉ Monteagudo was elected governor.

On July 31, 2011, the party modified its name to **Citizens' Movement** (*Movimiento Ciudadano*). The following year, it went from 6 seats in the Chamber of Deputies to 16, but dropped from 6 senators to 1. In 2015 the party increased its representation in the Chamber of Deputies by 10 seats, for a total of 26.

Leaders: Luis WALTON Aburto (President), Dante DELGADO Rannauro (Coordinator), Jesús Armando LOPEZ VELARDE CAMPA (Secretary General).

The **Social Encounter Party** (*Partido Encuentro Social*—PES), a conservative Christian grouping established in 2014, won 8 seats in the 2015 balloting.

For more information on minor or defunct parties, see the 2008, 2009, and 2013 *Handbooks*.

Paramilitary Groups:

Zapatista National Liberation Army (*Ejército Zapatista de Liberación Nacional*—EZLN). Initial accounts of the January 1994 uprising in Chiapas (see Political background, above) suggested that the rebels numbered upward of 1,000 men seeking economic relief for Mexico's "dispensable" indigenous groups. Ideologically, the EZLN was unique in neither invoking traditional Marxist jargon nor attempting to seize national power. In early 1996 the group announced the launching of a "sister organization," the **Zapatista National Liberation Front** (*Frente Zapatista de Liberación Nacional*—FZLN), which was not a "formal" political party and did not contest elections.

A march by EZLN leaders to Mexico City in February–March 2001 culminated in a controversial invitation to address the Congress of

Deputies on March 28. The EZLN urged passage of the Indigenous Rights Bill, although the Zapatistas ultimately rejected the version of the bill that was passed in late April as offering insufficient autonomy and land rights. As a consequence, the EZLN refused to negotiate with the Fox government.

In 2005 the group's spokesperson, known as "Subcomandante Marcos," declared that the group was entering mainstream politics; he was subsequently appointed coleader of a Chiapas "good government" municipal board. In 2006 he led a tour of Mexican cities to generate popular support ahead of the elections.

The EZLN seeks indigenous control over land and resources, most recently via lobbying efforts on the Internet. It has been less active nationally in recent years, though it remains an intact movement and a political force in several municipalities of Chiapas, relying on its skillful use of the media to garner support around the world. On May 24, 2014, Subcomandante Marcos announced he would henceforth be known as Subcomandante Insurgente Galeano, a reference to an EZLN member who was killed fighting a rival group on May 2.

Leader: Subcomandante MARCOS.

Popular Revolutionary Army (*Ejército Popular Revolucionario*—EPR). The EPR was apparently launched in 1994 as a coalition of a dozen-odd minor leftist factions allied with the peasant-based **Revolutionary Workers' Party and Clandestine Popular Union–Party of the Poor** (*Partido Revolucionario Obrerista y Clandestino de Unión Popular–Partido de los Pobres*—PROCUP-PDLP). PROCUP was founded in the 1970s by radicals under the leadership of Oaxaca University rector Felipe MARTÍNEZ Soriano, who has been imprisoned since 1990 for involvement in the killing of two security guards at a Mexican newspaper office. The PDLP, dating from 1967, was a largely moribund clandestine formation before being revived by merger with PROCUP. In 1991 PROCUP claimed responsibility for a series of bombings of the Mexico City offices of a number of international corporations and was charged in 1994 with the kidnapping of Alfred Harp Helu, the chair of Mexico's largest bank, for whose release his family paid a $30 million ransom.

During 1996 the EPR was reported to have killed 26 soldiers or police officers while extending its activities into more than half of Mexico's 31 states. At a secret press conference in August 1996 it announced formation of a 14-organization **Popular Democratic Revolutionary Party** (*Partido Democrático Popular Revolucionario*—PDPR) that would serve as its political wing. Three months earlier the PROCUP-PDLP reportedly had dissolved.

Relatively quiescent after 1997, the EPR resurfaced in May 2002 when it appeared responsible for the killing of two police officers 95 miles east of Acapulco. In 2004 President Fox indicated that the group was still active, while media reports suggested that it had spawned a number of splinter formations, particularly in the south. Between July and September 2007 the EPR claimed responsibility for massive bombings of natural gas pipelines, which resulted in thousands of people being evacuated and cost millions in damage to the economy. The group has carried out few armed actions since 2007, but it issues periodic political statements, including a 2009 endorsement of a small movement urging voters in the midterm elections to turn in blank ballots. A yearlong effort at mediation between the EPR and the government ended in April 2009 due to lack of progress. It supported the teachers strike in 2013.

In June 2013 a group called the **People's Revolutionary Army** (*Ejército Revolucionario del Pueblo—ERP*) announced it had broken away from the EPR because the latter group had strayed too far from its Marxist-Leninist roots. The EPR responded that the alleged rebels had never been part of the older group. Reports in 2014 indicated other breakaway factions of the EPR had formed. The EPR led demonstrations in Iguala after the disappearance of 43 students (see Current issues, above).

For information on the **Popular Insurgent Revolutionary Army** (*Ejército Revolucionario Insurgente Popular*—ERIP) and the **Zeta Killers** (*Mata Zetas*), see the 2014 *Handbook*.

For more information on guerilla groups, see the 2008 and 2009 *Handbooks*.

LEGISLATURE

The **Union Congress** (*Congreso de la Unión*) consists of a Senate and a Chamber of Deputies, both elected by popular vote. When Congress is not in session, limited legislative functions are performed by a Permanent Committee of 18 senators and 19 deputies elected by their respective houses. Legislators cannot serve consecutive terms.

Senate (*Cámara de Senadores*). The upper chamber contains 128 members, the number having been doubled with the election, for six-year terms, of 96 senators in 1994. In 1997, 32 senators were elected for three-year terms. In 2000 all 128 seats were renewed for the first time, half by majority vote in each state and the Federal District, one-quarter by assignment to the leading minority candidate in each of the 32 jurisdictions, and one-quarter by national proportional representation.

Following the most recent election on July 1, 2012, the seat distribution was as follows: the Institutional Revolutionary Party, 52 seats; National Action Party, 38; Democratic Revolutionary Party, 22; Mexican Green Ecologist Party, 9; Labor Party, 5; Citizens' Movement, 1; and New Alliance Party, 1.

President: Raúl CERVANTES Andrade (PRI).

Chamber of Deputies (*Cámara de Diputados*). The lower chamber presently contains 500 members elected for three-year terms, including 200 seats distributed on a proportional basis among parties winning more than 2 percent of the vote nationwide.

Following the most recent election on June 7, 2015, the seat distribution was as follows: Institutional Revolutionary Party, 203 seats; National Action Party, 108; Democratic Revolutionary Party, 56; Mexican Green Ecologist Party, 47; National Regeneration Movement, 35; Citizens' Movement, 26; New Alliance, 10; Social Encounter Party, 8; Labor Party, 6; and independents, 1.

President: Jésus ZAMBRANO Grijalva (PRD).

CABINET

[as of June 6, 2016]

President	Enrique Peña Nieto
Secretaries	
Agrarian Reform	Jorge Carlos Ramirez Marín
Agriculture, Livestock, Rural Development, Fisheries, and Food	José Calzada Rovirosa
Attorney General	Arely Gómez González [f]
Communications and Transport	Gerardo Ruiz Esparza
Economy	Ildefonso Guajardo Villarreal
Energy	Pedro Joaquín Coldwell
Environment and Natural Resources	Rafael Pacchiano Alamán
Federal Electricity Commission	Francisco Rojas Gutiérrez
Finance and Public Credit	Luis Videgaray Caso
Foreign Affairs	Claudia Ruiz Massieu Salinas [f]
Health	José Narro Robles
Interior	Miguel Ángel Osorio Chong
Labor and Social Welfare	Jesús Alfonso Navarrete Prida
National Defense	Salvador Cienfuegos Zepeda
Navy	Vidal Francisco Soberón Sanz
Pemex	Emilio Lozoya Austin
Public Education	Aurelio Nuño Mayer
Public Safety	Manuel Mondragón y Kalb
Social Development	José Antonio Meade Kuribreña
Tourism	Enrique de la Madrid Cordero

[f] = female

INTERGOVERNMENTAL REPRESENTATION

Ambassador to the U.S.: Carlos Manuel SADA Solana.

U.S. Ambassador to Mexico: Roberta JACOBSON.

Permanent Representative to the UN: Juan José Gómez CAMACHO.

IGO Memberships (Non-UN): APEC, EBRD, G-20, IADB, ICC, IOM, OAS, OECD, WTO.

For Further Reference:

Camp, Roderic Ai. *Politics in Mexico: Democratic Consolidation or Decline?* Oxford: Oxford University Press, 2013.

Doran, Marie-Christine. "Religion and Politics in Land Takeovers in Mexico: New Dimensions of 'Classical' Social Movements?" *Canadian Journal of Latin American and Caribbean Studies*. 39, no. 1 (2014): 72–92.

Morris, Stephen D. "Corruption, Drug Trafficking, and Violence in Mexico." *Brown Journal of World Affairs*. 18, no. 2 (Spring/Summer 2012): 29–43.

Tuckman, Jo. *Mexico: Democracy Interrupted.* New Haven, CT: Yale University Press, 2012.

FEDERATED STATES OF MICRONESIA

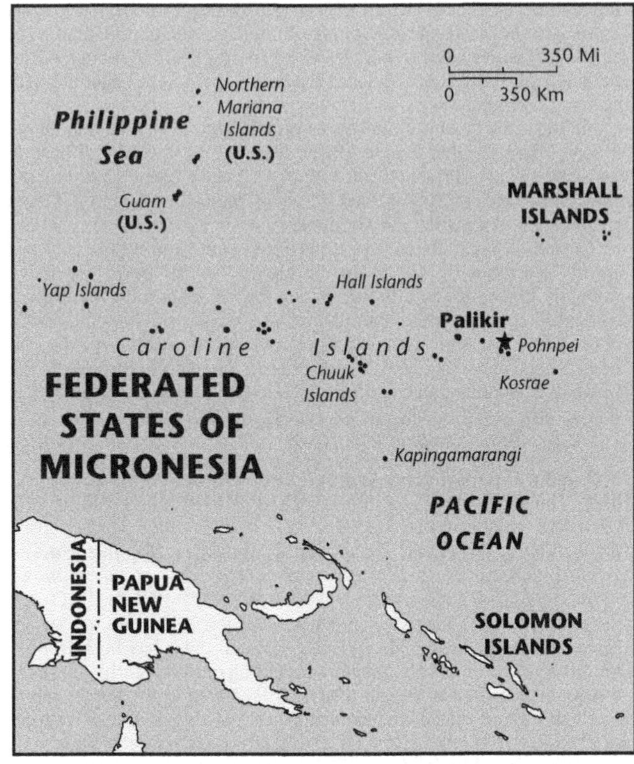

Political Status: Sovereign state in free association with the United States (which retains authority with regard to defense) since November 3, 1986.

Land Area: 271 sq. mi. (701 sq. km).

Population: 105,000 (2016E—UN); 104,719 (2016E—U.S. Census). (A significant number of FSM citizens reside in the U.S. territory of Guam or elsewhere in the United States.)

Major Urban Centers (2014E—UN): PALIKIR (capital); 7,000.

Official Language: English. The principal native languages are Chuukese, Kapingamarangi, Kosraean, Nukuoro, Pohnpeian, Ulithian, Woleaian, and Yapese.

Monetary Unit: U.S. Dollar (see the entry on United States for principal exchange rates).

President: Peter M. CHRISTIAN; elected by Congress on May 11, 2015, and sworn in for a four-year term on the same day, succeeding Emanuel "Manny" MORI, following the legislative elections on March 3.

Vice President: Yosiwo P. GEORGE; elected by Congress on May 11, 2015, and sworn in on the same day for a term concurrent with that of the president, succeeding Alik L. ALIK, following the legislative elections on March 3.

THE COUNTRY

The Federated States of Micronesia (FSM) comprises the archipelago of the Caroline Islands, some 300 miles to the east of the Philippines. The constituent states are the island groups (from west to east) of Yap, Chuuk (formerly Truk), Pohnpei (formerly Ponape), and Kosrae, each of which has its own indigenous language, with English as the official language of the Federation. Most inhabitants of the more than 600 islands are of either Micronesian or Polynesian extraction. Roman Catholicism predominates among the largely Christian population. Subsistence farming (important crops include bananas, taros, and yams) and fishing are the principal economic activities, with tourism of increasing importance. More than half of the taxpaying wage earners are government employees, with most of the remainder dependent on spending by either government or government workers. The paucity of job prospects has heightened emigration to the United States, where visas are not required for FSM citizens under the provisions of the Compact of Free Association with the United States. No women were elected to Congress in the 2015 balloting.

The International Monetary Fund (IMF) has warned that "achieving long-term economic stability has become more challenging" for the FSM, considering that Compact assistance (approximately $90 million in 2009) was scheduled to decline by $800,000 annually until 2023 (when grants were slated to end). In consonance with IMF recommendations, the government is pursuing tax reforms designed to enhance revenue while also emphasizing private-sector growth, particularly in regard to fisheries and tourism. In addition, the FSM has recently launched an offshore corporate registry.

GDP rose by less than 1 percent in the 2012 fiscal years as increased fishing revenues were mostly offset by declining construction. GDP fell by 4 percent in 2013, before rebounding in 2014 with 0.1 percent growth, and 0.3 percent growth the next year. The IMF estimated that GDP increased by 1 percent in 2016, while inflation was 1.9 percent. Micronesia ranked 123rd out of 189 countries in Human Development according to the UN in 2016. The World Bank ranked the country 148th out of 189 countries for ease of doing business because of issues in protecting contracts, protecting minority investors, and registering properties.

GOVERNMENT AND POLITICS

Political background. Purchased by Germany from Spain in 1899, the Carolines were seized in 1914 by Japan and were retained as part of the mandate awarded by the League of Nations to Japan in 1920. The islands were occupied by U.S. forces in World War II and (along with the Marshall and Northern Mariana Islands) became part of the U.S. Trust Territory of the Pacific in 1947. In 1965 a Congress of Micronesia was established, with the Carolines electing 14 of the 21 members of its House of Representatives. Following acceptance of a 1975 covenant authorizing creation of the Commonwealth of the Northern Mariana Islands, the remaining components of the Trust Territory were regrouped into six districts, four of which in July 1978 approved a constitution of the FSM that became effective on May 10, 1979. In October 1982 the FSM concluded a 15-year Compact of Free Association with the United States, which was declared to be in effect on November 3, 1986, following ratification by the U.S. Congress and final approval by the FSM government. Under the Compact (and its 2003 successor) the FSM is a sovereign entity, save with regard to defense; the FSM is also obligated to "consult" with Washington on major foreign policy matters.

On May 15, 1987, John R. HAGLELGAM was sworn in as the FSM's second president, succeeding Tosiwo NAKAYAMA. Haglelgam was unable to stand for a second term because of his failure to secure reelection to the FSM Congress on March 5, 1991, and on May 11 Bailey OLTER, formerly vice president under Nakayama, was elected as Haglelgam's successor. Olter was elected to a second term on May 11, 1995.

In November 1996 the Congress ruled that President Olter, who had recently suffered a stroke, was unable to fulfill his responsibilities and directed Vice President Jacob NENA to serve as acting president. Subsequently, it was determined that Olter would be unable to return to office, and on May 8, 1997, Nena was formally installed for the balance of Olter's four-year mandate. Olter died in February 1999.

On May 12, 1999, Vice President Leo A. FALCAM was elected to the presidency by the Congress, all 14 members of whom had been returned to office in nationwide balloting on March 2. However, both President Falcam and former president Nena lost their seats at the full legislative replenishment of March 4, 2003, and on May 10 the Congress elected Joseph J. URUSEMAL as chief executive.

Following a two-year extension of the 1986 Compact, a successor was signed on May 1, 2003, and approved by the U.S. Congress in November. The document provided for 20 more years of direct U.S. financial support in the form of annual grants (starting at about $77 million and decreasing by $800,000 annually until 2023) to subsidize the government's budget as well as $16 million annually for a trust fund to support the government after 2023. (The nonfinancial elements of the treaty have no expiration date.)

President Urusemal failed in a reelection bid after the congressional election of March 6, 2007. Emanuel (Manny) MORI, a longtime critic of the current Compact, was named to replace him on May 11. Although reports surfaced of intense backroom maneuvering on the matter, President Mori was ultimately reelected on May 11, 2011, without opposition in the formal vote in Congress.

Following legislative balloting on March 3, 2015, Peter M. CHRISTIAN was elected president on May 11, and sworn in that day. He named a cabinet on May 21 that was confirmed between May 30 and September 23.

Constitution and government. The 1979 constitution provides for a unicameral Congress of 14 members, referred to as senators. The president and vice president, who serve four-year terms, are selected by the Congress from among the four-year senators, the vacated seats being refilled by special election. The president may serve no more than two terms consecutively. The individual states have elected governors and legislatures, the latter encompassing a bicameral body of 38 members for Chuuk (a 10-member Senate and a 28-member House of Representatives) and unicameral bodies of 27, 14, and 10 members, respectively, for Pohnpei, Kosrae, and Yap. The state officials serve for four years (legislative terms on Chuuk and Pohnpei are staggered). Municipalities are governed by elected magistrates and councils, while villages follow traditional forms of rule.

State	*Area (sq. mi.)*	*Population (2010E)*
Chuuk	45.6	48,654
Kosrae	42.3	6,616
Pohnpei	132.4	34,000
Yap	46.7	11,377

In June 2014 President Mori urged that a referendum be held in conjunction with national elections in March 2015 regarding a proposal to make it easier to amend the constitution. Such revision could subsequently facilitate the adoption of a system for direct election of the president and vice president and other changes for which sentiment has reportedly been mounting recently.

Foreign relations. In December 1990 the UN Security Council formally abrogated the U.S. Trusteeship with respect to the FSM, the Northern Marianas, and the Marshall Islands, and in September 1991 both the Marshalls and the FSM were admitted to the United Nations. In June 1993 the FSM was admitted to the IMF and the World Bank. As in the case with the Marshall Islands, FSM's political autonomy is seemingly constricted by the U.S. retention of authority in defense matters and the U.S. right of "consultation" in foreign affairs.

Current issues. At present, the overwhelming concern is Micronesia's fate in the course of global warming. Insisting that his country is "on the verge of drowning" because of atolls being less than a meter above sea level, President Mori has joined with other island leaders in addressing the issue at the United Nations and elsewhere.

In 2012 the IMF warned that it currently appeared that the Compact Trust Fund would fall significantly short of the money it would need to support the FSM budget following the scheduled expiration of compact grants in 2023. Calling for greater attention to education and policies designed to promote the private sector, President Mori in 2013 proposed the convening of a constitutional convention to address, among other things, the "conflicting mandates" of the states and the federal government, which Mori characterized as hampering decisive economic action. He also argued that the strings attached to U.S. Compact aid were inappropriately infringing on the FSM's sovereignty over its internal affairs. Meanwhile, in reviewing conditions at the halfway mark of the current Compact, U.S. officials said that the emphasis on health and education had not produced significant demonstrable progress. Attention in 2014 turned to the Congressional elections due in March 2015 and the subsequent selection of a successor to Mori (constitutionally prohibited from seeking a third consecutive term). On April 1, 2015, super typhoon Maysak killed four and injured ten when it made landfall in Chuuk. The storm caused $8.5 million in damage.

POLITICAL PARTIES

There are, at present, no formal parties in the FSM, political activity tending to center on regional (state) alignments.

LEGISLATURE

The FSM **Congress** is a 14-member body, 4 of whose members are elected on a statewide basis (1 from each state) for four-year terms, while 10 (5 from Chuuk, 3 from Pohnpei, and 1 each from Kosrae and Yap) are selected for two-year terms in first-past-the-post voting in single-member districts delineated on a population basis.

Balloting for all 14 seats was held on March 8, 2011. In a referendum held at the same time, voters rejected a proposed amendment that would have made all legislative terms four years' duration. Elections for the 10 two-year seats were held on March 3, 2015.

Speaker: Westley W. SIMINA.

CABINET

[as of October 1, 2016]

Secretaries	
Director of the Environment and Emergency Management Office	Andrew R. Yatilman
Director of the Office of National Archives, Culture, and Historic Preservation	Rufino Mauricio
Education	Kalwin Kephas
Finance and Administration	Sihna N. Lawrence [f]
Foreign Affairs	Lorin S. Robert
Health and Social Services	Magdalena A. Walter [f]
Justice	Joses R. Gallen
Postmaster-General	Ginger Porter Mida [f]
Public Defender	Lorrie Johnson-Asher [f]
Resources and Development	Marion Henry
Transportation, Communication, and Infrastructure	Lukner Weilbacher

[f] = female

INTERGOVERNMENTAL REPRESENTATION

Ambassador to the U.S.: James NAICH (Chargé d'Affaires *ad interim*).

U.S. Ambassador to the Federated States of Micronesia: Robert RILEY.

Permanent Representative to the UN: Amatlain Elizabeth KABUA.

IGO Memberships (Non-UN): ADB, PIF.

For Further Reference:

Corbett, Jack. "Making Micronesia: A Political Biography of Tosiwo Nakayama." *The Journal of Pacific History* 49, no. 4 (2014): 513–515.

Fischer, Steven Roger. *A History of the Pacific Islands*. New York: Palgrave Macmillan, 2013.

Hezel, Francis X. *Making Sense of Micronesia: The Logic of Pacific Island Culture.* Honolulu: University of Hawaii Press, 2013.

MOLDOVA

Republic of Moldova
Republica Moldova

Note: Presidential elections were held on October 30, 2016, with runoff balloting on November 13. In the first round, Igor Dodon (Party of Socialists of the Republic of Moldova), won 48 percent of the vote, followed by Maia Sandu of the newly formed, pro-European, liberal Action and Solidarity Party, with 38.7 percent. There were seven other candidates, none of whom secured more than 6 percent of the vote. The two frontrunners advanced to the second round, where Dodon won 52.1 percent to 47.9 percent for Sandu. Opposition groups denounced the conduct of the elections, especially after revelations emerged that the voter rolls were larger than the total population of the country.

Political Status: Formerly the Moldavian Soviet Socialist Republic, a constituent republic of the Union of Soviet Socialist Republics; declared independence as the Republic of Moldova on August 27, 1991; became sovereign member of the Commonwealth of Independent States on December 21, 1991; new constitution approved on July 28, 1994, and entered into force on August 27.

Area: 13,000 sq. mi. (33,670 sq. km).

Population: 4,063,000 (2016E—Moldova); 3,510,485 (2016E—U.S. Census).

Major Urban Centers (2015E—Government): CHIŞINĂU (formerly Kishinev, 811,850), Bălţi (150,450), Tiraspol (135,000 [2014E]), Orhei (125,100), Cahul (124,600), Hînceşti (120,450), Ungheni (117,350), Tighina (92,000 [2014E]).

Official Language: Moldovan.

Monetary Unit: Moldovan leu (official rate October 1, 2016: 19.72 leu = $1US).

President: Nicolae TIMOFTI (ind.); sworn in for a four-year term on March 23, 2012, and assumed office on the same day, replacing Marian LUPU (Democratic Party); named acting president (due to his position as speaker of Parliament) by Parliament on December 30, 2010.

Prime Minister: Pavel FILIP (Democratic Party of Moldova); appointed by the president on January 15, 2016, and approved by Parliament, and sworn in on January 20; to succeed acting prime minister Gheorghe BREGA (Liberal Party). (See Current issues, below).

THE COUNTRY

Located in Eastern Europe, Moldova is bordered on the north, east, and south by Ukraine and on the west by Romania. The breakaway region of Transnistria (Transdniestria) lies between the Dnestr (Nistru) River and Ukraine. The 2004 census recorded the country as 78 percent Moldovan (compared to 64 percent in 1989, the last census to include Transnistria); 8 percent Ukrainian (14 percent); 6 percent Russian (13 percent); 4 percent Gagauz (4 percent), a Turkic people of Christian Orthodox faith; and 2 percent Bulgarian (2 percent).

A mild climate and fertile soil permit the cultivation of a wide variety of crops, including grains, sugar beets, fruits, and vegetables, with food processing being the leading industry. Metalworking and the manufacture of electrical equipment are also of importance. Excluding Transnistria, agriculture contributes approximately 14 percent of gross domestic product (GDP) and approximately 26 percent of employment, while industry accounts for 20 percent of GDP and 13 percent of employment. Principal exports are foodstuffs, beverages (notably wine), and tobacco. Russia was the leading trade partner in 2013, followed by Romania, Ukraine, Italy, and Germany.

Political and economic transition in the decade after 1989 yielded the largest decline in GDP in Eastern Europe, a fall of approximately 70 percent from the 1990 level. Inflation reached a high of 2,200 percent in 1992 before gradually falling to 115 percent in 1994. The economy was further shaken by the Russian financial crisis of 1998, the leu losing almost half its value in a single day in November, creating the most severe currency crisis since independence. The economy recovered in 2000, and late in the year, the International Monetary Fund (IMF) and World Bank approved a new civil code (adopted in 2002) favoring free-market principles.

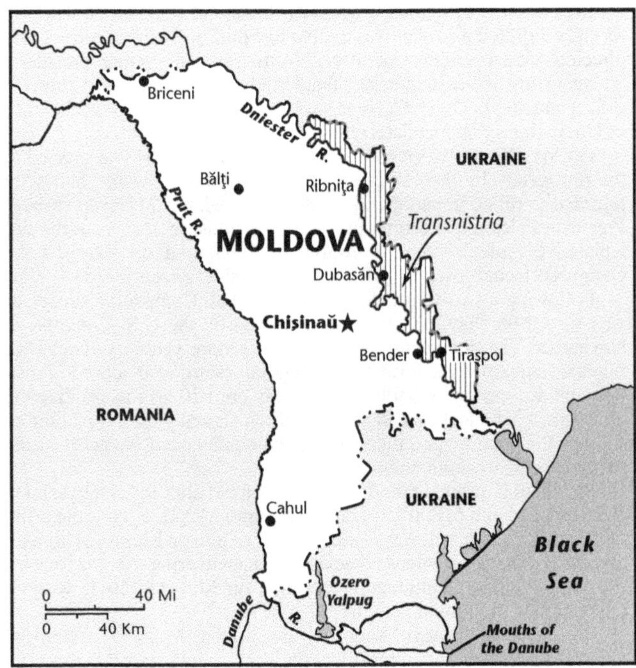

In January 2006 Russian energy giant Gazprom temporarily cut off natural gas deliveries to Moldova—which is almost completely dependent on its neighbors for energy—and doubled the price of gas. In March the Russian government banned imports of Moldovan wine, citing health and quality issues. The wine ban was particularly painful because, previously, Moldovan wine sales approached 15 percent of GNP, and it exported approximately 80 percent of its wine to Russia. (See the 2012 *Handbook* for details.)

Although the IMF expressed concern with the lack of structural reform, in 2006 it released a statement in which it noted, "Moldova's European aspirations have provided much-needed momentum to the authorities' structural reform efforts and commitment to combat corruption." The World Bank reported in 2006 that "GDP growth is no longer reducing poverty," particularly rural poverty. Roughly half the population lives off subsistence farming. Those who do produce a surplus have difficulty getting it to market, as the country's road network is deficient and agricultural purchase prices are low. Moreover, with an average wage of only about $129 per month, Moldova reportedly has the lowest standard of living in Europe. Inflation has remained high, averaging 16.6 percent annually from 1995 to 2008. One clear result of the economic difficulties is that 600,000 Moldovans (one in four adults) have left the country to look for work, principally in Russia and Italy. Remittances from workers abroad amounted to an estimated $950 million in 2007, accounting for over 35 percent of GDP.

In the first half of 2009 remittances fell by approximately 30 percent under the effects of the global financial crisis. That decline and a corresponding drop in consumer demand contributed to a 25 percent contraction in the manufacturing and construction sectors, although agriculture remained steady. GDP plummeted by 6 percent for the year, but annual growth averaged almost 7 in 2010–2011 in part due to an increase in remittances. GDP contracted by 0.7 percent in 2012, returning to 8.9 percent growth in 2013 and 4.6 percent in 2014. GDP contracted by 1 percent in 2015, but the IMF estimated that GDP grew by 3 percent in 2016. That year inflation rose by 4.3 percent, while unemployment was 6.3 percent, down from 7.5 percent the year before.

GOVERNMENT AND POLITICS

Political background. Historical Moldova lay between the frontiers of the Russian, Habsburg, and Ottoman empires and was the object of numerous invasions and territorial realignments, including incorporation in Greater Romania from 1918 to 1940. Present-day Moldova encompasses the territory of the pre-1940 Moldavian

Autonomous Soviet Socialist Republic, which was located within Ukraine and which was joined to all but the northern and southern portions of Bessarabia upon detachment of the latter from Romania in 1940. With its redrawn borders, the redefined Moldavian SSR became a constituent republic of the Soviet Union.

On July 29, 1989, Mircea SNEGUR was elected chair of the Presidium of the republican Supreme Soviet. Although a member of the Politburo of the Communist Party of Moldova (*Partidul Comunist din Moldova*—PCM), he subsequently endorsed the nationalist demands of the Popular Front of Moldova (*Frontul Popular din Moldova*—FPM), which had been launched earlier in the year. The language law of 1989 asserted a "Moldo-Romanian" identity, and in 1990 the Moldovan flag was adapted from the Romanian tricolor.

On August 19, 1990, the Turkic-speaking Gagauz minority in the southern part of the country responded to the prospect of union with Romania by announcing the formation of a "Republic of Gagauzia." On September 2 the Slavic majority in the eastern Dnestr valley followed suit, proclaiming a "Pridnestrovskian Moldavian Soviet Socialist Republic" (changing to Pridnestrovskian Moldavian Republic [*Pridnestrovskaia Moldavskaia Respublika*] in 1991, commonly called either Transnistria or Transdniestria in English). The Supreme Soviet thereupon went into emergency session, naming Snegur to the new post of executive president on September 3 and empowering him to introduce direct rule "in regions not obeying the constitution." Despite continued unrest, including a pitched battle between police and secessionist militia at a bridge over the Dnestr River on November 2, the situation eased late in the year after political intervention by Soviet President Mikhail Gorbachev.

On August 22, 1991, in the wake of the failed Moscow coup against Gorbachev, PCM first secretary Grigory YEREMEY resigned from the Politburo of the Communist Party of the Soviet Union (CPSU), and on August 23 President Snegur, who had opposed the Moscow hard-liners, effectively banned the PCM. On August 27 Moldova declared its independence and two days later established diplomatic relations with Romania. In October 1991 the leading pro-unification FPM faction came out in opposition to Snegur and called for a boycott of the presidential election set for December 8. Snegur was nevertheless reelected as the sole candidate in a turnout officially given as 82.9 percent, this time drawing his main political support from the pro-independence Agrarian Democratic Party of Moldova (*Partidul Democrat Agrar din Moldova*—PDAM).

In March 1992 ethnic conflict again erupted. Igor SMIRNOV, the president of Transnistria, called for mobilization of all men between ages 18 and 45. Concurrently, his deputy, Aleksandr KARAMAN, insisted that the only viable solution would be a confederal republic in which Moldovans, Russians, and Gagauz would have separate, autonomous territories. For his part, President Snegur offered special economic status to the Transnister region but rejected the concept of a separate republic. Local Red Army units stationed in the region intervened for Transnistria, escalating the conflict from September 1991 to July 1992. In July 1992 a cease-fire was signed and Russian Federation troops entered the region to act as monitors for the agreement.

Initial enthusiasm in Moldova and Romania for unification faded quickly, with public opinion polls in Moldova showing that no more than 10 percent of the population supported union. On January 7 President Snegur called for a referendum on unification to be held, appealing for strengthened Moldovan independence. The referendum split pro- and anti-unionist deputies, the referendum call ultimately being defeated by one vote. On August 3 Snegur was granted decree powers for the ensuing year to facilitate economic reforms, and in February 1994 his administration indicated that it sought accommodation with Transnistria on the basis of substantial autonomy for the region, including its own legislative body and the use of distinctive political symbols.

The parliamentary election of February 27, 1994, yielded an overall majority for the PDAM and was followed on March 6 by a referendum in which a reported 95.4 percent of participants voted for maintaining Moldova's separation from both Romania and Russia. A further national unity government under the continued premiership of the PDAM's Andrey SANGHELI obtained legislative approval on April 5, its first major act being the introduction of a new devolutionary constitution in August, effectively removing union with Romania as an option, except as a long-term aspiration.

Fortified by an IMF loan, the Moldovan government in March 1995 embarked on a major privatization program to dispose of some 1,500 state enterprises. However, resistance to privatization remained prevalent within the state bureaucracy, while opposition parties forecast an outbreak of widespread corruption. Principally because of such opposition within the PDAM, President Snegur in July launched the Party of Rebirth and Conciliation of Moldova (*Partidul Renaşterii şi Concilierii din Moldova*—PRCM).

Although Prime Minister Sangheli was able to announce on August 1, 1995, that the five-year Gagauz conflict was over (see Constitution and government, below), the Transnister problem remained more intractable. On December 24 a referendum in Transnister yielded an 82.7 percent majority in favor of a draft independence constitution and of separate membership in the Commonwealth of Independent States (CIS). However, on January 19, 1996, President Snegur secured the signatures of his Russian and Ukrainian counterparts on a joint statement asserting that the Transnister region was part of Moldova but should have special status. Further talks between Snegur and Smirnov culminated in an agreement on June 17 defining the region as "a state-territorial formation in the form of a republic within Moldova's internationally recognized borders." This tortuous wording appeared to satisfy both sides' core demands, although detailed implementation and ratification were expected to be difficult processes.

On the domestic political front, President Snegur launched his campaign for reelection in November 1996. A key feature of his platform was that Moldova should move to a more presidential form of government, particularly in respect to authority to appoint and dismiss ministers. The president faced obstruction from the opposition-dominated Parliament, which in February voted down a presidential proposal to change "Moldovan" to "Romanian" as the constitutional descriptor of the official language.

Backed by a PRCM-initiated "Civic Movement," Snegur headed the poll in the first round of presidential elections held on November 17, 1996, winning 38.7 percent of the vote against eight other candidates. In second place, with 27.7 percent, came Petru LUCINSCHI, the parliamentary speaker and unofficial PDAM candidate. Enlivened by a phone-tapping scandal and PDAM allegations that the president's supporters were attempting to rig the outcome, the second round of voting on December 1 featured a runoff between Snegur and Lucinschi, with the latter receiving the formal endorsement not only of the PDAM but also of the Party of Communists of the Republic of Moldova (*Partidul Comuniştilor din Republica Moldova*—PCRM). The outcome was a decisive victory for Lucinschi, who obtained 54 percent of the vote. After Lucinschi was inaugurated on January 15, 1997, he nominated Ion CIUBUC, an economist, to succeed Sangheli. The new prime minister pledged that his administration would focus on economic reforms.

Balloting for a new Parliament was held on March 22, 1998, with the PCRM winning a plurality of 40 seats, followed by the pro-Snegur Democratic Convention of Moldova (*Convenţia Democrată din Moldova*—CDM) with 26 seats, the pro-Lucinschi bloc For a Democratic and Prosperous Moldova (*Pentru o Moldovă Democratică şi Prosperă*—PMDP) with 24 seats, and the Party of Democratic Forces (*Partidul Forţelor Democratice*—PFD) with 11 seats. A center-right coalition consisting of the CDM, PMDP, and PFD, called the Alliance for Democracy and Reforms (*Alianţa pentru Democraţie şi Reforme*—ADR), formed a new government on April 21, with Ciubuc as premier. A growing economic crisis, however, led to Ciubuc's resignation on February 1, 1999. A new cabinet under Ion STURZA was approved on March 12, but it fell on November 9, when the Christian Democrats (*Frontul Popular Creştin Democrat*—FPCD), PCRM, and a handful of independents passed a vote of no confidence in the government's economic policies. (See the 2012 *Handbook* for details.)

A struggle between the president and the legislature ensued, with the latter rejecting two nominees for prime minister and Lucinschi not even submitting the name of his third choice when it became apparent that Parliament would again reject the cabinet. With the president having vowed to dissolve the legislature if it turned down another nominee, on December 21 Parliament approved a largely nonparty government led by Dumitru BRAGHIŞ, theretofore deputy minister for the economy and reform.

What remained of the former governing alliance, the ADR, broke apart in April 2000 when the principal component of the PMDP, Parliament Speaker Dumitru DIACOV's Movement for a Democratic and Prosperous Moldova (*Mişcarea o Moldovă Democratică şi Prosperă*—MMDP), announced its reconfiguration as the Democratic Party of Moldova (*Partidul Democrat din Moldova*—PDM) and its independence from President Lucinschi and his efforts to strengthen the presidency through constitutional amendment. The struggle over Moldova's system of government took a different direction in July, when Parliament, overriding Lucinschi's vehement veto, overwhelmingly passed constitutional changes that included indirect election of the president by the legislature. A corresponding election law promulgated in October mandated that a presidential candidate would need a three-fifths majority to secure a victory.

In December 2000 neither the PCRM's Vladimir VORONIN nor Pavel BARBALAT, chair of the Constitutional Court, succeeded in marshaling the 61 votes required to win the presidency. Barbalat, who was backed by Diacov's PDM, Snegur's CDM, and the Christian Democrats, repeatedly failed to break 40 votes, while Voronin came no closer than 59 (in a third ballot on December 6). A center-right parliamentary boycott prevented a quorum and thus a fourth ballot on December 21, and on December 26 the Constitutional Court ruled that President Lucinschi had the "right and duty" to order new elections. Accordingly, he dissolved Parliament on January 12, 2001, in preparation for a general election. On February 25 the PCRM won a clear majority of 71 seats on a 50.7 percent vote share. The only other formations to win seats were the new Braghiş Alliance (19 seats, 13.3 percent) and the Christian Democrats (11 seats, 8.3 percent). The PCRM landslide ensured the election of Voronin as Moldova's next president on April 4 and also gave it enough seats to amend the constitution unilaterally. On April 19 Parliament endorsed a new cabinet headed by Vasile TARLEV, a political independent.

In July 2004 the separatists in Transnistria raised tensions by shutting down schools in the region that taught Moldovan in the Latin script. Consequently Voronin broke off negotiations. In early August the separatists blocked rail lines between Transnistria and Moldova, and they subsequently announced that they were mobilizing reserves for the "Transnister Army." Smirnov collaterally declared that Transnistria "is marching on the road to setting up an independent, sovereign state." In October Russia stated that it would not leave Transnistria until the issue was resolved.

In the March 6, 2005, parliamentary elections, the PCRM failed to win a majority but, with 56 seats, remained the plurality party. Since the PCRM did not win the 61 seats required to elect a president, a successful opposition boycott of the subsequent presidential election would have meant, after two failed ballots, new parliamentary elections. Ultimately, however, enough members of the Democratic Moldova Bloc (*Blocul Electoral "Moldova Democrată"*—BMD) voted for Voronin for him to be reelected on the second ballot. Prime Minister Tarlev formed a new government later in April and indicated that he would trim the government's staff size by 70 percent.

Despite initial overtures to opposition parties, relations between the PCRM-led government and opposition parties worsened through 2005–2007. On October 13, 2005, in a strictly partisan vote, PCRM members of Parliament removed the immunity of three opposition members prior to charging them with abuse of office. In response, the Our Moldova Alliance (*Alianţa Moldova Noastră*—AMN), the main opposition party, on November 24 joined the Social Liberal Party (*Partidul Social-Liberal*—PSL) in calling (unsuccessfully) for the impeachment of President Voronin, charging him with "breaking laws, flouting a ruling of the European Court of Human Rights, offending the Romany ethnic minority with epithets used in relation to the opposition, and promoting his own candidate to the post of Chişinău mayor."

Legislation proposed by the Moldovan government in the spring of 2005 reportedly would have given Transnistria autonomous status within the Moldovan Republic, although banking, armed forces, customs, and foreign policy would have remained under Moldovan authority. This initiative did not progress significantly, and the government—with the support of the United States and the European Union (EU)—increased pressure on the separatists by gaining the agreement of Ukraine in March 2006 to refuse exports from Transnistria unless they were approved by the Moldovan customs. The separatist government, whose finances derive primarily from those exports, responded by instituting a blockade of train traffic at the border, which continued to be subject to transit disputes involving Russia as well as Moldova and Ukraine.

Local elections in 2007 (held in 2006 in autonomous Gagauzia) resulted in political setbacks for the PCRM, amid what the U.S. embassy termed "intimidation of candidates, unequal access to and coverage in the media for all parties, misuse of administrative resources, reports of improper campaigning near voting stations, government bias in favor of ruling-party candidates, and irregularities in voter lists." Particularly symbolic was the loss of the mayoral race in Chişinău to the Liberal Party (*Partidul Liberal*—PL) candidate, Dorin CHIRTOACĂ. Although the PDM and AMN saw only modest gains in the district elections, many of the smaller opposition political parties saw significant gains or obtained district seats for the first time, with nearly 30 percent of district seats held by members of the smaller parties or by independents. The Tarlev government subsequently became increasingly unpopular due to its problems in implementing economic and political reforms. Consequently, Tarlev stepped down as prime minister on March 19, 2008, stating the need for "new individuals" to lead the country. Deputy Prime Minister Zinaida GRECIANÎI subsequently became Moldova's first female prime minister.

The PCRM won 60 seats in the April 5, 2009, legislative balloting, leaving it 1 shy of the 61 seats (a three-fifths majority) needed to elect a president on its own. Consequently, balloting in Parliament on May 20 and June 3 failed to elect a president, necessitating a new legislative poll on July 29 at which the PCRM declined to 48 seats, compared to 53 seats for the opposition (the PDM, AMN, PL, and the recently formed Liberal Democratic Party of Moldova [*Partidului Liberal Democrat din Moldova*—PLDM]), which coalesced as the Alliance for European Integration (*Alianţa Pentru Integrare Europenă*—APIE) and pledged to form a new government.

Protesters (estimated at 15,000 in Chişinău alone) took to the streets throughout Moldova after the results of the April 2009 legislative elections were announced, claiming fraud on the part of the ruling PCRM. Part of the parliament building and the office of the president were burned. Several hundred protesters were injured in the subsequent police crackdown, and at least three died in custody.

The problems following the April 2009 elections appeared to undercut support for the PCRM in the July reballoting, especially after PCRM leader Marian LUPU defected, along with a number of other legislators, to the PDM. Eight years of communist rule came to an end with the installation of the APIE government in September under Vladimir FILAT, a prominent businessman who pledged to pursue further integration with the EU, strengthen ties with Romania, and seek to replace Russian troops in Transnistria with international peacekeepers. In response, Transnistrian leader Smirnov announced plans to expand his region's armed forces.

After the July 2009 elections, the new parliament was unable to elect a president of the republic in November or December as the PCRM boycotted the proceedings, thereby preventing Lupu, the APIE candidate, from securing the two-thirds majority required for election. No further presidential balloting could be held until after new legislative elections, which were constitutionally proscribed until at least July 2010 (one year from the last election).

President Voronin resigned effective September 11, 2009, and he was succeeded in an acting capacity by the PL's Mihai GHIMPU, who had recently been elected speaker of Parliament. At the request of the APIE, Ghimpu on September 17 nominated PLDM leader Vladimir Filat to form a new government, which as approved with 53 votes in Parliament on September 25, included members of the four APIE parties. However, Marian Lupu, the presidential candidate of APIE, failed to gain the 61 votes needed for election in ballots in the Parliament on November 10 and December 7, 2009. Consequently, acting president Ghimpu remained in the post.

Despite fierce opposition from the PCRM, a referendum to revise the constitution and allow for direct popular election of the president (and thus resolve the political deadlock) was held on September 5, 2010. Although 87.5 percent of those voting supported the change, the results of the initiative were declared invalid because turnout had been only 31 percent (33 percent was required). Consequently, acting president Ghimpu, in accordance with instructions from the Constitutional Court, announced that Parliament would be dissolved on September 28, 2010, and new elections would be held.

The PCRM again took the lead in the November 28, 2010, parliamentary election, winning 42 seats, compared with a combined 59 for APIE (now comprising the PLDM, PDM, and PL). Again due to the inability to indirectly elect a president, the new speaker of Parliament, Lupu, became acting president.

Local elections in 2011 broadly confirmed the existing political deadlock, although the larger political parties dominated the results, with the PCRM and APIE taking approximately 97 percent of all district seats. Chirtoacă was reelected as mayor of Chişinău in a tight race that saw him emerging as winner of the PCRM candidate by a margin of roughly 1 percent of all votes cast.

Transnistria held presidential elections in 2011; the Russian government notably withdrew its past support for Igor Smirnov, the president since 1990, and backed Anatoliy KAMINSKI of Renewal (*Obnovleniye*). The first round, on December 11, included three party candidates and three independent candidates. Yevgeny SHEVCHUK (ind.) received 38.6 percent of the vote and Kaminski (Renewal) 26.3, and both advanced to the second round; Smirnov placed third with 24.7 percent. In the second round, Shevchuk was elected with 73.9 percent over Kaminski, who obtained 19.7 percent of the vote.

In February 2011 the Moldovan Constitutional Court ruled that Parliament could schedule new elections given the "unique legal situation" of the lengthy acting presidency. Parliament subsequently called for a new presidential election, initially for November 18; when no candidates registered for that election, a second election was scheduled for December 16. Lupu was the only registered candidate. But as in 2009 and 2010, the ruling coalition was unable to win the necessary supermajority, obtaining 58 of the 61 votes needed, the PCRM having boycotted the voting. This second failed election should have resulted in early parliamentary elections in 2013; but on January 12, 2012, the Constitutional Court ruled that the December 16 balloting was unconstitutional, as some legislators had revealed their secret ballots to the media, and thus the attempt was nullified. A third round of voting was therefore permitted and held on March 16, 2012. Nicolae TIMOFTI (ind.) was elected with 62 votes when three former PCRM legislators who had previously defected to small socialist parties agreed to support him. This ended a period of 917 days during which Moldova lacked a president-elect.

Conflicts within the governing coalition (see Current events, below) led the PCRM and PDM to support a nonconfidence motion on March 5, 2013; Filat resigned effective March 8. President Timofti renominated Filat as prime minister on April 10, but the Constitutional Court on April 22 blocked the nomination due to the ongoing corruption investigations against members of his former cabinet. Reportedly fearing early elections in which polls predicted the PCRM would gain seats, the PDM and Liberal Reformist Party (*Partidul Liberal Reformator*—PLR), former PL legislators who had left to found a new party in 2012, agreed in May to form a coalition government under Iurie LEANCĂ of the PLDM. The PCRM boycotted the vote to approve the new cabinet, calling instead for early elections.

In the parliamentary election held on November 30, 2014, the newly formed pro-Russian Party of Socialists of the Republic of Moldova (*Partidul Socialiştilor din Republica Moldova*—PSRM) led the balloting with 20.5 percent of the vote, securing 25 seats in parliament. The remaining seats were distributed as follows: the PLDM, 23; the PCRM, 21; the PDM, 19; and the LP, 13. Multiple attempts to form a coalition government subsequently failed (see Current issues, below), and Gheorghe BREGA (LP) was appointed to lead a caretaker cabinet, which was sworn in on October 30, 2015. It was not until January 20, 2016, that Pavel FILIP (PDM) was sworn in as prime minister of a minority coalition government that included the PDM and PL.

Constitution and government. The 1994 constitution, replacing the 1977 Soviet-era text, described Moldova as a "presidential, parliamentary republic" based on political pluralism and "the preservation, development, and expression of ethnic and linguistic identity." Executive power continues to be vested in a president, who was directly elected until constitutional changes passed in July 2000 (over President Lucinschi's veto) transformed the country into a "parliamentary republic" and led to passage in September–October of a law establishing procedures for indirect election by the unicameral Parliament. (A three-fifths majority is required for a president to be elected. After two failed ballots, new legislative elections must be held, although only two legislative elections can be held in a single calendar year.) The president nominates the prime minister, subject to approval by the Parliament, which is elected for a four-year term. Passage of a nonconfidence motion in the Parliament forces the resignation of the Council of Ministers. Other constitutional clauses proclaim Moldova's permanent neutrality and proscribe the stationing of foreign troops on the national territory.

The 1994 constitution authorized "special status" for both the Gagauz region in the south and the Transnister region, where separatist activity had broken out in 1990. Statutes providing broad autonomy to Gagauz-Yeri (Gagauzia, *Găgăuzia*) went into effect in February 1995, with referendums the following month to determine which villages wished to be part of the special region. Subsequently, direct elections for a 35-member regional People's Assembly were held in May–June, as was the direct election of a regional executive leader (*bashkan*), who was authorized to carry out quasi-presidential responsibilities.

Meanwhile, the status of Transnistria remained unresolved. In December 1995 Transnistrians overwhelmingly endorsed an independence constitution, and in December 2006, 97 percent voted in a referendum to seek independence. In May 1997, however, the Moldovan and Transnister leaders, meeting in Moscow, agreed to participate in a single state, although the dynamics of the region's "special status" remained to be defined. In Kyiv, Ukraine, in July 1999 Smirnov and Lucinschi signed a declaration on normalizing relations that committed both sides to a single "economic, judicial, and social sphere within Moldova's existing borders." Nevertheless, subsequent claims by Transnistria that Chişinău ignored its needs and opinions soon led to a renewal of demands for independence. At present, a strong president who also serves as prime minister leads Transnistria's government; under changes introduced in 2000, a 43-member, unicameral Parliament replaced a bicameral legislature.

In January 2003 the government approved new legislation replacing 9 provinces and 2 autonomous regions introduced in 1999 with a structure that now encompasses 32 districts, 3 municipalities (Tighina and Bălţi as well as the capital), the Autonomous Territorial Unit of Gagauzia, and Transnistria. Local administrative units include communes and cities.

Although the constitution guarantees freedom of the press, onerous control was exercised by the PCRM prior to the 2009 ouster of President Voronin. (See the 2010 *Handbook* for details.) In 2016 Reporters Without Borders ranked the county as 76th out of 180 countries with respect to press freedoms. Censorship remains heavy in Russian-dominated Transnistria.

Foreign relations. Moldova's first international action following independence in 1991 was to establish diplomatic relations with Romania. On March 2 Moldova was admitted to the UN and on April 27 was formally offered membership in the IMF and World Bank. It also joined the Conference on (later Organization for) Security and Cooperation in Europe (CSCE/OSCE).

Possible union with Romania was placed on the agenda by the creation of a parliamentary-level National Council of Reunification in late 1991, but a growing preference in Moldova for independence meant that by mid-1993 reunification had ceased to be a practical political option. However, spurred by Romania's eagerness to join the North Atlantic Treaty Organization (NATO) and settle border issues, Moldova and Romania agreed in April 1997 to resume talks on a basic treaty, which was finally initialed on April 28, 2000, by the countries' foreign ministers. Despite years of further negotiation, the treaty remained unsigned, in part because Romania has refused to accept references to a separate Moldovan language.

On March 16, 1994, during a visit to Brussels for talks with officials from NATO and the EU, President Snegur signed NATO's Partnership for Peace, while the Moldovan Parliament on April 8 finally ratified membership in the CIS and its economic union. Although Moldovan participation in CIS military or monetary integration was ruled out, the CIS ratification indicated cautious alignment with Moscow, with the aim in particular of securing the long-sought departure of the Russian Fourteenth Army from Transnistria.

In July 1995 Moldova became the first CIS member to be admitted to the Council of Europe. In 1997 the government announced its support for negotiations with the EU toward associate membership, perhaps leading eventually to full membership. Regionally, in October 1997 Moldova joined Georgia, Ukraine, and Azerbaijan in forming the GUAM group.

Moldova subsequently made efforts to reach beyond purely regional issues. In September 2003, for example, it began participating in postwar security operations in Iraq at the invitation of the U.S. government. In addition, in January 2004 Moldova agreed to participate in UN peacekeeping operations, subsequently contributing soldiers to missions in Liberia, Côte D'Ivoire, Sudan, and Georgia.

In recent years Moldova's foreign relations have directly reflected its internal conflicts to an unusual degree. With large ethnic populations who identify with Romania and Russia, relations with those two countries have been at the forefront of Moldovan foreign policy. Relations with Romania were strained over suggestions by Moldovan President Voronin that "greater" Moldova included the Romanian province of Moldova. Romanian President Ion Iliescu, in January 2004, called the idea "a falsification of historical reality and an expression of revisionist inclinations."

Not coincidentally, Moldova's relations with Russia have often been the inverse of its relations with Romania. While Voronin (a former KBG officer) was considered pro-Russian when he first took office, he gradually adopted more anti-Russian positions, largely as a result of the conflict in Transnistria. In April 2004 Voronin emphasized that Moldova's relations with Russia were still good, with only the

Transnister issue being a problem. But Russia has repeatedly declined to sign a "Declaration on Stability and Security for the Republic of Moldova" sought by Voronin. Russia maintains that such a guarantee of Moldovan sovereignty would be possible only if Moldova guaranteed a peaceful settlement of the Transnister issue.

Moldova's desire for integration with the EU received a setback on March 10, 2004, when Ivan Borisavljevic, the European Commission's envoy to Moldova, said that there were serious obstacles on the road to accession, including the Transnistria conflict, corruption, poverty, and lack of genuine reforms. In February 2005 Moldova signed an "action plan" with the European Union (EU) to bring the country closer to EU standards. The action plan involved a wide range of political, economic, and judicial reforms.

Relations with Russia worsened in January 2006, when Russia cut off supplies of natural gas to Moldova after the latter declined to accept a 100 percent increase in prices. In mid-January, the two countries agreed on a less dramatic increase in prices. In March, however, the Russian government banned the import of wine from Moldova and Georgia, purportedly for health reasons. In fact, most analysts characterize Russia's move as retaliation for Moldova's and Georgia's position opposing Russia's entry into the World Trade Organization (WTO) until Russia stops supporting separatists in those two countries and removes troops from their territory. Relations improved in 2007 as both the Moldovan and international media reported rumors of feelers by both Moldova and Russia to resolve the Transnister problem.

Romania's accession to the EU on January 1, 2007, raised new issues with Moldova. Romanian President Traian Băsescu has urged Moldovan admission to the EU and offered Romanian assistance toward this goal. He stated in June 2007 that this would effectively "bring the Romanian people together under the umbrella of the European Union." Voronin, however, had declared in December 2006 that Romanian offers of assistance were "interference in the domestic affairs of a sovereign state." An agreement to open new Romanian consulates in the Moldovan towns of Bălți and Cahul was reversed in March 2007 by the Moldovan foreign ministry, which complained that Romania had released inflated figures regarding Moldovans seeking Romanian citizenship. Relations worsened in December 2007 with the expulsion of two Romanian diplomats and when Voronin and Romanian officials traded accusations over the continued delay in ratifying the basic treaty and border treaty between the two states. In July 2008 relations improved when it was announced that the Romanian consulate in Cahul would open in exchange for a Moldovan consulate in Iasi.

In March 2008 Moldovan media reported that the crucial issue in obtaining Russian support to resolve the Transnistrian conflict was Moscow's requirement for a formal repudiation of any future Moldovan membership in NATO. Voronin met with Smirnov in April 2008 for the first time in seven years, agreeing on further talks to "gradually" resolve the conflict. In the wake of the Russian–Georgian war of mid-2008, however, Smirnov in September called instead for Transnistria's formal independence and expressed confidence that Russia would support the "120,000 Russian citizens" living in Transnistria.

The pro-Western coalition government installed in September 2009 set further integration with the EU as one of its chief priorities in foreign affairs. Meanwhile, acting president Mihai Ghimpu, while acknowledging past personal convictions for a union with Romania, stressed that unification was not a goal for the new government. In response, Russian far-right political leader Vladimir Zhirinovsky called for immediate Russian recognition of the independence of Transnistria, a statement widely interpreted in Moldova as suggesting possible Russian opposition to continued EU expansion in the region. Romanian former foreign minister Adrian Cioroianu suggested that the Moldovan government effectively ignore the status of Transnistria while pursuing other aspects of European integration, this statement in turn seen as evidence of continued Romanian desire for unification.

In 2009 Romania modified its citizenship laws to allow foreigners to apply for naturalization if their grandparent or great-grandparent held Romanian citizenship. Roughly 17,000 Moldovans gained Romanian citizenship in this fashion in January–July 2010, and the Romanian government said that 800,000 applications remained pending. This policy was criticized by many political party leaders in Western Europe, who feared that hundreds of thousands of Moldovans might enter the EU workforce through a "loophole" if Romania is successful in its plan to join the Schengen Accord, which would allow visa-free travel for Romanian passport holders to the 25 EU countries.

The stalled negotiations between Romania and Moldova over the basic treaty were partially resolved with an April 2010 bilateral "strategic partnership" agreement pledging cooperation and a November 2010 border treaty. In May 2011 Romanian Foreign Minister Teodor Baconschi referred to the basic treaty as an "obsolete" concept.

Moldova and the EU concluded negotiations in June 2013 for a free trade agreement, despite objections from the Russian government. Moscow's decision to again ban the import of Molodvan wine in September 2013 was widely interpreted in domestic and international media as an effort to exert pressure on the issue. The Association Agreement with the EU was signed by Prime Minister Iurie Leancă on June 27, 2014, and ratified by Moldova on July 2 in a vote boycotted by the PCRM. In response, Russia banned imports of Moldovan fruit, cattle, and beef, raised import duties on a variety of goods, and threatened to cancel existing free trade agreements with Moldova.

Gagauzia held a referendum on February 2, 2014, on the question of EU accession. The results saw 98.4 percent of voters preferring closer relations with the Russian-led Eurasian Union as opposed to the EU and 98.9 percent agreeing that Gagauzia should seek independence if Moldova joins the EU.

The government of Moldova expressed concern regarding the status of Transnistria following the Russian annexation of Crimea in March 2014. The Supreme Council had formally requested on March 17 that the region be annexed to Russia, without response from Moscow. In April Transnistria requested Russian recognition of its independence.

Former Moldovan interim prime minister Natalia GHERMAN emerged in April 2016 as a candidate to be UN secretary general. In August an effort to mediate the status of Transnistria by German foreign minister and OSCE chair Frank-Walter Steinmeier during a visit to Moldova failed as separatist leaders continued to demand full independence, followed by annexation by Russia.

Current issues. The status of the Transnistria region has been a major focus of attention since independence. Chişinău has insisted that the region remain an integral part of Moldova, while Transnistrian leaders have fluctuated between demanding outright independence and proposing a confederal system that would grant the region autonomy. The presence of Russian troops in the region has complicated the issue (see Foreign relations, above). Moldovan leaders pursued "constructive dialogue" with Transnistrian leaders. The continued presence of Russian soldiers in the region, however, was seen as a continued violation of Moldova's neutral status. Tensions increased when Transnistrian leader Smirnov in February 2010 invited Russia to base missiles in Transnistria in response to Romania's agreement to host elements of a U.S. antimissile system.

A referendum was held on September 5, 2010, proposing two constitutional amendments: the direct election of the presidency and officially changing the name of the official language from "Moldovan" to "Romanian." Although 87.8 percent of those voting approved of the measures, voter turnout was only 30.3 percent, short of the 33.3 percent of eligible voters required to validate the election. When the December 28, 2010, legislative elections saw both the PCRM and the APIE fail to win the three-fifths of Parliament seats necessary to elect a president, Parliament again elected a speaker, who then assumed the role of acting president. The Constitutional Court, however, ruled in February 2011 that the inability to elect a president does not require a new, immediate round of parliamentary elections. Negotiations to amend or reform the electoral process for the presidency continued into 2012.

On July 13, 2012, Parliament banned the use of communist symbols, prompting protests by the PCRM and concerns in the domestic media that relations with Transnistria would grow further estranged.

Domestic media reported that the breakdown between PLDM and PDM was motivated at least in part by efforts by Filat to displace the PDM's control over the state's anticorruption institutions.

On December 5, 2013, the Constitutional Court ruled that the national language should be known as Romanian. The ruling argued that the country's Declaration of Independence (which uses the term *Romanian*) takes precedence over the constitution (which uses *Moldovan*). The PCRM protested against the change.

Following the November 2014 legislative elections, coalition negotiations failed to finalize a coalition government among the pro-European parties—the PLDM, PDM, and PL—and a succession of acting prime ministers lost confidence votes or were forced to resign: Chiril GABURICI (PLDM), in office from February 18, 2015–June 22; Natalia GHERMAN (PLDM), June 22–July 30; Valeriu STRELEȚ (PLDM), July 30–October 30; and Gheorghe BREGA (LP), October 30–January 20, 2016. On December 21, 2015, the president nominated Ion STURZA (ind.), but Parliament failed to act on his candidacy.

Finally, on January 15, the president nominated Pavel Filip (PDM), who was approved on January 20 and formed a PDM-PL cabinet.

Prior to the 2014 parliamentary elections, it was estimated that upwards of $1.5 billion went missing from three banks, which sparked protests and calls for an official inquiry in the fall of 2015.

The deadlock between the president and Parliament once again sparked protests in January 2016. Hundreds of people gathered outside of Parliament to demand an early election. The number of protestors grew to thousands and eventually broke through police barricades.

The Constitutional Court on March 4, 2016, reversed a 2000 amendment on the election of the president. The amendment, which empowered Parliament to elect the head of state, was overturned when 18 MPs of the LDPM filed a complaint. The court accepted the argument that the 2000 Parliament failed to request the opinion of the Constitutional Court throughout all drafts of the amendment. As such, the court voided the amendment and granted voters the right to elect the president.

POLITICAL PARTIES

Since independence, Moldovan parties have frequently formed electoral blocs to contest parliamentary elections, but none have lasted more than one national election cycle. (See the 2011 *Handbook* for details.) Moldova's unusually high bar for representation in Parliament (see Legislature, below, for details) helped encourage the formation of electoral blocs. In July 2003 the AMN was formed by merger of the **Social Democratic Alliance** (ASD), successor to the **Braghiş Alliance**; the Liberal Party (PL); and the **Alliance of Independents** (AI). In May 2004 the three primary center-left opposition parties—the AMN, the Democratic Party of Moldova (PDM), and the Social Liberal Party (PSL)—announced the formation of the **Democratic Moldova Bloc** (BMD). By January 2005, however, two months before the next legislative election, cracks were already showing in the alliance. Three members of the former Braghiş Alliance announced they were running on the Party of Communists (PCRM) list. The following October, 30 senior members of the AMN, including former prime minister Braghiş, left the party to form a new Party of Social Democracy (PDS).

Nine parties, 2 electoral blocs, and 12 independent candidates contested the March 2005 parliamentary elections, with only the PCRM, BMD, and Christian Democratic People's Party (PPCD) meeting the threshold for representation. Twelve parties and five independent candidates contested the April 2009 parliamentary election (recent electoral law changes having barred bloc participation), with the PCRM, the PLDM, AMN, and PL meeting the threshold. Following the failure by Parliament to elect a president, eight parties contested the new elections in July, with the PCRM, PLDM, AMN, PL, and PDM meeting the threshold. The PLDM, AMN, PL, and PDM subsequently formed a ruling government as the Alliance for European Integration (*Alianţa Pentru Integrare Europenă*—APIE). Early elections held in December 2010 saw 20 parties and 19 independent candidates compete, with only the PCRM, PLDM, PDM, and PL meeting the threshold. Of the 16 remaining parties, the **European Action Movement** (MAE) (since merged with the PL) took more than 1 percent of the vote.

The APIE ruling government (now minus the PL) thus continued in power, renamed as the Pro-European Coalition (*Coaliţia Pro-Europenă*—CPE).

In the November 2014 assembly elections, the PSRM, PLDM, PCRM, PDM, and LP secured representation.

Government and Government-Supportive Parties:

Democratic Party of Moldova (*Partidul Democrat din Moldova*—PDM). The PDM was established in April 2000 as successor to the movement "For a Democratic and Prosperous Moldova" (*Mişcarea "Pentru o Moldovă Democraticăşi Prosperă"*—MMDP). The centrist movement had been formed in February 1997 to promote the policies of President Lucinschi. Its leader, Dumitru Diacov, the former deputy speaker of the Parliament, had left the PDAM along with a group of other legislators in a policy dispute over support for the government.

In October 1999 the decision of four members of the MMDP's legislative delegation to sit as independents cost the government of Prime Minister Sturza its majority.

The formation of the PDM marked Speaker of Parliament Diacov's formal split with President Lucinschi, Diacov having strongly argued against the adoption of a presidential form of government. In 2001, running independently, the PDM failed to win any seats in Parliament. In the 2005 election the PDM won eight seats as a component of the BMD.

In February 2008 the PDM and the **Social Liberal Party** (*Partidul Social-Liberal*—PSL) announced a merger intended to create a unified opposition party to the PCRM. The PSL was formed in May 2001 under the leadership of Oleg Serebrian. In December 2002 it absorbed the **Party of Democratic Forces** (*Partidul Forţelor Democratice*—PFD), whose chair, Valeriu MATEI, had finished fifth in the first round of the 1996 presidential election. The center-right PSL favored domestic political reform and integration with the EU. It won three parliamentary seats in 2005.

In the April 2009 elections the PDM won only approximately 3 percent of the vote. However, the party's fortunes were transformed in June, following the dissolution of Parliament and announcement of new elections. Marian Lupu, a prominent member of the PCRM, left that party after stating that "reform from within was not possible." Lupu subsequently joined the PDM as de facto leader, bringing with him about a dozen sitting members of the PCRM parliamentary delegation and a substantial electoral base. Consequently, the PDM won 13 seats in the July balloting on a vote share of 12.5 percent. Subsequently, Lupu became the presidential candidate of the APIE for the balloting scheduled for late October, but he failed to gain the position when the APIE could not muster the required 61 votes.

In February 2010 as much as two-thirds of the membership of the Social Democratic Party (see below) reportedly left that party to join the PDM, which Lupu welcomed as a "consolidation" of the center-left.

In the December 2010 election the PDM took 12.7 percent of the vote and won 15 seats. Lupu was elected the same month as the speaker of parliament but was dismissed from the position on April 25, 2013 (see Current events, above). In the 2014 election, the PDM took 19 seats. PDM member Pavel FILIP was appointed prime minister on January 20, 2016.

Leaders: Pavel FILIP (Prime Minister), Marian LUPU (Chair), Dumitru DIACOV (Former Chair), Vlad PLAHOTNIUC (First Vice Chair), Oleg SEREBRIAN (Former Chair of the PSL).

Liberal Party (*Partidul Liberal*—PL). The PL (which should not be confused with the party of the same name that joined in forming the AMN in 2003; see below) was established in 1993 as the center-right **Party of Reform** (*Partidul Reformei*—PR), which changed its name to the PL in April 2005. The PL supports national unity, withdrawal of Russian forces, and integration into Western institutions.

The PR won 2.4 percent of the vote in the 1994 parliamentary election and 0.5 percent in 1998. In 2001 it joined the **National Romanian Party** (*Partidul Naţional Român*—PNR) in the Electoral Bloc **"Faith and Justice"** (*Blocul Electoral "Credinţaşi Dreptate"*—BECD), which won 0.7 percent. It did not compete in 2005. In June 2007 the PL's Dorin Chirtoacă, 28, unexpectedly won election as mayor in Chişinău.

In the April 2009 elections, the PL emerged as a significant political force, taking 13.1 percent of the vote and winning 15 seats. In the July balloting, it again secured 15 seats (on a vote share of 14.7 percent).

In the November 2010 elections, the PL took almost 10 percent of the vote and won 12 seats.

In March 2011 the **"European Action" Movement** (*Mişcarea "Acţiunea Europeana"*—MAE) merged with the PL. Founded in 2007, the MAE officially called for Moldovan integration into the EU. In the April 2009 election the MAE's candidate list won only 1 percent of the vote, and 1.2 percent of the vote in the December 2010 election.

Following the February 2013 cabinet crisis, a group of PL members formed the **Liberal Party Reform Council** (*Consiliul de Reformare a Partidului Liberal*—CRPL) in April 2013. The group subsequently split from the party, founding the PRL (see above).

In the 2014 elections, the PL took 13 seats in Parliament. Party member Gheorghe BREGA briefly served as prime minister from October 30, 2015, to January 20, 2016.

Leaders: Mihai GHIMPU (President); Dorin CHIRTOACĂ, Anatol ŞALARU (Senior Vice Presidents); Gheorghe BREGA (Former Prime Minister).

Liberal Democratic Party of Moldova (*Partidului Liberal Democrat din Moldova*—PLDM). The PLDM was founded in December 2007 by Vladimir Filat, a legislator who had left the PDM in September 2007, citing differences with the party leadership. In April 2008 the PLDM began a petition drive to change presidential elections to uninominal, direct elections, thereby confronting the PCRM and emerging as the most vocal opposition party. In the April 2009 elections the PLDM took 12.4 percent of the vote and won 15 seats. In the July balloting, the PDLM gained 18 seats on a vote share of 16.6 percent. In the November 2010 election the PLDM took 29.4 percent of the vote and won 32 seats.

On March 22, 2011, the PLDM signed an agreement to merge with the **Our Moldova Alliance** (*Alianţa Moldova Noastră*—AMN). The AMN was formed in July 2003 by the joining of three parties and was cochaired by former Prime Minister Dumitru Braghiş. (See this entry in the 2010 *Handbook* for an expanded history of the AMN.) Braghiş would leave in 2005 to found the Party of Social Democracy of Moldova. The AMN formed the core of the center-left Electoral Bloc "Democratic Moldova" (*Blocul Electoral "Moldova Democrată"*—BMD) in the 2005 parliamentary elections. The AMN won 9.8 percent of the vote and 11 seats in the April 2009 legislative elections but declined to a 7.4 percent vote share and 7 seats in the July balloting. In the 2014 election, the PLDM took 23 seats.

Leaders: Valeriu STRELEŢ (Acting Party President and Former Prime Minister), Iurie LEANCĂ (First Vice President of the Party and Former Prime Minister), Vladimir FILAT (Former Prime Minister).

Opposition Parties:

Party of Communists of the Republic of Moldova (*Partidul Comuniştilor din Republica Moldova*—PCRM). The PCRM is a successor to the Soviet-era **Communist Party of Moldova** (*Partidul Comunist din Moldova*—PCM). The latter was suspended in August 1991 but achieved legal status in September 1994 as the PCRM even though many former Communists had by then opted for the Socialist Party of Moldova (PSM, below). The party was not legalized until after the 1994 legislative balloting, but it subsequently attracted defectors from other parties.

In 1996 the PCRM sought to build an alliance of "patriotic popular forces" for the fall presidential election, in which party leader Vladimir Voronin finished third in the first round with 10.3 percent of the vote. The PCRM then backed the successful second-round candidacy of Petru Lucinschi and was awarded two ministries in the new government of Ion Ciubuc.

During the legislative campaign of late 1997 and early 1998 the PCRM called for the "rebirth of a socialist society," in which a "pluralist economy" would be supported by a "strengthened" state sector. Party leaders also expressed support for renewed linkage of the sovereign republics that had emerged following the breakup of the Soviet Union as well as close political and military ties with Russia. The PCRM led all parties in the March 1998 balloting with 30 percent of the vote, which earned it a plurality of 40 seats, including 9 non-PCRM supporters.

For the 1999 local elections it spearheaded formation of a **Communist, Agrarian, and Socialist Bloc** (*Blocul Comuniştilor, Agrarienilorşi Socialiştilor*—BCAS) that also finished first in total district and local council seats. Participants included the PDAM and the Party of Socialists (PSRM, below). In the 2001 election the PCRM won 71 seats, enabling it to elect its chair as president.

The PCRM did not fare as well in the 2005 parliamentary elections, winning only 56 seats. Lacking enough votes to ensure the reelection of Voronin as president, and threatened with a boycott of the presidential election by opposition parties, the PCRM reached out to members of the Democratic Moldova Bloc to gain enough votes to ensure Voronin's reelection. The 2007 local elections saw the PCRM weaken further, slipping from holding 615 district council seats nationwide to 465. Most notably, in Chişinău the PCRM lost the mayoral election. In 2008, however, the party and local coalition allies secured over a third of the seats for the People's Assembly in the autonomous region of Gagauzia, interpreted in the domestic press as arresting the party's decline.

The PCRM won 49.5 percent of the vote and 60 seats in the April 2009 parliamentary elections, falling one seat short of the three-fifths majority necessary to elect a president on its own. In the July balloting the PCRM declined to 44.7 percent of the vote and 48 seats, prompting Voronin's resignation from the presidency and the party's move into opposition status.

In the November 2010 elections, the PCRM won 39.3 percent of the vote and 42 seats in Parliament, again winning a plurality but isolated from the other parties in Parliament and thus not invited to form a government. Its position was weakened in November 2011 when a group of three MPs, including Igor DODON, PSRM leader Veronica ABRAMCIUC (of the PSRM, but who obtained her seat as a candidate on the PCRM list) and former prime minister Zinalda GRECEANII defected from the party and subsequently joined the PSRM. All voted for Timofti in the March 2012 elections, breaking the deadlock over the presidency.

In the 2014 elections, the PCRM took 21 seats.

Leaders: Vladimir VORONIN (Chair and Former President of the Republic), Maria POSTOICO (Parliamentary Leader), Marc TKACIUK (Secretary, PCRM Central Committee).

Party of Socialists of the Republic of Moldova (*Partidul Socialiştilor din Republica Moldova*—PSRM). Originally named the PSRM "Patria-Rodina" (the Romanian and Russian terms for *homeland*), the party was organized in 1997 by former PSM members. The party won only 0.6 percent of the national vote in the 1998 parliamentary election. For the February 2001 election it joined the Republican Party of Moldova (PRM, below) and the **Party of Progressive Forces of Moldova** (*Partidul Forţelor Progresiste din Moldova*—PFPM) in forming the **Unity Electoral Bloc** (*Blocul Electoral "Edinstvo"*). In January 2005 it formed the Electoral Bloc "Motherland" (*Blocul Electoral "Patria-Rodina"*—BEPR) with the PSM (below). The bloc advocated closer relations with Russia, self-determination for Transnistria, and elimination of the office of president. It opposed accession to the EU and closer relations with the West. The bloc earned only 5 percent of the vote in parliamentary elections in 2005, well below the threshold for representation.

For the 2007 local elections PSRM joined forces with the Social Movement *"Ravnopravie"* (MSPRR, above) in the Electoral Bloc *"Patria-Rodina–Ravnopravie."* In the 2009 and 2010 parliamentary elections, it supported the PCRM.

In November 2011, however, it broke with the PCRM, and subsequently gained parliamentary representation when sitting PCRM parliamentary deputies joined the party. This led to a subsequent conflict within the party leadership, with honorary chair Veronica AMBRACIUC reportedly removed in June 2013. The party reportedly shortened its name to PSRM at the same time.

In the 2014 elections, the PSRM took 25 seats.

Leader: Igor DODON (Chair).

Other Parties That Contested the 2010 or 2014 Legislative Elections:

Renaissance Party (*Partidul Renaştere/Vozrozhdenie*—PR). Established in September 2012 and registered in October, the PR was founded by former members of the PCRM. A self-identified socialist party, its program emphasizes social issues. The party's leaders included three sitting PCRM members of Parliament, which gave the PR immediate representation.

In February 2013 the PR announced it would form a coordinating body with the PSRM, Party "Moldova United" (PMUEM), and PPM (see below) to promote an alternative socialist platform in the country.

Leaders: Vadim MISHIN (Chair), Vasily TARLEV (Cochair and Former Prime Minister), Oleg BABENKO (Deputy Chair).

Democratic Action Party (*Partidul Acţiunea Democratică*—PAD). Founded by Mihai GODEA, a former PDLM member who had left that party in 2011 at the prospect that it might join the PCRM in forming a coalition government. He announced the formation of the PAD in July 2011. The PAD's program emphasizes the need for reform and integration into the EU. PAD secured just 0.2 percent of the vote in the 2014 parliamentary balloting.

Leader: Mihai GODEA (Chair).

Liberal Reformist Party (*Partidul Liberal Reformator*—PLR). The Liberal Party's conflicts with its partners in the APIE led a faction of the party, including seven members of parliament and two cabinet members, to publicly demand in April 2013 that the PL help form a new coalition government and not move into opposition. Several of these legislators were subsequently ejected from the party by the PL leadership. This faction formed a new party (fully constituted only in December 2013) while pledging support to the CPE coalition in May. The PLR gained immediate representation in parliament when the majority of the LP's delegation joined it. The party received 1.6 percent of the vote in the 2014 elections.

Leader: Ion HADÂRCA (Chair).

People's Democratic Party of Moldova (*Partidul Popular Democrat din Moldova*—PPDM). Registered as the **Humanist Party**

of Moldova (*Partidul Umanist din Moldova*—PUM) in February 2006. The party ran in the local elections of 2007 on a conservative platform that stressed the restoration of "human dignity," with attention to social morals, faith, and economic conditions in the country. The PUM did not register for the April 2009 elections, instead negotiating with the UCM for PUM members to be included on the UCM candidate list. The March 27, 2011, party congress adopted the present name.

Leader: Valeriu PASAT (Chair).

Christian Democratic People's Party (*Partidul Popular Creştin Democrat*—PPCD). A pro-Romanian party, the PPCD was known until December 1999 as the Christian Democratic People's Front (*Frontal Popular Creştin Democrat*—FPCD). The FPCD was a February 1992 continuation of the former Popular Front of Moldova (*Frontul Popular din Moldova*—FPM), which was formed in 1989 and became the dominant political group following the eclipse of the Communist Party of Moldova in mid-1991. The FPCD won nine parliamentary seats on a vote share of 7.3 percent in the February 1994 election, subsequently reiterating its commitment to eventual union with Romania.

The FPCD broke with the CDM alliance in March 1999 when it boycotted the confidence vote that installed the Sturza government. The FPCD insisted on four portfolios in the government instead of the two it was offered and, as a result, received none. In November it voted with the Communists against the Sturza government, and in December it supported the Braghiş cabinet.

At a December 1999 party congress the renamed PPCD deleted from its manifesto an insistence on Romanian national unity and instead called for Moldovan integration within Europe. In June 2000 the party's vice chair, Valentin DOLGANIUC, and a group of supporters resigned, accusing the party chair of creating an "atmosphere of intolerance and dictatorship" and of abandoning the party's principals through an alliance with the PCRM. Roşca subsequently commented that he viewed eventual unification with Romania as inevitable. The PPCD won 11 parliamentary seats in February 2001.

With the PCRM growing increasingly critical of Russia, the PPCD continued to move closer to the ruling party. Roşca even indicated in April 2005 that he would consider joining the cabinet. This led some party members to join other opposition parties, including, in December 2006, former party vice president Sergiu BURCA, who left for the PSL. After the 2005 elections PPCD seats in Parliament remained at 11; however, several deputies subsequently re-registered as independents.

The PPCD took 3.0 percent of the vote in the April 2009 elections and declined to 1.9 percent in July. In the November 2014 polling, the PPCD won 0.7 percent of the votes.

Leaders: Victor CIOBANU (President), Busila RADU (Vice President), Dinu ŢURCANU (Secretary General).

National Liberal Party (*Partidul Naţional Liberal*—PNL). The party was founded in 2006 to revive its namesake party of 1993, which in turn was an attempt to resurrect the traditions of the historical Romanian party of 1875–1947. The party platform supports classical liberal principles, integration into the EU and NATO, and unification with Romania. The PNL received 0.7 percent of the votes in the November 2014 balloting.

Leader: Vitalia PAVLICENCO (President).

Social Democratic Party (*Partidul Social Democrat*—PSD). This party was previously known as the Social Democratic Party of Moldova (*Partidul Social-Democrat din Moldova*—PSDM), one of many Moldovan parties to claim a social democratic orientation following independence. The PSDM contested the 1994 election as the core component of the Social Democratic Electoral Bloc (*Blocul Social-Democrat*—BSD), which secured 3.7 percent of the votes, barely missing the 4 percent threshold for parliamentary representation. In 1997 the party suffered a major split, when a wing supporting President Lucinschi separated and formed the United Social Democratic Party of Moldova (*Partidul Social-Democrat Unit din Moldova*—PSDUM) in conjunction with four other groups. In the 1998 election the PSDM, running on its own, won 1.9 percent of the vote, while the electoral alliance of the PSDUM and two other organizations received 1.3 percent. The PSDM subsequently reunited, and in 2001 it won 2.5 percent of the vote.

Prior to the March 2005 elections, the PSDM accused the ruling PCRM of illegally and unethically controlling the Central Election Commission and the country's media to block access by opposition parties. The commission rejected the PSDM charges. Running without an electoral bloc in 2005, the PSDM marginally improved its showing, earning 2.9 percent of the vote.

In June 2008 the PSDM merged with the Party of Social Democracy of Moldova (*Partidul Democraţiei Sociale din Moldova*—PDSM). Founded on April 15, 2006, and led by former Prime Minister Dumitru Braghiş, the PDSM was formed by disgruntled former members of Our Moldova Alliance. It adopted a social democratic agenda and advocated strong partnerships with the Russian Federation, the United States, and the EU. The party also called for closer relations with Romania and an ultimate withdrawal from the CIS. The PDSM's strong showing in the 2007 district elections left it the fourth-largest opposition party, albeit considerably behind the PDM, AMN, and PPCD.

Upon the 2008 merger of the PSDM and PDSM, the new grouping, which subsequently drew away a faction of the UCM (below) as well, was renamed the PSD, with Braghiş assuming leadership of the new party. In the April 2009 elections the PSD received 3.7 percent of the vote, failing to pass the threshold. In June the leadership of the PSD and UCM announced that the parties would merge by the end of 2009, calling for other centrist parties to join as well. The PSD won 1.9 percent of the vote in the July legislative poll. Following the failure of the party to gain parliamentary seats, Braghiş stepped down as party leader. In a party congress in April 2010, Braghiş stood as a candidate for party leadership but was defeated by Victor Şelin. (A number of PSD members had reportedly joined the PDM earlier in the year.)

Leaders: Victor ŞELIN (Chair), Sergiu COROPCEANU (Secretary General).

Republican Party of Moldova (*Partidul Republican din Moldova*—PRM). Established in 1999 under Ion CURTEAN, the PRM joined the PSRM in the *"Edinstvo"* electoral bloc for the 2001 parliamentary election. It won only 0.04 percent of the vote in 2005 and 0.09 percent of the vote in April 2009.

Leaders: Andrei STRATAN (Chair), Ion CURTEAN.

Conservative Party (*Partidul Conservator*—PC). Founded in 2006, the PC called for decentralization of governmental authority. It won 0.3 percent of the vote in the April 2009 elections.

Leader: Natalia NIRCA (Chair).

Party "Moldova United" (*Partidul "Moldova Unită–Edinaya Moldova"*—PMUEM). Originally founded in 2005 as the **Party of Spiritual Development "United Moldova"** (*Partidul Dezvoltării Spirituale" Moldova Unită*—PDSMU), the PDSMU called for, among other things, greater inclusiveness for women. In the April 2009 elections it won 0.2 percent of the vote. It did not formally contest the July balloting but encouraged party members to support the PSD. In February 2010 a party congress elected a new leadership and renamed the party as the PMUEM.

Leader: Vladimir ŢURCAN (Chair).

Ecologist Party of Moldova "Green Alliance" (*Partidul Ecologist "Alianţa Verde" din Moldova*—PEAVM). The PEAVM, which had participated in the 2007 elections on its own, ultimately withdrew from the April 2009 balloting, calling upon its supporters to vote for the PLDM. The PEAVM officially returned to the electoral arena for the July balloting, in which it won 0.4 percent of the vote. The party secured 0.09 percent of the vote in the November 2014 parliamentary balloting.

Leader: Vladimir BRAGA (President).

Republican Popular Party (*Partidul Popular Republican*—PPR). Founded in 1999 as the Peasants' Christian Democratic Party (*Partidul Ţărănesc Creştin Democrat din Moldova*—PŢCDM), the party changed its name at a party conference in May 2005 to the PPR. The party runs on a platform of improving conditions for the peasants of Moldova, in part through subsidized government loans. More specifically, it has called for a new Parliament of 51 members, each elected individually; for popular election of the president; and for a dramatic reduction in the size of government by cutting the number of ministries down to 6 at most.

The PŢCDM collected 1.4 percent of the vote in 2005. The PPR did not compete in 2009 but stated its support for the UCM.

Leader: Nicolae ANDRONIC (Chair).

Socio-Political Republican Movement "Equality" (*Mişcarea Social-Politică Republicană "Ravnopravie"*—MSPRR). A far-left party, the MSPRR advocates closer relations with Russia and Ukraine, seeks introduction of Russian as an official language, and opposes reunification with Romania. The party won 2.8 percent of the vote in the 2005 parliamentary elections (up from 0.4 percent in 2001), failing to win any seats.

In late 2008 talks were launched with the leadership of the UCM over a potential merger, but no accord was reached. However, the MSPRR in early 2009 announced its support for the UCM in the upcoming legislative 2009 elections, creating friction within the party that led to the ouster of Chair Valerii Klimenko in March. Some party members maintained that Klimenko remained the legal chair, however, and by early 2010 he had apparently regained control over the party.

Leader: Valerii KLIMENKO (Chair).

For Nation and Country Party (*Partidul Pentru Neamşi Tară*—PPNT). Founded in 2007 on a platform that stressed "social-liberal" values, modernization, and economic reform. It supported AMN in the 2009 elections but ran independently in November 2010. The party won 0.1 percent of the vote in the 2014 assembly elections.

Leader: Nicolae UŢICA (President).

Labour Party (*Partidul Muncii*—PM). The party was founded in 1999 as the **Labor Union "Motherland"** (*Uniunea Mundi "Patria-Rodina"*—UMPR) with a charter that called for the creation of a "social state" providing dignity and opportunity for all citizens. In 2007 the UMPR merged with an organization of Moldovans abroad, the *Asociaţia "Patria-Moldova"* to form **Motherland-Moldova** (*Patria-Moldova*—PM). The combined movement dissolved in 2009, and the UMPR subsequently changed its name to the Labour Party.

Leader: Gheorghe SIMA (President).

Patriots of Moldova (*Partidul "Patrioţii Moldovei"*—PPM). Founded in 2010, the PPM platform emphasizes independence from Romania, a distinctive national and linguistic character to Moldovans, and stronger relations with Ukraine. The party won 0.1 percent of the vote in 2014.

Leader: Mihail GARBUZ (President).

Roma Social-Political Movement of the Republic of Moldova (*Mişcarea social-politică a Romilor din Republica Moldova*—MRRM). Often referred to as the Roma Movement of Moldova in the domestic press, the MRRM was founded in 2010 on a platform that promotes both the values of Roma culture in Moldova and that the Roma are an "integral part" of the Moldovan people within a multiethnic framework.

Leader: Vasile DRANGOI (President).

Centrist Union of Moldova (*Uniunea Centristă din Moldova*—UCM). Founded in 2000 on a platform that called for adherence to the rule of law and creation of a civil society, it won one parliamentary seat in 2001 as part of the Braghiş Alliance but took only 0.8 percent of the vote in 2005. For the April 2009 elections, the UCM included members of the PLD and PUM on the UCM candidate list in an effort to combine the parties' support and pass the threshold into Parliament without violating the recent ban on electoral blocs. However, the UCM list secured only 2.8 percent of the vote. It did not contest the November 2010 election but did enter the 2011 local elections. It did contest the 2014 assembly balloting, where it gained 0.04 percent of the vote.

Leader: Mihai PETRACHE (Chair).

Other Parties:

Party of Law and Justice (*Partidul Legiişi Dreptăţii*—PLD). The PLD began in 1998 as the **Party of Social and Economic Justice** (*Partidul Dreptăţii Social-Economice din Moldova*—PDSEM). The party received less than 2 percent of the vote in 1998.

With Gen. Nicolae Alexei as its new leader, the PDSEM ran in the 2005 elections on a platform advocating European integration, closer relations with Romania, and popular election of the president. The party failed to improve on its previous performance, winning only 1.7 percent of the vote. The PLD did not register for the 2009 or 2010 legislative elections but did enter the 2011 local elections.

Leader: Gen. Nicolae ALEXEI.

Socialist Party of Moldova (*Partidul Socialist din Moldova*—PSM). Established in 1992 by former members of the proscribed Communist Party (PCM), the pro-Russian PSM ran for Parliament in 1994 as part of the PSMUE electoral bloc, winning 28 seats on a 21.8 percent vote share. The resultant Socialist Union (*Unitatea Socialistă*) parliamentary faction then aligned with the dominant PCRM. In 1996, however, the PSM fell into disarray over the presidential election, in which most of the leadership backed Prime Minister Sangheli but others preferred Petru Lucinschi. With a number of deputies having deserted the party and formed the PSRM, the four-party Socialist Union list won only 1.8 percent of the vote in 1998. In the 1999 local elections the PSM, running independently, fared no better. In 2001 the party joined the Braghiş Alliance.

In the 2007 local elections the PSM ran on its own in a limited number of city and village council races. The party leader, Victor Morev, was eventually accused of having illegally sold state property while mayor of Balti, and he reportedly fled the country to Russia.

Leader: Victor MOREV (Chair).

Other registered parties include the **Movement of Professionals "Hope"** (*Mişcarea Profesioniştilor "Speranţa-Nadezhda"*); the **Party for the Union of Moldova** (*Partidul Politic pentru Unirea Moldovei*); the **Social-Political Movement "New Force"** (*Mişcarea social-politică "Forţă Nouă"*); the **Green Ecologist Political Party** (*Partidul Politic Partidul Verde Ecologist*); the **New Historical Option Party** (*Partidul Politic Noua Opţiune Istorică*); the **"Our Home–Moldova" Party** (*Partidul politic "Casa Noastră–Moldova"*); the **Popular Anti-Mafia Movement** (*Partidul politic Mişcarea Populară Antimafie*); the **Popular Party of the Republic of Moldova** (*Partidul Politic Partidul Popular din Republica Moldova*); the **Democracy at Home Party** (*Partidul Politic "Democraţia Acasă"*); the **Popular Socialist Party of Moldova** (*Partidul Popular Socialist din Moldova*); the **Party of Regions of Moldova** (*Partidul Regiunilor din Moldova*); and the **People's Force Party** (*Partidul Politic Partidul Forţa*).

Transnistrian Parties:

Renewal (*Obnovleniye*). Established in 2000 as a nongovernmental organization, Renewal competed in the 2000 and 2005 Transnistrian parliamentary elections before becoming officially registered as a party in 2006. Having won 7 seats in 2000 (when most of the victors were officially nonpartisan, although supportive of President Smirnov), Renewal became the majority party in December 2005, winning 23 seats and gaining additional support from allied parties, which won 6 more. Probusiness in orientation, it has campaigned for full independence from Moldova; political reform, including adoption of a parliamentary rather than presidential system; and integration with Europe. In 2011 Russia supported Party Chair Anatoly KAMINSKY's campaign for the presidency; he won 26.3 percent of the vote in the first round and 19.7 percent in the second. Kaminsky resigned as speaker of Parliament and party leader in June 2012.

In late 2012 Renewal moved to oppose Transnistrian President Shevchuk, notably defeating the state budget proposed on December 2012 and similarly voting against finance and tax laws proposed in 2013.

Leader: Mikhail BURLA (Chair and Speaker of Parliament).

Republic (*Respublika*). Long the center of power in Transnistria, Republic began as a social association and emerged as the government party under the leadership of Igor Smirnov and Grigori MARACUTSA, Transnistria's president and parliamentary speaker, respectively. In the December 2005 election, however, Republic won only 13 seats, losing its majority status, after which Maracutsa was replaced as speaker.

Leaders: Gen. Aleksandr KOROLYOV, Vladimir RILYAKOV.

Breakthrough (*Proriv*). Founded in 2005 as a youth movement but registered as a political party in 2006, the party supports continued independence and closer relationships with Russia and Ukraine.

Leaders: Aleksandr GORELOVSKIY (President), Dmitry SOIN.

Transnistria's political party system is becoming increasingly complex, with more than half a dozen new parties registering in 2006–2007 alone. Some are closely associated with particular business interests. Among the more prominent of the current parties are the **Patriotic Party of Pridnestrovie** (*Partidul Patriotic din Pridnestrovie/Patrioticheskaya Partiya Pridnistrov'ya*—PPP), chaired by Oleg SMIRNOV, son of the former president; the **Social Democratic Party of Pridnestrovie** (*Partidul Soţial-Demokrat/Sotsial-Demokraticheskaya Partiya*—PSD/SDP), which, led by Aleksandr RADCHENKO, is the principal advocate of full union with Moldova; and the **Pridnestrovie Communist Party** (*Pridnestrovskaya Kommunisticheskaya Partiya*—PKP). Several other parties have close ties to established parties in Russia.

LEGISLATURE

In May 1991 the unicameral Supreme Soviet was redesignated as the **Parliament** (*Parlamentul*), which is elected for a four-year term by proportional representation from a single nationwide district. There are currently 101 members. Previously, the thresholds to gain representation were 6 percent for individual parties, 9 percent for two-party coalitions, and 12 percent for three-party blocs. Changes to the electoral code in 2008 banned coalitions, although some parties circumvented the ban in the April 2009 elections by having candidates from several parties run on the list of one of the parties. The thresholds were changed prior to the July 2009 balloting to 3 percent for independents and 5 percent for parties. A May 2013 law restored the threshold for parties to 6 percent.

Following the 2014 elections, the seats were distributed as follows: Party of Socialists of the Republic of Moldova, 25; Liberal Democratic Party of Moldova, 23; Party of Communists of the Republic of Moldova, 21; Democratic Party of Moldova, 19; and Liberal Party, 13.

Speaker: Andrian CANDU.

CABINET

[as of July 15, 2016]

Prime Minister	Pavel Filip (PDM)
Deputy Prime Ministers	Octavian Calmîc (ind.)
	Andrei Galbur (PL)
Deputy Prime Minister for Social Affairs	Gheorghe Brega (PL)
Deputy Prime Minister for Territorial Re-integration Affairs	Gheorghe Balan (ind.)
Ministers	
Agriculture and Processing Industry	Gheorghe Brega (PL)
Construction and Regional Development	Gheorghe Brega (PL)
Culture	Monica Babuc (PDM) [f]
Defense	Anatol Şalaru (PL)
Economy	Octavian Calmîc (ind.)
Education	Corina Fusu (PL) [f]
Environment	Valeriu Munteanu (PL)
External Affairs and European Integration	Andrei Galbur (PL)
Finance	Octavian Armasu (ind.)
Health	Ruxanda Glavan (PDM) [f]
Information Technology and Communications	Vasile Botnari (PDM)
Internal Affairs	Alexandru Jizdan (ind.)
Justice	Vladimir Cebotari (PDM)
Labor, Social Protection, Family, and Children	Stela Grigoraş (ind.) [f]
Transport and Roads	Iurie Chirinciuc (PL)
Youth and Sports	Victor Zubcu (PDM)

[f] = female

INTERGOVERNMENTAL REPRESENTATION

Ambassador to the U.S.: Tatiana SOLOMON (Chargé d'Afffaires *ad interim*).

U.S. Ambassador to Moldova: Jim PETTIT.

Permanent Representative to the UN: Vlad LUPAN.

IGO Memberships (Non-UN): CEUR, CIS, EBRD, ICC, IOM, OSCE, WTO.

For Further Reference:

Gosu, Armand. "Republic of Moldova: The Year 2015 in Politics." *Studia Politica: Romanian Political Science Review*. 16, no. 1 (January 2016): 21–51.

King, Charles. *The Moldavans: Romania, Russia, and the Politics of Culture*. Stanford, CA: Hoover Institution, 1999. Reprint, 2012.

Mamaliga, Ilie. "The Evolution of the Integration Process as Effect of the Treaties Signed between Republic of Moldova and European Union." *Acta Universitatis Danubius. Administratio* 6, no. 2 (July 2014): 20–29.

MONACO

Principality of Monaco
Principauté de Monaco

Political Status: Independent principality founded in the 13th century; constitutional monarchy since 1911; present constitution promulgated December 17, 1962 (amended in April 2002).

Area: 0.70 sq. mi. (1.81 sq. km).

Population: 38,000 (2016E—UN); 30,581 (2016E—U.S. Census).

Major Urban Center (2014E): MONACO-VILLE (1,151).

Official Language: French.

Monetary Unit: Euro (market rate October 1, 2016: 0.89 euro = $1US). Although not a member of the European Union (EU), Monaco was authorized by the EU to adopt the euro as its official currency and mint a limited supply of Monégasque euro coins.

Sovereign: Prince ALBERT II; acceded to the throne April 6, 2005, following the death of his father, Prince RAINIER III; formally installed in two-part process on July 12 and November 19, 2005.

Heir Presumptive: Hereditary Prince JACQUES.

Minister of State: Serge TELLE; assumed office February 1, 2016, following nomination by the sovereign to succeed Michel ROGER.

THE COUNTRY

A tiny but celebrated enclave on the Mediterranean coast nine miles from Nice, Monaco is surrounded on three sides by France. The principality is divided into four districts: Monaco-Ville (the capital, built on a rocky promontory about 200 feet above sea level), Monte Carlo (the tourist quarter), La Condamine (the business district around the port), and Fontvieille (the industrial district). A majority of the citizenry is of foreign origin, primarily French or Italian. Monégasques constitute approximately 19 percent of the population and speak their own language, a combination of French and Italian. Roman Catholicism is the state religion, and French is the official language, although other European languages are also spoken.

The principality's main sources of income are tourism, import-export trade, financial services, corporate and indirect taxes, and corporate research centers. Shipping is increasingly important, while gambling now accounts for no more than 4 percent of the country's income. In 2011 service industries accounted for 90 percent of GDP, and light industry, such as plastics, pharmaceuticals, glass, precision instruments, and cosmetics yielded about 10 percent of the GDP. Customs, postal services, telecommunications, and banking are governed by an economic union with France established in 1956.

Concerted land reclamation efforts begun in the 1960s succeeded in expanding the principality's total area by some 25 percent in the following 40 years, with some of the new acreage sold for private development consistent with the government's urban master plan.

In general, the principality's economic status reflects that of France and, indirectly, the European Union (EU). Monaco is also directly dependent on the French labor force; each business day an estimated 40,000 French workers cross the border, more than doubling the population. Per capita income is understood to be one of the highest in the world, and there is virtually no unemployment.

A period of stagnation in the mid-1990s was followed by significant recovery and sustained growth from 1997 until the global economy crisis in 2008. GDP declined by 11.5 percent in 2009 but rebounded with a 2.5 percent increase in 2010. Growth continued at 5.1 percent in 2011, 6.6 percent in 2012, 2.9 percent in 2013, and 7.2 percent in 2014.

GOVERNMENT AND POLITICS

Political background. Ruled by the Grimaldi family since 1297, the Principality of Monaco has maintained its separate identity in close association with France, under whose protection it was placed in 1861. A 1918 treaty stipulated that Monégasque policy had to conform with

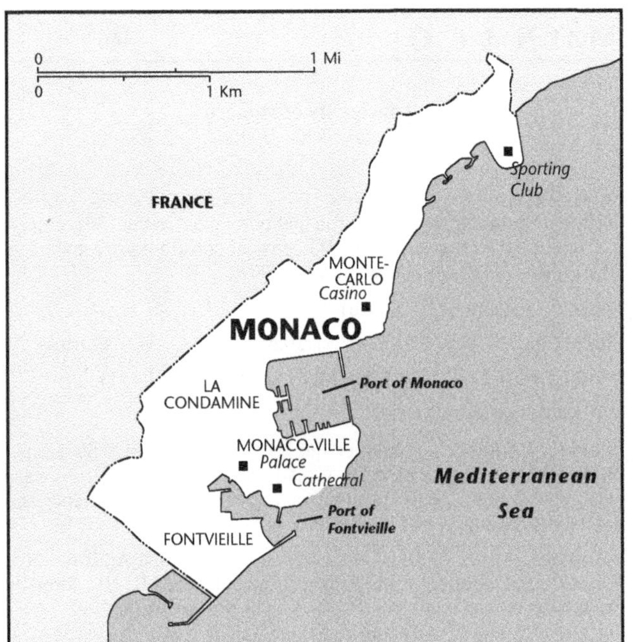

French political, military, naval, and economic interests. A further treaty of July 17, 1919, provided for Monaco's conversion to an autonomous state under French guidance should the reigning prince die without leaving a male heir. New conventions redefining the French–Monégasque relationship were signed in 1963 in response to the principality's status as a tax refuge, and the earlier treaties were superseded in 2005 (see Foreign relations, below, for details).

In the 1960s Prince RAINIER III, who had acceded to the throne in 1949, embarked on a three-year struggle with shipping magnate Aristotle S. Onassis for control of the *Société des Bains de Mer* (SBM), a corporation that owns the Monte Carlo Casino, main hotels, clubs, restaurants, and considerable Monégasque real estate. Monaco gained control of the company in 1967 by buying out Onassis's majority shareholdings.

World attention focused briefly on the principality again in 1982, following the death of Princess GRACE (the former American actress Grace Kelly) as the result of an automobile accident in the Côte d'Azur region. Subsequently, the passing of the princess was viewed as representing a fiscal as well as personal loss for Monégasques, whose economy, based in large part on tourism, had recently stagnated, with income from both real estate and gambling receding sharply over previous years. Other income sources include the annual Formula One Grand Prix, which brings in some $120 million, while the country's thriving contemporary art community is becoming a significant tourist draw.

Elections to the National Council in January 1993 appeared to mark a movement toward more competitive politics, although groupings remained electoral lists rather than parties as such. In December 1994 Paul DIJOUD (a former French ambassador to Mexico) was sworn in as Monaco's minister of state (chief minister) in succession to Jacques DUPONT. Dijoud was succeeded on February 3, 1997, by Michel LÉVÊQUE, another long-standing member of the French diplomatic corps who had most recently served as ambassador to Algeria. Elections on February 1 and 8, 1998, resulted in the capture of all council seats by the list of the National and Democratic Union (*Union Nationale et Démocratique*—UND), which had dominated every council election since its formation in 1962.

On January 1, 2000, Patrick LECLERCQ succeeded Michel Lévêque, who had retired as minister of state. Like his predecessors, Leclercq had a long history of diplomatic service to France, including, most recently, as ambassador to Spain.

The UND's long domination of the National Council came to a surprisingly dramatic end in the balloting of February 6, 2003, when it secured only 3 of the 24 seats in the National Council. The Union for Monaco (*Union pour Monaco*—UPM) list, presented by three allied parties, secured the other 21 seats. The balloting was widely viewed as a generational battle between the "young lion," Stéphane VALÉRI of the UPM coalition, and the UND's longtime leader, National Council President Jean-Louis CAMPORA, who had served in the council for 30 years. The overwhelming UPM victory was also attributed to the electorate's desire for "modernization."

Prince Rainer died on April 6, 2005, after an extended illness, and he was succeeded immediately by his son, ALBERT Alexandre Louis Pierre, who became Prince ALBERT II. Subsequently, the new sovereign named Jean-Paul PROUST, a former chief of police in Paris, to succeed Leclercq as minister of state.

The nation's ongoing positive economic performance helped the governing UPM secure 53 percent of the vote and 21 seats in the February 3, 2008, elections, compared to 40 percent for the UND-led Rally and Issues for Monaco and 7 percent for Monaco Together.

Jean-Paul Proust resigned as minister of state in March 2010 because of illness (he died on April 7). He was succeeded on March 29 by Michel ROGER, a French jurist, who was one of the seven members of the Monaco Supreme Court. His appointment disappointed those who had hoped that Prince Albert would appoint a native Monégasque.

On July 2, 2011, Prince Albert married his longtime companion, Charlene WITTSTOCK, 34, a former South African swimming champion. On August 31 Prince Andrea CASIRAGHI, son of Princess Caroline and second in line for the throne, married Colombian heiress Tatiana SANTO DOMINGO. On December 10 Princess Charlene gave birth to twins, GABRIELLA Thérèse and JACQUES Honoré Rainier, who became heir to the throne.

On December 16, 2015, Roger resigned due to illness and was replaced by French consul and ambassador to Monaco Serge TELLE, first on an interim basis and then permanently on February 1, 2016.

Constitution and government. As amended in 2002, the 1962 constitution (replacing the one of 1911) vests executive power in the hereditary prince or princess, grants universal suffrage, outlaws capital punishment, and guarantees the rights of association and trade unionism. The sovereign rules in conjunction with a minister of state, who is assisted by a cabinet (Council of Government), whose members, like the minister of state and all other palace personnel, are appointed by the sovereign.

Traditionally, the legislature (the National Council) has had few powers, although the 2002 constitutional amendments authorized the council to review budgets, introduce members' private bills, and ratify certain treaties and other international agreements. Advice on constitutional, treaty, and other matters may be offered by a 7-member Crown Council, while a 12-member State Council advises the sovereign in such areas as legislation, regulations, and law and order.

Municipal affairs in the four *quartiers* are conducted by a 15-member elected Communal Council (*Conseil Communal*), with the mayor of Monaco-Ville presiding. The judiciary includes a Supreme Court of five full and two deputy members, all named by the sovereign on the basis of nominations by the National Council and other institutions. In addition, a Review Court considers appeals based on alleged violations of law. At lower levels there are a district court, a labor court, a court of the first instance, and a court of appeals. The majority of judges are French nationals.

The 2002 amendments in part focused on succession to the throne, an issue that had come to the forefront because Prince Albert (Prince Rainier's son) had not married and thereby had no legitimate male heirs at the time. (He later acknowledged two illegitimate children, but they are precluded from the line of succession.) Under the 2002 revisions, which technically entered into effect upon French ratification in 2005 of a 2002 treaty (see Foreign relations, below), the long-standing principle of male primogeniture was modified to permit succession by a female sibling and her descendants in the event a reigning sovereign leaves no direct, legitimate male heir.

Given Monaco's small population and its location, most residents depend on French mass media for much of their information. A law on freedom of the media was passed in July 2005.

Foreign relations. Monaco's foreign relations were traditionally controlled by France, based on treaties from the early 1900s (see Political background, above, for details). However, those treaties were superseded by a new "Treaty adapting and confirming relations of friendship and co-operation between the French Republic and the Principality of Monaco," which was signed in Paris on October 24, 2002, and ratified by France on October 13, 2005. Most significantly, the new treaty ended Monaco's subservience to French policy, replacing it with the principle of sovereign equality in the context of historically "close and privileged relations." Furthermore, a new "Convention to adapt and develop administrative cooperation between the French Republic and the Principality," signed in November 2005 as a replacement for a 1930 convention, gave preference in senior government and civil service appointments to Monégasques. Consultation with Paris on major appointments remains the rule, but such senior positions as minister of state are no longer filled on a pro forma basis by French nationals. The principality participates indirectly in the EU by virtue of its customs union with France but has no plans to become a member. Prior to joining the United Nations (UN) in 1993, it maintained a Permanent Observer's office at UN headquarters in New York and had long belonged to a number of UN specialized agencies. The treaty also allowed other countries to accredit ambassadors to Monaco, rather than considering the principality to be a branch of the French government. The United States and Monaco upgraded from consular to full diplomatic relations in December 2006.

In 1994 Monaco signed an agreement with France providing for coordinated action against money laundering and requiring Monégasque banks and other institutions to report dubious financial transactions to the authorities. However, dissatisfaction with Monaco's progress in this regard surfaced in 1998 when young reformist judges alleged that the old guard was being lax in its prosecution. Consequently, overruling Prince Rainier, Paris appointed new prosecutors and chief judges. Stung by criticism (*Le Monde* characterized Monaco as a "refuge for cheats"), the government released a report in January 1999 denying that inappropriate activity was prevalent in the principality and attacking the "myth" of Monaco as a "superficial playground." In part, the report was seen as a component of the government's campaign to gain membership in the Council of Europe, which at first reportedly considered Monaco as neither fully sovereign nor sufficiently democratic. In October 2004, in consideration of the 2002 treaty revisions, an ongoing legal reform process, and the successful conduct of the 2003 legislative election under a new election law, Monaco was admitted to the Council of Europe.

Pressure on the principality increased in February 2008 after German officials bribed a bank official in Liechtenstein to release private bank records, which exposed many German nationals who were evading taxes. Monaco's practices fell under more scrutiny because Liechtenstein, in addition to Monaco, was among those cited by the Organization for Economic Cooperation and Development as retaining harmful tax policies. In March 2009 Monaco bowed to international pressure and agreed to follow OECD regulations on tax evasion. In return, the principality was removed from the "black list" and placed on a "gray list," pending implementation of reforms. It was removed from the list altogether in 2010.

By 2011 Monaco had signed agreements with 24 countries to exchange tax information. The banks in Monaco are under the watchful eye of the *Banque de France,* as well as the *Service d'Information et de Controle sur les Ciruits Financiers,* the French authority that monitors money laundering, terrorist financing, and corruption. Michel Roger, the minister of state, declared, "Today if you've got dirty money, Monaco is not the place to put it."

In March 2012, however, the Council of Europe's Group of States against Corruption (GRECO) criticized Monaco's efforts in revising its criminal code, noting that anticorruption laws still did not apply to senior government officials or to many foreign nationals.

Monaco has no income tax. When France's President François Hollande imposed a 75 percent tax on individuals making over €1 million per year, as promised in 2012, many French millionaires moved to Monaco. One unintended beneficiary was Monaco's national soccer team, which offered large, tax-free salaries to French team players. In November 2013 Monaco agreed to pay the French football league €50 million to settle a dispute over the tax-free salaries (league officials had threatened to suspend Monaco over what it described as an "unfair advantage").

In May 2014 Prince Albert received the Zayed International Prize for the Environment for his global leadership on environmental issues.

On April 15, 2016, Monaco and Belarus established diplomatic ties. On May 2 Hungary became the 130th country with diplomatic relations with Monaco.

Current issues. Under Prince Albert, Monaco began systematically (but slowly) reviewing and adopting some 200 Council of Europe conventions in an effort to cement its broader ties to Europe. The conventions, which cover legal, social, economic, institutional, and diplomatic concerns, also necessitated reform of many domestic laws and codes.

The Prince Albert II of Monaco Foundation was established in June 2006 to address climate change, biodiversity, and water shortages. The principality has funded research and sponsored international conferences on whaling, deforestation, and sustainable fishing. In March 2010 Monaco made a proposal to the 175-nation Convention on International Trade in Endangered Species to ban commercial trade in Atlantic bluefin-tuna fishing until the population level of the fish recovers. While most of the EU supported the ban, the proposal was voted down, with Japan playing a major role in marshaling opposition to it.

In January 2011, in response to the dismal GDP numbers for 2010, the prince appointed three new cabinet members, José BADIA for foreign affairs; Marie-Pierre GRAMAGLIA for public works, environment, and urban affairs; and Marco PICCININI for finance and the economy. As Monaco's former ambassador to India and China, Piccinini worked to attract banks and people from emerging countries, while improving banking transparency overall.

Along with banking reform, the government introduced new regulations on political funding. The July 2, 2012, Law on Campaign Finance established a €400,000 limit for each candidate and required candidates to submit an expense report to the Audit Committee within two months in order to receive reimbursement. (Candidates who pass a 5 percent threshold can be compensated for 25 percent of their expenses.)

Piccinini resigned in October to return to the private sector. Jean CASTELLINI, who had served in the cabinet in 2006–2007, was appointed minister of finance and economy.

The National Council election on February 13, 2013, gave a new alliance, Horizon Monaco (*Horizon Monaco*—HM), 20 of the 24 seats. Union for Monaco (*Union pour Monaco*—UPM), which had controlled the legislature since 2003, won only three seats. The remaining seat went to Renaissance, a new party representing workers from SBM. The country's main employer had registered a 40 percent drop in revenue since 2008, and employees feared possible layoffs or wage cuts.

In May bidding opened on a new land reclamation project that would increase the principality by 3 percent and include a 30–40 berth port. With an estimated €1 billion price tag, the reclamation project sets rigorous standards for sustainability and ecological soundness.

On June 18 the Venice Commission of the OSCE issued a sharply critical report on the balance of power in Monaco. It noted that the prince has ultimate control over executive, legislative, and judicial branches, while the National Council has little input on the composition of government or laws. "Monaco is not a parliamentary monarchy," the report concluded. "The Venice Commission strongly urges Monaco to adopt a new law on the independent functioning and organization of the National Council." Monegasque political leaders denounced the report for failing to consider the country's unique circumstances.

Following an altercation with Pierre Rainier CASIRAGHI at a New York nightclub in 2012, U.S. businessman Adam Hock was banned from Monaco when he attempted to entry the country on a yacht in July 2014. The original incident was reported to have been highly embarrassing to Prince Albert.

The government of Monaco established initiatives to promote the ownership of electric vehicles, including tax incentives, free charging stations, and free parking. These efforts raised the percentage of electric cars on Monaco's roads to 3 percent by June 2016, a record in Europe, where the average is 0.5 percent.

POLITICAL PARTIES

Although a party system is slowly developing, at present there is no political party law distinguishing parties from other associations. Nor is there public funding of parties except for small reimbursements to help cover election expenses. As explained by a 2007 report by the Monitoring Committee of the Council of Europe: "The primary function of a party in the Principality is not to attain power and thus enter government... but only to contribute to the management of the State's affairs whilst permanently seeking a compromise between the will of the Prince and the expectations of Monégasques as represented by the National Council."

In the absence of formal political parties, Monaco's politics were until recently dominated for nearly four decades by the **National and Democratic Union** (*Union Nationale et Démocratique*—UND). Formed in 1962 through the merger of the **National Union of Independents** (*Union Nationale des Indépendants*) and the **National Democratic Entente** (*Entente Nationale Démocratique*), the UND won all 18 National Council seats in the elections of 1968, 1978, 1983, and 1988. In

1993, when the UND captured 15 seats, it was sometimes informally referenced as the **Campora List** (*Liste Campora*), reflecting the leadership of Jean-Louis Campora, who was elected president of the new council to succeed long-term UND leader Jean-Charles REY. Two seats were also won in 1993 by the **Médecin List** (*Liste Médecin*), led by Jean-Louis MÉDECIN, the former mayor of Monaco-Ville. The UND list was credited with winning all the seats in the 1998 elections in competition with lists from the **National Union for the Future of Monaco** (*Union Nationale pour l'Avenir de Monaco*—UNAM) and the **Rally for the Monégasque Family** (*Rassemblement de la Famille Monégasque*—RFM).

In 2003 the UNAM, the **Promotion of the Monégasque Family** (*Promotion de la Famille Monégasque*—PFM, as the RFM had been renamed), and the **Union for the Principality** (*Union pour la Principauté*—UP) combined forces under an opposition Union for Monaco (*Union pour Monaco*—UPM) list. Led by former UND member Stéphane Valéri, now of the UP, the UPM won 21 of 24 seats, with the balance going to the UND list of the **Rally for Monaco** (*Rassemblement pour Monaco*—RPM).

In January 2006 the PFM, led by René GIORDANO, left the UPM. Also during 2006 UND councilor Christine PASQUIER-CIULLA formed her own **Monégasque Party** (*Parti Monégasque*—PM), while in September former UNAM vice chair Claude BOISSON and the UP's Vincent PALMARO established the **Principality, Ethics, and Progress** (*Principauté, Éthique, et Progrès*—PEP) party.

On February 3, 2008, the UPM, now comprising only the UP and the UNAM, repeated its 2003 win, securing 21 seats as Valéri urged voters to support the "evolution" of UPM programs. The conservative coalition called the **Rally and Issues for Monaco** (*Rassemblement et Enjeux pour Monaco*—REM), consisting of the RPM (led by Guy MAGNAN) and the **Values and Issues** (*Valeurs & Enjeux*) party (led by Laurent NOUVION) won 3 seats. A third coalition (**Monaco Together** [*Monaco Ensemble*—ME]), which included the PFM, **Monégasque Synergy** (*Synergie Monegasque*—SM), and the **Association of Non-Attached Monégasques** (*Association des Nom Inscrits Monégasques*—NIM), also took part in the election but won no seats with only about 7 percent of the vote. The PM did not participate in the election because it did not have a slate of at least 13 candidates as required by law. The PEP candidates ran under the banner of the RPM.

Three electoral alliances contested the February 13, 2013, election. **Horizon Monaco** (*Horizon Monaco*—HM) won a landslide victory, taking 20 seats in the National Council. Founded by Laurent Nouvion in September 2012, HM included members of REM, SM, and UP. The incumbent UPM took only three seats, while **Renaissance** (*Renaissance*), a new party founded in November 2012 to represent employees of SBN, captured 1 seat. Nouvion was subsequently elected president of the National Council.

LEGISLATURE

The **National Council** (*Conseil National*) is a 24-seat unicameral body elected via direct universal suffrage for a five-year term. Councilors are elected from one multimember national constituency, and voters can vote for up to 24 candidates. Sixteen seats are filled by the top vote-getters, with the balance then being chosen by proportional representation from those lists receiving at least 5 percent of the vote. (The proportional element was introduced in 2002 at the request of the Council of Europe.) In the most recent election on February 13, 2013, the seat distribution was as follows: Monaco Horizon, 20; Union for Monaco, 3; and Renaissance, 1. The next elections are scheduled for 2018.

President: Christophe STEINER (HM).

CABINET

[as of June 20, 2016]

Minister of State	Serge Telle
Councilors	
Finance and Economy	Jean Castellini
Foreign Affairs	Gilles Tonelli
Health and Social Affairs	Stéphane Valéri
Interior	Patrice Cellario
Public Works, Environment, and Urban Affairs	Marie-Pierre Gramaglia [f]

[f] = female

INTERGOVERNMENTAL REPRESENTATION

Monaco maintains consuls general in Washington, D.C., and New York, while the U.S. consul general in Nice, France, also services U.S. interests in Monaco.

Ambassador to the U.S.: Maguy MACCARIO DOYLE.

U.S. Ambassador to Monaco (resident in Paris): Uzra ZEYA (Chargé d'Affaires).

Permanent Representative to the UN: Isabelle F. PICCO.

IGO Memberships (Non-UN): CEUR, OSCE.

For Further Reference:

Braude, Mark. *Making Monte Carlo: A History of Speculation and Spectacle.* New York: Simon and Schuster, 2016.

Eccardt, Thomas. *Secrets of the Seven Smallest States of Europe: Andorra, Liechtenstein, Luxembourg, Malta, Monaco, San Marino and Vatican City.* New York: Hippocrane Books, 2004.

The Monegasque Institute of Statistics and Economic Studies. "Monaco Statistics." Accessed June 30, 2016. www.monacostatistics.mc.

MONGOLIA

Monggol Ulus

Political Status: Independent since 1921; Communist People's Republic established November 26, 1924; multi-party system introduced by constitutional amendment of May 11, 1990; current constitution adopted January 13, 1992, in effect from February 12.

Area: 604,247 sq. mi. (1,565,000 sq. km).

Population: 3,006,000 (2016E—UN); 3,031,330 (2016E—U.S. Census).

Major Urban Centers (2015E—UN): ULAANBAATAR (Ulan Bator, 1,379,631), Darkhan (100,443), Erdenet (95,000).

Monetary Unit: Tugrik (market rate October 1, 2016: 2,285.00 tugriks = $1US).

Official Language: Khalkha Mongol.

President: Tsakhiagiyn ELBEGDORJ (Democratic Party), popularly elected for a four-year term on May 24, 2009, and sworn in on June 18, succeeding Nambaryn ENKHBAYAR (Mongolian People's Revolutionary Party); reelected on June 26, 2013.

Prime Minister: Jargaltulga ERDENEBAT (Mongolian People's Party); became prime minister on July 7, 2016, succeeding Chimediin SAIKHANBILEG (Democratic Party).

THE COUNTRY

Traditionally known as Outer Mongolia (i.e., that portion of historic Mongolia lying north of the Gobi Desert), the present country of Mongolia occupies a vast area of steppe, mountain, and desert between the Russian Federation on the north and the People's Republic of China on the south. Khalkha Mongols make up 82 percent of the population. The remainder are other Mongol groups (often speaking their own dialects); Turkic-speaking peoples; and Chinese, Russian, and Tungusic minorities. Lamaist Buddhism is the prevalent faith, practiced by an estimated 40 percent of the population, even though its leadership was largely wiped out by antireligious activity in 1937–1939. Islam is practiced by the small Kazakh minority (4 percent), and there are also small numbers of Christians and shamanists. Some 51 percent of the active labor force is female. Women constitute 17.1 percent of the legislators (13 of 76 seats) elected in 2016, a dramatic increase from 2008 when they made up 4 percent of the legislature.

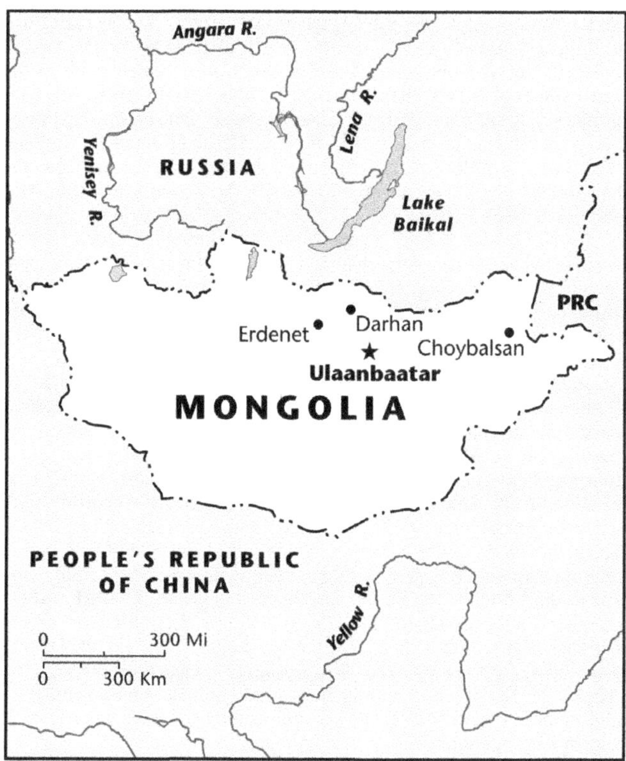

The Mongolian economy was traditionally pastoral, and agriculture, especially animal husbandry, continues to employ 34 percent of the active labor force. In addition, a significant proportion of the rural population is engaged in nonwage and subsistence level agriculture. The industrial sector is largely driven by ore extraction and processing, chiefly of copper and gold. One of the world's largest copper-molybdenum facilities is located in Erdenet, while initial production at the massive Oyu Tolgoi copper-gold mine began in 2013 and is expected to produce 450,000 tons annually at full production (see Current issues, below). Other mineral resources include uranium, fluorspar, coal, tungsten, and recently discovered petroleum. Mineral production has typically accounted for 60–67 percent of export earnings. Manufacturing is largely devoted to processing agricultural products into such goods as cashmere and textiles, the second most important export product. More than 32 percent of the population lives below the poverty line as of 2016.

The breakup of the Soviet Union precipitated a severe economic crisis in the first half of the 1990s. As Mongolia began privatizing state-owned enterprises, financial assistance from the West and international institutions helped support an economic recovery. GDP grew by an average of 8.8 percent from 2005 to 2008. In 2009, however, in the context of the global financial crisis, exports and commodity prices fell, contributing to a 1.2 percent loss in GDP. With copper prices recovering, and with international assistance from the International Monetary Fund (IMF) and elsewhere, Mongolia experienced a dramatic turnaround in 2010 when GDP grew by 6.4 percent. In 2014 GDP grew by 7.8 percent, while unemployment was 7.9 percent and inflation was 12.9 percent. In 2015 growth slowed to 2.3 percent, while unemployment rose to 8 percent and inflation dropped to 5.8 percent. Estimates for 2016 show growth of 0.4 percent, a slight drop in unemployment back to 7.9 percent, and a major drop in inflation to 1.9 percent. GDP per capita for 2016 was $5,276. In 2016 the World Bank ranked Mongolia 56th out of 189 countries in its annual ease of doing business survey.

GOVERNMENT AND POLITICS

Political background. The home of such legendary figures as Genghis Khan and Tamerlane, Mongolia fell under Chinese control in the 17th century and continued under Chinese suzerainty for over 200 years. The fall of the Manchu dynasty resulted in a brief period of independence from 1911 until 1919, when Chinese hegemony was reestablished. Two years later Mongolian revolutionary leaders Sukhe BATOR and Horloogiyn CHOYBALSAN (Khorloin CHOIBALSAN) defeated the Chinese with Soviet assistance and established permanent independence.

Initially, a constitutional monarchy was created under Jebtsun Damba KHUTUKHTU, but following his death in 1924 the Mongolian People's Party (founded in 1921) was renamed the Mongolian People's Revolutionary Party (MPRP) (in 2010, it reverted to MPP), and the Mongolian People's Republic was proclaimed as the first Communist state outside the Soviet Union. Rightist influences, including a major revolt in 1932, were suppressed, and Choybalsan gained the ascendancy in 1934–1939, after which he continued to dominate both party and government until his death in 1952.

Yumjaagiyn TSEDENBAL was named chair of the Council of Ministers in 1952 and, after a two-year period of apparent political eclipse, succeeded Dashiyn DAMBA as MPRP first secretary in 1958. In addition, in 1974 he was named chair of the Presidium of the People's Great Hural. In 1984 Tsedenbal was relieved of his government and party posts, reportedly because of failing health, with Jambyn BATMÖNH being named MPRP secretary general. Upon designation as Presidium chair in December, Batmönh relinquished the chair of the Council of Ministers to Dumajiyn SODNOM. Both were reconfirmed following the 19th MPRP Congress in 1986.

In obvious response to political change in Eastern Europe, the regime in December 1989 permitted the organization of an opposition Mongolian Democratic Union (MDU), and additional opposition groups emerged; starting in February 1990 some 300 MDU adherents organized the Mongolian Democratic Party (MDP).

At an MPRP Central Committee plenum in March 1990 the entire Politburo was replaced, with Gombojavyn OCHIRBAT succeeding Batmönh as party leader, Punsalmaagiyn OCHIRBAT (no relation to the party leader) succeeding Batmönh as head of state, and Sharavyn GUNGAADORJ replacing Sodnom as chair of the Council of Ministers.

In May 1990 the Great Hural approved constitutional amendments that formally abandoned the one-party system and provided for a proportionally elected standing body (Little Hural) to complement the existing legislature. At the ensuing election in July–August the MPRP won approximately four-fifths of the seats in the Great Hural and nearly two-thirds of those in the Little Hural, but a three-party opposition Coalition of Democratic Forces also won representation. A week later Dashiyn BYAMBASUREN succeeded Gungaadorj as chief of government (now termed prime minister) and on the following day named a "coalition" government that did not, however, include representatives of the MDP.

In June 1992, under a new constitution, an election for a reinstituted unicameral legislature saw the MPRP capturing 71 of 76 seats even though opposition parties won 40 percent of the vote. In July the Great Hural elected a free-market economist, Puntsagiyn JASRAY, as prime minister, and in August an all-MPRP administration was announced.

In April 1993 a special MPRP congress refused to nominate President Ochirbat for reelection, selecting instead Lodongiyn TUDEV, editor of the party newspaper *Ünen.* As a result, Ochirbat agreed to stand as joint candidate of the MSDP and the Mongolian National Democratic Party (MNDP), and in June he retained the presidency, winning 57.8 percent of the vote.

Elections in June 1996 marked the end of more than seven decades of communist rule. A recently organized Democratic Union (DU), led by the MNDP and the MSDP, defeated the MPRP by an unexpected two-to-one margin. Thirty days later the coalition's leader, Mendsaikhan ENKHSAIKHAN, formed a new government. However, the MPRP quickly regained a dominant position in the provincial and municipal elections of October. Moreover, the MPRP's Natsagiyn BAGABANDI overwhelmed incumbent president Ochirbat, the DU nominee, by 60.8 percent to 29.8 percent in the May 1997 presidential election.

In January 1998 the Great Hural approved a measure that would permit its members to serve concurrently as government ministers. In April the governing organs of the MNDP and MSDP both recommended that the DU chair, Tsakhiagiyn ELBEGDORJ of the MNDP, assume the prime ministership, leading Prime Minister Enkhsaikhan to tender his resignation. A week later, the Great Hural endorsed Elbegdorj by a vote of 61–5. For more than a month, however, parliamentary infighting led to rejection of several ministerial nominees, with the cabinet that was ultimately assembled consisting entirely of legislators.

In late May 1998 the MPRP precipitated a parliamentary crisis when its delegation began a boycott of the Great Hural following approval (subsequently rescinded) of a merger involving the bankrupt public Renovation Bank with a private bank. With the legislative process paralyzed by the boycott, in July the Great Hural passed a no-confidence motion 42–33, and as a consequence the prime minister resigned three months after taking office.

The DU leadership and the MPRP's Bagabandi were soon at loggerheads. The president repeatedly rejected the coalition's nominee for prime minister, Davaadorgjiyn GANBOLD of the MNDP, while the Great Hural rejected the DU nominee Rinchinnyamiin AMARJARGAL. Before the end of the month the president had rejected two additional nominees, while on October 2 the country was deeply shaken when an apparent MNDP compromise candidate, Sanjaasürengiyn ZORIG, who had been a principal leader of the prodemocracy movement in 1989–1990, was killed in his home. The political stalemate continued, with Ganbold again being rejected by the president for a seventh time, and the DU refusing to nominate any of six potential candidates deemed acceptable by Bagabandi.

On November 24, 1998, the Constitutional Court ruled for the second time in less than a month that the constitution prohibited members of the Great Hural from serving as prime minister or in the cabinet. The decision helped break the impasse, and on December 9, having received the imprimatur of both the DU and the president, Janlav NARANTSATSRALT, the mayor of Ulaanbaatar, was easily confirmed as prime minister. The Great Hural nevertheless rejected the majority of his initial cabinet nominees and withheld approval of the final four until January 1999.

Barely six months later, Narantsatsralt was accused of jeopardizing national interests in a letter he had sent, without prior ministerial consultation, to a Russian official regarding terms for the sale of Russia's share in the Erdenet copper-molybdenum joint venture. Having lost a legislative no-confidence vote 41–22 on July 23, Narantsatsralt resigned the following day. On July 30 the State Great Hural gave swift approval, this time, to President Bagabandi's prime ministerial nominee, Amarjargal, who resigned from the legislature and immediately won confirmation by a vote of 50–2. The cabinet approved on September 2 was substantially unchanged.

In the general election of July 2, 2000, the MPRP swept back into power, capturing 72 of the 76 seats in the State Great Hural. The sole MNDP seat was won by former prime minister Narantsatsralt, while the MSDP won none. Nambaryn ENKHBAYAR, chair of the MPRP and a member of the State Great Hural, was confirmed as prime minister on July 26, and an MPRP cabinet won legislative approval on August 9. The legitimacy of Enkhbayar's appointment was ultimately resolved in May 2001, when President Bagabandi accepted constitutional amendments permitting legislators to serve as cabinet members.

President Bagabandi won a second term in the election of May 20, 2001, taking 58 percent of the vote. His chief opponent was Radnaasümbereliyn GONCHIGDORJ, of the Democratic Party (DP), which had been formed the preceding December by merger of the MNDP, the MSDP, and three smaller parties.

In 2003 the DP and the Motherland–Mongolian Democratic New Socialist Party (M-MDNSP), led by gold magnate Badarch ERDENEBAT, formed the Motherland Democratic Coalition (MDC), which was joined by the Civil Will Republican Party (CWRP) in March 2004. In the June 27 parliamentary election the MDC won 34 seats, only 2 less than the governing MPRP. With neither group able to claim a majority in the legislature, protracted negotiations on forming a new government ensued. On August 13, 2004, the legislators unanimously elected the outgoing prime minister, Nambaryn Enkhbayar, as chair of the State Great Hural, and on August 20 former prime minister Tsakhiagiyn Elbegdorj of the DP/MDC was again appointed prime minister. It took another month for the MPRP and MDC to reach agreement on an equal division of cabinet posts, with a "Grand Coalition Government" subsequently sworn in on September 28. However, in December the M-MDNSP withdrew from the MDC, which soon led to the dissolution of the coalition and to the dismissal in February 2005 of the two M-MDNSP ministers.

With President Bagabandi prohibited from seeking a third term, the MPRP nominated Nambaryn Enkhbayar as its presidential candidate in the May 22, 2005, election. Enkhbayar won with 53.4 percent of the vote, defeating former prime minister Mendsaikhan Enkhsaikhan of the DP (19.7 percent) and three other candidates.

On January 11, 2006, all ten MPRP ministers resigned from the coalition cabinet, and two days later the State Great Hural voted to dissolve the government. Four key votes in favor of dissolution were cast by members of the DP, including Enkhsaikhan, former prime minister Janlav Narantsatsralt, and Mishig SONOMPIL. An effort by the MPRP to forge a "national unity" government was rejected by the DP, though Enkhsaikhan, Narantsatsralt, and Sonompil all accepted posts in the new cabinet of MPRP chair Miyegombo ENKHBOLD, who was confirmed as prime minister by the legislature on January 25. The three maverick ministers were expelled from the DP and formed the National New Party (NNP). Also joining the coalition government were the Motherland Party (formerly the MDNSP), the Republican Party (RP), and the People's Party (PP).

On November 5, 2007, Prime Minister Enkhbold resigned after he was ousted as MPRP party chair in October in favor of the incumbent secretary general, Sanj BAYAR. On November 22 the State Great Hural confirmed Bayar as prime minister, and he appointed a coalition cabinet including members of the Civil Will Party (CWP, formerly the CWRP), the NNP, and the RP.

In the aftermath of the legislative elections on June 29, 2008, DP leaders questioned the integrity of the vote, prompting a violent demonstration in Ulaanbaatar on July 1 that resulted in five deaths, the burning of the MPRP's headquarters, several hundred arrests, and a four-day state of emergency declared by President Enkhbayar. Official election results announced on July 14 gave the MPRP a majority, with ten seats unassigned pending recounts. Nine days later 25 of 27 DP deputies walked out of the opening session of the State Great Hural, making a quorum impossible and preventing new members from being sworn in. While the legislature was blocked, a group of MPRP and DP members acted as an interim government by consulting on urgent national affairs. After Prime Minister Bayar agreed to invite the DP into a coalition government, the DP legislators ended their walkout on August 28. Bayar was reappointed as prime minister on September 11 and named a new MPRP-DP government that received the Hural's approval on September 19.

In the presidential election on May 24, 2009, DP leader and former prime minister Tsakhiagiyn Elbegdorj, who also had the backing of the CWP and the Mongolian Green Party (MGP), defeated the incumbent Enkhbayar on a narrow vote share of 51 percent. Elbegdorj, the first non-MPRP president in the country's history, was sworn in for a four-year term on June 18.

Prime Minister Bayar, citing ill health, resigned from office on October 25, 2009. Four days later, the State Great Hural confirmed Minister of Foreign Affairs Sukhbaatar Batbold (MPRP) as his successor.

In legislative elections on June 28, 2012, the DP secured a plurality with 31 seats, followed by the MPP with 25 seats. DP chair Norovyn Altankhuyag became prime minister on August 8. He named a DP-led coalition cabinet that included members of the DP, the new Justice Coalition (see Political Parties, below), and the newly merged Civil Will–Green Party. The government was approved by the legislature on August 20.

On June 26, 2013, Elbegdorj was reelected, securing 50.9 percent of the vote to 42.5 percent for Badmaanyambuugiin BAT-ERDENE (MPP) and 6.6 percent for Natsag UDVAL (MPRP). Elbegdorj was sworn in on July 10. The minister of industry and agriculture resigned on May 22, 2014, and was replaced, on an acting basis, by the minister of mining. Altankhuyag was removed from office by parliament on November 5, and replaced on an acting basis the same day by Deputy Prime Minister Dendev TERBISHDAGYA (MPRP). Terbishdagya served as interim prime minister until Chimediin SAIKHANBILEG (DP), was named to the position on November 21, 2014 (see Current issues, below).

In elections on June 29, 2016, the MPP won a commanding majority of 65 seats, while the DP lost 25 seats to hold only 9. Jargaltulga ERDENEBAT (MPP) was elected prime minister on July 7. His initial cabinet proposal was rejected by the president on July 21, but revised lists were accepted July 22–23.

Constitution and government. The constitution adopted in 1960 left intact the guiding role of the MPRP, whose highly centralized leadership also dominated the state administration. The national legislature (People's Great Hural) was identified as the supreme organ of government, with the chair of its Presidium serving as head of state. Constitutional changes approved in 1990 included renunciation of the "guiding role" of the MPRP in favor of a multiparty system, conversion of the Presidium chair into a state presidency, and the creation of a vice presidency. Selected by the Great Hural, the vice president was to serve as ex officio chair of a new standing assembly (Little Hural).

The current constitution, adopted on January 13, 1992, returned legislative power to a single chamber, known as the State Great Hural, whose 76 members are elected by universal suffrage for four-year terms. The powers of the State Great Hural include appointing and dismissing the prime minister and other administrative officials. A popularly elected president serves as head of state for a four-year term; should no presidential candidate receive a majority of the votes cast, a two-way runoff is held. The president can veto legislative decisions (subject to override by a two-thirds majority), nominates the prime minister in consultation with the largest legislative party, and serves as commander-in-chief of the armed forces. A Supreme Court sits at the apex of the judicial system, while a Constitutional Court is charged with ensuring the "strict observance" of the basic law and with resolving constitutional disputes.

Mongolia is divided into 21 provinces (*aymguud* or *aimags*), each subdivided into counties and *baghs,* plus the capital city of Ulaanbaatar, subdivided into districts and *horoos.* At the provincial and capital level the prime minister appoints governors (*dzasag darga*) nominated by elected hurals. Each county (*soum*) and district (*khoron*) also elects a hural, while "General Meetings of Citizens" function at the lowest administrative tier. A local governor is nominated by each subdivision's legislative body and appointed by the governor of the next highest level.

The constitution guarantees freedom of the press and the right "to seek and receive information." However, journalists can be prosecuted for disclosing state secrets. The central government's leading newspapers were privatized in 1999. A 2005 law ordered the conversion of state-run broadcast outlets into public service companies, a process that was still underway as of 2016. In 2016 Reporters Without Borders ranked Mongolia 60th out of 180 countries in freedom of the press, citing issues such as defamation laws, self-censorship, and the lack of government transparency.

Foreign relations. Mongolia attempted to take a neutral stance in the early period of the Sino-Soviet dispute, but subsequently aligned with the Soviet Union, in part because of an inherited fear of Chinese hegemony and in part because of a dependence on Soviet military, economic, and cultural assistance. A member of the UN since 1961, it became a full member of the Soviet-dominated Council for Mutual Economic Assistance (CMEA) in 1962 and signed a treaty of friendship and mutual assistance with the Soviet Union in 1966. Relations with China began to thaw in 1985; a consular treaty signed the following year was the first since 1949.

In March 1989 Moscow announced that it would begin withdrawing its reported 50,000 troops from Mongolia, a process completed in September 1992. President Ochirbat visited Russia in January 1993 for talks with President Boris Yeltsin that yielded a treaty of friendship and cooperation, under which the two countries agreed to refrain from entering into military-political alliances aimed against each other.

Mongolia signed a friendship and cooperation treaty with China in 1994 (replacing a 1962 predecessor) during an official visit by Chinese premier Li Peng. Earlier that year Mongolia, China, and Russia had signed a tripartite pact defining their border junctures. China is Mongolia's largest foreign investor and receives roughly 70 percent of Mongolian exports. At the same time, Mongolia has become increasingly wary of China's growing economic power, which already dominates Mongolia's cashmere industry.

Since the Cold War ended, Mongolian foreign policy has been based on carefully balanced relations with Russia and China as well as "third neighbors," including the Western powers. Diplomatic relations with the United States were not established until 1987. In January 1991 President Ochirbat became the first Mongolian head of state to travel to the United States, where he met with President George H. W. Bush and signed a bilateral trade agreement. The nation was soon admitted into the Asian Development Bank along with the World Bank and the IMF. More recently, Mongolia has frequently been in accord with Washington on foreign policy matters, including the "war on terrorism."

In the mid-2000s Mongolian troops joined coalition forces in Iraq following the U.S.-led invasion in 2003, and Mongolia also deployed some military trainers to Afghanistan. Visits in 2005 by U.S. secretary of defense Donald Rumsfeld and President George W. Bush (the first sitting U.S. chief executive to do so) marked a significant shift in relations.

In 2008 enhanced economic cooperation between Mongolia and Russia was evidenced by Mongolia's importing almost all of its oil from Russia. In March 2009 Russian prime minister Vladimir Putin offered $300 million in credits to Mongolia's agriculture industry. In May the two nations agreed to develop a rail network extending to the Oyu Tolgoi and Tavan Tolgoi mines. Under the deal, Russian firms would receive licenses to mine both sites.

In October 2011 Germany and Mongolia signed a series of economic agreements to allow German companies to extract rare earth materials. In response to the growing number of foreign corporations operating in Mongolia, the legislature passed a measure in May 2012 that limited foreign ownership of mining firms to 49 percent for all companies worth at least $75 million.

In March 2013 Mongolia and Japan announced plans for a free trade agreement. In May Mongolia and Canada signed a defense cooperation agreement that expanded exchanges and training exercises between the two militaries. Also in May, during a state visit by Thai Prime Minister Yingluck Shinawatra, Mongolia and Thailand finalized an agreement designed to double trade between the two countries by 2017. In October President Elbegdorj became the first foreign head of state to visit North Korea since Kim Jong Un became that country's leader.

In February 2014 security officials denied a request by the United States to end a travel ban on Justin Kapla, a U.S. citizen and mining executive who was being held in Mongolia as a witness in a corruption case. Kapla was also accused of money laundering, but had not been formally charged. In June a joint South Korean–Mongolian ecological initiative announced plans to plant more than 3,000 hectares of trees in Mongolia. The effort was part of a ten-year, $13.4 million project to reserve desertification. On January 30, 2015, Kapla was imprisoned for tax evasion but was released on February 27 and returned to the United States.

Mongolia and Russia signed a strategic partnership accord in April 2016 to expand economic and political cooperation. In July Mongolia and South Korea began negotiations on a broad bilateral trade agreement.

Current issues. The Oyu Tolgoi (Turquoise Hill) copper-gold deposit, among the world's richest, was expected to create thousands of jobs and add 30 percent or more to Mongolia's GDP when fully operational. During the 2009 presidential campaign, both the DP and the MPRP pledged a proportion of mining profits to the Mongolian people. President Elbegdorj opposed taking an equity stake in Oyu Tolgoi, preferring to leave the industry in private hands, but in July DP lawmakers proposed a 34 percent stake for the government.

In August 2009 a special session of parliament overwhelmingly approved terms for the Oyu Tolgoi investment agreement, granting the government a 34 percent stake in the project, which is to be developed by Canada's Ivanhoe Mines and Australia's Rio Tinto, and repealing a 68 percent windfall profits tax. In September the finance minister announced that the government would create a sovereign wealth fund from its share of the revenues from Oyu Tolgoi. Government and industry representatives signed the agreement on October 6 in Ulaanbaatar. Nevertheless, the $5 billion project—the largest in Mongolian history—remained controversial. In April 2010 more than 5,000 demonstrators, reportedly mostly rural dwellers and the urban poor, protested over the profit distribution.

The projected expansion of the Tavan Tolgoi coal mine, with the world's largest deposit of coking coal for steel production, received parliamentary approval in August 2011 to offer new contracts to foreign firms. In January 2012 the DP withdrew from the MPP-led governing coalition ahead of national and local elections. The DP won the June balloting for the State Great Hural and formed a coalition government. Meanwhile, in August former president Enkhbayar was convicted on corruption charges and sentenced to four years in prison.

In October 2012 reports indicated that the government again launched negotiations to revise the Oyu Tolgoi contract with Rio Tinto. Also in October the falcon was named as the country's national bird (Mongolia is home to more than 6,800 falcons or about 45 percent of the world total). The designation was part of an effort to protect the raptor.

In January 2013 Mongolia conducted its first sovereign bond, raising $1.5 billion or 15 percent of GDP. In August Elbegdorj pardoned former president Enkhbayar. Also in August, the executive director of the state-owned company that held a 34 percent stake in Oyu Tolgi was replaced in what was reportedly an effort to improve relations with Rio Tinto.

In May 2014 the government promulgated an economic stimulus plan to cut government bureaucracy, improve infrastructure, and create two foreign economic zones. In June Rio Tinto cut 300 jobs from the Oyu Tolgi project. The next month, the government announced that Oyu Tolgi owed an unspecified amount of back taxes and penalties. In May 2015 an agreement was reached with Rio Tinto to restart the mine, and a $4.4 billion finance package was signed in December.

Prime Minister Altankhuyag gained parliamentary approval to reduce the number of cabinet positions from 16 to 13 in October 2014. In response, seven cabinet members resigned precipitating a political crisis that resulted in Altankhuyag's dismissal on November 5, following a vote of 34 to 32 in parliament. Deputy prime minister Dendev Terbishdagya (MPRP) was subsequently appointed acting prime minister.

On November 21, 2014, Terbishdagya was replaced by Chimediin Saikhanbileg (DP), who served until the elections of June 29, 2016. Twelve parties and 498 candidates participated in the balloting. The MPP won 65 seats; the DP, 9; the Mongolian People's Revolutionary Front, 1; and the final seat was won by an independent candidate.

POLITICAL PARTIES

On March 23, 1990, the People's Great Hural ended the monopoly held by the Mongolian People's Revolutionary Party (MPRP), and other parties quickly formed. By 2000 Mongolia had 24 registered parties.

Prior to the provincial and local elections held in October 2000, a significant coalescence of forces occurred. The principal opponents of the MPRP, which had been returned to power three months earlier, were a six-party **Coalition of Democratic Forces** (the "Big Six"), led by the Mongolian National Democratic Party (MNDP) and the Mongolian Social Democratic Party (MSDP), and another eight-party grouping led by the Civil Will Party (CWP) and the Mongolian Republican Party (MRP). In December 2000 the MNDP and MSDP led the formation of a new Democratic Party (DP).

In June 2003 the DP and the Motherland–Mongolian Democratic New Socialist Party (M-MDNSP) announced formation of the **Motherland Democratic Coalition**—MDC (*Ekh Oron Ardchilsan Evsel*), as a consequence of which the MPRP faced a unified front of the major opposition parties in the June 2004 election. The MDC won 44.7 percent of the national vote and emerged with sufficient seats to demand a role in the new government. In December 2004 the M-MDNSP (renamed Motherland in 2005) withdrew from the MDC, which disbanded.

Twelve parties and one coalition were registered for the June 2008 State Great Hural election, which, under a new proportional representation system with a 5 percent threshold, was dominated by the MPRP and the DP. In 2009, given that only parliamentary parties may nominate candidates for the state presidency, the presidential race was a contest between MPRP and DP contenders, as the only other parties in the State Great Hural, the CWP and the MGP, decided to back the DP's Elbegdorj rather than risk splitting the opposition.

Government Parties:

Mongolian People's Party—MPP (*Mongol Ardyn Nam*). Initially founded as the MPP in 1921, the party was renamed the **Mongolian People's Revolutionary Party**—MPRP (*Mongol Ardyn Khuv'sgalt Nam*) in 1924, before reverting to its original name in 2010. Organized along typical communist lines for nearly seven decades, its tightly centralized structure was nominally subject to party congresses meeting at five-year intervals. (For more on the party's history, see the 2013 *Handbook*.)

In 1993 the party's presidential candidate, Lodongiyn Tudev, editor of the party newspaper, lost to the incumbent, Punsalmaagiyn Ochirbat, who had maintained nominal MPRP membership despite being denied renomination and running as a joint candidate of the MNDP and MSDP. In a further setback, the MPRP's legislative representation plummeted to 25 seats in the 1996 election, a loss of 46 from its 1992 total. In 1997, however, the party's chair, Natsagiyn Bagabandi, won a landslide presidential victory, defeating President Ochirbat, who had formally resigned from the party to run as the DU candidate.

In 1999 a contemporary Mongolian People's Party (MPP), founded in 1991, merged with the MPRP, although a number of party dissidents continued to claim the MPP name.

In the July 2000 general election the MPRP won 72 of 76 seats in the State Great Hural, after which the party chair, Nambaryn Enkhbayar, won easy confirmation as prime minister. In local elections in October, the MPRP controlled all 21 provincial legislatures.

In June 2004 the party won 46.5 percent of the national vote but lost half its seats in the State Great Hural. Shy of a legislative majority, the MPRP courted the three parliamentary independents but was unsuccessful and therefore entered into negotiations with the opposition MDC for a coalition government. Ultimately, Prime Minister Enkhbayar agreed to step down and was elected chair of the legislature.

In May 2005 Enkhbayar was elected president, succeeding Bagabandi. A month later, following Enkhbayar's mandatory resignation as party chair, the MPRP elected Miyegombo Enkhbold, mayor of Ulaanbaatar, as his successor. Enkhbold became prime minister in January 2006 after ten MPRP ministers resigned from the Elbegdorj government, forcing its collapse. A wave of public protest followed, as the formerly communist MPRP stood accused of undermining democracy.

In June 2007 the MPRP's Tsend NYAMDORJ resigned as chair of the State Great Hural shortly after the Constitutional Court ruled that he had acted unconstitutionally in amending laws. At the party's congress in October, the secretary general, Sanj Bayar, successfully challenged Enkhbold for the party chair, winning 57 percent of the votes. As a consequence, Enkhbold resigned as prime minister and was succeeded by Bayar.

On July 1, 2008, the MPRP won a majority in legislative elections, but following accusations of vote fraud, an angry throng set fire to the MPRP headquarters in the capital. In the 2009 presidential election the MPRP was defeated for the first time since popular elections for that office began in 1990. President Enkhbayar's loss to the DP's Tsakhiagiyn Elbegdorj led to internal criticism of the party's strategy and turnover of its local leadership. Some younger party members sought to open the party to new reformist leadership and wider debate of strategy and policy. The party also considered adopting the name Mongolian Democratic Development Party but ultimately decided against a change.

On April 8, 2010, former prime minister Sanj BAYAR resigned as chair of the party and nominated in his place the current prime minister, Sukhbaatar Batbold, who easily won election.

In November 2010 the party was renamed the MPP. However, Enkhbayar disagreed with the decision and led a faction of the MPP into schism, founding a new organization, the new Mongolian People's Revolutionary Party (MPRP). After the MPP placed second in legislative balloting in June 2012, Batbold resigned as party leader and was replaced by Ulziisaikhan ENKHTUVSHIN.

The MPP nominated nationally famous wrestler Badmaanyambuugiin BAT-ERDENE as its 2013 presidential candidate. He placed second in the polling. Through 2014 the party employed a variety of legislative tactics, including boycotting votes and meetings, to block the governing coalition's economic program. The party returned to power in June 2016, winning 65 votes, and party member Jargaltulga ERDENEBAT became prime minister.

Leaders: Jargaltulga ERDENEBAT (Prime Minister), Myegombo ENKHBOLD (President of the Party), Ulziisaikhan ENKHTUVSHIN (Chair), Ukhnaa KHURELSUKH (General Secretary and Deputy Prime Minister).

Opposition Parties:

Democratic Party—DP (*Ardchilsan Nam*). The DP was formed on December 6, 2000, by the merger of six parties and groups: the **Mongolian National Democratic Party** (MNDP), which dated from the 1992 merger of four opposition parties, including the **Mongolian Democratic Party** (MDP) of Sanjaasürengiyn Zorig; the Mongolian Social Democratic Party (MSDP), which ultimately broke away and reregistered as a separate party in January 2005 (see below); the **Mongolian Democratic Party** (MDP), which traced its roots to Zorig's earlier MDP and which had been formed in January 2000 by disaffected members of the MNDP; the **Mongolian Democratic Renewal Party** (MDRP), which was founded in 1994 and participated in the "Big Six" coalition for the October 2000 provincial and local elections; the **Mongolian Religious Democratic Party** (MRDP), a Buddhist party that was established in 1990 and later participated in the DU coalition; and a faction of the **Mongolian Traditional United Party**—MTUP (*Mongolyn Ulamjlaliin Negdsen Nam*).

The DP's founding chair was the MNDP's Dambyn DORLIGJAV, a former minister of defense. The party's 2001 presidential candidate, former MSDP chair Radnaasümbereliyn Gonchigdorj, finished second, with 36.6 percent of the vote. In the June 2004 State Great Hural election the DP won 26 of the MDC's 35 seats. The MDC and the MPRP then formed a coalition government led by the DP's Tsakhiagiyn ELBEGDORJ. In December the DP's national committee voted to overhaul the party's leadership and replace former prime minister Mendsaikhan Enkhsaikhan with Gonchigdorj. Enkhsaikhan nevertheless remained the party's 2005 candidate for president, finishing second with 19.7 percent of the vote. In February 2006 Enkhsaikhan, former prime minister Janlav Narantsatsralt, and Mishig Sonompil were dismissed from the party after casting deciding votes against the Elbegdorj government and then accepting cabinet posts in the new MPRP government.

At the party congress on March 30–April 1, 2006, former prime minister Elbegdorj was elected chair over Erdeniin BAT-UUL and two other candidates. In November 2007 the DP was the sole parliamentary party to oppose the designation of the MPRP's Bayar as prime minister.

Following the 2008 election for the State Great Hural, Elbegdorj challenged the results and accused the MPRP of stealing the election. For weeks, a walkout by all but two of the party's legislators blocked the seating of a new parliament. However, while the legislature remained in limbo, members of the MPRP and DP worked as a de facto interim government, and the DP subsequently joined a new government with the MPRP in November.

Nonovyn Altankhuyag was elected party chair in 2008, Elbegdorj having stepped down in August. Elbegdorj subsequently was tapped as the party's flag bearer for the 2009 presidential election. He became the first Mongolian president from a party other than the MPRP.

The DP won balloting for the State Great Hural, securing 31 seats. Altankhuyag was appointed prime minister and named a coalition government that included all of the legislative parties except for the MPP. In May 2013 at a party congress, Elbegdorj was unanimously re-nominated as the DP's presidential candidate, and subsequently reelected president in June. In January 2014 the DP announced a controversial proposal to abolish political parties that were not represented in parliament. The DP won just 9 seats in the June 2016 parliamentary elections.

Leaders: Tsakhiagiyn ELBEGDORJ (President of the Republic), Nonovyn ALTANKHUYAG (Former Prime Minister and Party Chair), T. OYUNDARI (General Secretary), Zandaakhuu ENKHBOLD (Former Speaker of Parliament).

Mongolian People's Revolutionary Front—MPRP (*Mongol Ardiin Khuvsgalt Nam*). The MPRP was formed by former president Nambaryn Enkhbayar in 2010 with dissidents from the MPP. It joined the **Justice Coalition—**JC (*Shudarga Yos Evsel*) in an electoral coalition with the small **Mongolian National Democratic Party** (MNDP) for the 2012 legislative balloting. The MNDP was established as the **National New Party**—NNP (*Ündesnii Shine Nam*) by Janlav NARANTSATSRALT and Mendsaikhan Enkhsaikhan following their expulsion from the DP for joining the MPRP (now the MPP) government in February 2006. Narantsatsralt died in November 2007. In September 2011 the NNP voted to change its name to the Mongolian National Democratic Party. Enkhbayar was convicted of corruption in April 2012, but was released on bail on May 14 following a hunger strike, and was subsequently pardoned.

The JC secured 11 seats in the 2012 legislative balloting and was given three portfolios in the subsequent DP-led coalition government.

The MPRP nominated Natsag UDVAL as its presidential candidate. Although she placed third, Udval was the first woman presidential candidate in Mongolia. Meanwhile the MNDP supported the DP's Elbegdorj in the balloting, creating tensions within the coalition. Reports in 2014 indicated growing opposition within the coalition to the DP's economic stimulus program and the coalition dissolved.

The MPRP ran as a separate party in the June 2016 elections, when it won a single seat.

Leaders: Nambaryn ENKHBAYAR (Former President of the Republic and Chair), Dendev TERBISHDAGVA (Former Deputy Prime Minister), Natsagiin UDVAL (2013 presidential candidate).

Other Parties:

Civil Will–Green Party—CW-GP (*Irgenii Zorig—Nogoon Nam*). The center-left CW-GP was formed by a merger of the **Civil Will Party**—CWP (*Irgenii Zorig* Nam) and the **Mongolian Green Party**—MGP (*Mongol Nogoon Nam*) in March 2012. Sanjaasuren OYUN of the CWP was elected as the groupings first chair. The centrist CWP was registered in March 2000 under the leadership of Oyun, sister of the slain MNDP activist and cabinet member Sanjaasürengiyn Zorig. The CWP campaigned in coalition with the MGP for the July 2000 legislative election, with Oyun winning its only seat.

In September 2000 Oyun was elected chair of an eight-party opposition coalition to contest the October 2000 provincial and local elections. Participants included the Mongolian Republican Party (MRP), the Mongolian Liberal Democratic Party (MLDP), the Mongolian Civil Democratic New Liberal Party, and the Party for Mongolia (PM), which was established by Luvsandambyn DASHNYAM in 1998 and which agreed to join the CWP in December 2000. For the 2001 presidential election the CWP nominated Dashnyam, who captured only 3.5 percent of the vote.

In February 2002 the CWP and the MRP merged to form the **Civil Will Republican Party**—CWRP (*Irgenii Zorig Najramdakh Bügd Nam*), but they separated in December 2003 (see the RP, below), although the CWRP retained "Republican" in its name when it reregistered in April 2004. It then entered the national election campaign as part of the MDC, winning two State Great Hural seats. In January 2006 the party reestablished itself as the CWP.

Despite the objections of some members, in 2007 the party decided to join the MPRP-led coalition government. Oyun accepted the post of foreign minister under Prime Minister Bayar. She won the party's only seat in the 2008 parliamentary election. In the 2009 presidential election, the CWP supported Elbegdorj, Oyun expressing hope that he would help reconcile the nation's partisan divide.

The MGP was organized in 1990 as the political arm of the Mongolian Alliance of Greens. It competed as part of the DU in 1996 but failed to win any seats. For the July 2000 election it was allied with the CWP, but for the October provincial and local elections, the MGP participated in the six-party Coalition of Democratic Forces. Unlike its fellow coalition members, however, it later announced that its agenda prevented it from joining in the DP merger. In 2001 the MGP supported the presidential candidacy of the DP's Gonchigdorj. It ran six unsuccessful candidates for the State Great Hural in 2004.

In the 2008 elections for the State Great Hural, the MGP ran as part of the **Civil Alliance** (*Irgenii Evsel*), and its leader, Dangaasuren ENKHBAT, was declared the winner of a seat in Bayangol after a lengthy investigation of the vote. He quickly formed a Green Group in the State Great Hural to advocate for ecological approaches to the mining industry. In 2009 the Green Party supported the DP's Tsakhiagiyn Elbegdorj for president.

The CW-GP secured two seats in the 2012 parliamentary elections and joined the DP-led coalition government with Oyun appointed as minister of the environment. The CW-GP endorsed Elbegdorj of the DP in the 2013 presidential election. In June 2014 Environment Minister and party leader Sanjaasuren OYUN was elected as the inaugural president of the UN Environmental Assembly (see entry on the UN).

The party was banned from competing in the 2016 balloting because of flaws in its registration paperwork.

Leaders: Sanjaasuren OYUN (Founder), Sambuu DEMBEREL, Tserendorj GANKHUYAG.

Mongolian Social Democratic Party—MSDP (*Mongolyn Sotsial Ardchilsan Nam*). The MSDP called at its inaugural congress in March 1990 for a just and humane society patterned on the values espoused by social democratic parties in the West. The party's legislative representation fell from 7 (overall) in 1990 to 1 in 1992, but it won 12 State Great Hural seats in 1996 as part of the DU. One of its leaders, Radnaasümbereliyn Gonchigdorj, served as state vice president and chair of the State Great Hural before running as a DP candidate for president. The party lost all its State Great Hural seats in the July 2000 election and in September agreed to merge with the MNDP. The DP resulted in December.

In December 2004, however, objecting to DP policies, the MSDP separated from the DP. It was reregistered as a separate party on January 20, 2005, although the DP protested the restoration of the party's name. The MSDP held a party congress in March 2008 but did not field candidates in the elections for the State Great Hural. It failed to win seats in the 2012 or 2016 balloting.

Leaders: Adyagiin GANBAATAR (Chair), Ts. SAIKHANBILEG (Secretary General).

Motherland Party (*Ekh Oron Nam*). Motherland began as the **Mongolian Democratic New Socialist Party** (*Mongoliin Ardchilsan Shine Sotsialist Nam*—MDNSP). The MDNSP was organized in 1998 under the auspices of Badarch Erdenebat, the wealthy director general of the Erel Company. (For information on the early history of the party, see the 2014 *Handbook.*)

The M-MDNSP supported President Bagabandi's 2001 reelection but in June 2004 ran as part of the MDC, from which it withdrew at the end of December, in part because of Erdenebat's presidential aspirations. He served as minister of defense in the Elbegdorj cabinet until February 2005 and finished fourth, with 11.4 percent of the vote, in the May presidential election as candidate of Motherland, as the party had been renamed in January. Erdenebat served in the Enkhbold cabinet of 2006–2007 but lost his seat in parliament in the 2008 election. The party failed to secure any seats in the 2012 legislative elections. The party supported Tsakhiagiyn Elbegdorj of the DP in the 2013 presidential elections. The party did not compete in the 2016 balloting.

Leader: Badarch ERDENEBAT (Chair).

Republican Party—RP (*Bügd Najramdahk Nam*). The RP traces its origins to the 1992 launching of the **Mongolian Capitalists' Party**, which changed its name to the **Mongolian Republican Party** (MRP) in 1997.

In early 2002 the MRP merged with the CWP (above) to form the **Civil Will Republican Party** (CWRP), but the MRP reemerged as the RP in December 2003 because of its leaders' opposition to contesting the 2004 national election in alliance with the DP. Longtime leader Bazarsadiin JARGALSAIKHAN won the party's only seat in that polling.

In May 2005 Jargalsaikhan won 13.9 percent of the vote in the presidential election. He joined the Enkhbold coalition cabinet in January 2006 as minister of industry and commerce but left in February 2007 because of discontent with mining law reforms. The RP endorsed Elbegdorj in the 2013 presidential balloting. It secured 1.7 percent of the vote in the 2016 elections.

Leader: Bazarsadiin JARGALSAIKHAN.

For more information on the **Civil Movement Party** (CMP), please see the 2012 *Handbook.*

LEGISLATURE

State Great Hural (*Ulsyn Ikh Khural*). The 76 members of the Great Hural are popularly elected for four-year terms. In the election on June 28, 2012, Mongolia introduced a mixed system in which 48 seats were elected by majority vote in single-member districts and the remaining 28 elected through a proportional voting system based on party lists, with parties winning at least 5 percent of the national vote being awarded seats. Twenty percent of a party's candidates must be women. Ahead of the June 20, 2016, balloting, the proportional voting system was eliminated so that all districts used the first-past-the-post voting method. Following the June 29, 2016 elections, the seat distribution was as follows: Mongolian People's Party, 65 seats; Democratic Party, 9; Mongolian People's Revolutionary Front, 1; and independents, 1.

Chair: Myegombo ENKHBOLD.

CABINET

[as of September 16, 2016]

Prime Minister	Jargaltulga Erdenebat
Deputy Prime Minister	Ukhnaa Khurelsukh
Ministers	
Construction and Urban Development	Gombosuren Monkhbayar
Defense	Badmaanyambuugiin Bat-Erdene
Education and Science	Jamiyansuren Batsuri
Energy	Purevjav Gankhuu
Environment and Tourism	Dulamsuren Oyunkhorol [f]
Finance	Battogtokh Choijilsuren
Food, Agriculture, and Light Industry	Purev Sergelen
Foreign Affairs	Tsendiyn Munk-Orgil
Health	Aysuh Tsogtsetseg
Infrastructure Development	Dangaa Ganbat
Justice and Home Affairs	Sandag Byambatsogt
Labor	Nyamtaishir Nomtoibayar
Mining and Heavy Industry	Tsedev Dashdorj
Chief of Government Secretariat	Jamiyan Munkhbat

[f] = female

Note: All members of the cabinet belong to the MPP.

INTERGOVERNMENTAL REPRESENTATION

Ambassador to the U.S.: Bulgaa ALTANGEREL.

U.S. Ambassador to Mongolia: Jennifer Zimdahl GALT.

Permanent Representative to the UN: Sukhbold SUKHEE.

IGO Memberships (Non-UN): ADB, EBRD, ICC, IOM, NAM, SCO, WTO.

For Further Reference:

Addleton, John S. *Mongolia and the United States: A Diplomatic History*. Hong Kong: Hong Kong University Press. 2013.

Pederson, Morten Axel. *Not Quite Shamans: Spirit Worlds and Political Lives in Northern Mongolia.* Ithaca, NY: Cornell University Press, 2011.

Sabloff, Paula. *Does Everyone Want Democracy? Insights from Mongolia.* New York: Routledge, 2016.

MONTENEGRO

Republic of Montenegro
Republika Crna Gora

Note: In assembly elections on October 16, 2016, the Democratic Party of Socialists (DPS) won a plurality with 36 of 81 seats. In second place was an electoral alliance, the Democratic Front, led by the New Democratic Force, which won 18 seats. No other party or alliance secured more than 9 seats. After efforts by Prime Minister Milo Markovič (DPS) to create a governing coalition failed, the DPS formed a coalition government with four small parties under Deputy Prime Minister Dusko Markovic (DPS). Markovic was formally named prime minister on November 9, and his government approved by the legislature on November 28.

Political Status: An autonomous principality formally independent of the Ottoman Empire in 1878; declared a kingdom in 1910; incorporated as part of the Kingdom of the Serbs, Croats, and Slovenes, which was constituted as an independent monarchy on December 1, 1918, and formally renamed Yugoslavia on October 3, 1929; constituent republic of the communist Federal People's Republic of Yugoslavia instituted November 29, 1945, and then of the Socialist Federal Republic of Yugoslavia proclaimed April 7, 1963; constituent republic, along with Serbia, of the Federal Republic of Yugoslavia proclaimed April 27, 1992, and of the "state union" of Serbia and Montenegro established February 4, 2003, under new Constitutional Charter; Republic of Montenegro established June 3, 2006, following an independence referendum on May 21; new constitution adopted by the legislature (sitting as a Constituent Assembly) on October 19, 2007, and promulgated October 22.

Area: 5,333 sq. mi. (13,812 sq. km).

Population: 626,000 (2016E—UN); 644,578 (2016E—U.S. Census).

Major Urban Centers (2014E—UN): PODGORICA (formerly Titograd, 165,000).

Official Languages: Montenegrin; however, in areas established by national minorities, their languages (Albanian, Bosnian, Croatian, Serbian) are also accorded official status.

Monetary Unit: Euro (market rate October 1, 2016: 0.89 euro = $1US). The euro has been legal tender in Montenegro since January 1, 2002.

President: Filip VUJANOVIĆ (Democratic Party of Socialists of Montenegro); served as Montenegrin prime minister 1998–2002; elected chair of the Montenegrin Assembly on November 5, 2002, following the legislative election of October 20, and thus became acting president upon the resignation of President Milo DJUKANOVIĆ on November 25; elected president for a five-year term on May 11, 2003, and inaugurated June 13; reelected president in the first postindependence presidential election on April 6, 2008, and inaugurated on May 20; reelected again on April 7, 2013, and inaugurated on May 20.

Prime Minister: Milo DJUKANOVIĆ (Democratic Party of Socialists of Montenegro); nominated by the president on November 9, 2012, and confirmed by the legislature on December 4, succeeding Igor LUKŠIĆ (Democratic Party of Socialists of Montenegro).

THE COUNTRY

Montenegro is a Balkan republic, mostly mountainous, with a 180-mile coastline along the Adriatic Sea. The terrain, part of the

Karst Plateau, is renowned for its rugged scenery. The country is bordered by Albania to the south, Serbia and Kosovo to the east, and Bosnia and Herzegovina to the north. Per the results of the 2011 census, Montenegrins constitute 45 percent of the population, Serbs 28.7 percent, Bosniaks 8.7 percent, Albanians 4.9 percent, and various other ethnic groups (e.g., Croats and Roma) the remainder. Such categories obscure the complicated nature of identity, however, since ethnicity and "mother tongue" notably diverged on the census, particularly along the Montenegrin–Serbian divide (37 percent registering Montenegrin as their native language, 42.9 percent Serbian). Eastern Orthodox Christianity predominates, although there is a large Muslim minority (19.1 percent), a legacy of the Ottoman Empire.

Industrial production, which was badly damaged by the United Nations (UN) economic sanctions imposed against Yugoslavia in the 1990s, is concentrated in hydroelectricity generation; the extraction and processing of raw materials, especially bauxite, and also coal, lumber, and salt; and production of aluminum and steel. Processing of tobacco and food is also a major manufacturing activity. The industrial sector as a whole comprises 11 percent of GDP and employs approximately 21 percent of the total workforce, compared to 88 percent of GDP and 73 percent of employment for services. Only about 14 percent of the total area of the country is suitable for cultivation so that agriculture employs 6 percent of the workforce and contributes 1 percent to GDP. Tourism, concentrated along the Adriatic coastline, has been targeted for expansion.

Following independence, GDP grew at an annual rate of 7.6 percent from 2005 through 2008. Challenges include rebuilding neglected infrastructure, curbing public-sector corruption, boosting private-sector employment, and suppressing the enormous black-market sector that developed during the period of sanctions. Foreign investment, particularly in finance and tourism, has grown since independence, and in 2007 Montenegro had the third highest investment per capita ratio in Europe. The international financial crisis of 2008–2009 led to GDP contraction of 5.7 percent in 2009, fueled in part by the decline of the foreign-owned Kombinat Aluminijuma Podgorica aluminum processing facility, which in 2008 had accounted for 15 percent of the country's GDP. The economy had rebounded to 2.8 percent annual growth in 2010 and 2011. Economic development has addressed the widespread unemployment of the 1990s, although the official unemployment rate in June 2013 reached 13.1 percent. GDP contracted by almost 2.6 percent in 2012, but the International Monetary Fund (IMF) reported 3.3 percent growth in 2013, 1.2 percent growth in 2014, and 4.7 percent in 2015. The IMF estimated growth of 3.5 percent in 2016. Inflation that year was 1 percent, while GDP per capita was $7,104. In its annual ease of doing business survey in 2016, the World Bank ranked Montenegro 46th (between Italy and Cyprus) out of 189 countries.

GOVERNMENT AND POLITICS

Political background. Following centuries of struggle against the Ottoman Empire, an autonomous Montenegrin principality emerged over the 16th and 18th centuries. As with Serbia, in the 19th century Montenegro broke all but nominal ties to the Ottomans, finally achieving formal independence in 1878. The newly independent state was both an ally and rival to Serbia, with Prince (later, King) NIKOLA I himself hoping to unify Serbian-inhabited lands. Montenegro's incorporation on December 1, 1918, into the Kingdom of the Serbs, Croats, and Slovenes under the Serbian House of Karadjordjević led to a brief civil war. Montenegro was initially a constituent part of the kingdom, was later incorporated into the Banovina of Zeta in 1929 as part of King ALEKSANDAR'S efforts to reduce interethnic identities, then became a constituent republic of the Federal People's Republic of Yugoslavia in 1945 (see the Political background in the Serbia entry for details). As with other republics, Montenegro gained greater autonomy in the federal constitution of 1963 and following the death of Marshal Josip Broz TITO in 1980.

Economic ills set off a series of events that led to the dissolution of greater Yugoslavia into the independent states of Croatia, Slovenia, Bosnia and Herzegovina, and Macedonia, with only Serbia and Montenegro remaining in a diminished federation. In February 1992 Serbia and Montenegro agreed to join in upholding "the principles of a common state which would be a continuation of Yugoslavia." In April a rump Federal Assembly adopted the constitution of a new Federal Republic of Yugoslavia (FRY).

In 1996 the Democratic Party of Socialists of Montenegro (*Demokratska Partija Socijalista Crne Gore*—DPS) achieved a majority in elections for the separate Montenegrin Assembly. On July 15, 1997, Slobodan MILOŠEVIĆ, constitutionally barred from running for a third term as president of Serbia, was elected unopposed as the Yugoslav federal president. However, he continued to face electoral threats to his power. Montenegrin Prime Minister Milo DJUKANOVIĆ led a faction of the DPS against Milošević's local allies, culminating in Djukanović's victory over Bulatović in the second round of the 1997 presidential elections (see the 2011 *Handbook*).

The new president took office on January 13, 1998, despite violent protests by Bulatović supporters. Through mediation by Yugoslav Prime Minister Radoje KONTIĆ (a Montenegrin), on January 21 the demonstrators agreed to settle for early legislative elections in May 1998. A transitional government under the leadership of the DPS's Filip VUJANOVIĆ was appointed on February 4. It included 17 ministers from Djukanović's DPS faction, 7 from the opposition, and 4 independents; the Bulatović faction of the DPS as well as the pro-independence Liberal Alliance of Montenegro (*Liberalni Savez Crne Gore*—LSCG) refused to participate.

On May 19, 1998, former Montenegrin president Bulatović was named prime minister of Yugoslavia. On May 31, however, Montenegrin voters awarded 49.5 percent of the vote and a majority of seats in the Montenegrin Assembly to President Djukanović's For a Better Life electoral coalition, while Bulatović's recently organized Socialist People's Party of Montenegro (*Socijalistička Narodna Partija Crne Gore*—SNP) claimed 36 percent of the vote and emerged as the leading opposition party. Montenegro's interim prime minister, Vujanović, was reappointed on July 16 to head a government encompassing the three coalition partners: the DPS, the People's Party (*Narodna Stranka*—NS), and the Social Democratic Party of Montenegro (*Socijaldemokratska Partija Crne Gore*—SDP).

In 1999 Montenegrin president Djukanović continued his efforts to distance his administration from federal policies in regard to Kosovo, particularly "ethnic cleansing" of ethnic Albanians, which had precipitated military action by the United States and other North Atlantic Treaty Organization (NATO) countries (see the Serbia entry for details). Even though Montenegro was not exempt from the NATO air campaign, and despite rumors that the Serbian military was preparing to depose him, on April 21 Djukanović rejected orders that the Montenegrin police be placed under the command of the FRY army. Djukanović accused Milošević of using "the pretext of the defense of the country" to displace the civil government. Later, the republican government proposed replacing the federal republic with a looser association in which

Montenegro would set its own foreign and military policy and establish independent currency controls.

In July 2000 Milošević's allies pushed through the Federal Assembly constitutional changes designed to maintain his hold on power. The changes included directly electing the president, permitting the incumbent to serve two additional four-year terms, and putting organization of elections under the FRY instead of the individual republics. Although the Montenegrin Assembly described the changes as "illegal" and "a gross violation of the constitutional rights of the Republic of Montenegro," the legislators rejected a proposal for an immediate referendum on Montenegrin independence. In late July Milošević called elections for September, even though his presidential term would not expire until July 2001. The governing coalition in Montenegro quickly announced that it would boycott the balloting. The federal election of September 24 was followed by two weeks of turmoil that concluded with the demise of the Milošević regime and the inauguration on October 7 of Vojislav KOŠTUNICA.

On December 28, 2000, the NS withdrew from Montenegro's governing coalition in opposition to further movement toward independence. Four months later, President Djukanović entered the Montenegrin Assembly election of April 22, 2001, banking on a strong vote for separation from Serbia, but his DPS-SDP alliance failed to achieve more than a slight plurality against a coalition of the SNP, the NS, and the Serbian People's Party (*Srpska Narodna Stranka*—SNS). Three seats short of a majority, Djukanović turned to the Liberal Alliance, which agreed to extend external support to a new Vujanović cabinet, but the government's minority status soon forced the president to backtrack on plans for an immediate independence referendum.

On March 14, 2002, the governments of the Federal Republic of Yugoslavia and its two constituent republics announced an "agreement in principle" that would bring the history of Yugoslavia as such to an end, with its replacement by a "state union" to be called Serbia and Montenegro. Over the objections of parties that wanted a separate and independent Serbia, the Serbian legislature ratified the accord 149–79 on April 9. The same day, the Montenegrin legislature voted in favor of the agreement 58–11, despite strong opposition from the SDP and the previously government-supportive LSCG, both of which favored Montenegrin independence. Four SDP-affiliated ministers quickly resigned from the Montenegrin cabinet, and on April 19 Prime Minister Vujanović submitted his resignation, announcing that his government no longer commanded a legislative majority. At President Djukanović's request, Vujanović attempted to fashion another government, but he was unable to do so, and in July the president called for an early legislative election. Meanwhile, on May 31 both chambers of the Federal Assembly had approved the state union agreement by wide margins.

The Montenegrin Assembly election of October 20, 2002, saw a list headed by the DPS win 39 of 75 seats, compared to 30 for an opposition coalition. Following the election, caretaker Prime Minister Vujanović was elected speaker of the Montenegrin legislature. On November 25 Milo Djukanović resigned as president of Montenegro, and a day later Speaker Vujanović, in his new capacity as acting president, nominated Djukanović for the prime ministership (the office he had previously held from 1991 to 1998). Vujanović then ran in the Montenegrin presidential election of December 22. Although he won an overwhelming majority, an opposition boycott held the turnout under 50 percent, invalidating the results and forcing a similarly unsuccessful revote on February 9, 2003. In response, the Montenegrin Assembly eliminated the 50 percent requirement, and on May 11 Vujanović was elected president with 63 percent of the vote. Meanwhile, on January 8 Djukanović had been confirmed as prime minister.

On January 27 and 29, 2003, the Serbian and then the Montenegrin assemblies approved the Constitutional Charter for the state union of Serbia and Montenegro. The Federal Assembly concurred on February 4 (by votes of 26–7 in the upper chamber and 84–31 in the lower), thereby excising Yugoslavia from the political map. Under the charter a new state union assembly was elected by and from among the members of the FRY, Serbian, and Montenegrin legislatures, and the new assembly in turn elected the DPS's MAROVIĆ, the only candidate, as state union president and chair of the Council of Ministers on March 7.

Under their 2003 European Union (EU)-backed state union agreement, both Serbia and Montenegro had the right to vote on the question of independence in three years. On May 21, 2006, by a vote of 55.5 percent to 44.5 percent (half a percentage point above the EU threshold for approval), Montenegrins chose independence. Two weeks later, on June 3, the Montenegrin Assembly declared independence. On June 5, although many Serbians were unhappy with what they viewed as an abrupt divorce, the Serbian National Assembly declared Serbia to be the independent successor state to the state union, as had been agreed upon under the charter, and thereby extinguished the last remnants of the former Yugoslavia.

Opposition parties in Montenegro seized on cultural anxieties raised by the slim pro-independence margin. For example, petition drives demanding dual Montenegrin–Serbian citizenship sprang up soon after the votes were counted. Meanwhile, the pro-independence Bosniak and Albanian leadership was dismayed that the Constitutional Court had struck down the Minority Rights Act, which guaranteed seats in the assembly to minority groups based on their proportion in the population, even if they fell below the usual electoral threshold. The act had been passed just ten days before the referendum, after these leaders had made the bill a condition for their support of independence.

In the Montenegrin election of September 10, 2006, a coalition led by the DPS and SDP won a majority of 41 seats in the expanded 81-seat Montenegrin legislature. A multiparty opposition Serbian List, headed by the SNS, won 12 seats, while another ethnic Serbian coalition led by the SNP won 11. The new Movement for Change (*Pokret za Promjene*—PzP) also won 11 seats. On October 3 President Vujanović revealed that Prime Minister Djukanović had decided not to seek reappointment as prime minister, although he would remain at the helm of the DPS. A day later, Vujanović asked the minister of justice, Željko ŠTURANOVIĆ, to form a new government, and on November 10 the legislature confirmed the revamped Council of Ministers.

The closeness of the September 2006 assembly election left the legislature sharply divided on a number of hot-button issues for the minority communities, especially the Serb population. Their concerns, as reflected in the process of drafting a new constitution, included whether minority representation should be guaranteed not only in the legislature but also in the government bureaucracy and agencies, how much autonomy minorities would be accorded with respect to education and cultural matters, and whether Serbian should remain the official language. Disputes also raged over state symbols, including the national coat-of-arms, the national anthem, and the design of the flag. The 2007 constitution made Montenegrin the official language of the country. Polls in that year showed that over 50 percent of the country preferred to refer to the language as Serbian, a position backed by the pro-union opposition.

In early April 2007 the assembly, after a week of heated debate, adopted a constitutional draft that included alternatives proposed by minority representatives, and a period of "public debate" ensued. By August, however, neither the government majority nor the opposition appeared willing to compromise on the remaining issues. Apart from the concerns of the ethnic minority parties, the largest opposition party, the PzP, demanded that the government agree to a snap election upon adoption of the constitution. The DPS-SDP refused, but in the end the PzP and the BS voiced support for the proposed constitution, which, with 55 votes in favor and 21 against, achieved the two-thirds tally needed for passage. Most ethnic Albanian representatives abstained, while the Serbs voted in opposition.

On January 31, 2008, Prime Minister Šturanović resigned, citing health issues, and on February 20 President Vujanović once again nominated Milo Djukanović, who won confirmation on February 29. On April 6 Vujanović was reelected for another term in the first presidential elections since independence. In the first round of voting, Vujanović (51.9 percent of the vote) won an absolute majority over the Serb List candidate Andrija MANDIĆ (19.6 percent), PzP candidate Nebojša MEDOJEVIĆ (16.6 percent), and SNP candidate Srdjan MILIĆ (11.9 percent). Vujanović was inaugurated for his second term on May 21, 2008.

In June 2008 the SPD proposed that the capital be moved to the historic royal capital of Cetinje (recognized as such within the 2007 constitution), a move criticized by the SNS.

In January 2009 Prime Minister Djukanović proposed early elections although the sitting parliament had a year of its term remaining. Djukanović argued that new elections would provide a four-year mandate for a government to negotiate EU membership. The parliament voted for dissolution by a thin majority, the opposition arguing that the government hoped to use early elections to avoid voter retaliation for slowing economic growth.

In June 2009 a new Montenegrin Latin alphabet was announced as standard, replacing the existing Serbian Latin and Cyrillic alphabets; in July a new official standard for the language was announced.

In the parliamentary election of March 29, 2009, the Coalition for a European Montenegro (*Koalicija za Evropska Crna Gora*—KzECG) of the DPS, SDP, BS, and Croat Civic Initiative (*Hrvatska Gradjanska*

Inicijativa—HGI) won 48 out of 81 seats; they were subsequently joined in forming a government by the Democratic Union of Albanians (*Demokratska Unija Albanaca*—DUA/*Unioni Demokratih i Shqiptarëve*—UDSh), a small Albanian political party with 1 seat. The SNP led the opposition with 16 seats, while the New Serb Democracy (*Nova Srpska Demokracija*—NSD) won 8 and the PzP won 5, with the remaining 3 seats being split between small Albanian political parties. Djukanović was reconfirmed as prime minister on June 10.

On December 21, 2010, Djukanović resigned, stating that he had achieved his goals of creating a stable Montenegro and initiating accession into NATO and the EU. He was succeeded by Igor LUKŠIĆ on December 29.

A new electoral law (see Constitution and government, below) was passed in 2011, responding to the Constitutional Court's 2006 decision on the Minority Rights Act. The new law reserved five seats for minority parties but in a way interpreted by local analysts as reducing the influence of the ethnic Albanian minority.

On July 26, 2012, the ruling coalition voted to dissolve parliament. The government justified early elections by stressing the need to create a new government to respond to the challenges of EU accession. Local analysts have suggested it was timed to take place before unpopular austerity measures could diminish the popularity of the DPS.

In the parliamentary election of October 14, 2012, the KZECG, now comprised of the DPS, SDP, and the Liberal Party of Montenegro (*Liberalna Partija Crne Gore*—LPCG) won 39 out of 81 seats. They formed a government with the support of ethnic minority parties: the BS, with 3 seats, and the single seats each held by the HGI, Albanian Coalition (*Albanska Koalicija/Koalicioni Shqiptare*—AK/KS), and the New Democratic Force (*Nova Demokratska Snaga/Forca e Re Demokratike*—FORCA). The Democratic Front (*Demokratski front*—DF), a coalition including the NSD and PzP, led the opposition with 20 seats, the SNP won 9, and the newly formed Positive Montenegro (*Pozitivna Crna Gora*—PCG) won 7. Djukanović was again appointed prime minister, assuming office on December 4.

Vujanović's candidacy for a third term in the 2013 presidential elections was controversial because the constitution mandates a two-term limit. In February the SDP sided with the opposition and lodged a court challenge in the Constitutional Court. The court, however, ruled that the constitutional limit applies only to terms after the election of 2008. On April 7 Vujanović was reelected on the first round, with 51.2 percent of the vote, over the joint opposition candidate, Miodrag LEKIĆ (48.8 percent). The Constitutional Court rejected appeals by the opposition.

In June 2015 two cabinet ministers resigned from the SDP to form the Social Democrats of Montenegro (*Socijaldemokrate Crne Gore*—SD). The SDP threatened to join the opposition if the two former SDP ministers were not expelled, prompting a confidence vote in January 2016 that was won by the government. Djukanović then created a government of national unity with some of the main opposition parties, including the SDP (see Political Parties, below). The new cabinet was approved on May 19.

Constitution and government. At independence, Montenegrins had yet to craft a process for drafting and approving a new constitution for the republic. A parliamentary drafting committee, assisted by the OSCE, succeeded in enumerating a variety of basic rights, such as freedom of speech, press, assembly, and association as well as presumption of innocence and the right to a fair and public trial. The committee also laid out a governmental structure based on the division of powers among executive, legislative, and judicial branches, complete with a system of checks and balances. The new basic law was approved by the assembly, sitting as a Constituent Assembly, on October 19, 2007, and promulgated on October 22.

Under the constitution the president is elected for a five-year term. The term of the unicameral assembly, subject to early dissolution, is four years, with a 3 percent threshold to gain representation. Until 2011 the minority Albanian community was guaranteed representation with five seats allocated to a separate minority bloc. The electoral law was amended in September 2011, however. Five seats are now allocated for Albanian, Bosnian, and Croat minority parties. If no party for a given minority reaches the threshold of 3 percent, the threshold is reduced to 0.7 percent (except for the Croat minority, at 0.4 percent). Up to three seats per ethnic group may be gained through such lowered thresholds.

The government is headed by a prime minister nominated by the president and confirmed by the legislature. The judiciary includes a Constitutional Court and a Supreme Court. Local government is based on 21 municipalities.

Reporters Without Borders ranks Montenegro as 106th worldwide in 2016 in respect to press freedom, an improvement of 7 places since 2014. Threats of violence, arson, and the use of libel suits to intimidate the press have been reported by local journalists, and several physical attacks were reported in 2013 and 2014.

Foreign relations. As a constituent republic of the Federal Republic of Yugoslavia in the 1990s and then of the state union, Montenegro suffered from the international sanctions imposed because of the policies of the Slobodan Milošević era (see the entry on Serbia). Following the defeat of Milošević in 2000, the new Yugoslav government moved broadly to reestablish its international linkages. FRY was formally reintegrated into the UN on November 1 and into the Organization for Security and Cooperation in Europe (OSCE) on November 27. In April 2003 it joined the Council of Europe, and two months later it applied for membership in NATO's Partnership for Peace (PfP) program.

Just days after the declaration of independence, President Vujanović sent a letter to the UN seeking membership for Montenegro. The United States, the EU and its member nations, Russia, China, and many other governments quickly recognized Montenegrin independence shortly thereafter. The UN admitted Montenegro as its 192nd member on June 28, 2006, not long after Montenegro became the 56th member of the OSCE. It has subsequently been admitted to the International Monetary Fund, the World Bank, and other UN-related organizations, and in May 2007 it became the newest member of the Council of Europe. Two months earlier, Montenegro and the EU initialed a Stabilization and Association Agreement, regarded as the first step toward eventual EU membership. The Montenegrin government joined NATO's Partnership for Peace (PfP) program in December 2006 and applied for NATO membership on November 5, 2008. It formally began the EU integration process by applying for membership on December 15, 2008.

Despite both historical ties to Serbia and divided domestic popular opinion, the Montenegrin government recognized the independence of Kosovo on October 9, 2008. Serbia subsequently expelled the Montenegrin ambassador to Belgrade, with relations sinking to their lowest level since Montenegrin independence. Negotiations regarding dual citizenship, begun in October 2008, were one casualty of weakened relations, with talks continuing into 2009 with no resolution. The large number of Slavic Montenegrins identifying as ethnically Serbian makes the issue particularly sensitive for the DPS.

A Membership Action Plan was signed with NATO in December 2009, outlining the formal steps the country must take to join the alliance. In March 2010 Montenegro deployed soldiers for the NATO mission in Afghanistan, currently a force of 25 as of June 2014. The contribution sparked domestic opposition, but the government defended the policy as a demonstration of its commitment to NATO.

On May 1, 2010, Montenegro became an associate member of the EU. On December 17, 2010, Montenegro was granted candidate status in the EU. On October 12, 2011, the European Commission recommended that accession negotiations should be opened, while highlighting the need for further reform to combat corruption and organized crime. On April 29, 2012, Montenegro was admitted to the World Trade Organization (WTO). Accession negotiations with the EU opened on June 29, 2012.

On December 20, 2015, NATO extended an invitation to Montenegro to become the organization's 29th member. In Brussels, on May 19, 2016, foreign ministers signed the accession protocol with Prime Minister Djukanović watching. Russia continued to object to Montenegrin membership and threatened trade sanctions. Domestic opposition led to widespread protests (see Current issues, below). Through 2016 Montenegro remained on track to join the EU, with a goal of full membership in 2020.

Current issues. In August 2010 the government announced a new action plan to combat corruption, but opposition parties, domestic NGOs, and foreign observers criticized the plan as lacking clear goals and as having been devised without public input. The European Commission noted in November 2010 that "organized crime remains a problem" and that "corruption...constitutes a particularly serious problem."

The possibility of NATO membership has continued to be a polarizing issue. In a March 2014 opinion poll, 46 percent surveyed stated they approved joining the alliance (up from 31.2 percent in October 2009 surveys).

On July 16 the Assembly ratified a law that expands cooperation with NATO, including the opportunity to host military exercises. The opposition sharply criticized provisions in the law that allows that NATO personnel who commit a criminal act in Montenegro could only be tried in their home countries. NATO membership sparked protests in the streets of Podgorica in October 2015. Protesters reportedly threw fire bombs outside of the parliament, prompting the police to use teargas to disperse the crowd.

In July 2016 the government signed a €25 million deal with the German Development Bank as part of a broader €127 million project to improve power transmission by creating the Trans-Balkan Electricity Corridor.

POLITICAL PARTIES

In Montenegro, the Democratic Party of Socialists of Montenegro (DPS), successor to the League of Communists of Montenegro, has headed the government since the party's formation in the early 1990s, usually in alliance with the smaller Social Democratic Party of Montenegro (SDP). Other parties have proliferated, with 38 registered in 2009. Both the DPS and opposition parties have frequently turned to the use of coalitions.

For the October 2012 parliamentary election, five coalitions and eight individual parties offered candidate lists.

Government Parties:

Coalition for a European Montenegro (*Koalicija za Evropski Crna Gora*—KzECG). The KzECG is the latest variation in a series of coalitions led by the DPS starting in 1998, initially as an anti-Milošević grouping. In 2009 the coalition included the DPS, HGI, BS, and SDP. In the March 2009 elections the KzECG won 51.9 percent of the vote and 48 seats (47 in the national proportional vote, and 1 of the seats elected by the ethnic Albanian minority), securing a majority in parliament. In 2012 the minority parties chose to run independently, and the coalition included the DPS, SDP, and the LPCG. In the October 2012 elections, the KzECG won 46.3 percent of the vote and 39 seats.

Democratic Party of Socialists of Montenegro (*Demokratska Partija Socijalista Crne Gore*—DPS). The DPS is the successor to the **League of Communists of Montenegro.** In December 1992 it retained a majority in the Montenegrin legislative poll with 44 percent of the vote and finished fourth in the federal lower house. In November 1996 it increased its federal representation and maintained its majority at the republican level, winning 45 seats. Historically very close to Slobodan Milošević, the party suffered from intense internal squabbling as increasingly anti-Milošević Prime Minister Milo Djukanović narrowly beat Momir Bulatović in the 1997 Montenegrin presidential election and ousted him from the party leadership. The party split in January 1998, with the Bulatović faction forming the SNP (below).

In May 1998 the DPS won 30 of the **For a Better Life** (*Da Živimo Bolje*—DŽB) coalition's 42 legislative seats. Despite overtures from the anti-Milošević Democratic Opposition of Serbia alliance, the DPS chose to boycott the September 2000 federal elections, a major tactical error that left the anti-independence SNP in unchallenged control of the Montenegrin delegation to the federal Chamber of Citizens. In the April 2001 Montenegrin Assembly election the DPS-led **Victory Is Montenegro–Milo Djukanović Democratic Coalition** (*Pobjeda Je Crne Gore–Demokratska Koalicija Milo Djukanović*) coalition finished first, with 36 seats and 42 percent of the vote, but required the external support of the Liberal Alliance (see LPCG, below) to organize a government.

At the October 2002 republican election the DPS won 30 of the 39 seats (and 48 percent of the vote) won by the **Democratic List for European Montenegro–Milo Djukanović** (*Demokratska Lista za Evropsku Crnu Goru–Milo Djukanović*). An effort in late 2002 by President Djukanović and Prime Minister Filip Vujanović to, in effect, exchange jobs was finally accomplished in 2003. The DPS also held the office of state union president and was the leading Montenegrin party in the state union assembly, although it fully intended to lead Montenegro to independence.

The DPS introduced the independence referendum legislation in the assembly. After the Constitutional Court ruled the Minority Rights Act unconstitutional, the DPS leadership offered guaranteed slots in the assembly to several of the minority parties provided they join the DPS in an election coalition. It also promised to pursue legislation or a constitutional provision to undo the court ruling and reinstate the guaranteed legislative seats for ethnic minority parties.

In the September 2006 parliamentary election the DPS led the **Coalition for a European Montenegro–Milo Djukanović** (*Koalicija za Evropsku Crnu Goru–Milo Djukanović*), which also included the SDP and the Croat Civic Initiative, to a slim majority of 41 seats. In April 2008 the DPS candidate for the presidency, Filip Vujanović, was reelected in the first round with almost 52 percent of the vote, surprising analysts who had predicted two rounds of elections. In March 2009 the DPS won 35 seats as part of the Coalition for a European Montenegro list.

In early elections on October 14, 2012, the DPS won 30 seats again as part of the KzECG list. Djukanović accepted a new term as prime minister, while in the April 2013 presidential elections, DPS candidate Filip Vujanović was reelected to a third term with 51.2 percent of the vote.

Reports in June 2015 indicated a significant purge of senior party officials.

Leaders: Milo DJUKANOVIĆ (President of the Party and Prime Minister), Filip VUJANOVIĆ (President of the Republic and Vice President of the Party), Duško MARKOVIĆ (Deputy Prime Minister and Vice President of the Party), Igor LUKŠIĆ (Former Prime Minister).

Social Democratic Party of Montenegro (*Socijaldemokratska Partija Crne Gore*—SDP). Dating from the 1992 merger of three parties (two social democratic and one communist), the SDP was strongly pro-independence. It won one federal parliamentary seat in 1996. In the May 1998 Montenegrin legislative election, it won five seats as part of the For a Better Life coalition and joined the resultant government. It boycotted the 2000 federal election but again ran in coalition with the DPS in the April 2001 Montenegrin election. In October Ranko Krivokapić was elected party president, succeeding Žarko RAKČEVIĆ. In October 2002 the SDP won nine Montenegrin Assembly seats as part of the Democratic List. The SDP was once again in coalition with the DPS in 2006, both for the independence referendum and the September parliamentary election, at which it won seven seats. In the March 2009 elections the SDP won nine seats as part of the Coalition for a European Montenegro list; in the October 14, 2012, elections, the SDP again in the KzECG coalition won eight seats. In July 2015 SDP vice president Ivan BRAJOVIĆ left the party to form the Social Democrats of Montenegro (*Socijaldemokrate Crne Gore*—SD) (see below).

Leaders: Ranko KRIVOKAPIĆ (President of the Party); Vujica LAZOVIĆ, Rifat RASTODER, Raško KONJEVIĆ (Vice Presidents).

Liberal Party of Montenegro (*Liberalna Partija Crne Gore*—LPCG). The LPCG was established on October 31, 2004, under the leadership of Miodrag Živković, the former chair of the **Liberal Alliance of Montenegro** (*Liberalni Savez Crne Gore*—LSCG), following his expulsion from the LSCG in September.

Established in 1990 as a strong supporter of independence for Montenegro, the LSCG won 13 seats in the 1992 republican elections but failed to approach that total in subsequent contests. It won 6 seats in the April 2001 assembly election, after which it supported formation of a minority DPS-SDP government. Only a year later, however, it withdrew its support over objections to formation of the state union. In the resultant October 2002 Montenegrin election its representation fell to 4 seats, even though it had made major gains in municipal elections. In the May 2003 three-way republican presidential contest, Živković finished second, with 30 percent of the vote.

In 2004 the party split, largely over the issue of independence, leading to the Liberal Alliance chair's expulsion in September. On March 24, 2005, delegates to an extraordinary conference of the LSCG voted to end the Liberal Alliance party's existence. Longtime party leader Slavko PEROVIĆ condemned Montenegro's intelligentsia and opposition for abandoning their mission, and attacked the Djukanović regime as "mafia-ridden."

With the LSCG now defunct, LPCG leader Živković set his new party in support of independence but continued opposition to the alleged criminality and abuse of power by the Djukanović regime. (In July 2004 he had been found guilty of libeling the prime minister with salacious accusations.) It ran in alliance with the BS in 2006, winning only one seat.

For the 2009 elections the LPCG formed an electoral alliance with the **Democratic Center** (*Demokratskog Centra*—DC), the **For a Different Montenegro Coalition** (*Za Drugačiju Crnu Goru*—ZDCG). The ZDCG took 2.7 percent of the vote in the March 29, 2009, elections, failing to pass the threshold.

For the October 14, 2012, elections, the LPCG joined in coalition with the DPS and SDP, securing one seat.

Leaders: Andrija POPOVIĆ (Chair), Miodrag ŽIVKOVIĆ.

Bosniak Party (*Bošnjačka Stranka*—BS). The BS was established in February 2006 by merger of the **Bosniak Muslim Alliance**, the **International Democratic Union**, the **Bosniak Democratic Alternative**, and the **Party of National Equality**. With the independence referendum looming, the BS was seen as a vehicle for negotiating with both sides to achieve the most favorable terms for the Bosniak minority, which was split on the issue, in part because the Bosniak communities in the Sandžak region straddle the border between Serbia and Montenegro. In the end, the party chair, Rafet Husović, supported independence.

Afterwards, the BS rejected an overture by the DPS to join its coalition for the September 2006 parliamentary election and instead formed a coalition with the Liberal Party, the **Liberals and Bosniak Party–"Correct in the Past, Right in the Future"** (*Liberali i Bošnjačka Stranka–"Ispravni u Prošlosti, Pravi za Budnućnost"*), which won three seats.

Although not officially a party leader, the Sandžak politician Harun HADŽIĆ has been closely linked to the BS.

In the March 2009 elections, the BS won three seats as part of the KzECG list.

The BS ran independently in the October 14, 2012, elections, securing three seats with 4.2 percent of the vote.

Leaders: Rafet HUSOVIĆ (President and Minister for Regional Development), Suljo MUSTAFIĆ (Leader of Assembly Delegation).

New Democratic Force (*Nova Demokratska Snaga/Forca e Re Demokratike*—FORCA). FORCA was founded in October 2005 as a local ethnic Albanian political party in the coastal town of Ulcinj. FORCA subsequently expanded into other municipalities with a substantial ethnic Albanian minority. In the September 2006 parliamentary elections FORCA won 0.7 percent of the vote and no seats. In the March 29, 2009, elections, it won 1.9 percent of the vote and one of the seats elected by the ethnic Albanian minority.

For the October 14, 2012, elections, FORCA formed a coalition, the **Force for Unity** (*Forca za jedinstvo/Forca për Bashkim*—FzJ/FpB), with two smaller groups, the **Civic Initiative-Tuzi** and **Civil Movement "Perspective."** The coalition secured one of the minority seats, with 1.5 percent of the nationwide vote.

Leader: Nazif CUNGU (Chair).

Croat Civic Initiative (*Hrvatska Gradjanska Inicijativa*—HGI). The HGI was organized in 2002 prior to the October municipal elections in Tivat, in which it won four seats. The first Croat party to officially function in Montenegro since before World War II, it named Dalibor BURIĆ its first chair. It supported the independence referendum in 2006 and then in August agreed to join in the coalition formed by the DPS and SDP for the legislative election. It won one seat. Again competing with a DPS-led coalition in the March 2009 elections, the HGI won one seat as part of the coalition's list. In the October 14, 2012, elections it ran independently, securing one of the minority seats with 0.4 percent of the national vote.

Leader: Marija VUČINOVIĆ (President).

Albanian Coalition (*Albanska Koalicija/Koalicioni Shqiptare*—AK/KS). The AK/KS coalition includes the **Democratic Alliance in Montenegro** (*Demokratski Savez u Crnoj Gori/Lidhja Demokratike në Mal të Zi*—DSCG/LDMZ), the **Albanian Alternative** (*Albanska Alternativa/Alternativa Shqiptare*—AL/AS), and the **Democratic Party** (*Demokratska partija/Partia Demokratike*—DP/PD).

The DSCG and AL/AS each won a single parliamentary seat in the September 2006 parliamentary elections. For the March 2009 elections, the two parties formed the **Albanian List** (*Albanski List/Lista Shqiptare*—AL/LS), a coalition that won 0.9 percent of the national vote and secured a single seat in parliament from those elected by the ethnic Albanian minority.

Conflicting reports in 2011 and 2012 suggested the DP/PD had either merged or entered into an alliance with the **Albanian Coalition "Perspective"** (*Albanska Koalicija "Perspektiva"/Koalicioni Shqiptar "Perspektiva"*—AKP/KSP), a party founded in 2009 by dissident factions from several other parties and that had received 0.8 percent of the vote in the March 2009 elections, securing one of the minority seats in parliament.

In the October 14, 2012, elections, the AK/KS won one of the minority seats with 1.1 percent of the national vote.

Leader: Fatnur GJEKA (Chair).

Social Democrats of Montenegro (*Socijaldemokrate Crne Gore*—SD). The center-left SD was formed in July 2015 by defectors from the SPD, led by Ivan BRAJOVIĆ. It retained two cabinet posts in the DPS-led unity government.

Leader: Ivan BRAJOVIĆ.

Democratic Alliance (*Demokratski savez*—DEMOS). The center-right DEMOS split from the DF in 2015. Former DF leader Miodrag LEKIĆ left the party along with four parliamentarians. DEMOS joined the DPS-led unity government in May 2016.

Leader: Miodrag LEKIĆ.

United Reform Action (*Ujedinjena Reformska Akcija*—URA). The URA was established in March 2015 by defectors from the PCG and included two members of Parliament who were elected in 2012 from the PCG list. The URA joined the DPS-unity government in May 2016 but threatened to withdraw in August of that year.

Leader: Žarko RAKČEVIĆ.

Opposition Parties:

Democratic Front (*Demokratski front*—DF). Formed in July 2012 as an alliance of the opposition, the DF has a program that focuses on overturning the "authoritarian" rule of the DPS but also calls for anti-corruption reform, investigations into the privatization process, and the creation of a lustration commission. The DF includes the NSD, PzP and DSJ, and several small civic groups. In the October 14, 2012, elections, the DF secured 20 seats with 23.2 percent of the vote. Independent candidates affiliated with the DF but not with constituent parties were elected to six of those seats.

For the April 7, 2013, presidential elections, the DF along with the New Serb Democracy, Socialist People's Party, and Positive Montenegro joined to support the candidacy of Miodrag LEKIĆ as an independent opposition candidate. (Lekić, although president of the DF, was not a member of any of its constituent parties.)

Leader: Andrija MANDIĆ, Branko RADULOVIĆ, Nebojsa MEDOJEVIĆ, Milan KNEZEVIĆ, Vladisav BOJOVIĆ.

New Serb Democracy (*Nova Srpska Demokratija*—NSD). The NSD was formed in January 2009 as a merger between the **Serbian People's Party** (*Srpska Narodna Stranka*—SNS) and the **People's Socialist Party of Montenegro** (*Narodna Socijalistička Stranka Crne Gore*—NSS).

The Serbian People's Party was registered as a party in March 1998 by a dissident faction of the NS (below). Although the party supported the Milošević regime through the Kosovo crisis, some local party leaders refused to support the federal president's reelection in 2000. A party congress in February 2001 elected former NS leader Božidar Bojović as chair, succeeding Zelidrag NIKČEVIĆ. In October 2002 the SNS won six seats in the Montenegrin legislature. A year later Bojović was replaced by current leader Andrija Mandić and quickly formed the DSS.

The SNS joined the pro-union coalition in opposition to the 2006 independence referendum. Postreferendum news accounts alleged that SNS party members attributed the success of the referendum vote to the support of ethnic minority voters and therefore demonstrated increased hostility toward ethnic minorities, especially Bosniaks, in Serb-dominated areas.

After independence, SNS leaders positioned the party to advocate for policies aimed at protecting the status of Serbs in Montenegro. The SNS launched a petition drive advocating dual Serbian citizenship for Montenegrin Serbs, and party leaders publicly called for measures to preserve cultural autonomy and proportional representation in political institutions for Serbs. It parted ways with a key ally, the SNP, prior to the September 2006 election and instead headed the **Serbian List–Andrija Mandić** (*Srpska Lista–Andrija Mandić*), which included another frequent ally, the Montenegrin branch of the Serbian Radical Party (see SSR, below), as well as the Democratic Party of Unity (DSJ, below), the NSS, and a nongovernmental organization, the Serb National Council (*Srpsko Naradno Veće*—SNV). The SNS won 8 of the list's 12 seats, with each of the other four organizations in the coalition claiming 1. Mandić was reelected president in December 2006. As PzP president, he has endorsed strongly pro-Serbian policies, including opposition to the 2007 constitution (for formally changing the national language to Montenegrin from Serbian) and organizing rallies against any Montenegrin recognition of Kosovo's independence. Mandić himself has taken dual Montenegrin and Serbian citizenship. In the 2008 presidential elections the SNS-led Serbian List nominated Mandić as a common candidate, taking second place with almost a fifth of the vote. Following the government's decision to recognize an independent Kosovo in October 2008, the SNS led the Serbian List in a boycott of parliamentary functions.

The NSS was established in February 2001 by supporters of former FRY prime minister Momir Bulatović following his ouster from the SNP. The party failed to attract significant support in the April 2001 Montenegrin Assembly election, capturing less than 3 percent of the vote and therefore winning no seats. In 2002 it ran as a component of the Patriotic Coalition for Yugoslavia (*Patriotska Koalicija za Jugoslavia*—PK), which also included the Serbia-based Yugoslav United Left and Serbian Radical Party, but again failed to meet the 3 percent threshold. In 2006, as a component of the Serbian List, the NSS won one parliamentary seat.

The unified NSD won 9.2 percent of the vote in March 2009, securing eight seats.

In the October 14, 2012, elections, the NSD received eight seats from the coalition's total.

Leaders: Andrija MANDIĆ (President); Goran DANILOVIĆ (Deputy President); Emilo LABUDOVIĆ, Slaven RADULOVIĆ, Strahinja BULAJIĆ (Vice Presidents).

Movement for Change (*Pokret za Promjene*—PzP). The PzP began as a nongovernmental organization, the Group for Change (*Grupa za Promjene*—GzP), which was a significant participant in public discourse from its founding in 2002. Modeled on Serbia's G17 Plus think tank of economists, the GzP focused in part on ending corruption in the public sector, which it attributed primarily to the dominance of the DPS under Milo Djukanović. Its principal leaders, Executive Director Nebojša Medojević and Chair Svetozar JOVIĆEVIĆ, ranked among Montenegro's most respected public figures in the period leading up to independence. Many of its members appeared to support independence, but the GzP itself did not take a stand on the referendum.

Registered as a party in July 2006, the PzP surprised most observers by winning 11 legislative seats in September. As part of the opposition, it has frequently been allied with the leading Serbian parties, although it supported adoption of the 2007 constitution. Medojević, the party's candidate in the 2008 presidential elections, took third place with almost 17 percent of the vote in the first round. In the March 2009 elections the party took approximately 6 percent of the vote and 5 seats.

In the October 14, 2012, elections, the PzP received five seats from the coalition's total.

Leaders: Nebojša MEDOJEVIĆ (President); Branko RADULOVIĆ (Deputy President); Zoran MARSENIĆ, Branka BOŠNJAK, Koča PAVLOVIĆ, Veljko VASILJEVIĆ (Vice Presidents).

Democratic Party of Unity (*Demokratska Stranka Jedinstva*—DSJ). The DSJ is a new party registered in mid-2006 by Zoran ŽIŽIĆ, who was previously vice chair of the SNP. Žižić left the SNP when that party declined to join the Serbian List coalition in the run-up to the September 10 polls. Failing to reach a coalition accord with the SNP or the Serbian List, the DSJ did not enter the March 2009 elections. In the October 14, 2012, elections, the DSJ received a single seat from the coalition's total.

Leader: Zoran ŽIŽIĆ (Chair).

Socialist People's Party of Montenegro (*Socijalistička Narodna Partija Crne Gore*—SNP). The SNP was formed in early 1998 by Momir Bulatović following his rupture with the DPS. It held its first congress in March 1998. In the republican election of May 1998 the party came in second, with 29 seats.

Under FRY Prime Minister Bulatović, the party maintained strict support for Slobodan Milošević through the September 2000 election. Because the governing Montenegrin coalition boycotted the balloting, the SNP virtually swept the Montenegrin polls, winning 19 of the republic's 20 upper house seats and 28 seats in the lower house. With Bulatović having resigned the federal prime ministership following Milošević's concession, the party's vice chair, Zoran ŽIŽIĆ, was selected as his successor by newly installed President Koštunica in late October.

The chair passed from Momir Bulatović to an opponent, Predrag BULATOVIĆ (no relation), at a party congress in February 2001, after which the SNP formed the Together for Yugoslavia (*Zajedno za Jugoslaviju*) alliance with the SNS (see above) and the NS (see below) to contest the April Montenegrin legislative election, subsequently winning 30 seats with 38 percent of the vote. Following the June 2001 extradition to The Hague of Milošević to stand trial before the International Criminal Tribunal for the former Yugoslavia (ICTY), Prime Minister Žižić resigned in protest, but he was succeeded in mid-July by another SNP member, Dragiša Pešić, who remained in office until FRY was replaced by the state union. In the 2002 republican election the party won 19 of the 30 seats claimed by the Together for Changes coalition.

The SNP joined the other opposition parties in street protests against the DPS-SDP government throughout 2004 and the boycott of parliament in the same year. The SNP also spearheaded the pro-union coalition in opposition to the 2006 independence referendum. After the vote for independence, Predrag Bulatović steered the party toward a pragmatic "constructive dialogue" on post-independence platform issues, especially the need for a draft constitution, support for more democratic institutions, and engagement with the path toward European integration.

Negotiations toward a pre-election coalition with the other opposition parties were complicated by charges by SNP leaders of "poaching" tactics by the other opposition parties, especially the SNS, directed at SNP voters. In the end, the SNP and SNS formed separate coalitions, with the SNP leading the **SNP-NS-DSS Koalicija,** which won 11 parliamentary seats, 8 of them by the SNP. As a result of the poor showing, Bulatović resigned as chair in October. At the party's Fifth Congress, held in late November, Srdjan Milić defeated Dragiša Pešić and Borislav GLOBAREVIĆ for the leadership. Three deputy chairs were named in January 2007. Milić, nominated by the party for the 2008 presidential election, took almost 12 percent of the vote in the first round, placing fourth.

In the March 29, 2009, elections the SNP won 16.83 percent of the vote, for 16 seats in parliament.

In May 2010 the SNP led, along with the PzP and NSD, a broad coalition of 12 opposition parties to oppose the DPS in municipal elections. The coalition won only 2 of the 14 municipalities, highlighting the continued weakness of the opposition.

The SNP entered negotiations with the DF (see above) regarding an electoral coalition but was unable to secure an agreement on the future allocation of seats. In response, a dissident faction of the party left to join the DF.

In the October 14, 2012, elections, the SNP secured nine seats with 11.2 percent of the vote.

Leaders: Srdjan MILIĆ (President); Milorad BAKIĆ, Vasilije LALOŠEVIĆ, Neven GOŠOVIĆ, Radoman GOGIĆ (Vice Presidents).

Positive Montenegro (*Pozitivna Crna Gora*—PCG). The PCG was founded as a self-described "center-left" party in May 2012, advocating socioeconomic issues, anticorruption reform, and socially responsible environmental policies.

In the October 14, 2012, elections, the PCG secured seven seats with 8.4 percent of the vote. In 2015 defectors from the PCG created the **United Reform Action** (*Ujedinjena Reformska Akcija*—URA).

Leaders: Darko PAJOVIĆ (President), Azra JASAVIĆ (Deputy President and Deputy Prime Minister), Goran TUPONJA (Secretary General).

Other Parties That Contested the 2012 Elections:

Serbian Unity (*Srpska sloga*—SS). An electoral coalition formed in August 2012 for the October parliamentary elections and included the People's Party, the **Serbian Homeland Party** (*Otadžbinska srpska stranka*—OSS), the **Democratic Center of Boka** (*Demokratski Centar* Boke—DCB), the Montenegrin chapter of the **Serbian Radical Party** (*Srpska radikalna stranka*—SRS), and the **Serbian List** (*Srpska lista*—SL), a new party founded in January 2012.

In the October 14, 2012, elections, the SS won 1.5 percent of the vote, failing to pass the threshold.

People's Party (*Narodna Stranka*—NS). Historically an intensely pan-Serbian formation, the NS supported the maintenance of Montenegro's ties with Serbia. It won 14 seats and 13 percent of the vote in the December 1992 Montenegrin election. In November 1996 an NS coalition with the Liberal Alliance (see LPCG, below) called the People's Accord (*Narodna Sloga*) won 19 seats in the Montenegrin legislature as well as 8 federal seats. In March 1997 differences over continuing support for the coalition led supporters of the party's vice chair, Božidar Bojović, to attempt expulsion of the president, Novak KILIBARDA, who was moving closer toward accepting Montenegrin independence. Kilibarda's NS joined the DPS in forming the For a Better Life coalition shortly before the May 1998 Montenegrin election, in which it won 7 seats. In the same month the Bojović faction registered a new pro-Belgrade party, the SNS. Kilibarda joined the governing Montenegrin coalition as a deputy prime minister.

In March 2000, rejecting Kilibarda's pro-independence stance, the NS replaced him with Dragan ŠOĆ, the Montenegrin minister of justice. On December 28, objecting to the latest independence moves by President Djukanović, the NS left the governing coalition and subsequently allied itself with the SNP for the April 2001 election. (Kilibarda, meanwhile, had established the **People's Accord of Montenegro** [*Narodna Sloga Crne Gore*—NSCG], which has not played a notable role in Montenegrin politics.) In October 2002 it won five assembly seats as part of the Together for Changes coalition.

After independence, the NS leaders rebuffed SNS proposals for a Serbian List in favor of working to preserve the broader pro-union coalition with the SNP and DSS. In the September 2006 election the NS won 2 of the SNP-NS-DSS Coalition's 11 seats and then formed a 3-member parliamentary floor group with the DSS representative.

In February 2009 the NS formed an electoral alliance with the DSS, the **People's Coalition** (*Narodjačka Koalicija*—NK) but then failed to draw in the SNP or NSD. In the March 29, 2009, elections the NK took 2.9 percent of the vote, failing to pass the threshold.

Leader: Predrag POPOVIĆ (Chair).

Serbian National Alliance (*Srpski Nacionalni Savez*—SNS). The DSS formed this electoral alliance of Serbian parties in September 2012, along with the SSR and the **Serbian National Council** (*Srpskog narodno veće*—SNV). In the October 14, 2012, elections the SNS won 0.9 percent of the vote, failing to pass the threshold.

Democratic Serbian Party (*Demokratska Srpska Stranka*—DSS). This Montenegrin-based version of Serbia's DSS was launched by former NS and SNS party leader Božidar Bojović in December 2003. The DSS joined the opposition parties' street protests against the DPS-SDP government throughout 2004. The DSS also joined the pro-union coalition in opposition to the 2006 independence referendum. After the referendum DSS leaders rebuffed calls from the SNS for a Serbian list to contest the 2006 parliamentary elections, advocating instead for preservation of the larger pro-union coalition of parties.

Leaders: Ranko KADIĆ (Chair), Božidar BOJOVIĆ.

Party of Serb Radicals (*Stranka Srpskih Radikala*—SSR). The SSR began as the Montenegrin branch of Serbia's Serbian Radical Party (*Srpska Radikalna Stranka*—SRS), which was founded in February 1991 by Vojislav Šešelj, the radical pan-Serbian leader being tried by the ICTY for crimes against humanity.

The Montenegrin SRS joined the Serbian List in the run-up to the 2006 election and came away with one seat. In December it adopted its current name because the inclusion of Šešelj's name in the party's formal title violated Montenegro's law on political parties. Although legally independent of Serbia's SRS, the SSR leadership has stated that in all other respects they are the same. Confusingly, a party named the SRS registered in 2012 as part of the Serbian Unity coalition (see above).

In the March 2009 elections, the SSR headed a new **Serb National List** (*Srpska Nacionalna Lista*—SNL) coalition, with the SNV and a faction of the SNS. The coalition received 1.3 percent of the vote, failing to pass the threshold.

Leaders: Duško SEKULIĆ (Chair), Bojan STRUNJAŠ.

Democratic Union of Albanians (*Demokratska Unija Albanaca*—DUA/*Unioni Demokratih i Shqiptarëve*—UDSh). In the 2002 legislative election the DUA ran as the Democratic Coalition **"Albanians Together"** (*"Albanci Zajedno"*), which won two seats reserved for the Albanian community. The coalition included two other ethnic Albanian parties, the DSCG and the **Party for Democratic Prosperity**. In April 2001 the three had run independently, with the DUA and the DSCG each winning one seat.

In 2006 the DUA supported independence but chose to run alone in the parliamentary election, in which it won one seat and then joined the governing coalition. In the March 2009, elections the DUA again ran alone, winning 1.5 percent of the vote and one of the seats in parliament reserved for election by the ethnic Albanian minority.

In the October 2012 election, the DUA won 0.8 percent of the vote, failing to pass the threshold.

Leaders: Mehmed ZENKA (President), Ferhat DINOŠA (Honorary President).

Together (*Zajedno*). This coalition included the **Party of Pensioners and Disabled People of Montenegro** (*Stranka Penzionera i Invalida Crne Gore*) and the **Yugoslav Communist Party of Montenegro** (*Jugoslovenska Komunistička Partija Crne Gore*—JKPCG). In September 2009 the JKPCG merged with the **Montenegrin Communists** (*Crnogorski Komunisti*).

The coalition won 0.4 percent of the vote, failing to pass the threshold.

Albanian Youth Alliance (*Albanska omladinska alijansa/Aleanca Rinore e Shqiptarëve*—AOA/ARS). A newly founded citizen's initiative, the AOA/ARS received 0.2 percent of the vote, failing to pass the threshold.

Leader: Anton LULGJURAJ.

LEGISLATURE

Assembly of the Republic of Montenegro (*Skupština Republike Crne Gore*). The 81 members of the assembly (sometimes referred to as parliament) are elected to four-year terms by proportional representation. Parties must meet a 3 percent threshold to qualify for 76 national seats; the Albanian minority elects 5 other representatives. Results for the election of October 14, 2012, were as follows: Coalition for a European Montenegro, 39 seats (Democratic Party of Socialists of Montenegro, 30; Social Democratic Party, 8; Liberal Party of Montenegro, 1); Democratic Front, 20 (New Serb Democracy, 8; Movement for Changes, 5; Democratic Party of Unity, 1; independent, 6); Socialist People's Party of Montenegro, 9; Positive Montenegro, 7; Bosniak Party, 3; New Democratic Force, 1; Albanian Coalition, 1; and Croat Civic Initiative, 1.

President: Darko PAJOVIĆ.

CABINET

[as of July 15, 2016]

Prime Minister	Milo Djukanović (DPS)
Deputy Prime Minister for Economic Policy and Financial System	Vujica Lazović (SD)
Deputy Prime Minister for Political System, Foreign, and Interior Policy	Duško Marković (DPS)
Deputy Prime Minister for Regional Development	Rafet Husović (BS)
Deputy Prime Ministers	Petar Ivanovic (ind.) Azra Jasavić (PCG) [f]
Ministers	
Agriculture	Milenko Popović (ind.)
Culture	Pavle Goranović (ind.)
Defense	Milica Pejanović-Djurišić (DPS) [f]
Economy	Vladimir Kavarić (DPS)
Education and Sport	Predrag Bošković (DPS)
Finance	Rasko Konjević (SDP)
Foreign Affairs	(Vacant)
Health	Budmir Šegrt (DPS)
Human and Minority Rights	Suad Numanović (DPS)
Interior	Goran Danilović (DEMOS)
Justice	Zoran Pažin (ind.)
Labor and Social Welfare	Boris Marić (nominated by URA)
Science	Sanja Vlahović (DPS) [f]
Sustainable Development and Tourism	Branimir Gvozdenović (DPS)
Transportation and Maritime Affairs	Ivan Brajović (SD)
Without Portfolio	Marija Vučinović (HGI) [f]

[f] = female

INTERGOVERNMENTAL REPRESENTATION

Ambassador to the U.S.: Srdjan DARMANOVIĆ.

U.S. Ambassador to Montenegro: Margaret UYEHARA.

Permanent Representative to the UN: Željko PEROVIĆ.

IGO Memberships (Non-UN): EBRD, ICC, IOM, OSCE, WTO.

For Further Reference:

Dzankic, Jelena. "Citizenship between the 'Image of the Nation' and 'the Image of Politics': The Case of Montenegro." *Journal of Southeast European & Black Sea Studies* 14, no. 1 (March 2014): 43–64.

Jenne, Erin K., and Florian Bieber. "Situational Nationalism: Nation-building in the Balkans, Subversive Institutions and the Montenegrin Paradox." *Ethnopolitics* 13, no. 5 (October 2014): 431–460.

Prekic, Adnan. "The Religious Community and the Communist Regime in the Case of Montenegro, 1945–1955." *Journal for the Study of Religions & Ideologies* 15, no. 44 (Summer 2016): 111–136.

MOROCCO

Kingdom of Morocco
al-Mamlakat al-Maghribiyah

Political Status: Independent since March 2, 1956; constitutional monarchy established in 1962; present constitution approved by referendum on July 1, 2011.

Area: 274,461 sq. mi. (710,850 sq. km), including approximately 97,343 sq. mi. (252,120 sq. km) of Western Sahara, two-thirds of which was annexed in February 1976 and the remaining one-third claimed upon Mauritanian withdrawal in August 1979.

Population: 34,817,000 (2016E—UN); 33,655,786 (2016E—U.S. Census).

Major Urban Centers (2016E—UN): RABAT/SALE (2,004,000), Casablanca (3,544,000), FEZ (1,197,000), Marrakesh (1,168,000), Tangier (1,016,000).

Official Languages: Arabic and Tamazight.

Monetary Unit: Dirham (official rate October 1, 2016: 9.73 dirhams = $1US).

Sovereign: King MOHAMED VI became king on July 23, 1999, following the death of his father, HASSAN II.

Heir to the Throne: Crown Prince MOULAY HASSAN.

Prime Minister: Abdelillah BENKIRANE (Justice and Development Party), appointed on November 29, 2011, succeeding Abbas EL FASSI (*Istiqlal*); formed new government following legislative elections on October 7, 2016.

THE COUNTRY

Located at the northwest corner of Africa, Morocco combines a long Atlantic coastline and Mediterranean frontage facing Gibraltar and southern Spain. Bounded by Algeria on the northeast and (following annexation of the former Spanish Sahara) by Mauritania on the south, the country is topographically divided into a rich agricultural plain in the northwest and an infertile mountain and plateau region in the east that gradually falls into the Sahara in the south and southwest. The population is mostly Arabized Amazigh (Berber), with small French and Spanish minorities. Islam is the state religion. Most of the population adheres to the Sunni branch and follows the Maliki School. Moroccan Arabic is the spoken language of the majority, most others speaking one or more variations of Tamazight (Berber languages); Spanish is common in the northern regions and French among the educated elite. Women comprise 35 percent of the paid labor force, concentrated mainly in textile manufacture and domestic service; overall, one-third of the female population is engaged in unpaid family labor on agricultural estates. Increasing numbers of women from upper-income brackets have participated in local and national elections but have obtained minimal representation. In the 2009 local elections women gained just over 3,400 seats as the result of legislation that guaranteed women a minimum of 12 percent of the total seats. This was an increase in representation of 250 percent over the 2003 balloting. Following the 2016 parliamentary elections, women held 14 of 120 seats in the upper chamber (11.7 percent) and 81 of 395 seats in the lower chamber (20.5 percent). Past abuses of human rights, including the disappearance of dissenters, have diminished. The reform of the Personal Status Code (Moudawana) in 2004 improved the official legal status of women in Moroccan society. For example, the legal age for marriage rose from 15 to 18, but judges grant many exceptions, and child marriage is still common.

The agricultural sector employs approximately 39 percent of the population; important crops include cereals and grains, oilseeds, nuts, and citrus fruits. One of the world's leading exporters of phosphates, Morocco also has important deposits of lead, iron, cobalt, zinc, manganese, and silver; overall, mining accounts for about 45 percent of export receipts. The industrial sector emphasizes import substitution (textiles, chemicals, cement, plastics, machinery), while tourism and fishing are also major sources of income. Trade is strongly oriented toward France, whose economic influence has remained substantial. Since the early 1980s the economy has suffered from periodic droughts, declining world demand for phosphates, rapid urbanization, and high population growth. Unemployment remains a problem, with youth and talent seeking opportunity in Europe. Continued dependence on the agricultural sector of the economy remains a problem.

Living conditions remain low by regional standards, and wealth is poorly distributed. However, some developed (particularly European) countries consider Morocco, with its low inflation rate and cheap labor pool, a potential target for substantial investment. To encourage such interest, the government continues to privatize many state-run enterprises, address the literacy rate (67.1 percent, the lowest in the Arab world), and reform the stock market, tax system, and banking sector. However, the pace of reform remains somewhat sluggish.

A more costly wage structure and higher oil subsidies contributed to a rapidly rising budget deficit and a concurrent drop in the GDP growth rate to 1.2 percent in 2005. However, a 2004 free trade agreement with the United States (see Foreign relations, below) took effect in January 2006, improving prospects for increased direct foreign investment. Concurrently, Morocco's decision to allow private purchase of shares in the largest state-owned bank and the state telecommunications company further enhanced the climate for foreign capital. A widespread drought in 2007 hindered grain production that year and the following one.

Although in 2008 the agricultural sector recovered from the droughts of previous years, the worldwide economic crisis constrained growth as remittances from Moroccans living abroad declined by 9.7 percent, while exports were down 34 percent and imports fell by 23 percent. Nonetheless, GDP grew by 3.6 percent in 2010 and 5 percent in 2011. In August 2011 the European Union (EU) granted Morocco €185 million to support economic development and antipoverty programs. GDP grew by 5 percent in 2012, while inflation remained low at 1.3 percent. In 2012 the International Monetary Fund (IMF) provided Morocco a $6.2 billion line of credit in exchange for a pledge to reduce a range of consumer subsidies. In 2013 unemployment was 8.8 percent. GDP rose by 2.4 in 2014 and 4.5 percent in 2015. The IMF estimated GDP grew by 2.3 percent in 2016, while inflation was 1.5 percent, unemployment was 9.8 percent, and GDP per capita was $3,195. In 2016 the World Bank ranked Morocco 75th out of 185 countries in its annual survey on the ease of doing business, second only to Tunisia (74th) among the Maghreb states and a significant improvement from 97th in 2013.

GOVERNMENT AND POLITICS

Political background. Originally inhabited by Amazigh peoples, Morocco was successively conquered by the Phoenicians, Carthaginians, Romans, Byzantines, and Arabs. From 1912 to 1956 the country was subjected to de facto French and Spanish control, but the internal authority of the sultan was nominally respected. Under pressure by Moroccan nationalists, the French and Spanish relinquished their protectorates, and the country was reunified under Sultan MOHAMED V in 1956. Tangier, which had been under international administration since 1923, was ceded by Spain in 1969.

King Mohamed V tried to convert the hereditary sultanate into a modern constitutional monarchy but died before the process was

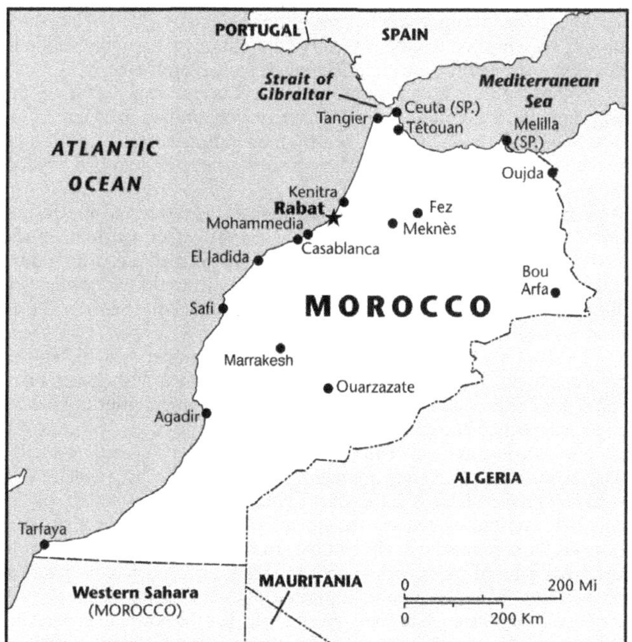

complete. It remained for his son, King HASSAN II, to implement his father's goal in a constitution adopted in December 1962. However, dissatisfaction with economic conditions and the social policy of the regime led to rioting at Casablanca in March 1965, and three months later the king assumed legislative and executive powers.

In June 1967 the king relinquished the post of prime minister, but the continued hostility of student and other elements led to frequent governmental changes. A new constitution, approved in July 1970, provided for a partial resumption of parliamentary government, strengthening of royal powers, and a limited role for political parties. Despite the opposition of major political groups, trade unions, and student organizations, an election for a new unicameral House of Representatives occurred on August 1970, yielding a progovernment majority. However, the king's failure to unify the country behind his programs was dramatically illustrated by abortive military revolts in 1971 and 1972.

Popular referendum overwhelmingly approved a new constitution in March 1972, but the parties refused to enter the government because of the monarch's reluctance to schedule legislative elections. After numerous delays, elections to communal and municipal councils finally took place in November 1976, to provincial and prefectural assemblies in January 1977, and to a reconstituted national House of Representatives in June 1977. On October 10 the leading parties agreed to participate in a "National Unity" cabinet headed by Ahmed OSMAN as prime minister.

Osman resigned on March 21, 1979, ostensibly to oversee reorganization of the proroyalist National Assembly of Independents (RNI), although the move was reported to have been precipitated by his handling of the lengthy dispute over the Western Sahara (see Disputed Territory, below). He was succeeded on March 22 by Maati BOUABID, a respected Casablanca attorney.

On May 30, 1980, a constitutional amendment extending the term of the House of Representatives from four to six years was approved by referendum, thus postponing new elections until 1983. The king indicated in June 1983 that the legislative poll, scheduled for early September, would be further postponed pending the results of a referendum in the Western Sahara to be sponsored by the Organization of African Unity (OAU, subsequently the African Union—AU). On November 30 a new "unity" cabinet headed by Mohamed Karim LAMRANI was announced, with Bouabid, who had organized a new moderate party eight months earlier, joining other party leaders in accepting appointment as ministers of state without portfolio.

The long-awaited legislative poll was finally held on September 14 and October 2, 1984, with Bouabid's Constitutional Union (UC) winning a plurality of both direct and indirectly elected seats, while four centrist parties collectively obtained a better than two-to-one majority. Following lengthy negotiations, a new coalition government, headed by Lamrani, was formed on April 11, 1985.

Although King Hassan appeared to remain popular with most of his subjects, domestic opposition leaders and Amnesty International continued to charge the government with human rights abuses and repression of dissent, including the alleged illegal detention and mistreatment of numerous leftists and Islamic extremists arrested in 1985 and 1986. On September 30, 1986, the king appointed Dr. Azzedine LARAKI, former national education minister, as prime minister, following Lamrani's resignation for health reasons.

Attributed in large measure to improvements in the economy, calm ensued, with domestic and international attention focusing primarily on the Western Sahara. Thus, a national referendum on December 1, 1989, overwhelmingly approved the king's proposal to postpone legislative elections due in 1990, ostensibly to permit participation by Western Saharans following a self-determination vote in the disputed territory.

In mid-1992, amid indications that the referendum might be delayed indefinitely or even abandoned, the government announced that forthcoming local and national elections would include the residents of Western Sahara as participants. On August 11 King Hassan reappointed Lamrani as prime minister and announced a "transitional cabinet" to serve until a postelection cabinet could be established under new constitutional provisions (see Constitution and government, below).

The basic law revisions were approved on September 4, 1992, by a national referendum, which the government hailed as a significant step in its ongoing democratization program. Widespread disbelief greeted the government's claim that 97.5 percent of the electorate had participated and that a 99.9 percent "yes" vote had been registered.

In balloting for directly elective house seats, delayed until June 25, 1993, the newly established Democratic Bloc (*Koutla*), a coalition of center-left opposition groups led by the old-guard *Istiqlal* party and the Socialist Union of Popular Forces (USFP), secured 99 seats. They won only 15 more in the September 17 voting in electoral colleges made up of local officials, trade unionists, and representatives of professional associations. Meanwhile, the National Entente (*Wifaq*), a group of center-right royalist parties, increased its representation from 116 in the first round of balloting to 195 after the second. The Democratic Bloc subsequently charged that the indirect election encompassed widespread fraud, an allegation that received some support from international observers.

Although King Hassan rejected the Democratic Bloc's demand that the results of the indirect poll be overturned, he did propose that the bloc participate in the formation of a new cabinet, the first of what the king envisioned as a series of alternating left-right governments. The offer was declined because of the monarch's insistence that he retain the right to appoint the prime minister and maintain de facto control of the foreign, justice, and interior portfolios. Consequently, Lamrani formed a new nonparty government on November 11.

With his poor health again cited as the official reason for the change, Lamrani was succeeded on May 25, 1994, by former foreign minister Abdellatif FILALI, a longtime close adviser to the king. On June 7 Filali presented the monarch with a ministerial list unchanged from that of his predecessor, while King Hassan continued to seek Democratic Bloc leadership of a new coalition government. The negotiations eventually collapsed in early 1995, in part because of the king's wish that Driss BASRI, long-term minister of state for interior and information, remain in the cabinet. The opposition parties had objected to Basri's influence for many years, charging that he had sanctioned human rights abuses and tolerated electoral fraud. Nonetheless, Basri retained the interior post on February 28 when Filali's new government, including 20 members of the National Entente, was announced.

Despite his failure to draw the leftist parties into the government, the king continued to pursue additional democratization, particularly regarding the proposed creation of an upper house of the legislature that, theoretically, would redistribute authority away from the monarchy to a certain degree. A reported 99.56 percent "yes" vote in a national referendum on September 13, 1996, affirmed the king's proposal. Most opposition parties endorsed the amendment (see Constitution and government, below).

Local elections occurred on June 13, 1997, with seats being distributed along a wide spectrum of parties with no apparent particular political dominance. Such was also the case with the November 14 balloting for a new House of Representatives as the *Koutla, Wifaq,* and a bloc of centrist parties each won about one-third of the seats. On the other hand, the indirect elections to the new House of Councilors revealed a decided tilt toward the *Wifaq,* not a surprising result considering its long-standing progovernment stance.

Continuing to pursue an alternating left-right series of governments, King Hassan was subsequently able to finally persuade the Democratic Bloc to assume cabinet control, and on February 4, 1998, he appointed Abderrahmane YOUSSOUFI of the USFP (which had won the most seats in the House of Representatives) as the next prime minister. As formed on March 14, the new cabinet included representatives from seven parties, although the King's supporters (most notably Basri) remained in several key posts.

King Hassan, whose health had been a concern since 1995, died of a heart attack on July 23, 1999; Crown Prince SIDI MOHAMED succeeded his father immediately. The official ceremony marking his enthronement as King MOHAMED VI took place on July 30. Shortly thereafter, Driss Basri, who was nicknamed "The Butcher" by human rights activists and had presided over a period of government crackdowns on the opposition, was dismissed as minister of the interior and moved to Paris. The new king confirmed his support for Prime Minister Youssoufi and his government. The cabinet was reshuffled on September 6, 2000, with Youssoufi retaining the top post, but the new king replaced him with an independent, Driss JETTOU, in 2002.

Palace officials were concerned by the rise of radical Islamists who were spurred on by the Iraq War. Several suicide attacks on one day in early 2003 in Casablanca killed more than 40 people. Some 2,000 Moroccans were convicted of the bombings, with several given death sentences and others long prison terms. A new antiterrorism law was swiftly passed amid concerns in the media that increased powers of detention and surveillance would erode the gains in human rights.

In 2005 a Moroccan truth commission—formally called the Equity and Reconciliation Commission (IER)—released its final report on alleged human rights abuses during the reign of King Hassan. The commission, described as the first of its kind in the Arab world, had been set up in January 2004. The commission reported that between independence in 1956 and the end of Hassan's rule in 1999, nearly 600 people were killed and that opposition activists were systematically suppressed, with numerous instances of torture and disappearances. Many prodemocracy activists, including the Moroccan Association for Human Rights, criticized the panel for its policy of withholding the names of those found responsible for the abuses and for not recommending prosecution of the perpetrators. The hearings were televised throughout the country, an event unprecedented in the region.

Parliamentary elections in September 2007 maintained a conservative government. After a record low turnout of 37 percent, the party *Istiqlal,* a member of the Democratic Bloc, took control. Abbass EL FASSI was appointed prime minister on September 19, 2007, and on October 15 formed a cabinet that reflected the king's desire for a moderately conservative, reformist government.

In January 2007 the militant Algerian organization *Groupe Salafiste pour la Predication et Combat* (GSPC) became Al-Qaida in the Islamic Maghreb (AQIM), suggesting potential regionwide cooperation among militant groups. Since then, the government has made several high-profile preventive arrests, reporting in July 2008 that it had found 55 terrorist cells since 2003. One such alleged cell included the Islamist political party the Civilized Alternative (*Al-Badil al-Hadari*). In February 2008 officials arrested 32 members of the group including leader Mustapha MOUATASSIME and revoked its legal status for suspected ties to clandestine extremist groups, including al-Qaida. Prior to local balloting in June 2009 the newly formed Party of Authenticity and Modernity (PAM), which included a number of members of the House of Representatives who had defected from other parties, announced it would join the opposition (see Political Parties, below). PAM placed first in the local elections, followed by *Istiqlal* in the contest to select more than 28,000 local councilors. During the balloting, Fatima Zahra Mansouri of the PAM became the first woman elected mayor of a major city, Marrakech, and only the second woman ever elected to lead a city in Morocco. Women won 12 percent of the seats in the balloting. In July there was a minor cabinet reshuffle which brought the Popular Movement (MP) into the government and expanded the number of ministers from the USFP and the RNI. The reshuffle was undertaken in order to maintain the government's majority in the legislature following the defection of deputies to PAM. As a result, the government had the support of 200 of the 325 deputies in the House. In regional balloting in September, the PAM won the chairpersonship of four of the eight regions. In indirect elections for one-third of the upper chamber in parliament, the PAM won 22 of 90 seats, followed by *Istiqlal* with 17 and the MP with 11.

There was a minor cabinet reshuffle in January 2010. That same month, the king created the Advisory Committee on Regionalization to develop recommendations to reform regional governments.

Following prodemocracy protests (see Current issues, below), the king appointed a committee to draft a new constitution in March 2011. The new basic law was approved by referendum on July 1 with 98.5 percent of the vote in favor (although some opposition groups boycotted the voting).

Early elections were held on November 25, 2011, and the Justice and Development Party (PJD) won a majority (see Current issues, below). PJD leader Abdelillah BENKIRANE formed a coalition government on January 3, 2012. *Istiqlal* withdrew from the government on July 8, 2013, and its ministers resigned from the cabinet on July 22 (see Current issues, below).

The PJD won a plurality of 125 seats in the October 7, 2016, legislative elections. Benkirane was appointed to form a new government three days later. Twelve ministers left the government after the balloting because they had been elected to the legislature.

Constitution and government. Morocco is a constitutional monarchy. The crown is hereditary and normally transmitted to the king's eldest son, who acts on the advice of a Regency Council if he accedes before age 20. The 2011 constitution reduces the monarch's authority. However, the king remains the commander in chief of the armed forces and has the power to declare a state of emergency, veto legislation, and initiate constitutional amendments. The king appoints the prime minister from the largest party in the legislature. Meanwhile, the prime minister has the power to appoint the cabinet and dissolve the assembly. The House of Representatives initiates legislation and confidence motions and launches investigations. The 2011 constitution also guaranteed freedom of expression and equality for men and women.

All members of the House of Representatives are now elected directly. Included in the new legislature's expanded authority is the power to censure the government and to dismiss cabinet members, although such decisions can still be overridden by the king. The upper house (House of Councilors) is elected indirectly from various local government bodies, professional associations, and employer and worker organizations.

The judicial system is headed by a Supreme Court (*Al-Makama al-Ulia*) and includes courts of appeal, regional tribunals, magistrates' courts, labor tribunals, and a special court to deal with corruption. All judges are appointed by the king on the advice of the Supreme Council of the Judiciary. The 2011 constitution established the judiciary as an independent branch of the government.

The country is currently divided into 49 provinces and prefectures (including four provinces in the Western Sahara), with further division into municipalities, autonomous centers, and rural communes. The king appoints all provincial governors, who are responsible to him. In addition, the basic law changes of September 1996 provided for 16 regional councils, with some members elected directly and others representing various professional organizations.

Moroccan newspapers have a reputation for being highly partisan and outspoken, although those incurring the displeasure of the state face reprisal, such as forced suspension, and government control has at times been highly restrictive. Following the enthronement of the reform-minded King Mohamed VI in 1999, the government somewhat relaxed its grip on the print media. However, domestic and international journalists' organizations criticized a libel law adopted in April 2002, accusing the government of eroding civil and press liberties by making it easier to file libel suits. In May 2006 Human Rights Watch issued a report critical of tightening controls on the press, citing recent harassment of independent news weeklies that had questioned government policies. Meanwhile, the government continued to arrest journalists for articles critical of the king. In October 2010 Morocco banned Al-Jazeera from broadcasting from Morocco after the Arab-language station carried reports critical of the kingdom's actions in the Western Sahara. In its 2016 annual index of freedom of the press, Reporters Without Borders ranked Morocco 131st out of 180 countries, its position unchanged from the previous year.

Foreign relations. A member of the UN and the Arab League, Morocco has been chosen on many occasions as a site for Arab and African Islamic conferences at all levels. It has generally adhered to a nonaligned policy, combining good relations with the West with support for African and especially Arab nationalism. Morocco has long courted economic ties with the European Union (EU, formerly the European Community—EC), although its request for EC membership was politely rebuffed in 1987 on geographic grounds. An association agreement was negotiated in 1995 and signed in 1996 with the EU, which reportedly had begun to perceive the kingdom as the linchpin of a European campaign to expand trade with North Africa. Morocco also joined the EU's European Neighborhood Policy and in this context developed an Action Plan, finalized in July 2005, which defined mutual priorities and objectives in the areas of political, economic, commercial, justice, security, and cultural cooperation. These objectives included negotiating an agreement on liberalized trade, pursuing legislative reform, applying human rights provisions, managing migration flows more effectively, and signing a readmission agreement with the EU and developing the energy sector. The action plan also called for an enhanced dialogue on combating terrorism.

In July 2008 France launched a new initiative, the Union for the Mediterranean, a regional group of European, Middle Eastern, and North African countries that gave Morocco a leading role. In addition, the Moroccan government has long been interested in formalizing its relationship to the EU as an advanced status partner, which would allow Moroccans greater access to EU labor markets. France strongly supported Morocco's bid and promoted its application.

Relations with the United States have been friendly, with U.S. administrations viewing Morocco as a conservative counter to northern Africa's more radical regimes. An agreement was signed in mid-1982 that sanctioned, subject to veto, the use of Moroccan air bases by U.S. forces in emergency situations. Periodic joint military exercises have since been conducted, with Washington serving as a prime supplier of equipment for Rabat's campaign in the Western Sahara. In 2004 the United States and Morocco signed a free trade agreement that went into effect in 2006. As a result, exports from Morocco to the United States increased from $445.8 million in 2005 to $878.5 million in 2008, while imports rose from $480.8 million to $1.44 billion. Morocco is a signatory to the U.S.-led Trans-Sahara Counterterrorism Initiative, a seven-year program worth $500 million, and the United States continues to view Morocco as a key ally in combating terrorism.

During early 1991 Rabat faced a delicate situation in regard to the Iraqi invasion of Kuwait the previous August. Many Arab capitals were critical of King Hassan for contributing 1,700 Moroccan troops to the U.S.-led Desert Shield deployment in Saudi Arabia and other Gulf states; domestic sentiment also appeared to be strongly tilted against Washington. However, the king defused the issue by permitting a huge pro-Iraq demonstration in the capital in early February and by expressing his personal sympathy for the Iraqi people during the Gulf war. His middle-of-the-road approach was widely applauded both at home and abroad.

A variety of issues complicate Morocco's role in regional affairs. Relations with Algeria and Mauritania have been marred by territorial disputes. (Until 1970 Morocco claimed all of Mauritania's territory.) The early 1970s brought cooperation with the two neighboring states in an effort to present a unified front against the retention by Spain of phosphate-rich Spanish Sahara, but by 1975 Morocco and Mauritania were ranged against Algeria on the issue. In an agreement reached in Madrid on November 14, 1975, Spain agreed to withdraw in favor of Morocco and Mauritania, who proceeded to occupy their assigned sectors (see map) on February 28, 1976, despite resistance from the Polisario Front, an Algerian-backed group that had proclaimed the establishment of an independent Saharan Arab Democratic Republic (SADR). Following Mauritanian renunciation of all claims to the territory in a peace accord with Polisario on August 5, 1979, Moroccan forces entered the southern sector, claiming it, too, as a Moroccan province.

Relations with Algeria were formally resumed in May 1988 prior to an Arab summit in Algiers on the uprising in the Israeli-occupied territories. The stage was thus set for diplomatic activity, which in the wake of first-ever talks between King Hassan and Polisario representatives in early 1989 appeared to offer the strongest possibility in more than a decade for settlement of the Western Sahara problem. Although little progress was achieved over the next seven years on a proposed UN-sponsored self-determination vote, a new UN mediation effort in 1997 rekindled hopes for a settlement (see Disputed Territory, below). Relations with Algeria improved further following the 1999 election of the new Algerian president, Abdelaziz Bouteflika, who suggested that bilateral affairs be handled independently of the conflict in the Western Sahara. Nevertheless, tensions between the two states persisted and the border remained closed from 1994. However, this rivalry does not prevent the two states from cooperating on common strategic concerns, such as security, including extradition of terrorist suspects and energy. In July 2008 Algerian officials announced that they would export electricity to Spain through a Moroccan pipeline and would be an energy provider to Morocco in emergencies. Long strained ties with Libya (which had been accused of complicity in several plots to overthrow the monarchy) began to improve with a state visit by Muammar Qadhafi to Rabat in mid-1983. The process of rapprochement culminated in a treaty of projected union signed by the two leaders at Oujda on August 13, 1984. An inaugural meeting of a joint parliamentary assembly was held in Rabat in July 1985, and commissions were set up to discuss political, military, economic, cultural, and technical cooperation. By February 1989 cordial relations paved the way for a summit in Marrakesh, during which Qadhafi joined other North African leaders in proclaiming the Arab Maghreb Union.

Morocco's attitude toward Israel has been markedly more moderate than that of many Arab states, in part because more than 500,000 Jews of Moroccan ancestry live in Israel. King Hassan was known to relish his conciliatory potential in the Middle East peace process and was believed to have assisted in the negotiations leading up to the Israeli/PLO agreement of September 1993. Israeli prime minister Yitzhak Rabin made a surprise visit to Rabat on his return from the historic signing in Washington, his talks with King Hassan being heralded as an important step toward the establishment of formal diplomatic relations between the two countries.

In late 2001 relations between Morocco and Spain were strained by disagreements over illegal immigration, fishing rights, and smuggling. In July 2002 the countries were involved in a brief military standoff over an uninhabited islet (called Perejil by Spain, Leila by Morocco, and claimed by both) off the coast of Ceuta. With U.S., EU, and Egyptian mediation, the two sides agreed to withdraw their troops from the islet and begin cooperating on various issues. The March 2004 bombings in Madrid, which were partly perpetrated by Moroccan immigrants, encouraged the states to coordinate security policy and exchange counterterrorism intelligence. Tensions eased dramatically when Spain's conservative government was replaced by the Spanish Socialist Workers Party in March 2004, but the relationship is still fragile. When Spain's King Juan Carlos visited Ceuta in November 2007, Morocco protested by recalling its ambassador from Spain.

In March 2009 Morocco broke off diplomatic relations with Iran, following statements by an Iranian official critical of Bahrain. The remarks prompted widespread outrage among Sunnis. The severance followed the recall of the Moroccan envoy to Iran in February because of that country's criticism of Morocco and reports in Rabat of Iranians endeavoring to undermine the monarchy. Also in March, Morocco expelled four foreign missionaries on the grounds they were illegally attempting to convert Muslims to Christianity.

Morocco withdrew from Libya's fortieth anniversary celebrations in September 2009 in protest over the appearance of Polisario leader Mohamed Abd al-Azziz (see Disputed Territory, below). However, the following month the two countries signed a range of bilateral economic agreements to expand cooperation in tourism, air travel, and various industries.

An agreement to expand economic cooperation between Morocco and Poland was signed during a visit by El Fassi to Poland in January 2010. In March the first EU–Morocco summit was held in Granada, Spain, to discuss closer economic and political collaboration. Moroccan activists periodically blockaded food shipments to the Spanish enclave of Melilla to protest reported instances of abuse by Spanish border guards through the summer of 2010. The king and Spanish prime minister met in September and pledged to reduce tensions. In December 2010 representatives from Morocco, Polisario, Algeria, and Mauritania resumed negotiations on the Western Sahara, the first direct talks since 2008.

In June 2011 a raid by Moroccans to secure a water reservoir that supplied water to Melilla led to protests from the Spanish government.

In the spring of 2012, high-level meetings with Algerian diplomats raised hopes the two countries might reopen their borders, reflecting a thaw in relations that some observers attributed to the need of both governments to deliver reforms. In October Spain and Morocco signed a series of confidence-building measures to improve cultural ties and economic cooperation.

Saudi Arabia provided Morocco $400 million in February 2013 for development projects. In March the EU announced it would begin negotiations with Morocco on a free trade agreement. During a state visit to Morocco by French president François Hollande in April, authorities signed a series of bilateral economic agreements. Also in April Canada announced it would provide up to $500 million to Morocco for infrastructure projects that utilized Canadian firms. In June the United Arab Emirates (UAE) agreed to provide Morocco with

$1.25 billion to promote sustainable economic development. The next month Morocco and the EU finalized a new four-year fishing agreement to allow European vessels to fish in Moroccan waters in exchange for a $53 million annual subsidy.

Continued tension in 2014 resulted in accusations between Algeria and Morocco of carrying out smear campaigns in the media. Foreign Minister Salaheddine MEZOUAR blamed Algeria for difficulties in the Arab Maghreb Union. Algeria remained steadfast in public support of the self-determination of the Sahrawi people of Western Sahara. Algeria also blames Morocco for not doing enough to stop the flow of drugs into Algeria. Algerian authorities seized 36 percent more Moroccan cannabis in the first half of 2014 than in 2013. The Spanish government announced in March that it would spend €2.1 million to fortify the borders of Ceuta and Melilla. In May more than 400 migrants made it over the towering fence between Morocco and Spain at Melilla.

The EU and Morocco agreed to postpone the fifth round of negotiations for a Deep and Comprehensive Free Trade Agreement (DCFTA) in July to allow Morocco to carry out studies in certain sectors covered by the DCFTA. Morocco has enjoyed Advanced Status within the European Union since 2008.

In August Morocco joined with Algeria, Egypt, Tunisia, and the United States in calling upon all parties in Libya to adopt an immediate ceasefire.

On August 11 and 12 temporary lapses in Moroccan security resulted in a dramatic, temporary rise in illegal migration from across the Straits of Gibraltar from Morocco to Spain. During the two-period, more migrants attempted to enter Spain than in all of 2013. Spanish officials speculated that heightened security around Ceuta and Melilla contributed to the influx at Gibraltar.

Morocco joined the Saudi-led military coalition fighting the Houthi rebels in Yemen in 2015. Morocco initially deployed aircraft and later approximately 1,500 ground troops to Yemen. In February 2016 Morocco announced it would back Saudi military intervention in Syria.

Current issues. Throughout February and March 2011, there were widespread prodemocracy demonstrations in Marrakesh and other major cities. The protests were led by a loose coalition known as the February 20 Movement. On April 28, 2011, a bomb killed 16 and injured more than 20 in Marrakesh. Also in April the king pardoned 96 political prisoners and reduced the sentences of 80 others. A new constitution that reduced the power of the king was overwhelmingly approved by a referendum in July. Despite the new constitution, antigovernment protests continued through the summer.

On October 28, 2012, Moroccan national Adil el-ATMANI was sentenced to death for his role in the bombing of a Marrakesh café that killed 17 people in April. Hakim DAH received a life sentence, and six others received two- to four-year sentences.

On November 25, 2011, early elections were held for the House of Representatives, which had been increased from 325 to 395 members (with 305 coming from party lists and the remaining 90 from national lists, two-thirds of which were reserved for women). The PJD secured a plurality with 107 seats, followed by the Independence Party, 60; and the National Assembly of Independents, 52. The turnout was 45.4 percent. On November 29 PJD leader Benkirane was named prime minister. On December 16 Benkirane signed a charter with *Istiqlal*, the Popular Movement, and the Party for Progress and Socialism for a coalition government that would command 217 of the 395 seats in the House of Representatives. On December 19 the new House elected *Istiqlal*'s Karim GHALLAB as its speaker.

On January 3 the king appointed a government under Benkirane as prime minister, who declared that his priorities would be eradication of shanty towns around cities and abject rural poverty.

Government representatives met with leaders from the Polisario Front for talks in New York on March 14, one month after Polisario leader Mohamed ABDELAZIZ warned that armed struggle might be resumed. The talks failed to make headway.

Later that month the government announced it had joined a defamation lawsuit filed by Moroccans in Austria against the Freedom Party of Austria over an election poster that featured the slogan "Love your native country rather than thieves from Morocco." On April 1 the party announced it would remove the posters. The next day the government announced that Thami Najim, a Danish national of Moroccan heritage, had been detained on charges of plotting to overthrow the Moroccan government. On April 24 the UN Security Council extended the mandate of the UN Mission for the Referendum in Western Sahara (MINURSO) until April 30, 2013, calling on both parties to continue negotiations. The next month, however, Morocco's government spokesman blamed UN envoy Christopher Ross for the lack of progress in negotiations, accusing him of bias and calling for his replacement.

On May 5, 2012, authorities announced they had broken up a "terrorist network" with ties to AQIM. On May 27 tens of thousands took part in a trade union rally in Casablanca, accusing Benkirane of failing to deliver promised reforms. On October 6 more than 2,300 judges held a demonstration at the main appeals court in Rabat, demanding that promised judicial reforms be implemented. On October 17 stone carvings in the Atlas Mountains, estimated to be more than 8,000 years old, were destroyed by Islamic militants who claimed the pagan artifacts were "idolatrous."

On July 9, 2013, *Istiqlal* withdrew from the governing coalition and the government. The party announced it sought to force Benkirane's resignation. Meanwhile the prime minister accused the Islamist party of attempting to sabotage reforms. In August reports indicated that the RNI agreed to join the government, thereby preserving the coalition and forestalling the need for early elections.

In January 2014, after two years of discussions, parliament unanimously amended an article in the penal code that allowed a rapist to escape prosecution if he married his victim. In May and June Moroccan authorities dismantled two terror recruitment networks based in Fez and on the Mediterranean coast. In August Moroccan authorities dismantled a third network recruiting volunteers to fight with the terrorist organization ISIS in Syria and Iraq. (See entries on Iraq and Syria in the 2014 *Handbook.*) The group operated in Tetouan, Fez, Fnideq, and nearby Ceuta. Morocco's Interior Ministry reported that 1,212 Moroccans belonged to terrorist groups in Iraq and Syria, including the Islamic State group. At least 100 were arrested on their return to Morocco.

In local and regional elections on September 4, 2015, the PJD won control of the majority of the country's cities, including Rabat, Casablanca, and Tangier. The PJD secured 174 seats on regional council, followed by PAM, 132; and the Independence Party, 119. In local elections, PAM won 6,655 seats, followed by the Independence Party, 5,106; and PJD, 5,021.

POLITICAL PARTIES

Governing Coalition:

Justice and Development Party (*Parti de la Justice et du Développement*—PJD). The PJD is an Islamist party formerly known as the **Popular Constitutional and Democratic Movement** (*Mouvement Populaire Constitutionnel et Démocratique*—MPCD). The MPCD was a splinter from the Popular Movement. It won three legislative seats in 1977 and none in 1984 or 1993. In June 1996 the moribund MPCD was rejuvenated by its merger with an unrecognized Islamist grouping known as **Reform and Renewal** (*Islah wa al-Tajdid*), led by Abdelillah Benkirane. The Islamists received three of the MPCD's secretariat seats, and Benkirane was generally acknowledged as the party's primary leader. He announced that his supporters had relinquished their "revolutionary ideas" and were now committed to "Islam, the constitutional monarchy, and nonviolence." The party won 9 seats in the House of Representatives in 1997, while Benkirane was successful in a by-election on April 30, 1999. The PJD gained in popularity, taking 42 seats in the House of Representatives in 2002. In local elections in 2003 it scaled back its proposed candidates to avoid alienating foreign investors with high-profile wins.

The PJD was expected to make major gains in the 2007 parliamentary elections, and many viewed the party as a test case for an Islamist parliamentary victory. While the party fielded candidates in just 50 constituencies in 2002, the PJD campaigned in 94 constituencies in the September elections. The party won the largest share of the vote but took only 46 legislative seats—6 fewer than *Istiqlal.* Despite its status as the second largest party, the PJD was not included in the governing coalition.

In July 2008 the party membership chose Abdelillah Benkirane, a well-known moderate and former leader of the Reform and Renewal party, as its new secretary general. Benkirane, who supports the monarchy, aimed to turn the party away from an overtly religious agenda.

The PJD came in sixth in local balloting in the June 2009 elections and secured only 5.5 percent of the seats, although the party did well in urban areas where it gained 16 percent of the posts. In June 2010 the leader of the PJD in parliament resigned over what he described as the marginalization of the legislature. The PJD supported ratification of the new constitution in the 2011 referendum.

In the 2011 elections, the party won by a considerable margin the largest share of votes, securing 107 seats in the new House. Benkirane was appointed prime minister in November 2011.

Reports indicated internal divisions within the party after the PJD leadership decided to not adopt an official position on the 2013 Egyptian coup (see entry on Egypt). In August PJD formed a ruling coalition with the **National Rally of Independents** (*Rassemblement National des Indépendants*—RNI, below).

Relations between the PJD and Amazigh groups grew tense throughout 2013 and 2014, and in August 2014 several Amazigh associations launched a public campaign calling for the dissolution of the PJD based on article 7 of the constitution of July 1, 2011, which states that no party may be founded on religious, linguistic, ethnic, or regional bases. In 2008 authorities dissolved the Amazigh Moroccan Democratic Party because of its ethno-linguistic foundation. The PJD have stated publicly since 2007 that the party is not an Islamist party, but rather a centrist party with an Islamist perspective. The Oneness and Reform Movement (*Mouvement Unicité et Réforme*—MUR), the explicitly religious branch of the PJD, held its 5th congress in Rabat in August.

The PJD won 31.7 percent of the vote in the 2016 legislative elections, securing 125 seats, and Benkirane was asked to form a new government.

Leader: Abdelillah BENKIRANE (Prime Minister and Secretary General of the Party).

Popular Movement (*Mouvement Populaire*—MP). Organized in 1958 as a monarchist party of Berber mountaineers, the MP was legally recognized in 1959. The MP was a major participant in government coalitions of the early 1960s. It secured the second-largest number of legislative seats in the election of June 1977 and was third ranked after the 1984 and 1993 elections. In October 1986 an extraordinary party congress voted to remove the MP's founder, Mahjoubi AHERDANE, from the post of secretary general, replacing him with Mohand LAENSER. Aherdane subsequently formed a new Berber party (see MNP, below). It is known to be loyal to the monarchy and still draws its support base from rural Berber areas. In the 2002 elections the MP won 27 seats and Laenser was named minister of agriculture. In 2006 the MP absorbed the **Popular National Movement** (*Mouvement National Populaire*—MNP) and the **Democratic Union** (*Union Démocratique*—UD), a center-leaning Berber party led by Bouazza IKKEN. In the 2007 elections the MP won 41 seats and became the third largest party in the House of Representatives. The MP won 2,213 seats in local council elections in June 2009. It joined the government following a cabinet reshuffle in July in which Laenser was appointed a minister of state without portfolio. The MP placed third in indirect elections for the House of Councilors with 11 seats. In the 2011 elections the party came in sixth, securing 32 seats. In 2012 Laenser was appointed interior minister. The MP held its 12th congress in June 2014. Attendees elected Fadili MOHAMED president of the National Council of the People's Movement.

The MP won 6.1 percent of the vote in the 2016 elections, securing 27 seats.

Leader: Mohand LAENSER (Interior Minister and Secretary General).

Party of Progress and Socialism (*Parti du Progrès et du Socialisme*—PPS). The PPS is the successor to the **Moroccan Communist Party** (*Parti Communiste Marocain*), which was banned in 1952; the **Party of Liberation and Socialism** (*Parti de la Libération et du Socialisme*), which was banned in 1969; and the **Party of Progress and Socialism** (*Parti du Progrès et du Socialisme*—PPS), which obtained legal status in 1974. The single PPS representative in the 1977 chamber, Ali YATA, was the first communist to win election to a Moroccan legislature. The fourth national congress, held in July 1987 in Casablanca, although strongly supportive of the government's position on the Western Sahara, criticized the administration's recent decisions to privatize some state enterprises and implement other economic liberalization measures required by the International Monetary Fund. However, by mid-1991 the PPS was reported to be fully converted to *perestroika,* a stance that had apparently earned the party additional support within the Moroccan middle class. In late 1993 Yata unsuccessfully urged his Democratic Bloc partners to compromise with King Hassan in formation of a new government.

Ali Yata, who had been reelected to his post of PRP secretary general in mid-1995, died in August 1997 after being struck by a car. Ismail Alaoui was elected as the new secretary general. In March 2002 the PPS and the PSD (see USFP, below) announced that they had launched the **Socialist Alliance** (*Alliance Socialiste*) and that they were planning to cooperate in the legislative poll in September. In that election the PPS collected only 11 seats. The PPS won 1,102 seats in local balloting in June 2009. It also secured two seats in the upper chamber of the parliament in the October balloting. In April 2011 the PPS announced that it had established a formal relationship with the Communist Party of China. In the 2011 elections the party secured 18 seats. It joined the PJD-led government and received four cabinet posts. In November 2013 the PPS issued a press release announcing the celebration of the 70th anniversary of the founding of the party. The PPS won 3 percent of the vote in 2016, gaining 12 seats.

Leaders: Mohammed Nabil BENABDELLAH (Minister of Housing and Urban Planning and Secretary General), Ismail ALAOUI.

National Assembly of Independents (*Rassemblement National des Indépendants*—RNI). The RNI was launched at a Constitutive Congress held October 6–9, 1978. Although branded by a left-wing spokesperson as a "king's party," it claimed to hold the allegiance of 141 of 264 deputies in the 1977 chamber. Subsequent defections and other disagreements, both internal and with the king, resulted in the party's designation as the "official" opposition in late 1981. It won 61 house seats in 1984, thereafter returning to a posture of solid support for the king and the government. RNI leader Ahmed Osman, a former prime minister and former president of the House of Representatives, is one of the country's best-known politicians and is also the son-in-law of the former king. Previously affiliated with the National Entente, the RNI participated (as did the MNP) in the November 1997 elections as an unaligned "centrist" party (winning 46 seats) and subsequently agreed to join the *Koutla*-led coalition government named in early 1998. In 2002 RNI won 41 seats. RNI sustained few losses in the 2007 elections and emerged with 39 seats.

In April 2007 Ahmed Osman was ousted by younger members who organized an extraordinary congress and demanded a successor be found. In May 2007 Mustafa MANSOUI was elected as the new president after Ahmed Osman agreed not to nominate himself again. Mansouri became the speaker of the House of Representatives in October 2007.

The RNI placed third in local balloting in June 2009 with 4,112 seats, or 14 percent of all positions. It was fifth in the indirect balloting for the upper chamber of the parliament with 9 seats. In September 2009 Salaheddine Mezouar challenged Mansouri's leadership, leading to Mansouri's resignation as party leader and speaker of the House of Representatives in January 2010. The RNI endorsed the 2011 constitution. In the 2011 elections RNI finished third, securing 52 seats.

Following the withdrawal of *Istiqlal* from the PJD-led government, the RNI's national committee voted on August 2, 2013, to join the governing coalition. The RNI earned 9.4 percent of the vote in the 2016 legislative elections and 37 seats.

Leader: Salaheddine MEZOUAR (Minister of Foreign Affairs and Cooperation and Chair).

Other Parties:

Independence Party (*Parti de l'Istiqlal*—*Istiqlal*). Founded in 1943, *Istiqlal* provided most of the nation's leadership before independence. It split in 1959, and its members were relieved of governmental responsibilities in 1963. Once a firm supporter of the throne, the party now displays a reformist attitude and only supports the king on selected issues. Stressing the need for better standards of living and equal rights for all Moroccans, it has challenged the government regarding alleged human rights abuses. In July 1970 *Istiqlal* formed a National Front with the **National Union of Popular Forces** (*Union Nationale des Forces Populaires*—UNFP) but ran alone in the election of June 1977, when it emerged as the then-leading party. It suffered heavy losses in both the 1983 municipal elections and the 1984 legislative balloting. (See the 2014 *Handbook* for details about *Istiqlal* activity between 1984 and 2009.)

The party placed second in local balloting in June 2009 and secured 5,292 seats (19 percent) on local and regional councils. It also placed second in balloting, winning 17 (one-third) of the seats in the upper chamber of the parliament in October. The party led efforts to enact the new constitution in the 2011 referendum. In the 2011 elections, the party finished second, securing 60 seats. At the party conference on September 24, 2012, Hamid CHABAT, a former mechanic, was elected as the party's secretary general, narrowly beating rival Abdelouahed al-FASSI, son of party founder Allal FASSI. Observers described

Chabat's meritocratic rise as evidence of a newly emergent democratic trend in a party whose leadership was traditionally chosen by a small cast of senior leaders.

At a party congress in May 2013, 870 of 976 delegates voted for *Istiqlal* to withdraw from its coalition with the PJD and join the opposition. Party member Mohamed EL OUAFA, the minister of education, initially refused to resign from the cabinet but ultimately left office in July 2013. In August 2014 *Istiqlal* and the USFP (see below) submitted a memorandum to the minister of the interior proposing that voting in the 2015 elections be made mandatory.

In the 2015 legislative polling, *Istiqlal* secured 11.7 percent of the vote and 46 seats.

Leaders: Hamid CHABAT (Secretary General), Hachmi EL FILALI, Abou Bakr KADIRI, Abdelkrim GHALLAB, Mohamed BOUCETTA, M'hamed DOUIRI (Presidential Council).

Socialist Union of Popular Forces (*Union Socialiste des Forces Populaire*—USFP). The USFP was organized in September 1974 by the UNFP-Rabat Section, which had disassociated itself from the Casablanca Section in July 1972 and was accused by the government of involvement in a Libyan-aided plot to overthrow King Hassan in March 1973. The USFP subsequently called for political democratization, nationalization of major industries, thorough reform of the nation's social and administrative structures, and the cessation of what it believed to be human rights abuses by the government. It secured the third-largest number of legislative seats in the election of June 1977 but withdrew from the House in October 1981 in protest at the extension of the parliamentary term. A year later it announced that it would return for the duration of the session ending in May 1983 so that it could participate in the forthcoming electoral campaigns. The majority of nearly 100 political prisoners released during July–August 1980 were USFP members, most of whom had been incarcerated for alleged antigovernment activities in 1973–1977.

After 52 of its 104 candidates (the USFP also supported 118 *Istiqlal* candidates) won seats in the June 1993 *Majlis* balloting, the union was reportedly divided on whether to accept King Hassan's offer to participate in a coalition government, the dispute ultimately being resolved in favor of the rejectionists. Subsequently, the USFP was awarded only four additional house seats in the September indirect elections. First Secretary Abderrahmane Youssoufi resigned his post and departed for France in protest over irregularities surrounding the process. The party also continued to denounce the harassment of prominent USFP member Noubir EL-AMAOUI, secretary general of the **Democratic Confederation of Labor** (*Confédération Démocratique du Travail*), who had recently served 14 months in prison for insulting and slandering the government in a magazine interview.

Youssoufi returned from his self-imposed exile in April 1995, apparently in response to overtures from King Hassan, who was again attempting to persuade leftist parties to join a coalition government. Although observers suggested that the USFP would soon redefine the party platform and possibly select new leaders, a July 1996 congress simply reconfirmed the current political bureau. Meanwhile, one USFP faction was reportedly attempting to "re-radicalize" the party under the direction of Mohamed BASRI, a longtime influential opposition leader. In June 1995 Basri returned from 28 years in exile, during which he had been sentenced (in absentia) to death three times.

The USFP was the leading party in the November 1997 house balloting, securing 57 seats and distancing itself somewhat from its *Koutla* partner *Istiqlal*. Subsequently, King Hassan named 74-year-old Youssoufi (once again being referenced as the USFP first secretary) to lead a new coalition government, although many younger USFP members reportedly opposed the party's participation. Internal dissent continued, as some radical members charged Youssoufi and the party administration with acting timidly in government and failing to push for further reforms in state institutions. Younger party members reportedly voiced demands for a leadership change in the party congress in March 2001. However, Youssoufi managed to retain his post, prompting some members to leave the party to form the **National Ittihadi Congress** (CNI, below). USFP was the leading party in the 2002 elections, winning 50 seats. In 2003 Youssoufi resigned, and Mohamed EL YAZGHI took over as first secretary. In 2005 the **Socialist Democratic Party** (*Parti Socialiste et Démocratique*—PSD), which had won 6 seats in the 2002 balloting, merged with the USFP. USFP came in with the largest losses in the 2007 elections; it won only 38 seats, down from 50 seats in 2007. In December of 2007 El Yazghi resigned his party leadership post following disagreements over the 2008 budget. Abdelwahed Radi and Fathallah OUALALOU ran for first secretary, and Radi was elected at a party congress in November 2008.

In local balloting in June 2009 the USFP won 3,266 seats, or 11.6 percent of the total, while in balloting for the House of Councilors, the party placed fourth with 10 seats. Radi urged USFP supporters to vote "yes" in the 2011 constitutional referendum. In the 2011 elections the party came in fifth, securing 39 seats. At a party congress in December 2012, Driss Lachgar was elected first secretary. Lachgar's political rival, Ahmed ZAIDI contested the election and formed the group *Démocratie et Ouverture* within the USFP in early 2014. In August Zaidi signed a petition denouncing Lachgar's control of the party.

The USFP won 20 seats in the 2016 balloting, with 5.1 percent of the vote.

Leader: Driss LACHGAR (First Secretary).

Party of Authenticity and Modernity (*Parti Authenticité et Modernité*—PAM). PAM was formed in August 2008 by Fouad El Himma, a childhood friend of Mohamed VI who had previously led another coalition, the **Movement for All Democrats** (*Mouvement pour tous les Démocrates*—MTD). PAM was created by a merger of five smaller parties: Alliance of Freedom (*Alliance des Libertés*—ADL), the Citizens' Initiatives for Development (*Initiatives Citoyennes pour le Développement*—ICD), the Covenant Party (*Al Ahd*), the Party of Environment and Development (*Parti de l'Environnement et du Développement*—PED, see Defunct Parties, below), and the National Democratic Party (PND, below). Its stated purpose is to limit the fragmentation of the Moroccan political environment and prevent the rise of Islamist parties.

PAM integrated the PED in 2008. In January 2009 the PND (see below) withdrew from the PAM after the party failed to win any seats in by-elections the previous September. PAM joined the opposition prior to the June local elections, reportedly as a means to demonstrate its independence from the monarchy. The grouping placed first in the balloting and secured 21.5 percent of the seats. It then won control of four of the eight regions in regional balloting in September. By the end of 2009 some 89 deputies in the House of Representatives had switched their allegiance to PAM, making the party the largest in the chamber. PAM secretary general Mohammed Cheikh BIADILLAH was elected speaker of the House of Councilors in October after balloting for one-third of the seats in the chamber in which PAM placed first with 22 seats. In the 2011 elections PAM formed an alliance with seven other parties of different political leanings and finished fourth, securing 47 seats.

Following the withdrawal of *Istiqlal* from the PJD-led government in 2013, the PAM rebuffed an offer to join the governing coalition. In August 2014 PAM joined *Istiqlal* to propose legislation for limited legalization of cannabis in some areas of Morocco.

PAM became the second-largest party in Parliament following the 2016 elections, with 102 seats and 25.8 percent of the vote.

Leader: Ilyas El OMARI.

National Democratic Party (*Parti National Démocrate*—PND). The PND was founded as the **Democratic Independents** (*Indépendants Démocrates*—ID) in April 1981 by 59 former RNI deputies in the House of Representatives. At the party's first congress on June 11–13, 1982, its secretary general, Mohamed Arsalane al-JADIDI, affirmed the PND's loyalty to the monarchy while castigating the RNI for not providing an effective counterweight to the "old" parties. In the 2007 elections the party ran its candidates with the Covenant Party. Together they won 14 legislative seats. The PND was one of the founding parties of the PAM in 2008, but then withdrew in January 2009 over leadership issues. The party did not win any seats in the 2011 elections.

Leaders: Abdallah KADIRI, Thami KHYARI (Secretary General).

Constitutional Union (*Union Constitutionelle*—UC). Founded in 1983 by Maati Bouabid, UC is a moderate party that emphasizes economic self-sufficiency. Said to have royal support, the party won 83 house seats in 1984. UC's representation fell to 54 seats in 1993, although it retained a slim plurality and one of its members was elected president of the new house. Bouabid died in November 1996, exacerbating problems within a party described as already in disarray. UC was the second leading party in the November 1997 house balloting, winning 50 seats, but dropped to 16 in 2002. In the 2007 elections UC won 27 seats. In the June 2009 local elections the UC won 1,307 seats. The UC gained 1 seat in the House of Councilors in the October 2010 balloting for one-third of the chamber. It was staunchly supportive of the 2011 constitutional reforms. After the 2011 elections, the UC won 23 seats in the lower house. In the 2016 legislative balloting, the UC won 4.8 percent of the vote and 19 seats.

Leader: Mohamed ABIED (Secretary General).

Democratic and Social Movement (*Mouvement Démocratique et Social*—MDS). Launched in June 1996 (as the **National Democratic and Social Movement**) by MNP dissidents, the right-wing Berber MDS is led by a former policeman. The party held seven seats following the 2002 balloting for the House of Representatives. The party had nine seats after the 2007 elections, but lost seven in the 2011 elections. The MDS opposed the expansion of the UN mission in the Sahara in 2013. The party won three seats in the 2016 parliamentary polling.

Leader: Mahmoud ARCHANE (Secretary General).

Other parties that won seats in 2016 legislative elections include the **Federation of the Democratic Left,** which secured two seats; the **Union and Democracy Party** (*Parti de l'Unité et de la Démocratie*—PUD), one seat; and the **Green Left Party** (*Partie Gauche Verte*—PGV), one seat.

Other Parties and Groups:

Democratic Forces Front (*Front des Forces Démocratiques*—FFD). Launched in 1997 by PRP dissidents, the FFD won nine seats in the November house balloting, and its leader was named to the March 1998 cabinet. In 2007 the party again won nine seats. It has endeavored unsuccessfully to enact legislation to abolish the death penalty in Morocco. The FFD secured one seat in the upper chamber of parliament following the 2010 balloting. Party founder Thami KHYARI died in 2013.

Leader: VACANT (National Secretary).

Other parties, a number of which won seats in 2002, 2006, 2007, or 2015, include the **Action Party** (*Parti de l'Action*—PA), led by Mohammed EL IDRISSI; the small but longstanding **Democratic Party for Independence** (*Parti Démocratique pour l'Indépendance* or *Parti de la Choura et de l'Istiqlal,* or *Choura*—PDI), led by Abdelwahed MAACH; the **Moroccan Liberal Party** (*Parti Marocain Libéral*—PML), led by Mohammed ZIANE; the **National Ittihadi Congress** (*Congrès National Ittihadi*—CNI), a breakaway group from the USFP led by Abdelmajid BOUZOUBAA; the **National Party for Unity and Solidarity** (*Parti National pour l'Unité et la Solidarité*—PNUS), led by Muhammad ASMAR; the **Party of Citizens' Forces** (*Parti des Forces Citoyennes*—PFC), led by Abderrahim LAHJOUJI; the **Party of Reform and Development** (*Parti de la Réforme et du Développement*—PRD), led by former RNI member Abderrahmane EL KOHEN; the **Party of Renewal and Equity** (*Parti du Renouveau et de l'Equité*—PRE), led by Chakir ACHEHBAR; the **Renaissance and Virtue Party** *(Parti de la Renaissance et de la Vertu),* an Islamist party set up in December 2005 by a former member of the PJD, led by Mohamed KHALIDI; the **Covenant Party** (*Parti Al Ahd*), which was established in 2002 by Nyib Al UAZZANI (for more on the history of the party, see the 2014 *Handbook*); and the **Social Center Party** (*Parti du Centre Social*—PCS), led by Lachen MADIH.

For more information on the **Popular National Movement** (*Mouvement National Populaire*—MNP) and groups active through the 1990s, see the 2008 *Handbook.* For information on other parties, including **Alliance of Freedom** (*Alliance des Libertés*—ADL), **Citizens' Initiatives for Development** (*Initiatives Citoyennes pour le Développement*—ICD), **Unified Socialist Party** (*Parti Socialiste Unifié*—PSU), **National Congress Party** (*Congrès National Ittihadi*—CNI), **Party of the Democratic Socialist Avant-Garde** (*Parti de l'Avant-Garde Démocratique Socialiste*—PADS), and **Workers' Party** *(Parti Travailliste)* see the 2014 *Handbook.*

Defunct Parties:

For information on defunct parties, including the **Party of Environment and Development** (*Parti de l'Environnement et du Développement*—PED) see the 2014 *Handbook.*

Clandestine Groups:

Justice and Welfare (*Adl wa-al-Ihsan*). The country's leading radical Islamist organization, *Adl wa-al-Ihsan* was formed in 1980. Although denied legal party status in 1981, it was informally tolerated until a mid-1989 crackdown, during which its founder, Sheikh Abd Assalam Yassine, was placed under house arrest and other members were imprisoned. The government formally outlawed the group in January 1990; two months later, five of its most prominent members were given two-year prison terms, and Yassine's house detention was extended, touching off large-scale street disturbances in Rabat. Although the other detainees were released in early 1992, Yassine remained under house arrest, with King Hassan describing extremism as a threat to Moroccan stability. An estimated 100 members of *Adl wa-al-Ihsan* were reportedly among the prisoners pardoned in mid-1994, although Yassine was pointedly not among them. He was finally released from house arrest in December 1995 but was soon thereafter placed under "police protection" for apparently having criticized the government too strenuously. (Among Yassine's transgressions, in the eyes of the government, was his failure to acknowledge King Hassan as the nation's supreme religious leader.) His house arrest prompted protest demonstrations in 1998 by his supporters, whom the government also charged with responsibility for recent protests among university students and a mass demonstration in late December 1998 protesting U.S.–UK air strikes against Iraq. Although the group remained proscribed, Yassine was released from house arrest in May 2000. Based on Yassine's rejection of violence, the government tolerated the group's activities. However, in May 2006 the government arrested hundreds of *Adl wa-al-Ihsan* members across the country, apparently in reaction to rumors that the party had planned an uprising. Those rounded up were later freed, but party members claimed that materials such as computers and books had been seized from party offices.

Subsequently the authorities continued to put pressure on the party. In July 2006 *Adl wa-al-Ihsan* member Hayat Bouida was allegedly abducted and tortured for three hours by six intelligence agents in Safi, a city 300 kilometers south of Casablanca. In May 2007 she was stabbed by two intelligence agents in front of her house. In March 2008 more than 20 members of the group were arrested and several were prosecuted. In July 2009 eight members of the group were arrested for illegal activities. By 2010 authorities estimated that there were approximately 200,000 members of *Adl wa-al-Ihsani* throughout Morocco. In June 2010 seven officials of the group were arrested for belonging to an illegal group. The group was one of the leading organizers of antiregime protests in February and March 2011. It opposed the 2011 constitution, asserting that it did not do enough to reform the government and it called for an end to electoral quotas for women. Since Yassine's death in December 2012, his daughter Nadia YASSINE has assumed a leadership role in the organization. In 2013 reports indicated that *Adl wa-al-Ihsan* rebuffed a government offer to register the grouping as a political party. In December 2015 Moroccan billionaire Said ALOUANI was arrested and charged with supporting terrorism for financing *Adl wa-al-Ihsan*, al-Qaida, and the Islamic State of Iraq and Syria.

Leaders: Mohammed ABBADI, Fathallah ARSLANE (Spokesperson).

LEGISLATURE

The constitutional amendments of September 1996 provided for a bicameral **Parliament** (*Barlaman*) comprising an indirectly elected House of Councilors and a directly elected House of Representatives. Previously, the legislature had consisted of a unicameral House of Representatives, two-thirds of whose members were directly elected with the remainder being selected by an electoral college of government, professional, and labor representatives.

House of Councilors (*Majlis al-Mustasharin*). The upper house consists of 120 members indirectly elected for nine-year terms (one-third of the house is renewed every three years) by local councils, regional councils, and professional organizations. Following the election to renew one-third of the house on October 2, 2015, the distribution of seats was as follows: *Istiqlal* won 24 seats; Authenticity and Modernity Party, 23; Party of Justice and Development, 12; Popular Movement, 20; National Assembly of Independents, 8; Socialist Union of Popular Forces, 5; Constitutional Union, 3; Party of Progress and Socialism, 2; Party of Reform and Development, 1; Covenant Party, 1; independents, 8; and various labor organizations, 20.

Speaker: Hakim BENCHAMACH.

House of Representatives (*Majlis al-Nawwab*). The lower house has 395 members directly elected on a proportional basis for five-year terms. Following legislative elections on October 7, 2016, the distribution of seats was the following: Party of Justice and Development, 125 seats; Authenticity and Modernity Party, 102; *Istiqlal*, 46; National Assembly of Independents, 37; Popular Movement, 27; Socialist Union of Popular Forces, 20; Constitutional Union, 19; Party of Progress and Socialism, 12; Democratic and Social Movement, 3; Federation of the Democratic Left, 2; Union and Democracy Party, 1; and Green Left Party, 1.

Speaker: Rachid Talbi ALAMI.

CABINET

[as of October 7, 2016]

Prime Minister	Abdelillah Benkirane (PJD)
Minister of State	(Vacant)
Ministers	
Agriculture, Rural Development, and Marine Fisheries	Aziz Akhenouch (ind.)
Budget	Mohamed Boussaid (Acting) (ind.)
Civil Service and Administrative Reform	Driss Merroun (Acting) (MP)
Communication, Government Spokesperson	Bassima Hakkaoui (Acting) (PJD) [f]
Culture	Mohamed Amine Sbihi (PPS)
Economy and Finance	Mohamed Boussaid (RNI)
Energy, Mining, Water, and Environment	Moulay Hafid Elalamy (RNI)
Equipment, Transport, and Logistics	Mohamed Boussaid (Acting) (RNI)
External Trade	Moulay Hafid Elalamy (Acting) (RNI)
Foreign Affairs and Cooperation	Salaheddine Mezouar (RNI)
General Secretary of the Government	Driss Dahak (ind.)
Habous (Religious Endowments) and Islamic Affairs	Ahmed Toufiq (ind.)
Handicrafts and Social and Solidarity Economy	Fatema Marouane (RNI) [f]
Health	El Houssaine Louardi (PPS)
Higher Education and Scientific Research	Jamila el Moussali (PJD) [f] (Acting)
Housing and Urban Planning	Mohammed Nabil Benabdellah (PPS)
Industry, Trade, and Digital Technologies	Moulay Hafid Elalamy (RNI)
Interior	Mohamed Hassad (ind.)
Justice	Mustafa Ramid (PJD)
Labor and Social Affairs	Abdessiam Seddiki (PPS)
Moroccans Living Abroad and Migration	Anis Birou (ind.)
National Education and Professional Training	Rachid Belmokhtar (ind.)
Relations with Parliament	Mohamed el Ouafa (Acting) (ind.)
Solidarity, Women, Family, and Social Development	Bassima Hakkaoui (PJD) [f]
Tourism	Aziz Akhenouch (Acting) (ind.)
Urban Affairs	Driss Merroun (MP)
Youth and Sports	Berjaoui Khalid (Acting) (MP)
Ministers Delegate (Ministries)	
Environment	Hakima el Haité (MP) [f]
General Affairs and Governance	Mohamed el Ouafa (ind.)
Higher Education	Jamila el Moussali (PJD) [f]
Interior	Charki Draiss (ind.)
National Defense	Abdellatif Loudiyi (ind.)
National Education	Berjaoui Khalid (MP)
Small Enterprises and Integration of the Informal Sector	Mamoun Bouhadhoud (RNI)
Water	Charafat Afilal (PPS) [f]

[f] = female

INTERGOVERNMENTAL REPRESENTATION

Ambassador to the U.S.: Mohammed Rachad BOUHLAL.

U.S. Ambassador to Morocco: Stephanie MILEY (Chargé d'Affaires).

Permanent Representative to the UN: Omar HILALE.

IGO Memberships (Non-UN): AfDB, EBRD, IOM, LAS, NAM, OIC, WTO.

For Further Reference:

Elliott, Katja Zvan. *Modernizing Patriarchy: The Politics of Women's Rights in Morocco.* Austin: University of Texas Press, 2015.

Spiegel, Avi Max. *Young Islam: The Politics of Religion in Morocco and the Arab World.* Princeton, NJ: Princeton University Press, 2015.

Willis, Michael. *Politics and Power in the Maghreb: Algeria, Tunisia, and Morocco from Independence to the Arab Spring.* Oxford: Oxford University Press, 2014.

DISPUTED TERRITORY

Western Sahara. Spain annexed the region known since 1976 as Western Sahara in two stages: the coastal area in 1884 and the interior in 1934. In 1957, the year after Morocco attained full independence, Rabat renewed a claim to the territory, sending irregulars to attack inland positions. In 1958, however, French and Spanish troops succeeded in quelling the attacks, with Madrid formally uniting Saguia el Hamra and Rio de Oro, the two historical components of the territory, as the province of Spanish Sahara. Mauritanian independence in 1960 led to territorial claims by Nouakchott, with the situation being further complicated in 1963 by the discovery of one of the world's richest phosphate deposits at Bu Craa. During the next dozen years, Morocco attempted to pressure Spain into relinquishing its claim through a combination of diplomatic initiatives (the UN first called for a referendum on self-determination for the Sahrawi people in 1966), direct support for guerrilla groups, and a legal challenge in the International Court of Justice (ICJ).

Increasing insurgency led Spain in May 1975 to announce that it intended to withdraw from Spanish Sahara. In November King Hassan ordered some 300,000 unarmed Moroccans, in what became known as the Green March, to enter the territory. Although Spain strongly objected to the action, a tripartite agreement with Morocco and Mauritania was concluded in Madrid on November 14. As a result, Spanish Sahara ceased to be a province of Spain at the end of the year; Spanish troops withdrew shortly thereafter, and Morocco and Mauritania assumed responsibility for Western Sahara on February 28, 1976. On April 14 Rabat and Nouakchott reached an agreement under which Morocco claimed the northern two-thirds of the region and Mauritania claimed the southern one-third.

Popular Front for the Liberation of Saguia el Hamra and Rio de Oro (Polisario, see below) led opposition to the partition. Polisario formally proclaimed a government-in-exile of the Sahrawi Arab Democratic Republic (SADR) in February 1976, headed by Mohamed Lamine OULD AHMED as prime minister. Whereas Polisario had originally been based in Mauritania, its political leadership was subsequently relocated to Algeria, with its guerrilla units, recruited largely from nomadic tribes indigenous to the region, establishing secure bases there. Neither Rabat nor Nouakchott wished to precipitate a wider conflict by operating on Algerian soil, which permitted Polisario to concentrate militarily against the weaker of the two occupying regimes and thus to aid in the overthrow of Mauritania's Moktar Ould Daddah in July 1978. On August 5, 1979, Mauritania concluded a peace agreement with Polisario in Algiers, but Morocco responded by annexing the southern third of Western Sahara. Meanwhile, Polisario launched its first raids into Morocco, while continuing a diplomatic offensive that by the end of 1980 had resulted in some 45 countries according recognition to the SADR.

At an OAU Council of Ministers meeting in Addis Ababa, Ethiopia, on February 22, 1982, a SADR delegation was, for the first time, seated, following a controversial ruling by the organization's secretary general that provoked a walkout by 18 member states, including Morocco. For the same reason, a quorum could not be declared for the next scheduled Council of Ministers meeting in Tripoli, Libya, on July 26, or for the 19th OAU summit, which was to have convened in Tripoli

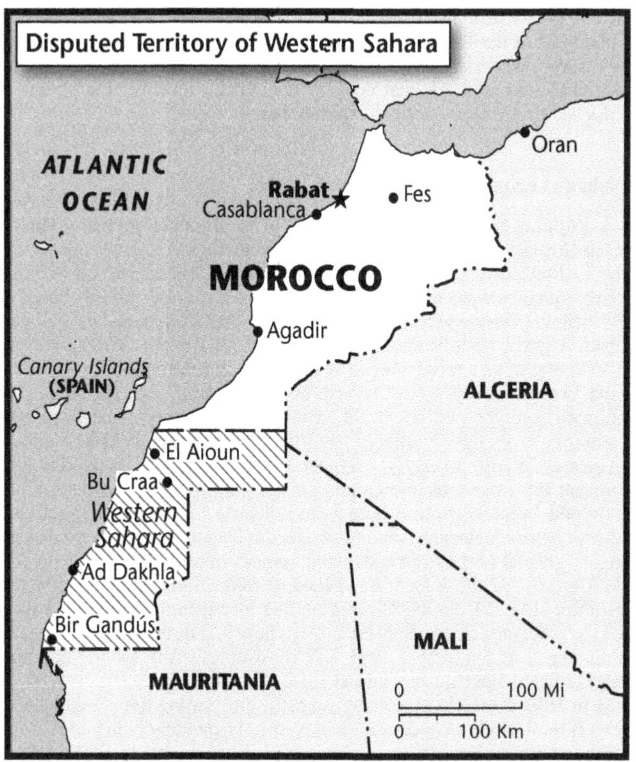

on August 5. An attempt to reconvene both meetings in November, following the voluntary and temporary withdrawal of the SADR, also failed because of the Western Sahara impasse, coupled with disagreement over the composition of a delegation from Chad. Another temporary withdrawal of the SADR allowed the OAU to convene the long-delayed summit in Addis Ababa in May 1983 at which it was decided to oversee a referendum in the region by the end of the year. Morocco's refusal to meet directly with Polisario representatives forced postponement of the poll, while the 1984 Treaty of Oujda with Libya effectively reduced support for the front's military forces. Subsequently, Moroccan soldiers crossed briefly into Algerian soil in "pursuit" of guerrillas, while extending the area under Moroccan control by 4,000 square miles. The seating of a SADR delegation at the twentieth OAU summit in November 1985 and the election of Polisario Secretary General Mohamed Abd al-AZZIZ as an OAU vice president prompted Morocco's withdrawal from the organization.

At the sixth triennial Polisario congress, held in "liberated territory" in December 1985, Abd al-Azziz was reelected secretary general; he subsequently appointed a new 13-member SADR government that included himself as president, with Ould Ahmed continuing as prime minister. The following May a series of "proximity talks" involving Moroccan and Polisario representatives concluded at UN headquarters in New York with no discernible change in the territorial impasse. Subsequently, Rabat began construction of more than 1,200 miles of fortified sand walls, called berms that forced the rebels back toward the Algerian and Mauritanian borders. Polisario, while conceding little likelihood of victory by its 30,000 fighters over an estimated 120,000 to 140,000 Moroccan soldiers, nonetheless continued its attacks, hoping that the economic strain of a war of attrition would induce King Hassan to enter into direct negotiations—a position endorsed by a 98–0 vote of the forty-first UN General Assembly. The UN also offered to administer the Western Sahara on an interim basis pending a popular referendum, but Rabat insisted that its forces remain in place. In 1987 the SADR reported an assassination attempt against Abd al-Azziz, alleging Moroccan complicity. Rabat denied the allegation and suggested that SADR dissidents may have been responsible.

Following the resumption of relations between Rabat and Algiers in May 1988, which some observers attributed in part to diminishing Algerian support for Polisario, progress appeared to be developing toward a negotiated settlement of the militarily stalemated conflict. On August 30, shortly after a new SADR government had been announced with Mahfoud Ali BEIBA taking over as prime minister, both sides announced their "conditional" endorsement of a UN-sponsored peace plan that called for a cease-fire and introduction of a UN peacekeeping force to oversee the long-discussed self-determination referendum. However, agreement was lacking on the qualifications of those who would be permitted to participate in the referendum and whether Moroccan troops would remain in the area prior to the vote. Underlining the fragility of the negotiations, Polisario launched one of its largest attacks in September before calling a cease-fire on December 30, pending face-to-face talks with King Hassan in January 1989. Although the talks eventually broke down, the cease-fire continued throughout most of the year as UN Secretary General Javier Pérez de Cuéllar attempted to mediate an agreement on referendum details. However, Polisario, accusing Rabat of delaying tactics, initiated a series of attacks in October, subsequent fighting being described as some of the most intense to date in the conflict. Another temporary truce was implemented in March 1990, and in June the UN Security Council formally authorized creation of a Western Saharan mission to supervise the proposed referendum. However, it was not until April 29, 1991, that the Security Council endorsed direct UN sponsorship of the poll, with the General Assembly approving a budget of $180 million, plus $34 million in voluntary contributions, for a UN Mission for the Referendum in Western Sahara (referenced by its French acronym, MINURSO). The mission's charge included the identification of bona fide inhabitants of the territory, the assembly of a voting list, the establishment of polling stations, and supervision of the balloting itself. The plan appeared to be in jeopardy when fierce fighting broke out in August between Moroccan and Polisario forces prior to the proposed deployment of MINURSO peacekeeping troops; however, both sides honored the UN's formal cease-fire date of September 6.

By early 1992 the broader dimensions of the Western Sahara conflict had significantly changed. The collapse of the Soviet Union and heightened internal problems for Polisario's principal backers, Algeria and Libya, created financial and supply problems for the rebels. At midyear it was estimated that more than 1,000 rank and file had joined a number of dissident leaders in defecting to Morocco. Meanwhile, Morocco had moved tens of thousands of settlers into the disputed territory, thereby diluting potential electoral support for Polisario. In addition, the proposed self-determination referendum, which the UN had planned to conduct in February, had been postponed indefinitely over the issue of voter eligibility, Polisario leaders charging that UN representatives had compromised their impartiality through secret dealings with Rabat. An unprecedented meeting, brokered by the UN at Laayoune between Moroccan and Polisario representatives, ended on July 19, 1993, without substantial progress. The main difficulty lay in a dispute about voting lists, Polisario insisting they should be based on a census taken in 1974 and Morocco arguing that they should be enlarged to include the names of some 100,000 individuals subsequently settling in the territory.

A second round of face-to-face talks, scheduled for October 1993, was cancelled at the last moment when Polisario objected to the presence of recent defectors from the front on the Moroccan negotiating team. Although the prospects for agreement on electoral eligibility were regarded as slight, MINURSO began identifying voters in June 1994 with the hope that balloting could be conducted in October 1995. Registration proceeded slowly, however, and UN officials in early 1995 protested that the Moroccan government was interfering in their operations. In April, UN Secretary General Boutros Boutros-Ghali reluctantly postponed the referendum again, sentiment reportedly growing within the UN Security Council to withdraw MINURSO if genuine progress was not achieved shortly.

In May 1996 the Security Council ordered a reduction in MINURSO personnel, UN officials declaring an impasse in the voter identification dispute and observers suggesting that hostilities could easily break out once again. However, face-to-face contacts between Polisario and Moroccan officials resumed in September, but no genuine progress ensued. It was reported that only 60,000 potential voters had been approved, with the cases of some 150,000 other "applicants" remaining unresolved at the end of the year.

New UN secretary general Kofi Annan made the relaunching of the UN initiative in Morocco one of his priorities in early 1997 and appointed former U.S. secretary of state James Baker as his personal envoy on the matter. Baker's mediation led to face-to-face talks between Polisario and representatives of the Moroccan government, culminating in the announcement of a breakthrough in September. Essentially, the two sides agreed to revive the 1991 plan with the goal of conducting the self-determination referendum in December 1998.

They also accepted UN supervision in the region pending the referendum and agreed to the repatriation of refugees under the auspices of the UN High Commissioner for Refugees. MINURSO resumed the identification of voters in December 1997; however, the process subsequently slowed, with most observers concluding that the Moroccan government bore primary responsibility for the foot-dragging. Annan his final push for a resolution in early 1999, calling for the resumption of voter registration at midyear leading up to a referendum by the end of July 2000.

Police suppressed several pro-independence riots in Western Sahara in September 1999. Authorities beat and arrested scores of demonstrators. UN special envoy Baker noted in April 2000 that he remained pessimistic about the prospects of a resolution of the conflict, citing Morocco's insistence that Moroccan settlers in Western Sahara be eligible in the proposed referendum. In September 2001 Polisario rejected Baker's proposal to grant the Western Sahara political autonomy rather than hold an independence referendum. Interest in oil drilling in the region reportedly further complicated the matter. In November 2002 King Mohamed described the notion of a self-determination referendum as obsolete. In mid-2004 the UN Security Council adopted a resolution urging Morocco and Polisario to accept the UN plan to grant Western Sahara self-government. Morocco rejected the proposal and continued to insist that the area be granted autonomy within the framework of Moroccan sovereignty. In August 2005 Polisario released 404 Moroccan prisoners, the last of the soldiers it had captured in fighting. The front said it hoped that the gesture would lead to Moroccan reciprocity and then a peace settlement. In November 2005 the king renewed his call for autonomy for the region within the framework of Moroccan sovereignty, but the Polisario Front quickly rebuffed what it referred to as the king's intransigence.

The stalemate lasted into 2006. Morocco continued to administer the annexed territory as four provinces: three established in 1976 (Boujdour, Es-Smara, Laayoune) and one in 1979 (Oued ed-Dahab). The SADR administers four Algerian camps, which house an estimated 165,000 Sahrawis, and claims to represent some 83,000 others who remain in the Western Sahara. Morocco has called for the relocation of the Sahrawis to a third country.

In April 2007 the Moroccan government submitted a proposal called the "Moroccan Initiative for Negotiating an Autonomy Status for the Sahara," to UN Secretary General, Ban Ki-Moon. Under this proposal the territory would become an autonomous region and would enjoy a measure of self-government but within the framework of the kingdom's sovereignty and national unity. The idea of autonomy was encouraged by both the United States and France, who viewed it as the most workable solution to the crisis. At the same time, however, Polisario submitted its own proposal to the UN, called "Proposal of the Frente Polisario for a Mutually Acceptable Political Solution Assuring the Self-Determination of the People of Western Sahara," which called for full self-determination through a free referendum with independence as an option. Morocco and Polisario agreed to attend UN-sponsored talks in June 2007, a groundbreaking development given that this was the first time in ten years that the two sides had sat down at the same table. In 2008 the UN envoy was quoted saying that independence was not an option for the Western Sahara, a comment that had the Polisario Front and the Algerian government crying foul. In April 2008 the UN renewed its mission in the region for another year, and the stalemate that had persisted in the last three attempts at negotiation between the parties continued. In August 2009 Morocco resumed informal negotiations with the Polisario Front under UN sponsorship. However, Algeria subsequently accused Morocco of responsibility for delaying the resumption of official talks. On October 7, 2010, the Polisario Front's top police officer, Mustapha Salma SIDI MOULOUD, was arrested after he made public comments supportive of a Moroccan compromise autonomy plan for the region. Rioting that month led to a raid by Moroccan security forces in November. The raid killed 12 in the disputed area around Laayoune. In June 2011 a Moroccan judge ordered the release of 37 people who had been arrested during the incident. Reports in 2013 indicated that Islamist militants from Mali had established bases in the Western Sahara. In February 2013 Morocco sentenced 25 human rights activists to varying prison terms for their participation in a November 2010 protest. The sentences were widely condemned by the international community. Despite the presence of drilling ships off the coast of Western Sahara in 2014, actual oil production is a long way off. It is unclear the extent to which oil production could complicate negotiations. Polisario leaders again expressed dissatisfaction with UN Special Envoy for Western Sahara Christopher Ross. Polisario leaders also expressed frustration with the premature dismissal of the Head of the MINURSO, German diplomat Wolfgang Weisbrod-Weber. Following a state visit to Tanzania in November by King Mohammed VI, that country announced its formal support for Morocco's position on the Western Sahara.

Sahrawi Front:

Popular Front for the Liberation of Saguia el Hamra and Rio de Oro (*Frente Popular para la Liberación de Saguia el Hamra y Rio de Oro*—Polisario). Established in 1973 to win independence for Spanish (subsequently Western) Sahara, the Polisario Front was initially based in Mauritania, but since the mid-1970s its political leadership has operated from Algeria. In consonance with recent developments throughout the world, the once strongly socialist Polisario currently promises to institute a market economy in "the future Sahrawi state," except in regard to mineral reserves (which would remain state property). The front also supports "eventual" multipartyism, its 1991 congress, held in Tindouf, Algeria, pledging to draft a "democratic and pluralistic" constitution to present for a national referendum should the proposed self-determination vote in the Western Sahara go in Polisario's favor. In other activity, the Congress reelected longtime leader Mohamed Abd al-Azziz as secretary general of the front and thereby president of the SADR. However, in August 1992 the defection to Morocco of the SADR foreign minister, Brahim HAKIM, served to point out the increasingly tenuous position of the rebel movement. Subsequently, a new SADR government in exile announced in September 1993 was most noteworthy for the appointment of hard-liner Brahim GHALI as defense minister.

In 1995 Polisario reportedly was still threatening to resume hostilities if the UN plan collapsed. However, it was widely believed that the front's military capacity had by then diminished to about 6,000 soldiers.

The Ninth Polisario Congress, held August 20–27, 1995, reelected Abd al-Azziz as secretary general and urged the international community to pressure the Moroccan government regarding its perceived stonewalling. In September a new SADR government was announced under the leadership of Mahfoud Ali Larous Beiba, a former SADR health minister. On October 12 the first session of a SADR National Assembly was convened in Tindouf, its 101 members having been elected via secret ballot at local and regional "conferences." A new SADR government was named on January 21, 1998, although Beiba remained as prime minister and a number of incumbents were reappointed. Beiba was succeeded in 1999 by Bouchraya Hamoudi Bayoun, who was in turn succeeded in 2003 by Abdelkader Taleb Oumar.

In the summer and fall of 2005, many Sahrawis had begun referring to their campaign against Morocco as an "*intifada,*" and Abd al-Azziz called for assistance from South Africa's Nelson Mandela and U.S. president George W. Bush in resolving the Western Sahara standoff.

In 2008 SADR announced that it sought bids for offshore oil exploration, but it received little foreign interest because of concerns over the long-term legal status of any contracts.

In August 2010 Antigua and Barbuda, Grenada, Saint Kitts and Nevis, and St. Lucia withdrew their recognition of SADR after a Moroccan diplomatic effort. In June 2011 Polisario attempted unsuccessfully to block an EU–Moroccan fisheries agreement. Meanwhile, in July Morocco and Polisario conducted a series of informal negotiations in New York under the auspices of the UN. Polisario denied reports in 2013 that its youth wing had connections with AQIM. In June 2014 several soldiers defected from Polisario to join the opposition youth group Youth Movement for Change. The group objects to the humanitarian conditions of refugees in Tindouf and accused Polisario leadership of embezzling international aid meant for refugees. In July, SADR, through the representation of Permanent Representative to the AU, Lamine BAALI, participated in the 7th Conference of African Ministers in Charge of Integration.

Abd al-Azziz died of cancer on May 31, 2016. In July former secretary general and defense minister Brahim Ghali was elected president of the SADR and secretary general of Polisario with 1,766 of 1,895 votes.

Secretary General: Brahim GHALI (President of the SADR).
Prime Minister of the SADR: Abdelkader Taleb OUMAR.

INTERGOVERNMENTAL REPRESENTATION

Polisario Front Representative to the UN: Ahmed BUKHARI.

MOZAMBIQUE

Republic of Mozambique
República de Moçambique

Political Status: Former Portuguese dependency; became independent as the People's Republic of Mozambique on June 25, 1975; present name adopted in constitution that came into effect on November 30, 1990.

Area: 309,494 sq. mi. (801,590 sq. km).

Population: 28,751,000 (2016E—UN); 25,930,150 (2016E—U.S. Census).

Major Urban Center (2016E—UN): MAPUTO (1,203,000, urban area).

Official Language: Portuguese (a number of African languages are also spoken).

Monetary Unit: Metical (market rate October 1, 2016: 78.08 meticals = $1US). The "new metical" was introduced in 2006 at the rate of 1 new metical = 1,000 old meticals.

President: Filipe NYUSI (Mozambique Liberation Front); elected on October 15, 2014, and inaugurated on January 15, 2014, to succeed Armando Emilio GUEBUZA (Mozambique Liberation Front).

Prime Minister: Carlos Agostinho do ROSÁRIO (Mozambique Liberation Front); appointed by the president on January 17, 2014, to succeed Alberto Clementino VAQUINA (Mozambique Liberation Front).

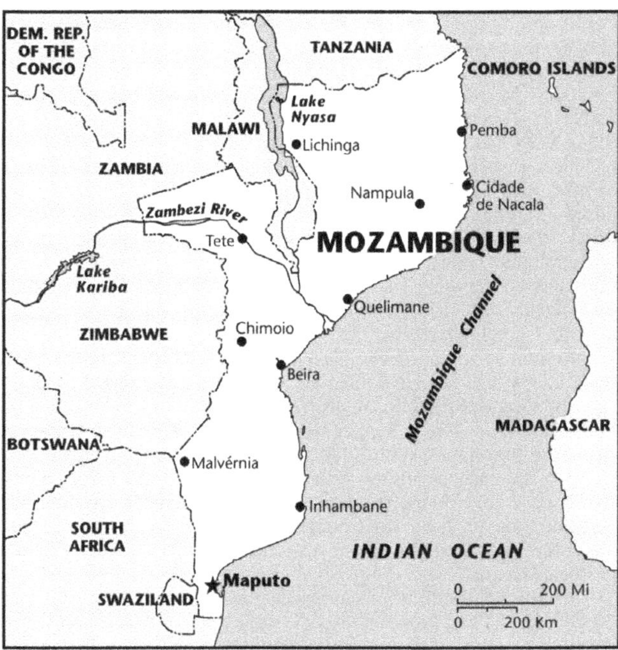

THE COUNTRY

Mozambique lies on the southeast coast of Africa, its contiguous neighbors being Tanzania on the north; Malawi and Zambia on the northwest; and Zimbabwe, South Africa, and Swaziland on the west and south. Mozambique's varied terrain comprises coastal lowlands, central plateaus, and mountains along the western frontier. The country is bisected by the Zambezi River, which flows southeastward from the Zambia-Zimbabwe border. The population, while primarily of Bantu stock, is divided into several dozen tribal groups, most speaking distinct local languages or dialects. About 55 percent of the population is Christian, and approximately 18 percent is Muslim, while about one-quarter of the population practices traditional religions. Women constitute 48 percent of the labor force, primarily in the agricultural sector; there are a number of female ministers in the current cabinet and 98 members of the assembly are women (39.2 percent).

Agriculture remains the mainstay of the economy, employing two-thirds of the workforce and providing the principal cultivated exports: cashew nuts, cotton, sugar, and tea. Seafood is also an important export. Following independence, agricultural output declined—particularly in production of sugar and cotton as well as of such minerals as coal and copper—as the government introduced pervasive state control and the Portuguese community, which possessed most of the country's technical and managerial expertise, left the country. In the early 1980s, however, the government began to encourage limited private ownership, foreign investment, and the development of family-owned and operated farms. For the most part, industry has been limited to processing agricultural commodities, although significant deposits of natural gas, as well as bauxite, iron, manganese, tantalite, uranium, and other ores, await exploitation.

Mozambique remained among the lowest-ranked nations regarding development, and poverty was widespread, much of the population living in small villages lacking electricity or running water. (For information on Mozambique's economy prior to 2000, see the 2011 *Handbook.*) Nonetheless, fueled by foreign aid, from 2000 through 2010, GDP grew an average of 7.9 percent per year, while inflation averaged 10.5 percent.

In 2008 the government announced a $3 billion effort, funded mainly by foreign investments, to develop Mozambique as a tourist destination. Through 2008 the World Bank provided $60 million annually for 17 infrastructure projects. Meanwhile, Portugal cancelled Mozambique's $390 million debt, while Ireland pledged $290 million over a four-year period for poverty reduction. The 2008–2009 global economic downturn slowed GDP growth slightly as foreign investment was reduced, but higher agricultural output offset the economic decline. In June 2009 the European Commission agreed to provide $598 million in aid to Mozambique, while the World Bank and other donors pledged $446 million to improve health care. In October 2010 the World Bank announced it would provide $143 million to expand water and sewage systems in the country's largest cities. GDP grew by 7.3 percent in 2011, mainly on the strength of expanded exports as well as foreign aid, which accounted for 15 percent of GDP. The economy grew by about 7.5 percent in 2012, according to the International Monetary Fund (IMF), which praised the government for policies that brought down inflation to 2.1 percent in 2012. Nonetheless, unemployment was almost 20 percent and as high as 60 percent in some areas.

Mozambique is considered to be on the verge of a multi-billion dollar energy boom—in hydropower, coal mining and electricity production, and offshore natural gas deposits—that could end the country's dependence on foreign aid, drastically reducing the influence of foreign donor governments. But questions remain whether the state has the capacity to manage these new investments and prevent corruption. Investments will depend on access to infrastructure that is regulated by inefficient monopolies and is further hampered by labor constraints in overwhelmed building and service companies. In June 2013 the 19 countries and international agencies that provide the bulk of Mozambique's foreign aid agreed to give $580 million for 2014 but insisted on increased transparency in government and state industries. The 2014 UN Human Development Report ranked Mozambique 178th out of 187 countries.

In 2013 GDP rose by 7.2 percent, and by 7.8 percent in 2014 and 2015. GDP was estimated to have expanded by 7.9 percent in 2016, while inflation was 5.6 percent. GDP per capita that year was $681. In 2016 the World Bank rated Mozambique as 133rd out of 189 nations in its survey on the ease of doing business, a rise from 2013 when the country ranked 146th out of 185 countries.

GOVERNMENT AND POLITICS

Political background. Portuguese hegemony was established early in the 16th century, when Mozambican coastal settlements became ports of call for traders from the Far East. However, it was not until the Berlin Congress of 1884–1885 that Portuguese supremacy was formally acknowledged by the European powers. In 1952 the colony of Mozambique became an Overseas Province and, as such, was constitutionally incorporated into Portugal. In 1964 armed resistance to

Portuguese rule was initiated by the Mozambique Liberation Front (*Frente de Libertação de Moçambique*—Frelimo), led by Dr. Eduardo MONDLANE until his assassination by Portuguese agents in 1969. Following Mondlane's death, Samora MACHEL and Marcelino DOS SANTOS overcame a bid for control by Frelimo Vice President Uriah SIMANGO and were installed as the movement's president and vice president, respectively. After the 1974 coup in Lisbon, negotiations in Lusaka, Zambia, called for the formation of a new government composed of Frelimo and Portuguese elements and for complete independence in mid-1975. The agreement was challenged by leaders of the white minority, who attempted to establish a white provisional government under right-wing leadership. After the collapse of this rebellion on September 10, 1974, most of the territory's 250,000 whites migrated to Portugal or South Africa.

On June 25, 1975, Mozambique became an independent "people's republic," with Machel assuming the presidency. Elections of Frelimo-sponsored candidates to local, district, provincial, and national assemblies were held during September–December 1977. In an apparent easing of its commitment to Marxist centralism, the government took steps in the early 1980s to separate government and party cadres. However, a government reorganization in March 1986 reestablished party domination, with the Council of Ministers being divided into three sections, each directed by a senior member of the Frelimo Political Bureau.

On July 26, 1986, Mário Fernandes da Graça MACHUNGO, an economist who had overseen recent liberalization of the economy, was sworn in as prime minister, a newly created post designed to permit President Machel to concentrate on defense of the regime against the Mozambique National Resistance (*Resistência Nacional Moçambicana*—Renamo), which had grown from a relatively isolated opponent to an insurgent force operating in all ten provinces. Machel, who had remained a widely respected leader despite the country's myriad problems, died in a plane crash on October 19 and was succeeded on November 6 by his longtime associate, Foreign Affairs Minister Joaquim Alberto CHISSANO. Chissano extended the economic liberalization policies initiated by his predecessor, overtures to the West for emergency and development aid generally being well received. However, domestic progress remained severely constrained by the ongoing civil war.

Frelimo abandoned its commitment to Marxism-Leninism in July 1989. A year later, direct talks with Renamo representatives were launched in Rome, Italy. On November 2, 1990, following extensive National Assembly debate, a new, pluralistic constitution was adopted. Subsequently, a tenuous cease-fire negotiated with Renamo on December 1 broke down, the rebels withdrawing from the Rome talks. The talks resumed in May 1991, and five months later the rebels agreed to halt armed activity, to drop demands for a UN transitional government, and to recognize the government's authority. For its part, the government agreed to procedures by which Renamo could function as a political party following a formal cease-fire.

After several weeks of deadlock in the ninth round of the Rome talks, the parties finally agreed on a protocol, which was signed March 12, 1992. It provided for election to the Assembly of the Republic by proportional representation; the holding of simultaneous legislative and presidential balloting; the formation of a National Electoral Commission, one-third of whose members would be named by Renamo; and government assistance to Renamo in establishing itself as a political grouping in every provincial capital. After another delay, the round continued with a June 10 agreement on the formation of a unified, nonpartisan army; the specifics of a cease-fire; and transitory arrangements before the general election. On August 5 Chissano and Renamo leader Gen. Afonso DHLAKAMA held their first ever face-to-face meeting, and on August 7 they reached an accord on a cease-fire and electoral preparations. Subsequently, despite reports of Renamo intransigence and an increasingly restive national army, Chissano and the rebel leader signed a peace treaty in Rome on October 4, ending the 16-year conflict. Included in the treaty were provisions for a cease-fire, multiparty elections within a year, the establishment of a 30,000-member army drawn equally from the existing forces, a political amnesty, and Western-financed repatriation of refugees. Five days later the assembly approved the treaty and the launching of the UN's Operation in Mozambique (*Operação des Nações Unidas em Moçambique*—ONUMOZ), a peacekeeping force with responsibility for disarming both combatants, integrating troops into the new armed forces, organizing elections, and securing trade routes.

In April 1993 the UN Security Council voiced "serious concern" over implementation of the October 1992 accord because of a shortfall in funds for deployment of peacekeeping troops and the withdrawal of Renamo members from the cease-fire and control commissions established under the treaty. Renamo subsequently indicated that it would not return to the commissions until a number of logistical problems had been resolved and some $15 million to support its political activities had been received.

On June 3, 1993, the commissions resumed meeting, and on June 21 the disarmament program was launched. Two months later the Joint Commission for the Formation of the Mozambique Defense Armed Forces announced that it had reached agreement on creation of the inclusive Mozambique Defense Armed Forces. In addition, an August 27–September 3 meeting between Chissano and Dhlakama, their first since 1992, yielded an accord on territorial administration, following Renamo's retreat from insistence that it be given jurisdiction over the provinces it controlled. At a further meeting on October 16–20 the two agreed on the establishment of a 20-member electoral commission (to be composed of ten government appointees, seven Renamo officials, and three from other opposition parties). Thereafter, the peace process continued to advance as the government and Renamo settled electoral law differences and formally agreed to a demobilization plan that would commence on November 30 and continue for six months.

By mid-January 1994 over 50 percent of the rebels were reported to have arrived at demobilization sites. By contrast, the government was widely criticized for a compliance level of only 19 percent. Nonetheless, President Chissano, responding to a Security Council call for a transfer of power to democratically elected officials by the end of November, announced that the country's first multiparty balloting would take place on October 27–28.

At the long-deferred balloting (extended by one day to October 29), President Chissano was a clear victor, polling 53.7 percent of the vote, compared to 33.7 percent for his principal opponent, Renamo's Dhlakama. While the legislative outcome was much closer (129–112), no opposition members were named to the government subsequently formed under former foreign minister Pascoal Manuel MOCUMBI.

Under pressure from the opposition and international donors to broaden its definition of what constituted a viable polling district, the assembly, with Renamo support, approved a constitutional amendment in November 1996 that provided for the establishment of a local government electoral system wherein communities with a functioning administration and a "reasonable" local tax base would participate in polling. In early 1997 Renamo reversed itself, threatening to stalemate the assembly and boycott elections if the scope of the polling was not expanded. Nevertheless, in March 1997 the assembly approved the creation of a nine-member, bipartisan national elections commission, which it charged with preparing for balloting. In June it was announced that elections would be held in 23 cities and 10 towns (one in each of the provinces) in December, one year after originally scheduled. Balloting was subsequently postponed until May 1998 and, once again, in March 1998 to June 30.

In April 1998 the partners in the Coordinating Council of the Opposition formally announced their intention to boycott the local polling, citing the government's unwillingness to allow their representatives to participate in the commission that was investigating alleged electoral roll fraud. The opposition's subsequent efforts to garner support for their boycott plans appeared to have succeeded dramatically, as on June 30 less than 20 percent of the electorate was reported to have participated in the balloting. In the immediate aftermath of the elections, during which Frelimo candidates easily overwhelmed a field of independent competitors, the opposition declared the polling "null and void" and threatened to launch a civil disobedience campaign if the results were upheld. Subsequently, however, the Renamo-led opposition announced that it would not hinder the efforts of the newly elected officials, asserting that it was turning its attention to preparing for general elections in 1999.

Chissano once again defeated Dhlakama (52.3–47.7 percent) in the presidential poll conducted on December 3–5, 1999, while Frelimo won 133 seats in the concurrent assembly balloting, compared to 117 seats for Renamo and its recently formed opposition alliance called the Renamo/Electoral Union (Renamo/*União Electoral*—Renamo/UE). After the Supreme Court rejected a Renamo/UE call for nullification of the results, Chissano was sworn in for another five-year term on January 15, 2000. Two days later he reappointed Mocumbi to head a new all-Frelimo cabinet, which was described as bringing "fresh blood" into the government while retaining the "tested core" of the previous administration.

Tension between the government and the opposition rose significantly in November 2000, when more than 40 people were killed during countrywide protest demonstrations called by Renamo. Although it was later announced that the Chissano and Dhlakama had agreed to form consultative "working committees," and the government pledged to consider Renamo's preferences in appointing governors in the disputed provinces, the exact form of this accommodation remained unclear. Dhlakama also shied away from formally recognizing the president, acknowledging only that Chissano "was *de facto* governing the country." Analysts noted that Dhlakama's subsequently muted rhetoric could be attributed in part to problems he was facing within his own party (see Renamo under Political Parties, below).

In February 2003 Renamo announced that it would run alone in upcoming municipal elections, thereby leading ten other opposition parties to form a new electoral coalition—the Movement for Change and Good Governance (*Movimento para a Mudança e Boa Governação*—MBG)—to oppose Frelimo and Renamo. In the municipal elections held on November 19, 2003, Frelimo won 28 mayoral posts and a majority of council posts in 29 municipalities, while Renamo won 5 mayor's races and council majorities in 4 municipalities (its best showing in municipal elections since multiparty elections were implemented). Although there was low voter turnout (estimated at 24.2 percent) and Renamo complained of irregularities, monitors from the European Union (EU) judged the elections free and fair, and the Constitutional Council confirmed the results in January 2004.

On February 19, 2004, former World Bank economist and Finance Minister Luisa Dias DIOGO was appointed prime minister. (Mocumbi had earlier announced his plans to retire from the premiership to take a UN job.) Diogo became the country's first female prime minister. Analysts suggested that she was appointed ahead of presidential and legislative elections in an effort to reinvigorate Frelimo and demonstrate a commitment by the party to economic reform.

Chissano having announced in 2001 that he would not seek reelection in 2004, Frelimo chose Armando GUEBUZA as its presidential candidate. In balloting on December 1–2, Guebuza won 63.7 percent of the vote. His closest rival was Dhlakama, who received 31.7 percent of the vote. In concurrent legislative balloting, Frelimo won 62 percent of the vote and 160 seats, while Renamo won 29.7 percent and 90 seats. None of the other 23 parties received more than 2 percent of the vote. Both the presidential and legislative elections were heavily criticized by the opposition and international observers. Renamo protested to the Constitutional Council, and its deputies initially refused to take their seats in the assembly. Nonetheless, on January 20, 2005, the council certified the results. Diogo was reappointed as prime minister on February 3, and she subsequently formed a new cabinet of Frelimo appointees.

During the 2004 presidential campaign, divisions within Frelimo emerged between the supporters of Armando Guebuza (the Frelimo candidate) and Chissano. The new cabinet appointed following Guebuza's victory contained many new members and appeared to represent an attempt by the new president to break with Frelimo's "old guard." In addition to purging many "*Chissanoistas*" from their former posts throughout government ranks, Guebuza also launched a broad anticorruption initiative that often focused on members of the former administration. (Guebuza described the "remoralization" of government as his top priority.) Tensions between Frelimo and Renamo also remained high, although Dhlakama (who continued to refuse to accept the validity of the 2004 election results) agreed to take his seat on the new Council of State in December 2005. Underscoring the ongoing friction, a bipartisan assembly commission, established in 2005 to propose electoral law reforms, disbanded in April 2006 without reaching agreement.

In March 2007 Guebuza conducted two cabinet reshuffles in an effort to improve the government's popularity. In particular, Guebuza replaced his brother-in-law, Defense Minister Gen. (Ret.) Tobias DAI, who had been heavily criticized following an explosion at a military facility. The president named as Transport and Communications minister Paulo ZUCULA, whose management of relief efforts following heavy flooding in January and February was widely acclaimed.

In local and regional elections in November 2008, Frelimo won 42 of the 43 mayoral contests and secured majorities on all 43 municipal councils. Renamo protested the results, which were judged as generally free and fair by both domestic and international observers. The constitutional court rejected the challenge and certified the results.

Presidential, legislative, and provincial elections were held on October 28, 2009. Many opposition candidates and parties were barred from participation, and both domestic and international observers criticized the conduct of the polling. Guebuza was reelected with 75 percent of the vote, Dhlakama placed second with 16 percent, and Daviz Simango of the Mozambique Democratic Movement (*Movimento Democrático de Moçambique*—MDM) secured 8.6 percent. In the assembly balloting, Frelimo increased its majority from 160 to 191 seats. Renamo placed second with 51 seats, and the MDM gained 8. In the provincial balloting, Frelimo secured 703 seats; Renamo, 83; the MDM, 24; and the Party for Peace, Democracy, and Development (*Partido para a Paz, Democracia, e Desenvolvimento*—PPDD), 2. After he was inaugurated, Guebuza appointed a largely reshuffled cabinet and named Aires Bonifacio ALI, then minister of education and culture, as prime minister. In October Ali conducted a minor cabinet reshuffle, replacing four ministers.

In May opposition parties in the assembly held a brief boycott as the legislature began to consider amendments to the country's constitution. In August the assembly and the cabinet approved a new austerity measure designed to reduce Mozambique's growing budget deficit, which rose to 5.4 percent of the GDP in 2010. Previous efforts to reduce government spending had resulted in riots and demonstrations.

In April 2008 Amnesty International issued a report that criticized the Mozambican police for excessive force and extrajudicial killings. Continuing internal strife among the opposition parties was instrumental in Frelimo's sweep of the 2009 presidential, legislative, and provincial balloting. In the polling, Guebuza was reelected with 75 percent of the vote, and Frelimo increased its majority in the assembly and among the provincial councils. MDM and Renamo candidates were banned by the election commission in many districts or faced restrictions on campaigning, and six candidates from smaller parties were banned from running for the presidency. International observers criticized the balloting for irregularities. Renamo rejected the results and called for new balloting. In response, some international donor states cut aid to the government.

Ali was dismissed as prime minister on October 8, 2012, and was immediately replaced by Alberto Clementino VAQUINA (see Current issues, below). Guebuza concurrently conducted a minor cabinet reshuffle.

Filipe NYUSI (Frelimo) won presidential balloting on October 15 with 57.1 percent of the vote. In concurrent legislative balloting, Frelimo won a reduced majority of 144 seats, followed by Renamo with 89, and the MDM with 17 seats. Renamo disputed the results of both the legislative and presidential balloting (see Current issues, below). Nyusi was sworn in on January 15, 2015, and named a reduced cabinet of 22 ministers led by Carlos Agostinho do ROSÁRIO (Frelimo). The cabinet was dominated by Frelimo members who were allies or associates of Nyusi.

Constitution and government. The 1975 constitution characterized the People's Republic of Mozambique as a "popular democratic state" while reserving for Frelimo "the directing power of the state and society," with decisions taken by party organs to be regarded as binding on all government officials. A subsequent constitution, adopted in August 1978, set as a national objective "the construction of the material and ideological bases for a socialist society." The president of Frelimo served as president of the republic and chief of the armed forces, while an indirectly elected People's Assembly was designated as the "supreme organ of state power."

The basic law approved by the assembly in November 1990 contained no reference to Frelimo or leadership of the working class, while "People's" was dropped from the state name. It provided for a popularly elected president serving a maximum of two five-year terms. The Council of Ministers continued to be headed by a presidentially appointed prime minister, with national legislators selected on a proportional basis in multiparty balloting. In addition to freedom of association and of the press, the new document guaranteed various human and civil rights, including the right to private property and the right to strike. A Supreme Court heads an independent judiciary.

A number of constitutional amendments were approved by the Assembly of the Republic in November 2004, although most of the basic elements of the 1990 text remained intact. (The president continued to hold the power to appoint the prime minister, cabinet ministers, and provincial governors.) The amendments reaffirmed the authority of the Constitutional Council (established in 2003) to rule on the constitutionality of legislation and to validate election results. Other changes provided for an Ombudsman (appointed by a two-third's majority in the assembly) to investigate allegations of misconduct by state officials, for the election of provincial assemblies (beginning in 2008), and for the establishment of an advisory Council of State (comprised of automatic members [such as former presidents, former assembly presidents, and the runner-up in the most recent presidential election], as well as members appointed by the president and the assembly). Although the new council was given no formal decision-making authority, the president was required to consult with the council on a broad range of matters, including the conduct of elections. The basic law revisions also removed the president's immunity from prosecution by authorizing impeachment by a vote of two-thirds of the assembly.

The governors of the country's ten provinces are appointed by the president, who may annul the decisions of provincial, district, and local assemblies. The city of Maputo (which has provincial status) is under the administrative direction of a City Council chair. Legislation in 2006 provided for the creation of elected assemblies for the ten provinces, the size of the assemblies to be determined by population. In 2008 the number of municipalities with elected mayors and assemblies was increased from 33 to 43.

After having maintained strict control of the media since independence, the government in 1990 permitted substantial press liberalization. In late 1991 a press law was ratified, giving existing publications six months to reregister in accordance with new provisions, including revised ownership rules. Reporters Without Borders ranked Mozambique as 87th out of 180 countries in its 2016 Press Freedom Index, a considerable improvement from 2010 when the country ranked 135th out of 178 states.

Foreign relations. Avowedly Marxist in orientation until mid-1989, the Frelimo government was for many years the beneficiary of substantial economic, technical, and security support from the Soviet Union, Cuba, East Germany, and other Moscow-line states. However, links with the West began to increase in 1979. The UK and Brazil extended credit, and in 1982 Portugal resumed relations that had ceased in 1977 as a result of the nationalization of Portuguese holdings. Relations with the United States, troubled since 1977 by charges of human rights abuses, reached a nadir in 1981 with the expulsion of all U.S. embassy personnel for alleged espionage. Relations were reestablished in July 1983, and President Machel made a state visit to Washington in September 1985, securing economic aid and exploring the possibility of military assistance. President Chissano was similarly received in March 1990 by U.S. president George H. W. Bush, who promised an unspecified amount of U.S. aid for reconstruction and development. Meanwhile, in 1984 Mozambique had been admitted to the IMF and World Bank, signifying a desire on Maputo's part to become a more active participant in the world economy.

Despite its prominence as one of the Front-Line States committed to majority rule in southern Africa, Mozambique maintained economic links to white-dominated South Africa as a matter of "realistic policy," with some 40,000 Mozambicans employed in South African mines and considerable revenue derived from cooperation in transport and hydroelectric power. However, relations were severely strained by South African support for the Renamo insurgents in the 1980s. In a 1984 nonaggression pact, the "Nkomati Accord," South Africa agreed to stop aiding Renamo in return for Mozambique's pledge not to support the African National Congress (ANC) in its guerrilla campaign against the South African minority government. The accord proved ineffective, however, as growing rebel activity fostered Mozambican suspicion of continued destabilization attempts by its white-ruled neighbor. In August 1987 the two countries agreed that the pact should be reactivated, prompting an unprecedented meeting between President Chissano and South African president Botha in September 1988, at which Botha again promised not to support the insurgents. In 1990 President Chissano announced that he was convinced that the new government in Pretoria had indeed halted its support of Renamo and that the two countries could now concentrate on economic cooperation.

The civil war also dominated Maputo's relations elsewhere in the region. The Zimbabwean government, declaring "If Mozambique falls, we fall," sent an estimated 10,000 troops to combat the Renamo rebels, particularly in the transport corridor to Beira, which played a central role in the Front-Line States' effort to reduce dependence on South African trade routes. In December 1986 Tanzanian president Mwinyi also agreed to make troops available to Mozambique, as did Malawi following a dispute over alleged Renamo bases within its borders (see entry on Malawi). In 1992 Zimbabwean president Robert Mugabe, along with Italian officials, played a major role in brokering the peace accord that was signed in Rome in October.

By early 1993 approximately 1.7 million Mozambicans had taken refuge in neighboring countries, Malawi housing 1.1 million. On June 12 Mozambique and the UN High Commission for Refugees (UNHCR) formally inaugurated a repatriation operation (beginning with exiles in Zimbabwe), which observers described as the largest ever in Africa, and by August 19 Mozambique had signed repatriation agreements with Malawi, Swaziland, and Zambia. The repatriation program was formally terminated on November 21, 1995, at which time the UNHCR announced that more than 1 million refugees had returned home.

The most surprising foreign policy development of 1995 was Mozambique's admission to the Commonwealth as the group's 53rd member. Its entry on a unique and special case basis had been urged by its anglophone neighbors as a means of enhancing regional trade, most importantly in cashew nuts, which critics insisted was effectively controlled by Indian and Pakistani interests.

In 1996 Mozambique negotiated security agreements with Malawi, Swaziland, and Zimbabwe in an effort to squelch the border violence attributed to *Chimwenje,* a shadowy grouping of Zimbabwean dissidents who were allegedly led and trained by former Renamo militiamen from bases along their shared borders. (For more information on *Chimwenje,* see entry on Zimbabwe.) Meanwhile, following approximately a year of negotiations, Mozambique signed an agreement with South Africa in May that provided South African farmers with access to Mozambican agricultural land. The deal was opposed by both Renamo leaders and Frelimo activists, who charged that "exporting white farmers to Mozambique" was favored by South Africa's ANC as a means of freeing up land for black settlement. At the same time, South Africa and Mozambique inaugurated the Maputo Corridor Development Project with the aim of redeveloping the trade route between Johannesburg and Maputo and refurbishing the latter's harbor. In 2002 the government initiated a program to resettle white farmers from Zimbabwe whose land had been expropriated.

Relations between Mozambique and the United States have improved in the 2000s. In 2002 Chissano, along with the leaders of Botswana and Angola, met with U.S. president George W. Bush in Washington, D.C., in a summit on development of the region. Mozambique is part of the U.S. Africa Growth and Opportunity Act (AGOA) that offers preferential trade opportunities to African states. Relations with European states also remained strong, with both France and Russia agreeing in 2002 to cancel portions of Mozambique's debt. Meanwhile the EU increased direct annual aid to Mozambique to $131 million per year through 2007.

In 2002 and 2003 Mozambique conducted a series of cooperative military exercises with Portugal. (The two countries also have an agreement whereby soldiers from Mozambique are trained in Portugal.) Although the relationship between the two countries subsequently remained essentially strong, friction developed in 2005 over the proposed takeover by Mozambique of a hydroelectric plant on the Zambesi River for which the Portuguese government held 85 percent financial responsibility. New President Guebuza refused to accept the amount of back debt that Portugal demanded be paid by Mozambique prior to the transfer of ownership, and, although a tentative agreement was announced in late 2005, it was not implemented until Mozambique paid Portugal $700 million in November 2007. Meanwhile, the Guebuza administration reached out to a broad range of other potential donors for assistance, achieving success most notably with China, Germany, and India. China agreed in 2007 to give Mozambique $2.5 million in military equipment and to provide training for Mozambican military officers annually at Chinese military academies.

In 2007 South Africa decided to reopen an investigation into the 1986 death of President Machel because of suspicions that the apartheid regime had been involved in the plane crash that had killed the Mozambique leader. Meanwhile, a South African soldier was killed along with five Mozambicans in June while participating in a joint operation to destroy mines and leftover military ordnance from Mozambique's civil war.

Political violence against Zimbabweans in South Africa led more than 10,000 refugees to flee to refugee camps in Mozambique in May 2008. In December Mozambique and China signed an agreement to increase military cooperation and collaboration. Meanwhile, China granted Mozambique $1.5 million to upgrade its military equipment.

Mozambique and Portugal signed an agreement in February 2009 to expand cooperation in the areas of law enforcement and criminal justice. Also in February Mozambique and India signed two new economic agreements and India granted Mozambique a $25 million line of credit to improve industry and infrastructure. A further accord, to increase cooperation in economic development, was signed in September 2010 between the two countries. In December 2010 diplomatic cables released by WikiLeaks revealed the increasing concern of the United States over the rise in drug trafficking in Mozambique. The documents also highlighted connections between the drug trade and some Frelimo officials. In June the United States listed prominent Mozambican businessman Mahamed Bachir SULEMAN as an international drug kingpin and requested assistance from the government in investigating him.

The UK announced in April 2011 that it would provide $538 million over four years to improve health and education in Mozambique. In June Mozambique and South Africa signed an agreement to cooperate on antipiracy measures, including joint naval patrols and intelligence collaboration. The Frelimo government announced in August that it would not ratify the ICC treaty until further study had been undertaken. Critics charged that government officials were afraid that they would be charged by the ICC for recent incidents, including the response to the September 2010 riots.

Mozambique and Zambia finalized an agreement to demarcate most of their mutual borders in August 2012 after a year's negotiations. Several disputed areas remained with both countries pledging further talks. In September China announced that it would provide $25 million in poverty-reduction assistance to Mozambique. This was in addition to $500 million in economic aid already pledged over a five-year period. In December Zimbabwe deployed more than 1,000 troops along the border with Mozambique in response to reported incursions by Renamo rebels.

In January 2013 Spain announced that it would be forced to cut aid to Mozambique as a result of financial pressures. The following month Mozambique and Thailand signed an accord to expand trade and commerce between the two nations. South Africa announced in May that it would increase border security with Mozambique following an increase in poaching of rhinos (see entry on South Africa). In June Mozambique and Japan signed an accord to promote investment. The agreement was the first of its kind between Japan and a sub-Saharan African country.

The African Development Banks announced in October 2014 that it would provide Mozambique with $59 million to support the government's annual budget. This was in addition to a $60 million line of credit to be used for economic development. The support was reportedly a reward for the conduct of the 2014 balloting, although international election observers criticized the conduct of the polls (see Current issues, below). The G-19, a group of nineteen donor states to Mozambique, became the G-15, after Belgium, the Netherlands, Norway, and Spain withdrew, citing a lack of democratization. Also in October Mozambique and Kenya signed a historic trade deal to dramatically reduce restrictions on air travel between the two nations.

Fighting between government troops and Renamo militias in July 2015 prompted a wave of some 11,000 refugees to flee to Malawi (see Current issues, below, and entry on Malawi) by May 2016. The refugees reported abuse at the hands of government soldiers. Fighting in the north also prompted Zimbabwe to institute new border controls to prevent Renamo groups from seeking shelter from Mozambican government forces.

In June 2016 China announced it would forgive about $5 million of Mozambique's debt.

Current issues. In August 2011 Afonso Dhlakama announced Renamo was setting up new military barracks, ostensibly in response to Frelimo violations of the demobilization clause of the peace accord, and threatened to set up a parallel government. In November a commission was launched to update the constitution, which critics said Guebuza might use to secure a third term. Renamo refused to fill its 6 of 17 seats on the commission.

Several Frelimo mayors resigned in the run-up to December 7 by-elections, amid reports that the party was afraid of losing future elections following anticorruption protests in some towns. Renamo boycotted the polls, saying that no free voting would happen under a Frelimo government. The outcome of the mayoral elections in the three northern cities saw the Frelimo candidate defeated by the MDM's Manuel de ARAUJO in the city of Quelimane, bolstering the sense that MDM might overtake Renamo as the main opposition party. In subsequent months a leaked report from the national police on why Frelimo lost the election created a stir, describing how an elite police force raided MDM property without warrants and how officials otherwise obstructed opposition staff and candidates.

By late 2012 proposals for anticorruption laws demanded by foreign aid donors were bogged down by procedural issues as officials labored to put off action until after the 2014 elections. These include conflict of interest reforms that could reportedly jeopardize legislators' lucrative business interests. At a Frelimo party congress in September, Ali lost his seat on Frelimo's governing committee (see Political Parties, below). Guebuza responded by dismissing the prime minister and replacing him with Alberto VAQUINO, a popular governor who was elected to the Frelimo executive.

Flooding in Maputo and southern areas of Mozambique killed 55 and displaced more than 169,000 in January 2013. In April clashes between opposition groups and security forces in the Sofala left seven dead and more than a score injured. Meanwhile Renamo officials threatened to boycott municipal elections in protest of new electoral laws that the party claimed inappropriately favored Frelimo (see Political Parties, below). Renewed fighting between Renamo and government forces continued into June. The passage of new measures on conflicts of interest led to the resignation of more than 30 Frelimo parliamentarians and party officials in May. The new law banned public servants from collecting both their government salary and pay from private or state firms.

Increased fighting between Renamo and Frelimo in October prompted the latter to declare that the 1992 peace accord was "over." Dhlakama subsequently went into hiding. In local balloting in December, Frelimo won in most of the 53 municipalities. However, the MDM surprised observers by winning mayoral posts in the major port cities of Beira and Quelimane. Renamo boycotted the elections. Fighting continued into 2014 as Renamo, with an estimated 1,000 fighters, was able to conduct an effective and disruptive guerilla campaign.

Ahead of national elections, Frelimo and Renamo signed a ceasefire on August 24, 2014. Under the terms of the agreements, fighters on both sides were granted amnesty, and some 200 Renamo prisoners were released. In addition, a small international monitoring force led by Botswana was scheduled to be deployed. In balloting on October 15, Frelimo candidate Felipe Nyusi was elected president, while his party again won a majority in the legislature. Renamo and the MDM both rejected the results, alleging massive fraud and pointing to turnout numbers that in some areas exceeded 100 percent of registered voters and highlighting reports of missing ballot boxes in opposition strongholds.

Renamo boycotted the assembly after the 2014 balloting. Party members only assumed their seats on February 11, 2015, after Frelimo agreed to changes that would give more power to regional governments. However, the assembly rejected, along party lines, proposed legislation to grant more power to provincial governments. The failure of successive devolution plans led Renamo to withdraw from ongoing peace negotiations in August. Meanwhile, renewed fighting was reported in the northern province of Tete between government forces and Renamo militias.

Reports in April 2016 indicated that the government had issued more than $1.4 billion in undisclosed loans in the final years of Guebuza's presidency to businesses and firms with ties to Frelimo officials. The loans brought Mozambique's total foreign debt to $9.9 billion or more than 100 percent of GDP. The revelations led the IMF and the United Kingdom to suspend aid to Mozambique. There was growing scrutiny from foreign donors, including the United States and Germany, and calls for independent audits of the finance ministry.

POLITICAL PARTIES

For its first 15 years of independence Mozambique was a one-party state in which Frelimo was constitutionally empowered to guide the operations of government at all levels. However, a constitutional revision in October 1990 guaranteed freedom of association, with subsequent legislation establishing the criteria for party legalization. Some 29 parties or alliances contested the 2014 legislative elections. The electoral commission rejected eight candidates ahead of the 2014 presidential balloting, leaving only the candidates of Frelimo, Renamo, and the MDM, to run for the presidency.

Government Party:

Mozambique Liberation Front (*Frente de Libertação de Moçambique*—Frelimo). Founded in 1962 by the union of three nationalist parties and led by Dr. Eduardo Mondlane until his death in 1969, Frelimo engaged in armed resistance to Portuguese rule from 1964 to 1974, when agreement on independence was reached. At its third national congress in 1977, the front was designated a Marxist-Leninist party (directed by a Central Committee, a Political Bureau, and a Secretariat), but at the fourth party congress in 1983 economic philosophy began to shift toward the encouragement of free-market activity. Following the death of Samora Machel in October 1986, the Central Committee designated his longtime associate, Joaquim Alberto Chissano, as its political leader.

Frelimo retreated even further from Marxist doctrine at the group's fifth congress in 1989. The party opened its membership to many formerly excluded groups, such as private property owners, the business community, Christians, Muslims, and traditionalists. The congress also called for a negotiated settlement with Renamo, bureaucratic reform, and emphasis on family farming rather than state agriculture.

Although President Chissano easily defeated Renamo's Afonso Dhlakama in the 1994 election, Frelimo as a party performed much more poorly, barely securing a majority of legislative seats. On a regional basis the results were quite mixed, the party substantially outpolling Renamo in the south, while being decisively defeated in the center and trailing marginally in the north.

In what was described as a break with "old guard" leadership, five of the Frelimo Central Committee's six members were replaced on July 24, 1995, and Manuel Tome was appointed as the party's new secretary general. In spite of these changes, corruption charges continued to dog the party. Observers attributed Frelimo's subsequent endorsement of a proposal to limit the geographic scope of municipal elections to weak support beyond its southern base. Challenged only by small opposition groups and independent candidates, Frelimo dominated balloting for local posts in June 1998. It secured 48.5 percent of the vote and 133 seats in the December 1999 legislative balloting.

During a party congress in June 2002, Chissano was reelected as Frelimo chair. However, former parliamentary leader Armando Guebuza was elected as the new secretary general and the party's 2004 presidential candidate despite the fact that Chissano had supported Herder MUTEIA for the post. Guebuza was elected president in the 2004 balloting, and Frelimo increased its seats in the assembly to 160. Significant friction was subsequently reported between President Guebuza and former members of the Chissano administration.

Guebuza further consolidated his control over Frelimo at a party congress in November 2006. His close supporters gained dominance of the 160-member party central commission and the 17-member political commission, the main decision-making body of Frelimo. Meanwhile, Guebuza loyalist Filipe Paunde was elected general secretary of the party. A party congress in July 2008 chose candidates to compete in municipal and regional elections. Reports indicated that the majority of candidates were Guebuza supporters. In September Guebuza was chosen as Frelimo's presidential candidate for the 2009 balloting at a party contest where the incumbent ran unopposed. Guebuza was reelected in the October 2009 balloting and Frelimo increased its seats in the assembly to 191. In January Guebuza replaced prime minister Luisa Dais DIOGO, who was seen as a possible successor to the president and the leader of the Chissano wing of the party, with Aires Bonifacio Ali, a close Guebuza ally. Tensions within the party led to the resignation of three Frelimo mayors in August 2011. Reports indicated that the trio were members of the Chissano wing of the party who were ousted to make way for pro-Guebuza candidates ahead of the 2013 balloting.

By December 2011, with Guebuza's futile efforts to change the constitution to allow a third term, contenders were reportedly jockeying to succeed him. There is also said to be growing resentment within the party against a group of Guebuza's associates and their families who have benefited financially from his tenure and were accelerating the accumulation of wealth in advance of his departure. Guebuza was reelected as party leader at the September 23–29, 2012, party congress. However Ali lost his position on the 17-member of the political committee in what was seen as a defeat for Guebuza, who was subsequently forced to dismiss the prime minister. Alberto Clementino VAQUINA, a close Guebuza ally, became prime minister.

Defense Minister Filipe Nyusi was selected as the Renamo presidential candidate in March 2014, and Elisha Machava became secretary general of the party. Nyusi went on to win the October balloting with 57.1 percent of the vote, while the party secured 55.9 percent of the vote and 144 seats in the assembly. Nyusi was formally elected Frelimo's chair at a party conference on March 29, 2015, in what reports indicate was an effort to broaden his power within the party.

Leaders: Felipe NYUSI (President of the Republic), Carlos Agostinho do ROSÁRIO (Prime Minister), Armando GUEBUZA (Former President of the Republic), Joaquim Alberto CHISSANO (Former President of the Republic and Honorary Party President), Verónica Nataniel MACAMO (President of the Assembly), Elisha MACHAVA (General Secretary).

Opposition Parties:

Mozambique National Resistance—MNR (*Resistência Nacional Moçambicana*—Renamo). Also known as the *Movimento Nacional da Resistência de Moçambique* (MNRM) and as the André Group, after its late founder, André Matade MATSANGAI, Renamo was formed in the early 1970s primarily as an intelligence network within Mozambique for the white Rhodesian government of Ian Smith. Following Rhodesia's transition to majority rule as "Zimbabwe" in 1980, Renamo developed into a widespread anti-Frelimo insurgency, relying on financial support from Portuguese expatriates and, until the early 1990s, substantial military aid from South Africa. The 20,000-member Renamo army, comprising Portuguese and other mercenaries, Frelimo defectors, and numerous recruits from the Shona-speaking Ndau ethnic group, operated mainly in rural areas, where it interdicted transport corridors and sabotaged food production. Widely condemned for terrorist tactics, including indiscriminate killing and mutilation of civilians, Renamo, although largely stalemating the government militarily, generally failed to gain external recognition. In an apparent attempt to foster its nationalist image, Renamo launched an "Africanization" program in 1987 that included replacements for white Portuguese at its Lisbon-based headquarters. Further image-building took place at the 1989 Renamo congress, which revamped the movement's internal bodies. The congress also declared that Renamo was no longer intent on overthrowing the government but was seeking instead a peace settlement under which it could participate as a recognized "political force" in free elections resulting from constitutional revision. However, the Renamo leadership appeared disconcerted when, in 1990, the government agreed to hold such elections. Thereafter, despite a December 1, 1990, cease-fire, Renamo's military activities continued, thus supporting a widely held view that apart from its advocacy of a multiparty system the group lacked a political agenda.

When rebel strikes coincided with the reopening of peace talks in March and May 1991, there was speculation that party president Gen. Afonso Dhlakama had lost control over some of his forces. Thereafter, in negotiations with the government in Rome, Renamo, weakened by dwindling finances and pressed by South Africa, the UK, and the United States to negotiate seriously, signed the first of a series of concessionary protocols. By mid-1992 it was apparent that the lengthy rebellion was drawing to a close.

While Dhlakama failed in his bid to win the presidency from Chissano in December 1994, the results of the legislative poll left Renamo only marginally second to Frelimo. In May 1995 President Chissano stated that, while Dhlakama could not be styled leader of the opposition (because he was not an elected member of the People's Assembly), he would be accorded "dignified status."

Although Renamo's legislative initiatives were blocked in the Frelimo-controlled assembly in 1995–1996, observers credited Dhlakama with continuing to enhance both the group's and his own political viability. In November 1996 Renamo legislators reportedly gave unanimous support to a constitutional amendment altering local election laws. In early 1997, however, the party reversed itself, threatening to boycott upcoming balloting unless the 1996 bill was repealed. Amid escalating tensions, the party organized nationwide antigovernment demonstrations in May 1997.

Although Renamo officials publicly insisted that they had no interest in returning to an armed struggle, arson attacks and disruption of the water supply were reported in July 1997. Subsequently, Dhlakama denounced the government's use of force to suppress the unrest.

Citing the need for the party to be "more flexible," Dhlakama forced the ouster of Secretary General Jose de CASTRO and Assistant Secretary General Albino FAIFE in January 1998. João Alexandre was subsequently named to Castro's former post.

In mid-1999 the **Mozambique National Resistance/Electoral Union** (*Resistência Nacional Moçambicana/União Electoral*—Renamo/UE) was formed. The Renamo/UE electoral alliance secured 38.8 percent of the vote and 117 seats in the December legislative balloting, a surprisingly good result in the opinion of most analysts after what was generally viewed as a minimalist campaign that lacked a coherent platform. Collaterally, Renamo/UE presidential candidate Afonso Dhlakama won 47.7 percent of the votes in the presidential balloting in 1999.

A split was reported in 2000 between those Renamo members, including a number of legislators, who appeared to be interested in negotiating a settlement with Frelimo, and those led by Dhlakama, who at midyear were still refusing to accept the results of the December 1999 legislative and presidential elections. In September 2000 the party's former legislative leader, Raul DOMINGOS, was expelled for "having collaborated with Frelimo" and for "corruption" during secret talks he allegedly held with the government. (Some analysts noted that Domingos had previously been seen as a possible successor to Dhlakama.)

Despite facing increasing dissent within the party, Dhlakama nevertheless was reelected as Renamo's president in November 2001. At a subsequent party congress, a ten-member political committee was created as a means to decentralize party leadership and broaden the party's appeal. Renamo contested municipal elections independently in 2003, but revived the Renamo/UE alliance in the 2004 presidential elections. The alliance was hurt by the defection of Renamo members to form the Party for Peace, Development, and Democracy (see below) and the loss of Unamo (see below). Dhlakama again ran as the party's candidate, receiving 31.7 percent of the vote. The Renamo-led electoral alliance won 29.7 percent of the vote in the concurrent legislative elections, its representation declining from 117 to 90 seats in the assembly. Renamo deputies initially boycotted the assembly to protest perceived irregularities in the polling, but, after the Constitutional Council upheld the results, the deputies were seated in January 2005.

A number of regional and local Renamo leaders reportedly defected to Frelimo in 2006. Partially in response to losses within the party, the senior Renamo leadership decided to contest upcoming regional and local elections without its coalition partners in an effort to gain greater representation at the provincial and municipal levels. In July 2007 the Renamo/UE electoral alliance ended. Some members of the grouping subsequently formed a new coalition, the **Electoral Union Coalition** (*Coligação União Eleitoral*—UE). Nonetheless, the member parties pledged to continue political cooperation in opposition to Frelimo. Prior to the 2008 local elections party leaders decided against allowing Daviz Simango, the popular mayor of Beira, from seeking reelection. Simango led a mass defection from Renamo. Reports indicated that at least ten Renamo deputies in the assembly resigned from the party. Simango campaigned as an independent and won another term and subsequently launched a new party, the **Mozambique Democratic Movement** (*Movimento Democrático de Moçambique*—MDM).

Led by Sebastiao JANOTA and Saimon MUTERO, a group of Renamo dissidents formed a splinter group, the **Renamo National Salvation Junta** (*Junta Nacional de Salvação da Renamo*—JNSR) in 2008. The JNSR reportedly sought to replace Dhlakama and institute a number of party reforms, including greater financial transparency and openness in internal Renamo elections. Dhlakama was chosen as Renamo's candidate for the 2009 presidential balloting. He placed second with 16.4 percent of the vote. Renamo had its worst electoral performance in flawed legislative balloting, dropping to 51 seats in the assembly.

In July 2011 Dhlakama publicly renounced violence and pledged not to engage in armed struggle in the future. However, the following month, Renamo began constructing "barracks" for former rebels in areas that had been Renamo strongholds. Opposition to a new electoral law in April 2013 led to renewed clashes between Renamo and government forces. Reports indicated that as many as 300 Renamo members were arrested that month. Meanwhile the party endeavored to both boycott and disrupt the 2013 municipal polling. Following a low-intensity insurgency in the first half of 2014, Renamo signed a new peace accord with the government in August to allow national elections in October. In that balloting Dhlakama placed second in the presidential election with 36.6 percent of the vote, while the party secured 32.5 percent of the vote, and 89 seats in the Assembly.

New fighting between government forces and Renamo broke out in July 2015. On October 9 Dhlakama was briefly detained by security forces at his home. On January 20, 2016, Renamo secretary general, Manuel BISSOPO, was shot twice, and a bodyguard was killed in an attack that the party blamed on Frelimo.

Leaders: Gen. Afonso Macacho Marceta DHLAKAMA (President and 2014 presidential candidate), Fernando MAZANGA (Spokesperson), João ALEXANDRE (Former Secretary General), Manuel BISSOPO (Secretary General).

Mozambique Democratic Movement (*Movimento Democrático de Moçambique*—MDM). The MDM was formed in 2009 by former Renamo members led by Daviz Simango. Simango was elected mayor of Beira as an independent in 2008. The MDM drew support from independents and former opposition members. Reports indicated that at least four Renamo deputies in the assembly had defected to the MDM. Simango was the MDM presidential candidate for 2009 and placed third in the balloting with 8.6 percent of the vote. The MDM received 3.9 percent of the vote in the assembly balloting and secured eight seats. In April 2011 MDM secretary general Ismael MUSSA resigned. He was replaced by Bernabé NKOMO. At a party congress in December 2012, Simango was reelected MDM president. Simango was the party's 2014 presidential candidate. He placed third with 6.4 percent of the vote. Meanwhile, the MDM secured 8.4 percent of the vote in legislative balloting, and 17 Assembly seats. The party supported the Renamo proposal to grant more autonomy to regional governments.

Leaders: Daviz SIMANGO (2014 presidential candidate), Luis BOAVIDA (Secretary General).

Other Parties and Groups:

Party for Peace, Democracy, and Development (*Partido para a Paz, Democracia, e Desenvolvimento*—PPDD). Formed in 2003 by disaffected members of Renamo, including Raul Domingos, the PPDD is a liberal party that promotes nonpartisanship in public administration. At the first party congress on October 4, 2003, Domingos was nominated to run for the presidency in 2004. He placed third in the balloting with 2.7 percent of the vote. The PPDD also came in third in the concurrent legislative elections with 2 percent of the vote. Most analysts believe that the PPDD pulled votes away from Renamo. The party hoped to continue to build its base through provincial and municipal elections in 2008 and then challenge Renamo as the main opposition party. In 2008 the ruling Senegalese Democratic Party (PDS) pledged to provide monetary and technical assistance to the PPDD in the 2008 local elections and the 2009 legislative balloting. The PPDD participated in the 2008 municipal balloting, placing third, behind Frelimo and Renamo, in overall votes. Following the local elections, Domingos reportedly offered to merge the PPDD with Renamo if Afonso Dhlakama resigned as leader of Renamo. The PPDD failed to secure any seats in the 2009 balloting for the national legislature, but it gained two seats in the concurrent provincial assembly elections. The party failed to secure representation in the national Assembly in the 2014 balloting.

Leader: Raul DOMINGOS.

Green Party of Mozambique (PVM). Formed in 1997, the PVM (also known as *Os Verdes* [The Greens]) split into two factions prior to the 1999 elections, one supportive of membership in Renamo/UE and the other committed to an independent campaign. In 2004 the independent faction gained 0.3 percent in legislative elections, and in 2009 it secured 0.5 percent in the assembly polling. The party again secured less than 1 percent of the vote in the 2014 balloting.

Leader: Armando Bruno João SAPEMBE.

Other minor parties that participated in the 2009 or 2014 assembly balloting but failed to gain seats include the **Party for Liberty and Development** (*Partido de Liberdade e Desenvolvimento*—PLD), formed in June 2009 and led by Caetano SABINDE; the **Party of Freedom and Solidarity** (*Partido de Solidariedade e Liberdade*), formed in 2004 and led by Carlos Inácio COELHO; the **National Reconciliation Party** (PARENA), led by André José BALATE; the **Mozambique Independents Alliance** (*Aliança Independente de Moçambique*—ALIMO), a breakaway faction of Pimo (see below) led by Khalid Hussein SIDET; the **Ecological Party–Land Movement** (*Partido Ecologista–Movimento da Terra*), led by João Pedro MASSANGO; the **Party of Union for Mundança** (*Partido de União para Mundança*—UM); **Patriotic Movement for Democracy** (*Movimento Patriótico para Democracia*—MPD), created in 2009 by Matias Dianhane BANZE; the **Union of Mozambican Democrats–Popular Party** (*União dos Democratas de Moçambique–Partido Popular*—UDM-PT), led by José Ricardo VIANA; the **National Party of Workers and Peasants** (*Partido Nacional dos Operários e Camponeses*—PANAOC); the **Popular Democratic Party** (*Partido Popular Democrático*—PPD); the **Electoral Union Coalition** (*Coligação União Eleitoral*—UE); the **Labor Party** (*Partido Trabalhista*—PT), led by Miguel MABOTE; and the **Social Democratic Reconciliation Party** (*Partido de Reconciliação Democrática Social*—PRDS). None of the parties received more than 0.5 percent of the vote.

Independent Party of Mozambique (*Partido Independente de Moçambique*—Pimo). Described as a "thinly disguised Islamic party," Pimo won 1.2 percent of the legislative vote in 1994 and 0.7 percent in 1999. Pimo leader Yaqub Sibinde attempted to run for president in 1999, but his nomination was declared invalid by the Supreme Court. In 2003 Pimo won three posts in municipal elections in predominately Islamic areas. In 2004 Sibinde ran for the presidency and received 0.9 percent of the vote. In the concurrent legislative elections, Pimo received 0.6 percent of the vote. In 2006 Sibinde was reported to have formed an opposition alliance of 18 minor parties called the **Constructive Opposition Bloc**. Besides Pimo, other members of the bloc included the PT and Panamo. Pimo gained one council seat in the 2008 municipal elections but failed to register candidates for the 2009 assembly elections. Pimo led an unsuccessful effort in 2011 to reform electoral practices ahead of balloting in 2013. In 2012 Sibinde was appointed a special advisor to the government on Islamic affairs. In 2014 Pimo endorsed Frelimo's Nyusi for the presidency, after Sibinde's candidacy was rejected for not securing the minimum 10,000 signatures to run. Pimo supported Renamo's call for greater regional autonomy in 2015.

Leaders: Yaqub Neves Salomão SIBINDE, Magalhaes IBRAMURGY (General Secretary).

Social, Liberal, and Democratic Party (*Partido Social, Liberal e Democrático*—PSLD). The PSLD was formed by former Palmo leader Casimiro Nhamithambo, who complained of the parent group "lacking democracy." The PSLD, also referenced by the initials SOL, was a founding member in early 1999 of the Mozambican Opposition Union (*União Moçambicana da Oposição*—UMO), which its supporters hoped would serve as an electoral front for as many as a dozen parties. Nhamithambo initially served as the UMO secretary general, but he resigned from that post later in the year as the result of friction with Wehia RIPUA, the leader of another UMO component, the **Mozambique Democratic Party** (*Partido Democrático de Mocambique*—Pademo). Although Nhamithambo announced at that time that the PSLD would remain in UMO despite the dispute, the PSLD ultimately contested the December 2000 legislative poll on its own, winning 2 percent of the vote. (Only three groups finally ran under the UMO banner: Pademo, the **Democratic Congress Party** [*Partido do Congresso Democrático*—Pacode], and the **Democratic Party for the Reconciliation of Mozambique**. Meanwhile, UMO supported Renamo's Afonso Dhlakama in the presidential race after Ripua's candidacy was disallowed due to faulty nomination papers.) In 2004 the PSLD won 0.5 percent of the legislative vote, but its candidate list was rejected by the electoral commission prior to the 2009 elections. The party's candidate list was approved in the 2014 balloting, but the PSLD failed to secure any seats.

Leader: Casimiro Miguel NHAMITHAMBO.

Social Broadening Party of Mozambique (*Partido de Ampliação Social de Moçambique*—Pasomo). Pasomo won 0.1 percent of the legislative vote in 1999 and 0.5 percent in 2004. It did not qualify for the 2009 assembly balloting. It did contest the 2014 balloting, but failed to win any seats in the national Assembly.

Leader: Helder Francisco CAMPIRA.

United National Coalition of the Opposition (*Coligação União Nacional de Oposição*—UNO). In 2008 the **Liberal Front** (*Frente Liberal*—FL) and PARENA formed the **National Democratic Alliance** (*Alianca Nacional Democrática*—AND) to compete in the municipal elections. AND also included two other small parties, the **Democratic Reconciliation Party** (*Partido de Reconcilliação Democrática*—PAREDE), led by Joaquina Joaaquim NOTICO, and the **Independent Social-Democratic Party** (PASDI). The coalition was reshuffled and reformed ahead of the 2009 balloting as the UNO and included PAREDE, PASDI, and the Mozambican Social Democratic Party (*Partido Moçambicano da Social Democracia*—PMSD).

Mozambican Social Democratic Party (*Partido Moçambicano da Social Democracia*—PMSD). The PMSD was launched as political heir to the Mozambican Nationalist Movement (*Movimento Nacionalista Moçambicana*—Monamo) at the conclusion of Monamo's first congress in May 1992. Monamo had been founded in 1979 by exiled former Frelimo members led by Máximo Dias, who in 1973–1974 had attempted to persuade the Lisbon government to negotiate with the insurgents. In the late 1980s Monamo merged with the West German-based Mozambique National Independent Committee (*Comité Nacional Independente de Moçambique*—Conimo) to form the Mozambican Political Union (*União Política Moçambicana*—Upomo). In 1989 the group called for an immediate cease-fire under UN auspices, the departure of foreign troops, and the holding of national elections. Upomo operated until adoption of the 1990 constitution, after which Dias returned to Mozambique and Monamo reportedly decided to seek legal party status on its own. (Despite the formal change of name in 1992, the Monamo acronym continues in use.)

In 2006 Dias reportedly threatened to leave the Renamo/UE coalition because of the dominance of Renamo. In July 2007 Dias announced that he intended to dissolve Monamo/PMSD and create a new humanitarian nongovernmental organization. However, Monamo/PMSD contested the 2008 local balloting, led by Dias, and subsequently formed the UNO ahead of the legislative balloting.

Leader: Dr. Máximo Diogo José DIAS (Secretary General).

Patriotic Action Front (*Frente de Acção Patriótica*—FAP). Founded in 1991, FAP was a proponent in 1992 of delaying multiparty elections and naming a two-year transitional government. Ahead of the 2008 municipal elections, FAP announced it would not run any of its own members, and would support the Renamo candidates.

Leaders: José Carlos PALAÇO (President), Raulda CONCEIÇÃO (Secretary General).

United Front of Mozambique–Democratic Convergence Party (*Frente Unida de Moçambique–Partido de Convergência Democrática*—Fumo-PCD). Linked to Germany's Christian Democrats, Fumo-PCD held its inaugural congress in Maputo in January 1993. The party secured 1.4 percent of the legislative votes in 1994. It joined the Renamo/UE in 1999 despite the objection of Fumo-PCD founder Domingos Arouca, who resigned from the party's presidency in protest. A June 2000 Fumo-PCD congress offered Arouca the position of "honorary president," but he angrily refused the post. The death of Arouca on January 3, 2009, at age 80, reportedly enhanced party president Jose Samo GUDO's control over Fumo-PCD. Fumo-PCD did not run any candidates in the 2008 local elections.

Leaders: Jose Samo GUDO (President), Pedro LOFORTE (Secretary General).

Mozambican National Union (*União Nacional Moçambicana*—Unamo). Reportedly then in control of three battalions of rebel fighters in Zambezia province, Unamo was formed in 1987 by a Renamo breakaway faction. Subsequently, some of its leaders appeared to be operating from Malawi, while others established an office in Lisbon. Political leaders returned from exile in 1990 in anticipation of Unamo being recognized as a legal party, spokespersons indicating it would participate in upcoming legislative contests but would endorse President Chissano in his reelection bid.

In 1992 Unamo was the first opposition party granted legal status. However, in August party president Carlos Alexandre Reis was imprisoned for financial crimes for which he had been convicted and sentenced in absentia seven years earlier.

In April 1994 Unamo was alleged to be financing Rombezia, an armed group in northern Mozambique led by Manuel ROCHA and Octavio CUSTODIO, which was descended from the African National Union of Rombezia (*União Nacional Africana da Rombezia*—UNAR). UNAR was believed to have been formed by the Portuguese secret police in the 1960s to promote an independent state in the Rovuma and Zambezia provinces (which gave the grouping its name).

Unamo secured only 0.7 percent of the vote in the 1994 legislative balloting and subsequently announced it was forming the extraparliamentary **United Salvation Front** (*Frente Unida de Salvação*—FUS) with the PSLD, PT, Pacode, Pimo, the Mozambique People's Progress Party (PPPM), and the **Democratic Renewal Party** (PRD). However, in 1999 Unamo chose to participate in the Renamo/UE, while the other FUS members either ran alone or joined different coalitions. In 2004, however, Unamo joined the electoral coalition, the Movement for Change and Good Governance (*Movimento para a Mudança e Boa Governação*—MGB), while Reis ran as the Unamo candidate for the presidency. He received 0.9 percent of the vote. In the 2008 local elections, Unamo secured one council seat. It appealed the election results, alleging fraud, but Unamo's bid for new balloting was rejected by the constitutional court.

Leaders: Carlos Alexandre REIS (President), Florencia João Da SILVA (Secretary General).

For more information on the **National Convention Party** (*Partido de Convenção Nacional*—PCN) or the **United Democratic Front** (*Frente Democrática Unida*—FDU), see the 2011 *Handbook*.

Other minor parties that were registered at the time of the 2009 or 2014 assembly elections included the **Progressive Unity Party** (*Partido de União Progressista*—PUP), led by Pedro LANGA; the **Democratic Conservative Party** (*Partido Conservador Democrático*—PCD), formed in 2004 and led by Gonçalvos MAGAGULE; the **United Party for Democratic Freedom** (*Partido Unido de Moçambique e de Liberdade Democrática*—PUMILD), formed in 2007 and led by Leonardo Francisco CUMBE; the **Mozambique People's Progress Party** (*Partido de Progresso do Povo Moçambicano*—PPPM); the **Congress of**

United Democrats (*Congresso dos Democratas Unios*—CDU), formed in January 2002 by António PALANGE following his expulsion from Palmo; the **African Conservative Party** (*Partido Africano Conservador*—PAC), created in 2003 and led by Alexandre PANONE; the **Party of All Mozambican Nationalists** (*Partido de Todos os Nativos Moçambicanos*—Partonamo); the **National Democratic Party of Mozambique** (*Partido Democrático Nacional de Moçambique*—PDNM); and the **United Democratic Front** (*Frente Democrática Unida*—UDF), established in 1995 and led by Janerio Mariano PORDINA.

Minor parties that competed in the 2008 or 2013 municipal balloting included the **Group for Democracy in Beira** (*Grupo para a Democracia de Beira*—GDB), an independent local grouping in Beria, which won seven council seats in the 2008 balloting; the **Natives and Residents of Manhica** (*Naturais e Residentes da Vila da Mahiça*—NATURMA); **Together for the City** (*Juntos pela Cidade*—JPC), a regional grouping that ran only in Maputo; the **Group for Change in Marromeu** (*Grupo para Mundança de Marromeu*—GMM), active only in Marromeu; and the **Organization of Independent Candidates of Nacala** (*Organização dos Candidatos Independentes de Nacala*—OCINA).

For information on the **Democratic Alliance of Veterans for Development** (*Aliança Democrática de Antigos Combatentes para o Desenvolvimento*—ADACD) and the **Democratic Union** (*União Democrática*—UD), see the 2014 *Handbook*.

LEGISLATURE

A **People's Assembly** (*Assembleia Popular*), consisting of Frelimo's then 57-member Central Committee, was accorded legislative status in an uncontested election in December 1977. The body was increased to 210 members in April 1983 by the addition of government ministers and vice ministers, provincial governors, representatives of the military and of each province, and ten other citizens. While its term was not constitutionally specified, the original mandate was set by law at five years. The lengthy poll eventually conducted in August–December 1986 was for 250 deputies, indirectly elected by provincial assemblies from a list of 299 candidates presented by Frelimo. The name of the body was changed to the Assembly of the Republic in the 1990 constitution, which also provided for future elections to be conducted by direct universal suffrage on a multiparty basis.

Assembly of the Republic (*Assembleia da República*). The current legislature is a unicameral body of 250 members elected on a proportional basis for five-year terms. Parties must secure 5 percent of the vote on a nationwide basis to gain representation. In the balloting of October 15, 2014, Frelimo won 144 seats; Renamo/EU, 89; and Mozambique Democratic Movement, 17.

President: Verónica Nataniel MACAMO.

CABINET

[as of September 1, 2016]

Prime Minister	Carlos Agostinho do Rosário
Ministers	
Agriculture and Rural Development	José Pacheco
Culture and Tourism	Silva Armando Dunduro
Education and Human Development	Luis Antonio Ferrao
Finance and Economy	Adriano Afonso Maleiane
Foreign Affairs and Cooperation	Oldemiro Balói
Health	Nazira Karimo Vali Abdula [f]
Industry and Commerce	Ernesto Max Elias Tonela
Interior	Jaime Basilio Monteiro
Justice and Constitutional and Religious Affairs	Isaque Chande
Labor, Employment and Social Security	Vitória Dias Diogo [f]
Land, Environment, and Rural Development	Celso Ismael Correia
Mineral Resources and Energy	Pedro Conceição Couto
National Defense	Atanasio Salvador Ntumuke
President's Office, Chief of Staff	Adelaide Amurane [f]
Public Works, Housing, and Water Resources	Carlos Bonete Martinho
Science, Technology, and Higher Education	Jorge Penicela Nhambiu
Sea, Inland Waters, and Fisheries	Agostinho Salvador Mondlane
State Administration	Carmelita Namashalua [f]
Transport and Communications	Carlos Alberto Fortes Mesquita
War Veterans' Affairs	Eusebio Lambo Gumbiwa
Women, Children, and Social Welfare	Cidalia Oliveira [f]
Youth and Sports	Alberto Hawa Januario Nkutumula

[f] = female

Note: All of the above are members of the Mozambique Liberation Front.

INTERGOVERNMENTAL REPRESENTATION

Ambassador to the U.S.: Carlos DOS SANTOS.

U.S. Ambassador to Mozambique: H. Dean PITTMAN.

Permanent Representative to the UN: António GUMENDE.

IGO Memberships (Non-UN): AfDB, AU, NAM, OIC, SADC, WTO.

For Further Reference:

Cabrita, Joao. *Mozambique: The Tortuous Road to Democracy.* New York: Palgrave, 2000.

Pitcher, M. Anne. *Transforming Mozambique: The Politics of Privatization, 1975–2000.* Cambridge: Cambridge University Press, 2002.

Sheldon, Kathleen. *Pounders of Grain: A History of Women, Work, and Politics in Mozambique.* Portsmouth, NH: Heinemann, 2002.

West, Harry. *Kupilikula: Governance and the Invisible Realm in Mozambique.* Chicago: University of Chicago Press, 2005.

MYANMAR (BURMA)

Republic of the Union of Myanmar
Pyihtaungsu Thamada Myanmar Naingngandaw

Political Status: Independent republic established January 4, 1948; military-backed regime instituted March 2, 1962; one-party constitution of January 4, 1974, abrogated upon direct assumption of power by the military on September 18, 1988, at which time the words "Socialist Republic" (*Socialist Thamada*) were dropped from the country's official name; official title in English changed from Union of Burma to Union of Myanmar on May 27, 1989; new republican constitution ratified through referendum of May 10 and 24, 2008, and promulgated May 29.

Area: 261,789 sq. mi. (678,033 sq. km).

Population: 54,363,000 (2016E—UN); 56,890,000 (2016E—U.S. Census).

Major Urban Centers (2016—UN): NAYPYIDAW (NAY PYI TAW, 1,045,000); Yangon (Rangoon, 4,904,000), Mandalay (1,196,000). In November 2005 the military regime began moving government offices to the vicinity of Pyinmana, 320 miles north of Yangon, the former capital. The newly built capital was officially designated Naypyidaw on March 27, 2006. City population estimates vary widely.

Official Language: Myanmar (Burmese).

Monetary Unit: Kyat (official rate October 1, 2016: 1,263.50 kyats = $1US). Exchange rate quoted here is set by the Myanmar government; black market rates can vary significantly.

President: HTIN Kyaw (National League for Democracy); elected by the Electoral College on March 15, 2016, and sworn in for a five-year term on March 30, to succeed Lt. Gen. (Ret.) THEIN SEIN (Union Solidarity and Development Party).

First Vice President: Lt. Gen. (Ret.) MYINT Swe (Union Solidarity and Development Party); elected by the Electoral College on March 15, 2016, and sworn in for a term concurrent with that of the president on March 30, to succeed SAI Mauk Kham (Union Solidarity and Development Party).

Second Vice President: Maj. (Ret.) Henry VAN THIO (National League for Democracy); elected by the Electoral College on March 15, 2016, and sworn in for a term concurrent with that of the president on March 30, to succeed Adm. (Ret.) NYAN Tun (Union Solidarity and Development Party).

THE COUNTRY

Myanmar, the largest country on the Southeast Asian mainland, has an extensive coastline running along the Bay of Bengal and the Andaman Sea. It shares a land border with Bangladesh and India in the west, China in the north, and Laos and Thailand in the east. Dominating the topography are tropical rain forests, plains, and mountains that rim the frontiers of the east, west, and north. Nearly three-quarters of the population is concentrated in the Irrawaddy (Ayeyawady) basin in the south.

More than 70 percent of the country's inhabitants are Burman. Karens (Kayins, about 7 percent) are dispersed over southern and eastern Myanmar, while Shans (9 percent), Thai in origin, are localized on the eastern plateau; Chins, Kachins, Mons, and Rakhines (Arakanese), totaling about 1 million, are found in the north and northeast. In addition, about 400,000 Chinese and 120,000 Indians and Bangladeshi are concentrated primarily in the urban areas. The various ethnic groups speak many languages and dialects, but the official Myanmar (Burmese), which is related to Tibeto-Chinese, is spoken by the clear majority. About 90 percent of the population professes Theravada Buddhism, the state religion; minority religions include Islam (4 percent), Christianity (4 percent), Hinduism (3 percent), and animism. Women make up an estimated 46 percent of the active labor force. Female representation in the military-dominated government is rare. Following the 2010 elections, women held 26 seats in the House of Representatives (6 percent) and 4 seats in the House of Nationalities (1.8 percent). After the 2016 elections, the Inter-Parliamentary Union ranked Myanmar 155th out of 191 countries for women's representation in Parliament with 43 seats (9.9 percent) in the House of Representatives and 23 (10.3 percent) in the House of Nationals.

Although the country is rich in largely unexploited mineral resources (including hydrocarbons, silver, zinc, copper, lead, nickel, antimony, tin, and tungsten), its economy is heavily dependent on agriculture, which accounts for 44 percent of GDP and employs nearly two-thirds of the labor force. Teak and other hardwoods, and pulses and beans are among the major exports, and agriprocessing remains the leading industry, although production of textiles and garments has become more important as a source of export earnings. Production of natural gas from offshore fields is expanding; base metals, ores, and gemstones also contribute to national income. Overall, the industrial sector contributes about 20 percent of GDP. There is also a thriving trade in opium, grown primarily in the "Golden Triangle" at the border juncture with Laos and Thailand, and in methamphetamines.

On May 3, 2008, Cyclone Nargis hit Myanmar's Irrawaddy region. By May 15 the UN estimated the number of severely affected people to be between 1.6 million and 2.5 million. In late June Myanmar raised the death toll to 84,500, with another 53,800 missing. A subsequent report from the Association of Southeast Asian Nations (ASEAN) put the cost of reconstruction and relief at $1 billion. Despite international criticism of the junta's response to the disaster, which initially included denying visas to foreign aid workers, the UN reported on July 10 that a total of 50 countries had pledged around $175 million to support relief, recovery, and rehabilitation efforts, with the United Kingdom and United States the largest donors.

In 2011 GDP grew by 5.9 percent and 7.3 percent in 2012 as economic reforms led to increased foreign investment and industrial production. Two major new natural gas production fields, which would double energy exports, were expected to be operational in 2014. In 2013 GDP grew by 7.5 percent, while inflation was 5.8 percent, and unemployment, 4 percent. In January 2014 the World Bank announced $2 billion in loans and grants after resuming lending to Myanmar. GDP grew by 8.7 percent in 2014, 7 percent in 2015, and 8.6 percent in 2016. The inflation rate was 9.6 percent in 2016, while GDP per capita was $1,416. The World Bank ranked Myanmar at 170th out of 190 countries in ease of doing business, among the lowest in the world, while the UN Human Development Report rated the country 148th its 2016 index.

GOVERNMENT AND POLITICS

Political background. Modern Burma was incorporated into British India as a result of the Anglo-Burmese wars of 1824–1886 but in 1937 was separated from India and granted limited self-government. During World War II Japan occupied the country and gave it nominal independence under a puppet regime led by anti-British nationalists, who subsequently transferred their loyalties to the Allied war effort.

The Anti-Fascist People's Freedom League (AFPFL), a coalition of nationalist forces, emerged as the principal political organization in 1945. Under the AFPFL, various groups and regions joined to form the Union of Burma, which gained full independence from the British in January 1948 and for a decade maintained a parliamentary democracy that was headed for most of that period by Prime Minister U NU. In May 1958 the AFPFL dissolved into factional groups, precipitating a political crisis that, four months later, forced Nu to resign in favor of a caretaker government headed by Gen. NE WIN, commander-in-chief of the armed forces.

The Nu faction of the AFPFL returned to power under the name of the Union Party in elections in 1960. However, problems involving internal security, national unity, and economic development led Ne Win to mount a coup d'état in March 1962, after which a Revolutionary Council of senior army officers ran the government. A Burma Socialist Program Party (BSPP) was launched by the council the following July. In January 1974, after 12 years of army rule, the Ne Win government adopted a new constitution and revived the legislature as a single-chambered People's Assembly.

In February 1977 Prime Minister SEIN WIN was among those denied reelection to the party's Central Committee. In March a new cabinet was organized with MAUNG MAUNG KHA as prime minister, and a new People's Assembly was elected in January 1978.

At the BSPP's fourth congress in August 1981, Ne Win announced his intention to resign as president while retaining his post as party chair. Following a legislative election in October, the assembly approved San Yu as his successor. Serious student-led disturbances erupted in the capital in 1988, leading to an extraordinary BSPP congress that concluded with both Ne Win and San Yu resigning from the party leadership. In July the People's Assembly named the new BSPP chair, SEIN LWIN, to succeed San Yu as state president, while Maung Maung Kha stepped down as prime minister in favor of TUN TIN. Student leaders thereupon mounted a campaign to press for President Sein Lwin's resignation, which culminated in a popular outpouring of more than 100,000 demonstrators in Yangon. Shortly thereafter, Sein Lwin was replaced as both president and party chair by the attorney general, Dr. MAUNG MAUNG. Like his predecessors, Maung Maung was a longtime associate of Ne Win.

On September 18, 1988, the military again seized power. The president was relieved, and army commander, Gen. SAW MAUNG, assumed the chair of a new State Law and Order Restoration Council (SLORC). The Defense Service Intelligence director, Brig. Gen. KHIN NYUNT, assumed the post of SLORC first secretary. On September 21 Saw Maung became prime minister, presiding over a new cabinet composed, with one exception, of military figures. Although few restrictions were placed on the formation of opposition parties, many of their supporters were severely repressed, and all public gatherings of more than four individuals were banned.

The February 1989 electoral campaign for a new People's Assembly was largely a contest between the government's National Unity Party (NUP, successor to the BSPP) and the National League for Democracy (NLD), led by AUNG SAN SUU KYI, the daughter of the "founder of modern Burma," AUNG SAN, who had been assassinated in 1947 on the eve of independence. On May 27, 1990, voters awarded a massive victory to the NLD, which secured more than 80 percent of the seats. Humiliated by the NUP's showing, 2.1 percent of the seats, the SLORC leadership refused to let the assembly convene and began systematic delegalization of opposition parties.

In October 1991 Aung San Suu Kyi was awarded the Nobel Peace Prize, which focused world attention on the repressive policies of the SLORC and triggered a wave of domestic demonstrations on behalf of the opposition leader, who had been held in detention since July 1989. The government responded by shutting down universities, arresting numerous protestors, and mounting a dry-season campaign against dissident minorities, especially Karen insurgents on the Thai border.

In April 1992 Saw Maung, who was reported to be in poor mental health, was succeeded as prime minister and SLORC chair by Gen. THAN SHWE. In May the SLORC announced that a "coordination meeting" would be convened to pave the way for a National Convention to draft a new constitution. Most opposition groups were excluded from the preparatory process for the convention, which opened in January 1993. In July 1995 Aung San Suu Kyi was freed, but in November the NLD delegation (only 86 members out of 703) pulled out of the National Convention, insisting that the body had displayed scant interest in democratic reform. In March 1996 the convention began what would turn out to be an eight-year hiatus.

In advance of a planned NLD congress in May 1996, the government arrested some 260 party members, limiting the number of attendees to 18. Some 500–800 NLD supporters were arrested when they attempted to hold another congress at Suu Kyi's house in September. In early December weeklong demonstrations in Yangon and Mandalay prompted the government to close the universities once again and reimpose Suu Kyi's house arrest. In late September 1997 the NLD held its first authorized congress since 1995, with Suu Kyi in attendance, but the event had no appreciable effect on the government's underlying strategy of arresting and imprisoning NLD activists.

During the mid-1990s the SLORC had mounted a series of successful attacks on longtime insurgents. In January 1995 the military captured Manerplaw, the headquarters of the rebel Karen National Union (KNU), which was followed by the fall of the KNU's last stronghold in Kawmoora, on the Thai border. In March Gen. BO MYA resigned as commander of the Karen National Army (KNA), although continuing as chair of the KNU. Also in March, the Karenni National Progressive Party (KNPP) abandoned its armed struggle, leading SLORC officials to claim that 14 of 16 rebel groups had now laid down their arms. Most of the remaining military opposition came from the Mong Tai Army (MTA) of Shan drug warlord KHUN SA. Eight months later Khun Sa announced his "retirement" as MTA chief, and in January 1996 his troops began their formal surrender. In April the government announced that Khun Sa would neither be tried for his crimes nor extradited to the United States to face charges of drug trafficking. In early 1997 negotiations between the regime and the KNU collapsed, and government forces immediately launched a lengthy offensive against the remaining rebel bases, forcing thousands of refugees to flee into Thailand.

On November 15, 1997, the SLORC was dissolved and immediately replaced by the "permanent" State Peace and Development Council (SPDC), which thereupon announced a cabinet reshuffling. Subsequently, Khin Nyunt ordered the detention of a number of former cabinet officials and their supporters on corruption charges.

Although the SPDC approved an NLD party congress held in May 1998 at Aung San Suu Kyi's residence, the military blocked attempts by the NLD leader to visit supporters outside the capital. In September Suu Kyi and nine other activists carried out a threat to initiate a "People's Parliament." Calling themselves the Committee Representing Elected Lawmakers, they declared all junta laws and proclamations invalid, demanded the release of all political prisoners, and stated their intention to act as a parliament until the Constituent Assembly elected in 1990 was allowed to meet. Meanwhile, the SPDC continued what had become its biggest crackdown against the opposition since early in the decade. By October nearly 900 NLD members had been detained. In August–September 2000 Aung San Suu Kyi twice tried to venture outside Yangon but was again prevented from doing so.

In November 2001 the government hierarchy underwent its most significant changes since the formation of the SPDC four years earlier. SPDC Secretary WIN MYINT was dismissed, as were the three deputy prime ministers. Several additional cabinet changes were announced, and 10 of 12 regional military commanders were reassigned. Although the SPDC did not explain its actions, observers concluded that the changes had served to strengthen the hands of Than Shwe and SPDC vice chair Sr. Gen. MAUNG AYE.

During the same period a UN special envoy to Myanmar, Malaysian diplomat Razali Ismail, was attempting to facilitate prisoner releases and discussions between the opposition and the SPDC. The military regime had begun releasing detained NLD members, but at the end of the year an estimated 1,500 political prisoners continued in custody. On May 6, 2002, Suu Kyi was unconditionally released from house arrest.

Two months earlier, in March 2002, the SPDC had reported the discovery of a planned coup led by Ne Win's son-in-law AYE ZAW WIN. Ne Win and his daughter SANDAR WIN, wife of the alleged ringleader, were placed under house arrest. In September Aye Zaw Win and his three sons were sentenced to hang for treason. Ne Win, age 91, died in December 2002.

On May 30, 2003, a convoy carrying Aung San Suu Kyi and supporters was attacked near Mandalay. The attack, reportedly by a mob of up to 2,000, was orchestrated by the government-supportive Union Solidarity and Development Association (USDA). Shortly after, the NLD leader was placed in "protective custody" until transferred to her home on September 26. The regime's actions provoked widespread international outrage.

On August 25, 2003, the SPDC announced a major cabinet reshuffle that saw Than Shwe turn over the prime ministership to Khin Nyunt, who was replaced as SPDC first secretary by the former second secretary, Lt. Gen. SOE WIN. Five days later the new prime minister announced that the long-adjourned National Convention would reconvene as the first element of a "seven-step road map" to democracy that would also include a referendum on a new constitution, legislative elections, and the selection of state leaders by the resultant People's Assembly.

The National Convention reconvened on May 17, 2004, with SPDC second secretary Lt. Gen. THEIN SEIN as chair. The 1,088 delegates included representatives of political parties, ethnic groups ("national races"), workers, farmers, the intelligentsia, and state service personnel, plus "invited delegates" from state "Special Regions" and former insurgent groups that had "exchanged arms for peace." Conspicuously absent were NLD representatives, who refused to participate until the regime released Aung San Suu Kyi and NLD vice chair TIN OO from house arrest.

On October 19, 2004, Prime Minister Khin Nyunt was "permitted to retire" and reportedly placed under house arrest. Soe Win assumed the cabinet leadership, and Thein Sein was elevated to SPDC first secretary. The SPDC began another major reorganization of the military command structure as well as a purge of the military intelligence apparatus, previously headed by Khin Nyunt, who was convicted of corruption and bribery in July 2005.

In late 2006 the KNU demanded that the military halt an offensive in the east that had brought an end to a two-year-old de facto cease-fire and had reportedly displaced 10,000 Karens. (In March the Norwegian Refugee Council had estimated that Myanmar had 540,000 internally displaced people, the largest number of any country in Asia.) The government justified its offensive against the KNU and other ethnic groups as a response to a number of small bomb blasts, which were also blamed on exile groups. The most serious incident occurred on May 7,

2005, in the capital; according to official sources, three bombs killed 19 people and injured 150.

On May 18, 2007, with Soe Win undergoing medical treatment, Thein Sein became acting prime minister. He officially succeeded the deceased Soe Win on October 24, when the SPDC also announced the appointment of Lt. Gen. TIN AUNG MYINT OO as SPDC first secretary.

On August 15, 2007, the SPDC announced major price hikes for fuels, triggering a series of protests led initially by the 88 Generation Students group. As September approached, Buddhist monks increasingly took control of what gradually became the first public uprising against the government since 1988. Antigovernment protests spread across the urban landscape, with some 100,000 people demonstrating. On September 25 the SPDC imposed a curfew, outlawed gatherings of more than five people, and sent troops and the police into the streets to quell demonstrations. USDA-organized militias—the *Swan-ar Shin* (Masters of Force)—also clashed with the protesters. Between September 26 and 28, the government reported the deaths of 10 demonstrators and the arrest of some 2,100. The country's principal Internet service provider was shut down, as were all cellular telephone networks. By September 30, with government forces having raided and cordoned off several monasteries in Yangon, the protest movement had succumbed.

Efforts by UN under-secretary general for political affairs Ibrahim Gambari to bring the government and the opposition to the negotiating table met with scant success until late October 2007. The curfew and ban on assembly were lifted on October 20, and within a week a government representative had met with Aung San Suu Kyi. On November 8 Gambari released a statement on behalf of Suu Kyi, who indicated she was "ready to cooperate with the government in order to make this process of dialogue a success." Nevertheless, no progress was made during a series of meetings between the government and Suu Kyi.

Although Suu Kyi's annually renewed house arrest technically expired in May 2009, at that time she was being held at Insein Prison in Yangon since being formally charged earlier in the month with harboring for two days an uninvited American who had swum to her lakeside home. Suu Kyi was convicted on August 11 and sentenced to three years in prison, but Gen. Than Shwe commuted the sentence to another 18 months under house arrest.

Meanwhile, the government pushed forward with its "Road Map for Democracy." Between July 18 and September 3, 2007, a final National Convention session completed "basic principles" for a new constitution. A 54-member, government-appointed State Constitution Drafting Commission then produced a complete text that was published on April 9, 2008, approved by 92 percent of those voting in a referendum on May 10 and 24, and promulgated by the SPDC on May 29. Under the Referendum Law for the Approval of the Draft Constitution, anybody who publicly critiqued the referendum faced a fine and a three-year prison sentence.

Prior to elections, scheduled for November 2010, several dozen new or reorganized political parties were registered, the most prominent of the progovernment parties being the USDA-backed Union Solidarity and Development Party (USDP), headed by Prime Minister Thein Sein. As required under the new constitution, he and several dozen other government ministers and SPDC members resigned their military commissions to run for office. Among the prodemocracy parties, the NLD, faced with having to expel Suu Kyi in order to register, instead chose forced dissolution, although some senior members rejected the NLD's call for an election boycott and registered as the National Democratic Force (NDF).

In the November 7, 2010, elections, the USDP secured 259 of the 330 elective seats in the People's Assembly, 129 of the 168 elective seats in the National Assembly, and a large majority of seats in the 14 state and regional parliaments. The leading opposition group, the Shan Nationalities Democratic Party (SNDP), won 18 seats in the lower house, where the NDF came away with only 8. Even before the official results were announced, however, world attention turned to the release of Aung San Suu Kyi on November 13, at the expiration of her most recent period of house arrest.

Thein Sein was elected president by the Electoral College on February 4, 2011. He subsequently named a new cabinet, which was approved by the assembly and sworn in on March 30. On March 30 the SPDC was officially abolished. However, former SPDC chair Than Shwe and other senior members of the group were appointed to a new body, the State Supreme Council. Reports described the council as an extra-constitutional grouping created to preserve the influence of the military within the government.

The NLD won 38 of 39 seats in by-elections in April 2012 (see Current issues, below). The vacancies were created when elected members resigned their seats to take government posts. First vice president TIN AUNG MYINT OO, regarded as a hardliner, resigned on May 3. He was replaced by Adm. (Ret.) NYAN Tun, a reformer, who was elected on August 16. A cabinet reshuffle began on August 29 and ended September 4. Thirteen ministries were involved in the reshuffle in which conservative ministers were replaced by reformers.

On March 20, 2013, the Union Parliament voted to create a commission to recommend revisions to the constitution, including the removal of the mandate that 25 percent of seats of the legislature be reserved for the military and prohibitions against foreign spouses or children for presidential candidates (a clause created to prevent Suu Kyi, whose husband was a British citizen, from running for the presidency). In June 2014 a parliamentary committee voted to retain the restriction that would effectively bar Suu Kyi from the 2016 presidential balloting.

The NLD won a majority in the November 8, 2015, legislative balloting, securing 255 seats in the lower chamber and 135 in the upper house. The USDP finished second with 30 seats in the lower house and 11 in the upper chamber in addition to those appointed by the military. Because Suu Kyi was banned from the presidency, the NLD nominated HTIN Kyaw (NLD) and Maj. (Ret.) Henry VAN THIO. Htin was elected president on March 15, 2016, while Lt. Gen. (Ret.) MYINT Swe (USDP) and Van Thio were elected first and second vice president, respectively. Htin formed a government that included representatives of previously marginalized minority groups. The cabinet was approved on March 24, and Htin was sworn in on March 30, becoming the first democratically elected president in more than 50 years. Suu Kyi was appointed as state councilor, a post roughly equal to prime minister (see Current issues, below).

Constitution and government. The 1974 constitution was adopted with the stated objective of making Burma a "Socialist Republic" under one-party rule. It provided for a unicameral People's Assembly as the supreme organ of state authority and for a State Council comprising 14 representatives from the country's major political subdivisions plus 15 additional members (including the prime minister) elected from the assembly. The State Council and its chair, who was also state president, served four-year terms, concurrent with that of the assembly. The prime minister was designated by the Council of Ministers, which was elected by the assembly from its own membership, following nomination by the State Council. All of these institutions were abolished upon direct assumption of power by the military in September 1988.

A new constitution was promulgated on May 29, 2008, following passage with 92 percent voter support, according to the SPDC. In addition to creating a republic, the constitution provides for a multiparty political system, the election of a bicameral Union Parliament, the indirect election of a president, and establishment of an independent judiciary. It also ensures a "national political leadership role" for the military, which it recognizes as the ultimate protector of the constitution and accords "the right to independently administer and adjudicate all affairs of the armed forces." In both houses of the Union Parliament and in the country's 14 state and regional assemblies, 25 percent of the seats are reserved for military designees.

The president is elected by members of the Union Parliament sitting as a tripartite Electoral College comprising (1) representatives of the states and divisions, with an equal number from each; (2) representatives elected from township constituencies on the basis of population; and (3) members of the defense services. The three groups each select a vice president, with the one who then receives the most votes from the full Electoral College assuming the executive presidency for a five-year term; the other two vice presidents serve a concurrent term. The president may be impeached for treason, breach of the constitution, misconduct, or "inefficient discharge of duties." Impeachment requires support by two-thirds of the full membership of both parliamentary houses.

With the concurrence of the Union Parliament, which can only reject the nominees for cause, the president is empowered to name government ministers and the justices of the supreme court. The president also names the commander-in-chief of the defense services, with the "proposal and approval" of the National Defense and Security Council (NDSC). The 11-member NDSC comprises the president and the 2 vice presidents; the speakers of the upper and lower houses; the commander-in-chief and his deputy; the minister of foreign affairs; and the ministers of defense, home affairs, and border affairs, all three of whom must be army officers. Thus, the military holds at least six seats on the NDSC. In the event of a national emergency, the president turns authority over to the commander-in-chief, who may rule with full presidential, legislative, and judicial powers and may suspend the rights of citizens. Following termination of the emergency, the NDSC is responsible for running the government until the conclusion of new elections, which must be held within six months.

The Supreme Court sits at the apex of the judiciary, followed by a system of high courts in the states and regions, courts of self-administered zones and divisions, and district and township courts. The constitution also provides for separate courts-martial to adjudicate defense service personnel. A Constitutional Tribunal is responsible for interpreting the constitution, reviewing the constitutionality of legislation, reviewing the actions of executive authorities, and resolving constitutional disputes between jurisdictions. Constitutional amendment requires 75 percent support from the Union Parliament, with the added proviso that amendments to specified sections of the basic law must then receive the assent of half of all eligible voters in a referendum.

Local government is based primarily on seven states (Chin, Kachin, Kayah, Kayin, Mon, Rakhine, Shan) and seven regions (Ayeyawady, Bago, Magway, Mandalay, Sagaing, Tanintharyi, Yangon), plus the Union Territory of Naypyidaw. The states and regions (previously called divisions) are divided into townships, which are subdivided into urban wards and village tracts. The 2008 constitution also recognizes five "self-administered zones" (Danu, Kokang, Naga, Palaung, and Pa-O) and one "self-administered division" (Wa), each comprising specified townships within a particular state or region. Each state and region elects an assembly. The executive is headed by a chief minister, who is nominated by the president and approved by the respective legislature. The union territory is directly administered by the president.

Government control of the media has loosened. In December 2012 the government announced that privately owned newspapers would be allowed for the first time in 50 years, starting in April 2013. Also, on January 16, 2013, the law forbidding criticism of the military was repealed. A new, less restrictive media law was enacted in March 2014. Nonetheless, journalists continue to face extensive censorship and violence. In March 2015, after the arrests of 127 students (see Current issues, below), several newspapers ran blacked-out spaces on their front pages to protest police attacks against journalists and to highlight the lack of freedom of the press. On March 18, 2015, two journalists from the *Myanmar Post* were sentenced to two months in prison for allegedly misquoting a military legislator. In 2016 Reporters Without Borders ranked Myanmar 143rd out of 180 countries in freedom of the press, a rise from 169th in 2012.

Foreign relations. Nonalignment was the cornerstone of Burmese foreign policy from 1948 through the end of the Cold War in the early 1990s, and until quite recently the country's participation in most intergovernmental organizations, including the UN and its specialized agencies, was marginal. In 1979 Burma announced its withdrawal from the Nonaligned Movement. In 1992, however, it rejoined the existing group. In 1997 Myanmar was admitted to ASEAN, partly in an effort by neighboring states to foster "constructive engagement" with the SPDC.

In 1949 Burma became the first noncommunist country to recognize the People's Republic of China. The two signed a Treaty of Friendship and Mutual Nonaggression in 1960, following settlement of a long-standing border dispute. By 1967, however, leftist terrorism, aimed at instituting a Chinese-style "Cultural Revolution," led to a severe deterioration in Sino-Burmese relations that lasted into the next decade.

Relations with Bangladesh worsened in mid-1978 because of an exodus from Burma of some 200,000 Rohingya Muslims who, according to Dhaka, had been subjected to an "extermination campaign." Later, it appeared that Muslim leaders had encouraged the flight in part to publicize their desire to establish the Rakhine (Arakan) region as an Islamic state; meanwhile, the number of refugees living in makeshift camps on the Bangladeshi side of the border had reportedly risen to more than 260,000 by March 1992. Repatriations began in September 1992; however, many Rohingyas were reluctant to return, while some of those who did were reported to be members of a terrorist Rohingya Solidarity Organization (*Kalarzo*) that was responsible for the killing of 16 Myanmar troops in May 1994. By September 1995 most refugees had been repatriated, although more than 20,000 remained in Bangladesh as of early 1998. Myanmar subsequently announced it would guarantee the safety of any additional voluntary returnees. In January 2000 Yangon rejected reentry for some 14,000 refugees, whom it claimed were not Myanmar, but in April 2004 the two governments agreed that the remaining Rohingyas would be repatriated. Nevertheless, most have refused to leave or have not received authorization from Myanmar. A dispute between Bangladesh and Myanmar over territorial boundaries in the Bay of Bengal also persists. Dating back to 1974, the dispute has taken on added significance because of possible oil and natural gas deposits under the sea.

In October 1994 Myanmar concluded a friendship pact with Thailand, but relations have remained cool. Insurgent refugee camps are still located on Thai soil, and Myanmar military forces have repeatedly crossed the border in pursuit of guerrillas. In October 1999 Thai authorities freed the five Myanmar perpetrators of a hostage incident at the Myanmar embassy in Bangkok, leading an angered SPDC to close the Thai-Myanmar border until late November. In contrast, in January 2000 Thailand earned the SPDC's praise for a swift, response when a small Kayinni group called God's Army took some 700 hostages at a hospital near the border (see Political Parties and Groups, below). In June 2001, four months after a cross-border clash led to a series of bilateral meetings, Myanmar and Thai leaders agreed to resolve border issues and to jointly fight drug production and smuggling. Difficulties continued into 2002, however, and the border was closed from May to October. In July 2003 the Thai government announced plans to relocate all Myanmar dissidents to refugee camps near the border. Largely as a result of the decades-old conflict with the KNU, some 400,000 Karens lived in refugee camps across the border in Thailand. (According to the Office of the UN High Commissioner for Refugees, between 2005 and 2008 some 30,000 Myanmar refugees were resettled from Thai camps, 21,500 of them in the United States.) In November 2010, immediately after Myanmar's national election, fighting between Karen insurgents and the government forces led an estimated 20,000 additional Myanmar refugees to flee across the border into Thailand, although as the violence diminished in the following days, they began returning to their homes.

In April 1997 the United States announced the imposition of economic sanctions against Myanmar, largely because of its repression of prodemocracy advocates. In 1998 the United States and Japan approved a grant of $3.8 million to the UN Drug Control Program to help eliminate opium poppy cultivation in Myanmar, but Washington continued its ten-year-old policy of refusing to make direct grants to the Yangon regime. In April 2000 the European Union (EU) announced that it was freezing assets of Myanmar officials in addition to increasing sanctions.

In mid-2000 the SPDC was condemned, not for the first time, by the International Labor Organization (ILO) for using forced labor and was also accused of having more child soldiers—at least 50,000, according to a Save the Children spokesperson—than any other country in the world. (For more on the relationship between the ILO and Myanmar, see the 2014 *Handbook.*)

Following the protests of 2007, further sanctions were applied by both the United States and the EU. On May 1, 2008, the U.S. Treasury froze the assets of state-owned firms in Myanmar, adding to the sanctions of October 2007 in which the Treasury froze the financial assets of members of the military regime. The EU added a ban on imports of timber, gemstones, and precious metals.

On September 29, 2006, for the first time in its history, the UN Security Council discussed human rights and internal developments in Myanmar. On January 12, 2007, however, Russia and China vetoed a Security Council resolution that called on the SPDC to release political prisoners, permit free expression and political activity, and end human rights violations and military action against ethnic minorities. The resolution had been sponsored by the United States and the United Kingdom.

On June 26–27, 2009, Ibrahim Gambari visited Myanmar for the eighth time in his capacity as special representative of the UN secretary general. On July 3–4 UN secretary general Ban Ki-moon paid a second visit to Myanmar—his first had come in the wake of Cyclone Nargis in 2008—at which time Sr. Gen. Than Shwe promised that the planned 2010 elections would be free and fair. The secretary general was not permitted to meet with Aung San Suu Kyi. In November U.S. president Barack Obama and Prime Minister Thein Sein met during a U.S.–ASEAN summit, marking the first time that a U.S. president and a junta leader had direct contact.

Renewed fighting in November 2010 in the northeast of Myanmar between ethnic Karens and government forces created an estimated 30,000 refugees, who fled into Thailand (see Current issues, below). In April 2011 the EU temporarily suspended some travel and economic sanctions against officials of the Myanmar government as an incentive for further democratization. In November Hilary Clinton became the first U.S. secretary of state to visit Myanmar since 1955.

In March 2012 the International Tribunal for the Law of the Sea ruled in favor of Bangladesh in a dispute with Myanmar over maritime claims in the Bay of Bengal, around St. Martin's Island.

In April 2012 Australia and the EU eased economic sanctions on Myanmar, after the election of Aung San Suu Kyi to the assembly (see Current issues, below). The prime minister of the United Kingdom, David Cameron, became the first Western leader to visit Myanmar since 1962. The following month the United States also relaxed trade sanctions and named its first ambassador to Myanmar since 1990. A succession of foreign leaders visited Myanmar, including President Barack Obama in November. Some nations offered new economic and development assistance: Japan agreed to write off $3.7 billion in debt, while Australia pledged to double its aid to $104 million per year. In November 2012 the World Bank announced it would lend to Myanmar for the first time since the 1980s. Meanwhile in 2012 the United States appointed its first ambassador to Myanmar since 1990.

In January 2013 the Asian Development Bank resumed operations in Myanmar with a 30-year, $512 million loan. In May Japan announced it would forgive Myanmar's remaining $1.7 billion in debt and provide a new $504 million economic development loan during a visit to Naypyitaw by Prime Minister Shinzo Abe, the first by a Japanese leader in 36 years. In June Coca-Cola announced a $200 million investment in Myanmar and the resumption of production in the country after more than 60 years. Meanwhile Myanmar and the United States finalized a trade treaty in May as President Sein became the first Myanmar leader to visit the White House since 1966. In September reports emerged that, in violation of an agreement with the United States, the government continued to import weapons from North Korea. Also in September, the government signed a series of agreements to grant inspectors from the International Atomic Energy Agency access to the country's nuclear facilities. On September 21 Myanmar and Angola established diplomatic relations. Through 2013, Thailand deported approximately 1,300 Rohingya refugees back to Myanmar. The refugees were fleeing ethnic violence (see Current issues, below).

In February 2014 the government suspended aid operations by the international group, Doctors Without Borders (*Médicins Sans Frontières*—MSF). The government claimed the group had made false reports about treating casualties of ethnic violence in the country. MSF was allowed to resume some operations on March 1, but not in the northwest of Myanmar. In May, tensions along the border between Myanmar and Bangladesh prompted the deployment of additional security forces by both nations.

U.S. president Obama visited Myanmar during the Ninth East Asia Summit on November 12 and 13, 2014, and met with Suu Kyi in Rangoon, where he criticized the provisions that prevented the opposition leader from being president. On December 29 the UN General Assembly adopted a nonbinding resolution urging full citizenship for the 1.3 million Rohingyas in the northwestern Arakan state.

In April 2015 India, Nepal, Bhutan, and Myanmar agreed to expand a 1972 trade deal.

The Rangoon Stock Exchange (YSX), Myanmar's first stock market, opened on December 9, with assistance from the Japan Exchange Group. Japan announced in November 2016 that it would provide $7.7 billion in aid to Myanmar over a five-year period to support economic development and reconciliation.

Current issues. In the week after the 2010 elections, attention increasingly turned toward Aung San Suu Kyi's residence in anticipation of the expiration of her latest period of house arrest. On November 13 crowds gathered in front of her house even before the announcement that she had been freed. Her release gave an immediate boost to prodemocracy advocates, and she wasted no time in championing their cause, delivering public addresses and media interviews in which she called for relegalizing the NLD and for peacefully pressuring the junta to open negotiations.

An estimated 2,200 political prisoners remained incarcerated in 2010. The SPDC periodically granted amnesty to thousands of prisoners —9,000 in September 2008, 7,100 in September 2009—but relatively few of them fell into the category of political prisoners. Among those currently serving sentences of more than 60 years are leaders of the September 2007 protests, including MIN KO NAING of the 88 Generation Students and ASHIN GAMBIRA of the Alliance of All Burmese Buddhist Monks.

During 2009 the SPDC continued a three-year military offensive against the KNU. There were reports of offenses against ethnic Chinese in northeastern Kokang, and a report by Human Rights Watch in January called attention to the plight of the Chin minority, adjacent to India, where army abuses were described as including forced labor, summary executions, torture, food shortages, and sexual exploitation. In April–May 2009 the junta approached a number of cease-fire groups with a proposal calling for them to operate as elements of a Border Guard Force (BGF) under the command of the army. Although a number of the cease-fire groups accepted the plan, others refused, concerned that the junta's intention was to neutralize them.

In June 2011 the construction of the $3.6 billion Myitsone Dam across the Irrawaddy River prompted a new round of fighting with the Karen Independence Organization (KIO) and other Karen groups. The KIO opposed the project because it would dislocate several thousand Karens. The strife displaced an estimated 15,000 civilians. On September 30, 2011, Thein Sein ordered an end to the construction in an effort to end the fighting. Fighting in the region in 2012 led the UN to suspend aid operations in northern Kachin.

On September 6, 2011, the government established a human rights commission to investigate complaints against the government. The following month, legislation was enacted to legalize trade unions for the first time since 1962. Concurrently, the government announced the release of more than 6,350 prisoners, including 220 political detainees.

Aung San Suu Kyi ended her boycott of elections and won a seat in the Assembly in by-elections on April 1, 2012. Her election prompted foreign governments to restore ties and assistance to the country. In June a state of emergency was declared in Rakhine (Arakan) state, following protracted sectarian violence between Buddhists and Muslims that left 78 dead and created more than 90,000 internally displaced persons. Also in June, the military announced the end to Myanmar's small nuclear program, which critics charged was designed to produce atomic weapons.

Following a ruling in March 2012 that limited the power of the legislature to investigate government agencies or ministers, the Union Parliament voted to impeach the constitutional court. The nine justices of the court subsequently resigned on September 6.

In January 2013 a 1988 law banning public gatherings of more than four people without a permit was repealed. On March 20, sectarian strife broke out between Buddhists and Muslims in Mandalay. The violence left more than 100 dead and prompted the deployment of military troops to restore order. More than 100,000 Muslims were resettled into camps, ostensibly for their safety. The UN and international rights groups called on the government to end the violence and reduce anti-Muslim discrimination. The government announced the release of 93 political prisoners in April. In June, despite ongoing negotiations, renewed fighting broke out between the KIO and government forces. Approximately 60,000 ethnic Kachins were displaced by the violence. On October 10 the government and the KIO agreed to a temporary ceasefire while negotiations for a permanent end to the fighting were launched with other insurgency groups. On November 2 leaders of 17 rebel groups endorsed a preliminary National Ceasefire Agreement (NCA). However, negotiations on a final NCA continued into 2014 under the auspices of the Union Peace Working Committee, comprised of rebel groups, civil society representatives, and government officials.

In January 2014 the UN reported that approximately 40 ethnic Rohingya Muslims were killed in ethnic clashes. The government denied the reports. Also in January, Thein Sein ordered the release of more than 13,700 prisoners in a broad amnesty. In February humanitarian groups called on the government to cease military operations against the Ta'ang National Liberation Army (TNLA) in Shan state. Fighting in the region created some 3,000 displaced persons. In March continuing ethnic conflict prompted the UN World Food Program to suspend operations in Arakan. Also, in March, the government implemented a ban on timber exports in an effort to slow deforestation.

On November 19, 2014, the KIO threatened to break off peace talks after 20 trainees were killed and another 40 injured by government artillery strikes near Laiza.

On February 1, 2015, the government agreed to meet with student leaders of the Action Committee on Democratic Education (ACDE) on an 11-point proposal to address concerns about restrictions on academic freedom. Riot police arrested 127 students on March 10 during violent clashes at Letpadan in protests about academic freedom.

Thein Sein declared a state of emergency and imposed martial law on February 17, 2015, in the remote region of Kokang in northeastern Shan state following clashes between the army and the Han Chinese Myanmar National Democratic Alliance Army (MNDAA), which killed at least 51 soldiers and 29 progovernment Kokang militia fighters, along with at least 130 MNDAA rebels and more than 100 civilians. The strife led more than 30,000 Kokang civilians to flee across the border to China. Fighting continued through May.

On October 15, 2015, the leaders of eight ethnic armed organizations signed the Nationwide Ceasefire Agreement (NCA) with the government in Naypyidaw. However, seven other groups rejected the peace agreement, including the KIO. A landslide near the Hpakant jade mine killed at least 113 migrant workers on November 21.

Despite the NCA, renewed fighting was reported in February 2016 between government forces and groups that had signed the peace deal.

POLITICAL PARTIES AND GROUPS

Following the 1962 coup, political parties continued to exist until March 1964, when the Revolutionary Council banned all but its own **Burma Socialist Program Party** (BSPP). During this period the Beijing-oriented **Burmese Communist Party** (BCP), which had been in open rebellion since 1948, and at least a score of ethnic insurgent groups continued to oppose the government. Following the September 1988 coup, the government rescinded the party ban, and the BSPP reorganized as the National Unity Party (NUP). By then, the BCP had diminished in importance. Ethnic opposition groups, in contrast, continued to control considerable territory, especially in the north and east.

The 2008 constitution provides for the formation of political parties within a "genuine and discipline-flourishing multiparty democratic system" (Chapter X). Party registrations may be revoked for receiving foreign assistance, abusing religion, or "directly or indirectly contacting or abetting" terrorists or insurgent groups in armed rebellion against the state. Members of the military are among those excluded from party membership. Under the Political Parties Registration Law, parties that did not seek reregistration were automatically dissolved. These included the NLD and the SNLD.

Competing in the November 2010 elections were 37 parties, about two-thirds of them based in ethnic communities. Many parties contested no more than a handful of seats at the national level, partly because of financial limitations, including having to pay a fee of 500,000 kyats (about $500) per candidate.

In December 2013 nine minor opposition parties agreed to form an electoral alliance, the **Freedom Democratic Alliance** (FDA) ahead of the 2015 elections. Among the members of the FDA were the National Democratic Force (NDF), the Democratic Party Myanmar (DPM), and the Chin Progressive Party (CPP).

Parties in the Union Parliament:

National League for Democracy (NLD). Registered as a political party in September 1988, the NLD was an outgrowth of the **Democracy and Peace (Interim) League** (DPIL), which had been formed by a number of leading dissidents a month earlier. Its founding president, AUNG GYI, withdrew to form the **Union National Democratic Party** (UNDP) after having called, unsuccessfully, for the expulsion from the DPIL of a number of alleged communists. (The UNDP was deregistered in 1992.)

Following her return to Myanmar in April 1988, the party's first general secretary, Aung San Suu Kyi, became the regime's most vocal and effective critic. Both she and fellow NLD leader Tin Oo were arrested in July 1989 and declared ineligible to compete in the May 1990 balloting, which produced an overwhelming victory for the NLD, tacitly allied with some 21 ethnic-based regional parties. The NLD's two other principal leaders, KYI MAUNG and CHIT KHAING, were arrested in September 1990.

In April 1991 the SLORC announced that the NLD's Central Committee had been "invalidated," thus technically removing the four leaders from their party positions. Kyi Maung and Tin Oo were released from prison in March 1995, while Suu Kyi was freed from house arrest in July. Kyi Maung left the NLD in 1997, reportedly because of a dispute with Suu Kyi.

In July 1997 SLORC leader Khin Nyunt met with NLD chair AUNG SHWE, and on September 27–28 NLD delegates were permitted to hold the group's first congress with Suu Kyi in attendance in two years. An authorized NLD Congress on May 27–28, 1998, at her residence was attended by 400 party members. In the following months, however, in response to the NLD's threat to call a "People's Parliament," the regime began a series of crackdowns against the party that included hundreds of detentions, closure of many local offices, and forced resignations. In all, tens of thousands of party members may have been forced to resign in 1998–1999. Suu Kyi was again placed under de facto house arrest from September 2000 until May 2002.

On May 30, 2003, following a violent attack on an NLD motorcade by government supporters, Suu Kyi was taken into "protective custody." An unclear number of NLD members—initial reports indicated 4, but some subsequent accounts said 60 or more—were killed by the mob. Suu Kyi's house arrest resumed on September 26. On April 13, 2004, Aung Shwe and Secretary General U LWIN were released, leaving Suu Kyi and Tin Oo as the only senior NLD members in detention. A month later the NLD refused to participate in the reconvened National Convention until both were freed.

As part of a wider amnesty for 9,000 prisoners, described by Amnesty International as mostly drug dealers and petty criminals, WIN TIN, one of the founders of the NLD, was released from prison in September 2008 along with several other NLD members. Described as Myanmar's longest-serving political prisoner, Win Tin had been incarcerated since 1989. Several dozen NLD members were among the 7,000 prisoners released in September 2009.

The 2008 constitution includes as a condition for presidential eligibility that a candidate as well as the individual's parents, spouse, and natural children and their spouses cannot owe allegiance to a foreign country. Because Suu Kyi's late husband, Michael Aris, was British, she is excluded from seeking the office. At the time of the constitutional referendum, both she and Tin Oo remained under house arrest. Suu Kyi's was not renewed in May 2009, but at the time she was being held in a prison after being charged with having harbored in her home an uninvited American. In August she was convicted, but a three-year prison sentence was commuted to another 18 months of house arrest. She lost all appeals of the verdict. Tin Oo was released from house arrest on February 13, 2010.

In April 2009 the NLD indicated that it would participate in the 2010 elections but only if the SPDC released all political prisoners, amended the 2008 constitution to meet democratic standards, and agreed to let the international community supervise the elections. It failed to reregister in 2010 and was therefore dissolved, although some members of the Central Executive Committee, rejecting Suu Kyi's call for an election boycott, organized the NDF. Shortly after her release from house arrest on November 13, Suu Kyi appealed against the party's dissolution to the Supreme Court. The high court rejected Suu Kyi's appeal on January 28, 2011. In December the NLD was reregistered as a political party.

Suu Kyi ended her electoral boycott and ran for office in the April 2012 by-elections. In the balloting, the NLD won 38 of 39 seats in the assembly and 4 of 5 seats in the upper chamber. Suu Kyi's reentry into politics paved the way for the easing of international sanctions on the country.

In March 2013 the NLD held its first national conference. Suu Kyi was reelected unanimously as NLD leader by the party's central committee. In 2014 the NLD spearheaded a petition, which reportedly garnered three million signatures, to abolish the military's de facto veto over constitutional change.

Suu Kyi drew international criticism in 2015 for remaining silent on the plight of the Rohingya refugee crisis. Reports indicated that Suu Kyi was reluctant to comment for fear of alienating her mainly Buddhist base.

In the November 2015 national elections, the NLD won 135 seats in the upper house vote and 255 seats in the lower chamber. HTIN Kyaw was elected president on March 15, 2016, while Suu Kyi reportedly asserted that she would be "above the president," making all important decisions in her capacity as state councilor.

Leaders: AUNG SAN SUU KYI (Chair), HTIN Kyaw (President of Republic), Maj. (Ret.) Henry VAN THIO (Vice President of the Republic), WIN Myint (Speaker of the House of Representatives).

Union Solidarity and Development Party (USDP). Registered in June 2010, the USDP sprang from the Union Solidarity and Development Association (USDA), a junta-supportive mass organization founded in 1993 and described by the *Far Eastern Economic Review* in 1998 as a more inclusive "quasi-political party established under the guise of a community-assistance organization." In May 2003 the USDA was accused of organizing the attack against Aung San Suu Kyi's motorcade, and it was subsequently used to suppress, sometimes violently, other antijunta activities. Sometimes referred to by the derogatory *Kyant Phut* (translatable as "monitor lizard" or, roughly, "stupid reptile"), the USDA had a reputed membership of some 23 million when it was dissolved in July 2010 in favor of the USDP, to which its assets were transferred. Most of the Thein Sein cabinet and many members of the SPDC joined the USDP after relinquishing their military commissions.

Before the November 2010 election it was widely expected that the USDP would win 80 percent of the elective seats in the new Union

Parliament, and it nearly equaled that forecast, taking 79.7 percent and 259 seats in the People's Assembly, and 76.8 percent and 129 seats in the National Assembly. It also won a large majority of seats in the state and regional parliaments. In 2013 Thein Sein announced that he would not seek reelection. Subsequently the speaker of the House of Representatives, Shwe MANN, a prominent reformer, declared his intention to be the USDP's 2015 presidential candidate.

The USDP only won 30 seats in the lower house and 11 seats in the upper house during the 2015 elections. Lt. Gen. (Ret.) MYINT Swe was elected vice president in March 2016.

Leaders: HTAY Than (Chair), MYAT Hein (Vice Chair), Lt. Gen. (Ret.) MYINT Swe (Vice President of the Republic), THET Naing Win (Secretary General).

Arakan National Party (ANP). Established on January 13, 2014, the ANP merged the **Rakhine Nationalities Development Party** (RNDP) and the **Arakan League for Democracy** (ALD). The ANP focuses on regional interests in the Rakhine state and Yangon region.

Officially registered in June 2010, the RNDP was a prodemocracy formation in the western state of Rakhine (Arakan). During the subsequent legislative election campaign it complained of harassment and other forms of intimidation by USDP members. Its general secretary was vice chair of the ALD when it won 11 seats in the 1990 Constituent Assembly. (Led by AYE THAR AUNG, who also served as secretary of the Committee Representing the People's Parliament, the ALD chose not to run in 2010.)

In the November 2010 elections the RNDP won 2.8 percent of the lower house vote, for nine seats, and 4.2 percent in the upper house, for seven seats, second to the USDP. Following violence in Rakhine in 2012, party leader Aye Maung participated in government-sponsored peace negotiations, although reports alleged that the RNDP was complicit in the strife. In June 2013 the RNDP and the ALD agreed to merge. In February 2014 Aye Maung survived an assassination attempt in Bukit Bintang when shots were fired at his car by a motorcycle.

The new ANP won 10 seats in the upper house and 12 seats in the lower house during the 2015 elections.

Leaders: AYE Maung (President), AYE Thar Aung (Chair).

Shan Nationalities League for Democracy (SNLD). Established in 1988, the SNLD won 23 seats in the 1990 Constituent Assembly balloting, second only to the NLD. Its leader, KHUN TUN OO, was a key opposition figure both in Shan State and on the national scene, where he participated in the "People's Parliament" and conferred repeatedly with UN and EU representatives. The SNLD refused to participate when the National Convention reconvened in May 2004.

In February 2005 Tun Oo and SAI SAW AUNG, the party's secretary, were among nearly a dozen individuals charged with treason, insurrection, and other offenses. In November Tun Oo was convicted and sentenced to spend the rest of his life in prison. Eight others also received lengthy sentences. The SNLD and NLD made a joint call for a "no" vote in the 2008 referendum on the new constitution and denounced the result. In May 2014 SNLD regional chair SAI JAN was arrested and charged with association with an unlawful group.

In the 2015 elections, the SNLD won 3 seats in the upper house and 12 in the lower house.

Leaders: KHUN HTUN OO (Chair), SAI NYUNT LWIN (Secretary General).

National Unity Party—NUP (*Taingyintha Silonenyinyutye* Party). An outgrowth of the former BSPP, the NUP was launched in September 1988. Unlike the practice under BSPP rule, members of the armed forces were specifically excluded from membership. The party won only 10 of 485 available seats in the Constituent Assembly election of May 1990.

The government-supportive NUP, reregistered in April 2010, is backed by business interests. Its chair is a former deputy commander in chief of the armed forces. In the 2010 balloting, it won 3.7 percent of the vote and 12 seats in the People's Assembly, plus 3 percent and 5 seats in the National Assembly. The NUP ran 23 candidates in the April 2012 by-elections but failed to secure any seats. In January 2014 the NUP announced that it hoped half of its candidates in the 2015 balloting would be women. NUP only won a single seat in the upper house during the 2015 elections.

Leaders: TUN YI (Chair), THAN TIN and KHIN MAUNG GYI (General Secretaries), HAN SHWE (Spokesperson).

Pa-O National Organization (PNO). The PNO, representing the Pa-O ethnic minority in the Pa-O Self-Administered Zone of Shan State, was registered in May 2010. Formed from one of the cease-fire groups and elements of the Union Pa-O National Organization, which had contested the 1990 election but was formally dissolved in September 2010 for failing to register, the PNO received at least tacit government support. It won three uncontested People's Assembly seats as well as one uncontested seat in the National Assembly. In the 2015 election PNO won one seat in the upper house and three in the lower house.

Leaders: AUNG KHAM HTI (Chair), KHUN SAN LWIN, MAI OHN KAING (Secretary General).

Wa Democratic Party (WDP). Registration of the WDP was approved in July 2010. Based in Shan State, the party has ties to the USDP. Its chair won a seat in the 1990 Constituent Assembly election as an NUP candidate. In November 2010 the WDP won two seats in the People's Assembly and one in the National Assembly. In 2013 the WDP refused to participate in an all-Shan state conference called by the SNLD. In the November 2015 balloting, the WDP won one seat in the House of Representatives.

Leaders: KHUN TUN LU (Chair), HSAI PAUNG NAP (General Secretary).

Taaung (Palaung) National Party (TNP). The TNP, which was registered in May 2010, represents the Taaung (Palaung) ethnic group based primarily in Shan State. Its chair served as leader of the Palaung State Liberation Army, which accepted a cease-fire with the junta in the early 1990s. At that time a Palaung Self-Administered Zone was established. In November 2010 the TNP claimed one seat in each house of the Parliament and four in the state parliament, all of them uncontested. In the November 2015 elections, the party won two seats in the upper house and one in the lower chamber.

Leaders: AIK MONE (Chair), TIN MAUNG, MAI OHN KAING (General Secretary).

Zomi Congress for Democracy (ZCD). The ZCD was initially established in 1988, as the **Zomi National Congress** (ZNC), to promote the unification of the Zomi people in India and Myanmar. It was abolished in 1992. The ZCD adopted its current name in 2012. In the November 2015 elections, the ZCD won two seats in each chamber of the national parliament.

Leader: Pu Chin SIAN THANG.

Kokang Democracy and Unity Party (KDUP). The KDUP, founded in 1988 and based in Shan State, competed in the 1990 election, subsequently participated in the National Convention, and was reregistered in May 2010. It represents ethnic Chinese in the self-administered Kokang zone. It failed to win any seats in the November 2010 elections but won one seat in the lower house in November 2015.

Leaders: LO Xingguang (Chair), YAN KYIN KAN (Vice Chair).

Minor parties that won seats at the national level in the 2015 elections included the **Mon National Party** (MNP), which won one seat in the upper chamber; the **Lisu National Development Party** (LNDP), which secured two seats in the lower chamber; and the **Kachin State Democracy Party** (KSDP), which won one seat in the lower house.

Other Parties Contesting the 2010 or 2015 Elections:

National Democratic Force (NDF). The NDF was registered in July 2010 by former members of the dissolved NLD's Central Executive Committee who objected to Aung San Suu Kyi's call to boycott the upcoming national elections. One of the leading prodemocracy parties to participate in the November election, the NDF put forward about 150 candidates for the Union Parliament. It won 2.5 percent of the vote and eight seats in the lower house, and 2.4 percent and four seats in the upper. In 2013 the NDF announced its support for constitutional changes that would allow Aung San Suu Kyi of the NLD to seek the presidency in 2015. In 2014 the NDF called for proportional voting to replace the current system of representation in Myanmar.

Leaders: THAN NYEIN (Chair), TIN AUNG AUNG (Vice Chair), KHIN MAUNG SWE, THEIN NYUNT (Spokesperson), SEIN WIN (Secretary).

All Mon Region Democracy Party (AMRDP). Campaigning on behalf of the Mon people in eastern Myanmar, the AMRDP was registered in May 2010. With the New Mon State Party (NMSP), a cease-fire group, having decided to boycott the November elections, the AMRDP was the only ethnic Mon party to compete. It won three seats (0.9 percent of the vote) in the People's Assembly but four seats (2.4 percent) in the National Assembly. In September 2012 the AMRDP agreed to merge with the small Mon Democracy Party (MDP); however, tensions between the two groupings had prevented the finalization of the merger until December 2013. The AMRDP failed to win a seat in either house in 2015 but held one seat in regional assembly.

Leaders: NGWE THEIN (Chair), HLA AUNG (Vice Chair).

Democratic Party Myanmar (DPM). Registered in May 2010, the DPM descends from the Democratic Party that was established by THU WAI in 1988 and that contested the 1990 election. In September 2009 MYA THAN THAN NU, daughter of the country's last elected prime minister, U Nu, and Nay Yee Ba Swe, daughter of former prime minister BA SWE (1956–1957), announced that they would organize a new Democratic Party to contest the legislative election scheduled for 2010. They were joined by CHO CHO KYAW NYEIN, daughter of former deputy prime minister KYAW NYEIN. The "three princesses," as they have been familiarly labeled, had all served time in prison or lived in exile.

The DPM, which alleged campaign and voting irregularities by the SPDC and the USDP, failed in its bid for seats in the Union Parliament but won three at the state/regional level in 2010. In December 2012 the DPM proposed the creation of a federal system similar to that of the United States.

In 2015 the DPM again failed to gain any seats in the national parliament but did win one at the regional level.

Leaders: THU WAI (Chair); MYA THAN THAN NU, NAY YEE BA SWE, and CHO CHO KYAW NYEIN (Joint Secretaries).

Lahu National Development Party (LNDP). Based in the Lahu tribe of eastern Shan State, the LNDP is one of the few extant parties that competed in 1990 and later participated in the National Convention. Government supportive, it condemned the NLD's announcement of the People's Parliament in 1998. It reregistered in April 2010 and won one state parliamentary seat in November. The LNDP won one regional seat in the 2015 balloting.

Leaders: KYAR HAR SHE (Chair), YAW THAT (Vice Chair).

Ethnic National Development Party (ENDP). Representing the Mara people in Chin State, the ENDP won one state-level parliamentary seat in November 2010.

Leaders: PU HIPA (President), VAN CING (Vice President).

Mro National Solidarity Organization (MNSO). Also known as the **Khami National Solidarity Organization,** the government-supportive MNSO is based in Rakhine and Chin states and claims to represent the interests of the Mro (Khami) ethnic group. It contested the 1990 Constituent Assembly election, winning one seat, and reregistered in April 2010. It won no seats in the November elections.

Leaders: SAN THAR AUNG (Chair), KYAW TUN KHAING (Vice Chair).

National Democratic Party for Development (NDPD). Despite being targeted by USDP members, the NDPD won two seats in the Rakhine state parliament in November 2010. The NDPD was highly critical of the government response to strife in Rakhine and claimed that casualty figures were substantially higher than official reports.

Leader: MAUNG MAUNG NI (Chair).

Shan Nationalities Democratic Party (SNDP). The prodemocracy SNDP was the successor to the Shan Nationalities League for Democracy (SNLD), which opposed the 2008 constitution, decided not to seek registration, and was dissolved by the election commission in September 2010. The SNLD (see above) had finished second in the 1990 Constituent Assembly election as an ally of the NLD. The SNDP's first chair, Sai Ai Pao, was the SNLP's secretary general.

Registered in May 2010, the SNDP, which is widely known as the White Tiger Party from its party emblem, focused its attention on winning Union Parliament seats in Shan State. In the lower house it finished second to the USDP overall, winning 5.5 percent of the vote and 18 seats. In the upper house it was less successful, taking 1.8 percent of the vote and winning 3 seats. It won an additional seat in the upper house in by-elections in April 2012.

The SNDP failed to win any seats at the national level in 2015 but won one state seat.

Leaders: SAI AI PAO (Chair), SAI HLA KYAW (General Secretary).

Chin National Party (CNP). Officially registered in May 2010, the CNP campaigned on behalf of the Chin people, calling for increased self-determination, economic development, and an end to arbitrary arrests and forced labor. The Union Election Commission censored part of the party's election manifest, including a call for religious freedom and the teaching of the Chin language.

In the November 2010 polling the CNP won 0.6 percent of the vote and two seats in the lower house, and 1.2 percent of the vote and two seats in the upper house. In June 2013 the CNP was reported to have merged with the Chin Progressive Party (see below).

Leaders: ZAM CIIN PAU (ZO ZAM) (Chair), CHAN HAY (Vice Chair), CEU BIK THAWNG (Secretary General).

Chin Progressive Party (CPP). Based in Chin State and Sagaing Division, the CPP registered in May 2010. Its leadership includes a number of former government workers as well as businessmen. Its goals include advancing economic development and the rights and cultural identity of ethnic Chin. In 2010 it won two seats in the People's Assembly (0.6 percent of the vote) but four in the National Assembly (2.4 percent).

Leaders: NOE THANG KUP (Chair), LAEL HTAN (Secretary).

Phalon-Sawaw Democratic Party (PSDP). Based in Kayin State and targeting ethnic Kayins, the PSDP registered in May 2010. Its election manifesto championed human rights, international peace, national unity, and overcoming oppression. The PSDP won two seats in the lower house and three in the upper in the November 2010 election.

Leaders: KHIN MAUNG MYINT (Chair), AUNG KYAW NAING (Vice Chair), KYI LIN (Secretary).

Inn National Development Party (INDP). Registration of the INDP was approved in June 2010. It ran in only one Shan State township, where the Intha ethnic group is centered. During the campaign the party accused SPDC officials of forcing civil servants to cast early ballots. The INDP won one seat in the People's Assembly.

Leaders: WIN MYINT (Chair), AUNG KYI WIN.

Kayin People's Party (KPP). Founded in 2001 and reregistered in May 2010, the KPP is led by Tun Aung Myint, a former naval commander, and Saw Simon Tha, a physician and peace negotiator who has been involved in discussions between the junta and Karen insurgents, including the Karen National Union (KNU, below). The party sought an alliance with the USDP before the November elections, when it won one seat in each house of the Union Parliament. KPP official Aloti SINGHA was arrested in February 2013 for allegedly harboring two KLO militants. In the 2015 balloting, the party won one seat in a regional assembly.

Leaders: TUN AUNG MYINT (Chair), SAW SIMON THA (First Vice Chair), SAW SAY WAH (General Secretary).

Unity and Democracy Party of Kachin State (UDPKS). Registered in August 2010, the projunta UDPKS was formed by a number of USDA members with connections to the military government. It won one seat in each house of the Union Parliament in November 2010 but only one seat at the regional level in November 2015.

Leaders: KHET HTEIN NAN (Chair); KHIN MAUNG LATT, AYE KYAW (Vice Chairs).

Kayin State Democracy and Development Party (KSDDP). The KSDDP was established by former members of cease-fire groups allied with the junta. Some of its members had reportedly belonged to the Democratic Karen Buddhist Association and the Karen Peace Force, both of which were splinters from the KNU (below). The new party was registered in August 2010 and won one seat in the upper house in November 2010 but only one seat at the state level in November 2015.

Leader: HTOO KYAW (Chair).

The following parties also ran for seats in the November 2010 elections but were unsuccessful: the **Democracy and Peace Party** (DPP), the **Kaman National Progressive Party** (KNPP), the **Kayin National Party** (KNP), the **Khami National Development Party** (KNDP), the **Modern People Party** (MPP), the **National Development and Peace Party** (NDPP), the **National Political Alliances League** (NPAL), the **Peace and Diversity Party** (PDP), the **Rakhine State National Force of Myanmar** (RSNF), the **United Democratic Party** (UnitedDP), the **Union Democratic Party** (UnionDP), the **Wa National Unity Party** (WNUP), and the **Wuntharnu NLD–Union of Myanmar** (WNLD).

Dissolved Parties:

In September 2010 the election commission announced that the following parties were dissolved: the **Shan State Kokang Democratic**

Party; the **Union Pa-O National Organization,** based in west-central Shan State; and the **Wa National Development Party.** At the same time, the following five parties, which had previously been registered, were dissolved for failing to submit complete candidate lists by the deadline: the **Mro National Party,** the **Myanmar Democracy Congress,** the **Myanmar New Social Party,** the **Regional Development Party (Pyay),** and the **Union Karen League.** Earlier, in July, the government had ruled the **Kachin State Progressive Party** ineligible for registration because of links to the Kachin Independence Organization (KIO), a cease-fire group that had rejected participation in the border guard force proposal.

For information on the **88 Generation Students,** the **88 Generation Student Youths (Union of Myanmar)** (88GSY), and the **Alliance of All Burmese Buddhist Monks** (AABBM), see the 2015 *Handbook.*

Cease-Fire Groups:

United Wa State Party (UWSP). The UWSP and the associated United Wa State Army (UWSA), founded in 1989 after Wa elements separated from the Communist Party of Burma, are reputedly the country's leading producer of opium, heroin, and methamphetamines. Reportedly numbering as many as 25,000, with another 10,000 in associated village militias, the UWSA has operated with considerable autonomy within the Golden Triangle area of Shan State, even before negotiating a cease-fire agreement with the junta. A leading ally is the smaller **National Democratic Alliance Army** (NDAA). Although the UWSP/UWSA leader, Bao Yuxiang, has asserted that poppy cultivation has been eliminated in the area under UWSA control, in November 2008 the U.S. State Department described the UWSA as the "largest and most powerful drug trafficking organization in Southeast Asia."

The UWSA has repeatedly rejected inclusion in the junta's Border Guard Force, and in November 2010 the UWSP refused to allow elections to take place in the area under its control. Reports in 2013 indicated that the UWSA had purchased missiles and other weaponry from China. In 2014 the UWSP agreed to be included on a government ceasefire commission.

Leader: BAO YUXIANG (PAU YU CHANG).

Cease-fire groups that have agreed to become part of the Border Guard Force (BGF) include the **Kachin Defense Force,** a splinter from the KIO's Kachin Independence Army (KIA); the **Karen Peace Force,** which split from the KNU in 1997; the **Karenni National People's Liberation Front,** a 1978 splinter from the KNPP; and the **New Democratic Army–Kachin,** which left the KIA in 1989. In August 2009 junta troops overran the **Myanmar National Democratic Alliance Army** (MNDAA) after the group rejected becoming part of the BGF, with the altercation resulting in the flight of some 37,000 Kokang refugees to China. The MNDAA, which separated from the Communist Party of Burma in 1989, has been replaced by a more compliant **Kokang Region Provisional Leading Committee.**

In addition to the UWSA and the NDAA, cease-fire groups that have rejected the government's BGF proposal include the **Kachin Independence Organization** (KIO), the **Karen National Liberation Army Peace Council,** the **New Mon State Party** (NMSP), the **Shan State Army–North** (SSA-N).

Insurgent Groups:

During the first half of the 1990s the military regime eliminated or arranged cease-fires with most of the country's longtime military insurgents, although negotiations with several groups subsequently broke down. (For a more complete accounting of insurgent groups active prior to 1995, see the 1993 and 1994–1995 editions of the *Handbook.*)

Karen National Union (KNU). With origins dating back to 1947, the KNU and its military wing, the **Karen National Liberation Army** (KNLA), was one of the more effective minority-based insurgent groups. The KNU declared a unilateral cease-fire in March 1995, following the loss of its Manerplaw headquarters in January and its base in Kawmoora a month later. In early 1997, however, talks between the KNU and the government broke down, with government troops quickly renewing their campaign against remaining KNU bases. At a ten-day party congress held in late January 2000, Bo Mya stepped down as KNU chair in favor of the party's former secretary general, SAW BA THEIN SIEN, who advocated for a political solution to the conflict.

A fringe KNU group, God's Army, took 700 hostages at a hospital in Ratchaburi, Thailand, in January 2000, demanding an end to an anti-Karen offensive in the Thailand–Myanmar border region. All 10 hostage-takers died in an assault by Thai forces a day later. Dating from 1997 and probably numbering no more than 150 men, the cultlike God's Army was ostensibly led by 12-year-old twins, Johnny and Luther HTOO. It apparently disbanded in October 2000, with the Htoo brothers being granted asylum in Thailand in January 2001.

At a congress held November 18–December 8, 2004, Bo Mya, reportedly in poor health, was replaced as vice chair but remained in charge of defense. A cease-fire came to an end after Khin Nyunt's removal from office in October 2004.

In May 2006 a renewed government offensive against KNU supporters drew widespread international criticism as well as calls for a new cease-fire and renewed negotiations. Bo Mya died on December 24, 2006. In February 2007 a KNU splinter led by HTAIN MAUNG signed a peace agreement with the government, and two months later reports surfaced of a major military defeat for the KNU.

On February 17, 2008, Secretary General PADOH MAHN SHA of the KNU was shot dead in his home. Thai police reported the assailants were Karen, although government culpability was suspected. In late 2008 the KNU elected its vice chair, Tamla Baw, as chair and his daughter, Zipporah SEIN, as secretary general.

Of the various groups that have split from the KNU, the most significant is the **Democratic Karen Buddhist Organization** (DKBO), which separated from the largely Christian KNU in 1994. With the support of government forces, the DKBO's military wing, the **Democratic Karen Buddhist Army** (DKBA), spearheaded several assaults in 1997–1998 on KNU refugee camps in Thailand. The KNU responded in March 1998 by attacking DKBA bases in Myanmar. As the **Democratic Karen/Kayin Buddhist Association,** the group was invited by the government to participate in the reconvened National Convention in 2004. More recently, a brigade of the DKBA led by SAW LAH PWE refused to function as a border guard force under the military, severed its association with the parent organization, and renewed armed attacks against junta forces. The first talks between the KNU and the DKBO since the 1994 split were reportedly held in October 1999. The rebellious faction, which was directly involved in the 2010 postelection fighting in Shan State that led to the temporary flight of some 20,000 refugees into Thailand, has reportedly joined forces with the KNLA in some areas. On April 7, 2012, the KNU and the government signed a 13-point peace plan. In December Gen. MUTU SAE POE was elected KNU chair, with former secretary general Zipporah Sein selected as vice chair. MUTU SAE POE and other KNU leaders met with President Thein Sein on June 3, 2014, to review the peace process.

Leaders: Gen. MUTU SAE POE (Chair), Zipporah SEIN (Vice Chair), SAW KWE HTOO (Secretary General).

Karenni National Progressive Party (KNPP). With a predominantly Kayinni membership, the KNPP was established in the mid-1950s. It concluded an agreement with the SLORC in March 1995 but in mid-1996 took up arms again and remained in active opposition in 2004, although two splinter groups, the **Kayinni National Progressive Party Dragon Group** and the **Kayinni National Progressive Party** (Hoya Splinter), had concluded cease-fire agreements with the SPDC and, on that basis, were invited to send delegates to the reconvened National Convention.

The KNPP held cease-fire discussions with the government in 2007 but failed to reach an agreement. In June 2007 it sponsored a meeting of ethnic groups that were still engaged in armed resistance. Among the attendees were the KNU and the Shan State Army–South (below). In the run-up to and in the aftermath of the November 2010 national election, the KNPP's military commander, Bee Htoo, asserted that half a dozen insurgent groups that rejected the 2008 constitution were in the process of forming an alliance to continue armed opposition to the government. Other participants included the KNU, the antijunta wing of the KIO, the NMSP, and the SSA-N.

Another cease-fire agreement was signed between the KNU and the government in March 2012, with a more formal accord finalized in June 2013. The new agreement included plans for demining and the resettlement of displaced Kayinnis.

Leaders: KHU HTE BU PEH, BEE HTOO (Commander of the Karenni Army).

Shan State Army–South (SSA-S). Dating from 1964, the Shan State Army established the **Shan State Progressive Party** (subsequently the Shan State Peacekeeping Council) in 1972, although the two later separated. In April 1998 Amnesty International, in a report quickly ridiculed by the SPDC, accused the Myanmar army of torturing or killing hundreds of Shans and forcing at least 300,000 to flee their homes in 1996–1997 as part of its effort to cut off support for the SSA. Although the SSA-North concluded a peace agreement with the SPDC, the SSA-South remained in militant opposition to the government.

During 2005 two cease-fire groups, the Shan State National Army (SSNA) and the Shan State Nationalities People's Liberation Organization (SNPLO) announced that they had ended their cooperation with the government and were joining the SSA insurgency. By the end of 2005, however, the SSNA had surrendered, as did the SNPLO in August 2008.

The SPDC declared the SSA-S to be a terrorist organization in August 2006. In mid-2009 there was considerably speculation that the SPDC, having achieved measurable gains in a recent offensive against ethnic Karens, was planning to launch a campaign against the SSA-S before the end of the year. Similar speculation followed the November 2010 national election.

A cease-fire was signed in January 2012. In June 2013 SSA commander Col. YAWD SERK urged other ethnic minorities to reach similar cease-fire accords with the government. In May 2014 security forces raided the offices of the SSA.

Leaders: Col. YAWD SERK (Commander), SAI LAO HSENG.

Among the other groups reputedly engaged in drug manufacture and trafficking is the **Shan United Revolutionary Party,** an offshoot of the Mong Tai Army that rejected the latter's surrender to government forces. In July 2008 a group calling itself the **Vigorous Burmese Student Warriors** (VBSW) claimed responsibility for a bomb that exploded outside a Yangon office of the USDA; it also claimed responsibility for a bomb in April 2010 that killed ten people.

Exile Groups:

A number of exile opposition groups currently function. Most supported the **National Coalition Government of the Union of Burma** (NCGUB), a shadow government that was established in 1991 but dissolved itself in 2012.

All Burma Student Democratic Front (ABSDF). The ABSDF was founded in 1988 by disaffected students. In March 1998 the Yangon regime accused the ABSDF of organizing a plot to assassinate government leaders and bomb government buildings and foreign embassies. The ABSDF denied the charge, responding that it had decided in 1997 to abandon armed conflict in favor of "nonviolent, political defiance." Earlier, ABSDF leader KO AUNG TUN was imprisoned for 15 years for writing a history of the Burmese student movement.

In September 2009 the ABSDF joined the 88 Generation Students and the All-Burma Monks' Alliance in a statement urging the junta to end its assaults against ethnic minority groups. In 2012 the ABSDF issued a formal apology for its role in political killings and torture in the 1990s. In September prominent ABSDF members, including former leader MOE THEE ZUN, returned to Myanmar. In May 2013 the government launched a new round of negotiations with the ABSDF. The organization was included as part of the Union Peace Working Committee, tasked to create a permanent ceasefire between the government and rebel groups.

Leaders: THAN KE (Chair), MYO WIN (Vice Chair), Sonny MAHINDER (General Secretary).

Other exile groups include the **Democratic Party for a New Society,** the **People's Defense Front,** the **Burma Women's Union,** and the **Network for Democracy and Development**. In February 2004 they joined with the ABSDF and a number of other groups to organize an umbrella **Democratic Alliance of Burma**. Additional formations include the **National Council of the Union of Burma** (NCUB), the **Federation of Trade Unions Burma** (FTUB), the **National League for Democracy–Liberated Areas** (NLD-LA), and the **U.S. Campaign for Burma**.

LEGISLATURE

The former People's Assembly (*Pyithu Hluttaw*), elected in November 1985, was abolished by the military government on September 18, 1988. In the election of May 27, 1990, 93 parties competed for 485 of 492 seats in a new Constituent Assembly (polling being barred in 7 constituencies for security reasons). The National League for Democracy won an overwhelming majority of 392 seats, compared to 10 for the government-backed National Unity Party. The military junta never permitted the assembly to convene. The 2008 constitution provides for a bicameral legislature, the **Union Parliament** (*Pyidaungsu Hluttaw*), in which all members serve five-year terms. Among those excluded from candidacy are civil servants, members of religious orders, employees of state-owned companies, and those who have criminal records.

House of Nationalities (*Amyotha Hluttaw*). The upper house comprises 224 members. The seven states and seven regions are equally represented by 12 directly elected members each, with an additional 56 seats (25 percent) reserved for members of the military, chosen by the commander in chief. In the election on November 8, 2015, the National Development Party won 135 seats; Union Solidarity and Development Party, 11; Arakan National Party, 10; Shan Nationalities League for Democracy, 3; Taaung (Palaung) National Party, 2; Zomi Congress for Democracy, 2; Mon National Party; National Unity Party, 1; Pa-O National Organization, 1; independents, 2.

Speaker: MAHN Win Khaing Than (NLD).

House of Representatives (*Pyithu Hluttaw*). The lower house comprises 440 members, of whom 330 are directly elected from township-based districts according to population; 110 seats (25 percent) are reserved for military appointees. The election on November 8, 2015, produced the following results: National Development Party, 255 seats; Union Solidarity and Development Party, 30; Arakan National Party, 12; Shan Nationalities League for Democracy, 12; Ta'ang National Party, 3; Pa-O National Organization, 3; Lisu National Development Party, 2; Zomi Congress for Democracy, 2; Kachin State Democracy Party, 1; Kokang Democracy and Unity Party, 1; and Wa Democratic Party, 1; and independents, 1. The security situation prevented voting in seven districts.

Speaker: WIN Myint (NLD).

CABINET

[as of November 12, 2016]

President	Htin Kyaw (NLD)
First Vice President	Lt. Gen. (Ret.) Myint Swe (USDP)
Second Vice President	Maj. (Ret.) Henry Van Thio (NLD)
Ministers	
Agriculture, Irrigation and Livestock	Aung Thu (NLD)
Attorney General	U Tun Tun Oo
Border Affairs	Lt. Gen. Ye Aung (Military)
Commander-in-Chief Air Force	Gen. Khin Aung Myint
Commander-in-Chief Navy	Vice Adm. Tin Aung San
Commerce	Than Myint (NLD)
Construction	U Win Khaing (ind.)
Defense	Lt. Gen. Sein Win (Military)
Education	Myo Thein Gyi (ind.)
Electricity	U Pyae Myint Htun (NLD)
Ethnic Affairs	Naing Thet Lwin (MNP)
Health	Myint Htwe (ind.)
Home Affairs	Lt. Gen. Kyaw Swe (Military)
Hotels and Tourism	U Ohn Maung (ind.)
Industry	U Khin Maung Cho (ind.)
Information	Pe Myint (ind.)
Labour, Immigration, and Population	Maj.-Gen. (Ret.) U Thein Swe (USDP)
Myanmar Defense Services	Senior Gen. Min Aung Hlaing (Military)
Natural Resources and Environment	U Ohn Win (ind.)
Office of the State Counsellor	U Kyaw Tint Swe (ind.)
Planning and Finance	U Kyaw Win (NLD)
Religious and Cultural Affairs	Brig.-Gen. (Ret.) Thura U Aung Ko (USDP)
Social Welfare, Relief, and Resettlement	Win Myat Aye (NLD)
Speaker of the House of Nationalities	U Mahn Win Khaing Than (NLD)

Speaker of the House of Representatives	U Win Myint (NLD)
State Counsellor and Minister of Foreign Affairs, Office of the President	Aung San Suu Kyi (NLD) [f]
Transport and Communication	U Thant Zin Maung (NLD)

[f] = female

INTERGOVERNMENTAL REPRESENTATION

Ambassador to the U.S.: U AUNG LYNN.

U.S. Ambassador to Myanmar (Burma): Scot MARCIEL.

Permanent Representative to the UN: Hau Do SUAN.

IGO Memberships (Non-UN): ADB, ASEAN, NAM, WTO.

For Further Reference:

Clapp, Priscilla A. *Securing a Democratic Future for Myanmar*. New York: Council on Foreign Relations Press, 2016.

Holliday, Ian. *Burma Redux: Global Justice and the Quest for Political Reform in Myanmar*. New York: Columbia University Press, 2012.

Than, Tharaphi. *Women in Modern Burma*. New York: Routledge, 2013.

Topich, William J., and Keith A. Leitich. *The History of Myanmar*. Santa Barbara, CA: ABC-CLIO, 2013.

NAMIBIA

Republic of Namibia

Political Status: Former German territory assigned to South Africa under League of Nations mandate in 1920; declared to be a United Nations responsibility by General Assembly resolution adopted October 27, 1966 (resolution not recognized by South Africa); subject to tripartite (Angolan-Cuban-South African) agreement concluded on December 22, 1988, providing for implementation from April 1, 1989, of Security Council Resolution 435 of 1978 (leading to UN-supervised elections on November 1 and independence thereafter); independence declared on March 21, 1990.

Area: 318,259 sq. mi. (824,292 sq. km).

Population: 2,514,000 (2016E—UN); 2,224,786 (2016E—U.S. Census). Both area and population figures include data for Walvis Bay (see Political background and Foreign relations, below).

Major Urban Center (2015E—UN.): WINDHOEK (368,000).

Official Language: English.

Monetary Unit: Namibian Dollar (official rate October 1, 2016: 13.72 dollars = $1US). Introduced on September 13, 1993, the Namibian dollar is at par with the South African rand, which is also legal tender in Namibia.

President: Hage GIENGOB (South West Africa People's Organization of Namibia); popularly elected on November 28, 2014, and inaugurated on March 21, 2015, for a five-year term; to succeed Hifikepunye POHAMBA (South West Africa People's Organization of Namibia).

Vice President: Nickey IYAMBO (South West People's Organization of Namibia); appointed by the president on March 21, 2015.

Prime Minister: Saara KUUGONGELWA-AMADHILA (South West Africa People's Organization of Namibia); appointed by the president on March 21, 2015; to succeed Hage GEINGOB (South West Africa People's Organization of Namibia).

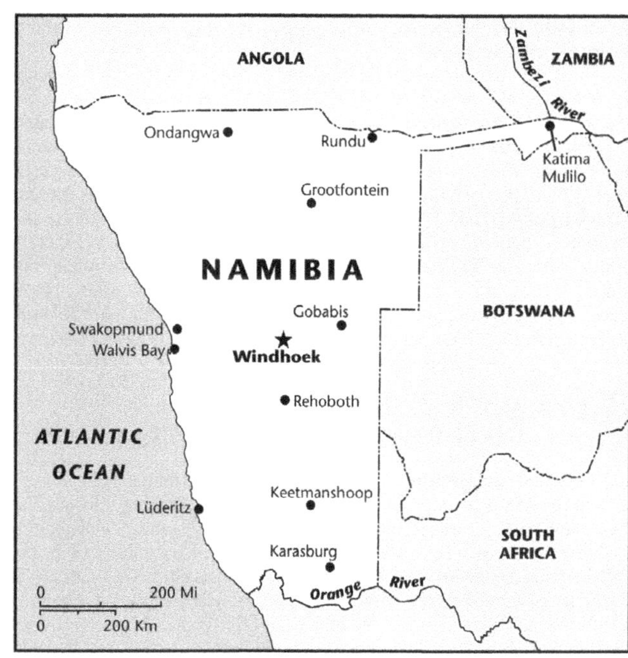

THE COUNTRY

Bordered on the north by Angola and Zambia, on the east by Botswana, on the southeast and south by South Africa, and on the west by the Atlantic Ocean, Namibia consists of a high plateau bounded by the uninhabited Namib Desert along the Atlantic coast, with more desert land in the interior. The inhabitants are of diversified origins, although the Ovambo constitute by far the largest ethnic group (approximately 49 percent of the population). A substantial exodus has reduced the white population, traditionally engaged in commercial farming and ranching, fish processing, and mineral exploitation, from approximately 12 percent to 6 percent. Other groups include the Kavango, the Herero, the Damara, the Nama, and those classified as "coloured." Although women continue to face a variety of discrimination in the economic and social sectors, strides have been made in politics. Namibia has among the highest percentage of elected women representatives in the world with 41.3 percent (43 of 104 seats) of the lower house and 23.8 percent (42 of 10 seats) of the upper house. There are just 4 women in the cabinet of 26 (15.4 percent), but the prime minister is female. The Inter-Parliamentary Union ranked Namibia at 11th out of 181 countries for women representation in government (tied with Iceland and Nicaragua). In the November 2015 elections for regional leaders, only 43 women were nominated among the 287 candidates to 121 regional constituency seats up for elections. Only 19 seats were won by women, a step backward for representation by women in Namibia. Namibia recently adopted a National Gender Policy calling for a 50–50 government representation for women.

The country is one of the world's largest producers of diamonds, which yield about half of export earnings, and uranium; copper, lead, zinc, tin, and other minerals are also available in extractable quantities. Foodstuffs, especially beef, are becoming a larger export market (see Current events, below). These resources yielded substantial economic growth during the 1970s; subsequently, falling mineral prices, extended periods of drought, and internal insecurity caused a severe recession, marked by 40–50 percent unemployment, 13–16 percent inflation, and severe budgetary problems. In July 1990 international donors committed $200 million to help offset a $270 million fiscal shortfall caused by South Africa's withdrawal from the economy. GDP growth averaged 5 percent annually in 1990–1993 and 3 percent annually in 1994–1999. Economic policies have focused on further exploitation of the country's rich fisheries, export manufacturing, promotion of private investment, and programs designed to ameliorate the severe maldistribution of wealth and continuing high unemployment rate. A 2002 agreement to allow Namibian craft to fish in South African territorial waters further expanded the sector.

Steady economic growth continued in the early 2000s, with GDP increasing by an average of 3–4 percent annually. Significantly, inflation fell to 5 percent by 2004 (from 8.8 percent in 1997) after the Bank of Namibia cut interest rates from 12.75 percent to 5 percent over a four-year period.

International firms have invested $800 million in the development of natural gas fields. Long-term plans are to use the fields to produce electricity for export to surrounding states, including South Africa. In an effort to reduce unemployment and poverty, the government launched a controversial land redistribution program in 2004 in order to increase farm ownership among black Namibians. (For details on land redistribution, see the 2011 *Handbook.*) Despite the economic challenges of an unemployment rate exceeding 20 percent and widespread poverty, real GDP growth averaged 4.2 percent in 2005–2007. While overall economic performance remained strong and debt declined, growth was insufficient to create new jobs. The International Monetary Fund (IMF) in 2007, while commending Namibia's overall economic progress, emphasized the need for authorities to develop the non-mining sector to help reduce poverty. The prevalence of HIV/AIDS, affecting an estimated 20 percent of the population, continued to be a major concern, though the outlook improved somewhat with the government's development of a strategy to address the disease. The IMF also cited progress in the implementation of education reforms, financial assistance to farmers in the wake of a major drought, and the establishment of an anticorruption commission. Economic growth contracted to an annual average of 1.5 percent over 2008–2009, owing in large part to a downturn in the mining sector as a consequence of the global financial crisis. Inflation fell from nearly 11 percent in 2008 to about 5 percent in 2010. The IMF noted that the banking sector in particular withstood well the adverse effects of the financial crisis. GDP grew by 6.6 percent in 2010 as the economy made a strong recovery, spurred by an increase in mineral exports, especially diamonds and uranium, and growth in domestic demand. In 2011 GDP growth slowed to an estimated 5.1 percent amid severe flooding in the north and a weaker global economy.

The IMF estimated that GDP grew by 5 percent in 2013, 4.3 percent in 2014, and 4.5 percent in 2015, while inflation was 6.5 percent, 6.1 percent, and 3.4 percent, respectively. Poverty remains significant. Over half of the population live in rural areas and live a subsistence agriculture lifestyle, skewing unemployment numbers. The UN estimated that approximately 55.8 percent of the population lives on less than $2 per day. GDP per capita in 2013 was $5,667, highlighting the economic inequities within Namibia. In its 2013 Human Development Index, the UN ranked Namibia 128th out of 186 countries, but improved slightly to 126th in 2015. Meanwhile, in 2016 continued concerns over corruption and government inefficiency led the World Bank to rank Namibia 101st out of 189 countries in its ease of doing business survey, a dramatic drop from 2006 when the country was rated 39th.

GOVERNMENT AND POLITICS

Political background. South West Africa came under German control in the 1880s, except for a small enclave at Walvis Bay, which had been annexed by the United Kingdom in 1878 and subsequently became a part of South Africa. Having occupied the whole of South West Africa during World War I, South Africa was granted a mandate in 1920 to govern the area under authority of the League of Nations. Declining to place the territory under the UN trusteeship system after World War II, South Africa asked the UN General Assembly in 1946 for permission to annex it; following denial of the request, Pretoria continued its rule on the strength of the original mandate.

Although the international status of the territory and the supervisory authority of the United Nations were repeatedly affirmed in advisory opinions of the International Court of Justice (ICJ), the court in 1966 declined on technical grounds to rule upon a formal complaint by Ethiopia and Liberia against South Africa's conduct in the territory. The UN General Assembly then terminated the mandate in a resolution of October 27, 1966, declaring that South Africa had failed to fulfill its obligations. A further resolution on May 19, 1967, established an 11-member UN Council for South West Africa, assisted by a UN commissioner, to administer the territory until independence (originally set for June 1968) and to prepare for the drafting of a constitution, the holding of an election, and the establishment of responsible government. The council was, however, refused entry by the South African government, which contended that termination of the mandate was invalid. South Africa subsequently disregarded a number of Security Council resolutions to relinquish the territory, including a unanimous resolution of December 1974 that gave it five months to initiate withdrawal from Namibia (the official name adopted on December 16, 1968, by the General Assembly).

Beginning in the mid-1960s, South Africa attempted to group the black population into a number of self-administering tribal homelands ("Bantustans"), in accordance with the so-called Odendaal Report of 1964. Ovamboland, the first functioning Bantustan, was established in October 1968, but its legitimacy was rejected by the UN Security Council. Fully implemented, the partition plan would have left approximately 88,000 whites as the largest ethnic group in two-thirds of the territory, with some 675,000 black inhabitants confined to the remaining third.

Both the Organization of African Unity (OAU, subsequently the African Union—AU) and the South West Africa People's Organization (SWAPO) consistently pressed for full and unconditional self-determination for Namibia. In May 1975, however, Prime Minister John Vorster of South Africa stated that while his government was prepared to "exchange ideas" with UN and OAU representatives, it was not willing to accede to the demand that it "acknowledge SWAPO as the sole representative of the Namibian people and enter into independence negotiations with the organization."

On September 1, 1975, the South African government convened a constitutional conference in Turnhalle, Windhoek, on the future of the territory. SWAPO and other independence groups boycotted the conference and organized demonstrations against it. As a result, the Ovambos, with approximately half of the territory's population, were represented by only 15 of 135 delegates. At the second session of the conference, held in March 1976, Chief Clemens KAPUUO, then leader of the Herero-based National United Democratic Organization, presented a draft constitution that called for a bicameral legislature encompassing a northern chamber of representatives from Bantu areas and a southern chamber that would include representatives from the coloured and white groups. During the third session of the conference in August, a plan was advanced for the creation of a multiracial interim government to prepare Namibia for independence by December 31, 1978. Despite continued opposition from SWAPO, the conference's constitution committee unanimously approved a resolution on December 3 that called for establishment of an interim government.

A draft constitution calling for representation of the territory's 11 major racial and ethnic groups was approved by the Turnhalle delegates on March 9, 1977, and was subsequently endorsed by 95 percent of the white voters in a referendum on May 17. However, it continued to be opposed by SWAPO as well as by a group of diplomats representing the five Western members of the UN Security Council (Canada, France, the Federal Republic of Germany, the United Kingdom, and the United States). The Western delegation visited Windhoek on May 7–10 and subsequently engaged in talks with South African prime minister Vorster in Cape Town, in the course of which it indicated that the Turnhalle formula was unacceptable because it was "predominantly ethnic, lacked neutrality, and appeared to prejudice the outcome of free elections." The group added, however, that the appointment of an administrator general by the South African government would not be opposed insofar as it gave promise of contributing to "an internationally acceptable solution to the Namibia question." For his part, Vorster, prior to the appointment of Marthinus T. STEYN as administrator general on July 6, agreed to abandon the Turnhalle proposal for an interim government, accept the appointment of a UN representative to ensure the impartiality of the constituent election in 1978, and initiate a withdrawal of South African troops to be completed by the time of independence. He insisted, however, that the South African government had no intention of abandoning its jurisdiction over Walvis Bay and certain islands off the South West African coast. (Governed as part of South Africa until 1922, when it was assigned to South West Africa for administrative purposes, Walvis Bay was reincorporated into South Africa's Cape Province in August 1977.)

During November and December 1977 representatives of the diplomatic group engaged in inconclusive discussions with leaders of SWAPO and of the black African "Front-Line States" (Angola, Botswana, Mozambique, Tanzania, and Zambia). The main problem concerned South African security forces within Namibia, SWAPO asserting that their continued presence would influence the outcome of the projected election despite a UN presence. Nonetheless, Administrator General Steyn moved energetically to dismantle the territory's apartheid system, including abolition of the pass laws and the Mixed Marriages Act, in preparation for the 1978 balloting.

On March 27, 1978, Chief Kapuuo, who had assumed the presidency of the Democratic Turnhalle Alliance (DTA, see Political Parties and Groups, below), was shot and killed by unknown assailants on the outskirts of Windhoek. The assassination removed from the scene the best-known tribal figure apart from SWAPO leader Sam NUJOMA, who denied that his group had been involved. Three days later the Western nations presented Prime Minister Vorster with revised proposals calling for a cease-fire between SWAPO guerrillas and the 18,000 South African troops in the territory. The latter force would be expected to gradually decrease to 1,500, with UN troops being positioned to maintain order in preparation for Constituent Assembly balloting. South Africa accepted the plan on April 25 after receiving assurances that the status of Walvis Bay would not be addressed until after the election, that the reduction of its military presence would be linked to "a complete cessation of hostilities," and that some of its troops might be permitted to remain after the election if the assembly so requested. On July 12 SWAPO agreed to the Western plan, which had also been endorsed by the Front-Line States. The UN Security Council approved the plan on July 27, but Pretoria reacted bitterly to an accompanying resolution calling for the early "reintegration" of Walvis Bay into South West Africa and subsequently announced that its own final approval would be deferred. In early September South African foreign minister P. W. Botha denounced the size of the proposed UN military force for the territory, and two weeks later he indicated that his government had reversed itself and would proceed with an election of its own before the end of the year. Undaunted, the Security Council on September 29 approved Resolution 435, which called for the formation of a 7,500-member UN Transitional Assistance Group (UNTAG) to oversee free and fair elections, while declaring "null and void" any unilateral action by "the illegal administration in Namibia in relation to the electoral process." Administrator General Steyn nonetheless proceeded to schedule balloting for a Constituent

Assembly, which on December 4–8, without SWAPO participation, gave the DTA 41 of 50 seats.

In May 1979 the South African government agreed to the Constituent Assembly's request that the body be reconstituted as a National Assembly, although without authority to alter the status of the territory. Collaterally, conflict between SWAPO guerrilla forces and South African troops intensified, the latter carrying out a number of preemptive raids on SWAPO bases in Angola and Zambia. By midyear negotiations between UN and South African representatives had not resumed. In an effort to break the deadlock, Angolan President António Agostinho Neto, a few weeks before his death in September, proposed the creation of a 60-mile-wide demilitarized zone along the Angolan–Namibian border to prevent incursions from either side. He also pledged that Angola would welcome a UN civilian presence to ensure that any guerrillas not wishing to return to Namibia to participate in an all-party election would be confined to their bases.

Although Pretoria agreed to "the concept" of a demilitarized zone, discussions during 1980 failed to yield agreement, and on November 24 UN secretary general Kurt Waldheim called for a meeting in Geneva in January 1981 to discuss all "practical proposals" that might break the lengthy impasse. Earlier, DTA spokesperson had urged repeal of the General Assembly's 1973 recognition of SWAPO, arguing that the root of the problem lay in the fact that "the UN is required to play a neutral role in respect of implementation but at the same time is the most ardent protagonist of SWAPO."

During 1981–1982 units of both the South West Africa Territorial Force (SWATF) and the South African Defence Force (SADF) conducted numerous "search and destroy" raids into Angola, Pretoria insisting that the withdrawal of Cuban troops from the latter country was a necessary precondition of its own withdrawal from Namibia and the implementation of a UN-supervised election. Thus, Prime Minister Botha declared at a Transvaal National Party congress in September 1982 that his government would never accede to Namibian independence unless "unequivocal agreement [could] first be reached" on the linkage issue. Subsequently, an Angolan spokesperson indicated that a partial withdrawal of Cuban forces was possible if Pretoria would agree to reduce the size of its military presence to 1,500 troops and discontinue incursions into his country. The overture prompted a secret but inconclusive series of talks between Angolan and South African ministerial delegations on the island of Sal in Cape Verde in early December, the South African foreign minister subsequently asserting that responsibility for a Cuban withdrawal was "the task of the Americans."

In November 1983 a Multi-Party Conference (MPC) of seven internal groups, including the DTA, was launched in Windhoek in an effort to overcome the standoff. Although the "Windhoek Declaration of Basic Principles" that was issued on February 24, 1984, did little more than reaffirm the essentials of the earlier UN plan, South African prime minister Botha announced in March that his government would be willing to enter into negotiations with all relevant parties to the dispute, including the Angolan government and UNITA, the Angolan rebel movement that enjoyed de facto SADF support. However, the overture was rejected by SWAPO on the ground that only Namibian factions should be involved in independence discussions. Collaterally, Angola offered to participate as an observer at direct negotiations between SWAPO and Pretoria. Two months later Zambian president Kenneth Kaunda and South West African administrator general Willem VAN NIEKERK jointly chaired a meeting in Lusaka that was attended by representatives of South Africa, SWAPO, and the MPC, while a meeting between van Niekerk and SWAPO president Nujoma was held in Cape Verde on July 25. Although unprecedented, the bilateral discussions also proved abortive, as did subsequent talks involving Washington, Luanda, SWAPO and/or Pretoria.

After lengthy discussion with the MPC, on June 17, 1985, Pretoria installed a Transitional Government of National Unity (TGNU), with a cabinet, 62-member legislature, and Constitutional Council of representatives from the MPC parties. Having largely excluded Ovambos, the new administration was estimated to command the support of perhaps 16 percent of the population and was further limited by Pretoria's retention of veto power over its decisions; not surprisingly, international support for the action was virtually nonexistent. While the TGNU's "interim" nature was stressed by Pretoria, which mandated a formal constitution within 18 months, stalled negotiations with Angola and continued SWAPO activity provoked South African intimations that the arrangement could lead to a permanent "regional alternative to independence."

In early 1986 Pretoria proposed that independence commence August 1, again contingent upon withdrawal of the Cubans from Angola. The renewed linkage stipulation, termed by the United Nations as "extraneous," prompted both Angola and SWAPO to reject the plan as nothing more than a "public relations exercise." In September a UN General Assembly Special Session on Namibia strongly condemned South Africa for effectively blocking implementation of the UN plan for Namibian independence and called for the imposition of mandatory sanctions against Pretoria; however, U.S. and UK vetoes precluded the passage of such resolutions by the Security Council.

During 1987 South Africa continued to seek Western recognition of the TGNU as a means of resolving the Namibian question. However, even within the TGNU, differences emerged regarding a draft constitution and the related question of new elections to second-tier legislative bodies.

In 1988 the long drawn-out dispute moved toward resolution. A series of U.S.-mediated negotiations among Angolan, Cuban, and South African representatives that commenced in London in May and continued in Cairo, New York, Geneva, and Brazzaville (Republic of the Congo) concluded at UN headquarters on December 22 with the signing of an accord that linked South African acceptance of Resolution 435/78 to the phased withdrawal, over a 30-month period, of Cuban troops from Angola. The agreement provided that the resolution would go into effect on April 1, 1989, with deployment of UNTAG (approximately 7,100 individuals from 22 countries). As ratified by the Security Council on February 16, the timetable further provided that South African troop strength would be reduced to 1,500 by July 1, followed by the election of a constituent assembly on November 1 and formal independence for the territory by April 1990.

Ten groups were registered to contest the slightly deferred Constituent Assembly election of November 7–11, 1989, with SWAPO winning 41 of 72 seats and the DTA winning 21. On February 16, 1990, the assembly elected Nujoma to the presidency of the new republic. He was sworn in by UN secretary general Pérez de Cuéllar during independence ceremonies on March 21, with Hage GEINGOB installed as prime minister of a 20-member cabinet.

In July 1993 Namibia and South Africa agreed to joint administration of Rooikop Airport at Walvis Bay, and on August 18 South African president F. W. de Klerk announced that his government had agreed to relinquish its claim to the port. The actual withdrawal on March 1, 1994, was hailed as completing the process of Namibian independence.

On July 18, 1994, Windhoek's already battered economic record was dealt a further blow when the auditor general released a report criticizing the Nujoma government for widespread financial mismanagement and accusing three ministries of criminal fraud. However, on December 6, one day before Namibia's first presidential and legislative elections since independence, South African president Nelson Mandela announced his country's plans to forgive Namibia's $190 million debt. Thereafter, propelled by Mandela's timely largesse and SWAPO's enduring image as the party of independence, President Nujoma and SWAPO legislative candidates easily outpaced the opposition in balloting on December 7–8, capturing approximately 76 percent of the presidential vote and 53 assembly seats. Nujoma's sole competitor, Mishake MUYONGO of the renamed DTA of Namibia (who received 23 percent of the vote), cited SWAPO's dominance in the north and declared that the elections left Namibia divided along ethnic lines. Although SWAPO captured the two-thirds assembly majority necessary to amend the constitution, Nujoma had announced earlier that any proposed changes would be submitted to popular referendum. SWAPO gained control of 27 of 45 local councils in the February 1998 balloting, followed by the DTA of Namibia with 9.

On October 16, 1998, the SWAPO-dominated National Assembly approved a constitutional amendment that granted President Nujoma the opportunity to compete for a third presidential term and increased the powers of the office. On October 30 the assembly voted against a DTA of Namibia proposal to hold a popular referendum on the bill, despite its earlier pledges to the contrary, and on November 19 the National Council also passed the third-term amendment, leaving final approval to Nujoma, who signed the bill into law in 1999. Despite continued opposition objections to the constitutional revamping, Nujoma was easily reelected for a third term in balloting on November 30–December 1, 1999, securing 76.8 percent of the vote, while SWAPO maintained its assembly dominance in concurrent legislative balloting. In late March 1999 Nujoma slightly reshuffled his government, appointing several prolabor deputy ministers in what observers described as an apparent attempt to counter the formation of a new party, the Congress of Democrats (CoD), by Ben ULENGA, a former independence fighter and trade unionist who had recently left SWAPO as the result of his opposition to the third term for Nujoma. The CoD, which called for an anticorruption drive among public officials and for the withdrawal of Namibian troops from the Democratic Republic of the Congo (DRC), was expected by some observers to offer SWAPO its first genuine electoral challenge. However, SWAPO easily maintained more than enough seats to permit constitutional revision at will.

Although President Nujoma volunteered in April 2001 to seek a fourth term if he believed that popular will favored such a decision, late in the year he announced that he had ruled out another term. Meanwhile, tension was reported between Nujoma and Prime Minister Geingob, resulting in the appointment of Theo-Ben GURIRAB to the premiership in August 2002. (Geingob declined Nujoma's offer of another cabinet post.)

In May 2004 a SWAPO party convention nominated Hifikepunye POHAMBA (the minister of lands, resettlement, and rehabilitation) as the party's presidential candidate in the November elections. Pohamba was challenged by six other candidates, including Ben Ulenga of the CoD. Pohamba received 76.3 percent of the vote in the November 15–16, 2004, elections, with his closest rival being Ulenga with 7.34 percent. None of the other candidates received more than 5.2 percent. In the concurrent legislative elections, SWAPO maintained its dominance, winning 55 of the 72 seats. Following the elections, a new cabinet composed of SWAPO members was chosen, with Nahas ANGULA, the former minister of higher education, training, and employment creation, as prime minister. Although the elections were initially described as free and fair by foreign observers, opposition groups took the electoral commission of Namibia to court over alleged irregularities. The charges were prompted by the discovery of uncounted ballots that had been removed from polling places. A recount in March 2005 confirmed the SWAPO victory, although opposition parties gained a small number of additional votes. In October 2006 a new ministry for veterans' affairs was created. The cabinet was reshuffled on April 8, 2008, and was again dominated by SWAPO members.

President Pohamba defeated 11 challengers in balloting on November 27–28, 2010, securing 75.25 percent of the vote. SWAPO also won 54 of the 72 directly elected seats in concurrent legislative elections. The SWAPO breakaway Rally for Democracy and Progress (RDP) was a distant second in both polls, with party leader Hidipo HAMUTENYA garnering 10.9 percent of the presidential vote, and the RDP winning eight assembly seats. Nevertheless, the relatively young RDP gained representation in the assembly for the first time. Nine opposition parties immediately criticized the results, which were announced six days after the poll, alleging irregularities with voter rolls and electoral procedures. The parties mounted a court challenge, which the high court dismissed on March 5, 2010, saying the applications were improperly presented to the court. The RDP members of parliament subsequently refused to attend the swearing-in ceremony and assume their seats. Pohamba and his new all-SWAPO cabinet were sworn in on March 21, with Angula again designated as prime minister.

On December 4, 2012, former prime minister Geingob was again named to that post in a major cabinet reshuffle that included the transfer of incumbent prime minister Angula to the defense portfolio (see Current issues, below). Also, Minister of Trade Calle SCHLETTWEIN became the first white cabinet minister since independence.

The constitution was amended on October 13, 2014, to increase the size of the assembly and national council (see Legislature, below) and to create a vice president position.

Geingob won 86.7 percent of the presidential election vote on November 28, 2014, followed distantly by McHenry VENAANI (DTA) with 5 percent and Hidipo HAMUTENYA (RDP) with 3.4 percent.

In concurrent legislative elections, SWAPO's dominance continued with 80 percent of the vote and 77 of the 96 seats won. SWAPO was followed by DTA with 5 seats (4.8 percent of vote) and the RDP with 3 seats (3.5 percent of vote), along with smaller parties that won 1 or 2 seats each. The election saw a 72 percent voter turnout. Geingob appointed Saara KUUGONGELWA-AMADHILA (SWAPO) as prime minister of a reshuffled cabinet. She became the first woman prime minister of the country.

Nickey IYAMBO (SWAPO) was appointed as the nation's inaugural vice president on March 21, 2015.

Constitution and government. On February 9, 1990, the Constituent Assembly approved a liberal democratic constitution that became effective at independence on March 21. The document provides for a multiparty republic with an executive president, selected initially by majority vote of the legislature (but by direct election thereafter) for a maximum of two five-year terms. (An amendment was approved in 1998 to permit incumbent President Nujoma to serve a third term, although the two-term limit will still exist for future presidents.) The bicameral legislature encompasses a National Assembly elected by proportional representation for a five-year term and a largely advisory National Council consisting of three members from each geographic region who are elected by regional councils for six-year terms. A Council of Traditional Leaders advises the president on the utilization and control of communal land. Provision is made for an independent judiciary, empowered to enforce a comprehensive and unamendable bill of rights, considered to be the centerpiece of the document. Capital punishment and detention without trial are outlawed. The basic law also calls for a strong affirmative action program. Freedom of the press is guaranteed. Reporters Without Borders ranked Namibia 17th out of 180 countries in 2016 in press freedom, continuing a streak of several years as the highest rated African country.

Regional and local units of elective government, delineated on a purely geographical basis, are to function "without any reference to the race, colour, or ethnic origin" of their inhabitants. In 2013 the number of regions was increased from thirteen to fourteen.

Foreign relations. At independence Namibia became the 50th member of the Commonwealth and shortly thereafter the 160th member of the United Nations. For economic reasons, it was deemed necessary to continue trading with South Africa; at the same time it viewed continuance of Pretoria's apartheid policies as precluding the establishment of normal diplomatic relations. Thus South Africa was permitted to maintain a mission in Windhoek that did not have the status of a full-fledged embassy.

In September 1990 it was reported that discussions (South Africa rejected the term "negotiations") had begun on the future status of South African-controlled Walvis Bay, title to which was claimed in both countries' constitutions. The talks continued in March 1991 without yielding agreement, Pretoria indicating that the only concession it would consider would be some form of joint administration of the enclave, but in November the two governments agreed to establish an interim joint administration committee. On August 21, 1992, the Walvis Bay Joint Administrative Body was formally launched. Meanwhile, neither government retreated from its territorial claim, with South Africa insisting that it would withhold a final decision until after it had formed a post-apartheid government. However, on August 16, 1993, in a major decision of the multiparty forum convened to decide on the future of South Africa, the South African government delegation agreed under pressure from the African National Congress and other participants to transfer the Walvis Bay enclave to Namibia. South Africa, however, refused in November 2000 to continue negotiations with Namibia on the precise position of the Orange River border between the two countries. In 2006 the two countries agreed to a draft plan for the use of water from the river, though agreement on the exact boundary had not been reached as of mid-2012.

A seemingly less consequential dispute with a neighboring country has turned on the status of Sedudu, a small island in the middle of the Chobe River along the southern border of Namibia's Caprivi Strip. The island had been assumed to be part of Botswana until 1992, when Namibia advanced a claim that yielded a number of armed skirmishes in the area. Following an unsuccessful mediation attempt by President Robert Mugabe of Zimbabwe, the two nations agreed in early 1995 to forward the dispute to the ICJ. On December 15, 1999, the ICJ ruled in favor of Botswana regarding Sedudu, and Namibia announced that it would accept the decision.

In an effort to end illegal trading across its border with Angola (which had been closed since September 1994), Windhoek ordered troops to fire at vehicles attempting to cross the frontier in 1995. Encountering continued insecurity along the border, Namibian authorities decided in September to create a "control unit" in support of defense and police efforts to monitor contraband traffic. On the other hand, a meeting between Namibian and Angolan officials in March 1996 was described as "positive," and in April Namibia welcomed the arrival of UN troops in southeastern Angola, suggesting that when the peacekeepers had established themselves, the border might be reopened. (The border was reopened in 1999.) In July 1997 an international human rights group accused the Nujoma administration of being responsible for the disappearance of over 1,700 Angolans since the 1994 crackdown.

In August 1998 President Nujoma confirmed that Namibian forces had been sent to the Democratic Republic of the Congo at the request of the DRC's president, Laurent Kabila, to fight Rwandan-backed rebels. While effectively acknowledging domestic critics' assertions that his office had acted unilaterally, Nujoma attributed his decision to join Angola and Zimbabwe in aiding the DRC to the "spirit of Pan-Africanism, brotherhood and international solidarity." Thereafter, in late October the DRC rebellion topped the agenda of Nujoma's summit with South African president Mandela. The latter had been a critic of involving the forces of the members of the Southern African Development Community (SADC) in the violence. The country's involvement with the conflict in DRC was widely criticized by the Namibian opposition during 1999 and 2000. Following the assassination of Kabila in 2001, Namibian troops were withdrawn under the auspices of a UN agreement.

In February 2001 Namibia joined Angola and Zambia in the establishment of a tripartite mechanism aimed at improving security along their mutual borders, Windhoek having continued to provide the Angolan government with military support in the campaign against UNITA. After the cease-fire agreement between the Angolan government and UNITA (see entry on Angola), the Namibian government began repatriating Angolan refugees, with 20,000 returned by the end of 2003.

In 2001 descendants of Hereros killed by the Germans during their occupation of the country filed a suit in the United States against the German government, seeking $2 billion in reparations. Although the suit was dismissed in 2004, Germany formally apologized for the role played by its colonial officials in the 1904–1907 Herero uprising against German rule. Germany also remained a leading Namibian donor.

Relations between Namibia and Brazil increased significantly during Nujoma's tenure as president. Brazilian companies were contracted to explore the edges of Namibia's continental shelf in order to determine the country's formal oceanic boundaries. In addition, under the terms of the 2002 Naval Cooperation Agreement, Brazil provided assistance to construct a naval port at Walvis Bay and to train Namibian naval officers in return for the purchase of Brazilian-built vessels for the Namibian navy. Namibia has also developed closer military ties with Russia. A 2001 bilateral military accord called for Russian technical and military assistance and the eventual purchase of Russian-built MiG fighters.

In late 2005, following President Pohamba's visit to Beijing, relations with China were enhanced as the two countries signed extradition and trade agreements, and China pledged continued economic and social assistance to Namibia. In 2006 Namibia and Zimbabwe signed extradition treaties to assist each other in legal and criminal matters.

Russian officials visited Namibia in 2007, resulting in discussions on a joint venture to produce and sell uranium to meet future needs in the development of nuclear power plants. North Korea also engaged in closer relations with Namibia, owing in part to the latter's uranium stores. (Namibia was the fifth-largest producer in the world). In March 2008 Kim Yom Nam, North Korea's second-most senior leader, attended the inauguration in Windhoek of the new presidential residence, built by North Korea at a cost of $125 million.

Relations with Germany deteriorated in 2010 when Namibia accused two political foundations reportedly linked to Germany's ruling party of seeking "regime change" after they clandestinely monitored Namibia's November 2009 elections and subsequently made reports critical of the elections. Nevertheless, Germany committed $168 million in development aid for 2011 and 2012, with a further $9.5 million in 2013. Namibia declined to recognize Libya's National Transitional Council or renew diplomatic relations pending democratic elections in Libya. In December Namibia declined a request by the SADC to provide troops for a multilateral peacekeeping force created in response to renewed fighting in the DRC.

In March 2013 the EU informed Namibia that it needed to conclude negotiations on an Economic Partnership Agreement (EPA) within 18 months or lose duty-free incentives with the Union. Namibia had refused to sign a draft EPA, arguing that it was economically disadvantageous. In May the government rejected a request from the DRC to establish fishing quotas in order to protect domestic fisheries in that country.

As part of broader negotiations between India and the Southern African Customs Union (SACU), which included Botswana, Lesotho, Namibia, South Africa, and Swaziland, India and Namibia signed a preferential trade agreement in February 2014. India also agreed to provide Namibia with $100 million in infrastructure grants. In March Namibia and Nigeria finalized an agreement to construct a $7 billion, joint oil refinery in Namibia. During a state visit to Swaziland in May, Namibian prime minister Pohamba pledged to increase economic cooperation between the two countries. In addition, the two countries signed ten other agreements to promote economic cooperation and collaboration on criminal justice issues.

On November 23, 2015, Namibia threatened to withdraw from the International Criminal Court (ICC), asserting that the ICC was biased and prosecuted African leaders at a higher rate than leaders in other regions.

German chancellor Angela Merkel formally apologized for her nation's attempted genocide of the Herero people of Namibia from 1904 to 1907. During that period approximately 85 percent of the Herero population was killed or displaced.

Current issues. Accusations of fraud and illegal practices were frequently exchanged between members of SWAPO and dissidents who broke away from the governing party to form the Rally for Democracy and Progress (RDP) in 2008. The former senior SWAPO members were reviled by the party, which purged its central committee of anyone whose name appeared on a list linked to the RDP (see Political Parties and Groups, below). Collaterally, in a move described as ushering in a new era in SWAPO's history, longtime SWAPO leader Sam Nujoma handed over party leadership to President Pohamba and lined up the president's likely successor by bringing former prime minister Hage Geingob back into the leadership fold as vice president of the party. Subsequently, attention in 2008 turned to the presidential and assembly elections in 2009; SWAPO initiated its campaign in April, stating its intention to increase its parliamentary seats from 55 to 71. A month earlier the elections commissioner and three of his top officials were suspended, critics claiming that now that the director was an impartial administrator, SWAPO had him removed. The elections director subsequently was reported to have joined the RDP. The dismissals led to the postponement of a local by-election that was deemed to be of special importance to SWAPO in one of its first contests against members of the breakaway RDP; however, SWAPO members secured all but one of the seats in the thrice-postponed by-election.

In December 2008 President Pohamba approved a 24 percent salary increase for all political office-holders, and in early 2009 he granted pay increases for civil servants, a move that was seen by some analysts as a "stimulus" to the economy during the global financial downturn. In March President Pohamba received SWAPO's bid to stand for reelection as president of the republic.

Meanwhile, widespread flooding over four months in early 2009 affected more than 200,000 people, with 102 reported dead and 82,000 in need of food aid due to the huge loss of crop land and livestock, particularly in the north. The government estimated it would need $240 million to clean up after the disaster, and the UN sought urgent funds to help flood victims.

As the 2009 elections drew near, more than a dozen parties signed up to contest the assembly poll, and 12 candidates were on the slate for the presidency. Only three opposition parties campaigned nationally—the RDP, DTA, and Congress of Democrats (CoD). Domestic attention was focused on the downturn in the economy, due in large part to a decline in diamond sales; in the political arena the RDP claimed that some 300 SWAPO members had threatened violence to keep the party from campaigning in one constituency. SWAPO, for its part, claimed harassment of its supporters by the RDP. Meanwhile, the CoD was reportedly riven by infighting, its leader having left to start the All People's Party (APP) a year earlier. About a month before the elections, the RDP and the CoD asked the state-owned broadcasting company to provide equal air time to all parties, a request that was met with the broadcaster's immediate cancellation of all free campaign air time. Subsequently, it was reported that SWAPO had garnered 82 percent of broadcast coverage, while the opposition's coverage was 4 percent. Following Pohamba and SWAPO's landslide victory on November 27–28, nine opposition parties challenged the results in court, primarily citing irregularities with the electoral register, though observers generally considered the polling to be free and fair.

As soon as Pohamba and his new government were sworn in on March 21, 2010, jockeying began among potential candidates for the 2014 elections, prompted by the president's appointment of Utoni NUJOMA, son of the country's first president Sam Nujoma, as minister for foreign affairs, reportedly in response to pressure from the elder Nujoma and his SWAPO allies. Already, pundits were pointing to former prime minister and SWAPO vice president Geingob and Deputy Prime Minister Hausiku as his likely rivals.

After the court's rejection of the opposition's legal challenge in March 2010, the RDP members of parliament began a boycott that lasted until October 2010, when the Supreme Court overturned its earlier ruling and agreed to hear the case. In the wake of the ruling,

SWAPO and the electoral commission were ordered to pay $146,000 in appeal costs, in addition to the opposition's legal costs. The same two judges who had originally dismissed the appeal on technical grounds were to decide the case; the RDP raised no objection. The ruling party was overwhelmingly successful in local and regional elections on November 26 and 27, winning 92 percent of the constituencies. The RDP was a distant second.

The legal challenges to the 2009 presidential elections were dismissed by the high court in February 2011 in a ruling that found "insufficient evidence to prove irregularities." In March the president declared a state of emergency in the wake of what he described as the worst flooding in the country's history. Aid organizations estimated that nearly 38,000 people were displaced.

The demise of Libya's Muammar al-Qadhafi alarmed Namibian leaders, and Defense Minister Charles NAMOLOH justified an increase in military expenditure in April 2011 by pointing out that Namibia, with its high inequality, could also be roiled by unrest.

Corruption continues to be a major issue. A long awaited trial for fraud against seven defendants with ties to senior members of SWAPO was delayed in June 2011, pending a ruling from the Supreme Court on a related constitutional challenge.

On March 28, 2012, Frans GOAGOSEB announced the dissolution of the Namibia Democratic Movement for Change (NDMC) party, which he founded in 2002 (the party received 0.5 percent of the vote in the 2004 legislative poll and 0.2 percent in the 2009 presidential election). In November, in order to overcome a budget deficit estimated to be $558.1 million, or 4.4 percent of GDP, the government for the first time offered bonds on the Johannesburg Stock Exchange. On December 4 Geingob was again appointed prime minister in a move that signaled he would be SWAPO's presidential candidate in 2014.

In May 2013 Pohamba recalled the nation's ambassadors and high commissioners and conducted a broad reshuffle of the nation's foreign service, including the appointment of a number of new diplomats. Also in May, Pohamba declared a nationwide emergency in response to a widespread drought.

In January 2014 conservationists strongly condemned the auction of a permit to hunt and kill an endangered black rhinoceros in Namibia. The permit sold for $350,000 and was conducted by the U.S.-based Dallas Safari Club, which pledged that the funding would go to support conservation efforts by the Namibian government. The episode was the first time a permit was issued outside of Namibia.

In April 2014 UNICEF published a report praising Namibia's efforts to reduce HIV/AIDS. The report noted that new HIV infections in Namibia fell from approximately 23,000 annually in 2001 to fewer than 10,000 per year by 2012. Nonetheless, Namibia continued to have one of the highest HIV infection rates in the world with 13.4 percent of the population HIV-positive. Namibia also dramatically reduced malaria deaths from 1,700 in 2001 to 36 in 2012. To support efforts to suppress HIV/AIDS, malaria, and tuberculosis, the Global Fund agreed to provide Namibia $111.3 million in 2014.

A major drought in 2015–2016 affected more than 600,000 Namibians and cost the government $66.4 million in emergency assistance. In regional and local balloting on November 27, 2015, SWAPO won 112 of 121 regional council seats and 277 of 378 local seats.

Namibia and the De Beers company signed a ten-year $4.9 billion agreement in May 2016 to facilitate the export of diamonds and other precious minerals. On July 15 Namibia became the first African country to be allowed to export beef to the United States and China. Exports were expected to rise to 5.7 million kg (12.6 million lbs.) per year.

POLITICAL PARTIES AND GROUPS

Government Party:

South West Africa People's Organization of Namibia (SWAPO). Consisting mainly of Ovambos and formerly known as the Ovambo People's Organization, SWAPO was the largest and most active South West African nationalist group and was recognized prior to independence by the United Nations as the "authentic representative of the Namibian people." Founded in 1958, it issued a call for independence in 1966 and subsequently initiated guerrilla activity in the north with the support of the OAU Liberation Committee. Further operations were conducted by the party's military wing, the People's Liberation Army of Namibia (PLAN), from bases in southern Angola. A legal "internal wing" engaged in political activity within Namibia, although it was the target of arrests and other forms of intimidation by police and South African military forces. SWAPO's co-founder, Andimba TOIVO JA TOIVO, was released from 16 years' imprisonment on March 1, 1984, and was immediately elected to the organization's newly created post of secretary general. In February 1988, at what was described as the largest such meeting in the movement's history, 130 delegates representing about 30 branches of SWAPO's internal wing reaffirmed their "unwavering confidence" in the exiled leadership of Sam Nujoma and their willingness to conclude a cease-fire in accordance with implementation of the UN independence plan. Nujoma returned to Namibia for the first time since 1960 on September 14, 1989, and was elected president of the new republic by the Constituent Assembly on February 16, 1990.

At a party congress in December 1991, the first since the group's inception, delegates reelected Nujoma and Rev. Hendrik Witbooi party president and vice president, respectively, while Moses GAROËB captured the secretary generalship from Toivo ja Toivo. The congress also elected a new Central Committee (enlarged from 38 to 67 members) and adopted a revised constitution, expunging references to the PLAN and changing descriptions of the group from a "liberation movement" to a "mass political party."

In presidential and legislative balloting in December 1994 President Nujoma and SWAPO legislative candidates captured approximately 70 percent of the vote. However, some internal friction was subsequently reported between Nujoma loyalists and the party's "pragmatists" over Nujoma's allegedly heavy-handed direction of party affairs. Thereafter, in what observers described as a possible shift of power to the group's younger leaders, in April 1996 Deputy Minister of Foreign Affairs Netumbo NANDI-NDAITWAH was named party secretary general. She replaced Garoëb, who had resigned days earlier.

In May 1997, at SWAPO's second congress since independence, party delegates adopted a resolution supporting amendment of the constitution to allow Nujoma a third presidential term. In addition, SWAPO vice president Witbooi retained his post, staving off a challenge by Prime Minister Hage Gottfried Geingob, while cabinet member and Nujoma confidante Hifikepunye Pohamba was elected secretary general.

On the eve of the extraordinary party congress of August 29–30, 1998, Ben Ulenga, Namibia's high commissioner to Britain and a SWAPO central committeeman, resigned from his overseas post to protest the plans to allow Nujoma a third term as well as the deployment of Namibian troops in the DRC. Ulenga's public denouncement of the Nujoma amendment, the first by a ranking SWAPO member, colored the late August proceedings, at which the congress rebuffed calls from party dissidents for a debate on the issue and formally approved the proposed bill. In November the party voted to suspend Ulenga, who had recently led "like-minded" colleagues in the formation of a self-described bipartisan grouping. (In early 1999 Ulenga launched the Congress of Democrats, below.)

Meanwhile, in regional council balloting in December 1998 SWAPO easily won the majority of the posts in polling marked by low voter turnout. In the legislative election in November–December 1999 the party got 76.1 percent of the vote and won 55 seats in the National Assembly, and Nujoma was reelected president with 76.8 percent of the vote.

At the August 2002 congress, the party's politburo underwent a significant change. Some analysts noted that new prime minister Theo-Ben Gurirab, new SWAPO vice president Hifikepunye Pohamba, and new secretary general Ngarikutuke TJIRIANGE were among the possible successors to Nujoma, who had announced in late 2001 that he would not seek a fourth presidential term.

In May 2004 Pohamba was chosen as Nujoma's successor at a party conference. Nujoma was reelected as party president for a three-year term. SWAPO was successful in the November legislative elections; Gurirab subsequently was elected speaker of the assembly, and Nahas Angula was appointed prime minister.

Party infighting erupted in 2005 after SWAPO secretary and deputy works minister Paulas KAPIA was accused in a scandal involving state funds (the opposition claimed Nujoma was involved as well; he denied the allegations). Kapia resigned his government post and his assembly seat, and was suspended from the party. Some observers suggested that it was President Pohamba who had forced the resignation of Kapia, a Nujoma protégé; subsequently, Nujoma returned Kapia to the party payroll. The rift between "Nujomaists" and backers of former foreign minister Hidipo Hamutenya, who took over Kapia's assembly seat, deepened after Jesaya NYAMU, a leading party member for some 40 years (and loyal to Hamutenya), was dismissed from the party in late

2005 for alleged "serious misconduct." The vote to oust him reportedly divided the party between backers of Nujoma and Hamutenya, with some observers speculating that Hamutenya might throw his support to Pohamba in an effort to remove Nujoma from the party presidency.

Nujoma retained party leadership in 2006, despite accusations by some party officials that the elections were fraudulent. Tensions increased in 2007, the rival factions now including those who backed Pohamba, in addition to supporters of Nujoma and Hamutenya. Because of the fractured party and lack of support from many cabinet ministers still loyal to Nujoma, observers said Pohamba was unable to lead the country effectively. Pohamba's uncertain status in the party contributed to the postponement of the next congress from midyear to November 2007. By the time the congress convened, however, Nujoma had decided to give up his party position after decades at the helm and to withdraw from active politics, thus handing off control to Pohamba (and to a slate of party officers tapped by Nujoma). The congress was also notable for the absence of party cofounder Toivo ja Toivo from the party's central committee, along with other high-ranking party members. (Though Toivo ja Toiva had been rumored at the time to have joined a new party started by Hamutenya and other dissidents—the Rally for Democracy and Progress—he denied it.) Reportedly, the list of breakaway RDP members had somehow been supplied to SWAPO, resulting in a great deal of acrimony toward the dissidents and the purge of the party's central committee in a scheme engineered by Nujoma to reward SWAPO loyalists. Collaterally, the startup of the RDP (see below) coincided with the election of the new SWAPO slate, including former prime minister Hage Geingob as the party's vice president. Pohamba was elected as party president, with Geingob, a political moderate, described as the likely successor to Pohamba as Namibia's president. (Geingob subsequently was given a ministerial post in 2008.) The party also elected its first female secretary general, justice minister Pendukeni IIVULA-ITHANA.

In the run-up to a by-election in the newly incorporated town of Omuthiya in early 2008, Pohamba called for a boycott of businesses owned by RDP members. SWAPO also postponed the by-election for several months, reportedly to fend off an initial electoral victory for the RDP, but also due to the dismissal of the elections commissioner over unspecified irregularities. SWAPO ultimately won the poll with a reported 90 percent of the vote.

In 2008 the elections director, Philemon KANIME, who had been a member of SWAPO for nearly 50 years, was suspended from his job (and subsequently not reappointed) after he had been accused of illegally registering the new RDP (below). Kanime then joined the RDP.

In 2009 SWAPO denied allegations of violence against the APP (below). In February the party suspended three members who were allegedly involved with the RDP. In March the party nominated President Pohamba as its standard-bearer in the November presidential elections, despite what were described as "behind the scenes" attempts to oust him. SWAPO won a landslide victory, claiming 75 percent of votes in both the legislative and presidential polls.

In March 2011 the central committee pledged that whoever was elected vice president at the party congress, regardless of tribe or gender, would become its flagbearer in the 2014 presidential election. Party officials said Pohamba would continue to head SWAPO. However, questions arose whether he would be able to complete his term after he suffered a mild stroke in July 2011. Changes to the party branch structure barred new branches from voting for delegates to the elective congress, which prompted nearly half of the 310 delegates at a November 2011 Women's Council conference in Caprivi to boycott the vote for a new regional executive. Jockeying and infighting increased through 2012, prompting Pohamba to appoint a commission to investigate the use of smear tactics. At a SWAPO congress in December, Pohamba was reelected party president. Geingob was again elected party vice president, and subsequently appointed prime minister, thereby confirming his place as Pohamba's successor.

In May 2013 in an apparent effort to bolster support for Geingob, 10 allies of the prime minister were elevated to SWAPO's party secretariat to replace supporters of Geingob's main rivals, Pendukeni Iivula-Ithana and Jerry EKANDJO. In 2014 SWAPO approved an internal policy that 50 percent of its candidates for elected office had to be women. In the November 2014 elections, Geingob was elected president, while the party secured 77 seats. In March 2015 Peter KATJAVIVI was elected speaker of parliament.

Leaders: Hage GEINGOB (President of the Republic and Party President), Peter KATJAVIVI (Speaker of the National Assembly), Nangolo MBUMBA (Secretary General).

Opposition Parties:

DTA of Namibia. The grouping known as the Democratic Turnhalle Alliance (DTA) until adoption of the abbreviated form in November 1991 was launched in the wake of the Turnhalle Conference as a multiracial coalition of European, coloured, and African groups. Advocating a constitutional arrangement that would provide for equal ethnic representation, the DTA obtained an overwhelming majority (41 of 50 seats) in the Constituent Assembly balloting of December 4–8, 1978, and was instrumental in organizing the Multi-Party Conference in 1983. Its core formations were the white-based Republican Party (RP), organized in October 1977 by dissident members of the then-dominant **South West Africa National Party** (SWANP), and the Herero-based National United Democratic Organization (NUDO), which had long advocated a federal solution as a means of opposing SWAPO domination. (For a list of other groups participating in the formation of the DTA, see the 1999 *Handbook.*)

At a Central Committee meeting on November 30, 1991, DTA officials announced the transformation of the coalition into an integrated political party. The committee also reelected the party leaders to permanent positions, adopted a new constitution, and announced that the group would thenceforth be known as the DTA of Namibia.

An intraparty chasm between former RP leader Dirk MUDGE and a faction led by party president Mishake MUYONGO and information secretary Andrew MATJILA widened in the wake of the DTA of Namibia's poor showing in regional and local council elections in November–December 1992. At a central committee meeting in February 1993, the Muyongo faction pressed Mudge to resign, arguing that his former ties to South Africa had contributed to the party's loss of electoral support from all but small-town whites and the Herero and Caprivi communities. In April Mudge announced that he would be vacating his parliamentary seat, insisting that he had made the decision for purely personal reasons and would retain the DTA of Namibia chair. In mid-1994 Matjila broke with the party, and less than a year later Mudge resigned his party post and bowed out of politics. Thereafter, in balloting in December, Muyongo secured only 23 percent of the presidential vote, while the party's parliamentary representation fell to 15 seats, the DTA of Namibia claiming that there had been widespread voting irregularities.

On August 25, 1998, the DTA of Namibia's Executive Committee suspended Muyongo from the party presidency and named Vice President Katuutire KAURA interim party leader after Muyongo called for the secession of the Caprivi Strip region from Namibia. Muyongo subsequently assumed control of the militant Caprivi Liberation Movement (see CLF, under Illegal Groups, below).

The legislative elections on November 30–December 1, 1999, proved nearly disastrous for the DTA of Namibia as the party secured less than half the seats it had won in 1994, winning only 9.5 percent of the vote and seven seats in the National Assembly. In the presidential election, Kaura received 9.6 percent of the vote. In early April 2000 the DTA of Namibia and the UDF formed an opposition coalition when the negotiations with the CoD broke down.

The DTA of Namibia won four seats in the 2004 legislative elections while its presidential candidate, again Kaura, placed third with 5.2 percent of the vote. The defections of DTA of Namibia members to the RP and NUDO hurt the party most in the December Regional Council elections, where voters split among the three parties, giving SWAPO its greatest success ever in such balloting. The DTA of Namibia secured two seats in the 2004 legislative balloting.

In 2005 Kaura was elected party president, and Alois GENDE won the post of secretary general over McHenry Venaani, 27, who had also challenged Kaura for the party presidency. Early in 2007 the DTA proposed a "grand coalition" of opposition parties, a notion that did not interest the RP, CoD or NUDO.

Venaani, a member of parliament, announced in March 2008 that he would not contest any party office at the central committee meeting to be held later in the year, citing his desire to keep the party unified. Rifts had begun to develop after constituents in the Kavango region called for Kaura to step down and expressed their support for Venaani. Two months earlier, party stalwart Rudolf KAMBURONA resigned from the DTA after 32 years, saying he wanted to concentrate on farming, rejecting speculation that he was going to join the RDP (below). Meanwhile, observers noted growing dissatisfaction within the party with Kaura's leadership. Nevertheless, Kaura was reelected along with other party leaders at the DTA congress in November 2008, the only surprise being the election of Venaani as secretary general, according to observers.

In January 2009 some tribal members claimed that the government had refused drought aid to tribe members who belonged to parties other than SWAPO. The government denied the allegations. Venaani also demanded that the agencies that distributed the food stop claiming that the relief came directly from SWAPO. In the November elections the party won two assembly seats. Presidential candidate Kaura came in a distant third with 3 percent of the vote. In 2012 Kaura announced he would not seek reelection as party leader in 2013.

In June 2013 the DTA called for the creation of an opposition coalition ahead of the 2014 national elections. Venaani was elected party president in 2013. Kaura was subsequently expelled from the party in February 2014 for publicly criticizing his successor, but apologized and was reinstated.

Venaani was the party's presidential candidate in the November 2014 balloting, placing second with 5 percent of the vote. The DTA won five seats in the concurrent legislative balloting. In November 2015 the DTA won 2 seats on regional councils and 41 in local councils.

At a party congress on July 4, 2016, Venaani was reelected president and Manuel NGARINGOMBE won the post of secretary general. A new party constitution was subsequently approved, and the DTA announced plans to create an opposition coalition to include the UDF and NUDO.

Leaders: McHenry VENAANI (President), Katuutire KAURA (Former President and 2004 and 2009 presidential candidate), Kazeongere TJEUNDO (Vice President), Jennifer VAN DEN HEEVER (Chair), Manuel NGARINGOMBE (Secretary General).

United Democratic Front (UDF). The UDF was led by Justus Garoëb, longtime head of the **Damara Council,** which withdrew from the MPC in March 1984; chair of the group was Reggie DIERGAARDT, leader of the **Labour Party,** a largely colored group that was expelled from the DTA in 1982 but participated in the MPC subsequent to its November 1983 meeting. Two small leftist groups were also Front members: the **Communist Party of Namibia** (CPN) and the Trotskyist Workers' Revolutionary Party (WRP, see below). The UDF ran a distant third in the November 1989 election, winning four assembly seats. In balloting during November–December 1992 the party was unable to lessen the gap between itself and the two major parties, capturing only 1 of 13 regional council seats.

In a November 1993 action opposed by other clan chiefs, UDF president Garoëb was enthroned as the king of Damara. Thereafter, observers attributed Garoëb's failure to participate in the December 1994 presidential balloting, despite a pledge to the contrary, to the UDF's poor financial condition. Meanwhile, the party, securing only 2 percent of the vote, lost two of its 4 assembly seats.

In late 1998 a UDF spokesperson denounced SWAPO's legislative efforts to grant Nujoma a third term. The UDF won two seats in the 1999 National Assembly election, while Garoëb secured 3 percent of the vote in the presidential poll.

In the 2004 presidential balloting Garoëb gained 3.8 percent of the vote, and the UDF won three seats in the assembly.

The UDF, along with several other opposition parties, was unsuccessful in calling for postponement of by-elections in one constituency in 2008 because of alleged irregularities.

In 2009 the party won two assembly seats; Garoëb placed fifth in presidential balloting with 2.4 percent of the vote. In February 2013 Garoëb announced he would not seek reelection as UDF leader at the party's November congress. He was replaced by Apius AUCHAB who received 214 votes, to 97 for Samson TJONGARERO.

The UDF won two seats in national elections in November 2014. In November 2015 it secured 4 seats on regional councils, and 21 on local bodies. In July 2016 the party agreed to join a DTA-led opposition alliance.

Leaders: Apius AUCHAB (President), Justus GAROËB (King of Damara, Former President of the Party, and 2004 and 2009 presidential candidate), Dudu MURORUA (Vice President), Elia GAWESEB (Secretary General).

National Unity Democratic Organization (NUDO). Led by the Herero High Chief, Kuaima RIRUAKO, former members of NUDO left the DTA of Namibia (and his seat in parliament) in 2003 to reestablish their Herero-based party. In the 2004 elections, NUDO secured 4.8 percent of the vote and three seats in the assembly. Riruako came in third with 5.2 percent of the vote in the presidential poll. Party leader Chief Kuaima Riruako resigned his National Assembly seat on February 1, 2008, saying he wanted to "focus his energies on other matters," including recruiting more supporters for NUDO across the country. He retained his post as party chair. In January 2009 a youth leader in the party called on the government to make an early announcement of the dates of the presidential and legislative elections, rather than waiting until the customary two months ahead of time, to give candidates and parties time to adequately prepare.

The 79-year-old Riruako died of natural causes on June 2, 2014, and was succeeded by Aser MBAI. The party won 2 assembly seats in the November 2014 elections. Mbai placed fourth in concurrent presidential balloting with 2.9 percent of the vote. NUDO won only 4 seats on regional councils and 11 seats in seven local authorities in the November 2015 elections. NUDO agreed to a united opposition coalition with the DTA and UDF on July 4, 2016.

Leaders: Aser MBAI (President), Meundju JAHANIKA (Secretary General).

Other Legislative Parties:

Rally for Democracy and Progress (RDP). One of three parties formed within months of each other in the run-up to the 2009 elections, the RDP was established on November 17, 2007, as a result of rifts within SWAPO. Former senior SWAPO members, including Hidipo Hamutenya and Jesaya Nyamu, both former ministers, and Kandi Hehova, a former chair of SWAPO's National Council, launched the party with pledges to eradicate poverty and unemployment and improve health and education services, areas in which they believed SWAPO had failed to make significant progress. They denied some analysts' description of RDP as a tribal party.

Another factor that observers said led to the formation of the new party was Hamutenya's dismissal from his ministerial post following his having contested the SWAPO presidency in 2004 against Pohamba. Hamutenya had been a SWAPO loyalist for 46 years, having served on SWAPO's central committee for 30 years.

In its first electoral test in a local by-election in April 2008, the party fared poorly; SWAPO won overwhelmingly. Another by-election in the new town of Omuthiya, which had been scheduled for February 2008, was postponed until late April, observers saying that SWAPO was trying to postpone a likely RDP victory. SWAPO did not want the RDP to win in its first contest (see SWAPO, above). Following a large RDP rally in July, the by-election was postponed again until September, the RDP winning only one seat while SWAPO won the remaining six. Observers described the defeat as a serious blow to the RDP, since most of its leaders are from Omuthiya and its surrounding regions. Subsequently, the RDP, alleging "political anarchy," called on the government to resign and hold early elections. Violence broke out in another constituency in November, when hundreds of SWAPO supporters allegedly prevented the RDP from holding a rally and several reportedly were beaten.

At the party's congress in December 2008, former foreign minister Hidipo Hamutenya, who had been dismissed by President Nujoma in 2004, was elected party president. As flagbearer in the 2009 presidential election, he placed a distant second with 10.9 percent of the vote. Though the party was widely regarded as SWAPO's biggest challenger and won the second-highest number of assembly seats (eight) to become the official opposition, it significantly trailed SWAPO's representation.

In April 2010 the party joined the general public outcry against a proposed 35 percent increase in electricity rates. In late 2010 the Republican Party (RP, below), led by member of parliament and 2004 and 2009 presidential candidate Henk MUDGE, announced it would merge with the RDP. Mudge gave up his assembly seat and his party fully in 2011 to complete the merger.

In 2014 Hamutenya was reelected as head of the party's national executive committee. He was the party's candidate in the November 2014 presidential balloting, placing third with 3.4 percent of the vote. The RDP also won three seats in the national assembly. On February 28, 2015, Hamutenya was forced to resign as RDP president. He subsequently rejoined SWAPO. The party secured 16 seats in local councils in polling in November.

Leaders: Steve NUJOMA (President), Steve BEZULDENHOUT (Vice Chair), Kandi HEHOVA, Jeremiah NAMBINGA (Information Secretary), Mike KAVETORA (Secretary General), Robert MATONGELA (council).

Republican Party (RP). Originally part of the DTA (above), the RP was reestablished as an independent party in 2003 under the leadership of Henk Mudge, the son of Dirk MUDGE, the leader of the former Republican Party within the DTA. The conservative RP won 1.9 percent of the vote in the 2004 elections and gained a seat in the assembly for the first time. In addition, the younger Mudge ran as a presidential candidate; he came in fifth with 2 percent of the vote. (For more on the history of the party, see the 2015 *Handbook.*)

In October 2008 the party claimed that four of its members, including Vice Chair Clara Gowases, were illegally arrested for distributing flyers urging voters to boycott an upcoming regional by-election. The party members were released after a few hours. The party subsequently boycotted the by-election.

In the 2009 assembly election the party won one seat; Henk Mudge received 1.2 percent of the vote in concurrent presidential balloting. He resigned his assembly seat and gave up the party presidency officially in 2011 to join the RDP. Though the parties were said to have merged, Clara Gowases replaced Mudge in the assembly and ascended to chair of the party.

Mudge was the party's candidate in the November 2014 presidential balloting. He won 1 percent of the vote, while the party won one seat in the assembly. The RP won no seats in the 2015 local elections.

Leaders: Clara GOWASES (Chair), Henk MUDGE (2015 and 2009 presidential candidate).

All People's Party (APP). Licensed on January 22, 2008, the APP was established ahead of the 2009 elections by former minister and former CoD secretary general Ignatius Shixwameni and his brother, Herbert Shixwameni, following the former's leadership dispute with CoD president Ben Ulenga. Other members were said to be defectors from SWAPO, DTA, and NUDO, with the party's stronghold in the northern Kavango region. The stated goals were to unite a broad, national base in a "truly democratic party" and to fight to wipe out poverty, unemployment, and inequality. If successful in presidential elections, the leaders pledged to set up a welfare state, providing free education and access to decent housing.

The party's first rally, held in March 2008, was reported to be a "huge success," with thousands attending in the Kavango region.

In the 2009 elections the party secured one assembly seat; Shixwameni won 1.2 percent in the presidential poll. Shixwameni was reelected party president at an APP congress in May 2013. Fifteen of the 31 members elected to the party's central committee were women. Shixwameni won 0.8 percent of the vote in the 2014 presidential election, while the party secured two assembly seats. The party also won four seats on local councils in 2015.

Leaders: Ignatius SHIXWAMENI (Party President and 2009 and 2014 presidential candidate), Madala NAUYOMA (Vice President), Mariska BRENDEL (Secretary General).

South West Africa National Union (SWANU). Formerly coordinating many of its activities with SWAPO's internal wing, the Herero-supported SWANU joined with the Damara Council and a number of smaller groups to form a multiracial coalition in support of the Western "contact group" solution to the Namibian problem. SWANU's president, Moses KATJIOUNGUA, participated in the 1983 MPC meeting and in September 1984 was reported to have been replaced as party leader by Kuzeeko Kangueehi, who indicated that the group would leave the MPC, with a view to possibly merge with SWAPO. In October, on the other hand, Katjioungua was again identified as holding the presidency, with Kangueehi described as the leader of a dissident faction (subsequently styled SWANU-Left). The incumbent's anti-SWAPO orientation was reflected by his inclusion in the "national unity" cabinet of 1985. A founding member of the Democratic Coalition of Namibia (DCN), SWANU abruptly dropped out of the grouping in November 1994 while Katjioungua stayed within the DCN. SWANU formed an electoral alliance with the Workers' Revolutionary Party (WRP, below), which received less than 0.5 percent of the vote in the legislative election on November 30–December 1, 1999.

SWANU secured less than 1 percent of the vote in the 2004 legislative elections.

At the party's congress in November 2007, Usutuaije Maamberua, a former finance secretary, was elected party president. In recent years the party has been campaigning for reparations from Germany for alleged atrocities committed under German rule more than 100 years ago, similar to reparations paid to Jewish people who suffered at the hands of the Nazis.

In advance of the 2009 parliamentary elections, SWANU presented its ten-point platform in February, calling for a "socialist, transformationist, revolutionary approach" to government. The party won one seat; in the concurrent presidential election, flagbearer Maamberua won 0.37 percent of the vote.

In 2013 Maamberua rejected calls from within the party for a new SWANU congress (the last all-party meeting was scheduled for 2009, but was also cancelled). Maamberua was named as the party's 2014 presidential candidate. He received 0.6 percent of the vote, and the party won one seat in the balloting.

Leaders: Usutuaije MAAMBERUA (President and 2009 and 2014 presidential candidate), Dr. Rihupisa KANDANDO (National Chair), Kuzeeko KANGUEEHI, Hitjevi Gerson VEII, Tangeni IYAMBO (Secretary General).

The **Workers' Revolutionary Party** (WRP), led by Attie BEUKES and Harry BOESAK, won two seats in the 2014 assembly balloting. (For more information on the original WRP, see the 2013 *Handbook.*)

The **United People's Movement** (UPM), formed in 2010 and led by Jan Johannes VAN WYK, won one assembly seat.

Other Parties That Contested the 2009 or 2014 Elections:

Congress of Democrats (CoD). The CoD was launched in March 1999 by former SWAPO stalwart Ben Ulenga, who had been suspended by SWAPO in 1998 after he criticized efforts to permit President Nujoma to run for a third term and had formed a grouping styled Forum for the Future. Included in the CoD's platform were calls for a smaller cabinet and the withdrawal of Namibian troops from the DRC. (For more on the history of the party, see the 2015 *Handbook.*) Factionalism within the party was reported in 2007, with some members continuing to call for new leadership following failed party elections in May. The election was declared void due to fraud and other irregularities (Ulenga defeated his challenger by 14 votes). Though Ulenga said he would step down based on what had happened during the party election, he apparently retained the leadership post amid the discord. Ignatius Shixwameni, leader of the main faction within the CoD and the party's secretary general, formed a splinter group that broke away in late 2007 and became the basis for the new All People's Party.

Kala GERTZE, one of the CoD's founding members and its secretary general from 2004–2007, died from asthma in March 2008. Infighting continued through July 2008, despite a High Court ruling that the party hold a congress in five months. The court subsequently ruled that if the two factions could not agree on a chairperson to oversee the party's elections, the Law Society of Namibia would appoint a candidate. Ultimately, Ulenga retained his post as party president, defeating Nora SCHIMMING-CHASE, a faction leader and the party's former vice president, in balloting at a party congress in November. Elma DIENDA, an assembly member who reportedly was a Schimming-Chase supporter, was elected party treasurer.

In 2009 the party secured one assembly seat; presidential candidate Ulenga received 0.7 percent of the vote. In December 2012 the CoD announced that it would delay a party congress scheduled for November 2013 to early 2014. In February 2014 Dienda left the CoD to join the DTA. Ulenga secured just 0.4 percent of the vote in the 2014 presidential balloting, while the party failed to secure any seats in the assembly. The COD only secured one seat, representing Gochas, in the November 2015 local elections.

Leaders: Ben ULENGA (President and 2004, 2009, and 2014 presidential candidate), Elma DIENDA (Treasurer), Gretchen BOOIS (Deputy Secretary General), Tsudao GURIRAB (Secretary General).

Monitor Action Group (MAG). A conservative, predominantly white grouping, the MAG won one assembly seat in December 1994. The MAG received 0.7 percent of the vote in the legislative election on November 30–December 1, 1999, and won one seat in the National Assembly.

In the 2004 polls Jacobus Pretorius received 1.2 percent of the presidential vote, while the party retained its single seat in the assembly.

The MAG did not field a presidential candidate in 2009 or 2014, nor did it receive enough votes to gain a seat in the assembly. In June MAG chair and former presidential candidate Pretorius announced his retirement from politics.

Leaders: Gernot SCHAAF (Acting Chair), Jurgie VILJOEN.

Democratic Party of Namibia (DPN). Formed in July 2008 by Solomon Dawid Isaacs, a former SWAMU member who lived in exile from the 1960s to 1978, the party's stated mission is to address the marginalization of minority groups, particularly in the south. Isaacs said the DPN supports equal distribution of wealth and redistribution of land or "regaining" ancestral lands.

Presidential candidate Isaacs won 0.2 percent of the vote in the 2009 election. The party did not field candidates in the assembly election, but continued to contest local balloting. The party received 0.1 percent of the vote in the 2014 national elections.

Leader: Solomon Dawid ISAACS (Acting Chair and 2009 presidential candidate).

Other parties that contested the 2014 assembly balloting (none gained representation), including the **Namibian Economic Freedom Fighters**, formed in 2010 and led by Epafras MUKWIILONGO, and the **Christian Democratic Voice.**

Other Parties and Groups:

Federal Convention of Namibia (FCN). Strongly opposed to the UN independence plan, the FCN was organized by J. G. A. (Hans) DIERGAARDT, a former minister of local government and leader of the **Rehoboth Free Democratic Party** (*Rehoboth Bevryder Demokratiese Party*—RBDP). The RBDP was an outgrowth of the former Rehoboth Liberation Front (RLF), which endorsed the partition of Namibia along ethnic lines and obtained one assembly seat in 1978 as representative of part of the Baster community, composed of Afrikaans-speaking people with European customs. (For more on the history of the party, see the 2015 *Handbook.*) The FCN won less than 0.5 percent of the vote in the 1999 legislative elections and won no seats. Diergaardt, party chair, died in 1998 at age 70.

Namibia Movement for Independent Candidates (NMIC). The NMIC was launched in July 1997 on a platform stressing the need to incorporate Namibian youths into the political process. In September 1998 NMIC became affiliated with the DTA of Namibia (above). Party leader Joseph Kauandenge subsequently had a leading role in several parties, most recently in the DMC and RP (above).

Illegal Groups:

Caprivi Liberation Front (CLF). Formed in 1994, the CLF has sought autonomy or independence for the Caprivi Strip, a narrow portion of northern Namibia that juts about 250 miles into central Africa, touching the borders of Angola, Botswana, Zambia, and Zimbabwe. The strip, theretofore part of the British protectorate of Bechuanaland (subsequently Botswana), was ceded to Germany, colonial ruler of South West Africa, in 1890 as part of a land swap that included Britain's assumption of control in Zanzibar. The region is part of the former ancestral kingdom of Barotseland, which also included portions of Zambia, Botswana, and Zimbabwe. In the 1970s and 1980s the strip was used by South African forces as a base for military activities against independence fighters in Namibia as well as against the Angolan government.

In 1998 the Namibian government reported that a security sweep had uncovered training bases in Caprivi for the CLF-affiliated Caprivi Liberation Army (CLA). Several thousand Caprivians subsequently fled to Botswana, including Mishake Muyongo, the CLF/CLA leader who been dismissed from both SWAPO and the DTA of Namibia for his secessionist sentiments. In early August 1999 a small group of alleged CLA members attacked security locations in the town of Katima Mulilo, the fighting leaving at least 16 dead. The insurgents were quickly routed, but the Namibian government declared a state of emergency in the region for three weeks and implemented what critics described as a heavy-handed crackdown that allegedly included the abuse of detainees. Among the factors reportedly fueling antigovernment sentiment among Caprivians (primarily from the Lozi ethnic group) is the political and economic dominance of Ovambos in Namibia.

In August 2007 ten men, all Namibian citizens, including CLF leader Mishake Muyongo, were found guilty of high treason in the 1999 attempt to overthrow the government in the Caprivi region and establish a separate state. The men were among alleged CLA members who crossed the border into Angola in 1998 to obtain arms, returning to CLA training camps in northern Namibia, according to the government. All of the men, claiming they were not Namibian, refused to recognize the court's authority. They were sentenced to prison terms ranging from 30 to 32 years, and all ten appealed their convictions. (Two other men accused in the same case were acquitted in June 2007.) In February 2009 police arrested Albius Moto LISELI, who they claimed was an associate of Muyongo and a participant in the insurgency. He was also charged with high treason. Another leader in the secessionist movement, John MABUKU, who had fled with Muyongo, died in exile in Botswana in 2008.

In June 2012 Prime Minister Angula offered to relaunch negotiations with Muyongo if the latter renounced his call for secession. However, the CLF leader rejected the overture and repeated his call for talks under the auspices of the UN. In June 2014 a retrial of the ten convicted of treason in 2007 began after they successfully appealed their convictions on the grounds that the judge in the trial should have recused himself.

On December 8, 2015, the trial for those arrested in 1999 CLA attack concluded. Initially there were 125 defendants: 30 were convicted, 32 were acquitted, 43 were released, and 20 died in custody.

Leader: Mishake MUYONGO (Leader in Exile in Denmark).

For more on the **United Democratic Party** (UDP), see the 2015 *Handbook*.

LEGISLATURE

The Namibian **Parliament** consists of an indirectly elected National Council and a National Assembly whose voting members are directly elected.

National Council. The largely advisory upper house is a 42-member body containing 3 members from each of 14 regional councils (including the governor or each region); the term of office is six years. The national body launched its first session on May 11, 1993, following regional and local elections on November 29–December 4, 1992. After SWAPO gained control of 12 of the 13 regional councils in balloting on November 27, 2015, the distribution of seats in the National Council was as follows: South West Africa People's Organization of Namibia, 40 seats; Democratic Turnhalle Alliance of Namibia, 1; and National Unity Democratic Organization, 1.

President: Margaret Natalie MENSAH-WILLIAMS.

National Assembly. The 72 members of the lower house were initially elected on November 7–11, 1989, to the Namibian Constituent Assembly, which at independence assumed the functions of an ordinary legislature with a five-year mandate. The size of chamber was expanded to 104 members, including 96 that are directly elected. Following the most recent balloting of November 28, 2014, the distribution of seats was as follows: the South West Africa People's Organization of Namibia, 77 seats; Democratic Turnhalle Alliance of Namibia, 5; Rally for Democracy and Progress, 3; All People's Party, 2; National Unity Democratic Organization, 2; United Democratic Front, 2; Worker's Revolutionary Party, 2; Republican Party, 1; United People's Movement, 1; and South West Africa National Union, 1. In addition to the elected members, up to 8 nonvoting members may be named by the president.

Speaker: Peter KATJAVIVI (SWAPO).

CABINET

[as of July 15, 2016]

Prime Minister	Saara Kuugongelwa-Amadhila [f]
Deputy Prime Minister	Netumbo Nandi-Ndaitwah [f]
Ministers	
Agriculture, Water, and Forestry	John Mutorwa
Attorney General	Albert Kawana
Defense	Penda Ya Ndokolo
Education	Katrina Hanse-Himarwa [f]
Environment and Tourism	Uahekua Herunga
Finance	Calle Schlettwein
Fisheries and Marine Resources	Bernard Esau
Gender Equality and Child Welfare	Doreen Sioka [f]
Health and Social Services	Bernard Haufiku
Higher Education, Training, and Innovation	Itah Kandji-Murangi
Home Affairs and Immigration	Pendukeni Iivula-Ithana [f]
Industrialization, Trade, and Small and Medium-sized Enterprise Development Communication Technology	Immanuel Ngatjizeko
Justice	Albert Kawana
Labor, Industrial Relations, and Employment Creation	Erkki Nghimtina

Land Reform	Utoni Nujoma
Mines and Energy	Obeth Kandjoze
National Planning Commission	Tom Alweendo
Poverty Eradication and Social Welfare	Zephania Kameeta
Presidential Affairs	Frans Kapofi
Public Enterprises	Leon Jooste
Safety and Security	Charles Namoloh
Urban and Rural Development	Sophia Shaningwa [f]
Works and Transport	Alpheus Naruseb
Youth, National Service, Sport, and Culture	Jerry Ekandjo

[f] = female

Note: All ministers are members of SWAPO.

INTERGOVERNMENTAL REPRESENTATION

Ambassador to the U.S.: Martin ANDJABA.

U.S. Ambassador to Namibia: Thomas F. DAUGHTON.

Permanent Representative to the UN: Neville Melvin GERTZE.

IGO Memberships (Non-UN): AfDB, AU, Comesa, CWTH, NAM, SADC, WTO.

For Further Reference:

Behr, Daniela, Roos Haer, and Daniela Kromrey. "What Is a Chief without Land? Impact of Land Reforms on Power Structures in Namibia." *Regional & Federal Studies* 25, no. 5 (2015): 455–472.

Cooper, Ian. "It's My Party: Opposition Politics, Party Motivation and Electoral Strategy in Namibia." *Journal of Southern African Studies* 40, no. 1 (2014): 111–127.

Melber, Henning. *Understanding Namibia: The Trials of Independence*. Oxford: Oxford University Press, 2015.

NAURU

Republic of Nauru
Naoero

Political Status: Independent republic since January 31, 1968; special membership in the Commonwealth changed to full membership on May 1, 1999.

Area: 8.2 sq. mi. (21.3 sq. km).

Population: 10,000 (2016E—UN); 9,591 (2016E—U.S. Census).

Major Urban Centers: None; the Domaneab ("meeting place of the people"), which is the site of the Nauru Local Government Council, is located in Uaboe District, while government offices are located in Yaren District.

Official Languages: Nauruan. English is widely spoken and is used for most governmental and commercial purposes.

Monetary Unit: Australian Dollar (market rate October 1, 2016: 1.30 Australian dollars = $1US).

President: Baron WAQA; elected by Parliament on June 11, 2013, following legislative elections on June 8, and inaugurated the same day to succeed Sprent DABWIDO; reelected on July 13, 2016.

THE COUNTRY

A very small and isolated coral island in the west-central Pacific, Nauru is located just south of the equator between the Marshall Islands and the Solomon Islands. The present population consists of approximately 60 percent indigenous Nauruans (a mixture of Micronesian, Melanesian, and Polynesian stocks), 25 percent other Pacific islanders, 8 percent Chinese, and 7 percent Caucasians (primarily from Australia). Habitation (served by a single main road) is mainly confined to a fertile strip of land along the coast ringing a central plateau composed of very high-grade phosphate deposits. For several decades this mineral wealth yielded one of the world's highest per capita incomes, which, however, declined from a peak of over $17,000 in 1975 to, by some estimates, less than $3,000 in 2007. In the midst of the decline, Nauru turned to offshore banking accounts, which, however, led to accusations by the Organization for Economic Cooperation and Development (OECD) and others that Nauru had become a center for tax evasion and money laundering.

Parliament passed an anti-money laundering bill in August 2001, but Nauru remained on the OECD's uncooperative list because of little concrete action against an estimated 400 shell banks. In March 2003 offshore banking was outlawed in Nauru, but the action failed to dispel recurrent charges of corruption that yielded an average of two executive turnovers a year in the period 1999–2004. It was not until May 2008 that the OECD indicated partial acceptance of the anticorruption effort by withdrawing two of its reporting and compliance conditions.

In mid-2012 the government announced that it believed that phosphate production ($59 million for the fiscal year ending in July 2012) could actually begin to expand again soon. Significant revenue was also anticipated from the controversial detention centers opened on Nauru by Australia to process asylum seekers (see Political background and Current issues, below) and a new regional fishing agreement. However, Nauru continued to struggle with a number of long-term issues, including high unemployment (as much as 40 percent according to some estimates), the threat of inundation from global warming, and a lack of arable land that has necessitated reliance on imports for 90 percent of the island's food. The government has recently introduced new income and business taxes in order to generate additional revenue, and in 2014 it was announced that Nauru had applied for membership in the International Monetary Fund and the World Bank. GDP grew by an average of 7.1 percent from 2009–2012, while inflation averaged 3.7 percent.

GOVERNMENT AND POLITICS

Political background. A former German colony, Nauru became a British League of Nations mandate in 1919, with Australia as the administering power. The Japanese occupied the island during World War II and transported most of the inhabitants to Truk, where fewer than two-thirds survived the hardships of forced labor. In 1947 Nauru was made a UN Trust Territory under joint administration of the United Kingdom, Australia, and New Zealand, with Australia again serving as de facto administering authority. Local self-government was gradually accelerated, and in 1966 elections were held for members of a Legislative Council that held jurisdiction over all matters except defense, external affairs, and the phosphate industry. Pursuant to that council's request for full independence, Australia adopted the Nauru Independence Act in November 1967, and the trusteeship agreement was formally terminated by the United Nations, effective January 31, 1968. The arrangements for independence were negotiated by a delegation led by Hammer DeROBURT, who had been head chief of Nauru since 1956 and who became the new republic's first president by legislative designation on May 18, 1968. Reelected in 1971 and 1973, President DeRoburt was replaced by Bernard DOWIYOGO following a legislative election in December 1976.

Although reconfirmed following a parliamentary election in November 1977, President Dowiyogo resigned in January 1978 because of a deadlock over budgetary legislation. He was immediately reelected, but he resigned again in mid-April after the opposition had blocked passage of a bill dealing with phosphate royalties. Dowiyogo was succeeded by Lagumot HARRIS, who in turn resigned on May 11 because of an impasse on an appropriations bill. Harris was succeeded, on the same day, by former president DeRoburt, apparently as the result of a temporary defection by an opposition representative.

President DeRoburt was reelected in 1980 and 1983, but he was forced to yield office temporarily to Kennan Ranibok ADEANG during a ten-day loss of his parliamentary majority in October 1986 and for a four-day period in the wake of an election on December 6. DeRoburt was sworn in for a ninth term on January 27, 1987, following redesignation by a new Parliament elected three days earlier.

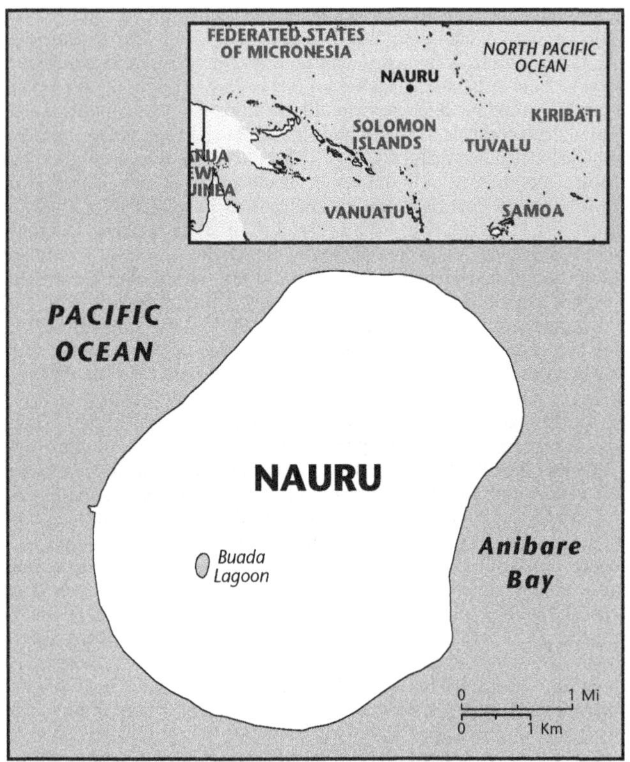

President DeRoburt again fell victim to a no-confidence vote on August 17, 1989, Kenas AROI being designated his successor. However, Aroi was obliged to resign on December 12 to seek medical treatment in Australia, and Dowiyogo returned for a third time as chief executive.

Legislative balloting on November 15, 1992, yielded a standoff between supporters of President Dowiyogo and Beraro DETUDAMO, a protégé of former president DeRoburt, who had died on July 15. After intense negotiations, Dowiyogo succeeded in forging a ten-member coalition of the nominally independent members.

On November 22, 1995, following a legislative poll the day before, Parliament reelected former president Lagumot Harris over Dowiyogo by a 9–8 vote. However, Dowiyogo was reappointed by Parliament on November 7, 1996, only to be ousted himself on November 26 in favor of Adeang, who in turn lost a confidence motion soon thereafter, prompting the appointment of Reuben KUN as acting president. Following new legislative elections on February 8, 1997, Kinza CLODUMAR, a former finance minister, was named president on February 12. He was ousted by a no-confidence vote on June 17, 1998, and was succeeded by Dowiyogo, who assumed office for a fifth term. Dowiyogo himself lost a no-confidence motion on April 27, 1999, and was succeeded by René HARRIS, a member of Parliament since 1977 and former head of Nauru's national phosphate corporation.

President Harris was reelected following legislative balloting on April 8, 2000, but he was obliged to resign on April 19 because of factional differences, with Dowiyogo being returned to office on April 20. Dowiyogo's sixth term in office ended with passage of a no-confidence motion on March 30, 2001, at which time René Harris resumed the presidency.

President Harris was defeated in a no-confidence vote on January 8, 2003, with Dowiyogo sworn in as his successor the following day. However, the Nauru Supreme Court (sitting in Australia) ruled that the vote for Dowiyogo was invalid because it had been called without the presence of Harris and his ministers. With the Harris group in attendance, the vote was split 9–9. Following a period of confusion that included Harris's return to the presidency for one day, Dowiyogo defeated Clodumar on a 9–8 vote and was reinvested on January 20. However, Dowiyogo died after undergoing heart surgery in Washington, D.C., on March 20, and he was succeeded on an acting basis by Derog GIOURA.

Another general election was held on May 3, 2003, and on May 29 Ludwig SCOTTY was installed as president. On August 8 Scotty was ousted and replaced by Harris; however, on June 22, 2004, Harris was in turn replaced by Scotty. On October 1 Scotty dissolved Parliament, and in the ensuing general election on October 23 he was accorded a new majority that permitted his reinvestiture. Scotty was again reconfirmed on August 28, 2007, following an early legislative poll on August 24, but he lost a no-confidence vote on December 18 and was succeeded the following day by Marcus STEPHEN.

President Stephen, after declaring a state of emergency because of a parliamentary impasse, survived a snap election on April 26, 2008, and he was reinvested on April 28. However, the legislative standoff continued through 2009, leading to a bizarre sequence of events in 2010. Stephen survived a no-confidence vote on February 18, and then attempted to secure passage of a constitutional amendment that, inter alia, would have provided for a popularly elected chief executive. Failing to obtain the bill's approval (see Constitution and government, below), Stephen called for an election on April 24, which yielded no change in parliamentary representation. On May 13 a new speaker, Godfrey THOMA, was named, after which the president proposed the creation of a 19th legislative seat to avoid a repeat of the earlier impasse. The effort failed, however, and Thoma resigned. Two legislators crossed the aisle on June 1 to elect Dominic TABUNA as Thoma's successor. However, Tabuna himself stepped down on June 3, and another election was held on June 19 that yielded one new legislator.

On July 5, 2010, Aloysius AMWAN was named speaker after securing a pledge from President Stephen that Stephen would stand down. Instead, the president, in an action ultimately securing judicial approval, subsequently removed Amwan from office, and on August 2 Stephen extended the state of emergency for another 21 days. On November 1 former president Ludwig Scotty accepted designation as speaker, thus eliminating the parliamentary deadlock by restoring the government's slim majority, and Stephen was again confirmed as president.

President Stephen resigned on November 10, 2011, in the face of a looming nonconfidence motion being promoted by opposition legislator David ADEANG, who reportedly questioned Stephen's interactions with foreign phosphate dealers. Frederick PITCHER, who had resigned from Stephen's cabinet earlier in the year but had remained a government supporter, was elected president the same day by a vote of 9–8 in Parliament. However, new president Pitcher described the criticism of Stephen as unwarranted and retained Stephen in his cabinet. Consequently, Adeang quickly announced his opposition to Pitcher, who lost a confidence vote on November 15 and was succeeded by Sprent DABWIDO, who was elected by the usual 9–8 vote after he switched his allegiance to the opposition. Dabwido appointed a number of opposition legislators, including Adeang, to his new cabinet with the stated hope of achieving the constitutional reform deemed critical in establishing political stability by eliminating the nation's "revolving door presidency." That concept failed, however, and on June 11, 2012, Dabwido dismissed the cabinet and brought former president Stephen and several of Stephen's former cabinet members back into the government. Dabwido was succeeded on June 11, 2013, by Baron WAQA following legislative elections that were held on June 8 in the wake of a complicated constitutional wrangle (see Current issues, below).

Legislative elections were held on July 9, 2016. Six of the members elected in the balloting were new. Waqa was reelected president on July 13 on a vote of 16–2. He conducted a minor cabinet reshuffle two days later.

Constitution and government. Nauru's constitution, adopted by an elected Constitutional Convention on January 29, 1968, and amended on May 17 of the same year, provides for a republic whose president combines the functions of head of state and chief of government. The unicameral Parliament selects the president (for a three-year term) from among its membership; the president in turn appoints a number of legislators to serve as a cabinet that is responsible to Parliament and is obligated to resign as a body in the event of a no-confidence vote.

The island is administratively divided into 14 districts, which are regrouped into 8 districts for electoral purposes. An elected Local Government Council of nine members (one of whom is designated Head Chief) shares administrative responsibilities with Parliament. The court system is headed by a Supreme Court.

In April 2007 voters went to the polls to elect members of a constitutional convention to debate the findings of an independent Commission on Constitutional Review appointed a year earlier to assess the country's 39-year-old basic law. The commission recommended that the president be popularly elected, that the legislative speaker not be a member of Parliament, that a Public Service Commission be established, that an independent director of audit be appointed, that judicial appeals to the High Court of Australia be abolished, and that the language in the basic law regarding human rights be expanded. After acceptance by the constitutional convention, the recommendations were unanimously approved by Parliament in August 2009. However, some of the proposed changes (most notably the one concerning the election of the president) required endorsement in a national referendum, and voters rejected them with a 67 percent "no" vote on February 27, 2010.

A constitutional reform package was narrowly rejected by Parliament in June 2012, but the government pledged to pursue the proposed changes as individual pieces of legislation. Consequently, in July the Parliament agreed to increase the number of legislators to 19 in order to resolve a problem associated with the provision that the speaker (chosen from the members of Parliament) votes only in case of a tie vote among the other legislators. (Prior to the membership expansion, in a Parliament divided politically on a 9–9 basis, the side electing the speaker paradoxically fell into minority status.)

Although Nauru has traditionally received a satisfactory rating regarding freedom of the press, complaints were lodged against the government in 2013–2014 for alleged interference in reporting on controversial issues, particularly in regard to the Australian detention centers in Nauru for asylum seekers. In that regard, the Nauruan government announced in early 2014 that a fee of $8,000 would be charged for any foreign journalists seeking an entry visa.

Foreign relations. Relations with the Commonwealth were initially defined by an agreement announced on November 29, 1968, whereby Nauru became a "special member" of the Commonwealth entitled to full participation in the organization's activities, except meetings of the heads of government. Nauru also maintains formal diplomatic relations with about a dozen foreign governments, primarily through representatives accredited to Australia and Fiji. Long a member of the UN Economic and Social Commission for Asia and the Pacific and of the South Pacific Forum (SPF, now the Pacific Islands Forum), Nauru acceded in August 1982 to the South Pacific Regional Trade Agreement, under which Australia and New Zealand had agreed to permit the duty-free entry of a wide variety of goods from SPF member countries. Its principal international tie, however, has been with the Commonwealth (in which Nauru was accorded full membership in 1999).

In January 1992 Nauru joined with sister island nations Kiribati and Tuvalu, and the New Zealand dependencies of the Cook Islands and Niue, to form a Small Island States (SIS) grouping to address a number of common concerns, including global warming, the negotiation of fishing rights in their 200-mile Exclusive Economic Zones, and the possibility of renting airspace to planes overflying their countries.

During 1995 Nauru adopted the hardest line of all regional countries in opposing France's decision to resume nuclear testing at Mururoa Atoll in September. Among other things, President Dowiyogo, who had previously supported New Zealand's World Court bid to stop the tests, traveled to Paris with other regional leaders in an unsuccessful effort to secure cancellation.

In January 1998, on the 30th anniversary of Nauru's independence, President Clodumar announced that the country would apply for membership in the United Nations. A formal request was issued in April 1999 with admittance to the world body in September.

In July 2002 Nauru and Taiwan ended two decades of diplomatic relations as the Harris government and China agreed to establish formal ties. Attempting to justify its about-face, the Nauruan administration cited the alleged interference of a Taiwanese envoy in a recent parliamentary by-election, although most observers attributed the shift to an expectation that Beijing would provide substantially more economic aid than Taipei.

Subsequently, Nauru entered into a series of agreements with Australia for the detention of large numbers of "boat people" whom Canberra did not wish to admit as refugees. The arrangements, part of Australia's "Pacific Solution" for migrants, were not intended to be permanent, and in late 2003 a group of detainees staged a hunger strike to press consideration of their claim by Canberra. The strike was called off in early 2004, after Australia agreed to review their cases and New Zealand said it would accept some of the refugees on humanitarian grounds. Subsequently, in another decision with broad economic implications, the Scotty administration in Nauru resumed relations with Taiwan in 2005, arguing that China had provided little aid since 2002.

Australia closed the detention center on Nauru in 2007, thereby negatively affecting Nauru's economy, which had benefited from payments of an estimated A$100 million over a six-year period. As a result, Canberra agreed to fund a limited resumption of phosphate mining and provide A$29 million in developmental assistance for fiscal 2009.

In late 2009 Nauru, apparently at Russia's request, became one of the few countries to formally recognize the independence of the Georgian breakaway republics of Abkhazia and South Ossetia. Reports subsequently surfaced that Russia had agreed to give Nauru $50 million for infrastructure improvement. Nauru's reputation for "checkbook diplomacy" was also underscored by allegations that government ministers and legislators were continuing to receive substantial monthly payments from Taiwan.

In the second half of 2011 discussion took place over the possible reopening of the Australian detention center in Nauru. Possibly to facilitate such a decision, in September Nauru became a party to the UN Convention on Refugees, which, among other things, sets minimum standards that would have to be met at the reopened center. (Activists argued that the earlier experience in Nauru had been "a disaster" marked by rampant human rights abuses.) Australia and Nauru concluded an agreement in mid-2012 to reestablish a "processing center" on Nauru for the asylum seekers, as the Australian government adopted the policy that none of the boat people would be allowed to settle in Australia. (See Current issues, below, for subsequent developments.)

The suspension of five opposition lawmakers in May 2014 (see Current issues, below), led New Zealand to suspend annual aid to Nauru in September.

In June 2015 Australia began a $42.2 million plan to transfer refugees from Nauru to Cambodia. The plan was criticized in both Australia and Nauru as only five refugees had been transferred by December 2015. In August 2016 the Australian government rejected a report by Amnesty International and Human Rights Watch that decried the conditions for refugees on Nauru and charged there was systemic abuse and neglect.

Current issues. President Dabwido dismissed two of his six cabinet ministers in early 2013, and two others resigned, leaving the Parliament fractionalized and the government ineffective. Consequently, Dabwido asked Speaker Ludwig Scotty to dissolve Parliament and set a date for early elections. Scotty, also citing "unruly" behavior on the part of some legislators, ordered the dissolution on April 1, refusing to permit debate on the matter. The lack of debate proved significant as opposition legislators demanded the opportunity to present a no-confidence motion against the Dabwido administration rather than proceed directly to elections. Based on their appeal, the Supreme Court overturned the initial dissolution decree and another announced by Scotty in mid-March. Godfrey THOMA was elected as the new speaker in April, and in May he reluctantly ordered another dissolution in the face of a continued boycott of proceedings by pro-Dabwido legislators. Thoma initially set the new elections for June 22, but on May 27 President Dabwido declared a state of emergency, arguing that the proposed date would compromise access to budget funds. Setting a new election for June 8, he also decreed a temporary ban on constitutional rulings from the Supreme Court and dismissed the speaker.

Seven of the 19 successful candidates in the June 8, 2013, legislative balloting were new to Parliament, suggesting potential relief from the country's longstanding political gridlock. Similar hopes were expressed when Baron Waqa, a former education minister, was subsequently elected president by a vote of 13–5 over Roland KUN (Dabwido did not run). Waqa called for better communication between the government and the populace, particularly in regard to the Australian detention/processing centers (see Foreign relations, above). That issue attracted even greater attention when asylum seekers at one of the two centers rioted at the end of July (causing an estimated $60 million in damage).

In accordance with a recently signed memorandum of understanding with Australia, the Nauruan administration in the second half of 2013 announced that asylum seekers granted formal refugee status would be allowed to resettle, at least temporarily, in Nauru. Opposition legislators argued that Nauru did not have the resources for such a resettlement program, despite $26 million in Australian assistance. They also strongly criticized Waqa's decision in early 2014 to dismiss and deport Nauru's only magistrate and to cancel the visa of the country's chief justice (both men are Australians). Waqa survived a nonconfidence motion on the matter by a vote of 11–7 on January 28, but tensions remained high in the Parliament, which in May ordered the suspension of three opposition legislators for discussing the detention centers too much with the foreign media. (The government argued that the negative press coverage was hindering development plans.) Two more opposition legislators were suspended in June for "unruly behavior."

As of mid-2014 nearly 100 asylum seekers had been granted formal refugee status by Nauru and given five-year residency visas, with government pledges to assist the refugees in finding employment on the island. Approximately 30 others had been denied refugee status, and preparations began to return them to their countries of origin. More than 1,200 claimants were still awaiting adjudication, and UN and other agencies urged the Nauruan government to permit international monitoring of conditions in the centers. For its part, the government called for less attention on the issue of asylum seekers and more on efforts to promote economic and social progress for Nauruan citizens, such as the recent establishment of the Nauru Trust Fund to be funded by, among other donors, Australia, China, and the Asian Development Bank, who would also assist in the administration of the fund.

On December 12, 2014, the Supreme Court dismissed an appeal by the five lawmakers suspended in May and June. In May 2015 Parliament passed a measure criminalizing hate speech and political speech that leads to violence or disorder. Critics argued the measure was designed to suppress dissent.

POLITICAL PARTIES

Although several loosely structured parties have been referenced since 1976 (see the 2014 *Handbook* for details), none of them appear to be operating currently.

LEGISLATURE

The unicameral **Parliament** comprises 19 members (raised from 18 in 2012) directly elected in eight districts for a three-year term, subject to dissolution. Voting is compulsory for those over 20 years of age. The speaker only votes in case of a tie vote among the other legislators. The most recent election was on July 9, 2016.

Speaker: Cyril BURAMAN.

CABINET

[as of August 15, 2016]

President	Baron Waqa
Ministers	
Assistant to the President	David Adeang
Climate Change	Baron Waqa
Commerce, Industry, and Environment	Baron Waqa
Education	Charmaine Scotty [f]
Finance and Sustainable Development	David Adeang
Fisheries	Valdon Dowiyogo
Foreign Affairs and Trade	Baron Waqa
Health	Valdon Dowiyogo
Home Affairs	Charmaine Scotty [f]
Justice	David Adeang
Land Management	Charmaine Scotty [f]
Multicultural Affairs	David Adeang
Nauru Rehabilitation Corporation	Aaron Cook
Nauru Royalties Trust	Shadlog Bernicke
Nauru Utilities Corporation	Aaron Cook
Police and Emergency Services	Baron Waqa
Public Service	Baron Waqa
Republic of Nauru Phosphate (RONPHOS)	Aaron Cook
Sports	Valdon Dowiyogo
Telecommunications	Shadlog Bernicke
Transport	Valdon Dowiyogo

[f] = female

INTERGOVERNMENTAL REPRESENTATION

Ambassador to the U.S. and Permanent Representative to the UN: Marlene MOSES.

U.S. Ambassador to Nauru (resident in Fiji): Judith CEFKIN.

IGO Memberships (Non-UN): ADB, CWTH, ICC, PIF.

For Further Reference:

Gleeson, Madeline. *Offshore: Behind the Wire on Manus and Nauru.* Sydney: University of New South Wales Press, 2016.

Isaacs, Mark. *The Undesirables: Inside Nauru.* Richmond, Victoria: Hardie Grant, 2014.

McDaniel, Carl, and John Gowdy. *Paradise for Sale: A Parable of Nature.* Berkeley: University of California Press, 2000.

NEPAL

Federal Democratic Republic of Nepal
Sanghiya Loktantrik Ganatantra Nepal

Political Status: Independent monarchy established 1769; limited constitutional system promulgated December 16, 1962; constitutional monarchy proclaimed under constitution of November 9, 1990; interim constitution promulgated January 15, 2007, changing country's official name from Kingdom of Nepal to State of Nepal; monarchy formally ended and federal democratic republic proclaimed May 28, 2008, by a Constituent Assembly; new constitution approved on September 20, 2015.

Area: 56,826 sq. mi. (147,181 sq. km).

Population: 28,851,000 (2016E—UN); 29,033,914 (2016E—U.S. Census).

Major Urban Center (2016E—UN): KATHMANDU (1,224,000).

Official Language: Nepali.

Monetary Unit: Nepalese Rupee (market rate October 1, 2016: 106.53 rupees = $1US).

President: Bidhya Devi BHANDARI (Communist Party of Nepal [Unified Marxist-Leninist]); elected by parliament on October 29, 2015, and sworn in on October 30; succeeding Ram Baran YADAV (Nepali Congress).

Vice President: Nanda Kishor PUN (Unified Communist Party of Nepal [Maoist]); elected by parliament on October 31, 2015; succeeding Paramananda JHA (Madhesi People's Rights Forum Nepal).

Prime Minister: Pushpa Kamal Dahal "PRACHANDA" (Unified Communist Party of Nepal [Maoist]); elected by parliament on August 3, 2016; succeeding Khadga Prasad Sharma OLI (Communist Party of Nepal [Unified Marxist-Leninist]).

THE COUNTRY

Landlocked between India and Tibet in the central Himalayas, Nepal encompasses three distinct geographic zones: a southern plain known as the Terai, a central hill region with many rivers and valleys, and a northern section dominated by the Himalaya Mountains. The country is inhabited by more than 50 tribes, who fall into two main ethnic groupings, Mongolian and Indo-Aryan. The majority of the population, particularly in the south, is Hindu in religion and linked in culture to India. The northern region, adjoining Tibet, is mainly Buddhist, but throughout the country Hindu and Buddhist practices have intermingled with each other and with shamanism.

Women's participation in government is relatively high. The Inter-Parliamentary Union (IPU) ranked Nepal in 2016 as 47th out of 181 countries in female representation, with women holding 175 of 595 seats in parliament (29.6 percent). Bidhya Devi BHANDARI became Nepal's first woman president in 2015, but there were no women in the cabinet.

With 50 percent illiteracy (higher for females), Nepal is considered one of the world's least developed nations. Moreover, Nepal suffers

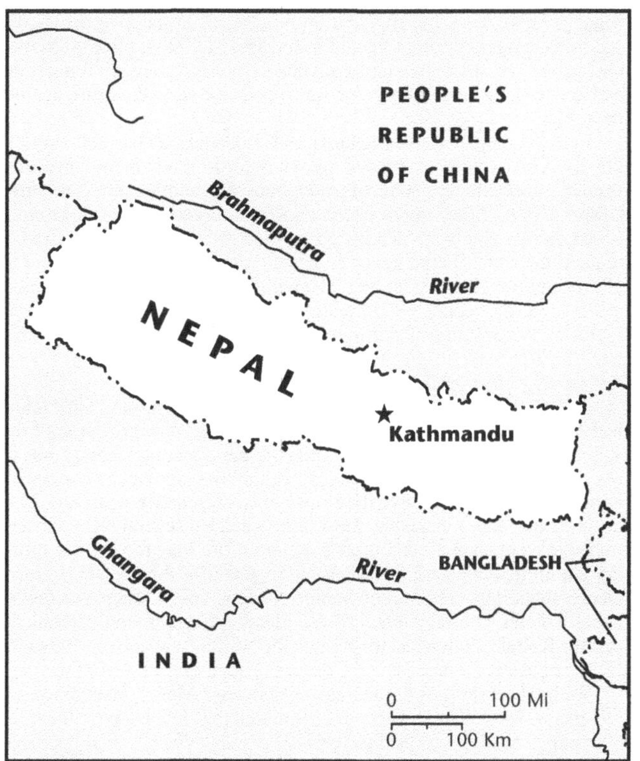

from a severely unequal distribution of wealth: according to some estimates, average income in the "hill country" is less than 10 percent that of the capital region.

Agriculture continues to employ 75 percent of the labor force and to account for about 35 percent of GDP. Industry, which contributes 16 percent of GDP, is oriented toward processed foods and other nondurable consumer goods, industrial development being hindered by rudimentary communication and transportation facilities. Natural resources include timber (despite extensive deforestation in some areas), mica, and coal, while there is increasing emphasis on the export potential of hydropower. At present, leading exports include woolen carpets, ready-made clothing, and such agricultural products as pulses, jute, and grain. Another significant source of foreign exchange is remittances from Nepalese employed abroad.

The Nepalese economy saw relatively consistent growth averaging 4.1 percent between 2000 and 2010. After posting robust growth of 4.6 percent in 2012, the economy slowed to 3 percent in 2013. The decline was in large part due to the impact of bad weather on agriculture, but also indicated the political difficulties in passing a budget. Growth of 5.4 percent in 2014 reflected recovery in the agriculture sector and increased public spending under the newly installed government, but slowed to 3.4 percent in 2015. Inflation was 8.3 percent in 2014, and 7 percent in 2015, but rose to 11.1 percent in 2016. Per-capita income is about $2,500, or $6.85, per day in 2015. The World Bank group ranked Nepal 99th out of 189 countries for ease of doing business in 2016, down from 94 in 2015.

GOVERNMENT AND POLITICS

Political background. Founded in 1769 by the Gurkha ruler Prithvi NARAYAN Shah as a kingdom comprising 46 previously sovereign principalities, Nepal was ruled by Narayan's descendants until the 1840s, when the Rana family established an autocratic system that, under hereditary prime ministers, lasted until 1951. A revolution in 1950, inspired in part by India's independence, restored the power of King TRIBHUVAN Bir Bikram Shah Dev and initiated a period of quasi-constitutional rule that continued after 1955 under the auspices of Tribhuvan's son, King MAHENDRA Bir Bikram Shah Dev.

A democratic constitution promulgated in 1959 paved the way for an election that brought to power the socialist-inclined Nepali Congress (NC) under Biseswar Prasad KOIRALA. In December 1960, however, the king charged the new government with misuse of power, dismissed and jailed its leaders, suspended the constitution, banned political parties, and assumed personal authority. A new constitution promulgated in 1962 and amended in 1967 established a tiered *panchayat* (assembly) system of representative bodies that was held to be more in keeping with Nepal's traditions. The nonparty system encountered persistent opposition, despite reconciliation efforts that included Koirala's release from detention.

King BIRENDRA Bir Bikram Shah Dev, who succeeded to the throne in 1972, accorded high priority to economic development but encountered difficulty in combining monarchial rule with pressures for political liberalization. In 1979, after prolonged demonstrations, King Birendra announced that a referendum would be held to determine whether the nation favored revision of the *panchayat* structure or its replacement by a multiparty system. In May 1980 Nepalese voters rejected reintroduction of a party system, and in December the king proclaimed a number of constitutional changes, including direct, nonparty election to the National Assembly.

In the wake of economic distress caused by the March 1989 lapse of crucial trade and transit treaties with India (see Foreign relations, below), the banned NC called for dissolution of the government. The NC and seven communist groups joined in February 1990 to form a Movement for the Restoration of Democracy that sought multiparty elections and an end to the *panchayat* system. In April King Birendra reluctantly agreed to the appointment of the NC president, Krishna Prasad BHATTARAI, to head an interim cabinet. In May the king declared an amnesty for all political prisoners (most of whom had campaigned for party legalization). Shortly thereafter, he approved the government's nominees to a Constitutional Recommendation Commission and in September accepted the commission's draft of a new basic law, formally promulgated on November 9.

On May 12, 1991, in the country's first multiparty general election since 1959, the NC won control of the new House of Representatives, although Bhattarai lost his seat. As a result, the party's strongly anti-communist general secretary, Girija Prasad KOIRALA (brother of the former prime minister), was named to head a new administration. In July 1994 Koirala submitted his resignation.

In the election held in November 1994 the Communist Party of Nepal (Unified Marxist-Leninist)—CPN (UML) won a plurality of 88 seats in the 205-member lower house, and its leader, Man Mohan ADHIKARI, was sworn in as prime minister. In June 1995, however, the NC tabled a no-confidence motion that the National Democratic Party (*Rastriya Prajatantra* Party—RPP), theretofore a crucial CPN (UML) ally, announced it would support. Two days later, at Adhikari's request, the king dissolved the National Assembly. The action was protested by the NC, the rightist RPP, and the royalist Nepali Goodwill Party (*Nepal Sadbhavana* Party—NSP), which collectively held 106 legislative seats. In August the Supreme Court ruled the action unconstitutional, and the prime minister resigned following rejection of a confidence motion in September. The NC's Sher Bahadur DEUBA then formed the country's first coalition administration, encompassing the NC, RPP, and NSP.

The Deuba coalition government remained vulnerable to potential shifting alliances, especially among the RPP ministers, and the prime minister resigned in March 1997, after losing a confidence motion by two votes. The king invited former prime minister Lokendra Bahadur CHAND (1983–1986, 1990) of the RPP to form a new government, which included the CPN (UML), RPP, and NSP. Following local elections in May, elements within the RPP as well as opposition parties charged the victorious CPN (UML) with having committed election fraud and other irregularities. By late September the RPP had split into factions led by Chand and former prime minister Surya Bahadur THAPA (1963–1964, 1965–1969, 1979–1983). When Chand lost a confidence motion in October, he resigned, and Thapa became prime minister for the fourth time, naming a new government that included the RPP and NSP. The NC subsequently joined the cabinet in another reshuffle, but the coalition remained unstable, and in January 1998 Thapa asked the king to dissolve the parliament and call new elections. The CPN (UML) and the Chand faction of the RPP objected and instead called for a special legislative session to consider a no-confidence motion. As a result, the RPP expelled the Chand group, which immediately formed a "New RPP." Meanwhile, the king had referred the issue to the Supreme Court, which in February recommended convening the House of Representatives. On February 20 the government survived a no-confidence motion by only three votes. In April, Prime Minister Thapa resigned in accordance with a power-sharing arrangement with the NC.

Former NC prime minister G. P. Koirala was sworn in on April 15, 1998, as the head of a three-person minority government, the NC being the plurality party in the House following a March split in the CPN (UML). The latter party had lost more than half its MPs to a new Communist Party of Nepal (Marxist-Leninist) (CPN [ML]) in a dispute over the water-sharing treaty concluded with India in 1996. On April 18 Koirala secured a confidence vote and three days later introduced an expanded cabinet.

A cabinet reshuffle in August 1998 marked formation of an NC-led coalition with the new CPN (ML), which had demanded in return for its support review of the 1950 Indo-Nepal Peace and Friendship Treaty; withdrawal of Indian troops from the disputed Kalapani border area, where they had been posted since the 1962 Sino-Indian war; and repatriation to Bhutan of the nearly 100,000 Bhutanese refugees of Nepali descent who had been sheltered in camps in southeast Nepal since 1990. In December, charging that the NC had failed to honor its commitment, the CPN (ML) withdrew from the government, prompting Prime Minister Koirala to recommend that the lower house be dissolved. The NC and the CPN (UML) then agreed to form an interim, pre-election government—Nepal's sixth in four years—that was sworn in with the additional participation of the NSP. The interim administration won a confidence vote in January 1999, and a day later the king dissolved the House of Representatives and announced that a general election would be held in May.

With the left split by the CPN (UML)-CPN (ML) rupture, and with Prime Minister Koirala having announced that he would step aside in favor of his longtime intraparty rival, former prime minister K. P. Bhattarai, the NC swept to victory in the May 3 and 17, 1999, election. The election had been conducted in two phases to ensure adequate security in the western and central regions, site of a Maoist "People's War" insurgency, which largely relied on support from the illiterate, impoverished peasantry in the hinterlands. With the NC having won a majority of 111 seats in the lower house, Bhattarai was sworn in as prime minister on May 31. Nevertheless, internecine warfare continued between NC president Koirala and Prime Minister Bhattarai, even though the two septuagenarians had committed to preparing a "younger generation" of leaders. On March 16, 2000, one day before a scheduled vote by the NC parliamentarians would have ousted him from office, Bhattarai announced to the lower house that he would submit his resignation to the king. On March 18 Koirala easily defeated former prime minister Deuba in the NC's first-ever open leadership election, and on March 20 the king appointed him prime minister for the fourth time.

In February 2001 Koirala included members of Deuba's NC faction in a reshuffled cabinet, but after two months of parliamentary boycotts and disruptions led by the opposition CPN (UML), King Birendra prorogued both houses of the legislature on April 5.

On June 1, 2001, Nepal experienced an unprecedented trauma when Crown Prince DIPENDRA Bikram Shah Dev killed most of the royal family, including King Birendra and Queen AISHWARYA, with an automatic weapon during a family get-together at the palace. Eight died immediately and two others, including Dipendra, who had shot himself, succumbed on June 4. Upon the death of Dipendra, who had been proclaimed king on June 2 despite his comatose state, Prince Regent GYANENDRA Bir Bikram Shah Dev, brother of King Birendra, ascended to the throne. The massacre had apparently originated in the late king and queen's persistent rejection of Dipendra's choice of a bride, whose ancestry they found wanting.

With the kingdom barely recovered from the June tragedy, Prime Minister Koirala resigned on July 19, 2001, having proved unable to quell the Maoist insurgency and to overcome corruption allegations. On July 22 King Gyanendra named the new NC leader, former prime minister Deuba, to head a new government that was sworn in four days later. Upon nomination, Prime Minister Deuba had identified resolving the insurgency as his highest priority, and on July 23 he declared a cease-fire with the rebels. By mid-August Deuba had announced an ambitious series of reforms, including a land redistribution plan to aid the poor (and undercut rural support for the Maoists), a proposal to make discrimination against Dalits (untouchables) a crime, establishment of a National Women's Commission to pursue gender equality, and forward movement on the previous administration's anticorruption bill. The measures, particularly land reform, drew opposition from within his party.

The opening of talks between the Communist Party of Nepal (Maoist) and the government on August 30, 2001, was preceded by mutual prisoner releases, but the two sides failed to make progress before a third round of talks collapsed on November 13. Shortly thereafter the Maoists broke the cease-fire, and on November 26 the king declared a state of emergency; promulgated a Terrorist and Disruptive Activities Ordinance, which defined terrorism and suspended many civil liberties; and for the first time authorized full mobilization of the army against the rebels.

In succeeding months casualties rapidly mounted, and on February 21, 2002, Deuba easily marshaled the two-thirds lower house majority needed to extend the state of emergency for another three months. Responding to criticism from the opposition as well as from international human rights advocates, on April 4 the government somewhat relaxed the state of emergency to permit greater press freedom and to allow public political meetings. Meanwhile, the Maoists widened their attacks on the country's infrastructure, including communications facilities, water supplies, dams, bridges, schools, and health clinics. By late May the death toll from the six-year insurgency had risen to 4,000–5,000, up from about 1,800 the preceding October.

In May 2002 Koirala supporters within the NC, charging that Deuba had failed to consult them before requesting a second extension of the state of emergency, prepared to join the parliamentary opposition in rejecting the proposal. Facing defeat, Prime Minister Deuba convinced King Gyanendra to dissolve the House of Representatives on May 22, a decision that was attacked by most parties and led several NC ministers to resign from Deuba's caretaker cabinet. In late May the NC disciplinary committee expelled Deuba from the party for three years. In turn, Deuba supporters called a convention for June 16–19 and proceeded to expel Koirala. On September 17 the Election Commission determined that the Koirala faction had the right to the NC title, and on September 23 Deuba registered a new Nepali Congress (Democratic)—NC(D).

With a backdrop of the increasingly intense Maoist insurgency, on October 4, 2002, King Gyanendra dismissed the Deuba government for "incompetence," postponed the early legislative election that had been scheduled for November 13, and temporarily assumed executive powers. On October 11 he named former prime minister L. B. Chand of the promonarchy RPP to head a nonparty government, which was then expanded in mid-November. After negotiations with the CPN (Maoist)—CPN-M broke down, Prime Minister Chand resigned on May 30, 2003.

On June 4, 2003, the king named as prime minister the RPP's S. B. Thapa (his fifth term) after rejecting the candidate of a five-party opposition Joint People's Movement (JPM), Madhav Kumar NEPAL, the CPN (UML)'s general secretary. Like its predecessor, the all-RPP cabinet introduced on June 1 was denounced as illegitimate by the NC, the CPN (UML), and the other JPM parties, who accused the king of undermining multiparty democracy through "regression." Many in the opposition advocated recalling the dismissed House of Representatives—although there was no constitutional provision for doing so—as well as forming an all-party government.

A third round of peace talks on August 17–19, 2003, made no significant progress as the Maoists continued to insist that a constituent assembly be elected to draft a new constitution. On August 27 the CPN-M leader, Pushpa Kamal DAHAL "Comrade PRACHANDA," issued a statement announcing an end to both the talks and the cease-fire, and in succeeding months the violence escalated once again as the insurgents demonstrated their ability to attack throughout the country. The CPN-M also continued its efforts to organize administrative machinery in the districts it claimed to control.

On May 7, 2004, Prime Minister Thapa resigned. On June 2 the king reappointed former prime minister Deuba—the country's 14th prime minister in 14 years. Shortly thereafter, the CPN (UML), contending that opposition-supported antigovernment street demonstrations were no longer "meaningful," withdrew from the JPM. On July 5 the Deuba cabinet was expanded to include the CPN (UML), the RPP, and the NSP, in addition to Deuba's NC(D).

At the beginning of 2005 the government remained in disarray. The NC had joined the CPN (UML) in calling for creation of a republic, while other parties had decided to support the Maoists' demand for election of a constituent assembly and their inclusion in an interim government. On February 1 King Gyanendra dismissed the Deuba government, reintroduced a state of emergency, placed many political leaders under house arrest, ordered the army into the streets of the capital, and suspended press and other freedoms. Having vowed to "restore peace and effective democracy in this country within the next three years," on February 2 he named a cabinet of loyalists under his leadership. Although the state of emergency was lifted on April 29, 2005, a number of civil restrictions remained in effect. The cabinet was expanded on July 15 by the addition of several other loyalists.

On May 8, 2005, the country's leading opposition parties announced formation of a "Seven-Party Alliance" (SPA), adopting a roadmap to the restoration of democracy that included reinstating the dissolved House of Representatives and forming a unity government. Participating in the SPA were the NC; the NC(D); the CPN (UML); the NSP (Anandi Devi), an NSP splinter formed in 2003; People's Front Nepal (*Janamorcha Nepal*—JMN); the Nepal Workers' and Peasants' Party (NWPP); and the United Left Front (ULF), at that time a five-party grouping of small communist parties. Together, the SPA parties had held all but about a dozen of the 205 seats in the dissolved House of Representatives.

Responding to prodemocracy overtures from the SPA, on September 3, 2005, the Maoists' Prachanda announced a three-month unilateral cease-fire. Subsequent talks between the SPA and the Maoists led to a November 22 announcement of a 12-point agreement designed to end the king's "autocracy" and move toward election of a constituent assembly. The cease-fire was extended on December 2 but ended on January 2, 2006, because of lack of response by the government.

Municipal elections on February 8, 2006, were boycotted by the SPA, while Maoist threats against candidates and voters contributed to a low turnout. With the Maoists in control of an estimated three-fourths of the countryside and with the roads into Kathmandu again blockaded, the SPA began a general strike on April 6. In the wake of public protests, King Gyanendra on April 24 announced that he would reinstate the House of Representatives and asked the SPA to assume responsibility "for taking the nation on the path to national unity and prosperity, while ensuring permanent peace and safeguarding multiparty democracy." On April 26 the SPA nominated veteran NC leader G. P. Koirala for prime minister, the same day the Maoists announced another cease-fire. The House of Representatives convened on April 28. Two days later, the House unanimously approved a resolution endorsing formation of a constituent assembly.

On May 18, 2006, the House of Representatives assumed all legislative powers; stripped most governmental rights and responsibilities from the king, including his role as commander in chief; and delegated executive authority to a Council of Ministers responsible to the House. In their first face-to-face meeting, held June 16, 2006, Prime Minister Koirala and Comrade Prachanda, joined by other Maoist negotiators and representatives of the SPA, concluded an agreement that called for implementing the November 2005 agreement and a cease-fire code of conduct that had been signed on May 26. The new agreement expressed a commitment to "democratic norms and values" and provided for the immediate drafting of an interim constitution, to be followed by formation of an interim government in which the CPN-M would participate. On November 28 the government and the CPN-M signed, along with a UN representative, a tripartite agreement calling for the Nepalese Army to return to barracks, for the 30,000–40,000 soldiers of the Maoist People's Liberation Army to be confined to several camps, and for a comparable number of arms from each side to be locked away under UN supervision. In all, more than 16,000 people died during the 1996–2006 Maoist insurgency, nearly half of them civilians, with another 1,200 listed as missing and over 70,000 displaced by the fighting. During the last years of the conflict, casualties and reports of human-rights violations by both sides escalated, and difficulties persisted even after the peace accord.

Following protracted negotiations, a draft interim constitution was approved by the SPA and the CPN-M in December 2006 and promulgated on January 15, 2007, by the House of Representatives. The legislature was immediately superseded by a unicameral Interim Legislature-Parliament of 330 members, including 83 representatives of the CPN-M. An Interim Council of Ministers, including Maoists, assumed office on April 1.

An election for a Constituent Assembly to draft a new constitution was set for November 22, 2007, having been postponed from June. However, on September 18 the Maoists resigned from the government over the issue of abolishing the monarchy, and their continuing demands for the declaration of a republic in advance of the referendum contributed to a further postponement of the polling. They subsequently rejoined the government in December, and on December 23, the CPN-M and the government parties signed an agreement that included support for establishing a federal democratic republic at the first meeting of the Constituent Assembly, once its 601 members were chosen. Meanwhile, five small royalist parties formed the United Inclusive Front to oppose the republican trend, and former prime minister Thapa of the RPP campaigned in favor of retaining the monarchy.

The elections to the Constituent Assembly were finally held on April 10, 2008, with the elections commission estimating voter turnout of 60 percent. Both first-past-the-post and proportional representation systems were employed, with the CPN-M winning the most seats (220). On May 28 the assembly voted 560–4 to abolish the monarchy and declared Nepal a federal democratic republic. King Gyanendra confirmed on June 2 that he would abdicate, and he left the palace on June 11. On June 26 Prime Minister Koirala resigned, effective upon the election of a president. On July 19 the assembly elected Paramananda JHA of the Madhesi People's Rights Forum (*Madheshi Janadhikar* Forum—MJF) as vice president, and two days later it chose Ram Baran YADAV (NC) as president. Yadav then asked the CPN-M to form a government, and Pushpa Kamal Dahal was named prime minister on August 18.

Dahal's brief tenure ended in May 2009 in the wake of turmoil over the reintegration of the Maoist People's Liberation Army (PLA), resulting in Dahal's firing the army chief of staff, Gen. Rookmangud KATAWAL, on May 3. On the same day, however, President Yadav overruled Dahal, who resigned on May 4. The Maoists, demanding that the assembly debate the president's action, subsequently obstructed parliament with walkouts and heckling, and slowed the economy with strikes and other demonstrations. With the Maoists boycotting the session, on May 23 the assembly elected Madhav Kumar Nepal of the CPN (UML) as prime minister of a coalition government that also included the NC and the newly formed Madhesi People's Rights Forum (*Madheshi Janadhikar* Forum [Democratic]—MJF-L) as its principal components. Prime Minister Nepal gradually filled out his new government with ministers from additional parties. Meanwhile, the CPN-M merged with smaller parties to create a new grouping, the United Communist Party of Nepal (Maoist)—UCPN-M (see Political Parties, below).

Faced with continuing obstruction by the Maoists, on May 28, 2010, the assembly extended by a year its own term as well as the deadlines for integrating the PLA and completing a new constitution. On June 30 Prime Minister Nepal resigned to make way for a consensus government, but he and his cabinet remained in place pending election of a new prime minister.

After seven months of negotiations, on February 3, 2011, Jhala Nath KHANAL (CPN [UML]) was elected prime minister and sworn into office three days later. However, tensions between Khanal and the UCPN-M, the largest party in the legislature, led to the latter's resignation on August 14. On August 28 Baburam Bhattarai (UCPN-M) was elected prime minister. He formed a coalition government that included the UCPN-M, the newly formed coalition, and the United Democratic Madhesi Front (UDMF). Meanwhile, the Constituent Assembly again extended its term on August 29.

On May 27, 2012, the Constituent Assembly dissolved when the deadline to draft the new Constitution passed. Prime Minister Bhattarai called for elections on November 21, but none were held. President Yadav repeatedly called on party leaders to establish an interim government, which was finally achieved in March when the four largest parties, the UCPN-M, UDMF, NC, and CPN (UML), agreed to appoint chief Justice Khil Raj REGMI leader of a nonpartisan election government.

Regmi was sworn in as interim prime minister on March 14, 2013. Three months later, he named November 19 for the next elections. In balloting for the Constituent Assembly, the NC won a clear majority and negotiated an alliance with the CPN (UML). Sushil KOIRALA of the NC was elected prime minister on February 10.

The Constituent Assembly failed to meet successive deadlines for a new constitution. However, on June 8, 2015, the major political parties of the assembly signed a 16-point accord on the framework for the constitution. The first draft of the new basic law was completed on June 30. Strikes and demonstrations against the draft occurred throughout August, with more than 100 arrested and 40 killed in clashes between protestors and security forces (see Foreign relations, below). Many Madhesis opposed the constitution because of perceptions that the new system would lead to underrepresentation in the parliament. Madhesis sought the creation of a second, predominately Madhesi, state in the new federal system. Meanwhile, another group in the Terai region, the Tharus, opposed the new borders because they would divide the people between two states. On September 20 the assembly endorsed the new constitution with 507 out of 598 legislators voting in favor of the document. On October 11, 2015, the Constituent Assembly changed its name to the Legislature-Parliament, as required by the constitution, and elected Khadga Prasad Sharma OLI (CPN [UML]) as prime minister on a vote of 338 to 249, over Koirala. Oli formed a coalition government, led by the CPN (UML). On October 16 Parliament elected its first female speaker, Onsari Gharti MAGAR (UCPN-M), who ran unopposed.

Bidya Devi BHANDARI (CPN [UML]) was elected president on October 29, 2015, becoming Nepal's first woman leader. She won with 327 votes to 214 for Kul Bahadur GURUN (NC). Nanda Kishor PUN (UCPN-M) was elected vice president on October 31 with 325 votes to 212 for Amiya Kumar YADAV (NC).

On August 3, 2016, Prachanda was elected prime minister for a second time. He appointed a coalition government that included the UCPN-M, the NC, the Communist Party of Nepal (United)—CPN (United), and the RPP.

Constitution and government. The *panchayat* system in operation prior to the May 1980 referendum provided for a hierarchically arranged parallel series of assemblies and councils encompassing four different levels: village (*gaun*) and town (*nagar*), district (*jilla*), zone (*anchal*), and national (*Rastriya Panchayat*). The members of the village and town assemblies were directly elected, members of the other bodies being indirectly elected by bodies directly below them in the hierarchy. The constitutional changes introduced in December 1980 provided for direct, rather than indirect, election to a nonpartisan National Assembly; designation of the prime minister by the assembly, rather than by the king; and parliamentary responsibility of cabinet members.

Under the 1990 constitution the remaining vestiges of the *panchayat* system were abandoned in favor of multiparty parliamentary government, with the king's role substantially curtailed. Executive powers were exercised jointly by the king and a Council of Ministers, the latter headed by a prime minister who, although named by the king, had to command a majority in the popularly elected lower house of Parliament, the House of Representatives. An upper chamber, the National Assembly, contained both indirectly elected and nominated members. The constitution could be amended by a two-thirds majority of the lower house, save for entrenched provisions dealing with such matters as human rights, the basic structure of the governmental system, and the rights of parties. Treaties and other major state agreements required approval by a two-thirds majority of both houses in joint session. The judicial hierarchy encompassed district courts, appellate courts, and a Supreme Court with powers of constitutional review.

The May 18, 2006, proclamation by the House of Representatives, which stripped King Gyanendra of his rights and powers, specified that the House was "sovereign... until another constitutional arrangement is made." Executive authority was delegated to the Council of Ministers, which was responsible to the House. The House also assumed full authority over the Nepalese Army (renamed from Royal Nepal Army), made the king's property and income subject to taxation, and declared Nepal to be a secular state. Further, the proclamation declared that the 1990 constitution and prevailing laws "shall be nullified to the extent of inconsistency" with the proclamation. An additional measure passed on June 10 specifically stripped the king of the veto and of his power to sign legislation into law.

The 167-article interim constitution adopted in January 2007 enumerated a wide range of "fundamental rights," including those of free expression, assembly, and equal protection. It endowed the Council of Ministers with executive authority and stated that "no power regarding the governance of the country shall be vested in the king," but it stopped short of naming the prime minister as head of state. The interim constitution also established a unicameral Interim Legislature-Parliament pending election of a Constituent Assembly tasked with determining the fate of the monarchy and drafting a permanent constitution. The existing judicial system was left in place. Amending the interim constitution required a two-thirds vote of the legislature, which in late December 2007 passed an amendment endorsing establishment of a federal republic. The Constituent Assembly, at its inaugural session on May 28, 2008, formally created the republic, abolishing the monarchy entirely after 239 years.

The Fifth Amendment to the interim constitution was approved by the Council of Ministers on June 25, 2008, and adopted by the Constituent Assembly on July 13. This provision allows for the formation of a government through a simple majority vote of the Constituent Assembly. It creates a national president and vice president, although their powers are not specified, executive power being vested in the prime minister. According to the amendment, the president, vice president, prime minister, and Constituent Assembly chair and vice chair are to be selected on the basis of a political understanding; however, if such understanding cannot be reached, they can be elected by a simple majority vote in the assembly. A Constituent Assembly majority is required to remove a prime minister from office through a no-confidence vote. The amendment also stipulates that the leader of the opposition shall be a member of the Constitutional Council, which is responsible for recommending appointees to key posts.

On September 20, 2015, the 2007 interim constitution was replaced by a permanent constitution. The new basic law was ratified by 90 percent (507 of 598) of the assembly. The constitution structured Nepal as a federal republic with seven provinces and 75 districts. The constitution guarantees gender equality and religious rights. The president is indirectly elected by an electoral college that is made up of members of Parliament and the provincial legislatures. The vice president is elected simultaneously and must be either a different gender or different ethnic group than the president. A new bicameral legislature, the Parliament, would be created (see Legislature, below).

The 1990 constitution endorsed freedom of the press, most importantly by outlawing prior censorship, although on occasion the government attempted to restrict independent media from disseminating news it considered sensationalist or unverified. During the Maoist insurgency a significant number were tortured or killed, either by the police and the military for supporting the Maoist cause or by Maoists for spying or other alleged offenses. The 2007 interim constitution lists freedom to publish and broadcast as a fundamental right. Dozens of journalists were threatened or attacked in 2012 by political groups unhappy with coverage leading up to the May 27 constitution vote (see Current issues, below). In 2016 Reporters Without Borders ranked Nepal 105th out of 180 countries in freedom of the press.

Foreign relations. Although historically influenced by Britain and subsequently by India, Nepal has endeavored to strengthen its independence, particularly after India's annexation of the adjacent state of Sikkim in 1975. Thus, Kathmandu adopted a policy of nonalignment and has sought a balance in regional relations. Nepalese leaders have moved to involve not only India and China, but also Bangladesh, Bhutan, and Pakistan in cooperative endeavors, with primary emphasis on water resource development.

In November 1979 a major issue in relations with China was apparently resolved when an agreement defining Nepal's northern frontier was signed, seen as a model for settling border disputes China had with India and Bhutan.

In 1989 Nepal and India reached an impasse over trade and transit agreements upon which the Nepalese economy was highly dependent. Factors influencing India's reluctance to renew the treaties included recent Nepalese arms purchases from China, the levying of a 55 percent tariff on Indian goods, and the enactment of legislation requiring non-Nepalese to obtain work permits. The agreements were revived following an announcement by Prime Minister Bhattarai in 1990 that his government had postponed receipt of the latest Chinese arms shipment.

In January 1996 the Nepalese and Indian foreign ministers signed an agreement in Kathmandu calling for a joint hydroelectric project in the Mahakali River basin. The $5 billion undertaking was bitterly opposed by a faction of the CPN (UML). The Indo-Nepal Mahakali Integrated Development Treaty was ratified in September.

In the 1990s successive governments expressed concern about an influx of ethnic Nepalese from nearby Bhutan. Although some claimed to be descendants of 19th-century settlers, Bhutanese authorities insisted that most had relocated to Bhutan in the 1980s and were illegal immigrants. An agreement was reached in April 1994 on how to categorize the more than 90,000 Bhutanese of Nepalese origin stranded in eastern Nepal. However, subsequent bilateral talks failed to resolve the dispute. As of April 2013 nearly 80,000 had been resettled from the camps, the majority in the United States. (For additional details, see the entry on Bhutan.)

On January 23, 2007, the UN Security Council established a UN Mission in Nepal (UNMIN) to help maintain the cease-fire, monitor sequestration of arms by the Maoists and the Nepalese Army, and oversee the Constituent Assembly election. The UNMIN mandate was repeatedly extended but expired on January 15, 2011. The UCPN-M sought to extend the mission but was blocked in the Constituent Assembly by opposition from the CPN (UML) and the NC, which both supported an immediate cessation of UNMIN.

In September 2012 the United States removed the Unified Communist Party of Nepal (Maoist) from its list of terrorist organizations, noting that the party had abandoned its militant past and was taking steps toward reconciliation.

New York-based rights group Human Rights Watch released a report in April 2014 revealing the extent to which China pressures Nepal regarding the treatment of Tibetan refugees, including limited movement, subjection to security forces, and keeping them under surveillance. An estimated 20,000 Tibetans live in Nepal.

During an August 2014 state visit, Indian prime minister Narendra Modi spoke in the Constituent Assembly and urged Nepalese lawmakers to continue the work of drafting the new constitution.

From April to December 2015 Nepal experienced a significant fuel shortage. Nepalese officials accused the Indian government of creating an unofficial blockade at border crossings. (India had voiced concerns that the new constitution was not broad based and that it discriminated against the Madhesi people, who had ethnic ties to India). Indian officials blamed the slowdown in deliveries on the reluctance of truck drivers to cross into Nepal, while violent protests against the constitution were ongoing and the Madhesi were blockading trade routes. Relations between the two nations improved dramatically, and fuel deliveries resumed after the adoption of a constitutional amendment designed to increase the representation of the Madhesis. Meanwhile, on November 5, 2015, Nepal and China agreed to open seven new border crossings between their countries.

Current issues. On May 3, 2012, Bhattarai's cabinet resigned after the leaders of the major political parties decided to form a new government under national consensus toward the goal of completing a new constitution by the May 27 deadline, a process hindered by failure to agree on the number, boundaries, and names of the country's states. The new national unity government, which included representatives from the country's major parties except the CPN (UML), the unity government failed to meet the deadline, and the legislature was disbanded upon the expiration of their term at midnight on May 27, without option for term extension. Nepal plunged into legal uncertainty, which Bhattarai tried to remedy by calling for elections to be held on November 22. Opposition political leaders meanwhile denounced the move as a power grab.

The UCPN-M ruling party split on June 19 when hard-line party member Mohan BAIDYA Kiran left to form the new Nepal Communist Party (Maoist—NCP-M). Thirty-three members of the UCPN-M defected to the NCP-M on August 25.

In late July Nepal's Election Commission announced confirmed that the country lacked the legal framework to hold legitimate elections on November 21, the date named by Bhattarai, although the elections were not officially postponed until November 20, after the CPN (UML) and the NC refused to take part in polling organized under Maoist leadership. President Yadav called for leaders of the parties to form a unity government by November 29, a deadline twice extended and ultimately unheeded.

Progress came in February 2013, when leaders of the UCPN-M, NC, CPN-UML, and UDMF began negotiating a plan for Chief Justice Khil Raj Regmi to lead a nonpartisan interim government until elections could be held. Talks were temporarily derailed when the UCPN-M demanded that amnesty for past crimes by Maoists be included in the agreement. In a marathon 13-hour session on March 13, the parties agreed to an 11-point pact, addressing the composition of a truth and reconciliation commission and integration of Maoist fighters into the national army, paving way for Regmi to take office on March 14, leading an 11-member cabinet, with the expectation that elections would be held by June 21 (viewed to be ambitious, given that the leading parties had not yet settled on a legal framework). His term ends upon the election of a new government, or in December 2013. The formation of the interim government generated significant opposition, some arguing it to be unconstitutional because it violated separation of powers. Led by the CPN-M, 22 parties protested Regmi's inauguration.

In mid-March the UCPN-M, NC, CPN-UML, and UDMF formed a "high level political committee," chaired on a one-month rotational basis by each party chief. The coalition was highly criticized from the outside as well as from within; in April CPN-UML member Pradip GYANWALI criticized the committee for unconstitutionally ruling the country and shutting other parties out.

Three months after taking office, the Regmi government announced in June that Constituent Assembly elections would take place on November 19, after the promulgation of an amendment removing the stipulation that parties must secure 1 percent of the vote to win a seat in the proportional representation system, a step reportedly taken to ensure all parties' participation in writing the constitution. Three parties—the CPN-M, the Federal Socialist Party Nepal, and the Madhesi Janaadhikar Forum–Nepal—vocally refused to participate in the election in protest of the installation of the Regmi government. By June the election commission reported that 11.7 million of an estimated 15.4 million eligible voters had already registered.

The week before elections were due to be held, the CPN-M announced a day-long general strike and subsequent transit strike to protest the polls. Nonetheless, balloting proceeded as scheduled on November 19 with 70 percent voter turnout, a record high. International observers praised the electoral process.

Two days after the elections, the UCPN-M called for a halt to vote counting, alleging the Election Commission and military had rigged the vote. Meanwhile, the NC, with a clear majority of 196 seats, set about attempting to negotiate a unity government.

On December 24 the NC and the CPN-UML agreed to form a board of inquiry to investigate electoral integrity, thereby appeasing the UCPN-M. The members of the Second Constituent Assembly were sworn in on January 21, 2014, and convened the following day. Sushil Koirala, a widely respected NC member, was elected prime minister by parliament on February 10 with more than two-thirds of the vote. He was sworn in the next day, but the CPN-UML boycotted the ceremony and backed out of the coalition government, protesting that Koirala did not award the powerful home ministry to the CPN-UML. On February 25 Koirala named an expanded cabinet, which included Bam Dev Guatam of the CPN-UML as deputy prime minister and heading the home portfolio.

On April 18, 2014, an avalanche on Mount Everest killed 16 Nepali Sherpas, leading to a suspension of the climbing season.

On September 22 activist Nanda Prasad ADHIKARI died after staging an 11-month hunger strike to protest the government for not providing justice for his son, who was kidnapped and then killed during the Maoist uprising. His wife, Ganga MAYA, who had started a hunger strike at the same time as her husband, continued her protest. On October 8 treason charges were filed at a special court against C.K. RAUT, who was charged with leading a secessionist campaign in the southern Madhesi region.

On April 25, 2015, a 7.5 magnitude earthquake struck 77 km (47.8 miles) northwest of Kathmandu, killing 8,617, injuring more than 22,000, and damaging more than 473,000 homes. The earthquake also triggered an avalanche on Mount Everest, killing 22. On May 12, 2015, another earthquake, 7.3 in magnitude, struck in the Dolakha Valley, one of 250 aftershocks from the April 25 quake. The May 12 earthquake killed 154. Due to the aftershocks, more than 800,000 homes were destroyed or damaged, including a series of cultural and world heritage landmarks. Rescue and recovery efforts were slowed by the rugged terrain and the aftershocks. On the anniversary of the disaster, there were widespread demonstrations against the government because of the slow pace of recovery. By June 2016 there were still more 600,000 Nepalese in temporary housing. International donors pledged significant aid. India led donors with $1 billion in cash and supplies, followed by the United Kingdom, with $130 million, and Germany, $68 million.

POLITICAL PARTIES

Political formations were banned by royal decree in 1960, although de facto party affiliations continued. The 1990 constitution prohibited restrictions on political parties. At the time of the 1999 election, there were 101 recognized parties, of which 30 offered candidates. Only six parties captured 3 percent or more of the vote, a requirement for designation as a "national party."

A total of 62 parties applied to the Election Commission for formal recognition prior to the assembly election. By late July 2007 about 40 had been registered and assigned election symbols. A total of 25 parties won seats in the Constituent Assembly, including several new parties. In the 2013 election only eight parties won seats in the Constituent Assembly.

Government Parties:

Nepali Congress (NC). Founded in 1947, the NC long sought abolition of the *panchayat* system and defied the regime by holding a national convention in Kathmandu in 1985, after which it launched a civil disobedience movement (*satyagraha*). Following the widespread popular agitation that began in February 1990, NC president K. P. Bhattarai was asked to head a coalition government pending nationwide balloting in May 1991. Although the NC won 110 of 205 seats in the house in 1991, Bhattarai failed to secure reelection and yielded the office of prime minister to G. P. Koirala, who served until 1994. Sher Bahadur Deuba served as prime minister in a coalition government from 1995 to 1997. Koirala returned as prime minister in April 1998, although his cabinet provoked considerable intraparty controversy over the inclusion of what some members considered "corrupt" ministers.

During the parliamentary campaign of 1999, Koirala stepped aside in favor of Bhattarai, who returned as prime minister when the NC won a clear majority of 111 seats in the House of Representatives. Conflict continued between Bhattarai and supporters of Koirala, who had retained the party presidency. Bhattarai resigned on March 16, 2000. Meeting two days later for the party's first open leadership election, the parliamentarians selected Koirala as their leader by a 69–43 vote over Deuba. Accordingly, King Birendra redesignated Koirala as prime minister on March 20.

On August 8, 2000, Koirala dismissed the minister of water resources, Khum Bahadur KHADKA, for calling for Koirala's resignation. Although Koirala beat back another challenge by Deuba's supporters at a party convention in January 2001, he resigned as prime minister on July 19. Deuba then defeated Secretary General Sushil Koirala, 72–40, for the party leadership and was designated prime minister by the king.

In the May 2002 the NC disciplinary committee expelled Deuba for failing to consult the party before seeking parliamentary extension of the country's state of emergency. Deuba's supporters then expelled Koirala at a "general convention" in June 16–19. Deuba to registered his faction as the Nepali Congress (Democratic)—NC(D), following a decision by the Election Commission that the Koirala faction held ownership of the name "Nepali Congress," taking 40 of the NC lower house representatives with him.

In the months following the king's October 2002 decisions to dissolve the House of Representatives and replace Prime Minister Deuba with the National Democratic Party's L. B. Chand, the NC joined the CPN (UML) and other, smaller parties in challenging the constitutionality of the moves. The NC was the prime mover in the formation of the JPM in April–May 2003 and of the SPA two years later. The NC(D) also joined the SPA. Deuba had been reappointed prime minister for the third time in June 2004, only to be dismissed once again on February 1, 2005, placed under house arrest, and convicted by a corruption commission. However, he was released in February 2006 and went on to regain leadership of the NC(D) parliamentary delegation.

With election of a Constituent Assembly in the offing, the NC and the NC(D) reunited on September 25, 2007. A collateral decision to support a republican form of government led former prime minister Bhattarai to resign from the party. The NC won 110 of 601 Constituent Assembly seats in April 2008. The party joined the coalition government headed by Madhav Kumar Nepal in May 2009. Koirala angered some in the party by nominating his daughter Sujata KOIRALA for the post of foreign minister. In June, in a contested election for leader of the party's parliamentary group, Ram Chandra Poudel defeated former prime minister Deuba. G. P. Koirala died on March 20, 2010, at the age of 86.

The party's 12th general convention, held in September 2010, marked a continuation of the struggle between the Koirala and Deuba factions. In the election for party president, Sushil Koirala defeated Deuba by a vote of 1,652–1,317. The Deuba faction also opposed the party's continuing support for its prime ministerial candidate, Ram Chandra Poudel.

In March 2013 Sushil Koirala put the party's support behind the interim government. A split between Koirala and Deuba, apparently resolved in February 2012 when the factions shared the task of appointing chiefs of sister organizations, resurfaced in 2013 when Deuba supporters bristled over party appointments by Koirala in May.

Following the Constituent Assembly balloting of November 2013, in which the NC won 196 seats, the largest share of directly elected seats, Sushil Koirala led efforts to build a unification government with support of all parties. Efforts were abandoned and in late January, the NC negotiated an alliance with the CPN (UML).

At the party's 13th convention in March 2016, Deuba was elected NC president.

Leaders: Sher Bahadur DEUBA (President of the Party and Former Prime Minister), Ram Chandra PAUDEL.

Communist Party of Nepal (Unified Marxist-Leninist) (CPN [UML]) (*Nepala Kamyunishta Parti [Ekikrit Marksbadi ra Leninbadi]*). Sometimes referred to as the United (or Unified) Communist Party of Nepal (UCPN), the CPN (UML) was formed in 1991 by the merger of two factions of the Communist Party of Nepal: the CPN (Marxist) and the CPN (M-L). In April 1990 the CPN (Marxist) and the CPN (ML) had joined with five other leftist formations, three pro-Soviet CPN factions, a pro-Chinese group, and the Nepal Workers' and Peasants' Party (below), in a United Leftist Front (ULF) in support of the restoration of democracy. This diverse grouping became moribund prior to the 1991 poll.

In May 1991 Man Mohan Adhikari was elected head of the CPN (UML) parliamentary group and, therefore, leader of the opposition. Following the November 1994 election, he was sworn in as prime minister of Nepal's first communist government, but he was obliged to resign after losing a no-confidence vote in September 1995. The CPN (UML) subsequently participated in the coalition government formed by Prime Minister Chand in March 1997, before joining that of Prime Minister Koirala in December 1998.

In March 1998 more than half the CPN (UML) legislators reorganized under the former CPN (ML) title to protest the 1996 water-sharing agreement with India. In February 2002 the bulk of the CPN (ML) members rejoined the parent party.

In the May 1999 election the CPN (UML) won 71 seats, down from the 88 it had claimed in 1994. In early 2001 the CPN (UML) was largely responsible for the legislative boycotts and disruptions that led the king to prorogue both houses of parliament in April.

Having left the JPM following Prime Minister Deuba's reappointment, in July 2004 the CPN (UML) joined an expanded, four-party cabinet, in which Bharat Mohan Adhikari served as deputy prime minister until the entire government was dismissed on February 1, 2005.

The party won the third highest number of seats in the Constituent Assembly election in April 2008, splitting the left-wing vote with the Maoists and other communist groupings. Jhalanath Khanal was elected party chair at a convention in February 2009, defeating K. P. Oli. The party left the Maoist-led government in May after Prime Minister Dahal, the Maoist leader, dismissed the army chief of staff without consulting the other government parties. When Dahal resigned, the CPN (UML) was invited to form a new government. M. K. Nepal was elected prime minister, and party members assumed several key ministries. The party subsequently was divided in its stance toward the Maoists, but in June 2010 Nepal offered his resignation to facilitate the formation of a consensus government. Khanal was elected prime minister in February 2011 but resigned that August, and the CPN (UML) joined the opposition.

In December 2012 the CPN (UML) joined calls from other opposition parties for the resignation of Prime Minister Bhattarai. Though initially split over the proposal for a Regmi-led interim government, the party eventually threw its support behind the measure on March 13, 2013. Days later, the party joined the three other largest parties in forming the HLPC.

The CPN (UML) secured the second largest vote share in the November 2013 elections, with a total of 175 seats. The party negotiated an alliance with the NC, on the terms that the CPN (UML) hold the Home Affairs portfolio in cabinet. At internal elections in July 2014, K. P. Sharma Oli was elected chair.

The UML was key in negotiating the new constitution ratified in October 2015. Also in October, the party's deputy leader, Bidhya Devi BHANDARI, was elected president.

Leader: Bidhya Devi BHANDARI (President of the Republic).

Unified Communist Party of Nepal (Maoist) (UCPN-M). Established in 1994 by a breakaway faction of the CPN (Unity Center), in 1996 the CPN-M launched the "People's War" insurgency, which continued and intensified for ten years. In August 2000 the Maoists announced that they had formed a People's Liberation Army (PLA). They also set up a United People's Revolutionary Council as a quasi-central government for the areas under its control.

Despite having rejected previous government overtures, in early 2000 the Maoists indicated they would be willing to open discussions related to a 32-point list of demands. At the first round of peace talks with the Deuba government on August 30, 2001, the Maoist representative Krishna Bahadur Mahara pressed for an end to the monarchy, the formation of an interim government, the establishment of a constituent assembly to draft a new constitution, and the release of all Maoist prisoners. No significant progress was made, and the insurgents abruptly ended a four-month-old cease-fire in November. A January–August 2003 cease-fire and the resultant peace talks also came to nothing, as the Maoists continued their insistence on elections for a constituent assembly. In the following 18 months the insurgency expanded its reach and its tactics, initiating general strikes and, on more than one occasion, blockading Kathmandu.

With opposition to King Gyanendra's "autocratic monarchy" mounting, secret talks between the CPN-M and the SPA began even before a unilateral Maoist cease-fire in September 2005. Further discussions then led to the November 2005 12-point plan for restoring democracy and bringing the CPN-M into the political mainstream. In early May 2006 one of the first measures of the new Koirala government was to end the party's proscription.

The June 16, 2006, eight-point agreement with the new government, accomplished following the first face-to-face meeting between Prime Minister Koirala and Prachanda, granted the Maoists much of what they had been seeking, including the election of a constituent assembly in the near future and a role in an interim government, while committing them to dissolving the rural governments they had formed and to permitting international supervision of their army and weapons prior to the election. A comprehensive peace agreement followed in November, ahead of the promulgation of the interim constitution on January 15, 2007. The CPN-M, effecting a transformation from a guerrilla army to a political party, joined the Interim Legislature-Parliament with 83 seats. In September 2007 the CPN-M withdrew its four ministers from the government, rejoining after securing a commitment from the Council of Ministers to support establishment of a republic.

The Maoists took first place in the election on April 10, 2008, securing 220 of the assembly's 575 elected seats. On August 15 the assembly elected Pushpa Kamal Dahal to the office of prime minister.

In January 2009 the CPN-M merged with the **Communist Party of Nepal (Unity Center *Mashal*)** (CPN [UCM]). (For a history of the latter party, see the People's Front Nepal, below.) Renaming itself the Unified Communist Party of Nepal (Maoist), the party formally renounced the "Prachandapath"—the leader's adaptation of Maoist principles to Nepalese conditions—as its guiding doctrine.

The party advocated for the integration into Nepal's army of its nearly 20,000 PLA combatants, who were confined to temporary quarters under UN monitoring. When President Yadav overturned Prime Minister Dahal's dismissal of the army chief of staff on May 3, 2009, Dahal claimed the move exceeded the president's constitutional authority and threatened civilian control of the military. He resigned the following day, and the party shifted to the opposition, launching intense protests. Maoist partisans stormed the Constituent Assembly on May 18 and boycotted the election for a new prime minister. Following Prime Minister Nepal's resignation at the end of June 2010, Dahal again stepped forward as a candidate for prime minister, but neither he nor anyone else was able to muster the necessary two-thirds support, and Dahal, under increasing criticism for questionable financial dealings, withdrew from consideration on September 26, after seven ballots.

Meanwhile, within the party, former party leader Matrika YADAV in 2009 rejected Dahal's deviation from the revolutionary path and organized a splinter party that adopted the UCPN-M's former name, the Communist Party of Nepal (Maoist). Mani THAPA formed the **Revolutionary Communist Party of Nepal** (RCPN). In November 2010, in the context of an ongoing party plenum, the hard-liner Mohan BAIDYA Kiran called for a renewal of the people's revolt, while Baburam Bhattarai advocated moderation. Both viewed Dahal as dictatorial and questioned his integrity. Bhattarai was elected prime minister in August 2011, after Dahal agreed to withdraw from balloting in the Constituent Assembly. The party split in June 2012, as the dissenting faction formed the Communist Party of Nepal (Maoist) (below).

In February 2013 Bhattarai agreed to resign as prime minister to make way for Chief Justice Regmi to lead the interim government, a decision backed by the party. In March the UCPN-M joined the NC, CPN-UML, and UDMF in forming the High Level Political Committee (HLPC). Both decisions spurred dissent within the party, with many concerned about the constitutionality of Regmi's government, and the exclusion of smaller parties from the committee.

Two days after election day on November 19, the UCPN-M called for vote counting to stop, alleging that the Election Commission and army had conspired to rig the election. Koirala appealed to Dahal to join a consensus government, but the UCPN-M boycotted meeting of all parties held on December 4. The NC and CPN-UML agreed to form a board of inquiry into the election process on December 24, satisfying UCPN-M demands, and the party agreed to sit in the CA as the opposition. The UCPN-M allied with six Madhesi parties in July 2014, including the MJF and the MJF-L (below).

In the November 2013 elections, the UCPN-M suffered a large defeat, winning just 80 seats and falling to a distant third behind NC's 196 and UML's 175 seats. On September 26, 2015, Baburam BHATTARAI, the vice chair of the party, announced he was leaving to create a new "political force." Dahal became prime minister of a coalition government in August 2016.

Leaders: Pushpa Kamal DAHAL "Comrade PRACHANDA" (Prime Minister and Chair of the Party), Nanda Kishor PUN (Chief Commander of PLA).

National Democratic Party (*Rastriya Prajatantra* Party—RPP). A monarchist party comprising largely former *panchayat* members and supporters, the RPP was formed in 1992 by the merger of two groups (both calling themselves the National Democratic Party), one led by S. B. Thapa and the other led by L. B. Chand. The unified RPP won 20 legislative seats in the 1994 election. It joined the government as a member of the NC-led coalition in September 1995. The demise of the coalition in March 1997 led to Chand's designation as prime minister in a CPN (UML)-RPP-NSP cabinet, which survived less than seven months before being replaced by an RPP-NSP (and subsequently NC) government under Thapa. In January 1998 the RPP expelled former prime minister Chand and nine supporters for threatening to back a no-confidence vote against Prime Minister Thapa, who had asked the king to dissolve the House of Representatives. The rebel group quickly formed a "New RPP," commonly called the RPP (Chand).

The RPP won 11 percent of the vote and 11 seats in the May 1999 election, while the RPP (Chand) claimed a meager 3 percent and no seats. The Thapa and Chand groups reunited in January 2000. In October 2002 the king reappointed Chand prime minister, but Chand resigned in May 2003 and was in turn replaced by former prime minister Thapa. The change further widened the rift between the Chand and Thapa factions in the party, and in December 2003 the RPP called for Thapa's resignation. Thapa resigned in May 2004.

By late 2004 the rupture within the RPP appeared complete. Thapa had stated his intention to form a new party, which was launched in March 2005 as the ***Rastriya Janshakti* Party** (RJP). (For more on the RJP's activities between 2005 and 2013, see the 2013 *Handbook*.) The departure of Thapa's supporters did not end the factionalism within the RPP. In September 2005 the RPP announced that it would support the "prodemocracy agitation" led by the SPA. In January 2006 President P. S. Rana ousted ten members of the party's central committee, including six cabinet ministers. The royalist dissidents ultimately formed the RPP (Nepal)—above.

With nine seats, the RPP became the largest opposition party in the Interim Legislature-Parliament. Party divisions, as well as the RPP's opposition to ending the monarchy, weakened its showing in the Constituent Assembly balloting; the party won eight seats. It joined the government in June 2009.

In May 2013 Thapa's RJP and the RPP merged, with Thapa assuming leadership of the unified party. The RPP won a total of 13 seats in the Consituent Assembly elections on November 19, 2013. Support for the ruling NC and CPN (UML) government earned the RPP two portfolios in Koirala's cabinet. Thapa resigned the chairmanship in June, and it rotated to Rana. The RPP joined the 2016 coalition government.

Leaders: Pashupati Shumsher RANA (Chair), Surya Bahadur THAPA (Former Prime Minister and Senior Leader), Lokendra Bahadur CHAND (Reclaiming Member and Former Prime Minister).

Other Legislative Parties:

National Democratic Party (Nepal) (*Rastriya Prajatantra* Party [Nepal]—RPP [Nepal]). The RPP (Nepal) began as a faction of the RPP (above) that approved participating in King Gyanendra's government after the king deposed the democratic government in 2005. In January 2007 it absorbed two other small parties: the ***Rastriya Prajatantra* Party (*Rastrabadi*)**—RPP (National Democratic Party [Nationalist]), led by Rajeshwor DEVKOTA, itself an earlier splinter from the RPP; and the ***Nepal Bidwat Parishad***, led by Jit Bahadur ARJEL.

At the inaugural session of the Constituent Assembly on May 28, 2008, the RPP (Nepal)'s four members cast the only votes against forming a republic. The right-wing party continued to favor popular referendums on restoring the monarchy and on whether Nepal should be a secular or a Hindu state.

The RPP (Nepal) won 24 seats in the 2013 general elections. On December 20 Tanka DHAKAL led a faction to leave the party, claiming party leader Kamal Thapa did not allot the proportional representation seats accurately. However, following the Election Commission's rejection of Dhakal's application to form a new party, the factions reunited in early 2014.

Leader: Kamal THAPA.

Madhesi People's Rights Forum (Nepal) (*Madheshi Janadhikar* Forum—MJF). The MJF began in 1997 as a civic organization advocating for the rights of the Madhesis—the indigenous people who make up the majority in Nepal's southern plain—to self-determination. An uprising and general strike in January 2007, protesting against the interim constitution, which the MJF said ignored the interests of the marginalized groups, escalated into violence resulting in some 50 deaths.

In August 2007, despite some factional opposition, the MJF signed an agreement with the government on 22 points. Later, the MJF declared that the government had failed to fulfill the terms of the agreement and called for militant protests around November 22, the scheduled date for the Constituent Assembly election. A second wave of violence arose in the Terai in February 2008.

After the uprising, the government agreed to UDMF demands, including the creation of an autonomous Madhesi state. In its first electoral contest the MJF won 52 seats, making it the fourth largest party in the assembly. It joined the Maoist-led government and party leader Upendra Yadav was named foreign minister.

Following Prime Minister Dahal's resignation in May 2009, the incoming prime minister Nepal offered the deputy prime minister position to Bijaya Kumar Gachchhadar, the leader of the MJF parliamentary group, without the approval of the MJF executive committee. This led to a bitter division, resulting in the expulsion of Gachchhadar and six others. Gachchhadar, however, claimed the support of the majority of the party's lawmakers. His faction continued to participate in the government and later received additional ministerial portfolios (see MJF-L, below). Yadav accused the leaders of the CPN (UML) and NC of intentionally provoking a split in the MJF and joined the opposition. In February 2008 the MJF and its breakaway factions joined with the *Sadbhavana* Party (SP, see below) and the *Terai Madhesh* Democratic Party (*Tarai Madhesh Loktantrik* Party—TMLP) (below) to form the **United Democratic Madhesi Front** (UDMF), which negotiated an agreement to join the UCPN-M government.

After movements in summer 2013 toward a unification of Madhesi parties, Yadav pulled the MJF out of negotiations with the TMLP (below), noting that an alliance of Madhesi parties should be policy based. In the general election of November 2013, the MJF won two seats and was allotted eight proportional seats.

Leader: Upendra YADAV (Chair).

Madhesi People's Rights Forum (Democratic) (*Madheshi Janadhikar* Forum [*Loktantrik*] (MJF-L). Formed by a fissure in the indigenous MJF (above), the MJF-L was established in mid-2009 after Bijaya Kumar Gachchhadar accepted the position of deputy prime minister under Madhav Kumar Nepal, without prior approval of MJF leadership. Gachchhadar, who had previously belonged to the NC and then the NC(D), refused to decline the high office and claimed leadership of the party, asserting that a majority of MJF Constituent Assembly members supported him. He and the other dissidents, who included 28 members of the Constituent Assembly, then formed the MJF-L. The MJF-L joined the UCPN-M coalition government in August 2011. Gachchhadar was reappointed deputy prime minister. In July 2012 central committee member Sanjay SHAH defected to join the *Sadbhavana* Party (below). The MJF-L won four elected and ten proportional seats in the 2013 balloting. In July 2014 the MJF-L joined five other Madhesi parties in allying with the UCPN-M.

Leader: Bijaya Kumar GACHCHHADAR (Chair).

***Rastriya Madhes Samajwadi* Party** (RMS. Formed in June 2012 by senior Madhesi leader Sharad Singh Bhandari, the RMS is a splinter group of the MJF-L. Nine party leaders, including Bhandari, were expelled by Deputy Prime Minister Gachchhadar when they refused to support the decision to back Bhattari's call for November 22 elections. In February 2013 Bhandari backed the interim government, arguing for it to remain nonpartisan. After initial efforts to form an encompassing Madhesi alliance failed, Bhandari participated in a last ditch effort in early November 2013 to forge and electoral alliance with the TMLP and the SP (both below) to promote the strongest Madhesi candidates. The party won three proportional seats in November 2013 balloting.

Leader: Sharad Singh BHANDARI (Chair).

***Terai Madhesh* Democratic Party** (*Tarai Madhesh Loktantrik* Party (TMLP). An ethnic and regional party founded in 2008 by former NC leader Mahanta Thakur, the TMLP demands that Madhesis be granted an autonomous province and that Madhesis and all ethnic groups be given proportional representation in all state organizations. In February 2008 the TMLP joined with the MJF and the SP to form the UDMF. The TMLP split in December 2010, with defecting members forming the ***Tarai Madhesh Loktantrik* Party (Nepal)**, led by Mahendra Raya YADAV (later dubbed the *Terai Madhes Sadbhavana* Party, below). The TMLP won 20 seats in the Constituent Assembly voting and joined the government in June 2009.

Ahead of the elections expected in November 2013, in June, Thakur urged Madhesi parties to unite in a single alliance, and resumed his effort, again unsuccessfully, two weeks before the election. In November 19 balloting, the TMLP secured a total of 11 seats.

Leader: Mahanta THAKUR (Chair).

***Sadbhavana* Party** (SP). The SP separated from the Nepal Goodwill Party (*Anandi Devi*) (NSP-A, below) in 2007, and in February 2008 it joined the MJF and the TMLP to form the UDMF.

The SP's leader, Rajendra Mahato, had been general secretary of NSP-A and a cabinet minister. Mahato announced his resignation from the interim parliament on January 19, 2008, accusing the government of ignoring the demands of the Madhesis. He was among nine SP members elected to the Constituent Assembly, and he was appointed minister of commerce in the Dahal cabinet. On May 3, 2009, the party withdrew from the Maoist-led government to protest the firing of the army chief of staff.

The party initially chose not to join Prime Minister Nepal's government, but in July 2009 Mahato joined the cabinet. The SP joined the 2011 UCPN-M government. Meanwhile, reports indicated the emergence of a breakaway faction of the party, calling itself the **Federal *Sadbhavana* Party** (FSP). A leader of the FSP, Anil Kumar Jha, was appointed minister of industry in the 2011 government. In January 2012 a faction of the party broke off to form the ***Rastriya Sadbhavana* Party**.

In July 2013 amid calls for unity among Madhesi parties in the November election, the SP sent a letter seeking unification with the UDMF, which ultimately did not succeed. The SP won one seat and five proportional seats in the November 2013 election. In July 2014 it joined a UCPN-M-led alliance.

Leaders: Rajendra MAHATO (Chair), Manish SUMAN (General Secretary).

Communist Party of Nepal (Marxist-Leninist) (CPN [ML]). On March 5, 1998, 46 of the CPN (UML)'s 89 house members, led by former deputy prime minister Bamdev Gautam and others, left the parent grouping and formed the CPN (ML), objecting to the water-sharing arrangements in the 1996 Indo-Nepal Mahakali Integrated Development Treaty. Describing the new formation's leaders voiced support for nationalism and democracy, and labeled the United States imperialist and India a "regional hegemonist."

The CPN (ML) joined the NC in the government of August–December 1998; its departure over policy differences guaranteed the administration's collapse. Despite winning 7 percent of the vote in May 1999, the party failed to capture any lower house seats. In August 2001 the CPN (ML) and the CPN (UML) agreed to discuss reunification and proceeded in February 2002. Some CPN (ML) leaders rejected reunification and restructured the party.

At a party convention in January 2007, a rift developed in the CPN (ML) central committee, with a faction led by Rishi Kattel subsequently helping to start a new party, the CPN (Unified)—see below.

The CPN (ML) formed the ULF with other CPN splinters and joined the Seven-Party Alliance in the Koirala government. Contesting independently for the Constituent Assembly in 2008, it won eight seats.

In August 2010 Jagat Bahadur BOGATI, objecting in part to General Secretary C. P. Mainali's decision not to support the Maoist's Dahal for prime minister, led a group of dissidents, including four Constituent Assembly members, to form a new party, the **Communist Party of Nepal (Marxist-Leninist-Samajwadi)** (CPN-ML [*Samajwadi*]).

In July 2013 CPN (ML) leaders met with the HLPC over concerns about the distribution of citizenship certificates. The CPN (ML) contested the November 2013 elections, winning five proportional seats in the Constituent Assembly.

Leaders: Chandra Prakash MAINALI (General Secretary), N. P. ACHARYA, Damber SHRESTHA.

Federal Socialist Party-Nepal (FSP [N]). Launched in November 2012 by Ashok Rai, the former vice chair of the CPN (UML), the FSP (N) advocates for a federalist system based on identity. In an effort to demonstrate commitment to inclusive democracy, the party committee includes members from Brahmin, Chhettri, Madhes, and Dalit communities. The party won five proportional seats in the Constituent Assembly.

Leader: Ashok RAI.

Communist Party of Nepal (United) (CPN [United]). The CPN (United) traces its origin to the pro-Moscow branch of the original

CPN, which was launched in 1949 but suffered repeated fractures beginning in 1982. In 1991 the CPN (Democratic), led by Bishnu Bahadur MANANDHAR; the CPN (Varma) of K. N. VARMA; and the **CPN (Amatya)**, led by Tulsi Lal AMATYA, formed a unified party, the CPN (United). In December 1993 Amatya broke from the CPN (United) and led his faction into the CPN (UML).

In 1998 the party formed a United Marxist Front (UMF) with the small CPN (Marxist), led by Prabhu Narayan CHAUDHARI. In 2001 the Varma faction joined the CPN (UML).

Although the CPN (United) and the CPN (Marxist) merged in September 2005, the party split in late 2006. The CPN (United) was reestablished in 2007 under the leadership of Chandra Dev Joshi. As part of the ULF, it joined the governing Seven-Party Alliance, but in 2008 the ULF was dissolved.

The CPN (United) won seats for five members in the Constituent Assembly. Party leader Ganesh Shah was given a ministry portfolio in the Maoist-led government. The party boycotted the election of a new prime minister in May 2009, but in July T. P. Sharma was appointed to Prime Minister Nepal's cabinet. The CPN (United) did not join the 2011 UCPN-M government. In February 2013 Joshi joined the chorus of opposition leaders calling for the resignation of Prime Minister Bhattarai. The CPN (United) secured three seats in the November 2013 elections.

Leaders: Chandra Dev JOSHI (President), Thakur Prasad SHARMA (Former Minister of Environment, Science, and Technology).

Terai Madhes Sadbhavana **Party** (TMSP). Originally launched as a splinter group from the TMDP led by Mahendra Prasad Yadav under the name ***Tarai Madhesh Loktantrik*** **Party (Nepal)**, the party later adopted the TMSP banner. The party won three seats in the Constituent Assembly.

Leader: Mahendra Prasad YADAV.

National People's Front (*Rastriya Janamorcha* (RJM). The RJM began as electoral front of the CPN (*Mashal*) in the 1990s. It merged with the political front of another CPN splinter in 2002 to form the People's Front Nepal (*Janamorcha Nepal*—JMN, above). After the JMN joined the governing Seven-Party Alliance in 2006, Chita Bahadur K. C. led a faction out of the party and reclaimed the name of the RJM. The party held three seats in the Interim Legislature-Parliament and won four seats in the 2008 Constituent Assembly. The current **CPN (*Mashal*)** is led by Mohan Bikram SINGH.

The RJM was the first party in the Constituent Assembly to oppose any type of federal structure for the Nepalese republic. The party advocates decentralization within the existing unitary system. In July 2010 the party expelled its general secretary, Dilaram ACHARYA, for breaking party discipline. Acharya thereupon announced the formation of ***Rastriya Janamorcha*** **(Nepal)** (RJM-N.

In May 2013 the RJM joined other fringe parties in calling for citizenship reform, and for removal of the provision requiring parties to demonstrate they have 10,000 voters. The RJM won three seats in November 2013 elections.

Leader: Chitra BAHADUR K. C. (Chair).

Nepal Workers' and Peasants' Party (NWPP [Nepal *Majdoor Kisan* Party]). An advocate for the poor and working people, the NWPP began as a Maoist formation but currently advocates nonalignment and a mixed economy. Most of the party's support lies in its stronghold in the Bhaktapur area. It doubled its lower house strength from two to four seats in 1994 but won only 1 in May 1999. The NWPP was a member of the Seven-Party Alliance but declined an invitation to join the government. It agreed to sign the December 2007 23-point agreement with the Maoists despite objections. It won four seats in the 2008 Constituent Assembly election.

In February 2009 the party proposed that Nepal's 14 existing zones become separate states in a federal structure with a president as head of state and government. The party won four seats in the 2013 Constituent Assembly elections.

Leader: Narayan Man BIJUKCHHE "Rohit".

National People's Liberation Party (*Rastriya Janamukti* Party). An ethnically based party founded in 1990 by the indigenous leaders M. S. Thapa and Gore Bahadur KHAPANGI, the party favors a federal system based on autonomous ethnic federal units. The party won two seats in the 2008 Constituent Assembly balloting, which it retained in the 2013 elections.

Leader: K. Suryavanshi MAGAR (General Secretary).

Dalit Janjati **Party** (DJP). The DJP is a party representing Dalits and other marginalized peoples. It held one seat the Constituent Assembly elected in 2008. The DJP won two seats in the general elections of November 2013.

Leader: Bishwendra PASAWAN.

Nepal Family Party (*Nepal Parivar Dal* (NPD). Founded on the vision of Nepal as a single family, the NPD is a utopian socialist party. It won one seat in the general elections of 2008. In the Constituent Assembly elections of 2013, the NPD won two seats.

Leader: Eknath DHAKAL.

Tharuhat Tarai **Party (Nepal)** (TTP [N]). Representing the ethnic Tharu community, the TTP (N) was founded in August 2011. One of the founders, Laxman THARU, was expelled from the party in October 2012 after he attempted to broker a merge of the party without party approval. The TTP (N) won two proportional seats in the November 2013 election.

Leader: Gopal DAHIT.

In addition, the following parties each won one Constituent Assembly seat: ***Sanghiya Sadbhawana*** **Party**, a Madhesi party led by Anil Kumar JHA; the **Khumbuwan National Front Nepal** (*Khumbuwan Rastriya Morcha Nepal*—KRMN), representing the Limbu population in the east, led by Ram Kumar RAI; the **Nepali People's Party** (*Nepali Janata Dal*—NJD), formed in 1995 with the goal of representing Dalits, Janjatis, and women, led by Hari Charan SHAH; the **Great Nepal Party** (*Akhanda Nepal* Party—ANP), a proponent of topography-based federalism led by Kumar Khadka; the ***Sanghiya Lokantrik Rastriya Manch*** **(*Tharuhat*)**; the ***Samajwadi Janata*** **Party**; the **Madhesi People's Rights Forum (Republic)** (*Madhesi Janadhikar* Forum [*Ganatantrik*]—MJF-G), an offshoot of the MJF formed in May 2011 by Jayaprakash Prasad Gupta; the ***Jana Jagaran*** **Party (Nepal)**, led by Lok Mani Dhakal; the ***Madesh Samata*** **Party Nepal**; and the **Nepa National Party** (*Nepa Rastriya* Party), an ethnonationalist party supporting the linguistic and cultural rights of the Newar community, led by Keshavman SHAKYA.

Other Parties:

People's Front Nepal (*Janamorcha Nepal* (JMN). The JMN began as the electoral front for the Communist Party of Nepal (Unity Center *Mashal*) (CPN [UCM]), the formation of which was announced in April 2002 by the leaders of the CPN (Unity Center) and the CPN (*Mashal*). Both parties traced their origins to the pro-Chinese CPN (Fourth Congress), which had been founded in India in 1974 but from which several *Mashal* (Torch) groups emerged in the 1980s. The CPN (Unity Center) was formed in 1990 from the merger of a CPN (Fourth Congress) rump, two *Mashal* factions, and the Nepal Proletarian Labor Organization. (See the 2014 *Handbook* for more on the JMN in the 1990s.)

The April 2002 decision to form the CPN (UCM) was followed in July by an announcement that the SJN and the RJM would also merge as the JMN. In 2006 the JMN became a member of the governing Seven-Party Alliance, a move that the CPN (UCM) rejected. The JMN (KC), led by Chitra Bahadur K. C., left the SPA and registered in 2007 as the reconstituted *Rastriya Janamorcha* (RJM, below). Another JMN faction, the JMN (Ale), led by Chitra Bahadur Ale, later joined in forming the CPN (Unified), also discussed below. A third JMN group, led by Amik SERCHAN, retained the JMN designation, remaining part of the SPA and, in April 2008, winning seven seats in the Constituent Assembly. In August 2008, however, Serchan's support for the election of President Yadav led to his ouster, with Lilamani POKHAREL becoming acting chair.

In January 2009 the CPN (UCM), led by General Secretary Narayan Kaji SHRESTHA, merged with the CPN (Maoist) to form the UCPN-M. Shrestha, Serchan, and Pokharel were all named to the UCPN-M Secretariat. Opponents of the merger then reconstituted the JMN.

In November 2012 the JMN joined 14 opposition parties in calling for the resignation of Prime Minister Bhattarai. The JMN contested the November 2013 elections but was unsuccessful.

Leaders: Dan Bahadur BISHWOKARMA (Chair), Man Bahadur SINGH, Bharat DAHAL, Sadhya Bahadur BHANDARI (General Secretary).

More than 90 other parties unsuccessfully contested the November 19, 2013, Constituent Assembly election. The following parties won more than 0.15 percent of the vote: ***Sanghiya Gantantrik Samajwedi*** **Party Nepal**; the **Nepal Communist Party**; the **Nepal *Yuwa Kisan***

Party; the **Nepal *Janata* Party**; the **Nepal *Sadbhawana* Party**; and the ***Khas Samabeshi Rashtriya* Party.**

Communist Party of Nepal (Maoist) (CPN-M). Former UCPN-M member and communist hard-liner Baidya, asserting the UCPN-M had strayed by accepting a parliamentary system, led a dissenting faction of the ruling Maoist party to form the CPN-M in June 2012. In August, 33 UCPN-M members publicly defected to the fledgling party, but stayed loyal to Bhattarai. The parties diverged in March 2013 when Baidya led 22 parties in protest against the installation of the Regmi government. In June the CPN-M led a 33-party alliance in agreeing to boycott the November elections. In August, the UCPN-M, NP, and CPN-UML agreed to hold ultimately unsuccessful talks with the CPN-M alliance. The coalition held strikes against the election beginning on November 11, some of which turned violent. The CPN-M boycotted the polls and rejected Koirala's offers in late November to include the party in an all-party government. However, the CPN-M and the UCPN-M showed signs of mending their divisions in March 2014 when they agreed to protest the government's attempts to hold local elections together.

Leaders: Mohan BAIDYA Kiran (Chair), Netra Bikram CHANDRA (Secretary).

Communist Party of Nepal (Unified) (CPN [Unified]). Formed in 2007, the CPN (Unified) brought together three splinter groups from other communist organizations: the Chitra Bahadur ALE wing of the JMN, the Rishi KATTEL wing of the CPN (ML), and the faction of the CPN (Marxist-Leninist-Maoist Center) led by Sitaram TAMANG. The new party assumed the two seats in the Interim Legislature-Parliament that had been assigned to the JMN (Ale) and subsequently won two seats in the Constituent Assembly. In April 2010 a faction led by Navaraj SUBEDI joined the UCPN-M.

Leaders: Ram Singh SHRIS, Mohan BIKRAM (General Secretary).

Nepal Goodwill Party (Anandi Devi) (*Nepali Sadbhavana* Party [Anandi Devi] (NSP [Anandi Devi] or NSP-A). The Nepal Goodwill Party was formed in the mid-1980s to promote the interests of the Madhesi inhabitants of the Terai. It sought redelineation of the southern constituencies on the basis of population and the granting of citizenship to all persons settled in Nepal before adoption of the 1990 constitution. The NSP won three House seats in 1994 after winning none in 1991 and was awarded one portfolio in the Deuba government of September 1995. In December 1998 the NSP entered the NC-CPN (UML) coalition administration as a junior partner. In the May 1999 election the NSP won five seats on a 3 percent vote share.

In January 2002 the party's founder and longtime president, Gajendra Narayan SINGH, died. Differences subsequently emerged over who should fill party posts. At a divisive national convention in March 2003 one faction supported Singh's widow, Anandi Devi SINGH, for the presidency, while another backed the acting president, Deputy Prime Minister Badri Prasad MANDAL. As a consequence, the party split. In April 2004 the Supreme Court upheld an August 2003 Election Commission decision that awarded the NSP title to the Mandal faction, with the other faction becoming the NSP (Anandi Devi).

In June 2007 the NSP and the NSP (Anandi Devi) reunited, retaining the latter designation. A faction led by cabinet minister Rajendra Mahato eventually splintered off under the designation the *Sadbhavana* Party (SP, above).

The party won only two seats in the 2008 Constituent Assembly election, after which factional disputes led to the apparent removal of an ailing Anandi Devi as chair by Shyam Sundar Gupta, a move rejected by the Sarita Giri faction. The party withdrew from the Maoist-led government in February 2009, after which the internal conflict intensified. The Gupta faction was recognized in May 2010 by the election commission, prompting Giri and Vice Chair Kushi Lal MANDAL to petition the Supreme Court for a stay. In July Giri charged Gupta and the party's secretary general, Yashwant Kumar SINGH, a nephew of Anandi Devi, with having abducted the honorary chair. The Giri faction supported the August 2011 UCPN-M government, and Giri became minister of labor and transportation. In June 2013 the Supreme Court settled the leadership issue, ruling that Giri is the chair of the party.

Leader: Sarita GIRI (Chair).

LEGISLATURE

The 1990 constitution provided for a bicameral Parliament (*Sansad*) consisting of a permanent upper house, the National Assembly (*Rastriya Sabha*), of 60 indirectly elected and appointed members, and a 205-member directly elected House of Representatives (*Pratinidhi Sabha*) with a five-year mandate. The proclamation of sovereignty by the House of Representatives on May 18, 2006, effectively suspended the National Assembly's governmental role. The lower house was dissolved by the king on May 22, 2002, and reinstated on April 28, 2006.

When the House promulgated the interim constitution on January 15, 2007, both houses of Parliament "automatically cease[d] to subsist." At the same time, a 330-member Interim Legislature-Parliament came into existence, encompassing a combination of 209 legislators from the previous Parliament—excluded were the king's nominees and those who had supported his assumption of power—plus party nominees. The three largest parties—the Nepali Congress, the Communist Party of Nepal (Unified Marxist-Leninist), and the Communist Party of Nepal (Maoist)—held roughly the same number of seats. Nine other parties were represented, including the Nepali Congress (Democratic), which reunited with the Nepali Congress in September.

As called for in the interim constitution, the tenure of the Interim Legislature-Parliament came to an end upon formation of the **Constituent Assembly**. In addition to drafting a new constitution, the assembly was to act as a unicameral legislature for two years, but in May 2010 the mandate was extended to May 2011. On May 28, 2012, Prime Minister Bhattarai called for elections on November 22, but the electoral law enacted for the first Constituent Assembly did not provide for second elections. Negotiations between political groups over the next year produced an interim government in March 2013 tasked with overseeing the next elections for a reduced 491-member Assembly. In June, elections were set for November 19. In September the government requested the membership return to the original 601 members: 240 directly elected in districts, through the "first-past-the-post" method; 335 elected by proportional representation on the basis of party lists; and 26 named by the Council of Ministers to represent indigenous and marginalized groups.

Under the 2015 constitution, a bicameral **Legislature-Parliament** (*Byabasthapika-Sansad*) would be created at the next elections. The upper house, the National Assembly, would consist of 59 members indirectly elected for six-year terms. Each province would elect eight members, with the remaining three appointed by the president. The lower chamber, the House of Representatives, would be comprised of 275 members, directly elected for a five-year term.

In the election on November 19, 2013, for 575 seats, the seat distribution was as follows: Nepali Congress, 196 seats; the Communist Party of Nepal (Unified Marxist-Leninist), 175; Unified Communist Party of Nepal (Maoist), 80; *Rastriya Prajatantra* Party Nepal, 24; Madhesi People's Rights Forum (Democratic), 14; National Democratic Party, 13; *Terai Madhesh* Democratic Party, 11; Madhesi People's Rights Forum, 10; *Sadbhavana* Party, 6; Communist Party of Nepal (Marxist-Leninist), 5; Federal Socialist Party, 5; Nepal Workers' and Peasants' Party, 4; *Terai Madhes Sadbhavana* Party, 4; *Rastriya Madhes Samajwadi* Party, 3; Nepal Family Party, 2; *Dalit Janjati* Party, 2; *Tharuwat Tarai* Party Nepal, 2; National People's Liberation Party, 2; *Sanghiya Sadbhawana* Party, Khumbuwan National Front Nepal, Nepali People's Party, Great Nepal Party, *Sanghiya Lokantrik Rastriya Manch* (*Tharuhat*), *Samajwadi Janata* Party, Madhesi People's Rights Forum (Republic), *Jana Jagaran* Party (Nepal), *Madesh Samata* Party Nepal, and Nepa National Party, 1 each; and independents, 2.

CABINET

[as of August 26, 2016]

Prime Minister	Pushpa Kamal Dahal "Prachanda" (UCPN-M)
Deputy Prime Minister, Finance	Krishna Bahadur Mahara (UCPN-M)
Deputy Prime Minister, Home Affairs	Bimalendra Nidhi (NC)
Ministers	
Agriculture Development	Gauri Shankar Chaudhari (UCPN-M)
Culture, Tourism, and Civil Aviation	Jeevan Bahadur Shahi (NC)

Commerce	Romi Gauchan Thakali (NC)
Cooperatives and Poverty Alleviation	Hridaya Ram Thani (NC)
Defense	Bal Krishna Khand (NC)
Education	Dhaniram Paudel (UCPN-M)
Energy	Janardan Sharma (UCPN-M)
Federal Affairs and Local Development	Hitraj Pandey (UCPN-M)
Foreign Affairs	Prakash Sharon Mahat (NC)
Forest and Soil Conservation	Shankar Bhandari (NC)
General Administration	Keshab Kumar Budhathoki (NC)
Health	Gagan Kumar Thapa (NC)
Industry	Nabindra Raj Joshi (NC)
Information and Communication	Surendra "Ram" Karki (UCPN-M)
Irrigation	Deepak Giri (NC)
Labor and Employment	Suryaman Gurung (NC)
Land Reform and Management	Bikram Panday (RPP)
Law, Justice, Parliamentary Affairs	Ajaya Shankar Nayak
Livestock Development	Pushpa Kamal Dahal "Prachanda" (UCPN-M)
Peace and Reconstruction	Sitadevi Yadav (NC) [f]
Physical Infrastructure and Transport	Ramesh Lekhak (NC)
Population and Environment	Jayadev Joshi (CNP[U])
Science and Technology	Pushpa Kamal Dahal "Prachanda" (UCPN-M)
Supplies	Deepak Bohara (NDP)
Urban Development	Arjun Narsingh K.C. (NC)
Water Supply and Sanitation	Prem Bahadur Singh (CPN [UML])
Women, Children, and Social Welfare	Kumar Khadka (ANP)
Youth and Sports	Daljit Shrepaili (UCPN-M)

[f] = female

INTERGOVERNMENTAL REPRESENTATION

Ambassador to the U.S.: Arjun Kumar KARKI.

U.S. Ambassador to Nepal: Alaina B. TEPLITZ.

Permanent Representative to the UN: Durga Prasad BHATTARAI.

IGO Memberships (Non-UN): ADB, IOM, NAM, SAARC, WTO.

For Further Reference:

DeVotta, Neil, ed. *An Introduction to South Asian Politics*. New York: Routledge, 2015.

Lawoti, Mahendra, and Susan Hangen. *Nationalism and Ethnic Conflict in Nepal: Identities and Mobilization after 1990*. New York: Routledge, 2013.

Malagodi, Mara. *Constitutional Nationalism and Legal Exclusion: Equality, Identity Politics, and Democracy in Nepal (1990–2007)*. Oxford: Oxford University Press, 2013.

Von Einsiedel, Sebastian, David M. Malone, and Suman Pradhan. *Nepal in Transition: From People's War to Fragile Peace*. Cambridge: Cambridge University Press, 2012.

NETHERLANDS

Kingdom of the Netherlands
Koninkrijk der Nederlanden

Political Status: Constitutional monarchy established 1814; under multiparty parliamentary system.

Area: 13,103 sq. mi. (33,936 sq. km).

Population: 16,980,000 (2016E—UN); 17,016,967 (2016E—U.S. Census).

Major Urban Centers (2013E): AMSTERDAM (799,000), Rotterdam (616,000), The Hague (seat of government, 506,000), Utrecht (322,000), Eindhoven (218,000).

Official Language: Dutch.

Monetary Unit: Euro (market rate October 1, 2016: 0.89 euro = $1US).

Sovereign: King WILLEM-ALEXANDER; ascended the throne April 30, 2013, upon the abdication of his mother, Queen BEATRIX Wilhelmina Armgard.

Heir Apparent: CATHARINA-AMALIA, Princess of Orange.

Prime Minister: Mark RUTTE (People's Party for Freedom and Democracy); sworn in as head of a two-party minority coalition on October 14, 2010, following the general election of June 9, succeeding Jan Peter BALKENENDE (Christian Democratic Appeal); sworn in as head of a two-party minority coalition on November 5, 2012, following the general election on September 12.

THE COUNTRY

Facing the North Sea between Belgium and Germany, the Netherlands (often called "Holland," from the name of one of its principal provinces) is noted for the dikes, canals, and reclaimed polder lands providing constant reminder that two-fifths of the country's land area lies below sea level. The largely homogeneous, Germanic population is divided principally between Catholics (31 percent) and Protestants (21 percent), with 40 percent declaring no religious affiliation. In 2013 women constituted 58 percent of the labor force, concentrated in the services sector. Women currently occupy 58 seats in the Second Chamber (38.7 percent) and 27 seats in the First Chamber (36 percent). Women chair both chambers, and head 5 of 13 ministries.

The Netherlands experienced rapid industrialization after World War II, although the industrial sector is now limited to approximately 22 percent of the labor force as compared with 74 percent in the services sector. The traditionally important agricultural sector employs fewer than 4 percent but is characterized by highly efficient methods of production, which are amply rewarded by the common agricultural policy of the European Union (EU, formerly the European Community—EC), of which the Netherlands was a founding member. Leading agricultural products include potatoes, vegetables, sugar beets, wheat, and pork. Since there are few natural resources except large natural gas deposits, most nonagricultural activity involves the processing of imported raw materials. Refined petroleum, chemicals, steel, textiles, and ships constitute the bulk of industrial output. Principal exports include machinery and transport equipment, chemicals and petroleum products, and food.

In the early 1980s the economy was stagnating under the influence of persistently high budget deficits necessitated, in part, by the nation's extensive welfare system. However, a labor/business pact in 1982 established the basis for significant governmental cost-cutting, private-sector promotion, wage moderation, and more flexible employment regulations. As a result, the economy grew steadily, rising from an average of 1.9 percent in the late 1980s to 4.1 percent in 1998. The Netherlands easily met the economic criteria required to participate in the EU's new Economic and Monetary Union (EMU) on January 1, 1999.

However, the budget surplus of the late 1990s (which had permitted tax reduction) was replaced by a deficit that reached 3.3 percent of GDP in 2004, thereby creating difficulty for the administration regarding EMU fiscal guidelines. The economy began a recovery in 2004, only to fall into recession in the second quarter of 2008 as a result of the global financial crisis, to which Netherlands was particularly vulnerable because of its robust financial sector and international connections. A slow and fragile economic recovery began in 2010 with GDP growing by 1.8 percent, driven mostly by exports. GDP grew 0.9 percent in 2011, but dropped 0.9 percent in 2012. GDP fell again in 2013, declining by 0.8 percent. Inflation rose by 2.6 percent, while unemployment grew for the second year in a row, rising to 6.9 percent. Growth returned in 2014, as GDP expanded by 0.9 percent, and then 1.6 percent in 2015 and 2016. Inflation was –0.1 percent in 2015, and then 0.9 percent in 2016. Unemployment declined from 7.2 percent in 2015 to 7 percent

the next year. GDP per capita in 2016 was $45,202. In 2016 the World Bank's annual report on the ease of doing business index ranked the Netherlands 28th out of 189 countries, one notch below France.

GOVERNMENT AND POLITICS

Political background. Having declared independence from Spain in 1581 at the time of the Counter Reformation, the United Provinces of the Netherlands were ruled by hereditary *stadhouders* (governors) of the House of Orange until the present constitutional monarchy was established under the same house at the close of the Napoleonic period. Queen JULIANA, who had succeeded her mother, WILHELMINA, in 1948, abdicated in favor of her daughter BEATRIX in April 1980.

Following World War II the Netherlands was governed by a succession of coalition governments in which the large Catholic People's Party (*Katholieke Volkspartif*—KVP) typically played a pivotal role prior to its merger into the more inclusive Christian Democratic Appeal (*Christen-Democratisch Appèl*—CDA) in 1980. Coalitions between the KVP and the Labor Party (*Partij van de Arbeid*—PvdA) were the rule until 1958, when the latter went into opposition, the KVP continuing to govern in alliance with smaller parties of generally moderate outlook. A center-right coalition headed by Petrus J. S. DE JONG assumed office in April 1967 and was followed by an expanded center-right government formed under Barend W. BIESHEUVEL in 1971.

The inability of the Biesheuvel government to cope with pressing economic problems led to its early demise in July 1972 and to an election four months later. A 163-day interregnum then ensued before a PvdA-led government organized in May 1973 by Johannes (Joop) M. DEN UYL emerged as the first Dutch administration dominated by the political left. It survived until March 1977, when it collapsed in the wake of a bitter dispute between PvdA and CDA leaders over compensation for expropriated land. After another extended interregnum (the longest in the nation's history), Andreas A. M. VAN AGT succeeded in organizing a government of his CDA and the People's Party for Freedom and Democracy (*Volkspartif voor Vrijheid en Democratie*—VVD) in late December.

In the election of May 1981 the center-right coalition lost its legislative majority and was replaced by a grouping that included the CDA, PvdA, and center-left Democrats 66 (*Democraten 66*—D66), with van Agt continuing as prime minister. The comfortable legislative majority thus achieved was offset by sharp differences over both defense and economic policy, and the new government collapsed in May 1982. The principal result of balloting in September was a loss of 11 seats by the D66 and a gain of 10 by the VVD. Ruud F. M. LUBBERS was installed as head of another center-right government in November following his succession to the CDA leadership in October. Contrary to opinion poll predictions, the CDA won a plurality in the lower house election of May 1986, Lubbers being returned as head of a new center-right government in July.

Lubbers was forced to resign on May 2, 1989, following coalition disagreement over funding for an ambitious environmental plan, although he remained in office in a caretaker's capacity pending new elections. Because of its perceived anti-environmental posture, the VVD's parliamentary representation dropped from 27 to 22 seats in the balloting on September 6, with the PvdA becoming the CDA's partner in a new center-left administration sworn in on November 7 under Lubbers's leadership. His continuation in office was made possible by a commitment to the PvdA to increase antipollution and social welfare expenditures, financed largely by the imposition of a "carbon dioxide" tax on business firms and a freeze on defense spending in 1991. While the subsequent course of events in Eastern Europe permitted an actual cutback in projected military expenses, the overall economic situation deteriorated.

The May 1994 general election marked the withdrawal from Dutch politics of Prime Minister Lubbers, who failed to gain the presidency of the European Commission in June. (The U.S. government vetoed his candidacy for the post of secretary general of the North American Treaty Organization [NATO] in 1995, but Lubbers was named to head the UN Office of the High Commissioner for Refugees in 2000.) The CDA campaign in 1994 was headed by Elco BRINKMAN, party leader in the Second Chamber. With Lubbers's departure, the CDA suffered its worst-ever defeat, losing a third of its support. The PvdA also lost ground, but it replaced the CDA as the largest parliamentary party, while substantial gains were registered by the VVD and D66. Far-right and far-left parties also gained seats, and two new pensioners' movements made their chamber debuts. In light of the new parliamentary arithmetic, the outcome of lengthy postelection negotiations was, as expected, the formation in August 1994 of a three-party coalition of the PvdA, VVD, and D66, with Willem "Wim" KOK becoming the first Labor prime minister since 1977.

With the government having received wide international praise for the "Dutch model" of sustained economic growth, substantial job creation, and an effective social services sector, the PvdA and the VVD improved their positions in the May 6, 1998, Second Chamber elections, although the D66 slipped significantly. The new government announced by Kok on August 3 comprised six ministers each from the PvdA and the VVD and three from the D66, with the coalition controlling 97 of the 150 seats in the *Tweede Kamer.*

On May 19, 1999, the cabinet resigned following the defeat by one vote in the *Eerste Kamer* of a bill sponsored by the D66 that would have permitted national "corrective referendums" to veto certain economic and social legislative decisions. However, on June 2 the three parties agreed to resume the coalition and to back a revised "consultative referendum" bill under which referendum results would not be binding.

Although the three-party governing coalition flirted with collapse in May 1999, two years of relative stability followed.

At the same time, the Netherlands attracted international attention frequently in the past, for legalizing controversial social practices. In 2001 it became the world's first country to permit same-sex marriages, and in 2002 a law legalizing euthanasia entered into effect. The Dutch euthanasia law made headlines again in February 2012 when Prince Johan Friso suffered a severe brain injury while skiing in Austria. He remains on life support with little hope of recovery at a London hospital, a situation criticized by Dutch euthanasia advocates.

On August 26, 2001, Prime Minister Kok confirmed that he would not seek reelection, so the party turned to its parliamentary leader, Ad MELKERT, to lead it into the 2002 elections. Kok and his cabinet resigned on April 16, 2002, in response to a report that criticized the Dutch military for failing to prevent the July 1995 massacre at the Bosnian "safe haven" of Srebrenica. The government continued to serve in a caretaker capacity until the May general election.

Events prior to the May 15, 2002, balloting for the *Tweede Kamer* were dominated by the sudden emergence of the flamboyant Pim FORTUYN, whose promotion of a populist mix of liberal policies (such as the improvement of public services) and rightist positions (such as heavy curbs on immigration and restrictions on rights for ethnic minorities) had struck a chord within a Dutch population increasingly concerned over deteriorating economic conditions and rising crime. Following Fortuyn's assassination on May 6 by an animal rights and environmental activist, consideration was given to postponing the balloting. However, all the major party leaders consented to proceeding as scheduled. The List Pim Fortuyn (*Lijst Pim Fortuyn*—LPF) won 26 seats and joined the CDA (43 seats) and VVD (24 seats) in a center-right coalition government installed on July 22 under the leadership of Jan Peter BALKENENDE of the CDA.

The coalition government resigned on October 16, 2002, as a result of differences over the proposed expansion of the EU, a power struggle within the LPF, and increasing economic difficulties, which prompted early elections on January 22, 2003, at which the CDA again achieved a slim plurality (44 seats versus 42 for the PvdA). The CDA initially sought to form a coalition with the PvdA, but negotiations fell apart due primarily to personal animosity between the leaders of the parties.

A CDA/VVD/D66 coalition was announced on May 27, with Balkenende retaining the premiership and promising a crackdown on drug trafficking and other crimes. Although the LPF seat total fell to 8 in the January balloting and the party lost its cabinet status, some of its proposals regarding immigration and crime had become official government policy. Prime Minister Balkenende's administration also tried to combat a burgeoning fiscal crisis through proposed liberalization of labor regulations and reductions in longstanding welfare and pension benefits.

The intertwined issues of immigration and rising anti-Muslim sentiment moved dramatically to the forefront again in November 2004 when Theo van GOGH, a filmmaker who had recently released a movie that focused on Islam's treatment of women, was assassinated, allegedly by an Islamic radical. In early 2005 the government announced that stricter qualifications would be imposed on potential immigrants regarding their knowledge of the nation's history and culture. Concurrently, an extensive campaign to combat terrorism was launched, and a number of alleged Islamic militants were either arrested or deported. The immigration and terrorism issues were widely believed to have been major factors in the 61.5 percent "no" vote registered by the Dutch electorate in a national referendum in June on the question of whether the proposed new EU constitution should be approved. (The government and most major parties had called for a "yes" vote.)

In May 2006 Immigration and Integration Minister Rita Verdonk of the VVD announced that she was considering revoking the citizenship of Ayaan HIRSI ALI, a member of the legislature and an immigrant from Somalia, for having allegedly lied on her application for asylum. After public uproar, the government ultimately decided to allow Hirsi Ali to retain her Dutch citizenship, though she had already resigned her legislative seat and accepted a job at the American Enterprise Institute, a conservative think tank in the United States. The D66 party, the smallest member of the governing coalition, demanded the resignation of Verdonk in exchange for its continuing participation in the government. Verdonk was also under fire from D66 for her proposals to require Dutch to be the only language spoken in the streets of Holland. When Verdonk refused to resign, the D66 on June 29 left the coalition; Prime Minister Balkenende consequently announced the resignation of his government and set the stage for new elections to be held approximately a year early. Former Prime Minister Ruud Lubbers was called on to negotiate a new government, and within a week an interim minority government comprising the CDA and VVD was installed to begin work on the 2007 budget.

Although many analysts had predicted a major defeat for the CDA, the party lost only three of its seats in the November 22, 2006, *Tweede Kamer* balloting, while the PvdA lost nine of its seats. Most electoral gains were registered on the extremes, as the extreme-left Socialist Party (*Socialistische Party*—SP) won 25 seats (up from 9 in 2003) and new extreme right-wing Party for Freedom (*Party voor de Vrijheid*—PVV) won 9 seats. The PVV was led by Geert WILDERS, who continued the anti-immigrant, anti-Islam beliefs espoused by the late Fortuyn (see Current issues, below). After more than two months of negotiations, Balkenende was able to construct a broad-spectrum coalition government comprising the CDA, PvdA, and the Christian Union (*ChristenUnie*—CU), which was installed on February 22, 2007.

The PVV continued to rise in popularity, stunning many analysts by finishing second in the European Parliament elections in June 2009 with 17 percent of the vote. Although the CDA led all parties in that balloting with 19 percent of the vote, the three-party governing coalition lost 6 of the 16 seats it had previously held.

The Balkenende government fell on February 20, 2010, after the PvdA pulled out of the three-party coalition over the government's extension of the Dutch mission in Afghanistan. The governing coalition had previously agreed that Dutch troops would be withdrawn from the Afghan province of Uruzgan in 2010; however, Prime Minister Balkenende opted to consider further extension of the mission after receiving a request by NATO in early 2010. On February 21 Balkenende stated that his caretaker CDA-CU government had no authority to accept NATO's request for an extension and, consequently, that troops would be removed on schedule in August 2010. Left without a governing majority, the CDA and the CU formed a minority caretaker government and scheduled a new election for June 9.

In voting on June 9, 2010, the VVD became the largest party in the legislature with 31 of the 150 seats. Under Cohen's leadership, the PvdA performed better than expected, finishing second with 30 seats. The PVV became the third-largest party with 25 seats, a gain of 16. The big loser was the CDA, which fell from first to fourth largest. While the Socialist Party won only 15 seats, down from 25, the Green Left and the D66 both saw their vote and seat shares increase, each winning 10 seats.

In view of preelection speculation that the PVV would hold enough seats to influence the formation of the next governing coalition, discussion about including the PVV in government had begun during the campaign. Many of PVV leader Wilders's xenophobic policy proposals, such as a tax on headscarves worn by Muslim women and a ban on the Koran, were thought to be too extreme to warrant serious consideration by the other parties, although no party expressly ruled out forming a coalition with the PVV. In the early weeks of the electoral campaign, Wilders announced that he was willing to compromise on any issue except his opposition to an increase in the retirement age. After the ballots were counted, Wilders announced that he would be willing to compromise even on the retirement issue.

Coalition negotiations focused principally on whether the PVV would participate in government, play a critical but subsidiary role as a government-supportive party, or be excluded entirely. Combined, the VVD and CDA controlled only 52 of the legislature's 150 seats. With the support of the 24 PVV legislators, the three parties would control a bare majority of 76 seats putting the PVV in a critical, if not pivotal, position.

After four months of negotiations, in late September 2010 Rutte proposed that the VVD and CDA form a two-party minority government, with a supporting role for the PVV. The agreement secured unanimous approval from VVD and PVV legislators, but CDA legislators forced the party leadership to put the PVV's proposed role to a vote in their party congress, which ultimately acquiesced to the coalition arrangement in October.

The Rutte government primarily focused on bringing the national deficit below the 3 percent of GDP EU threshold through budget cuts and other austerity measures. The new government also proposed to reduce the size of the legislature and the number of governmental ministries, and to increase the retirement age. The PVV's influence was demonstrated through proposed restrictions on non-EU migrants, a tightening of asylum measures, a ban on headscarves for political and judicial officials, and a general ban on the full-length Islamic burka.

The government collapsed in April 2012 (see Current issues, below), triggering elections on September 12, 2012. Prime Minister Rutte's VVD finished first, with 41 seats, followed closely by the PvdA with 38. Voters rejected the anti-Europe rhetoric of the PVV, which won only 15 seats, down from 24. The new VVD-PvdA government was sworn in on November 5.

Following the precedent of her mother and grandmother, on January 28, 2013, Queen Beatrix announced her intention to abdicate in favor of her eldest son, Willem-Alexander. The new king was inaugurated on April 30.

In October 2014 Foreign Minister Frans TIMMERMANS (PvdA) became a member of the European Commission. He was replaced by Bert KOENDERS (PvdA), who had been a UN special envoy to Mali. The minister for security and justice and the secretary of state for that portfolio were replaced in March 2015 (see Current issues, below). In First Chamber elections in May, the VVD was first with 13 seats, followed by the CDA with 12 (see Political Parties, below).

Constitution and government. Originally adopted in 1814–1815, the Netherlands' constitution has been progressively amended to incorporate the features of a modern democratic welfare state in which the sovereign exercises strictly limited powers. Under a special Statute of December 29, 1954, the Kingdom of the Netherlands was described as including not only the Netherlands proper but also the fully autonomous overseas territories of the Netherlands Antilles and Suriname, the latter ultimately becoming independent in 1975. On January 1, 1986, the island of Aruba formally withdrew from the Antilles federation, becoming a separate, self-governing member of the kingdom.

Political power centers in the parliament, or States General (*Staten Generaal*), consisting of an indirectly elected Senate or First Chamber (*Eerste Kamer*) and a more powerful, directly elected House of

Representatives or Second Chamber (*Tweede Kamer*). Either or both chambers may be dissolved by the sovereign prior to the holding of a new election. Executive authority is vested in a Council of Ministers (*Ministerraad*) appointed by the sovereign but responsible to the States General. An advisory Council of State (*Raad van State*), comprised of the queen and crown prince plus a number of councillors appointed by the queen upon nomination by the Second Chamber, is consulted by the executive on legislative and administrative policy. The judicial system is headed by a Supreme Court and includes five courts of appeal, 19 district courts, and 62 cantonal courts.

For administrative purposes the Netherlands is divided into 12 provinces, the most recent, Flevoland, having been created on January 1, 1986, from land formed under the more than half-century-old Zuider Zee reclamation project. Each province has its own elected council, which elects an executive, and a sovereign commissioner appointed by the queen. At the local level there are approximately 640 municipalities, each with a council that designates aldermen to share executive responsibilities with a crown-appointed burgomaster.

Under the arrangements providing for the dissolution of the Netherlands Antilles in October 2010, the islands of Bonaire, Saba, and St. Eustatius became "special municipalities" within the Netherlands. The islands were expected to retain their elected Island Councils.

Newspapers are free from censorship and published by independent commercial establishments, with strict separation between managerial and editorial boards. Reports Without Borders ranked the Netherlands 2nd of 180 countries in its 2016 Index of Press Freedom.

Foreign relations. Officially neutral before World War II, the Netherlands reversed its foreign policy as a result of the German occupation of 1940–1945 and became an active participant in the subsequent evolution of the Western community through the Benelux Union, NATO, the Western European Union, the EC/EU, and other West European and Atlantic organizations. A founding member of the UN, the Netherlands also belongs to all of the UN's specialized agencies. The country's principal foreign policy problems in the postwar period stemmed from the 1945–1949 transition to independence of the Netherlands East Indies (Indonesia); Jakarta's formal annexation in 1969 of West New Guinea (Irian Jaya); and continued pressure, including numerous acts of terrorism, by South Moluccan expatriates seeking Dutch aid in the effort to separate their homeland from Indonesia.

On December 15, 1992, the States General completed its ratification of the EC's Maastricht Treaty on economic and political union. However, the Netherlands' enthusiasm for European integration did not extend to participation in the "Eurocorps" military force inaugurated by France and Germany in 1992. Instead, the Netherlands on March 30, 1994, signed an agreement with Germany providing for the creation of a 30,000-strong Dutch–German joint force that would be fully integrated into NATO and open to other NATO members. The new joint force was formally inaugurated in August 1995, with staff headquarters in Münster, Germany.

Amsterdam took offense in November 1995 when the U.S. government vetoed the candidacy of former prime minister Ruud Lubbers for the post of NATO secretary general, reportedly because of Lubbers's record of concern about German dominance in Europe. Nevertheless, the Netherlands, which had previously committed troops to peacekeeping efforts in Bosnia, assigned 2,100 troops to the NATO-commanded International Force (IFOR) under the Dayton peace accords. The Kok administration also supported NATO action against Yugoslavia in early 1999.

The Hague is home to the International Court of Justice and the UN-sponsored International Criminal Tribunals for the former Yugoslavia and Rwanda (see the discussion under the UN Security Council). A Dutch air base also served as the trial site for two Libyans accused of the 1988 bombing of Pan Am Flight 103 over Lockerbie, Scotland; the Dutch government had permitted the base to be regarded as Scottish territory for the duration of the trial, which concluded with one guilty verdict and one acquittal in early 2001.

Although the Netherlands had contributed naval resources to the U.S.-led UN coalition in the 1991 Gulf War, support for the U.S./UK-led invasion of Iraq in 2003 was tepid (at best) in many quarters. Although the government initially deployed 1,700 troops to the Iraqi campaign, those forces were withdrawn in 2005. However, in February 2006 the Dutch parliament bowed to entreaties of U.S. and NATO officials and agreed to send up to 1,700 troops to Afghanistan as part of a NATO reconstruction mission. Those troops were withdrawn at the end of the mission in August 2010.

Dutch voters took a dramatic step back from European integration when a larger-than-expected 61.5 percent of voters rejected the EU constitution in a referendum in June 2006. Prime Minister Balkenende's government had conducted a campaign in favor of the treaty, and Balkenende subsequently announced that any future consideration was to take place in the legislature rather than by referendum. The government announced approval of the treaty in July 2008 after both houses of parliament provided large majorities voting in support.

In January 2011 the government sent 545 Dutch personnel and four F-16 fighter jets to Afghanistan but only after Green Left party leaders extracted a written guarantee from the Afghan government that Dutch-trained personnel would not be used in military action.

In January Finance Minister Jeroen DIJSSELBLOEM was named chairman of the Eurogroup, the association of all EU finance members, replacing Luxembourg's Jean-Claude Juncker.

Royal Dutch Shell signed a production agreement with the Ukrainian government in January 2013 to develop the Yuzivska gas field in eastern Ukraine. The company was forced to suspend its Arctic drilling program in February 2013, however, after one of its ships ran aground off the Alaskan coast. The incident was the latest in a series of expensive mishaps in the first major effort to tap potentially lucrative Arctic oil deposits. The United States will not allow Shell to resume without new safety measures.

The Ministry of Foreign Trade and Development Cooperation shifted its foreign aid program in early 2013, moving to support Dutch investments in foreign countries rather than awarding cash grants. For example, in April, the Dutch government gave Tanzania $164 million to help construct a new airport terminal using a Dutch construction company.

Foreign Minister Frans TIMMERMANS concluded an agreement with Venezuela in June to provide greater economic cooperation between the two countries. In August Timmermans unveiled a list of 54 policy areas that the Netherlands wanted to remain under national, not EU, purview. In September the Dutch government apologized for summary executions in Indonesia during that country's struggle for independence (1945–1949).

In November 2013 the Netherlands filed suit against Russia at the International Tribunal for the Law of the Sea in an effort to compel Moscow to release the Greenpeace vessel *Artic Sunrise,* which had been seized in September. The vessel was registered in the Netherlands and two of its crew were Dutch. Russia released the ship in June 2014.

Following the passage of an anti-homosexuality law in Uganda in February 2014, the Netherlands suspended aid to the country. Representatives of the Netherlands and Kuwait signed an accord to increase environmental cooperation in 2014. Saudi Arabia threatened to impose sanctions on the Netherlands in May after Dutch rightwing politician Geert Wilders distributed stickers to his supporters with the message "Islam is a lie, Muhammad a criminal, the Koran is poison" super-imposed on a Saudi flag.

In November 2015 the European Commission (EC) ruled that the Netherlands had illegally created tax incentives for the U.S. coffee chain Starbucks, and ordered the firm to pay the country $32.7 million in back-taxes. The Netherlands appealed the decision.

On April 6, 2016, Dutch voters voted "no" in a nonbinding referendum on the association agreement between the EU and Ukraine (see entry on Ukraine). The margin was 61 percent against and 38.2 percent in favor, with a turnout of 32.3 percent. Parliament voted 75–71 to move forward with the agreement on April 19, but Prime Minister Rutte subsequently stated that he did not believe the country could ratify the accord in light of the referendum.

Current issues. In March and April 2012 the government spent seven weeks trying to adopt a budget that would cut €16 billion and bring the budget deficit below 3 percent of GDP, the EU target. Possible solutions on the table included higher taxes, raising the retirement age from 65 to 67, and charging for prescription medications. Consumer spending continued to contract, as homeowners struggled to pay down mortgages.

On April 21, 2012, the far-right wing PVV, refusing to raise the retirement age, withdrew its support from the government. Unable to create a new coalition, Prime Minister Rutte submitted his resignation on April 23, triggering new elections. Rutte and Finance Minister Jan KEES DE JAEGER (CDA) quickly put together a five-party coalition (VVD, CDA, D66, CU, GL) to serve as a caretaker government and to pass a budget by April 27.

The Dutch parliament ratified the establishment of the European Stability Mechanism (ESM) in April 2012. The Netherlands was the fifth-largest donor, contributing €700 billion to the bail out. Wilders filed suit, asking a Dutch court to overturn the parliamentary vote so that the new parliament due to be elected in September would take up the issue. A court rejected his argument on June 1.

The government nationalized SNS Reaal on February 1, 2013, injecting €3.7 billion to keep the bank solvent and prevent it from further damaging the national financial system.

In March 2013 the government announced that an additional €4 billion in austerity cuts were needed, as revised estimates put the budget deficit for 2013 at 3.3 percent of GDP. However, the ruling coalition faced stiff opposition to the proposal, especially in the Senate, where it did not have a majority. D66 demanded the reinstatement of €200 million in education spending, while the CU insisted the government abandon plans to make illegal immigration a criminal offense. In April the government announced it had reached a "social accord" with labor that would postpone difficult decisions on spending cuts until the fall and changes to unemployment benefits until 2016.

By August 2013 the Dutch economy had contracted for six consecutive quarters and the country was poised to miss the 3 percent deficit limit in 2014. EU officials ordered an additional €6 billion in spending cuts and taxes increases, which led labor unions to pull out of the social accord. Voters, weary of continued austerity, began to turn away from the ruling parties and the PVV's favorability ratings rose.

In his first annual address to parliament, King Willem-Alexander on September 17 announced that the Dutch welfare model was no longer viable and that in the new "participatory society," citizens would have to assume more responsibility for their healthcare, pensions, and other social benefits. In October the government was able to secure a budget deal with center-right opposition parties, including the D66, the CU, and the Political Reformed Party (*Staatkundig Gereformeerde Partij*—SGP). The budget contained the €6 billion in austerity measures, but reduced the impact on some social programs. It projected a budget deficit of 3.2 percent for 2014.

In municipal elections on March 19, 2014, the CDA received the largest share of the vote with 14 percent. The PvdA's vote share fell to 10 percent, while the VVD's declined to 12 percent. Following the balloting, PvdV leader Wilders created a furor during a celebratory speech in which he asked supporters if they wanted more or "fewer Moroccans" in the Netherlands. After the crowd began chanting "fewer," Wilders pledged to "take care of that." The speech created a backlash which hurt the party in the 2014 EU parliamentary elections (see Political Parties, below). In the EU balloting, the CDA won five seats, followed by D66 and the PVV, each with four.

In May 2015 the government approved a partial ban on wearing veils that covered a person's face, a law directed at Islamic garb, such as the burqa. The ban applied to public spaces, such as schools and hospitals where security concerns necessitated being able to identify a person's face.

On January 13, 2016, Khadija ARIB (PvdA) was elected speaker of the lower house after Anouchka van MILTENBURG (VVD) resigned on December 12, 2015, in the midst of a scandal that had earlier caused the resignation of Security and Justice Minister Ivo OPSTELTEN (VVD) in March 2015. The scandal involved the 2001 return of 4.7 million guilders to a convicted drug dealer by prosecutors without the involvement of superiors and the tax service, and the subsequent effort to hide the payment.

POLITICAL PARTIES

The growth of the Dutch multiparty system, which emerged from the tendency of political parties to reflect the interests of particular religious and economic groups, has been reinforced by the use of proportional representation. Twenty-one parties contested the 2012 *Tweede Kamer* elections; 11 won seats.

Government Parties:

People's Party for Freedom and Democracy (*Volkspartij voor Vrijheid en Democratie*—VVD). The forerunners of the VVD included the prewar Liberal State and Liberal Democratic parties. Organized in 1948, the party drew its major support from upper-class businesspeople and middle-class, white-collar workers. Although it accepted social welfare measures, the VVD was conservative in outlook and strongly favored free enterprise and separation of church and state.

The party lost ground in both the 1986 and 1989 elections, on the latter occasion going into opposition for the first time since 1982. In the May 1994 balloting, however, the VVD advanced from 14.6 to 19.9 percent of the vote and then entered into a governing coalition with the PvdA and D66 in August. The VVD struck a popular chord with its tough line on immigration and asylum seekers, overtaking the CDA as the strongest party in provincial elections in March 1995. The VVD's Second Chamber seat total rose from 31 to 38 in the May 1998 poll (based on 25 percent of the vote), although it fell to second place behind the CDA in the provincial elections of March 1999. The rise of the LPF (below) cost the VVD in the May 2002 general election, at which VVD representation fell to 23 seats.

Jozias van AARTSEN became party leader when the VVD joined the coalition government in July 2002 and former party leader Garrit ZALM left the post to become minister of finance. Van Aartsen resigned his position after the party performed poorly in the municipal elections of March 2006, and Mark Rutte was elected new party leader on May 31, defeating Immigration and Integration Minister Rita Verdonk for the post.

Verdonk was at the center of the controversy that brought down the government in late June 2006, as the D66 left in protest over her actions in the Hirsi Ali affair (see Political background, above). Although the VVD remained a partner in the interim minority government that followed, the November election saw the VVD vote share drop to 14.7 percent and its seat total to fall to 22, a loss of 6. Verdonk stirred another government crisis in December 2006, and when she continued to press her anti-immigrant criticisms of the VVD, the party expelled her in September 2007. Rather than resign her parliamentary seat, she decided to sit as an independent and subsequently formed a new political group called Proud of the Netherlands (see below).

In the 2010 legislative balloting the VVD for the first time became the largest party in the *Tweede Kamer,* winning 31 seats on 20.5 percent of the vote. The party campaigned on a program of tough fiscal austerity measures and immigration restrictions. Under the continuing leadership of Mark Rutte, the VVD entered into a minority government coalition with the CDA, with pledged support from the PVV.

Following the collapse of the government in April 2012 over EU-mandated budget cuts, Rutte remained as caretaker prime minister and led his party in the September parliamentary election. The VVD won 41 seats on a 26.6 percent vote share, and Ruute formed a majority government with the Labor Party.

In the May 2014 EU elections, the VVD secured three seats. In June Henry Keizer was elected party chair. In the 2015 provincial balloting, the VVD won 89 seats, and then secured 13 seats in the Senate.

Leaders: Mark RUTTE (Prime Minister), Loek HERMANS (Senate Leader) Halbe ZIJLSTRA (House of Representatives Leader), Henry KEIZER (President), Jeanette BALJEU (First Vice President), Robert REIBESTEIN (Second Vice President), Stephanie TER BORG (General Secretary).

Labor Party (*Partij van de Arbeid*—PvdA). The Labor Party was formed in 1946 by a union of the former **Socialist Democratic Workers' Party** with left-wing Liberals and progressive Catholics and Protestants. It favored democratic socialism and was a strong supporter of the UN and European integration. The party program stressed the importance of equality of economic benefits, greater consultation in decision making, and reduced defense spending. In October 1977, against the advice of its leadership, the party's national congress voted in favor of the establishment of a republican form of government for the Netherlands. During the same period, the PvdA strongly opposed both nuclear power generation and the deployment of cruise missiles. Subsequent policy considerations focused on employment; strengthening social security, health care, and education; transport infrastructure; and debt reduction.

In the May 1994 general election, the PvdA slipped from 31.9 to 24.0 percent of the vote but overtook the CDA as the largest Second Chamber party with 37 seats. It won 45 seats (on a 29 percent vote share) in May 1998. The PvdA's seat total slipped badly to 23 in the May 2002 balloting for the *Tweede Kamer,* but the party rebounded to 42 seats in January 2003, making it the second largest party in the country.

In municipal elections in March 2006, the PvdA showed a sharp increase in support, raising its share of the vote by 7.6 percent to 23.4 percent from the 2002 elections. Some analysts predicted that the PvdA would be the main beneficiary of the resignation in June 2006 of the Balkenende government, since recent opinion polls projected that the PvdA would win the largest share of parliamentary seats if a snap election were held. Those forecasts proved premature, however. With the economy rebounding and the CDA losing only 3 seats in the November election, the PvdA lost 9 seats. However, its 33-seat total kept it as the second largest party in the parliament, which was enough to make it the most viable partner for the CDA in the new government.

In February 2010 the PvdA withdrew from government in opposition to Prime Minister Balkenende's agreement to extend the Dutch mission in Afghanistan beyond previously agreed upon terms, prompting a call for new elections in June. Job Cohen, the former mayor of Amsterdam, was selected to lead the PvdA in the election campaign. Running on a platform of multiculturalism and opposition to other parties' plans for strong austerity measures, the PvdA held its position as the second-largest party in the *Tweede Kamer,* winning 30 seats on 19.6 percent of the vote. The party's policy disagreements with the other major parties led Cohen to give only fleeting consideration to reaching an agreement to have the PvdA participate in a new government. PvdA lost considerable popular support while out of the government and did not have a strategy for dealing with the far-right PVV. Cohen resigned on February 20, 2012.

A PvdA party congress elected Diederik Samsom as chair of the parliamentary group on March 21, 2012. He opted not to join the five-party caretaker government and argued that the 3 percent deficit target would disproportionately hit Labor's constituents. The PvdA finished second in the September election, winning 38 seats with 24.8 percent of votes. Samsom agreed to be the junior partner in a majority government with the VVD.

In the March 2014 municipal elections, the PvdA lost control of Amsterdam for the first time in 60 years, as voters turned to more centrist parties. In the May EU balloting, the party won three seats. In the 2015 balloting, the PvdA won 63 provincial seats, and 8 Senate seats.

In 2016 party member Khadija ARIB was elected speaker of the lower house, becoming the first Muslim and immigrant to hold the office.

Leaders: Diederik SAMSOM (Party Leader), Hans SPEKMAN (Party Chair), Lodewijk ASSCHER (Deputy Prime Minister).

Opposition Parties:

Party for Freedom (*Party voor de Vrijheid*—PVV). The PVV grew out of a one-man faction in the *Tweede Kamer* in 2004 by Geert Wilders, who had resigned from the VVD in a dispute with party leaders over Turkey's possible entry into the EU but had refused to resign his legislative seat. Wilders subsequently continued to promote anti-immigration policies and other right-wing causes. For the 2006 legislative poll, the Euro-skeptic PVV presented itself as a free-market, low-tax party and an advocate of conformity to Judeo-Christian cultural traditions. The PVV surprised observers by securing nine seats in the *Tweede Kamer* on a vote share of 5.9 percent.

Wilders burst onto the political scene by focusing on immigration issues, especially with respect to Muslims. *Fitna,* his 2008 short film, portrays the Koran as a source of violence and terrorism. After Dutch television refused to air the film, Wilders released it on the Internet, leading to the closing of the Dutch embassy in Afghanistan and calls for boycotts of Dutch products. The film drew little reaction from Dutch Muslims, but the government put Wilders on trial for inciting hatred and discrimination against Muslims. (Wilders was acquitted of all charges in June 2011.)

Even though the PVV had called for the European Parliament to be dissolved, the party presented candidates for the elections to that body for the first time in June 2009. In a surprising outcome, the PVV finished second in that balloting with 17 percent of the vote, securing 4 of 25 seats. Wilders' hate speech trial began in January 2010 but was aborted in the autumn (after Wilders successfully pressed a charge of judicial bias) and scheduled for retrial. The final court verdict was announced in June 2011 and cleared Wilders of all charges against him. The court concluded that while Wilders's remarks were "insulting," they were protected under the country's freedom of speech laws and were aimed mostly at Islam as a religion rather than the Muslim population.

With concerns over immigration on the rise, the Wilders-led PVV surpassed expectations by becoming the third-largest party in the *Tweede Kamer* in the June 2010 poll, winning 24 seats on 15.5 percent of the vote. Holding a significant share of the seats, Wilders made it clear that he would be willing to compromise on his policy positions in order to be part of a government arrangement. In October the PVV entered into a government-supportive role with the minority VVD-CDA coalition through an agreement that contained policy plans aimed at restricting immigration and tightening integration policies, including a ban on the Islamic burka.

In April 2012 Wilders and the PVV brought down the ruling VVD/CDA coalition by refusing to vote budget cuts needed to meet EU-imposed fiscal targets. Instead, Wilders advocated quitting the EU and readopting the guilder as its own currency.

Members of the PVV parliamentary faction have complained about a perceived lack of democracy within the party. Between April and July 2012, three PVV MPs quit, calling Wilders a dictator. Hero BRINKMAN formed his own political party (see below), while Wim KORTENOEVEN and Marcial HERNANDEZ tweeted their resignations as Wilders unveiled the PVV campaign platform ("Out of the morass, out of the euro, out of the EU!") during a press conference. The PVV dropped from 24 seats to 15 in the September parliamentary elections, but its popularity revived in early 2013. In November Wilders created a bilateral alliance with France's National Front for 2014 EU parliamentary elections.

Wilders controversial call for "fewer Moroccans" in March 2014 prompted six party members, including two parliamentarians and the leader of the PVV's EU parliamentary group, to resign. Reports indicated the comments also hurt the party in the 2014 EU elections, where the PVV's vote share declined by 3.5 percent to 13.3 percent from the last elections. The party did maintain its four seats. The party won 9 seats in the Senate in 2015, and 66 provincial seats.

Leaders: Geert WILDERS (Chair and Parliamentary Chair), Fleur AGEMA (Parliamentary Vice Chair), Martin BOSMA (Group Secretary).

Socialist Party (*Socialistische Partij*—SP). The left-wing SP increased its vote share from 0.4 percent in 1989 to 1.3 percent in the May 1994 Second Chamber poll, returning two deputies. In preparation for the May 1998 elections, party leaders argued that there was "too much poverty" in the country and criticized a perceived widening of the gap between the rich and poor. It won 3.5 percent of the votes, for five seats. The SP also offered a progressive agenda, in contrast to the LPF, for the 2002 and 2003 elections for the *Tweede Kamer,* securing nine seats both times. In 2005 the SP opposed the proposed new EU constitution.

The SP won 5.7 percent of the votes in the March 2006 municipal elections (more than doubling its number of seats). In the 2006 *Tweede Kamer* election the SP won 25 seats, a gain of 16, making it the third largest party in that chamber. The party dropped to fifth largest following the June 2010 general election, at which it won 15 seats on 9.8 percent of the vote.

The SP was leading public opinion polls going into the September 2012 parliamentary elections, and it was projected to take 32 seats. However, on election day the SP secured only 15 seats with a 9.7 share of the vote, finishing fourth overall. In the 2014 EU elections, the SP won 9.6 percent of the vote and 2 seats. The SP secured 9 seats in the May 2015 Senate polling, and 70 seats in provincial elections.

Leaders: Emile ROEMER (Parliamentary Chair), Jan MARIJNISSEN (Chair); Hans van HEIJNINGEN (General Secretary).

Christian Democratic Appeal (*Christen-Democratisch Appèl*—CDA). Party organization in the Netherlands has long embraced a distinction between confessional and secular parties, although the former experienced a gradual erosion in electoral support. Partly in an effort to counter the anticonfessional trend, the CDA was organized in December 1976 as an unprecedented alliance of the **Catholic People's Party** (*Katholieke Volkspartij*—KVP) and two Protestant groups, the **Anti-Revolutionary Party** (*Anti-Revolutionaire Partij*—ARP) and the **Christian Historical Union** (*Christelijk-Historische Unie*—CHU). The KVP was founded in 1945 as a centrist party supported primarily by Roman Catholic businesspeople, farmers, and some workers. It endorsed many social welfare programs while favoring close cooperation between spiritual and secular forces in the community. The ARP, founded in 1879, was the nation's oldest political organization, drawing its principal strength from Calvinist businesspeople, white-collar workers, and farmers. The CHU was formed in 1908 by a dissident faction of the ARP. Traditionally more centrist than the parent party, it shared the ARP's Calvinist outlook.

The three constituent parties, which had presented joint lists at the May 1977 parliamentary election, agreed in October 1980 to merge into a unified political grouping. Led by Ruud Lubbers, the CDA obtained a plurality of legislative seats in both 1986 and 1989, aligning itself with the Liberals on the earlier occasion and with Labor on the latter. Under the new leadership of Elco Brinkman for the May 1994 poll, the CDA lost a third of its support (falling from 35.3 to 22.2 percent of the vote) and was reduced to the status of second strongest Second Chamber party. Brinkman resigned as CDA leader in August.

A period of "uncertainty and wrangling" developed within the CDA in the wake of the 1994 electoral decline, the right wing appearing to gain ascendancy in 1997 with selection of Jaap de HOOP SCHEFFER as new party leader. In the May 1998 Second Chamber balloting, the CDA slipped to 29 seats (down from 34) on a vote share of 18.4 percent, although it rebounded strongly to finish first in the March 1999 provincial elections and, thus, in selection of the new First Chamber two months later. De Hoop Scheffer resigned as parliamentary leader in September 2001, citing inadequate support from the party. He was succeeded by Jan Peter Balkenende.

Positioning itself as a "reasoned choice" between the radically conservative LPF (below) and the social-democratic PvdA, the CDA led all parties by securing 43 seats in the May 2002 election to the *Tweede Kamer.* Balkenende subsequently formed a coalition government with the LPF and VVD, but the government collapsed three months later due to divisions within the LPF. Balkenende formed another coalition (this time with the VVD and the D66) following the January 2003 general election, in which the CDA again finished first with 44 seats.

In municipal elections in March 2006, the CDA showed a moderate loss of support, winning 16.9 percent of the vote, a drop of 3.4 percent over the 2002 elections, apparently as a result of an underperforming economy and unpopular pension and health care reforms.

After the June 29, 2006, cabinet crisis and the installation of a minority interim government of the CDA and VVD on July 7, new elections were held in November. The CDA won 26.5 percent of the vote and 41 seats. Balkenende formed a new government in coalition with PvdA and CU in February 2007. Following the break-up of the governing coalition in February 2010, the CDA suffered its worst-ever results (only 21 seats on a vote share of 13.6 percent) in the June elections. Balkenende resigned as CDA leader immediately after the balloting and was replaced by Maxime Verhagen on June 10.

Negotiations over a new government formation became prolonged as CDA legislators debated whether and how to align with a VVD-led administration that would grant an influential role to the right-wing PVV. The CDA leadership left the decision to approve a VVD-CDA minority government with pledged support from the PVV to its party congress. The congress approved the initiative on a 68 percent vote in favor (a smaller majority than expected), and the CDA became the junior government party on October 14. Verhagen asked to be removed from the CDA list for the September 2012 election, citing the need for a break from politics.

The CDA plummeted from junior government partner to fifth place in the September 2012 elections, dropping from 21 seats to only 13 on an 8.5 vote share. However, the party rebounded in the 2014 municipal balloting with 14 percent of the vote. In the 2014 EU elections, the CDA won 5 seats, with 15 percent of the vote. The CDA won 12 seats in the 2015 Senate elections, and 89 seats in provincial polling.

Leaders: Ruth PEETOM (Party Chair), Sybrand VAN HAERSMA BUMA (Parliamentary Chair), Mijam STERK (Parliamentary Vice Chair).

Democrats 66 (*Democraten 66*—D66). Formed in 1966 as a left-of-center party, the D66 favored the dropping of proportional representation and the direct election of the prime minister. Its stand on other domestic and foreign policy questions was similar to that of the PvdA. It changed its name from Democrats '66 to Democrats 66 in 1986. The party's lower house representation rose from 9 seats in 1986 to 12 in 1989, the latter figure being doubled in 1994 on a vote share of 15.5 percent.

In May 1999 the D66 caused the near collapse of the government when its proposal for "corrective referendums" (to override certain parliamentary decisions) was defeated by one vote in the upper house. The matter was resolved in early June when the D66 accepted a compromise that opened the way for nonbinding referendums.

The D66's representation fell to 7 seats in the May 2002 Second Chamber balloting, down from 14 in 1998. Although the party secured only 6 seats in the January 2003 election, the D66 became something of a "kingmaker" when it provided the necessary legislative majority for the new coalition government led by the CDA and the VVD.

The D66 withdrew its support for the Balkenende coalition government in June 2006, resulting in the collapse of the government. The immediate cause of the party's withdrawal was the failure of the VVD's Rita Verdonk to resign as immigration minister (see Current issues for details), but the party also objected to the Balkenende government's support for sending additional Dutch troops to Afghanistan.

The D66's electoral decline continued in the 2006 legislative poll, in which it won only three seats on a 2 percent vote share. However, the party rebounded to win ten seats on 7 percent of the vote in the June 2010 general elections. In 2013 Fleur Gräper-van Koolwijk became party chair.

The party won a dozen seats—a gain of two—in September 2012. The D66 received 12 percent of the vote in the 2014 municipal elections, and received the most local council seats in Amsterdam, The Hague, and Utrecht. In subsequent EU elections, the D66 secured four seats. D66 secured 10 Senate seats and 67 provincial seats in the 2015 elections.

Leaders: Alexander PECHTOLD (Parliamentary Chair), Letty DEMMERS (Chair), Thom de GRAFF (Senate Leader).

Christian Union (*ChristenUnie*—CU). The Christian Union dates from January 2000, when the **Reformational Political Federation** (*Reformatorische Politieke Federatie*—RPF) and the **Reformed Political Union** (*Gereformeerd Politiek Verbond*—GPV) agreed to unify. Appealing to both Calvinists and interdenominational Christians, the RPF had been formed in 1975; it obtained two Second Chamber seats in 1981 and 1982, one in 1986 and 1989, and three in 1994 and 1998. Established in 1948, the more conservative, Calvinist GPV long supported a strong defense policy and the Atlantic alliance but opposed any subordination to a supranational governmental body. It won two Second Chamber seats in each of the last three general elections prior to the launching of the CU.

Following the merger, the Christian Union controlled four seats in the First Chamber and five seats in the Second Chamber. The GPV and RPF factions in the Second Chamber formally merged in March 2001. The Christian Union won three seats in the *Tweede Kamer* in 2002 as well as 2003. After winning nearly 4 percent of the vote and six seats in the *Tweede Kamer* in November 2006, the CU joined the Balkenende-led governing coalition. The CU stayed on as a partner in the caretaker government after the PvdA withdrew from the coalition in February 2010. The CU thereafter won five seats on 3.2 percent of the vote in the June balloting but did not retain a position in government. It similarly secured five seats on 3.1 percent of the vote in September 2012. Long-time chair Peter BLOKHUIS retired in 2012.

The CU campaigned with the SGP (see below) in the 2014 EU elections. The alliance won two seats. The party won 3 seats in the Senate and 29 seats in provincial councils in the 2015 elections.

Leaders: Gert-Jan SEGERS (Parliamentary Leader), Piet ADEMA (Chair).

Political Reformed Party (*Staatkundig Gereformeerde Partij*—SGP). Dating from 1918, the SGP is an extreme right-wing Calvinist party that bases its political and social outlook on its own interpretation of the Bible. It advocates strong legal enforcement, including the use of the death penalty, and is against supranational government, which it feels opens society to corrupting influences. Since 1993 women have been banned from active membership.

The SGP retained its existing three Second Chamber seats in the 1989 election but slipped to two in May 1994 before rebounding to three in 1998. It frequently cooperated with the GPV and RPF (see Christian Union, above), including presentation of joint lists for European Parliament balloting. The SGP won two seats in the *Tweede Kamer* in 2002, 2003, 2006, and 2010 (on 1.7 percent of the vote in the latter). It picked up a third seat in 2012, with 2.1 percent of the vote. The SGP and the CU campaigned together for the 2014 EU balloting, winning two seats. The SGP won 18 provincial seats and 2 Senate seats in the 2015 polling.

Leaders: C. G. "Kees" van der STAAIJ (Parliamentary Chair), Adrie VAN HETEREN (Chair).

Green Left (*GroenLinks*—GL). The GL was organized as an electoral coalition prior to the 1989 balloting by the **Evangelical People's Party** (*Evangelische Volkspartij*—EVP), the **Radical Political Party** (*Politieke Partij Radikalen*—PPR), the **Pacifist Socialist Party** (*Pacifistisch Socialistische Partij*—PSP), and the **Netherlands Communist Party** (*Communistische Partij van Nederland*—CPN). It became a permanent party in 1991, when each of its constituent groups voted to disband. The party seeks to establish a country that is sustainable and socially minded.

The GL more than doubled its previous representation when it won 11 *Tweede Kamer* seats on a 7.3 percent vote share in 1998. After the GL won ten seats in the 2002 elections, its representation fell to eight seats in 2003 and seven in 2006. The GL's seat share increased to ten, on 6.7 percent of the vote, in the June 2010 balloting, but it dropped back to four seats, on 2.3 percent of the vote, in September 2012. The party elected a new slate of leaders in March 2013. In the 2014 EU polling, the GL won two seats, a loss of one from the previous balloting. The GL won 30 provincial seats and 4 Senate seats in 2015.

Leaders: Bram VAN OJIK (Parliamentary Chair), Rik GRASHOFF (Chair).

Party for the Animals (*Party voor de Dieren*—PvdD). Founded in 2002 as an advocate for animal rights, the party won 0.5 percent of the *Tweede Kamer* vote in 2003. However, it secured two seats in the Second Chamber in 2006, (on a vote share of 1.8 percent, thus becoming the first party principally devoted to animal welfare to gain entry into parliament. The party retained its two seats in the June 2010 election, on 1.3 percent of the vote, and again in September 2012 on 1.9 percent of the vote. In EU balloting in 2014, the PvdD won one seat. It won 18 provincial seats and 2 seats in the Senate in 2015.

Leaders: Marianne THIEME (Leader), Luuk FOLKERTS (Chair).

50Plus Party (*50 Plus Partij*). 50Plus was established in 2009 to advocate for pension reform, including cost of living increases, tax rates, rent freezes, and retirement age. The party calls upon the government to create a cabinet-level post for senior citizens affairs. The president of 50Plus is Jan Nagel, who served in the Dutch Senate for six years as a member of the PvdA. The party has a hotline that provides advice to patients whose prescriptions are not covered under current insurance programs. 50Plus has one seat in the Senate (held by Nagel) and nine provincial office holders. It entered the *Tweed Kamer* in September 2012, winning two seats on 1.9 percent of the vote. The party won 3.7 percent of the vote in the 2014 EU balloting, but no seats. In 2015 the party won 14 seats on provincial councils and 2 seats in the Senate.

Leaders: Jan NAGEL (Chair), Maurice KOOPMAN (First Vice Chair), Hylke TEN CATE (Secretary).

Other Parties That Contested the 2012 Elections:

Democratic Political Turning Point (*Het Demokratisch Politiek Keerpunt*—DPK) formed by the June 2012 merger of Hero Brinkman's **Independent Citizen's Party** and the Rita Verdonk's **Proud of the Netherlands Party** (TON). Brinkman had been a member of the extremist PVV and won a parliamentary seat in 2010 as an independent. He resigned from the PVV on March 20, 2012, complaining that the party structure was not democratic. Verdonk, the minister of immigration and integration from 2003 to 2006, set up her own party in 2010 after losing a bid to lead the VVD to Mark Rutte.

Leaders: Hero BRINKMAN (Chair), Rita VERDONK.

Other parties and lists that unsuccessfully contested the 2012 elections to the *Tweede Kamer,* or the 2014 EU parliament balloting, included the **Pirate Party** (*Piratenpartij*—PiratenP), led by Dirk POOT; the **Party for Human and Spirit** (*Partij voor Mens en Spirit*—MenS), led by Lea MANDERS; **Sovereign Independent Pioneers** (*Soeverein Onafhankelijke Pioniers Nederland*—SOPN), led by Johan OLDENKAMP; **Party of the Future** (*Partij van de Toekomst*—PvdT), led by Johan VLEMMIX; **Libertarian Party** (*Libertarische Partij*—LP), led by Toine MANDERS; **Netherlands Local** (*Nederland Lokaal*—NL), led by Ton SCHIJVENAARS; **Liberal Democratic Party** (*Liberaal Democratische Partij*—LibDem), founded by Samuel VAN TUYLL VAN SEROOSKERKEN; **Anti-Europe Party** (*Anti Europa Partij*—AeuP), led by Arnold REINTEN; the **Political Party NXD** (*Politieke Partij* NXD) of Anil SAMLAL; **Article 50** (*Artikel 50*), led by Daniël VAN DER STOEP; and **The Greens** (*De Groenen*), founded in 1983 as a federation of local conservative parties, and led by Paul FRERIKS.

For more on **Transparent Europe,** see the 2014 *Handbook.* For a list of other small parties that were active in the 1990s and/or early 2000s, see the 2007 *Handbook.*

LEGISLATURE

The **States General** (*Staten Generaal*) is a bicameral body consisting of an indirectly elected First Chamber and a directly elected Second Chamber.

First Chamber (*Eerste Kamer*). The 75 members of the upper house are indirectly elected by the country's 12 provincial councils for four-year terms. Elections to the First Chamber on May 26, 2015, gave the People's Party for Freedom and Democracy 13 seats; Christian Democratic Appeal, 12; Democrats 66, 10; Freedom Party, 9; Socialist Party, 9; Labor Party, 8; Green Left, 4; Christian Union, 3; Political Reformed Party, 2; 50Plus Party, 2; Party for the Animals, 2; and Independent Senate Group, 1.

President: Ankie BROEKER-KNOL (VVD).

Second Chamber (*Tweede Kamer*). The lower house consists of 150 members directly elected (in a single nationwide district under a pure proportional representation system) for four years, subject to dissolution and, under certain circumstances, term extension. The threshold for a party or list to secure representation is 0.67 percent of the national vote. Following the most recent election of September 12, 2012, the People's Party for Freedom and Democracy held 41 seats; Labor Party, 38; Party for Freedom, 15; Socialist Party, 15; Christian Democratic Appeal, 13; Democrats 66, 12; Christian Union, 5; Green Left, 4; Political Reformed Party, 3; Party for the Animals, 2; and 50Plus Party, 2.

Chair: Khadija ARIB (PvdA).

CABINET

[as of October 15, 2016]

Prime Minister	Mark Rutte (VVD)
Deputy Prime Minister	Lodewijk Asscher (PvdA)
Ministers	
Defense	Jeanine Hennis-Plasschaert (VVD) [f]
Economic Affairs	Henk Kamp (VVD)
Education, Culture, and Science	Jet Bussemaker (PvdA) [f]
Finance	Jeroen Dijsselbloem (PvdA)
Foreign Affairs	Bert Koenders (PvdA)
Foreign Trade and Development Cooperation	Lilianne Ploumen (PvdA) [f]
General Affairs	Mark Rutte (VVD)
Health, Welfare, and Sport	Edith Schippers (VVD) [f]
Housing and the Central Government Sector	Stef Blok (VVD)
Infrastructure and the Environment	Melanie Schultz van Haegen-Mass Geesteranus (VVD) [f]
Interior and Kingdom Relations	Ronald Plasterk (PvdA)
Security and Justice	Ard van der Steur (VVD)
Social Affairs and Employment	Lodewijk Asscher (PvdA)
Secretaries of State	
Agriculture and Economic Affairs	Martjin van Dam (PvdA)
Education, Culture and Science	Sander Dekker (VVD)
Finance	Eric Wiebes (VVD)
Health, Welfare, and Sport	Martin van Rijn (PvdA)
Infrastructure and the Environment	Sharon Dijlsma (PvdA) [f]
Security and Justice	Klaas Dijkhoff (VVD)
Social Affairs and Employment	Jetta Klijnsma (PvdA [f]

[f] = female

INTERGOVERNMENTAL REPRESENTATION

Ambassador to the U.S.: Hendrik Jan Jurriaan SCHUWER.

U.S. Ambassador to the Netherlands: Shawn CROWLEY (Chargé d'Affaires).

Permanent Representative to the UN: Karel VAN OOSTEROM.

IGO Memberships (Non-UN): ADB, AfDB, CEUR, EBRD, EIB, EU, IADB, IEA, ICC, IOM, NATO, OECD, OSCE, WTO.

For Further Reference:

Andeweg, Rudy, and Galen Irwin. *Governance and Politics of the Netherlands.* 4th ed. New York: Palgrave Macmillan, 2014.

Arblaster, Paul. *A History of the Low Countries.* 2nd ed. New York: Palgrave Macmillan, 2012.
Coates, Ben. *Why the Dutch Are Different: Into the Hidden Heart of the Netherlands.* London: Nicholas Brealey, 2015.

ARUBA

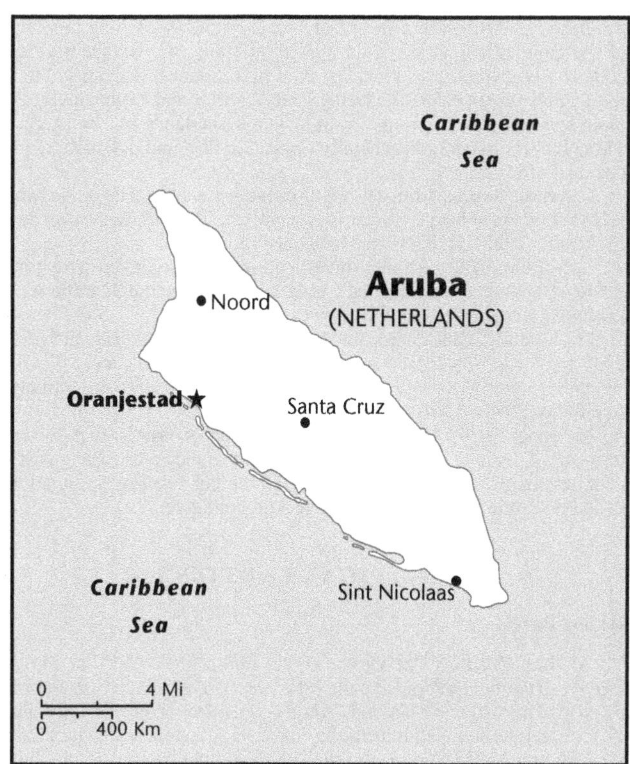

Political Status: Formerly part of the Netherlands Antilles; became autonomous in internal affairs on January 1, 1986.

Area: 74.5 sq. mi. (193 sq. km).

Population: 104,000 (2016E—UN); 113,648 (2016E—U.S. Census).

Major Urban Center (2014E—UN): ORANJESTAD (29,000).

Official Language: Dutch. English, Spanish, and Papiamento (an Antillean hybrid of mainly Portuguese and Spanish that is common to the Leeward Islands) are also spoken.

Monetary Unit: Aruban Guilder (official rate October 1, 2016: 1.79 guilders = $1US). The guilder (also called the florin) is at par with the Netherlands Antilles guilder, which is pegged to the U.S. dollar.

Sovereign: King WILLEM-ALEXANDER.

Governor: Fredis J. (Freddy) REFUNJOL; invested on May 7, 2004, succeeding Olindo KOOLMAN.

Prime Minister: Michiel "Mike" Godfried EMAN (Aruban People's Party); sworn in on October 30, 2009, following legislative election of September 24, succeeding Nelson Orlando ODUBER (People's Electoral Movement, *Movimento Electoral di Pueblo*—MEP); reelected on September 27, 2013.

THE COUNTRY

Aruba is a Caribbean island situated approximately 16 miles off the northeast coast of Venezuela and 50 miles west of Curaçao. Like other former Dutch dependencies in the area, its population is largely of mixed African ancestry, with minorities of Carib Indian and European extraction. Roman Catholicism is the dominant religion. Tourism is presently of primary economic importance, making up 85 percent of the GDP in 2015. From 2006 to 2008 a recovery in tourism, along with what the International Monetary Fund (IMF) defined as "robust" activity in the construction and utility sectors, contributed to an economic rebound. However, the impact of the recent global economic crisis was severe; the IMF estimated a cumulative GDP contraction of 15 percent in 2009 and 2010. The island's only oil refinery, which was a significant source of income, ceased operations in March 2012, triggering an economic decline of more than 1 percent. A strong recovery in 2013 of 4.8 percent, according to the IMF, weakened the following year to GDP growth of just 1.1 percent. In 2014 public debt surpassed 80 percent of GDP. In 2015 GDP grew by 2.3 percent, and was estimated by the IMF to be 1.8 percent in 2016.

GOVERNMENT AND POLITICS

Political background. Like Curaçao and Bonaire, Aruba became a Dutch possession in 1634 and remained so, save for a brief period of British control during the Napoleonic wars, until participating in constitutional equality with the Netherlands as part of the Netherlands Antilles in 1954.

However, a majority of the islanders disliked perceived political and economic domination by Curaçao and entered into lengthy discussions with Dutch authorities that resulted in the achievement of formal parity with the Netherlands and Netherlands Antilles, under the Dutch crown, on January 1, 1986. Upon the assumption of domestic autonomy, the assets and liabilities of Aruba and the five remaining members of the federation were divided in the ratio 30–70, Aruba agreeing to retain economic and political links to the Netherlands Antilles at the ministerial level for a ten-year period. (Full independence was initially projected for 1996 but tentative agreement was reached in July 1990 for the island to maintain its existing status indefinitely. References to the 1996 independence date were removed from the related constitutional documents completely in April 1995.)

Pre-autonomy balloting on November 22, 1985, yielded victory for a four-party coalition headed by John Hendrik Albert (Henny) EMAN of the center-right Aruba People's Party (AVP) over the MEP, then led by "the architect of Aruba's transition to...eventual independence," Gilberto (Betico) CROES. Following the election of January 7, 1989, a three-party government was formed, led by the MEP's Nelson ODUBER. The coalition continued in office after the election of January 8, 1993. Oduber resigned on April 17, 1994, after disagreements with his coalition partners. Eman headed a new government coalition that included the small Aruban Liberal Organization (OLA) following a general election on July 29.

The legislature was dissolved on September 15, 1997, in the wake of a coalition. In a December 12 general election, the parliamentary distribution remained unchanged. Negotiations continued until April 16, 1998, when the AVP and the OLA agreed on a new government.

The AVP/OLA government again collapsed in June 2001 when the two OLA members resigned after voicing objections to the AVP's plan to convert the tourism ministry into a semiprivate agency. In early elections held on September 28, the MEP won a majority of 12 seats. MEP leader Oduber returned to the prime minister's post on October 30. Oduber remained in office following the election of September 23, 2005, at which the MEP retained control with 11 seats. On the basis of a 12-seat AVP victory in the most recent election of September 8, 2009, Michiel (Mike) EMAN, the youngest brother of former prime minister Henny Eman, was named to form a new government.

Seven parties contested the September 27, 2013, general elections. The AVP, led by Eman, won 13 seats with 58 percent of the vote, a solid victory over the MEP's 7 seats, with 30 percent of the vote. Eman was sworn in for his second term on October 30 along with a reshuffled AVP cabinet.

Constitution and government. The Dutch sovereign is titular head of state and is represented in Aruba by an appointed governor. Domestic affairs are the responsibility of the prime minister and other members of the Council of Ministers, appointed with the advice and approval of a unicameral *Staten* (legislature) of 21 deputies. Control of foreign affairs and defense is vested in the Council of Ministers in The Hague, with the Department of Foreign Affairs in Aruba working in conjunction with the Ministry of Foreign Affairs in The Hague.

Similarly, an Aruban minister plenipotentiary sits as a voting member of the Council of Ministers on matters affecting the island. Judicial authority is exercised by a local court of first instance, with appeal to a joint Court of Appeal of the Netherlands Antilles and Aruba, and ultimate appeal to the Supreme Court of the Netherlands in The Hague. Though press freedom is generally respected, libel and defamation are criminal offenses.

Current issues. Minister Plenipotentiary to the Hague Edwin ABATH resigned his post in early November 2013 and was succeeded by Alfonso BOEKHOUDT on November 15.

In March 2014 a criminal investigation team began investigating money laundering in Aruba and Curaçao involving some $2 million of illegal cigarettes allegedly linked to Colombia's FARC.

On June 11, 2016, authorities from Aruba and Venezuela, and officials from two oil companies, Petróleos de Venezuela and CITGO Aruba, announced an agreement to reopen a the closed Valero refinery to produce 209,000 barrels per day.

In June 2016 Otmar ODUBAR, Aruba's tourism minister, announced plans to introduce legislation that would restrict the growth of all-inclusive resorts. The Caribbean Hotel and Tourism Association called on Prime Minister Eman to reject the initiative.

POLITICAL PARTIES

Ruling Party:

Aruban People's Party (*Arubaanse Volkspartij*—AVP/*Partido di Pueplo Arubano*—PPA). Like the MEP, the AVP advocated separation of Aruba from the Netherlands Antilles. A member of the Christian Democrat International, it formed a coalition government that included the PPA and AND (below) after the 1985 balloting but was forced into opposition in 1989. Though its vote share exceeded that of the MEP in 1993, they tied with 9 seats each. It formed a new government in coalition with the OLA (below) after the 1994 election, which was revived in May 1998 but fell in June 2001. In the September election it won 6 *Staten* seats, adding 2 more in 2005. It returned to power with a majority of 12 seats in 2009, and added a seat in 2013 balloting.

Leader: Michiel "Mike" Godfried EMAN (Party Leader).

Parliamentary Parties:

People's Electoral Movement (*Movimiento Electoral di Pueblo*—MEP). Founded in 1971 and a member of the Socialist International, the MEP was in the forefront of the struggle for self-government. It won a plurality of ten *Staten* seats in 1989. Two were lost in 1993, but the MEP formed a governing coalition with the AND and PPA (below) prior to the withdrawal of both in April 1994. In 2001 the MEP won 12 seats, 1 of which was lost in 2005. It fell to a minority of 8 seats in 2009. In July 2011 a major party leader, Booshi WEVER, announced his resignation from the party leadership because of a lack of confidence in the party's political leader, Nelson Oduber. The MEP won 7 seats in September 2013 balloting. That year, Evelyn WEVER-CROES was elected party chair.

Leaders: Evelyn WEVER-CROES (Chair), Nelson Orlando ODUBER (Former Prime Minister).

Real Democracy (*Democracia Real*—DR). Launched in 2004, the DR failed to secure legislative representation in 2005 but won one seat in 2009. With 8 percent of the vote, the DR maintained its single seat in 2013 balloting.

Leader: Andin BIKKER (Party Leader).

Other Parties Contesting the 2013 General Election:

Aruban Patriotic Party (*Arubaanse Patriottische Partij*—APP/*Partido Patriótico Arubano*—PPA). Organized in 1949, the PPA is a social-democratic group that has opposed full independence for the island. It won two parliamentary seats in 2001 but lost both in 2005, and again was unsuccessful in 2013.

Leader: Benedict "Benny" Jocelyn Montgomery NISBETT.

Network of Eternal Democracy (*Red Eternal Democratico*—RED). The RED won one seat in the 2005 election, but lost in 2009. It contested unsuccessfully in 2013.

Leader: Armando "Rudy" LAMPE.

Also contesting the 2013 elections were the **United Christians Reinforcing Aruba's Potential** (*Cristiannan Uni Reforzando Potencial*—CURPA); the **Independent Social Movement/Aruban Liberal Organization** (Organisatie Liberaal Arubaanse/*Organisacion Liberal Arubano/Organisashion pa Liberashou di Aruba*—OLA) led by Glenbert François CROES; and the **Aruban Patriotic Movement** (*Movimento Patriotico Arubana*—MPA), led by Monica ARENDS-KOCK, who has been described as Aruba's first female party leader.

Other parties include the **National Democratic Action** (*Acción Democratico Nacional*—AND), led by Pedro Charro KELLY; the **Aruban Democratic Alliance** (*Aliansa Democratico Arubano*—ADA), led by Robert Frederick WEVER; and the **Concentration for the Liberation of Aruba** (*Conscientisacion y Liberacion Arubano*—CLA), led by Mariano Duvert BLUME.

LEGISLATURE

The unicameral **States** (*Staten*) consists of 21 members elected for four-year terms, subject to dissolution. In the most recent balloting, held on September 27, 2013, the Aruban People's Party won 13 seats; the People's Electoral Movement, 7; Real Democracy, 1.

Chair: M. J. LOPEZ-TROMP.

CABINET

[as of June 21, 2016]

Prime Minister	Michiel Godfried Eman
Vice Prime Minister	Mike Eric de Meza
Ministers	
Economic Affairs, Communications, Energy, and Environment	Mike Eric de Meza
Education, Family Policy, and Adult Education	Michelle Hooyboer-Winklaar [f]
Finance and Government Organization	Angel Roald Bermudez
General Affairs and Sustainable Development	Michiel Godfried Eman
Justice	Arthur Lawrence Dowers
Public Health, Elderly Care, and Sports	Carlos Alex Schwengle
Regional Planning, Infrastructure, and Integration	Oslin Benito Sevinger
Social Affairs, Youth Policy, and Labor	Pauldrick François Teodoric Croes
Tourism, Transportation, Culture, and Primary Sector	Otmar Enrique Oduber
Minister Plenipotentiary in the Hague	Alfonso Boekhoudt
Minister Plenipotentiary in Washington, D.C.	Jocelyne Croes [f]

[f] = female

Note: All cabinet members are affiliated with the AVP.

INTERGOVERNMENTAL REPRESENTATION

Foreign relations are for the most part conducted through the Netherlands Ministry of Foreign Affairs in The Hague, although there is a Minister Plenipotentiary in the Netherlands Embassy in Washington, D.C., and the United States maintains a Consulate General's Office in Curaçao that also serves Aruba.

For Further Reference:

Government of Aruba. "Aruba Gobierno." Accessed August 19, 2016. www.government.aw.

Haanappel, Peter, Ejan Mackaay, Hans Warendorf, and Richard Thomas, trans. *The Civil Code of the Netherlands Antilles and Aruba.* The Hague, Netherlands: Kluwer Law, 2002.

Minto-Coy, Indianna D., and Evan M. Berman, eds. *Public Administration and Policy in the Caribbean.* Boca Raton, FL: CRC Press, 2015.

CURAÇAO

Country of Curaçao
Land Curaçao (Dutch)
Pais Kòrsou (Papiamento)

Political Status: Former Dutch dependency; from 1948 a component of the Netherlands Antilles, which became autonomous in internal affairs, under charter of the Kingdom of the Netherlands, effective December 29, 1954; achieved separate autonomous status in internal affairs upon dissolution of the Netherlands Antilles on October 10, 2010.

Area: 171 sq. mi. (444 sq. km).

Population: 159,000 (2016E—UN); 149,035 (2016E—U.S. Census).

Major Urban Center (2015E—UN): WILLEMSTAD (145,000, urban area).

Official Languages: Dutch, English, and Papiamento (an Antillean hybrid, principally of Portuguese and Spanish).

Monetary Unit: Netherlands Antilles Guilder (official rate October 1, 2016: 1.81 guilders = $1US). The guilder is pegged to the U.S. dollar. A new Caribbean guilder, likewise pegged to the dollar, was to be introduced jointly by St. Maarten and Curaçao in January 2012. However, no progress had been achieved on the currency as of mid-2016.

Sovereign: King WILLEM-ALEXANDER.

Governor: Lucille GEORGE-WOUT; nominated by the Council of Ministers of Curaçao in August 2013, appointed by the Netherlands Council of Ministers on November 1; sworn in by the king on November 4, 2013, effective November 8; succeeding Dr. Fritz M. de los SANTOS GOEDGEDRAG, who resigned on November 24, 2012, due to health issues.

Prime Minister: Ben WHITEMAN (Sovereign People), sworn in on September 1, 2015, after Ivar ASJES (Sovereign People) resigned on August 31 (see Government and Politics, below).

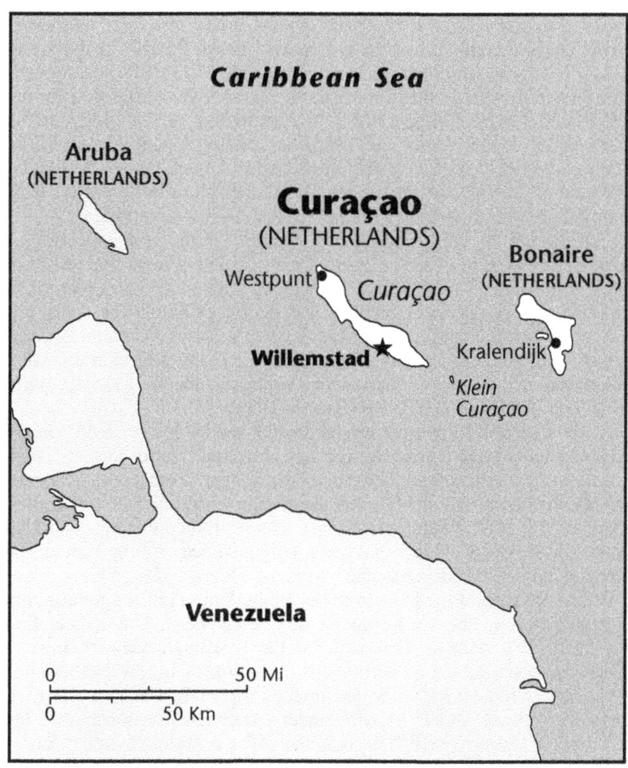

THE COUNTRY

Only 40 miles off the coast of Venezuela in the southern arc of the Lesser Antilles, the Caribbean island of Curaçao lies east of Aruba and west of Bonaire. The Country of Curaçao also includes the small, uninhabited island of Little Curaçao. Approximately 85 percent of the population is of mixed African ancestry, the remainder being of Carib Indian and European derivation. Roman Catholicism is professed by 85 percent of the population, which also includes various Protestant denominations and a small Jewish population. (Curaçao is home to the oldest continuous Jewish congregation in the Americas, dating from 1651.) Some 85 percent of the population speaks Papiamento, but many also speak English, Spanish, or Dutch.

The economy was initially dependent on salt refining and, given the island's superior deepwater ports, trade (including the slave trade). Since 1920 the principal industry has been petroleum refining and transshipment, followed by tourism and offshore finance in later decades. Agriculture, accounting for only 1 percent of GDP, is restrained by poor soil and little rainfall. Services provide 85 percent of GDP and employ the large majority of the labor force. Since the 2009 international financial crisis, when GDP declined by 0.2 percent, Curaçao has struggled. In 2011, with unemployment at about 12 percent, the economy contracted by 0.6 percent, and GDP remained stagnant in 2012. In December 2012 the Dutch government expressed its concern for Curaçao's public finances, predicting the budget shortfall would increase to $236.5 million by 2015. Accordingly, Curaçao's GDP grew by an average of less than 1 percent annually from 2013–2015. By 2015 unemployment was estimated to be 11.7 percent.

GOVERNMENT AND POLITICS

Political background. Sighted by the Spanish in 1499 and claimed by the Dutch in 1634, Curaçao subsequently served as the region's principal slave-trading port. From the late 17th century until the Dutch firmly established ownership in 1815, possession of the island was frequently contested by Britain and France as well as the Netherlands. In 1828 Curaçao became part of the Dutch West Indies, along with the South American territory of Dutch Guiana, the nearby islands of Aruba and Bonaire, and the northern Leeward Islands of St. Eustatius and Saba plus the southern third of St. Maarten (the northern two-thirds, St. Martin, is a French possession). Having been administered for over a century as a colonial dependency, in 1954 the six island jurisdictions, known collectively since 1948 as the Netherlands Antilles, were granted constitutional equality with the Netherlands and Suriname (the former Dutch Guiana) as an autonomous component of the Kingdom of the Netherlands. In 1975 Suriname achieved full independence, and in 1986 Aruba became a separate, largely autonomous "country" within the kingdom.

Given the geographical range of the Netherlands Antilles, political differences were largely island-based, necessitating highly unstable coalition governments that rival parties from the most populous islands, Aruba and Curaçao, tended to dominate. Aruba's departure on January 1, 1986, resulted in an Antillean legislature, the States (*Staten*), in which Curaçao was assigned 14 of the 22 seats, compared to 3 for St. Maarten, 3 for Bonaire, and 1 each for St. Eustatius and Saba. Thus, the Curaçao-based rival New Antilles Movement (*Movimentu Antiá Nobo*—MAN), National People's Party (*Partido Nashonal di Pueblo*—PNP), Workers' Liberation Front (*Frente Obrero de Liberashon*—FOL), and (from 1994) Restructured Antilles Party (*Partido Antiá Restrukturá*—PAR) became the leading parties in a series of coalition governments that also included various smaller parties from the other, less-populous Antilles jurisdictions. The same parties also dominated Curaçao's local legislature, the 21-member Island Council.

In the November 1985 election for the Netherlands Antilles *Staten,* Maria LIBERIA-PETERS of the PNP, the Antilles's first female prime minister, was defeated in an election held in preparation for Aruba's departure on January 1, with former prime minister Dominico MARTINA (MAN) then forming a new administration. Between December 1987 and March 1988, however, Martina lost the backing of the 3 representatives from St. Maarten and another from Curaçao's FOL, and he was forced from office in favor of Liberia-Peters, who returned in May as head of a new coalition that claimed the support of 13 of 22 *Staten* members.

In a referendum on November 19, 1993, 73 percent of Curaçao voters rejected a government-backed proposal that the island seek special autonomy status similar to that of Aruba; 8 percent favored incorporation into the Netherlands and only 1 percent endorsed full independence. Two of the PNP's non-Curaçao partners withdrew from the government coalition, forcing Liberia-Peters's resignation. The PNP justice minister, Susanne CAMELIA-RÖMER, became acting prime minister, and in late December she was succeeded by the PNP's Alejandro Felippe PAULA, a professor of sociology at the University of the Netherlands Antilles, pending a general election in February 1994. At the polls, the recently organized PAR, led by Miguel POURIER, secured an eight-member plurality of *Staten* seats and in late March formed a broad-based coalition government.

Although the PAR maintained a plurality in the *Staten* election of January 1998, it lost four of its eight seats on a vote share that fell from nearly 40 percent to less than 19 percent. Invited by the governor to form a new government, Pourier was unable to attract the necessary support from the ten other legislative groups. While Pourier's government continued in a caretaker capacity, lengthy negotiations were launched on a variety of alternatives, which in June yielded a six-party coalition headed by the PNP's Camelia-Römer.

The Camelia-Römer government collapsed in October 1999 amid a dispute concerning a national recovery plan, and Pourier formed a new coalition government in November. Benefiting from continued economic difficulties, the FOL led all groups in the *Staten* election of January 18, 2002, winning five seats. However, the FOL was excluded from the six-party cabinet that was finally installed on June 3 under the leadership of the PAR's Etienne YS.

The absence of the FOL from the Netherlands Antilles government became more of an issue following the Curaçao Island Council election of April 2003, when the FOL won 8 of the 21 seats. In May 2003 Prime Minister Ys resigned to permit the formation of a new Netherlands Antilles government that would include the FOL. Because the FOL leader, Anthony GODETT, was under indictment for corruption, the FOL's Bernhard KOMPROE assumed office as acting prime minister on July 22, and on August 11 Mirna LUISA-GODETT, Anthony Godett's sister, was in turn sworn in as Komproe's successor.

In December 2003 Anthony Godett was convicted of forgery, bribery, and money laundering and sentenced to prison. Two of the FOL's partners thereupon withdrew from the government, leaving the coalition temporarily without a majority in the *Staten;* however, the coalition was strengthened shortly thereafter with the addition of parties from Bonaire and St. Maarten. On April 6, 2004, the government again collapsed when the PNP refused to continue with Komproe as justice minister. Luisa-Godett resigned, with the PAR's Etienne Ys returning as prime minister on June 3.

On April 8, 2005, 68 percent of Curaçao's voters endorsed autonomous status for the island within the Kingdom of the Netherlands. As a result, on November 26 the five constituent islands and the kingdom's government agreed that the Netherlands Antilles would dissolve by July 2007, with Curaçao and St. Maarten (whose voters had expressed support for autonomy in a 2000 referendum) achieving "country" status, like Aruba, and with Bonaire, Saba, and St. Eustatius becoming "Kingdom Islands" (*Koninkrijkseilanden*) with the status of special municipalities within the Netherlands proper.

In November 2006, however, Curaçao's Island Council voted to reject the 2005 agreement, under which The Hague would retain control of defense, foreign policy, and law enforcement. As a result, the date for its implementation was put back to December 15, 2008, to permit reevaluation of the objectionable provisions. The other four islands appeared, in general, to be satisfied with the proposed restructuring.

Meanwhile, in the Netherlands Antilles *Staten* election of January 27, 2006, the PAR had won five seats and the MAN, three, with the PAR's Emily DE JONGH-ELHAGE being sworn in as prime minister on March 26. On April 20, 2007, the two parties again finished first and second, respectively, in an election for Curaçao's Island Council, with the PAR winning seven seats and the MAN, five.

In late 2007 the Dutch government expressed doubt that the deadline for constitutional changes for Curaçao and St. Maarten autonomy could be met. In April 2008 The Hague formally declared that it was no longer realistic. A new target of early 2010 was advanced, coincident with expiration of the Antillean legislative term. On May 15, 2009, Curaçao voters narrowly approved a nonbinding referendum acquiescing to the retention of substantial economic control by The Hague in return for Dutch assumption of a major portion of Curaçao's foreign debt, thus clearing the way for political autonomy in 2010.

Further delays in implementing the planned dissolution of the Netherlands Antilles necessitated a final election for its *Staten.* In balloting on January 22, 2010, nine parties divided the 22 seats, with the PAR adding 1 to its 2006 tally, for a total of 6. Of the other successful Curaçao parties, a three-party Change List (*Lista di Kambio*), headed by the MAN, won 5 seats, while the Sovereign People (*Pueblo Soberano*) took 2 and the PNP, 1. Prime Minister de Jongh-Elhage, with support from other islands, then succeeded in forging another multiparty coalition whose principal task became clearing the way for the dissolution of the Netherlands Antilles.

On June 19, 2010, Curaçao's Island Council failed to muster the two-thirds vote needed to approve a constitution for the Country of Curaçao. Under the kingdom charter, this necessitated a new council election before a second vote, in which a simple majority would prevail. On the weekend of June 26–27 the governor dissolved the council and called for an election, which was held on August 27. The PAR won eight seats, while the newly organized Movement for the Future of Curaçao (*Movementu Futuro Kòrsou*—MFK) won five; the Sovereign People (*Pueblo Soberano*—PS), four; the MAN, two; the FOL, one; and the PNP, one. In a quick series of actions on September 4, the leader of the MFK, Gerrit SCHOTTE, completed a coalition agreement with the PS and MAN, the new Island Council convened and approved the constitution by a 15–6 vote, and the legislators appointed a new Executive Council to serve until dissolution of the Netherlands Antilles.

On October 10, 2010, the Country of Curaçao came into existence. The Island Council automatically became the new *Staten* of Curaçao, and Gerrit SCHOTTE took office as Curaçao's first prime minister, heading an MFK-PS-MAN Council of Ministers. After the MFK lost its majority when a minister left the party, Schotte dissolved parliament on August 3, 2012, and called for early elections in October. Later in August, 12 parliamentarians petitioned Governor Frits GOEDGEDRAG to form an interim cabinet. Goedgedrag appointed former Lieutenant Governor Stanley BETRIAN to create a temporary government.

A total of eight parties contested the October 2012 elections, with six winning seats. The PS won a narrow majority in balloting on October 19, and after several months of negotiations, established a coalition government with the PAIS and the PNP (see Current issues, below). Four days after the general election, Governor Goedgedrag submitted his resignation, effective November 24, 2012, because of health problems. Adele Van der PLUIJM-VREDE served on an acting basis for almost a year. Lucille GEORGE-WOUT was nominated in August 2013, approved by the Netherlands Council of Ministers on November 1, sworn in by the king on November 4, and installed on November 8, becoming the first woman to hold the post.

Daniel HODGE of the PS on December 31 became leader of a transitional government. He dissolved his cabinet three months later on March 27, 2013. On June 7 PS-leader Ivar ASJES was sworn in as prime minister. In late December 2013 Asjes completed his cabinet, assigning the vacant Education portfolio to the PS's Irene DICK.

Asjes resigned as prime minister on August 31, 2015, after losing the support of the PS in Parliament. He was replaced by the minister of health, Ben WHITEMAN (PS), who was sworn in on September 1. Whiteman initially agreed to serve as interim prime minister for three months but then agreed to remain in place until new elections, scheduled for September 2016. On November 9 independent member of Parliament Marilyn MOSES withdrew from the governing coalition, ending its majority. However, Whiteman was able to form a new PS-led coalition which included its contemporary partners and the Restructured Antilles Party (*Partido Antiá Restrukturá*—PAR).

Constitution and government. Under the 2010 constitution the Dutch sovereign, the titular head of state, is represented in Curaçao by an appointed governor. Domestic affairs are the responsibility of the prime minister and other members of the Council of Ministers, appointed with the advice and approval of the unicameral legislature, the States of Curaçao (*Staten van Curaçao*). Elections to the *Staten* are held every four years, subject to dissolution. A Council of Advice, whose members are appointed by government decree, reviews proposed legislation and administrative orders and may offer advice to the government. The constitution also provides for an ombudsperson. Control of foreign affairs and defense remains vested in the Council of Ministers in The Hague, where a minister plenipotentiary from Curaçao advises on matters relevant to Curaçao. Judicial authority is exercised by a Court of First Instance and by a Common Court (for Aruba, Curaçao, St. Maarten, and the special municipalities of Bonaire, St. Eustatius, and Saba), whose members are appointed by the queen. Ultimate appeal is to the Supreme Court of the Netherlands in The Hague. The constitution may be amended by a two-thirds vote of the Curaçao legislature, subject to the subsequent approval of the Dutch government.

Current issues. In elections on October 19, 2012, the PS won five seats with 22.7 percent of the vote, narrowly defeating the leading MFK, which also won five seats but with 21.2 percent. After attempts to negotiate a coalition government, former prime minister and MFK leader Gerrit Schotte withdrew his party, halting efforts to form the new leadership. Eventually, a PS-led coalition secured 11 of 21 seats in the assembly with the PAIS, the PNP, and former PAR-member Glenn SULVARAN. On December 31 Daniel Hodge was sworn in as prime minister, followed by his cabinet on January 2, 2013, to serve for a transitional period of three to six months. On March 27, 2013, Prime Minister Hodge and his cabinet resigned, citing that his leadership was intended to be short-term. PS leader Ivar Asjes assumed the office of prime minister on June 7, 2013.

Helmin WIELS, the leader of the PS, was shot dead on May 5, 2013. Wiels had been a major player in forming the leading coalition. It was unclear whether his assassination was politically motivated or linked to his outspoken opposition to organized crime.

After an April 2014 meeting, Asjes and St. Maarten prime minister Sarah Wescot-Williams announced desire to abolish the countries' shared central bank to establish their own individual ones.

Former prime minister Schotte and his long-term girlfriend were arrested on May 20, 2014, as suspects in a money laundering operation. He was released one week later but was convicted of money laundering and bribery in March 2016 and sentenced to three years in prison.

After his resignation as prime minister, Asjes formed a new political grouping, the Party for Curaçao (*Partido Pro Korsou*—PPK). By July 2016 19 parties had registered for the 2016 elections.

POLITICAL PARTIES

Governing Coalition:

Sovereign People (*Pueblo Soberano*—PS). Founded in 2006 as a left-of-center, progressive party, the pro-independence PS won one seat in Curaçao's Island Council election of April 2007, two in the Netherlands Antilles *Staten* election of January 2010, and four in the August 2010 Island Council election. Its representatives voted against the Curaçao draft constitution, but the party agreed to join the MFK-led government in September 2010. The PS has called for an end to U.S. military use of an air base on the island. The PS secured a narrow majority with 22.6 percent and five seats in polling on October 19, 2012.

Following the murder of party president and founder Helmin Wiels on May 5, 2013, internal tensions emerged within the party, with members of the parliamentary party calling for the committee members to step down. On May 15 Ivar Asjes assumed party leadership. Subsequently, PS opponents criticized the group for straying from its central mission, complete independence. A group of former PS members, led by Wiels' brother, Aubert, announced in April 2014 that they would launch a new formation called 1 Team Magno (*1 Tim Magno*) dedicated to the true ideals of the late party president. Jaime CÓRDOBA was elected chair of the PS in December 2015.

Leaders: Ben WHITEMAN (Prime Minister), Jaime CÓRDOBA (Chair).

Social Progress and Innovation Party (*Partido Adelanto i Inovashon Soshul*—PAIS). The PAIS was registered in 2010 by Alex Rosario, a former PNP member and finance official. The PAIS won 3 percent of the Curaçao Island Council vote and no seats in August 2010. In October 2012 the PAIS secured four seats and 17.7 percent of the vote.

Leaders: Mike FRANCO (Party President), Alex ROSARIO (Political Leader).

National People's Party (*Partido Nashonal di Pueblo*—PNP/ *Nationale Volkspartij*). The right-of-center PNP served as the core of the governing coalition in the Netherlands Antilles from 1988 to 1993. Its leader, Maria Liberia-Peters, was obliged to step down as prime minister as a result of the November 1993 referendum result, and its *Staten* representation dropped from seven to three seats in February 1994, before rising to four in January 1998. In May 1998–November 1999 Susanne Camelia-Römer headed the Antilles government. The PNP secured three seats in 2002, one of which was lost in 2006. In January 2010 the PNP won only one seat. It also claimed one seat, on 6 percent of the vote, in the August 2010 Curaçao Island Council election, a loss of one seat from 2007. In the October 2012 elections, the PNP secured one seat and 5.9 percent of the vote.

Leaders: Humphrey DAVELAAR (Party Leader), Gisette SEFERINA (Chair).

Restructured Antilles Party (*Partido Antiá Restrukturá*—PAR). The PAR is a social-Christian formation launched in the wake of the November 1993 referendum. It became the leading party of the Netherlands Antilles government coalition formed after the 1994 election, in which it won 8 of 22 *Staten* seats. It was reduced to a minority of 4 seats in 1998 and secured the same number in 2002, with 1 additional seat added in 2006, at which time it became the plurality party and headed a multiparty governing coalition under Prime Minister Emily de Jongh-Elhage. The PAR picked up an additional *Staten* seat in January 2010, thereby retaining its plurality in the final Netherlands Antilles *Staten*.

In Curaçao's Island Council, the PAR finished second to the FOL in the May 2003 election, when it won 5 of 21 seats, but claimed a plurality of 7 seats in the April 2007 election and 8 in August 2010 (with 30 percent of the vote). Despite obtaining a plurality of votes, the PAR became the main party of the opposition after the creation of an MFK-led coalition.

In balloting of October 19, 2012, the PAR secured 4 seats and 19.7 percent of the vote. After the party withdrew from coalition negotiations with the PS, member Glenn SULVARAN severed ties with the PAR to independently join the leading coalition.

With the establishment of the Whiteman cabinet in 2015, the PAR joined the government for the first time in five years.

Leader: Emily DE JONGH-ELHAGE (Political Leader).

Other Parliamentary Parties:

Movement for the Future of Curaçao (*Movementu Futuro Kòrsou*—MFK). The MFK was organized by Gerrit Schotte in July 2010. He had previously been affiliated with the FOL (below) and had also been a founder of the **Patriotic Movement of Curaçao** (*Movementu Patriotiko Kòrsou*—MPK). In August 2010, in its first electoral contest, the MFK won 21 percent of the vote and five seats in Curaçao's Island Council, after which Schotte negotiated a coalition agreement with the PS (above) and MAN (below). In late September he was asked by the governor of Curaçao to form the Country of Curaçao's first Council of Ministers, which took office on October 10. The MFK lost power in the October 2012 elections, coming in second with 21.2 percent of the vote and winning five seats. Following the arrest of Schotte in May 2014 (see Current issues, above), the party stood behind their leader.

Leaders: Gerrit SCHOTTE (Former Prime Minister and Party Leader), Dean ROZIER (Chair).

New Antilles Movement (*Movishon Antiá Nobo/Movimentu Antiyas Nobo*—MAN). The MAN is a left-of-center member of the Socialist International that served as the core of the Dominico Martina administrations of 1982–1984 and 1985–1988 in the Netherlands Antilles, although holding only four *Staten* seats on the latter occasion. Its representation in the *Staten* dropped to two seats in 1990, both of which were retained in 1994 and 1998. The party failed to gain representation in 2002 but won three seats in 2006, and in January 2010 it led the three-party **Change List** (*Lista di Kambio*), which also included the **Upwards Curaçao** (*Forsa Kòrsou*), led by Nelson NAVARRO, and **Not One Step Back** (*Niun Paso Atras*), led by Carlos MONK. The Change List came in second, with five *Staten* seats.

As for recent Curaçao Island Council elections, the MAN finished with 19 percent of the vote and five seats in April 2007 but in August 2010 saw its support drop to 9 percent and two seats. It was awarded two ministerial posts in the Schotte cabinet. Member Eugene CLEOPA left the party in September 2012 but retained his seat in parliament. In the October 2012 election, the MAN won two seats and 19.7 percent of the vote.

Leader: Hensley KOEIMAN (Party President).

Other Parties:

Workers' Liberation Front of 30 May (*Frente Obrero di Liberashon 30 di Mei*—FOL). A Marxist group, the FOL entered the 1990 Netherlands Antilles election in coalition with the **Independent Social** (*Soshal Independiente*—SI), which had been formed in 1986 by a group of PNP dissidents. The two groups also presented joint candidates in the January 1998 balloting (as the **Social Independence–Workers' Liberation Front**—SIFOL), winning two seats. The FOL left the

Netherlands Antilles government coalition in mid-2001 as a result of tension between FOL leader Anthony Godett and the administration regarding budget cuts. The FOL was the top vote-getter in the 2002 Antilles election, winning five legislative seats on a vote share of 23 percent, but Godett was precluded from installation as prime minister because of his indictment (and later conviction) for bribery, fraud, and money laundering. In September 2005 the High Court in The Hague upheld a 15-month prison sentence for Godett.

An Antilles government under Godett's sister, Mirna Luisa-Godett, fell in the wake of Godett's conviction, and in 2006 the FOL won only two *Staten* seats. In 2010 the FOL lost both Netherlands Antilles *Staten* seats and one of its Curaçao Island Council seats.

In the 2012 elections, 29 FOL candidates contested, but the party did not secure any seats. Godett subsequently resigned from party leadership.

Democrat Laboral. In the October 2012 general election, the Labor Party Popular Crusade (PLKP) and the Democratic Party–Curaçao (DP) (both below) combined. Twenty-nine candidates ran, winning 1.3 percent of the vote and no seats.

Labor Party Popular Crusade (*Partido Laboral Krusada Popular*—PLKP). A trade union-based group launched in 1997, the PLKP won three seats in the 1998 Netherlands Antilles legislative election. It joined the subsequent cabinet led by the PNP's Susanne Camelia-Römer but withdrew in 1999 and was not included in the PAR-led cabinet of November 1999. The PLKP rejoined the government in June 2002, having secured 12.1 percent of the vote and two seats in the January legislative poll; it lost both seats in 2006. Although it held three Curaçao Island Council seats after the May 2003 election, the PLKP was later weakened by a split that produced the Social Labor Movement (*Movementu Social Laboral*—MSL), and in the 2007 election it failed to retain council representation.

The PLKP won only 1 percent of the Curaçao Island Council vote in August 2010.

Leader: Errol GOELOE (Party Leader).

Democratic Party–Curaçao (*Partido Democraat—DP*). Prior to the 1985 election the DP was primarily Curaçao-based, with a Dutch-speaking branch on Bonaire and English-speaking branches on St. Maarten and St. Eustatius. In 2010 it won no seats in either the January Netherlands Antilles vote or the August Curaçao Island Council vote. In the latter, it won 4 percent of the vote.

Leader: Norberto RIBERIO (Political Leader).

LEGISLATURE

The unicameral **States of Curaçao** (*Staten van Curaçao*) consists of 21 members elected by proportional representation for four-year terms, subject to dissolution. In the election held October 19, 2012, for the Curaçao Island Council, Sovereign People won 5 seats; the Movement for the Future of Curaçao (MFK), 5; Social Progress and Innovation Party, 4; Restructured Antilles Party, 4; New Antilles Movement, 2; and National People's Party, 1.

Chair: Mike FRANCO.

CABINET

[as of June 23, 2016]

Prime Minister	Bernard Whiteman (PS)
Ministers	
Economic Development	Eugene P. Rhuggenaath (PAR)
Education, Science, Culture, and Sports	Irene Dick (PS) [f]
Finance	Jose Jardim (ind.)
General Affairs and International Affairs	Bernard Whiteman (PS)
Government Policy, Planning, and Services	Etienne van der Horst (PAIS)
Health, Environment, and Nature	M.A. Victorina (PS)
Justice	Nelson Navarro (PAIS)
Social Development, Labor, and Welfare	R.D. Larmonie-Cecilia (PS) [f]
Traffic, Transport, and Urban Planning	Suzanne Camelia-Römer (PNP) [f]
Minister Plenipotentiary to The Hague	Marvelyne Wiels (PS) [f]

[f] = female

INTERGOVERNMENTAL REPRESENTATION

Foreign relations are for the most part conducted through the Dutch Ministry of Foreign Affairs in The Hague, although the United States maintains a Consulate General's Office in Curaçao.

For Further Reference:

Central Bureau of Statistics Curaçao. Accessed August 19, 2016. www.cbs.cw.

Goslinga, Cornelius. *A Short History of the Netherlands Antilles and Surinam.* New York: Springer, 1979.

Government of Curaçao. Accessed June 30, 2016. www.gobiernu.cw.

ST. MAARTEN

Country of Saint Maarten
Land Sint Maarten

Note: In the St. Maarten general election on September 26, 2016, the United Peoples (UP) won 29.1 percent of the vote and five seats, while the National Alliance (NA) secured 26.6 percent of the vote and five seats. The United St. Maarten Party (USP) received 19.6 percent of the vote and three seats, and the Democratic Party of St. Maarten (DP) received 12.8 percent of the vote and two seats. The outcome allowed the governing coalition of the NA, USP, and DP, under Prime Minister William Martin (NA), to remain in office.

Political Status: Former Dutch dependency; from 1948 a component of the Netherlands Antilles, which became autonomous in internal affairs, under charter of the Kingdom of the Netherlands, effective December 29, 1954; achieved separate autonomous status in internal affairs upon dissolution of the Netherlands Antilles on October 10, 2010.

Area: 13.1 sq. mi. (34 sq. km).

Population: 40,000 (2016E—UN); 41,486 (2016E—U.S. Census).

Major Urban Centers (2010E): PHILIPSBURG (1,228), Lower Prince's Quarters (8,123).

Official Languages: Dutch and English.

Monetary Unit: Netherlands Antilles Guilder (official rate October 1, 2016: 1.81 guilders = $1US). The guilder is pegged to the U.S. dollar. A new Caribbean guilder, likewise pegged to the dollar, was to be introduced jointly by St. Maarten and Curaçao in January 2012. However, no progress had been achieved on the currency as of mid-2016.

Sovereign: King WILLEM-ALEXANDER.

Governor: Eugene HOLIDAY; nominated by the St. Maarten Executive Council in June 2010 and approved by the Netherlands Council of Ministers on September 7; sworn in by the Queen BEATRIX for a six-year term on September 30, 2010, effective October 10.

Prime Minister: William MARLIN (National Alliance); named prime minister–designate by coalition agreement concluded on September 30, 2015, and took the oath of office on November 19, succeeding Marcel GUMBS (United People's Party).

THE COUNTRY

Located 160 miles east of the island of Puerto Rico in the Leeward Islands of the Lesser Antilles, between the British overseas territory of Anguilla to the north and the French overseas collectivity of

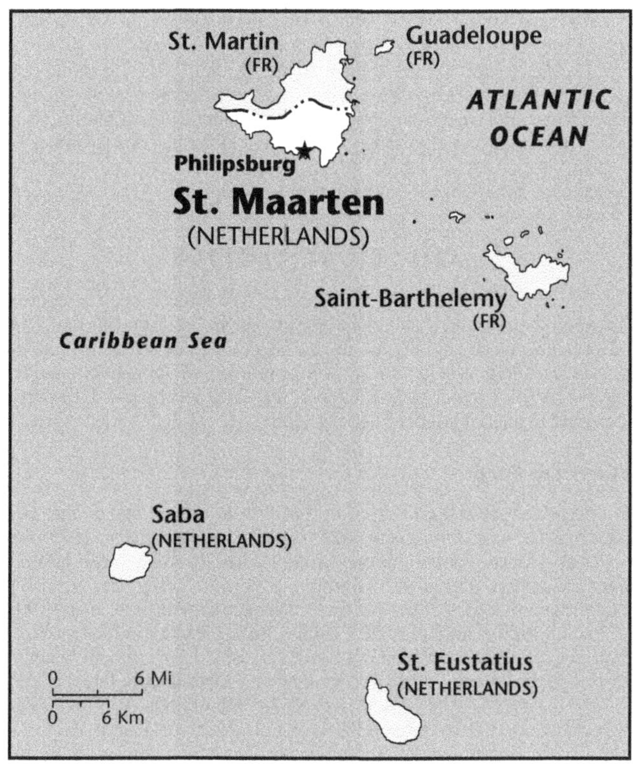

St. Barthelemy to the southeast, St. Maarten occupies the southern third of a small Caribbean island that is shared by the French overseas collectivity of St. Martin. About two-thirds of the population, which is of mixed African, Carib Indian, and European ancestry, speak English; less than 5 percent speak Dutch. Roman Catholicism and Protestantism are the principal religions. The economy was traditionally dependent on the export of salt, the only significant onshore natural resource. However, salt production declined by the mid-20th century, after which tourism became increasingly important. Only 10 percent of the land is arable, and most farming is at the subsistence level, despite some earlier plantation production of sugarcane.

Tourism currently accounts for over 80 percent of GDP and employment, with small-scale industry contributing another 15 percent. Remittances from abroad are another significant source of island income. According to the Sint Maarten Department of Economic Affairs, GDP grew by 1 percent in 2013, 1.6 percent in 2014, and 1.3 percent in 2015. Unemployment remained steady from 2013 to 2014 at 9.2 percent, before falling to 8.5 percent in 2015.

GOVERNMENT AND POLITICS

Political background. Discovered by the Spanish at the time of Christopher Columbus, the island of St. Martin/St. Maarten saw its first French settlers arrive in 1628, and they were soon joined by the Dutch, who in 1634 proclaimed the Leeward Islands as possessions. A brief period of Spanish occupation followed. In 1648 the French and Dutch concluded the Treaty of Mt. Concordia, which divided the island between them, although it took another two centuries for the arrangement to be firmly established. In 1828 St. Maarten became part of the Dutch West Indies, along with the nearby islands of St. Eustatius and Saba; the islands of Aruba, Bonaire, and Curaçao in the southern arc of the Lesser Antilles; and the South American territory of Dutch Guiana. Having been administered for over a century as a colonial dependency, in 1954 the six island colonies, known collectively since 1948 as the Netherlands Antilles, were granted constitutional equality with the Netherlands and Suriname (the former Dutch Guiana) as an autonomous component of the Kingdom of the Netherlands. In 1975 Suriname achieved full independence, and in 1986 Aruba became a largely autonomous "country" within the kingdom.

Given the geographical range of the Netherlands Antilles, political differences were largely island-based, necessitating highly unstable coalition governments that rival parties from the most populous islands, Aruba and Curaçao, tended to dominate. Aruba's departure on January 1, 1986, resulted in an Antillean legislature, the States (*Staten*), in which Curaçao was assigned 14 of the 22 seats, compared to 3 for St. Maarten, 3 for Bonaire, and 1 each for St. Eustatius and Saba. Thus, the Curaçao-based rival New Antilles Movement (*Movimentu Antiá Nobo*—MAN), National People's Party (*Partido Nashonal di Pueblo*—PNP), Workers' Liberation Front (*Fronte Obrero de Liberashon*—FOL), and (from 1994) Restructured Antilles Party (*Partido Antiá Restrukturá*—PAR) became the leading parties in a series of coalition governments that at various times also included the St. Maarten-based Democratic Party of St. Maarten (*Democratische Partij Sint Maarten*—DP-StM or DP) and the Sint Maarten People's Alliance (SPA). In 2002 the SPA and the National Progressive Party (NPA) formed the National Alliance (NA), led by William MARLIN, which won 1 *Staten* seat in 2002 and 2 in 2006.

On the island of St. Maarten, from 1954 local politics were dominated by the DP's Claude WATHEY, an outspoken advocate for independence who in 1992 objected when the Netherlands imposed stricter financial supervision on the island. In 1993 a criminal investigation into these matters implicated Wathey and several other prominent island figures. Wathey, although charged in 1994 with corruption and criminal conspiracy, was ultimately convicted only of perjury.

In a referendum on October 14, 1994, voters on St. Maarten indicated a preference (by 59 percent of the vote) for remaining within the Netherlands Antilles. Another 32 percent voted to become an autonomous "country" within the Dutch kingdom, while only a few backed the other two options, namely closer ties to the Netherlands or independence.

From 1994 until 1999, the DP's leading role on St. Maarten was challenged by the SPA, which led to a series of unstable administrations. In the Island Council election of May 1999, however, the DP, now led by Sarah WESCOT-WILLIAMS, won 7 of the 11 seats.

In a June 23, 2000, referendum, some 70 percent of the voters supported withdrawal from the Netherlands Antilles. In April 2005 Curaçao's voters registered similar sentiments, and on November 26, 2005, the five constituent islands and the kingdom's government agreed that the Netherlands Antilles would dissolve by July 2007, with Curaçao and St. Maarten achieving autonomous country status, like Aruba, and with Bonaire, Saba, and St. Eustatius becoming municipalities within the Netherlands proper.

Mainly because of objections from Curaçao's Island Council regarding The Hague's retaining control of defense, foreign policy, and law enforcement, implementation of the dissolution was delayed beyond 2007. In April 2008 the Dutch government formally declared that even the new deadline of December 15, 2008, could not be met. A new target of early 2010 was advanced, coincident with expiration of the Antillean legislative term.

In May 2003 the DP had retained six seats on the St. Maarten's Island Council, to four for the NA and one for the People's Progressive Party. In April 2007 the election split gave the DP six seats and the NA five, but in November 2008 the DP lost its one-seat majority when Labor Commissioner Louie LAVEIST resigned from the St. Maarten Executive Council and left the party after being charged with corruption. Laveist retained his Island Council seat, however, which left the DP and NA with five seats each. Following Laveist's May 2009 conviction for bribery, forgery, and fraud (which the Common Court of Justice of Aruba and the Netherlands Antilles later overturned), he resigned from the Island Council. Subsequent efforts by the DP and NA to form a joint national government failed when the DP objected to the NA's demands that it be accorded a majority of Executive Council posts and that the NA's Marlin be named head of that council. In June the NA gained the support of Theo HEYLIGER, a member of the Island Council who until then had belonged to the DP, and formed a new government headed by Marlin.

Delays in implementing the planned January 2010 dissolution of the Netherlands Antilles necessitated a final election for its *Staten.* In balloting held on January 22, 2010, the NA won all three seats from St. Maarten—the first time since the 1960s that the DP had failed to claim at least one seat—and then gave its support to the incumbent prime minister, Emily de Jongh-Elhage of Curaçao's PAR, in her successful effort to forge a multiparty coalition.

On July 21, 2010, the St. Maarten Island Council adopted a constitution that would enter into force upon dissolution of the Netherlands Antilles, and on September 17 the island's voters cast ballots for a 15-member States of St. Maarten (successor to the Island Council) that would convene on October 10, 2010, the new date for dissolution.

The NA won a plurality of 7 seats in the September poll, with Theo Heyliger's new United People's (UP) party taking 6 and the DP being reduced to 2.

On September 23, 2010, the UP and the DP concluded a governing accord that awarded the DP the prime ministership and one additional cabinet post. DP party leader Sarah Wescot-Williams took her oath of office as prime minister, heading a seven-member UP-DP cabinet, on October 10, when the island officially became the Country of St. Maarten.

The UP-DP coalition lost its legislative majority in April 2012 when two independent members of parliament formed a new legislative bloc with a member of the UP and signed an agreement with the NA. The government resigned on May 8 and Wescot-Williams formed a new coalition government, with the NA and DP. The NA's William Marlin became deputy prime minister. The second Wescot-Williams cabinet was installed on May 21.

On May 4, 2013, one independent and two DP parliamentarians withdrew their support from the ruling NA-DP coalition, citing discontent over a proposed Department of Justice complex, and caused the collapse of the second Wescot-Williams cabinet. Three days later, five NA ministers, led by Vice Prime Minister Marlin, submitted a concept national decree to Governor Eugene HOLIDAY calling for an early election to be held on July 26. Wescot-Williams instead negotiated a new UP-DP-Independent coalition. The new cabinet took office on June 14.

The UP won the largest share of seats (seven) in the August 29, 2014, elections. However, earlier that week, UP leader Heyliger emerged as the main suspect in a 2010 vote-buying case, which was later dismissed because of prosecutorial missteps. The UP seemed to be forced into the opposition when the NA, the DP, and the United Sint Maarten Party (USP) formed a coalition. On September 2 Governor Holiday appointed the NA's Marlin formateur, tasked with naming a new cabinet. The coalition was cast into question later in the month, when Cornelius de WEEVER defected from the DP to support the UP, thereby giving the latter party an absolute majority. On October 8 eight members of parliament signed a UP–de Weever governing accord.

The new governing coalition continued to be the subject of intense scrutiny from the Dutch government, which on October 18, 2014, instructed Governor Holiday to refrain from formalizing the appointments of Heyliger as prime minister and his cabinet until each appointee underwent criminal background screenings. Heyliger withdrew as prime minister designate, and Marcel GUMBS of the UP was finally able to form a new government on December 19, 2014.

On October 1, 2015, the Council of Ministers under Marcel Gumbs fell after two members of the UP defected and joined a no-confidence vote. A new eight-member coalition, the "Red, White, and Blue Coalition," was formed under the NA's Marlin, who became prime minister on November 19. The new alliance included the NA, the DP, the USP, and two independents. (See Current issues, below.)

Constitution and government. Under the 2010 constitution, the Dutch sovereign, the titular head of state, is represented in St. Maarten by an appointed governor. Domestic affairs are the responsibility of the prime minister and other members of the Council of Ministers (direct institutional successor to the island's Executive Council), which is appointed with the advice and approval of the unicameral legislature, the States of St. Maarten (*Staten van Sint Maarten*). Elections to the *Staten* are held every four years, subject to dissolution. A Council of Advice, whose members are appointed by government decree, reviews proposed legislation and administrative orders and may offer advice to the government. The constitution also provides for an ombudsperson and a General Audit Chamber. Control of foreign affairs and defense remains vested in the Council of Ministers in The Hague, where a minister plenipotentiary from St. Maarten advises on matters relevant to St. Maarten. Judicial authority is exercised by a Court of First Instance and by a Common Court (for Aruba, Curaçao, St. Maarten, and the special municipalities of Bonaire, St. Eustatius, and Saba), whose members are appointed by the queen. Ultimate appeal is to the Supreme Court of the Netherlands in The Hague. In addition, St. Maarten has a Constitutional Court to examine the constitutionality of legislation and government actions. The constitution may be amended by a two-thirds vote of the St. Maarten legislature, subject to the subsequent approval of the Dutch government. Freedom of expression is constitutionally protected.

Dutch Prime Minister Mark Ruute visited St. Maarten in July 2013 and instructed Governor Holiday to investigate corruption allegations against the government. Prime Minister Wescot-Williams denounced the move as outside intrusion but invited Transparency International to review the situation.

Current issues. In July 2011 St. Maarten made a request for associate membership in the Caribbean Community (Caricom).

The defection of two UP members in October 2015 led to the collapse of the Marcel Gumbs's cabinet and the installation of the NA-led Red, White, and Blue Coalition government under William Marlin. In an effort to capitalize on the apparent weakness of the UP, on December 14 Marlin presented a decree for new elections. The governor set September 26, 2016, as the date for new balloting.

POLITICAL PARTIES

Since 1990 politics on St. Maarten has largely been a contest between the dominant Democratic Party of St. Maarten (DP) and the National Alliance (NA) or its predecessor, the Sint Maarten Political Alliance (SPA), despite the frequent presence of short-lived smaller parties. A third major political force, the United People's (UP) party, emerged in the September 2010 balloting.

Governing Parties:

National Alliance (NA). The NA traces its origins to the Sint Maarten Patriotic Movement (SPM), which was formed in 1979, initially as a loose grouping in opposition to the DP, and evolved into the **Sint Maarten Patriotic Alliance** (SPA) in 1990. In the 1990 Netherlands Antilles *Staten* poll the SPM captured one seat. In the 1991 Island Council election the SPA doubled its representation from two of nine seats to four, after which it formed an island government in coalition with the recently organized **Progressive Democratic Party** (PDP) of DP dissidents. The SPA increased its Netherlands Antilles *Staten* representation to two seats in 1994, one of which was lost in 1998. For the 2002 Netherlands Antilles election the SPA joined with the **National Progressive Party** (NPP) to form the NA, which secured one seat under the leadership of William Marlin.

In May 2003 the NA won four Island Council seats, and it increased its total to five of 11 in April 2007. In June 2009 the NA formed its first island government in ten years through the support of Louie Laveist, a DP dissenter. In November 2009 the party held its first formal congress.

The NA won all three St. Maarten seats in the final Netherlands Antilles parliamentary election in January 2010. It won a plurality of seven seats in the new 15-member St. Maarten *Staten* in September, but a UP-DP coalition, with eight seats, formed the Country of St. Maarten's first government. In April 2012 the NA regained a legislative majority and formed a coalition with the DP and three independent members of parliament, however the party returned to the backbench in May 2013 when a new DP-led coalition came to power. Jeffrey RICHARDSON, formerly of the Concordia Political Alliance (see the 2014 *Handbook*), joined the NA in July 2014. The NA won four seats in balloting on August 29, 2014. On November 19 it formed a governing coalition with the DP and USP, titled the United Democratic Alliance, or the **Red, White, and Blue Coalition**, with Marlin as prime minister.

Leaders: William MARLIN (Prime Minister and Party President), Silveria JACOBS (Vice President).

Democratic Party of St. Maarten (*Democratische Partij Sint Maarten*—DP-StM or DP). The DP began in the mid-1980s as an English-speaking branch of the **Democratic Party–Curaçao** (*Democratische Partij–Curaçao*). Under the leadership of Claude Wathey, who supported independence, the DP dominated island politics into the 1990s. Another DP leader, Louis C. GUMBS, resigned in 1991 to stand for an Island Council seat as a candidate of the Progressive Democratic Party (PDP), launched by a group of DP dissidents. The party lost one of its two *Staten* seats in 1994, its leadership passing thereafter from Wathey to Sarah Wescot-Williams (formerly of the PDP). Wathey died in 1998.

The DP's representation in the Netherlands Antilles legislature fell from 2 seats in 2002 to 1 in 2006, but it nevertheless remained the leading party in the St. Maarten Island Council, winning 7 of 11 seats in 1999, 6 in 2003, and 6 in 2007. In January 2010, however, it failed to win any seats in the Netherlands Antilles election, and in September it took only 2 of 15 seats in the new St. Maarten *Staten.* With UP support, DP leader Wescot-Williams became the Country of St. Maarten's first prime minister. The DP-UP coalition lost its majority in 2012, leading Wescot-Williams to negotiate a new coalition with the NA. In 2013, after another parliamentary power shift, the DP-NA leadership dissolved and the DP remained in power by establishing a new coalition with the UP. Hasani Brendan Ellis became DP president at a party congress in April 2014. The DP won two seats in August 2014 balloting and joined the NA-led government in 2015. Meanwhile, Wescott-Williams was elected speaker of the parliament in October 2015.

Leaders: Sarah WESCOT-WILLIAMS (Former Prime Minister, Speaker of the States, and Party Leader), Hasani Brendan ELLIS (President).

United St. Maarten Party (USP). The USP was launched in December 2013 by Frans Richardson. In August 2014 balloting, the new party won two seats and joined the NA-led United Democratic Alliance in 2015.

Leaders: Frans RICHARDSON (Party Founder), Cecil NICHOLAS (Party President).

Opposition Party:

United Peoples (UP). Launched in late July 2010 by former DP member Theo Heyliger (a former member of the island's Executive Council), the UP formed an alliance with the NA on a platform of unity, fighting crime, creating jobs, and investing in youth and their education. In late July, Gracita ARRINDELL, theretofore the leader of the PPA (below), announced her resignation from that party and her collateral decision to join the UP.

In September 2010 the UP won 6 of 15 seats in the new *Staten,* after which it formed a coalition government with the DP. In 2012 the DP-UP coalition lost power when the UP's Romaine Laville left the party to form a bloc with the NA. The UP returned to power in June 2013 when a new governing coalition was formed. In the August 2014 general elections, the UP won the largest bloc with seven seats, and the defection of Cornelius de Weever in late September gave the party an absolute majority of eight seats. A government was formed under the UP's Marcel GUMBS, but the coalition fell following a no-confidence vote on October 1, 2015, and the defection of two UP legislators.

Leaders: Theodore HEYLIGER (Party Leader), Marcel GUMBS (Former Prime Minister).

Other Parties:

One Sint Maarten People Party (OSPP). Formed under the leadership of Lenny Priest in August 2013, the OSPP campaigned against government corruption. Nine candidates contested the 2014 general election, but the new party won no representation.

Leader: Lenny PRIEST (Party Leader).

Social Reform Party (SRP). The SRP was launched by Jacinto Mock in 2013, building a platform based on human rights and good governance. The party unsuccessfully contested the 2014 elections.

Leader: Jacinto MOCK (Party Leader).

For information on the **People's Progressive Alliance** (PPA), see the 2014 *Handbook.*

LEGISLATURE

The unicameral **States of St. Maarten** (*Staten van Sint Maarten*) consists of 15 members (often styled senators) elected by proportional representation for four-year terms, subject to dissolution. Following the election on August 29, 2014, the makeup of the *Staten* was as follows: United People's Party, 7 seats; National Alliance, 4; Democratic Party of Sint Maarten, 2; and United Sint Maarten Party, 2.

President: Sarah A. WESCOTT-WILLIAMS.

CABINET

[as of June 22, 2016]

Prime Minister	William Marlin (NA)
Ministers	
Education, Culture, Youth, and Sports Affairs	Silveria Jacobs (NA) [f]
Finance	Richard Gibson
General Affairs	William Marlin (NA)
Health, Social Development, and Labor	Emil Lee
Housing and Spatial Planning, Environment, and Infrastructure	Angel C. Meyers
Justice	Edson G. Kirindongo
Tourism, Economic Affairs, Transport, and Telecommunications	Irania Arrindell [f]
Minister Plenipotentiary to The Hague	Henrietta Doran-York [f]

[f] = female

INTERGOVERNMENTAL REPRESENTATION

Foreign relations are for the most part conducted through the Dutch Ministry of Foreign Affairs in The Hague. St. Maarten is represented by attachés in various Dutch embassies and consulates, including those in Cuba, Dominican Republic, Trinidad and Tobago, Venezuela, and the United States (Washington, D.C., and Miami, Florida).

For Further Reference:

Department of Statistics: Sint Maarten. Accessed August 19, 2016. http://stat.gov.sx.

Goslinga, Cornelius. *A Short History of the Netherlands Antilles and Surinam.* New York: Springer, 1979.

Government of Sint Maarten official website. Accessed August 19, 2016. www.sintmaartengov.org.

NEW ZEALAND

Aotearoa

Political Status: Constitutional democracy with Queen Elizabeth II as titular head of state; formally independent since 1947.

Area: 104,454 sq. mi. (270,534 sq. km).

Population: 4,565,000 (2016E—UN); 4,474,549 (2016E—U.S. Census.

Major Urban Centers (2016E): WELLINGTON (383,000), Auckland (1,344,000), Christchurch (351,200).

Official Languages: English, Maori.

Monetary Unit: New Zealand Dollar (market rate October 1, 2016: 1.37 dollars = $1US).

Sovereign: Queen ELIZABETH II.

Governor General: General Sir Jerry MATAPARAI, named by Queen Elizabeth II on March 7, 2011. (See Government and Politics, below.)

Prime Minister: John Phillip KEY (National Party), named by the governor general to form a new government following the parliamentary election of November 8, 2008, and sworn in on November 19. Sworn in again on December 13, 2011, and for the third time on October 8, 2014.

THE COUNTRY

Located approximately 1,200 miles southeast of Australia in the southern Pacific Ocean, New Zealand is the most physically isolated of the world's economically developed countries. The two main islands (North Island and South Island), separated by the Cook Strait, extend nearly 1,000 miles on a northeast-southwest axis. They exhibit considerable topographical diversity, ranging from fertile plains to high mountains, but enjoy a relatively temperate climate. The 2013 census found that the majority of the population (74 percent) was of European extraction, and the Maori, descendants of the original Polynesian settlers, constituted almost 15 percent. Smaller ethnic groups included Asians (11.8 percent) and Pacific island peoples (7.4 percent). The Anglican, Roman Catholic, and Presbyterian churches predominate. Women constituted

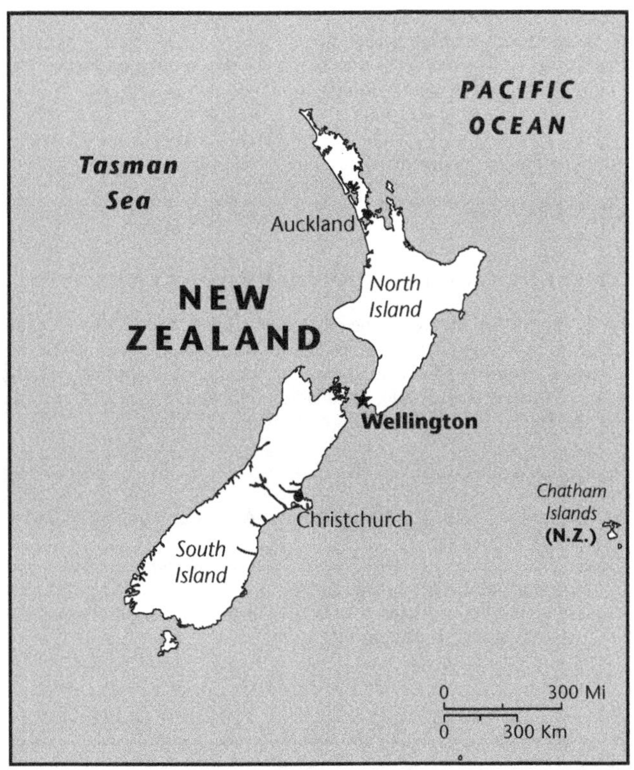

over 46 percent of the active labor force, primarily in wholesale and retail trade, health and social work, and education. Female representation in the House of Representatives (Parliament) elected in September 2014 totaled 37 out of 121 MPs.

The service sector is the largest contributor to the GDP, just over 70 percent in 2011, employing 74 percent of the workforce. Although the agricultural sector employs less than 10 percent of the labor force, it remains the basis of the country's wealth. Dairy products, meat, forest products, fish, fruits and vegetables, wine, and wool provide over half of New Zealand's merchandise export earnings. The manufacturing sector employs 19 percent of the workforce and contributes a quarter of the GDP, with processing of foods, wood and paper products, aluminum, and chemicals ranking among the leading industries. Exports of machinery, transport and marine equipment, chemical products, and metals have become important earners. Since the mid-1970s, efforts have focused on the exploitation of natural gas, oil, coal, and lignite deposits, as well as hydroelectric capacity, and in 2013 crude oil constituted the fourth most valuable export by value. Top trading partners are China, Australia, the United States, Japan, South Korea, and Great Britain. In the 1990s tourism surpassed dairy exports to emerge as New Zealand's most valuable source of foreign exchange.

From 1999 through 2004 GDP growth averaged about 4 percent annually, but a downturn in primary production and overseas earnings and a weakening of housing, finance, and retail markets dragged the economy into recession and the GDP shrank by 1.7 percent in 2009. Two devastating earthquakes in Christchurch, among other natural disasters, slowed recovery despite high overseas earnings for commodities. The International Monetary Fund (IMF) forecast a GDP growth rate of 2.5 percent in 2016. Net foreign debt declined from 71 percent of GDP in 2012 to 67 percent in 2016, and unemployment declined to 5.3 percent as of 2015. Thus, while the IMF expects the New Zealand economy to grow, it cautions such growth will be gradual.

GOVERNMENT AND POLITICS

Political background. New Zealand's link to Europe began with a landfall by the Dutch mariner Abel Tasman in 1642, but settlement by the English did not begin until the 18th century. In 1840 British sovereignty was formally accepted by Maori chieftains, who signed the Treaty of Waitangi. Recurrent disputes between the settlers and the Maori were not resolved, however, until the defeat of the latter in the land wars of the 1860s. Granted self-government in 1852 and dominion status in 1907, New Zealand became an independent member of the Commonwealth upon accession to the Statute of Westminster in 1947.

Through the mid-20th century both of the main political parties, National and Labour, endorsed a protected economy and extensive programs of social welfare. The more conservative National Party, which was in power from 1960 to 1972 under the leadership of Keith J. HOLYOAKE and then John R. MARSHALL, was succeeded in government by the Labour Party in 1972, led by Norman E. KIRK and, upon Kirk's death in August 1974, by Wallace E. ROWLING. Labour was succeeded in turn by National, led by Robert MULDOON, in 1975. Thereafter, the two major parties alternated in power: Labour in 1984, National in 1990, Labour in 1999, and National in 2008, albeit each needing the support of minor parties. The adoption of a proportional representation electoral system, first employed in the 1996 election, enabled smaller parties, disadvantaged by the traditional first-past-the-post system, to win seats, and NZ First, Alliance, Green, ACT, Maori, United NZ, and Progressive candidates subsequently took their places in the House. (See the 2010 *Handbook* for details.)

Following the election of 1999, Labour Party leader Helen CLARK, New Zealand's first elected woman prime minister, was sworn in on December 10 at the head of a minority government. Alliance leader James (Jim) ANDERTON negotiated with Clark a novel coalition agreement permitting "public differentiation between the parties in speech and vote" when they disagreed and was rewarded with the deputy prime ministership. This established a formula employed by subsequent minority governments, allowing Labour to govern following the elections of 2002 and 2005 and National to govern after the elections of 2008 and 2011 although neither party achieved a majority of seats.

Controversy had erupted in 2004 over a bill that would ensure state ownership of New Zealand's shorelines. The legislation, the Foreshore and Seabed Bill, was adamantly opposed by most Maori leaders, who viewed it as truncating tribal rights. Despite opposition by the National, United Future, and Maori parties, the Foreshore and Seabed Bill was enacted into law in November. (For more on opposition to the bill, see Maori party, below, and also the 2011 *Handbook*.)

Uninspiring leadership, alleged contact with a religious sect, and admitted marital infidelity by Don BRASJ hampered the National Party until a new leader, John Phillip KEY, was chosen in November 2006, whereupon National began a steady rise in the polls. By 2008 economic issues (jobs, taxes, property values) rose to the top of the list of public worries. The economy in 2006 and 2007 had grown on the strength of high agricultural export earnings and a strong dollar, but it turned downward in 2008 as energy and food import prices rose, the dollar and property values weakened, credit tightened, and financial institutions declared bankruptcy, with thousands of investors losing their savings. Labour was widely blamed despite its prudent financial management, accumulation of a budget surplus, and partial repayment of overseas debt. (For discussion of contentious political issues of 2007–2010, see the 2014 *Handbook*.)

In the general election of November 8, 2008, the National Party won 44.9 percent of the popular vote and 58 seats in the House of Representatives, followed by Labour's 34.0 percent and 43 seats, thus neither commanding a majority of seats. The third-ranked party, the Greens, won 6.7 percent of the vote and 9 seats, but these seats, combined with Labor's 43 seats, failed to outnumber National's 58 seats. In the end, ACT New Zealand (5 seats), the Maori Party (5 seats), and United Future New Zealand (1 seat) pledged their support in confidence and budget votes to a National-led minority government. The new government led by Prime Minister John Key was sworn in on November 19 and comprised 23 ministers in the cabinet, all National MPs, and 8 ministers outside the cabinet, including 3 from National, 2 from ACT, 2 from Maori, and 1 from United Future. On election night Helen Clark announced her resignation as party leader. Phil GOFF was subsequently chosen by Labour as Clark's successor, thereby becoming leader of the opposition in the House. Clark resigned her Mount Albert parliamentary seat in April 2009 to take up the post of administrator of the United Nations Development Program. Winston PETERS, Clark's erstwhile minister of foreign affairs, was embroiled in a secret campaign donations exposé and lost his seat, as did all his NZ First Party colleagues.

Public criticism of abuse by parliamentarians of their housing and travel allowances erupted in mid-2009 and continued into 2010 driven by media exposés, obliging several MPs, including leaders of the National, ACT, and Green parties, to repay excess claims and inducing the prime minister to counsel his ministers to exercise spending restraint. Allegations that National MP Pansy WONG had used her travel privileges to further her husband's business interests in China led to her resignation from Parliament in December. She was followed in March 2012 by Nick SMITH who, as accident compensation minister, intervened improperly in a friend's case.

As the 2011 election approached, political issues dividing the parties included representation of Maori and other ethnic minorities in the decision-making processes of the Auckland "supercity," legislation on the legal drinking age and sentencing and parole of violent offenders, the financing of facilities for the 2011 Rugby World Cup, approval of sales of dairy farms to China-based corporations, and concessions for off-shore oil and gas drilling. National's proposal to sell minority shareholdings in four energy companies and Air New Zealand attracted opposition from the public and all other parties save ACT and United Future. The November 26 election was marked by a record low voter turnout of 68.8 percent. National won 47.3 percent of the vote and 59 seats in the House but fell short of an outright majority, so entered into supply and confidence agreement with ACT and United Future (one MP each) and the Maori Party (three MPs) to form a minority government. An accompanying referendum on the electoral system saw 57.8 percent of voters opting to retain the MMP system, which was reviewed in 2012 without significant change.

In the September 20, 2014, general election, the National Party won 47 percent of the vote and 60 seats in the House. The New Zealand Labour Party won 25.1 percent of the vote and 32 seats, while the Green Party garnered 10.7 percent of the popular vote, thereby retaining their 14 seats. The ACT, United Future, and Maori parties also won seats. In the balloting, National failed to win an outright majority and once again entered into a supply and confidence agreement with ACT and United Future (one MP each) and the Maori Party (two seats) to form a minority government. Key announced a new cabinet on October 6. A minor cabinet reshuffle was announced on December 7.

Patsy REDDY was named as the governor general designate to succeed Sir Jerry MATAPARAI, and was scheduled to be sworn in on September 1, 2016.

Constitution and government. New Zealand's political system, historically patterned on the British model, has no consolidated written constitution. As in other Commonwealth states that have retained allegiance to the queen, the monarch is represented by a governor general, now a New Zealand citizen, who performs the largely ceremonial functions of chief of state. The only legally recognized executive body is the Executive Council, which includes the governor general and all government ministers. De facto executive authority is vested in the cabinet, headed by the prime minister, under a system of parliamentary responsibility. The national legislature, the House of Representatives, popularly referred to as Parliament, is elected through a combination of single-seat local constituencies and a nation-wide party list. Some constituency seats are filled from a separate electoral roll on which Maori may choose to be registered. The judicial system is headed by a High Court, a Court of Appeal, and the Supreme Court, with district courts and justices of the peace functioning at lower levels.

Local administration is based on 16 regions. Four (Nelson City, Gisborne, Tasman, and Marlborough) are defined as unitary authorities, whereas the other 12 are subdivided into 57 districts and 16 cities. In addition, the remote, sparsely populated Chatham Islands, some 500 miles east of Christchurch, have unitary status. Each local unit is governed by an elected council headed by a chair or mayor, and advised by elected community boards in some urban areas.

Constitutional change appeared imminent when Prime Minister Clark said in February 2002 that New Zealand would "inevitably" become a republic. A step in that direction was taken in October 2003 when the House of Representatives, over opposition by National, passed a bill ending the right of final legal appeal to the Privy Council in London and creating a national Supreme Court, which began hearing cases in July 2004. The government also discontinued awarding knighthoods to meritorious citizens, opting instead for nonmonarchical honors. National upon assuming office in 2008 reinstated royal honors, and subsequently, republicanism faded as a political issue.

New Zealand has traditionally had few restrictions on the press. In Reporters Without Borders's 2016 ranking of press freedom in 180 countries, New Zealand ranked 5th.

Foreign relations. New Zealand has traditionally maintained preferential trading and defense relations with its nearest neighbor, Australia, and has supported collective security through the United Nations, the ANZUS treaty with Australia and the United States, and the Five Power Defense Arrangements with Australia, Malaysia, Singapore, and the United Kingdom. Wellington has also engaged in regional security consultations in the Association of Southeast Asian Nations Regional Forum (ARF). New Zealand is an active member of the Commonwealth (of which former foreign minister Don McKINNON was secretary general from 2000 to 2008), and of the Pacific Islands Forum, having hosted its inaugural meeting in Auckland in 1971 and a 40th anniversary meeting in 2011.

In February 1985 the Labour government led by David LANGE refused entry to a U.S. Navy warship alleged to be capable of carrying nuclear weapons. Wishing to deter similar ship visit bans by other allies, the Ronald Reagan administration discontinued bilateral exercises, intelligence sharing, and cabinet-level diplomatic intercourse. In June 1987 New Zealand's Parliament approved a Nuclear Free Zone, Disarmament, and Arms Control Act that legally prohibited the entry of nuclear-armed or nuclear-powered ships into New Zealand waters, whereupon Secretary of State George Schultz suspended U.S. security commitments and declared ANZUS "inoperative" with respect to New Zealand. A decade of cool relations followed.

In September 1999, to prepare for the UN-backed peacekeeping mission in East Timor (to which New Zealand committed some 800 troops), U.S. president Bill Clinton announced that the U.S. ban on military exercises with New Zealand would be waived for this and other multilateral operations. In 2001 the Clark government strongly endorsed the U.S.-led "war on terrorism" and dispatched troops to Afghanistan in support of the U.S.-led Operation Enduring Freedom. In March 2002 Prime Minister Clark was invited to meet with U.S. president George W. Bush, the first consultation with a Labour leader since the mid-1980s. The Clark government refused to participate in the 2003 invasion of Iraq, but troop contributions to Afghanistan, counterterrorism patrols in the Persian Gulf, assistance in negotiations with North Korea, and participation in the U.S.-led Proliferation Security Initiative earned goodwill in Washington. Secretary of State Condoleezza Rice paid an official visit in July 2008, signaling that the unresolved nuclear ship disagreement would no longer impede high-level relations.

Following two meetings with U.S. president Barack Obama, Key in August 2009 announced the deployment of 70 Special Air Service combat troops to Afghanistan in addition to the 140 NZ Defence Force personnel and civilian specialists serving as a Provincial Reconstruction Team that had begun in 2003. The decision was supported by the National and ACT parties but contested by all the other parties in the House. Key also welcomed indications by assistant secretary of state Kurt Campbell that training opportunities for New Zealand troops with their American counterparts were to be expanded, and New Zealand was subsequently invited to participate in the multinational Rim of the Pacific (RIMPAC) exercise, which took place in July 2012. U.S. secretary of state Hillary Clinton visited in November 2010 and with Prime Minister Key signed the Wellington Declaration, signaling a return of close relations, including full restoration of intelligence sharing. At the invitation of President Obama, Key visited the White House in July 2011 and conferred with top U.S. leaders and officials. In June 2012 the defense ministers of the two governments signed a defense cooperation agreement called the Washington Declaration covering maritime security, antipiracy, counterterrorism, peacekeeping, and disaster relief. Secretary of Defense Chuck Hagel announced in October 2013 the full restoration of bilateral military exercise relations.

In 2011 Key also visited leaders in Britain, Europe, and Asia and hosted South Pacific, American, European Union, and Asian leaders and the UN secretary general at the Pacific Island Forum's 40th-anniversary summit in Auckland in September. New Zealand has played an active part in South Pacific development and Asia-Pacific economic and political cooperation, with its initiatives including successful mediation of the Bougainville separatist conflict in Papua New Guinea in 1996 and dispatch of troops and police to support the elected government of the Solomon Islands in 2003. Wellington was quick to impose sanctions on the military junta of Fiji following the December 2006 coup, as it had done in response to coups in 1987 and 2000; these sanctions were selectively eased in 2013 in step with the Fiji military leader's preparations to hold an election in 2014.

Since 1989 New Zealand has been active in the 21-nation Asia-Pacific Economic Cooperation (APEC) forum, and from 2006 New Zealand has participated in the East Asian Summit meetings, which proponents hope will evolve into a 16-nation Asia-wide trade liberalization pact. Starting in 2000 New Zealand diplomats negotiated free-trade agreements with Singapore, then with Chile and Brunei, which culminated in July 2005 with the signing of the Trans-Pacific Strategic Economic Partnership Agreement (TPPA or P-4). New Zealand's free trade negotiations with China came to fruition in the New Zealand–China Free Trade Agreement signed April 7, 2008, China's first with a developed country. China in 2014 became New Zealand's most valuable trade partner. Free trade agreements with Malaysia and Hong Kong and with the Association of Southeast Asian Nations (ASEAN) followed, and negotiations or studies with South Korea, India, the Gulf Cooperation Council, and Russia were undertaken, and a free trade agreement with Taiwan was signed in July 2013. Negotiations for a 12-member Trans Pacific Partnership (TPP) trade agreement including New Zealand, the United States, Canada, Australia, and eight Asian and Latin American governments progressed, with completion forecast for early 2015.

The Defence White Paper issued in November 2010 reaffirmed New Zealand's commitment to the defense of Australia and the Pacific islands; security cooperation with the United States, Britain, Singapore, and Malaysia; and peacekeeping under United Nations auspices. Peacekeeping commitments in Solomon Islands, Timor-Leste, and Afghanistan were concluded in 2013 but in September 2014, 123 Defence Force personnel remained deployed abroad in nine peacekeeping and other missions in ten countries.

In 2014 New Zealand was elected a nonpermanent member of the UN Security Council for a two-year term.

The New Zealand government announced in February 2015 the deployment of 143 troops to Iraq as part of a two-year training mission. New Zealand suspended aid to Nauru in September (see entry on Nauru).

The final text of the TPP was signed in Auckland on February 4, 2016. In April former prime minister Helen CLARK officially declared her candidacy for the position of UN secretary general. In May New Zealand and Iran finalized an agreement to enhance agricultural cooperation and expand trade.

Current issues. Controversy over the government's asset sale plans continued in 2013. The Maori Council asserted traditional ownership rights over watercourses, briefly holding up the sale of hydropower company shares. The government's issue of Mighty River Power shares to the public went ahead in May and those of Meridian Energy in October. Despite the success of a Green Party petition opposing asset sales triggering a referendum in December, the government sold Air New Zealand shares in November. Meanwhile, a Shanghai firm's bid to buy a set of dairy farms was opposed by the Labour Party and temporarily held up by court action by a New Zealand bidder, and the Labour Party proposed setting limits on foreign purchases of residential properties; neither initiative succeeded. Other controversies included the following: Maori and environmentalists' objections to exploration of offshore sites for oil and gas wells and proposals to facilitate oil extraction by injection of water at high pressure, called "fracking"; the government's revising of its target for greenhouse gas emissions reduction from 10 percent to 5 percent; and bills in Parliament to detain mass asylum seekers (passed in June 2013), legalize same-sex marriages (passed in August), augment the surveillance powers of the Government Communications Security Bureau (passed in August), extend paid parental leave, raise the retirement age, and restrict welfare. Relations with Australia were disturbed by the inability of long-term New Zealand residents and tax payers in Australia to obtain welfare benefits. The combat deaths of five soldiers in Afghanistan, and allegations of violations of international law by Special Air Service personnel, stimulated adverse media and public comment and the prime minister brought forward the end date of the Provincial Reconstruction Team's deployment from September to April 2013 but kept a small contingent of soldiers in Afghanistan on training and liaison duties. He also travelled to Asia, Europe, and New York to promote New Zealand's bid in October 2014 for election to a nonpermanent seat on the UN Security Council, visited the White House, and hosted Japan's prime minister and China's president.

Cabinet resignations punctuated 2013 and 2014. Peter DUNN, leader of National's coalition partner United Future, lost his revenue portfolio in 2013 for allegedly leaking information to a journalist. John BANKS, leader of the ACT, another coalition partner, resigned his portfolios in October to stand trial for alleged electoral fraud and, upon conviction in 2014, resigned from Parliament. Customs minister Maurice WILLIAMSON resigned in May 2014 after intervening in a police investigation and Justice Minister Judith COLLINS stood down in August following allegations she intervened in an enquiry by the head of the Serious Fraud Office.

The 2014 electoral campaign debate focused on taxes (which Labour wanted to increase by instituting capital gains and high-income tax rates), providing affordable housing in Auckland, restricting foreigners' purchases of property, relieving child poverty, and protecting the environment. In August investigative journalist Nikki HAGAR published *Dirty Politics,* a book alleging cabinet ministers' and prime ministerial office staffers' improper contacts with political bloggers and disclosure of confidential information for political advantage. Media attention to these allegations, and subsequent allegations that the Key government was condoning mass surveillance of New Zealanders' electronic communications, overshadowed debate on substantive issues.

On September 1, 2015, the government announced four potential designs for a new flag. A fifth was added on September 23, following a petition drive. A national referendum was conducted from November 20 to December 11 to choose one of the designs, which then advanced to a second referendum against the current flag. In balloting from March 3–24, 2016, voters endorsed keeping the current flag, 56.7 percent to 43.3 percent.

POLITICAL PARTIES

A two-party system has long characterized New Zealand politics, with conservative and liberal policies offered by the National and Labour parties, respectively. Differences between the two narrowed considerably after World War II, and even more so with the initiation of policies by the Labour Party after its election in 1984 that introduced liberalization and deregulation reforms similar to those advocated by the National Party, thus attenuating New Zealand's long-standing protectionist and welfare state policies.

The potential for smaller parties to form and play a significant role in politics was enhanced by the adoption in the 1996 election of a mixed member proportional representation system (MMP) similar to Germany's. In the general election in November 2011, 13 parties offered party lists (down from 19 in 2008), of which 8 won seats. In the 2014 election 15 parties sponsored candidates, of which 7 won seats.

Governing Parties:

New Zealand National Party (National Party). Founded in 1936 as a union of the earlier Reform and Liberal Parties, the National Party controlled the government from 1960 to 1972, 1975 to 1984, 1990 to 1999, and 2008 to the present. A party of the center-right drawing its strength from well-off rural and suburban areas, National was traditionally committed to the support of personal initiative, private enterprise, and minimum government regulation. However, the distinction between right and left blurred as Labour shifted to free-market policies, and the 1975–1984 National government led by Sir Robert Muldoon endorsed selective state intervention in the economy, including subsidies for farmers.

While National won a landslide victory over Labour in 1990, Bolger's young populist colleague Winston Peters overtook him in popularity, and the two became rivals. Bolger dismissed Peters as Maori affairs minister in late 1991 for alleged disloyalty and a year later excluded him from the party's parliamentary caucus. Peters responded by resigning his seat and humiliated the government by winning a by-election under the banner of his newly established NZ First Party.

The National Party won a bare majority of 50 of the 99 legislative seats in the 1993 balloting, but the defection of Ross MEURANT in September 1994 to form the **Right of Centre Party** eliminated this margin, obliging Bolger to form a coalition with the new party. In the 1996 election National won a plurality of 44 out of 120 seats, sufficient for it to form a coalition government with NZ First, with Peters as deputy prime minister. In November 1997 Bolger was supplanted as party leader by Jenny SHIPLEY, the leader of the party's right wing, who was named prime minister in December, the first woman to achieve this office.

NZ First left the coalition in August 1998, but Shipley survived until the November 1999 election, which National lost to Labour. Shipley resigned her party leadership post in October 2001 and was succeeded by Bill ENGLISH, a former minister of health, who was then ousted in November 2003 by Don Brash, a former governor of the Reserve Bank of New Zealand who had joined the party only three years before. In the July 2002 election the party's list vote share plummeted to 20.9 percent, with only 27 seats won, a record low. In November 2006 Brash, whose leadership was tarnished by public gaffes, marital infidelity, and alleged links to a secretive right-wing Christian organization, resigned as party leader and was succeeded by former international currency trader John Key.

The November 8, 2008, election produced a plurality for National of 58 seats with 44.3 percent of the total vote and enabled Key to form a coalition government. Despite resignations in 2009 and 2010 by National MPs Richard WORTH and Pansy Wong for alleged misconduct, and in the face of the economic recession, John Key's vigorous response to the South Canterbury Finance collapse and the Christchurch earthquakes and his cordial meetings with President Obama contributed to Key's personal popularity and helped win National 47.3 percent of the vote and a record 59 seats in the November 2011 election despite a campaign marked by few divisive issues and a record low voter turnout. National achieved victory again in 2014, winning 47.4 percent of the vote and sending 60 MPs to Parliament.

Leaders: John KEY (Party Leader and Prime Minister), Bill ENGLISH (Deputy Leader and Deputy Prime Minister), Peter GOODFELLOW (President), Gerry BROWNLEE (Leader of the House), David CARTER (Speaker of the House).

Maori Party. Tariana TURIA, a former Labour MP and associate minister for Maori affairs, established the Maori Party in June 2004. She had left Labour in May to protest the government's Foreshore and Seabed Bill, which she saw as a betrayal of Maori customary rights. Under the new banner of the Maori Party, Turia won a parliamentary by-election for her old seat in July, taking some 90 percent of the vote.

Partly as a consequence of the demise of its rivals *Mana Maori Motuhake* (Maori Self-Determination) and the *Mana Maori* Movement, the Maori Party won four Maori-roll seats in the 2005 election.

In the November 2008 election the Maori Party contested all seven Maori seats (and a number of general seats besides) and succeeded in winning five of them with 2.4 percent of the total vote. To build a governing coalition, National offered Turia and her co-leader Pita SHARPLES ministerial portfolios (outside cabinet) and pledged to review Labour's Foreshore and Seabed Act. Turia and Sharples protested Prime Minister Key's June 2010 proposal to repeal the act and at the same time curb certain Maori customary rights, but they were persuaded to continue supporting the National-led government until the next election. In August Maori Party MP Hone HARAWIRA provoked criticism for announcing his disapproval of his children's dating *pakeha* (people of European decent). In September Harawira threatened to vote against the Marine and Coastal Area (Takutai Moana) Bill negotiated by his party with the National-led government. Facing criticism from Turia and Sharples, he resigned from the party in February 2011, resigned from Parliament in May, formed a new party called Mana in June, and on June 25 won the subsequent by-election in the Te Tai Tokerau electorate, defeating the Maori Party and Labour Party challengers. Rahui KATENE lost the Te Tai Tonga seat to the Labour challenger, reducing the Maori Party to 3 MPs. Turia and Sharples pledged to support a National-led minority government and were given the portfolios (outside cabinet) of Disability Issues and Maori Affairs, respectively. Both stood down after the 2014 election and drafted Te Ururoa Flavell as the next Maori Party leader. Flavell won his electorate seat and brought one list MP with him to Parliament.

As a result, the Maori Party lost one seat in the 2014 election, but still maintained their place in the government.

Leaders: Te Ururoa FLAVELL, Marama FOX (Co-Leaders); Tukoroirangi MORGAN (President).

ACT New Zealand (ACT). Founded in 1994 as the political arm of the Association of Consumers and Taxpayers, ACT advocates tax reduction, welfare reform, school choice, health care reform, and termination of Waitangi Tribunal claims. One of the party's founders, Sir Roger DOUGLAS, was a former Labour finance minister and the architect of the deregulatory and free-market reforms introduced in 1985.

The party won eight seats in the 1996 election and nine in the 1999 election and provided crucial confidence votes to Prime Minister Shipley's minority government. In 2002 ACT retained its nine seats on the basis of a 7.1 percent share of the party list vote.

But with public support for ACT falling below 3 percent, Richard PREBBLE stepped down as party leader in April 2004 and Rodney HIDE won a four-way battle for the leadership. In September 2005 the party won only 1.5 percent of the party list vote but thanks to Hide's constituency victory ACT was eligible for one list seat, which was taken by Heather ROY. Sir Roger Douglas contested the 2008 election as a list candidate, ranked third behind Hide and Roy; he was elected but not awarded a ministerial portfolio because of Prime Minister Key's adamant refusal to work with him. Hide and Roy were awarded portfolios (outside cabinet) in the new National-led government. In August 2010 Roy, critical of Hide's leadership, was dismissed as deputy leader by the ACT caucus and was replaced by John Boscawen.

Former National Party leader Don Brash successfully seized the leadership of ACT in April 2011 and then named former Auckland mayor John Banks to contest the Eden electorate in place of Rodney Hide, who was voted out of the leadership and resigned from Parliament after the 2011 election. All sitting ACT MPs subsequently declined to stand in the 2011 election. ACT's popularity thereupon sank and by election night November 26 stood at 1.1 percent, with only Banks winning his constituency seat. Brash then resigned as leader, deputy leader John Boscawen foreshadowed his retirement at the next election, and Banks began negotiations to support a National-led government in supply and confidence, for which he was rewarded with the portfolios of Regulatory Reform and Small Business, both outside cabinet. In October 2013 Banks resigned his portfolios to stand trial for alleged electoral fraud during his 2010 Auckland mayoral bid; he was convicted in August 2014. In his place Jamie Whyte was chosen as ACT leader. ACT sponsored 41 candidates for the September election but only 1, David SEYMOUR, won a seat. Upon Whyte's resignation in October, Seymour became the head of the ACT party. As leader of one of the government's support parties, he was appointed Parliamentary Under Secretary for Education and Regulatory Reform.

Leaders: David SEYMOUR (Leader), Kenneth WANG (Deputy Leader), John THOMSON (Party President), Beth HOULBROOKE (Vice President), Lindsay FERGUSSON (Treasurer).

United Future New Zealand (United Future). United Future was formed in 2000 by the merger of **United New Zealand** (United NZ) and **Future New Zealand** (Future NZ). (See the 2010 *Handbook* for background details on these parties.)

In its first national election in July 2002, United Future won eight House seats and agreed to support Helen Clark's Labour-Progressive coalition. In 2005 the party won only three seats, but these proved crucial in Labour's effort to remain in power, as a consequence of which Dunne was awarded the post of minister of revenue.

In the 2008 election Dunne again won his electorate seat, but he was the sole surviving MP for United Future. Nevertheless, he was kept on by Prime Minister Key as minister of revenue (outside cabinet). United Future's popularity remained low, registering just 0.6 percent in the November 2011 election, but Dunne retained his constituency seat and was reinstated as minister for revenue in the new National-led government. The Electoral Commission deregistered United Future on May 31, 2013, for insufficient membership; although the party was reregistered on August 13, Dunne lost his revenue portfolio to National's Tod McCLAY. Nevertheless Dunne's electorate returned him to Parliament in the 2014 election where he again supported the National-led government.

Leaders: Peter DUNNE (Party Leader and Former Minister of Revenue), Judy TURNER (Deputy Leader), Damian LIGHT (Party President), Ronald GARROD (Secretary-General).

Opposition Party:

New Zealand Labour Party (Labour Party). Founded in 1916 and in power 1935–1949, 1957–1960, 1972–1975, and 1984–1990, the Labour Party initiated much of the legislation that created the New Zealand welfare state. However, in a radical policy shift compelled by international economic changes, the post-1984 Labour administration of David Lange introduced free-market policies, including privatization of state enterprises, deregulation of commercial activities, and elimination of subsidies. The party nonetheless maintained its traditional antimilitary and antinuclear postures and in 1985 prohibited a visit by a U.S. warship, precipitating a curtailment of bilateral defense relations by Washington. Labour was reelected in 1987 but in 1989 the increasingly unpopular Lange resigned in favor of Geoffrey PALMER, who was in turn succeeded by Michael "Mike" MOORE in 1990. The party's legislative representation fell to an all-time low of 28 seats in the 1990 election, but it staged a recovery to 45 seats out of 99 in 1993.

In December 1993 a Labour caucus ousted Moore in favor of his deputy, Helen Clark, a leader of the party's left wing. In the 1994 and 1996 elections Labour lost seats and remained in opposition. Labour recovered in the 1999 election, taking 38.7 percent of the list vote and gaining 49 seats. Clark negotiated a coalition with the Alliance (10 seats) and secured support on crucial votes from the Greens, and thus became New Zealand's first elected woman prime minister.

The collapse of the Alliance led to an early election in July 2002, in which Labour retained its plurality, winning 52 seats (including all 7

Maori roll seats) on the strength of 45 percent of the electorate votes and 41 percent of the party list votes. Clark then negotiated a coalition with the former Alliance leader Jim Anderton's new Progressives and a cooperation agreement with United Future that assured her new government a working majority. In late 2004 Labour lost the 7 Maori members, who left to form a new Maori Party (see above). In September 2005, although its electorate vote dropped to 40 percent, Labour won a plurality of 50 seats, just ahead of the rival Nationals, formed another coalition with Jim Anderton's Progressives, and gained sufficient support from United Future and New Zealand First to form a minority government.

Labour contested the election of November 2008 with a new front bench and relatively unknown candidates, winning only 34 percent of the vote and 43 seats. On election night as the result became clear, Helen Clark unexpectedly announced her retirement as Labour leader. She subsequently retired from Parliament to head the United Nations Development Program. The party's nomination for her seat went to David Shearer, a former UN official who had served in Iraq. Shearer won the by-election of June 13, 2009, with 63.3 percent of the vote.

In March 2009 Phil Goff was unanimously chosen to lead the party and Annette KING became his deputy. Party president Mike WILLIAMS stepped down and union secretary Andrew LITTLE was elected in his place; he was succeeded in 2010 by Moira COATSWORTH. In mid-2010 Labour's Shane JONES was demoted from his shadow ministership as a result of parliamentary allowance spending abuses, and in October Chris CARTER was expelled from the Labour Party for undermining Phil Goff's leadership. A promising young MP, Darren HUGHES, resigned from Parliament in March 2011 following allegations of sexual misconduct. By August Labour's popularity sagged to 30 percent in polls, and Phil Goff's desirability as preferred prime minister declined to 12 percent. The November election found Labour's vote reduced to 27.5 percent and Parliamentary seats to 34, whereupon Goff and King offered their resignations as leader and deputy, and the Labour caucus elected David Shearer and Grant ROBERTSON in their place. In 2012 and 2013 neither the party nor the leader polled well, and in August 2013 Shearer resigned, to be replaced by David Cunliff. David Parker was chosen as deputy leader and shadow finance minister. Labour's advocacy of a capital gains tax and higher taxes on upper income earners, and Cunliff's sometimes lackluster leadership, proved unpopular, and in the 2014 election the party won only 25.1 percent of the vote and 32 seats, its worst performance since 1922. As a result, Cunliff resigned in October and in November Little was elected as party leader. Labour announced in May 2016 that it would form an alliance with the Greens in an effort to defeat the National Party in the 2017 elections.

Leaders: Andrew LITTLE (Party Leader and Leader of the Opposition), Annette KING (Deputy Party Leader), Nigel HAWORTH (President), Andrew KIRTON (Secretary-General).

Other Parties in Parliament:

Green Party of Aotearoa (Greens). Founded in 1972 as the **New Zealand Values Party,** the country's left-oriented environmental party adopted its present name in 1988. In addition to environmental and conservation concerns, it advocates disarmament, pacifism, and devolution of power to the people and opposes free trade agreements. In 1991 the Greens entered an alliance with New Labour and other small groups, which gained three legislative seats in the 1996 balloting.

In the 1999 election the Greens, contesting independently, won seven seats in the House. Because the Labour-Alliance coalition failed to gain a majority, the incoming Clark minority government appealed for Green support, which it got for crucial votes, although a formal cooperation agreement was never concluded.

In the 2002 election the Green seats rose to nine, but Prime Minister Clark rejected their demand for a blanket moratorium on genetically modified organisms, so the Greens went into opposition. In September 2005 the Greens won six seats and again, while remaining outside the new Labour-led minority government, agreed not to oppose it on confidence votes, enabling Clark to remain prime minister.

The Greens surged to 6.7 percent in the November election, winning nine seats and placing third behind National and Labour and well ahead of ACT. Labour's attempt to build a new coalition failed, and the Greens moved to the opposition benches again. The Greens' most popular activist, Jeanette FITZSIMONS, retired from co-leadership in June 2009, and the party chose Metiria TUREI as the new co-leader. Russel NORMAN replaced the late Rod DONALD as the male co-leader. On election night November 26, 2011, the Greens attracted 11 percent of the party vote to send 14 list members to Parliament despite winning no constituency seats. Despite skillful and principled campaigning in the 2014 election he party again won just 14 seats in Parliament.

While the Greens enjoyed some electoral success in the 2014 election, former party leader Norman stepped down, resigning from the Parliament. He was replaced by James SHAW in 2015.

Leaders: James SHAW, Metiria TUREI (Co-Leaders); Debs MARTIN, John RANTA (Co-Conveners).

New Zealand First Party (NZ First). The right-wing populist NZ First was launched in July 1993 by the flamboyant former Maori affairs minister, Winston Peters, who had been ejected from the National Party caucus earlier in the year. Forcing a by-election by resigning from the House, he retained his seat with a massive 11,000-vote majority in the Tauranga electorate and subsequently attracted much public approval for his allegations of corruption in the Cook Islands (see Related Territories, below). NZ First won only 2 seats in the 1993 election but improved to 17 seats (including all 5 Maori roll seats) in the 1996 election, enabling Peters to negotiate a coalition agreement with the National Party whereby he was named deputy prime minister and treasurer. However, his rapid elevation generated opposition within National Party ranks.

On August 14, 1998, a day after calling Prime Minister Shipley "devious" and "untrustworthy" on the floor of the House, Peters was sacked and NZ First moved into opposition. Several members subsequently formed the short-lived **Mauri Pacific** (Spirit of the Pacific) party, which failed to win any House seats in 1999 and was dissolved in 2001. NZ First failed to reach the 5 percent threshold in the 1999 national election, but Peters retained his Tauranga seat (by 63 votes), and this enabled NZ First to claim four additional party list seats.

In the 2002 election NZ First appealed to anticrime, anti-immigration, and anti-Maori sentiments and took 10.4 percent of the party list vote, to surge to 13 House seats, but the party remained in opposition. In the 2005 election the party declined to only 7 list seats on a 5.7 percent vote share and Peters lost his Tauranga seat to a National candidate. But Peters, elected on the party list, then negotiated a "supply and confidence agreement" with Labour that made him minister of foreign affairs, although he remained outside cabinet and able to criticize the government. Subsequent allegations that he had accepted secret donations from wealthy business interests damaged his credibility, and in August 2008 Prime Minister Clark suspended him as minister of foreign affairs. Parliament passed a motion of censure three weeks later. Peters was ultimately cleared by the Serious Fraud Office, but meanwhile, NZ First had slumped in the polls and won only 4.1 percent of the vote. Furthermore, Peters lost his constituency race, so the party was excluded from the new Parliament altogether. The party continued to attract a small but loyal following Peters' return to campaigning in the 2011 election run-up revived it; despite winning no constituencies NZ First garnered 6.8 percent of the party vote and sent 8 MPs to Parliament. Peters declined to enter into negotiations with either National or Labour, opting again to position his party on the opposition benches. The party's position improved in the 2014 election, winning 8.9 percent of the vote and sending 12 members to Parliament, but failed to hold the balance of power because the National Party was able to form a government without NZ First participation.

Leaders: Winston PETERS (Leader), Ron MARK (Deputy Leader), Brent CATCHPOLE (President).

Other Parties:

Mana Movement (Mana). Registered on June 24, 2011, by Hone Harawira, following his resignation from the Maori Party (above), the party championed the redressing of Maori grievances. It objected particularly to the compromises made by the Maori Party in the Marine and Coastal Area (Takutai Moana) Act. Its leader forced a by-election by resigning from Parliament and then successfully contested the Te Tai Tokerau seat against Labour and Maori Party rivals and returned to Parliament on the opposition benches. Despite attracting high-profile personalities John MINTO and Sue BRADFORD as members, it remained a one-person ethnic protest party, gaining only 1.0 percent of the party vote in the November 2011 election despite Harawira's constituency victory. In July 2014 Mana merged with the Internet Party to form the Internet Mana Party (below).

Leaders: Hone HARAWIRA (Leader), Lisa McNAB (President), Gerard HEHIR (Party Secretary).

Internet Mana Party. On July 24, 2014, Harawira joined with the Internet Party (registered May 13, 2014) led by union activist and former Alliance MP Laila Harre to register the Internet Mana party. It was financed by immigrant German internet millionaire Kim Dotcom. The composite party, promoting Maori and youth values and advocating free internet access for all citizens, fielded 32 candidates in the 2014 election. But the party gained only 1.3 percent of the vote and Harawira lost his Te Tai Tokerau seat to the Labour candidate. Without a single member in Parliament, the future of Internet Mana appeared in doubt.

Leaders: Hone HARAWIRA (Leader), Leila HARRE (Deputy Leader), Gerald HEHIR (Secretary).

Conservative Party. Launched in July 2011, the Conservative Party is led by Auckland property developer Colin CRAIG. It espouses lower taxes, minimum government, strict law enforcement and sentencing of convicted persons, opposition to asset sales and the Emission Trading Act, and family and Christian values. In the 2011 election it fielded a full slate of 60 candidates and garnered 2.8 percent of the party vote but failed to reach the 5 percent threshold or win the Rodney seat contested by Craig and won no parliamentary seats. In the 2014 election it sponsored 20 candidates and won 4.1 percent of the vote but fell short of the 5 percent threshold so gained no seats in Parliament.

In November 2015 Craig resigned as a result of inflammatory remarks he made in a televised interview.

Leader: Kevin STITT (National Administrator).

The Alliance. The Alliance was launched in 1991 as a coalition of five parties—the **New Labour Party**, the ***Mana Motuhake***, the **New Zealand Democratic Party**, the **Green Party of Aotearoa**, and the **Liberal Party**—on a platform calling for preservation of the welfare state and an end to the free-market policies of the two major parties. It won 2 seats in 1993 and in the 1996 campaign won 13 seats. However, in late 1997 the Greens left the Alliance and in early 1998 the Liberal Party dissolved.

Nevertheless in the November 1999 election the Alliance captured ten seats and worked out a power-sharing arrangement with Labour that permitted separate stances on issues affecting the "distinctive political identity" of each party. The new Labour-led cabinet included four Alliance ministers and a fifth minister for consumer affairs and customs outside cabinet. However, in 2002 a sharp division between the Alliance caucus and the party leadership headed by Matt McCARTEN led to the expulsion of Anderton and six other MPs who had supported the government's decision to participate in U.S.-led military operations in Afghanistan.

In the July 2002 election, called early because of the split, the Alliance was ousted from the House, having won only 1.3 percent of the party list vote. In December 2002 *Mana Motuhake* formally left the Alliance and dissolved in 2005. In subsequent elections the Alliance won 0.07 percent of the vote in 2005, 0.08 percent in 2008, and 0.05 percent in 2011 and no seats; it did not contest the 2014 election.

Leaders: Kay MURRAY (Co-Leader and Treasurer), Kevin CAMPBELL (Co-Leader), Tom DOWIE (President), Andrew McKENZIE (General Secretary).

Jim Anderton's Progressive Party (Progressives). When divisions over defense policy and relations with the United States split the Alliance coalition party in April–May 2002, its former leader and the sitting deputy prime minister organized his own "Jim Anderton's Progressive Coalition," which was registered as a party by the Electoral Commission in June 2002. In the July 2002 election the Progressive Coalition attracted only 1.7 percent of the party list vote but claimed one additional proportional seat on the strength of Anderton's constituency seat victory. Anderton retained his agriculture and other ministerial portfolios, but not his position as deputy prime minister, in the new Clark minority government.

In April 2004 the Progressive Coalition was formally reregistered as the Progressive Party, adopting its current name in July 2005. In the 2005 election Anderton retained his seat, but the party's 1.2 percent party list vote did not entitle it to another seat. In the 2008 election Anderton again won his electorate seat, but his party garnered only 0.9 percent of the vote, and Anderton moved to the opposition seats with Labour and the Greens. In October 2010 Anderton ran unsuccessfully for the mayoralty of Christchurch and then retired from Parliament after the 2011 election. His party did not contest that poll and was deregistered on March 9, 2012.

Leaders: Jim ANDERTON (Leader), Matt ROBSON (Deputy Leader), Phil CLEARWATER (General Secretary).

New Zealand Democratic Party for Social Credit (Democrats for Social Credit). Established in May 1953 as the Social Credit Political League, the party campaigned largely on a platform that promoted economic sovereignty, small business, worker shareholding and participation in management, tax and banking reform, public ownership of utilities, and introduction of a "Universal Basic Income." Social Credit subsequently proposed a defense posture of "armed neutrality" and a nuclear-free zone.

Leader Bruce BEETHAM held a seat in the House from 1978 until 1987, but his party secured no representation for a decade until winning two seats as part of the Alliance in 1996. It retained both in 1999. When the Alliance split in 2002, the party joined Jim Anderton's Progressive Coalition but won no seats in the July 2002 House election. At a party conference three months later the party opted to separate from the Progressives.

The party adopted its present name in July 2005 but won only 0.1 percent of the party list vote that year, 0.05 percent of the vote in 2008, and 0.08 percent in 2011, and won no seats. It fielded 35 candidates for the 2014 election, winning just 0.08 percent of the vote and no seats.

Leaders: Stephanie de RUYTER (Leader), Chris LEITCH (Deputy Leader), John PEMBERTON (President).

New Zealand Independent Coalition (NZIC). A new party registered on July 24, 2014, NZIC is centered on former TV weather presenter and independent MP Brendan Horan who was expelled from the New Zealand First party in December 2012 for allegedly misappropriating money from his mother's estate and gambling. He remained in Parliament as an independent and his party sponsored ten candidates in the 2014 election, but won no seats in the September poll.

Leaders: Brendan HORAN (Leader), Michael O'NEILL (Deputy Leader), Helen ANDERSON (Party Secretary).

1Law4All. Registered in July 2014, this party's core policies are to abolish the separate Maori electoral role, reserved parliamentary seats, and other Maori privileges and remove the Treaty of Waitangi from New Zealand law. It fielded no candidates for the 2014 election.

Leaders: Tom JOHNSON (Acting Leader), Crispin CALDICOTT (Registered Officer).

Ban 1080. Registered in August 2014, this new single-issue party campaigned against the widespread use by the Department of Conservation of 1080 poison to control the possum pest threat to native forests. It fielded nine candidates but won no seats in the 2014 election.

Leaders: Bill WALLACE, Mike DOWNARD (Co-Leaders); David HECTOR (Party Secretary).

The following parties contested the 2008, 2011, or 2014 election without success, and nine were subsequently deregistered. The **Kiwi Party** (registered February 15, 2008; Larry BALDOCK, leader; Gordon COPELAND, president; Simonne DYER, secretary), which successfully led the petition initiative to force the August 21, 2009, referendum on the "anti-smacking" bill, won 0.5 percent. It did not contest the 2011 election and was deregistered on February 8, 2012. The **Aotearoa Legalize Cannabis Party** (Julian CRAWFORD, leader; ABE GRAY, deputy leader; Kevin O'CONNELL, president; Irinka BRITNELL, secretary) won 0.4 percent in 2008, 0.5 percent in 2011, and 0.4 percent in 2014. The **Libertarianz** (Richard McGRATH, leader; Sean FITZPATRICK, deputy leader; Craig MILMINE, president; Robert PALMER, secretary), a radical minimum-government party founded in 1996, won 0.05 percent of the vote in 2008 and 0.07 percent in 2011. The **Workers Party of New Zealand** (registered October 3, 2008; Philip FERGUSON, national organizer; Daphna WHITMORE, national secretary), which won 0.04 percent, is a descendent of numerous small leftist parties, most recently the **Anti-Capitalist Alliance** (2002–2006); it was deregistered in May 2011. The **New Citizen Party**, aspiring to represent recent Asian migrants, was registered on November 25, 2010, with Kevin LIU as party secretary but did not contest the 2011 election and was deregistered on February 29, 2012.The **Bill and Ben Party** (registered July 29, 2008; Ben BOYCE and Jamie LINEHAM, co-leaders; Andrew ROBINSON, secretary), a "joke party" led by two TV satirists, won 0.6 percent of the vote in 2008; it was deregistered in April 2010. The **Family Party** (registered December 17, 2007; Richard LEWIS, leader; Paul ADAMS, deputy leader; Elias KANARIS, president; Anne WILLIAMSON, secretary), which won 0.4 percent of the vote, descended from two fundamentalist parties, the **New Zealand Family Rights Protection Party** (registered March 2005 and deregistered September 2007) and **Destiny New Zealand** (registered July 2003 and deregistered in October 2007); it was deregistered in April 2010. The **New Zealand Pacific Party** (Philip FIELD, leader; Ropeti GAFA, interim secretary) won 0.4 percent; it was deregistered in August 2010. The **RAM–Residents Action Movement** (Grant BROOKES, chair; Elaine BLADE, vice chair; Elliott BLADE, secretary) won 0.02 percent; it was deregistered in April 2010. The **Republic of New Zealand Party** (Kerry BEVIN, leader; Richard NIGHTINGALE, secretary), which won 0.01 percent, was registered in July 2005 and deregistered on June 30, 2009. The **New World Order Party**, founded in 2006 and registered in May 2008 (Nathan Lee COUPER, President and Secretary), was deregistered in June 2011. The Electoral Commission registered the logo of an aspiring party, **Thrive New Zealand**, which promotes citizens' referenda and direct democracy, on August 28, 2013, but registration was not achieved by the time of the 2014 election.

For more information on the **Civilian Party**, see the 2015 *Handbook.*

LEGISLATURE

The former bicameral General Assembly of New Zealand became a unicameral body in 1950 with the abolition of its upper chamber, the Legislative Council. Now called the **House of Representatives** (although popularly called Parliament and its delegates referred to as members of Parliament, or MPs), the body currently consists of 120 members elected by universal suffrage for a three-year term, subject to dissolution. Under a partially proportional system (mixed member proportional, or MMP) introduced in 1996, 71 members are elected from single-member constituencies by majority vote (including 7 elected by voters on a separate Maori electoral roll) and at least 50 from party lists to ensure proportional representation for those parties winning at least one constituency or obtaining at least 5 percent of the national vote.

In the election of September 17, 2005, the new Maori Party won 1 more electorate seat than would otherwise have been awarded on the basis of the party list vote. Under New Zealand's MMP electoral system, this "overhang" seat meant that the House had 121 seats (69 electorate seats and 52 party list seats). The 2008 election produced an "overhang" of 2 Maori seats and a House of 122 members. These were distributed as follows: National Party, 58 (constituency seats 41, party list seats 17); Labour Party, 43 (21, 22); Green Party of Aotearoa, 9 (0, 9); ACT New Zealand, 5 (1, 4); Maori Party, 5 (5, 0); Jim Anderton's Progressive Party, 1 (1, 0), United Future New Zealand, 1 (1, 0). The October 2010 expulsion of Chris Carter reduced the Labour caucus to 42, the June 2011 resignation of Hone Harawira to win a by-election seat under the Mana Party label reduced the Maori Party caucus to 4, and the July resignation of John CARTER to become High Commissioner to Cook Islands reduced the National caucus to 57 and the number of legislative seats to 121.

The election of November 26, 2011, returned the following parties to the House: National 59 (constituency seats 40, list seats 19); Labour 34 (23, 11); Green 14 (0, 8); NZ First 8 (0, 8); Maori 3 (3, 0); Act 1 (1, 0); Mana 1 (1, 0); United Future 1 (1, 0). The Maori Party's three constituency victories with only 1.3 percent of party vote produced an "overhang" of 2 and a House of 122 seats. The election of September 20, 2014, resulted in a House of 121 MPs and the following party distribution: National (constituency seats 41, list seats 19), Labour (27, 5), Green (0, 14), NZ First (0, 11), Maori (1, 1), United Future (1, 0), ACT (1, 0). The new MPs included 37 women, 18 Maori, 7 Pacific islanders, 3 Indians, 2 Chinese, 5 gays, and 1 deaf MP.

Speaker: David CARTER.

CABINET

[as of August 14, 2016]

Prime Minister, Tourism, National Security, and Intelligence	John Key
Deputy Prime Minister, Finance	Bill English
Ministers in Cabinet	
Accident Compensation Commission, Civil Defence, Youth	Nikki Kaye [f]
Arts, Culture, and Heritage, Conservation, Senior Citizens	Maggie Barry
Attorney General, Treaty of Waitangi Negotiations, New Zealand Security Intelligence Service, Government Communications Security Bureau	Christopher Findlayson
Climate Change Issues, Social Housing, State Services	Paula Bennett [f]
Corrections, Police	Judith Collins
Economic Development, Regulatory Reform, Science and Innovation, Tertiary Education, Skills and Employment	Steven Joyce
Education	Hekia Parata [f]
Energy and Resources, Transport	Simon Bridges
Environment, Building and Housing	Nick Smith
Ethnic Communities, Local Government, Pacific Peoples	Peseta Sam Lotu-Iiga
Foreign Affairs	Murray McCully
Greater Christchurch Regeneration, Defence	Gerry Brownlee
Health, Sport and Recreation	Jonathan Coleman
Immigration, Revenue, Workplace Relations and Safety	Michael Woodhouse
Justice, Courts, Broadcasting, Communications	Amy Adams [f]
Primary Industries, Racing	Nathan Guy
Social Development	Anne Tolley [f]
State Owned Enterprises, Trade	Todd McClay
Ministers outside Cabinet	
Commerce, Consumer Affairs	Paul Goldsmith
Community and Voluntary Sector, Food Safety	Jo Goodhew [f]
Customs, Disability Issues	Nicky Wagner [f]
Land Information, Women	Louise Upston [f]
Small Business, Statistics, Veterans' Affairs	Craig Foss
Support Party Ministers	
Internal Affairs	Peter Dunne
Maori Development, Whanau Ora	Te Ururoa Flavell (Maori Party)

[f] = female

Note: Unless otherwise noted, all ministers belong to the National Party.

INTERGOVERNMENTAL REPRESENTATION

Ambassador to the U.S.: Tim GROSER.

U.S. Ambassador to New Zealand: Candy GREEN (Chargé d'Affaires).

Permanent Representative to the UN: Gerard VAN BOHEMEN.

IGO Memberships (Non-UN): ADB, APEC, CWTH, ICC, IEA, IOM, OECD, PIF, WTO.

For Further Reference:

Fischer, David Hackett. *Fairness and Freedom: A History of Two Open Societies, New Zealand and the United States.* Oxford: Oxford University Press, 2012.

Grant, David. *The Totara: The Life and Times of Norman Kirk.* Auckland: Random House New Zealand, 2014.

Jones, Carwyn. *New Treaty, New Tradition: Reconciling New Zealand and Maori Law.* Vancouver: University of British Columbia, 2016.

Stenson, Marcia. *The Treaty: Every New Zealander's Guide to the Treaty of Waitangi.* Auckland: Random House New Zealand, 2012.

RELATED TERRITORIES

New Zealand has links to two self-governing territories in free association, the Cook Islands and Niue, and administers two dependent territories, Tokelau and Ross Dependency.

Cook Islands. Located some 1,700 miles northeast of New Zealand and administered by that country from 1901 to 1965, Cook Islands is now a self-governing political entity recognizing Queen Elizabeth II (represented by New Zealand's governor general) as its sovereign and constitutionally linked in free association with New Zealand. The islands have a land area of 90 square miles (234 sq. km) and are divided between a smaller, poorer, northern group and a larger, more fertile, southern group. The most populous island, Rarotonga, is the site of the capital, Avarua. The islands' total resident population of 21,000 (2016E—UN) consists almost entirely of Polynesians who are New Zealand citizens. In 2006, 58,011 Cook Islanders resided in New Zealand, with another 15,000 in Australia, and their remittances are a significant source of income for the territory. Exports include fish, pearls, tropical fruits, and handicrafts, while tourism is the source of over 75 percent of foreign earnings. Offshore banking and the sale of fishing licenses to foreign ships also contribute income. Future prospects include mining of undersea mineral nodules. Cook Islands annually receives more than $20 million from an integrated New Zealand and Australia development cooperation program, supplemented by project and relief aid from Japan, France, the European Union, China, and the Asian Development Bank (ADB).

In June 2000 the Cook Islands was named by the Organization for Economic Cooperation and Development (OECD) as 1 of 35 uncooperative tax havens and by the international Financial Action Task Force on Money Laundering (FATF) as 1 of 15 noncooperative countries and territories. In 2002 the Cook government undertook remedial action and in 2005 was removed from the FATF list, having satisfied demands for tighter controls.

Self-government with an elected Legislative Assembly (commonly called the Parliament) and a premier (prime minister, since 1981) elected by the Parliament was instituted in 1965, with New Zealand obligated by legislation to assist in external and defense affairs when requested. A hereditary House of Ariki, with up to 15 members, serves as an upper legislative chamber, advising on customary matters and land use. In 2004 Parliament voted to drop the seat for voters overseas, reduce the size of the legislature to 24, and shorten the legislative term from five to four years.

Over the past 30 years political power has swung between the **Cook Islands Party** (CIP), which dates from 1965, and the **Democratic Party** (DP), founded in 1971 and named the Democratic Alliance Party (DAP) until 2003, often entailing coalition governments (for details, see the 2010 *Handbook*). The political landscape stabilized in 2004 when, following formation of a new grouping called *Demo Tumu* (subsequently renamed Cook Islands First) by defectors from the CIP and the DP, Jim MARURAI was elected prime minister. Marurai shored up his leadership by including CIP and DP leaders in his cabinet. After losing his majority in Parliament in 2006, he called a snap election that concluded with the DP holding 15 seats; CIP, 8; and a CIP-aligned independent, 1. Marurai was reinstated as prime minister, with Terepai MAOATE as his deputy and Wilkie RASMUSSEN as minister of foreign affairs. The CIP's Tom MASTERS became leader of the opposition.

In a cabinet reshuffle in November 2009 Marurai sacked Maoate, brought in Robert WIGMORE as deputy prime minister and foreign minister, and moved Rasmussen to the finance portfolio. In July 2010 Marurai, facing serious opposition from the CIP, held on as prime minister by refusing to convene Parliament except for a session to pass the budget. The election of November 17 brought the CIP to power with 44.5 percent of the vote and 16 seats to the DP's 8 seats. Henry PUNA, leader of the CIP since 2006, became prime minister, and Mapu TAIA, DP, became speaker of Parliament. In 2012 senior politician Norman GEORGE resigned from the CIP to re-join the DP and challenged the constitutionality of the Electoral Amendment Act 2007 preventing parliamentarians from changing parties, and in August 2013 Minister of Marine Resources Teina BISHOP stood down amid allegations of fraudulent practices regarding granting of fishing licenses to Chinese-flagged boats.

Internationally, the Cook Islands is a member of the Pacific Community, the Smaller Island States subgroup (with Kiribati, Nauru, Niue, and Tuvalu) within the Pacific Islands Forum, various UN agencies, and the ADB, and is engaged in negotiations to augment the Pacific Agreement on Closer Economic Relations that includes Australia, New Zealand, and the Forum governments. In 2009 Marurai and Prime Minister John Key announced completion of a tax information exchange agreement, further dispelling lingering allegations of tax evasion. A similar agreement was negotiated with Australia. Cook Islands in April petitioned the UN Commission on the Limits of the Continental Shelf (CLCS) to extend its Exclusive Economic Zone by 400,000 sq. km, and in July 2011 Minister for Minerals and Natural Resources Tom Masters announced plans to begin issuing deep-sea mining exploration licenses in 2013. This was followed in June 2012 by legislation under the Cook Islands Seabed Mining Act 2009 establishing Cook Island jurisdiction over resources in its EEZ and in August by an agreement with neighboring Kiribati, Niue, and Tokelau demarcating their respective maritime boundaries. The budget for 2012–2013 foreshadowed a surplus made possible by new taxes on imported tobacco and beverages and tourism activities and foreign grants and loans of NZ$48 million, including NZ$4 million from China. The ratio of debt to GDP was forecast to rise to 33 percent in 2013–2014 reflecting borrowing from the ADB and China for infrastructural improvements. New Zealand's aid in the period 2013–2015 included NZ$12 million annually for economic growth and infrastructure, NZ$4 million for health and education, and NZ$1.6 million for governance improvement, a projected three-year total of NZ$57 million. Australia contributed another NZ$5 million annually. In 2013 New Zealand and China commenced a joint water reticulation project, a first for both governments. The July 9, 2014, election returned Puna to power with 13 Cook Island Party representatives; the Democratic Party won 8 seats and the new One Cook Island Party won 2. In September construction began on a New Zealand-European Union funded renewable energy project for outer islands valued at $16.8 million. In June 2015 the government announced its intention to seek full UN membership but pledged that membership would not change its relationship with New Zealand.

New Zealand High Commissioner: John CARTER.
Prime Minister: Henry PUNA.
Queen's Representative: Tom J. MARSTERS.

Niue. An island of 100 square miles (259 sq. km), Niue is the largest and westernmost of the Cook Islands but has been administered separately since 1903. The territory obtained self-government in 1974, with a premier heading a 4-member cabinet and a Legislative Assembly (*Fono*) of 20 members, 6 elected from a common roll and 14 chosen by villages, serving three-year terms. It is now a self-governing political entity recognizing Queen Elizabeth II, represented by New Zealand's governor general, as its sovereign and is constitutionally linked in free association with New Zealand. Niueans have New Zealand citizenship, and New Zealand is obligated by legislation to assist Niue with foreign affairs and defense when requested. The capital is Alofi.

Niue's resident population has declined almost continuously from 5,194 in 1966 to 1,740 in 2006 and an estimated 1,300 in 2013. According to the 2006 census, 22,473 Niueans resided in New Zealand, and their overseas remittances constitute a major source of the island's income. Other economic resources include annual budgetary and project aid from New Zealand, loans from international agencies, and export sales of noni juice, fish, taro, honey, and vanilla. A small tourism industry attracted some 3,500 tourists in 2007, but numbers remain low due to limited hotel facilities and airline flights. Arrivals are also affected by the threat of cyclones. Recent efforts to increase the island's income have included leasing its telephone area code for sex-related and other services, selling its postal code ("NU") for Internet domain addresses, and investigating prospects for commercial fishing. Internationally, Niue participates in the Pacific Community, the Smaller Island States subgroup (with the Cook Islands, Kiribati, Nauru, and Tuvalu) within the Pacific Islands Forum, the UN Educational, Scientific, and Cultural Organization (UNESCO), the World Health Organization (WHO), and the UN Food and Agricultural Organization and has economic and trade agreements with New Zealand, Australia, the European Union, and the other Pacific islands.

Niue's first and longest-serving premier Sir Robert R. REX died in December 1992, and a Legislative Assembly election in February 1993 brought Frank LUI to the premiership. The period 1994–2004 saw a divided assembly and a series of inconclusive no-confidence motions as the Niue People's Party (NPP) disintegrated. (See the 2010 *Handbook* for details.)

In June 2002 the legislature repealed a controversial 1994 act that had permitted the licensing of offshore banks. Never as lucrative as hoped, this banking legislation had contributed to Niue's designation in 2000 by the international FATF as noncompliant in fighting money laundering. Collaterally, the OECD had labeled Niue as 1 of 35 jurisdictions considered to be an uncooperative tax haven. By the end of 2002 Niue had taken sufficient corrective actions to warrant removal from both lists.

With the NPP having dissolved in 2003, all candidates in the election of 2005 ran as independents. Veteran politician Young VIVIAN retained the premiership. In early March 2007 he easily survived a no-confidence motion, 12–7, despite a financial crisis that had necessitated a cut in civil service pay as well as other major spending reductions. Following the June 2008 general election, Toke TALAGI secured 14 assembly votes to Vivian's 5 to take the premiership. The May 2011 election produced a similar result, with Talagi gaining 11 votes to 8 for challenger Togia SIONEHOLO.

In the 2014 general election, Talagi retained his premiership, winning 12 of the seats in the Niuean Assembly.

To increase fiscal security, the governments of Niue, New Zealand, and Australia in 2006 established a Niue International Trust Fund, which is now valued at nearly NZ$40. In 2009 Talagi hosted a visit by Prime Minister John Key, at which time he urged speedier release of NZ$2 million earmarked for tourism development under the 2004 Halavaka Agreement, criticized micromanagement of aid by Wellington, and hinted that he was prepared to talk with China, with which Niue had established diplomatic relations in 2008, if New Zealand did not look after the island's needs. In 2010 the two governments agreed on a five-year aid plan under which New Zealand was to provide nearly NZ$20 million per year for tourism and infrastructure development and administrative capacity building. The aid allocation for 2014 was NZ$13 million. Meanwhile, China in January 2011 made a grant of NZ$1.5 million to finance purchase of 25 tractors and in August undertook discussions to provide solar panels to be funded by New Zealand aid. In April 2012 Niue ratified the Comprehensive Nuclear Test Ban Treaty, and in June Premier Talagi announced plans to issue licenses to foreign firms to explore for gold and copper. The Niue Treaty Subsidiary Agreement providing a legal framework for Pacific island government cooperation in fisheries management came into effect in August 2014. In May 2015 Japan recognized Niue and established diplomatic relations through its embassy in New Zealand.

New Zealand High Commissioner: Ross ARDEN.

Premier: Toke TALAGI.

Tokelau. A group of three atolls (Atafu, Fakaofo, and Nukunonu) north of Samoa with an area of 4 square miles (10.4 sq. km), the Tokelaus were originally claimed by the United States in the Guano Islands Act 1856, but the claim was never acted on. The atolls were subsequently administered by Great Britain and, from 1923, New Zealand, and were included within New Zealand's territorial boundaries by legislation enacted in 1948. The United States ceded claims to the three main atolls in 1979 but incorporated Swain's Island (Olohega) into American Samoa, creating the potential for dispute if Tokelau becomes independent in the future. The islands have limited economic viability, the principal income sources being annual budget and project aid from New Zealand; remittances from Tokelauans working overseas; the export of coconut, copra, and tuna; the sale of stamps, handicrafts, and souvenir coins; and the sale of fishing licenses to foreign fleets. In 2004 an International Trust Fund for Tokelau was established in 2004, which is now valued at over NZ$70 million. Tokelau has a resident population of 1,000 (2016E—UN), while several thousand Tokelauans reside in New Zealand, Sydney, Samoa, and Hawaii.

Tokelau is now a non–self-governing territory of New Zealand and remains on the agenda of the UN Special Committee on Decolonization. In UN-supervised referenda in 2006 and 2007 Tokelauans rejected the option of independence, with many anxious that New Zealand would not sustain its present financial commitment and extension of citizenship if Tokelau became independent. Consequently Tokelauans remain New Zealand citizens, use the New Zealand dollar as their currency, and rely on New Zealand for the conduct of their foreign affairs and defense. Tokelau is a member of the Pacific Community Secretariat, an observer in the Pacific Island Forum, and an associate member of the WHO and UNESCO.

Each of the atolls elects for a three-year term a *faipule,* whose duties include executive and judicial responsibilities. As each atoll's highest elected official, the *faipule* advises the territory's New Zealand–appointed administrator, who represents the crown and is responsible to New Zealand's Ministry of Foreign Affairs and Trade. Each atoll also has a Council of Elders (*Taupulega*) and an elected mayor (*pulenuku*), and together the *faipule* and the mayors constitute the Council for the Ongoing Government. The government is chaired for a one-year term by the *Ulu-O-Tokelau,* the titular head of the territory, which rotates among the three *faipule.* The 23 members of the *Fono,* which includes the *faipule* and the *pulenuku,* are elected for three-year terms, most recently in January 2008. In April 2010 the *faipule,* led by Foua TOLOA on behalf of the *Fono,* declared Tokelau's exclusive economic zone waters as a whale sanctuary, the 11th to be so declared in the Pacific.

The election of January 2011 resulted in replacement of two of the three *faipule* and installation of new members in the *Fono.* New Zealand aid for 2013 was estimated at NZ$20 million, supplemented by technical exchanges, telecommunications assistance, information sharing, maritime surveillance, and visits by Navy ships whose personnel contribute small scale health and construction projects. In 2012 New Zealand initiated a NZ$9 million solar panel project to make Tokelau the first nation entirely powered by solar power, eliminating a NZ$1 million diesel fuel import bill and in 2013 carried out a project to conserve fresh water. Kuresa NASAU in February 2014 became the head of government in rotation.

Administrator: Jonathan KINGS.

Head of Government: Siopili PEREZ

Faipule (Titular Heads of *Tokelau's* three atolls): Foua TOLOA (Fakaofo), Keli KOLOI (Atafu), Salesio LUI (Nukunonu).

Ross Dependency. A large, wedge-shaped portion of the Antarctic Continent, the Ross Dependency extends from 160 degrees east to 150 degrees west longitude and has an estimated area of 160,000 square miles (414,400 sq. km). It includes the Ross Ice Shelf, the Balleny Islands, and Scott Island. Although the Ross Dependency has been administered by New Zealand since 1923, the Antarctic Treaty of 1959 puts New Zealand's claim, as well as all other states' claims, in abeyance. Nevertheless, New Zealand criminal law and conservation laws and other legislation are recognized as valid in the territory, which in 1977 was extended 200 nautical miles into the Southern Ocean by the Territorial Sea and Exclusive Economic Zone Act. A permit is required from the Ministry of Foreign Affairs and Trade to visit the territory or from the Ministry of Fisheries to conduct fishing activities. In accordance with the Antarctica (Environmental Protection) Act 1994, mineral prospecting and mining is prohibited. The territory, in accordance with the Antarctic Treaty, is a conventional and nuclear-weapons-free zone.

New Zealand maintains a permanent scientific research station in the territory called Scott Base, serviced by Royal New Zealand Air Force aircraft, and cooperates with the U.S. National Science Foundation, which maintains the McMurdo scientific station nearby. New Zealand designates senior staff at Scott Base as officers of the government, empowering them to administer New Zealand law in the dependency. Any person born in the Ross Dependency becomes a New Zealand citizen. Since 1988, in an effort to stop illegal fishing in the Ross Sea, surveillance of the area has been exercised by patrols undertaken periodically by air force planes and navy vessels, in coordination with similar surveillance by Australian planes and ships. The 2002 Statement of Strategic Interest stressed New Zealand's environmental stewardship of the region. The November 2010 Defence White Paper echoed warnings by conservationists in calling attention to the vulnerability of the Antarctic landmass and seas to unscrupulous resource exploitation. Meetings of the Commission for the Conservation of Antarctic Marine Living Resources in 2013 and 2014 considered a joint New Zealand–United States proposal to establish a 2.27 million square kilometer marine protected area in the Ross Sea but failed to reach a decision because of Russian objections.

NICARAGUA

Republic of Nicaragua
República de Nicaragua

Note: National elections for the presidency and the assembly were held on November 6, 2016. José Daniel Ortega Saavedra of the Sandinista National Liberation Front (FSLN) was reelected for a third consecutive term as president with 72.4 percent of the vote. His closest opponent, Maximino Rodriguez, of the Constitutionalist Liberal Party (PLC) secured 15 percent, followed by four other candidates. Ortega's running mate was his wife, Rosario Murillo (FSLN). In balloting for the unicameral legislature, the FSLN won 71 seats, followed by the PLC, 14; the Independent Liberal Party, 2; the Nicaraguan Liberal Alliance, 2; the Conservative Party of Nicaragua, 1; the Alliance for the Republic, 1; and the newly formed indigenous grouping, the Sons of Mother Earth (YATAMA), 1. Opposition groups widely decried the polling as corrupt and fraudulent after anti-regime candidates were barred from campaigning and foreign election observers were banned.

Political Status: Independence originally proclaimed 1821; separate republic established 1838; provisional junta installed July 19, 1979; present constitution adopted November 19, 1986, in effect from January 9, 1987.

Area: 50,193 sq. mi. (130,000 sq. km).

Population: 6,150,000 (2016E—UN); 5,966,798 (2016E—U.S. Census).

Major Urban Center (2015E—UN): MANAGUA (956,000).

Official Language: Spanish.

Monetary Unit: Córdoba Oro (principal rate October 1, 2016: 28.76 córdobas = $1US).

President: Daniel ORTEGA Saavedra (Sandinista National Liberation Front); served as president 1985–1990; reelected on November 5, 2006, and inaugurated for a five-year term on January 10, 2007, succeeding Enrique BOLAÑOS Geyer (Grand Liberal Union); reelected on November 6, 2011, and inaugurated on January 10, 2012, for an unprecedented third term.

Vice President: Omar HALLESLEVENS Acevedo (Sandinista National Liberation Front); elected on November 6, 2011, and inaugurated, for a term concurrent with that of the president on January 10, 2012, succeeding Jaime Rene MORALES Carazo (Sandinista National Liberation Front).

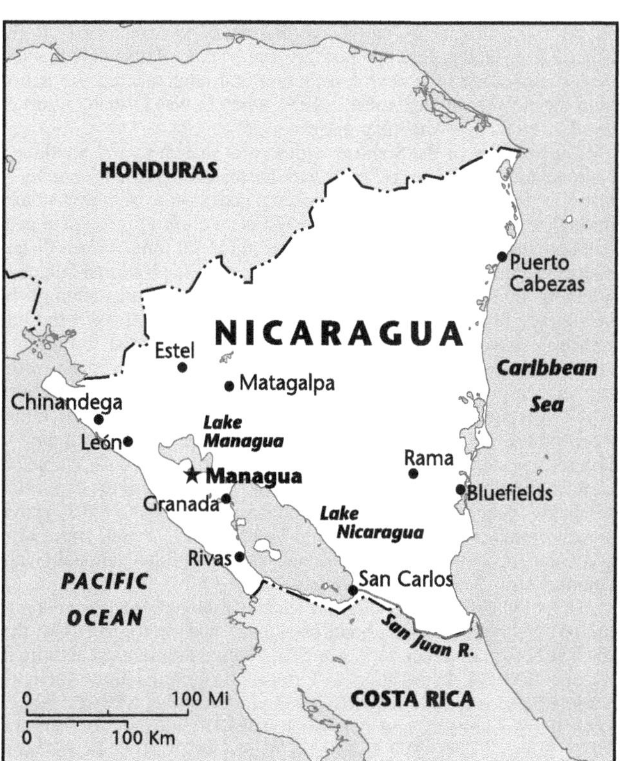

THE COUNTRY

Bounded by Honduras on the north and west and by Costa Rica on the south, Nicaragua is the largest but, apart from Belize, the least densely populated of the seven Central American states. Its numerous mountains are interspersed with extensive lowlands that make it a potential site for an interoceanic canal. The population is predominantly (69 percent) mestizo (mixed Indian and European), with smaller groups of whites (17 percent), blacks (9 percent), and Indians (5 percent). Although freedom of worship is constitutionally recognized, 58.5 percent of the inhabitants adhere to Roman Catholicism, followed by 21.6 percent who are Evangelical.

There were approximately 3 million people in the Nicaraguan labor force as of 2013. Women comprise about 47 percent of the labor force and are concentrated in domestic service, teaching, and market vending; in recent years, female participation has greatly increased, particularly in agriculture (under the Sandinista regime women also constituted 40 percent of the armed forces and nearly half of the civil militia). Women are also well represented in the cabinet.

Services account for 56.8 percent of Nicaragua's GDP, followed by industry at 25.9 percent and agriculture at 17.3 percent. Agricultural exports, however, account for about 75 percent of the country's export revenue; the biggest single export being coffee, worth $342 million in 2010, most of which was exported to the United States. The UN Food and Agriculture Organization (FAO) commended Nicaragua in April 2013 for reducing the undernourished citizens from 55.1 percent in 1990 and 20.1 percent in 2010. The extraction of mineral resources (including silver, gold, lead, gypsum, and zinc) is also important.

The Nicaraguan economy has been battered by numerous natural and human-inflicted disasters in the past decades, including a disastrous earthquake that struck Managua in December 1972. The final phase of the anti-Somoza rebellion in 1978–1979 also severely disrupted development, as did the U.S. economic blockade of the Sandinista regime and support of the antigovernment rebels throughout the 1980s, which together culminated in a more than 12 percent contraction of the country's economy in 1988.

Economic recovery in the 1990s was halted by Hurricane Mitch in October 1998, which left more than 4,000 people dead and destroyed or damaged about 36,000 homes. Hurricane Felix, on September 4, 2007, destroyed or damaged more than 19,000 homes. While social indicators had improved over the previous two decades, 42.5 percent of the population lived at or below the poverty line in 2009.

The economy contracted as a result of the global economic downturn, but budgetary reforms and reductions in spending helped GDP grow 4.5 percent in 2010, 4.7 percent in 2011, 3 percent in 2012, and 4.6 percent in 2013. Unemployment has stagnated averaging 8.2 percent in 2009 to 8 percent in 2012. Remittances added $1.014 billion in 2012, mostly from Nicaraguan residents in the United States and Costa Rica. Venezuela provides cheap oil to Nicaragua, as well as about $500 million annually through the Bolivarian Alliance for the Americas programs. Much of this money comes from Venezuela and is used for social programs administered through Ortega's office and therefore not tracked through Nicaragua's official budget sheet. Venezuelan aid is expected to decline in the near term decreasing 4.3 percent between 2013 and 2012.

A priority of the Ortega government has been to increase access to electricity, which it claims has expanded from 53 percent of the country in 2006 to 67 percent in 2011, and reduce Nicaragua's dependence on foreign oil, which accounts for almost 70 percent of energy production. Foreign direct investment in the country doubled from 2010 to 2011 to $1 billion and jumped to $1.5 billion in 2013, before falling to $840 million in 2014. GDP grew by 4.5 percent in 2014, and 4.6 percent in 2015. In 2016 GDP expanded by 4.3 percent, while inflation was 7 percent, and GDP per capita $2,049.

GOVERNMENT AND POLITICS

Political background. Nicaraguan politics following the country's liberation from Spanish rule in 1821 was long dominated by a power struggle between leaders of the Liberal and Conservative parties, punctuated by periods of U.S. intervention, which was virtually continuous during 1912–1925 and 1927–1933. A Liberal Party victory in a U.S.-supervised election in 1928 paved the way for the assumption of power by Gen. Anastasio SOMOZA García, who ruled the country as president from 1937 until his assassination in September 1956.

Political power remained in the hands of the Somoza family under the Liberal Party presidencies of Luis SOMOZA Debayle, the dictator's elder son (1956–1963); René SCHICK Gutiérrez (1963–1966); Lorenzo GUERRERO Gutiérrez (1966–1967); and Gen. Anastasio SOMOZA Debayle (1967–1972), the younger son of the late dictator. Constitutionally barred from a second term, Somoza Debayle arranged an interim collegial executive (consisting of two members of the Liberal Party and one member of the Conservative Party) that oversaw the promulgation of a new constitution and administered the nation until the election of September 1, 1974, when he was formally returned to office by an overwhelming margin.

The stability of the Somoza regime was shaken by the Sandinista National Liberation Front (*Frente Sandinista de Liberación Nacional*—FSLN or Sandinistas), which launched a series of coordinated attacks throughout the country in October 1977 in an effort to instigate a general uprising. While the immediate effort failed, far more serious disturbances erupted in 1978, including occupation of the National Palace in Managua by FSLN rebels on August 22 and a major escalation of the insurgency in early September. During the first half of 1979 the tide turned decisively in favor of the Sandinistas, who by the end of June controlled most of the major towns as well as the slum district of the capital. Despite 12 days of intense bombardment of FSLN positions within Managua, government forces were unable to regain the initiative, and on July 17 General Somoza left the country after resigning in favor of an interim president, Dr. Francisco URCUYO Maliaños. Confronted with a bid by Urcuyo to remain in office until the expiration of his predecessor's term in 1981, three members of the FSLN provisional junta flew from Costa Rica to León on July 18 and, amid some confusion, accepted the unconditional surrender of the National Guard commander in Managua the following day.

Daniel ORTEGA Saavedra, the leader of the five-man junta and of the FSLN's nine-member Directorate, announced in August 1980 that the FSLN would remain in power until 1985, with electoral activity to resume in 1984. In addition to Ortega, the original junta included Violeta Barrios de CHAMORRO, Moisés HASSAN Morales, Sergio RAMÍREZ Mercado, and Alfonso ROBELO Callejas. On May 18, 1980, Rafael CORDOVA Rivas and Arturo José CRUZ Porras were named to succeed Chamorro and Robelo, who had resigned on April 19 and 22, respectively. On March 4, 1981, Hassan and Cruz also resigned, Ortega being named coordinator of the remaining three-member group.

On September 17, 1980, former president Somoza was assassinated in a bazooka attack on his limousine in central Asunción, Paraguay. (In early 1999 the former chief of state security during the Sandinista regime reportedly acknowledged his agency's responsibility for the attack.)

In early 1984, under diplomatic pressure from Western countries and military pressure from U.S.-backed insurgent (contra) forces, the junta adjusted its electoral timetable to permit both presidential and legislative balloting the following November. Although attempts by the regime to reach procedural agreement with the opposition failed (most of the latter's larger parties withdrawing from the campaign), the November 4 election was contested by a number of small non-Sandinista groups. In balloting described as exemplary by international observers (who nonetheless objected to preelection censorship and harassment of opposition candidates), Ortega won 67 percent of the presidential vote, while the FSLN gained a similar percentage of seats in a National Constituent Assembly, which approved a new basic law on November 19, 1986.

After extensive negotiations, a preliminary peace agreement for the region, based in part on proposals advanced by President Oscar Arias Sánchez of Costa Rica, was approved by the five Central American chief executives in Guatemala, on August 7, 1987. In accordance with the agreement, talks between the Sandinista government and contra leaders were initiated in January 1988 that failed to yield a definitive cease-fire agreement, although most of the rebel forces had quit Nicaragua for Honduras by mid-August because of a failure to secure further military aid from the United States. Subsequently, the Central American presidents, during a meeting in El Salvador, on February 13–14, 1989, agreed on a program of Nicaraguan electoral reform that would permit opposition parties unimpeded access to nationwide balloting no later than February 25, 1990, while the U.S. Congress in mid-April approved a $49.7 million package of nonlethal aid for the contras over the ensuing 10 months.

Although public opinion polls had suggested that the FSLN enjoyed a substantial lead in the 1990 elections, Chamorro, heading a National Opposition Union (UNO) coalition, defeated Ortega by a 15 percent margin in the February presidential poll, with the UNO capturing 51 of 92 assembly seats. Following her inauguration in April, President Chamorro was confronted with a perilously weak economy reeling from numerous clashes between peasants who had benefited from the Sandinista land policies and demobilized contras pressing for promised land and monetary compensation. Chamorro responded by naming a number of influential contras to government positions, while retaining her predecessor's brother, Cdr. (thereafter Gen.) Humberto ORTEGA Saavedra as chief of the armed forces. These actions, in addition to continuance of a social pact (*concertación*) with the FSLN led Vice President Virgilio GODOY Reyes' conservative UNO bloc to adopt a posture of de facto opposition. The complexity of the new alignment was evidenced by the January 1991 balloting for president of the National Assembly (*Asamblea Nacional*): former contra leader and presidential adviser Alfredo CESAR Aguirre, with the backing of both Sandinista and moderate UNO members, defeated incumbent Míriam ARGUELLO Morales, a conservative hard-liner from the UNO party supported by Godoy.

On January 9, 1993, a cabinet reshuffle was announced that for the first time awarded a portfolio (tourism) to a Sandinista, while a new assembly, dominated by Sandinistas and the ex-UNO Center Group, was convened, which proceeded to elect Gustavo TABLADA Zelaya, a former communist, as its presiding officer. By now the breach between Chamorro and her former coalition supporters was such that some UNO leaders called for shortening her term of office, and in late February General Ortega charged Vice President Godoy and former assembly president César with encouraging a resurgence of contra activity in the north to create sufficient unrest to cause the government's collapse. The UNO hardliners responded by organizing a series of mass demonstrations against the president's "cogovernment" with her former adversaries.

Following an abortive effort by Chamorro to launch a national dialogue on the issues dividing the country, a remarkable series of tit-for-tat military actions erupted. On July 21–22, 1993, nearly 50 people were killed when a group of 150 demobilized contras, known as recompas, seized control of the northern town of Estelí, plundering three local banks before being routed by government troops. On August 19 right-wing recontras took 42 hostages in an attack on another northern town, El Zúngana; in retaliation a recompa unit stormed the Managua offices of the UNO, taking captive an equal number of individuals, including Godoy and César. All of the hostages were released within days, following intervention by the Organization of American States (OAS).

On September 2, 1993, President Chamorro angered her FSLN supporters by announcing that General Ortega would be removed as military chief in 1994; the pledge did not, however, mollify her UNO critics, who called for his immediate dismissal. During the following week General Ortega and Vice President Godoy held two private meetings that led to an unprecedented series of talks between FSLN and UNO representatives in October and November on proposals for constitutional reform.

By early 1994 a new legislative majority had emerged in the form of a working alliance between the FSLN, the Center Group, and the Christian Democratic Union (UDC), which advanced the process of constitutional revision by lifting a requirement that amendments be approved by two successive assembly sessions. Subsequently, General Ortega, in response to continuing pressure to step down, indicated that he would not do so until a new military statute had been enacted that placed nomination to his office in the hands of a Military Council (*Consejo Militar*). On May 18 President Chamorro stated that Ortega would retire on February 21, 1995. The announcement came one day before submitting to the assembly her proposals for military reform, which did not call for subordination of the military to civilian control and did not provide for a ministry of defense.

Meanwhile, the FSLN had encountered an identity crisis because of General Ortega's continuing governmental role. Ortega was seen as moving to the right in a possible bid to gain the presidency in 1996. This led to the formation of a centrist faction within the FSLN National Directorate that, while distancing itself from a hard-line leftist minority, sought "a basic reordering of the economy" along genuinely social-democratic lines. Disarray within the Sandinista leadership was also seen in a growing cleavage between Ortega and the party's relatively moderate legislative leader, former vice president Sergio Ramírez. Significantly, one of the constitutional reforms endorsed by Ramírez would restrict a president to a single term, which would deny the former chief executive an opportunity to vindicate himself for his 1989 loss to Chamorro. Ortega subsequently repositioned himself to the left of his party's mainstream, urging opposition to economic restructuring and occasionally endorsing violence to oppose privatization by the Chamorro administration. His new hard-line posture won the day at an extraordinary FSLN congress in May 1994 and secured the dismissal of Ramírez as FSLN legislative leader in September. However, Ortega was unable to prevent the election of another moderate, Dora María TÉLLEZ, as Ramírez's assembly bloc successor.

On September 2, 1994, a new military code was approved that limited the armed forces chief to a single five-year term and prohibited appointment of relatives of the president to the post. On the other hand, the military would continue to nominate its commander. Subsequently, the Military Council proposed Maj. Gen. Joaquín CUADRA Lacayo to succeed Gen. Humberto Ortega on February 21, 1995.

In November 1994 the National Assembly approved a lengthy series of constitutional amendments (see Constitution and government, below), significantly altering the distribution of power between the executive and legislative branches in favor of the latter. The changes were strongly opposed by President Chamorro and by the orthodox wing of the Sandinistas, which supported a new effort by Míriam Argüello to recapture the assembly presidency in January 1995. Argüello was, however, unable to deny reelection to the reformist Luis Humberto GUZMÁN, and on February 17 the assembly published the constitutional revisions after Chamorro had refused to do so. The conflict intensified further on April 6, when the legislature named 5 new Supreme Court justices (2 to replace members whose terms had expired and 3 to expand the size of the Court from 9 to 12 under a provision of the amended basic law). On May 8, following presidential repudiation of the appointments, the court, without ruling on the substance of the constitutional changes, declared the amendments null and void in the absence of executive promulgation. However, on June 15, in the wake of mediation by Cardinal Miguel OBANDO y Bravo, then the archbishop of Managua, the lengthy impasse was broken with Chamorro's acceptance of the constitutional reform package, which was promulgated on July 4. An agreement on the new Supreme Court justices followed on July 21.

By early 1995 campaigning for the 1996 election by Nicaragua's more than two dozen parties was effectively under way. One of the leading candidates, Presidency Minister Antonio LACAYO Oyanguren, indicated that he might divorce his wife, Cristiana CHAMORRO, so as to comply with the new constitutional requirement that blood and marriage relatives serving heads of state be disqualified. Other likely contenders were Daniel Ortega Saavedra and Sergio Ramírez of the deeply divided FSLN and, on the right, Managua Mayor Arnaldo ALEMÁN Lacayo, representing the largely reunited Liberals. On December 6, 1995, legislative passage of a new general election law included a provision for a presidential runoff if no candidate gained at least 45 percent of the vote.

On July 6, 1996, the Supreme Electoral Council (*Consejo Supremo Electoral*—CSE) formally declared Antonio Lacayo ineligible for the presidency; the council also disqualified Alvaro ROBELO of the conservative Nicaraguan Alliance (AN) and Edén PASTORA Gómez of the Democratic Action Party (PAD) for having acquired, respectively, Italian and Costa Rican citizenship.

In the balloting of October 10, 1996, Alemán Lacayo emerged as the clear victor in the presidential race, although the FSLN insisted that his official tally of 51 percent was fraudulently inflated. The legislative outcome was far less simple, as Alemán's Liberal coalition was held to a plurality of 42 seats, while the runner-up FSLN gained 36.

With Alemán ineligible for reelection in 2001, Enrique BOLAÑOS Geyer, who had resigned as vice president in October 2000 to qualify as a presidential candidate, won the Constitutionalist Liberal Party (*Partido Liberal Constitucionalista*—PLC) nomination and garnered 56.1 percent of the vote to defeat Daniel Ortega Saavedra in the FSLN leader's third nationwide effort on November 4. Alemán supporters subsequently secured his election as president of the National Assembly, a post that he was obliged to relinquish on September 19, 2002, amid mounting evidence of corruption during his tenure as chief executive. On December 7, 2003, Alemán was convicted of fraud, money laundering, and the theft of state funds and received a 20-year sentence.

In late 2003 Alemán, who continued as Liberal leader despite his imprisonment, joined forces with Ortega, thus splitting the party into pro- and anti-Bolaños factions. The president responded by forming a new party, the Grand Liberal Union (GUL), which joined with five minor groups in an Alliance for the Republic (*Alianza por la República*—APRE) to contest the November 2004 municipal elections.

The FSLN swept the November 7, 2004, local balloting, winning more than 90 of 152 mayoralties, including 15 of 17 capitals, on a 45 percent vote share. The PLC won 41 mayoralties and only 1 capital, while the APRE took 5 mayoralties and 1 capital. Following the election, the FSLN and PLC concluded a power-sharing pact under which the two would alternate the presidency, beginning with whoever won the next election, with guarantees to the other of a share of high-level government positions.

Ortega made a comeback in his fourth bid for the presidency on November 5, 2006, with 38 percent of the vote. Eduardo MONTEALEGRE of the Nicaraguan Liberal Alliance (*Alianza Liberal Nicaragüense*—ALN) placed second, with 28.3 percent, followed by the PLC's José RIZO with 27.1 percent. In concurrent legislative balloting, the FSLN secured a plurality of 38 seats, followed by the PLC and the ALN. The cabinet was reshuffled on January 10, 2007.

Political infighting and tensions dominated the government in 2007, when the PLC and the ALN formed an electoral alliance in July, in direct opposition to a similar effort between the FSLN and the PLC. However, the PLC-ALN alliance fell apart ahead of the 2008 municipal elections because the PLC refused to break with the FSLN. This resulted in a rift in the ALN, with the party dismissing Montealegre, who formed his own party, Let's Go with Eduardo (*Vamos con Eduardo*—VCE), which aligned with the PLC, the small Independent Liberal Party (*Partido Liberal Independiente*—PLI), and the Central American Unity Party (*Partido Unidad de Central America*—PUCA). The rift healed in time for the PLC to name Montealegre as its candidate for mayor of Managua in the November 2008 municipal elections. Montealegre lost that election amid allegations of fraud and vote- rigging, and a recount, which was not monitored by outside observers, also drew heavy criticism. The results gave a narrow victory (51.3 percent) to world boxing champion and FSLN candidate Alex ARGÜELLO, who unexpectedly died in 2009 at age 38.

Meanwhile, the principal opposition parties in the National Assembly staged several walkouts in 2008 to protest Ortega's governing style. Opponents called their coalition the "Block against the Dictatorship" and criticized Ortega's increasingly hostile reaction toward the United States and excessively close ties to Venezuela and Iran. The Civil Society Coordinating Committee, composed of numerous nongovernmental organizations, demonstrated against Ortega on July 17, 2008, the first major protest since he took office. The FSLN responded two days later, on the 29th anniversary of the Sandinista revolution, with a progovernment demonstration by tens of thousands of people, including the presidents of Venezuela and Paraguay.

High food prices continued to be a major challenge in 2009, as poverty affected thousands more Nicaraguans. The government sought international donor aid and initiated a Zero Hunger Program in March in efforts to mitigate effects from the global financial crisis. Meanwhile, President Ortega proposed constitutional reforms that included, among other things, the elimination of presidential term limits and the possibility of a recall referendum on elected officials.

Facing insurmountable opposition from the PLC, Ortega took his proposed term-limit revision to the judiciary. On October 19, 2009, the CSJ lifted the constitution's ban that prevented a president from serving two consecutive terms in office. Many observers called the decision illegal, saying that only the legislature was invested with the power to strike down the prohibition. Both supporters and opponents of the Ortega administration took to the streets of Managua on November 21 in mass protests over Ortega's initiative.

On January 9, 2010, Ortega again appeared to challenge the constitutional separation of powers by promulgating a decree that extended the mandates of sitting judicial and election officials who were scheduled to be replaced but for whom replacements had not been approved by the deadlocked legislature. Ortega unilaterally continued the terms of 25 officials, saying that he did not want to see a power vacuum form.

Opposition legislators with the PLC, the ALN, the Sandinista Renovation Movement (*Movimiento de Renovación Sandinista*—MRS), and the VCE boycotted the legislature in protest over Ortega's decree to extend terms for a number of officials, preventing it from convening. However, observers said the opposition was unable to muster a unified front due to interference by influential former president and PLC leader Arnoldo Alemán, who held a decade-old power-sharing pact with Ortega. In April 2010 the CSJ president, a PLC ally, refused to recognize two magistrates (aligned with the FSLN) who had attempted to retain their expiring positions in accordance with Ortega's decree. Later that month the opposition tried to convene the assembly after the nearly two-month boycott in order to overturn the decree. However, they were stopped by hundreds of Ortega supporters blocking access to the capitol building. Legislators then attempted to convene the assembly at a hotel but were attacked with rocks and fireworks, which injured three PLC politicians. The next day FSLN supporters held 18 opposition party members hostage and set two vehicles on fire. Ortega endorsed the violence as a "simple, legitimate expression of the people." A number of civil society groups, the OAS, and the United States voiced strong concerns over the violence and erosion of the political process in Nicaragua. The congress convened on April 22 under heavy police protection but did not open debate on the decree, instead ratifying two uncontroversial international loans.

On June 28, 2010, at least nine people were injured when FSLN supporters joined police to storm the mayor's office in the opposition-held central Nicaraguan city of Boaco. The group ejected the mayor, who voiced opposition to Ortega's reelection bid and who was aligned with Eduardo Montealegre's opposition VCE. The CSE validated the ejection by installing a new mayor. The move was the fifth removal of mayors who did not support Ortega's bid for another term as president and, combined with the alleged skullduggery of the 2008 municipal elections, pointed to an offensive campaign by the president against local governments.

Following maneuvering in August 2010 that left a majority of CSJ magistrates allied with the FSLN, the court ruled in September that Ortega's January decree to continue the mandates of judiciary officials was legal. The CSJ then ruled that Ortega's push to end presidential term limits, which was endorsed in October 2009 by the CSJ's constitutional chamber, was also legal on the grounds that the ban on running for office consecutively was an infringement of human rights against the president. In September Ortega ordered a reprinting of the constitution that included his January decree. The opposition protested, arguing that the printing amounted to a change in the constitution and thus required a two-thirds majority vote in the assembly. On September 22 the opposition—the PLC, the ALN, the MRS, and the VCE—began an indefinite boycott of the legislature in protest. The new version of the constitution was approved in the assembly on October 5 in what opposition leaders characterized as an illegal vote.

The Supreme Court endorsed Ortega's bid for an unprecedented third term as president, and on November 6, 2011, Ortega defeated Fabio GADEA (Independent Liberal Party) and Arnoldo Alemán (Constitutionalist Liberal Party). However, some of the president's closest allies appeared uncomfortable with his disregard for the constitution. Vice President Jaime Rene MORALES Carazo declined to stay on for Ortega's third term, a move regarded as indicating his disapproval. Instead, Ortega selected Omar HALLESLEVENS Acevedo as his running mate, raising some concerns that he might again turn to the military to enforce his rule.

In simultaneous parliamentary elections, the FSLN increased its existing majority, capturing a commanding 63 seats. The PLI won 27 seats, while the PLC garnered only 2. Monitors from the Organization of American States reported many irregularities.

The new parliament began its term on January 10, 2012. With the additional seats picked up in November, the FSLN had a supermajority in the National Assembly, so dissenting voices from opposition parties can easily be squelched. The opposition MPs unanimously voted against Ortega's 2012 budget, for example, but it still easily passed. With municipal elections scheduled for November, in May the National Assembly tripled the number of municipal councilors from 2,178 to 6,534.

The CSE made questionable calls about which parties qualified for the municipal elections. The UDC, now an independent party that has attracted disillusioned FSLN members, was disqualified; with the CSE announcing the UDC had valid candidates in only 73 percent of municipalities, below the 80 percent threshold. Yet APRE, which mustered less than 10,000 votes in 2011, was declared valid in 98 percent of municipalities. The PCN and ALN also had astonishingly high registration levels. Some analysts suggested that Ortega was using Somoza's *zancudismo* (bloodsucker) strategy—a collection of "fake" opposition parties to create the appearance of democracy.

In November 4 municipal elections, the Sandinistas won about 75 percent of the vote, increases its control from 109 municipalities to 134 out of a total 153 and sparking charges of fraud by opposition parties. The PLI won 13 races, followed by the regional party Yátama (3), PLC (2), and Liberal Alliance (1). The Organization of American States expressed support for the elections, but the U.S. State Department issued a statement expressing concern with voting irregularities. Three people were killed in clashes between Sandinistas and the opposition. The PLI and PLC appealed the results in five races but were rebuffed by the CSE.

Members of the FSLN marches have staged several protests in 2012, upset that the party apparatus, headed by Ortega's wife, Rosario MURILLO, selected local candidates without consulting them.

Ortega named a new minister for mines and energy on January 13, 2015.

Constitution and government. The constitution approved by a National Constituent Assembly in November 1986 provided for a president, vice president, and National Assembly elected for six-year terms (later changed to five-year terms, concurrent with that of the president). The assembly contains 90 members directly elected by proportional balloting in regional districts, with additional seats for unsuccessful presidential candidates securing a minimum number of votes. The assembly may be expanded in accordance with population growth, while its acts may be vetoed, in whole or in part, by the president within 15 days of their approval. The judiciary encompasses a Supreme Court of at least seven judges elected for six-year terms by the National Assembly, in addition to appellate and municipal courts.

The country is divided into 15 departments and two largely indigenous, self-governing areas, the North Atlantic Autonomous Region (RAAN) and the South Atlantic Autonomous Region (RAAS). Municipalities are governed by elected councils.

On November 24, 1994, the assembly approved a series of constitutional amendments that provided for increased legislative authority vis-à-vis the president, whose term was reduced from six years to five, with a ban on relatives of a serving president standing for the office. In addition, both the president and National Assembly were authorized to introduce tax measures and to share responsibility for appointing Supreme Court justices, the comptroller general, and the president and vice president of the national bank. Other provisions guaranteed the rights of primary and secondary education and free health care for all citizens, provided greater independence for the judiciary, increased civilian control over the military, eliminated conscription, and recognized the rights of indigenous populations on both the east and west coasts.

In late January 2000 President Alemán signed into law another round of constitutional changes, including a reduction from 45 to 35 percent in the vote share required for presidential election; legislative life tenure for himself, with a two-thirds vote required for removal of immunity from prosecution; the appointment of five permanent members of the State Comptroller's Office from a list approved by the president and the assembly; an increase in the number of Supreme Court justices to 16 from 12; an increase in the membership of the Supreme Electoral Council to seven from five; and the deregistration of political parties securing less than 4 percent of the vote. In addition, President Alemán advocated holding a constitutional assembly election in place of the presidential poll scheduled for 2001, but he failed to secure sufficient legislative support for the proposal.

In late 2004 the National Assembly approved a new package of constitutional reforms that included legislative ratification of ministerial and ambassadorial appointments and lowered to a simple majority (from two-thirds) the vote needed to overturn a presidential veto. The package was struck down by the Central American Court of Justice on March 29, 2005, on the ground that it should have been submitted to a constituent assembly. However, Nicaragua's Supreme Court of Justice (CSJ) approved the changes on March 30, arguing that the regional court lacked jurisdiction because of a protocol approved by the Central American presidents in December that banned it from intervening in intrapower disputes in member states.

Beginning in 2009, President Ortega began calling for the abolition of the constitutional ban on presidential term limits and for a measure designed to wrest control of some legislative power from the National Assembly, where his FSLN held a minority of seats (see Current issues, below). Two actions drew the most attention: a CSJ ruling that abolished the ban on a president running for office for two consecutive terms and Ortega's decree that the expiring terms of judicial and electoral officials be extended in the face of legislative gridlock on new appointments (see Currents issues, below). In 2014 the assembly formally voted to abolish presidential term limits, on a vote of 64–25.

The Somoza regime severely constricted the media, while the subsequent Sandinista government also suspended several publications. Acceding to opposition demands, a press law stipulating that all printed matter must reflect "legitimate concern for the defense of the conquests of the revolution" was rescinded before President Ortega's departure from office in 1990. Reporters Without Borders described the relationship between the current Ortega administration and the privately owned press as "conflictual," resulting in a number of reported incidents of government attempts to pressure journalists. In 2016 Nicaragua was listed as 75th out of 180 countries in the Reporters Without Borders annual ranking of press freedom.

Foreign relations. The conservative and generally pro-U.S. outlook of the Somoza regime was reflected in a favorable attitude toward North American investment and a strongly pro-Western, anti-communist position in the UN, OAS, and other international bodies. The United States, for its part, did not publicly call for the resignation of General Somoza until June 20, 1979, and subsequently appealed for an OAS peacekeeping presence to ensure that a successor government would include moderate representatives from what it deemed acceptable to "all major elements of Nicaraguan society." Although the idea was rejected by both the OAS and the FSLN, the United States played a key role in the events leading to Somoza's departure, and the administration of President Jimmy Carter extended reconstruction aid to the new Managua government in October 1980. By contrast, President Ronald Reagan was deeply committed to support of the largely Honduran-based rebel contras, despite a conspicuous lack of enthusiasm for such a policy by many U.S. members of Congress.

Regional attitudes toward the contra insurgency were mixed, most South American countries professing neutrality, although Managua–Quito relations were broken in 1985 after then Ecuadorian president Febres Cordero called Nicaragua "a bonfire in Central America." Subsequently, members of the Contadora Group (Colombia, Mexico, Panama, and Venezuela) and the Lima Group (Argentina, Brazil, Peru, and Uruguay) met intermittently with Central American leaders in an effort to broker the conflict, although neither bloc directly influenced the accords of August 1987 and February 1989.

In April 1991 President Chamorro became the first Nicaraguan head of state in more than 50 years to make an official visit to Washington, D.C., where she was warmly received and addressed a joint session of the U.S. Congress. In sharp contrast, an August 1992 report issued by a top aide of U.S. senator Jesse Helms charged the Chamorro government with being controlled by "communists, terrorists, thugs, robbers and assassins" and recommended the discontinuance of aid to Nicaragua pending a number of changes, including the replacement of all Sandinista army and police personnel by former contras and the return of properties belonging to Nicaraguans living in the United States (many of whom were supporters of the former Somoza regime).

Regionally, Nicaragua called in May 1991 for deferment on formal admission to the new Central American Parliament (*Parlamento Centroamericano*—Parlacen) on the grounds that it lacked the resources for an early referendum on the matter. In October 1992 Nicaraguan authorities accused Costa Rica of contaminating the San Juan River by sanctioning the use of highly toxic pesticides on its banana plantations. A month later, in the first such meeting since the end of the Sandinista-contra war, General Ortega traveled to Honduras, where he conferred with his counterpart, Gen. Luis Alonso Discua Elvir, on collaborative efforts to limit the use of their countries "for illegal drug, arms, cattle, or fish trafficking."

During a summit meeting in Managua on April 22, 1993, Nicaragua joined its three northern neighbors (El Salvador, Guatemala, and Honduras), which had previously undertaken a *Triángulo Norte* free trade initiative, in launching the *Grupo América Central 4* (AC-4), which was viewed as paving the way for a free trade zone throughout the isthmus. The process was further advanced during a five-member regional summit in Guatemala City on October 27–29, 1993, following inauguration of the headquarters of the Central American Integration System (SICA, under the Central American Common Market—CACM).

A long-dormant territorial dispute with Colombia was rekindled in April 1995 with Nicaragua's seizure of two Colombian fishing vessels and the alleged violation of its airspace by three Colombian aircraft. At issue was Nicaragua's 1980 revocation of a 1928 treaty, by which Nicaragua, under reported U.S. pressure, ceded ownership of certain Caribbean islands to its neighbor in compensation for construction of the interoceanic canal through Panama.

In November 1995 Nicaragua and Costa Rica agreed to regularize the status of 50,000 Nicaraguans working illegally in Costa Rica. Under the accord, the workers would be given special Nicaraguan passports, while work permits would be issued by Costa Rican authorities once worker employment had been certified.

Relations with Honduras, complicated during the 1980s by the presence of several thousand mainly former Somoza supporters, exiled in Honduran border camps, were exacerbated in early 1995 by the eruption of a "shrimp war" in the Gulf of Fonseca. Tensions were reignited in May and August 1997 following the Nicaraguan navy's seizure of numerous Honduran fishing boats that had reportedly strayed into Nicaraguan waters.

In August 1998 Nicaragua rescinded an agreement that had been concluded only a month earlier with Costa Rica for free navigation, including police patrols, along the San Juan River because of opposition claims that Nicaragua had ceded sovereignty to its neighbor. The dispute was temporarily abated by a new agreement in mid-2000 that restored Costa Rica's right to the patrols as long as Nicaragua received prior notification of their movements. However, in 2005 Costa Rica filed suit at the International Court of Justice (ICJ) against Nicaragua for a judgment on Costa Rica's navigational rights on the San Juan River (see below for subsequent developments).

A crisis with Honduras erupted in November 1999, following ratification by the Honduran legislature of a 1986 maritime border treaty with Colombia that involved 50,000 square miles of coastal waters, portions of which were alleged to have been forcibly ceded to Colombia during the U.S. occupation of Nicaragua in the 1920s. In reprisal, Nicaragua imposed a 35 percent duty on all goods imported from Honduras. In June 2001 the two countries accepted an OAS-brokered pact that allowed OAS observers to monitor activities along both land and marine borders. However, friction continued into 2002, with periodic seizures of Honduran boats in alleged Nicaraguan waters and Nicaragua authorizing oil prospecting in the region. In March 2003 the Nicaraguan assembly suspended the 35-percent tariff.

Relations with the United States warmed in 2004 when President Bolaños announced that all surface-to-air missiles remaining in Nicaragua from its conflict with U.S.-backed rebels would be destroyed. He destroyed about 1,000 of the missiles. (In 2008 President Ortega refused to destroy all of the missiles, despite ongoing pressure from the United States.)

In 2005 Nicaragua, Costa Rica, El Salvador, Guatemala, Honduras, and the Dominican Republic signed a wide-ranging free trade agreement known as CAFTA-DR with the United States. In 2006 Ortega signed a treaty incorporating Nicaragua into the Bolivarian Alternative for the Americas (ALBA), Venezuelan President Hugo Chávez's alternative to U.S.-led free trade agreements. Nicaragua and Venezuela signed a number of other accords, including one that canceled Nicaragua's $38 million debt with Venezuela and one that allowed Venezuela to build a $2.5 billion oil refinery in Nicaragua. Ortega also reestablished relations with Cuba and Iran.

Nicaragua and Costa Rica in recent years have disputed a 170-square-mile strip of poorly demarcated swampland on the southern shore of Lake Nicaragua. The 5,000 impoverished residents of the area have rejected the claims of both governments, seeking instead an independent "Republic of Airrecú." Tensions with Costa Rica heightened in June 2008, when Costa Rica rejected a request from Nicaragua that it halt development of an open-pit gold mine several miles from the San Juan River.

Relations with the United States cooled through mid-2008, as President Ortega criticized a loan from the U.S. Agency for International Development (USAID) to 16 nongovernmental organizations to promote citizen participation in the November municipal elections.

In the midst of a regional dispute in March 2008 prompted by a Colombian raid inside Ecuador against guerilla fighters, Nicaragua briefly suspended diplomatic relations with Colombia.

In mid-2009 Nicaragua, like most of its neighbors, supported ousted Honduran president Manuel Zelaya and his efforts to negotiate his return to power from Nicaragua. Nicaragua further refused to allow the use of its airspace by de facto Honduran leader Roberto Micheletti. The presence of Zelaya in Nicaragua spurred tensions between the FSLN and its opponents, and threatened long-standing bilateral agreements between Nicaragua and Honduras.

Relations with the United States and the European Union deteriorated in mid-2009 amid accusations of fraud regarding municipal elections, resulting in both major donors indefinitely suspending millions of dollars in aid to Nicaragua. Washington eliminated a $64 million development aid program following the less than free and fair 2010 regional elections.

In July 2009 the ICJ released its judgment on the case brought before it by Costa Rica in 2005 pertaining to navigation rights on the San Juan River. In a decision that offered partial victories to both sides, the court ruled that Costa Rica had commercial navigation rights on the river but that Nicaragua could require that Costa Rican vessels stop at Nicaraguan border posts. Although the court ruled that the river belonged entirely to Nicaragua, it also stated that official Costa Rican vessels could use the river "in specific situations" to provide essential services to its citizens but not for police functions or to move border personnel between posts.

The Ortega administration's dredging project on a section of the San Juan River, which began in October 2010, brought Nicaragua back into conflict with Costa Rica over their respective border demarcations. Both sides said they would appeal to the OAS, the UN Security Council, and the ICJ. In December Costa Rican president Laura Chinchilla announced the deployment of more police to the border area and said relations between the two countries had fallen "to a minimum."

Relations with Washington cooled again in early 2011, when the state department cables released by WikiLeaks revealed activities by the U.S. Chamber of Commerce, a nongovernmental group that promotes

American corporate interests, in support of Ortega's opponents in recent years. On April 8 the state department criticized Nicaragua in its annual human rights report, charging the government with corruption and harassment of media and nongovernmental groups. At a July rally celebrating the 50th anniversary of the FSLN, Ortega proposed a referendum to enable citizens to decide whether to seek compensation from the United States for its "dirty war" against the Sandinistas during the 1980s. The International Court of Justice in The Hague had ruled in favor of the suit in 1986, but the United States ignored the ruling by the UN court, which it does not recognize.

The ICJ ruled in Nicaragua's favor on November 19, 2012, granting it 75,000 square kilometers of the Caribbean Sea previously claimed by Colombia. Nicaragua's plans to prospect for oil in the region could threaten the Seaflower biosphere reserve. The map change could cause a surge in drug trafficking, as Nicaragua does not have adequate naval capacity to fully patrol the area. In September 2013 Ortega asked the ICJ to formally demarcate the maritime border between Nicaragua and Colombia and to extend Nicaragua's claim by 150 nautical miles.

In August 2013 tensions increased with Costa Rica after President Ortega threatened to seek justice from the ICJ over the Costa Rican province of Guanacaste, annexed in 1824. This was in retaliation for ongoing disputes related to the 2012 ruling against Nicaragua concerning some contested wetlands along the border, as well as continuing disputes over resource and mineral rights in waters off their shared coasts. This preceded an October complaint that Nicaragua continued to develop the Isla Portillos, violating a 2012 ICJ ruling. In November the ICJ ordered Nicaragua to fill in a trench designed to divert water from the San Juan River shared with Costa Rica.

Russian president Putin visited the state in July 2014 as part of his efforts to rekindle relationships across Latin America.

In a ruling on December 16, 2015, the ICJ affirmed that Costa Rica had sovereignty over the Isla Portillos wetlands (see entry on Costa Rica). Ortega responded by declaring that the ruling allowed for a new page in relations between the two nations.

In August 2016 the World Bank announced it would support a program to expand broadband Internet access to more than 180,000 people across Nicaragua.

Current issues. Murillo launched a signature program, "Vivir Bonito" (Live Nicely) in March 2012. The campaign seeks to create a civil society by encouraging citizens to be orderly and patriotic, to respect authority, and to volunteer in their communities. In the first phase, teachers are to issue report cards on the behavior of their students' parents on these performance standards. Critics decried the program as an invasion of privacy, and 20 percent of teachers boycotted weekend training sessions.

With the prolonged illness and March 2013 death of Venezuelan patron Hugo Chávez, Ortega's focus has been on securing alternative sources of funding. An extended credit facility agreement with the International Monetary Fund (IMF) expired in December 2011 and had not been renewed as of mid-2013. Russia also continues to provide assistance, including military equipment, training, and counter-narcotics operations. The Russian general staff chief Colonel-General Valery Gerasimov paid an official three-day visit to Nicaragua in April.

In May Ortega confirmed that in September 2012 he had granted a 99-year concession to the Hong Kong Nicaragua Development (HKND) company for an ambitious $40 billion project to build a canal to connect the Atlantic and Pacific Oceans through Nicaragua. The waterway project, which would be twice the size of the Panama Canal, also includes a high-speech railroad, airports, and an oil pipeline. The shadowy HKND, believed to be a front for the Chinese government, was granted a range of tax breaks and exemptions from labor laws. The news upset local investors, neighboring countries, and environmental groups. In July 2014 the state approved the 172-mile proposed route that will take it through Lake Nicaragua. The plan is to finish the project by 2019 with operations beginning in 2020. Chinese investor Wang Jing is financing the project and announced a start date of December 2014.

A June 2014 report discussed a severe threat to the Nicaraguan coffee industry that accounts for over half of their exports. A fungus that is difficult to remove has infected many of the country's coffee plantations, which may impact half the nation's coffee production. Meanwhile, Nicaragua experienced a record drought throughout 2014 severely impacting the growing season increasing food shortage issues across the region.

In April 2016 there were widespread protests against the Nicaraguan Canal by opposition groups that asserted the project would disrupt rural communities and damage the environment. As of August 2016, the canal project had been put on hold after Jing lost billions of dollars in the 2015–2016 Chinese stock market crash (see entry on China).

Through 2015 and 2016, opposition groups held demonstrations in favor of electoral reforms before national elections scheduled for November 2016. In July the protests turned violent, and police broke up demonstrations in Managua, arresting dozens. Prodemocracy groups decried a decision by Ortega to not allow international elections observers to monitor the polling. There were also reports that at least 12 foreign journalists had been expelled from the country.

POLITICAL PARTIES AND GROUPS

Historically, the Liberal and Conservative parties dominated Nicaraguan politics in what was essentially a two-party system. During most of the Somoza era (1936–1974), the heir to the liberal tradition, the **Nationalist Liberal Party** (*Partido Liberal Nacionalista de Nicaragua*—PLN), enjoyed a monopoly of power, while in mid-1978 the **Nicaraguan Conservative Party** (*Partido Conservador Nicaragüense*—PCN) joined other opposition groups in a **Broad Opposition Front** (*Frente Amplio de Oposición*—FAO) that called for the president's resignation and the creation of a government of national unity. Following the Sandinista victory, the principal internal groupings were the FSLN-led **Patriotic Front for the Revolution** (*Frente Patriótico para la Revolución*—FPR) and a series of opposition center-right coalitions. (For details on the principal electoral alliances formed before the 2011 election, see the 2010 *Handbook.*)

Following the FSLN's landslide victories in 2011 and 2012, opposition groups began intensive discussions about creating a united opposition party ahead of the March 2014 elections for the assemblies in the North and South Atlantic Autonomous Regions (which were postponed in November 2012) and especially in time for presidential and legislative elections in 2016. Several parties split over whether or not to embrace this strategy.

In August 2013 leaders of the Independent Liberal Party (*Partido Liberal Independiente*—PLI), Sandinista Renewal Movement (*Movimiento de Renovación Sandinista*—MRS), and Constitutionalist Liberal Party (*Partido Liberal Constitucionalista*—PLC) created the **United for the Republic** (UNIR) coalition.

Government Party:

Sandinista National Liberation Front (*Frente Sandinista de Liberación Nacional*—FSLN). The FSLN was established in 1961 as a Castroite guerrilla group named after Augusto César Sandino, a prominent rebel during the U.S. occupation of the 1920s. The FSLN displayed a remarkable capacity for survival, despite numerous eradication campaigns during the later years of the Somoza regime, in the course of which much of its original leadership was killed. In 1975 it split into three factions: two small Marxist groupings, the Protracted People's War (*Guerra Popular Prolongada*—GPP), and the Proletarian Tendency (*Tendencia Proletaria*), and a larger, less extreme Third Party (*Terceristas*), a nonideological, anti-Somoza formation supported by peasants, students, and upper-class intellectuals. The three groups coordinated their activities during the 1978 offensive and were equally represented in the nine-member Joint National Directorate. Although the July 1979 junta was largely *tercerista*-dominated, the subsequent withdrawal of a number of moderates yielded a more distinctly leftist thrust to the party leadership, hard-liner Bayardo ARCE reportedly characterizing the November 1984 balloting as "a bother." In an August 1985 reorganization of the Directorate, its Political Commission was replaced by a five-member Executive Commission, chaired by Daniel Ortega Saavedra, with Arce as his deputy.

Following the unexpected Sandinista defeat in February 1990, Ortega pledged to "obey the popular mandate" and participated in the inauguration of Violeta Barrios de Chamorro on April 25. In conformity with a postelectoral agreement precluding the holding of party office by military personnel, his brother Gen. Humberto Ortega withdrew as a member of the FSLN Executive after being named the armed forces commander by the new president.

The 581 delegates to the first FSLN congress on July 19–21, 1991, reaffirmed the Front's commitment to socialism, while confessing to a variety of mistakes during its period of rule. Former president Ortega was elected to the new post of general secretary, while seven former *comandantes* of the previous leadership were elected to a new nine-member National Directorate that also included former Nicaraguan vice president Sergio Ramírez Mercado.

A pronounced intraparty split emerged before an extraordinary FSLN congress on May 20–22, 1994, the reflection primarily of an "orthodox" faction headed by Ortega and a moderate "renewalist" faction headed by Ramírez, with party treasurer Henry RUIZ Hernández leading an avowedly centrist unity grouping. The Ortega faction emerged victorious, gaining eight seats on an expanded Directorate, against four for the renewalists and three for the centrists. However, public opinion polls had shown Ramírez to be much stronger than Ortega as a potential presidential candidate.

Ramírez served in the National Assembly as Ortega's alternate; thus, in September 1994, the former president was able to oust him as legislative bloc leader by reclaiming the seat. However, the FSLN delegation proceeded to elect a moderate, Dora María Téllez, as its new leader rather than Ortega, thus formalizing a cleavage between the Front's legislative members and its National Directorate. In early 1995 Ramírez, Téllez, and approximately three-quarters of the Sandinista legislative delegation withdrew from the FSLN to form the MRS (below).

In November 1995 Ortega surprised observers by announcing that he would seek his party's nomination for reelection to the post that he had lost to Chamorro five-and-a-half years earlier. In the October 1996 balloting he lost to the AL's Alemán Lacayo by more than 13 percent of the popular vote.

Ortega was reelected FSLN general secretary at a party congress in May 1998, and on January 21, 2001, defeated two other candidates, Alejandro MARTINEZ Cuenca and Víctor HUGO Tinoco, for the party's 2001 presidential endorsement.

Defeated in his third presidential bid on November 4, 2001, Ortega nonetheless retained leadership of the FSLN at its third congress in March 2002, during which the group's 205-member assembly was supplanted by a 40-member Board of Directors headed by an 8-member Executive Commission. The move was seen as concentrating power among Ortega supporters, thus limiting intraparty dissent.

In late 2004 the FSLN concluded a power-sharing pact with the PLC (see Political background, above). However, the prospect of an FSLN victory in the 2006 balloting was seemingly diminished by the expulsion from the party in February 2005 of Ortega's leading rival, former Managua mayor Herty Lewites, who had been leading Ortega in the opinion polls (see MRS, below).

His critics notwithstanding, Ortega was returned to the presidency after a 16-year hiatus on November 6, 2006. Ortega's close win and the FSLN's plurality in the National Assembly have forced the FSLN to continue its agreement, commonly referred to as "the pact," with the PLC. In the 2008 municipal elections the party was accused of widespread fraud which resulted in successful bids for more than 40 mayoral seats.

In October 2009 the Supreme Court revoked a constitutional ban on the reelection of incumbent presidents and of those who have served two terms, opening the way for Ortega to run for president again. On February 26, 2011, the FSLN nominated Ortega as its candidate in the November 6, 2011, presidential elections. Dissident Sandinistas, denouncing Ortega for what they called a power grab, promptly declared February 26 a day of "shame and rage." On March 18 Ortega announced that his running mate for the vice presidency would be Gen. (Ret.) Omar Halleslevens Acevedo. Ortega easily won a third term with 62.46 percent of the vote, while the party received a supermajority of 63 seats in the National Assembly. The party won 134 of the 153 municipal seats contested in November 2012.

In 2016 Ortega announced that his wife, Rosario MURILLO, would be his running mate in the 2016 presidential balloting.

Leaders: Daniel ORTEGA Saavedra (President of the Republic and General Secretary of the Party), Jacinto SUÁREZ (Deputy General Secretary).

Other Legislative Parties:

Independent Liberal Party (*Partido Liberal Independiente*—PLI). Organized in 1944 by a non-*somocista* group calling for a return to the traditional principles of the PLN, the PLI participated in the Broad Opposition Front before the 1979 coup. Subsequently led by postcoup labor minister Virgilio Godoy Reyes, it was a member of the Patriotic Front, but following *Coordinadora*'s withdrawal, it became the most vocal opposition formation of the 1984 campaign. The party was a founding member of the UNO in 1989, Godoy Reyes becoming its most conspicuous leader. Having endorsed Godoy Reyes as its 1996 presidential candidate, the PLI was the only Liberal group not to have joined the ALN before the October poll. The PLI entered into an alliance with the PLC and Let's Go with Eduardo, the movement formed by Eduardo Montealegre, in November 2008, but failed to win any seats. For the 2011 election, the PLI formed an alliance, **Nicaraguan Unity for Hope** (*Unidad Nicaragüense por la Esperanza*—UNE), with the MRS, the **Citizens' Action Party** (*Partido Acción Ciudadana*—PAC), and the **Coastal Unity Movement** (*Movimiento de Unidad Costeña*—PAC) around the presidential candidacy of Fabio GADEA Mantilla, who finished second to Ortega, with 31 percent of the vote. The PLI also finished second, behind the FSLN, with 26 seats. It won 13 municipal seats in November 2012.

In June 2016 the Supreme Court removed Montealegre as the leader of the PLI, thereby preventing him from contesting the presidency. The court turned control of the party over to Pedro REYES Valle, an ally of President Ortega. Sixteen PLI members were expelled from the legislature for refusing to recognize the new party leader.

Leaders: Pedro REYES Valle (President), Roberto SÁNCHEZ Cordero (General Secretary).

Constitutionalist Liberal Party (*Partido Liberal Constitucionalista*—PLC). The PLC originated in 1968 as a spin-off of the Somoza-era PLN. It was subsequently affiliated with the UNO and in 1996 constituted the core of the AL.

Although retaining the presidency and securing a majority of legislative seats in 2001, the party became deeply divided between supporters of President Bolaños and former president Alemán, as a result of which Bolaños launched a separate grouping, the Grand Liberal Union (GUL) in early 2004.

Following his imprisonment in late 2003, Alemán delegated the party presidency to his wife, María Fernánda Flores. Reacting to the move, three members of the party directorate, including National Secretary René HERRERA, resigned in protest.

In January 2005 Eduardo Montealegre Rivas (see ALN, below) was expelled from the party for refusing to resign his cabinet post as secretary to the presidency after President Bolaños had endorsed corruption proceedings against his predecessor.

The PLC's José RIZO placed third in the 2006 presidential balloting with 27.1 percent of the vote. In concurrent legislative elections, the PLC won 25 seats, the second-largest number behind the FSLN.

The party supported the FSLN on key issues in 2008 but formed an alliance with several small parties to field candidates in the 2008 municipal elections. The PLC endorsed Montealegre's candidacy for the mayorship of Managua after he lost a leadership battle in the ALN.

In January 2009 the Supreme Court overturned former president Alemán's conviction on charges of fraud, money laundering, and corruption. (Alemán had been sentenced to 20 years in prison in December 2003 for stealing more than $35 million of state money for personal use.) Alemán ran as the party's presidential candidate in 2011, with support from the Conservative Party of Nicaragua and the Indigenous Multiethnic Party (see below), receiving 5.9 percent of the vote. The PLC received 6.4 percent of the vote and two legislative seats in the 2011 election. It also won two municipal seats in November 2012.

Leaders: Maria HAYDEE Osuna (Chair), Miguel ROSALES (Secretary General).

Other Parties That Contested the 2011 Elections:

The **Nicaraguan Liberal Alliance** (*Alianza Liberal Nicaragüense*—ALN) and **Alliance for the Republic** (*Alianza por la República*—APRE) both fielded candidates for the 2011 elections but won less than 1 percent of the vote. Their leaders have moved on to other political groupings, and the two alliances appear defunct. For details on their past, see the 2013 *Handbook*.

Other Parties:

Sandinista Renewal Movement (*Movimiento de Renovación Sandinista*—MRS). The MRS was launched in January 1995 by former Sandinista legislative leader Sergio RAMÍREZ Mercado and the renewalist majority of the FSLN National Assembly delegation. Members of the MRS strongly opposed Chamorro's efforts to secure an enhanced role for the presidency in the 1995 constitutional reforms. Ramírez Mercado, the party's 1996 presidential candidate, subsequently withdrew from an active role in partisan politics and was highly critical of a 2001 electoral alliance with the FSLN. In early 2006 the

MRS announced FSLN dissident Herty LEWITES as its candidate for the upcoming presidential election. However, Lewites, considered one of the top three presidential contenders, died in early July.

Since December 2006 the MRS has been in alliance with the **Nicaraguan Socialist Party** (*Partido Socialista Nicaragüense*—PSN), the **Autonomous Women's Movement** (*El Movimiento Autónomo de Mujeres*—MAM), and the **CREA Movement** (*El Movimiento CREA*). The MRS was barred from running in the 2008 elections after the Supreme Electoral Council revoked its registration in June 2008 on a technicality.

The MRS joined the PLI to form an alliance around the candidacy of Fabio Gadea for the 2011 presidential poll (see below).

Leaders: Ana Margarita VIJIL Gurdián (President), Víctor Hugo TINOCO (Vice President).

Conservative Party of Nicaragua (*Partido Conservador de Nicaragua*—PCN). Formed in emulation of Nicaragua's historic Conservative Party, the current PCN resulted from a 1992 merger of the **Democratic Conservative Party** (*Partido Conservador Demócrata*—PCD) with two smaller formations, the **Conservative Social Party** (*Partido Social Conservador*—PSC) and the **Conservative Party of Labor** (*Partido Conservador Laborista*—PCL).

Launched in 1979 by supporters of the traditional PCN, the PCD had long been deeply divided, with one of its leaders, Rafael Cordova Rives, joining the junta in May 1980 while most others were in exile. The party was a surprising first runner-up in the 1984 balloting, winning 14 legislative seats and a 14 percent vote share for its presidential candidate; rent by further defection, including formation of the PANC, the party secured no representation in 1990 but won 3 seats on a fifth-place finish in 1996.

The Conservatives, who have undergone several changes in their top leadership, including the February 2001 resignation of Pedro SOLORZANO Castillo as president, saw their poll numbers diminish in the run-up to the November 2001 elections when their presidential nominee, Noel VIDAURRE Argüello, and his running mate, Carlos TUNNERMAN Bernheim, withdrew on July 18 because of policy differences with other party leaders. Earlier in the year, the PCN's initial choice for the vice presidency, former defense minister José Antonio ALVARADO, had withdrawn because of continuing controversy over his citizenship. On July 31 the party announced a new ticket headed by Alberto Saborío Morales, whose standing in the polls fell below 5 percent in September. He won only 1.4 percent of the vote on November 4, while the party's legislative representation dropped from three to two.

For the 2006 campaign, the PCN joined in supporting the presidential candidacy of PLC dissident Eduardo Montealegre Rivas under a grouping styled the **Liberal Nicaraguan–Conservative Party Alliance** (*Alianza Liberal Nicaragüense–Partido Conservador*—ALN-PC). The PCN lost its registration as a valid party in June 2008 for failing to meet the threshold for candidates in municipal elections. It formed an electoral alliance with the PLC and the **Indigenous Multiethnic Party** in support of Arnoldo Alemán for the 2011 presidential election.

Leaders: Alejandro César BOLAÑOS Davis (President), Maritza BRENES (Vice President), Magda BRIONES (Political Secretary).

Christian Democratic Union (*Unión Demócrata Cristiana*—UDC). The UDC was formed in early 1993 by merger of two former UNO members, the **Social Christian Popular Party** (*Partido Popular Social Cristiano*—PPSC) and the **Democratic Party of National Confidence** (*Partido Democrático de Confianza Nacional*—PDCN), both of which had been formed (in 1976 and 1988, respectively) by dissidents from the PSCN. The UDC joined with the FSLN in a new coalition, **United Nicaragua Triumphs** (*Unidad Nicaragua Triunfa*—UNT), to contest the 2008 municipal elections, but separated from the FSLN in 2012 so that Augustín Jarquin Anaya could run for mayor of Managua in 2012 against an FSLN candidate. Instead, the party was controversially disqualified over registration regulations.

Leader: Augustín JARQUIN Anaya.

There are a number of small indigenously-based political parties in the Atlantic Coast region, including: **Misatán,** a pro-Sandinista Indian movement led by Rufino LUCAS WILFRED; the northern-based **Yátama,** a member of the FSLN's electoral coalition for the 2008 municipal elections, and a former contra group led by Brooklyn RIVERA Bryan, who was named by President Chamorro as cabinet-level head of a new Institute for the Development of the Autonomous Regions of the Caribbean Coast; the right-wing **Coastal Democratic Alliance,** led by RAAS coordinator Alvin GUTHRIE; the **Multiethnic Indigenous Party** (*Partido Indigenista Multiétnico*—PIM), led by Carla WHITE Hodgson; the **Central American Unity Party** (*Partido Unionista Centroamericano*—PUCA); the **Multiethnic Party for Caribbean Coastal Unity** (PAMUC); the **Union of Nicaraguan Coastal Indians** (KISAN), led by Roger GERMAN; the **Coastal Authentic Autonomy Movement;** and the Corn Island–based **Island Youth Movement.** The PAMUC and the PIM were disqualified by the Supreme Electoral Council in June 2008 for failing to field candidates in at least 80 percent of electoral districts.

For a list of groups active prior to the 2006 elections, see the 2006 *Handbook.*

LEGISLATURE

The previously bicameral Congress (*Congreso*) was dissolved following installation of the provisional junta in July 1979. A 47-member Council of State (*Consejo de Estado*), representing various Sandinista, labor, and other organizations, was sworn in May 4, 1980, to serve in a quasi-legislative capacity.

Under the constitution promulgated in 1987 and amended in 1994, the **National Assembly** (*Asamblea Nacional*) was established, with 90 members popularly elected for five-year terms on a proportional representation basis from party lists, 20 from a nationwide constituency and 70 from multi-member constituencies. Two additional seats are reserved for the outgoing president of the republic and the second-place finisher in the most recent election.

After the most recent election on November 6, 2011, the seat distribution was as follows: the Sandinista National Liberation Front, 62; Liberal Independent Party, 26; and Constitutionalist Liberal Party, 2. (One seat was reserved for 2011 runner-up presidential candidate Fabio Gadea Mantilla of the PLI. One seat is also reserved for the outgoing president, but since President Ortega was reelected, the seat was given to his deputy, Jaime Rene Morales Carazo of the FSLN.)

President: Gustavo PORRAS Cortés.

CABINET

[as of September 28, 2016]

President	Daniel Ortega Saavedra
Vice President	Omar Halleslevens Acevedo
Ministers	
Agriculture and Forestry	Edward Francisco Centeno Gadea
Development, Industry, and Commerce	Orlando Solórzano Delgadillo
Education, Culture, and Sports	Miriam Raúdez Rodriguez [f]
Energy and Mines	Salvador Mansell Castrillo
Environment and Natural Resources	Juana Argeñal Sandoval [f]
Family, Youth, and Children	Marcia Ramirez Mercado [f]
Finance and Public Credit	Ivan Acosta Montalván
Foreign Affairs	Samuel Santos López
Health	Sonia Castro González [f]
Interior	Ana Isabel Morales Mazún [f]
Labor	Alba Luz Torres Briones [f]
Secretary General of Defense	Martha Elena Ruiz Sevilla [f]
Tourism	Mayra Salinas [f]
Transportation and Infrastructure	Pablo Fernández Martínez Espinosa

[f] = female

INTERGOVERNMENTAL REPRESENTATION

Ambassador to the U.S.: Francisco Obadiah CAMPBELL HOOKER.

U.S. Ambassador to Nicaragua: Laura Farnsworth DOGU.

Permanent Representative to the UN: María RUBIALES DE CHAMORRO.

IGO Memberships (Non-UN): IADB, IOM, NAM, OAS, WTO.

For Further Reference:

Booth, John A., and Patricia Bayer Richard. "Revolution's Legacy: Residual Effects on Nicaraguan Participation and Attitudes in Comparative Context." *Latin American Politics & Society* 48, no. 2 (Summer 2006): 117–140.

Chavez, Daniel. *Nicaragua and the Politics of Utopia: Development and Culture in the Modern State.* Nashville, TN: Vanderbilt University Press, 2015.

Close, David. *Nicaragua: Navigating the Politics of Democracy.* Boulder, CO: Lynne Rienner, 2016.

NIGER

Republic of Niger
République du Niger

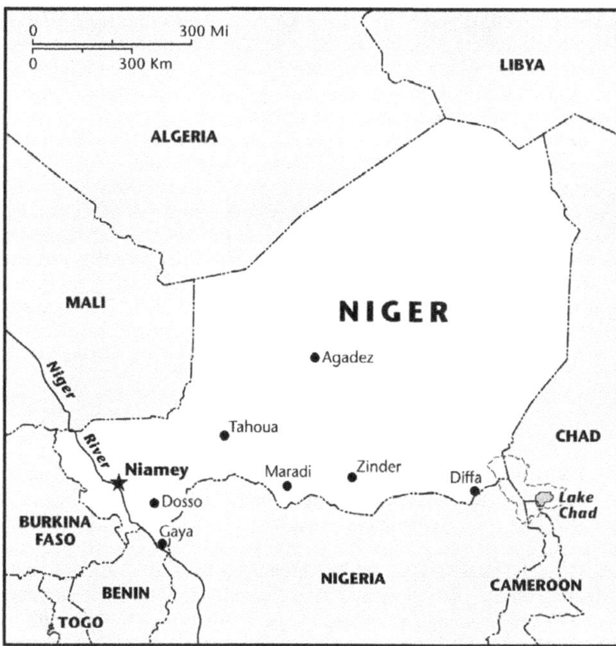

Political Status: Former French dependency; independence declared August 3, 1960; military regime established April 15, 1974; constitution of September 1989, providing for single-party military/civilian government, suspended on August 4, 1991, by a National Consultative Conference that had declared itself a sovereign body on July 30; multiparty constitution of December 27, 1992, suspended by military coup on January 27, 1996; new constitution adopted on May 22, 1996, following approval by national referendum on May 12; constitution suspended by the military-based National Reconciliation Council on April 11, 1999; new multiparty constitution providing for return of civilian government approved by national referendum on July 18, 1999, and promulgated on August 9; new constitution approved by national referendum on August 4, 2009, suspended by military coup on February 18, 2010; new constitution providing for return of civilian government approved by national referendum on October 31, 2010.

Area: 489,189 sq. mi. (1,267,000 sq. km).

Population: 20,715,000 (2016E—UN); 18,638,600 (2016E—U.S. Census).

Major Urban Center (2016E—UN): NIAMEY (1,125,000).

Official Language: French.

Monetary Unit: CFA Franc (official rate October 1, 2016: 592.38 CFA francs = $1US). The CFA franc, formerly pegged to the French franc, is now permanently pegged to the euro at 655.957 CFA francs = 1 euro.

President: Mahamadou ISSOUFOU (Nigerien Party for Democracy and Socialism–*Tarayya*), elected for a five-year term in runoff balloting on March 12, 2011, and sworn in on April 7 to succeed Lt. Gen. Salou DIJBO (Council for the Restoration of Democracy) who led military coup on February 18, 2010, that ousted President Mamadou TANDJA (National Movement for a Developing Society–Victory); reelected in runoff balloting on March 20, 2016.

Prime Minister: Brigi RAFINI (Nigerien Party for Democracy and Socialism–*Tarayya*), appointed by the president on April 7, 2011, to succeed Mahamadou DANDA; reappointed by the president on April 2, 2016, following presidential balloting on March 20.

THE COUNTRY

A vast landlocked country on the southern border of the Sahara, Niger is largely desert in the north and arable savanna in the more populous southland, which extends from the Niger River to Lake Chad. The population includes numerous tribes of two main ethnic groups: Hausa-Fulani and Zarma Songhay. About two-thirds of the population is Hausa; in the north are the nomadic Tuareg, Toubou, and Peulh groups. The population is largely (85 percent) Muslim, with smaller groups of animists and Christians. While French is the official language, Hausa is the language of trade and commerce and is constitutionally classified, along with Arabic and five other tribal languages, as a "national" language. Women constitute a minority of the labor force, excluding unpaid family workers. Following balloting in 2011, women held 15 of 113 seats in the Assembly (13.3 percent).

Agriculture and stock raising occupy 90 percent of the work force, the chief products being millet and sorghum for domestic consumption and peanuts, vegetables, and live cattle for export. The country's major exports are cotton and uranium, of which Niger is one of the world's top five producers. Coal, phosphates, iron ore, gold, and petroleum have also been discovered, but their exploitation awaits development of a more adequate transportation and communication infrastructure. Niger's economy declined in the 1980s, with agriculture suffering from both floods and drought. Also, a decrease during the decade in uranium demand contributed to a severe trade imbalance and mounting foreign debt. The introduction of austerity measures, while generating substantial social unrest, yielded assistance from the International Monetary Fund (IMF) and debt rescheduling from the Paris Club. In June 1996 the IMF approved a new three-year loan to facilitate further structural adjustments.

The government's economic policies in 1996–1998, which focused on privatization of state-run enterprises, were described as "broadly satisfactory," with GDP growth rising from 2.8 percent in 1997 to 10.4 percent in 1998. However, political turmoil and an eight-month imposition of military rule following the assassination of President Maïnassara halted economic progress, as some external financing was frozen and domestic arrears (including the payment of civil service salaries) accumulated. GDP, which had contracted by 0.6 percent in 1999, grew by an average of about 1.5 percent per year between 2001 and 2003 in view of returned support from the IMF and World Bank, which endorsed the new government's commitment to structural reform and financial transparency. Drought and widespread devastation by locusts in 2004 weakened the economy and resulted in a lack of trade and subsequent GDP growth of less than 1 percent. Because of progress the country made in economic reforms, however, the IMF provided substantial debt relief at the end of 2005, noting that Niger remains one of the poorest countries in the world. Though annual GDP growth contracted from 6.8 percent to 3.2 percent in 2007, the IMF noted strong performance in the mining sector and stable growth in the agriculture sector. The United States approved $1.4 million in poverty reduction assistance in 2007, and additional international debt relief was reported by the IMF to be "yielding results," particularly in health and education services and in the rural sector. Annual GDP growth averaged 3.5 percent in 2008–2009, owing in large part to greater mining production and an increase in investments in mining, oil, and infrastructure, as well as a strong yield in the agriculture sector. Also in 2009, the IMF approved an additional $15 million in poverty reduction funds for Niger.

In the wake of the political crisis and coup in 2010, coupled with poor agricultural performance and flooding that contributed to famine, Niger withstood the economic shocks with support from the IMF. The European Union also was prepared to resume aid. The IMF noted that the economic reforms following the coup focused on transparency in public finance management. GDP growth of about 5 percent was recorded in 2011; annual growth of 8.5 percent was forecast for 2012. Fund managers cited factors including foreign investment in infrastructure and $112 million from the United States for improved food security and to help bolster uranium mining. The World Bank also gave Niger $110 million to finance two water and sanitation projects.

Growth slowed through the second half of 2011, owing to a decline in agricultural production under less-than-average rainfall in the Sahel. Consequently, according to the IMF, growth was estimated at only 1.5 percent (down from a projected 4 percent). As almost half of the population might be affected by food shortages, the government requested donor support for food aid programs. In 2014 GDP was 6.9 percent, down from 11.2 percent in 2012. Inflation rose by 2.7 percent, up from a low 0.5 percent in 2012. GDP expansion continued in 2015, but slowed slightly to 4.6 percent, before rebounding and rising by 5.4 percent in 2016. Inflation that year was 1.8 percent, while GDP per capita was $429.

GOVERNMENT AND POLITICS

Political background. Niger was an object of centuries-old contention among different African peoples. The French first made contact in the late 19th century. Military conquest of the area began prior to 1900 and lasted until 1922, when Niger became a French colony. Political evolution began under a constitution granted by France in 1946, with Niger becoming a self-governing republic within the French Community in 1958 and attaining full independence in August 1960. Although its membership in the community subsequently lapsed, Niger has retained close economic and political ties with its former colonial ruler.

The banning of the Marxist-oriented *Sawaba* (Freedom) Party in 1959 converted Niger into a one-party state under the Niger Progressive Party (*Parti Progressiste Nigérien*—PPN), headed by President Hamani DIORI, a member of the Djerma tribe. Thereafter, Djibo BAKARY led *Sawaba* elements to continue their opposition activity from abroad, with terrorist incursions in 1964 and 1965 that included an attempt on the president's life. The Diori government, carefully balanced to represent ethnic and regional groupings, was reelected in 1965 and 1970 by overwhelming majorities but proved incapable of coping with the effects of the prolonged Sahelian drought of 1968–1974. As a result, Diori was overthrown on April 15, 1974, by a military coup led by Gen. Seyni KOUNTCHÉ and Maj. Sani Souna SIDO, who then established themselves as president and vice president, respectively, of a Supreme Military Council (*Conseil Militaire Suprême*—CMS). On August 2, 1975, Kountché announced that Sido and a number of others, including Bakary, had been arrested for attempting to organize a second coup.

A National Development Council (*Conseil National pour le Développement*—CND), initially established in July 1974 with an appointive membership, was assigned quasi-leadership status in August 1983, following indirect election of 150 delegates. Earlier, on January 24, Oumarou MAMANE had been appointed to the newly created post of prime minister; on August 3 he was named president of the reconstituted CND. Hamid ALGABID replaced him as prime minister on November 14.

President Kountché died in a Paris hospital on November 10, 1987, after a lengthy illness. He was immediately succeeded by the army chief of staff, Col. Ali SAIBOU. After being formally invested by the CMS on November 14, the new president named Algabid to head an otherwise substantially new government.

On August 2, 1988, following a July 15 cabinet reorganization that included the return of Mamane as prime minister, Saibou announced the formation of a National Movement for a Developing Society (*Mouvement National pour une Société de Développement*—MNSD) as the "final step in normalization of Niger's politics." The CND, whose constituent functions had been reaffirmed by Saibou in December 1987, was given the task of further defining the role of the MNSD.

Adding to the complexity of the restructuring process was General Saibou's declaration on January 1, 1989, that the initial congress of the MNSD would elect the membership of a Supreme Council of National Orientation (*Conseil Suprême de la Orientation Nationale*—CSON) to replace the CMS, while the CND would become an advisory Economic and Social Council (*Conseil Economique et Social*—CES). On May 17 Saibou was elected president of the CSON, thereby becoming, under a new constitution approved in September, the sole candidate for election as head of state on December 10. Saibou was credited with more than 99 percent of the votes, as was the single list of 93 MNSD candidates concurrently elected to the new National Assembly.

The post of prime minister was eliminated upon the formation of a new government on December 20, 1989. However, it was reestablished in a March 2, 1990, reshuffle precipitated by student-government confrontations in Niamey; Aliou MAHAMIDOU, a government industrial executive, was named to the position. Three months later, the CSON committed itself to "political pluralism," and in mid-November, after encountering further dissatisfaction with his policies, Saibou announced that a National Consultative Conference would convene to consider constitutional reform.

The conference opened on July 29, 1991, with delegates from 24 political groups and 69 mass organizations in attendance. After declaring its sovereignty and electing André SALIFOU as chair, the conference suspended the constitution on August 9 and transferred all but ceremonial presidential powers from Saibou to Salifou. It was decided at the time that Prime Minister Mahamidou would remain in office. However, on November 1, in the wake of an inquiry into the May 1990 massacre of Tuareg nomads by government troops, Amadou CHEIFFOU was named to succeed Mahamidou for a 15-month transition to multiparty balloting scheduled for January 31, 1993. On November 2 the conference appointed a 15-member High Council of the Republic (*Haut Conseil de la République*—HCR), chaired by Salifou, to serve as a constituent assembly and provisional legislature for the duration of the transitional period. The following day the conference voted to disband the HCR in favor of another form of transitional government.

Cheiffou announced the creation of a transitional government on November 4, 1991, which was then dissolved on March 23, 1992, in the wake of a failed military coup on February 28; a new cabinet was named on March 27. In early July Cheiffou survived a nonconfidence motion triggered by a mid-June decision to recognize Taiwan in exchange for an economic aid package, an arrangement that the HCR branded as contravening National Conference resolutions. The split between Cheiffou and the HCR proved short-lived, as the two agreed at an August 7 meeting to reconcile their differences. Meanwhile, preparations for a constitutional referendum and multiparty election proceeded haltingly. The new constitution was finally approved on December 26 by 89 percent of referendum voters, despite observations that the polling was marred by irregularities.

In late December 1992 the government admitted it had lost control over troops assigned to the northeastern Tuareg region where the insurgent Front for the Liberation of Air and Azaouad (*Front de Libération de l'Aïr et l'Azaouad*—FLAA) had resumed activity, further complicating the transitional process. Seven months earlier, the government had responded to the FLAA capture of some 28 military personnel and two officials of the recently restyled National Movement for a Developing Society-Victory (*Mouvement National pour une Société de Développement-Nassara*—MNSD-*Nassara*) by giving the army control of security in the region, a decision criticized by local Tuareg officials as equivalent to imposing a state of emergency. Frustrated by the rebels' unwillingness to release their prisoners, the army, apparently without government approval, arrested 186 alleged FLAA rebels and supporters, including a number of prominent Tuareg members of the transitional administration. Tuareg officials denounced a subsequent soldiers-for-civilians exchange offer and appealed to the UN for assistance. A Niamey offer to create a "forum for national reconciliation" in November was rebuffed by the Tuaregs, who questioned the government's ability to provide for their safety.

Following a National Assembly election on February 14, 1993, the MNSD-*Nassara,* with a plurality of 29 seats, appeared likely to form a coalition with one or more of its competitors, as a means of retaining control of the government. However, two days later, nine opposition parties, decrying the possibility of MNSD-*Nassara* controlling 50 assembly seats and continuing its rule, formed a majoritarian Alliance of Forces of Change (AFC). In the first round of presidential balloting on February 27 MNSD-*Nassara* candidate Mamadou TANDJA led the eight-candidate field with 34.2 percent of the vote, followed by Mahamane OUSMANE of the Democratic and Social Convention-*Rahama* (*Convention Démocrate et Sociale-Rahama*—CDS-*Rahama*), with 26.6 percent. However, in the second round on March 27, Ousmane was able to surpass Tandja with 54.4 percent of the vote, thanks to solid AFC backing; he was sworn in for a five-year term on April 16. The next day Mahamadou ISSOUFOU, leader of the Nigerien Party for Democracy and Socialism–*Tarayya* (*Parti Nigerien pour la Démocratie et le Socialism–Tarayya*—PNDS-*Tarayya*), was appointed prime minister. Issoufou named a cabinet on May 23.

In early 1994 opposition legislators launched a boycott against the assembly, but all 33 were arrested for advocating civil disobedience following violent antigovernment demonstrations on April 16–17. Among those incarcerated for their roles in the unrest were Tandja and the leaders of two theretofore AFC parties, André Salifou of the Union of Democratic Patriots and Progressives–*Chamoua* (UPDP-*Chamoua*) and Issoufou ASSOUMANE of the Democratic Union of Progressive Forces–*Sawaba* (UDFP-*Sawaba*). Their defection lent credence to reports of discord within the AFC, apparently stemming from the president's poorly received efforts to seize Mahamadou Issoufou's prime ministerial powers.

The AFC lost its assembly majority on September 25, 1994, when the PNDS-*Tarayya* broke with the coalition, complaining it had been marginalized by the CDS-*Rahama*. Prime Minister Issoufou resigned on September 28, and Ousmane named CDS-*Rahama* cabinet minister Abdoulaye SOULEY as the new head of government the same day. However, on October 16, two days after the MNDS-*Nassara* and PNDS-*Tarayya* had successfully orchestrated an assembly nonconfidence vote, the 11-day-old Souley government was forced to dissolve. The following day Ousmane reappointed Souley, who proffered the same cabinet. A second nonconfidence vote ensued and, faced with the choice of appointing a prime minister from the new parliamentary majority or dissolving the National Assembly and holding a new legislative election, Ousmane chose the latter.

On January 9, 1995, three days before the election, the MNSD-*Nassara* coalition threatened a boycott due to alleged voter registration fraud and the assassination of an opposition candidate, Seydou Dan DJOUMA. Nevertheless, the coalition participated in the poll and captured 43 legislative seats; AFC-affiliated groups secured the remaining 40. Ousmane ignored MNSD-*Nassara*'s request that he name Hama AMADOU as prime minister, despite the party's assembly majority, and instead appointed another MNSD-*Nassara* member, Amadou Boubacar CISSÉ, on February 8. Two days later the MNSD-*Nassara* expelled Cissé, and on February 20 the assembly voted to censure the new prime minister. The following day Ousmane dismissed Cissé and appointed Amadou, who subsequently formed a cabinet drawn from supporters of the new governing coalition.

Despite differences within the Tuareg leadership, a final peace accord was signed on April 25, 1995. On June 12 the National Assembly unanimously decided to grant full amnesty to all participants of the civil war. Meanwhile, political turmoil continued in Niamey as the AFC, which had earlier accused the MNSD-*Nassara* and its partners of "monstrous irregularities" during the January polling, criticized Prime Minister Amadou's new government for failing to represent "half of the population." Ousmane refused Amadou's call for a cabinet meeting on July 6, in an apparent attempt to avert a vote on his own non-cabinet appointments. Amadou contended that Ousmane lacked the authority to name government officials and responded by ordering riot police to prevent Ousmane-appointed administrators from entering their offices. Despite subsequent negotiations, Amadou dismissed the officials in question on August 1; however, a Niamey court immediately reinstated them. On August 4 the prime minister held a cabinet meeting without Ousmane, who promptly declared all cabinet decisions "null and void."

In early October 1995 opposition parliamentarians aligned with Ousmane declared that the prime minister had deliberately violated the constitution by convening the cabinet without presidential approval and called for his censure. However, their attempt to pass a nonconfidence motion on October 8 failed (in part because some members boycotted the vote to protest the absence of the assembly speaker). In November international mediators met with the president and prime minister in what was described as a successful attempt to end the constitutional impasse, although the question of who controlled government appointments remained unresolved.

On January 27, 1996, at least ten people were killed in a military coup directed by Army Chief of Staff Col. Ibrahim Baré MAÏNASSARA, who claimed that he had acted to end the "absurd, irrational, and personalized crisis" gripping the Nigerien government. Following seizure of the presidential palace and assembly building, Maïnassara announced the "dismissal" of the president and prime minister (both of whom had been arrested), the dissolution of the assembly, suspension of political party activity, and his own installation as chair of the National Salvation Council (*Conseil pour le Salut National*—CSN), an 11-member military body organized to govern until a civilian government could be reestablished. On January 30 the CSN designated Boukari ADJI, vice governor of the Central Bank of West African States (BCEAO), as prime minister.

In February 1996 Maïnassara appointed a 100-member Committee of Wisemen to act as an advisory council and a 32-member Coordinating Committee for the Democratic Renewal to supervise the restoration of a democratic government and draft a new constitution. At a meeting chaired by Maïnassara on February 12, Ousmane and Amadou publicly acknowledged the "constitutional problems" that had prompted the coup and endorsed the CSN's early governing efforts.

On February 17, 1996, the CSN announced a timetable for the return to a democratically elected government, which called for a constitutional referendum in September and presidential and legislative elections by the end of the year. However, under pressure from France, which on March 6 became the first international donor to renew ties with the junta, the CSN released a revised timetable that moved the schedule up by three months. On March 27 the regime established a transitional legislature, the National Forum for Democratic Renewal, consisting of members from the Committee of Wisemen and the Coordinating Committee, as well as former National Assemblymen. The National Forum met for the first time on April 1 and six days later it approved a draft constitution that included provisions for a second legislative body (a Senate), as well as a government wherein the prime minister would be accountable to the president. On April 19 the National Forum released yet another transitional timetable, rescheduling the constitutional referendum to May 12, presidential balloting to July 7, and legislative elections to September 22.

The constitutional referendum was approved on May 12, 1996, by 92 percent of the voters—though the election was poorly attended. Maïnassara revoked the ban on political parties May 19, and lifted the state of emergency four days later.

In balloting July 7–8, 1996, Brig. Gen. Maïnassara (who was promoted on May 14) captured the presidency, securing 52 percent of the vote, according to government figures. However, the election was marred by the junta's termination of the Independent National Electoral Commission (CENI) on the second day of voting and installation of a National Electoral Commission (CNE) filled with Maïnassara's supporters. Dismissing the regime's claim that it had dissolved the CENI to end the "corruption" of ballots by opposition activists, Maïnassara's top three challengers (former president Ousmane, MNSD-*Nassara* chair Mamadou Tandja, and former National Assembly president Mahamadou Issoufou) filed a petition to have the results overturned. (Ousmane had been credited with 19.75 percent of the vote, Tandja 15.65 percent, and Issoufou 7.6 percent. The fifth candidate, Moumouni DJERMAKOYE of the Nigerien Alliance for Democracy and Progress–*Zaman Lahiya* (*Alliance Nigérienne pour la Démocratie et le Progrès–Zaman Lahiya*—ANDP-*Zaman Lahiya*), secured 4.8 of the vote; he did not formally contest the results.) The Supreme Court officially validated Maïnassara's electoral victory July 21, and on August 23 the new president named a cabinet, again led by Prime Minister Adji, which included no military officials.

Following his inauguration on August 7, 1996, President Maïnassara attempted to negotiate an agreement that would prompt angry opposition groups to participate in upcoming legislative elections. Among other things, he dissolved the CNE on August 30 and announced the formation of a new electoral commission. However, the opposition, most of which coalesced in September as the Front for the Restoration and Defense of Democracy (*Front pour la Restauration et la Défense de la Démocratie*—FRDD), demanded that the members of the CENI be reappointed and that other measures be taken to ensure fair elections. Unconvinced of the regime's democratic intentions, the FRDD ultimately boycotted the balloting for a new National Assembly held on November 23, paving the way for the National Union of Independents for Democratic Renewal (UNIRD), which had recently been established by supporters of resident Maïnassara, to win 59 of the 83 seats. Declaring the transition to civilian government complete, Maïnassara dissolved the CSN on December 12. On December 21 he appointed a new government, headed, ironically, by Amadou Cissé, whose attempted appointment to the premiership in February 1995 had triggered the constitutional crisis leading up to the January 1996 coup.

Antigovernment sentiment culminated in large-scale demonstrations in the capital in early January 1997. Maïnassara responded with a crackdown that resulted in the arrest of the FRDD leaders; however, the detainees were released after ten days, regional leaders having apparently persuaded the president to adopt a less harsh approach.

On March 31, 1997, Maïnassara dissolved the Cissé government in response to the opposition's agreement to set aside its preconditions for entering into negotiations (i.e. dissolution of the assembly and organization of fresh elections) and accept cabinet postings. However, talks between the two sides quickly broke down, and no opposition members were included in the government named on June 13. The opposition rejected subsequent government entreaties, and unrest was reported throughout the country. Consequently, on November 24 Maïnassara again dismissed the Cissé government, accusing it of "incompetency" and failing to ease political tensions.

On November 27, 1997, Ibrahim Assane MAYAKI was named to replace Cissé, and on December 1 a new government was appointed.

Despite Maïnassara's pledge to include opposition figures in the new cabinet, only one minister, Tuareg leader Rhissa ag BOULA, came from outside the pro-presidential coalition of parties. Moreover, a number of Cissé ministers were reappointed.

Opposition candidates captured a majority of the contested seats in local, municipal, and regional balloting on February 7, 1999. Heightened government-opposition tension was consequently reported in Niamey after the Supreme Court (acting, according to the opposition, under pressure from the administration) ordered extensive repolling in early April.

On April 9, 1999, President Maïnassara was assassinated at the Niamey airport upon returning from a trip to Mecca, reportedly by members of the presidential guard. Troops immediately took control of the capital, and Prime Minister Mayaki dissolved the assembly, suspended political party activities, and asserted that he and his cabinet would continue governing until a "unity" government was formed. After two days of uncertainty, however, junior army officers announced on April 11 that they had assumed power and formed a National Reconciliation Council (*Conseil de Réconciliation Nationale*—CRN), whose chair, Maj. Daouda Malam WANKÉ (theretofore commander of the presidential guard), was also named head of state. The junta suspended the constitution and formally dissolved the government and Supreme Court. In addition, the results of the February elections were annulled. At the same time, the military announced a nine-month transitional plan that would culminate in the inauguration of an elected president. On April 16, 1999, the CRN named an interim government that included Wanké as the head of government, Mayaki in a diminished prime ministerial role, and a number of FRDD ministers.

A new constitution, designed, among other things, to resolve the presidential/prime-ministerial power-sharing confusion of the early to mid-1990s, was approved by 90 percent of the vote in a national referendum on July 18, 1999, although turnout was estimated at only 32 percent. Seven candidates ran in the presidential election on October 17, and in runoff balloting on November 24 Mamadou Tandja of MNSD-*Nassara* defeated Mahamdou Issoufou of PNDS-*Tarayya*, 60 percent to 40 percent. The MNSD-*Nassara* also secured a plurality in new assembly balloting on November 24, and in coalition with the CDS-*Rahama* controlled a comfortable majority of 55 legislative seats. Tandja was inaugurated on December 22 and, upon the recommendation of the assembly, named fellow party member Hama Amadou as prime minister on December 31. In addition to the MNSD-*Nassara* and CDS-*Rahama*, the new cabinet announced on January 5, 2000, included representatives of two small, nonlegislative parties—the Union of Popular Forces for Democracy and Progress-*Sawaba* (*Union des Forces Populaires pour la Démocratie et le Progrès-Sawaba*—UFPDP-*Sawaba*) and the Party for National Unity and Development-*Salama* (*Parti pour l'Unité Nationale et la Développement-Salama*—PUND-*Salama*)—as well as two leaders of former Tuareg rebel organizations. However, in a reshuffle on September 17, 2001, the ministers from the UFPDP-*Sawaba* and PUND-*Salama* were dropped from the cabinet.

The country's first municipal elections, postponed from May 4, 2004, were successfully held on July 24, 2004, with councilors elected to represent 206 communities.

Tandja was reelected in 2004, after winning the first round of balloting on November 16 and easily defeating Issoufou in second-round balloting on December 4 with 65.5 percent of the vote. He named a new cabinet on December 30, which included five women and retained Amadou as prime minister. The assembly, also elected on December 4, seated seven members from a new party formed earlier in the year by former transitional leader Cheiffou: the Social Democratic Rally-*Gaskiya* (*Rassemblement pour Sociale Democrate*—RSD-*Gaskiya*). In the wake of the dismissal of two cabinet ministers in 2006 in connection with a corruption scandal involving two ministers accused of embezzling more than $1 million in 2006, the parliament backed a no-confidence vote on May 31, 2007 that dissolved the government and forced the resignation of Prime Minister Amadou on June 1 based on delegates' allegations of Prime Minister Amadou's complicity. President Tandja's appointment of equipment minister Seini OUMAROU as prime minister on June 3 was initially rejected by the parliament, and the opposition refused to participate in a proposed unity government. However, Oumarou was sworn in on June 7 and a new government was installed on June 9, comprising members of the MNSD-*Nassara,* the CDS-*Rahama,* and the Democratic Rally of the People–*Jama'a* (*Rassemblement Démocratique du Peuple–Jama'a*—RDP-*Jama'a*), but no members of the opposition. The cabinet included eight women and a former Tuareg rebel leader, Issad KATO.

The immediate issue of concern in the wake of the government shake-up was the renewed violence in the north by a new Tuareg rebel group, the Movement of Nigeriens for Justice (Mouvement des Nigériens pour la Justice—MNJ), which had emerged in February 2007 (see Rebel Groups, below). In June the government moved 4,000 troops to the northern region to confront the rebels, who were demanding that the government use more of the country's uranium profits to improve the living conditions in the north and that the president fulfill the terms of the 1995 peace agreement.

Fighting continued in 2008, but President Tandja steadfastly refused to acknowledge the rebels, who had widened their base of support to include the Toubou and some Tuaregs from neighboring Mali. Meanwhile, international human rights groups reported that 20,000 people had been displaced by the fighting. In June the rebels kidnapped four French employees of a nuclear power company, releasing them days later. The rebels announced that their reason for such actions was to pressure the governments of Niger and France to enter negotiations to end the conflict. That same month, news reports surfaced that MNJ leader Acharif had been killed by government forces. Meanwhile political turmoil heightened following the arrest of former prime minister Hama Amadou on corruption charges. Widely viewed as President Tandja's likely successor, Amadou denied that he had embezzled state funds, claiming he was being targeted to prevent him from seeking the presidency in 2009. Amadou was removed as party leader of the MNSD as a consequence of the corruption charges and his subsequent imprisonment. In November 2008 the president extended a state of emergency that had been effect since August 2007 in response to the continuing conflict with Tuareg rebels in the north. The measure enhanced the powers of the armed forces in the region.

Amadou was released after ten months, in April 2009, and he left Niger to seek medical treatment. In May 2009 a presidential decree extended the state of emergency for another three months. The cabinet was reshuffled on May 14, 2009, when the president dismissed ministers from two parties that opposed his plan for a constitutional referendum—the RDP-*Jama'a* and the ANDP-*Zaman Lahiya*—and replaced them with members of the MNSD. He also replaced the justice minister without explanation. On May 26 the president dissolved parliament following a Constitutional Court ruling the previous day rejecting his proposal for a referendum that, if approved, would change the constitution to allow him to seek a third five-year term.

In June the president dissolved the Constitutional Court and assumed emergency powers, announcing that the referendum would be held on August 4. The new constitution, which removed presidential term limits, was approved by voters (see Constitution and government, below). Opposition parties protested and later announced they would boycott National Assembly elections scheduled for October. On August 19 the government stepped down to allow the president to name a new government, but he reappointed all members the same day. On September 24 Prime Minister Oumarou resigned to seek election to parliament (he returned to the post following the poll). Interior Minister Albadé ABOUBA served as interim prime minister.

In controversial parliamentary balloting on October 20, 2009, the MNSD-*Nassara* secured a majority, winning 76 of 113 seats, and for the first time, independents won representation. One seat was subsequently annulled. Months of political turmoil followed, and on February 18, 2010, soldiers led by Lt. Gen. Salou DJIBO stormed the presidential residence in a violent coup and assumed power. Djibo, the head of the Council for the Restoration of Democracy (*Conseil Suprême pour la Restauration de la Democratie*—CSRD), on February 19 suspended the constitution and dissolved parliament. Former president Tandja and many of his ministers were detained under house arrest. On February 23, Djibo named a new prime minister, Mahamadou DANDA, who had served as a minister in the transitional government following the 1999 coup. On March 1 Djibo formed a transitional government comprising 20 members, primarily technocrats, as well as five military officers. Five women were also given portfolios. The cabinet was reshuffled on October 10. Following an alleged October 22 coup attempt, four officers were arrested. A national referendum on a new constitution to restore civilian governance was approved by 93.5 percent of voters on October 31. In December Tandja was charged with misappropriation of state funds and moved to a prison near Niamey, ignoring an ECOWAS ruling that had ordered his release a month earlier.

The junta moved forward with plans for civilian rule by paving the way for multiparty presidential and parliamentary elections on January 31, 2011, despite protests from opposition party leaders, who claimed there were problems with the voter rolls and sought a postponement. The PNDS-*Tarayya* secured a plurality of seats, followed by strong showings by the MNSD-*Nassara* and the newly formed Nigerien Democratic

Movement for an African Federation–*Lumana* (*Mouvement Démocratique Nigérien pour une Fédération Africaine–Lumana*—MODEN-*Lumana* FA/Niger) of Hama Amadou. Five other parties won representation, and four women secured seats. In the first round of presidential balloting, former Tandja opponent Mahamadou ISSOUFOU of the PNDS-*Tarayya* was the top vote getter among the ten candidates but fell short of the threshold to avoid a runoff with former prime minister Oumarou of the MNSD-*Nassara*. Ahead of the March 12 presidential runoff, Issoufou formed alliances with several other candidates, most notably Amadou, whose MODEN-*Lumana* FA/Niger had won a third of the seats in municipal elections on January 8. Issoufou handily defeated Omarou in the runoff with 58 percent of the vote. He was sworn in on April 7 and the same day, in what was viewed as a significant effort toward reconciliation, appointed a Tuareg, Brigi RAFINI as prime minister. Over the years, Rafini, a former government minister, had been a member of several parties, including the RDP-*Jama'a,* of which he was a founder, before joining the PNDS-*Tarayya*. A new government, dominated by the PNDS-*Tarayya* but including members of the parties that had supported Issoufou in the runoff and six women, was appointed on April 21. Former prime minister and presidential challenger Amadou Cissé and CDS-*Rahama* dissident Abdou LABO were appointed as two of the three ministers of state. Omarou was invited to join the government, but he declined.

On August 13, 2013, Issoufou reshuffled the cabinet, bringing in members of the opposition to form a unity government.

In legislative balloting on February 21, 2016, the PNDS-*Tarayya* obtained a plurality with 75 seats, followed by the MODEN-*Lumana* FA/Niger with 25 seats, and the MNSD with 20, among other parties. In all, parties supportive of the president won 118 seats. In concurrent presidential polling, Issoufou won 48.5 percent in the first round and advanced to a runoff election with second-place finisher Amadou of MODEN-*Lumana* FA/Niger, who had secured 17.8 percent. In the second round of balloting on March 20, Issoufou won 92.5 percent of the vote after Amadou publicly withdrew from the election on March 9, citing irregularities. Meanwhile, Amadou remained incarcerated (see Current issues, below). Opposition parties boycotted the second round, but Amadou's name remained on the ballot. Issoufou reappointed Rafini as prime minister on April 2, and a reshuffled unity government was named on April 11. Most opposition parties declined the president's invitation to join the cabinet.

Constitution and government. In January 1984 President Kountché created a National Charter Commission, largely comprised of CND members, to develop a constitutional framework that was ultimately endorsed in a national referendum on June 14, 1987. On December 17 of the same year, General Saibou announced the formation of a national "reflection committee" to finalize guidelines for the new basic law, which was approved by popular referendum on September 24, 1989. Capping the government structure was the CSON, whose 67 civilian and military members (14 serving as a National Executive Bureau) were elected by the MNSD and whose president became sole candidate for election to the presidency of the republic. The 1989 document, which also provided for a National Assembly of 93 MNSD-approved members and for a judiciary headed by a presidentially appointed Supreme Court, was suspended by the National Conference on August 9, 1991.

By mid-1992 the presidency had been reduced to an essentially symbolic institution, as true executive power was exercised by the prime minister who until early 1993 answered to a quasi-legislative High Council of the Republic (HCR). One of the functions of the HCR was to oversee the drafting of the new basic law, which was approved by national referendum on December 27, 1993. The document provided for a directly elected president to serve a once-renewable five-year term. A presidentially nominated prime minister is responsible to a unicameral National Assembly whose members are also elected for five-year terms.

Upon its ascension to power in early 1996 the CSN military regime suspended the 1993 document and appointed a commission to draft a new charter. The new constitution, which was approved by national referendum on May 12, 1996, featured an executive branch headed by a powerful president, thus clearly distinguishing itself from its predecessors. Meanwhile, in early June the regime created a ten-member High Court of Justice and granted it sole authority to prosecute the president and government members.

The 1996 basic law was suspended by the CRN on April 11, 1999, and an interim Consultative Council (*Conseil Consultative*—CC) was appointed in May by the new military head of state, Maj. Daouda Malam Wanké, to draft yet another constitution. As approved in a national referendum on July 18, the new basic law accorded strong power to the president to prevent a reoccurrence of the difficulties experienced in interpreting the 1993 document with regard to the authority of the prime minister versus the president.

A new constitution was promulgated on August 18, 2009, following a referendum on August 4 that was approved by 92.5 percent of voters. The new charter granted the president an extension beyond his second five-year term (ending in December 2009) and the right to seek unlimited reelection. Following the coup of February 18, 2010, the constitution was suspended. A new constitution limiting the presidential mandate to two five-year terms and granting amnesty to coup leaders was approved by voters on October 31 and signed by head of state Lt. Gen. Salou Djibo on November 25, following validation by the Constitutional Court a day earlier. The charter was promulgated on November 30. The new constitution guaranteed freedom of the press. In 2016 Reporters Without Borders ranked Niger 52nd out of 180 countries.

Foreign relations. Prior to the 1974 coup Niger pursued a moderate line in foreign affairs, avoiding involvement in East–West issues and generally maintaining friendly relations with neighboring states. The Kountché government established diplomatic links with a number of communist states, including China and the Soviet Union, and adopted a conservative posture in regional affairs, including a diplomatic rupture with Libya from January 1981 to March 1982. Tripoli was periodically charged thereafter with backing anti-Niamey forces, including those involved in a late 1983 coup attempt and northern Tuareg rebel activity in 1985 and 1990. However, a bilateral security agreement in December 1990 eased tensions between Niger and Libya.

Niamey's relations with neighboring Algeria and Mali have been complicated since October 1991 by the resurgence of militant Tuareg activities across their shared borders. In March 1992 a meeting between Prime Minister Cheiffou and Tuareg officials in Algeria yielded a two-week truce. However, the truce was allowed to lapse, and in February 1993 Nigerien and Malian troops clashed, after reportedly mistaking each other for Tuareg units. The January 1996 military coup in Niger drew condemnation from both regional and international observers, with France, the European Union, and the United States suspending aid payments. Although Paris resumed cooperation in March 1996, Washington reiterated its stance following the controversial July presidential elections.

A number of regional and other international capitals condemned the military takeover in April 1999; France, for example, promptly broke off its relations with Niger and suspended all aid. Such pressure was considered influential in the subsequent quick return to civilian rule, after which normal international relations were reestablished and external financial assistance was resumed.

In May 2000 a long-standing dispute between Niger and Benin over ownership of Lete Island and a number of smaller islands in the Niger River resurfaced. After mediation by the Organization of African Unity (OAU, subsequently the African Union [AU]) failed to produce successful border delineation, the case was submitted to the International Court of Justice (ICJ). In 2005 the ICJ ruled that 16 of the 25 disputed islands, including Lete, belonged to Niger. In 2007 Niger officially took ownership of Lete Island. In 2007 Benin officially took possession of nine other islands it was awarded by the ICJ's ruling.

Longtime tensions between Niger and Burkina Faso escalated in 2007, each accusing the other's security forces of crossing the border to rob villagers. Local officials called for a jointly controlled buffer zone, and the two countries agreed to ask the ICJ to mediate the dispute.

Relations with France were strained in 2007 following the deportation of a French journalist from Niger after his imprisonment for filming a documentary on Tuareg rebels. Questions about the role of French uranium-mining company Areva also played a part in the deterioration of ties with France (see Current issues, below).

China, meanwhile, maintained warm relations with Niger in 2007, the former having opened what was described as a "vast new embassy" in Niamey and having secured a number of uranium prospecting licenses. In September 2007 President Tandja and officials of the Chinese Communist Party met in Niger and agreed to foster cooperation between the two governments; they signed an oil production agreement in 2008. In 2009 China loaned Niger $95 million for a uranium mining project owned in partnership between the two countries.

During the political crisis in President Tandja's government in 2009, ECOWAS offered the government and the opposition a "road map" for resolving differences. Despite objections by ECOWAS, Tandja followed through with plans for a controversial constitutional referendum in August. ECOWAS immediately suspended Niger after the national poll.

Following the February 2010 coup, ECOWAS condemned the junta's action as an unconstitutional "ascension to power."

Seven foreign nationals, including five from France, all of whom worked for French companies, were kidnapped near a northern Nigerien mining town in September 2010. The French government subsequently deployed military personnel, aircraft, and weapons to help find the hostages. Al-Qaida in the Islamic Maghreb (AQIM) claimed responsibility for the abductions. Three of the hostages were released in February 2011, and French president Nicolas Sarkozy thanked the authorities in Niger for their efforts in the matter. In a separate incident reported in February, a French Niger national was executed by his kidnappers after he was abducted in January. Around the same time, the U.S. Peace Corps withdrew its volunteers from the country, citing security concerns, marking the first time the agency had ceased operations there since 1962.

In April 2011 Niger called for donor aid to help some 59,000 Africans—many of them Nigeriens—who fled the Libyan civil war.

In August 2012 Niger joined Algeria, Burkina Faso, and Mauritania in the creation of a 45,000 member "hot pursuit" force to combat terrorism and cross-border incursions. Officials from China and Niger announced in September a loan offer of $1.1 billion for infrastructure projects, including airport terminals, a light rail line for the capital, and improving the country's internet capability.

Reports in January 2013 indicated that Niger had granted the United States permission to establish a drone base in the country. In Niamey, U.S. and French forces set up neighboring drone hangars to conduct reconnaissance flights over Mali. In addition, Niger agreed to contribute 675 troops to the AU-led intervention force in Mali. The International Court of Justice ruled in April on a border dispute between Niger and Burkina Faso. The ruling finalized the border along 380 km (236 miles). In August Niger and Mauritania signed a defense cooperation accord.

Niger extradited former Libyan leader Muammar al-Qadhafi's son al-Saadi to Libya on March 6, 2014. He was transferred to a prison in Tripoli. Al-Saadi had fled Libya in 2011 and had been under house arrest in Niger since then.

In late June several Nigeriens were arrested for alleged involvement with an international baby trafficking ring between Nigeria, Benin, and Niger (see Current issues, below).

French president François Hollande announced that France would again bulk up its forces in West Africa in July. Under Operation Barkhane (a term for a crescent-shaped sand dune), France was preparing for permanent deployment of 3,000 troops at bases in Mali, Chad, Niger, and Burkina Faso. In September the United States announced that the U.S. military was preparing to open a second drone base in Niger in the desert city of Agadez to track Takfiri militant groups, insurgents, arms traffickers, and drug smugglers. The deal between the United States and Niger stipulated that the United States is only to fly unarmed drones out of the base for reconnaissance missions.

French forces conducted offensive operations in northern Niger in September and October 2014, destroying an AQIM weapons convoy and capturing Abu Aasim el-MOUHAJIR, an AQIM commander. Boko Haram attacks in neighboring Nigeria were estimated to have caused more than 100,000 to flee into Niger by the end of 2014. Meanwhile, a joint repatriation program between Niger and Algeria began to move the first of some 3,000 refugees back to Algeria in December 2014.

Attacks by Boko Haram on the towns of Bosso and Diffa in northern Niger in February 2015 left dozens of civilians dead, while the Nigerien military reported 109 militants had been killed. Following the strikes, Issoufou announced in February that Niger would contribute 750 troops to a regional force fighting the extremist group. Continued attacks during the summer of 2015 killed approximately 200 civilians, and security forces reportedly killed 67 militants. In October the United States deployed 30 troops to Niger to train security forces and provided $36 million in military equipment, including 30 vehicles and 2 reconnaissance aircraft.

Current issues. In the run-up to the 2009 elections, scheduled for November–December, President Tandja said he would not seek a third term (a third term would require a constitutional amendment), but he changed his mind in early May. With several parties voicing their opposition to Tandja's proposed constitutional revision allowing him to seek a third term, the president removed several cabinet members whose parties objected to the referendum. Days later the Constitutional Court, having taken up the issue after it was referred by parliament, ruled that the president "cannot undertake to change the constitution without violating his oath of office." The next day, Tandja dissolved parliament, a move that meant he could avoid having to appear before the High Court of Justice on charges of high treason, observers said. The high court judge, Moumouni Adamou DJERMAKOYE of the pro-government ANDP-*Zaman Lahiya,* had recently warned that the proposed referendum would divide the country. The president's plan drew international protests as well, the United States calling the proposed referendum "a setback for democracy," and the Economic Community of West African States (ECOWAS) threatening sanctions. Tandja, however, rejected the criticism and defied the Constitutional Court and the National Assembly by going forward with plans for the referendum, scheduled for August 4. In June protesters led by Mahamadou Issoufou of the PNDS-*Tarayya* announced they would defy the government ban on demonstrations. Subsequently, more than 230 parties and groups under the umbrella Front for Defense of Democracy (FDD) held a series of protests to counter what they claimed was the president's plan to "install absolute power." On June 26 the president dissolved the government and assumed emergency powers. Several days later he dissolved the Constitutional Court and suspended a television station that aired opposition views. On July 3 the president appointed a new Constitutional Court, which was widely criticized; ten days later the country's attorneys went on strike in protest. Following a controversial referendum in August, in which nearly 93 percent of voters approved constitutional amendments that removed presidential term limits, ECOWAS offered to help negotiate a resolution to the political crisis that ensued, recommending a power-sharing arrangement. Meanwhile, Issoufou was arrested, charged with misappropriation of funds, and released on bail. He left the country on October 29, the day controversial parliamentary elections were held, but he returned the following day, saying he would cooperate with the judiciary. In results announced in early November, the MNSD regained the majority it had lost in 2004. ECOWAS immediately suspended Niger for not postponing the poll. Domestic dissent continued over the president's enhanced authority, the unrest exacerbated by famine and a lack of progress toward a resolution proposed by ECOWAS. On a positive note, late in the year Tuareg rebels in Niger and in neighboring Mali agreed to disarm as a result of peace talks brokered by Libyan leader Muammar al-Qadhafi.

"So chaotic and tense" had the last year been, according to *Africa Research Bulletin,* some 10,000 opposition demonstrators protested in Niamey on February 14, 2010. Four days later, in what was described as an "audacious daylight attack," soldiers stormed the presidential palace, engaged in a four-hour gun battle in which ten people were killed, and overthrew the government. President Tandja and his cabinet were arrested, the constitution was suspended, and parliament was dissolved by the junta, styled as the Council for the Restoration of Democracy—CSRD. The action was immediately condemned by the AU, France, and the UN, while the United States issued more vague comments urging "a speedy return to democracy." Junta leader Lt. Gen. Salou Djibo subsequently appointed Mahamadou Danda as interim prime minister and on March 1 named a transitional government dominated by technocrats. Meanwhile, though some ministers were released from custody, Tandja and his key officials remained under house arrest on the grounds of the presidential compound. The junta announced that it would hold elections following a transitional period, and that its members, along with police, customs officers, and others, would not be allowed to participate. Further, governors, district administrators, and tribal chiefs were banned from participating in political activity. On March 12 Djibo appointed military officers as governors of seven of the eight regions, replacing civilians in the posts. In response to international pressure, Djibo met with representatives of political parties and civil societies to discuss a scheme for successful political transition. Subsequently, he formed a Consultative Council from a cross-section of society to assist in the transition, naming as its head Marou AMADOU, the former president of a civil association, United Front for the Safety of Democracy (FUSAD), which had opposed Tandja's constitutional reform in 2009. (Marou Amadou had been arrested repeatedly during the Tandja regime for his opposition stance.) While the coup was reported to have the approval of a majority of the populace, Djibo, for his part, requested that the public refrain from demonstrations of support in order to "maintain a spirit of neutrality." Meanwhile, that same month former prime minister and former MNSD stalwart Hama Amadou returned from exile in France and formed a new political party, the MODEN-*Lumana* FA/Niger (see Political Parties, below).

In April 2010 the junta announced a schedule for returning to civilian rule, with presidential elections set for December 26, and a second round, if needed, on January 26, 2011, with democracy to be restored by March 1, 2011. In May the junta acknowledged the alarming food shortage in the country (20 percent of the population reportedly had food for only ten days), something former president Tandja had refused to do. Junta leaders also vowed to clean up corruption as reports surfaced of alleged kickbacks to Tandja's allies in exchange for mining contracts. In early October two high-ranking junta members were arrested for an alleged plot to overthrow Djibo when he was out of the country in September. Another military officer was fired from the cabinet. No reason was given. Progress was made toward restoring civilian rule after a new constitution was overwhelmingly approved in a national referendum on October 31and subsequently validated by the Constitutional Court and signed by Djibo. The new charter limits the presidential mandate to two five-year terms and grants amnesty to those involved in the February coup. The junta announced a new schedule for ending the transitional period, with parliamentary and presidential elections now set for January 31, 2011, and a second round of presidential balloting, if needed, on March 12, 2011, with a new president to be inaugurated on April 6. On November 8 the ECOWAS court ruled that Tandja should be released from what it deemed was illegal detention and urged junta leaders to respect its decision. A group of opposition parties issued a statement calling for Tandja to remain in custody and be charged with high treason. The junta rejected the ECOWAS court's ruling and called for Tandja to be charged with high treason. In December the State Court lifted Tandja's presidential immunity, and he was charged with misappropriating $1 million in state funds. He was then transferred from house arrest to a prison near Niamey and was scheduled to stand trial in May 2011.

The junta rejected a demand by nine of the ten presidential candidates that the election be postponed due to their concerns about complaints lodged against the national electoral commission. Meanwhile, four of the presidential candidates—Issoufou, Mahamane Ousmane of the CDS-*Rahama,* Amadou Cissé, now of the Union for Democracy and the Republic–*Tabbat* (*Union pour la Démocratie et la République–Tabbat*—UDR-*Tabbat*), and Hama Amadou—had formed an electoral alliance, styled as the Coordination of Democratic Forces for the Republic (*Coordination des Forces pour la Démocratie et la République*—CFDR). However, shortly before the election, another coalition was formed, including two candidates who switched allegiance (Amadou and Ousmane) to join the National Reconciliation Alliance against Issoufou. Following the latter's success in the first round of balloting, Amadou threw his new party's support behind the PNDS-*Tarayya* candidate. The PNDS fell short of a majority in concurrent legislative balloting, but Issoufou handily defeated Oumarou in second-round voting on March 12. After naming a Tuareg as his prime minister, Issoufou made further conciliatory moves by offering Oumarou a ministerial post (which the MNSD leader turned down) and by including presidential challengers Mahamane Ousmane and Amadou Cissé, as well as CDS-*Rahama* dissident Abdou Labo in his new government. The cabinet also included members of the UDR-*Tabbat,* which had endorsed his candidacy. Marou Amadou, a key opponent of Tandja's constitutional reforms in 2009, was appointed minister of justice. One of the new president's first acts was to bestow the country's highest award upon coup leader Lieutenant General Djibo. Issoufou pledged to provide water and help improve the agriculture sector, to waive school fees for children up to age 16, and to provide an additional 2,500 classrooms and teachers, among other things.

In a move that seemed to take many observers by surprise, the country's appeals court in May 2011 dismissed all corruption charges against Tandja and ordered his release from prison. The decision was based on the law that prohibits Niger from trying a head of state after he has left office, which observers said was meant to prevent politically motivated cases from being brought against deposed leaders. Upon his release, the former president was greeted by thousands of cheering supporters.

In 2011–2012 the situation in Niger was strained by the arrival of groups displaced by neighboring conflicts: some 200,000 Nigerian migrant workers passing from Libya through Agadez; several hundred men carrying weapons procured in Libya en route to Mali; and at least 20,000 refugees fleeing the instability in Mali. The government feared events could inspire an uprising from its own Tuareg population.

In a national broadcast on Aug. 9, 2011, Issoufou announced that ten people had been arrested for their involvement in a failed coup attempt scheduled for July 12–13.

In September 2011 Saadi Qadhafi, the son of Libya's ex-ruler, turned up in the northern town of Agadez in a convoy, prompting accusations of Niger's complicity from Libya's National Transitional Council. Issoufou's decision to grant him asylum the next month, which some observers attributed to a sense of personal obligation stemming from Qadhafi's funding of his past campaigns, further angered the NTC. In February Saadi was placed under de facto house arrest after he caused a diplomatic headache for his host by announcing in a phone call interview with Al Arabiya news channel that he was in touch with insurgents in Libya and claiming there would be a new rebellion against the NTC.

Fourteen people were killed and 13 arrested on November 6 when troops engaged a convoy of gunmen outside the northern town of Assamaka near the borders with Algeria and Mali. Local sources reported the gunmen included Libyans and Tuaregs from Mali, likely Qadhafi loyalists fleeing the conflict. Also in November, five aid workers who had been kidnapped by an Islamic group, the Movement for Oneness and Jihad in West Africa (MUJAO), were freed during a military operation. A sixth hostage was killed during rescue.

On May 23, 2013, attacks on a uranium complex and a military base left 35 dead. The strikes were blamed on AQIM. The following month, militants staged a jail break that freed 22, including several prominent AQIM leaders.

On May 19, 2014, unidentified individuals fired shots into the home of an MP close to PNDS. Three days later, unknown individuals threw a Molotov cocktail at PNDS headquarters. On June 5 government officials placed six MODEN members in custody on charges of plotting against the security of the state. The Court of Appeal of Niamey released them on August 26. The accused are all close to Hama Amadou.

Meanwhile, 17 people, 12 of them women, were arrested in late June for their suspected involvement in a baby-trafficking ring between Nigeria, Benin, and Niger. One of Amadou's wives is among the 17 people. In August Ben Omar authorized a politically charged investigation into Amadou's alleged involvement in the trafficking ring. Subsequently Amadou fled Niger to Burkina Faso and ultimately France allegedly to escape the investigation. He was removed from his post as speaker of the Assembly. The remand of Agriculture Minister Abdou Labo on August 30 was also thought to be politically motivated. The opposition, including CDS, denounced the investigation as a breach of parliamentary rules, which forbid an office of the National Assembly to deliver a deputy to justice or to have him arrested. However, on September 4 the Constitutional Court determined that when parliament is not in session, it is lawful to authorize the arrest of a member. In November Amadou SALIFOU (MNSD) was elected speaker of the Assembly to replace Amadou, who returned to Niger and was arrested.

On December 17, 2015, Issoufou announced on television that security forces had stopped an alleged coup, and arrested nine military officers. Thirteen additional arrests were made in January 2016. Despite his incarceration, Amadou was allowed to run for the presidency in February 2016. He placed second in the first round of balloting behind Issoufou, but then withdrew from the runoff balloting because opposition groups claimed electoral fraud in both the legislative and presidential balloting.

POLITICAL PARTIES

Political parties were not permitted in Niger during the more than 13 years of the Kountché regime. The National Movement for a Developing Society (MNSD, below) was established as a government formation in 1988, and some 15 parties received provisional recognition in the five months following President Saibou's November 1990 acceptance of a multiparty system. All party activity was suspended in the wake of the January 1996 coup, but the ban was soon lifted on May 19. However, the new standards guiding party formations and activities were described as restrictive. Nevertheless, numerous coalitions were formed in 1996–1998, though alliances continued changing. Most notably, the once powerful **Alliance of Forces of Change** (*Alliance des Forces de Changement*—AFC) appeared to have collapsed by the late 1990s. (For further information on the AFC, see the 1998 *Handbook.*)

Political party activity was suspended immediately following the April 1999 military takeover; however, within days of President Maïnassara's death the leading opposition groups announced their intention to cooperate with the military junta, and the suspension was lifted.

In March 2000 the PNDS-*Tarayya,* RDP-*Jama'a,* ANDP-*Zaman Lahiya,* and a number of smaller parties formed a loose antigovernment coalition called the **Coordination of Democratic Forces** (*Coordination des Forces Démocratiques*—CFD). In response the MNDS-*Nassara* and several allies, including the CDS-*Rahama,* announced the creation of an **Alliance of Democratic Forces** (*Alliance des Forces Démocratiques*—AFD) in July. The ANDP-*Zaman Lahia* joined the AFD coalition on July 8, 2002.

Prior to the 2004 legislative elections, the PNDS-*Tarayya* formed electoral coalitions with several parties: the PPN/RDA and the PNA-*Al Ouma;* and the UNI/UDR-*Tabbat.*

Government and Government-Supportive Parties:

Nigerien Party for Democracy and Socialism–*Tarayya* (*Parti Nigerien pour la Démocratie et le Socialism–Tarayya*—PNDS-*Tarayya*). In the legislative election of February 1993, the PNDS-*Tarayya*, then affiliated with the AFC, won 13 seats. Having gained only a 16 percent vote share in the first round of 1993 presidential balloting, party leader and presidential candidate Mahamadou Issoufou was eliminated from the runoff election; he was subsequently named prime minister. (For information about party history before 2007, see the 2014 *Handbook*).

In 2007 the party's secretary general, Alou Bozari, joined numerous parties in the northern region in calling for an immediate cease-fire between government troops and Tuareg rebels.

The party opposed the president's constitutional referendum in 2009 and organized a massive, peaceful protest in May that included civil rights groups, trade unions, students, and supporters of former prime minister Amadou. Issoufou was arrested in October on charges of misappropriation of funds. He left the country but then returned the day after parliamentary elections and vowed to cooperate with the authorities. Following the 2010 coup that ousted Tandja, the PNDS nominated Issoufou as its flag bearer for the 2011 presidential election. The PNDS won 34 seats in the concurrent parliamentary election. Issoufou stepped down as party president after his election, in keeping with the requirement that the head of state not be involved in party politics. Party vice president Mohamed Bazoum, who assumed the leadership position, was appointed minister of state for foreign affairs in the new government. The party's secretary of state, Foumakoye Gado, was appointed minister of mines, and then minister of petroleum and energy. The 6th ordinary party congress took place in late December 2013. Members elected Bazoum head of the party.

On May 19 unidentified individuals fired shots into the home of Mohamed BEN OMAR, an MP close to PNDS. Three days later, unknown individuals threw a Molotov cocktail at PNDS headquarters, injuring three people. In June government officials arrested six members of MODEN for the attacks (see Current issues, above).

On November 7, 2015, incumbent president Issoufou was elected as the party's presidential candidate. Issoufou was reelected in March 2016. Meanwhile, the party won 75 seats in the February 2016 Assembly elections with 35.7 percent of the vote.

Leaders: Mohamed BAZOUM (President), Foumakoye GADO (Vice President), Hassoumi MASSAOUDOU (Secretary General), Kalla ANKOURAO (Deputy Secretary General).

Democratic Rally of the People–*Jama'a* (*Rassemblement Démocratique du Peuple–Jama'a*—RDP-*Jama'a*). The RDP-*Jama'a* held its inaugural congress on August 14–19, 1997, and was the party of then-President Maïnassara. Thereafter, the party emerged as the leader of a loose coalition of parties that supported the president. At local and municipal polling in early 1999, the RDP-*Jama'a* reportedly captured the largest number of seats; however, the military junta that came to power in April nullified the balloting.

Intraparty fighting erupted over the choice of a 1999 presidential nominee, leading former Prime Minister Amadou Boubacar Cissé and his supporters to leave the party. Meanwhile, Hamid Algabid of the RDP-*Jama'a* won 10.9 percent of the vote in the first round of presidential balloting and supported Mahamadou Issoufou of the PNDS-*Tarayya* in the second round. In the first round of presidential elections in 2004, Algabid won only 4.9 percent of the vote, finishing in last place. He supported Tandja in the second round. The party won only six seats in the assembly elections of 2004.

Disagreements within the party led to the departure of Secretary General Abdourahamane SEYDOU in 2008.

The party opposed the president's proposed constitutional referendum early in 2009 unless it also included a measure that would abolish amnesty for those who had been involved in the assassination of President Maïnassara, but in midyear it unexpectedly dropped the conditional demand and supported the referendum.

The party won seven seats in the October 2009 assembly elections.

In the first round of presidential balloting in 2011 the RDP-*Jama'a* backed the MNSD-*Nassara*'s Seini Oumarou, but it joined several other parties in supporting Issoufou over Oumarou in the second round. In the National Assembly elections the RDP-*Jama'a* won seven seats. In August 2013 RDP-member Chaïbou Dan Inna was named minister of vocational and technical education.

The RDP-*Jama'a* endorsed Issoufou in the 2016 presidential election, while it won three seats in the Assembly polling with 2.4 percent of the vote.

Leader: Hamid ALGABID (Chair and 1999 and 2004 presidential candidate).

Democratic and Social Convention–*Rahama* (*Convention Démocrate et Sociale–Rahama*—CDS-*Rahama*). In the legislative balloting of February 1993 CDS-*Rahama* captured 22 seats, the most by any opposition party. Its candidate Mahamane Ousmane who had finished second in the first round of balloting, captured the presidency with 54.4 percent of the vote in the second round of presidential balloting on March 27. In January 1995 the party increased its assembly representation to 24 seats. Ousmane was ousted from office in the January 1996 coup; his bid to regain the presidency in the July balloting fell short as he came in second (at least according to government tallies) with 19.8 percent of the vote. He finished a close third in the first round of presidential balloting in 1999 with 22.5 percent of the vote. The CDS-*Rahama* subsequently threw its support behind Mamadou Tandja of the MNSD-*Nassara* for the second round. In the 2004 presidential balloting Ousmane was again third in the first round of voting and again threw his support behind Tandja in the second round. CDS-*Rahama* won 22 seats in the assembly balloting of 2004.

Though the party had been supportive of President Tandja, in 2009 it opposed his plan for a constitutional referendum, saying Niger's "political and institutional stability" would be threatened. The CDS-*Rahama* agreed with the court ruling that the referendum was unconstitutional. Further, party leader Mahamane Ousmane had been speaker of the assembly when Tandja dissolved parliament in May. In June the party withdrew its eight ministers from the government in protest and subsequently formed an opposition coalition styled the **Movement for Defense and Democracy** (*Mouvement pour le défense et le démocratie*—MDD) with five minor parties.

The party failed to win seats in the October 2009 parliamentary election.

In 2011 Ousmane finished fourth in the presidential balloting with 8.4 percent of the vote. The party won three seats in the concurrent parliamentary election and dissident Abdou Labo, who went against the party and backed Issoufou in the presidential runoff, was appointed to the new government. In August 2013 Labo was appointed minister of state.

In February 2014 CDS was involved in talks with MNSD and MODEN to form an opposition coalition ahead of the 2016 presidential elections. The two wings of CDS (one led by Mahamane Ousmane and one by Abdou Labo) formed a reconciliation committee in March 2014 that called on the party to hold a party congress as soon as possible to work past internal differences. Ousmane did not participate in the reconciliation committee and refused to schedule a party congress despite being legally required to do so as party leader. On June 23 the Labo wing filed a complaint against Ousmane, and the prosecutor lifted Ousmane's immunity. The party congress, attended by 664 delegates, took place September 6–7. No clear leadership decisions had been reached by late September.

On November 14, 2015, Labo was chosen as the CDS candidate for the 2016 balloting. Ousmane defected to the Nigerien Movement for Democratic Renewal (*Mouvement Nigérien pour le Renouveau Démocratique–Hankuri,* MNRD-*Hankuri,* see below). Labo was seventh with 2.1 percent of the vote. The CDS secured 2.4 percent of the vote in the legislative polling, and three seats.

Leaders: Abdou LABO (2016 presidential candidate), Nabram ISSOUFOU, Maïdagi ALLAMBEY.

Nigerien Democratic Movement for an African Federation–*Lumana* (*Mouvement Démocratique Nigérien pour une Fédération Africaine-Lumana*—MODEN-*Lumana* FA/Niger). Founded in early 2010 by Hama Amadou, the embattled former MNSD-*Nassara* chair who was imprisoned in 2008 and former prime minister in the Ousmane government in 1995, the MODEN party's motto is liberty, justice, and progress. The party nominated Amadou in November as its flag bearer in the 2011 presidential election. Ahead of the election in January, MODEN was among the three parties that formed the umbrella Alliance for National Reconciliation to support whichever party's candidate reached the second round. Following Amadou's third-place showing in the first round with just under 20 percent of the vote, MODEN, citing its commitment to the political and institutional stability of the country, changed course and backed Issoufou in the second round. The party won the third highest number of seats—23—in the 2011 parliamentary election, and in April Amadou was elected speaker of the National Assembly. In spring 2012 a scandal followed

Lumana MP, Zakou DJIBO, and seven other MPs suspected of embezzling $3 million. Citing the importance of *Lumana*'s support for the governing coalition, observers said Issoufou appeared politically hamstrung, unwilling to lift Djibo's parliamentary immunity and so open to criticism from the opposition, which took the case to the Constitutional Court and threatened to accuse Issoufou of perjury. In August 2013 the party suspended its involvement in the coalition government, asserting that the number of cabinet posts it held were "inadequate."

By February 2014 two wings of MODEN emerged, one led by Amadou and the other led by party secretary general Omar Hamidou TCHIANA, who refused to leave the government. On June 5, 2014, government officials placed six MODEN members in custody on charges of plotting against the security of the state. The Court of Appeal of Niamey released them on August 26. The accused include two former ministers, Abdoulrahame Seydou (Sport) and Soumana SANDA (Health), and former mayor of central Niamey, Oumarou Moumouni DOGARI, all close to Hama Amadou. That same month, Amadou fled Niger to Burkina Faso and ultimately France to escape an investigation into his alleged involvement in a baby trafficking ring (see Current issues, above).

Amadou was chosen as the party's presidential candidate in November 2015, despite his incarceration (see Current issues). The Tchiana wing of the party backed incumbent President Issoufou. Amadou placed second in the first round of balloting on February 21, 2016, with 17.7 percent of the vote. However, he withdrew from the second round, and his faction urged its members to boycott the election. In the February Assembly balloting, the party was second with 12.9 percent of the vote and 25 seats. The party initially boycotted parliament, but members took their seats in May. Tchiana remained in the cabinet and was made a minister of state.

Leaders: Hama AMADOU (President of the Party, Speaker of the National Assembly, and 2011 and 2016 presidential candidate), Salissou Mamadou HABI (Vice President), Noma OUMAROU (Second Vice President), Almoustapha CISSÉ (Treasurer), Ali GAZAGAZA (Deputy Secretary General), Omar Hamidou TCHIANA (Secretary General).

Union for Democracy and the Republic–*Tabbat* (*Union pour la Démocratie et la République–Tabbat*—UDR-*Tabbat*), founded in 1999 by former prime minister and 2011 presidential candidate Amadou Boubacar Cissé, formerly of the RDP-*Jama'a*. The UDR-*Tabbat* won six seats in the 2011 parliamentary elections, and Cissé was appointed one of three ministers of state in the new government. Cissé was the party's 2016 candidate, garnering 1.5 percent of the vote. The UDR-*Tabbat* won two seats in the Assembly elections, but Cissé did not rejoin the government.

Leader: Amadou Boubacar CISSÉ (Party Leader and 2016 presidential candidate).

Other Legislative Parties:

National Movement for a Developing Society–Victory (*Mouvement National pour une Societé de Développement–Nassara*—MNSD-*Nassara*). General Saibou announced the formation of the MNSD on August 2, 1988. Rejecting calls for a multiparty system, he claimed that the new group would allow for the "plural expression of opinions and ideological sensibilities," while paving the way for the normalization of politics in Niger.

General Saibou was reelected MNSD chair at a party congress on March 12–18, 1991, during which a transition to a multiparty system was formally endorsed. The military also announced its withdrawal from politics, and the MNSD added the Hausa word *Nassara* (Victory) to its name. On July 12, just as the party prepared to enter the competitive arena, Saibou resigned his chairmanship, citing a need to serve in a nonpartisan capacity. (For information about party history before 1999, see the 2014 *Handbook*)

Tandja again took the lead in the presidential elections of 2004, taking 40.7 percent of the vote in the first round of balloting on November 16. He retained his post in the second round of balloting on December 4 with a resounding victory (65.5 percent of the vote) by striking alliances with ANDP-*Zaman Lahiya* candidate Moumouni Djermakoye (who was fifth in the first-round balloting) and Amadou Cheiffou of the Rally for Social Democracy-*Gaskiya,* who ran as an independent (fourth in the first round), and gaining the support of the CDS's Ousmane, who garnered just 24.6 percent of votes in the first round, and Hamid Algabid of the Democratic Rally of the People-*Jama'a* (sixth place in the first round). The MNSD-*Nassara* captured 47 legislative seats, a gain of 9 from the previous elections, though it failed to gain an absolute majority of the expanded 113-member assembly (see Legislature, below). The legislative election coincided with the second round of presidential elections on December 4.

In 2008 former prime minister and party chair Hama Amadou was arrested on charges of corruption and subsequently imprisoned, galvanizing his supporters in the party and creating a rift with the backers of President Tandja. The Amadou faction, who viewed him as Tandja's likely successor, also denounced the violence that they alleged had been used against them. Meanwhile, tensions were exacerbated when, at a special congress in February 2009, Amadou was replaced as party chair by Prime Minister Oumarou after Tandja pushed forth a constitutional referendum in an effort to allow him to run for a third term in balloting at the end of the year. (Amadou's backers opposed the proposal.) Shortly thereafter, eight members, including five assembly members—all Amadou supporters—were expelled from the party. The party then named five replacement assembly deputies.

In the 2009 elections the MNSD won 76 assembly seats.

Following the February 2010 coup, party secretary general Albadé Abouba, along with other high-ranking government members, was detained. Though other ministers were quickly released, Abouba, who was a minister at the time of the coup, was kept under house arrest. Despite repeated party protests, junta leaders said he would not be released. Former party secretary general Salissou Mamadou HABI left the MNSD in March 2010 to join Hama Amadou's MODEN-*Lumana* FA/Niger.

The party won 25 seats in the January 2011 parliamentary elections. Abouba was released on March 4 after 379 days in detention with no charges having been brought against him. On March 12 Oumarou, who was backed by the Alliance for National Reconciliation, lost to Issoufou by 16 percentage points in the second-round presidential balloting.

In August 2013 members of MNSD joined the unity government. Abouba was appointed a minister of state, and party members were given three other ministries. However, the MNSD subsequently announced it would boycott the government. Party divisions resulted in two factions emerging by February 2014, one led by Oumarou, the other by Abouba.

Oumarou was the official MNSD candidate in the 2016 presidential election. He placed third with 12.1 percent of the vote, and his party secured 10.3 percent of the vote and 20 seats in the Assembly balloting.

Leaders: Seini OUMAROU (Former Prime Minister and Party Chair, 2011 presidential candidate), Albadé ABOUBA (Secretary General).

Nigerien Movement for Democratic Renewal (*Mouvement Nigérien pour le Renouveau Démocratique*—MNRD-*Hankuri*). The MNRD-*Hankuri* was founded in 2009, but did not contest elections nationally until 2016. That year the party formed an electoral alliance with the **Nigerien Social Democratic Party–*Alhéri*** (*Parti Social Démocrate du Niger–Alhéri*—PSDN-*Alhéri*) that had been established in 1992, but had only limited electoral success. (For more on the PSDN, see the 2013 *Handbook.*) The alliance put forth former president Mahamane Ousmane as its presidential candidate in 2016. He received 6.3 percent of the vote in the first round of balloting. The alliance won 4.2 percent of the vote in the Assembly elections, securing six seats.

Leader: Mahamane OUSMANE (Former Speaker of the National Assembly, Former President of the Republic, and President of the Party).

Nigerien Alliance for Democracy and Progress–*Zaman Lahiya* (*Alliance Nigérienne pour la Démocratie et le Progrès–Zaman Lahiya*—ANDP-*Zaman Lahiya*). On August 28, 1992, ANDP-*Zaman Lahiya* vice president Birgi RAFFINI, a former Saibou government official, was arrested during an army crackdown on suspected **Front for the Liberation of Air and Azaouad** (*Front de Libération de l'Aïr et l'Azaouad*—FLAA) rebels and sympathizers. He was released in early 1993, and his party won 11 seats in legislative balloting that February. ANDP-*Zaman Lahiya*'s candidate, Moumouni Adamou Djermakoye, secured only 15 percent of the vote in the first round of presidential balloting, but his support for the CDS-*Rahama*'s Ousmane was described as pivotal to Ousmane's presidential victory. In April Djermakoye was named National Assembly president. The party's legislative representation fell to 9 seats in January 1995.

In the July 1996 presidential balloting Djermakoye received only 4.8 percent of the vote, finishing last in the five-candidate field. The ANDP-*Zaman Lahiya* was the only major party not to boycott the November 1996 elections, in which it secured eight seats.

In 1998 the ANDP-*Zaman Lahiya* joined the PUND-*Salama* and the PNA (see below) to form a pro-Maïnassara group called the Alliance of Democratic Social Forces (*Alliance des Forces Démocratiques et Sociales*—AFDS). Djermakoye won 7.7 percent of the votes in the first round of presidential balloting in 1999 and endorsed Mahamadou Issoufou of the PNDS-*Tarayya* in the second round. The ANDP-*Zaman Lahiya* agreed to join the progovernment Alliance of Democratic Forces in 2002.

In 2004 presidential candidate Djermakoye received only 6.1 percent of the vote in the first round of balloting, the fifth of six candidates. Since his party belonged to the ruling coalition, his support in the second round likely went to Tandja. ANDP-*Zaman Lahiya* won five seats in the assembly election of 2004.

Despite his support for the president in the past, Djermakoye warned in 2009 that the country "will be split in two" if the president's proposed constitutional referendum were approved. Djermakoye died as he was about to address an opposition rally in June.

The party failed to win seats in the October 2009 parliamentary election. In January 2010 a divided party elected Kindo HAMANI as its interim leader. However, a former MNSD member, Amadou BAGNOU, appeared on television a day later, claiming to be the party's president. In July, Moussa Moumouni Djermakoye, brother of the deceased party leader, was elected party president. He subsequently represented the party in the 2011 presidential election, in which he finished sixth in the first round, with 4 percent of the vote. He backed Issoufou in the second round. The party won eight seats in the 2011 parliamentary election. In August 2013 two party members were appointed to the cabinet, Saley SEYDOU (minister of transport) and Abdoulkarim Dan MALLAM (minister of youth, sports, and culture).

In the 2016 legislative elections, the party won four seats with 3 percent of the vote.

Leader: Moussa Moumouni DJERMAKOYE (President and 2011 presidential candidate).

Patriotic Movement for the Republic (*Mouvement Patriotique pour la Republique*—MPR-*Jamhuriyai*). The MPR was established in October 2015 by defectors from the MNSD. The party did not field a presidential candidate in 2016, but 7.1 percent of the vote in the Assembly balloting and 13 seats.

Leader: Albadé ABOUBA.

Nigerien Patriotic Movement (*Mouvement Patriotique Nigérien*, MPN-*Kishin Kassa*). The MPN-*Kishin Kassa* was founded in November 2015 by renegades from the PNDS, led by Ibrahim YACOUBA. Yacouba was the party's presidential candidate in 2016, but only received 4.3 percent of the vote. The party won 3.3 percent of the vote and five seats.

Leader: Ibrahim YACOUBA.

Other legislative parties include the **Union of Independent Nigeriens** (UNI), led by Amadou Djibo ALI.

Social Democratic Rally–*Gaskiya* (*Rassemblement pour Sociale Democrate–Gaskiya*—RSD-*Gaskiya*). The RSD-*Gaskiya* split off from CDS in January 2004. Amadou Cheiffou, a former transitional prime minister from 1991 to 1993 and party founder, ran as an independent presidential candidate in 2004, receiving only 6.3 percent of the vote in the first round of balloting. However, the new party did win seven seats in the assembly and subsequent representation in the cabinet of President Tandje.

In 2009 the RSD-*Gaskiya* was one of only a few parties that supported President Tandja's plan for a constitutional referendum with the aim of ending presidential term limits. The party won 15 seats in the October assembly elections. In August 2013 RSD member Yahouza Sadissou was appointed minister of communications.

Cheiffou was the party's candidate in the 2016 presidential polling, winning 1.8 percent. The party secured 2.9 percent of the vote in the legislative balloting and four seats.

Leaders: Amadou CHEIFFOU (Former Prime Minister and 2004 and 2016 presidential candidate), Mahamadou Ali TCHÉMOGO (Secretary General).

Other parties that won seats in the 2016 elections included the **Congress for the Republic** (*Congrès Pour la République*—CPR-*Inganc*), founded in 2014 and led by 2016 presidential candidate Maradi Kassoum MOCTAR, which won three seats; the **Alliance of Movements for the Emergence of Niger** (*Alliance des Mouvements pour l'Emergence du Niger—AMEN AMIN*), established in 2015 by Oumarou Harridou Ladan TCHIANA, which won three seats; the **Alliance for Democratic Renewal** (*Alliance pour le Renouveau Démocratique-Adaltchi-Mutunchi*—ARD-*Adaltchi-Mutunchi*), led by 2011 presidential candidate Issoufou Ousmane OUBANDAWAKI, which secured 2 seats; the **Social Democratic Party** (*Parti Sociale Démocrate*, PSD-*Bassira*), created in 2015 by Mohamed Ben OMAR, which won two seats; and the **Democratic Alliance for Niger** (*Alliance Démocratique pour le Niger*—ADN-*Fusaha*), established in 2014 by Habi Mahamadou SALISSOU, which won 1 seat.

Other Parties:

Niger Party for Self-Management (*Parti Nigérien pour l'Autogestion–Al Ouma*—PNA-*Al Ouma*). Former CDS vice chair Sanoussi JACKOU formed the PNA in early 1997. It supported Mamadou Tandja in the 1999 presidential balloting despite its previous affiliation with the AFDS. Chair Jackou received a four-month suspended prison sentence in May 2002 after he was accused of slander and inciting racial hatred. In January 2005 he was released after serving a one-month prison sentence for insulting an ethnic group during a radio broadcast.

In the 2004 legislative elections the PNA was allied in various coalitions along with PNDS-*Tarayya.*

Ahead of the 2009 elections the party participated in protests organized by the umbrella Front for Defense of Democracy (FDD) against President Tandja's constitutional referendum. The party contested the October parliamentary elections alone and won one seat. In the 2016 Assembly elections, the party won only 0.5 percent of the vote and no seats.

Leader: Sanoussi JACKOU.

Nigerien Democratic Front–*Mutunci* (*Front Démocratique Nigerien–Mutunci*—FDN-*Mutunci*). The launching of the FDN-*Mutunci* in late January 1995 represented a redefinition of the **Nigerien Progressive Party** (*Parti Progressiste Nigerien*—PPN), which had previously operated as the local section of the African Democratic Rally (*Rassemblement Démocratique Africaine*—RDA) under the PPN/RDA rubric. The new name was adopted shortly after the group withdrew from the AFC, as it was being increasingly dominated by CDS-*Rahama*. The platform advanced by the FDN-*Mutunci* calls for the "preservation" of Niger's sovereignty and the "strengthening of national cohesion." The party won one seat in the January 1995 balloting and none in November 1996.

Ide OUMAROU was elected chair of FDN-*Mutunci* at a party congress in October 1998. Thereafter, he announced that the group (still widely referred to as the PPN/RDA) would align itself with parties supporting President Maïnassara. It ran in coalition with smaller parties for the 2004 assembly elections.

Former party chair Ide Oumarou died in February 2002. At the time of his death he had been vying with RDA leader Abdoulaye Hamani DIORI, son of the country's first president, to be chair of the party. In 2004 the PPN/RDA contested the assembly elections in separate alliances with the PNDS-*Tarayya* and with the PNDS-*Tarayya* and the PNA-*Al Ouma*.

Diori opposed President Tandja's attempt to extend his term by amending the constitution prior to the 2010 coup, and in the 2011 presidential election, Diori backed Issoufou. On April 7 he was appointed as special counsel to the president in the new government, but he died at age 65 on April 25. In August 2013 PPN/RDA member Maïkibi Kadidiatou DAN DOBI was appointed minister of population, promotion of women, and protection of children.

Leaders: Dan Dicko Dan KOULODO (Former Chair), Oumarou Garba YOUSSOUFOU (1993 presidential candidate), Léopold KAZIENDE.

Union of Popular Forces for Democracy and Progress–*Sawaba* (*Union des Forces Populaires pour la Démocratie et le Progrès–Sawaba*—UFPDP-*Sawaba*). The UFPDP-*Sawaba* is an offshoot of the UDN-*Sawaba*. It was led by Djibo Bakary, a 74-year-old former prime minister and former opponent of President Diori, from May 1957 to December 1958. He was unanimously elected party president in February 1992. Running on a platform calling for national unity and increased dialogue with the Tuareg rebels, Bakary captured 1.68 percent of the presidential vote in February 1993. The party lost both of its former legislative seats in January 1995 and was equally unsuccessful in the November 1996 balloting. Bakary died in 1998.

The UFPDP-*Sawaba* supported Mamadou Tandja in the 1999 presidential poll and was rewarded with a cabinet seat in the January 2000 government. However, the UFPDP-*Sawaba* minister, Issoufou Assoumane, was not reappointed in the September 2001 reshuffle; he formed a new political party in 2001 called the **Union of Nigerien Democrats and Socialists** (*Union des démocrates et socialistes nigériens*—UDSN-*Talaka*), which in 2009 opposed President Tandja's plans to hold a constitutional referendum.

Union for Democracy and Social Progress–*Amana* (*Union pour la Démocratie et le Progrès Social–Amana*—UDPS-*Amana*). On August 28, 1992, (then) UDPS-*Amana* leader Akoli Daouel was imprisoned during the army's crackdown on suspected Tuareg dissidents. He was released in 1993 and later joined the PUND-*Salama*.

A deadly grenade attack on a UDPS-*Amana* meeting at Agades in October 1994 was blamed on Tuaregs angered by ongoing negotiations with the government. Thereafter, in the legislative balloting of January 1995, the party doubled its parliamentary representation to two seats.

Although technically an opposition grouping, the UDPS-*Amana* was awarded a cabinet portfolio by Prime Minister Amadou in February 1995. However, under pressure from opposition allies, who termed the appointment "regrettable," the minister was expelled from the party. The UDPS-*Amana* won three seats in the November 1996 assembly elections. Rhissa ag Boula, formerly with the ORA, joined the UDPS-*Amana* in August 2005. President Tandja met with Boula a few times in 2006 to discuss ways to prevent the Tuareg uprisings in neighboring Mali from spilling over into Niger. In a televised debate in 2007 Rhissa ag Boula expressed concerns over what he described as the "increasing anti-Tuareg xenophobia" and the government's failures to follow through on all aspects of the 1995 peace agreement.

Though he had been involved in the peace process in 2009, Rhissa ag Boula rejoined an MNJ faction abroad, known as the **Front of Forces for Rectification** (*Front des forces de redressement*—FFR). He was arrested and imprisoned by the junta upon his return to Niger following the February 2010 coup. The party secured just 0.1 percent of the vote in the 2016 balloting.

Leaders: Almoctar ICHA, Mohamed ABDULLAHI, Mohamed MOUSSAL, Rhissa ag BOULA.

Other parties include the **Rally of Nigerien Patriots–*Al Kalami***, founded in May 2009 by Ousmane Issoufou OUBANDAWAKI; the **Workers' Movement Party–*Albarka***—PMT-*Albarka*, led by Abdoulkarim MAMALO; and **Revolutionary-Social Democracy** (*Mouvement Socio-Révolutionnaire pour la Démocratie–Damana*—MSRD-*Damana*), led by Ibrahima Saidou MAIGA.

For a listing of minor parties dating to the early 2000s, see the 2009 *Handbook*. For more information on the **Front for the Liberation of Tamoust** (*Front pour la Libération de Tamoust*—FLT), and the **Party for National Unity and Development–*Salama*** (*Parti pour l'Unité Nationale et la Développement–Salama*—PUND-*Salama*), see the 2013 *Handbook*.

Former Rebel Groups:

Organization of the Armed Resistance (*Organisation de la Résistance Armée*—ORA). ORA emerged in March 1995 upon the temporary demise of the CRA (see below) when the FLAA withdrew from the coalition. Successful implementation of a final peace agreement, signed by Rhissa ag Boula on behalf of the ORA on April 25, 1995, was viewed as depending on the resolution of differences between the FLAA and CRA chair Mano Dayak. In June the ORA denounced the inclusion of the so-called self-defense groups in the proposed amnesty, arguing that the groups were responsible for attacks on Tuareg civilians.

At the end of 1996 the Popular Front for the Liberation of the Sahara (*Front Populaire pour la Libération de la Sahara*—FPLS, below) and the **Revolutionary Army of the Liberation of Northern Niger** (*Armée Révolutionaire de Libération du Nord Niger*—ARLNN) reportedly left ORA to join the new UFRA (below) in an attempt to "rationalize" the Tuareg leadership situation. At that point it was not clear if Boula's FLAA would maintain the ORA structure, as FLAA appeared to be the dominant, and perhaps only, component in the ORA. Furthermore, the FLAA also appeared to have distanced itself from the 1995 accord. Such concerns were at least temporarily eased in September 1996 when the ORA reportedly integrated a number of its fighters into the government's newly formed "peacekeeping detachment." (In 1998 the ORA and the CRA turned in their weapons when parliament granted amnesty to the rebel groups in March.) In 1997 Boula was named to the Mayaki government. He remained in the new governments announced in January 2000 and September 2001 but was dismissed from his post as tourism minister in the Tandja government on February 13, 2004. Boula was then arrested and jailed for his alleged involvement in the assassination of a militant member of the ruling party, MNSD-*Nassara,* in January. He was released in March 2005, allegedly after his brother, rebel leader Mohamed ag Boula, claimed he would not release four kidnapped soldiers until his brother was freed. (The hostages returned home in February 2005 after Libya helped secure their release.) Rhissa ag Boula left the ORA in August 2005 and became a leader of the UDPS-*Amana*; he was reported to be living in exile in France. In 2008 he was sentenced to death in absentia by a Nigerien court for the alleged assassination plot dating to 2004. (See Union for Democracy and Social Progress–*Amana*, above.)

Leader: Attaher ABDOULMOUMINE.

Popular Front for the Liberation of the Sahara (*Front Populaire pour la Libération de la Sahara*—FPLS). The FPLS was launched on January 28, 1994, by Mohamed Anako and Issad Kato, who pledged to cooperate with existing Tuareg groups. In April 1999 Anako was reportedly appointed minister without portfolio and special adviser to head of state Maj. Daouda Wanké, a move some observers said was meant to avert further violence following Wanké's ascension after the assassination of President Maïnassara. Issad Kato, who had reestablished relations with the government, was named animal resources minister in 2007. Mohamed Anako in 2007 headed the Nigerien Commission for Peace, which called for dialogue with the Tuareg rebels, and was said to be an adviser to President Tandja.

Coordination of Armed Resistance (*Coordination de la Résistance Armée*—CRA). Originally formed in January 1994 by the FLAA, FPLS, ARLNN, and FLT, the CRA met in Tenere in early February to elect an executive bureau and draft a platform calling for the creation of an autonomous Tuareg territory and Tuareg representation in the armed forces, government, and National Assembly. The coalition participated in talks with the government in Ouagadougou, Burkina Faso, in late February and in Paris in June, which ultimately resulted in a preliminary peace accord on October 9.

The CRA splintered in March 1995 following a disagreement between FLAA leader Boula and CRA chair Mano DAYAK over the latter's approach to renewed peace negotiations. Immediately thereafter, Boula reorganized the CRA members, including the Dayak-led FLT, under the ORA banner; however, in June the FLT withdrew from the coalition. In July Dayak announced that he had revived the CRA; he would no longer respect the peace agreement and further negotiations would have to include his new Toubou and Arab allies (see FARS, below).

In October 1995 FLT militants were accused of violating the peace accord; however, Dayak continued to negotiate with the government, and CRA officials pledged to proceed with peace talks following his death in a plane crash in December. Thereafter, at a summit of the leaders of the Tuareg and Toubou fronts in Kawar on March 8, 1996, the CRA agreed to recognize the 1995 peace accord and joined the others in declaring a unilateral cease-fire as a sign of support for the military regime. Consequently, the junta offered to include the CRA in its "application" of the treaty, and the group signed the accord on April 2.

A split between the CRA and the ORA was reported in November 1996, with the emergence of the new UFRA. Included in the "new" CRA were a number of Toubou and Arab autonomous movements based in the southeast who had complained of being ignored by the peace process.

Leaders: Mohamed AOUTCHEKI Kriska (FLT), Mohammed AKOTE.

For more information on the **Democratic Renewal Front** (*Front Démocratique pour le Renouvellement*—FDR), see the 2015 *Handbook*.

Rebel Groups:

Armed Revolutionary Forces of the Sahara (*Forces Armées Révolutionnaires de la Sahara*—FARS). The primarily Toubou and Arab FARS gained international attention in February 1997 for kidnapping a Canadian aid worker and three Nigerien security officials in an effort to dramatize demands for an inquiry into the death of 14 FARS fighters in a clash with government forces the month before. Following peaceful resolution of that crisis, the FARS signed a cease-fire agreement with the government in June; however, that accord proved short-lived, and the FARS was subsequently reported to have formed an alliance with the UFRA before the latter grouping disarmed in 1998.

In September 2001 the government launched a major crackdown that, among other things, resulted in the death of a FARS leader, Chahayi BARKAYE. In an effort to establish peace, France agreed to help finance the reintegration of some 250 FARS rebels into the northern region of Bilma.

FARS reemerged in 2006 when the group kidnapped and later released 11 tourists in protest against what the group claimed was the ongoing marginalization of the Toubous.

Leaders: Barka OUARDOUGOU, Boubacar Mohamed SOGOMA.

Movement of Nigeriens for Justice (*Mouvement des Nigériens pour la Justice*—MNJ). The Tuareg rebel group was not widely known until after it launched an attack against an army post near the northern town of Iferouane in February 2007. Following a series of attacks over the next several months against army installations, uranium mining sites, Red Cross convoys, and a northern airport, for which the MNJ claimed responsibility, the government refused to acknowledge the group's existence, instead blaming "bandits" and "drug traffickers." The MNJ accused the government of not upholding the tenets of the 1995 peace agreement with the Tuaregs, and called for more economic development in the north, including more equitable distribution of uranium profits; greater representation of Tuaregs in the government, the army, and the police; and government recognition of the MNJ (see Current issues, above). The MNJ reported in mid-2007 that some 700 army deserters had joined its group, including one high-ranking officer. It also claimed to have drawn support from Arabs, Fulani, and Toubou, as well as Tuaregs in Mali, the latter forming a group called the Niger-Mali Tuareg Alliance. In 2008 MNJ leaders stepped up their attacks, including strikes against uranium and oil interests. In June it was reported that MNJ vice president Mohamed Acharif had been killed by Nigerien soldiers. Throughout the year, the group continued to engage in fighting with government forces, but in September the rebels agreed to lay down their arms in a peace deal negotiated by Libya's leader Muammar al-Qadhafi.

Leaders: Agali ag ALAMBO (President), Moktar ROMAN (Spokesperson).

LEGISLATURE

The unicameral **National Assembly** (*Assemblée Nationale*) was enlarged from 113 to 171 members in 2016. Members are directly elected for five-year terms: 158 from 8 multimember constituencies using a proportional representation system. Eight seats are elected from special constituencies reserved for ethnic minorities, while five seats are for Nigeriens abroad (one for each continent). Both the minority and expatriate seats are elected through a first-past-the-post system.

The assembly elected in January 1995 was dissolved by the National Salvation Council on January 27, 1996, and replaced on March 27 by a 600-member transitional body known as the National Forum for Democratic Renewal, which included former assemblymen as well as members of various advisory groups supportive of the new military regime. Balloting for a new assembly was held on November 23, though it was boycotted by most major opposition groups.

On April 10, 1999, Prime Minister Mayaki suspended the assembly in the wake of the assassination of President Maïnassara. Balloting to refill the body was held on November 24, 1999.

In balloting on October 20, 2009, the National Movement for a Developing Society–Victory won an overwhelming majority of seats. Parliament was dissolved following the military coup of February 18, 2010. The new constitution promulgated in November restored a unicameral parliament.

Following the most recent election on February 21, 2016, the seat distribution was as follows: Nigerien Party for Democracy and Socialism–*Tarayya,* 75; Nigerien Democratic Movement for an African Federation–*Lumana,* 25; National Movement for a Developing Society–Victory, 20; Patriotic Movement for the Republic, 13; Nigerien Movement for Democratic Renewal–Party for Socialism and Democracy in Niger, 6; Nigerien Patriotic Movement, 5; Nigerien Alliance for Democracy and Progress–*Zaman Lahiya,* 4; Social Democratic Rally, 4; Democratic and Social Convention–*Rahama,* 3; Congress for the Republic, 3; Democratic Rally of the People–*Jama'a,* 3; Alliance of Movements for the Emergence of Niger, 3; Union for Democracy and the Republic–*Tabbat,* 2; Alliance for Democratic Renewal, 2; Social Democratic Party, 2; and Democratic Alliance for Niger, 1.

Speaker: Ousseini TINNI (PNDS-*Tarayya*).

CABINET

[as of September 25, 2016]

President	Mahamadou Issoufou
Prime Minister	Brigi Rafini (PNDS-*Tarayya*) PNDS)
Council of Ministers	
Civil Service and Administrative Reform	Waziri Maman Laouan
Commerce and Promotion of the Private Sector	Alma Oumarou (MNSD)
Communications	Amina Moumouni [f]
Community Development and Regional Planning	Djika Rakiatou Bako [f]
Cultural Renaissance, Arts, and Social Modernization	Assoumana Mallam Issa (PNDS-*Tarayya*)
Employment, Labor, and Social Security	Chaoulani Zénaba [f]
Energy and Oil	Pierre Foumakoye Gado (PNDS-*Tarayya*)
Entrepreneurship of Youth	Ibrahim Issifi Sadou
Environment and Sustainable Development	Wassalké Boukari (MNSD)
Equipment	Kadi Abdoulaye
Finance	Saidou Sidibé (PNDS-*Tarayya*)
Foreign Affairs, Cooperation, African Integration and Nigeriens Abroad	Ibrahim Yacouba
Higher Education, Scientific Research, and Innovation	Mohamed Ben Omar
Humanitarian Action and Disaster Management	Magagi Laouan
Justice and Keeper of the Seals	Marou Amadou (PNDS-*Tarayya*)
Lands and Urban Development	Moctar Kassoum
Mines and Industry	Hassane Barazé Moussa
National Defense	Massoudou Hassoumi (PNDS-*Tarayya*)
Office of the President	Ouhoumoudou Mahamadou (PNDS-*Tarayya*)
Planning	Kané Aïchatou Boulama [f]
Population	Kaffa Rékiatou Jackou [f]
Posts, Telecommunications, and the Digital Economy	Yahouza Sadissou
Primary Education, Literacy, and Promotion of National Languages	Daouda Marthé
Professional and Technical Education	Amani Abdou
Public Health	Kalla Moutari
Relations with Institutions	Barkaï Issouf
Secondary Education	Sani Abdourahamane
Tourism and Handicrafts	Sani Maïgochi
Towns and Urban Planning	Habi Mahamane Salissou (MNSD)
Water Management and Sanitation	Barmou Salifou
Youth and Sports	Salissou Ada
Ministers of State	
Agriculture	Albadé Abouba (MNSD)
Interior, Public Security, Decentralization, and Religious and Customary Affairs	Bazoum Mohamed (PNDS-*Tarayya*)
Transport	Omar Hamidou Tchiana (MODEN-*Lumana* FA/Niger)

[f] = female

INTERGOVERNMENTAL REPRESENTATION

Ambassador to the U.S.: Hassana ALIDOU.

U.S. Ambassador to Niger: Eunice S. REDDICK.

Permanent Representative to the UN: Abdallah WAFY.

IGO Memberships (Non-UN): AfDB, AU, ECOWAS, IOM, NAM, OIC, WTO.

For Further Reference:

Decalo, Samuel. *Historical Dictionary of Niger.* 3rd ed. Lanham, MD: Scarecrow Press, 1997.

Jenkins, Mark. *To Timbuktu: A Journey down the Niger.* New York: Modern Times, 2008.

Toynbee, Arnold J. *Between Niger and Nile.* Oxford: Oxford University Press, 1965.

NIGERIA

Federal Republic of Nigeria

Political Status: Independent member of the Commonwealth since 1960; republic established in 1963; civilian government suspended as the result of military coups in January and July 1966; executive presidential system established under constitution effective October 1, 1979; under military rule following successive coups of December 31, 1983, and August 27, 1985; constitution of Third Republic promulgated May 3, 1989; existing state organs dissolved following military takeover of November 17, 1993; 1979 constitution restored and Provisional Ruling Council established on November 21, 1993; current constitution entered into effect May 29, 1999, with installation of new civilian government.

Area: 356,667 sq. mi. (923,768 sq. km).

Population: 186,988,000 (2016E—UN); 186,053,386 (2016E—U.S. Census).

Major Urban Centers (2016E—UN): ABUJA (2,586,000), Lagos (13,661,000), Kano (3,676,000), Ibadan (3,243,000), Port Harcourt (2,465,000), Benin City (1,543,000), Onitsha (1,165,000), Kaduna (1,064,000).

Official Language: English (the leading indigenous languages are Hausa, Igbo, and Yoruba).

Monetary Unit: Naira (official rate October 1, 2016: 315.00 naira = $1US).

President: Muhammadu BUHARI (All Progressives Congress); elected on March 28–29, 2015, and sworn in for a four-year term on May 29, to succeed Goodluck JONATHAN (People's Democratic Party).

Vice President: Yemi OSINBAJO (All Progressives Congress); elected along with the president on March 28–29, 2015, and sworn in on May 20, for a term concurrent with the president, succeeding Namadi SAMBO (People's Democratic Party).

THE COUNTRY

The most populous country in Africa and one of the most richly endowed in natural resources, Nigeria extends from the inner corner of the Gulf of Guinea to the border of Niger in the north and to Lake Chad in the northeast. Included within its boundaries is the northern section of the former United Nations Trust Territory of British Cameroons, whose inhabitants voted to join Nigeria in a UN–sponsored plebiscite in 1961. Nigeria's topography ranges from swampy lowland along the coast, through tropical rain forest and open plateau country, to semidesert conditions in the far north. The ethnic pattern is similarly varied, with tribal groups speaking more than 250 languages. The Hausa, Fulani, and other Islamic peoples in the north; the mixed Christian and Islamic Yoruba in the west; and the predominantly Christian Ibo in the east are the most populous groups. Nearly half the population is Muslim, with 40 percent Christian and the remainder adhering to traditional religious practices. Numerous traditional rulers retain considerable influence, particularly in rural areas. Women are responsible for the bulk of subsistence farming, and their participation in the paid work force (about 36 percent) is concentrated in sales and crafts. Following the 2015 legislative elections, women held 20 out of 360 seats (5.6 percent) in the House of Representatives and 7 out of 109 (6.4 percent) in the Senate.

Nigeria's natural resources include petroleum and natural gas, hydroelectric power, and commercially exploitable deposits of tin, coal, and columbite. Oil production of 2.5–2.7 million barrels per day accounts for an estimated 95 percent of exports and provides 80 percent of the government's revenue; some 60–90 percent of Nigerian crude, considered ideal for gasoline production, is exported to the United States. The leading cash crops are cocoa, peanuts, palm products, and cotton, with timber and fish also important.

High oil prices provided significant additional resources in 2004–2005 for the government, which, among other things, established a $6 billion "emergency fund." (For an overview of the Nigerian economy prior to 2004, see the 2013 *Handbook.*) Late in the year, the Paris Club of creditor nations accepted an agreement under which Nigeria could fulfill its obligation to them by paying only $12 billion of the $30 billion owed. In April 2006 Nigeria made its final payment to the Paris Club.

GDP rose by an average of 11 percent per year between 2000 and 2008 (primarily as a result of higher oil prices and significant growth in the non-oil sector), while inflation averaged 12.3 percent and unemployment 20 percent. A modest increase in foreign investment also contributed to the improved economic outlook, as did significant advances in the telecommunication and financial sectors. However, intensified antigovernment activity in the oil-rich Niger Delta subsequently continued to constrain oil production, while most analysts concluded that corruption remained entrenched throughout all levels of government and business, hampering efforts to reduce the 70 percent poverty level. In 2008 the government began to implement IMF-recommended reforms to the banking and fuel sectors. In 2009 Nigeria conducted an audit of the nation's 24 major banks and found 10 were significantly undercapitalized, prompting the central bank to put more than $6 billion into the institutions to keep them solvent (see Current issues, below). In May 2010 the World Bank agreed to loan Nigeria $915 million for infrastructure improvements, while a $23 billion oil investment deal to build new refineries was finalized between Nigeria and China. In 2012 GDP rose by 6.3 percent and inflation increased by 12.2 percent. Estimates were that the unemployment rate exceeded 22 percent. In 2012 Nigeria announced an ambitious program to expand oil production to 4 million barrels per day (see Current issues, below). However, reports indicated in 2013 that as much as 400,000 barrels per day were lost to theft or waste and that as much as $100 billion in oil revenues had been illicitly diverted since 2002.

In 2013 GDP grew by 5.4 percent, while inflation was 8.5 percent. Unemployment was unofficially estimated to be around 24 percent. In 2014 GDP rose by 6.3 percent before slowing to a 2.7 percent increase in 2015 as a result of declining oil prices. GDP expanded by 3.2 percent in 2016. Inflation in 2016 was 10.4 percent, while GDP per capita was $2,929, and official unemployment was 10 percent. In its 2014 annual report on the ease of doing business index, the World Bank ranked Nigeria 169th out of 189 countries in terms of conducting commerce, a sharp decline from 131st the previous year in 2013, and the country remained in 169th place in 2016.

GOVERNMENT AND POLITICS

Political background. Brought under British control during the 19th century, Nigeria was organized as a British colony and protectorate in 1914, became a self-governing federation in 1954, and achieved independence within the Commonwealth on October 1, 1960. Under the guidance of its first prime minister, Sir Abubaker Tafawa BALEWA, Nigeria became a republic three years later, with the former governor general, Dr. Nnamdi AZIKIWE of the Ibo tribe, as president. The original federation consisted of three regions (northern, western, and eastern); a fourth region (the midwestern) was created in 1963.

Independent Nigeria experienced underlying tensions resulting from ethnic, religious, and regional cleavages. Weakened by strife and tainted by corruption, the federal government was overthrown on January 15, 1966, in a coup that cost the lives of Prime Minister Balewa and other northern political leaders and resulted in the establishment of a Supreme Military Council (SMC) headed by Maj. Gen. Johnson T. U. AGUIYI-IRONSI, the Ibo commander of the army. Resentment on the part of northern Muslims toward the predominantly Ibo leadership and

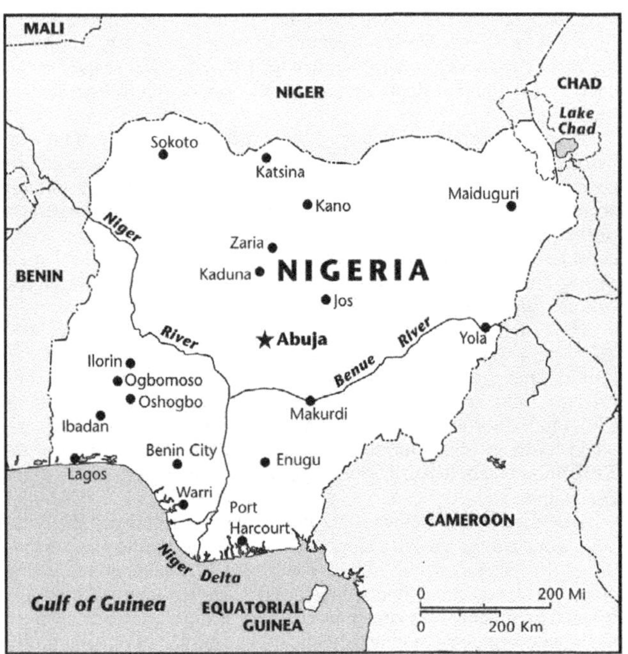

its subsequent attempt to establish a unitary state resulted on July 29 in a second coup, led by a northerner, Col. (later Gen.) Yakubu GOWON. Events surrounding the first coup had already raised ethnic hostility to the boiling point, and thousands of Ibo who had settled in the north were massacred before and after the second coup, while hundreds of thousands began a mass flight back to their homeland at the urging of eastern leaders.

Subsequent plans for a constitutional revision that would calm Ibo apprehensions while preserving the unity of the country were blocked by the refusal of the Eastern Region's military governor, Lt. Col. Odumegwu OJUKWU, to accept anything less than complete regional autonomy. Attempts at conciliation having failed, Colonel Gowon, as head of the federal military government, announced his assumption of emergency powers and the reorganization of Nigeria's four regions into 12 states on May 28, 1967. Intended to equalize treatment of various areas and ethnic groups throughout the country, the move was also designed to increase the influence of the Eastern Region's non-Ibo inhabitants. The Eastern Region responded on May 30 by declaring independence as the Republic of Biafra, with Ojukwu as head of state. Refusing to recognize the secession, the federal government initiated hostilities against Biafra on July 6. Peace plans were subsequently proposed by London, the Commonwealth, and the Organization of African Unity (OAU, subsequently the African Union—AU). However, Ojukwu rejected them repeatedly on the ground that they failed to guarantee Biafra's future as a "sovereign and independent state." Limited external support, mainly from France, began to arrive in late 1968 and enabled Biafra to continue fighting despite the loss of most non-Ibo territory, massive casualties, and a growing threat of mass starvation. A series of military defeats in late 1969 and early 1970 finally resulted in surrender of the rebel forces on January 15, 1970.

The immediate postwar period was one of remarkable reconciliation, as General Gowon moved to reintegrate Ibo elements into Nigerian life. Not only were Ibo brought back into the civil service and the military, but the federal government also launched a major reconstruction of the devastated eastern area. Normal political life remained suspended, however, and on July 29, 1975, while Gowon was attending an OAU meeting in Kampala, Uganda, his government was overthrown in a bloodless coup led by Brig. (later Gen.) Murtala Ramat MUHAMMAD. In October the SMC charged a 50-member committee with drafting a new constitution that would embrace an "executive presidential system."

General Muhammad was assassinated on February 13, 1976, during an abortive coup apparently provoked by his campaign to wipe out widespread government corruption. He was succeeded as head of state and chair of the SMC by Lt. Gen. (later Gen.) Olusegun OBASANJO, who had been chief of staff of the armed forces since the 1975 coup.

A National Constituent Assembly met in 1977 to consider the constitution proposed by the committee established two years earlier. The assembly endorsed a draft on June 5, 1978, although the SMC made a number of changes before the new basic law was promulgated on September 21, at which time Nigeria's 12-year-old state of emergency was terminated and the ban on political parties was lifted.

Elections were contested in mid-1979 by five parties that had been approved by the Federal Electoral Commission (Fedeco) as being sufficiently national in representation. Balloting commenced on July 7 for the election of federal senators and continued, on successive weekends, with the election of federal representatives, state legislators, and state governors, culminating on August 11 with the election of Alhaji Shehu SHAGARI and Dr. Alex EKWUEME of the National Party of Nigeria (NPN) as federal president and vice president, respectively. Following judicial resolution of a complaint that the NPN candidates had not obtained a required 25 percent of the vote in 13 of the 19 states, the two leaders were inaugurated on October 1.

By 1983 public confidence in the civilian regime had waned in the face of sharply diminished oil income, massive government overspending, and widespread evidence of official corruption. Nonetheless, the personally popular Shagari easily won reelection in the presidential balloting of August 4. Subsequent rounds of the five-week election process, marred by evidence of electoral fraud and by rioting in Oyo and Ondo states, left the ruling NPN in control of 13 state houses, 13 governorships, and both houses of the National Constituent Assembly. However, the economy continued to decline after the balloting, with an austerity budget adopted in November further deepening public discontent. On December 31 a group of senior military officers (most of whom had served under Obasanjo) seized power. On January 3, 1984, Maj. Gen. Muhammadu BUHARI, formerly Obasanjo's oil minister, was sworn in as chair of a new SMC, which launched a "war against indiscipline," reintroduced the death penalty, and established several special tribunals that moved vigorously in convicting numerous individuals, including leading politicians, of embezzlement and other offenses.

In the wake of increasing political repression and a steadily worsening economy, Major General Buhari and his armed forces chief of staff, Maj. Gen. Tunde IDIAGBON, were deposed by senior members of the SMC on August 27, 1985. The ensuing administration, headed by Maj. Gen. (later Gen.) Ibrahim BABANGIDA as chair of a new Armed Forces Ruling Council (AFRC), abolished a number of decrees limiting press freedom, released numerous political detainees, and initially adopted a more open style of government that included the solicitation of public opinion on future political development. However, there was a countercoup attempt late in the year by a group of disgruntled officers, several of whom were executed in March 1986.

In September 1987 the Babangida regime announced a five-year transition to civilian government, including the promulgation of a new constitution, lifting of the ban on political parties in 1989, gubernatorial and state legislative elections in 1990, and federal legislative and presidential elections in 1992. To guard against tribal and religious fractionalization, the AFRC adopted the recommendation of a university-dominated "Political Bureau" that only two political parties be sanctioned. Late in 1987 Babangida announced that most former and current leaders, including himself and the rest of the AFRC, would be barred from running in forthcoming elections. Local nonparty elections were held on December 12, 1987; however, many of the results from that poll were invalidated, and further balloting was conducted on March 26, 1988.

In May 1989 General Babangida lifted the ban on party politics, calling on parties to register with the National Electoral Commission (NEC) and announcing details of a draft constitution that had been presented to him in April by the National Constituent Assembly. Although more than 50 parties were reportedly interested in securing recognition, a short enrollment period and a complex application process limited the number of actual petitioners to 13, 6 of which were subsequently recommended to the AFRC for further reduction to 2. However, on October 7, amid reports of the arrest of members of "illegal" parties, Babangida cited "factionalism" and "failing marks" on preregistration examinations as reasons for dissolving all 13 parties and substituting in their place the regime-sponsored Social Democratic Party (SDP) and National Republican Convention (NRC).

In January 1990 General Babangida canceled state visits to Italy and the United States in the wake of widespread unrest provoked by a December 29 reshuffle of senior military and civilian officials. The tension culminated in a coup attempt on April 22 in Lagos by middle-ranked army officers, with at least 30 persons being killed in heavy fighting. On August 30 General Babangida announced another extensive cabinet reshuffle and the appointment of Vice Admiral Augustus

AIKHOMU to the newly created position of vice president of the republic. Shortly thereafter, in furtherance of General Babangida's plan to "demilitarize" politics, Aikhomu and a number of other senior government leaders retired from military service, while ten military state governors were replaced by civilian deputies pending the upcoming gubernatorial elections. Meanwhile, organization of the SDP and NRC continued under stringent government supervision, with two-party local elections being held on December 8.

Neither of the parties secured a clear advantage in the 1990 local poll or in gubernatorial and state assembly elections in December 1991, although the SDP won control of both the Senate and House of Representatives in National Constituent Assembly balloting on July 4, 1992. Party presidential primaries (on August 7 and again on September 12, 19, and 26) were invalidated on grounds of widespread irregularities, with presidential balloting originally slated for December 5 being rescheduled to June 1993. Concurrently, General Babangida announced that the AFRC would be replaced by a National Defense and Security Council (NDSC) and that the existing Council of Ministers would be abolished in favor of a civilian Transitional Council to pave the way for the planned installation of a new government in August 1993. On December 15, 1992, Chief Ernest Adegunle SHONEKAN was named to chair the Transitional Council, which, along with the NDSC, was formally installed on January 4, 1993.

The long-delayed presidential balloting was held on June 12, 1993, with the SDP candidate, reputed billionaire Moshood Kashimawo Olawale "MKO" ABIOLA, appearing to be the winner over the NRC's Bashir Othma TOFA. However, on June 16 the NEC bowed to a court order restraining it from announcing the outcome. The two parties thereupon agreed to form an interim coalition government if General Babangida would authorize a return to civilian rule by the previously agreed upon date of August 27. The general's response being negative, serious rioting erupted in Lagos on July 5, followed by the announcement that a new election, from which the earlier candidates would be excluded, would take place on July 31. Not surprisingly, this plan was scuttled, with Babangida naming Shonekan as head of an Interim National Government (ING) before stepping down as president on August 26. On September 19 the NEC announced that new presidential and local elections would be held on February 19, 1994. However, on November 10 the Federal High Court unexpectedly pronounced the ING unconstitutional, and on November 17 Shonekan resigned in favor of a new military administration headed by Defense Minister Sani Abacha, who had long been viewed as the "power behind the throne" of both the Babangida and Shonekan governments. Subsequently, Abacha formally dissolved both the ING and the National Constituent Assembly, banned the SDP and NRC, and, on November 24, announced the formation of a Provisional Ruling Council (PRC) comprising senior military figures and several members of a new cabinet-level Federal Executive Council (FEC).

On April 22, 1994, the Abacha regime outlined the first phase of a political transition program that called for the convening of a constitutional conference to prepare a draft basic law for approval by the PRC. Elections were held nationwide in May to select the conference participants, although the balloting was boycotted by a number of prodemocracy groups as well as organizations representing southern interests. On June 22, 1994, Moshood Abiola, who, based on the 1993 poll, had declared himself president 11 days earlier, emerged from hiding to address a rally in Lagos; he was arrested the following day for treason. On June 27 General Abacha opened a National Constitutional Conference (NCC), which was promptly adjourned for two weeks because of "logistical problems." Subsequently a large number of strikes erupted to protest Abiola's arrest and resumption of the NCC. The most serious of the stoppages was by the oil unions, whose resistance crumbled in late August after the PRC had replaced their leaders with military-appointed administrators. On September 6, 1994, the PRC issued several new decrees that restricted the media and precluded legal challenges to action taken by the regime in regard to "the maintenance of law and order." Further underscoring the regime's hard-line approach, the new 25-member PRC formed on September 27 contained only military officers, even though 4 of the 11 members on the previous council had been civilians. Meanwhile, NCC sessions continued, and in October the conference gave its preliminary endorsement to a draft constitution (see Constitution and government, below). In addition, the NCC in December formally notified the military that the conference expected the transition to a civilian government to be accomplished by January 1, 1996. Initially appearing to support that schedule, the PRC dissolved the FEC on February 8, 1995, so that members of the council could "prepare for their upcoming political careers." However, the new FEC, which was appointed on March 20, reportedly favored an extension of military control, the apparent policy change being attributed to turbulence surrounding the recent arrest of a group of military officers and civilians in connection with an alleged coup plot. Consequently, on April 25 the NCC reversed its earlier decision regarding the deadline for a return to civilian government and approved a new resolution granting the Abacha regime what amounted to an open-ended tenure. As a result, the final NCC report, submitted to Abacha on June 27, contained the draft of a new basic law but no proposed timetable for its implementation.

The international criticism prompted by the apparent retrenchment on democratization intensified sharply when minority rights activist Kenule SARO-WIWA and other members of the Movement for the Survival of the Ogoni People (MOSOP) were hung on November 10, 1995, soon after their conviction on what were perceived outside the government to be highly dubious murder charges. However, the regime angrily rejected what it termed external meddling in its domestic affairs and refused to reevaluate its proposed timetable, which called for the government to turn authority over to an elected civilian government on October 1, 1998. (See Current issues in the Nigeria entry in the 2007 *Handbook* for details.)

Consequently, Nigeria entered 1996 regarded internationally as a "pariah state," and developments over the next year did little to alter that situation. The government refused to permit Commonwealth representatives into the country until November and, even then, blocked access to prisoners such as former president Obasanjo (jailed since March 1995 on what most analysts considered spurious coup plot charges) and Mobiola. In addition, following a fact-finding mission to Nigeria in March, the UN Human Rights Committee accused the government, already considered one of the most repressive in Nigeria's history, of a wide range of abuses.

Local elections were held on March 16, 1996, although political parties remained proscribed. The campaign period was limited to only five days, and balloting was conducted by having voters line up behind their preferred candidate, a practice long criticized by prodemocracy activists. Facing ongoing internal and external pressure, the government in June issued regulations for the proposed legalization of a limited number of political parties, five of which were recognized in September, although the initiative elicited only scorn from prodemocracy groups. Six new states were established on October 1, and the government announced that 183 additional municipalities would be created for the next local elections, with balloting to be conducted on a limited multiparty basis.

Two bomb attacks in Lagos killed several soldiers and wounded more than 30 other people in January and February 1997; no groups claimed responsibility. The government subsequently intensified its crackdown on opposition groups, among other things charging Nobel Prize winner Wole SOYINKA (in self-imposed exile) and 14 other dissidents with treason in March. Spokespersons for the regime linked several subsequent attacks to the National Democratic Coalition (NADECO), although impartial observers strongly questioned any such connection and suggested the government was merely attempting to silence some of its more effective critics. Harassment was also reported of journalists who questioned the regime. New local elections were held on March 15, 1997, followed by balloting for state assemblies on December 6. Meanwhile, on November 17 President Abacha announced that the cabinet had been dissolved, a number of incumbent senior ministers being left out of the new government appointed on December 18.

In national legislative elections on April 25, 1998, the United Nigeria Congress Party (UNCP) reportedly captured the majority of the seats. Voter turnout was described as scant (as little as 10 percent in some areas), with many Nigerians apparently heeding the opposition's call for a boycott of the contest. Meanwhile, Abacha was reportedly named as the candidate of all the legal parties for the upcoming presidential election. On June 8 Abacha died of an apparent heart attack, and the following day Gen. Abdulsalam ABUBAKAR was sworn in as his replacement. Opposition militants derided Abubakar's inaugural pledge to adhere to his predecessor's transitional program, and in mid-June government troops forcibly broke up an opposition demonstration. Thereafter, Abubakar approved the release of dozens of political prisoners, and in early July UN secretary general Kofi Annan announced that the regime was preparing to release all political prisoners, including Abiola, who had reportedly agreed to relinquish his claim to the presidency. However, on July 7 (the eve of his release) Abiola fell ill during a meeting with a high-level U.S. mission and died. On July 8 General Abubakar dissolved the five legal parties as well as the government that had been named by General Abacha. Two weeks later Abubakar called for the creation of an "unfettered" democracy and announced that he would soon release all political prisoners and allow the free formation of political parties. To that end, in early August the regime appointed a 14-member electoral commission, the Independent National Electoral Commission (INEC), which it charged with overseeing a transitional schedule expected to culminate in the return to civilian rule in May 1999. On August 21 Abubakar named a new cabinet, which included only five holdovers from the Abacha government. Four days later, the INEC released an electoral timetable calling for local elections in December, gubernatorial polling in January 1999, and legislative and presidential balloting on February 20 and 27, respectively. Twenty-five political groups applied for provisional legal status between August 27 and September 5, and nine were subsequently registered. However, in local elections in December only three of those parties—the People's Democratic Party (PDP), the All People's Party (APP), and the Alliance for Democracy (AD)—secured the minimum vote tally (at least 5 percent in 24 of the 36 states) required to maintain their legal status and continue on to the next electoral stages. The PDP, under the leadership of General Obasanjo, led all parties in the local balloting with approximately 60 percent of the vote.

In gubernatorial elections held January 9–30, 1999, the PDP once again overwhelmed its competitors, capturing 21 of the 36 state houses (unrest in the state of Bayelsa had forced officials to postpone balloting there from January 9 to January 30). Seeking to prevent further PDP domination, the APP and AD subsequently announced their intention to form an electoral alliance and forward a joint candidate for president. On February 5 the INEC ruled that such an alliance would be illegal; however, faced with an APP/AD threat to boycott further elections, the commission subsequently reversed itself, although it precluded the two groups from using a single symbol on ballot papers.

The PDP won approximately two-thirds of the seats in both the Senate and House of Representatives in poorly attended legislative polling on February 20, 1999. In presidential balloting on February 27, General Obasanjo completed the sweep for the PDP, capturing 62.8 percent of the vote and easily defeating Samuel Oluyemisi "Olu" FALAE, the APP/AD candidate. International observers asserted that the elections "generally" reflected the "will of the people" but refused to describe them as free and fair because both sides appeared to have tried to rig the balloting. Obasanjo was sworn in on May 29, and on the same day the new constitution (signed by General Abubakar on May 5) also came into effect. On June 28 Obasanjo swore in a new 47-member cabinet, claiming the large size was necessary to represent Nigeria's ethnic and regional diversity. The government included representatives from all 36 states as well as ministers from all three registered parties.

The incoming Obasanjo administration and PDP-dominated legislature confronted economic, political, and social problems of immense proportions in 1999. Among the most pressing issues awaiting the new government were violent political and social unrest in the economically critical oil-producing regions, a decayed infrastructure, and a treasury depleted by corruption. As a first step in his anticorruption program, Obasanjo in June expelled 60 senior military officers and suspended all contracts negotiated by the Abacha government.

Ethnic tensions in the oil-producing Niger Delta escalated throughout the fall of 1999, resulting in the deployment of 2,000 government troops to the state of Bayelsa. Political discord increased significantly in June 2001 when religious and ethnic conflict between Christians and Muslims in the northern state of Bauchi left 1,000 dead. Another 1,000 were killed in continuing violence in the region before the end of the year. One area of dispute involved Muslim efforts to implement sharia (Islamic religious law) in the region. (A dozen northern states instituted sharia, despite opposition from the federal government.) In addition, a series of general strikes by oil workers threatened to disrupt production.

The registration of political parties having begun in 2002, multiparty legislative and presidential elections were held on April 12, 2003. The PDP again won a commanding majority in both the House of Representatives and the Senate, its strongest opposition coming from the All Nigeria People's Party (ANPP), the successor to the APP. Gubernatorial races were also held on April 19, and the PDP secured 29 of the 36 governorships. In addition, the PDP also won about two-thirds of the total seats in the state assemblies in elections held May 3.

President Obasanjo was reelected with 62 percent of the vote in balloting on April 19, 2003, that was contested by 20 candidates. His closest rival was former SMC chair Buhari, with 32 percent; no other candidate received more than 3.5 percent of the vote. Buhari challenged the results, but the federal Court of Appeal ruled in favor of Obasanjo, who was inaugurated on May 29. However, it was not until July 17 that Obasanjo was able to form a new federal government.

President Obasanjo's second term was initially marked by efforts at economic reform and a broad range of anticorruption campaigns, but strikes and other problems in the petroleum sector continued to constrain the government's efforts. On May 18, 2004, because of the escalating violence between Christians and Muslims in the region, Obasanjo declared a state of emergency for Plateau State and ordered the federal government to take control from the state governor and assembly, the first time that the federal government had taken over a state since 1962. A similar state of emergency was also declared in Ekiti in October 2006.

The government convened a National Political Reforms Conference (NPRC) in February 2005 in an effort to ease tensions among the regions. After contentious debate, the conference in April issued a report that called for increased oil revenues to be allocated to southern and eastern regions and rejected the proposed revision of the constitution to permit Obasanjo to run for a third term. The latter issue was permanently put to rest in May 2006 when the Senate blocked an amendment presented by supporters of a third term. (Obasanjo agreed to abide by that ruling.)

The other dominant issue in late 2005 and early 2006 was sustained severe discord in the oil-rich Niger Delta region. Two groups—the Niger Delta's People's Volunteer Force (NDPVF) and the Movement for the Emancipation of the Niger Delta (MEND)—claimed responsibility for a number of attacks on pipelines and kidnappings designed to disrupt production. Their goals were greater autonomy for the region and compensation for environmental damage done by oil companies in the state of Bayelsa. In June 2006 MEND declared a "cease-fire" after a Nigerian court ordered Shell (the country's largest oil producer) to pay $1.5 billion for environmental "reparations." However, MEND conducted new attacks in August. In response to the continued unrest, federal security forces launched an offensive in the region that led to more than 100 arrests but did not substantially reduce the level of violence.

A political feud between President Obasanjo and Vice President Atiku ABUBAKAR over control of the PDP led the president in September 2006 to ask the Senate to impeach Abubakar on corruption charges. The High Court in November blocked the impeachment effort, thereby apparently permitting Abubakar to become a candidate for the 2007 presidential election. However, the PDP subsequently nominated Umar YAR'ADUA, a relative unknown within the party, fueling speculation that Obasanjo had orchestrated the nomination. (Abubakar subsequently left the PDP to stand as the candidate of a new small party called the Action Congress of Nigeria [ACN].)

In January 2007 President Obasanjo announced a major cabinet reshuffle in which a number of ministries were eliminated. The initiative was presented as a means of streamlining the government and reducing corruption, with a view toward enhancing the ruling party's domestic approval in advance of the 2007 elections.

The PDP dominated the elections for governorships and state assemblies on April 14, 2007, as well as the federal balloting for the Senate and House of Representatives on April 21. Also on April 21, Umaru Musa Yar'Adua, nominated by the PDP after efforts to revise the constitution to permit President Obasanjo to run for a third term were blocked, handily won the presidential poll, securing more than 70 percent of the vote. International and domestic observers strongly criticized the elections for fraud at the local, state, and national levels. The courts subsequently ordered new balloting for a number of offices, but a special tribunal in February 2008 upheld the presidential results.

Following Yar'Adua's inauguration on May 29, 2007, the new president formed what he described as a new "government of national unity" on July 26. Although dominated by the PDP, the new cabinet was noteworthy for the inclusion of independents and members of the ANNP and several other new small parties.

The new government's first year in office was marked by an anticorruption campaign that snared a number of officials from the Obasanjo administration. Yar'Adua initiated a major cabinet reshuffle in October 2008 and finalized the new government in December. Another, minor, reshuffle occurred in July 2009, as part of a broader anti-corruption campaign by the government that included a program to spend more than $2 billion to reform the federal security forces (see Current issues, below). Yar'Adua left Nigeria for medical treatment in Saudi Arabia for a heart condition on November 23. He remained hospitalized out of the country until February of the next year.

On February 9 the Assembly enacted legislation that made Vice President Goodluck JONATHAN acting president in light of Yar'Adua's continuing medical problems. Jonathan appointed a new cabinet on April 6. Yar'Adua died on May 5, and Jonathan was sworn in as president the following day to complete the remainder of the former president's term (see Current issues, below). The governor of Kaduna, Namadi SAMBO of the PDP, was appointed vice president.

Jonathan was elected for a full term in the first round of presidential balloting on April 16, 2011. In legislative balloting that began on April 9 the PDP maintained a commanding majority in the Senate, with 71 seats, followed by the Action Congress of Nigeria (ACN) with 18 seats (no other party secured more than 8 seats). In the House of Representatives the PDP secured a reduced majority with 202 seats, followed by the CAN, 66 seats, and the CPC, 35 (see Current issues, below). The PDP also won 18 of the 26 gubernatorial elections. Jonathan finalized a new government on July 14.

In March 2012 five gubernatorial elections were held after the Supreme Court ruled in January that the terms of the governors had expired in 2011. All of the governors had been originally elected in 2007 but were forced to compete in new elections in 2008 because of irregularities in the balloting. All of the governors were members of the PDP. Four were reelected. The fifth stood down, but another PDP candidate won the balloting. The president conducted a minor cabinet reshuffle on May 24. Another minor reshuffle occurred on October 31. On February 4, 2013, Kabiru Saminu TURAKI was appointed a minister in the office of the presidency and tasked to oversee the government response to rising Islamic extremism (see Current issues, below). In December six ministers and three ministers of state were dismissed in a cabinet reshuffle. Their replacements were confirmed in February 2014. Between February and March 2014, three additional ministers and a secretary of state were dismissed.

Elections were postponed from February 14, 2015, because of technical difficulties with voter identification cards and violence by *Boko Haram* (see Current issues, below). In balloting on March 28–29, 2015, former dictator Mohammadu Buhari (APC) defeated President Jonathan, with 54 percent of the vote to the incumbent's 45 percent, in a surprise victory. There were 12 other minor candidates, none of whom received more than 0.2 percent of the vote. In concurrent legislative elections, the APC won 225 seats in the House of Representatives, followed by the PDP with 125, among other parties. In the Senate, the APC secured 60 seats and the PDP, 49. The APC also won 19 governorships to 7 for the PDP. Buhari named an APC cabinet in September and gained Senate approval in October. The ministers took office on November 11.

Constitution and government. In February 1976 it was announced that the 12 states created in 1967 would be expanded to 19 to alleviate the domination of subunits by traditional ethnic and religious groups. A centrally located area of some 3,000 square miles was also designated as a federal capital territory, with the federal administration to be transferred (a process declared completed in late 1991) from Lagos to the new capital of Abuja. New states were progressively added, bringing the total to 36. (See the 2013 *Handbook* for more information.) In 1996 it was also announced that 183 new municipalities would be established, bringing the total to 776.

Region (Pre-1967)	*State (1967)*	*State (1987)*	*State and Capital (1996)*	*Population (2006C)*
Northern	Benue Plateau	Benue	Benue (Makurdi)	4,219,244
			Kogi (Lokoja) †*	3,278,487
		Plateau	Plateau (Jos)	3,178,712
			Nassatawa (Lafia) ‡	1,863,275
	Kano	Kano	Kano (Kano)	9,383,682
			Jigawa (Dutse) †	4,348,649
	Kwara	Kwara	Kwara (Ilorin)	2,371,089
	North-Central	Kaduna	Kaduna (Kaduna)	6,066,562
		Katsina	Katsina (Katsina)	5,792,578
	North-Eastern	Bauchi	Bauchi (Bauchi)	4,676,465
			Gombe (Gombe) ‡	2,353,879
		Borno	Borno (Maiduguri)	4,151,193
			Yobe (Damaturu) †	2,321,591
		Gongola	Adamawa (Yola) †	3,168,101
			Taraba (Jalingo) †	2,300,736
	North-Western	Niger	Niger (Minna)	3,950,249
		Sokoto	Sokoto (Sokoto)	3,696,999
			Kebbi (Birnin Kebbi) ‡	3,238,628
			Zamfara (Gusau) ‡	3,259,846
Eastern	East-Central	Anambra	Anambra (Akwa)	4,182,032
			Enugu (Enugu) †	3,257,298
		Imo	Imo (Owerri)	3,934,899
			Abia (Umuahia) †	2,833,999
			Ebonyi (Abakaliki) ‡**	2,173,501
	Rivers	Rivers	Rivers (Port Harcourt)	5,185,400
			Bayelsa (Yenagoa) ‡	1,703,358
	South-Eastern	Cross River	Cross River (Calabar)	2,888,966
		Akwa Ibom	Akwa Ibom (Uyo)	3,920,208
Mid-Western	Mid-Western	Bendel	Delta (Asaba) †	4,098,391
			Edo (Benin) †	3,218,332
Western	Lagos	Lagos	Lagos (Ikeja)	9,013,534
	Western	Ogun	Ogun (Abeokuta)	3,728,098
		Ondo	Ondo (Akure)	3,441,024
			Ekiti (Ado-Ekiti) ‡	2,384,212
		Oyo	Oyo (Ibadan)	5,591,589
			Osun (Oshogbo) †	3,423,535
			Abuja, Federal Capital Territory	1,405,201

Notes: † created in 1991; ‡ created in 1996; *also includes territory from Kwara; **also includes territory from Enugu.

The 1979 constitution established a U.S.-style federal system with powers divided among three federal branches (executive, legislative, and judicial) and between federal and state governments. Executive authority at the national level was vested in a president and vice president who ran on a joint ticket and served four-year terms. To be declared the victor on a first ballot, a presidential candidate was required to win a plurality of the national popular vote and at least one-quarter of the vote in two-thirds of the (then) 19 states. Legislative power was invested in a bicameral National Assembly comprising a 95-member Senate and a 449-member House of Representatives.

Upon assuming power on December 31, 1983, the Supreme Military Council (SMC) suspended those portions of the constitution "relating to all elective and appointive offices and representative institutions." A constitutional modification decree issued in January 1984 established a Federal Military Government encompassing the SMC; a National Council of States, headed by the chair of the SMC and including the military governors of the 19 states, the chief of staff of the armed forces, the inspector-general of police, and the attorney general; and a cabinet-level Federal Executive Council (FEC). The decree also provided for state executive councils headed by the military governors. Following the coup of August 1985, the SMC was renamed the Armed Forces Ruling Council (AFRC), and the FEC was renamed the National Council of Ministers. The chair of the AFRC was empowered to serve as both the head of state and chief executive. However, responsibility for "civilian political affairs" was delegated to a chief of general staff. Following the AFRC's announcement in September

1987 of a five-year schedule for return to civilian government, a 46-member Constitution Review Committee was created to prepare a revision of the 1979 basic law.

In May 1988 a 567-member Constituent Assembly was established to complete the work of the Constitution Review Committee. The most controversial issue faced by the assembly was the proposed institution of sharia, which was not favored by Muslim president Babangida or the Christian population. Unable to reach agreement, the assembly provided two separate and divergent submissions on the matter, which the president stated the AFRC would review in the context of "the national interest."

The draft constitution of the "Third Republic," presented to the AFRC by the Constituent Assembly in April 1989, mirrored the 1979 basic law with the notable addition of anticorruption measures and extension of the presidential term to six years. The document took no position on sharia, as Babangida claimed the issue would constrain debate on other provisions and should be addressed separately at a future time. The existing judiciary was left largely intact, although it was enjoined from challenging or interpreting "this or any other decree" of the AFRC.

A new National Assembly was elected on July 4, 1992, and convened on December 5. Presidential balloting was, however, deferred until June 12, 1993, with a return to constitutional government scheduled for the following August 27. In the meantime, a Transitional Council, with a chair as nominal head of government, was designated to serve in a quasi-executive capacity. The system nonetheless remained tutelary, since both legislative and executive actions were subject to review by the president and the military-civilian National Defense and Security Council (NDSC). Coincident with President Babangida's resignation in 1993, the Transitional Council was abolished, not in favor of a constitutional government but of an Interim National Government (ING), which was in turn superseded by the Provisional Ruling Council (PRC)/Federal Executive Council (FEC) in November.

The 369 participants in the constitutional conference that convened on June 27, 1994, had been selected in widely boycotted balloting on May 23 and 28 from a list of PRC-approved candidates. The conference's recommendations were formally submitted to the PRC on June 27, 1995, and the provisions in the new proposed basic law called for a presidency that would rotate between the north and the south, the election of three vice presidents, the creation of several new states, and the installation of a transition civilian government pending new national elections. However, many of the 1995 document's provisions were not included in the draft charter released by the Abubakar regime for comments in September 1998. The new draft more resembled the 1979 constitution, providing for a strong, executive president responsible for nominating a cabinet subject to senate approval. At the state level, power was vested in a popularly elected governor and the state legislature. In early 1999 the regime announced that it had agreed on details of the new constitution, which was promulgated into law in May. The 1999 document codified a federal system comprising 36 states and the federal capital territory. The states were divided into 776 local government districts and municipalities. The term of office for the president and the two-house legislature (both elected by universal suffrage) was set at four years, renewable only once for the president.

Prior to the scheduled 2011 elections, the Assembly approved a constitutional change in October 2010 that required national elections to be held between 30 and 150 days prior to the May inauguration date (see Current issues, below).

Nigerian journalists have been significantly affected by the violence that pervades political life, suffering, according to watchdog organizations, beatings and arrests at the hands of local, regional, and national officials who operate for the most part with impunity. "Abusive judicial procedures" are also often initiated against journalists for articles that have irked authorities, according to Reporters Without Borders, which has characterized the State Security Service as a "press freedom predator." The group ranked Nigeria 116th out of 180 countries in terms of freedom of the press in 2016.

Foreign relations. As a member of the United Nations, the Commonwealth, and the OAU following independence, Nigeria adhered to a policy of nonalignment, opposition to colonialism, and support for liberation movements in all white-dominated African territories. (For more information on the history of Nigerian Foreign relations, see the 2012 *Handbook.*) At the regional level, Nigeria was the prime mover in negotiations leading to the establishment in 1975 of the Economic Community of West African States (ECOWAS) and spearheaded the ECOWAS military and political involvement in Liberia in 1990 and Sierra Leone in 1998.

Benin and Cameroon have challenged Nigerian territorial claims along the Benin-Nigeria border and in offshore waters, respectively. In 1989 President Babangida sought to repair relations that had been strained by expulsion of illegal aliens by the Shagira regime, primarily by providing Benin with financial assistance. Cameroon and Nigeria continued to assert rival claims to the Bakassi Peninsula, several deaths having been reported during military clashes in 1994 in that oil-rich region. Briefs in the case were submitted to the International Court of Justice (ICJ) during the first half of 1995, but tension stemming from the dispute subsequently remained high. Seeking to repair relations even as legal wrangling over the region continued, president-elect Obasanjo visited Cameroon in early 1999.

In 2002 the ICJ ruled in favor of Cameroon in the border dispute. The governments of both Cameroon and Nigeria subsequently entered into the UN-brokered talks to implement the decision. By 2003 Nigeria had turned over more than 30 small villages to Cameroon in exchange for control of a small area. A second round of territorial exchange occurred in July 2004, and diplomatic relations were also restored between the two countries. However, in September the Obasanjo administration refused to participate in a third round of land exchange, which led to a new UN mediation effort (see entry on Cameroon). (In 2006 Obasanjo signed a UN-brokered agreement regarding a final settlement.)

Relations with Benin were also strengthened in the early 2000s. Joint border patrols were initiated in 2002 between the two states, which subsequently agreed to redraw their borders. Three areas claimed by Nigeria were turned over to Nigeria in return for its release of seven areas claimed by Benin. In addition, in May 2003 Nigeria and Benin agreed, along with Ghana and Togo, to the construction of a 1,000-kilometer pipeline to transship oil. In 2006 Obasanjo signed a UN-brokered agreement regarding a final settlement.

Relations between Nigeria and the United Kingdom, weakened by the flight to Britain of a number of political associates of former president Shagari, were formally suspended in mid-1984, when British police arrested a Nigerian diplomat and expelled two others for the attempted kidnapping of former transport minister Umaru DIKKO, who was under indictment in Nigeria for diversion of public funds. Full relations with the United Kingdom resumed in February 1986, with Dikko being denied asylum in early 1989.

Despite Nigeria's admission to full membership in the Organization of the Islamic Conference (OIC) in 1986, intense Christian opposition, prompted the country to formally repudiate its links to the conference in 1991, although the OIC continued to list Nigeria as one of its members. Muslims objected strenuously to the 1991 reversal of an 18-year lapse in relations with Israel, although the Babangida regime two years earlier had recognized the Palestinian claim to statehood.

In February 1998 Nigerian troops were at the vanguard of the ECOWAS Monitoring Group (Ecomog) that invaded Freetown, Sierra Leone, in an effort to restore to power the democratically elected government of Ahmed Tejan Kabbah. (Kabbah had been forced into exile in the aftermath of the military coup [see entry on Sierra Leone for further details].)

In 2003 Liberian leader Charles Taylor accepted a Nigerian proposal whereby he received asylum in Nigeria in exchange for surrendering power. Taylor left Liberia for Nigeria in August 2003 and settled in Calabar. Nigeria then contributed 1,500 troops to the UN-sponsored peacekeeping mission to Liberia in October 2003.

The new civilian regime installed in 1999 received much international praise for its attempt to eliminate widespread corruption and its commitment to democratic practices. Among other things, the United States restored military ties and announced that Nigeria would receive $10 million in military aid. In addition, a U.S.–Nigerian committee was established in 2005 to address regional security issues as well as to combat violence in Nigeria's oil-producing areas.

In March former Liberian leader Taylor tried to flee from Nigeria when it became apparent that President Obasanjo planned to extradite him. However, Taylor was captured and turned over to a special UN court for trial on charges of having committed war crimes. In June Nigeria withdrew its citizens from the Bakassi Peninsula as part of an additional UN-sponsored border agreement with Cameroon. Nigeria also relocated 13 villages located along its border with Niger to move them from disputed territory. In November Nigeria finalized an agreement under which South Korea agreed to spend $10 billion on Nigerian railways in return for preferential treatment in regard to future oil contracts. In February 2007 Nigeria, Benin, and Togo signed an agreement to increase security and economic cooperation, in part through the proposed creation of a three-state common market.

Nigeria formally handed over the Bakassi Peninsula to Cameroon in August 2008. (Some 100,000 of the approximately 300,000 residents on the peninsula [most of whom consider themselves Nigerian] had reportedly already relocated to Nigeria proper.) Following the demarcation of the maritime border between Nigeria and Cameroon, the two countries agreed to work together to develop what were expected to be rich offshore oilfields.

In May 2009 the U.S. firm Halliburton revealed that it had paid several million dollars in bribes to Nigerian officials in exchange for energy contracts worth more than $6 billion. The revelations prompted the government to establish investigations in several large agreements with foreign firms. Nigeria and Russia signed a joint agreement in June, worth $2.5 billion, to expand Nigeria's gas production capabilities. Also in June, China and Nigeria finalized a broad accord to improve the quality and safety of products imported from China. In July the EU pledged more than $110 million in development aid to the Niger Delta. In November the EU and Nigeria agreed to a $1 billion accord to promote development in the Niger Delta and to fund peace-building measures. On November 20 a Swiss court ordered more than $350 million in assets owned by the son of former president Abacha seized as part of an ongoing investigation into corruption that had already returned more than $700 million to Nigeria. In August 2010 the Nigerian government filed suit against U.S. energy company Halliburton for bribes paid to Nigerian officials between 1996 and 2005.

On August 25, 2011, a car bomb exploded at the UN office in Lagos, killing 18 and wounding more than 60. The attack was blamed on a new Islamic extremist group, *Boko Haram* (see Current issues, below). Also in August, a British court ordered the Anglo-Dutch oil firm Shell to establish a $410 billion trust fund to compensate the Ogoni people for environmental damage from oil spills.

Continuing unrest (see Current issues, below) in northern Nigeria in December 2011 prompted Jonathan to close the borders with Niger and Chad after evidence revealed that militants were launching attacks from bases in the two countries. On March 8, 2012, British and Nigerian special operations forces attempted to rescue a British and an Italian hostage who had been abducted by *Boko Haram.* Both hostages were killed in the raid. In response to increased *Boko Haram* attacks, the United States announced new intelligence and security cooperation with the Nigerian government. Relations between Nigeria and the UK were reported to have become strained after the Nigerian Senate passed a measure that criminalized gay marriage. Also in 2012, Nigeria and China announced a joint venture to construct three new refineries in Lagos.

Relations between Nigeria and Saudi Arabia deteriorated sharply in September 2012 when Saudi officials deported more than 600 Nigerian women pilgrims for travelling without "a male guardian." In response, Nigeria cancelled flights to Saudi Arabia and argued that an existing bilateral agreement exempted its citizens from the rule.

Nigeria deployed 900 troops to Mali in January 2013 as part of an ECOWAS force, the African International Support Missions to Mali (AFISMA) (see entry on Mali). AFISMA was commanded by a Nigerian general. The intervention in Mali followed growing reports that *Boko Haram* fighters had established bases there. In April seven French hostages were released by *Boko Haram,* reportedly in exchange for a $3.15 million ransom. The French government denied any ransom had been paid. Also in April, Nigeria and Austria signed an accord to promote investment between the nations. The next month, Nigeria and Cuba signed a treaty to expand sports cooperation between the two countries. In November the United States formally designated *Boko Haram* a terrorist organization.

Nigeria was elected as a non-permanent member of the UN Security Council for a term that began January 1, 2014. Nigeria rejected an ECOWAS economic partnership agreement (EPA) with the EU in March. The accord would have granted ECOWAS states immediate access to EU markets. In return, the EU would gain access to 75 percent of the region's markets over a 20-year period. The EU would also offer $8.9 billion to mitigate any immediate negative consequences of the EPA. Although the majority of ECOWAS states favored the EPA, Nigerian officials asserted it would result in job losses and reduced government revenue. In June officials from Nigeria and Pakistan signed four accords to increase security and counter-terrorism cooperation between the two countries.

In January 2015 Royal Dutch Shell agreed to clean up areas of the Niger Delta that were contaminated by oil spills in 2008. Shell also announced it would pay $86 million in reparations to the Bodo community, which was affected by the spills. Nigeria signed an $80 billion agreement with the Russian energy firm Rosatom in April for the construction of four nuclear power plants in the country. Rosatom estimated that it would have the first plant completed in 2025.

The World Bank provided Nigeria with $1.5 billion in 2015 as part of an effort to keep the government solvent in response to declining oil prices. In addition, the World Bank pledged to provide $2 billion to rebuild areas impacted by the *Boko Haram* insurgency.

Current issues. A 2009 government offensive against MEND fighters left hundreds dead, including civilians, and led MEND to launch retaliatory strikes against oil facilities. On June 8, 2009, Royal Dutch Shell consented to pay $15.5 million to people along the Niger delta to settle court cases brought against the energy giant. Also in June, Yar'Adua announced an amnesty program and 60-day ceasefire for MEND fighters (see Political parties, below). Meanwhile fighting in July between government forces and an Islamic militant group alternatively known as *Al Sunna Wal Jamma* or *Boko Haram* left more than 700 dead and thousands displaced. Police captured group's leader Mohammad Yusuf, who subsequently died in custody. Audits in August revealed widespread corruption in the financial sector and led the Central Bank to replace the heads of five of the nation's largest banks. The investigations were in response to bad loans and other problems that caused the Nigerian stock market to lose 65 percent of its value between March 2008 and March 2009. In response, the Central Bank allocated more than $6 billion to shore up the banking sector.

Yar'Adua fell ill in November 2009 because of a heart condition and died on May 5, 2010. Vice President Goodluck Jonathan was appointed to replace the ailing chief executive. Jonathan dismissed the cabinet on March 17 and appointed a new government the following month. Reports indicated that the new cabinet had been purged of Yar'Adua loyalists. Jonathan was inaugurated to serve the remainder of Yar'Adua's term on May 6. Reports that Jonathan, a southern Christian, would seek reelection, prompted protests and condemnation among northern Muslims since within the PDP the presidency unofficially rotated between the six regions of the country, and Yar'Adua was a northern Muslim. Also in May, police in the UAE arrested former Delta governor James IBORI who was wanted for corruption and embezzlement. The arrest was reportedly part of a broader anticorruption campaign by Jonathan (Ibori subsequently pled guilty to ten counts of corruption and was sentenced to 13 years imprisonment).

Renewed fighting in 2010 in Jos left more than 600 dead. Meanwhile, in March, MEND announced an end to a cease-fire followed by two car bombings in Warri. Jonathan dismissed the head of the election commission in April because of charges related to fraud during the 2007 elections. Bombings in Abuja on October 1, 2010, the national independence day holiday, killed 12 and were widely blamed on MEND.

Presidential and legislative elections scheduled for January 2011 were postponed until April following negotiations between the national electoral commission and political parties. The change required a constitutional amendment, approved on October 28, 2010, which reduced the amount of time between balloting and the inauguration of officials.

In late 2010 *Boko Haram* launched a campaign of bombings and assassinations against the government and Christian targets. Described as the "Nigerian Taliban," the group was reported to have established ties with al-Qaida. Attacks in the northern areas of the country led to the deployment of more than 400 security personnel in October 2010. In June 2011 a series of *Boko Haram* attacks killed more than 50 Nigerians.

In national elections on April 16, 2011, Jonathan was elected president with 58.9 percent of the vote. His closest rival was Buhari with 32 percent (no other candidate received more than 6 percent of the vote). In balloting on April 9 and 26, 2011, the PDP secured majorities in both houses of the legislature in balloting that domestic and international observers described as among the freest and fairest in recent Nigerian history. The northern areas of the country were wracked by postelection violence as supporters of Buhari and other opposition candidates rejected the results and protested what they perceived to be Jonathan's violation of the unofficial rotation of the presidency between the north and south. More than 500 were killed in the strife, which led to the deployment of additional security forces and curfews in five states. In October, three former governors were arrested on charges of embezzling more than $615 million while in office. In November, 65 people were killed in a series of coordinated bombings by *Boko Haram.*

On January 20, 2012, *Boko Haram* militants killed 185 people in Kano. Also in January Jonathan announced that the government would end a popular fuel subsidy, asserting that Nigeria could no longer afford the costs of the program. The announcement prompted widespread protests and a partial reversal of the order, which reduced the subsidy by 50 percent. By June attacks on energy production facilities by MEND and *Boko Haram* had reduced oil output to 2.7 million barrels per day, far below the government's goal of 3.7 million barrels per day for 2012. Meanwhile, severe flooding—said to be the worst in 50 years—killed more than 300 people and displaced more than two million people.

More than 800 people were killed in *Boko Haram* attacks between 2012 and 2013. Meanwhile, there was a growing number of civilian casualties as fighting between the extremist group and security forces intensified. The government launched an investigation into the deaths of 228 people who were killed during an anti-*Boko Haram* operation in Baga in April 2013. Meanwhile, government efforts to negotiate with the group were rebuffed. By the summer of 2013, the conflict had produced an estimated 20,000 internally displaced persons. Jonathan declared states of emergency in the northern states of Adamawa, Borno, and Yobe and dispatched additional military troops.

An explosion and fire at a refinery on June 19, 2013, at Bodo forced Shell to stop operations and cut production by 150,000 barrels per day. Company officials blamed the accident on efforts to steal oil, while community leaders blamed Shell. A simmering political feud between Jonathan and the governor of Rivers State, Rotimi AMAECHI (PDP), erupted in July, when rival backers of the two leaders fought each other in Port Harcourt, prompting the deployment of security forces. Amaechi has emerged as the most visible opponent to Jonathan's reelection efforts within the PDP.

In a series of attacks in late October and early November 2013, *Boko Haram* militants killed more than 70 in the northeastern region of the country. In response, the legislature approved the extension of states of emergency in Adamawa, Borno, and Yobe.

In January 2014 Jonathan replaced the nation's senior military figures. The changes were reportedly part of an effort to increase the competency of the military in the ongoing conflict with *Boko Haram.* Over one two-day period in February alone, more than 100 people were killed in *Boko Haram* attacks.

On January 13, 2014, Jonathan signed into a law a measure criminalizing same-sex marriages, civil unions, membership in homosexual organizations, and public displays of same-sex relationships. On February 20, the president dismissed Lamido SANUSI, the governor of Nigeria's central bank. Sanusi pledged to fight the dismissal which he described as retribution for publicizing some $20 billion in fraud committed by the state oil company. Sanusi subsequently became emir of Kano in what was described as a rebuff to the regime.

On April 14, 2014, *Boko Haram* abducted more than 250 schoolgirls in Chibok. Subsequent reports indicated that the girls were being forced to convert to Islam and some sold as child brides. In June an additional 91 women and children were kidnapped in the region. The attacks prompted the closure of schools throughout the northern regions of the country. Multiple nations offered assistance in the search of the abductees. For instance, the United States deployed military and law enforcement officers, as well as aerial drones. Reports indicated that as of July 2014, more than 4,000 people had been killed in *Boko Haram* attacks and government security operations since 2010. Seven cabinet ministers resigned in October 2014 to contest gubernatorial elections scheduled for 2015.

A major government military offensive against *Boko Haram* in April 2015 overran 13 insurgent camps in the Sambisa Forest in northeastern Nigeria. One result of the campaign was the rescue of 200 girls and 93 women, including most of the kidnapped Chibok schoolgirls. Despite the offensive, *Boko Haram* continued attacks in other parts of the country, killing more than 40 civilians in Gubio, in the Borno state, during an attack on May 23 in which the terrorist group destroyed more than 400 homes.

In May 2015 the government announced that its budget, at $22.6 billion, would be 3.2 percent less than the previous year because of falling oil prices. Before he left office at the end of May, President Jonathan signed into law a measure banning female genital mutilation.

A series of attacks by *Boko Haram* in June 2015, including suicide bombings, killed more than 150. Meanwhile, as part of an effort to reduce corruption, Buhari disbanded the board of the Nigerian National Petroleum Corporation on June 26.

The government's budget for 2016, announced in December 2015, was $30.3 billion. In December 2015 a UN report found that the *Boko Haram* insurgency had led to the closure of more than 2,000 schools in Nigeria. The Islamic Movement in Nigeria (IMN) asserted that security forces had massacred 270 members on December 13–14. Government reports put the number of dead at 60 and claimed that the IMN had attempted to assassinate the Nigeria army's chief of staff.

More than 150 suspected *Boko Haram* insurgents were arrested in January 2016, and the army announced that the group no longer held any significant territory in the country. Nonetheless, terrorist attacks by *Boko Haram* continued through 2016.

POLITICAL PARTIES AND GROUPS

In June 1995 General Abacha announced that the ban on "political activity" had been lifted, although "rallies and campaigns" remained restricted and other constraints continued as a consequence of the country's severe political turmoil. (See the 2011 *Handbook* for information on political parties prior to 1995.) In April 1998 all 5 current legal parties nominated Abacha to be their presidential candidate in balloting then scheduled for August. However, following Abacha's death in June, his successor, General Abubakar, dissolved the 5 parties and called on political associations to register with the newly created Independent National Electoral Commission (INEC). Between August 27 and September 9, 25 political groups applied to the INEC for provisional legal status. Only 9 of the applicants met the baseline qualifications, including maintaining functional offices in 24 states. In local elections in December only 3 of those groups—the People's Democratic Party (PDP), the All People's Party (APP), and the Alliance for Democracy (AD)—secured the voting tally necessary to maintain their legal status and move on to legislative and presidential elections. The other 6 groups were reportedly deregistered. Three new parties—the National Democratic Party (NDP), the United Nigeria People's Party (UNPP), and All Progressive Grand Alliance (APGA)—were registered in June 2002, and by 2010 some 50 parties had been legalized. Propresidential parties created an electoral alliance, the Patriotic Electoral Alliance of Nigeria (PEAN), ahead of the planned 2011 balloting. Members of PEAN included a number of small parties, such as Accord, the Nigerian People's Congress, and the Advanced Congress of Democrats (ACD). PEAN supported incumbent president Jonathan's election bid.

Legislative Parties:

People's Democratic Party (PDP). The PDP was formed in Lagos in August 1998 as an umbrella for more than 60 organizations, including many from the so-called Group of 34, which registered among its leaders traditional chiefs, businesspeople, academicians, and a strong contingent of retired generals. Alex EKWUEME, a former national vice president, and Jerry GANA emerged from the PDP's inaugural meetings as the group's chair and second in command, respectively. The party presented a platform that reflected its broad political base, advocating the "guided" deregulation of the economy, respect for human rights, and improved funding for health care and education.

In late October 1998 Gen. Olesegun Obasanjo, the military head of state between 1976 and 1979, joined the PDP. With Obasanjo at the helm, the party subsequently swept local and gubernatorial elections, won a majority in the assembly, and in February 1999 captured the national presidency.

In January 2003 the PDP elected Obasanjo as its presidential candidate for the upcoming elections, which he won with 62 percent of the vote. The PDP also retained its majorities in the federal Senate and House of Representatives and among state governors and state assemblies.

A feud developed in 2005 between President Obasanjo and Vice President Atiku Abubakar over the proposed constitutional amendment to permit Obasanjo to seek a third term (see Current issues, above). The split also appeared to reflect the schism between the party's founding members ("concerned elders") led by Abubakar and the "progressive faction" led by Obasanjo. A party congress elected Ahmadu ALI as the PDP chair, and Obasanjo's supporters blamed Ali for the defeat of the constitutional amendment that would have allowed Obasanjo a third term. Subsequently, a PDP faction led by Solomon LAR declared itself the real leadership of the party and sued for access to the PDP assets.

Abubakar was suspended from the PDP in September 2006 for "antiparty activities," and he subsequently joined the new Action Congress of Nigeria (below). In December a PDP congress chose Umaru Yar'Adua as its presidential candidate. He easily secured the presidency (with more than 70 percent of the vote) in the April 2007 balloting, while the PDP also dominated the federal legislative polls and secured 27 of 36 state governorships.

Although Yar'Adua had been characterized as Obasanjo's handpicked successor, significant infighting was subsequently reported between supporters of the two leaders, particularly because the new government's anticorruption campaign focused on many officials from Obasanjo's administration. Obasanjo backed Sam EGWU to be the new PDP leader, but Egwu was defeated for the post by Vincent Ogbulafor at the PDP convention in March 2008. Ogbulafor, a former PDP general secretary, was considered a compromise candidate who reportedly faced a difficult task in reunifying the party. Between 2007 and 2009 a number of members of the All Nigeria People's Party defected to the PDP, including two sitting governors, Aliyu Mahmud SHINKAFI of Zamfara and Isa YUGUDA of Bauchi.

Jonathan declared his intent to seek the party's nomination for the January 2011 presidential race. He was challenged by former president Ibrahim Babangida and former vice president Atiku Abubakar. A bitter internal dispute emerged within the PDP over the selection of delegates to the party's nominating convention, with Jonathan and his supporters arguing that current office holders be allowed to serve as delegates, while Babangida's adherents opposed the change. As a result, primaries planned for October 2010 were postponed until January 14, 2011. Jonathan won the PDP primary and was victorious in the general election, winning a full term in balloting on April 16. Meanwhile, the PDP secured reduced majorities in the house and Senate in legislative polling.

At a party congress on March 24, 2012, Alhaji Bamangar TUKUR, a close ally of Jonathon, was elected party chair. Meanwhile, in April Obasanjo resigned as chair of the PDP board of trustees. In June 2013 Tukur survived an effort among the PDP's executive committee to replace him. In August seven PDP governors announced they were leaving the PDP. Five of the group subsequently joined the APC.

On January 16, 2014, Tukur resigned and was replaced by former Bauchi governor Adamu MU'AZU.

Jonathan was defeated in his reelection bid in balloting in March 2015, while the party lost control of both chambers of Parliament, securing 125 seats in the House, and 49 in the Senate. After the elections, Party Leader Mu'azu resigned and was replaced on an acting basis by Deputy Chair Uche SECONDUS.

Leaders: Goodluck JONATHAN (Former President of the Republic, Gen. Olesegun OBASANJO (Former Chair of the PDP Board of Trustees and Former President of the Republic), Uche SECONDUS (Acting Chair), Olagunsoye OYINLOLA (General Secretary).

All Progressives Congress (APC). The APC was formed in February 2013 by a merger of four opposition parties, the **Congress for Progressive Change** (CPC), the **All Nigeria People's Party** (ANPP), and the **Action Congress of Nigeria** (ACN). (For more information on the history of these parties, see the 2014 *Handbook*.) The mainly Muslim, centrist CPC was formed in 2009 by supporters of former general Muhammadu BUHARI. The party's main strength was in the north. Many of the original CPC leadership consisted of former members of the ANPP. Buhari was the party's 2011 presidential candidate. He placed second in the balloting with 32 percent of the vote, while the CPC was placed third in the Senate and house balloting. The party also secured one governorship.

The ANPP was a successor to the All People's Party (APP), a center-right grouping established in September 1998 by some 14 Ibo and Hausa-Fulani political associations. ANPP presidential candidate Ibrahim SHERARAU placed fourth in the balloting with 2.4 percent of the vote in the 2011 elections. Meanwhile, the party ANPP won three governorships, 7 Senate seats, and 25 seats in the House. On June 26, 2012, the chair of the ANPP in the Rivers State, Julius NWAOFU, was assassinated. Through 2013 *Boko Haram* conducted a series of attacks on ANPP officials.

The ACN was originally formed as the Action Congress (AC) in 2006 by dissidents from the AD, Justice Party, ACD, and other smaller parties. In 2010 the AC changed its name to the Action Congress of Nigeria (ACN). The ACN won three governorships in the 2011 elections. It was second in the legislative balloting, while the party's presidential candidate, Nuhu RIBADU, placed third in the presidential election, with 5.4 percent of the vote.

The APC grouping described itself as a progressive socialist party, and Bisi AKANDE of the ACN was elected its first chair. Defections from the PDP brought the number of APC legislators in the House to 172, compared with 171 for the PDP.

In February PDP founding member Atiku ABUBAKAR joined the APC. In June, John Odigie OYEGUN, a Christian, was elected chair in what was reportedly an attempt to broaden the appeal of the party in the South.

Former military dictator Mohammadu BUHARI was the APC's 2015 presidential candidate. He won the balloting with 54 percent of the vote. In concurrent legislative elections, the APC gained majorities in both houses of Parliament, with 225 in the House, and 60 in the Senate. Buhari's victory marked the first time that the PDP had been defeated at the national level in more than 20 years.

Leaders: Mohammadu BUHARI (President of the Republic), Yemi OSINBAJO (Vice President of the Republic), John Odigie OYEGUN (Chair).

Accord. Formed in 2006 by Ikra Bilbis, a former member of the PDP, Accord maintained close ties with the PDP, and President Obasanjo appointed Bilbis to a cabinet post in 2006. Accord supported PDP candidate Yar'Adua in the 2007 presidential election. Reports in 2009 indicated that many members of Accord joined the PDP. Accord won five seats in the 2011 House elections. A report in July 2014 indicated that more than 1,000 members of Accord had defected en masse to other parties. Nonetheless, the party secured one seat in the 2015 House elections. Accord's 2015 presidential candidate, Tunde ANIFOWOSE-KELANI, won just 0.1 percent of the vote.

Leaders: Muhammad Lawal MALADO (Chair), Suleiman ISIYAKU (National Secretary).

All Progressive Grand Alliance (APGA). Launched in April 2002, the APGA is led by a prominent chief of the southern Igbo ethnic group, Chekwas Okorie. However, its founders criticized those who branded the APGA as an "Igbo party," arguing instead that it intended to represent "all the marginalized people of Nigeria." Okorie came in third in presidential balloting in 2003 with 3.3 percent of the vote. The party also gained two seats in the house but none in the Senate in 2003.

A faction of the party led by Chief Victor Umeh claimed to be the legitimate leader of the APGA in 2005–2006, and the INEC recognized the claim in 2007. However, Okorie challenged the INEC decision in the courts, but his suit was rejected in 2008. The APGA won one governorship in 2007. At a gathering in 2009, Okorie's faction reelected him as chair and expelled Umeh, along with Governor Peter Obi. However, the faction led by Umeh and Obi refused to recognize the authority of the convention, and Umeh was ultimately recognized by the national election commission as the party leader.

The APGA won one governorship in the 2011 balloting and six seats in the House. Reports in 2012 indicated that continued infighting between Umeh and Obi led to a significant decline in APGA membership. Although the APGA was part of the negotiations to form the APC, the party ultimately rejected the merger, although a small faction did join the new grouping.

In the 2015 election, the party won five House seats.

Leaders: Chief Victor UMEH (Chair), Sani SHINKAFI (National Secretary), Peter OBI.

Other parties that secured representation in the legislature in the 2015 balloting included the **Labour Party**, formed in 2002 and led by Alhaji Abdulkadir ABDULSALAM; and the **Social Democratic Party** (SDP), a revived version of the party that included 13 constituent groupings. Both parties secured one seat.

Other Parties That Contested the 2011 or 2015 Elections:

Progressive People's Alliance (PPA). The PPA was formed in 2003, and the party's candidate—Orji Uzor KALU (a former PDP member)—won the gubernatorial election in Abia that year. Kalu served until 2007 but was indicted after he left office on charges of corruption. In 2007 the PPA won the gubernatorial elections in Abia and Imo. After the 2007 legislative elections the PPA joined the PDP-led national unity government. In 2009 the governor and deputy governor of Imo, both members of the PPA, defected to the PDP, leading the PPA to launch a legal challenge against the right of the former members to remain in office. The PPA failed to secure any seats in the 2011 legislative elections. In June 2013 the PPA voted to change its name to the All Progressive People Alliance (APPA). Reports in 2014 indicated that the party was in negotiations to merge with the APGA.

Leader: Peter Ojonugwa AMEH (Chair).

United Nigeria People's Party (UNPP). The UNPP is a successor to the United Nigeria Democratic Party (UNDP), which was launched in August 2001 by, among others, former members of the PDP and supporters of former president Babangida. The UNDP changed its name to the UNPP in May 2002 to avoid confusion with the UN Development Program (also UNDP). The UNPP subsequently was splintered by a proposed merger with the APP; although some UNPP members joined the new ANPP, a rump UNPP continued to operate. Jim NWOBODO, the UNPP candidate in the 2003 presidential poll, secured 0.4 percent of the vote. In the concurrent legislative balloting, the UNPP secured 2.7 percent of the vote in the Senate (but no seats) and 2.8 percent of the vote and two seats in the house.

In 2006 it was reported that many members of the UNPP had defected to the newly formed Movement for Restoration and Defense of Democracy (MRDD, below). The UNPP did not secure any seats in the 2011 legislative balloting. In 2012 former deputy governor and

UNPP official Alhaji Musa Adebayo AYENI won, and a number of supporters defected to the ACN. The UNPP was deregistered by the national election commission in December 2012. In 2014 the UNPP announced it would merge with the PDP.

Leaders: Mallem Salek JAMBO (Chair), Ukeje NWOKEFORO (National Secretary).

People's Redemption Party (PRP). The PRP was formed in 2002 under the leadership of Balarabe Musa, who was also the party's unsuccessful presidential candidate in 2003. The PRP won one seat in the House in 2003 but failed to gain representation in 2007. The PRP launched a series of efforts to form an electoral coalition with parties such as the PPA ahead of the 2011 elections, but it declined to join the PEAN. The PRP failed to secure any seats in the 2011 House or Senate elections. In 2012 the PRP filed suit with the electoral commission over government plans to deregister the party because of a lack of electoral success and the low number of candidates it fielded. The PRP joined several other deregistered parties in a lawsuit against the electoral commission in 2014, in order to participate in the 2015 balloting.

Leaders: Balarabe MUSA (Chair), Dr. Ngozi OKAFOR (National Secretary).

Advanced Congress of Democrats (ACD). The ACD was formed in April 2005 to oppose President Obasanjo's bid for a third presidential term. The party attracted a number of elected officials at the state and national level, including members of the House and Senate, as well as senior PDP figures, including a former chair of the PDP, Audu OGBEH. The party mainly comprises northerners and is essentially an anti-PDP formation. The ACD reportedly attracted members from other parties, principally the AD, but failed to gain representation in the 2007 federal elections. The ACD announced in 2010 that it would support incumbent president Jonathan of the PDP in the 2011 elections. It ran only four candidates in the 2011 house balloting and failed to secure any seats. The ACD announced in April 2013 that it was forming an opposition coalition ahead of the 2015 balloting.

Leaders: Yusuf BUBA (Chair), Kenneth KALU (National Secretary), Lawal KAITA (Former Governor of Kaduna), Ghali Umar NA'ABA (Former President of the House of Representatives).

The parties participating in the 2011 elections included, among others (all received less than 1 percent of the vote and no representation in the legislature) the **People's Salvation Party** (PSP), created in 2002 and led by Lawal MAITURARE; the **National Conscience Party** (NCP), formed in October 1994, and currently led by Osagie OBAYUWANA; the **Justice Party** (JP), led by former NADECO member Ralph OBIOHA; the **Movement for Democracy and Justice** (MDJ), led by J. O. OSULA; the **People's Mandate Party** (PMP), led by Edward OPARAOJI and 2011 presidential candidate, Nwadike CHIKEZIE; the **New Nigeria Peoples' Party** (NNPP), chaired by B. O. ANIEBONAM; the **United Democratic Party** (UDP), formed in 1998 and led by Umaru DIKKO; the **Democratic Party Alliance** (DPA), a "progressive" party formed in November 2006 by Ulu FALAYE; the **Nigeria People's Congress** (NPC), led by Ngozi EMIONA and Brimmy Asekharuagbom OLAGHERE (2007 presidential candidate); the **African Democratic Congress** (ADC), formed in 2006 by Chief Okewo OSUI, which ran Peter NWANGWU as its 2011 presidential candidate; the **Fresh Democrats,** established in 2006 under the leadership of Chris Okotie (2007 and 2011 presidential candidate); the **People's Progressive Party** (PPP), led by 2011 presidential candidate Lawson Igboanugo AROH; the **People for Democratic Change** (PDC), led by 2011 presidential contender Mahmud WAZIRI; and the **Mega-Progressive People's Party** (MPPP), who ran Rasheed SHITTA-BEY as its 2011 presidential candidate.

Other parties that secured representation in the legislature in the 2011 balloting included the **Democratic People's Party** (DPP), which had been formed in 2006 by dissidents from the ANPP, led by Jeremiah USENI, and which secured two seats in the House and one in the Senate; and the **People's Party of Nigeria** (PPN), led by Abiodun ODUSANYA, which won two seats in the House.

For information on the **Movement for Restoration and Defense of Democracy** (MRDD) and the **National Democratic Party** (NDP), see the 2012 *Handbook.*

Other Groups:

National Democratic Coalition (NADECO). Organized in May 1994 by a group of former politicians, retired military officers, and human rights activists, NADECO demanded that the Abacha regime yield to an interim government led by Moshood Abiola, the apparent winner in the aborted 1993 presidential election. As in the case of other prominent antigovernment figures, several NADECO leaders were temporarily detained, including the revered 87-year-old ex-governor of Ondo, Michael AJASIN.

Wole Soyinka, the prominent exiled critic of the government who was involved in the reported formation of several external groups, was identified as a NADECO leader in 1997. (See the National Liberation Council of Nigeria in the 2007 *Handbook.*) Soyinka (in absentia) and other NADECO supporters were charged with treason in March 1997 for their antiregime activities. In early May 1998 NADECO's secretary general, Ayo Opadokum, was among 20 opposition activists arrested when a rally in Ibadan turned violent.

Beginning in mid-1998 the Abubakar regime released a number of opposition figures and was reportedly preparing to release Moshood Abiola when Abiola died. In October Soyinka, who had been a leading advocate for Abiola's release, returned from exile, where most recently he had been calling for the formation of a South African–style human rights tribunal to investigate the alleged abuses of Nigeria's military regimes. Subsequently, NADECO Chair Ndubuisi Kanu stated that the organization would resume its role as unofficial opposition, although it would not assume the status of political party. In 2009 a NADECO convention endorsed a call for a new constitution that emphasized regional autonomy. In September 2010 Soyinka reportedly formed a new political party, the **Democratic Front for a People's Federation** (DFPF). In 2012 Kanu called on Jonathan to engage in a national dialogue to end sectarian violence.

Leaders: Commodore Ndubuisi KANU (Chair), Bolaji AKINYEMI, Wole SOYINKA, Ayo OPADOKUM (Secretary General).

Movement for the Survival of the Ogoni People (MOSOP). MOSOP pressed the government for years on the rights of the indigenous Ogoni ethnic group in oil-rich southwestern Nigeria. Having previously suggested that a self-determination referendum would be appropriate, MOSOP has more recently concentrated on forcing the government to share the oil wealth more equitably with the local population.

Kenule SARO-WIWA (a well-known author, minority rights activist, and longtime MOSOP leader) was arrested in 1994 on murder charges involving the death of four progovernment Ogoni leaders. Saro-Wiwa vehemently denied the charges, calling them a blatant attempt by the Abacha regime to silence his criticism. Most internal and external observers remained extremely skeptical of Saro-Wiwa's guilt, and Western and African capitals urged his release. However, Saro-Wiwa and eight others were found guilty by a special military tribunal in late October 1996 and, following ratification of the sentences by the PRC, were hanged on November 10. The executions prompted an international outcry that contributed significantly to the government's sustained isolation in 1996–1998. MOSOP subsequently attempted to change the constitution so that the presidency would rotate on a regional basis. In 2009 MOSOP was divided by a leadership crisis in which one faction supported Ledum Mitee and another Goodluck DIIGBO, following a December 2008 congress in which Mitee was reelected chair. In 2011 the rivalry between Mitee and Diigbo was reported to have split the grouping. In 2013 MOSOP organized demonstrations in Bori to protest the government's failure to implement UN environmental recommendations. In 2014 MOSOP called on the government to negotiate a cease-fire with *Boko Haram.*

Leader: Ledum MITEE.

Movement for the Actualization of the Sovereign State of Biafra (MASSOB). An Ibo group formed by lawyer and activist Ralph Uwazurike in 1999, MASSOB advocates the secession of Biafra and is opposed to the introduction of sharia in northern states. In October 2005 Uwazurike and 6 members of MASSOB were arrested on charges of treason and organizing an illegal organization. In 2009 MASSOB announced that after years of boycotting elections, it would participate in regional balloting in 2010 and support APGA candidates. In July 2010, 68 members of MASSOB were arrested for illegal demonstrations. In 2013 ten MASSOB members were arrested following clashes with police in Nnobi. Police in March 2014 arrested three alleged MASSOB members and charged them with the bombing of the Biafra state house. In November 2016 the Nigerian military launched an offensive to suppress MASSOB separatists in Biafra.

Leader: Ralph UWAZURIKE.

O'odua People's Congress (OPC). The OPC is a militant organization that advocates secession for the Yoruba ethnic group. Some members of the OPC reportedly support the spread of sharia in northern states in the hope that the issue will further divide the country and thereby make Yoruba secession easier to obtain. Attacks by OPC members in October 2008 left six dead and more than a score injured. Seven members of the OPC were arrested in November 2010 for arms smuggling.

Movement for the Emancipation of the Niger Delta (MEND), which emerged in early 2006 when it conducted a series of attacks on oil production facilities. MEND was subsequently believed responsible for the kidnapping of a number of foreign oil workers. It demanded compensation from foreign oil companies for environmental damage done in the Niger Delta as well as more equitable distribution of oil revenue to the Delta inhabitants. MEND reportedly finances its operations through large-scale bunkering of oil.

In May 2007 MEND announced a cease-fire after new president Yar'Adua pledged to develop a revenue-sharing plan and to accord greater autonomy to the Niger Delta. The reconciliation was reportedly facilitated by new vice president Jonathan, who, like many MEND members, is a member of the Ijaw ethnic group. Although federal military forces were deployed into the region to confront other rebel forces, the MEND cease-fire appeared to hold into September. However, MEND subsequently resumed its attacks on oil facilities and kidnapping of oil workers after MEND leader Henry OKAH (who reportedly also uses the nom de guerre of Jomo Gbomo) was arrested in Angola on gun-running charges and was extradited to Nigeria to face trial for treason, terrorism, and arms smuggling. (A Nigerian court in May 2008 ruled that Okah's trial would be conducted in secret.) After a series of deadly incidents, MEND, reportedly interested in improving its image and differentiating itself from the numerous militias (described by some as "criminal gangs") operating in the Delta, announced another cease-fire in late June. However, hostilities erupted again in September, rebel attacks on deepwater oil platforms (previously considered safe) having prompted significant production shutdowns. In spite of a two-month government amnesty program in April 2009, MEND launched a series of new attacks on oil facilities and pipelines in the region causing more than $60 million in damage and reducing oil output by 20 percent. In July Okah accepted a government pardon and was freed from custody and went into exile in South Africa. Meanwhile, a new rebel leader, Government EKPEMUPOLO "Tompolo," emerged as one of the main MEND leaders and was the subject of a government manhunt and offensive through the summer before also accepting the amnesty in October, along with other MEND leaders Victor Ben EBIKABOWEI, Ateke TOM, and Farah DAGOGO. Following the October 2010 Abuja bombings, Okah was arrested in South Africa. In November 2010 MEND kidnapped seven foreign oil workers in Akwa Ibom state. Meanwhile, in March 2011 MEND and the Nigerian government launched a new round of negotiations. On February 5, 2012, MEND destroyed an oil pipeline in Bayelsa.

Okah was convicted of terrorism in South Africa in January 2013 and sentenced to 24 years in prison. The conviction sparked a new wave of MEND attacks, including a strike that killed 12 police officers in Azuzama in April and a bombing in July that destroyed an oil pipeline. In March 2014 MEND claimed responsibility for an attack on a Shell facility in the Delta. In November 2016 the Nigerian military launched aerial attacks on MEND camps, killing more than 30.

Boko Haram. Formally known as the **Congregation and People Committed to the Propagation of the Prophet's Teachings and Jihad,** *Boko Haram* (loosely translated as "Western education is sinful") was established in Northern Nigeria in 2001 by Mohammed YUSUF to spread sharia. It subsequently evolved into an Islamic terrorist organization. Estimates are that the conflict between *Boko Haram* and the Nigerian government killed more than 14,000 since 2001. Western intelligence agencies have linked *Boko Haram* with other extremist groups, including al-Qaida in the Islamic Maghreb. The group was consistently rejected efforts by the government to negotiate. Members of *Boko Haram* broke away in January 2012 to form another militant group, the **Vanguard for the Protection of Muslims in Black Lands** (*Ansaru*), led by Abu Usmatul AL-ANSARI. The new grouping was reportedly critical of *Boko Haram* for its attacks on Muslims.

In October 2012 top *Boko Haram* commander Shuaibu Mohammed BAMA was captured by security forces. After a state of emergency was declared in northern Nigerian states in May 2013, reports indicated that many *Boko Haram* fighters had fled into Mali. However, international military intervention in Mali prompted a reverse movement of militants. Through 2013 and into 2014, the group increasingly targeted Christian churches and villages. Reports in 2014 indicated that the group had between 4,000 and 5,000 active fighters.

More than 5,000 people were released by the military from *Boko Haram* camps in Borno in June 2016. In August the Nigerian military claimed that *Boko Haram* leader Abubakar SHEKAU had been killed, along with as many as 300 fighters in aerial attacks on their camp in Borno, but reports were not confirmed.

Leader: Abubakar SHEKAU.

For more information on the **People's Democratic Congress** (PDC), the **People's Liberation Party** (PLP), the **Liberal Democrats** (LD), **Movement for National Reconciliation,** the **National Democratic Movement** (NDM), the **New Democratic Party** (NDP), the **Nigerian People's Movement,** the **United Action for Democracy** (UAD), the **South-South Liberation Movement,** the **Ijaw Youth Organization,** the **Federated Niger Delta Izon Communities** (FNDIC), the **Rivers' States Coalition,** and the **Niger Delta's People's Volunteer Force** (NDPVF), see the 2011 *Handbook.*

For information on the **Arewa People's Congress** (APC), the **United Democratic Forum** (UDF), the **Alliance for Democracy** (AD), the **Eastern Mandate Union**, the **National Democratic Movement** (NDM), the **Northern Elders' Forum**, the **United Democratic Congress**, the **Fourth Dimension**, the **National Solidarity Party** (NSP), and the **Social Democratic Mega-Party** (SDMP), see the 2012 *Handbook.*

LEGISLATURE

The **National Assembly,** encompassing a Senate and a House of Representatives, was dissolved in December 1983. It was revived under the 1989 constitution, with an election of members to four-year terms in both houses on July 4, 1992. However, the new body did not convene until December 5 and was again dissolved in the wake of the November 1993 coup, with new elections held on April 25, 1998.

Senate. The upper chamber consists of 109 seats: 3 from each state and 1 from the Federal Capital Territory of Abuja. Members serve four-year terms. Following the balloting of March 28–29, 2015, the seats were distributed as follows: All Progressives Congress, 60 seats; and People's Democratic Party, 49.

President: Olubukola Abubakar SARAKI.

House of Representatives. The lower house consists of 360 seats, with the number of seats per state being apportioned on the basis of population. Members serve four-year terms. Following the balloting of March 28–29, 2015, the seats were distributed as follows: All Progressives Congress, 225 seats; People's Democratic Party, 125; All Progressive Grand Alliance, 5; Accord, 1; Labour Party, 1; Social Democratic Party, 1; and the remaining 2 seats to be decided in by-elections.

President: Yakubu DOGARA.

CABINET

[as of December 15, 2016]

President	Muhammadu Buhari
Vice President	Yemi Osinbajo
Federal Executive Councilors	
Agriculture and Rural Development	Audu Ogbeh
Aviation	Hadi Sirika
Budget and National Planning	Udoma Udo-Udoma
Communications	Adebayo Shittu
Culture and Information	Lai Mohammed
Defense	Brig. Gen (Ret.) Muhammad Mansur Dan-Ali
Education	Mallam Adamu Adamu
Environment	Amina Mohammed [f]
Federal Capital Territory	Mohammed Musa Bello
Finance	Kemi Adeosun [f]
Foreign Affairs	Geoffrey Onyeama

Health	Isaac Adewole Folorunso
Internal Affairs	Lt. Gen. Abdulrahman Dambazau
Justice and Attorney General	Abubakar Malami
Labor	Chris Ngige
Mines and Steel Development	John Kayode Fayemi
Niger Delta Region	Usani Uguru Usani
Petroleum	Muhammadu Buhari
Power, Works, and Housing	Babatunde Raji Fashola
Science and Technology	Ogbonnaya Onu
Trade, Industry, and Investment	Enyinnaya Okechukwu Enelemah
Transport	Rotimi Amaechi
Water Resources	Sueiman Adamu Kazaure
Women Affairs	Aisha Jumai Alhassan [f]
Youth and Sports	Solomon Dalong
Ministers of State	
Agriculture and Natural Resources	Heineken Lokpobiri
Budget and National Planning	Zainab Ahmed [f]
Education	Anthony Gozie
Environment	Ibrahim Usman Jibril
Foreign Affairs	Khadijat Bukar Abba-Ibrahim [f]
Health	Osagie Ehanire
Labor and Employment	(Vacant)
Mines and Steel	Bawa Bawa Abubakar
Niger Delta Affairs	Claudius Omoleye Daramola
Petroleum	Ibe Kachikwu
Power, Works, and Housing	Baba Shehuri Mustapha
Trade, Investment, and Industry	Aisha Abubakar [f]

[f] = female

INTERGOVERNMENTAL REPRESENTATION

Ambassador to the U.S.: Hakeem BALOGUN (Chargé d'Affaires).

U.S. Ambassador to Nigeria: W. Stuart SYMINGTON.

Permanent Representative to the UN: Joy OGWU.

IGO Memberships (Non-UN): AfDB, AU, CWTH, ECOWAS, ICC, IOM, NAM, OPEC, WTO.

For Further Reference:

Bourne, Richard. *Nigeria: A New History of a Turbulent Century.* London: Zed Book, 2015.

Elaigwu, J. Isawa. *The Politics of Federalism in Nigeria.* London: Adonis and Abbey, 2007.

Kendhammer, Brandon. *Muslims Talking Politics: Framing Islam, Democracy, and Law in Northern Nigeria.* Chicago: University of Chicago Press, 2016.

NORWAY

Kingdom of Norway
Kongeriket Norge

Political Status: Constitutional monarchy established in 1905; under multiparty parliamentary system.

Area: 149,115 sq. mi. (386,209 sq. km), including Svalbard and Jan Mayen (see Related Territories).

Population: 5,272,000 (2016E—UN); 5,265,158 (2016E—U.S. Census).

Major Urban Centers (2016E): OSLO (658,000), Bergen (269,000), Trondheim (184,000), Stavanger (131,000).

Official Language: Norwegian.

Monetary Unit: Krone (official rate October 1, 2016: 7.98 kroner = $1US).

Sovereign: King HARALD V; succeeded to the throne January 17, 1991, upon the death of his father, King OLAV V.

Heir to the Throne: Crown Prince HAAKON Magnus, son of the king.

Prime Minister: Erna SOLBERG (Conservative Party); appointed by the king on October 16, 2013, succeeding Jens STOLTENBERG (Norwegian Labor Party), who had submitted his resignation on the same day, following the election of September 9.

THE COUNTRY

A land of fjords and rugged mountains bisected by the Arctic Circle, Norway is the fifth-largest country in Western Europe but the second-lowest in population density, after Iceland. In addition to borders with its two Scandinavian neighbors, Sweden and Finland, Norway has also had a common border in the far north with the Soviet Union/Russia since 1944. Three-fourths of the land area is unsuitable for cultivation or habitation, and the population, homogeneous except for asylum-seekers and foreign workers, is heavily concentrated in the southern sector and along the Atlantic seaboard. For generations, the population was homogeneous except for a small Sámi (Lapp) minority of approximately 40,000 in the north. Immigrants from developing countries have flocked to Norway in recent years and now make up almost 15 percent of the population—double that number in Oslo. For historical reasons the Norwegian language exists in two forms: the Danish-inspired *Bokmål* as well as *Nynorsk,* a traditional spoken tongue with a comparatively recent written form; in addition, the Sámi speak their own language, a member of the Finno-Ugrian group. The state-supported Evangelical Lutheran Church commands the allegiance of 82.1 percent of the population, although a recent survey concluded that only 10 percent of those members attend religious services or other church-related activities more than once a month.

Women constitute 47.2 percent of the active labor force, concentrated in the health and social services sector, wholesale and retail trade, and education. Just under 40 percent of the national legislators elected in 2013 were women, and no Norwegian government has been formed since 1986 with less than 40 percent women. Both the World Economic Forum and the United Nations (UN) Development Program rank Norway second in terms of economic and political gender equality. In 2013 parliament passed legislation to include women in military conscription. The Inter-Parliamentary Union ranks Norway at 15th among the 181 surveyed countries for female representation, with women comprising 39.6 percent of the members of parliament (67 of the 169 seats). In 2016, 9 of the 19 members of the cabinet were women, including the prime minister.

The Norwegian merchant fleet is one of the world's ten largest (by country of owner) and, prior to the discovery of North Sea oil, was the country's leading foreign-exchange earner. Norway continues to export considerable amounts of such traditional commodities as fish and forest products, although the agricultural sector as a whole now contributes only 1 percent of GDP. Norway was the world's second-largest exporter of natural gas and seventh-largest crude oil exporter, and the country has Western Europe's largest petroleum reserves, located in the Norwegian and Barents Seas as well as the North Sea. In addition, the development of hydroelectric power in recent decades has made Norway one of the largest exporters of aluminum and nitrogen products in Western Europe. Since exports and foreign services, including shipping, account for roughly 40 percent of the GNP, the economy is heavily influenced by fluctuations in the world market. Oil and natural gas production have made Norway one of the world's most affluent countries, but production peaked in 2004 and new reserves must be found.

Norway has felt few direct effects of the global financial crisis or eurozone crisis, thanks to injecting a large fiscal stimulus and buoyancy in the hydrocarbon sector. GDP growth was 0.7 in 2010, 1.7 percent in 2011, 3.0 percent in 2012, 1 percent in 2013, 2.2 percent in 2014, and 1 percent in 2015. Norway has one of the lowest unemployment rates in Europe, ranging from 3.2 percent to 4.4 percent for 2009–2015. Norway offered a $9.2 billion loan to the International Monetary Fund (IMF) in April 2012 to be used in global economic stability programs. In 2016 GDP grew by an estimated 1.6 percent, inflation was 2.3 percent, and unemployment of 3.9 percent. Norway continues to be the highest-rated country on the UN's human development index with a per-capita income of $68,400 in 2015.

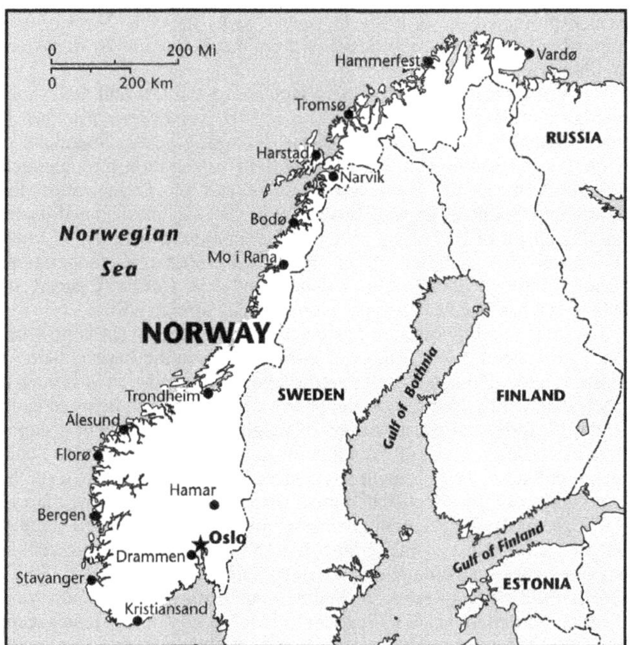

GOVERNMENT AND POLITICS

Political background. Although independent in its early period, Norway came under Danish rule in 1380. A period of de facto independence began in January 1814 but ended nine months later, when the legislature (*Storting*) accepted the Swedish monarch as king of Norway. Norway remained a territory under the Swedish Crown until 1905, when the union was peacefully dissolved and the Norwegians elected a sovereign from the Danish royal house. Though Norway avoided involvement in World War I, it was occupied from 1940 to 1945 by Nazi Germany, which sponsored the infamous puppet regime of Vidkun QUISLING, while the legitimate government functioned in exile in London.

Norway's first postwar election continued the prewar ascendancy of the Norwegian Labor Party (*Det Norske Arbeiderparti*—DNA), and a government was formed in 1945 under Prime Minister Einar GERHARDSEN. Labor continued in the majority until 1961 and then maintained a minority government until 1965, when a coalition of nonsocialist parties took control under Per BORTEN, leader of the Center Party (*Senterpartiet*—Sp). The Borten government was forced to resign in 1971, following disclosure that the prime minister had deliberately leaked information on negotiations for entering the European Community (EC, later the European Union—EU). A Labor government under Trygve BRATTELI subsequently came to power but was forced from office in September 1972, when EC membership was rejected in a national referendum by 53.5 to 46.5 percent of participants. However, when a coalition government under Lars KORVALD of the Christian People's Party (*Kristelig Folkeparti*—KrF) failed to win the September 1973 general election, Bratteli returned as head of a minority government. Upon stepping down, Bratteli was succeeded in January 1976 by Labor's Odvar NORDLI. In the election of September 1977, Labor and its ally, the Socialist Left Party (*Sosialistisk Venstreparti*—SV), obtained a combined majority of one seat over four nonsocialist parties, enabling Nordli to continue in office.

Prime Minister Nordli resigned for health reasons in February 1981 and was succeeded by Gro Harlem BRUNDTLAND, the country's first female chief executive. However, in September her first minority government fell in the wake of a 10-seat loss at the polls by Labor, and in October Kåre WILLOCH formed a minority administration led by the Conservative Party (*Høyre*) with the legislative support of the KrF and the Sp. Responding to the recessionary effects of Willoch's economic policies, voters nearly unseated the government in September 1985; the three ruling parties obtained a total of 78 seats, as opposed to 77 for Labor and the SV, making the 2 seats won by the right-wing Progress Party (*Fremskrittspartiet*—Frp) key to the balance of power.

In April 1986 the Willoch government lost a confidence vote on a proposed gas tax increase when the anti-tax Frp voted with the opposition. In the first change in power without an intervening election in 23 years, Brundtland returned as head of another minority Labor administration. In the parliamentary poll of September 1989 the Labor and Conservative parties both lost ground, with the Conservatives, under Jan P. SYSE, forming a new minority administration in coalition with the KrF and Sp. The resignation of the Syse government in late 1990 was forced by the Center Party's objection to the proposed signing of a European Economic Area (EEA) agreement (see entry on the European Free Trade Association—EFTA) that would have necessitated revision of Norwegian laws restricting foreign ownership of industrial and financial institutions.

The Center Party agreed to support Labor's return to power under Brundtland in December, when she pledged to prioritize domestic control over natural resources and economic activities. Norway signed the EEA Treaty in May 1992, after securing additional clauses designed to meet its concerns.

Controversy over Norway's renewed application for EC/EU membership, approved by the *Storting* in November 1992, dominated the general election of September 1993. The Labor and Conservative Parties favored accession (although the former was deeply divided over the issue), whereas the Center, Socialist Left, Christian People's, and Progress Parties were opposed. The results were far from definitive: Labor and the Center Party gained seats, while the other parties lost ground. Brundtland subsequently formed another Labor minority government, although the anti-EU parties had sufficient collective strength to deny the government the three-quarters majority required for approval of formal accession. Thus, the question was put to a referendum at which voters had to weigh whether accession provisions had sufficiently resolved questions regarding such key issues as the future of Norway's oil and gas reserves, access to Norway's fisheries, and safeguards for Norwegian farmers (among the most heavily subsidized in the world). On November 28, 1994, the Norwegian electorate again rejected EU membership, this time by a margin of 52.2 to 47.8 percent. Having acknowledged the outcome as a major defeat, Prime Minister Brundtland decided to negotiate appropriate changes to the EEA Treaty that would continue to apply to Norway as a non-EU member.

Brundtland stepped down in October 1996, and Labor entered the September 1997 election under the leadership of Thorbjørn JAGLAND, who had promised during the campaign to resign if his party polled less than the 36.9 percent of the vote it had received in 1993. Although Labor won 65 seats, compared to 25 each for the KrF and the Frp and 23 for the Conservatives, Jagland narrowly missed his self-imposed target and submitted his resignation in October. KrF leader Kjell Magne BONDEVIK subsequently formed a new minority government (42 seats) comprised of the KrF, the Sp, and the Liberal Party (*Venstre*–V). Bondevik submitted his resignation in March 2000 after losing a vote of confidence triggered by the government's objections to proposed construction of two gas-fired power stations. Labor's Jens STOLTENBERG was subsequently named head of an all-Labor, minority government.

The election of September 10, 2001, saw Labor narrowly retain its plurality, but with only 43 seats—its worst election returns in nearly a century. As a result, Kjell Bondevik returned to office at the head of a center-right minority coalition of the KrF, the Conservatives, and the Liberals. Controlling only 62 of the *Storting*'s 165 seats, the government required external support from the Frp, which had won 26 seats in the election.

The Labor Party's promise to increase welfare spending and reverse the tax reforms and other conservative policies initiated by prime minister Bondevik resonated with voters and led to a dramatic victory for Labor in the September 12, 2005, election. Labor captured 61 seats and in partnership with the Socialist Left (15 seats) and Center (11 seats) parties established a red-green majority of 87 seats. The election also saw the populist Progress Party become the principal opposition by outpolling the Conservatives, 38 seats to 23.

Reinstalled on October 17, 2005, as head of Norway's first majority government in two decades, Jens Stoltenberg drew upon the country's immense oil wealth to swing the domestic agenda to the left. The government rejected calls for another referendum on EU membership despite public opinion polls that indicated approximately 50 percent support for accession. Some analysts questioned how long the three-party government coalition would survive. That concern was reinforced by the September 2007 municipal and county elections. Although Labor improved on its 2003 performance and the Center Party basically held even, the Socialist Left took a drubbing, losing nearly half its support. The Frp's vote share also dropped from 22 percent in the 2005 national election to under 18 percent in the 2007 balloting, while the Conservatives staged a comeback, climbing from 14 to 19 percent.

In June 2007 the *Storting* approved a major consolidation within the domestic oil industry—Statoil's purchase of the oil and gas operations of

Norsk Hydro, the petroleum and aluminum giant, for $30 billion. The state now owns a 67 percent interest in the world's largest offshore oil producer.

The economy and immigration dominated the run-up to the September 15, 2009, parliamentary election. The Stoltenberg government increased public spending by temporarily exceeding the 4 percent ceiling on using the country's oil revenues. The main challenge to the government came from the Frp, which campaigned on a platform calling for tax cuts, privatization, and tighter immigration controls. Although the election results marked a new electoral high for the Frp in votes and seats, center-right parties declared they would not join an Frp-led coalition. Instead, the relatively stable economy, coupled with Stoltenberg's personal popularity, resulted in an increase of 3 seats for the DNA. The red-green DNA-led coalition claimed 86 of the 169 seats, marking the first time in 16 years that an incumbent government won reelection and the first time since 1969 that a government maintained a majority after an election.

Amid declining popularity of the DNA, Stoltenberg shuffled his cabinet in September 2012. He changed the ministers of labor and social inclusion, health, defense, foreign affairs, and culture. Hadia TAJIK, the new minister of culture, became both the youngest and the first Muslim to serve in the Norwegian Cabinet. The Center and SV reshuffled their ministers earlier in the year.

In the 2013 election, a conservative four-party coalition won control of the *Stortinget* (Parliament), with 96 of its 169 seats. Conservative Party leader Erna SOLBERG formed a minority government with the Progress Party. Stotenberg's Labor Party won 55 seats and 73 total for his coalition. Solberg appointed women to half of her cabinet to ensure gender equality. To deal with a growing refugee crisis, Solberg created a new minister of immigration and integration on December 16, 2014.

Constitution and government. The Eidsvold Convention, one of the oldest written constitutions in Europe, was adopted by Norway on May 17, 1814. Executive power is exercised on behalf of the sovereign by a Council of State (*Statsråd*), which is headed by a prime minister and is responsible to the *Storting*. Should the cabinet resign on a vote of no confidence, the chair of the party holding the largest number of seats (exclusive of the defeated party) is asked to form a new government.

The members of the *Storting* are elected by universal suffrage and proportional representation for four-year terms. There are no by-elections, and the body is not subject to dissolution. Until October 1, 2009, the *Storting* operated as a modified bicameral assembly by electing one-fourth of its members to serve as an upper chamber (*Lagting*), while the remainder served as a lower chamber (*Odelsting*). Legislative proposals were considered separately by the two, but most other matters were dealt with by the *Storting* as a whole. The division proved largely meaningless in recent years as the party division in the chambers was the same, and legislation approved by the *Odelsting* was routinely rubber-stamped by the *Lagting*. In February 2007 the *Storting* approved a constitutional amendment, by a vote of 159–1, to dissolve the *Lagting* following the 2009 election.

The judicial system consists of district courts (*tingrett*), courts of appeal (*lagmannsrettene*), and a Supreme Court of Justice (*Høyesterett*). Judges are appointed by the king on advice from the Ministry of Justice. In addition to the regular courts, there are three special judicial institutions: a High Court of the Realm (*Riksrett*), consisting of the members of the Supreme Court and lay justices, which adjudicates charges against senior government officials; a Labor Relations Court (*Arbeidsretten*), which handles all matters concerning relations between employer and employee in both private and public sectors; and, in each community, a Conciliation Council (*Forliksråd*), to which most civil disputes are brought prior to formal legal action.

Local government is based on 19 counties (*fylker*), with Oslo, the capital, serving as one of the counties; in each county, the central government is represented by an appointed governor (*fylkesmann*). The County Council (*Fylkestinget*), which elects a board and a chair, is the representative institution at the county level. The basic units of local government are urban municipalities and rural communes, each of which is administered by an elected council (*Kommunestyre*), a board, and a mayor.

In 1987, following nearly a decade of agitation by the country's then approximately 20,000 Laplanders, agreement was reached on the establishment of a Sámi Parliament (*Sámediggi*) as replacement for the former Norwegian Sámi Council, which had been viewed as an inadequate defender of Sámi interests. The 43-member legislature has been granted authority in certain areas, such as the future of the Sámi language, the preservation of Sámi culture, and the determination of land use in Sámi-populated areas. It also has advisory functions in such areas as regional control of natural resources. Elections are held in tandem with balloting for the *Storting*.

Freedom of the press is constitutionally guaranteed. As in many other countries, media ownership has become more concentrated, which prompted the *Storting* to enact checks in 1998. Norway was ranked 3rd out of 180 countries in terms of media freedom by Reporters Without Borders in 2016.

Foreign relations. A founding member of the UN and the homeland of its first secretary general, Trygve LIE, Norway was also one of the original members of the North Atlantic Treaty Organization (NATO) and has been a leader in Western cooperation through such organizations as the Council of Europe and the Organization for Economic Cooperation and Development. Norway participated in the establishment of EFTA but, in national referendums held in 1972 and 1994, rejected membership in the EC/EU. Regional cooperation, mainly through the Nordic Council and the Nordic Council of Ministers, has also been a major element in its foreign policy.

A long-standing concern has been a dispute with what is now the Russian Federation regarding ocean-bed claims in the Barents Sea. At issue is a 60,000-square-mile area of potentially oil-rich continental shelf claimed by Norway on the basis of a median line between each country's territorial coasts and by its neighbor on the basis of a sector line extending northward from a point just east of their mainland border. A collateral disagreement has centered on fishing rights in a southern "grey zone" of the disputed area, where 200-mile limits overlap. A 1977 provisional agreement governing joint fishing in an area slightly larger than the "grey zone" proper has subsequently been renewed on an annual basis pending resolution of the larger controversy.

In 1992 Norway attracted international criticism by withdrawing from the International Whaling Commission (IWC) rather than accept an IWC ban on commercial whaling; a month later it joined with Iceland, the Faroe Islands, and Greenland to establish the pro-whaling North Atlantic Marine Mammals Commission. In 1993 foreign disapproval grew when Norwegian vessels resumed commercial whaling despite U.S. threats of trade sanctions and EU warnings that whaling was incompatible with membership.

Seeking to promote peaceful regional cooperation in the post-Soviet era, Norway became a founding member of the ten-nation Council of the Baltic Sea States in 1992 and also joined the Barents Euro-Arctic Council set up in 1993 by the five Nordic countries and Russia and the Arctic Council established in 1996 with the five Nordic countries plus Finland, Iceland, and Sweden as members. Meanwhile, Norway had not only endorsed the EEA Treaty but had also, in 1992, accepted associate membership of the Western European Union (WEU), thereby seeking to demonstrate the pro-European axis of its foreign policy. Norway has also actively promoted peace in the wider international sphere, most dramatically through its participation in the negotiations that concluded with the 1993 Oslo Accord between Israel and the Palestinians.

Norway became enmeshed in an acrimonious fisheries dispute with Iceland in 1994, arising mainly from the latter's determination to fish in the waters around the Norwegian Svalbard islands. In November 1997 Norway concluded an agreement with Iceland and Denmark (on behalf of Greenland) establishing fishing limits in the region. Fishing issues periodically resurface, with Norway typically letting the EU take the lead in negotiations with Reykjavík.

Norway's commitment to NATO has included deploying troops in peacekeeping operations in Bosnia, Kosovo, and Afghanistan. Although Norway initially pledged $74 million to aid the reconstruction of Iraq and sent 150 troops to support peacekeeping efforts there, Prime Minister Bondevik described the Iraq war as "regrettable and sad." Prime Minister Stoltenberg recalled the remaining contingent of Norwegian troops from Iraq shortly after winning the September 2005 parliamentary election.

Norway irritated the United States and some of its European neighbors with the passage of an ethical code for investments by the country's Government Pension Fund. By law, the fund, pooled from more than $300 billion in oil exports, must be invested outside Norway. The ethical code requires investments to be made only in "socially responsible" companies, blacklisting U.S. companies including General Dynamics, Boeing, Lockheed Martin, and Northrop Grumman.

Tensions between Russia and Norway increased as a result of Moscow's decision in October 2006 to forbid Norway, along with other countries, from developing Russia's natural gas fields in the Barents Sea. Norway's Statoil took a 24 percent stake in Russia's Shtokman field, one of the world's largest, but it pulled out of the project in August 2012 and wrote off its $335 million investment. At a meeting in Greenland in May 2008, Norway and Russia joined Canada, Denmark, and the United States in agreeing to use existing international laws to resolve Arctic disputes. In November 2010 Norway joined the other seven members of the Arctic Council in the signing of the Council's first binding international treaty, which established a permanent secretariat in Tromso, Norway. After 40 years of intransigence, Norway and Russia arrived at a provisional agreement on the Arctic maritime border in 2010, granting a nearly 50–50 split of the disputed area. The agreement was finalized in a treaty signed September 15, 2011. Now Norway plans to begin prospecting the southeastern Barents region.

Under tighter immigration restrictions passed in January 2012, Norway cracked down on individuals whose requests for asylum had been denied. Prime Minister Stoltenberg ordered the deportation of more than 1,000 Ethiopians, including 450 children born and raised in Norway. Many of the Ethiopians faced likely imprisonment and possible torture upon their return. Other ethnic groups were also frightened by the policy shift, with one Sri Lankan immigrant immolating herself and her 20-month-old son in protest. On July 12, 2013, the European Court of Human Rights ruled against Stoltenberg, saying the practice of returning child asylum-seekers was illegal.

Norway's attempt to become the first European country to forge a bilateral trade agreement with China had stalled when the Nobel committee awarded the 2010 Nobel Peace Prize to Chinese dissident Liu Xiao Bo. China subsequently cancelled a series of trade talks and block salmon shipments, despite the Norwegian government's insistence that it had no influence on the committee's decision. Beijing refused to issue a visa to former prime minister Kjell Magne Bondevik in June 2012 so that the ordained minister could attend a meeting of the World Council of Churches. In December 2013 a Norwegian art museum and Chinese businessman Huang Nubo struck a deal to return to China marble columns from the Beijing Old Summer Palace that had been acquired in the late 19th century by a Norwegian cavalryman. While both parties insist the deal was nongovernmental, the artifacts carry strong national significance, and the exchange was expected to warm Sino-Norwegian relations.

Following the annexation of Crimea by Russia in March 2014, Oslo condemned the move by its arctic neighbor, and at that time, temporarily suspended joint military exercises with Russian troops. In May Defense Minister Ine Eriksen SOEREIDE warned NATO to be wary of Russian activity in the Arctic.

Ahead of a May 2014 trip to Oslo by the Dalai Lama to commemorate the 25th anniversary of his Nobel Peace Prize, China condemned the visit. Norwegian leaders, wary of deepening the diplomatic crisis, capitulated to Chinese pressures and refused meetings with the exiled Tibetan spiritual leader. Critics spoke out against the snub as cowardice on behalf of government officials. Prime Minister Solberg defended the move, saying it was in an effort to thaw relations with China.

Former prime minister Jens Stoltenberg took office as the secretary general of NATO on October 1, 2014.

In July 2016 Norway announced it would contribute 200 soldiers as part of a 4,000-member NATO force to be deployed in Poland and the Baltic states as a deterrent against Russia. The deployment was scheduled to begin in 2017.

Current issues. On July 22, 2011, a bomb exploded in downtown Oslo, killing 8 and damaging government buildings, and 68 people were shot to death at a youth camp run by the ruling DNA. Anders Behring Breivik, a Norwegian citizen, far-right extremist, and former member of the Progress Party, admitted to being the perpetrator of both attacks. Breivik received the maximum prison sentence in August 2012.

Political fallout from the Breivik attack began in the September 2011 local elections. The far-right Progress Party dropped from 18 percent to 11 percent of the vote, while the DNA's showing rose from 29.6 percent in 2007 to 31.6 percent. Anger focused on Justice Minister Knut Storberget and security services chief Janne Kristiansen, leading them to resign in November 2011 and January 2012, respectively. Public opinion switched to Stoltenberg, however, on August 13, 2012, when the government-appointed independent commission investigating the attacks released a scathing report citing numerous lapses in security and communications, and blaming the high death toll on incompetence.

Stoltenberg has taken a hard-line stance toward the domestic petroleum industry. Aware of their sector's importance, oil and gas workers struck for higher wages in 2012, the government responded with a lockout and binding arbitration. Norway's oil wages are 69 percent above the EU average, driving up wages across the board and undermining competitiveness. To appease Center's agricultural constituents, the government imposed higher meat and cheese tariffs in November 2012.

On January 16, 2013, Islamist militants attacked a gas-processing plant in Algeria, killing dozens, including five Norwegian Statoil employees. The insurgents were believed to have entered Algeria from Mali. Defense Minister Anne-Grete STRØM-ERICHSEN (DNA) announced on June 4 that Norway would contribute 25 troops to the UN peacekeeping mission in Mali. The news came as a surprise, as the SV, DNA's pacifist junior partner, had been vehemently against any involvement.

Parliamentary elections were held on September 9, 2013. Health care, education, and immigration dominated the campaign, with parties differing over how best to use the country's oil revenue fund. Stoltenberg's coalition fractured ahead of the election over how to balance industrialization and environmental concerns. Distancing itself from Labor, the Center Party's 2013 congress ended with calls for Norway to leave the Schengen area and the European Economic Area. The Conservatives stressed improving competitiveness through education, innovation, and privatizing some health care services.

Voters in 12 municipalities, about 250,000 residents, were able to vote online. A coalition of 4 conservative parties, led by Erna Solberg, won 96 seats in the *Stortinget*, comfortably exceeding the 85 needed for a majority. Solberg's Conservatives won 48 seats, followed by the Progress Party with 29, the Christian Democrats with 10, and the Liberals with 9. The populist Progress Party has never been in government before, and even with its toned-down anti-immigration rhetoric, the Christian Democrats and Liberals were reluctant to join a coalition that included them. On September 30 Solberg announced she was forming a minority government with the Progress Party, winning its support after agreeing to halt Arctic oil exploration and to tighten asylum policies.

In January 2014 the Norwegian government began taking steps toward privatizing state-owned real estate company, Entra Holding AS. The Conservatives have long pushed to reduce direct state ownership, and took further steps in May when the government signaled plans to include divestiture from eight companies in the 2015 budget. In two companies, telecommunications company Telenor ASA and defense contractor Kongsberg Gruppen SA, the government will retain a "blocking minority." Liberals have come out in support. On October 14 Norway expanded compulsory military service to include women, making it the first NATO nation to have peacetime conscription of its full population.

In response to a growing number of migrants (see entry on the EU), on October 8, 2015, Norway implemented a five-year limitation on asylum seekers. In November Norway imposed temporary border controls, which were subsequently extended through May 2016.

In January 2016 Norway began the deportation of an estimated 5,000 migrants who had illegally crossed into the country or had been denied asylum. The country's immigration directorate reported that it had granted asylum to 18,431 people in 2015 out of 31,145 applications.

In June 2016 Parliament enacted legislation requiring the country to become carbon neutral by 2030, two decades sooner than required by the 2016 Paris Climate Agreement (see entry on the United Nations).

POLITICAL PARTIES

Government Parties:

Conservative Party (*Høyre*—H). The oldest of the contemporary Norwegian parties (founded in 1884), the *Høyre* (literally "Right") advocates a "modern, progressive conservatism" emphasizing private investment, elimination of government control in the semipublic industries, lower taxes, and a revised tax structure that would benefit business. It has long favored a strong defense policy.

Although the party's parliamentary representation declined from 50 seats in 1985 to 37 in 1989, it succeeded in forming a short-lived minority coalition administration under Jan Syse—the party's sole prime minister, Kåre Willoch, left office in 1986. In the September 1993 election the pro-EU Conservatives slumped from 37 seats to 28. The national leadership frequently backed the minority Labor government. In 1997 the party decline continued as it won only 23 seats. In 2001 it resurged, winning 38 seats, but its chair, Jan PETERSEN, yielded to KrF insistence that Kjell Bondevik be prime minister of any KrF-Conservative-Liberal government.

Although the party captured only 23 seats in the 2005 election, in 2006 it opted to maintain its leadership, reelecting Erna Solberg as chair. It won the September 2007 elections 19 percent of the vote. The Conservative vote share rebounded to 17.2 percent in 2009, increasing the party's seat total from 23 to 30, but still 11 seats behind the Frp. Public opinion polling a month after the election showed the Conservatives pulling ahead of the Frp for the first time in several years.

Campaigning on a platform of lower taxes, economic diversification, and privatization, Solberg led the Conservatives to victory in 2013, winning 48 seats—placing it second behind Labor—but head of a four-party coalition that secured a majority of 96 seats. Solberg formed a minority government with the Progress Party. In local balloting on September 14, 2015, the party was second with 23.2 percent of the vote.

Leaders: Erna SOLBERG (Prime Minister and Chair), Jan Tore SANNER (First Vice Chair), Bent HØIE (Second Vice Chair), Lars Arne RYSSDAL (Secretary General).

Progress Party (*Fremskrittspartiet*—Frp). A libertarian group founded by Anders LANGE in 1974, the anti-EU Progress Party was known until 1977 as **Anders Lange's Party for a Strong Reduction in Taxes, Rates, and Public Intervention** (*Anders Langes Parti til Sterk Nedsettelse av Skatter, Avgifter, og Offentlige Inngrep*). Although it lost 2 of its 4 seats in the 1985 balloting, the Frp was subsequently invited to join the ruling coalition to offset the Conservatives' losses. Declining to do so, the party held a subsequent balance of power in the *Storting* and provided the crucial votes needed to defeat the Willoch government in April 1986. In the 1989 parliamentary poll the Frp emerged as the third largest party, with 22 *Storting* seats, but in 1993 it suffered a major reverse, winning only 10. In 1997 the Frp regained its strength by winning 25 seats and a 15.3 percent share of the vote, second only to Labour. The Frp opposes fishing and agriculture subsidies, but supports dismantling the welfare state and restrictions on immigration.

Less than a year before the September 2001 election, polls showed the Frp as the country's most popular party, but that changed in February 2001 when party members, including its second most influential leader, Terje SÖVIKNES, were implicated in a sex scandal. Meanwhile, the party was also being torn by sharp differences between its more moderate elements and its more overtly fascistic and racist wing. In the end, the party registered a modest loss in vote share, to 14.7 percent, and won 26 seats.

Entering the September 2005 election, the Frp positioned itself as an outside party and campaigned both in defense of a strong welfare state and for radical tax cuts. It was rewarded with 22 percent of the vote and 38 seats, supplanting the Conservatives as the leading opposition party. In May 2006 Siv Jensen—the first woman to lead the party—was elected chair. Under her leadership the party took an increasingly hard line against immigrants, especially Muslim immigrants.

In the September 2007 local elections the Frp won about 18 percent of the vote, below its 2005 vote share and a percentage point behind the Conservatives. The Frp continued to make electoral progress in the September 2009 balloting, increasing its vote share to a best-ever 22.9 percent and winning 41 seats. The party's popularity dropped initially following the in the wake of Anders Behring Breivik's murder spree in 2011 (Breivik, who had once been a member of the Frp, attacked the Labor Party because he believed that its promotion of multiculturalism had allowed a Muslim "demographic jihad" threatening Norway's national identity), but it recovered and finished third in the 2013 parliamentary election, winning 29 seats. It entered government for the first time in coalition with the Conservative Party. Members of the Frp expressed concern over the coalition's 2014 initiative to reduce government share in certain companies, primarily the defense firm Kongsberg Gruppen. In local elections in September 2015, the party was third with 9.5 percent of the vote.

Leaders: Siv JENSEN (Chair), Per SANDBERG (First Vice Chair), Ketil Solvik OLSEN (Second Vice Chair), Finn Egil HOLM (Secretary General).

Other Parliamentary Parties:

Norwegian Labor Party (*Det Norske Arbeiderparti*—DNA). Organized in 1887, Labor has been the strongest party in Norway since 1927. Its program of democratic socialism resembles those of other Scandinavian Social Democratic parties. Its longest-serving post-World War II prime ministers have been Einar Gerhardsen, who served three times (for a total of over 17 years), between 1945 and 1965, and Gro Harlem Brundtland, who also served three times (for some 10 years), between 1981 and 1996.

In June 1994 a special Labor conference decided by a 2–1 majority to back EU accession in the November referendum, although substantial rank-and-file Labor opposition to membership contributed to the eventual "no" vote. When Brundtland decided to retire as prime minister in 1996, she handed over leadership to Thorbjørn Jagland. The party leadership seemed open to finding private sector solutions for the problems of the welfare state, alienating some of its more left-wing supporters. Labor also remained a firm backer of NATO.

Jagland resigned as prime minister after the 1997 legislative election. Even though Labor had won a plurality of 65 seats, it fell short of his prediction. Labor's vote share declined in municipal balloting in September 1999 and February 2000, but the fall of the Bondevik coalition government in March 2000 led to formation of a Labor minority government under Jens Stoltenberg. After Labor won a dismal 43 *Storting* seats in the September 2001 election, Stoltenberg resigned as prime minister and became party chair, replacing Jagland, in November 2002.

Building on positive results in the September 2003 local elections, Stoltenberg negotiated a red-green alliance with the Center and Socialist Left Parties that, led by Labor's 61 seats at the September 2005 election, permitted Stoltenberg to reclaim the office of prime minister. In the September 2007 local elections Labor increased its vote share over 2003 by about 2 percent, to 30 percent of the total. Even more impressive was Labor's 35.4 percent vote share in the September 2009 general election. Its 64 seats allowed the Stoltenberg-headed, Labor-led coalition to continue its majority status. Labor dropped 9 seats in 2013 and lost control of the *Stortinget.* Stoltenberg tendered his resignation on October 14, after completing the 2014 budget. In March 2014 he was appointed NATO secretary general. Jonas Gahr STØRE was elected party leader in internal balloting on June 14, 2014.

Labor led the 2015 local polling with 33 percent of the vote.

Leaders: Jonas Gahr STØRE (Party Leader), Helga PEDERSEN (Deputy Leader), Raymond JOHANSEN (General Secretary).

Christian People's Party (*Kristelig Folkeparti*—KrF or KFp). Also known as the **Christian Democratic Party**, the KrF was created in 1933 with the primary objective of maintaining the principles of Christianity in public life. In addition to support for most Conservative policies, the KrF's agenda subsequently centered on introduction of anti-abortion legislation and increased trade with developing countries. In the 1989 election its legislative strength dropped from 16 to 14 seats, falling further by 1 seat in 1993, when it campaigned against EU membership. The party nearly doubled its representation in September 1997, going up to 25 seats. Joining with the Liberal and Center Parties to form a minority coalition government in October, the KrF was permitted to select the new prime minister—former deputy prime minister and foreign affairs minister Kjell Bondevik—because it held the largest deputy bloc of the three. Bondevik resigned as prime minister in March 2000 following defeat of a government bill in the *Storting.* Although the party finished with only 22 seats after the September 2001 election, Bondevik returned to the prime ministership. Following a poor performance by the KrF in the September 2003 local elections, Valgerd Svarstad HAUGLAND resigned after nearly nine years as KrF chair; she was succeeded in 2004 by Health Minister Dagfinn Høybråten, a strong opponent of EU membership.

Under Bondevik, Norway enjoyed strong economic growth. Moreover, inflation remained largely in check while interest rates declined sharply. However, Bondevik's insistence on a conservative fiscal policy and tax cuts seemed out of step with the general public, which favored higher levels of public sector spending. In 2005 the KrF won less than 7 percent of the votes cast and only 11 seats. Bondevik announced his retirement from politics shortly after the election. In the September 2009 parliamentary balloting, the KrF vote share fell back to 5.5 percent (good for 10 seats), its worst showing since shortly after the party was formed in the 1930s. It polled a similar 5.6 percent in 2013, again taking 10 seats. The party won 5.4 percent of the vote in the 2015 local elections.

Leaders: Knut Arild HAREIDE (Chair); Dagun ERIKSEN, Bjørg Tysdal MOE (Deputy Chairs); Hans Olaf SYVERSEN (Parliamentary Leader); Knut JAHR (Secretary General); Andreas Haug LØLAND (International Secretary).

Center Party (*Senterpartiet*—Sp). Formed in 1920 to promote the interests of agriculture and forestry, the Sp was originally known as the Agrarian Party. In the late 1980s it began to take steps to broaden its appeal, changing its name, stressing ecological issues, and advocating reduced workdays for families with small children. Not surprisingly, it also championed the post-1975 government policy of bringing farmers' incomes up to the level of industrial workers, although it remained conservative on some economic, social, and religious matters.

Campaigning on a strongly anti-EU ticket, the Sp made major gains in the September 1993 election, increasing its representation from 11 to 32 seats. In the new *Storting* the Sp often backed the minority Labor government, although in June 1996 the party issued a joint statement with Christian People's and Liberal Parties envisaging a nonsocialist coalition after the 1997 election. In 1997 the Sp dropped back to 11 seats, although its vision of a center-liberal coalition government became a reality the following month.

Anne Enger LAHNSTEIN, Sp chair for 16 years, resigned her party post (but not her cabinet position) in March 1999 and was succeeded by

Odd Roger ENOKSEN. In the 2001 election the party won ten *Storting* seats, remaining in opposition. Åslaug HAGA assumed the party's leadership in 2005 and entered into the red-green alliance with the Labor and Center Parties. By doing so, she further moved the party to a centrist position, supporting, for example, oil production in the Barents Sea (under strict environmental standards) and further participation in the global markets. Some members of the party charged that Haga abandoned farmers and the party's traditional agricultural values. In the September 2007 local elections the Sp won about 8 percent of the total vote, as it had in 2003.

After receiving fierce criticism over allegations that she had obtained illegal building permits for her family's homes, Haga resigned her party leadership and ministerial positions in mid-June 2008. She was replaced on a temporary basis by Deputy Leader Lars Peder Brekk until the party elected Liv Signe Navarsete as its new leader in September. Under Navarsete's leadership the Sp held onto its 11 seats (on a vote share of 6.2 percent) in the September 2009 election, which allowed it to continue as a junior partner in the Labor-led majority coalition, despite misgivings about Labor's intention to keep open the possibility of more off-shore oil exploration. The party dropped from 11 seats to 10 in the 2013 election. Navarsete resigned in January 2014. At an extraordinary general meeting on April 7, Trygve Slagsvold Vedum was elected unopposed to the post. Deputy leader Ola Borten MOE was reelected as deputy leader in a divisive battle. The party secured 8.5 percent of the vote in the 2015 local elections.

Leaders: Trygve Slagsvold VEDUM (Party Leader), Ola Borten MOE (Deputy Leader), Knut OLSEN (Secretary General).

Liberal Party (*Venstre*—V). Formed in 1884, the Liberal Party (*venstre* means "left"), like the Sp, currently stresses ecological issues, while in economic policy it stands between the Conservative and Labor Parties. The Liberals lost their two remaining parliamentary seats in 1985. In June 1988 the **Liberal People's Party** (*Det Liberale Folkepartiet*—DLF), which had been formed in 1972 by Liberal dissidents who favored Norway's entrance into the EC and had lost its only parliamentary seat in 1977, rejoined the parent party. After failing to regain *Storting* representation in 1989, the Liberals won 1 seat in 1993 and took 6 seats in 1997, joining the subsequent KrF-led coalition government until its dissolution in March 2000. *Venstre* won only 2 seats in 2001 but again joined Prime Minister Bondevik's governing coalition. In the September 2005 elections the party made its best showing since 1972, winning almost 6 percent of the vote and capturing 10 seats, but the success was short-lived. Ahead of the September 2009 parliamentary election, leader Lars SPONHEIM ruled out his party's participation in any government that included the Progressives. The party won only 3.9 percent of the vote and 2 seats. Sponheim resigned after the election, and Trine Skei Grande, one of the party's two parliamentarians, was elected party leader in April 2010. *Venstre* won 9 seats in 2013 as part of Erna Solberg's conservative coalition. The party won 5.5 percent of the vote in the 2015 local elections.

Leaders: Trine Skei GRANDE (Leader); Ola ELVESTUEN, Terje BREVIK (Deputy Leaders).

Socialist Left Party (*Sosialistisk Venstreparti*—SV). Organized prior to the 1973 election as the **Socialist Electoral Association** (*Sosialistisk Valgforbund*), the SV was until late 1975 a coalition of the Norwegian Communist Party (below), the **Socialist People's Party** (*Sosialistisk Folkeparti*—SF), and the **Democratic Socialist/ Labor Movement Information Committee against Norwegian Membership in the Common Market** (*Demokratiske Sosialister/ Arbeiderbevegelsens Informasjonskomite mot Norsk Medlemskap i EF*—DS/AIK). At a congress held in Trondheim in March 1975, the members of the coalition committed themselves to the formation of the new party, although dissolution of the constituent parties was not mandatory until the end of 1976. In November 1975 the Communist Party decided against dissolution, and in the September 1977 election the SV, damaged in August when two of its deputies leaked a secret parliamentary report on defense negotiations with the United States, retained only 2 of the 16 seats formerly held by the Socialist alliance. The party nonetheless provided the Nordli government with the crucial support needed to maintain a slim parliamentary majority prior to the 1981 balloting, in which it won 2 additional seats. In 1989 the party raised its parliamentary representation from 6 to 17 seats before slipping back to 13 in 1993.

The SV campaigned against EU accession in the November 1994 referendum. In April 1996 SV leader Erik SOLHEIM accused Labor and its Center parliamentary allies of "Americanizing" Norway by a combination of tax cuts for the rich and welfare benefit cuts for the poor. The SV faltered in the 1997 election, dropping from 13 seats to 9. It has toned down its anti-NATO rhetoric in recent years and is now a strong advocate for Norway's "international responsibilities," including foreign aid. The SV more than doubled its representation in the September 2001 election, winning 23 seats.

Looking to build upon its 2001 success, the SV continued to move toward more centrist positions and joined Labor and the Center Party to form the red-green alliance in the September 2005 election. As a requirement for joining the alliance, the SV agreed to set aside its long-standing demand that Norway withdraw from NATO and muted much of its anti-U.S. rhetoric. However, it retained only 15 seats. In 2006–2007 the SV grew more critical of the government's environmental policies and the country's continuing presence in Afghanistan. In the September 2007 local elections the SV won only 6 percent of the vote, about half of its 2003 share. Its electoral fortunes also fell in the 2009 parliamentary balloting, in which it won only 6.2 percent of the vote and 11 seats. The SV subsequently kept its minor coalition partner role in government, but only after agreeing to the Labor Party positions on tightening restrictions on asylum seekers and keeping open the possibility of more off-shore oil exploration. Long-time party leader Kristin HALVORSEN stepped down as party chair on March 10, 2012. She was succeeded by Audun Lysbakken, the former minister of children, equality, and social inclusion. Lysbakken had resigned that post just five days earlier amid charges of channeling public funds to charity groups linked to him, but he was the only candidate for the job. The party dropped from 11 seats to 7 in the 2013 elections. In local balloting in 2015, the party secured 4.1 percent of the vote.

Leaders: Audun LYSBAKKEN (Party Chair), Bård Vegar SOLHJELL (Deputy Chair and Parliamentary Leader), Inga Marte THORKILDSEN (Deputy Chair), Silje Schei TVEITDAL (Secretary General), Lene Aure HANSEN (International Secretary).

Green Party (*Miljøpartiet De Grønne*—MDG). Norway's Green Party was established in 1988 by consolidating many local movements. It advocates a "caring society in ecological balance" and is especially concerned with the environmental impact of Norway's petroleum industry. The party received only 0.3 percent of the vote in 2009, its first run for the *Stortinget*, but won representation in 18 city councils in 2011, including Oslo, Bergen, Trondheim, and Stavanger. It won its first national seat in 2013, with 2.8 percent of the vote. It also won 4.2 percent of the vote in the 2015 local polls.

Spokespersons: Hilde OPUKU, Rasmus HANSSON (Spokespersons); Lars GAUPSET (Party Secretary).

Other Parties Contesting the 2013 Elections:

Red (*Rødt*). Red was formed in March 2007 by merger of the **Red Electoral Alliance** (*Rød Valgallianse*—RV) and the **Workers' Communist Party** (*Arbeidernes Kommunistparti*—AKP). The RV had been formed in 1973 as an electoral front for the Maoist AKP but subsequently grew to include a substantial number of self-described "independent socialists." Prior to the 1989 elections the RV joined with the Norwegian Communist Party (NKP, above) in the FMS. Returning to a separate status, in 1993 the RV won 1.1 percent of the vote and one *Storting* seat, which it lost in 1997. In 2005 the RV won only 1.2 percent of the vote and again failed to capture any seats. Torstein DAHLE was reelected party president in 2005 and then leader of the newly formed Red. He was able to lead the party to a slight increase in vote support in the September 2009 balloting, but the RV's 1.4 percent of the vote entitled it to no seats. It dropped to 1.1 percent in 2013 but secured 2 percent in the 2015 local balloting.

Leaders: Torstein DAHLE (Leader); Marie Sneve MARTINUSSEN, Marielle LERAAND (Deputy Leaders); Mari ELFRING (Secretary).

The only other parties to achieve at least 0.1 percent in 2013 were the **The Christians** (*De Kristne*), with 0.6 percent; the **Pensioners' Party** (*Pensjonistpartiet*—Pp), 0.4 percent; the **Pirate Party of Norway** (*Piratpartiet Norge*), 0.3 percent; the **Coastal Party** (*Kystpartiet*), **Democrats in Norway** (*Demokratene i Norge*), and the **Christian Unity Party** (*Kristent Samlingsparth*); each polled 0.1 percent.

Norwegian Communist Party (*Norges Kommunistiske Parti*—NKP). The NKP held 11 *Storting* seats in 1945 but lost all of them by 1961. In March 1975 it participated in the initial formation of the

Socialist Left Party, but the following November it voted at an extraordinary congress against its own dissolution. Prior to the 1989 election it joined with the Red Electoral Alliance (see Red, above) to form the **Local List for Environment and Solidarity** (*Fylkeslistene for Miljø og Solidaritet*—FMS), which failed to secure representation. The party chose not to contest the 1993 election and obtained only 0.1 percent of the vote or less in 1997, 2001, 2005, and 2009. It received 611 votes in 2013.

Leader: Runa EVENSEN.

LEGISLATURE

The ***Stortinget*** (also frequently rendered as *Storting*) is a unicameral parliament whose members are elected to four-year terms by universal suffrage and party-list proportional representation from 19 multimember (3 to 16 seats each) constituencies (corresponding to the 19 counties). (Of the 169 members, 150 are elected based solely on results within each constituency. The other 19 sears [one in each constituency] serve as "top up" or compensatory seats and are distributed according to nationwide vote percentages for parties.) From 1814 through mid-2009 it divided itself for certain purposes into two chambers by electing one-fourth of its members to an upper chamber (*Lagting*), while the remaining members constituted a lower chamber (*Odelsting*). Each *ting* named its own president; the president of the *Storting* served for the duration of its term, and the presidents of the two chambers were chosen annually. The *Lagting* sat for the last time in June 2009, and the dual chamber structure was officially dissolved on October 1.

In the most recent election on September 9, 2013, the Norwegian Labor Party won 55 seats; Conservative Party, 48; Progress Party, 29; Christian People's Party, 10; Center Party, 10; Liberal Party, 9; Socialist Left Party, 7; and Green Party, 1.

President of the Storting: Olemic THOMMESSEN.

CABINET

[as of August 18, 2016]

Prime Minister	Erna Solberg (H) [f]
Ministers	
Agriculture and Food	Jon Georg Dale (Frp)
Children, Equality, and Social Inclusion	Solveig Horne (Frp) [f]
Climate and Environment	Vidar Helgesen (H)
Culture	Linda Cathrine Hofstad Helleland (H) [f]
Defense	Ine Marie Eriksen Søreide (H) [f]
Education, Research, and Higher Education	Torbjørn Røe Isaksen (H)
Environment	Tine Sundtoft (H) [f]
EU Affairs	Elisabeth Aspaker (H) [f]
Finance	Siv Jensen (Frp) [f]
Fisheries	Per Sandberg (H)
Foreign Affairs	Børge Brende (H)
Health and Care Services	Bent Høie (H)
Immigration and Integration	Sylvi Listhaug (FrP) [f]
Justice and Public Security	Anders Anundsen (Frp)
Labor and Social Affairs	Anniken Hauglie (Frp) [f]
Local Government and Regional Development	Jan Tore Sanner (H)
Petroleum and Energy	Tord Lien (Frp)
Trade and Industry	Monica Mæland (H) [f]
Transport and Communications	Ketil Solvik-Olsen (Frp)

[f] = female

INTERGOVERNMENTAL REPRESENTATION

Ambassador to the U.S.: Kare R. AAS.

U.S. Ambassador to Norway: Jim DeHART (Chargé d'Affaires *ad interim*).

Permanent Representative to the UN: Geir O. PEDERSEN.

IGO Memberships (Non-UN): ADB, AfDB, CEUR, EBRD, EFTA, IADB, ICC, IEA, IOM, NATO, OECD, OSCE, WTO.

For Further Reference:

Brundtland, Gro Harlem. *Madam Prime Minister: A Life in Power and Politics.* New York: Farrar, Straus and Giroux, 2002.

Sejersted, Francis. *The Age of Social Democracy: Norway and Sweden in the Twentieth Century.* Princeton, NJ: Princeton University Press, 2011.

Taulbee, James Larry, Ann Kelleher, and Peter C. Grosvenor. *Norway's Peace Policy: Soft Power in a Turbulent World.* New York: Palgrave Macmillan, 2014.

RELATED TERRITORIES

Norway's principal overseas territories are the islands of the Svalbard group and Jan Mayen, both of which are legally incorporated into the Norwegian state. In addition, Norway has two dependencies in southern waters, Bouvet Island and Peter I Island, and claims a sector of Antarctica.

Svalbard. Svalbard is the group name given to all the islands in the Arctic Ocean between 74° and 81° north latitude and 10° and 35° east longitude, Spitzbergen being the most important island in the group. Svalbard has a land area of 23,957 square miles (62,049 sq. km); its resident population is approximately 2,640 (2012E), of whom some 1,600 are Norwegians, most of the remainder being Russians.

The islands were placed under Norwegian sovereignty by the 1920 Svalbard Treaty, the 39 signatories of which are entitled to exploit Svalbard's natural resources, although only Norwegian and Soviet/Russian companies have done so. Coal mining is the major activity in the area; oil and gas exploration began in the late 1980s. In 1993 the government and four Norwegian universities established at the largest settlement, Longyearbyen, the University Center in Svalbard, which hosts domestic and international researchers and students. More recently, tourism has been gaining in importance.

In 2007 construction began on the Svalbard International Seed Vault on Spitzbergen. The vault, positioned 120 meters inside a mountain, will store seeds from all known varieties of food crops as protection against their loss.

Governor: Odd Olsen INGERØ.

Jan Mayen. Jan Mayen is an island of 144 square miles (373 sq. km) located in the Norwegian Sea, 555 nautical miles from Tromsø. It was incorporated as part of the Kingdom of Norway in 1930. A meteorological station was established on the island during World War II, with navigational and radio facilities added thereafter. There are no permanent inhabitants.

Bouvet Island (*Bouvetøya*). Located in the South Atlantic, Bouvet Island has an area of 22 square miles (58 sq. km) and is uninhabited. It became a Norwegian dependency in 1930 and was declared to be a nature reserve in 1971.

Peter I Island (*Peter I Øy*). Situated some 250 miles off the Antarctic continent in the Bellingshausen Sea, Peter I Island has an area of 96 square miles (249 sq. km) and became a Norwegian dependency in 1933. It is uninhabited.

Queen Maud Land (*Dronning Maud Land*). The Norwegian-claimed sector of Antarctica, Queen Maud Land, extends from 20° west longitude to 45° east longitude. Its legal status has been placed in suspense under terms of the 1959 Antarctic Treaty.

OMAN

Sultanate of Oman
Sultanat Uman

Political Status: Independent sultanate recognized December 20, 1951; present regime instituted July 23, 1970; new "basic law" decreed on November 6, 1996.

Area: 119,500 sq. mi. (309,500 sq. km).

Population: 4,655,000 (2016E—UN); 3,355,262 (2016E—U.S. Census).

Major Urban Center (2015E—UN): MUSCAT (838,000, urban area).

Official Language: Arabic.

Monetary Unit: Oman Rial (official rate October 1, 2016: 0.39 rial = $1US).

Head of State and Government: Sultan Qabus bin Said Al SAID; assumed power July 23, 1970, in a coup d'état that deposed his father, Sultan Said bin Taymur Al SAID.

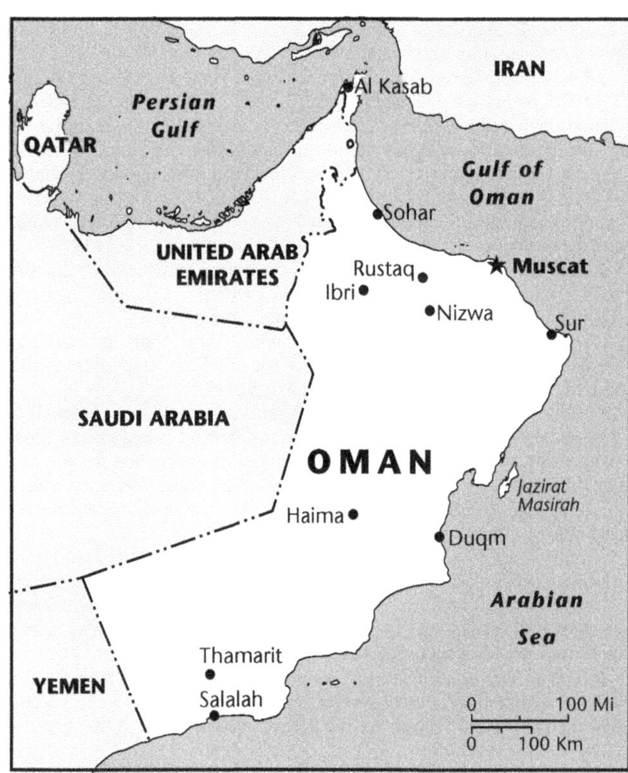

THE COUNTRY

The Sultanate of Oman (known prior to August 1970 as Muscat and Oman), which occupies the southeast portion of the Arabian Peninsula and a number of offshore islands, is bounded by the United Arab Emirates on the northwest, Saudi Arabia on the west, and Yemen on the extreme southwest. A small, noncontiguous area at the tip of the Musandam Peninsula extends northward into the Strait of Hormuz, through which much of the world's ocean-shipped oil passes. Although the Omani population is predominantly Arab (divided into an estimated 200 tribes), small communities of Iranians, Baluchis, Indians, East Africans, and Pakistanis are also found. Ibadhi Muslims constitute up to 75 percent of the population; most of the remainders are Wahhabis of the Sunni branch, although there is a small Shiite population. In addition to Arabic, English, Farsi, and Urdu, several Indian dialects are spoken.

Prior to 1970 the Sultanate was an isolated, essentially medieval state without roads, electricity, or significant educational and health facilities; social behavior was dictated by a repressive and reclusive sultan. However, following his overthrow in 1970, the country underwent rapid modernization, fueled by soaring oil revenue. Oman currently provides free medical facilities, housing assistance for most of its citizens, and schooling, with a 97 percent enrollment rate for primary school aged children in 2011, according to the World Bank. Economic growth has been concentrated in the coastal cities with an accompanying construction boom relying on a large foreign workforce. However, under a government program designed to reduce migration to urban areas, services have been extended to most of the vast rural interior. Growing access to education (more than 40 percent of Omani students are female) has reduced the once high illiteracy rate among women. Women have visible roles in both private and public sectors in part because of the relatively moderate (in regional terms) stance of the sultan.

Although much of the labor force works in agriculture, most food must be imported; dates, nuts, limes, and fish are exported. Cattle are bred extensively in the southern province of Dhofar, and Omani camels are prized throughout Arabia. Foreign workers are estimated to be 40 percent of the population. Since petroleum production began in 1967, the Sultanate has become heavily dependent on oil revenue, which, at a production rate of more than 700,000 barrels per day, accounts for more than 70 percent of government revenue and 40 percent of GDP. However, liquefied natural gas continues to be a rapidly growing segment of the economy. In a further effort to offset the nation's dependence on oil, the government has launched a program of economic diversification, intended to encourage foreign investment, promote small-scale private industry, and enhance the fledgling tourism sector. Recent initiatives include changes in investment law to permit Omani companies to be owned by non-nationals. The government of Oman has also undertaken a number of large infrastructure projects, including the construction of the giant maritime trans-shipment terminal at the port of Mina Raysut, and development of gas exports.

Oman's decision in 2008 to continue its monetary peg to the U.S. dollar rather than join a monetary union with the Gulf Cooperation Council (GCC) was commended by fund managers, though they acknowledged that the peg was among the chief reasons for rising inflation in the sultanate. In the wake of the global economic crisis in 2009, the government said it would increase spending by 11 percent to help offset declining oil revenues. Annual GDP growth remained robust, averaging 4.4 percent from 2008 to 2011, even as oil reserves (and output) declined. The estimated real GDP growth rate for 2013 was 4.2 percent. Increases in tourism, direct foreign investment, oil prices, and public spending helped bolster the economy, which IMF managers said had weathered the global economic crisis well. Economic growth of 2.9 percent in 2014 reflected a slight decrease in fiscal surpluses. In 2016 annual GDP growth was estimated to have dipped to 3.1 percent, largely the result of a marked drop in the price of the oil on which the Omani economy is disproportionately reliant. Inflation that year was 2.6 percent, while GDP per capita was $15,796.

GOVERNMENT AND POLITICS

Political background. Conquered by the Portuguese in 1508, the Omanis successfully revolted in 1650 and subsequently extended their domain as far south as Zanzibar. A brief period of Iranian intrusion (1741–1743) was followed in 1798 by the establishment of a treaty of friendship with Great Britain; thereafter, the British played a protective role, although formally recognizing the Sultanate's independence in 1951.

Oman is home of the Ibadhi sect, centered in Nazwa, which evolved from the egalitarian Kharijite movement of early Islam. During much of the twentieth century, Omani politics centered on an intrasect rivalry between imams, who controlled the interior, and sultans of the Said dynasty, who ruled over the coastal cities of Muscat and Muttrah, although the Treaty of Sib, concluded in 1920, acknowledged the nation's indivisibility. On the death of the incumbent imam in 1954, Sultan Said bin Taymur Al SAID attempted, without success, to secure election as his successor. However, revolts against the sultan by the new imam's followers were ended with British help in 1959, thus cementing the sultan's authority over the entire country. The foreign presence having become the subject of a number of UN debates, the remaining British bases were closed in 1977, although a number of British officers remained attached to the Omani armed forces.

The conservative and isolationist Sultan Said was ousted on July 23, 1970, by his son, Qabus bin Said Al SAID. The former sultan fled to London, where he died in 1972. Qabus, whose takeover was supported by the British, soon began efforts to modernize the country, but his request for cooperation from rebel groups who had opposed his father evoked little positive response. In 1971–1972 two left-wing guerrilla groups merged to form the Popular Front for the Liberation of Oman and the Arabian Gulf (renamed in July 1974 as the Popular Front for the Liberation of Oman—PFLO), which continued resistance to the sultan's regime, primarily from bases in the (then) People's Democratic Republic of Yemen (South Yemen). Qabus maintained his superiority with military assistance from Saudi Arabia, Jordan, Iran, and Pakistan, and in December 1975 he asserted that the rebellion had been crushed, and a formal cease-fire was announced in March 1976.

Although the sultan subsequently stated his desire to introduce democratic reforms, a Consultative Assembly established in 1981 consisted entirely of appointed members, and Oman remained for all practical purposes an absolute monarchy. In November 1990 the sultan announced plans for a Consultative Council of regional representatives in an effort to provide for more citizen participation.

On November 6, 1996, Sultan Qabus issued "The Basic Law of the Sultanate of Oman," the nation's first quasi-constitutional document. Although it confirmed the final authority of the sultan in all government matters, it also codified the responsibilities of the Council of Ministers and provided for a second consultative body, the Council of State (see Legislature, below). Subsequently, following preliminary balloting for a new Consultative Council on October 16, 1997, Sultan Qabus reshuffled his cabinet on December 16, designating several "young technocrats" as new ministers.

New elections to the Consultative Council were held on September 14, 2000, successful candidates for the first time not being subject to approval by the sultan. The Omani government continued to pursue "quiet progress" toward political liberalization by mandating that 30 percent of the electors in the electoral college be women. As it turned out, only two women candidates were successful in the elections of October 4, 2003, the first time that all citizens could participate. Members were elected to four-year terms in the first balloting open to all citizens.

In the October 27, 2007, Consultative Council elections, no women won seats, marking the first time in many years that the assembly was without female representation. The cabinet was reshuffled on September 9, 2007, and the manpower minister was replaced in September 2008. The minister of health was replaced in March 2010.

Beginning with protests in Tunisia in December 2010, the so-called Arab Spring uprisings spread quickly throughout North Africa and the Middle East, erupting in Oman in late February, driven by high unemployment and a young population, more than half of which is under age 30. On the second day of demonstrations in the port town of Sohar, police shot and killed two protesters. Sultan Qabus responded quickly, reshuffling the cabinet, granting pay raises to civil servants, pledging to create 50,000 public sector jobs, and ceding some lawmaking powers to the Consultative Council. Though demonstrations continued in various parts of the country with activists calling for democratic reforms and an end to corruption, the protests were generally much smaller in number than in other countries in the region in 2010–2011. Sultan Qabus, for his part, authorized a $2.6 billion social spending package, including financial assistance to military and civil service employees and an increase in the minimum wage. After making minor changes to the cabinet on February 27, 2011, Sultan Qabus orchestrated a major reshuffle on March 7 in response to ongoing protests. Amnesty International published a report on March 31, 2011, lambasting Omani authorities for their treatment of protesters. Protests continued into April, and clashes left a total of five people dead.

In response to the Arab Spring uprisings, in September Qabus called for Consultative Council elections to be held on October 15, 2011. For the first time, candidates were allowed to conduct advertising campaigns on billboards, posters, banners, and in newspapers. Voter registration was reported to be at an all-time high of more than 522,000 citizens, and voter turnout was 76 percent. On February 29, 2012, the sultan announced the second major cabinet reshuffle in a year, replacing the justice and information portfolios.

The 2016 budget, adopted in December 2015, raised the corporate tax rate from 12 to 15 percent and cut subsidies, including fuel subsidies, in an effort to reduce a deficit estimated to be more than 8 percent of GDP.

Constitution and government. Lagging behind most other Arab states in this regard, Oman until recently had no constitution or other fundamental law, absolute power resting with the sultan, who ruled by decree. However, on November 6, 1996, Sultan Qabus issued "The Basic Law of the Sultanate of Oman," formally confirming the government's status as a hereditary Sultanate—an "independent, Arab, Islamic, fully sovereign state" for which *sharia* (Islamic religious law) is the "basis for legislation." Total authority for the issuance of legislation remains with the sultan, designated as head of state and commander in chief of the armed forces. The "ruling family council" is authorized to appoint a successor should the position of sultan become vacant. The sultan rules with the assistance of a Council of Ministers, whose members he appoints. The first woman was appointed to the cabinet in 2004. The sultan may appoint a prime minister but is not so required. Consultation is also provided by the Oman Council, comprising a new Council of State and the Consultative Council (see Legislature, below). The basic law can be revised only by decree of the sultan. Among other things, the basic law provides for freedom of opinion, expression, and association "within the limits of the law."

The sultanate ranked 125th out of 180 countries in the 2016 annual press freedom index by Reporters Without Borders. At least 50 bloggers were prosecuted for cybercrime in 2012, and the trend continued into the following year when a blogger was arrested for Facebook posts in May, and an author sentenced to prison in June for selling books on the 2011 protests.

The judicial system is also based on *sharia* and is administered by judges (*qadis*) appointed by the minister of justice. Appeals are heard in Muscat. In remote areas the law is based on tribal custom. Administratively, the country is divided into nine regions in the north and one province in the south (Dhofar). Governors (*walis*) posted in the country's 59 *wilayah*s (administrative districts) work largely through tribal authorities and are responsible for maintaining local security, settling minor disputes, and collecting taxes. In December 2012 municipal council elections were held for the first time (see Current issues, below).

Foreign relations. Reversing the isolationist policy of his father, Sultan Qabus has fostered diplomatic relations with most Arab and industrialized countries. Britain has been deeply involved in Omani affairs since 1798, while the United States and the Sultanate signed their first treaty of friendship and navigation in 1833. In recent years Japan has also become a major trading partner. Diplomatic relations were established with the People's Republic of China in 1978 and with the Soviet Union in September 1985. In June 198– the Sultanate signed a military cooperation agreement with France.

Despite its importance as an oil-producing state, Oman is not a member of either the Organization of Petroleum Exporting Countries (OPEC) or the Organization of Arab Petroleum Exporting Countries (OAPEC). However, since the late 1980s it has cooperated with OPEC regarding production quotas.

Relations with the more radical Arab states, already cool, were not improved by Sultan Qabus's endorsement of the Egyptian-Israeli peace treaty of March 1979. However, Oman broke off relations with Israel in the wake of the intifada. In June 1980, after statements by Sultan Qabus opposing what he viewed as Soviet efforts to destabilize the Middle East, Muscat granted the United States access to Omani air and naval facilities in return for economic and security assistance. Oman has remained a U.S. military base since, supporting American military operations in the Middle East in the 1990s.

Long-standing tension with the (then) People's Democratic Republic of Yemen, occasioned largely by that country's support of the sultan's opponents in Dhofar, moderated substantially at an October 1982 "reconciliation" summit, which was followed by an exchange of ambassadors in late 1983. After a cooperation pact in October 1988, Oman concluded a formal border agreement with the Republic of Yemen in 1997.

After the September 11, 2001, terrorist attacks against the United States, Oman and Saudi Arabia issued a joint statement calling for greater cooperation in combating terrorism, and Oman was later described as highly cooperative in the U.S.-led "war on terrorism." In 2006 the United States signed a free trade agreement with Oman.

Oman considers Iran's nuclear power an asset to the region inasmuch as there is a peaceful application of the technology. In March 2008 U.S. vice president Dick Cheney visited Oman to discuss Iran's nuclear program, an issue of heightened international concern and of particular significance for Oman, given its "guardianship" with Iran over the Strait of Hormuz.

In January 2009 Oman, along with several other Arab nations, sent tons of food and medical supplies to Gaza during the fighting between Israel and Hamas (see entry on Palestinian Authority/Palestine Liberation Organization for details). In February Oman and Russia discussed expanding bilateral ties. The relationship with India strengthened in 2010 with announcements of a joint investment fund of $100 million, a higher education initiative, and a joint military exercise planned for 2011.

Oman was among several nations that did not attend the 2010 Arab League summit in Libya, observers citing objections to remarks made earlier at the UN by Libyan leader Muammar al-Qadhafi, among other issues. Late in the year Oman and Pakistan agreed to boost economic ties.

Immigration issues received attention in 2010 when in May the government agreed to take back deported Bangladeshi workers who could prove that they did not violate immigration law. The action came after a meeting between the sultan and the Bangladeshi ambassador in the wake of reports that Oman had recently deported some 10,000 Bangladeshi, 17,000 Pakistani, and 26,000 Indian workers.

The arrest of seven Omani fishermen by an Irani navy vessel in Iranian waters in May 2012 strained relations between the countries. The Omani embassy in Tehran arranged for their release.

In May 2012 Oman ordered its embassy staff to temporarily evacuate Sana'a, the capital of Yemen, due to death threats from an unknown group related to the continuing civil conflict in that country.

In December 2012 India moved to sign a mutual cooperation treaty with Qatar to ensure collaboration in prevention, investigation, and prosecution of crime, and the subsequent judicial process.

Oman moved to improve bilateral ties with Turkey and Uzbekistan and established relations with Bangladesh in April 2013. During a meeting in Tehran in August, Omani officials offered to reprise its mediator role in negotiations between Iran and the United States but were rebuffed. In November Nepal opened an embassy in Muscat.

With the backing of the United States, Oman quietly emerged as a mediator in the ongoing Syrian civil war in December 2013, hosting talks between regime officials and delegates from some anti-regime factions.

Oman and Iran deepened their alliance in 2014, holding joint military exercises in April. Oman renewed support for Palestine during the July 2014 fighting with Israel, delivering trucks of humanitarian aid to Gaza. Oman also played a central role in facilitating the start of the negotiation process that resulted in a July 2015 deal between the P5+1 (United Nations Security Council Permanent Five members: China, France, Russia, United Kingdom, and United States + Germany) and Iran (see entry on Iran). Officials from Iran and the United States met secretly in Muscat multiple times between July 2012 and March 2013, paving the way to the start of the P5+1 negotiation process in November 2013. Oman also supported U.S. president Barack Obama's request to accept ten Yemeni detainees from the Guantánamo Bay Detention Center in January 2016.

Current issues. Popular unrest resurged in the spring of 2012 after contract workers of Petroleum Development Oman went on what the Omani government regarded as an illegal strike for higher wages in May. Three men were arrested after going to an oilfield to show solidarity with the strikers. The government dismissed 400 PDO workers, but they were later reinstated.

Local municipal elections were held for the first time in December 2012. Some 1,475 candidates contested the 192 seats on 61 councils. Of the 46 women who ran, 4 were elected. Though largely symbolic because the council has no executive powers, the elections were seen as a step toward democracy.

In an effort to combat unemployment and make private sector jobs more attractive, the sultan issued a decree effective July 2013 for the minimum wage to rise by 60 percent (the second increase in as many years) and for a reduction of foreign workers to 33 percent of the population.

Oman orchestrated a crackdown on corruption in the oil sector in 2014. In January the former director of Galfar Engineering and Contracting was convicted of bribing Petroleum Development Oman. Several other high-level Omani and foreign business leaders subsequently faced corruption charges, including former commerce minister Mohammad bin Nasir Al KHUSAIBI, who was convicted in May. Meanwhile, beginning in March 2014, the Omani police arrested and deported thousands of "infiltrators," chiefly illegal foreign laborers and narcotics smugglers. Sultan Qabus's health was a significant concern since an eight-month stay in Germany for unspecified medical tests between the summer of 2014 and the winter of 2014–2015 and a return visit for the same purpose from February–March 2016. However, Oman's health minister, Ahmed bin Muhammad bin Obaid al-Saeedi, indicated in a June 2016 statement that the sultan was in good health and even presided over a cabinet meeting soon after his return to Oman in April.

POLITICAL PARTIES

There are no political parties in Oman. Most opposition elements previously were represented by the **Popular Front for the Liberation of Oman** (PFLO), although there has been no reference to PFLO activity for many years. (See the 1999 edition of the *Handbook* for a history of the PFLO.)

LEGISLATURE

The basic law decreed by the sultan in November 1996 provided for a consultative **Oman Council,** consisting of a new, appointed Council of State and the existing Consultative Council.

Council of State (*Majlis al-Dawlah*). Considered roughly the equivalent of an upper house in a bicameral legislature, the Council of State was expected to debate policy issues at the request of the sultan, although the extent of its authority and its relationship to the Consultative Council remained unclear. On December 16, 1997, Sultan Qabus appointed 41 members (including four women) from among prominent regional figures to the first Council of State. In 2006 the council had 59 members, 9 of whom were women, all serving four-year terms. On November 4, 2007, a total of 70 members, including 14 women, were appointed by royal decree. Following Consultative Council elections in October 2011, the sultan appointed 15 women to the council. The membership of the body was expanded to 83 in 2015 for a term that runs through 2019.

President: Yahya bin Mafouz al-MUNTHERI.

Consultative Council (*Majlis al-Shura*). The former Consultative Assembly, established in 1981, was replaced on December 21, 1991, by the Consultative Council, an advisory body appointed by the sultan (or his designee) from candidates presented by local "dignitaries" and "people of valued opinion and experience." The council is authorized to propose legislation to the government but has no formal lawmaking role. The initial council consisted of 59 regular members (one from each *wilayah*) and a speaker who served three-year terms. In 1994 the council was expanded to 80 regular members (two from each *wilayah* with a population over 30,000 and one from each of the other *wilayahs*) and a president. For the first time women were allowed to stand as candidates (albeit only from six constituencies in or around Muscat), and two women were among those seated at the new council's inaugural session on December 26, 1994. The council was expanded to 82 members in 1997, and women from all of Oman were allowed to stand as candidates and participate in the preliminary balloting for the new council on October 16. An "electoral college" of 51,000 people (all approved by the government, primarily based on literacy requirements) elected 164 potential council members from among 736 candidates (also all approved by the government). Final selections were made in December by the sultan, who had essentially been presented with 2 candidates from which to choose for each seat.

On October 4, 2003, an expanded council of 83 members was elected to serve a four-year term. This was the first ballot open to all citizens. The president of the council, appointed by the sultan, serves as the 84th member. In the balloting on October 27, 2007, those elected were reported by the government to have strong tribal connections or were prominent businesspeople. None of the 21 women who contested were elected. In the elections of October 15, 2011, there were 1,133 candidates, including 77 women, and voting generally lined up with tribal loyalties. Those elected included 3 activists from the prodemocracy movement and 1 woman. Khalid al-Mawali was elected chair of the council on October 29, the first time the chair had been elected and not appointed by Sultan Said. He was reelected on November 4, 2015.

President: Khalid al-MAWALI.

CABINET

[as of August 15, 2016]

Prime Minister	Sultan Qabus bin Said al-Said
Deputy Prime Minister for Cabinet Affairs	Said Fahd bin Mahmud al-Said
Secretary General of the Cabinet	Sheikh al-Fadhl bin Muhammad bin Amed al-Harthy
Ministers	
Agriculture and Fisheries	Fuad bin Jaafar bin Muhammad al-Sajwani
Civil Service	Sheikh Khalid bin Omar bin Said al-Marhoon
Commerce and Industry	Ali bin Masoud bin Ali Sunaidy
Defense	Said Badr bin Saud al-Busaidi
Diwan of Royal Court	Said Khalid bin Hilal al-Busaidi
Education	Madeeha bint Ahmed bin Nassir al-Shibaniyah [f]
Environment and Climate Affairs	Sheikh Muhammad bin Salim bin Said al-Toobi
Finance	Darwish bin Ismaeel bin Ali al-Balushi
Foreign Affairs	Yusuf bin Alawi bin Abdallah
Health	Dr. Ahmed bin Muhammad bin Obaid al-Saeedi
Heritage and Culture	Haitham bin Tariq al-Said
Higher Education	Rawya bint Saud al-Busaidi [f]
Housing	Saif al-Shabibi
Information	Abdulmunim bin Mansour bin Said al-Hasani
Interior	Said Hamud bin Faisal al-Busaidi
Justice	Abdulmalik bin Abdallah bin Ali al-Khalili
Legal Affairs	Abdullah bin Muhammad bin Said al-Saeedi
Manpower	Abdullah bin Nasser bin Abdullah al-Bakri
Personal Representative of the Sultan	Said Thuwainy bin Shihab al-Said
Petroleum and Gas	Dr. Muhammad bin Hamad al-Rumhi
Regional Municipalities and Water	Ahmed bin Abdullah bin Muhammad al-Shuhi
Religious Trusts (*Awqaf*) and Islamic Affairs	Abdullah bin Muhammad al-Salimi
Royal Office Affairs	Lt. Gen. Sultan bin Muhammad al-Nuamani
Social Development	Muhammad bin Said bin Saif al-Kalbani
Sports	Saad bin Muhammad bin Said al Mardhouf al-Saadi
Tourism	Ahmed bin Nasser bin Hamad al-Mehrzi
Transportation and Communications	Ahmed bin Muhammad bin Salim al-Futaisi
Ministers of State	
Governor of the Capital	Sayyid Saud bin Hilal bin Hamad al-Busaidi
Governor of Dhofar	Said Muhammad bin Sultan bin Hamud al-Busaidi

[f] = female

INTERGOVERNMENTAL REPRESENTATION

Ambassador to the U.S.: Hunaina Sultan al-MUGHAIRY.

U.S. Ambassador to Oman: Marc SIEVERS.

Permanent Representative to the UN: Khalifa Ali Issa al-HARTHY.

IGO Memberships (Non-UN): GCC, LAS, NAM, OIC, WTO.

For Further Reference:

Besant, John. *Oman: The True Life Drama and Intrigue of an Arab State*. New York: Mainstream Publishing, 2002.

Jones, Jeremy, and Nicholas Ridout. *A History of Modern Oman*. Cambridge: Cambridge University Press, 2015.

Valeri, Marc. *Oman: Politics and Society in the Qaboos State*. New York: Oxford University Press, 2009.

PAKISTAN

Islamic Republic of Pakistan
Islami Jamhuria-e-Pakistan

Political Status: Formally became independent on August 14, 1947; republic established on March 23, 1956; national territory confined to former West Pakistan with de facto independence of Bangladesh (former East Pakistan) on December 16, 1971; independence of Bangladesh formally recognized on February 22, 1974; martial law regime instituted following military coup of July 5, 1977; modified version of 1973 constitution introduced on March 2, 1985; martial law officially lifted December 30, 1985; constitution suspended and state of emergency imposed on October 14, 1999, following military coup of October 12; constitution restored on November 16, 2002, as amended by Legal Framework Order (LFO) promulgated on August 21; 17th constitutional amendment, containing many of the LFO provisions, approved by Parliament on December 29–30, 2003, and signed by the president on December 31; LFO abolished by passage of the 18th constitutional amendment in Parliament and 1973 constitution restored on April 15, 2010.

Area: 310,402 sq. mi. (803,943 sq. km), excluding Jammu and Kashmir, of which approximately 32,200 sq. mi. (83,400 sq. km) are presently administered by Pakistan.

Population: 192,827,000 (2016E—UN); 201,995,540 (2016E—U.S. Census).

Major Urban Centers (2016E—UN): ISLAMABAD (1,433,000), Karachi (17,121,000), Lahore (8,990,000), Faisalabad (3,677,000), Rawalpindi (2,582,000), Gujranwala (2,193,000), Multan (1,969,000), Hyderabad (1,812,000), Peshawar (1,787,000).

National Language: Urdu. The 1973 constitution identified Urdu as the "national language" but added that "arrangements shall be made for its being used for official and other purposes within fifteen years from the commencing day." In the meantime, English "may be used for official purposes." As of 2011 the clause requiring adoption of Urdu as an official language had not yet been implemented. Each province may also identify and promote its own "provincial language," and all have done so.

Monetary Unit: Pakistani Rupee (market rate October 1, 2016: 104.46 rupees = $1US).

President: Mamnoon HUSSAIN (Pakistan Muslim League–Nawaz); elected for a five-year term by combined votes of Parliament and the four provincial assemblies on July 30, 2013, and sworn in on September 9, succeeding Asif Ali ZARDARI (Pakistan People's Party).

Prime Minister: Muhammad Nawaz SHARIF (Pakistan Muslim League–Nawaz); elected by the National Assembly on June 5, 2013; succeeding acting prime minister Mir Hazar Khan KHOSO (ind.) who had been sworn in on March 25.

THE COUNTRY

Located in the northwest of the Indian subcontinent, Pakistan extends from the Arabian Sea a thousand miles northward across eastern plains to the Hindu Kush and the foothills of the Himalayas. The racial stock is primarily Aryan, with traces of Dravidian. The dominant language is Punjabi (50 percent), followed by Pushtu, Sindhi, Saraiki, Urdu, Gujarati, and Baluchi. English is widely spoken in business and government. Islam, the state religion, is professed by over 95 percent of the people; Christians and Hindus constitute most of the balance. Women make up only 21 percent of the active labor force, but many others participate in unpaid agricultural work. In addition, women are often engaged in home-based or cottage industries. Female participation in government has been constrained by Islamic precepts in the past, although Benazir BHUTTO was the Muslim world's first woman prime minister (1988–1990, 1993–1996). Only about half the adult population is literate—less in the case of women.

Much of the country consists of mountains and deserts, but some of the most fertile and best-irrigated land in the subcontinent is provided by the Indus River system. Agriculture continues to employ more than 45 percent of the active labor force, the principal crops being cotton, wheat, rice, sugarcane, and maize. In addition, the western province of Baluchistan supplies a rich crop of fruits and dates. The agricultural sector contributes about 22 percent of gross domestic product (GDP), while industry accounts for 23.6 percent of GDP and just under 20 percent of employment. Though it is not heavily endowed in mineral resources, the country extracts petroleum, natural gas, iron, limestone, rock salt, gypsum, and coal. Manufacturing includes production of cotton and other textile yarns and fabrics, clothing and accessories, cement, and sugar and other foodstuffs. Pakistan's exports also include fruits, seafood, carpets, and handicrafts.

In 2000 the newly installed government privatized nonstrategic, state-owned enterprises, improving tax collection, and cutting nonessential spending as components of an economic program partly designed to secure additional assistance from the International Monetary Fund. Fueled in large part by some $5.5 billion in U.S. aid since late 2001, growth peaked mid-decade at 7.7 percent before dropping to 2 percent in 2008 and 2009 in response to global economic conditions. Inflation surged to 20.8 percent in 2009 in response to rising commodity prices. In November 2008 the International Monetary Fund (IMF) approved $7.6 billion in stabilization funding, which was raised in August 2009 to $11.3 billion. The country also saw a large inflow of foreign aid to counter and rebuild from the catastrophic flooding it experienced in 2010, with promised international funding totaling more than $4 billion as of September that year. Aid from the United States, a crucial donor, was cut by $800 million following the death of Osama bin Laden in Pakistan in May 2011 (see Foreign relations, below). In 2010 GDP expanded by 4.8 percent, while inflation grew by 10.1 percent. The economy expanded by 3 percent in 2011, while inflation accelerated to 13.6 percent. In 2012 GDP grew by 3.7 percent, and inflation declined to 11 percent. In December 2012, the World Bank announced a $5.5 billion. In 2013 GDP grew by 3.7 percent. The inflation rate continued to moderate, slowing to 7.4 percent, while unemployment was 6.1 percent. GDP per capita that year was $1,279. In September 2013 the IMF announced a $6.6 billion loan to Pakistan.

GDP rose by 4 percent in 2014, 4.2 percent in 2015, and 4.5 percent in 2016. Inflation was 3.3 percent, while unemployment was 6 percent. The World Bank ranked Pakistan 138th out of 189 countries in its 2016 annual ease of conducting business survey.

GOVERNMENT AND POLITICS

Political background. Subjected to strong Islamic influences from the 7th century onward, the area that comprises the present state of Pakistan and former East Pakistan (now Bangladesh) became part of British India during the 18th and 19th centuries and contained most of India's Muslim population. First articulated in the early 1930s, the idea of a separate Muslim state was endorsed in 1940 by the All-India Muslim League, the major Muslim political party. After the league swept the 1946–1947 election, the British accepted partition and Parliament passed the Indian Independence Act, which incorporated the principle of a separate Pakistan. Transfer of power occurred on August 14, 1947, with the new state formally coming into existence at the stroke of midnight, August 15. Mohammad Ali JINNAH, head of the All-India Muslim League, became independent Pakistan's first governor general.

India's Muslim-majority provinces and princely states were given the option of remaining in India or joining Pakistan. Sindh, Khyber Pakhtunkhwa (formerly the North-West Frontier Province [NWFP] until it was renamed in 2010), Baluchistan, and three-fifths of the Punjab accordingly combined to form what became West Pakistan, while a part of Assam and two-thirds of Bengal became East Pakistan. The Hindu maharaja of the predominantly Muslim state of Jammu and Kashmir subsequently acceded to India, but Pakistan challenged the action by sending troops into the territory; resultant fighting between Indian and Pakistani forces was halted by a UN cease-fire on January 1, 1949, leaving Pakistan in control of territory west and north of the cease-fire line. Communal rioting and population movements stemming from partition caused further embitterment between the two countries.

In March 1956 the tie to the British Crown was broken with implementation of a republican constitution, under which Iskander Ali MIRZA served as Pakistan's first president. In October 1958, however, Mirza abrogated the constitution, declared martial law, dismissed the national and provincial governments, and dissolved all political parties. Field Marshal Mohammad Ayub KHAN, appointed supreme commander of the armed forces and chief martial law administrator, took over the presidency from Mirza and was confirmed in office by a national referendum of "basic democrats" in February 1960.

Constitutional government, under a presidential system based on indirect election, was restored in June 1962, with Ayub Khan continuing to rule until March 1969, when, in the context of mounting political and economic disorder, he resigned. Gen. Agha Mohammad Yahya KHAN, army commander in chief, thereupon assumed authority as chief martial law administrator, suspended the constitution, dismissed the national and provincial assemblies, and took office as president.

Normal political activity resumed in 1970, the major unresolved issue being East Pakistani complaints of underrepresentation in the central government and an inadequate share of central revenues. In preparing for the nation's first direct election on the basis of universal suffrage (ultimately held in December 1970 and January 1971), efforts were made to assuage the long-standing political discontent in the more populous East Pakistan by allotting it majority representation in the new assembly, rather than, as in the previous legislature, mere parity with West Pakistan. Of the 300 seats up for direct election (162 from East Pakistan, 138 from West Pakistan), Sheikh Mujibur RAHMAN's East Pakistani *Awami* League won 160 and the Pakistan People's Party (PPP), 82.

After repeated postponements of the assembly opening, originally scheduled to take place in Dacca (East Pakistan) in March 1971, the government banned the *Awami* League and announced in August the disqualification of 79 of its representatives. By-elections to the vacated seats, scheduled for December, were prevented by the outbreak of war between Pakistan and India in late November and the occupation of East Pakistan by Bengali guerrilla and Indian military forces. Following the surrender of some 90,000 of its troops, Pakistan on December 17 agreed to a cease-fire on the western front. Yahya Khan stepped down as president three days later and was replaced by Zulfikar Ali BHUTTO as president and chief martial law administrator. In July 1972 President Bhutto and Indian prime minister Indira Gandhi met in Simla, India, and agreed to negotiate outstanding differences. As a result, all occupied areas along the western border were exchanged, except in Kashmir, where a new Line of Control (LoC) was drawn. In July 1973 the National Assembly granted Bhutto the authority to recognize Bangladesh, and in August a new constitution was adopted. The speaker of the assembly, Fazal Elahi CHAUDHRY, was elected president of Pakistan, and Bhutto was designated prime minister.

A general election held in March 1977 resulted in an overwhelming victory for the ruling PPP; however, the opposition Pakistan National Alliance (PNA) denounced the returns as fraudulent and initiated a series of strikes and demonstrations that led to outbreaks of violence throughout the country. Faced with impending civil war, the army mounted a coup on July 5 that resulted in the arrest of many leading politicians, including Prime Minister Bhutto, and the imposition of martial law under Gen. Mohammad ZIA ul-Haq. Shortly after President Chaudhry's term expired in August 1978, General Zia assumed the presidency, announcing that he would yield to a regularly elected successor following a legislative election in 1979.

In April 1979, despite worldwide appeals for clemency, former prime minister Bhutto was hanged. Riots immediately erupted in most of the country's urban areas, and PNA representatives withdrew from the government. Later in the year, Zia postponed elections, banned all forms of party activity, and imposed strict censorship on the communications media.

An interim constitution promulgated in March 1981 provided for the eventual restoration of representative institutions "in conformity with Islam," while the formation the same year of the PPP-led Movement for the Restoration of Democracy (MRD) created a force against both the regime and right-wing Islamic parties. In late 1984 the president announced a referendum on an "Islamization" program, endorsement of which would also grant him an additional five-year presidential term. In the wake of an MRD call for a referendum boycott, the size of the turnout was hotly disputed, estimates ranging from as low as 15 percent to as high as 65 percent. Nevertheless, citing an overwhelming margin of approval, Zia scheduled parliamentary elections on a nonparty basis for February 1985. Despite another opposition call for a boycott, five incumbent ministers and a number of others associated with the martial law regime lost their bids for parliamentary seats. As a result, the president dissolved the cabinet and designated Mohammad Khan JUNEJO, of the center-right Pakistan Muslim League (PML), as the country's first prime minister in eight years. In the absence of legal parties, the assembly divided into two camps—a government-supportive Official Parliamentary Group (OPG) and an opposition Independent Parliamentary Group (IPG).

In October 1985 the assembly approved a political parties law despite objections by President Zia, who continued to view a multiparty system as "un-Islamic." Dissent immediately ensued within the MRD; some components—including the PML and the moderate *Jamaat-e-Islami,* which controlled the OPG and IPG, respectively—announced their intention to register, while others termed the entire exercise fraudulent and continued to press for fresh elections under a fully restored 1973 constitution. Without responding to the pressure, Zia proceeded with the scheduled termination of martial law on December 30.

In what was dubbed a "constitutional coup," in May 1988 President Zia abruptly dismissed the Junejo government because of alleged corruption. He also dissolved the National Assembly, the provincial assemblies, and local governments. In June he appointed a PML-dominated caretaker administration headed by himself and in July announced that "free, fair, and independent" elections to the national and provincial assemblies would be held on November 16 and 19, respectively.

On August 17, 1988, General Zia, the U.S. ambassador, and a number of senior military officers were killed in a plane crash in southeastern Punjab. Immediately afterward the Senate chair, Ghulam Ishaq KHAN, was sworn in as acting president and announced the formation of a caretaker Emergency National Council to rule the country pending the November elections. The PPP secured a substantial plurality in the National Assembly poll but achieved only second place in three of the four provincial elections. Nonetheless, in what some viewed as a political "deal," on December 1 Ishaq Khan formally appointed as prime minister Benazir BHUTTO, daughter of the executed prime minister, and was himself elected to a five-year term as president on December 12.

By 1990 relations between the president and the prime minister became increasingly strained. Accusing her government of corruption, abuse of power, and various other unconstitutional and illegal acts, President Khan dismissed Bhutto on August 6, 1990, appointing as her interim successor Ghulam Mustafa JATOI, leader of the Islamic Democratic Alliance (IDA), a somewhat disparate coalition of conservative anti-Bhutto groups that had been organized two years earlier. Two months later the PPP was decisively defeated in national and provincial elections, including a loss in its traditional stronghold of Sindh. On November 6 the IDA's Mohammad Nawaz SHARIF was sworn in as Pakistan's first Punjabi prime minister.

On April 18, 1993, in the wake of a failed effort by Nawaz Sharif to curtail the president's constitutional power, Ishaq Khan dismissed the Sharif government, naming Balkh Sher MAZARI, a dissident member of Sharif's PML, as acting prime minister. In May, however, the Supreme Court reinstated Sharif, thereby canceling a general election that had been scheduled for July. The action failed to resolve the widening split within the PML, and on July 18, following intervention by the recently appointed army chief of staff, Gen. Abdul WAHEED, both the president and prime minister stepped down. Ishaq Khan was succeeded, on an acting basis, by Senate chair Wasim SAJJAD. A relatively unknown former World Bank vice president, Moeenuddin Ahmad QURESHI, succeeded Nawaz Sharif.

Nawaz Sharif attempted to regain power as leader of the PML's largest faction, the PML-Nawaz (PML-N). Although the PML-N outpolled the PPP 41–38 percent in the National Assembly election of October 1993, the latter gained a plurality of seats (86, as opposed to 72 for Sharif supporters), and Bhutto was returned to office. In electoral college balloting for president in November, the PPP's Sardar Farooq Ahmad Khan LEGHARI defeated the acting incumbent.

In July 1996, in the wake of increased tension with India over Kashmir and heightened domestic unrest on the part of Islamic fundamentalists and activists of the *Muhajir Qaumi* Movement (MQM), 13 opposition parties announced an alliance to topple Bhutto. On July 31 the prime minister greatly enlarged her cabinet. Among 14 new appointees was her controversial husband, Asif Ali ZARDARI, who, in his first ministerial assignment, was named to head an investment portfolio. In September the prime minister's estranged brother, Murtaza BHUTTO, was one of seven breakaway PPP faction members killed in a gunfight outside Murtaza's Karachi home.

Citing evidence of corruption, intimidation of the judiciary, misdirection of the economy, and failure to maintain law and order, President Leghari on November 5, 1996, dismissed Prime Minister Bhutto, naming Malek Meraj KHALID, a former legislative speaker and long-estranged Bhutto confidant, as her successor in a caretaker capacity pending election of a new National Assembly in February 1997. In the interim, President Leghari announced formation of a Council for Defense and National Security (CDNS) comprising himself, the prime minister, several cabinet ministers, and the heads of the branches of the armed forces.

Voter turnout was low for the February 1997 legislative election, in which the PML-N swept to power by securing 134 of the 207 seats, compared to 19 seats for Bhutto's PPP. The PML-N subsequently invited a number of smaller parties to join the governing coalition, giving it more than the two-thirds majority required for constitutional amendment. Following the installation of a new cabinet on February 26, Prime Minister Sharif quickly oversaw the abolition of the CDNS and directed constitutional revision that, among other things, removed the president's authority to dismiss the prime minister and assembly at will and to appoint military leaders.

In the wake of renewed violence in Karachi (much of it perpetrated by rival MQM factions) as well as conflict between minority Shiite and majority Sunni Muslim militants in Punjab, a new antiterrorism bill was adopted in August 1997, granting sweeping new powers to security forces and establishing special courts to try terrorism cases. The collateral usurpation of judicial power exacerbated tension between the government and the judiciary. On December 2, calling Sharif an "elected dictator," Leghari resigned rather than comply with the prime minister's order to swear in a new acting chief justice. On December 31 a Sharif ally, Mohammad Rafiq TARAR, was elected president by an overwhelming majority of electors.

There was an upsurge in religious, ethnic, and political violence through 1998. In August the Sharif administration's failure to contain the violence led the principal MQM faction to withdraw its support for the government, which in February had already lost a leading ally when the *Awami* National Party (ANP) left the cabinet because of the prime minister's reluctance to endorse renaming the NWFP as Pakhtoonkhwa (Land of the Pakhtoon). Demands for greater provincial autonomy also continued to gather momentum in Khyber Pakhtunkhwa and elsewhere.

To the surprise of many observers, on October 7, 1998, Gen. Jehangir KARAMAT, chair of the joint chiefs of staff, resigned, two days after calling for greater military participation in the government and criticizing the prime minister for his administration's economic shortcomings and its inability to stem domestic disorder. On April 9, 1999, Prime Minister Sharif named Karamat's replacement as army chief of staff, Gen. Pervez MUSHARRAF.

On October 12, 1999, while attending a conference in Sri Lanka, General Musharraf was alerted by supporters within the army that Sharif was replacing him. Musharraf immediately flew back to Pakistan on a commercial flight, but, on the prime minister's order, his plane was denied permission to land in Karachi, whereupon the army moved in and secured the airport. At the same time, the military arrested Sharif and his cabinet. On October 14 Musharraf proclaimed a state of emergency (but not martial law), suspended the constitution, and named himself "chief executive" of Pakistan. President Tarar continued in office. On October 25 the chief executive named the initial civilian members of a governing National Security Council (NSC), which also included, ex officio, the naval and air force chiefs. President Tarar swore in the civilian members of the NSC and a nonparty cabinet on November 6.

Ruling unanimously on May 12, 2000, the Supreme Court legitimized the October 1999 coup as justified and necessary to end political corruption and lawlessness, despite being "extra-constitutional." It also ruled that democratic national and provincial assembly elections should be held no later than October 2002. On August 15 the NSC was reconstituted to include four civilian ministers, and the cabinet was expanded.

On April 6, 2000, an antiterrorism court sentenced Nawaz Sharif to life imprisonment following his conviction for hijacking and terrorism in connection with his refusal to let General Musharraf's plane land. The terrorism conviction was ultimately overturned on appeal, and on December 10 Musharraf granted a pardon to Nawaz Sharif, who flew into exile.

On June 20, 2001, General Musharraf dismissed President Tarar, assumed the presidency himself, dissolved both houses of Parliament, and also disbanded all provincial legislatures. In an apparent effort to legitimize his standing, General Musharraf called an April 30, 2002, referendum in which voters were asked to extend his presidency for another five years, to support economic reforms as well as a crackdown on Islamic extremists. Although 97.7 percent of those casting ballots reportedly voted "yes," the referendum was replete with irregularities, and the outcome was rejected by the boycotting Alliance for the Restoration of Democracy (ARD), an umbrella grouping of more than a dozen opposition parties, including the PPP and the PML-N.

In August–December 2001, searching for domestic stability as well as increased international legitimacy following the September 11 al-Qaida attacks on the United States, Musharraf began freezing assets and detaining the leaders of militant Islamic groups. On January 12, 2002, in what was widely regarded as a landmark speech, Musharraf rejected the "intolerance and hatred" of extreme sectarianism; banned a number of militant Islamic political parties and groups (see Banned and Other Extremist Organizations, below); stated that all fundamentalist Islamic schools (madrasas) would be brought under government supervision to ensure that they adopted adequate educational goals.

On August 21, 2002, President Musharraf promulgated a controversial Legal Framework Order (LFO) that incorporated 29 constitutional amendments, including the creation of a permanent NSC to institutionalize a governmental role for the military leadership. The LFO also enlarged both houses of Parliament and gave the president sweeping powers, including the right to dismiss the cabinet, dissolve the National Assembly, appoint provincial governors if he saw fit, name Supreme Court judges, and unilaterally increase his term of office.

An election for the 272 directly elective seats in Pakistan's reconfigured, 342-seat National Assembly took place on October 10, 2002, with the Musharraf-supportive *Qaid-i-Azam* faction of the PML (PML-Q) finishing ahead of the newly registered PPP Parliamentarians (PPPP) and the *Muttahida Majlis-e-Amal* (MMA), an Islamic coalition. Most international observers regarded the electoral process as seriously deficient in meeting democratic standards. When the 60 seats reserved for women and 10 seats reserved for religious minorities were distributed at the end of the month, the PML-Q held a plurality of 118 seats, followed by the PPPP with 81 and the MMA with 60.

In simultaneous provincial assembly elections, the PML-Q won in Punjab and the MMA assumed control in Khyber Pakhtunkhwa (formerly known as the NWFP), with the two parties forming coalition administrations in Baluchistan and, in conjunction with smaller parties, in Sindh. Immediately upon assuming power in Khyber Pakhtunkhwa, the MMA government announced that it would impose Islamic law in the province. Efforts by Musharraf and the United States to track down al-Qaida terrorist network members and the deposed Taliban regime in neighboring Afghanistan were set back by the MMA's success in Khyber Pakhtunkhwa. The MMA opposed both Islamabad's participation in the U.S.-led "war on terrorism" and the consequent presence of U.S. forces on Pakistani soil.

At the central level, over the next several weeks the PML-Q and PPPP jockeyed for MMA support in an effort to establish a governing coalition, but neither succeeded. The process culminated on November 21, 2002, when the National Assembly confirmed Zafarullah Khan JAMALI of the PML-Q as prime minister after he secured the backing of several small parties and ten dissenters within the PPPP, who organized as the PPP (Patriots). Runner-up in the voting was the MMA's Fazlur RAHMAN, followed by the PPPP's Shah Mahmood QURESHI.

During the following year the National Assembly was unable to overcome the obstructive tactics of LFO opponents, including the PPPP and MMA, who also demanded that President Musharraf resign as chief of the army staff. Indirect elections to the Senate were held on February 25 and 27, 2003, with the PML-Q again attaining a plurality, but the opposition parties extended their LFO protest into a Senate boycott. The stalemate over the LFO was not resolved until late December, when Musharraf announced an agreement with the MMA under which he would step down as army chief by December 2004, submit to a vote of confidence by Parliament, and permit review by the Supreme Court of any presidential decision to dissolve the National Assembly. In addition, it was agreed that the NSC would be established by legislative act, not by constitutional amendment. With the deadlock broken, on December 29 the National Assembly voted, 248–0, to incorporate most LFO provisions as the 17th amendment to the constitution, although the PPPP and the PML-N walked out of the session. By a vote of 72–0 the Senate approved the amendment the following day. On January 1, 2004, Musharraf received a vote of confidence from both houses, 191–0 in the assembly (the MMA abstaining and ARD boycotting), and 56–1 in the Senate, as well as from the provincial assemblies. A bill establishing a 13-member NSC, to include the chiefs of the army, navy, and air force, was signed into law by the president on April 19.

On June 26, 2004, Prime Minister Jamali resigned under pressure from President Musharraf. Chaudhry Shujaat HUSSAIN, leader of the largely reunited PML (minus the PML-N), was confirmed as an interim successor on June 29 and sworn in on June 30. He was expected to serve until Finance Minister Shaukat AZIZ won a National Assembly seat, thereby making him eligible for designation as prime minister. Following a by-election victory on August 18, Aziz won assembly approval as prime minister on August 28 and assumed office on August 29.

On November 30, 2004, Mohammadmian SOOMRO, chair of the Senate and acting president during a trip abroad by General Musharraf, signed into law a bill permitting Musharraf to continue as both army chief of staff and president. The new law, which proponents justified as necessary to maintain stability in the face of terrorism and subversion, was attacked by the MMA as a betrayal of its December 2003 pact with Musharraf.

On May 14, 2006, meeting in London, former prime ministers Benazir Bhutto and Nawaz Sharif signed a Charter of Democracy, which decried "the erosion of the federation's unity" and "the military's subordination of all state institutions." The charter called for repealing the LFO and the 17th constitutional amendment, establishing a Federal Constitutional Court to resolve constitutional issues, providing for minority representation in the Senate, releasing all political prisoners and permitting the return of political exiles, installing neutral caretaker governments prior to national elections, and creating a Defense Cabinet Committee (in place of the NSC) that would exert control over the military and its nuclear capability.

In September 2006 the government concluded an agreement with tribal leaders in the Federally Administered Tribal Area (FATA) of North Waziristan that tacitly acknowledged the failure of the military and security agencies to bring the region under its control despite years of efforts. In effect, the government turned control of the agency over to tribal leaders. Modeled on a pact that Musharraf had concluded in February 2005 in South Waziristan, the agreement called for Islamabad to withdraw an estimated 70,000 troops, release prisoners, and provide amnesty to Taliban and tribal militants, in return for which the tribal leaders agreed to end attacks against army and law enforcement personnel, to prevent the Taliban from launching attacks into Afghanistan, and to expel foreigners who failed to honor the agreement.

On March 8, 2007, President Musharraf set off a political firestorm by suspending Chief Justice Iftikhar Mohammed CHAUDHRY on grounds of misconduct and abuse of authority. With the presidential term set to expire in November, Musharraf apparently perceived Chaudhry as an obstacle to his reelection. Musharraf wanted the sitting national and provincial legislators—the same ones who had confirmed him in January 2004—to authorize another term, and without his first stepping down as army chief. The opposition, arguing that any such procedure would be antidemocratic and unconstitutional, pledged to appeal to the Supreme Court, which, under Chaudhry, had previously demonstrated its independence. In response to Chaudhry's dismissal, dozens of judges tendered their resignations, while the opposition and the legal establishment condemned the action as an attack on judicial independence. The crisis widened on May 12–13, when members of the government-supportive MQM clashed with Chaudhry supporters in the streets of Karachi, leaving more than 40 people dead. On July 20 Chaudhry was reinstated by the Supreme Court, which unanimously ruled Musharraf's action illegal.

Less than a week earlier, tribal militants in North Waziristan, responding to the storming by security forces of Islamabad's Red Mosque (*Lal Masjid*), canceled the September 2006 agreement with the government. The Red Mosque assault concluded a July 3–11, 2007, siege that had been precipitated by clashes with militant students, who for six months had been aggressively promoting Islamization in the capital, sometimes by attacking noncompliant civilians. Following unsuccessful negotiations with the students and their clerical mentors, military personnel cleared the mosque and adjacent madrasas in a prolonged assault that cost more than 100 lives. Among those killed in the fighting was the radical cleric Abdul Rashid GHAZI. Although President Musharraf's decision to storm the mosque won considerable praise in the West and from domestic secularists, Islamists increased suicide bombings, ambushes, and other attacks.

On August 23, 2007, the Supreme Court ruled that former prime minister Nawaz Sharif could not be prevented "from returning to his motherland." Nevertheless, when he flew into Islamabad on September 10, the government detained him at the airport and within hours deported him to Saudi Arabia. Four days later, Benazir Bhutto, in the context of negotiations with Musharraf on power-sharing arrangements, announced that she planned to return to Pakistan in October.

With Chief Justice Chaudhry having recused himself, the Supreme Court ruled 6–3 on September 28, 2007, that President Musharraf could stand for reelection while still serving as army chief. Although Musharraf had stated that, should he win reelection, he would resign from the military before inauguration, most of the opposition declared that it would boycott the presidential voting. On October 6 an electoral college of Parliament and the four provincial assemblies reelected Musharraf to a five-year term by a margin of 671–8 against token opposition from a former judge, Wajihuadin AHMAD. A day earlier, however, the Supreme Court had announced that the results could not be declared official until it had ruled on opposition challenges.

Although power-sharing discussions with former prime minister Bhutto remained incomplete, on October 5, 2007, Musharraf promulgated a National Reconciliation Ordinance (NRO) that quashed corruption charges—including 11, involving some $1.5 billion, against Bhutto and her husband, Asif Ali Zardari—targeting politicians for illegalities allegedly committed during 1986–1999. On October 18 Bhutto ended eight years in exile, returning to Karachi. The triumphal occasion turned grim, however, when suicide bombers attacked her motorcade from the airport, killing 145 and wounding more than 200 others.

On November 3, 2007, citing the need to combat rising Islamic extremism, Musharraf, in his capacity as chief of the army staff, suspended the constitution and declared a state of emergency. Chief Justice Chaudhry was immediately dismissed, while most of his fellow justices resigned or refused to take a new oath under a provisional constitutional order. The emergency declaration provoked demonstrations by many of those associated with the July protests. More than 5,000 activists were temporarily jailed in the following days, and Bhutto was twice placed under house arrest.

On November 16, 2007, a day after the completion of the 2002–2007 legislative term, Musharraf swore in a caretaker government headed by Senate Chair Mohammadmian Soomro, an ally. On November 22 the Supreme Court, now packed with Musharraf supporters, dismissed the last of four opposition petitions challenging Musharraf's reelection, which paved the way for his stepping down as chief of the army staff on November 28 and his taking the presidential oath of office as a civilian on November 29. Shortly before, he had designated Gen. Ashfaq KAYANI, a former head of the Inter-Services Intelligence (ISI) agency, as his military successor.

On November 25, 2007, opposition demands for restoration of the constitution had been further strengthened by the successful return to Pakistan of Nawaz Sharif, following intervention on his behalf by the king of Saudi Arabia. Nevertheless, it appeared unlikely that the courts would lift the prohibition against his directly participating in the legislative election that had been scheduled for January 8, 2008.

Former prime minister Benazir Bhutto was assassinated by Islamist extremists while leaving a campaign rally in Rawalpindi on December 27, 2007. Shortly after, her 19-year-old son, Bilawal Bhutto ZARDARI, a college student in the United Kingdom, was named titular head of the PPP, while her husband, Asif Ali Zardari, was given responsibility for running day-to-day party operations. On January 2, 2008, citing the violent disturbances that had followed Bhutto's death, the Pakistan Election Commission briefly postponed the National Assembly election. The PPP, the PML-N, and other opposition parties objected to the decision. (A UN commission investigating Bhutto's assassination concluded in April 2010 that her death could have been prevented if authorities had provided the proper level of security.)

Voters went to the polls instead on February 18, 2008, and gave the PPP (still technically running as the PPPP) a plurality of 124 seats. The PML-N finished second, with 91 seats, while the PML-Q (officially listed on the ballot simply as the PML) came in a distant third, with 54 seats. On March 25 a PPP vice chair, Syed Yousaf Raza GILANI, was sworn in as prime minister of a multiparty government led by the PPP and PML-N. One provision of their coalition agreement called for reinstating the dismissed judges, but the government's failure to do so led Nawaz Sharif to announce the withdrawal of the PML-N ministers on May 12.

Facing pending impeachment over allegedly unconstitutional acts, including the 1999 coup and the November 2007 state of emergency, President Musharraf resigned on August 18, 2008. A week later, Nawaz Sharif took the PML-N into opposition because the PPP had not reinstated 63 dismissed judges and had proposed Zardari, rather than a nonpartisan, as Musharraf's successor. Most parties nevertheless coalesced around Zardari, who was elected president on September 6 with 482 of 700 possible electoral college votes. Zardari took the oath of office on September 9. On November 3 Prime Minister Gilani not only filled the cabinet posts that had been vacated by the PML-N withdrawal but announced one of the largest cabinets in the country's history, which was further expanded when the MQM joined the government in January 2009.

Meanwhile, in the wake of the Red Mosque siege in July 2007 and the failed peace agreements in North and South Waziristan, a dozen or more militant Islamic groups came together under the framework of the *Tehrik-e-Taliban* Pakistan (TTP), led by Baitullah MEHSUD. Although the TTP operated throughout the FATA and Khyber Pakhtunkhwa, in 2008 the Swat valley in Khyber Pakhtunkhwa's Malakand division emerged as a focus of militant activity. In an effort to disrupt the government and inculcate strict adherence to Islamic law, the TTP executed dozens of opponents and alleged government collaborators, destroyed more than 180 schools (most of which had been educating girls), and by early 2009 controlled up to 90 percent of the valley. On February 13 the Khyber Pakhtunkhwa government and the leader of the pro-Taliban *Tehrik-e-Nifaz-e-Shariat-e-Muhammadi* (TNSM), cleric Sufi MOHAMMED, signed an agreement on adoption of sharia throughout Malakand that was approved by the National Assembly and then signed into law by President Zardari on April 13, despite protests from the MQM. By then, up to 1,500 people, many of them bystanders, had been killed in the conflict.

On March 17, 2009, the Gilani government reinstated Chief Justice Chaudhry, four other Supreme Court judges, and six provincial high court judges. The move, spurred by a Karachi-to-Islamabad protest caravan by lawyers and other activists, was seen as a victory for Nawaz Sharif. Furthermore, on May 26 the Supreme Court overturned a February ruling that, citing earlier criminal convictions, had barred Nawaz Sharif from seeking office and had forced his brother, Mohammad Shahbaz SHARIF, to step down temporarily as chief minister of Punjab.

By May 2009 it had become apparent that the February peace agreement in Khyber Pakhtunkhwa was illusory, as the TTP, led locally by Maulana FAZULLAH, a son-in-law of Sufi Mohammad, continued to extend its reach beyond Swat. As a consequence, the Pakistani military, which was already fighting for control in the FATA's Bajaur Agency and elsewhere, launched a concerted effort to end the Taliban threat in Malakand. By late June most of Swat had been secured and impressive gains had been registered in other districts, in part with the cooperation of local militias. The military undertook a long-anticipated ground campaign against the TTP in South Waziristan in October 2009.

In September 2010 the Supreme Court reopened corruption cases against high-level politicians, including President Zardari, after a December 2009 ruling declared a 2007 general immunity from prosecution instituted by former president Musharraf was unconstitutional (see Constitution and government, below). The high court's call joined with growing government pressure for Swiss authorities to reopen money-laundering cases against Zardari that had been suspended in 2008 because of the immunity order. The Swiss cases involved an alleged $12 million in bribes paid to Zardari and his late wife Benazir Bhutto by companies to win contracts in Pakistan throughout the 1990s. The allegations led to calls for his removal from office. Musharraf, living in self-imposed exile in London, announced in September that he would soon launch a new party called the All Pakistan Muslim League to contest the general election in 2013 (see Current issues, below).

The cabinet was reshuffled and expanded in April 2012. On April 26 the high court convicted Gilani of contempt of court for failing to pursue prosecution of Zardari (Gilani argued in vain that the president was immune from prosecution). On June 19 the court ruled that Gilani's conviction made him ineligible to serve in the legislature and, therefore, to be prime minister. Three days later, Zardari named Makhdoom SHAHABUDDIN as prime minister, but the appointee was arrested over alleged drug trafficking, leading to speculation that the courts and the military were endeavoring to end the PPP government. On June 22 Water and Power Minister Raja Pervaiz ASHRAF was designated prime minister and confirmed the same day. A reshuffled cabinet was approved on June 26.

Ashraf's PPP-led government was the first civilian government in Pakistani history to complete its full term and turn over power. In accordance with the constitution, the assembly was dissolved on March 16, 2013, in preparation for new elections. Mir Hazar Khan KHOSO (independent) was sworn in along with a caretaker government on March 25. The PML-N won a plurality in the May 11 assembly balloting and, with allied parties, was able to secure a majority in the chamber (see Current issues, below). On June 5 Nawaz Sharif was elected prime minister and formed a mainly PML-N cabinet two days later. Mamnoon HUSSAIN (PML-N) was subsequently elected president by the parliament and was sworn in on September 9. There were minor cabinet reshuffles in November and December.

MQM lawmakers in the National Assembly, Senate, and the Sind regional assembly resigned in August 2015 to protest a government-backed paramilitary offensive in Karachi. The PML-N leadership vowed not to accept the resignations, but instead negotiate a solution to the crisis.

Member of Parliament Sardar Ayaz SADIQ (PML-N) was elected speaker of the National Assembly on November 11, 2015.

Constitution and government. Between 1947 and 1973 Pakistan adopted three permanent and four interim constitutions. In August 1973 a presidential system introduced by Ayub Khan was replaced by a parliamentary form of government. Following General Zia's assumption of power in 1977, a series of martial law decrees and an interim constitution promulgated in March 1981 progressively increased the powers of the president, as did various revisions accompanying official restoration of the 1973 document in March 1985. Constitutional changes introduced in April 1997 revoked major provisions of the 1985 revisions, reducing the president to little more than a figurehead.

On October 15, 1999, General Musharraf, who had suspended the constitution and assumed the title of chief executive the previous day, issued Provisional Constitution Order No. 1 of 1999, which specified that Pakistan would continue to be governed, "as nearly as may be," in accordance with the constitution. The order also restricted the president to acting on the advice of the chief executive and mandated the continued functioning of the existing court system, with the proviso that no court could act against the chief executive, his orders, or his appointees. The order left intact all fundamental constitutional rights, such as freedom of the press, not in conflict with the state of emergency.

The LFO instituted by General Musharraf in August 2002, effective from October 12, incorporated 29 constitutional changes, enhancing presidential power, enlarging both houses of Parliament, and creating as a permanent body a civilian-military National Security Council (NSC). The LFO also disqualified convicted criminals from running for the legislature, thereby ensuring that neither Benazir Bhutto nor Nawaz Sharif could stand in the October 2002 election. Opposition to promulgation of the LFO ultimately led to a December 2003 compromise under which most of the LFO provisions were enacted as the 17th amendment to the constitution. The NSC provision was removed, however, and enacted by law in April 2004.

In November 2006 the Khyber Pakhtunkhwa legislature passed an Islamic accountability law, but President Musharraf successfully petitioned the Supreme Court for a stay. In August the court had thrown out 20 subsections of a previous law authorizing clerics to oversee media content and social behavior, including interactions between the sexes. The central government had argued that the law overstepped constitutional bounds. A collateral debate focused on a national Protection of Women Bill, which was ultimately signed into law on December 1 despite fierce opposition from all but the most moderate Islamic organizations. Under the new law rape cases were assigned to civil rather than religious courts and for the first time permitted conviction on the basis of forensic and circumstantial evidence rather than on the testimony of male witnesses.

A number of ordinances brought into being in 2007 under former president Musharraf expired in November 2009, including presidential control of Pakistan's nuclear weapons arsenal, which subsequently transferred to the authority of the prime minister. Musharraf's NRO, which granted amnesty to late prime minister Benazir Bhutto, her husband and current president Zardari, and nearly 8,000 other officials who faced prosecution for corruption, also expired without extension. The Supreme Court ruled in December that the NRO was unconstitutional and ordered corruption cases voided by the ordinance, including those against Zardari, be reopened. The corruption charges involved many members of the PPP, including several cabinet ministers. The attorney general resigned in April 2010, citing obstruction of criminal investigations into the corruption cases.

In April 2010 the federal legislature passed a bill that restored the 1973 constitution and repealed former president Musharraf's 2003 LFO. On April 15 the Senate unanimously passed the 18th constitutional amendment bill, which contained 102 clauses, after earlier unanimous passage of the bill in the National Assembly on April 8. The changes transferred power from the president to the prime minister to dismiss the National Assembly and to name the armed services chiefs and the elections commissioner, while also empowering an independent commission to appoint judges. The bill gave the prime minister and provincial chief ministers the power to dissolve provincial assemblies, and eliminated the two-term-limit imposed on the prime minister. Reinstatement of the old governing laws rescinded most of the powers that had been accumulated in the office of the presidency and left the position largely ceremonial. One clause also renamed the NWFP as the Khyber Pakhtunkhwa, doing away with a vestige of British colonial rule. The portion of the amendment that created the commission to appoint judges was challenged in the Supreme Court on grounds that it impeded judicial independence.

The current constitution mandates that the president, who serves a five-year term, is chosen by vote of Parliament and the four provincial assemblies sitting jointly as an electoral college. The bicameral Parliament includes an indirectly elected Senate and a popularly elected National Assembly; the latter includes reserved seats for women and religious minorities, and it has sole jurisdiction over money bills. Sitting in joint session, Parliament may by a simple majority enact bills that have been returned to it by the president. The prime minister, who must be a member of the National Assembly, may be removed by a majority vote of the house's total membership; the president may be removed by a two-thirds vote of the full Parliament.

The judicial system includes a Supreme Court, a Federal Shariat Court to examine the conformity of laws with Islam, high courts in each of the four provinces (Baluchistan, North-West Frontier, Punjab, and Sindh), and a number of antiterrorism courts authorized by legislation in 1997. The assembly approved measures in 1991 that called for formal appeal to the Koran as the country's supreme law and mandated the death penalty for blasphemy.

Centrally appointed governors head provincial administrations. Each province also has an elected Provincial Assembly and a Council of Ministers led by the prime minister, the latter named by the governor. Central appointees govern the Federal Capital Territory and the Federally Administered Tribal Areas (FATA), which are located between Khyber Pakhtunkhwa and Afghanistan. The seven FATA agencies, roughly from north to south, are Bajaur, Mahmand, Khyber, Orakzai, Kurram, North Waziristan, and South Waziristan. Pakistan also administers parts of disputed Kashmir, and in 2009, Gilgit-Baltistan was granted self-governance (see Related Territories, below).

A Federal Legislative List defines the exclusive authority of the center; there also is a Concurrent Legislative List, with residual authority assigned to the provinces. To safeguard provincial rights, a Council of Common Interests is mandated, comprising the chief ministers of the four provinces plus four federal ministers.

Pakistan is one of the most dangerous countries in the world for journalists. The constitution guarantees press freedom, but formal censorship has been imposed during periods of martial law and states of emergency. The imposition of sharia law in the Swat Valley and other areas of the country had a significant impact on press freedom. The country was ranked 147th out of 180 countries in the 2016 press freedom index by Reporters Without Borders.

Foreign relations. Relations between India and Pakistan reflect a centuries-old rivalry based on mutual suspicion between Hindus and Muslims. Widespread communal rioting and competing claims to Jammu and Kashmir accompanied the British withdrawal in 1947. Relations improved in 1960 with an agreement on joint use of the waters of the Indus River basin, but continuing conflict over Kashmir and the Rann of Kutch on the Indian Ocean involved the two countries in armed hostilities in 1965, followed by a withdrawal to previous positions, in conformity with the Tashkent Agreement negotiated with Soviet assistance in January 1966. After another period of somewhat improved relations, the internal crisis in East Pakistan, accompanied by India's open support of the Bengali cause, led to further hostilities in 1971.

Following recognition by Pakistan of independent Bangladesh, bilateral negotiations with India were renewed, and a number of major issues were resolved by the return of prisoners of war, a mutual withdrawal from occupied territory, and the demarcation of a new LoC in Kashmir. Further steps toward normalization were partially offset by Pakistani concern over India's detonation of a nuclear device in May 1974, and formal diplomatic ties were not resumed until July 1976.

A rapprochement followed General Zia's death in August 1988 but abruptly ended in early 1990 as Kashmir became the scene of escalating violence on the part of Muslim separatists. By April thousands of residents had fled to Pakistan from the Indian-controlled Kashmir valley.

On April 6, 1998, Pakistan test fired its first domestically produced medium-range surface-to-surface missile, which provoked immediate criticism from India's recently installed Vajpayee administration. Then on May 11 and 13 India exploded five nuclear weapons in underground testing, prompting Pakistan to respond on May 28 and 30 with six nuclear tests of its own. The international community quickly condemned the tests, and a number of countries imposed economic sanctions against both governments. Shortly after, however, Prime Ministers Sharif and Vajpayee adopted less belligerent stances, meeting during the July session of the South Asian Association for Regional Cooperation (SAARC) in Colombo, Sri Lanka, and again in September in New York, where they announced renewed talks on Kashmir and other matters.

Although the Kashmir talks produced no tangible results, the prime ministers met again in February 1999 in Lahore. The resulting Lahore Declaration included pledges by both administrations to reduce the possibility of accidental nuclear war.

On October 1, 1999, militants carried out an assault on the state assembly building in Srinagar, the summer capital of the Indian State of Jammu and Kashmir, resulting in nearly 40 deaths. Charging that Pakistan had failed to stop terrorist infiltrators, India ordered additional troops to Kashmir, with Pakistan responding in kind. On December 13 terrorists attacked India's Parliament, leaving 14 dead, including the terrorists, and by May 2002, when three gunmen stormed a Kashmiri army base and left nearly three dozen dead, India and Pakistan had a combined million troops or more stationed along the LoC. Diplomatic intervention, led by the United States, ultimately helped to diffuse the immediate situation.

When Prime Minister Vajpayee called on April 18, 2003, for "open dialogue" with Pakistan, Islamabad announced its willingness to cooperate, which led to a mutual deepening of diplomatic relations. On November 26 the two governments instituted a cease-fire, the first in 14 years, between Pakistani and Indian forces in the disputed border region. The cease-fire was followed by an announcement at the January 4–6, 2004, SAARC session that the two governments would undertake "composite talks" on bilateral issues, and in late June 2005 Prime Minister Aziz described the peace process as "irreversible." Nevertheless, scant progress was made in the following six years, in large part because of terrorist attacks within India by Islamist groups with Pakistani connections (see Current issues, below). The most dramatic recent instance occurred on November 26–29, 2008, when a ten-person assault team attacked predetermined targets in Mumbai, leaving 163 people dead and another 300 hurt. All of the assailants, including the lone survivor, Ajmal Amir AMIN (Ajmal Kasab), were ultimately shown to have Pakistani addresses. On February 12, 2009, Islamabad admitted that "some part of the conspiracy" had been planned in Pakistan. Attention focused on the *Lashkar-i-Taiba* (LiT), whose chief of operations, Zaki-ur-Rehman LAKHVI, was alleged to be the mastermind behind the Mumbai attack. On November 19 a special antiterrorism court indicted Lakhvi and six others. (On May 3, 2010, Amin was found guilty for his part in the Mumbai shootings and sentenced to death by an Indian special court.)

Relations with Bangladesh have improved considerably in recent years, although no formula has yet been found for relocating some 300,000 Biharis, most of whom have been living in over 100 camps in the former East Pakistan since the 1972 breakup. An agreement in August 1992 led to the airlifting of an initial contingent to Lahore in early 1993, but the Bhutto government suspended the program later in the year. Although Pakistan recommitted itself in early 1998 to resettling the Biharis, no substantive move toward that goal had been achieved by May 2008, when the Bangladeshi High Court approved offering citizenship to some 150,000 Biharis who were minors in 1971 as well as all those born since then.

Although Pakistan and Afghanistan had long been at odds over the latter's commitment to the creation of an independent Pushtunistan out of a major part of Pakistan's NWFP, Islamabad reacted strongly to the Soviet invasion of its neighbor in 1979, providing Muslim rebel groups (*mujahidin*) with weapons and supplies for continued operations against the Soviet-backed regime. Support for the rebels occasionally provoked bombing raids in the area of Peshawar, the Khyber Pakhtunkhwa capital, and the presence of more than 3.5 million Afghan refugees proved economically burdensome.

Following the Soviet departure, which was completed in early 1989, Pakistan supported the installation of an interim coalition government in Kabul. Kabul later accused Islamabad of supporting the fundamentalist Taliban militia, which Pakistan recognized as Afghanistan's government shortly after it took power in September 1996.

Following the U.S.-led ouster of the Taliban in 2001, relations with Kabul have been complicated by the fact that Islamic fundamentalists, having been permitted to establish education and training camps in the Peshawar area during the Afghan revolution, became increasingly active within Pakistan itself, particularly in FATA and Khyber Pakhtunkhwa as well as within the divided Kashmir. Relations with Afghanistan were frayed from early 2006, when President Hamid Karzai accused Pakistan of failing to secure Pakistan's side of the border and of not curbing Pakistani-based al-Qaida and Taliban militants.

U.S.–Pakistani relations have been dominated by counterterrorism since the mid-1990s. In February 1995, the government permitted U.S. agents to join in the apprehension of Ramzi Ahmed YOUSEF, the suspected mastermind of the 1993 World Trade Center bombing in New York, and then approved his prompt extradition. Following the September 11, 2001, assaults on the United States, relations with the new U.S. administration were significantly strengthened by Pakistan's assistance in fighting al-Qaida and the Taliban. In early 2002 the Musharraf regime reacted swiftly to the murder of the American journalist Daniel Pearl in Pakistan. The principal suspect, Ahmad Omar SHAIKH, a UK national, was captured in February and later sentenced to death. Despite Pakistan's decision not to back the 2003 U.S. invasion of Iraq, the Bush administration continued to praise and support Musharraf. Not even a public admission in February 2004 by Abdul Qadeer KHAN, the former head of Pakistan's nuclear weapons program, that he had passed nuclear secrets to Iran, Libya, and North Korea damaged the U.S. Pakistani relationship. Musharraf immediately pardoned Khan, a national hero, without protest from Washington. (The International Atomic Energy Agency subsequently speculated that Khan's revelations were merely the "tip of the iceberg" in an operation that also involved the sale of nuclear components in a number of countries.) In March U.S. secretary of state Colin Powell, making his fourth visit to Pakistan, announced that Pakistan was regarded as a "major non-NATO ally," and a week later U.S. president Bush lifted the few remaining sanctions imposed after the 1998 nuclear tests and the 1999 coup. Pakistan has handed over hundreds of suspected al-Qaida operatives. Additionally, its armed forces have also launched major offensives against tribal Islamists, al-Qaida, and Taliban elements in Khyber Pakhtunkhwa and especially in FATA. The central government regained control of the Swat Valley following an offensive in 2009, though the slow distribution of aid money hampered subsequent progress.

In March 2009 the administration of U.S. president Barack Obama acknowledged that stemming the flow of militants back and forth across the Afghan–Pakistani border required Pakistan's active participation. As an incentive, President Obama proposed a five-year civilian aid package of $7.5 billion. When the U.S. Congress passed the aid bill in October, however, it met fierce criticism from some Pakistanis, who claimed that it would permit U.S. interference in Pakistan's civilian and military affairs. The bill requires the secretary of state to certify that Pakistan is participating in counterterrorism, maintaining civilian authority over the military, safeguarding its nuclear arsenal, and meeting international nonproliferation standards.

Relations deteriorated, however, following the discovery in May 2011 that Osama bin Laden had been hiding for years in a compound that was at walking distance from an elite Pakistani military academy in Abbottabad. After his death on May 20, the U.S. authorities openly questioned whether Pakistan was both willing and capable of cooperating with counterterrorism efforts. Despite the embarrassment for the military, much of the scrutiny focused on the Inter-Services Intelligence (ISI), which has long been viewed as holding an ambivalent position toward militant groups. The ISI remains deeply suspicious of India and thus has been known to police local and regional militants only haphazardly, allowing them some support in the event that they are needed to respond to a hypothetical attack by India. Although the United States had accepted this partial cooperation for years, it suspended $800 million, or one-third, of its military aid to Pakistan in July 2011.

U.S. secretary of state Hillary Clinton visited Pakistan in October 2011 and called for a new "partnership" between the two countries. She also revealed that the ISI had facilitated negotiations between the United States and the terrorist Haqqani network (see entry on Afghanistan). Meanwhile, on October 24 Pakistan was elected for a two-year term on the UN Security Council.

In November 2011 Pakistan's ambassador to the United States, Hussain HAQQANI, was forced to resign after allegations surfaced that he sought U.S. assistance in curbing the power of the Pakistani military. Tensions with the United States increased dramatically following a U.S. air strike on November 26 that killed 24 Pakistani soldiers along the Afghan border. In response to the incident, Pakistan closed North Atlantic Treaty Organization (NATO) supply lines into Afghanistan. Pakistan also ordered the withdrawal of U.S. forces from the Shamsi airbase in Baluchistan.

In April 2012 Pakistan deported to Saudi Arabia three of bin Laden's widows and 11 of his children. In June, after 45 days of negotiations, U.S. diplomats left Pakistan with no resolution to the dispute over the closure of NATO supply routes through Pakistan. Meanwhile, U.S. drone strikes continued including three in June that killed 27, including 16 suspected militants. In October Kabul accused Islamabad of violating a bilateral transport treaty by denying or delaying cargo bound for Afghanistan. Pakistan denied the allegations.

In January 2013 a series of skirmishes and artillery exchanges across the LoC left three Pakistani and two Indian soldiers dead. Reports indicated that tension had increased dramatically after India built two new military bunkers in a disputed area. By month's end Pakistani and Indian military officials had launched negotiations to forestall additional fighting. On March 11, 2013, the presidents of Pakistan and Iran attended the ceremonial opening of a $7.6 billion gas pipeline from Iran. The pipeline was seen as a diplomatic snub to the United States, which endeavored to block its construction.

In August 2013 Pakistan approved the Convention on the Transfer of Sentenced Prisoners. The accord allowed the EU and the United States to extradite convicted prisoners back to Pakistan. Also in August, Pakistan and India exchanged artillery across the LoC following an ambush in which five Indian soldiers were killed by suspected Islamic militants.

On September 3, 2013, Islamic militant Abu Jarara al-YEMINI was captured by Saudi special forces units in a raid on Murree and taken to Saudi Arabia, reportedly without the knowledge of the Pakistani government. Following a visit by Prime Minister Sharif to Washington, D.C., in October, the United States released more than $1.5 billion in assistance that had been suspended. During the trip, the United States also pledged only to conduct future drone strikes as a last resort and to take additional steps to minimize civilian casualties.

In March 2014 a Sunni militant group, the Army of Justice (*Jaish al-Adl*) executed five Iranian border guards in Pakistan. Pakistani security forces did manage to free 11 other hostages that had been captured by the group. In May Pakistan and Iran agreed to establish a military hotline to prevent escalation of border incidents.

In April 2015 President Xi Jingping became the first Chinese head of state to visit Pakistan since 2006. During his visit, the two countries announced that China would invest $45 billion in infrastructure projects, including energy production and distribution, and the construction of highways and railways. Reports in April revealed that Pakistan had arranged to buy eight submarines from China to augment its current fleet of five French-built submarines as part of a strategic effort to balance Indian naval dominance in the region.

On April 10, 2015, a joint session of the legislature voted to reject a call by Saudi Arabia for Pakistan to participate in the Saudi-led coalition that was fighting Houthi rebels in Yemen (see entry on Yemen). Meanwhile, India launched an official protest over the April release of Lakhvi on bail, the alleged mastermind of the 2008 Mumbai attacks.

The United States announced in August 2016 that it would withhold $300 million in military aid for Pakistan because of that country's failure to take stronger action to suppress the Haqqani network.

Current issues. A January 2010 report found 3,021 civilians had been killed in Pakistan in 2009 and 7,334 had been injured over the course of 2,586 terrorist, sectarian, and insurgent attacks. The numbers killed rose 48 percent over the previous year. The report said the total of dead rose to more than 12,000 in 2009 if those killed in military action or U.S. drone attacks were included. The killings continued into 2011.

This situation is further complicated by tacit support for selected rebel groups by the ISI and sympathizers within the military. This issue is muted in Pakistan, as several journalists have been pressured to self-censor following apparent assassinations of colleagues who were critical towards the security apparatus. Security in Karachi, Pakistan's most important port city and the center of commercial and industrial operations, has been particularly affected. Rival criminal organizations claiming affiliation with Pakistan's opposing political parties, including the PPP, the MQM, and the ANP, have contributed to increasing violence, with over 300 people killed in gang-related violence in July 2011 alone. Violence increased after the crackdown in the FATA from October 2009, which upset the city's ethnic balance as migrating Pashtuns from the Afghan border areas, commonly represented by the ANP, reduced the proportion of the dominant Mujhairs, who are affiliated with the MQM. The PPP, which is associated with Sindhi people, along with the ANP, have attempted to reduce the influence of the MQM in the city. Local critics posited in late 2011 that the NRO had enabled corrupt officials to continue governing, notwithstanding their inability to secure the country's eroding semblance of order (see PPP under Political Parties and Groups, below).

The MQM left the coalition in June 2011. The grouping refused to agree to delay elections in Karachi in a bid to increase the number of PPP seats at its expense. Campaigning has increased across the country, with voters in the FATA hailing amendments to the Victorian-era Frontier Crimes Regulations (FCR), which outlawed the mass arrest of entire tribes or appropriation of business in retaliation for the act of a single individual. The FCR had previously been used by local governments to deter would-be rivals from campaigning. Flooding in August and September killed more than 430 and affected an estimated 5 million. On December 6 Zardari traveled to the United Arab Emirates (UAE) for medical treatment following what was described as a "minor heart attack."

In Senate elections on March 2, 2012, the PPP won 19 of 54 seats, followed by the PML-N, 14, and the ANP, 12. The election was seen as a strong popular endorsement of the PPP. A government offensive in the FATA in April resulted in more than 250,000 internally displaced persons who fled to other provinces. On April 20 an airliner crashed near Karachi, killing all 127 aboard. In May Shakil AFRIDI, who had assisted the United States in locating bin Laden, was arrested, tried, convicted, and sentenced to 33 years in prison. The conviction was protested by the United States. (In August 2013 the conviction was overturned on appeal, but Afridi remained in prison on unrelated murder charges). In September 2012 protests swept across the region against the movie *The Innocence of Muslims,* which ridiculed Islam and the Prophet Muhammad. At least 25 were killed in clashes with security forces.

On October 9, 2012, Malala YOUSAFZAI, a schoolgirl who had risen to prominence as an education activist, was shot by Taliban militants in an assassination attempt. The attack was met by international condemnation and sparked a significant domestic backlash against the Taliban in Pakistan. Yousafzai was flown to the United Kingdom for treatment and recovery. Meanwhile, massive flooding in four provinces killed 422, destroyed some 275,000 homes, and affected more than 4.5 million people. In December the government and international health groups suspended a polio vaccine program after suspected Taliban militants killed eight healthcare workers.

The government of Baluchistan was dismissed on January 13, 2013, following massive demonstrations in protest of rising sectarian violence in the province. Two bombings on January 10 killed 86 and wounded more than 100. On January 15 the Supreme Court issued arrest warrants for Prime Minister Ashraf and 15 other officials on corruption charges. However, Ashraf was not arrested and denounced the charges as politically motivated to undermine the PPP ahead of future assembly balloting.

Musharraf returned to Pakistan in March 2013 in an effort to relaunch his political career through a new grouping, the All Pakistan Muslim League. However, on April 16, a court rejected his political candidacy for the assembly. Three days later, the former ruler was placed under house arrest while he awaited trial on treason and other charges. A major military offensive against the Taliban in the Tirah Valley in April killed more than 100 militants and displaced over 43,000. A major earthquake on April 16 in Baluchistan killed 36, injured over 300, and left more than 19,000 homeless.

In assembly balloting on May 11, 2013, PML-N and its allies fell six votes short of a majority but were able to form a coalition with support from 19 independents. Nawaz Sharif was subsequently elected prime minister by the assembly. In August the coalition was bolstered when the JUI-F joined the government.

An all-parties conference on September 9, 2013, endorsed a government proposal to launch direct talks with the Taliban. Meanwhile a government offensive in early September reestablished control over much of the Tirah Valley for the first time since the 1990s. On September 22 two suicide bombers attacked a Christian church in Peshawar, killing 85 and wounding more than 150 in the most severe attack against Christians in recent years. An earthquake in Baluchistan on September 24 killed 407 and left 300,000 homeless. In December the High Court overturned an appeals court decision that had declared unconstitutional a measure criminalizing homosexual activity.

A study in the medical journal *Lancet* found that the number of HIV/AIDS infections was increasing in Pakistan at an annual rate of 11 percent. In February the government launched cease-fire talks with the TTP in Islamabad. The following month, the TTP announced a one-month cease-fire in exchange for a government pledge to end air strikes on militant positions. Meanwhile, also in February, the treason trial of Musharraf began. In April the TTP resumed attacks, but pledged to continue negotiations with the government.

Seven TTP extremists attacked an Army-run school in Peshawar on December 16, 2014, killing 132 children and 9 teachers, and injuring 124. The killing of children was condemned throughout the political spectrum, with the prime minister vowing to eradicate the TTP and declaring an end to any efforts to reconcile with moderate elements of the group. On December 17 Sharif announced that he was lifting the moratorium on the death penalty and that the military had begun "massive" airstrikes on TTP bases. However, TTP attacks on Shia mosques in January and February 2015 killed 80 and injured 50.

In June 2015 reports emerged that eight of the ten TTP members who were accused of the 2012 attack on Nobel Prize laureate and teenage activist Malala Yousafzai had been acquitted at a secret trial in April.

A proposal by the ruling PMD-N to ban child marriages by raising the minimum age to marry, from 16 years to 18 years, was withdrawn from parliament on January 15, 2016, after the Council of Islamic Ideology ruled that the measure was "un-Islamic." Also on January 15 the government reported that a program to resettle families in the war-torn areas of the FATA had returned 265,214 families, with 182,330 remaining to be returned.

Musharraf was permitted to leave Pakistan after a travel ban was lifted by the Supreme Court in March 2016. Musharraf travelled to Dubai for medical treatment. On March 28 in Lahore, 72 people were killed and more than 320 injured by a suicide bomber who targeted Christians. An al-Qaida–affiliated group, *Jamaat-ul-Ahrar,* claimed responsibility for the attack. In October Islamic State (IS) terrorists attacked a police academy in Quetta, killing 59 and injuring more than 100. The following month the IS claimed responsibility for a bombing in Baluchistan, which killed 52 and injured more than 80. The attacks highlighted the growing threat of the terrorist organization in Pakistan, although security officials remained reluctant to acknowledge the presence of the IS.

POLITICAL PARTIES AND GROUPS

Political activity has often been restricted in independent Pakistan. Banned in 1958, parties were permitted to resume activity in 1962. The Pakistan Muslim League (PML), successor to Mohammad Ali Jinnah's All-India Muslim League, continued its dominance during Ayub Khan's tenure. The election of December 1970 provided a major impetus to the reemergence of parties. The PML's supremacy ended with the rise of Zulfikar Ali Bhutto's Pakistan People's Party (PPP) in West Pakistan and the ***Awami* League** in East Pakistan (now Bangladesh). In the election of March 1977, the PPP faced a coalition of opposition parties organized as the **Pakistan National Alliance** (PNA). In October 1979 all formal party activity was again proscribed.

In February 1981 nine parties agreed to form a joint **Movement for the Restoration of Democracy** (MRD), of which the most important component was the PPP under the leadership of Begum Nusrat Bhutto and her daughter, Benazir Bhutto. The composition of the alliance changed several times thereafter, although it remained the largest opposition grouping for the balance of the Zia era. (For an overview of party politics from 1980 to 2008, see the 2011 *Handbook.*)

Prior to the February 2008 election, Pakistan had 110 registered parties and coalitions. Most of the APDM parties chose to boycott the February 2008 election, the most notable exception being the PML-N.

In all, 46 parties contested the election. In the 2013 assembly balloting, 111 parties participated in the balloting.

Government Parties:

Pakistan Muslim League–Nawaz (PML-N). Under the leadership of former Punjab chief minister and then prime minister Mohammad Nawaz Sharif, the PML-N emerged from the PML-Junejo Group in 1993 and quickly established itself as the dominant PML grouping. In 1997 the PML-N won a parliamentary majority under Nawaz Sharif. Following the October 1999 coup, the PML-N established a 15-member Coordination Committee to consider party reorganization. It did not, however, call for the immediate restoration of the Sharif government, having concluded that directly confronting the military would be inadvisable.

As a condition of his release from prison in December 2000, Sharif agreed to abandon politics for at least two decades, although he continued to exert considerable influence from exile. In May 2004 his brother, Shahbaz, having received a favorable ruling from the Supreme Court on his right to return, attempted to end his four-year exile but was immediately ushered back out of the country by officials.

At the October 2002 National Assembly election, the PML-N ran as part of ARD, winning 19 seats. A year later the party's acting president, Javed Hashmi, was arrested for distributing a letter, allegedly written by army officers, that was critical of President Musharraf. Despite widespread expressions of outrage from ARD and other elements of the opposition, Hashmi was convicted in April 2004 of treason, mutiny, and forgery. In August he was put forward as the opposition candidate for prime minister.

In August 2007 Hashmi was freed on bail by the Supreme Court after nearly four years' incarceration. Late in the same month, the justices also ruled that Nawaz Sharif could return from exile, but his attempt to do so on September 10 was thwarted by the government, which ordered him detained at the airport, served him an arrest warrant for corruption and money laundering, and immediately deported him to Saudi Arabia. Nawaz Sharif returned again on November 25, following the intervention of Saudi Arabia's king, and was greeted by thousands of supporters.

In the February 2008 National Assembly election, PML-N candidates won 91 seats, the vast majority from Punjab. Nawaz Sharif was prevented from running by earlier corruption convictions. Afterward, the PML-N formed a governing coalition with the PPP, but it withdrew its ministers in May, primarily because of differences with the PPP over reinstatement of the Supreme Court justices and other judges that had been dismissed by President Musharraf. The PML-N joined the opposition in August that year. Its candidate for president, Saeeduzzaman SIDDIQUI, finished second in September 2008.

The PML-N placed second in Senate balloting in March 2012, gaining 8 seats, for a total of 14. In 2012 Hashmi defected to the PTI (see below). In the 2013 assembly elections, the party secured 166 seats, and Nawar Sharif was elected prime minister of a coalition government. In May 2013 the **National People's Party** (NPP) merged with the PML-N. The NPP was formed in 1986 by a group of PPP moderates led by former Sindh chief minister Ghulam Mustafa. The NPP won three seats in the 2013 assembly balloting. (For more information on the NPP, see the 2014 *Handbook.*)

Nawaz Sharif was reelected party leader in October 2016.

Leaders: Mohammad Nawaz SHARIF (Prime Minister and Party Leader), Mamnoon HUSSAIN (President of the Republic), Raja ZAFAR-UL-HAQ (Chair), Iqbal Zafar JHAGRA (Secretary General).

***Jamiat-Ulema-e-Islam* Fazlur Rahman Group**—JUI-F (Assembly of Islamic Clergy Fazlur Rahman Group). The *Jamiat-Ulema-e-Islam* was founded in 1950 as a progressive formation committed to constitutional government guided by Sunni Islamic principles. In 1988 the JUI's Darkhwasty Group withdrew from the IDA to reunite with the parent formation, although a faction headed by Maulana Sami ul-Haq remained within the government coalition until November 1991. Factionalization subsequently remained a problem, with Sami ul-Haq heading one group, the *Jamiat-Ulema-e-Islam* Sami ul-Haq Group (JUI-S), and Fazlur Rahman heading another, the JUI-F. The latter, which won two National Assembly seats from Baluchistan in 1997, emerged as the dominant faction. Fazlur Rahman supported Afghanistan's Taliban and, following the 1999 coup, condemned ousted Prime Minister Sharif's "lust for unlimited powers." He was placed under house arrest in October 2001, at the opening of the U.S.-led military campaign in Afghanistan.

In the 2002 National Assembly election, the JUI-F claimed the most MMA seats. The *Muttahida Majlis-e-Amal* (United Council for Action), organized in June 2001 by the JUI-F and five other Islamic parties, campaigned on a platform that included restoration of the constitution, creation of an Islamic state, and resolution of the Kashmir issue through negotiation. All of the constituent parties opposed General Musharraf's decision to join the U.S.-led "war on terrorism" and to permit U.S. forces to operate from Pakistani soil. Having won 60 seats in the National Assembly, the MMA was courted by both the PML-Q and the PPPP (with which it had little in common ideologically) to form a coalition government, but it rejected both. Its firm opposition to the 2002 Legal Framework Order was largely responsible for the yearlong stalemate in the National Assembly, until an agreement was reached with President Musharraf in December 2003.

Although the MMA was chaired from its inception by the moderate Maulana Shah Ahmad Noorani Siddiqui of the JUP (below) until his death in December 2003, the leaders of the two largest member parties—the JUI-F's Fazlur Rahman and Qazi Hussain Ahmad of the JIP (below)—exerted more influence. One contentious issue was the JIP's objections to participation in President Musharraf's National Security Council. As leader of the opposition, the JUI-F's Fazlur Rahman held a seat on the council, as did JUI-F member Akram Khan Durrani, who was at that time the chief minister of Khyber Pakhtunkhwa.

In July 2007 the MMA participated in the anti-Musharraf All Parties Conference and joined in forming the APDM, but the alliance subsequently split over whether to boycott the February 2008 election. The JUI-F chose to contest the election, in which it ran under the MMA banner, taking 2.2 percent of the vote, winning 7 seats, and then joining the PPP-led government. At the same time, however, it was soundly defeated in the Khyber Pakhtunkhwa legislative election, winning only 14 of 124 seats. Following the 2009 Senate election, it held 10 seats in the upper house. In April 2012 the JUI-F began a boycott of parliamentary committees over a disagreement with the PPP about the suspension of NATO's supply routes through Pakistan.

The party secured 15 seats in the 2013 assembly balloting and joined the governing coalition in August. The party was given one cabinet post in the PML-N-led government. Reports in June 2014 indicated growing dissatisfaction between the JUI-F and the PML-N over security policies led the smaller grouping to threaten to withdraw from the government.

The JUI-F led efforts in April 2016 to defeat PML-N proposals to outlaw honor killings and strengthen laws against sexual abuse of women.

Leaders: Maulana Fazlur RAHMAN, Akram Khan DURRANI (Minister of Communications and Former Chief Minister of NWFP), Hafiz Hussein AHMAD.

Pakistan Muslim League–Functional (PML-F). The PML-F was established by longtime PML leader Pir Sahib Pagaro, who broke from the PML in mid-1992. In 2002 the PML-F won five National Assembly seats and one in the Senate.

Although Pagaro initially appeared willing to participate in the reunification of the various PML parties with the dominant PML-Q in 2004, he soon retreated from that position. In 2005 the largely reunited PML indicated that it regarded the PML-F as a separate, allied party. In February 2008 the PML-F won five National Assembly seats, and two months later Pagaro indicated that he was considering unification with the PML-Q. Nevertheless, in November 2008 the PML-F joined the cabinet.

Jehangir Khan Tareen, an erstwhile party parliamentary leader, announced the possible launch of a new "party of the clean" in September 2011. The new party would focus on uniting electable, ethical politicians opposed to the corruption of establishment parties. In October 2012 the PML-F announced that it would not participate in an electoral alliance with the PPP in future balloting. Instead, the grouping joined the PML-N in an electoral alliance for the 2013 assembly elections and won six seats. The PML-F was given one cabinet seat in the subsequent PNL-N-led cabinet. In 2014 the PML-F and the PML-N launched merger discussions.

Leaders: Pir Sahib PAGARA, Haji Khuda Bux RAJAR (Minister of Narcotics), Jehangir Khan TAREEN.

Other Parties Represented in the National Assembly:

Pakistan People's Party (PPP). An Islamic socialist party founded in 1967 by Zulfikar Ali Bhutto, the PPP held a majority of seats in the National Assembly truncated by the independence of Bangladesh in

1971. Officially credited with winning 155 of 200 assembly seats in the election of March 1977, it was the primary target of a postcoup decree in October that banned all groups whose ideology could be construed as prejudicial to national security.

Bhutto was executed in April 1979, the party leadership being assumed by his widow and daughter Benazir, both of whom, after being under house arrest for several years, went into exile in London. After having briefly returned to Pakistan in July 1985 to preside over the burial of her brother, Shahnawaz, Benazir Bhutto again returned in April 1986. The PPP won a sizable plurality (92 of 205 contested seats) in the National Assembly election of November 1988, and Bhutto became prime minister. She remained in office until dismissed in August 1990. The party's legislative strength was then cut by more than half in the October general election (for which it joined with a number of smaller groups to campaign as the People's Democratic Alliance—PDA). It regained its plurality in 1993, with Ms. Bhutto being reinstalled as prime minister.

In December 1993 the PPP's Executive Council ousted Prime Minister Bhutto's mother, Begum Nusrat BHUTTO, as party cochair. The action was the product of estrangement between the two over the political role of Benazir's brother, Murtaza Bhutto, who had returned from exile in November to take up a seat in the Sindh provincial legislature. In March 1995 he announced the formation of a breakaway faction of the PPP, but he died in a firefight with gunmen in September 1996. Following the ouster of Prime Minister Bhutto in November, her husband, Asif Ali Zardari, was charged with complicity in the killing. Meanwhile, Benazir Bhutto was meeting with leaders of smaller opposition parties, which ultimately led to the formation of the PAI alliance in February 1998.

Earlier, at the end of 1996, allegations about the death of Murtaza Bhutto led his widow, Ghinwa BHUTTO, to form the **Pakistan People's Party–Shaheed Bhutto** (PPP-SB) to challenge Benazir Bhutto's hold on the party. The subsequent national legislative campaign in early 1997 contained an added element of personal hostility between the two women, although both suffered disastrous defeats in the election.

During 1998–1999 new corruption allegations or charges were repeatedly brought against Benazir Bhutto and her husband. Bhutto's political viability suffered a major blow in April 1999 when a Lahore court sentenced her and her husband to five years in prison, disqualified them from public office for five years, and fined them $8.6 million for corruption and abuse of power. Bhutto asserted from England that she would appeal the conviction to the Supreme Court, which in April 2001 threw out the decision and ordered a retrial because of apparent government involvement in the verdict.

In March 1999 the party leadership elected the former prime minister chair for life, a decision reiterated by a party convention in September 2000 in defiance of the government's August announcement that convicted criminals could not hold party offices. Bhutto remained in self-imposed exile, the Musharraf regime having refused to lift outstanding arrest warrants.

To get around a proscription against the electoral participation of any party having a convicted criminal as an officeholder, the PPP organized the legally separate **Pakistan People's Party Parliamentarians** (PPPP) in August 2002. Two months after its formation, the PPPP won 81 National Assembly seats, but in November it suffered the defection of 10 representatives who supported the installation of the Jamali government. (The move was possible because the antidefection clause of the constitution remained suspended.) The defectors then organized under Rao Sikander IQBAL as the **Pakistan People's Party (Patriots),** which merged with the PPP–Sherpao, a 1999 splinter (see QWP, below), in June 2004. The new organization was then registered by the Election Commission as the "official" PPP. Bhutto's PPP immediately appealed the Election Commission's decision on the grounds that use of the PPP name by another party would deceive and defraud the electorate. Iqbal and his supporters joined the PML-Q before the 2008 general election, for which the PPP–Sherpao was separately registered.

On July 27, 2007, President Musharraf and Benazir Bhutto met in Abu Dhabi in the context of ongoing discussions between the government and her representatives on a power-sharing arrangement. Bhutto returned to Pakistan on October 18, following Musharraf's promulgation of the NRO that freed her from prosecution, but the imposition in November of a state of emergency resulted in her calling, while under house arrest, for Musharraf's resignation. Following Bhutto's assassination on December 27, she was succeeded as party chair by a teenaged son, Bilawal, with Asif Zardari handling the party's day-to-day affairs.

In the February 2008 election, the PPP, running as the still-registered PPPP, won 30.6 percent of the vote and a plurality of 124 seats. (Zardari was prevented from running by earlier corruption convictions.) It then forged a coalition agreement with the PML-N and several smaller parties, after which the PPP vice chair, Yousaf Raza Gilani, was elected as prime minister. Following President Musharraf's August resignation, Zardari emerged as the leading candidate for the presidency, even though the PML-N had withdrawn from the coalition. Zardari was elected president on September 6. In the March 2009 election for one-half of the Senate, the PPP claimed nearly half the seats and thereby surpassed the PML-Q as the plurality party in the upper house.

In March 2010 the Supreme Court demanded the chairman of the National Accountability Bureau reopen hundreds of corruption cases, many involving PPP officials that were stopped by Musharraf's 2007 NRO (see Political background, above). In 2011 the PPP was also criticized for deteriorating public security, notably in the Sindh province and its increasingly turbulent capital, Karachi. The minister for Sindh, Dr. Zulfiqar MIRZA, a senior PPP member, resigned from all of his government posts in August 2011. He accused his own party of failing to take adequate measures to stem the violence. Also in 2011, PPP Executive Committee Member Shah Memood QURESHI left the PPP to join the **Pakistan *Tehrik-e-Insaaf*** (PTI). Following the dismissal of Gilani as prime minister in June, PPP member Raja Pervaiz ASHRAF succeeded him. At a party congress in January 2013, Makhdoom Amin Fahim was elected party president, and Ashraf was elected secretary general. In the 2013 balloting, the PPP secured a disappointing 42 seats but remained the majority party in Azad Kashmir, Gilgit-Baltistan, and Sindh.

In January 2014 Safdar ABBASI, a former aide to Benazir Bhutto, left the party to form a new grouping, the **Pakistan People's Party Workers** (PPP Workers). The PPP's victory in a by-election in Karachi in November 2016 was reportedly an indication of the growing popuarity of the party.

Leaders: Bilawal Zardari BHUTTO (Chair), Makhdoom Amin FAHIM (Party President), Asif Ali ZARDARI (Former President of Pakistan and Cochair of the PPP), Raja Pervaiz ASHRAF (Former Prime Minister and Secretary General), Syed Yousaf Raza GILANI (Former Prime Minister and PPP Vice Chair).

Pakistan Movement for Justice (Pakistan *Tehreek-e-Insaf*—PTI). The PTI is a centrist grouping founded by popular cricket captain Imran Khan in 1996. It gained one seat in the assembly elections in 2002 but boycotted the 2008 polling. The party surprised pundits in the 2013 balloting by placing second in the election with 16.9 percent of the vote and third in seats with 35. The party also formed a coalition government to govern Khyber Pakhtunkhwa province. In November 2013 members of the PTI initiated an unofficial blockade of routes used to supply NATO forces in Afghanistan in protest of U.S. drone strikes. The blockade was ended in February 2014 after the government intervened. The party began a boycott of parliament in October 2016 in protest of a failure of the justice system to investigate charges of corruption against the prime minister and his family related to the "Panama Papers" (see entry on Panama). A partial suspension of the boycott was announced after 53 days.

Leaders: Imran KHAN (Chair), Javed HASHMI (President), Jenhangir Khan TAREEN (Secretary General).

***Muttahida Qaumi* Movement**—MQM (Nationalist People's Movement). Organized in 1981 as the ***Muhajir* National Movement,** at that time the MQM was primarily concerned with the rights of postpartition migrants to Pakistan, whom it wanted to see recognized as constituting a "fifth nationality." Originally backed by Zia ul-Haq as a counter to Zulfikar Bhutto's Sindh-based PPP, the party became the third largest National Assembly grouping, with 13 seats, after the 1988 election. It was subsequently allied, at different times, with both the PPP and the PML.

The assassination of party chair Azim Ahmad TARIQ in May 1993 exacerbated a violent cleavage that had emerged within the group the year before, the principal leaders being Altaf Hussain (MQM-Altaf), who is now a citizen of the United Kingdom, and Afaq Ahmed of the MQM-*Haqiqi* (below). Although the party boycotted the National Assembly election in 1993, it was runner-up to the PPP in the Sindh provincial elections. In 1994 Altaf Hussain and two of his senior associates were sentenced in absentia to 27-year prison terms for terrorism, but in 1997 the convictions were quashed.

In February 1997 the MQM-Altaf, under the banner of the ***Haq Parast* Group,** won 12 National Assembly seats, all from Sindh, and thereafter entered a governing alliance with the PML-N at both provincial and national levels. Also in 1997 the party changed its name from *Muhajir* to *Muttahida* to indicate that its interests had broadened to encompass Pakistanis in general rather than only the Muslim migrants from India.

In August 1998 the MQM announced its intention to withdraw from the governing coalitions, in part because the Nawaz Sharif administration had not done enough to stem the increasingly violent clashes in Karachi between the MQM-Altaf and the MQM-*Haqiqi,* the latter functioning primarily as a collection of urban street fighters. When Islamabad responded to the violence by dismissing the Sindh provincial government and imposing federal rule, Altaf Hussain loyalists accused the Nawaz Sharif government of trying to take away the party's power base. In 1999 a number of party leaders broke with Hussain and threatened to form a separate party unless he adopted a stronger stance toward autonomy for Sindh.

In the 2002 National Assembly election, the MQM won 17 seats, after which it joined the Jamali government. In July 2006, however, it threatened to pull its ministers from the cabinet and to leave the Sindh government because President Musharraf would not fire the Sindh chief minister. The crisis was resolved a week later, and the MQM remained in the government.

In the February 2008 election, the MQM-Altaf won 7.4 percent of the vote and a total of 25 National Assembly seats. The MQM did not immediately join the Gilani cabinet, reportedly because the party demanded more posts than were offered. It eventually joined the government in January 2009 and June 2011.

In 2010 and 2011 party supporters in Karachi were involved in political violence against ethnic Pashtuns and the ANP. Raza HAIDER, an MQM leader and lawmaker in the Sindh Assembly, was gunned down in Karachi in a drive-by shooting that was part of the violence that left at least 37 people dead in August. In October 2011 the MQM announced it would join the PPP-led government, but later rejected the coalition agreement. In the 2013 assembly balloting, the MQM won 23 seats.

Hussain was arrested in London on charges of money laundering on June 3, 2014, but released on bail three days later. MQM official Gulfraz KHATTK was arrested in October 2016, prompting the party to warn of a possible boycott of the national and regional legislatures.

Leaders: Altaf HUSSAIN (President), Babar GHAURI (Parliamentary Leader of the Party).

Pakistan Muslim League (PML-Q). Officially registered in 2004 as the PML, the current party continues to be interchangeably identified as the **Pakistan Muslim League–*Qaid-i-Azam*** ("Father of the Nation," a reference to Mohammad Ali Jinnah) or PML-Q.

The complicated history of the PML began in 1962 when it was launched as successor to the pre-independence **All-India Muslim League**. Long riven by essentially personalist factions, it split over participation in the February 1985 election. A Chatta Group, led by Kawaja KHAIRUDDIN, joined the MRD's boycott call, while the mainstream, led by Pir Sahib PAGARO, participated in the election "under protest" and won 27 seats. Mohammad Khan Junejo, a longtime party member, became prime minister.

The PML split again in August 1988, with an army-supported faction of Zia loyalists (the PML-Fida) emerging under Fida Mohammad KHAN. The party reunited as a component of the IDA prior to the November balloting, in which the IDA routed the PPP, Mohammad Nawaz Sharif of the PML thereupon being named prime minister. Pagaro formed his own party, the PML–Functional (see PML-F, above), in mid-1992.

In May 1993, two months after Junejo's death, the Junejo group split into a majority (Nawaz or PML-N) faction headed by Nawaz Sharif and a rump (Junejo or PML-J) faction led by Hamid Nasir CHATTA. The latter joined the Bhutto government following the October 1993 election, while the PML-N became the core of the parliamentary opposition.

Following the elections of February 1997 in which it won a majority of the assembly seats, the PML-N took power. The party remained prone to factionalism, however, with the PML-J and a Qasim Group (PML-Qasim) joining the opposition PAI alliance upon its formation in 1998. Following the October 1999 coup, another faction, the PML-Q, was formed with the tacit support of the military and became the party most closely associated with President Musharraf.

Entering the 2002 election, the PML-Q was allied with the National Alliance (NA) in the Grand National Alliance. The PML-N ran as part of the ARD. The PML-J, although still separate, appeared to be drawing closer to the PML-Q. Also running independently were the PML-F; the PML–Zia ul-Haq (PML-Z), which had been formed by the son of the late president in August 2002; and the PML-Jinnah, which had been established in 1998 following a factional dispute within the PML-J. Electoral results gave the PML-Q, 118 seats; PML-F, 5; PML-J, 3; and PML-Z, 1.

With the PML-Q in the ascendancy, holding a plurality of seats in both houses of parliament and dominating the government, efforts to unite the PML factions gathered strength in 2003, leading to the announcement in May 2004 of a "united PML," excluding only the PML-N. In August, however, objecting in particular to the leadership of Chaudhry Shujaat Hussain, Pir Sahib Pagaro declared that he intended to restore the PML-F's separate standing.

Days after the formation of the "united PML," the NA parties, which had won 16 seats in the October 2002 election, announced that they were merging with the PML. (One of the founding NA parties, the Sindh National Front, had already withdrawn from the alliance.) The **Sindh Democratic Alliance** (SDA), led by Arbab Ghulam RAHIM (chief minister of Sindh since June 2004), had been launched in September–October 2001 and had already established a working relationship at the provincial level with the PML-Q. The **Millat Party** (MP) had been launched in August 1998 by former president Sardar Farooq Ahmad Khan Leghari. There was, however, opposition to the merger within the other NA parties. In the end, the National People's Party (NPP) and the *Awami* National Party (ANP, below) retained separate identities.

In mid-June 2004 the election commission approved the merger of the PML-F, PML-J, PML-Jinnah, PML-Z, and SDA into the PML-Q and the redesignation of the latter as, simply, the PML, although the PML-Q designation is still commonly used (in part, to distinguish it from the PML-N). Formal incorporation of the MP followed.

In 2005 vocal opposition surfaced to the continued leadership of the party president, Shujaat Hussain, and to the prominent role of the Punjab chief minister, Chaudhry Pervez ELAHI, who allegedly ignored the recommendations of National Assembly representatives in choosing candidates for local council elections. The "forward bloc" dissident group, numbering about 30 members of the National Assembly, was led by Mian Riaz Hussain PIRZADA, Farooq Amjad MIR, and Mazhan QURESHI. In May 2006 President Musharraf, looking toward the next general election, asked Shujaat Hussain to form a dispute resolution board to resolve the differences. Nevertheless, Pirzada, in particular, continued to object to many of President Musharraf's decisions, including the dismissal of the Supreme Court judges and the imposition of a state of emergency in November 2007.

In the February 2008 National Assembly election, the PML finished third, with 23 percent of the vote and a total of 54 seats. Those defeated for reelection included Shujaat Hussain. In March the PML candidate for prime minister, Pervez Elahi, finished a distant second, with 42 votes. In May former senior vice president Manzoor Ahmad WATTOO (previously leader of the PML-Jinnah) joined the PPP.

At the same time, dissatisfaction with the continued dominance of Shujaat Hussein and Pervez Elahi led a group of dissidents to form a **Like-Minded Bloc** within the PML. In October 2008 the bloc called for new party elections, charging that Shujaat Hussain failed to consult with the party's executive and working committees and that his failure of leadership had left the PML out of the Baluchistan provincial government despite its having won a legislative plurality. With Shujaat Hussain virtually guaranteed reelection, the bloc then boycotted the July 2009 party election. Two months later, it announced its own leadership as Hamid Nasir Chatta, chair; Salim SAIFULLAH, president; and Humayan Akhtar KHAN, secretary general.

On June 25, 2012, PML-Q leader Chaudhry Pervaiz Elahi was appointed deputy prime minister. In the 2013 assembly balloting, the PML-Q secured two seats. Following the balloting, the PML-Q endeavored to form an opposition alliance against the PML-N. Reports in April 2016 indicated that a number of defectors from the PML-N and the PPP had joined the PML-Q.

Leaders: Chaudhry Shujaat HUSSAIN (President), Chaudhry Pervaiz ELAHI (Former Deputy Prime Minister), Wasim SAJJAD (Leader of the Opposition in the Senate), Aleem ADIL Sheikh (Chair), Mushahid HUSSAIN Syed (Secretary General and 2008 presidential candidate).

***Awami* National Party** (ANP). The ANP was formed in July 1986 by four left-of-center groups: the **National Democratic Party** (NDP), a group of Pakistan National Party (PNP) dissidents led by Latif AFRIDI, elements of the *Awami Tehrik* (PAT, below), and the ***Mazdoor Kissan* Party** (MKP). As originally constituted under the direction of Pushtoon leader Khan Abdul WALI KHAN, the ANP was unusual in that each of its constituent groups drew its primary support from a different province.

The NDP had been organized in 1975 upon proscription of the National *Awami* Party, a remnant of the National *Awami* Party of Bangladesh that, under the leadership of Wali Khan, was allegedly involved in terrorist activity aimed at secession of Baluchistan and Khyber

Pakhtunkhwa. A founding component of the PNA, the NDP withdrew in 1978, and in 1979 a group of dissidents left to form the PNP.

The ANP won three assembly seats in October 1993 and ten seats—all from Khyber Pakhtunkhwa—in February 1997. A year later the ANP terminated its alliance with the governing PML-N because of the latter's refusal to support the redesignation of the NWFP as Khyber Pakhtunkhwa, the area's precolonial name. Later in 1998 the ANP was a prime mover in formation of the PONM opposition alliance, but it parted ways in 1999 with what it considered the PONM's unrealistic goals for national reconfiguration.

The ANP failed to win representation in the National Assembly election of 2002 but won two Senate seats in February 2003. The party's founder, Khan Abdul Wali Khan, died in January 2006.

In June 2006 the central party leadership endorsed the Charter of Democracy proposed by former prime ministers Bhutto and Nawaz Sharif. In the same month, the National *Awami* Party (NAP), a 2000 offshoot led by Arbab Ayub JAN and Sharif KHATTAK, reunited with the parent party.

In February 2008 the ANP won 13 National Assembly seats and also won control of the Khyber Pakhtunkhwa legislature. It then joined the PPP, PML-N, and JUI-F in forming a central government. In March 2009 it won 5 Senate seats, for a total of 6.

A prominent NWFP legislator, Alamzeb KHAN, was killed by a roadside bomb in Peshawar in February 2009, and party supporters engaged in violent confrontations with supporters of MQM in Karachi throughout 2011. In Senate elections in March 2012, the ANP placed third, raising its representation to 12. In the 2013 assembly balloting, the ANP only won one seat. In March 2014 the ANP formed an electoral alliance with the JUI-F.

Leaders: Asfandyar WALI KHAN (President), Haji Muhammad ADIL (Senior Vice President), Zahir Khan OCH (First Deputy Vice President), Bushra GOHAR (Second Deputy Vice President).

***Jamaat-e-Islami* Pakistan** (JIP). Organized in 1941, the *Jamaat-e-Islami* (Islamic Assembly) is a right-wing fundamentalist group that has called for an Islamic state based on a national rather than a purely communalistic consensus. The group participated in formation of the IDA in 1988 but withdrew in 1992, in part because the coalition had failed to implement a promised Islamization program. In 1993 it was instrumental in launching a **Pakistan Islamic Front** (PIF), which won only three seats in the October legislative poll. Although the JIP held no national legislative seats following the 1997 election, it remained politically influential. It welcomed the October 1999 coup but called for setting up a caretaker civilian government.

One of the two largest parties in the MMA, the JIP increasingly differed with the JUI-F (above) after the 2002 general election, threatening the MMA's effectiveness. One contentious issue was the JIP's objections to the JUI-F's participation in President Musharraf's National Security Council. In 2008 the JIP boycotted the general election.

In March 2009 the JIP elected its secretary general, Syed Munawwar Hassan, to a five-year term as chair.

Officially a branch of the *Jamiat-e-Islami* in Pakistan but so independent that it might well be considered a separate movement, the **Jammu and Kashmir *Jamiat-e-Islami*** was active in electoral politics by 1970 and even participated to a limited degree in Indian *Lok Sabha* and provincial elections. In 1997 the party denied that it was the political wing of the militant *Hizb-ul-Mujaheddin,* and in October 40 of its members challenged the militant campaign as not contributing to the goal of an independent Kashmir.

In the 2012 Senate elections, the JIP lost its representation in the upper chamber. In the 2013 assembly polling, the party secured four seats. In April 2014 Sirajul HAQ was elected leader of the party.

Leaders: Sirajul HAQ (Chair), Qazi Hussain AHMAD (Former Chair), Liaqat BALOCH (Secretary General).

Baluchistan National Party–*Awami* (BNP-A). One of several rival political formations in Baluchistan, the BNP was formed by the 1997 merger of the **Baluchistan National Movement** (Mengal Group) and the **Pakistan National Party of Mir Ghaus Baksh Bizenjo**. It won three National Assembly seats that year and initially backed the Nawaz Sharif government, but it later withdrew its support. The party soon split into factions. In the 2002 National Assembly election the BNP–Mengal (below) won one seat; in the 2003 Senate election the BNP–Mengal and the BNP-A each won one. Also in 2003, another BNP faction led by Abdul HAYEE Baloch joined in forming the National Party (NP, below).

In the February 2008 National Assembly election, the BNP-A won one seat. In July it won a second Senate seat in a by-election necessitated by the resignation of the BNP–Mengal senator. The BNP-A joined the government in November 2008 and added a third Senate seat in 2009.

The BNP-A called upon the government to deploy troops to troubled cities, including Karachi, in response to the ethnically motivated killings of Baloch people in 2011. In a separate development the party dismissed Sen. Muhammad Ali Rind in response to his conviction for electoral fraud in August that year. In September 2012 local party official Jihadul Islam ZIA was killed in a bomb attack in Jessore. In the 2013 assembly elections, the BNP-A secured one seat.

Leader: Akhtar MENGAL (President).

***Pakhtoonkhwa Milli Awami* Party** (PkMAP). Drawing its support mainly from the Pakhtoon ethnic group in Khyber Pakhtunkhwa, the PkMAP has campaigned for greater regional autonomy. It elected three National Assembly members in 1993 but none in 1997. In 1998 it participated in formation of the PONM opposition alliance.

In the 2002 National Assembly election, the PkMAP won one seat; in 2003 it won two Senate seats, picking up a third in 2006. The party's chair, Mahmood Khan Achakzai, was elected president of the PONM in June 2006 and then became convener of the APDM. He has used that platform to demand a separate province for Pukhtuns. After the March 2009 Senate election, the PkMAP held only one seat in the upper house, which it lost after the 2012 balloting. In the 2013 general elections, the PkMAP won four seats in the assembly.

Leaders: Mahmood Khan ACHAKZAI (Chair), Sen. Abdul Rahim Khan MANDOKHEL.

***Qaumi Watan* Party** (QWP). The QWP was initially formed as the **Pakistan People's Party–Sherpao** (PPP-S). It was established by Aftab Ahmad Khan Sherpao following Benazir Bhutto's 1999 decision to dismiss him as PPP senior vice president for breaking party discipline over political developments involving the Khyber Pakhtunkhwa government. In the 2002 general election, the PPP–Sherpao won two seats in the Senate and two in the National Assembly. A June 2004 merger with the progovernment PPP (Patriots) resulted in a decision by the Election Commission to assign the unified party the PPP designation—Benazir Bhutto's PPP had been deregistered—but the issue of who held title to the name became moot after Bhutto's return to Pakistan in 2007 and the decision of the PPP (Patriots) leaders to join the PML-Q.

In April, and again in December 2007, Aftab Sherpao was the apparent intended target of suicide bombings that killed a total of some 80 people. The PPP-S ran independently in the 2008 National Assembly election, retaining one assembly seat. It secured one seat in the 2013 assembly elections. Two QWP ministers in Khyber Pakhtunkhwa Assembly were dismissed for corruption in November 2013.

Leader: Aftab Ahmad Khan SHERPAO.

National Party (NP). The NP was formed in 2003 by merger of the leading faction of the **Baluchistan National Movement** (BNM), led by Abdul Hayee Baloch, and the **Baluchistan National Democratic Party** (BNDP), led by Hasil Bizenjo and Sardar Sanaullah ZEHRI. Competing primarily against supporters of the BNP, the NP has had little electoral success at the national level. It currently holds two Senate seats.

As a member of the APDM, the NP chose to boycott the February 2008 National Assembly election, but Senior Vice President Zehri objected, formed a **National Party Parliamentarians** (NPP) group, and won a seat in the Baluchistan Assembly.

In April 2009 Ghulam Muhammad BALOCH, president of the BNM and secretary general of the eight-party **Baluchistan National Front** (BNF), was killed along with another BNM leader and the head of the **Baloch Republican Party** (BRP), Sher Mohammad BALOCH. The execution-style deaths led to rioting and antigovernment demonstrations in Baluchistan, although it was unclear who was responsible for the murders.

The NP announced in 2012 that it would contest future assembly elections and not repeat its 2008 boycott. It won one assembly seat in 2013. In May 2016 the party's secretary general Senator Hasil Khan BIZENJO was appointed minister of human rights.

Leaders: Abdul HAYEE Baloch, Sen. Abdul MALIK (President), Sen. Hasil Khan BIZENJO (Secretary General).

The following parties secured one seat in the assembly (all received less than one percent of the vote): the **Pakistan Muslim League–Zia ul-Haq** (PML-Z), led by Ijaz ul-HAQ; ***Awami* Muslim League,** founded in 2008 and led by Sheikh Rashid AHMED; ***Awami Jamhuri Ittehad* Pakistan; All Pakistan National Muslim League,** founded by former president Perez MUSHARRAFF; and the **Baluchistan National Party–Mengal** (BNP-M), led by Araullah MENGAL.

Other Parties:

Jamiat Ulema-e-Pakistan—JUP (Assembly of Pakistani Clergy). Founded in 1968, the JUP is a popular Islamic group that withdrew from the PNA in 1978. Its president, Maulana Shah Ahmed NOORANI, was among those failing to secure an assembly slot in 1988; its secretary general, Maulana Abdul Sattar Khan NIAZI, quit the Nawaz Sharif cabinet in 1991 after being criticized by the prime minister for not supporting government policies on the Gulf war against Iraq. The party subsequently split into four factions, including those led by Noorani and Niazi. Niazi died in May 2001 and Noorani, in December 2003.

In May 2006 the JUP-Niazi, which supported the ARD, indicated that it would sign the Charter of Democracy that had been drafted by former prime ministers Bhutto and Nawaz Sharif. In March 2008 the president of the JUP-Noorani, Muhammad Anas Noorani, announced that he was stepping down. His successor, Abu al-Khair Zubair, later led an unsuccessful effort to reconcile the leaders of the JUI-F and JIP in the hope of revitalizing the MMA.

In May 2009 the JUP joined in forming the **Sunni Ittehad Council** (SIC), a group of eight moderate Sunni parties that strongly opposed the Taliban but also called for the withdrawal of U.S. forces from Afghanistan and an end to missile attacks from unmanned drones. The JUP's Fazal Kareem was named SIC chair. Another SIC founder, cleric and religious scholar Sarfraz Ahmed NAEEMI, was assassinated by a Taliban suicide bomber in June. Another former JUP official, Maulana SALIMULLAH, was killed in May 2011.

The JUP organized protests in September 2012 against the anti-Islamic film *The Innocence of Muslims*. In February 2014 six factions of the JUP agreed to integrate with the JUP-Noorani.

Leaders: Abu al-Khair Muhammad ZUBAIR (President, JUP-Noorani), Muhammad Anas NOORANI (JUP-Noorani), Pir Syed Anis HAIDER Shah (President, JUP-Niazi), Muhammad Fazal KAREEM (President, JUP-FK), Saleem Ullah KHAN (President, JUP-*Nifaz-i-Shariat*).

***Jamhoori Watan* Party**—JWP (Republican National Party). A successor to the **Baluchistan National Alliance** (BNA), the JWP is active at both provincial and national levels. The JWP, which was formed in 1990 by Nawab Akbar BUGTI, won two seats from Baluchistan in the 1997 National Assembly election and as of early 1999 held five Senate seats.

The death of the JWP's prominent founder in an August 2006 military operation precipitated widespread rioting, and the first anniversary of his death was observed by a general strike across Baluchistan. By then, the party had split into two factions, the more radical of which was led by a grandson of Akbar Bugti, Baramdagh BUGTI, who is also a leader of the separatist Baluchistan Republican Army.

The JWP boycotted the 2008 National Assembly election. In August 2011 the party supported a general strike in observance of the fifth anniversary of the death of Baloch leader Nawab Akbar BUGTI. Bugti's grandson was killed in violence in Karachi in 2011. In 2012, Bugti called for the creation of a broad opposition coalition. The JWP boycotted regional balloting in 2014.

Leaders: Nawabzada Talal Akbar BUGTI (President), Sen. Shahid Hassan BUGTI, Shah Zain BUGTI.

Markazi Jamiat-e-Ahle Hadith (MJAH). A militant Sunni group with a number of factions, the MJAH has close ties to former prime minister Nawaz Sharif. Originally a component of the MMA, it withdrew when the latter decided to function as an electoral alliance for the 2002 National Assembly election, although it later returned. The leader of the most prominent faction, Sajid Mir, was reelected in 2009 to a Punjab seat in the Senate with the endorsement of the PML-N.

Leader: Sajid MIR.

Among the more than 100 parties that participated in the 2013 balloting were (all received less than 0.5 percent of the vote) the **Bahawalpur National *Awami* Party,** formed in 2010 by Nawab Salahuddin ABBASI; **Sindh United Party**, led by Syed Jalal Mahmood SHAH; **Movement for the Protection of Pakistan** (*Tehreek-e-Tahaffuz-e-Pakistan*-TTP), led by Abdul Qadeer KHAN; **Pakistan Muslim League–J**; the ***Awami Jamhuri Ittehad* Pakistan,** led by Shahram KHAN; the **Pakistan National Muslim League**; and the **Sunni Ittehad Council.**

For further information on the ***Awami Qiadat* Party** (AQP), ***Jamiat-Ulema-e-Islam* Sami ul-Haq Group** (JUI-S), ***Khaksar Tehrik*, *Muhajir Qaumi* Movement–*Haqiqi*** (MQM-*Haqiqi*), **Pakistan *Awami Tehrik*** (PAT), the **Pakistan Democratic Party** (PDP), the **Sindh National Front** (SNF), and ***Tehrik-e-Istiqlal* Pakistan,** see the 2009 *Handbook.*

Banned and Other Extremist Organizations:

***Tehrik-e-Taliban* Pakistan** (TTP). The TTP is an umbrella for radical groups that support strict adherence to sharia, oppose the presence of Western forces in Afghanistan, and have conducted attacks directed against the Pakistani military, police, and civilian government. Although Afghanistan's Taliban government had adherents and supporters in Pakistan's FATA and NWFP even before the United States launched its attack on Afghanistan in October 2001, the TTP as it currently functions probably dates from late 2007, when Baitullah Mehsud convinced a dozen or so jihadist and Islamist organizations to accept a degree of central coordination. Based in South Waziristan, Mehsud's home base, the TTP is directly linked to **al-Qaida** (see the entry on Afghanistan). Al-Qaida was banned by Pakistan in 2003, as was the TTP in August 2008.

With Mehsud as its most vocal presence, the TTP quickly extended its reach in the FATA, but its greatest impact occurred in Khyber Pakhtunkhwa's Swat valley, where its violent actions included bombings, assassinations, and the burning of girls' schools. In an effort to end the violence, in February 2009 the Khyber Pakhtunkhwa government agreed to the adoption of sharia in the Malakand division. The central government accepted the pact in April, by which time the TTP was reportedly already establishing its own sharia courts. In June militia leader Qari ZAINUDDIN, who had broken from Mehsud in 2008 and later rejected the use of suicide bombers, was assassinated. By then, the government, responding to continuing TTP violence, had already discarded the February pact and was engaged in a new military offensive.

Meanwhile, in March 2009 the United States had placed a $5 million bounty on Mehsud, who was described as a "key al-Qaida facilitator" and who was believed to have directed the assassination of former prime minister Bhutto. On August 5 a missile launched from an unmanned NATO drone mortally wounded Mehsud, who succumbed later in the month and was succeeded by Hakimullah MEHSUD and Waliur Rehman. Hakimullah is believed to have close ties to *Sipah-i-Sahaba* (SSP) and *Lashkar-i-Jhangvi* (LiJ) (below) as well as al-Qaida.

Maulana FAZLULLAH, a son-in-law of Sufi Muhammad of the TNSM (below) and a leader of the TTP in Swat, was arrested in early September 2009 during the continuing military offensive. The Pakistani government later announced a $5 million bounty for information leading to the capture or death of Hakimullah. On October 17 the government sent some 30,000 troops on a military offensive into the FATA against the TTP after weeks of bombing militant strongholds by the air force. The group retaliated with violence in cities around Pakistan. On December 28 a TTP suicide bomber attacked a Shia Muslim procession in Karachi, killing more than 40, injuring 100, and setting off riots and widespread arson in the city. Hakimullah Mehsud and another TTP commander were thought to have died of their injuries after one of two U.S. drone aircraft missile strikes in January. In April 2010 the TTP took responsibility for a heavily armed attack against the U.S. consulate in Peshawar. Hakimullah showed up in a video in May threatening that TTP militants would soon strike within the United States hours after the group claimed responsibility for a failed car-bombing of New York City's Times Square. In May Afghan police claimed Fazlullah had been killed as he led 500 Pakistani Taliban in fighting in Nuristan Province. It became clear to Pakistani government officials that the offensive against the TTP served only to disperse militants from the FATA around the country, and by July 2010 the TTP were returning to that area, the Swat Valley, and also making inroads in eastern Punjab province.

In September that year, the U.S. government added the TTP to its list of foreign terrorist organizations and offered a bounty of $5 million for the capture of Hakimullah and Rehman. The same month the TTP carried out a series of 3 suicide attacks in Lahore, killing more than 30 and injuring hundreds more. The attacks were aimed at the city's Shi'ite population and triggered riots as citizens vented frustration at the city's security forces, who had been unable to stem a dozen such attacks that had occurred in Lahore since March. The TTP claimed responsibility for a subsequent attack on a bus carrying students from an exclusive English-language school near Peshawar in September 2011.

TTP strikes in February 2012, including suicide attacks, killed more than 100. Security forces reported the deaths of 50 TTP militants in fighting during the same period. On April 15 a TTP attack on a prison in Bannu freed more than 380 prisoners, including more than 20 militants.

In an effort to support Afghan negotiations with the Taliban, on December 31 Pakistan released four senior members of the Afghan Taliban. A U.S. drone strike killed Hakimullah on November 1, 2013. A week later, the TTP announced that Mullah FAZULLAH had become the new leader of the organization.

Reports in 2015 indicated that a growing number of TTP fighters had traveled to Syria to fight against the regime in that country's civil war.

Leaders: Mullah FAZLULLAH, Waliur REHMAN, Maulvi OMAR.

Lashkar-i-Taiba—LiT (Army of the Pure). LiT was established in 1993 by Hafiz Muhammad Sayeed and Zafar IQBAL as the military wing of an above-ground religious group, the *Markaz ad-Dawa Wal Irshad* (Center for Religious Learning and Propagation), which was formed in 1986 to organize Pakistani Sunni militants participating in the Afghan revolution. The *Markaz* was officially dissolved in December 2001 and all its assets transferred to the new ***Jamaat-ud-Dawa***—JuD (Party for Religious Propagation) in an effort to avoid proscription. The LiT was banned by Pakistan in January 2002. The JuD was placed on a "watch list" by the Pakistani government in November 2003 and banned in December 2008 because of links to terrorists who had carried out attacks in Mumbai, India, a month earlier.

The LiT, which may be the largest Pakistan-based militant group seeking separation of Jammu and Kashmir from India, with bases in Azad Kashmir and near the LoC, has claimed responsibility for and been implicated in innumerable attacks within Kashmir and elsewhere. Following a series of transport blasts that killed several hundred people in Mumbai, India, in July 2006, the Indian government placed suspicion on LiT, which denied involvement. LiT has also been active in a number of other conflict areas, including Bosnia and Herzegovina, Chechnya, Iraq, and Southeast Asia.

The LiT chief of operations, Zaki-ur-Rehman Lakhvi, has been described as the mastermind of the November 2008 Mumbai assault, which was carried out by Pakistani nationals linked to the LiT. In December Lakhvi, Sayeed, and dozens of other leaders of the LiT and the JuD were detained, but in June 2009 the Lahore High Court ordered Sayeed's release from house arrest on the grounds that his detention was without constitutional grounds. In October the court dismissed the case. Lakhvi and six others were indicted by an antiterrorism court on November 25.

In an effort to circumvent its proscription, the JuD has reportedly reorganized as the ***Tehrik-e-Tahafuz Qibla Awal*** (Movement for the Safeguarding of the First Center of Prayer).

In April 2012 the United States offered a $10 million reward for the capture of Sayeed. Reports in September 2013 indicated the central government was investigating the transfer of provincial funds to support the LiT's nonmilitary activities.

Lakhvia was released on bail in April 2015.

Leaders: Hafiz Mohammed SAYEED, Zaki-ur-Rehman LAKHVI (Chief of Operations), Haji Muhammad ASHRAF (Chief of Finance).

Sipah-i-Sahaba—SiS (Guardians of the Friends of the Prophet). The SiS is a militant Sunni group founded in 1982 as a JUI breakaway by Maulana Haq Nawaz JHANGVI, who was later murdered. It has close connections to the extremist ***Lashkar-i-Jhangvi*** (LiJ) and the equally militant TNSM (below), both of which have been involved in sectarian bloodshed. The SiS was banned in 2002.

An SiS leader, Asif RAMZI, who had been linked to the kidnapping and murder of American journalist Daniel Pearl, was killed in a bomb explosion in December 2002. ATTAULLAH, an alleged LiJ leader, was sentenced to death in September 2003. Another alleged LiJ member was also sentenced to death in June 2005 for his involvement in the bombing of Shia mosques that killed 45 in May 2004.

In October 2003 SiS leader Muhammad Azam TARIQ, who had won election to the National Assembly a year earlier as an independent while still in prison, was assassinated, allegedly by members of the Shiite TJP (see TiP, below). Earlier, the SiS had been renamed the ***Millat-i-Islamia* Pakistan** (MIP) to circumvent a government ban, but the MIP was then proscribed in November 2003. The United States has placed both SiS and the LiJ on its list of terrorist organizations; both have direct links to al-Qaida, and LiJ was thought to have linked up with the TTJ in February 2010. More than 200 SiS members were arrested during protests in September 2012 during protests against the film *The Innocence of Muslims.*

Leaders: Maulana Muhammad Ahmad LUDHIANVI, Ghulam Mustafa JADOON, Abid PARACHA, Ibrahim QASIMI.

Tehrik-e-Nifaz-e-Shariat-e-Mohammadi—TNSM (Mohammedan Movement for the Enforcement of Islamic Law). The TNSM, a fundamentalist group established in 1992 by Sufi Muhammad, was blamed by the government for the deaths of 11 persons in May 1994 and of 10 more the following November as the result of tribal demands in the northern Malakand division for the introduction of Islamic law. The TNSM responded to the August 1998 U.S. missile attack against terrorist camps in Afghanistan by organizing a rally in Peshawar at which it threatened to lay siege to U.S. property and kidnap Americans. In response to the 2001 onset of U.S.-led efforts to oust al-Qaida and the Taliban from Afghanistan, the TNSM helped recruit thousands of activists to fight the Western forces. The TNSM was then banned in January 2002.

After six years in prison, Sufi Muhammad was released in April 2008, which also saw the TNSM and the recently installed ANP-led NWFP government reach a peace agreement. A further agreement in February 2009 permitted the application of sharia in Malakand division, including Swat. The agreement was signed by President Zardari on April 13, after adoption by National Assembly. Nevertheless, continuing militant activity in the region led in May to a renewed effort by the Pakistani military to recover control of Malakand, with Sufi Muhammad and his three sons detained in July. The group continued to plan attacks in 2011. In September 2012 the government was forced to drop terrorism cases against Sufi Muhammad and a dozen TNSM figures. Nineteen other charges against Sufi Muhammad remained, with 13 ongoing in August 2013. In November 2013 Muhammad was released.

Leader: Sufi MUHAMMAD.

Other proscribed organizations include ***Harkat-ul-Mujaheddin al-Alami*** (HMA); ***Islami Tehrik-i-Pakistan*** (TiP), led by Allama Sajid Ali NAQVI and Abdul Jalil NAQVI; ***Jaish-e-Muhammad Mujaheddin-e-Tanzeem*** (JMMT or JeM), led Maulana Masood AZHAR and Abdul RAUF; **Baluchistan National Army** (BLA), led by Brahamdagh Khan BUGTI; ***Lashkar-e-Islam*** (LeI), formed in 2004 by Munir SHAKIRA; and ***Ansar-ul-Islam*** (AuI), established by Saifullah SAIFI.

Banned groups based in the Khyber and Bajaur agencies of the FATA have links to the TTP but have frequently clashed with each other. In April 2008 the LeI branch in Bajaur Agency, led by Wali REHMAN, reportedly changed its name to ***Jaish-e-Islami,*** while Mengal Bagh stated in August 2009 that he had renamed the LeI as the ***Tehrik Lashkar-e-Islam.*** Pakistan has also banned the ***Al Akhtar* Trust** and the ***Al Rasheed* Trust,** both based in Karachi and involved in financing terrorist groups, as well as the ***Hizb-ut-Tahrir.***

LEGISLATURE

The **Parliament** (*Majlis-e-Shoora*), also known as the Federal Legislature, is a bicameral body consisting of the president, an indirectly elected Senate, and a directly elected National Assembly. Both were suspended by proclamation of Chief Executive Musharraf on October 15, 1999, and dissolved by him on June 20, 2001. Elections to expanded lower and upper houses were held in October 2002 and February 2003, respectively.

Senate. The current upper house comprises 100 members: 22 elected by each of the four provincial legislatures (14 general seats, 4 reserved for women, and 4 reserved for technocrats/*ulema*), plus 8 from the Federally Administered Tribal Areas (FATA) and 4 from the Federal Capital (2 general, 1 woman, 1 technocrat/*aalim*). FATA and Federal Capital senators are chosen by the National Assembly members of their respective jurisdictions. Senatorial terms are six years, with one-half of the body retiring every three years, although the election of February 24 and 27, 2003, was for the full, reconfigured house. The most recent election was held March 2, 2012, for 54 seats. After the election, the Pakistan People's Party Parliamentarians held 41 seats; Pakistan Muslim League–Nawaz, 14; *Awami* National Party, 12; *Jamiat-Ulema-e-Islam* Fazlur Rahman Group, 7; *Muttahida Qaumi* Movement, 7; Baluchistan National Party–*Awami*, 4; Pakistan Muslim League–*Qaid-i-Azam*, 4; Pakistan Muslim League, Pakistan Muslim League–Functional, and National Party, 1 each; independents, 12.

Chair: Syed Nayyer Hussain BOKHARI.

National Assembly. Serving a five-year term, subject to premature dissolution, the current National Assembly has 342 seats: 272 directly elected in single-member constituencies; 60 seats reserved for women, distributed proportionally according to party seats won in provincial assemblies; and 10 seats designated for members of religious minorities (4 Christian; 4 Hindu; 1 Sikh, Buddhist, or Parsi; 1 Qadiani), distributed proportionally to parties based on the directly elected National Assembly seat totals. The most recent election for the directly elected seats took place on May 11, 2013. The final results were as follows: the Pakistan Muslim League–Nawaz won 166 seats (126 directly elected, 34 seats reserved for women, 6 seats reserved for minorities); the Pakistan People's Party Parliamentarians, 42 (33, 8, 1); Pakistan Movement for Justice, 35 (28, 6, 1); *Muttahida Qaumi* Movement, 23 (18, 4, 1); *Jamiat-Ulema-e-Islam* Fazlur Rahman Group, 15 (11, 3, 1); Pakistan Muslim League–Functional, 6 (5, 1, 0); *Jamiat-Ulema-e-Islam*, 4 (3, 1, 0); *Pakhtoonkhwa Milli Awami* Party, 4 (3, 1, 0); National People's Party, 3 (2, 1, 0); Pakistan Muslim League, 2 (2, 0, 0); Pakistan Muslim League–Z, *Awami* Muslim League, *Awami Jamhuri Ittehad Pakistan*, *Awami* National Party, Baluchistan National Party–*Awami*, All Pakistan Muslim League, *Qaumi Watan*, and National Party each secured 1 directly elected seat; independents, 27. Nine elections were scheduled to be redone. All 10 representatives elected from FATA are categorized as independents, but in the past the majority has supported Islamic parties.

Speaker: Sardar Ayaz SADIQ (PML-N).

CABINET

[as of November 30, 2016]

Prime Minister	Muhammad Nawaz Sharif
Federal Ministers	
Climate Change	Zahid Hamid
Commerce	Khurram Dastgir Khan
Defense	Mohammad Asif
Defense Production	Tanveer Hussain
Finance, Revenue, Planning and Development, Economic Affairs, and Statistics	Mohammad Ishaq Dar
Housing and Works	Akram Khan Durrani (JUI-F)
Human Rights	Kamran Michael
Industry and Production	Ghulam Murtaza Khan Jatoi
Information and Broadcasting	Muhammad Nawaz Sharif
Inter-Provincial Coordination	Riaz Hussain Pirzada
Interior and Narcotics Control	Nisar Ali Khan
Kashmir Affairs and Gilgit-Baltistan	Muhammad Barjees Tahir
Law and Justice	Zahid Hamid
National Food Security and Research	Sikandar Hayat Bosan
Overseas Pakistanis and Human Resources	Sadaruddin Shah Rashdi (PML-F)
Petroleum and Natural Resources	Khagan Abbasi
Planning and Development	Ahsan Iqbal
Ports and Shipping	Hasil Khan Bizenjo (NP)
Railways	Saad Rafiq
Religious Affairs and Interfaith Harmony	Sardar Muhammad Yousuf
Science and Technology	Tanveer Hussain
States and Frontier Regions	Gen. (Ret.) Abdul Qadir Baloch
Textile Industry	Abbas Khan Afridi (ind.)
Water and Power	Mohammad Asif
Ministers of State	
Capital Administration and Development	Tariq Fazal Chaudhary
Communications	(Vacant)
Education, Training, and Standards in Higher Education	Muhammad Baligh Ur Rehman
Information and Broadcasting	Marriyum Aurangzeb [f]
Information Technology and Telecommunications	Anusha Rahman Ahmad Khan [f]
National Health Services, Regulation, and Coordination	Saira Afzal Tarar [f]
Parliamentary Affairs	Aftab Ahmad
Postal Services	Abdul GHafoor Haideri (JUI-F)
Privatization	Mohammad Zubair
Religious Affairs and Interfaith Harmony	Muhammad Amin Ul-Hasant
Water and Power	Abid Ser Ali

[f] = female

Note: Except where noted all are members of the PML-N.

INTERGOVERNMENTAL REPRESENTATION

Ambassador to the U.S.: Jalil Abbas JILANI.

U.S. Ambassador to Pakistan: David HALE.

Permanent Representative to the UN: Maleeha LODHI.

IGO Memberships (Non-UN): ADB, IOM, NAM, OIC, SAARC, SCO, WTO.

For Further Reference:

Jaffrelot, Christophe. *Pakistan at the Crossroads: Domestic Dynamics and External Pressures.* New York: Columbia University Press, 2016.

Lieven, Anatol. *Pakistan: A Hard Country.* New York: PublicAffairs, 2011.

Shah, Aqil. *The Army and Democracy: Military Politics in Pakistan.* Cambridge, MA: Harvard University Press, 2014.

RELATED TERRITORIES

The precise status of predominantly Muslim Jammu and Kashmir has remained unresolved since the 1949 cease-fire, which divided the territory into Indian- and Pakistani-administered sectors. While India has claimed the entire area as a state of the Indian Union, Pakistan has never regarded the portion under its control as an integral part of Pakistan. Rather, it has administered Azad Kashmir and the Gilgit-Baltistan (known as the Northern Areas until September 2009) as de facto dependencies for whose defense and foreign affairs it is responsible.

Azad Kashmir. Formally called Azad (Free) Jammu and Kashmir, the smaller (4,200 sq. mi.) but more populous (estimated at 3,623,000 in 2006) of the Jammu and Kashmir regions administered by Pakistan is a narrow strip of territory lying along the northeastern border adjacent to Rawalpindi and Islamabad. It is divided into eight districts (Bagh, Bhimber, Kotli, Mirpur, Muzaffarabad, Neelum, Poonch, and Sudhnoti). Muzaffarabad City serves as the territory's capital. An Interim Constitution Act of 1974 provided for a Legislative Assembly, now comprising 49 members—41 directly elected plus 5 women and single representatives for technocrats, overseas Kashmiris, and *mashaikh* (Muslim spiritual leaders), all named by those directly elected. The principal executive body is the Azad Kashmir Council, which is chaired by the prime minister of Pakistan and also includes the president of Azad Kashmir as vice chair, the prime minister of Azad Kashmir or his designee, six members elected by the Legislative Assembly, and five federal ministers.

In the June 1996 Legislative Assembly election, the governing **All Jammu and Kashmir Muslim Conference** (also known simply as the Muslim Conference—MC) suffered an unprecedented drubbing by candidates from the Azad Kashmir affiliate of the PPP, and on July 30 Sultan MAHMOOD CHAUDHRY, president of the Azad Kashmir PPP, was sworn in as prime minister, replacing the MC's Sardar Abdul QAYYUM Khan. Except for a brief period in 1990, the MC had been in power for 13 years. On August 12, President Sikander HAYAT Khan, also of the MC, lost a no-confidence motion in the assembly, in which the PPP now controlled more than three-fourths of the seats. On August 25, Mohammad IBRAHIM Khan was sworn in as his successor. The transition marked the fourth time the octogenarian Ibrahim had assumed the presidency.

The MC turned the tables on the PPP in the July 5, 2001, election, winning 25 out of 40 directly elected seats to the PPP's 8 and then picking up 5 more of the reserved seats. The PPP ended up with a total of 9 seats and the PML, 8. When the new legislature convened, Sikander Hayat defeated the incumbent by a vote of 30–17 and thereby returned as prime minister.

Seventeen parties contested the legislative election of July 11, 2006, in which the MC won 22 of 41 elective seats (after a revote in

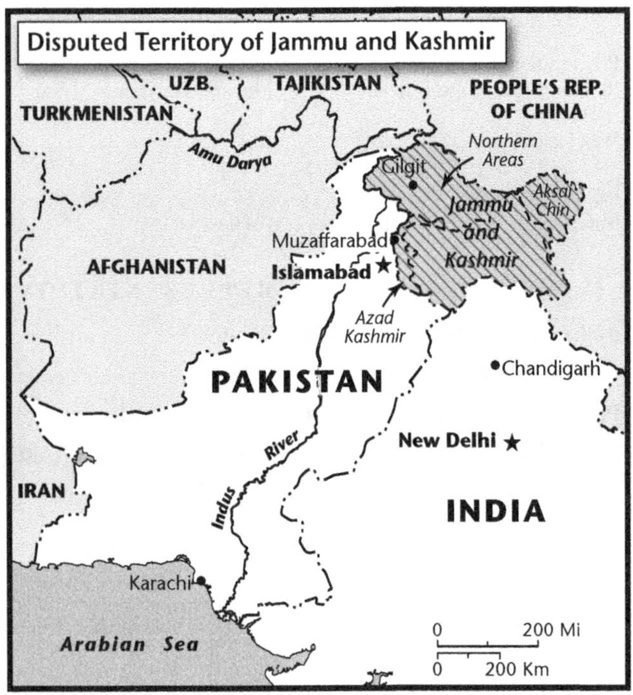

one district) and quickly gained the support of several independents. The PPP Azad Kashmir, led by Sahibzada Ishaq ZAFAR, won 7 seats; a PML alliance, 4; the MQM, 2; and Sardar Khalid IBRAHIM Khan's **Jammu and Kashmir People's Party,** 1. Immediately after the election the MMA, which had fielded a large slate of unsuccessful candidates, led a chorus of opposition parties in accusing the central government of vote-rigging, particularly in refugee camps set up in the wake of a devastating October 8, 2005, earthquake, which affected some 2,800 villages in Azad Kashmir and Khyber Pakhtunkhwa, killed more than 73,000 people, and left 3.3 million homeless. On July 22 the MC added 6 of the 8 reserved seats to its total, with the others going to the PPP and the JUI.

With Sikander Hayat having chosen not to seek reelection to the Legislative Assembly, the MC proposed Sardar ATTIQUE AHMED Khan, son of Sardar Abdul Qayyum, as prime minister, and he was sworn in on July 24, 2006. Three days later, the new legislature elected the MC's Raja Zulqarnain Khan as president by a vote of 40–8 over the PPP Azad Kashmir candidate, Sardar QAMAR-U-ZAMAN.

A September 2006 report by Human Rights Watch labeled the Azad Kashmir government a "façade" dominated by Islamabad, the military, and the intelligence services. The report further alleged that free expression has been routinely curtailed and torture allowed. Open advocates of Kashmiri independence are not allowed to seek public office and often face persecution.

In the following two years a split within the MC widened. An anti-Attique Ahmed faction, the Forward Bloc, accused the prime minister of nepotism, mismanagement, malfeasance, and a lack of transparency. On January 6, 2009, a combination of the Forward Bloc, led by Raja FAROOQ HAIDER Khan, and the opposition passed a no-confidence motion against Attique Ahmed and endorsed as his successor Sardar Muhammad YAQOOB Khan, who had been elected in 2006 as an independent. The rift in the MC was subsequently repaired, however, and on October 14 Yaqoob Khan resigned rather than face a no-confidence vote in the Legislative Assembly. On October 22 Farooq Haider, by a vote of 29–19, defeated Yaqoob Khan and was sworn in as prime minister. Yaqoob Khan had been backed by a four-party alliance of the Azad Kashmir PPP, the MQM, Sultan Mahmood Chaudhry's **Jammu and Kashmir People's Muslim League,** and a so-called Friends Group of dissident MC members. In 2011 Chaudhry Abdul MAJID (PPP) was elected prime minister of Azad Kashmir.

An avalanche in the northernmost area of the region killed 124 Pakistani soldiers and 15 civilians on April 7, 2012.

In elections on July 21, 2016, the PML-N won 31 seats, followed by the PPP with 3; MC, 3; PTI, 2; Azad Jammu and Kashmir People's Party, 1; and independent, 1. Farooq Haider KHAN (PML-N) became prime minister of the region on July 31, while Masood KHAN (PML-N) was elected president on August 16.

President: Masood KHAN (PML-N).

Prime Minister: Farooq Haider KHAN (PML-N).

Gilgit-Baltistan. Gilgit-Baltistan, which was called the Northern Areas from 1970 until September 2009, encompasses approximately 28,000 square miles, with a population (2006E) of 970,000. The region has served as the principal conduit for supplying troops and matériel to the Line of Control, facing Indian Kashmir. Pakistan's overland route to China, the Karakoram Highway, also traverses the region, which currently comprises seven districts: Astore, Diamir, Ghanche, Ghizar, Gilgit, Hunza-Nagar, and Skardu. Approximately half the population is Shiite, with the other half divided between Sunnis and Ismailis. The region has frequently seen outbreaks of sectarian violence involving Sunni and Shiite groups.

In early October 1999 the Sharif administration announced that party-based elections would be held on November 3 for a Northern Areas Legislative Council having the same powers as provincial assemblies. (For more information, see the 2014 *Handbook.*) The announcement marked a significant departure in that the government had previously argued that no permanent institutions could be established until the fate of the entire Jammu and Kashmir was determined through a UN-sponsored plebiscite.

Although the October 1999 military coup in Islamabad intervened, the November election took place as scheduled. Of the leading parties, the PML won 6 seats (5 more than it had previously held); the PPP, 6; and the *Tehrik-e-Jafariya-e-Pakistan* (TJP), 6. Voter turnout was very low, which analysts attributed in part to the council's severely limited role. After the 5 seats reserved for women were finally filled nearly nine months later, a PML-TJP alliance controlled 19 of the 29 seats. As a result, the PML's Sahib KHAN was elected speaker of the council and the TJP's Fida Muhammad NASHAD became deputy chief executive, second in the governmental hierarchy to the federal minister for Kashmir and the Northern Areas.

At the Northern Areas Legislative Council election of October 12, 2004, the PML-Q and PPP Parliamentarians (PPPP) each won 6 of the 24 directly elective seats, and the PML-N won 2, the balance being claimed by independents, 8 of whom then aligned with the PML-Q. When the 12 reserved seats (including 6 for women), all chosen by the elected members, were finally filled on March 22, 2006, the PML-Q picked up 10 of them, with independents claiming the remaining 2. The PPPP immediately protested that the election had been rigged and argued that seats should have been assigned on a proportional basis.

In October 2007 President Musharraf announced a Northern Areas reform package that called for creation of a seventh district (Hunza-Nagar); conversion of the Northern Areas Legislative Council to the Northern Areas Legislative Assembly (NALA), to be chaired by the minister of Kashmir and Northern Areas affairs; and elevation of the office of deputy chief executive to that of chief executive. A new chief executive, Ghazanfar ALI KHAN (PPP), with enhanced administrative powers, was sworn in on January 4, 2008.

On September 7, 2009, President Zardari signed the Gilgit-Baltistan (Empowerment and Self-Government) Order 2009, which had been passed by Parliament in late August. The order, in addition to changing the region's name, provided for a level of autonomy comparable to that of Azad Kashmir, which prompted some Kashmiri activists to charge that Islamabad was making Gilgit-Baltistan a de facto province of Pakistan. Under the order, Islamabad's principal representative is a governor appointed by the president of Pakistan on the advice of the prime minister. The territory's Legislative Assembly comprises 33 members—24 directly elected plus 9 named to reserved seats (6 women and 3 professionals). A chief minister and his cabinet are responsible to the Legislative Assembly, which has significantly expanded powers. An executive Gilgit-Baltistan Council is chaired by the prime minister of Pakistan, with the governor as vice chair. Also sitting on the council are the chief minister of Gilgit-Baltistan, 6 members elected from the Legislative Assembly, and 6 representatives of the central government (ministers or members of Parliament). A Supreme Appellate Court is to sit at the apex of the independent judicial system.

The first election for the new Legislative Assembly was held on November 12, 2009. The PPP was initially credited with winning 11 seats; the PML-N, 2; the PML-Q, 2; the JUI-F, 1; the MQM, 1, and independents, 4. (Polling in one district was postponed due to the death of a candidate, and disruptions at some polling stations in two other districts necessitated partial revotes.) The PML-N and other parties immediately rejected the results as the product of irregularities and of favoritism on the part of the acting governor, PPP minister Qamar Zaman Qaira. A group of NGOs monitoring the elections found widespread irregularities and flaws in the election procedures. By late November, however, the PPP claimed the support of 17 legislators, including 3 of the independents and the JUI-F member, and anticipated gaining additional seats when the 9 nonelected members were chosen. The PPP's nominee for chief minister, party chair Syed Mehdi Shah, was confirmed by the full Legislative Assembly on December 12.

Among the groups attacking the 2009 Gilgit-Baltistan Order was the **Balawaristan National Front** (BNF), chaired by Abdul Hamid KHAN. The BNF has called for self-rule and elections to a constituent assembly that would then draft a constitution.

On March 23, 2010, Dr. Shama Khalid was sworn in to office as the first governor of Gilgit-Baltistan after being selected by President Zardari. Khalid was also the country's first female governor. She died in office from cancer on September 15, 2010, and was replaced by acting governor Wazir BAIG (PPP) and then Pir Karam Ali Shah in January 2011.

In April 2012, after a grenade attack killed 14 Sunnis, sectarian violence spread through the region, prompting the deployment of government security units. In response to rising food costs, Islamabad increased the region's wheat subsidy by $4.5 million.

In balloting in June 2015, the PML-N won 22 seats in the assembly and Hafiz Hafeesur REHMAN (PML-N) became chief minister. Ghazanfar Ali KHAN (PML-N) was appointed governor of the region on November 24, 2015.

Governor: Ghazanfar Ali KHAN (PML-N).

Chief Minister: Hafiz Hafeesur REHMAN (PML-N).

PALAU

Republic of Palau
Belu'u era Belau

Political Status: Former U.S. Trust Territory; became sovereign state in free association with the United States on October 1, 1994.

Land Area: 178 sq. mi. (461 sq. km).

Population: 22,000 (2016E—UN); 21,347 (2016E—U.S. Census). Approximately 6,000 residents are nonnationals.

Major Urban Center (2012E): MELEKEOK (299), Koror (10,600). Melekeok, located on the largely undeveloped northern island of Babeldaob, replaced Koror as Palau's capital in October 2006.

Official Languages: English, Palauan.

Monetary Unit: U.S. Dollar (see U.S. article for principal exchange rates).

President: Thomas REMENGESAU Jr. (nonparty); elected on November 6, 2012, and inaugurated for a four-year term on January 17, 2013, succeeding Johnson TORIBIONG (nonparty); reelected on November 1, 2016.

Vice President: Antonio BELLS; elected on November 6, 2012, for a term concurrent with that of the president, succeeding Kerai MARIUR (nonparty); reelected on November 1, 2016, for a term concurrent with the president.

THE COUNTRY

Palau encompasses a chain of more than 200 Pacific islands and islets at the western extremity of the Carolines, some 720 miles southwest of Guam and 500 miles east of the Philippines. The population in 2012 was approximately 72 percent Palauan, 15 percent Filipino, 5 percent Chinese, and the remainder divided among smaller groups. Both Palauan and English are spoken, and Roman Catholicism is the principal religion. Following the November 2016 elections, there were no women in the congress.

The climate is tropical with quite heavy rainfall. Fishing and tourism are the leading economic sectors, with the United States pledging approximately $650 million in aid over a 15-year period as part of a trusteeship settlement that became effective on October 1, 1994. Because of the aid, Palau's nominal GDP grew by 24.3 percent in fiscal year 1994–1995 but declined sharply thereafter. From 2000 to 2008, GDP growth registered about 2.2 percent annually, before falling by 4.6 percent in 2009. GDP grew by 0.3 percent in 2010. A surge in tourist arrivals initiated a strong recovery in 2011, with a GDP growth of 5.8 percent. The International Monetary Fund (IMF) reported that GDP grew by 4 percent in 2012, but declined by 0.2 percent the following year as the country went into a recession. Growth returned in 2014 when GDP expanded by 4.2 percent, rising by 9.4 percent in 2015, and an estimated 2 percent in 2016. Inflation in 2012 was 5.4 percent, 2.8 percent in 2013, –7.2 percent in 2014, and –0.1 percent in 2015. GDP per capita was $11,021 in 2015. The IMF has expressed concern about the fiscal adjustment that will be required when U.S. grant assistance ends in 2024 (see Current issues, below). Meanwhile, in 2016 the World Bank ranked Palau 136th in its annual ease of conducting business survey out of 189 countries.

GOVERNMENT AND POLITICS

Political background. Purchased by Germany from Spain in 1889, the Palau group was among the insular territories seized by Japan in 1914 and retained as part of the mandate awarded by the League of Nations in 1920. The islands were occupied by U.S. forces near the end of World War II and became part of the U.S. Trust Territory of the Pacific in 1947. A republican constitution was adopted by referendum in October 1979, and on January 1, 1981, Haruo I. REMELIK was inaugurated as the country's first president. On November 30, 1984, Remelik was elected to a second four-year term on a platform that called for early implementation of a 1980 Compact of Free Association with the United States. Remelik was assassinated on June 30, 1985, and in a special election on August 28 Lazarus SALII defeated Acting President Alfonso OITERONG in balloting for Remelik's successor.

The Palauan Compact, including provision for substantial U.S. aid, required that the republic provide facilities for U.S. conventional and nuclear forces. After failed attempts to pass the Palauan Compact because of the controversial nuclear weapons clause, President Salii, who had received assurances that Washington would not "use, test, store, or dispose of nuclear, toxic, chemical, gas, or biological weapons on the islands," suggested that only a simple majority was needed for approval of the compact. His position was challenged by the islands' ranking chief, who obtained a favorable appellate ruling by the Palauan Supreme Court on September 17.

After two more failed attempts to pass the compact in December 1986 and June 1987, a referendum on amending the constitution to suspend the applicability of its antinuclear clause to the compact was held on August 4, which resulted in 71 percent approval, with majorities in 14 of the 16 states. The vote was hailed by the government, which contended that amending (as distinguished from overriding a constitutional proscription) required only a simple majority overall, coupled with majorities in at least 12 states. The constitutional issue seemingly having been resolved, a sixth plebiscite (yielding 73 percent approval) was held on August 21, with the Palauan legislature voting on August 27 to approve the compact. On April 22, acting on a refiled opposition suit, the islands' Supreme Court trial division ruled that the August 4 referendum was invalid.

On August 20, 1988, President Salii was found dead in his office from an apparently self-inflicted gunshot wound, and Vice President Thomas REMENGESAU was subsequently sworn in to serve for the rest of the year, pending the results of November's regularly scheduled presidential election. Shortly thereafter, the appellate division of the Supreme Court upheld the April decision invalidating the 1987 compact voting. While ruling that a special referendum on constitutional revision could be called at any time, the court declared that the proposed amendment must first be approved by 75 percent majorities in both houses of parliament or be requested by a petition signed by at least 25 percent of the electorate.

In balloting on November 2 Ngiratkel ETPISON, who appeared to enjoy the backing of many former Salii supporters, was elected president from among seven candidates. After another failed vote in 1990, the issue was referred back to Washington with a demand to reduce the length of the compact, but this was rejected by U.S. president George H. W. Bush. President Etpison thereupon called for a threshold vote on July 13 but was again rebuffed by the court, which ruled that prior congressional approval was required. In August the legislators responded by placing the matter on the ballot for the general election of November 4.

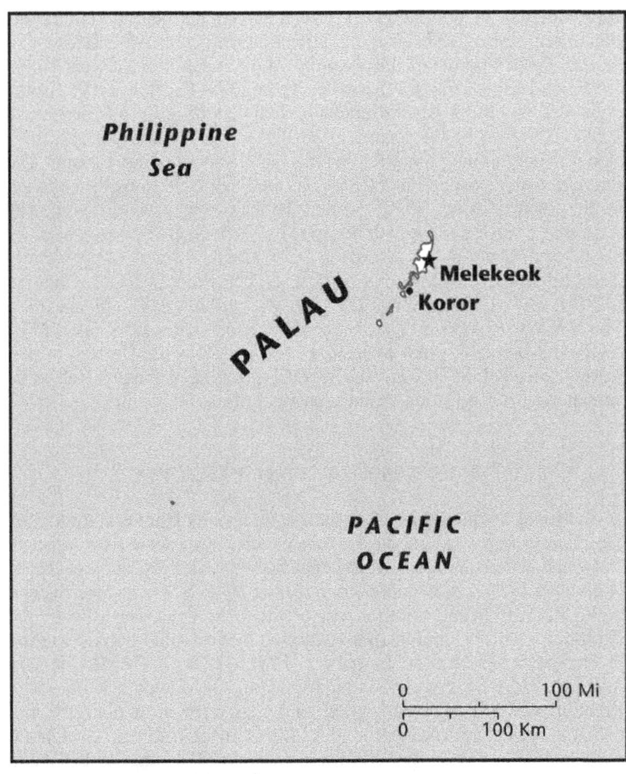

For the 1992 presidential balloting, Etpison was defeated in a primary that resulted from abandonment of the earlier first-past-the-post system, and on November 3 the incumbent vice president, Kuniwo NAKAMURA, defeated Johnson TORIBIONG by a slim 50.7 percent majority. More important, the amendment to reduce the threshold required to alter the antinuclear provision of the constitution was approved by the voters. This cleared the way for approval of the compact by 64 percent of the participants on November 9, 1993. In September 1994 the Palauan Supreme Court dismissed an appeal challenging the validity of the 1993 vote, and on October 1, 1994, independence was formally proclaimed. (For more on the process by which the Palauan Compact was passed, see the 2011 *Handbook.*)

Benefiting from an economic upswing based on the infusion of U.S. compact funds, in addition to a "look north" policy that had attracted significant Japanese, Filipino, and Taiwanese investment, President Nakamura won reelection on November 6, 1996, easily defeating the mayor of Koror, Paramount Chief Ibedul Yutaka GIBBONS, by a 2–1 margin.

In voting on November 7, 2000, Vice President REMENGESAU Jr. was elected president, defeating Sen. Peter SUGIYAMA. Running separately, Sen. Sandra PIERANTOZZI defeated her nephew, Alan REID, for the vice presidency even though Reid had been endorsed by outgoing President Nakamura.

President Remengesau was accorded a second term in the election of November 2, 2004, although Vice President Pierantozzi was defeated by Elias Camsek CHIN. The vice-presidential outcome led to a constitutional amendment (approved in 2004) that the president and vice president thereafter be elected as a team.

On November 4, 2008, Johnson Toribiong defeated Chin with a presidential vote share of 51.2 percent.

In November 2009 former president Remengesau was found guilty of violating Palau's fiscal disclosure law and was assessed a fine of $156,000 on December 28.

Remengesau won presidential balloting on November 6, 2012, with 58 percent of the vote to Toribiong's 42 percent. The campaign focused on management of the trust (see Current issues, below). Antonio Bells was concurrently elected vice president. Most members of the subsequent cabinet were approved by April 2013.

Remengesau was reelected on November 1, 2016, in extremely close voting that he won by 255 votes. His opponent was his brother-in-law, Senator Surangle WHIPPS Jr. Bells, who was reelected vice president.

Constitution and government. Under the Compact of Free Association, Palau is a fully sovereign state, save with regard to defense, which was to remain a U.S. responsibility for at least a 15-year period; it was also obligated to "consult" with Washington regarding major foreign policy matters. For the first decade of independence, its constitution provided for a president and vice president elected on separate tickets for four-year terms after having been selected (since 1992) by primaries replacing a first-past-the-post system. This was replaced in 2004 by a requirement that the two offices be filled on a single ticket. The bicameral National Congress consists of a Senate currently composed of 14 members elected on a population basis (9 from Koror, 4 from the northern islands, 1 from the southern islands), and a House of Delegates, encompassing one representative from each of the republic's 16 states (a proposal to abandon bicameralism in favor of a unicameral legislature was rejected by voters in 2004). There is also a 16-member Council of Chiefs to advise the government on matters of tribal laws and customs. The judicial system consists of a Supreme Court (including both Trial and Appellate Divisions), a National Court, and a Court of Common Pleas. In late 2007 a Senate bill was introduced that would create a court to deal with land, property, and other issues governed by traditional principles.

Each of the states (Aimeliik, Airai, Angaur, Kayangel, Koror, Melekeok, Ngaraard, Ngardmau, Ngaremlengui, Ngatpang, Ngchesar, Ngerchelong, Ngiwal, Peleliu, Sonsorol, and Tobi) elects its own governor and legislature. Palauans, on a per capita basis, have been termed "the most governed people on earth."

In addition to the measures referenced above, three constitutional amendments were approved in 2004: the holding of dual U.S.–Palau citizenship, a limitation of three four-year terms for legislators, and a cap on congressional salaries. In addition to the amendments passed in 2004, a second constitutional convention was held in 2005. During the convention, some 24 changes to the constitution were approved. Among these changes were establishing the joint election of president and vice president, setting a specific date for the inauguration of new members of Congress, and a constitutional ban on same-sex marriage. These changes were approved by the citizens of Palau in 2008 in a referendum held concurrently with the state's general elections.

Foreign relations. Palau was admitted to the United Nations on December 15, 1994. It participates in the Pacific Islands Forum and a number of other intergovernmental organizations. Following independence, the government opened embassies in Tokyo and Washington. In 2004, on the other hand, President announced that Palau was withdrawing from the G-77 group of developing countries (which it had joined two years before) on the grounds that it had been ineffective in lobbying on environmental issues, such as global warming.

In 1999 diplomatic relations were established with Taiwan, a linkage that critics subsequently urged the Remengesau administration to abandon in favor of ties with the People's Republic of China. (For more on relations with Taiwan, see the 2012 *Handbook.*)

The establishment of diplomatic relations with Russia in late 2006 was followed by an upsurge in tourists that prompted an increase in Russian-speaking staff by resort owners.

In April 2012 relations with China were strained after Palau marine police killed a Chinese fisherman suspected of illegal fishing and arrested 25 others.

In December 2012 Palau voted against observer status for the Palestinian Authority in the UN (see entry on Palestine). In June 2013 Palau and Tuvalu became the first Pacific countries to sign the UN Small Arms Treaty (see entry on the UN).

In April 2014 the Asia Development Bank agreed to loan Palau $28.8 million to upgrade its sewage system. In May eight Vietnamese fishermen were sentenced each to a one-year suspended sentence for fishing in Palau's protected marine zone. In both 2015 and 2016 Vietnamese boats were burned in protests against illegal fishing near Palau.

Current issues. In February 2009, with the value of Palau's Trust Fund having lost approximately 40 percent of its value because of the U.S. recession, President Toribiong called for renegotiation of the compact's funding provisions. Washington was reported to have offered up to $200 million in long-term financial assistance if Koror would accept 17 Chinese Muslims detained at Guantánamo Bay. Six arrived in Palau in November 2009. Although officials denied any connection, a one-year extension of U.S. financial assistance was negotiated for October 2009–October 2010.

On the 15th anniversary of the Palauan Compact in September 2009, a review was established in accordance with the initial compact. The United States reached an agreement with Palau in September 2010 to extend aid in the amount of $250 million to the country until 2024.

The agreement was signed by both sides; it remained unapproved by the U.S. Senate as of July 2013. Also in September Palau became the first nation to ban commercial shark fishing in its waters.

In May 2011 Palau overdrew its financial aid from the United States. The United States had placed a $5 million borrowing limit on the island's U.S.-funded trust fund until the approval of the aid agreement by the U.S. Congress. Palau had withdrawn $7 million from the fund, causing the U.S. Department of the Interior to demand that Palau repay the $2 million excess.

With the compact still awaiting approval from the U.S. Congress, the United States extended more than $13 million in aid to Palau for 2012.

In March 2012 five senators filed two lawsuits against Toribiong, charging him with personal liability for the $2 million in overspending and alleging that he misused $500,000 in U.S. funding for the resettlement of the Chinese Muslim detainees, half of which was used to renovate a building owned by his relative for their housing.

In 2013 audits indicated that the trust had been overdrawn again in 2012, by $2 million, leading to delays in the release of $13.2 million in U.S. aid. The creation of a special prosecutor was approved in July, but nominees to the post were repeatedly rejected by the Senate until 2015.

Remengesau announced in February 2014 that Palau's 200-mile exclusive economic zone would become a marine sanctuary where commercial fishing would be banned. Attorney General Victoria ROE announced her resignation in April. In May Remengesau utilized his presidential authority to reduce a supplemental spending bill from $1.09 million to $861,000 in an attempt to balance the budget for the last quarter of the fiscal year.

In January 2016 the Senate passed a law offering financial incentives for families to have more children in an effort to counter high emigration rates.

POLITICAL PARTIES

Traditionally there were no formal parties in Palau. However, an antinuclear **Coalition for Open, Honest, and Just Government** emerged to oppose the Compact of Free Association, which was defended by a Ta Belau Party, led by Kuniwo Nakamura. Subsequently, a **Palau National Party** was launched by (then) opposition leader Johnson Toribiong. However, there is no indication that any of them currently exists.

LEGISLATURE

The **Palau National Congress** (*Olbiil Era Kelulau,* which translates literally as "House of Whispered Decisions") is a bicameral body, both of whose chambers have four-year mandates (there is a three-term limit). Balloting was last held on November 1, 2016.

Senate. The upper house currently consists of 11 members, selected in a nationwide election.
President: Elias Camsek CHIN.

House of Delegates. The lower house contains 16 members, one from each of Palau's states.
Speaker: Sabino ANASTACIO.

CABINET

[as of October 15, 2016]

President	Thomas Remengesau Jr.
Vice President	Antonio Bells
Ministers	
Attorney General	John Bradley
Community and Cultural Affairs	Baklai Temengil [f]
Education	Sinton Soalablai
Finance	Elbuchel Sadang
Health	Greg Ngirmang
Justice	Antonio Bells
Natural Resources, Environment, and Tourism	Fleming Umiich Sengebau
Public Infrastructure, Industries, and Commerce	Charles Obichang
Special Prosecutor	Steven Killelea
State	William Kuartei

[f] = female

INTERGOVERNMENTAL REPRESENTATION

Ambassador to the U.S.: Hersey KYOTA.

U.S. Ambassador to Palau: Amy Jane HYATT.

Permanent Representative to the UN: Caleb OTTO.

IGO Memberships (Non-UN): ADB, PIF.

For Further Reference:

Shuster, Donald R., Peter Larmour, and Karin von Strokirch, eds. *Leadership in the Pacific Islands: Tradition and the Future*. Canberra, Australia: National Center for Development Studies, 1998.

Wilson, Lynn. *Speaking to Power: Gender and Politics in the Western Pacific.* New York: Routledge, 1995.

Veenendaal, Wouter P. "How Democracy Functions without Parties: The Republic of Palau." *Party Politics* (November 2013).

PANAMA

Republic of Panama
República de Panamá

Political Status: Became independent of Spain as part of Colombia (New Granada) in 1819; independent republic proclaimed on November 3, 1903; present constitution, adopted on September 13, 1972, substantially revised on April 24, 1983.

Area: 29,208 sq. mi. (75,650 sq. km).

Population: 3,990,000 (2016E—UN); 3,705,246 (2016E—U.S. Census).

Major Urban Centers (2014E): PANAMA (also known as Panama City, 1,025,425), San Miguelito (350,949).

Official Language: Spanish.

Monetary Unit: Balboa (official rate October 1, 2016: 1.00 balboa = $1US). The balboa is at par with the U.S. dollar, which is also acceptable as legal tender.

President: Juan Carlos VARELA (Pro-Panamanian Party); elected on May 4, 2014, and inaugurated on July 1 for a five-year term, succeeding Ricardo MARTINELLI Berrocal (Democratic Change Party).

Vice President: Isabel SAINT MALO de Alvarado (ind.); elected on May 4, 2014, and inaugurated on July 1 for a term concurrent with that of the president, succeeding Juan Carlos VARELA (Pro-Panamanian Party).

THE COUNTRY

Situated on the predominantly mountainous isthmus that links North and South America, Panama has the second-smallest population of any Latin American country but ranks comparatively high in per capita wealth and social amenities, due mainly to the economic stimulus imparted by the Panama Canal, the interoceanic canal built in 1904–1914 that cuts across the country's midsection. Population density is not high, although nearly one-fourth of the people live in Panama City and Colón. About 70 percent of the populace is of mixed Caucasian, Indian, and African descent; pure Caucasian is estimated at 9 percent and pure African at 14 percent, the balance being of Indian ancestry and

other origins. Roman Catholicism is professed by approximately 85 percent of the people, but other faiths are permitted. In 2012 women constituted 37.2 percent of the workforce; female participation in government has traditionally been minimal, although the president in 1999–2004 was a woman (the first in the nation's history). In 2014 three of the 15 cabinet ministers were women. Law 22, passed on July 14, 1997, required that 30 percent of candidates nominated by parties be women. There were nine women in the 71-member National Assembly elected in 2014.

Panama's shipping fleet is the largest in the world by virtue of flag-of-convenience registrations. It is also one of the world's most important centers of entrepôt activity, its economy being heavily dependent on international commerce and transit trade. Since 1970, when a new banking law went into effect, it has become a leading Spanish-language and offshore banking center. The service sector now accounts for 80 percent of GDP and employs almost 74 percent of the workforce. Bananas remain the most important export, followed by shrimp and other seafood, clothing, sugar, and coffee.

Economic performance was mixed throughout the 1990s but began a steady march upward beginning in 2002, averaging 7.4 percent growth annually through the next seven years. With the impact of the global downturn, expansion fell to 3.2 percent in 2009. However, International Monetary Fund (IMF) managers said the country's banking system had "weathered the global financial crisis relatively well." In March 2010 the Martinelli administration introduced reforms raising the value-added tax by 2 percent, abolishing 30 taxes and updating the fiscal code. In 2010 the IMF forecast that Panama's economy would post the fastest expansion in Central America through at least 2015, spurred by the robust services sector and the economic injection caused by upgrading the Panama Canal. After posting consistent growth of 10.8 percent in 2011 and 10.7 percent in 2012, GDP expansion slowed slightly to 8.4 percent in 2013, which the IMF attributed as a typical decline because of decreased capital spending. Though GDP growth slowed to 6.2 percent in 2014, the IMF noted the positive impact of public and private investment. Inflation was 4.8 percent that year, with unemployment of 4.2 percent. In 2015 GDP grew by 6.1 percent, rising to 6.4 percent in 2016. Inflation was 2 percent in 2016, while unemployment was 4.1 percent and GDP per capita was $12,621. In 2016 the World Bank's annual ease of conducting business survey ranked Panama 69th out of 189 nations, second only to Coast Rica (58th) among Central American countries.

GOVERNMENT AND POLITICS

Political background. After renouncing Spanish rule in 1821, Panama remained a part of Colombia until 1903, when a U.S.-supported revolt resulted in the proclamation of an independent republic. Shortly thereafter, Panama and the United States signed a treaty in which the latter guaranteed the independence of Panama while obtaining "in perpetuity" the use, occupation, and control of a zone for the construction, operation, and protection of an interoceanic canal. Panama also received a down payment of $10 million and subsequent annual payments of $250,000.

In the absence of strongly rooted political institutions, governmental authority was exercised in the ensuing decades by a few leading families engaged in shifting alliances and cliques. Following World War II, however, Panamanian politics were increasingly dominated by nationalist discontent inspired by U.S. control of the canal and the exclusive jurisdiction exercised by the United States in the Canal Zone. Despite increases in U.S. annuity payments and piecemeal efforts to meet Panamanian complaints, serious riots within the zone in January 1964 yielded a temporary rupture in diplomatic relations with Washington. Following their restoration in April, the two countries agreed to renegotiate the treaty relationship, but progress was impeded by internal unrest in Panama as well as by political opposition within the United States.

In early 1968 the outgoing president, Marco A. ROBLES, became involved in a major constitutional conflict with the National Assembly over his attempt to designate an administrative candidate, David SAMUDIO, for the presidential election of May 12. Samudio was defeated in the voting by Arnulfo ARIAS Madrid, a veteran politician who had already been twice elected and twice deposed (in 1941 and 1951). Inaugurated for the third time on October 1, Arias initiated a shake-up of the National Guard, a body that served both as an army and police force, and guard officers who felt threatened by his policies again overthrew him on October 11–12. Col. José María PINILLA and Col. Bolívar URRUTIA Parilla were installed at the head of a Provisional Junta Government, which suspended vital parts of the constitution and normal political processes, promised a cleanup of political life, and indicated that a new election would be held without military participation in 1970. Real power, however, was exercised by the high command of the National Guard under the leadership of then colonel Omar TORRIJOS Herrera and Col. Boris N. MARTÍNEZ, his chief of staff. Martínez was relieved of his command and exiled in February 1969, leaving Torrijos in undisputed control of the military. In December 1969 Pinilla and Urrutia attempted to purge Torrijos; they failed, however, and were subsequently replaced by two civilians, Demetrio Rasilio LAKAS Bahas and Arturo SUCRE Pereira, as president and vice president. On July 15, 1975, Sucre resigned for health reasons and was succeeded by Gerardo GONZÁLEZ Vernaza, the former minister of agricultural and livestock development.

Politics in the wake of the 1968 coup focused primarily on two issues: renegotiation of the Canal Zone treaty and the long-promised reactivation of normal political processes. Nationalist sentiments put increasing pressure on the United States to relinquish control over the Canal Zone, while a partial return to normalcy occurred in 1972 with the nonpartisan election of an Assembly of Community Representatives. The assembly's primary function was to legitimize existing arrangements, and one of its first acts was the formal designation of General Torrijos as "Supreme Leader of the Panamanian Revolution."

Following a legislative election on August 6, 1978, General Torrijos announced that he would withdraw as head of government and would refrain from seeking the presidency for the 1978–1984 term. On October 11 the National Assembly designated two of his supporters, Arístides ROYO and Ricardo de la ESPRIELLA, as president and vice president, respectively.

During 1979 political parties were authorized to apply for official recognition, although the leading opposition party and a number of smaller groups refused to participate in balloting on September 28, 1980, to elect one-third of an expanded Legislative Council (theretofore primarily identifiable as a nonsessional committee of the National Assembly).

General Torrijos was killed in a plane crash on July 31, 1981 and on August 1 was succeeded as National Guard commander by Col. Florencio FLORES Aguilar. On March 3, 1982, Colonel Flores retired in favor of Gen. Rubén Darío PAREDES, who was widely regarded as a leading presidential contender and who was due to retire from the military on

September 11. Under pressure from Paredes, President Royo resigned on July 30, allegedly for health reasons, in favor of Vice President de la Espriella, who reaffirmed an earlier pledge that "clean and honest" elections would be held in 1984. On September 6 it was announced that Paredes had acceded to requests from the president and the military high command to remain in his post beyond the mandated retirement date.

On April 24, 1983, a series of constitutional amendments (see below) were approved in a national referendum, paving the way for a return to full civilian rule, and on August 12 General Paredes retired as military commander in favor of Gen. Manuel Antonio NORIEGA Morena to accept presidential nomination by the *torrijista* Democratic Revolutionary Party (*Partido Revolucionario Democrático*—PRD). Because of widespread opposition to his candidacy, he was, however, forced to step down as PRD standard-bearer in September.

On February 13, 1984, following designation of Nicolás ARDITO Barletta as the nominee of a PRD-backed electoral coalition called the National Democratic Union (*Unión Nacional Democrática*—Unade), President de la Espriella was obliged to resign in a second "constitutional coup." Vice President Jorge ILLUECA, who was identified with more leftist elements within the PRD, succeeded him.

On May 6, 1984, Panama conducted its first direct presidential balloting in 15 years. From a field of seven candidates, Unade's Ardito Barletta narrowly defeated former president Arias Madrid amid outbreaks of violence and allegations of vote-rigging. The new chief executive assumed office on October 11, pledging to alleviate the country's ailing economy, expose corruption, and keep the military out of politics. The legislative election, held concurrently with the presidential poll, also yielded victory for the six-party Unade coalition, which took 40 of the 67 National Assembly seats.

In the second such action in 18 months, Ardito Barletta resigned on September 27, 1985, being succeeded the following day by First Vice President Eric Arturo DELVALLE Henríquez. The move was reportedly dictated by General Noriega, who had warned a month earlier that the country's political situation was "out of control and anarchic." During his year in office, Ardito had drawn criticism for a series of economic austerity measures, although the more proximate cause of his downfall appeared to be an effort by the military to deflect attention from the "Spadafora scandal," involving the death of former health minister Hugo SPADAFORA, whose decapitated body had been found near the Costa Rican border on September 14. After leaving the government in 1978, Spadafora had joined the *sandinista* forces opposing Nicaraguan dictator Anastasio Somoza but subsequently shifted his allegiance to the *contra* group led by Edén Pastora. Spadafora had publicly accused General Noriega of involvement in the drug trade, and opposition groups charged that the president's resignation had been forced in the wake of a decision to appoint an independent investigative committee to examine the circumstances surrounding the murder.

In June 1986 the *New York Times* published a series of reports that charged General Noriega with electoral fraud, money-laundering, drug trafficking, clandestine arms trading, and the sale of high-technology equipment to Cuba. Noriega vehemently denied the charges and insisted that they were part of a campaign aimed at blocking Panama's assumption of control of the Panama Canal in the year 1999. A year later, in apparent retaliation for his forced retirement as military chief of staff, Col. Roberto DÍAZ Herrera issued a barrage of accusations in support of the *Times* reports, also charging his superior with complicity in the 1981 death of General Torrijos. Popular unrest was fanned by the National Antimilitarist Crusade (*Cruzada Civilista Nacional*—CCN), a newly formed middle-class group with opposition party and church support. In July Vice President Roderick ESQUIVEL joined in an opposition call for an independent commission to investigate Díaz's claims. Although Díaz issued a retraction late in the year, a U.S. federal grand jury handed down indictments on February 4, 1988, charging Noriega and 14 others with drug trafficking. On February 25 President Delvalle, who had previously supported Noriega, announced his intention to dismiss the general, but the following day, based on the grounds that he had exceeded his constitutional authority, he was himself dismissed by the National Assembly, which named Education Minister Manuel SOLIS Palma as his acting successor. Delvalle, whom the United States and a number of Latin American countries continued to recognize as chief executive, escaped from house arrest, went into hiding, and announced that he would continue to struggle against the Noriega "puppet regime." Subsequently, Panamanian assets in U.S. banks were frozen, further exacerbating a financial crisis stemming from the fact that the U.S. dollar was, for all practical purposes, the only circulating currency. On March 16 Noriega's forces put down a coup attempt by midlevel dissident officers, while a general strike called by the CCN five days later collapsed following the arrest of numerous opposition leaders and journalists on March 29.

Despite internal political resistance and continued economic pressure by the United States, Noriega clung to power during the ensuing year, amid preparations for national elections on May 7, 1989, in which, contrary to expectations, the general did not run. In the wake of the balloting, despite evidence of massive government fraud, it became clear that the regime's nominee, Carlos DUQUE Jaén, had been substantially outpolled by the opposition candidate, Guillermo ENDARA Galimany (Arias Madrid having died the previous August), and on May 10 the Electoral Commission nullified the results because of "obstruction by foreigners" and a "lack of voting sheets [that] made it impossible to proclaim winners."

On September 1, 1989, when Delvalle's term would have ended, Francisco RODRÍGUEZ, a longtime associate of General Noriega, was sworn in as president after designation by the Council of State, a body composed of senior military and civilian officials. Little more than a month later, on October 3 Noriega put down a violent coup attempt led by Maj. Moisés GIROLDI Vega, who, with a number of fellow conspirators, was summarily executed. On December 15 a revived National Assembly of Community Representatives elevated Noriega to the all-inclusive title conferred earlier on General Torrijos and accorded him sweeping powers to deal with what was termed "a state of war" with the United States. Washington responded on December 20 with U.S. troops attacking Panamanian Defense Forces in Panama City and elsewhere, forcing Noriega to take refuge in the Vatican Embassy, from which he voluntarily emerged on January 3, 1990. Immediately taken into custody, he was flown to the United States for trial on drug trafficking and other charges for which he was ultimately convicted on April 9, 1992. Meanwhile, on December 21, 1989, Guillermo Endara, head of the four-party Democratic Alliance of Civil Opposition (*Alianza Democrática de Oposición Civilista*—ADOC) that included the Christian Democratic Party (*Partido Demócrata Cristiano*—PDC), the National Republican Liberal Movement (*Movimento Liberal Republicano Nacional*—Molirena), the Authentic Liberal Party (*Partido Liberal Autenico*—PLA), and his Arnulfist Party (*Partido Arnufista*—PA), had been declared the winner of the May 7 election and was formally invested as Panamanian president. Concurrently, the PDC's Ricardo ARIAS Calderón and Molirena's Guillermo FORD Boyd were reconfirmed as first and second vice presidents, respectively.

Throughout 1991 President Endara's political influence eroded dramatically. In April Vice President Arias and four other PDC ministers left the government after being charged by Endara with a variety of hostile acts, including the operation of a domestic spy operation with the help of former Noriega supporters. Subsequently, Arias (who retained his elective post) branded the government's increasingly unpopular austerity measures as "senseless," although he refused to endorse a plebiscite on continuance of the Endara presidency on the grounds that it would "weaken the democratic process." On September 1 the PLA's Arnulfo ESCALONA lost a bid for the assembly presidency to fellow PLA member Marco AMEGLIO, who had aligned himself with the opposition. However, the most embarrassing reversal for Endara came on September 30, when Mireya MOSCOSO de Gruber, the widow of former president Arias Madrid, defeated Endara's candidate, Francisco ARTOLA, for the presidency of the PA.

The election of May 8, 1994, was largely a contest between a United People (*Pueblo Unido*) coalition of the PRD plus two minor parties, and a similar three-party Democratic Alliance (*Alianza Democrática*) led by the PA. In the presidential race the PRD's Ernesto PÉREZ Balladares defeated the PA's Moscoso by an unexpectedly close vote margin of 3.7 percent, while the PRD won a plurality of 31 assembly seats to the PA's 15. The new president's cabinet, sworn in with Pérez on September 1, was PRD-dominated but included a number of independents and opposition figures in accordance with a campaign pledge to form a coalition administration.

With President Pérez excluded from seeking a second term, Martín TORRIJOS Espino, Gen. Omar Torrijos's son, won a PRD presidential primary on October 25, 1998, but he was defeated on May 2, 1999, by Moscoso at the head of an *Arnulfista*-led populist coalition that included Molirena, the National Renovation Movement (*Movimiento de Renovación Nacional*—Morena), and the recently registered Democratic Change (*Cambio Democrático*—CD). The PA-led alliance failed, however, to capture a majority in simultaneous balloting for the assembly, in which the PRD-led New Nation coalition won 41 seats. Thus, Moscoso courted additional support from the PDC and two erstwhile New Nation organizations, the Solidarity Party (*Partido Solidaridad*—PS) and the National Liberal Party (*Partido Liberal Nacional*—PLN). By her September 1 inauguration she had cobbled together a working parliamentary majority of 1 seat, but it lasted only until August 2000, when the PRD and the PDC (subsequently renamed the Popular Party) agreed to cooperate in the assembly. With the further addition of two PS legislators, the opposition controlled 38 seats by September 2001.

The PRD's Martín Torrijos was elected president with 47.4 percent of the votes on May 2, 2004. The PRD-led New Nation also secured a substantial legislative majority, while the PRD won control of most municipalities (including the country's five largest) and an overwhelming majority of communal assemblies. The most surprising result of the presidential poll was the second-place finish (30.9 percent) by the PS candidate, former president Endara, who had left the PA in the wake of Moscoso's ascendancy. By contrast, the PA candidate, José Miguel ALEMÁN, captured only 16.4 percent of the vote. Following constitutional revisions approved in 2004 that abolished the post of second vice president (see Constitution and government, below), the PRD's Rubén AROSEMENA was the last to hold the post. He subsequently was named minister of the presidency.

Despite the strong GDP growth in 2007, the economy, particularly the rising cost of living, remained the primary concern of Panamanians in the final year of President Torrijos's tenure, as well as the most prominent issue of the subsequent presidential campaign. In the run-up to the 2009 elections, President Torrijos reshuffled the cabinet in May 2008, as ministers resigned in advance of presidential and legislative balloting, and others were dismissed because of involvement in a scandal.

Increasing crime rates, drug trafficking, and violent conflicts near the Colombian border became major domestic concerns in 2008, leading to a change in police commissioners. The legislature in June voted to give President Torrijos two months to rule by decree on security matters. Subsequently, the president's orders created new agencies for air and naval service, border security, national defense, and intelligence. Critics argued that the new bodies—especially the border security force—would too closely resemble Panama's army, abolished under a 1995 constitutional amendment. President Torrijos submitted approval of these new security measures to the legislature, which quickly approved them.

Three days before the May 3, 2009, presidential elections, the Supreme Court overturned rules barring independent candidates from running.

In December 2008 the Alliance for Change (*Alianza por el Cambio*—AC) coalition began forming around businessman Ricardo MARTINELLI, a CD member, when the Molirena party broke from a brief alliance with the PP, whose candidate, Juan Carlos VARELA, was struggling in the polls. On January 28, 2009, Martinelli struck an agreement allowing the PP to join the broad opposition coalition, which was then given the AC name, and PP candidate Varela became Martinelli's running mate. Meanwhile, the PRD government was enjoying relatively high approval ratings, though Martinelli dominated the issue of crime, which polling showed to be a rapidly growing domestic concern. Observers said the government's failure to curb crime and improve the economy, along with the controversial security measures, worked to Martinelli's advantage. A proposal by Martinelli for a $1 billion subway system to help relieve traffic congestion was also well received.

On May 3 Martinelli won a landslide victory, becoming the first presidential candidate in modern Panamanian history to win an absolute majority of the votes (59.97 percent). His closest challenger was the PRD's Balbina HERRERA, with 37.7 percent. Former president Guillermo Endara of the Moral Vanguard of the Homeland (*Vanguardia Moral de la Patria*—VM) won just 2.3 percent. In concurrent legislative elections, the AC won a majority of seats, while the PRD lost 15 seats. The PRD also lost the mayorship of Panama City to the Pro-Panamanian Party (*Partido Panameñista*—PP), though it won 62 of 75 mayoralties and more than half of municipal council seats nationwide in 2009.

President Martinelli named a new government, dominated by CD and PP members, on May 10, 2009. The new government drew heavily from the business community and members of the AC coalition. Figuring most prominently were the PP's Varela as foreign minister in addition to his post as vice president; banker Alberto VALLARINO, whom Varela had defeated for the PP presidential nomination in 2008, as minister of economy and finance; and José Raúl MULINO of the small Patriotic Union Party (*Partido Unión Patriótica*—PUP) as interior and justice minister.

Thousands of indigenous citizens organized by the National Mobilization of Indigenous, Peasants and People (*Movilización Nacional, Indígena, Campesina y Popular*) protested in September and October 2009 for more rights and against government policies allowing development on indigenous lands.

Panama, a growing transit point for the distribution of cocaine and heroin, opened the first of 11 new air and sea bases in December 2009 to combat organized crime. The country's overall crime situation also worsened, which led the Martinelli government to launch a raft of new security laws including reducing the age of criminal responsibility to 12 years old and bolstering recruitment into the police forces. The country, traditionally one of the safest in the region, saw a dramatic surge in its homicide rate to 23.2 per 100,000 in 2009. President Martinelli was criticized in December 2009 when he appointed two close allies as Supreme Court justices.

In January 2010 former leader Manuel Noriega's appeal against extradition from the United States to France, where he had been convicted in absentia in 1999 on money-laundering charges, was denied. Noriega was sent to France in April after U.S. secretary of state Hillary Clinton approved the extradition. A new trial in France in June led to a seven-year sentence on money-laundering charges. In December 2011 Noriega returned to Panama to serve the rest of his sentence.

On May 24, 2010, Vice President Juan Carlos Varela delivered a formal apology on behalf of the state for crimes committed under the military dictatorship era of 1968–1989. It was Panama's first formal recognition of crimes committed under military rule.

Following the dissolution of the AC in 2011, the CD secured a parliamentary majority, as 17 members defected to the CD since the 2009 elections. Prompted by a corruption scandal, Martinelli conducted a cabinet reshuffle in August 2012.

In the elections of May 4, 2014, Vice President Varela won the presidency, contesting as the candidate of the PP and the Popular Party. (See Current issues, below, for more on the 2014 presidential and legislative elections.) There was a minor cabinet reshuffle in June 2016.

Constitution and government. The constitutional arrangements of 1972 called for executive authority to be vested in a president and vice president designated by a popularly elected Assembly of Community Representatives for terms concurrent with the latter's six-year span. Under a series of amendments approved by national referendum on April 24, 1983, the 1972 document was substantially revised. The major changes included direct election of the president for a five-year term, the creation of a second vice presidency, a ban on political activity by members of the National Guard, and abolition of the National Assembly of Community Representatives in favor of a more compact National Assembly (see Legislature, below). Under an earlier amendment introduced by General Paredes in October 1982, provincial governors and mayors, all theretofore presidential appointees, were made subject to popular election.

Headed by a nine-member Supreme Court, the judicial system embraces Superior District tribunals and Circuit and Municipal courts. The country is divided into nine provinces and one special (Indian) territory, the smallest administrative units, *corregimientos,* forming the basis of the electoral system.

The Technical Judicial Police supplemented a Public Force that encompassed the National Police, National Air Service, and National Maritime Service in early 1991. In 1992 the National Assembly endorsed the constitutional abolition of an armed defense force, an action that was reversed by popular referendum on November 15, but revived by President Endara in August 1994 and accorded formal ratification by the post-Endara assembly on October 4.

A package of constitutional reforms backed by President-elect Torrijos was approved by the legislature in mid-2004. Among the changes were a two-month limit on the transitional period between governments; establishment of a Constituent Assembly to consider constitutional revisions; reduction of the National Assembly from 78 to 71 seats; and abolition of the position of second vice-president.

On March 31, 2010, the parliament approved the reorganization of the Ministry of Interior and Justice into two separate entities: the Ministry of the Interior and the Ministry of Public Safety.

The constitution of Panama guarantees freedom of speech and of the press without censorship, but adds "there exist legal responsibilities when one of these media launch attacks against people's reputation or honor, or against social security or public order." A revised penal code passed in 2007 abolished "gag laws" that had made it a criminal offense to defame or libel state officials. Panama ranked 87th out of 180 countries in the 2014 Reporters Without Borders press freedom index, a climb of 24 spots as misuse of judicial action against journalists declined but fell back slightly to 91st in 2016.

Foreign relations. Panama is a member of the United Nations and many of its specialized agencies, as well as of the Organization of American States (OAS) and other regional bodies. Though not a member of the now-moribund Organization of Central American States (ODECA), Panama was active in some of the organization's affiliated institutions and participated in a number of regional peace initiatives in the 1980s sponsored by the Contadora Group, of which it was a founding member. However, the government, expressing an interest in joining the North American free trade agreement (FTA), in the early 1990s did not pursue economic integration with its Central American neighbors with enthusiasm.

The country's principal external problems have traditionally centered on the Canal Zone and its complex and sensitive relationship with the United States because of the latter's presence in the zone (see Panama Canal Zone, below). This relationship was again strained in 1987 when the administration of Ronald Reagan committed itself to the support of Noriega's domestic opponents—a policy complicated by evidence that the general had previously been associated with the U.S. Central Intelligence Agency (CIA) in a variety of clandestine operations. The United States refused to recognize the appointment of Solís Palma as acting president in February 1988 or of Rodríguez in September 1989 and intervened militarily to oust Noriega the following December (see Political background, above). Subsequently, the United States strongly supported the reconstruction efforts of the Endara administration, although the U.S. aid package of $420 million was estimated to be substantially less than half of the loss attributable to the invasion. As a result, an OAS body, the Inter-American Human Rights Commission (IAHRC), agreed in October 1993 to look into compensation claims of $1.2 billion advanced by 285 Panamanian families. However, the action was complicated by the fact that the United States, while a member of the OAS, had not ratified the IAHRC accord and hence remained technically outside its jurisdiction.

During 1996 Panama became increasingly concerned about an influx of Colombians, including left-wing guerrillas and right-wing paramilitaries, in the remote Darién region. In mid-July troops were dispatched to curb unrest in the area, which had been infiltrated by Colombian rebels and drug traffickers and served as a sanctuary for refugees.

In August 2004 Cuba and Venezuela broke off relations with Panama after outgoing President Moscoso pardoned four men convicted of plotting to assassinate Cuba's president, Fidel Castro, because the men would be executed if they were extradited. Subsequently, President Torrijos said that that he disagreed with his predecessor's action, and relations with Cuba were restored.

The September 2007 release of former dictator Manuel Noriega caused disagreement between the United States and Panama. Panama wanted him returned as a prisoner of war, while Washington, believing that he would be accorded light treatment in his homeland, preferred extradition to France, where Noriega had been convicted of a number of criminal offenses. Ultimately, it was decided that Noriega would remain in a U.S. prison until all appeal routes had been exhausted. That year, the United States and Panama signed a Trade Promotion Agreement (TPA), which the Panamanian government immediately approved, but the measure was held up by the U.S. Congress. Meanwhile, Panama established bilateral FTAs with Chile, Costa Rica, and Honduras. In 2008 the United States funded Panamanian police in an effort to fight crime and drug trafficking.

Relations with Cuba were enhanced in January 2009 when the two signed a trade agreement to more than double Panama's exports to Cuba. In March President Torrijos traveled to Guatemala to sign another agreement in an effort to cushion both countries from the global economic slowdown and to fight drugs and crime. A Guatemala–Panama FTA was implemented in June.

Canada and Panama completed negotiations for an FTA in August 2009. Though signed in May 2010, the agreement stalled in Canadian Parliament in 2012.

In November 2009 the recently elected Martinelli administration began efforts to meet international tax standards to change Panama's image as an international tax haven. With the promise of a U.S.–Panama FTA in the balance, the government signed the first of 12 accords with other countries to increase tax transparency, improve the sharing of fiscal information, and end double taxation. The efforts combined with domestic tax reforms to push Panama's credit rating higher into an investment-grade bracket.

Ties between Panama and its southern neighbor Colombia grew stronger with the 2009 election of Martinelli, who shared similar right-wing ideology to Colombian president Alvaro Uribe and his successor Juan Manuel Santos. In January 2010 the countries revealed a new military alliance to combat drug trafficking and the paramilitary Revolutionary Armed Forces of Colombia (*Fuerzas Armadas Revolucionarias de Colombia*—FARC), which had entered Panama with Colombia's successful effort to push the group to its periphery. But the relationship with Colombia came under strain when in late 2010 the Panamanian government granted asylum to a former director of the Colombian intelligence service who had fled the country after being named a suspect in a wiretapping scandal. The Santos administration reacted angrily both for not being made aware of the asylum request when it was made and for the Panamanians granting it. Both countries played down the diplomatic row and focused attention on the joint fight against the FARC.

Panama submitted a formal request to withdraw from the Central American Parliament (Parlacen), a regional legislative body dedicated to fostering cooperation among its members. In October 2010 the Central American Court of Justice ruled that Panama could not legally withdraw from Parlacen without approval from the regional body's other member states. Panama rejected the ruling, arguing that the court did not have jurisdiction over the country's membership because the Panamanian legislature never ratified Parlacen's founding documents. In November the country formally withdrew from Parlacen.

Panama and the United States signed a tax information exchange agreement (TIEA) in April 2011 to improve information sharing between the two countries, a necessary step before the U.S. Congress would ratify the FTA that had been held up since 2007. Panama was removed from the Organization for Economic Cooperation and Development's list of tax havens in July, after it signed a TIEA with France, bringing the total number of such agreements it had signed with other countries to 12, the minimum international standard. The U.S. Congress passed the Panama–U.S. FTA on October 12, 2011.

In July 2012, after "months of negotiations," Martinelli formally recognized the Taiwanese ambassador, seven months after the latter took up his post—reportedly in retaliation for a meeting that took place between Vice President Varela and Taiwan's foreign minister, which inspired accusations that Taiwan was meddling in Panama's affairs.

Originally set to take effect on October 1, 2012, the Panama–U.S. FTA was postponed until October 31 awaiting ratification of amendments to the agreement by the Panamanian parliament. A December clash between the FARC and Panama's National Border Service left one insurgent dead and resulted in seven arrests.

In July 2013 Panamanian authorities seized a North Korean–flagged ship found to be carrying 25 containers of Cuban obsolete military hardware, including fighter aircrafts, anti-aircraft systems, and missiles, which Havana said were being sent for repair. In August, North Korea appealed to Panama for a bilateral settlement of the issue. Though Panama was pursuing charges against the 35-member crew for endangering collective Panamanian security by failing to declare the weapons, the foreign ministry made clear that the matter would be handled by the United Nations. Later that month, the foreign ministry quoted an unpublished UN report that the ship was an "undoubted violation" of the arms embargo on North Korea.

On September 20, 2013, Panama signed an FTA with Colombia, part of Panama's effort to join the Pacific Alliance regional trade bloc. The agreement came shortly after the two countries had gone to the World Trade Organization (WTO) over a dispute regarding taxation of Asian textiles imported to Colombia from Panama's tax-free zone.

After Pyongyang had paid a $700,000 fine, the North Korean ship was released to return to Cuba with its cargo in February 2014. Three crew members were held on arms trafficking charges.

On March 5, 2014, Venezuelan president Nicolas Maduro expelled Panama's ambassador to Caracas along with three other diplomats, accusing them of conspiring against his government. The severing of diplomatic and economic ties came against the backdrop of months of antigovernment protests in Venezuela. Maduro alleged the United States was behind moves by Panama and the OAS to intervene in Venezuela. Diplomatic relations were restored in June 2014.

The revelations of the "Panama Papers" (see Current issues, below) in April 2016 prompted France to include Panama on a list of countries "not cooperating" in international efforts to reduce money laundering. In response, President Varela pledged to implement unspecified retaliatory measures. By May Panama had agreed to new tax treaties with 30 countries, with agreements with Austria, Bahrain, Belgium, Colombia, Germany, and Vietnam awaiting ratification and negotiations ongoing with Australia, India, and Japan.

Current issues. After changes to mining laws in February 2011 prompted violent nationwide protests that left several protesters dead, the government repealed a set of recently enacted laws in March.

The approved and then quashed laws would have opened Panama's mining industry to foreign government investment. Indigenous and environmental protesters said the change would put more land under exploitation, including ancestral territory held sacred by indigenous groups. Both highly unpopular and eventually repealed laws gave new talking points to the corruption-wracked and floundering opposition PRD, which backed the indigenous groups, and the umbrella leftist and labor group National Front for the Defense of Social and Economic Rights (*Frente Nacional por la Defensa de los Derechos Economicos y Sociales Panama*—Frenadeso), which moved to register as a political party in 2011. The nascent party was calling itself the Broad Front for Democracy (*El Frente Amplio por la Democracia*—FAD) as it began collecting voter signatures in late August.

Shifts within political parties and within the AC coalition turned into a political crisis in mid-2011 (see Political Parties, below). The PRD—hit by corruption allegations and looming criminal investigations—went into a freefall that included massive losses to party membership and defections from its congressional delegation to other parties, primarily the CD. Earlier, the PUP had voted to merge with the CD, while Molirena's leadership signaled it would also fold into the ruling party. The realignment helped the ambitions of Martinelli's CD both within its own coalition and to build majorities with other parties to enact its legislative agenda. But the PP, led by Vice President Varela, moved farther apart from the CD on presidential election proposals such as immediate reelection and holding runoffs, and the coalition all but disintegrated as of late August. At the same time, Martinelli claimed that Varela, who was also Panama's foreign minister, was spending too much time on his 2014 candidacy and fired him from that post on August 30. Fellow PP finance and housing ministers resigned in solidarity on August 31.

In September 2011 opposition lawmakers said they would challenge a bill, passed by Congress, replacing Panama's previous electoral system with a two-stage one, providing for a presidential runoff if a presidential candidate received less than 50 percent of votes. Critics said the bill was unconstitutional.

In June 2012 Martinelli announced plans to sell government shares in state-owned telecom companies, which the opposition claimed would be used to fund a reelection bid—forbidden under the present constitution. Martinelli withdrew the proposal after Congress was briefly suspended to reduce tensions between opposition and progovernment legislators, street protests drew thousands. Faced with declining popularity, in February 2012 Martinelli signed a statement committing not to seek reelection in 2014.

At the Summit of the Americas in Cartagena in April 2012, Martinelli was among a number of Latin American leaders to criticize the United States about its war on drugs strategy by favoring decriminalization.

Following the political crisis of 2011, the CD secured a majority in the National Assembly, gaining 17 additional seats since the 2009 elections (see Political Parties, below). However, corruption scandals continued to mar Martinelli. In July 2012 one of his closest advisers, Minister of the Presidency Demetrio Papadimitriu, resigned over his role in a corrupt land titling deal. Martinelli conducted a cabinet reshuffle in August, replacing five ministers.

In September 2012 the parliament approved a controversial electoral reform package with a 40 to 22 majority. The legislation, which allows for independent candidates but does not introduce a cap on campaign funding, prompted street protests. Deadly protests erupted on October 19 against controversial legislation that allowed the sale of public land plots from the Colón free trade zone to private parties, with protesters afraid the law would cut jobs and run them out of the area. A week later, parliament repealed the law, marking the fourth time Martinelli backtracked immediately after rushing through legislation.

Juan Carlos NAVARRO became the PRD presidential candidate in March 2013, the same month Vice President Varela won the PP nomination amid some controversy. José Domingo ARIAS won the CD nomination after a contentious race concluded in May. Arias led the ruling party, continuing its coalition with Molirena, to campaign on its record in power. Meanwhile, Varela, who was backed by a PP–Popular Party coalition called People First (*El Pueblo Primero*), worked to distance himself from the party of his former running mate, attacking government corruption and pledging to increase transparency. Navarro ran on social programs, pledging to improve education and to fight the rising crime rate.

Seven candidates contested the presidential balloting on May 4, 2014, including three independents. Varela won with 39.1 percent of the vote, a solid lead over the runner-up, Arias, with 31.4 percent. In concurrent balloting, the Alliance for Change won the largest share of the Assembly with 32 seats. However, the People First coalition, with a total of 13 seats, negotiated an alliance with the PRD, holding 25 seats, to form a minority government.

Varela, who assumed office on July 1, 2014, named a PP-dominated cabinet. However, he retained Roberto ROY, the minister of Canal Affairs from Martinelli's administration.

In 2014 an investigation was initiated into the inner workings of Mossack Fonseca, a Panamanian private law firm. The search produced 11.5 million leaked documents detailing the creation of offshore accounts and the transfer of assets by Mossack Fonseca for clients. The International Consortium of Investigative Journalists began releasing the documents in April 2016. The leaks were dubbed the "Panama Papers." Some of the accounts and transfers were illegal, others were unethical or unseemly, and the revelations led to scandals in several countries and the resignation of a number of international leaders, including the prime minister of Iceland (see entry on Iceland). In response, Panama enacted a number of measures, including the creation of investigatory bodies and the establishment of a special tribunal.

POLITICAL PARTIES

Government Parties:

Democratic Revolutionary Party (*Partido Revolucionario Democrático*—PRD). The PRD was initially a left-of-center *torrijista* group organized as a government-supportive party in 1978. It obtained 10 of 19 elective seats in the 1980 Legislative Council balloting.

In May 1982 the PRD secretary-general, Gerardo González Vernaza, was replaced by Dr. Ernesto Pérez Balladares, a former financial adviser to General Torrijos. In November Pérez Balladares resigned in the wake of a dispute between left- and right-wing factions within the party, subsequent speculation being that General Rubén Paredes, commander of the National Guard, would be the country's 1984 presidential candidate. Paredes announced as a candidate in mid-1983 before accepting retirement from military service, and was reported to have been nominated by the party in August. In the face of opposition to his candidacy, he announced his withdrawal from politics in September but later ran as a nominee of the **National People's Party** (*Partido Nacionalista Popular*—PNP), which was deregistered in late 1984. The PRD named Nicolás Ardito Barletta, then World Bank regional vice president for Latin America, as its candidate after formation of the progovernment **National Democratic Union** (*Unión Nacional Democrática*—Unade) coalition in February 1984. Elected chief executive in May 1984, Ardito Barletta resigned on September 27, 1985, and was succeeded by First Vice President Eric Delvalle, who was himself dismissed by the National Assembly in February 1988.

In early 1990 a new group of PRD leaders emerged, distancing themselves from Noriega and offering themselves as a "loyal opposition" to the Endara regime, which it nonetheless characterized as being responsible for the U.S. invasion. As the party's nominee in 1994, Pérez Balladares captured the presidency on a 33.2 percent vote share, while the PRD won a plurality of 31 legislative seats at the head of a **United People** (*Pueblo Unido*) coalition that also included the **Republican Liberal Party** (*Partido Liberal Republicano*—Libre) and the right-wing **Labor Party** (*Partido Laborista*—Pala), both of which were later deregistered for failing to meet a 5 percent vote threshold.

In primary balloting on October 25, 1998, the PRD named Martín Torrijos Espino, the son of Gen. Omar Torrijos, as its presidential standard-bearer in 1999. Torrijos led the **New Nation** (*Nueva Nación*) coalition, also referenced as **New Motherland** (*Patria Nueva*—PN), which included the PRD, **Solidarity Party** (*Partido Solidaridad*—PS), **National Liberal Party** (*Partido Liberal Nacional*—PLN), and elements of the **Motherland Movement** (*Movimiento Papá Egoró*—MPE). (For additional information on the MPE, which lost its registration in 1999, see the 2008 *Handbook.*) The alliance won a majority (41 seats) in the Legislative Assembly in 1999 but failed to capture the presidency. Torrijos returned as the PRD candidate in 2004, leading the reconstituted New Nation alliance, and winning the presidency by a substantial margin. The party won a majority of the legislature with 41 seats.

In 2008 the PRD nominated Balbina Herrera, a former mayor of San Miguelito, as its 2009 presidential candidate in a closely fought primary victory over Juan Carlos Navarro, the mayor of Panama City. Herrera led **A Country for Everyone** (*Un País para Todos*), a coalition of the PRD, Popular Party, and PL.

Herrera ran as a left-of-center candidate, promising more social expenditure. Herrera's campaign was damaged by a 2009 statement by a jailed Colombian pyramid-scheme manager and accused money-launderer that he had contributed $3 million to Herrera's campaign and another $3 million to that of the PRD's Panama City mayoral candidate, Roberto VELÁSQUEZ. The remarks were said to have contributed to both candidates' failed bids for office. She finished second behind Ricardo Martinelli with 37.7 percent of votes. The PRD was the largest single vote-getter in the legislative elections, with 34.6 percent of all votes. The party won 26 seats, 15 less than it won in 2004.

On October 5, 2009, the PRD's national executive committee resigned en masse to "renovate and rejuvenate" the party after its defeat in the elections. Declining membership was another consequence of the party's internal crisis; the almost 635,000 constituents on 2009 voter rolls slid to 464,000 by June 2011. The threat of criminal prosecutions over corruption and the decreasing public support for the party caused seven legislators to abandon the PRD's ranks and join other parties as of September 2011.

In August 2012 Juan Carlos Navarro was elected secretary general in a landslide against incumbent Mitchel DOENS at a party conference. Beating 17 other candidates, Navarro secured the party's nomination for 2014 presidential candidate with 94 percent of the vote by internal balloting in March 2013. He called for creation of a Ministry of Indigenous Affairs and pledged to ease tensions with organized labor and indigenous leaders. The PRD contested the May 2014 elections without a coalition. Navarro came in third with 28.1 percent of the presidential vote. Meanwhile, the party won 25 legislative seats. The PRD and the PP (below) subsequently negotiated a legislative alliance. About half of the PRD central committee, including Navarro, resigned on July 15 in an effort to bring fresh leadership to the party after two presidential losses.

In July 2015 PRD member Rubén de LEÓN Sánchez was elected president of the Assembly and was reelected in July 2016.

A media investigation in February 2016 found that the PRD numbered 447,830 members, an increase of 1,414, at a time when most other parties saw significant declines.

Leaders: Benicio ROBINSON (President of the Party), Rubén de LEÓN Sánchez (President of the National Assembly), Juan Carlos NAVARRO (2014 presidential candidate), Martín TORRIJOS Espino (Former President of the Republic).

People First (*El Pueblo Primero*). The People First alliance formed on August 25, 2013, when the Popular Party voted to back the PP's Juan Carlos Varela for president. The alliance together won 13 seats and negotiated a governing alliance with the PRD.

Pro-Panamanian Party (*Partido Panameñista*—PP). The PP is the rubric adopted in 1995 by the **Arnulfist Party** (*Partido Arnulfista*—PA), which was legalized in 1990. The PA originated from the mainstream of the **Authentic Panamanian Party** (*Partido Panameñista Auténtico*—PPA), itself an outgrowth of the original *Partido Panameñista,* which supported the three abortive presidencies of Arnulfo Arias Madrid. Following Arias's death in August 1988, the PPA split into factions, a minority headed by Hildebrando NICOSIA seeking to achieve a "national union" with the Noriega-backed regime.

For the 1994 elections, the PA formed a **Democratic Alliance** (*Alianza Democrática*) with two minor parties, the **Authentic Liberal Party** (*Partido Liberal Auténtico*—PLA), and the **Independent Democratic Union** (*Unión Democrática Independiente*—UDI). The PA won 15 of the alliance's 20 legislative seats, while its presidential candidate, Mireya Moscoso de Gruber, finished a close second. (The PLA and the UDI were subsequently deregistered for failing to obtain at least a 5 percent vote share in the legislative balloting.)

In mid-1996 the PA formed a strategic alliance with Molirena, Morena, and the PDC to oppose what they termed was the government's lack of leadership. In September 1996 Mireya Moscoso de Gruber, the widow of former president Arias, was reelected president of the party. In 1997 the PA, Molirena, the PDC, and Morena grouping was expanded to include the **Civil Renovation Party** (*Partido Renovación Civilista*—PRC), the Gloria Young faction of the MPE, and the PNP in a **National Front for the Defense of Democracy** (*Frente Nacional por la Defensa de Democracia*—FNDD) to oppose a reelection bid by President Peréz Balladares. Moscoso de Gruber won the national presidency in 1999, but her party's candidate, José Miguel ALEMAN, ran a poor third in 2004.

In January 2005 the party dropped its PA designation in favor of the historical PP label. In March Moscoso de Gruber was forced to resign as the PP's leader, ostensibly because of the party's poor showing in the 2004 balloting but also in the wake of corruption charges having recently been brought against her.

The PP nominated Juan Carlos Varela as its presidential candidate for 2009. Varela had fallen out with the party in the late 1990s after he ran the losing primary campaign of Alberto VALLARINO Clément against Moscoso. However, Varela returned to the party in 2003. In January 2009 Varela, trailing in the polls, threw his support behind the CD's Martinelli and subsequently became Martinelli's running mate and vice president of Panama when the coalition won. The PP won 21 seats in the legislature but subsequently lost 1 seat to a defection as of September 2011 and several others to the CD. After it became clear that the AC would be splitting, the PP leadership in mid-2011 began asserting that the party would become a voice of strong opposition to the CD. In March 2013 Varela secured the 2014 presidential nomination with 99 percent of the vote; however, just one-quarter of party members voted in the primary, and detractors began an effort to collect signatures to remove Varela, calling his candidacy "very weak."

Despite early lack of support from within the party, Varela proved to be a popular candidate, running on a platform of improving government dialogue and quality of life. With the backing of the Popular Party, an electoral alliance known as People First formed in August 2013, he won the presidency in May 2014 with 39.1 percent of the vote. In concurrent balloting, the PP won 12 seats. Subsequently, the PP allied with the PRD to create a minority government.

Leaders: Juan Carlos VARELA (President of the Republic and President of the Party), Alcibiades VÁSQUEZ (Secretary General and Vice President of the Republic), Alberto VALLARINO Clément (Vice President).

Popular Party (*Partido Popular*). The Popular Party adopted its current name in 2001, having previously been called the **Christian Democratic Party** (*Partido Demócrata Cristiano*—PDC). The PDC participated in the 1980 balloting, winning two council seats. Named a vice-presidential candidate in 1984, PDC leader Ricardo Arias Calderón was viewed as a likely successor to Arias Madrid as principal spokesperson for the opposition and was **Democratic Alliance of Civil Opposition** (*Alianza Democrática de Oposición Civilista*—ADOC) vice-presidential candidate in 1989.

Possessing a plurality within the assembly, the PDC was estranged from its coalition partners in September 1990, when the latter joined with the opposition PRD to reject its nominees for chamber officials; despite the rebuff, the party stayed within ADOC until April 1991, when its ministerial delegation was ousted by President Endara for displaying "disloyalty and arrogance." Arias Calderón resigned as first vice president of the republic in December 1992. The party secured only one assembly seat in 1994.

With Alberto Vallarino, a prominent banker who had run in the 1994 presidential race again serving as its standard-bearer, the PDC contested the May 1999 elections in an **Opposition Action** (*Acción Opositora*) coalition that included the PRC, which secured one of the group's five seats, and the **Liberal Party** (*Partido Liberal*—PL) and PNP, neither of which won representation.

As the junior partner in Torrijos's 2004 New Nation coalition, the Popular Party obtained one assembly seat. In 2008 the party announced that it intended to remain in the coalition for the 2009 elections. Again, it won one assembly seat with 2.6 percent of the vote.

In August 2013 the Popular Party voted to form an electoral alliance with the PP in support of Vice President Varela for the 2014 presidential election. Meanwhile, Aníbal CULIOLIS led Popular Party members who did not support the alliance to form a faction called the **Movement for Panama Greens and Independents** (*Movimiento Verdes e Independientes por Panamá*). The Popular Party helped boost the Varela to victory, and secured representation in the new cabinet. Meanwhile, the party won one seat in the assembly.

Leaders: Milton Cohen HENRÍQUEZ Sasso (President of the Party), Daniel BREA (Vice President), José RAMOS (Secretary General).

Other Legislative Parties:

Alliance for Change (*Alianza por el Cambio*—AC). The AC was formed in January 2009 after the PP became the fourth—and largest—party to support Martinelli. The coalition's parties share a 42-seat majority in the legislature. The alliance was damaged in 2009 when several members, including Martinelli's cousin, were implicated in corruption scandals. It came under further stress when the CD (below) proposed a bill in January 2011 that would allow the president to stand for reelection. The PP had previously agreed to support the CD's Martinelli in 2009 in return for the PP heading up the AC coalition ticket in the 2014 elections. The bill was defeated in the committee. The two parties pulled further apart because of Martinelli's continuing quest to amend election laws so that political contests would include runoffs.

But defections to the CD by legislators from other parties, particularly the PRD, caused the fragile coalition's numbers to swell. Then, in March, the PUP (see CD, below) voted to merge with the CD. The relative strengths of the CD and PP within the AC switched with the defections and merger, and so did the dynamics of power, with the CD no longer reliant on the PP to wield a majority for legislative action. As a result, the CD reneged on agreements with the PP and installed a CD politician as the president of the National Assembly, a seat that was supposed to be rotated between the two parties. The coalition dissolved in September 2011.

With Martinelli restricted from seeking another term in 2014, the CD and Molerina formalized their alliance for 2014 in December 2013 and backed José Domingo Arias. Together, the parties won 32 assembly seats in May 2014 balloting. However, in early July 2014 Molerina dissolved the alliance.

Democratic Change (*Cambio Democrático*—CD). The CD was initially registered in 1998 as a breakaway group from the PRD, its main campaign opposing corruption. Initially it ran as the Democratic Party, winning two legislative seats in 1999 as a minor party in the coalition, along with the PP and Molirena, which supported President Moscoso. As the CD, it won three seats in 2004.

In 2009 the CD won 17 seats, making it the third-largest vote getter in the country, and its leader, Ricardo Martinelli, secured the presidency of the republic. The party's membership increased by 20 percent by the end of 2009 with the popularity of the new president. The party's legislative delegation attracted a number of defectors subsequent to the elections, and by October 2011, the party had 36 seats in total, giving it an absolute majority in the National Assembly.

In July 2011 the Panamanian electoral authorities approved the incorporation of the small **Patriotic Union Party** (*Partido Unión Patriótica*—PUP) into the CD. The PUP, founded in 2006 as a result of a merger of the PLN and the PS, won 6.4 percent of the vote and four seats in the 2009 elections. (For more on the PUP, see the 2013 *Handbook*.) In March 2011 the PUP voted to be incorporated within the CD, which brought the CD's voter rolls up to more than 380,000 members, an increase of more than three times over the party's size in 2008, and as of June 2012 it had more than 473,000 members.

A heated campaign for the 2014 presidential candidacy culminated on May 13, 2013, when former housing minister José Domingo Arias secured 67.5 percent of the vote. Arias ran a campaign based on the ruling party's record, promising to continue the record of expanding public works and infrastructure. The party selected President Martinelli's wife, Marta LINARES, as Arias's running mate in January 2014.

In the May 2014 balloting, Arias lost the presidency to Varela, winning 31.4 percent of the vote. Meanwhile, the party won 30 seats, the largest vote share, but the CD was precluded from continuing leadership in the assembly by a PRD-PP alliance.

A 2016 newspaper report asserted that the CD had lost 30,000 members from 2014 to 2015.

Leaders: Ricardo MARTINELLI Berrocal (President of the Party and Former President of the Republic); José Domingo ARIAS (2014 presidential candidate); Roberto HENRIQUEZ, Aníbal Galindo NAVARRO, Mario MILLER, Rogelio BARUCO Mojica, Dario RUBEN Campos (Vice Presidents of the Party).

Nationalist Republican Liberal Movement (*Movimiento Liberal Republicano Nacionalista*—Molirena). Molirena is a relatively small conservative grouping that was legally recognized in 1981. Its legislative representation increased from 14 to 16 as a result of the partial election of January 27, 1991, but fell to 5 in 1994 and to 3 in 1999. It won 4 seats as a member of the ***Visión*** coalition in 2004.

In the run-up to the 2009 elections, Molirena endorsed the PP's Juan Carlos Varela for president but backed off in late December 2008 when Varela lagged in the polls. Molirena subsequently endorsed Ricardo Martinelli in January 2009, shortly before the PP itself followed suit. In the 2009 elections, the party won 3.4 percent of the vote and two seats in the legislature, but one seat was lost to defection in September 2011. As an imminent AC split became apparent in 2011, Molirena's leadership moved for a merge with the CD, following suit with the PUP. However, election authorities rejected the first vote in July 2011 because it was not done by secret ballot; subsequently, a split emerged within the party among the founders, who did not support a merge, and the leadership. Morilena, an ally of Martinelli's CD, has been absorbing former members of the PP following the AC split, and its total membership reached 100,000 in May 2012.

In February 2013 Party President Sergio González announced that Molirena would not hold primary elections and would support the CD's 2014 presidential candidate. Tensions with the party's founders continued, and in May, the leadership began removal proceedings against party founder Olimpo SÁEZ, alleging he collaborated with organizations opposed to the party. He was expelled in August.

Morilena formalized its continued electoral alliance with the CD in December 2013. It secured two seats in the May 2014 balloting. However, in early July, the small party dissolved the alliance with the CD, saying the partnership was intended to last just through the election.

The party was reported to have lost 6,000 members from 2014 to 2015.

Leaders: Francisco "Pancho" ALEMAN (President), Guillermo QUIJANO, Rubén DARÍO Carles, Gisela CHUNG (Founders of the Party).

Other Parties That Contested the 2014 Elections:

Broad Front for Democracy (*El Frente Amplio por la Democracia*—FAD). Born from the umbrella leftist and labor group National Front for the Defense of Social and Economic Rights (*Frente Nacional por la Defensa de los Derechos Economicos y Sociales Panama*—Frenadeso), the FAD began collecting signatures to register as a political party in August 2011. In June 2013 the party was officially recognized by the Electoral Tribunal and in August held its first congress and announced its participation in the 2014 general election. At a party congress in November 2013, the FAD nominated Genaro LÓPEZ presidential candidate with 71 percent of the internal vote. López received 0.6 percent of the vote in the May 2014 general elections. The FAD won no assembly seats. The party failed to meet the minimum vote totals necessary for official recognition in the 2014 balloting and was deregistered.

Leaders: Genaro LÓPEZ (2014 presidential candidate), Ignacio IRIBERRI (Chair).

Other Groups:

Moral Vanguard of the Homeland (*Vanguardia Moral de la Patria*—VM). The VM was a center-right party founded in November 2007 by former President Guillermo Endara after he broke with the PS. (He ran under the PS flag in the 2004 presidential election, finishing second to Torrijos with 30.9 percent of votes.) The VM did not participate in a coalition in 2009, and it failed to win a legislative seat. Former president Endara won 2.3 percent of the vote in the presidential election, finishing a distant third. Endara died on September 28, 2009, at the age of 73. The party failed to meet the required minimum percentage of total votes cast and was dissolved by the election authorities.

Leaders: Guillermo ENDARA Galimany (President of the Party and 2009 presidential candidate), Menalco SOLIS (First Vice President), Ana Mae DIAZ de Endara (Secretary General).

Alternative Grassroots Party (*Partido Alternativa Popular*—PAP). The PAP is a center-left party that was registered in August 2007 to compete in the 2009 election. However, its registration remained under review by the Electoral Tribunal, preventing it from participating in the 2009 poll, and in January 2011 the authorities stripped the PAP of recognition as a party in formation.

Leaders: Raúl GONZÁLEZ (Sub-Secretary), Olmedo Ernesto BELUCHE Velasquez (Secretary General).

LEGISLATURE

Before 1984 the Panamanian legislature consisted of an elected 505-member National Assembly of Community Representatives (*Asamblea Nacional de Representantes de Corregimientos*), which met on average only one month a year, and a de facto upper house, the

National Legislative Council (*Consejo Nacional de Legislación*), consisting of 19 elected members and 37 appointed from the assembly. Under a constitutional revision approved in April 1983, the *Asamblea Nacional* was abolished, while the council was converted into a smaller, fully elected Legislative Assembly.

National Assembly (*Asamblea Nacional*). The present assembly consists of 71 members elected for five-year terms. The number of seats was reduced from 78 as part of a 2004 constitutional reform.

Following the most recent election on May 4, 2014, the distribution of seats was as follows: Alliance for Change, 32 seats (Democratic Change, 30; Nationalist Republican Liberal Movement, 2); Democratic Revolutionary Party, 25; People First, 13 (Pro-Panama Party, 12; Popular Party, 1); and independent, 1.

President: Rubén de LEÓN Sánchez (PRD).

CABINET

[as of September 15, 2016]

President	Juan Carlos Varela (PP)
Vice President	Isabel Saint Malo de Alvarado (ind.) [f]
Ministers	
Agricultural Development	Jorge Arango Arias (PP)
Canal Affairs	Roberto Roy (CD)
Commerce and Industry	Melitón Arrocha (PP)
Economy and Finance	Dulcidio de la Guardia (PP)
Education	Marcela Paredes de Vásquez (PP) [f]
Environment and Sustainable Development	Mirei Endara [f]
Foreign Relations	Isabel Saint Malo de Alvarado (ind.) [f]
Health	Miguel Antonio Mayo (PP)
Housing and Territorial Management	Mario Etchelecu (PP)
Ministry of Government	Milton Henríquez (Popular)
Labor	Luis Ernesto Carles (PP)
Presidency	Álvaro Aleman (PP)
Public Works	Ramón Arosemana (PP)
Security	Rodolfo Aguilera Franceschi (PP)
Social Development	Alcibíades Vásquez (PP)

[f] = female

INTERGOVERNMENTAL REPRESENTATION

Ambassador to the U.S.: Emanuel GONZALEZ Revilla.

U.S. Ambassador to Panama: John D. FEELEY.

Permanent Representative to the UN: Laura Elena FLORES Herrera.

IGO Memberships (Non-UN): IADB, ICC, IOM, NAM, OAS, WTO.

For Further Reference:

Carse, Ashley. *Beyond the Big Ditch: Politics, Ecology, and Infrastructure at the Panama Canal.* Cambridge, MA: MIT Press, 2014.

Porter, Casey, ed. *Panama Canal Expansion: Issues and Potential Effects.* New York: Nova Science, 2014.

Sanchez, Peter. *Panama Lost? U.S. Hegemony, Democracy, and the Canal.* Gainesville: University Press of Florida, 2008.

PANAMA CANAL ZONE

Bisecting Panama in a southwesterly direction from the Atlantic to the Pacific, the Canal Zone served historically for the protection of the interoceanic waterway completed by the United States in 1914. Occupation, use, and control of a 553-square-mile area extending about five miles on either side of the canal were granted to the United States in perpetuity by Panama in a treaty concluded in 1903. Following nationalist riots within the zone in 1964, the two countries in 1967 negotiated a new draft treaty that would have replaced the 1903 accord, recognized Panamanian sovereignty in the zone, and enabled Panama to participate in the management of the canal. In 1970, however, following a change in government, Panama declared the draft to be unacceptable. After further extended negotiations, U.S. and Panamanian representatives reached agreement on an amended accord that was incorporated into two treaties signed in Washington, D.C., on September 7, 1977. Endorsed by Panama in a plebiscite on October 23, the treaties were barely approved by the U.S. Senate on March 16 and April 18, 1978. U.S. president Jimmy Carter subsequently exchanged documents of ratification during a state visit to Panama on June 16.

The first treaty provided for a phased assumption of control of the canal and the Canal Zone by Panama, beginning six months after ratification and concluding in the year 2000. Panama would assume general territorial jurisdiction, although until December 31, 1999, the United States would maintain control of all installations needed to operate and defend the canal. Until 1990 the canal administrator would be American, while his deputy would be Panamanian; from 1990 to 1999, the administrator would be Panamanian, with an American deputy.

The second treaty declared that "the canal, as an international transit waterway, shall be permanently neutral." It also provided that "tolls and other charges... shall be just, reasonable and equitable" and that "vessels of war and auxiliary vessels of all nations shall at all times be entitled to transit the canal, irrespective of their internal operation, means of propulsion, origin, destination, or armament."

Implementation of the treaties was delayed because of a U.S. Senate stipulation that ratification would not be deemed complete until the passage of enabling legislation by the Congress or until March 31, 1979, whichever came first. Thus it was not until October 1, 1979, that the American flag was lowered within the Canal Zone and administrative authority for the canal formally transferred to a binational Panama Canal Commission.

In early 1980, despite a significant increase in revenue accruing to Panama under the new arrangement, President Royo formally complained to the United States about a "unilateral" provision of the enabling legislation that effectively brought the commission under the control of the U.S. Defense Department. Subsequently, in the wake of an assessment that the existing facility, which was unable to offer transit to vessels in excess of 75,000 tons, would be obsolete by the year 2000, Royo and a group of high-level advisers visited Japan to discuss the possibility of Japanese involvement in the building of a new sea-level waterway.

During a meeting in Panama City in December 1982, the feasibility of a new waterway was further discussed by Panamanian, Japanese, and U.S. representatives. Earlier, a 9.8 percent increase in canal tolls had been agreed on to offset an anticipated shortfall of up to $5 million a month after the opening of a new trans-isthmian oil pipeline.

In mid-1984 the canal again became the focus for anti-U.S. sentiment, following U.S. reluctance to provide a major portion of the $400 million to $600 million needed to widen the waterway on the grounds that it would be unlikely to recover its investment before full reversion in the year 2000. Late in the year, however, the United States and Japan agreed to a four-year program to consider canal improvements, not excluding the possibility of constructing a new facility to accommodate ships of up to 300,000 tons.

In June 1986 a tripartite commission, composed of Panamanian, Japanese, and U.S. representatives, began a projected four-year study on the feasibility of measures to upgrade or augment the existing facility, including improved pipeline, highway, and rail transport across the isthmus. The commission was also charged with undertaking an analysis of world shipping requirements in the 21st century and drafting recommendations on U.S.–Panamanian relations on expiration of the present canal treaties.

In July 1988 Panama refused to send delegates to a scheduled Canal Commission board meeting because of U.S. economic pressure against the Noriega regime and the U.S. rejection of representatives appointed by the Solis Palma administration. However, the problems were resolved by the overthrow of Noriega in December 1989 and the long-time Panamanian deputy administrator, Fernando Manfredo BERNAL became acting administrator on January 1, 1990. On April 30, during a visit by President Endara to Washington, D.C., President George H. W. Bush endorsed the appointment for a regular term of Gilberto GUARDIA Fábrega, who was formally approved by the U.S. Senate on September 11. Meanwhile, doubts arose as to the Panamanian government's ability to administer and defend the canal after December 31, 1999, then Government and Justice Minister Ricardo Arias Calderón having conceded in August that "a military defense [of the waterway] similar to the proportions of the United States is outside the practical and economic scope of Panama."

In early 1993 the Panamanian Legislative Assembly approved the establishment of an autonomous Interoceanic Region Authority (*Autoridad de la Regón Interoceánica*—ARI) to administer canal-related property acquired from the United States under the 1977 treaties. However, its future was clouded in late 1994 by a proposed constitutional amendment that would create a new Panama Canal Authority (*Autoridad del Canal de Panama*—ACP). Critics charged that the move was linked to a proposal before the U.S. Senate authorizing the formation of a corporation to administer the canal as a private undertaking.

In early September 1995 the U.S. Armed Forces' Southern Command said it would withdraw from the country and turn over two of its bases, Fort Davis and Fort Gulik, to the government of Panama. Shortly after, President Balladares met with President Bill Clinton in Washington, D.C., to discuss "maintaining some degree of U.S. military presence after the year 2000." A month later an opinion poll indicated that 86 percent of Panamanians wanted at least some bases to remain under U.S. control. On September 25, 1997, the U.S. Southern Command quit Panama, leaving five of eight bases for Panama (two more bases were relinquished in 1998). During 1998 labor unions expressed concern over the imminent privatization of canal services and attendant job losses after the U.S. pullout. Opinion polls indicated that nearly three-quarters of Panamanians supported the continued presence of the U.S. military. But the United States formally handed over administration of the canal to Panama in December 1999 after it vacated the last U.S. installation, Howard Air Force Base. The canal administrator later announced that technical proposals for constructing a new set of locks to accommodate ships up to 150,000 tons would be presented by the ACP to a canal advisory group representing 12 of the waterway's principal users. While the cost of the upgrade was estimated at $3 billion to $6 billion, experts insisted that demand would outstrip the existing system's capacity by 2010.

By mid-2003 estimates of canal expansion costs had risen to $4 billion to $8 billion, with no decision as to which of several options might be adopted. The most viable, large-scale widening of the facility was bitterly opposed by *campesinos* on both shores, while funding sources were far from clear.

In April 2006 the government announced its intention to invest $5.25 billion, obtained largely from increased toll charges, in an eight-year project to expand the canal and construct a new set of locks 40 percent wider and 60 percent longer than the existing locks. The undertaking, approved in a national referendum on October 22, 2006, was officially launched on September 3, 2007, and was expected to be completed by 2014. Once complete the expansion was expected to double the tonnage of cargo that could pass through the canal every year to 600 million tons.

Three international consortia submitted bids in March 2009 for the largest single construction project, the $3.2 billion design and construction of two new locks.

The ACP reported annual totals for fiscal year 2008–2009 that were largely untouched by the global economic downturn. It awarded the last of four major excavation contracts in January 2010, and as of June around 100 contracts had been awarded for the expansion project. In July 700 workers, who were employed with the consortium that won the largest contract to build two new locks, went on a week-long strike, demanding a repeal of new labor and environmental regulations pushed through by the Martinelli government.

As of November 2010 the canal authority had awarded contracts totaling $4.2 billion. Cargo tonnage moving through the canal in 2011 was estimated to be more than 15 million tons above what was predicted at the start of the fiscal year, and this prompted the ACP to release a record fiscal 2012 budget of nearly $293 million.

Engineer Jorge Luis Quijano assumed administration over the canal in September 2012. In February 2013 the canal expansion reached the halfway point, signifying that the inauguration date would likely be postponed from October 2014 until April 2015 (a result of a seven-month delay in cement pouring in 2011). The delay does not make a proposed canal project in Nicaragua any more likely. (For more on the proposed Nicaraguan canal, see the entry on Nicaragua.)

In July 2013 Panamanian authorities halted a North Korean ship found to be carrying Cuban weapons as it passed through the canal (see Foreign relations, above).

By the end of 2013 the canal expansion project had gone over budget by $1.6 billion. *Grupo Unido por el Canal* (GUPC), the Spanish-led team of international companies behind the expansion of the canal, gave a 21-day deadline beginning on December 30 for the ACP to pay the difference. When the ACP refused, likening the demand to blackmail, the companies halted work on the project in February for two weeks. After a series of negotiations, the dispute was resolved in mid-March, with a new projected completion date of December 2015. The expansion project concluded with the reopening of the canal in June 2016, two years later than the original completion date and at a total cost of $5.25 billion.

Panama Authority Chair: Roberto ROY.

Panama Canal Administrator: Jorge Luis QUIJANO.

PAPUA NEW GUINEA

Independent State of Papua New Guinea
Gau Hedinarai ai Papua-Matamata Guinea (Hari-Motu)
Independen Stet bilong Papua Niugini (Tok Pisin)

Note: The literal translation of *Gau Hedinarai* is "entity of the people," hence the official title in Hari-Motu could be "Republic of Papua New Guinea."

Political Status: Former Australian-administered territory; achieved internal self-government on December 1, 1973, and full independence within the Commonwealth on September 16, 1975, under constitution of August 15.

Area: 178,259 sq. mi. (461,691 sq. km).

Population: 7,776,000 (2016E—UN); 6,791,317 (2016—U.S. Census).

Major Urban Centers (2015E): PORT MORESBY (metropolitan area, 345,000), Lae (78,038), Mt Hagen (27,789).

Official Languages: English, Tok Pisin, Hari-Motu.

Monetary Unit: Kina (market rate October 1, 2016: 3.17 kina = $1US).

Sovereign: Queen ELIZABETH II.

Governor General: Sir Michael OGIO; elected by the National Parliament on January 14, 2011, sworn in on January 25, and installed for a six-year term after formal appointment by the Queen on April 26, succeeding Sir Paulias MATANE, who served from 2004 until December 10, 2010, with Jeffrey NAPE serving as acting governor general in the interim.

Prime Minister: Peter O'NEILL (People's National Congress); elected by parliament and sworn in by the governor general on August 2, 2011, and elected by parliament and sworn in for a second term on August 3, 2012, succeeding Sir Michael SOMARE (National Alliance Party), who served from September 1975 to March 1980, from August 1982 to November 1985, and from August 2004 to December 13, 2010. Sam ABAL served as acting prime minister in the interim.

THE COUNTRY

Situated between Australia and the Equator in the southwest Pacific, Papua New Guinea (PNG) consists of the eastern half of the island of New Guinea and numerous adjacent islands, including those of the Bismarck Archipelago as well as part of the Solomon group. It shares its only land border with the Indonesian province of Papua. The indigenous inhabitants, mainly of Melanesian ethnic origin, comprise over 1,000 tribes that speak more than 700 languages, of which English and two pidgins, Tok Pisin and Hari-Motu, have become lingua franca and accorded official status. Although animism and traditional beliefs are widespread among the predominantly rural population, Christianity, encouraged by foreign missionaries, is the dominant formal religion, with Protestant denominations in the majority. While females are reported to constitute more than 40 percent of the labor force, most are engaged in subsistence agriculture, and make up only 30 percent of the wage sector. Female representation in formal elected bodies is minimal, but women's councils are active at both the national and provincial levels, and enjoy social status and government recognition and funding. In 2016 the Inter-Parliamentary Union ranked PNG among the lowest in women's representation in

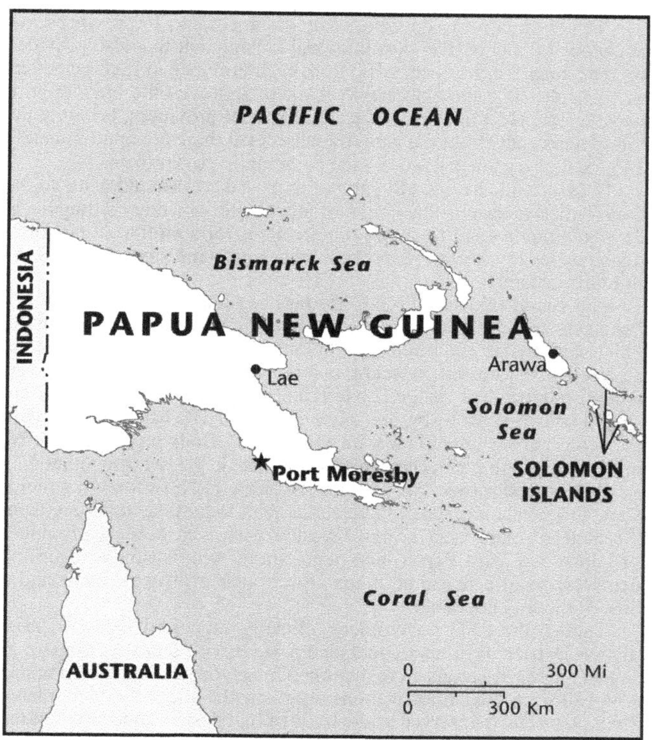

parliament at 183rd out of 191 countries. Women held only 3 of 111 seats in the legislature (2.7 percent).

Much of the country's terrain consists of dense tropical forests and inland mountain ranges separated by grassland valleys. The climate is monsoonal. Roughly 70 percent of the population relies on subsistence farming and hunting and lives in primitive conditions, although some rural modernization has been achieved with government support; only 20 percent of the labor force is employed in the formal sector. PNG is rich in natural resources and exports of gold, copper, and oil comprised nearly 70 percent of foreign earnings in 2013, with agricultural, forestry and fisheries products comprising the balance; natural gas exports are expected to go on stream in 2014. Australia is the principal trading partner, followed by Japan, China, and Malaysia.

Real economic growth, according to the World Bank, averaged 5 percent during 1990–1996. However, falling mineral prices, lagging private investment, sagging demand from Asia, the aftermath of the Bougainville insurrection, a prolonged drought, and three severe tsunamis slowed the economy for half a decade. Rising commodity prices and energy exports brought the GDP growth rate up to a peak of 8.9 percent in 2008, after which it eased to 6.0 percent in 2009. Distribution of wealth is uneven, unemployment remains high at nearly 80 percent in urban areas, the population below the poverty line was 37 percent in 2015, and malnutrition and hunger have been reported. The United Nations Development Program (UNDP) in 2014 ranked PNG 157th out of 187 countries on the "Human Development Index." *Joint United Nations Program on HIV/AIDS* (UNAIDS) reported in June 2014 that 90 percent of HIV/AIDS cases in the Pacific region are found in PNG. Government corruption, urban crime, and tribal vendettas have combined to discourage international investment, entrepreneurialism, and tourism despite the attractiveness of the country's natural wealth.

The International Monetary Fund (IMF) estimated GDP growth at 8.5 percent in 2014, rising to 9 percent in 2015, but then moderating to 3.1 percent in 2016. GDP per capita in 2016 was $1,974. Inflation averaged 6 percent between 2013 and 2016.

GOVERNMENT AND POLITICS

Political background. Sighted in 1526 by a Portuguese navigator who gave it the name Papua ("woolly haired"), the island of New Guinea was colonized over the centuries by a succession of European and Asian nations, including Portugal, Netherlands, Great Britain, Germany, and Japan. Indonesia, the most recent colonizer, retains the western half, now designated the provinces of Papua and West Papua. In 1906 the British New Guinea southern sector of the eastern half, renamed the Territory of Papua, was transferred to Australia. Northeast New Guinea, formerly a German colony, was assigned to Australia as a League of Nations mandate in 1920. Parts of both sectors were occupied by Japanese forces from 1942 to 1945, after which Australia reassumed control. Australia unified the northern and southern sectors administratively prior to granting independence to Papua New Guinea in 1975.

Representative government was initiated by the election of a House of Assembly in 1964, and in 1968 the Administrator's Executive Council admitted a majority of assembly members. The territory achieved independence on September 16, 1975, and the former chief minister Michael T. SOMARE assumed the office of prime minister. Somare was immediately confronted by a unilateral declaration of independence by secessionist leaders of a "Republic of the North Solomons" in the island province of Bougainville. They were aggrieved by unequal revenue sharing of the proceeds from the Panguna copper mine, but were pacified by a revised formula and the granting of substantial autonomy to the provincial government in August 1976.

After the nation's first post-independence election for the National Parliament in June-July 1977, Somare's Papua and Niugini Union Pati (Pangu), the People's Progress Party (PPP), and a number of independents formed a coalition government with Somare confirmed as prime minister. But in March 1980 the Somare government, now including the United Party (UP), collapsed in the face of a no-confidence vote led by the PPP. A new coalition led by Sir Julius CHAN governed for two years, but in August 1982 Somare returned as prime minister for a further three years. His coalition was weakened by the withdrawal of Deputy Prime Minister Paias WINGTI, who then, in November 1985, defeated Somare in a vote of no confidence and became prime minister, serving three years. He was replaced in June 1988 by Rabbie NAMALIU (Pangu), who led the country at the head of a succession of coalition governments for the following 14 years. The election of June 1992 produced a new coalition led by Wingti, but in 1994 the Supreme Court ordered a new election that led to a PPP-Pangu coalition under Sir Julius Chan, who assumed the prime ministership, to be succeeded by Bill SKATE in 1997. (For details, see the 2010 *Handbook.*)

In May 1989 the Bougainville copper mine suspended operations in the face of sabotage by local landowners frustrated at the lack of compensation for despoliation of their lands and rivers. A full-scale secessionist movement broke out in midyear, led by the Bougainville Revolutionary Army (BRA) under the leadership of a former land surveyor, Francis ONA, who on May 17, 1990, declared Bougainville's independence.

Prime Minister Bill Skate's negotiations with the Bougainville rebels yielded a truce in October 1997, stabilized by a Truce Monitoring Group led by New Zealand with Australian, Fijian, Tongan, and Vanuatu support. A peace treaty followed on January 23, 1998, as did a series of agreements to implement Bougainville's political autonomy and consider eventual independence for the island. Despite ongoing political turmoil and legal disputes, an election for a Bougainville People's Congress (BPC) was held in May 1999. In August 2001 agreement was reached to create an interim provincial government with an autonomous police force. Subsequently a Bougainville Constituent Assembly approved a draft constitution, and on January 14, 2005, power was formally handed over to Governor John MOMIS. In May–June 2005 Bougainville conducted a peaceful election that brought Kabui to the presidency, backed by his Bougainville People's Congress Party (BPCP) with a majority of legislative seats. The legislative elections of June–July 2007 saw 77 of the 109 parliamentary seats change hands and the rival National Alliance Party win a plurality with 27 seats. President Kabui died on June 7, 2008, and was succeeded pro tem by his vice president, John TABINAMAN. In December James TANIS was elected as the interim president, taking office on January 6, 2009.

Meanwhile, in Port Moresby, Prime Minister Chan's secret contract with Sandline International to deploy mercenary soldiers to quell the Bougainville insurgency led to his defeat in parliament in July 1997. He was succeeded by Port Moresby Mayor Bill Skate and then in 1999 by the PDM Leader Sir Mekere MORAUTA, who presided for a further four years despite intermittent challenges and political turmoil.

The election of June 2002 yielded a plurality of 20 parliamentary seats for NA, and Somare was designated prime minister a third time in August. Skillful manipulation of a succession of broad coalitions and abrupt cabinet reshuffles and adjournments of parliament kept Somare in office until 2010. (See the 2014 *Handbook* for details.)

But Somare's leadership became untenable in July when three of his ministers, Beldan NAMAH, Charles ABEL, and Ano PALA, announced their support for an opposition motion of no confidence. Soon thereafter Somare was indicted on charges of tax evasion and other illegal activity. He resigned on December 13, 2010, surrendering the prime ministership to Sam ABAL. He was found guilty on April 4, 2011, of tax evasion and electoral funding irregularities and suspended from parliament for two weeks; he announced his retirement on June 30. On July 4 Somare's son, Arthur, minister for state enterprises and regarded as a contender for the prime ministership, was suspended from office.

Prime Minister Abal's erratic leadership, including his summary dismissal of his foreign minister and treasury minister, led to his suspension from the National Alliance party in July, and on August 2, he was defeated in parliament by former treasurer Peter O'Neill, who was elected prime minister by a vote of 70–24. The new prime minister appointed a cabinet representing 5 political parties and 21 independents. The new government announced reform measures, including the sale of a controversial government executive aircraft, investigation of alleged corruption in the National Planning Department, and initiatives to raise the minimum wage and give ownership of subsurface minerals to traditional landowners.

On December 12, 2011, the Supreme Court ruled O'Neill's August election invalid, whereupon Governor General Ogio announced that Somare was still prime minister and swore him in. O'Neil, backed by parliament, refused to step aside, and on December 19, Governor General Ogio reversed himself and declared O'Neill was still the prime minister. Somare, having named a new cabinet, police chief, and army chief, vowed to fight for reinstatement. In January 2012 retired colonel Yaura SASA staged an abortive mutiny and declared his support for Somare but surrendered after a week and was arrested; his followers were granted amnesty on January 30. O'Neill resumed his leadership as prime minister, but on May 21 the Supreme Court ruled that Somare was still legally prime minister. O'Neill disputed the court's authority to make a decision on political leadership and took his case to parliament, where he was again elected as the prime minister on May 30, whereupon he called a general election.

On November 27, 2014, Chief Justice Sir Salamo INJIA appointed a leadership tribunal headed by retired New Zealand judge Sir Peter Blanchard to investigate government corruption (see Current events, below). Meanwhile, a succession of members of parliament and government officials were found guilty of various forms of corruption and bribery in 2014 and 2015, including Vice Minister of Trade Ronny KNIGHT, former National Planning Minister Paul TIENSTEN, and Minister of Culture, Arts, and Tourism Boka KONDRA.

The Supreme Court on September 7, 2015, declared that amendments enacted in 2013 were unconstitutional, including measures to extend the government's grace period of immunity for votes of no confidence from 18 months to 30 months and reduce the minimum time for parliament to be seated from 63 days to 40 days before an immunity vote could be called.

From May 11–23, 2015, elections were held in Bougainville. Incumbent president John MORRIS of the New Bougainville Party (NBP) was reelected with 53 percent of the vote. Concurrent balloting was conducted to replace one-third of the seats of the Bougainville legislature.

O'Neill's government survived a no-confidence vote on July 21, 2016. However, the prime minister subsequently reshuffled the cabinet to improve the government's relations with parliament.

Constitution and government. Under the 1975 constitution, which can be amended by a two-thirds legislative majority, executive functions are performed by a National Executive Council that includes a governor general, nominated by the council itself to represent the Crown for a six-year term; a prime minister, appointed by the governor general on advice of the legislature; and other ministers who are designated on advice of the prime minister and must total no fewer than six and no more than one-quarter the number of legislators. The unicameral National Parliament normally sits for a five-year term, dissolution not being mandated in the wake of a no-confidence vote (which can be called by 10 percent of the members) if an alternative prime minister (previously designated by the leader of the opposition) succeeds in securing a majority. The judicial system encompasses a Supreme Court that acts as the final court of appeal, a National Court, and lesser courts (currently including district, local, warden, and children's courts) as established by the legislature.

A 1977 initiative to decentralize government into 19 provinces was abandoned under a 1995 constitutional amendment that also provided for a regional assembly member from each province to become governor. In July 2009 the National Parliament approved the upgrading of two regions, Hela and Jiwaka, to the status of provinces, bringing the total number to 21. At the subprovincial level there are approximately 145 local government councils and community governments.

In July 2013 the O'Neill cabinet proposed two amendments to the constitution to specify the length of annual parliamentary sittings—40 days minimum—and to stiffen requirements for a motion of no confidence in the government—three months' notice and signatures by one-third of parliamentarians.

The island of Bougainville, formerly called the North Solomons Province, achieved its current status of Autonomous Bougainville Government (ABG) on January 14, 2005, with its own constitution; an elected legislature and president; taxing, judiciary, and policing power; and an independent budget. External security and foreign policy are shared with Port Moresby, and since 2010 the ABG has consulted with the central government in a Joint Supervisory Body regarding a referendum on possible independence, whose date is yet to be negotiated.

Foreign relations. Two issues have shaped PNG's foreign policies since independence: sensitive relations with Indonesia stemming from the status of Irian Jaya (formerly West New Guinea, now the provinces of Papua and West Papua) and negotiations with Australia regarding demarcation of a maritime boundary through the Torres Strait and a host of security concerns.

Though the PNG government officially supported Jakarta's jurisdiction in Irian Jaya, and concluded a Status of Forces Agreement in January 1992, relations were disturbed by advocates of a "free Papua" who called on the United Nations to review the allegedly manipulated 1969 plebiscite that served as the basis of Indonesia's annexation of the mineral-rich territory. More than 10,000 refugees have entered PNG from the Indonesian side since 1983, fleeing violence and alleging persecution by Indonesian authorities. PNG's maintenance of border refugee camps was denounced by Jakarta, who suspected that they were sources of aid for rebels of the Free Papua Movement, now part of a recently organized umbrella organization, the West Papua National Coalition for Liberation. Closure of the camps in 2002 to ease tensions with Indonesia led to new squatter camps springing up, and PNG's attempts to repatriate rebels have not stemmed the influx. In May 2008 PNG blocked a move in the Melanesian Spearhead Group (see below) to grant observer status to the Papuan separatists, and in March 2009 it announced the creation of a civilian Border Development Authority with a budget of $28 million to bring order to the border region. Nevertheless, armed clashes in Papua and border incursions by Indonesian forces in pursuit of rebels, most recently by a platoon of troops in July 2008 and a police officer in June 2009, and PNG's refusal in June 2011 to extradite rebels to Indonesia, continued to disturb PNG-Indonesia relations and retard tourism and cross-border economic activity. Working relations were restored by a visit in March 2010 by Indonesia's president, during which Somare reaffirmed PNG's recognition of Papua and West Papua as integral parts of Indonesia and the two leaders signed agreements on improved defense cooperation, double taxation relief, and agricultural cooperation. Eleven further agreements—on cooperation in labor, tourism, sport, education, air transport, mining, and energy—and an extradition treaty were concluded in June 2013 during a visit by Prime Minister Peter O'Neill to Jakarta. Governor General Ogio announced his intention to attend President-Elect Jakowi WIDODO's inauguration in October 2014 and invited Widodo to visit PNG in early 2015.

Shortly after independence from Australia, the PNG government attempted to negotiate a boundary in the Torres Strait based on the equidistance principle. Canberra objected that this would remove the Torres Strait islands from the state of Queensland's jurisdiction. In a treaty concluded in 1985 the two governments compromised on a complex formula involving (1) an exclusive economic zone (EEZ) seabed line running south of a number of islands and reefs that would nevertheless remain Australian territories, and (2) a protected zone to which citizens of each country would have access. In 2008 the two governments agreed to extend a moratorium on drilling in the strait to protect its ecosystem.

Australia continues to be a crucial partner, not only as PNG's principal trading partner but also as the largest source of aid and technical assistance. Canberra's Partnership for Development aid package, budgeted at A$577.1 million in 2014–2015, focuses on health, HIV/AIDS, education, transport, good governance, and law and justice. Prime ministers and ministers meet regularly in the Australia–Papua New Guinea

Ministerial Forum. Australian-listed investors include Oil Search Ltd., Lihir Gold Ltd. (major shareholder Rio Tinto), Highlands Pacific Ltd., Coca Cola Amatil, Campbell Australia Ltd., and Nestle Australia.

In response to security concerns, Australia has provided extensive training, equipment, and weapons to the PNGDF and the police. The secondment of Australian defense and police officers, however, has provoked nationalist opposition by Port Moresby officials, as has Canberra's "Pacific Policy" of deflecting intercepted Middle East "boat people" to Manus Island for refugee processing. The Manus camp was closed in 2008, but Prime Minister O'Neill in August 2012 accepted Australia's request to reopen it and on July 19, 2013, despite criticism by the UN High Commission for Refugees, the International Organization for Migration, and Australian human rights groups, signed the Regional Resettlement Arrangement between Australia and PNG formalizing the transfer of intercepted asylum seekers to Manus for processing and possible permanent resettlement in PNG. This and other agreements were encompassed in an omnibus PNG-Australia Partnership declared by the two prime ministers on May 10.

After independence PNG conducted an uneasy relationship with the governments of both the People's Republic of China (PRC) and the Republic of China (ROC) on Taiwan, initially granting formal diplomatic recognition to the PRC but also hosting a trade office sponsored by Taiwan's ROC government. In 2008 Beijing approved PNG as a "Chinese industrial zone," reflecting China's status as a significant investor in mining ventures. Prime Minister Somare visited Beijing in April 2009 and military chief Commodore Peter HAU in June reaffirmed PNG's commitment to its military exchange program with China, which has emerged as PNG's second most valuable trading partner and a growing source of investment and aid. Visits by potential investors from Shanghai followed in 2009 and 2010. In November 2009 PNG signed three bilateral agreements gaining, among other things, a concessional loan facility with the China Exim Bank worth $123 million, and in October 2010 PNG signed an agreement with the Shenyang Corporation for International Economic and Technical Cooperation (SCIETC) to construct a Pacific Marine Industrial Zone in Madang valued at $79 million.

Ethnic rioting broke out in Lae in May 2009, directed against Chinese shops and Chinese nickel miners for alleged unfair prices and discrimination in favor of Chinese workers in violation of PNG employment law. Attacks on Chinese in August 2008 and again in August 2014 at the Ramu Nico nickel mine, and another occurred in July 2009 at Popondetta, an oil palm-growing center, inducing the Chinese embassy to express "grave concern" about the safety of Chinese nationals and businesses. China's rising purchases of PNG hardwoods became controversial following revelations by international environmentalists of rapid and often illegal deforestation allegedly conducted by unscrupulous Chinese and Malaysian entrepreneurs with the connivance of corrupt PNG officials.

Relations with the neighboring Solomon Islands became tense upon the outbreak of the uprising on Bougainville in 1989 because the rebellious province is closer geographically and ethnically to the Solomon Islands than to the PNG mainland. In late 1991 Honiara's provincial affairs minister called for Bougainville's independence or its merger with the Solomons, and Solomon Islanders were reported to be smuggling supplies to the beleaguered Bougainvilleans in defiance of the PNG blockade. The peace agreement with the Bougainville leaders eased tensions between Port Moresby and Honiara, and in July 2003 the Solomon Islands National Parliament approved the participation of PNG personnel in the Regional Assistance Mission to Solomon Islands (RAMSI) to restore law and order in the wake of interethnic violence. In May 2009 PNG joined with the Solomon Islands and Federated States of Micronesia to submit to the United Nations a joint claim to the Ontong Java continental shelf, which would extend their economic zones into a pocket currently regarded as international waters. Port Moresby and Honiara also cooperated, with other Pacific island states, in initiatives to curb bottom trawling and tuna poaching in their adjoining EEZ waters.

As a member of the Pacific Islands Forum (PIF), PNG has championed self-determination for French Overseas Territories, particularly New Caledonia. In 1985 PNG joined with Solomon Islands, Vanuatu, and Fiji in the "Melanesian Spearhead Group," a caucus within the PIF to coordinate policy on regional issues with a view to possible formation of a Melanesian free trade zone. In 2009 PNG and other Spearhead members publicly supported Vanuatu's claim to Matthew and Hunter islands, two rocky outcrops north of New Caledonia claimed also by France. In 2012 PNG and its neighbors established a Melanesian Spearhead Group Police Formed Unit to promote regional security and engage in peacekeeping activities abroad.

PNG also participates in Association of Southeast Asian Nations (ASEAN) meetings as an observer, having acceded to ASEAN's 1976 Treaty of Amity and Cooperation in December 1987, and aspires to full membership. Shinzo Abe became the first Japanese prime minister to visit PNG in three decades when he arrived in July 2014 to commemorate soldiers fallen in World War II, acknowledge the start of LNG exports to Japan, and to announce a three-year aid package worth Y20 billion (US$195,121,000).

Relations with the United States have been continuous but not always harmonious since independence in 1975. A dispute over tuna fishing rights was settled by negotiation in 1987 of the U.S.–Pacific Islands Multilateral Fisheries Treaty. While bilateral trade volume is small, U.S. aid is substantial, directed to health (particularly to combat HIV/AIDS), education (particularly of women), rural development (particularly food and forestry), and the training of civil servants, police, and PNGDF military personnel. U.S. based energy and mineral consortia led by ExxonMobil and Rio Tinto have made major investments. Secretary of State Hillary Clinton visited PNG in November 2010, pledged closer partnership, and announced new aid initiatives, and United States Agency for International Development (USAID) opened a Pacific Regional Office in Port Moresby in October 2011. In 2012 a dispute arose over payment for access to PNG and neighboring waters by U.S. tuna boats.

From independence PNG has maintained diplomatic, trade, and aid relations with leading European governments, particularly the United Kingdom and Germany, from which it receives aid. In July 2009 it entered into an interim Economic Partnership Agreement (EPA) with the European Union (EU) which grants PNG fish exports continued preferential access to the European market and facilitates EU aid projects but is due to expire in late 2014.

The PNG government imposed a travel ban on Australians going to Bougainville on May 13, 2015, after news emerged that Australia planned to establish a consulate in Buka, Bougainville, without notifying the PNG. On May 26 the two governments announced the incident was a misunderstanding and the travel ban was ended.

Current issues. The 2012 election took place June 23–July 17 with 3,435 candidates in 46 political parties contesting 111 National Parliament seats. Ninety-five candidates from 21 parties and 16 independents won seats. Prime Minister Peter O'Neill on August 9 named 33 ministers representing 9 political parties and 1 independent to his new cabinet. Parliament in February had declined to pass a bill to establish 22 seats reserved for women. Only three women were elected to the current parliament, but Prime Minister O'Neill appointed one, Loujaya TONI, to the new cabinet and another, Delilah GORE, later.

PNG's central government budget for 2013 forecast expenditures of a record 10.8 billion kina and included allocations for free education and hospital care as well as funding for transport and road infrastructure. Revenues, buoyed in 2011 by rising international prices of gold, copper, and gas and by investments anticipating the massive ExxonMobil LNG project, declined sharply in 2012 as world commodity prices sagged. Treasurer Don POLYE in July 2013 reported that the tax take had fallen by over 5 percent and that the budget deficit could reach 7.2 percent of GDP by year's end.

Corruption in government continued to retard economic development. In 2013 Transparency International ranked PNG 144th out of 177 countries. In August Prime Minister O'Neill took steps to set up an Independent Commission Against Corruption and provide more funding for the Task Force Sweep anticorruption unit. In August 2014 the National Court ordered a recount of the 2013 Madang by-election, placing Minister for Petroleum and Energy Nixon DUBAN's seat in jeopardy. Despite PNG's establishment of a national human rights commission in 2010, the U.S. State Department identified several categories of persistent human rights violations, including police abuse of detainees, poor prison conditions, infringement of privacy rights, discrimination against women, and ineffective enforcement of labor laws, and placed PNG in the bottom tier of its annual human trafficking classification alongside Sudan and Zimbabwe. The O'Neill government responded by passing the People Smuggling and Trafficking in Persons Act in July 2013. PNG was ranked 44th out of 180 countries by Reporters Without Borders in 2014, but fell to 55th place in 2016.

Cabinet turnover continued when O'Neill sacked William DUMA, Mark MAIPAKAI, and Don Polye in March 2014. Upon the resignation of Community Development Minister Loujaya KOUZA to chair the Lae City Commission, O'Neill in August reinstated Duma to the Transport portfolio and assigned Malakai TABAR to the Higher Education portfolio and Delilah Gore to the Community Development portfolio. O'Neill's leadership came under scrutiny when the Ombudsman Commission on August 13 cited him for misconduct in office and referred the case to the public prosecutor. In June O'Neill had disbanded the anticorruption task force sweep after it issued a warrant for his arrest, sacked its chair Sam KOIM, and dismissed Attorney General Kerenga KUA, replacing him with Ano Pala. The National Court in July reinstated the task force. In August the Registrar of Political Parties announced changes to the Organic Law on the Integrity of Political Parties and Candidates to restrain MPs from changing political parties during a parliamentary term. In May 2010 veteran leader John Momis won the presidential election for the autonomous Bougainville government (ABG). Sworn in on June 15, he declared his three priorities to be sequestering weapons, improving governance, and attracting foreign investment. Port Moresby in April 2011 announced a 500 million kina ($39 million) five-year grant to Bougainville for roads, health, education, and law and order reform, but ABG minister for finance Albert PENGHU in July 2013 complained that 188 million kina earmarked for Bougainville were being withheld by the central government. Meanwhile, despite national government leaders' denial of the legal competence of the ABG to make agreements with foreign firms, Bougainville officials began exploratory talks with Bougainville Copper Limited and other firms to encourage resumption of mining and palm oil planting. In June 2013 landowners in Wakunai, Panguna, and Kieta declared their support for reopening the mine, but the secessionist Me'ekamui Movement, led by Philip MIRIORI, declared it would oppose any deals until Bougainville achieved full independence. In August 2014 the ABG parliament passed the Bougainville Mining (Transitional Arrangements) Bill asserting the ABG's authority in consultation with customary landowners to regulate all mining in the autonomous region.

On October 2, 2014, the Supreme Court ruled that the police lacked the power to execute the June arrest warrant against O'Neill.

On December 2015 water rationing started in Port Moresby because of an ongoing drought. Water was turned on for six hours, and then off for the same period throughout the day.

POLITICAL PARTIES

At the time of the July 2012 election, the Integrity of Political Parties and Candidates Commission listed 46 parties registered by the Registrar of Parties of which 21 secured one or more seats. It also listed 26 deregistered parties.

Government Parties:

People's National Congress (PNC). Launched in early 1993 by a group of independent MPs, the original PNC merged in April 1998 with the **Christian Century Party** (CCP) and a number of smaller formations to form the **PNG First Party** (PNGFP) led by Prime Minister Skate. In June 1999 the PNGFP split; 22 PNG First MPs remained with the restored PNC, and 11 moved to the revived National Party. By mid-2001 the party held only about half a dozen seats in parliament and then won only three seats in 2002. It secured three ministerial portfolios in the new Somare government, but all were ousted in May 2004.

The PNC fortunes declined further when Skate was expelled from the party in early 2005 and party (and opposition) leader Peter O'Neill was arrested in August 2005 on charges of misappropriating funds. The PNC won four legislative seats in 2007 and joined the Somare government with one cabinet post—public service—going to O'Neill. O'Neill was elected prime minister in July 2011 and again in August 2012, his party having won a plurality of 27 seats in the election. Twelve other PNC members were appointed to the new cabinet.

Leaders: Peter O'NEILL (Prime Minister), Simon KORAWA (President), Jonathan OATA (Secretary General).

Triumph Heritage Empowerment Party (THE). Founded January 23, 2012, by Don Polye and members of the Polye faction that broke away from the National Alliance Party (NA, below), THE espouses Christian and family values, environmental sustainability, multiculturalism, better working conditions, and a moderate foreign policy. THE won 10.8 percent of the vote in the 2012 parliamentary election and entered into coalition with PNC, gaining four portfolios in the O'Neill cabinet, including Don Polye as Treasury minister until he was dismissed in March 2014. THE leader Don POLYE was elected leader of the parliamentary opposition on December 2, 2014.

Leaders: Don POLYE (Leader), Douglas TOMURIESA (President), James KIELE (General Secretary).

National Alliance Party (NA). NA was founded by Bernard NAROKOBI in 1995 on an anticorruption platform. Michael Somare, who had been associated with the **People's National Alliance** (PNA), the Bougainville-based Melanesian Alliance Party (MAP, below), the **Movement for Greater Autonomy** (MGA), and the **People's Action Party** (PAP, below), soon became its leading member and prime minister and secured the inclusion of the NA in every subsequent cabinet. The traditional NA leadership balance of four deputy prime ministers, one each for Papua, the Madang-Sepic region, the highlands, and the islands, was disrupted by Somare's numerous patronage appointments, with Polye and other highlanders emerging stronger.

Somare's temporary departure from office in December 2010 in the face of accusations of financial irregularities and his subsequent absence for medical treatment brought Sam Abal to party leadership. But, Abal's assertive style split the NA party between the Abal and Polye factions, induced the party's national executive to suspend his membership, and led parliament to vote him out of power in July 2011, whereupon Abal became leader of an opposition faction of the NA. Polye subsequently left to found the Triumph Heritage Empowerment Party (THE, above), and Patrick PRUAITCH was chosen as the new party leader. In August 2012 three NA members, Pruaitch, Jim SIMATAB, and Kerenga KUA, were invited into the new O'Neill cabinet. Somare resigned from the NAP over differences of leadership in the ruling coalition in 2015.

Leaders: Patrick PRUAITCH (Leader), Simon KAIWI (President), Joyce GRANT (General Secretary).

United Resources Party (URP). Organized in early December 1997 by defectors from other parties, URP advocated a greater voice for resource owners and resource-rich provinces. After its launching, it joined, then withdrew from, the Skate administration. In December 1999 the party leaders extended their support to the Morauta government. Peter IPATAS, governor of Enga Province, defected to the PDM in April 2001. The URP won five seats in 2007 and seven in 2012, joining the governing coalition in each case. URP members in the O'Neill cabinet include Steven KAMA, Fabian POK, and William DUMA.

Leaders: William DUMA (2012–2014 Minister of Petroleum and Energy, Minister of Transport), Ken YAPANE (President), Peter KOIM (Secretary General).

People's Party (PP). The party was founded in 2006 by the governor of Enga Province since 1997, Peter Ipatas, a member of the PDM until 2005 and then briefly of the NA. The PP is based in PNG's most rugged inland province and represents the interests of the central highlands. It won 3 of the 109 seats in the election of 2007. In July 2010 veteran politician John PUNDARI, previously a member of the Advance PNG and PDM parties and who served in 1999–2001 as house speaker, minister of foreign affairs, and deputy prime minister, was appointed minister for mining in the expanded Somare cabinet. The party won 6 seats in the 2012 parliamentary election, and members Pundari and Davies STEVEN were invited into the O'Neill cabinet. The party retained one portfolio after the July 2016 cabinet reshuffle.

Leaders: Sam BASIL (Leader), Douglas IVARATO (President), Willie PALMERS (Secretary General).

People's Progress Party (PPP). The PPP was formed in 1976 and alternated between government participation and opposition for the next ten years. Sir Julius Chan led the party to victory in 1985 and became prime minister but moved to the opposition benches from July 1988 to June 1992 until rejoining the government under Paius Wingti. In 1993, PPP withdrew from the governing coalition with the PDM and revived its earlier alliance with Pangu, whereupon Chan returned as prime minister. Although PPP members continued in the Skate cabinet after the election of 1997, Chan lost his seat. The PPP withdrew from the Skate administration in October 1998, joined the Morauta government in July 1999, but suffered party leader Michael NALI's dismissal as trade and industry minister in November 2000. In 2001 Sir Julius rejoined the party leadership in preparation for the 2002 general election. The party won nine seats and joined the Somare administration but went into opposition when Chan failed in the challenge to Somare in 2007. The PPP won six parliamentary seats in 2012, and Byron CHAN and Ben MICAH were invited into the O'Neill cabinet. Micah resigned as minister of petroleum and energy in July 2016 and left the PPP to join the opposition.

Leaders: Sir Julius CHAN (Member of Parliament, Former Prime Minister), Byron CHAN (Minister of Mining), Brown SINAMOI (President), Philip KUWIMB (Secretary General).

People's Democratic Movement (PDM). The PDM was organized by former Deputy Prime Minister Paias Wingti, who broke with Pangu in March 1985. PDM formed a government in November and Wingti remained in office following the 1987 election but was defeated in a nonconfidence vote on July 4, 1988. Wingti returned in July 1992 as head of a coalition government that included the PPP. However, the PPP withdrew in August 1994 and Wingti lost the prime ministership, but during the next eight years, led by Bill Skate, then Mekere Morauta, the PDM participated in shifting governing coalitions. In May 2000 most of the **Advance PNG Party** (APNGP) was absorbed by the PDM, which thereupon claimed a majority in the national legislature. After the 2007 election, the PDM joined the National Alliance coalition government and party leader Michael Ogio was rewarded with the ministry of higher education, research, science and technology. On July 29, 2008, PDM MP John BOITO moved to the opposition benches in protest over the adjournment of parliament for four months. Ogio was elected PNG's governor general on January 14, 2011. In August 2012 Boito was appointed minister of internal security in the new O'Neill cabinet.

Leaders: Geoffrey BULL (President), Ezekiel PAWAI (Secretary General).

United Party (UP). UP is a highlands-based party organized in 1969. It was opposed to early independence. It entered the government in coalition with Pangu in November 1978. After March 1980 many of its members joined the Chan majority. After losses in the balloting of June 1982, it rejoined forces with the Pangu-led government but returned to opposition in April 1985.

The UP won only two legislative seats at the 1997 election but subsequently saw its delegation swell to more than a dozen. Prime Minister Morauta brought the UP into his coalition, but by May 2001 its ministers had been dismissed and defections had claimed most of its MPs. It won three seats in 2002, one of which was lost in 2007. The UP subsequently joined the Somare-led government, and leader Bob DADAE was given the defense portfolio. The party won only one seat in the 2012 election, but Rimbink PATO was offered a portfolio in the O'Neill cabinet.

Leaders: Chris KOPYOTO (President), Mathew TASO (Secretary General), Rimbink PATO (Minister of Foreign Affairs and Immigration).

Social Democratic Party (SDP). The SDP was launched on February 27, 2010, under the label **United Democratic Front** until July. It was led by Powes PARKOP, governor of the National Capital District, whose platform includes a campaign against corruption and elite power politics. SDP won three seats in the 2012 election, and Justin TKATCHENKO was awarded the portfolio of sports and Pacific games in the O'Neill cabinet.

Leaders: Wesley SANARUP (President), David Dom KUA (Secretary General), Powes PARKOP (NCD Governor).

Papua New Guinea Party (PNGP). Sir Mekere Morauta formed the PNGP in 2003 after being ousted as leader of the PDM after losing the 2002 election. Three of PNGP's members, though not Morauta himself, joined the Somare government in May 2004. The PNGP won eight seats in the 2007 election to become the second largest party in parliament, and Morauta was elected leader of the opposition. For his role in helping unseat Acting Prime Minister Abel, Morauta was given the portfolio of state enterprises in the O'Neill cabinet in August 2011 and was appointed minster for state enterprises in the August 2012 O'Neill cabinet, his party having won eight seats in parliament. Belden Namah, deputy prime minister in the 2011 O'Neill cabinet, was dropped from the August 2012 O'Neill cabinet whereupon he joined Pangu (below) and became Leader of the Opposition. In August 2014 Deputy Leader of the Opposition Sam BASIL resigned from PNGP and joined Pangu.

Leaders: Philip ELEDUME (President), Tom KUKHANG (General Secretary), Sir Mekere MORAUTA (Former Prime Minister).

Indigenous People's Party (IPP). A new party registered in 2012 and based in Lae, IPP champions PNG's ethnic minorities. Party leader Loujaya TONI is one of only three female members of parliament and one of two females in the current cabinet.

Leaders: John TEKWIE (President), Augustine SASAKING (General Secretary), Loujaya TONI (Minister for Religion, Youth, and Community Development).

Opposition Parties:

Papua and Niugini Union Pati (Pangu). The urban-based Pangu was organized in 1967 to represent the pro-independence movement. It was the senior component of the **National Coalition** that secured the largest number of legislative seats in the 1977 election. It moved into opposition following parliamentary defeat of the Somare government in March 1980 but returned to power after the election of June 1982 and the redesignation of Somare as prime minister in August. Despite Somare's ouster and Wingti's defection, the party secured a plurality of 26 assembly seats in the election of November 1987. Pangu suffered the worst defeat of the 1992 balloting, losing half of its 30 sitting members. Pangu returned to government in 1994 in a coalition with the PPP and other parties, with Sir Julius Chan, then Bill Skate, as prime minister. It joined the Morauta government in September 1999 and continued as part of the Somare administration after the 2002 and 2007 elections. Leader Andrew KUMBAKOR was awarded the housing and urban development portfolio after the 2007 election, and Philemon EMBEL was subsequently appointed minister for sport and constitutional matters. Pangu leaders Ken FEARWEATHER and Waka GOI were appointed ministers in the O'Neill cabinet in August 2011 but dropped from the August 2012 cabinet, which contained no Pangu members, the party having won only one seat in the 2012 election. The party was given one portfolio in the July 2016 reshuffle.

Leaders: Bendan NAMAH (Leader of the Opposition), Milo TIMINI (President), Morris DOGIMAI (Secretary General).

Melanesian Liberal Party (MLP). The MLP was formed in early 2007 by Dr. Allan MARAT and, in the June–July 2007 election, won two seats. Marat joined Somare's NA-led coalition government and was awarded the justice portfolio. In May 2010, Marat publicly disagreed with government policy and was dismissed by Somare, whereupon the MLP party went into opposition. The MLP won two seats in the 2012 election.

Leaders: Lui POE (President), Gabriel BUAKIA (Secretary General), Alan MARAT (Member of Parliament and Former Prime Minister).

Other Opposition Parties in Parliament:

Coalition for Reform, 2 seats; **People's Movement for Change,** 2; **People's United Assembly Party,** 2; **New Generation Party,** 1; **Our Development Party,** 1; **PNG Constitutional Democratic Party,** 1; **PNG Country Party,** 1; **Stars Alliance,** 1; and **United Party,** 1.

Parties Winning No Seats in 2012:

Melanesian Alliance Party (MAP). Led by Dame Carol Kidu, the MAP (not to be confused with the earlier Bougainville-based MAP of Fr. John Momis) appealed to the urban women's vote. In the 2007 election it returned a single MP, Dame Kidu, the only woman in parliament, who joined Somare's coalition government as minister of community development, religion, and sports. It won no portfolios in the August 2011 O'Neill cabinet and no seats in the 2012 election.

Leaders: Dame Carol KIDU (Leader), Simon EYORK (President), Nick KLAPAT (Secretary General).

People's Action Party (PAP). PAP was formed on December 4, 1986, by the then forestry minister Ted DIRO as a right-of-center party. After a hiatus, Diro returned to the cabinet as minister without portfolio in April 1988. PAP's founding president, Vincent ERI, was named governor general in early 1990. Diro was convicted of corruption in September 1991, and the new PAP leader, Akoka DOI, failed to be reelected in 1992. The PAP was accorded five cabinet posts in the 2002 Somare government. In the 2007 election the party won six seats and was awarded two ministerial posts: correctional services for Tony AIMO and fisheries and marine resources for Ben SEMRI. Aimo, held responsible for several prison breakouts, was dropped from the government in January 2010 but in May was reinstated by

Somare to shore up the governing coalition; he and his party colleagues were excluded from the O'Neill government that was formed in August 2011 and won no seats in the 2012 election.

Leaders: Mark SARONG (President), Simon BOLE (Secretary General).

People's Labor Party (PLP). Launched in 2001 by Peter YAMA, the PLP won five parliamentary seats in 2002 and held the housing portfolio in the Somare administration until January 2004. The party won only two seats in the 2007 election and joined the opposition coalition led by Sir Mekere Morauta (PNGP) but won no seats in the 2012 election.

Leaders: Thomas TULIN (President), Michael KONDAI (Secretary General).

Rural Development Party (RDP). Winning three seats in the 2007 election, this party's base of support lies to the east of the capital, in Milne Bay and Manus, where its leader served as provincial governor. RDP joined the government when Moses MALADINA was appointed minister of state for constitutional matters by Somare in July 2010. Malanda was invited into the August 2011 O'Neill cabinet. In 2012 the RDP won no seats and no portfolios.

Leaders: John ROBIN (President), Bafike KONRUI (Secretary General), Moses MALADINA (former Minister for Implementation and Rural Development).

Other Parties without Seats in Parliament:

Christian Democratic Party, Kingdom First Party, League for Democracy Party, Mama Papa Graun Pati, Mapai Levites Party, National Conservative Party, National Front Party, New Dawn Transformation Party, Pan Melanesian Congress Party, PNG Greens Party, PNG National Party, People's Action Party, People's First Party, People's Freedom Party, People's Heritage Party, People's Labour Party, People's Resource Awareness Party, PNG Labour Party, PNG Conservative Party, PNG Country Party, PNG Destiny Party, PNG New Vision Party, Republican Party, Rural Development Party, and **Transform PNG Party.**

Bougainville Parties:

Bougainville parties include the **Bougainville Independence Movement** (BIM), formed in April 2005 by current leader James TANIS, former president of autonomous Bougainville, and supported by former rebel leader Francis Ona; the **Bougainville Labour Party** (BLP), led by lawyer Thomas TAMUSIO; the **Bougainville People's Congress Party** (BPCP), led by provincial president Joseph Kabui until his death in 2008; and the **New Bougainville Party** (NBP), founded in April 2005 by former island governor and current provincial president John MORRIS and now led by Ezekiel MASATT. A shadowy group based on remnants of the Panguna Landowners' Association and the Bougainville Revolutionary Army, called variously **Original Me'ekumi, Me'ekamui Tribal Nation, Me'ekumi Defence Force or Me'ekumi Government of Unity,** led by Philip Miriori, asserted itself in 2011 but was not recognized by either the Bougainville or the national government. (For further details on inactive political parties, see the 2011 *Handbook.*)

LEGISLATURE

The unicameral **National Parliament** was called the House of Assembly (*Bese Taubadadia Hegogo*) before independence. It currently consists of 111 members (90 from open and 21 from provincial electorates) elected to five-year terms by universal adult suffrage. Traditionally, candidates were not obligated to declare party affiliation, and postelectoral realignments were common; however, controversial legislation passed in December 2000 required future candidates to declare their affiliations and then, if elected, to maintain them or face expulsion. In 2007 the limited preferential voting system was employed for the first time, replacing the first-past-the-post system.

The following was the distribution of seats after the balloting of June 23–July 17, 2012: People's National Congress Party, 27 seats; Independents, 16; Triumph Heritage Empowerment Party, 12; PNG Party, 8; National Alliance, 7; United Resources Party, 7; People's Progress Party, 6; People's Party, 6; Social Democrat Party, 3; People's Movement for Change, 2; People's United Assembly Party, 2; People's Democratic Movement, 2; Coalition for Reform, 2; Melanesian Liberal Party, 2; New Generation Party, 2; Indigenous People's Party, 1; Our Development Party, 1; Pangu Party, 1; PNG Constitutional Democratic Party, 1; PNG Country Party, 1; Stars Alliance, 1; United Party, 1.

Speaker: Theodore Zibang ZURENUOC.

CABINET

[as of October 15, 2016]

Prime Minister	Peter O'Neill (PNC)
Deputy Prime Minister	Leo Dion (THE)
Ministers	
Agriculture and Livestock	Tommy Tomscoll (PDMP)
Autonomous Regions	Peter O'Neill (PNC)
Civil Aviation	Steven Davis (NAP)
Communication and Information Technology	Jimmy Miringtoro (PNC)
Community Development, Youth, and Religion	Delilah Gore (THE) [f]
Correctional Services	Jim Simatab (NAP)
Defense	Fabian Pok (URP)
Education	Nick Kuman (PNC)
Environment and Conservation	John Pundari (PP)
Finance	James Marape (PNC)
Fisheries and Marine Resources	Mao Zeming (PNC)
Foreign Affairs and Immigration	Rimbink Pato (UP)
Forests and Climate Change	Douglas Tomuriesa (PNC)
Health and HIV/AIDS	Michael Bill Malabag (PNC)
Higher Education, Research, Science, and Technology	Francis Marus (Pangu)
Housing and Urban Development	Paul Isikiel (PNC)
Intergovernmental Relations	Leo Dion (THE)
Justice, Attorney General	Ano Pala (PNC)
Labor and Industrial Relations	Benjamin Poponawa (THE)
Lands and Physical Planning	Benny Allan (PNC)
Mining	Byron Chan (PPP)
National Planning	Charles Abel (PNC)
Petroleum and Energy	Nixon Duban (PNC)
Police	Robert Atiyafa (PNC)
Public Enterprise and State Investment	William Duma (URP)
Public Service	Puka Temu (ODP)
Sports and Pacific Games	Justin Tkatchenko (SDP)
State Enterprises	Mekere Morauta (PNGP)
Trade, Commerce and Industry	Richard Maru (ind.)
Transport	William Duma (URP)
Treasury	Patrick Pruaitch (NA)
Without Portfolio	Boka Kondra (PNC)
Works and Implementation	Francis Awesa (PNC)

[f] = female

INTERGOVERNMENTAL REPRESENTATION

Ambassador to the U.S.: Rupa MULINA.

U.S. Ambassador to Papua New Guinea: Catherine EBERT-GRAY.

Permanent Representative to the UN: Max Hufanen RAI.

IGO Memberships (Non-UN): ADB, APEC, CWTH, MSG, PIF, WTO.

For Further Reference:

Bossip, Joseph. *Major Impediments to the Development of Papua New Guinea. Non-communicable Diseases (Lifestyle) Disease, High Illiteracy Rate, Corruption and Landowner Compensation (Conflict)*. Germany: GRIN Verlag, 2016.

Dinnen, Sinclair. *Law and Order in a Weak State: Crime and Politics Pacific Islands Studies.* Honolulu: University of Hawaii Press, 2001.

Sillitoe, Paul. *A Place against Time: Land and Environment in the Papua New Guinea Highlands*. New York: Routledge, 2013.
Wanek, Alexander. *The State and Its Enemies in Papua New Guinea*. New York: Routledge, 2013.
Woolford, Don. *Papua New Guinea: Initiation and Independence*. Brisbane: University of Queensland Press, 2013.

PARAGUAY

Republic of Paraguay
República del Paraguay (Spanish)
Tetã Paraguái (Guaraní)

Political Status: Independent since 1811; under presidential rule established in 1844; present constitution promulgated on June 20, 1992.

Area: 157,047 sq. mi. (406,752 sq. km).

Population: 6,725,000 (2016E—UN); 6,783,272 (2015E—U.S. Census).

Major Urban Centers (2016E—UN): ASUNCIÓN (2,406,000, metropolitan area)

Official Languages: Spanish, Guaraní.

Monetary Unit: Guaraní (market rate October 1, 2016: 5,555.04 guaraníes = $1US).

President: Horacio CARTES (National Republican Association–Colorado Party); elected on April 21, 2013, and sworn in on August 15, 2013, succeeding Luis Federico FRANCO Gómez (Patriotic Alliance for Change/Authentic Radical Liberal Party).

Vice President: Juan AFARA Marques (National Republican Association–Colorado Party); elected on April 21, 2013, and sworn in on August 15, 2013, succeeding Oscar Amancio DENIS (Authentic Radical Liberal Party).

THE COUNTRY

A landlocked, semitropical country wedged between Argentina, Bolivia, and Brazil, the Republic of Paraguay takes its name from the river that divides the fertile grasslands of the east ("Oriental") from the drier, less hospitable Chaco region of the west ("Occidental"). The population is 95 percent *mestizo,* mainly of Spanish and Indian origin, although successive waves of immigration have brought settlers from all parts of the globe, including Japan and Korea. Spanish is the official language; however, 90 percent of the population also speaks Guaraní, the language of most of the indigenous inhabitants. Approximately 89 percent of the population adheres to Roman Catholicism, the established religion, while about 7 percent practices other forms of Christianity. Women constitute 40 percent of the labor force, concentrated primarily in the informal sector, manufacturing, and domestic service. Women have played a greater role in politics in recent years, but remain a minority in that sphere.

With 77 percent of the land owned by 1 percent of the population and without an adequate transportation network, Paraguayan development has long been impeded. Agriculture and cattle-raising constitute the basis of the economy; soybeans, beef, cotton, and vegetable oils are the main exports. Industry is largely confined to processing agricultural, animal, and timber products, but there is a small consumer-goods industry. The government is presently embarked on exploitation of the vast hydroelectric potential of the Paraná River. The Itaipú Dam, the world's second largest and jointly constructed with Brazil, was opened in November 1982. The Yacyretá Dam, the globe's twelfth biggest and developed together with Argentina, entered full operation in 1998. As a result, Paraguay is now one of the world's leading exporters of electricity.

Paraguay is one of the world's most unequal societies in terms of income distribution. Inequities in the distribution of land, education, and wealth have fueled ongoing tensions and a climate of social mistrust. More than one-third of the Paraguayan labor force has either been unemployed or underemployed in the last decade. In 2010 one out of five Paraguayans lived in extreme poverty, while 35 percent of the population lived below the national poverty line. Health coverage in Paraguay remains one of the poorest in the Western Hemisphere. Though illiteracy has dropped to 5.4 percent of the adult population, functional illiteracy remains high. Among neighboring countries, only Bolivia's per capita GDP of $1,973 was below that of Paraguay's at $2,860 in 2010.

Paraguay's GDP rose by an average of 2.8 percent from 2000–2008. (For an overview of Paraguay's economy prior to 2000, see the 2011 *Handbook.*) In 2009 the World Bank approved $600 million in grants and loans to Paraguay to mitigate the impact of the economic downturn, which caused GDP to decline by 4 percent. The following year, influx of aid and the largest soy crop in the country's history led to a spectacular GDP growth of 13.1 percent. GDP shrank by 1.2 percent in 2012, due largely to a drought that devastated soybean production. Under a stimulus implemented in 2012, spending was reduced. The IMF reported a strong recovery of 14.2 percent in 2013, reflecting higher exports as the agricultural sector recovered. Continued successes in agriculture, as well as new investment in infrastructure, were expected to fuel economic growth of 4.4 percent in 2014. Inflation was 5 percent, while unemployment was steady at 5.5 percent. GDP grew by 4 percent in 2015 and 2016. In 2016 inflation was 4.5 percent, unemployment was 5.5 percent, and GDP per capita was $4,504. The World Bank rated Paraguay as 100th out of 189 countries in its 2016 annual ease of business survey.

GOVERNMENT AND POLITICS

Political background. Paraguay gained independence from Spain in 1811 but was slow to assume the contours of a modern state. Its initial years of independence were marked by a succession of strong, authoritarian leaders, the most famous of whom was José Gaspar RODRIGUEZ de Francia. Known as "El Supremo," Rodriguez ruled Paraguay from 1814 until 1840, during which time he sought to isolate the country from the outside world by expelling foreigners and cutting off communications. In 1865–1870 Paraguay fought the combined forces of Argentina, Brazil, and Uruguay in the War of the Triple Alliance, which claimed the lives of approximately half of the country's population and the vast majority of its males. From 1880 to 1904 the country was ruled by a series of Colorado Party (*Partido*

Colorado—PC) presidents, while the Liberals ruled for most of the period from 1904 to 1940. A three-year war against Bolivia over the Chaco territory ended in 1935, with Paraguay winning the greater part of the disputed region.

For more than half a century two men dominated the political scene: the dictatorial Gen. Higinio MORÍNIGO (1940–1947) and the equally authoritarian Gen. Alfredo STROESSNER, who came to power in 1954 through a military coup against President Federico CHÁVEZ. Initially elected to fill the balance of Chávez's unexpired term, Stroessner was subsequently reelected to successive five-year terms, the last on February 14, 1988. Stroessner was overthrown on February 3, 1989, in a coup led by Gen. Andrés RODRIGUEZ Pedotti, who was elected on May 1 to serve the balance of the existing presidential term. In simultaneous balloting, the Colorados retained their existing majorities in both houses of Congress.

At municipal balloting on May 26, 1991, the Colorados lost the race for the Asunción mayorship to the labor-backed Asunción for All (*Asunción para Todos*), while their traditional liberal opponents won in 43 other municipalities. The faction-ridden ruling party recovered to win 122 of 198 National Constituent Assembly seats on December 1. After six months of extensive debate, the assembly produced the draft of a new basic law, which became effective on its acceptance by the president on June 22, 1992.

Despite a heated challenge for the 1993 Colorado presidential nomination from Dr. Luis María ARGAÑA, Juan Carlos WASMOSY was named the party's standard-bearer at a convention in February, amid serious charges of fraud. The Colorado Party won pluralities in both houses of Congress in the May 9 presidential election with overt military support and widespread use of state resources to finance its campaign.

In early 1995 a rift developed between President Wasmosy and the self-styled military "strongman," Gen. Lino César OVIEDO Silva. In mid-May Oviedo was induced to join Wasmosy in an agreement with the congressional opposition that provided for the "temporary suspension" of party memberships held by army and police personnel.

In late April 1996 General Oviedo resigned from the army for violating a constitutional ban on its members' involvement in politics. Prior to his departure, though, the general threatened to bring down the Wasmosy government. The coup attempt, however, was thwarted as a result of intense international pressure and divisions within the military. Oviedo's subsequent appointment to head the Ministry of Defense was canceled soon thereafter amid strong congressional and street opposition. Oviedo went on to form his own Colorado Party faction (see Political Parties, below).

On September 7, 1997, Oviedo outpaced Argaña and Wasmosy's candidate, Finance Minister Carlos Alberto FACETTI, to win the Colorado presidential primary, with nearly 37 percent of the vote, close to Argaña's 35 percent and well above Facetti's 22 percent. Oviedo's victory triggered fears within the political and military establishment, which prompted an alliance between Wasmosy and Argaña aimed at stopping the former general's presidential bid. Oviedo's victory was challenged in the courts following *argañista* complaints of fraud.

On October 3 Wasmosy ordered Oviedo's disciplinary arrest under military law for "insults" leveled against the president, including the charge that he was a "thief." Wasmosy's efforts to postpone the May 10, 1998, presidential elections were rebuffed at various times by the political opposition and leading foreign ambassadors, notably between December 1997 and March 1998.

On December 12 Oviedo turned himself in to serve the 30-day sentence ordered by the president. Although Oviedo on December 29 became the legally recognized Colorado standard-bearer, a special military tribunal ordered that his incarceration continue indefinitely, pending further investigation of the abortive 1996 coup.

On April 17, 1998, the Supreme Court upheld a second sentence of ten years imposed on Oviedo in March, and his registration as Colorado standard-bearer was nullified the next day. His vice-presidential running mate, Raúl CUBAS Grau, was subsequently named his successor and went on to defeat opposition candidate Domingo LAÍNO in presidential balloting on May 10.

Three days after taking power, Cubas ordered Oviedo's release on a legal technicality. The measure elicited great controversy. Under an alliance of *argañistas,* with the opposition PLRA and the National Encounter Party (PEN), the National Congress challenged Cubas's decision in the courts.

On December 2, 1998, the Supreme Court annulled Cubas's release of Oviedo and ordered that the former general be returned to jail. However, Cubas issued a statement two days later rejecting the court's decision. The court, again unsuccessfully, directed Cubas to order Oviedo back to jail in February 1999, and Congress held preliminary discussions on impeachment proceedings. Although some observers initially believed Cubas might survive a congressional vote, the political landscape was dramatically altered on March 23 when Argaña was shot to death in Asunción by a professional hit squad. Suspicion of possible involvement immediately fell on Oviedo, and demonstrators poured into the streets of the capital to demand the president's resignation. After four days of protest in front of the National Congress, seven antigovernment demonstrators were killed by *oviedista* sniper fire and more than 150 protestors were wounded. The massacre took place while demonstrators were protecting the Congress from Oviedo supporters bent on blocking impeachment proceedings against Cubas.

Under intense international pressure, Cubas resigned on March 28, 1999, only hours before the Senate's final vote on his removal. He was succeeded within hours by Luis GONZÁLEZ Macchi, the *argañista* president of the Senate. On March 30 González Macchi appointed a "national unity" government, which included two members each from the PLRA and PEN. Meanwhile, Oviedo fled to Argentina and Cubas to Brazil. In late April the Supreme Court ruled that González Macchi was entitled to serve out the remainder of Cubas's term (until 2003) and directed that a new vice president be elected later in the year, a decision later postponed by the Supreme Electoral Court until August 13, 2000.

Subsequently, the Colorados indicated that they would contest the poll, despite a national unity agreement that the post be awarded to the opposition. As a result, the PLRA withdrew from the ruling coalition in February 2000, depriving the government of its legislative majority. González Macchi suppressed a botched coup attempt by Oviedo stalwarts in May 2000, an event that prompted Oviedo's arrest by Brazilian authorities the following month.

Liberal candidate Julio César FRANCO narrowly bested the Colorado nominee, Félix ARGAÑA (son of the former vice president), in the August balloting. President González Macchi's tenure was beset with corruption scandals, which prompted the PLRA to launch several efforts to impeach González Macchi, the last of which failed by a handful of votes in the Senate in February 2003.

In 2002 the *oviedistas* withdrew from the PC, with Oviedo announcing from Brazil, where he was then under detention, that he intended to return to Paraguay and seek the presidency in 2003. Meanwhile, opposition pressure against President González Macchi continued, fueled in part by the filing in April of formal charges against him for the diversion of about $16 million in public funds into a U.S. bank account. In addition to having immunity from prosecution while in office, the president retained enough support in the Chamber of Deputies to prevent the two-thirds vote needed to impeach him. Over the next six months, however, a series of sometimes violent antigovernment, anticorruption demonstrations took place, with supporters of González Macchi insisting that they were orchestrated by Oviedo and Vice President Franco. (In 2006 González Macchi was sentenced to eight years in prison; the ruling, though, was overturned later by the Court of Appeals.)

In the election of April 27, 2003, Nicanor DUARTE Frutos of the Colorado Party was elected president with 38.3 percent of the vote. The Colorados secured only pluralities in the Senate (16 of 45 seats) and the Chamber of Deputies (37 of 80 seats). Following his inauguration, President Duarte enjoyed initial popularity, stemming in part from his opposition to the privatization of state-owned enterprises and support for land reform. On August 15, 2003, President Duarte reached an agreement with the opposition to change six members of the Supreme Court. The Duarte administration stabilized Paraguay's rocky economy after reaching a stand-by agreement with the International Monetary Fund in December 2003, and initiated various administrative and tax reforms to increase public revenue. Duarte's reformist impetus, however, began to lose traction in 2004 in the face of mounting social discontent and conflict in the countryside. That year, landless peasants occupied 74 large properties, leading to 1,156 arrests among rural activists and the murder of five landless peasants.

Disenchantment with the Duarte administration increased after 2005. The May resignation of Duarte's independent and well-reputed finance minister signaled the political limits of Duarte's promise to modernize and clean up the Paraguayan state.

In February 2006 President Duarte resumed formal leadership of the Colorados, arguing that a constitutional ban on his holding any office other than the presidency applied only to governmental posts. He also indicated that he would seek a Constitutional Court ruling validating the action. In the meantime, he delegated interim leadership of the party to José Alberto ALDERETE. Three months earlier Duarte had appealed for constitutional reform in a move widely interpreted as clearing the way for a reelection bid by revoking the one-term limitation. His congressional critics, led by the PLRA, responded with a threat of impeachment, but they clearly lacked the required two-thirds majority in both chambers. In May 2007 Duarte, facing pressure even within the Colorado Party, announced that he had given up on his effort to challenge the one-term limitation.

With Duarte out of the race, Oviedo, who had returned to Paraguay in late June 2004, fixated on the presidency. Upon his return, he was held in a military prison to serve the sentence issued in early 1998 for his April 1996 coup attempt. He was released on parole in early September 2007, as result of a Supreme Court decision that was widely perceived to have been engineered by Duarte, in hopes of splitting the broad anti-Colorado coalition formed in support of a presidential bid by Fernando LUGO, a progressive Catholic bishop. On October 31 the Supreme Court annulled Oviedo's sentence for the 1996 coup attempt, which allowed him to launch his own presidential candidacy through the National Union of Ethical Citizens (*Unión Nacional de Ciudadanos Éticos*—UNACE).

Meanwhile, Duarte decided to support Blanca OVELAR de Duarte, his minister of education and culture, rebuffing Vice President Luis CASTIGLIONI Soria and the Colorado Party president Alderete, who both expected his endorsement. Castiglioni and Alderete went on to form their own movements to bid for the Colorado presidential slot.

In December 2007 Ovelar defeated Castiglioni for the Colorado nomination by less than 5,000 votes. Castiglioni and his supporters refused to recognize Ovelar's victory. However, the Colorado Party proclaimed Ovelar its standard-bearer in January 2008; she thereby became the first woman to head the presidential ticket of a major party.

Meanwhile, Lugo had become the opposition's main hope for defeating the ruling Colorado Party, after serving as the main speaker at an anti-Duarte demonstration attended by 40,000 people in late March 2006. Lugo helped to forge a broad coalition in September 2007 called the Patriotic Alliance for Change (*Alianza Patriotica para el Cambio*—APC) and, after resigning from the priesthood (the constitution forbids religious leaders from holding political office), defeated five other candidates (including Oviedo and Ovelar of the Colorado Party) in the presidential election of April 20, 2008. The results in the concurrent congressional and gubernatorial elections were essentially split, although the Colorado Party remained small pluralities in both legislative chambers.

On April 16, 2009, Lugo conducted a minor cabinet reshuffle and replaced four ministers in an effort to enhance the popularity of the government following an inability to enact promised reforms because of legislative resistance. Later that month he reached outside of the APC and chose Hector LACOGNATA of the Beloved Homeland Party (*Partido Patria Querida*—PPQ) to replace the foreign minister, who had resigned, in an effort to broaden his support within the Congress. He also supported the election of Miguel CARRIZOSA Galiano of the PPQ as president of the Senate. However, the effort led to the withdrawal of the PLRA from the APC (see Political Parties, below). The PLRA did maintain its three cabinet positions and continued to support the government.

In April 2010 Congress enacted legislation allowing the government to declare a state of emergency in five departments as part of a broader effort to suppress the Paraguayan People's Army (*Ejército del Pueblo Paraguayo*—EPP), which was behind a series of high-profile murders and kidnappings. On July 29 EPP leader Severiano MARTÍNEZ was killed in fighting with security forces.

In municipal elections on November 7, 2010, the Colorado Party secured 139 of the country's 238 municipalities. The party won the mayorship of the national capital and those of the capitals of 14 of Paraguay's 17 departments. The victory was seen as a major defeat for Lugo and the APC.

On June 22, 2012, the Senate voted to impeach President Lugo. Vice President Luis Federico FRANCO was immediately sworn in as president. Elections proceeded on schedule on April 21, 2013. In the wake of Lugo's impeachment, leftist parties fell into disarray, paving the way for political newcomer Horacio CARTES of the Colorado Party to win a decisive victory and for the party to secure majorities in both legislative houses. (For more on Lugo's impeachment and the 2013 election, see Current issues, below.)

Cartes completed his cabinet in April 2014 when Guillermo SOSA was sworn in as minister of labor. The cabinet was reshuffled in January 2015, and the defense minister was replaced in November of that year. The agriculture minister was replaced in January 2016, as was the minister of education and culture in May of that year.

Constitution and government. The 1992 constitution established an important break from the 1967 constitution. While maintaining the country's presidential system and a two-chamber legislature, the current constitution upholds basic democratic guarantees of association and expression, and improved the rights of women and indigenous people. The legislative branch was strengthened and various provisions were included to enhance judicial independence, including a Council of Magistrates responsible for screening nominations to the Supreme Court and appointing judges to the appellate and lower courts.

The new constitution introduced the post of vice president, to be elected along with the president by simple plurality (thus denying the opposition an opportunity to join forces in a runoff), and limited the president to a single five-year term. In a rebuff to the military, the constitutional assembly prohibited the chief executive from transferring his or her powers as commander-in-chief to another and instituted elections for the governors and council members of the country's departments. Strong guarantees for private property rights were established at the expense of constitutional provisions in favor of land reform.

For administrative purposes Paraguay is divided into 17 departments (exclusive of the capital), which are subdivided into a total of 230 municipalities.

The judicial system encompasses justices of the peace, courts of the first instance, appellate courts, and, at the apex, the Supreme Court of Justice. Despite significant reforms undertaken after 1995, including the overhaul of all judges, public opinion continues to view the judiciary as a corrupt institution.

Newspapers did not enjoy complete freedom of the press, and a number ceased publication during the Stroessner era. Freedom of the press is constitutionally guaranteed, but it is common for reporters to be threatened, both legally and violently. Following the ouster of President Lugo in 2012, media outlets faced intimidation for their reporting. From 2013 to 2016, Paraguay declined 20 spots to 111th of 180 countries in the Reporters Without Borders press freedom index (see Current issues, below).

Foreign relations. A member of the United Nations, the Organization of American States, the Latin American Integration Association, and other regional organizations, Paraguay traditionally maintained a strongly anti-leftist foreign policy, including a suspension of relations with Nicaragua in 1980 following the assassination in Asunción of former Nicaraguan president Anastasio Somoza Debayle. Paraguay began to soften its approach to foreign policy with the reestablishment of diplomatic ties with Cuba in 1996.

Relations with neighboring regimes have been relatively cordial. In March 1991 Paraguay joined Brazil, Argentina, and Uruguay to establish the Southern Cone Common Market (*Mercado Común del Cono Sur*—Mercosur). Periodic disagreements with Brazil and Argentina over hydroelectric issues have flared. At the Itaipú Dam, an unfair pricing system has provoked repeated demands by successive governments to renegotiate the 1973 Itaipú treaty with Brazil.

Relations with the United States improved after Stroessner's demise. Paraguay had been a close ally during the Cold War, but repeated human rights violations and allegations of high-level Paraguayan involvement in narcotics trafficking strained relations between both countries, especially after 1977. The United States government helped prevent a coup against General Oviedo in 1996, and thereafter began to press Paraguay to curb illicit economic practices, notably in the realm of intellectual property violations and drug trafficking.

Following September 11, 2001, the shared border of Paraguay, Brazil, and Argentina became a leading point of concern for United States policymakers, who viewed the area as a haven for money laundering, arms and drug trafficking, and Islamist militants. The United States provided Paraguay with technical assistance, equipment, and training to strengthen counternarcotics operations. In July 2003 the U.S. government suspended all military aid to Paraguay as a result of the country's refusal to grant immunity to U.S. citizens in legal cases involving the International Court of Justice in The Hague.

Enhanced democratic stability in Paraguay and closer relations with neighboring leftist governments reduced the traditional influence exercised by the United States in Paraguayan foreign policy. In 2004 Paraguay was one of twelve nations to join the newly-created Union of South American Nations (*Unión de Naciones Suramericanas*—UNASUR), designed to bring together MERCOSUR and the Andean Community. However, the Congress failed to ratify the organization's treaty. In July 2009 Paraguay and Brazil signed an accord that settled a long-running dispute over the operations of the bilateral Itaipu hydroelectric plant.

In August 2010 the government had to withdraw a bill supporting Venezuelan membership in MERCOSUR after opposition parties mustered the votes to defeat the measure. Opposition to Venezuelan membership was led by Vice President Luis Federico Franco Gómez, creating a dispute with Lugo, who campaigned heavily in favor of extending membership. All members of the organization except Paraguay and Brazil had already approved Venezuela's entry into the trade bloc. Meanwhile, Paraguay rejected participation in the U.S.-sponsored military program New Horizons 2010, which offered training and equipment to countries in the region. In September Paraguay joined with other South American nations to create the Bank of the South (*Banco del Sur*) to reduce the influence of institutions such as the IMF and the World Bank.

In a sign of improving cooperation with the United States in counternarcotics efforts, Paraguay extradited three Lebanese nationals to the United States to face drug-trafficking charges in February 2011. In May the Brazilian legislature approved the increase in payments for energy from the Itaipú Dam from $120 million per year to $360 million. A visit by the Iranian foreign minister in August led to increased economic ties between the two nations. That month, Congress officially approved the UNASUR treaty, and membership was finalized with the president's signature in September. Paraguayan authorities began meetings with Brazilian officials in November 2011 to develop a program jointly to fight organized crime and corruption.

The impeachment of Lugo in June 2012 strained relations throughout the region; Mercosur and UNASUR suspended Paraguay, and several Latin American countries withdrew their ambassadors. Tension ran particularly high with Venezuela, which had cut off oil shipments following Lugo's impeachment, and in October Venezuela expelled all Paraguayan diplomats. In November Paraguay's foreign ministry stated that the country would not facilitate electoral observers from neighboring countries but ultimately agreed to a mission from UNASUR. In April 2013 president-elect Cartes signaled his interest in joining the Pacific Alliance, the regional trade bloc formed in June 2012.

Mercosur allowed Paraguay to rejoin in August 2013 after Cartes's inauguration. Wishing to smooth tensions with the group, Cartes insisted on waiting for congressional approval of Venezuela's Mercosur membership. On December 18, 2013, Congress voted to approve Venezuela's membership.

On January 3, 2014, Paraguay and Brazil announced plans to build a bridge connecting the Brazilian city of Foz do Iguaçu with the Paraguayan city Presidente Franco.

On July 18, 2014, Cartes signed an agreement with Uruguayan president Jose Mujica toward cooperation in developing a deepwater port. In addition to signaling tighter bilateral relations between neighbors, the agreement could lead to less trade reliance on Argentina.

In August 2015 Paraguay protested an incursion into its territory by Brazilian military forces that were in pursuit of suspected smugglers.

In June 2016 Paraguay announced its opposition to Venezuela assuming the rotating chair of Mercosur over concerns about democracy in that country. Paraguay joined Argentina and Brazil in issuing a consensus statement opposing Venezuelan leadership (see entry on Mercosur).

Current issues. In June 2012 a dispute broke out between police forces and landless farmers over an attempt by authorities to remove some 150 farmers from part of a privately owned estate. Advocates for the farmers asserted that the land should have been part of an agrarian reform program, pointing to Lugo's unfulfilled campaign promise to enact reform to serve Paraguay's 87,000 landless farm families. Lugo ordered the army to intervene on June 15 and, in the ensuing clashes, 6 police officers and 11 farmers were killed. The interior minister and the chief of police resigned.

Opponents of Lugo seized upon the incident, and the lower chamber of Paraguay's Congress voted to impeach the president less than a week later. The following day, on June 22, the Senate held a public impeachment trial, spearheaded by the majority Colorado Party, which accused Lugo of malfeasance. Lugo, who was given two hours to present a defense, did not attend, sending lawyers instead to ask for 18 days so he could prepare his case. The request was dismissed and the Senate voted 39–4 in favor of the impeachment. Vice President Franco was subsequently sworn in as president. The power transfer was widely denounced as a parliamentary coup.

Lugo initially accepted the ouster but reversed his position shortly afterward. He formed a parallel cabinet and, in September, received the official support of the PDC.

The electoral court announced in August 2012 that elections would be held on April 21, 2013. Eleven presidential candidates contested. In December, the Colorado Party confirmed Horacio Cartes, a tobacco magnate who was investigated by the United States in 2000 for drug trafficking, as the nominee, the PLRA selected Efrain ALEGRE, and in January, Lino OVIEDO of UNACE launched his campaign. UNACE was jolted on February 2 when Oviedo died in a helicopter crash. Instead of selecting a new candidate, UNACE and the PLRA opened discussions on forming an alliance. Initial efforts were abandoned, but in April, UNACE agreed to promote Alegre. Cartes won the election decisively, securing 48.5 percent of the vote; Alegre followed with 39 percent. The Colorado Party retained its majority in both legislative chambers, securing 45 seats in the lower house and 19 in the senate; the PLRA followed, with 26 seats and 13 seats, respectively. Cartes was inaugurated on August 15, 2013, at which time he named his cabinet.

A week later, Congress approved a law expanding President Cartes's ability to mobilize the army in a police capacity after an EPP attack on August 18 left four security officers and one police officer dead, marking the beginning of a period of increased EPP actions against large landowners.

On October 1 the government announced plans to cut 15,000 public sector jobs, saying salaries account for some 80 percent of Paraguay's budget. The PLRA led protests in Asunción on October 17.

During an army mission against EPP units in December 2013, EPP guerrilla fighters ambushed soldiers. One soldier was killed and another severely injured in the attack. In early July 2014 the EPP used bombs to attack electricity infrastructure, cutting power for an estimated 765,000 people.

In 2014 three journalists were murdered. In April of that year the Inter-American Commission requested that Paraguay take stronger action to prevent attacks on journalists and to investigate and prosecute those who infringe on reporters' freedom of speech and the press.

In an effort to combat corruption, in September 2014 the Access to Public Information and Transparency Law was passed, granting all citizens of Paraguay access to government financial records. In February 2016 the president ordered all government agencies to publish the names, salaries, and qualifications of all their employees in a further effort to reduce corruption.

In December 2015 massive flooding forced the evacuation of more than 90,000 in and around the capital.

POLITICAL PARTIES

Paraguay's two traditional political organizations were the now-divided Liberal Party, which was last in power in 1940, and the National Republican Association (Colorado Party), which dominated the political scene from 1947 and sponsored the successive presidential candidacies of Gen. Alfredo Stroessner. In addition to these two traditional parties, Paraguay has a number of smaller, independent parties and political movements, ranging from right to left positions on the political spectrum.

Government Party:

National Republican Association–Colorado Party (*Asociación Nacional Republicana–Partido Colorado*—ANR-PC). Formed in 1887, the mainstream of the Colorado Party has long been conservative in outlook and consistently supported Gen. Stroessner for more than three decades. The party has, however, been subject to factionalism. (For a discussion of its shifting "currents" before 1991, see the 1990 *Handbook*.)

During the run-up to municipal elections in May 1991, the principal internal groupings were three *tradicionalista* alignments: the highly conservative *Tradicionalistas Autónomos,* led by then acting party president Dr. Luis María Argaña; the moderately liberal *Movimiento Tradicionalista Democrático,* led by Blás RIQUELME; and the centrist *Tradicionalismo Renovador,* led by Angel Roberto SEIFART. Following the municipal balloting the *democráticos* and the *renovadors* joined forces as the *Tradicionalismo Renovador Democrático* (Trardem), which commanded a majority at an extraordinary party convention on July 15–19. Subsequently, Trardem and the *autónomos* ran joint lists in Colorado balloting on October 6 to pick candidates for the forthcoming Constituent Assembly elections, winning all of the contests.

Other party factions included the *Frente Democrático* (FD), led by Waldino Ramón LOVERA; the strongly renewalist *Coloradismo Democrático* (Codem), led by Miguel Angel GONZALEZ Casabianca; and the youthful *Nueva Generación* (NG), led by Enrique RIERA Jr. In

1993 Colorado dissident Leandro PRIETO Yegros campaigned for the presidency under the banner of a Progressive Social Movement (*Movimiento Social Progresista*—MSP), but the electoral tribunal rejected his candidacy.

At a Colorado convention in February 1993 the military-backed Juan Carlos Wasmosy defeated Argaña for the party's presidential nomination. Following the election, Argaña's faction, now styled the Colorado Reconciliation Movement (*Movimiento Reconciliación Colorada*—MRC), held a majority of the party's seats in the Chamber of Deputies and formed a legislative bloc with the PLRA and PEN. In late 1994, after three generals had accused Wasmosy of intraparty vote rigging, *argañistas* formally challenged the validity of the president's incumbency by calling for his impeachment. (For more information on the alliance formed between the *argañistas* and *oviedistas* in early 1995, see the 2008 *Handbook.*)

In May 1996, following his forced retirement from the army, Oviedo launched a PC faction styled the National Union of Ethical Colorados (*Unión Nacional de Colorados Éticos*—UNACE, below). Meanwhile, in an April 28 election for the party leadership, Argaña secured an easy victory of 55 percent over Seifart (35 percent) and Riquelme (8 percent).

Despite his status as a coup suspect (see Political background, above), General Oviedo was elected Colorado presidential candidate in September 1997. Following Oviedo's preclusion from the 1998 presidential poll by the Supreme Court, he was replaced as the Colorado standard-bearer by Raúl Cubas Grau, previously the vice-presidential candidate and a close ally of Oviedo. Argaña became the vice-presidential candidate. Intense conflict subsequently persisted between the *argañistas* and the Cubas/Oviedo faction. In mid-March the *oviedistas* took control of the Colorado headquarters in Asunción after the *argañistas* had postponed the scheduled election of new party leaders. Shortly thereafter, Argaña was assassinated, leading to the ouster of President Cubas and elevation of Luis González Macchito the national presidency. González was succeeded by Nicanor Duarte Frutos in April 2003. Duarte, Argaña's running mate in the 1997 Colorado presidential primaries, became the Colorado standard-bearer after defeating Osvaldo DOMINGUEZ Dibb, who contested the result of the December 22, 2002, primaries. The Colorado Party went on to win the April 27 presidential contest by a 13 percent advantage over the PLRA.

In a February 19, 2006, internal party election Duarte was challenged again by Dominguez, but Duarte won. Alfredo Stroessner died in Brazil on August 16 of that year. His grandson, Alfredo "Goli" DOMINGUEZ Stroessner, who prefers to be known as Alfredo STROESSNER, assumed leadership of the *neostronista* faction.

Duarte's exploration of a possible constitutional change to permit him to run for another presidential term caused further turmoil in the party. Vice President Luis Alberto Castiglioni announced plans to seek the party's presidential nomination himself. In May Duarte withdrew his name and backed Education and Finance Minister Blanca Ovelar de Duarte for the nomination. Castiglioni, supported within the party by the Colorado Vanguard Movement (*Movimiento Vanguardia Colorado*—MVC), resigned as vice president in early October to contest the 2008 elections but lost a close primary vote to Ovelar in December. Castiglioni and his supporters alleged fraud. When Ovelar finished second in the April 2008 presidential poll with 30.7 percent of the vote, Castiglioni promised to launch a "true" Colorado Party and demanded immediate leadership elections. However, competing claims for the party's presidency remained in a legal imbroglio through November. The party was also reportedly split by a decision by Duarte's backers to provide legislative support for the new Lugo government. (The Castiglioni camp declined Lugo's offer.) Meanwhile, Duarte, to his consternation, was seated (because of his status as a past president) as a nonvoting member of the Senate, despite the fact that he had been elected as a regular member in the April balloting.) Duarte, maintaining that his Senate bid had been approved by the Supreme Election Tribunal, appealed to the Supreme Court, which ruled in his favor in November 2011.

The ANR-PC played a leading role in the June 2012 impeachment of President Lugo. Businessman and political newcomer Hugo Cartes secured the party's presidential nomination in December with 59.6 percent of the vote, a solid victory over runner-up Javier Zacaría IRÚN. Cartes won a decisive victory in April 2013, with 48.5 percent of the vote. The party retained majorities in both legislative houses.

On February 3, 2014, in a speech commemorating the 25th anniversary of the end of Stroessner's regime, president of Congress Julio César VELÁZQUEZ admitted that the ANR-PC was the "main political support" of the regime, and said it was a "mistake." Later that month, President Cartes made moves to ease friction with is party. Party members were reportedly resentful of Cartes's decision to forgo ANR-PC officials for outside technical experts to fill his cabinet.

In July 2015 Hercules Pedro ALLIANA was elected party president.

Leaders: Hugo CARTES (President of the Republic), Hercules Pedro ALLIANA (President of the Party), Nicanor DUARTE Frutos (Former President of the Republic and Leader of the *Movimiento Progresista Colorado*), Luis Alberto CASTIGLIONI (Former Vice President of the Republic and Leader of the MVC).

Other Legislative Parties:

Authentic Radical Liberal Party (*Partido Liberal Radical Auténtico*—PLRA). Paraguay's historical **Liberal Party** (*Partido Liberal*—PL) was founded in 1887 and legally proscribed in 1942. The party was legally reestablished in 1961, but most of its members left in the same year to form the **Radical Liberal Party** (*Partido Liberal Radical*—PLR). In 1977 a majority of PL and PLR members withdrew from their organizations to form the **Unified Liberal Party** (*Partido Liberal Unificado*—PLU). The government, however, refused to legalize the new grouping, continuing instead to recognize a rump of the PLR. The PLRA was formed in 1978 by a group of center-left PLU dissidents, many of whom had been subjected to police harassment after the 1978 election. (For PLRA history between 1978 and 1996, see the 2013 *Handbook.*)

In November 1996 the PLRA's Martín BURT, running with the support of PEN (below), was elected mayor of Asunción. He subsequently heralded that outcome as an example of how cooperation between the two leading opposition parties might defeat the Colorados in 1998, and in August 1997, the PLRA joined with PEN in a **Democratic Alliance** (*Alianza Democrática*—AD) to contest the general election of May 1998. The PLRA was awarded two seats in the national unity government installed in March 1999. It withdrew from the González administration on February 6, 2000. In March 2002 the party's president, Miguel Abdón SAGUIER, was ousted in favor of legislator Oscar Denis.

Having won the vice presidency in August 2000, Julio César Franco resigned the office in October 2002 to meet a legal requirement that presidential candidates vacate their governmental positions six months before the scheduled balloting. The PLRA attempted to form an opposition Power Front 2003 (*Frente Poder 2003*) and subsequently attempted two other alliances. Obliged to run alone, the PLRA finished second in both the presidential and the legislative races.

In October 2005 longtime party icon Domingo Laíno and a number of others were temporarily expelled from the PLRA for actions that appeared to make them de facto allies of the ruling Colorados.

After leading the formation of the CN in 2006, the PLRA in January 2007 announced plans for PLRA president Frederico FRANCO (the brother of Julio César Franco) to serve as the PLRA's nominee in what it hoped would be a multiparty primary to determine the opposition's presidential candidate for 2008. In a very close vote, the PLRA in June endorsed Fernando Lugo, who agreed to allow the PLRA to select his running mate. In a very close primary election for the vice-presidential slot in December, Franco defeated Sen. Carlos MATEO Balmelli. However, the party remained factionalized. Some components complained that the party was not sufficiently represented in Lugo's government. Franco stepped aside as party leader, and Antonio Gustavo CARDOZA became acting PLRA leader.

The PLRA left the APC in 2009 over frustration with Lugo's efforts to reach out to the opposition. In June 2011 following a cabinet reshuffle, members of the PLRA called for Lugo's resignation. Franco assumed the presidency upon the ouster of Lugo in June 2012.

Ahead of the 2013 presidential election, the PLRA officially allied with the PDP in April 2012 and the PEN in October. In a December primary election, Efraín Alegre secured the party nomination for presidency. Following the February death of UNACE presidential candidate Lino Oviedo, the PLRA attempted to form an alliance. Though discussions were abandoned in February, in early April UNACE agreed to promote Alegre. In April 21 balloting, Alegre came in second with 39 percent of the vote. The PLRA won 26 seats in the lower house and 13 in the Senate. Shortly after the elections, party president Blás LLANO tendered his resignation. Miguel Abdón Saguier officially assumed the post in July 2013.

Leaders: Miguel Abdón SAGUIER (President of the Party); Efraían ALEGRE (2013 presidential candidate); Rolando Aníbal FRANCO Gomez, Luis Alberto WAGNER Lezcano (Vice Presidents).

Progressive Democratic Party (*Partido Democrata Progresista*—PDP). The PDP was founded by dissident members of the PPS in 2007. Party leader Rafael Augusto FILIZZOLA Serra served as interior minister in the Lugo government but was dismissed in June 2011 after Lugo charged that the minister's presidential aspirations interfered with his official duties. The PDP subsequently left the FG. In April 2012 the PDP and the PLRA formalized their alliance, paving the way for Filizzola to take the vice presidential slot on the Alegre ticket. The PDP secured three Senate seats in April 2013 balloting. In 2015 Filizzola was again elected PDP president.

Leader: Rafael Augusto FILIZZOLA Serra (PDP President and 2013 vice presidential candidate).

National Encounter Party (*Partido Encuentro Nacional*—PEN). PEN was organized in mid-1992 as a somewhat loose alignment of supporters of independent presidential candidate Guillermo Caballero VARGAS, who consistently led in the public opinion polls until the eve of the 1993 balloting. The group, which included elements of the PRF and PDC as well as Carlos Filizzola's CPT, won eight seats in each legislative house and subsequently entered into an opposition pact with the Liberals, which was reaffirmed for Asunción's mayoral contest in November 1996. PEN agreed to support the PLRA candidate after public opinion polls showed him ahead of the other contenders. PEN accepted two cabinet posts in the national unity government installed in March 1999. A week earlier Filizzola had lost the party presidency to Eúclides ACEVEDO. PEN's Diego Abente BRUN ran a distant fifth in the 2003 presidential race, while none of the party's candidates won congressional representation.

In April 2012 party president Fernando Camacho announced his candidacy for the FG presidential nomination. However, in October, the PEN formalized a split with the FG and threw support behind the Alegre–Filizzola ticket. The PEN won two Chamber seats and one Senate seat in the April 2013 balloting.

Leaders: Fernando CAMACHO (President), Hermann RATZLAFF (Vice President).

Guasú Front (Frente Guasú—FG). The FG was formed in March 2010 when the **Patriotic Alliance for Change** (*Alianza Patriotica para el Cambio*—APC), led by then-president Fernando Lugo, entered an alliance with the **Unitary Space–People's Congress** (*Espacio Unitario–Congreso Popular*—EU-CP), a movement created by leftist leaders in June 2009. The APC is an outgrowth of the **National Concertation** (*Concertación Nacional*—CN), a broad coalition formed in September 2006 with the aim of ending the Colorado Party's 60-year dominance of Paraguayan politics. The CN comprised the PLRA, PPS, PEN, PPQ, and UNACE, as well as additional leftist and civil organizations. (For more on the CN, see the 2013 *Handbook.*)

Dissension within the CN emerged in early 2007 over the question of how to pick a candidate for the 2008 presidential elections, resulting in the eventual withdrawal of the UNACE and PPQ (the second and third largest parties in the opposition camp) in September, after the PRLA and five smaller parties (the PPS, PEN, PDC, PRF, and the **Socialist Party** [*Partido Socialista*—PS]) had named Lugo as presidential nominee.

The APC was launched on September 18, 2007, by the PRLA, PPS, PEN, PDP, PRF, PDC, PPT, the **Broad Front** (*Frente Amplio*—FA), and other groups, including the influential social movement **Social and Popular Bloc** (*Bloque Social y Popular*). Lugo, whose concern for the impoverished peasantry had earned him the nickname "Red Bishop," was elected president of the republic under the APC rubric with 40.8 percent of the vote in the April 2008 election. The APC component parties presented their own candidates in the concurrent congressional balloting. In July 2009 the PLRA officially withdrew from the APC. Efforts to change the constitution to allow Lugo to seek a second term further divided members of the APC.

Meanwhile, the EU-CP launched in June 2009 under the leadership of *campesino* leader Elvio BENÍTEZ as a progressive alternative to challenge the traditional parties. The movement united some 19 small leftist parties, including the **Paraguayan Communist Party** (*Partido Communista Paraguayo*—PCP), the **Popular Socialist Convergence Party** (*Partido Convergencia Popular Socialista*—PCPS), and the **Popular Patriotic Movement** (*Movimiento Patriótico y Popular*—MPP).

In March 2010 Lugo's APC and the EU-CP officially merged under the FG banner.

Following Lugo's impeachment in June 2012, the former president was appointed leader of the FG coalition with unanimous support. A rift formed within the party the following month when Mario FERREIRO, who had announced his candidacy for the 2013 presidential race, did not secure the FG nomination and formed a new coalition, taking the PDC and several other parties with him (see Avanza País, below). In January 2013 the coalition confirmed Aníbal CARRILLO as presidential candidate. In April 21 balloting, Carrillo secured 3.5 percent of the vote. The FG won five Senate seats and one Chamber seat. Lugo won one of the Senate seats.

Leader: Fernando LUGO (Former President of the Republic).

Country in Solidarity Party (*Partido País Solidario*—PPS). The PPS was formed in 2001 by Carlos Filizzola, who had led PEN from its formation until losing a leadership election in March 1999. Earlier, he had headed the **Asunción for Everybody** (*Asunción para Todos*—APT), winning the capital's mayoralty in 1991, and then the **Constitution for Everybody** (*Constitución para Todos*—CPT). A joint secretary of the labor confederation *Central Unitaria de Trabajadores,* he had been imprisoned several times by the Stroessner regime for supporting peasant land seizures. Filizzola lost the Asunción mayoral election of November 2001 despite PLRA support. The party won two Senate and two Chamber seats in 2003. However, it suffered a split in 2007 (which led to the creation of the PDP, above) and retained only one Senate seat in 2008. The PPS was a leading force in an unsuccessful petition for a referendum to abolish the one-term presidential limit. Filizzola was elected to the Senate in the 2013 election.

Leaders: Carlos FILIZZOLA (President), Jorge GIUCICH (Vice President).

Popular Tekojojá Party (*Partido Popular Tekojojá*—PPT). The PPT was established in December 2006 by left-wing social and political activists in support of Fernando Lugo's presidential candidacy. Party leader Aníbal CARRILLO Iramain accepted a government post in the ministry of health as part of the Lugo government, but resigned in 2009 and was replaced by Esperanza MARTÍNEZ, who left office when Franco became president. Carrillo won the FG presidential nomination in January 2013 internal balloting.

Leader: Aníbal CARRILLO Iramain (President).

Forward Country (*Avanza País*—AP). The AP formed in October 2012 when Mario Ferreira led a splinter group of six left-wing parties off former president Lugo's FG. The **Movement Towards Socialism Party** (*Partido del Movimiento al Socialismo*—P-MAS, led by Camilo SOARES), one of the founding members of the APC, joined the new movement. In April 2013 balloting, Ferreira came in third place in the presidential race, securing 6.2 percent of the vote. The alliance won two seats in both legislative houses.

Leader: Mario FERREIRA (2013 presidential candidate).

Christian Democratic Party (*Partido Demócrata Cristiano*—PDC). The PDC, which was refused recognition by the Electoral Commission from 1971 through 1988, is the furthest left of the non-Communist groupings and one of the smallest of Paraguay's political parties. The party won only 1 percent of the vote in 1989. It secured one Constituent Assembly seat in 1991, none thereafter.

In September 2012 the Paraguayan PDC released a statement that the party, with the support of parallel groups in other Latin American countries, did not recognize the Franco government.

Leader: Alba Cristaldo ESPINOLA (President).

Other members of the AP include the small leftist **February Revolutionary Party** (*Partido Revolucionario Febrerista*—PRF) (see the 2011 *Handbook* for more information); the Democratic **Unity for Victory Movement** (*Movimiento Unidad Democrática para la Victoria*—MUDV); the **April 20 Political Movement** (*Movimiento Político 20 de Abril*—M-20A), a pro-Lugo movement created in 2010 and led by Miguel LOPEZ PERITO; and the **Paraguay Tekopyahú Party** (*Partido Paraguay Tekopyahú*—PPT).

National Union of Ethical Citizens (*Unión Nacional de Ciudadanos Éticos*—UNACE). The present UNACE (sometimes identified as the UNACE Party, or PUNACE) began as the ANR-PC's *Unión Nacional de Colorados Éticos* faction, which Lino Oviedo had launched in 1996. In March 2002, while under arrest in Brazil, Oviedo announced that he intended to sever his faction's links to the Colorados, return to Paraguay, and establish a new party as a vehicle for a presidential bid in 2003. However, the Supreme Court invalidated any candidacy by the general. His surrogate, Sen. Guillermo Sánchez Guffanti, received 13.5 percent of the popular vote. In September 2007 Oviedo was released from prison. The Supreme Court subsequently annulled his sentence for the April 2006 coup attempt, allowing him to present a presidential bid in April 2008, in which he obtained 22 percent of the vote.

Oviedo launched his campaign for the April 2013 presidential election in January. Weeks later, on February 2, he was killed in a helicopter crash. Soon thereafter, UNACE opened discussions with the PLRA over forming a possible alliance, which subsequently dissolved. In early April the parties reached an agreement to promote PLRA presidential candidate Efraín Alegre. Nonetheless, Lino Oviedo Sanchez, who assumed the UNACE nomination after the death of his uncle and namesake, received 0.8 percent of the vote on April 21. UNACE secured two Senate and two Chamber seats.

Leader: Lino OVIEDO Sanchez (2013 presidential candidate).

Beloved Homeland Party (*Partido Patria Querida*—PPQ). The PPQ was launched in early 2002 by Catholic businessman Pedro FADUL Niella, who launched an anticorruption campaign for the 2003 elections, in which he received 21.3 percent of the presidential vote, while the PPQ won nine seats in the Chamber of Deputies and seven in the Senate. Fadul subsequently initiated the abortive call for President Duarte's impeachment in November 2005.

The PPQ broke away from the CN, the broad anti-Colorado coalition, in July 2007 after Fernando Lugo agreed to have a PLRA running mate and the CN's proposed primary system was eliminated. Fadul subsequently ran as the PPQ presidential candidate in 2008, but he won only 2.4 percent of the votes. The PPQ won four Senate seats and three in the Chamber of Deputies, one of which was belonged to Orlando PENNER Dirksen of the **Departmental Alliance of Boquerón** (*Alianza Departamental de Boquerón*—ADB), a regional political movement comprising the PPQ, PEN, and PLRA.

The PPC selected Miguel Carrizosa as 2013 presidential candidate in September 2011. Sebastian ACHA assumed party leadership in internal elections in December 2012. Carrizosa won 1.2 percent of the vote in April 2013, and the party secured one Chamber seat.

Leaders: Sebastian ACHA (Party President), Miguel CARRIZOSA (First Vice President and 2013 presidential candidate).

Chaqueña Passion Alliance (*Alianza Pasión Chaqueña*). The Chaqueña Passion Alliance secured one seat in the Chamber of Deputies in April 2013 balloting.

Other Parties Contesting the 2013 Elections:

Minor political parties and movements that participated in the 2013 elections, individually or as part of coalitions, included **Paraguayan Humanist Party** (*Partido Humanista Paraguayo*—PHP), whose presidential candidate Roberto FERREIRA won 0.2 percent of the vote; **Kuña Pyrenda Movement** (*Movimiento Kuña Pyrenda*—MKP), whose presidential candidate, Lilian SOTO, won 0.2 percent; **Workers' Party** (*Partido de los Trabajadores*—PT), whose presidential candidate, Eduardo ARCE, won 0.1 percent; **White Party** (*Partido Blanco*), whose presidential candidate, Ricardo ALMADA, won 0.1 percent; **Free Homeland Party** (*Partido Patria Libre*—PPL), whose presidential candidate Atanasio GALEANO, won 0.1 percent of the vote; **Youth Party** (*Partido de la Juventud*); **Independent Constitutionalist Movement** (*Independiente Constitucionalista en Alianza*); and **Civic Awakening Movement** (*Movimiento Depertar Ciudadano*).

LEGISLATURE

The bicameral **National Congress** (*Congreso Nacional*) currently consists of a Senate and a Chamber of Deputies, both elected concurrently with the president for five-year terms.

Senate (*Cámara de Senadores*). The upper house comprises 45 members who are directly elected via party-list proportional balloting in one nationwide constituency, plus former presidents of the republic, who serve as senators for life but without voting power. In the most recent election of April 21, 2013, the Colorado Party won 19 seats; Authentic Radical Liberal Party, 13; Guasú Front, 5; Progressive Democratic Party, 3; Forward Country, 2; National Union of Ethical Citizens, 2; and National Encounter Party, 1.

President: Blás Antonio LLANO.

Chamber of Deputies (*Cámara de Diputados*). The lower house comprises 80 members who are directly elected via party-list proportional balloting in 18 multimember constituencies (the country's 17 departments plus the capital). Following the most recent election of April 21, 2013, election officials listed the following distribution of seats: Colorado Party, 45 seats; Authentic Radical Liberal Party, 26; National Union of Ethical Citizens, 2; Forward Country, 2; National Encounter Party, 2; Beloved Homeland Movement, 1; Guasú Front, 1; and Chaqueña Passion Alliance, 1.

President: Hugo Adalberto VELÁZQUEZ Moreno.

CABINET

[as of September 15, 2016]

President	Horacio Cartes
Vice President	Juan Afara Marques
Ministers	
Agriculture and Livestock	Juan Carlos Baruja
Education	Enrique Riera Escudero
Finance	Santiago Peña
Foreign Relations	Eladio Loizaga
Health and Social Welfare	Antonio Barrios
Industry and Trade	Gustavo Leite
Interior	Francisco de Vargas
Justice	Carla Bacigalupo [f]
Labor, Employment, and Security	Guillermo Sosa
National Defense	Diagnese Martínez
Public Works and Communications	Ramón Jiménez Gaona
Women's Affairs	Ana María Baiardi [f]

[f] = female

INTERGOVERNMENTAL REPRESENTATION

Ambassador to the U.S.: Germán ROJAS.

U.S. Ambassador to Paraguay: Leslie Ann BASSETT.

Permanent Representative to the UN: Federico Alberto GONZÁLEZ.

IGO Memberships (Non-UN): IADB, IOM, Mercosur, OAS, WTO.

For Further Reference:

Grassi, Davide. "Democracy and Social Welfare in Uruguay and Paraguay." *Latin American Politics & Society* 56, no. 1 (Spring 2014): 120–143.

Hetherington, Kregg. *Guerilla Auditors: The Politics of Transparency in Neoliberal Paraguay.* Durham, NC: Duke University Press, 2011.

Lambert, Peter, and Andrew Nickson, eds. *The Paraguay Reader: History, Culture, Politics.* Durham, NC: Duke University Press, 2012.

PERU

Republic of Peru
República del Perú

Political Status: Independent republic proclaimed 1821; military rule imposed on October 3, 1968; constitutional government restored on July 28, 1980; national emergency declared in wake of army-backed "presidential coup" on April 5, 1992; present constitution effective from December 29, 1993.

Area: 496,222 sq. mi. (1,285,216 sq. km).

Population: 31,774,000 (2016E—UN); 30,741,062 (2016E—U.S. Census).

Major Urban Center (2015E—UN): LIMA (metropolitan area, 9,897,000), Arequipa (850,000).

Official Languages: Spanish, Quechua.

Monetary Unit: New Sol (market rate October 1, 2016: 3.38 new sols = $1US).

President: Pedro Pablo KUCZYNSKI (Peruvians for Change); elected in runoff balloting on June 5, 2016, and sworn in on July 28, to succeed Ollanta Moisés HUMALA Tasso (Peruvian Nationalist Party).

First Vice President: Martin VIZCARRA Cornejo (Peruvians for Change); elected on June 5, 2016, and sworn in on July 28 for a term concurrent with that of the president, to succeed Marisol ESPINOZA (Peruvian Nationalist Party).

Second Vice President: Mercedes ARAOZ Fernandez (ind.); elected on June 5, 2016, and sworn in on July 28 for a term concurrent with that of the president, to Omar CHEHADE (Peruvian Nationalist Party), who resigned on January 16, 2012.

President of the Council of Ministers (Prime Minister): Fernando ZAVALA Lombardi (ind.) appointed by the president and sworn in on July 28, 2016, succeeding Juan Federico JIMÉNEZ Mayor (ind.).

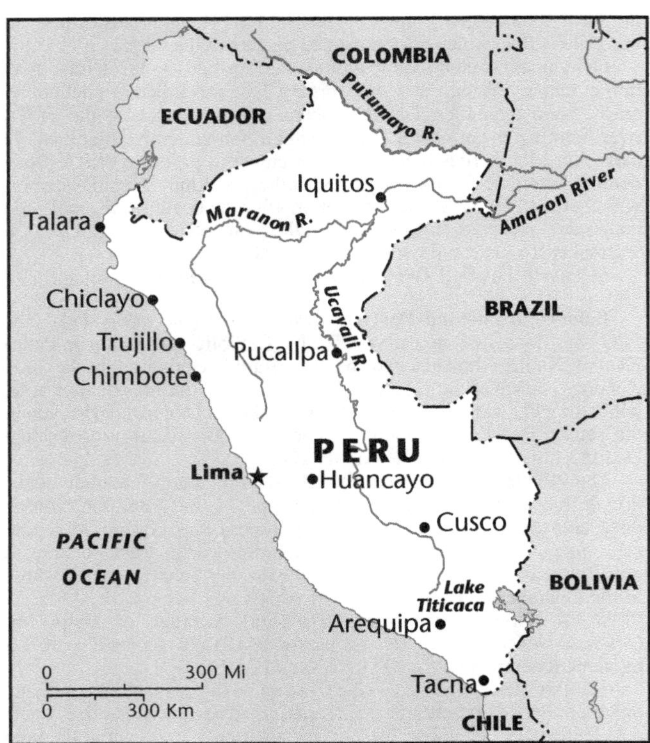

THE COUNTRY

The third-largest country in South America and the second after Chile in the length of its Pacific coastline, Peru comprises three distinct geographical areas: a narrow coastal plain; the high sierra of the Andes; and an inland area of wooded foothills, tropical rain forests, and lowlands that includes the headwaters of the Amazon River. While it contains only 30 percent of the population, the coastal area is the commercial and industrial center. Roman Catholicism is the state religion, and Spanish has traditionally been the official language, although Quechua (recognized as an official language in 1975) and Aymará are commonly spoken by Peruvian Indians. Of Inca descent, Indians constitute 46 percent of the population but remain largely unintegrated with the white (10 percent) and *mestizo* (44 percent) groups. Women constitute approximately 45 percent of the labor force, primarily in agriculture, with smaller groups in domestic service and the informal trading sector; female participation in government is minimal, save at the national level, where women constituted 36 of the 130 legislators (27.7 percent) elected in 2016.

The Peruvian economy depends heavily on the extraction of rich and varied mineral resources, the most important being copper, silver, zinc, lead, and iron. Petroleum, which was discovered in the country's northeastern jungle region in 1971, is being extensively exploited. The agricultural sector employs approximately 40 percent of the labor force and embraces three main types of activity: commercial agriculture, subsistence agriculture, and fishing. The most important legal commodities are coffee, cotton, sugar, fish, and fishmeal, with coca production the major component of the underground economy.

Like most of its neighbors, Peru faced economic adversity in the 1980s, and in August 1985 the International Monetary Fund (IMF) declared the government ineligible for further credit after it had embarked on a somewhat unorthodox recovery program (see Political background, below). Overall, gross domestic product (GDP) rose from 1990 to 2000 at an average of 3.2 percent per year, although widespread poverty showed little improvement. From 2001 to 2008 it marched upward at an average rate of 5.9 percent before the global economic crisis caused expansion to slow to 0.9 percent in 2009. Inflation held within the single-digit range since falling there in 1997, and the unemployment rate averaged 8.7 percent from 1999 to 2009. Peru's GDP growth averaged 7 percent from 2010 through 2012. GDP grew by 6.3 percent in 2013. With a decrease in domestic confidence, alongside deceleration of trade with major partners like China, GDP growth was 6.1 percent in 2014. Inflation was 2.3 percent and unemployment 6.8 percent. GDP expanded by 3.3 percent in 2015, and 3.7 percent in 2016. Inflation that year was 3.1 percent, while GDP per capita was $5,513 and unemployment was 6 percent. The World Bank ranked Peru 50th out of 189 countries in its 2016 annual ease of doing business survey, just behind its southern neighbor Chile (48th).

GOVERNMENT AND POLITICS

Political background. The heartland of the Inca Empire conquered by Francisco Pizarro in the 16th century, Peru held a preeminent place in the Spanish colonial system until its liberation by José de SAN MARTIN and Simón BOLIVAR in 1821–1824. Its subsequent history has been marked by frequent alternations of constitutional civilian and extra constitutional military rule.

The civilian government of José Luis BUSTAMANTE, elected in 1945, was overthrown in 1948 by Gen. Manuel A. ODRIA, who held the presidency until 1956. Manuel PRADO y Ugarteche, elected in 1956 with the backing of the left-of-center American Popular Revolutionary Alliance (APRA), presided over a democratic regime that lasted until 1962, when a new military coup blocked the choice of *Aprista* leader Víctor Raúl HAYA DE LA TORRE as president. An election in 1963 restored constitutional government under Fernando BELAÚNDE Terry of the Popular Action (AP) party. With the support of the now defunct Christian Democratic Party (PDC), Belaúnde, although hampered by an opposition-controlled Congress and an economic crisis at the end of 1967, implemented economic and social reforms. Faced with dwindling political support, his government was ousted in October 1968 in a bloodless coup led by Div. Gen. Juan VELASCO Alvarado, who assumed the presidency, dissolved the Congress, and formed a military-dominated leftist administration committed to a participatory, cooperative-based model that was known after mid-1974 as the Inca Plan. Formally titled the Plan of the Revolutionary Government of the Armed Forces, it aimed at a "Social Proprietorship" (*Propiedad Social*) in which virtually all enterprises—industrial, commercial, and agricultural—would be either state-owned or worker-owned and would be managed collectively.

Amid growing evidence of discontent within the armed forces, Velasco Alvarado was overthrown in August 1975 by Div. Gen. Francisco MORALES BERMÚDEZ Cerruti, who had served as prime minister since the preceding February and initially pledged to continue his predecessor's policies in a "second phase of the revolution" that would make the Inca reforms "irreversible." Despite the existence of well-entrenched rightist sentiment within the military, Div. Gen. Oscar VARGAS Prieto, who had succeeded Morales Bermúdez as prime minister in September 1975, was replaced in January 1976 by a leftist, Gen. Jorge FERNÁNDEZ Maldonado, who was put forward as a figure capable of maintaining the policies of the revolution in the midst of growing economic difficulty. Under the new administration, Peru's National Planning Institute (INP) prepared a replacement for the Inca Plan known as the *Plan Túpac Amaru.* The document was, however, considered too radical by rightist elements. Its principal authors were deported as part of a move to clear the INP of "left-wing infiltrators," and Fernández Maldonado was replaced in July 1976 by the conservative Gen. Guillermo ARBULÚ

Galliani, following the declaration of a state of emergency to cope with rioting occasioned by a series of austerity measures.

Gen. Oscar MOLINA Pallochia was designated to succeed Arbulú Galliani after the latter's retirement in January 1978, while on June 18, in Peru's first nationwide balloting in 15 years, a 100-member Constituent Assembly was elected to draft a new constitution. The assembly completed its work in July 1979, paving the way for presidential and congressional elections in May 1980, at which Belaúnde Terry's AP scored an impressive victory.

By 1985 economic conditions had plummeted, yielding massive inflation, underemployment estimated to encompass 60 percent of the workforce, and negative per capita GDP growth. As a result, the AP was decisively defeated in the election of April 14, Javier ALVA Orlandini running fourth behind APRA's Alan GARCÍA Pérez; Alfonso BARRANTES Lingán, the popular Marxist mayor of Lima; and Luis BEDOYA Reyes, of the recently organized Democratic Convergence (Conde). APRA fell marginally short of a majority in the presidential poll, but second-round balloting was avoided by Barrantes's withdrawal, and García was sworn in on July 28 as, at age 36, the youngest chief executive in Latin America.

In May 1986 the García administration reversed an earlier position and agreed to pay IMF arrears, but after unilaterally rolling over repayment of approximately $940 million in short-term debt, the country was cut off from further access to IMF resources. Concurrently, intense negotiations were launched with the country's more than 270 foreign creditor banks to secure 15-year to 20-year refinancing on the basis of a medium-term economic program intended to reduce the country's dependence on food imports and restructure Peruvian industry, in a manner reminiscent of the Inca Plan, toward basic needs and vertical integration. The audacious effort was buoyed by short-term evidence of recovery. Aided by the upswing, APRA secured an unprecedented 53 percent of the vote at municipal elections in November 1986, winning 18 of 24 departmental capitals.

By mid-1987 the recovery had run its course, with increased inflationary pressure and a visible slackening of the 8.5 percent GDP growth registered in 1986. On June 29 García's second vice president, Luis ALVA Castro, who had served additionally as prime minister, resigned the latter post in the wake of a well-publicized rivalry with the president, leaving economic policy in the hands of the chief executive and a group styled "the bold ones" (*los audaces*), who in late July announced that the state would assume control of the country's financial system. Although bitterly condemned by the affected institutions and their right-wing political supporters, a somewhat modified version of the initial expropriation bill was promulgated in October. The action was followed by a return to triple-digit inflation, and in mid-December the government announced a currency devaluation of 39.4 percent.

During 1988 virtually all efforts by President García to reverse the country's plunge into fiscal chaos proved fruitless. An attempt at midyear to formulate an agreement (*concertación*) between business and labor (and subsequently with rightist and leftist political opponents) elicited scant response, and in September the administration introduced a "shock program" that included a 100 percent currency devaluation, a 100–200 percent increase in food prices, and a 120-day price freeze in the wake of a 150 percent increase in the minimum wage. However, the inflationary surge continued, necessitating a further 50 percent devaluation and the appointment in December of the government's fifth finance minister in less than four years. On several occasions there was evidence of García's desire to abandon the presidency, including indications that he might not be adverse to military intervention—a prospect that the armed forces, with no apparent solution to the nation's problems within their grasp, seemed unwilling to implement.

Events continued on an erratic course during 1989. The leftist alliance virtually collapsed, with the popularity of the fledgling right-wing contender, novelist Mario VARGAS Llosa, far outdistancing that of the leftist alliance's leading aspirant, Barrantes Lingán, by early May. Despite a clear lead in opinion polls for most of the year-long campaign, Vargas Llosa failed to gain a majority in presidential balloting on April 8, 1990, and was defeated in a runoff on June 10 by a late entrant, Alberto Keinya FUJIMORI, of the recently organized Change 90 (*Cambio 90*) movement.

Assuming office on July 28, 1990, Fujimori startled both domestic and foreign observers by a series of initiatives that were at once wide-ranging and controversial. He installed a supporter of Vargas Llosa, Juan Carlos HURTADO Miller, as both prime minister and finance minister, and embarked on an austerity program that was not only at variance with his campaign promises, but more severe than that advocated by his opponent. His cabinet included two active-duty army officers (appointed after the virtually unprecedented cashiering of both the air force and navy commanders), three left-wingers (one of whom resigned in late October), and a number of independents. He instituted corruption proceedings against 700 members of the judiciary, discharged 350 police officers, and publicly disagreed with the United States on antidrug policy (insisting on free-market enticement of farmers away from coca production rather than crop eradication). By mid-November his audacity had reaped visible benefits: the army appeared to be a staunch ally; triple-digit monthly inflation had eased dramatically; a near-empty treasury had been replenished with reserves of about $500 million; payment on portions of the foreign debt had been resumed; and in his attitude toward the church and judiciary, Fujimori, according to a *Washington Post* report, had "taken positions that [struck] a chord in a society long disenchanted with institutional failures."

In April 1991 the Shining Path (*Sendero Luminoso*), a guerrilla organization, launched a new wave of attacks, and Fujimori felt obliged to replace his interior minister, Gen. Adolfo ALVARADO, whose anti-insurgency policies had drawn increasing criticism. Concurrently, the administration announced that it planned a fourfold increase in the number of its rural self-defense patrols (*rondas campesinas*) while moving to establish similar units in urban areas (*rondas urbanes civiles*). In June 1991 Congress granted the president emergency powers to deal with the escalating guerrilla activity as well as drug-related terrorism, and in July Fujimori felt obliged to reverse himself and conclude an antidrug accord with the United States.

On April 5, 1992, after what appeared to have been extensive consultation with the military, Fujimori seized extraconstitutional power in a dramatic self-coup (*autogolpe*). Announcing the formation of an Emergency Government of National Reconstruction, the president dissolved Congress, launched a reorganization of the judicial and penal systems, and declared that he would take "drastic action" against both the *Sendero Luminoso* and drug traffickers.

In response to the coup, a number of senior officials resigned, with Education Minister Oscar DE LA PUENTE Raygada being named prime minister. On November 13 three retired army generals who had served in the military household of the García administration mounted an unsuccessful attempt to overthrow Fujimori and hand over the presidency to First Vice President Máximo SAN ROMÁN Caceras.

With most major opposition groups as nonparticipants, Fujimori supporters captured a majority of seats in balloting on November 22, 1992, for a Democratic Constituent Congress (CCD), which was charged with drafting a new constitution. Earlier, the president had indicated that the CCD would not be superseded by a democratically constituted successor in April 1993 as initially announced, but would remain in office for the duration of his term (that is, to mid-1995). Municipal elections (postponed from October 1992) were, however, held on February 7, 1993, with both the regime and the traditional parties losing ground to locally based independent movements.

Meanwhile, on September 12, 1992, Peru's most celebrated outlaw, *Sendero Luminoso* leader Manuel Abimael GUZMÁN Reinoso, was captured in Lima after a 12-year national search. On October 17 five other members of the organization's Central Committee were also apprehended, offering hope that the antirebel campaign might be drawing to a conclusion.

Approval of the new constitution in December 1993 made it possible for Fujimori to present himself as a candidate for reelection in 1995. Given the success of his economic policies, he appeared to be an odds-on favorite before indications in early 1994 that Javier PÉREZ de Cuéllar might oppose him. Initially, polls showed the former UN secretary general leading Fujimori, but by not announcing his candidacy until late August, Pérez de Cuéllar gradually fell behind by about 15 percentage points.

With an ease that reportedly surprised the incumbent himself, Fujimori won nearly two-thirds of the valid votes in presidential balloting on April 9, 1995. Equally surprising was the showing of his ruling coalition (*Cambio 90–Nueva Mayoría*), which won 67 of 120 congressional seats with 51.5 percent of the vote, humbling the leading "traditional" parties, none of whom surpassed the 5 percent threshold needed to retain legal registration.

Growing concern about Peru's economic future, stemming in part from a proposed privatization of the state oil company, *Petroperú,* led to a decline in the president's popularity to 60 percent by late February 1996. On May 31 *Petroperú* was formally put up for sale, with the president's rating reportedly dropping to less than 56 percent shortly thereafter. Nevertheless, the Congress on August 23 paved the way for Fujimori to stand for a third term by voting, after a heated debate, that his initial incumbency was excluded from an existing two-term limit since it began under the previous constitution.

On December 17, 1996, about 25 members of the Túpac Amaru Revolutionary Movement (MRTA, below) stormed a reception at the Japanese embassy in Lima, taking nearly 600 guests prisoner. In the course of intense negotiations all but 83 were released by the end of the month. However, Fujimori rejected concessions in the form of economic policy changes and the release and safe passage out of the country of imprisoned MRTA members. As a result, the siege continued for 126 days, the longest in Latin American history, ending with an assault on the complex by Peruvian commandos April 22, 1997, during which all of the rebels were killed. In the wake of the crisis Fujimori's popularity, which had crested at 70 percent, plummeted to a low of 27 percent, in part because of a move by the government-controlled Congress to dismiss three members of the Constitutional Tribunal who had voted against the president's bid to seek a third term; by midyear his popularity had declined even further because of unsubstantiated charges that Fujimori had been born in Japan, rather than in Peru, as had long been alleged.

On June 4, 1998, Alberto PANDOLFI Arbulú resigned as prime minister and, somewhat surprisingly, was succeeded by Javier VALLE Riestra, a prominent defender of human rights who had publicly opposed Fujimori's reelection. Punctuated by clashes with military and governmental hard-liners, Valle Riestra's tenure lasted only two months, his predecessor, Pandolfi Arbulú, being reinvested as prime minister on August 21. Pandolfi Arbulú resigned again, on January 4, 1999, and Víctor JOY WAY Rojas, the president of Congress and a trusted Fujimori lieutenant, was named his successor. The cabinet resigned en masse on April 14 after the new labor and social promotion minister charged that corruption was rife in the customs system. Many of the ministers were reappointed the following day, although the one who made the accusations and four of his "technocrat" colleagues did not return. On October 8 Joy Way stepped down as prime minister to stand for reelection to Congress and was succeeded by Alberto BUSTAMANTE Belaúnde.

In late December 1999 the National Election Board accepted Fujimori's argument that he was not bound by the two-term limit because he had assumed office before adoption of the current constitution. In mid-March 2000, despite remarkable polling gains, the leading opposition candidate, Alejandro TOLEDO Manrique, threatened to withdraw from presidential contention because of anticipated fraud. However, he remained in the race and at first-round balloting on April 8 was officially credited with a vote share of 40.3 percent, as contrasted with 49.8 for the incumbent. Unable to secure postponement of the runoff scheduled for May 28, Toledo pulled out, urging his followers to abstain. The appeal was only partially successful: Fujimori won 50.3 percent in the "uncontested" second poll and Toledo 16.2 percent, with 32.5 percent of the ballots nullified.

The concluding months of 2000 yielded a remarkable turnabout in Peruvian politics. On September 16 a videotape surfaced that allegedly showed Fujimori's intelligence chief, Vladimiro MONTESINOS, offering a bribe to an opposition member of Congress. Two days later, Fujimori announced that he would call for a new presidential poll, at which he would not stand as a candidate. Collaterally, defections from Fujimori's Peru 2000 coalition cost him his legislative majority. On September 25 Montesinos flew to Panama, and on October 12 the government ordered that the National Intelligence Service be disbanded. On November 20 Fujimori, who had taken up residence in Japan, tendered his resignation. However, the Congress countered with a declaration that the office was vacant because the president had become "morally unfit." Meanwhile, both the first and second vice presidents had resigned, and on November 22 the recently installed congressional president, Valentín PANIAGUA Corazo, was sworn in as interim chief executive. On November 23 a new cabinet took office with Javier Pérez de Cuéllar as prime minister.

In the first-round presidential poll of April 8, 2001, Toledo again failed to secure a majority but went on to defeat former president Alan García Pérez by a narrow margin (53.1 to 46.9 percent) in a runoff on June 3. Subsequently, he named Roberto DAÑINO to head a cabinet composed, with one exception, of members from his Peru Possible grouping, which had won a plurality of 45 legislative seats in April. On July 12, 2002, with the government ministers divided over privatization policy, Toledo shuffled the cabinet, replacing Dañino with Luis SOLARI de la Fuente. Solari lasted until June 2003, after widespread public disturbances in the wake of a teachers' strike had led Toledo to proclaim a state of emergency. Beatrix MERINO Lucero succeeded him. Merino, a highly popular and seemingly incorruptible tax lawyer, held office for only six months before succumbing to a whisper campaign that involved rumors of influence peddling as well as supposed homosexuality. Carlos FERRERO Costa took her seat on December 15. Ferrero, after having served as president of Congress, became Toledo's fourth prime minister in 30 months. Ferrero resigned on August 11, 2005, in the wake of ordinances by two regional governors legalizing coca cultivation, and was succeeded by Economy Minister Pedro Pablo KUCZYNSKI.

The Toledo presidency was characterized by relative social peace and higher economic growth rates than Peru had seen since the 1970s. The president, however, consistently rated among Latin America's least popular; Toledo spent many of his years in office with an approval rating at or below 20 percent. The president's inner circle was hit by corruption allegations, while poll respondents generally regarded Toledo as lacking a work ethic and being unaware of voters' priorities. Leading the list of these concerns were corruption, steadily rising crime rates, and frustration with the unequal distribution of wealth generated by recent economic growth.

Discontent was plainly visible in the 2006 presidential campaign. The candidate who most closely identified herself with Toledo's policies, conservative one-time front-runner Lourdes FLORES Nano, finished third in first-round balloting on April 9. The first-round winner was Ollanta HUMALA, an intensely nationalistic retired army officer, who led the field with 30.6 percent of the vote. Former president García, leading a new party, the Peruvian Aprista Party (*Partido Aprista Peruano*—PAP), defeated Humala 44.5 to 55.4 percent in a runoff on June 4. Humala's Union for Peru (UPP) won a plurality (45 of 120) of legislative seats.

Five months later, on November 19, 2006, the PAP was trounced in municipal and regional elections, winning only 2 (down from 12) of the country's 25 regional governments. PAP also failed to unseat Lima Mayor Luis CASTAÑEDO Lossio of the National Unity (*Unidad Nacional*—UN) coalition. The only consolation PAP could take from the voting was that no other party fared better, including Humala's UPP/Peru Nationalist Party (PNP), which failed to win a single regional presidency. "Independent" candidates, many of them powerful local political bosses, won 20 of the regional presidencies, along with 112 of 195 provinces.

The return of Alan García to the Peruvian presidency in 2006 was surprising in view of the disastrous outcome of his previous incumbency. Equally surprising was the emergence of Ollanta Humala as his principal rival. Humala, who sought to emulate the success of Evo Morales, his ethnically based Bolivian counterpart, had difficulty in distancing himself from the shadow of Hugo Chávez, while García's victory would not have been possible without the support of the third-ranked contender, Lourdes Flores. Overall, García won only 9 departments, compared to his opponent's share of 15, although most of the latter were in the less densely populated, impoverished, central and southern highlands, where Humala had hoped to launch his "great transformation."

Significantly, Keiko Fujimori, the daughter of the former president, won election to Congress in 2006, winning more votes than any other candidate. Even as the ex-president neared an extradition decision in Santiago, García's Aprista bloc entered into what some regarded to be an unofficial alliance with pro-Fujimori political movements. Fujimori's Alliance for the Future Party was the only one to join in García's failed attempt, in late 2006 and early 2007, to institute the death penalty in terrorism cases. President García's dependence on the pro-Fujimori bloc to advance his legislative agenda opened him to charges of insufficiently supporting Fujimori's prosecution for human rights crimes. Opposition politicians speculated in July that García had granted Fujimori a "golden jail" in exchange for his legislative bloc's support for PAP legislator Javier VELÁSQUEZ Quesquen's candidacy for president of the Congress.

In April 2007 García chose a hard-line response to disputes with coca farmers in the highlands, who had organized strikes and blockades to protest the forcible eradication of their crops. With much of the chamber abstaining on April 26, 2007, the Congress gave the president the authority to rule by decree on issues relating to drug trafficking, terrorism, and organized crime. Human rights defenders assailed the decrees, which included a prohibition on local officials participating in strikes and an automatic pardon for security personnel who injure or kill strikers while "fulfilling their duty."

On August 15, 2007, an 8.0 magnitude earthquake devastated a region in southern Peru centered on the city of Pisco, killing more than 500 people. President García received high marks for his personal, highly visible response to the disaster, though many voiced discontent at the confused, improvised nature of the rescue and rebuilding efforts he led.

The Fujimori trial dominated the country's political discourse during 2008. In December 2007, Fujimori was sentenced to six years in prison for illegally ordering the search and seizure of his shadowy former intelligence chief, Vladimiro Montesinos. He then went on to face human rights charges, beginning with two massacres committed by a government death squad in the early 1990s.

As the findings of a groundbreaking 2003 truth commission report continued to reverberate, human rights were a major topic of debate in 2007 and 2008. Human rights defenders argued that the PAP and pro-Fujimori political blocs wished to remove Peru from the Inter-American Human Rights Court, a body of the Organization of American States (OAS) that, on two occasions, has required the Peruvian government to pay damages to the relatives of massacred *Sendero Luminoso* guerrillas and sympathizers. In May 2008 Vice President Luis GIAMPETRI Rojas called publicly for Peru's withdrawal from the court. The PAP and pro-Fujimori blocs also collaborated in late 2006 on controversial legislation that placed strict regulations on the financing and activities of nongovernmental organizations (NGOs). In May 2008, after APRODEH, one of Peru's main human rights groups, recommended that the European Union (EU) remove the nearly defunct MRTA guerrillas from its list of international terrorist groups, President García called APRODEH "traitors to the country" and ordered an investigation of its financing. That month, media reports alleged that the government had set up an intelligence group *Comando Canela* to infiltrate nongovernmental human rights defender groups and others engaged in social protest.

During his first year in office, García's approval ratings consistently hovered around 50 percent, but by July 2008, they had fallen to 26 percent. Economic growth and reduced poverty levels helped the president, though good economic news was far scarcer in the impoverished regions where Humala was popular. Inflation, which was expected to reach 7 percent in 2008, was an increasing concern as higher food and fuel prices disproportionately impacted the poor. Public security became a principal complaint as citizen concerns increased about worsening crime, particularly by drug-related organizations, prompting the García government to give the armed forces a greater internal crime-fighting role. Meanwhile, remnants of *Sendero Luminoso* and other narco-criminal gangs were responsible for sporadic acts of violence in the countryside, including ambushes that killed police and officials involved in coca leaf regulation in December 2006 and April 2007 as well as an attack on a rural police station in November 2007. About 42 Peruvian antinarcotics police or coca eradicators were killed from January 2007 to July 2009.

On May 13, 2008, President García created a new cabinet-level environment ministry and named Antonio BRACK Egg to head it.

In October a scandal emerged from the revelation of audiotapes documenting a top state oil-licensing official and a PAP politician discussing plans to steer contracts to a Norwegian petroleum company in exchange for bribes. On October 9 the entire cabinet tendered its resignation over the matter. García's new prime minister, leftist politician Yehude SIMON Munaro of the Peruvian Humanist Movement Party (*Partido Movimiento Humanista Peruano*—PMHP), assembled a new cabinet on October 14, keeping ten of the ministers and replacing six.

On April 7, 2009, Peru's Supreme Court convicted 70-year-old former president Alberto Fujimori and sentenced him to 25 years in prison for his role in two massacres carried out by the Grupo Colina death squad, among other abuses. On May 16, 2009, President García declared a 30-day state of emergency in several Amazon-basin provinces, sending the armed forces to help the police deal with a growing wave of indigenous groups' protests, which had begun a month earlier and had grown to include about 30,000 people blockading roads, rivers, and pipelines. The protesters were opposing additional decrees, among a number that President García had issued in 2007, shortly before U.S. ratification of the countries' free trade agreement, to ease foreign investment in sectors such as energy, mining, and forestry. Violence erupted in Bagua, Amazonas, on June 5, as clashes between indigenous protesters and police claimed at least 33 lives, including 24 police officers. Indigenous leaders claimed that their death toll was higher and that police had fired on them from helicopters. Congress sought a censure vote on June 30 against Prime Minister Simon and Interior Minister Mercedes CABANILLAS for their handling of the matter; the vote failed only because 11 pro-Humala legislators were under suspension for their earlier role in a raucous protest in the Congress in support of the indigenous cause. While they survived the censure vote, Simon, Cabanillas, and several other cabinet ministers were drummed out less than two weeks later amid a cabinet shake-up that saw Simon replaced with Congressional President Velásquez of the PAP, and Cabanillas replaced with independent politician Octavio SALAZAR. Salazar became the García government's fourth interior minister in a 12-month period. Velásquez retained nine ministers and replaced seven.

In September 2009 the government created a commission to investigate events surrounding May's indigenous uprising in Bagua with the aim of creating a consensual plan of development for the region and reconciling the indigenous population with the government. On September 30 seven and a half years were added on to former president Alberto Fujimori's prison sentence when he was found guilty of wire-tapping the phones of journalists, businesspeople, and politicians; bribing 12 legislators to get them to join his Peru 2000 alliance; and bribing members of the news media for favorable coverage.

The commission released its report in January 2010, stating that the government had misjudged animosity to the opening of the region to private investment. Indigenous rights umbrella group Interethnic Association for the Development of the Peruvian Rainforest (*Asociación Interétnica de Desarrollo de la Selva Peruana*—AIDESEP), which was one of the organizers of the protests and whose members sat on the commission, said the report had failed to investigate the incident deeply enough. In February the government, under pressure from AIDESEP, indefinitely suspended a company's exploratory mining activities in the Amazon region to avert more confrontation. In May Congress approved a law that required the government to consult indigenous communities on state business that affects their lands and traditions. The same month, authorities arrested and charged Alberto PIZANGO Chota, the leader of AIDESEP, for fomenting the June 2009 violence between indigenous protestors and authorities.

Two drug reports released in 2010 criticized Peru's efforts to control cocaine coming out of the country, which in 2009 was the world's second-largest producer of coca and its drug derivative. U.S. government and UN analyses found that Peru had seized fewer drugs in 2009 than in 2008, cocaine-manufacturing potential had increased, and coca acreage had expanded by 45 percent over the decade.

The specter of the deadly Bagua protests reappeared in April 2010, when two separate groups blocked the Pan-American Highway in southern Peru in protest to changes in mining laws and a proposed copper mine. Thousands of informal miners in Arequipa protested new mining exclusion zones and a prohibition on unregulated gold panning and river dredging. Five protestors were killed in clashes with police. Another protest occurred in the same department over a major copper mining project. Both protests ended after the government agreed to include local citizens in decisions concerning the region.

As García's term neared its end in the April 2011 presidential and congressional elections, his approval ratings dropped to 11 percent in some districts—the lowest in his cohort of South American leaders. Though his work saving and shoring up the Peruvian economy brought plaudits from world leaders and international organizations, at home he dealt with anger over the handling of indigenous and worker protests that led to killings in the street, natural gas supply insecurity that led to Lima running out of liquefied petroleum gas in July 2010, increasing *Sendero* attacks against the military, and more cocaine production under his watch that brought pressure from foreign governments and the UN (see Current events, below).

The president of the council of ministers Velásquez resigned on September 13, 2010. Minister of Education José Antonio CHANG Escobedo was named the new president of a reshuffled council on September 14. Chang resigned on March 18, 2011, and was replaced by Justice Minister Rosario FERNÁNDEZ Figueroa the following day.

Prior to the national elections in April 2011, five main electoral coalitions emerged. Humala's PNP joined with four other left-wing parties to create the Peru Wins Alliance (*Alianza Gana Perú*). Keiko FUJIMORI, daughter of the former president, formed a center-right coalition, Force 2011 (*Fuerza 2011*), which included the National Renewal (*Renovación Nacional—Renovación*). The other electoral alliances included the National Solidarity Alliance (*Alianza Solidaridad Nacional*), led by former Lima mayor Luís CASTAÑADA Lossio; Alliance for the Great Change (*Alianza por el Gran Cambio*), under former prime minister Kuczynski; and the centrist Peru Possible (*Perú Posible*), which supported the presidential candidacy of former president Toledo.

In legislative balloting on April 10, 2011, the Peru Wins Alliance won a plurality with 47 seats. After no candidate received more than half the total votes in the concurrent presidential balloting on April 10, a runoff election was held on June 5 between the two front-runners, Humala and Keiko Fujimori. In one of the most highly polarized and contested elections in Peruvian history, Humala won with 51.5 percent of the vote to Fujimori's 48.5 percent. Humala was sworn in on July 28 for a five-year term. He appointed political independent Salomón LERNER Ghitis as prime minister of a PNP-dominated cabinet, which was sworn in on July 28.

The first year of Humala's presidency was fraught with problems. Lerner unexpectedly resigned in December 2011 over his mishandling of a mining dispute. Interior Minister Oscar VALDÉS took the post, only to step down in July 2012, prompting a cabinet reshuffle in which 10 out of 19 ministers were replaced, and Juan JIMÉNEZ Mayor, previously minister of justice, became prime minister. Jiménez resigned on October 30, 2013, after making controversial comments likening crime to mere "hysteria." Humala then appointed César VILLANEUVA, who served until February 24, 2014, when he left office after butting heads with Finance Minister Luis Miguel CASTILLA over plans to raise the minimum wage. René CORNEJO then assumed office for a term cut short by a scandal involving a staffer trying to discredit an opposition politician. On July 22 Ana del Rosario JARA Velásquez, a staunch Humala supporter, became prime minister. The post of second vice president remained vacant following Omar CHEHADE resigned in January 2012.

The cabinet was extensively reshuffled on February 24, 2015, in the wake of a scandal involving domestic spying by the nation's intelligence service (see Current issues, below). On March 30 Congress voted to censure Prime Minister Jara over the espionage scandal. Jara and the government resigned on April 2, and she was replaced by Pedro CATERIANO (PNP).

In national elections on April 10, 2016, Popular Force won a clear majority in Congress with 73 seats. In the concurrent presidential polling, Keiko Fujimori was first with 39.9 percent of the vote and former prime minister Kuczynski was second with 21.1 percent. The two advanced to runoff balloting on June 5. Kuczynski won with 50.1 percent of the vote to Fujimori's 49.9 percent. Kuczynski named Fernando ZAVALA Lombardi (independent) as prime minister on July 10. Zavala and his cabinet were sworn in on July 28.

Constitution and government. On December 29, 1993, the "Fujimori constitution," which had been approved by a slim 52.2 percent in an October 31 referendum, came into effect. The principal departures from its 1979 predecessor were supersession of the former bicameral legislature by a unicameral body and the lifting of a ban on presidential reelection. (Although the new basic law provided for only one five-year renewal, it was subsequently argued that Fujimori's incumbency could extend to 2005, as his previous election was under the old constitution.) In addition, the president's authority was significantly enhanced, including the redesignation of control over military appointments as an executive rather than a legislative prerogative. The death penalty was restored for convicted terrorists, although assumed not to be applicable to persons currently incarcerated, while a number of social amenities were abolished, including free university education and a right to job security.

In April 2003 Congress overwhelmingly endorsed restoration of the country's two-chamber legislature, composed of a 150-member lower house and a 50-member Senate. It was argued that the lower chamber would cater to the interests of the various departments and the upper would focus on issues of national concern. The action was never implemented; in 2005 Toledo tried to restore the Senate but lacked the necessary two-thirds majority. In mid-2007 the legislature's constitutional committee approved a proposal to leave the lower house at 120 members and add a 50-member Senate. This proposal failed to pass.

The country's judicial system is headed by a Supreme Court and includes 18 district courts in addition to a nine-member Constitutional Court and a National Council for the judiciary. In March 1987 President García promulgated legislation that divided the country's 25 departments into 12 regions, each with an assembly of provincial mayors, popularly elected representatives, and delegates of various institutions.

In September 2009 the Congress approved a bill to increase the number of seats in the legislature from 120 to 130, effective after the next election in 2011. The constitutional change was approved by a two-thirds majority of legislators, meaning a referendum on the matter was unnecessary. The reform was brought forward to decrease the high number of citizens being represented by each representative.

The press is primarily privately owned. There are reports of intimidation against journalists, including violence against journalists reporting on the mining protests in the first half of 2012. In its 2016 annual index on press freedom, Reporters Without Borders ranked Peru 84th out of 180 countries, a significant improvement from 2014 when the country was 104th.

Foreign relations. Peruvian foreign policy stresses protection of its sovereignty and its natural resources. After the 1968 coup the military government expanded contacts with Communist countries, including the Soviet Union, the People's Republic of China, and Cuba. Its relations with neighboring states, though troubled at times by frequent regime changes, are generally equable, apart from a traditional suspicion of Chile and a long-standing border dispute with Ecuador that yielded overt conflict in January–February 1981 and a renewed flare-up in late January 1995 when its neighbor charged Peru with "launching a massive offensive." Peru claimed that Argentina illegally sold arms to Ecuador in the second dispute, damaging relations between the two for decades. The more recent fighting gave way to a cease-fire on February 13, after a Peruvian announcement that it had recaptured the last Ecuadorian outpost on its territory, and to another on March 1, following a brief, but intense, resumption of fighting. On July 26 the two countries agreed to demilitarize more than 200 square miles of the disputed territory, while President Fujimori attended a Rio Group (*Grupo de Rio*) summit in Quito, Ecuador, in September, during which he surprised observers by extending an unofficial invitation to Ecuadorian President Sixto Durán-Ballén to visit Peru.

A seemingly more definitive event was an agreement reached in Rio de Janeiro on January 19, 1998, on a timetable for a peace treaty. The accord called for the establishment of four commissions dealing with major aspects of the controversy, including one centering on the thorniest issue: border demarcation. The lengthy dispute was formally settled with a "global and definitive" accord signed by Fujimori and his Ecuadorian counterpart in Brasília on October 26, 1998. While the disputed territory was awarded to Peru, control (but not sovereignty) of the principal town of Tiwintza, in addition to a corridor from the border, was assigned to Ecuador, which was also granted free navigation along the Amazon and the right to establish two port facilities within Peruvian territory. Provision was also made for linkup between the two countries' electrical grids and oil pipelines. On June 1, 2007, President García met Ecuadorian president Rafael Correa in the northern Peruvian town of Tumbes. García said that Peru had "no territorial or maritime claim to make with Ecuador," and Correa described relations as the "best... in the history of the two countries." The two countries' foreign and defense ministers met in February 2008, signing accords establishing a binational confidence-building and security commission. In November 2012 Ecuador and Peru signed a maritime border treaty addressing their claims to the Gulf of Guayaquil, paving the way for bilateral exploration of hydrocarbon deposits.

Long-standing differences with Chile were largely resolved in November 1999 during a state visit by Fujimori to Santiago (the first by a Peruvian leader since the war of the Pacific in 1879–1883). However, a new flare-up occurred in early 2004 with the killing by Chilean marines of a Peruvian national after Chile had heightened border security against illegal immigrants seeking Chilean employment. Lima became frustrated in 2005 by its inability to secure the extradition of former president Fujimori, who had been arrested in Chile in November 2005 after his return from Japan to seek the Peruvian presidency. Under house arrest, Fujimori's fate was determined by Chile's Supreme Court, which heard his case in August 2007 and extradited him to Peru on September 22, based on 7 of the original 13 charges. Relations chilled further in November 2005, when the Peruvian Congress passed a bill claiming sovereignty over 15,000 square miles of Pacific waters controlled by Chile.

Peru's relations with Venezuela have been troubled since the 2006 presidential campaign, when Venezuelan president Hugo Chávez was widely accused of interference in internal affairs with his vocal endorsements of Humala. Opponents alleged that Humala's campaign was receiving financial support from Caracas, which he denied. The two countries recalled their ambassadors in April 2006, only to restore them in March 2007. Peruvian sensitivity to perceived Venezuelan meddling has remained high, however. Strong concerns have been raised about health care programs and the opening of offices of the Venezuelan-supported ALBA (Bolivarian Alternative for Latin America) movement in several regions of Peru. An investigative commission established in 2008 to investigate the financing of so-called "ALBA houses" released a strongly worded report in March 2009 recommending that the 148 existing "ALBA houses" be closed, characterizing them as a tool of foreign political infiltration. However, the step was not taken, because of support for the program in Peru's provinces and to the political fallout of June indigenous protests that ended in violence.

Relations with neighboring Bolivia worsened in 2008, as Presidents Alán García and Evo Morales—a close ally of Venezuela's Chávez—traded periodic criticisms and insults. Though the substance tended to be disagreements over free trade and Venezuelan influence, the bickering reached its nadir in June, when Morales said García was "very fat and not very anti-imperialist." Peru briefly recalled its ambassador from Bolivia.

Relations with the United States had been strained by recurrent controversies over the expropriation of U.S. businesses, the seizure of U.S. fishing boats accused of violating Peru's territorial waters, and the degree of U.S. involvement in combating the narcotics trade. In April 2001 a Peruvian jet downed a civilian aircraft carrying U.S. missionaries, killing a woman and her infant daughter, after a CIA-contracted surveillance plane had mistakenly identified it as engaged in drug smuggling. International attention had been drawn to the case of a U.S. journalist, Lori Berenson, who was convicted in 1996 of aiding the MRTA guerrillas. Initially sentenced to prison by a secret military court, Berenson was reconvicted by a civilian court in June 2001, with an appeal rejected by the Supreme Court in February 2002. Relations with the United States were jarred in August 2003 when the U.S. Export-Import Bank refused, on environmental grounds, to issue loan guarantees for a controversial trans-Amazon natural gas pipeline; however, in September the Inter-American Development Bank, with the U.S. representative abstaining, approved a loan package for the project, which was then 70 percent completed.

Peru remains the world's second-largest producer, after Colombia, of coca, the plant used to make cocaine. Police estimate that a large number of small narcotrafficking organizations, most with ties to Mexican, Colombian, and Brazilian cartels, operate in Peru. Though U.S. and UN measurements have found coca cultivation in Peru to have increased by about one-third since 1999, Washington has generally praised Lima's commitment to eradication and interdiction. In May 2007, in part to placate the U.S. government, President García fired his agriculture minister, Juan José SALAZAR, who had taken a conciliatory attitude toward the country's organized coca growers' organizations who wished to see assistance in marketing the leaf for legal purposes.

President García courted the favor of the U.S. government. He traveled to the United States on several occasions to urge the Democratic Party leadership in the U.S. Congress to ratify a free trade agreement (FTA) that President George W. Bush and the Toledo government signed in April 2006. The agreement was ratified in December 2007, after passing the House by a 285–132 vote and the Senate by a 77–18 vote.

García's government sought tighter trade ties with Brazil, with a May 2008 agreement for petrochemical investments and a September 2008 offer from García to set up "a sort of bilateral free trade agreement." Peru's trade push continued with the November 2008 hosting, in Lima, of the fifteenth meeting of the 21-member Asia-Pacific Economic Forum (APEC). During his stay in Lima, Chinese president Hu Jintao signed ten accords for new investment in Peru. An FTA between the two was signed in Beijing in April 2009 and went into effect in March 2010.

Peru's relations with Venezuela and Bolivia remained poor in 2009. Manuel Rosales, President Hugo Chávez's main opponent in Venezuela's 2006 presidential elections, took up residence in Lima in April 2009. Peru gave asylum in May 2009 to a top minister of the Bolivian Gonzalo Sánchez de Lozada government in power from 2002 until 2003. A month later, after Bolivian president Evo Morales expressed solidarity with indigenous protesters clashing with Peruvian police and accused the government of "genocide," the García government recalled its ambassador from La Paz.

Relations with Chile reached a new low in November 2009 after the arrest by Peruvian authorities of a Peruvian air-force officer whom the government accused of spying for Chile. A Peruvian court put out an arrest order for two Chilean military officers for paying the Peruvian officer to reveal sensitive information. Peruvian officials reprimanded Chile, which denied the spying charge. Also in November, President García sent envoys to neighboring countries to boost his proposal that the 12 member nations of the Union of South American Nations (Unasur) cut military spending by 3 percent and arms purchases by 15 percent and create a regional peacekeeping force. The savings would be used to cut poverty and fight global warming. The president came under criticism on the seeming incongruence between his arms de-escalation and his 2010 budget, which included a 27 percent increase in defense spending over 2009.

In March 2010 Peru received Argentine president Cristina Fernández Kirchner on the first official state visit by that country's chief executive in 16 years. The two presidents signed a number of bilateral trade agreements. Meanwhile, Brazil and Peru drew closer in June 2010 when the two countries' presidents signed bilateral cooperation agreements covering science and technology, border integration, agricultural production, and water resources.

In June 2012 Peru and Colombia signed a FTA with the EU, which was ratified by the European Parliament in December and will gradually eliminate tariffs on products and services.

On January 27, 2014, the International Court of Justice (ICJ) delivered its decision on the maritime border dispute between Chile and Peru, which had been presented before the court in 2009 and 2010. The ICJ ruling awarded about 8,000 of the 14,700 disputed square miles to Peru. Neither party can appeal the decision.

On February 21, 2015, Peru's ambassador to Chile was recalled in the wake of espionage allegations involving two Peruvian naval non-commissioned officers who had been charged with spying for Chile.

Peru and China announced in November 2016 that the two countries would upgrade and expand their existing free trade agreement.

Current issues. The Peru Wins Alliance won the legislative balloting on April 10, 2011, but failed to gain an absolute majority in the Congress. Discussions to form a governing coalition with former president Toledo's Peru Possible Alliance fell apart in July. However, a subsequent Peru Wins Alliance government included some members of Peru Possible. Ten candidates contested the concurrent presidential balloting on April 10. No candidate won an absolute majority, and Humala (Peru Wins) and Keiko Fujimori (Force 2011) advanced to runoff balloting on June 5. Humala narrowly won the polling and was sworn in on July 28. He appointed a cabinet dominated by moderates in an effort to assuage fears that he would implement a radical, antimarket economic and social agenda that would scare off foreign investment.

A wave of resignations in late 2011 brought turnover within the government. On December 5 Second Vice President Omar CHEHADE's seat in the Congress was suspended by a vote of the legislature. Facing corruption accusations, Chehade refused to resign the vice presidency despite increasing pressure by the legislature and calls by the president to leave office. The crisis highlighted the inability of the president to remove either of the vice presidents. Five days later, Prime Minister Salomón Lerner Ghitis resigned over the government's mishandling of a mining dispute. Humala appointed Minister of the Interior Oscar Valdés in his place and reshuffled the cabinet at that time. Chehade finally caved to pressure the following month, handing in his resignation from the vice presidency on January 17, 2012, but he retained his seat in Congress. As of September 2013, the second vice presidency remains vacant.

In February the Peruvian government confirmed the capture of Florindo Flores, known as "Comrade Artemio," the last member of the Shining Path's central committee who had not yet been killed or imprisoned. Two months later, Humala declared the Shining Path "defeated" upon the capture of Freddy Arenas, known as Braulio, the leader in the Alto Huallaga Valley. The blow proved not to be fatal to the remnants of the organization, however. Later that month, Shining Path rebels captured several gas workers in Cusco (reports varied from 30 to 36 captives). In response, the government deployed 1,500 troops, the largest military action against the Shining Path since the 1990s. Between April and May the group killed nine Peruvian police officers. Estimated to be about 500 people strong, the group was nowhere near as large as it was at its peak; however, the resurgence of activity was surprising to many who considered it near extinction. Meanwhile, the Maoist group's political arm, Movadef, also began to reemerge, with reports that rallies were held in poor neighborhoods and on university campuses in September. The government blocked the group from registering as a political party in an effort to prevent its growth.

In May 2012 Humala declared a state of emergency after eight days of protests over Xstrata's proposed expansion of the Tintaya copper mine in Cusco. Two people were killed and at least 50, including 30 police officers, were injured in the clash. Shortly after the 30-day state of emergency in Cusco ended in June, conflict erupted over the $4.8 billion Conga gold mine in Cajamarca, with locals protesting that the mine would contaminate the water. On July 3 the government declared a state of emergency in the region, the second use of the measure in just five weeks. Five civilians were killed as the protests escalated.

Following the government's crackdown on the demonstrations, several prominent members of Congress called for Prime Minister Valdés' resignation, arguing that he should have encouraged mediation rather than force. On July 23 Valdés stepped down as part of the second cabinet reshuffle in the first year of Humala's presidency, and Juan Jiménez was appointed in his place.

In October 2012 Alberto Fujimori, currently serving a 25-year sentence for corruption and human rights violations, filed a petition for amnesty on humanitarian grounds because of poor health. Humala rejected the request in June 2013, in line with a recommendation by a presidential commission, noting that the illness is not terminal. The decision led to greater political tension with the main opposition party Fuerza Popular (formerly Fuerza 2011), led by Keiko FUJIMORI.

Humala announced in January 2013 the establishment of a new body to combat high-level political corruption, comprising the president of national congress, cabinet heads, and judicial leaders.

In July 2013 Shining Path founder Florindo FLORES was sentenced to life in prison. The following month, three rebels were killed by security forces. On July 17 Congress appointed an ombudsman, six members to the Constitutional Court, and three new Central Reserve Bank directors, all candidates selected by the leading congressional parties. The vote stirred controversy, attracting criticism for threatening the political independence of the institutions. Several thousand marched in protest, and on July 24 Congress rescinded the appointments.

Prime Minister Jiménez resigned on October 29, 2013, following controversial comments he made about crime and citizen safety and was succeeded by César Villanueva. Villanueva's term came to an abrupt end in February 2014 when he and Finance Minister Luis Miguel Castilla butted heads over plans to raise the minimum wage. Both resigned, but President Humala reappointed Castillo days later, when René Cornejo was installed as prime minister. It took the new cabinet three attempts to find the support in Congress to pass the necessary confidence vote in March. A mass arrest of 28 people with ties to *Sendero Luminoso* marked a victory for the government in April 2014. Cornejo's term as prime minister was cut short in July when he resigned over allegations that his staff tried to orchestrate a smear campaign. Ana Jara became Humala's third prime minister in less than a year.

On January 8, 2015, former president Fujimori was sentenced to eight years in prison and fined $1 million for corruption. Revelations emerged in January that the nation's national intelligence service had illegally spied on Humala's political opponents. On February 9 Humala announced that the intelligence service was to undergo wide-ranging reforms over a 180-day period while the agency's day-to-day operations would be partially suspended. Humala then reshuffled the cabinet in an effort to restore public confidence in his government. However, in the midst of the espionage scandal, reports emerged that his wife was under investigation for money laundering and corruption after prosecutors reopened a case from 2009.

Humala declared a 45-day state of emergency in the Callao region in response to growing crime and lawlessness. More than 2,000 police officers were deployed to the province, and 300 suspected gang members and criminals were arrested.

POLITICAL PARTIES AND GROUPS

Most of the political parties active before the 1968 coup were of comparatively recent vintage, the principal exception being the Peruvian affiliate of APRA (PAP, below), which was alternately outlawed and legalized beginning in the early 1930s. While failing to capture the presidency until 1985, it contributed to the success of other candidates and was the nucleus of a powerful opposition coalition that controlled both houses of Congress during Belaúnde's 1963–1968 presidency.

During the decade after 1968, the status of the parties fluctuated, many being permitted a semilegal existence while denied an opportunity to engage in electoral activity. Most, except those of the extreme left, were allowed to register before the Constituent Assembly election of June 1978, with further relaxation occurring before the presidential and legislative balloting of May 1980, in which 20 groups participated. By contrast, only 9 groups presented candidates in 1985, with the PAP, the IU, the Democratic Convergence, and the AP collectively capturing 96.9 percent of the valid votes.

Virtually all of the major opposition parties either boycotted or failed to qualify for the Democratic Constituent Congress election of November 22, 1992, at which the regime-supportive C-90–NM won a majority of seats, with the remainder scattered among 8 other parties. Subsequent elections were contested by an average of more than 20 parties or party coalitions.

Presidential Party:

Peruvians for Change (*Peruanos Por el Kambio*—PPK). The center-right PPK was formed in October 2014 to support the presidential campaign of former prime minister Pedro Pablo Kuczynski. The grouping was a revival of the **Alliance for the Great Change** (*Alianza Por El Gran Cambio*), which had been established in 2010 to support Kuczynski. Kuczynski placed fourth in that year's balloting, while the alliance secured 12 seats. Following divisions within the alliance over the election of officers for the Constitutional Court, five Congress members defected, marking the departure of the **National Restoration** (*Restauracion Nacional*—RN) and the **Humanist Party** (*Partido Humanista*). Left with seven seats, the alliance regrouped under the banner **PPC–APP,** led by Alberto Beingolea. The PPC–APP continued to support the Peru Wins Alliance and helped the government survive a March 2014 confidence vote.

In the April 2016 national elections, the PPK won 18 seats with 16.5 percent of the vote. Kuczynski won runoff balloting in June to become president.

Leaders: Pedro Pablo KUCZYNSKI (President of the Republic), Gilbert VIOLETA (Party President).

Regional Union (*Unión Regional*). The Regional Union parliamentary bloc formed in July 2013 with three defectors from the Alliance for the Great Change and five from Peru Possible. The group often takes an opposition stance. In early August 2014 two key Regional Union members reportedly defected and joined the Peru Wins Alliance.

Leader: Cecilia TAIT.

Other Legislative Parties:

Broad Front (*Frente Amplio*—FA). Also known as the **Broad Front for Justice, Life and Liberty** (*El Frente Amplio por Justicia, Vida y Libertad*—FA), the FA was established in June 2013. Veronika MENDOZA was elected as the Front's presidential candidate in 2016. She was third with 18.7 percent of the vote in the April balloting, while the party was second in the congressional elections with 20 seats, and 13.9 percent of the vote.

Leader: Veronika MENDOZA (2016 presidential candidate).

Alliance for the Progress of Peru (*Alianza para el Progreso del Perú*). The center-right alliance was created in 2015 to contest the April 2016 national elections by the Alliance for Progress (*Alianza para el Progreso*—APP), We Are Peru (*Somos Perú*), and National Restoration (*Restauracion Nacional*—RN). The grouping won 9.2 percent of the vote and nine seats in the 2016 congressional elections. Party leader César ACUÑA Peralta was disqualified from the 2016 presidential election.

Leader: César ACUÑA Peralta.

Alliance for Progress (*Alianza para el Progreso*—APP). Established in 2001 by César Acuña Peralta, the APP joined the Alliance for Great Change in 2010.

Leader: César ACUÑA Peralta.

We Are Peru (*Somos Perú*). *Somos Perú* is an outgrowth of the *Somos Lima* movement, organized by former independent Alberto Andrade Carmona after his capture of the Lima mayorship in November 1995. The party's supporters include some former members of the defunct right-wing **Solidarity and Democracy** (*Solidaridad y Democracia*—Sode), which had been led by Javier SILVA Ruete. In early 1999 Andrade led in public opinion polls for the 2000 presidential election but dropped to a distant third in the balloting of April 2000. For the 2001 presidential poll it joined with the CD in supporting the candidacy of Jorge SANTISTEVAN de Noriega. In March 2013 Fernando Andrade, brother of the late party founder, was elected party president, after Alberto Andrade's wife was kept off the ballot by a controversial technicality.

Leaders: Fernando ANDRADE (Party President), Alberto ANDRADE Carmona (2000 presidential candidate).

National Restoration (*Restauracion Nacional*—RN). The RN is a small formation led by evangelicals. It won two legislative seats in 2006, finishing seventh with 4 percent of the votes cast. After a poor showing in the 2006 local elections—in which most of the party's few winning candidates were not from an evangelical background—the party expelled its leader Humberto Lay Sun in early 2007. Later that year, however, Lay Sun reestablished himself as the party's leader. It joined the Alliance for the Great Change in

2010; however, in July 2013 Lay withdrew the RN from the Alliance and put support behind the Regional Union, reportedly to focus on the political work within the party.

Leader: Humberto LAY SUN.

Popular Action (*Acción Popular*—AP). Founded by Fernando Belaúnde TERRY in 1956, the moderately rightist AP captured the presidency in 1963 and served as the government party until the 1968 coup. Democratic, nationalist, and dedicated to the extension of social services, AP sought to mobilize public energies for development on Peru's terms. After the 1968 coup, the party split, a mainstream faction remaining loyal to Belaúnde and another, headed by former vice president Edgardo SEONE Corrales, collaborating with the military junta. Belaúnde was returned to office in the 1980 election, winning 45.4 percent of the votes cast, while the AP captured 98 of 180 Chamber seats and 26 of 60 seats in the Senate. However, in a massive voter reversal, the party won only one provincial city in the municipal elections in November 1983 and ran fourth in the 1985 balloting, obtaining only 10 Chamber and 5 Senate seats. The party supported Vargas LLOSA for the presidency in 1990 as a member of the Democratic Front. A shadow of its former self, the AP won only 4 congressional seats in 1995, while its presidential candidate, Raúl Diez CANSECO, drew a vote share of 1.6 percent. In April 2000 AP presidential candidate, Víctor Andrés García Belaúnde, secured a minuscule 0.4 percent of the vote, while the party's legislative representation dropped to 3 seats. It won an equal number in 2001. Former leader Terry died in June 2002. AP candidates accounted for 4 of the 5 seats won by the FC coalition in the 2006 legislative elections. The party joined the **Peru Possible** (*Perú Posible*) electoral alliance for the 2011 national elections.

In the 2016 elections, AP candidate Alfred BARNECHEA was fourth in the presidential balloting with 7 percent of the vote. The party won 7.2 percent of the vote and five seats in that year's congressional polling.

Leaders: Mesias GUERVARA (President), Alfred BARNECHEA (2016 presidential candidate).

Popular Force (*Fuerza Popular*). The right-wing **Force 2011** (*Fuerza 2011*) was formed in 2010 to support the presidential candidacy of Keiko Fujimori, the daughter of the former president. Force 2011 was the successor to the **Alliance for the Future** (*Alianza por el Futuro*—AF), formed in 2005 as a coalition of the two pro-Fujimori groups below, in anticipation that the former president's attempt to reenter the country and seek reelection as head of his party (see *Sí Cumple,* below) would be denied. The group finished fourth and won 13 legislative seats in 2006, including 1 by Keiko Fujimori, who received more votes than any other single legislative candidate. Alberto Fujimori's extradition and trial was an uncomfortable topic for Peruvian politicians. In July 2008 *Fujimorista* support proved crucial to the election of the PAP's Javier Velásquez to the presidency of the Congress; opposition figures alleged that the vote coincided with a relaxing of the conditions of Fujimori's imprisonment. Leading legislator Keiko Fujimori declared her intention in 2008 to fuse the pro-Fujimori parties into a single entity, Fuerza 2011, to compete in the 2011 presidential and congressional elections. Keiko Fujimori was selected as the alliance's presidential candidate for the 2011 election, campaigning on bolstering foreign investment and a transparent tax system. She was placed second in the presidential balloting, and Force 2011 placed second in the legislative polling with 37 seats.

In January 2013 Keiko Fujimori announced the party would be renamed Popular Force. In April 2014 a new executive committee was elected. Keiko Fujimori was again the party's presidential candidate in the 2016 elections. She was second in runoff balloting with 49.9 percent of the vote. The party won a majority in Congress with 73 seats and 36.3 percent of the vote.

Leaders: Keiko FUJIMORI (Party Leader and 2011 and 2016 presidential candidate), Joaquín RAMÍREZ (Secretary General), Martha Gladys CHÁVEZ Cossio (2005 presidential candidate).

New Majority (*Nueva Mayoría*—NM). The NM was launched in 1992 by a group of independents who presented a joint list with *Cambio 90* for the 1992 and 1995 polls, participated in the *Perú 2000* coalition, and remained allied with C90 in 2001. By 2006 the C90 designation had given way to NM.

Leader: Martha Gladys CHÁVEZ Cossio (2005 presidential candidate).

He Delivers (*Sí Cumple*). *Sí Cumple* was founded by former president Alberto Fujimori in 1998 as *Vamos Vecino* (Let's Go Neighbor), adopting its current name in 2005. In 2000 the party joined with C90 and the NM in a Peru 2000 Alliance to support Fujimori's reelection. In 2005 the group again joined with C90 and NM in *Aliaga Sí Cumple,* but the action was rejected by the National Jury of Elections and the other two groups contesting the 2006 poll as the Alliance for the Future (see Popular Force, above).

Leaders: Alberto FUJIMORI (Former President of the Republic, imprisoned), Absalón VASQUEZ, Carlos ORELLANA Quintanilla (Secretary General).

National Renewal (*Renovación Nacional—Renovación*). This rightist party was founded by Rafael Rey in 1992. It formed part of the UN coalition in the 2001 and 2006 elections. It split with UN later in 2006 and spent two years as part of the **Parliamentary Alliance** until it joined the newly formed GANA in 2008. Rey has served in the García government as minister of production, ambassador to Italy (briefly in 2009), and minister of defense. Rey was one of Fujimori's vice-presidential candidates in 2011.

Leader: Rafael REY (President and 2011 vice-presidential candidate).

Popular Alliance (*Alianza Popular*). The centrist Alliance was formed in December 2015 to support the candidacy of former president Alan García Pérez in the 2016 presidential balloting. Garcia secured 5.8 percent of the vote, while the Alliance won 8.3 percent of the vote in concurrent legislative elections, and five seats. The Alliance was dissolved following the elections.

Peruvian Aprista Party (*Partido Aprista Peruano*—PAP). The PAP was launched in 1930 as the Peruvian affiliate of the region-wide **American Popular Revolutionary Alliance** (*Alianza Popular Revolucionaria Americana*—APRA), formed six years earlier in Mexico. APRA was initially a radical left-wing movement. Its Peruvian branch (also frequently referenced as APRA) was not legalized until 1945. It mellowed into a mildly left-of-center, middle-class grouping with a strong labor base. Despite long-standing antagonism between the PAP and the military, its principal figure, Víctor Raúl Haya de la Torre, was permitted to return from exile in 1969 and was designated president of the Constituent Assembly after the party had won a substantial plurality in the election of June 18, 1978. Following his death in August 1979, Armando VILLANUEVA del Campo assumed party leadership. Decisively defeated in the 1980 balloting, the party split into a left-wing faction headed by Villanueva and a right-wing faction headed by second vice-presidential candidate Andrés TOWNSEND Ezcurra, who was formally expelled from the party in January 1981 and later formed the **Hayista Bases Movement** (*Movimiento de Bases Hayista*—MBH).

While he remained an influential party figure, Villanueva's control of the organization ended in 1983 with the rise of Alan García Pérez, a centrist, who in 1985 became the first Aprista leader to assume the presidency of the republic. The party swept municipal elections in November 1986. Unable to resolve the country's burgeoning economic problems, García suffered a dramatic loss in popular support during 1988 and resigned the party presidency at a congress in late December, with the office itself being abolished. The delegates then installed former prime minister Luis Alva Castro as general secretary. Alva Castro placed third in the 1990 presidential race.

Following the 1992 coup, former president García was granted political asylum in Colombia, which in early 1993 rejected a request by the Fujimori government that he be extradited to face charges of personal enrichment while in office. The Aprista leadership stripped García of his position as secretary general, and named a tripartite interim secretariat consisting of an *alanista,* former prime minister Villanueva; a García opponent, Alva Castro; and an "equidistant" chair, Luis Alberto SÁNCHEZ. The more radical ***Generación en Marcha*** "renewalist" and ***Nueva Generación*** leaders pressed for a party plenum to elect new officials.

In November 1993 García announced that he had applied for Colombian citizenship, and in August 1994 resigned his "secretary general in exile" title, after a secret Cayman Islands bank account in the name of a fugitive businessman to whom he was linked was discovered. Agustin MANTILLA Campos, elected secretary general in August 1994, and Mercedes Cabanillas, the party's 1995 standard-bearer, were both *alanistas.*

Winning less than 5 percent of the April 1995 balloting, the party needed to collect 100,000 signatures to avoid deregistration. Germán PARRA Herrera became head of an "action command" charged with reorganizing the party. He later resigned in October, claiming that other party members were refusing to recognize the gravity of the crisis. The party leadership subsequently reverted to Alva Castro, assisted by a political commission.

In early 2001 the Supreme Court revoked a sentence for corruption that had been passed against García in absentia, saying that the statute of limitations had run its course. The former president subsequently returned for a reelection bid, losing to Alejandro Toledo Manrique of Peru Possible in the second-round poll of June 3.

At the first-round presidential poll of April 19, 2006, García placed second with a 24.3 percent vote share but went on to defeat Ollanta Humala of the UPP (below) in a runoff on June 4. The PAP received the second-largest vote percentage in the 2006 legislative elections, with 20.6 percent of the total valid votes cast, only 0.6 percentage points behind the UPP. Its legislators hold 36 congressional seats. The PAP fared poorly in November 2006 municipal and regional elections, but the party maintained the presidency of Peru's Congress in 2007–2009, with support from the pro-Fujimori Alliance for the Future and Humala's UPP. A string of high-profile corruption scandals in 2010 involving members of PAP, including the party's two cosecretaries general, brought into doubt its prospects for local and regional elections in 2010 and national balloting in 2011. President García had not yet settled on a potential successor to be the party's presidential candidate as of the latter half of 2010, but his prime minister, Javier Velásquez Quesquén, resigned on September 13 and became the PAP's vice-presidential candidate. Mercedes ARAÓZ Fernández was chosen as the PAP's presidential candidate. She withdrew from the campaign on January 17, citing lack of support in opinion polls. García ran unsuccessfully for the presidency in 2016, placing fifth.

Leaders: Alan Gabriel Ludwig GARCÍA Pérez (Former President of the Republic and President of the Party), Jorge Alfonso Alejandro DEL CASTILLO Gálvez (Former Prime Minister and Secretary General), Ángel Javier VELÁSQUEZ Quesquén (Former Prime Minister and President of Political Committee).

Christian People's Party (*Partido Popular Cristiano*—PPC). The PPC was formed in the wake of the split in the now defunct PDC in 1967, with Luis Bedoya Reyes leading a conservative faction out of the parent group. The party was runner-up to the PAP in the Constituent Assembly election of June 1978 and was placed third in the 1980 presidential and legislative races, after which it joined the Belaúnde government by accepting two ministerial appointments. For the 1985 balloting it formed an alliance with Townsend Ezcurra's MBH, styled the **Democratic Convergence** (*Convergencia Democrática*—Conde), which secured 7 Senate and 12 Chamber seats. It participated in the 1990 campaign as a member of Fredemo, which won a plurality of one-third in each house of Congress. Initially endorsing its secretary general for the 1995 presidential race, it subsequently backed the UPP's Pérez de Cuéllar. In the congressional poll it won only 3 seats, none of which was retained in 2000.

For the 2001 campaign, it served as the core of the UN coalition, which included the National Solidarity Party (PSN), National Restoration (RN), and *Renovación*. The UN secured 15 congressional seats, while its leader, Lourdes Flores Nano, placed third in the presidential race. Led by Flores, the PPC again participated in the UN coalition in 2006, with Flores finishing third in the first round of presidential voting despite leading in the pre-election polls. With 15.3 percent of the vote and 17 congressional seats, the UN finished third.

The UN political bloc effectively disbanded in August 2008, with Lourdes Flores citing ideological differences with the PSN and its leader, Lima mayor Luis CASTAÑEDA, whom she accused of being too accommodating to the García government. The UN continues to exist in name as a legislative grouping of PPC members and a handful of independent legislators, totaling 13 seats in the Congress. The party selected Flores to be its presidential candidate for the 2011 election, but owing to a weak showing in polls, she withdrew. Two legislators defected from the party in August 2013.

Leaders: Raúl CASTRO Stagnaro (President of the Party), Rafael YAMASHIRO Oré (Secretary General).

Other Parties Contesting the 2011 or 2016 Elections:

Peru Possible (*Perú Posible*). *Perú Posible* leader Alejandro Toledo entered the 1995 presidential race as organizer of a group styled Possible Nation (*País Posible*), which joined with the **Democratic Coordination** (*Coordinadora Democrática*—Code) in an alignment registered as *Code–País Posible*. The renamed formation was credited with a second-place legislative finish (29 seats) in 2000, Toledo himself withdrawing from the presidential runoff of May 28 because of anticipated fraud. He secured a 53.1 percent victory in the second-round balloting on June 3, 2001. A group of *Perú Posible* dissidents subsequently organized as **Peru Now** (*Perú Ahora*). Running without a coalition, the party fared poorly in the 2006 elections; it decided not to field a presidential candidate, and its candidates for the legislature received only 4.1 percent of the votes cast, finishing sixth and winning only 2 seats. The party made a similarly poor showing in the 2006 municipal and regional elections. Toledo ran as the party's presidential candidate in the 2011 election. After he came in third in the presidential elections, Toledo supported Humala of the Peru Wins Alliance in the runoff balloting. (For information on the **Peru Possible** [*Perú Posible*] electoral alliance, see the 2015 *Handbook.*)

In the 2016 national elections, Toledo was the party's standard-bearer, winning 1.3 percent of the vote in the presidential balloting, while the grouping secured 2.4 percent of the vote in the congressional elections and no seats.

Leaders: Alejandro TOLDEDO Manrique (President of the Party and Former President of the Republic), Luis SOLARI de la Fuente (Former Prime Minister).

Peru Wins Alliance (*Alianza Gana Perú*). Formed in 2010 to support the presidential candidacy of Ollanta Humala, the left-wing Peru Wins Alliance was the successor of the **Nationalist Union Party for Peru** (*Partido Nacionalista Unión por el Perú*—PNUP). The PNUP was launched by Humala in late 2005 as a coalition of the UPP and PNP. Thereafter, it was frequently referenced as the UPP or the UPP/PNP rather than the PNUP, as the two parties maintained distinct identities. The coalition was the largest vote-getter in the 2006 legislative elections, with 21.2 percent of valid votes. Internal dissent caused two new parties, the Popular Bloc (*Bloque Popular*—BP, below) and Democratic Commitment (*Compromiso Democrático*—CD, below), to splinter from the UPP in 2008. In 2010 Humala formed the Peru Wins Alliance with the PNP and four other left-wing parties. In balloting on April 10, 2011, the Peru Wins Alliance secured congressional 47 seats. Humala won the presidency with a bare majority of 51.5 percent in a June 5 runoff election. Though negotiations to gain an absolute majority by forming an alliance with Peru Possible dissolved, several Peru Possible members were appointed in the Peru Wins Alliance government.

A trilateral effort to unite with Peru Possible and Popular Force to elect the Constitutional Court in July 2013 (see Current issues, above) dissolved. However, both parties helped the Peru Wins Alliance survive a confidence vote in March 2014. Ana María SOLÓRZANO was elected president of Congress by a narrow margin in July 2014.

Leader: Lt. Col. (Ret.) Ollanta HUMALA Tasso (Former President of the Republic).

Peru Nationalist Party (*Partido Nacionalista Peruano*—PNP). The PNP is the political arm of the Etnocacerista Movement (*Movimiento Etnocacerista*—ME), founded by former army major Antauro HUMALA, Ollanta Humala's younger brother, who participated in an abortive uprising against former president Fujimori. The ME is an openly racist, anti-white formation, claiming to reflect the Incan moral code of Marshal Andrés CACERES, a hero of the 19th-century war with Chile. In mid-2009 the PNP had 23 seats in the Congress, making it the largest party in the bloc supporting Ollanta Humala. In September 2009 the PNP legislators were alone in opposing the expansion of the Congress from 120 members to 130, arguing that it would lead to more inefficiency and unnecessary expense. Humala won reelection as party leader at a party congress in late December 2013 but urged that his wife, Nadine HEREDIA, be appointed to the post instead. She took over leadership on December 30. Heredia was subsequently investigated over allegations of money laundering and corruption stemming from contributions she received in 2006.

In August 2016 Humala again became president of the party, pledging to run for the presidency in 2021.

Leaders: Ollanta HUMALA Tasso (Former President of the Republic), Nadine HEREDIA (Party Leader).

Socialist Party of Peru (*Partido Socialista del Perú*—PSP). The PSP is a left-wing party organized in 1979. It ran in 1995 under the **Opening for a National Development–Socialist Party** (*Apertura para el Desarrollo Nacional–Partido Socialista*) list but won only 0.3 percent of the legislative vote.

During the 1990s PSP leader Javier Diez Canseco was a vigorous opponent of the Fujimori regime and, as a member of Congress, participated in investigations of alleged human rights violations by members of both the Shining Path and the Peruvian Armed Forces. The PSP joined the Peru Win Alliance ahead of the 2011 balloting.

Leaders: Javier DIEZ Canseco (2006 presidential candidate), Julio Sergio CASTRO Gomez, Aída García NARANJO Morales (Secretary General).

Other parties in the Peru Wins Alliance include the **Peruvian Communist Party** (*Partido Comunista Peruano*—PCP), the **Revolutionary Socialist Party** (*Partido Socialista Revolucionario*—PSR), and the **Political Movement Socialist Voice** (*Movimiento Politico Voz Socialista*).

Humanist Party (*Partido Humanista*). The Humanist Party's leader and sole legislator Yehude Simon defected from the Alliance for the Great Change in 2013, citing ideological differences. The Humanist Party rejected offers from the Peru Wins Alliance, opting to remain independent. The Humanist Party entered negotiations to form an alliance with Peru Possible in November 2013, and Simon officially joined the ranks in July 2014. It ran as an independent party in 2016, with Simon as its presidential candidate. However, he withdrew his candidacy before the balloting.

Leader: Yehude SIMON.

National Solidarity Alliance (*Alianza Solidaridad Nacional*). The National Solidarity Alliance is a center-right grouping that was created in 2010. In addition to the parties below, the small **Always Together** (*Siempre Unidos*) also joined the alliance. The alliance's 2011 presidential candidate was former Lima mayor Luís Castañeda Lossio. The alliance gained nine seats in the 2011 elections. After he was eliminated from the runoff balloting, Castañeda endorsed Keiko Fujimori of Force 2011. Enrique WONG defected from the Alliance for the Great Change in July 2013, joining the NSA.

For the 2016 balloting, the National Solidarity Party (*Partido de Solidaridad Nacional*—PSN) and Union for Peru (*Unión por el Perú*—UPP) again agreed to form an alliance. However, the grouping withdrew its candidates prior to the balloting because of low polling.

Leader: Luís CASTAÑEDA Lossio (2011 presidential candidate).

National Solidarity Party (*Partido de Solidaridad Nacional*—PSN). Formally registered in early 1999, the PSN served in 2000 as the vehicle for the presidential campaign of Luís Castañeda Lossio. During the 2001 campaign Castañeda withdrew in favor of the UN's Flores Nano. In October 2005 Castañeda announced he would not contend for the position in 2006. Flores Nano split with the PSN in 2008, accusing Castañeda of supporting the García government in exchange for central government funding of municipal projects in Lima. Castañeda initially led the field of 2011 presidential candidates in polls but was placed fifth in the balloting.

Leaders: Luís CASTAÑEDA Lossio (President of the Party, Former Mayor of Lima, and 2000 and 2011 presidential candidate), Jose LUNA Gálvez (Secretary General).

Union for Peru (*Unión por el Perú*—UPP). The UPP was formed as a campaign vehicle for Javier Pérez de Cuéllar following the announcement by the former UN secretary general on August 18, 1994, that he would stand for the presidency in 1995. The UPP candidate ran a distant second to Fujimori, with 21.8 percent of the vote. Though the UPP secured just 0.3 percent in the presidential election of April 2000, Pérez de Cuéllar was named prime minister in the Paniagua administration of November 2000.

Pérez de Cuéllar withdrew from the party following the designation of Humala as its 2006 standard bearer. The UPP received the largest percentage of voting in the 2006 legislative elections, with 21.2 percent of the total valid votes cast.

Leaders: Eduardo ESPINOZA Ramos (President), Aldo Vladimiro ESTRADA Choque (First Vice President), José VEGA Antonio (Secretary General).

Perú Patria Segura.* Change 90** (*Cambio 90*—C90), as *Perú Patria Segura* was originally named, was organized before the 1990 campaign as a political vehicle for Alberto Fujimori. While Fujimori secured a majority of the second-round presidential votes, C90 ran third in both upper and lower house legislative contests. Before the 1992 election, it formed a coalition with the *Nueva Mayoría* (above), which won a 55 percent majority of CCD seats on a vote share of 38 percent. In 1995 Fujimori was reelected with 64.3 percent of the vote, while the ruling coalition decimated the traditional parties by securing 51.4 percent of the valid ballots. For the 2000 balloting C90 headed a coalition styled ***Perú 2000 and was credited with winning 52 of 120 congressional seats. It was reduced to 3 seats in 2001. By the 2006 elections C90 had largely given way to the *Nueva Mayoría* among the pro-Fujimori bloc. The remaining C90 members refused to endorse Keiko Fujimori and instead joined the National Solidarity Alliance. In December 2013 Renzo REGGIARDO announced the reorganization of the C90 under the *Perú Patria Segura* banner, formalizing the split with Fujimori.

Leader: Renzo REGGIARDO.

Other parties that participated in the 2016 balloting included the **Hope Front** (*Frente Esperanza*), which won 1.2 percent of the vote in the congressional balloting, and whose presidential candidate Fernando OLIVERA, secured 1.3 percent of the vote; and **Direct Democracy** (*Democracia Directa*), which received 4.3 percent of the vote. **Developing Peru** (*Progresando Perú*) and the **Order Party** (*Partido Político Orden*) both received less than 1 percent of the vote and no seats in Congress.

Parties in the 2011 national elections included the following (unless noted otherwise, the parties received less than 1 percent of the vote): **Radical Change** (*Cambio Radical*), which received 2.7 percent of the vote in the legislative balloting; the **Fonavist Party** (*Fonavistas Des Perú*), which secured 1.3 percent of the vote; the **Forward Party** (*Partido Politico Adelante*); the **Decentralist Party Social Force** (*Partido Decentralista Fuerza Social*); the **National Force Party** (*Partido Fuerza Nacional*); the **National Awakening Party** (*Partido Despertar Nacional*); and the **Justice, Technology, Ecology Party** (*Justicia, Tenologia, Ecologia*), whose presidential candidate, Humberto PINAZO, was placed sixth in the 2011 presidential balloting.

Other Parties:

National Coordination of Independents (*Coordinadora Nacional de Independientes*—CNI). The CNI, a grouping of independents organized before the 2006 elections, ran as part of the Center Front coalition (see *Alianza,* above). The CNI failed to elect any of its candidates to Peru's Congress in 2006. In January 2010 former prime minister Pedro Pablo KUCZYNSKI announced that he was considering running in the 2011 presidential election under the CNI banner, but instead he ran as the candidate for the Alliance for the Great Change.

Leaders: Drago Guillermo KISIC Wagner, Gonzálo AGUIRRE Arriz.

Independent Moralizing Front (*Frente Independiente Moralizador*—FIM). The FIM was launched before the 1995 election by Luis Fernando Olivera Vega, a former investigator for the state prosecutor's office who had pursued a six-year crusade to bring former president Alan García to trial for alleged misdeeds while in office. The party won 6 congressional seats in 1995, 9 in 2000, and 11 in 2001. Olivera finished fourth, with 9.9 percent of the vote, in the 2001 presidential balloting. The party briefly endorsed Peru Possible candidates in 2006, then chose to run its own candidates. Olivera ultimately dropped out of the presidential balloting to focus on the legislative campaign. Neither he nor other FIM candidates won any seats.

Leader: Luis Fernando OLIVERA Vega (2001 presidential candidate).

Decentralizing Coalition (*Concertación Decentralista*—CD). The center-left CD was formed before the 2006 election as a coalition of the **Party for Social Democracy–Compromise Peru** (*Partido por la Democracia Social–Compromiso Perú*) and the **Peruvian Humanist Movement Party** (*Partido Movimiento Humanista Peruano*—PMHP). The party has since been inactive.

Leader: Susana María del Carmen VILLARÁN de la Puente (President and 2006 presidential candidate).

Democratic Force (*Fuerza Democrática*—FA). The FA was launched in 1998 to compete at the municipal level. It won a small number of local positions in 2006, mainly in Peru's remote Amazon basin region.

Leader: Alberto BOREA.

Popular Agricultural Front of Peru (*Frente Popular Agrícola del Perú*—Frepap). In the 1995 election Frepap was known as the **Peruvian Agricultural and Popular Front** (*Frente Agrícola y

Popular del Perú—FAPP). It won two congressional seats in 2000 and none in 2001 or 2006.

Leader: Alfredo GÁLVEZ (2006 presidential candidate).

Country Project (*Proyecto Pais*—PP). The PP is a "law and order" group founded in 1998 by Marco Antonio Arrunategui Cevallos.

Leader: Marco Antonio ARRUNATEGUI Cevallos (2001 and 2006 presidential candidate).

Andean Renaissance (*Renacimiento Andino*—RA). The RA was launched in 2001 by Ciro Alfredo Gálvez Herrera, who won less than 1 percent of the vote that year. It withdrew from the 2006 presidential election to avoid drawing support from Lourdes Flores.

Leader: Ciro Alfredo GÁLVEZ Herrera (2001 and 2006 presidential candidate).

Popular Bloc (*Bloque Popular*—BP). On August 6, 2008, after a series of disagreements with the UPP, particularly over leading UPP members' support of PAP legislators to serve as president of the Congress, a group of eight more radical legislators split from the party and declared themselves the **Patriotic Peruvian Unity–Popular Bloc.**

Leader: Antonio LEÓN (Spokesperson).

Democratic Commitment (*Compromiso Democrático*—CD). Twelve days after the BP split from the UPP, another group of three UPP legislators followed suit, citing similar disagreements, and formed the CD.

Leader: Washington ZEBALLOS Gámez (Coordinator).

Also participating in the 2006 poll were the **National Justice Party** (*Partido Justicia Nacional*—PJN), led by Jamie SALINAS; **Advance the Country—Social Integration Party** (*Avanza País—Partido de Integración Social*—AP-PIS), led by Ulisés HUMALA, Ollanta Humala's brother; the **New Left Movement** (*Movimiento Nueva Izquierdo*—MNI), led by Alberto MORENO; the **With Force Peru** (*Con Fuerza Perú*—CFP), led by Pedro KOECHLIN Von Stein; **Peru Now** (*Perú Ahora*), led by Luis GUERRERO Figueroa; the **Democratic Reconstruction** (*Reconstrucción Democrática*—RD); the **Peruvian Resurgence** (*Resurgimiento Peruano*—RP); the **And It's Called Peru** (*Y se llama Perú*); and the **Let's Make Progress Peru** (*Progresemos Perú*—PP).

Land and Liberty (*Tierra y Libertad*—TL) is a new left-wing movement founded on June 30, 2009, in the wake of clashes with indigenous protesters (see Current issues, above), by Catholic priest Marco ARANA and Pedro FRANCKE. Arana launched an unsuccessful campaign for the 2011 presidential race on his foundation of liberation theology, arguing for environmental rights and social justice.

Leaders: Marco ARANA, Pedro FRANCKE.

Guerrilla and Terrorist Organizations:

Shining Path (*Sendero Luminoso*). The *Sendero Luminoso* (also translated as "Luminous Path") originated at Ayacucho University as a small Maoist group led by a former philosophy instructor Dr. Manuel Abimael Guzmán Reinoso. During 1980 it was involved in a number of bombings in Lima, Ayacucho, Cuzco, and other provincial towns in southern Peru, causing property damage only. About 170 of its followers were arrested in October 1980 and January 1981, but most were freed in a daring raid on the Ayacucho police barracks in March 1982. Thereafter, guerrilla activity in the region intensified, including the assassination of a number of local officials and alleged police informants. While the insurgency appeared to remain localized (apart from sporadic terrorist attacks in Lima), the government felt obliged to order a major sweep through the affected provinces by 1,500 military and police units at the end of the year. Subsequently, the rebellion showed no sign of diminishing, despite the imposition of military rule in the departments of Ayacucho, Apurímac, Huancavelica, Huánuco, and part of San Martín. By late 1987 more than 10,000 deaths, on both sides, had been reported since the insurgency began, and the organization, estimated to encompass at least 3,000 members, had become increasingly active in urban areas. Its reputed second-in-command, Osman MOROTE Barrionuevo, was captured by Lima police in June 1988 and subsequently sentenced to 15 years' imprisonment. The insurgency intensified during 1989 as the nation's economy approached collapse; however, its adherents were surprisingly unsuccessful in a campaign to limit participation at municipal elections in November. Guzmán himself was captured in Lima on September 12, 1992, and sentenced by a secret military tribunal to life imprisonment, while his principal deputy, Edmundo Daniel Cox Beauzeville, was apprehended in August 1993.

In January 1994 it was reported that *Sendero Luminoso* had split into two factions, one loyal to the imprisoned Guzmán and another, styled the **Red Path** (*Sendero Rojo*), committed to continuing the rebellion under the leadership of Oscar Ramírez Durand (a.k.a. "Camarada Feliciano"). By March, however, nearly 4,100 alleged *senderistas* had surrendered under a 1992 "Repentance Law," while a number of Ramírez's lieutenants were apprehended during the ensuing three months. By midyear, while 66 of the country's 155 provinces remained under a state of emergency, guerrilla activity was reported to be confined largely to three areas: some marginal districts of the capital, the highlands of Lima department, and the Huallaga valley jungle region. In August 1997 *Sendero Luminoso* guerrillas captured about 30 oil workers in a remote jungle area 200 miles east of Lima; two days later the hostages were released after their French-based employer sent supplies of food, medicine, and clothing. The deputy leader of *Sendero Rojo,* Pedro Domingo QUINTEROS Ayllón (also known as "Camarada Luis"), was captured in April 1998, while the senior military leader, Juan Carlos RIOS, was arrested in December, by which time the grouping was described as "largely impotent" as the result of the government's campaign. Ramírez Durand, the formation's last major leader, was captured in July 1999 and sentenced to life imprisonment.

Bomb attacks in March 2002, preceding a visit to Lima by U.S. president George W. Bush, were attributed to a *Sendero Luminoso* faction. From mid-2003, *Sendero* activity was conducted by apparently drastically depleted guerrilla units.

A retrial of Guzmán and his lieutenants began in November 2004 after a constitutional tribunal overturned their original convictions on the grounds that they should have been tried in a civilian rather than a military court. However, the proceedings collapsed when two of the three presiding judges stepped down because of involvement in earlier rulings. A second retrial opened in Lima in September 2005. On October 13, 2006, Guzmán and several lieutenants were sentenced to life in prison for "aggravated terrorism."

Sendero activity continued in 2007 and 2008, including two ambushes on police and civilians as well as a November 2007 attack that destroyed a police station in Apurímac. Most analysts believed the group had less than 500 members and depended almost entirely on the cocaine trade.

Sendero activity increased significantly in 2008, particularly in the Upper Huallaga and Apurimac and Ene Valley (VRAE) regions, with military casualties totaling 25, the largest figure since the early 1990s. The group's VRAE faction, led by "Comrade JOSÉ," is called the Principal Regional Committee and rejects both founder Guzmán and any possibility of negotiation. "Comrade ARTEMIO," the Sendero leader in the Upper Huallaga and a member of the group since the 1980s, made periodic offers of negotiation, which the García government rejected.

On September 3, 2009, the group attacked and downed an air-force helicopter (responding to an ambush that wounded three soldiers earlier that day) in the central highlands Junín region, killing three troops and wounding five others. *Sendero* killed more than 40 members of the military and police in 2009, leading to a warning that it was increasing its firepower and capabilities.

Sendero leaders confirmed that the group intended to compete in municipal and regional elections in 2010 and 2011's national balloting, signaling intentions to make the organization an explicitly political one, a shift evident in the militant activities of the previous decade, which targeted military and police. In September 2011 military units were deployed in the Vrae region following fresh *Sendero* attacks. Just three months into his presidency, Humala declared a state of emergency in five provinces. In February 2012 Peruvian troops captured Comrade Artemio, the last remaining member of the central committee who had not been arrested or killed. He was sentenced to life in prison in July 2013. The following month, three rebels were killed by security forces. Guzmán, already serving a life sentence, stood trial again in January 2014 for his role in a 1992 bombing. In April 2014 Peruvian officials arrested 28 people with links to *Sendero* on drug trafficking and terrorism charges. The mass arrest, the culmination of a two-year investigation, was praised by the United States and other international observers.

The United States named *Sendero* as a narcotics trafficking organization on June 1, 2015, and froze the assets of the group's leaders.

Leaders: "Comrade JOSÉ" (Principal Regional Committee), "Comrade ARTEMIO" (imprisoned), "Comrade Miriam" Elena

IPARRAGUIRRE (imprisoned), Manuel Abimael GUZMÁN Reinoso (imprisoned), Edmundo Daniel COX Beauzeville (imprisoned), Margie Evelyn CLAVO Peralta (imprisoned), Oscar RAMÍREZ Durand (*Sendero Rojo,* imprisoned).

See the 2010 *Handbook* for information on the now-defunct **Túpac Amaru Revolutionary Movement** (*Movimiento Revolucionario Túpac Amaru*—MRTA).

LEGISLATURE

The bicameral Congress (*Congreso*), established under the 1979 constitution, encompassed a Senate and a Chamber of Deputies, both elected for five-year terms by universal adult suffrage. The Congress elected in 1990 was declared by President Fujimori to have been dissolved, as of April 6, 1992. In its place a unicameral Democratic Constituent Congress (*Congreso Constituyente Democrático*—CCD) was established, elections to which were conducted on November 22, 1992. The CCD gave way, in turn, to a new unicameral Congress elected on April 9, 1995. Subsequent elections were held on April 9, 2000; on April 8, 2001 (following a premature dissolution); on April 9, 2006; and on April 10, 2011.

Congress (*Congreso*). The Congress had 120 members, who, before 2001, were selected by proportional vote from a single national list but now represent geographic constituencies. Ahead of the 2011 elections, the number of seats was increased to 130.

Following the most recent elections on April 10, 2016, the seat distribution was as follows: Popular Force, 73 seats; Broad Front, 20; Peruvians for Change, 18; Alliance for the Progress of Peru, 9; Popular Alliance, 5; and Popular Action, 5.

President: Luz Filomena SALGADO Rubianes.

CABINET

[as of November 25, 2016]

President of Council of Ministers	Fernando Zavala Lombardi
Ministers	
Agriculture and Irrigation	José Hernández
Culture	Jorge Nieto
Defense	Mariano González
Economy and Finance	Alfredo Thorne
Education	Jaime Saavedra Chanduví
Energy and Mines	Gonzalo Tamayo
Environment	Elsa Galarza [f]
Foreign Relations	Ricardo Luna
Foreign Trade and Tourism	Eduardo Ferreyros Küppers
Health	Patricia García [f]
Housing, Construction, and Sanitation	Edmer Trujillo
Interior	Carlos Basombrío
Justice	Marisol Pérez Tello [f]
Labor and Employment	Alfonso Grados
Production (Fisheries and Industry)	Bruno Giuffra
Social Development and Inclusion	Cayetana Aljovín Gazzani [f]
Transport and Communications	Martín Vizcarra Cornejo
Women's Affairs and Vulnerable Populations	Ana María Romero [f]

[f] = female

INTERGOVERNMENTAL REPRESENTATION

Ambassador to the U.S.: Carlos PAREJA.

U.S. Ambassador to Peru: Brian A. NICHOLS.

Permanent Representative to the UN: Gustavo Adolfo MEZA-CUADRA Velásquez.

IGO Memberships (Non-UN): APEC, IADB, ICC, IOM, Mercosur, NAM, OAS, WTO.

For Further Reference:

Crabtree, John, and Francisco Durand. *Peru: Elite Power and Political Capture.* London: Zed Books, 2017.

Greene, Shane. *Customizing Indigeneity: Paths to a Visionary Politics in Peru.* Stanford, CA: Stanford University Press, 2009.

Starn, Orin, Carlos Ivan Degregori, and Robin Kirk, eds. *The Peru Reader: History, Culture, Politics.* 2nd ed. Durham, NC: Duke University Press, 2005.

PHILIPPINES

Republic of the Philippines
Republika ng Pilipinas

Political Status: Independent republic since July 4, 1946; currently under constitution adopted by referendum of February 2, 1987, effective from February 11.

Area: 115,830 sq. mi. (300,000 sq. km).

Population: 102,250,000 (2016E—UN); 102,624,209 (2016E—U.S. Census).

Major Urban Centers (2016E—UN): METRO MANILA (13,131,000), Davao City (1,662,000), Cebu City (923,000).

Official Languages: Filipino and English.

Monetary Unit: Philippine Peso (market rate October 1, 2016: 48.47 pesos = $1US).

President: Rodrigo DUTERTE (Philippine Democratic Party–Laban); popularly elected on May 9, 2016, and inaugurated on June 30 for a fixed six-year term; succeeding Benigno S. AQUINO III (Liberal Party).

Vice President: Leni ROBREDO (Liberal Party); elected for a six-year term on May 9, 2016, and sworn in on June 30, succeeding Jejomar C. BINAY (Philippine Democratic Party–Laban).

THE COUNTRY

Strategically located along the southeast rim of Asia, the Philippine archipelago embraces over 7,000 islands stretching in a north-south direction for over 1,000 miles. The largest and most important of the islands are Luzon in the north and sparsely populated Mindanao in the south. The inhabitants, predominantly of Malay stock, are 83 percent Roman Catholic, although a politically significant Muslim minority (5 percent) is concentrated in the south. The country is not linguistically unified; English and Spanish are used concurrently with local languages and dialects, although Pilipino, based on the Tagalog spoken in the Manila area, has been promoted as a national language. Women, who constitute about 38 percent of the active labor force, have been prominent in journalism and politics. Women made up 30 percent of the representatives in the lower house of Congress and 25 percent of the Senate following the May 2016 elections). According to a report from the World Economic Forum in 2014, the Philippines ranked ninth out of 142 countries in gender equality.

Rice for domestic consumption and wood, sugar, and coconut products for export were traditionally mainstays of the economy. Although agriculture continues to employ about 35 percent of the labor force, it now accounts for only 15 percent of GDP, compared to about 30 percent for industry and 55 percent for services. Well over half of the country's exports by value are electronics; garments, other manufactures, minerals and mineral products, coconut products, sugar cane, and bananas also rank among the leading exports. The mining industry has benefited from investment in recent years. Remittances from as many as ten million overseas workers (over one quarter of the country's labor force) are a leading source of foreign exchange. The Philippines had significant GDP growth through the 2000s. However, poverty and income inequality remain persistent problems, creating an instability exacerbated by rising food prices during the global financial crisis of

2008–2009. Despite rising remittance inflows, domestic consumption fell sharply in 2009. The Philippine economy grew by just 1.1 percent in 2009 but rose by 7.6 percent in 2010, 3.9 percent in 2011, and 6.5 percent in 2012 due to increasing investor confidence and a recovery in the global economy. According to the International Monetary Fund (IMF), GDP grew by 7.2 percent in 2013, inflation was 2.9 percent, and unemployment was 7.1 percent. GDP grew by 6.1 percent in 2014, rising to 6.7 percent in 2015, and slowly slightly to 6.3 percent in 2016. That year inflation was 2.8 percent, while unemployment was 6 percent, and GDP per capita was $3,284. In 2016 the World Bank ranked the Philippines 103th out of 180 countries in its annual report on the ease of doing business index, a ranking far below neighboring states, including as Singapore (1st), Malaysia (18th), and Vietnam (90th).

GOVERNMENT AND POLITICS

Political background. Claimed for Spain by Ferdinand Magellan in 1521 and ruled by that country until occupied by the United States during the Spanish–American War of 1898, the Philippines became a self-governing commonwealth under U.S. tutelage in 1935 and gained independence on July 4, 1946. Manuel ROXAS, first president of the new republic (1946–1948), took office during the onset of an armed uprising by Communist-led Hukbalahap guerrillas in central Luzon that continued under his successor, the Liberal Elpidio QUIRINO (1948–1953). Quirino's secretary of national defense, Ramon MAGSAYSAY, initiated an effective program of military action and rural rehabilitation designed to pacify the Huks, and he was able to complete this process after his election to the presidency on the *Nacionalista* Party ticket in 1953. Magsaysay also dealt strongly with bureaucratic corruption and did much to restore popular faith in government, but his accidental death in 1957 led to a loss of reformist momentum and a revival of corruption under his *Nacionalista* successor, Carlos P. GARCIA (1957–1961). Efforts toward economic and social reform were renewed by Liberal President Diosdado MACAPAGAL (1961–1965).

The election, under *Nacionalista* auspices, of former Liberal leader Ferdinand E. MARCOS in 1965 was accompanied by pledges of support for the reform movement, but discontent with prevailing conditions of poverty, unemployment, inflation, and corruption fostered a climate of violence that included the activities of the Maoist New People's Army (NPA), which was founded in 1969, and a persistent struggle between Muslim elements and government forces on Mindanao and in Sulu Province. In some areas Muslims sought to drive out Christian settlers from the north, but as antigovernment activities expanded under the direction of the Moro National Liberation Front (MNLF), Muslim leaders increasingly called for regional autonomy or outright independence.

In the midst of a rapidly deteriorating political situation, a Constitutional Convention began work on a new constitution in July 1971, but its deliberations were curtailed by a declaration of martial law in September 1972. Strict censorship immediately followed, as did widespread arrests of suspected subversives and political opponents of the regime, most notably Liberal Party (LP) leader Benigno S. AQUINO Jr. The new constitution, which provided for a parliamentary form of government, was declared ratified in January 1973; concurrently, Marcos assumed the additional post of prime minister and announced that the selection of an interim National Assembly called for by the constitution would be deferred.

Following talks in early 1975 between representatives of the Philippine government and the MNLF, the Muslims dropped their demand for partition of the republic, while the government agreed to an integration of rebel units into the Philippine armed forces. President Marcos ordered a suspension of military operations in the south in late 1976, following a cease-fire agreement signed in Tripoli, Libya, with representatives of the moderate MNLF faction. In accordance with the agreement, a referendum was held in April 1977 on the establishment of an autonomous Muslim region. Most Muslims boycotted the polls, however, and the proposal was defeated by an overwhelming majority of those participating. Meanwhile, in 1973 the Communist Party of the Philippines–Marxist-Leninist (CPP) and its military wing, the NPA, had joined with other leftist Marcos opponents to organize a National Democratic Front (NDF).

Amid charges of widespread voting irregularity, particularly in the Manila area, the interim National Assembly was elected in April 1978. The president's recently organized New Society Movement (*Kilusan Bagong Lipunan*—KBL) was officially credited with winning 151 of 165 elective seats.

Martial law was lifted in January 1981, prior to the April adoption by plebiscite of a series of constitutional changes that included direct presidential election. In nationwide balloting in June Marcos was overwhelmingly reelected to a six-year term.

In the first full election to a unicameral National Assembly in May 1984, opposition candidates claimed approximately one-third of the seats. Despite the lifting of martial law, the Marcos regime continued to rule by decree. Opposition feeling had already been inflamed by the assassination of Benigno Aquino upon his return from the United States in August 1983, which precipitated 18 months of often violent antiregime demonstrations. In October 1984 a government commission of inquiry concluded that ultimate responsibility for Aquino's death lay with the armed forces chief of staff, Gen. Fabian VER, who was thereupon temporarily suspended from his duties. (In December 1985, having been acquitted of conspiracy in the assassination, he was reinstated.)

A year later, in the face of mounting support for Corazon AQUINO as political surrogate for her slain husband, Marcos announced that a premature presidential election would be held in early 1986 to "restore confidence" in his administration. Mrs. Aquino filed as the sole opposition candidate for the presidency, with Salvador H. LAUREL as her running mate. The election in February was conducted amid allegations by both opposition leaders and foreign observers of manifest government fraud; Aquino was named the victor by an independent citizens' watchdog group, while official figures attesting to the president's reelection were accepted by the National Assembly. With both candidates thus claiming victory, Aquino called for an expanded program of strikes, boycotts, and civil disobedience to "bring down the usurper."

The turning point came on February 22, 1986, when Defense Secretary Juan Ponce ENRILE and Lt. Gen. Fidel V. RAMOS, the leader of an anticorruption campaign within the military, declared their allegiance to Aquino. Ramos quickly joined troops loyal to him at Camp Crame, the national police headquarters. In response to an appeal from Cardinal Jaime SIN to protect the rebels, the base was surrounded by thousands of Philippine citizens in what became known as the first "People Power" rally. Subsequently, much of the media passed to opposition control, while the military, including the palace guard, experienced mass defections. On February 26, a day after the swearing in of both presidential claimants, Marcos and his immediate entourage departed for exile in Hawaii.

In March 1986 the new chief executive dissolved the National Assembly by suspending the 1973 constitution, presenting in its place an interim document "under which our battered nation can shelter."

In February 1987 more than 80 percent of those voting approved a new U.S.-style constitution, under which President Aquino and Vice President Laurel would remain in office until 1992. In the subsequent congressional election, Aquino supporters won more than 80 percent of 200 directly elective seats in the House of Representatives and defeated opposition candidates in 22 of 24 Senate races.

The Aquino government survived six coup attempts, the most serious of which erupted in December 1989, with the seizure by rebel troops of two military installations in Manila followed by an air attack on the presidential palace. Despite U.S. air support of the government, the insurgency was not completely crushed for ten days, in the course of which 119 persons died and more than 600 were wounded.

Seven candidates vied for the presidency in May 1992, with Aquino-endorsed Fidel Ramos turning back strong challenges by political newcomer Miriam DEFENSOR-SANTIAGO and conservative businessman Eduardo COJUANGCO of the National People's Coalition (NPC). Ramos's People Power–National Union of Christian Democrats (*Lakas*-NUCD) emerged as the principal victor in the May 1995 legislative poll, winning approximately two-thirds of the lower house seats.

In September 1992 the MNLF had rejected an offer of amnesty until the government implemented its 1976 pledge to sanction the creation of semiautonomous political structures for the Mindanao region. In November 1993 the two sides concluded a three-month truce agreement, which was followed by the signing of a cease-fire in January 1994 and a formal peace agreement in September 1996. That month, the MNLF's Nur MISUARI was elected unopposed as governor of the Autonomous Region of Muslim Mindanao (ARMM), encompassing the four provinces—Sulu, the Tawi Tawi island group, and the mainland provinces of Maguindanao and Lanao del Sur—then controlled by the MNLF. Meanwhile, 7,500 of the MNLF's 16,000-member military would be incorporated into the national army and police. The peace agreement was immediately rejected by the more militant Moro Islamic Liberation Front (MILF) and by hard-line MNLF splinters.

Political developments in 1997 were dominated by preparations for the 1998 presidential election. In June a Supreme Court decision scuttled a campaign by a group of President Ramos's supporters to amend the constitution so that he could run for a second term. Also in June, Vice President Joseph E. ESTRADA, a former film actor and the leading contender for the presidency, formed a three-party electoral coalition called the Struggle for the Nationalist Filipino Masses (*Laban ng Makabayang Masang Pilipino*—LAMMP), which included his own Party of the Filipino Masses (*Partido ng Masang Pilipino*—PMP), the NPC, and the Democratic Filipino Struggle (*Laban ng Demokratikong Pilipino*—LDP). In December Estrada selected the LDP's Edgardo ANGARA as his running mate. Estrada won the May 11, 1998, presidential election with 39.9 percent of the vote in a field of ten candidates, with Gloria MACAPAGAL-ARROYO, backed by Ramos's *Lakas*-NUCD, easily winning the vice presidency over Angara. The LAMMP electoral coalition, which later merged to become the Party of the Philippine Masses (*Lapian ng Masang Pilipino*—LAMP), also swept to victory in the House of Representatives and won a majority of the open seats in the Senate. Estrada thus held a firm base of support in the Congress despite opposition from most of the business community and the Catholic hierarchy, which called him morally unfit for office.

A year into his term Estrada's popularity dropped dramatically in response to his ultimately unsuccessful effort to introduce constitutional changes that would have opened the economy to increased foreign investment. His administration was further damaged by allegations of corruption, cronyism, and mismanagement. In October 2000 Luis SINGSON, governor of Ilocos Sur, charged that he had transmitted to President Estrada some $8.6 million in illegal gambling payoffs and another $2.8 million in provincial tobacco taxes. On October 12 Vice President MACAPAGAL-ARROYO resigned from the cabinet amid opposition calls for Estrada to resign. By the end of the month the vice president was at the front of a "united opposition" that included most of the opposition political parties, led by *Lakas*-NUCD.

On November 4, 2000, a rally organized by Cardinal Sin drew tens of thousands of anti-Estrada demonstrators into the streets of Manila. Proclaiming his innocence, Estrada asked the House to move quickly on an impeachment complaint that had been introduced in October. On November 13, arguing that more than one-third of the House membership had signed the impeachment complaint, Speaker of the House Manuel VILLAR Jr. ordered, without a formal committee vote or a floor debate, that the articles of impeachment be forwarded to the Senate for trial.

The Senate trial opened on December 7, 2000, but adjourned on January 17, 2001, a day after the Senate voted 11–10 not to admit evidence proving, according to the prosecution, that Estrada held secret bank accounts under aliases. In response, the Senate president and the House prosecutors resigned, an estimated 500,000 people took to Manila's streets in "People Power II" demonstrations, most of the cabinet joined the opposition, and the police and military withdrew their support from Estrada. On January 19 the Supreme Court, acting extraconstitutionally, ruled the presidency vacant, and Estrada abandoned the presidential palace, although he refused to resign. Macapagal-Arroyo took the oath of office as president on January 20.

On April 25, 2001, Estrada was arrested and charged with economic plunder, his immunity from prosecution having been lifted by the Supreme Court. At that time a unanimous court had also confirmed the legitimacy of the Macapagal-Arroyo presidency, asserting that Estrada "by his acts and statements" had resigned. In legislative elections held on May 14, Macapagal-Arroyo's *Lakas*-NUCD and its immediate allies won a plurality in the House of Representatives.

Upon taking office Macapagal-Arroyo had moved quickly to open discussions with Communist and Muslim insurgents, with mixed results. Since 1992 the Communist-led NDF had engaged in a series of on-again, off-again talks with successive administrations, but without resolving the conflict, which was estimated to have cost 40,000–50,000 lives since the late 1960s. Negotiations were renewed in April 2001 in Oslo, Norway, but in June the government suspended the process indefinitely in response to the NPA's alleged involvement in the assassination of a congressman. At the same time, the Macapagal-Arroyo administration opened peace talks with the MILF in June in Tripoli. A preliminary peace agreement was announced two days later. On August 7, despite the condemnation of Muslim rejectionists, the MILF signed a more formal cease-fire in Kuala Lumpur, Malaysia, but continued to engage in sporadic military activity. In July 2003 the government and the MILF initiated a new cease-fire that paved the way for a series of informal meetings. More formal peace talks, held in Kuala Lumpur, resumed in April 2005. Meanwhile, under the sponsorship of the Organization of the Islamic Conference (OIC), members of an International Monitoring Team from Malaysia, Brunei, and Libya had taken up their posts in Mindanao. (Japan joined the group in July 2006, in a nonmilitary advisory role, and Norway joined in 2010.)

In December 2002 Macapagal-Arroyo had stated that she would not seek election to a full term as president, but she reversed herself in October 2003, asserting that she needed a full term to implement the necessary political and economic reforms. Her vice president, Teofisto GUINGONA of *Lakas*-NUCD, who had already distanced himself from the president on a number of issues, responded that she had been an ineffective leader, failing to root out corruption and to end the Muslim rebellion in the south.

With general elections approaching, in December 2003 the LDP, the Filipino Democratic Party–Laban (*Partido Demokratikong Pilipinos*–Laban—PDP-Laban), and Estrada's Force of the Filipino Masses (*Puwersa ng Masang Pilipino*—PMP, as the Party of the Filipino Masses was now known) established an opposition alliance, the Coalition of the United Filipinos (*Koalisyon ng Nagkakaisang Pilipino*—KNP). A month later the *Lakas*–Christian Muslim Democrats (*Lakas*-CMD, the reconfigured *Lakas*-NUCD) led the formation of a second major electoral alliance, the Coalition for Truth and Experience for the Future (*Koalisyon ng Katapatan at Karanasan sa Kinabukasan*—K4), which also included the NPC, the LP, and several smaller parties.

In the presidential election on May 20, 2004, Macapagal-Arroyo won 40 percent of the vote against four other candidates, chiefly the KNP's Fernando POE Jr., a film actor and friend of former president Estrada. Poe won 35.5 percent of the vote. The vice presidency was won by former news anchor Sen. Noli DE CASTRO of the *Lakas*-CMD, who defeated another former news anchor, the KNP's Sen. Loren LEGARDA. In congressional contests the K4 parties won 7 of the 12 contested Senate seats and a clear majority in the House of Representatives. Although Poe and his supporters, claiming fraud, refused to accept the presidential results, a joint session of Congress officially named Macapagal-Arroyo the winner on June 24, and she was sworn in on June 30.

On February 11–14, 2004, Manila and the NDF had reopened peace talks in Oslo, and additional rounds were held in March–April and June. An August session was canceled by the NDF, however, in part because the government had not attempted to convince the United States, Canada, Australia, and the European Union (EU) to remove the NDF, CPP, and NPA from their lists of foreign terrorist organizations.

In July 2005 President Macapagal-Arroyo included in her annual State of the Nation address to Congress a constitutional reform proposal that called for replacing the existing "dysfunctional" presidential system with a unicameral parliamentary form of government headed by a prime minister. Such a "charter change" could be implemented by an elected constitutional convention or by Congress's sitting as a constituent assembly. The Senate's opposition to forming a constituent assembly led the government to begin circulating a "people's initiative" petition that, with sufficient signatures (from at least 12 percent of the voters, including a minimum of 3 percent in each congressional district) could have put the charter change proposal to the voters in a referendum. In October, however, a divided Supreme Court ruled that a plebiscite could not be employed to make such major constitutional revisions. The charter change initiative was shelved but remained high on Macapagal-Arroyo's agenda.

On July 8–11, 2005, a dozen cabinet members and senior aides resigned and called for President Macapagal-Arroyo to do likewise over allegations of vote-rigging during the 2004 presidential election (during the vote count she had spoken with an election official) and illegal gambling payoffs to members of her immediate family. The president refused to step down and told her opponents to "take your grievances to Congress," where they could pursue impeachment. On July 20 a formal impeachment motion was introduced in the House of Representatives, where the removal effort split the LP. On August 31 the House's Justice Committee rejected the complaint 48–4, and a week later, with 79 votes needed to pursue impeachment, only 51 House members voted against accepting the committee report.

Opposition to the president nevertheless persisted, and on February 24, 2006, she declared a state of emergency in response to the discovery of an alleged coup plot by elements of the armed forces. The state of emergency was lifted on March 3, four days after charges were filed against 16 individuals. On August 24 another effort to impeach the president, citing abuse of her authority and other offenses, was ended by a 173–32 vote of the House.

The May 14, 2007, election for the House of Representatives and half the Senate saw *Lakas*-CMD and its allies, including Kampi and the NPC, win a convincing majority in the lower house. Control of the Senate swung to the opposition, now led by the LP and the NP, but candidates backed by the progovernment caucus won election as Senate president and majority leader.

On September 12, 2007, former president Estrada was convicted of plunder and sentenced to life in prison. Not long after, however, the government initiated talks with Estrada on a conditional pardon, which was granted by Macapagal-Arroyo on October 26.

The nation's two strongest parties, *Lakas*-CMD and Kampi, agreed to merge in June 2008, and the formal merger was completed on May 28, 2009. The new *Lakas* Kampi CMD, the nation's largest party by far, appeared poised to make a strong run in the 2010 elections, but the party was wracked by internal divisions and its presidential candidate, former defense minister Gilbert TEODORO, never entered the top tier. Sen. Benigno AQUINO III of the LP, the only son of Benigno and Corazon Aquino, won a decisive victory in the polling on May 10, 2010, and formed a majority coalition in the new parliament.

In legislative elections on May 13, 2013, the LP won a plurality in the House, followed by the NPC (see Current issues, below). Meanwhile, pro-presidential parties secured an absolute majority in elections for one half of the Senate seats. In December 2013, in the aftermath of Typhoon Yolanda (Haiyan) (see Current issues, below), the president appointed Panfilo LACSON as a special assistant in charge of rehabilitation and recovery.

In national elections on May 9, 2016, Rodrigo DUTERTE (PDP-Laban) won the presidential balloting with 39 percent of the vote. He was inaugurated on June 30, and a new cabinet took office the same day. Leni ROBREDO (LP) was concurrently elected vice president. In concurrent legislative polling, the LP was first with a plurality of 115 seats in the House.

Constitution and government. The basic law approved on February 2, 1987, supplanting the "Freedom Constitution" of March 1986, contains broad civil rights guarantees, denies the military any form of political activity save voting, prohibits abortion, authorizes local autonomy for Muslim-dominated areas, calls for a "nuclear-free" policy (save where the national interest dictates otherwise), and requires legislative concurrence for the leasing of Filipino territory to foreign powers.

In April 2006 the Supreme Court declared unconstitutional a "calibrated preemptive response" (CPR) policy introduced "in lieu of maximum tolerance" toward rallies and public demonstrations. In its ruling the court stated that the CPR "has no place in our legal firmament and must be struck down as a darkness that shrouds freedom. It merely confuses our people and is used by some police agents to justify abuses." In the same decision the court also rejected a "no permit, no rally" policy but added that local governments could restrict permitless demonstrations to designated "freedom parks." The court further stated that officials could deny permits "only on the ground of clear and present danger to public order, public safety, public convenience, public morals or public health."

The constitution provides for a directly elected president serving a single six-year term in conjunction with a separately elected vice president; a bicameral Congress consisting of a Senate and a House of Representatives (with senators and representatives who may serve no more than two and three terms, respectively); and an independent judiciary headed by a Supreme Court. The president is specifically enjoined from imposing martial law for more than a 60-day period without legislative approval. The House of Representatives may impeach the chief executive if one-third of its membership concurs, with a two-thirds vote of the Senate then needed for conviction.

Administratively, the country encompasses 17 regions, 82 provinces, over 130 cities, 1,500 municipalities, and nearly 42,000 local authorities (*barangays*). In November 1975 an enlarged Metropolitan Manila was created by merging the city with 16 surrounding communities, including the official capital, Quezon City. The new metropolis, with a total population of more than 5 million, is governed by a Metropolitan Manila Commission. The Autonomous Region of Muslim Mindanao (ARMM) currently includes the provinces of Basilan, Lanao del Sur, Maguindanao, Sulu, and Tawi Tawi, plus Marawi City. An agreement negotiated with Muslim rebels to expand the "ancestral domain" of Philippine Muslims was struck down by the Supreme Court in October 2008 (see Current issues, below).

Freedom of the press is guaranteed by the constitution, but in the wake of the February 2006 state of emergency the government, in an effort to reduce the incidence of negative news reports about its activities, employed pressure tactics that included, according to the *International Herald Tribune,* "warnings, watch lists, surveillance, court cases, harassment lawsuits and threats of arrest on charges of sedition." Moreover, the climate of violence fostered by the Communist and Islamic insurgencies has made the Philippines the second deadliest country for journalists, after Iraq. In 2016 Reporters Without Borders ranked the Philippines 138th out of 180 countries in freedom of the press, an increase from 149th in 2014.

Foreign relations. Following independence, Philippine foreign policy was based on strong opposition to communism, close alliance with the United States, and active participation in the United Nations and its related agencies. The Philippines also joined various regional organizations, such as the Association of Southeast Asian Nations (ASEAN) and the Asian Development Bank (ADB). After the Vietnam War, however, uncertainty about the U.S. role in Southeast Asia spurred greater independence in foreign policy, and diplomatic and trade relations were established with several Communist states, including the People's Republic of China, the Soviet Union, and Vietnam.

A major issue for Corazon Aquino's government concerned U.S. financial assistance during the remaining years of the 1947 treaty that provided for U.S. use of six military installations, including Clark Air Base and Subic Bay Naval Station, the two largest U.S. overseas installations. Following the eruption of Mount Pinatubo in June 1991, however, the U.S. Defense Department announced that, because of the magnitude of cleanup costs, no attempt would be made to reopen Clark, which had been engulfed in volcanic ash. Negotiations to extend the Subic Bay lease ultimately broke down, with formal "disestablishment" being proclaimed in September 1992.

In January 1998, despite nationalist and leftist opposition, Manila and Washington signed a controversial Visiting Forces Agreement (VFA) that would permit large-scale joint military exercises, allow U.S. warships in Philippine waters, and accord legal standing to visiting U.S. forces. The Philippine Senate approved the pact in May 1999, prompting the formal withdrawal of the Communist NDF from peace negotiations with the government. The first joint military exercises under the VFA were held in February 2000. In November 2002, in the context of the U.S.-led "war on terrorism," the two governments signed a Mutual Logistics Support Agreement, which permits the United States to position communications and other nonlethal equipment in the Philippines. In March 2003, during a visit by President Macapagal-Arroyo to Washington, U.S. president George W. Bush declared the Philippines to be a "major non-NATO ally." These ties were reaffirmed in August 2009 when Macapagal-Arroyo met with U.S. president Barack Obama at the White House.

In February 1994, at the conclusion of the first U.S. court case involving alleged human rights violations in another country, a federal jury in Honolulu, Hawaii, ordered the estate of the late President Marcos to pay damages of some $2.5 billion to thousands of individuals said to have suffered under his rule. To settle the claim, in February 1999 the Marcos family agreed to pay $150 million to some 10,000 victims. In July 2004 the Hawaii district court ordered $40 million in hidden assets to be paid out, but Manila appealed the decision on the grounds that "all decisions on ill-gotten wealth lie within the sovereign prerogative of the Philippines." In May 2006 a U.S. appeals court backed the Hawaii court's decision. In 1998 the Swiss Supreme Court had rejected a final appeal by Marcos family representatives that would have prevented the return to the Philippine government of $590 million from the former president's Swiss bank accounts.

Relations between Manila and its ASEAN partners have typically been stable. Nevertheless, a vexing regional issue concerns competing claims to the Spratly Islands in the South China Sea, which sit astride vital shipping lanes, support a major fishing industry, and may contain significant oil and natural gas deposits. In addition to the Philippines, the claimants include China, Taiwan, and three other members of ASEAN (Brunei, Malaysia, and Vietnam). Since 1995 China and the Philippines have had numerous clashes over fishing rights and construction on various reefs and shoals. In March 1999 the Chinese and Philippine foreign ministers, conferring in Manila, agreed to "exercise joint restraint" in the Spratlys, although China continued to oppose a Philippine proposal for international mediation. Altercations also occurred with Malaysia and Vietnam in 1999. A visit by President Estrada to China in May 2000 concluded with both countries repeating their intentions to settle the dispute peacefully. In September 2004 the Philippine and Chinese state oil companies announced that they would jointly conduct a seismic study to determine if oil and natural gas are present in the Spratlys. In March 2005 they and Vietnam's counterpart agreed to a tripartite Joint Marine Seismic Undertaking. The Philippines codified its territorial claims, including its claim to the Spratly Islands, by approving "baselines" legislation in March 2009. China protested the law and sent a military patrol boat into the area days later. As the diplomatic issue heated up following an ASEAN regional forum in 2010, some Filipino commentators urged the state to make its military presence in the region more credible to back up its policy concerning the South China Sea.

Over the past decade, Malaysia has helped broker peace talks between the Philippine government and the MILF, leading to the Memorandum of Agreement on Ancestral Domain that was invalidated by the Supreme Court in October 2008 (see Current issues, below). On April 24, 2012, the Philippine government and MILF signed a new ten-point peace plan following talks in Malaysia (see Current issues, below).

In January 2012 the United States and the Philippines launched negotiations on increased defense ties, including the possible restoration of U.S. military bases in the Philippines. In April a Philippine naval vessel stopped two Chinese fishing vessels in the disputed waters on the Scarborough Shoal. China dispatched two patrol ships to the area, while the Philippines deployed another vessel. A standoff ensued until June 18, when both nations withdrew their naval units ostensibly because of the onset of typhoon season. China and the Philippines both continued to assert sovereignty over the area. In September, in a symbolic measure, the Philippines renamed areas of the South China Sea as the West Philippine Sea.

In January 2013 the Philippines announced it would refer its maritime dispute with China over the Spratly Islands for international arbitration under the UN Convention on the Law of the Sea. On January 31 the United States issued an apology to the Philippines for the wreck of a U.S. naval minesweeper that ran aground in the Tubbataha Reefs Natural Park, a UN-world heritage site. The United States also announced it would dismantle the ship. However, in April the United States refused to pay a $1.4 million fine for the incident. Meanwhile, a Chinese fishing vessel ran aground on the reefs on April 8, and the crew was charged with poaching after officials discovered 10 tons of endangered scaly anteater meat aboard.

In March 2013 fighting broke out between approximately 200 members of a Filipino militia group, the Royal Army of the Sulu Sultanate, and Malaysian security forces in Saban, Malaysia. At least 90 were killed in the violence, which prompted the Malaysian government to deploy some 5,000 soldiers to disperse the Filipinos. Reports indicated that more than 4,000 ethnic Filipinos who lived in Saban fled back to the Philippines to avoid reprisals. Philippine President Aquino condemned the violence but maintained a claim to the territory.

In February 2014 the Philippines filed a formal protest with China after Chinese naval vessels fired water cannons on Filipino fishermen near the disputed Scarborough Shoal. Continuing tensions with China prompted the Philippines and the United States to sign a new, ten-year defense accord, which granted Washington the ability to construct facilities on Philippine military bases and pre-position military equipment.

France provided the Philippines a $150 million loan in June 2014 to support decentralization reforms designed to empower local governments. Also in June Singapore formally endorsed the claims of the Philippines in the South China Sea. In July the Philippines and Australia finalized an accord to combat human trafficking, following the revision of a series of domestic laws against human trafficking in the Philippines.

On July 12, 2016, the Permanent Court of Arbitration at The International Tribunal in The Hague ruled in favor of the Philippines in a dispute with China over territory in the South China Sea. The court asserted that "there was no evidence that China has historically exercised exclusive control over the waters or their resources." China, however, immediately rejected the ruling on the grounds that, among others, the arbitration process was unilateral by the Philippines. China refused to be part of the case and continued to proclaim that it only accepted bilateral dialogue with the Philippines over the disputed waters.

On September 5, 2016, President Duterte made highly insulting comments about U.S. president Barack Obama that led to the latter's cancellation of a scheduled meeting with his Philippine counterpart during a summit in Laos. Four days later, the Philippines and Indonesia announced an agreement to suppress terrorism in south Philippines. Later that month, Japan agreed to provide the Philippines with maritime patrolling vessels, including ten small-sized and two large-sized patrol ships and up to five secondhand surveillance aircraft.

In October 2016, during a diplomatic visit to Beijing, China, Duterte provoked alarm within both his government and the United States with comments indicating that he planned a "separation" from Washington. Duterte later indicated that his comments were taken out of context and what he meant was that the Philippines would pursue a more independent foreign policy. While in Beijing, the Philippine president secured an agreement to allow his country's fishing fleet some access to disputed maritime areas under the control of China. On October 26 Duterte asserted that the Philippines could not be treated like a "doormat," and he wanted foreign troops withdrawn from his country within years. He also claimed he was cancelling joint U.S.–Philippine military patrols.

Current issues. On August 1, 2009, former president Corazon Aquino died. More than 200,000 people lined the streets of Manila to glimpse her casket before it was laid to rest beside the grave of her husband, Benigno Aquino Jr. The funeral electrified the opposition. In a country whose politics are dominated by dynastic families, the outpouring of love for the departed "Cory" Aquino transformed into a movement to draft her son, Benigno Aquino III, for the presidency. Aquino, a backbench LP senator with a relatively low profile, wavered at first, but after Sen. Manuel ROXAS II, already nominated as the LP's candidate, withdrew from the race on September 1, "Noynoy" Aquino announced his candidacy eight days later, with Roxas as his running mate.

Noynoy Aquino campaigned on his family's legacy and an anticorruption platform. The issue of corruption worked to Aquino's advantage, since his two principal rivals, former House speaker Manuel Villar of the NP and former president Estrada of the PMP (who had defied a condition of his 2007 pardon by running for office again), were both alleged to have enriched themselves illicitly while in power. In addition, the Philippines introduced nationwide computerized voting in the 2010 general election. Relatively few glitches marred the May 10, 2010, balloting. Aquino won handily with 42 percent of the vote to Estrada's 26.3 percent and Villar's 15.4 percent. Jejomar BINAY of PDP-Laban narrowly defeated Roxas for the vice presidency. In August 2011 it was announced that former president, and now member of Congress, Macapagal-Arroyo had been barred from traveling abroad due to pending corruption charges. She faced "plunder charges" as she allegedly illegally misused tens of millions of dollars of government funds for her election campaign. Additionally, she faced separate charges that she did not remit $1.7 million in taxes on the sale of a government lot. There were also allegations that she used $17 million of state fertilizer funds for her 2004 reelection campaign. Macapagal-Arroyo's spokesperson claimed the charges were politically motivated. (For separate information on political violence during the campaign, see the 2014 *Handbook.*)

In his first executive order following his inauguration on June 30, President Aquino established a truth commission to investigate and "bring necessary closure to allegations of official wrongdoing and impunity" during the prior administration.

On the island of Mindanao, the October 2008 Supreme Court decision nullifying the government's negotiated agreement with the MILF created a serious setback in the peace process. On July 16 of that year the administration announced that it had reached a peace agreement with the MILF, after three years of talks brokered by Malaysia. The Memorandum of Agreement on Ancestral Domain (MOA-AD) would create an autonomous Muslim homeland much larger than the current Autonomous Region in Muslim Mindanao (ARMM). Fearing that the pact would lead the separatists to declare an independent state, several Philippine politicians brought suit. On August 4, one day before the scheduled signing ceremony in Kuala Lumpur, the Supreme Court issued a temporary restraining order against accession to the MOA-AD. Several violent raids by MILF fighters followed; citing these incidents, the Macapagal-Arroyo administration backed away from the agreement, amid sharp criticism for failing to consult with lawmakers during the negotiations. In an 8–7 decision, on October 14 the court ruled that the administration had exceeded its constitutional authority by negotiating the document in full knowledge that it would require amending the constitution.

Numerous clashes in the succeeding months resulted in hundreds of deaths and more than a half million refugees. Despite a loss of confidence, both sides prepared to resume talks. The president ordered a suspension of military operations in July 2009, days before her final State of the Nation address, and MILF swiftly followed suit. Administration officials said the government aimed to finalize peace agreements with both the Muslim MILF rebels and the Communist forces of the NDF before the end of Macapagal-Arroyo's term, but the president was unable to meet either of these goals.

On August 4, 2011, MILF chairperson Al-Haj MURAD Ebrahim and President Benigno Aquino had a meeting at Narita, Japan, to discuss self-determination for Bangsamoro. Meanwhile, on November 18 Macapagal-Arroyo was arrested for electoral fraud. In February she pleaded not guilty to the charges. Typhoon Washi hit Mindanao on December 16–18. The storm killed 1,249, with more than 60,000 left homeless.

The government and MILF signed a peace accord on April 24, 2012, in Malaysia. The agreement endorsed the creation of a new political body to replace the ARMM and offer greater autonomy to the region. Nonetheless, sporadic fighting continued between government forces and MILF. A further ceasefire was signed in October. Meanwhile, on May 29 the Senate voted to impeach Supreme Court Chief Justice Renato CORONA for failing to disclose $2.4 million in assets. The Senate failed to convict the chief justice on concurrent charges that he obstructed efforts to prosecute Macapagal-Arroyo.

On July 30, 2012, Typhoon Saola hit the island of Luzon, killing 50. A week later, tropical storm Haiku again devastated Luzon, killing at least 65 and leaving more than 646,000 homeless.

In April 2013 MILF accused security forces of carrying out a series of attacks, but the government asserted that the strikes had been aimed at the *Abu Sayyaf* Group. The LP won House elections on May 13, securing 112 seats, followed by the NPC with 43, and the newly formed National Unity Party with 24. The LP also won the majority of governorships, securing 38 of the country's 80, compared to the NPC's 13 and the NP's 10, among others. Although the government reported that the elections were relatively peaceful, 46 people were killed in election-related violence.

In November 2013 Super Typhoon Yolanda (Haiyan) struck the Philippines with an estimated loss of life of more than 6,000 and an estimated population of over four million displaced. The typhoon struck the agricultural heartland of the Philippines but spared most of the industrial base. The aftermath of the event resulted in widespread looting and violence; the government response was criticized for failing to deliver humanitarian aid and security in a timely manner. In December Aquino announced a four-year, $8.2 billion reconstruction initiative for the regions damaged by the storm.

On March 27, 2014, a comprehensive peace accord between the government and MILF was signed in Manila. The agreement created the Bangsamoro autonomous region to replace the ARMM and committed to approximately 12,000 MILF fighters to disarm.

In April 2014 the government announced that it could only account for $14.8 million of an estimated $600 million in foreign aid for Typhoon Yolanda. Officials announced new measures to track funds and a series of audits to account for the missing monies. Typhoon Glenda (Rammasun) struck the Philippines on July 15, 2014. The storm killed 98 and caused $250 million in damage, including cutting power for more than 25 million people.

On January 25, 2015, 43 Philippine elite Special Action Force members were killed during a clash with MILF and the Bangsamoro Islamic Freedom Fighters (BIFF). On September 21 the kidnapping of Norwegian Kjartan Sekkingstad and Canadians Robert Hall and John Ridsdel by *Abu Sayyaf* militants on Samal Island led to a massive, but unsuccessful, search by the Philippine security forces.

On October 18, 2015, Typhoon Koppu (Lando) made landfall in the Aurora province in the northern Philippines. The excessive rainfall caused floods in the Cagayan River valley, one of the most important agricultural areas of the Philippines, with damages estimated at $135 million. Typhoon Melor (Nona) swept through the northern provinces on December 24, killing 42 and prompting the evacuation of 750,000. More than 279,000 homes were damaged by the storm.

On Mar 26, 2016, *Abu Sayyaf* kidnapped ten Indonesian sailors in Sulu.

The Supreme Court, on July 19, 2016, dismissed the plunder case filed against former president Macapagal-Arroyo. On September 17, after a series of negotiations between the government and *Abu Sayyaf*, Sekkingstad and three of the ten Indonesian sailors were released.

Newly elected president Duterte initiated a harsh crackdown on drug trafficking in line with his campaign promises of reducing crime and drug-trafficking. From July 1–September 18, 2016, reports indicated that more than 3,800 people had been killed by the Philippine police and vigilantes. The violence led an estimated 600,000 drug dealers and users to surrender to the authorities; however, the campaign raised wide concern from the United Nations, the EU, and the United States that the killings gravely violated basic human rights. President Duterte refused to attempt to restrain the extrajudicial killings.

POLITICAL PARTIES AND GROUPS

From 1946 until the imposition of martial law by Ferdinand Marcos in 1972, political control oscillated between the *Nacionalista* Party (NP), founded in 1907, and the Liberal Party (LP), organized by slightly left-of-center elements that split from the *Nacionalistas* in 1946. Since martial law was lifted in 1978, Filipino parties have tended to form loose and shifting coalitions around electoral campaigns. Some parties and coalitions jointly endorse legislative candidates with other national parties or with small local or regional parties. Party platforms and ideologies are relatively loose and it is common for politicians to switch parties, sometimes during campaign season. Parties often contain members belonging to both the pro-administration and opposition blocs in Congress. In addition, the party-list system guarantees significant parliamentary representation for minority constituencies.

For details on the principal electoral alliances formed prior to the most recent campaigns, see the 2010 and 2014 *Handbooks.*

Presidential Party:

Philippine Democratic Party–Laban (*Partido Demokratikong Pilipinas–Lakas ng Bayan*—PDP-Laban). The current PDP-Laban constitutes the branch of the original PDP-Laban that refused to join in formation of the LDP (see below) in 1988. In 2004 it won two lower house seats as a component of the Coalition of the United Filipinos (*Koalisyon ng Nagkakaisang Pilipino*—KNP) alliance. In 2005–2006 party leader Aquilino Pimentel Jr. was one of the more outspoken voices demanding President Macapagal-Arroyo's resignation.

In the 2007 election, the PDP-Laban won three House seats. Two PDP-Laban members entered the 2010 presidential contest: Jejomar "Jojo" Binay, mayor of Makati, and Senator Ana Consuelo "Jamby" Madrigal. The latter, a wealthy senator, left the party to run as an independent. Binay switched to the vice presidential race, as running mate of the PMP's Joseph Estrada. Binay's victory brought hopes for a revival of the party to its former heights during the Corazon Aquino era. The PDP-Laban joined with the PMP in the UNA. Binay was selected as the president of the UNA. In February 2014 Binay left the

PDP–Laban to launch a new political grouping that would remain within the UNA. Meanwhile, the PDP–Laban announced it would leave the UNA after Binay's departure.

Party leader Rodrigo Duterte was elected president of the Philippines on May 9, 2016, with 39 percent of the vote. While the party only won three seats in the concurrent House balloting, and one Senate seat, reports indicate that a number of defectors from other groupings transferred to the PDP-Laban. The party also formed a coalition with the LP and other groupings to give it approximately 200 seats in the House (see LP below).

Leaders: Rodrigo DUTERTE (President of the Philippines and Party Chair), Pantaleon ÁLVAREZ (Party Secretary General and Speaker of the House), Aquilino PIMENTEL III (Senate President and President of the Party).

Other National Congressional Parties:

Liberal Party (LP). The LP was organized in 1946 by a group of centrist *Nacionalista* dissidents. Formerly a member of **United Nationalist Democratic Organization** (UNIDO), its congressional delegation after the 1987 election encompassed 8 senators and 42 representatives. Subsequently, it divided into a pro-Aquino mainstream faction headed by Jovito SALONGA and a more rightist group headed by Eva KALAW.

Manila mayor Alfredo LIM was the party's 1998 "law-and-order candidate" for president and ran with the endorsement of former president Corazon Aquino. Lim won only 8.7 percent of the vote, and the LP captured 14 House seats. The party subsequently entered a "strategic" coalition with the **Party of the Philippine Masses** (*Lapian ng Masang Pilipino*—LAMP). In January 2000 Lim joined the Estrada cabinet.

Although the LP was also divided over the Estrada impeachment question, most of the party leadership ended up calling for the president's resignation. The LP won 21 lower house seats in May 2001. It supported President Macapagal-Arroyo's reelection in 2004 and participated in the K4, winning more than two dozen seats in the House of Representatives, as well as 2 in the Senate.

The 2005 presidential impeachment battle effectively split the LP. In March 2006 a faction led by Manila mayor Jose ATIENZA, supporting Macapagal-Arroyo, ousted Senate president Franklin DRILON as party leader, but the Drilon faction met shortly thereafter and expelled Atienza and cabinet member Michael DEFENSOR. Drilon subsequently asked the Commission on Elections to decide the issue. In July Drilon stepped down as Senate president. On November 26 the party's Executive Council appointed Manuel ROXAS II as party president. In April 2007 the Supreme Court sided with the Drilon faction. In the May election, the party won 23 House seats to lead the opposition and retained 4 Senate seats.

Senator Manuel Roxas II at first appeared set to become the party's standard-bearer in the 2010 presidential election, but the death of Corazon Aquino on August 1, 2009, caused a shift in the political winds, sparking a public clamor for Benigno Aquino III to enter the race. Roxas withdrew his previously declared candidacy to make way for his Senate colleague. "Noynoy" Aquino accepted the challenge days later, taking Roxas as his running mate and vowing to restore clean government to the nation. As the campaign got underway, several prominent leaders bolted their parties to join the Aquino campaign, including Sen. Francis "Chiz" ESCUDERO (from the NPC, below) and former Quezon City mayor Feliciano "Sonny" BELMONTE Jr. (from *Lakas* Kampi CMD). Aquino vaulted ahead of his rivals and marched to a decisive victory in the presidential race; Roxas narrowly lost the vice presidential contest to Jejomar Binay. The LP made dramatic gains in the House of Representatives, becoming the second largest party behind *Lakas* Kampi CMD, and entering a majority coalition with other parties (including many lawmakers from *Lakas*) to elect Belmonte as speaker. In June 2012 Sarangani Governor Miguel Rene DOMINGUEZ defected from *Lakas* and joined the Liberal Party.

In the May 2013 national elections, the LP became the largest party in the House. In concurrent local balloting, the LP won 33.4 percent of the vote and pluralities or majorities of seats on 45 percent of the provincial boards. Reports in 2014 indicated that Roxas was the clear frontrunner to be the party's candidate in the 2016 presidential elections.

In the May 2016 national elections, the LP remained the largest party in the House, with 115 seats, and increased its seats in the Senate to 6. Roxas, the LP presidential candidate, was second with 23.5 percent of the vote, but the party's vice presidential candidate, Leni ROBREDO, won her election with 35.1 percent.

The LP joined the PDP-Laban coalition after the election. However, an estimated 30 party members refused to back the PDP-Laban and remained part of the opposition.

Leaders: Benigno C. AQUINO III (Former President of the Republic and Executive Vice President of the Party), Sen. Franklin DRILON (Chair), Manuel ROXAS II (Secretary of the Interior and Local Government and Party President), Joseph Emilio ABAYA (Secretary of Transport and Communications and Secretary General of the Party).

***Lakas* Kampi Christian Muslim Democrats** (*Lakas-Kabalikat ng Malayang Pilipino ng Kristiyano at Muslim Demokrata*—*Lakas* Kampi CMD). Two of the largest Filipino parties, ***Lakas*-CMD** and **Alliance of Free Filipinos** (*Kabalikat ng Malayang Pilipino*—Kampi), completed a merger in 2009. *Lakas*-CMD traces its origin to the **People Power Party** (*Partido Lakas ng Tao*—PPP) that was founded by presidential hopeful Fidel Ramos in January 1992, two months after he had left the dominant LDP because of its decision to designate Ramon Mitra as its nominee. In early February the formation was redesignated as EDSA-LDP (EDSA being an acronym for *Epifanio de los Santo Avenue*, the location of the first "People Power" rally in 1986). Subsequently, *Lakas ng EDSA* (EDSA Power) joined in a coalition with the **National Union of Christian Democrats** (NUCD), led by Raul MANGLAPUS, who had previously led the pre-1972 Christian Socialist Movement.

While *Lakas*-NUCD won only 51 of 201 lower house seats in the 1992 election, its ranks were subsequently swelled by defections from other parliamentary groups, including, most notably, the LDP. In mid-1994, by contrast, it lost a number of House supporters, most prominently its majority leader, Ronaldo Zamora. It captured an overwhelming majority of House seats in 1995. In June 1997 the Supreme Court ruled that Ramos could not run for reelection, and in December he backed Jose de Venecia, Speaker of the House of Representatives.

To enhance his party's chances at the polls, Ramos engineered an electoral alliance with the moderate **United Muslim Democratic Party** (UMDP) of Mindanao and with Kampi, which had been organized in 1997 by José Cojuangco and others to support the presidential aspirations of Gloria Macapagal-Arroyo, daughter of former president Diosdado Macapagal. Although opinion polls indicated that Macapagal-Arroyo was running second only to Joseph Estrada among presidential contenders, she agreed to unite Kampi with *Lakas*-NUCD and to serve as de Venecia's running mate.

In May 1998 de Venecia finished second, with 15.9 percent of the presidential vote, while Macapagal-Arroyo won the vice presidency with a 47 percent share and subsequently agreed to join the cabinet as secretary of social welfare and development. Following her victory, Kampi remained in existence, although most of its members were also affiliated with *Lakas*-NUCD. Although the *Lakas*-NUCD won 5 Senate seats and 50 House seats, its effectiveness as the leading opposition party was soon weakened by defections to President Estrada's LAMP. The situation was reversed following Estrada's departure from office in January 2001, and the *Lakas*-NUCD emerged from the May 2001 election with a plurality of some 85 seats (including those won by *Lakas* candidates with other endorsements).

President Macapagal-Arroyo was named chair of the party in June 2002, at which time she proposed adopting a new, consolidated name. Accordingly, in October the party leadership approved the change to *Lakas*-CMD.

In October 2003 Macapagal-Arroyo reversed a 2002 decision not to seek election to a full term in 2004, which resulted in the departure from the party of Vice President Teofisto Guingona, who had been *Lakas*-CMD's president. In the May 2004 balloting Macapagal-Arroyo won a full term, with 40 percent of the vote, against four other contenders. At the same time, the party and its K4 allies (including Kampi) captured sufficient seats to maintain a government majority in the Senate and swept to an easy victory in the House of Representatives. The K4's apparent unity subsequently suffered a significant setback in the House, however, when several dozen members, dissatisfied with the House leadership and the divvying up of key committee assignments, declared allegiance to a revitalized Kampi.

In May 2007 *Lakas*-CMD won a plurality of seats in the House of Representatives and, in partnership with second-place finisher Kampi, the NPC, and others, held a majority. De Venecia was ousted from his position as House Speaker on January 28, 2008, and from the party presidency on March 10. Prospero NOGRALES succeeded him in both posts.

A formal agreement on the merger of *Lakas*-CMD and Kampi was signed in Davao City on June 18, 2008, and announced by President

Macapagal-Arroyo. The process of integrating the nation's two largest parties on the regional level was completed at a ceremony in Manila on May 28, 2009. The merger left *Lakas* Kampi CMD with a majority in the House of Representatives and control of more than half the nation's governorships. The party claimed more than five million members.

At a party convention in Manila on November 19, 2009, *Lakas* Kampi CMD nominated the former defense minister Gilbert TEODORO as its 2010 presidential bet. President Macapagal-Arroyo surrendered the party chair to the youthful Teodoro, who had departed from the NPC the previous July to join *Lakas*. However, the party was losing far more members through defections than it was gaining.

In late March 2010 Teodoro surprised onlookers by resigning as chair of the party, claiming a need to set aside administrative duties in order to concentrate on his own lagging campaign. Observers noted disarray in the nation's dominant party, especially at the local and regional levels, where candidates were complaining of insufficient support from the party apparatus. Interim party chair Amelita VILLAROSA had to fend off questions about the imminent disintegration of *Lakas*, especially when House Speaker Prospero Nograles announced he was leaving the party in April. (Nograles changed his mind the next day.)

Lakas led all parties in the 2010 general election, winning 93 House seats, but defections and internal divisions made the party weaker than those numbers suggested. In a party caucus shortly following the election, outgoing president Macapagal-Arroyo, who had won her race to enter Congress from Pampanga, assumed the party presidency once again. A sizable majority of the *Lakas* delegation declared support for the incoming administration, allowing the LP to elect former *Lakas* stalwart Feliciano "Sonny" Belmonte as speaker. Subsequently, a large number of *Lakas* representatives defected to other parties, including the LP, or joined a new grouping, the National Unity Party (NUP) (see below).

In February 2013 Ferdinand Martin ROMUALDEZ succeeded Macapagal-Arroyo as party leader. Following the May balloting, there were calls within the party for Romualdez to resign after *Lakas* only secured 14 seats in the House balloting, a decline of 4 from the previous election.

In 2014 Party Chair Ramon REVILLA Jr. was one of three senators charged with corruption.

In the May 2016 elections, the *Lakas*-CMD did not gain any seats in the Senate but won 4 in the House, along with one provincial governorship and three vice-governorships. After the election, *Lakas* entered into a coalition agreement with the NUP to support President Duterte and the PDP-Laban.

Leaders: Ferdinand Martin ROMUALDEZ (President), Ramon REVILLA Jr. (Chair of the Party), Arthur DEFENSOR (Executive Vice President), Fidel V. RAMOS, Gloria MACAPAGAL-ARROYO (Chairs Emeritus).

Nationalist People's Coalition (NPC). The NPC was formed prior to the 1992 balloting by right-wing elements of both the Liberal and *Nacionalista* parties under the leadership of President Aquino's estranged cousin and former Marcos business confidant, Eduardo Cojuangco. Although Cojuangco finished third in the 1992 presidential poll, NPC candidate Joseph Estrada won the vice presidency on a 33 percent vote share.

The NPC remained in opposition during the Ramos presidency, joining the **Struggle for the Nationalist Filipino Masses** (*Laban ng Makabayang Masang Pilipino*—LAMMP) coalition upon its formation in June 1997. In December, however, NPC President Ernesto Maceda was ousted as Senate president and, blaming Estrada and LDP leader Edgardo Angara, apparently sidetracked a planned formal merger of the three LAMMP parties.

The NPC remained allied with President Estrada until his departure from office in January 2001, after which it agreed to cooperate with President Macapagal-Arroyo's administration. In the May 2001 lower house election the NPC finished second to *Lakas*-NUCD.

As the 2004 elections approached, the NPC was divided over support for Macapagal-Arroyo's reelection bid. As a result, some members supported her principal opponent, Fernando Poe Jr., and ran for Congress as participants in the opposition KNP alliance, while the majority participated in the K4 alliance. In the election the NPC won over 50 House seats. In 2007 it finished third, but with only 28 seats.

Senator Francis "Chiz" Escudero, expected to run for president in 2010, quit the NPC in October 2009 and declined to run as an independent. His Senate colleague Loren Legarda, Poe's running mate in the 2004 election, declared her candidacy first for the top job, then shifted course toward the vice president's office. Legarda, a former anchorwoman known for her environmental advocacy, became the running mate of Sen. Manuel VILLAR of the NP (below). The rival LP brought a successful suit to stop the NP and NPC from formalizing their uneasy coalition. The NPC secured 29 House seats in the 2010 polling and added several more through defections from other parties. The party joined the majority bloc in Congress with the promise of holding onto several committee chairpersonships and campaigned with the LP in the 2013 Senate elections. The NPC placed second in the 2013 House balloting with 43 seats and third in local government balloting, with 100 of the 926 council seats up for election. In June 2014 five provincial board members from Pangasinian resigned from the NPC over what they cited was a lack of consultation between national party leaders and local officials.

In the May 2016 elections, the NPC earned 42 seats in the House and 3 in the Senate, becoming the second-largest grouping in both chambers.

Leaders: Faustino DY Jr. (Chair), Frisco SAN JUAN (President), Michael John DUAVIT (Secretary-General), Eduardo COJUANGCO (Chair Emeritus).

***Nacionalista* Party** (NP). Essentially the right wing of the Philippines' oldest party (formed in 1907), the *Nacionalistas* had been reduced by 1988 to a relatively minor formation within the **Grand Alliance for Democracy** (GAD), which had been organized by former defense minister Juan Ponce Enrile, prior to the 1987 congressional election as an anti-Aquino and anticommunist formation. The GAD also included the now-defunct Mindanao Alliance and the Philippine Democratic Socialist Party (PDSP). In February 1990 Enrile was arrested on charges of involvement in the December 1989 coup attempt, but the Supreme Court subsequently ordered the more serious charges reduced, and Enrile quickly returned to politics.

As the party's 1992 presidential candidate, Vice President Salvador Laurel ran eighth with a vote share of only 3.4 percent. In 1998 Enrile, who had been expelled from the party by Laurel in 1991, ran for president as an independent, capturing 1.4 percent of the vote. For the 1998 elections the NP was allied with the *Lakas*-NUCD and subsequently supported the removal of President Estrada.

Although allied with *Lakas*-CMD in 2004's K4 alliance, the NP ran in 2007 as part of the **Genuine Opposition** (GO) coalition. It won ten House seats and held four Senate seats. However, its leader, Manuel Villar Jr., was subsequently able to retain the role of Senate president only because he received the support of the pro-Macapagal-Arroyo senators. He later lost their backing and ceded the Senate presidency to Juan Ponce Enrile in November 2008. The Senate's ethics committee investigated and finally cleared Villar of corruption charges in 2009, after accusations that he had directed extra government funds to a road project traversing his own property.

Despite the scandal, Villar topped polls as the 2010 presidential race got underway and outspent his opponents in the campaign's early months, but he was unable to stop the meteoric rise of Benigno Aquino III. Villar chose the NPC's Loren Legarda as his running mate. Villar finished a distant third in the balloting. In the general election, the NP gained 12 House seats.

In balloting in 2013, the NP won 17 seats in the House, 6 governorships, and 106 seats on regional councils. Reports in 2014 indicated that General Secretary of the Party Alan Peter CAYETANO intended to seek the NP nomination for the 2016 presidential elections.

In the May 2016 elections, the NP won 3 seats in the Senate, 24 seats in the House of Representatives, and 9 provincial governorships. It joined the PDP-Laban–led majority in the House.

Leaders: Sen. Manuel VILLAR Jr. (President of the Party), Sen. Alan Peter CAYETANO (Secretary General).

United Nationalist Alliance (UNA). The UNA was an electoral coalition formed in 2012 by the PMP (below) and the PDP-Laban (above). A number of smaller or regional parties joined the grouping before the 2013 national elections. In the May balloting, world-famous boxer Manny PACQUIAO was reelected to Congress as a representative from Sarangani; his **People's Champ Movement** was part of the UNA. The UNA secured 5 Senate seats, 8 seats in the House, 4 governorships, and 47 seats on local councils.

On July 1, 2015, Jejomar BINAY announced his bid for the presidency and chose Gringo HONASAN as his running mate. Binay lost the presidential campaign in the May 2016 election. In the same election, the UNA gained 1 seat in the Senate and 11 seats in the House.

Leaders: Jejomar BINAY (President of the Party), Gringo HONASAN (Party Vice President), Joseph ESTRADA (Chair).

Democratic Filipino Struggle (*Laban ng Demokratikong Pilipino*—LDP). Formally established in September 1988, the LDP constituted a merger of the Filipino Democratic Party–Laban (*Partido Demokratikong Pilipinas–Lakas ng Bayan*—PDP-Laban) and the **People's Struggle** (*Lakas ng Bansa*). The PDP, launched in 1982 by former members of the Mindanao Alliance, had joined with the **People's Power** (*Lakas ng Bayan*—Laban), nominally led by Benigno Aquino Jr. until his death in August 1983, to form the PDP-Laban. (Part of the PDP-Laban formation, led by Aquilino Pimentel, refused to enter the LDP and maintains a separate identity—see PDP-Laban, above.) The People's Struggle had been formed in 1987 by a nephew of Corazon Aquino.

Following the May 1995 election, at which the LDP was nominally allied with *Lakas*-NUCD, the LDP split, Edgardo ANGARA, the LDP chair, going into opposition after being ousted as Senate president in favor of Neptali GONZALES, also of the LDP. As a result, elements of the LDP ended up on both sides of the political aisle. In May 1996, however, the LDP severed its remaining coalition links. Five months later Gonzales, a strong supporter of President Ramos, was himself removed as Senate leader.

The LDP won 22 House seats (1 in coalition with the NPC) in the May 2001 election. Earlier in the year a faction known as the "Conscience Bloc" abandoned the party because of its support for pro-Estrada candidates. Most of the dissenters ultimately joined the *Lakas*-NUCD.

In 2004 the party was divided over the presidential contest, with supporters of party leader Edgardo Angara constituting the backbone of the KNP and backing its nominee, actor Fernando Poe Jr., who finished second, with 36.5 percent of the vote. A smaller LDP faction headed by Agapito "Butz" AQUINO supported the candidacy of Sen. Panfilo Lacson, who finished third, with 10.9 percent of the vote. (Poe died on December 14, 2004, three days after suffering a stroke.)

Angara reaffirmed his control of the party at a March 2005 national congress. Senator Angara won reelection in 2007 and the LDP took three House seats. Angara and his son, Juan Edgardo Angara, a House member from the Aurora district, were the only party members elected to Congress in 2010. The party endorsed the vice-presidential bid of the NPC's Loren Legarda.

In the 2013 elections, the LDP won one Senate seat, two House seats, and four spots on provincial councils.

In the 2016 elections, the LDP won two seats in the House.

Leaders: Edgardo ANGARA (Chair), Juan Edgardo ANGARA (Secretary General).

National Unity Party (*Partido Ng Pambansang Pagkakaisa*—NUP). The NUP was formed by disaffected members of *Lakas*-CMD in 2011. The **Populist Party** was split in the 2013 elections, with the party formally supporting the LP, but a large number of members reportedly backing the UNA. In the 2013 balloting, the NUP secured 24 seats in the House, 8 governorships, and 73 seats on local councils.

In the May 2016 election, the NUP won 27 seats in the House of Representatives.

Leaders: Feliciano BELMONTE Jr. (Honorary Chair), Pablo GARCIA (Chair), Rodolfo ANTONINO (President), Elpidio BARZAGA Jr. (Vice President), Roger MERCADO (Secretary General).

Other Parties Winning Seats in 2016:

***Akbayan*! Citizens' Action Party** (*Akbayan*). *Akbayan* was formed in January 1998 as an electoral coalition of various leftist groups, including splinters from the Communist Party of the Philippines (CPP, below) and the **Metro Manila-Rizal Regional Party Committee** (*Komite ng Rehiyon ng Manila-Rizal*—KRMR). In the May 1998 election it won one party-list seat. In May 2001 it again won sufficient support for one seat, while in 2004 it captured 6.7 percent of the vote and was awarded three seats. In 2007 it held one seat, but gained another in April 2009 following the Supreme Court's party-list reallocation (see Legislature, below). Walden BELLO, an academic and well-known globalization critic, joined the lower house and won a full term in 2010. In 2013 the party won two seats in the House.

In the May 2016 elections, *Akbayan* gained one seat in the Senate but won no seats in the House.

Leaders: Risa HONTIVEROS-BARAQUEL, Walden BELLO (Members of the House of Representatives).

Bayan Muna* Party.** The leftist *Bayan Muna* (People First), which descends from the Communist-affiliated **New Nationalist Alliance** (*Bagong Alyansang Makabayan*—Bayan), was the most successful of the party-list groups in 2001 and 2004, winning three House seats in both elections. In 2004 the government charged that it and two associated party-list organizations—the **Gabriela Women's Party** (GWP), led by Liza LARGOLA-MAZA, and the ***Anakpawis (Toiling Masses), previously led by the late Crispin BELTRAN—had channeled money to Communists. Party leader Satur OCAMPO campo had also been associated with the NDF (below).

Among those arrested in connection with the alleged coup plot against Macapagal-Arroyo in February 2006 were the six party-list members from *Bayan Muna, Anakpawis,* and the GWP. The six, minus Beltran, who had already been arrested, initially sought sanctuary in the House complex, Batasan, and were therefore dubbed the "Batasan 5." In July 2007 the Supreme Court dismissed the charges against all six. *Bayan Muna, Anakpawis*, and the GWP formed the core of a new progressive coalition, ***Makabayan***, which ran a slate of Senate candidates in 2010. *Bayan Muna* won two party-list House seats in 2010. In 2014 the party joined a group of left-wing leaders in filing an impeachment complaint against the president for signing the revised U.S.–Philippine defense accord.

In the May 2016 elections, *Bayan Muna* won one seat in the House.

Leaders: Satur OCAMPO, Teodoro CASIÑO Jr.

For a complete list of the groups that won party-list seats in the House of Representatives in 2016, see the Legislature section, below.

For more information on the **Philippine Democratic Socialist Party** (*Partido Demokratiko Sosyalista ng Pilipinas*—PDSP), see the 2013 *Handbook*.

Other Parties:

Force of the Filipino Masses (*Puwersa ng Masang Pilipino*—PMP). The PMP was founded as the **Party of the Filipino Masses** (*Partido ng Masang Pilipino*—PMP) in the early 1990s by Joseph Estrada, a former Liberal, to support his presidential aspirations. He ran as the vice presidential candidate of the NPC in 1992, but by 1998 the rejuvenated PMP claimed 5 million members and Estrada was elected. The PMP was virtually eliminated as an electoral force in the May 2001 election, although Estrada's wife, Luisa EJERCITO-ESTRADA, won election to the Senate as a PMP candidate.

With his trial ongoing, former president Estrada continued to hold sway over the PMP (now known as the Force of the Filipino Masses) as the 2004 elections approached. In December 2003 the PMP joined in formation with the KNP and supported presidential aspirant Fernando Poe Jr. After the May 2004 balloting, the PMP claimed several House seats, while Estrada's son José joined his mother in the Senate. According to reports, in September 2004 the former president rejected a proposal by LDP opposition leader Edgardo Angara to merge the PMP into the LDP.

In August 2005 Juan Ponce Enrile, the chair of the party, took the unorthodox step of joining the majority in the Senate. Enrile stated at the time that former president Estrada had approved the move. In 2007 the PMP won four House seats. Shortly thereafter, Enrile and Jose Estrada were criticized by much of the opposition for joining the pro–Macapagal-Arroyo senators in supporting the NP's Manuel Villar Jr. for Senate president. The mayor of Manila, Alfredo Lim, was appointed party president in 2007, but removed from the position in August 2008.

As the 2010 presidential race heated up, Estrada repeatedly stated that he was willing to offer himself as a candidate if the opposition could not unite behind a single contender. It became increasingly clear that the former president, known in headlines as "Erap," intended to seek the office again, even though his pledge not to do so had been instrumental in obtaining his 2007 pardon. Estrada declared his candidacy, with the PMP's backing, in October 2009. The Commission on Elections (COMELEC) dismissed three petitions filed to prevent his candidacy. The former movie star proved to have enduring popularity, finishing second in the 2010 balloting with 26 percent of the vote. His running mate, Jejomar BINAY of PDP-Laban, won the vice presidency. The PMP won five House seats in 2010 and retained its two Senate seats, with Enrile winning a second term as Senate president. Ahead of the 2013 Senate elections, the PMP joined with the PDP-Laban to form the United Nationalist Alliance (UNA). Estrada was selected as the chair of the UNA. In May 2013 Estrada was elected mayor of Manila.

The party won no seats in the Senate or House in the 2016 congressional elections.

Leaders: Joseph ESTRADA (Chair of the Party and Former President of the Republic), Sen. Juan Ponce ENRILE, José "Jinggoy" ESTRADA.

People's Reform Party (PRP). The PRP was the nominal party vehicle for the 1992 presidential bid of political independent Miriam Defensor-Santiago, who campaigned with sufficient vigor on an anti-corruption platform to gain a 19.7 percent vote share as runner-up to Fidel Ramos. Senator Defensor-Santiago proved less successful in 1998, winning only 3 percent of the presidential vote. She was one of President Estrada's strongest Senate supporters before and after his November 2000 impeachment. In May 2001 she lost her reelection bid.

Defensor-Santiago was expected to seek another Senate term in 2004 as an opposition candidate, but she ultimately gained the endorsement of the government-supportive K4. After winning, she had a falling out with the *Lakas*-CMD and declared herself an independent. Later, however, she repaired relations with the administration and spoke in favor of constitutional reform. One of the most colorful politicians in the Philippines, Defensor-Santiago, was reelected in 2010 with the third-highest vote total among Senate candidates and reelected again in 2013. In July 2014 it was reported that Defensor-Santiago had lung cancer.

In the May 2016 elections, the PRP lost its only seat in the House of Representatives.

Leader: Miriam DEFENSOR-SANTIAGO.

Communist Groups:

National Democratic Front (NDF). The NDF was launched by the Communist Party of the Philippines (CPP, below) in April 1973 in an effort to unite Communist, labor, and Christian opponents of the Marcos regime, which declared it illegal. It encompasses more than a dozen "revolutionary allied organizations," most prominently the CPP and the CPP's military wing, the New People's Army (NPA). After decades of fighting and multiple failed ceasefires, on March 16, 1998, in The Hague, representatives from the government and the NDF signed a Comprehensive Agreement on Respect for Human Rights and International Humanitarian Law (CARHRIHL). (For more information on the history of the NDF, see the 2013 *Handbook.*)

In July 2006, responding to President Macapagal-Arroyo's directive that the police join with the armed forces to pursue all-out war against the NPA, NDF leader Luis Jalandoni called for renewed peace talks. With military operations against the NPA continuing, in October 2007 the government indicated that a cease-fire would have to be established before peace talks could resume. NDF leaders expressed willingness to reopen talks, accusing the government of closing the door to further negotiations by imposing preconditions such as disarmament and demobilization.

In May 2009 the government announced the expected resumption of peace talks with the rebels. Under a restored security agreement, NDF negotiator Luis Jalandoni briefly returned from exile in July. Two detained rebel "consultants" were freed in August, but the delay in releasing more threatened to scuttle the revival of the peace process. Peace negotiations resumed in September 2012 but were suspended in February 2013 by the government citing a lack of progress. The NDF released four kidnapped police officers in July 2014 after the government agreed to a five-day cease-fire.

On May 26, 2016, President Duterte indicated that he would open cabinet positions to NDF nominees. On August 26 the government and the NDF agreed to indefinitely extend a cease-fire to allow further negotiations.

Leaders: Luis JALANDONI (Chair of the NDF Negotiating Panel), Fidel AGCAOILI (Spokesperson for Negotiating Panel), José María SISON (Political Consultant).

Communist Party of the Philippines–Marxist-Leninist (CPP-ML or CPP). The CPP was launched as a Maoist formation in 1968, with the New People's Army (NPA) established as its military wing in early 1969. Between 1986 and 1991, many of its leaders were captured by government forces, including NPA commander Romulo KINTANAR, who was released in 1992, abandoned the guerrilla movement, and was assassinated in January 2003. José María Sison (who reportedly uses the pseudonym Armando Liwanag) was reelected party chair at a Central Committee meeting in September 1992, although he had been an exile in the Netherlands since his release by the Aquino government in 1986. A number of splinter groups subsequently left the CPP (see below).

The NPA numbers some 5,000 rural-based guerrillas, down from a peak of 25,000 in 1987; it is strongest in northeast and central Luzon, in the Samar provinces of the Visayas, and in southern Mindanao, although at various times it has undertaken insurgent activity in well over three-quarters of the country's provinces. In March 1999 the NPA announced that it had established an alliance with the MILF (below). In October 2002 the government declared the CPP to be a terrorist organization.

In 2004 hard-liners attacked Sison for supporting electoral candidates through a number of party-list organizations, including the *Bayan Muna* Party. In the 2010 election campaign, a coalition of leftist party-list groups ran two Senate candidates on the *Nacionalista* Party slate; they were defeated. Some press reports suggested a growing divide between the exiled Sison and hardline leaders Benito and Wilma TIAMZON.

Meanwhile, the NPA and government forces continued to clash. President Macapagal-Arroyo vowed to defeat the NPA by the end of her term in 2010. While the military fell short of this goal, it claimed it had reduced the NPA to a small "spent force" in several regions. Skirmishes and ambushes continued after the Aquino administration took office. In September 2012 an NPA grenade attack in Davao City injured 47 at a circus. In August 2013 Philippine security forces captured a major NPA camp in Northern Samar.

In March 2014 security forces arrested Vice Chair Benito E. Tiamzon and his wife Wilma, the secretary general of the CPP, on murder charges. They were released in August 2016.

On September 26, 2016, President Duterte met with the couple in an effort to promote peace. The same day, the CPP released two government captives.

Leaders: José María SISON (Chair, in exile), Benito E. TIAMZON (Vice Chair), Wilma TIAMZON (Secretary General), Gregorio ROSAL (Spokesperson).

For more information on the **Filipino Workers' Party** (*Partido ng Manggagawang Pilipino*—PMP), see the 2009 *Handbook*. For information on the **Revolutionary Workers' Party–Philippines** (*Rebolusyonaryong Partido ng Manggagawa–Pilipinas*—RPMP), see the 2012 *Handbook*. See the 2013 *Handbook* for more information on other recently active Communist splinter parties including the **Marxist-Leninist Party of the Philippines** (MLPP), **Metro Manila-Rizal Regional Party Committee** (*Komite ng Rehiyon ng Manila-Rizal*—KRMR), and **Revolutionary Worker's Party–Mindanao** (*Rebolusyonaryong Partido ng Manggagawa–Mindanao*—RPM-M).

Southern-Based Muslim Groups:

Moro National Liberation Front (MNLF). In separatist rebellion since 1974 on behalf of Mindanao's Muslim communities, the MNLF split in 1975 into Libyan-backed and Egyptian-backed factions, the latter subsequently calling itself the Moro Islamic Liberation Front (MILF, below). Originally the stronger of the two guerrilla armies, MNLF forces had dwindled by 1986 to one-third their original size, and in early 1987 the MNLF leader, Nur Misuari, tentatively agreed to drop his demands for an independent southern state in favor of autonomy. A January 1994 cease-fire and a subsequent peace agreement directly led to Misuari's election as governor of the Autonomous Region of Muslim Mindanao (ARMM) on September 9, 1996, although hard-line MNLF splinters and the MILF rejected the arrangement.

In April 2001 the MNLF Central Committee voted to remove Misuari as chair, citing a lack of progress during his tenure as governor of the ARMM. He was replaced by a "Council of 15" but refused to acknowledge the decision. In August the government named the MNLF general secretary, Muslimin Sema, to replace him as head of the Southern Philippines Council for Peace and Development (SPCPD), and in October he was derecognized by the OIC. On November 19 Misuari loyalists broke the MNLF's five-year-old cease-fire in a series of attacks on Jolo Island. Arrested on November 24 while attempting to enter Malaysia, Misuari was later extradited to the Philippines to face charges of rebellion. On November 26 the MNLF's Parouk Hussin was elected to succeed Misuari as ARMM governor.

In February 2006 the MNLF elected Nur Misuari to return as chair (despite his continuing detention), only to remove him again from that position in April 2008. In June 2009 the MNLF declared it would boycott the upcoming ARMM elections to demonstrate its dissatisfaction with the implementation of the 1996 peace accord. On April 20, 2010, in Tripoli, following talks facilitated by the OIC, the MNLF and the Philippine government signed a Memorandum of Understanding on implementation of the 1996 peace agreement. The memorandum called for the creation of the Bangsamoro Development Assistance Fund, instituted the previous month by President Macapagal-Arroyo through an executive order, with an initial disbursement of 100 million pesos. In August 2013 Misuari symbolically declared independence from the Philippines but pledged to pursue the goal peacefully.

Reports in 2014 indicated that approximately 1,000 MILF fighters, led by Senior Commander Ustad ZAMSODIN, defected to the MNLF rather than accept a comprehensive peace accord with the government.

On July 26, 2016, both the MNLF and MILF announced their support for peace negotiations between the Muslim insurgent groups and Duterte's government.

On September 2, 2016, four MNLF fighters were killed in a clash with *Abu Sayaaf* in Sulu as part of a joint offensive with the government against the terrorist group.

Leaders: Nur MISUARI (Chair), Muslimin SEMA (Central Committee Chairperson and Mayor of Cotabato City), Abdul SAHRIN (Secretary General), Parouk HUSSIN.

Moro Islamic Liberation Front (MILF). The MILF was launched as a fundamentalist faction within the MNLF, with Hashim Salamat, a Cairo-trained *ulema* (Islamic religious leader), as deputy to Nur Misuari. It split from the parent group in 1978, adopting the MILF name in 1980. Estimates of the size of its military wing, the **Bangsamoro Islamic Armed Forces**, vary widely, from a Philippine government assessment of 10,000 to an MILF claim of 120,000.

In opposing the September 1996 peace agreement, the MILF indicated that it would settle for nothing less than full independence for Muslim-dominated areas.

In December 1997 MILF leader Salamat returned from 20 years of exile in Libya, and in March 1998 the government and the MILF reached agreement on setting up a quick-response team to prevent future altercations from escalating. In March 1999 Hashim Salamat and the MNLF's Nur Misuari reportedly conferred for the first time in 21 years.

Intermittent formal peace talks, interrupted by suspensions and punctuated by continuing hostilities, continued into 2000. In August the MILF indefinitely suspended talks following a series of military defeats, including the loss of its headquarters at Camp Abubaker in July. Salamat responded by calling for a *jihad* (holy war) against the government and insisted that any further peace talks should take place abroad, in a Muslim country. Negotiations in Tripoli in June 2001 quickly led to a peace pact that was formalized in Kuala Lumpur in August. At the same time, the MILF and the MNLF concluded a "framework of unity" agreement.

Although the MILF condemned the subsequent participation of U.S. troops in the *Balikatan* military exercises, in a meeting with government representatives in Putrajaya, Malaysia, in May 2002 it agreed to assist in eliminating such criminal activities as kidnapping for ransom. The MILF also accepted responsibility for distributing funds to be provided by Manila as reparations for damages attributable to the 2000 military campaign in Mindanao.

In March 2003 the MILF and the Communist NPA announced a "tactical" alliance that stopped short of actual military cooperation. Later in the same month, the MILF agreed to resume peace negotiations with the government, but continuing military activity by the MILF led the Macapagal-Arroyo administration to cancel talks and to reject a cease-fire offer. On June 23 MILF Chair Salamat stated that the MILF renounced terrorism and denied any terrorist links, despite numerous reports that members of the regional *Jemaah Islamiah* (JI) network had infiltrated the MILF. Salamat's statement undoubtedly contributed to the government's decision to reverse itself and accept a cease-fire from July 19. Although it was not made public until August 5, 2003, Hashim Salamat died suddenly on July 13, 2003, and was soon succeeded by the vice chair for military affairs, Murad Ebrahim.

A series of informal meetings concluded in February 2004 with an announcement that formal peace talks would open in Kuala Lumpur. That year Manila complied with two MILF preconditions: the dropping of charges against MILF members for a series of bombings near Davao Airport and government withdrawal from a captured MILF complex in Buliok. October witnessed the deployment of some 50 Malaysian troops, the core of an International Monitoring Team offered by members of the OIC. Exploratory peace talks resumed in April–June 2005.

Negotiations with the government resulted in a Memorandum of Understanding on Ancestral Domain (MOA-AD), announced on July 16, 2008. The Philippine Supreme Court declared the agreement unconstitutional on October 14, and MILF responded by going on an offensive that led to nearly a half-million displaced people on Mindanao. The government declared a unilateral ceasefire in July 2009, and the MILF agreed to return to the negotiating table (see Current issues). The Macapagal-Arroyo administration was unable to arrive at a new agreement with the MILF before leaving office. On May 3, 2012, Aleem Abdul Azis MIMBANTAS, a MILF cofounder and the organization's current vice chair for military operations, died of a heart attack. Reports in July 2013 indicated renewed fighting between MILF and the MNLF in North Cotabato. The strife displaced more than 2,000 villagers.

Following the signing of a comprehensive peace agreement with the government in March 2014, a breakaway faction of MILF, the **Bangsamoro Islamic Freedom Fighters** (BIFF), vowed to continue the armed struggle.

Leaders: Al-Haj MURAD Ebrahim (Chair), Ghazali JAAFAR (Vice Chair for Political Affairs), Mohaqher IQBAL, Jun MANTAWIL (Head, Peace Panel Secretariat), Muhammad AMEEN (Chairperson, Central Committee Secretariat).

Abu Sayyaf. The most radical of the fundamentalist Muslim insurgent groups, *Abu Sayyaf* (Bearers of the Sword) has continued its activities despite an August 1994 announcement by Manila that the rebels, including their leader, Brahama SALI, had been "annihilated." Although the MILF had earlier condemned the group as a terrorist organization at odds with the precepts of Islam, *Abu Sayyaf* reportedly agreed in September 1996 to operate under MILF command in opposition to the government's accord with the MNLF. In December 1998 the authorities announced that *Abu Sayyaf*'s leader, Abdurajak Abubakar JANJALANI, had been killed by government forces. In contrast to the MILF, *Abu Sayyaf* is believed to number no more than a few hundred guerrillas.

After more than a year of relative quiescence, *Abu Sayyaf* dramatically resurfaced in March–April 2000 with the kidnapping of more than 50 Philippine hostages on the southern island of Basilan and more than 20 others from the Malaysian resort island of Sipadan, off the Borneo coast. Half a dozen of the Basilan hostages were reportedly executed. Most of the Sipadan hostages were ultimately ransomed for some $17.5 million, in part through the intercession of Libya. In 2001 *Abu Sayyaf* renewed its kidnapping activities, abducting dozens of people and beheading a number of them.

In May 2002 the United States offered a $5 million reward leading to the apprehension of five *Abu Sayyaf* leaders; the Philippine government already had in place its own bounty program, which had contributed in July 2001 to the capture of a principal leader, Najmi SABDULA "Commander Global." In December 2003 another *Abu Sayyaf* commander, Ghalib ANDANG "Commander Robot," was captured by government forces. The United States, noting the organization's apparent links to the Indonesian-based JI as well as al-Qaida, added *Abu Sayyaf* to its list of foreign terrorist organizations.

A February 2004 *Abu Sayyaf* bombing of a Manila ferry cost more than 100 lives. In August 2004 a Basilan court sentenced 17 members to death for the 2002 kidnappings.

A failed prison break on March 14–15, 2005, resulted in over two dozen deaths. Those killed included Najmi Sabdula and Ghalib Andang. Since then, *Abu Sayyaf* has continued its bombings and kidnappings, although none on the scale evidenced earlier. At the same time, the Philippine military has stepped up its attacks, aided by intelligence data from U.S. military personnel. In September 2006 *Abu Sayyaf*'s leader, Khaddafy JANJALANI, was killed, as was another commander, Abu SULAIMAN, in January 2007. Five months later the Philippine military announced that Yasser Igasan had succeeded Janjalani. In June 2008 the group kidnapped well-known television journalist Ces Drilon and her crew, releasing them nine days later. Kidnappings, beheadings, and attacks by *Abu Sayyaf* and military efforts to capture the militants were ongoing through 2013. For instance, an *Abu Sayyaf* attack in August 2013 killed one soldier and seven militants in Basilan. In June 2014 seven government troops and ten *Abu Sayyaf* militants were killed in fighting in Sulu province.

On July 23, 2014, Isnilon HAPILON, an *Abu Sayyaf* leader, pledged allegiance to the Islamic State of Iraq and Syria (ISIS). In September Hapilon's faction launched a series of terrorist attacks in the name of ISIS.

In November 2015 a 74-year-old Korean hostage held by the *Abu Sayyaf* was found dead in Sulu.

Responding to a military assault by the government, *Abu Sayyaf* bombed a market in Davao City on September 2, 2016, killing more than 15.

Leader: Yasser IGASAN.

See the 2013 *Handbook* for more information on the **Rajah Solaiman Movement** (RSM) and the so-called **Pentagon Group.**

LEGISLATURE

The 1987 constitution provides for a bicameral **Congress of the Philippines,** encompassing a Senate and a House of Representatives.

Senate. The upper house consists of 24 at-large members who may serve no more than two six-year terms. Half of the body is elected every three years; voters may cast as many votes as there are seats to be filled.

Due to the upper house's small size, senators are often elected less by party affiliation than by personal following. In the May 2016 elections, the Liberal Party won 2 seats; Nationalist People's Coalition, 1; and Citizens' Action Party, 1.

Following the 2016 election, the party breakdown for the Senate was as follows: Liberal Party, 6 seats; United National Alliance, 4; Nationalist People's Coalition, 3; Nationalist Party, 3; Democratic Filipino Struggle, 1; Philippine Democratic Party–Laban, 1.

President: Aquilino PIMENTEL III.

House of Representatives. The lower house includes a maximum of 292 members, of whom the majority is directly elected from legislative districts. A maximum of 20 percent of the members are elected via "a party-list system of registered national, regional, and sectoral parties or organizations." Each voter may cast a ballot for both a district representative and a party-list group. For each party-list seat, an organization must receive at least 2 percent of the total party-list votes cast, but no group may exceed three seats. (For 2013 the Commission on Elections accredited 150 party-list organizations.) In April 2009 a Philippine Supreme Court decision (*Banat vs. Comelec*) changed the formula for allocating party-list seats in the House, mandating the maximum number of party-list representatives be seated. All representatives serve for three years, with no member to be reelected more than twice.

The most recent election was held May 2016. Of the 238 district seats, the Liberal Party won 115 seats; Nationalist People's Coalition, 42; National Unity Party, 23; National Party, 24; United Nationalist Alliance, 11; *Lakas* Kampi Christian Muslim Democrats, 4; Philippine Democratic Party–Laban, 3; Democratic Filipino Struggle, 2; Progress for Manilans, 2; *Aksyon Demokratiko* (Democratic Action), 1; Force of the Villagers, 1; Voice of the Masses Party, 1; People's Chap Movement (PCM), 1; Hope for Bukidnon, 1; Caring Love, 1; Forward San Joseans (ASJ), 1; and Partner of the Nation for Progress, 1.

In the May 2016 elections, 46 parties and other organizations were awarded a total of 59 party-list seats, giving the House a total membership (counting district and party-list seats) of 297. The Ako Bicol Political Party won three seats while each of the following won two seats: *Abono,* Gabriela Women's Party, Cooperative NATCCO Network Party (Coop-NATCCO), One Patriotic Coalition of Marginalized Nationals (1PACMAN), Act Teachers Party-List (Act Teachers), Coalition of Associations of Senior Citizens in the Philippines (Senior Citizens), *Kabalikat ng Mamamayan* (KABAYAN), *Agri-Agra na Reporma para sa Magsasaka ng Philipinas Movement* (AGRI), *Puwersa ng Bayaning Atleta* (PBA), *Buhay Hayaan Yumabong* (BUHAY), and *Anak Mindanao* (AMIN). Each of the following won one seat: 1st Consumers Alliance for Rural Energy (1-Care); Advocacy for Teacher Empowerment Through Action, Cooperation and Harmony Towards Educational Reforms (A TEACHER); Agricultural Sectoral Alliance of the Philippines, Inc. (AGAP); the *Bayan Muna* Party; Akbayan Citizens' Action Party; An Waray; Citizens Battle Against Corruption (CIBAC); Alliance of Concerned Teachers; Luzon Farmers Party (Butil); Advocacy for Social Empowerment and Nation Building Through Easing Poverty (KALINGA); LPG Marketers Association (LPGMA); Youth Against Corruption and Poverty (YACAP); *Alyansa ng mga Batayang Sektor* (ABS); *Ang Partido Ng Mga Pilipinong Marino* (ANGKLA); Democratic Independent Workers' Association (DIWA); *Kabataan; Anakpawis; Ang Asosasyon Sang Mangunuma Nga Bisaya-Owa Mangunguma* (AAMBIS-OWA); Social Amelioration and Genuine Intervention on Poverty (SAGIP); *Agbiag!* Party List; Ang National Coalition of Indigenous Peoples Action (ANAC-IP); Trade Union Congress Party (TUCP); Abang Lingkod, Inc.; Alliance of Organizations, Networks, and Associations of the Philippines, Inc. (ALONA); Acts-Overseas Filipino Workers Coalition of Organizations (ACTS-OFW); *Ang Kabuhayan*; Ang Mata'y Alagaan (MATA); Bagong Henerasyon (BH); Ating Agapay Sentrong Samahan ng mga Obrero, Inc. (AASENSO); *Serbisyo sa Bayan* Party (SBP); *Magdalo Para sa Pilipino* (MAGDALO); *Una ang Edukasyon;* Manila Teachers' Savings and Loan Association, Inc. (MANILA TEACHERS); *Kusug Tausug;* and *Aangat Tayo.*

Speaker: Pantaleon ÁLVAREZ.

CABINET

[as of September 1, 2016]

President	Rodrigo Duterte (PDP-Laban)
Vice President	Leni Robredo (LP) [f]
Secretaries	
Agrarian Reform	Rafael Mariano
Agriculture	Manny Piñol
Budget and Management	Benjamin Diokno
Education	Leonor Briones [f]
Energy	Alfonso Cusi
Environment and Natural Resources	Regina Paz L. Lopez [f]
Finance	Carlos Dominguez III
Foreign Affairs	Perfecto Yasay Jr.
Health	Paulyn Jean Rosell-Ubial [f]
Information and Communication Technology	Rodolfo Salalima
Interior and Local Government	Mike Sueno
Justice	Vitaliano Aguirre
Labor and Employment	Silvestre Bello III
National Defense	Delfin Lorenzana
National Economic Development Authority	Ernesto Pernia
Public Works and Highways	Mark Villar
Science and Technology	Fortunato de la Peña
Social Welfare and Development	Judy Taguiwalo [f]
Tourism	Wanda Corazon Teo [f]
Trade and Industry	Ramon Lopez
Transportation and Communications	Art Tugade
Cabinet Secretary	Leoncio Evasco Jr.
Executive Secretary	Salvador Medialdea

[f] = female

INTERGOVERNMENTAL REPRESENTATION

Ambassador to the U.S.: Patrick A. CHUASOTO (Chargé d'Affaires *ad interim*).

U.S. Ambassador to the Philippines: Sung Y. KIM.

Permanent Representative to the UN: Lourdes Ortiz YPARRAGUIRRE.

IGO Memberships (Non-UN): ADB, APEC, ASEAN, IOM, ICC, NAM, WTO.

For Further Reference:

Kerkvliet, Benedict J. Tria. *Everyday Politics in the Philippines: Class and Status Relations in a Central Luzon Village.* Lanham, MD: Rowman & Littlefield, 2002.

Tabajen, Rhene C., and Erlinda B. Pulma. *Philippines Politics and Government.* Pasay City, Philippines: JSF Publishing, 2016.

White, Lynn T., III. *Philippine Politics: Possibilities and Problems in a Localist Democracy.* New York: Routledge, 2014.

POLAND

Polish Republic
Rzeczypospolita Polska

Political Status: Independent state reconstituted 1918; Communist-ruled People's Republic established 1947; constitution of July 22, 1952, substantially revised in accordance with intraparty agreement of April 5, 1989, with further amendments on December 29, including name change to Polish Republic; new interim "small" constitution introduced December 8, 1992; permanent "large" constitution approved by national referendum on May 25, 1997, effective October 17, 1997.

Area: 120,725 sq. mi. (312,677 sq. km).

Population: 38,593,000 (2016E—UN); 38,523,261 (2016E—U.S. Census).

Major Urban Centers (2015E—UN): WARSAW (1,722,000), Kraków (760,000), Łódź (70319,000), Wrocław (628,000), Poznań (545,000), Gdańsk (460,000), Szczecin (407,000).

Official Language: Polish.

Monetary Unit: Złoty (market rate October 1, 2016: 3.82 złotys = $1US). After Poland joined the European Union in May 2004, the Polish government announced that it hoped to adopt the euro as Poland's national currency by 2007. However, the target date was subsequently pushed back.

President: Andrez DUDA (elected as a member of Law and Justice); elected on May 24, 2015, and inaugurated on August 6; to succeed Bronisław KOMOROWSKI (elected as a member of Civic Platform). (Presidents are constitutionally required to resign their party affiliations upon inauguration.)

Prime Minister: Beata SZYDLO (Law and Justice) nominated by the president on October 27, 2015, to succeed Donald TUSK (Civic Platform) following the legislative elections of October 25, 2015, and inaugurated (along with her new cabinet) on November 18.

THE COUNTRY

A land of plains, rivers, and forests, Poland has been troubled throughout its history by a lack of firm natural boundaries to demarcate its territory from that of powerful neighbors of both East and West. Its present borders reflect major post–World War II adjustments that involved the loss of some 70,000 square miles of former Polish territory to the former Soviet Union and the acquisition of some 40,000 square miles of previously German territory along the country's northern and western frontiers, the latter accompanied by the expulsion of most ethnic Germans and resettlement of the area by Poles. These changes, following the Nazi liquidation of most of Poland's prewar Jewish population, left the country 96 percent Polish in ethnic composition and 90 percent Roman Catholic in religious faith.

Poland's economy underwent dramatic changes in the years after World War II, including a large-scale shift of the workforce into the industrial sector. A resource base that included coal, copper, and natural gas deposits contributed to significant expansion in the fertilizer, petrochemical, machinery, electronic, and shipbuilding industries, placing Poland among the world's dozen leading industrial nations. Attempts to collectivize agriculture proved largely unsuccessful, with 80 percent of cultivated land remaining in private hands, and the lack of agricultural modernization contributed to periodic agricultural shortages, which in turn, contributed to consumer unrest. The communist government sought Western loans to finance industrial improvements but often could not keep up with payments, allowing interest to accumulate at $1 billion each year.

On October 22, 1978, Cardinal Karol WOJTYŁA, archbishop of Kraków, was invested as the 264th pope of the Roman Catholic Church. The first Pole ever selected for the office, Pope JOHN PAUL II was regarded as a politically astute advocate of church independence who had worked successfully within the strictures of a Communist regime. During a June 2–10, 1979, visit by the pope to his homeland, he was greeted by crowds estimated at 6 million. In 1980, Polish Primate Cardinal Stefan WYSZYŃSKI played a key role in moderating the policies of the country's newly formed free labor unions while helping persuade the Communist leadership to grant them official recognition. Cardinal Wyszyński died on May 28, 1981, and he was succeeded as primate on July 7 by Archbishop Józef GLEMP, whose efforts to emulate his predecessor were interrupted by the imposition of martial law on December 13. The result was a worsening in church–state relations that continued until May 1989, when the Polish *Sejm* voted to extend legal recognition to the church for the first time since 1944. Two months later, Poland and the Holy See established diplomatic relations.

Limited political reforms were introduced in 1988, eventually leading to roundtable discussions between the government and Solidarity. (For more on the history of the economy, see the 2015 *Handbook*.) Over a matter of months, the two sides negotiated open elections for a new, multiparty government in July 1989. The political and economic transitions were difficult; gross domestic product (GDP) contracted nearly 20 percent, and annual inflation hit 120 percent in 1991–1992, prior to the resumption of growth in 1993. Inflation averaged approximately 5 percent annually in 1998–2004, while unemployment rose steadily from a low of about 10 percent in 1998 to a high of 20 percent in 2003–2004.

Poland was the largest of the ten new members to join the European Union (EU) in May 2004, and a year later much of the country was reportedly content with the EU developments to date. Farmers, initially concerned that subsidies in other EU countries would undercut Polish productivity, reported increased exports.

Poland was the only country in the EU to register consistent economic growth during the 2008–2012 financial crisis, averaging 3.52 percent, primarily because its large domestic market made it less dependent on exports than some of its neighbors. Poland has a large number of small businesses (2.3 million) that have helped support the domestic economy, but 55 percent of its exports go to EU member states. The government also took steps to maintain confidence by such measures as strengthening household deposit insurance, obtaining a $20.5 billion precautionary loan from the IMF, and increasing fiscal stimulus to the economy. Inflation averaged 3.5 percent, while unemployment hovered around 9.2 percent. Poland's debt to GDP ratio remained high, holding near 51 percent since 2011, slightly exceeding EU limits and nearing a constitutionally imposed debt barrier of 60 percent. Poland's economy slowed in 2013 as exports to its neighbors dwindled. Economists predicted a recession, rising unemployment, and growing budget deficits, as slowing sales would cut into tax revenue. In 2013 the government also received an additional IMF line of credit for $33.8 billion. GDP growth declined to 1.3 percent in 2013, but recovered to 3.3 percent in 2014, growing slowly to 3.6 percent in 2015, with estimated growth of 3.5 percent for 2016. The IMF cautioned that Poland's strong ties to the EU and Russia make it vulnerable to external volatility, particularly with ongoing conflict over Ukraine. Inflation remained low, at 1.8 percent in 2016, while unemployment dropped from 11 percent in 2013 to an estimated seven percent in 2016.

GOVERNMENT AND POLITICS

Political background. Tracing its origins as a Christian nation to 966 A.D., Poland became an influential kingdom in late medieval and early modern times, functioning as an elective monarchy until its liquidation by Austria, Prussia, and Russia in the successive partitions of 1772, 1793, and 1795. Its reemergence as an independent republic at the close of World War I was followed in 1926 by the establishment of a military dictatorship headed initially by Marshal Józef PIŁ SUDSKI. The first direct victim of Nazi aggression in World War II, Poland was jointly occupied by Germany and the USSR, coming under full German control with the outbreak of German–Soviet hostilities in June 1941.

After the end of the war in 1945, a Communist-controlled "Polish Committee of National Liberation," established under Soviet auspices in Lublin in 1944, merged with a splinter group of the anti-Communist Polish government-in-exile in London to form a Provisional Government of National Unity. The new government was headed by Polish Socialist Party (*Polska Partia Socjalistyczna*—PPS) leader Edward OSÓBKA-MORAWSKI, with Władysław GOMUŁKA, head of the (Communist) Polish Workers' Party (*Polska Partia Robotnicza*—PPR), and Stanisław MIKOŁAJCZYK, chair of the Polish Peasants' Party (*Partia Stronnictwo Ludowe*—PSL), as vice premiers. Communist tactics in liberated Poland prevented the holding of free elections as envisaged at the Yalta Conference in February 1945. Instead, the election that was ultimately held in 1947 represented the final step in the establishment of control by the PPR, which forced the PPS into a 1948 merger as the Polish United Workers' Party (*Polska Zjednoczona Partia Robotnicza*—PZPR).

Poland's Communist regime was thereafter subjected to periodic crises resulting from far-ranging political and economic problems, accompanied by subservience to Moscow and the use of Stalinist methods to consolidate the regime. In 1948 Gomułka was accused of "rightist and nationalist deviations," which led to his replacement by Bolesław BIERUT and his subsequent imprisonment (1951–1954). By 1956, however, post-Stalin liberalization was generating political turmoil, precipitated by the sudden death of Bierut in Moscow and "bread and freedom" riots in Poznań, and Gomułka returned to the leadership of the PZPR as the symbol of a "Polish path to socialism." The new regime initially yielded a measure of political stability, but by the mid-1960s Gomułka was confronted with growing dissent among intellectuals in addition to factional rivalry within the party leadership. As a result, Gomułka-inspired anti-Semitic and anti-intellectual campaigns were mounted in 1967–1968, yielding the mass emigration of some 18,000 Polish Jews (out of an estimated 25,000) by 1971. Drastic price increases caused a serious outbreak of workers' riots in December 1970, which, although primarily economic in nature, provoked a political crisis that led to the replacement of Gomułka as PZPR first secretary by Edward GIEREK.

Following a parliamentary election on March 23, 1980, a new austerity program was announced that called for a reduction in imports, improved industrial efficiency, and the gradual withdrawal of food subsidies. Workers responded by demanding wage adjustments and calling strikes, which by August had assumed an overtly political character, with employees demanding that they be allowed to establish "workers' committees" to replace the PZPR-dominated, government-controlled official trade unions. Among those marshaling support for the strikers was the Committee for Social Self-Defense (*Komitet Samoobrony Społeczej*—KSS), the largest of a number of recently established dissident groups.

On August 14, 1980, the 17,000 workers at the Lenin Shipyard in Gdańsk went on strike, occupied the grounds, and issued a list of demands that included the right to organize independent unions. Three days later, workers from a score of industries in the area of the Baltic port presented an expanded list of 16 demands that called for recognition of the right of all workers to strike, abolition of censorship, and release of political prisoners. In an emergency session also held on August 17, the PZPR Politburo agreed to open negotiations with the strikers, eventually consenting to meet with delegates of the Gdańsk interfactory committee headed by Lech WAŁĘSA, a former shipyard worker who had helped organize the 1970 demonstrations. On August 30 strike settlements were completed and the *Sejm* approved the 21-point Gdańsk Agreement, which was signed by Wałęsa and the government on August 31. While recognizing the position of the PZPR as the "leading force" in society, the unprecedented document stated, "It has been found necessary to call up new, self-governing trade unions which would become authentic representatives of the working class."

Although most workers along the Baltic coast returned to their jobs on September 1, 1980, strikes continued to break out in other areas, particularly the coal-mining and copper-mining region of Silesia, and on September 6, First Secretary Gierek resigned in favor of Stanisław KANIA. On September 15 the government announced registration procedures for independent unions to file with the Warsaw provincial court. Three days later, 250 representatives of new labor groups established a "National Committee of Solidarity" (*Solidarność*) in Gdańsk with Wałęsa as chair, and on September 24 the organization applied for registration as the Independent Self-Governing Trade Union Solidarity. The court objected, however, to its proposed governing statutes, particularly the absence of any specific reference to the PZPR as the country's leading political force. Not until November 10—two days before a threatened strike by Solidarity—did the Supreme Court, ruling in the union's favor, remove amendments imposed by the lower court, the union accepting as an annex a statement of the party's role. By December some 40 free trade unions had been registered, while on January 1, 1981, the official Central Council of Trade Unions was dissolved.

The unprecedented events of 1980 yielded sharp cleavages between Wałęsa and radical elements within Solidarity and between moderate and hard-line factions of the PZPR. Fueled by the success of the registration campaign, labor unrest increased further in early 1981, accompanied by appeals from the private agricultural sector for recognition of a "Rural Solidarity." Amid growing indications of concern by other Eastern-bloc states, the minister of defense, Gen. Wojciech JARUZELSKI, was appointed chair of the Council of Ministers on February 11. Initially welcomed in his new role by most Poles, including the moderate Solidarity leadership, Jaruzelski attempted to initiate a dialogue with nonparty groups and introduced a ten-point economic program designed to promote recovery and counter "false anarchistic paths contrary to socialism." The situation again worsened following a resumption of government action against dissident groups, although the Independent Self-Governing Trade Union for Private Farmers–Solidarity (Rural Solidarity), which claimed between 2.5 and 3.5 million members, was officially registered on May 12.

At a delayed extraordinary PZPR congress that convened on July 14, 1981, in Warsaw, more than 93 percent of those attending were new delegates selected in unprecedented secret balloting at the local level. As a consequence, very few renominations were entered for outgoing Central Committee members, while only four former members were reelected to the Politburo. Stanisław Kania was, however, retained as first secretary in the first secret, multicandidate balloting for the office in PZPR history.

Despite evidence of government displeasure at its increasingly political posture, Solidarity held its first national congress in Gdańsk on September 5–10 and September 25–October 7, 1981. After reelecting Wałęsa as its chair, the union approved numerous resolutions, including a call for wide-ranging changes in the structure of trade-union activity. First Secretary Kania resigned at the conclusion of a PZPR Central Committee plenary session on October 18 and was immediately replaced by General Jaruzelski, who on October 28, made a number of changes in the membership of both the Politburo and Secretariat. Collaterally, Jaruzelski moved to expand the role of the army in maintaining public order.

During the remaining weeks of 1981 relations between the government and Solidarity progressively worsened. On December 11 the union announced that it would conduct a national referendum on January 15, 1982, that was expected to yield an expression of no confidence in the Jaruzelski regime. The government responded by arresting most of the Solidarity leadership, including Wałęsa. On December 13 the Council of State declared martial law under a Military Committee for National Salvation headed by Jaruzelski. The committee effectively banned all organized nongovernmental activity except for religious observances and established summary trial courts for those charged with violation of martial law regulations.

On October 8, 1982, the *Sejm* approved legislation that formally dissolved all existing trade unions and set guidelines for new government-controlled organizations to replace them. The measures were widely condemned by the Catholic Church and other groups, and Solidarity's underground leadership called for a nationwide protest strike on November 10. However, the appeal yielded only limited public support, and Wałęsa was released from detention two days later. On December 18, the *Sejm* suspended (but did not lift) martial law.

On July 21, 1983, State Council Chair Henryk JABŁOŃSKY announced the formal lifting of martial law and the dissolution of the Military Committee for National Salvation. Four months later a National Defense Committee, chaired by General Jaruzelski, was vested with overall responsibility for both defense and state security.

Following *Sejm* elections in October 1985, General Jaruzelski succeeded the aging Jabłońsky as head of state, relinquishing the chair of the Council of Ministers to Zbigniew MESSNER, who entered office as part of a major realignment that substantially increased the government's technocratic thrust. Jaruzelski was reelected PZPR first secretary at the party's tenth congress in mid-1986, during which nearly three-quarters of the Central Committee's incumbents were replaced.

In October 1987 Jaruzelski presented to the PZPR Central Committee a number of proposed economic and political reforms that far outstripped Mikhail Gorbachev's "restructuring" agenda for the Soviet Union. Central to their implementation, however, was a strict austerity program that included massive price increases and was bitterly opposed by the outlawed Solidarity leadership. Even though voters rejected the proposals in a remarkable referendum on November 29, the government indicated that it would proceed with their implementation, albeit at a slower pace than had originally been contemplated.

New work stoppages erupted in Kraków in late April 1988 and quickly spread to other cities, including Gdańsk, before being quelled by security forces. On August 22 emergency measures were formally invoked to put down a further wave of strikes, and six days later the PZPR Central Committee approved a plan for broad-based talks to address the country's economic and social ills. Although the government stated that "illegal organizations" would be excluded from such discussions, a series of meetings were held between Solidarity leader Wałęsa and Interior Minister Czesław KISZCZAK. On September 19, however, the Messner government resigned after being castigated by both party and official trade union leaders for economic mismanagement. Mieczysław RAKOWSKI, a leading author of the March 1981 economic program, was named prime minister on September 26.

In the wake of further party leadership changes on December 21, 1988, which included the removal of six Politburo hard-liners, a new round of discussions with representatives of the still-outlawed Solidarity was launched on February 6, 1989. The talks resulted in the signing on April 5 of three comprehensive agreements providing for the legalization of Solidarity and its rural counterpart; political reforms that included the right of free speech and association, democratic election to state bodies, and judicial independence; and economic liberalization. The accords paved the way for parliamentary balloting on June 4 and 18, at which Solidarity captured all of the 161 non-reserved seats in the 460-member *Sejm* and 99 of 100 seats in the newly established Senate.

On July 25, 1989, six days after General Jaruzelski was elected president of the republic by the barest of legislative margins, Solidarity rebuffed his effort to secure a PZPR-dominated "grand coalition" government. On August 2 the *Sejm* approved Jaruzelski's choice of General Kiszczak to succeed Rakowski as prime minister; however, opposition agreement on a cabinet proved lacking, and Kiszczak was forced to step down in favor of Solidarity's Tadeusz MAZOWIECKI, who succeeded in forming a four-party administration on September 12 that included only four Communists (although the PZPR was, by prior agreement, awarded both the interior and defense portfolios).

On December 29, 1989, the *Sejm* approved a number of constitutional amendments, including a change in the country name from "People's Republic of Poland" to "Polish Republic," termination of the Communist Party's "leading role" in state and society, and deletion of the requirement that Poland must have a "socialist economic system." Subsequently, on January 29, 1990, formal Communist involvement in Polish politics ended when the PZPR voted to disband in favor of a new entity to be known as Social Democracy of the Republic of Poland (*Socjaldemokracja Rzeczypospolitej Polskiej*—SdRP).

In the face of widespread opposition to his status as a holdover from the Communist era, President Jaruzelski on September 19, 1990, proposed a series of constitutional amendments that would permit him to resign in favor of a popularly elected successor. At first-round balloting on November 25 Wałęsa led a field of six candidates with a 40 percent vote share; in the second round on December 9, he defeated émigré businessman Stanisław TYMIŃSKI by a near three-to-one margin, and he was sworn in for a five-year term on December 22. On January 4, 1991, the president's nominee, Jan Krzysztof BIELECKI, won parliamentary approval as prime minister, with the *Sejm* formally endorsing his ministerial slate on January 12.

In June 1991, amid mounting opposition to government economic policy, President Wałęsa twice vetoed bills calling for a form of proportional representation that he insisted would weaken Parliament by admitting a multiplicity of parties, but he was eventually defeated by legislative override on June 28. As predicted, the ensuing poll of October 27 yielded a severely fragmented lower house, with the Democratic Union (*Unia Demokratyczna*—UD) winning the most seats but no party securing more than 13 percent of the vote. A lengthy period of consultation followed, during which Wałęsa offered to serve as his own prime minister. Unable to secure the reappointment of Bielecki, the president was ultimately obliged to settle on a critic of his free-market strategy, Jan OLSZEWSKI, who narrowly succeeded in forming a government on December 23. Four days earlier Wałęsa had been forced to withdraw a group of proposed constitutional amendments that would have given him authority to appoint and dismiss ministers and to veto parliamentary no-confidence motions, while authorizing a simple rather than a two-thirds *Sejm* majority to enact legislation.

The government was weakened in May 1992 by the successive resignations of the economy and defense ministers, the latter in the wake of allegations he had made concerning the military's involvement in politics. Far more contentious, however, was legislative authorization on May 28 to release secret police files of individuals who had reportedly collaborated with the Communist regime. The action had long been sought by the right-of-center Olszewski government but had been resisted as a violation of human rights by the center-left parties, which insisted that many of the dossiers had been deliberately falsified by departing members of the security forces. Olszewski's subsequent publication of a list of alleged collaborators generated widespread outrage, not least from President Wałęsa, who publicly called for the prime minister's dismissal, and on June 5 the *Sejm* approved a no-confidence motion by an overwhelming margin.

On June 6, 1992, the *Sejm* endorsed Waldemar PAWLAK, the relatively obscure leader of the PSL, as new prime minister. However, Pawlak was unable, during the ensuing month, to muster sufficient parliamentary support to form a government and was obliged to resign. On July 6 the UD's Hanna SUCHOCKA was confirmed as Poland's first female prime minister, and five days later she secured *Sejm* approval of a new coalition administration, which included seven parties with ministerial posts and several others pledged to give it parliamentary support. Committed to speedier transition to a market economy, Suchocka's government relaunched the privatization program and secured the reactivation of International Monetary Fund (IMF) credit facilities that had been suspended since 1991. However, Suchocka's austerity policies, including a firm stand against striking coal miners and rail workers, incurred widespread opposition from Solidarity deputies, and on May 28, 1993, her government fell by one vote over a continued tight budget. President Wałęsa responded by refusing to accept the prime minister's resignation, asking Suchocka to remain in office on a caretaker basis pending a new election.

The balloting of September 19, 1993, yielded a pronounced swing to the left, with the SdRP-dominated Democratic Left Alliance (*SojuszLewicy Democratycznej*—SLD) winning 37 percent of the legislative seats and the PSL winning 29 percent. Five weeks later, on October 26, the two groups formed a coalition government headed by the PSL's Pawlak.

Conflict between the presidency and the ruling coalition intensified in October 1994, when the government rejected President Wałęsa's dismissal of the defense minister and the legislature voted by a large majority to urge the president to cease interfering in the democratic process. Wałęsa responded by denouncing the Pawlak government and calling for stronger presidential powers; the controversial defense minister was forced out the following month. The crisis deepened in January 1995 amid various policy differences between the president and his government, which culminated in Pawlak's resignation on February 7, after the president had threatened parliamentary dissolution. Collateral strains between the two coalition parties were resolved sufficiently to enable the SLD's Józef OLEKSY, a Communist-era minister, to be sworn in on March 6 as prime minister of a continued SLD-PSL coalition, albeit with half of its members new appointees.

Despite the relative failure of a 1993 effort to form a "presidential" party styled the Nonparty Bloc in Support of Reform (*Bezpartyjny Blok Wspierania Reform*—BBWR), Wałęsa in April 1995 confirmed his candidacy for a second presidential term. His main opponents were Aleksander KWAŚNIEWSKI of the SLD/SdRP, Jacek KUROŃ of the center-right Freedom Union (*Unia Wolności*—UW), and former prime ministers Olszewski and Pawlak. In the first round of balloting on November 5 Kwaśniewski took a narrow lead, with 35.1 percent against 33.1 percent for Wałęsa. In the runoff contest on November 19, Kwaśniewski won 51.7 percent to 48.3 percent for Wałęsa, even though most of the other first-round candidates and center-right parties had thrown their support behind Wałęsa.

Sworn in on December 22, 1995, Kwaśniewski quickly lost his prime minister, Oleksy, who resigned on January 24, 1996, over allegations (later dismissed) that he had passed information to the Soviet, later Russian, intelligence service. He was replaced on February 8 by Włodzimierz CIMOSZEWICZ of the SLD, heading a further coalition of the SLD and PSL that included six independents.

In preparation for the 1997 legislative elections Solidarity in June 1996 began organizing small center-right parties into the Solidarity Electoral Action (*Akcja Wyborcza Solidarność*—AWS), which ultimately became a coalition of some 36 parties and groups. Despite President Kwaśniewski's popularity and four years of economic growth, the AWS won 201 seats against 164 for the SLD in the balloting on September 21, 1997. The AWS's success was attributed to its alignment with the Catholic Church and its appeal to lingering resentment against the ex-Communists. After protracted negotiations, the AWS signed a coalition agreement with the UW on October 20 and formed a new government on October 31, with Jerzy BUZEK of the leading AWS party, the Social Movement–Solidarity Electoral Action (*Ruch Społeczny–Akija Wyborcza Solidarność*—RS-AWS), as prime minister.

In 1998 and early 1999, Warsaw's imminent entry into the North Atlantic Treaty Organization (NATO) and its preparations for accession to the EU had far-reaching effects on both foreign and domestic policies. With Poland about to become the eastern front line of NATO and the EU, Warsaw was under pressure to tighten its eastern borders, which increased tension with Belarus and raised concerns in Ukraine. Warsaw sought to reassure its former Soviet bloc neighbors and held talks to improve relations with Germany, with whom it hoped to tie up lingering postwar issues, particularly compensation for deported Poles used by the Nazi regime as slave laborers. Poland formally entered NATO on March 12, 1999.

On the domestic front, reforms designed to prepare for EU accession created labor unrest with political fallout. Privatization plans and other reforms, some of which raised the prospects of huge job losses, caused strikes in the coal mining, steel, railway, and defense industries. In trying to curb subsidies and protectionist tariffs, the government alienated farmers, who, under the leadership of radical unionist Andrzej LEPPER of the Self-Defense of the Polish Republic (*Samoobrona Rzeczypospolitej Polskiej*), blocked roads throughout the nation in a series of disruptive protests, the most serious of which began in December 1998 and extended into 1999. At the beginning of 1999 the government was also confronted by opposition to a series of health care reforms, introduction of which led to physician resignations, more strikes, and public confusion. The crisis in health care also contributed to a potential rift in the governing coalition, but the AWS managed to mollify its junior partner, the UW, in late January, in part by dismissing a deputy health minister. The UW nevertheless continued to criticize its senior partner for what it saw as half-hearted pursuit of free-market policies, particularly privatization. Meanwhile, public opinion polls registered increasing dissatisfaction with the AWS and growing support for the leftist SLD.

Policy and leadership differences within the government continued to cause persistent internal friction, and on October 11, 1999, in an effort to stabilize the situation, the AWS and the UW signed a renegotiated coalition agreement. Nevertheless, on June 6, 2000, objecting to Buzek's continuation as prime minister as well as to the inability of the AWS to exert discipline over its disparate components, the UW formally withdrew. The move left the AWS in charge of a minority government, although it continued to receive regular UW support in Parliament and survived until the legislative term ended in 2001.

On October 8, 2000, President Kwaśniewski won reelection with 53.9 percent of the vote against 11 other active candidates. Second place (17.3 percent) went to an independent, Andrzej OLECHOWSKI, who had previously been associated with the AWS, while Solidarity's Marian KRZAKLEWSKI, despite AWS backing, finished third (15.6 percent). Former president Wałęsa managed only 1 percent of the vote, finishing seventh.

In December 2000 Solidarity announced that it was withdrawing from active politics and turned over to Prime Minister Buzek's RS-AWS its voting rights in the AWS, which was rapidly disintegrating as its various leaders and parties sought to position themselves as the best center-right alternative to the SLD for upcoming parliamentary elections. In the *Sejm* and Senate elections on September 23, 2001, a coalition of the SLD and the much smaller Union of Labor (*Unia Pracy*—UP) claimed a plurality of 216 seats in the lower house and an overwhelming majority in the upper, while Buzek's new coalition, the Solidarity Electoral Action of the Right (*Akcja Wyborcza Solidarność Prawicy*—AWSP), failed to meet the 8 percent coalition threshold for *Sejm* representation. The UW also lost all representation in the *Sejm* as three new formations—the Civic Platform (*Platforma Obywatelska*—PO), with 65 seats; Law and Justice (*Prawo i Sprawieliwość*—PiS), with 44; and the League of Polish Families (*Liga Polskich Rodzin*—LPR), with 38—split much of the center-right vote. Andrzej Lepper's populist *Samoobrona* entered the *Sejm,* finishing third, with 53 seats.

On October 9, 2001, the SLD/UP completed a coalition agreement with the rural PSL that permitted the SLD's Leszek MILLER, an electrician who had risen through the ranks of the PZPR and the SdRP, to become prime minister of an SLD-dominated cabinet on October 19, concurrent with the opening of the new parliamentary session.

In early March 2003 the PSL left the governing coalition following a disagreement with the SLD over a tax initiative. The government was therefore left with a minority of only 212 seats (of 460) in the *Sejm,* a situation that was only partially eased by addition of the newly formed, but now-defunct, Peasant Democratic Party (*Partia Ludowe Democratyczna*—PLD) to the coalition from late March until January 2004. The government remained stressed on several fronts, and Miller announced his resignation on May 2, 2004, only one day after Poland had acceded to the EU. President Kwaśniewski immediately designated "technocrat" Marek BELKA of the SLD to succeed Miller, but Belka lost a confirmation vote on May 14 in the *Sejm,* which was then constitutionally permitted to present its own candidate. When the *Sejm* failed to act in that regard, the president reappointed Belka on June 11, and he and his SLD/UP cabinet were confirmed by the *Sejm* on June 24. Marek Belka was immediately regarded as, at best, a caretaker leader of a dying government, a perception underscored by the poor performance of the SLD and UP in the June European Parliament balloting.

In the legislative elections on September 25, 2005, the PiS led all parties by securing 155 seats in the *Sejm,* followed by the PO with 133 seats and *Samoobrona* with 56. The SLD was relegated to fourth place with 55 seats. Given the recent wave of scandals, the dramatic decline of the SLD was not unexpected. However, the plurality achieved by the rightist PiS surprised observers across Europe. On September 27, the PiS named Kazimierz MARCINKIEWICZ as its choice for prime minister and sought to form a coalition government with the PO.

The first round of presidential elections was held on October 9, 2005, with a field of 12 candidates. Donald TUSK of the PO won 36.3 percent of the vote, followed by Lech KACZYŃSKI of the PiS with 33.1 percent. In the runoff on October 23, 2005, Kaczyński bested Tusk 54 percent to 46 percent to gain the presidency.

President Kwásniewski on October 24, 2005, formally designated Marcinkiewicz to form a new government. However, the PiS/PO talks collapsed, and Marcinkiewicz was sworn in as head of a minority PiS government on October 31, depending on the support of two diverse "fringe parties"—*Samoobrona* and the LPR—to maintain a legislative majority. On November 10 the government won a vote of confidence in the 460-seat *Sejm* with 272 votes, thanks to support from *Samoobrona* and the LPR. The PiS ascendancy was completed with Kaczyński's inauguration on December 23. Subsequently, in a May 5, 2006, reshuffle, the LPR and *Samoobrona* formally joined the government, their leaders being named deputy ministers. However, following a series of disputes between Prime Minister Marcinkiewicz and President Kaczyński and his twin brother Jarosław KACZYŃSKI (the chair of the PiS) over privatization and the campaign to remove former Communists from all levels of government, Marcinkiewicz resigned on July 10. President Kaczyński immediately named his brother as prime minister–designate, and Jarosław Kaczyński was sworn in as prime minister on July 14 to head an essentially unchanged cabinet. The PiS/LPR/*Samoobrona* government won a vote of confidence in the *Sejm* on July 19 with 240 votes.

The gap between the goals of PiS and its coalition partners widened throughout 2006–2007, particularly as the Kaczyński brothers began to pursue their policies of lustration, fiscal discipline, and anticorruption more vigorously, dismissing *Samoobrona* Chair Andrzej Lepper on two occasions. *Samoobrona* was also compromised by the findings of the Central Anti-Corruption Bureau (*Centralne Biuro Antykorupcyjne*—CBA), an institution whose formation was promised in the PiS campaign platform. Critics later alleged that the CBA had focused primarily on political rivals of the ruling party. As one of its conditions for allowing allies to remain in government during the crisis of July 2007, the PiS insisted that junior coalition partners refrain from investigating the controversial agency. The combination of demands for unconditional compliance with the PiS, or "loyalty conditions," and a lack of promised evidence regarding the charges against Lepper precipitated *Samoobrona*'s break with the government. The coalition crisis endured for several weeks, prompting a PiS meeting with its rival, the center-right PO, in August, after which early elections were scheduled for the fall, two years ahead of schedule.

Snap legislative elections on October 21, 2007, resulted in a pronounced victory for the PO, whose chair, Donald Tusk, formed a centrist government on November 16 comprising the PO and the PSL. In the *Sejm,* the PO won 209 seats, and its coalition partner, the PSL, won 31. The Law and Justice party took 166, while the Left and Democrats garnered only 53. In the Senate, the PO obtained a clear majority, winning 60 of the 100 seats. The PiS took 39, and 1 seat went to an independent.

The decisive victory for the europhile PO in the 2007 legislative poll neutralized Prime Minister Kaczyński's bid to strengthen his power. Turnout was one of the largest in history, and the PO surge was attributed in part to its support among young voters. By 2008, Prime Minister Tusk was ranked in public opinion polls as Poland's most trusted politician, while his rival Lech Kaczyński was among the least trusted. However, restricted spending remained necessary to reduce the deficit, which threatened to damage his popularity and his alliance with the PSL. Energy problems also provided cause for concern. Poland has the largest coal reserves in the EU and generates 95 percent of its electricity from coal. However, stringent EU carbon emission standards would raise electricity rates astronomically if Poland were forced to conform to them. Consequently, Poland in 2009 announced plans to build a nuclear energy plant.

The PO received a vote of confidence from the Polish electorate in elections for the European Parliament that were held on June 7, 2009, winning 44.4 percent of the vote and obtaining 25 seats. Jerzy Buzek, a PO member, was subsequently elected president of the European Parliament, becoming the first Eastern European to hold that office.

The plane crash of April 10, 2010, that killed 96 people (many from the Polish political elite) represented one of the most devastating political catastrophes any country has ever faced. In addition to President Lech Kaczyński and his wife, 18 members of parliament, including 3 deputy speakers, died. Also among the victims were Sławomir SKRZYPEK, the president of the National Bank of Poland; Franciszek GĄGOR, chief of the general staff of the Polish Armed Forces; Vice Admiral Andrzej KARWETA, the commander in chief of the Polish Navy; and a host of other dignitaries. The plane was on its way to Smolensk, Russia, to attend a memorial service marking the massacre of around 22,000 Polish nationals by Soviet authorities in 1940. The event was to be a milestone in Polish–Russian relations, as the Soviets had once blamed the atrocity on the Nazis, and Russia had not acknowledged Soviet responsibility until 1990. The offices of the victims of the crash were subsequently filled with calm deliberation, and the accident precipitated neither a national nor an international crisis in spite of the many conspiracy theories that arose after the tragedy.

The early presidential election of June–July 2010 was widely viewed as a referendum on the PO's performance, and PO candidate Bronisław Komorowski, the speaker of the *Sejm,* was expected to secure an easy victory. However, the election results were closer than expected because Komorowski proved to be a poor campaigner and Jarosław Kaczyński a surprisingly good one. Nevertheless, with Komorowski's ultimate success, the PO held control of both the executive and legislative branches of government. Its victory was expected to mean closer ties with its partners in the EU as well as with Russia.

On October 9, 2011, Poland held elections for both the Senate and the *Sejm,* the upper and lower houses of parliament. The ruling coalition, consisting of the dominant PO and the Polish Peasants' Party (*Partia Stronnictwo Ludowe*—PSL), made history by becoming the first government to win reelection since the fall of communism in 1989. Prime Minister Donald Tusk returned to office by stressing that Poland was the only European nation not to fall into recession during the ongoing global economic crisis and that Poland needed continuity in order to continue growing. The PO won 207 seats in the *Sejm,* and the PSL won 28 seats, for a coalition total of 235 (51 percent) of the 460 seats. The PO won 63 of the 100 seats in the Senate. Discouragingly, turnout was only 48.9 percent.

The Law and Justice Party (*Prawo i Sprawieliwość*—PiS) of former prime minister Jarosław Kaczyński won 157 seats in the *Sejm,* down 8 from the previous election. The success of the new party Palikot's Movement was a surprise. It won 40 seats in the *Sejm,* taking third place. It was headed by a charismatic vodka entrepreneur, Janusz Palikot, who ran an anticlerical campaign, supporting abortion on demand, homosexual civil unions, and legalizing marijuana. He appealed to young people and the supporters of the Democratic Left Alliance (*SojuszLewicy Democratycznej*—SLD), which won only 27 seats in this election, down dramatically from the 55 it had won in 2007.

Unlike his EU neighbors, Tusk did not have to face voters after imposing a tough austerity package onto an already suffering population. In May 2012 the *Sejm* voted to raise the retirement age, from 60 for women and 65 for men, to 67 years for both, deferring pension costs. Tusk also planned to deregulate some 200 professions, such as cab drivers, with the goal of creating 100,000 jobs. Tusk also planned to invest in infrastructure projects, including railways, road construction, power plants, and shale-gas exploration.

In November 2013 Tusk conducted a cabinet reshuffle, citing the "need for new energy." The biggest surprise was the firing of long-serving finance minister Jacek ROSTOWSKI.

As high unemployment rates continued into the next year, the PO's slipping popularity became evident in the May 2014 elections for European Parliament, in which the PO won 19 seats, tying with the PiS.

On May 10, 2015, Andrez DUDA (PiS) won the first round of presidential balloting with 34.8 percent of the vote, while PO-backed incumbent Komorowski came in second with 33.8 percent. Duda won the second round of balloting on May 24 with 51.5 percent of the vote. The October parliamentary elections continued the PiS resurgence, with 235 seats, while the PO was second with 138 seats. Beata SZYDLO (PiS) was nominated as prime minister on October 27 and named a new cabinet on November 9 (see Current issues, below).

Constitution and government. The constitutional changes of April 1989 provided for a bicameral legislature that incorporated the existing 460-member *Sejm* as its lower chamber and added a 100-member upper chamber (Senate). For the June 1989 balloting it was specified that all of the Senate seats would be free and contested, while 65 percent (299) of the lower house seats would be reserved for the PZPR and its allies (35 on a noncontested "National List" basis). All seats at subsequent elections were to be open and contested. Initially, the combined houses were empowered to elect a state president for a six-year term; however, constitutional changes prior to the December 1990 poll provided for a popularly elected president serving a five-year term. A new "small" constitution became effective on December 8, 1992, having been signed by President Wałęsa on November 17. It redefined the powers of, and relations between, the legislature, presidency, and government. A new "large" constitution, including a charter of liberties and human rights, was approved by a popular referendum on May 25, 1997, by a vote of 56.8 percent.

Parliament sits for a four-year term, save that the *Sejm* may dissolve itself (and by such action end the Senate term) by a two-thirds majority, assuming a quorum of at least 50 percent. The president has widespread authority in foreign and defense matters, with decrees in other areas requiring countersignature by a prime minister who is nominated by the president but must be confirmed by the *Sejm.* The prime minister appoints other ministers, while the president names military leaders and high-level judges. The president may veto legislation but can be overridden by a three-fifths majority of the lower house. There is a Constitutional Tribunal, whose members are appointed by the *Sejm,* while the regular judiciary has three tiers: regional courts, provincial courts, and a Supreme Court.

As a result of constitutional and administrative reforms in 1975, the number of provinces (voivodships, or *województwa*) was increased from 22 to 49. However, in July 1998, following a contentious debate over boundaries, Parliament reduced the number to 16 (4 more than the government initially proposed). The reduction was part of a package of administrative reforms that also created a "middle tier" of 65 cities and 308 districts (*powiats*) and, in furtherance of decentralization, assigned authority for regional economic development to the voivodships. At the local level, there are nearly 2,500 communes (*gminas*). The prime minister appoints provincial governors (*wojewodowie*); provincial assemblies as well as executives and legislative organs at the lower levels are elected.

Although the leading organs were under government control, the Polish press for most of the Communist era was livelier than in other East European countries, the regime making little effort to halt publication of "uncensored" (*samizdat*) publications, many of which were openly distributed prior to the imposition of martial law in late 1981, when strict censorship was imposed. Many state-controlled newspapers and magazines were privatized following the collapse of the Communist regime, and freedom of the press was subsequently protected for the most part. Reporters Without Borders ranked Poland 19th out of 180 for 2014. However, government response to leaked tapes in June 2014 sparked criticism over media freedom leading to a 2016 ranking of 47th out of 180 countries, a 29 point loss of status reflecting concerns over a new media law enabling the government to appoint and dismiss the heads of the state radio and TV broadcast media, which came into effect in January 2016.

Foreign relations. During most of the postwar era, Polish foreign policy supported the stationing of Soviet troops in Poland as well as Polish participation in the Warsaw Pact and the Council for Mutual Economic Assistance. The events of the first half of 1980 elicited harsh criticism from the Soviet Union, Czechoslovakia, and East Germany while prompting expressions of concern in the West that the Warsaw Pact might intervene militarily, as it had in Hungary in 1956 and in Czechoslovakia in 1968. Predictably, the Soviet Union and most Eastern-bloc countries endorsed the Polish government's crackdown of December 1981. Western disapproval was alleviated by the lifting of martial law in mid-1983, and Washington withdrew its opposition to Polish membership in the IMF at the end of 1984, facilitating the country's admission to that agency and its sister institution, the World Bank, in June 1986.

In February 1990, Prime Minister Mazowiecki traveled to Moscow for talks with President Gorbachev, reiterating Polish concern that a newly unified Germany might attempt to reclaim land ceded to Poland after World War II. These fears were allayed by the outcome of "two-plus-four" talks between the two Germanys and World War II's victorious powers in July, which yielded a treaty between Bonn and Warsaw on November 14 that confirmed Poland's western border at the Oder and Neisse rivers. Poland's other major foreign policy concern was alleviated when the last Russian military contingent withdrew on September 17, 1993.

On May 21–23, 1992, during President Wałęsa's first visit to Moscow, a friendship and cooperation treaty was concluded that subsequently generated widespread resentment in Poland for its failure to address the issue of Russian responsibility for Stalinist atrocities during World War II. In October this source of strain was reduced when Moscow, bringing to an end over 50 years of false denials, admitted that the former Communist regime had ordered the execution of some 26,000 captured Polish army personnel in Katyn forest in 1940.

On November 2, 1992, Poland's National Defense Committee adopted a new policy based on the assumption that Poland had no natural enemies and no territorial claims on neighboring states. Longer-term security was seen as lying in a Euro-Atlantic system involving Polish membership in NATO. The main thrust of Polish foreign policy, however, was toward membership in the European Community (EC, subsequently the EU). To this end, Poland helped establish a series of new, transitional international groupings of post-communist countries, including the Central European Free Trade Area (CEFTA) treaty with Czechoslovakia and Hungary in 1991 and the Central European Initiative (CEI).

Having joined NATO's Partnership for Peace in February 1994, Poland on April 8 followed Hungary's lead in formally applying for admission to the EU. A month later, on May 9, it was one of nine former Communist states to become an "associate partner" of the Western European Union (WEU). Despite the Western thrust, which included a warm reception for U.S. President Clinton during an address to the *Sejm* on July 7, Poland also sought improved relations with Russia and the other members of the Commonwealth of Independent States (CIS). The motivation for the latter was largely economic: relatively stiff tariffs had generated a deficit in trade with the EU countries, whereas Poland had previously maintained a trade surplus with the Soviet Union. In December 1997 EU leaders agreed to open entry negotiations with Poland and five other nations, and the first formal talks were held in November 1998.

Under an agreement signed in Paris on July 11, 1996, Poland became the third ex-Communist state (after the Czech Republic and Hungary) to gain full membership in the Organization for Economic Cooperation and Development (OECD). The signing coincided with the end of an official visit to the United States by President Kwaśniewski, during which he received assurances of U.S. support for Poland's accession to NATO. Meanwhile, Poland had assigned 700 troops to the NATO-commanded International Force (IFOR) deployed in Bosnia under the Dayton peace agreements. At the Madrid summit meeting in July 1997, NATO leaders invited Poland and two other former Warsaw Pact nations (the Czech Republic and Hungary) to join the alliance. They became members on March 12, 1999, at ceremonies celebrating NATO's 50th anniversary in Independence, Missouri.

Poland was one of the more supportive countries of the U.S./UK-led invasion of Iraq in early 2003, lending some 2,400 troops to the campaign. In April 2003, Prime Minister Miller endorsed a plan for Poland to buy 48 U.S. fighter planes for an estimated $3.5 billion as part of a 15-year military upgrade program. Prime Minister Donald Tusk ended the mission to Iraq in October 2008, which had dwindled to 900 troops largely involved in training and humanitarian work.

On June 7–8, 2003, Polish voters endorsed their country's proposed accession to the EU by a 58.9 percent "yes" vote in a national referendum. Poland joined nine other states as new EU members on May 1, 2004.

Tensions rose between Germany and Poland in late 2004 over the issue of reparations from World War II and its aftermath. Representatives of Germans who had been deported from former German territory in 1945–1946 after the territory was incorporated into Poland renewed their campaign for compensation in 2004. In return, Poland threatened to seek reparations from Germany for damage inflicted during the war.

The PiS minority cabinet and the subsequent PiS-led coalition that emerged from the 2005 elections adopted a nationalistic, euroskeptic approach toward foreign policy. Among other things, other European countries reportedly objected to the new Polish administration's blockage of cross-border takeovers of Polish state-run enterprises slated for privatization. In addition, the EU specifically noted Poland in a resolution condemning perceived growing racism and ultranationalism throughout the continent. Of particular concern to the EU was the inclusion of the LPR in the Polish cabinet in 2006. The Polish legislature, in turn, issued a counter-resolution condemning the EU resolution.

Relations with the EU worsened during Germany's subsequent presidency of the EU, as the PiS coalition argued against reduced voting representation for Poland in a treaty meant to replace the EU constitution rejected by French and Dutch voters in 2005. Prime Minister Kaczyński famously asserted in a June 2007 radio interview that Poland's population-based representation would be greater if its people had not been decimated by Germany and Russia during World War II. Poland's government also charged that Germany was undermining European energy security by cooperating with Russia in the construction of a Baltic pipeline.

Following his election in October 2007, Prime Minister Donald Tusk adopted a more europhilic stance, meeting with Angela Merkel in Berlin in December 2007 and hosting a one-day summit with Nicolas Sarkozy in Warsaw in May 2008. In December 2007 he visited EU headquarters in Brussels and declared his will to "defend European interests." Poland and Sweden launched an Eastern Partnership in 2009, a regional association under EU auspices that would work to bring Ukraine, Moldova, Georgia, Armenia, and Azerbaijan into a closer relationship with the EU. Tusk, however, declined to sign the EU Charter of Fundamental Rights, noting that it could compel Poland to recognize the claims of Germans forced from their homes following postwar border changes and because of its stance on gay rights and other social issues that he considered antithetical to Poland's more conservative public opinion. President Kaczyński remained opposed to the EU and refused to sign the ratification of the Lisbon Treaty, which had passed both houses of parliament in April.

Since the political ascendancy of the PO, Prime Minister Tusk has made a concerted effort to forge closer relations with all of Poland's neighbors. In 2009 Poland and Ukraine signed an agreement to make border crossings easier for people living near the frontier.

In September 2009 the U.S. president Barack Obama administration reversed a George W. Bush administration plan to deploy a missile shield in Poland. The decision was popular among the Polish public, but Foreign Minister Radosław SIKORSKI commented that the action created a "credibility problem" for the United States. Sikorski's criticism resonated with the U.S. government, and in October it was announced that Poland could still host U.S. missiles, although not ones that could be converted to offensive nuclear weapons or otherwise pose a threat to Russia. That announcement was followed in December with an agreement to place mobile Patriot missiles and 100 to 150 U.S. soldiers at Morag, Poland, which is about 35 miles from the Russian base at Kaliningrad. Russia complained that it could not understand the necessity "to create the impression as if Poland is bracing itself against Russia."

The troops and missiles arrived in Poland in May 2010, and Russia replied by deploying an antiaircraft missile installation to Kaliningrad.

The presence of Polish troops in Afghanistan was an issue in the 2010 presidential election. Komorowski argued that Poland's deployment of 2,500 soldiers achieved nothing and squandered funds that Poland needed to modernize its military. In July Foreign Minister Radosław Sikorski visited Afghanistan and stated, "We would like to withdraw our brigade at the end of 2012 and possibly continue to support Afghans in some other form." In 2011 Poland declined to participate in the NATO alliance against Libya, although it was willing to send humanitarian aid. It claimed that its pilots were not yet trained well enough in flying F-16s to contribute effectively and it would be prohibitively expensive.

The April 2010 plane crash in Russia that killed 96 people including dozens of Polish officials briefly improved relations with Russia. Prime Minister Putin was compassionate, bringing roses to the crash site and accompanying the body of President Kaczyński back to Warsaw. Russia also declared a national day of mourning to honor the dead. A week after the misfortune Russian television showed the Polish film *Katyn* to a national audience, most of which were unfamiliar with the Soviet atrocity and the related ongoing anger among Poles. The warming trend cooled in January 2011 when the official Russian report attributed the crash to an error of the Polish pilots, who were under pressure to land in unsafe conditions. In July the Polish report gave some responsibility for the crash to the Russian air traffic controllers but ascribed most of the blame to Polish officials and procedures. Polish minister of defense Bogdan KLICH resigned after the report was issued because his department trained the pilots.

In May 2011 President Obama visited Poland at the end of a six-day trip to Europe. He praised Poland as a democratic model for the emerging Arab states and supported legislation that would make it easier for Poles to obtain visas to the United States. He also promised that the Poles would not suffer from his reset of U.S. relations with Russia, endorsing an agreement, which was signed in June, to station U.S. air force personnel and planes in Poland to train Polish pilots. However, in May 2012 Obama mistakenly used the phrase "Polish death camps" when speaking of Nazi camps located in Poland. The gaffe outraged many Poles, despite Obama's quick apology.

In 2011 Poland's relations with Western Europe, especially Germany, were positive. Tusk, who spoke fluent German, had a warm relationship with Merkel. At their meeting in Warsaw in June Merkel promised that if the Nord Stream pipeline caused problems of access to Polish Baltic ports, Germany would bury them deeper. Tusk noted that trade between German and Poland was 1 billion euros greater than trade between Russia and Germany. Both countries decided not to engage in military activity in Libya. In June 2011 Tusk also met with Sarkozy in Paris, where the French president promised to support Poland during its EU presidency and vowed not to interfere with Poland's shale gas extraction, although the practice has been banned by the French parliament.

Poland held the rotating presidency of the EU for the second half of 2011, but since it did not use the euro, Warsaw was left out of many critical negotiations about the economic crisis.

Revelations that Poland allowed the United States to use its territory to incarcerate and interrogate terror suspects from 2001 to 2004 sparked controversy. After an investigation, on January 10, 2012, former interior minister and secret services chief Zbigniew SIEMIATKOWSKI was indicted for false imprisonment. Poland was the first EU member state to indict an official in this matter.

Relations with Lithuania became strained due to a decision to drop Polish-language classes in Lithuanian schools and limit the use of Polish in public areas. Warsaw insists that would deprive Lithuania's Polish ethnic group of a basic right. The new Lithuanian government elected in October 2012 was more amenable to Polish language use.

Poland sent 20 troops to Mali in April 2013 as part of an EU training mission. Meanwhile, Warsaw withdrew its troops from Afghanistan in 2014. The Polish military base in Ghazni province was renovated for use as a geology and mining university.

Protests began in Kiev, Ukraine, in November 2013 and, as the security situation escalated over subsequent month, Poland assumed a special role in the Ukrainian crisis. While tensions over Ukraine escalated between the EU and Russia, Poland emerged as the EU mediator with its neighbor. In January 2014 Polish officials warned that escalation of violence in Ukraine could cause turbulence in Europe and could spark mass emigration. As Moscow became more assertive in Ukraine, Poland and its other former Soviet neighbors fretted about the implications for the region. On April 1, 2014, Poland asked NATO to deploy 10,000 troops to reinforce the border. The Pentagon responded by holding small ground-force exercises in Poland and Estonia late that month. Also in April, Poland campaigned for a European energy union, which would allow the EU to negotiate contracts on behalf of all member states with energy companies. As of June 2016 some 4,100 Ukrainians had applied for refugee status in Poland. (See the Ukraine entry in the 2015 *Handbook* for more on the 2013–2014 crisis.)

On June 3, 2014, President Obama kicked off a four-day tour of Europe in Warsaw, where he announced a $1 billion security plan to beef up military presence in Eastern Europe. Some military assets, including Patriot air defense missile batteries, were deployed to Poland in 2015 and 2016. Concurrently, an increase in rotational military deployments and combined training exercises in Poland and the Baltic states has increased the U.S. role in the region.

Poland opposed proposals by the UK in December 2015 to suspend social benefits for new EU migrants as part of the negotiations to avoid a British exit ("Brexit") from the EU (see entry on the United Kingdom). The government opposed changes that would have deprived segments of the large Polish community in the UK from work-related benefits, such as unemployment or health insurance.

Current issues. The question of whether Poland should join the eurozone dominated political discussion in 2013. The country should have fulfilled all of the Maastricht criteria and been eligible to adopt the euro in 2015. The *Sejm* endorsed the EU Fiscal Compact by a vote of 282 to 155 on February 20, which President Komorowski ratified on February 28. The PiS asked the constitutional tribunal to review the matter, arguing that approval needed a two-thirds majority to give budgetary control to an external power. All parties agree that a constitutional amendment must be enacted before Poland joins the eurozone, as Article 227 gives the National Bank of Poland exclusive control over printing and regulating the national currency. Tusk and the PO favored changing the constitution immediately, so that, "When the eurozone resolves its problems we should be ready to join it." However, the PO-PSL government did not have the two-thirds majority in the Sejm needed to pass a constitutional amendment. The PiS insisted on a popular referendum on when to change currency before any constitutional amendment. In March 2013 Tusk offered a compromise to the PiS, agreeing to a referendum if the PiS in return for the party's backing to change the constitution. However, polls show that two-thirds of Poles don't support the euro, largely deterred by the ongoing financial crisis in core eurozone states since 2008.

Spring 2013 saw several adjustments in the cabinet. Tusk sacked Treasury Minister Mikolaj BUDZANOWSKI in April for failing to disclose a pipeline expansion deal with Russia's Gazprom. Justice Minister Jarosław GOWIN was fired on April 29 for suggesting that Polish fertility clinics were selling embryos. By June, popular support for the PO dropped to 27 percent, behind the PiS at 30 percent. Support for the PSL sunk below the 5 percent threshold for entering the *Sejm*.

As the economy slowed, the defense ministry slashed spending for 2014 by 10 percent. Events in Ukraine, and tensions with Russia, saw a reverse of this policy, with an 18 percent increase in spending for 2015. The lead-up to the May 2014 European Parliament elections saw the emergence of new political groupings, including Europa Plus and the Poland Together Jarosława Gowin (*Polska Razem Jarosława Gowina*—PRJG), the new initiative of the former justice minister. The PO's diminishing popularity was made evident by the results; the ruling party secured 32.1 percent of the vote, a fractional lead over the PiS's 31.8 percent. Both parties won 19 seats, followed by the SLD with five seats, and the KNP and PSL with four each. Poland's voter turnout was 22.7 percent, half of the European average. Meanwhile, Poland was on-trend with the rest of the regional body, seeing a sharp rise in popularity of conservative and anti-EU groupings.

The PO's crisis worsened on June 14, 2014, when the weekly magazine *Wprost* published a transcript of a tape allegedly recorded one year earlier in which Interior Minister Bartlomiej SIENKIEWICZ, who was replaced in the November 2013 cabinet reshuffle (see Political background, above), asked the head of Poland's central bank for support in the 2015 elections. The bank is required by law to be independent of the government, but defended both men in the recording and dismissed the leak as an attempted coup. On June 22 Tusk said that he was considering calling early elections if the scandal did not subside. A raid by security forces on the magazine offices that week to seize the tapes escalated the controversy, as did a second leak, in which two cabinet officials called Poland's alliance with the United States "worthless." Tusk surprised his parliamentary opponents on

June 26 by calling a vote of confidence in his government. With the support of the PSL, which had been negotiated the day before, the administration survived the vote, 237 to 203.

In presidential elections on May 10, and 24, 2015, PiS candidate Andrej Duda beat sitting president Komorowski. The victory was due to a combination of fatigue with the Komorowski administration as well as fears over immigration and tension with Russia. Beata Szyldo, who had managed the Duda campaign, became the PiS candidate for the prime ministership, which she won when the Senate and the *Sejm* held elections on October 25, 2015. The PiS secured 37.6 percent of the vote and 235 seats. The government party, PO, came in second with 24.1 percent and 138 seats. A new, openly right-wing party, Kukiz' 15, came in third with 8.8 percent and 42 seats. For the first time in Europe since 1993, both major parties fielded female candidates. Szydło was sworn in as the head of a one-party PiS cabinet, the first time since 1989 that an absolute majority was achieved.

The PiS government, which gained office on a Eurosceptic platform, did not stop accession talks to join the eurozone. In September 2015 Finance Minister Mateusz SZCZUREK noted that the 2004 calculus for joining the euro had "changed," and the government needed more discussion.

POLITICAL PARTIES AND GROUPS

Government Party:

Law and Justice (*Prawo i Sprawiedliwość*—PiS). Drawn primarily from conservative elements of the Christian National Union (ZChN), the SKL, and the **Republican League** (*Liga Republikańska*—LR) of Mariusz KAMIŃSKI, the PiS was organized in March 2001 under the leadership of Jarosław Kaczyński, a former editor of *Tygodnik Solidarność* (*Solidarity Weekly*) and a longtime supporter of Lech Wałęsa. In its Christian-democratic orientation the PiS resembled an earlier Kaczyński formation, the now-defunct Center Alliance (*Porozumienie Centrum*—PC; see SKL-RNP, below), which had been organized in 1991 and had then formed the core of a **Center Citizens' Alliance** (*Porozumienie Obywatelskie Centrum*—POC) that secured 44 *Sejm* seats the following October. In January 1998 Kaczyński resigned after eight years as PC chair because of the party's decision to remain in the AWS.

Registered as a party in June 2001, the PiS gained additional support through the presence of Kaczyński's twin brother, Lech Kaczyński, a former justice minister who brought to the party his reputation as an anticorruption, anticrime campaigner as well as one of Poland's most popular politicians. At the September 2001 elections the PiS won 44 seats in the *Sejm,* based on 9.5 percent of the vote.

In April 2002 the PiS and the **Alliance of the Right** (*Przymierze Prawicy*—PP) announced their pending merger. The PP (not to be confused with the Polish Agreement [PP], below, under the LPR) had been established in March 2001 by Minister of Culture Kazimierz UJAZDOWSKI and former members of the AWS-affiliated SKL and ZChN, including the latter's ex-chair, Marian PIŁKA. Ujazdowski, a close ally of Lech Kaczyński, had headed the Conservative Coalition (*Koalicja Konserwatywna*—KK) before its merger with the SKL in early 1999.

The PiS consistently opposed the economic policies of the Miller administration, and the Kaczyński brothers regularly accused government officials of corruption. That stance appeared to resonate with the public, which accorded the PiS a third-place finish in the June 2004 balloting for the European Parliament.

The PiS's share of seats in the *Sejm* increased from 44 in 2001 to 155 in the 2005 elections. The party also won the presidency and a plurality of seats in the Senate. The PiS subsequently formed an unsteady coalition with two populist parties, *Samoobrona* and the LPR, hoping to establish a leading Christian-democratic conservative party by coopting smaller factions. While the PiS performed well in regional assembly elections in 2006, taking 25.1 percent of total votes, it was eclipsed by the PO (below), which also took the mayoralty of Warsaw from PiS control. The PiS-led coalition faced a succession of crises in 2007, as public support flowed from *Samoobrona* and the LPR to the PO. Dwindling poll numbers were exacerbated by seemingly excessive PiS-led corruption investigations of government officials, which in July 2007 resulted in the president's controversial dismissals of several cabinet ministers, including Andrzej Lepper, the agricultural minister and *Samoobrona* chair. Following a breakdown in negotiations toward continuing the current coalition, PiS leaders asserted that the *Sejm* might be dissolved and early elections held. The final blow to the coalition appeared to come with the dismissal of Interior Minister Janusz KACZMAREK on August 8 for alleged leaks that purportedly undermined ongoing investigations of Lepper. The PiS subsequently agreed with the PO to hold snap elections in the fall. Despite having hoped for a renewed mandate, the PiS was ousted from power following the October 21 poll, in which it finished second to the PO with 166 seats on a 32.1 percent vote share. Nevertheless, President Kaczyński indicated that he intended to utilize the leverage left to him in his position, exerting some control over defense, economic, and foreign affairs through his veto power. The party spent most of 2008 on the defensive but sent a representative (an invited guest) to the U.S. Democratic National Convention in Denver, with hopes of learning campaign techniques that could be applied in Poland. The PiS came in second to the PO in the European Parliament elections that were held in June 2009, electing 15 members, who plan to group with conservatives from 7 other countries to form a conservative coalition.

In January 2010 the PiS suffered a further setback when seven of its members in the *Sejm* bolted from the party to form a short-lived new party called **Poland Plus.** (See the 2013 *Handbook* for details.) Subsequently, the plane crash in April that took the life of President Kaczyński and the failure of his brother to beat the PO candidate in the special presidential election meant that the party lost the right to veto legislation.

The PiS performed poorly in the November 2010 regional elections, winning 81 seats less than the PO, and dissatisfaction within its ranks became open. Seven members who were unhappy with the party's leadership left to form a new party, Poland Comes First (*Polska jest Najważniejsz*—PJN, see below). Kaczyński has criticized the Tusk administration for its handling of the plane crash that killed his brother and promised to make it an issue during the campaign.

PiS placed second in the October 9, 2011, parliamentary elections, with 30 percent of the vote. It received 157 seats in the *Sejm*, down from 166 in 2007, and 31 in the Senate, down from 39 in 2007. Seventeen influential party members blamed the disappointing results—a sixth consecutive loss—on Kaczyński's leadership style and ultimately left the PiS to form a new party, **United Poland** (see below).

The PiS benefited from fatigue with the ruling party in the May 2014 European elections, placing a close second to the PO, though tying in securing 19 seats. This was followed by the party's presidential victory of May 2015, which it won with 51.5 percent of the vote. The party's success culminated with the October 2015 parliamentary elections, in which the PiS won 61 seats in the Senate and 235 seats in the *Sejm.*

Leaders: Jarosław KACZYŃSKI (Former Prime Minister and Party President), Beata SZYDŁO (Prime Minister), Mariusz KAMINSKI, Adam LIPIŃSKI, Antoni MARCIEREWICZ (Vice Presidents of the Party).

Opposition Parties:

Civic Platform (*Platforma Obywatelska*—PO). The PO was organized in January 2001 at the initiative of three prominent politicians: former presidential candidate Andrzej Olechowski, who, running as an independent, had finished second in the 2000 poll with 17 percent of the vote; Donald Tusk, formerly of the Freedom Union (*Unia Wolnósci*—UW, below); and former AWS leader and *Sejm* Speaker Maciej PŁAŻYŃSKI. The new formation's liberal, free-market orientation soon attracted other disparate elements, including much of the previously AWS-supportive **Conservative Peasant Party** and the extreme right-wing Realpolitik Union (UPR). (For additional information on the UPR, see the 2007 *Handbook.*) For the 2001 Senate campaign, the PO joined the Solidarity Electoral Action of the Right (*Akcja Wyborcza Solidarność Prawicy*—AWSP), the UW, and Law and Justice (PiS, above) in a **Senate Bloc 2001** (*Bloc Senat 2001*) in an unsuccessful effort to prevent the SLD from gaining a majority. In the concurrent *Sejm* election the PO finished second, with 12.7 percent of the vote and 65 seats, although a number of deputies elected on its list, including eight from the SKL, chose to sit in the lower house as members of other parliamentary groups.

The PO, which had entered the 2001 elections as a "group of voters," was registered as a political party in March 2002. In April 2003 PO Chair Maciej PŁAŻYŃSKI resigned to protest the centrist party's failure to adopt his rightist policies. The PO led all parties in the balloting for the Polish seats in the European Parliament in June 2004.

In the 2005 parliamentary elections, the PO won the second largest block of seats with 133, more than doubling the 65 seats that it won in 2001. Initially, the party was thought to be in a position to partner with the PiS to form the government, but talks collapsed.

The PO's candidate, Donald Tusk, came in first in the first round of presidential polling in October 2005 but lost to the PiS candidate in the second round. Enjoying a strong 27.2 percent vote share in the 2006 regional elections, the Civic Platform secured the coveted mayoralty of Warsaw. After a meeting with the PiS in August 2006, the PO announced support for early elections, pledging to work with the government to pass critical EU legislation before the next poll.

Early parliamentary elections in October 2007 yielded a substantial plurality for the PO in the *Sejm* (on a 41.5 percent vote share) and a three-fifths majority in the Senate. In spite of difficult economic conditions the party did extremely well in the elections for the European parliament in June 2009, gaining 44.4 percent of the vote and half of the 50 seats allotted to Poland. In order to show its commitment to Europe, a PO candidate, who subsequently won a seat in Gdańsk, debated two of his rivals in English. On July 3, 2010, Tomasz Tomczykiewicz was elected head of the PO's parliamentary caucus, replacing Grzegorz Schetyna, who was elected speaker of the *Sejm*.

In November 2010 the PO won 222 seats in regional assemblies. The PiS was second with 141 seats. The party also was the top vote getter in the October 9, 2011, parliamentary election. With 39.2 percent of the vote, the PO received 207 seats in the *Sejm* and 63 in the Senate, down slightly from 209 and 60 in 2007. To shore up his position, Tusk moved elections for party chair from 2014 to August 2013. Gowin challenged Tusk in the PO's August 2013 leadership election but failed to unseat the prime minister; Tusk received 79.4 percent of the vote, compared to Gowin's 20.4 percent. Gowin went on to found Poland Together Jarosława Gowin (*Polska Razem Jarosława Gowina*—PRJG, below).

Party support slumped, largely due to high unemployment rates, ahead of the May 2014 European parliament elections, in which the PO won a slender victory over the PiS. Confidence further deteriorated in June when tapes of high-level party officials were leaked. The party's position eroded further when it lost the presidential election in May 2015 and the parliamentary elections in October of that year. Former PO leader, Donald TUSK, who became president of the European Council in 2014, remains the party's most visible figure. Ewa KOPACZ, who served as prime minister until her loss in the November 2015 elections, relinquished her role as party leader on December 31, 2015, to Grzegorz SCHETYNA.

Leaders: Grzegorz SCHETYNA (Chair), Hanna GRONKIEWICZ-WALTZ (Vice Chair and Mayor of Warsaw).

Polish Peasants' Party (*Polskie Stronnictwo Ludowe*—PSL). The original PSL was organized in 1945 by Stanisław Mikołajczyk after the leadership of the traditional **Peasant Party** (*Stronnictwo Ludowe*—SL), founded in 1895, had opted for close cooperation with the postwar Communist regime. In November 1949, following Mikołajczyk's repudiation by leftist members, the two groups merged as the **United Peasants' Party** (*Zjednoczone Stronnictwo Ludowe*—ZSL), which became part of the Communist-dominated FJN.

In August 1989 a group of rural activists met in Warsaw to revive the PSL on the basis of its 1946 program. (Party leaders subsequently insisted that the Polish name of the party should more appropriately be translated as Polish People's Party, a usage that has recently gained wide acceptance.) In November the ZSL reorganized into two parties, the **PSL-Rebirth** (PSL-*Odrodzenie*—PSL-O) and the **PSL-*Wilnanóv*** (PSL-W). Six months later, the present PSL emerged from a unification congress of the PSL-O, part of the PSL-W, and some members of the **PSL-*Solidarność***, which had been formed by former Rural Solidarity members in 1989. The PSL's principal support came from small farmers who opposed the introduction of large-scale agricultural enterprises on the U.S. model.

At the 1991 election, the PSL was the core of a **Peasant Coalition** (*Sojusz Programowy*) that won 48 *Sejm* seats. Running alone, it secured 132 seats in 1993 and formed a governing coalition with the SLD. Amid frequent strains between the coalition parties, the PSL deputy president was dismissed as chair of the *Sejm*'s privatization committee in November 1994 on the grounds that he had tried to block or slow down the sell-off of state enterprises.

The PSL lost considerable ground in the 1997 balloting, dropping from 132 seats to 27 on a 7.3 percent vote share. Party leader Jarosław Kalinowski finished fourth, with 6 percent of the vote, in the 2000 presidential election. In September 2001 the party won 9 percent of the *Sejm* vote, for 42 seats, as a result of which it negotiated a governing coalition with the larger SLD/UP alliance. However, Prime Minister Miller of the SLD forced the PSL to leave the government in April 2003 after the PSL voted against its coalition partners on a contentious road tax measure.

The PSL secured only 25 seats in the 2005 *Sejm* balloting (on a vote share of 7 percent), but it won 13.2 percent of the vote in the 2006 regional elections. After securing 8.9 percent of the vote in the October 2007 *Sejm* balloting, the PSL moved into a surprisingly strong government position, as its 31 seats were necessary to provide the PO-led coalition cabinet with a legislative majority. Party leader Waldemar Pawlak, who is also deputy prime minister and minister of the economy, has been a good partner, but the party's performance in the 2009 European Parliament elections, where it won only 7 percent of the vote and 3 seats, weakened its position in the coalition. Pawlak ran in the first round of the 2010 presidential elections, but he garnered only 1.75 percent of the vote. Yet in local elections in 2010 the party won 93 seats, coming in third behind the PO and PiS. The party came in fourth in the 2011 elections, with 8.4 percent of the vote. It lost three seats in the *Sejm* (from 31 to 28) but secured two seats in the Senate after having nonce since 2007. The PO and PSL again formed the governing coalition. On November 17, 2012, Janusz Piechociński upset Pawlak, 547 votes to 530, to become party chair. Pawlak immediately resigned from the cabinet. Piechociński began to construct a center-right group with Poland Comes First (*Polska jest Najważniejsz*—PJN), announcing in January 2013 intentions to contest the European parliamentary elections together. The alliance subsequently dissolved, and the PSL won four seats in the May 2014 balloting. In the 2015 parliamentary elections, the PSL lost one of its two senate seats, as well as 12 seats in the *Sejm*, reducing it to 16 seats and knocking it out of the ruling coalition. One victim of the defeat was Janusz PIECHOCIŃSKI, who resigned on November 7 as party leader to be replaced by Władysław KOSINIAK-KAMYSZ.

Leaders: Władysław KOSINIAK-KAMYSZ (Chair); Hetman KRYZYSZTOF (Vice Chair and Member of the European Parliament); Jarubas ADAM, Dariusz KLIMCZAK, Adam STRUZIK (Vice Chairs); Andrej MARIAN GRZYB, Piotr ZGORZELSKI (Secretaries).

Kukiz'15 (K'15). Kukiz'15 was founded in 2015 as a right-wing political party dedicated to "destroying particracy." It did not formally register as a party. Nevertheless, the "movement," in coordination with the far right **National Movement** (*Ruch Narodowy*), worked together to contest the 2015 elections, with a focus on replacing the proportional representation electoral system with single-member constituencies that would provide for direct representation and minimize the role of party leaders. The movement was led and inspired by right-wing politician Pawel KUKIZ, a popular musician and anticlerical (but pro-Catholic) social conservative with a nationalist agenda. Kukiz came in third in the first round of the May 2015 presidential elections with 21 percent of the vote. In the November 2015 parliamentary elections, the party won 8.8 percent of the vote and 42 seats in the *Sejm*, making it the third-largest party in Poland. Five of those seats are held by members of the National Movement.

Leaders: Pawel KUKIZ (Chair).

Modern (*Nowoczesna*—N). The liberal Modern Party was founded in May 2015 by Ryszard PETRU, a former World Bank economist. In the 2015 legislative balloting, Modern secured 7.6 percent of the vote and 28 seats.

Leader: Ryszard PETRU (Chair).

German Minority of Lower Silesia (*Mniejszość Niemiecka Slaska Opolskiego*—MNSO). Representing ethnic Germans in western and northern Poland, the MNSO list won seven seats in the October 1991 balloting, four of which were retained in 1993. It won two seats in 1997, 2001, and 2005 under rules that exempt national minority parties from the 5 percent threshold. (Both deputies were from the largest German association—the German Social and Cultural Society of Opole Silesia [*Towarzystwo Spoleczno-Kulturalne Niemcówna Slasku Opolskim*—TSKN].) Ethnic rights issues having apparently faded in relevance following the recent adoption of EU legislation guaranteeing minority rights; the party won one seat in the 2007 *Sejm* balloting on a 0.2 percent vote share. The German minority's former representative to the *Sejm*—Henryk KROLL—who had been elected to the *Sejm* five times between 1991 and 2005, was elected in 2009 to the European Parliament as a representative of the German minority in Poland. The party won a single seat in the *Sejm* in October 2011 and retained it in the 2015 elections.

Leader: Ryszard GALLA (Chair and Parliamentary Leader).

Other Parties That Contested the 2015 Elections:

United Poland (*Solidarna Polska*—SP). Following the PiS loss in the October 9, 2011, parliamentary election, Deputy Chair Zbigniew Ziobro accused Kaczyński of having a controlling style that damaged the party. Ziobro, a member of the European Parliament and former minister of justice in Poland, and PiS strategist, formed a new parliamentary political bloc, United Poland. Sixteen MPs and 1 senator took up his cause when Ziobro and 2 other MEPs were expelled from the PiS on November 4. By spring, the SP had 20 MPs, 2 senators, and 4 MEPs, who turned it into a formal political party on March 24, 2012. Members elected Ziobro as the party chair and announced a platform that favored taxing wealthy individuals and large businesses, banning abortion and euthanasia, and opposing nuclear power. They did not, however, rule out a future coalition with the PiS, describing the two groups as the "two lungs" of Polish conservative politics. In the European parliamentary balloting of May 2014, the SP won 4 percent of the vote, but failed to secure any seats. In the October 2015 elections, the party won no seats.

Leaders: Zbigniew ZIOBRO (Chair), Jacek KURSKI, Beata KEMPA (Vice Chairs).

United Left (*Zjednoczona Lewica*—ZL) ZL was a temporary electoral alliance that existed from July 2015 to February 2016. It was established to contest the October 2015 elections but failed to secure any seats. The alliance consisted of the Democratic Left Alliance (SLD), Your Movement (TR), Polish Socialist Party (PPS), Labor United (UP), and the Greens (PZ). It secured 7.6 percent of the vote in the 2015 elections. Reports in 2016 indicated the alliance had been disbanded.

Leader: Barbara NOWACKA (Chair).

Democratic Left Alliance (*Sojusz Lewicy Democratycznej*—SLD). The SLD was launched prior to the 1991 election as a coalition of the **Social Democracy of the Republic of Poland** (*Socjaldemokracja Rzeczypospolitej Polskiej*—SdRP) and the previously Communist-dominated **All Poland Trade Unions Alliance** (*Ogólnopolskie Porozumienie Związków Zawodowych*—OPZZ). The SdRP had been established on January 29, 1990, upon formal dissolution of the Polish **United Workers' Party** (*Polska Zjednoczona Partia Robotnicza*—PZPR). Formed in 1948 by merger of the (Communist) **Polish Workers' Party** (*Polska Partia Robotnicza*—PPR) and the Polish Socialist Party (*Polska Partia Socjalistyczna*—PPS, below), the PZPR claimed approximately 3 million members prior to the events of 1980–1981, as a result of which enrollment declined by nearly 800,000.

At the December 1990 presidential poll, the candidate backed by the SdRP, Włodzimierz CIMOSZEWICZ, placed fourth, with 9.2 percent of the vote; by contrast, the SLD was runner-up in the 1991 *Sejm* balloting and then became the largest *Sejm* formation in 1993 by increasing its representation from 60 to 171. Announced in May 1995, the presidential candidacy of SLD/SdRP leader Aleksander Kwaśniewski was subsequently endorsed by some 30 parties and groups, sufficient to yield a comfortable three-point margin of victory for him in the second round of the November balloting. Although the SLD improved its vote share from 1993, it actually won fewer seats (164) in 1997, when it was unable to withstand the pro-Catholic Church, anti-Communist campaign of the AWS. However, following the local elections of October 1998, the SLD controlled 9 of the nation's 16 provinces, having won a vote share of 32 percent.

Józef Oleksy became SdRP chair in January 1996, after Kwaśniewski won the 1995 presidential election. After the 1997 election the party chose Leszek Miller to replace Oleksy, who had not run for reelection. Miller's easy victory over Wiesław KACZMAREK, a former economics minister, was considered a blow to reformers who wanted further distance from the party's Communist origins.

The SLD was transformed into a political party announced in April 1999, after which the SdRP dissolved, and in July Miller formally took over the leadership of the SLD. Two other coalition partners, the PPS and the **Movement of Polish Working People** (RLP), chose to remain distinct from the new party. All three parties endorsed President Kwaśniewski for reelection in 2000, and on October 8 he claimed a first-round victory against 11 other candidates, winning 53.9 percent of the vote.

In preparation for the September 2001 parliamentary elections the SLD and the Union of Labor (*Unia Pracy*—UP, below) forged an electoral coalition (*Koalicja Sojuszu Lewicky Demokratycznej i Unii Pracy*) that captured 41 percent of the national vote and 216 seats, 15 short of a majority. Miller thereupon negotiated a coalition with the PSL (above) and became prime minister. The SLD/UP coalition had even greater success in the majoritarian Senate contest, winning 75 of 100 seats. However, the SLD's popularity subsequently declined amid discontent in some quarters over government austerity measures and disputes among government coalition parties. Miller resigned as SLD president in March 2004, although one of his close allies, Krzysztof JANIK, was elected to succeed him. Miller also resigned as prime minister on May 2, his replacement, Marek Belka, only achieving confirmation as a caretaker prime minister until the 2005 parliamentary balloting after pledging to undo some of the economic measures adopted by the Miller administration. The SLD (weakened by the defection of a group of legislators in March) managed only a fifth-place finish (again in alliance with the UP) in the June 2004 elections to the European Parliament. Subsequently, Janik was defeated in December in his bid for reelection as SLD leader by former prime minister Oleksy, although Oleksy came under intense scrutiny regarding allegations concerning his activities during Communist rule. The SLD was repudiated at the ballot box in 2005 when it saw its number of seats in the *Sejm* drop to 55. Oleksy was replaced as party leader by Wojciech OLEJNICZAK on May 29, 2005. The party regrouped in 2006 as part of an electoral coalition with the SDPL, UP, and PD, sharing in the collective 14.2 percent of votes taken by the coalition in the November regional elections. Along with the PiS, the SLD had its financial records for the previous cycle rejected by the State Election Commission due to the party having apparently accepted campaign donations in violation of electoral law. Its disappointing showing in the 2007 election caused the replacement of Olejniczak as party leader by Grzegorz NAPIERALSKI on May 31, 2008, but their popularity has continued to decline. Party member Marek Siwiec was elected as a vice president of the last European parliament.

The SLD won only seven seats in the 2009 EU elections in which the SLD ran in a coalition with UP. Napieralski came in a distant third (13.7 percent) behind the PiS and PO candidates in the first round of the June 2010 presidential election. He had been chosen to represent the party in April after Jerzy SZMAJDZIŃSKI was killed in the plane crash of April 10. In the local elections of November 2010 the SLD came fourth, trailing the PO, the PiS, and the PSL. Napieralski again led the party in the October 2011 elections, where it ran a list of younger candidates in the hope of appealing to youth. When the party won only 27 seats in the *Sejm*, Napieralski was sacked. Miller was brought back as party chair. In February 2013 Kwaśniewski created a new center-left political movement, Europa Plus, with several small parties to challenge the recent dominance of the PO and PiS, and to prioritize introducing the euro. However, the SLD left the alliance on February 7, 2014, and contested the election alone, winning five seats with 9.4 percent of the vote. The party secured no seats in the 2015 elections.

Leaders: Leszek MILLER (Chair and Former Prime Minister), Krzysztof GAWKOWSKI (Secretary General).

Your Movement (*Twój Ruch*—TR). **Palikot's Movement** (*Ruch Palikota*—RP) was founded as a progressive, anticlerical party by Janus Palikot, a flamboyant entrepreneur and defector from the PO. The RP platform supported abortion on demand, homosexual civil unions, and the legalizing of marijuana. It placed a surprising third, taking 10 percent of the vote and 40 seats in the *Sejm*. It did not participate in the Senate race. Slawomir KOPYCINSKI, elected to the *Sejm* on the SLD list, later changed his affiliation to RP. On October 6, 2013, the RP officially relaunched as the TR. For the 2014 European elections, the TR formed the **Europa Plus** coalition with the SLD (below) and several other left-leaning parties. However, the coalition dissolved following the 2014 European elections, in which Europa Plus secured just 3.6 percent of the vote. The party won no seats in the 2015 elections.

Leader: Barbara NOWACZKA (Chair).

Union of Labor (*Unia Pracy*—UP). Known as **Labor Solidarity** (*Solidarność Pracy*—SP) in 1991, when it won 4 *Sejm* seats as a left-wing faction of the original Solidarity movement, the UP captured 41 seats in 1993. With a 4.7 percent vote share in 1997, the UP failed to meet the 5 percent threshold and thus retained no seats. Key members, who include representatives of the Belarusan minority, subsequently were reported to have joined the UW (see below) early in 1998. The UP was part of the Social Alliance in the October 1998 local elections.

The UP concluded an electoral coalition with the SLD for the 2001 legislative contests and, following the alliance's success at the polls, joined the new administration under Prime Minister Miller. Izabela JARUGA-NOWACKA was elected president of the UP at an April 2004 party congress, and she joined the new government formed by the

SLD's Marek Belka in May as a deputy prime minister. The UP again presented joint candidates with the SLD in the June 2004 balloting for the European Parliament.

Even running in coalition with the SDPL, the UP was unable to win a seat in the 2005 elections, after having won 16 in the 2001 contests. Not a single UP candidate was elected. In 2008 the UP and the SLD signed an agreement to cooperate in attempting to collaborate to achieve a left-wing political agenda, and they ran together as a coalition in the 2009 elections for the European Parliament, gaining 12.3 percent of the vote and 7 seats.

Going into the 2011 parliamentary election, the UP had acquired three members in the *Sejm* in spite of its failure to win a seat in the 2007 election. Two members of the SDPL splinter group defected to the UP in 2009, and one of the UP's members took the oath of office as a legislator in May to succeed an SLD legislator who was killed in the plane crash of April. The two former SDPL members, however, again defected this time from the UP to the PO in May 2011. The UP unsuccessfully ran one candidate under the SDL banner in the October elections and failed to win any seats in the 2015 elections, in spite of its temporary alliance with the United Left electoral block.

Leaders: Waldemar WITKOWSKI (President), Adam GIEREK (Vice President for International Affairs), Arkadiusz HORONZIAK, Jan LUS, Catherine MATUSZEWSKA (Vice Presidents).

Polish Socialist Party (*Polska Partia Socjalistyczna*—PPS). Founded in 1892, the PPS went underground during World War II and provided Poland's first postwar prime minister. Although only a small faction was pro-Communist, the party was formally merged with the Communist PPR in 1948 to form the PZPR. The party was revived in 1987 and in March 1990 sponsored a congress of non-Communist leftists. Weakened by internal strife, the PPS failed to secure *Sejm* representation in 1991 or 1993. In February 1996, the two main PPS factions unified under the leadership of 82-year-old Jan MULAK. He was unanimously replaced by Piotr IKONOWICZ at a party congress in April 1998. Although it had been a member of the SLD coalition, in 1999, the PPS did not enter the new SLD party. Ikonowicz won only 0.2 percent of the vote in the 2000 presidential election. In 2003 Ikonowicz formed a new party (see New Left, below), and he was succeeded as PPS chair by Andrzej ZIEMSKI, who pledged to "moderate" the PPS to appeal to a broader range of voters. The PPS ran on a common ballot with the Polish Pensioners' Party and the Center-Left of the Republic of Poland for European parliamentary elections in 2003 and 2004. Members of the PPS were invited in 2007 to join the new LiD, which remains a group far from the mainstream of Polish politics. In 2010 it made a point of neither running its own candidate nor endorsing any other candidates in the presidential elections, nor did it participate in the 2011 parliamentary election.

Leaders: Boguslaw GORSKI (President), Gregory ILNICKI, Lukasz SZYMANSKI (Vice Presidents).

The **Greens 2004** (*Zieloni 2004*), a member of the European Green Party, was first registered in 2004. It ran in the 2009 European parliamentary elections in the coalition Agreement for the Future with the SD and SDPL.

Leaders: Małgorzata TRACZ, Marek KOSSAKOWSKI.

Self-Defense of the Polish Republic Party (*Partia Samoobrona Rzeczypospolitej Polskiej*). Popularly known as *Samoobrona,* this party has its base in the agrarian trade union of the same name. Formed in 1993, the union encompassed about half a million mostly rural members, although the much smaller party initially also attracted a high percentage of businesspersons disaffected from the rest of the political establishment. Generally regarded as the most militant of Poland's three principal farmers' unions, *Samoobrona* did not become a significant parliamentary force until the 2001 national election, at which the party won 10.2 percent of the vote and 53 seats in the *Sejm.* Following *Samoobrona* success at the polls in 2001, Andrzej Lepper was named vice marshal of the lower house, but he was removed from the post in late November, partly as a consequence of provocative statements made against other national figures. On January 25, 2002, the house revoked his parliamentary immunity, and five days later he was fined by an appeals court for defamatory statements made against President Kwaśniewski and others in 1999. In February 2002 Lepper was charged with seven additional counts of slander. However, the charges appeared to enhance Lepper's popularity.

In 2006 *Samoobrona* (whose support fell to 5.6 percent of the vote in the 2006 regional elections) joined the PiS and the League of Polish Families (*Liga Polskich Rodzin*—LPR, below) to form a coalition government, with Lepper named deputy prime minister. Lepper was subsequently dismissed in July 2007 in the face of corruption allegations.

Samoobrona and the LPR in July 2007 announced formation of an electoral alliance called the **League and Self-Defense** (*Liga i Samoobrona*—LiS) in preparation for possible early elections. The LiS pledged to challenge Poland's adoption of the new EU treaty proposed in 2007, rejecting the "loyalty conditions" endorsed by the PiS as necessary to preserve the coalition. The alliance did not last long, and both parties eventually decided to contest the October balloting on their own and the LiS was disbanded. Samoobrona secured only 1.5 percent in the 2007 *Sejm* elections and did not win a seat. Its performance in the 2009 elections for the European parliament was equally unimpressive, winning only 1.5 percent of the vote and no seats. The party's chair Andrzej Lepper ran in the first round of the presidential elections in 2010, but obtained only 1.3 percent of the vote. On August 4, 2011, Lepper was found hanging in his office, an apparent suicide. It was blamed on financial troubles and his conviction for soliciting sex in exchange for a job in the party. The party received less than 10,000 votes in October 2011. Andrzej PROCHON was elected party chair in March 2012, then replaced by Lech Kuropatwinski in August 2012. After initial discussion of an alliance with the PSL, *Samoobrona* contested the 2014 European elections alone, registering just 0.04 percent. The party won no seats in the 2015 elections.

Leader: Lech KUROPATWINSKI (Chair).

Congress of the New Right (*Kongres Nowej Prawwicy*—KNP) is a free market, Eurosceptic party that was founded in March 2011 by Janusz Ryszard KORWIN-MIKKE, a libertarian conservative who received 2.5 percent of the vote in the first round of the presidential poll. It represents a merger of the UPR and WIP. The party secured 35,169 votes in October 2011, or 1.1 percent of those cast. KNP's anti-euro platform proved popular in the 2014 European elections as the small party won four seats with 7.2 percent. In the 2015 elections the party lost its representation in the *Sejm* and the Senate, earning only 0.03 percent of the vote.

Leader: Michal MARUSIK.

Poland Together Jarosława Gowin (*Polska Razem Jarosława Gowina*—PRJG). Founded by former justice minister Jarosława Gowin in December 2013, the conservative PRJG grew out of the PJN (below). Although the PRJG did not secure any seats in the 2014 European elections, it did win 3.2 percent of the vote. The party joined with the Law and Justice Party for the 2015 election cycles, and while it retained a separate identity, its actual independence from the PiS was uncertain.

Leader: Jarosława GOWIN.

Other Parties:

Poland Comes First (*Polska jest Najważniejsz*—PJN). Founded by disgruntled members of PiS, including 4 former PP members, PJN counted 18 MPs and 1 senator ahead of the October 2011 parliamentary election. However, key members switched affiliation before election day. The most high-profile defector was Chair Joanna KLUZIK-ROSTKOWSKA, who went over to the PO. The center-right party received 2.2 percent of the votes in October 2011 and failed to cross the threshold for seats. In December 2013 the PJN was officially absorbed into the PRJG.

Polish Labor Party/August 80 (*Polska Partia Pracy-Sierpien 80*—PPP). The **Polish Labor Party** emerged for the 2007 *Sejm* elections, where it received 0.8 percent of votes. It did no better in the European parliamentary elections of 2009 when it also took 0.7 percent of the vote under the leadership of Bogusław Zbigniew ZIĘTEK. Ziętek ran for president in 2010, receiving 0.2 percent of the vote in the first round. The party polled 0.55 percent in the 2011 parliamentary election. Chair Bogusław Zbigniew Zietik resigned in April 2013, and the PPP joined Europa Plus.

Republic Right Party (*Prawica Rzeczypospolitej*—PRP). The Republic Right Party is an antiabortion party that won 2 percent of the vote in the 2009 EU elections. In 2010 it ran Marek JUREK, a former speaker of the *Sejm,* as its candidate in the presidential elections. He received 1 percent of the vote in the first round. The party ran for the *Sejm* in October 2011 and received 35,169 votes for 0.2 percent. Ahead of the 2014 European elections, the PRP allied with the PiS. Jurek secured a seat in the May balloting.

Leader: Marek JUREK.

Democratic Party (*Partia Demokratyczna*—PD). A promarket, pro-European grouping hoping to attract centrist support, the PD was launched in the first half of 2005 by Jerzy Hausner (former SLD deputy prime minister) and Władysław Frasyniuk of the UW. Hausner had recently quit the SLD after his proposal to cut the federal budget had been rejected.

The PD took 2.5 percent of the vote in the 2005 parliamentary elections before joining the LiD umbrella for the 2007 balloting, when it gained 3 of the LiD's 53 seats. The PD ran in coalition with the SDPL and the Greens in the 2009 elections for the European Parliament, but the coalition gained only 2.4 percent of the vote. The PD supported the PO's Bronisław Komorowski in both rounds of the 2010 presidential elections. (The PD should not be confused with the long-standing party of the same name; see SD, below.) They did not participate in the October 2011 elections. The PD joined the Europa Plus alliance to contest the May 2014 European elections. They did not participate in the 2015 elections.

Leaders: Andrzej CELINSKI (Chair), Elizabeth BINCZYCKA (Vice Chair).

Polish Social Democracy Party (*Socjaldemokracja Polska*—SDPL). The SDPL was formed in March 2004 by Marek Borowski (a former speaker of the *Sejm*) and some 22 other SLD deputies seeking to distance themselves from the administration of Prime Minister Miller. Although the SDPL declined formal coalition status in the government formed by the SLD's Marek Belka in June 2004, an SDPL member was named minister of health, and the SDPL pledged to support the caretaker government in the legislature until the 2005 elections.

In 2005 the SDPL ran in coalition with the UP and failed to gain seats in the legislature. The SDLP continued to garner low returns with a 3.9 percent vote share in the 2006 regional elections. It competed in the 2007 election as part of the LiD coalition, securing 10 of the LiD's 53 seats.

Eight of the SDPL's legislators subsequently broke with the SLD and in 2009 formed their own parliamentary caucus, calling itself **Social Democracy of Poland–New Left** (*Socjaldemoracja Polska-Nowa Lewica*—SDPL-NL). The SDPL competed in the 2009 elections for the European Parliament in a coalition with the PD and the Greens but failed to gain a seat. The party's vice chair and spokesperson Arkadius KASZNIA ran under the PO list in the October 2011 elections, but he did not win a seat. In June 2013 it joined the Europa Plus alliance for the 2014 European election, though departed the coalition in February 2014, and did not contest elections in 2015. Marek BOROWSKI, who maintains his membership in the party, successfully ran for the 2015 *Sejm* elections as an independent candidate.

Leaders: Wojciech FILEMONOWICZ (Chair), Arkadiusz KASZNIA (Vice Chair).

League of Polish Families (*Liga Polskich Rodzin*—LPR). Initially formed as a "group of voters," the LPR brought together an assortment of nationalist, predominantly anti-EU and Catholic groups, many of them associated with *Radio Maryja.* Registered as a party on May 30, 2001, the LPR was headed by Antoni MACIERWICZ, a former interior minister whose efforts to expose former Communist collaborators contributed to the fall of the Olszewski government in 1992. In February 1993 Macierewicz launched the now-defunct right-wing **Christian National Movement–Polish Action** (*Ruch Chrześcijańsko-Narodowe-Akcja Polska*—RChN-AP), and in 1995 he participated in the formation of the now-defunct Movement for the Reconstruction of Poland (Ruch Odbudowy Polski—ROP). He broke from the ROP in late 1997 and established the Catholic National Movement for the Reconstruction of Poland, which in May 1998 shortened its name to the Catholic National Movement (*Ruch Katolicko-Narodowy*—RKN) and then joined the AWS. Another LPR founder, Jan ŁOPUSZAŃSKI of the **Polish Agreement** (*Porozumienie Polskie*—PP) had won 0.8 percent of the vote in the 2000 presidential race.

For the 2001 legislative elections, the LPR list included not only members of the PP but also members of the **National Party** (*Stronnictwo Narodowe*—SN) and the ROP. The SN dated from the December 1999 merger of Bogusław KOWALSKI'S **National Democratic Party** (*Stronnictwo Narodowo Demokratyczne*—SND) and an existing SN. In the 2000 presidential election campaign, the SN had been a leading supporter of Gen. Tadeusz WILESKI, who won 0.2 percent of the vote.

In September 2001 the LPR won 9 percent of the vote and 38 seats in the *Sejm.* Within six months, however, significant differences had emerged within the parliamentary delegation. In April 2002 Macierewicz and Jan Łopuszański both reportedly resigned from the party Presidium, and Macierewicz and four other disaffected LPR deputies subsequently resumed coordination under the RKN rubric. Macierewicz served as one of the main opponents to EU membership in the run-up to the 2003 referendum on the issue.

The LPR became part of the government in May 2006, but popular support for the party dwindled, as evidenced by its 4.7 percent vote share in regional elections later that year. Influential Catholic media owner Father Tadeusz RYDZYK publicly urged the coalition to continue, as LPR voters had been wooed away by the PiS's increasingly conservative stance, dampening the LPR's prospects for the next election cycle. Nevertheless, LPR Chair Giertych resigned his position as national education minister in July 2007, with *Samoobrona* and the LPR subsequently announcing plans (eventually aborted) to present candidates on a common LiS ballot in the next parliamentary poll.

Damaged by public discontent with the ruling party and a tumultuous summer, as well as isolated xenophobic incidents involving LPR members, support for the party dipped to 1.3 percent in the October 2007 parliamentary balloting. Giertych announced that he would resign as chair following the party's loss of parliamentary representation. In 2009, their candidates ran as members of the Libertas party in the European parliamentary elections. None was elected.

Leaders: Witold BAŁAŻAK (Chair), Zenon MROCZKOWSKI (Chair of Political Council).

Polish Peasant Party (SKL, also known as the **Conservative-Peasant Party–New Poland Movement** [*Stronnictwo Konserwatywno-Ludowe–Ruch Nowej Polsi*—SKL-RNP]). The SKL-RNP was established in January 2002 by merger of the SKL and the **Polish Party of Christian Democrats** (*Porozumienie Polskich Chrześcijańskich Demokratów*—PPChD).

Founded in January 1997, the SKL united two small right-wing parties, the **Conservative Party** (*Partia Konserwatywna*—PK), which had been launched in December 1992 by amalgamation of the **Forum of the Democratic Right** (*Forum Prawicy Demokratycznej*—FPD) the **Peasant-Christian Alliance** (*Stronnictwo Ludowo-Chrześcijańskie*—SLCh), and others. The SKL's founding members included ex-ministers Jan Maria ROKITA and Bronisław KOMOROWSKI and elements of the Christian Democratic Labor Party (*Chrześcijańska Demokracja Stronnictwo Pracy*—ChDSP). (For additional information on the ChDSP, see the 2007 *Handbook.*) At the SKL party congress in late February 1998, two groups joined the SKL: the **Party of Republicans** (*Partia Republikanów*—PR), led by Jerzy EYSYMONTT, and the **Integrative Initiative** (*Inicjatywa Integracyjna*—II) faction of the **Center Alliance** (*Porozumienie Centrum*—PC), led by Wojciech DOBRZYŃSKI. In February 1999 the **Conservative Coalition** (*Koalicja Konserwatywna*—KK) of Kazimierz Ujazdowski also joined the SKL.

In September 1999 what remained of the Center Alliance, which dated from 1991, and the Christian Democratic Party (*Partia Chrześcijańskich Demokratów*—PChD) announced their merger as the PPChD under Antoni TOKARCZUK, previously the PC chair. Also joining the new formation were the **100 Movement** (*Ruch 100*), which had been founded by former foreign minister Andrzej Olechowski, now of the PO; the **Polish Peasants' Party–Peasant Alliance** (*Polskie Stronnictwo Ludowe–Porozumienie Ludowe*—PSL-PL); and the **Movement for the Republic** (*Ruch dla Rzeczypospolitej*—RdR), which traced its origins to the 1992 formation of the **Christian Democratic Forum** (*Forum Chrześcijańsko-Demokratyczne*—FChD) by supporters of ousted prime minister Jan Olszewski. In April 2001 the PPChD added to its ranks the **Electoral Solidarity** (*Solidarni w Wyborach*—SwW) of Jerzy GWIŻDŻ. Later in the same month, the PPChD aligned itself with Prime Minister Buzek's efforts to reshape the AWS. The failure of Buzek's AWSP coalition at the September 2001 poll ultimately led the PPChD to seek a stronger alliance, which led to the 2002 merger with the SKL.

In March 2001 the SKL announced that it would leave the government and enter the Civic Platform (PO) in preparation for the September 2001 legislative elections. Following the balloting, however, a number of deputies who had been elected on the PO list established themselves as a separate SKL parliamentary group. In January 2002, the party split over the question of the PO affiliation. One faction, led by Jan Maria Rokita, opted to remain with the PO, and another, led by Artur BALAZS, instead approved the merger with the PPChD and the creation of the SKL-RNP. The latter was subsequently largely absorbed into the PiS but found its position there increasingly awkward, unsuccessfully pressuring the PiS-led coalition to tighten abortion laws in early 2007. In August 2007 the SKL-RNP reformed itself and now uses the simpler name of Polish Peasant Party (*Stronnictwo Konserwatywno-Ludowe*—SKL). It supported Bronisław Komorowski in the 2010 presidential elections. At a party congress that was held on June 18, 2011, however, the party decided to work closely with the new party PJN, but that party collapsed before election day. Instead, party leader Marek Zagorski unsuccessfully ran for a seat under the PiS banner. Ahead of the 2014 European elections the SKL-RNP joined the PRJG (above). The party did not contest the 2015 elections.

Leader: Marek ZAGORSKI (Chair).

Democratic Party (*Stronnictwo Demokratyczne*—SD). Recruiting its members predominantly from among professional and intellectual ranks, the SD was founded in 1939 as a non-Marxist group and was a Front party during the Communist era. In mid-1989 the party abandoned its alliance with the Communists and, in September, accepted three portfolios in the Solidarity-led Mazowiecki government. Thereafter, it was seemingly unable to decide what its political profile should be, securing only one *Sejm* seat in the 1991 balloting and none in 1993 or 1997. In 2001 the SD ran in conjunction with the SLD. In June 2002, at the party's 20th congress, delegates replaced Jan KLIMEK as party chair, citing the party's weak performance under his leadership. (The SD should not be confused with the PD [above] that was launched in early 2005.) In the European parliamentary elections of 2002, the SD garnered only 0.3 percent of the vote. In 2005 it formed a coalition with the SDPL but attained only 0.2 percent of the vote. In 2009 the SD formed a coalition with the Greens and the SDPL called Agreement for the Future, which gained 2.4 percent of the vote in elections for the European Parliament. The SD ran former finance minister Andrzej OLECHOWSKI in the first round of the 2010 presidential elections. He obtained only 1.4 percent of the vote, however, and both Olechowski and party chair Pawel Piskorski supported Bronisław Komorowski, the PO candidate, in the second round. Piskorski was briefly removed from office by the regional court over legal issues in Warsaw, but then he was reinstated in March 2011, although the forgery charges still loomed. The party did not run an independent list of candidates in the October 2011 elections. The SD contested the European elections of 2014 as part of Europa Plus but did not contest the 2015 elections.

Leader: Pawel PISKORSKI (Chair).

The Left and Democrats (*Lewica i Demokraci*—LiD). Hoping to take advantage of instability within the PiS-led government coalition, former president Aleksander Kwaśniewski announced the formation of the LiD, a center-left coalition, in September 2006. It consisted of the Democratic Left Alliance (*Sojusz Lewicy Democratycznej*—SLD), the Polish Social Democracy Party (Socjaldemokracja Polska—SDPL), the Democratic Party (*Partia Demokratyczna*—PD, and the Union of Labor (*Unia Pracy*—UP, above). The alliance aimed to create an alternative to the PiS in the upcoming early elections and reportedly approached the PO about the possibility of creating a common ballot. Kwaśniewski, who was credited with modernizing social democracy in Poland, opposed the Kaczyński ambition of purging former communists from government. The LiD received 13.15 percent of votes in the 2007 *Sejm* elections, giving it 53 seats out of 460. The LiD coalition was formally dissolved after the election, but a coalition of 43 legislators (comprising members of the SLD and UP and former members of the SDPL) formed a parliamentary caucus called simply the Left (Lewica).

In preparation for the 2005 general election, a number of new parties emerged, including the **Center Party** (*Centrum*), a pro-EU grouping that received 0.2 percent of votes in that election and supported the PO in the 2007 election under the leadership of Dr. Zbigniew RELIGA, an internationally renowned heart surgeon; and the **New Left** (*Nowa Lewica*—NL), a left-wing "anticapitalist" grouping established in 2003 by former PPS leader Piotr IKONOWICZ, which held demonstrations against the missile shield in August 2008.

Other parties participating in the 2005 *Sejm* balloting included the **Polish National Party** (*Polska Partia Narodowa*—PPN), led by nationalist and xenophobe Leszek BUBEL, with 0.3 percent of votes; the **National Civic Coalition** (*Ogólnopolska Koalicja Obywatelska*—OKO), a collection of 140 social organizations and unions, with 0.1 percent of votes; the **Polish Dignity and Work Confederation** (*Polska Konfederacja-Godność i Praca*—PKGiP), with 0.07 percent of votes; the **Labor Party** (*Stronnictwa Pracy*—RS), with 0.01 percent of votes; and **Social Rescuers** (*Społeczni Ratownicy*—SR), a party in favor of expanded welfare benefits, with 0.01 percent of votes.

New parties participating in the 2007 *Sejm* elections included the **Women's Party** (*Komitet Wyborczy Partii Kobiet*—PK), which gained only 0.3 percent of the vote and subsequently did not compete in the 2009 elections for the European parliament.

The pan-European **Libertas** party, which was started by Irishman Declan GANLEY in 2009, presented candidates in Poland for the 2009 European parliamentary elections. In Poland, it consisted of 3 members of the Libertas party, 57 independent candidates, and 67 members from six other parties. These consisted of **Forward Poland** (*Naprzód Polsko*—NP, **Polish People's Party "Piast"** (*Polskie Stronnictwo Ludowe "Piast"*—PSL Piast, **Party of Regions** (*Partia Regionów*—PR), League of Polish Families (*Liga Polskich Rodzin*—LPR, above), **National Polish Organization-Polish League** (*Organizacja Narodu Polskiego-Liga Polska*—ONP-LP), and the Christian National Union (*Zjednoczenie Chrześcijańsko-Narodowe*—ZChN, below). Libertas, which was organized in opposition to the Lisbon Treaty, gained only 1.1 percent of the vote and no seats. Another party that participating in the 2009 EU elections included the **Republic Right Party** (*Prawica Rzeczypospolitej*—PRP), an antiabortion party that won 2 percent of the vote. The right-wing **Realpolitik Union** (*Unia Polityki Realnej*—UPR) won 1.1 percent of the vote in the 2009 European Parliament balloting.

For more information on the **Peasant Democratic Party** (*Partia Ludowe Democratyczna*—PLD), the **Movement for the Reconstruction of Poland** (*Ruch Odbudowy Polski*—ROP), and smaller parties active during the 2005 balloting, see the 2008 *Handbook*.

The 2010 presidential election saw the rise of the **Liberty and Rule of Law Party** (*Wolność i Praworządność*—WIP), which was founded by Janusz KORWIN-MIKKE, Meanwhile, a hero of the original Solidarity movement—Kornel MORAWIECKI—ran as a candidate of a party that he founded in 1982 called **Fighting Solidarity** (*Solidarność Walcząca*—SW). He received 0.1 percent of the vote in the first round of balloting.

For information on the defunct parties—**Social Movement, Christian National Union, Freedom Union,** and the **Christian Democratic Party of the Third Republic**—see the 2011 *Handbook*.

LEGISLATURE

Under Communist rule, the 460 members of the *Sejm* (Diet or Parliament) were elected via direct universal suffrage from candidate lists strictly controlled by the Front of National Unity and its successor, the Patriotic Movement for National Rebirth. Following extensive government/Solidarity negotiations, a bicameral legislature was established in 1989 that incorporated the existing *Sejm* and added a 100-member Senate, each serving four-year terms, subject to dissolution. Only a portion of the *Sejm* seats were open to opposition candidates in the 1989 balloting, although subsequent elections have been conducted on a fully open basis. As codified in the 1997 constitution, when sitting together, the *Sejm* and the Senate constitute the **National Assembly** (*Zgromadzenie Narodowe*).

Senate (*Senat*). The upper house comprises 100 members elected under a majoritarian system from 40 multimember constituencies. The Senate cannot initiate legislation but has the power of veto over the *Sejm,* which the latter can overturn only by a two-thirds majority. Following the most recent election of October 25, 2015, the distribution of seats was as follows: Law and Justice, 61; Civic Platform, 34; independent, 4; and Polish People's Party, 1.

Speaker: Stanslaw KARCZEWSKI (PiS).

Sejm. The lower house comprises 460 members elected from 41 multimember constituencies under a proportional system (revised in 2001) in which parties (save for national minority groups) must gain 5 percent of the vote and coalitions need 8 percent to qualify for lower house seats. The distribution following the election of October 25, 2015, was as follows: Law and Justice, 235; Civic Platform, 138; Kukiz'15, 42; Modern, 28; Polish Peasants' Party, 16; and German Minority of Lower Silesia, 1.

Marshal: Marek KUCHCINSKI (PiS).

CABINET

[as of July 1, 2016]

President	Andrez Duda (PiS)
Prime Minister	Beata Szydło (PiS)[f]
Deputy Prime Ministers	Piotr Gliński (PiS)
	Mateusz Morawiecki (PiS)
	Jarosław Gowin (PT)
Ministers	
Agriculture and Rural Development	Krzysztof Jurgiel (PiS)
Culture and National Heritage	Piotr Gliński (PiS)
Economy	Marek Gróbarczy (PiS)
Environment	Jan Szyszko (PiS)
Finance	Paweł Szałamacha (PiS)
Foreign Affairs	Witold Waszczykowski (PiS)
Health	Konstanty Radziwiłł (PT)
Infrastructure and Development	Mateusz Morawiecki (PT)
Interior and Special Intelligence Services	Mariusz Błaszczak (PiS)
Justice	Zbigniew Ziobro (PiS)
Labor and Social Policy	Elżbieta Rafalska (PiS) [f]
National Defense	Antoni Maciarewicz (PiS)
National Education	Anna Zalewska (PiS) [f]
Public Administration and Digitalization	Anna Streżyńska (ind.) [f]
Science and Higher Education	Jarosław Gowin (PT)
Sports and Tourism	Witold Bańka (PiS)
Treasury	Dawid Jackiewicz (PiS)

[f] = female

INTERGOVERNMENTAL REPRESENTATION

Ambassador to the U.S: Piotr WILCZEK.

U.S. Ambassador to Poland: Paul W. JONES.

Permanent Representative to the UN: Bogusłąw WINID.

IGO Memberships (Non-UN): CEUR, EBRD, EIB, EU, ICC, IEA, IOM, NATO, OECD, OSCE, WTO.

For Further Reference:

Coppen, Luke. "Sorry, Bono, but 'Hyper-nationalists' Aren't Running Poland." *The Spectator,* May 21, 2016.

Holzer, Jan. *Challenges to Democracies in East Central Europe.* New York: Routledge, 2016.

Krafczyk, Eva. "History Becomes a Battleground of Polish Politics." *Deutsche Press-Agentur* (February 24, 2016).

Millard, Francis. *Polish Politics and Society.* New York: Routledge, 1999.

Szczerbiak, Aleks. "What Does Pawel Kukiz's Election Success Mean for Polish Politics?" *The Polish Politics Blog*, May 14, 2015. http://blogs.lse.ac.uk/europpblog/2015/05/15/what-does-pawel-kukizs-election-success-mean-for-polish-politics.

PORTUGAL

Portuguese Republic
República Portuguesa

Political Status: Independent republic proclaimed on October 5, 1910; corporative constitution of March 19, 1933, suspended following military coup of April 25, 1974; present constitution promulgated on April 2, 1976, with effect from April 25.

Area: 35,553 sq. mi. (92,082 sq. km).

Population: 10,304,000 (2016E—UN); 10,833,816 (2016E—U.S. Census).

Major Urban Centers (urban area, 2016E—UN): LISBON (2,902,000), Porto (Oporto, 1,304,000).

Official Language: Portuguese.

Monetary Unit: Euro (market rate October 1, 2016: 0.89 euro = $1US).

President: Marcelo REBELO DE SOUSA (Social Democratic Party); elected on January 24, 2016, and inaugurated on March 9, for a five-year term; succeeding Aníbal CAVACO SILVA (Social Democratic Party).

Prime Minister: António COSTA (Socialist Party); designated by the president on November 23, 2015, and sworn in on November 26; succeeding Pedro Passos COELHO (Social Democratic Party) whose government lost a confidence vote on November 10, 2015.

THE COUNTRY

Known in antiquity as Lusitania, Portugal overlooks the Atlantic along the western face of the Iberian Peninsula, while including politically the Azores and the Madeira Islands in the Atlantic. Mainland Portugal is divided by the Tagus River into a mountainous northern section and a southern section of rolling plains whose geography and climate are akin to those of northern Africa. The population, a blend of ancient Celtic, Iberian, Latin, Teutonic, and Moorish elements, with a recent admixture of African and other immigrants, is culturally homogeneous and almost wholly affiliated with the Roman Catholic Church, which traditionally exercised commanding social and political influence. Portuguese, the official language, is spoken by virtually all of the population. Women comprise 44 percent of the official labor force, concentrated in agriculture and domestic service; female representation in government and politics—despite the participation of a few prominent women, including former prime minister Maria de Lourdes PINTASILGO—averages less than 10 percent. Although the legislature rejected a mandate that women be allotted 25 percent of all posts in the Portuguese Assembly as well as in the Portuguese delegation to the European Parliament, all of the major parties volunteered to observe the proposed quota. (As of 2016, women held 34.8 percent of seats in the national legislature or 80 of 230 seats.)

The economy, one of the least modernized in Europe, retains a somewhat paternalistic structure characterized by limited social services and per capita gross domestic product (GDP) of $20,700 in 2013. Although agriculture accounts for about 39.7 percent of the land area, it contributes only 2.3 percent of GDP. Industry, consisting primarily of small manufacturing firms, employs some 28.5 percent of the labor force and contributes 23 percent of GDP. Exports include machinery and tools as well as such traditional goods as textiles, clothing, fish products, cork, and olive oil, of which Portugal is one of the world's largest producers. The European Union (EU) accounts for three-quarters of Portugal's imports and exports. The service sector, including tourism and retail, has become Portugal's largest employer. The government has successfully recruited investment into renewable energy industries in an effort to offset Portugal's dependence on foreign sources of oil and natural gas. The government plan called for Portugal to produce more than 60 percent of its electricity from renewable sources by 2020, far more than the EU target of 20 percent. Already home to Europe's largest onshore wind farm, Portugal's first floating offshore wind turbine began producing electricity in 2012.

By 2008, falling demand for goods and services, including a 20.8 percent decrease in exports, pushed Portugal's economy into negative economic growth. (For an overview of the economy prior to 2008, see the 2013 *Handbook.*) In 2009 GDP declined by 2.9 percent, while inflation was –0.9 percent. Unemployment rose to 9.5 percent and the government deficit rose sharply to 9.4 percent of GDP, prompting warnings from the EU and International Monetary Fund (IMF) and the implementation of an austerity plan. Lisbon requested a debt bailout in 2011, as the country slid into a recession. GDP declined by 1.3 percent in 2011 and a further 3.2 percent in 2012. Inflation rose 2.8 percent in 2012 and just 0.4 percent in 2013, while unemployment was 15.6 percent and 15.3 percent, respectively. GDP continued to decline in 2013, falling by 1.1 percent. Unemployment rose to 13.9 percent in 2014 and

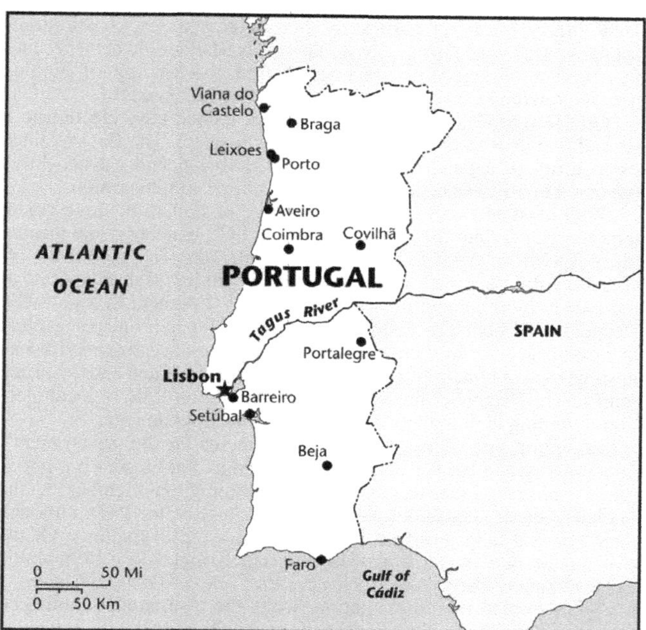

dropped slightly to 12.6 percent in 2015. GPD growth rate was 0.9 percent in 2014 and 1.5 percent in 2015. The World Bank ranked Portugal 31st of 189 countries in its 2014 annual report and 23rd in its 2016 annual report on the ease of doing business.

GOVERNMENT AND POLITICS

Political background. As one of the great European monarchies of late medieval and early modern times, Portugal initiated the age of discovery and colonization and acquired a far-flung colonial empire that was one of the last to be abandoned. Interrupted by a period of Spanish rule from 1580 to 1640, the Portuguese monarchy endured until 1910, when a bloodless revolution initiated a republican era marked by chronic instability and recurrent violence. A military revolt in 1926 prepared the way for the presidency of Marshal António CARMONA (1926–1951) and the assumption of governmental authority by António de Oliveira SALAZAR, an economics professor who became finance minister in 1928 and served as prime minister from 1932 until his replacement because of illness in 1968. Salazar, mistrustful of democratic and socialist ideologies and influenced by Italian fascism, established economic and political stability, and in 1933 he introduced a "corporative" constitution designed to serve as the basis of a new Portuguese State (*Estado Novo*). With the support of the Catholic Church, the army, and his National Union, the only authorized political movement, Salazar completely dominated Portuguese political life and reduced the presidency to an auxiliary institution.

The later years of Salazar's regime were marked by rising, though largely ineffectual, domestic discontent and growing restiveness in the Overseas Territories. Elections were frequently boycotted by the opposition, and direct presidential elections were eliminated following a vigorous but unsuccessful opposition campaign by Gen. Humberto DELGADO in 1958. Overseas, the provinces of Goa, Damão, and Diu were seized by India in 1961; in the same year, a revolt broke out in Angola, while independence movements became active in Portuguese Guinea in 1962 and in Mozambique in 1964. Attempts to suppress the insurrections resulted in severe economic strain as well as increasing political isolation and repeated condemnation by the United Nations (UN).

The crisis created by Salazar's nearly fatal illness in September 1968 was alleviated by the selection of Marcello CAETANO, a close associate, as the new prime minister. Although he permitted a measure of cautious liberalization, including some relaxation of secret police activity and the return from exile of the Socialist Party (*Partido Socialista*—PS) leader Mário SOARES, Caetano preserved the main outlines of Salazar's policy both in metropolitan Portugal and overseas.

Prior to the parliamentary election of October 1969, opposition parties were legalized, but they were again outlawed after a campaign in which the official National Union won all 130 seats in the National Assembly. The atmosphere of repression eased again after the adoption in 1971 of constitutional legislation expanding the power of the enlarged National Assembly, granting limited autonomy to the Overseas Territories, abolishing press censorship, and permitting religious freedom. Nevertheless, in the legislative election of October 1973 the ruling Popular National Action (successor to the National Union) won all 150 seats, including 34 representing the Overseas Territories.

In a bloodless coup on April 24, 1974, a group of mainly left-wing military officers calling themselves the Armed Forces Movement (*Movimento das Forças Armadas*—MFA) seized power, ending more than 40 years of civilian dictatorship. The president and prime minister were arrested and flown to Brazil, where they were granted political asylum. The leader of the "Junta of National Salvation," Gen. António Sebastião Ribeiro de SPÍNOLA, assumed the presidency, and on May 15 a center-left cabinet was sworn in with Adelino de PALMA CARLOS as prime minister. After a dispute with the reconstituted Council of State as to the extent of his powers, Palma Carlos resigned on July 9 and was replaced by Gen. Vasco dos Santos GONÇALVES, whose administration recognized the right of the Overseas Territories to "self-determination" and independence. On September 30 General Spínola also resigned, leaving power in the hands of leftist military officers and civilians. The new president, Gen. Francisco da COSTA GOMES, subsequently reappointed General Gonçalves as prime minister.

In May 1974 Costa Gomes declared that the new government was prepared to offer a cease-fire in Angola, Mozambique, and Portuguese Guinea, with the guerrilla organizations being permitted to organize political parties and participate in democratic elections. As a result of the initiative, negotiations were undertaken that led to the independence of Guinea-Bissau (formerly Portuguese Guinea) in September and independence for Mozambique, São Tomé and Principe, and Cape Verde the following year. Although negotiations with Angolan leaders were complicated by the presence of a sizable white minority and by the existence of three major insurgent groups, the formation of a united front by the insurgents opened the way for independence. The front subsequently collapsed, but Portugal withdrew from Angola on the agreed date of November 11, 1975.

On March 11, 1975, right-wing military elements, reportedly acting at the instigation of former president Spínola, attempted to overthrow the government. When the coup failed, General Spínola flew to Brazil, and the Junta of National Salvation was dissolved in favor of a Supreme Revolutionary Council (SRC). The latter, sworn in by President Costa Gomes on March 17, was given full executive and legislative powers for the purpose of "directing and executing the revolutionary program in Portugal." One-third of the cabinet announced on March 25 was comprised of military officers, in addition to representatives of the main political parties.

In a Constituent Assembly election on April 25, 1975, the Socialists received 38 percent of the total vote, compared with 26 percent for the Popular Democrats and less than 13 percent for the Communists. The first session of the assembly was convened on June 2, with the Socialists holding 116 of the 250 seats. Despite their commanding legislative strength, the Socialists and Popular Democrats subsequently announced their intention to resign from the government, in part because of a Communist takeover of the Socialist newspaper *República*, and on July 31 a new, essentially nonparty cabinet was formed. However, increasing opposition to Communist influence led, on August 29, to the resignation of Prime Minister Gonçalves and the appointment of Adm. José Baptista Pinheiro de AZEVEDO as head of a new cabinet (the sixth since the 1974 coup) comprising representatives of the three leading parties, as well as of the Armed Forces Movement.

In mid-November 1975 a Communist-led labor union general strike in Lisbon was followed on November 26 by an uprising of leftist military units that was crushed by loyalist troops. Although the SRC had previously rebuked Azevedo for his conduct during the strike, the coup's failure was seen as a major defeat for the Communists, and in mid-December, following designation of a new army chief of staff, the council ordered a major reorganization of the armed forces, emphasizing military discipline and the exclusion of the military from party politics.

The new constitution came into effect on April 25, 1976, and an election to the Assembly of the Republic was held the same day. The Socialists remained the largest party but again failed to win an absolute majority. On June 27 Gen. António dos Santos Ramalho EANES, a nonparty candidate supported by the Socialists, Popular Democrats, and Social Democrats, was elected to a five-year term as president. The election was a further setback for the Communists, whose candidate, Octávio PATO, finished third, behind far-left candidate Maj. Otelo SARAIVA DE CARVALHO. Three weeks later, on July 16, Soares was invested as prime minister, heading a Socialist minority government that was, however, endorsed by the other two parties in the presidential election coalition.

Having lost a crucial assembly vote on an economic austerity plan, Soares was forced to resign on December 8, 1977, though he was subsequently able to return as head of a governmental coalition with the conservative Social Democratic Center (*Centro Democrático Social*—CDS) on January 30, 1978. On July 27, however, President Eanes dismissed Soares after the CDS ministers had resigned over disagreements on agricultural and health policies, leaving the Socialists without a working legislative majority. His successor, Alfredo NOBRE DA COSTA, was in turn forced to resign on September 14 following legislative rejection of an essentially nonparty program. A new government, largely composed of independents, was eventually confirmed on November 22 with Dr. Carlos Alberto da MOTA PINTO, a former member of the Social Democratic Party (*Partido Social Democrata*—PSD, the renamed Popular Democratic Party), as prime minister.

Having witnessed assembly rejection of his proposed budget on three occasions since March, Prime Minister Mota Pinto resigned on June 6, 1979. On July 19 Maria de Lourdes Pintasilgo, a member of several previous post-1974 governments, was named to head a caretaker, nonparty government, pending an early legislative election. The balloting of December 2 confirmed Portugal's move toward the extremes of the political spectrum. Francisco SÁ CARNEIRO, a conservative Social Democrat who in July had formed a Democratic Alliance (*Aliança Democrática*—AD) with the Center Democrats, Monarchists, and disaffected Socialists, led his electoral coalition to a clear majority and was named on December 29 to organize a new government—the 12th since 1974—that was sworn in on January 3, 1980. The Alliance was returned to office with an increased majority at the second legislative election within a year on October 5, 1980.

Prime Minister Sá Carneiro was killed in a plane crash on December 4 and was succeeded as PSD leader and prime minister by Dr. Francisco Pinto BALSEMÃO, who proceeded to organize a new AD cabinet that was sworn in on January 5, 1981. Balsemão continued as head of a reorganized administration on September 1, 1982, prior to resigning on December 19, 1982.

In a general election on April 25, 1983, the Socialists obtained a substantial plurality, enabling Soares to form a cabinet of nine Socialists, seven Social Democrats, and one independent that assumed office on June 9. However, severe economic difficulties eroded the popularity of the Socialists, while the coalition partners disagreed on the extent of proposed austerity measures. On June 4, 1985, PSD parliamentary leader Aníbal CAVACO SILVA announced his party's withdrawal from the government, although agreeing to a postponement until the signature on June 12 of Portugal's entry accord with the EC. Two days later, Soares was named to head a caretaker administration pending a new election, while declaring himself a candidate for the forthcoming presidential poll.

The October 6, 1985, legislative balloting dealt a serious blow to the Socialists, whose representation was cut nearly in half. The largest vote share, 30 percent, went to the PSD, and Cavaco Silva formed a minority government based on his party's assembly plurality on November 6. The PSD's preferred presidential candidate, the Christian Democrat Diogo FREITAS DO AMARAL, captured nearly half the vote in the initial presidential balloting on January 23, 1986, out of a field of four candidates; however, an unusual coalition of the Socialists, the pro-Eanes Democratic Renewal Party (*Partido Renovador Democrático*—PRD), and the Communist-led United People's Alliance (*Aliança Povo Unido*—APU) succeeded in electing Soares, the remaining center-left candidate, with 51 percent of the vote in the February 16 runoff. Soares, the first civilian head of state in 60 years, was sworn in as Eanes's successor on March 9.

President Soares dissolved the assembly on April 28, 1987, following the April 3 defeat of the Cavaco Silva government on a censure motion that had charged the administration with mismanagement of the economy. In elections on July 19, the Social Democrats became the first party in 13 years to win an absolute majority of legislative seats. The incumbent prime minister returned to office on August 17 as head of an all-PSD government. Following his reconfirmation, Cavaco Silva moved to privatize state-owned firms and to reverse a number of post-1974 measures aimed at agricultural collectivization. In November 1988 the two leading parties reached agreement on constitutional changes that would strip the basic law of its Marxist elements, reduce the number of legislative deputies, permit the holding of binding national referenda, and accelerate the privatization process.

On January 13, 1991, President Soares gained easy election to a second five-year term on a 70.4 percent vote share. The PSD retained its majority in legislative balloting on October 6 and Cavaco Silva remained in office as head of a slightly modified administration.

With most economic indicators positive or stable, the government took the escudo into the broad band of the EC's exchange rate mechanism (ERM) on April 6, 1992. Five months later it was thrown off course by the European monetary crisis, which led to devaluations of the escudo by 6 percent in November and by 7 percent in May 1993. Deepening economic recession and assorted political problems resulted in a sharp decline in the government's standing, accompanied by an upsurge of "cohabitation" tensions between the president and the prime minister. In December the Socialists outpolled the PSD in local elections, winning their highest-ever share of a nationwide vote.

Recession and rising unemployment increased the government's unpopularity and led Cavaco Silva to resign as PSD leader but not as prime minister, in January 1995. In balloting on October 1, the Socialists made substantial gains at the expense of the PSD, although their 112-seat tally left them just short of an overall majority. Of the two smaller parties that won seats, the center-right Social Democratic Center–Popular Party (*Centro Democrático Social–Partido Popular*—CDS-PP) trebled its representation, while the Communist-dominated Unitary Democratic Coalition (*Coligação Democrática Unitária*—CDU) lost ground. The Socialist leader, António GUTERRES, accordingly formed a minority government at the end of October that was expected to have CDU external support on most issues.

In a presidential election on January 14, 1996, the Socialist candidate and former mayor of Lisbon, Jorge SAMPAIO, scored a comfortable first-round victory, taking 53.8 percent of the vote against 46.2 percent for the PSD's Cavaco Silva. Sampaio was sworn in for a five-year term on March 9. The Socialists extended a string of electoral victories thereafter, unexpectedly adding 3 seats in the assembly election of October 10, 1999 (for a total of 115, exactly half the membership), and retaining the presidency in balloting on January 14, 2001. In the latter contest, President Sampaio won 55.8 percent of the vote, versus 34.5 percent for the PSD's candidate, Joaquim FERREIRA DO AMARAL.

The PS suffered significant losses in municipal elections on December 16, 2001, and the following day Prime Minister Guterres announced his resignation. On December 28 President Sampaio, following the unanimous advice of the Council of State, dissolved the assembly in preparation for national legislative balloting in March.

In assembly balloting on March 17, 2002, the PSD secured 40.2 percent of the vote and 105 seats, followed by the Socialists (37.9 percent of the vote and 96 seats). On March 28 President Sampaio named José Manuel Durão BARROSO of the PSD to form a new government, and the next day Barroso signed a coalition pact with the CDS-PP, which was given three ministerial posts in the new government appointed on April 6.

Strengthened by their victory in the June 2004 European Parliament elections, the PS and other opposition parties demanded early elections when Prime Minister Barroso resigned on July 5 to become president of the European Commission. Instead, President Sampaio opted to pursue "stability" by appointing Pedro SANTANA LOPES of the PSD to succeed Barroso.

In light of the continued decline in popular support for the governing coalition, Sampaio dissolved the assembly on December 10, 2004, and directed that new elections be held on February 20, 2005, at which time the PS gained its first legislative majority (121 seats) since independence. Consequently, the new government installed on March 12 under the PS's José SÓCRATES included only PS members and a number of independents. Sócrates focused on improving Portugal's economy through public sector reforms. Decreased pension benefits, a reduction in the number of public sector workers, and spending cuts sparked widespread criticism.

After months of protests against Sócrates's austerity measures, voters on January 22, 2006, elected former prime minister Cavaco Silva to a five-year term as president. Cavaco Silva, who won 50.6 percent of the vote to defeat five left and center-left opponents, including PS member Manuel ALEGRE, who ran as an independent, and former president and official PS candidate Mário Soares, became the first center-right president to serve since the restoration of democracy in 1974. Although the Socialist Sócrates supported Soares for president, Cavaco

Silva declared his intention to maintain a positive "dialogue" with the Socialist government and refrained from exercising his veto power to block government-supported bills, including a controversial law permitting abortion during the first 10 weeks of gestation.

Despite opposition, in November 2006 the governing PS pushed through its austerity budget for 2007, aimed at enabling Portugal to meet the EU deadline for reducing the budget deficit from 4.6 percent of GDP to 3 percent by 2008. The government exceeded its goal, shrinking the deficit to 2.6 percent of GDP, and broadened its reform efforts to include education, health care, and labor. In May 2008 the parliament approved a controversial measure standardizing the Portuguese language among the seven Portuguese-speaking countries by adopting Brazilian spelling.

In an effort to win support before national elections scheduled on September 27, 2009, the PS in January issued an election platform that included a €200 subsidy for each child born in Portugal, mirroring similar measures introduced in other European countries with falling birth rates. However, widespread discontent with the government, especially its austerity measures amid a steep recession, led to a shift in the Portuguese delegation to the European Parliament in elections held on June 7, 2009. The opposition PSD won 8 of 22 seats, the PS won 7, and the Left Bloc won 3, marking a shift in the parties' fortunes. Preelection tensions mounted on July 2, when Finance Minister Manuel PINHO was forced to resign after insulting a Communist deputy during a parliamentary debate.

On election day, the PS won a leading 97 seats, but the loss of 24 seats from its 2005 total left it well short of a majority in the 230-seat legislature. Allegations that the prime minister's office had bugged the president's offices emerged in the midst of the September balloting, making it impossible for Sócrates to negotiate a coalition agreement with any other party. Instead, Sócrates formed a minority PS government that was sworn in on October 26. In December the EU and IMF warned the government of the need to reduce a record deficit of more than 9 percent of GDP.

In March 2010 credit agencies downgraded Portugal's bond rating because of the deficit and national debt. In March the assembly enacted a four-year austerity program that included a wage freeze for government employees, cuts to the military and public services, and tax increases. Civil servants protested the cuts through a series of one-day strikes though the spring. Portugal's credit rating was further downgraded in December 2010.

In February 2011 the European Central Bank intervened to purchase Portuguese bonds as concerns mounted that the country would be forced to seek a bailout similar to those negotiated by Greece and Ireland with the IMF and EU (see the entries on Greece and Ireland). The Sócrates government developed a new austerity package in an effort to satisfy EU requirements for financial aid. However, the new economic program was defeated in the assembly in March. Sócrates resigned, and new elections were scheduled for June.

In balloting on January 23, 2011, incumbent president Silva was reelected with 52.9 percent of the vote in the first round of balloting, defeating Manuel Alegre (PS), who secured 19.8 percent, independent candidate Fernando NOBRE with 14.1 percent, and a number of minor candidates. Opposition parties voted against a new economic program on March 23 in a no-confidence measure. Sócrates subsequently resigned, and new elections were called for June 5. The PSD won a plurality of 108 seats in the legislature in the balloting, and party leader Pedro Passos COELHO formed a coalition government with the CDS-PP on June 21. The 12-member cabinet was considerably smaller than previous governments. In July 2013 Coehho conducted a cabinet reshuffle after the CDS-PP threatened to withdraw from the government in protest of the extensions of austerity measures.

Several members of the cabinet resigned in July 2013 in opposition to austerity measures. President Aníbal Cavaco Silva called the political parties together, including the opposition PS, to construct a "National Salvation Plan" that would work out the details through the bailout period. The talks failed, but the government members returned to their posts. In early October 2013 the troika insisted on keeping the 2014 target for deficit reduction and demanded government spending cuts.

Austerity played a major role in the local elections of 2013, where the opposition PS won 30 percent more of the mayoral elections than the PSD-led government in the worst polling for PSD in decades. However, the PSD-led government managed to meet the financial bailout terms and exit the program in May 2014 (see Foreign relations, below).

In balloting on October 4, 2015, PSD and the CDS-PP formed an electoral coalition, securing 107 seats and forming a minority government on October 27. However, the government fell following a confidence vote on November 10. The PS, which won 86 seats in the elections, was then able to form a coalition government with the BE (19 seats) and the CDU (17 seats) on November 25.

In presidential polling on January 24, 2016, Marcelo REBELO DE SOUSA (PSD) won with 52 percent of the vote, followed by independent António Sampaio DA NÓVOA (ind.), with 22.9 percent, and eight others.

Constitution and government. The constitution of April 25, 1976, stemmed from a constitutional agreement concluded two months earlier by the leading parties and Costa Gomes in his capacity as chief of state and president of the SRC (subsequently the Council of the Revolution). Under the pact (which superseded an earlier agreement of April 1975), the council, while formally designated as the most important government organ after the presidency, became, in large part, a consultative body with powers of absolute veto only in regard to defense policy. The third most important organ, the Assembly of the Republic, was empowered to override the council (on nonmilitary matters) and the president by a two-thirds majority.

A series of constitutional reforms that came into effect in October 1982 abolished the Council of the Revolution and distributed its powers among a Supreme Council of National Defense, a 13-member Constitutional Tribunal, and an advisory Council of State of 16 members (plus national presidents elected since adoption of the existing basic law): five named by the president, five named by the assembly, and six ex officio (the prime minister; the national ombudsman; and the presidents of the assembly, the Supreme Court, and the regional governments of the Azores and the Madeira Islands).

The president, elected for a five-year term, serves as military chief of staff and as chair of the Council of State and appoints the prime minister, who is responsible to both the head of state and the assembly. Portugal's judicial system, based on European civil law and heavily influenced by the French model, includes, in addition to the Constitutional Tribunal, a Supreme Court, courts of appeal, and district courts as well as military courts and a Court of Audit.

Administratively, metropolitan Portugal is divided into 18 districts (each headed by a governor appointed by the minister of the interior), which are subdivided into 275 municipalities and more than 4,000 parochial authorities. The Azores and the Madeira Islands are governed separately as Autonomous Regions, each with an elected Regional Assembly and municipal subdivisions (a total of 30). In both regions the central government has been represented since March 2006 by a "representative of the republic" (previously called a minister of the republic), who is appointed by the president.

Portugal's constitution guarantees freedom of the press and free speech. All newspapers are privately owned. In 2014 Reporters Without Borders ranked Portugal 30th out of 180 countries in freedom of the press and 23rd in 2016.

Foreign relations. Allied with England since 1373, Portugal nevertheless declared itself neutral in World War II. It currently participates in the North Atlantic Treaty Organization (NATO) and the OECD as well as in the UN and its specialized agencies. It became a member of the Council of Europe in September 1976 and, after years of negotiation, joined Spain in gaining admission to the EC on January 1, 1986.

The country's foreign policy efforts prior to the 1974 coup were directed primarily to retention of its overseas territories at a time when other European powers had largely divested themselves of colonial possessions. Subsequent to the 1974 coup, its African problems were significantly alleviated by the independence of Guinea-Bissau (formerly Portuguese Guinea) in 1974 and of Angola, Cape Verde, Mozambique, and São Tomé and Principe in 1975.

In late 1975 a dispute arose with Indonesia regarding the status of Portuguese Timor, the country's only remaining Asian possession except for Macao. On December 8 Indonesian foreign minister Adam Malik announced that pro-Indonesian parties in the Portuguese (eastern) sector of the island had set up a provisional government and that Indonesian military units had occupied Dili, the capital. Portugal promptly severed diplomatic relations with Indonesia, which had also announced the annexation of Ocussi Ambeno, a small Portuguese enclave on the northern coast of West Timor. On July 17, 1976, Jakarta proclaimed the formal incorporation of the remainder of Timor into Indonesia, although the UN continued to regard Portugal as the territory's legitimate administrative power.

Lisbon's objection to Indonesian control of East Timor was again manifested in the recall of its ambassador to Australia in August 1985, after Australian prime minister Bob Hawke had endorsed his predecessor's acceptance of the takeover. Relations with Canberra were further strained in 1989 when Australia concluded a treaty with Indonesia providing for the division of offshore oil resources in the Timor Gap. Claiming that Indonesia's illegal occupation of East Timor rendered the treaty invalid under international law, Portugal in 1991 took the matter to the International Court of Justice (ICJ). In June 1995, however, the ICJ ruled that it had no jurisdiction on the 1989 treaty, as it was precluded from giving a ruling on the legality of Indonesia's annexation of East Timor by Indonesia's nonrecognition of the court's jurisdiction in the matter and because Indonesia was not a party to the case brought by Portugal. UN-prompted "dialogue" between the Portuguese and Indonesian foreign ministers on the East Timor question made no substantive progress in 1995, with Portugal finding little merit in an Indonesian proposal that each side should establish "interest sections" in third-country embassies in Lisbon and Jakarta. Diplomatic relations were not restored with Indonesia until late 1999, following Jakarta's acceptance of an independence referendum in East Timor, which achieved independence as the Democratic Republic of Timor-Leste on May 20, 2002.

In early 1988 Portugal called for a "thorough overhaul" of a mutual defense treaty that permitted the United States to use Lajes air base in the Azores. Although the agreement was not due to expire until 1991, it included a provision for military aid, which the U.S. Congress had sharply reduced in approving the administration's foreign assistance budget for the year. The dispute was eventually settled in January 1989, with Washington pledging to increase levels of both military and economic compensation. An agreement granting a further extension on U.S. use of the Lajes base was signed in Lisbon on June 1, 1995.

In 1989 it was agreed that regular consultative meetings of the foreign ministers of Portugal and the five lusophone African countries would be convened to promote the latter's economic development. In 1991 the six countries plus Brazil agreed upon linguistic standardization, while plans were initiated for a common television satellite channel. Further meetings of the seven Portuguese-speaking states in the early 1990s led to the formal establishment in July 1996 of the Community of Portuguese Speaking Countries (CPLP), with a total population of some 200 million Portuguese speakers (80 percent of them in Brazil). Meanwhile, Portuguese diplomacy had scored a major success in brokering the 1991 Escuril Accord between the warring factions of post-independence Angola.

The 1991 Maastricht Treaty on the economic and political union of what became the EU was ratified by the Portuguese Assembly on December 10, 1992, by a large majority. Two days later the EU's Edinburgh summit agreed to set up a "cohesion fund" for its four poorest members, of which Portugal was one. Portugal was a founding member of the EU's Schengen zone in March 1995 and the Economic and Monetary Union (EMU) on January 1, 1999.

Portugal has been largely supportive of further European integration and supported Germany's 2007 successful rejection of an effort by Poland to allow a minority of EU states to delay EU legislation against the majority's wishes.

The Barroso administration vigorously supported the U.S.-led campaign in Iraq in 2003, committing troops to the overthrow of Saddam Hussein and to subsequent security and reconstruction efforts. Responding to increasing public opposition to the war in Iraq and acting on a campaign promise, new Prime Minister Sócrates withdrew Portugal's 120 troops from Iraq in February 2005. Portugal also participated in NATO peacekeeping efforts in Afghanistan. In March 2009 Lisbon signed an agreement with the United States to install a climate observatory on the island of Graciosa in the Azores, and in June the government agreed to accept two to three detainees from the controversial U.S. prison camp at Guantánamo Bay, Cuba.

In September 2009 Barroso was reelected as head of the European Commission for a second five-year term by a vote of 382 to 219, with 117 deputies abstaining.

In February 2010 Portugal announced it would increase its troop deployment in Afghanistan to 250 soldiers. Meanwhile, in August Portugal and Indonesia signed an accord to increase bilateral cooperation. During a state visit in November, Chinese president Hu Jintao signed a range of bilateral cultural, economic, and educational agreements with Sócrates.

High unemployment in 2012 prompted a 40 percent increase in the number of Portuguese immigrants to the former colonies of Angola and Brazil (see Current issues, below). By 2011 there were 100,000 Portuguese with work permits in Angola and 328,860 in Brazil.

In April 2012 the assembly approved the EU Treaty on Stability, Coordination, and Governance in the Economic and Monetary Union. As part of the continuing effort to reduce government spending, the cabinet reduced military spending by 3.9 percent for 2012 (see Current issues, below).

In September 2013 Portugal announced it would seek to establish an exclusive economic zone around the uninhabited Savage Islands in the Atlantic. Spain opposed the effort. Portugal and Turkey finalized a defense industry cooperation agreement. In December officials in Guinea Bissau forced a Portuguese national airline carrier to transport 74 refugees to Lisbon. Portuguese officials asserted that the refugees did not have proper documentation and temporarily suspended flights to Guinea Bissau.

On February 16, 2015, the Eurogroup of the eurozone finance ministers approved Portugal's €14 billion EU-IMF early payoff plan to allow the country to exit oversight procedures put in place as part of the 2011 bailout initiative. In June Portugal and the Aga Khan signed a historic agreement to allow the Ismaili Shia leader to establish its formal seat in the country, the home of the largest group of Ismaili Muslims in the EU.

Current issues. On April 6, 2011, Portugal formally requested a debt bailout from the EU after yields on Portuguese bonds soared to new records. In May the EU and IMF agreed to provide Portugal with €78 billion over three years to service debt payments in exchange for additional austerity measures. Popular discontent with the government's management of the economy manifested itself in the June legislative balloting, in which the PS had its worst showing in more than 20 years. The PSD won a plurality in the parliament and formed a coalition government with the CDS-PP, with Pedro Passos Coelho of the PSD as prime minister. The new cabinet immediately began to implement the unpopular cuts to public sector salaries and social programs demanded by the EU and IMF.

In early 2012 the government announced that it had reached 60 percent of its EU-IMF mandated privatization goals and was on track to complete the requirement by 2014. Although Portugal consistently met its bailout goals, austerity measures were blamed for a high unemployment rate, which reached 14.9, the highest level ever recorded. Budget-squeezed citizens cut back on consumption, forcing the government to reduce revenue expectations. Tax revenue fell 3.5 percent in the first half of 2012, putting the target budget deficit of 4.5 percent of GDP out of reach. In an effort to increase competiveness, the government suspended 4 of the nation's 14 national holidays for a five-year period.

Amid widespread protests in September, the government abandoned plans to raise employee social security contributions from 11 percent to 18 percent. That month international lenders relaxed the 2012 deficit goal to 5 percent and the 2013 goal from 3 to 4.5 percent. In November the government adopted another austerity-focused budget for 2013 that included tax hikes equivalent to a month's salary for the average citizen. Workers in Portugal and Spain staged an unprecedented joint general strike on November 14. Privatization of state assets, such as the national airline and airport operator, brought in €6.4 billion, easily meeting the €5.5 billion by 2013 target.

Anti-austerity protests spread across the country on March 2, 2013, as unemployment neared 18 percent. Two days later, the Constitutional Court struck down four of the nine austerity measures in the 2013 budget. Justices ruled that cutting wages, benefits, and bonuses for civil servants constituted discrimination. The rejected measures left a €1.4 billion hole in the budget that had to be plugged to receive the next bailout payment. Portugal was granted a seven-year extension on repaying its emergency loans. Also, the budget deficit target for 2013 was raised to 5.5 percent of GDP.

A cabinet reshuffle occurred on April 13, following the resignation of Parliamentary Affairs Secretary Miguel RELVAS, who was discovered to have falsified his university degree. On April 23 Economy Minister Alvaro Santos PEREIRA announced a far-reaching stimulus package to encourage business, including a reduction in the business tax. The revised budget, issued in June, extended the workweek from 35 hours to 40 and increased employee contributions for health insurance.

Finance Minister Vitor GASPAR resigned on July 1, 2013, and Prime Minister Passos Coelho nominated Gaspar's deputy, Maria Luis ALBUQUERQUE (independent), as his replacement, indicating an ongoing commitment to austerity. But this prompted the resignation of CDS-PP leader, Foreign Minister Paulo PORTAS, who insisted the government needed a new economic policy. Passos Coelho refused to accept Portas's resignation. To keep his coalition together and forestall new elections, he promoted Portas to deputy prime minister—a title not used for nearly 30 years. Passos Coelho completed this cabinet shuffle, his seventh, on July 23. Unemployment fell from 17.6 percent in June to 16.5 percent in July, but the PSD still suffered heavy losses in the September 29 local elections, gaining only 26.5 percent of the overall popular vote and losing 34 mayoral seats and 137 councilors.

In January 2014 Cavaco Silva announced that economic growth had returned and Portugal was no longer in recession, with GDP growing by 1.6 percent in the final quarter of 2013. Estimates were that GDP would grow by 1.4 percent in 2014. Meanwhile the government was able to raise €3.3 billion in bonds, almost half the amount needed for 2014 in what analysts described as a "successful" return to credit markets. In May the Constitutional Court again declared that reductions in civil service wages, pensions, and health care were unconstitutional. The ruling created a €1.1 budget shortfall and prompted the government to announce the possibility of tax increases. Portugal formally exited the bailout program in May. In July credit firm Moody's upgraded Portugal's debt rating to Ba1 from Ba2.

In October 2014 the Espírito Santo Financial Group (ESFG) and its subsidiary, Espírito Santo Financière, filed for bankruptcy after being denied creditor protection by a Luxembourg court. ESFG held 25 percent of Banco Espírito Santo (BES), which was bailed out in May 2014. Meanwhile, investigations into BES led to police raids of 41 locations, seizing more than 5 million documents. BES and Banco Novo were under investigation of systematic corruption.

Former prime minister Sócrates was arrested over corruption charges and money laundering on November 21, 2014. In March 2015 reports indicated that former prime minister Coelho owed back taxes and social security contributions on unreported earnings from 2003 to 2007 that totaled greater than €10,000, including fines.

POLITICAL PARTIES

Government Parties:

Socialist Party (*Partido Socialista*—PS). Organized in 1973 as heir to the former **Portuguese Socialist Action** (*Acção Socialista Portuguesa*—ASP), the PS won a substantial plurality (38 percent) of the vote in the election of April 1975 and 35 percent a year later, remaining in power under Mário Soares until July 1978. In the December 1979 balloting the PS lost 33 of the 107 assembly seats it had won in 1976. It secured a plurality of 101 seats in 1983, with Soares being redesignated prime minister on June 9 and continuing in office until forced into caretaker status by the withdrawal of the Social Democrats (PSD) from the government coalition in July 1985. The party won only 57 seats in the October election, although Soares succeeded in winning the state presidency in February 1986, at which time he resigned as PS secretary general.

A party congress in June approved wide-ranging changes aimed at democratizing the party's structure and deleted all references to Marxism in its Declaration of Principles, committing the organization to an "open economy where private, public, and social institutions can coexist." The party's legislative strength gained only marginally (from 57 to 60 seats) in the balloting of July 16, 1987, but it secured 72 seats in the election of October 6, 1991.

Remaining in the opposition, the party elected António Guterres as its leader in February 1992 and registered its best ever national vote in the December 1993 local elections. In the general election of October 1995 the PS won 112 assembly seats, with Guterres forming a minority government. In 1996 the PS's Jorge Sampaio captured the national presidency with a majority in the first round. In the October 1999 legislative election the PS fell just short of a legislative majority, winning 115 seats in the 230-seat chamber. President Sampaio continued the party's string of successes in January 2001, easily winning reelection. However, the PS did poorly in the December 2001 municipal elections, setting the stage for Guterres's resignation as prime minister and the PS's fall from national power in 2002. Eduardo FERRO RODRIGUES, a former minister in Guterres's 1995 cabinet, was elected in January to succeed Guterres as PS secretary general and thereby the party's candidate for prime ministership. However, Rodrigues resigned the leadership in July 2004 to protest President Sampaio's decision not to call early elections following the resignation of Prime Minister Barroso. Former environment minister José Sócrates was elected as the new PS leader in late 2004, and having attempted to move the PS "to the center," he led the party to a resounding legislative victory in February 2005.

In September 2005 Manuel Alegre, a member of the assembly who had lost the race for party leader to Sócrates in 2004, announced that he would seek the presidency in 2006, even though the official socialist endorsement had gone to 81-year-old former president Soares. At the January 2006 polls Alegre finished second, with 20.7 percent of the vote, while Soares came in third, with 14.3 percent.

While in power, the PS focused on improving economic efficiency, especially through labor market reforms, spending cuts, and a reduction in public sector employment. The party's loss of 5 seats in the European Parliament in the June 2009 election suggested a narrowing of public support. Although the PS remained the largest party in the assembly after the September legislative balloting, the party lost 24 seats. Nonetheless, Sócrates formed a new minority government.

Alegre placed second in 2011 presidential election, with 19.7 percent of the vote. Sócrates lost a no-confidence vote in March and resigned as prime minister. In legislative balloting in June the PS fell to 74 seats. Maria de Belém Roseira was elected party president in September 2011, with 746 of 788 votes.

The party placed first in EU balloting in 2014 with 31.5 percent of the vote and 8 seats. In the October 4, 2015, legislative elections, the PS won 86 seats and eventually formed a coalition government with António COSTA as prime minister. On November 29 Carlos CÉSAR became party president.

Leaders: António COSTA (Prime Minister), Carlos CÉSAR (President of the Party), Jorge SAMPAIO (Former President of the Republic), António GUTERRES (UN High Commissioner for Refugees and Former Prime Minister), José SÓCRATES (Former Prime Minister).

Unified Democratic Coalition (*Coligação Democrática Unitária*—CDU). Prior to the 1979 election, the Portuguese Communist Party (PCP, below) joined with the **Popular Democratic Movement** (*Movimento Democrático Popular*—MDP) in an electoral coalition known as the **United People's Alliance** (*Aliança Povo Unido*—APU). The APU won 47 legislative seats in 1979, 41 in 1980, and 38 in 1985, its constituent formations having campaigned separately in 1983. In the 1986 presidential race, the party formally endorsed independent Maria de Lourdes Pintasilgo, with some dissidents supporting Francisco Salgado ZENHA of the now-defunct **Democratic Renewal Party** (*Partido Renovador Democrático*—PRD); following the elimination of both from the runoff, a special Communist Party congress on February 2, 1986, urged Alliance supporters to "hold their nose, ignore the photograph," and vote for Soares.

Disturbed by allegations that it was merely a PCP front, the MDP withdrew from the Alliance in November 1986. The APU was thereupon dissolved in favor of the CDU, which embraced the PCP; a group of MDP dissidents calling themselves **Democratic Intervention** (*Intervenção Democrática*—ID), which effectively superseded the MDP; an environmentalist formation, The Greens (*Os Verdes*, below); and a number of independent leftists. The new group obtained 31 assembly seats in 1987, 7 fewer than the APU in 1985. In October 1991, having lauded the attempted hard-line coup in the Soviet Union two months earlier, the CDU's legislative representation was further reduced to 17. It slipped to 15 seats in the October 1995 legislative election but then added 2 more in 1999. The coalition received 14 seats in 2005 and 15 seats in 2009. During the 2011 election, the coalition took 16 seats: 14 for the PCP and 2 for PEV. CDU candidate Francisco LOPES placed fourth in the 2011 presidential election, with 7.1 percent of the vote. The CDU secured 3 seats in the 2014 EU parliamentary balloting. In the October 4, 2015, legislative elections, the CDU won 17 seats and subsequently joined the PS-led government.

Leader: Jerónimo Carvalho DE SOUSA.

Portuguese Communist Party (*Partido Comunista Português*—PCP). Founded in 1921 and historically one of the most Stalinist of the West European Communist parties, the PCP was the dominant force within both the military and the government in the year following the 1974 coup. Its influence waned during the latter half of 1975, particularly following the abortive rebellion of November 26, and its legislative strength dropped to fourth place in April 1976, prior to organization of the APU. The party made limited concessions to Soviet-style liberalization at its 12th congress in December 1988 by endorsing freedom of the press and multiparty politics. At a special congress called in May 1990, however, the PCP returned to a hard-line posture. It enjoys widespread support in rural and industrial areas.

In the 1999 assembly election, the PCP won 15 of the CDU's 17 seats. Its 2001 presidential candidate, António SIMÕES DE ABREU, finished third, with only 5 percent of the vote. In 2005 the party's assembly representation dropped to 12 (and later to 11 when a PCP delegate became unaffiliated in November 2007) but rose to 13 in 2009.

In 2006 presidential candidate Jerónimo Carvalho De Sousa finished fourth, with 8.6 percent of the vote. The party gained 14 seats in elections in June 2011. The PCP won all 3 of the CDU's seats in the 2014 EU elections and 15 seats in the 2015 federal chamber balloting.

Leaders: Jerónimo Carvalho DE SOUSA (General Secretary), Bernardino SOARES (Parliamentary Leader).

Ecologist Party "The Greens" (*Partido Ecologista "Os Verdes"*—PEV). The PEV began in 1982 as the **Portuguese Ecologist Movement**—"The Greens" Party (*Movimento Ecologista Português—Partido "Os Verdes"*). In the October 1999 election the party won two of the CDU's legislative seats. The PEV subsequently was described as having shifted its emphasis from purely Portuguese environmental issues to broader European concerns.

The Greens won two seats in each of the 2005, 2009, and 2011 legislative elections. None of the Greens candidates won seats in the 2014 EU elections, but two won seats in the 2015 legislative elections.

Leader: Heloísa APOLÓNIA (Parliamentary Leader).

Left Bloc (*Bloco de Esquerda*—BE). The BE held its first national convention in February 1999. The alliance included the socialist **Politics XXI** (*Politica XXI*), the Trotskyite **Revolutionary Left Front** (*Frente da Esquerda Revolucionária*—FER), the Marxist-Leninist **Popular Democratic Union** (*União Democrática Popular*—UDP), and the small Trotskyite **Revolutionary Socialist Party** (*Partido Socialista Revolucionário*—PSR). The BE won 2.4 percent of the vote and two seats in the general election of October 1999. Its 2001 presidential contender, Fernando ROSAS, won 3 percent. The BE, which presents itself as a mainstream, progressive alternative to the PCP, lost two of its constituent parties with the November 2005 dissolution of the UDP and FER. BE leader Francisco LOUÇÃ finished fifth in the 2006 presidential election, with 5.3 percent of the vote. The BE tripled its presence in the Portuguese delegation to the European Parliament in the June 2009 election to that body, from one to three seats, a result that analysts attributed to public frustration over the government's austerity measures. The BE also benefited from voter dissatisfaction with the PS government in the 2009 legislative balloting when the party doubled its representation to 16 seats in the Assembly. The BE supported PS candidate Manuel Alegre in the 2011 presidential balloting. In legislative elections in June the BE lost half its seats, falling to 8, prompting Louçã to step down as leader. The BE led a series of strikes and protests against austerity measures in 2012. The BE secured 1 seat in the 2014 EU balloting. In the October 4, 2015, legislative elections, BE won 19 seats and joined the PS-led coalition government.

Leaders: Catarina MARTINS (Leader of the Party), Luís FAZENDA (General Secretary).

Other Legislative Parties:

Social Democratic Party (*Partido Social Democrata*—PSD). The PSD was founded in 1974 as the **Popular Democratic Party** (*Partido Popular Democrático*—PPD), under which name it won 26 percent of the vote for the Constituent Assembly on April 25, 1975, and 24 percent in the Assembly of the Republic election a year later. Although it initially advocated a number of left-of-center policies, including the nationalization of key sectors of the economy, a number of leftists withdrew in 1976, and the remainder of the party moved noticeably to the right.

An April 1979 disagreement over leadership opposition to the Socialist government's proposed budget led to a walkout of 40 PSD deputies prior to a final assembly vote. Shortly thereafter, 37 of the 73 PSD deputies withdrew and announced that they would sit in the assembly as the **Association of Independent Social Democrats** (*Associação dos Sociais Democratas Independentes*—ASDI). The party's losses were more than recouped in the December election, however, when the PSD-led alliance won a three-seat majority, as a result of which the party president, Francisco Sá Carneiro, was named prime minister. Francisco Pinto Balsemão was designated party leader in December 1980, following Sá Carneiro's death, and he became prime minister in January 1981.

In early 1983, following the formal designation of a three-member leadership at a party congress in late February, Balsemão was effectively succeeded by Carlos Mota PINTO. The party was runner-up to the PS at the April election, winning 75 assembly seats. In June 1985 Aníbal Cavaco Silva, who had succeeded Mota Pinto as PSD leader the previous month, withdrew from the ruling coalition and formed a minority government after the party had gained a slim plurality in legislative balloting in October. Defeated in a censure vote in April 1987, the PSD became the first party since 1974 to win an absolute majority of seats in the ensuing legislative poll in July. It retained control with a slightly reduced majority of 135 of 230 seats in 1991. A subsequent slide in the PSD's standing, including losses at the 1994 election for the European Parliament, compelled Cavaco Silva to vacate the party leadership in January 1995. At the same time, he hoped to position himself for a presidential challenge.

Under the new leadership of Joaquim Fernando NOGUEIRA, the party was defeated in the October 1995 general election, retaining only 88 seats on a 34 percent vote share. In the January 1996 presidential balloting, moreover, Cavaco Silva was defeated by the socialist candidate in the first round. The party's response at the end of March was to elect as its new leader Marcelo REBELO DE SOUSA, a media personality on the party's liberal wing who had not held ministerial office during the period of PSD rule.

In early 1998 the PSD and CDS-PP (below) formed an electoral alliance, styled the AD, with the stated aim of presenting a single list for the upcoming European Parliament and national legislative elections. The AD Pact was formally ratified in February 1999; however, it collapsed the following month, and immediately thereafter Rebelo de Sousa resigned as leader of the PSD. His successor, José Manuel Durão Barroso, a former foreign affairs minister, led the party in the October 1999 election, but the PSD lost 7 of its 88 seats. In 2001 it failed to unseat President Sampaio, with its candidate, Joaquim Martins Ferreira do Amaral, finishing a distant second (34.5 percent of the vote).

Barroso was named prime minister following the March 2002 legislative balloting, at which the PSD won a plurality of 105 seats. He resigned as prime minister in July 2004 to become president of the European Commission. Pedro Santana Lopes succeeded Barroso as prime minister until the February 2005 legislative poll, in which the PSD fell to 75 seats. Santana Lopes resigned as PSD leader in April. In the 2006 presidential contest, Cavaco Silva won 50.6 percent of the vote, and avoided a runoff. In October 2007 the party chose member of parliament Luís Filipe MENEZES, a vocal critic of the government's austerity measures, to lead the PSD. Unable to mount a strong challenge to the government, Menezes resigned seven months later and was succeeded by former finance minister Manuela Ferreira LEITE on May 31, 2008.

The PSD gained one additional seat in the European Parliament in June 2009, bringing its total to eight. It also increased its representation in the assembly by six seats in the subsequent legislative balloting. Barroso was reelected president of the European Commission in September.

Cavaco was reelected president in January 2011. The PSD won 108 seats in legislative balloting in June and Pedro Passos Coelho formed a government with the CDS-PP.

The PSD and the CDS-PP contested the 2014 EU elections as a coalition. The grouping won seven seats, six of which were secured by the PSD. In the October 4, 2015, legislative elections, the **Portugal Ahead** (*Portugal à Frente*—Pàf) coalition of the PSD and the CDS-PP won 107 seats. In January 2016 Marcelo REBELO DE SOUSA was elected president of Portugal, reversing recent electoral declines.

Leaders: Marcelo REBELO DE SOUSA (President of the Republic), Aníbal CAVACO SILVA (Former President), Pedro Passos COELHO (Former Prime Minister and Chair), Pedro SANTANA LOPES (Former Prime Minister), José Manuel Durão BARROSO (Former European Commission President and Former Prime Minister).

Social Democratic Center–Popular Party (*Centro Democrático Social–Partido Popular*—CDS-PP). This right-of-center Christian democratic party was founded in 1974 as the CDS. The name was changed to the CDS-PP in 1993. The party is strongest in the northern part of the country, and a number of its members were named to key government posts following the 1979 and 1980 legislative elections. Despite the party's having lost 8 of 30 assembly seats in the October 1985 election, its presidential candidate, Diogo Freitas do Amaral, won 46 percent of the vote in first-round presidential balloting in January 1986, but he lost to former prime minister Soares (PS) in the runoff. Freitas do Amaral resigned the CDS presidency after the 1991 election, in which the party won only five assembly seats. Standing on an anti-EU platform, the CDS-PP gained ground in the October 1995 national election, winning 15 seats on a vote share of 9.1 percent.

Despite having repulsed a leadership challenge by Paulo Portas, Manuel MONTEIRO resigned as CDS-PP president in September 1996 in protest against internal party feuding. He subsequently agreed to return as president, although he announced he would not run again in the party congress scheduled for March 1998. As promised, Monteiro left his party post in March, and in subsequent intraparty balloting Portas finally secured the presidency. A principal architect of the 1998 PSD/CDS-PP electoral alliance, Portas nevertheless quickly grew disenchanted with the PSD leadership, and just prior to the AD's dissolution, the PSD's Rebelo de Sousa accused Portas of publicizing confidential information. Despite a reduced vote share of 8.3 percent, the party retained its 15 assembly seats at the October 1999 election. In 2001 it endorsed President Sampaio for reelection.

Portas resigned as the CDS-PP leader in April 2005, two months after the party won only 12 assembly seats, but he regained the leadership in April 2007. The CDS-PP presence in the assembly dropped to 11 after a party member joined an unaffiliated group on December 17, 2008. The CDS-PP maintained its 2 seats in the EU Parliament balloting in 2009 but gained 9 seats in that year's legislative elections to bring its total to 21.

The CDS-PP supported Cavaco Silva of the PSD in presidential balloting in January 2011. The CDS-PP placed third in the June assembly balloting with 24 seats. It subsequently formed a coalition government with the PSD but grew uneasy at repeated tax increases. Portas was promoted from minister of state for foreign affairs to deputy prime minister in July 2013, to keep the governing coalition intact. In an electoral alliance with the PSD, the CDS-PP won 1 seat in the 2014 EU elections and 18 in the 2015 federal chamber balloting. In March 2016 Assunção CRISTAS was elected party leader.

Leaders: Assunção CRISTAS (Chair), Nuno MELO, Adolfo Mesquita NUNES, Cecília MEIRELES (Vice Presidents).

Other parties that won seats in the 2015 federal chamber balloting included the **People-Animals-Nature** (*Pessoas-Animais-Natureza*—PAN), founded in 2009, which won one seat.

Other Parties That Contested the 2011 or 2014 Elections:

Parties that contested the June 2011 assembly balloting but failed to win a seat included the **Portuguese Workers' Communist Party/ Reorganizative Movement of the Party of the Proletariat** (*Partido Comunista dos Trabalhadores Portugueses/Movimento Reorganizativo do Partido do Proletariado*—PCTP/MRPP), a Maoist party led by Garcia PEREIRA; the **New Democracy Party** (*Partido da Nova Democracia*—PND), a conservative party founded in 2003 by its current leader, former CDS-PP president Manuel Monteiro; the center-left **Humanist Party** (*Partido Humanista*—PH), led by Luís Filipe GUERRA; the neo-fascist **National Renewal Party** (*Partido Nacional Renovador*—PNR), led by José PINTO-COELHO; the Trotskyite **United Socialist Workers' Party** (*Partido Operário de Unidade Socialista*—POUS), formed in 1976 and led by Aniceto BARBOSA; and the **Atlantic Democratic Party** (*Partido Democrático do Atlântico*—PDA), a grouping based in the Azores and the Madeira Islands and led by José VENTURA; the **Hope for Portugal Movement** (*Movimento Esperança Portugal*—MEP), a centrist party founded by businessman Rui MARQUES in 2008; the **People's Monarchist Party** (*Partido Popular Monárquico*—PPM), founded in 1974; the green, center-right **Earth Party** (*Partido da Terra*—MPT), founded in 1993; the **Labor Party** (*Partido Trabalhista*); the small **Pro-Life Party;** and the ***Livre*** **Party**, formed in 2013.

LEGISLATURE

The unicameral **Assembly of the Republic** (*Assembleia da República*) consists of 230 members elected for four-year terms (subject to dissolution) via proportional representation. (Four seats are elected by Portuguese living abroad.)

In the most recent balloting on October 4, 2015, the seat distribution was as follows: Portugal Ahead, 107 seats (the Social Democratic Party, 89 seats; the Social Democratic Center–Popular Party, 18); the Socialist Party, 86; the Left Bloc, 19; the Unified Democratic Coalition, 17 (Portuguese Communist Party, 15; Ecologist Party "The Greens," 2), and People-Animals-Nature,1.

President: Maria da ASSUNÇÃO ESTEVES.

CABINET

[as of August 20, 2016]

Prime Minister	António Costa (PS)
Ministers	
Assistant Minister	Eduardo Cabrita
Agriculture, Forestry, and Rural Development	Luís Capoulas Santos
Culture	Luís Filipe Castro Mendes
Economy	Manuel Caldeira Cabral
Education	Tiago Brandão Rodrigues
Environment	João Pedro Matos Fernandes
Finance	Mário Centeno
Foreign Affairs	Augusto Santos Silva
Health	Adalberto Campos Fernandes
Internal Administration	Constança Urbano de Sousa [f]
Justice	Francisca van Dunem [f]
Labour, Solidarity, and Social Security	José Antonio Vieira da Silva
National Defense	José Alberto Azeredo Lopes
Planning and Infrastructure	Pedro Marques
Presidency and Administrative Modernization	Maria Manuel Leitão Marques [f]
Science, Technology, and Higher Education	Manuel Heitor
The Sea	Ana Paula Vitorino [f]

[f] = female

INTERGOVERNMENTAL REPRESENTATION

Ambassador to the U.S.: Domingos Fezas VITAL.

U.S. Ambassador to Portugal: Herro MUSTAFA (Chargé d'Affaires).

Permanent Representative to the UN: José DE MENDONÇA E MOURA.

IGO Memberships (Non-UN): ADB, AfDB, CEUR, EBRD, EIB, EU, IADB, ICC, IEA, IOM, NATO, OECD, OSCE, WTO.

For Further Reference:

Chilcote, Ronald H., Stylianos Hadjiyannis, Fred A. Lopez III, Daniel Nataf, and Elizabeth Sammis. *Transitions from Dictatorship to Democracy: Comparative Studies of Spain, Portugal and Greece.* Abingdon, UK: Taylor & Francis, 2015.

Magone, José M. *Politics in Contemporary Portugal: Democracy Evolving.* Boulder, CO: Lynne Rienner, 2014.

Maxwell, Kenneth. *The Making of Portuguese Democracy.* Cambridge: Cambridge University Press, 1997.

Pridham, Geoffrey, ed. *The New Mediterranean Democracies: Regime Transition in Spain, Greece and Portugal.* New York: Routledge, 2016.

RELATED TERRITORIES

The Azores and the Madeira Islands have long been construed as insular components of metropolitan Portugal and, as such, were legally distinct from a group of Portuguese possessions whose status was changed in 1951 from that of "Colonies" to "Overseas Territories." Of the latter, the South Asian enclaves of Goa, Damão, and Diu were annexed by India in 1961; Portuguese Guinea became independent as Guinea-Bissau in 1974; and Angola, the Cape Verde Islands, Mozambique, and São Tomé and Principe became independent in 1975. Portuguese Timor (East Timor) was annexed by Indonesia on July 17, 1976, but the action was never recognized by Portugal, and diplomatic relations with Jakarta were not restored until late 1999, after the Indonesian government had accepted the results of the August 1999 independence referendum in East Timor (now Timor-Leste). Macao, which had been defined as a "collective entity" (*pessoa colectiva*) under a governing statute promulgated on February 17, 1976, reverted to Chinese sovereignty in 1999 (see entry on China). Under the 1976 constitution, the Azores and Madeira are defined as autonomous regions.

Azores (*Açores*). The Azores comprise three distinct groups of islands located in the Atlantic Ocean about 800 miles west of mainland Portugal. The most easterly of the islands are São Miguel and Santa Maria; the most westerly and least densely populated are Corvo and Flores; Fayal, Graciosa, Pico, São Jorge, and Terceira are in the center. There are three political districts, the capitals and chief seaports of which are Ponta Delgada (São Miguel), Horta (Fayal), and Angra do Heroísmo (Terceira). The islands' total area is 890 square miles (2,305 sq. km), and their resident population (2006E) is 244,100.

Following the 1974 coup, significant separatist sentiment emerged, particularly on Terceira, whose residents feared that the left-wing government at Lisbon might close the U.S. military base at Lajes. In August 1975 a recently organized **Azorean Liberation Front** (*Frente de Libertação dos Açores*—FLA) announced its opposition to continued rule from the mainland. Following the resignation of three appointed governors, the Portuguese government surrendered control of the islands' internal administration to local political leaders and in April 1976 provided for an elected Regional Assembly.

In March 1991 FLA leader José de ALMEIDA was acquitted of treason charges on the grounds that there was insufficient evidence of his having incited others to violence. In assembly balloting on October 11, 1992, the Social Democratic Party (PSD) regained its majority, winning 28 of 51 seats. The PSD and the Socialist Party (PS) each won 24 seats in the October 3, 1996, balloting, with the Popular Party (PP) gaining 2 seats and the Portuguese Communist Party (PCP), 1. In the election of October 15, 2000, the PS claimed a majority of 30 seats, while the PSD dropped to 18. The PP and the Unitary Democratic Coalition (the PCP and the Greens) each won 2 seats. The PS advanced to 44 of 52 seats in the assembly balloting of October 17, 2004. In October 2008 balloting, the PS kept its majority in the assembly, winning 30 of 57 seats, followed by the PSD with 18; the CDS-PP, 5; the Left Bloc, 2; the PCP-PEV, 1; and the PPM, 1.

Two candidates from the PS, and one from the PSD, from the Azores won seats in the National Assembly in the June 2011 Portuguese election. The PS continued its dominance in the October 14, 2012, local election, winning 31 seats, followed by the PSD (20), and CDS-PP (3). President César retired after 16 years in office and was succeeded by Vasco Alves CORDEIRO (PS). In November 2013 Cordeiro traveled to Washington, D.C., in an effort to convince U.S. lawmakers not to reduce the garrison at Lajes military base. The Azores signed an agreement with Bermuda to expand tourism and air travel in 2016.

President of the Regional Government: Vasco Alves CORDEIRO (PS).

Representative of the Republic: Pedro Manuel Alves dos Reis CATARINO.

Madeira Islands (*Ilhas da Madeira*). The Madeira Islands consist of Madeira and Porto Santo islands and the uninhabited islets of Desertas and Salvages. Lying west of Casablanca, Morocco, some 500 miles southwest of the Portuguese mainland, they have a total area of 308 square miles (797 sq. km) and a resident population (2006E) of 240,000. The capital is Funchal, on Madeira Island.

As in the case of the Azores, separatist sentiment exists, the **Madeira Archipelago Liberation Front** (*Frente de Libertação de Arquipélago da Madeira*—FLAM), which advocated independence from Portugal and possible federation with the Azores and the Spanish Canaries, claiming on August 29, 1975, to have established a provisional government. However, both the government that was installed on October 1, 1976, and the elected Regional Assembly that was convened on October 23 were pledged to maintain ties to the mainland.

In balloting on October 15, 2000, the Social Democratic Party (PSD) won its seventh regional election in a row, claiming 41 of the 61 seats in the assembly. The Socialist Party (PS) won only 13 seats and the Popular Party (PP), 3. Alberto João Jardim of the PSD has served as regional president for nearly a quarter of a century. The PSD won 44 of 68 assembly seats in balloting on October 17, 2004. In the February 2005 Portuguese election, three PS and three PS candidates from the Madeira Islands won seats in the National Assembly.

On February 19, 2007, President Jardim resigned to protest a new, government-supported law on regional financing that would reduce aid levels from the central government to Madeira. The resignation prompted early elections on May 6, which Jardim won easily. The government rejected his call to rescind the law, but a court ruling in September forced it to do so.

A February 2010 storm, described as the worst in a century, caused extensive flooding and landslides. More than 50 people were killed and there was extensive property damage. The Portuguese government initiated a program to repair homes and build replacement dwellings. Madeira's debt reached €6 billion in 2012, largely government loans matched by the EU. The PSD won 25 of 47 seats in balloting in October 2011, and Jardim was reelected. In 2014 Madeira assumed an additional €854.1 million in debt with Lisbon's backing to cover its financial obligations. Deadly wildfires affected the island in August 2016, killing four and displacing more than 1,000 people.

President of the Regional Government: Alberto João JARDIM (PSD).

Representative of the Republic: Antero Alves MONTEIRO DINIZ.

QATAR

State of Qatar
Dawlat al-Qatar

Political Status: Traditional sheikhdom; proclaimed fully independent September 1, 1971; first permanent constitution, approved in referendum of April 29, 2003, went into effect on June 8, 2004.

Area: 4,247 sq. mi. (11,000 sq. km).

Population: 2,291,000 (2016E—UN); 2,258,263 (2016E—U.S. Census), including nonnationals, who constitute more than two-thirds of the resident population.

Major Urban Centers (2015E—UN): DOHA (718,000) (al-Dawhah, 353,000), Rayyan (677,000).

Official Language: Arabic.

Monetary Unit: Qatar Riyal (official rate October 1, 2016: 3.64 riyals = $1US).

Sovereign (Emir): Sheik Tamim ibn Hamad al-THANI; assumed power on June 25, 2013, upon the abdication of his father Sheikh Hamad ibn Khalifa al-THANI, who assumed leadership on June 27, 1995.

Heir to the Throne: Abdullah bin Hamad bin Khalifa al-THANI; appointed deputy emir and heir on November 11, 2014.

Prime Minister: Sheikh Abdullah ibn Nasser ibn Khalifa al-THANI, appointed by the emir on June 27, 2013, succeeding Sheikh Hamad ibn Jasim ibn Jabir al-THANI.

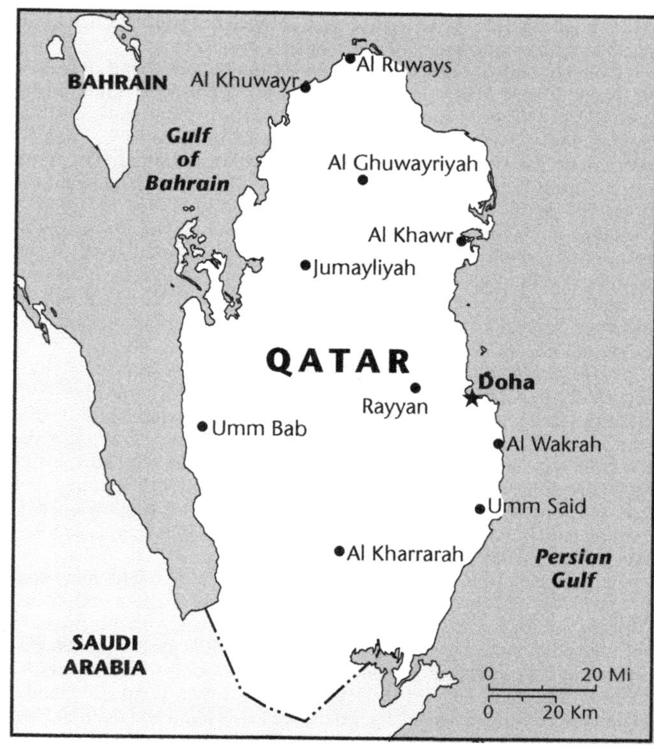

THE COUNTRY

A flat, barren, peninsular projection into the Persian Gulf from the Saudi Arabian mainland, Qatar consists largely of sand and rock. The climate is quite warm with very little rainfall, and the lack of fresh water has led to a reliance on desalination techniques. The population is almost entirely Arab, but indigenous Qataris (mainly Sunni Muslims of the conservative Wahhabi sect) comprise substantially less than a majority, as thousands have flocked from abroad to cash in on Qatar's booming economy; the nonindigenous groups include Pakistanis, Iranians, Indians, and Palestinians. The percentage of women in the workforce grew substantially in the 1990s, and religious and governmental strictures upon women are less severe than in most other Gulf states. In 2013 one female minister served in the cabinet: Hessa Sultan al-Jaber, Minister of Communications and Information Technology. Most women continue to wear veils in public, accept arranged marriages, and generally defer to the wishes of the male members of their families. Qatari culture as a whole continues to reflect the long history of "feudal tribal autocracy" and the "puritanical" (in the eyes of many Western observers) nature of Wahhabism, which is also practiced in Saudi Arabia, Qatar's influential neighbor.

The economy remains largely dependent on revenue from oil and natural gas, which have been produced for export since 1949 and under local production and marketing control since 1977. During the oil boom years of the 1970s, Qatar became one of the world's wealthiest nations. The sheikhdom was therefore able to develop a modern infrastructure, emphasizing schools, hospitals, roads, communication facilities, and water and electric plants.

Qatar is also home to the world's third-largest reserves of liquid natural gas. (For more on the history of the Qatari economy, see the 2015 *Handbook*.)

The Qatari government continued to emphasize diversification, announcing plans in 2008 to transform Qatar's economy from one based on oil production to one "that has knowledge as its mainstay." It has invested heavily in education, including Doha's multibillion-dollar Education City. The financial forecast remained positive, despite high inflation. Annual GDP growth of 14.9 percent was recorded for 2008–2011, driven by a significant expansion in the production of liquefied natural gas, as well as growth in the non-hydrocarbon sector. The International Monetary Fund (IMF) commended Qatar for "successfully steering the economy through the global financial crisis." With a self-imposed moratorium on increased oil production, growth slowed to 6.6 percent in 2012 and slipped further to 5.2 percent in 2013. Inflation was 1.9 percent. Unemployment of Qataris dropped to 3.1 percent in 2012 from 3.9 percent the previous year, according to government statistics. GDP growth in 2014 remained steady at 5 percent, with the IMF noting in an annual report that non-hydrocarbon sectors now account for one-half of the economy. Inflation rose to 4 percent, reflecting increased housing demand. In 2015 GDP growth slowed to 3.6 percent, largely as a result of a marked decrease in the price of oil, on which the Qatari economy remained disproportionately reliant. The IMF estimated that GDP grew by 6.5 percent in 2016, while inflation was 2.7 percent, and GDP per capita remained among the highest in the world at $79,500.

GOVERNMENT AND POLITICS

Political background. Qatar was dominated by Bahrain until 1868 and by the Ottoman Turks from 1878 through World War I, until it entered into treaty relations with Great Britain in 1916. Under the treaty, Qatar stipulated that it would not conclude agreements with other foreign governments without British consent; in return, Britain agreed to provide for the defense of the sheikhdom. When the British government announced in 1968 that it intended to withdraw from the Persian Gulf by 1971, Qatar attempted to associate itself with Bahrain and the Trucial Sheikhdoms in a Federation of Arab Emirates. Qatar declared independence when it became apparent that agreement on the structure of the proposed federation could not be obtained; its independence was realized in 1971.

The new state was governed initially by Sheikh Ahmad ibn Ali ibn Abdallah al-THANI, who proved to be an inattentive sovereign. In February 1972 his cousin, Prime Minister Sheikh Khalifa ibn Hamad al-THANI, deposed Sheikh Ahmad in a bloodless coup approved by the royal family. Although modernist elements subsequently emerged, the sheikhdom remained a virtually absolute monarch with close relatives of the emir occupying senior government posts.

In May 1989 Sheikh Hamad ibn Khalifa al-THANI, the emir's heir apparent, was named head of the newly formed Supreme Council for Planning, which was commissioned to oversee Qatar's resource development projects. The government's economic efforts gained additional momentum on July 18 when the first cabinet reshuffling since 1978 resulted in the replacement of seven elderly ministers.

Like its Arab neighbors, Qatar faced international and domestic pressure for political reform following the 1990–1991 Gulf crisis, which drew Western attention on the dearth of democratic institutions in the region. The issue came to a head in early 1992 when 50 prominent Qataris expressed "concern and disappointment" over the ruling family's "abuse of power" and called for economic and educational reform, ultimately demanding the abolition of the Consultative Council in favor of a true legislative body. The government responded harshly to the criticism and briefly detained some of the petitioners, muting calls for democratization. However, reformists considered it a positive step when nonrelatives of the royal family assumed several key ministerial positions in the cabinet reshuffle of September 1, 1992.

Though Qataris liked Sheikh Khalifa on a personal level, they reportedly believed he was allowing Qatar to slip behind other Gulf countries in economic and political progress. They expressed little dissent when Sheikh Hamad deposed his father on June 27, 1995, while the emir was on a private visit to Switzerland. Sheikh Hamad consolidated his authority and reorganized the cabinet on July 11, naming himself as prime minister and defense minister. (Sheikh Khalifa lived in Europe until he returned to Qatar for the first time since he was deposed on October 14, 2004, to attend his wife's funeral.)

In February 1996 the government announced that it had uncovered a coup plot, and those arrested reportedly included army and police officers. Although Sheikh Khalifa strongly denied any involvement in the alleged plot, he argued that it indicated popular support for his reinstatement. The government concluded an out-of-court financial settlement with Sheikh Khalifa in October 1996, which permitted Sheikh Hamad to establish a sense of permanence to his reign and facilitated an at least partial reconciliation between father and son. In November 1997 some 110 people, including many military officers, were tried for alleged participation in the February 1996 coup attempt. While 85 of the defendants were acquitted in February 2000, about 30 were convicted and received sentences of either life in prison or death. An appeals court upheld their sentences in May 2001. Meanwhile, Sheikh Hamad had gained broader support from the populace and continued to promote his liberalized administration as a potential model for other countries in the region where long-standing regimes have resisted political and economic reform.

On October 22, 1996, Sheikh Hamad appointed his third son, Sheikh Jassim ibn Hamad al-THANI, as crown prince and his heir apparent. Six days later the emir appointed his younger brother, Sheikh Abdallah ibn Khalifa al-THANI, as prime minister to the government named on October 20, which included a number of younger ministers.

On March 8, 1999, the nation's first elections were held for the transitional Consultative Central Municipal Council, which the government established to introduce representative popular elections in the country. In July a committee newly appointed by the emir held its first meeting to draft a constitution that would ultimately provide for a popularly elected legislature. In 2002 Qatar established a national human rights committee.

The crown prince relinquished his position on August 5, 2003, to his younger brother, Sheikh Tamim ibn Hamad al-THANI. In September the emir conferred the title of deputy prime minister upon two of his ministers, and the new crown prince also was named commander in chief of the armed forces. Sheikh Hamad also appointed the first woman to the Qatari cabinet, Sheikha Ahmad al-MAHMUD, in 2003 (see Cabinet, below).

Sheikh Abdallah ibn Khalifa al-Thani resigned as prime minister on April 3, 2007, and was replaced the same day by Sheikh Hamad ibn Jasim ibn Jabir al-Thani. The new prime minister was sworn in along with a reshuffled cabinet on April 3.

The cabinet was enlarged and reshuffled on July 2, 2008, with a second woman named to a ministerial post. Both women were replaced in a cabinet reshuffle on April 29, 2009. Three ministers were replaced in April and June 2010. The minister of energy and industry was replaced on January 18, 2011, by the minister of state for energy and industry, though the former retained his post as deputy prime minister.

On June 25, 2013, Sheikh Hamad abdicated the throne and Sheikh Tamim assumed power. The following day, he installed a new cabinet, naming Sheikh Abdullah ibn Nasser ibn Khalifa al-THANI as prime minister (see Current issues, below). On November 11, 2014, the emir named his half-brother, Abdullah bin Hamad bin Khalifa al-THANI, deputy emir and heir.

In January 2016 the government was reshuffled, with new ministries created and others consolidated.

Constitution and government. Qatar employs traditional patterns of authority, onto which a limited number of modern governmental institutions have been grafted. The provisional constitution of 1970 provided for a Council of Ministers, headed by an appointed prime minister, and an Advisory Council (Consultative Council) of 20 (subsequently 35) members. Three of the Advisory Council members were to be appointed and the rest elected, although national elections were not held. The judicial system embraces five secular courts (two criminal as well as civil, labor, and appeal) and religious courts, which apply Islamic law (sharia).

In November 1998 Sheikh Hamad announced that a constitutional committee would draft a new permanent basic law, one that should provide for a directly elected National Assembly to replace the Consultative Council. The emir announced that all Qataris over 18, including women, would be permitted to vote, while those over 25, also including women, would be allowed to run for the new legislative body. The new constitution, promulgated on June 8, 2004, after gaining overwhelming approval by voters (96.6 percent) in a national referendum on April 29, 2003, identifies Islam as the state religion. However, officials say Islamic law only "inspires" the new charter and is not the only source for its content. Under the new charter, the emir retains executive powers, including control over general policy and the appointment of a prime minister and cabinet. The new constitution also states that 30 of 45 members of the Consultative Council will be elected, the remainder appointed by the emir. In 2011 the emir announced that elections would take place in 2013, but they were indefinitely postponed upon his abdication (see Current issues, below).

In 2016 Reporters Without Borders ranked Qatar as 117th out of 180 countries for press freedom. The country's newspapers are largely owned by members of the royal family, stifling journalistic criticism of the government.

Foreign relations. Until 1971 Qatar's foreign relations were administered by Britain. Since reaching independence it has pursued a policy of nonalignment in foreign affairs as a member of the United Nations (UN), the Arab League, and the Organization of Petroleum Exporting Countries (OPEC).

In 1981 Qatar joined with five other Gulf states (Bahrain, Kuwait, Oman, Saudi Arabia, and the United Arab Emirates) in establishing the Gulf Cooperation Council (GCC) and has since participated in joint military maneuvers and the formation of economic cooperation agreements, though territorial disputes sporadically threatened GCC unity. In April 1986 fighting nearly erupted between Qatari and Bahraini troops over a small, uninhabited island, Fasht al-Dibal, which Bahrain had reclaimed from an underlying coral reef. Although Qatar acquiesced to temporary Bahraini control of the island, sovereignty remained in question. In mid-1991, Qatar asked the International Court of Justice (ICJ) to rule on Fasht al-Dibal as well as several other contested Bahraini-controlled islands. In 1997 GCC mediation between Qatar and Bahrain resulted in an agreement to open embassies in each other's capitals and await the ICJ ruling. Ultimately, in 2001, the ICJ awarded the disputed islands to Bahrain while reaffirming Qatar's sovereignty over the town of Zubara and its surrounding territory (which Bahrain had claimed as part of the case). Relations between the two countries have warmed, and in 2006, they signed a deal to begin construction of a causeway connecting them.

Another long-simmering dispute erupted in violence in late September 1992 when two Qatari border guards were killed in a confrontation along the border with Saudi Arabia. Saudi leaders dismissed the incident as an inconsequential clash among Bedouin tribes, but Qatar reacted with hostility, boycotting several GCC ministerial sessions and reportedly threatening to quit the organization altogether. After years of negotiations, Qatar accepted Saudi Arabia's demands and a final agreement on land and sea border demarcation was signed in June 1999.

The sheikhdom denounced the August 1990 Iraqi invasion of Kuwait and responded further by offering its territory as a base for allied forces, expelling PLO representatives, and taking part in joint military exercises. At the GCC's December summit Qatar supported the "Doha Declaration," which called for a plan to prevent a repetition of Iraqi aggression, the departure of "friendly" forces upon the resolution of the crisis, and an Iranian role in security arrangements. In early 1991 Qatari forces (composed primarily of foreigners) participated in allied air and ground actions. Qatar remained closely aligned with the other GCC states on most security issues following the war and signed a defense agreement with the United States in June 1992 in the wake of similar U.S. pacts with Bahrain and Kuwait.

Meanwhile, Qatar, without GCC support, moved to improve relations with Iran for regional stability. In May 1992, Doha signed a number of agreements with Tehran, calling for peaceful negotiations to resolve the Iranian nuclear issue.

Qatar has also adopted a more lenient posture than most of its GCC partners regarding Iraq, calling in early 1995 for UN sanctions against Iraq to be lifted for humanitarian reasons. However, in the wake of the brief crisis generated by the massing of Iraqi troops near the Kuwaiti border in October 1994, Doha agreed to let the U.S. permanently store its armor in Qatar.

In the early 21st century, Qatar became an important American ally in the Middle East. In mid-2000, the United States financed and built a massive staging area for its ground troops in eastern Qatar, which later became the U.S. Central Command site in the 2003 invasion of Iraq.

On the second anniversary of the U.S.–Iraqi invasion in March 2005, a car bomb exploded in a Qatari theater frequented by Westerners. It was the first incident of its kind in Qatar. An Egyptian expatriate with alleged al-Qaida links was later blamed in the attack.

Qatar made efforts "to bring Israel into the Gulf" as a contribution to the Middle East peace process. In May 2005, Israel agreed to Qatar's unprecedented request for support of Doha's candidacy for a rotating seat in the UN Security Council. The request marked the first time an Arab state had sought Israel's help in such a matter, and signaled the potential for increasingly positive relations between the two countries. In early 2006, however, Qatar was among 14 Arab nations attending a summit in Damascus to discuss tightening the boycott against Israel. Qatar allowed the governing Palestinian group, Hamas, to have an office in Doha in 2006 and pledged $50 million in aid to Hamas, despite pressure from the United States not to help the anti-Israel group financially.

In late 2008, Russia and Qatar announced that they were setting up an OPEC-style cartel, along with Iran, for natural gas. The three countries were reported to control 60 percent of the world's gas reserves.

Though Qatar has no diplomatic relationship with Israel, Israeli foreign minister Tzipi Livni visited Doha in April 2008, at the invitation of the emir, to lobby for Arab states' ties with Israel and for support against Iran's nuclear program. Her trip came in the wake of Qatar's offer in February to help broker a peace agreement between Israel and Hamas. Following Israel's attacks on Gaza in response to Hamas's launching rockets into southern Israel in late 2008 and early 2009, Qatar closed Israel's trade office in Doha and cut off all economic and political ties with the state.

In a move that reportedly surprised Qatari officials, Ethiopia in April 2008 suspended diplomatic relations with Qatar, claiming that media outlets in Qatar were supporting terrorism in Ethiopia and Somalia in the wake of Ethiopia's failed efforts to drive out Islamists who had gained control in Somalia.

Despite the International Criminal Court's (ICC) appeal to Qatar to cooperate with an arrest warrant against Sudan's President Beshir for alleged war crimes, Qatari officials invited Beshir and did not detain him when he arrived for a 2009 visit. (Qatar is not a signatory to the agreement that dates to the establishment of the ICC.) Subsequently, Arab leaders in the summer rejected the ICC's arrest warrant, calling for it to be annulled.

In May 2010 Israel rejected Qatar's offer to reestablish trade relations between the two countries, provisioned on permission for Qatar to import materials into Gaza. Following Israel's attack on a flotilla bound for Gaza on May 31, Qatar backed a proposed UN Security Council resolution condemning Israel's action.

China and Qatar in 2011 pledged to expand energy cooperation.

During the so-called "Arab Spring" that same year, Qatar expressed its support to the Syrian president in the wake of mass antigovernment protests, though it later reversed its position to publicly oppose Bashar al Assad. In early 2011 Qatar tried to resolve a government crisis in Lebanon but was thwarted by Hezbollah. In August Qatar closed its Damascus embassy and threw support behind the opposition Syrian National Council, calling for a peaceful transfer of power. Qatar participated in the Arab League's peace initiative in Syria, with very limited success. Prime Minister Hamad ibn Jasim ibn Jabir al-Thani called for the Syrian opposition to be armed. Qatar's assertiveness in Syria has heightened tensions with Iran.

Qatar joined the NATO effort in Libya from March through October 2011 and was the first Arab country to recognize the authority of the Libyan rebels, winning the praise of Western leaders. However, Qatar supported Saudi Arabia in sending troops to defend Bahrain's minority Sunni king against the protesting Shiite majority, and, in May, deported a Libya woman who took refuge in Qatar after alleged sexual assault by Libyan government forces.

In May 2011 Qatar withdrew from the GCC's initiative to secure the resignation of Yemeni president Ali Abdullah Saleh, saying that "the intensity of the conflict" and "a lack of wisdom" in Yemen made mediation by the GCC impossible. Saleh, who saw Qatar as a hostile party and Qatar-based television channel Al-Jazeera as a supporter of the Yemeni opposition, welcomed Qatar's withdrawal.

A visit by Pakistan President Asif Ali Zardari in November 2012 resulted in an effort to improve bilateral economic and trade relations between the two countries.

In January 2012 a spokesman for Afghanistan's Taliban movement announced that it had reached an agreement to open a representative office in Doha, a move meant to foster "negotiations with the international community." In June 2013 the Taliban opened their first official foreign office in Doha, expected to usher in talks with the United States, Pakistan, and the Afghan government led by Hamid Karzai. However, talks stalled almost immediately when Karzai and the United States objected to the display of the Taliban flag and a plaque reading the "Islamic Emirate of Afghanistan" (used when the Taliban rose to power in the 1990s). Upon their removal by Qatari officials, Taliban representatives, some 20 of whom are said to be in Qatar, refused to enter the office. Little progress has been made since.

Qatar's continued support for Islamist groups, primarily Egypt's Muslim Brotherhood, has stirred controversy with other GCC states, which view such movements as threats to stability. On March 5, 2014, Bahrain, Saudi Araba, and the United Arab Emirates withdrew their ambassadors from Doha, claiming Qatar's policies interfered in their domestic affairs. The three countries said Sheikh Tamim failed to comply with a November 2013 GCC pact pertaining to extradition agreements. Egypt withdrew its ambassador the following day. On April 17 Doha reached a tentative agreement with the GCC, though relations remained icy. Qatar deported more than a dozen Islamist leaders to Libya in late April, likely an effort to warm ties with other GCC states.

In late May 2014 Qatar helped broker a deal between the United States and the Taliban in which one American captive was released in exchange for five Guantanamo Bay detainees. Additionally, Qatar volunteered to oversee the released Taliban captives to ensure they do not resume fighting or be allowed to make speeches, give interviews or communicate with their compatriots in Afghanistan. The al-Thani regime also facilitated meetings between Iran and Hamas in Doha in March 2015.

Qatar joined the Saudi-led anti-Houthi coalition fighting in Yemen in 2015 (see entry on Yemen). In September 2016 the government announced that three of its soldiers had been killed fighting in Yemen.

Current issues. In November 2012 Qatari poet Mohammad al-AJAMI was sentenced to life in prison for insulting the emir in a poem he recited in Egypt in 2010 that was later posted online. The ruling was internationally condemned, and, upon appeal in February 2013, the sentence was reduced to 15 years.

In a televised speech on June 25, 2013, Sheikh Hamad abdicated, transferring power to his 33-year-old son, Sheikh Tamim. The move was seen as a challenge to the region's monarchical traditions, where power is transferred only by death or palace coup. Sheikh Hamad handed the reins to his son, noting the shift represents "a new era where young leadership hoists the banner." No official explanation for the elder emir's abdication was given, but it was widely reported that he suffers from chronic medical problems. On June 26 Sheikh Tamim appointed his new cabinet, with former minister of state for internal affairs Sheikh Abdullah ibn Nasser ibn Khalifa al-Thani serving as prime minister. The cabinet includes the second woman to serve at the ministerial level in Qatar, Hessa Sultan al-JABER.

Meanwhile, the transfer of power further postponed Consultative Council elections. In May 2008 the council established direct elections for two-thirds of the 45-member body. No elections were scheduled at the time, and the emir extended the members' terms for two years in July, and then, in 2010, renewed the extension for three years. In November 2011, responding in part to the year's Arab Spring protests, the emir promised elections by the end of 2013. Complicated by the emir's abdication, the promise went unfulfilled both in 2013 and again in 2016.

Preparations for the 2022 FIFA World Cup brought international attention to labor standards in Qatar. After British newspaper *The Guardian* published a report in September 2013 comparing conditions to "modern-day slavery," human rights group Amnesty International released a paper detailing the scope of Qatar's foreign labor market. In May 2014 Qatar moved to make changes to regulations on foreign laborers, including relaxing requirements that workers must seek employers' permission to change jobs or leave the country, but international rights groups said the reforms did not go far enough. Further complicating domestic and international political matters for Doha were allegations in 2015 of bribery of FIFA officials associated with the awarding of the World Cup to Qatar, prompting international investigations that could result in the country losing the rights to host the games. Qatar's spending on the games, including construction of new facilities, was estimated to be more than $200 billion.

POLITICAL PARTIES

The constitution promulgated on June 8, 2004 (see Constitution and government, above), does not provide for the formation of political parties.

LEGISLATURE

The **Consultative Council** (*Majlis al-Shura*), created in 1972, was increased from 20 members to 30 in 1975 and to 35 in 1988. The present council consists exclusively of the emir's appointees, most of them named in 1972 and subsequently reappointed. Arrangements for a partially elected National Assembly are included in the new constitution that was promulgated in June 2004 (see Constitution and government, above). On June 27, 2006, the emir appointed 35 members for a term of one-year to the Consultative Council. On July 2, 2007, the emir extended the term of Consultative Council members, though the length of the new term was unclear. On July 2, 2008, another decree of the emir extended the members' terms to June 30, 2010. The terms were renewed for three more years in 2010 and again in 2013 and 2016.

Speaker: Muhammad ibn Mubarak al-KHALIFI.

CABINET

[as of August 15, 2016]

Prime Minister	Sheikh Abdullah ibn Nasser ibn Khalifa al-Thani
Deputy Prime Minister	Ahmed ibn Abdullah ibn Zaid al-Mahmud
Ministers	
Administrative Development	Issa Saad al-Jafali al-Nuaimi
Awqaf and Islamic Affairs	Ghaith Mubarak Ali Omran al-Kuwari
Communications and Information Technology	Hessa Sultan al-Jaber [f]
Culture and Sports	Salah ibn Ghanem ibn Nasser al-Ali
Development Planning and Statistics	Saleh Mohamed Salem al-Nabit
Economy and Trade	Sheikh Ahmed ibn Jassim ibn Mohamed al-Thani
Education and Higher Education	Mohammed Abdul Wahed Ali al-Hammadi
Energy and Industry	Muhammad ibn Saleh al-Sada
Environment	Ahmed Amer Mohamed al-Humaidi
Finance	Ali Sherif al-Emadi
Foreign Affairs	Sheikh Mohamed ibn Abdulrahman al-Thani
Interior	Sheikh Abdullah ibn Nasser ibn Khalifa al-Thani
Justice	Hassan Lahdan Saqr al-Mohannadi
Labor and Social Affairs	Abdullah Saleh Mubarak al-Khulaifi
Municipality and Environment	Mohamed ibn Abdullah al-Rumaihi
Public Health	Hanan Mohamed al-Kuwari
Transport and Communications	Jassim Seif Ahmed al-Sulaiti
Ministers of State	
Cabinet Affairs	Ahmed ibn Abdullah ibn Zaid al-Mahmud
Defense Affairs	Khalid ibn Ali al-Attiyah

[f] = female

INTERGOVERNMENTAL REPRESENTATION

Ambassador to the U.S.: Mohamad Jaham A.A. al-KUWARI.

U.S. Ambassador to Qatar: Dana Shell SMITH.

Permanent Representative to the UN: Alya Ahmed Saif al-THANI.

IGO Memberships (Non-UN): GCC, NAM, OPEC, OIC, WTO.

For Further Reference:

Fromherz, Allen J. *Qatar: A Modern History*. Washington, DC: Georgetown University Press, 2012.

Kamrava, Mehran. *Qatar: Small State, Big Politics*. Ithaca, NY: Cornell University Press, 2015.

Ulrichsen, Kristian Coates. *Qatar and the Arab Spring*. New York: Oxford University Press, 2015.

ROMANIA

România

Note: Legislative elections on December 11, 2016, were won by the Social Democratic Party (PSD), which retained pluralities in both chambers of parliament. The PSD secured 154 seats in the House of Deputies, and 67 in the Senate. In second place was the National Liberal Party (PNL) with 69 seats in the House and 30 in the Senate, while the newly formed Save Romania Union, won 30 seats in the House and 13 in the Senate, becoming the third-largest parliamentary grouping. Nineteen other parties secured seats in either the House or Senate. PSD leader Liviu Dragnea was tasked to form a new coalition government, and negotiations were ongoing through December 2016. PNL leader Alina Gorghiu resigned as party chair following the balloting.

Political Status: Independence established 1878; People's Republic proclaimed December 30, 1947; designated a Socialist Republic by constitution adopted August 21, 1965; redesignated as Romania in December 1989; presidential multiparty constitution approved in referendum of December 8, 1991.

Area: 91,699 sq. mi. (237,500 sq. km).

Population: 19,373,000 (2016E—UN); 21,599,736 (2016E—U.S. Census).

Major Urban Centers (2012E—UN): BUCHAREST (București, 1,912,515), Cluj-Napoca (303,047), Timişoara (306,462), Iaşi (318,871), Constanţa (297,503), Craiova (293,567), Galaţi (286,530), Braşov (275,514).

Official Language: Romanian.

Monetary Unit: New Leu (market rate October 1, 2016: 3.96 new lei = $1US). The new leu was introduced on July 1, 2005, at the rate of 1 new leu = 10,000 old lei.

President: Klaus IOHANNIS (formerly National Liberal Party, currently independent as constitutionally required); elected in second-round balloting on November 16, 2014, and inaugurated for a five-year term on December 21 in succession to Traian BĂSESCU (elected as the candidate of the Democratic Party).

Chair of the Council of Ministers (Prime Minister): Dacian CIOLOŞ (ind.); designated by the president on November 10, 2015, and sworn in on November 17, to succeed Victor PONTA (Social Democratic Party), who resigned on November 4. (See Current issues, below.)

THE COUNTRY

Shaped by the geographic influence of the Carpathian Mountains and the Danube River, Romania occupies the northeastern quarter of the Balkan Peninsula. It served historically both as an outpost of Latin civilization and as a natural gateway for Russian expansion into southeastern Europe. Some 83 percent of the population is ethnically Romanian, claiming descent from the Romanized Dacians of ancient times. There are also some 1.2 million Magyars (Hungarians), situated mostly in Transylvanian lands acquired from the Austro-Hungarian Empire after World War I. A sizeable German community that totaled approximately one-half million after World War II has dwindled because of emigration. Traditionally, the Romanian (Eastern) Orthodox Church has been the largest religious community. Female participation in political affairs increased significantly under the former Communist regime, but the membership of Parliament in 2012 was only 11.5 percent women (7.4 percent in the Senate and 13.3 percent in the Chamber of Deputies).

Although one of the world's pioneer oil producers, Romania was long a predominantly agricultural country and continues to be largely self-sufficient in food production. After World War II most acreage was brought under the control of collective and state farms, while the agricultural component of the workforce dropped sharply from 65 percent in 1960 as the result of an emphasis on industrial development—particularly in metals, machinery, chemicals, and construction materials—under a series of five-year plans. Agriculture continues to account for about 6 percent of gross domestic product (GDP) and to employ about 30 percent of the labor force. Most farms have now been reprivatized. Leading crops include grains, potatoes, apples, and wine grapes. Industry contributes almost 30 percent of GDP. Major exports include electrical machinery, clothing, and light machinery. The leading trading partners are Germany, Italy, Hungary, and France.

Following the overthrow of the Ceauşescu regime in December 1989 and the new administration's espousal of a free-market orientation, Romania suffered serious economic reversals: a 33 percent contraction of GDP from 1990 to 1993, inflation averaging 140 percent per annum, currency depreciation of 97 percent, and an increase in official unemployment to over 10 percent of the labor force. Improvement from 1994 to 1996 was disrupted by GDP contraction and high inflation during economic crisis of 1997–1999, but this was followed by a high average annual GDP growth rate of 5.9 percent in 2001–2008, placing it among the fastest-growing economies in the region. The IMF reported significant privatization progress, liberalization of the electricity and gas markets, and modernization of the mining sector. Romania's accession to the European Union (EU) at the beginning of 2007 assisted continued growth.

Until recently, the main problems facing successive governments have been corruption and the large trade and budget deficits. However, those issues have been overshadowed since mid-2008 by domestic economic concerns, which played a significant role in that year's legislative campaign. The government estimated that GDP contracted by 7.2 percent in 2009 under the influence of the global economic downturn, while unemployment reached 7.6 percent by the end of the year. The IMF reported a further 1.2 percent decline in GDP in 2010, but GDP grew by an average of 2.1 percent annually in 2011 through 2013. GDP grew by 3 percent in 2014, 3.7 percent in 2015, and 4.2 percent in 2016. Inflation was –0.4 percent in 2016, while unemployment was 6.4 percent and GDP per capita was $9,157. In its 2016 annual survey on the ease of conducting business, the World Bank ranked Romania 37th out of 189 countries, between the Czech Republic (36th) and Bulgaria (38th).

GOVERNMENT AND POLITICS

Political background. The twin principalities of Walachia and Moldavia were conquered by the Ottoman Turks in 1504. The principalities were unified in 1859 and became the core of the Romanian state. Recognized as independent at the Berlin Congress in 1878, Romania made large territorial gains as one of the victorious powers in World War I but lost substantial areas to Hungary (Northern Transylvania), to the Soviet Union (Bessarabia and Northern Bukovina), and to Bulgaria (Southern Dobruja) in 1940 under threats from its neighbors and pressure from Nazi Germany. The young King MIHAI (Michael), who took advantage of the entry of Soviet troops in 1944 to dismiss the pro-German regime and switch to the Allied side, was forced in 1945 to accept a Communist-led coalition government under Dr. Petru GROZA. Following rigged elections in 1946, the king abdicated in 1947. The Paris peace treaty in 1947 restored Northern Transylvania to Romania, but not the other territories lost in 1940. Thereafter, the Communists proceeded to eliminate the remnants of the traditional parties, and in 1952, after a series of internal purges, Gheorghe GHEORGHIU-DEJ emerged as the unchallenged party leader.

Following a decade of rigidity, Romania embarked in the early 1960s on a policy of increased independence from the Soviet Union in both military and economic affairs. This policy was continued and intensified under Nicolae CEAUŞESCU, who succeeded to leadership of the Romanian Communist Party (*Partidul Comunist Român*—PCR) on Gheorghiu-Dej's death in 1965 and became president of the Council of State in 1967. While maintaining relatively strict controls at home, the Ceauşescu regime consistently advocated maximum autonomy in international Communist affairs.

In November 1989 Romania appeared impervious to the winds of change sweeping over most other East European Communist regimes. Thus, the 14th PCR congress met without incident on November 20–24, and Ceauşescu made a state visit to Iran on December 19–20. During his absence, long-simmering unrest among ethnic Hungarians in the western city of Timişoara led to a bloody confrontation between police and antigovernment demonstrators. The protests quickly spread to other cities, and on December 21 an angry crowd jeered the president during what had been planned as a progovernment rally in Bucharest. By the following day army units had joined in a full-scale revolt, with a group known as the National Salvation Front (*Frontul Salvării Naţionale*—FSN) announcing that it had formed a provisional government. Unlike other East European revolutions, Romania's overthrow of Communist rule involved fierce fighting, in Bucharest and other cities, with many civilian casualties. On December 25 Ceauşescu and his wife Elena, who had been captured after fleeing the capital, were executed following a secret trial that had pronounced them guilty of genocide and the embezzlement of more than $1 billion. On December 26 Ion ILIESCU was sworn in as provisional head of state, with Petre ROMAN, a fellow member of the PCR *nomenklatura,* being named prime minister. The FSN quickly came under attack as a thinly disguised extension of the former regime, and on February 1, 1990, it agreed to share power with 29 other groups in a coalition styled the Provisional Council for National Unity (*Consiliul Provizoriu de Uniune Naţională*—CPUN).

In presidential and legislative elections (the latter involving 6,719 candidates) on May 20, 1990, Iliescu won 85.1 percent of the presidential vote, while the FSN secured 67 and 66.3 percent of the votes for the upper and lower houses of Parliament, respectively. The balloting went ahead despite demonstrations by opposition parties claiming that they had been accorded insufficient time to organize. The protesters were eventually evicted from Bucharest's University Square in mid-June by thousands of club-wielding coal miners summoned to the capital by the president. On June 20 Iliescu was formally invested for a two-year term as president, with Roman continuing as prime minister.

Following his reappointment, Roman declared that he would pursue a "historic transition from a supercentralized economy to a market economy" and asserted that only "shock therapy" could save the rapidly deteriorating economy from disaster. Thus, prices of essential goods doubled as the result of sharp cuts in state subsidies in April 1991, while a drastic revision of the foreign investment code, urged by the IMF, offered non-Romanian companies full ownership, capital protection, repatriation of profits, and multiyear tax concessions.

Despite rapidly eroding support for the government by mid-1991, the reforms continued unabated, including the enactment of legislation in August that authorized the privatization of all state enterprises except utilities. For their part, the miners responded to soaring inflation by returning to Bucharest in September for three days of violent demonstrations, and on October 1 it was announced that Theodor STOLOJAN, the nonparty finance minister, had been asked to form a new government. By December it was clear that President Iliescu and former prime minister Roman were engaged in a struggle for control of the FSN. Iliescu supporters, formally organized from April 1992 as the Democratic National Salvation Front (*Frontul Democrat al Salvării Naţionale*—FDSN), gained parliamentary support for simultaneous legislative and presidential elections in September, at which Roman's forces were decisively routed.

At his reinvestiture on October 30, President Iliescu endorsed further progress toward pluralism and a market economy, despite having long been accused by opponents of foot-dragging on both counts. Fourteen days later, a deeply divided Parliament ended a five-week impasse by agreeing to the formation of a government led by Nicolae VĂCĂROIU, a relatively unknown tax official then without party affiliation, who proceeded to combine liberal reform with "special care" for its social consequences. In July 1993 the FDSN absorbed three other progovernment parties and adopted a new name, the Social Democracy Party of Romania (*Partidul Democraţiei Sociale din România*—PDSR), which Văcăroiu later joined.

Despite deepening economic misery, the Văcăroiu government endured, with support from the (ex-Communist) Socialist Labor Party (*Partidul Socialist al Muncii*—PSM), the far-right Greater Romania Party (*Partidul România Mare*—PRM), and (after 1994) the rightist Romanian National Unity Party (*Partidul Unităţii Naţionale Române*—PUNR). In the course of 1995, however, the PDSR's relations with all three coalition partners deteriorated sharply, with the PRM and PSM leaving the government alliance in October, with the PUNR's exit confirmed in September 1996.

In the first round of presidential balloting held on November 3, 1996, incumbent Iliescu (PDSR) headed the poll against 15 other candidates, winning 32.3 percent of the vote. However, he was closely followed by the CDR candidate, Emil CONSTANTINESCU, with 28.2 percent, while Petre Roman, standing for the Social Democratic Union (*Uniunea Social Democrată*—USD), came in third with 20.5 percent. The USD and most other opposition parties then swung behind the CDR candidate for the runoff polling on November 17. As a result, Constantinescu won a decisive victory over Iliescu by 53.5 percent to 46.5 percent, the incumbent having been weighed down not only by Romania's economic and social deterioration, but also by evidence of abuse of power and pervasive corruption within ruling circles. In legislative balloting also held on November 3, the CDR won pluralities in both the Senate and the Chamber of Deputies, with the USD also polling strongly as the third grouping, after the PDSR.

Interparty talks following the elections yielded the signature of an agreement on December 6, 1996, providing for Victor CIORBEA, the youthful CDR mayor of Bucharest, to head a majority coalition government with the USD and the Hungarian Democratic Union of Romania (*Uniunea Democrată a Maghiarilor din România*—UDMR), the latter representing Romania's ethnic Hungarian minority. Accorded a 316–152 endorsement by a joint session of the two legislative houses on December 11, the new administration was sworn in the following day.

Ciorbea's government found it difficult to implement the reforms required to resolve Romania's economic problems. Coalition members, particularly the CDR's Christian and Democratic National Peasants' Party (*Partidul Naţional Ţărănesc Creştin şi Democrat*—PNŢCD) and the USD's Democratic Party (*Partidul Democrat*—PD, an FSN descendant), generally were unable to compromise. In the wake of persistent feuding and public discord, the cabinet was reshuffled in December, with a number of independents being appointed. On January 14, 1998, the PD withdrew its support from Ciorbea and threatened to quit the government if he did not resign and if no agreement was reached within the coalition on a reform program by March 31. On February 5 the PD's five cabinet ministers resigned, and a new coalition agreement was approved, the open ministerial posts going to the PNŢCD, the National Liberal Party (*Partidul Naţional Liberal*—PNL), and the Civic Alliance Party (*Partidul Alianţa Civică*—PAC). After three months of political instability, Ciorbea resigned on March 30.

On April 2, 1998, President Constantinescu named Radu VASILE, the general secretary of the PNŢCD, to replace Ciorbea; Vasile and his cabinet were sworn in on April 15. The new government included members from the PNŢCD, PD, UDMR, PNL, Romanian Social Democratic Party (*Partidul Social Democrat Român*—PSDR), and Romania's Alternative Party (*Partidul Alternativa României*—PAR). However, in October PAR quit the coalition government in protest over the slow pace of economic reform.

Himself an economist, Vasile promised to strengthen the market economy by accelerating privatization efforts, and in December 1998 he restructured the government, reducing the number of ministries to quicken the pace of reform. In early 1999, however, his plans were set back by a miners' strike in the Jiu Valley that escalated into Romania's worst civil disorder since 1991. In mid-January the government reached a compromise with the leader of the miners' union, Miron COZMA, agreeing to abandon immediate plans to close unprofitable coal mines. The agreement averted a potential armed conflict between security forces and 20,000 strikers, but in mid-February Cozma and several hundred others were arrested as he led 2,000 miners toward Bucharest in protest against his recent sentencing to 18 years in prison for his role in the September 1991 riots.

With inflation and unemployment at unacceptable levels, and with the leu having fallen by more than one-third of its value between January and mid-March 1999, general dissatisfaction with the state of the economy continued to grow. Squabbling within the governing coalition also persisted, hindering progress on reform measures, and by December Vasile had lost the support of his own PNŢCD, whose ministers, constituting the majority of the cabinet, resigned. On December 13 President Constantinescu dismissed Vasile, with Mugur ISĂRESCU, the governor of Romania's central bank, appointed on December 16 as the new prime minister. Isărescu and a largely unchanged Council of Ministers received the legislature's approbation on December 21.

The final years of the CDR-led government were marked by political infighting and a resultant inability to establish a course that would resolve Romania's economic difficulties. At the same time, the country continued to grapple with the legacy of the Ceauşescu era. The government decided to release files held by the former secret police, the *Securitate,* and supported measures covering restitution for personal property, farmland, and forests.

After mid-2000, with presidential and legislative elections approaching, the political alliance behind the governing coalition gradually dissolved. In August 2000 the PNŢCD and several allied parties reconstituted the CDR as the CDR 2000, but minus one of its previous principal components, the PNL. The PD, UDMR, and PNL prepared to contest the elections independently, while in September the PSDR left the government and formed an alliance with the PDSR. The legislative election of November 26 saw the PDSR capture a large plurality in both parliamentary houses, with the xenophobic PRM, in the election's most startling development, rising to second place with 20 percent of the vote and with the enfeebled CDR 2000 failing to meet the threshold for representation. In the presidential contest, former president Iliescu of the PDSR easily defeated the PRM's Corneliu VADIM TUDOR in a two-way runoff on December 10. (President Constantinescu had decided not to seek a second term, describing Romania's political parties as conducting "a blind struggle" for power.) Iliescu assumed office on December 21. His choice for prime minister, Adrian NĂSTASE, was confirmed by the Parliament and sworn in on December 28 at the head of a minority government dominated by the PDSR, with external backing from the PNL and the UDMR. On June 16, 2001, the PDSR and the PSDR completed their merger as the Social Democratic Party (*Partidul Social Democrat*—PSD).

At legislative balloting on November 28, 2004, the PSD, and its ally in the National Union coalition, the Humanist Party of Romania (*Partidul Umanist din România*—PUR), secured a plurality of 132 seats in the Chamber of Deputies. Following closely (with 112 seats) was the Justice and Truth Alliance (*Alianţa Dreptate şi Adevăr*—ADA), which had been formed in 2003 by the PNL and the PD. In concurrent first-round presidential balloting, Prime Minister Năstase led 12 candidates with 41 percent of the vote. The ADA's Traian BĂSESCU finished second with 34 percent of the vote, followed by the PRM's Vadim Tudor with 12.6 percent.

In the presidential runoff on December 12, 2004, Băsescu scored a surprising victory over Năstase, securing 51.2 percent of the vote. Observers were surprised by Năstase's loss since as prime minister he had successfully negotiated accession to NATO, overseen progress toward European Union (EU) membership, and adopted policies that contributed to economic improvement. However, Băsescu was aided among voters still concerned about corruption by his reputation for rectitude as mayor of Bucharest. On December 28 the Parliament, by a vote of 265–200, approved a cabinet (led by Călin POPESCU-TĂRICEANU of the PNL) comprising the PNL, PD, UDMR, and PUR (which had split from the PSD).

In April 2005 Romania signed an accession treaty with the EU calling for Romania to become a member in January 2007, although analysts noted that significant reform was still required. Complicating matters at midyear was reported friction between the president and the prime minister on a number of issues.

The Conservative Party (*Partidul Conservator*—PC, as PUR had been renamed) left the government in December 2006 after a series of disagreements within the coalition over a number of issues. (Several PC leaders were also facing corruption investigations.) The government's legislative majority was also compromised by the defections of a number of PNL deputies to a new party (the Democratic Liberal Party [*Partidul Liberal Democrat*—PLD]) formed by former prime minister Stolojan and other PNL dissidents. Nevertheless, Prime Minister Popescu-Tăriceanu declined to call new elections, in part, apparently, in an effort to maintain stability in advance of the January 1, 2007, accession to the EU.

An even stronger threat to the government arose when the ADA was dissolved and the PD withdrew from the cabinet on April 1, 2007. However, on the following day Prime Minister Popescu-Tăriceanu named a new minority government comprising the PNL and UDMR, which was easily approved by the assembled Parliament on April 5, thanks primarily to support from the PSD. Turmoil nevertheless continued as the Parliament, at the prime minister's urging, on April 19 voted 322–108 to suspend President Băsescu and conduct a referendum on his possible permanent removal from office for alleged violation of the constitution in regard to the extent of presidential authority. Nicolae VĂCĂROIU, the chair of the Senate, served as acting president until the May 19 referendum, in which nearly 75 percent of the voters rejected the proposed removal of the president, who resumed his duties on May 23.

Another national referendum was held on November 25, 2007, concerning changes in the national electoral system supported by President Băsescu, who favored decentralizing the government and making Parliament more responsive to constituents by, among other things, introducing a majoritarian element to the legislative balloting. The proposal received an 80 percent endorsement in the referendum, although the results were ruled invalid due to insufficient turnout. Nevertheless, spurred by the debate, Parliament approved new electoral arrangements in March 2008. (See Legislature, below, for details.)

In the campaign for the November 2008 parliamentary elections, wage levels and domestic economic concerns emerged as significant factors. The PSD and PD-L, among others, sponsored legislation before the election promising wage hikes of up to 50 percent for civil servants, subsequently promising expenditures on infrastructure to stimulate the economy and to address regional disparities in regard to development. However, Prime Minister Popescu-Tăriceanu refused to implement the proposals, arguing that the budget lacked the necessary resources. In the November 30, 2008, elections the Democratic-Liberal Party (*Partidul Democrat-Liberal*—PD-L), a recent merger of the PD and PLD, secured 115 seats in the Chamber of Deputies, compared to 114 for the alliance of the PSD and PC. The PNL won 65 seats and the UDMR 22, while the PRM failed to pass the threshold. The close results led to calls for a "Grand Coalition" between the PD-L and PSD. However, the first attempt at forming the new government was disrupted when prime minister designate Theodor Stolojan of the PD-L withdrew his name from consideration, citing the need for a "younger generation" to assume governmental responsibility. The PD-L's Emil BOC, the mayor of Cluj-Napoca, subsequently formed the coalition, which was approved by a vote of 324–115 in Parliament on December 22.

The June 7, 2009, European Parliament elections were conducted by nationwide proportional representation. The alliance of the PSD and PC won a plurality of 31.1 percent of the vote and 11 of the country's 33 seats. The PD-L finished second with 29.7 percent of the vote and 10 seats, followed by the PNL with 14.5 percent of the vote and 5 seats, and the UDMR with 8.9 percent of the vote and 3 seats. The PRM won 8.7 percent of the vote and 3 seats, and independent candidate Elena BĂSESCU (President Băsescu's daughter) won a seat with 4.2 percent of the vote. The close results in the second round of the presidential elections of December 6, 2009, plus the fact that exit polls had indicated a lead for the PSD's Mircea GEOANĂ led to accusations of fraud against Băsescu and the PD-L. Although the Constitutional Court certified Băsescu's reelection, the PSD did not withdraw its allegations.

The ministers from the Social Democratic Party (PSD) resigned from the cabinet on October 1, 2009, to protest the recent dismissal of Administration and Interior Minister Dan Nica, who had reportedly speculated about the possibility of fraud in the upcoming presidential poll. Without PSD support, the government of Prime Minister Emil Boc collapsed on October 13, when it lost a confidence motion by a vote of 254–176 in the Chamber of Deputies. Independent Lucian Croitoru and Liviu Negoiţă of the Democratic-Liberal Party (PD-L) successively failed to win legislative support for their proposed cabinets, and Boc on December 23 formed a new minority government comprising the PD-L, the Hungarian Democratic Union of Romania, independents, and rogue members of the PSD and National Liberal party who subsequently formed the National Union for the Progress of Romania (*Uniunea Naţională pentru Progresul României*—UNPR). The new government was approved by a 276–135 legislative vote. Meanwhile, President Traian Băsescu had been sworn in for another five-year term on December 21 after winning a runoff on December 6 with 50.3 percent of the vote against PSD chair Mircea Geoană.

Protests in January 2012 (see Current issues, below) led to the resignation of Boc on February 6, 2012, and the announcement of a new government by Mihai Razvan UNGUREANU on February 9, again a coalition of the PD-L, UDMR, and UNPR. However, a vote of no confidence in the government on April 27 succeeded after a series of defections by PD-L legislators to the Social Liberal Union (*Uniunea Social Liberală*—USL), a coalition of the PSD, PC and PNL. Victor PONTA of the PSD was then asked to form a government. On May 7 Ponta formed a government of the PSD, PNL, and PC. Following a failed effort to impeach Băsescu in June through August 2012, however, Ponta announced a significant reshuffle of the cabinet in August to "restore credibility" in the government.

In the December 9, 2012, elections the USL (now including the UNPR) secured 273 seats in the Chamber of Deputies, compared to 56 for the Right Romania Alliance (*Alianța România Dreaptă*—ARD), an electoral alliance of the PD-L, PNŢCD, Civic Force (*Forța Civică*—FC) and Romanian National Party (*Partidul Național Român*—PNR). Also in the opposition was the newly formed People's Party-Dan Diaconescu (*Partidul Poporului-Dan Diaconescu*—PP-DD), with 47 Chamber seats and the UDMR with 18.

In February 2012 the PNL withdrew from the government and moved to the opposition, citing an inability to work with Ponta as prime minister. On May 4 the parliament approved a new Ponta-led government of the PSD, PC, UNPR, and UDMR.

Ponta secured 40.3 percent of the vote in the first round of presidential balloting on November 2, 2016, followed by Klaus IOHANNIS (National Liberal Party) with 30.4 percent of the vote. The two advanced to runoff polling that was won by Iohannis with 54.4 percent of the vote. He was inaugurated on December 21, while Ponta remained prime minister.

On November 4, 2015, Ponta was forced to resign amidst widespread protests over a corruption scandal (see Current issues, below). Dacian CIOLOŞ (independent) was appointed to succeed Ponta on November 10, and his mainly technocrat government was sworn in on November 17. New elections were scheduled for December.

Constitution and government. Upon assuming power in late 1989, the FSN suspended the constitution of 1974 and declared its support for a multiparty system and a market economy. The balloting of May 20, 1990, was for a president and a bicameral Parliament, the latter being empowered to draft a new constitution within 18 months, with new elections to follow within 12 months. A revised basic law providing for a strong presidency, political pluralism, human rights guarantees, and a commitment to market freedom was approved by Parliament (sitting as a Constituent Assembly) on November 21, 1991, and ratified by referendum on December 8.

A national referendum held October 18–19, 2003, approved (by a 90 percent "yes" vote in a 55.7 percent turnout) a number of constitutional amendments designed for the most part to facilitate Romania's planned accession to the EU. Among other things, the changes strengthened the protection of human rights (most notably for minority groups) and property rights. In addition, the presidential term was extended from four to five years.

Administratively, Romania is divided into 41 counties plus the city of Bucharest, in addition to a large number of towns and villages. A prefect represents the central government in each county, which elects its own council. Mayors and councils are elected at the lower level.

Reporters Without Borders ranked Romania as 49th out of 180 countries in its 2016 Press Freedom Index, the second-highest ranking in the Balkans, behind Slovenia (40th).

Foreign relations. Romania during its first 15 years as a Communist state cooperated fully with the Soviet Union both in bilateral relations and as a member of the Council for Mutual Economic Assistance, the Warsaw Pact, and the United Nations. However, serious differences with Moscow arose in the early 1960s over the issue of East European economic integration, leading in 1964 to a formal rejection by Romania of all Soviet schemes of supranational planning and interference in the affairs of other Communist countries. Subsequently, Romania followed an independent line in many areas of foreign policy, refusing to participate in the 1968 Warsaw Pact intervention in Czechoslovakia, rejecting efforts to isolate Communist China, and remaining the only Soviet-bloc nation to continue diplomatic relations with both Egypt and Israel. Prior to the admission of Hungary in 1982, Romania was the only Eastern-bloc state to belong to the World Bank and the IMF.

A constant regional theme of Romania's external relations in the early 1990s was discord with Hungary over the status of Romania's substantial ethnic Hungarian minority population, concentrated in Transylvania. Tension mounted when the ultranationalist Gheorghe FUNAR, presidential candidate of the Romanian National Unity Party (*Partidul Unității Naționale Române*—PUNR), was elected mayor of Cluj-Napoca in Transylvania in February 1992, with subsequent restrictions on "anti-Romanian" public meetings. Collaterally, the central government named ethnic Romanians to replace ethnic Hungarian prefects in the two Hungarian-majority counties, the resultant outrage being only partially eased by the appointment of two prefects for each county, one Hungarian and one Romanian.

A second major preoccupation of post-Communist Romania has been the position of Moldova (the former Moldavian Soviet Socialist Republic), once the bulk of Romanian-ruled Bessarabia and inhabited predominantly by ethnic Romanians. On September 3, 1991, the Romanian Parliament adopted a resolution endorsing an August 27 declaration of independence by Moldova. On November 2, during a visit to Bucharest, Moldovan prime minister Valeriu Muravschi expressed the hope that intergovernmental exchanges could "speed up the process of [his country's] integration with Romania."

Advancing the concept of "two republics, one nation," the Romanian and Moldovan governments took a gradualist approach to unification and from May 1992 engaged in protracted diplomatic efforts with Russia and Ukraine to bring about a lasting cessation of hostilities between the warring ethnic groups in Moldova. (On the other hand, the Moldovan election of February 1994 yielding a legislative majority for proindependence parties represented a rebuff to the reunification effort.)

Romania was a founding member of the Black Sea Economic Cooperation (BSEC) grouping launched in June 1992, and on February 1, 1993, Romania signed an association agreement with the European Community (EC, subsequently the EU). However, its continuing problems in gaining international acceptance were highlighted by the refusal of the United States to extend most-favored-nation trade status until October 1993, although Washington had joined Western European governments in applauding the overthrow of the Ceauşescu regime.

In September 1993 the Parliamentary Assembly of the Council of Europe approved the admission of Romania to the organization. Subsequently, on January 26, 1994, Romania became the first former Communist state to join NATO's Partnership for Peace program, pursuant to its aim of eventual full NATO membership as well as accession to the EU. In the latter context, Romania in mid-1994 secured an EU pledge that it would be treated on a par with the four Visegrád states (Czech Republic, Hungary, Poland, Slovakia) also seeking membership. (On June 22, 1995, Romania became the third ex-Communist state [after Hungary and Poland] to submit a formal application for EU membership, although it was not invited to open accession negotiations until December 1999.)

The June 1994 advent of a Socialist government in Hungary led to an improvement in Bucharest–Budapest relations, including a visit to Hungary by the Romanian foreign minister in September. Nevertheless, difficulties continued, occasioned by such events as passage in the Romanian Parliament of legislation regulating Hungarian-language education and the display of the flag or the singing of the anthem of another state. In a new initiative in September 1995, the Romanian government submitted three draft documents to Hungary covering reconciliation between the two countries, bilateral cooperation, and a code of behavior on treatment of ethnic minorities. Although the response in Budapest was cool, Bucharest persisted, with the result that a 1996 bilateral treaty saw both sides make concessions on the minority question. Hungary renounced any claim to Romanian territory populated by ethnic Hungarians, and Romania undertook to guarantee ethnic minority rights within its borders. Although the treaty commanded majority support in both national legislatures, it attracted fierce criticism from nationalist parties in both Hungary and Romania.

Romanian–Hungarian relations continued to improve after the election of President Constantinescu in November 1996, and in February 1997 the defense ministers of the two countries met and agreed on the formation of a joint peacekeeping force, a move that was seen as enhancing both nations' prospects for gaining entry into NATO. In March Prime Minister Ciorbea, in the first visit of a Romanian prime minister to Hungary since 1989, signed five agreements. The following month President Arpád Göncz became the first Hungarian head of state to visit Romania, while in June the two nations signed a friendship treaty, confirming existing borders.

Despite support from France, Italy, and Spain, Romania's request to be included in the first-round expansion of NATO was blocked in 1997 by the United States, with U.S. defense secretary William Cohen explaining that Washington had said "not yet" rather than simply "no." The rejection was seen as a desire by the United States to placate a nervous Russia and to delay admission until democracy and free-market reforms in Romania had become irreversible. In July U.S. president Clinton, in the first visit to Romania by an American president in more than 20 years, praised the Romanians and encouraged them to stay their course.

Romania became a member of the Central European Free Trade Agreement (CEFTA) on July 1, 1997, expecting to regain access to Eastern and Central European markets as well as to enhance its prospects for NATO membership (see Poland, Foreign relations, for more on CEFTA). A month earlier, the presidents of Ukraine and Romania had signed a friendship treaty, calling existing borders "inviolable" despite earlier friction over the status of Northern Bukovina and Southern Bessarabia, both of which Romania had been compelled to cede to the USSR in June 1940. Related issues of national identity delayed conclusion of a basic treaty with Russia until 2003, as had Romania's demand that Russia return the state treasury that has been held in Moscow since its delivery there for safekeeping during World War I.

A trip to Romania in May 1999 by John Paul II was the first visit by a Roman Catholic pope to a country with an Orthodox majority since the Great Schism of 1054. Although restricted to Bucharest, the pope was warmly greeted by the patriarch of the Romanian Orthodox Church, TEOCTIST.

A basic treaty between Romania and Moldova was initialed on April 28, 2000, but neither country's legislature ratified the agreement. Subsequently, in November 2002 Romania and Hungary signed an agreement defining the future course of their bilateral partnership and guaranteeing each other support for EU membership.

In 2003 Romania was included in the "second wave" of candidates for membership in NATO, to which it formally acceded in March 2004 along with six other countries. Earlier, Romania had contributed a contingent of noncombat troops to the U.S.–UK–led operation in Iraq, withdrawing in 2009.

In October 2005 Romania and Hungary signed a number of potentially significant agreements providing for cooperation in environmental protection, law enforcement, border security, joint defense programs, and cultural and educational exchanges. The two countries also pledged to pursue common economic policies.

Romania acceded to the EU on January 1, 2007. However, Romania pledged to continue reforms, particularly judicial reforms and anticorruption measures, as specified by the European Commission Mechanism for Cooperation and Verification.

Tensions grew in 2007 concerning the large expatriate Romanian community in Italy. Among other things, widespread protests, including violent attacks on Romanian immigrants, broke out in Italy when an Italian woman was allegedly murdered by a Romanian citizen. The Italian government responded by using emergency measures to expel some Romanian citizens, drawing expressions of concern from the Romanian government. Many of those expelled were of Roma origin, highlighting problems of minority relations in both Italy and Romania.

The International Court of Justice in February 2009 resolved Romania's ongoing territorial dispute with Ukraine over the disposition of Serpents' Island (transferred at Soviet insistence in 1948) and related maritime borders. Some 9,700 square kilometers of maritime waters were slated to be transferred to Romanian sovereignty, an area that was believed to have significant oil and gas reserves.

In campaigning for the June 2009 European Parliament elections, the PD-L and PSD both proposed changes to Romanian citizenship laws to provide citizenship to ethnic Romanians living in the Republic of Moldova. EU officials subsequently criticized such rhetoric as offering blanket Romanian citizenship (and, consequently, EU citizenship) to Moldovans, leading the Romanian foreign ministry to repudiate such proposals. The PNL subsequently called for the relaxation of visa regimes and border controls with Moldova.

Ties between Romania and Moldova improved after the Moldovan elections of September 2009 led to the end of the Vladimir Voronin presidency. In November Romania relaxed its visa regime to allow Moldovan residents living in villages and towns within 30 kilometers of the border to enter without a visa, a category that extends to nearly half of the country's population. In January 2010 Băsescu offered Moldova €100 million in economic aid, further pledging to support Moldova's entry into the EU on a timeframe comparable to that of candidate countries in the western Balkans.

Relations with Russia saw considerable friction in 2011, chiefly due to Romania's offer to provide a site for U.S. SM-3 missile interceptors at Deveselu air base (formally signing an agreement in September). The use of anti-Russian rhetoric in domestic populist political appeals has also played a factor, such as Băsescu's statement on June 22, 2011, that he agreed with Romania's participation in the 1941 German-led invasion of the Soviet Union so far as it was driven by the desire to regain Moldova, ceded to the Soviets in 1940.

After the outbreak of fighting by pro-Russian armed separatists in Ukraine in February 2014, Romanian leaders expressed concern that these groups might seek to link with Transnistrian separatists in Moldova. In April, Prime Minister Ponta announced a 10 percent increase in the military budget for the next year, with further increases to 2017 until the budget reaches 2 percent of GDP.

In January 2015 the European Court of Human Rights ruled that Romania had violated the rights of 37 Roma when security forces used "excessive" force in suppressing protests in Transylvania. The Roma were awarded €192,000 in damages.

President Iohannis promulgated a new security strategy on June 22, 2015, that called for closer integration with NATO and the EU. On September 8 Iohannis rejected an EU quota that would have required Romania to accept 4,646 migrants (see entry on the EU). The president argued that Romania could only accept 1,785 refugees because of the limited resources of the country. In December a U.S. antimissile defense system was launched at a NATO base in Deveselu and was expected to be fully operational by the end of 2016. Russia condemned the facility, which the United States and Romania asserted was designed to protect from missile attacks from Iran or North Korea, not Russia.

Current issues. In May 2010 the government embraced a series of austerity measures to gain access to an IMF loan, cutting salaries of state employees by 25 percent and raising the value-added tax on goods from 19 to 24 percent. A second series of initiatives in September 2010 raised the retirement age to 65 years (up from 63.5 years for men and 59.5 years for women) and lowered health care and social spending. The changes prompted widespread protests.

Although the European Commission in July 2011 praised Romania for its continued efforts to stem corruption, the report also underlined the need for further reform by 2012 to meet the guidelines laid out at Romania's accession to the EU. Issues of state corruption were underscored by the dismissal in February 2011 of Radu MĂRGINEAN, the head of the National Customs Authority, after his indictment on charges of taking bribes. Concern by other EU members over Romanian border controls and bribery of border guards was a significant factor in the decision in June 2011 to delay Romania's entry to the Schengen area, which waives border controls between members. The PSD and PD-L, however, have issued frequent and mutual recriminations that anticorruption efforts are being used for political purposes.

New austerity measures, particularly controversial measures to reform and privatize health care, sparked significant protests in several Romanian cities over January 12 through January 15, 2012. As many as 20,000 protested over the issue in Bucharest, joined by protesters concerned over a variety of issues, including shale gas fracking, the proposed Roşia Montană gold mine, and corruption. In response, Prime Minister Boc resigned on February 5.

In June 2012 tensions between Băsescu and Prime Minister Ponta erupted into an open clash over which figure had the legal right to represent Romania in the June 28, 2012, meeting of the European Council, with Parliament backing Ponta in a 249–30 vote. Subsequent developments heightened the political tensions. On June 19 Ponta was formally accused of plagiarizing his 2003 doctoral dissertation; then on June 20 former PSD leader Adrian Năstase attempted suicide when police attempted to arrest him to serve a two-year prison sentence for corruption. Ponta subsequently charged Băsescu with motivating the charges against himself and Năstase.

On June 27 the Constitutional Court ruled that Băsescu should attend the European Council, but the government delayed publishing the verdict and confirmed Ponta's attendance, leading Băsescu to publicly concede. The conflict, and particularly the Ponta government's use of emergency legislation during the crisis (for example, limiting the oversight of the Constitutional Court on parliamentary decisions), led to domestic and international criticism that Ponta was undermining the democratic process.

On July 6 Parliament voted 256–114 to suspend Băsescu, then voting 242–0 (the opposition boycotting the vote) to call for a public referendum to impeach Băsescu. The referendum on July 29 saw 88.7 percent of voters vote to impeach, but with only 46.2 percent of voters turning out, the Constitutional Court ruled on August 21, 2012, that the vote was invalid having failed to reach the specified 50 percent + 1 threshold. On August 27 Băsescu was reinstated.

In March 2013 the EU again postponed Romanian accession to the Schengen Zone, citing corruption issues. The decision raised concerns that the 2014 deadline to open the EU labor market to Romanians could be similarly postponed.

In April 2013 Ponta withdrew the government's target date of 2015 for joining the eurozone. No new target was offered, although Ponta states adoption of the Euro remains a "fundamental objective."

On May 20, 2013, the Romanian Supreme Court sentenced politician George BECALI and former Minister of Defense Victor BABIUC to prison terms for fraud related to the exchange of state land in the late 1990s.

The two-thirds parliamentary majority won by the USL in the December 2012 elections has opened the possibility for constitutional revision. In May 2013 a parliamentary constitution commission was created, which drafted a series of amendments. Many revisions provoked controversy, including proposals to limit the powers of the president; to redefine administrative boundaries, creating 7 or 8 economic regions that would encompass the present 41 counties; for the prime minister to represent Romania in EU bodies (overturning the 2012 Constitutional Court decision); to define marriage as solely between a man and a woman; and to restore the coat of arms to the national flag. The Constitutional Court of Romania ruled, in February 2014, that elements of the draft-proposed constitution were unconstitutional. In an opinion solicited by the Romanian government, the Council of Europe's Venice Commission for Democracy Through Law similarly suggested in February the need for revisions.

In July 2013 Băsescu threatened to call a new referendum on restructuring parliament if parliament did not take steps to fulfill the 2009 referendum.

On July 12 PNL member and minister of transport Relu FENECHIU was convicted of corruption and sentenced to five years in prison, the first minister to be convicted while in office. In October Romanian prosecutors charged 75 officials, including Vice Prime Minister Liviu DRAGNEA, with falsifying voter data in the 2012 referendum.

On January 1, 2014, EU labor markets opened to Romanian citizens. However, Romanian accession to the Schengen Zone has continued to be delayed amid allegations that it has not done enough to secure its borders and address corruption.

In July 2014 a former Communist-era prison official went on trial, charged with crimes against humanity. The trial has divided Romanian public opinion on whether to expand lustration and investigations of Communist-era officials.

On June 5, 2015, revelations emerged that Prime Minister Ponta was under investigation for corruption that allegedly occurred in 2007–2008. Ponta was suspected of forgery, money laundering, and tax evasion in connection with Ponta's relationship with former transport minister Don SOVA (PSD), who had been forced to resign amid abuse of office charges. The president called on Ponta to resign, but the prime minister refused. He survived a no-confidence vote on June 12, and took a three-week leave of absence, while Deputy Prime Minister Gabriel OPREA (independent) served as acting chief executive. Meanwhile there were widespread protests and demonstrations. In July Ponta resigned as leader of the PSD and was formally charged with corruption the next day.

On November 4, 2015, a fire swept through the Colectiv nightclub in Bucharest, killing 60 and injuring 147. The tragedy prompted more protests against the government. Ponta resigned on November 4 and was succeeded by Dacian Cioloş at the head of a technocrat government.

In January 2016 former deputy prime minister Oprea was charged with abuse of office for providing police escorts, without authorization, for prosecutor general Tiberiu NITU. Niu resigned on February 3. On June 13, Chamber speaker Valeriu ZGONEA (PSD) was removed as speaker after he was expelled from his party for calling for the resignation of the PSD's leader Liviu DRAGNEA after the latter's conviction on corruption charges (see Political Parties, below). Florin IORDACHE was appointed interim speaker.

POLITICAL PARTIES

Until late 1989 Romania's political system was based on the controlling position of the **Romanian Communist Party** (*Partidul Comunist Român*—PCR). Founded in 1921, the PCR changed its name to the **Romanian Workers' Party** (*Partidul Muncitoresc Român*—PMR) in 1948 after a merger with the left-wing Social Democrats, but the party reassumed its original name at the ninth party congress in 1965. Identified by the constitution as "the leading political force of the whole society," the PCR exercised its authority with the aid of the **Front of Socialist Democracy and Unity** (*Frontul Democraţiei şi Unităţii Socialiste*—FDUS), which prepared the approved list of candidates for election to the Grand National Assembly and other bodies.

Following the rebellion of December 22, the new government of Ion Iliescu declared that the question of banning the PCR would be decided by a popular referendum on January 28, 1990. However, on January 19 the ruling National Salvation Front (*Frontul Salvării Naţionale*—FSN) announced that the decision to schedule the referendum had been "a political mistake," with the result that the party quickly ceased to exist as an organized force.

Eleven parties and alliances and 31 independent candidates participated in the November 2008 elections, a significant decrease from the nearly 50 parties that registered in 2004.

Government Parties:

Social Liberal Union (*Uniunea Social Liberală*—USL). In April 2008 the PSD and the PC announced the formation of a common parliamentary group and a "permanent" electoral alliance, the **Social Democratic Party + Conservative Party Alliance** (*Alianţa Politică Partidul Social Democrat + Partidul Conservator*—PSD+CP). In January 2011 the PC formed an additional alliance with the PNL, the **Center Right Alliance** (*Alianţa de Centru Dreapta*—ACD). In February 2011 the three parties clarified the relationship: the ACD and the PSD comprised the **Social-Liberal Union** (*Uniunea Social Liberală*—USL). The fall of the Urgureanu government in April 2012 brought the USL coalition into government. The USL emerged as the winner in the June 2012 local elections, obtaining 42 percent of town hall seats and 50 percent of county councils. In July 2012 the PSD and the UNPR announced formation of the **Center Left Alliance** (*Alianţa de Centru Strânga*—ACS), bringing the UNPR into the USL. In the December 2012 legislative elections, the USL secured 122 Senate with 60 percent of the vote, and 273 Chamber seats with 58.6 percent of the vote. In February 2014 the PNL withdrew from the coalition and moved to the opposition, fracturing the alliance. The PSD, PC, and UNPR competed in the June 2014 European Parliament election in an alliance, reviving the previously used name of **Social Democratic Union** (*Uniunea Social Democrată*—USD). The USD won 37.6 percent of the popular vote and 16 European Parliament seats.

Center Left Alliance (*Alianţa de Centru Strânga*—ACS). The PSD and UNPR announced an electoral alliance in July 2012, but before the December elections expanded this into a proposed merger between the two parties. Reportedly, tensions between the parties at the local level meant the merger has been indefinitely postponed.

Social Democratic Party (*Partidul Social Democrat*—PSD). The PSD was formally established on June 6, 2001, by merger of the **Social Democracy Party of Romania** (*Partidul Democraţiei Sociale din România*—PDSR) and the much smaller **Romanian Social Democratic Party** (*Partidul Social Democrat Român*—PSDR). The two had envisaged their eventual merger in a September 2000 electoral agreement establishing the three-party **Social Democratic Pole of Romania** (*Polul Democrat-Social din România*—PDSR) in partnership with the Humanist Party of Romania (now the PC, see below).

The PDSR had been formed as the "presidential" party on July 10, 1993, by the renaming of the Democratic National Salvation Front (FDSN) and its absorption of the **Romanian Socialist Democratic Party** (*Partidul Socialist Democrat Român*—PSDR), the **Cooperative Party** (*Partidul Cooperatist*—PC), and the **Republican Party** (*Partidul Republican*—PR). Less reform-oriented than their colleagues, a number of pro-Iliescu chamber deputies, had withdrawn from the FSN in March 1992 and registered as the FDSN in April. The new formation won a plurality of seats in both houses of Parliament in the September 1992 balloting and secured the reelection of Iliescu at the second-round presidential poll of October 11. The Socialist Democrats were a leftist formation that had once been closely allied with the FSN. A centrist party favoring free enterprise, the PR was formed in 1991 by merger of an existing Republican Party and the Social Liberal Party–20 May.

Having previously headed a minority government, the PDSR in August 1994 drew the right-wing PUNR (see Conservative Party, below) into a coalition that continued to attract external support from the Greater Romania Party (PRM) and the Socialist Labor Party (PSM). However, increasing strains resulted in all three withdrawing their support from the government between October 1995 and September 1996, after which the PDSR was technically reduced to minority status in the Chamber of Deputies. Hitherto identified as a nonparty technocrat, Prime Minister Nicolae Văcăroiu announced his adhesion to the PDSR in May 1996. In local elections the following month the PDSR saw its support decline, with former tennis champion Ilie NĂSTASE failing in a bid for the Bucharest mayoralty.

In the November 1996 balloting, Iliescu suffered a second-round defeat in his presidential reelection bid, while the PDSR fell to second place in the legislature (with 21.5 percent of the lower house vote) and went into opposition, whereupon Iliescu assumed the formal party leadership. As the party attempted to regroup in 1997, tensions emerged among the leadership. At the PDSR national conference in June reformers led by former foreign minister Teodor Meleşcanu criticized Iliescu for failing to dissociate the party from corrupt elements. After the conference Meleşcanu and others resigned from the PDSR and formed the Alliance for Romania (ApR; see PNL, below). In June 1999, however, the party agreed to absorb a PUNR splinter, the Alliance for Romanians' Unity Party (PAUR; see PC, below).

The left-of-center PSDR descended from the historic party founded in 1893 but was forced to merge with the Communist Party in 1948. Following its re-forming in late 1989, several competing groups claimed the inheritance, a court subsequently awarding the PSDR designation to the main faction, which had Socialist International recognition. Standing on the Democratic Convention of Romania (CDR) ticket in the 1992 balloting, the PSDR won 10 chamber seats and 1 in the Senate. While maintaining its links with some CDR parties for the November 1996 elections, the PSDR established a formal electoral alliance, the Social Democratic Union (*Uniunea Social Democrată*—USD), with the Democratic Party–National Salvation Front (see PD, below), winning 10 of the USD's 53 chamber seats and 1 of its 23 Senate seats. The USD subsequently agreed to join Victor Ciorbea's CDR-led coalition government.

In July 2000 the PSDR approved a merger with the **Socialist Party** (*Partidul Socialist*—PS), led by unsuccessful 1996 presidential candidate Tudor MOHORA, while on September 7 it not only agreed to an alliance with the opposition PDSR for the November elections, but to join the PDSR, after the elections, in forming the PSD. Accordingly, on September 8 it formally withdrew from the governing coalition. The agreement with the PDSR prompted longtime party leader Sergiu CUNESCU to resign, asserting that the PSDR had committed "self-enslavery" to an organization that was guilty of "confiscating the revolution" after 1990.

The Social Democratic Pole's 2000 presidential candidate, Ion Iliescu, finished first in the November 26 presidential contest, with 36.5 percent of the vote, and then defeated the Greater Romania Party's Vadim Tudor in the runoff on December 10, taking a 66.8 percent vote share. In the November legislative contests the alliance won 36.6 percent of the vote in the Chamber of Deputies, for a plurality of 155 seats, and 37 percent in the Senate, for a plurality of 65 seats. The minority government installed under Adrian Năstase on December 28 included one minister from the PSDR and one from PUR.

An extraordinary PDSR party conference held in January 2001 unanimously elected Prime Minister Năstase as chair, President Iliescu having resigned in accordance with a constitutional dictate. Upon formation of the PSD, Năstase remained chair.

In November 2001 the **Party of Moldovans** (*Partidul Moldovenilor*—PM) merged into the PSD. The PM had been organized by the mayor of Iaşi, Constantin SIMIRAD, as a vehicle for forging closer ties between Moldova and Romania. Despite discussions with the PNL in early 2000, the PM had chosen to join the CDR 2000 for the general election in November. In 2003 the PSD absorbed the **Socialist Labor Party** (*Partidul Socialist al Muncii*—PSM) and the **National Revival Socialist Party** (*Partidul Socialist al Renaşterii Naţionale*—PSRN).

The PSD participated in the 2004 UN alliance with PUR, securing a plurality of legislative seats. However, the PSD was forced into opposition when PUR and the UDMR agreed to join the ADA in a new coalition government. Adrian Năstase was narrowly defeated as the UN candidate in the 2004 presidential poll. He subsequently resigned from all party leadership posts in the wake of a corruption scandal.

Although still formally classified as an opposition party, the PSD agreed in April 2007 to support the new PNL/UDMR government in the legislature as necessary to ensure the coalition's continuation until the 2008 general elections. Although the PSD+PC won a plurality of votes in the November 2008 elections (33.1 percent in the Chamber of Deputies and 34.2 percent in the Senate), it received fewer seats (114 in the chamber, 49 in the Senate) than the PD-L. It therefore surrendered (albeit reluctantly) the lead in forming a new government to the PD-L. In December 2008 the PSD agreed to join a coalition government with the PD-L, stipulating that the new government not include the UDMR. On October 1, 2009, Interior Minister Dan Nica of the PSD was dismissed following his charge that fraud had been committed in the June European Parliamentary elections and that fraud was planned for the upcoming Romanian presidential elections. The PSD withdrew from the coalition in response to Nica's dismissal, leading to a lengthy cabinet crisis.

In the 2009 presidential elections the PSD nominated chair Mircea Geoană, who received 31.2 percent of the ballot (good for second place) in the first round and 49.7 percent in the second. (The results were challenged by the PSD as fraudulent.) In the wake of the defeat, a party congress in February 2010 replaced Geoană as chair with Victor Ponta.

As part of the USL in the December 2012 legislative elections, the PSD received 51 Senate seats and 149 Chamber seats.

Following allegations of corruption, Ponta resigned as party leader in July 2015, and then as prime minister in November. He was replaced as party leader by Liviu DRAGNEA, who had in turn been convicted of corruption in May 2015 and subsequently given a two-year suspended sentence.

Leaders: Liviu DRAGNEA (President), Mircea GEOANĂ (Former President of the Party and 2009 presidential candidate), Ion ILIESCU (Honorary President of the Party and Former President of Romania), Adrian NASTASE (Former Prime Minister), Ecaterina ANDRONESCU, Dan NICA.

National Union for the Progress of Romania (*Uniunea Naţională pentru Progresul României*—UNPR). Formed in March 2010 by members of parliament of the PSD and PNL that broke away to support President Băsescu, initially as independent deputies. The UNPR immediately joined the ruling coalition. In 2011 the UNPR absorbed the **National Initiative Party** (*Partidul Iniţiativa Naţională*—PIN), an offshoot of the PD. In 2012 the UNPR passed into the opposition, but following the June 2012 local elections, it formed an alliance with the PSD and shifted to support the government.

As part of the USL in the December 2012 legislative elections, the UNPR received five Senate seats and ten Chamber seats. In February 2016 the UNPR and the PSD agreed to cooperate in future local elections. However, in July reports indicated that the party had merged with the People's Movement Party (*Partidul Mişcarea Populară*—PMP) (see below).

Conservative Party (*Partidul Conservator*—PC). The PC is a successor to the **Humanist Party of Romania** (*Partidul Umanist din România*—PUR), which had been formed in the early 1990s and had subsequently called for adoption of a "third way" that rejected both doctrinaire socialism and "market fundamentalism." PUR allied with the PSD in 2000 as part of the Social Democratic Pole (see PSD, above, for details). As a result, it subsequently gained legislative seats and representation in the PSD-led cabinet.

For the 2004 legislative elections, PUR again presented joint lists with the PSD through the National Union (*Uniunea Naţională*—UN). However, following that balloting, PUR deserted the UN to join the new government led by the ADA.

In May 2005 PUR's national convention voted to adopt the PC rubric, although leaders stated that the change did not indicate a revision of what they now declared to be the party's long-standing devotion to conservative doctrine.

In February 2006 the PC merged with the **Romanian National Unity Party** (*Partidul Unității Naționale Române*—PUNR). The PUNR was organized in 1990 as the political arm of the nationalist Romanian Hearth (*Vatra Românească*). It ran fifth in the 1992 parliamentary balloting on a hard-right ticket, securing 30 Chamber and 14 Senate seats on an 8 percent vote share, and was eventually co-opted into the government coalition in August 1994. Problems with coalition partners and internal dissent with party leader Gheorghe FUNAR (the mayor of Cluj-Napoca in Transylvania) weakened the PUNR. Funar was expelled as party leader in 1997, only to launch the rival **Alliance for Romanians' Unity Party** (*Partidul Alianței pentru Unitatea Românilor*—PAUR), which subsequently joined the PDSR. (Funar himself would join the PRM.) (For additional information on the PUNR, see the 2008 *Handbook.*)

Gheorghe COPOS, a state minister (vice prime minister) in the ADA-led coalition government, resigned his cabinet post in June 2006 following his reported indictment on tax evasion charges. Although the PC, claiming ideological differences with the PNL, subsequently left the government, it continued to support the administration in the legislature on a case-by-case basis.

In April 2008 the PC announced a political alliance with the PSD, receiving four of the alliance's seats in the Chamber of Deputies and one in the Senate in the November elections. It did not, however, receive cabinet positions in the subsequent coalition government between the PD-L and PSD.

In January 2011 the PC formed an alliance with the PNL, the **Center Right Alliance** (*Alianța de Centru Dreapta*—ACD), within the broader framework of the USL.

As part of the USL in the December 2012 legislative elections, the PC received eight Senate seats and 13 Chamber seats. The party reportedly merged with the **Liberal Reformist Party** (*Partidul Liberal Reformator*—PLR) in June 2015 to create a new grouping, the **Alliance of Liberals and Democrats** (*Alianța Liberalilor și Democraților*—ALDE).

Leaders: Daniel CONSTANTIN (President), Dan VOICULESCU (Founding President).

Hungarian Democratic Union of Romania (*Uniunea Democrată a Maghiarilor din România*—UDMR/*Romániai Magyar Demokrata Szövetség*—RMDSz). Representing Romania's Hungarian minority, the newly organized UDMR placed second in the legislative poll of May 1990, winning 29 chamber and 12 Senate seats, despite a mere 7.2 percent vote share; it slipped to fifth in 1992 (with a slightly increased vote share), winning 27 chamber and 12 Senate seats.

Following the resignation of Géza DOMOKOS as UDMR president, the moderate Béla Marko was elected to the post in January 1993 after protestant bishop Lászlo TÖKÉS, a radical, had withdrawn his candidacy to accept appointment as honorary president. In mid-1995 the UDMR was rebuffed in efforts to establish political cooperation with other opposition parties, who claimed that it had become a party of extreme nationalism, favoring immediate local and regional autonomy for the Hungarian community. However, after the UDMR had won 25 chamber and 11 Senate seats in November 1996, it was accepted as a member of the CDR-led coalition government.

The UDMR's role in the coalition was frequently strained in subsequent years over Hungarian-language and minority education issues. The organization nevertheless remained part of the successor administrations of Radu Vasile and Mugur Isărescu. In the election of November 2000 it won 27 seats in the chamber and 12 in the Senate, while its presidential candidate, György FRUNDA, finished fifth, with 6.2 percent of the national vote. In late December the party extended its external support to the PDSR-led minority government of Prime Minister Năstase, which had indicated it would quickly move forward on legislation designed to permit wider use of ethnic languages in localities and to resolve the status of property confiscated during the Communist era.

In 2003 the UDMR suffered a setback when several dissident groups announced their "independence" to protest what they considered the "betrayal" of party principles through continued association with the PSD. Bishop Tökés resigned as the UDMR's honorary president at the 2003 party congress, and several splinter groups, the **Reformist Bloc** (*Blocul Reformist*—BR) and the **Hungarian Civic Union** (*Uniunea Civică Maghiară*—UCM), were formed at or subsequently to the congress.

The UDMR won 22 seats in the Chamber and 10 in the Senate in November 2004, and its decision to join the ADA-led coalition in December 2004 was considered crucial to the establishment of a legislative majority for the cabinet.

In the November 2007 European Parliament elections, Tökés won a seat running as an independent candidate. UDMR leaders accused Tökés of colluding with the PD-L to split the Hungarian vote.

The UDMR argued that the new electoral laws of 2008 would weaken the proportional voice of ethnic Hungarians in national elections. Despite these fears, the UDMR took 22 seats in the Chamber and 9 in the Senate in the November balloting. At the insistence of the PSD, the UDMR was excluded from the new ruling coalition, and the UDMR moved into the opposition for the first time since 1996. In the 2009 presidential elections the UDMR nominated Hunor Kelemen, who received 3.8 percent of the ballot in the first round. He supported the PSD's Geoană in the second round. Following the election, the UDMR successfully negotiated entry into a new PD-L–led government.

In May 2011 Tibor TORÓ led a faction of the party to form the **Hungarian People's Party in Transylvania** (*Partidul Popular Maghiar din Transilvania/Erdélyi Magyar Néppárt*—PPMT/EMN), campaigning for greater autonomy. It contested the December 2012 elections but failed to win any seats.

In the December 2012 legislative elections, the UDMR won 9 Senate seats with 5.3 percent of the vote, and 18 Chamber seats with 5.2 percent of the vote.

In the May 2014 European Parliament elections, the UDMR won two seats with 6.3 percent of the vote.

Following the collapse of the ruling government in early 2014, the UDMR joined a new PSD-led coalition in May 4. Kelemen was the UDMR candidate for the presidency in 2014. He received 3.5 percent of the vote.

Leaders: Hunor KELEMEN (Executive President and 2009 presidential candidate), László BORBÉLY (Vice President), Péter KOVÁCS (Secretary General), Béla MARKO (Former President of the Party and 2004 presidential candidate).

Opposition Parties:

Right Romania Alliance (*Alianța România Dreaptă*—ARD). An electoral alliance registered on September 15, 2013, that comprised the PD-L, PNȚCD, PNR, and the **Center-Right Civic Initiative** (*Inițiativa Civică de Centru-Dreapta*—ICCD), founded in July 2012 by Former Prime Minister Mihai Ungureanu. It later expanded to include the **Civic Force** (*Forța Civică*—FC). In the December 2012 elections, the alliance secured 24 Senate seats with 16.7 percent of the vote, and 56 Chamber seats with 16.5 percent of the vote.

Leader: Mihai Răzvan UNGUREANU.

Democratic-Liberal Party (*Partidul Democrat-Liberal*—PD-L). The PD-L was formed in January 2008 by the merger of the PD and the PLD. Although the PD and PLD had defined themselves as social-democratic parties, the PD-L has been described as a "populist" and centrist formation. The new party led the June 2008 local elections with 28 percent of the vote and took (barely) the leading role in parliament with 115 seats in the Chamber of Deputies and 51 in the Senate in the November national balloting. After the PD-L's initial discussions to form a coalition with the UDMR and PNL broke down over the latter's insistence on holding the position of prime minister, a collaboration protocol between the PD-L and PSD was signed instead in December 2008, despite significant tensions between the two parties and an anticipated clash in the upcoming presidential election between Băsescu and Mircea Geoană of the PSD. After the PSD withdrew from the cabinet in October 2009, the PD-L supported the reelection campaign of Băsescu, who received 32.4 percent of the vote in the first round of balloting on November 22, finishing first among the 12 candidates. Băsescu was credited with 50.3 percent of the vote in the runoff against Geoană on December 6.

The PD-L's poor showing in the June 2012 local elections (winning 13 percent of the vote to 51 percent for the USL) led to an extraordinary congress that replaced the senior leadership of the party.

As part of the ARD in the December 2012 legislative elections, the PD-L received 22 Senate seats and 52 Chamber seats.

In March 2013 a party congress reelected BLAGA despite significant opposition within the party. In July 2013 a faction of the party led by Eugen TOMAC and affiliated with Traian Băsescu broke away to form the People's Movement Party (*Partidul Miscarea Populara*—PMP, below).

In the May 2014 European Parliament election, the PD-L won five seats with 12.2 percent of the vote. This represents half the seats the party won in the 2009 election.

After several months of negotiations, in July 2014, a joint congress of the PD-L and PNL agreed to a merger of the two parties, reportedly to be completed by the end of the year, to continue under the PNL name.

Leaders: Vasile BLAGA (President), Catalin PREDOIUP, Anca BOAGIU, Dorin FLOREA, Liviu NEGOITA, Andreea PAUL (Senior Vice Presidents), Goerge FLUTUR (General Secretary).

Democratic Party (*Partidul Democrat*—PD). The PD was the direct descendant of the **National Salvation Front** (FSN), which was described as a "self-appointed" group that assumed governmental power following the overthrow of the Ceaușescu regime. Claiming initially to be a supraparty formation, the front reorganized as a party in February 1990 and, as such, swept the balloting of May 20. Ion Iliescu subsequently stepped down as FSN president to serve as head of state but later emerged as de facto leader of the Democratic National Salvation Front (FDSN), which opposed rapid economic reform.

At its first national convention held March 16–17, 1991, the FSN, despite criticism from the Iliescu faction, approved a free-market reform program titled "A Future for Romania" that was presented by Prime Minister Petre Roman, who replaced Iliescu as party president its second convention in March 1992. With the FDSN faction having separated from the FSN, the FSN ran a distant fourth in the national presidential poll of September 1992, Roman having declined to stand as its candidate; in the legislative balloting the FSN was limited to third place behind the FDSN and CDR, winning 10 percent of the vote.

In May 1993 the FSN reconstituted itself as the **Democratic Party–National Salvation Front** (*Partidul Democrat–Frontul Salvării Naționale*—PD-FSN), and in October 1994 it absorbed the **Democratic Party of Labor** (*Partidul Democrat al Muncii*—PDM). In February 1996 Roman accepted nomination as the PD-FSN candidate in the November presidential election, proclaiming his intention to stand on a social-democratic platform. For the accompanying legislative balloting the PD-FSN not only entered into the Social Democratic Union (USD) with the PSDR, but also sought to rally other proreform groupings under its banner. These efforts yielded third place for Roman in the presidential contest, while the PD-FSN won 43 chamber and 22 Senate seats in the legislative balloting.

As part of the Ciorbea government the PD, which had dropped the FSN designation, frequently tussled with the PNȚCD (below), particularly over the forced resignation in early 1998 of PD minister of transport Traian Băsescu, who had called for more rapid economic reform. The PD was at the center of governmental turmoil until Ciorbea's resignation in March 1998. The PD subsequently supported both the Vasile and Isărescu administrations, with Petre Roman becoming foreign minister in the latter.

In the November 2000 election the PD finished third, declining to 31 seats in the Chamber of Deputies and 13 in the Senate, and then moved into the opposition when the new Parliament convened. Among the successful senatorial candidates on the PD list was former prime minister Radu Vasile, who, having been expelled from the PNȚCD in early 2000, accepted an invitation to bring his supporters into Cornel BRAHAS's **Party of the Romanian Right** (*Partidul Dreapta Româneasca*—PDR). After overcoming a court challenge from opponents within the PDR, the expanded party then reregistered under Vasile's chairship as the **Romanian People's Party** (*Partidul Popular din România*—PPDR), which espoused authoritarianism, opposed multiculturalism, and described suspicion of foreigners as "a natural instinct."

Roman, who had finished the 2000 presidential race in sixth place with 3.0 percent of the vote, subsequently proposed establishing a center-right "Alternative 2004" of the PD, the Alliance for Romania (ApR), and the National Alliance (PUNR-PRN). However, at an extraordinary national convention the following May, he was replaced as chair by Traian Băsescu, recently elected as mayor of Bucharest. In 2003 Roman left to form the **Democratic Front of Romania Party** (*Partidul Frontul Democrat din România*—PFDR).

Between June and September 2001 the PD absorbed the National Alliance, formation of which had been announced in late July 2000 by the Romanian National Unity Party (PUNR) and the Romanian National Party (*Partidul Național Român*—PNR). In the November 2000 election the grouping—formally on the ballot as the **National Alliance Party** (*Partidul Alianța Națională* [PUNR-PNR])—won only 1.4 percent of the vote in each house, and in February 2001 the former PUNR leadership indicated its intention to reregister their organization as a separate entity.

The PNR had been founded in March 1998 by the merger of the **New Romania Party** (*Partidul "Noua Românie"*—PNR) of Ovidiu TRAZNEA and the **Agrarian Democratic Party of Romania** (*Partidul Democrat Agrar din România*—PDAR) of Mihai BERCA, with the **Christian Liberal Party** (*Partidul Liberal Creștin*—PLC) joining soon after. The PDAR, an agricultural workers' party launched in 1990 on a nationalist platform, later served as a governing partner of the PDSR, but it withdrew from the alliance in April 1994 in protest over a bill introducing an IMF-mandated land tax. For the 1996 presidential election the PDAR initially nominated Ion COJA, a literature professor and prominent anti-Semite who had temporarily broken with the PUNR. However, the PDAR ultimately joined the Humanist Party (PUR) and the Ecologist Movement (MER) in the unsuccessful National Union of the Center (UNC) alliance, which backed Ion Pop de POPA as its presidential candidate.

In September 1999 Viorel CATARAMĂ resigned as PNR chair, ostensibly to distance the party from a failed company that he had led. His interim replacement, Virgil MĂGUREANU, a former director of the Romanian intelligence service, was elected chair in February 2000. Catarama ultimately joined the ApR (which merged with the PNL in 2002), while Măgureanu led the PNR into the National Alliance, and then the alliance, minus the PUNR, into the PD.

Traian Băsescu, then mayor of Bucharest and chair of the PD, became the ADA's successful presidential candidate in 2004. He was succeeded as PD chair by Emil Boc, who in 2005 convinced the delegates at a PD national convention to adopt a platform favoring promarket economic policies, a shift to the center from its former left-leaning doctrine.

After the dissolution of the ADA coalition in the spring of 2007, the PD left the government and became an opposition party to the new PNL-led cabinet.

Democratic Liberal Party (*Partidul Liberal Democrat*—PLD). The PLD was formed by former prime minister Theodor Stolojan and other PNL dissenters in December 2006. It was reported that some 30 legislators had defected from the PNL to the PLD, along with approximately 11,500 PNL members. Stolojan, an aide to President Băsescu, attacked the PNL leaders as "oil tycoons," and pledged to cooperate with the PD in reviving the ADA's center-right principles. Dissidents from the PLD formed the People's Movement Party (*Partidul Mișcarea Populară*—PMP) (see below).

Civic Force (*Forța Civică*—FC). Founded in 2004 as the **Christian Party** (*Partidul Creștin*), it took its present name in 2008. It contested the 2009 European Parliament elections but failed to pass the threshold. During negotiations to join the ARD in 2012, it became a "political wing" for the ICCD (see ARD, above) and elected Mihai Ungureanu as party present on September 7.

As part of the ARD in the December 2012 legislative elections, the FC received one Senate seat and three Chamber seats.

Leaders: Mihai Răzvan UNGUREANU (President), Adrian IURAȘCU (First Vice President).

Christian and Democratic National Peasants' Party (*Partidul Național Țărănesc Creștin și Democrat*—PNȚCD). Founded in the prewar period and banned by the Communists, the National Peasants' Party under its veteran leader, Ion PUIU, refused to cooperate with the FSN because of the large number of former

Communist officials within its ranks. Prior to the 1990 election members of the "historic" PNŢ agreed to merge with a younger group of Christian Democrats as the PNŢCD, with the leadership going to Corneliu COPOSU, another party veteran, who had spent 17 years in jail during the Communist era.

The PNŢCD was one of the core components of the Democratic Convention of Romania (*Conventia Democrata Romana*—CDR), an anti-FSN alliance launched prior to the local elections of February 1992 as a successor to the eight-party Democratic Union (*Uniunea Democrata*—UD) that had been formed in 1990. Embracing some 18 parties and organizations, the CDR ran second to the FDSN (see PDSR) in the 1992 parliamentary balloting (winning a 20 percent vote share), while its nominee, Emil Constantinescu, was runner-up to Ion Iliescu in the presidential poll. The ethnic Hungarian UDMR was also affiliated, although it presented a separate list in the 1992 election.

The PNŢCD's Coposu died in November 1995 and was succeeded in January 1996 by Ion DIACONESCU, who defeated Vice President Ion RAŢIU for the post. In the November legislative balloting the promarket PNŢCD was returned as substantially the largest CDR component party, therefore providing the prime minister in the resultant CDR-led coalition government.

Constantinescu again ran for the presidency in 1996, pledging to accelerate the privatization program and encourage domestic and foreign investment in Romania's economy. His candidacy, which had been proposed by the PNŢCD, provoked some opposition within the CDR. Nevertheless, Constantinescu was a strong second in the presidential balloting in November and comfortably defeated President Iliescu in the runoff. In simultaneous legislative elections, the CDR won pluralities in both the Senate (53 seats) and the chamber (122 seats), with vote shares of 30.7 and 30.2 percent, respectively.

At the time, the center-right CDR included the PNŢCD, the National Liberal Party (PNL, below), the PNL–Democratic Convention (PNL-CD), **Romania's Alternative Party** (PAR), the Romanian Ecologist Party (PER), and the **Ecological Federation of Romania** (FER). In conjunction with the UDMR and the two-party Social Democratic Union (USD), the CDR formed a majority coalition under the PNŢCD's Victor Ciorbea. The CDR remained the core of the government under his successors, Radu Vasile of the PNŢCD and then Mugur Isărescu (nonparty), but by mid-2000 the PNL was preparing to contest the upcoming presidential and legislative elections on its own. PAR had already withdrawn in October 1998.

In April 1998 Victor Ciorbea was succeeded as prime minister by the PNŢCD's Radu Vasile, who was in turn replaced in December 1999 by an independent, Mugur Isărescu. The party subsequently decided to support Isărescu's presidential candidacy in 2000, although several members left in August in support of the PNL candidate, former prime minister Theodor Stolojan. Now known as the CDR 2000, the alliance was formally reconstituted on August 31, 2000, under a protocol signed by the PNŢCD, the **Union of Rightist Forces** (UFD, successor to PAR), and FER. Subsequently joining were Ciorbea's new Christian Democratic National Alliance (ANCD; see below), the **Traditional National Liberal Party** (PNL-T), and the Party of Moldovans (PM). (The PM ultimately merged into the PSD in November 2001.)

In the November 2000 general elections the CDR 2000 was wiped out, winning barely 5 percent of the vote in each house and, as a consequence, no seats. Prime Minister Isărescu, who had received the alliance's endorsement for president, finished fourth in the contest, with 9.5 percent of the vote.

The disastrous showing of the CDR 2000 and the PNŢCD in the November 2000 election led the party's entire leadership to resign, with an interim governing board under Constantin Dudu IONESCU being elected on December 2, pending a party congress in early 2001. At the January session the party elected as chair Andrei MARGA, who defeated Ionescu on a third ballot.

In April 1999 Ciorbea had led a faction out of the PNŢCD and formed the **Christian Democratic National Alliance** (*Alianţa Naţională Creştin-Democrată*—ANCD). With neither party having won parliamentary seats in November 2000, the ANCD rejoined the parent organization in March 2001. The reunification rapidly led to yet another fissure, however, with Marga resigning as chair and being replaced by Ciorbea in early July. The opposing factions subsequently held competing extraordinary congresses, with Ciorbea being confirmed as chair by the first, on August 14. The forces loyal to Marga held their congress August 17–19 and then, on October 20 established the Popular Christian Party (PPC).

Following a poor showing by the PNŢCD in the mid-2004 local elections, Ciorbea relinquished the party leadership to Gheorghe CIUHANDU, who had just been elected mayor of Timişoara. After another dismal performance in the December 2004 legislative poll (1.85 percent of the vote in the balloting for the Chamber of Deputies), it was reported in 2005 that the party was soliciting consolidation with other centrist parties. In June 2007 the party entered the Center-Right Poll alliance with the PNL and AP, subsequently electing Marian Petre Miluţ as chair. In view of the PNŢCD's poor standing in public opinion polls, the party supported the PNL's parliamentary list in the 2008 elections, but without a formal political alliance in which the PNŢCD would receive a proportion of the legislative seats. Instead, several party members (including Aurelian Pavelescu) ran as candidates on the PNL list. Party leadership defended this approach as providing time for reorganization of the party, but the agreement, as well as broader criticism of Miluţ's leadership, led to a revolt in 2009 by the regional party leadership in Cluj and Bucharest counties, including Radu SÂRBU and Gheorghe CIUHANDU, who threatened legal action to gain control over the national leadership. In June 2009 the PNŢCD participated in Romania's European Parliament elections but failed to win any seats. Party congresses were held by the rival factions in July and September 2010, respectively, electing as chairs Aurelian Pavelescu and Radu Sârbu, both of whom claimed legitimacy as the rightful leader of the party as legal action continued. Each faction held separate extraordinary congresses in June 2011, at which the Pavelescu faction elected a new leader, Vasile Lupu; the Sârbu faction elected Victor Ciorbea, who was recognized by court officials in September 2011 as the leader of the registered PNŢCD.

As part of the ARD in the December 2012 legislative elections, the PNŢCD received one Senate seat and one Chamber seat.

Divisions within the party continued into 2014, with the Lupu faction condemning the April 2013 congress, which elected Aurelian Pavelescu as party president. The party supported Elena UDREA of the PMP for the presidency in 2014.

Leaders: Aurelian PAVELESCU (President, contested), Vasile LUPU (President, contested), Radu SÂRBU.

National Liberal Party (*Partidul Naţional Liberal*—PNL). Founded in the mid-19th century but banned by the Communists in 1947, the PNL was reconstituted in 1990 as a right-of-center party that, in addition to supporting a free-market economy, endorsed resumption of the throne by the exiled King Mihai. A founding member of the Democratic Convention (*Convenţia Democrată Româna*—CDR), the PNL withdrew from the alliance in April 1992. Two splinter groups, the party's Youth Wing and the PNL–Democratic Convention (*Partidul Naţional Liberal–Convenţia Democrată*—PNL-CD), the latter led by Nicolae CERVENI, refused to endorse the action and remained affiliated with the CDR. Some of the youth wing members later helped form the Liberal Party 1993 (*Partidul Liberal 1993*—PL-93), although others, grouped as the New Liberal Party (*Noul Partid Liberal*—NPL), rejoined the PNL at a February 1993 PNL "unification" congress. Ironically, the 1993 congress ultimately led to formation of a third major splinter when the election of Mircea IONESCU-QUINTUS as chair was contested by his predecessor, Radu CÂMPEANU, who went on to form the **PNL-Câmpeanu** (PNL-C).

Having failed to win any seats in the Chamber of Deputies in September 1992, the PNL later reestablished a presence in that house through absorption in May 1995 of the PL-93's Political Liberal Group (*Grupul Politic Liberal*) and the Group for Liberal Unification (*Grupul pentru Unificarea Liberală*) of the Civic Alliance Party (*Partidul Alianţa Civică*—PAC), although chamber rules to inhibit floor crossing meant that the dozen or so PNL representatives were technically classified as independents. (PAC was an outgrowth of the still active **Civic Alliance** [*Alianţa Civică*—AC], which had been organized in November 1990 by a group of trade unionists and intellectuals to provide an extraparliamentary umbrella for post-Communist opposition groups, in partial emulation of East Germany's New Forum and Czechoslovakia's Civic Forum. At its second congress in July 1991 the AC had voted to establish PAC as its electoral affiliate under the leadership of literary critic Nicolae MANOLESCU. In the 1992 general election PAC had won 13 seats in the Chamber of Deputies and 7 in the Senate as a component of the CDR.)

The PNL rejoined the CDR in time for the November 1996 election and won 25 seats in the chamber and 17 in the Senate. The PNL-CD took 5 seats in the lower house and 4 in the upper, but the PL-93, having left the CDR in 1995, won no seats as part of the **National Liberal Alliance** (*Alianța Națională Liberală*—ANL), which it had formed with PAC.

In February 1997 PNL-CD dissidents, with unofficial support from the CDR, suspended Nicolae Cerveni as chair because of his efforts to join forces with liberals outside the CDR. In June Cerveni loyalists in the PNL-CD united with the PL-93 to form the Liberal Party (*Partidul Liberal*—PL), chaired by Cerveni. Subsequently, in February 1998 PAC merged with the PNL.

In March 1998 the PL and the PNL-Câmpeanu formed an umbrella group called the **Liberal Federation** (*Federația Liberală*—FL), but differences over the PL's relationship to the PNL and the CDR soon led to a bifurcation of the PL, with Cerveni heading one faction and Dinu PATRICIU, the former PL-93 chair, and his supporters constituting another. In May the Cerveni PL was renamed the **Romanian Liberal Democratic Party** (*Partidul Liberal Democrat Român*—PLDR), while in July 1999 the Patriciu PL was absorbed by the PNL. At the same time, the PNL-CD and PL-93 ceased to exist. In May 1999 Cerveni agreed to merge his party with the Romanian National Party (PNR; see PD, above), but differences soon emerged and Cerveni competed for the presidency in November 2000 as the candidate of the PLDR, finishing last among 12 contenders. Like the PLDR, the PNL-Câmpeanu, running independently, failed to win representation in either house in 2000.

As the 2000 general election approached, the PNL, increasingly dominated by Deputy Chair Valeriu STOICA, distanced itself from the CDR, and in June 2000 it offered its own candidates in local elections, placing fourth in terms of mayoral victories. When the party formally abandoned the CDR shortly thereafter, Stoica attempted to forge ties to the Alliance for Romania (*Alianța pentru România*—ApR), but many party members objected, Nicolae Manolescu being the most prominent member to resign as a consequence. In the 2000 presidential contest the PNL endorsed former prime minister Theodor Stolojan, but a group headed by Minister of Finance Decebal Traian REMEȘ, accusing the party of a leftward drift, denounced the selection and left to establish a new party that was registered in October as the **National Liberal Party–Traditional** (*Partidul Național Liberal–Tradițional*—PNL-T). At the November balloting Stolojan finished third, with 11.8 percent of the vote, while the party won 30 seats in the chamber and 13 in the Senate.

A party congress in February 2001 elected Stoica as PNL chair, the octogenarian Ionescu-Quintus having decided to step down. The following November, the ApR signed a merger agreement with the PNL, and the two united under the PNL rubric on January 19, 2002.

The ApR, a center-left party founded in August 1997, had been formed by reformers who had split off from the PDSR. Led by Teodor Meleșcanu, the ApR regarded itself as a "nonconfrontational" opposition party. It claimed 13 deputies in the chamber and 2 senators upon its formation, but in the November 2000 election it failed at the polls, taking only about 4 percent of the vote for each house. Meleșcanu finished seventh in the concurrent presidential balloting, with 1.9 percent of the vote. Prior to the election the ApR had discussed an alliance with the PNL, but the overtures fell through, in part because the PNL refused to accept the ApR leader as its presidential candidate. Because of the ApR's dismal electoral showing, the entire leadership stepped down in early December 2000. At a party conference in March 2001, however, Meleșcanu was returned to office, and the party redefined itself as "social-liberal" (center-right) in orientation. A social democratic (center-left) faction strongly opposed the redefinition, and subsequent efforts by Meleșcanu to negotiate an alliance with the Democratic Party (DP) failed to bear fruit. However, talks with the PNL proved more fruitful, and in 2002 the ApR merged with the PNL, Meleșcanu becoming vice president of the PNL.

With the goal of reuniting all the liberal factions under one banner, in April 2002 the PNL-C absorbed the PNL-T, led by Decebal Traian Remeș. In June the Cerveni wing of the liberal movement (the PLDR) also merged into the PNL-C. At that point, there were only two major liberal groupings—the PNL and the PNL-C. Final consolidation was achieved at the end of 2003 when the PNL-C merged into the PNL. Meanwhile, by that time the Union of Rightist Forces (*Uniunea Forțelor de Dreapta*—UFD) had also merged with the PNL. (See the 2000–2002 *Handbook* for additional information on the UFD.)

In November 2003 the PNL launched the Justice and Truth Alliance (*Alianța Dreptate și Adevăr*–ADA) with the PD (below), with the goal of presenting a strong opposition front to the PSD-led governing coalition. The ADA pledged to combat corruption, restore the independence of the judiciary, protect property rights, pursue EU membership, and adopt promarket economic reforms. PNL chair Theodor Stolojan resigned the party leadership and canceled plans to seek the ADA's presidential nomination due to health reasons, and the PNL supported the PD's Traian Băsescu, who was elected president in second-round balloting in December 2004. Subsequently, the ADA (which had finished second in the November legislative balloting to the PSD/PUR alliance) formed a coalition government with PUR and the UDMR, with new PNL leader Călin Popescu-Tăriceanu as prime minister.

The PNL and the PD presented separate candidate lists for the June 2004 local elections (except in Cluj and Bucharest, where joint lists were used). Analysts subsequently described the ADA as "walking a thin line" in representing the sometimes diverse aspirations of the PNL and PD while remaining sufficiently strong as an alliance. The PNL suffered severe factionalization in the second half of 2006 when a number of prominent members, including Stolojan, strongly criticized the policies and governing approach of Prime Minister Popescu-Tăriceanu. Stolojan and others were expelled from the PNL in October and subsequently formed the PLD, taking nearly 30 PNL legislators with them.

Although there had been talk of a formal merger of the PNL and the PD, the ADA collapsed in the spring of 2007 and the PD moved into opposition. In June 2007 the PNL announced the formation with the PNȚCD and the Popular Action (*Acțiunea Populară*—AP) of a new alliance called the Center-Right Pole (*Polul de Centru-Dreapta*), dedicated to representing the interests of the middle class and supporting liberal, Christian-democratic values. In 2008 the PNL formally absorbed the AP, which had been formed in mid-2003 by supporters of former president Emil Constantinescu, who was named chair of the new party even though he had announced his retirement from politics following his 2000 presidential defeat. Upon the AP's incorporation into the PNL, Constantinescu stated that the leadership and members of the AP would correct "false attitudes" within the PNL and strengthen the party's conservative wing.

Crin Antonescu assumed party leadership in March 2009 and was nominated for the 2009 presidential elections. He received 20 percent of the ballot in the first round and supported the PSD's Geoană in the second round.

On February 5, 2011, the PNL joined the PSD and the CP in a political alliance, the USL (above).

As part of the USL in the December 2012 legislative elections, the PNL received 51 Senate seats and 101 Chamber seats.

In February 2014 the PNL withdrew from USL and from the ruling coalition, entering the opposition. In response, a group of PNL parliamentarians, led by Călin Popescu-Tăriceanu, split from the party to found the **Liberal Reformist Party** (*Partidul Liberal Reformator*—PLR). The party moved further to the right in May 2014, when it was announced that the PNL would seek a merger with the PD-L.

In the May 2014 European Parliament election, the PNL won six seats with 15 percent of the popular vote.

In June 2014 a party congress elected Klaus Iohannis as party chair on a platform that pledged to oppose collaboration with the PSD.

On July 26 a joint congress of the PNL and PD-L reportedly approved a merger between the two parties, which would be named the PNL.

Party leader Iohannis was elected president in runoff polling on November 16, 2014. In December Alina GORGHIU became president of the party.

Leaders: Alina GORGHIU (President), Mircea IONESCU-QUINTUS (Honorary Chair), Rareș MĂNESCU (Secretary General), Crin ANTONESCU.

People's Party-Dan Diaconescu (*Partidul Poporului-Dan Diaconescu*—PP-DD). Founded in September 2011 by Dan DIACONESCU, owner of the former OTV television station. The PP-DD offered a populist slate that included raising pension levels, restructuring taxation, eliminating salaries for members of parliament and top government officials, and offering cash grants both to Romanians who start businesses and to emigrants who return to Romania.

In the December 2012 legislative elections, the PP-DD won 21 Senate seats with 14.6 percent of the vote, and 47 Chamber seats with 14 percent of the vote. By June 2013, however, over a fifth of the PP-DD's members of parliament (two senators and 16 deputies) had left to sit as independents or to join other parties;

OTV was shut down in January 2013 after failing to pay fines levied by state agencies for violations of broadcasting legislation. In December, Diaconescu was found guilty of blackmail and sentenced to three years in prison. Both acts weakened the party, which saw the further defections by its parliamentary delegation.

Leaders: Simona MAN (Chair), Dan DIACONESCU (Honorary President).

Ethnic Minority Legislative Parties:

Eighteen legislative seats are reserved for ethnic parties in Romania; following the 2012 legislative elections, the parties listed below secured representation.

Roma Party "Pro-Europe" (*Partida Romilor "Pro-Europa"*—PRPE). Representing Romania's substantial Roma (Gypsy) population, the Roma Party (*Partida Romilor*—PR) in March 1996 launched an electoral coalition with 11 other Roma groups with the aim of maximizing the impact of the Roma vote in the fall legislative elections. In 2000 the party won only 0.6 percent of the vote for the Chamber of Deputies but claimed one minority seat. The PR is frequently referred to under the rubric **Social Democratic Roma Party of Romania** (*Partida Romilor Social Democrată din România*—PRSDR).

Leaders: Nicolae PĂUN (President), Ivan GHEORGHE (Vice President).

Smaller parties include the **Association of Italians of Romania** (*Asociaţia Italienilor din România*—RO.AS.IT.), the **Association League of Albanians of Romania** (*Asociaţia Liga Albanezilor din România*—ALAR), the **Association of Macedonians of Romania** (*Asociaţia Macedonenilor din România*—AMR), the **Bulgarian Union of the Banat-Romania** (*Uniunea Bulgară din Banat-România*—UBBR), the **Cultural Union of Rusyns of Romania** (*Uniunea Culturală a Rutenilor din România*—UCRR), the **Democratic Forum of Germans in Romania** (*Forumul Democrat al Germanilor din România*—FDGR), the **Democratic Union of Slovaks and Czechs in Romania** (*Uniunea Democratică a Slovacilor şi Cehilor din România*—UDSCR), the **Democratic Union of Turco-Islamic Tatars of Romania** (*Uniunea Democrată a Tătarilor Turco-Musulmani din România*—UDTTMR), the **Federation of Jewish Communities of Romania** (*Federaţia Comunităţilor Evreieşti din România*—FCER), the **Greek Union of Romania** (*Uniunea Elenă din România*—UER), the **Lipovan Russian Community of Romania** (*Comunitatea Ruşilor Lipoveni din România*—CRLR), the **Turkish Democratic Union of Romania** (*Uniunea Democrată Turcă din România*—UDTR), the **Union of Armenians of Romania** (*Uniunea Armenilor din România*—UAR), the **Union of Croatians of Romania** (*Uniunea Croaţilor din România*—UCR), the **Union of Poles of Romania "Polish Home"** (*Uniunea Polonezilor din România "Dom Polski"*—UPR), the **Union of Serbs of Romania** (*Uniunea Sârbilor din România*—USR), and the **Union of Ukrainians of Romania** (*Uniunea Ucrainenilor din România*—UUR).

Other Parties Contesting the 2012 Legislative Elections:

Greater Romania Party (*Partidul România Mare*—PRM). The political wing of the extreme nationalist Greater Romania movement, the PRM won a 4 percent vote share in the 1992 legislative balloting. In a March 1993 speech, Corneliu Vadim Tudor praised Nicolae Ceauşescu as a Romanian patriot and portrayed his 1989 overthrow as an "armed attack" by Hungary and the former Soviet Union. From mid-1994 the PRM gave external support to the incumbent government coalition but terminated the arrangement in October 1995 amid much acrimony. Tudor was subsequently named as the PRM's candidate in the November 1996 presidential election, although by vote of the Senate in April he lost his parliamentary immunity and faced possible legal proceedings on over a dozen assorted accusations. Also in April a PRM congress adopted a "blitz strategy" to be followed if the party came to power, including the banning of the ethnic Hungarian UDMR, strict control of foreign investment, and confiscation of "illegally acquired" property.

In early September 1996 the PRM absorbed the small Romanian Party for a New Society (*Partidul Român pentru Noua Societate*—PRNS), led by Gen. Victor VOICHIŢA. It nevertheless managed only 4.5 percent of the lower house vote in the November election, for 19 chamber and 8 Senate seats. Tudor finished fifth in the presidential race, winning 4.7 percent of the vote.

In September 1997 Tudor canceled plans for an alliance with the PDSR, saying PDSR leader Ion Iliescu's unification effort was designed to return him as head of state. In February 1998 the PRM signed a protocol with Gheorghe Funar's wing of the PUNR, which envisioned the establishment of a Great Alliance for the Resurrection of the Fatherland. The alliance's agenda included a new government and outlawing of the UDMR. Subsequently, however, Funar and his supporters were forced from the PUNR, and he eventually joined the PRM leadership.

In early 1999 Tudor publicly supported the Jiu Valley miners' strike, but he subsequently expelled the miners' leader, Miron Cozma, from the PRM for bringing the party into "disrepute." Meanwhile, the Senate suspended Tudor for his having supported the strikers.

The November 2000 elections constituted a major advance for the PRM, which saw its legislative representation jump to 84 seats in the lower house and 37 in the upper, second only to the PDSR; the party's vote share of 19.5 percent in the chamber and 21 percent in the Senate was more than a fourfold increase over its 1996 results. In the presidential race, Tudor won 28.3 percent of the first-round vote and advanced to a runoff against the PDSR's Iliescu, who, with support from all the other leading parties, prevailed two-to-one over the PRM leader. During the campaign and afterward, Tudor showed no inclination to tone down his ultranationalist, anti-Hungarian, anti-Roma, anti-Semitic, populist rhetoric, asserting, for example, that Ceauşescu had been "one of the world's great statesmen" and that the IMF and the World Bank were blackmailing Romania, demanding poisonous policy changes in return for vitally needed loans and credits. In the following two years the party lost more than a dozen chamber deputies as well as other defectors dissatisfied with Tudor's authoritarian leadership and the party's far-right rhetoric. Principal benefactors were the joint PSD-PUR parliamentary faction (which picked up about a dozen seats), the new **Socialist Party of National Revival,** and the **Romanian Socialist Party.**

Prior to the 2004 elections Tudor expressed remorse for his past actions and recanted previous attacks on various minority groups. He subsequently finished third in the first round of presidential balloting in December, while the PRM secured 48 seats in the Chamber of Deputies.

In March 2005 Tudor issued a surprise announcement that he was stepping down as PRM leader in favor of Corneliu CIONTU, hitherto deputy chair. It was subsequently reported that the PRM had changed its name to the **Popular Greater Romania Party** (*Partidul Popular România Mare*—PPRM) and had adopted a more moderate centrist platform. Tudor returned to the forefront in June and convinced the party's National Council to rescind the name change, return him to his leadership post, and force Ciontu from the party. The PRM subsequently lost roughly half of its members to the PC. Its rump agreed in April 2007 to support the new PNL/UDMR minority government as needed in the legislature to maintain government stability.

In the 2008 legislative elections the PRM did not pass the threshold for legislative representation and failed to take any seats in the Chamber of Deputies or Senate for the first time since 1996. The defeat led to an unprecedented agreement with the PNG-CD (below) to combine electoral lists for the June 2009 balloting for Romanian delegates to the European Parliament, with Tudor taking one of the three seats won by the alliance.

In the 2009 presidential elections the PRM nominated Tudor, who received 5.6 percent of the ballot in the first round and called upon PRM members to boycott the second round.

In the December 2012 parliamentary elections, the PRM received 1.5 percent of the ballot in the Senate elections and 1.2 percent in the Chamber, failing to win any seats. Tudor subsequently blamed the defeat on the rise of the PP-DD, which he argued was a surrogate created by other parties to weaken the PRM.

A party congress in July 2013 voted to eject Tudor from the party and elected Gheorghe FUNAR as chair. Tudor contested the move and filed legal appeals in August to overturn the decision. Tudor was the party's presidential candidate in November 2014, winning 3.7 percent of the vote. Tudor died on September 14, 2015.

Leader: Emil STRAINU (Chair).

Romanian Ecologist Party (*Partidul Ecologist Român*—PER). The PER is an ecological group founded in 1978 in opposition to Socialist-era economic development. In 1989 it was registered as a political party with a substantially smaller membership than the **Ecologist Movement of Romania** (*Mişcarea Ecologistă din România*) with which it cooperated in 1992. Standing in its own right as a CDR party in 1996, it won five chamber seats and one in the Senate.

For the November 2000 parliamentary elections PER spearheaded formation of an alliance called the **Romanian Ecologist Pole** (*Polul Ecologist din România*) that also included the smaller **Green Alternative Party–Ecologists** (*Partidul Alternativa Verde–Ecologiştii*—PAVE) and the **Romanian Ecologist Convention Party** (*Partidul Convenţia Ecologistă din România*—PCER). The alliance offered a joint candidate list that polled less than 1 percent of the vote in each house. In early 2003 it was reported that the PER, PAVE, and PCER had merged under the PER rubric. In 2008 the PER created an electoral alliance with the Green Party to form the electoral alliance **Green Ecologist Party** (*Partidul Verde Ecologist*), which failed to reach the electoral threshold.

In the 2009 presidential elections the PER nominated Ovidiu Cristian Iane, who was credited with 0.2 percent of the vote in the first round.

In the December 2012 parliamentary elections, the PER received 0.8 percent of the ballot in the Senate elections and 0.5 percent in the Chamber, failing to win any seats. William BRINZĂ was the party's 2014 presidential candidate. He secured 0.5 percent of the vote.

Leaders: Dănuţ POP (President), Mircea COSEA (Honorary President), Ovidiu-Cristian IANE (2009 presidential candidate).

Other parties participating in the 2012 legislative balloting included the **People's Party** (*Partidul Popular*—PP); the **Socialist Alliance Party** (*Partidul Alianţa Socialistă*—PAS); **The Popular Party for Social Protection** (*Partidul Popular şi al Protecţiei Sociale*—PPPS), formerly the **Romanian Party of Pensioners** (*Partidul Pensionarilor din România*—PPR); and the **Christian Democratic National Party** (*Partidul Naţional Democrat Creştin*—PNDC).

Other Parties That Contested the 2008 Legislative Elections:

New Generation Party–Christian Democrat (*Partidul Noua Generaţie–Creştin Democrat*—PNG-CD). The New Generation Party (PNG) was launched in 2000 under the leadership of Virel LIS, the former mayor of Bucharest. However, Lis subsequently left the party, and the leadership mantle eventually passed to George Becali, the owner of a prominent soccer club. Campaigning on a center-right platform, Becali secured 1.8 percent of the vote in the first round of the December 2004 presidential balloting. In April 2006 the party changed its name to the PNG-CD.

The PNG-CD won less than 3 percent of the vote in the 2008 balloting for the Senate and Chamber of Deputies, failing to reach the electoral thresholds. Consequently, merger talks were launched with the PD-L in early 2009, but Becali's subsequent arrest on charges of kidnapping (allegedly, thieves who had earlier stolen his car) led to a cessation of the talks. Cooperation with the PRM in the 2009 European Parliament elections, in which Becali won a seat, reignited speculation of a merger of the two significant far-right parties.

In the 2009 presidential elections the PNG-CD nominated Becali, who received 1.9 percent of the ballot in the first round and supported the PSD's Geoană in the second round.

The PNG-CD contested the 2012 local elections but did not nominate candidates for the 2012 legislative elections. Becali reportedly attempted to negotiate a merger of the PNG-CD with the PNL in 2012. Although this was declined by the PNL, he joined the latter party and won a parliamentary seat. On May 29, 2013, however, he was found guilty of fraud and sentenced to three years, losing his parliamentary seat.

Leader: George BECALI (President).

Other Parties:

People's Movement Party (*Partidul Miscarea Populara*—PMP). Founded by supporters of Traian Băsescu after his break with the PD-L leadership in March 2013, the PMP was registered as a political party in June 2013. The PMP won two seats in the May 2014 European Parliament elections with 6.2 percent of the vote. Party leader Elena UDREA was the PMP candidate in the November 2014 elections. She received 5.2 percent of the vote. Udrea was arrested on suspicion of money laundering and hiding assets. The UNPR merged with the PMP in July 2016.

Leaders: Elena UDREA (Chair), Theodor PALEOLOGU, Emil BOC (Former Prime Minister), Elena BĂSESCU.

LEGISLATURE

The present Romanian legislature is a bicameral **Parliament** (*Parlament*) consisting of a Senate and a Chamber of Deputies, each with a four-year term. Elections from 1990 to 2004 were conducted via proportional representation on the basis of party lists. However, a complicated (and confusing to most analysts) system (combining majoritarian and proportional elements) was adopted by Parliament in March 2008, and then further modified in July 2012.

Voters now cast a single ballot for candidates within 311 single-member districts ("colleges") for the Chamber of Deputies and 135 for the Senate, these districts distributed across the 41 counties, Bucharest and a special district for nonresident Romanians. Candidates who receive more than 50 percent of the vote in a district are elected automatically. The remaining seats (including the supplemental seats) are distributed proportionately to parties that achieve the necessary threshold for representation (5 percent of the total national vote for single parties, 8 percent for two-party alliances, 9 percent for three-party alliances, and 10 percent for alliances of four or more parties), first within the 43 electoral counties and then at the national level. Additional seats can then be added to ensure the proportional representation of coalitions and parties; in December 2012 an additional 97 deputy and 39 Senate seats were thus created.

A national referendum on November 22, 2009, had endorsed a proposal from President Băsescu to combine the two houses of Parliament into a 300-seat unicameral legislature. However, further legislation has not been enacted to make the change.

Senate (*Senat*). The upper house currently comprises 176 members elected from 135 districts (two single-seat districts are reserved for nonresident Romanians), with 39 "supplementary" seats added to ensure proportional representation.

Following the elections of December 9, 2012, the alliance of the Social Liberal Union won 122 seats (Social Democratic Party, 58; National Liberal Party, 51; Conservative Party, 8; and National Union for the Progress of Romania, 5); Right Romania Alliance, 24 (Democratic Liberal Party, 22; Civil Force, 1; and Christian-Democratic National Peasants' Party, 1); People's Party-Dan Diaconescu, 21; and the Hungarian Democratic Union of Romania, 9.

Chair: Călin POPESCU-TĂRICEANU.

Chamber of Deputies (*Camera Deputaţilor*). The lower house currently comprises 412 members elected from 315 districts (4 single-seat districts are reserved for nonresident Romanians), with 79 seats added to ensure proportional representation. Organizations representing the following 18 ethnic communities are also given seats (assuming that no members of the ethnic community had otherwise been elected): Albanians, Armenians, Bulgarians, Croats, Czechs and Slovaks, Germans, Greeks, Italians, Jews, Lipovan Russians, Poles, Roma, Ruthenians, Serbs, Slav Macedonians, Turko-Muslim Tatars, Turks, and Ukrainians. Voting for the minority seats is via nationwide balloting for each ethnic community, the party securing a plurality of votes for each community claiming that community's seat.

Following the elections of December 9, 2012, the alliance of the Social Liberal Union won 273 seats (Social Democratic Party, 149; National Liberal Party, 101; Conservative Party, 13; and National Union for the Progress of Romania, 10); Right Romania Alliance, 56 (Democratic Liberal Party, 52; Civil Force, 3; and Christian-Democratic National Peasants' Party, 1); the People's Party-Dan Diaconescu, 47; and Hungarian Democratic Union of Romania, 18.

Chair: Florin IORDACHE (Acting).

CABINET

[as of November 27, 2016]

Prime Minister	Dacian Cioloş (ind.)
Vice Prime Minister	Costin Borc
Vice Prime Minister	Vasile Dîncu
Ministers	
Agriculture and Rural Development	Achim Irimescu
Culture	Corina Şuteu [f]
Economy, Commerce, and Tourism	Costain Borc
Education and Scientific Research	Mircea Dumitru
Energy	Victor Vlad Grigorsecu
Environment, Water, and Forests	Cristina Paşca Palmer [f]
European Funds	Dragoş Cristian Dinu
Foreign Affairs	Lazăr Comănescu
Health	Vlad Voiculescu
Information Society and Communications	Delia Popescu [f]
Internal Affairs	Ioan Dragoş Tudorache
Justice	Raluca Alexandra Prună [f]
Labor, Family, Social Protection, and Elderly	Dragoş Nicolae Pîslaru
National Defense	Mihnea Ioan Motoc
Prime Minister's Office	Paul Gheorghiu
Public Consultation and Civic Dialogue	Victoria-Violeta Alexandru [f]
Public Finance	Anca Dana Dragu [f]
Regional Development and Public Administration	Vasile Dîncu
Transport	Petru Sorin Buşe
Youth and Sports	Elisabeta Lipă [f]
Ministers Delegate	
Parliament Liaison	Ciprian Bucur
Romanians Abroad and Liaison with Moldova	Maria Ligor [f]

[f] = female

INTERGOVERNMENTAL REPRESENTATION

Ambassador to the U.S.: George Cristian MAIOR.

U.S. Ambassador to Romania: Hans G. KLEMM.

Permanent Representative to the UN: Ion JINGA.

IGO Memberships (Non-UN): CEUR, EBRD, EIB, ICC, IOM, NATO, OSCE, WTO.

For Further Reference:

Abraham, Florin. *Romania since the Second World War: A Political, Social, and Economic History.* New York: Bloomsbury, 2017.

Kaplan, Robert. *In Europe's Shadow: Two Cold Wars and a Thirty-Year Journey through Romania and Beyond.* New York: Random House, 2016.

Moscovici, Claudia. *Velvet Totalitarianism: Post-Stalinist Romania.* Lanham, MD: University Press of America, 2009.

RUSSIA

Russian Federation/Russia
Rossiiskaya Federatsiya/Rossiya

Political Status: Formerly the Russian Soviet Federative Socialist Republic (RSFSR), a constituent republic of the Union of Soviet Socialist Republics (USSR); present official designations adopted on April 17, 1992; current constitution approved by referendum of December 12, 1993.

Area: 6,592,800 sq. mi. (17,075,400 sq. km).

Population: 143,440,000 (2016E—UN); 142,355,415 (2016E—U.S. Census).

Major Urban Centers (2016E—UN): MOSCOW (12,260,000), St. Petersburg (formerly Leningrad, 5,001,000), Novosibirsk (1,498,000), Yekaterinburg (formerly Sverdlovsk, 1,381,000), Nizhny Novgorod (formerly Gorky, 1,200,000), Samara (formerly Kuibyshev, 1,162,000), Omsk (1,161,000), Chelyabinsk (1,160,000), Kazan (1,096,000), Rostov-na-Donu (1,095,000), Ufa (1,069,000), Volgograd (1,020,000), Krasnoyarsk (1,013,000).

Official Languages: Russian, in addition to languages recognized by the constituent republics and autonomous areas.

Monetary Unit: Ruble (official rate October 1, 2016: 62.88 rubles = $1US).

President: Vladimir PUTIN (United Russia); elected on March 4, 2012, and inaugurated for a four-year term on May 7, succeeding Dmitri MEDVEDEV (United Russia).

Chair of the Government (Prime Minister): Dmitri MEDVEDEV (United Russia); nominated by the president on May 7, 2012, and approved by the State Duma on May 8 to succeed Vladimir PUTIN.

THE COUNTRY

The world's largest country, with more than three-quarters of the former Soviet Union's land mass (though little more than half of its population), the Russian Federation stretches for more than 5,000 miles from the Baltic Sea in the west to the Pacific Ocean in the east. Its contiguous neighbors lie along an arc that encompasses Norway and Finland in the northwest; Estonia, Latvia, Lithuania, Poland, and Belarus in the west; Ukraine in the southwest; and Georgia, Azerbaijan, Kazakhstan, Mongolia, China, and North Korea in the south. Although there are upward of 100 nationalities, approximately 80 percent of the population is Russian. There are also many millions of ethnic Russians living in the "near abroad" of the other ex-Soviet republics. Women make up about 49 percent of the active labor force but remain underrepresented in government. Following legislative elections on September 18, 2016, women held 57 seats in the Duma (12.7 percent).

Russia possesses a highly diversified economy, including major manufacturing centers in the northwestern, central European, and Ural mountain regions; substantial hydroelectric capacity in the Volga River basin and Siberia; and widespread reserves of oil, natural gas, coal, gold, industrial diamonds, and other minerals.

Following the collapse of the Soviet Union in 1991, a commitment to radical economic reform became the centerpiece of Russian government policy, including price liberalization, currency convertibility, privatization, and encouragement of foreign investment. However, the rapid change to a free market system over nearly a decade led to economic collapse, forcing millions into poverty. Annual gross domestic product (GDP) contracted an average of nearly 14 percent between 1992 and 1995, and the inflation rate soared to 1,350 percent in 1992 before easing to 131 percent in 1995. Meanwhile, due to a currency crisis in October 1994, the ruble was valued at around 4,000 to the U.S. dollar (compared with an official one-to-one rate five years earlier), with further depreciation taking the rate above 5,500 by late 1996. Corruption was rampant, and billions in cash and other assets were reportedly taken out of the country.

The economy began to recover in 1997 as GDP increased by 0.4 percent, and currency reform at the end of the year led to a revaluation of the ruble (about 6 rubles to 1 U.S. dollar).

In August 1998 the economy was severely weakened due to low oil prices globally, a continuing East Asian financial crisis, and Russia's unmanageable debt. The ruble lost 70 percent of its value by the first quarter of 1999. In late April 1999 the International Monetary Fund (IMF), which had suspended loan disbursements to Russia the previous August, agreed to provide $4.5 billion to cover part of the country's massive debt servicing. Annual growth of 5.4 percent was recorded,

owing in large part to progress in the country's conversion to a market economy.

From 2000 to 2007 annual average GDP growth was a robust 7.2 percent, due in large part to a boom in world oil prices and the increased competitiveness of the ruble. Inflation remained in double digits.

The 2008 global financial crisis, including a steep decline in oil prices, contributed significantly to the Russian economic crisis of 2008–2009. Other contributing factors included a decrease in exports, the republic's weak banking system, mortgage defaults and a credit crisis, and the flight of many foreign investors as a result of the fighting in Georgia. (For details, see the 2011 *Handbook.*) Subsequently, in 2009 the Russian economy experienced its steepest decline in 15 years, with annual GDP contracting 7.8 percent from the 5.2 percent recorded in 2008. Double-digit declines were registered in the manufacturing, construction, and tourism sectors. To combat the contraction, the government initiated a large stimulus program and cut interest rates ten times. The approach was considered effective for the most part. However, the unemployment rate in 2009 averaged 8.4 percent, and the inflation rate was 11.7 percent.

Increased domestic spending and investment helped achieve restored economic growth, with annual GDP growth of 4.1 percent over 2010–2012. Inflation slowed to 6.9 percent in 2010, slowing further to 5.1 percent in 2012. The IMF emphasized that the country's high commodity prices created "an opportunity to embark on bold and decisive reforms" and urged authorities to implement measures to create a more favorable climate for investment and economic diversification. GDP growth slowed to 1.3 percent in 2013. The GDP growth in 2014 was a mere 0.8 percent, although following the 2014 crisis in Ukraine, the Russian Economic Ministry had forecasted slower levels of growth due in part to Western economic sanctions (see Current issues, below). In 2015 the GDP fell 3.8 percent, and the IMF estimated that in 2016 the GDP fell a further 1.8 percent. In 2016 inflation was 8.4 percent, while unemployment was 6.5 percent, and GDP per capita was $7,743. In its annual ease of conducting business survey, the World Bank ranked Russia 51st out of 189 countries, a decline from 40th in 2013, mainly as the result of growing corruption and government inefficiency.

GOVERNMENT AND POLITICS

Political background. Russia's early national history was that of a series of small medieval fiefs that gradually united under the leadership of the grand dukes of Moscow in the 15th and 16th centuries, expanding into a vast but unstable empire that collapsed midway through World War I. Military defeat and rising social unrest resulting from that conflict led directly to the "February" Revolution of 1917, which resulted in the abdication of Tsar NICHOLAS II (March 15, 1917, by the Western calendar), and the formation of a provisional government whose best-remembered leader was Aleksandr F. KERENSKY. Unable to cope with the country's mounting social, political, economic, and military problems, the provisional government was forcibly overthrown in the "October" Revolution of November 7, 1917, by the Bolshevik wing of the Russian Social Democratic Party under Vladimir Ilyich LENIN. The new Soviet regime—so called because it based its power on the support of newly formed workers,' peasants,' and soldiers' councils, or "soviets"—proceeded under Lenin's guidance to proclaim a dictatorship of the proletariat; to nationalize land, means of production, banks, and railroads; and to establish on July 10, 1918, a socialist state known as the Russian Soviet Federative Socialist Republic (RSFSR).

Draconian peace terms imposed by the Central Powers under the Brest-Litovsk Treaty of March 3, 1918, were invalidated by that alliance's eventual defeat in the west, but civil war between the Bolsheviks and the Whites, compounded by foreign intervention in Russia, lasted until 1922. Other Soviet Republics that had meanwhile been established in Ukraine, Byelorussia, and Transcaucasia joined with the RSFSR by treaty in 1922 to establish the Union of Soviet Socialist Republics (USSR), whose first constitution was adopted on July 6, 1923. The Central Asian territories of Turkmenistan and Uzbekistan became constituent republics in 1925, followed by Tajikistan in 1929 and Kazakhstan and Kyrgyzstan in 1936, at which time dissolution of the Transcaucasian SSR yielded separate union status for Armenia, Azerbaijan, and Georgia. The Estonian, Latvian, Lithuanian, and Moldavian SSRs were formally proclaimed in 1940.

Lenin's death in 1924 had been followed by struggles within the leadership of the ruling Communist Party before Joseph Vissarionovich STALIN emerged in the later 1920s as the unchallenged dictator of the party and country. There followed an era characterized by extremes: forced industrialization that began with the First Five-Year Plan in 1928; all-out collectivization in agriculture commencing 1929–1930; and far-reaching political and military purges from 1936 to 1938. The conclusion in August 1939, on the eve of World War II, of a ten-year nonaggression pact with Nazi Germany enabled Soviet military power to expand Soviet frontiers at the expense of Poland, Finland, Romania, and the Baltic states of Estonia, Latvia, and Lithuania. Nazi–Soviet collaboration came to an abrupt end when German forces attacked the USSR on June 22, 1941. The subsequent years of heavy fighting, which cost the USSR an estimated 20 million lives and left widespread devastation in European Russia, eliminated the military power of Germany and ultimately enabled the USSR to extend its influence into the heart of Europe.

Stalin's death in March 1953 initiated a new period of political maneuvering among his successors. The post of chair of the Council of Ministers, held successively by Georgy M. MALENKOV (1953–1955) and Nikolai A. BULGANIN (1955–1958), was assumed in March 1958 by Nikita S. KHRUSHCHEV, who had become first secretary of the Soviet Communist Party in September 1953. Khrushchev's denunciation of Stalin's despotism at the 20th Communist Party of the Soviet Union (CPSU) Congress in February 1956 gave impetus to a policy of "de-Stalinization" in the USSR and Eastern Europe, while emphasis in Soviet foreign policy shifted from military confrontation to "competitive coexistence," symbolized by a growing foreign aid program and by such achievements as the launching of the world's first artificial satellite, *Sputnik,* in 1957. Khrushchev's policies nevertheless contributed to a series of sharp crises within and beyond the Communist world. An incipient liberalization movement in Hungary was crushed by Soviet armed forces in 1956, relations with Communist China deteriorated, and recurrent challenges to the West culminated in a defeat for Soviet aims in the confrontation with the United States over Soviet missiles in Cuba in October 1962.

Khrushchev's erratic performance resulted in his dismissal in October 1964 and the substitution of collective rule, under which Leonid I. BREZHNEV became head of the CPSU and Aleksei N. KOSYGIN became chair of the Council of Ministers. In 1965 Nikolai V. PODGORNY succeeded Anastas I. MIKOYAN as chair of the Presidium of the Supreme Soviet and thereby as nominal head of state, while Brezhnev clearly emerged from the 24th party congress in 1971 as first among equals. His position as CPSU general secretary was reconfirmed at the 25th and 26th congresses in 1976 and 1981. In June 1977 the Supreme Soviet designated Secretary Brezhnev to succeed Podgorny as chair of the Presidium.

In October 1980 Kosygin asked to be relieved of his duties as chair of the Council of Ministers because of declining health, and he was replaced by First Deputy Chair Nikolai TIKHONOV. Of more far-reaching consequence was the death of Brezhnev in November 1982 and his replacement as party secretary by Yuri V. ANDROPOV, who had previously served as head of the KGB, the Soviet intelligence and internal security agency. Andropov was named chair of the Presidium in June 1983 but died in February 1984. He was succeeded as CPSU general secretary and, two months later, as head of state by Konstantin Y. CHERNENKO.

Long reputed to be in failing health and widely viewed as having been elevated to the top leadership on a "caretaker" basis, Chernenko died in March 1985. As evidence that the succession had already been agreed upon, the relatively young (54-year-old) Mikhail S. GORBACHEV was named general secretary on the following day. The Presidium chairship remained temporarily vacant.

During the ensuing four years, wide-ranging personnel changes occurred in both the party and the government. In July 1985 the long-time foreign minister, Andrei A. GROMYKO, was named Presidium chair, while Nikolai I. RYZHKOV replaced the aging Tikhonov as chair of the Council of Ministers in September. In October 1988 Secretary Gorbachev was elected to the additional post of Presidium chair, with Gromyko moving into retirement. Two months later extensive constitutional revisions introduced a new parliamentary system, competitive elections, heightened judicial independence, and other changes in keeping with Gorbachev's policies of openness (glasnost), restructuring (perestroika), and greater democracy.

In May 1989 a new, supra-legislative Congress of People's Deputies elected Gorbachev to a five-year term as chair of a restructured Supreme Soviet, with Anatoly I. LUKYANOV (vice chair of the Presidium since October) redesignated as Gorbachev's deputy. Following further constitutional amendments in December 1989 and March 1990 that sanctioned a multiparty system, increased the scope of direct elections, and broadened the rights of private property and enterprise, the Congress named Gorbachev in March 1990 to the new post of Union president. Concurrently, it elected Lukyanov chair of the Supreme Soviet.

In June 1990 the Russian Federation issued a declaration asserting the primacy of the RSFSR constitution within its territorial limits. The document also asserted a right to engage in foreign relations and "freely leave the USSR" in accordance with procedures set forth in Union law. Earlier, on the basis of constitutional reforms approved at the Union level in 1988, the Russian Federation had emulated the central USSR administration by establishing a two-tiered legislative system consisting of a Congress of People's Deputies and a bicameral Supreme Soviet elected by the Congress. On May 29, 1990, the 1,068 Congress deputies, who had been elected in competitive balloting on March 4, elected Boris YELTSIN as chair of the RSFSR Supreme Soviet, and hence, de facto president of the federation.

On July 20, 1990, Yeltsin announced a "500-day" drive toward a market economy within the federation, which subsequently became the core of an all-Union plan that secured approval in weakened form three months later. In mid-November, following a meeting with USSR President Gorbachev, Yeltsin called for a central "coalition government of national unity" as a prelude to further Union negotiations.

During the fall and winter of 1990–1991 conservative forces (principally elements of the administrative and Communist Party bureaucracies, the army, the interior police, and the KGB) ranged themselves against Gorbachev's pluralist measures. For a time, the Soviet leader appeared to offer little resistance to the backlash, but a six-month lapse into authoritarianism ended dramatically in April 1991 with a much-heralded "nine-plus-one" conference, at which the participating republics (with Armenia, Georgia, Moldova, and the Baltic states not attending) endorsed a new Union Treaty that called for extensive decentralization in social, political, and economic spheres. Under the plan, a new constitution would be drafted for a "Union of Soviet Sovereign Republics."

At a nonbinding referendum on the draft of the Union Treaty on March 17, 1991, RSFSR voters had registered 71.3 percent approval, with 69.9 percent also endorsing the creation of a directly elected RSFSR presidency. On April 5 the republican Congress voted to create the office, and on June 12 Yeltsin defeated five other candidates, including former Soviet ministerial chair Nikolai Ryzhkov, for the presidency, with Aleksandr RUTSKOI elected vice president.

During the week of August 19, 1991, a self-proclaimed State Committee for the State of Emergency (SCSE), led by Soviet Vice President Gennadi YANAYEV, responded to Gorbachev's reforms and the new Union proposal by launching an attempted coup. With RSFSR President Yeltsin in the forefront of the opposition, the coup quickly failed and USSR President Gorbachev resumed constitutional authority. By the end of the month, however, most of the republican parties had renounced the authority of the CPSU, Ukraine had declared its independence, and Yeltsin had called upon Gorbachev to recognize the independence of Estonia, Latvia, and Lithuania.

On September 6, 1991, Moscow accepted the withdrawal of the Baltic states. The remaining 12 republics, during a meeting at Alma-Ata (Almaty), Kazakhstan, held October 1–2, endorsed a plan for what Gorbachev characterized as a union of "confederal democratic states." However, in a referendum on December 1 Ukrainians overwhelmingly endorsed complete independence, and one week later in Brest, Belarus, both Russia and Belarus joined Ukraine in proclaiming the demise of the Soviet Union. On December 21 Russia and 10 of its sister republics (with Georgia not participating) proclaimed the formation of the Commonwealth of Independent States (CIS—see entry under Intergovernmental Organizations), and four days later Gorbachev, the last president of the USSR, resigned.

Meanwhile, in mid-July 1991 the RSFSR Congress of People's Deputies had encountered an impasse over the selection of Yeltsin's successor as chair of the Russian Supreme Soviet. When no candidate managed to muster a majority in six rounds of voting, the former deputy chair, Ruslan KHASBULATOV, who had been accused of an excessively authoritarian leadership style, was named acting chair. Two months later a dispute broke out in the Supreme Soviet over an attempt by the president to augment his executive powers, and on September 27 Ivan SILAYEV resigned as chair of the Council of Ministers. In late October Khasbulatov was confirmed as Supreme Soviet chair and Yeltsin personally took over Silayev's responsibilities, while continuing to press for enhanced capacity to move forward with his economic reforms. On November 1 the added powers were approved, as was authority to suspend the actions of the presidents of the autonomous republics within the RSFSR. On November 6 Yeltsin was formally invested as chair of the Council of Ministers. On the same day he issued a decree banning both the Union and the republican Communist parties and nationalizing their assets.

The abolition of most price controls and other "shock therapy" economic measures in 1992 intensified a clash between ministers and legislators, with Khasbulatov warning that the federation could encounter "a catastrophic decline in living standards, famine [and] social upheaval." The cabinet responded by submitting its resignation on April 12, with members withdrawing en masse from the Congress of People's Deputies. In the end, after defeating a proposal by Khasbulatov that would have stripped the president of most of his powers, the deputies adopted a declaration that permitted a resumption of governmental activity, with an architect of the Yeltsin reform program, Finance Minister Yegor GAIDAR, being named acting chair of the Council of Ministers on June 15. Yeltsin's victory was, however, less than total. He failed in a bid to further augment his executive powers and was precluded from effectively moving on land reform, most notably in regard to privatization.

During the final months of 1992 Yeltsin was forced into an increasingly defensive posture on domestic policy. In December Yeltsin was obliged to abandon Gaidar, his leading reform advocate, and accept as prime minister Viktor S. CHERNOMYRDIN, previously in charge of the state fuel-energy complex. In early 1993 the contest between Yeltsin and Khasbulatov intensified, with the former campaigning for an April referendum on major provisions of a new constitution and the latter calling for early parliamentary and presidential elections in 1994. On March 28, 1993, during an emergency Ninth Congress, a motion to dismiss Yeltsin secured a substantial majority, but not the two-thirds required for implementation; a similar motion to dismiss Khasbulatov, which required only a simple majority, also failed. The Congress then proceeded to authorize an April 25 referendum at which the voters simultaneously voiced support for Yeltsin and his socioeconomic policies as well as for early legislative elections. (See the 2013 *Handbook* for details of this phase of the conflict between Yeltsin and Khasbulatov.)

Two days before the referendum Yeltsin had unveiled his draft constitution, which called for a strong presidency, a bicameral legislature, and an independent judiciary. Not unexpectedly, the document was rejected on May 7, 1993, by the Supreme Soviet's Constitutional Commission, which preferred a parliament with expanded powers, including the capacity to reject government appointments. Undaunted, the president on June 5 convened a 700-member constitutional conference, which approved his draft on July 12.

Yeltsin's renewed ascendancy was demonstrated on September 16, 1993, by the reappointment of Gaidar as deputy prime minister and economics minister. Moreover, in actions that were immediately repudiated by the Constitutional Court, the president on September 21 issued a decree on constitutional reform, suspended both the Congress of People's Deputies and the Supreme Soviet, called for the election of a new bicameral legislature on December 11–12, and announced that presidential balloting would take place on June 12, 1994. The Congress, assembling in an emergency session, responded by voting to impeach the president and named the conservative Rutskoi, whom Yeltsin had suspended as vice president on September 1, as his successor.

Yeltsin thereupon mounted a series of measures against his legislative opponents that culminated in the House of Soviets ("White House") being sealed off by some 2,000 troops on September 27, 1993. A number of armed clashes followed, with the anti-Yeltsin leaders surrendering on the evening of October 4 after government forces had stormed the building. Overall, the fighting cost some 140 lives, while several hundred people were injured. As the power struggle drew to a close, Yeltsin announced that the December 12 elections would be augmented to include a referendum on the new constitution. However, the proposal for an early presidential election was abandoned.

In polling on December 12, 1993, for the State Duma, the lower house of the new Federal Assembly, the pro-reform Russia's Choice list won a plurality of seats but was strongly challenged by both right-wing and left-wing opponents. At the same time, 58.4 percent of participating voters approved the new constitution. The most startling success was that of the neofascist Liberal Democratic Party of Russia (*Liberalno-Demokraticheskaya Partiya Rossii*—LDPR), led by Vladimir ZHIRINOVSKY, which secured the largest share (22.8 percent) in the party preference poll and finished second overall in the State Duma race, with 64 of 450 seats.

Events in early 1994 illustrated Yeltsin's increased political vulnerability as a result of the 1993 election. In January both Gaidar and the reformist finance minister, Boris FEDOROV, resigned after failing to secure a number of objectives. A month later the State Duma voted to grant amnesty not only to the leaders of the October 1993 parliamentary maneuverings but also to those involved in the August 1991 coup attempt. Yeltsin responded on April 28 by concluding a two-year Treaty on Civil Accord with 245 political and social groups. The document specified, among other things, that controversial constitutional changes would be avoided, that there would be no early elections, that local self-government would be strengthened, and that the rights of ethnic minorities would be supported. Signatories of the document included not only arch-reformer Gaidar but also Zhirinovsky, whereas some rightists, notably former vice president Rutskoi, denounced it as unconstitutional.

The Treaty on Civil Accord yielded a measure of political stability for the Chernomyrdin government, while steps were taken to reduce the potential for presidential/ministerial tension. At the same time, the slowdown in the pace of economic reform attracted growing criticism from Gaidar, whose party was renamed Russia's Democratic Choice (*Demokraticheskii Vybor Rossii*—DVR) in June 1994. In October the government was jarred by a major currency crisis that halved the external value of the ruble and led, a month later, to a major reshuffle of economic portfolios.

The Russian government made some progress in 1994 in improving relations with its more fractious constituent republics, concluding accords with Tatarstan in February and with Bashkortostan in August that provided for substantial home rule. However, the self-declared "independent" Republic of Chechnya in the Caucasus proved to be obdurate. In the wake of mounting tensions Russian forces launched a full-scale invasion of the territory on December 11 with the aim of restoring central government authority. Despite fierce Chechen resistance, the Russians finally captured the capital, Grozny, on February 6, 1995, and thereafter extended their control to other population centers.

The invasion of Chechnya dominated Russian politics in the first half of 1995. The action was strongly supported by the nationalist right but opposed by important elements of the centrist/reformist parties that had usually backed the Yeltsin administration, notably Gaidar's DVR. Ministry of Defense figures in late February 1995 put the number of dead and missing Russian soldiers at about 1,500, but independent observers estimated that some 10,000 Russians might have been killed and that Chechen civilian deaths totaled 25,000 in Grozny alone. International criticism of the action was particularly strong in the Islamic world—the Chechens being predominantly Muslim—and was heightened by Red Cross reports that Russian soldiers had massacred at least 250 civilians during an April assault on the village of Samashki in western Chechnya. Moreover, it appeared that a protracted guerrilla war was a prospect, since the self-styled Chechen "president," Gen. Dzhokhar DUDAYEV, had gone underground with a considerable military entourage. In June 1995 a band of Chechen gunmen seized a hospital in the southern Russian town of Budennovsk, holding more than 1,000 people hostage for five days until securing safe passage back to Chechnya in return for the hostages' release. At least 120 people died in the crisis, including about 30 casualties when Russian forces tried unsuccessfully to storm the hospital.

The Chechen attack was perceived as humiliating for Russia and provoked a parliamentary motion of no confidence in the government, directed mainly at the three "power" ministers of defense, interior, and security—all Yeltsin supporters—rather than at Prime Minister Chernomyrdin, who had negotiated the hostages' release. On June 21 the motion was carried by 241 votes to 72, but the result was nonbinding under the constitution unless repeated within three months. With Yeltsin's announcement that several senior ministers and officials would be dismissed, a second motion at the beginning of July failed to obtain the requisite majority. Russian and Chechen negotiators eventually signed a cease-fire agreement on July 30, but general hostilities resumed in October amid continued wrangling over the future political status of Chechnya.

Party politics from mid-1995 focused on the forthcoming legislative and presidential elections, scheduled for December 1995 and June 1996, respectively. New parties, alliances, and realignments proliferated, including the launching in May of Our Home Is Russia (*Nash Dom–Rossiya*—NDR) by Prime Minister Chernomyrdin. Several prominent figures declared their presidential candidacies, including Zhirinovsky on the far right and Gennadi ZYUGANOV of the Communist Party of the Russian Federation (*Kommunisticheskaya Partiya Rossiiskoi Federatsii*—KPRF). Despite health problems, President Yeltsin subsequently confirmed his candidacy for election to a second term.

The outcome of the State Duma election on December 17, 1995, was a significant victory for the KPRF, which won a plurality of 157 of the 450 seats with 22.3 percent of the party list vote, more than double the tally of the second-place NDR, which managed only 55 seats. In third place came the LDPR with 51 seats, while the reformist Yavlinsky-Boldyrev-Lukin Bloc (*Yabloko*), with 45 seats, was the only other list to achieve the 5 percent threshold for the allocation of proportional seats. In the constituency section, however, a total of 19 other groupings won representation.

President Yeltsin responded to the Communist/conservative electoral advance by making major government changes in January 1996. Several prominent reformers were dropped, including privatization architect Anatoly CHUBAIS as first deputy premier. Andrei KOZYREV was replaced as foreign minister by Yevgeni PRIMAKOV, hitherto chief of foreign intelligence and known to be much less pro-Western than his predecessor. These changes and a collateral slowdown in the privatization program found favor with the dominant KPRF contingent in the State Duma.

Held on June 16, 1996, the first round of the presidential balloting found Yeltsin heading the field of ten candidates with 35.3 percent of the vote, but only narrowly ahead of Zyuganov, who obtained 32 percent. In third place, with 14.5 percent, was Gen. (Ret.) Aleksandr LEBED, the former Russian military commander in the separatist Moldovan region of Transnistria, standing as the candidate of the nationalist Congress of Russian Communities (*Kongress Russkikh Obshchin*—KRO), while Grigori YAVLINSKY (*Yabloko*) and Zhirinovsky (LDPR) trailed. Within two days of the polling Yeltsin had forged an alliance with Lebed, who was appointed secretary of the National Security Council. With Lebed's endorsement in the runoff ballot on July 3, Yeltsin won a decisive victory over Zyuganov by a margin of 53.7 to 40.3 percent. Reinaugurated on August 9, President Yeltsin immediately reappointed Chernomyrdin as prime minister, at the head of a reshaped government in which pro-reform elements regained some of the ground lost in the January reshuffle. In addition, Anatoly Chubais assumed the key post of presidential chief of staff at a time of mounting concern about the president's health.

In Chechnya, the collapse of the cease-fire in October 1995 was followed in January 1996 by major hostage seizures by Chechen rebels. Russian peace overtures were assisted by the death of Chechen leader Dudayev in a Russian rocket attack in April, following which his successor, Zelimkhan YANDARBIYEV, concluded a cease-fire agreement with President Yeltsin. The May cease-fire again broke down with Yeltsin's reelection, but efforts by the new presidential security adviser, General Lebed, yielded a new agreement on August 31 that provided for the withdrawal of Russian and rebel forces from Grozny. Following Yeltsin's dismissal of Lebed in October, on grounds that he had proved to be a disruptive influence, the Russian president concluded yet another peace agreement with the Chechen leadership. The November accord provided for a complete Russian military withdrawal before the holding of presidential and parliamentary elections in Chechnya on January 27, 1997.

The winner in the presidential election was the most moderate of the candidates, Aslan MASKHADOV, who nevertheless continued to favor complete independence. In May Maskhadov and Yeltsin signed a peace treaty that rejected the use of force and postponed final resolution of Chechen-Russian relations to the year 2001. The situation nevertheless remained precarious as Chechen field commanders and extralegal groups continued to engage in abductions, politically motivated murders, and skirmishes with Russian troops along the Chechen frontier.

President Yeltsin underwent heart bypass surgery in November 1996 and spent most of the next several months in the hospital, prompting questions about his health that dominated the political scene into 1997. Attempts at impeachment by the opposition KPRF and LDPR over the health issue failed to pass constitutional muster, however, and in March Yeltsin significantly restructured the government, bringing in two noted reformers: Anatoly Chubais as a first deputy prime minister (the position from which he had been dismissed in January 1996) and the youthful governor of Nizhny Novgorod, Boris NEMTSOV. In November 1997 Chubais was dismissed as finance minister (but retained as deputy prime minister) following revelations that he had received money for his contribution to a book on privatization in Russia, a scandal widely linked to rivalry between financial conglomerates over the spoils of privatization.

Apparently determined to end infighting within the cabinet and to forge ahead with economic reform despite such adverse signs as a falling stock market and continuing wage arrears, on March 23, 1998, Yeltsin dismissed the government and named Sergei KIRIYENKO, a young reformer, as prime minister. Facing a threat of dissolution by the president after having rejected the nomination twice, the Duma finally approved Kiriyenko on April 24. His tenure proved to be short, however, as Russia's economic plight deepened, precipitated by falling oil prices on world markets and the impact of the recent East Asian financial turmoil. The crisis led on August 17 to a major devaluation of the ruble, the suspension of foreign debt payments, and the rescheduling of domestic short-term debt. Six days later, having dismissed Kiriyenko, Yeltsin nominated a former prime minister, Viktor Chernomyrdin, as his successor. However, the Duma twice rejected the nomination and Chernomyrdin withdrew his candidacy. On September 10 Yeltsin proposed in his stead a political veteran, Foreign Minister Primakov, who, with the support of the KPRF, won easy confirmation the following day.

Primakov's accomplishments included initiating an anticorruption campaign that targeted the "oligarchs," businessmen with powerful political connections who had made fortunes since the breakup of the Soviet Union, largely through the auction of state-owned enterprises in the mid-1990s. A principal target, Boris BEREZOVSKY, had close connections to Yeltsin's entourage ("the family"), and accusations surfaced that the president himself may have been involved, at least indirectly, in illegal business dealings.

On May 12, 1999, Yeltsin dismissed Primakov, who, at the time, had been considered the front-runner to succeed Yeltsin at the expiration of the presidential term in 2000. Primakov's replacement, First Deputy Prime Minister Sergei STEPASHIN, was confirmed by the State Duma on May 19 and thus became Russia's fourth prime minister in 14 months.

On August 9, 1999, Yeltsin once again dismissed his prime minister, designating as Stepashin's successor Vladimir PUTIN, theretofore head of the Federal Security Service (successor to the KGB) and secretary of the Security Council. Furthermore, Yeltsin identified Putin as his preferred presidential successor. The State Duma approved Putin's appointment as prime minister on August 16.

Speaking to the legislature before the confirmation vote, Putin not only outlined his government's economic goals, but also asserted that he would restore order to the North Caucasus and Chechnya. In early February 1999 Chechnya's President Maskhadov, under pressure from opposition field commanders, had issued a decree ordering an immediate transition to Islamic law (sharia), curtailed the legislature's powers, and created a commission to draft an Islamic constitution. On February 9 the field commanders set up a *Shura* (Islamic Council) and subsequently elected Shamil BASAYEV as its leader. On March 19 the instability of the entire North Caucasus region was exacerbated by a bombing in Vladikavkaz, the capital of North Ossetia, which killed at least 50 and wounded 100.

In early August 1999 Chechen rebels commanded by Basayev and Jordanian-born Omar ibn al-KHATTAB invaded Dagestan, capturing several border villages and declaring an independent Islamic state. Federal and Dagestani forces began a counteroffensive and within two weeks forced the insurgents to withdraw. On August 16 President Maskhadov declared a state of emergency in Chechnya, but the situation continued to deteriorate. When several massive bomb blasts in Moscow and elsewhere in August–September killed nearly 300 people, suspicion immediately fell on Chechen terrorists. Additional incursions into Dagestan prompted tighter security measures, and Russian forces renewed the push into Chechnya.

By late October 1999 nearly 200,000 civilians had fled the fighting, many into neighboring Ingushetia. Emphasizing air power and artillery in an effort to minimize Russian casualties, the strong military response served to strengthen Prime Minister Putin's standing in the polls. The government asserted that its intention was to convince the entire North Caucasus region—the Republics of Karachayevo-Cherkessia and North Ossetia as well as Chechnya, Dagestan, and Ingushetia—that Moscow would exert its full force to maintain central authority and defeat terrorism.

In the December 18, 1999, State Duma polling, the KPRF again won a plurality (113 seats on a 24 percent vote share), but, more significantly, the combined success of several recently formed, increasingly pro-Putin blocs secured a majority for the government. Two of the new electoral alliances, Unity (*Edinstvo*) and the Union of Right Forces (*Soyuz Pravyh Sil*—SPS), had been endorsed by Putin. A third, the Fatherland–All Russia bloc (*Otechestvo–Vsya Rossiya*—OVR), led by former prime minister Primakov and Moscow's mayor, Yuri LUZHKOV, found itself undercut by Putin's popularity. Most of the more than 100 representatives elected as independents soon joined progovernment parliamentary factions and deputies' groups.

With Putin's standing secured, President Yeltsin unexpectedly resigned on December 31, 1999, the prime minister thereby becoming acting president pending an election to be held within three months. Putin quickly decreed immunity from prosecution for Yeltsin, although not for "family" members. (Yeltsin died of heart failure on April 23, 2007.) In the presidential election on March 26, 2000, Putin secured 52.9 percent of the vote. Among the ten challengers, the KPRF's Zyuganov finished second, with 29.2 percent. Both former prime minister Primakov and Mayor Luzhkov of the Fatherland declined to run, given Putin's certain victory. Putin was inaugurated on May 7, and he nominated Mikhail KASYANOV as prime minister three days later. The State Duma approved the nomination on May 17 and over the next several days confirmed a revamped cabinet that featured, most notably, major changes in the structure and leadership of economic ministries.

Putin continued to take a hard line toward the Chechen rebels, Russian forces taking control of Grozny in February 2000, months after federal forces had advanced into the city with the support of pro-Russian Chechen contingents. The remaining Chechen rebels retreated, amid heavy casualties, to the southern mountains. At the same time charges of human rights abuses by Russian troops escalated, especially in "filtration camps" established to weed out belligerents. On April 25 the United Nations Commission on Human Rights voted to condemn a "disproportionate and indiscriminate use of Russian military forces." By then, pro-Russian Chechen officials were increasingly being targeted for assassination by the rebels, who also continued guerrilla assaults on Russian troops.

President Putin soon initiated steps to consolidate Moscow's authority, issuing a decree on May 13, 2000, establishing seven federal "superdistricts" to be funded by Moscow and headed by presidentially appointed envoys empowered to ensure regional compliance with federal law. The president also secured the authority to dismiss regional leaders for violating federal law (see Constitution and government, below).

On June 8, 2002, President Putin imposed direct rule on Chechnya and four days later named Mufti Akhmed KADYROV as acting head of administration.

In July 2001 Unity, All Russia, and Fatherland organized an alliance that was registered in December as Unity and Fatherland–United Russia (*Edinstvo i Otechestvo–Edinaya Rossiya*), and two months later the members of all three voted to dissolve as separate entities. On the right, many of the SPS participants had also merged into a single party, while on the left the continued domination of the KPRF was called into question by factional disputes as the 2003 State Duma election approached. At the December 7 poll the Putin-supportive United Russia won a majority of seats, while the KPRF lost support to a recently organized Motherland–People's Patriotic Union (*Rodina–Narodno-Patrioticheskii Soyuz*) electoral bloc. In a major setback, neither the SPS nor *Yabloko* met the 5 percent threshold for claiming proportional seats, while the LDPR doubled its representation to 36 seats. When the State Duma convened, the United Russia parliamentary faction surpassed the two-thirds majority needed to approve constitutional changes.

On February 24, 2004, three weeks before the presidential election, President Putin dismissed the Kasyanov government and on March 1 named Mikhail FRADKOV, Russia's ambassador to the European Union (EU) and considered an "outsider," as prime minister. Confirmed by the legislature on March 5, Fradkov completed his streamlined cabinet on March 9. Five days later Putin, running as an independent, easily won reelection, capturing 71.3 percent of the vote, defeating five challengers, the closest of whom, the KPRF's Nikolai KHARITONOV, won 13.7 percent. Required by the constitution to resign following the May 7 presidential inauguration, Fradkov was immediately reappointed by Putin and confirmed on May 12.

In 2002 the frequent suicide bombings and hostage taking in Chechnya continued to draw international attention. On October 23 separatists seized more than 800 hostages at a Moscow theater. An attack by Russian special forces on October 26 not only killed all the rebels but also resulted in the deaths of some 130 hostages. Two months later suicide bombers attacked the administrative headquarters in Grozny, killing 80 and wounding 150. In 2003, from May to August, suicide bombers, some of them women, included in their targets a music festival in Moscow, government buildings and a religious festival in Chechnya, and a military hospital in North Ossetia.

On March 23, 2003, a reported 96 percent of Chechen voters endorsed a draft constitution for a self-ruling republic with an elected legislature and president. Akhmed Kadyrov won the Chechen presidential election on October 3 with more than 80 percent of the vote, his principal rivals having withdrawn. He was assassinated by Chechen Islamists in Grozny in 2004. Prime Minister Sergei ABRAMOV, who had been in office less than two months, became acting president. On August 29 Maj. Gen. Alu ALKHANOV, theretofore the Chechen interior minister, was elected president with 74 percent of the vote. His principal rival, Chechen businessman Malik SAIDULLAYEV, was denied a place on the ballot due to a technicality. On September 1, 2004, some 30 rebels, reportedly including several operatives linked to the al-Qaida network, invaded a school at Beslan, North Ossetia, and took 1,200 teachers, parents, and children hostage. Two days later nearly 340 hostages died during a rescue mission.

President Putin continued to consolidate his authority, as in 2005 he tightened requirements for registration of political parties; eliminated single-mandate legislative districts beginning with the 2007 State Duma election; and raised to 7 percent the vote threshold needed for parties to claim lower house seats. Putin claimed that by switching to proportional representation for legislative elections, the party system would be strengthened since there would be fewer parties in the lower house. Putin's consolidation of power was interpreted by some observers as marking the ascendancy of the *siloviki* (roughly, the powerful), individuals with a background in the Soviet KGB or the Russian security and military services, at the expense of former president Yeltsin's "family"—particularly some of the oligarchs who had amassed fortunes through the sale of state assets in the 1990s. Early targets included Vladimir GUSINSKY, owner of Russia's largest independent media conglomerate, Media-MOST, which had angered the government with its unfavorable coverage of the war in Chechnya. Gusinsky, fleeing charges of tax evasion, relocated to Israel, while Media-MOST fell under the control of Gazprom, the state-owned natural gas company. Mikhail KHODORKOVSKY, the chief executive officer of a leading energy company, Yukos, was convicted of tax evasion and fraud in May 2005 and sentenced to nine years in prison. (Yukos was dismantled in 2007, furthering the government's aim of regaining a controlling share of the country's natural resources and other critical industries, such as pipelines, rail transport, shipping, and nuclear energy.)

The Chechen separatists suffered a significant blow on March 8, 2005, when Aslan Maskhadov died during an operation by the Federal Security Service. Two days later the separatist Chechen State Defense Committee announced that Abdul-Khalim SADULAYEV had succeeded Maskhadov as its chair. Moscow increased its control over the Chechen republic through the parliamentary elections called for November 27, 2005, which were widely criticized for irregularities and low turnout. The United Russia party was declared to have won 61 percent of the vote, giving it majorities in both upper and lower chambers.

In March 2006 pro-Moscow warlord Ramzan KADYROV, leader of a private army of thousands of irregular troops and son of slain president Akhmed Kadyrov, was approved as prime minister in a unanimous vote of the People's Assembly of Chechnya, succeeding Sergei Abramov, who had resigned in February. In mid-June Abdul-Khalim Sadulayev was killed in a Russian police operation. His deputy, Doku UMAROV, assumed the separatist leadership. On July 10 Shamil BASAYEV, the Chechen separatist leader who had claimed responsibility for attacks that killed hundreds of Russian civilians in the past decade, including the Beslan school massacre, died when a nearby truck carrying dynamite blew up.

In February 2007 Ramzan Kadyrov was appointed acting president of Chechnya, Alkhanov having been named federal deputy minister of justice in a cabinet reshuffle. On March 2 Kadyrov was elected president, and in April named a cousin, Odes BAYSULTANOV, as prime minister. By then, with the separatist leadership having been decimated, the pace and severity of separatist attacks had diminished.

On September 12, 2007, President Putin accepted the resignation of Prime Minister Fradkov, and according to law, the cabinet was dismissed. Fradkov remained as acting prime minister until Putin nominated Viktor ZUBKOV as his successor on September 14. Zubkov had been serving as first deputy finance minister and chair of the committee responsible for combating money laundering. On October 6 Putin appointed Fradkov as head of the Foreign Intelligence Service.

In the December 2, 2007, legislative elections, in which 11 parties participated, United Russia won 64.3 percent of the vote and 315 of the legislature's 450 seats. The KPRF, as expected, finished second, with 11.6 percent and 57 seats. Shortly after the election, President Putin, who was barred constitutionally from seeking a third consecutive term, announced his support for First Deputy Prime Minister Dmitri MEDVEDEV in the 2008 presidential election. Medvedev, in turn, indicated that if elected, he intended to nominate Putin as prime minister. All four pro-Kremlin parties—United Russia, Just Russia, Agrarian Party of Russia (*Agrarnaya Partiya Rossii*—APR), and Civil Force (*Grazhdanskaya Sila*—GS)—endorsed Medvedev as well. The Russian Ecological Party "The Greens" (*Rossiiskaya Ekologicheskaya Partiya "Zelenye"*—REP) also backed Medvedev.

In the election on March 2, 2008, Medvedev, who officially is an independent, received 70.3 percent of the vote, defeating Gennadi Zyuganov of the KPRF, with 20.0 percent of the vote; Vladimir Zhirinovsky of the LDPR, with 9.5 percent; and Andrei Bogdanov of the DPR, with 1.3 percent. As expected, Medvedev appointed Putin prime minister. Putin named a new cabinet on May 12. A minor reshuffle occurred in October.

One minister was replaced on March 12, 2009, and a ninth deputy chair of the Council of Ministers was appointed on January 19, 2010. Another deputy chair resigned on October 21 in order to contest the Moscow mayoral election.

In August 2011 the governor of St. Petersburg resigned in advance of filling the post of speaker of the Federation Council, which had been vacated by the resignation (under pressure by United Russia) of the previous speaker on May 18. Valentina MATVIYENKO, a senior member of United Russia, was installed as speaker on September 21.

The long-serving finance minister resigned on September 27, 2011, after refusing to withdraw the remarks he had made days earlier in the wake of Prime Minister Putin's announcement that he would seek reelection as president in 2012 and that Medvedev would stand on the United Russia ticket in the December parliamentary elections and would likely be prime minister. Aleksei KUDRIN, who was also a deputy prime minister, had said during a trip to Washington that he would refuse to serve under Medvedev.

The December 4, 2011, legislative elections included seven registered parties. United Russia won 49.3 percent of the vote and 238 of the legislature's 450 seats. The KPRF took second place, with 19.2 percent and 92 seats. United Russia secured a majority and the mandate to form a government, but it did lose the two-thirds constitutional majority it had previously enjoyed, while the three parliamentary opposition parties all gained seats. There were, subsequently, numerous protests against perceived flaws in the election (see Current issues, below).

In the presidential election on March 4, 2012, Putin received 63.6 percent of the vote, defeating Gennady Zyuganov of the KPRF, with

17.2 percent of the vote; Mikhail Prokhorov, an independent, with 7.9 percent; Vladimir Zhirinovsky of the LDPR, with 6.2 percent; and Sergey MIRONOV of A Just Russia with 3.9 percent. Putin appointed Medvedev as prime minister, as he suggested in September 2011, and Medvedev named a new cabinet on May 15, 2012.

But Putin's new term of office saw the replacement of several key cabinet members. Oleg GOVORUN, minister for regional development and widely seen as an ally of Medvedev, was dismissed on October 17, 2012, after public criticism by Putin the preceding month. Putin dismissed defense minister and long-time ally Anatoly SERDYUKOV on November 6, 2012, after the police began a corruption investigation of how the defense ministry had privatized ministry land. Most notably, on May 8, 2013, Deputy Prime Minister Vladislav SURKOV resigned a day after Putin criticized his performance. The resignation was interpreted by the local media as a possible sign of a rift between Putin and Medvedev. Surkov, a former key political advisor of Putin, had distanced himself during the December 2011 elections.

In legislative balloting on September 18, 2016, United Russia expanded its majority by securing 343 seats, followed by the KPRF with 42, a loss of more than half its seats. The voting was sharply criticized by opposition groups who claimed that the government limited their media access and engaged in voter fraud and other electoral irregularities. On October 19 Vitaly MUTKO, the minister of sport, youth, and tourism, was appointed as a deputy prime minister. The appointment raised the number of deputy prime ministers to nine.

Constitution and government. Under the 1993 constitution the Federation president "determine[s] guidelines for the domestic and foreign policy of the state." Directly elected for no more than two consecutive four-year terms, the president nominates the chair of government (the prime minister) as well as higher court judges; in addition, he serves as commander in chief of the armed forces, appoints and dismisses the top military commanders, and may issue decrees carrying the force of law. He may reject an initial vote of nonconfidence and upon the repassage of such a measure within three months may call for dissolution of the legislature and new elections. The current basic law makes no provision for a vice president. The president's main advisory body on security issues is the Security Council, whose powers were substantially strengthened by presidential decree in July 1996.

The bicameral Federal Assembly consists of the State Duma and, as an upper house, the Federation Council. The Duma votes on the president's nominee as government chair as well as his choices for other high positions. Legislation must first be approved by majority vote of the entire Duma; rejection by the upper house requires a two-thirds vote of the entire Duma to override. Measures vetoed by the president require approval by two-thirds of both houses. The Federation Council comprises two representatives from each of Russia's 83 territorial components (85, including the Republic of Crimea and the federal city of Sevastopol)—prior to 2002, the governing executive (governor or, in the case of republics, president) and the leader of the assembly. On August 7, 2000, however, President Putin signed into law a measure stripping regional officials of their ex officio seats and of their immunity from prosecution. With full effect from January 2002, the regional executives each appoint one member to the council (with legislative concurrence), and each territorial assembly elects a legislative representative. The Federation Council's powers include review of martial law and emergency decrees.

The judicial system includes a Constitutional Court, a Supreme Court, a Supreme Arbitration Court, and lesser federal entities as determined by law. Between 2001 and 2002 Russia introduced codes permitting the sale and private ownership of land, although the sale of agricultural land to foreigners and to companies with majority foreign ownership was prohibited. In July 2002 a new "Western-style" criminal code instituted a jury system nationwide for serious offenses, required police to obtain court warrants for arrests and searches, and set a 48-hour limit on detentions.

Local self-government is conducted through referenda, elections, and other means, with appropriate "consideration for historical and other local traditions." Mergers of territorial units have been encouraged by the central government as part of a larger plan to consolidate the federal structure, ostensibly to streamline public administration, but apparently also as a way to diminish the political authority of the often restless ethnic areas. Prior to the annexation of Crimea in 2014, the federation encompassed 21 republics (*respubliki*), nine territories (*kraia*), 46 regions (*oblasti*), the Jewish autonomous region (*avtonomnaya oblast*) of Birobijan, four autonomous areas (*avtonomnie okruga*), and two "cities of federal importance" (Moscow and St. Petersburg). (See the 2013 *Handbook* for recent changes to administrative divisions.)

By decree, on May 13, 2000, President Putin established seven federal districts—Central, Far Eastern, North Caucasus (renamed Southern by decree on June 23), Northwest, Siberian, Ural, and Volga—to oversee regional compliance with federal law. (An eighth, the North Caucasian Federal District, was created in January 2010 by dividing the Southern district. Crimea became a ninth district on March 21, 2014, after its agreement of unification with Russia.) Later, in conjunction with the reform of the Federation Council, Putin signed into law measures intended to restructure the federal relationship, one giving the president authority to dismiss regional heads who violate federal law and the other permitting regional executives to remove local officials for similar cause. On September 1, again by decree, President Putin established a consultative State Council of the Russian Federation, to ensure that executives from all territorial subdivisions have an institutional voice in Moscow. Chaired by the president, the State Council has a seven-member Presidium consisting of a presidentially appointed representative from each of the "super-districts." Serving six-month terms, the appointees are chosen by rotation from among the leaders of Russia's constituent republics and regions. Legislation passed in 2004 brought an end to the election of regional governors and republican presidents, who are now appointed by the federation president with the concurrence of the legislature of the particular jurisdiction.

All mass media are licensed by the government, and most of the country's leading newspapers and broadcasting outlets are owned by companies close to the government or in which the government has majority ownership. Foreign ownership of broadcast media was prohibited by a 2011 law.

Reporters Without Borders listed Russia as 148th out of 180 countries in its 2016 Press Freedom Index, pointing to media-self censorship, the, "arbitrary" applications of anti-extremism legislation, the continued repression of protests against the government, laws enacted in 2013 that penalize statements "insulting" to religious belief, and a ban on "propaganda" promoting "nontraditional sexual relations." A February 2014 law allows the government to block websites, and a law passed in May requires Russian bloggers and other content providers who register more than 3,000 daily site visitors to register with the government.

Foreign relations. The Russian Federation was generally accepted as successor to the Soviet Union in respect to the latter's international commitments and affiliations, including membership in the United Nations and the Conference on (later Organization for) Security and Cooperation in Europe (CSCE/OSCE). It also assumed the Soviet Union's obligations under international and bilateral treaties, such as those on arms control with the United States.

Russian troops remained deployed in several areas of the "near abroad" following the disintegration of the Soviet Union. When Georgia declared its independence in 1991 after the collapse of the Soviet Union, two of its regions, South Ossetia and the Abkhaz Republic, now commonly known as Abkhazia, took up arms to gain autonomy. Hundreds were killed and hundreds of thousands displaced as independence fighters engaged Georgian troops. In summer 1992 Russian peacekeepers were deployed in South Ossetia, achieving an end to the violence but leaving the issue of sovereignty unresolved.

In June 1992 Russia was formally admitted to membership in the IMF and the World Bank.

In August 1992 tension between Russia and Ukraine eased in the wake of an agreement to place the former Soviet Black Sea fleet under joint command pending implementation of a June accord to divide the ships equally and jointly finance their bases. At a CIS meeting in 1994 the two countries agreed that 15 to 20 percent of the fleet's 800-plus ships would be retained by Ukraine, with Russia "purchasing" the remainder of Ukraine's share.

In the course of a summit in Washington in 1992, Presidents Yeltsin and George H. W. Bush concluded agreements on most-favored-nation trade status and a major extension of the 1991 Strategic Arms Reduction Treaty (START). Under the START II accord, each nation would be limited to 3,000–3,500 long-range weapons (down from 11,000–12,000 on the eve of START I), while all land-based multiple warhead missiles would be banned. In November 1992 the Supreme Soviet ratified the 1991 START I accord with the United States, although an exchange of ratification documents was deferred until Belarus, Kazakhstan, and Ukraine had signed the 1968 Nuclear Non-Proliferation Treaty (NPT) and agreement had been reached on the disposition of nuclear arms in their possession. (Under a protocol to START I signed in Lisbon in

May 1992, the three ex-Soviet republics had agreed that Russia should be the sole nuclear power in the CIS.) By late 1993 Belarus and Kazakhstan had completed these procedures; Ukraine acceded to the NPT in December 1994.

With regard to areas of the "near abroad" populated by ethnic Russian minorities, the Yeltsin administration firmly opposed the demands of right-wing nationalists that they be brought under Russian sovereignty. At the same time, it insisted that the rights of Russian minorities must be fully respected by the governments concerned. Thus, in October 1992 Yeltsin suspended the withdrawal of Russian troops from the three Baltic states, citing "profound concern over the numerous infringements of rights of the Russian-speaking population" in Latvia and Estonia, in particular. However, Western pressure and assurances on ethnic Russian rights yielded the withdrawal of Russian forces from Lithuania by August 1993 and from Estonia and Latvia a year later, subject to Russian retention of certain defense facilities for a specified period.

Russian negotiators facilitated a cease-fire agreement between Georgia and the Abkhaz Republic in April 1994. Both South Ossetia and Abkhazia have operated as de facto independent states since then, and Russia has provided both regions with peacekeeping troops, financial support, and Russian passports.

The rapid transformation of Russia's external relations was highlighted in June 1994 when Russia acceded in principle to the North Atlantic Treaty Organization's (NATO's) Partnership for Peace (PfP) program for former Soviet-bloc and neutral European states, and also signed a new partnership and cooperation agreement with the EU.

In September 1994 President Jiang Zemin became the first senior Chinese leader to visit Moscow since 1957. Agreements signed on September 3 resolved most bilateral border demarcation disputes and committed each never to use force against the other. Further visits to Moscow by Chinese president Jiang in May 1995 and by Premier Li Peng in June continued the rapprochement, which was consolidated by President Yeltsin's April 1996 visit to Beijing. Troop reductions on the Sino-Russian border were agreed to as part of a new "strategic partnership."

Efforts at improving ties with Japan were long stalled due to a dispute over the four southern Kurile Islands seized by the Soviet Union at the end of World War II (see the Foreign relations section of the entry on Japan). In November 1997 President Yeltsin and Japanese Prime Minister Ryutaro Hashimoto pledged to sign a treaty by 2000 that would settle the dispute and normalize relations. The two leaders also concluded a fishing agreement covering the Kurile Islands and agreed to further economic cooperation. (The dispute remained unresolved in 2014, despite an April 2013 trip to Moscow by Japanese Prime Minister Shinzo Abe.)

The dominant foreign policy issue in 1997 was the proposed admission of former Warsaw Pact members Poland, the Czech Republic, and Hungary into an expanded NATO, despite Russian objections and its previous threat to withdraw from the 1990 Conventional Forces in Europe (CFE) treaty. Negotiations held in Moscow in May led to an accord, signed in Paris on May 27, known as the Founding Act. While Russia had sought a treaty, rather than a nonbinding accord, it accepted an agreement to strengthen the OSCE, acquiesced on the need for revisions to the CFE treaty, and received a pledge, but not a guarantee, from NATO that the Western alliance would not place nuclear weapons on the territory of any new member states. While the NATO Founding Act did not give Russia a veto over future NATO decisions, as Yeltsin had desired, a Russian-NATO joint council has afforded Russia a voice in NATO decisions. Russia also received a number of economic concessions, including enhanced status in the Group of Seven (G-7). (In 1998 Russia became a full participant, and the G-7 officially became the G-8.) In addition, Washington pledged to support eventual Russian accession to the World Trade Organization (WTO).

On July 23, 1997, in Vienna 16 NATO and 14 former Warsaw Pact states agreed "in principle" on a new draft CFE accord that set national rather than bloc limitations on conventional armed forces, as Russia's objections to the 1990 CFE treaty had rested on a desire to limit NATO deployments in the former Warsaw Pact countries.

Agreements concluded in May 1997 permitted Russia to lease half of the Ukrainian naval base at Sevastopol for a period of 20 years and also signified Russian recognition of Crimea and Sevastopol as Ukrainian territory.

Related to the eastward expansion of NATO, Yeltsin advocated closer linkages with CIS member states, in particular regarding economic, political, and military ties between Russia and Belarus. In June 1997 the legislatures of both countries ratified a Charter of the Union, which set out a plan for greater integration (see entry on Belarus). On December 25, 1998, Yeltsin and Belarusan President Alyaksandr Lukashenka agreed to set up an integrated monetary system and customs policies and form a common leadership while retaining national sovereignty. Modeled on the EU, a formal Union Treaty was signed in Moscow on December 8, 1999, and unanimously ratified on December 22 by the upper houses of both countries.

Russian contingents have participated in several peacekeeping missions, including a UN-sponsored force in Bosnia and Herzegovina and a CIS contingent in Tajikistan. In the confrontation between Yugoslavia and NATO over the Kosovo question in 1998–1999, Moscow took a pro-Belgrade stance, owing in large part to the strong cultural ties between Russians and Yugoslavia's Serbs. Despite Russian anger over the bombing campaign against Yugoslavia in March 1999, in the aftermath Russian troops were successfully stationed alongside NATO-led peacekeepers in Kosovo.

In 2000 Russia announced its withdrawal from the 1992 Bishkek Treaty on visa-free travel among CIS members, citing threats posed by international terrorism, crime, and drug trafficking.

On April 14, 2000, the State Duma, at the urging of President-elect Vladimir Putin, ratified START II and on April 22 approved the 1996 Comprehensive Test Ban Treaty. At the same time, however, the legislature also endorsed a revised military doctrine authorizing use of nuclear weapons "if the very existence of the country" were in jeopardy.

A visit by U.S. president Bill Clinton to Russia in June 2000 produced a bilateral agreement on the disposal of weapons-grade plutonium and on setting up an early-warning center—the first permanent U.S.-Russian military operation—to reduce the risk of accidental nuclear war.

In July 2000 the government introduced a new foreign policy doctrine favoring pragmatism, cooperation with NATO, closer ties with China and India, and "active dialogue" with the United States. Moscow and Washington differed, however, over the contemplated U.S. limited missile defense plan, with Russian officials charging that the proposed warhead intercept system would violate the 1972 Anti-Ballistic Missile (ABM) Treaty. The United States formally withdrew from the ABM Treaty in 2002, straining relations with Russia.

In a meeting in Moscow on May 24, 2002, Presidents Putin and George W. Bush signed the Treaty of Moscow (the Strategic Offensive Reductions Treaty—SORT), committing both countries to reducing nuclear stockpiles by two-thirds over the next decade. Other summit concerns included improved cooperation in counterterrorism and in trade relations, particularly with regard to the energy sector.

On May 28, 2002, in Rome, Italy, NATO and Russia signed Rome Declaration, establishing a NATO–Russia Council for the purpose of discussing nonproliferation, combating terrorism, and peacekeeping. On May 29, at a Russian–EU summit in Moscow, the EU recognized Russia as a market economy, as did the United States shortly thereafter, thereby advancing Russia's efforts to enter the WTO.

In September 2003 Kazakhstan and Ukraine joined Russia and Belarus in signing a treaty intended to create a Single Economic Space, which includes a free trade zone and greater coordination of economic policy.

In October 2004 the legislature ratified the Kyoto Protocol, aimed at combating global warming. Although President Putin had expressed reservations as to whether the protocol was in Russia's best interests, ratification became central to establishing closer relations with the EU.

In 2005 China and Russia held their first joint military exercises.

Following severe reductions in gas shipments to the Ukraine in 2006 over a debt dispute, the crisis was ultimately resolved peacefully, but tensions between the two countries remained, owing in part to Russia's opposition to Ukraine's goal of joining NATO and the EU.

Russia's relations with the United Kingdom in 2006 suffered in the wake of the murder of former security agent Aleksandr LITVINENKO, a vocal critic of President Putin, who had defected. Litvinenko died in London in November of poisoning by radioactive polonium-210. Russia refused to extradite Andrei LUGOVOI, an LDPR member of the State Duma and the principal target of the British investigation, and instead attempted to implicate the exiled Boris Berezovsky in Litvinenko's poisoning. Relations with the United Kingdom subsequently remained tense. (Russia has continued to reject requests to extradite Lugovoi.)

At a Russia–EU summit in May 2007, leaders addressed criticism of Russia's human rights record, especially in Chechnya, and the future status of Kosovo, among other issues. Russia continued to reject Kosovar independence without Serbian approval even after Kosovo declared independence in February 2008. Western recognition of Kosovo was viewed by some analysts as one of the provocations leading to Russia's recognition of South Ossetia and Abkhazia in Georgia, a staunch Western ally.

Russia continued to struggle against U.S. plans to deploy a defensive missile shield in Europe, which would include placing intercept missiles in Poland and a radar installation in the Czech Republic. Though the United States claimed that the shield would not target Russia and its purpose was to protect against "rogue" states such as Iran, Russia viewed the shield as a national security threat. Putin threatened to retarget Russian missiles on Europe if the missile defense system was deployed. Further, in July 2007 Putin announced that Russia intended to suspend its participation in the CFE Treaty, partly over the proposed missile shield and partly because some NATO members had never ratified the revised treaty.

Differences between Russia and the United States persisted over Iran's efforts to develop nuclear power, which would give it the capacity to enrich uranium for weapons. In 2007, when Iran reportedly violated requirements of the Non-Proliferation Treaty, the United States and other Western countries attempted to force Iran to dismantle its nuclear programs with threats of sanctions. Russia has consistently voted against sanctions against Iran in the UN Security Council, claiming that all states have a right to develop nuclear energy. Amid heightened tensions between the United States and Iran, Putin traveled to Tehran and met with President Mahmoud Ahmadinejad in October 2007, marking the first visit by a Russian or Soviet leader to Iran since 1943.

Following Russian occupation of South Ossetia and Abkhazia in August 2008, Russia recognized the provinces as independent.

U.S. president Barack Obama moved to "reset" relations with Russia in July 2009, when he met in Moscow with President Medvedev and Prime Minister Putin, both sides pledging cooperation. The two countries agreed to further reduce nuclear arsenals and resume military contacts that had been suspended during Russia's war with Georgia. Also, Russia agreed to open its airspace to allow U.S. troops and weapons to be transported to Afghanistan.

Relations with Belarus deteriorated in 2009, when a dispute was revived after President Lukashenka told his government the country must no longer rely on Russia. Putin subsequently pledged to continue to provide financial support to Belarus. The two countries ultimately reached an agreement on oil supplies in January 2010, but in June Russia dramatically cut gas supplies to Belarus. However, the matter was resolved in a few days when both sides agreed to repay the debts they owed to each other.

The election of Viktor Yanukovych as president of Ukraine in February 2010 brought an improvement in relations. In April agreements were reached on the cost of Russian gas supplies to the Ukraine, which will receive a rebate on prices until 2019. Collaterally, Ukraine granted permission to Russia to station its Black Sea Fleet at Sevastopol until 2042.

In March 2010 Russia and the United States agreed to the New START Treaty, which provides for both sides to ultimately reduce their deployments to no more than 1,550 strategic warheads and 700 launchers. The treaty was ratified by the U.S. Senate in December 2010. (It was signed by President Obama on February 2, 2011.)

Tensions with Poland heightened following a plane crash near Smolensk, Russia, in April 2010, which killed the Polish president, among other leading Polish political figures who were traveling to a ceremony honoring Polish soldiers killed by the Soviets in the Katyn Massacre during World War II. Russia and Poland subsequently sparred over how to assess blame for the crash. (See the 2013 *Handbook* for details.) Ultimately, however, the event resulted in warming relations between the two countries, as the Russian president and prime minister expressed their condolences and announced a national day of mourning. The gesture of President Putin laying flowers at the crash site and paying tribute alongside Polish prime minister Donald Tusk was reported to have contributed greatly to an enhanced opinion of the Russian leader by the Polish public and helped ease tensions. In November the State Duma passed a resolution stating that the Soviet leader Josef Stalin—not Nazi Germany as had previously been claimed—was responsible for the Katyn Massacre.

In June 2010 Russia was one of five countries that agreed to sanctions against Iran for its nuclear program. Russia's acquiescence was widely attributed to its better relations with the United States.

In 2011 relations between the United States and Russia remained cordial, and in the wake of the uprising against Libyan leader Muammar Qadhafi, Medvedev shifted his position after meeting with President Obama and agreed that the dictator must relinquish control. Also, Russia allowed the United States to transport military equipment over its territory to Afghanistan. After the outbreak of the Syrian civil war, however, Russia has blocked UN resolutions that would impose sanctions on the government of Bashar Al-Assad, a position that continued into 2013.

Trade with Germany increased significantly in 2011, and in June a German company agreed to develop a multimillion-dollar combat training center in Russia. During Medvedev's trip to Germany in July, the two countries signed a number of agreements on culture, politics, science, and economics.

The Eurasian Economic Space, consisting of Belarus, Kazakhstan, and Russia, went into effect on January 1, 2012, creating a single market between the three countries overseen by the Eurasian Commission. This builds on their 2010 customs union, and it is the foundation for the November 18, 2011, agreement to establish a Eurasian Union by 2015, roughly modeled on the EU. Tajikistan and Kyrgyzstan have both expressed interest in joining.

In August 2012 Russia joined the WTO.

In July 2013 Russia disputed Western claims that the Syrian government had used chemical weapons against its own people. In August a foreign ministry spokesman suggested that rebels had used the weapons as a "provocation" to draw in international intervention, a position that Putin restated in a September 11 editorial in *The New York Times*. In September Russian leaders argued for a negotiated surrender of all Syrian chemical weapons as a way to avoid U.S. military intervention.

Relations with the United States were further complicated by the flight of Edward Snowden to Moscow on June 23. Snowden, a civilian contractor for the U.S. National Security Agency who exposed U.S. Internet and telephone surveillance programs, received temporary asylum in Russia on August 1.

Russia brought economic pressure to bear on several neighboring states in 2013. Energy prices for Armenia were raised in June 2013 and extensive customs checks were briefly declared for all Ukrainian goods entering Russia in August. Both policies were seen as linked to Armenia and Ukraine's efforts to negotiate Association Agreements with the EU, including expanded trade links. In September Russia briefly imposed a ban on imports of Moldovan wine for the second time in seven years.

Moscow announced a ban on Moldovan wine in September 2013, an act widely interpreted as an effort to exert pressure against Moldova's Association Agreement with the EU, a free trade pact.

In November 2013 Ukraine noted publicly that its delay in achieving preconditions for its own Association Agreement with the EU was due in part to Russian concerns, sparking protests. In December Russia offered a $15 billion loan and discounts on natural gas to bolster the Yanukovych government. Continued protests, however, helped spark the Ukrainian Revolution on February 18, 2014. On February 22 the Ukrainian parliament voted to impeach Yanukovych, although the motion lacked the required three-quarters supermajority.

Pro-Russian protests began in Crimea on February 23 and escalated into open clashes by February 27, when armed groups seized government buildings. On February 28 soldiers in unmarked uniforms took control of the airports in Simferopol and Sevastopol. Ukraine has claimed that these were Russian personnel; following a March 1 request by new Crimean Prime Minister Sergei AKSYNOV that Russia assist with security, troops, ships, and aircraft with Russian markings intervened in Crimea. On March 16 Crimea held a referendum on whether to unite with Russia; 83 percent of possible voters took part, with 96.8 percent voting in favor of union. On March 21 Putin signed a Treaty of Accession of the Republic of Crimea to Russia, with Crimea becoming a federal district of the Russian Federation.

In response to the Crimean crisis, in March the EU, United States, Canada, and Japan, among other countries, imposed targeted sanctions on Russian individuals and institutions. On March 24 Russia was suspended from the G-8.

Pro-Russian protests had similarly emerged in eastern Ukraine in early March. On April 7 pro-Russian groups declared a People's Republic of Donetsk and clashed with police. On April 8 separatists declared a Lugansk People's Republic. Fighting escalated over the following weeks. On May 11 both regions held referendums, with majorities supporting union with Russia. Meanwhile, the United States and EU broadened sanctions, imposing bans on travel and on financial transactions with individuals and companies seen as supportive of Putin's actions in Ukraine.

In May Russia signed an agreement with China to construct the world's longest natural gas pipeline and provide $400 billion in natural gas over 30 years.

On May 29, 2014, Putin signed the Eurasian Economic Union Treaty, deepening the economic union among Russia, Belarus, and Kazakhstan. If ratified by the parliament of each state, it will go into effect on January 1, 2015.

As fighting continued in eastern Ukraine in June, Ukraine and the United States accused Russia of providing tanks, artillery, heavy weapons, and supplies to separatist groups.

Moldova signed its Association Agreement with the EU in early July. Subsequently, Russia announced a ban on imports of Moldovan fruit and beef and raised tariffs on a variety of Moldovan goods.

On July 17 Malaysia Airlines Flight 17 was lost over an area in Ukraine controlled by separatists, with all 298 crew and passengers killed. Ukraine and the United States have subsequently alleged that separatist groups shot it down with a surface-to-air missile; Russian officials and media outlets have accused Ukraine of the act. (The preliminary report by the Dutch air safety board, released in September, states that the cause of the crash was due to collision with "high-energy objects" from outside the aircraft, consistent with an antiaircraft missile.)

Over July and August, the EU, United States, Japan, Norway, and Switzerland expanded sanctions several times in the wake of the Flight 17 disaster. By July 31 the EU had announced a halt on financial transactions and credit to all government majority-owned banks in Russia as well as the energy and defense industries. Meanwhile, the United States accused Russia of violating the Intermediate-Range Nuclear Forces Treaty by testing a new ground-launched cruise missile. In response, Russia banned imports of agricultural products from the EU, United States, Canada, Australia, and Norway for one year.

In August Ukraine accused Russia of firing artillery and air strikes across the border to support separatists, of providing tanks and heavy weaponry, and also that Russian troops had crossed the border to intervene in the conflict.

A cease-fire was announced in eastern Ukraine on September 3, although subsequently, it was sporadically violated. Despite the agreement, on September 12 the United States and EU announced further sanctions that would end finance, technology sales, and support for Russian deepwater, Arctic, offshore, shale oil and gas exploration and would further increase limits on Russian banks.

Increased tensions between Russia and the West led to new deployments of NATO forces in eastern European members of NATO in 2015. In response, in March 2015 Russia halted all participation in the CFE Treaty.

In September 2015 Syria formally requested military assistance from Russia, and the Duma approved airstrikes on the Islamic State and other anti-regime fighters. The United States and other Western powers criticized Russian aerial attacks on pro-Western opposition groups; however, Russian intervention appeared to stabilize the regime and change the course of the conflict (see entry on Syria). On November 24 a Turkish fighter jet shot down a Russian aircraft that violated the country's airspace, causing a diplomatic crisis between the two countries. Meanwhile, Russia also began to deploy the first of approximately 4,000 ground forces to Syria.

The United Kingdom published a report in January 2016, linking the 2006 poisoning of Litvinenko to two Russian security agents, acting under the orders of Putin. Russia rejected the findings and threatened to implement sanctions against those involved in the investigation.

In March 2016 Russia announced that it was withdrawing its ground forces from Syria, although it continued airstrikes. Reports indicated that between September 2015 and September 2016, Russian airstrikes killed at least 5,500 anti-government fighters and 3,800 civilians.

Current issues. Political uncertainty increasingly drew domestic attention, as speculation about the future leadership of the country centered on whether Prime Minister Putin would seek reelection or whether President Medvedev would stand for a second term. Analysts saw divisions between Putin and his supporters, who sought greater state control, and Medvedev and his backers, who favored more modernization and liberal political policies. Putin ended the speculation with an announcement on September 24 that he would contest the 2012 presidential election and that Medvedev, in turn, was likely to become prime minister. Some observers said that a Putin presidency raised concerns about further economic stagnation, as in 2011 alone, there had been some $70 billion leaving the country as investors shied away due to the political uncertainty.

The 2011 parliamentary elections were widely criticized as fraudulent by opposition parties and media, a charge partially supported by an OSCE report that stated that "there was no real competition" in the election. Protests in Moscow on December 5, 2011, grew by December 10 into the largest protests since the 1990s, spreading to St. Petersburg, Novosibirsk, Yekaterinburg, and almost 90 other towns and cities across Russia. Protesters demanded an annulment of the elections, official investigations into voting fraud, greater liberty to register parties, and new elections. Subsequent protests on December 24 and February 4, 2012, were even larger and marked by large counter-protests in support of the government. New rounds of protests broke out on March 5, in reaction to Putin's reelection, and May 6, the day before his inauguration. The May protest in Moscow was marred by clashes between police and protestors and the reported arrest of hundreds; prior to an additional round of protests on June 12, new laws on demonstrations went into effect that allow protestors engaging in unauthorized demonstrations to be fined or jailed.

A series of smaller terrorist attacks continued into 2012, chiefly in Chechnya and Dagestan. The most significant was a pair of bombings on May 3 in the capital of Dagestan that killed 13 and injured 130, but four other reported attacks (three in August 2012 alone) killed 25 people.

On August 17, 2012, three members of the Russian female punk band Pussy Riot were found guilty of "hooliganism" and sentenced to two years of labor in a penal colony for performing an anti-Putin protest song on February 21, 2012, in Moscow Cathedral of Christ the Savior. Their trial gathered international attention and helped spark a new major protest by opposition parties on September 12. (One of the three was released on a suspended sentence in October 2012, while the others were released in December 2013 as part of an amnesty.)

Opposition protests continued, with significant rallies on December 15, 2012, January 13, 2013 (in response to a recent law banning U.S. citizens from adopting Russian children), and May 6. The government has continued to take action against protest organizers. Opposition activist Sergei Udaltsov, who helped organize protests in 2011 and 2012, was charged with organizing "mass disorder" and placed under house arrest in February 2013. On July 18, 2013, opposition leader Aleksei NAVALNY was convicted of embezzlement and sentenced to five years' imprisonment. Despite the conviction, Navalny competed in the September 8, 2013, Moscow mayoral election, placing second with 27.2 percent of the vote (to 51.4 percent for Sergey Sobyanin, a member of United Russia).

In June 2013 the Duma adopted a law prohibiting the distribution to minors of "propaganda" that advocates "non-traditional sexual relations," and included provisions allowing the police to expel or detain "pro-gay" foreigners. In July a law was passed banning the adoption of Russian-born children by anyone from a country that allows same-sex marriage. The policies came under international scrutiny in the wake of the upcoming Olympic games in Sochi.

In August 2013 the Russian government began a popularly received roundup of illegal immigrants, mostly from Central Asia and Vietnam. The policy, triggered by the widely reported July 27 assault on a police officer in a Moscow open-air market by the family of an ethnic Dagestani detainee, had led to the arrest of nearly 5,000 illegal immigrants by mid-September.

A suicide bombing in Volgograd in October killed 7 and injured 36, while two further bombings in late December killed 34. All three incidents were attributed to Islamist terror groups from Dagestan.

In February 2014 a new electoral law was approved by parliament, returning a mixed electoral system. Half of the Duma will now be elected in single-mandate districts, while the threshold for proportional representation has been reduced from 7 to 5 percent.

Also in February, eight defendants charged with violence against police in the 2011 protests were sentenced, with seven receiving prison terms. Police detained hundreds of protestors after the sentences were announced, including Navalny.

Economic sanctions against Russia by the U.S., EU, and other nations in response to the 2014 Ukraine crisis were widely reported in the international media to potentially slow Russian growth and fuel inflation. Real wages in Russia fell 4 percent in 2014 and then 9 percent in 2015 as a result of the sanctions and declining oil prices.

A new law enacted on December 31, 2015, gave security officials the right to enter residences or businesses without a warrant and to use force, including deadly force, in order to prevent possible terrorist attacks or other imminent threats. Critics charged that the measure would be used to repress opponents of the regime.

In February 2016 the government announced plans to partially privatize seven state-owned companies, including Aeroflot, the Russian state airline. The privatization was expected to raise $15.5 billion to be used to offset budget shortfalls from low oil prices and economic sanctions.

A new bill that required all cellular and Internet providers to hold communication data for six months and store metadata for three years was introduced in December 2016. The law also banned preaching, praying, and proselytizing outside of religious institutions and other specifically designated places. It also rendered as a crime the failure to report to law enforcement any and all instances of others planning, carrying out, or having already carried out any crimes and criminal liability. The proposed law met with sharp criticism from the media and opposition group outcry over a provision that would enable the government to strip citizenship from Russian nationals, something forbidden by the constitution. The controversial citizenship provision was removed before the final vote. Named for its author, Irina YAROVAYA, the Yarovaya Bill was signed into law on July 7, 2016, by Putin.

In July 2016 the World Anti-Doping Agency issued a highly critical report that detailed widespread use of performance-enhancing drugs by Russian athletes. The International Olympic Committee met to discuss banning Russia from the 2016 Summer Games in Rio de Janeiro, but instead ruled that Russian athletes would have to prove they had not used enhancing drugs. Of 389 Russians originally scheduled to compete in the Olympics, 111 were banned from participation.

POLITICAL PARTIES AND GROUPS

The advent of political pluralism in the Soviet Union in 1990 and the suspension of the CPSU in August 1991 stimulated the emergence of over 200 parties, most of which did not survive in the successor Russian Federation. Some three dozen formations were active in the run-up to the December 1993 legislative elections; ten ultimately gained representation in the State Duma. Thereafter, the party scene was characterized by frequent realignments and new formations, particularly among the pro-market and centrist groupings broadly supportive of the Yeltsin administration. The launching in May 1995 of the center-right Our Home Is Russia (*Nash Dom–Rossiya*—NDR) formation as the "government" party and concurrent moves to form a center-left opposition bloc were seen as an attempt by the political establishment to create a two-party system that would exclude from power the ultranationalists on the far right and the revived Communists on the reactionary left. However, both camps retained sizeable popular constituencies in the complex party maneuverings preceding the legislative balloting of December 17, 1995, at which more than 40 parties, movements, and alliances offered candidates.

As of January 1, 1999, the Ministry of Justice reported 141 registered political organizations, more than 40 of which had sought official status during December 1998 to meet the eligibility deadline for the December 1999 legislative election. However, electoral laws permitted a political formation registered for less than a full year to contest the election if it constituted an alliance of at least two legally registered parties or movements. In the end, 26 organizations qualified for the election, including several alliances formed in 1999. Of the four most important groups active in September 2000, only the Communist Party of the Russian Federation (KPRF) predated 1998, the other three being the Putin-backed Unity, the left-centrist Fatherland, and the right-centrist Union of Right Forces (SPS).

At the beginning of 2001 there were 56 registered parties and 156 other political groups, but a law passed by both houses of the Federal Assembly in June and subsequently signed by President Putin rewrote registration requirements to the detriment of small parties. The law stipulated that to compete nationally parties must have at least 10,000 members, with no fewer than 100 members registered in each of 45 or more of the country's then 89 regions and republics.

The new parties law accelerated a process of political consolidation that had begun in anticipation of its passage. In May 2001, with most of its constituent groups having agreed to a formal merger, the SPS held a congress to authorize its restructuring as a unified party. A second congress in December confirmed the decision, and it was officially registered as such in March 2002. In July 2001 Unity, All Russia, and Fatherland had formed an alliance that was registered in December as the Unity and Fatherland–United Russia; its central component organizations voted to dissolve as separate entities in February 2002, by which time United Russia was already being referred to in some circles as the latest "party of power." Consolidations were also taking place among Russia's less significant parties.

For the State Duma election of December 2003 a total of 44 parties were eligible to present candidate lists for the proportional component. (Twenty public associations were also eligible, but only as members of electoral blocs.) In the end, 18 individual parties and 5 electoral blocs competed, with only 3 parties and 1 bloc meeting the 5 percent threshold for proportional seats: United Russia, the KPRF, the far-right Liberal Democratic Party of Russia (LDPR), and the Motherland–People's Patriotic Union bloc, elements of which subsequently united as the Motherland party. (For a complete discussion of parties and blocs that contested the 2003 election, see the 2005–2006 or 2007 *Handbook.*)

Shortly after the 2003 election, President Putin, backed by United Russia's overwhelming majority faction in the State Duma, began passing legislation intended to eliminate Russia's many medium-sized and small parties before the December 2007 election. For a party to register, it must now have at least 50,000 members, with at least 500 members in each of half the country's regions and 250 in each of the rest. Parties failing to meet the membership test must reregister as public organizations rather than parties or be disbanded by the courts. Single-mandate districts have been eliminated, and the threshold for winning proportional seats now stands at 7 percent of the total national vote. Parties and associations are no longer allowed to form electoral blocs, and members of one party are prohibited from appearing on the candidate list of another party, although individuals without a current party affiliation may be included. Except for those parties that won list seats in the preceding State Duma, parties must pay a deposit of $2.35 million (refundable for those winning at least 4 percent of the 2007 vote) or submit 200,000 supporting signatures; if more than 5 percent of a party's signatures are declared invalid, the party is disqualified. In addition, "none of the above" has been eliminated as a ballot option; it had frequently been used to cast a protest vote. Minimum turnout requirements for national elections have been eliminated, and lawmakers who switch parties after election are to be stripped of their seats.

In the run-up to the 2007 State Duma election, the Patriots of Russia (PR) formed a coalition with the Party of Russia's Rebirth (PVR). The Russian Ecological Party ("The Greens") was disqualified for allegedly faking signatures. While 11 registered parties were deemed eligible for the December election, only 4 reached the 7 percent threshold for election: United Russia, the KPRF, the LDPR, and Just Russia.

In May 2011 Prime Minister Putin established what he said was a new political movement, styled as the All Russian Popular Front, to bring together, with United Russia, "all people who are united by a common desire to strengthen our country," ahead of the December 2011 legislative and March 2012 presidential elections.

Governing Party:

United Russia (*Edinaya Rossiya*). In July 2001 **Unity** (*Edinstvo*), **All Russia** (*Vsya Rossiya*), and **Fatherland** (*Otechestvo*) organized an alliance that was registered in December as **Unity and Fatherland–United Russia** (*Edinstvo i Otechestvo–Edinaya Rossiya*). The members of all three then voted in February 2002 to dissolve as separate entities.

The Unity bloc, also known as the Inter-Regional Movement "Unity" (*Mezhregionalnoye Dvizhenie "Edinstvo"—Medved* [Bear]), had been announced in September 1999 by nearly three dozen leaders of regions and republics (some of whom later withdrew their support) to contest the State Duma elections in December. Backed by President Yeltsin and Prime Minister Putin as a counter to the **Fatherland–All Russia** bloc, Unity offered no ideological platform and was described by some commentators as a "virtual party."

Apparently benefiting from Putin's prosecution of the war in Chechnya and his accompanying rise in popularity, Unity finished second to the KPRF in the December 1999 federal election, winning 23 percent of the vote and 73 seats. In May 2000, with President Putin in attendance, Unity held its founding congress as a political party. On the same day former prime minister Viktor Chernomyrdin's **Our Home Is Russia** (*Nash Dom–Rossiya*—NDR), having won only 1.2 percent of the party list vote and 8 constituency seats at the most recent State Duma election, voted to disband in favor of Unity.

Little more than a year earlier, in April 1999 the organizing committee of All Russia had met in an effort to establish in the Federal Assembly a regionalist power bloc dominated by various regional governors and presidents. Two days later it allied with the Fatherland movement, which had been founded in late 1998 by Yuri Luzhkov, the mayor of Moscow. The resultant Fatherland–All Russia (*Otechestvo–Vsya Rossiya*—OVR) won 13 percent of the party list vote and 66 seats at the December State Duma election.

In April 2001 the Unity faction in the State Duma and the Fatherland–All Russia faction announced that they would work together with the goal of forming a unified party. Within days, two additional parliamentary factions, Russia's Regions and the People's Deputies, had agreed to cooperate with them on selected issues, thereby—at least on paper—creating a 234-seat majority bloc in the State Duma.

In the December 2003 parliamentary election, the unified party, now known as United Russia (sometimes translated as Unified Russia), with President Putin's backing, was the clear victor, winning 36.6 percent of the proportional vote and a slim majority of the filled seats. More important, it soon attracted additional support from independents and other parties, enabling its Duma faction to chair all committees and to surpass the two-thirds threshold for making constitutional changes.

United Russia has emerged as the vehicle for what Putin's supporters label "reform" (and his detractors, authoritarianism). It espouses "social conservatism"—a blend of market economics, promotion of the middle class, nationalism, and support for social order and stability. There has, however, been tension between the party's more rightist market forces and those committed to a more "social orientation," some of whom strongly objected to a Putin initiative that replaced guaranteed social service benefits with cash payments.

United Russia extended its political control in March 2006, winning 55 percent of the vote in eight regional and republican legislative elections. In March 2007 it took 46 percent in winning control in 13 out of 14 legislatures.

Prior to the December 2007 legislative election, United Russia continued to pick up adherents as smaller parties dissolved. Speaking at a party congress on October 1, 2007, President Putin announced that he had agreed to head the party's candidate list and would consider leading the party and serving as prime minister following the end of his presidential term in 2008. In the December election, United Russia won 64.3 percent of the vote. A month before the election, the **Agrarian Party of Russia** (*Agrarnaya Partiya Rossii*—APR), which had been aligned with the Communists, merged with United Russia. (See the 2009 *Handbook* for details on the APR.) Also in 2008, United Russia shortened its name by dropping the "All Russia" rubric.

Following the election of President Medvedev in 2008, whose candidacy was supported by United Russia, Putin, as had been expected, was named prime minister. In April Putin was elected to a four-year term in the newly created post of chair of the party. The party's strength was further consolidated by its victories in most of the March 2009 mayoral elections and in the regional elections of October. Following a series of televised political party debates in mid-2009, United Russia was reported to have achieved its highest-ever popularity rating of 58 percent. Earlier in the year the mayor of Smolensk was dismissed from the party allegedly because of the poor state of infrastructure in his district. However, observers said the party was backing another mayoral candidate, and when the incumbent defiantly added his name to the ballot, he was expelled.

United Russia was concerned about its relatively poor showing in the regional and municipal elections of March 2010. Consequently, the party began to hold mass meetings and to seek new candidates for leadership, particularly on the local level, while also looking for projects to help economic development, especially in Siberia.

United Russia held national party primaries in July 2011 to increase the number of candidates for the December election to the Duma and perhaps increase the party's appeal, which had been waning. The party was suffering from a reputation for corruption and authoritarianism; further, the Communist Party accused it of using state funds to finance the primaries.

In September 2011, at a party convention in Moscow, Medvedev announced that he would defer to Putin as the party's flag bearer in the 2012 presidential election. If Putin were to be elected, Medvedev would become prime minister.

In the December 4, 2011, parliamentary election, United Russia won 49.3 percent of the popular vote, securing 238 seats. In the presidential election on March 4, 2012, Putin received 63.6 percent of the vote, easily defeating Gennady Zyuganov of the KPRF, who was second with 17.2 percent. Following Putin's election, on May 26 Medvedev was announced as the new leader of the party.

In legislative elections on September 18, 2016, United Russia received 54.2 percent of the vote and expanded its majority in the Duma to 343 seats.

Leaders: Dmitry MEDVEDEV (Chair and Prime Minister), Vladimir PUTIN (President), Boris GRYZLOV, Mintimer SHAIMIEV, Sergei SHOIGU, Andrei VOROBYOV, Andrei ISAEV, Sergei NEVEROV (Secretary).

Other Parties in the State Duma:

Communist Party of the Russian Federation (*Kommunisticheskaya Partiya Rossiiskoi Federatsii*—KPRF). The KPRF is a late 1992 revival of the former **Communist Party of the Soviet Union**—CPSU (*Kommunisticheskaya Partiya Sovetskogo Soyuza*—KPSS), which was suspended in August 1991 and then banned in November 1991. The KPRF ran third in the legislative poll of December 1993 and thereafter generally opposed the Yeltsin administration, although in January 1995 a Communist was appointed justice minister. At the December 1995 State Duma election the KPRF won a plurality of 157 of the 450 seats, including 99 from a 22.3 percent share of the proportional vote.

KPRF leader Gennadi Zyuganov contested the mid-1996 presidential election on a platform deploring the erosion of Russia's industrial base by IMF-imposed policies and promising to restore economic sovereignty. He finished a close second to President Yeltsin in the first round on June 16, with 32 percent of the vote, but lost to the incumbent in the runoff on July 3, taking 40.3 percent of the vote. The KPRF then sought to consolidate the left-wing and conservative backing obtained by Zyuganov, initiating the formation in August of the opposition People's Patriotic Union of Russia (NPSR—see Patriots of Russia, below).

After having unsuccessfully attempted to forge a **"For Victory"** (*Za Pobedu*—ZP) electoral coalition of Communists, Agrarians, and others to contest the December 1999 State Duma balloting, the KPRF basically ran independently, with "For Victory" reduced to little more than a slogan. As in 1995, it won a plurality, taking 114 seats and a party list vote share of 24 percent. Three months later Zyuganov again finished second, with 29 percent of the vote, in the presidential contest.

In May 2002 the party's Central Committee expelled three leading members who refused to resign from leadership posts in the State Duma after the ascendant United Russia won committee chairs away from the KPRF. The most prominent dissenter was the chair of the Duma, Gennadi Seleznev, who subsequently built his patriotic Russia movement (*Rossiya*) into the Party of Russia's Rebirth (PVR).

At the December 2003 State Duma election the KPRF saw its support halved—to 12.6 percent of the proportional vote and a total of only 52 seats—in part because a significant fraction of the leftist vote was won by the new Motherland coalition. Sergei Glazyev, a former Communist who had sought an electoral alliance with the KPRF before forming the Motherland coalition, was one of several prominent leftists who had grown disenchanted with Zyuganov's continuing leadership, which led, in mid-2004, to further ruptures. In July supporters of Zyuganov and Vladimir TIKHONOV held competing congresses, with the Ministry of Justice ultimately ruling in Zyuganov's favor. Tikhonov went on to form the **All-Russian Communist Party of the Future** (*Vserossiiskaya Kommunisticheskaya Partiya Budushchego*—VKPB). Zyuganov also lost the support of Gennadi Semigin, chair of the NPSR, who was expelled from the KPRF and later formed the Patriots of Russia.

The KPRF's 2004 presidential candidate, Nikolai Kharitonov, finished second, with 13.7 percent of the vote.

The KPRF has subsequently led opposition to a number of President Putin's initiatives, including changes to social benefits policies. In March 2006 the KPRF came in second in six of eight regions holding legislative elections, improving its representation in five regions due in part to the fact that competing leftist party *Rodina* was excluded from the balloting in all but one of the regions. In March 2007 the KPRF received 16 percent of the vote in 14 regional and republican legislative elections.

In the December 2007 State Duma election the KPRF received 11.6 percent of the votes. Zyuganov stood as the party's presidential candidate for the third time on March 2, 2008, finishing second with 17.8 percent.

The KPRF fared poorly in the regional and municipal elections of October 2009, gaining only 5.3 percent of the vote nationwide.

However, it was the only other party besides United Russia to win seats in the Moscow Duma (3 of 35 seats).

In the December 4, 2011, parliamentary election, the KPRF won 19.2 percent of the popular vote, securing 92 seats. In the March 4, 2012, presidential election, KPRF candidate Gennady Zyuganov won 17.2 percent of the popular vote, placing second.

In the September 2016 Duma elections, the KPRF won 13.3 percent of the vote and 42 seats, a loss of 50 from the previous election.

Leaders: Gennadi ZYUGANOV (Chair and 2012 presidential candidate), Vladimir Stepanovich NIKITIN, Ivan MELNIKOV (Deputy Chair), Vladimir KASHIN (Deputy Chair), Nikolai AREFIEV.

A Just Russia (*Spravedlivaya Rossiya*—SR). (*Spravedlivaya Rossiya* is usually translated as "A Just Russia," but at times the party is called "Fair Russia.") A Just Russia was established in October 2006 by the merger of three parties: Motherland (later reformed, see Motherland, below), the Russian Party of Life, and the Russian Party of Pensioners. Also joining, in April 2007, was the People's Party of the Russian Federation (NPRF).

Motherland (*Rodina*) had originated as the **Party of Russian Regions** (*Partiya Rossiiskih Regionov*—PRR), which joined the Party of National Rebirth "People's Will", the Socialist United Party of Russia (Spiritual Heritage) (*Sotsialisticheskaya Edinaya Partiya Rossii [Dukhovnoe Nasledie]*—SEPR), and smaller groups in forming the **Motherland–People's Patriotic Union** (*Rodina–Narodno-Patrioticheskii Soyuz*) electoral bloc in September 2003. Appealing to the patriotic left, the Motherland bloc surprised most observers by drawing support from the Communists and winning 9 percent of the proportional vote and a total of 36 State Duma seats in December.

The bloc's principal organizers, Sergei GLAZYEV and Dmitri ROGOZIN, had been associated with a number of political formations since the breakup of the Soviet Union, including the Congress of Russian Communities (*Kongress Russkikh Obshchin*—KRO), a moderately nationalist movement that dated from 1995. Much of the KRO's membership had followed Rogozin into the NPRF after its formation in 2001. Glazyev later became the chair of the SEPR, founded in March 2002 by merger of the Socialist Party of Russia (*Sotsialisticheskaya Partiya Rossii*—SPR) and Alexei PODBEREZKIN's Spiritual Heritage (*Dukhovnoe Nasledie*), which dated from 1996 and 1995, respectively. For the 2003 elections Glazyev had approached the KPRF about an alliance but was turned down, leading to his involvement in forming the *Rodina* alliance with Rogozin.

Soon after the unexpected success of the Motherland–People's Patriotic Union in December 2003, their ideological differences and competing political ambitions caused a rupture between Glazyev and Rogozin. In February 2004 Rogozin engineered the renaming of the PRR as the *Rodina* party, after which Glazyev, who had decided to run against President Putin, was removed from the leadership. As an independent, Glazyev finished third, with 4.1 percent of the vote, in the March 2004 balloting. Three months later his new public-political organization, For a Decent Life (*Za Dostoinuyu Zhizn*—ZDZ), based on a loyal SEPR faction and various other elements of the Motherland coalition, was denied registration by the Ministry of Justice. In March 2006 Rogozin announced his resignation from all senior party posts but remained a member of *Rodina* until formation of A Just Russia. In 2007 he formed the Great Russia (*Velikaya Rossiya*—VR) party. Glazyev, who initially supported formation of A Just Russia, later announced his retirement from politics.

The **Russian Party of Life** (*Rossiiskaya Partiya Zhizni*—RPZh) was established in 2002 by Sergei Mironov, chair of the Federation Council. Centrist in nature, the RPZh focused on quality-of-life issues. For the 2003 State Duma election the RPZh forged an electoral bloc with the Party of Russia's Rebirth (PVR), but the bloc won only 1.9 percent of the proportional vote and 3 constituency seats. Mironov won less than 1 percent of the vote as a candidate for president in 2004.

The **Russian Party of Pensioners** (*Rossiiskaya Partiya Pensionerov*—RPP) dated from 1997. It contested the 2003 State Duma elections in a bloc with the Party of Social Justice (PSS, below), winning 3.1 percent of the vote but no seats, which contributed to the suspension of the party's chair, Sergei ATROSHENKO in January 2004. He was succeeded by Valery GARTUNG, initially in an acting capacity. In October the RPP joined in forming the Patriots of Russia coalition, but it remained separate from the subsequently organized Patriots of Russia party. In February 2005 Gartung broke with United Russia's parliamentary faction, primarily because of his opposition to President Putin's plan to replace guaranteed social service benefits with monetary payments (the so-called cash-for-benefits reform), which was widely viewed as adversely affecting pensioners. Seemingly as a direct result of this action, it was discovered that Gartung's election as party leader involved irregularities, which ultimately cost him the post that autumn.

The **People's Party of the Russian Federation** (*Narodnaya Partiya Rossiiskoi Federatsii*—NPRF), formed from Gennadi RAIKOV's preexisting People's Deputy group in the State Duma, was registered as a party in October 2001. At the December 2003 elections it won only 1.2 percent of the proportional vote but 17 district seats. Its deputies then elected to sit in the United Russia parliamentary faction. Citing his duties in the Duma, Raikov stepped down as party chair in April 2004 and has most recently served on the Central Electoral Commission.

At a January 2005 party congress the NPRF adopted a more social-democratic platform and criticized Putin's cash-for-benefits reform. The party leadership later threatened to pull its deputies from the United Russia deputy group, but in May the majority of the NPRF's 17 deputies instead opted to join United Russia to ensure their inclusion on the United Russia party list for the 2007 Duma election. Party chief Gennadi Gudkov later attempted to unite various leftist parties, but the effort failed and he joined A Just Russia in March 2007, a month before the NPRF was deregistered by the courts.

Since its formation, A Just Russia has remained generally supportive of President Putin's policies while attempting to establish itself as the country's principal alternative to United Russia. Its candidate list for the 2007 State Duma election included various prominent figures whose parties had failed to meet the new stringent registration requirements, including Oleg SHEIN of the **Russian Labor Party** (*Rossiiskaya Partiya Truda*—RPT) and Ivan GRACHEV of the **Development of Enterprise** (*Razvitie Predprinimatelstva*—RP), a business-oriented party that was formed in 1998 and won 1 constituency seat in the 2003 State Duma election. A Just Russia received 7.8 percent of the vote in the December 2007 State Duma election.

In 2008 the **Russian Ecological Party "The Greens"** (*Rossiiskaya Ekologicheskaya Partiya "Zelenye"*—REP "The Greens") and the SEPR merged with A Just Russia, as did the **Party of Social Justice** (*Partiya Sotsialnoi Spravedlivosti*—PSS). (For details on these parties, see the 2009 *Handbook.*)

In February 2010 United Russia agreed to coordinate its actions with A Just Russia in support of Just Russia's Sergey Mironov in his role as chair of the Federation Council. However, prior to the March local elections, the LDPR, KPRF, and A Just Russia agreed to combine efforts against United Russia by refraining from campaigning against each other. Consequently, A Just Russia won several mayoral elections.

In April 2011 a party congress elected Nikolai LEVICHEV as chair. In May 2011 Mironov was sacked as chair of the Federation Council, resulting in the party's losing much of its financial and administrative resources. In June, A Just Russia declared that it would not support the candidate (ultimately, Putin) from United Russia in the 2012 presidential elections.

In the December 4, 2011, parliamentary election, A Just Russia won 13.2 percent of the popular vote, securing 64 seats. REP "The Greens," however, had received no seats in the December 2011 election in the lists of A Just Russia and accordingly withdrew and reestablished itself as an independent party in February 2012.

In the March 4, 2012, presidential election, A Just Russia candidate Sergei Mironov won 3.9 percent of the popular vote, placing fifth.

On September 14, 2012, A Just Russia parliamentary deputy Gennady Gudkov was expelled from the Duma, leading to accusations by the party that United Russia was attempting to repress the opposition. On September 29, defectors from A Just Russia reformed *Rodina* as a separate party (see Motherland, below).

On October 27, 2013, Mironov was again elected as party chair.

The party lost 41 seats in the September 2016 Duma balloting, securing 6.2 percent of the vote and 23 seats.

Leaders: Sergey MIRONOV (Chair and 2012 presidential candidate), Nikolai LEVICHEV, Aleksandr BABAKOV.

Political Party LDPR (*Politicheskaya partiya LDPR*). Founded as the **Liberal Democratic Party of Russia** (*Liberalno-demokraticheskaya Partiya Rossii*), the LDPR took its current name, based on its former acronym, at its December 2012 congress. The far-right LDPR was launched in Moscow in March 1990 as an all-Union grouping. Its leader, the xenophobic Vladimir Zhirinovsky, drew over 6 million votes (7.8 percent) in the 1991 presidential poll. Zhirinovsky had made a number of extravagant promises, such as providing each Russian with cheap vodka and launching a campaign to reconquer

Finland. The party was officially banned in August 1992 on grounds that it had falsified its membership lists; however, it was permitted to contest the 1993 legislative poll, at which it ran second to Russia's Choice overall, while heading the party list returns with 22.8 percent of the national vote.

Although Zhirinovsky signed the April 1994 Treaty on Civil Accord between President Yeltsin and more than 200 political groups, his increasingly controversial utterances caused him to be shunned by the political establishment, including his own natural allies. In the December 1995 legislative balloting the LDPR slipped to 11.4 percent of the proportional vote, coming in third with 51 seats. In the mid-1996 presidential contest, Zhirinovsky managed only fifth place in the first round, with 5.7 percent of the vote. The LDPR continued to fare poorly in regional elections in 1997.

In October 1999 the Central Electoral Commission disqualified the LDPR party list from the December State Duma election because two of its top three candidates—one of whom was being investigated for money laundering—had not fully declared their assets. Zhirinovsky cobbled together an alternative list, the Zhirinovsky Bloc (*Blok Zhirinovskogo*), based on the small affiliated Spiritual Revival of Russia Party (*Partiya Duhovnogo Vozrozhdeniya Rossii*—PDVR), led by his half-sister Lyubov ZHIRINOVSKAYA and Oleg FINKO, and the Russia Free Youth Union (*Rossiiskii Soyuz Svobodnoi Molodezhi*—RSSM), led by Yegor SOLOMATIN. The bloc won a 6 percent party list vote share and 17 seats at the election. In the March 2000 presidential contest Zhirinovsky polled 2.7 percent of the vote, for fifth place.

At the December 2003 State Duma election the LDPR finished with an unexpected 11.5 percent of the proportional vote and a total of 36 seats. This momentum did not last, however. Zhirinovsky, acknowledging President Putin's insurmountable lead going into the 2004 presidential election, chose not to run. The party's candidate, Oleg MALYSHKIN, finished fifth with 2 percent of the vote. The LDPR did not reach the threshold for winning seats in two of eight regions holding legislative elections in March 2006, and lost significant ground in the other 6. In March 2007 it won only 9 percent of the total vote in the 14 regions and republics holding elections. In the December 2007 State Duma election, the LDPR won 8 percent of the vote. In the March 2008 presidential election, Zhirinovsky finished third with 9.5 percent.

In 2009 President Medvedev said that although the LDPR was an opposition party, he was certain compromise and cooperation were possible, the LDPR having often voted with United Russia in the past. The LDPR won 4.1 percent of the vote in the regional and municipal elections of October 2009, and it finished third behind United Russia and the Communists in local elections of March 2010.

In June 2011 Zhirinovsky called for repeal of anti-extremist legislation.

In the December 4, 2011, parliamentary election, the LDPR won 11.7 percent of the popular vote, securing 56 seats. In the March 4, 2012, presidential election, LDPR candidate Vladimir Zhirinovsky won 6.2 percent of the popular vote, placing fourth.

The LDPR won 13.1 percent of the vote in the September 2016 national legislative elections, securing 39 seats.

Leaders: Vladimir ZHIRINOVSKY (Chair and 2012 presidential candidate), Igor LEBEDEV, Vasily ZHURKO, Oleg LAVROV, Alexei OSTROVSKY, Maxim ROHMISTROV.

Motherland (*Rodina*). The far-right *Rodina* was founded in 2003, but merged with two other parties to form A Just Russia (above) in 2006. Dissidents from A Just Russia reformed *Rodina* on September 29, 2012, under the leadership of Aleksey ZHURAVLYOV. The party won one seat in the September 2016 Duma balloting.

Leader: Aleksey ZHURAVLYOV.

Civic Platform (*Grazhdanskaya Platforma*). Civic Platform was founded on June 4, 2012, by billionaire Mikhail PROKHOROV as a pro-business, centrist opposition party. Prokhorov resigned from the party in February 2015 after members participated in a pro-Putin rally in Moscow and Rifat SHAYKHUTDINOV succeeded him. The party won one seat in the September 2016 Duma elections.

Leader: Rifat SHAYKHUTDINOV.

Other Parties That Contested the 2011 State Duma Election:

Yabloko. Formally the **Russian Democratic Party *"Yabloko"*** (*Rossiiskaya Demokraticheskaya Partiya "Yabloko"*), *Yabloko* descends from the Yavlinsky-Boldyrev-Lukin Bloc, an electoral grouping formed in October 1993 by economist Grigori Yavlinsky, scientist Yuri BOLDYREV, and former ambassador to the United States Vladimir LUKIN, who, while endorsing market reforms, opposed what they viewed as Yeltsin's "shock therapy." In December 1993 the grouping won 7.8 percent of the party list vote. Boldyrev left the party in 1994. (In 1999 he formed an electoral bloc with the KRO—see A Just Russia, above.) Yabloko's name (which translates as "Apple") comes from an acronym of the three figures' names (Ya-B-L-oko).

Yabloko finished fourth in the December 1995 legislative balloting, winning 45 seats. In the mid-1996 presidential contest Yavlinsky placed fourth in the first round, winning 7.3 percent of the vote and then giving qualified endorsement to Boris Yeltsin in the runoff balloting. Debates over the 1997 and 1998 budgets showed *Yabloko,* rather than the Communists or the nationalists, to be the most uncompromising opponent of the government's spending plans.

At the 1999 State Duma elections *Yabloko* won 21 seats. During the campaign it had been the only major party to criticize the government's conduct of the war in Chechnya, particularly the bombing of Grozny. Yavlinsky finished third, with 5.8 percent of the vote, in the March 2000 presidential election.

At the 2003 lower house election *Yabloko* won only 4.3 percent of the proportional vote and 4 seats. The poor showing of both *Yabloko* and the Union of Right Forces (SPS, see Party of Growth, below) rekindled discussions, first broached in 2000, of a merger, although Yavlinsky had significant differences with SPS leader Anatoly Chubais. In July 2004 Yavlinsky won reelection as party head over Yuri KUZNETSOV, who had advocated an alliance with the SPS. In the March 2006 regional elections *Yabloko* and the SPS, running as an electoral alliance, failed to win any legislative seats, and in June the *Yabloko* party congress voted not to pursue the merger. In the December 2007 State Duma election, Yabloko failed to reach the 7 percent threshold and lost its representation in the lower house. In a statement on election day, Yavlinsky claimed that the election had been rigged.

After 15 years as *Yabloko*'s leader, Yavlinsky stepped down on June 21, 2008, though he remained influential within the party. Sergei Mitrokhin, the leader of the party's Moscow branch, took over as party chair.

In January 2009 the party protested as illegal the arrests of its members who demonstrated in memory of slain journalists and liberal public figures. Another party activist was arrested at a demonstration in April.

Yabloko won only 4 seats of the more than 42,000 seats available nationally in the October 2009 regional and municipal elections and complained of fraud. (Mitrokhin stated that according to official returns *Yabloko* received no ballots in the precinct in which he and his family vote.) The March 2010 local elections were also dismal for the party, their candidates having been barred from competing in the Sverdlovsk and Kaluga regions because a large number of the signatures on the petitions for registration had been declared invalid.

In the December 4, 2011, parliamentary election, Yabloko won 3.4 percent of the popular vote, failing to pass the 7 percent threshold and gain representation.

Yabloko opposed the 2014 annexation of the Crimea. In the September 2016 Duma elections, the party received just 2 percent of the vote, again failing the secure presentation in the legislature.

Leaders: Sergei MITROKHIN (Chair), Alexei ARBATOV (Vice Chair), Mikhail AMOSOV, Elena DUBROVINA, Sergei V. IVANENKO (Treasurer).

Patriots of Russia (*Patrioty Rossii*—PR). Founder and former Communist Gennadi Semigin announced formation of the PR as a unified political party in April 2005. The previous October Semigin had spearheaded formation of a PR coalition encompassing ten predominantly leftist parties and movements, including his own **People's Patriotic Union of Russia** (*Narodno-Patrioticheskii Soyuz Rossii*—NPSR), which had been organized in 1996 by the KPRF's Gennadi Zyuganov as a means of consolidating left-wing, nationalist parties and movements. Zyuganov had lost control of the NPSR in mid-2004, however, during the dispute over leadership of the KPRF. Other initial participants in the PR coalition included the All-Russian Communist Party of the Future (VKPB; see under KPRF, above); the Eurasian Party–Union of Russian Patriots (EP-SPR); the National-Patriotic Forces of the Russian Federation (*Natsionalno-Patrioticheskii Sil Rossiiskoi Federatsii*—NPSRF), led by Shmidt DZOBLAEV; the Party of

Russia's Rebirth (PVR); the Party of Workers' Self-Government (*Partiya Samoypravleniya Trudyashchikhsya*—PST), founded in 1995 by Svyatoslav FYODOROV, who finished sixth in the 1996 presidential election; the People's Patriotic Party of Russia (NPPR); the Russian Party of Pensioners (RPP; see under A Just Russia, above), a wing of the Russian Labor Party (RPT) led by Sergei KHRAMOV; and the Union of People for Education and Science (*Soyuz Liudei za Obrazovanie i Nauku*—SLON), led by Vyacheslav IGRUNOV, one of the original *Yabloko* leaders. The PR also claimed the support of some 30 public organizations.

The PR took part in five of the eight races to regional legislatures in March 2006, passing the 5 percent threshold to win seats in the parliaments of the Kaliningrad and Orenburg regions. It had scant success in the March 2007 regional elections, and received less than 0.9 percent of the vote in the December 2007 State Duma election, failing to win any legislative seats.

The **Party of Russia's Rebirth** (*Partiya Vozrozhdeniya Rossii*—PVR), led by Gennadi SELEZNEV, and the **Party of Peace and Unity** (*Partiya Mira i Edinstva*—PME), led by Sazhi UMALATOVA, merged with the PR in 2008. (See the 2009 *Handbook* for details on the PVR and the PME.)

The PR won only 6 out of more than 42,000 seats contested in the October 2009 regional and municipal elections, and in February 2010 party spokesperson Nadezhda Korneeva complained of the elaborate and expensive process required to gather signatures in order to have candidates compete in an election.

In the December 4, 2011, parliamentary election, the PR won 1 percent of the popular vote, failing to pass the 7 percent threshold to gain representation. It also failed to gain any seats in the September 2016 balloting, winning 0.6 percent of the vote.

Leaders: Gennadi SEMIGIN (Chair), Nadezhda KORNEEVA (Vice Chair).

Party of Growth (*Partiya Rosta*). The party was formerly known as **Right Cause** (*Pravoye Delo*—PD). The pro-business liberal Right Cause was formed in November 2008 by the merger of the **Union of Right Forces** (*Soyuz Pravyh Sil*—SPS), led by Leonid GOZMAN; **Civil Force** (*Grazhdanskaya Sila*—GS), led by Mikhail BARSHCHEVSKY; and **Democratic Party of Russia** (*Demokraticheskaya Partiya Rossii*—DPR), led by Andrei BOGDANOV. (See the 2009 *Handbook* for details on these three parties.) It was officially registered on February 18, 2009, becoming only the second new party to obtain registration in recent years (the other was A Just Russia). Right Cause promotes a civil society based on democratic principles and the rule of law, and it urges political and public freedom, along with free and fair elections. Its critics, however, have accused the party of being too closely aligned with President Medvedev and Prime Minister Putin and more or less controlled by the Kremlin.

Rifts in the party over the tripartite leadership and a campaign platform were reported in 2009, and it won only a few seats nationwide in the October regional and municipal elections. Following another self-acknowledged "dismal" performance in the March 2010 local polls, the party appeared to be in a state of disorganization and in danger of collapse.

In June 2011 Mikhail PROKHOROV, described as the third richest man in Russia, was named party leader. However, rifts within the party had deepened by September, resulting in the ouster of Prokhorov as party chair because of his leadership style, followed by the resignations of several senior leaders. Some observers claimed the party was deliberately riven by Kremlin loyalists, who feared Prokhorov's potential as a political force. Prokhorov subsequently insisted that the party return $22.8 million in party investments that were intended for the parliamentary campaign. (Prokhorov subsequently stood in the March 4, 2012, presidential election as an independent, winning 7.9 percent of the vote and placing third.)

In the December 4, 2011, parliamentary election, Right Cause won 0.6 percent of the popular vote, failing to pass the 7 percent threshold to gain representation.

In March 2016 the Right Cause party officially changed its name to the Party of Growth. In the September Duma balloting, the party won 0.7 percent of the vote.

Leader: Boris TITOV (Chair).

For information on parties that have been dissolved or denied registration, see the 2011 and 2012 *Handbooks*.

Other Political Organizations:

Russian Opposition Coordination Council (*Koordinatsionnyi Sovet Rossiiskaya Oppositsii*—KSRO). In June 2012 activists involved in the ongoing protest movement triggered by the 2011 elections created a council to unify the aims and actions of the disparate opposition groups. Elections of 45 council members were held on October 20–22. In October 2013 the council ended its term of office without setting elections for a new board, leading state-owned media outlets to announce that the KSRO had ceased to exist.

Leaders: Alexei NAVALNY, Gennady GUDKOV, Sergei UDALTSOV, Garry KASPAROV, Andrey PIONTKOVSKY, Yevgeniya CHIRIKOVA, Ilya YASHIN, Boris NEMTSOV, Oleg KASHIN.

The Other Russia (*Drugaya Rossiya*—DR). A forum organized in July 2006 by opponents of President Putin, the DR brought together a philosophically incongruous assortment of former government figures, human rights activists, communists, and nationalists. Organizers included former prime minister Mikhail Kasyanov of the **People's Democratic Union** (*Narodno-Demokraticheskii Soyuz*—NDS), a movement formed in March 2006 to unite left-wing and prodemocracy forces beneath a single banner; among the other NDS leaders were Irina Khakamada, SPS (above) founder and 2004 independent presidential candidate, and Ivan STARIKOV. Participants in the Other Russia also included former chess champion Garry Kasparov, founder in 2005 of the centrist **United Civic Front** (*Obyedinyonny Grazhdansky Front*—OGF); the writer Eduard Limonov, whose radical **National Bolshevik Party** (*Natsional-Bolshevistskaya Partiya*—NBP) had been banned as an extremist organization; and Vladimir Ryzhvov of the **Republican Party of Russia** (*Respublikanskaya Partiya Rossii*—RPR). From December 2006 the principal DR tactic was to convene opposition rallies in major cities. The protests have often been dispersed by the police, with resultant arrests.

In September 2007 differences between Kasparov supporters and Kasyanov led Kasyanov to work outside the forum. He announced formation of **People for Democracy and Justice** (*Narod za demokratiyu i spravedlivost*—NDS) and was nominated as a candidate for the presidential election in December. He was then disqualified by the Central Election Commission, which claimed a large number of his 2 million supporting signatures were invalid. In October DR elements nominated Kasparov as their 2008 presidential candidate. Kasparov withdrew from the presidential election in December. In March 2010 Kasparov was a signatory to a petition circulated by "Putin Must Go," which calls for the resignation of Putin from the government in the interest of creating a free society.

An attempt by Kasyanov, Boris Nemtsov, and others to register a new party, the **People's Freedom Party,** was rejected by the justice ministry in June 2011, but organizers continued to hold rallies pushing their antityranny, anticorruption platform. They further declared that the December 2011 legislative elections would be illegitimate without the party's representation on the ballot.

Leaders: Garry KASPAROV, Eduard LIMONOV.

LEGISLATURE

The 1993 constitution provides for a **Federal Assembly** (*Federalnoe Sobranie*) consisting of a Federation Council and a State Duma. The normal term for each is four years.

Federation Council (*Sovet Federatsii*). The upper house comprises two representatives from each of Russia's constitutionally recognized territorial units (89 units in 2003, declining to 83 in March 2008, and increasing to 85 after the 2014 annexation of Crimea). Each jurisdiction returns two members, one selected by the unit's executive and one by the unit's legislature. (Prior to January 2002, the chief executive and legislative chair of each unit had served ex officio.) Most members are designated as independents, but a majority supports United Russia.

Chair: Valentina MATVIYENKO.

State Duma (*Gosudarstvennaya Duma*). The lower house is a 450-member body. In the election of December 7, 2003, half of the seats were filled from single-member constituencies and half by proportional representation from party lists obtaining a minimum of 5 percent of the vote. Following repeat elections in several districts and significant realignments due to parliamentary factions, the 447 filled seats of the 2003–2007 Duma fell into bloc alignments as follows:

United Russia, 306; Communist Party, 52; Motherland, 38; Liberal Democratic Party of Russia, 36; unaffiliated, 15.

In accordance with a law adopted in 2005, State Duma elections starting in 2007 were conducted on a party-list proportional representation basis. Following the September 18, 2016, election, the seat distribution was as follows: United Russia, 343 seats; Communist Party of the Russian Federation, 42; Political Party LDPR, 39; A Just Russia, 23; Motherland, 1; Civic Platform, 1; and independents, 1.

Chair: Vyacheslav VOLODIN.

CABINET

[as of November 30, 2016]

Prime Minister	Dmitry Medvedev
First Deputy Prime Ministers	Igor Shuvalov
Deputy Prime Ministers	Olga Golodets [f]
	Arkady Dvorkovich
	Dmitry Rogozin
	Alexander Khloponin
	Dmitry Kozak
	Yury Turtnev
	Sergei Prikhodko
	Vitaly Mutko
Ministers	
Agriculture	Alexander Tkachev
Civil Defense, Emergencies, and Disaster Relief	Vladimir Puchkov
Communications and Mass Media	Nikolai Nikiforov
Construction, Housing, and Utilities	Mikhail Men
Culture	Vladimir Medinsky
Defense	Sergei Shoigu
Development of the Russian Far East	Alexander Galushka
Economic Development	Maxim Oreshkin
Education and Science	Olga Vasilyeva [f]
Energy	Alexander Novak
Finance	Anton Siluanov
Foreign Affairs	Sergei Lavrov
Health	Veronika Skvortsova [f]
Industry and Trade	Denis Manturov
Interior	Vladimir Kolokoltsev
Justice	Alexander Konovalov
Labor and Social Security	Maxim Topilin
Natural Resources and Environmental Protection	Sergei Donskoi
North Caucasus Affairs	Lev Kuznetsov
Open Government Affairs	Mikhail Abyzov
Sport, Youth, and Tourism	Pavel Kolobkov
Transportation	Maxim Sokolov

[f] = female

INTERGOVERNMENTAL REPRESENTATION

Ambassador to the U.S.: Sergey Ivanovich KISLYAK.

U.S. Ambassador to Russia: John F. TEFFT.

Permanent Representative to the UN: Vitaly Ivanovich CHURKIN.

IGO Memberships (Non-UN): APEC, CEUR, CIS, EBRD, OSCE, WTO.

For Further Reference:

McDougal, Trevor. "A New Imperialism? Evaluating Russia's Acquisition of Crimea in the Context of National and International Law." *Brigham Young University Law Review* 2015, no. 6 (May 22, 2016): 1847–1887.

Monaghan, Andrew. *The New Politics of Russia: Interpreting Change.* Manchester: Manchester University Press, 2016.

Ostrovsky, Arkady. *The Invention of Russia: From Gorbachev's Freedom to Putin's War.* New York: Viking, 2015.

RWANDA

Republic of Rwanda
République Rwandaise (French)
Republika y'u Rwanda (Kinyarwanda)

Political Status: Republic proclaimed January 28, 1961; independent since July 1, 1962; multiparty constitution adopted June 10, 1991, but full implementation blocked by ethnic-based fighting; peace agreement signed August 4, 1993, in Arusha, Tanzania, providing for transitional government and multiparty elections by 1995; twenty-two month transitional period announced January 5, 1994; new transitional government installed on July 19, 1994, by the Rwandan Patriotic Front (FPR) after taking military control in the wake of genocide of April 1994; new constitution (providing for a four-year, FPR-led transitional government but including provisions of the 1991 basic law and the 1993 Arusha peace agreement) adopted by the Transitional National Assembly on May 5, 1995; transitional period extended by the FPR for four years on June 8, 1999; new constitution providing for full transition to civilian rule adopted on June 4, 2003, following a national referendum on May 26.

Area: 10,169 sq. mi. (26,338 sq. km).

Population: 11,883,000 (2016E—UN); 12,998,423 (2016E—U.S. Census).

Major Urban Center (2016E—UN): KIGALI (1,293,000, urban area).

Official Languages: English, French, Kinyarwanda.

Monetary Unit: Rwandan Franc (official rate October 1, 2016: 805.71 francs = $1US).

President: Maj. Gen. Paul KAGAME (Rwandan Patriotic Front); named acting president by the Supreme Court on March 24, 2000, following the resignation the previous day of Pasteur BIZIMUNGU (Rwandan Patriotic Front); elected in a permanent position by the combined Transitional National Assembly and cabinet on April 17, 2000, and inaugurated on April 22; reelected by popular vote on August 25, 2003, and inaugurated for a seven-year term on September 12; reelected for a second seven-year term on August 9, 2010.

Prime Minister: Anastase MUREKEZI (Social Democratic Party); appointed by the president on July 23, 2014, to replace Pierre Damien HABUMUREMYI (Rwandan Patriotic Front).

THE COUNTRY

Situated in the heart of Africa (adjacent to Burundi, Tanzania, Uganda, and the Democratic Republic of the Congo), Rwanda consists mainly of grassy uplands and hills endowed with a temperate climate. The population comprises three main ethnic groups: the Hutu, or Bahutu (84 percent); the Tutsi, or Batutsi (15 percent); and the Twa, or pygmies (1 percent). Approximately 57 percent of the population is Roman Catholic, with Protestant (37 percent) and Muslim (5 percent) minorities. In addition to English, French, and Kinyarwanda (the three official languages), Kiswahili is widely spoken. Women account for about half of the labor force, primarily as unpaid agricultural workers on family plots; female representation in government and party posts is minimal, though the 2003 constitution called for increased participation by women in all levels of government, civil service, and policy-making. By 2008 the World Bank estimated that women owned 41 percent of Rwandan businesses, the highest percentage in Africa. Women also won a majority of seats in the 2013 legislative balloting with 51 of 80 posts. With women accounting for 63.8 percent of the seats, Rwanda is the only country in the world where women outnumber men in the legislature.

Rwanda has been hindered by high population growth (it is one of the most densely populated states in Africa), inadequate transportation facilities, distance from accessible ports, and the ravages of civil war. Services account for 43.6 percent of gross domestic product (GDP), followed by agriculture, 42.1 percent, and industry, 14.3 percent. Approximately 80 percent of the population is employed in agriculture. Coffee is the leading cash crop and

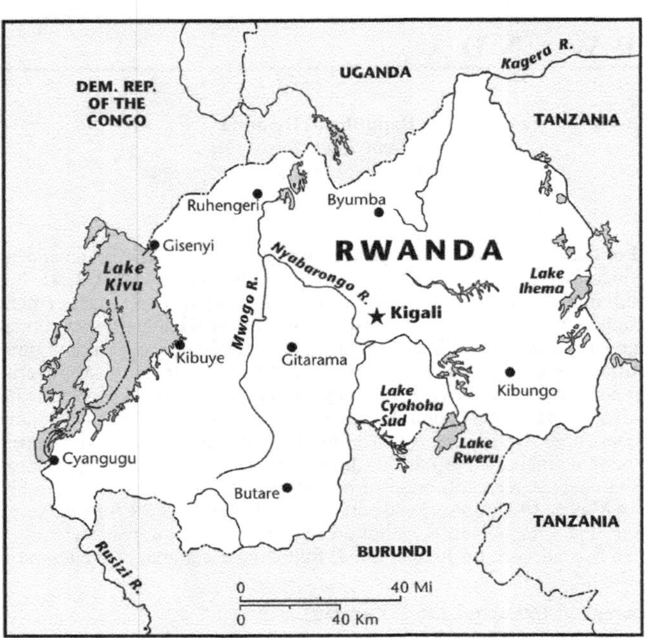

principal source of foreign exchange, although tea cultivation is expanding. Industry is concentrated in food processing and nondurable consumer goods, but the mining of cassiterite and wolframite ore is also important.

Despite the subsequent problems associated with civil war and the massive displacement and return of perhaps 2 million Rwandans, as of mid-2002 Rwanda was continuing to make considerable progress in rebuilding its economy. (For information on the economy prior to 2002, see the 2010 *Handbook.*) Reinforcing the country's economic infrastructure subsequently became the primary focus of governmental policy, which attracted substantial donor assistance.

Rwanda's GDP growth averaged 8.1 percent from 2002 through 2008, and the government was credited with continued liberalization of the economy and retrenchment in public spending. In 2005 the International Monetary Fund (IMF) and World Bank announced that Rwanda had met the requirements for large-scale debt reduction through the Heavily Indebted Poor Countries (HIPC) initiative which allowed the country to write off $1 billion of its $1.4 billion in foreign debt. Subsequently, Rwanda's entry into the East African Community (EAC) in July 2007 was expected to further accelerate development by, among other things, opening neighboring markets to Rwandan goods.

The country passed a milestone when its domestic government revenues exceeded foreign aid for the first time since the 1994 genocide. The global economic crisis caused a decline in agricultural exports in 2009 and GDP growth slowed to 4.1 percent. In 2010 GDP grew by 6.5 percent, while inflation was 2.3 percent. In 2011 GDP grew by 8.6 percent, owing to increased agricultural output, strong exports, and domestic demand. High food and fuel prices, as well as an accommodative monetary policy, drove inflation to its peak of 8.3 percent by the end of 2011. A household expenditure survey released in February 2012 showed substantial progress in poverty reduction over the previous five years across all provinces, particularly outside the capital. The IMF reported that GDP grew by an average of 6.7 percent between 2012 and 2015, while inflation averaged 3.8 percent. GDP expanded by an estimated 7 percent in 2016, and inflation was 4.4 percent. GDP per capita was $815.53 that year. In June 2014 the journal *Foreign Policy* ranked Rwanda second only to Botswana for foreign investment in Africa. In 2015 the EU and Rwanda finalized a €460 million aid program to improve power production and distribution. Japan also announced the resumption of aid to Rwanda after a 26-year hiatus. In its 2016 annual report on the ease of doing business index, the World Bank ranked Rwanda 62nd out of 189 countries, the highest ranking among continental African countries.

GOVERNMENT AND POLITICS

Political background. Like Burundi, Rwanda was long a feudal monarchy ruled by nobles of the Tutsi tribe. A German protectorate from 1899 to 1916, it constituted the northern half of the Belgian mandate of Ruanda-Urundi after World War I and of the Belgian-administered trust territory of the same name after World War II. Resistance to the Tutsi monarchy by the more numerous Hutus intensified in the 1950s and culminated in November 1959 in a bloody revolt that overthrew the monarchy and led to the emigration of thousands of Tutsis. The Party of the Movement for Hutu Emancipation (*Parti du Mouvement de l'Émancipation Hutu*—Parmehutu), founded by Grégoire KAYIBANDA, won an overwhelming electoral victory in 1960, and Rwanda proclaimed itself a republic on January 28, 1961, under the leadership of Dominique MBONYUMUTWA. Since the United Nations did not recognize the action, new elections were held under UN auspices in September 1961, with the Hutu party repeating its victory. Kayibanda was accordingly designated president on October 26, 1961, and trusteeship status was formally terminated on July 1, 1962. Subsequently, Tutsi émigrés invaded the country in an attempt to restore the monarchy; their defeat in December 1963 set off mass reprisals against the remaining Tutsis, resulting in 10,000 to 15,000 deaths and the flight of 150,000 to 200,000 Tutsis to neighboring countries.

The Hutu-dominated government consolidated its position in the elections of 1965 and 1969. Moreover, with President Kayibanda legally barred from seeking another term in the approaching 1973 election, the constitution was altered to assure continuance of the existing regime. The change fanned hostility between political elements from the northern region and those from the southern and central regions, the latter having dominated the government since independence. Beginning in February 1973 at the National University in Butare, renewed Hutu moves against the Tutsis spread quickly to other areas. The government did not attempt to quell the actions of the extremists, and continued instability raised the prospect of another tribal bloodbath or even war with Tutsi-ruled Burundi. In this context, a bloodless coup took place on July 5, 1973.

The new government, under Maj. Gen. Juvénal HABYARIMANA, moved quickly to dissolve the legislature, ban political organizations, and suspend portions of the constitution. A civilian-military government, composed largely of young technocrats, was subsequently installed, and it established a more centralized administrative system. A regime supportive National Revolutionary Movement for Development (*Mouvement Républicain National pour le Développement*—MRND) was organized in mid-1976 and was accorded formal status as the sole legal party under a new constitution adopted by referendum on December 17, 1978. Subsequently, it was announced that the same poll had confirmed Habyarimana for an additional five-year term as president.

In 1980 the administration declared that it had foiled a coup attempt allegedly involving current and former government officials, including Maj. Théonaste LIZINDE, who had recently been removed as security chief after being charged with corruption. Lizinde received a death sentence, which was subsequently commuted to life imprisonment.

Single-party legislative balloting was conducted in 1981, 1983, and on December 26, 1988. Habyarimana, the sole candidate, was accorded additional five-year terms as president by means of referendums in 1983 and on December 19, 1988. In July 1990 Habyarimana called for the drafting by 1992 of a new national charter, which would separate governmental and MRND powers, reduce the size of the bureaucracy, and establish guidelines for the creation of a multiparty system. However, political reform was delayed by an October 1990 invasion from bases in Uganda of the Tutsi-dominated Rwandan Patriotic Front (*Front Patriotique Rwandais*—FPR), obliging the government to call in French, Belgian, and Zairean troops to help repel an FPR advance on Kigali. In March 1991 a cease-fire was negotiated, although fighting continued intermittently thereafter.

On April 6, 1991, a National Synthesis Commission was charged with revising the constitution, and a draft charter was completed on April 30. On June 2 the president announced the legalization of multiparty politics, and the revised constitution was adopted on June 10, one year ahead of schedule. (Earlier, plans for a national referendum were reportedly abandoned for economic reasons.) On October 12 Justice Minister Sylvestre NSANZIMANA was named to the newly created post of prime minister, and on December 30 he announced the installation of a bipartisan administration drawn from what was now termed the National Republican Movement for Democracy and Development (*Mouvement Républicain National pour la Démocratie et le Développement*—MRNDD) and the Christian Democratic Party (*Parti Démocratique Chrétien*—PDC), one of a number of newly registered formations.

In April 1992 the Social Democratic Party (*Parti Social Démocrate*—PSD), Liberal Party (*Parti Liberal*—PL), and Republican Democratic Party (*Parti Démocratique Républicain*—MDR), which had refused to enter the government unless an opposition leader was named prime minister, agreed to join an expanded five-party administration headed by the MDR's Dismas NSENGIYAREMYE pending legislative balloting within a year. In early June the new administration's plan to expedite a debate on a national conference and then hold general elections was foiled when the FPR ejected government forces from a large area of northern Rwanda and threatened to continue its advance unless granted a role in the administration. During preliminary talks held June 5–7 in Paris, the FPR and the government agreed to revive the March 1991 cease-fire and hold a full-scale peace conference.

The first round of talks held July 10–14, 1992, in Arusha, Tanzania, with Western and regional observers in attendance, yielded a truce and a new cease-fire to take effect July 19 and 31, respectively. Thereafter, despite reports of continued fighting, negotiations continued, and on October 31 a power-sharing protocol was announced. On January 10, 1993, following two months of debate on the composition of a transitional government, a formal peace agreement was signed that would give the FPR, MDR, PDC, PL, and PSD a majority of seats in the cabinet and National Assembly. The MRNDD, which was assigned six cabinet seats, and a weakened presidency, denounced the agreement, saying that it categorically refused to participate in the future broad-based transitional government. By early February more than 300 people, predominantly Tutsis, had reportedly been killed in violent anti-accord demonstrations allegedly orchestrated by the MRNDD and the Coalition for the Defense of the Republic (*Coalition pour la Défense de la République*—CDR), an openly anti-Tutsi group, which had been excluded from the government. In response to continuing violence, the FPR announced that it was withdrawing from peace negotiations, and on February 8 it launched an attack on government forces in northern Rwanda near the site of a recent Tutsi massacre. However, the deployment of additional French troops (bringing their number to 600), officially to protect foreign nationals, enabled the regime to survive.

Following further negotiations with the FPR in Arusha in March 1993, Habyarimana was able in July to appoint a new coalition government of the same five internal parties, although this time with a more accommodating faction of the MDR, headed by Agathe UWILINGIYIMANA as prime minister. Renewed Arusha talks subsequently yielded a new 300-page treaty that was signed by President Habyarimana and FPR chair Alexis KANYERENGWE on August 4. Under the new accord, a Hutu prime minister acceptable to both sides would be named and the FPR would be allocated 5 of 21 cabinet posts in a government to be installed by September 10, with multiparty presidential and legislative elections to be held by mid-1995. In addition, a united military force would be formed, 40 percent of which would be Tutsi and 60 percent Hutu. Earlier, on June 22, the UN Security Council had voted to establish a UN Observer Mission Uganda–Rwanda (UNOMUR) to verify that no external military assistance was reaching the FPR. In accordance with the August agreement, the Security Council voted on October 4 to establish a UN Assistance Mission in Rwanda (UNAMIR), which was mandated to monitor the cease-fire and to contribute to security and national rehabilitation in the run-up to the planned elections.

Bickering among the Rwandan parties and delays in UNAMIR deployment made it impossible to meet a September 1993 deadline for the start of the transitional period or a revised target date of December 31. Thus, a new timetable was announced by Habyarimana when, on January 5, 1994, he assumed the presidency for a 22-month transitional period preparatory to multiparty elections in October 1995. However, intense criticism from both the FPR and the internal prodemocracy parties forced the president to postpone the designation of a transitional government and interim legislature. The assassination by unknown assailants on February 21 of PSD leader and government minister Félicien GATABAZI, a Hutu who had promoted rapprochement with the FPR, provoked a new crisis. On February 22 Habyarimana declared an indefinite extension of the transitional phase amid street clashes in which the chair of the Hutu CDR, Martin BUCYANA, was slain by a mob of PSD supporters.

Previous violence in Rwanda paled in significance compared with the wholesale slaughter that followed the death of Habyarimana on April 6, 1994. Both he and President Ntaryamira of Burundi died when their plane was shot down on approach to Kigali airport. The reaction of Hutu militants in Rwanda, led by the Presidential Guard and CDR militia, was to embark on an orgy of killing, not only of Tutsis but also of Hutus believed to favor accommodation with the FPR. Among those murdered within hours of the president's death were Prime Minister Uwilingiyimana and members of her family, at least one minister, Constitutional Court chair Joseph KAVAUNGANDA, and ten Belgian soldiers of the UNAMIR force.

As prescribed by the constitution, the president of the National Development Council, Theodore SINDIKUBWABO, assumed the presidency on April 9, 1994, appointing an interim government headed by Jean KAMBANDA as prime minister and including the five parties represented in the previous coalition. Although a broader-based transitional administration was promised within six weeks, the FPR rejected the legitimacy of the new government (claiming that the presidency should have passed to the president of the yet-to-be-inaugurated transitional legislature) and declared a new military offensive. On April 12, as FPR forces closed in on Kigali, the new government fled to Gitarama, some 30 miles to the south. Meanwhile, French, Belgian, and U.S. troops had been deployed in Rwanda to evacuate foreign nationals. On April 14, upon completion of the transfer of the foreign nationals, Belgium withdrew its 420-strong contingent from UNAMIR. That action, coupled with the failure of UN mediators to arrange a lasting cease-fire, prompted the UN Security Council, in a controversial decision on April 22, to vote unanimously for a reduction of UNAMIR from 2,500 to 270 personnel.

The FPR offensive and the effective absence of an international military presence served to incite the Hutu militants in Rwanda to even greater savagery against the Tutsi minority and presumed Hutu opponents. Gangs of machete-wielding soldiers and militia members reportedly roamed the countryside, engaging in systematic and indiscriminate slaughter of men, women, and children. Although numbers were impossible to verify, the death toll was estimated to be at least 200,000 by late April and perhaps as high as 800,000—a scale of killing officially described by the UN as genocidal. The carnage caused a mass exodus from the country, both of surviving Tutsis and of Hutus fearing FPR vengeance. By early May some 1.5 million refugees had crossed into neighboring countries, creating one of the most severe humanitarian crises ever to afflict independent Africa.

Following widespread criticism of its April 22 decision, the UN Security Council on May 17, 1994, reversed itself by approving the creation of a UNAMIR II force of 5,500 troops, while embargoing arms supplies to the Rwandan combatants. Mainly at U.S. insistence, however, only 150 unarmed observers were initially dispatched, followed by an 800-strong Ghanaian contingent charged with securing Kigali airport. Deployment of the bulk of the force was contingent on a further report from the UN secretary general on its duration, mandate, and composition, and on the attitude of the warring factions to a heightened UN presence. The immediate reaction of the FPR to the UN decision was one of suspicion that UNAMIR II would forestall its imminent military victory. On May 30, with FPR forces controlling portions of Kigali, UN mediators succeeded in bringing about talks between government and rebel representatives. However, little of substance resulted from these and subsequent meetings, while a cease-fire agreement signed under the auspices of the Organization of African Unity (OAU, subsequently the African Union—AU) in Tunisia on June 14 was equally ineffectual. Accounts continued to emerge from Rwanda of atrocities, some allegedly committed by advancing FPR forces. Especially deplored in the West was the murder on June 9 by FPR soldiers (later described as "renegades" by the FPR leadership) of the (Hutu) archbishop of Kigali, two Hutu bishops, and ten Catholic priests.

The UN Security Council on June 9, 1994, unanimously extended the UNAMIR mandate for a six-month period and approved the speedy deployment of two further battalions, which were to protect civilians in Rwanda and facilitate the international relief effort. However, difficulties and delays in assembling and equipping the UNAMIR force (most of which was to be provided by African states) led France to propose on June 15 that it should dispatch 2,500 troops pending the arrival of the enlarged UNAMIR contingent. The Security Council endorsed the French proposal on June 22 (albeit with five members abstaining), and French troops (supported by a small Senegalese contingent) arrived in Rwanda the next day. The result was the establishment of a large "safe area" southeast of Lake Kivu for surviving Tutsis as well as for Hutus fleeing the advancing FPR forces.

The FPR leadership expressed strong opposition to the French deployment, disputing the French claim to nonpartisanship in the conflict in light of the French record of support for the Hutu-based Habyarimana regime. Moving quickly to consolidate its position, the FPR completed its capture of Kigali on July 4, 1994, and two weeks later declared itself the victor in the civil war. On July 19 the FPR installed a new transitional government, with a moderate Hutu, Pasteur BIZIMUNGU, as president, and another Hutu, Faustin TWAGIRAMUNGU (the opposition's nominee for the post following the August 1993 agreement) as prime minister. The FPR military commander, Maj. Gen. Paul KAGAME, became vice president and defense minister, while Tutsis took most of the remaining portfolios. In addition to the FPR and MDR, the PDC, PL, and PSD were represented in the new administration, while the MRNDD and CDR were excluded.

Because of widespread reports of mass killings, the Office of the UN High Commissioner for Refugees (UNHCR) in September 1994 suspended its policy of encouraging Rwandan refugees in Zaire to return home, and on November 8 the Security Council established an International Criminal Tribunal for Rwanda (ICTR) to prosecute those responsible for genocide "and other serious violations of international humanitarian law." Subsequently, the 70-member Transitional National Assembly provided for under the 1993 Arusha agreement convened in Kigali on December 12 (see Legislature, below).

On April 22, 1995, the image of the FPR-controlled government was severely tarnished by the Tutsi-dominated army's massacre of some 2,000 Hutus in the Kibeho refugee camp near Gikongoro. The universally condemned action slowed the voluntary return of Rwandans from Zaire, in addition to setting back efforts to secure badly needed international aid. This and other atrocities by the victorious Tutsis were reportedly the reason for the resignation of Prime Minister Twagiramungu on August 28, with Pierre-Célestin RWIGEMA, the relatively obscure primary and secondary education minister, being named three days later as Twagiramungu's successor and the head of a government which included a number of new Tutsi members in posts formerly assigned to Hutus.

By the end of 1997 an estimated 1.5 million refugees had returned, but the FPR regime still fell short of fulfilling what it had delineated as one of the top prerequisites for national reconciliation—resolution of the judicial process for the tens of thousands of predominantly Hutu prisoners imprisoned (in reportedly subhuman conditions) for their alleged roles in the 1994 genocide. In fact, the FPR continued to be plagued by charges, largely unsubstantiated, that the Tutsi-controlled military was engaging in its own campaign of revenge killings. Meanwhile, the ICTR—26 justices assigned to more than 100,000 cases—proceeded at a glacial pace, hampered, according to a January 1998 UN internal investigation, by a mismanaged judicial system. By the end of 1997, three years after the massacres, the ICTR had not convicted a single defendant. Kigali's judicial efforts, which disposed of fewer than 300 cases in 1997, also foundered when a plea-bargaining program failed to break the logjam, causing observers to note that, barring new developments, most prisoners would die in prison long before their cases could come to trial.

Meanwhile, the toll from ethnic conflict increased in the second half of 1997 (with at least 6,000 more murders during the year, according to UN monitors) as Hutu guerrillas grew in strength and began making daylight raids, particularly in the northwest, where they had wide popular support. Although the guerrillas appeared to have no hope of a military victory, their attacks seemed aimed at making Rwanda ungovernable.

During ICTR testimony in February 1998 the former UNAMIR commander in Rwanda said he had advised the UN leadership of the impending genocide and asked for authorization (never granted) to prevent it. Similarly, a report by the Belgian parliament released in February 1998 claimed the Belgian, French, and U.S. governments also had credible advance warning of the genocide. U.S. president Bill Clinton visited Rwanda in March as part of an African tour, and he acknowledged that the United States and other Western nations had been slow to react to the developments of 1994. (In July 2000 an OAU panel strongly criticized the United States, France, Belgium, the UN, and others—including church groups—for failing to prevent or stop the genocide and called for a "significant level of reparations.")

In April 1998 Rwanda publicly executed 22 persons convicted of murders committed during 1994, and by June thousands of other prisoners had pleaded guilty, apparently to avoid death sentences. In early September the ICTR (recently expanded by the UN in response to widespread criticism) issued its first guilty verdict. Shortly thereafter, the tribunal sentenced former interim prime minister Jean Kambanda to life in prison following his conviction on genocide charges. (Kambanda had admitted his guilt earlier and had reportedly provided evidence against other officials.)

Despite the ongoing judicial quagmire, a degree of normalcy had returned to Rwanda by early 1999, as evidenced by the successful completion of nonparty local elections in March, the first balloting since 1988. At the same time, however, instability persisted near the DRC border, hundreds of thousands of civilians having moved into camps protected by government troops. International attention also remained focused on the Rwandan government's significant role in the DRC civil war (see entry on the DRC). Under those circumstances, it was not surprising that the transitional government in July extended its mandate for four more years, with FPR leaders concluding that security conditions did not permit the organization of multiparty elections.

Major General Kagame remained the most powerful figure in the administration, and on March 24, 2000, he moved into the presidency following the resignation of President Bizimungu. Earlier, on March 8, Bernard MAKUSA, a relatively unknown former ambassador to Burundi and Germany, was appointed to succeed Rwigema as prime minister.

Prime Minister Rwigema's resignation in late February 2000 was attributed to his deteriorating relationship with the Transitional National Assembly (which was investigating alleged financial improprieties on the part of government officials) as well as conflict with other MDR leaders. Likewise, an intraparty power struggle in the FPR apparently contributed to the resignation of President Bizimungu in March. The installation of Major General Kagame as president merely formalized his already de facto authority. Kagame called upon all Rwandan refugees to return home and pledged to pursue national reconciliation, although his status as the nation's first Tutsi president since independence created additional unease for those already concerned over the lack of Hutu representation in government. That worry was not alleviated by the March 2001 district elections, in which party activity was again barred and most of the successful candidates appeared to be aligned with the FPR.

The return to normality continued with the government in December 2001 adopting a new flag, national anthem, and national seal. However, Hutu groups continued to assert periodic discrimination and retaliation by the FPR-dominated government. Domestically, hopes for Tutsi–Hutu reconciliation rested, in part, on the reestablishment in early 2002 of the traditional *gacaca* system, in which elected village judges were to adjudicate the cases of some 90,000 detainees still facing charges relating to the events of 1994. (Most of the other cases, involving those accused of ordering mass killings or participating in rapes, were to be handled by the normal court system. Meanwhile, the "masterminds" of the genocide still faced trial at the ICTR, which as of April 2002 had arrested 60 of the 75 people who had been indicted so far. Only eight convictions had been achieved by that time, although a number of high-profile cases were on the docket for the remainder of the year.)

In January 2003 the government ordered the release of 40,000 detainees but reserved the right to arrest the released people if new evidence emerged. By the end of the year some 25,000 had been released. Survivor groups severely criticized the measure, claiming that many involved in the genocide were being released. Meanwhile, the *gacaca* courts began to adjudicate an increasing number of cases. In August 2003 one *gacaca* court convicted 105 people in a mass two-day trial.

In April 2003 the Transitional National Assembly approved a new draft constitution that was put before voters in a national referendum on May 26, 2003. The new basic law was approved by a 93.4 percent vote and became effective June 4. Among other provisions, the constitution created a bicameral legislature and provided for direct election of the president. In an effort to prevent further ethnic conflict, the constitution also prohibited any parties based solely on race, gender, or religion. However, some opposition parties and international human rights groups charged that this provision was enacted to reinforce the political domination of the FPR.

Prior to the presidential elections, the constitutional court ruled that the MDR and the PDC were illegal parties because of their role in the events of 1994. Consequently, the MDR candidate—former prime minister Twagiramungu—and the PDC candidate—Jean-Népomuscéne NAYINZIRA—were forced to run as independents. In the balloting on August 25, 2003, Kagame was elected with 95.1 percent of the vote, followed by Twagiramungu with 3.6 percent and Nayinzira with 1.3 percent.

Legislative balloting took place September 29–30 and October 2, 2003. Of the 53 directly contested seats, a coalition led by the FPR secured 40 seats; the PSD, 7; and the PL, 6. Makusa was reappointed prime minister and formed a new unity government on October 19. The government included representatives of all 7 parties that secured representation in the Chamber of Deputies. Kagame carried out several cabinet reorganizations, including a major reshuffle on March 7, 2008, in which 5 new ministers were appointed, and 11 had their portfolios changed.

By March 2005 the ICTR had convicted 22 defendants and acquitted 3. In addition to complaints about the continued slow pace of case resolution, criticism emanated from Rwandan Hutus over the fact that no Tutsis had been indicted by the ICTR, despite Hutu assertions that revenge killings and other atrocities had been committed by Tutsis from the FPR in 1994. Meanwhile, the *gacaca* courts faced a backlog of some 95,000 cases by the end of the year. Tension also arose from the release of documents from the Kambanda trial that appeared to support Tutsi arguments that the Hutu attacks in 1994 had been well coordinated and discussed in advance at high levels of government.

In an effort to promote national reconciliation, more than 9,000 prisoners who had been accused of participation in the 1994 genocide were released in February 2007. Although none of those released had faced charges of so-called major crimes, genocide victims' groups still criticized the action. In April former president Bizimungu was also pardoned. Meanwhile, former Maj. Gen. Laurent MUNYAKAZI became the most senior military figure to be convicted when he was found guilty of 13 counts of genocide by a Rwandan court. He was sentenced to life in prison.

A 2007 controversial family planning law met with widespread opposition in the Catholic community. It limited couples to three children in an effort to slow population growth. Meanwhile, the death penalty was abolished in June and replaced by life imprisonment.

In the 2008 legislative elections, the FPR again formed an electoral coalition. The grouping won 42 seats in the direct elections, while the Social Democratic Party secured 7, and the Liberal Party, 4. The main opposition groups boycotted the elections, but international observers declared the elections free and fair and noted that the National Election Commission had implemented all of the reforms recommended after the 2003 polling. In balloting for the Chamber of Deputies in October 2008, women secured 45 posts, or more than 56 percent of the seats, making Rwanda the first country to have a majority female legislative chamber. Rwanda was also the first country to meet the AU's Protocol to the African Charter on the Rights of Women in Africa, which called for countries to have 50 percent of their legislature made up of women deputies. The FPR-led coalition led won the legislative balloting and Kagame subsequently reappointed Makusa as prime minister of a coalition government that included only minor alterations from the previous cabinet.

Kagame carried out a major cabinet reshuffle on November 29, 2009. Kagame won presidential balloting on August 9, 2010, with more than 90 percent of the vote against three candidates from progovernment parties. Leading opposition leaders were barred from entering the race. On September 14 Kagame reappointed Makusa as prime minister and renewed the existing cabinet.

On May 7, 2011, Kagame conducted a cabinet reshuffle and reduced the number of portfolios in the government. Pierre Damien HABUMUREMYI was appointed by the president on October 6, to succeed Makusa as prime minister.

Kagame undertook a cabinet reshuffle on February 25, 2013, which included the appointment of three additional ministers of state. In the September 16–18, Chamber of Deputies balloting, the FPR and its allies again won a majority, with 41 votes (see Political Parties, below); followed by the PSD, 7; and the PL, 5 (see Current issues, below). On July 23, 2014, Anastase MUREKEZI (PSD) was appointed prime minister. The cabinet was reshuffled the next day.

On July 14, 2014, the legislature approved amending the constitution to abolish presidential term limits and allow Kagame to seek a third stint in office. Draft amendments to the constitution were approved by parliament in November 2015 and a national referendum on the issue was held on December 18. Voters overwhelmingly approved the constitutional change, by 98.3 percent.

Constitution and government. On June 10, 1991, President Habyarimana signed into law a new constitution distinguished by the introduction of a multiparty system and the separation of executive, legislative, and judiciary powers. (For information on the 1971 constitution, see the 2014 *Handbook*.) Under the 1991 constitution, executive powers were shared by the president and a presidentially appointed prime minister, who named his own cabinet. In addition, the legislature's presiding officer was empowered to serve as interim president if the incumbent left the country or became incapacitated. The constitution also stated that while political party formations could organize along ethnic and tribal lines, they had to be open to all.

On May 5, 1995, the Transitional National Assembly that had convened five months earlier adopted a new constitution incorporating the essentials of the 1991 document as well as elements of the 1993 power-sharing peace agreement. On June 8, 1999, the transition period, initially scheduled to expire in 1999, was extended to 2003.

The new constitution adopted on June 4, 2003, created a bicameral legislature and provided for a directly elected president. A clause that limited presidents to two seven-year terms was abolished in December 2015. Amendments to the constitution in October 2005 reduced the number of provinces from 12 to 5, the number of districts from 106 to 30, and the number of "sectors" (local administrative units) from 1,545 to 416. The consolidation was seen as a way to save money and streamline government. In February 2006 the language in the constitution regarding property rights was strengthened to assist returning refugees in recovering their property. In July 2008 the constitution was amended to ensure that the country's budgetary process was in accordance with requirements of the EAC. Amendments also clarified the duties of some cabinet ministers, changed the title of the country's senior military officer to chief of the defense staff, and granted perpetual immunity to former presidents of the republic.

The judiciary, headed by a Supreme Court, includes magistrates, prefectural, and appeals courts; a Court of Accounts; a Court of Cassation; and a Constitutional Court composed of the Court of Cassation and a Council of State. The president and vice president of the Supreme Court are elected by the Senate. In 2008 the tenure of judges was reduced from lifetime appointments to four-year periods, followed by a legislative review and potential reappointment.

On August 14, 1991, the legislature adopted a press law guaranteeing, with certain restrictions, a free press. Most papers stopped publishing as the result of the 1994 genocide, although the situation has since returned to normal. The press is generally considered to be supportive of the government and exercises a degree of self-censorship in that regard. In March 2013 a new law eliminated restrictions on print media, although some constraints remained on broadcast journalism. In its annual index on press freedom in 2016, the journalism watchdog group Reporters Without Borders ranked Rwanda 161st of 180 countries.

Foreign relations. Under President Kayibanda, Rwandan foreign policy exhibited a generally pro-Western bias but did not exclude relations with a number of communist countries, including the Soviet Union and the People's Republic of China. Following the 1973 coup, however, the country took a pronounced "anti-imperialist" turn; Rwanda became the first African nation to break relations with Israel as a result of the October 1973 Arab–Israeli war, and it also contributed to the support of liberation movements in southern Africa. At the same time, President Habyarimana initiated a policy of "opening" (*l'ouverture*) with adjacent countries. Despite a tradition of ethnic conflict between Burundi's ruling Tutsis and Rwanda's ruling Hutus, a number of commercial, cultural, and economic agreements were concluded during a visit by Burundian president Michel Micombero in June 1976, while similar agreements were subsequently negotiated with Tanzania and Côte d'Ivoire. Burundi, Rwanda, and Zaire established the Economic Community of the Great Lakes Countries in 1976.

Relations with Uganda were strained for several decades following independence by large numbers of refugees crossing the border in both directions to escape tribal-based hostilities. (For more on relations between the countries from 1985 to 1995, see the 2012 *Handbook*.)

In 1995 and 1996 Rwanda's foreign relations continued to be defined by the encampment of an estimated 2 million Rwandans outside its borders. In August 1995 the UN lifted its embargo on the sale of weapons to Rwanda after months of lobbying by Rwanda, which claimed that members of the former Hutu government now exiled in Zaire were engaging in cross-border guerrilla attacks. In response to the end of the embargo, Kinshasa launched a violent and unsuccessful repatriation program, claiming that Kigali was preparing to attack the refugee camps. A subsequent repatriation attempt in February 1996 strained relations even further, and throughout the first half of 1996 the two capitals accused each other of employing "destabilization" tactics. Meanwhile, in mid-April the FPR cheered the withdrawal of the last UN peacekeepers from Rwanda. (The Tutsi regime held the UN forces responsible for both allegedly collaborating in the 1994 genocide and undermining the regime's attempts to govern.) During the second half of 1996 a stunning sequence of events in Burundi, Zaire, and Tanzania, respectively, resulted in the repatriation of approximately 650,000 refugees to

Rwanda. In Burundi the military coup by Tutsi officers in late July reportedly sparked fear of reprisal attacks among the refugees, and, following the departure of 130,000 people, Bujumbura on August 27 announced the closing of the last of Burundi's camps. Thereafter, in mid-November, several hundred thousand refugees were reported to have fled back across the border from their encampments in eastern Zaire after an allegedly Kigali-funded rebellion on behalf of Zairean Tutsis, the Banyamulenge, resulted in the rout of Zairean troops and Rwandan Hutu militiamen who had been seeking to establish a "Hutuland" in the region. In December Tanzanian government forces, with the tacit and unprecedented approval of the UNHCR, forcibly repatriated over 200,000 refugees to Rwanda.

In 1997 Rwanda, along with five other nations, supported the forces of Laurent Kabila in Zaire, hoping a rebel victory there would enable Rwanda to close the rear bases of the Hutu guerrillas as well as the camps where they sought refuge. After the Kabila victory, the refugee camps along the border were closed, but guerrillas drifted across into Rwanda with returning refugees and regrouped in Rwanda. Meanwhile, Rwandan government forces that had crossed the border into the former Zaire (now known as the Democratic Republic of the Congo, or DRC) remained in two provinces, North and South Kivu, in a de facto occupation apparently with Kabila's tacit approval. Relations between Kinshasa and Kigali subsequently deteriorated, as Kabila distanced himself from Tutsi influence, prompting hostility among the Banyamulenge Tutsis in the eastern portion of the DRC, as Zaire had been renamed. In July 1998 Kabila announced an end to military cooperation with Rwanda, and in August a full-fledged rebellion broke out against his administration (see the entry on the DRC). By November Rwanda acknowledged that its troops were allied with the anti-Kabila rebels, claiming that the DRC government was rearming the Hutus responsible for the 1994 genocide.

In an unexpected turn of events, forces from Rwanda and Uganda, previously allied in support of anti-Kabila rebels in the DRC, clashed in northeast DRC in August 1999, with underlying factors apparently including support for different anti-Kabila factions in the DRC and perhaps most importantly, rivalry regarding eventual preeminence in the region. Fighting between the Rwandan and Ugandan troops erupted again in the spring of 2000.

In November 2001 Kagame began a series of meetings with the leader of Uganda, president Museveni. Following mediation efforts by South Africa and the United Kingdom, in 2003 the two governments agreed to take stronger action to prevent rebels and dissident groups from crossing each other's borders and initiating conflicts. In addition, the two heads of state agreed on the voluntary repatriation of 26,000 Rwandans remaining in refugee camps in Uganda. In July 2002 a separate peace accord was signed in Pretoria, South Africa, between Rwanda and the DRC. By October all 23,400 Rwandan troops had withdrawn from the DRC, and in September 2003 the two countries reestablished diplomatic relations.

In 2005 the government deployed 2,000 troops to the UN peacekeeping mission in Darfur, Sudan.

Burundi and Rwanda established a joint committee to resolve border issues in August 2006. Subsequently, Rwanda and Uganda agreed to increase security cooperation to suppress Hutu militias operating in the border regions of the two countries.

In November 2006 a French judge issued an international arrest warrant for nine senior Rwandan officials on charges that they had been involved in the downing of President Habyarimana's plane in 1994. All nine were close allies of Kagame. The Rwandan government adamantly rejected the charges and broke off diplomatic relations with France. Rwanda also closed its embassy in Paris and opened a new one in Sweden. Meanwhile, there were large demonstrations against France in Rwanda, including one in Kigali involving more than 25,000 people. During local trials in Rwanda, new allegations emerged that French military officers had ignored calls to help victims of the genocide. A memorandum of understanding between Rwanda and the UK led to the arrest of four genocide suspects in London in December 2006. Rwanda subsequently applied for membership in the Commonwealth as a manifestation of the country's growing ties with the UK.

In April 2007 the UN lifted the arms embargo that had been in place against Rwanda since 1994, and in July Rwanda became a member of the EAC. As part of the accession agreement, other EAC members reduced tariffs on Rwandan agricultural exports. The Rwandan government also initiated a program to change the language of instruction from French to English. Officially this was part of a broader effort to integrate into the EAC, but it also indicated the continuing tense relations between Rwanda and France. French president Nicholas Sarkozy visited Rwanda in October in an effort to improve relations between the two countries. In November, an agreement was reached between Rwanda and the DRC to disarm the Hutu resistance group, the Democratic Forces for the Liberation of Rwanda (*Forces Démocratiques pour la Libération du Rwanda*—FDLR), and to suppress other armed groups in both countries. The agreement was followed by a DRC offensive against the FDLR. Kagame attended the meeting of heads of state of the Commonwealth in November, and the country began negotiations to join the organization.

During the crisis in Zimbabwe (see the entry on Zimbabwe), Kagame emerged as one of the foremost critics of President Robert Mugabe and a proponent for new elections in that country. In March Rwanda and the UN finalized an agreement whereby those convicted by the ITCR would be allowed to serve their sentences in Rwanda. In August a commission created by the Rwandan government charged various French officials, including former president Francois Mitterrand, with complicity in the 1994 genocide. The French government rejected the accusations.

Joint Rwanda–DRC military operations against the FDLR in 2008 and 2009, resulted in a number of the rebel group's top leaders being killed or captured and allowed for the return of more than 2,000 Hutu refugees. In January 2009 it was reported that Rwanda arrested the leader of the DRC Tutsi rebel group, the National Congress for the Defense of the People (*Congrès National pour la Dèfense du Peuple*—CNDP) that had been supported by Rwanda. The CNDP had split into rival factions with one group, led by Bosco NTAGANDA, signing a cease-fire with the DRC in January. Rwanda reportedly backed the Ntaganda faction. In April Rwanda and Uganda signed an agreement to return more than 20,000 Rwandan refugees. The UNHCR pledged aid and material support to facilitate the resettlement. At the November 2009 meeting of the Commonwealth, Rwanda was formally admitted to the organization as its 54th member.

In January 2010 publication of a government report absolved France of any role in the 1994 assassination of Habyarimana (see Current issues, below). Relations between Rwanda and France subsequently improved significantly. French president Sarkozy, during a trip to Rwanda, in February acknowledged that actions by his country contributed to the genocide. Following a meeting between high-ranking military officials, Rwanda and China announced closer security ties. In June 2010 Rwanda and South Africa recalled their respective ambassadors after an aborted assassination attempt against the Rwandan opposition figure Kayumba NYAMWASA. In August Ugandan authorities arrested fugitive Hutu leader Augustin NKUNDABAZUNGU and extradited him to Rwanda to stand trial for genocide related to the 1994 civil war.

In October a report by the UN accused Rwandan troops of committing crimes against humanity, including rape and extrajudicial killings, during the 1990s. The Rwandan government rejected the report and threatened to withdraw its peacekeeping forces from Sudan. Intervention by UN Secretary General Ban Ki-moon defused the crisis. Also in October the French authorities arrested Callixte MBARUSHIMANA, a leader of the FDLR. He was subsequently turned over to the International Criminal Court on charges of war crimes (in December 2011 the ICC freed Mbarushimana for lack of evidence).

In late May 2012, a leaked UN report claimed Rwandan authorities were complicit in the recruitment of Rwandans to fight with rebels who broke away from the control of Congo's national army in April. In late June the United Nations published its full investigation into Rwanda's involvement with the M23 rebel group in eastern Congo, documenting numerous violations of international law and UN resolutions (see entry on the DRC). In addition to sending troops and arms to the fight, the report claimed that Rwandan officials had encouraged the secession of North and South Kivu and may have tried to sponsor a rebellion in South Kivu. In response, the United States and other donors announced the suspension of aid. (For more information, see the 2014 *Handbook.*) Despite the controversy, on October 18, Rwanda was elected to a nonpermanent seat on the UN Security Council. Meanwhile, Rwanda announced it would withdraw its remaining forces in the DRC.

On February 1, 2013, Germany restored aid to Rwanda. Also in February, Rwanda and the Netherlands pledged to further increase collaboration following the signing of an aviation treaty. That month Rwanda, the DRC, and Uganda, signed a conservation treaty to encourage wildlife preservation. In June Rwanda signed an agricultural cooperation agreement with Ethiopia, followed by a broader trade accord in August. In December, reports indicated that Rwanda had ended its support for the M23 rebels in the DRC.

In June 2014 there were a series of border clashes between Rwanda and the DRC. At least five DRC soldiers were killed in the skirmishes. Both countries accused the other of violating their respective territories. In July Rwanda and Equatorial Guinea signed a broad cooperation pact on areas ranging from the economy to security to transport. The accord was heralded as the onset of close relations between the two nations. Also in July Rwanda and the Czech Republic signed a defense accord.

In October 2014 regulators in Rwanda suspended the broadcast of the BBC after a controversial documentary aired that was critical of the government's narrative of the genocide. There were widespread protests against the film, and the parliament adopted a resolution in November supporting the suspension and calling for the producers of the documentary to be tried for genocide denial. In December Belgium announced it was withholding €40 million in aid because of Rwanda's failure to meet media freedom goals as stipulated in a 2011 agreement.

The chief of Rwanda's intelligence service, Lt. Gen. Emmanuel Karenzi KARAKE, was arrested on June 20, 2015, in London in response to an EU arrest warrant on charges that he was involved in the murder of three Spanish aid workers in 1997. Karake was granted bail, and the EU extradition request was denied by a UK court on August 10.

In June 2016 Israeli prime minister Benjamin Netanyahu made a state visit to Rwanda and signed a number of cooperative agreements on agriculture and technical assistance in a sign of growing ties between the two nations.

Current issues. In January 2009 Agnes NTAMABYALIRO became the first former government minister of the 1994 Hutu cabinet to be tried and sentenced in Rwanda for her part in the 1994 genocide. In June a *gacaca* court sentenced senator Stanley SAFARI, the leader of the Prosperity and Solidarity Party (PSP), to life in prison for his role in the genocide and the PSP leader subsequently fled to Uganda to avoid detention. The Senate subsequently expelled Safari from the chamber. In December 2009 the UN extended the mandate of the ICTR through 2012 and approved the appointment of additional judges to address the backlog of cases. Meanwhile Ephrem NKEZABERA was convicted and sentenced to 30 years of imprisonment for involvement in the genocide.

On January 11, 2010, an independent commission led by Jean MUTSINZI issued a comprehensive report on the 1994 genocide. The report blamed the 1994 assassinations of the Rwandan and Burundian presidents on a small group of Hutu officials. In March Agathe HABYARIMANA, the widow of the assassinated former president, was arrested outside Paris on a warrant issued by Rwanda on charges of involvement in genocide. In April Victoire INGABIRE, leader of the United Democratic Forces (*Forces Democratiques Unifiées*—FDU-Inkingi) and her party's presidential candidate, was arrested on charges of genocide denial and illegally working with the FDLR (in October 2012 she was sentenced to eight years in prison).

Former army chief of staff and opposition leader Kayumba Nyamwasa was wounded in an assassination attempt in Johannesburg on June 19, 2010. Reports initially blamed Rwandan intelligence agents, but six people were subsequently arrested in the attack. Meanwhile, opposition newspaper editor Jean-Léonard RUGAMBAGE was killed on June 24. On July 13 André Kagwa RWISEREKA, the vice president of the Democratic Green Party of Rwanda (*Parti Democratique Vert du Rwanda*), was murdered and beheaded. Kagame was reelected on August 9 in balloting described by international observers as free and fair. However, opposition parties rejected the balloting. In June 2011 Pauline NYIRAMASUHUKO became the first woman to be convicted of genocide and incitement to rape by the ICTR. She was sentenced to life in prison.

On January 11, 2012, two French judges cleared the FPR of shooting down the plane carrying Habyarimana, and they agreed with a team of British experts that the missiles were fired from a camp under the control of the Rwandan army. The decision angered Kagame's critics in France and Rwanda. In December 2012 Augustin NGIRABATWARE, former minister of planning and cooperation, was convicted by the ICTR of genocide. He was the last person to be tried by the ICTR, which did continue to hear appeals.

On September 16–18, 2013, elections for the Chambers of Deputies were held. There was minor violence prior to the balloting, including two grenade attacks in Kigali that killed two and injured 14, and was blamed on the FDLR. The FPR-led alliance won an absolute majority of 41 seats in the 80-member chamber, in balloting that was criticized by opposition groups who claimed that their supporters faced harassment and intimidation at polling centers.

On March 4, 2014, opposition figure Nyamwasa survived another assassination attempt in South Africa. South Africa responded by expelling three Rwandan diplomats. Kigali then expelled six South African diplomats. Also in March, Pascal SIMBIKANGWA, Rwanda's chief intelligence official in 1994, was found guilty of genocide by a French court and sentenced to 25 years in prison.

On December 30, 2015, Jean Bosco UWINKINDI was found guilty of genocide and sentenced to life in prison by the Rwandan high court. Uwinkindi's case became the first to be transferred from the ICTR to Rwanda's national court system.

POLITICAL PARTIES

A one-party state after the 1973 coup, Rwanda adopted a multiparty constitution on June 10, 1991. Under the terms of the 2003 constitution, the government has the power to ban political parties that might advocate civic unrest or exacerbate ethnic differences. Using this provision, the government banned the MDR, PDC, and several smaller parties prior to the 2003 elections (see below). Prior to the 2008 legislative elections, it was announced that the same parties that formed an FPR-led grouping in the 2003 balloting would campaign as an electoral coalition. The parties included the FPR, the PDC, the **Islamic Democratic Party** (*Parti Démocratique Islamique*—PDI), the **Rwandan Socialist Party** (*Parti Socialiste Rwandais*—PSR), and the **Rwandan People's Democratic Union** (*Union Démocratique du Peuple Rwandais*—UDPR). The Party for Progress and Concord (*Parti pour le Progrès et la Concorde*—PPC) and the **Prosperity and Solidarity Party** (*Parti de la Solidarité et du Progrès*—PSP) also joined the FPR-led coalition. Reports in 2010 indicated that three small parties, the **United Democratic Forces** (*Forces Democratiques Unifiées*—FDU-Inkingi), the **Democratic Green Party of Rwanda** (*Parti Democratique Vert du Rwanda*), and **Social Party Imberakuri** (*Parti Social Imberakuri*—PS Imberakuri), formed an opposition coalition, the Permanent Consultative Council of Opposition Parties.

Government and Progovernment Parties:

Rwandan Patriotic Front (*Front Patriotique Rwandais*—FPR). Currently the dominant political force in Rwanda, the FPR is a largely Tutsi formation that invaded Rwanda in October 1990 from Uganda under the command of Rwandan refugees who were formerly officers in the Ugandan armed forces. However, most of the original leadership, including FPR founder Fred RWIGYEMA, were killed in fighting with government troops in late 1990 and early 1991.

Buoyed by a series of stunning victories in early June 1992, which yielded control of much of northern Rwanda, the FPR called on the Rwandan government to integrate FPR members into both the military and the government, reduce the president's power, allow all refugees to return, and hold multiparty elections. The FPR signed the Arusha peace agreement on August 4, 1993, but implementation was subject to repeated delays. The massacres of Tutsis and moderate Hutus, which followed the death of President Habyarimana in April 1994, impelled the FPR to launch a new offensive, which brought it to power three months later. The victory was attributed largely to the military leadership of Maj. Gen. Paul Kagame. Kagame consolidated his power when he was elected FPR president in February 1998 and president of the republic in March 2000. Kagame was subsequently reelected president for a seven-year term in 2003. During legislative elections, the FPR led an electoral coalition that received 73.8 percent of the vote and 40 seats. (The FPR gained 33 seats alone.) The FPR conducted elections in July 2007 for local and regional party organizations. Allies of Kagame won the majority of posts.

In 2008 the party vehemently rejected the 40 arrest warrants issued by a Spanish judge for FPR members who were currently military or government officials (see Current issues, above). In elections for the Chamber of Deputies, the FPR again led a coalition of progovernment parties. The coalition won 78.8 percent of the vote and 42 of the directly elected seats. The FPR had to replace one of its deputies in the assembly, Beatrice NIRIERE, after she was convicted of genocide in June 2009.

Kagame was reelected president with 93.1 percent of the vote in balloting on August 9, 2010. In October Kagame publicly rejected speculation that he would attempt to change the constitution in order to seek a third term. In legislative balloting in September 2013, the FPR-led coalition won 76.2 percent of the vote and renewed its majority in the Chamber. Kagame was reelected party chair in December with 99.5 percent of the vote.

After Parliament and a national referendum altered the constitution to remove presidential term limits, Kagame announced on January 1, 2016, that he would seek a third term.

Leaders: Maj. Gen. Paul KAGAME (President of the Republic and Chair of the Party), Christophe BAZIVAMO (Vice Chair), Col. Alexis KANYARENGWE (Former President of the Front), Francois NGARAMBE (Secretary General).

Christian Democratic Party/Centrist Democratic Party (*Parti Démocratique Chrétien*—PDC). The PDC accepted one cabinet post in the governments of December 1991 and April 1992. A PDC member also served in the Makusa government until March 2001. Prior to the 2003 presidential elections, the PDC was banned since the Constitution forbade religious parties. It reconstituted itself as the **Centrist Democratic Party** (*Parti Démocrate Centriste*—PDC) before legislative elections, and the reconstituted PDC joined the FPR-led coalition. It won three seats. Former PDC president Jean-Népomuscéne Nayinzira placed third in the national presidential polling in 2003. Party leader Alfred Mukezamfura was elected speaker of the Chamber of Deputies in 2003, but he fell ill in September 2007 and was temporarily replaced, before resuming his duties. Mukezamfura announced in August 2008 that he would not seek reelection to the Chamber of Deputies, but that the PDC would join the FPR-led electoral coalition. In June 2009 Agnes MUKABARABGA was elected chair of the PDC at a party congress. The PDC supported Kagame in the 2010 presidential elections and was part of the FPR-led electoral coalition in the 2013 legislative balloting (the PDC won one seat in the polling). The party announced in February 2016 that it was adopting Pan-Africanism as one of its priorities.

Leaders: Agnes MUKABARABGA (Chair), Alfred MUKEZ AMFURA (Former Speaker of the Chamber of Deputies).

Party for Progress and Concord (*Parti pour le Progrès et la Concorde*—PPC). The PPC was formed in 2003 after the MDR was outlawed. It is comprised mainly of Hutus. In the 2003 legislative elections, the PPC received 2.2 percent of the vote, below the 5 percent threshold needed for representation. Party leader Alivera MUKABARAMBA was the PPC's 2003 presidential candidate. She was appointed to the Senate in 2003. In February 2008 an internal split emerged in the PPC. Christian MARARA claimed to be president of the PPC after the group's leadership dismissed him and affirmed Mukabaramba as party president. The PPC joined the FPR-led coalition for the 2008 assembly balloting. Mukabaramba was the PPC candidate in the 2010 presidential elections but received less than 1 percent of the vote. She was appointed minister of state for community development and social affairs in 2011. The PPC remained part of the FPR-led alliance in the 2013 legislative balloting and won one seat. Mukabaramba retained her portfolio in the 2014 cabinet reshuffle.

Leaders: Alivera MUKABARAMBA (Minister of State for Social Affairs, Party President, and 2003 and 2010 presidential candidate), Etienne NIYONZIMA (Vice President).

Ideal Democratic Party (*Parti Démocratique Idéal*—PDI). Originally formed in 1992 as the **Islamic Democratic Party** (*Parti Démocratique Islamique*—PDI), the PDI changed its title in 2003 in response to a constitutional ban on religious parties and as part of a broader effort to attract voters. The PDI joined the FPR-led coalition in the 2003 and 2008 legislative elections. PDI party leader Sheikh Mussa HARERIMANA was appointed interior minister after the 2003 balloting. The PDI backed Kagame in the 2010 presidential polling, and Harerimana was reappointed interior minister. The PDI won one seat as part of the FPR coalition in the 2013 elections. Harerimana retained his position following the 2014 cabinet realignment. In February 2014 he was elected head of the Consultative Forum for Political Parties, an umbrella organization of parties in Rwanda.

Leader: Sheikh Mussa HARERIMANA (Chair).

Other members of either the 2008 or 2103 FPR-led electoral coalition, which all supported Kagame in the 2010 presidential elections, included the **Rwandan Socialist Party** (*Parti Socialiste Rwandais*—PSR), a workers' rights party launched in 1991, which was led by Medard RUTIJANWA and which won one seat in 2013; **Rwandan People's Democratic Union** (*Union Démocratique du Peuple Rwandais*—UDPR), formed in 1992 and led by Gonzague RWIGEMA; and the **Prosperity and Solidarity Party** (*Parti de la Solidarité et du Progrès*—PSP), led by Stanley SAFARI (see Current issues, above).

Social Democratic Party (*Parti Social-Démocrate*—PSD). One of the first three opposition parties to be recognized under the 1991 constitution, the PSD was one of several prodemocracy parties that accepted cabinet posts from April 1992, and in August 1993 it was a signatory of the Arusha peace agreement. The assassination of its leader, Félicien GATABAZI, in February 1994 sparked the violence in Rwanda, which escalated to genocidal proportions from April onward. Following the death of President Habyarimana two months later, PSD president Frederic NZAMURAMBAHO and vice president Felicien NGANGO also died. The PSD's Juvénal Nksui, then Speaker of the assembly, was sacked by the legislature in March 1997 and accused of incompetence after failing to sign into law a bill passed by the assembly that would make the president accountable to it. The PSD won 6 seats in the 2003 legislative elections. Party leader Vincent Biruta was elected to the Senate and was subsequently elected Speaker of that body. The PSD participated in the subsequent Kagame unity government. Prior to the September 2008 legislative elections, the PSD announced an electoral list that included 64 candidates. It declined an invitation to join the FPR-led coalition. In the balloting, the PSD won 13.1 percent of the vote and 7 seats in the assembly. Jean Damascene NTAWUKURIRYAYO was the PSD presidential candidate in 2010. He placed second to Kagame with 5.2 percent of the vote but was subsequently elected president of the Senate. Biruta was appointed minister of education in the FPR-led cabinet. In January 2011 the PSD member of Parliament Jacqueline MUKAKANYAMUGENGE was elected to chair the National Consultative Forum for Political Organizations, an umbrella group of Rwandan political parties.

In the 2013 legislative balloting, the PSD secured 13 percent of the vote and seven seats. In July 2014 Anastase MUREKEZI was appointed prime minister. In 2015 two PSD members of parliament resigned, reportedly for "personal reasons." Nonetheless, the resignations prompted speculation of dissent within the party.

Leaders: Anastase MUREKEZI (Prime Minister), Vincent BIRUTA (Chair and Minister of Education), Juvénal NKSUI (Former Speaker of the Assembly), Jean Damascene NTAWUKURIRYAYO (President of the Senate and 2010 presidential candidate).

Liberal Party (*Parti Liberal*—PL). Joining the MDR and PSD in refusing to enter the Nsanzimana government of December 1991, the PL accepted three cabinet posts under the MDR's Dismas Nsengiyaremye in April 1992 and also participated in subsequent coalitions, becoming as a consequence split into progovernment and antigovernment factions. The latter joined the government installed by the FPR following its military victory in July 1994. The PL's Joseph SEBARENZI became speaker of the assembly when that body sacked Juvénal Nksui (see PSD, above); however, Sebarenzi resigned his speaker's position in January 2000 amid a power struggle within the party and in the face of parliamentary criticism. He was subsequently reported to have assumed self-imposed exile in the United States. Prosper Higiro became party chair in 2001. In the 2003 elections, the PL secured seven seats. The PL was given a cabinet post in the subsequent Kagame unity government.

Following elections for regional party officials in August 2007, the PL was divided by a power struggle. The party leadership expelled two of its parliamentarians and five other party officials after they accused senior PL officials of corruption in the party's September 2007 leadership election, which was won by Protais MITALI. The members appealed their expulsion, but on November 9 the high court rejected their appeal, and the party replaced the parliamentarians. The PL ran 62 candidates in the 2008 legislative elections. Most of the candidates were reported to be members of the Mitali-led faction of the party. The PL secured 7.5 percent of the vote and four seats in the assembly. Mitali was reappointed minister of youth in the subsequent FPR-led government and appointed minister of sports and culture following subsequent cabinet reshuffles. Higiro was the PL candidate in the 2010 presidential balloting. He received 1.4 percent of the vote.

The PL received 9 percent of the vote in the 2013 legislative elections and five seats. Party member Donatille MUKABALISA was elected speaker of the assembly in October 2013. Mitali was reelected party leader in March 2014. He subsequently lost his cabinet post in the July reshuffle but was named ambassador to Ethiopia.

Leaders: Protais MITALI (President of the Party), Leopold NDORUHIRWE (General Secretary), Donatille MUKABALISA (Speaker of the Chamber of Deputies), Prosper HIGIRO (Vice President of the Senate).

Other Parties and Groups:

Social Party Imberakuri (*Parti Social Imberakuri*—PS Imberakuri). Formed in 2008 by Bernard NTAGANDA, the party emerged as one of the main opposition groupings. In 2009 reports indicated that the party split between Ntaganda and former party vice president Christine MUKABUNANI. Ntaganda sought to campaign against Kagame in the 2010 presidential elections. However, he was arrested in June for his role in what the government described as illegal demonstrations. In 2011 reports indicated that dissidents loyal to Ntaganda had created a new grouping. The party participated in the 2013 assembly elections but failed to secure any seats with only 0.6 percent of the vote. Ntaganda was released from prison in June 2014.

Leaders: Bernard NTAGANDA, Christine MUKABUNANI.

Republican Democratic Movement (*Mouvement Démocratique Républicain*—MDR). A predominantly Hutu party, the MDR drew its support from the central Rwandan capital region. Prior to the 2003 legislative elections the National Assembly voted to dissolve the MDR under the terms of the 2003 constitution. Former MDR member Twagiramungu ran for the presidency in 2003 and placed third. Subsequently, many members of the MDR joined the new Hutu-based party, the Party for Progress and Concord (*Parti pour le Progrès et la Concorde*—PPC). For more information on the MDR, see the 2009 *Handbook*.

Resistance Forces for Democracy (*Forces de Résistance pour la Démocratie*—FRD). The FRD was launched by former Hutu prime minister Faustin TWAGIRAMUNGU and former interior minister Seth SENDASHONGHA in Brussels on March 26, 1996, following their breaks from the MDR and FPR, respectively. The new party's platform called for the ouster of the Tutsi regime (which the FRD cited as an unbreachable impediment to the return of Rwanda's primarily Hutu refugees) and the drafting of a new power-sharing constitution based on the 1993 Arusha peace agreement. Furthermore, the FRD accused the FPR regime of engaging in genocide against the Hutu population. Party leader Sendashongha was in exile in Nairobi when he was assassinated in May 1998. Moderates had wanted Sendashongha to return to Kigali to lead reconciliation efforts. Twagiramungu strongly criticized President Kagame's call in April 2000 for exiles to return to Rwanda, charging that Kagame was attempting to cover up his "crimes against humanity." Nonetheless, Twagiramungu returned to Rwanda in June 2003 and launched a bid for the presidency as an independent. He placed second in the balloting but challenged the results. His challenge was overturned by the Supreme Court. Reports indicated in 2013 that Twagiramungu had formed a new political grouping, the Rwandan Dream Initiative—Rwanda Rwiza. Twagiramungu subsequently was reported to have formed an opposition coalition, including the FDLR, in Belgium. In January 2016 Twagiramungu threatened in a Facebook post to launch an armed insurrection if the government impeded the return of Hutu refugees.

Leader: Faustin TWAGIRAMUNGU (Former Prime Minister).

Democratic Forces for the Liberation of Rwanda (*Forces Démocratiques pour la Libération du Rwanda*—FDLR). Described in 2004 and early 2005 as one of the last major organized resistance groups outside Rwanda, the Hutu FDLR was accused by some Western leaders of involvement in the killing of civilians in the DRC. In March 2005 the FDLR formally apologized for its role in the 1994 killings in Rwanda. In April 2005 the FDLR declared it was disarming, and the leadership announced the group's intention to return to Rwanda from the DRC and to try to establish a legal political movement.

FDLR leader Ignace MURWANASHYAKA was arrested in Germany in April 2006 on alleged immigration violations. The Rwandan government asked for his extradition, but the German government refused the request. In November 2007 the DRC and Rwanda signed an agreement to disarm the FDLR (see Foreign relations, above). In December the United States announced an effort to initiate sanctions against the FDLR through the UN. In 2008 the UN estimated that approximately 6,000 FDLR fighters remained, but more than 1,000 surrendered or were killed during a joint DRC–Rwandan offensive in December 2008 and January 2009. In 2010 an amnesty program was credited with encouraging the repatriation of more than 200 FDLR fighters and their families. The FDLR was blamed for a number of terrorist attacks from 2010 through 2013 (see Current issues, above). In September 2011 DRC security forces killed 40 FDLR fighters in the Talama region. Reports in 2013 from former FDLR fighters accused the DRC of supporting some FDLR militias. An October 2013 UN report praised Rwanda for its efforts to reintegrate FDLR militias into society, noting that since 2004 more than 10,000 FDLR fighters had been demobilized and rehabilitated. Reports in 2014 indicated that FDLR fighters in the DRC had approached the UN with an offer to initiate cease-fire negotiations. However, fighting continued and the DRC and UN forces launched a major offensive against the FDLR in May 2016.

Leader: Ignace MURWANASHYAKA.

The Dutch-based **United Democratic Forces** (*Forces Democratiques Unifiées*—FDU-Inkingi), led by Victoire INGABIRE, absorbed the **Rally for Return and Democracy** (*Rassemblement pour la Démocratie et le Retour*—RDR) in 2006. (See the 2013 *Handbook* for more information on the RDR.) The FDU-Inkingi attempted to compete in the 2010 presidential balloting, but Ingabire was arrested (see Current issues, above). The **Democratic Green Party of Rwanda** (*Parti Democratique Vert du Rwanda*) was formed in 2009 and led by Frank HABBINEZA. The party was denied official registration prior to the 2010 presidential balloting but was registered in August 2013, too late for that year's legislative election. In 2015 it unsuccessfully sued to prevent the abolition of presidential term limits.

For more information on the **Party for Democracy and Renewal** (*Parti pour la Démocratie et le Renouveau*—PDR), see the 2013 *Handbook*.

LEGISLATURE

Prior to the resumption of hostilities between the Rwandan armed forces and the Rwandan Patriotic Front in April 1994, the legislature consisted of a unicameral National Development Council (*Conseil pour le Développement National*) of 70 members elected on December 26, 1988, from 140 candidates nominated by the MRND. Under the terms of the power-sharing agreement reached by the government and FPR on January 10, 1993, and confirmed by the Arusha peace agreement of August 4, 1993, a transitional legislative body was formally launched on December 12, 1994.

Under the terms of the 2003 constitution, a bicameral **Parliament** (*Inteko Ishinga Amategeko*) was created.

Senate. The Senate (*Umutwe wa Sena*) consists of 26 indirectly elected members who serve eight-year terms. Twelve senators are elected by regional councils; 8 are appointed by the president; 4 are elected by a regulatory forum of the country's political parties; and the remaining 2 are elected by university staffs and faculty. In addition, former presidents of the republic can request to be members of the Senate. The first senators were sworn in on October 10, 2003.

President: Bernard MAKUZA (ind.).

Chamber of Deputies. The lower house (*Umutwe w'Abadepite*) consists of 80 members who serve five-year terms. Fifty-three are directly elected by a system of proportional representation in which parties must achieve a 5 percent threshold to gain representation. Two deputies are elected by the National Youth Council and one by the Federation of the Associations of the Disabled. The remaining 24 deputies are elected by a joint council, which includes representatives from provincial, district, and city governments, as well as members of the executive committees of women's groups at various regional levels. In balloting for the 53 directly elected members of the Chamber of Deputies from September 16–18, 2013, the Rwandan Patriotic Front-led coalition won 41 seats; Social Democratic Party, 7; and Liberal Party, 5.

Speaker: Donatille MUKABALISA (PL).

CABINET

[as of February 1, 2017]

Prime Minister	Anastase Murekezi (PSD)
Ministers	
Agriculture and Animal Resources	Geraldine Mukeshimana [f]
Cabinet Affairs	Stella Ford Mugabo [f]
Chief Executive Officer of the Rwandan Development Board	Francis Gatare
Defense	Gen. James Kabarebe
Disaster Management and Refugee Affairs	Serafine Mukantabana (ind.) [f]

East African Community	François Kanimba
Education	Papias Musafiri
Finance and Economic Planning	Claver Gatete (ind.)
Foreign Affairs and Cooperation	Louise Mushikiwabo (ind.) [f]
Gender and Family Promotion	Esperance Nyirasafari [f]
Health	Diane Gashumba [f]
Infrastructure	James Musoni
Justice, Attorney General	Johnston Busingye (ind.)
Local Government	Francis Kaboneka
Natural Resources, Lands, Forestry, Environment, and Mines	Vincent Biruta (PSD)
Office of the President	Venantia Tugireyezu [f]
Public Service and Labor	Judith Uwizeye [f]
Sports and Culture	Julienne Uwacu [f]
Trade and Industry	François Kanimba
Youth and Information Communication Technology	Jean Philbert Nsengimana
Ministers of State	
Agriculture	Fulgence Nsengiyumva
Constitution and Legal Affairs	Evode Uwizeyimana
Economic Planning	Uzziel Ndagijimana
Energy and Water	Germaine Kamayirese [f]
Primary and Secondary Education	Isaac Munyakazi
Public Health and Primary Healthcare	Patrick Ndimubanzi
Social Affairs	Alvera Mukabaramba (PPC) [f]
Socio-economic Development	Vincent Munyeshyaka
Technical and Vocational Education	Olivier Rwamukwaya
Transport	Alexis Nzahabwanimana

[f] = female

Note: Unless indicated, cabinet officials belong to the FPR.

INTERGOVERNMENTAL REPRESENTATION

Ambassador to the U.S.: Mathilde MUKANTABANA.

U.S. Ambassador to Rwanda: Erica J. BARKS-RUGGLES.

Permanent Representative to the UN: Valentine RUGWABIZA.

IGO Memberships (Non-UN): AfDB, AU, Comesa, CWTH, IOM, NAM, WTO.

For Further Reference:

Barnett, Michael. *Eyewitness to a Genocide: The United Nations and Rwanda.* Ithaca, NY: Cornell University Press, 2002.

Ensign, Margee, and William Bertrand. *Rwanda: History and Hope.* Lanham, MD: University Press of America, 2010.

Gourevitch, Philip. *We Wish to Inform You That Tomorrow We Will Be Killed with Our Families.* New York: Farrar, Straus and Giroux, 1999.

Kinzer, Stephen. *A Thousand Hills: Rwanda's Rebirth and the Man Who Dreamed It.* Hoboken, NJ: John Wiley, 2008.

ST. KITTS AND NEVIS

Federation of Saint Kitts and Nevis
Federation of Saint Christopher and Nevis

Note: Both versions of the name are official, although "Federation of Saint Kitts and Nevis" is preferred.

Political Status: Former British dependency; joined West Indies Associated States in 1967; independent member of the Commonwealth since September 19, 1983.

Area: 101 sq. mi. (262 sq. km), encompassing Saint Christopher (65 sq. mi.) and Nevis (36 sq. mi.).

Population: 56,000 (2016E—UN); 52,329 (2016E—U.S. Census).

Major Urban Center (2014E—UN): BASSETERRE (14,000).

Official Language: English.

Monetary Unit: East Caribbean Dollar (market rate October 1, 2016: 2.69 dollars = $1US).

Sovereign: Queen ELIZABETH II.

Governor General: Sir Samuel Weymouth Tapley SEATON; sworn in on May 19, 2015, succeeding Sir Edmund Wickham LAWRENCE.

Prime Minister: Timothy HARRIS (People's Labour Party); sworn in on February 18, 2015, succeeding Denzil Llewellyn DOUGLAS (St. Kitts-Nevis Labour Party), following the election of February 16, 2015.

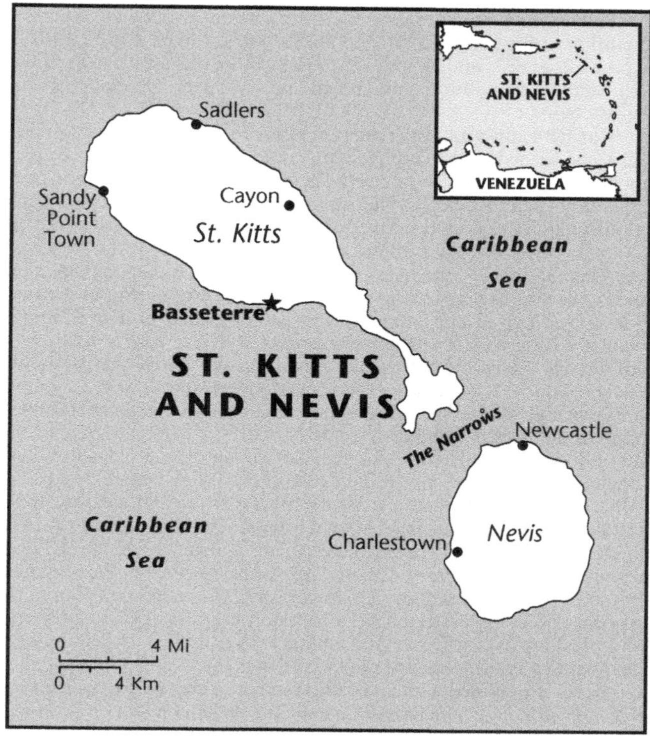

THE COUNTRY

Conventionally styled St. Kitts-Nevis, Saint Christopher and Nevis form part of the northern Leeward Islands group of the Eastern Caribbean. The population is largely of African descent and the religion primarily Anglican. The economy is dependent on tourism, with several hotels currently under construction; agriculture on the large island is devoted primarily to sugarcane and its derivatives, and on Nevis to coconuts and vegetables. Recent economic planning has focused on the promotion of small-scale local industry and agricultural diversification to reduce the islands' dependence on food imports and fluctuating sugar prices.

In October 1993 St. Kitts-Nevis graduated from concessionary loan financing by the World Bank, with future loans to be at commercial rates; however, the islands were dealt serious blows by two major hurricanes in the 1990s causing more than $500 million in damage. Following severe contraction of 4.2 percent in 2009 during the global financial crisis, the St. Kitts-Nevis economy was slow to recover. After three years of near stagnation, measures taken under the guidance of the IMF, including a 2011 stand-by arrangement and the implementation of a value-added tax, yielded growth of 1.9 percent in 2013. The following year saw growth of 3.3 percent. The St. Kitts-Nevis cabinet returned a $40 million unused installment of the stand-by agreement to the IMF in May 2014, part of a new effort toward reduced spending and borrowing. GDP expanded by 3.5 percent in 2015 and 3 percent in 2016. That year inflation was 2 percent, while GDP per capita was $15,095.

GOVERNMENT AND POLITICS

Political background. Although one of the smallest territories of the West Indies, St. Kitts was Britain's first colony in the region, settled in 1623. Ownership was disputed with France until 1783, when Britain acquired undisputed title in the Treaty of Versailles. The tripartite entity encompassing St. Kitts, Nevis, and the northern island of Anguilla entered the West Indies Federation in 1952 and was granted internal autonomy as a member of the West Indies Associated States in February 1967. Three months later Anguilla repudiated government from Basseterre and in 1976 was accorded a separate constitution that reconfirmed its status as a dependency of the United Kingdom (see United Kingdom: Related Territories).

The parliamentary election of February 18, 1980, yielded the first defeat of the St. Kitts Labour Party (SKLP) in nearly three decades and the formation of a government under Dr. Kennedy A. SIMMONDS of the People's Action Movement (PAM), with the support of the Nevis Reformation Party (NRP). Despite protests by the SKLP, the Simmonds government issued a white paper on a proposed federal constitution in July 1982. A revised version of the document, which formed the basis of discussions in London the following December, was endorsed by the St. Kitts-Nevis House of Assembly in March 1983 and secured the approval of the British Parliament in early May. Formal independence followed on September 19.

The PAM-NRP coalition maintained its majority until 1993. The election of November 29, 1993, yielded four seats each for the PAM and SKNLP (Nevis having been added to the opposition party's name), with the NRP losing one of its remaining seats to its Nevis-based opponent, the Concerned Citizens' Movement (CCM). The governor general on December 1 asked Simmonds to continue as head of a PAM-NRP minority government.

Political, religious, business, and labor leaders agreed at a "forum for national unity" on November 12, 1994, that all parties represented in the National Assembly would be permitted to participate in key government decisions and that the next general election would be held by November 1995, three years ahead of schedule. However, Prime Minister Simmonds scheduled the poll even earlier, on July 3. He lost his own seat in a seven-to-one SKNLP victory on St. Kitts; consequently, Denzil DOUGLAS was installed as head of a new government on July 7. Douglas retained office in an early election on March 6, 2000, the SKNLP gaining an additional legislative seat for a majority of eight.

In early elections in October 2004, the SKNLP majority declined to seven seats. A further SKNLP decline to six seats on January 25, 2010, did not preclude the formation of a fourth Douglas administration.

In the July 2011 Nevis Island Administration general election, the NRP retained its slender majority over the CCM. Two seats were won by a narrow margin of fewer than 35 votes. The CCM filed an election petition, and the High Court voided the results for one district on March 21, 2012. The Eastern Caribbean Supreme Court upheld the decision. Rather than hold a constitutionally mandated by-election, the Nevis parliament was dissolved November 8. In January 22, 2013, balloting, the CCM defeated the NRP.

Sir Edmund Wickham LAWRENCE was sworn in as governor general on January 2, 2013, following Sir Cuthbert SEBASTIAN's retirement.

In balloting on February 16, 2015, Team Unity—an electoral coalition of the PAM, CCM, and the People's Labour Party (PLP)—won with seven seats. Timothy HARRIS (PLP) was sworn in as prime minister of a coalition government on February 18 (see Current issues, below).

Constitution and government. The 1983 constitution describes St. Kitts-Nevis as a "sovereign democratic federal state" whose ceremonial head, the British monarch, is represented by a governor general of local citizenship. The governor general appoints as prime minister an individual commanding a parliamentary majority and, on the latter's advice, other ministers, all of whom, except for the attorney general, must be members of the legislature. He also appoints, on the advice of the government, a deputy governor general for the island of Nevis. Legislative matters are entrusted to a unicameral National Assembly, 11 of whose members (styled "representatives") are directly elected for five-year terms from single-member constituencies (8 on St. Kitts and 3 on Nevis). After consulting with the prime minister and the leader of the opposition, the governor general may appoint additional members (styled "senators") who can number no more than two-thirds of the elected membership. Constitutional amendments require approval by two-thirds of the representatives, while certain entrenched provisions must also be endorsed by two-thirds of the valid votes in a national referendum. The highest court—apart from the right of appeal, in certain circumstances, to the Judicial Committee of the Privy Council in London—is the West Indies Supreme Court (based on St. Lucia), which includes a Court of Appeal and a High Court, one of whose judges resides on St. Kitts and presides over a Court of Summary Jurisdiction. District courts deal with petty offenses and minor civil actions.

Nevis is provided with an island Assembly, currently consisting of five elected and three nominated members (the latter not to exceed two-thirds of the former); in addition, the governor general appoints a premier and two other members of the Nevis Assembly to serve as a Nevis Island Administration. Most importantly, the Nevis Islanders have the right of secession from St. Kitts, if a bill to such effect is approved by two-thirds of their elected legislators and endorsed by two-thirds of those voting on the matter in an island referendum.

In late July 1995, following his installation as prime minister, Denzil Douglas announced that he intended to introduce a constitutional reform that would provide separate governments for St. Kitts and Nevis. Having discussed the matter with then Nevis premier Vance AMORY, he pledged to draw on both local and international expertise to draw up a document that would be acceptable to residents of both islands. The overture notwithstanding, Amory in June 1996 initiated secession proceedings, Douglas characterizing the action as indicating that the Nevis leader had "no other issue of note to bring to the people." Nonetheless, the inhabitants of the smaller island had long chafed at alleged policy discrimination by the federal government at Basseterre. Involved were a variety of complaints ranging from slow response to a proposed upgrading of public services and fears of exclusion from offshore banking opportunities.

Efforts by regional representatives to mediate the dispute having failed, the Nevis Assembly voted unanimously on October 13, 1997, for secession, opposition members indicating their support "on principle." In August 1998, however, only 61.8 percent of Nevis voters in an island referendum backed secession, thus defeating the measure because it failed to gain the constitutionally required two-thirds majority.

The St. Kitts-Nevis constitution provides for freedom of speech, and freedom of the press is generally respected in privately owned media, though opposition parties claimed the government-run TV and radio stations unfairly favored the SKNLP in the 2010 election.

Foreign relations. At independence, St. Kitts-Nevis became an independent member of the Commonwealth and shortly thereafter was admitted to the United Nations. It joined the Organization of American States (OAS) in March 1984. Regionally, it is a member of the Association of Caribbean States (ACS), the Caribbean Community and Common Market (Caricom), and the Organization of Eastern Caribbean States (OECS). Most of its bilateral aid has come from Britain, which, at independence, provided a special grant-loan package of £10 million for capital projects and technical cooperation. The Simmonds government endorsed the U.S. intervention in Grenada in October 1983, subsequently receiving modest military assistance from the United States in support of its small voluntary defense force.

In June 2010 St. Kitts became the 17th signatory of the Tax Information Exchange Agreement (TIEA) with Canada. In February 2011 St. Kitts-Nevis approved an agreement with India. (For more, see the 2014 *Handbook.*)

St. Kitts-Nevis signed a treaty in January 2011 with the other countries of the OECS to form an economic union to allow easier movement of people and goods between member states. In 2012 the Douglas government renewed commitment to fully embrace the Caribbean Court of Justice (CCJ) as the highest appellate court, replacing the London-based privy court, along with the other members of the OECS. No action had been taken as of mid-2013.

In January 2014 St. Kitts and Nevis indicated intent to join the Venezuela-led Bolivarian Alliance for the Peoples of Our Americas (ALBA).

St. Kitts-Nevis citizenship-by-investment program came under fire in March 2014 when three Iranian sanction evaders were found to have acquired passports through legal channels. In June the United States and Canada encouraged St. Kitts-Nevis to tighten security around the program.

On April 12, 2016, St. Kitts-Nevis and Mongolia established diplomatic relations. St. Kitts-Nevis signed an agreement with Germany on September 19 to enhance cooperation in civil and criminal tax matters. Ten days later, St. Kitts-Nevis established diplomatic relations with Saudi Arabia.

Current issues. In December 2012 opposition leader Mark BRANTLEY filed a no-confidence motion against the SKNLP government, which was tabled. Prime Minister Douglas dismissed Agriculture Minister Timothy HARRIS in January for opposing a bill to increase the number of senators in the Assembly; Deputy Prime Minister Sam Condor resigned over the matter days later. In March Harris and Condor joined the PAM-CCM bloc in voicing support for the still-tabled no confidence motion (giving it majority support). In April the opposition appealed to the High Court to force a vote on the no-confidence motion, which was withdrawn in July after the Douglas administration noted that a vote would not occur until legal proceedings concluded. Condor and Harris launched the PLP in June. In July the opposition filed a new no-confidence motion. In August 2013 Brantley announced that the PAM, CCM, and PLP would form a unity platform.

The opposition again brought the tabled no-confidence motion to court in November 2013. Protests over the matter escalated in early 2014, when a series of arson attacks targeted government buildings. On January 5 fires destroyed the Venezuelan embassy and damaged the offices of the OAS, and, on January 17, damaged a treasury building. On February 12 the court ruled that the no-confidence motion could be allowed, and the PAM-CCM-PLP coalition wrote to Governor General Lawrence the next day to indicate Douglas had lost majority support. A meeting with Speaker Curtis MARTIN in early March failed to produce movement on the motion. The opposition filed a third no-confidence motion in September 2014.

The February 2015 electoral victory of Team Unity (see Political background, above) ended two decades of rule by the SKNLP and brought to a close the 20-year-long tenure of Douglas as prime minister.

POLITICAL PARTIES

Government Parties:

Concerned Citizens' Movement (CCM). The CCM is a Nevis-based party that in 1987 captured one local assembly seat and in 1989 one National Assembly seat from the NRP. It won control of Nevis on June 1, 1992, by securing three of five assembly seats, retaining them on February 24, 1997. It increased its National Assembly representation from one to two in 1993, retaining both in 1995, 2000, 2004, and 2010. In the balloting for the Nevis Assembly in September 2001, the CCM secured four of the five elected seats, two of which were lost in July 2006. In the July 2011 Nevis Assembly elections, the CCM retained its two seats in what was one of the closest elections in the island's history, with two of five seats decided by fewer than 35 votes. In the early election in January 2013, the CCM won three seats and Vance Amory assumed premiership. The CCM allied with the PAM and PLP (both below) in July 2013 to form the Team Unity coalition.

In the 2015 balloting, the CCM won 13 percent of the vote and two seats.

Leaders: Vance W. AMORY (Party Leader), Mark BRANTLEY (Deputy Leader), Stedmond TROSS (Chair).

People's Action Movement (PAM). The PAM is a moderately left-of-center party formed in 1965. It won only three of nine elective seats in the 1980 preindependence balloting, but with the support of two members from Nevis was able to force resignation of the existing Labour government. It captured six of the eight seats from St. Kitts in June 1984; it retained all six seats in 1989 but slipped to four in 1993. Although finishing second in the popular vote, the PAM, despite SKNLP objections, retained office in coalition with the NRP. It won only one legislative seat in the July 1995 election, which was lost in the March 2000 poll but regained in 2004. The PAM secured two seats in January 2010. In internal elections in September 2012, Shawn Richards became party leader. A PAM faction reportedly expelled for speaking out about party corruption formed the National Integrity Party in April 2013. The Team Unity platform with the PLP and the CCM was formalized at the PAM annual meeting in May 2014. PAM won 27.9 percent of the vote in the 2015 elections and four seats. Richards was appointed a deputy prime minister in the subsequent Team Unity government.

Leaders: Shawn K. RICHARDS (Deputy Prime Minister and Party Leader), Jonel POWELL (Deputy Leader), Valentine LINDSAY (Chair).

People's Labour Party (PLP). Former SKNLP members Timothy Harris and Sam Condor launched the PLP in June 2013 as an alternative to the leading party. The PLP joined the Team Unity coalition with the PAM and CCM for the 2015 elections. The PLP won one seat in that balloting with 9 percent of the vote. After Team Unity won the polling, Harris was named prime minister.

Leaders: Timothy HARRIS (Prime Minister and Party Leader), Sam CONDOR (Chair).

Opposition Parties:

St. Kitts-Nevis Labour Party (SKNLP). What was then styled the **St. Kitts Labour Party** (SKLP) was organized as a socialist party in 1932. Long the dominant grouping on St. Kitts, it won seven of nine Assembly seats in 1971 and retained a plurality of four in 1980 but was forced from office by the PAM-NRP coalition. The party initially opposed federal status for Nevis, claiming that it made Nevis "more equal" than St. Kitts; however, this position was reversed following the SKLP's crushing defeat in the 1984 election. Youth leader Henry BROWNE succeeded Moore. Though it increased its Assembly representation from two to four in 1993, it was unable to persuade the CCM (above) to join a government coalition. The party swept to victory on July 3, 1995, winning seven of eight seats on St. Kitts. It added the eighth seat in the election of March 6, 2000, but returned to seven in 2004. An additional seat was lost in January 2010, leaving the SKNLP with a bare majority. Prime Minister Douglas was reelected for a 22nd consecutive year as Labour Party leader.

Cracks within the SKNLP emerged in January 2013 leading Sam Condor and Timothy Harris to leave the government and party, and in June, launch the PLP. The SKNLP elected their replacements at a party conference in May. Condor and Harris were officially expelled from the SKNLP at the party congress in May 2014.

The SKNLP won 39.3 percent of the vote in the 2015 balloting and three seats.

Leaders: Dr. Denzil Llewellyn DOUGLAS (Former Prime Minister), Nigel CARTY (Deputy Political Leader), Marcella LIBURD (Chair).

Nevis Reformation Party (NRP). Organized in 1970, the NRP had, before 1980, campaigned for Nevis's secession from St. Kitts. It won two National Assembly seats in 1980 and participated in the independence discussions that led to the formation of the federal state. It captured all three seats from Nevis in 1984, after having won all five seats to the Nevis Island assembly in August 1983; it lost one of the latter in December 1987 and one of the former in March 1989, both to the CCM. In the Nevis election of June 1, 1992, it retained only two assembly seats. It lost one of two National Assembly seats in November 1993, with no change in 1995, 2000, 2004, and 2010.

Following the 1997 Nevis poll, in which the NRP retained two seats, former premier Simeon DANIEL stated that he would not contest future elections. The NRP lost one of its two seats in balloting for the Nevis assembly in September 2001 but secured three seats (a majority) in July 2006. In 2010 NRP parliamentary representative Patrice NISBETT became the first NRP member of the federal cabinet. In the 2011 balloting for the Nevis assembly, the NRP retained its three seats in one of the closest elections in Nevis's history. In August 2012 the court nullified Hensley Daniel's 14-vote victory. Joseph Parry called for general elections (rather than by-elections). In January 2013 balloting, the NRP lost its majority, winning two seats. The NRP secured one seat in the 2015 elections with 10.8 percent of the vote.

Leader: Joseph W. PARRY (Former Premier of Nevis and President of the Party).

For more information on the **National Integrity Party** (NIP) and the **United National Empowerment Party** (UNEP), see the 2015 *Handbook.*

LEGISLATURE

The unicameral **National Assembly** presently consists of 11 elected members, plus 3 appointed senators (two-thirds by the government, one-third by the opposition) and the attorney general, if he or she is not already a member of parliament. The legislative mandate is five years, subject to dissolution. In the most recent balloting of February 16, 2015, the People's Action Movement elected 4 members; St. Kitts-Nevis Labour Party, 3; Concerned Citizens' Movement, 2; People's Labour Party, 1; and Nevis Reformation Party, 1.

Speaker: Franklin BRAND.

CABINET

[as of October 15, 2016]

Prime Minister	Timothy Harris (PLP)
Deputy Prime Minister	Shawn Richards (PAM)
Ministers	
Attorney General	Vincent Byron (PAM)
Agriculture, Health and National Health Insurance, Human Settlements, Community Development, Gender Affairs, Social Services, and Lands and Cooperatives	Eugene Hamilton (PAM)
Finance, Sustainable Development, People Empowerment, National Security, and Constituency Empowerment	Timothy Harris (PLP)
Education, Youth, Sport, and Culture	Shawn Richards (PAM)
Foreign Affairs and Aviation	Mark Brantley (CCM)
International Trade, Industry, Commerce, and Tourism	Lindsay Grant (PAM)
Justice, Legal Affairs, and Communications	Vincent Byron (PAM)
Nevis Affairs, Labour, Social Security, and Ecclesiastical Affairs	Vance Winkworth Amory (CCM)
Public Infrastructure, Posts, Urban Development, and Transport	Ian "Patches" Liburd (PAM)
Minister of State	
Health, Community Development, Gender Affairs, and Social Services	Wendy Colleen Phillips (PAM) [f]

[f] = female

INTERGOVERNMENTAL REPRESENTATION

Ambassador to the U.S.: Thelma Patricia Phillip BROWN.

U.S. Ambassador to St. Kitts-Nevis (resident in Barbados): Linda Swartz TAGLIATELA.

Permanent Representative to the UN: Sam Terrance CONDOR.

IGO Memberships (Non-UN): Caricom, CWTH, ICC, IOM, OAS, WTO.

For Further Reference:

Cox-Alomar, Rafael. "Revisiting the Transatlantic Triangle: The Decolonisation of the British Caribbean in Light of the Anglo-American Special Relationship." *Diplomacy & Statecraft* 15, no. 2 (June 2004): 353–373.

Dyde, Brian. *Out of Crowded Vagueness: A History of the Islands of St. Kitts, Nevis, and Anguilla.* Oxford: Macmillan, 2005.

Hubbard, Vincent. *A History of St. Kitts: The Sweet Trade.* Oxford: Macmillan, 2002.

ST. LUCIA

Saint Lucia

Political Status: Former British dependency; joined West Indies Associated States in 1967; independent member of the Commonwealth since February 22, 1979.

Area: 238 sq. mi. (616 sq. km).

Population: 186,000 (2016E—UN); 164,464 (2016E—U.S. Census).

Major Urban Center (2014E—UN): CASTRIES (22,000).

Official Language: English.

Monetary Unit: East Caribbean Dollar (official rate October 1, 2016: 2.69 dollars = $1US).

Sovereign: Queen ELIZABETH II.

Governor General: Dame Pearlette LOUISY; sworn in September 17, 1997, succeeding Sir W. George MALLET.

Prime Minister: Allen CHASTANET (St. Lucia Labour Party); sworn in on December 6, 2011, succeeding Stevenson KING (United Workers' Party) following the election of November 28.

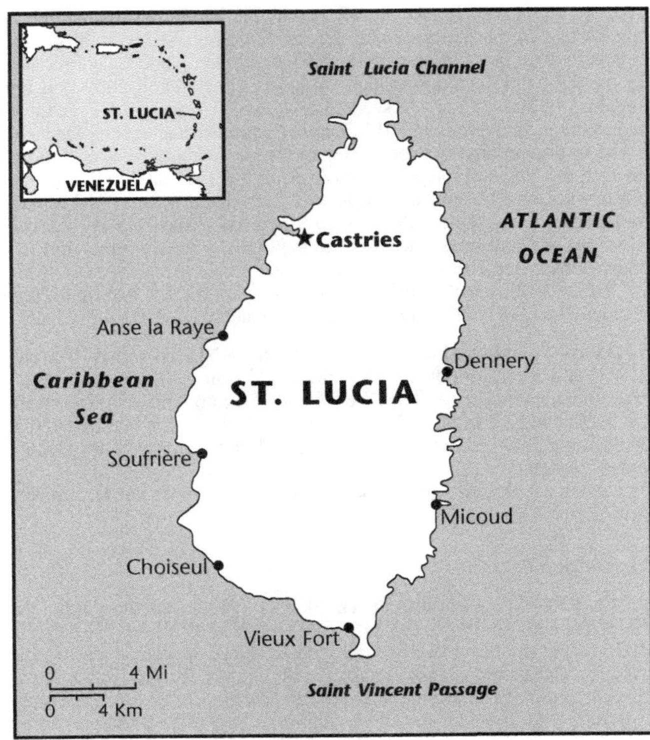

THE COUNTRY

The second largest of the former West Indies Associated States, St. Lucia lies between Martinique and St. Vincent in the Windward Islands chain of the eastern Caribbean. As in the case of adjacent territories, most of the inhabitants are descendants of West African slaves who were brought as plantation laborers in the 17th and 18th centuries. Following the conclusion of a treaty with the indigenous Carib Indians in 1660, France settled the island and significant traces of French culture remain despite undisputed British control after 1803. At least 80 percent of the population is Roman Catholic.

The principal economic sectors are agriculture, with bananas and coconuts as the leading export items; tourism, which has been growing rapidly in recent years; and manufacturing, which currently embraces more than 40 relatively diversified enterprises. Despite satisfactory infrastructural development and significant geothermal energy potential, the economy has been hampered by rapid population growth, which has yielded widespread unemployment. (For more on the economy of the 1980s and 1990s, see the 2012 *Handbook.*)

Following a recession of 4.8 percent in 2001, St. Lucia enjoyed growth through the decade until the impacts of the global recession in 2009 caused the GDP to slow to 0.4 percent. Hurricane Tomas devastated the country in October 2010, causing an estimated $336 million in damage. Subsequently, unemployment rose to 24.5 percent, up from 14 percent in 2006. Economic growth floundered in recent years, averaging 0.4 percent between 2010 and 2012, reflecting low tourism rates, an outbreak of banana leaf disease, and the introduction of a value-added tax (VAT) in October 2012. In 2014 GDP declined 1.1 percent, while inflation was 2.5 percent. In 2015 GDP growth resumed at 1.8 percent and then 1.4 percent in 2016. Inflation was 2.4 percent in 2016, while GDP per capita was $8,501.

GOVERNMENT AND POLITICS

Political background. Administered after 1833 as part of the British Leeward Islands, St. Lucia was incorporated in 1940 into the Windward Islands group, which also included Dominica, Grenada, and St. Vincent. It participated in the Federation of the West Indies from 1958 to 1962 and became one of the six internally self-governing West Indies Associated States in March 1967. St. Lucia, under Premier John G. M. COMPTON of the long-dominant United Workers' Party (UWP), applied for independence under a provision of the West Indies Act of 1966 requiring only that an Order in Council be laid before the British Parliament. After initially calling for a referendum, the opposition St. Lucia Labour Party (SLP), led by Allan LOUISY, participated in a constitutional conference held in London in July 1978. Following approval of the proposed constitution by the St. Lucia House of Assembly on October 24 and a draft termination order by both houses of Parliament in December, independence within the Commonwealth was proclaimed on February 22, 1979, with Premier Compton assuming the office of prime minister. Compton was succeeded by Louisy following a landslide victory by the leftist-oriented SLP on July 2, 1979.

In the wake of mounting conflict between the prime minister and a radical SLP faction led by Foreign Minister George ODLUM, Louisy resigned on April 30, 1981, paving way for centrist Winston CENAC. After Cenac was forced to step down on January 16, 1982, the governor general named Michael PILGRIM to head an all-party administration pending a general election on May 3 in which Compton's UWP secured a decisive victory, sweeping all but three parliamentary seats. Retaining control by one seat in the balloting of April 6, 1987, Compton called for a second election only three weeks later, which yielded the same outcome.

Buoyed by a resilient economy and campaigning on the slogan "Keep St. Lucia in good hands," Compton led the UWP to an 11–6 victory over the SLP in parliamentary balloting on April 27, 1992. He retired on March 31, 1996, and was succeeded by his recently designated party successor, Dr. Vaughan A. LEWIS, on April 2. Compton, however, returned as party leader in mid-1998.

In the election of May 23, 1997, the SLP crushed the UWP, 16–1, winning 61.3 percent of the valid votes under its new leader, Kenny D. ANTHONY. Anthony called early assembly elections for December 3, 2001, the SLP securing 14 seats compared to 3 for the UWP.

In another reversal, on December 11, 2006, the UWP regained power with 11 seats to the SLP's 6. The 82-year-old Compton was invested for the fifth time as prime minister. Following Compton's death less than a year later on September 7, 2007, Stevenson KING, who had served as acting prime minister since May 1, 2007, was named prime minister. (For more on King's cabinet, see the 2012 *Handbook.*)

Ahead of the November 2011 elections, two UWP parliamentarians resigned in protest of government policies. Meanwhile, controversy brewed over a revelation published in a Trinidadian newspaper in July 2011 alleging that Taiwan spent $3.8 million in an effort to keep the UWP in power (see Current Affairs, below). Against a backdrop of economic stagnation and an unemployment rate over 20 percent, both the UWP and SLP platforms touted job creation. The SLP returned to power with 11 seats, claiming victory over the UWP's 6. Kenny Anthony was sworn in on December 6 to serve his third term as prime minister.

Legislative elections were held in Saint Lucia on June 6, 2016. The UWP won 11 seats, while the SLP secured 6. UWP leader Allen CHASTANET was sworn in as prime minister on the following day.

Constitution and government. Under the 1979 constitution, the St. Lucia Parliament consists of "Her Majesty, a Senate and a House of Assembly." The queen, as titular head of state, is represented locally by a governor general whose emergency powers are subject to legislative review. Senators are appointed, serve only for the duration of a given Parliament, may not introduce money bills, and can only delay other legislation. The size of the Assembly is not fixed, although the present house has not been expanded beyond the preindependence membership of 17. The prime minister must be a member of the Assembly and command a majority therein; other ministers are appointed on the prime minister's advice from either of the two houses. Appointments to various public commissions, as well as the designation of a parliamentary ombudsman, require consultation with the leader of the opposition. The judicial system includes membership in the Eastern Caribbean Supreme Court, with appeals from its Court of Appeal transferred from the Judicial Committee of the Privy Council in London to the Caribbean Court of Justice upon the latter's launching in April 2005.

In 1985 the Compton government announced a plan to divide the island into eight regions, each with its own council and administrative services; implementation of the decentralization plan began in December 1985 and was completed the following year.

Calls for a number of constitutional changes, including abandonment of the link to the British Crown, were made to a Constitutional Reform Commission in early 2009. In March 2009 the Constitutional Reform Commission received submissions from individuals and organizations seeking changes in the island's basic law, including calls for the adoption of a republican form of government, a fixed date for general elections, changes in the appointment and function of the Senate, and expansion of the Bill of Rights to encompass education, health, and protection of the environment. The commission submitted its report to parliament in September 2012 and was tabled by Prime Minister Anthony in April 2013. Debate was expected during the next parliamentary session.

Freedom of speech is constitutionally guaranteed, and libel was removed from the criminal code in 2006.

Foreign relations. In May 1982 Prime Minister Compton reaffirmed his earlier wariness of Havana while indicating that his administration would cooperate with all regional governments participating in the Organization of Eastern Caribbean States (OECS), established in June 1981. In May 1987 Compton joined with James Mitchell of St. Vincent in urging that the seven OECS members work toward the formation of a single unitary state. Prime Minister Vere C. Bird Sr. of Antigua criticized the proposal as neocolonial, while other regional leaders showed only modest support.

Given the apparent failure of the OECS unification scheme, St. Lucia joined with its Windward Island neighbors (Dominica, Grenada, and St. Vincent and the Grenadines) in an effort to launch a less inclusive grouping. In September 1991 agreement was reached on a federal system with a common legislature and executive. Prime Minister Compton sought a structure of association that would not require modification of the participants' constitutions.

Prime Minister Compton denied after the December 2006 election that his administration sought refreshed ties with Taiwan, which would come at the expense of severing relations with the People's Republic of China. However, early the next year, the government invited a Taiwanese delegation to examine how "the interests of both parties could be advanced." Four months later, the Taiwanese flag was again raised in Castries, casting the diplomatic relationship with China into turmoil and stirring domestic controversy over the way the matter was handled.

St. Lucia joined with the five other OECS member states to officially create the OECS Economic Union on January 21, 2011. The accord provided a framework for an OECS Commission, an executive body with decision-making capability. A multilateral decision was finalized concerning the allowance of free movement of people and goods amongst OECS states, and the measure took effect on August 1 of that year. In January 2012 St. Lucia joined the OECS states in affirming commitment to fully embrace the jurisdiction of the Caribbean Court of Justice (CCJ), replacing the London-based Privy Court as the highest appeals court in the region.

The relationship between Taiwan and St. Lucia was complicated by revelations of the so-called Red Envelope Affair, in which the Taiwanese ambassador allegedly distributed $37,000 to each UWP candidate before the 2011 election. Nonetheless, Prime Minister Anthony in September 2012 announced St. Lucia would maintain diplomatic ties with Taiwan while also seeking to maintain economic and other ties with China.

Canada revoked visa-free entry for St. Lucian citizens in September 2012, citing concerns over the reliable authenticity of St. Lucian passports.

During a state visit to Cuba in May 2013, Prime Minister Anthony reinforced the strength of the relationship between the countries. That month, the Eastern Caribbean Supreme Court of Appeals ruled St. Lucia could adopt the CCJ without a referendum. In July Prime Minister Anthony began the process of negotiating the terms of adoption with the opposition UWP.

St. Lucia fully acceded the Bolivarian Alliance for the Americas (ALBA) in August 2013 despite UWP concerns that membership in the Venezuelan-led regional organization would damage relations with the United States.

Severe flooding in late December 2013 caused an estimated $99 million of damage to St. Lucia. Caricom neighbors offered financial support, as did the European Union and the World Bank in early 2014.

In March 2014 Caricom leaders decided to consider legalizing medical marijuana. St. Lucian national security minister Phillip LA CORBINIERE immediately spoke out against the proposal. In April Prime Minister Anthony urged regional cohesion as the debate proceeded.

A visit from the Malaysian foreign minister in May 2014 to seek St. Lucian support for Malaysia's bid to join the UN Security Council also produced discussions on increasing bilateral arrangements between the two countries.

On June 4, 2015, St. Lucia established an embassy in Taiwan. St. Lucia was the first of the Caricom community to have an embassy in Asia.

Current issues. Stephenson King's administration appeared reluctant to press for implementation of a VAT, to which it had long been committed, apparently reflective of concerns within the business community as to which lesser levies (ranging from personal taxes to import duties) the VAT would supersede. Prime Minister Anthony inherited King's VAT proposal, and the VAT was implemented on October 1, 2012.

Public sector workers went on strike in March 2013 as the government refused to meet union demands of a salary increase of at least 6 percent, citing the country's "unsustainable" debt. While some unions within the umbrella organization agreed to the 4 percent raise, other groups maintained the strike for three weeks at an estimated cost of $1.1 million.

The murder of a British tourist on January 17, 2014, prompted a strong reaction from the government to curb crime levels. Anti-gang legislation, which had been introduced in 2013, received renewed support and was passed in May.

Ongoing financial struggles dominated the 2014 political agenda, as the previous year ended with soaring unemployment of 24.9 percent. Eager to avoid consulting the IMF, Anthony undertook a string of measures designed to increase revenue and decrease public debt. In the 2014–2015 budget proposed in April 2014, Anthony announced intent to reduce corporate taxation. In early May the Anthony administration began meetings with unions to negotiate salary cuts. When the proposals were rejected, Anthony announced in June that the government may consider layoffs in the public sector.

Since taking office in June 2016, the Chastanet administration has reported that members of the civil service have resisted and undermined new policies. In particular, multiple diplomats and members of the senior diplomatic staff had "no quit" clauses in their contracts, making their replacement extraordinarily difficult and leading to a high level of intransigence over new policies.

POLITICAL PARTIES

Government Party:

United Workers' Party (UWP). The UWP was organized in 1964 by members of the former **National Labour Movement** and the **People's Progressive Party**. The party's basically moderate leader, Sir John G. M. Compton, served as chief minister from 1964 to 1967 and as premier from 1967 to 1979, becoming prime minister upon independence. Decisively defeated in July 1979, the UWP returned to power on May 3, 1982. It obtained a bare majority of one assembly seat in the election of April 6, 1987, and failed to improve its standing in a second election on April 30. By contrast, the party won a healthy margin of five seats in April 1992. In January 1996 Compton retired as party leader in favor of

Dr. Vaughan Lewis, who succeeded as prime minister on April 2 before the election of May 23, 1997, in which the party secured only one seat.

Morella Joseph, a retired school principal, was elected unopposed as the UWP party leader at the October 2000 annual convention. Despite an increase in UWP representation to three seats with a vote share of 36.6 percent in the 2001 election, Joseph resigned and was replaced on an interim basis by Marius Wilson. In mid-2004 the parliamentary leader of the opposition, Marcus NICHOLS, was sacked after calling for UWP leader Lewis to resign. In March 2005 former prime minister Compton came out of political retirement to defeat Lewis for the UWP leadership. In May 2007 Stevenson King was appointed acting prime minister when Prime Minister Crompton was incapacitated because of illness. Upon Crompton's death on September 7, 2007, King was named prime minister and was elected party leader at the 2007 UWP annual convention.

In January 2011 Member of Parliament Jeannine COMPTON-ANTOINE, daughter of party founder and former prime minister John G. M. Compton, resigned from the UWP.

In internal elections of July 2013, former tourism minister Allen Chastanet won a decisive victory for party leadership, defeating King, 264 to 99. Since Chastanet did not hold a seat in parliament, King served as opposition leader until mid-January 2014, when he was ousted amid reports of party infighting. Gale RIGOBERT assumed the post on February 1.

In the June 2016 elections, the UWP won 54.8 percent of the vote and 11 seats. Chastanet became prime minister on June 7.

Leaders: Allen CHASTANET (Prime Minister and Party Leader), Gale RIGOBERT, Ezekial JOSEPH (Chair).

Opposition Party:

St. Lucia Labour Party (SLP). The SLP is a left-of-center party formed in 1946. After boycotting the independence ceremonies because they were not immediately preceded by balloting for a new assembly, it won a landslide victory in the election of July 2, 1979. Party leader Allan Louisy resigned as prime minister in April 1981 because of intraparty conflict with "new Left" advocate George Odlum, who subsequently withdrew to form the **Progressive Labour Party** (PLP) in opposition to the government of Louisy's successor, Winston Cenac. At its 1984 annual convention, the SLP named Castries businessman Julian HUNTE party leader. The party was unable to secure a majority in either of the 1987 elections and secured only 6 of 17 seats in 1992. Hunte resigned his leadership post in February 1996 because of the party's poor showing in a Castries by-election and was succeeded in March by Kenny Anthony.

Anthony led the SLP to a near sweep (16 of 17 assembly seats) in the election of May 23, 1997, resulting in his appointment as prime minister. George Odlum joined the subsequent cabinet as minister of foreign affairs and international trade. However, he left the government in March 2001 after announcing that he would not stand as an SLP candidate in the 2001 balloting. The SLP maintained a strong showing in the 2001 election, capturing 14 seats. After losing control of the government 6 seats to the UWP's 11 in 2006, Anthony led the party to victory in the 2011 elections, unseating the UWP by winning a 5-seat majority.

In legislative elections in June 2016, the SLP won 44.1 percent of the vote and six seats. After its defeat, former prime minister Anthony resigned as party leader and was replaced by his deputy, Phillip J. PIERRE.

Leaders: Phillip J. PIERRE (Political Leader), Kenny Davis ANTHONY (Former Prime Minister)

Other Parties:

Lucian People's Movement (LPM). Created in 2010 as a third party alternative to the SLP and the UWP, the LPM is devoted to promoting equity, social equality, and increased standards of living for all of St. Lucia's citizens. It appeals to democratic tools, such as referendum, to accurately gage the will of the people in their governance. The LPM places a heavy influence on youth as the future of the nation and accordingly desires to incorporate youth into the decision making of the government. Six candidates ran without success in 2011. In July 2013 the LPM urged the government to hold a referendum on the CCJ (see Foreign relations, above). The LPM won only 0.2 percent of the vote in the June 2016 election.

Leader: Therold PRUDENT.

National Democratic Movement (NDM). The NDM was created in 2004. Five candidates ran unsuccessfully in the 2011 election. The party did not field candidates in 2016.

Leader: Ausbert D'AUVERGNE.

An additional party, the **Lucian Greens,** headed by Andre DeCaires, unsuccessfully contested the 2011 election in three districts.

LEGISLATURE

The **Parliament** of St. Lucia consists of an appointed Senate and an elected House of Assembly, each with a normal term of five years, subject to dissolution.

Senate. The upper house encompasses 11 members, of whom 6 are appointed on the advice of the prime minister, 3 on the advice of the leader of the opposition, and 2 after consultation with religious, economic, and social groups.

President: Andy DANIEL.

House of Assembly. The lower house presently consists of 17 directly elected members plus an appointed speaker. In the election of June 6, 2016, the St. Lucia Labour Party won 6 seats, and the United Workers' Party, 11.

Speaker: Leonne THEODORE-JOHN.

CABINET

[as of October 15, 2016]

Prime Minister	Allen Chastanet
Ministers	
Agriculture, Fisheries, Physical Planning, Natural Resources, and Cooperatives	Ezechial Joseph
Economic Development, Housing, Urban Renewal, Transport, and Civil Aviation	Guy Joseph
Education, Innovation, Gender Relations, and Sustainable Development	Gale Rigobert [f]
Equality, Social Justice, Empowerment, Youth Development, Sports, Culture, and Local Government	Lenard Montoute
Finance, Economic Growth, Job Creation, External Affairs, and Public Service	Allen Chastanet
Health and Wellness	Mary Isaac [f]
Home Affairs and National Security	Hermangild Francis
Infrastructure, Ports, Energy, and Labor	Stephenson King
Justice and Attorney General	Stephen Julien

[f] = female

Note: All members belong to UWP.

INTERGOVERNMENTAL REPRESENTATION

Ambassador to the U.S.: Elizabeth DARIUS-CLARKE.

U.S. Ambassador to St. Lucia (resident in Barbados): Linda Swartz TAGLIATELA.

Permanent Representative to the UN: Menissa RAMBALLY.

IGO Memberships (Non-UN): ALBA, Caricom, CWTH, ICC, IOM, NAM, OAS, WTO.

For Further Reference:

Hamsen, Jolien, Guy Ellis, Cape Moule, and Robert Devaux. *A History of St. Lucia.* St. Lucia: Lighthouse Road Publication, 2014.

Sutton, Paul. *Dual Legacies in the Contemporary Caribbean: Continuing Aspects of British and French Dominion.* London: Franc Cass, 1986.

Tennyson, S. D. Joseph. *Decolonization in St. Lucia: Politics and Global Neoliberalism, 1945–2010.* Jackson: University Press of Mississippi, 2011.

ST. VINCENT AND THE GRENADINES

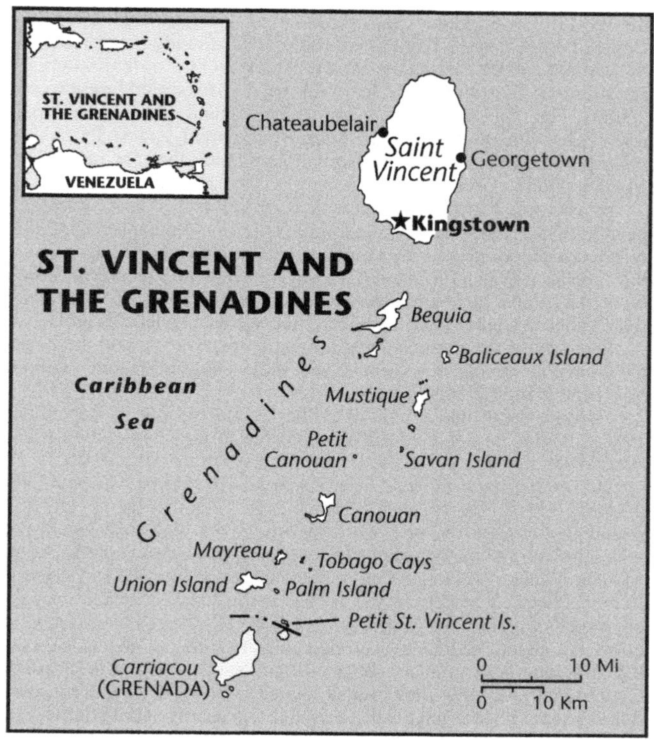

Political Status: Former British dependency; joined West Indies Associated States in 1967; independent member of the Commonwealth since October 27, 1979.

Area: 150 sq. mi. (389 sq. km), including the Grenadine dependencies, which encompass 17 sq. mi. (44 sq. km).

Population: 110,000 (2016E—UN); 102,350 (2016E—U.S. Census).

Major Urban Center (2014E—UN): KINGSTOWN (27,000).

Official Language: English.

Monetary Unit: East Caribbean Dollar (market rate October 1, 2016: 2.69 EC dollars = $1US).

Sovereign: Queen ELIZABETH II.

Governor General: Sir Frederick Nathaniel BALLANTYNE; sworn in on September 2, 2002, after being appointed by the Queen following the death of Sir Charles James ANTROBUS on June 3. (Deputy Governor General Monica DACON had served in an acting capacity during the interim period.)

Prime Minister: Dr. Ralph E. GONSALVES (Unity Labour Party); sworn in March 29, 2001, following the election of March 28 in succession to Arnhim EUSTACE (New Democratic Party); remained in office following elections of December 7, 2005, December 13, 2010, and December 9, 2015.

THE COUNTRY

St. Vincent and the Grenadines (comprising some 32 islands and keys) is located in the Windward group of the eastern Caribbean, south of St. Lucia and west of Barbados. Its jurisdiction encompasses the northern Grenadine islets of Beguia, Canouan, Mayreau, Mustique, Prune Island, Petit St. Vincent, and Union Island, the southern portion of the Grenadines chain being part of Grenada. The population is mainly of African and mixed origin, with small numbers of Asians, Caribs, and Europeans. The economy is based almost entirely on tourism (the leading earner of foreign exchange) and agriculture, with bananas, arrowroot, and coconuts being the principal export commodities. An extended series of volcanic eruptions in April 1979 caused massive devastation and necessitated temporary evacuation of the northern two-thirds of the main island, although substantial recovery was registered by early 1984.

GDP contracted for several years in the wake of the 2008 global financial crisis, which, among other things, depressed tourism and foreign investment. Recovery was subsequently compromised by natural disasters, prompting assistance from the International Monetary Fund (IMF), which called for structural reforms such as improved tax compliance, reduced government spending, and promotion of the private sector. Modest growth was achieved in 2012 and 2013, although severe flooding at the end of 2013 undercut short-term economic prospects (see Current issues, below). GDP expanded by 1.1 percent in 2014, 2.1 percent in 2015, and 3.1 percent in 2016. That year, inflation grew by 0.9 percent, while GDP per capita was $7,195.

GOVERNMENT AND POLITICS

Political background. Claimed by both Great Britain and France during the 17th and 18th centuries, St. Vincent was definitively assigned to the former by the Treaty of Versailles in 1783. Fifty years later, the islands became part of the general government of Barbados and the Windward Islands. After the separation of Barbados and the Windward Islands in 1885, the territory covering St. Vincent and the Grenadines was administered from Grenada. A founding member in 1958 of the Federation of the West Indies (which dissolved in 1962), St. Vincent and the Grenadines joined the West Indies Associated States in 1969 as an internally self-governing territory with a right of unilateral termination, which was exercised on October 27, 1979. After the state's admission to the Commonwealth as a special member in 1979, Sir Sydney GUN-MUNRO, the former governor, assumed the titular role of governor general, while Premier Robert Milton CATO became prime minister. Cato continued in office after balloting on December 5, in which his St. Vincent Labour Party (SVLP) captured 11 of 13 elective parliamentary seats.

In the election of July 25, 1984, the SVLP was defeated by the New Democratic Party (NDP), whose nine-member majority forced the resignation of Prime Minister Cato in favor of former premier James F. MITCHELL. The NDP swept the balloting of May 20, 1989, the country thereby becoming bereft of an elected opposition. The NDP continued in office by winning 12 of 15 elective seats on February 21, 1994, before being reduced to a bare majority of 8 seats on June 18, 1998. Arnhim EUSTACE, theretofore finance minister, succeeded Mitchell as prime minister upon the latter's retirement on October 27, 2000.

In accordance with an agreement reached the previous year, early elections were held on March 28, 2001. The center-left Unity Labour Party (ULP, a successor, in part, to the SVLP) captured 12 elective seats to the NDP's 3. ULP leader Ralph GONSALVES was appointed prime minister on March 29, and he announced a ULP cabinet on April 2, thus ending 16 years of uninterrupted NDP control. Gonsalves remained in office after the election of December 7, 2005, which yielded no change in the legislative distribution. Gonsalves also retained his post as head of a new cabinet formed on December 19, 2010, although the ULP's majority over the NDP had fallen to a single seat in the legislative balloting of December 13, in part as a result of recent economic shocks.

The ULP won eight seats in the December 9, 2015, elections, while the NDP secured seven. Gonsalves remained prime minister and named a reshuffled cabinet on December 16.

Constitution and government. The constitution adopted at independence in 1979 provides for a governor general who acts on behalf of the British Crown and who appoints as prime minister the individual best able to command a majority within the legislature. Other cabinet members are appointed on the advice of the prime minister. Legislative authority is exercised by a unicameral House of Assembly. The highest court—apart from a right of appeal in certain circumstances to the Judicial Committee of the Privy Council in London—is the West Indies Supreme Court (based in St. Lucia), which includes a Court of Appeal and a High Court, one of whose judges is resident in St. Vincent and the Grenadines and presides over a Court of Summary Jurisdiction. District Courts deal with petty offenses and minor civil actions. The main island of St. Vincent is divided into five local parishes (Charlotte, St. George, St. Andrew, St. David, and St. Patrick); a sixth parish covers all of the Grenadine islands that are part of St. Vincent and the Grenadines.

In what was considered a major setback to the ULP government, 55 percent of the voters in a national referendum on November 25, 2009, rejected a proposed new constitution that, among other things, would have replaced Queen Elizabeth II as head of state with a president chosen by the legislature and would have replaced the UK's Privy Council with the Caribbean Court of Justice as the country's final appellate court.

Freedom of the press is constitutionally guaranteed, and the country's several private newspapers and radio stations operate without government interference.

Foreign relations. Admitted to the United Nations in September 1980, St. Vincent obtained full membership in the Commonwealth in June 1985.

One of the more moderate Caribbean leaders, Prime Minister Cato declared during independence ceremonies in 1979 that his government would "not succumb to pressure from any power bloc" and would not seek admission to the Nonaligned Movement because such participation "is to be aligned." Although Cato assisted in establishing the U.S.-backed Regional Security System (RSS), his successor, James Mitchell, strongly opposed "militarization" of the region and in 1986 helped block the U.S. effort to upgrade the RSS to a stronger alignment that would have established a centralized military force to fight "subversion" in the Eastern Caribbean. In July 1996, however, he agreed to the conclusion of an extradition treaty with Washington that was aimed primarily at drug traffickers.

While opposing military enhancement, Mitchell was long viewed as the "father" of regional political integration. Following failure by the seven-member Organization of Eastern Caribbean States (OECS) to move toward a single unitary state, he advocated unification of St. Vincent and the Grenadines with the neighboring Windward Island states of Dominica, Grenada, and St. Lucia. However, the third session of a Regional Constituent Assembly that convened in Roseau, Dominica, in September 1991 could reach agreement only on a federal system, preliminary approval for which was to be sought by referendums (never held) in the four nations.

St. Vincent and the Grenadines is one of about two dozen (mainly small) countries maintaining relations with Taiwan, which has provided financing for a variety of projects. Other sources of external aid for St. Vincent and the Grenadines are the United Kingdom, Canada, and the United States, which contribute both bilaterally and through donations to the World Bank, the United Nations Development Programme, and the Caribbean Development Bank. In addition, a $7 million aid package was negotiated with Iran in 2008.

St. Vincent and the Grenadines distanced itself from the United States somewhat with a declaration by Prime Minister Gonsalves in early 2009 that his country would join the Bolivarian Alternative for the Americas (ALBA), launched by Venezuelan president Hugo Chávez as a counter to the U.S.-backed Free Trade Area of the Americas. In addition, unlike several of its Caribbean neighbors, St. Vincent and the Grenadines initially did little to assist the campaign organized by the Organization for Economic Cooperation and Development (OECD) to eliminate tax havens.

Prime Minister Gonsalves warmly welcomed integrationist initiatives in 2011–2012 within the OECS, including the implementation of the free movement of nationals among the member countries and progress toward economic union. He also strongly criticized the lack of similar progress within the Caribbean Community and the Common Market (Caricom), while continuing to promote ALBA as an important regional grouping. Earlier, Iranian President Mahmoud Ahmadinejad had praised St. Vincent and the Grenadines for having resisted the "bullying" of Western states.

The government's stance in regard to OECD demands about tax havens has softened recently, and in April 2012 Gonsalves announced the completion of the first phase of efforts to improve the regulatory framework of the nation's financial sector in consonance with OECD guidelines. In addition, bilateral agreements have been concluded regarding the exchange of tax information with many countries, including France, which in 2012 removed St. Vincent and the Grenadines from its blacklist in that regard.

In March 2013 Gonsalves urged the creation of a Caribbean-wide initiative to seek reparations from the United Kingdom for Britain's role in the slave trade in the region and for the "theft" of land during colonial rule.

In August 2016 the NDP pledged to cut ties with Taiwan if elected, prompting Gonsalves to publicly reaffirm relations with the Republic of China.

Current issues. Heavy rains in late December 2013 produced severe flooding and landslides that destroyed many homes, widely damaged roads and bridges, and disrupted water supplies. Analysts estimated the damage at more than $120 million, not including the short-term impact on tourism. Meanwhile, the opening of the country's new $280 million international airport was postponed until at least early 2015. For his part, Prime Minister Gonsalves continued to call for "more mature, more profound regionalism" in dealing with disaster mitigation, transportation, climate change, drug trafficking, and economic doldrums.

In 2016 a controversial draft law was introduced that would permit prison sentences of up to two years for online defamation. The measure was opposed by journalists and the opposition.

POLITICAL PARTIES

Government Party:

Unity Labour Party (ULP). The ULP was formed in October 1994 by the merger of two opposition groups, the **St. Vincent and Grenadines Labour Party** (SVGLP) and the **Movement for National Unity** (MNU).

The SVGLP was launched in 1955 as the **St. Vincent Labour Party** (SVLP), a moderate socialist formation that obtained 10 of 13 elective legislative seats in the preindependence balloting of 1974 and 11 seats in the first postindependence poll in December 1979. The party was forced into opposition after winning only 4 seats in 1984. Soon afterward, former prime minister Robert Cato, whose relatively advanced age of 69 and recent ill health were viewed as contributing factors in the election reversal, announced his retirement from politics. Hudson TANNIS was elected party leader at a special congress in January 1985. His rival for the party leadership, Sir Vincent Ian BEACHE, was later elected parliamentary opposition leader, indicating continued competition for control of the SVLP before Tannis's death in a plane crash in August 1986. Beache retired in September 1992, Stanley JOHN being elected his successor.

The MNU had been organized as a moderate leftist grouping by Ralph Gonsalves following his withdrawal from the **United People's Movement** (UPM) in 1992. (Once described as "the leading Marxist theoretician in the Caribbean," Gonsalves had organized the UPM as a coalition of left-wing groups before the 1979 election.)

In September 1993 the SVGLP initially rejected an MNU proposal to conclude an anti-NDP alliance for the next general election; however, such an alliance, formed in January 1994, won three seats in the February 21 poll. After the election Beache returned to lead the SVLP/MNU coalition and subsequently the ULP (as leader of the opposition). He resigned as leader of the ULP in December 1998, being succeeded by Gonsalves, whose political views had moderated noticeably.

Despite earlier internal disputes, the ULP won an overwhelming victory in the March 2001 legislative balloting. It retained its 12-seat majority in the December 2005 legislative poll and was credited with 51 percent of the vote in securing a bare majority of 8 seats in the December 2010 elections, having campaigned on a platform stressing job creation and expanded social programs.

In September 2013 Camillo Gonsalves (the prime minister's son), theretofore the nation's permanent representative to the United Nations, was appointed minister of foreign affairs, foreign trade, information technology, and consumer affairs and was also appointed as a ULP senator in the assembly. In 2014 Ralph Gonsalves (67) implied that the next legislative campaign would be his last as ULP leader.

In the 2015 elections, the ULP won 52.3 percent of the vote and eight seats. Gonsalves was reappointed prime minister. His son was named minister of economic planning.

Leaders: Dr. Ralph E. GONSALVES (Leader and Prime Minister), Louis STRAKER (Deputy Prime Minister), Edwin SNAGG (Chair), Audrey GITTENS-GILKES (Deputy Chair), Julian FRANCIS (Secretary General).

Opposition Party:

New Democratic Party (NDP). The NDP is a centrist grouping formed in 1975. It became the formal opposition party after the 1979 election, although it had captured only two legislative seats and NDP leader James Mitchell had lost his bid for reelection after abandoning his traditional seat from Beguia for a main-island constituency. Subsequently, Mitchell's successor from the Grenadines resigned, permitting Mitchell to regain the seat in a by-election in June 1980. Following a thorough reorganization, the NDP, campaigning in July 1984 under the slogan "Time for a Change," won 9 of the (then) 13 elective assembly seats; it captured all 15 such seats in May 1989, with a vote share of 66.2 percent. In February 1994 it dropped to 12 seats on a vote share of 54.5 percent.

Mitchell resigned as prime minister in October 2000 and was succeeded by Finance Minister Arnhim Eustace, who led the party to defeat in March 2001 and December 2005. The NDP closed significantly on the ULP by securing 49 percent of the vote (good for 7 of the assembly's 15 elected seats) in the December 2010 elections. The NDP campaign manifesto emphasized the pursuit of foreign investment and characterized the ULP government as corrupt and too closely aligned with leftist governments in the region. In the 2015 balloting, the NDP secured 47.4 percent of the vote and seven seats.

Leaders: Arnhim Ulric EUSTACE (Former Prime Minister, President of the Party, and Leader of the Opposition); Linton LEWIS (Chair); St. Clair LEACOCK, Goodwin FRIDAY (Vice Presidents); Sir James F. MITCHELL (Former Prime Minister and Former President of the Party); Allan CRUICKSHANK (Secretary General).

Other Party Contesting the 2015 Election:

Democratic Republican Party (DRP). The DRP was established on August 23, 2012, by Anesia BAPTISTE. In the 2015 elections, the party won 0.2 percent of the vote.

Leader: Anesia BAPTISTE.

St. Vincent and the Grenadines Green Party (SVGGP). Launched in January 2005, the Green Party won no seats in the 2005 balloting or in the 2010 poll, in which it was credited with 0.2 percent of the vote. The SVGGP won 0.1 percent of the vote in 2015.

Leaders: Ivan O'NEAL (Leader), Don O'NEAL, Ordan O. GRAHAM (Secretary).

Other Parties:

People's Progressive Movement (PPM). The PPM was launched on August 13, 2000, by former members of the ULP (above), including Ormiston "Ken" BOYEA, who had battled with ULP leader Ralph Gonsalves. The PPM presented 11 candidates in the March 2001 balloting but won no seats, securing only 2.6 percent of the vote. The PPM is now defunct.

Leaders: Ormiston "Ken" BOYEA, Stanley "Stalley" JOHN.

For more information on the **People's Movement for Change** (PMC), see the 2015 *Handbook.*

LEGISLATURE

The unicameral **House of Assembly** currently consists of 6 appointed senators (4 appointed by the government party and 2 by the opposition) and 15 representatives elected from single-member constituencies for five-year terms, subject to dissolution. The speaker of the assembly and the attorney general serve as ex officio members, with the right to vote except on financial or constitutional matters. In the most recent balloting of December 9, 2015, the Unity Labour Party won 8 of the elective seats and the New Democratic Party, 7.

Speaker: Jomo Sanga THOMAS.

CABINET

[as of October 15, 2016]

Prime Minister	Ralph E. Gonsalves
Deputy Prime Minister	Louis Straker
Ministers	
Agriculture, Industry, Forestry, Fisheries, and Rural Transformation	Saboto Caesar
Economic Planning	Camillo Gonsalves
Finance	Ralph E. Gonsalves
Foreign Affairs, Foreign Trade, Information Technology, and Consumer Affairs	Louis Straker
Grenadine Affairs	Ralph E. Gonsalves
Health, Wellness, and the Environment	Robert Luke Brown
Housing, Informal Human Settlements, Physical Planning, and Lands and Surveys	Montgomery Daniel
Legal Affairs	Ralph E. Gonsalves
National Mobilization, Social Development, Family, Gender Affairs, Persons with Disabilities, and Youth	Frederick A. Stephenson
National Reconciliation, Education, and Ecclesiastical Affairs	St. Clair Prince
National Security and Air and Sea Port Development	Ralph E. Gonsalves
Tourism, Sports, and Culture	Cecil McKie
Transport, Works, Urban Development, and Local Government	Julian Francis
Attorney General	Judith S. Jones-Morgan [f]

[f] = female

Note: All members of the cabinet belong to the ULP.

INTERGOVERNMENTAL REPRESENTATION

Ambassador to the U.S.: Lou-Anne Gaylene GILCHRIST.

U.S. Ambassador to St. Vincent (resident in Barbados): Linda Swartz TAGLIATELA.

Permanent Representative to the UN: Inga Rhonda KING.

IGO Memberships (Non-UN): Caricom, CWTH, ICC, IOM, NAM, WTO.

For Further Reference:

Grossman, Lawrence. *The Political Ecology of Bananas: Contract Farming, Peasants, and Agrarian Change in the Eastern Caribbean.* Chapel Hill: University of North Carolina Press, 1998.

Samuel, Vin G. *The Life and Times of Dr. John Parmenas Eustace.* Princeton, NJ: Hairoun Publishers, 2006.

Sutty, Lesley. *St. Vincent and the Grenadines.* Oxford: Macmillan, 1994.

SAMOA

Independent State of Samoa
Sa 'oloto Tuto 'atasi o Samoa

Note: There is considerable confusion regarding Samoan proper names, the initial component being generally accorded benchmark status and, with some exceptions, utilized herein as such.

Political Status: Gained independence (as Western Samoa) on January 1, 1962; member of the Commonwealth since 1970; current name adopted in 1997; under mixed political system approximating a constitutional monarchy.

Area: 1,097 sq. mi. (2,842 sq. km).

Population: 195,000 (2016E—UN); 198,926 (2016E—U.S. Census).

Major Urban Center (2014E—UN): APIA (37,000).

Official Languages: English, Samoan.

Monetary Unit: Tala (market rate October 1, 2016: 2.50 tala = $1US).

Head of State: Tui Atua TUPUA Tamasese Taisi Efi; elected by the Legislative Assembly and installed for a five-year term on June 20, 2007, succeeding Susuga MALIETOA Tanumafili II, who had died on May 12; reelected July 20, 2012, and sworn in for a second five-year term on July 25.

Prime Minister: TUILAEPA Lupesoliai Neioti Aiono Sailele Malielegaoi (Human Rights Protection Party); confirmed by the Legislative Assembly on November 23, 1998, following the resignation of TOFILAU Eti Alesana (Human Rights Protection Party); continued in office following the elections of March 2, 2001, March 31, 2006, March 4, 2011, and March 4, 2016.

THE COUNTRY

What was formerly called Western Samoa consists of two volcanic islands (Savai'i and Upolu) and several minor islets located east of Fiji and west of American Samoa in the south-central Pacific. The country enjoys a tropical climate and good volcanic soils, but rugged topography limits the cultivated and populated areas to the lowlands and coastal fringes. The Christian, highly literate Samoans are representatives of the second-largest ethnic group of Polynesia. They have had lengthy contact with the West but retain their traditional social structure, which is based on an extended family grouping known as the *aiga,* whose chief, or *matai,* also serves as the *aiga's* political representative.

The economy is largely based on subsistence agriculture (which involves two-thirds of the labor force) and fishing (which accounts for 60 percent of exports), supplemented by the production of coconut oil, coffee, and bananas for export. (Cocoa was an increasingly important cash crop in the 1980s but is currently limited primarily to domestic consumption.) Basic raw materials are lacking, and the country suffers from a chronic trade deficit, part of which is offset by tourism (20 percent of GDP), remittances (25 percent of GDP) from Samoans living in New Zealand and the United States, and foreign aid.

Economic improvement in the 1990s was attributed, in part, to government initiatives to support the private sector, which included tax breaks for foreign investors, modernization of customs procedures, and reduction of import tariffs. The government also privatized some state-run enterprises while promoting the fledgling offshore banking sector. Efforts to improve oversight of offshore facilities followed criticism in June 2001 from the Organization for Economic Cooperation and Development, which included Samoa on a list of jurisdictions with questionable tax policies. Although formally deleted from the list a year later, Samoa continued to attract attention as a tax haven.

After a decade of steady growth, GDP plummeted by more than 5 percent in 2009 as a result of the global economic crisis and a massive tsunami in September that inflicted unprecedented damage on physical infrastructure and killed more than 180 people. In part due to post-tsunami reconstruction and a government stimulus program, GDP rose by more than 2 percent in 2011 and 2012.

In March 2012 the World Bank announced it would provide $100 million in grants and concessionary lending over the next five years. An economic boost was also anticipated from Samoa's accession to the World Trade Organization (WTO) the following May. However, the economy suffered another severe shock when Cyclone Evan hit in December (see Current issues, below). Real GDP declined slightly in fiscal year 2012–2013, but an increase of 1.9 percent was projected for fiscal year 2013–2014, thanks, in part, to emergency assistance from the International Monetary Fund (IMF). GDP grew by 2.8 percent in 2015, and 1.4 percent in 2016. Inflation in 2016 was 2.2 percent, while GDP per capita was $4,613.

GOVERNMENT AND POLITICS

Political background. An object of missionary interest since the 1830s, the Samoan Islands came under joint British, German, and American supervision in 1889 but were politically divided as a consequence of an 1899 treaty whereby the United States annexed Eastern (American) Samoa, while Western Samoa became a German protectorate. New Zealand occupied Western Samoa during World War I and acquired subsequent control of the territory under a League of Nations mandate. Opposition to the New Zealand administration resulted in the formation in Western Samoa of a nationalist organization known as the "Mau," which was active between 1927 and 1936.

Following World War II a Samoan request for independence was rejected, and Western Samoa continued under New Zealand administration as a United Nations Trust Territory. However, political evolution subsequently gained momentum. Cabinet government was introduced in 1959; a new constitution, adopted in 1960, was approved by plebiscite in 1961; and the country became fully independent by agreement with New Zealand and the United Nations on January 1, 1962. The largely ceremonial position of head of state was at first held jointly by the representatives of two of the four royal lines (the Tuiaana/Tuiatua and the Malietoa), but one of the incumbents died in 1963.

The first government after independence, headed by Prime Minister FIAME Mata'afa, lasted through 1970, when it was replaced by an administration headed by Tupua TAMASESE Lealofi IV. The Tamasese regime was succeeded in 1973 by another Fiame government, although Tamasese returned as acting prime minister to serve the remainder of Fiame's term upon the latter's death in May 1975. In March 1976, following a legislative election in which more than half of the incumbents lost their seats, TUPUOLA Taisi Efi became the first prime minister who was not a *Tama Aiga* ("Royal Son") from one of the four leading families. After balloting on February 24, 1979, that again saw more than half of the incumbents defeated, Tupuola was redesignated prime minister following legislative endorsement by a vote of 24–23.

In the election of February 27, 1982, the islands' first formally constituted political group, the Human Rights Protection Party (HRPP), won a plurality of 22 parliamentary seats, and, after a lengthy period of consultation with independent members, it organized a government under VA'AI Kolone on April 13. However, the party lost its 1-seat majority in late June upon the ouster of a member found guilty of electoral malpractice, and on September 18 Va'ai's seat was vacated by the Supreme Court on similar grounds. Former prime minister Tupuola was thereupon returned to office, although his attempt to form a coalition government was rebuffed by the HRPP, which argued that the court had exceeded its authority in its expulsion orders. Upon rejection of a budget bill, Tupuola was again forced to resign, and the new HRPP leader, TOFILAU Eti Alesana, succeeded him on December 30, the party having regained its majority in special elections to refill the vacated seats. In mid-1984 opposition leader Tupuola was designated a *Tama Aiga* in succession to his cousin, former prime minister Tamasese Lealofi IV; thenceforth Tupuola was addressed as Tui Atua TUPUA Tamasese Efi.

The HRPP captured 31 of 47 assembly seats in the election of February 22, 1985, Tofilau Eti being redesignated prime minister after former prime minister Va'ai Kolone had withdrawn a bid to recover the party leadership. Despite his party's technical majority, Tofilau was forced to resign on December 27, 1985, after members of the HRPP joined with the opposition (now including Va'ai) to defeat the 1986 budget bill on a 27–19 vote. During the following week a new coalition government headed by Va'ai was formed, the head of state having rejected a request to dissolve the assembly.

The results of the extremely close election of February 26, 1988, were not announced until the new assembly convened on April 7, at which time the HRPP was declared to have obtained a bare majority of 24 seats, with Tofilau Eti returning as prime minister. By late summer, following a number of Supreme Court rulings on electoral challenges and a series of special elections, the HRPP's representation had increased to 27.

In a popular referendum on October 29, 1990, voters by a narrow margin indicated that they favored the adoption of universal suffrage for all persons age 21 and above (albeit with only chiefs eligible as candidates), while rejecting by a 3–2 margin the proposed establishment of an upper chamber reserved for *matai.* Under the new procedure the HRPP won an increased majority of 30 seats (1 of which was subsequently vacated) in the election of April 5, 1991, with Tofilau Eti forming a new government on May 14.

In early 1994 the introduction of a value-added tax (VAT) on goods and services generated a series of demonstrations and protest marches. The HRPP responded by expelling 3 antitax members, thereby reducing its position (in the wake of several 1993 defections) to a legislative plurality of 23 seats. However, by March 1995, after special elections and other realignments, the HRPP had regained a majority of 33.

In the election of April 26, 1996, HRPP government representation declined to 22 seats, with a loss of 3 cabinet members and the assembly speaker. However, Tofilau Eti retained office by a 34–14 vote on May 17, with a number of independents entering the HRPP to establish its majority once more.

In early 1997 Prime Minister Tofilau Eti introduced a constitutional amendment, which was subsequently approved, to change the country's name from Western Samoa to Samoa. The change was bitterly opposed by American Samoans, who were, however, unable to secure a reversal.

Tofilau Eti, who had long been in ill health, resigned as prime minister in favor of his deputy, TUILAEPA Sailele Malielegaoi, on November 23, 1998, and died four months later. Prime Minister Tuilaepa was returned to office following the legislative election of March 2, 2001, although the HRPP required the adherence of independents to secure his confirmation and establish a working majority in the Legislative Assembly. Tuilaepa was returned with a far more commanding majority of 33 after the election of March 31, 2006.

Prior to his death at age 95 on May 12, 2007, MALIETOA Tanumafili II had been recognized as the world's oldest surviving head of state, having served since Samoa's independence in 1962. He was succeeded on May 12 by former prime minister Tui Atua Tupua Tamasese Efi, the first head of state to be elected for a five-year term rather than for life (see Constitution and government, below).

Although it faced a significant challenge from the recently formed Tautua Samoa Party (TSP), which accused the government of financial mismanagement, the HRPP retained a clear majority in the March 4, 2011, legislative poll. Prime Minister Tuilaepa named nine new ministers to the cabinet appointed on March 19.

Head of State Tupua was reelected unopposed for a second five-year term on July 20, 2012. The HRPP won 35 seats in the March 2016 balloting. The cabinet was reshuffled on March 18, and again on July 1.

Constitution and government. As defined by the constitution of October 28, 1960, Samoa's political institutions combine the forms of British-style parliamentary democracy with elements of the traditional Samoan social structure. The head of state (*O le Ao o le Malo*) performs the duties of a constitutional sovereign. The constitution provides for the head of state to be elected by the Legislative Assembly (*Fono Aoao Faitulafono*) for a five-year term, although special arrangements were made for the position initially to be shared by representatives of two of the four royal lines, who were designated for life. (One died in 1963, but the second served until 2007, following which the *Fono* elected the head of state for a five-year term for the first time.) The head of state appoints the prime minister upon the recommendation of the assembly; the prime minister appoints the members of the cabinet, who are drawn from the assembly and are responsible to that body. Traditionally, most members of the legislature were indirectly elected by *matai,* or family heads, whose number was increased by one-third to 16,000 in a series of controversial appointments before the 1985 balloting; direct election was limited to two special representatives chosen by universal adult suffrage of persons outside the *matai* system.

A measure calling for universal suffrage (without a universal right of candidacy) for all *Fono* seats was rejected by the assembly in 1981. However, with chiefly titles being created at a rate exceeding that of population growth and with some individuals holding multiple titles (each carrying an electoral vote), the *matai* system came under mounting criticism. Given the increasingly prevalent practice of bestowing titles for political purposes, universal suffrage (endorsed in an October 1990 referendum), ironically, came to be viewed as a means of maintaining historic Samoan values.

The judicial system is headed by a Supreme Court and includes a Court of Appeal, magistrates' courts, a special Land and Titles Court for dealing with disputes over customary land and Samoan titles and recently established Family and Youth Courts.

For the most part, local government is carried out through the *matai* system and includes the institution of the village *fono,* or council. There are some part-time government officials who operate in rural areas.

Freedom of the press is constitutionally guaranteed, although instances of implicit censorship or of contempt citations against journalists have occurred in the past. Calling the media "weak" in regard to professional standards, Prime Minister Tuilaepa in 2012 proposed the establishment of a media regulatory body. However, some Samoan journalists in 2013–2014 described the proposed council as an inappropriate attempt by the government to further control an already constrained media.

Foreign relations. Samoa has established diplomatic relations with more than two dozen other countries (including the People's Republic of China), most of which conduct relations with Apia through diplomats accredited to New Zealand. Although not choosing to apply for UN membership until 1976, Western Samoa had previously joined a number of UN subsidiary agencies and other international organizations, including the World Health Organization, the IMF, and the World Bank.

Relations with the country's principal trading partner, New Zealand, which had been cordial since independence, cooled in 1978 and 1979 as a result of Wellington's attempt to expel some 200 Samoan "overstayers" who had expected to be granted New Zealand citizenship. Subsequently, the Judicial Committee of the Privy Council in London ruled that all Western Samoans born between 1928 and 1949 (when New Zealand passed legislation separating its citizenship from that of Britain), as well as their children, were entitled to New Zealand citizenship. However, the decision was effectively invalidated by an agreement concluded in mid-1982 by Prime Minister Va'ai Kolone and New Zealand prime minister Robert Muldoon whereby only the estimated 50,000 Samoans resident in New Zealand could claim such citizenship. The accord was widely criticized within Western Samoa, then opposition leader Tupuola Efi chastising the Samoan government for abrogating "a basic tenet of the Anglo-Saxon legal heritage that the right to legal citizenship can only be surrendered by personal choice." A related issue arose in early 1989, when Wellington announced that it might terminate a special immigration quota for Samoans on the ground that the immigrants were contributing to New Zealand's high rate of unemployment. The dispute was partially resolved at midyear with a statement from Prime Minister David Lange that the quota would remain, with a stricter application of its rules. Subsequently, in September 1991 the Western Samoan government indicated that it would not seek amnesty from Wellington for 7,500 overstayers, following assurances by New Zealand authorities that their appeal rights would be protected.

Visa overstayers from Samoa subsequently continued to generate discussion in American Samoa, where it was estimated that some two-thirds of the territory's inhabitants were nonnative. However, the problem was not viewed as seriously as elsewhere because of the shared cultural identity of the two island peoples; their shared identity was, however, central to American Samoa's strong objection to adoption of the unqualified name "Samoa" by its western neighbor in 1997.

As with a number of other financially strapped countries, accusations have been made of the illegal sale of Samoan passports to Chinese nationals. Former prime minister Tofilau Eti denied any knowledge of such a practice, although a number of individuals were formally indicted in the matter. Major Chinese officials have recently made well-publicized visits to Samoa, often in connection with the announcement of development assistance, and Prime Minister Tuilaepa has praised China for providing aid with "no strings attached," unlike Western donors.

At the end of 2011 Samoa "moved" west of the international dateline so that it would be more closely aligned in regard to time with its trading partners in Asia and Australasia. The government acknowledged that the dateline decision was only the latest in a series of measures underscoring the decline of U.S. influence in the region recently. Among other things, Prime Minister Tuilaepa argued that the peaceful conditions of the South Pacific had resulted in reduced U.S. attention. However, in marking the nation's 50th independence anniversary in May 2012, he expressed confidence that Samoa's accession to the WTO would promote increased trade with American Samoa.

The release of the "Panama Papers" in May 2016 (see entry on Panama) highlighted Samoa's role as an offshore tax haven. The leaked documents revealed that more than 5,000 companies or trusts had been created in Samoa by a Panamanian law firm implicated in leaks. The EU granted Samoa €20.2 million in assistance to improve sanitation and access to clean water in June. Also in June the World Bank announced a $25 million grant to upgrade Samoa's main airport.

Current issues. Cyclone Evan struck the island of Upolu (home to 70 percent of the population) in December 2012, causing flash floods, crop destruction, and widespread dislocation. Observers described the damage from the storm as at least as bad as that from the 2009 tsunami, with many schools and other buildings being destroyed. Assistance from donor countries and international financial organizations subsequently helped the tourism, housing, and agricultural sectors to recover. However, the IMF and World Bank cautioned that increased government spending, while appropriate during reconstruction, had nearly doubled Samoa's external debt and would require fiscal consolidation soon on the part of the administration.

Prime Minister Tuilaepa took over the finance portfolio in April 2014 after Finance Minister MUAGUTUTAGATA Peter Ah Him resigned under pressure following allegations of inappropriate spending in his previous post of minister of works, transport, and agriculture. (Tuilaepa had resisted dismissing the minister for more than a year despite a highly critical auditor's report in the matter.) Opposition leaders also challenged a proposal from the prime minister in July that constitutional amendments be adopted, which critics charged would effectively give the ruling party greater power in the selections of the head of state and speaker of the legislature.

In January 2015 the *Fona* rejected recommendations from the 2014 auditor's report. In February Muagututagata was convicted of two of four counts of forgery and misconduct. FIAME Naomi MATA'AFA (HRPP) became Samoa's first woman deputy prime minister on March 6, 2016, and on August 27 MATA Tuatagaloa became the first female to serve as a permanent justice on the country's Supreme Court.

POLITICAL PARTIES

Although there traditionally had been no political parties in Western Samoa, the Human Rights Protection Party was formed following the 1979 election. Other parties followed, including several short-lived groups formed during the 1990s. (See the 2012 *Handbook* for details.)

Governing Party:

Human Rights Protection Party (HRPP). The HRPP was organized by Va'ai Kolone following the 1979 election to oppose the reconfirmation of Tupuola Efi as prime minister. The new party subsequently claimed the support of a near majority of legislators. It won 22 of 47 seats in the February 1982 balloting and, after protracted negotiation with independent members, secured a 1-seat majority that permitted the installation of a Va'ai Kolone government on April 13. As a result of legal actions in late June and mid-September, 2 seats, including the prime minister's, were lost, Va'ai temporarily turning the party leadership over to Tofilau Eti Alesana, who was able to form a new HRPP government at the end of the year. Va'ai, who had regained his legislative seat in a by-election, failed in his effort to regain the HRPP leadership prior to the February 1985 election. He consequently resigned from the HRPP, moving into opposition (formally as an independent).

Tofilau Eti led the HRPP to a landslide 31–16 victory in the election of February 22, 1985, but the HRPP lost control of the government in December by defection of its members to the opposition. (Va'ai Kolone returned to the premiership with the support of Tupuola's **Christian Democratic Party** [see SDUP, below].) Tofilau Eti gained a new term as prime minister by the barest possible legislative majority in April 1988, and he formed a drastically restructured government following the election of April 5, 1991. Reversing a previous announcement that he would retire, Tofilau Eti easily won reelection in 1996. His party was less successful, however, declining to a plurality of 22 seats before regaining a majority with the conversion of independents.

Tofilau Eti's successor as prime minister, Tuilaepa Malielegaoi, carried the party to a plurality in the March 2001 election, after which the HRPP attracted enough independents to claim a majority of 28 seats when the new Legislative Assembly convened. It gained 2 additional seats as a result of subsequent special elections.

The HRPP led the balloting of March 31, 2006, securing 33 seats and, with the support of five members who had campaigned as independents, holding a commanding legislative majority. Defections reduced the HRPP's majority to 30 seats (plus the continued support of five independents) prior to the March 2011 assembly poll, in which the HRPP secured 28 seats (augmented by 1 following by-elections in August).

Significant dissent was reported within the HRPP in 2013–2014 concerning the prime minister's handling of a report that was critical of the fiscal management of the then finance minister while he was in a previous cabinet post. It was reported that 21 HRPP legislators signed a letter calling for the minister's dismissal prior to his resignation in April 2014. The HRPP won 57.3 percent of the vote in 2016 and 35 seats.

Leaders: TUILAEPA Sailele Malielegaoi (Prime Minister), FIAME Naomi MATA'AFA (Deputy Prime Minister), Laulu Dan STANLEY (General Secretary).

Parliamentary Opposition:

Tautua Samoa Party (TSP). Formation of the TSP was announced in December 2008 by nine members of the Legislative Assembly (including two members who had resigned from the HRPP in April and a number of members formerly from the SNDP [see SDUP, below]). The seats of the nine legislators were promptly declared vacant by the speaker because the legislators had violated Statutory Orders by establishing a new party prior to parliamentary dissolution. Samoa's Supreme Court subsequently ruled that the expulsion of the nine was invalid, but the *Fono* passed new legislation requiring that any legislator who switched allegiance to a different party (regardless of whether it was officially registered or not) lose his or her seat. The TSP (registered in November 2009) subsequently claimed the allegiance of 11 legislators, who formally continued to sit as independents.

The TSP, criticizing the government's handling of the 2009 tsunami, won 13 seats in the March 2011 legislative poll, including a seat for TSP leader VA'AI Papu Vailupe. However, Va'ai was subsequently charged with bribery and lost his seat, which was secured by the HRPP in the August by-election. (Va'ai was convicted in May 2012.)

TSP president VA'AELUA Eti Alesana died in October 2011. He was succeeded by Leatinu'u Salote Lesa, one of the few women in Samoa to hold a position of significant political influence. In January 2015 TSP's parliamentary leader was suspended from the *Fono.* The party won just two seats in the March 2016 polling.

Leaders: LEATINU'U Salote Lesa (President), PALUSALUE Faapo II (Leader of the Opposition and Former President of the Party), A'EAU Peniamina Leavi (Deputy Leader of the Opposition), LEALAILEPULE Rimoni Aiafi (Founder and Former Chair), VA'AI Papu Vailupe (Former President).

Other Parties:

Samoa Democratic United Party (SDUP). The SDUP was formed in 2003 by the merger of the **Samoan National Development Party** (SNDP) and the **Samoan United Independent Party** (SUIP) following disqualification of the SNDP for allegedly providing the Interparliamentary Union with false information about the government.

The SDNP was an outgrowth, at least in part, of the **Christian Democratic Party** (CDP), which supported Tupuola Taisi Tufuga Efi, who served as prime minister for two consecutive terms in 1976–1982. Tupuola became leader of the opposition following the 1982 election, and the CDP secured 16 seats in the 1985 balloting. Late in the year, the CDP joined with 11 HRPP defectors to defeat the budget proposed by Prime Minister Tofilau and to support the return of former HRPP prime minister Va'ai Kolone to the premiership, despite Va'ai's earlier opposition to Tupuola. The coalition of the CDP and the HRPP defectors was formalized by the launching of the SDNP after the 1988 election, in which the HRPP returned to power. The small Samoa National Party also participated in the formation of the SNDP, which was led by Tupuola (by then referenced as Tui Atua Tupua Tamasese Efi following his designation as a *Tama Aiga* in 1984). The SNDP slipped to 14 seats in 1991 and 13 in 1996.

The SUIP was registered as a party before the March 2001 election, in which it initially claimed 13 seats after the balloting; however, the number fell to 7 following recounts and defections to the HRPP. Meanwhile, the SNDP was credited with winning 13 seats in that poll and proceeded to fashion a coalition with the SUIP. Before the opening of the new legislative session the coalition claimed to have sufficient support to form a new government, but it ended up 4 seats short of a majority, with 21. Asiata Saleimoa Va'ai, a son of former prime minister Va'ai Kolone (who had died shortly after the election), was initially selected as leader of the opposition in the *Fono,* but he voluntarily surrendered the post to Le MAMEA Ropati Mualia, who had replaced Tupua as leader of the larger SNDP. (Tupua was elected head of state in 2007.) However, in September 2006 Mamea left the SDUP to sit as an independent, with Asiata resuming the role of opposition leader (until his death in 2010).

The SDUP secured 13 seats in the 2007 legislative poll but subsequently disintegrated under the influence of ongoing leadership battles. A number of SNDP legislators joined the TSP (above), while Mamea secured a *Fono* seat in 2011 on the HRPP ticket and was named minister of agriculture and fisheries in the new cabinet.

People's Party (PP). The PP, a successor to a civic group called People Against Switching Sides (PASS), was launched in July 2008 and held its first convention two months later. Its immediate objective was revocation of the controversial Road Transport Reform Bill that in September 2009, amid much acrimony, changed road driving from right to left, in accordance with the procedure in Australia and New Zealand. The PP insisted the change would generate an increase in highway accidents.

Leader: MAPOSUA Teleafoa Punafelutu Solomona Toailoa (President).

Samoan Christian Party (SCP). Also referenced simply as the Christian Party (CP), the SCP is primarily a women's party.

Leader: Tuala TIRESA Malietoa.

For more information on the **Samoan Progressive Political Party** (SPPP), ***Faamatai* Party** (FP), the ***Pati Samoa Aoao*** (PSA), and the **Samoa United People's Party** (SUPP), **Samoan Party** (SP), and the **United Samoa People's Party**, see the 2015 *Handbook.*

LEGISLATURE

In November 1991 the term of the unicameral **Legislative Assembly** (*Fono Aoao Faitulafono*) was changed from three to five years (subject to dissolution), with 2 seats being added to the existing 47. Currently, 47 *matai* are elected from territorial constituencies (6 multimember, 35 single-member) by universal suffrage of all persons age 21 and above, with an additional 2 members elected (in 1 multimember constituency) by and from those ("part-Samoans" and non-Samoans) outside the *matai* system. In 2013 the assembly approved a bill mandating that at least 10 percent of the membership of subsequent assemblies be female (there are currently two female legislators). If fewer than five women are elected outright in future polls, additional women (up to five) will be accorded seats based on the number of votes they received in the general election. Consequently, subsequent assemblies could comprise as many as 54 members.

In 2014 the government proposed the elimination of the 2 seats elected by and from those outside the *matai* system in favor of 2 additional regular seats in urban areas. In the most recent balloting on March 4, 2016, the results were as follows: the Human Rights Protection Party, 35; the Tautua Samoa Party, 2; and independents, 13 (twelve of the independents were reportedly aligned with the HRPP).

Speaker: TOLEAFOA Faafisi.

CABINET

[as of August 1, 2016]

Prime Minister	Tuilaepa Lupesoliai Sailele Malielegaoi
Deputy Prime Minister	Fiame Naomi Mata'afa [f]
Ministers	
Agriculture and Fisheries	La'aulialemaliestoa Polataivao Leuatea
Commerce, Industry, Trade, and Labor	Lautafi Fio Selafi Purcell
Communication and Information Technology	Afamasaga Lepuiai Rico Tupa'i
Education, Sports, and Culture	Loau Sola Keneti Sio
Finance	Sili Epa Tuioti
Foreign Affairs and Trade	Tuilaepa Lupesoliai Sailele Malielegaoi
Health	Talalelei Tuitama
Justice and Courts Administration	Fa'aolesā Katopau Ainu'u
Natural Resources and Environment	Fiame Naomi Mata'afa [f]
Police, Prisons, and Fire Service	Sala Fata Pinati
Public Enterprises	Lautafi Tio Selafi Purcell
Revenue	Tialavea Feo Leniu Tionisio Hunt
Women's Affairs and Community and Social Development	Faimalōtoa Kika Iemainma Stowers [f]
Works, Transport, and Infrastructure	Papaliltele Niko Lee Hang

[f] = female

INTERGOVERNMENTAL REPRESENTATION

Ambassador to the U.S. and Permanent Representative to the UN: Ali'ioaiga Feturi ELISAIA.

U.S. Ambassador to Samoa: Angelina M WILKINSON (Chargé d'Affaires).

IGO Memberships (Non-UN): ADB, CWTH, ICC, IOM, PIF, WTO.

For Further Reference:

Meleisea, Malama. *The Making of Modern Samoa: Traditional Authority and Colonial Administration in the History of Western Samoa.* Suva: University of the South Pacific, 1987.

Samoa. "Government of Samoa." www.samoagovt.ws.

Thode-Arora, Hilke. *From Samoa with Love: Retracing the Footsteps.* Chicago: Hirmer, 2014.

SAN MARINO

Republic of San Marino
Repubblica di San Marino

Political Status: Independent republic dating from the early Middle Ages; under multiparty parliamentary regime.

Area: 23.6 sq. mi. (61 sq. km).

Population: 32,000 (2016E—UN); 33,000 (2016E—U.S. Census).

Major Urban Center (2014E—UN): SAN MARINO (4,000).

Official Language: Italian.

Monetary Unit: Euro (market rate October 1, 2016: 0.89 euro = $1 US). (Although San Marino is not a member of the European Union [EU], it has negotiated a monetary agreement with the EU to permit usage of the euro as the national currency.)

Captains Regent: Massimo Andrea UGOLINI (San Marino Christian Democratic Party) and Gian Nicola BERTI (We Sammarinese); inaugurated on April 1, 2016, to succeed Lorella STEFANELLI (San Marino Christian Democratic Party) and Nicola RENZI (Popular Alliance). (Captains regent are elected every six months, in March and September.)

THE COUNTRY

An enclave within the Italian province of Emilia-Romagna, San Marino is the world's oldest and second-smallest republic (after Nauru). Its terrain is mountainous, the highest point being Mount Titano, on the western slope of which is located the city of San Marino. The Sammarinese are ethnically and culturally Italian, but their long history has created a strong sense of separate identity and independence. The population enjoys one of the highest rates of life expectancy in the world, supported by extensive social benefits provided by the government. The principal economic activities are tourism (some 2 million tourists visit annually), light manufacturing (39.2 percent of GDP in 2016), and service-related industries (60.7 percent of GDP in 2016), especially nonresident banking and financial services (known, until recently, for strict secrecy laws that attracted many foreign depositors, especially from Italy). Agriculture employs less than 1 percent of the workforce; olives and wine grapes rank with various grains as important crops. Wine, textiles, varnishes, ceramics, woolen goods, furniture, and building stone are chief exports. Traditional sources of income include the sale of coins and postage stamps and an annual budget subsidy from the Italian government.

By virtue of its economic union with Italy, San Marino became part of the European Economic Community (EEC) in the 1950s. It now has a separate customs union and cooperation agreement with the European Union (EU). Gross domestic product (GDP) rose by an average of 7 percent annually throughout the 1990s, while expansion in the tourism industry contributed to an influx of cross-border workers (nearly one-fourth of the labor force). Growth was robust in 2006 and 2007, thanks largely to a series of regulatory reforms, spending cuts, and initiatives to boost competitiveness in services. However, the global recession began to take a severe toll on San Marino in 2008, as focus intensified on San Marino's status as a tax haven. Italian measures (see Current issues, below) in particular contributed to a major outflow of nonresident deposits from Sammarinese banks while also compromising exports from San Marino. GDP had declined by more than 35 percent cumulatively by 2014, while unemployment had risen to 8 percent (up from 3 percent in 2007) and inflation to 8 percent. In 2015 GDP slowed its fall to a decline of less than 1 percent, with unemployment at 8.4 percent and inflation at 0.4 percent. In 2016 estimates showed continued improvement, with GDP rising by 1.1 percent, unemployment dropping to 7.9 percent, and inflation rising to just under 1 percent. In 2014 the International Monetary Fund (IMF) reported that "deep restructuring" had led to "stabilization" in the banking sector and had improved prospects for recovery, adding in 2016 that increasing diversification of the service and banking sector was needed.

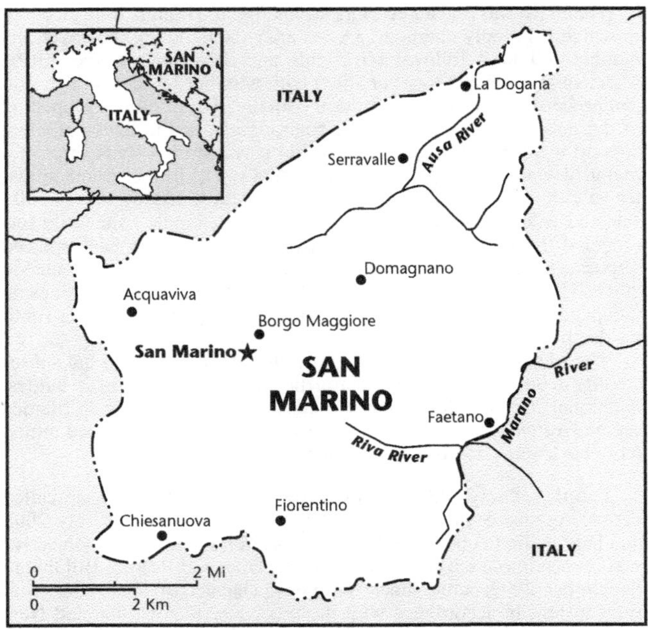

GOVERNMENT AND POLITICS

Political background. Reputedly founded in 301 A.D., San Marino is the sole survivor of the numerous independent states that existed in Italy prior to unification in the 19th century. A treaty of friendship and cooperation was concluded with the Kingdom of Italy in 1862, and it has subsequently been renewed and amended at varying intervals.

A coalition of Communists (*Partito Comunista Sammarinese*—PCS) and Socialists (*Partito Socialista Sammarinese*—PSS) controlled the government from 1945 until 1957, when, because of defections from its ranks, the coalition lost its majority to an opposition alliance composed mainly of Christian Democrats and Social Democrats. The San Marino Christian Democratic Party (*Partito Democratico Cristiano Sammarinese*—PDCS) was the plurality party in the elections of 1959, 1964, and 1969, but it required the continuing support of the San Marino Independent Social Democratic Party (*Partito Socialista Democratico Indipendente Sammarinese*—PSDIS) to ensure a governing majority. The coalition split over economic policy in January 1973, enabling the Socialists to return to power in alliance with the Christian Democrats. In the September 1974 election (the first in which women were allowed to present themselves as candidates for the country's legislative body—the Grand and General Council), the Christian Democrats and the Social Democrats maintained government control, although they each lost two seats, while the Communists and the Socialists experienced small gains.

In November 1977 the Socialists withdrew from the government, accusing the Christian Democrats of being bereft of ideas for resolving the country's economic difficulties. Following a lengthy impasse marked by successive failures of the Christian Democrats, Communists, and Socialists to form a new government, a premature general election was held in May 1978, but the balance of legislative power remained virtually unchanged. Subsequently, the Christian Democrats again failed to secure a governing mandate, and in July a "Government of Democratic Collaboration" involving the Communists, Socialists, and the Socialist Unity Party (*Partito Socialista Unitario*—PSU, principal successor to the PSDIS) was approved by a single-vote parliamentary majority. The other PSDIS successor, the San Marino Social Democratic Party (*Partito Socialista Democratico Sammarinese*—PSDS), joined the governing coalition in 1982 but returned to opposition after the May 1983 election, in which the ruling parties gained an additional council seat. The leftist government fell in June 1986, when the Communist and Socialist Unity parties withdrew over foreign policy and other issues. In late July the council, by a 39–13 vote, approved a new program advanced by the Christian Democratic and Communist parties, the first such coalition in the country's history. The coalition was renewed in June 1988, following a general election in May in which the governing parties gained four seats at the expense of a divided Socialist opposition. In 1990 the PCS, responding to recent events in Eastern Europe, recast itself as the San Marino Progressive Democratic Party (*Partito Progressista Democratico Sammarinese*—PPDS).

On February 24, 1992, the Christian Democrats withdrew from their coalition with the PPDS and forged a new ruling alliance with the recently reunified Socialists. The outcome of the May 30, 1993, election was notable for the emergence of three smaller parties, although the ruling center-left coalition of the Christian Democrats (PDCS) and the Socialists (PSS) retained a comfortable majority in the Grand and General Council. The coalition was renewed following the May 1998 legislative elections.

In February 2000 the Socialists withdrew from the government because of policy differences. The Christian Democrats then turned to the PPDS to ensure a new legislative majority, and on March 28 a government of the Christian Democrats, the Progressive Democrats (PPDS), and the Socialists for Reform (*Socialisti per le Riforme*—SpR) assumed office. In February 2001, after the Christian Democrats rebuffed efforts to introduce measures aimed at tightening the country's financial and tax regulations, another crisis ensued, leading to premature dissolution of the legislature on March 11.

As in 1998, the 2001 pre-election debate raised questions about the republic's relationship with the EU, which centered on San Marino's status as a tax haven. The EU, which in November 2000 had proposed an open exchange of information on nonresident investment accounts, maintained that financial secrecy in San Marino created an uneven playing field in the markets, eroded the tax bases of EU members, and facilitated fraud. Indeed, Italian tax officials had launched raids throughout San Marino in July 1998 to snare tax evaders, estimated to have been costing Rome $600 million annually.

The legislative election held on June 10, 2001, resulted in only minor changes in the makeup of the Grand and General Council. The PDCS remained in the plurality, claiming 25 seats on a vote share of 41.5 percent, while the PSS took 15 seats on 24.2 percent of the vote. Third place (20.8 percent of the vote and 12 seats) went to the newly organized Party of Democrats (*Partito dei Democratici*—PdD), successor to the PPDS, the SpR, and Ideas in Motion (*Idee in Movimento*—IM). Following the election, the PDCS and PSS established a new coalition, but the PSS withdrew on June 5, 2002. Subsequently, the PSS, the PdD, and the small San Marino Popular Democratic Alliance (*Alleanza Popolare dei Democratici Sammarinesi*—APDS) formed a new government that excluded the Christian Democrats. However, that government collapsed in December and was replaced with a PSS/PDCS coalition; the PdD rejoined the government in December 2003.

Following the election of June 4, 2006, a center-left coalition government was formed by the recently established Party of Socialists and Democrats (*Partito dei Socialisti e dei Democratici*—PSD), which resulted from the merger of the PSS and PdD; the Popular Alliance (*Alleanza Popolare*—AP, as the APDS had been renamed); and the small United Left (*Sinistra Unita*—SU) alliance. Under heavy criticism from the PDCS, which had been excluded from the center-left coalition despite winning a plurality of seats in the council, the government lost a confidence vote and resigned on October 29, 2007. It was replaced on November 28 by a coalition that included the previous government parties (PSD, AP, and SU) and the Center Democrats (*Democratici di Centro*—DdC), a new party founded by former Christian Democrats who had quit over the PDCS's inability to exert influence in the council. Also in 2007, another group of PDCS defectors, critical of the party's inability to attract moderates, founded yet another new party, Euro-Populars for San Marino (*Europopolari per San Marino*—EpS).The center-left coalition subsequently was unable to garner enough consensus to surmount legislative gridlock, and the government collapsed on July 9, 2008.

The center-right returned to power following early elections on November 9, 2008, winning 35 seats on the council as the Pact for San Marino (*Patto per San Marino*) coalition, compared with 25 for the center-left opposition coalition, Reforms and Liberty (*Riforme e Libertà*). The most vexing problem faced by the new government was the status of San Marino's banks in light of growing international pressure on so-called tax havens to become significantly more transparent in regard to foreign deposits. Although the Organization for Economic Cooperation and Development (OECD) in 2009 removed San Marino from its list of uncooperative states in regard to the exchange of financial information among nations, Italy continued to accuse San Marino of providing Italians with broad opportunities to avoid paying Italian taxes. When Italy offered its citizens an amnesty in 2010 regarding back taxes if foreign deposits were "repatriated" to Italian banks, it was estimated that some 5 billion euros in deposits were switched from San Marino to Italy. Italy also decreed in mid-2010 that any transactions conducted in San Marino totaling more than 5,000 euros would have to be reported to Italian tax authorities, which the government of San Marino characterized as an attempted "trade embargo" by Italy (the recipient of 95 percent of San Marino's exports) against San Marino.

The government's legislative support had fallen by mid-2012, in part due to severe economic decline. Consequently, early elections were held on November 11, 2012, with a ticket comprising the PDCS, AP, and PSD securing 35 seats and subsequently forming a government on December 5.

Claudio FELICI (PSD), first appointed as finance minister in December 2012, resigned on October 15, and was replaced by Giancarlo CAPICCHIONI (PSD) on October 22.

Constitution and government. Although a document dating from 1600 is sometimes referenced as San Marino's constitution, it is perhaps more accurate to say the republic has a "constitutional tradition" that is hundreds of years old rather than a formal constitution. Legislative power is vested in the Grand and General Council (*Consiglio Grande e Generale*) of 60 members directly elected for five-year terms, subject to dissolution. A 10-member Congress of State (*Congresso di Stato*), or cabinet, is elected by the Grand and General Council for the duration of its term. Two members of the council are designated for six-month terms as captains regent (*capitani reggenti*), who serve as the heads of state but under normal circumstances do not set policy; both have equal power. Each is eligible for reelection three years after the expiration of his or her term. The judicial system encompasses justices of the peace (the only level not entrusted to Italian personnel); a law commissioner and assistant law commissioner, who deal with both civil and criminal cases; a criminal judge of the Primary Court of Claims (involving penalties greater than three years); two Appeals Court judges; and a Council of Twelve (*Consiglio dei XII*), which serves as a final court of appeals in civil cases only.

Administratively, San Marino is divided into nine districts called castles (*castelli*), each of which is directed by an elected Castle Board led by the captain of the castle, both serving five-year terms (increased from two years in 1994).

Although San Marino has no formal constitution, freedom of expression is protected by legal precedent and, more explicitly, by the Declaration of the Rights of Citizens and the Fundamental Principles of the Juridical Order of San Marino, issued by the Grand and Central Council on July 12, 1974. Newspapers and periodicals are published primarily by the government, political parties, or trade unions.

Foreign relations. On March 2, 1992, San Marino was admitted to full United Nations membership, having previously been accorded observer status, and in September it became a member of the IMF. The republic is also a member of other international organizations, including the Conference on (later Organization for) Security and Cooperation in Europe, in whose review sessions it has been an active participant.

San Marino's relations with Italy (raised to the ambassadorial level in 1979) are governed by a series of treaties and conventions establishing a customs union, regulating public-service facilities, and defining general principles of good neighborly relations. Despite San Marino's staunchly reiterated independence, its reliance on Italy for a variety of necessities, ranging from daily newspapers to currency, provides little evidence that it will break with a tradition of alignment with Italian social and political processes.

On December 9, 2015, San Marino signed an agreement with the EU to increase financial transparency by sharing bank records in an effort to reduce tax evasion.

Current issues. In March 2012 San Marino pledged to adopt EU guidelines on certain bank regulations designed, among other things, to combat money laundering, and it concluded a treaty with Italy in June providing for "data-sharing" regarding bank accounts. San Marino emphasized its hope that the financial sector would soon experience a resurgence following adoption of all international standards. In part in an effort to achieve "national unity" to deal with, among other things, the ongoing deep recession, the PDCS (the majority partner in the incumbent government) agreed to participate in the San Marino Common Good coalition in the early elections of November 2012 along with the PSD (until then the major opposition party).

Although the EU had already indicated reluctance to offer full accession to microstates such as San Marino, a referendum was held on October 20, 2013, in San Marino to determine the electorate's sentiment in regard to applying for EU membership. A yes vote of 50.3 percent was reported, but the proposal did not achieve the required 32 percent of all eligible voters (turnout was only 43 percent) and therefore failed. In 2014 the government announced that its priorities included widening the tax base to relieve pressure on the national budget and improving infrastructure to further promote the already robust tourism sector.

A report in 2016 found that San Marino was the only country in Europe with more vehicles than people (1,139 vehicles for every 1,000 people). The report prompted environmental groups to advocate for new restrictions on passenger traffic in the country.

POLITICAL PARTIES

San Marino's older political parties traditionally had close ties with and resembled corresponding parties in Italy, although recent mergers and name changes have led to more distinct identities for the parties in San Marino. Electoral law revision was proposed following the 2006 legislative balloting to permit parties to form coalitions for subsequent polls, with the hope that "fragmentation" in the Grand and General Council would give way to something similar to a two-party (or at least a two-coalition) system. The change was approved in 2007, with subsequent changes in 2008 establishing a complicated threshold structure (see Legislature, below, for details) and requiring coalitions to present their proposed governments and policy plans prior to the balloting, with no significant changes being permitted through a coalition's term in office.

Two coalitions were formed prior to the November 2008 legislative poll, the first to be conducted under the new electoral law. They were the **Pact for San Marino** (*Patto per San Marino*), which included the PDCS and its affiliated parties (the **Euro-Populars for San Marino**

[*Europopolari per San Marino*—EpS] and the AeL), AP, **Freedom List** (*Listadella Libertà*—LdL) (comprising the NPS and NS), and USDM (comprising the San Marino Populars and the ANS); and **Reforms and Liberty** (*Riforme e Libertà*), which included the PSD list (comprising the PSD and the SpL), SU (comprising the **San Marino Communist Refoundation** [*Rifondazione Comunista Sammarinese*—RCS] and **Left Party–Free Port** [*Partito della Sinistra–Zona Franca*—ZF]), and **Center Democrats** (*Democratici di Centro*—DdC). The center-left Reforms and Liberty campaigned on a platform calling for increased social benefits and additional cooperation with Italy in regard to banking and tax issues. The center-right Pact for San Marino promised to promote domestic political stability and stronger ties with the EU. The Pact for San Marino parties secured 35 seats (on a vote share of 54 percent), with the remaining 25 seats going to Reforms and Liberty (46 percent). The primary reason for the Pact for San Marino's victory appeared to be its inclusion of the AP, which had previously been aligned in the center-left government with the PSD and SU.

Three individual parties and three coalitions (significantly altered from 2008) contested the November 2012 legislative balloting. The coalitions were the **San Marino Common Good** (*San Marino Bene Commune*), comprising the PDCS-NS joint list, PSD, and AP; the **Agreement for the Country** (*Intera Per Il Paese*), comprising the PS, UPR, and Moderate Sammarinese; and **Active Citizenship** (*Cittadinanza Attiva*), comprising the SU and Civic Movement 10.

Government Parties:

San Marino Christian Democratic Party (*Partito Democratico Cristiano Sammarinese*—PDCS). Catholic and conservative in outlook, the PDCS was established in 1948 and first came to power in 1957. In recent years it has been the strongest party in the Grand and General Council, winning at least 18 seats in every election since 1974. It ruled as the senior partner in coalitions with the Socialist Party of San Marino (PSS) from 1973 until the latter's withdrawal in December 1977, at which time the PDCS was unable to organize a new government majority and went into opposition. The PDCS returned to power in an unprecedented coalition with the Communist Party (subsequently the **San Marino Progressive Democratic Party** [PPDS]) in July 1986, from which it withdrew in February 1992 to revive the alliance with the PSS. The PDCS again won a plurality in the 1993 balloting, following which its coalition with the PSS was continued.

The PDCS lost 1 of its 26 seats in the legislative election of May 1998. The subsequent collapse in 2000 of the PDCS-PSS coalition led the PDCS to reunite with the PPDS in a tripartite coalition that also included the Socialists for Reform (*Socialisti per le Riforme*—SpR; see PSD, below). Although the PDCS retained its 25 seats in the June 2001 election, a revived PDCS-PSS coalition government lasted only one year, and the PDCS was forced into opposition. In the June 2006 election the PDCS won 21 seats, more than any other party, but not enough to outweigh the combined strength of 32 seats won by the center-left governing coalition. The PDCS subsequently lost 9 council seats due to resignations from the party (5 to the EpS and 4 to the DdC [see UPR, below, for both]). The PDCS list, which included the candidates from the EpS and the new AeL (below), secured 22 of the seats won by the Pact for San Marino in the November 2008 election. However, three legislators left the PDCS/EpS/AeL parliamentary group in September 2010 to form an autonomous legislative faction. The new grouping was initially viewed as a de facto component of the majority, but one of the three defectors subsequently became an official independent, while the other two aligned with the opposition DdC.

In the 2012 elections the PDCS, We Sammarinese, and the PSD ran on a combined ticket, with the merged PDCS-PSD winning 18 seats.

Leaders: Marco GATTI (Political Secretary), Luigi MAZZA (Parliamentary Leader), Antonio CECCOLI (President), Teodora LONFERNINI (State Secretary).

We Sammarinese (*Noi Sammarinesi*—NS). Founded in 2006, the NS defined itself as defending the republic's traditional values. It won 2.5 percent of the vote and one seat on the council in 2006 and presented its candidates on the **Freedom List** (*Listadella Libertà*—LdL) with the NPS (see PS, below) in 2008 as part of the Pact for San Marino. The LdL secured 4 of the Pact's 35 seats in that poll. For the 2012 poll the NS participated in a joint list with the PDCS within the San Marino Common Good coalition, winning 3 seats.

Leaders: Marco ARZILLI, Maria Luisa BERTI (Coordinator), Gabrielle BUCCI.

Party of Socialists and Democrats (*Partito dei Socialisti e dei Democratici*—PSD). The PSD was founded on February 25, 2005, as a merger of the leftist **Socialist Party of San Marino** (*Partito Socialista Sammarinese*—PSS) and the **Party of Democrats** (*Partito dei Democratici*—PdD), both of which were participating in a governing coalition that also included the PDCS. (The PSD's Italian counterpart is the Democratic Party.)

The PSS and the **San Marino Communist Party** (*Partito Comunista Sammarinese*—PCS) ruled jointly during 1945–1957. In 1973 the PSS returned to power upon forming a coalition government with the Christian Democrats that was continued after the 1974 election, in which the PSS won eight council seats. (The coalition gained an additional representative when the **San Marino Independent Social Democratic Party** [*Partito Socialista Democratico Indipendente Sammarinese*—PSDIS], originally a right-wing splinter from the PSS, split in 1975.) In November 1977, however, the PSS withdrew from the coalition, precipitating the fall of the PDCS-led administration. The PSS went on to win eight council seats in 1978 and nine in 1983, entering the government on both occasions. However, the unprecedented PDCS-PCS coalition formed in July 1986 excluded the PSS.

In 1990 the **Socialist Unity Party** (*Partito Socialista Unitario*—PSU), the more extreme remnant of the PSDIS, reunited with the PSS, which revived its coalition government with the Christian Democrats in February 1992. In the May 1998 balloting the PSS retained its 14 legislative seats, continuing as the junior coalition partner until withdrawing from the government in February 2000. After winning 15 seats in June 2001, the PSS reentered a PDCS-led coalition. A year later it joined the PdD and APDS in a left-leaning government.

The PdD was established in March 2001 by merger of three groups: the PPDS (see PDCS, above)); **Ideas in Motion** (*Idee in Movimento*—IM); and the **Reformist Democrats and Socialists** (*Riformisti Democratici e Socialisti*), led by Emma ROSSI. In the context of the political upheaval of late 1989 in Eastern Europe, the PPDS had been formally launched on April 15, 1990, as heir to the PCS), which had won 18 legislative seats in 1988. The PCS, a nominally independent offshoot of the Italian Communist Party, had generally followed the line of its Italian counterpart.

The PPDS was forced into opposition following the breakup of its coalition with the Christian Democrats in early 1992, and it fell back to 11 legislative seats in 1993. For the May 1998 election it formed a joint list with the IM and others that retained 11 seats on 18.6 percent of the vote. The February 2000 departure of the PSS from the government enabled the PPDS to reestablish a coalition with the Christian Democrats in March, but the resultant government collapsed a year later.

Meanwhile, the leftist IM had been established in 1998 by Alessandro ROSSI as principal successor to the Democratic Movement (*Movimento Democratico*—MD); following the 1998 election, the nascent IM extended its support to the newly formed PDCS-PPDS government. The MD had been formed in 1990 by members of the **San Marino Social Democratic Party** (*Partito Socialista Democratico Sammarinese*—PSDS), the most moderate of San Marino's several socialist parties and itself a partial successor to the PSDIS, which had bifurcated in 1975. In the 1993 general election the MD had won three seats. Emma Rossi's reformist group was largely a continuation of the **Socialists for Reform** (*Socialisti per le Riforme*—SpR), which she had formed in 1998 after quitting the PSS on the ground that it had become too closely aligned with the PDCS. The SpR won two seats in the 1998 poll. In March 2000 Rossi entered the newly formed government coalition.

Formation of the PdD was announced in preparation for the premature election of June 2001. Having won 12 seats in that poll, the PdD joined the PSS and the APDS in a new coalition government in mid-2002.

Following its formation in 2005, the PSD won 31.8 percent of the vote and 20 seats in the 2006 legislative poll. (The PSD total was 7 fewer than the total won in the previous election by its constituent parties [the PSS and PdD].) On July 12 the PSD formed a center-left governing coalition with the AP and SU that controlled 32 seats in the legislature until it fell on October 29, 2007. The PSD led a successor coalition government with the AP, the SU, and the DdC from November 28, 2007, to July 9, 2008.

The PSD list (which included candidates from the SpL [below]) secured 32 percent of the vote and 18 of the 25 seats won by the Reforms and Liberty coalition in the November 2008 legislative poll. However, citing the need for a new group in the Grand and General Council to promote traditional socialist values, PSD secretary Paride Andreoli and seven other PSD council members left the party and the Reforms and Liberty coalition on July 1, 2009, to form the PSRS (see PS, below). The move reduced the number of Reforms and Liberty seats in the council to 17 and PSD seats to 10, threw the opposition coalition into disarray, and prompted a number of other PSD members to resign.

Despite having previously been highly critical of the PDCS-led government (particularly in regard to slow progress in the reform of bank secrecy laws), the PSD opted to join the PDCS, NS, and AP in the "national unity" ticket presented under the San Marino Common Good electoral umbrella for the 2012 legislative poll. Denise BRONZETTI, theretofore president of the PSD and a former captain regent of the republic, resigned from the PSD in September 2013 and subsequently sat as an independent in the Grand and Central Council.

Leaders: Paride ANDREOLI (President), Beluzzi IRO (Parliamentary Leader), Marina LAZZARINI (Secretary).

Popular Alliance (*Alleanza Popolare*—AP). This centrist, liberal party, formerly known as the **San Marino Popular Democratic Alliance for the Republic** (*Alleanza Popolare dei Democratici Sammarinesi per la Repubblica*—APDS), was formed prior to the 1993 election under the leadership of former Christian Democrats. The APDS won four Grand and General Council seats in 1993 and six seats in 1998. In 2001 it slipped to five seats. In 2006 the party, by that time known as the AP, won 12.1 percent of the vote and seven seats, making it the third-largest party in the council.

Amid mounting discord with the United Left (SU, below), one of the AP's partners in the governing center-left coalition that collapsed in 2008, the AP joined the center-right Pact for San Marino for the November 2008 election. It won 11.5 percent of the vote and 7 of that Pact's 35 seats and 4 of the 35 seats secured by the San Marino Common Good coalition in 2012.

Leaders: Gabriele GATTI (President), Nicola RENZI (Coordinator).

Opposition Parties:

Socialist Party (*Partito Socialista*—PS). Formed in March 2012 by the **New Socialist Party** (*Nuovo Partito Socialista*—NPS) and the **San Marino Socialist Reformist Party** (*Partito Socialista Riformista Sammarinese*—PSRS), the PS secured 7 of the 12 seats won by the Agreement for the Country coalition in the November legislative balloting.

The social-democratic NPS had been founded in November 2005 by defectors from the PSD to protest what they perceived as corruption in the PSD-led government and to restore what the leaders of the new party described as traditional socialist values. The NPS won 5.4 percent of the vote and 3 seats in the 2006 election and was part of the opposition to the PSD-SU-AP governing coalition that collapsed in 2008. In advance of the 2008 election, the NPS formed an electoral list called the Freedom List (*Listadella Libertà*—LdL) with the NS.

Founded on July 1, 2009, by eight defectors from the PSD as a new opposition group in the Grand and General Council, the PSRS was formally launched as a new political party shortly thereafter.

The PS won 7 seats as part of the Agreement for the Country coalition (12 seats total) in the 2012 elections.

Leaders: Augusto CASALI (President), Paride ANDREOLI (Parliamentary Leader), Simone CELLI (Secretary).

Union for the Republic (*Unione per la Repubblica*—UPR). The UPR is an outgrowth, at least in part, of the **Center Democrats** (*Democratici di Centro*—DdC), a Catholic, populist movement founded in March 2007 by four defectors from the PDCS who were frustrated by the PDCS's poor showing in the 2006 elections. The defectors, including sitting Captain Regent Rosa Zafferani, resigned from the PDCS, but not from the legislature, in an effort to promote the DdC as a more viable centrist party. In November the DdC joined the center-left governing coalition.

In November 2008 the DdC won 4.9 percent of the vote and two council seats as a component of the Reform and Liberty coalition. In March 2011 the two DdC parliamentarians joined with the three defectors from the government to form the UPR faction in the council. The UPR subsequently became a formal party with the inclusion of the Euro-Populars for San Marino (*Europopolari per San Marino*—EpS).

The centrist EpS had been formed in July 2007 by former PDCS political secretary Marino Menicucci and several other prominent PDCS members who had resigned from the PDCS in 2006, citing the party's inability to adapt to the changing political climate and the need to widen its base of support to include moderates. However, the EpS realigned with the PDCS for the 2008 elections, and the EpS candidates ran on the PDCS list.

Legislator Gian Marco Marcucci, the leader of the EpS, resigned from his position as minister for labor, cooperation, and postal service relations in March 2011 and subsequently joined the new opposition parliamentary faction formed with the DdC.

The UPR secured 5 of the 12 seats won by the Agreement for the Country coalition in the November 2012 legislative balloting.

Leaders: Marco PODESCHI, Gian Marco MARCUCCI, William GIARDI (Parliamentary Leader), Lorenzo LONFERNINI (Coordinator).

United Left (*Sinistra Unita*—SU). The leftist SU political alliance was formed in 2005 by the **San Marino Communist Refoundation** (*Rifondazione Comunista Sammarinese*—RCS) and the **Left Party–Free Port** (*Partito della Sinistra–Zona Franca*—ZF). In the 2006 legislative poll the SU won 8.7 percent of the vote and five seats. It retained its five seats in 2008 as a component of the Reforms and Liberty coalition and in 2012 as a component of the Active Citizenship coalition. The other 2012 electoral coalition member, **Civic Movement 10** (*Movimento Civico 10*—Civico 10) led by Andrea ZAFFERANI (Parliamentary Leader) and Marco ROSSI, won four seats.

Leaders: Gastone PASOLINI (President), Alessandro ROSSI (Former Captain Regent), Francesca MICHELOTTI (Parliamentary Leader), Ivan FOSCHI (Former RCS Leader), Roberto TAMAGNINI (ZF Coordinator), Angelo DELLA VALLE (RCS Secretary).

Renewal, Equity, Transparency, and Eco-sustainability Civic Movement (*Rinnovamento, Equità, Transparenza, Ecosostenibilità Movimento Civico*—RETE Movement). Recently formed by activist groups concerned with, among other things, the environment, civil rights, and the arts, the RETE Movement, competing on its own, won four seats on a vote share of 6.3 percent in the November 2012 legislative poll.

Leaders: Gloria ARCANGELONI (President), Roberto CIAVATTA (Parliamentary Leader).

Other Parties:

Moderate Sammarinese (*Moderati Sammarinese*). This party is an outgrowth of the **San Marino Populars** (*Popolari Sammarinese*), a centrist, Catholic party that was founded in 2003 and that won 2.4 percent of the vote and one seat on the Grand and General Council in 2006. The San Marino Populars formed an electoral list called the San Marino Union of Moderates (*Unione Sammarinese dei Moderati*—USDM) with the ANS (below) prior to the November 2008 legislative poll, at which the USDM won 4.2 percent of the vote and 2 of the 35 seats secured by the Pact for San Marino. However, legislative cooperation between the San Marino Populars and the ANS declined in 2011, and members of the San Marino Populars formed Moderate Sammarinese to participate in the Agreement for the Country Coalition for the November 2012 legislative elections. Candidates from Moderate Sammarinese did not secure any of the coalition's 12 seats.

Leader: Angela VENTURINI.

Arengo and Freedom (*Arengo e Libertà*—AeL). The center-left AeL was founded in September 2008 by council members Fabio Berardi and Nadia Ottaviani, who left the PSD because they thought the party had moved too far to the left. The AeL was named for the assembly (*Arengo*) that ruled San Marino during the Middle Ages. The new party presented its candidates for the 2008 elections on the PDCS list. There was no reference to the AeL in regard to the 2012 balloting.

Leaders: Fabio BERARDI, Nadia OTTAVIANA.

San Marino National Alliance (*Alleanza Nazionale Sammarinese*—ANS). The right-wing ANS, founded in 2001 and linked to the Italian post-fascist National Alliance (*Alleanza Nazionale*), won one seat in the June 2001 council election. In 2006 it won 2.3 percent of the vote and retained its seat on the council. In 2008 the ANS presented its candidates with the San Marino Populars on the USDM list (a component of the Pact for San Marino). There was no reference to the ANS in regard to the 2012 elections.

Leaders: Glauco SANSOVINI (Political Secretary), Ennio Vittorio PELLANDRA (President).

Sammarinese for Freedom (*Sammarinesi per la Libertà*—SpL). Founded in 2002, the center-left SpL won 1.8 percent of the vote and one council seat in 2006. It participated in the PSD electoral list for the 2008 poll as a member of the Reforms and Liberty coalition. A report in 2012 indicated that the SpL had expressed interest in the formation of the Socialist Party.

Leaders: Giuseppe ROSSI (President), Monica BOLLINI.

New parties that ran unsuccessfully in the 2012 legislative elections include **San Marino 3.0** (led by Simone DELLA VALLE and Mickael BORKHOLZ), which received 1.8 percent of the vote; and **For San Marino** (*Per San Marino*), which received 2.8 percent of the vote under the leadership of Emilio DELLA BALDE and Alvara SELVA.

LEGISLATURE

The **Grand and General Council** (*Consiglio Grande e Generale*) is a unicameral body consisting of 60 members elected on a proportional basis for five-year terms (subject to dissolution) by direct popular vote in a single nationwide constituency. The captains regent serve as presiding officers.

Electoral law revisions following the 2006 poll permitted parties to form coalitions for subsequent elections (see Political Parties, above). In addition, a minimum threshold of 3.5 percent was established for a party or coalition to secure representation in most cases. (Lower thresholds are possible depending on how many lists are presented in any given election and how many parties participate in a list.) Finally, "bonus seats" were authorized to ensure that the leading coalition secures at least 35 seats.

Following the most recent election on November 11, 2012, the seat distribution was as follows: the San Marino Common Good coalition, 35 (the joint list of the San Marino Christian Democratic Party [PDCS] and We Sammarinese [NS], 21 [PDCS, 18; NS, 3]; the Party of Socialists and Democrats [PSD], 10); Popular Alliance, 4; Agreement for the Country coalition, 12 (the Socialist Party, 7; the Union for the Republic, 5); Active Citizenship coalition, 9 (United Left [SU], 5; Civic Movement 10, 4); and Renewal, Equity, Transparency, and Ecosustainability Civic Movement, 4. One legislator formerly from the PSD and one formerly from the SU were listed as independents as of the fall of 2014.

Speakers (Captains Regent of the Republic): Marino RICCARDI, Fabio BERARDI (until April 1, 2017).

CABINET

[as of October 7, 2016]

Captains Regent	Marino Riccardi (PSD) Fabio Berardi (AeL)
Secretaries of State	
Education, Culture, the University, Scientific Research, Social Affairs, and Gender Equality	Giuseppe Maria Morganti (PSD)
Finance and Budget, Posts, and Relations with the Philatelic and Numismatic State Corporation	Gian Carlo Capicchioni (PSD)
Foreign and Political Affairs	Pasquale Valentini (PDCS)
Health and Social Security, National Insurance, Family, and Economic Planning	Francesco Mussoni (PDCS)
Industry, Crafts, Trade, Transportation, and Research	Marco Arzilli (NS)
Internal Affairs, Civil Service, Justice, and Relations with Township Councils	Gian Carlo Venturini (PDCS)
Labor, Cooperation, and Information	Iro Belluzi (PSD)
Territory and Environment, Agriculture, Telecommunications, International Economic Cooperation, Civil Protection, and Relations with the Public Works State Corporation	Antonella Mularoni (AP) [f]
Tourism, Sports, and Relations with the Public Utilities State Corporation	Teodoro Lonfernini (PDCS)

[f] = female

INTERGOVERNMENTAL REPRESENTATION

Ambassador to the U.S.: Damiano BELEFFI (Chargé d'Affaires *ad interim*).

U.S. Ambassador to San Marino (resident in Italy): Kelly DEGNAN (Chargé d'Affaires *ad interim*).

Permanent Representative to the UN: Damiano BELEFFI.

IGO Memberships (Non-UN): CEUR, ICC, OSCE.

For Further Reference:

Eccardt, Thomas M. *Secrets of the Seven Smallest States of Europe.* New York: Hippocrene Books. 2004.

Edwards, Adrian, and Chris Michaelides. *San Marino.* Santa Barbara, CA: ABC-CLIO Press, 1996.

SÃO TOMÉ AND PRÍNCIPE

Democratic Republic of São Tomé and Príncipe
República Democrática de São Tomé e Príncipe

Political Status: Achieved independence from Portugal on July 12, 1975; constitution of November 5, 1975, revised in December 1982, October 1987, August 1990, and March 2003; currently under multiparty mixed presidential-parliamentary system.

Area: 387 sq. mi. (1,001 sq. km).

Population: 194,000 (2016E—UN); 197,541 (2016E—U.S. Census).

Major Urban Center (2014E—UN): SÃO TOMÉ (71,000).

Official Language: Portuguese.

Monetary Unit: Dobra (market rate October 1, 2016: 21,795.50 dobras = $1US).

President: Evaristo CARVALHO (Independent Democratic Action); directly elected in runoff balloting on August 7, 2016, and sworn in for a five-year term on September 3, succeeding Manuel PINTO DA COSTA (ind.), who boycotted the August 7 balloting. (See Government and Politics, below.)

Prime Minister: Patrice Emery TROVOADA (Independent Democratic Action); appointed by the president on November 25, 2014, and inaugurated (along with his new cabinet) on November 29 in succession to Gabriel Arcanjo FERREIRA DA COSTA (Union for Democracy and Development).

THE COUNTRY

Located in the Gulf of Guinea some 125 miles off the coast of Gabon, São Tomé and Príncipe consists of a small archipelago of two main islands (after which the country is named) and four islets: Cabras, Gago Coutinho, Pedras Tinhosas, and Rôlas. Volcanic in origin, the islands exhibit numerous craters and lava flows; the climate is warm and humid most of the year. The indigenous inhabitants are primarily descended from plantation laborers imported from the African mainland. The Portuguese population, estimated at more than 3,000 before independence in 1975, subsequently declined substantially. Roman Catholicism is the principal religion. Women constitute about one-third of the economically active population and hold a limited number of leadership positions in politics and government. Ten women were elected to the National Assembly in 2010.

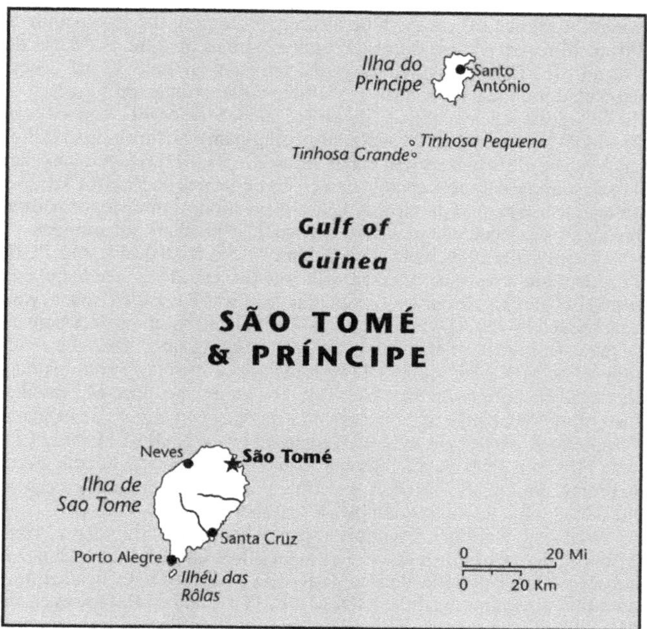

São Tomé and Príncipe was once the world's leading producer of cocoa, although production has declined. Tourism and construction also contribute significantly to the economy, and the government hopes that oil revenues from the Gulf of Guinea will boost the nation's finances. (São Tomé and Príncipe shares with Nigeria an economic development zone that was believed initially to hold more than 11 billion barrels of crude oil. Exploration began in 2006, but results to date have been discouraging.) Most food is imported, often in the form of donations, with copra, coffee, palm kernels, sugar, and bananas being produced domestically. Consumables dominate the small industrial sector, and the country relies heavily on foreign aid, which provides approximately 80 percent of the government's budget.

The flight of Portuguese managers and skilled labor at independence took a toll on the economy, as did cyclical droughts and, beginning in 1980, low world cocoa prices. The government began moving away from a Marxist orientation in the mid-1980s and subsequently began to emphasize economic denationalization (most importantly in the cocoa industry), foreign investment, reduction of subsidies, currency devaluation, and other liberalization measures that won the support of the International Monetary Fund (IMF) and World Bank. In addition, the administration tried to diversify the economy by developing fishing and tourism.

In 2009 the IMF approved $3.8 million in assistance for the following three years to support the government's economic reforms (including improvements in the banking sector) and efforts to reduce poverty, which reportedly affects more than one-half of the population. The IMF in 2012 continued to praise the government for its "fiscal prudence" and probusiness regulatory reforms and approved another three-year, $3.9 million program.

The World Bank announced grants of $5.5 million in mid-2013 to support the government's efforts to, among other things, improve the investment climate. However, analysts subsequently predicted that it would be unlikely that oil would start flowing anytime soon in view of the fact that most of the initial exploratory blocks had been abandoned. Business leaders also described progress on the proposed deepwater port in Fernão Dias on São Tomé as sluggish.

GDP growth of 4 percent was reported for 2013, with inflation registering 7.1 percent. In 2014 the IMF urged the government to "reenergize" its structural reform efforts. GDP grew by 4.5 percent in 2014 and 5 percent in 2015. In 2016 the IMF estimated that GDP expanded by 5.2 percent, while inflation grew by 5 percent. GDP per capita that year was $2,038. In its annual ease of doing business survey, the World Bank ranked the country 166th out of 189 nations.

GOVERNMENT AND POLITICS

Political background. Discovered by Portuguese explorers in 1471, the islands of São Tomé and Príncipe separately became Portuguese territories in 1552–1523 and, collectively, an Overseas Province of Portugal in 1951. Nationalistic sentiment became apparent in 1960 with the formation of the Committee for the Liberation of São Tomé and Príncipe (*Comité de Libertação de São Tomé e Príncipe*—CLSTP). In 1972 the CLSTP became the Movement for the Liberation of São Tomé and Príncipe (*Movimento de Libertação de São Tomé e Príncipe*—MLSTP), which quickly became the leading advocate of independence from Portugal. Based in Gabon under the leadership of Manuel PINTO DA COSTA, the MLSTP carried out a variety of underground activities, particularly in support of protests by African workers against low wages in São Tomé and Príncipe.

In 1973 the Organization of African Unity (OAU, subsequently the African Union—AU) recognized the MLSTP, and Portugal granted the country local autonomy. After the 1974 military coup in Lisbon, the Portuguese government began negotiations with the MLSTP, which it recognized as the sole official representative for the islands. The two agreed in November 1974 that independence would be proclaimed on July 12, 1975, and that a transitional government would be formed under MLSTP leadership until that time. Installed on December 21, 1974, the transitional government council comprised four members appointed by the MLSTP and one by Portugal. Upon independence, Pinto da Costa assumed the presidency and promptly designated his MLSTP associate, Miguel Anjos da Cunha Lisboa TROVOADA, as prime minister. In December 1978, however, Trovoada was relieved of his duties, and in October 1979 he was arrested on charges that he had been involved in a projected coup, one of a series that Pinto da Costa claimed to have foiled with the aid of Angolan troops. The president subsequently served as both head of state and chief executive without serious domestic challenge, despite Trovoada's release in 1981. In late 1987 the government, which had already introduced many economic liberalization measures, launched a political liberalization campaign as well (see Constitution and government, below). One of the first official changes was the revival of the office of prime minister; Celestino ROCHA DA COSTA was appointed to the post in January 1988.

The reform process culminated in an August 1990 referendum that endorsed abandonment of the country's single-party system, and on January 20, 1991, the recently legalized Party of Democratic Convergence (*Partido de Convergência Democrática*—PCD) outdistanced the restyled MLSTP–Social Democratic Party (MLSTP–*Partido Social Democrata*—MLSPT-PSD) by winning 33 of 55 seats in the new National Assembly. On February 8 PCD general secretary Daniel Lima dos Santos DAIO was named to head a new government, and on March 3 former prime minister Trovoada secured election as head of state. (Incumbent president Pinto da Costa had earlier announced his retirement from public life, although he subsequently returned to politics [see below].)

Prime Minister Daio was dismissed on April 22, 1992, in favor of his finance minister, Norberto José d'Alva COSTA ALEGRE. Despite an MLSTP-PSD call for a unity government, the cabinet announced by Costa Alegre on May 16 was composed solely of PCD members.

On July 2, 1994, President Trovoada sacked Prime Minister Costa Alegre in favor of Evaristo CARVALHO, who, although a PCD member, had long been close to the president. Four days later Carvalho was expelled from the PCD, which called for a new presidential election. Trovoada responded by appointing a Carvalho-recommended government of "presidential friends." On July 10, after the PCD had announced that it intended to introduce a motion declaring the new administration unconstitutional, Trovoada dissolved the National Assembly and called for new elections.

In legislative balloting on October 2, 1994, the MLSTP-PSD returned to power with the capture of a near-majoritarian 27 seats, while the PCD and President Trovoada's recently legalized Independent Democratic Action (*Ação Democrática Independente*—ADI) each secured 14 seats. On October 25 Trovoada appointed MLSTP-PSD secretary general Carlos Alberto Dias Monteiro DA GRAÇA as prime minister. Although da Graça had pledged to form a government of "national union," he named a cabinet dominated by MLSTP-PSD members on October 28.

On August 16, 1995, a group of Cuban-trained rebel soldiers led by Lt. Orlando das NEVES stormed the presidential palace, taking President Trovoada prisoner. However, Trovoada resumed his duties a week later after issuing a pardon to the officers who had seized him. Among the concessions reportedly made to secure Trovoada's release were pledges to name the long-anticipated unity government and restructure the military.

After the MLSTP-PSD, ADI, and the Opposition Democratic Coalition (*Coligação Democrática da Oposição*—Codo) had signed a cooperation pact on December 29, 1995, MLSTP-PSD deputy secretary general Armindo Vaz de ALMEIDA on January 5, 1996, formed a cabinet that included seven members from the MLSTP-PSD, four from the ADI, and one from Codo, despite Codo's lack of legislative representation.

In delayed first-round presidential balloting on June 30, 1996, incumbent president Trovoada led a five-man field with 40.9 percent of the vote, followed by former president Pinto da Costa (39.1 percent), the PCD's Alda BANDEIRA (14.6 percent), former prime minister da Graça, and Armindo TOMBA, an anticorruption journalist. In the run-off on July 21, Trovoada defeated Pinto da Costa by 52–48 percent.

On September 20, 1996, an assembly nonconfidence motion reportedly orchestrated by the assembly president, Fortunato PIRES, forced the resignation of the Almeida government. Subsequent MLSTP-PSD efforts to have Pires appointed to the premiership were blocked by Trovoada and the ADI, however, and on November 13 Trovoada appointed MLSTP-PSD deputy secretary general Raúl Bragança NETO as prime minister. On November 28 Neto named a government that included six MLSTP-PSD ministers, three from the PCD, and one independent.

The MLSTP-PSD won 31 legislative seats in polling on November 8, 1998, with the ADI improving to 16 seats and the PCD falling to 8. The MLSTP-PSD subsequently nominated Guilherme POSSER DA COSTA, a former foreign minister and ambassador, to be the next prime minister, and Posser da Costa and his MLSTP-PSD government were sworn in on January 5, 1999.

In first-round presidential balloting on July 29, 2001, ADI candidate Fradique de MENEZES (56.3 percent of the vote) defeated former president Manuel Pinto da Costa (38.4 percent) and three minor candidates. Subsequently, several attempts to form a "cohabitation" government failed, in part because President Menezes rejected cabinet recommendations from the MLSTD-PSD. Menezes, who was inaugurated in September, consequently dismissed Prime Minister Posser da Costa and his cabinet and named former prime minister Carvalho to head a "presidential initiative" government including members from the ADI and the PCD. Calling the minority government "unconstitutional," the MLSTP-PSD walked out of the assembly, initiating a political crisis that prompted President Menezes to dissolve the assembly on December 7 and call for early elections. Concurrently, it was reported that the leading political parties had agreed to allocate cabinet posts according to the seats won by each party in the new legislative balloting.

In the assembly poll on March 3, 2002, the MLSTP-PSD secured a 1-seat plurality of 24 seats over the new electoral coalition formed by the PCD and the recently launched, pro-Menezes Democratic Movement Force for Change–Liberal Party (*Movimento Democrático Força da Mudança–Partido Liberal*—MDFM-PL). On March 26 the president appointed Gabriel COSTA (a former leader of the MLSTP-PSD but now an independent described as "close" to the MDFM–PL) as the new prime minister. The cabinet that took office in April contained, according to the previously determined proportion, members of the MLSTP-PSD, the coalition of the MDFM-PL and the PCD, and the new Uê Kédadji alliance that had been formed by the ADI, Codo, and others prior to the assembly poll, at which the alliance had captured third place with 8 seats.

Following a dispute between Prime Minister Costa and Defense Minister Victor MONTEIRO, President Menezes dismissed Costa and the rest of the cabinet on September 27, 2002. On October 3 the president appointed Maria das NEVES de Souza (MLSTP-PSD) as the new prime minister. On October 6 das Neves announced her new cabinet, which again included members of her own party, the coalition of the MDFM-PL and PCD, and the Uê Kédadji alliance.

In 2003 the potential windfall from oil exploration raised concerns regarding government accountability and corruption. In June a military group briefly deposed President Menezes while he was in Nigeria, but he returned to office on July 23 after successful negotiations with the rebels. Among other things, the assembly agreed to a deal arranged by international negotiators to grant amnesty to the junta and to the political group linked to it, the Christian Democratic Front (*Frente Democrática Cristã*—FDC). However, the fractious debate over energy resources, which inspired the coup, continued over the terms of a contract with a Nigerian company involved in the Joint Development Zone (JDZ).

President Menezes appointed Damiao ALMEIDA as prime minister on September 17, 2003, and a reshuffled cabinet made up of the MLSTP-PSD and ADI was sworn in the next day. The award of five blocs of the JDZ to international oil companies in May 2005 caused disagreement in the government's inner circles, and Patrice TROVOADA, an oil broker and the son of the former president, was dismissed as oil adviser to the president. Menezes then flew to Nigeria, where he signed off on the bloc awards, prompting the resignation of Prime Minister Almeida and the entire cabinet on June 3. Maria do Carmo SILVEIRA was named prime minister on June 7, and a new cabinet, dominated by the MLSTP-PSD, was appointed on June 8.

In legislative elections on March 26, 2006, MDFM-PL supporters of President Menezes won 23 seats, surprising many by finishing ahead of the MLSTP-PSD, whose seat count fell to 20. The ADI secured the other 11 seats. Menezes subsequently named Tomé Soares da VERA CRUZ—an engineer who had previously held the position of minister of natural resources—as head of a new minority MDFM-PL/PCD government.

On July 30, 2006, with the backing of the MDFM-PL and PCD, President Menezes was reelected with 60.6 percent of the vote in the first round of balloting. Menezes's main opponent was Patrice Trovoada, who was backed by the ADI and the MLSTP-PSD and received 38.8 percent of the vote. In August, in the first regional balloting since 1992, the coalition of the MDFM-PL and PCD won majorities in six of seven districts that held elections, with the MLSTP-PSD winning the other. Meanwhile, the Union for Change and Progress in Príncipe (*União para Mudança e Progresso do Príncipe*—UMPP), supported by the MDFM-PL and PCD, won all seven seats in the regional assembly of Príncipe in concurrent balloting. José CASSANDRA, the UMPP leader, subsequently became president of the regional assembly on October 5.

When the National Assembly rejected his proposed budget, Prime Minister Vera Cruz resigned in February 2008, and President Menezes subsequently appointed Patrice Trovoada of the ADI to head a new coalition government of the MDFM-PL, PCD, and ADI. However, on May 30 the government suffered a vote of no confidence in the assembly when the PCD voted with the opposition. Consequently, on June 10 Menezes appointed Joachim Rafael BRANCO of the MLSTP-PSD as prime minister. The new government sworn in on June 21 included the MDFM-PL, PCD, and MLSTP-PSD.

In December 2009 President Menenzes was elected president of the MDFM-PL, but the MLSTP-PSD and PCD criticized his elevation in the party as illegal and asked the Constitutional Court for a ruling. (The constitution forbids a sitting president from engaging in "other political activities.") As a result, the MDFM-PL announced it was leaving the government, although several MDFM-PL ministers reportedly indicated a desire to resist that decision. On January 12, 2010, Branco announced a new minority cabinet comprising the MLSTP-PSD and the PCD. Menezes subsequently withdrew from his party responsibilities (see section on the MDFM-PL, below).

The ADI won a plurality of 26 seats in the August 1, 2010, assembly balloting, while the MDFM-PL, running on its own, plummeted to only 1 seat. ADI leader Trovoada formed a minority government (comprising only ADI members and independents) on August 14. Subsequent legislative action remained constrained by interparty friction, particularly between the ADI and the MLSTP-PSD, which had contributed to decades of political instability (18 prime ministers since 1991).

Ten candidates—seven running as independents—contested the first round of presidential elections on July 17, 2011. Former president Manuel Pinta da Costa, running as an independent after failing to secure the nomination from the MLSTP-PSD, finished first with 35.8 percent of the vote, followed by the ADI's former prime minister Evaristo Carvalho (the speaker of the National Assembly) with 21.8 percent. Pinto da Costa won a narrow victory with 52.9 percent of the vote in the second round on August 7. He was sworn in on September 3, 20 years after he had last held the office. Pinto da Costa, 74, pledged to fight poverty and corruption in response to growing popular frustration over those issues. Although much presidential authority had been shifted to the prime minister since Pinto da Costa had last held office two decades earlier, some observers worried about a possible return to the authoritarian approach that had marked Pinto da Costa's previous presidency.

All the non-ADI legislative parties participated in a mass "Save Democracy" demonstration in October 2012, as Prime Minister Trovoada's critics accused him of hard-line tactics against the opposition, manipulation of the media, and a lack of transparency in regard to various financial dealings.

Although Prime Minister Trovoada reportedly retained substantial popular support, he lost a confidence motion in the assembly on November 28, 2012, when all the non-ADI legislators supported the government's ouster. President Pinto da Costa dismissed Prime Minister Trovoada and his cabinet on December 4, and former Prime Minister Gabriel Costa subsequently formed a new government that included the, PCD, and the MDFM-PL, but not the disgruntled ADI.

In the October 12, 2014, elections to the National Assembly, ADI won 33 seats; the MSLPT-PSD, 16; the PCD, 5; and the Union for

Democracy and Development (*União para Democracia e Desenvolvimento*—UDD), 1. Former prime minister Trovoada returned to the premiership as head of a new ADI-dominated cabinet that was installed on November 29.

In the first round of presidential balloting on July 17, 2016, former prime minister Carvalho was initially reported to have won outright with 50.1 percent of the vote. However, four days after the balloting, the election commission issued a recount that left Carvalho with 49.9 percent, necessitating a runoff with incumbent president Pinto da Costa, who was second with 24.8 percent. On August 1 Pinto da Costa withdrew from the runoff, asserting that the original polling was tainted. Carvalho subsequently ran unopposed in the second round on August 7 and succeeded Pinto da Costa.

Constitution and government. The constitution, as revised in 1982, identified the MLSTP as the "directing political force" for the country, provided for an indirectly elected National Popular Assembly as the supreme organ of state, and conferred broad powers on a president, who was named by the assembly for a five-year term. In October 1987 the MLSTP Central Committee proposed a number of constitutional changes as part of a broad democratization program. Theretofore elected by the People's District Assemblies from candidates nominated by an MLSTP-dominated Candidature Commission, legislators would now be chosen by direct and universal suffrage. Independent candidates would be permitted in addition to candidates presented by the party and "recognized organizations," such as trade unions or youth groups. The president would be elected by popular vote rather than being designated by the assembly; however, only the MLSTP president (elected by secret ballot at a party congress) could stand as a candidate. In the course of approving the reform program, the assembly provided for the restoration of a presidentially appointed prime minister.

As a consequence of an August 1990 referendum, a multiparty system was introduced, together with multicandidature and popular balloting for legislators and the president. In addition, the president was limited to two five-year terms. The National Assembly conferred local autonomy upon Príncipe in 1994, and elections were held there in March 1995 for a seven-member regional assembly and a five-member regional government (headed by a president). The new bodies were installed April 29, 1995.

In November 2002 the assembly endorsed constitutional revision designed to diminish presidential power. Despite the objections of President Menezes, the changes took effect in March 2003. Among other things, the new basic law eliminated the president's right to veto constitutional amendments and provided for the establishment of two new bodies—an advisory Council of State and a Constitutional Tribunal.

The judiciary is headed by a Supreme Court, whose members are designated by and are responsible to the assembly. Administratively, the country is divided into two provinces (coterminous with each of the main islands) and 12 counties (11 of which are located on São Tomé).

São Tomé and Príncipe's constitution protects free speech and freedom of the press. Among other things, opposition groups and parties are guaranteed access to state-controlled radio and television.

Foreign relations. Despite the exodus of much of the country's Portuguese population from 1974 to 1975, São Tomé and Príncipe continued to maintain an active commercial trade with the former colonial power. Following independence, diplomatic relations were established with the Soviet Union and the Eastern-bloc countries as well as the major Western states and other former Portuguese dependencies in Africa, most notably Angola. In 1978 some 1,000 troops from Angola, augmented by a small contingent from Guinea-Bissau, were dispatched to São Tomé to guard against what President Pinto da Costa claimed to be a series of coup plots by expatriates in Angola, Gabon, and Portugal. However, most of the troops were withdrawn by the mid-1980s as part of a rapprochement with the West.

Ties with nearby Francophone nations subsequently grew, and France became São Tomé and Príncipe's leading trade partner. The county has also enjoyed significant aid from Taiwan, which São Tomé and Príncipe recognized in 1997.

In November 1999 São Tomé and Príncipe joined six of its Gulf of Guinea neighbors in agreeing to establish the Gulf of Guinea Commission (GGC) to coordinate "cooperation and development" in the oil- and fish-rich region. In early 2001 São Tomé and Príncipe reached an accord with Nigeria to establish the JDZ in disputed waters in the Gulf of Guinea; however, in May 2005 tensions arose between the two countries over operating rights in the zone. Cooperation subsequently appeared back on track, and in 2007 São Tomé and Príncipe and Nigeria created a joint military commission to enhance bilateral security cooperation. Nigeria also supported São Tomé and Príncipe by selling it subsidized oil and providing a $30 million credit line. (In May 2009 the Nigerian legislature approved a $10 million interest-free loan for São Tomé and Príncipe to be paid back over six years with revenue from the JDZ.)

The United States has provided training to local security forces and has assisted in numerous infrastructure projects in the islands. The two countries conducted a joint military training exercise in March 2007, and in May 2007 the United States announced that it would assist São Tomé and Príncipe in coastal security to protect oil shipments passing through the Gulf of Guinea.

Despite the nation's diplomatic ties with Taiwan, the government announced an agreement in late 2013 for the People's Republic of China to promote development in São Tomé and Príncipe.

São Tomé and Príncipe announced in July 2015 that citizens of the EU and the United States would be allowed entry into the country without a visa.

Current issues. Prime Minister Trovoada decried his dismissal by the president in early December 2012 as "illegitimate," and the ADI refused to nominate another candidate for the premiership, calling instead for new elections. Meanwhile, new Prime Minister Gabriel Costa was viewed as a "consensus builder" whose government would at least enjoy a relatively collegial relationship with the president.

The government announced a budget of $154 million for 2015, with $60 million from domestic revenue and the remainder financed by foreign aid and donations, including $10.2 million from the UN Development Program. In July 2015 the IMF announced a $3.2 million credit to support public finances.

In February 2016 São Tomé and Príncipe was one of 13 African countries to receive the African Leaders Malaria Alliance (ALMA) award for efforts to eradicate the disease. The country reduced its number of malaria infections from more than 54,000 in 2004 to 9,261 in 2013.

POLITICAL PARTIES

Government Party:

Independent Democratic Action (*Ação Democrática Independente*—ADI). Formed in 1992 under the leadership of President Miguel Trovoada's political advisor, Gabriel Costa, the ADI participated in municipal elections that year as an "independent group." It was legally registered in early 1994 and won 14 seats in the 1994 assembly balloting and 16 in 1998, claiming irregularities in the latter poll. In 2000 the ADI formed an electoral alliance with the PCD, Codo, UNDP, and PPP called the "Democratic Platform," which backed ADI candidate Fradique de Menezes in the 2001 presidential election. The ADI subsequently formed a coalition government with the PCD. However, Menezes later fell into disagreement with pro-Trovoada factions within the ADI, and his allies formed the MDFM-PL (below). Meanwhile, Costa objected to the elevation of Patrice Trovoada, son of the former president, to ADI leader and left the party, eventually founding the UDD (below).

The ADI participated in the UK coalition (below) from late 2001 until early 2006 but won 11 seats on its own in the March 2006 legislative election. Party secretary general Patrice Trovoada, the son of the former president, became prime minister for a short time in the first half of 2008 but was unable to hold the fledgling coalition together. Calling for fresh legislative elections, the ADI rejected the negotiations that brought about Prime Minister Branco's coalition government in June 2008. The ADI subsequently maintained the position that Branco's government was unconstitutional. Trovoada was named prime minister again after the ADI secured a plurality of 26 seats (on a vote share of 42 percent) in the 2010 assembly balloting.

Party secretary general Evaristo Carvalho lost in the 2011 runoff presidential balloting to Manuel Pinta da Costa with 47.1 percent of the vote. Trovoada was dismissed as prime minister in December 2012, but regained the position after the ADI won legislative elections in October 2014. In that balloting, the ADI secured an absolute majority with 49.8 percent of the vote and 33 seats. Carvalho was elected president in August 2016.

Leaders: Patrice TROVOADA (Prime Minister and Chair), Evaristo CARVALHO (President of the Republic and 2011 presidential candidate), Levy NAZARÉ (Secretary General).

Opposition Parties:

Movement for the Liberation of São Tomé and Príncipe–Social Democratic Party (*Movimento de Libertação de São Tomé e Príncipe–Partido Social Democrata*—MLSTP-PSD). An outgrowth of an earlier **Committee for the Liberation of São Tomé and Príncipe** (*Comité de Libertação de São Tomé e Príncipe*—CLSTP), the MLSTP was founded in 1972 and became the leading force in the campaign for independence from Portugal. At its first congress in 1978, the movement defined itself as a "revolutionary front of democratic, anti-neocolonialist, and anti-imperialist forces"; however, it did not formally adopt Marxism-Leninism despite that ideology's influence on its leaders and their economic policies. The MLSTP was the country's only authorized political group until the adoption of a multiparty system in August 1990. Two months later, President Manuel Pinto da Costa retired from leadership of what had been redesignated the MLSTP-PSD.

Pinto da Costa returned to political activity in 1996 and was elected to the party presidency in May 1998, prompting the resignation of Francisco Pires, a senior MLSTP-PSD leader who decried Pinto da Costa's "authoritarianism." Promising to reverse the country's declining economic conditions, the MLSTP-PSD secured a majority of assembly seats in the November election. However, Pinto da Costa was defeated in his bid for the presidency in 2001, and the MLSTP-PSD was excluded from the new government. In February 2005 former prime minister and party vice president Guilherme Posser da Costa replaced Pinto da Costa as the party's president. In June 2005 the MLSTP-PSD threatened to resign from the government, but the party subsequently agreed to form a new government to avoid early elections. Party member Maria do Carmo Silveira became the new prime minister and finance minister.

In the March 2006 legislative elections, the MLSTP-PSD won 20 seats, finishing second behind the coalition of the MDFM-PL and PCD. In the July presidential election, the MLSTP-PSD chose not to field its own candidate, instead supporting the ADI's Patrice Trovoada. In regional balloting in August 2006, the MLSTP-PSD won a majority in only one of seven districts. In light of that poor showing, party president Posser da Costa resigned the party leadership post; he was replaced in February 2007 by Joaquim Rafael Branco, a party veteran who promised to rebuild the base before the next legislative elections in 2010. Following the collapse of the short-lived Trovoada government in May 2008, Branco was named to head a new coalition government. He lost the premiership following the August 2010 assembly balloting, in which the MLSTP-PSD won 21 seats (on a vote share of 33 percent) to finish second to the surging ADI.

In January 2011 businessman Aurélio Martins was elected party president over rival Jorge Amado. Martins subsequently became the party's flagbearer for the July presidential elections, while former party leader Pinto da Costa, as well as party stalwarts Maria das Neves and Elsa PINTO, ran as independents. Eventual winner Pinto da Costa received 35.8 percent of the first-round vote, while das Neves secured 13.9 percent, Pinto 4.6 percent, and Martins 4.1 percent. Jorge Amado was elected as the new party president at the MLSTP-PSD congress in June 2012. He was a prominent leader in the demonstrations in October that contributed to the downfall of the Trovoada government.

Former prime minister and longtime MLSTP-PSD stalwart Joaquin Rafael Branco left the party in early 2014 and subsequently helped found the PEPS (below). In the 2014 legislative balloting, the party was second with 24.7 percent of the vote and 16 seats. Martins was elected party chair in November 2015.

Former prime minister Maria das NEVES de Souza was the party's presidential candidate in 2016. She placed third with 24.3 percent of the vote in the first round of voting.

Leaders: Aurélio MARTINS (Former President, Party Chair, and 2011 presidential candidate), Guilherme POSSER DA COSTA (Former Prime Minister), Armindo Vaz de ALMEIDA (Former Prime Minister), Osvaldo VAZ, Fernando MAQUENGO (Secretary General).

Party of Democratic Convergence (*Partido de Convergência Democrática*—PCD). The PCD was launched in 1987, initially as an underground movement styled after the **Reflection Group** (*Grupo de Reflexão*—GR), which surfaced as an open opposition formation following the introduction of multiparty politics in August 1990.

In early 1996 the PCD refused to participate in the new government. Subsequently, it named party president Alda Bandeira de Conceicão as its presidential candidate; following his third-place finish in the first round of presidential polling in June, the PCD supported Miguel Trovoada in the second round.

In the November 1998 legislative polling, the PCD's representation fell from 14 to 8 seats. The PCD supported the ADI's candidate in the 2001 presidential election, and the PCD was given posts in the new cabinet in September 2001. In 2002 and again in 2006, the PCD entered into an electoral alliance with the MDFM-PL. Running on its own in the 2010 assembly poll, the PCD finished third, securing 7 seats on a vote share of 13.9 percent.

In the 2011 presidential election, Delfim Neves, party secretary general, received 13.9 percent of the vote in the first round, finishing fourth. In the 2014 legislative elections, the party won 11 percent of the vote and 5 seats.

Leaders: Xavier MENDES (President), António DIAS (2014 candidate for prime minister), Daniel Lima dos Santos DAIO (Former Prime Minister), Alda BANDEIRA de Conceicão (1996 presidential candidate), Delfim NEVES (2011 presidential candidate and Secretary General).

Union for Democracy and Development (*União para Democracia e Desenvolvimento*—UDD). Launched by ADI dissidents, including ADI cofounder Gabriel Costa, the UDD (also referenced as the **Union of Democrats for Citizenship and Development** [*União dos Democrats para e Cidadania e* Desenvolvimento—UDCD]) secured 2.4 percent of the vote in the March 2006 legislative poll and 1.2 percent (and again no seats) in 2010. In the 2014 balloting, the UDD won 1.9 percent of the vote and 1 seat.

Leaders: Manuel DIOGO (President), Gabriel COSTA (Former Prime Minister and Vice President of the Party).

Other Parties and Groups:

Democratic Movement Force for Change–Liberal Party (*Movimento Democrático Força de Mudança–Partido Liberal*—MDFM-PL). The MDFM-PL was formed in late 2001 by former members of the ADI close to President Menezes and later established an electoral alliance with the PCD for legislative balloting in 2002. That alliance won the largest number of seats (23) in the March 2006 election and went on to win majorities in six of seven districts in regional voting in August. In July President Menezes easily won reelection with more than 60 percent of the vote in the first round.

The MDFM-PL participated in the brief Trovoada government of February–May 2008 and in the subsequent Branco cabinet. However, apparently at Menezes's direction, the MDFM-PL officially withdrew from the government in late 2009. Menezes had been elected president of the MDFM-PL at an extraordinary congress in December 2009 and had indicated he would become prime minister if the party won the upcoming assembly poll. However, the leaders of other parties charged that Menezes's elevation to the MDFM-PL presidency was a violation of the constitutional provision that the president of the republic may not engage in "other public activity." When the legal community appeared to side with his critics, Menezes in January 2010 announced he was relinquishing the party's leadership responsibilities to MDFM-PL vice president Joao Costa Alegre. Running on its own in the August assembly poll, the MDFM-PL secured only one seat on a vote share of 7.3 percent, and, after Menezes left office in 2011, the party was described by one analyst as "in the political graveyard." The MDFM-PL supported Delfim Neves of the PCD in the 2011 presidential race. The party won 3.3 percent of the vote in the 2014 assembly elections and no seats.

Leaders: Fradique de MENEZES (Former President of the Republic and 2014 candidate for prime minister), João COSTA ALEGRE (Acting President of the Party), Tomé Soares da VERA CRUZ (Secretary General).

New Way Movement (*Movimento Novo Rumo*—NR). The NR won one seat (from Príncipe) in the March 2006 assembly elections but did not join the new coalition government.

Leader: João GOMES.

Opposition Democratic Coalition (*Coligação Democrática da Oposição*—Codo). Codo was launched in March 1986 as an alliance of two Lisbon-based opposition groups—the **Independent Democratic Union of São Tomé and Príncipe** (*União Democrática Independente de São Tomé e Príncipe*—UDISTP) and the **São Tomé and Príncipe National Resistance Front** (*Frente da Resistência Nacional de São*

Tomé e Príncipe—FRNSTP)—to combat what they called the "totalitarianism" of the Pinto da Costa government. Although the UDISTP previously had stated that it would reach its goals through "peaceful means," its association with the FRNSTP, generally considered a more radical group, led to a Codo posture that did not rule out "recourse to armed struggle."

Codo was one of the key components of the *Uê Kédadji* (UK) alliance established in late 2001. Other UK members included the **National Union for Democracy and Progress** (*União Nacional para a Democracia e Progresso*—UNDP), led by Manuel Paixao LIMA; the **People's Progress Party** (*Partida Progresso do Povo*—PPP), led by Francisco SILVA; and the **Democratic Renovation Party** (*Partido da Renovaçáo Democrática*—PRD), led by Armindo GRAÇA. The UNDP and the PPP had been recognized in September 1998 and were part of the Democratic Platform that supported the ADI candidate in the 2001 presidential balloting. After the 2002 balloting, the UK held eight seats in the legislature, but the ADI left the alliance in early 2006. In February 2006 the **Social Renovation Party** (*Partido Social Renovado*—PSR), led by Hamilton VAZ, joined the UK, which failed to win any seats in the 2006 legislative elections. The UNDP ran on its own in 2010 and 2014, and the Codo Party–Movement of National Resurgence (*Partido Codo–Movimento de Ressurgimento*) also participated unsuccessfully (under the leadership of longtime Codo stalwart Manuel Neves e SILVA) in the 2010 and 2014 polls, with Adjair GARCIA serving as its candidate for prime minister in 2014.

Union for Change and Progress in Príncipe (*União para Mudança e Progresso do Príncipe*—UMPP). The UMPP was founded by José Cassandra, an ally of former Prime Minister Vera Cruz. The party won control of the regional assembly in Príncipe in the 2006 balloting, and Cassandra was subsequently elected president of that assembly, promising to increase development of the island and to decrease its dependence on the island of São Tomé. Cassandra and other party leaders subsequently threatened to resign from the regional assembly if the central government on São Tomé did not reverse its decision to delay municipal and regional elections originally scheduled for August 2009. Cassandra was reelected regional president in the July 25, 2010, municipal and regional elections, which were dominated by the MLSTP-PSD. Cassandra had the support of the ADI, the PCD, and the MDFM-PL.

In early 2012 the UMPP urged the residents of Príncipe to participate in protest demonstrations against the national government's decision not to ratify an investment agreement recently negotiated between the regional government and a prominent South African financier. The UMPP and others argued that political and business leaders on São Tomé were envious of the investment accord, which called for development of a "luxury eco-tourism" project on Príncipe.

The UMPP reportedly formed an electoral alliance with the UDD (above) for the October 2014 municipal elections in Príncipe.

Leader: José CASSANDRA.

Christian Democratic Front (*Frente Democrática Cristã*—FDC). The FDC leader, Arlécio Costa, first became known for his role in fighting for the apartheid government in South Africa in the 1980s as commander of the South African military's Buffalo Battalion. FDC members were also implicated in a coup attempt in São Tomé and Príncipe in 2003 and subsequently maintained an uneasy relationship with the government.

Costa and some 30 others were arrested in February 2009 for allegedly plotting a coup. About half of the detainees were released in August, but Costa and others were convicted later in the year for illegal arms possession and "acts amounting to rebellion." Costa was released in January 2010 as part of President Menezes's yearly amnesty. The party secured just 0.1 percent of the vote in the 2014 balloting.

Leaders: Arlécio COSTA, Amilton BARBOSA.

Other recently active groups include the **São Tomé Workers' Party** (*Partido Trabalhista São Tomense*—PTS), led by Anacleto ROLIM; the **Democratic Alliance for the Development of Príncipe** (*Aliança Democrática para Desenvolvimento do Príncipe*—ADDP), a regional party in Príncipe supported by the MLSTP-PSD; the **Renaissance Movement of Agua Grande,** which won two seats in regional elections in Príncipe in August 2006, the **Socialist Movement** (*Movimento Socialista*—MS), led by Gilberto Gil UMBELINA; the **Labor Party of São Tomé and Príncipe**, led by economist Hugo MENEZES; the **National Platform for Development** (*Plataforma Nacional para o Desenvolvimento*—PND), formed in 2014 by ADI dissidents, including Antonio Quintas AGUIAR; and the **Party for Stability and Social Progress** (*Partido de Estabilidade e Progresso Social*—PEPS), which presented former ADI leader Joaquim Rafael Branco as its 2014 candidate for prime minister.

LEGISLATURE

Formerly an indirectly elected National Popular Assembly (*Assembleia Popular Nacional*) of 40 members, the current **National Assembly** (*Assembleia Nacional*) is a unicameral body of 55 members directly elected via proportional representation (primarily from party lists, although independent candidates are permitted) for four-year terms from seven multimember constituencies.

Following the most recent balloting of October 12, 2014, the seat distribution was as follows: Independent Democratic Action, 33 seats; Movement for the Liberation of São Tomé and Príncipe–Social Democratic Party, 16; Party of Democratic Convergence, 5; and Union for Democracy and Development, 1.

President: José da Graco DIOGO (ADI).

CABINET

[as of August 15, 2016]

Prime Minister	Patrice Trovoada
Ministers	
Agriculture and Rural Development	Teodorico de Campos
Defense and the Sea	Carlos Olímpio Stock
Economy and International Cooperation	Agostinho Quaresma dos Santos Afonso Fernandes
Education, Culture, and Science	Olinto Silva e Sousa Daio
Finance and Public Administration	Américo d'Oliveira Ramos
Foreign Affairs and Communities	Manuel Salvador dos Ramos
Health and Social Affairs	Maria de Jesus Trovoada dos Santos [f]
Infrastructure, Natural Resources, and the Environment	Carlos Manuel Vila Nova
Internal Affairs	Arlindo Ramos
Justice and Human Rights	(Vacant)
Labor and Social Affairs	Carlos Alberto Pires Gomes
Presidency and Parliamentary Affairs	Afonso da Graca Varela da Silva
Youth and Sports	Marcelino Leal Sanches

[f] = female

Note: All members of the cabinet belong to the Independent Democratic Action party.

INTERGOVERNMENTAL REPRESENTATION

Ambassador to the U.S. and Permanent Representative to the UN: Carlos Filomeno Agostinho DAS NEVES.

U.S. Ambassador to São Tomé and Príncipe (resident in Gabon): Cynthia AKUETTEH.

IGO Memberships (Non-UN): AfDB, AU, IOM, NAM.

For Further Reference:

Francisco, Albertino, and Nujoma Agostinho. *Exorcising Devils from the Throne: São Tomé and Príncipe in the Chaos of Democratization.* New York: Algora Publishing, 2011.

Hodges, Tony, and Malyn Newitt. *São Tomé and Príncipe: From Plantation Colony to Microstate.* Boulder, CO: Westview Press, 1988.

Seibert, Gerhard. *Comrades, Clients, and Cousins: Colonialism, Socialism, and Democratization in São Tomé and Príncipe.* 2nd ed. Leiden, Netherlands: Brill Academic Publishers, 2006.

SAUDI ARABIA

Kingdom of Saudi Arabia
al-Mamlakah al-Arabiyah al-Saudiyah

Political Status: Unified kingdom established September 23, 1932; under absolute monarchical system; Basic Law of Government based on Islamic law promulgated by royal decree on March 1, 1992.

Area: 829,995 sq. mi. (2,149,690 sq. km).

Population: 32,158,000 (2016E—UN); 28,160,273 (2016E—U.S. Census). Foreign nationals constitute approximately one quarter of both figures.

Major Urban Centers (2016E—UN): RIYADH (royal capital, 6,540,000), Jiddah (administrative capital, 4,161,000), Makkah (Mecca, 1,799,000), Medina (1,303,000).

Official Language: Arabic.

Monetary Unit: Riyal (market rate October 1, 2016: 3.75 riyals = $1US).

Ruler and Prime Minister: King Salman ibn Abd al-Aziz Al SAUD; confirmed on January 23, 2015, by the royal court upon the death of King Abdallah ibn Abd al-Aziz Al SAUD.

Heir Apparent: Crown Prince Mohammed ibn Nayif ibn Abd al-Aziz Al SAUD; appointed crown prince and heir to the throne on April 29, 2015, to succeed Prince Muqrin ibn Abd al-Aziz Al SAUD (see Government and Politics, below).

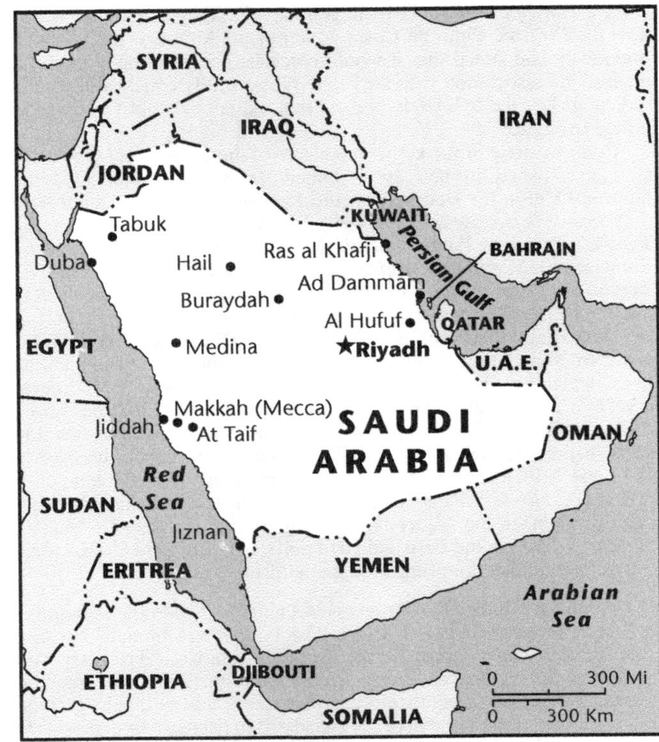

THE COUNTRY

A vast, largely desert country occupying the greater part of the Arabian Peninsula, the Kingdom of Saudi Arabia exhibits both traditional and contemporary lifestyles. Frontiers were poorly defined for many years, and no census was undertaken prior to 1974. Some 85 percent of the indigenous inhabitants, who have traditionally adhered to patriarchal forms of social organization, are Sunni Muslim of the conservative Wahhabi sect. The Shiite population (15 percent) is located primarily in the east. Despite a strict interpretation of Islam, female participation in the paid labor force has tripled to 15 percent over the last two decades. Mecca and Medina, the two holiest cities of Islam and the goals of an annual pilgrimage by Muslims from all over the world, lie within the western region known as the Hijaz, where the commercial and administrative center of Jiddah is also located.

Saudi Arabia is the leading exporter of oil and possesses the world's largest known petroleum reserves (estimated at upward of 200 billion barrels), which have made it one of the world's richest nations. The government acquired full interest in the Arabian-American Oil Company (Aramco) in 1980. Dramatic surges in oil revenue permitted heightened expenditures after 1973 that focused on the development of airports, seaports, and roads, as well as the modernization of medical, educational, and telecommunications systems. In addition, large-scale irrigation projects and heavy price subsidies yielded agricultural self-sufficiency in a country that once produced only 10 percent of its food needs. Vast sums were also committed to armaments, particularly modern fighter planes, missiles, and air defense systems.

Because of a reversal in oil prices and substantial support to Iraq in its eight-year war with Iran, the Saudis experienced a major recession in the early 1980s. An economic revival was sparked in the early 1990s, however, by increased oil production as an offshoot of Iraq's invasion of Kuwait in 1991. Subsequently, concern over falling cash reserves and growing external debt prompted substantial budgetary retrenchment, including reductions in the traditionally high subsidies upon which Saudis had come to rely. The government also introduced programs designed to help move Saudis into private-sector jobs, which are held primarily by foreign workers.

Generally higher oil prices in 1996 and 1997 permitted a return to moderately expansive budgets, with emphasis being placed on infrastructure designed to promote private-sector development. However, financial difficulties returned in 1998 as the result of a sharp drop in oil prices and the effects of the Asian economic crisis. In July 2003 the government bolstered its "Saudization" effort to help reduce unemployment, most significantly by replacing 17,800 foreign white-collar workers with Saudis. Unemployment, widely estimated at nearly 30 percent (though the government says it is in the single digits), has been a particular problem among those under age 20, a group that constitutes more than half the population.

As a result of the U.S. war in Iraq since 2003, Saudi oil prices and production increased significantly. In September 2003 Russia and Saudi Arabia agreed to a landmark deal paving the way for a multibillion-dollar Saudi investment in the Russian oil industry, thus ensuring long-term capacity for both. As a result of surging economic growth, the kingdom has improved roads, schools, and hospitals. It has also continued to move ahead with privatization efforts and in 2006 opened its stock market to foreign investors. Annual gross domestic product (GDP) growth averaged 5.2 percent in 2006–2008 but contracted to less than 1 percent in 2009 due to a dramatic decline in the price of oil during the global economic crisis. Meanwhile, authorities drew from the country's $400 billion reserves to fund key projects and maintain growth in the wake of the worldwide financial turmoil, and the International Monetary Fund (IMF) praised the government's efforts to diversify. Annual growth accelerated to an average 7.6 percent in 2010–2012, owing in large part to a rebound in the private sector, boosted by government spending, and growth in the non-oil sector. Growth of 4.4 percent in 2013 was buoyed by strong performance in the non-oil sector, which continued into 2014, when GDP expansion averaged 3.6 percent. GDP expanded by 3.4 percent in 2015 and 1.2 percent in 2016. In 2016 inflation was 3.7 percent, while GDP per capita was $19,312. The World Bank ranked Saudi Arabia 82nd, between Guatemala (81st) and Ukraine (83rd), out of 189 countries in its annual ease of doing business survey.

GOVERNMENT AND POLITICS

Political background. Founded in 1932, the Kingdom of Saudi Arabia was largely the creation of King Abd al-Aziz Al SAUD (Ibn Saud), who devoted 30 years to reestablishing the power his ancestors had held in the 18th and 19th centuries. Oil concessions were granted in the 1930s to what later became Aramco, but large-scale production did not begin until the late 1940s.

Ibn Saud was succeeded in 1953 by an ineffectual son, Saud ibn Abd al-Aziz Al SAUD, who was persuaded by family influence in 1958 to delegate control to his younger brother, Crown Prince Faysal (Faisal) ibn Abd al-Aziz Al SAUD. Faysal began a modernization program, abolished slavery, curbed royal extravagance, adopted sound fiscal policies, and personally assumed the functions of prime minister prior to the formal deposition of King Saud on November 2, 1964. Faysal was assassinated by one of his nephews, Prince Faysal ibn Musaid ibn Abd al-Aziz Al SAUD, while holding court in Riyadh on March 25, 1975, and was immediately succeeded by his brother, Crown Prince Khalid ibn Abd al-Aziz Al SAUD.

Despite a number of coup attempts, the most important occurring in mid-1969 following the discovery of a widespread conspiracy involving civilian and military elements, internal stability has tended to prevail under the monarchy. The regime was visibly shaken, however, in late 1979 when several hundred Muslim extremists seized the Grand Mosque in Mecca during the annual pilgrimage. Under the leadership of a *mahdi* (messiah), the men involved in the takeover called for an end to corruption and monarchical rule, and for a return to strict Islamic precepts. They held parts of the complex for two weeks; several hundred casualties resulted among the insurgents, hostages, and government forces. Citizens of several other predominantly Muslim countries, including Egypt and South Yemen, were among the 63 participants publicly beheaded on January 9, 1980, for their role in the seizure. Collaterally, the Shiite minority initiated antigovernment demonstrations in eastern areas of the kingdom.

King Khalid died on June 13, 1982, and was immediately succeeded as monarch and prime minister by his half-brother and heir, Crown Prince Fahd ibn Abd al-Aziz Al SAUD. On the same day, Prince Abdallah ibn Abd al-Aziz Al SAUD was designated heir to the throne and first deputy prime minister. King Fahd's rule subsequently encountered potential instability, with declining oil revenues threatening social programs, and a radical Islamic movement, supported by Iran, attempting to undermine the regime diplomatically and militarily.

King Fahd's decision in August 1990 to request Western and regional, assistance in defending Saudi Arabia's border against the possibility of an Iraqi invasion was widely supported within the kingdom. However, the presence of Western forces and media resulted in intense scrutiny of Saudi government and society, raising questions about the nation's inability to defend itself despite massive defense expenditures; generating calls for modernization of the political system, which the king answered by promising reforms; and eliciting signs of dissent, including a quickly suppressed, but highly publicized protest by Saudi women for greater personal liberties. The government also faced growing pressure from Islamists, even though the regime was already considered one of the most conservative in the Arab world because of its active enforcement of Islamic interdictions. In May 1991 Islamist leaders sent a highly publicized letter to King Fahd demanding 12 reforms, including extended implementation of sharia and creation of an independent consultative council that would be responsible for domestic and foreign policy. King Fahd issued royal decrees on March 1, 1992, creating Saudi Arabia's first written rules of governance and providing for the formation of a national Consultative Council. But, he rejected the notion that "the prevailing democratic system in the world" was suitable for Saudi Arabia and insisted that no elections would be in the offing.

In September 1992 Islamist leaders again formally challenged government policy, this time in a "memorandum" to religious leaders that was viewed as "more defiant and bolder" than the 1991 document. The action was followed in May 1993 by the establishment of a Committee for the Defense of Legitimate Rights (CDLR; see Political Groups, below). However, the government quickly declared the organization illegal, with King Fahd warning the Islamists to cease distributing antigovernment material and using mosques as "political pulpits."

The most conspicuous result of a July 1993 cabinet reshuffle was the creation of a new Ministry of Islamic Guidance, which was seen as an attempt to buttress the kingdom's "religious establishment" against Islamist pressure within the Shiite and Sunni populations. The following month the king appointed the members of the national Consultative Council. The council consisted entirely of men, none drawn from the royal family, representing a broad social spectrum. Although the government heralded the inauguration of the council in December 1993 as a major advance, some observers derided it as a "public relations exercise," noting that council sessions would not be open to the public and that topics for debate required advance approval by the king.

Questions also surrounded the king's October 1994 appointment of the new Supreme Council on Islamic Affairs, which was dominated by members of the royal family and technocrats owing their livelihood to the government. The new body was viewed as a further effort by the monarchy to undercut the appeal of the Islamists, who had been pressing for further Islamization of government policy and a curtailment of Western ties since the 1990–1991 Gulf crisis and war.

On August 2, 1995, in the most sweeping ministerial shakeup in two decades, no less than 13 portfolios, including those of finance, industry, and petroleum, changed hands, with many political veterans being succeeded by younger, Western-educated technocrats. While members of the royal family were left in charge of several key ministries (notably defense, interior, and foreign affairs), the obvious intent was to improve efficiency by bringing in a new generation of officials.

King Fahd was hospitalized in early November 1995, suffering from what was widely reported but never officially confirmed to be a stroke. On January 1, 1996, he formally transferred responsibility for "affairs of state" to Crown Prince Abdallah, interpreted by many observers to be a step toward permanent succession, but King Fahd formally reassumed full authority on February 22.

An explosion near a U.S. Air Force building, the Khobar Towers, in Dhahran in June 1996 killed 19 U.S. servicemen and wounded 350, prompting the transfer of American forces to more secure desert bases. Meanwhile, in what was seen as a related development, the Saudi government launched a crackdown on Shiite dissidents in the east, where antimonarchical and anti-Western sentiment appeared to be the strongest. Members of a pro-Iran Shiite group were later accused by the United States of being responsible for the attack (see Political Groups, below).

A cabinet reshuffle was announced on June 6, 1999, with members of the ruling family retaining six key posts. A Supreme Economic Council was established in August to oversee proposed reform in non-oil sectors, and a Supreme Council for Petroleum and Mineral Affairs was created in January 2000. By 2003 major reforms had begun to take shape. In an unprecedented move in January of that year, Crown Prince Abdallah met with reformists, some of whom the government had jailed in the 1990s for advocating reforms. Government representatives also met for the first time on Saudi soil with a UN human rights group, and in October, for the first time a woman was named dean at a major university. The most stunning news, however, came on October 13, 2003, when the government announced that it would hold nationwide elections for municipal councils in 2004 (postponed to 2005), to be followed by elections for city councilors and, ultimately, members of the Consultative Council. The announcement coincided with the country's first human rights conference, held in Riyadh, October 13–15.

King Fahd granted greater legislative powers to the Consultative Council in November 2003, effectively shifting some influence from the cabinet to the legislative body. The reforms followed in the wake of increasing pressure from "liberals," but more significantly after an attack in May 2003 on a luxury residential compound that killed 35 and wounded hundreds (see Foreign relations, below). The government, which came under increasing pressure from the United States to undertake social and political reforms, in 2003, approved direct elections for half of the seats of the 178 municipal councils, though women were not allowed to vote. The first municipal elections in more than 30 years were held February 10–April 21, 2005. Islamists won the vast majority of seats.

King Fahd died on August 1, 2005, at age 82 after a 23-year reign. He was immediately succeeded by 82-year-old Crown Prince Abdallah, his half-brother. Sultan ibn Abd al-Aziz Al SAUD, the longtime defense minister, replaced Abdallah as crown prince—while continuing to hold the defense portfolio and several other positions.

After an unprecedented visit to the Vatican by King Abdallah in November 2007, Saudi authorities reportedly held secret talks with the Vatican regarding the opening of the first Roman Catholic church in the kingdom, which historically has banned all Christian denominations.

In his first major cabinet reshuffle, King Abdallah appointed several reformers and dismissed "reactionaries," according to news reports, in new appointments announced February 14, 2009. The king appointed the first female cabinet member, naming her to the post of deputy minister for girls' education—making her the kingdom's highest-ranking female political figure ever. Some analysts said the king's most far-reaching change was his reconfiguration of the Grand Ulema Council, the country's premier religious body, to include more moderates. Further, the king appointed as head of the Supreme Judicial Council the former chair of the Consultative Council, Salih ibn HUMAYD, who was seen as more likely to advance the king's reforms than his predecessor. In addition, the head of the "notoriously strict" religious police was replaced with a more moderate figure, according to published reports. In March, the king delayed the next municipal elections for at least two years in an effort to grant more power to the local councils and to expand the electoral process. The government explained the postponement as having "extended the mandate" of the sitting councils by two years while necessary changes to the law were prepared. On March 28 Prince Nayif ibn Abd al-Aziz AL SAUD was sworn in as second deputy prime minister, placing him third in line for the throne behind the king and the crown prince.

Issues related to terrorism and security dominated 2010, as in December, the intelligence director announced a special security unit to combat terrorism. The launch of the new security team was preceded in November by announcements of the arrests of some 146 al-Qaida militants over the past eight months.

Prince Nayif became deputy prime minister and crown prince upon the death of Crown Prince Sultan on September 22, 2011. Nayif died on June 16, 2012, and Salman ibn Abd al-Aziz Al SAUD became the next in line to the throne.

On March 26, 2011, King Abdallah established a new ministry of housing. On September 25, he granted women the right to vote and to run in future municipal elections. He appointed 30 women to the Consultative council in January 2013 (see Current issues, below).

King Abdallah died on January 23, 2015, at age 90 and was immediately succeeded by Crown Prince Salman ibn Abd al-Aziz al Saud, who also assumed the post of prime minister. Prince Muqrin ibn Abd al-Aziz AL SAUD was concurrently appointed crown prince, heir to the throne, and deputy prime minister. King Salman appointed a new cabinet, which was sworn in on February 1. On April 29 the king replaced Crown Prince Muqrin with his nephew Mohammed ibn Nayif ibn Abd al-Aziz Al SAUD. The king's son, Mohammad ibn Salman ibn Abd al-Aziz Al SAUD, was concurrently named deputy crown prince and second deputy prime minister.

A cabinet reshuffle was carried out on May 8, 2016, replacing almost all of the remaining ministers from King Abdallah's reign.

Constitution and government. Saudi Arabia is a traditional monarchy with all power ultimately vested in the king, who is also the country's supreme religious leader. The kingdom held its first national municipal elections in some 30 years in 2005, though women continued to be disenfranchised. There are no political parties in Saudi Arabia, and legislation is by royal decree, though in 2004 King Fahd granted a greater legislative role to the Consultative Council, shifting some influence from the cabinet. In recent years an attempt was made to modernize the machinery of government by creating ministries to manage affairs of state. However, the king serves additionally as prime minister, and many sensitive cabinet posts are held by members of the royal family, often for long periods of time. The judicial system, encompassing summary and general courts, a Court of Cassation, and a Supreme Council of Justice, is largely based on Islamic religious law (sharia), but tribal and customary law are also applied. Sweeping judicial reforms were announced on April 3, 2005, including establishment of a Supreme Court and appeals courts in the 13 provinces.

For administrative purposes Saudi Arabia is divided into 13 provinces or regions, each headed by a governor appointed by the king. In April 1994 the provinces were subdivided into 103 governorates. The principal urban areas have half-elected, half-appointed municipal councils, while villages and tribes are governed by sheikhs in conjunction with legal advisers and other community leaders.

On March 1, 1992, King Fahd authorized the creation of a 60-member national Consultative Council (*Majlis al-Shura*) headed by a chair (speaker) appointed by the king to a four-year term. The *Majlis* (inaugurated on December 29, 1993) was empowered to initiate laws, review domestic and foreign policies, and scrutinize budgets "in the tradition of Islamic consultation." Council membership was raised to 90 in 1997 and to 120 in 2001. In late 1993 the king also issued a decree authorizing the formation of consultative councils in each province, encompassing the provincial governor and at least ten appointed individuals. Another decree codified a "basic system of government" based on Islamic law. The 83-article document is widely described as the country's first written constitution, which went beyond previous unwritten conventions by guaranteeing individual rights. It also formally delineated the rules of succession, institutionalizing the king's unilateral authority to designate (and dismiss) his heir, a son or grandson of King Abd al-Aziz Al Saud, who died in 1953.

In October 1994 King Fahd appointed the Supreme Council on Islamic Affairs to review educational, economic, and foreign policies to ensure that they were conducted in concert with Islamic precepts.

On October 20, 2006, the king issued a new law establishing a committee made up of the sons and grandsons of King Fahd to choose future kings and crown princes. The changes do not go into effect until the current crown prince becomes king (see Current issues, below). On October 1, 2007, King Abdallah issued a decree approving the formation of a supreme court, special tribunals for labor and commercial disputes, and appeals courts—all in accordance with Islamic law.

The king renewed the Consultative Council on February 28, 2009, appointing 150 members to four-year terms.

In the wake of Arab Spring movements, Saudi Arabian authorities further tightened laws prohibiting criticism of the government. The Ministry of Culture and Information heavily censors print and broadcast media. Reporters Without Borders ranked Saudi Arabia 165th of 180 countries for press freedom in 2016.

In May 2014 a Saudi Arabian cleric issued an edict saying that online chats between men and women were religiously forbidden.

Foreign relations. Since the late 1950s, Saudi Arabia has stood as the leading conservative power in the Arab world. The early 1960s were marked by hostility toward Egypt over North Yemen, with Riyadh supporting the royalists and Cairo backing the ultimately victorious republicans during the civil war that broke out in 1962. By 1969, however, Saudi Arabia had become a prime mover behind the pan-Islamic movement and subsequently sought to mediate such disputes as the Lebanese conflict in 1976 and the Iran–Iraq war. An influential member of the Organization of the Petroleum Exporting Countries (OPEC), the kingdom was long a restraining influence on oil price increases. Since the U.S.-led invasion of Iraq in 2003, Saudi Arabia, a swing producer, has been authorized by OPEC to continue to boost production to meet global demand.

The Saudis provided financial support for other Arab countries involved in the 1967 and 1973 Arab–Israeli conflicts and broke diplomatic relations with Cairo in April 1979 to oppose the Egyptian–Israeli peace treaty. Otherwise, the kingdom has been generally allied with the United States. The outbreak of war between Iraq and Iran in September 1980 prompted the Carter administration, which earlier in the year had rejected a Saudi request for assistance in upgrading its military capability, to announce the "temporary deployment" of four Airborne Warning and Control Systems (AWAC aircraft), a decision influenced by Riyadh's support of Washington's plan to increase U.S. military presence in the Gulf region upon the 1979 Soviet intervention in Afghanistan. Despite Israel's objections, the Reagan administration secured Senate approval in October 1981 of a major package of arms sales to Saudi Arabia that included five surveillance aircraft, although delivery did not commence until mid-1986 because of controversy over U.S. supervisory rights. Earlier, the Saudis had indicated a willingness to allow American use of bases in the kingdom in the event of Soviet military action in the Gulf. As the U.S. Iran-contra scandal unfolded in late 1986 and 1987, it was alleged that the Saudis had agreed to aid anticommunist resistance groups around the world as part of the AWAC purchase deal, ultimately making some $32 million available to the Nicaraguan rebels between July 1984 and March 1985. In July 1988 relations were further strained when Riyadh, citing congressional delays and other "embarrassments" caused by Washington's criticism of Chinese missile imports, purchased $25 billion of British armaments, thus undercutting reliance on the United States as its leading military supplier.

During 1987 and 1988 the Iran–Iraq war yielded continued political tension between revolutionary Tehran and pro–Western Riyadh. In July 1987 the seizure of Mecca's Grand Mosque by Muslim extremists resulted in the death of an estimated 400 Iranian pilgrims; subsequently, Iranian officials called for the immediate "uprooting" of the Saudi royal family, while King Fahd, supported by most of the Arab states, vowed to continue as "custodian" of Islam's holy shrines. In April 1988, citing the Mecca riot and increasing Iranian attacks on its shipping vessels, Saudi Arabia became the first member of the Gulf Cooperation Council (GCC) to sever diplomatic relations with Tehran. The Khomeini regime's subsequent decision to forbid its citizens from participating in the 1988 pilgrimage was seen as an attempt to discredit Saudi administration of the holy cities. Diplomatic relations were restored in March 1991 upon the rise of more moderate Irani leadership.

Relations with the Soviet Union, which were suspended in 1938, briefly saw potential for improvement when Foreign Minister Saud al-Faisal visited Moscow in 1982. After Moscow's 1988 announcement that it would withdraw from Afghanistan—Riyadh long having been a highly vocal supporter of the rebel president-in-exile, Sibgahatullah Mojaddidi—resolution of the impasse became possible. Diplomatic relations were restored in 1990, the same year ties were established with China. In 1992 the kingdom moved quickly to establish ties with the Commonwealth of Independent States (CIS), offering economic aid and pursuing private-sector ties. Particular attention was given to the Central Asian republics, where the Saudis were expected to vie with Turkey and Iran for influence.

In March 1989 Iraqi and Saudi officials signed a mutual noninterference pact. However, in the wake of Iraq's invasion of Kuwait on

August 2, 1990, and amid reports that Iraqi troops were massing on the Saudi border, the Saudi government criticized the invasion as "vile aggression," and called for international assistance to prevent further Iraqi gains. The ensuing buildup of Western and regional forces along the Saudi border with Kuwait caused a rupture in relations with pro-Iraqi leaders of Yemen, Jordan, and the Palestine Liberation Organization (PLO). On September 19 Riyadh rescinded special privileges for Yemeni and PLO workers, prompting repatriation of more than half of the 1.5 million Yemeni citizens in the kingdom. Oil deliveries to Jordan were suspended, Jordanian diplomats were expelled, and the Saudi ambassador to Amman was recalled. Meanwhile, the Saudi government moved to reimburse and reward its allies, particularly Egypt and Syria. The kingdom's most dramatic Gulf crisis decision, however, was to acknowledge its effective alliance with the United States, which responded by promising to sell the Saudis $20 billion in armaments. Saudi Arabia played a pivotal role in the U.S.-led coalition against Iraq during the 1991 war.

After the Gulf war, the Saudi government allowed U.S. troops to remain in the kingdom, angering many, including Osama bin Laden and his supporters. During the buildup to the 2003 U.S. invasion of Iraq, King Fahd announced that the kingdom would not participate in a war against Iraq. However, U.S. forces were eventually allowed to deploy to Saudi Arabia prior to the war. After the May 12, 2003, suicide bombings of a compound in Riyadh that killed 35 and wounded hundreds, Riyadh became more attuned to the U.S. war on terror, with the government declaring its own such war in August 2003.

In June 2005 some 57 Islamic nations—Saudi Arabia among them—met in Yemen and agreed to fight terrorism, now a defining issue in the Middle East. Analysts said that Riyadh was concerned that sectarian violence between Sunnis and Shiites in Iraq might make its way into Saudi Arabia if armed militants gained support from Shiite hardliners in the kingdom.

Saudi Arabia's relations with North Yemen and South Yemen and, since 1990, the unified Republic of Yemen have often been strained, particularly regarding border demarcations. In March 2005 the two countries signed a border agreement, influenced by their desire to halt the flow of weapons and drug smuggling and an increasing number of terrorist suspects. In April Yemen and Saudi Arabia held their first joint military exercise.

Saudi Arabia has played a role in supporting a negotiated settlement between Israel and the Palestinians, at times acceding to foreign pressure. In early 1993 the Saudis responded favorably to a U.S. request for resumption of aid to the PLO as an inducement to the Palestinians to rejoin stalled peace talks with Israel. Riyadh also underscored its backing for the regional peace process the following September, when it convinced the GCC countries to end their long-standing boycott of companies doing business with Israel (see entry on the Arab League for details). In 2003 Crown Prince Abdallah presented the Arab League with an initiative for peace with Israel in return for its withdrawal from occupied territories. (The following day, however, Israel launched a massive invasion to reoccupy the West Bank.) When Saudi Arabia was granted membership in the World Trade Organization (WTO) in December 2005, the kingdom granted assurances that it had ended its trade boycott against Israel, though later acknowledged that it had lifted only "certain aspects" of the boycott. In February 2006 Riyadh joined other Arab countries in rejecting a U.S. request that they cut off aid to Hamas (which won election to the new Palestinian government a month earlier). The kingdom has continued to support what it has described as the legitimate rights of Palestinians.

In February 2007 Saudi Arabia invited the leaders of Hamas and Fatah to a summit in Mecca, where the warring Palestinian factions agreed to form a unity government (which subsequently failed). Shortly after the Mecca meeting, Riyadh hosted an Arab League summit that renewed the peace initiative, offering Israel normalized ties with Arab states if it would agree to return to its pre-1967 borders. Following the collapse of the peace deal and a visit in August by U.S. secretary of state Condoleezza Rice and U.S. defense secretary Robert Gates, Saudi Arabia agreed to send its foreign minister to the U.S.-sponsored Middle East peace conference in Annapolis, Maryland, in November—its participation seen as bolstering President George W. Bush's initiative at a time when U.S. standing in the region was at a low point.

Relations with Syria deteriorated in 2008, with Saudi Arabia ultimately joining Egypt, Jordan, and Lebanon in boycotting an Arab summit in Damascus following Syria's failure to help facilitate the election of a new government in Lebanon. Riyadh grew increasingly concerned over the tumultuous events in Beirut (see entry on Lebanon), calling on "all regional sides to respect the sovereignty and independence of Lebanon," with particular references to Syria and Iran. Tensions with Iran heightened following Saudi Arabia's describing Hezbollah's military attacks in Lebanon as a "coup" backed by Iran, highlighting Saudi Arabia's efforts to counter Iran's growing Shiite influence in the region. Meanwhile, the kingdom strengthened ties with the United States, signing agreements in May to broaden counterterrorism efforts and bolster peaceful nuclear cooperation, among other things. In addition, President Bush pledged to push for a $20 billion arms deal for Saudi Arabia, despite the objections of Israel and some members of the U.S. Congress. Meanwhile, relations with Syria warmed somewhat following a visit by President Bashar al-Assad to Saudi Arabia in March. Seven months later, King Abdallah, made a "highly symbolic" visit to Syria to ease tensions. The king and President Assad agreed to work toward closer ties between their countries. (For more on Saudi Arabia's counterterrorism efforts and oil policies in 2007–2008, see the 2013 *Handbook*.)

Agreements on security issues strengthened with Yemen in 2009 as a result of that country's crackdown in particular on al-Qaida terrorists, who were reported to be using Yemen as a staging ground for radical Islamist activities. In November Yemen's war against Huthi rebels spilled over into Saudi Arabia when the rebels killed a Saudi border official. The rebels accused Saudi Arabia of allowing Yemeni government forces to attack them from a Saudi military base.

In January 2010 Saudi authorities held talks with Iran in an effort to repatriate the 17-year-old daughter of Osama bin Laden.

A long-simmering dispute with the United Arab Emirates (UAE) over maritime and land borders erupted in April 2010, when vessels from both countries exchanged gunfire. Subsequently, two Saudi border guards arrested by the UAE were released. Despite an accord signed by the two countries in 1974 that supposedly resolved the matter, Abu Dhabi resented that the pact put a huge oilfield in Saudi territory.

In July 2010 King Abdallah visited Jordan, Syria, and Egypt in an effort to bolster Arab unity in the region. In September reports revealed details of what was said to be the largest single arms sale ever by the United States to Saudi Arabia, totaling some $67 billion over 10 years.

In 2011 Saudi Arabia and Pakistan agreed to enhance ties, and Saudi Arabia established a diplomatic mission in Cuba. Relations with Iran were strained after Saudi Arabia sent troops into Bahrain to back the Sunni king against antigovernment demonstrators.

The June 2012 execution of four Iranians for drug trafficking caused diplomatic tensions, which were resolved with a treaty in July addressing the repatriation of criminals between the two countries. In January 2013 Sri Lanka withdrew its envoy in Saudi Arabia in protest after a Sri Lankan nanny was executed because of the death of an infant in her care.

Saudi Arabia established itself as the main outside support for antigovernment fighters in Syria in 2013. The kingdom financed a major purchase of weaponry from Croatia to arm Syrian rebels in February. In June Saudi authorities called for a ban on supplying arms to the Syrian government and condemned the role of Iran and Hezbollah in the civil war.

In late March 2013, in an effort to lower unemployment rates, Saudi Arabia began deporting Yemenis and other foreign workers, estimated to number around 9 million. After two weeks, in which time Yemen reported some 20,000 had returned, the policy was revised to give a three-month grace period. However, mass deportations resumed in November 2013, after the expiration of the amnesty period.

Meanwhile, the typically smooth relationship with the United States frayed that month as Riyadh objected to Washington's newly softened approach to Iran's nuclear program. U.S. secretary of state John Kerry visited Saudi Arabia in November and again in early January 2014. On March 28 and 29 President Barack Obama visited in a continued effort to placate Riyadh. An indicator of thawing relations between Saudi Arabia and Iran came in May 2014, when the kingdom extended an invitation to Iranian foreign minister Mohammad Javad Zayif.

The expanded activity of the Islamic State of Iraq and Syria (ISIS) in the region in June 2014 prompted a strong reaction from the Saudi government. A Sunni movement hitherto chiefly active as a player in the ongoing Syrian civil war, ISIS invaded the Iraqi city of Mosul on June 6. Later that month, King Abdullah gave assurances to U.S. officials that he would reverse his noninterventionist policy toward Iraq and would assert his influence to attempt to install a multi-sect government. On July 1 Saudi Arabia gave $500 million to the United Nations (UN) to aid Iraqis displaced by the Sunni insurgency. Further, in August Saudi Arabia gave an unprecedented sum of $100 million to a UN counterterrorism agency.

In September 2014 Saudi Arabia agreed to an American initiative to provide training grounds to Syrian opposition fighters. Saudi Arabia formed a coalition to intervene in Yemen's civil war in March 2015 to fight Iranian-backed Shia Houthi rebels (see entry on Yemen). The kingdom and its allies conducted air strikes and deployed troops. In December Saudi Arabia announced the formation of another coalition of 34 Muslim states to fight the Islamic State in Iraq, Libya, and Syria.

As global oil prices declined from $100 per barrel in 2014 to below $30 in January 2016, Saudi Arabia rebuffed calls to reduce production in an effort to drive new producers out of the market (see entry on the Organization of Petroleum Exporting Countries). In September 2016 Saudi Arabia agreed to cut production.

In October 2016 the U.S. Congress passed a measure, over the veto of President Obama, giving families of those killed in the September 11, 2001, terrorist attacks the ability to file suit against Saudi Arabia for any possible role in the strikes. The measure was strongly condemned by the Saudi government.

Current issues. As the so-called Arab Spring of political unrest unfolded in early 2011, Saudi Arabia found itself caught up in the tumultuous events in the neighboring countries. When antigovernment protests in Tunisia escalated in January and spread across the country, President Zine Ben Ali deployed troops to curb the demonstrations and on January 14 fled to Saudi Arabia, where he was granted refuge. In February, majority Shiites rebelled against minority Sunni rule in Bahrain, where the royal family was supported by Saudi Arabia. The repressive tactics of Yemen's president Ali Abdullah Saleh continued against the protesters, and in April Saudi Arabia and the UAE sent some 1,500 troops to back up the Bahraini forces. On April 18 opposition activists in Bahrain claimed that the Saudi-backed Bahraini troops had demolished or desecrated seven Shiite mosques and many prayer centers and shrines. On April 23 President Saleh, under intense domestic and international pressure, agreed to accept a plan for his departure brokered by Saudi Arabia and the other GCC member countries. Meanwhile, that same month, Tunisia sought to extradite President Ben Ali from Saudi Arabia. (He was sentenced in absentia in July to 15 years' imprisonment.)

While political turmoil churned the region, the Saudi monarchy focused mainly on domestic issues, though it wasn't fully spared its own homegrown protests. The king had poured $130 billion into the economy in June 2010 to boost the salaries of civil servants, build houses, and finance religious organizations, among other things, effectively quelling most of the opposition. In July 2011 the council passed legislation asserting the government's determination to prevent the Arab Spring from spilling over into Saudi Arabia. Saudi authorities were granted sweeping new powers to combat sedition, allowing for one-year detention without trial, secret trials, the tapping of phones, and extrajudicial searching of homes.

In summer 2011 a small group of women demanded that the law be changed to allow them to drive, a cause that was publicly endorsed by U.S. secretary of state Hillary Clinton. The woman who had started the "movement" on Facebook was arrested after she posted a video of herself. Her sentence of nine days in jail was seen as surprisingly harsh and taken as a warning that the monarchy was sending a message against any type of movement organized via social media. On February 5, 2012, a group of women filed a lawsuit against the traffic department for refusing to issue drivers licenses to women. Meanwhile, the Consultative Council recommended that women be allowed to vote and be candidates in municipal elections, and King Abdallah decreed on September 25, 2011, that women would be given the vote and the right to run for election to local councils in the 2015 elections. He also announced that they would be eligible to be appointed to the Consultative Council. On September 29 the long-delayed municipal council elections were held. Turnout among the still-all-male electorate was low, possibly because of the presumed powerlessness of the councils. Half of the council's membership was filled, with the other half to be appointed.

In February 2012 two men were killed and several were wounded when police opened fire on Shiite demonstrators in Al-Qatif, a coastal town in the Eastern Province. (Public gatherings are illegal, though social media have gained significant momentum.) Small-scale, protests cropped up sporadically throughout the year: in July a government crackdown on Shiite protesters in Eastern Province reportedly left 14 injured; relatives of political prisoners demonstrated in September in Riyadh, with dozens detained; a similar protest of about 40 people took place outside the Saudi Human Rights Commission in November.

A recent change of faces in the Cabinet indicates the passing of the torch to the younger generation of Saudi leaders. In November 2012 Prince Mohammad ibn Nayef ibn Abd al-Aziz Al Saud was appointed minister of the interior, succeeding his uncle, who resigned after just five months in office.

In January 2013 King Abdallah appointed 30 women to the Consultative Council and decreed that henceforth 20 percent of council members must be women. Though in many ways an unprecedented move, female councilors will be segregated with their own door and seating area. Prince Muqrin, the former head of Saudi intelligence, was named second deputy prime minister in February 2013, making the 67-year-old third in line for the throne. In May King Abdallah elevated the department of the National Guard to the cabinet and named his son Prince Miteb to the post. Governorships of Riyadh and Eastern Province were also passed down to younger members.

On March 7, 2014, the kingdom declared the Muslim Brotherhood, originally an Egypt-based movement that had gained support around the region, a terrorist organization. At the same time, a new list of banned groups was issued, which included, among others, ISIS, the Al-Nusra Front, and "Saudi Hezbollah."

As a virus with no cure, known as Middle East respiratory syndrome (MERS), spread through the region, Health Minister Abdullah al RABEEAH was removed from his post. Labor Minister Adel FAKIEH assumed responsibilities.

In early May 2014, 62 people accused of having ties to terrorist organizations in Yemen and Syria were arrested for planning attacks against the government and foreign interests.

On December 12, 2015, municipal elections for 284 councils were held. It was the first election that women were allowed to vote and seek office, and 20 women won seats.

Due to declining revenues from oil sales, Saudi Arabia borrowed $10 billion from foreign investors in April 2016. The country then issued more than $17.5 billion in bonds in October.

POLITICAL GROUPS

There are no political parties, as such, in Saudi Arabia.

Committee for the Defense of Legitimate Rights (CDLR). The CDLR was formed in May 1993 by several prominent Islamists who described the grouping as the kingdom's first human rights organization. However, the government charged that the CDLR was in reality a vehicle for extending fundamentalist criticism of the monarchy, which had been on the rise since the Gulf crisis. Consequently, the CDLR was ordered to disband only two weeks after its creation; in addition, CDLR leader Muhammad al-MASARI and some 1,000 followers were arrested, and a number of CDLR supporters were fired from their government positions. After his release the following November, al-Masari moved to London, where the CDLR was reestablished in April 1994 as an exile organization. The committee subsequently issued numerous communiqués criticizing the Saudi regime's human rights and economic policies. Although accused by Riyadh of attempting to promote "destabilization" so as to facilitate elimination of the monarchy in favor of a fundamentalist regime, CDLR leaders took no official antimonarchical stance and steadfastly avowed a policy of nonviolence. However, the CDLR remained critical of what it alleged to be widespread corruption within the ruling family and direct in its call for imposition of strict Islamic rule in the kingdom. (In 1998 the Saudi government released Sheikh Sulaymah al-RUSHUDI, reportedly one of the founders of the CDLR.)

In 1996 a conflict was reported between CDLR leaders Muhammad al-Masari and Saad al-FAQIH, with the latter forming a breakaway grouping called the **Movement for Islamic Reform in Arabia** (MIRA). Subsequent activity has been minimal on the part of both groups, although in 2003 MIRA led an unprecedented demonstration in Riyadh. MIRA's antigovernment Website in March 2005 posted an audiotape purporting to represent the new al-Qaida leader in Saudi Arabia. According to MIRA, he was killed in April 2005. A year later, Abd al Aziz al SHANBARI, a former Saudi dissident who had been affiliated with MIRA, denounced the group during a meeting with King Abdallah. Al Shanbari returned to Saudi Arabia after two years in exile in London, reportedly having made some sort of private arrangement with the king. MIRA reportedly operates out of London.

MIRA's Website in 2006 addressed the new succession law issued by the king, claiming that the real aim of the law was to exclude Prince Nayif ibn Abd al-Aziz Al SAUD, the interior minister and a brother of King Fahd, from ascending the throne because of Nayif's alleged defiance of many of the king's orders and pressure from U.S. officials who were said to be dissatisfied with the level of cooperation from Nayif. In 2007 MIRA started television broadcasts via satellite from London.

In 2010 Muhammad al-MASARI, formerly described as leader of the CDLR, was reported to be the head of a group called the **Party for Islamic Renewal**, based in London.

Reform Movement. A loosely organized Shiite grouping, the Reform Movement (also referenced as the **Islamic Revolutionary Organization in the Arabian Peninsula**) originally operated out of London and Damascus, its activities including publication of the *Arabian Peninsula,* a newsletter critical of, among other things, the Saudi government's human rights record. In late 1993 the movement's leaders agreed to discontinue its attacks on the government in return for the release of Shiite dissidents from prison and permission for Shiite expatriates to return to Saudi Arabia. However, some members reportedly remained in "revolutionary" mode and opposed to the proposed reconciliation pact. A number of Shiites were arrested in the government crackdown that followed the 1996 bombing in Dhahran, prompting observers to suggest that the agreement with the Reform Movement had collapsed. However, little formal activity was subsequently reported on behalf of the movement, though it continues to press for change and its members are routinely arrested, convicted, and jailed. The leader, Sheikh Hassan al-Safar, was reportedly living in exile in Damascus in 1993. At some point al-Safar, a cleric, returned to the Shiite-dominated area of eastern Saudi Arabia. In 2003 al-Safar was among those invited to participate in the king's "national dialogue" in Mecca, where measures to counter extremism were among the topics. It was reported to be the first such gathering in the country to include Shiites and Sunnis, and observers made note of the fact that leaders from the two main religious branches were seen together on television.

Leader: Sheikh Hassan al-SAFAR.

LEGISLATURE

On March 1, 1992, King Fahd decreed that a **Consultative Council** (*Majlis al-Shura*) of 60 members (plus a speaker) would be appointed within six months. In accordance with the decree, a speaker was named the following September. Other members were not appointed until August 20, 1993, and the council convened on December 29. Upon the expiration of the first term of the council in July 1997, King Fahd increased its membership to 90 for the subsequent four-year term. Membership increased to 120 for the new council appointed on May 24, 2001, and the council was renewed on April 11, 2005. The king appointed an expanded 150-member council on February 28, 2009. In January 2013 King Abdallah decreed that 20 percent of the council members must be women and appointed 30 women to the council (see Current issues, above).

Chair: Abdullah Al ASHAIKH.

CABINET

[as of November 18, 2016]

Prime Minister	King Salman ibn Abd al-Aziz Al Saud
Deputy Prime Minister	Prince Mohammed ibn Nayif ibn Abd al-Aziz Al Saud
Second Deputy Prime Minister	Prince Mohammad ibn Salman ibn Abd al-Aziz Al Saud
Ministers	
Civil Service	Khalid ibn Abdullah al-Araj
Commerce and Industry	Majed ibn Abdullah ibn Abd al-Aziz al-Jadaan
Communications and Information Technology	Mohammad ibn Ibrahim al-Suwaiyel
Culture and Information	Aded ibn Zaid al-Turaifi
Defense and Aviation	Prince Mohammad ibn Salman ibn Abd al-Aziz Al Saud
Economy and Planning	Abel ibn Mohammed ibn Abdulgader Fakieh
Education	Ahmed ibn Mohammed al-Issa
Energy, Industry, and Mineral Resources	Khalid ibn Abdul Aziz al-Falih
Environment, Water, and Agriculture	Abdul Rahman ibn Abdul Mohsen al-Fadhli
Finance	Mohammed ibn Abdullah ibn Abdul Aziz al-Jadaan
Foreign Affairs	Adel ibn Ahmed al-Jubeir
Health	Tawfeeq ibn Faozan ibn Mohammed al-Rabee'a
Housing	Majid ibn Abdullah ibn Hamad al-Hugail
Interior	Prince Mohammed ibn Nayif ibn Abd al-Aziz Al Saud
Islamic Affairs, Endowments, Call, and Guidance	Salih ibn Abd al-Aziz Mohammed ibn Ibrahim al-Shaikh
Justice	Walid ibn Mohammed ibn Saleh al-Samaani
Labor	Mujref ibn Saad al-Haqbani
Municipal and Rural Affairs	Abdul Lateef ibn Abdul Malik ibn Omar al-Sheikh
National Guard	Prince Miteb ibn Abdullah ibn Abd al-Aziz Al Saud
Pilgrimage	Mohammed Saleh ibn Taher Bentin
Transport	Sulaiman ibn Abdullah al-Hamdan
Ministers of State	
Advisor to the King	Prince Mansour ibn Miteb Abd al-Aziz Al Saud
Arab Gulf Affairs	Thamer al-Sabhan
Head of Royal Court	Khalid ibn Abdulrahman al-Issa
Shura Affairs	Mohammed ibn Faisal ibn Jaber Abu Saq
Without Portfolio	Musaid ibn Muhammad al-Ayban
	Mohammed ibn Abdulmalik ibn Abdullah al-Sheikh
	Mutlaab ibn Abdallah al-Nafissa
	Essam ibn Saad ibn Saeed
	Ibrahim ibn Abd al-Aziz al-Assaf
	Saad ibn Khalid ibn Saadallah al-Jabri

INTERGOVERNMENTAL REPRESENTATION

Ambassador to the U.S.: Prince Abdullah bin Faisal bin TURKI.

U.S. Ambassador to Saudi Arabia: Christopher HENZEL (Chargé d'Affaires).

Permanent Representative to the UN: Abdallah Yahya A. al-MOUALLIMI.

IGO Memberships (Non-UN): AfDB, GCC, LAS, NAM, OIC, OPEC, WTO.

For Further Reference:

Aarts, Paul, and Carolien Roelants. *Saudi Arabia: A Kingdom in Peril.* London: C. Hurst, 2015.

Fandy, Mamoun. *Saudi Arabia and the Politics of Dissent.* New York: Palgrave, 1999.

Mabon, Simon. *Saudi Arabia & Iran: Power and Rivalry in the Middle East.* London: I. B. Taurus, 2013.

SENEGAL

Republic of Senegal
République du Sénégal

Political Status: Former French dependency, independent since August 20, 1960; presidential system established under constitution promulgated March 7, 1963; Senegalese-Gambian Confederation of Senegambia, formed with effect from February 1, 1982, dissolved as of September 30, 1989.

Area: 75,750 sq. mi. (196,192 sq. km).

Population: 15,590,000 (2016E—UN); 14,320,055 (2016—U.S. Census).

Major Urban Center (urban area, 2015E—UN): DAKAR (3,653,000).

Official Language: French.

Monetary Unit: CFA Franc (official rate October 1, 2016: 592.38 francs = $1US). The CFA franc, previously pegged to the French franc, is now permanently pegged to the euro at 655.93 francs = 1 euro.

President: Macky SALL (APR-*Yakaar*); elected in second-round balloting on March 18, 2012, and inaugurated for a seven-year term on April 2, in succession to Abdoulaye WADE (Senegalese Democratic Party).

Prime Minister: Mohammed Abdallah DIONE (ind.); appointed by the president on July 6, 2014, to succeed Aminata TOURE (Alliance for the Republic).

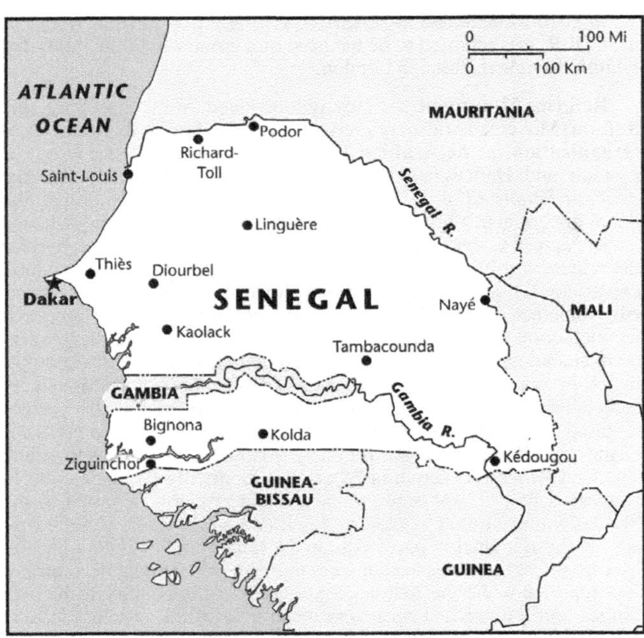

THE COUNTRY

Senegal is situated on the bulge of West Africa between Mauritania on the north, Mali on the east, and Guinea and Guinea-Bissau on the south. Gambia forms an enclave extending into Senegal's territory for 200 miles along one of the area's four major rivers. The predominantly flat or rolling savanna country in Senegal has a population of varied ethnic backgrounds, with the Wolof, whose language is widely used commercially, being the largest group. French, the official language, is spoken only by a literate minority. More than 94 percent of the population is Muslim, the remainder being animist or Christian. Islamic "brotherhoods" exercise significant economic and political influence throughout the country, most of them espousing what Western observers would describe as a moderate version of Islam. The illiteracy rate fell below 50 percent in 2015. In addition, it is estimated that about 46 percent of the population lives in poverty. In 2015 the UN Human Development Index ranked Senegal 170th out of 186 nations. Women have made significant political strides in recent years. In the 2012 elections, women secured 64 of 150 seats in the assembly or 42.7 percent, the seventh highest percentage in the world. Women also held 40 seats in the Senate (40 percent) before it was abolished in September that year.

GDP grew by an average of more than 5 percent annually from 1996 to 2008, earning praise from the International Monetary Fund (IMF) and World Bank, while inflation averaged less than 4 percent. (For an overview of the economy prior to 2008, see the 2014 *Handbook*.) At the same time, Senegal entered the new millennium with an economy that remained peasant-based and stressed by unequal distribution of wealth, high unemployment, an external debt of $3.5 billion, and deteriorating social services. Nonetheless, Senegal subsequently experienced steady, if modest, economic growth, which was accompanied by low inflation. As a result of sound fiscal policy, the government was also able to lower deficits and increase tax revenue.

The global economic crisis slowed Senegal's economy in 2009 because of declines in commodity exports and decreases in remittances. GDP growth was 2.1 percent for the year, while inflation was –1.7 percent. In September 2009, Senegal concluded an agreement with the Millennium Challenge Corporation to provide $540 million in funding for road construction and irrigation projects. Inflation remained steady at 1.1 percent in 2013. GDP grew by 4.5 percent in 2014, increasing to 6.5 percent for 2015 and 2016. Inflation expanded by 1.6 percent in 2016 and GDP per capita rose to $1,457. In its annual report on the ease of doing business index for 2016, the World Bank ranked Senegal 153rd out of 189 countries.

GOVERNMENT AND POLITICS

Political background. Under French influence since the 17th century, Senegal became a French colony in 1920 and a self-governing member of the French Community in November 1958. In January 1959 it joined with the adjacent French Soudan (now Mali) to form the Federation of Mali, which became fully independent within the Community on June 20, 1960. Two months later Senegal seceded from the federation, and the separate Republic of Senegal was proclaimed on September 5. President Léopold Sédar SENGHOR, a well-known poet and the leader of Senegal's strongest political party, the Senegalese Progressive Union (*Union Progressiste Sénégalaise*—UPS), governed initially under a parliamentary system in which political rival Mamadou DIA was prime minister. An unsuccessful coup in December 1962 resulted in Dia's arrest and imprisonment (until his release in 1974) and the establishment by Senghor of a presidential form of government under his exclusive direction. In an election held under violent conditions on December 1, 1963, Senghor retained the presidency, and his party won all of the seats in the National Assembly, as it also did in the elections of 1968 and 1973.

In response to demands for political and constitutional reform, Senghor in early 1970 reinstituted the post of prime minister, while a constitutional amendment adopted in 1976 sanctioned three political parties, the ideology of each being prescribed by law. In early 1979 a fourth, essentially conservative, party was also accorded recognition. Additional parties were legalized under legislation enacted in April 1981.

Although he had been overwhelmingly reelected to a fourth five-year term on February 26, 1978, President Senghor resigned on December 31, 1980, and, as prescribed by the constitution, he was succeeded by Prime Minister Abdou DIOUF. Coalitions remained prohibited in national balloting on February 27, 1983. Diouf was reelected with 83 percent of the vote, and the ruling Socialist Party (*Parti Socialiste*—PS) captured 111 of 120 assembly seats. In the subsequent poll of February 28, 1988, Diouf was reelected by a reported 73 percent of the vote, with the PS being awarded 103 assembly seats. However, controversy surrounding this election, and its aftermath tarnished Senegal's long-standing democratic reputation.

While the major opposition parties boycotted local elections in November 1990, a number of their leaders, including Abdoulaye WADE, Diouf's principal opponent in the 1982 and 1988 presidential campaigns, were named to a government headed by Habib THIAM on April 7, 1991. However, in October 1992 Wade and three other cabinet members from Wade's Senegalese Democratic Party (*Parti Démocratique Sénégalais*—PDS) resigned from the government, claiming they had been marginalized by their PS colleagues and included in only "trivial" decision making.

In first-round balloting on February 21, 1993, President Diouf was credited with winning 58 percent of the valid vote, thus eliminating the need for a second round. Wade was runner-up with a vote share of 32 percent. In the legislative poll of May 9, the PS won a reduced majority of 84 assembly seats, with the PDS securing 27 seats.

On May 15, 1993, the Constitutional Council's vice president, Babacar SEYE, was assassinated by a group identifying themselves as the People's Army. On May 16 Wade and a number of his PDS colleagues were detained after one of the alleged conspirators, Cledor SENE, claimed to be acting on their orders. On June 7, Sene recanted his story and publicly apologized to Wade for attempting to "decapitate" the PDS. Thereafter, relations between the government and the opposition grew increasingly acrimonious, as two PDS deputies, Mody SY and Samuel SARR, remained imprisoned for alleged involvement in the assassination, and the PDS mounted a demonstration in late July on behalf of their release. On August 24, the National Assembly further aggravated the situation by approving an emergency economic austerity plan that called for cuts in civil service salaries. Implementation of the measure was subsequently temporarily suspended following a general strike on September 2. In early October, Wade and his wife, Viviane WADE, who had previously been released, were rearrested for their alleged involvement in Seye's assassination, and on November 5 more than 130 opposition activists were arrested for participating in an antigovernment rally organized by the PDS and the African Party for Democracy and Socialism/*And Jëf* (*Parti Africain pour la Démocratie et le Socialisme/And Jëf*—PADS/AJ). Violent clashes erupted during a demonstration against the effects of the mid-January 1994 CFA devaluation, and the government moved quickly to indict Abdoulaye Wade and Landing SAVANE, leader of the PADS/AJ, for "breach against the state security," a charge for which 73 others were also being detained. However, on May 26 the Wades and their fellow PDS members were cleared of involvement in the Seye assassination, and at midyear Sy and Sarr were released after launching hunger strikes. In August Wade and Savane were acquitted of the February charges. In October three people were sentenced for their roles in Seye's assassination, although no motive was revealed.

In March 1995 the Diouf administration scored what appeared to be a major political victory when Wade accepted a cabinet-level post. As a result, the government contained three of the four leading groups previously aligned as regime opponents. In addition, although Wade had previously refused to enter the government unless the PDS was given half the posts in a 20-member cabinet, he now agreed to accept only 5 portfolios in a 33-member cabinet. A number of opposition parties, including the PDS, the PADS/AJ, and the Movement for Socialism and Unity (*Mouvement pour le Socialisme et l'Unité*—MSU), operated in a loose coalition called Uniting to Change Senegal until that grouping's demise following the PDS's decision to join the government in 1995.

Amid reports of increasing violations of a two-year-old cease-fire between the government and secessionist Casamance rebels in southern Senegal, security forces in May 1995 arrested Fr. Augustin DIAMACOUNE Senghor, leader of the Movement of Democratic Forces of Casamance (*Mouvement des Forces Démocratiques de la Casamance*—MFDC). Full-scale fighting erupted following Diamacoune's detention, and in mid-June the cease-fire was formally abandoned. In September the government attempted to start peace talks in Ziguinchor, but fighting continued as MFDC militants refused to negotiate until Diamacoune, who had been placed under house arrest, was freed. In response to the release of a number of his associates in early December, Diamacoune called for an end to the uprising, and on December 30 charges against him were dropped. The following day Diouf announced the creation of a parliamentary upper house, a Senate, which he described as the first step in an effort to decentralize power through a process of "regionalization."

In early 1996 the Diouf administration announced that independent candidates would be prohibited from participating in the rural, regional, and municipal elections scheduled for November. Grassroots groups and small opposition parties then accused Diouf of retreating from his pledge to decentralize power. Meanwhile, electoral preparations were threatened by the renewal of Casamance rebel activity, and in May the president's party rebuffed proposals to form an independent electoral commission. In balloting on November 24 the PS won what was described as a landslide victory, although voter turnout was reported at only about 50 percent and opposition parties criticized some aspects of the way the elections were conducted.

In March 1997 President Diouf convened a conference to review the 1996 elections with the purported aim of improving polling procedures. However, 19 opposition parties accused the PS of attempting to dominate the proceedings and withdrew from the conference in May. In August the Diouf administration, in an abrupt about-face, announced that it would establish an independent electoral commission, the National Elections Observatory (*Observatoire National des Elections*—ONEL) and published a draft electoral reform document that opposition leaders described as meeting "80 percent" of their demands.

After the PDS withdrew from the government in March 1998, it spearheaded the formation of an Alliance of Forces for Change (*Alliance des Forces pour le Changement*—AFC), which also included the PADS/AJ and Independence and Labor Party (*Parti de l'Indépendance et du Travail*—PIT). In legislative balloting on May 25, 1998, PS candidates dominated an 18-party field, winning 93 seats in the expanded 140-member assembly; the PS's nearest two competitors, the PDS and the newly formed Union for Democratic Renewal (*Union pour le Renouveau Démocratique*—URD), secured 23 and 11 seats, respectively. Although the PDS, URD, and four other parties petitioned to have the polling results overturned because of alleged fraudulent tallying, the ONEL and international observers described the elections as generally free and fair. On July 3 Diouf named Mamadou Lamine LOUM to replace Thiam as prime minister, and the following day a new cabinet that included only one non-PS member was announced.

In August 1998 the PS-dominated assembly voted 93–1 to abolish the limit on presidential terms, thereby permitting the Diouf presidency to continue past 2000. All but two opposition legislators boycotted the session, and the following day all of the leading opposition politicians condemned the assembly vote at an unprecedented joint news conference.

Elections to fill the legislature's newly formed upper house, or Senate, were held on January 24, 1999, candidates affiliated with the PS winning all 45 elective seats. The AFC was superseded in late 1999 by the formation of an opposition coalition known as Alternance 2000 to challenge the PS in the 2000 presidential balloting. The new coalition, which endorsed Abdoulaye Wade of the PDS in the first round of the presidential election, was dominated by the PDS but also included, among other groupings, the PADS/AJ, MSU, PIT, Democratic League–Labor Party Movement (*Ligue Démocratique–Mouvement pour le Parti du Travail*—LD-MPT), and the Action Front for Renewal/The Way (*Front d'Action pour le Renouveau/Yoon Wi*—FAR/Yoon Wi). In early 2000 Alternance 2000 joined with a number of other opposition groupings to form the Front for Fair and Transparent Elections (*Front pour la Régularité et la Transparence des Elections*—FRTE) to combat what the members perceived to be efforts by the PS to sabotage the election. The FRTE was not an electoral coalition; several members, including Alternance 2000, the Alliance of Forces for Progress (*Alliance des Forces pour le Progrès*—AFP), and the URD, presented their own presidential candidates in the first round.

Eight candidates contested the first round of presidential balloting on February 27, 2000, with Diouf securing 43 percent of the vote and Wade 30 percent. Following the first round of presidential balloting, a number of groups previously aligned in the FRTE (including Alternance 2000, the AFP and the CDP) formed the Front for Change (*Front pour l'Alternance*—FAL) to support Wade in the second round after the PDS/Alternance 2000 leader promised that his victory would be followed by installation of a coalition government. Meanwhile President Diouf of the PS was also endorsed in his reelection bid by a coalition called the Patriotic Convergence (*Convergence Patriotique*—CP). Wade won the second round, 58.7 to 41.3 percent. Following his inauguration on April 1, Wade appointed Moustapha NIASSE of the AFP as prime minister to head a coalition cabinet that also included the PADS/AJ, the PIT, and the LD-MPT.

As promised during the 2000 presidential campaign, the PDS and its allies presented a number of constitutional amendments for a national referendum on January 7, 2001. The measures, which abolished the presidentially appointed Senate and otherwise reduced the president's authority, were approved by 94 percent of the voters in a reported 66 percent turnout.

Invoking a provision in the new basic law that authorized the president to call for new legislative elections after the most recently elected assembly had served for at least two years, Wade dissolved the assembly on February 15, 2001, and ordered new elections for April 29. Meanwhile, friction grew between Wade and Niasse, and the prime minister left his post (having either resigned or been dismissed, depending on whose account was accurate) on March 3. He was succeeded by Mame Madiou BOYE, an independent who had been serving as justice minister; Boye thereby became Senegal's first female prime minister.

The FAL essentially collapsed when Niasse resigned as prime minister and the AFP cabinet members also left the government. Consequently, the PDS organized the *Sopi* (Wolof for "Change") Coalition, which ultimately included upward of 40 smaller groups, to contest the April 29, 2001, assembly balloting. Meanwhile, the AFP, PIT, and a number of other opposition parties formed a loose preelection coalition called the Front for Defense of Democracy (*Front pour la Défence de la Démocratie*—FDD), under the leadership of the PIT's Amath DANSOKHO. The *Sopi* Coalition was credited with winning 89 of the legislative seats. The new government named by Boye on May 12 was again led by the PDS and several of its smaller electoral partners.

Subsequently, opposition parties (including the PS, AFP, URD, and PIT) organized a Permanent Framework for Consultation (*Cadre Permanent de Concertation*—CPC) to work against the policies of the PDS-led government. In response, the PDS organized a grouping known as the Convergence of Actions around the President for the 21st

Century (*Convergence des Actions autour du Président en Perspective du 21ème Siècle*—CAP-21). The CAP-21, which included the PADS/AJ, the LD-MPT, and some 20 other smaller groups, contested the May 2002 municipal balloting as an electoral coalition, as did the CPC.

On November 4, 2002, President Wade dismissed Prime Minister Boye in the wake of a ferry disaster that claimed 1,200 lives and attracted intense international scrutiny. Wade appointed Idrissa SECK, his chief of cabinet, to form a new government. However, in August 2003 the Seck government resigned in response to growing public discontent with the inquiry into the ferry's sinking and negative reaction to the government's response to recent severe flooding. Seck was reappointed prime minister and was asked to develop a government of national unity, but most opposition parties declined to join the government, which remained largely dominated by propresidential parties. Tensions between Wade and Seck resulted in the latter's dismissal as prime minister on April 21, 2004. Former interior minister Macky SALL was named the next day to lead a reshuffled cabinet, while Seck was subsequently charged with subversion and embezzlement and kicked out of the PDS.

On July 15, 2005, former prime minister Seck was arrested and charged with embezzlement and later with endangering national security. In August the assembly voted to strip Seck of immunity and forced him to appear before a special anticorruption court. The court dismissed the embezzlement and subversion charges, and the former prime minister was released from prison in February 2006. Seck continued to face a minor charge of overspending government funds; however, his release allowed him to launch his 2007 presidential campaign.

In late 2005 legislative elections scheduled for May 2006 were postponed until June 2007, ostensibly to save money by combining the polling with presidential elections. Wade redirected the $13 million allocated for the 2006 balloting to help relocate Senegalese displaced by flooding. Opposition leaders met in Dakar in December 2005 and issued a joint statement condemning the postponement. Meanwhile, in spite of his age, Wade announced his intention to campaign for reelection.

Seck ran against Wade in the 2007 presidential elections, which were marked by violent clashes between the supporters of the two candidates. Wade received 55.9 percent of the vote in the first round of voting on February 25, followed by Seck (running as the candidate of a new party called The Nation) with 14.9 percent and Ousmane Tanor DIENG of the PS with 13.6 percent. None of the other 12 candidates received more than 6 percent of the vote. After Wade was sworn in on April 3, the Sall government resigned, but it was immediately reappointed by the president.

Citing irregularities in the presidential balloting, many opposition parties boycotted the June 2007 legislative elections, in which the propresidential *Sopi* 2007 Coalition won 131 seats and no other party secured more than 3 seats. Wade subsequently appointed independent Cheikh Hadjibou SOUMARÉ as prime minister of a cabinet dominated by the PDS, while Sall was elected speaker of the National Assembly. In balloting for the Senate in August the PDS won 34 of the elected seats, while the African Party for Democracy and Socialism/*And Jëf* won 1. Wade appointed the remaining 65 seats in September. Wade ally and mayor of Dakar, Pape DIOP was subsequently elected speaker of the Senate. A major cabinet reshuffle in December reduced the number of members from 38 to 28 in an effort to streamline the government. Wade faced significant criticism as 8 of the dismissed ministers were women.

The PS and other opposition groups announced that they would participate in local and regional elections scheduled for May 18, 2008. However, the assembly postponed the balloting until March 2009. The action led to protests by the opposition, especially after the assembly enacted legislation in May 2008 to consolidate the number of local and regional offices. In October the terms of office of speaker in both the Senate and Assembly were reduced from five years to one year.

In January 2009 Diadji DIOUF, a well-known gay rights activist, and eight others were tried and convicted of homosexuality. They were each sentenced to eight years in prison. International and domestic human rights groups condemned the trial and sentence. Diouf was released after five months and left Senegal.

Despite a series of cabinet reshuffles in late 2008 and early 2009 as part of an effort to enhance the popularity of the government, in balloting for local and municipal offices on March 22, opposition parties won the majority of posts. These wins included a number of seats in areas that were strongholds for the ruling *Sopi* Coalition. The defeat was the first broad electoral loss for Wade's coalition since 2000. The deteriorating economy and rising costs were reportedly responsible for the *Sopi* Coalition's electoral losses. *Sopi* faced a coalition of opposition groups, United to Boost Senegal (see Political Parties, below). Wade's coalition even lost control of the governing council of Dakar, and opposition leader Khalifa SALL was elected mayor of the capital city.

Following the losses, Wade replaced Soumaré as prime minister on April 30 with a close political ally, Souleymane Ndéné NDIAYE. Ndiaye reshuffled the cabinet and formed a new government on May 1. Wade's son Karim WADE was subsequently appointed to a cabinet post, leading to speculation that he was being groomed to succeed his father. In June, the assembly approved the creation of the post of vice president, a post that remained vacant through 2009.President Wade conducted more cabinet reshuffles through 2009 and 2010. A massive 160-foot statue was unveiled at independence celebrations in April 2010. The $27 million cost of the monument drew criticism from opposition groups and public protests. On October 5, 2010, the president dismissed Samuel SARR, the minister of energy, following widespread power outages and concurrent public protests and demonstrations. Wade appointed his son Karim to replace Sarr and ordered audits of the national electric company and changes in personnel. Reports indicated that the appointment was a further signal that the younger Wade was being groomed to take over the presidency in the future. Wade reshuffled the cabinet again on January 25, 2011, and on May 7.

Former prime minister Sall won the presidential election in run-off balloting on March 18, 2012 (see Current issues, below). Sall was the candidate of the Alliance for the Republic–Hope (*Alliance pour le République–Yaakar*—APR-*Yakaar*). Sall appointed independent Abdoul MBAYE prime minister of a coalition cabinet that was significantly smaller than its predecessor. The APR-*Yakaar* subsequently formed an electoral coalition, United in Hope (*Benno Bokk Yakaar*), which won 119 seats out of 150 in balloting for the National Assembly on July 1. On October 29, the cabinet underwent a major reshuffle, including the addition of five ministries.

After Sall dismissed Abdoul Mbaye for undisclosed reasons, on September 1, 2013, human rights activist Aminata TOURE of the Alliance for the Republic party became prime minister. She appointed a cabinet of 28 men and 4 women ministers. When her party failed to win any seats in local balloting in June 2014, Sall requested that Touré step down.

In July 2014 in-coming prime minister Mohamed Abdallah DIONE appointed his new cabinet, increasing the number to 33.

On March 20, 2016, voters in Senegal approved a referendum that reduced the presidential term to five years as part of a broader series of proposed constitutional changes, including formal recognition of the leader of the opposition in the assembly, and expanded powers for local governments. The referendum passed on a vote of 62.6 percent in favor, and 37.4 percent opposed. The shortened presidential term was scheduled to go into effect in 2019.

Constitution and government. Senegal is administratively divided into eleven regions, each headed by a presidentially appointed governor who is assisted by an elected Regional Assembly; the regions are divided into departments. The constitution provides for a president elected by direct universal suffrage, with runoff balloting for the two top contenders if none secures an absolute majority. Under amendments approved in 1991, presidents were limited to two terms, although the incumbent (Abdou Diouf), already elected twice, was permitted to stand one more time. An amendment in 1993 extended presidential terms to seven years, but a referendum in 2016 reduced the term to five years, beginning in 2019. The two-term restriction was formally abandoned in 1998, thereby permitting Diouf to contest the 2000 balloting as well. Amendments in 2001 reimposed the two-term limit and returned the length of the term to five years. In 2008, the presidential term was again extended to seven years, to take effect after the 2012 balloting. The president appoints the prime minister (the office having been abolished in 1983 and revived in 1991), who in turn appoints the Council of Ministers in consultation with the president.

Legislative power was vested in a unicameral National Assembly until December 31, 1995, when President Diouf announced the creation of a Senate to act as an upper house. The first Senate was elected in January 1999, but that body was abolished in the 2001 constitutional amendments. Under initial procedures, half of the assembly members were elected from Senegal's departments on a "first past the post" basis, the other half by proportional representation from a national list. However, electoral changes adopted in 1989 provided that national lists would be dropped from future elections, with all members being chosen on a departmental basis. Only parties registered at least four months before an election were allowed to participate; neither independent candidacies nor opposition coalitions were permitted. However, the combination of departmental and national lists was reestablished for the April 2001 assembly election in accordance with the January constitutional revisions. Party restrictions were also lifted as were barriers to electoral coalitions. The principal judicial organs, under a system revised in 1992, include a Constitutional Council, one of whose functions is to rule on electoral issues; a Council of State; a Court of Cassation; and a Court of Appeal; with magistrate courts at the local level. In addition, a High Court of Justice, chosen by the assembly from among its own membership, is responsible for impeachment proceedings. Elections for municipal and rural community councilors were held in May 2002.

In January 2007 the National Assembly voted to reinstate the Senate, and elections for the chamber were held in August. In 2008 the presidential term of office was extended from five to seven years.

The National Commission for Institutional Reform (CNRI) submitted its report to President Sall on February 13, 2014. Unexpectedly, the commission presented a complete new draft constitution to accompany the report. CNRI's draft constitution of 154 articles, which maintains a semi-presidential system, received a mixed reception. Sall's party, the APR, claimed the CNRI overstepped its mandate. Specifically, the APR opposed the constitutional provision that would inhibit the president from retaining the chairmanship of his party.

Newspapers are subject to government censorship and regulation, although a number of opposition papers appeared in the 1990s, some evading official registration by means of irregular publication, and restrictions have eased significantly in recent years. Prior to the 2007 elections, the government reportedly forced the closure of some private radio stations, seized editions of newspapers, and detained journalists who were critical of the regime. In its 2016 press freedom index, media organization Reporters Without Borders ranked Senegal 65th out of 180 countries, a slight regression over 2014, when Senegal was ranked 62nd.

Foreign relations. Formally nonaligned, Senegal has retained especially close political, cultural, and economic ties with France. An active advocate of West African cooperation, it has participated in such regional groupings as the Economic Community of West African States, the Permanent Inter-State Committee on Drought Control in the Sahel, and the Organization for the Development of the Senegal River. (The members of the latter are Mali and Mauritania.) Regional relations improved substantially as the result of a "reconciliation" pact signed in Monrovia, Liberia, in March 1978, ending five years of friction with Guinea and Côte d'Ivoire.

Under President Senghor, Senegal maintained a generally conservative posture in African affairs, refusing to recognize Angola because of the presence of Cuban troops there, supporting Morocco against the claims of the insurgent Polisario Front in the Western Sahara, and breaking relations with Libya in mid-1980 because of that country's alleged efforts to destabilize the governments of Chad, Mali, and Niger, as well as Senegal. Reflecting the "spirit of our new diplomacy"—essentially an effort to introduce greater flexibility in its relations with other African governments—Dakar announced in February 1982 that it would reverse its long-standing support of the Angolan resistance movement and recognize the *Mouvement Populaire de Libération de l'Azawad* (MPLA) government in Luanda. Ties with Algeria were strengthened in the course of reciprocal visits by the respective heads of state in 1984 and 1985; relations with Libya eased as the result of a visit by Colonel Muammar Qadhafi in December 1985 and were formally restored in November 1988.

In light of the unusual geographic relationship between the two countries, one of Senegal's most prominent regional concerns has been its association with Gambia. A 1967 treaty provided for cooperation in foreign affairs, development of the Gambia River basin, and, most important, defense. Consequently, Senegalese troops were dispatched to Banjul, Gambia, in October 1980 amid rumors of Libyan involvement in a projected coup and again in July 1981 when an uprising threatened to topple the Jawara administration (see article on Gambia). The latter incident was followed by an agreement to establish a Confederation of Senegambia, completed on February 1, 1982. Although the component states remained politically independent entities, the Confederation agreement called for the integration of security forces, the establishment of an economic and monetary union, and the coordination of policies in foreign affairs, internal communications, and other areas. A joint Council of Ministers and an appointed Confederal Assembly were established, and it was agreed that the presidents of Senegal and Gambia would serve as president and vice president, respectively, of the confederation. In practical terms, however, little progress was made in actualizing the confederation. Many Gambians criticized what was perceived as an unequal relationship, while Gambian government and business leaders questioned the wisdom of their country's proposed entrance into the franc zone. Economic union was also hindered by the fact that Gambia had long favored liberal trade policies in contrast to Senegal's imposition of high protective tariffs. In August 1989, Senegal unilaterally withdrew some of its troops from Gambia, and President Diouf declared that the confederation, having "failed in its purpose," should be "frozen." Gambian President Jawara responded by suggesting it be terminated completely, and a protocol was quickly negotiated formally dissolving the grouping as of September 30. Despite a presidential summit in December 1989, relations remained cool through 1990 as Senegal enacted trade sanctions aimed at stemming the importation of foreign goods via its relatively duty-free neighbor. In January 1991 the two countries moved to reestablish bilateral links by the conclusion of a treaty of friendship and cooperation. As finalized in June, the treaty provided for annual summits and the establishment of joint commissions to ensure implementation of summit agreements.

In May 1989 the third conference of francophone heads of state met in Dakar amid deepening hostility between Senegal and Mauritania that had been triggered by a dispute on April 9 over farming rights along their border. Rioting in both Dakar and Nouakchott ensued, causing death or injury to several hundred people and the cross-repatriation of an estimated 150,000–300,000, including a substantial number of Moors, who had dominated the crucial small-business retail sector in the Senegalese capital. The situation continued in crisis for the balance of the year. Relations remained broken, with a continuing exodus (forced, according to Senegalese charges) of blacks from Mauritania to Senegal; Nouakchott announced preparations for a possible war. In January 1990 border forces exchanged artillery fire across the Senegal River, but diplomatic efforts, led by Organization of African Unity (OAU, subsequently the African Union—AU) president Hosni Mubarak, helped avert additional violence. By early 1991 relations had again deteriorated, as Nouackchott accused Senegal of aiding antigovernment rebels and Dakar charged Mauritania with arming Casamance separatists with Iraqi weapons. Meanwhile, relations with Guinea-Bissau, already strained by Bissau's refusal to recognize a July 1989 international court decision favoring Senegal in their maritime border dispute, were exacerbated by a clash in May 1991 that left 17 dead and by reports that Bissau was also supporting the Casamance rebels.

A May 1991 rapprochement between Dakar and the Casamance insurgents had a positive effect on relations with both Guinea-Bissau and Mauritania. The choice of the former as the site for the signing of a cease-fire agreement signaled a further lessening of tensions, and on July 18, an agreement to reopen the Senegalese-Mauritanian border paved the way for restoration of diplomatic relations on April 23, 1992. However, on December 12 tension again flared with the bombing by Senegalese forces of alleged Casamance bases in northern Guinea-Bissau. Four days later the Senegalese government offered its apologies after Bissau had protested the violation of its border, and on December 22 it was reported that Casamance leader Diamacoune had been expelled from Guinea-Bissau.

In May 1994 Dakar demanded the withdrawal of Iran's ambassador, accusing Tehran of supporting the activities of the Islamic fundamentalist movement in Senegal. Fear of the spread of Islamic fundamentalism also dominated a meeting among Senegal, Mali, and Mauritania in January 1995, with the three agreeing to "combat fanaticism in all its forms." On February 10 Senegalese aircraft bombed a suspected Casamance rebel base in Guinea-Bissau, Dakar ignoring Bissau's subsequent demand for an explanation of the attack. However, in September Dakar and Bissau signed a security cooperation pact, and in December the prospect of closer relations improved markedly when Bissau agreed to withdraw its earlier objections to the 1989 court ruling on their shared maritime border. In 1996 Senegal continued to enjoy improved relations with its neighbors, signing cooperation agreements with Guinea, Guinea-Bissau, Mali, and Mauritania. On a less positive note, efforts to repatriate the Mauritanian refugees residing in Senegal since 1989 were only haltingly successful.

In June 1998 President Diouf deployed troops to Guinea-Bissau to shore up the embattled government there, underlining Dakar's concern that the Casamance region in Senegal would erupt in violence if the pro-Casamance Bissaun rebels secured power in Guinea-Bissau (see entry on Guinea-Bissau). The administration's military strategy initially drew widespread support; however, by August opposition leaders had begun to question the effort. In March 1999 the last of the Senegalese troops were withdrawn. In 2001 armed forces from Guinea-Bissau destroyed the main Casamance rebel bases in that country. In 2002 separatist groups launched a new round of negotiations with the Senegalese government following the appointment of a new government peace commission. The government committed to a number of infrastructure programs in the province and released some government-held rebels on bail. In response the rebels adopted a cease-fire, although rebels opposed to the negotiations continued to launch minor attacks.

Wade maintained close ties with France but also reached out to other major powers. In February 2002 he hosted Tony Blair, the first British prime minister to visit Senegal. During the meeting Blair pledged support for the New Partnership for Africa's Development (NEPAD), an organization launched through the OAU in October 2001 to promote socioeconomic recovery in Africa. In April 2002 Wade hosted the first major NEPAD conference. Wade also worked to improve relations with the United States and met with U.S. president George W. Bush in Senegal in July 2003. In addition, Senegal pledged to cooperate with the United States in the global war on terrorism. In 2003 Wade angered France by his refusal to condemn the U.S.-led war in Iraq.

On December 30, 2004, the government and the main rebel group in Casamance, the MFDC, signed a comprehensive peace settlement, although some minor rebel factions continued to fight the central government. (In March 2006 fighting between competing factions of the MFDC displaced 5,000 civilians along the border between Senegal and Guinea-Bissau.)

Tensions emerged in 2005 over a Gambian decision to double the tariff on ferry traffic on the Gambia River, which prompted Wade to close border crossings. The dispute was later resolved with a 15 percent reduction in the tariffs.

In October 2005 Senegal reestablished diplomatic relations with the People's Republic of China, ending Senegal's long-standing recognition of Taiwan. Economic relations between Dakar and Beijing were the main reason for the action, as trade between the two countries had increased by 25 percent per year since 2003.

Renewed fighting in Casamance between rival wings of the MFDC in September 2006 created 15,000 refugees, and at least 5,000 people fled across the border into Gambia. In December, Senegal and Gambia launched new talks to resolve tensions over the presence of Senegalese rebel bases in Gambia. In July 2007 the government announced that it would try former Chadian president Hisséne Habré (see entry on Chad), in custody in Senegal, on charges of murder and torture following a request for such a trial from the AU. In April 2008 the National Assembly amended the constitution to allow Habré's trial on retroactive charges of crimes against humanity.

In 2006 Senegal and Spain agreed to joint patrols of Senegalese waters to deter illegal immigration to the Canary Islands. Senegal also reached an immigration agreement with France that eased restrictions on Senegalese immigrating to France but also simplified repatriation for illegal immigrants.

France announced in October 2007 that it would resume development loans to Senegal for the first time in 17 years. Senegal agreed in November to a governance program sponsored by the IMF. Under the terms of the initiative, the IMF provided technical advice and assistance on monetary and fiscal policy. In December Morocco recalled its ambassador to Senegal over remarks made by a member of the assembly that supported independence for the Western Sahara. Diplomatic ties were restored the following month.

In March 2008 Wade helped negotiate a nonaggression pact between Sudan and Chad. Also in March Senegal hosted the meeting of the Organization of Islamic States (OIC) in Dakar. South Africa and Senegal signed a bilateral trade agreement in April in what was reported to be a sign of growing ties between the two nations. In November Senegal deployed troops along its border with Guinea Bissau in response to an attempted coup.

In February 2009 Belgium filed a motion before the International Court of Justice in an effort to force Senegal to try former Chadian president Habré. Senegal had reportedly delayed prosecution because of the costs associated with a trial. During a visit to Senegal by Chinese president Hu Jintao, a number of new bilateral economic agreements were signed. In May Wade helped negotiate an agreement to allow elections in Mauritania in July 2009, following a 2008 coup.

Following the January 2010 Haiti earthquake, Wade offered to allow survivors of the disaster to resettle in Senegal and provided $1 million in aid for the country. In June France withdrew 900 of its 1,200 troops from Senegal and turned three military facilities over to the Senegalese. The remaining French soldiers continued the long-standing training mission in the country. Meanwhile, in September Senegal joined five other West African nations in a multilateral agreement, sponsored by Norway, to delineate the maritime borders of the nations. In 2010 China and Senegal signed two economic agreements whereby Chinese firms were awarded contracts to modernize Senegal's aging power system (see Current issues, below). In addition, in December China provided 50 vehicles to the Senegalese government. By the end of 2010 trade between the two countries had reached $459 million annually, and there was more than $1.5 billion in infrastructure agreements in place. In 2011 Senegal cut ties with Iran after the discovery of Iranian-supplied arms in the hands of Casamance rebels. In September, Sierra Leone opened an embassy in Dakar, three years after the restoration of ties with Senegal.

In August 2012 the United States announced that it would expand military cooperation with Senegal, including an increase in joint training exercises. Also in August, Senegal signed an accord with the AU to create a special court to try Habré, following a ruling from the ICJ that Senegal either extradite the former Chadian leader or prosecute him. In September, a Gambian opposition group, the National Transitional Council of the Gambia, was launched in Dakar. Also that month, Senegal banned certain classes of supertrawlers from fishing in Senegalese waters following reports of overfishing.

In January 2013 Senegal agreed to contribute 500 troops to the ECOWAS-led peacekeeping force in Mali, the African International Support Mission to Mali (AFISMA). As the fighting in Mali escalated (see entry on Mali), Senegal increased security throughout the country and deployed additional forces along the border with Mali. In August Senegal and Chad finalized an agreement to finally allow the trial of Habré to begin.

In September 2014 it was reported that thousands of child beggars live in the streets of Dakar. Poor parents from rural areas in Senegal, Guinea, Mali, and Guinea Bissau send their children to the city to attend classrooms called *daaras* to receive Islamic religious instruction. To provide for the upkeep of the daaras, the instructors, called marabouts, send the pupils to beg on the streets for food, clothing, and money. A 2010 Human Rights Watch report compared the child beggars to modern-day slaves. Sall's government entered into a partnership with international organizations to modernize daaras in order to improve the living conditions. Conflict in Mali and Guinea Bissau has prevented the government from repatriating pupils from those countries.

Reports in August 2015 that Senegalese soldiers had crossed into territory claimed by Gambia prompted a series of high-level talks to resolve border tensions. Negotiations continued through 2016. Meanwhile, Senegal and Ukraine finalized a treaty on military cooperation in December.

A group of about 70 Senegalese migrants who had become stranded in Benin were returned to Senegal with the aid of the UN in January 2016. Also in January Canada announced the deployment of about 100 special operations forces to Senegal to train regional military forces in counterterrorism operations. Continuing tensions led to border closures between Senegal and Gambia from February until May. In April Senegal agreed to accept to two Libyan detainees from the U.S. facility at Guantánamo Bay.

Current issues. Riots and protests swept the capital and other major cities on June 22 and 23, 2011, after Wade introduced a constitutional amendment that would have lowered the threshold to win a presidential election, without a runoff, from 50 percent to 25 percent. The measure was perceived as a ploy by the president to ease his reelection bid. The demonstrations left more than 100 injured and led the government to deploy military forces. A second measure to create an elected vice president also met with widespread opposition as most assumed that Wade would name his son Karim as his vice-presidential running mate. The violence prompted Wade to withdraw the measures. On June 28 new rioting commenced following widespread power outages that left some areas of Dakar without electricity for more than 30 hours. Power availability improved after the government tapped an emergency fund to buy additional diesel fuel for power plants. A new, loose coalition of opposition parties and civil society groups, known as the June 23 Movement, emerged following the riots. The group sought to prevent Wade from seeking a third term as president and later rallied behind opposition figures in the 2012 balloting.

On January 27, 2012, a court ruled that Wade's first term did not count toward the two-term limit because the constitution was amended in 2001, after he had initially been elected. The decision, which allowed Wade to run in the February balloting, was met with widespread protests and violence. Wade placed first among 14 candidates with 34.8 percent of the vote, followed by former prime minister Sall, with 26.6 percent. The two advanced to run-off balloting that was won by Sall, with 65.8 percent of the vote, after opposition leaders rallied behind the challenger. In April riots swept through Dakar following the arrest of Cheikh Bethio THIOUNE, a leader of the Islamist Mouride Sufi Brotherhood on murder charges after his followers beat and killed two youths. Sall's APR-*Yakaar*-led coalition, United in Hope, went on to win legislative balloting in July. In September the assembly voted to abolish the Senate rather than hold new elections. In October Sall replaced Minister of the Interior Mbaye NDIAYE over his management of the protests.

Sall was praised by international observers for his anticorruption efforts, including the creation in January 2013 of a new office to investigate and prosecute malfeasance in office. Sall signed a series of emergency decrees that allowed the government to spend more than $200 million on a range of security and infrastructure projects without parliamentary approval. Opposition groups decried the spending as an effort to bolster the president's popularity and argued that the funds were being used for non-emergencies. The dispute led to the passage of a revised finance law in July 2013.

From the beginning of Sall's time in office, criticism has emerged about the role of his wife, Marième FAYE SALL. Critics refer to the couple's joint leadership as the "Faye-Sall Dynasty" and the "fayesallisation of the state". Conspicuously, several candidates running in the municipal elections in June 2014 were relatives of the Salls. In July Minister of Culture Mbagnick Ndiaye caused the first lady considerable embarrassment when he told the media that he and Minister of Sport Matar Ba owed their appointments to her. The apparent nepotism of the Sall regime echoes former president Wade's attempt to groom his son for leadership.

On May 1, 2014, a cease-fire seemingly brought an end to the Casamance rebellion, following a series of secret peace talks held at the Vatican.

Despite the outbreak of the disease in neighboring Guinea, the government of Senegal reported on October 17 that the Ebola virus had been contained. One person, a Guinean national, was diagnosed with the virus but recovered from it.

In May 2016 President Sall called for the National Assembly to draft a new constitution for Senegal, with 15 major issues to be reformed, including alterations in how the assembly was elected and public financing of campaigns.

POLITICAL PARTIES

In March 1976 the National Assembly approved a constitutional amendment authorizing three political parties. (For more on the development of the three parties, see the 2013 *Handbook*.) In early 1979 the amendment was altered to permit the legal establishment of a fourth, essentially right-wing, party—the Senegalese Republican Movement. In April 1981 the assembly removed the remaining restrictions on party activity.

For the 2007 presidential and legislative elections, pro-presidential parties ran as the *Sopi* 2007 Coalition. Leading opposition parties boycotted the legislative balloting under the ***Siggil Sénégal Front***, while a number of other parties formed coalitions for the polling. For the 2009 local elections, 79 parties were registered. A new opposition coalition, **United to Boost Senegal** (*Benno Siggil Senegaal*—BSS), brought together 35 opposition parties prior to the municipal balloting. The BSS was led by former PS parliamentarian, Khalifa Sall, and it included a number of parties that had boycotted the 2007 legislative elections, including the PS, the PIT, and the PPS. The BSS won a number of key constituencies in the elections. Ahead of the 2012 balloting, a number of parties in the BSS broke away to form the United in Hope Coalition (*Benno Bokk Yakaar*—BBY) coalition in 2012.

In the 2012 balloting, 24 parties or groupings fielded candidates. New electoral laws required that women comprise at least 50 percent of party lists.

Government and Government-Supportive Parties:

United in Hope Coalition (*Benno Bokk Yakaar*—BBY). The pro-Mackey Sall coalition was formed in 2012 by opposition parties in an effort to end the political dominance of the PDS. United in Hope won 119 seats in the 2012 assembly balloting. Tensions within the coalition were reported ahead of local balloting in June 2014, casting doubts on the ability of Sall to maintain all parties in the grouping. Tension persisted, and low numbers of BBY candidates were elected, prompting media reports to pronounce the death of the coalition. The coalition campaigned in support of the 2016 referendum on constitutional changes.

Leaders: Moustapha DIAKHATE (President), Mackey SALL (President of the Republic), Moustapha NIASSE (Speaker of the Assembly).

Alliance for the Republic–Hope (*Alliance pour la République–Yaakar*—APR-*Yakaar*). The APR-*Yakaar* was formed in 2008 by former prime minister Mackey SALL to oppose Wade and the PDS. Sall won the 2012 presidential balloting and the APR-*Yakaar* formed the United in Hope coalition to contest legislative balloting that year. APR suffered a heavy defeat after the June 2014 municipal elections.

Leader: Mackey SALL (President of the Republic).

Alliance of Forces for Progress (*Alliance des Forces pour le Progrès*—AFP). Formed by Moustapha Niasse in the fall of 1999 after he had left the PS, the AFP supported Abdoulaye Wade in the second round of the 2000 presidential election, after Niasse had finished third in the first round with 16.7 percent. Under an apparent electoral agreement with Wade, Niasse was named prime minister in Wade's first cabinet, but he subsequently quit that post in early 2001. The AFP, some of whose support comes from the Tidjane Islamic Brotherhood, competed alone in the 2001 legislative elections, finishing second to the *Sopi* Coalition.

Niasse was the AFP's 2007 presidential candidate and placed fourth in the balloting. The AFP joined the opposition boycott of that year's legislative polling. In 2008 Niasse led a failed effort by opposition parties to replace the national election commission, seen as being dominated by the PDS, with an independent agency. The AFP joined the BSS coalition for the 2009 local elections. Niasse placed third in the first round of presidential balloting in 2012 and then supported Sall in the second round. Niasse was elected speaker of the assembly in July 2012. The AFP was given two posts in the October 2012 cabinet. BBY-endorsed joint AFP-APR lists were unsuccessful in the 2014 municipal elections largely because of competing lists from within the BBY coalition.

Leader: Moustapha NIASSE (Speaker of the Assembly and Former Prime Minister).

Socialist Party (*Parti Socialiste*—PS). Known until December 1976 as the **Senegalese Progressive Union** (*Union Progressiste Sénégalaise*—UPS), the PS consistently held a preponderance of seats in the National Assembly until 2001. A moderate Francophile party long identified with the cause of Senegalese independence, the UPS, was founded by Léopold Senghor in 1949 in a secession from the dominant local branch of the French Socialist Party. From 1963 to 1974, it was the only legal party in Senegal; it absorbed the only significant opposition grouping, the leftist ***Parti de Regroupement Africain-Sénégal*** (PRA) in 1966 in furtherance of Senghor's "national reconciliation" policy. In early 1981, following his resignation of the presidency, Senghor withdrew as party secretary general. During an extraordinary conference in March 1989, the PS voted to assign internal authority to a ten-member Executive Committee that was directed to recruit new members and assist in "rejuvenation" of the party. At the PS congress in 1990, Abdou Diouf was reappointed secretary general and given unchecked control of a restructured, "nonhierarchical," 30-member Politburo.

The PS experienced unprecedented levels of intraparty violence prior to its 1996 congress, spurring a call from Diouf for "reconciliation." Meanwhile, Diouf and Ousmane Tanor Dieng were elected to the newly created party presidency and executive secretaryship, respectively, with the latter assuming administrative responsibilities previously assigned to the secretary general.

In March 1998 a PS faction, led by Djibo KA, broke off from the party and formed the URD (see below). Among the reasons cited for Ka's decision was Diouf's reported elevation of Dieng to the status of heir apparent.

Another prominent PS member, Moustapha Niasse, left the PS after 40 years to form the AFP (see below), the recent departures contributing to Diouf's failure in his 2000 reelection bid. Although Diouf was reconfirmed as the PS leader at an October 2000 congress, he subsequently announced plans to retire from politics.

The PS led the opposition to the 2006 postponement of legislative elections and tried to rally opposition parties. It was also reportedly active in unsuccessful efforts to form an opposition electoral coalition ahead of the 2007 balloting. Dieng was the party's candidate in the presidential polling, placing third. The PS boycotted the 2007 legislative balloting. Dieng was formally elected party leader in October. The PS agreed to participate in local and regional elections in 2008, in which it gained mayoral posts and majorities on councils in a number of areas. The PS was instrumental in the creation of the opposition BSS coalition and sought to use the grouping as a potential base for an alliance ahead of future legislative balloting. Dieng placed fourth in the first round of presidential balloting in 2012 and then supported Sall in the second round. On May 24, 2014, PS held elections for secretary general of the party. The party's 15th ordinary congress took place from June 6 to 7. The party supported a "yes" vote in the 2016 referendum.

Leaders: Ousmane Tanor DIENG (Chair and 2012 presidential candidate), Abdou DIOUF (Former President of the Republic), Mamadou Lamine LOUM (Former Prime Minister), Cheikh Abdoul Khadre CISSOKHO (Former National Assembly President).

Democratic League–Labor Party Movement (*Ligue Démocratique–Mouvement pour le Parti du Travail*—LD-MPT). A self-proclaimed independent Marxist group with links to Senegal's leading teachers' union, the LD-MPT contested both the 1983 and 1984 elections. At its second congress in December 1986, the League's Secretary General Abdoulaye Bathily called for "disorganized alliances" among opposition parties and advanced an economic "alternative to the recipes of the International Monetary Fund and the World Bank" as a means of establishing a socialist society. The party supported PDS candidate Abdoulaye Wade in the 1988 presidential poll but presented its own legislative candidates, securing no seats on a 1.4 percent vote share.

In April 1988 LD-MPT's Bathily was given a suspended sentence for having organized an illegal antigovernment demonstration, while five other party activists were indicted on similar charges late in the year. In 1990 Bathily intensified his criticism of the Diouf administration's policies and called for a non-Diouf "unity" government. Thereafter, despite the co-option of a number of opposition colleagues, Bathily initially refused Diouf's offer of a cabinet portfolio, citing Dakar's repressive policies in Casamance. However, Bathily ultimately agreed to become environment minister in June 1993, with the party being awarded a second portfolio in August 1995. Following the May 1998 legislative poll (in which it won three seats), the LD-MPT declined to participate in the next government. Instead, it proposed the formation of a unified opposition front against the PS and President Diouf. In the 2001 legislative balloting, 6 of the 89 successful candidates from the *Sopi* Coalition were identified as LD-MPT members. Two LD-MPT deputies briefly served in the government in 2005 before disputes with Wade led to their dismissal during a cabinet reshuffle.

Bathily was the LD-MPT's presidential candidate in 2007 (he received 2.2 percent of the vote). The LD-MPT boycotted the 2007 legislative election. The LD-MPT participated in the postponed 2009 local and regional elections as a member of the PS-led opposition BSS grouping. Bathily supported Sall in the 2012 balloting. He was appointed as the UN Deputy Special Representative for the world body's peacekeeping mission in Mali (MINUSMA) in July 2013. On July 7, 2014, at the 7th LD-MPT party congress, members voted for Mamadou NDOYE, a former Minister of Education, to take over party leadership. Bathily became the Special Representative for Central Africa and Head of the United Nations Regional Office for Central Africa (UNOCA) in Gabon in April 2014,

Leader: Mamadou NDOYE (Secretary General).

Independence and Labor Party (*Parti de l'Indépendance et du Travail*—PIT). Organized by a group of PAI dissidents and permitted to register in 1981, the PIT was recognized by Moscow as Senegal's official Communist Party. It contested both the 1983 and 1984 elections but won no assembly or town council seats. The party joined the LD-MPT in supporting PDS presidential candidate Wade in 1988, while its legislative candidates won only 0.8 percent of the vote and no seats. The PIT secretary general was among those arrested after the elections, but the charges were later dismissed. In mid-1989 the PIT entered into negotiations with the ruling Socialist Party, and the party was awarded two portfolios in the cabinet reshuffle of August 1995. However, both ministers were ousted a month later in the wake of a PIT Central Committee statement critical of the Diouf administration.

The PIT was a member of Alternance 2000 in support of the 2000 presidential bid of Abdoulaye Wade, and the party's secretary general, Amath Dansokho, served in the first Wade cabinet. However, the two leaders subsequently quarreled, and Dansokho resigned from the government in early 2001. Dansokho was briefly arrested in July 2005 for making antigovernment statements. The PIT participated in the 2007 boycott of legislative elections but took part in the local elections that were postponed until 2009. The PIT was a member of the BSS coalition during the balloting; however, a dispute within the PIT led Dansokho to withdraw his mayoral candidacy for Kedougou. The PIT supported Sall in the 2012 presidential balloting and subsequently joined the United in Hope Coalition. Dansokho was named leader of the opposition grouping, M23. In 2014 the party was still active and working to refine its message and political strategy.

Leader: Amath DANSOKHO (Secretary General).

Opposition Parties:

Senegalese Democratic Party (*Parti Démocratique Sénégalais*—PDS). The PDS was launched in October 1974 as a youth-oriented opposition group to implement the pluralistic democracy guaranteed by the Senegalese constitution. Although standing to the left of President Senghor on certain issues, it was required by the constitutional amendment of March 1976 to adopt a formal position to the right of the government party. Having charged fraud in both the 1980 and 1983 legislative elections (although the PDS was one of two opposition parties to gain representation on the latter occasion), PDS leaders participated in the 1984 municipal boycott and asserted their regret at having campaigned in 1983. Following the return from abroad of party leader Abdoulaye Wade in early 1985, the PDS led a number of mass prayer demonstrations for radical change, with Wade calling for "a transitional government of national unity."

As the major force in Senegal's growing opposition movement, the PDS appeared to pose a genuine threat to the PS in the 1988 legislative and presidential campaigns, partly as a result of its alliance with the LD-MPT and the PIT (above). Although presidential candidate Wade was officially credited with 26 percent of the vote, widespread indications of electoral abuse suggested that his actual total may have been higher.

In 1991 Wade attributed his acceptance of a cabinet post to fears that continued opposition activity would destabilize the country. However, Wade resigned from the government in October 1992 in what was viewed as an attempt to recapture the allegiance of PDS members estranged by his alliance with Diouf. Shortly thereafter Wade announced that the party would present candidates at the forthcoming legislative poll and entered the presidential contest in which he ran second to the incumbent, with a 32 percent share of the vote.

In July 1993 the PDS, ignoring a government ban, organized a demonstration for the release of jailed party deputies Mody Sy and Samuel Sarr, both of whom had been held since mid-May for their alleged involvement in the assassination of the Constitutional Council's vice president. On October 1 Wade, who had himself been detained for two days after the assassination, was arrested along with his wife for their alleged roles in the killing. Within days a number of other prominent PDS leaders, including Abdoulaye FAYE and Ousmane NGOM, were also implicated in the assassination.

On November 5, 1993, a number of party members were arrested for leading antigovernment demonstrations, and on February 18, 1994, Wade was reimprisoned for his participation in rioting, which erupted following the devaluation of the CFA franc. At a perfunctory military trial on February 24, Wade was convicted of a "breach against state security." However, on May 26 charges against him and his associates in connection with the 1993 assassination were dropped. Wade was one of five PDS leaders to accept cabinet portfolios in August 1995.

In March 1998 the PDS withdrew from the government and legislature after the PS legislators increased the size of the latter. At the same time Wade reportedly predicted that the PDS would win as many as 80 seats in the May polling. However, the party fell far short of such expectations, securing just 23 seats. In July Wade resigned his assembly post, saying that he would focus his efforts on resolving the PDS's intraparty disputes.

Wade finished second with 31 percent of the vote in the first round of presidential balloting in February 2000. However, after securing the support of most of the other first-round runners-up, Wade went on to defeat President Diouf in the second round in March with 58.7 percent of the vote, setting the stage, in conjunction with the PDS legislative victory in April 2001, for one of the continent's most remarkably peaceful shifts in political power.

In April 2002 the **Party for Progress and Citizenship** (*Parti pour le Progrès et la Citoyenneté*—PPC) agreed to merge with the PDS. The PPC, formed in 2001 by Mbaye Jacques DIOP after he quit the PS, had secured one seat in the 2001 legislative balloting. The **Senegalese Democratic Party–Renewal** (*Parti Démocratique Sénégalais–Rénovation*—PDS-R) also merged with the PDS. The PDS-R was originally organized in June 1987 by an anti-Wade faction within the PDS that announced as its goal the establishment of a "truly secular and pluralist democracy." PDS-R candidates secured minuscule legislative vote shares in the 1988 and 1993 elections, while supporting Diouf for president on both occasions. Serigne Lamine DIOP, the PDS-R secretary general, was named minister of justice and keeper of the seals in the Loum government formed in July 1998, the party having secured one seat in the May legislative balloting. In 2003 the **Senegalese Liberal Party** (*Parti Libéral Sénégalais*—PLS) merged with the PDS. The PLS had been formed in June 1998 by Ousmane Ngom and a number of other party leaders who left the PDS after they failed to gain central committee posts in their former party. At the group's founding meeting, Ngom described the PLS as a vehicle of "liberalism" and denounced Wade's rule of the PDS as monarchical.

In April 2005, 14 PDS members of parliament announced their intention to leave the party and form a new group, the Forces of Change. After it was ruled that the 14 would have to resign their seats and campaign in special elections, they returned to the PDS. In May the Convention of Democrats and Patriots (*Convention des Démocrates et des Patriotes*—CDP) merged with the PDS. Also known as *Garab-Gi* ("The Cure"), the CDP was founded in May 1992 by Iba Der THIAM, a former education minister and UNESCO Executive Council member. In December 1994 the CDP and the RND (below) issued a joint statement rejecting the Uniting to Change coalition's call for the drafting of a national consensus program, describing it as a self-serving PDS maneuver. However, after Thiam secured 1.2 percent of the vote in the first round of the 2000 presidential poll, he threw his support behind Wade in the second round, becoming the coordinator of the FAL. The CDP, noted for its antipoverty platform and, more recently, an increasingly Islamic orientation, secured one seat as a member of the *Sopi* Coalition in the 2001 legislative balloting before joining the PDS.

Wade's main political rival within the PDS, Idrissa Seck, was dismissed as prime minister in April 2004. In August, Seck was also dismissed from his post as PDS executive secretary, and he and several of his supporters were expelled from the party. In November 2007 former prime minister Macky SALL, and then speaker of the assembly, was dismissed from his post as a deputy secretary general of the party, reportedly because he was perceived to be a threat to plans for Wade's son to be the future leader of the party. In November 2008 Sall was voted out of the speakership by the PDS. Sall subsequently formed a new political party, **Alliance for the Republic–Hope** (*Alliance pour le République–Yaakar*—APR-*Yakaar*, see above), which joined the BSS opposition coalition in the 2009 local elections. Reports indicated that three factions had emerged within the party: the first led by Karim WADE, the second supportive of Pape Dion, and the third under former presidential advisor Moustapha DIAKHATE.

Wade reconciled with Seck in an effort to consolidate the party ahead of municipal elections in 2009, but the party suffered significant losses, including the defeat of Senate Speaker Pape Diop in his reelection bid as mayor of Dakar.

Wade announced in July 2010 that he intended to run for the presidency again in 2012. This set off a constitutional debate and disagreements within the party since presidents were limited to two terms. However, Wade's supporters within the PDS argued that since the term of office had been changed from five years to seven years, the incumbent had not served two full terms. In April 2011 Seck was expelled from the party after he announced his public opposition to Wade's 2012 presidential candidacy. Seck subsequently launched an independent presidential campaign.

Wade lost the 2012 presidential election, and the PDS only secured 12 seats in the subsequent assembly balloting after a group of dissidents broke from the party to form the United for a Common Vision Coalition (*Bokk Gis Gis*).

In April 2013 Karim Wade was arrested on corruption charges that much of his estimated personal fortune of $1.4 billion was illicitly gained through misuse of office. The arrest prompted protests and demonstrations in Dakar by the PDS.

Authorities arrested PDS party member Samuel Amète Sarr in August 2014 for libeling Sall after he accused Sall on social media of financial misconduct. In September tensions mounted between PIT and PDS leadership. Wade declared that a member of his family would lead Senegal in 2017 and PIT leader Dansokho accused Wade of having plotted a coup during the 2012 elections.

On June 23, 2016, Karim Wade received a presidential pardon and was released from prison. He was subsequently named as the party's candidate for the 2019 presidential elections.

Leaders: Abdoulaye WADE (Secretary General of the Party and Former President of the Republic), Pape DIOP (Speaker of the Senate).

African Party for Democracy and Socialism/*And Jëf* (*Parti Africain pour la Démocratie et le Socialisme/And Jëf*—PADS/AJ). The PADS/AJ was formed in 1991 by merger of the **Revolutionary Movement for the New Democracy** (*Mouvement Révolutionnaire pour la Démocratie Nouvelle*—MRDN) and two other left-wing groups, the **People's Democratic Union** (*Union pour la Démocratie Populaire*—UDP) and the **Socialist Workers' Organization** (*Organisation Socialiste des Travailleurs*—OST).

Also known as *And Jëf,* a Wolof expression meaning "to unite for a purpose," the MRDN was a populist southern party of the extreme left that included former socialists and Maoists. It was permitted to register in June 1981 but joined the 1983 and 1984 election boycotts. The UDP was organized in 1981 by a pro-Albanian MRDN splinter group, while the OST was a small Marxist-Leninist formation launched in 1982.

Landing Savane ran a distant third as the 1993 presidential nominee of the PADS/AJ. For the May legislative balloting, the party participated with the RND (see below) in a **Let Us Unite** (*Jappoo Liggeeyal*) **Senegal** coalition that won three assembly seats. In November Savane was arrested for organizing a demonstration against the Diouf administration's economic austerity program. Given a suspended sentence for the incident, the PADS leader was rearrested in February 1994 and, along with Wade, he was subsequently convicted of provoking antigovernment riots.

The PADS/AJ captured four seats in the 1998 legislative balloting; subsequently, it cooperated with the PIT and PLS to run a joint slate of candidates in the January 1999 Senate elections under the banner of "*And Fippu.*" After supporting Abdoulaye Wade of the PDS in the 2000 presidential campaign, the PADS/AJ secured two seats in the 2001 legislative poll and joined the PDS-led parliamentary faction. Savane and Mamadou DIOP were given posts in subsequent PDS-led governments.

Savane was the PADS/AJ candidate in the 2007 presidential election, in which he secured a little more than 2 percent of the vote. The PADS/AJ was the main component of the **Build Senegal Together** (*And Defar Sénégal*) coalition that secured three seats in the assembly in 2007. In 2007, divisions within the party emerged between the supporters of Savané and a group led by Madièye MBODJ that criticized the leadership for abandoning the core principles of the party. PADS/AJ won one senate seat in the 2007 balloting. In 2008 Savané was appointed a minister of state and party official Mamadou Diop DECROIX was appointed commerce minister. Following the 2009 municipal elections, both Savané and Diop lost their positions during a cabinet reshuffle. Subsequently under Savané the PADS/AJ joined the BBY coalition and Decroix moved into the opposition. Decroix was expelled from the party in 2009 during an internal feud with Savané. Decroix rejoined the party in 2012 and took over the leadership.

The PADS/AJ supported Sall in the 2012 presidential balloting and won one seat in the July legislative polling. PADS/AJ joined the **Patriotic Front for the Defense of the Republic** (Front Patriotique pour la Défense de la République—FPDR) coalition, and in September 2014, Decroix met with the opposition grouping M23 leader Mamadou Mbodj.

Leader: Mamadou Diop DECROIX (Secretary General).

Union for Democratic Renewal (*Union pour le Renouveau Démocratique*—URD). The URD, originally styled the **Democratic Renewal** (*Renouveau Démocratique*—RD), was formed by former interior minister Djibo Ka in November 1997 to act as a reform group within the PS; however, in December, Ka and ten of his dissident colleagues were suspended from the PS for three months. Subsequently, Ka declared his intention to forward an independent list of candidates for legislative balloting in May 1998. In March 1998 the PS rejected Ka's list, and on April 1 he resigned from the group and formally launched the URD. Having emerged from the 1998 legislative polling with 11 seats, the URD presented Ka as its candidate in the first round of the 2000 presidential election. He finished fourth and surprisingly threw his support to Abdou Diouf in the second round. A split in the URD regarding that decision (one faction joined the *Sopi* Coalition) apparently contributed to the URD's decline to three seats following the 2001 legislative poll.

Ka was appointed minister of state for fisheries in the Sall government and reappointed to a post in the Soumaré cabinet. Following a 2007 cabinet reshuffle, Ka became minister of state for the environment and protection of nature, reservoirs, and artificial lakes. He retained that post in the new government formed after the 2009 municipal elections and in subsequent cabinet reshuffles through the summer of 2011. Ka won the URD's sole seat in the 2012 legislative balloting. Once in the assembly, he declined to join the formal opposition grouping. In March 2014 a power struggle emerged between Ka and URD communications officer and leader of the youth section Badara POUYE.

Leader: Djibo KA (Secretary General and 2000 presidential candidate).

Other parties that won seats in the 2012 Assembly elections included: **United for a Common Vision Coalition** (*Bokk Gis Gis*); the **Citizen Movement for Reform** (*Mouvement Citoyen pour la Réforme Nationale*—MCRN); the **Republican Movement for Socialism and Democracy** (*Mouvement Républicain pour le Socialisme et la

Démocratie—MRSD); the **Party for Truth and Development** (*Parti pour la Vérité et le Développement*—PVD), led by Kara MBACKE; the **Senegalese Patriotic Movement** (*Sénégalais Mouvement Patriotique*—SMP); **Patriotic Convergence for Justice and Equity** (*Convergence Patriotique pour la Justice et l'Équité*—CPJE-Nay Leer); the **Party for the Emergence of Citizens** (*Parti pour l'Émergence de Citoyens*—Tekki 2012); ***Deggo Souxali Transport ak Commerce***; the **Enlighten the People** (*Leeral Askanwi*).

Other Parties Contesting the 2012 Legislative Elections:

Other parties that contested the 2012 Assembly elections (none received more than 1 percent of the vote), included: the **Rally of Ecologists of Senegal** (*Rassemblement des Écologists du Sénégal*—RES), led by Ousmane Sow HUCHARD; the **Democratic Alliance** (*Alliance Démocratique*); the **Authentic Socialist Party** (*Parti Socialiste-Authentique*—PS-A), led by Souty TOURÉ; the **Allied Coalition of the People** (*Coalition Alliée du Peuple*—CAP 21); the **And Taxawal Askan Wi Coalition**, led by Abdourahim AGNE; the **Lii Dal Na Xel Coalition;** and the **Booloo Taxawu Askan Wi Coalition.**

Other Parties and Groups:

Smaller pro-Wade formations include the **Senegalese Democratic Rally** (*Rassemblement Démocratique Sénegalais*—RDS); the **Union of Senegalese Patriots**; the **Popular Democratic Rally** (*Rassemblement Démocratique Populaire*—RDP); the **Democratic Union for Federalism/Mboloomi** (*Union Démocratique pour le Fédéralisme/Mboloomi*—UDF/Mboloomi); and the **Union for Democratic Renewal/Front for Change** (*Union pour le Renouveau Démocratique/Front pour l'Alternance*—URD/FAL).

Front for Socialism and Democracy–Unite and Correct (*Front pour le Socialisme et la Démocratie–Benno Jubël*—FSD-JB). Launched under the direction of a prominent Muslim leader, Cheikh Abdoulaye Dieye, the FSD-JB captured one seat in the 1998 legislative balloting on a platform emphasizing care for the elderly and women. Dieye captured 1 percent of the first-round vote in the 2000 presidential election, and the FSD-JB subsequently joined the FAL. Cheikh Bamba DIEYE succeeded his father as party leader following the former's death in 2002.

The younger Dieye received less than 1 percent of the vote in the 2007 presidential balloting, while the party gained one seat in the assembly in 2007. The FSD-JB participated in the opposition BSS coalition in the 2009 municipal elections, in which party leader Dieye was elected mayor of Saint-Louis. Dieye publicly opposed the proposed constitutional amendment to create an elected vice president. Dieye placed sixth in presidential balloting in 2012. Dieye was appointed minister of communication and information technology in October 2012. Dieye was not reelected mayor of Saint Louis in June 2014, and in August Mayor Mansour FAYE accused Dieye of providing salaries to 121 phantom employees. Dieye denied the accusation.

Leader: Cheikh Bamba DIEYE (2007 and 2012 presidential candidate).

Alliance *Jëf Jël*. Formerly known as the **Alliance for Progress and Justice/*Jëf Jël***, this grouping adopted its current name at a party congress in June 2000. Party leader Talla Sylla placed eighth in the 2007 presidential balloting, but was the sole party member elected to the National Assembly. He subsequently announced his intention to retire as party president in June for health reasons but has remained at the helm of the party after he emerged as one of the most visible leaders of the opposition. The party joined the BSS coalition for the 2009 local elections. The party joined the small Benno Alliance 2012 and supported Abdou Latif COULIBALY for the 2012 presidential election, but the candidate withdrew a month before the balloting. In July 2014 Sylla was elected mayor of Thiès. *Jëf Jël* was also a member of the **Action for the Renaissance** coalition (*Action pour la Renaissance/Wallu Askanu Senegal*—AR/WA Senegal, also called *Aar Senegaal*). In August *Jëf Jël* joined the And Defar Coalition of Thiès alongside Rewmi leader Idrissa Seck.

Leaders: Talla SYLLA (President), Moussa TINE.

National Democratic Rally (*Rassemblement National Démocratique*—RND). Established in February 1976, the RND described itself as a "party of the masses." It applied, without success, for recognition in September 1977, and two years later its founder, Cheikh Anta DIOP (who died in 1986), was ordered to stand trial for engaging in unauthorized party activity. The RND was legalized in June 1981; it subsequently repeatedly criticized the government for its position on Chad and for its "systematic alignment with the positions of France and the United States." Evincing an anti-Wade orientation, the RND retained its single legislative seat in 2001, although it garnered only 0.7 percent of the vote. In June 2006 the party's sole deputy in the assembly resigned in protest over the postponement of legislative elections. The party boycotted the 2007 elections. After the boycott, Diouf was reported to have announced his retirement from politics. The RND was a member of the BSS coalition in the 2009 balloting. In February 2014 RND spoke out against the findings presented in a report published by the National Commission for Institutional Reform's (CNRI) (see Constitution and government, above).

Leader: Dialo DIOP (Secretary General).

Other parties that gained seats in the 2007 election include the **Rally for the People** (*Rassemblement pour le Peuple*—RP); the **Reform Movement for Social Development** (*Mouvement de la Réforme pour le Développement Social*—MRDS), led by Mbaye NIANG, which initially joined the BSS in the 2009 municipal balloting but withdrew from the coalition prior to the elections because of differences with the PS; **Convergence for Renewal and Citizenship** (*La Convergence pour le Renouveau et la Citoyenneté*—CRC), led by Aliou DIA; the **National Patriotic Union** (*Union Nationale Patriotique*—UNP), led by Me Ndèye FATOU TOURÉ; and the **Social Democrat Party–The Sun** (*Parti Social-Démocrate–Jant Bi*—PSD-JB), led by Mamour CISSE.

Other parties include the **Party of Renewal and Citizenship** (*Parti de la Renaissance et de la Citoyenneté*—PRC); the **Assembly of African Workers–Senegal** (*Rassemblement des Travailleurs Africains–Sénégal*—RTA-S), a social-democratic party recognized in March 1997 and a member of the BSS coalition in 2009; the **Movement for Democracy and Socialism/*Naxx Jarinu*** (*Mouvement pour la Démocratie et le Socialisme/Naxx Jarinu*—MDS/NJ); the **Union for the Republic** (*Union pour la République*—UPR); the **Social Democratic Party/*Jant-Bi***; the **Democratic Union of Progressive Patriotic Forces** (*Union Démocratique des Forces Progressistes Patriotiques*—UDFP); the **Citizens' Movement for a Democracy of Development** (*Mouvement des Citoyens pour une Démocratie de Développement*); the **Action Front for Renewal/The Way** (*Front d'Action pour le Renouveau/Yoon Wi*—FAR/*Yoon Wi*), led by Bathie SECK; the **Gainde Centrist Bloc** (*Bloc des Gainde Centristes*—BGC); the **Reform Party** (*Parti de la Réforme*—PR); the **Rally for Unity and Peace** (*Rassemblement pour l'Unité et la Paix*—RUP); **The Nation** (*Rewmi*), formed by former Prime Minister Idrissa SECK, who placed second in national polling as the party's 2007 presidential candidate (*Rewmi* boycotted the 2007 legislative elections) and fifth in the 2012 presidential balloting; and the **Senegalese People's Party** (*Parti Populaire Sénégalais*—PPS), which was legalized in 1981 and was part of the BSS coalition in the 2009 local elections.

For information on the **Senegalese Democratic Union–Renewal** (*Union Démocratique Sénégalais–Rénovation*—UDS-R), the **Senegalese Republican Movement** (*Mouvement Républicain Sénégalais*—MRS), and the **Party for the African Renaissance** (*Parti pour la Renaissance Africaine*—PARENA), see the 2009 *Handbook*. For more on the **Action for National Development** (*Action pour le Développement National*—ADN), **Senegalese Republican Party** (*Parti Sénégalais Républicain*—PSR), the **Engagement and Reconstruction of Senegal Coalition** (*Takku Defaraat Sénégal*), **The Field** (*Waar Wi*), and the **Senegalese Patriotic Rally** (*Rassemblement Patriotique Sénégalais–Jammi Rewmi*—RPS-JR), see the 2012 *Handbook*. For information on the **Movement for Socialism and Unity** (*Mouvement pour le Socialisme et l'Unité*—MSU); and **African Independence Party** (*Parti Africain de l'Indépendance*—PAI), see the 2014 *Handbook*.

Illegal Groups:

Movement of Democratic Forces of Casamance (*Mouvement des Forces Démocratiques de la Casamance*—MFDC). The MFDC was launched as a clandestine grouping advocating the secession of the Casamance region of southern Senegal. Many supporters, including MFDC leader Fr. Augustin Diamacoune Senghor, were jailed following demonstrations in the provincial capital of Ziguinchor in the early 1980s, and another 152 people were arrested in 1986 for allegedly attending a secret MFDC meeting. Diamacoune and most of the other detainees were subsequently released. However, new MFDC-army clashes were reported in late 1988.

In mid-1990 Diamacoune and most other MFDC civilian leaders were arrested or forced into exile following a resurgence of separatist violence spearheaded by *Attika* ("Fighter"), the MFDC's military wing. The uprising, which the separatists claimed was the result of their being economically and socially marginalized, continued through late 1990. However, in May 1991, following a series of secret meetings with ethnic Diola parliamentarians negotiating on Diouf's behalf, MFDC leaders agreed to a cease-fire and disarmament. Reports of the negotiations supported observers' suspicions that the separatists encompassed a limited number (300–500) of ethnic Diolas.

In April and May 1992 renewed separatist activity was attributed to a militant MFDC splinter and despite an escalating verbal confrontation between Dakar and the MFDC leadership over the military's allegedly heavy-handed response to the violence, the Diouf administration, as late as September, absolved the MFDC leadership of blame for the cease-fire breakdown.

On July 8, 1993, the MFDC signed a cease-fire agreement with the government that included provisions for further negotiations, a bilateral prisoner release, the deployment of French military observers, and the establishment of a refugee repatriation program. However, renewed clashes were reported three days later, and open fighting resumed following the government's killing of an MFDC activist in September. Thereafter, no serious cease-fire violations were reported until January 1995, when a pro-independence faction led by Léopold SANIA rejected the peace accord and resumed guerrilla activities.

In April 1995 the government deployed an additional 1,000 troops in the Casamance region in response to persistent breaches of the cease-fire, including the disappearance of 4 French tourists who were assumed to have been kidnapped by the MFDC. In late April the government announced the arrest of some 50 suspected activists, including Father Diamacoune, and in mid-July the separatists formally abandoned the cease-fire. While Diamacoune's imprisonment served as a rallying point for MFDC faithful during the 1995 crisis, his influence with party militants reportedly had already begun to wane. Subsequently, despite his declaration of a unilateral cease-fire in January 1996, rebel attacks continued throughout the first half of the year.

Fierce fighting broke out in August 1997 as the government responded to renewed rebel activity with a massive offensive, and by late September more than 100 people were reported dead. Meanwhile, the fighting widened the split in the MFDC between the hard-line northern wing, led by Mamadou SANE, and Diamacoune's predominantly southern followers, who were described as prepared to abandon their demand for independence in return for a government promise to speed development of the region. In early 1998 the two factions were reported to be in open conflict. Furthermore, troops from Guinea-Bissau were reportedly laying siege to Sane's longtime safe havens within Bissau's border.

In March 1998 the government claimed to have killed 50 MFDC fighters preparing to attack a village near Ziguinchor. Thereafter, fighting was reported throughout the region during the run-up to legislative polling; however, the government deployed a large number of forces to the area for the balloting period, and few incidents were reported.

Amid reports that the MFDC was preparing to enter into negotiations with the Diouf administration, the group's military and political leaders met in Banjul, Gambia, in April 1999. However, on April 30, 17 people were reported killed in a clash between the rebels and government forces, thus underscoring continued reports that the movement was splintered.

Some MFDC fighters were reported to have disarmed in mid-1999, and another questionable cease-fire was announced late in the year. However, the leadership dispute within the MFDC continued, as did the low-level war between rebels and government troops. Additional negotiations were launched in December 2000, new Senegalese President Abdoulaye Wade having declared resolution of the conflict a top priority for his government. A peace pact was again announced in March 2001. It also appeared that Diamacoune and his supporters had renounced their secessionist stance and instead had agreed to pursue greater autonomy for the region while remaining a part of Senegal. The accord was greeted hopefully by many observers, especially following a face-to-face meeting between Wade and Diamacoune and the MFDC's call for fighters to lay down their guns for the April national legislative balloting. Banditry and sporadic killings continued, however, precluding finalization of a permanent settlement.

At a mid-2001 MFDC congress, Diamacoune became the group's president, a role considered more ceremonial in nature than his previous post. Meanwhile, Sidi Badji, a hard-liner rival to Diamacoune, was reportedly named head of military affairs. Badji subsequently claimed the secretary general's position, and the power struggle between his "radical" faction (which also included military commander Salif SADIO) and Diamacoune's "peacemaking" faction continued into mid-2002. On September 19, 2004, Diamacoune became honorary president, while Biagui became the effective leader of the MFDC.

The MFDC signed a peace agreement with the government on December 30, 2004, and it announced plans to reestablish itself as a legitimate political party and contest legislative elections in 2007. However, in March 2006 the Sadio-led faction of the MFDC initiated attacks against other MFDC groupings. In response, security forces from Guinea-Bissau launched an offensive against MFDC positions in an attempt to end the factional fighting.

On January 14, 2007, Diamacoune died of natural causes in a Paris hospital, creating an unresolved internal struggle over the leadership of the MFDC. In December a faction of the MFDC assassinated a presidential envoy during negotiations over Casamance. The attack was condemned by most of the leadership of the MFDC. There was sporadic fighting between the MFDC and government forces in May 2008. During summer 2009 there was a significant increase in violence in the region, which reports attributed to younger members of the MFDC who opposed a settlement with the government. In response, in March 2010 the Senegalese military launched a new campaign in the region. That month, Cesar Atoute BADIATE, the leader of one MFDC faction agreed to talks with the government as long as they were hosted by a neutral country. However, other MFDC leaders rejected negotiations. In August Wade formally requested that Gambia assume a formal role in a negotiated settlement with the MFDC. Meanwhile, new fighting erupted in August in Diango between the MFDC and government security forces.

After the election of Sall in 2012, the MFDC announced it was willing to reenter negotiations with the government; however, new fighting broke out in July along the Gambian border. In July the MFDC freed nine hostages who were working as part of a demining operation. They had been captured in May. Following negotiations with Senegal in August, Gambia announced it would pardon two suspected Senegalese MFDC members who had been sentenced to death. Suspected MFDC members kidnapped and subsequently released nine community public health workers and a soldier Bafata on border with Guinea Bissau on August 26, 2014. Following secret talks at the Vatican, Badji signed a cease-fire agreement on May 1, 2014.

Leaders: Mamadou SANE, Sidi BADJI, Jean-Marie BIAGUI (Secretary General).

LEGISLATURE

The **Parliament** consists of a National Assembly, which was established in 1963, and a Senate, which was established in 1999, abolished in 2001, and reestablished in 2007.

Senate. Legislation adopted by the assembly in January 2007 mandated the reestablishment of the upper house, the Senate, with 100 members serving five-year terms. Of these 100 senators, 35 (one from each district) are indirectly elected for five-year terms by members of regional, rural, and municipal councils. The remaining 65 senators are appointed by the president.

In balloting (boycotted by most of the main opposition parties) for the 35 elected senators on August 19, 2007, the Senegalese Democratic Party (PDS) won 34 seats, and the African Party for Democracy and Socialism/*And Jëf* won 1. President Wade appointed the remaining 65 members on September 21; most were members of the PDS, although the appointees reportedly included members of opposition parties and a number of independents. In September 2012 MPs voted to abolish the senate to free $15 million for flood assistance and flood prevention. It has not been reestablished.

National Assembly. The assembly currently consists of 150 members, 90 elected on a majoritarian basis at the department level and 60 elected on a proportional basis from national party lists. (The assembly voted in November 2006 to increase its size from 120 to 150 members.) Members serve five-year terms, although the assembly is subject to presidential dissolution after two years.

In the most recent balloting of July 1, 2012, the United in Hope Coalition won 119 seats; the Senegalese Democratic Party, 12; United for a Common Vision Coalition, 4; Citizen Movement for National Reform, 4; Republican Movement for Socialism and Democracy, 2; Party for Truth and Development, 2; Union for Democratic Renewal, 1; Senegalese Patriotic Movement, 1; Patriotic Convergence for Justice and Equity, 1; Party for the Emergence of Citizens, 1; *Deggo Souxali Transport ak Commerce*, 1; Enlighten the People, 1; and African Party for Democracy and Socialism/*And Jëf*, 1.

President: Moustapha NIASSE.

CABINET

[as of July 1, 2016]

Prime Minister	Mohammed Abdallah Dione (ind.)
Ministers	
African Integration Project of NEPAD and the Promotion of Good Governance	Khadim Diop
Agriculture and Rural Equipment	Papa Abdoulaye Seck
Armed Forces	Augustin Tine
Commerce, Informal Sector, and Handicrafts	Alioune Sarr
Culture and Communication	Mbagnick Ndiaye
Education	Serigne Mbaye Thiam
Energy and Renewable Energy Development	Maïmouna Ndoye Seck [f]
Environment and Sustainable Development	Abdoulaye Baldé
Finance, Planning, and Economy	Amadou Ba
Fisheries and Maritime Affairs	Oumar Guèye
Foreign Affairs and Senegalese Abroad	Mankeur Ndiaye
Health and Social Action	Awa Marie Coll Seck [f]
Higher Education and Research	Marie-Tew Niane [f]
Industry and Mines	Ngouille Aly Ndiaye
Infrastructure and Land Transport	Mansour Elimane Kane
Interior and Public Security	Abdoulaye Daouda Diallo
Investment Promotion and Development of State Tele-Services	Khoudia Mbaye [f]
Justice	Sidiki Kaba
Livestock	Aminata Mbengue Ndiaye [f]
Planning and Local Government	Oumar Youm
Posts and Telecommunications	Abdoul Yaya Kane
Professional Training, Apprenticeships, and Handicrafts	Mamadou Talla
Public Service, Labor, and Relations with Institutions	Mansour Sy
Public Service Rationalization	Viviane Laure Elisabeth Bampassy [f]
Sport	Matar Ba
Tourism and Air Transport	Abdoulaye Diouf Sarr
Urban Renewal, Living Environment, and Housing	Diene Farba Sarr
Water and Sanitation	Mansour Faye
Women, Family, and Childhood	Mariama Sarr [f]
Youth, Training, and Employment	Mame Mbaye Niang
Ministers Delegate	
Economy and Finance, in Charge of Budget	Birima Mangara
Urban Renewal, Housing and the Living Environment	Fatou Tambedou [f]
Women, Family and Childhood, Head of Microfinance and Solidarity Economy Department	Moustapha Diop

[f] = female

INTERGOVERNMENTAL REPRESENTATION

Ambassador to the U.S.: Babacar DIAGNE.

U.S. Ambassador to Senegal: James Peter ZUMWALT.

Permanent Representative to the UN: Fodé SECK.

IGO Memberships (Non-UN): AfDB, AU, ECOWAS, ICC, IOM, NAM, OIC, WTO.

For Further Reference:

Diouf, Mamadou. *Tolerance, Democracy, and Sufis in Senegal.* New York: Columbia University Press, 2013.

Jones, Holly. *The Métis of Senegal: Urban Life and Politics in French West Africa.* Bloomington: Indiana University Press, 2013.

Theobald, Anne. "Successful or Failed Rebellion? The Casamance Conflict from a Framing Perspective." *Civil Wars*. 17, no. 2 (June 2015), 181–200.

SERBIA

Republic of Serbia
Republika Srbija

Political Status: Incorporated in the Kingdom of the Serbs, Croats, and Slovenes, which was constituted as an independent monarchy on December 1, 1918, and formally renamed Yugoslavia on October 3, 1929; became constituent republic of the communist Federal People's Republic of Yugoslavia, instituted November 29, 1945, and then of the Socialist Federal Republic of Yugoslavia, proclaimed April 7, 1963; continued as constituent republic, along with Montenegro, of the Federal Republic of Yugoslavia (FRY), proclaimed April 27, 1992; included in the "state union" of Serbia and Montenegro, established February 4, 2003, under new Constitutional Charter; proclaimed as the independent Republic of Serbia on June 5, 2006, following Montenegro's declaration of independence on June 3; currently governed under new constitution approved by referendum on October 28–29, 2006, and formally adopted by the National Assembly on November 8. (Serbia's Autonomous Province of Kosovo and Metohija was placed under administration of the United Nations Interim Administrative Mission in Kosovo with effect from June 14, 1999, by authorization of United Nations Security Council Resolution 1244. The autonomous province declared independence as the Republic of Kosovo on February 17, 2008, an action unrecognized by Serbia, which labeled it as illegal and in violation of international principles of sovereignty and territorial integrity.)

Area: 34,116 sq. mi. (88,361 sq. km). Included are the autonomous provinces of Kosovo and Metohija, 4,211 sq. mi. (10,908 sq. km), and Vojvodina, 8,304 sq. mi. (21,506 sq. km).

Population: 8,813,000 (2016E—UN, includes Kosovo and Metohija); 7,143,921 (2016E—U.S. Census).

Major Urban Centers (2014E—UN): BELGRADE (1,363,611), Novi Sad (Vojvodina, 284,230), Niš (186,568).

Official Languages: Serbian. National minorities may officially use their languages in localities where they comprise at least 15 percent of the population.

Monetary Unit: Dinar (market rate October 1, 2016: 109.49 dinars = $1US).

President: Tomislav NIKOLIĆ (elected as the candidate of the Serbian Progressive Party, from which he resigned following his election); elected in second-round voting on May 20, 2012, and inaugurated for a five-year term on May 31, succeeding Boris TADIĆ (Democratic Party), who resigned on April 5, 2012. Slavica DJUKIĆ-DEJANOVIĆ (Socialist Party of Serbia) served as acting president between April 5 and May 31.

Prime Minister: Aleksandar VUČIĆ (Serbian Progressive Party); nominated by the president April 22, 2014, following the National

Assembly election of March 16; confirmed by the National Assembly on April 27, succeeding Ivica DAČIĆ (Serbian Socialist Party); nominated for a second term by the president on May 23, 2016, following the National Assembly elections of April 24; confirmed by the National Assembly on August 11.

THE COUNTRY

The Republic of Serbia, encompassing approximately 35 percent of pre-1992 Yugoslavia's area, is a landlocked Balkan state. While it has a Serb ethnic majority of 83 percent, Serbs are unevenly distributed. There have been particularly destabilizing effects in Serbia's Kosovo and Metohija Province, more than 90 percent of whose 2.2 million inhabitants are ethnic Albanians, and in the Sandžak region of western Serbia, where half the population are Bosniak Muslims. Serbia's Vojvodina Province, in the north, has a notable ethnic Hungarian minority (some 4 percent of the country's total population). Eastern Orthodox Christianity predominates, with regional Muslim and Roman Catholic Vojvodina minorities.

Mostly underdeveloped before World War II, Yugoslavia, comprising six constituent republics (Bosnia and Herzegovina, Croatia, Macedonia, Montenegro, Serbia, and Slovenia), made rapid advances after 1945 under a Communist regime that applied pragmatic and flexible methods of economic management.

Political transition and the outbreak of regional conflict in mid-1991 caused the economy to deteriorate rapidly, the decline being aggravated by the imposition of economic sanctions against the new Federal Republic of Yugoslavia (FRY, encompassing the constituent republics of Serbia and Montenegro) by the United Nations from May 1992 until November 1995. Substantial currency devaluations were undertaken in early 1992, with inflation soaring to a historically unprecedented rate of 1 million percent a month by December 1993. The "super dinar," introduced in January 1994, was valued at 13 million old dinars and had the effect of ending hyperinflation. The GDP of Serbia and Montenegro declined by more than 40 percent in the period 1990–1995. For the rest of the decade, growth averaged only about 2 percent annually.

Beginning in early 1998, escalating violence in Kosovo led to a renewal of international sanctions and then to a bombing campaign conducted by the North Atlantic Treaty Organization (NATO) in March–June 1999, severely damaging Serbia's economic infrastructure. In late September the government claimed that the NATO air war had caused $100 billion in damage, compared to the $30 billion to $50 billion estimated by international sources. According to FRY government figures, GDP declined by 16 percent in 1999 because of the Kosovo conflict but increased by 5 percent in 2000. (Beginning in 2000 basic economic statistics have excluded Kosovo.) Output nevertheless stood at only half of its 1989 level, and 30 percent of the labor force was unemployed. From 2006 to 2008, GDP grew at an average of 5.8 percent. In 2009 GDP fell by 4 percent due to reductions in trade, consumer demand, output, and fiscal revenues during the global economic downturn, but annual average growth of 1.3 percent returned in 2010–2011.

In 2013 Serbia's agricultural sector accounted for about 8 percent of GDP and employed about 24 percent of the active labor force. Leading crops include wheat, maize, sunflowers, and sugar beets. Industry contributed about 32 percent of GDP and engaged 17 percent of workers. Major exports have included iron and steel, rubber, textiles, agricultural products, and nonferrous metals.

Inflation has averaged more than 10 percent annually from 2006 through 2011. Unemployment has eased from 1999 levels, but has remained either near or higher than 20 percent from 2010 through 2016. GDP contracted in 2012 by 1.5 percent, rebounding to 2.6 percent growth in 2013 but falling once again by 1.8 percent in 2014. The International Monetary Fund (IMF) estimated GDP fell by 0.5 percent in 2015 and grew by 1.5 percent in 2016. In 2016 inflation was estimated to be 4 percent, while GDP per capita was $21,960.

GOVERNMENT AND POLITICS

Political background. The Kingdom of the Serbs, Croats, and Slovenes, was formed on December 1, 1918, under the Serbian House of Karadjordjević. Uniting the independent kingdoms of Serbia and Montenegro with the Croatian, Dalmatian, and Bosnian and Herzegovinian territories previously ruled by Austria-Hungary, the new entity (formally renamed Yugoslavia on October 3, 1929) was ruled between World Wars I and II as a highly centralized, Serb-dominated state in which the Croats became an increasingly disaffected minority. The Serb–Croat antagonism, which caused many Croats to sympathize with Nazi Germany and Fascist Italy, continued even after the two Axis powers attacked and occupied the country in April 1941 and set up a pro-Axis puppet state of Croatia that included most of Bosnia and Herzegovina.

Wartime resistance to the Axis was led by two rival groups, the pro-royalist Chetniks, under Gen. Draža MIHAILOVIĆ, and the Communist-inspired Partisans, led by Marshal Josip Broz TITO, a Croat who sought to enlist all the country's national groups in the liberation struggle. The Partisans' greater effectiveness in opposing the occupation forces and securing Allied aid paved the way for their assumption of power at the end of the war. In March 1945 Tito became prime minister in a government of national unity; eight months later, on November 29, the monarchy was abolished and a Federal People's Republic of Yugoslavia, based on the equality of the country's principal national groups, was proclaimed. On January 14, 1953, under a new constitution, Tito was elected president of the republic.

Yugoslavia developed along orthodox Communist lines until 1948, when its refusal to submit to Soviet directives led to its expulsion from the Communist bloc and the imposition of a political and economic blockade by the Soviet Union and its East European allies. Aided by Western arms and economic support, Yugoslavia maintained its autonomy throughout the Stalin era and by the late 1950s had achieved a partial reconciliation with the Soviet-led Warsaw Pact states, although it still insisted on complete independence and the right to find its own "road to socialism." A federal constitution promulgated in 1963 consolidated the system of "social self-management" by attempting to draw the people into economic and administrative decision-making at all levels; it also expanded the independence of the judiciary, increased the responsibilities of the federal legislature and those of the country's six constituent republics and two autonomous provinces (Kosovo and Metohija, and Vojvodina), and widened freedom of choice in elections.

In May 1980 Marshal Tito, president for life of the republic and of the League of Communists of Yugoslavia (*Savez Komunista Jugoslavija*—SKJ), died at age 87. The leadership of state and party thereupon passed to collegial executives—the eight-member State Presidency and the eight-member Presidium of the SKJ Central Committee. Yugoslavia's six republics and two autonomous provinces were equally represented in both. Through the 1980s the president of the State Presidency and the president of the Presidium rotated on an annual basis.

During 1990 both the federal government and the SKJ experienced acute crises as economic ills exacerbated long-standing political animosities. An SKJ congress that convened in January 1990 was forced to adjourn because of a split over introduction of a multiparty system. Croatia and Slovenia both subsequently conducted open legislative elections in which the SKJ's republic-level affiliates were defeated.

The situation was further aggravated in May when the hard-line Borisav JOVIĆ of Serbia became president of the State Presidency.

In July 1990 Slovenia and Macedonia declared their "full sovereignty" within Yugoslavia, while Croatia approved constitutional changes having much the same effect. In Serbia, a majority of voters endorsed a new Serbian constitution that, contrary to the federal document, effectively stripped the provinces of Kosovo and Vojvodina of autonomous status. Concurrently, ethnic Albanian delegates to the Kosovo Assembly declared their province independent of Serbia and a constituent republic of the Yugoslav federation. Serbia responded three days later by dissolving the Kosovo legislature. In a series of multiparty elections during November and December, former Communists won overwhelmingly in Serbia and Montenegro but were decisively defeated in Bosnia and Herzegovina.

The elections occurred at a time of mounting confrontation between the government of Croatia and the Serb-dominated Yugoslav National Army (*Jugoslovenske Narodne Armije*—JNA). In January 1991 Croatia and Slovenia concluded a mutual defense pact. In February the Slovene Assembly voted for phased secession from the federation. Shortly thereafter, the Serb-populated regions of Croatia opted for effective secession from that republic, prior to proclaiming at year's end a self-styled "Republic of Serbian Krajina."

In June 1991 the presidents of the six constituent republics were reported to have agreed to a plan whereby the republics would retain sovereignty within Yugoslavia but would not seek international recognition as independent states. However, the relatively prosperous Slovenes subsequently indicated their unwillingness to continue financial support for the less-developed republics, while Croatia feared that its sizable Serbian minority would force geographic dismemberment if it remained in the federation. As a result, the two western republics declared their independence on June 25.

That the federation had in fact expired was quickly apparent in the failure of the JNA to mount real opposition to Slovenia's secession, while JNA engagement in Croatia was mainly directed to backing local Serbs against Croatian government forces. By late August 1991 the conflict had cost Croatia nearly one-third of its territory, although some was later retaken. On September 8 Macedonians voted overwhelmingly in favor of establishing a sovereign and independent Macedonia. Bosnia and Herzegovina followed suit, issuing a declaration of sovereignty on October 15. On December 5 Croatia's Stjepan MESIĆ resigned as president of the State Presidency, stating, "Yugoslavia no longer exists." The Croatian Assembly backdated the action to October 8, when its declaration of independence formally came into effect.

On January 15, 1992, one day after the advance contingent of a UN peacekeeping force had arrived in Yugoslavia, the European Community (EC, subsequently the European Union—EU) recognized the independence of Croatia and Slovenia. In contrast, on February 12 Serbia and Montenegro agreed to join in upholding "the principles of a common state which would be a continuation of Yugoslavia." In a referendum held February 29–March 1, Bosnia and Herzegovina opted for independence, and on March 26 Macedonia moved in the same direction by securing the withdrawal of JNA forces from its territory.

On April 27, 1992, a rump Federal Assembly adopted the constitution of a new Federal Republic of Yugoslavia (FRY), under which elections for a successor assembly were held in Serbia and Montenegro in May. The Socialist Party of Serbia (*Socijalistička Partija Srbije*—SPS), led by the president of Serbia, Slobodan MILOŠEVIĆ, won a slim majority in the new lower house, the Chamber of Citizens, in part because opposition elements, including the new Democratic Movement of Serbia coalition (*Demokratska Pokret Srbije*—Depos) boycotted the balloting. On June 15 the assembly elected Dobrica ĆOSIĆ, a well-known writer and political independent, as federal president. Under the new basic law, Ćosić, a Serb, was obligated to name a Montenegrin to the post of prime minister; however, in an unusual move apparently instigated by Milošević in the hope of currying favor in Washington, Ćosić nominated Milan PANIĆ, a wealthy U.S. citizen born in Serbia, who was formally confirmed by the assembly in July.

Milošević soon became increasingly critical of Panić, who, despite his questionable residential qualifications, then ran against Milošević in the Serbian presidential election in December 1992 but was soundly defeated. In the simultaneous legislative election Milošević's SPS maintained its dominance of the Serbian National Assembly. Although the SPS lost ground in the FRY's Federal Assembly, the hard-liners and anti-Panić forces were sufficiently strong to secure the overwhelming passage of a nonconfidence motion against the prime minister.

Amid uncertainty stemming from Panić's refusal to resign, his deputy, Radoje KONTIĆ of Montenegro, was named prime minister in February 1993. Thereafter, as the FRY's international isolation increased because of its involvement in the worsening ethnic conflict in Bosnia and Herzegovina, the ire of the Serbian hard-liners focused on the nonparty federal president, Ćosić, replacing him in June with the chair of the Serbian legislature, Zoran LILIĆ (see the 2012 *Handbook* for details).

Thereafter, Milošević was increasingly aligned with the "greater Serbia" school, although international pressure had obliged him in early May 1993 to accept the Vance-Owen plan for the cantonization of Bosnia and Herzegovina. Milošević was bitterly denounced for his action by the leader of the ultranationalist Serbian Radical Party (*Srpska Radikalna Stranka*—SRS), Vojislav ŠEŠELJ, whose call for a nonconfidence vote forced dissolution of the Serbian National Assembly in October. In the resultant December election, the SPS increased its strength in the 250-member body from 101 to 123 seats, while SRS representation declined from 73 to 39 in a contest that nevertheless saw a marked shift to right-wing nationalist attitudes among the opposition parties. Postelection negotiations led to the formation in March 1994 of a Serbian "cabinet of economists" that was headed by Mirko MARJANOVIĆ (SPS) and also included representation for the New Democracy (*Nova Demokratija*—ND) party.

In 1995 a major offensive by Croatian government forces had recovered most of the "Republic of Serbian Krajina" by early August (see the entry on Croatia). In Yugoslavia, this provoked a storm of criticism directed against Milošević by hard-line Serb leaders. Political difficulties were compounded by the flight of an estimated 200,000 Serbian refugees from Krajina, most of them into Yugoslavia, where many supported opposition demands for the government's ouster. Milošević's muted response to the Croat successes (and to subsequent advances by allied Muslim and Croat forces in Bosnia) was widely seen as in line with his recent policy of distancing the Belgrade government from the Croatian and Bosnian Serbs, in part to secure a settlement that would fully lift UN sanctions on Yugoslavia (see Foreign relations, below).

Serbian relations with the province of Kosovo remained in a state of crisis in 1995 and 1996 as ethnic Albanians, resisting Serbian attempts to impose political, social, and educational control, established an underground administration. Elections to the Kosovo Assembly in May 1992, won by the pro-independence Democratic League of Kosovo (*Lidhja Demokratike e Kosovës*—LDK), had been condemned as illegal by Belgrade, which had officially dissolved the body in 1990. Nevertheless, the LDK leader, Ibrahim RUGOVA, was proclaimed president of a self-declared "Republic of Kosovo," which secured international recognition only from Albania. The local situation deteriorated in December 1994, when Serbian security forces carried out the most sweeping wave of arrests since 1990 in an effort to eliminate the unauthorized police force created by the ethnic Albanians. Tension intensified further in mid-1995 when the Belgrade government announced that Serb refugees from Krajina would be resettled in Kosovo with the aim of redressing the province's ethnic imbalance.

Elections in November 1996 took place amid increasing voter dissatisfaction with government mismanagement, crime, and corruption, as well as with the lack of economic improvement following the suspension a year earlier of UN sanctions. In the election for the federal Chamber of Citizens an SPS-led alliance won 64 of the 138 seats, with the government-aligned Democratic Party of Socialists of Montenegro (*Demokratska Partija Socijalista Crne Gore*—DPSCG) adding another 20 seats. SRS representation fell to 16, while the Together (*Zajedno*) coalition of moderate opposition parties obtained a disappointing 22 seats in the federal contest. In contrast, in mid-November, following a second-round election for local assemblies, the opposition parties claimed victory in most of Serbia's cities, including Belgrade. The SPS-controlled courts and electoral commissions quickly annulled the municipal results, alleging irregularities. In response, the opposition parties, joined by students and later the Serbian Orthodox Church and teachers, staged mass demonstrations of up to 250,000 people in the streets of Belgrade. After 88 days of marches, Milošević, in February 1997, finally felt compelled to have the Serbian National Assembly confirm the opposition victories.

Once in office, however, the opposition found its hands tied, the pro-Milošević bureaucracy having collaborated with departing SPS politicians in the mass transfer of government property from localities to the SPS-dominated Serbian republic. Moreover, by summer the *Zajedno* coalition had collapsed, its constituent parties having failed to agree on a common candidate to oppose Milošević for the presidency of Yugoslavia. (He was constitutionally barred from running for a third term as president of Serbia.) Thus, in July 1997 the federal legislature elected an unopposed Milošević as federal president. Two months later, in Serbia's parliamentary elections, Milošević's SPS and allies won a plurality of seats but were faced with having to rely on either the second-place SRS or the third-place opposition Serbian Renewal Movement (*Srpski Pokret Obnove*—SPO) for a parliamentary majority. After months of negotiations, in March 1998 the SPS and an ally, the Yugoslav Left (*Jugoslovenska Levica*—JUL), formed a government with the SRS under the continued leadership of Prime Minister Marjanović.

In the first round of the Serbian presidential election (held in tandem with the September 1997 parliamentary election), no candidate had won an absolute majority, forcing a runoff between Milošević's hand-picked SPS candidate, Zoran Lilić, and SRS leader Vojislav Šešelj. The results of the October 1997 second round favored Šešelj but were annulled by law as turnout had fallen below 50 percent. New first-round elections were held in early December, with Šešelj facing six candidates, including the SPS's Milan MILUTINOVIĆ. In the runoff two weeks later, Milutinović handily defeated Šešelj with 59 percent of the vote. The election was subsequently characterized as "fundamentally flawed" by the Conference on (later Organization for) Security and Cooperation in Europe (CSCE/OSCE).

Having fallen out of favor with President Milošević, in May 1998 the federal prime minister, Radoje Kontić, after more than five years in office, lost a confidence vote in the upper chamber of the Federal Assembly and was succeeded by Milošević ally and former Montenegrin president Momir BULATOVIĆ of the recently organized Socialist People's Party of Montenegro (*Socijalistička Narodna Partija Crne Gore*—SNPCG). In October 1997 Bulatović had lost a close bid for reelection as Montenegro's president, largely because of a split between pro- and anti-Milošević forces in his previous party, the DPSCG.

By this point, tensions had worsened in Kosovo. Following the murder of four Serbian policemen in February 1998 by members of the separatist Kosovo Liberation Army (KLA), a retaliatory security operation killed 24 ethnic Albanian villagers, many apparently by summary execution. Later in March, ethnic Albanians, in addition to casting ballots for the shadow "Republic of Kosovo" legislature, reelected the LDK's Ibrahim Rugova as shadow president (see entry on Kosovo).

With daily demonstrations continuing in the province, U.S. diplomats succeeded in convincing Milošević and Rugova to meet for the first time in May 1998. Although both sides agreed to initiate weekly talks in Priština, the violence in Kosovo continued to escalate over October to January 1999, despite a cease-fire in December and Milošević's agreement to withdraw in the face of imminent NATO air strikes. In February 1999, peace talks between Serbian officials and ethnic Albanians—including KLA representatives—opened in Rambouillet, France. Cosponsored by France and the United States, the negotiations were aimed at almost complete administrative autonomy for the province with the end of hostilities to be overseen by NATO troops. In March the Kosovar delegation signed the pact, but the Serbian delegation continued to reject the presence of NATO peacekeepers (see entry on Kosovo).

On March 24, 1999, NATO forces from eight countries initiated Operation Allied Force, the most extensive air campaign in Europe since the close of World War II. Serbian forces stepped up a widespread campaign of "ethnic cleansing" that saw the entire Albanian population forced from some cities and villages, creating an immediate refugee crisis at the borders of Albania and Macedonia. By the end of April the refugee exodus was swelling toward 750,000, with additional hundreds of thousands displaced within the province itself.

The main Serbian opposition parties, a number of which had earlier joined various nongovernmental organizations in an umbrella grouping, the Alliance for Change (*Savez za Promene*—SZP), were largely silenced by the country's war footing. The loudest dissenting voice was that of Deputy Prime Minister Vuk DRAŠKOVIĆ of the SPO. Having joined the government in January in a show of national solidarity, he was dismissed in late April for having stated that the populace should be told, contrary to government contentions, "that NATO is not facing a breakdown, that Russia will not help Yugoslavia militarily, and that world public opinion is against us." In Montenegro, President Milo DJUKANOVIĆ (Bulatović's successor) continued his efforts to distance his administration from federal policies. Even though Montenegro was not exempt from the NATO air campaign, and despite rumors that the Serbian military was preparing to depose him, Djukanović rejected orders that the Montenegrin police be placed under the command of the army. Djukanović accused Milošević of using "the pretext of the defense of the country" to displace the civil government.

On May 6, 1999, the Group of Seven countries plus Russia (G-8) proposed a peace plan providing for "deployment in Kosovo of effective international civil and security presences" and formation of an interim provincial administration under the UN Security Council. On June 3 President Milošević accepted the terms of an amended peace agreement offered by President Martii Ahtisaari of Finland and Russia's Viktor Chernomyrdin, including the deployment in Kosovo—but not in the rest of Serbia—of a UN-sponsored, NATO-dominated peacekeeping contingent (Kosovo Force, or KFOR) expected to number some 50,000 troops. The agreement also called for the complete withdrawal of the Serb army, police, and paramilitary forces from Kosovo.

On June 10, 1999, NATO suspended its bombing campaign and the UN Security Council adopted Resolution 1244, authorizing international troop deployment and the establishment of an interim civilian administration in Kosovo. The resolution also reaffirmed Yugoslavia's "sovereignty and territorial integrity" but echoed previous calls for "substantial autonomy and meaningful self-administration in Kosovo." The agreement was widely, though often reluctantly, accepted by most of the opposition, including Serbian nationalists, the principal exception being the SRS, which protested by announcing its withdrawal from the coalition government in Serbia. (The withdrawal was technically prohibited by Serbian president Milutinović because of the state of war.) Meanwhile, on May 27 the International Criminal Tribunal for the former Yugoslavia (ICTY) had indicted Milošević and four others, including the interior minister and army chief of staff, for crimes against humanity related to events in Kosovo.

On June 14, 1999, the UN Security Council received a plan for the civil Kosovo administration that included a new UN Interim Administration in Kosovo (UNMIK). On June 20, with the Yugoslav army having completely withdrawn from Kosovo, NATO formally concluded its bombing campaign. On the same day NATO and the KLA signed an agreement providing for KLA demilitarization. Most of the 1 million or more Kosovo Albanian refugees and displaced persons were already returning to their homes, contributing to the collateral flight from the province of ethnic Serbs, many of whom feared reprisals.

In December 1999 UNMIK announced formation of an Interim Administrative Council (IAC) of Rugova, the KLA's Hashim THAÇI, and Rexhep QOSJA of the United Democratic Movement (*Lëvizja Bashimit Demokratike*—LBD); a fourth seat on the IAC was reserved for a representative of the Serb community, which refused to participate. By then, forensic specialists from the international war crimes tribunal had already exhumed thousands of Albanian bodies from mass graves in Kosovo. (Late in the year, the Albanian death toll was estimated at 4,000–5,000, considerably less than originally projected.)

A federal cabinet reshuffle in August 1999 saw the addition of SRS ministers to the Bulatović administration in an effort to shore up support for Milošević. Political opposition to Milošević nevertheless continued to mount. In January 2000 the SPO's Drašković joined his principal opposition rival, Zoran DJINDJIĆ of the Democratic Party (*Demokratska Stranka*—DS), in forging a unified strategy that was signed by 16 opposition parties.

On April 18, 2000, the Eurocorps, with troop contingents from Germany, Spain, France, Belgium, and Luxembourg, took over control of the Kosovo peacekeeping effort from NATO, but KFOR was encountering increasing difficulty in preventing violent clashes between Albanian and Serb communities. The climate of violence was not, however, limited to Kosovo: in February the Yugoslav defense minister, Pavle BULATOVIĆ, had been assassinated in Belgrade, and in June the SPO's Drašković was wounded in Montenegro.

In a gambit designed to maintain Milošević's hold on power, on July 6, 2000, the SPS pushed through the Federal Assembly constitutional changes authorizing direct election of the president and of the upper legislative house. With most of the opposition continuing a boycott of parliament, the proposals easily received the necessary two-thirds support. The changes, in addition to permitting the incumbent to serve two additional four-year terms, put organization of elections under the FRY instead of the individual republics. On July 8 the Montenegrin assembly described the changes as illegal and "a gross violation of the constitutional rights of the Republic of Montenegro."

On July 27, 2000, Milošević called elections for September, even though his presidential term would not expire until July 2001. The governing coalition in Montenegro quickly announced that it would boycott the balloting. On August 7 the Democratic Opposition of Serbia (*Demokratske Opozicije Srbije*—DOS), ultimately encompassing some 18 parties and a trade union association, nominated Vojislav KOŠTUNICA, leader of the Democratic Party of Serbia (*Demokratska Stranka Srbije*—DSS), as their joint presidential candidate. The SPO, running independently, nominated the mayor of Belgrade, Vojislav MIHAJLOVIĆ, raising the prospect of a split in the opposition vote.

Despite allegations of vote rigging and other irregularities committed by Milošević's supporters, Koštunica emerged from the September 24, 2000, presidential election as the likely leader, although the SPS initially claimed otherwise. In the legislative contests, the DOS won a plurality in the lower house, but the electoral boycott by Montenegro's governing parties left the balance of power in the hands of the pro-Milošević SNPCG. On September 26 the government-controlled election commission admitted that Koštunica held the lead in the presidential tally, but with less than the 50 percent needed to avoid a runoff with Milošević. Rejecting the commission's count, Koštunica refused to participate in a second round of voting scheduled for October 8.

In the following days, massive street demonstrations called for Milošević to step down, the Serb Orthodox Church began referring to Koštunica as the president, the Yugoslav army made it clear that it would not intervene, and ultranationalist SRS leader Vojislav Šešelj announced that he, too, would support Koštunica's claim to the presidency. On October 4, 2000, the Constitutional Court annulled the presidential poll, but two days later, with the country in the grip of a general strike and with pro-DOS demonstrators in Belgrade having burned the Federal Assembly and other buildings, the court reversed itself and declared that Koštunica had won 50.2 percent of the vote (some sources put the total at 55–56 percent). On the same day Milošević conceded, and the new president took office on October 7.

Faced with mounting opposition, the SPS-led government of Serbia resigned on October 21, 2000. The SPS's Milomir MINIĆ assumed office as prime minister on October 24 at the head of a transitional cabinet of the SPS, DOS, and SPO, pending a Serbian National Assembly election set for December 23. On November 4 the Federal Assembly confirmed the nomination of Zoran ŽIŽIĆ of the SNPCG as federal prime minister, Momir Bulatović having resigned on October 9. The Žižić cabinet included an equal number of ministers from the SNPCG and the DOS, plus two reform-oriented, nominally unaffiliated economists with strong ties to the DOS.

At the Serbian republican election in December 2000, the DOS handily defeated Milošević's SPS, winning 176 of the National Assembly's 250 seats, with 64 percent of the vote. On January 25, 2001, Zoran Djindjić of the DS took office as prime minister of Serbia, heading a new DOS-dominated Serbian cabinet that also included independents and members of the DOS-supportive G17 Plus economic think tank.

On April 1, 2001, after a violent standoff outside the former president's villa, Serbian police arrested Milošević on charges of corruption and abuse of power. A debate continued over where he should be tried. Some members of the federal administration called for surrendering him to the ICTY, even though President Koštunica opposed any such action in the absence of legislation or a constitutional change authorizing extradition. In the Federal Assembly, efforts to pass extradition legislation were repeatedly stymied by the SNPCG. As a consequence, on June 23 the majority of the federal cabinet—minus the absent Prime Minister Žižić and all but one SNPCG minister—issued a decree on cooperation with the war crimes tribunal. On June 28, the FRY Constitutional Court stayed the decree pending determination of its constitutionality, but Serbian prime minister Djindjić and his cabinet, meeting in an emergency session and in near unanimity, discredited the court and refused to accept the stay. Justifying their action under a provision of the Serbian constitution that allowed the Serbian government to act unilaterally and temporarily on behalf of the whole country if federal authorities were unable to do so, the Serbian authorities immediately surrendered Milošević to UN representatives, who flew him to the Netherlands. (On March 11, 2006, 444 days into his trial before the ICTY, Milošević would be found dead of a heart attack in his cell.) In reaction, FRY prime minister Žižić resigned on June 29, although he remained in a caretaker capacity until the confirmation on July 17 of Dragiša PEŠIĆ, also of the SNPCG.

In the context of a growing rivalry between Federal president Koštunica and Serbian prime minister Djindjić, Koštunica's DSS withdrew from the Serbian coalition government on August 17, 2001, ostensibly over the government's inaction in fighting organized crime. The increasing distance between the DSS and the DOS culminated on June 12, 2002, when the DSS withdrew from the Serbian legislature in protest of a government effort to replace 21 DSS deputies for absenteeism and to distribute some of their seats to other parties.

On March 14, 2002, the governments of Serbia, Montenegro, and the FRY announced an "agreement in principle" that would replace Yugoslavia with a "state union" to be called Serbia and Montenegro. Over the objections of parties that wanted a separate and independent Serbia, the Serbian legislature ratified the accord 149–79 on April 9. The same day, the Montenegrin legislature voted in favor of the agreement 58–11, but dissatisfaction on the part of proindependence parties soon cost the Montenegrin government its majority. On May 31 both chambers of the Federal Assembly approved the state union agreement by wide margins.

In August 2002, with the federal presidency certain to be replaced by a much weaker union presidency, federal president Koštunica entered the race for the Serbian presidency. In the September 29 election he won a leading 31 percent of the vote. Second place, with 27 percent, went to Miroljub LABUS, the federal deputy prime minister and the hand-picked candidate of Serbian prime minister Djindjić. In a runoff election on October 13 Koštunica took about 67 percent of the vote, but the turnout fell under 50 percent, invalidating the results. A repeat election on December 8, which pitted Koštunica against the SRS's Vojislav Šešelj and one other candidate, met the same fate, leaving Serbia without an elected president when Milutinović's term expired near the end of the month.

On January 27 and 29, 2003, the Serbian and then the Montenegrin assemblies approved a Constitutional Charter for the state union of Serbia and Montenegro. The Federal Assembly concurred on February 4 (by votes of 26–7 in the upper chamber and 84–31 in the lower), thereby excising Yugoslavia from the political map. Under the charter a new state union Assembly of Serbia and Montenegro was elected by and from among the members of the FRY, Serbian, and Montenegrin legislatures, and on March 7 the new assembly in turn elected the DPSCG's Svetozar MAROVIĆ, the only candidate, as state union president and chair of the Council of Ministers.

Five days later Serbian prime minister Zoran Djindjić was assassinated by an organized Belgrade criminal gang, the Zemun Clan, many of whose members had served in Milošević's Special Operations Unit, the so-called Red Berets. (In May 2007 a dozen defendants were convicted in connection with the assassination and sentenced to prison terms of between 8 and 37 years.) Djindjić was succeeded in an acting capacity by Deputy Prime Minister Nebojša ČOVIĆ of the DOS-affiliated Democratic Alternative (*Demokratska Alternativa*—DA), with the Serbian legislature then confirming the DS's Zoran ŽIVKOVIĆ as the new prime minister on March 18, 2003.

Later in 2003 the DOS-led government of the Serbian Republic lost its legislative majority, precipitating an early National Assembly election on December 28. With the DOS alliance having dissolved, the ultranationalist SRS won a plurality of 82 seats but was unable to form a government. Thus, Vojislav Koštunica, who had stepped down as the last president of the FRY on March 3, 2003, was named Serbian prime minister-designate on February 20, 2004, by Dragan MARŠIĆANIN—the second of three acting Serbian presidents following the expiration of Milutinović's term in 2002. On March 3, 2004, the newly elected Serbian legislature confirmed Koštunica as the head of a minority government that included his DSS, the allied SPO and New Serbia (*Nova Srbija*—NS), and the G17 Plus. Because of its minority status, the new government depended on parliamentary support from the SPS.

In February 2004, three months after another invalidated Serbian presidential election, the Serbian Assembly eliminated the 50 percent turnout requirement. In a fresh election on June 13 Tomislav NIKOLIĆ of the ultranationalist SRS finished first, with 31 percent of the vote, against a dozen other candidates, including the DS's Boris TADIĆ (28 percent) and independent businessman Bogoljub KARIĆ (18 percent). In runoff balloting on June 27, however, Tadić, having gained the support of most mainstream parties, won 54 percent to Nikolić's 46 percent, and he was inaugurated as Serbian president on July 11.

Under their 2003 EU-backed state union agreement, both Serbia and Montenegro had the right to vote on the question of independence in three years. On May 21, 2006, by a half a percentage point above the EU-set threshold of 55 percent for approval, Montenegro's voters chose separation from Serbia, and on June 3 the Montenegrin assembly passed a declaration of independence. Although many Serbians were unhappy with what they viewed as an abrupt divorce, on June 5 the Serbian National Assembly declared Serbia to be the independent successor state to the state union, as had been agreed upon under the charter, and thereby extinguished the last remnants of the former Yugoslavia. The two new countries then began the process of disentangling their institutions.

Independent Serbia's adoption of a new constitution, which was approved by 96.6 percent of those voting in a referendum on October 28–29, 2006, prepared the way for election of a new National Assembly on January 21, 2007. The SRS again won a plurality, 81 of 250 seats, but protracted negotiations among the other leading parties led to formation of a coalition by the DS, DSS, NS (now allied with the DSS), and the G17 Plus, which together commanded 130 seats. The new government, once again headed by Prime Minister Koštunica, took office on May 15.

Meanwhile, Kosovo, still under UNMIK administration, continued to press for independence from Serbia. Under a May 2001 Constitutional Framework for Provisional Self-Government, UNMIK had created "provisional institutions of self-government," lending legitimacy to Kosovo's presidency, government, and assembly. Following President Rugova's death from cancer on February 10, 2006, the Kosovar legislature elected the LDK's Fatmir SEJDIU as president, with Agim ÇEKU then being named prime minister in an effort to provide stronger leadership during UN-mediated negotiations over Kosovo's future political status.

On March 26, 2007, having abandoned futile efforts to achieve a compromise between the Serbian and Kosovar governments, UN special envoy Martii Ahtisaari submitted to the UN Security Council his plan for Kosovo's "supervised independence." The Ahtisaari plan gave considerable attention to the status of the minority Serb population. (Only a fraction of the estimated 200,000 Serbs who had fled Kosovo since 1999 had returned.) Serbs would be granted broad governmental powers in six municipalities, each of which could receive direct aid from Serbia. In addition, Serbs and other minorities would be guaranteed seats in the legislature. Although the Kosovo assembly voted its approval of the Ahtisaari plan in early April 2007, Serbia rejected it.

Given a December 2007 deadline for reaching a final decision on Kosovo's future, representatives of Serbia and Kosovo, including both presidents and both prime ministers, met in New York on September 28 for face-to-face discussions. Between then and November 26 five additional negotiating rounds were held. Serbia's final offer of self-government except in foreign relations, defense, and border control was rejected by Kosovo, the only significant point of agreement being that both would avoid threats and violence.

On November 17, 2007, the PDK won a plurality in an election for the Assembly of Kosovo. On January 9, 2008, the new legislature reelected Fatmir Sejdiu as president and then endorsed Hashim Thaçi as prime minister of a coalition cabinet comprising ministers from the PDK and the LDK, as well as two Serbs and a Turk.

In the presidential election on January 20, 2008, the SRS's Tomislav Nikolić led in the first round of voting, winning 40.0 percent in a nine-way contest. The incumbent, Boris Tadić, finished second, with 35.4 percent, but went on to win reelection in the February 3 runoff, with 50.3 percent versus Nikolić's 48.0 percent. Prime Minister Koštunica, taking a harder line than the president on Kosovar independence and EU integration, had refused to support Tadić.

On February 17, 2008, Prime Minister Thaçi declared Kosovo to be "proud, independent, and free." The unilateral declaration was immediately condemned as illegal by Serbia. Addressing the UN Security Council on February 18, President Tadić asserted that Kosovo's action violated guarantees of sovereignty and territorial integrity contained in the UN charter. Protests by ethnic Serbs on both sides of the Kosovo border erupted, and in Belgrade tens of thousands of sometimes-violent demonstrators took to the streets on February 21.

On March 8, 2008, having vowed that he would not support further negotiations with the EU until it accepted that Kosovo remained part of Serbia, Prime Minister Koštunica announced that the government coalition had collapsed, and five days later President Tadić dissolved the National Assembly. The resultant May 11 election saw Tadić's For a European Serbia (*Za Evropsku Srbiju*—ZES) coalition, led by the DS and G17 Plus, win 102 seats, to 78 for the SRS and 30 for Koštunica's coalition of the DSS and NS. Negotiations on forming a new coalition government concluded on June 26 with the announcement that the ZES would be joined by the SPS and several smaller parties. On July 7 the National Assembly confirmed a new cabinet headed by the DS's Mirko CVETKOVIĆ, theretofore the minister of finance.

As a step toward preparing for EU membership, in 2009, the National Assembly passed a regionalization bill to consolidate the country's 29 districts into development regions based on EU standards. Concerns about further ethnic partition and strife contributed to opposition from the SRS and other nationalist parties. The government reassured critics that regional boundaries would be determined on a statistical basis and would avoid ethnic homogeneity.

President Tadić resigned on April 5, 2012, ten months before his term was slated to expire, allowing the presidential and parliamentary elections to be run concurrently, in hopes of boosting the fortunes of the DS.

The May 6, 2012, parliamentary election saw the Nikolić's Let's Get Serbia Moving (*Pokrenimo Serbiju*—PS) coalition, led by the SNS, win 73 seats with 24 percent of the vote, and Tadić's Choice For a Better Life (*Izbor za Bolji Život*—IzBZ) won 67 seats with 22 percent of the vote. In the subsequent negotiations to form a government, the SPS emerged as a key player, their own coalition having secured 44 seats with 14.5 percent of the vote. The SPS agreed on May 9 that they would support the DS in forming a government, pending the results of the second round of the presidential elections.

Meanwhile, the incumbent, Boris Tadić, won 25.3 percent of the vote in a 12-way contest. The SNS's Tomislav Nikolić finished second, winning 25.0 percent but went on to win in the second round with 49.5 percent to Tadić's 47.3 percent.

Following Nikolić's election, the SPS shifted to negotiate with the SNS; the government subsequently announced on July 23 included the SPS, SNS, URS (a coalition group led by G17 Plus), United Pensioners of Serbia (PUPS), SDPS, DS, and NS.

Conflicts within the ruling coalition had emerged by January 2013. In July Prime Minister Ivica DAČIĆ (SPS) demanded the ouster of the URS from the government; the resulting conflict between the SPS and SNS threatened to shatter the government and trigger early elections. In August a compromise created a new cabinet joined by a slate of nonparty experts. The URS moved to the opposition, but the SPO and DHSS supported the cabinet reshuffle, which was approved on September 3.

Buoyed by strong public support following the announcement that Serbia would begin accession talks with the EU, the SNS called for early parliament elections in December 2013. President Nikolić dissolved the National Assembly on January 29, announcing a general election on March 16.

Boris Tadić, who left the DS after elections were announced and founded the New Democratic Party, sought to form a grand coalition of opposition parties to oppose both the SNS and the DS but was unable to reach agreement between with LDP and URS.

The March 16, 2014, parliamentary election saw The Future That We Believe (*Budućnost u kolu verujemo*—BKV) coalition, led by the SNS, win 158 seats with 48.4 percent of the vote, followed by a coalition of the SPS, PUPS, and United Serbia JS, which won 44 seats with 13.5 percent of the vote. With 134 seats, the SNS could have ruled alone but subsequently formed a government that included the SPS, SDPS, New Serbia (*Nova Srbija*—NS), and the Socialist Movement (PS), with Aleksandar VUČIĆ (SNS) as prime minister.

Vučić called snap elections for April 24, 2016, in an effort to prolong his government, which was in the midst of negotiating EU membership (see Current issues, below). In the balloting, the SNS-led, nine-party coalition, Aleksandar Vučič–Serbia Wins, secured 131 seats. Vučić was reappointed prime minister on May 23, but it took until August 8 to finalize the coalition government, which was dominated by the SNS but included the SPS, SDPS, PS, PUPS, and independents.

Constitution and government. Yugoslavia under successive postwar constitutions remained a Communist one-party state until the emergence of a variety of opposition groups at the republican level in early 1990. The constitution of the Federal Republic of Yugoslavia, adopted in 1992, provided for a bicameral Federal Assembly, encompassing a Chamber of Republics (with equal representation for Serbia and Montenegro) and a Chamber of Citizens apportioned on the basis of population. The federal president was elected to a four-year term by the assembly until July 2000, when constitutional changes instituted direct elections for the presidency as well as for the Chamber of Republics. The president was expected to nominate a prime minister from the other constituent republic.

The Constitutional Charter of the state union of Serbia and Montenegro (including Serbia's Autonomous Province of Vojvodina and Autonomous Province of Kosovo and Metohija) was formally adopted in February 2003 and lasted until both countries chose independence in 2006. It established a presidency with circumscribed powers, although the head of state also served as chair of the Council of Ministers. The president was elected for a single four-year term by the unicameral legislature, the Assembly of Serbia and Montenegro, comprising 91 Serbian and 35 Montenegrin deputies. Each of the constituent republics had a popularly elected president and unicameral assembly, with a prime minister nominated by the former and confirmed by the latter.

Serbia's 2006 constitution retains a mixed presidential-parliamentary system. The president, elected by majority vote, serves a five-year, once-renewable term. The National Assembly, elected by proportional representation, also serves a five-year term, subject to dissolution. The president proposes a prime minister, who is approved by the legislature along with a cabinet. The president may return legislation to the National Assembly for reconsideration but, following repeat passage by a majority of the whole legislature, must then promulgate the resultant law. The president may also dissolve the National Assembly "upon the elaborated proposal of the Government."

A Supreme Court of Cassation sits at the apex of the judicial system. The National Assembly elects the president of the Supreme Court (for a nonrenewable five-year term) and first-time judges (for terms of three years). The latter may then be given permanent tenure by a High Judicial Council, an autonomous body elected by the National Assembly. There is also an autonomous Constitutional Court, whose authority extends to such matters as the constitutionality of laws, intergovernmental disputes, and compatibility of ratified treaties with the constitution. Local jurisdictions include 29 districts (5 in Kosovo), municipalities, towns, and the capital of Belgrade. A law passed in 2009 and amended in 2010 created five statistical development regions: Belgrade, Kosovo and Metohija, Southern and Eastern Serbia, Šumadija and Western Serbia, and Vojvodina.

The constitution begins by affirming the "equality of all citizens and ethnic communities in Serbia" and adds that Kosovo and Metohija is "an integral part of the territory of Serbia," albeit with "substantial autonomy." Vojvodina is also recognized as an autonomous province. Despite Kosovo's February 2008 unilateral declaration of independence, Serb representatives from 26 municipalities from the mainly northern, Serb-dominated areas of Kosovo convened in May in Mitrovica as a 45-member Assembly of the Community of the Municipalities of the Autonomous Province of Kosovo and Metohija. (See the 2012 *Handbook* for details.)

In August 2009 the National Assembly adopted amendments to the Public Information Law that established heavy fines on journalists and media outlets for publishing false or libelous information. Media associations and watchdogs criticized the changes as likely to result in self-censorship and the closure of electronic and print outlets that are found to violate the law. In 2013 Freedom House described the press in Serbia as only "partially free" due to widespread corruption, laws which restrict media freedom, and economic and political pressure. In 2016 Reporters Without Borders ranked Serbia 59th out of 180 countries in its press freedom index, a decline of 5 places since 2014.

Foreign relations. Following the 1948 break with Moscow, Yugoslav foreign policy concentrated on maintaining the country's independence from both major power blocs. The Tito regime consistently advocated peace, disarmament, détente, and aid to anticolonial and developmental struggles of third world countries. Along with Egypt's Nasser and India's Nehru, Tito was considered a founder of the Nonaligned Movement.

Federal Yugoslavia was ostracized by much of the international community because of military action in support of Serbs in Croatia and in Bosnia and Herzegovina. The Bosnian conflict led to UN Security Council sanctions on May 30, 1992, as well as an EC trade embargo and the dispatch of NATO and Western European Union military units to enforce these sanctions. By the end of 1992, Yugoslavia was suspended from the IMF, the OSCE, and the Central European Initiative. (See entry on Yugoslavia in the 2011 *Handbook* for details.)

Intensified UN sanctions on the FRY compelled the Belgrade government to take an overtly stronger line with the Bosnian Serbs following the tabling of new peace proposals—the so-called Stoltenberg-Owen plan—in July 1994 by the Contact Group (of the UK, France, Germany, Russia, and the United States, together with the UN and EU). When the Bosnian Serbs rejected the plan, Belgrade's response was to announce the severance of all political and economic ties with the Bosnian Serbs and to agree to the deployment of international observers on the Yugoslav-Bosnian border to monitor compliance with the official blockade.

Belgrade's reward was UN Security Council approval on September 24, 1994, of a selective suspension of sanctions. Following the intensification of NATO aerial attacks in late August 1995, the Bosnian and Croatian Serb leaders were pressured into accepting the primary role of the Serbian president Milošević in peace negotiations. As a result, after three weeks of intense negotiations between the protagonists conducted under U.S. sponsorship in Dayton, Ohio, a peace agreement was concluded on November 21, 1995 (see entry on Bosnia and Herzegovina), and initialed on behalf of Yugoslavia and the Bosnian Serbs by Milošević. Suspended the following day, UN sanctions against Belgrade were formally lifted by a unanimous Security Council vote on October 1, 1996 (although FRY assets remained frozen because of disputes and claims from other Yugoslav successor states).

Beginning in February 1998, however, Serbian police and military actions in Kosovo again put Yugoslavia at odds with much of the rest of the world, and on March 31 the UN Security Council imposed an arms embargo on Yugoslavia. From April to June the Contact Group, which now included Italy, met several times, with only Russia dissenting from the imposition of various economic sanctions. A September UN Security Council called for a cease-fire and condemned the "excessive and indiscriminate use of force" by the Serb military and security units. In November Belgrade barred members of the UN war crimes tribunal from entering Kosovo to investigate allegations of extrajudicial killings, prompting the U.S. president of the tribunal to brand Yugoslavia as a "rogue state, one that holds the international rule of law in contempt."

Although Yugoslavia stated during the February 1999 peace talks in Rambouillet, France, that it was prepared to consider regional autonomy for Kosovo, it continued to reject a NATO presence on its soil. Immediately following the start of the NATO bombing campaign on March 24, 1999, Belgrade declared a state of war and broke diplomatic relations with France, Germany, the UK, and the United States. Relations with all four were restored in November 2000 as Yugoslavia, now headed by Vojislav Koštunica, moved broadly to reestablish its international linkages. The FRY was formally reintegrated into the UN on November 1 and into the OSCE on November 27. On May 25, 2001, meeting in Vienna, the FRY and the other four Yugoslav successor states reached agreement on the division of assets from the former Yugoslavia. In April 2003 the FRY joined the Council of Europe.

A 2004 report by the government acknowledged Serbian involvement in the 1995 massacre of some 8,000 Muslim men and boys outside Srebrenica, Bosnia and Herzegovina. During a visit to Bosnia and Herzegovina in December 2004, President Tadić drew considerable international attention by apologizing "to all against whom a crime was committed in the name of the Serbian people."

On February 26, 2007, the International Court of Justice (ICJ), ruling in a case brought against the Federal Republic of Yugoslavia in 1993, concluded that Serbia was not responsible for genocide committed in Bosnia and Herzegovina during that country's conflict and did not owe reparations. The court severely criticized Serbia, however, for neglecting its obligations under the Convention on the Prevention and Punishment of the Crime of Genocide, both by failing to prevent the 1995 Srebrenica massacre in Bosnia and by failing to cooperate fully with the ICTY.

Prior to Montenegro's declaration of independence, the state union's ambitions to join the EU were complicated by the differences between the Serbian and Montenegrin currency, customs, and market regimes. Negotiations with the EU on a Stabilization and Association Agreement (SAA) as a precursor to EU membership primarily stalled, however, because of Serbia's testy relationship with the ICTY and the unresolved status of Kosovo. At the ICTY, the trial of former Serbian president Milan Milutinović began in July 2006, while that of SRS ultranationalist leader Vojislav Šešelj began in November 2007. Milutinović and Šešelj had surrendered to the ICTY in January and February 2003, respectively, to defend themselves against charges that included crimes against humanity and violations of the conventions of war. Although a number of once-prominent Serbian military leaders had also voluntarily surrendered to the ICTY in 2004 and 2005, the prosecutors in The Hague, Netherlands, continued to insist that Belgrade had not rigorously pursued Radovan KARADŽIĆ and Ratko MLADIĆ, the most notorious Bosnian Serb commanders. Some human rights advocates charged that Serbia was actively protecting the two, who were under indictment for genocide, crimes against humanity, and war crimes. The Serbian government denied the accusations, even though Prime Minister Koštunica consistently argued that Serbians suspected of criminal acts during the Croatian, Bosnian, and Kosovar conflicts should be tried by a Serbian war crimes court.

The matter of cooperation with the ICTY had also delayed consideration by NATO of Serbia's participation in its Partnership for Peace (PfP) program. PfP membership was eventually offered by NATO in November 2006.

In December 2007, despite negotiations led by a troika of mediators representing the EU, Russia, and the United States, the deadline passed for Serbia and Kosovo to reach an accommodation on Kosovo's future status. Kosovo's February 2008 unilateral declaration of independence was quickly recognized by France, Germany, the UK, and the United States, among other countries, prompting some Serb nationalists to call for breaking off diplomatic relations with those states and to withdraw from an SAA with the EU that had been initialed on November 7, 2007. Nevertheless, the SAA was signed on April 29, 2008, two weeks before the legislative election that President Tadić described as setting out a "clear European path for Serbia." As of July 2013, 103 countries and Taiwan had recognized the Republic of Kosovo.

On March 30, 2010, the Serbian parliament passed a resolution condemning and apologizing for the massacre of 8,000 Muslims at Srebrenica in 1995. President Tadić on July 11 attended the commemoration of the 15th anniversary of the Srebrenica massacre. Taken together, the two events constituted an unprecedented recognition by the Serbian state of the crimes committed during the conflict in Bosnia.

The May 26, 2011, arrest of Ratko Mladić and July 20, 2011, detainment of Goran HADŽIĆ, a Croatian Serb who acted as president of the "Republic of Serbian Krajina," meant that the Serbian authorities had captured the last two ethnic Serbian fugitives from ICTY indictments. The step was praised by the European Commission and by EU officials as demonstrating the "determination and commitment" of Serbia to pursue the rule of law and as an important step in Serbia's goal of joining the EU. On March 1, 2012, Serbia moved to full candidate status for accession to the EU.

On April 17, 2013, Serbia and Kosovo accepted a 15-point draft document to normalize their relations. Much of the document addressed the status of the Mitrovica region, including provisions that local Serbian communities would retain significant autonomy. The EU had helped broker the negotiations and hailed Serbia's participation as a key step in moving toward accession. In September Serbia dismantled the assemblies in the Mitrovica region as part of the agreement.

In December 2013 the Council of Europe approved opening accession talks with Serbia. Talks began on January 21, 2014.

In the wake of the crises in Crimea and Ukraine in 2014, Serbia remained one of few European countries to not impose economic sanctions against Russia. In August the EU called on Serbia to refrain from increasing agricultural exports to Russia after Moscow announced bans on agricultural imports from the United States and various EU member states.

In August the presidents of Serbia, Bosnia and Herzegovina, Croatia, and Montenegro signed a declaration pledging to strengthen the search for missing persons from the wars of the 1990s. On September 1 the Croatian government warned it would block EU accession for the other signatory states if they fail to pass on all information regarding missing Croats.

In February 2016 Serbia announced new border controls in an effort to limit the flow of refugees from the Middle East and North Africa using the country to travel to the EU (see entry on the EU). Along with Slovenia and Macedonia, Serbia set a cap of 580 migrants per day and increased border security. Between January and July 2016, Serbia registered 102,000 migrants, most of whom had crossed over from Bulgaria. Since 2014 estimates were that more than 600,000 migrants had crossed through Serbia into the EU.

Following Croatian approval, on July 18, 2016, Serbia opened Chapters 23 and 24 in the county's ascension talks at the third Serbia–EU Intergovernmental Conference (IGC).

Current issues. The two principal issues that continue to face Serbia are the status of Kosovo and the country's relationship with the EU. None of the major Serbian parties, let alone the government, has dared characterize Kosovo's independence as a fait accompli, but entry into the EU undoubtedly depends on how the Kosovo question is resolved.

On July 21, 2008, a Serbian security team arrested Radovan Karadžić in a Belgrade suburb, and on the following day a judge ordered his transfer to The Hague to stand trial. Meanwhile, the ICTY has continued its activities. The trial of former Yugoslav army chief of staff Momčilo PERIŠIĆ, who had surrendered to the ICTY in 2005, opened in October 2008 and entered the defense phase in February 2010. Perišić faced 13 charges related to war crimes and crimes against humanity committed in 1993–1995 in Bosnia and Croatia. He was found guilty on September 6, 2011, and sentenced to 27 years, but on February 28, 2013, the Appeals Chamber overturned the verdict and acquitted him. On February 26, 2009, former Serbian president Milan Milutinović was acquitted of similar charges against him, although five codefendants were found guilty and sentenced to between 15 and 22 years in prison. The trial of SRS leader Vojislav Šešelj was interrupted in February 2009 when prosecutors alleged intimidation of witnesses. In July Šešelj was found guilty of contempt of court and sentenced to 15 months in prison for having revealed the names of three protected witnesses. The original trial was again interrupted in 2010 by further alleged intimidation of witnesses and another trial for contempt in February 2011 and a third trial in June 2012. The trial entered its closing arguments in March 2013, but Šešelj successfully appealed in December 2013 to have one of his judges dismissed over allegations of bias. Šešelj then appealed to have the trial dismissed after a new judge was appointed, adding to trial delays; the appeal was finally denied in June 2014. War crimes trials conducted by Serbia itself also continued. As of November 2010, 49 people had been convicted and more than 50 others were on trial.

On June 22, 2010, the ICJ issued an advisory opinion that found that Kosovo's 2008 declaration of independence did not violate international law. The Serbian government in response noted that the ICJ opinion did not recognize Kosovo's right to independence but merely that the "technical content" of the declaration did not violate international law. On September 9 Serbia dropped its formal complaint to the UN regarding the unilateral nature of the declaration and called for EU-facilitated direct dialogue with Kosovo. However, Tadić reaffirmed in 2010 that Serbia will not recognize the independence of Kosovo.

In November 2010 the EC praised Serbia's commitment to regional reconciliation and combating organized crime but stressed that EU candidate status would first require the country to be "more co-operative towards independent Kosovo" and undertake judicial reform. Underscoring the problem were clashes between Kosovo border police and Serb protestors in June 2011, when the former attempted to establish Prishtina's control over parts of the northern border between Serb-inhabited Kosovo and Serbia. On August 23, 2011, the German chancellor, Angela Merkel, stated that Serbia must shut down the "parallel structures" of administration it operates in northern Kosovo before it could gain EU candidate status. Protests against the extension of Pristina's control into the Mitrovica region continued through August and September, leading to clashes between the protestors and KFOR personnel.

On August 25 President Tadić stated that Serbia's commitment to joining the EU does not come at the price of abandoning Kosovo and Metohija, leading to criticism from within his party and from allied parties that he risked the loss of EU candidacy status.

Corruption emerged as a prominent theme in the May 2012 legislative elections, with Deputy Prime Minister Aleksandar VUČIĆ leading the government's anticorruption efforts. A series of high-profile arrests were subsequently made, including the November 26, 2012, arrest of former minister of agriculture Saša DRAGIN and the December 12, 2012, arrest of Miroslav MIŠKOVIĆ, the richest businessman in Serbia. Both arrests were related to accusations of fraud in the privatization of state-owned companies.

In April 2014 Vučić announced a series of austerity measures and reforms intended to reduce public-sector expenses, encourage foreign investments, and meet EU standards in regulation of the private sector.

In August the OSCE's Rule of Law and Human Rights Department alleged that Serbia was failing to prosecute suspects of war crimes; Vučić responded that such trials were the responsibility of the ICTY. In September the Serbian government stated it supported the formation of a special court to investigate war crimes committed in Kosovo, following calls by the EU in June and by the United Nations Security Council in August for such.

In December 2015 police launched a massive anticorruption campaign that resulted in the arrests of more than 80 people in 20 separate criminal cases involving more than €100 million in financial improprieties. Included among those detained was a former minister of agriculture. Reports indicated that the investigations and subsequent arrests were part of a broader effort to demonstrate the government's commitment to reduce corruption, a key demand in its negotiations with the EU.

On March 31, 2016, Šešelj was acquitted on all counts of war crimes and crimes against humanity by the ICTY in a two-to-one decision. Following his victory in the April 2016 polling, Vučić appointed Ana BRNABIĆ (independent) as the minister for regional development and local self-government. Brnabić became the first openly gay cabinet minister in Serbian history.

POLITICAL PARTIES

For four-and-a-half decades after World War II, Yugoslavia's only authorized political party was the Communist Party, which was redesignated as the **League of Communists of Yugoslavia** (*Savez Komunista Jugoslavija*—SKJ) in 1952. Political control was also exercised by its "front" organization, the **Socialist Alliance of the Working People of Yugoslavia** (*Socijalistički Savez Radnog Naroda Jugoslavije*—SSRNJ). The collapse of Communist rule in 1989–1990 led to the formation of a large number of successor and other parties, including several "federal" groupings that sought, without success, to preserve the Yugoslav federation (see the 1994–1995 *Handbook*).

Until late 2000, the dominant party in Serbia and at the federal level was Slobodan Milošević's Socialist Party of Serbia (SPS). Beginning in 1992 a number of opposition coalitions attempted to dislodge the SPS and its allies. The **Democratic Movement of Serbia** (*Demokratska Pokret Srbije*—Depos) was formed in May 1992 as an alliance whose principal members were the Serbian Renewal Movement (SPO), **New Democracy** (ND, subsequently the Serbian Liberals), and, following its separation from the Democratic Party (DS), Vojislav Koštunica's Democratic Party of Serbia (DSS). Depos quickly fractured, however, although the SPO and the ND, joined by the **Civic Alliance of Serbia** (GSS; see the Liberal Democratic Party, below), attempted to rejuvenate the alliance (dubbed Depos II) prior to the December 1993 Serbian Assembly election, in which it won 45 seats. In February 1994 the ND decided to support the Serbian government, and that, coupled with a move to the right by the SPO, brought an end to Depos.

In early 1996 the **Together** (*Zajedno*) coalition was established by the SPO, DS, and GSS, which were later joined by the **Democratic Center** (DC; see the DS, below) and, at the federal level, the DSS. The alliance captured a disappointing 22 seats in the federal poll of November 1996 but was far more successful in municipal elections later in the month, although the federal government did not acknowledge the victories for several months. Thereafter, with Serbian legislative elections approaching, relations between the SPO and its partners turned acrimonious, and in mid-1997 *Zajedno* collapsed.

A more inclusive **Alliance for Change** (*Savez za Promene*—SZP) originated in a June 1998 agreement by half a dozen parties to adopt a uniform opposition strategy. Among the initial participants were the DS, the GSS, and the Christian Democratic Party of Serbia (DHSS). Organizations joining later included the DC, the Democratic Party of Vojvodina Hungarians (DSVM), the New Serbia (*Nova Srbija*—NS, see below), the Association of Free and Independent Trade Unions (*Asocijacija Slobodnih i Nezavisnih Sindikata*—ASNS), some 20 smaller parties, and various civic groups.

A smaller opposition grouping, the **Alliance of Democratic Parties** (*Savez Demokratskih Partija*—SDP), had been organized in October 1997 by the Alliance of Vojvodina Hungarians (SVM), the League of Vojvodina Social Democrats (LSV), the **Reformist Democratic Party of Vojvodina** (RDSV, subsequently the RVSP—see the Vojvodina Party, below), the **Sandžak Coalition** (KS), the Social Democratic Union (SDU), and the **Šumadija Coalition** (*Koalicija Šumadija*—KŠ).

The SZP and SDP, often in conjunction with the SPO, organized or participated in a number of anti-Milošević demonstrations and, beginning in September 1999, a series of opposition roundtables. These led to a January 10, 2000, meeting at which 16 opposition party leaders, spearheaded by the SPO's Vuk Drašković and the DS's Zoran Djindjić, committed their organizations to a joint strategy for forcing early elections. Following the July adoption by the Milošević-controlled Federal Assembly of constitutional changes permitting direct election of the president and the upper house, the opposition prepared for the September 24 federal elections by attempting to forge a comprehensive electoral alliance. Although the SPO and many less-influential parties ultimately chose to remain independent, the unification effort culminated in formation of the **Democratic Opposition of Serbia** (*Demokratske Opozicije Srbije*—DOS), which nominated the DSS's Koštunica for the presidency. By the time of the September balloting the DOS encompassed 18 parties (plus the ASNS), among them the DS, DSS, GSS, NS, and the 6 SDP parties. The DOS followed up its federal victories in September by winning 176 of the 250 seats in the December Serbian National Assembly election. By the time of the December 2003 Serbian election, however, the cumbersome DOS had dissolved.

For the March 2014 Serbian national election, 19 parties and coalitions offered party lists, up from 18 in 2012 but down from 22 in May 2008. The leading coalition, BKV, included as the principal participant Aleksanda Vučić's SNS. Other significant coalitions were formed by the SPS, PUPS, and JS; by the New Democratic Party and five smaller parties; and by the LDP and SDU. A 5 percent threshold for seats continued in effect except for ethnic minority parties, which needed only 0.4 percent of the vote to obtain a seat. Three such parties or coalitions won a total of 11 seats. A plethora of other minor organizations exist, many with a predominantly regional or ethnic character. A 2011 law requires that 30 percent of National Assembly seats must be held by women; following the 2016 elections, women held 85 seats (34 percent).

Government Parties:

Aleksandar Vučić–Serbia Wins (*Srbija* Pobeđuje—SP). The coalition was a rebranding of the 2014 grouping, **The Future That We Believe** (*Budućnost u kolu verujemo*—BKV). The SP was formed to support Prime Minister Aleksandar VUČIĆ's (SNS) election campaign in the April 2016 balloting.

The BKV was a continuation of the 2012 electoral coalition **Let's Get Serbia Moving** (*Pokrenimo Serbiju*—PS), the BKV retained the SNS and NS, while adding the SDPS, the SPO, and Aleksandar VULIN's **Socialist Movement** (*Pokret Socijalista*—PS). Most of the smaller parties from the 2012 coalition were not officially registered as participating in the BKV, but the final electoral list did include candidates from Bogoljub KARIĆ's **Strength of Serbia Movement** (*Pokret "Snaga Serbije"*—PSS), **the Serbian Association of Small and Medium Companies and Entrepreneurs** (*Asocijacija Malih i Srednjih Preduzeća i Preduzetnika Srbije*—AMSPPS), **the Association of Refugees in Serbia** (*Stvaranje Udruženje Izbeglica u Srbiji*—SUIS), the **People's Peasant Party** (*Narodna Seljačka Stranka*—NSS), and the **Bosniak People's Party** (*Bošnjačka Narodna Stranka*—BNS).

In 2012 the PS had won 73 seats with 24 percent of the vote in the May 6, 2012, elections; in the subsequent distribution of seats, the NS received 55 seats, the NS received 8, the PSS received 2 seats, and each smaller party (except the Vlach Unity Movement) received 1 seat. After the elections, the coalition was retained as a parliamentary group, with the exception of the NS, which formed its own group.

In 2014 the BKV won 158 seats with 48.4 percent of the vote in the parliamentary elections on March 16, 2014; in the subsequent distribution of seats, the SNS received 134 seats, the SDPS 10, the NS 6, the SPO 5, the PS 2, and the DHSS 1.

The SP included parties from the BKV, such as the SNS, SDPS, PUPS, NS, SPO, PS, and PSS, along with the **Independent Democratic Party of Serbia** (*Nezavisna Demokratska stranka Srbije*—NDSS) and the **Serbian People's Party**—SPP (*Srpska narodna stranka*).

In the April 24, 2016, legislative elections, the SP secured 131 seats with 48.3 percent of the vote. The seats were won by the following parties: the SNS had 96; the SDPS, 10; PUPS, 9; NS, 5; SPO, 3; PS, 3; PSS, 2; NDSS, 2; and the SPP, 1.

Serbian Progressive Party (*Srpska Napredna Stranka*—SNS). The SNS was formed in September 2008 by a group of SRS members, including about 20 members of the National Assembly, who broke with party policy because they supported greater European integration, including EU membership. The dissenters, led by former SRS presidential candidate Tomislav Nikolić, were expelled by the SRS leadership, prompting formation of a separate faction in the National Assembly, the Go, Serbia! (*Napred Srbijo*) deputy group, and confirmation of their intention to establish a new "radical" party. Apart from the issue of closer ties to Western Europe, the SNS remains ideologically nationalistic, supporting the integrity of the state and rejecting independence for Kosovo. It also advocates military neutrality and support for ethnic Serbs throughout the former Yugoslavia.

The SNS nominated Tomislav Nikolić as its candidate for the 2012 presidential elections. Nikolić won 25.1 percent of the vote in the first round on May 6 and won the second round on May 20 with 49.5 percent of the vote. Nikolić stood down as party leader on May 24. He was replaced by Aleksandar VUČIĆ, who became prime minister in 2014.

Leaders: Aleksandar VUČIĆ (Prime Minister and President of the Party), Tomislav NIKOLIĆ (President of the Republic and Former President of the Party), Jorgovanka TABAKOVIĆ (Vice-President), Maja GOJKOVIĆ (President of Parliament).

New Serbia (*Nova Srbija*—NS). The NS was organized following the expulsion of Čačak's controversial mayor, Velimir Ilić, from the SPO in 1998 and his subsequent departure from **Serbia-Together** (*Srbija-Zajedno*), an SPO offshoot.

The NS joined the Alliance for Change and then the DOS. In November 2003 Ilić ran third in the invalidated Serbian presidential election. A month later the NS and the SPO ran as a coalition in balloting for the Serbian legislature, with the NS being awarded nine seats.

In November 2006, the NS allied with the DSS in preparation for the 2007 National Assembly election, in which the NS won 10 seats. Ilić finished third, with 7.4 percent of the vote, in the first round of the

2008 presidential contest. In May it won 9 National Assembly seats and then formed its own deputy group. Despite joining the SNS in electoral coalitions in 2012, 2014, and 2016, it has retained its deputy group.
Leader: Velimir ILIĆ (President).

Social Democratic Party of Serbia (*Socijaldemokratska Partija Srbije*—SDPS). Formation of the SDPS was announced in August 2009 by Rasim Ljajić. Ljajić stated that the SDPS was an effort to unite various social democratic parties, including his own **Sandžak Democratic Party**, the **Social Democratic Party of Nebojša Čović** (SDP), and the **Independent Social Democrats** (*Nezavisni Socijaldemokrata*—NSD), led by Zoran DRAGIŠIĆ. The SDPS was registered in October.

The SDP had been established in April 2002 by merger of one wing of **Social Democracy** (*Socijaldemokratija*—SD), led by Slobodan ORLIĆ, and the Social Democratic Union (SDU, below), led by Žarko KORAĆ. The SD-SDU merger proved short-lived: In March 2003 the SDU was reestablished as a separate party, with the rump group retaining the SDP name. (In June 2002 the SD wing loyal to party founder Vuk OBRADOVIĆ had won title to the SD name in the courts.)

In October 2003 the SDP withdrew its support for the DOS-led Serbian government, which contributed to the collapse of the government and accelerated the alliance's disintegration. In the December 2003 parliamentary election the SDP candidates joined the G17 Plus electoral list, winning three seats.

In September 2004 Nebojša Čović's Democratic Alternative (*Demokratska Alternativa*—DA) merged into the SDP. The DA, dating from 1997, had participated in the Alliance for Change but departed and formed the DAN Coalition with the New Democracy and the Democratic Center (see DS, below) in late 1999 before joining the DOS in 2000. In the December 2003 Serbian legislative election, the DA won only 2.2 percent of the vote and no seats.

In August 2005 Prime Minister Koštunica asked the SDP to leave the government after two of its three assembly members voted against privatization of the state oil and gas company. Party chair Čović, who had been serving as head of the Serbia and Montenegro Coordination Center for Kosovo, was then dismissed, and the party formally entered the opposition. Minister of Labor Slobodan LALOVIĆ sided with the government and left the party. In 2007 the SDP joined forces with the PUPS (see under SPS, above), but the coalition won only 3.1 percent of the vote and therefore failed to meet the threshold for representation.

The NSD was established by Zoran Dragišić, a security analyst, in January 2008. The new party drew most of its members from what remained of the SD, then led by Nanad VUKASOVIĆ.

In 2009 the SDPS fully merged with the **Sandžak Democratic Party** (*Sandžačka Demokratska Partija*—SDP). The SDP was founded as a result of factional strife within the Sandžak SDA (see Leading Sandžak Parties, below) and was founded in October 2000. It participated unsuccessfully in the 2003 Serbian legislative election, although Ljajić as leader of the SDP received a cabinet position in 2006. (See the 2012 *Handbook* for details.) In 2007, running on the DS list, the SDP was awarded three National Assembly seats. It received four in 2008 as part of the ZES.

In 2012 the SDPS joined the Choice for a Better Life coalition (see DS, below), and received nine of the seats won by the coalition. The SDPS subsequently left the coalition and joined the SNS-led government in July 2012, forming its own progovernment deputy group.

The SDPS was part of the SNS-led coalition in the 2016 balloting, and Ljajić was again appointed deputy prime minister.
Leaders: Rasim LJAJIĆ (Deputy Prime Minister, Minister of Trade, Tourism, and Telecommunications, and President of the Party), Miorad MIJATOVIĆ (Leader of Deputy Group).

Serbian Renewal Movement (*Srpski Pokret Obnove*—SPO). The SPO was founded in March 1990 as a merger of four parties, most notably those led by Vojislav Šešelj and Vuk Drašković. In less than three months, however, internal squabbling led to the departure of Šešelj to found a new party, the SRS (below). Without Šešelj the SPO moderated its extreme nationalism and participated in the Depos coalitions in 1992 and 1993. During this time, Drašković spoke out against war crimes, and as a result, he and his wife Danica were arrested and allegedly beaten by Serbian police. Following the disappointing showing of *Zajedno* in the 1996 federal election, the SPO was the sole opposition party to contest the 1997 Serbian elections for both parliament and the presidency, finishing third in both contests.

In January 1999 Drašković joined Prime Minister Bulatović's government as a deputy prime minister, but his show of national solidarity ended three months later when comments made contrary to policy led to his dismissal. The other three SPO ministers immediately resigned.

In 2000 the SPO remained aloof from the DOS alliance—a move that Drašković subsequently acknowledged as a mistake. In the September elections the SPO won only one upper house seat, while its presidential candidate, Vojislav Mihajlović, the mayor of Belgrade, took only 3 percent of the vote. In the December election for the Serbian assembly, the SPO won less than 4 percent of the vote and no seats. Drašković subsequently voiced support for reestablishing Serbia as a constitutional parliamentary monarchy.

For the 2003 Serbian legislative election, the SPO joined forces with NS, winning 13 of the coalition's 22 seats (based on a 7.7 percent vote share). Intraparty differences led in 2005 to formation of the Serbian Democratic Renewal Movement (SDPO) by 9 of the SPO's deputies. In 2007 the SPO list, which included members of the Serbian Liberals and the People's Peasant Party, won only 3.3 percent of the vote and thus no National Assembly seats. In the May 2008 election, the SPO ran as part of the ZES and was awarded 4 seats.

The SPO joined the Turn Around electoral coalition (see Jovanović Coalition, below) for the May 2012 legislative elections, winning four seats. Following the election, it left the alliance and formed a deputy group with the DHSS. In September 2013 the SPO supported the new cabinet proposed by Ivica Dačić, although the parties did not join the government. Following the March 2014 elections and the April 2016 balloting, the SPO did not join the coalition cabinets but supported Aleksandar Vučić's governments.
Leader: Vuk DRAŠKOVIĆ (President).

Party of United Pensioners of Serbia (*Partija Ujedinjenih Penzionera Srbije*—PUPS). PUPS was a center-left party founded in 2005 by Jovan KRKOBABIĆ. After Krkobabić died on June 28, 2014, his son, Milan KRKOBABIĆ, became party leader. PUPS joined the SNS-led coalition in the 2016 balloting and joined the subsequent coalition government. Krkobabić was appointed a minister without portfolio.
Leader: Milan KRKOBABIĆ (Minister without Portfolio).

Other parliamentary parties that were part of the Aleksandar Vučić–Serbia Wins coalition were the **Independent Democratic Party of Serbia** (*Nezavisna Demokratska stranka Srbije*—NDSS) and the **Serbian People's Party**—SPP (*Srpska narodna stranka*), led by Nenad POPOVIĆ.

Christian Democratic Party of Serbia (*Demohrišćanska Stranka Srbije*—DHSS). The DHSS dates from 1997, when a dispute with Vojislav Koštunica led a number of DSS members to leave the party under the former DSS vice president, Vladan BATIĆ. He subsequently served as coordinator of the Alliance for Change and as a principal leader of the DOS.

At the December 2003 Serbian legislative election, the DHSS headed the Independent Serbia *(Samostalna Srbija)* list, which won 1.1 percent of the vote. In 2007 DHSS candidates were included on the coalition list headed by the LDP and GSS; the DHSS was awarded one seat.

In February 2008 the DHSS blamed the Koštunica government for instigating the Belgrade riots ("an act of state terrorism") that followed Kosovo's unilateral declaration of independence. In May the party again ran on the LDP list, with Batić claiming the party's sole seat.

In May 2010 the **My Serbia Movement** (*Pokret Moja Srbija*) merged with the DHSS. The My Serbia Movement had participated in the 2008 elections but failed to gain seats.

The DHSS joined the Choice for a Better Life electoral coalition (see DS, below) in the 2012 legislative election, securing one seat. Following the elections, however, it formed a deputy group with the SPO (above). The DHSS, like the SPO, supported but did not join the Ivica Dačić cabinet in 2013 and the Aleksandar Vučić cabinet in 2014.
Leader: Olgica BATIĆ (President).

Socialist Party of Serbia (*Socijalistička Partija Srbije*—SPS). The SPS was formed in July 1990 by consolidation of the former **League of Communists of Serbia** and its associated **Socialist Alliance**. The party won 194 of 250 seats in the Serbian Assembly in December 1990, while its leader, Slobodan Milošević, defeated 30 other candidates in retaining the Serbian presidency with a 65 percent vote share. The SPS won a narrow majority (73 of 138 seats) in the federal Chamber of Citizens in May 1992. Following the imposition of UN sanctions on May 30, anti-Milošević social democrats within the party formed several splinter groups; however, Milošević remained firmly in charge and was reelected in December, when the party also retained its pluralities in both the federal and the republican assemblies.

Thereafter, the SPS moved closer to the ultranationalist SRS (below), with which it cooperated to oust President Ćosić from the FRY presidency in June 1993. Four months later the SRS terminated the relationship, prior to the Serbian legislative poll in December, in which the SPS won 123 seats. In late 1995 Milošević dismissed several hard-line nationalists in the SPS leadership who were critical of the Dayton peace accord. Subsequently, an SPS-led electoral alliance, the **Joint List**, dominated federal parliamentary elections in November 1996 as well as the September 1997 presidential and legislative elections in Serbia. The Joint List also included the ND and the **Yugoslav Left** (*Jugoslovenska Levica*—JUL), an umbrella grouping of some two dozen communist and other leftist organizations led by Mirjana MARKOVIĆ, Milošević's wife.

At the federal presidential election of September 2000 President Milošević finished second, with some 35 to 37 percent of the vote, although he refused to acknowledge his loss to the DOS's Koštunica until early October. In simultaneous parliamentary elections, the SPS-JUL alliance saw its seat total in the lower house drop to 44, while it won only 7 of Serbia's 20 seats in the newly elective upper house. Although the SPS continued to control the republican government and legislature in Serbia, the success of the DOS precipitated a premature dissolution of the Serbian National Assembly in late October and the swearing in of an interim coalition government of the SPS, DOS, and SPO, pending an election in late December. In the meantime, a defiant Milošević was reelected party chair at a party congress in November.

The erosion of public support for the SPS continued in the December 2000 Serbian Assembly balloting. The SPS won only 37 seats, in contrast to the 86 won in 1997 as part of the Joint List with the JUL and ND. In the December 2003 election, it won only 7.7 percent of the votes, good for 22 seats. Milošević, despite being on trial in The Hague, remained the SPS chair until his death in 2006.

Struggles over leadership of the SPS began after Milošević's death. The infighting undermined party unity in the assembly; this threatened the government, which depended on SPS support. In December 2006 the party elected Ivica Dačić over Milorad VUČELIĆ as successor to the late president. In the January 2007 election the SPS won just 5.6 percent of the vote and 16 seats. A year later, its presidential candidate, Milutin Mrkonjić, finished fourth, with 6.0 percent of the vote in the first round.

In the May 2008 legislative election the SPS ran in coalition with PUPS (see above) and the **United Serbia** (*Jedinstvena Srbija*—JS), winning 12 of the alliance's 20 seats. The PUPS won 5 seats and then established its own deputy group, led by Momo ČOLAKOVIĆ, in the National Assembly. The JS won 3 seats, while 1 seat went to an SPS electoral partner, the **Movement of Veterans of Serbia** (*Pokret Veterana Srbije*—PVS).

In the May 2012 legislative election, the SPS again ran in coalition with the PUPS and the JS; the coalition won 44 seats with 14.5 percent of the vote. The SPS won 24 seats, with 1 additional seat being allocated to the PVS, led by Saša DUJOVIĆ. The PUPS, led by Jovan KRKOBABIĆ, won 12 seats. The JS, led by Dragan MARKOVIĆ, won 7 seats. Both the PUPS and JS established their own deputy groups in parliament. In the 2012 presidential election, the coalition supported Dačić, who secured 14.2 percent of the vote in the first round, taking third place and failing to advance to the second round.

The SPS won 13.5 percent of the vote in the 2014 balloting and 25 seats. In the 2016 elections, it ran in a coalition with the JS and **Greens of Serbia** (*Zeleni Srbije*—ZS), led by Ivan KARIĆ. In that polling, the SPS secured 11 percent of the vote and 21 seats. The SPS joined the SNS-led coalition government, and Dačić was appointed first deputy prime minister.

Leaders: Ivica DAČIĆ (First Deputy Prime Minister and Party President), Aleksandar ANTIĆ (Deputy President), Milutin MRKONJIĆ (Honorary President).

Opposition Parties:

Democratic Party (*Demokratska Stranka*—DS). The descendant of a post–World War I governing democratic party, the DS was revived in December 1989 and held a constituent convention in February 1990. A centrist party committed to a democratic multiparty system, human rights, and a free press, the DS boycotted the May 1992 Federal Assembly election. Its reluctance to join the opposition coalition Depos in 1992 resulted in a party split, with the departing faction, the DSS, joining the alliance. Building on its modest success in the December 1992 balloting, the DS won 29 Serbian Assembly seats a year later as the party's turn toward nationalism won it surreptitious support from the Milošević-run media. At the head of the nationalist faction was Zoran Djindjić, who led the electoral campaign and in 1994 was elected party president.

The party returned to active opposition in 1996 by joining *Zajedno.* The SPO's withdrawal in mid-1977 meant the demise of *Zajedno,* and the DS boycotted the 1997 Serbian elections. In 1998 Djindjić joined a number of other opposition politicians in announcing formation of the Alliance for Change (SZP). In 2000 Djindjić was a leading participant in the formation of the DOS as well as coordinator of the SZP. As prime minister of Serbia, he led the more reform-minded majority within the DOS, often in opposition to his chief rival, Vojislav Koštunica of the DSS. Djindjić was assassinated on March 12, 2003. A week later Zoran Živković was confirmed as prime minister.

Following the breakup of the DOS, the DS ran independently in the Serbian legislative election of December 2003, although various candidates from other parties, including the Civic Alliance of Serbia (GSS) and the DC, were included on the DS electoral list. The DS's Boris Tadić was elected president of Serbia in June 2004.

In January 2005 the DC merged into the DS. Following its formation in 1995, the DC had participated in both the Depos and the *Zajedno* opposition alliances before forming the DAN Coalition (*Koalicija DAN*) in late 1999 with New Democracy (*Nova Demokratija*—ND; renamed the Serbian Liberals [*Liberali Srbije*—LS] in 2003) and the Democratic Alternative (DA). All three DAN parties then joined the DOS in 2000. The DC's Mićunović ran as the DOS candidate in the invalidated Serbian presidential election of November 2003, finishing second. In the 2003 Serbian National Assembly election, five DC candidates on the DS electoral list were awarded seats.

Following the separation of Serbia and Montenegro, and with an eye toward the growing popularity of the SRS, Tadić backed a call for early elections. In the January 2007 election the DS list won 64 seats, including 3 awarded to the Sandžak Democratic Party and 1 to the Democratic Alliance of Croats in Vojvodina. It then formed a coalition government with the DSS, the NS, and G17 Plus. Tadić later confirmed his intention to seek reelection as president in January 2008. Although he finished second to the SRS candidate in the first round, with 35.4 percent of the vote, he won the February runoff, with 50.3 percent.

Following the withdrawal of the DSS from the government in March 2008 and the consequent dissolution of the National Assembly, the DS formed the ZES coalition to contest the May legislative election, in which its list won 64 of the alliance's 102 seats.

The DS was one of the key parties in the electoral coalition **Choice for a Better Life** (*Izbor za Bolji Život*—IzBZ). Announced on March 16, 2012, this coalition also included the SDPS, the DHSS, the League of Social Democrats of Vojvodina (LSV; see Leading Vojvodina Parties, the Democratic Alliance of Croats in Vojvodina). The ISPO, led by Srdjan SREĆKOVIĆ, was formed in February 2012 by a faction of the SPO (see above). The IzBZ won 67 seats with 22.1 percent of the vote in the May 6, 2012, parliamentary election. In the subsequent allocation of the coalition's seats, the DS received 49, the SDPS 9, the LSV 5, and the ZS, DHSS, DSHV, and ISPO 1 seat each. The SDPS subsequently broke with the coalition in the negotiations over the new government, while the DHSS formed a deputy group with the SPO (see above).

Following the May 6, 2012, parliamentary elections, the DS received 49 seats from the 67 won by the IzBZ coalition. As presidential candidate, Tadić took first place in the first round of the presidential election with 25.3 percent but lost the second round with 47.3 percent to 49.5 percent for Tomislav Nikolić. In August, dissatisfaction with election results led elements of the party, including Deputy President Dragan DJILAS, to call for significant reforms by the leadership or risk a split. Tadić stepped down as party leader in November, and a party congress the same month elected Djilas as party leader.

In September 2013 Djilas was recalled from his position as mayor of Belgrade, a post he had held since 2008, by a majority vote of the city council initiated by the SNS.

Tadić sought to regain the presidency of the party in the January 2014 party congress. After Djilas's reelection, in February 2014, Tadić announced his resignation from the DS, citing disagreements with the party leadership, and founded the New Democratic Party (*Nova Demokratska Stranka*—NDS, see SDS, below).

The DS was supported in an electoral alliance by several smaller parties, including **Rich Serbia** (*Bogata Srbija*—BS), led by Zaharije TRNAVCEVIĆ and the **Vojvodina Party** (see Leading Vojvodina Parties, below).

In the early parliamentary elections held on March 16, 2014, the DS won 19 seats with 6 percent of the vote. In response to the defeat, a party council elected Bojan PATIĆ as the new party president in June 2014.

The party led the For a Just Serbia alliance in the 2016 polling. The coalition included the **New Party** (*Nova Stranka*), the Democratic Alliance of Croats in Vojvodina (*Demokratski Savez Hrvata u Vojvodini*—DSHV) (see below), **Together for Serbia** (*Zajedno za* Srbiju—ZZS), led by Blagoje BRADIĆ, and **Together for Šumadija** (*Zajedno za Šumadiju*). The DS won 12 seats in the balloting, while the coalition secured 16.

Leaders: Bojan PATIĆ (President), Gordana COMIĆ (Deputy President), Balsa BOZOVIĆ (Secretary General), Dragan DJILAS.

Social Democratic Party (*Socijaldemokratska Stranka*—SDS). Boris Tadić resigned from the DS (above) in February 2014. Lacking time to register a new party prior to the March 16 early elections, Tadić negotiated an agreement with the Greens of Serbia (*Zeleni Srbije*—ZS), previously a part of the Choice for a Better Life coalition (see DS, above), in which it secured 1 seat.

Tadić and his faction from the DS joined the ZS, with Tadić assuming the presidency of the combined party, known as the **New Democratic Party–The Greens** (*Nova Demokratska Stranka–Zeleni*). The coalition then entered into an electoral alliance with the ZZS, the **Democratic Left of Roma** (*Demokratska Levica Roma*—DLR), led by Jovan DAMJANOVIĆ; **Together for Vojovdina** (*Zajedno za Vojvodinu*—ZZV); the LSV and DZVM/VMDK (see Leading Vojvodina Parties, below).

In the March 16, 2014, legislative elections the alliance won 18 seats with 5.7 percent of the vote. In the subsequent distribution of votes the NDS received 10 seats; the LSV, 6; the ZZS, 1; and the ZS, 1. The NDS, ZZS and Greens formed a joint parliamentary deputy group.

Following the election, Tadić and his faction subsequently seceded from the alliance, founding the **New Democratic Party** (*Nova Demokratska Stranka*—NDS), registering the party in August 2014. In October of that year, the name of the party was changed to the SDS. It won 5 seats in the 2016 parliamentary balloting, as part of the Alliance for a Better Serbia, with the **League of Vojvodina Social Democrats** (*Liga Socijaldemokrata Vojvodine*—LSV), and the **Liberal Democratic Party** (*Liberalno Demokratska Partija*—LDP, see below). The coalition won 13 seats.

Leader: Boris TADIĆ (President).

Liberal Democratic Party (*Liberalno Demokratska Partija*—LDP). The LDP was formed in 2005 by a dissenting faction of the DS following the ouster from the leadership of the LDP's founder, Čedomir Jovanović. It ran in the 2007 legislative election in coalition with the **Civic Alliance of Serbia** (*Gradjanski Savez Srbije*—GSS), the Social Democratic Union (SDU, below), and the League of Social Democrats of Vojvodina (LSV, below). The coalition won 15 seats, 5 of which were assigned to the LDP. In April 2007 the GSS merged into the LDP.

The GSS, founded in 1992 by antiwar activist Dr. Vesna PEŠIĆ, never achieved notable success in the polls despite participating in Depos, *Zajedno,* the Alliance for Change, and the DOS. In December 2003 GSS candidates for the Serbian legislature ran on the DS electoral list, ending up with five seats. In the following year a number of GSS leaders, including the party's president, Goran SVILANOVIĆ, resigned and joined the DS.

In the 2008 presidential election, Jovanović finished with 5.3 percent of the vote. In May the LDP list won 5.2 percent of the National Assembly vote, for 13 seats, including 1 for the SDU and 1 for the Christian Democratic Party of Serbia (below).

The LDP received 11 seats in the distribution by the Turn Around coalition following the May 6, 2012, parliamentary election. Jovanović was again nominated for the 2012 presidential election, receiving 5 percent of the vote in the first round, placing sixth.

The LDP joined the Alliance for a Better Serbia in the 2016 balloting, securing four seats.

Leaders: Čedomir JOVANOVIĆ (President), Nenad MILIĆ (Deputy President).

Serbian Radical Party (*Srpska Radikalna Stranka*—SRS). Founded in 1991 and runner-up to the SPS in the federal lower house elections of May and December 1992, the SRS advocates a "Greater Serbia." It withdrew its support of the SPS at both the republican and federal levels in September 1993 and mounted a campaign to undercut the ruling party in the run-up to the 1993 legislative election, in which, however, its representation dropped from 73 to 39 seats.

In 1994 the SRS abolished its paramilitary wing, the Serbian Chetnik Movement, following charges that it was guilty of war crimes in Croatia during 1991 and 1992. It was also implicated in the Bosnia and Herzegovina conflict. Party leader Vojislav Šešelj was given a four-month prison sentence in September 1994 for repeated acts of violence in the assembly. In opposition to his continuing leadership, party dissidents left to form a new party, the **Radical Party of the Left Nikola Pašić** (*Radikolna Stranka Levice Nikola Pašić*—RSLNP), but had no success in the polls.

In the November 1996 federal election SRS lower house representation slipped further, to 16 seats. In the first runoff of the 1997 Serbian presidential election, Šešelj appeared to have beaten SPS candidate Zoran Lilić, but due to a low turnout the election was invalidated. Šešelj ultimately lost to new SPS candidate Milan Milutinović in December, though the official count and turnout levels were questionable. In the parliamentary election, the SRS, attacking Milošević as the cause of Serbia's woes, finished a strong second with 82 seats. As a result, the SPS approached the SRS about joining the Serbian government, with Šešelj being named a deputy prime minister in March 1998. The SRS was the only prominent Serb party to reject the June 1999 Kosovo peace plan.

At the federal level, the SRS 2000 presidential candidate, Tomislav Nikolić, finished third, with 6 percent of the vote, while the party captured only 5 seats in the lower house and 2 in the upper. In the December 2000 Serbian National Assembly election the SRS finished third, with 23 seats, a loss of 59.

In February 2003 Vojislav Šešelj surrendered to ICTY authorities to face charges that included crimes against humanity from 1991 to 1995. In December, with the DOS having dissolved, the SRS won a leading 27.6 percent of the vote and 82 seats in the National Assembly, far outdistancing the second-place DSS. Although the victory also gave the SRS a plurality of 30 indirectly elected seats in the new state union assembly, the party was unable to muster enough additional support to form a government in Serbia. Nikolić finished first in the June 2004 first-round voting for president of Serbia but was defeated in the second round, winning 46 percent of the vote.

In November 2006, in the midst of a four-week hunger strike, Vojislav Šešelj refused to appear at the opening of his trial in The Hague. A month earlier, the SRS had reelected him as leader. In January 2007 the SRS again emerged from the legislative election with a plurality, 81 seats based on a 28.6 percent vote share.

In late December 2007 the SRS absorbed the **Serbian Unity Party** (*Stranka Srpskog Jedinstva*—SSJ), an ultranationalist group launched prior to the December 1992 election, with the reported support of President Milošević, as a counter to the SRS. Its leader, Željko RAŽNJATOVIĆ "Arkan," a commander of the paramilitary Tigers group, had been linked in press reports to a variety of atrocities in Bosnia and Croatia. In March 1999 the ICTY announced that it had sent Belgrade a warrant for Arkan, who was killed by masked gunmen in January 2000. The hard-line stance of the SSJ won it 14 seats in the December 2000 Serbian Assembly election. In 2003 it ran under the banner of the unsuccessful ZNJ electoral list. Its chair, Borislav PELEVIĆ, ran for president in 2004.

In the January 2008 presidential race, Nikolić again led after the first round but lost in the runoff, with 48 percent of the vote. In the May National Assembly election, the SRS increased its vote share to 29.5 percent but won 3 fewer seats, finishing second to the ZES coalition. Four months later the party split over the issue of EU integration. Nikolić and others who supported eventual EU membership were expelled from the SRS, having been branded by Šešelj as traitors and "Western puppets." The departure of Nikolić and his supporters, including the SRS's general secretary, Aleksandar Vučić, reduced the SRS contingent in the National Assembly to 57 seats. In late September Nikolić formed the Serbian Progressive Party (SNS, above).

In July 2009 the ICTY sentenced Vojislav Šešelj to 15 months in jail for contempt of court after he revealed the identities of three protected witnesses. He was charged with contempt a second time in February 2010 and a third time in July 2011. As of October 2011 his trial for crimes against humanity had not concluded, delayed in part due to Šešelj's apparent poor health and to repeated accusations that Šešelj has publicly revealed the names of prosecution witnesses.

In the May 2012 parliamentary election, the SRS won 4.6 percent of the vote, failing to clear the threshold and winning no seats in parliament. Jadranka ŠEŠELJ, wife of the party leader, was the SRS's presidential candidate in the May 2012 presidential election, winning 3.8 percent of the vote and failing to advance to the second round.

In the March 2014 legislative election, the SRS won 2 percent of the vote, again failing to clear the threshold. However, in April 2016 the party won 8.1 percent of the vote and 22 seats.

Leaders: Vojislav ŠEŠELJ (President), Gordana POP-LAZIĆ.

Enough is Enough (*Dosta je Bilo*–"Restart"). Founded in January 2014 by Saša RADULOVIĆ, the liberal, reform party failed to gain any seats in the 2014 assembly balloting, with just 2.1 percent of the vote. However, it secured 6 percent, and 16 seats, in the 2016 elections.

Leader: Saša RADULOVIĆ.

Doors (*Pokret Dveri*—PD). A conservative, nationalist political movement, the PD has been notable in organizing opposition to Gay Pride events in Belgrade. Registering as a political party prior to the May 2012 parliamentary election, it received 4.4 percent of the vote and failed to gain representation. In the March 2014 election, it received 3.6 percent of the vote, again failing to pass the threshold. The PD ran in the 2016 elections in a coalition with the Democratic Party of Serbia (*Demokratska Stranka Srbije*—DSS, see below). The coalition won 13 seats, of which the PD secured 7.

Leaders: Boško OBRADOVIĆ, Vladan GLIŠIĆ, Branimir NEŠIĆ, Srdjan NOGO, Zoran RADOJIČIĆ, Danilo TVRDIŠIĆ, Radovan TVRDIŠIĆ (Leadership Council).

Democratic Party of Serbia (*Demokratska Stranka Srbije*—DSS). The DSS was established shortly before the December 1992 election by a dissident faction of the Democratic Party that wished to join the Depos opposition bloc in that contest. Under Vojislav Koštunica it later swung further to the right than its parent.

Standing on its own in the December 1993 Serbian Assembly election, the DSS won seven seats. Although a constituent of the *Zajedno* alliance in the November 1996 election, in which it won four seats, the DSS ran separately in some municipalities in the subsequent local balloting. Like the DS, it boycotted the 1997 Serbian elections.

In August 2000 Koštunica emerged as the consensus DOS presidential candidate to oppose Slobodan Milošević, and he was declared the winner of the September election in early October. Subsequently, the conservative Koštunica had differences with the DOS majority, not least over the handling of Milošević.

In August 2001 the DSS withdrew from the Serbian government, which it accused of failing to address the problem of organized crime. Relations with the DOS and, more specifically, the DS continued to worsen thereafter, and in December the DSS's Dragan Maršićanin was forced out as speaker of the Serbian National Assembly after being accused of vote rigging. With the rivalry between DS leader Djindjić and Koštunica heating up, the DSS in effect withdrew from the DOS.

Koštunica was denied the Serbian presidency in 2002 when a low voter turnout invalidated elections in October and December. Having led the DSS to a second-place finish, with 17.7 percent of the vote and 53 seats, in the Serbian legislative election of December 2003, he was confirmed as the head of a minority government in March 2004. For the December election the DSS had included on its electoral list a handful of candidates from several small parties, including the People's Democratic Party (*Narodna Demokratska Stranka*—NDS), led by Slobodan VUKSANOVIĆ, which then merged into the DSS in October 2004.

In November 2006, looking toward the January 2007 general election, the DSS formed an alliance with New Serbia (*Nova Srbija*—NS, above). The coalition won 47 seats, including the DSS's 33 and the NS's 10. Also awarded 2 seats each on the DSS-NS list were the Serbian Democratic Renewal Movement (SDPO, below) and the United Serbia (see SPS, above). For the January 2008 presidential contest the DSS supported Velimir Ilić of the NS. In May 2008 a coalition of the DSS and the NS won 30 seats (21 for the DSS) on an 11.6 percent vote share. The DSS, adamantly opposed to Kosovo's independence and its recognition by the majority of EU members, joined the opposition.

In the May 6, 2012, election, the DSS won 21 seats with 7 percent of the vote. Koštunica secured 7.4 percent of the vote in the first round of the presidential election, taking fourth place and failing to advance to the second round.

Following the 2012 election, Koštunica emerged as Serbia's leading Euroskeptic. The DSS position has shifted to oppose membership in either the EU or NATO. In early 2014 he called for a public referendum on whether Serbia should join the EU.

In early legislative elections of March 16, 2014, the DSS received 4.2 percent of the vote, failing to pass the threshold to gain representation. The DSS ran in a coalition with the PD in 2016, winning 6 seats.

Leaders: Sanda Rašković IVIĆ (Former Prime Minister of Serbia and President of the Party), Dragan JOČIĆ (Vice President).

In addition to those already mentioned, four ethnic minority parties won seats in the April 2016 legislative election. The **Alliance of Vojvodina Hungarians** (see Leading Vojvodina Parties, SVM, below) won 4 seats; the **Bosniak Democratic Community of Sandžak** (*Bošnjačka Demokratska Zajednica Sandžaka*—BDZS, see Jovanović Coalition, below), 2 seats; the Albanian **Party for Democratic Action** (*Partia për Veprim Demokratik/Parija za Demokratsko Delovanje*—PPVD/PZDD), led by Riza HALIMI, 1 seat; and the **Green Party** (*Zelena Stranka*—ZES), 1 seat.

Other Parties That Contested the 2014 or 2016 Elections:

United Regions of Serbia (*Ujedinjeni Regioni Srbije*—URS). The URS is a party that emerged from the merger of G17 Plus and coalition partners in April 2013.

The **G17 Plus** originated in a think tank of reform-minded, nonparty economists that participated in the FRY and Serbian cabinets following the ouster of Slobodan Milošević. It was established as a political party in December 2002 under the leadership of Miroljub Labus, former FRY deputy prime minister. (For more on the history of the G17, see the 2015 *Handbook*.)

The G17 Plus founded a political coalition, the **United Regions of Serbia,** on May 16, 2010, with Together for Šumadija and six smaller parties: the **People's Party** (*Narodna Partija*—NP), the **Coalition for Pirot** (*Koalicija za Pirot*—KZP), **I Live for Krajina** (*Živim za Krajinu*—ZZK), the **Bunjevac Party** (*Bunjevačka Partija*—BP), the **Sandžak People's Party** (*Sandžačka Narodna Partija*—SNP), and the **Vlach People's Party** (*Vlaška Demokratska Stranka*—VDS). In the May 6, 2012, parliamentary election, the URS won 16 seats with 5.5 percent of the vote; in the subsequent distribution of seats, G17 Plus received 10, the ZZSh 2, the NP 2, and the ZZK and KZP each won 1 seat. In June 2012 the NP was expelled from the coalition after it was revealed they were negotiating a coalition agreement with the Democratic Party.

The NP subsequently formed a progovernment deputy group along with the Party of Democratic Action Sandžak (see Leading Sandžak Parties, SDA Sandžak, below) and the **Rich in Serbia** (*Bogata Serbija*—BS).

In the 2012 presidential election, the URS supported Zoran STANKOVIĆ of the G17 Plus. In the first round, he secured 6.6 percent of the vote, placing fifth and failing to advance to the second round.

In May 2013 the G17 Plus merged with the URS, transforming the latter into a political party.

In the March 16, 2014, early parliamentary election, the URS received 3 percent of the vote, failing to pass the threshold for representation.

In November 2015 the URS was removed from the political party's register and dissolved.

Leaders: Mladjan DINKIĆ (President), Veroljub STEVANOVIĆ (Deputy President), Suzana GRUBJEŠIĆ and Verica KALANOVIĆ (Vice Presidents).

Together for Šumadija (*Zajedno za Šumadiju*—ZZSh). Originally formed as part of the *Zajedno* coalition, this group won the 1996 local elections in Kagujevac, the fourth-largest city in Serbia. By 2002, it had evolved into a regional party, **Together for Kragujevac** (*Zajedno za Kragujevac*—ZZK). The party platform stresses economic revival, membership in the EU, and decentralization of government power—decrying what it terms the "Belgradization" of Serbia and subordination of regional interests to those of the capital. In 2008, the party received two parliamentary seats as part of a coalition with G17 Plus and subsequently was refounded as the ZZSh on June 10, 2008. In 2012 it again received two seats as part of the URS.

Leader: Veroljub STEVANOVIĆ.

Jovanović Coalition. This coalition of the LDP, the SDU, and the **Bosniak Democratic Community of Sandžak** (*Bošnjačka Demokratska Zajednica Sandžaka*—BDZS) is led by Jahja FEHRATOVIĆ. The coalition was supported by the **Association of Free and Independent Trade Unions** (*Asocijacija Samostalnih i*

Nezavisnih Sindikata—ASNS), led by Ranka SAVIĆ. The coalition is a partial continuation of the 2012 coalition **Turn Around** (*Preokret*). In 2016 the BDZS ran independently and won 2 seats with 0.9 percent of the vote.

The origins of Turn Around lie in a joint statement by the LDP, SPO, and SDU on November 5, 2011, that the government will have to adopt new policies (e.g., "turn around" policy) given the reality of Kosovo's secession if Serbia is to obtain EU membership. On March 11, 2012, a formal coalition between the three parties was announced, which further included Rich Serbia, the ASNS, the Vojvodina Party, the **Democratic Party of Sandžak** (see Leading Sandžak Parties, below), **the Green Ecological Party-Green** (*Zelena Ekološka Partija-Zeleni*—ZEPZ), and **the Party of Bulgarians from Serbia** (*Partija Bugara Srbije*—PBS). In the May 6, 2012, parliamentary election, Turn Around won 19 seats with 6.5 percent of the vote; in the subsequent distribution of seats, the LDP received 11 seats, the SPO 4, the SDU 1, the BS 1, the ASNS 1, with 1 seat allocated to a nonparty candidate. The SPO subsequently formed a deputy group with the DHSS, and the BS formed a group with the NP, with the remaining deputies in an LDP-led group.

The 2014 electoral alliance received 3.4 percent of the vote, failing to pass the threshold and achieve representation. It was not continued for the 2016 balloting.

Social Democratic Union (*Socijaldemokratska Unija*—SDU). The SDU was formed by a former associate of the Civic Alliance, Žarko Korać. He was also linked to the student-led Resistance (*Otpor*), which repeatedly took to the streets in opposition to the Milošević regime. The SDU participated in the DOS alliance in 2000.

Following an abortive merger with a wing of Social Democracy in 2002, the SDU reemerged as a separate party in March 2003. In the December 2003 Serbian National Assembly election its candidates ran on the DS electoral list, ending up with one seat. In 2007 it competed in coalition with the LDP, GSS, and LSV and was awarded one seat. In 2008, once again allied with the LDP, it again received one seat. In the 2016 balloting, the party failed to win any seats.

Leader: Miloš ADAMOVIĆ (President).

Other unsuccessful parties/electoral lists contesting the March 2014 election include **Third Serbia** (*Treći Srbija*—TS), led by Aleksandar PROTIĆ; and the **Patriotic Front** (*Patriotski Front*—PF), led by Borsilav PELEVIĆ.

Other Parties That Contested the 2012 Election:

Unsuccessful parties/electoral lists contesting the May 2012 election included Zoranom DRAGIŠIĆEM's **Movement of Workers and Peasants** (*Pokret Radnika i Seljaka*—PRS), the **Communist Party** (*Komunistička Partija*—KP), and Milan VIŠNJIĆ's **Reformist Party** (*Reformistička Stranka*—RS).

Leading Sandžak Parties:

Party of Democratic Action Sandžak (*Stranka Demokratske Akcije Sandžaka*—SDA Sandžak). Linked to the Party of Democratic Action in Bosnia and Herzegovina, the ethnically Bosniac SDA has distinct organizations based in the Albanian/Muslim communities of the Sandžak region (in southwestern Serbia, adjacent to Montenegro), Montenegro, Preševo, and Kosovo.

In 1995 conflicts between factions led by the chair of the SDA Sandžak, Sulejman Ugljanin, and by the party's secretary general, Rasim Ljajić, fragmented the group into five similarly named Sandžak parties. Ugljanin would continue at the head of what he deemed the "true" SDA Sandžak and organized a three-party coalition, the **Sandžak List Dr. Sulejman Ugljanin** (*Koalicija "Lista za Sandžak Dr. Sulejman Ugljanin"*—LZS), which won a seat in the November election for the federal legislature and three seats in the Serbian Assembly in 1997. In 2000 Ljajić's SDA Sandžak adopted the name Sandžak Democratic Party (SDP; see SDPS, above), which remains the principal regional rival of Ugljanin's SDA.

For the 2003 Serbian election various participants in the Sandžak List, including the **Bosniac Democratic Party of Sandžak** (*Bošnjačke Demokratske Stranke Sandžaka*—BDSS), led by Esad DŽUDŽEVIĆ, and Bajram OMERAGIĆ's **Social Liberal Party of Sandžak** (*Socijalno-Liberalna Stranka Sandžaka*—SLSS), were included on the DS party list. In 2007 the Sandžak List, which won two National Assembly seats, also included the **Sandžak Reformists** (*Reformisti Sandžaka*—RS). In 2008 the LZS was renamed the **Bosniac List for a European Sandžak** (*Bošnjačka Lista za Evropski Sandžak*), which again won two seats, one for the BDSS and one for the SLSS.

Ugljanin, who accepted appointment to the Cvetković cabinet after the 2008 election, has also chaired the Bosniac National Council of Sandžak (*Bošnjačko Nacionalno Vijeće Sandžaka*—BNVS), which claims to be the highest representative body of Bosniacs in the region.

In the May 6, 2012, election, the SDA Sandžak won two seats in parliament as a minority list.

In the March 16, 2014, early legislative election, the SDA Sandžak won three seats in parliament as a minority list. The party won two seats in the 2016 balloting with 0.8 percent of the vote.

Leader: Sulejman UGLJANIN (President).

Leading Vojvodina Parties:

League of Vojvodina Social Democrats (*Liga Socijaldemokrata Vojvodine*—LSV). The moderate left-wing LSV was a founding member of the Vojvodina Coalition (see the Vojvodina Party, below) and continues to support autonomy for the region. The party competed in the September election as part of the DOS alliance.

In 2004 the LSV led formation of the **Coalition "Together for Vojvodina"** (*Koalicija "Zajedno za Vojvodinu"*), which won seven seats in that year's Vojvodina Assembly election. After the election the LSV joined the DS-led provincial government. For the 2007 National Assembly election the LSV ran in coalition with the LDP, GSS, and SDU and claimed four seats.

For the May 2008 National Assembly election, the LSV ran as part of the ZES, winning five seats. For the provincial election, however, it again led a Together for Vojvodina Coalition, which won six seats.

The LSV was part of the IzBZ coalition (see above) in the May 2012 election, receiving five seats in the subsequent distribution.

For the early parliamentary elections held on March 16, 2014, the LSV joined the coalition led by the NDS (see SDS, above), receiving six seats. It was part of the SDS-led Alliance for a Better Serbia in 2016, securing 4 seats.

Leaders: Nenad ČANAK (Chair), Bojan KOSTREŠ (Deputy Chair).

Alliance of Vojvodina Hungarians (*Savez Vojvodjanskih Madjara/Vajdasági Magyar Szövetség*—SVM/VMSZ). Founded in 1994 as an offshoot of the DZVM (below), this minority party won 3 seats in the 1996 federal election and 4 in the 1997 Serbian election. It joined the DOS in 2000 but nevertheless offered a separate candidate list in several constituencies, winning 1 lower house seat in the September federal election and, in conjunction with the DOS, an overwhelming majority of seats in the Vojvodina Assembly election of September–October. In the 2004 provincial election the SVM finished third, with 11 seats, far behind the DS's 38 and the SRS's 35. It suffered similar losses in local council elections but joined in forming a DS-led provincial government.

In the 2007 national election, the SVM won three seats. In May 2008, the party ran at the national and provincial levels as part of the **Hungarian Coalition** (*Madjarska Koalicija*—MK) along with the DZVM and the DSVM (below). The MK won four National Assembly seats and nine in the 120-member Vojvodina Assembly, where the ZES won a majority. In January the SVM's chair, István Pásztor, had won 2.3 percent of the first-round vote for president.

In the May 6, 2012, parliamentary election, the SVM won five seats from the minority list (with 1.8 percent of the national vote).

In the March 16, 2014, parliamentary election, the SVM won six seats with 2.1 percent of the vote. The party secured four seats in the 2016 balloting as part of a coalition with the Democratic Party of Vojvodina Hungarians (*Vajdasági Magyar Demokrata Párt/ Demokratska Stranka Vojvodjanskih Madjara*—VMDP/DSVM, see below).

Leaders: Jósef KASZA (Honorary President), István PÁSZTOR (President), Károly PÁL (Executive Vice President).

Democratic Community of Vojvodina Hungarians (*/Vajdasági Magyarok Demokratikus Közössége/ Demokratska Zajednica Vojvodjanskih Madjara*—VMDK/DZVM). The VMDK was formed in 1990 to represent the interests of the ethnic Hungarian population of Vojvodina. In the December 1993 regional elections the VMDK leader, Andraš Agošton, disclosed that pro-autonomy Hungarian organizations in Vojvodina had been financed from Hungary. Agošton was replaced as chair in 1996 and organized the VMDP (below) in 1997. Remaining aloof from the DOS, the party failed to win any seats in the Vojvodina Assembly election in September–October 2000.

For the 2007 national election, the DZVM joined forces with the DSVM in the Coalition of Hungarian Unity (*Koalicija Madjarska Sloga*—KMS), which won less than the 0.4 percent threshold for minority parties. In May 2008 it competed as part of the MK. The party's longtime leader, Sándor PÁL, died in July 2010.

Leader: Áron CSONKA (Chair).

Democratic Party of Vojvodina Hungarians (*Vajdasági Magyar Demokrata Párt/Demokratska Stranka Vojvodjanskih Madjara*—VMDP/DSVM). The VMDP was formed in 1997 by András ÁGOSTON, former chair of the VMDK. The party did not join the DOS in 2000. It won one Vojvodina Assembly seat in 2004. It joined the VMDK in 2007's KMS alliance and in 2008 participated in the MK. The VMDP joined the SVM in an alliance for the 2016 balloting but failed to win any of its own seats.

Leader: András ÁGOSTON.

Democratic Alliance of Croats in Vojvodina (*Demokratski Savez Hrvata u Vojvodini*—DSHV). Founded in 1990, the DSHV represents the small ethnic Croat minority in Vojvodina. For the 2004 Vojvodina election it cooperated with the SVM. In the January 2007 National Assembly election its candidates ran on the DS list and received one seat. In 2008, running with the ZES, it again claimed 1 seat. In 2012 it again claimed one seat, running with the IzBZ. In 2016 the party was part of the For a Just Serbia coalition but failed to win any seats of its own.

Leader: Petar KUNTIĆ (Chair).

Vojvodina Party (*Vojvodjanska Partija*—VP). Formation of the Vojvodina Party was accomplished in June 2005 by the merger of half a dozen small parties. (For details, see the 2014 *Handbook*.) A principal goal of the new formation was full autonomy for the province.

At the 2007 National Assembly election, the VP headed a Coalition "Vojvodina Parties" (*Koalicija "Vojvodjanske Partije"*) that failed to win representation. In 2008, running independently, it took only 0.1 percent of the vote. In 2012 it ran as part of the Turn Around coalition but received no seats.

Leader: Aleksandar ODŽIĆ.

Kosovo Parties:

Ethnic Albanian parties in Kosovo uniformly refused to participate in national elections, and most ethnic Serb parties in Kosovo have boycotted Kosovar elections. Kosovo parliamentary elections were held on June 8, 2014. The **Democratic Party of Kosovo**, led by former Kosovo Liberation Army head Hashim THAÇI, won a plurality of 37 seats in the Assembly of Kosovo. The **Democratic League of Kosovo,** led by President Fatmir SEJDIU, finished second, with 30 seats. Other parties passing the 5 percent minimum threshold for proportional seats were ***Vetëndosje***, with 16 seats; the **Alliance for the Future of Kosovo,** 11; and the Civic Initiative for Kosov, 6. Ten minority parties split the remaining 20 seats, including 9 seats for the **Serbian List**.

For a full discussion of these and other parties, see the entry on Kosovo.

Other Ethnic or Regional Parties:

In the 2007 National Assembly election, the **Roma Party** (*Romska Partija*—RP), led by Šajn SRDJAN, and the **Union of Roma in Serbia** (*Unija Roma Srbije*—URoS), led by Rajko DJURIĆ, each received one seat. Neither was successful in May 2008. The URoS did not compete in the 2012 elections, but the RP received one seat in 2012 as part of the PS coalition (see above). **None of the Above** (*Nijedan od Ponudjenih Odgovora*—NOPO), a party representing the Vlach minority, won 1 seat in the 2012 elections, as did the **Coalition of Albanians from the Preševo Valley** (*Koalicija Albanaca Preševske Doline*—KAPD). The KAPD had been formed by two ethnic parties based in the southern localities of Preševo, Bujanovac, and Medvedja: the **Democratic Action Party** (*Partija za Demokratskoe Delovanje/Partia për Veprim Demokratik*—PDD/PVD), led by Riza HALIMI, and the **Democratic Union of the Valley** (*Demokratske Unije Doline*—DUD), led by Skender DESTANI. In 2007 the two were the first ethnic Albanian parties to contest a national election since 1993.

Ethnic parties that completed unsuccessfully in the March 2014 legislative election include the **Montenegrin Party** (*Crnogorska Partija*—CP), led by Nenad SATEVOVIĆI; a coalition between the ethnic Ruthene **Rusin Democratic Party** (*Rusinska Demokratska Stranka*—RDS) and the **Slovak Democratic Party** (*Slovachka Demokraticka Stranka*—SDS); the **Russian Party** (*Ruska Stranka*—RS); and the coalition **All Together** (*Sve Zajedno*), which included the **Bosnian Democratic Union** (*Bošnjačka Demokratska Zajednica*—BDZ), the **Hungarian Civic Alliance** (*Magyar Polgári Szövettség/Gradjanski Savez Madjara*—MPSz/GSM), the **Democratic Union of Croats** (*Demokratska Zajednica Hrvata*—DZH), the **Hungarian Hope Movement** (*Magyar Remény Mozgalom/Pokret Madjarske Nade*—MRM/PMN), and the **Hungarian Unity Party** (*Magyar Egység Párt/Stranska Madjarskog Jedinstva*—MEP/SMJ).

LEGISLATURE

The **Serbian National Assembly** (*Narodna Skupština Srbije*) comprises 250 members elected to four-year terms by proportional representation. In general, party lists must meet a 5 percent threshold to qualify for seats, except that minority parties are awarded a seat for each 0.4 percent of the vote they receive. In the most recent election, held April 24, 2016, Aleksandar Vučič–Serbia Wins coalition won 131 seats (Serbian Progressive Party, 96; Social Democratic Party, 10; Party of United Pensioners of Serbia, 9; New Serbia, 5; Serbian Renewal Movement, 3; Socialist Movement, 3; Strength of Serbia Movement, 2; Independent Democratic Party of Serbia, 2; and Serbian People's Party, 1); Socialist Party of Serbia–United Serbia–Greens of Serbia coalition, 29 (Socialist Party of Serbia, 21; United Serbia, 6; Greens of Serbia, 2); Serb Radical Party, 22; Enough Is Enough, 16; For a Just Serbia, 16 (Democratic Party, 12; Together for Serbia, 2; New Party, 1; and Together for Šumadija, 1); Alliance for a Better Serbia, 13 (Social Democratic Party, 5; Liberal Democratic Party, 4; and League of Social Democrats of Vojvodina, 4); Doors–Democratic Party of Serbia Coalition (Doors, 7; Democratic Party of Serbia, 6); the Alliance for Vojvodina Hungarians, 4; Bosniak Democratic Community of Sandžak, 2; the Party of Democratic Action of Sandžak, 2; the Party for Democratic Action, 1; and the Green Party, 1.

President: Maja GOJKOVIĆ (SNS).

CABINET

[as of August 15, 2016]

Prime Minister	Aleksandar Vučić (SNS)
First Deputy Prime Minister	Ivica Dačić (SPS)
Deputy Prime Ministers	Zorana Mihajlović (SNS) [f] Rasim Ljajić (SDPS) Nebojša Stefanović (SNS)
Ministers	
Agriculture and Environmental Protection	Branislav Nedimović (SNS)
Construction, Transport, and Infrastructure	Zorana Mihajlović (SNS) [f]
Culture and Media	Vladan Vukosavljević (ind.)
Defense	Zoran Djordjević (SNS)
Economy	Goran Knezević (SNS)
Education and Science	Mladen Sarcević (ind.)
Finance	Dušan Vujović (ind.)
Foreign Affairs	Ivica Dačić (SPS)
Health	Zlatibor Lončar (SNS)
Interior	Nebojša Stefanović (SNS)
Justice	Nela Kuburović (ind.) [f]
Labor, Employment, Veteran, and Social Affairs	Aleksandar Vulin (PS)
Mining and Energy	Aleksandar Antić (SPS)
Regional Development and Local Self-Government	Ana Brnabić (ind.) [f]
Trade, Tourism, and Telecommunications	Rasim Ljajić (SDPS)
Youth and Sport	Vanja Udovičić (ind.)

Without Portfolio	Milan Krkobabić (PUPS) Jadranka Joksimović (SNS) [f] Slavica Đukic-Dejanović (SPS) [f]

[f] = female

INTERGOVERNMENTAL REPRESENTATION

Ambassador to the U.S.: Djerdj MATKOVIĆ.

U.S. Ambassador to Serbia: Kyle Randolph SCOTT.

Ambassador to the UN: Milan MILANOVIĆ.

IGO Memberships (Non-UN): CEUR, EBRD, ICC, IOM, OSCE.

For Further Reference:

Babić, Marko. "Defining Political Extremism in the Balkans. The Case of Serbia." *International Studies: Interdisciplinary Political & Cultural Journal* 17, no. 1 (December 2015): 73–90.

Greenberg, Jessica. *After the Revolution: Youth, Democracy, and the Politics of Disappointment in Serbia*. Stanford, CA: Stanford University Press, 2014.

Thomas, Robert. *The Politics of Serbia in the 1990s*. New York: Columbia University Press, 1999.

SEYCHELLES

Republic of Seychelles
Repiblik Sesel
République des Seychelles

Political Status: Independent member of the Commonwealth since June 29, 1976; present constitution approved by referendum of June 18, 1993.

Area: 171 sq. mi. (429 sq. km).

Resident Population: 97,000 (2016E—UN); 93,186 (2016E—U.S. Census); some 30,000 Seychellois live abroad, mainly in Australia and the United Kingdom.

Major Urban Center (2014E—UN): VICTORIA (26,000).

National Languages: Creole, English, French.

Monetary Unit: Seychellois Rupee (market rate October 1, 2016: 13.35 rupees = $1US).

President: Daniel FAURE (People's Party); elevated (from vice president) to the presidency on October 16, 2016, following the resignation of James Alix MICHEL (Seychelles People's Progressive Front).

Vice President: Vincent MERITON (People's Party); appointed by the president on October 28, 2016, to succeed Daniel FAURE (People's Party) who was elevated to the presidency on October 16.

THE COUNTRY

The Seychelles archipelago consists of some 115 islands in the Indian Ocean about 600 miles northeast of Madagascar. More than 85 percent of the population is concentrated on the largest island, Mahé, which has an area of approximately 55 square miles (142 sq. km); most of the remainder is distributed between the two northern islands of Praslin and La Digue. Most Seychellois are of mixed French-African descent and adhere to Roman Catholicism. There are small minority groups of Indians and Chinese. Nearly 98 percent of adult women are classified as "economically active," largely in subsistence agriculture; women are more likely than men to be literate. Following the September 2016 elections, women held seven seats in the National Assembly (21.2 percent).

Tourism is a significant source of national income and employs about 30 percent of the labor force. Small-scale industries provide about one-quarter of GDP, while the fishing sector produces about 30 percent of export earnings. The economy is also underpinned by a growing offshore banking sector. There has been cautious hope of finding oil, with a U.S. firm awarded a bid to drill south of the islands in 2005.

In 2001 the Seychelles agreed to make changes and was added to the list of Organization for Economic Cooperation and Development (OECD) countries committing to eliminating harmful tax practices.

Following the Indian Ocean tsunami in December 2004, the Paris Club canceled Seychelles's debt. The government began soliciting foreign investment for the tourism sector and promoted the Seychelles as a provider of offshore financial services, but the International Monetary Fund (IMF) reported there was little activity in that area due to the lack of financial supervision.

On the heels of the mid-2000s tsunami, the global financial crisis of 2008–2009 hit the islands hard. In December 2009 the IMF approved $31 million under a stand-by arrangement to support Seychelles's economic program in 2010–2012. Annual growth for 2010 was 5.6 percent, reflecting a rebound in tourism. The IMF commended authorities for modernizing the tax system, including progress toward initiating a value-added tax in 2012. The IMF completed its fourth review of the finance program in January 2012, allowing for the disbursement of an additional $4.7 million.

According to the IMF, growth slipped to 2.8 percent in 2012, down from 5 percent the previous year, in part because of the slowdown in tourism due to the 2010 European debt crisis. Tensions in the oil markets and depreciation of the Euro against the dollar also contributed to negative growth. In April 2012 the World Bank announced a $21 million Country Partnership Strategy with the Seychelles, designed to reduce the country's vulnerability to economic shocks, and in October, the IMF extended the support program until December 2013. Slight recovery in 2013 brought GDP growth of 3.2 percent. In March 2014 the IMF and the Seychelles negotiated a successor three-year arrangement that would make some $17.8 million in funds available to the islands. That year, growth was at 6.2 percent, with inflation and unemployment rates down to 1.4 and 3 percent, respectively. GDP expanded by 4.4 percent in 2015 and 3.3 percent in 2016. Inflation was 2.1 percent in 2016, while unemployment was 2.7 percent, and GDP per capita was $15,400.

GOVERNMENT AND POLITICS

Political background. Following a half-century of French rule, the Seychelles became a British possession under the Treaty of Paris in 1814. Originally administered from Mauritius, it became a Crown Colony in 1903. A partially elected governing council was established in 1967, and limited self-government under a chief minister was introduced in 1970. Following a constitutional conference in London in March 1975, the legislative assembly established in 1970 was increased from 15 to 25 members, the 10 new members being nominated by the two parties in the government coalition. Concurrent with the achievement of independence on June 29, 1976, the former chief minister, James R. MANCHAM, was designated president, and the former leader of the opposition, France Albert RENÉ, became prime minister.

On June 5, 1977, while the president was attending a Commonwealth conference in London, the government was overthrown in a near-bloodless coup that installed René as the new head of state. In balloting on June 23–26, 1979, conducted under a single-party socialist constitution adopted on March 26, René was confirmed in office for a five-year term. After assuming power, President René encountered a series of external and internal challenges to his authority.

In November 1979 he announced the discovery of an antigovernment plot "sponsored from abroad" that allegedly involved ousted president Mancham and a force of mercenaries based in Durban, South Africa. About 85–100 people were arrested in the wake of the allegations including the head of the country's immigration service. A potentially more serious threat was averted in November 1981 with the detection at Mahé's Pointe Larue airport of a group of mercenaries led by the celebrated Col. Michael "Mad Mike" Hoare, an Irishman who had been involved in a number of African destabilization efforts during the previous two decades. In the course of a pitched battle with units of the Seychelles People's Defence Force (SPDF), some 45 of the invaders commandeered an Air India Boeing 707 and ordered the pilot to fly them to Durban, where they eventually surrendered to South African police. Released on bail in early December, the mercenaries were rearrested on

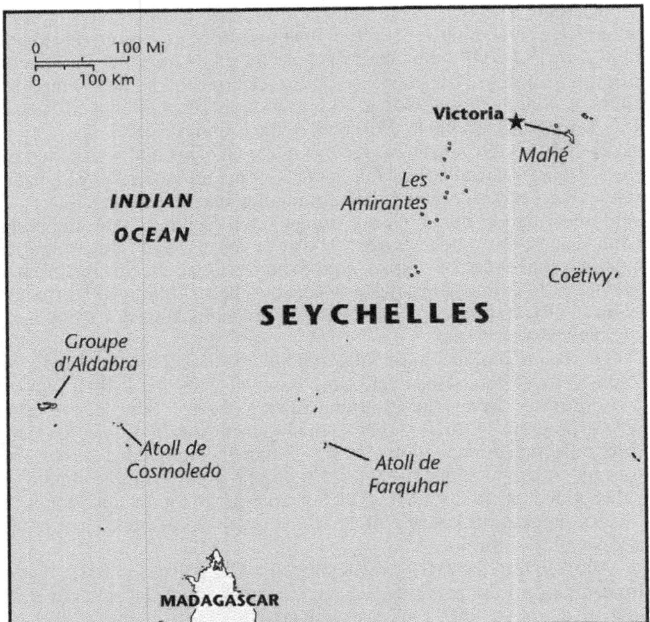

January 5, 1982, in the wake of mounting international criticism. Most were given modest jail sentences under the South African Civil Aviation Offenses Act, Colonel Hoare ultimately being released in May 1985.

In August 1982 some 150 lower-ranked members of the SPDF seized key installations on Mahé in an abortive protest against alleged ill-treatment by senior military officials, while in September 1986 a number of army officers loyal to the minister of defense, Col. Ogilvy BERLOUIS, were charged with plotting to assassinate the president. In London, the exiled Seychelles National Movement (*Mouvement National Seychellois*—MNS) claimed knowledge of the 1986 plot, saying that the principals had been divided as to its implementation; subsequently, Colonel Berlouis resigned his post and left the country for Britain.

Despite exile opposition calls for a boycott, President René was reelected by a reported 92.6 percent of the vote on June 17, 1984, after having announced that those failing to participate would lose their right to public assistance. The National Assembly was subsequently replenished in single-party balloting on December 5, 1987, while the president was accorded a third term on June 9–11, 1989. Over the next two years, President René made tentative steps toward political change.

In November 1990 President René commented favorably on the possibility of a reform referendum, although with reference only to the conduct of intraparty affairs. In March 1991 he was further reported to favor limited administrative decentralization through the reestablishment of district councils, whose members would, however, have to be supporters of the ruling Seychelles People's Progressive Front (SPPF).

On September 12, 1991, the assembly approved a Local Government Bill that provided for the multiple candidature, one-party election of local councils, whose heads were to meet with the Central Committee of the SPPF to rule on the desirability of a referendum on constitutional revision. However, in a remarkable turnabout on December 3, an extraordinary SPPF congress (meeting with the council heads elected two days earlier and identified as constituting a new assembly) voted unanimously to endorse an unexpected proposal by René to introduce a pluralist system. Under the plan, opposition parties would be permitted to register by January 1992 and a Constituent Committee would be elected by proportional representation in July to draft a new constitution. The president had also called on political exiles to return to the Seychelles, provided they retract their "accusations" against his regime.

In the Constituent Committee balloting on July 26, 1992, the SPPF won 14 seats on the basis of a 58.4 percent vote share, while the Democratic Party (DP) of former president Mancham was awarded 8 seats on the basis of a 33.7 percent share; no other groups secured representation.

The DP eventually boycotted the following constitutional proceedings after accusing the SPPF of "bulldozer tactics," and the SPPF delegation (which constituted a quorum) continued alone. On October 6 the opposition set out specific objectives, which included the termination of links between the SPPF and the armed forces and a halt to state funding for the SPPF.

In the face of opposition criticism, the draft constitution secured the approval of only 53.7 percent of the votes cast (60 percent being needed for acceptance) at the referendum of November 15, 1992. The DP thereupon returned to the Constituent Committee and participated in the approval on May 7, 1993, of a revised draft that received popular endorsement by 73.6 percent of participating voters on June 18. (For more on the 1992 constitution, see the 2012 *Handbook*.)

New presidential and assembly elections were held on March 20–22, 1998, with President René and the SPPF again winning by convincing margins. René was reelected with 67 percent of the vote, 7 points higher than he had scored in the 1993 election; in addition, James MICHEL, whom René had appointed as vice president the previous year, was elected as René's running mate. René's nearest competitor was Rev. Wavel RAMKALAWAN, leader of the United Opposition (UO), who secured 20 percent of the vote, while former president Mancham of the DP finished with 14 percent. The DP also fared poorly in the assembly balloting, winning only one seat (down from the five they had held previously). Meanwhile, the SPPF, with 30 legislative seats, improved its total by 3 from 1993; the UO became the main opposition party, such as it was, with 3 assembly seats.

Following the approval by the National Assembly in 2000 of a constitutional amendment allowing the president to call presidential elections separately from legislative elections, René called for an early presidential poll on August 31–September 2, 2001. Once again facing Ramkalawan (representing the Seychelles National Party [SNP], as the UO had been renamed), René was reelected with 54.2 percent of the vote. Ramkalawan, however, significantly improved his vote share to 45 percent, partly because of Mancham's decision not to run. The cabinet announced by René on September 5 included reshuffled assignments but no new members.

In October 2002 the assembly voted to dissolve and hold new legislative balloting on December 4–6. Although the SPPF retained its majority (23 of 34 seats on a 54 percent vote share), the SNP improved from 3 to 11 seats (on a 40 percent vote share).

President René, citing the fact that he was "getting older," resigned the presidency on March 31, 2004, and Michel was inaugurated as his successor on April 14. Joseph BELMONT, a cabinet member since 1982, was confirmed as vice president by the assembly on April 16. Initial objection to Michel's appointment on behalf of the SNP subsided and his leadership was accepted. An opposition (SNP) motion to dissolve the assembly to allow for parliamentary elections at the same time as presidential balloting in 2006—a year ahead of schedule—was rejected by the full body in May 2006. Presidential elections subsequently were held July 28–30, 2006, in which the incumbent Michel and running mate Vice President Belmont garnered 53.7 percent of the votes, defeating the SNP's Ramkalawan and running mate Annette GEORGES (45.7 percent of the vote), and independent Philippe BOULLÉ (0.6 percent). A reshuffled cabinet was sworn in on August 9, 2006.

Following a violent confrontation with police in October 2006 over a law banning political parties and religious groups from owning radio stations, the 11 opposition legislators boycotted parliament, and their five-month absence prompted President Michel to dissolve the National Assembly in March 2007, setting the stage for early legislative elections on May 10–12. The SNP on March 27 formed an electoral alliance with the DP. The ruling SPPF retained its 23-seat majority with a 57 percent vote share; the DP-SNP coalition won 11 seats on a vote share of 43 percent. The president reshuffled the cabinet on July 3.

Vice President Belmont chaired a constitutional review committee in 2008. The constitution review panel, then chaired by Francis CHANG-SAM, turned its recommendations in to President Michel in April 2010, and the president subsequently asked the attorney general to begin the process to update the charter. The government posted the review on its Website and invited the public to submit comments. The authorities said a national consultation exercise would be conducted in 2011.

On June 8, 2010, the president announced a major reshuffle of the cabinet and named a new vice president, Daniel FAURE, in light of the retirement of Vice President Belmont at the end of June after more than 40 years of public service. The new, restructured government and the new vice president took office on July 1, following approval by the National Assembly.

President Michel was reelected in balloting on May 19–21, 2011 (several days were set to accommodate the distances across the archipelago), with 55.4 percent of the vote, defeating perennial candidate Wavel Ramkalawan, who secured 41.4 percent. Philippe Boullé was a distant third with 1.7 percent, followed by the DP's Ralph VOLCERE with 1.5 percent. The president and Vice President Faure were sworn in on May 23, 2011.

President Michel dissolved the National Assembly in July 2011 after the SNP boycotted most the assembly's sessions. The SNP, the NDP, and the Seychelles Freedom Party also boycotted the resulting legislative elections to protest the systematic use of state resources by the ruling party. Consequently, the SPPF won all 31 directly elected seats and 6 of the 7 proportional seats. The newly formed Popular Democratic Movement (PDM) gained the remaining proportional seat (see Current issues, below).

President Michel announced a restructuring of ministries on February 29, 2012, and named a reshuffled cabinet on March 7, appointing several new ministers and creating the Ministry of Tourism and Culture. Former Indian archipelago central bank governor, Pierre LAPORTE, was appointed Minister of Finance.

In presidential balloting on December 3–5, 2015, Michel was first with 47.8 percent of the vote, followed by the SNP's Ramkalawan with 33.9 percent. The two advanced to runoff polling on December 16–18, which was won by Michel with 50.2 percent of the vote (winning by just 193 votes). Ramkalawan bitterly denounced the results and demanded a recount, but Michel was sworn in on December 20.

Ahead of legislative balloting on September 8–10, 2016, four opposition parties formed the Seychelles Democratic Alliance (*Linyon Demokratik Seselwa*—LDS), led by the SNP. In the elections, the LDS won 19 seats to 14 for the PP. Michel announced his resignation on September 27 and was replaced by Faure on October 16. On October 28 Faure conducted a major cabinet reshuffle.

Constitution and government. The 1993 constitution provides for a multiparty presidential system, under which the chief executive is elected for a thrice-renewable five-year term. Legislative authority is vested in a unicameral National Assembly. Constitutional amendments introduced in July 1996, following their adoption by an SPPF congress in late May, created the post of vice president and also increased the number of directly elective seats in the assembly from 22 to 25, while reducing the proportional seats to a maximum of 10 subject to a threshold of 10 percent of the vote.

The judiciary encompasses a Court of Appeal, a Supreme Court (part of which sits as a Constitutional Court), an Industrial Court, and magistrates' courts. Local government, seemingly necessary for geographic reasons, was abolished in 1971 following problems growing out of a district council system that had been introduced in 1948. However, the councils were revived in 1991.

The constitution provides for freedom of expression, though within limits. The minister of information can prohibit the broadcast of material counter to "national interest." State media hold a virtual monopoly, as private media have not flourished. In 2016 the media watchdog Reporters Without Borders ranked Seychelles 92nd out of 180 countries in terms of press freedom.

Foreign relations. The main objectives of the Seychelles foreign policy following independence were the "return" of a number of small islands and island groups administered since 1965 as part of the British Indian Ocean Territory and designation of the Indian Ocean as a "zone of peace." In March 1976, prior to debate on the Seychelles independence bill in the House of Commons, the British government indicated that arrangements had been made for the return to the Seychelles of the islands of Aldabra, Desroches, and Farquhar; however, the Chagos Archipelago would remain as the sole component of the British Indian Ocean Territory. Included in the archipelago was Diego Garcia, where the United States, under an agreement concluded with Britain in 1972, maintained military and communications facilities. There was also a U.S. space-tracking station on the island of Mahé, where, despite the Diego Garcia issue, relations between American personnel and the Seychellois were relatively cordial. In July 1989, while visiting Washington, President René agreed to a five-year extension of the station's lease, which in 1984 provided 5 percent of the state's revenue. In 1995 Washington announced it was closing the Mahé station in a cost-cutting move and transferring its activity to a new facility on Diego Garcia.

Relations between the Seychelles and South Africa were by no means enhanced as a result of the 1981 coup attempt on Mahé. Colonel Hoare and the other defendants, tried under air piracy charges, argued that South Africa's National Intelligence Service (NIS) had full knowledge of the plot, and the trial judge conceded that it would be naïve to assume otherwise as one of the mercenaries was a former NIS agent. South African prime minister P. W. Botha did not dispute this finding but argued that "neither the South African Government, the Cabinet, nor the State Security Council" had been informed and that, therefore, no authorization had been given. Significantly, 34 of the mercenaries convicted on the air piracy charges were given time off for good behavior and released on November 27, 1982, after spending only four months in prison. But by early 1992 relations between the two countries had warmed, permitting the establishment of consular and trade (though not ambassadorial) relations.

In mid-1988 the Seychelles established diplomatic relations with Mauritius and the Comoros. The three, along with Madagascar and France (representing Réunion), are members of the Indian Ocean Commission (IOC) set up in 1982 to promote regional cooperation and economic development.

Relations with the United States cooled in 1996 following the closure of the U.S. embassy in Victoria (responsibility for the Seychelles transferring to the U.S. ambassador to Mauritius). In addition, a U.S. State Department report in March criticized the Seychelles's human rights record, referring to the ruling party's "pervasive system of political patronage and control over government jobs, contracts, and resources." In the wake of increasing global terrorist attacks, the United States in 2005 pledged continued support to the Seychelles military. Washington reportedly valued the Seychelles geographical location for transit for U.S. shops, though also viewed the islands as a potential transfer point by terrorists seeking access to Africa.

Although the Seychelles agreed to a regional free trade pact with the European Union (EU) in 2007, it was one of several African countries that in 2008 rejected participation in a free trade zone and a customs union as proposed by the Common Market for Eastern and Southern Africa (Comesa).

Attention turned in 2009 to the growing problem of piracy, the Seychelles having arrested more than a dozen suspected pirates early in the year. The Seychelles allowed EU troops on the islands and expanded its military cooperation with the United States, China, France, and the United Arab Emirates in intensified efforts to combat piracy. Reports late in the year indicated that hijackings had increased, despite the deployment of what had now become an international armada in coastal waters. By 2010 the Seychelles had become a hub for antipiracy action as it boosted surveillance with the help of the U.S. government in providing an unarmed aerial vehicle.

Strengthened relations with China, which the Seychelles had been fostering for several years, led to China's pledging $6 million for development projects in the islands in May 2010.

In July 2010—in the first such ruling in the islands—the government sentenced 11 Somali pirates to ten years in jail for attacking a coast guard vessel inside territorial waters. Piracy continued to be a high-priority issue in 2011, when the Seychelles changed its laws to allow pirates captured anywhere beyond its territorial waters to be prosecuted. In February, 10 Somalis who had seized a fishing boat with 7 Seychellois on board in November 2010 were sentenced to 20 years in jail on two counts of piracy. The Somalis were sent back to Somalia in accordance with an agreement between the two countries. In 2011 the Seychelles signed an agreement with Denmark to fight piracy in the Indian Ocean, and with international support, the country remained a hub for combating piracy.

China announced in December 2011 that it would accept the Seychelles's offer of establishing a naval refueling port on Mahé (China's first overseas military base) to support its antipiracy operations. In 2011 China and Seychelles also renewed a defense agreement signed in 2004, under which China provides training and equipment to Seychellois military personnel.

In February 2012 India and Seychelles signed a pact to install a surveillance system in the Seychelles's exclusive economic zone to combat piracy and terrorism. India has since deployed several ships to the Seychelles, and the two nations are discussing further bilateral cooperation in defense, including the training of experts and police. In April India signed a $75 million credit line and grant agreement with the Seychelles.

Seychelles joined the Combined Maritime Forces, an antipiracy alliance of 26 countries. Seychelles and Qatar in November 2012 iterated an interest in strengthening ties between the two countries.

In April 2013 Seychelles granted asylum to Sakhr el-Materi, son-in-law of deposed Tunisian leader Zine al-Abidine Ben Ali, who was convicted of corruption in absentia in Tunisian court. Seychelles did not comply with Tunisian extradition requests, claiming that there were no conditions for a free and fair trial.

In November 2013 the OECD included the Seychelles on a list of countries that had not done enough to implement global tax standards. During a meeting in June 2014 to formalize a Joint Cooperation Agreement with Kenya, leaders from the two countries spoke out against terrorism travel warnings issued by European and North American countries. The Seychelles in August 2014 joined nine other African countries in pledging personnel and equipment to the 5,000-strong East Africa Standby Force.

The Seychelles finalized a bilateral trade agreement with the United States in September 2014, paving the way for a full ascension to the World Trade Organization in April 2015. In August 2015 the Seychelles and India signed an agreement to share the financial information of citizens in an effort to reduce tax evasion and money laundering. Also in August, the two countries finalized an agreement to allow India access to the maritime economic zone of the Seychelles.

Current issues. Following his reelection to a second term in May 2011, President Michel called for a bipartisan effort toward a "new Seychelles." Though some opposition members claimed there were electoral violations, the polling was declared free and fair by observers, who recommended equal access to the state media by all candidates.

Due to a boycott of the legislative elections, the SPPF initially won all the seats in the National Assembly, prompting concern from other parties and observers about the country returning to one-party rule. The newly formed People's Democratic Movement, founded by former SNP member Daniel Pierre in August 2011, won 9.6 percent of votes nationwide, but the Electoral Commission declared this was not enough to claim a proportionally allocated seat. The MDP contested the outcome and was eventually awarded the seat by the Court of Appeals, a decision that was criticized by the SPPF. The SNP and the other political parties called for electoral reform as proposed by the Electoral Commission. In May 2012 the first piece of legislation for the Electoral Reform Process was sent to the Cabinet. The proposed Public Assembly Act would eliminate the current requirement that political parties request permission from the Commissioner of Police before holding a meeting; parties still, however, would be required to notify the Commissioner five days in advance.

The island nation continued to be a venue for prosecuting piracy in 2012. In January 15 Somali pirates who had hijacked an Iranian ship were captured by the U.S. Navy and, in March, were transferred from Djibouti to the Seychelles to stand trial.

Meanwhile, in two separate incidents in December 2011 and April 2012, U.S.-operated unarmed aerial vehicles (or "drones") crashed near or on the Seychelles. U.S. officials said unmanned aerial vehicles are being operated from the island to track pirates in the Indian Ocean.

In January 2013 Seychelles won an award recognizing its efforts toward protection of the ozone layer. The Seychelles was among the first countries to ratify the Montreal Protocol.

Following a two-year moratorium, the Seychelles reopened bidding for oil and gas exploration rights in its exclusive economic zone in June 2013. Meanwhile, antipiracy efforts continued through 2013, with a conviction of 11 pirates, likely of Somali origin, in October.

In April 2016 the assembly approved a measure to limit presidents to two terms in office. The measure would become effective with the next presidential election.

POLITICAL PARTIES

Prior to the 1977 coup, government was shared by the centrist **Seychelles Democratic Party** (SDP), led by President James R. Mancham, and the left-of-center **Seychelles People's United Party** (SPUP), headed by Prime Minister France René. Following the coup, René stated that the SDP "has not been banned, it has simply disappeared." The government-supportive Seychelles People's Progressive Front (SPPF) was the sole legal party from June 1978 until January 1991, following which other parties, including Mancham's Democratic Party, were recognized. Provision was also made for the financial support of parties from public funds.

Government Party:

People's Party (*Parti Lepep*—PL). The PL was originally organized as the **Seychelles People's Progressive Front**—SPPF (*Front Populaire Progressiste des Seychelles*) in early 1978 as successor to the SPUP. Like its predecessor, it advocated a broad spectrum of "progressive" policies while attempting to cultivate relations with Catholic clergy sympathetic to its approach to social issues. Upon the retirement of Secretary General Guy SINON in May 1984, President René was named to succeed him as head of an expanded secretariat of 13 members, René's former position as party president being abolished.

Delegates to the party's congress in 1991 approved a Central Committee declaration that "the SPPF believes in the one-party system and in the socialist option" but left open the possibility of a future referendum on multipartyism. It also endorsed revival of an earlier system of party-controlled elective district councils, prior to approving a return to political pluralism at an extraordinary congress in December (see Political background, above). René was reelected as party chair during the annual SPPF conference on April 3, 2005, even though many observers had expected him to vacate the post following his resignation as president of the republic in 2004.

In June 2009, upon the 45th anniversary of the party's founding, René relinquished party leadership to President Michel. Finance Minister Daniel Faure became secretary general. That year, the party adopted the People's Party banner. Faure was appointed vice president in 2010. At a party congress in March 2014, the PL attempted to woo prominent businesspeople, including several known to support the opposition. In June 2014, the PL celebrated its 50th anniversary.

Michel was reelected president in December 2015 but resigned after the party lost its majority in legislative balloting in September 2016, when the PL won 49.2 percent of the vote and 14 seats. Michel subsequently resigned and was replaced by Vice President Faure, while Vincent MERITONE was appointed vice president.

Leaders: Daniel FAURE (President of the Republic and President of the Party), Vincent MERITONE (Vice President of the Republic), Joseph BELMONT (Former Vice President of the Republic), France Albert RENÉ (Former President of the Republic and Chair of the Party).

Opposition Parties:

Seychelles Democratic Alliance (*Linyon Demokratik Seselwa*—LDS). The LDS was formed in 2015 by four opposition parties: the Seychelles National Party (SNP, below), the Seselwa United Party (SUP, below), **Seychellois Alliance** (*Lalyans Seselwa*—LS), and the **Seychelles Party for Social Justice and Democracy** (SPSD), led by Alexia AMESBURY. The constituent parties supported their individual candidates in that year's presidential polling but united for the 2016 legislative balloting in which the coalition won 49.6 percent of the vote and 19 seats, giving the opposition a legislative majority for the first time in more than two decades. Patrick PILLAY of the LS was elected speaker of the assembly on September 27.

Leader: Rev. Wavel RAMKALAWAN (SNP).

Seychelles National Party (SNP). The SNP is the successor to the **United Opposition** (UO), which changed its name at a July 1998 congress. The UO had been formed by the three parties immediately below to oppose the 1993 constitution in both its original and final forms. Its candidate, Philip BOULLÉ, ran a distant third in the presidential balloting of July 23, and the party won only one proportionally allocated seat. Boullé retired from politics in 1995 (see National Alliance Party, below). In September 1995 Rev. Wavel Ramkalawan defeated Gabriel Hoareau of the MNS for the party presidency. Ramkalawan finished second in the 1998 presidential election with 20 percent of the vote. With three seats, the UO became the lead opposition group. At the July 1998 congress, the party adopted the SNP rubric.

In the 2001 presidential election, Ramkalawan received 45 percent of the vote in his loss to President René. While relations between Ramkalawan and René appeared to improve during the 2002 parliamentary elections, government forces cracked down on an SNP demonstration in July 2003. The SNP won 11 seats in the December 2002 legislative elections.

Ramkalawan, with a 45.7 percent vote share and an endorsement by the DP, failed to defeat James Michel in the July 2006 presidential election. In October 2006 Ramkalawan reportedly was among those arrested during a demonstration protesting a law banning political parties and religious groups from owning radio stations. In March 2007 the SNP and the DP formed an electoral alliance for the May legislative elections, the coalition retaining 11 opposition seats.

Following published attacks on SNP leaders, the party's secretary general Roger Mancienne, who owned a printing company, stopped printing the DP's newspaper, *Le Nouveau Seychelles Weekly*, which he said his company had agreed to publish "in support of freedom of expression and the work of the opposition." The newspaper's editor responded that those involved in politics should be ready to accept criticism.

Ramkalawan again failed in his bid for the presidency in 2011, when Michel was reelected. Following Michel's reelection, Ramkalawan called for a boycott of the 2011 National Assembly elections over "deficiencies in political and electoral conditions," and some former members of the party broke away to form the Popular Democratic Movement (PDM) in order to field an opposition to the ruling PL.

Leaders: Rev. Wavel RAMKALAWAN (President of the Party and 1998, 2001, 2006, 2011, and 2016 presidential candidate), Bryan JULIE (Treasurer), Nicolas PREA (Secretary General).

Seychelles Party (*Parti Seselwa*—PS). Led by Jean-François Ferrari, son of Maxime FERRARI (former foreign minister and leader of the RPSD), and formerly referenced most frequently by its French rubric, *Parti Seychellois,* the free enterprise-oriented PS was, prior to its legalization, the domestic clandestine affiliate of the RPSD/UDF. Jean-François Ferrari, publisher of the opposition weekly *Regar,* was among those arrested in the July 2003 crackdown.

Leaders: Rev. Wavel RAMKALAWAN, Jean-François FERRARI (Secretary).

Seychelles National Movement (*Mouvement National Seychellois*—MNS). The MNS was originally formed in Brussels in 1984 as an affiliate of the Resistance Movement (*Mouvement pour la Résistance*—MPR).

Leaders: Gabriel (Gaby) HOAREAU (President), Robert FRICHOT (Vice President), Terry SANDAPIN (Secretary).

National Alliance Party (NAP). The NAP was organized in early 1992 by Philippe Boullé and Kathleen Pillay, a former leader of the United Democratic Front (UDF). Boulle later ran as the UO's presidential candidate in balloting in 1993 and announced his retirement in 1995 from active politics. However, he ran as an independent candidate in presidential balloting in 2001, securing only 0.9 percent of the vote, and again in 2006, winning a mere 0.6 percent. In 2011 he secured 1.7 percent of the vote, again as an independent candidate.

Leader: Kathleen PILLAY (Secretary).

Seselwa United Party (SUP). The **Democratic Party** (DP), as the SUP was originally named, was legalized in March 1992 as a revival of the former SDP. Its leader, Sir James Mancham, returned from exile on April 12, 1992. Subsequently, the DP and the SPPF were viewed as the country's two principal political "currents."

Mancham was reelected party leader at an extraordinary party congress on March 18, 1995, from which his intraparty opponents were excluded. DP dissident Christopher Gill, expelled for complaining about Mancham's "tightfisted" control, founded the short-lived New Democratic Party in 1995 before joining the SPPF in 1997, despite his previous criticism of the René government. The DP secured only one seat in the 1998 elections, while Mancham won only 14 percent of the vote in the Presidential election. The DP lost its seat in the National Assembly in the 2002 election, polling only 3.1 percent. Mancham retired as party leader in January 2005, although he subsequently was reportedly involved in planning a conference of opposition leaders designed to promote "reconciliation."

In 2006 the DP supported the SNP's Ramkalawan in the presidential election. In 2007 the DP contested the National Assembly elections in a coalition with the SNP, winning 11 seats.

In March 2009 it was reported that Ralph Volcere was elected party president following the resignation of Paul CHOW. The Party changed its name to New Democratic Party in June 2009 but is distinct from Gill's New Democratic Party. Following the 2011 presidential election, in which Volcere finished a distant fourth with just 1.5 percent of the vote, he offered to resign as party president, but the party's executive committee rejected the offer, and Volcere remained party leader. In 2011 the DP boycotted the National Assembly elections and adopted the banner the New Democratic Party. Two years later, the name changed to the Seselwa United Party. Volcere resigned as party leader in April 2014. The SUP committee named Robert ERNESTA to fill the post.

Leaders: Robert ERNESTA (President of the Party), Sir James R. MANCHAM (Former President of the Republic).

Other Parties:

Popular Democratic Movement (PDM). Registered with the Electoral Commission in August 2011, the PDM (initially named the **Popular Democratic Party**) was hurriedly formed by breakaway members of the SNP following the party's boycott of the 2011 National Assembly elections. The PDM was the only opposition party that fielded candidates and was awarded one proportionally elected seat. Party leader David PIERRE was the PDM presidential candidate in 2015. He received 2.1 percent of the vote. The party did not secure any seats in the 2016 balloting.

Leaders: David PIERRE (Party Leader and Former Deputy Secretary General of the SNP), Francesca MONNAIE (Secretary General).

Seychelles Freedom Party (SFP). The SFP was registered in August 2011. It was founded by Christopher GILL, formerly of the Democratic Party (see also SUP, above). In the mid-1990s, Gill formed a breakaway New Democratic Party but then later joined the SPPF in 1997. Gill tried to register the party under the name ***Mouvman Seselwa Rasin*** (Seychelles Roots Movement), but the name was deemed too xenophobic by authorities. The SFP campaigns against what it perceives as unfair rights and privileges, like tax breaks and land ownership enjoyed by wealthy foreigners. The party has been accused of inciting racism. Gill's SFP, along with the SNP and DP, boycotted the 2011 National Assembly elections and, like the SNP, pushes for electoral reform and the de-linking of the state and the ruling party.

Leader: Christopher GILL.

Other Parties and Groups:

The only other party to present candidates in the 2002 assembly balloting was the **Social Democratic Alliance**, which fielded one candidate. However, several independent candidates contested the elections.

A British-based organization known simply as the **Resistance Movement** (*Mouvement pour la Résistance*—MPR) appeared to have been implicated in the November 1981 coup attempt, while a South African-based **Seychelles Popular Anti-Marxist Front** (SPAMF) announced late in the year that it had known of the mercenary effort but had declined to participate on the ground that it was unworkable. A third group, the **Seychelles Liberation Committee** (*Comité de la Libération Seychelles*—CLS) was launched in Paris in 1979. In November 1985 MPR leader Gérard HOAREAU was assassinated outside his London residence by an unknown assailant. Former president Mancham charged the René government with the killing, which was vehemently denied by a spokesperson for the Seychelles embassy.

During a speech before a House of Commons committee in February 1990 Mancham invited all of the exile groups to join him in a **Crusade for Democracy in Seychelles** (CDS) and subsequently called for the formation of an opposition **United Democratic Front** (UDF). A less conservative London exile, former foreign minister Maxime Ferrari, displayed ambivalence toward the Mancham overture and in December 1990 launched a **Rally of the Seychelles People for Democracy** (*Rassemblement du Peuähple Seychellois pour la Démocratie*—RPSD) that, somewhat unrealistically, appeared to seek common ground between Mancham and René. Ferrari returned to the Seychelles in 1991.

LEGISLATURE

The unicameral **National Assembly** (*Assemblée Nationale*) has 25 directly contested seats from 25 single-member constituencies, plus up to 10 seats allocated on a proportional basis to parties winning at least 10 percent of the vote. (A party gets one proportional seat for each 10 percent of the vote it receives in the balloting for the directly contested seats.) The term of office is five years. The results of the most recent elections on September 8–10, 2016, were as follows: Seychelles Democratic Alliance, 19 seats (15 directly contested, 4 proportional); People's Party, 14 (10, 4).

Speaker: Patrick PILLAY (LDS).

CABINET

[as of November 20, 2016]

President	Daniel Faure
Vice President	Vincent Meriton

Ministers

Agriculture and Fisheries	Michael Benstrong
Defense, Legal Affairs, Public Administration, and Foreign Affairs	Daniel Faure
Education and Human Resources Development	Joel Morgan
Employment, Entrepreneurship, and Business Innovation	Wallace Cosgrow
Environment, Energy, and Climate Change	Didier Dogley
Finance, Trade, and Economic Planning	Peter Larose
Habitat, Infrastructure, and Land Transport	Charles Bastienne
Health and Social Services	Jean-Paul Adam
Home Affairs, in Charge of Immigration, Prisons, and Police (Internal Affairs and Transport)	Mitcy Larue [f]
Information, Blue Economy, Investment and Industry, Information Communication Technology, Disaster Risk Management, Civil Society and Religious Affairs, and the Inner and Outer Islands	Vincent Meriton
Local Government	Macsuzy Mondon [f]
Tourism, Civil Aviation, Ports and Marine	Alain St. Ange
Youth, Sports, and Culture	Idith Alexander [f]

[f] = female

INTERGOVERNMENTAL REPRESENTATION

Ambassador to the U.S. and Permanent Representative to the UN: Marie-Louise Cecile POTTER.

U.S. Ambassador to the Seychelles and Mauritius: Melanie ZIMMERMAN (Chargé D'Affaires).

IGO Memberships (Non-UN): AfDB, AU, Comesa, CWTH, NAM, WTO.

For Further Reference:

Hoare, Mike. *The Seychelles Affair.* Reprint; Boulder, CO: Paladin Press, 2008.

Scarr, Deryck. *Seychelles since 1770: History of a Slave and Post-Slave Society.* Trenton, NJ: Africa World Press, 1999.

Shillington, Kevin. *Albert René: The Father of Modern Seychelles, a Biography.* Crawley: University of Western Australia Publishing, 2014.

SIERRA LEONE

Republic of Sierra Leone

Political Status: Independent member of the Commonwealth since April 27, 1961; republic proclaimed April 19, 1971; one-party constitution adopted June 1978; multiparty constitution approved by popular referendum on August 23–30, 1991, with effect from September 24; government overthrown in military coup of April 29, 1992; ruling military council overthrown and replaced by "reconstituted" military council on January 16, 1996; democratically elected president inaugurated on March 29, 1996; government overthrown in military coup of May 25, 1997; ruling military council forcibly removed by regional forces on February 13, 1998; previously elected government reinstalled on March 10, 1998; July 1999 Lomé peace accord and UN peacekeepers unable to halt ongoing violence; cease-fire agreed between government and insurgents on May 16, 2001; previously elected president and majority party won elections of May 14, 2002.

Area: 27,699 sq. mi. (71,740 sq. km).

Population: 6,592,000 (2016E—UN); 6,018,888 (2016E—U.S. Census).

Major Urban Center (2016E—UN): FREETOWN (1,029,000).

Official Language: English.

Monetary Unit: Leone (market rate October 1, 2016: 5,639.50 leones = $1US).

President: Ernest Bai KOROMA (All People's Congress), elected in second-round balloting on September 8, 2007, and sworn in for a five-year term on September 17 to succeed Ahmad Tejan KABBAH (Sierra Leone People's Party); reelected on November 17, 2012, and sworn in on November 23.

Vice President: Victor FOH (All People's Congress), appointed by the president and sworn in on March 19, 2015, following the March 17 dismissal of Sahr SAM-SUMANA (All People's Congress). (See Government and Politics, below.)

THE COUNTRY

The West African nation of Sierra Leone ("lion mountain"), facing the South Atlantic and nearly surrounded by the Republic of Guinea on the northwest, north, and east, encompasses three geographic regions: a peninsula in the west; a western coastal region, which consists of mangrove swamps and a coastal plain; and a plateau in the east and northeast. The indigenous inhabitants range over 12 principal tribal groups, the most important being the Mende in the south and the Temne in the north. There are also numerous Creole descendants of freed slaves. A variety of tribal languages are spoken, with Krio, a form of pidgin English, serving as a lingua franca. Approximately 70 percent of the population is Muslim, mainly in the north, while 21 percent is Christian, mainly in the south and west. Traditional religions are common and often blended with other faiths.

The agricultural sector of the economy employs about two-thirds of the workforce. Rice is the main subsistence crop, while cocoa, coffee, and palm kernels are the leading agricultural exports. Gold, bauxite, and rutile are among the minerals extracted, with a diamond reserve providing approximately 55 percent of export earnings in 2013. The International Monetary Fund (IMF), the World Bank group, and the European Community/Union (EC/EU) have been among the international agencies extending recent aid in support of efforts to revive an economy that has deteriorated markedly since the mid-1970s. (For more on the economy between the 1970s and 1990s, see the 2012 and 2015 *Handbooks*.)

Diamond mining, the country's third-largest employer, has been a prime beneficiary of the cessation of hostilities. The smuggling of "blood diamonds," a key feature of the civil war, was curbed somewhat by a United Nations diamond embargo on Sierra Leone in 2000 and a subsequent diamond-certification scheme known as the Kimberley process. Since then, the government has regained partial control over the diamond trade; however, smuggling continued to be a problem.

Economic growth improved in 2005–2006, with a decline in inflation (to 9.5 percent) and increased foreign investment in oil and mining. The IMF approved a new three-year poverty reduction program for Sierra Leone, citing the government's "considerable progress" toward economic stability and addressing widespread poverty. (The IMF noted that 80 percent of the population lives on less than $1US per day.) The fund urged the government to enforce tax regulations, accelerate privatization efforts, and diversify and expand exports to bolster revenue. In 2006 the country qualified for $994 million in debt relief under the Heavily Indebted Poor Countries (HIPC) initiative.

The return of "peace and stability" to Sierra Leone contributed to robust economic growth of about 5.5 annually in 2008, according to the IMF, which continued to press for increased spending to help relieve pervasive poverty and for the acceleration of structural reforms. Annual growth was 5.3 percent in 2010, while inflation soared to 17.8 percent "reflecting largely the challenges associated with the new goods and services tax," according to the IMF. Gross domestic product (GDP) grew by 6 percent in 2011, while inflation rose to 18.5 percent, owing in large part to foreign investment in the mining sector and expansion in construction. GDP soared by 15.2 percent in 2012 and 16.3 percent

the following year, mainly on increased foreign investment in the mineral sector and economic assistance. In 2013 the IMF approved a $40.3 million credit to support economic reforms. Inflation slowed to 13.8 percent in 2012 and 9.7 percent in 2013. The economy contracted sharply in 2015, with GDP falling by 12. 8 percent (see Current issues, below). Recovery began in 2016 when GDP grew by an estimated 8.4 percent, while inflation was 11.8 percent. GDP per capita that year was $799.85. Poverty remained prevalent, and the UN ranked Sierra Leone 181st out of 188 countries in its 2014 Human Development Index.

GOVERNMENT AND POLITICS

Political background. Growing out of a coastal settlement established by English interests in the 18th century as a haven for freed slaves, Sierra Leone became independent within the Commonwealth in 1961. Political leadership from 1961 to 1967 was exercised exclusively through the Sierra Leone People's Party (SLPP), a predominantly Mende grouping led successively by Sir Milton MARGAI and his half-brother, Sir Albert M. MARGAI. Attempts to establish a one-party system under the SLPP were successfully resisted by the opposition All People's Congress (APC), a predominantly Temne formation headed by Dr. Siaka P. STEVENS, a militant trade-union leader belonging to the smaller Limba tribe.

Following an unexpectedly strong showing by the APC in the election of 1967, Stevens was appointed prime minister, but he was prevented from taking office by Brig. David LANSANA's declaration of martial law on March 21. Two days later, Lt. Col. Andrew JUXON-SMITH assumed the leadership of a National Reformation Council (NRC) that suspended the constitution, dissolved the parties, and ruled for the ensuing 13 months. The NRC was itself overthrown in April 1968 by a group of noncommissioned officers, the Anti-Corruption Revolutionary Movement, which restored civilian government with Stevens as prime minister.

The ensuing decade was marked by a series of coup attempts and government harassment of political opponents. In 1973 official intimidation contributed to an SLPP boycott of the general election, with the APC winning all but one of the seats in the House of Representatives. In 1975 six civilians and two soldiers were executed in Freetown after being convicted of an attempt to assassinate (then) Finance Minister Christian KAMARA-TAYLOR and take over the government. Under a new constitution adopted by referendum in June 1978, Sierra Leone became a one-party state; President Stevens was reinvested for a seven-year term on June 14.

In early 1985, the president announced his intention to retire, naming army commander Maj. Gen. Joseph Saidu MOMOH as his successor. The new president was confirmed in single-party balloting on October 1; Stevens transferred power to him on November 28, although formal swearing-in ceremonies were not held until January 26, 1986. The House of Representatives was renewed in a multicandidate, one-party poll held on May 29–30, a year prior to expiry of its normal term.

Enthusiasm over Momoh's accession subsided when a campaign to "instill military discipline" in fighting corruption and managing the economy failed to yield tangible results. By mid-1990, the Momoh regime's inability to check inflation, generate the funds for civil service salary payments, or maintain basic services had provoked widespread civil unrest and calls for the adoption of a new, multiparty constitution. Consequently, at an extraordinary APC meeting in August, President Momoh named economist Peter TUCKER to head a National Constitution Review Commission to explore government reorganization along "democratic lines." (At the same time, Momoh described multiparty activity as incompatible with Sierra Leone's tribal structures and widespread illiteracy.)

In late March 1991, less than a week after having reiterated his opposition to the idea, Momoh announced that he welcomed the introduction of a multiparty system. Two months later, the Tucker Commission submitted its report, and in early June the life of the existing House of Representatives was extended to enable it to approve a pluralistic basic law. On July 2, following intense debate both within and outside the government, the House of Representatives ratified the new constitution, and on August 23–30 the document was approved by popular referendum; more than 60 percent of the 2.5 million participants reportedly favored its enactment. On September 23 President Momoh named a transitional government to rule until multiparty elections, tentatively scheduled for late 1992. One day later, the constitution was promulgated, and on September 30 the ban on political parties was officially lifted.

On April 29, 1992, army units, angered at a lack of pay and the failure of the government to provide them equipment to end a 13-week rebellion in eastern Sierra Leone, ousted President Momoh, who flew to exile in Guinea. On May 1 Capt. Valentine Strasser and (then) Lt. Solomon Anthony James MUSA were named chair and vice chair, respectively, of a National Provisional Ruling Council (NPRC), which suspended the constitution and ruled by decree. On May 2 the NPRC appointed a 19-member government, which included several members of the NPRC and six civilians. Two days later the NPRC dissolved the legislature and suspended political activity. On July 14 Captain Strasser announced that the NPRC would thenceforth be known as the Supreme Council of State (SCS) and would no longer be involved in day-to-day administration. Concurrently, ministers were redesignated as secretaries of state, with Musa serving in the quasi-prime ministerial post of chief secretary. In October a 15-member advisory council was established with a mandate to work out a return to multipartyism, with an emphasis on involving citizens in the democratization process.

In mid-December 1992 the regime established a special military tribunal "in the interest of maintaining peace, security, and public order." On December 28 government troops violently repulsed an alleged coup attempt by the so-called Anti-Corruption Revolutionary Movement (ACRM), a grouping of pro-Momoh civilians and military personnel (some of whom were already incarcerated). On December 30, following a summary military trial, 26 people (9 ACRM members and 17 others who had been convicted of high treason for their involvement in an earlier incident) were executed. The executions drew international condemnation; several Western donors announced suspension of aid payments.

On April 29, 1993, Strasser announced the commencement of a three-year transition period to culminate in multiparty elections. In addition, the chair promised to launch an inquiry into the special military tribunal's activities and to ease some security measures.

In a government reshuffle on July 5, 1993, Capt. Julius Maada BIO replaced Musa as SCS vice chair and chief secretary. Musa's dismissal came amid reports that he had clashed with Strasser about the return to multipartyism and that he harbored his own presidential ambitions. In December Dr. James JONAH was appointed chair of the newly established Interim National Electoral Commission (INEC), which had been charged with preparing for presidential and legislative elections tentatively scheduled for 1995.

In 1994 the Strasser regime's credibility was impaired by its inability to suppress the Revolutionary United Front (RUF, below), a Sierra Leonean offshoot of Charles Taylor's National Patriotic Front of Liberia (NPFL, see entry on Liberia) led by Foday Sankannah SANKOH; the Strasser regime claimed the RUF had been organized to punish Sierra Leone for its peacekeeping role in Liberia. By midyear, RUF-related violence was reportedly responsible for the deaths of hundreds of individuals and the dislocation of thousands. Consequently, in July the State Advisory Council, noting that "local people must be collaborating" with the insurgents, announced the creation of a National Security Council charged with ending the hostilities. Thereafter, despite reports that most of the country was "lawless," the government released a draft constitution in October, which included provisions for a return to civilian rule by 1996.

On November 12, 1994, the junta executed 12 soldiers in an apparent attempt to intimidate the so-called "sobels" (soldiers during the day, rebels at night) whom observers described as increasingly beyond Freetown's control. On November 25, bolstered by reports that an offensive had severely weakened the rebels, the Strasser government called on the RUF to begin negotiations on a peace accord and cease-fire, pledging that they would be allowed to form a political party in preparation for multiparty elections. The RUF, which had gained international attention two weeks earlier when it kidnapped two British citizens, initially rejected the offer but on December 4 met with government negotiators for discussions, which were described as "frank." However, the rebels' kidnapping campaign continued into 1995; they reportedly seized an additional 15 foreigners by February. (All of the hostages were eventually handed over to International Red Cross representatives on April 20.)

On March 31, 1995, Captain Strasser announced a major government restructuring, under which Health and Social Services Secretary Lt. Col. Akim GIBRIL would become chief secretary in place of Bio, who remained SCS vice chair while assuming the position of chief of the defense staff "to provide additional mettle" to the armed forces in their campaign against the RUF. On April 27 Strasser promised to lift the ban on political parties and relinquish power to a democratically elected president in January 1996. He also offered the RUF a truce to negotiate an end to the conflict that had claimed some 5,000 lives since 1991. On May 18 he asked the Economic Community of West African States (ECOWAS) to broker negotiations with the rebels; however, the RUF rejected the initiative, calling instead for Strasser to convene a sovereign national conference to decide the future of the country.

On June 21, 1995, the regime lifted the ban on political parties, but two days later it issued a list of 57 people, headed by former president Momoh, who were ineligible to compete in the upcoming balloting. On August 18 the government convened a National Consultative Conference; however, despite its earlier entreaties, the RUF refused to attend. Among the rulings adopted by the conference were the postponement of balloting until February 1996 and the organization of simultaneous presidential and legislative polling.

On October 3, 1995, a coup attempt led by at least eight senior military officers was quashed by troops loyal to Strasser, who was out of the country. The failed uprising highlighted the growing chasm in the SCS between those who opposed the return to a civilian government and its advocates, purportedly led by Strasser.

On January 16, 1996, Strasser was overthrown by his second-in-command, Brigadier General Bio, who announced that he would lead a "Reconstituted" Supreme Council of the State (RSCS). At his inauguration the following day, Bio promised to continue preparations for "transparent, free, and fair" elections and urged the RUF to begin peace talks. In response, the RUF announced a one-week, unconditional cease-fire and called for postponement of the elections, saying it would not negotiate with a civilian government.

In the first round of legislative and presidential balloting on February 26–27, 1996, held under provisions of the 1991 constitution, the SLPP captured 36.1 percent of the vote, easily outpacing the United People's Party (UNPP, below), which finished second with 21.6 percent, and 11 other parties. Meanwhile, SLPP presidential candidate Ahmad Tejan KABBAH and UNPP leader John KARIFA-SMART finished first and second, respectively, in their 12-candidate race. However, because neither captured a majority, a second round of balloting was held on March 15, with Kabbah winning with 59.5 percent of the vote.

The Kabbah administration moved quickly to build on the peace initiative its predecessor had begun with the RUF, and on April 23, 1996, agreement was reached between Kabbah and Sankoh on a "definitive" cease-fire and the establishment of committees to draft disarmament and peace accords. On May 30 Freetown announced that it had reached agreement with the RUF on 26 of 28 articles in a proposed peace plan, leaving unresolved only the timetable for the withdrawal of foreign troops and the establishment of a national debt commission. However, the rebels continued to refuse to recognize the Kabbah government publicly and insisted that the cease-fire was only provisional. At the same time, the administration's announced intention to reduce the military ranks from 18,000 to approximately 4,000 added the threat of yet another military coup to a domestic security landscape already populated by RUF dissidents, "sobels," and escaped prisoners.

On September 8, 1996, at least six soldiers were arrested after senior military officials were alerted to their alleged plans to overthrow the government, and within a week 150 more soldiers were purged in response to an executive order demanding the dismissal of suspected dissidents. Meanwhile, a series of clashes between government forces and rebels in the east threatened the six-month-old cease-fire. However, when government troops reportedly gained the upper hand on the battlefield, President Kabbah and RUF leader Sankoh signed a peace treaty in Abidjan, Côte d'Ivoire, on November 30. Highlighting the accord were provisions for the immediate end to hostilities, the demobilization and disarmament of the RUF, and the integration of rebel soldiers into the national army. Furthermore, the agreement entitled the RUF to transform itself into a legal political party.

Sporadic fighting was reported throughout late 1996 and early 1997; the RUF and government accused each other of violating the peace accord. In addition, clashes were reported between alleged "sobels" and ethnic Kamajor militiamen allied with the president. On March 12 the RUF's Sankoh was detained in Nigeria, and on March 15 he was dismissed from the RUF by senior party officials who accused him of blocking implementation of the peace accord. Subsequently, Sankoh's supporters threatened to attack Freetown unless he was returned from Lagos.

On May 25, 1997, junior army officers fighting alongside RUF militants overran the prison where the defendants in the September 1996 coup plot were being held. Subsequently, under the leadership of one of the freed prisoners, Maj. Johnny Paul KOROMA, the combined forces took control of Freetown and overthrew the government (with Kabbah fleeing to Guinea). On May 28 the military junta abolished the constitution and banned political parties. Meanwhile, 300,000 people reportedly fled the country amid heavy fighting between the junta's forces and Nigerian-led ECOWAS troops, who had launched a countercoup offensive. On June 1 the junta established a 20-member Armed Forces Revolutionary Council (AFRC) and named Koroma its chair. Unable to dislodge the rebel soldiers, the Economic Community of West African States Monitoring Group (Ecomog) announced a cease-fire on June 2. Nevertheless, regional and international observers vowed not to let the coup stand and refused to recognize the Koroma regime.

On June 17, 1997, Major Koroma was sworn in as the leader of the AFRC, and he subsequently agreed to participate in internationally mediated negotiations. However, the talks were promptly abandoned after the junta leader demanded a four-year term. Frustrated with Koroma's intransigence, ECOWAS officials tightened sanctions against the AFRC in late August, and on September 2, Ecomog forces bombed Freetown in an effort to enforce an embargo on imported goods. Furthermore, on October 8 the UN Security Council adopted a resolution empowering Ecomog forces to enforce oil and arms sanctions against the regime. On October 24, under pressure of heavy shelling, AFRC negotiators agreed to a peace plan that included provisions for a disarmament process (beginning December 1), Kabbah's reinstallment on April 22, 1998, immunity for the junta's forces, and a future government role for RUF leader Sankoh. Despite the accord, clashes continued between the AFRC and Ecomog forces, and in mid-December 1997 Koroma asserted that the timetable for implementing the pact would be delayed.

Following a week of particularly intense fighting, Ecomog forces captured Freetown on February 13, 1998. On February 17 ECOWAS announced the formation of an interim "special supervision committee," headed by Vice President Albert DEMBY and the Nigerian leader of the Ecomog forces, Col. Maxwell Khobe. On February 20, 25 of the AFRC leaders were captured as they attempted to escape into Liberia (Johnny Paul Koroma is widely believed to be dead). President Kabbah was officially reinstated on March 10 and promptly named a 15-member cabinet.

As of March 1998, Ecomog-directed, propresidential forces reportedly controlled 90 percent of Sierra Leone. In addition to attempting to wrest control of the remainder of the country from the remnants of the combined AFRC-RUF forces, the reinstalled Kabbah government faced a myriad of other challenges, including resurrecting a devastated economy; reintegrating tens of thousands of dislocated and homeless citizens; and reestablishing relations with Sankoh and the RUF, many of whose fighters reportedly had hidden their weapons when confronted by the Ecomog offensive. Meanwhile, the Kabbah administration pressed ahead with legal actions against former Koroma coup members and their alleged collaborators. In

October Freetown ignored observers' calls for leniency and executed 24 people for treasonous acts, including Koroma's brother, Brig. Gen. Samuel KOROMA. On October 23 Sankoh, who had been returned for trial from Nigeria in July, was sentenced to death for similar offenses. (Collaterally, on November 5 former president Momoh received a ten-year jail term for his ties to Koroma, who remained a fugitive.) Following Sankoh's sentencing, a dramatic upsurge in rebel attacks against civilians was reported; thousands subsequently fled to the capital to escape a campaign marked by atrocities. Despite initial depictions of the violence as being the rebels' last gasp, the RUF and its AFRC military allies advanced to within striking distance of Freetown by December.

In late December 1998 RUF commander Sam BOCKARIE rejected calls for a cease-fire, and on January 6, 1999, the rebels invaded the capital. Approximately 5,000 people were killed before Ecomog troops regained control of the city in mid-month. Thereafter, President Kabbah agreed to let Sankoh participate in cease-fire negotiations; however, apparently emboldened by reports of Ecomog gains elsewhere in the country, Kabbah insisted that the rebels respect the dictates of the 1996 peace accord. Consequently, negotiations proceeded fitfully through February and early March. On March 16 Bockarie broke off talks, reportedly suspecting the government of employing delaying tactics while it won back territory. Subsequently, the Kabbah administration came under pressure from its two largest military backers, the United Kingdom and Nigeria, to seek a negotiated end to its "unwinnable" war.

On May 18, 1999, President Kabbah and rebel leader Sankoh signed an agreement in Togo calling for a cease-fire effective May 25, and a formal peace accord was signed in July. The agreement promised to give the RUF and the AFRC four key government posts and extended total amnesty to RUF and AFRC leaders, including Sankoh, as well as former head of state Momoh, who had been charged with collaborating with the AFRC junta. Amid reports of internal divisions, the RUF and the AFRC agreed to demobilize and disarm and also dropped their demands for an immediate withdrawal of Ecomog troops. The AFRC wing that accepted Koroma's call to stop violence immediately was then reincorporated into the political arena. In October the UN Security Council authorized the United Nations Mission in Sierra Leone (UNAMSIL) to replace the Ecomog troops gradually. In November Sankoh was given powers equivalent to those of vice president, and the RUF and the AFRC were allocated nonsenior cabinet posts. Concurrently, the RUF decided to transform itself into a registered political party, adopting the rubric Revolutionary United Front Party (RUFP). However, the issues of demobilization and disarmament created problems during much of early 2000, and in May the peace agreement broke down as UNAMSIL was moving to replace the Ecomog troops. RUF fighters and some renegade AFRC militia (linked with Eddie KANNEH's wing, which was uneasy with Koroma's call to stop the violence) attacked UNAMSIL detachments, and 19 civilians were killed by Sankoh's bodyguards during a demonstration in front of his residence. Although Sankoh fled the country following the incident, he was apprehended in Nigeria on May 17. Due to advances by UNAMSIL, the progovernment Kamajor militia (styled as the Civil Defense Force [CDF]), Guinean forces opposed to the RUF, and renegade AFRC forces, the rebels were on the defensive for much of the year. In November the RUF agreed once again to commit itself to the peace process and to disarm its troops and relinquish most of its territory to government and UNAMSIL control. In February 2001 Kabbah asked the National Assembly to postpone the presidential and legislative elections due to be held in February and March because of the "uncertain security situation." He also reshuffled his cabinet to include some opposition figures.

As Liberian president Charles Taylor tried to distance himself from the RUF in an effort to clean up his country's image as a protector of the rebels, the RUF signed a peace agreement in May 2001 and another cease-fire was implemented. In August it was announced that elections were expected to be held in June 2002 under a "constituency electoral system," although in September the National Electoral Commission advised the assembly to adopt a proportional representation system instead. Despite criticism from the opposition that Kabbah was trying to eliminate his potential rivals in the coming elections, as well as fears that some RUF forces might resume fighting, the country appeared to be moving toward normalization.

At a dramatic weapons-burning ceremony on January 18, 2002, which marked the completion of the disarmament process, President Kabbah declared the "war is over," and the four-year state of emergency was formally lifted on March 1. (An estimated 50,000 people died as a result of the conflict.) In presidential balloting on May 14, President Kabbah was elected to another four-year term by securing more than 70 percent of the vote against eight opponents. (Kabbah's running mate, Solomon BEREWA, the sitting minister of justice and attorney general and also from the SLPP, was elected to the vice presidency in succession to Albert Joe Demby, who had been dropped from the ticket at the SLPP congress in March.) In concurrent voting for the National Assembly, which had been expanded to 112 members elected on a proportional basis, the SLPP secured the majority of seats, followed by the All People's Congress (APC). A small number of seats were won by the Peace and Liberation Party (PLP); the RUF failed to win any seats. A new cabinet of the SLPP and two independents was sworn in on July 9, the independents subsequently joining the SLPP.

After the elections, international troops who had overseen the cease-fire ending Sierra Leone's civil war began to withdraw. In 2005 UNAMSIL forces were replaced by a small contingent of military advisers—the United Nations Integrated Office in Sierra Leone (UNIOSL)—charged with monitoring the security situation and guarding the war crimes tribunal (see Current issues, below).

The cabinet was reshuffled on September 6, 2005, all ministers representing the SLPP.

The APC was victorious in the parliamentary and presidential elections of 2007, unseating the governing SLPP, as the APC secured 40.7 percent of the seats in first-past-the-post legislative elections on August 11, followed by the SLPP with 39.5 percent and the newly formed People's Movement for Democratic Change (PMDC), an SLPP breakaway party, with 15.4 percent. Among the 572 candidates vying for 112 parliamentary seats, none was chosen from four other parties contesting the elections, nor were any independent candidates successful. In the first round of presidential balloting on August 11, APC chair Ernest Bai Koroma's vote share of 44.3 percent and Solomon Berewa's 38.3 percent as the SLPP candidate led five other contenders (from the PMDC, the Convention People's Party—CPP, the NDA, PLP, and UNPP). Since neither Koroma nor Berewa secured the 55 percent required for election, a runoff was held on September 8, in which Koroma won 54.6 percent to Berewa's 45.4 percent. President Koroma and his running mate, Sahr SAM-SUMANA, were sworn in on September 17. The president named a new APC-dominated cabinet, which included four members of the PMDC but none from the SLPP, on October 8 and October 16.

Among Koroma's first acts as president was the invocation of a "certificate of emergency," which granted him the authority to push laws through the National Assembly, most notably one giving prosecutorial powers to the Anti-Corruption Commission (ACC). Among Koroma's reform efforts, he also pledged to support efforts to restore electricity and a policy of "zero tolerance" for corruption. (For more on Koroma's reforms, see the 2014 *Handbook*.)

In 2007 legislation was approved granting unprecedented rights to women. New laws made domestic violence a crime, allowed women to inherit property, and protected young women against forced marriage. Other new laws prohibited exploitative labor practices and set up national agencies to protect the rights of children.

On July 5, 2008, local elections were held without incident, the first such balloting since the country's civil war ended. In a further sign of peace and stability, the UN's Integrated Office in Sierra Leone (Uniosil), was established as a follow-up to UN peacekeepers and began working on good governance and human rights issues.

The cabinet was reshuffled on February 27, 2009, with the replacement of 9 of 20 ministers, including, most notably, the appointment of the former central bank governor as finance minister. Observers said the appointment was significant as the government struggled to deal with the slumping economy. Furthermore, analysts said, the reshuffle was necessary in the wake of corruption scandals in the ministries of mines, energy, and transport. The minister for health and sanitation was suspended in November after being indicted on corruption charges (he was subsequently convicted). That portfolio fell under the supervision of Vice President Sam-Sumana. The minister of state in the office of the vice president was replaced the same day.

Attention in early 2009 quickly turned to what was reported as the worst political violence in the country since 2007, when supporters of the APC and the SLPP attacked each other over a period of five days in March. Thousands of youthful fighters took to the streets; the SLPP's headquarters were ransacked, and women were reported to have been sexually assaulted inside the headquarters building. Two radio stations accused of inflaming tensions were indefinitely suspended by the government. Meanwhile, the APC was angered by the reappearance in the

SLPP leadership of former NPRC members, including its secretary general, John BENJAMIN, and both the SLPP and the APC reportedly used "youth protection squads" that included former fighters. The fragility of the political situation prompted intercession by the UN, which mediated a peace agreement between the two parties in April.

A long-standing trial of war criminals concluded in April 2009 when the special court in Sierra Leone convicted three RUF leaders (see Political Parties, below) and imposed lengthy sentences. Of added significance, the court also determined that it was the AFRC that was responsible for a February 1999 invasion of Freetown in which 6,000 people died. In that case, the court determined that the RUF was not involved in the atrocities. The court made a point of highlighting that the AFRC and army dissidents had a major role in war crimes, not just the RUF as many believed. Further, the court set forth five new violations of international humanitarian law: forced marriage, sexual slavery, enlisting child soldiers under the age of 15, attacks on peacekeepers, and acts of terrorism against civilians.

Drug trafficking, in conjunction with corruption and a high unemployment rate among youth, was described in 2009 as the "main destabilizing force" in the country, as well as in neighboring West African nations, as they became transit points for the smuggling of cocaine from South America to Europe. On a positive note, the government's Anti-Corruption Act, adopted in 2008, granted more powers to the Anti-Corruption Commission (ACC) to review ministries, among other things. Despite efforts to fight corruption, however, the Koroma administration continued to lose support, as the opposition rallied against the replacement of some 200 government workers from the southeast region with appointees from Koroma's home region in the northwest, and as the economic recovery was deemed to be too slow. A positive development was the restoration of electric power to much of the capital in November, when the Bumbuna dam came online after nearly 40 years of construction. At the end of October the Special Court for Sierra Leone, which was hearing war crimes cases, upheld the sentences of former RUF interim leader Issa SESAY and two other high-ranking members (see Political Parties, below). In December eight men who had been found guilty in the UN-backed war crimes court were transferred to prisons in Rwanda because no facilities in Sierra Leone met the required international standards.

On March 15, 2010, the marine resources minister was removed as a result of corruption charges and replaced by the minister of presidential and parliamentary affairs. The cabinet was extensively reshuffled on December 4, dominated by members of the APC and a few from the PMDC. The foreign affairs minister was a member of the SLPP, but he was immediately suspended by the party and officially resigned from the SLPP on February 9, 2011.

In elections held on November 17, 2012, Koroma won a second term as president, defeating opponent Julius Maada Bio (Sierra Leone People's Party) and seven other candidates. The APC also strengthened its parliamentary majority, winning 67 seats to the SLPP's 42 seats. No other parties secured seats in the parliament. Koroma named a reshuffled cabinet over the next three months.

On March 6, 2015, Vice President Sahr SAM-SUMANA was expelled from the APC for a variety of alleged offenses, including falsifying his academic credentials and endeavoring to establish a new political party (see Political Parties, below). Eight days later, Sam-Sumana sought asylum in the U.S. embassy in Freetown, claiming his life was in danger. On March 17 Koroma dismissed Sam-Sumana as vice president for abandoning his position to seek refuge in the United States and for not belonging to any official party. The president then appointed Victor FOH (APC) vice president. Sam-Sumana and opposition groups asserted the dismissal was unconstitutional and unsuccessfully challenged the action in court. Concurrent with the replacement of the vice president, Koroma conducted a cabinet reshuffle. Another major reshuffle occurred in December (see Political Parties, below).

Constitution and government. The 1991 constitution provided for a popularly elected executive president who could serve for no more than two five-year terms; a parliament whose members could not serve simultaneously as ministers; and a State Advisory Council composed of 12 paramount chiefs (one from each local district) and ten "emergent citizens" nominated by the president. There was no limit on the number of political parties, provided they met basic requirements. The judicial system included a Supreme Court and a Court of Appeal, as well as a lower tier of high, magistrates', and native courts.

Following the establishment of the NPRC in 1992, the constitution was suspended, and on July 14 the Supreme Council of State (as the NPRC was subsequently named) called for the designation of three SCS members as "principal liaison officers," each of whom would oversee a number of government departments (successors to the former ministries). The department heads were to be styled secretaries of state under a chief who would report to the SCS. Meanwhile, the SCS had assumed a quasi-legislative function by the issuance of decrees. In 1993 the Strasser regime named a national advisory council to prepare a draft document as the basis for a new constitution (with the aim of holding a referendum in 1995). The draft, published in September 1994, included stipulations that future presidents be at least 40 years old and native-born Sierra Leoneans. It also included provisions for restoring basic human rights, guaranteeing freedom of expression, establishing a unicameral legislature, and empowering parliament to remove a president who became mentally or physically incapacitated, or who was dishonest.

On February 7, 2002, the constitution was amended in accordance with the Electoral Laws Act of 2002 adopted by parliament to provide for a party-list proportional voting system for the National Assembly. In October 2006 the government established the Constitutional Review Committee to consider changes to the charter (see Current issues, below). The constitution was amended in 2007 in accordance with the Electoral Laws Act of 2002 to provide for a first-past-the-post voting system for the National Assembly.

Freedom of the press is guaranteed, and a new press law was enacted in 2013 to increase government transparency. However, in November 2013 two journalists were charged with libel for publishing an article critical of the president. Reporters Without Borders ranked Sierra Leone 83rd out of 180 countries in media freedom in 2016, down from 61st in 2013.

Sierra Leone is administratively divided into three provinces (Northern, Eastern, Southern) in addition to a Western Area that includes Freetown. The provinces are subdivided into 12 districts and 147 chiefdoms.

Foreign relations. Sierra Leone has long subscribed to a generally pro-Western foreign policy, while maintaining diplomatic relations with the former Soviet Union, several East European countries, the People's Republic of China, and North Korea. Regionally, it has been an active participant in the Organization of African Unity (OAU, subsequently the African Union—AU) and a long-standing member of OAU committees established to resolve the disputes in Chad and the Western Sahara. Traditionally cordial relations with bordering states were strained by the overthrow of civilian governments in Liberia and Guinea; however, the three countries signed a security agreement in September 1986 and revived the Mano River Union plan for economic cooperation. In early 1989, continuing efforts by Freetown to "intensify existing friendly relations" with regional neighbors led to the establishment of joint economic and social commissions with Nigeria and Togo.

Civil war in neighboring Liberia topped Freetown's foreign policy agenda in 1990 as ECOWAS's peacekeeping forces, including Sierra Leonean troops, were dispatched from Freetown. In November Momoh described the influx of Liberian refugees as "stretching thin" his government's resources and characterized Liberian rebel leader Charles Taylor, who had threatened retaliation for Sierra Leone's involvement, as "ungrateful." In March 1991 Taylor, angered by Freetown's participation in the ECOWAS operation, began launching raids into Sierra Leone, and Nigeria and Guinea were reported in mid-April to have dispatched troops to aid in repulsing the intruders. Meanwhile, Freetown also accused Libya, Burkina Faso, and Côte d'Ivoire of aiding the rebels.

By early November 1991, the government and its allies claimed to have routed the guerrillas, and Guinean forces began their withdrawal. However, a cease-fire signed earlier in Côte d'Ivoire proved short-lived; in December Taylor charged Freetown with backing incursions by the Liberian United Movement for Freedom and Democracy (ULIMO), a group linked to the deposed Doe regime. ULIMO admitted to having engaged Taylor's forces but denied being based in Sierra Leone.

During the second half of 1992, Captain Strasser reportedly developed close ties with Nigerian military leader General Babangida, who in early 1993 agreed to provide Sierra Leone with military advisers. Subsequently, Sierra Leone and ULIMO forces were reported to have participated in joint operations against RUF rebels.

In March 1994 the Strasser government pressed Ecomog commanders to establish a buffer zone along its shared border with Liberia, citing increased rebel activity as well as the volatility of Liberia's disarmament process. One month later, the Strasser government expelled Germany's ambassador to Freetown, claiming that his "undiplomatic" behavior, including meetings with Liberia's Taylor, were undermining Sierra Leone's interests and threatening relations between the two countries. However, other reports linked the German's ouster to his defense of a Sierra Leonean journalist who had been arrested for criticizing Strasser. In September 1995 seven Guinean soldiers, stationed in Sierra Leone to fulfill a defense pact between the two nations, were killed during a clash with the RUF.

In mid-1998 the UN Security Council announced the establishment of a United Nations Observer Mission in Sierra Leone (UNOMSIL) which it charged with overseeing peacekeeping efforts. In February 1999 UNOMSIL personnel accused Nigerian members of Ecomog of executing civilians suspected of aiding the antigovernment insurgents. Subsequently, observers in Lagos reported that support for continued involvement in Sierra Leone had reached a new low. Meanwhile, Liberia, Libya, and Burkina Faso were alleged to be supplying the rebels with armaments and refuge. Following the May 1999 agreement between Sierra Leone and the RUF, the Liberian border was reopened in May, and in December Sierra Leone and Liberia established a joint security committee.

However, with the breakdown of the agreement and the resumption of violence in May 2000, Sierra Leone's relations with all three countries suspected of helping the RUF deteriorated once again. Although the Mano River Union summit held in May and attended by Sierra Leone, Liberia, Guinea, and Mali "deplored the attacks by the RUF," Kabbah's government and much of the international community continued to charge Liberia with assisting the rebels. With the RUF rebels crossing into the Guinean territory, and the Guinean president Lasana Conté accusing Sierra Leonean and Liberian refugees in his country of assisting the rebels, the Mano River region became a crisis zone and the scene of a severe refugee tragedy.

After the fighting in Liberia's Lofa county intensified in early 2001, Liberian president Taylor renewed his claim that the Sierra Leonean and Guinean authorities were assisting the Liberian rebels. In March the ambassadors of Sierra Leone and Guinea were expelled from Liberia. Relations improved following a new peace agreement between Sierra Leone and the RUF in May 2001.

In 2006 Sierra Leone became a full member of the Community of Sahel and Saharan States (CEN-SAD). On June 4, 2007, Sierra Leone and Liberia reached a border agreement, culminating in the reopening on June 7 of the Mano River bridge connecting the two countries. Peace talks continued at another Mano River Union summit in July.

In May 2008, during a summit in Monrovia, Sierra Leone and Guinea joined with their Liberian host in pledging that the Mano River Union, soon to include Côte d'Ivoire, would sustain peace and security in the region. In August the UN Security Council approved the transition of UNOMSIL to a smaller mission, the UN Integrated Peacebuilding Office in Sierra Leone (UNIPSIL). Also in 2008 relations with China were strengthened as the two countries signed a cooperation agreement following China's granting of interest-free loans to Sierra Leone to help rebuild its war-torn economy. The leaders of China and Sierra Leone agreed in 2009 to enhance bilateral relations.

In April 2009 former British prime minister Tony Blair visited Sierra Leone on a trip designed to promote tourism in the country, and the United Kingdom promised aid of nearly $71 million in 2010. In October Sierra Leone prepared to send its first troops to join a UN peacekeeping mission in Sudan. Britain provided financial assistance for the restructuring of Sierra Leone's significantly reduced army.

The first group of U.S. Peace Corps volunteers since 1994 arrived in Sierra Leone in June 2010.

In February 2012 the UN recalled its representative in Sierra Leone, Michael von der SCHULENBURG, after Koroma complained that the diplomat inappropriately supported the SLPP in upcoming elections. Schulenburg denied the charge.

In April 2012 former Liberian leader Taylor was convicted of war crimes (see entry on Liberia) and sentenced to 50 years in prison. Also in April, Sierra Leone announced it would deploy 850 troops as part of the African Union (AU) peacekeeping force in Somalia. Sierra Leone and Sri Lanka established full diplomatic relations with each other in 2012, while Sierra Leone and the United States finalized an open skies agreement that year in an effort to increase air traffic between the two countries. In September, under pressure from the United States, the Koroma government deregistered ten Iranian ships that had been using Sierra Leonean registration to evade international sanctions on oil sales from the Islamic republic.

In March 2013 the UN Security Council approved an extension of UNIPSIL until March 2014 and announced that the mission would cease on that date. The United Kingdom was Sierra Leone's largest donor in 2013, providing $115 million in aid. Meanwhile, Japan announced $15.1 million in aid to upgrade the nation's utilities in December 2013.

On March 31, 2014, UNIPSIL completed its mission in Sierra Leone. In May the EU announced a €107 million project to improve roads between Sierra Leone and Liberia. Because of an outbreak of the deadly Ebola virus (see Current issues, below), in August a number of countries issued travel warnings, while international air carriers, including British Airways, suspended flights to Sierra Leone and other countries in the region.

In November 2015 Koroma announced that the government was abandoning a plan to construct a new international airport under pressure from the IMF. The IMF had threatened to withhold access to $67 million in assistance designated for Sierra Leone if the government moved ahead with the project, which IMF officials had warned could cost the country 11 percent of its GDP. However, reports indicated that Koroma continued negotiations with Chinese officials in an effort to secure capital and additional funding beyond a $315 million loan from the Chinese Import–Export Bank that had already been pledged to fund the project.

Current issues. In January 2010 the Koroma government took control of the logging industry, reportedly to help restore depleted forests, and banned the transport and export of lumber. On September 29 the UN Security Council lifted all sanctions it had imposed on Sierra Leone in 1997 as a result of the civil war and related atrocities. The move, which allowed for the free flow of goods and services, was hailed as opening the way for economic recovery and stimulating trade, investment, and tourism.

In January 2011 the government addressed a long-standing issue by paying out $1.4 million to families of soldiers said to be missing in action during the conflict that ended in 2002. Meanwhile, a British team began helping to train Sierra Leone's reorganized armed forces, pared down from 13,500 in 2007 to 8,500. Tensions increased in May when the government slashed the gas subsidy by half, reportedly resulting in a 30 percent increase in price at the pump. Analysts said the cut was meant to provide revenue to help pay off the government's external debt, but it was alleged that a large portion of the money was used by the APC for the country's Golden Jubilee anniversary celebration of independence. On a positive note, the government stepped up efforts to involve more women in governance, an initiative also backed by the SLPP, and established the All Political Parties Women's Association–Sierra Leone (APPWA-SL) to encourage active participation by women. Subsequently, the government said it would implement measures to ensure that women represented 30 percent of public and private sector jobs.

In August 2012 allegations emerged that Vice President Sam-Sumana had used foreign commercial funds to support the APC in the 2007 election. Also in August, a cholera outbreak prompted Koroma to declare a nationwide state of emergency. By the end of the month, reports indicated that more than 230 had died from the disease, which had sickened more than 14,000.

Koroma was easily reelected in the November balloting, defeating eight other candidates. Meanwhile the APC expanded its parliamentary majority. International observers reported the balloting was generally free and credible, but they noted some irregularities and delays in vote counting.

In January 2013 protests and demonstrations against widespread fuel shortages occurred in Freetown following the disruption of petroleum from Benin and Côte d'Ivoire. In March the ACC charged 29 government officials with corruption in a scandal over the misappropriation of vaccines.

Koroma dismissed his chief of staff Richard KONTEH on June 10, 2014, over a controversial mining and logging agreement. Konteh and two other officials were subsequently charged with corruption. Also in June the government declared a state of emergency in the Kailahun district because of an outbreak of Ebola. Schools were closed and public gatherings banned. By August there were more than 700 cases of the disease reported in Sierra Leone and 334 fatalities. The disease was present in all 12 districts in the country, and the government deployed troops to enforce emergency measures.

Sierra Leone was not declared Ebola free until November 7, 2015. The disease killed 4,216. The government faced substantial domestic criticism for its response to the disease, including charges that it was ill prepared for the outbreak and that graft and corruption undermined its response efforts. A report by the government's auditor general estimated that more than $30 million had been lost in waste and fraud.

A 2015 census was heavily criticized by opposition parties for reportedly inflating population figures within districts dominated by the ruling APC. In December 2015 Parliament enacted legislation legalizing abortion.

The impact of the Ebola outbreak combined with falling iron prices led to a dramatic economic decline in 2015, with GDP shrinking by 12.8 percent. All four of the nation's largest mines suspended production of iron and other precious minerals during the height of the Ebola epidemic, and two of the larger mining companies went bankrupt. By 2016 only one major mine, the Chinese-owned facility at Tonkolili, had resumed operations and only then after a major restructuring that cut production costs.

In January 2016 two new case of Ebola were reported in Sierra Leone, but no new cases were found beyond those through March of that year. New cases of the virus in Liberia in March prompted health warnings in Sierra Leone and border closures. An unexpected side effect of the Ebola crisis was a baby boom in Sierra Leone. In 2016 reports indicted a 65 percent rise in teenage pregnancies in the country.

POLITICAL PARTIES

During Sierra Leone's first 17 years of independence, the principal political groupings were the Sierra Leone People's Party (SLPP), strongest in the Mende area of the south, and the All People's Congress (APC), based in the Temne region of the north. The SLPP dominated from 1961 to 1967 and the APC from 1967 to 1978, when it was accorded monopoly status. Following adoption of the 1991 constitution, a number of new parties emerged, most of which were accorded legal recognition prior to the suspension of political activity in May 1992.

By late 1992 the regime had released the majority of the political figures detained in the aftermath of the coup, the most prominent of whom included SLPP leader Salia JUSU-SHERRIFF and **National Action Party** (NAP) co-founder Dr. Sheka KANU.

The ban on political party activity was rescinded on June 21, 1995, in preparation for elections promised by early 1996. In August the Interim National Electoral Commission granted provisional registration certificates to approximately 15 groups, 11 of which were granted permission in November to participate in the upcoming elections.

Political parties were banned by the Koroma military junta upon its seizure of power in May 1997. Following his reinstallation in March 1998, President Kabbah authorized parties to resume their activities. His decision to include representatives from only four groups in his reshuffled government was criticized by his opponents, who had expected a more inclusive cabinet.

Following the July 1999 peace and power-sharing agreement, Kabbah reshuffled his cabinet in November, and the rebels (the RUF and AFRC) were given four nonsenior posts. After the resumption of fighting in May 2000, however, three rebel ministers were jailed. In March 2001 Kabbah reshuffled his cabinet to replace retiring and jailed rebel ministers. In an effort described as "forming a more inclusive national unity government" but criticized by opponents as "trying to silence and co-opt" his rivals, Kabbah appointed four new ministers. Three came from the opposition **National Unity Party** (NUP), People's Democratic Party (PDP), and United National People's Party (UNPP) to supplement Kabbah's SLPP-dominated government (which had also included civilians); one minister came from the **Democratic Center Party** (DCP). The latter party, chaired by Aiah Abu KOROMA, reportedly dissolved in 2002 after pledging its support to Kabbah. However, the UNPP, NUP, and PDP announced they were not supporting Kabbah's rule by joining the government but were merely trying to help the country in difficult times. (In 2003, however, NUP leader John BENJAMIN joined the SLPP, following the party's former chair, Dr. John KARIMU, who had defected in 2001.) Indeed, the APC, People's Democratic Alliance (PDA), People's National Convention (PNC), People's Progressive Party (PPP), PDP, and UNPP had formed an opposition alliance styled as the **Grand Alliance** (GA) in August 2000. A number of smaller parties reportedly joined the GA later. Although the GA members announced they would "unite under a single political party in due course," by mid-2001, various internal rifts seemed to have rendered that aim difficult to achieve. The APC and UNPP subsequently left the alliance.

In the May 14, 2002, balloting, 11 parties presented candidates for the presidency, and 12 parties were represented in the legislative contest. Seven political parties participated in the 2007 parliamentary and presidential elections, while ten took part in the 2012 balloting.

Government Parties:

All People's Congress (APC). Leftist and republican in outlook, the APC was formed in 1960 by Dr. Siaka Probyn Stevens in a split with a dissident group headed at that time by Albert M. Margai. Although strongest in Temne territory, the party was not exclusively tribal in character, drawing its support from wage-earning and lower-middle-class elements in both Temne and non-Temne areas. The APC won all but one of the legislative seats in the 1973 election, which was boycotted by the opposition SLPP; it won all but 15 seats in 1977 and was constitutionally unopposed in 1982 and 1986. At the conclusion of an APC conference in August 1985, despite strong support for (then) first vice president Sorie KOROMA, Maj. Gen. Joseph Momoh was nominated as the sole candidate to succeed Stevens as president of the republic. While yielding the post of secretary general to Momoh, Stevens retained the title of chair, as well as the primary loyalty of much of the party's membership, until his death in June 1988. Momoh was reelected unopposed to the party's top post at the tenth APC conference in January 1989, which also yielded abandonment of the positions of chair and vice chair and adoption of a demanding "Code of Conduct" for political leaders and public servants.

At an APC Central Committee and Governing Council joint session on August 17–20, 1990, President Momoh, pressured by calls for political reform, proposed an "overhauling" of Sierra Leone's political system. However, his support in March 1991 for the adoption of a multiparty constitution generated deep fissures within the party. In mid-July two of its leaders resigned their posts, and ten others were suspended for criticizing the document that was approved in late August. In early 1992 the party further redefined its policies and principles, and, by providing for rank-and-file balloting, underwent sweeping personnel changes.

APC presidential candidate Edward Mohammed Turay captured just 5.1 percent of the vote in 1996 balloting, while the party finished fourth in the legislative contest. In March 2002 Ernest Bai Koroma was elected party president and chosen as the party's candidate for president in the 2002 elections. Koroma won 22.3 percent of the vote, and the party finished second in the legislative election, winning 27 seats, including a seat won by Koroma. Rifts in the party resulted in Koroma's losing the top party post in June 2005, but he was reinstated in September and subsequently ran unopposed for the party leadership. Tensions within the party eased as Koroma was tapped to represent the APC in the 2007 presidential election, securing his victory in two rounds of voting. His win came as a surprise to observers, who had forecast victory by Koroma's main challenger, Vice President Berewa of the long-governing SLPP. But Koroma's leadership in the party reportedly helped it regain support in the north, its traditional stronghold, and the APC also benefited from newfound support in the south in the runoff, with backing from the PMDC (below), which split the SLPP's support in that region. Also adding to Koroma's popularity, according to *Africa Confidential*, was the fact that "voters seem to think that since he already made so much money (in insurance), he would be less corrupt in power."

In May 2008 the party was said to have lost favor with some members in the wake of reports that the government had shut down the radio station of the SLPP. Soon thereafter, the station was cleared of four charges of misconduct.

Following the peace agreement between the APC and the SLPP in April 2009, SLPP leader John Benjamin, in a show of support for stability, spoke at the APC congress shortly thereafter. President Koroma was reelected party leader, as well as its presidential candidate at a congress in April 2012. Koroma won the November presidential election with 58.7 percent of the vote, while the APC expanded its majority in parliament, securing 67 seats with 53.7 percent of the vote. Reports in 2014 indicated growing tension between Koroma and Vice President Sahr SAM-SUMANA as the former tacitly supported amending the constitution to allow a third term. Sam-Sumana was dismissed in March 2015 from the party and the vice presidency. Koroma conducted a government reshuffle in December 2015 in which a number of close allies were appointed to senior positions in a reported effort to enhance his political base prior to launching a bid for a third term.

Leaders: Ernest Bai KOROMA (President of the Republic, Party Leader, and 2002, 2007, and 2012 presidential candidate), Victor CHUKUMA-JOHNSON (Chair), Edward Mohammed TURAY (1996 presidential candidate), Victor FOH (Secretary General).

Opposition Party:

Sierra Leone People's Party (SLPP). Led by former second vice president Salia JUSU-SHERIFF, whose identification with the Momoh regime was viewed as a political liability, the SLPP was launched as a revival of the party outlawed in 1978.

Ahmad Tejan Kabbah, a 64-year-old veteran politician and former UN development worker, emerged as the SLPP's presidential candidate after an intraparty contest with Charles Margai in early 1996. Subsequently, in the February 1996 parliamentary balloting, the SLPP secured 10 more seats than its nearest competitor while its allies (the PDP, APC, NUP, and DCP) gained an additional 24 seats.

In mid-1998, Kabbah reportedly signaled that he would not seek another term in office. Among those cited by observers as potential successors were Margai, cabinet member Harry WILL, and Sam Hinga Norman, whose command of Kamajor militias had won him wide acclaim. Kabbah reversed his previous announcement, however, during a period of peace, which was followed by a resumption of violence and another time of peace from 1999 to 2001, when he won enough support to ensure another election victory for himself and his party in 2002. Former military leader Julius Bio returned to Sierra Leone in 2004 after ten years in exile and reportedly stated his interest in party leadership while condemning the current regime for its alleged corruption and incompetence. Margai left the party in 2005 after losing the leadership post—and, thus, the opportunity to be the party's presidential candidate—to Solomon Berewa, who *Africa Confidential* said was "generally referred to as President Number Two" because Kabbah delegated many official duties to him. Margai then formed the PMDC (above) with other SLPP defectors. Bio, for his part, announced he would not follow Margai and reiterated his support for the SLPP.

Kabbah, who observers said was increasingly unpopular at home and abroad, was barred by the constitution from seeking a third term as president, paving the way for the nomination of Vice President Berewa as the party's standard-bearer in the 2007 election. Berewa chose as his running mate Momodu KOROMA, the minister of foreign affairs, widely known as a Kabbah loyalist. Observers explained Berewa's selection as one of demographics: since Berewa is from the southeast, it was important for him to choose a running mate from the north, where the APC's Ernest Koroma had a stronghold. Though Momodu Koroma was born in the south, his father is a northerner like Kabbah. Party stalwarts reportedly opposed the selection of Koroma, based on his ties to Kabbah and on speculation that Berewa, 67 and in ill health, might not survive a first term.

Though Berewa, described as a shrewd politician, was seen by many as the near-certain successor to Kabbah, the 2007 presidential election proved to be an upset victory for the APC's candidate, bolstered in large part by support from Margai's SLPP-breakaway PMDC, which split the vote in the south. Berewa, who observers said symbolized continuity (versus the change promised by the APC's Koroma), lost in the runoff with 45.4 percent versus Koroma's 54.6 percent. Berewa subsequently resigned as party leader, the post being assumed by U. N. S. JAH.

In 2008 tensions heightened between the SLPP and the APC in advance of local elections in July, with the SLPP threatening to boycott the balloting unless ECOWAS replaced the elections commission as organizer of the poll. (The SLPP had accused the commission of improper conduct during the 2007 elections.) The SLPP ultimately participated, but it fared poorly, leading to discord within the ranks. In early 2009 party veteran John Benjamin was elected chair, and the party began to formulate its strategy ahead of the 2012 general elections. In April the party signed a peace agreement with the APC in the wake of violent confrontations involving both parties in March (see Current issues, above).

Party members began vying for position in early 2010 to become the SLPP's candidate in the 2012 presidential election, as in March 23 members made their intentions known. However, in May Alpha Osman TIMBO, a former labor minister, declared himself the flag bearer, purportedly to mend divisions within the party. In June another long-time party member, Umaru DUMBUYA, who had worked as a prison guard in the United States for many years, said he intended to be the flag bearer. Ultimately, 19 challengers stepped forward but their bids were halted in May 2011 when one of the candidates, Bu-Buakei JABBI, took the party to court, claiming the leadership could not hold an election because its tenure had expired. The Supreme Court ruled in his favor. The court also granted the party the right to appeal a Court of Appeal ruling regarding the voiding of several hundred votes in the 2007 presidential runoff election.

Rifts continued to develop in mid-2011, as Brigadier General Bio, a rival of Benjamin's dating to the 1990s, put himself forth as the main presidential candidate of the SLPP. On July 20 the Supreme Court lifted the injunction against the party holding a congress, and when the SLPP convened on July 29–31, Bio secured the presidential nomination with 238 of 602 votes. His closest rival was Usman Boie KAMARA with 186 votes. Timbo received 44 votes and Dumbuya, 2, while Jabbi received just 1 vote. Bio was allied with Abass BUNDU, who lost his bid at the helm to Benjamin, who did not contest the presidential bid. In November 2011 Bio chose Kadi SESAY, a well-known feminist and human rights advocate, as his running mate for the 2012 balloting. Bio lost that election to incumbent president Koroma of the APC, securing 37.4 percent of the vote. Meanwhile Kamara defected to the APC and was appointed to a cabinet post following the November balloting. In August 2013 Sumanoh KAPEN, close ally of Bio, was elected party chair.

On March 13, 2014, Kabbah died of natural causes at age 82.

Osman Karankay CONTEH won a by-election for the SLPP in Port Loko in July 2016, with 68.8 percent of the vote.

Leaders: Sumanoh KAPEN (Chair), Solomon BEREWA (Former Vice President of the Republic and 2007 presidential candidate), Sulaiman Banja TEJANSIE (Secretary General).

Other Parties That Contested the 2012 Elections:

People's Movement for Democratic Change (PMDC). Registered by the government in April 2006, the PMDC was founded by Charles Margai, who left the SLPP after he lost his bid for the chairship, to promote a civilian, democratic government. Margai was arrested in 2006 on a variety of charges related to disorderly behavior against the government and was later released on bail. Several student members reportedly defected to the SLPP in mid-2007, and in midyear Margai was slated as the PMDC's presidential candidate. His defection from the SLPP caused the former governing party to lose a significant number of votes in 2007 in the south and southeast regions of the country, particularly among younger voters, who make up 56 percent of the electorate.

Following the first-round balloting in the 2007 presidential election, in which Margai secured just 13.9 percent of the vote, he backed Ernest Bai Koroma in the runoff. The new president subsequently named four PMDC members to his cabinet, including party co-founder Moses Moisa-Kapu. In the concurrent parliamentary elections, the PMDC secured a small number of seats, trailing the APC and the SLPP.

Rifts reportedly began developing between the PMDC and the APC in early 2008 when Margai accused the new APC government of "chronic tribalism." Merger talks with the SLPP later in the year did not come to fruition at a time when the PMDC was widely reported to be in disarray. Subsequently, in 2009 the national women's leader of the party blamed Margai for bringing about the "disintegration" of the PMDC. However, in February President Koroma included PMDC members in his reshuffled cabinet. Meanwhile, rifts within the party deepened, and in January 2010 more than 600 members reportedly defected to the APC. More defections, this time to the SLPP, were reported in September. Margai again publicly lashed out at the APC in October, claiming that President Koroma gave former party chair Mohamed Bangura $300,000 to form a new political party. Bangura, who was suspended in July for three years for allegedly offending the values of the party, denied that he had been given any money. Bangura and others in the party who had protested his suspension called for Margai to step down from the helm, but a court ruling upheld Bangura's suspension, and Margai retained his post. Bangura subsequently formed a new party, the United Democratic Movement (UDM), in 2011 (see below).

In July 2011 Margai shocked party members with the remarks he made at the SLPP party congress indicating that the PMDC would align with the SLPP during presidential and parliamentary elections in 2012 and that he aimed to remove the APC from power. The PMDC immediately issued a statement condemning Margai for his comments and vowing that the party would remain united and "focused on its political objectives for the 2012 elections." In September 2012 Margai was reelected party leader. Margai placed third the November presidential election, securing just 1.3 percent of the vote. The PMDC received just 3.2 percent of the vote in concurrent legislative balloting and failed to gain any seats in the parliament. Margai was briefly detained in May 2013 for making threatening statements about the first lady in relation to a land dispute. In October 2015 the chief justice of the Supreme Court filed a complaint with the nation's legal council against Margai for publicly alleging that the members of the high court had been bribed by the president.

Leaders: Charles MARGAI (President of the Party and 2007 presidential candidate), Moses MOISA-KAPU, Ansu LANSANA, William A. B. TUCKER (Secretary General).

National Democratic Alliance (NDA). The NDA fielded candidates for the legislature but not the presidency in 2002. The party reconvened in 2005 after having been inactive for several years.

In 2007 the NDA formed an alliance with the PLP to back Vice President Solomon Berewa of the SLPP in the presidential runoff election. The NDA's candidate, Amadu Jalloh, finished fifth, with about 1 percent of the vote, in the first round of balloting. The NDA did not field a candidate in the 2012 presidential balloting. It received 1.3 percent of the vote in the assembly elections and no seats. In 2015 Jalloh was appointed to lead a reconciliation committee with the party in an effort to end infighting.

Leaders: Ansu MASSAQUOI (Chair), Amadu JALLOH (2007 presidential candidate), Saa Mackaimekoe FAMANDA (Secretary General).

Peace and Liberation Party (PLP). Established in 2001, the PLP was led by the former AFRC leader Johnny Paul Koroma. It was linked with the Grassroots Awareness movement, one of many peace promotion organizations. In the May 2002 elections, Koroma came in third in the presidential race, while the party won 3.6 percent of the vote—and two seats—in the legislative contest. Though Koroma was indicted in 2003, he remained the party's leader, the party spokesperson said in 2007. However, it was later reported that Koroma was dead.

In the 2007 presidential election, Kandeh Baba CONTEH came in sixth in the first round, with 0.6 percent of the vote.

The PLP was ruled ineligible to participate in the 2008 local elections. Conteh was the party's presidential candidate in the 2012 elections. He placed seventh with 0.3 percent of the vote. The PLP secured just 0.1 percent of the vote in the legislative elections. In 2014 the PLP joined other parties in quarterly meetings to reduce tensions in an initiative launched by Koroma.

Leaders: Kandeh Baba CONTEH (2007 and 2012 presidential candidate), Darlington MORRISON (Chair), Bai MORROW, Amadu BAH (Spokesperson).

United National People's Party (UNPP). The UNPP secured 17 seats behind a 21 percent vote tally in the February 1996 balloting. Meanwhile, its leader, banker John KARIFA-SMART, placed second in concurrent presidential balloting. In March 1997 Karifa-Smart was charged with contempt and suspended from the assembly. He also unsuccessfully attempted in April 2001 to expel some legislators from the party due to differences on certain policies. Karifa-Smart came in last, with 1 percent of the vote, in the May 2002 presidential election, and the UNPP failed to win any seats in the legislative contest, with 1.3 percent of the vote. Following the election, a cabinet minister who had been a member of the UNPP joined the SLPP. In May 2005 the UNPP joined in coalition with the National Unity Movement (NUM, below) in advance of the next presidential elections. It backed out of a so-called merger with the RUF after some of the latter's leaders were charged with war crimes.

Karifa-Smart retired from politics in 2006, and Abdul Kadi Karim was elected as party leader and 2007 presidential candidate. He came in last with 0.4 percent of votes. In 2008 the party was one of three ruled ineligible to take part in local elections in March.

James Obai FULLAH emerged as the UNPP's presidential candidate in the 2012 elections. He came in ninth (last) with 0.2 percent of the vote. The UNPP secured just 0.2 percent of the vote in assembly balloting. In 2013 Fullah was suspended by the party's executive committee but challenged the action in court.

Leaders: James Obai FULLAH (Party Leader and 2012 presidential candidate), Abdul Kadi KARIM (2007 presidential candidate), Mohamed Husman FORNAH (Chair), Osman CONTEH (Secretary General).

People's Democratic Party (PDP). The PDP was characterized by *West Africa* as the "loudest" of the new parties, whose "main handicap is the uncharismatic quality" of its leader, former information minister Thaimu BANGURA. In September 1991 Bangura had been named chair of a United Front of Political Movements (UNIFORM), a six-party opposition formation that was subsequently dissolved.

In the February 1996 balloting, Bangura placed third in the presidential contest, with 16.1 percent of the vote, and the party won 12 seats. Subsequently, as an apparent reward for supporting Kabbah in the second round of presidential balloting, the PDP secured three cabinet portfolios.

Bangura died in March 1999. Following infighting between Osman Kamara and former NPRC member Abdul Rahman KAMARA to replace Bangura, Osman Kamara was elected chair. Abdul Rahman Kamara quit the party to form his own organization, the **People's Democratic Alliance** (PDA) in November. In a cabinet reshuffle in March 2001, Osman Kamara was given the post of the trade and industry minister, although he claimed that the PDP was still an opposition party. He was subsequently replaced. The PDP, with 1 percent of the vote, failed to win a seat in the legislative election of May 2002. Following the election, one cabinet member affiliated with the PDP subsequently joined the SLPP. The party did not present a presidential candidate but came out in support of Kabbah. Several party officials were expelled in 2006 for alleged financial malfeasance. The party did not participate in the 2007 elections.

In May 2009 there was speculation that former APC minister of transport and aviation, Kemoh SESAY, was planning to revive and lead the PDP. Sesay was dismissed in the cabinet reshuffle of February 2009 because of suspicions related to a cocaine deal.

In September the party elected Gibrilla KAMARA as its 2012 presidential candidate and the PDP leader. He placed sixth in the November polling with 0.4 percent of the vote. The PDP received 0.4 percent of the vote in the concurrent legislative balloting.

Leader: Gibrilla KAMARA (Secretary General and 2012 presidential candidate).

Revolutionary United Front (RUF). The RUF surfaced in early 1991 as a group of Sierra Leone dissidents who had joined forces with Liberian guerrillas loyal to Charles Taylor along the Sierra Leone–Liberia border, where diamond smuggling had been estimated to yield some $100 million annually. In July 1992 the rebels rejected an appeal by the Strasser regime to surrender and negotiate a resolution of their estrangement from Freetown, demanding instead a national interim government and free democratic elections.

In August 1993 the RUF was described as "unorganized" amid indications that attempts had been made to oust its leader, Foday Sankannah Sankoh (who earlier was rumored to have died). On December 30 Sankoh's personal bodyguards surrendered when government troops overran Pujehin, and in early 1994 the RUF leader was reported to have barely escaped arrest during fighting at Kailahun, which resulted in the further capture of elite rebel troops.

Thereafter, although estimates of the actual number of RUF members fluctuated between 100 and 1,000, the group, which had reportedly broken into four units, was credited with orchestrating military activities in over two-thirds of the country. By October 1994 some observers suggested that the government's war with the rebels was nearly concluded. However, in early November the RUF appeared to be invigorated when its seizure of two British nationals drew international attention, and on November 28 the rebels rejected Freetown's cease-fire entreaties, saying it would only negotiate with the British government.

On January 18–20, 1995, the RUF captured two of the country's most important mines; however, the rebels suffered numerous casualties in a government counter-offensive that dislodged the insurgents. Subsequently, the RUF requested that the International Committee of the Red Cross act as a mediator in the conflict.

Confronted with a reorganized Sierra Leonean Army and near starvation conditions in areas under their control, RUF political leaders in September 1995 reportedly sought a dialogue with Freetown. However, rebel military activities continued unabated, underscoring the reported split between RUF moderates and militants.

Following the overthrow of the Strasser regime in mid-January 1996, the RUF announced a one-week unconditional cease-fire, and on February 25 the rebels held their first direct talks with the new government in Côte d'Ivoire, where they unsuccessfully sought a delay in nationwide elections. Subsequently, the rebels were blamed for disrupting polling in a number of regions. At a meeting with Brigadier General Bio on March 24, Sankoh agreed to a cease-fire but refused to recognize the civilian government-elect. Thereafter, the Kabbah government expressed "cautious optimism" following a meeting between Sankoh and the new president on April 22–23, which yielded a "definitive" cease-fire. The final accord signed on November 30 permitted the RUF to begin functioning as a political movement immediately, with the understanding that it would apply for formal party recognition within 30 days.

Subsequently, implementation of the peace pact stalled because Sankoh refused to meet with officials seeking to finalize the scheduling of the RUF's disarmament and reintegration, and in early 1997 the government accused Sankoh of failing to meet his responsibilities as dictated by the accord. Following a meeting with Nigerian officials, Sankoh was arrested in Lagos on March 12. Three days later, a senior RUF official,

Philip Sylvester PALMER, announced that Sankoh had been dismissed from the RUF for "thwarting the peace process." The arrest and ouster of Sankoh (an "international conspiracy" according to his followers) sparked fierce internecine fighting between his loyalists and opponents.

RUF militants played a major role in the fighting, which led to President Kabbah's overthrow in May 1997, and in June at least three RUF representatives were included in the AFRC. Moreover, the AFRC's exhaustive diplomatic efforts to win Sankoh's freedom from detention in Nigeria fueled reports that the RUF was steering the junta's activities. During negotiations with the AFRC in late 1997, representatives of the Kabbah administration agreed to find a role for Sankoh upon their proposed reinstallation in Freetown. Meanwhile, RUF fighters who had aligned with rebel soldiers were being targeted by Ecomog troops.

Following the peace agreement with the government in July 1999, the RUF was promised cabinet posts, and Sankoh was given powers equivalent to those of vice president. In the meantime, the RUF decided to transform itself into a registered political party (the RUFP). However, after the breakdown of the agreement and the resumption of fighting in May 2000, Sankoh was jailed, and Issa Sesay replaced him as the interim leader. In June the government asked the UN to set up a special court to try Sankoh and other RUF officials for "war crimes."

Before and after the RUF's announcement of commitment to the peace process once again in May 2001, there were signs of a split within the organization. Reportedly, the faction for continuing the war, represented by an uneasy coalition of Sam Bockarie and Dennis Superman Mingo, was in conflict with the official leadership of Sesay and the faction committed to the peace process.

The RUFP's presidential candidate, Alimamy Pallo BANGURA, came in fourth, with 1.7 percent of the vote, in May 2002, while the party won 2.2 percent of the vote—and no seats—in the legislative contest.

Sesay, who had been indicted on war crimes charges by the special court, was replaced as interim leader in January 2005 by Peter VANDY. The following month, however, Vandy resigned from the party and joined the SLPP, declaring his belief in the SLPP as the party of reconciliation and multiparty democracy. In early 2006 Sesay was in detention on war crimes charges. Meanwhile, party official Omrie Golley was charged in 2006 with plotting to overthrow the government. Former presidential candidate Bangura resigned from the party in 2006.

In 2007 Secretary General Jonathan Kposowa said the party would not contest the upcoming presidential and parliamentary elections because of a lack of financial support.

The war crimes trial of Sesay and other RUF leaders, which began in mid-2008, concluded in March 2009 with the convictions of Sesay, Morris KALLON, and Augustine GBAO on 14 to 16 charges of war crimes and crimes against humanity. Sesay was sentenced in April to 52 years in prison, Kallon received a 40-year sentence, and Gbao received 25 years. (The court did not have the authority to impose life sentences.) In October the court upheld the sentences for Sesay, Kallon, and Gbao.

In August 2010, at the trial of former Liberian president Charles Taylor, Sesay (a defense witness for Taylor) apologized to the people of Sierra Leone for his role in the war. In September 2012 Eldred Collins was elected the leader of the RUFP and became the party's 2012 presidential candidate. Collins secured 0.6 percent of the vote while the RUF received 0.6 percent in the legislative polling.

Leaders: Eldred COLLINS (Party Leader and 2012 presidential candidate), Issa SESAY (in detention), Gibril MASSAQUOI (Spokesperson), Dennis Superman MINGO, Omrie GOLLEY (Peace and Political Council Chair; in detention), Jonathan KPOSOWA (Secretary General).

United Democratic Movement (UDM). With the goal of contesting the 2012 elections, the UDM was established by former PMDC chair Mohamed Bangura in early 2011. The party received its official legal approval on May 31. Bangura was the UDM presidential candidate in 2012. He received 0.2 percent of the vote, while the UDM received 0.6 percent in the concurrent assembly elections.

Leader: Martin BANGURA (Party Chair and 2012 presidential candidate).

Citizens Democratic Party (CDP). Led by Joshua Albert Carew, the party's 2012 presidential candidate, the CDP secured 0.4 percent of the vote in the 2012 legislative elections.

Leader: Joshua Albert CAREW (Chair and 2012 presidential candidate).

Other Parties and Groups:

Other groups include the **People's Progressive Party** (PPP), led by former ECOWAS executive secretary Dr. Abass Bundu who was a 1996 presidential candidate but in 2007 was said to be in the SLPP camp; the **People's National Convention** (PNC), led by 1996 presidential candidate Edward KARGBO, reported in 2002 to be retired; the **National Unity Movement** (NUM), led by Sam LEIGH, which formed a political alliance with the UNPP in 2005; the **National Alliance Democratic Party** (NADP), an opposition party based in the United States and led by Mohamed Yahya SILLAH; the **Sierra Leoneans Advocate for Progress** (SLAP), led by Christian JOHNSON and Jon KANU; and the **Liberal Democratic Party** (LDP) and the **Sierra Leone Socialist Party** (SLSP), both organized in 2000.

For more on the **Convention People's Party** (CPP), and the **Citizens United for Peace and Progress** (CUPP), see the 2012 *Handbook.* For information on the **Movement for Progress** (MOP), see the 2013 *Handbook.*

LEGISLATURE

The Sierra Leone **National Assembly** is a 124-member unicameral body. In accordance with the Electoral Laws Act of 2002, a constitutional amendment was enacted on February 7, 2002, providing for 112 assembly members to be elected on a party-list proportional basis (5 percent threshold required) from 12 multimember constituencies for five-year terms. In addition, 12 seats are filled by paramount chiefs, representing the 12 provincial districts.

In the most recent election of November 17, 2012, the All People's Congress won 67 seats, and the Sierra Leone People's Party, 42 (three seats remained undecided as of June 20, 2013). The 12 seats for paramount chiefs were filled on December 7, 2012.

Speaker: Sheku Badara Bashiru "S.B.B." DUMBUYA (APC).

CABINET

[as of July 30, 2016]

President	Ernest Bai Koroma
Vice President	Victor Foh
Ministers	
Agriculture, Food Security, and Forestry	Monty Jones
Defense	Ernest Bai Koroma (Acting)
Education, Science, and Technology	Minkailu Bah
Energy	Henry Macauley
Finance and Development	Momodu Kargbo
Foreign Affairs	Samura Kamara
Health and Sanitation	Abu Bakarr Fofanah
Information and Communications	Mohamed Bangura
Internal Affairs	Maj. (Ret.) Alfred Palo Conteh
Justice and Attorney General	Joseph Kamara
Labor and Social Security	Matthew Teambo
Lands, Country Planning, and Environment	Finda Diana Konomanyi [f]
Local Government and Rural Development	Maya Kaikai
Marine Resources and Fisheries	Elizabeth Mans [f]
Mineral Resources	Minkailu Mansaray
Political and Public Affairs	Nanette Thomas [f]
Resident Minister, East	Karamoh Kabba
Resident Minister, North	Alie Kamara
Resident Minister, South	Muctarr Conteh
Social Welfare, Gender, and Children's Affairs	Sylvia Blyden [f]
Sports	Ahmed Khanou
Tourism and Cultural Affairs	Sidi Yahya Tunis
Trade and Industry	Capt. Momodu Allieu Pat-Sowe

Transport and Aviation	Leonard Balogun Koroma
Water Resources	Momodu Maligie
Works and Housing and Infrastructural Development	Ibrahim Kemoh Sesay
Youth	Bai Mamoud Bangura

[f] = female

INTERGOVERNMENTAL REPRESENTATION

Ambassador to the U.S.: Bockari K. STEVENS.

U.S. Ambassador to Sierra Leone: John HOOVER.

Permanent Representative to the UN: Adikalie Foday SUMAH.

IGO Memberships (Non-UN): AfDB, AU, CWTH, ECOWAS, IOM, NAM, OIC, WTO.

For Further Reference:

Denov, Myriam. *Child Soldiers: Sierra Leone's Revolutionary United Front.* Cambridge: Cambridge University Press, 2010.

Harris, David. *Sierra Leone: A Political History.* Oxford: Oxford University Press, 2014.

Reno, David. *Corruption and State Politics in Sierra Leone.* Cambridge: Cambridge University Press, 1995. Reprinted, 2009.

Zack-Williams, Tunde, ed. *When the State Fails: Studies on Intervention in the Sierra Leone Civil War.* London: Pluto Press, 2012.

SINGAPORE

Republic of Singapore
Xinjiapo Gongheguo (Chinese)
Republik Singapura (Malay)
Singapur Kutiyarasu (Tamil)

Political Status: Attained self-rule within the British Commonwealth June 3, 1959; joined in formation of Malaysia on September 16, 1963; independent republic since August 9, 1965.

Area: 246 sq. mi. (636 sq. km), including adjacent islets that encompass some 15 sq. mi. (39 sq. km).

Population: 5,697,000 (2016E—UN); 5,781,728 (2016E—U.S. Census).

Major Urban Center (2016E—UN): SINGAPORE (5,717,000).

Official Languages: Chinese (Mandarin is the preferred form), English, Malay, Tamil.

Monetary Unit: Singapore Dollar (market rate October 1, 2016: 1.36 dollars = $1US).

President: Tony TAN Keng Yam (nonparty); declared president-elect on August 27, 2011; inaugurated on September 1 for a six-year term, following presidential elections on August 27, 2011, succeeding Sellapan Ramanathan NATHAN (nonparty).

Prime Minister: LEE Hsien Loong (People's Action Party); sworn in on August 12, 2004, upon the resignation of GOH Chok Tong (People's Action Party); continued in office following the election on May 7, 2011, and on September 11, 2015.

THE COUNTRY

Joined to the southern tip of the Malay Peninsula by a three-quarter-mile-long causeway, Singapore consists of a single large island, on which the city of Singapore is located, and about 50 adjacent islets. Situated at the crossroads of Southeast Asian trade routes, the country is one of the world's most densely populated, with two-thirds of the population—about 74 percent ethnic Chinese, 13 percent Malay, and 9 percent Indian and Pakistani—residing in Singapore City. Religious divisions follow ethnic divisions: the Malays and Pakistanis are overwhelmingly Muslim, the Indians are Hindu, and the Chinese include Buddhists, Christians, Taoists, and Confucianists. Women constitute 43 percent of the active labor force and 23.8 percent of the members of parliament.

Singapore's economy has traditionally been geared to the entrepôt trade, with a heavy emphasis on the processing and transshipment of petroleum, rubber, timber, and other regional products, and on related banking, shipping, insurance, and storage services. In addition, tourism has become a significant source of earnings. In all, services account for 75 percent of gross domestic product (GDP) and employ 76 percent of the labor force. Singapore is a leading oil-refining hub and a "global operations center" for more than 3,500 multinational firms. (For more information on Singapore's economy, see the 2010 *Handbook.*) Singapore is now a major producer of computer-related electronics as well as pharmaceuticals. Manufacturing as a whole contributes 25 percent of GDP and employs 17 percent of the active labor force.

For 2005–2008 average annual GDP growth was 7.5 percent. Following a record downturn in the first half of 2009, the economy quickly recovered and GDP growth rebounded to 14.7 percent in 2010 as a result of renewed exports. Government gross debt has steadily decreased since 2009, when it totaled 105 percent of GDP, falling to 96.2 percent in 2010 and 93.4 percent in 2011. In 2012 GDP grew by 1.3 percent, and the government again posted a surplus, $3.9 billion or 1.1 percent of GDP. In 2013 GDP rose by 4.1 percent, while inflation was 2.4 percent and unemployment was 1.9 percent. In 2014 GDP rose by 3.2 percent, while inflation was 1.2 percent, and unemployment 1.9 percent. The next year, growth slowed to 2 percent, while inflation dropped to –0.5 percent, but unemployment remained steady. The IMF projected slowed growth to 1.7 percent in 2016, while inflation remained negative at –0.2 percent, and unemployment ticked up slightly to 2 percent. GDP per capita for 2015 was $53,604. In 2016, once again, the World Bank ranked Singapore first in its annual report on the ease of doing business index.

GOVERNMENT AND POLITICS

Political background. Established as a trading station by Sir Stamford RAFFLES in 1819, purchased by Great Britain in 1824, and subsequently organized as part of the Straits Settlements (with Penang and Malacca), Singapore became a crown colony in 1867. It was occupied by the Japanese in World War II but achieved internal self-rule within the Commonwealth on June 3, 1959. Led by LEE Kuan Yew of the People's Action Party (PAP), it joined in 1963 with the Federation of Malaya, Sarawak, and Sabah to form Malaysia. Malay opinion subsequently became alarmed by the efforts of Lee and his largely Chinese party to extend their influence into other parts of Malaysia, and Singapore was consequently excluded on August 9, 1965.

As a fully independent state, Singapore adopted a republican form of government. The PAP, which had been seriously challenged in the early 1960s by the more radical Socialist Front (*Barisan Sosialis*), subsequently consolidated its position, obtaining a monopoly of all legislative seats in the four elections from 1968 through 1980 and then losing no more than two seats through 1988. By then, Prime Minister Lee had made a strong effort to bring "second-liners" (second-generation leaders) into government and the PAP hierarchy.

In October 1989 Lee, having become the world's longest-serving prime minister, confirmed reports that he planned to step down as prime minister. In November 1990 GOH Chok Tong formally succeeded Lee, who nevertheless retained backstage power in the post of senior minister and, until 1992, as PAP secretary general.

Although retaining its political dominance, the PAP was jolted by the outcome of an early election called by Goh for August 1991: The opposition captured four seats while the ruling party's popular support fell to a 23-year low of 61 percent. In response, the prime minister undertook a September cabinet shakeup that dispensed with most of his second-generation colleagues in favor of a third-generation cohort, including his predecessor's son, LEE Hsien Loong. Conscious that the anti-PAP vote had secured inadequate representation, and in an apparent effort to undermine by-election campaigns by the opposition, the government approved a 1992 parliamentary recommendation that six nonelected persons should become MPs, as allowed under a 1990 constitutional amendment.

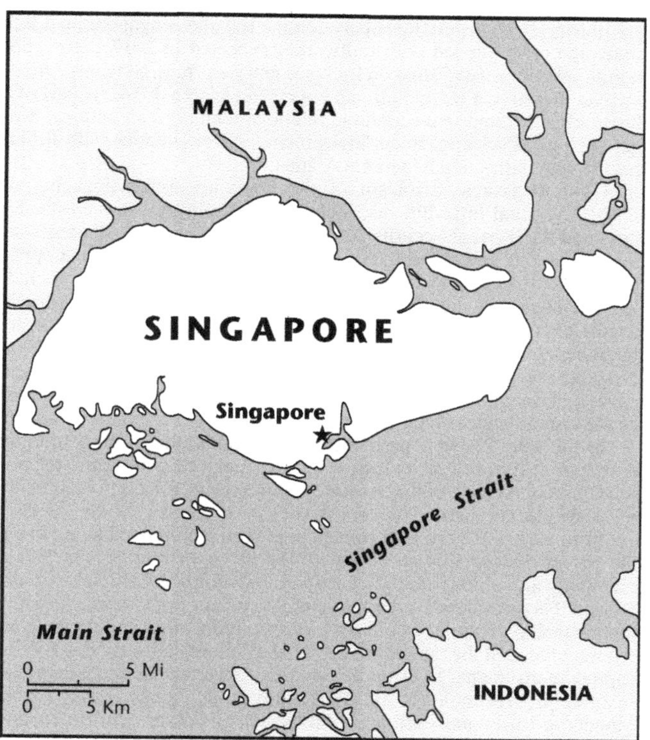

In the legislative election of January 1997, the PAP won 81 of 83 seats with about 65 percent of the popular vote. The following May, J. B. JEYARETNAM, secretary general of the Workers' Party (WP) and a longtime opponent of Lee Kuan Yew and the PAP, was awarded a non-constituency seat to bring the opposition total up to the constitutionally mandated minimum of three.

In July 1999 ONG Teng Cheong, who had been installed in 1993 as Singapore's first popularly elected president, announced that he would not seek reelection. S. R. NATHAN, a former military intelligence official and ambassador to the United States, was designated president-elect on August 18 by the Presidential Elections Commission, which had declared that the two other potential nominees did not meet the standards for office. On September 1 Nathan took the oath of office.

Hoping to forestall negative political consequences of an economic downturn, in October 2001, Prime Minister Goh announced an early legislative election for November 3. Earlier, four opposition parties had organized a Singapore Democratic Alliance (SDA), but the PAP nevertheless retained its stranglehold on Parliament, winning 82 elective seats, compared to 1 for the SDA and 1 for the WP.

On August 17, 2003, Prime Minister Goh confirmed what had long been anticipated in announcing the appointment of Deputy Prime Minister Lee Hsien Loong, officially taking over on August 12, 2004.

On April 20, 2006, Parliament was dissolved and an early election called on May 6. Although the PAP experienced a drop to 67 percent in overall support compared with 75 percent in 2001, it again won 82 seats. On May 7, 2011, the PAP received its lowest level of popular support since 1965, taking 60.1 percent of the vote in the general election, which cost the party one seat. Loong continued to occupy the office of prime minister after the general election in May (see Current issues, below), which was followed by the election of Tony TAN Keng Yam (ind.) as president on August 27, 2011.

On August 1, 2012, Loong announced a cabinet reform whereby the ministry of community development, youth, and sport and the ministry of information, communication, and the arts would be reconfigured to create three new portfolios beginning in November.

On January 14, 2013, Halimah YACOB (PAP) became the first woman elected speaker of Singapore's parliament. In April 2014 the acting ministers of culture, community and youth, and manpower were confirmed for their posts. Between April and May 2015, there was a minor cabinet reshuffle. In parliamentary elections on September 11, 2015, the PAP won 83 seats. Loong remained as prime minister and conducted a major cabinet reshuffle on September 28.

Constitution and government. Singapore's current basic law has evolved since 1959, with amendments necessitated by its temporary Malaysian affiliation and the subsequent adoption of republican status. The executive branch is headed by a president with limited powers—the chief executive's principal role is to safeguard the country's financial reserves—and a presidentially designated prime minister, who must command a parliamentary majority and who selects a cabinet that is collectively responsible to the Parliament. A Presidential Elections Commission is responsible for vetting presidential nominees, who must have sufficient governmental or corporate experience and be able to demonstrate "good integrity, character, and reputation." A Presidential Council for Minority Rights reviews legislation (except money bills or security-related legislation) to ensure racial and religious nondiscrimination.

The unicameral legislature is elected by universal suffrage and compulsory voting for a maximum term of five years. Under 1984 and 2010 constitutional amendments, up to nine non-constituency seats (originally six) may be awarded to ensure opposition representation in Parliament, with the precise minimum number of opposition seats (currently three) determined by electoral law. Should fewer than three members of the opposition win election, the requisite number of non-constituency seats are awarded to the opposition candidate(s) who came closest to winning. In addition, 1990 and 1997 constitutional amendments authorize the president, based on recommendations from a Special Select Committee of Parliament, to name up to nine (originally six) similarly constrained "nonpolitical Singaporeans." A 2010 amendment made the nonpolitical appointee system permanent. Nonelected members are not permitted, however, to vote on key measures, such as money bills, nonconfidence motions, and constitutional amendments.

Singapore's Supreme Court encompasses a High Court and a Court of Appeal. Since 1994 the Court of Appeal has served as the highest appellate court, replacing in that capacity the Judicial Committee of the UK Privy Council. Subordinate courts include district and magistrate's courts.

Even before independence, Singapore was administered as a unified city-state, local government bodies having been absorbed by departments of the central government in 1959. In 1960 Parliament created a People's Association (PA), a statutory board chaired by the prime minister and led by a chief executive director. Its goals have included achieving multiracial harmony, advancing social cohesion, and organizing community work. As such, it has sponsored residential committees, a Social Development Service, volunteer and grassroots organizations, community clubs, and youth programs, among other bodies and activities. The PA is also responsible for appointing members of Community Development Councils (CDCs). In 2000 Prime Minister Goh stated that the government planned to give the CDCs greater authority, responsibilities, and funding, in order to decentralize delivery of various services and other government functions. At present, the country's 23 electoral constituencies are grouped into five regions, each of which has an appointed mayor (a member of Parliament) and a CDC of roughly 12 to 80 councilors drawn from among community leaders, administrators, and professionals.

The domestic press has long been free in principle although restrained in practice by government ownership or control of major outlets, continuous monitoring, and periodic crackdowns for exceeding official perceptions of acceptable criticism. The government has also taken action against a number of foreign publications, several of which have been forced to apologize for articles and to make civil payments to government officials for critical stories. Internet sites posting political or religious content must register. In 2016 Reporters Without Borders ranked Singapore 154th out of 180 countries in press freedom, down four levels since 2015 and a significant decline from 135th in 2012.

Foreign relations. Singapore joined the United Nations in 1965 and in 1967 helped found the Association of Southeast Asian Nations (ASEAN). Upon the departure of most British defense forces in 1971, Singapore became a member of the Five Power Defense Arrangement (along with Britain, Australia, New Zealand, and Malaysia), a regional security system that calls for the maintenance of Commonwealth forces in Singapore.

Following independence, Singapore's relations with its immediate neighbors were initially tense. However, in 1989 Malaysia and Singapore held their first joint military exercises since 1965, and the Lee government signed defense agreements with both Malaysia and Indonesia. In early 1992, however, Singapore–Malaysia relations were strained when a visit to Singapore by U.S. president George H. W. Bush produced an agreement on relocating a U.S. naval logistical command headquarters from Subic Bay, Philippines, to Singapore.

In 1998 Singapore and Malaysia agreed to submit to the International Court of Justice (ICJ) competing claims to the islet of Pedra Blanca (Pulau Batu Putih), although a formal agreement to that effect was not signed until February 2003. Eight months later the International Tribunal for the Law of the Sea ruled against Malaysia and in favor of Singapore's right to conduct land reclamation on Pulau Tekong Island. In January 2005 the neighbors reached a "mutually acceptable and beneficial solution" to the dispute. In May 2008 the ICJ ruled in favor of Singapore's claim to Pedra Blanca but gave the nearby Middle Rocks to Malaysia.

In September 2001 Singapore and Malaysia signed an agreement on settling their differences over water supplies, transport links, the right of Singapore's aircraft to enter Malaysian airspace, and other matters. In December 2004, the two countries began new talks, which focused on releasing Malaysian workers' pension funds held by Singapore and on building a bridge to replace the outdated causeway that connects Singapore to the mainland. In April 2006, however, Malaysia scrapped plans for the bridge, construction of which Singapore continued to link to restoration of full airspace rights as well as to a 20-year commitment from Malaysia for 1 billion cubic meters of sand for reclamation. In May 2010 Prime Minister Lee and Prime Minister Najib Razak of Malaysia agreed to resolve differences over rail stations and transit. In 2011, however, disputes persisted with Malaysia over delivering freshwater to Singapore, Singapore's extensive land reclamation works, bridge construction, and maritime boundaries in the Johor and Singapore Straits. (For more information on Singapore's relationship with regional countries, see the 2010 *Handbook.*)

In 2006 Singapore and Indonesia signed an agreement on establishing special economic zones on three nearby Indonesian islands, the principal purpose being to attract investment capital from Singapore. In February 2007 the two signed a joint defense cooperation agreement and Singapore agreed to an extradition treaty, although opposition in the Indonesian legislature forced President Susilo Yudhoyono's government to postpone ratification efforts. In March 2009 Indonesia's minister of defense described the defense agreement and the treaty as "frozen" but assigned responsibility for the impasse to Singapore, which, he said, was concerned that the extradition pact might require the return of not only fugitives to Indonesia, but also their funds. More recently, in August 2010 the two countries' foreign ministers concluded an agreement defining the maritime border in the western Singapore Strait. (For more information on Singapore's relationship with Indonesia prior to 2006, see the 2010 *Handbook.*)

The government supported the U.S.-led invasion of Iraq in March 2003 and committed a landing ship (LST) and a handful of support aircraft, but no combat troops, to the multinational operation.

Effective January 2010, Singapore and five other ASEAN states (Brunei, Indonesia, Malaysia, Philippines, and Thailand) inaugurated a trade agreement with China under which 90 percent of mutual trade was tariff-free. The resultant trade zone is the largest in the world in terms of overall population and third, behind the European Union and the North American Free Trade Association, in terms of potential value. Territorial disputes in the South China Sea between China and several ASEAN countries surfaced in 2010 and 2011. Foreign ministers from Singapore and Cambodia jointly urged a peaceful solution in October 2011. Also in October, Singapore donated 45 military patrol boats to Thailand.

The United States announced the deployment of three additional naval vessels to Singapore in 2012. The increased cooperation was reported to be a reaction to the rising Chinese military presence in the region. In April 2012 Singapore agreed to contribute $4 billion to the $430 billion International Monetary Fund (IMF) emergency fund used to support eurozone bailout programs. In December Singapore finalized negotiations with the EU over a free trade agreement.

In December 2013 Singapore and Taiwan finalized a free trade accord.

In February 2014 Singapore withdrew invitations to an air show from 100 Indonesian military officers after Indonesia named a naval vessel for two of its soldiers who had carried out a bomb attack in Singapore in 1965. In July Vietnam apologized to Singapore after workers destroyed equipment and looted facilities at three Singapore-run industrial parks in Vietnam during a series of anti-Chinese riots.

In November 2014 Singapore announced it would contribute logistics personnel to the U.S.-led coalition conducting airstrikes against the Islamic State in Syria and Iraq.

In May 2015 negotiations between the EU and Singapore on a free trade agreement ended with ratification expected in 2017. After economic sanctions were lifted on Iran (see entry on Iran), Singapore finalized an investment treaty with the country in March 2016. As part of a broad effort to improve economic relations with African nations, Singapore signed bilateral trade, investment, and tax treaties with Ethiopia, Mozambique, and Nigeria in August.

Current issues. Criticism of the government remains circumscribed by legal impediments, including the country's severe slander laws and the Internal Security Act (ISA). Moreover, the PAP continues to use lawsuits and the threat of consequent bankruptcy against opponents. The ISA has also been used to detain suspected terrorists, including members of the *Jemaah Islamiah* (JI), the Indonesian-based terrorist network that has called for creation of a regional Muslim state. In September 2010 Indonesia extradited Mas Salamat KASTARI to Singapore to face charges involving a plot to hijack an aircraft and crash it at Singapore's international airport. Kastari has been described as the former leader of Singapore's JI branch.

In the May 7, 2011, parliamentary elections, the overwhelmingly dominant PAP received its lowest level of support in 46 years, reflecting voter concerns over the economy. Nonetheless, the party secured 81 of the 87 elected seats.

In January 2012 the government approved recommendations to cut the pay of ministers by an average of 36 percent (Singapore's cabinet members are among the highest-paid government officials in the world). The president's salary would also be cut by 51 percent, while members of parliament would see 3 percent reductions. In July the government reduced the number of criminal offences that were eligible for capital punishment. In August two new universities, the Singapore Institute of Technology and SIM University, opened. They were Singapore's fifth and sixth universities and part of an effort to expand the number of graduating high-school Singaporeans able to enter university in the city state from 27 percent to 40 percent.

In response to growing international criticism, a new law in March 2013 mandated that domestic workers such as maids and housekeepers be given at least one day off per week; at the time, estimates were that fewer than 10 percent of household workers were given one day off per week.

In late June 2013 activist and former SDP treasurer Vincent WIJEYSINGHA became Singapore's first openly homosexual politician. By August Wijeysingha had resigned from the SDP to focus full-time on activism related to civil liberties and human rights. In September, 14 people were arrested in Singapore for involvement in a criminal syndicate that fixed the scores of more than 100 football games around the world. In December rioting broke out between ethnic Indians and Chinese. Twenty-seven Indian immigrants were arrested, while 52 were deported. The government instituted a ban on alcohol in the mainly Indian district where the rioting occurred.

In October 2014 the Supreme Court rejected an appeal that argued that national laws that criminalized homosexual sex were discriminatory and unconstitutional.

Former prime minister Lee Kuan Yew died on March 23, 2015, at age 91. The government ordered a week of mourning, and more than 100,000 people attended his state funeral.

POLITICAL PARTIES

Since Singapore achieved self-rule in 1959, the People's Action Party (PAP) has never been out of power. Newly registered parties continue to show low membership.

Governing Party:

People's Action Party (PAP). Organized as a radical socialist party in 1954, the PAP has been Singapore's ruling party since 1959. Some of its more militant leaders were arrested by the British in 1957, and other radicals split off in 1961 to form the Socialist Front (see under WP, below). What remained was the more moderate, anti-Communist wing of the original party, which has supported a pragmatic program emphasizing social welfare and economic development.

Despite its legislative dominance, the party's share of the total vote declined steadily from 78 percent in 1980 to 61 percent in 1991. It rebounded to a 65 percent share in January 1997, when the PAP won 81 of 83 parliamentary seats, and to nearly 75 percent in 2001, when it won 82 of 84 seats. Prime Minister Goh soon announced that a

"People's Action Forum" of 20 MPs would be set up as an internal opposition to encourage debate within the PAP.

Under the leadership of Goh's successor, Lee Hsien Loong, the PAP's support declined to 67 percent of the vote and 82 elective seats in the May 2006 election and again in May 2011, with 60.1 percent of the vote and 81 of 87 seats. Loong was appointed chair of the Government of Singapore Investment Corporation (GIC) in June 2011.

In January 2013 the PAP suffered its second by-election defeat since the 2011 polling, reducing its majority to 80 seats. In December the PAP adopted a resolution to create a "fair and just" multiethnic society in what was described as an effort to attract new voters ahead of legislative elections.

The PAP won 69.8 percent of the vote and 83 seats in the September 2015 parliamentary balloting.

Leaders: LEE Hsien Loong (Prime Minister and Secretary General of the Party), TEO Chee Hean (Assistant Secretary General and Deputy Prime Minister), KHAW Boon Wan (Chair and Minister for Transport), YAACOB Ibrahim (Vice Chair and Minister for Communications and Information).

Parliamentary Opposition:

Workers' Party—WP (*Parti Pekerja*). Founded in 1957 and reorganized in 1971, the WP long advocated a more democratic constitution and closer relations with Malaysia. In its early years a number of WP leaders were arrested for alleged pro-Communist activities, and in 1978 its secretary general, Joshua Benjamin Jeyaretnam, was convicted of having committed "a very grave slander" against Prime Minister Lee. In a by-election in October 1981, the Sri Lankan-born Jeyaretnam became the first opposition member of Parliament since 1968. Despite having previously been acquitted of making a false declaration about party finances, Jeyaretnam and the party chair, WONG Hong Toy, were retried in September 1985. Jeyaretnam was fined and imprisoned for one month in late 1986, which cost him his legislative seat.

Prior to the 1988 election, the Socialist Front (*Barisan Sosialis*) and the **Singapore United Front**—SUF (*Barisan Bersatu Singapura*) merged with the WP. Formed in 1961 by a group of pro-Beijing PAP militants under the leadership of trade unionist LIM Chin Siong, the *Barisan Sosialis* was the leading opposition party until 1966, when 11 members resigned their seats and 2 went underground. The SUF, organized in 1973, ran third in 1984 but won no legislative seats. In 1989 Singapore's most celebrated political prisoner, former *Barisan Sosialis* leader CHIA Thye Poh, was released after 23 years' detention. Remaining restrictions imposed on Chia's political activity were finally lifted in 1998.

The WP elected one MP in 1991 and again in January 1997. In May 1997 Secretary General Jeyaretnam was awarded a non-constituency seat, even though he and fellow WP candidate TANG Liang Hong had been sued by Prime Minister Goh and other PAP members for defaming them during the election campaign. Claiming his life had been threatened, Tang fled abroad, and in March he was found guilty in absentia and ordered to pay heavy damages. Late in 1997 the government issued a warrant for his arrest on tax evasion charges. Jeyaretnam also lost his case, and in July 1998 a court not only dismissed his appeal but also raised the damage award. A subsequent report indicated that Jeyaretnam had agreed to pay some $61,500 in installments to avoid bankruptcy and forfeiture of his seat in Parliament.

In May 1999 the Court of Appeal dismissed a request by the WP to throw out a defamation award of more than $150,000 won by a group called the Tamil Language Committee, which had sued over an article in the party newsletter. The septuagenarian Jeyaretnam himself lost an appeal of a bankruptcy order in July 2001 and was thereby forced to vacate his parliamentary seat. Citing lack of support for his case, he resigned from the WP before the November 2001 election, at which the party again won one seat. In April 2002 Jeyaretnam publicly apologized for his 1997 remarks, in return for which the government dropped seven other lawsuits against him.

In 2003 Sylvia Lim was elected to chair the party, thereby becoming the first woman to assume that role. In the 2006 election the WP won one seat. Lim claimed a second, non-constituency seat. In June 2008 she was reelected chair. In May 2011 the WP secured six seats. In February 2012 WP MP Yaw SHIN Leong resigned. In the subsequent by-election, the WP retained the seat and won a second by-election in January 2013.

The WP won six seats in the 2015 elections, and gained two non-constituency memberships.

Leaders: Sylvia LIM Swee Lian (Chair), Mohammed Faisal bin Abdul MANAP (Vice Chair), LOW Thia Khiang (Leader of the Opposition and Secretary General of the Party).

Singapore Democratic Alliance (SDA). Formation of the four-party SDA was announced on July 28, 2001. In the November 2001 election it won only one seat but was later awarded an additional non-constituency seat. In May 2006 it retained only its electoral seat.

In January 2007 the National Solidarity Party (NSP, below) withdrew from the SDA, which consisted of the Singapore People's Party (SPP), the Singapore Malay National Organization (PKMS), and the Singapore Justice Party (SJP). The SDA's Executive Council was most recently elected in January 2009. In February 2011 the SDA's council voted to relieve Chiam See Tong of the SPP of his role as chair, following which Chiam announced that his party was withdrawing from the SDA.

In March 2013 the dormant **Democratic Progressive Party** was revived and agreed to join the SDA. Party leader Desmond LIM Bak Chuan placed fourth in the 2013 by-election for Punggol East. The SDA participated in the 2015 elections but did not gain any seats.

Leader: Desmond LIM Bak Chuan (Secretary General).

Singapore Malay National Organization (*Pertubuhan Kebangsaan Melayu Singapura*—PKMS). Originally an affiliate of the United Malays National Organization in Malaysia, the PKMS assumed its present name in 1967. It supports Malay interests, racial harmony, national unity, and "the advancement of Islam without interfering in the affairs of other religions." In 1999 it called for government creation of a "supervisory council" charged with eliminating racial discrimination.

In recent years, the party has suffered from a number of intra-party disputes. In September 2006 the party's sitting president and vice president, Borhan Ariffin and MUHAMMAD Ali Aman, were ousted in a party election but then challenged the results. In January 2007 the courts ruled that a new election should be held by the following September. That election concluded with the apparent reelection of the unopposed sitting president, Osman Hassan, and other officers. Borhan's supporters again challenged the results, however, with the Registrar of Societies refusing to recognize the outcome of the election until its validity was examined by the courts.

The factional dispute continued into 2008, when an extraordinary general meeting in November elected a new slate of officers, led by Borhan. The Osman faction refused, however, to acknowledge the legitimacy of the election, and in September 2009, when a group of Borhan supporters attempted to enter the party headquarters, a riot ensued. The police arrested 21 individuals. Each side accused the other of misusing party funds and violating the party constitution.

Following an August 7, 2010, general meeting, the Borhan faction asked the Registrar of Societies to resolve the dispute with the Osman faction. Meeting a day later, the Osman faction elected Ali Asjadi to assume the presidency, with Osman taking on the role of chief adviser. On August 10 the High Court ordered the Borhan faction to turn over the keys to party headquarters to its rival, but Borhan announced his intention to appeal the decision. Still a member party of SDA, PKMS also maintains ties with UMNO Malaysia. In October 2011 Asjadi was convicted of selling contraband cigarettes and sentenced to 30 months in prison. He was subsequently expelled from the party and Deputy President ABU Mohmed was made acting leader of the PKMS. In 2013 a former member of the PKMS executive committee, Sulaiman GANI, was convicted of stealing jewelry from Asjadi and sentenced to seven months in prison.

At a party conference in April 2016, Abu was reelected.

Leaders: ABU Mohmed (President); Ismail YACOOB (Deputy President); Malik ISMAIL, Kuswadi ATNAWI (Vice Presidents); Muhammad Hairullah AHMAD (Secretary General).

Singapore People's Party (SPP). A moderate breakaway faction of the SDP (below), the SPP was registered in November 1994. In January 1997 the party won one seat, tying the WP for opposition representation in the Parliament. The SPP's sole seat was held by Chiam See Tong, a longtime legislator who joined the party in 1996 after losing a power struggle in the SDP (below).

In 2010 Chiam indicated that he favored his wife, Lina CHIAM, as his successor rather than his longtime assistant, Desmond Lim. At the same time, Chiam supported, but Lim opposed, accepting the Reform Party (below) into the SDA. Lina Chiam is now the SPP's sole representative and serves as a Non-Constituency MP (NCMP), often emphasizing her role as "a voice for other opposition parties."

In January 2012, after six SPP central executive committee members resigned, a new central body was elected. In January 2013 SPP member Benjamin PWEE left the party to relaunch the Democratic Progressive Party. Lina Chiam became chair of the party in 2013. The party did not win seats in the 2015 elections, coming in third with 3.1 percent of the votes, but it retained a non-constituency membership.

Leaders: CHIAM See Tong (Secretary General); Lina CHIAM (Chair); Han JOOK KUANG, Williamson LEE, Shahir bin SHAFIE (Council Members); Yong SENG FATT (Treasurer).

Other Opposition Parties:

Singapore Justice Party (SJP). The SJP is a small group organized in 1972. It has contested only a handful of parliamentary seats, none since 1991. Internal disputes weakened the party, but when the SDP's Chiam See Tong became SPP's leader in 1997, several SJP members joined SPP. In 2001 SJP and others became an inaugural component of SDA. After the SPP pulled out of SDA in 2011, ex-SJP member Desmond Lim resigned from SPP in order to stay within SDA. The party did not participate in the 2015 elections.

Leaders: Habibi binte JOHARI (Chair), AMINUDDIN bin Ami (Secretary General).

National Solidarity Party—NSP (*Parti Perpaduan Nasional*). Conceived in April 1986 by a group of former SDP and SUF leaders, the NSP gained its first legislative representative when Steve Chia Kiah Hong was named a non-constituency member after the 2001 election. In December 2003 Chia resigned as NSP secretary general because of admitted sexual peccadilloes, but he was reelected to the vacant post in July 2005 and continues to serve on the party's governing council.

A founding member of the SDA, the NSP left the alliance in January 2007. The "amicable parting" was intended to afford the party room to "maneuver, reengineer, and rebuild." In the May 7, 2011, elections it fielded the largest number of candidates. A new central executive committee was elected in April 2013, with party president Sebastian Teo reelected. In October Jeannette CHONG-ARULDOSS was elected secretary general of the party. The party participated in the 2015 elections but failed to win any seats. Several senior members of the party resigned, including then–Secretary General, Hazel POA.

Leaders: Sebastian TEO (President), Abdul RASHEED (Vice Chairman), Lim TEAN (Secretary General).

Reform Party (RP). The RP was launched in early 2008 by Ng Teck Siong and longtime Workers' Party stalwart J. B. Jeyaretnam, who had recently emerged from bankruptcy, on a platform that included abolition of the death penalty and of the ISA. One of the government's staunchest critics as well as an advocate for multiparty democracy, Jeyaretnam, 82, died in September 2008. In April 2009 a son, Kenneth, stepped into the leadership, and, Ng Teck Siong, following a vote of no confidence by the Central Executive Committee, resigned as chair. (In 2010, Ng formed the Socialist Front, see below.)

At its May 2010 annual meeting the RP conditionally approved joining the SDA, but some members of the alliance's leadership objected to what it perceived not as negotiating points but as unreasonable demands by the RP. Discussions on the potential affiliation subsequently resumed. In the 2011 general election many RP members defected to the NSP. Discussions on a possible alliance with SDA and SPP also broke down. The RP candidate received less than 1 percent of the vote in the January 2013 Punggoi East by-election. In May 2014 the RP called on the government to reduce Singapore's dependence on foreign workers.

The RP participated in the 2015 elections but failed to win seats, securing only 2.6 percent of the vote.

Leaders: Andy ZHU (Chair), Kenneth JEYARETNAM (Secretary General).

Singapore Democratic Party (SDP). Organized in 1980 by Chiam See Tong, the SDP attracted liberal-minded Singaporeans seeking a degree of formal opposition to the PAP. Chiam won one of the two seats lost by the PAP in 1984; the seat was retained in 1988. The party won three parliamentary seats in 1991, but in June 1993 Chiam resigned as the SDP secretary general and later joined the SPP.

Having been targeted by the PAP, the SDP lost all its seats in the 1997 parliamentary elections. Four years later, despite attracting about 8 percent of the vote, the SDP failed to win any seats. It had campaigned on a "Singaporeans First" platform that blamed foreign workers for rising unemployment.

Since 1999 party leader Chee Soon Juan has been repeatedly fined and jailed for offenses that have included making unlicensed public policy speeches, illegally selling a book he had written, and defaming government officials, including the current prime minister and his two predecessors. Forced into bankruptcy in 2006, Chee was thereby disqualified to run for Parliament in May. In November he was jailed for five weeks for refusing to pay a fine of S$5,000 imposed for speaking in public without a permit during the parliamentary election campaign. Also sentenced to jail were party leaders Ghandi Ambalam and YAP Keng Ho. Earlier in the year, longtime party leader Wong Hong Toy (previously a leader of the WP) resigned as assistant secretary general because of policy differences with Chee.

Chee has since been charged with additional offenses, including leading an illegal march in September 2007, attempting in October 2007 to deliver to the prime minister's office a petition regarding Singapore's relationship with Myanmar's ruling junta, and holding an illegal assembly outside Parliament in March 2008 to protest rising prices. In June 2008 he and his sister, CHEE Siok Chin, served 12-day and 10-day sentences, respectively, for contempt of court during a defamation proceeding. In December 2009 they and party chair Gandhi Ambalam served a week in jail rather than pay a fine for having distributed fliers without a permit in 2006. As of October 2010 several court cases and appeals involving the party leaders were pending, and ultimately Chee went bankrupt, foreshadowing an unstable future for the party. Negotiations between the SDP and the WP on fielding joint candidates in by-elections failed in 2013. In October 2013 Jeffrey GEORGE was elected party chair, but was replaced on November 4, 2015, by Wong SOUK YEE, following the former's arrest on drug charges. The party won no seats in the 2015 elections.

Leaders: Wong Souk Yee (Chair), John TAN (Vice Chair), CHEE Soon Juan (Secretary General), Christopher ANG (Assistant Secretary General).

Socialist Front—SF (*Angkatan Sosialis*). The SF was established and registered in September 2010 at the instigation of Ng Teck Siong, who had previously belonged to the SDP, the WP, and the RP. He left the RP in April 2009 after a vote of no confidence in his leadership. During the May 7, 2011, elections party leaders were divided over whether to contest the balloting, further dividing what many viewed as a short-lived party. The SF did not participate in the 2015 elections.

Leaders: NG Teck Siong (Chair), CHIA Ti Lik (Secretary General).

Other parties that participated in the 2015 balloting included the anti-immigrant **Singaporeans First** (SF), formed in August 2014 and led by Ang Yong GUAN, and the **People's Power Party** (PPP), established in 2015 and led by Syafarin SARIF.

For information on the **United Singapore Democrats** (USD), see the 2012 *Handbook*.

LEGISLATURE

The unicameral **Parliament** currently includes 89 members directly elected (from a mix of group representation and single-member constituencies) for five-year terms, subject to dissolution. In the general election of September 11, 2016, the PAP took 83 seats, while the WP won 6. Currently, the Parliament comprises 89 members of Parliament (MPs), 3 non-constituency members of Parliament (NCMPs), and 9 nominated members of Parliament (NMPs), who are appointed once Parliament convenes.

Speaker: Halimah YACOB.

CABINET

[as of October 1, 2016]

Prime Minister	Lee Hsien Loong
Deputy Prime Ministers	Rear Adm. (Ret.) Teo Chee Hean Tharman Shanmugaratnam

Ministers

Communications and Information	Yaacob Ibrahim
Culture, Community, and Youth	Grace Fu Hai Yien [f]
Defense	Ng Eng Heng
Education	Ong Ye Kung
Environment and Water Resources	Masagos Zulkifli
Finance	Heng Swee Keat
Foreign Affairs	Vivian Balakrishnan
Health	Gan Kim Yong
Home Affairs and Law	Kasiviswanathan Shanmugam
Industry	S. Iswaran
Manpower	Lim Swee Say
National Development	Lawrence Wong
National Security, Coordinating Minister	Rear Adm. (Ret.) Teo Chee Hean
Prime Minister's Office	Maj. Gen. (Ret.) Chan
Social and Family Development	Tan Chuan-Jin
Trade	Lim Hng Kiang
Transport	Khaw Boon Wan

[f] = female

INTERGOVERNMENTAL REPRESENTATION

Ambassador to the U.S.: Ashok Kumar MIRPURI.

U.S. Ambassador to Singapore: Stephanie SYPTAK-RAMNATH (Charge d'Affaires *ad interim*).

Permanent Representative to the UN: Burhanudeen GAFOOR.

IGO Memberships (Non-UN): ADB, AOSIS, APEC, ASEAN, CWTH, NAM, WTO.

For Further Reference:

Acharya, Amitav. *Singapore's Foreign Policy: The Search for Regional Order*. Singapore: World Scientific Publishing Company, 2007.

Barr, Michael D. *The Ruling Elites of Singapore: Networks of Power and Influence*. London: I. B. Tauris, 2013.

Lim, Jason. *Singapore: Negotiating State and Society, 1965–2015*. New York: Routledge, 2016.

SLOVAKIA

Slovak Republic
Slovenská Republika

Political Status: Slovak Republic proclaimed upon separation of the constituent components of the Czech and Slovak Federative Republic (see article on Czech Republic) on January 1, 1993.

Area: 18,933 sq. mi. (49,035 sq. km).

Population: 5,429,000 (2016E—UN); 5,445,802 (2016E—U.S. Census).

Major Urban Centers (2014E—UN): BRATISLAVA (418,534), Košice (239,631).

Official Language: Slovak.

Monetary Unit: Euro (market rate October 1, 2016: 0.89 euro = $1US). The monetary unit was the koruna until Slovakia adopted the euro on January 1, 2009, at an exchange rate of 30.1260 koruny = 1 euro. (The official rate of the koruna on December 31, 2008, was 21.45 koruny = $1US.)

President: Andrej KISKA (ind.); popularly elected in runoff balloting on March 29, 2014, and inaugurated on June 15 for a five-year term, succeeding Ivan GAŠPAROVIČ (originally elected as the candidate of the People's Union–Movement for Democracy).

Prime Minister: Robert FICO (Direction–Social Democracy) designated by the president on March 15, 2012, to form a new government following the legislative elections of March 10 and formally appointed by the president on April 4 to head a new government in succession to Iveta RADIČOVÁ (Slovak Democratic and Christian Union); designated by the president on March 9, 2016, following legislative elections on March 5, 2016, and sworn in on March 23.

THE COUNTRY

Situated in the geographical center of Europe, Slovakia consists of some 40 percent of the area of the former Czechoslovak federation. It is bounded by the Czech Republic to the west, Poland to the north, Ukraine to the east, Hungary to the south, and Austria to the southwest. A former province of the Hungarian-ruled part of the Austro-Hungarian Empire, the country's population is 86 percent Slovak and 10 percent Hungarian (Magyar), with small minorities of Czechs, Roma (Gypsies), Ruthenes, and Ukrainians. Approximately 69 percent of the population is Roman Catholic, the other Christian denominations include Protestant (11 percent) and Greek–Catholic (Orthodox-rite Christians who acknowledge the hierarchy of the Catholic Church; 4 percent). Women continued to be underrepresented in government and industry. Following the March 2016 legislative balloting, women held 30 of 150 seats in the National Council (20 percent).

A substantial proportion of former Czechoslovakia's heavy industry is located in Slovakia. Industry as a whole accounted for 35.5 percent of gross domestic product (GDP) in 2011. The principal manufactures include machinery, chemicals, plastics, and processed foods; Slovakia is also the world's biggest per capita car producer. The agricultural sector contributes less than 4 percent of GDP; its leading crops are wheat, other grains, and sugar beets. Leading trade partners include Germany, the Czech Republic, Russia, Italy, and Poland.

Long less affluent than Bohemia and Moravia, reform efforts in the immediate post-Communist period in Slovakia accentuated economic differences with the Czech Republic, fueling pressure for political separation on January 1, 1993. State control and central planning were much more entrenched in the Slovak bureaucracy, which continued to be dominated by officials who had prospered under the previous regime. In 1993 Slovakia's estimated per capita GNP was only $1,500, as contrasted with $2,500 in the Czech lands, with Slovak GDP falling by an estimated 5 percent during the year; at the same time, unemployment and inflation in Slovakia rose well above Czech levels, to 15 percent and around 25 percent, respectively.

After lackluster economic performance until the installation in 1998 of a center-right administration that implemented numerous reforms, Slovakia was described as one of Central Europe's brightest economic performers upon its accession to the European Union (EU) in 2004. Slovakia joined the European Exchange Rate Mechanism II agreement on November 28, 2005, a key step toward entry into the Eurozone.

The country achieved a long-standing objective by adopting the euro in January 2009. However, that success was partially overshadowed by the impact of the global financial crisis, with unemployment surpassing 12 percent in 2009. GDP fell by 4.7 percent. In 2010 strong exports helped lift the country out of recession. GDP growth was 3.5 in 2011 and 2 for 2012. Inflation dipped from 4 percent in 2011 to 3.7 percent, while unemployment rose from 13.7 percent in 2011 to 14 percent in 2012. In 2013 GDP grew by 0.9 percent, while inflation was 1.5 percent and unemployment was 14.2 percent. In 2015 GDP grew by 3.6 percent, inflation was –0.3 percent, and unemployment was 11.5 percent. In 2016 GDP increased by 3.4 percent, while inflation was 0.2 percent and unemployment was 10.4 percent. In its 2016 annual report on the ease of doing business index, the World Bank ranked Slovakia 29th out of 189 countries. GDP per capita that year was $15,917.

GOVERNMENT AND POLITICS

Political background. Founded in 1918, Czechoslovakia was considered to be the most politically mature and democratically governed of the new states of Eastern Europe, but it was dismembered following the 1938 Munich agreement. The preponderant role of Soviet military forces in liberating the country at the close of World War II enabled the Communists to gain a leading position in the postwar cabinet headed by strongly pro-Soviet Premier Zdeněk FIERLINGER, although President Eduard BENEŠ was perceived as

nonaligned. Communist control was consolidated in February 1948, and, under Marxist-Leninist precepts, Czech-Slovak differences officially ceased to exist, the two ethnic groups being charged with building socialism in amity and cooperation. (For subsequent political developments during the Communist era, see the entry on the Czech Republic.)

Communist power in Czechoslovakia crumbled in late 1989. On November 20, one day after formation of the opposition Civic Forum (*Občanské Fórum*—OF), 250,000 antiregime demonstrators marched in Prague, and 24 hours later government leaders held initial discussions with Forum representatives. On November 22 the widely admired Alexander DUBČEK (who had attempted to introduce "socialism with a human face" while serving as leader of the Czechoslovakian Communist Party in the "Prague Spring" of 1968) returned to the limelight with an address before an enthusiastic rally in Bratislava. Following a nationwide strike on November 28 (preceded by a three-day rally of 500,000 in Prague), the regime accepted loss of its monopoly status, and on December 7 Prime Minister Ladislav ADAMEC quit in favor of the little-known Marián ČALFA. On December 10 President Gustáv HUSÁK resigned after swearing in the first non–Communist-dominated government in 41 years, with the Federal Assembly naming Václav HAVEL as his successor on December 29. The Civic Forum and its Slovak counterpart, Public Against Violence (*Verejnost Proti Násili*—VPN), won a majority of federal legislative seats in nationwide balloting on June 8 and 9, 1990, with Čalfa (who had resigned from the Communist Party on January 18) forming a new government on June 27 and Havel being elected to a regular two-year term as president on July 5.

During 1991 the anti-Communist coalition, its major objective achieved, crumbled into less-inclusive party formations. The Civic Forum gave rise to two Czech groups in February, while in Slovakia the VPN assumed a new identity, the Civic Democratic Union–Public Against Violence (*Občanská Demokratická Únie–Verejnost Proti Násili*—ODU-VPN), in October after having been substantially weakened by the defection of a Slovak separatist faction, the Movement for a Democratic Slovakia (*Hnutie za Demokratické Slovensko*—HZDS). In November negotiations between federal and republican leaders over the country's future political status collapsed, with the Federal Assembly becoming deadlocked over the issue of a referendum on separate Czech and Slovak states.

On March 3, 1992, the Federal Assembly presidium scheduled a general election (coinciding with elections to the Czech and Slovak National Councils) for June 5–6, and on April 14 Havel announced that he would seek a further term as president. By then, however, a contest between Czech Finance Minister Václav KLAUS and former Slovak prime minister Vladimír MEČIAR had emerged as the major determinant of federal politics, Klaus favoring a right-of-center liberal economic policy with rapid privatization and Mečiar preferring a slower transition to capitalism. The two remained in firm control of their respective regions in the election of June 5–6, after which Mečiar returned to the post of Slovak prime minister, from which he had been dismissed in April 1991. Paralleling their differing economic outlooks, the Czech and Slovak leaders entertained divergent views as to the federation's political future. Klaus insisted that Czechoslovakia should remain a state with strong central authority or divide into separate entities, while Mečiar favored a weakened central government with most powers assigned to the individual republics. In the end, the death knell of the combined state was sounded by successful Slovak opposition in the assembly to the reelection of Havel as federal president on July 3. Thereafter, events moved quickly toward formal dissolution, with agreement being reached between the two governments by the end of August and the Slovak National Council adopting an independent constitution on September 1. Ironically, public opinion in both regions opposed separation. Thus, Klaus and Mečiar were obliged to act through the Federal Assembly, 183 of whose deputies (3 more than the required minimum) on November 25 endorsed the breakup with effect from January 1, 1993.

The Mečiar government of independent Slovakia quickly came under criticism for its alleged dictatorial tendencies and its reluctance to tackle the entrenched position of former Communists in the state bureaucracy. The election of Michal KOVÁČ as president on February 15, 1993, added to the divisions in the ruling HZDS. Although Kováč, a former reform Communist, was then backed by Mečiar, his postelection offer to resign from the HZDS highlighted an internal rift between the prime minister and leading cabinet colleagues. In a cabinet reshuffle in March, Mečiar ejected his main HZDS opponent, Foreign Minister and Deputy Prime Minister Milan KŇAŽKO, who promptly defected from the party to found a new group, the Alliance of Democrats of the Slovak Republic (*Aliancia Demokratov Slovenskej Republiky*—ADSR). Mečiar also insisted on appointing a former Communist military officer, Imrich ANDREJČÁK, as defense minister. The one ministerial representative of the Slovak National Party (*Slovenská Národná Strana*—SNS) thereupon resigned in protest, although the SNS, a strongly nationalistic formation with an anti-Hungarian orientation, announced that it would continue to support the government.

Mečiar governed the country for the next seven months as head of a minority government, failing during this period to entice the (ex-Communist) Party of the Democratic Left (*Strana Demokratickej L'avice*—SDL'; see *Smer,* below) to join his administration. In October 1993 the HZDS-SNS coalition was formally revived, this time with the junior partner holding several key portfolios. However, divisions within both ruling parties became irresolvable in early 1994, and defections led to Mečiar's defeat in a parliamentary nonconfidence vote on March 11. Mečiar resigned three days later and was replaced as prime minister on March 16 by Jozef MORAVČÍK, who had resigned as foreign minister the previous month and had set up a new party opposed to the HZDS. He formed a center-left coalition, headed by his Democratic Union of Slovakia (*Demokratická Únia Slovenska*—DÚS) and including the SDL'.

The ouster of the Mečiar government, described as a "parliamentary putsch" by the former prime minister, served to enflame political antagonisms in the run-up to the election. Particularly venomous were relations between Mečiar and President Kováč, whose open criticism of the HZDS leader had been a major cause of the government's collapse. Nevertheless, in legislative balloting on September 30–October 1, 1994, Mečiar and the HZDS won a plurality, campaigning on a populist platform that appealed to the large rural population. Despite an economic upturn under the Moravčík government, the new DÚS could manage only fifth place, being outpolled by the center-left Common Choice bloc (headed by the SDL'), the Hungarian Coalition (*Mad'arská Koalícia*—MK), and the Christian Democratic Movement (*Křest'ansko-demokratické Hnutie*—KDH). Six weeks later, on December 13, Mečiar embarked upon his third term as prime minister, heading a "red-brown" coalition of the HZDS, the far-right SNS, and the now-defunct leftist Association of Workers of Slovakia (*Združenie Robotníkov Slovenska*—ZRS) that commanded 83 of the 150 legislative seats. (For more background on the ZRS, see the 2007 *Handbook.*)

In March 1995 tensions between Mečiar and President Kováč flared when the latter delayed a bill transferring overall control of the national intelligence agency, the Slovak Information Service (*Slovenská

Informačna Služba—SIS), from the presidency to the government. Although the president signed the bill on April 8, following its readoption by the legislature, the National Council on May 5 passed a motion censuring him for mismanagement of the SIS. The 80-vote tally in favor was below the two-thirds majority required to remove the president; nevertheless, Mečiar backed an HZDS executive call for Kováč's resignation and urged his expulsion from the party. The following month the prime minister called for a national referendum to decide whether Kováč should continue in office, while on June 23 the National Council voted to strip the president of his duties as commander in chief and to transfer them to the government.

Early in 1997 the opposition completed a petition drive to hold a referendum on instituting direct presidential elections, but the government suspended the referendum on April 22, claiming that the constitution could only be changed by the parliament. On May 22 the Constitutional Court ruled that the referendum would be legal, but the government asserted that the result would not be binding and, therefore, should not appear on the same ballot as a separate referendum on whether the Slovak Republic should join NATO. On the eve of the referendum the interior minister, Gustáv KRAJČÍ, ordered new ballots to be printed without the presidential question, creating voter confusion and provoking a boycott. As a result, the turnout was less than 10 percent, invalidating the results.

As was widely expected, in early 1998 the legislature failed to elect a new president, no candidate being able to command the required three-fifths majority. When President Kováč's term expired on March 2, the constitution authorized Prime Minister Mečiar to assume various presidential powers. He quickly dismissed nearly half of the government's overseas ambassadors and canceled further referendums on NATO membership and direct presidential elections. By then, Mečiar had already been attacked for alleged intimidation of the media, abuse of police powers, and the apparent enrichment of cronies through the sale of state-run enterprises. Popular support for his administration continued to decline as the HZDS repeatedly blocked the National Council from selecting a new president and also, in May, changed the electoral law to make it more difficult for small parties to win seats in the legislature (see Constitution and government, below).

In the National Council election of September 25–26, 1998, the HZDS secured only 27 percent of the vote. Although it retained a slim plurality of seats (43, down from 61 in 1994), its only potential coalition partner was the SNS, with 15 seats, the ZRS having failed to achieve representation. Consequently, the newly formed Slovak Democratic Coalition (*Slovenská Demokratická Koalícia*—SDK) allied with the SDL', the Party of the Hungarian Coalition (*Strana Mad'arskej Koalície*—SMK), and the Party of Civic Understanding (*Strana Občianskeho Porozumenia*—SOP) to form a new government on October 30 under the leadership of the SDK's Mikuláš Dzurinda. Dzurinda quickly pledged to repair the nation's international image in order to attract foreign investment and enhance chances for EU and NATO accession. Domestic reform included curtailment of strictures on the media and unions as well as the appointment of an ethnic Hungarian to the newly created post of deputy prime minister for human and minority rights.

In January 1999 the new legislature resolved the presidential impasse by approving the long-delayed constitutional amendment to provide for the direct election of the president. The governing coalition nominated SOP leader Rudolf SCHUSTER, the mayor of Košice (and a former prominent member of the Czechoslovakian Communist Party), as its candidate for the May 15 presidential election. Schuster was initially expected to face the strongest opposition from former president Kováč and actress and former ambassador Magda VÁŠÁRYOVÁ, both of whom ran as nonparty, or "civic," candidates. However, in early April former prime minister Mečiar, who had left the public arena following his regime's 1998 loss, reappeared to announce that he had accepted the nomination of the HZDS for the post, immediately positioning himself as Schuster's primary opponent. On May 15 Schuster garnered 47.4 percent of the vote, shy of the 50 percent needed for an outright victory despite Kováč's late withdrawal in his favor. In runoff balloting on May 29 against Mečiar, who had claimed second place with 37.2 percent support, Schuster won 57.2 percent and was therefore inaugurated on June 15.

The apparent stability of the multiparty Dzurinda government during its first two years in office belied the tensions in the underlying political party structure. In January 2000, acknowledging that the SDK would not outlive the current legislative term, Dzurinda announced that he planned to organize a new party, the Slovak Democratic and Christian Union (*Slovenská Demokratická Kresťanská Únia*—SDKÚ), in preparation for the 2002 election. By the end of the year the Christian Democrats and others had formally withdrawn from the SDK (see Political Parties and Groups, below), although not from the government.

The HZDS led all parties with a plurality of 36 seats in the September 20–21, 2002, legislative balloting followed by the SDKÚ with 28 and the recently formed Direction (*Smer*). Despite the HZDS's plurality, Dzurinda was subsequently able to form a new government comprised of the SDKÚ, SMK, KDH, and the recently formed New Citizen's Alliance (*Alliancia Nového Občana*—ANO). The coalition fell to minority status in September 2003, when seven SDKÚ legislators left the party.

The first round of new presidential balloting was held on April 3, 2004, with Mečiar leading all candidates with 32.7 percent of the vote, followed by Ivan GAŠPAROVIČ of the new People's Union–Movement for Democracy (*L'udová Únia–Hnutie za Demokraciu*—L'U-HZD) with 22.3 percent and the SDKÚ's Eduard KUKAN with 22.1 percent. In the runoff election on April 17, Gašparovič defeated Mečiar with a 59.1 to 40.1 percent vote share.

Dzurinda's minority coalition government collapsed in February 2006 upon the KDH's decision to quit the cabinet in a dispute over abortion policy. (The KDH had unsuccessfully promoted legislation that would have allowed hospital workers to decline to assist in abortions because of their religious beliefs.)

Early legislative elections were held on June 17, 2006, with Direction–Social Democracy (*Smer–Sociálna Demokracia,* formed in 2005 via the merger of *Smer,* the SDL,' and several other parties) leading all parties with 50 seats after campaigning on a populist platform of reduced taxes, increased social spending, ending privatization of state-run enterprises, and withdrawal from Iraq. *Smer* leader Robert FICO on July 4 formed a coalition government comprised of *Smer,* the far-right SNS, and the renamed People's Party–HZDS (*L'udová Strana–HZDS*—L'S-HZDS). The coalition government maintained a comfortable majority in the National Council, with 85 of the 150 seats. A strong economy allowed Fico to maintain high approval ratings, mixing populist slogans with modest reform, such as eliminating a nominal but unpopular fee for accessing the healthcare system, while generally not reversing the Dzurinda reforms.

Following the 2006 elections, Prime Minister Fico criticized the country's media for a lack of professionalism in reporting, claiming it showed bias in favor of opposition parties and special interests. A new "Right of Reply" media law proposed in April 2007 required media to allow interested parties to respond to published material (whether true or not) and promised the Ministry of Culture powers to sanction publishers. The proposal drew domestic and international allegations that the government sought merely to limit media criticism and that the law fell out of line with Western European practices. To prevent the law from passing, opposition parties—the SDKU, KDS, and KDH—tied their support of the EU Lisbon treaty to revisions to the new law, invoking criticisms of the law supplied by the OSCE. In April 2008, however, Fico broke the opposition alliance against the media bill, pushing through the controversial proposal by drawing KDH support for the governing coalition's position on the Lisbon treaty. This KDH "betrayal" was symptomatic of a general fragmentation of Slovak center-right politics in 2008, a consequence of which was the formation in July of a new political party, the Conservative Democrats of Slovakia (*Konzervatívni Demokrati Slovenska*—KDS), by four former KDH deputies (see Political Parties and Groups, below).

Meanwhile, in November 2007 it had emerged that Branislav BRIZA, deputy director of a Ministry of Agriculture agency—the Slovak Land Fund (SPF)—and an HZDS appointee, had authorized a cut-price land sale to a company alleged to be close to Vladimír Mečiar. Fico responded by calling for the resignations of Briza and Miroslav JURENA, agriculture minister and deputy leader of the HZDS. Meanwhile, Mečiar not only backed Jurena, but also called for the director of the SPF, a *Smer* appointee, to resign. The situation finally deescalated when Mečiar consented to Jurena's replacement by another deputy from his party. While his statements at the time suggested that Mečiar was considering suspending the coalition upon the EU's approval of Slovakia's euro bid, the coalition remained steady even following the euro assessment. The coalition weathered several other major cabinet resignations and reshuffles in 2008.

Presidential elections were held on March 21, 2009, with Gašparovič (supported by *Smer,* the SNS, and the Movement for Democracy [*Hnutie za Demokarciu*—HZD]) leading all candidates with 46.7 percent of the vote. He was followed by Iveta RADIČOVÁ of the SDKÚ–Democratic Party (SDKÚ–*Demokratická Strana*—SDKÚ-DS, formed in 2006 when the SDKÚ merged with the DS) with 38.1 percent. (Radičová was also supported by the SMK, KDH, and the small Civic Conservative Party [*Občianska Konzervativna Strana*—OKS].) Five other candidates received support in the single digits. In the runoff balloting on April 4, Gašparovič defeated Radičová with a 55.5 to 44.5 percent vote share.

Slovakia's European Parliament election on June 6, 2009, demonstrated *Smer*'s continued popularity and roughly paralleled the 2006 parliamentary elections. The 13 seats were distributed as follows: *Smer,* 5; SDKÚ-DS, 2; SMK, 2; KDH, 2; L'S-HZDS, 1; and SNS, 1.

In legislative elections on June 12, 2010, *Smer* placed first and increased its seats in the parliament from 50 to 62, still short of a majority. In the balloting, women secured 24 seats, or 16 percent of the total. One of parties in the Fico government, the L'S-HZDS, failed to secure any seats in the National Council, while another partner, the SNS, lost more than half its seats. Consequently, although *Smer* increased its representation in the parliament, Fico was unable to negotiate a new coalition. Iveta RADIČOVÁ, of the SDKÚ-DS, was subsequently named to organize a government and she concluded a coalition agreement on June 28 between her party, and three other center-right parties, the KDH, the Freedom and Solidarity (*Sloboda a Solidarita*—SaS), and the Bridge (*Most–Híd*—MH). The resultant government had the support of 79 deputies and was sworn in on July 9. It survived a no-confidence vote on August 10. The ministry of the environment, which had been consolidated into another ministry, was reestablished in November. The budget deficit rose to 7.9 percent of GDP in 2010 as the Radičová government endeavored to stimulate the economy and was forced to expand unemployment benefits.

A September 19, 2010, national referendum on reducing the number of deputies in parliament from 150 to 100, failed because only 22.8 percent of voters participated, less than the 50 percent required.

Rising unemployment was one of the main reasons for the defeat of the SDKÚ-DS in local elections on November 27. In the balloting, among formal parties, the SDKÚ-DS was placed third with 159 mayoral posts, behind *Smer*, with 599 posts, and the KDH, with 161. However, independent candidates won 979 mayorships in what was reported to be a broad rejection of established parties.

In October 2011 the ruling coalition fell apart after the SaS refused to support Slovakian approval for the European financial stability accord. In early elections on March 10, 2012, *Smer* won an absolute majority with 83 seats (see Current issues, below). Fico subsequently formed a new government composed of *Smer* members and three independents.

Independent candidate Andrej Kiska won runoff balloting for the presidency on March 29, 2014, defeating Fico (see Current issues, below). Kiska was inaugurated on June 15.

In the March 5, 2016, parliamentary elections, *Smer* lost its majority, but maintained a plurality with 49 seats. Fico negotiated a coalition agreement with the MH, SNS, and the newly formed Network (*Sieť*) on March 16, and was sworn in along with his government on March 23.

Constitution and government. The constitution of the Slovak Republic came into effect on January 1, 1993, on dissolution of the Czechoslovak federation. It defines Slovakia as a unitary state with a unicameral legislature, the 150-member National Council of the Slovak Republic, which sits for a maximum term of four years. Elections are by proportional representation. Prior to passage of a May 1998 electoral reform, individual parties were required to obtain at least 5 percent of the national vote to claim council seats, while alliances of two or three parties needed at least 7 percent, and alliances of four or more parties, at least 10 percent. Under the amended law, however, all parties, regardless of their participation in coalitions, are required to meet a 5 percent threshold, as a result of which numerous previously allied organizations merged before the September 1998 election (see Political Parties and Groups, below).

In another major change, a January 1999 constitutional amendment introduced direct presidential elections. Previously, the National Council chose the president by secret ballot, a three-fifths majority being required for election. The president serves a five-year term and performs a largely ceremonial role, although legislation and treaties require presidential approval and the president may dissolve the National Council and declare a state of emergency. In addition, the president appoints the prime minister and, on the latter's recommendation, other government ministers, who are collectively responsible to the legislature. A set of amendments were passed in 2001 to address prerequisites required for membership in NATO and the EU (see Current issues, below).

Under legislation enacted in 1996, Slovakia is divided into eight regions (Bratislava, Trnava, Nitra, Trenčín, Žilina, Banská Bystrica, Prešov, and Košice), which are themselves divided into 79 districts. Regional officials were nominated at the federal level until 2002 (see Current issues, below); district officials are elected.

A feature of the Slovak constitution is its guarantee of the rights of ethnic minorities, including freedom to choose national identity and prohibition of enforced assimilation and discrimination. Under associated legislation, use of minority languages in dealings with public authorities is guaranteed in administrative areas where a minority forms 20 percent or more of the total population.

Earlier, the National Council had decreed that Czechoslovak federal law would continue to apply in Slovakia but that, in cases of conflict between Slovak and federal law, the former would prevail. In addition, following the deletion from the Czechoslovak constitution in December 1989 of the guarantee of Communist power, a systematic revision of legal codes had been initiated to reestablish "fundamental legal norms." A revision of the criminal law included abolition of the death penalty and provision of a full guarantee of judicial review, while a law on judicial rehabilitation facilitated the quashing of nearly all of the political trials of the Communist era. Commercial and civil law revisions established the supremacy of the courts in making decisions relating to rights, and property rights were reinstituted.

Freedom of the press is constitutionally guaranteed. In 2016 Reporters Without Borders ranked Slovakia 12th out of 180 countries in its annual index of press freedom.

Foreign relations. On December 21, 1992, the "Visegrád" countries (Poland, Hungary, and Czechoslovakia) concluded a Central European Free Trade Agreement (CEFTA), to which the Czech and Slovak republics were deemed to have acceded at their attainment of separate sovereignty on January 1, 1993. (For additional information on CEFTA, see Foreign relations in the entry on Poland.) On December 30 the International Monetary Fund (IMF) decided to admit both the Czech and Slovak republics as full members, effective January 1. On January 19, 1993, the UN General Assembly admitted the two republics to membership, dividing between them their seats on various subsidiary organs held by the former Czechoslovakia. The two states also became separate members of the Council of Europe, the Conference on (later known as Organization for Security and Cooperation in Europe (CSCE/OSCE), and the European Bank for Reconstruction and Development (EBRD), sovereign Slovakia having declared its intention to honor and fulfill all the international treaties and obligations entered into by the Czechoslovak federation. In October 1993 agreements were signed with the EU transferring the latter's 1991 association agreement with Czechoslovakia to the two successor states in renegotiated form. (For foreign relations of the former federative republic prior to December 31, 1992, see the entry on the Czech Republic.)

As part of its orientation toward the West, Slovakia in February 1994 joined NATO's Partnership for Peace program for former Communist and neutral states, becoming in addition an associate partner of the Western European Union (WEU) in May. Shortly thereafter, it signed military cooperation agreements with Germany and France, receiving from both countries assurances of support for eventual Slovakian membership in NATO and the EU.

Following the breakup of Czechoslovakia, the Slovak government applied itself to the implementation of some 30 treaties and agreements designed to regulate relations with the Czech Republic, but some aspects of the separation (including the division of federal property, debt settlement, and border arrangements) proved difficult to finalize. A temporary currency union between the two states was terminated on February 8, 1993, accompanied by a dramatic slump in bilateral trade despite the commitment of both sides to a customs union. In 1994 Slovak–Czech trade began to recover, while the Moravčík government upon assuming office in March sought improved relations by moving quickly to conclude an agreement with Prague on police and customs arrangements.

The Czech government's unilateral decision in June 1995 to terminate the payments clearance system operating with Slovakia drew strong condemnation from Bratislava, where Czech charges of Slovak noncompliance with its rules were rejected. The premiers of the two countries met at a CEFTA summit in Brno, Czech Republic, on September 11, when a mutual desire to preserve the Czech-Slovak customs union was expressed. In January 1996 Bratislava and Prague signed a treaty defining the 155-mile Slovak–Czech border and involving land exchanges totaling some 6,000 acres in resolution of outstanding claims. Remaining property and debt disputes were resolved at prime ministerial meetings in November 1999 and May 2000.

Slovakia's relations with neighboring Hungary have long been colored by the presence of a 600,000-strong ethnic Hungarian minority: allegations of official discrimination against it inevitably draw the attention of the Budapest government, which regards itself as the protector of Magyars beyond its borders. Under the 1992–1994 Mečiar government, the influence of the nationalist SNS contributed to a worsening of relations with the ethnic Hungarian community. The Moravčík government took a more conciliatory line and also sought to improve relations with Budapest later in 1994.

A long-negotiated treaty of friendship and cooperation was signed in Paris on March 19, 1995, by the Slovak and Hungarian prime ministers that recognized the rights of national minorities and enjoined their protection, while declaring the Slovakian–Hungarian border to be "inviolable." The treaty was ratified by the Slovak legislature on March 27, 1996. A remaining disagreement involves the controversial Gabčíkovo-Nagymaros dam being built by Slovakia on the Danube. In early 1999 tentative agreement was reportedly reached for joint operation of the dam and the discontinuation of plans to build another on the Danube, but no final resolution followed. In September 2000 UN secretary general Kofi Annan apparently offered to mediate the dispute, but Prime Minister Dzurinda rejected the offer as unnecessary.

On June 27, 1995, Slovakia formally submitted an application for full EU membership, and it subsequently expressed its desire to join NATO. However, in July 1997 the Madrid summit of NATO leaders did not include Slovakia among the three former Warsaw Pact nations, including the Czech Republic, invited to join the alliance. Neither was Slovakia numbered in December among the six nations invited to begin formal membership discussions with the EU, though it remained one of five East European countries expected to participate in a "second wave" of expansion. The decisions were reportedly based on political grounds, including the perceived lack of democratic reforms in Slovakia and its treatment of ethnic Hungarians. The change of government in the fall of 1998 improved Slovakia's prospects for EU and NATO accession, as new prime minister Dzurinda indicated his desire to redirect the nation's focus away from Russia and Ukraine (his predecessor's favored direction) and toward the West. Slovakia's standing with regard to NATO admission was also improved by the government's support for the 1999 air campaign against Yugoslavia.

Slovakia was invited on July 28, 2000, to join the Organization for Economic Cooperation and Development (OECD), which the Dzurinda government viewed as further recognition of the country's readiness for full integration with Western institutions. Slovakia was formally invited in November 2002 to begin membership negotiations with NATO. In what was seen as a related development, Slovakia and a group of other Eastern European countries publicly endorsed the stance of U.S. president George W. Bush regarding Iraq in early 2003. On April 10 the National Council approved NATO accession by a vote of 124–11, and in June Slovakia sent some 100 military engineers to support the U.S.-led coalition in Iraq (despite the fact that polls indicated that 75 percent of Slovakia's population opposed the war). Slovakia officially joined NATO with six other new members on March 29, 2004. EU accession followed on May 1, a national referendum on May 16–17, 2003, having approved EU membership by a 94 percent "yes" vote, albeit with a modest turnout of only 52 percent.

Prime Minister Dzurinda's defeat in the legislative balloting of June 2006 was initially seen as a possible setback in the country's goal of adopting the euro on January 1, 2009. However, in July new prime minister Robert Fico announced that he would support the 2009 schedule. Twelve months later the EU ratified Slovakia's entry into the euro area on the existing schedule, despite the European Central Bank's "considerable concerns" voiced in May 2008 that Slovak inflation could rise more than the euro average. On December 21, 2007, Slovakia was one of nine new countries incorporated into the Schengen Agreement, Europe's free movement zone.

Following his alliance with the HZDS (led by the former authoritarian Vladimír Mečiar) and the SNS (led by Ján SLOTA, a politician known for his xenophobic rhetoric), Fico's *Smer* party found itself excluded from the Party of European Socialists (PES), the social democratic grouping in the European Parliament. In November 2007 PES head Hannes Swoboda visited Slovakia to monitor minority issues and concluded that Slota's inflammatory statements against ethnic Hungarians caused real damage to Slovakia's international standing. *Smer* was reinstated by the PES in early 2008 after Fico and Slota reaffirmed their commitment to human rights. But in April the Slovak government further tarnished its image in Europe by approving a controversial media law (see Current issues), despite objections from the Organization for Security and Cooperation in Europe (OSCE).

Tensions with Hungary increased in September 2007, when the Slovak parliament approved a declaration on the inviolability of the Beneš decrees. Enacted in the 1940s by the Czechoslovak government-in-exile, this series of laws forced thousands of ethnic Hungarians out of the country following World War II. In September 2008 Hungarian prime minister Ferenc Gyurcsány agreed to an official visit to Slovakia to help ease bilateral tensions, having refused a similar invitation in October 2007. However, Fico's coalition arrangement with the nationalist SNS continued to strain relations, while anxiety about Hungarian irredentism has prevented the Slovak government from recognizing the unilateral declaration of independence by Kosovo.

During Fico's first stint as prime minister, Slovakia recast its bilateral relationships with both the United States and Russia. In a break with the pro-American stance of his predecessor, the prime minister withdrew the majority of Slovakia's small contingent in Iraq in early 2007 and made visits to Libya, Venezuela, and the Cuban embassy in Bratislava. Meanwhile, in anticipation of the renegotiation of its gas supply contract with Russian gas monopoly Gazprom at the end of 2008, Slovakia signaled that its support of Russia was on the upswing. "We consider [Russia] a reliable partner," said Slovak foreign minister Ján Kubiš. In an apparent contradiction of the official Slovak line on Kosovar independence, the official reaction to the August 2008 conflict between Russia and Georgia over South Ossetia set Slovakia apart from the pro-Georgian stances taken by its neighbors Poland and the Czech Republic, with Deputy Prime Minister Dušan Čaplovič declaring that South Ossetia should be allowed a chance at independence.

Tension between Slovakia and Hungary continued to worsen, and the European Commission in November 2008 expressed concern over the nature of political discourse in both countries. The Slovak State Language Act of June 2009 was criticized by Hungarian government officials. In turn, Hungarian president László Sólyom was denied permission to enter Slovakia in August to participate in a celebration of St. Stephen's Day, the Hungarian national holiday.

Slovakia and Russia signed a series of accords on economic cooperation in energy and transport on April 7, 2010. In May Slovakia and Moldova signed an agreement to increase bilateral diplomatic cooperation and ease travel barriers between the two nations. In July Slovakia agreed to provide €4.3 billion to the €750 billion EU stabilization fund, but rejected participation in the separate €110 billion EU-led bailout program for Greece. Slovakia strongly condemned the expulsion of the Roma from France in September 2010 (see entry on France) and called for intervention by the European Commission.

When Hungary extended citizenship to Hungarians living abroad in spring 2010, the Fico government passed a controversial law banning dual citizenship, effective July 17, 2010.

In November 2011 Estonia opened its first consul in Slovakia. In June 2012 Slovakia announced that it could not continue with decommissioning two nuclear power plants without additional funding from the EU, which had already provided €115 million.

Fico has not resumed the open confrontations with Hungary and policy tilt toward Russia that characterized his first time as prime minister, although he has promoted Russia's membership in the OECD. Slovakia opened an embassy in Tunisia in late 2012 and is advising the Tunisian government on the democratic transition process.

President Gašparovič met with his Hungarian counterpart in Budapest on February 19, 2013, the first presidential summit in nine years. In December Slovakia agreed to resettle three ethnic Uighurs who had been held by the United States at its detention center in Guantánamo Bay. The country had previously accepted three other Uighurs in 2009 after China pressured other nations not to accept them (see entry on China).

Slovakia began reselling gas, originally imported from Russia, to Ukraine in May 2014, after securing permission from Moscow. Slovakia and the Czech Republic agreed to cooperate on air defense, including joint purchases of equipment such as radars, in June. The following month Slovakia and Vietnam signed an economic agreement designed to enhance trade.

In September 2014 Slovakia announced its diplomatic support for the U.S.-led coalition fighting the Islamic State in Syria and Iraq, and provided $25,000 to support Kurdish fighters.

In May 2015 Slovakia, Hungary, Romania, and Bulgaria signed an agreement to integrate their natural gas networks in an effort to reduce their dependency on imports from Russia.

In July 2016 Slovakia assumed the presidency of the EU. In September the country held an emergency summit to begin crafting responses to the United Kingdom's referendum to leave the EU (see entry on the United Kingdom). EU leaders also agreed at the meeting to create an EU military operations headquarters and to deploy EU border police to the Turkish–Bulgarian border to help address the migrant crisis. Slovakia was unable to gain consensus on its bid to eliminate sanctions on Russia (see entry on Russia).

Current issues. In late June 2009 amendments to Slovakia's State Language Act were passed to formalize the use of Slovak in official communication. The SMK criticized the law as restricting the use of the Hungarian language and discriminating against the ethnic Hungarian minority. Analysts noted that although the practical implication of the law may be minor, it served to create populist platforms for its sponsors in government ahead of the 2010 parliamentary campaigns. In September more than 10,000 ethnic Hungarians protested the measure in the town of Dunajska Streda.

In June 2011 the assembly overrode a veto by President Gašparovič on a Hungarian language bill. The measure reduced from 20 to 15 percent the minimum ethnic population required in a municipality for the official use of a minority language, including Hungarian, German, Roma, and Ruthenian.

On October 11, 2011, the governing coalition lost its majority in parliament when the SaS withdrew over opposition to the government-backed EU fiscal and stability pact. Radičová gained approval of the measure by agreeing to a *Smer* demand for early elections in March 2012. Meanwhile, on November 23 Defense Minister Lubomir GALKO resigned following revelations that military intelligence had wiretapped three journalists. On November 28 a state of emergency was declared throughout the country after more than 2,400 doctors resigned in a dispute over pay.

In December 2011 revelations emerged that the financial firm Penta had bribed members of the SDKÚ-DS-led coalition government in the early 2000s in exchange for privatization contracts. The so-called Gorilla scandal was followed by the "Sea Flower" affair in January 2013, in which MPs were allegedly paid to vote for Jozef ČENTÉŠ, the government coalition's candidate for prosecutor-general in 2011. Together, the scandals seriously undermined the Radičová government ahead of the early elections. The newly formed conservative **Ordinary People and Independent Personalities** (*Obyčajní L'udia a Nezávislé Osobnosti*—OL'aNO) was one of several parties to campaign on anti-corruption platforms.

In January and February 2012 international credit agencies downgraded Slovakia's bond ratings in light of rising debt.

In early elections on March 10, 2012, *Smer* won 44 percent of the vote, enough for a majority 83 seats. *Smer* thus became the first party in Slovakia's history to rule without a coalition. All other parties took less than 9 percent of the vote, with seats allocated as follows: KDH, 16; OL'aNO, 16; MH, 13; SDKU-DS, 11; and SaS, 11. Former prime minister and Smer leader Robert Fico formed a center-left majority government with three independent members. Fico pledged to create a social dialog to find less painful ways to bring the deficit below 3 percent of GDP in 2013, raised the corporate tax rate, and canceled the previous government's 19 percent flat tax. He also announced that Slovakia would no longer be the euro zone's troublemaker and immediately approved the EU's expanded stability facilty. The SDKU-DS, KDH, and MH subsequently allied in parliament as the People's Platform.

In July 2012 Archbishop Róbert BEZÁK of Trnava was fired by Pope Benedict XVI. No explanation was given by the Vatican, but in December 2012 a fraud investigation was launched against Bezák's predecessor, Archbishop Jan SOKOL. Critics suggested that Sokol's allies were behind Bezák's sacking. Sokol is no stranger to controversy, after it was revealed in January 2007 that he had worked for the Secret Service (*Štátna Bezpečnosú*—ŠtB). Earlier that month, he had praised the wartime pro-German government of Archbishop Jozef Tiso, drawing protests from Slovakia's Jewish community. (For more on allegations of ŠtB collaboration, see the 2013 *Handbook*.)

In January 2013 the opposition introduced a motion to impeach President Gašparovič. At issue was the president's refusal to appoint Čentéš as attorney general. Although parliament nominated Čentéš in 2011, Gašparovič refused the appointment, due to rumors of vote buying (the "Sea Flower" affair). Only 45 MPs voted for the impeachment motion, half of the 90 needed to move the issue to the Constitutional Court.

In June 2013 parliament nominated Jaromir CIZNAR as prosecutor general, although many opposition parties denounced the vote as anti-constitutional. Gašparovič subsequently appointed Ciznar in July.

Fico eased some minority concerns when he signed a Memorandum of Mutual Cooperation with his Hungarian counterpart on July 2, 2013. The two leaders agreed to upgrade roads and increase border crossings.

Andrej Kiska, an independent with no political experience, surprised the establishment by placing second out of 15 in the first round of presidential balloting on March 15, with 24 percent of the vote behind Fico, who secured 28 percent. Subsequently the majority of the other candidates endorsed Kiska, who touted his independence. In run-off balloting on March 29, Kiska won 59.4 percent of the vote to Fico's 40.6 percent. Kiska became the first Slovak president who had not been a past member of the Communist Party.

On April 21, 2015, Economy and Construction Minister Pavol PAVLIS resigned after revelations emerged that his brother-in-law had illicitly received lucrative state contracts.

POLITICAL PARTIES AND GROUPS

From 1948 to 1989 Czechoslovakia displayed the façade of a multi-party system through the National Front of the Czechoslovak Socialist Republic (*Národní Fronta*—ČSR), which was controlled by the Communist Party. The Front became moribund in late 1989, as most popular sentiment coalesced behind the recently organized coalition of the **Civic Forum** (*Občanské Fórum*—OF) in the Czech lands and its Slovak counterpart, the **Public Against Violence** (*Verejnost Proti Násili*—VPN), which swept the legislative balloting of June 8–9, 1990. The Movement for a Democratic Slovakia (HZDS) emerged as a new party under the Slovak prime minister, Vladimír Mečiar, on June 22, 1991. (For more on the evolution of parties in Slovakia, see the 2014 *Handbook.*) Twenty-three parties were registered to compete in the March 5, 2016, parliamentary balloting.

Government Parties:

Direction–Social Democracy (*Smer–Sociálna Demokracia—Smer*). Following the Communist defeat in late 1989, elements of the Communist Party of Slovakia (*Komunistická Strana Slovenska*—KSS) reestablished themselves as the Party of the Democratic Left (*Strana* Demokratickej *L'avice*—SDL') in 1990. By 1994, the party had emerged as the strongest component of a new center-left coalition but was unable to transform this into electoral success. Disputes over whether or not to join the HZDS in a coalition divided the party resulted in the emergence of Jozeph MIGAŠ as the party's chair, with several factions breaking away to form new parties.

Smer was formally established on December 11, 1999, by former members of the SDL,' and quickly emerged as a potentially significant force for the 2002 election due to the strength of its leader's popularity. Robert Fico, previously an SDL' deputy chair, organized *Smer* as a center-left, third-way party supporting EU accession, political reform, and caution with regard to majority foreign ownership of key industries. In late 2000 opinion polls ranked Fico as the country's most trustworthy and popular politician.

Smer won 13.5 percent of the vote and 25 seats in the September 2002 general election and subsequently served as one of the strongest left-leaning opponents of the Dzurinda government. *Smer* supported Ivan Gašparovič of the HZDS in his successful run for president in 2004.

In early 2005 *Smer* merged with the SDL', the Social Democratic Party of Slovakia (*Sociálnodemokratická Strana Slovenska*—SDSS), and the Social Democratic Alternative (*Sociálnodemokratická Alternatíva*—SDA), a small party formed by former SDL' ministers that had competed unsuccessfully in the 2002 legislative poll. (For information on the historically significant SDSS, see the 2006 *Handbook.*) The SDL' had been heir to the Communist Party of Slovakia (*Komunistická Strana Slovenska*—KSS), originally formed in 1939 but subsequently absorbed by the Communist Party of Czechoslovakia. The SDL' was reestablished in 1989, and in October 1990 its majority wing renamed itself the Communist Party of Slovakia–Party of the Democratic Left, which became simply Party of the Democratic Left later in the year.

The SDL' ran third in Slovakian local elections in November 1990 and second in the June 1992 general election. In 1993 it resisted overtures from the then-ruling HZDS to join the government, and in March

1994 it became the strongest component of a new center-left coalition. For the general election in fall 1994, it headed the Common Choice (SV) alliance, which won 18 seats (13 filled by members of the SDL', which had won 29 seats in 1992). The failure of the SDL' to emulate the recent electoral success of other East European ex-Communist parties was attributed in part to the preference of the old Slovak *nomenklatura* for Mečiar's HZDS.

From 1995 the SDL' experienced internal strife over whether to join the coalition government, as proposed by the HZDS. The election of compromise candidate Jozef Migaš as party leader in April 1996 (in succession to Peter WEISS) failed to end the dissension, which intensified when the SDL' leadership gave qualified external support to the government during a midyear cabinet crisis. Having finished third in the 1998 legislative election with 23 seats, the SDL' signed a coalition agreement under which it accepted six ministerial portfolios, compared with nine for the SDK, three for the SMK, and two for the SOP. Migaš was reelected chair at a July 2000 party conference despite considerable dissension over antigovernment statements, including his support for a no-confidence motion in April. On December 16, 2000, the SDL' minister of defense, Pavol KANIS, announced that he would shortly leave the cabinet, primarily over allegations concerning the financing of a luxury villa he had built.

The new 2005 grouping, which also reportedly attracted former members of the SOP, adopted the Direction–Social Democracy rubric, although it continued to be routinely referenced as simply *Smer*. The party secured a plurality of 29.1 percent of the legislative vote in 2006 and formed a government in coalition with two junior parties, the SNS and the HZDS. Since his election in 2006, Fico has consolidated his position within *Smer*, displacing rivals such as Monika FLAŠIKOVÁ-BEŇOVÁ (who was demoted from a deputy chair position in August 2006 after criticizing the coalition agreement with the SNS). The small **Left Bloc** (*L'avicový Blok*—L'B) merged with *Smer* in 2008.

Smer backed Ivan Gašparovič in his 2009 reelection bid, with the president going so far at some rallies as to identify his campaign with *Smer*'s political future. Although *Smer* won a plurality in the June 2010 legislative balloting, it could not negotiate a coalition government. In the March 2012 parliamentary elections, *Smer* secured 34.8 percent of the vote and 83 seats. Fico subsequently formed a new government.

Fico placed second in presidential runoff balloting on March 29, 2014. In balloting for the EU parliament, *Smer* placed first with 24 percent of the vote and four seats.

Smer won 28.3 percent of the vote in the 2016 legislative balloting but lost 34 seats, securing a plurality with 49 seats. Following the election, Fico negotiated a coalition government, which was sworn in on March 23.

Leaders: Robert FICO (Chair and Prime Minister), Robert KALIŇÁK, Pavol PASKA, Dusan CAPLOVIC, Peter PELLEGRINI, Marek MAD'ARIČ, Dušan ČAPLOVIČ, and Peter KAŽIMÍR (Vice Chairs).

Slovak National Party (*Slovenská Národná Strana*—SNS). Founded in December 1989, the SNS is an intensely nationalist and anti-Hungarian formation defining itself as Christian, national, and social. In the 1990 National Council balloting it received 13.9 percent of the vote but took only 7.9 percent in June 1992, after which it entered into a coalition with the HZDS. It continued to support the government after the resignation of its sole minister in March 1993 and in October resumed formal coalition status, obtaining several key ministries. Its moderate wing, led by Chair L'udovit Černák, broke away in February 1994 (see NDS-NA, under SDKÚ-DS, below), and the SNS went into opposition after the fall of the Mečiar government in March. In May the SNS Central Council decided that only ethnic Slovaks could be members of the party, which was awarded two portfolios in the coalition formed in December 1994 after winning 9 seats in the preceding election. The party advocated a "no" vote on the NATO referendum of May 1997 and joined the ZRS in backing President Mečiar's proposal for a "voluntary exchange of minorities" between Slovakia and Hungary. Its legislative representation rose to 14 in 1998 after securing 9 percent of votes.

On June 27, 1998, the **Slovak Green Alternative** (*Slovenská Zelených Alternatíva*—SZA), led by Zora LAZAROVÁ, merged into the SNS. (For the 1994 election the SZA had participated in a joint list with the HZDS, drawing some environmental support away from the SZS.) On the same day the **Christian Social Union** (*Křest'anská Socialná Únia*—KSÚ) ratified a merger agreement signed in May by the SNS's Ján Slota and the KSÚ Chair Viliam OBERHAUSER.

In the 1999 presidential election, Slota drew only 2.5 percent of the popular vote, in fifth place, and at a party congress in September he lost his chairship. In March 2000 the SNS renewed its alliance with the HZDS, the two parties agreeing to work together in parliament and in an effort to force an early election. Unlike the HZDS, the SNS opposed NATO membership.

In September 2000 the National Council stripped an SNS MP, Vít'azoslav MORIC, of parliamentary immunity, and in early October he was charged with inciting ethnic and racial hatred for having proposed that "unadaptable Gypsies" be sent to "reservations." The charges were subsequently dropped.

Slota and a number of his supporters were expelled from the SNS in late 2001. They subsequently announced the establishment of a "Real SNS," although the selection of that name was challenged by the SNS proper. The Real SNS was credited with 3.7 percent of the legislative vote in 2002, while the SNS was credited with 3.3 percent. The two factions reunited in April 2005, restoring Slota as leader. The SNS was surprisingly successful in the 2006 legislative poll, securing 20 seats on a vote share of 11.7 percent. However, in a political upset on December 2, 2006, Slota's reelection as mayor of Žilina failed, despite its status as a political stronghold of the SNS. Subsequent polls revealed public frustration with Slota for his perceived failure to establish transparency in decision making.

In 2006 SNS joined *Smer* and the L'S-HZDS in Fico's center-left governing coalition, a move that increased tensions with Hungary and contributed to a rift between the Slovak government and the social democratic faction of the European Parliament (see Foreign relations). The SNS demonstrated its role as a generally pliant coalition partner by accepting three successive requests from Fico in 2008 and 2009 that SNS environment ministers resign after criticism was raised regarding the disbursement of environmental-related government contracts. Fico subsequently withdrew the ministry of the environment from the purview of the SNS. The SNS joined *Smer* in supporting President Gašparovič's 2009 reelection bid. The earlier scandals undermined support for the SNS in the 2010 Council balloting and the party only secured 5.1 percent of the vote, reducing its seats in the parliament from 20 to 9. In July 2011 the SNS signed a memorandum of understanding with the far-right Austrian Freedom Party to oppose Turkey's bid for EU membership.

Following the party's disastrous showing in the March 2012 balloting, 4.6 percent of the vote and no seats, Slota was replaced as party chair by his deputy, Andrej Danko. The SNS secured 3.6 percent of the vote in the 2014 EU balloting and no seats.

The party made a strong comeback following its poor showing in the 2012 elections, winning 8.6 percent of the vote in 2016 and securing 15 seats in the legislature. Following the election, the party joined the *Smer*-led governing coalition. On March 23, 2016, Danko was elected speaker of the National Council.

Leaders: Andrej DANKO (Chair); Jaroslav PASKA (First Deputy Chair); Eva SMOLIKOVA, Anton MUGS, Stefan ZELNIK, Cyril LESKO (Deputy Chairs).

Bridge (*Most–Híd*—MH). This party was founded in June 2009 by Béla Bugár, the former president of the SMK. The party's name, which translates as "bridge" in both Hungarian and Slovak, is symbolic of its platform. Bugár described the MH as a moderate formation representing the interests of the ethnic Hungarian minority in cooperation with Slovak parties. The small **Civic Conservative Party** (*Občianska Konzervatívna Strana*—OKS) joined in an electoral alliance with the MH for the 2010 Council elections. The grouping placed fifth in the balloting with 8.1 percent of the vote and 14 seats in the parliament. The MH joined the SDKÚ-DS-led government and party Vice President Rudolf Chmel was appointed a deputy prime minister. In the March 2012 polling, the MH won 6.9 percent of the vote and 13 seats. In the 2014 presidential polling, the MH endorsed Pavol Hrušovský of the KDH. The MH was eighth in the 2014 EU elections with 5.8 percent of the vote and one seat.

In the March 2016 parliamentary balloting, the party won 6.5 percent of the vote and secured 11 seats. Following the election, MH joined the *Smer*-led governing coalition and received three cabinet positions.

Leader: Béla BUGÁR (President).

Network (*Siet'*). This party was founded by Radoslav PROCHÁZKA, a former member of the KDH, in June 2014. The party received 5.6 percent of the vote in the 2016 parliamentary elections and secured ten seats in the legislature. After becoming part of the *Smer*-led governing coalition, the party began to splinter. Procházka was replaced by Roman BRECELY in August 2016, while eight of the party's members of parliament reportedly defected to the MH.

Leader: Roman BRECELY.

Opposition Parties:

Freedom and Solidarity (*Sloboda a Solidarita*—SaS). Founded in February 2009 by economist Richard Sulík, the SaS called for economic and social liberalism. It won 4.7 percent of the vote in the June European Parliament elections. The SaS placed third in the June 2010 legislative balloting with 12.1 percent of the vote, and it secured 22 seats. Sulík was elected speaker of the National Council on July 8, and the SaS joined the SDKÚ-DS–led coalition government. The SaS split with its coalition partners and opposed a second EU bailout package for Greece in 2011. In the 2012 parliamentary balloting, the SaS was sixth with 5.9 percent of the vote and 11 seats. The party split in March 2013 when Jozef KOLLAR failed to unseat Richard Sulik as chair and left to form a civic association, Liberal Agreement, that later joined the New Majority party. Four MPs also quit the party. The party was seventh in the 2014 EU balloting with 6.5 percent of the vote and one seat. In the 2016 legislative elections, the party was second, securing 12.1 percent of the vote and 21 seats in parliament.

Leader: Richard SULIK (Chair and Former Speaker of the National Assembly).

Ordinary People and Independent Personalities (*Obyčajní Ľudia a Nezávislé Osobnosti*—OĽaNO). The OĽaNO, a conservative grouping, was founded in October 2011 by Igor MATOVIČ, a former members of the SaS. The party placed third in the March 2012 elections with 8.6 percent of the vote and 16 seats. Peter POLLAK become the country's only Roma member of parliament and the government's commissioner for the Roma community. In the 2014 EU polling, the party placed fourth with 7.5 percent of the vote and one seat. In the 2016 parliamentary elections, the party once again received the third-most votes, winning 11 percent of the vote and securing 19 seats in the legislature.

Leader: Igor MATOVIČ.

We Are Family (*Sme Rodina*). This party was formed in November 2015 by Boris KOLLÁR. In the party's first parliamentary election in 2016, it won 6.6 percent of the vote and secured 11 seats in the legislature.

Leader: Boris KOLLÁR.

Kotleba–People's Party Our Slovakia *(Kotleba–Ľudová strana Naše Slovensko)*. This party, formerly **People's Party–Our Slovakia** (*Ľudová strana–Naše Slovensko*—ĽSNS), is a far-right party. While failing to win seats in the 2012 parliamentary election because the party did not cross the 5 percent electoral threshold, in the 2016 election the party won the fifth-most amount of votes, winning 8 percent of the vote and securing 14 seats in parliament.

Leader: Marian KOTLEBA.

Other Parties Contesting the 2012, 2014, and 2016 Elections:

Christian Democratic Movement (Křest'anskodemokratické Hnutie—KDH). Previously a partner of the Czech Christian Democrats, the KDH presented its own list in Slovakia for the 1990 poll. Its chair, Ján ČARNOGURSKÝ, served as Slovakian prime minister following Mečiar's dismissal in April 1991. The party went into opposition after the June 1992 election but returned to government in the center-left coalition formed in March 1994. Polling a creditable 10.1 percent and winning 17 seats in the fall election, the KDH again went into opposition and subsequently rejected cooperation overtures from the ruling HZDS. In late 1996, the KDH joined with the DÚS and DS to form the Blue opposition alliance, named after the color of the EU flag to demonstrate the participants' pro-Europeanism.

Following the 1998 election, the KDH strongly argued for maintaining its separate identity within the SDK. In response to the formation of the SDKÚ (an obvious rival for Christian Democratic support), the KDH withdrew from the SDK in November 2000, taking with it nine members of the National Council. Late in the month, however, it officially joined the governing coalition. A month earlier, Čarnogurský had resigned the party chairship after ten years in office.

The KDH secured 8.3 percent of the votes in the 2002 legislative poll, while its presidential candidate, legislator František MIKLOŠKO, won 6.5 percent of the votes in the first round of balloting in April 2004. In February 2006, the party left the government coalition due to objections to an international treaty signed between Slovakia and the Holy See. The KDH won 8.3 percent of the vote in the 2006 legislative poll.

On February 21, 2008, four prominent members of the KDH left the party, citing dissatisfaction with its deviation from Christian Democratic ideals. On July 15 the four members submitted a successful petition to the Interior Ministry to form a new party, the Conservative Democrats of Slovakia (KDS, below).

In the 2009 presidential elections, the KDH supported SDKÚ-DS candidate Iveta Radičová as part of a broader strategy of cooperation with other opposition parties. In September 2009 the party elected a new leader, Ján Figel, who pledged to reverse the party's declining fortunes. The party secured 16 seats in the June 2010 legislative balloting and subsequently joined the Radičová coalition government. Figel' was appointed a deputy prime minister. The KDH placed second in assembly balloting in March 2012 with 8.8 percent of the vote and 16 seats. Former interior minister Daniel LIPŠIC and Jana ZITNANSKA left the KDH in 2013 to form the New Majority (Nová Väčšina) party (see below). Radoslav PROCHAZKA established a separate Alfa platform and then quit the party in February.

Čarnogurský ran as independent in the 2014 presidential elections. He received 0.6 percent of the vote. The KDH candidate was Pavol HRUŠOVSKÝ, who secured 3.3 percent of the vote. In EU balloting the KDH placed second with 13.2 percent of the vote and two seats. In the 2016 parliamentary elections, the party received just 5 percent of the vote and did not win any seats in parliament for the first time since the party's inception in 1990.

Leaders: Ján FIGEĽ (Chair and Former EU Commissioner); Pavol ABRHAN, Peter BELINSKY, Julius BROCK, John HUDACKY, Milos MORAVCIK, Miroslava SZITOVÁ (Deputy Chairs); Ján ČARNOGURSKÝ (Former Prime Minister and Member of the Presidency of the Party); Pavol HRUŠOVSKÝ (Former Chair, Former Speaker of the National Council, and 2014 presidential candidate).

Slovak Democratic and Christian Union–Democratic Party (*Slovenská Demokratická Krest'anská Únia–Demokratická Strana*—SDKÚ-DS). Officially registered as a party on February 14, 2000, by Prime Minister Dzurinda (formerly of the KDH), the SDKÚ held its initial congress on November 18–19, 2000. Some 19 deputies and numerous government ministers affiliated with the **Slovak Democratic Coalition** (*Slovenská Demokratická Koalicia*—SDK) had pledged allegiance to it by the end of the year. The SDK had emerged in 1997 as a loose, philosophically diverse coalition of opposition parties—including the SDSS; the SZS; the DÚ, which dissolved in favor of the SDKÚ; the KDH; and DS, both of which withdrew in late 2000. In February 1998 the SDK evolved into an electoral alliance, and four months later, it officially registered as a unified party to ensure that none of its constituent organizations would fail to meet the new 5 percent threshold for claiming National Council seats. As a result, the SDK secured 42 seats in the September 1998 legislative balloting (on 26 percent of the votes) and led the subsequent coalition government. Following the withdrawal of the KDH and DS in late 2000, the SDK deputies numbered 27, including those who had announced support for the new SDKÚ and 2 (including former DÚ deputy chair and Velvet Revolution leader Ján BUDAJ) who had recently formed the **Liberal Democratic Union** (*Liberálnodemokratická Únia*—LDÚ).

On August 26, 2000, the **Democratic Union** (*Demokratická Únia*—DÚ, one of the founding members of the SDK, officially dissolved to join the SDKÚ, as did the minor **Slovak Union of Small Tradesmen, Entrepreneurs, and Farmers** (*Únie Živnostníkov, Podnikatel'ov a Rolníkov*—ÚŽPR) on June 30. (The ÚŽPR, led by Pavol PROKOPOVIĆ, had cooperated with the SDK in the 1998 election, contributing one seat to the alliance.) The DÚ had been founded at a Bratislava congress on April 23, 1994, as a merger of two components of the coalition government that came to power the previous month: the **Democratic Union of Slovakia** (DÚS), led by Prime Minister Jozef Moravčík, which had originated in February as a breakaway group of the then-ruling HZDS called the Alternative of Political Realism; and the **Alliance of Democrats of the Slovak Republic** (*Aliancia Demokratov Slovenské Republiky*—ADSR), another HZDS splinter group formed in June 1993 by Milan Kňažko, who had been ousted as foreign minister three months earlier. Commanding the support of 18 members of the National Council at the time of the merger, the DÚS adopted a centrist orientation and sought to build an alliance of similar formations for the fall 1994 general election. It largely failed to do so, attracting only the **National Democratic Party–New Alternative** (*Národná Demokratická Strana–Nová Alternatíva*—NDS-NA) onto its list, which polled an 8.6 percent vote share and won 15 seats. Founded in March 1994 by a moderate faction of the SNS and led by L'udovit ČERNÁK, the NDS-NA was formally absorbed by the DÚS in early 1995. In 1998, the DÚS won 12 of the SDK's 42 National Council seats.

The SDK officially dissolved in 2001; some core components formally transferred their allegiance to the SKDÚ, while the DS, SDSS, SZS, and KDH continued as independent parties. Following the 2002 legislative balloting (in which the SDKÚ finished second to the HZDS with 28 seats and a 19 percent vote share), Prime Minister Dzurinda was again asked to head a coalition government.

Following his dismissal as defense minister in September 2003, SDKÚ legislator Ivan ŠIMKO launched the Free Forum (below), the defections throwing the SDKÚ coalition into the status of a minority government. Continuing the SDKÚ slide, Eduard Kukan finished third (with 22.1 percent of the vote) as the party's candidate in the first round of presidential balloting in April 2004.

In January 2006 the SDKÚ merged with the **Democratic Party** (*Demokraticka Strana*—DS), the new grouping adopting the SDKÚ-DS rubric. (For information on the DS, see the 2006 *Handbook.*) In the legislative election of June 2006, Prime Minister Dzurinda and the SDKÚ-DS lost to Robert Fico's *Smer,* 29.1 percent to 18.4 percent. Dzurinda said that his reforms "should continue," a rather unlikely prospect as they were one of the main causes of the voters' desire for a change in government. Opinion polls in August 2007 continued to list Dzurinda as one of the least popular political figures in the country, while Deputy Chair Iveta Radičová polled as the third "most trusted" politician.

The SDKÚ-DS declined by 1,300 members in 2007, a 15 percent loss, and in March 2008, the party ejected 14 members for challenging the leadership of Dzurinda. In July 2008 Radičová called for a "restructuring" of the party and its communications strategy.

Despite divisions on several issues, in May 2008 the SDKÚ-DS and KDH announced a common strategy for the 2010 parliamentary election, an agreement that initially excluded the SMK. Dzurinda, however, suggested that the SMK partnership would eventually resume, specifically in the three parties' backing (along with the OKS, below) of a single candidate, Radičová, to challenge popular incumbent Ivan Gašparovič in the 2009 presidential election. Radičová won 38.1 percent of the vote in the first round of balloting on March 21 and 44.5 percent in the second round on April 4. Despite her loss, analysts characterized her performance as a substantial personal victory, and there was widespread speculation she might emerge as leader of the party, although she chose not to challenge Dzurinda for leadership in party primaries in May. Although, the SDKÚ-DS placed second in legislative balloting in June 2010, Radičová formed a center-right coalition government.

Following legislative elections in March 2012, Radičová resigned from the party. In that balloting, the party placed fifth with 6.1 percent of the vote and 11 seats. The huge defeat led to the election of a new leadership team at the May 2012 party congress, where Pavol Frešo, president of the Bratislava Self-Governing Region, narrowly defeated former justice minister Lucia ALITNANSKA. Miroslav BEBLAVY and Alitnanska established their own platform, "We Are Creating Slovakia."

The party supported Pavol Hrušovský of the KDH in the 2014 presidential balloting. In EU elections, the SDKÚ-DS was third with 7.8 percent of the vote and two seats. In the 2016 parliamentary elections, the party only received 0.3 percent of the vote and failed to win any seats. Following the election, Frešo stepped down as the leader of the party and was replaced by Andrew MATTHIAS.

Leader: Andrew MATTHIAS (Chair).

Party of the Hungarian Community (*Strana Mad'arskej Koalície*—SMK/*Magyar Koalíció Partja*—MKP). The SMK was established in June 1998 as an outgrowth of the **Hungarian Coalition** (*Mad'arská Koalícia*—MK). Based in Slovakia's 600,000-strong ethnic Hungarian population, the MK had been formed for the 1994 national election by three parties, of which the first two had presented a joint list in the 1990 and 1992 elections, winning 7.4 percent of the vote on the latter occasion. In the 1994 balloting, the three-party alliance came in third place with 17 seats on a 10.2 percent vote share. The ethnic Hungarian parties were the only groups in favor of across-the-board support of NATO in the 1997 referendum, endorsing membership as well as the deployment of nuclear weapons and placement of foreign military bases in Slovakia. In September they called upon Prime Minister Mečiar to resign over his suggestion that Hungary and Slovakia "exchange" minorities, which had reminded them of the postwar deportations 50 years ago. The SMK captured 15 National Council seats in the September 1998 election, in which it won 9.1 percent of the vote.

In August 2000 the party called for establishment of a self-governing region in the south, threatening to withdraw its support for the Dzurinda government. The call came in the context of national plans to establish new local administrative boundaries, creating 12 regions from the current 8. Ethnic Hungarians objected, in particular, to division of the Komárno region, fearing a dilution of their political power.

The SMK secured 11.7 percent of the vote in the 2006 legislative balloting. New party elections in March 31, 2007, ousted Béla Bugár from the chair in favor of former deputy prime minister Pál Csáky.

In the 2009 presidential election, the SMK supported SDKÚ candidate Iveta Radičová. In the 2010 legislative elections, the SMK lost support to another Hungarian party, the Bridge (above). In the balloting, the SMK received 4.3 percent of the vote and no representation in the Council. Because of the poor electoral showing, the senior party leadership resigned on June 13. The SMK secured 4.4 percent in local balloting in November. In Council elections in March 2012, the SMK failed to gain any seats. Gyula BÁRDOS was the SMK's candidate in the 2014 presidential elections, and he received 5.1 percent of the vote. The party secured 6.5 percent of the vote in EU balloting that year but lost its one seat. In the 2016 legislative elections, the party received 4 percent of the vote and failed to secure any seats in parliament.

Leaders: József BERÉNYI (Chair), László SZIGETI (Vice Chair).

People's Party–Movement for a Democratic Slovakia (*L'udová Strana–Hnutie za Demokratické Slovensko*—L'S-HZDS). The L'S-HZDS and its original version, HZDS, dominated Slovak politics in the 1990s and served in the Fico government of 2006–2010. Party leader Vladimir Mečiar served three terms as prime minister. However, its popularity plummeted and membership fragmented after 2006, and the party was shut out of parliament in the 2010 and 2012 elections, taking barely 1 percent of the vote in 2012. Mečiar resigned as party chair in May 2012. Although the party has one MEP, Sergej KOZLÍK, it has effectively dissolved. (For more on L'S-HZDS, see the 2013 *Handbook.*)

Communist Party of Slovakia (*Komunistická Strana Slovenska*—KSS). Descended from the original Slovak Communist Party founded in 1939, the present KSS consists of the Marxist-Leninist minority that rejected transitioning to the democratic socialist SDL' in 1990. The party won a 2.7 percent vote share in the 1994 legislative balloting and 2.8 percent in 1998. In 1999 its candidate for president attracted only 0.5 percent of the vote. The KSS improved to 6.3 percent of the vote (and 11 seats) in the 2002 legislative poll. However, it failed to secure representation in 2006 on a vote share of 3.9 percent.

On August 12, 2008, an unaffiliated candidate, Milan SIDOR began collecting signatures in preparation for a presidential bid with the support of the KSS. Earlier, in April, KSS member and former MP Dagmara BOLLOVÁ left the party in order to launch an independent run for the presidency. Bollová took 1.1 percent and Sidor 1.1 percent of the vote in the first round of balloting in March 2009. In the 2010 and 2012 legislative balloting, the KSS received less than 1 percent of the vote. Ján JURIŠTA was the KSS presidential candidate in 2014. He received 0.6 percent of the vote. The party won just 1.5 percent of the vote in the 2014 EU elections. In the 2016 parliamentary elections, the party received 0.6 percent of the vote and did not secure any seats.

Leader: Jozef HRDLIČKA (Chair).

Green Party (*Strana Zelených*—SZ). Founded in December 1989 as the **Green Party in Slovakia** (*Strana Zelených na Slovensku*—SZS), the SZ failed to secure federal parliamentary representation in 1990 but obtained six seats in the Slovak National Council. Having lost all six in the 1992 balloting, the party regained two seats in 1994 as part of the Common Choice coalition. In 1998 the Greens won three SDK seats, agreeing in late 2000 to work with the newly formed LDÚ on leftist concerns. The SZ adopted its current designation in January 2006.

In a move that was widely seen as a means for *Smer* to improve its environmental credentials, in March 2008 the SZ signed an agreement with *Smer,* pledging to cooperate on drawing up environmental legislation.

However, Fico and (then) SZ Chair Pavel PETRIK denied that the agreement was a step on the road to a merger. The SZ won 2.1 percent of the vote in the 2009 European Parliament elections but only 0.4 percent in the 2012 Council elections. The SZ secured just 0.5 percent of the vote in the 2014 EU balloting. The SZ secured only 0.7 percent of the vote in Slovakia's 2016 parliamentary elections and did not win any seats.

Leaders: Peter PILINSKÝ (Chair), Ivan HIRLÄNDER (Deputy Chair), Martin JÓNA (Secretary).

Among the small parties that unsuccessfully contested the 2016 legislative election was **Chance** (*Šanca*) led by Eva BABITZOVÁ; **Courage** (*Odvaha*), led by Stanislav MARTINČKO, a party that seeks to increase economic and political cooperation between Slovakia and Russia; **Direct Democracy** (*Priama Demokracia*), led by Robert BENO; **DEFIANCE-Labor Party** (*VZDOR-strana práce*); **Democrats Slovakia-*Ľudo Kaník*** (*Demokrati Slovenska-Ľudo Kaník*); and **Strana TIP,** led by Tomáš HUDEC, a party that received only 0.7 percent of the vote and was quickly dissolved following the election.

Several new parties contested the 2014 EU parliamentary balloting, including: the **New Majority** (*Nová Väčšina*), led by Daniel Lipšic, which secured one seat in the EU parliament; and the **People's Party–Our Slovakia** (*Ľudová Strana–Naše Slovensko*—ĽSNS), a far-right party that failed to win representation in the EU parliament, but whose leader, Marian KOTLEBA, had been elected governor of Banska Bystrica in November 2013.

For more information on the **New Citizens' Alliance** (*Alliancia Nového Občana*—ANO), the **Liberal Party** (*Liberálna Strana*—LS), and the **Party of Civic Understanding** (*Strana Občianskeho Porozumenia*—SOP), see the 2009 *Handbook.* For information on the **Conservative Democrats of Slovakia** (*Konzervatívni Demokrati Slovenska*—KDS); the **Free Forum** (*Slobodné Fórum*—SF); the **Romany Civic Initiative** (*Rómska Občanská Iniciatíva*—ROI); and the **Romany Initiative of Slovakia** (*Rómska Iniciatíva Slovenska*—RIS), see the 2012 *Handbook.*

See the 2015 *Handbook* for more information on the **Movement for Democracy** (*Hnutie za Demokraciu*—HZD); the **Party of the Democratic Left** (*Strana Demokratickej Lavice*—SDL); the **Party of the Slovak Roma Union** (*Strana Romské Unie na Slovensku*—SRUS); the **99 Percent–Civic Voice** (*99%–Občiansky Hlas*); the **Free Forum** (*Slobodné Fórum*—SF); and the **Free Word Party of Nora Mojsejová** (*Strana Slobodné Slovo–Nory Mojsejovej*—SSS).

LEGISLATURE

The unicameral **National Council of the Slovak Republic** (*Národná Rada Slovenské Republiky*) consists of 150 members directly elected via proportional representation in one countrywide constituency for four-year terms. Parties must secure at least 5 percent of the vote to achieve representation. Following the most recent balloting of March 5, 2016, the seats were distributed as follows: Direction–Social Democracy, 49 seats; Freedom and Solidarity, 21; Ordinary People and Independent Personalities, 19; Slovak National Party, 15; Kotleba–People's Party Our Slovakia, 14; Bridge 11; We Are Family, 11; and Network, 10.

Speaker: Andrej DANKO (SNS).

CABINET

[as of November 6, 2016]

Prime Minister	Robert Fico
Deputy Prime Ministers	Peter Pellegrini
Ministers	
Agriculture and Regional Development	Gabriela Matečná (ind.) [f]
Culture and Tourism	Marek Maďarič
Defense	Lt. Gen. Peter Gajdoš (ind.)
Economy and Construction	Peter Žiga
Education, Science, Research, and Sport	Peter Plavčan (ind.)
Environment	László Solymos (*Most–Híd*)
Finance	Peter Kažimír
Foreign Affairs	Miroslav Lajčák (ind.)
Health	Tomáš Drucker (ind.)
Interior	Robert Kaliňák
Justice	Lucia Žitňanská (*Most–Híd*) [f]
Labor, Social Affairs, and Family	Ján Richter
Transport, Posts, and Telecommunications	Roman Brecely (Network)

[f] = female

Note: Unless indicted, all ministers belong to *Smer*.

INTERGOVERNMENTAL REPRESENTATION

Ambassador to the U.S.: Peter KMEC.

U.S. Ambassador to the Slovak Republic: Adam STERLING.

Permanent Representative to the UN: František RUŽIČKA.

IGO Memberships (Non-UN): CEUR, EBRD, EIB, EU, ICC, IOM, NATO, OECD, OSCE, WTO.

For Further Reference:

Baldersheim, Harald, and Jozef Bátora, eds. *The Governance of Small States in Turbulent Times: The Exemplary Cases of Norway and Slovakia.* Berlin: Barbara Budrich Publishers, 2012.

Csergo, Zsuzsa. *Talk of the Nation: Language and Conflict in Romania and Slovakia.* Ithaca, NY: Cornell University Press, 2007.

Hacker, Paul. *Slovakia on the Road to Independence.* University Park: Pennsylvania State University Press, 2010.

SLOVENIA

Republic of Slovenia
Republika Slovenija

Political Status: Former constituent republic of the Socialist Federal Republic of Yugoslavia; independence declared June 25, 1991, on the basis of a referendum held December 23, 1990; present constitution adopted December 23, 1991.

Area: 7,818 sq. mi. (20,251 sq. km).

Population: 2,069,000 (2016E—UN); 1,978,029 (2016E—U.S. Census).

Major Urban Centers (2014E—UN, urban area): LJUBLJANA (279,000), Maribor (109,000).

Official Language: Slovene.

Monetary Unit: Euro (market rate October 1, 2016: 0.89 euro = $1US). Slovenia adopted the euro as its official currency on January 1, 2007. Its former currency was the tolar.

President: Borut PAHOR (Social Democrats); elected on December 2, 2012, in the second round of presidential balloting and inaugurated on December 22; succeeding Danilo TÜRK (nonparty).

President of the Executive Council (Prime Minister): Miro CERAR (Modern Center Party); nominated by the president on August 19, 2014, following legislative elections on July 13; sworn in, along with a new cabinet, on September 18; succeeding Alenka BRATUŠEK (Positive Slovenia).

THE COUNTRY

Located in the extreme northwest of post–World War II Yugoslavia, with a short Adriatic coastline south of Trieste, Slovenia is bordered on the west by Italy, on the south and east by Croatia, on the northeast by

Hungary, and on the north by Austria. The population is predominantly Slovene (83.1 percent), with small Croat, Serb, Magyar (Hungarian), and Italian minorities. About 58 percent of the population is Roman Catholic. Women and men are equal participants in the labor force. Following the elections in 2012 and 2014, women made up 2.5 percent (3 members) of the National Council and 35.6 percent (32 members) of the National Assembly.

Leading manufactures include transport equipment, textiles, and chemicals and pharmaceuticals. Tourism is another significant contributor to the economy. The European Union (EU) now accounts for about two-thirds of trade, with Germany and Italy in the lead.

In March 2003 Slovenian voters approved a referendum on EU membership, and the country formally joined the organization on May 1, 2004. (For information on Slovenia's economy prior to 2004, see the 2014 *Handbook.*) Between 2000 and 2008, gross domestic product (GDP) growth averaged 4.3 percent, while inflation averaged 5.3 percent and unemployment 6 percent. In January 2007 Slovenia became the first Eastern or Central European state to adopt the euro as its currency. The economy went into recession in the last quarter of 2008, and GDP declined by 7.8 percent in 2009 because of the global economic slowdown. That year inflation fell to less than 1 percent but unemployment rose from 4.4 percent to 9.2 percent. Meanwhile, the deficit expanded in 2009 because of lower tax revenues and increased public spending. In 2010 GDP grew 1.2 percent, while the following year, the country fell in to recession as GDP fell by 0.2 percent, followed by –2.5 percent in 2012. Inflation was 1.8 percent in 2011 and 2.6 in 2012, while unemployment rose from 8.1 percent in 2011 to 11 percent in 2012. GDP declined again in 2013, falling by 1.1 percent. Inflation that year was 1.6 percent, while unemployment remained high at 10.4 percent. Government debt rose from 54.3 percent of GDP to 73 percent from 2012–2013. GDP rose by 3 percent in 2014 and 2.9 percent in 2015. The IMF estimated that GDP increased by 1.9 percent in 2016, while inflation was just 0.1 percent and unemployment 7.9 percent. GDP per capita fell from a high of $24,050 in 2014 to $21,209 in 2016. In 2016 the World Bank ranked Slovenia 29th out of 189 countries (and 16th among EU states) in its annual report on the ease of doing business index.

GOVERNMENT AND POLITICS

Political background. Previously consisting of a number of Austrian crown lands, modern Slovenia was included in the Kingdom of the Serbs, Croats, and Slovenes, which was officially renamed Yugoslavia in October 1929. During World War II it was divided between Germany, Hungary, and Italy, and in 1945 it became a constituent republic of the Yugoslavian federation.

After 45 years of Communist one-party rule, a six-party Democratic Opposition of Slovenia (*Demokratične Opozicije Slovenije*—Demos) obtained a majority of legislative seats in the tricameral Slovenian Assembly in balloting on April 8 and 22, 1990, with Demos leader Lojze PETERLE being named president of the Executive Council (prime minister) on May 16. However, in the contest for president of the republic the former Communist leader, Milan KUČAN, outpolled three competitors by winning 44.5 percent of the vote in the first round and defeated the runner-up, Demos candidate Jože PUČNIK, with a 58.7 percent vote share in the second. On July 2 the assembly issued a declaration of full sovereignty for the Slovene Republic, and in a referendum on December 23 an overwhelming majority of voters opted for independence.

On February 20, 1991, the assembly approved a resolution announcing the phased "dissociation of Slovenia from Yugoslavia," and on June 25 Slovenia joined neighboring Croatia in issuing a formal declaration of independence. A brief war ensued with federal Yugoslav forces, resulting in the withdrawal of the latter after ten days of relatively minor skirmishing. Having achieved its primary objective, the Demos coalition proved unstable and was formally dissolved in December 1991. This left what became the Party of Democratic Reform (*Stranka Demokratične Prenove*—SDP) and the Liberal Democratic Party (*Liberalna Demokratična Slovenije*—LDS)—with the former having descended from the League of Communists and the latter from the former Communist youth organization—more strongly represented than any other grouping. Even so, Peterle, leader of the conservative Slovenian Christian Democrats (*Slovenski Krščanski Demokrati*—SKD), remained premier.

In early 1992 the government encountered criticism for the slow pace of economic reform, and on April 22 Peterle was obliged to resign upon passage of a parliamentary vote of no confidence. The assembly thereupon named Janez DRNOVŠEK of the LDS to form a new government, which, after being installed on May 14, announced a program that included reducing inflation and unemployment, privatizing the economy, and establishing linkages with international financial institutions.

The LDS became the strongest parliamentary party in the first postindependence general election, held on December 6, 1992, with the SKD taking second place. In simultaneous presidential balloting, Kučan, abandoning his party affiliation, was returned for a five-year term by 63.8 percent of the vote against seven other candidates. The governmental outcome was the formation of a new center-left coalition under the continued incumbency of Drnovšek, with Peterle as deputy premier and foreign minister.

The new Drnovšek government reaffirmed its commitment to the "Economic Policy Program" aimed at galvanizing the private sector, reforming fiscal legislation, restructuring the banking system, and rehabilitating state-owned enterprises. However, it took a cautious line in its economic reform, preferring to adapt existing structures rather than abolish them. Observers noted that the center-left cabinet included former Communists in all the key economic portfolios. Moreover, President Kučan, once Slovenia's Communist leader, retained considerable personal influence (and public popularity), even though the 1991 constitution reduced the presidency to a largely symbolic role.

In June 1993 the president and various ministers became involved in a major arms-trading scandal when some 120 tons of weaponry were discovered at Ljubljana's Maribor airport, apparently en route from Saudi Arabia to the Bosnian Muslims in contravention of a United Nations (UN) embargo. Amid conflicting allegations as to who had instigated the shipment, the affair became a power struggle between Defense Minister Janez JANŠA of the Social Democratic Party of Slovenia (*Socialdemokratična Stranka Slovenije*—SDS) and President Kučan, with the former depicting the episode as characteristic of the corrupt practices surrounding the ex-Communist ruling clique. The confrontation persisted until March 1994, when reported misconduct by military police under the defense minister's authority prompted the prime minister to dismiss Janša from the government, whereupon the SDS joined the opposition.

The transfer to opposition of the SDS was not seen as affecting survival of the Drnovšek government, which continued to command a parliamentary majority. Indeed, prior to the ouster Drnovšek had consolidated his assembly support by restructuring the LDS, now called the Liberal Democracy of Slovenia (*Liberalna Demokracija Slovenije*—LDS), to include elements of three smaller parties, two with parliamentary representation.

The SKD's participation in the ruling coalition became strained in 1994, culminating in the resignation of Peterle from his government posts in September to protest the selection of an LDS deputy to be the new president of the National Assembly. Other Christian Democrats continued to hold important portfolios, however, and the government remained secure in the National Assembly. More ominous for the LDS was the withdrawal of the United List of Social Democrats (*Združena Lista Socialnih Demokratov*—ZLSD) from the coalition in January 1996 (in protest against the prime minister's move to dismiss a ZLSD minister), while in May a parliamentary nonconfidence vote against the foreign minister, Zoran THALER, obliged Drnovšek to make a new appointment to the post.

In assembly balloting on November 10, 1996, the LDS remained the largest single party but fell back to 25 seats out of 90, while a center-right Slovenian Spring (*Slovenije Pomladi*—SP) alliance of the Slovenian People's Party (*Slovenska Ljudska Stranka*—SLS), the SDS, and the SKD won a combined total of 45 seats. Drnovšek was asked to remain as head of a caretaker government, and he immediately announced his intention to form a new government comprised of the LDS and the other non-SP parties. However, the 45–45 parliamentary split between the SP and the LDS-allied parties delayed not only the quick formation of a new government, but also the election of a permanent prime minister. The latter stalemate was finally broken in early January 1997 when an SKD deputy announced support for Drnovšek, who was reelected on January 9 by a vote of 46–44. Nevertheless, wrangling over the formation of a new cabinet continued for some seven weeks until the SLS broke with the SP to participate with the LDS and the small Slovenian Democratic Party of Pensioners (*Demokratična Stranka Upokojencev Slovenije*—DeSUS) in a government approved on February 27. President Kučan won reelection on November 23, 1997, taking 55 percent of the vote in a field of eight candidates in the first-round balloting, thereby avoiding a runoff.

Drnovšek survived two nonconfidence votes in May and December 1998, both relating to claims by opposition leader Janša that the prime minister knew about a secret 1995 security agreement with Israel and failed in his constitutional duty to make it public. In the December election the opposition could muster only 24 votes in the 90-seat National Assembly.

On March 15, 2000, nine SLS ministers announced that they would leave the government on April 15, at which time the SLS and the SKD would merge in preparation for an autumn general election. With the SLS controlling 19 of the government's 49 seats in the National Assembly, Prime Minister Drnovšek faced the imminent demise of his government. On April 3 he proposed adding eight nonparty experts to the cabinet, but lack of support forced his resignation on April 8. The unified center-right SLS+SKD Slovenian People's Party (*SLS+SKD Slovenska Ljudska Stranka*—SLS+SKD) put forward Andrej BAJUK as his successor, but Bajuk, an economist with the Inter-American Development Bank who had spent all but a fraction of his life abroad, twice failed to win majority support in the legislature, obtaining 44 votes on April 20—2 shy of the required 46—and then 43 on April 26. Following negotiation of a coalition agreement with the SDS, Bajuk won confirmation, 46–44, on May 3, although on May 23 the legislature split evenly on his proposed cabinet, which did not win approval until June 7, also by a 46–44 vote. The new government included eight SLS+SKD ministers, five SDS ministers, and five independents.

The government suffered a serious rupture in late July 2000 when the majority of the SLS+SKD, but not Prime Minister Bajuk, reversed course and joined the LDS in backing retention of proportional representation in the National Assembly. (In a 1996 binding referendum the public had endorsed a majoritarian system, but the legislature had failed to enact the change because of opposition from the left.) As a result, the SDS ended its agreement with the SLS+SKD, and on July 27 President Kučan called an election for October. In the interim, Prime Minister Bajuk left the SLS+SKD and formed the New Slovenia–Christian People's Party (*Nova Slovenija–Krščanska Ljudska Stranka*—NSi), which quickly formed an electoral coalition with the SDS.

In the October 15, 2000, balloting the LDS won a plurality of 34 seats. Prime Minister Drnovšek returned to power in November as the head of a four-party coalition that also included the ZLSD, the SLS+SKD, and the DeSUS. Easily confirmed by the National Assembly on November 17, Drnovšek fashioned a restructured cabinet comprised of nine LDS ministers and three each from the ZLSD and the SLS+SKD. In addition, the ZLSD chair, Borut PAHOR, took over as president of the legislature.

In runoff balloting on December 1, 2002, Prime Minister Drnovšek won the presidency of Slovenia, capturing about 56.5 percent of the vote against Barbara BREZIGAR, a state prosecutor. Drnovšek resigned as prime minister the next day, and on December 6 President Kučan (who had been barred from seeking a third term) nominated Finance Minister Anton ROP (LDS) as the new prime minister. Confirmed by the National Assembly on December 19, Rop and his cabinet took office on December 20. President Drnovšek was sworn in on December 22 and assumed his duties the following day.

In November 2002 Slovenia was invited to join the North Atlantic Treaty Organization (NATO) along with six other countries, and in December 2002 Slovenia was one of ten countries that were offered EU membership. At a national referendum on March 23, 2003, voters approved entry into both organizations. EU membership was approved by 89.6 percent of the voters, while NATO membership was supported by 66.1 percent. On March 29, 2004, Slovenia joined NATO, and on May 1 it became a member of the EU.

In 2004 the assembly enacted controversial legislation to grant Slovenian citizenship to refugees from the former Yugoslavia. Opposition groups argued against the measure, which undermined public support for the LDS-led government and prompted the SLS (the SLS+SKD having returned to the SLS rubric) to withdraw from the government on April 7, 2004. The issue was also prominent in European parliamentary elections on June 13, 2004, in which the opposition NSi received 23.5 percent of the vote and two seats, while an alliance of the LDS and the DeSUS secured 21.9 percent and two seats; the SDS, 17.7 percent and two seats; and the ZLSD, 14.2 percent and one seat. Previously, on February 26, 2004, the National Assembly had approved legislation that required 40 percent of party candidates for the EU seats to be female.

In addition to the unpopular citizenship policy, the ruling coalition faced problems over internal strife surrounding the 2004 legislative elections. On June 24 Rop requested that the assembly approve a no-confidence vote for Foreign Minister Dimitrij RUPEL, whom the prime minister accused of cooperating with the opposition. The assembly removed Rupel through such a vote on July 5 (Rupel subsequently joined the SDS).

In the legislative elections on October 3, 2004, the SDS became the largest party in the legislature when it received 29.1 percent of the vote and 29 seats in the assembly, while the LDS only secured 22.8 percent and 23 seats. SDS leader Janša was subsequently nominated by the president to form a government, and his new cabinet, which included the SDS, NSi, DeSUS, and SLS, was approved by the assembly on December 3. His government initiated a range of economic reforms, including tax reductions. However, its privatization program subsequently stalled, and the government faced calls from the EU and the IMF to reduce state involvement in the banking and financial sectors. Nevertheless, Slovenia was praised by the EU for its management of the adoption of the euro in 2007.

President Drnovšek announced that he would not seek reelection due to ill health in February 2007. (Drnovšek died on February 23, 2008, of cancer.) Seven candidates contested the first round of presidential balloting on October 21. Former prime minister Lojze Peterle, an independent supported by the SDS, the SLS, and the NSi, placed first with 28.7 percent of the vote. Independent Danilo TÜRK came in second with 24.5 percent of the vote. Türk was endorsed by the SD, DeSUS, Active Slovenia (*Aktivna Slovenia*—AS), and For Real (*Zares*). In the second round of polling on November 11, Türk won with 68 percent of the vote to Peterle's 32 percent. He assumed office on December 22. Meanwhile, the endorsement of Türk by the DeSUS, a member of the SDS-led government, led Janša to call for a confidence vote after the election. On November 19 the Janša government won the confidence vote by a margin of 51 to 33 votes as the DeSUS continued to support the government. The prime minister and new president subsequently pledged to work together as Slovenia assumed the rotating presidency of the EU.

In September 2008 Janša survived another confidence vote following allegations of corruption. (See the 2014 *Handbook* for more information.) The SD received 30.5 percent of the vote and 29 seats, followed by the ruling SDS with 29.3 percent and 28 seats in assembly balloting on September 21. Negotiations on a government continued until November 3, when Borut Pahor (SD) was nominated as prime minister of an SD-led coalition government supported by 50 deputies in the assembly.

In April 2009 the Pahor government announced deep cuts in defense spending to shift resources to social programs as a recession cut government revenues. In elections for the European Parliament on June 7, the SDS retained its two seats, while the SD gained one to bring its total to two. The NSi, the LDS, and *Zares* each secured one seat in the balloting, which saw a voter turnout rate of 28.3 percent and reflected the continuing division of public sentiment between parties of the left and right. In November the new government announced that Slovenia would construct a second nuclear power plant that would become operational between 2020 and 2025.

On January 26, 2010, Karl ERJAVEC, the chair of DeSUS and the minister of the environment and physical planning, resigned after losing a confidence vote requested by Pahor. The prime minister requested the motion after he accused the minister of inefficiency and poor management. Three other ministers resigned in 2010.

In April 2011 DeSUS withdrew from Pahor's coalition government, and the following month, *Zares* pulled out. The loss of the two partners left the government with only 33 votes in the assembly. Following the loss of a confidence vote in September, Pahor announced that he would remain at the head of a minority government until early elections on December 4, 2011. In balloting on December 4, 2011, the newly formed center-left Positive Slovenia (*Pozitivna Slovenija*—PS) placed first with 28 seats but was unable to form a government. Instead, Janša negotiated a center-right coalition government that included the SDS, SLS, NSi, DeSUS, and the new Civic List (*Državljanska Lista*—DL). The new government was approved on February 10, 2012.

Presidential elections on November 11, 2012, were expected to give President Türk a second term, but he unexpectedly placed second, with 36 percent of the vote, behind Pahor, with 40 percent. Pahor soundly defeated Türk 67.4 percent to 32.6 percent in the December 2 runoff, results widely interpreted as criticism of Janša's austerity program. At 49, Pohor became Slovenia's youngest president.

Janša's government lost a no-confidence vote on February 27, 2013 (see Current issues, below). Alenka Bratušek (Positive Slovenia) was nominated prime minister of a PS–SD government, which was approved by the parliament on March 20. Bratušek became the first female prime minister of Slovenia. However, she resigned on May 5, 2014, after being ousted as leader of the PS (see Political parties, below). In early elections on July 13, a new grouping, the Party of Miro Cerar (*Stranka Mira Cerarja*—SMC [later Modern Center Party]), formed by law professor Miro Cerar, won 36 seats, followed by the SDS with 21, and DeSUS with 10 (see Current issues, below). Cerar was appointed prime minister on August 19 and formed a coalition government of the SMC, DeSUS, and the SD, which was approved on September 18. Three deputy prime ministers, one each from the CMC, DeSUS, and SD, were appointed on October 2.

The prime minister requested the resignation of Defense Minister Janko VEBER (SD) on April 8, 2015. Veber refused to resign but was dismissed following a vote of Parliament on April 9. Andreja KATIČ (SD) was appointed to replace Veber on April 21.

Constitution and government. The Slovenian elections of April 1990 were the first to be freely contested in former Yugoslavia in 51 years. The current constitution was adopted on December 23, 1991, and was amended by the Constitutional Act of July 14, 1997, and the Constitutional Act of July 25, 2000.

The head of state is the president, who is directly elected for a five-year term but has a largely ceremonial role. The principal executive officer is the prime minister, who is designated (and may be removed) by the National Assembly.

The 1991 document endorses basic human rights on the European model, one of the aims of the drafters having been to demonstrate Slovenia's suitability for admittance into European democratic organizations. The judiciary includes district and regional courts, with a Supreme Court at the apex. Administratively, Slovenia encompasses 210 municipalities, each consisting of 1 or more of the country's approximately 2,700 cadastral communities. Municipalities may choose to form larger districts (*upravne enote*), of which there are currently 58. Eleven large municipalities have been granted "urban status," which allows them greater autonomy. On June 22, 2008, Slovenians voted in favor of the creation of 13 regions in a nonbinding referendum that was marred by low voter turnout of 10.9 percent.

In 2004 the assembly passed legislation, requested by the Supreme Court, which granted citizenship to residents of Slovenia who had immigrated from other areas of the former Yugoslavia and who had lost their legal status because they failed to apply for citizenship within a six-month grace period following Slovenian independence. (This group became known as the "erased" since they were struck from the census records and therefore were ineligible for government benefits and services.) Conservative and opposition parties forced a national referendum on the issue, and on April 4, 2004, voters overwhelmingly rejected the citizenship law with 94 percent voting against amnesty. The government and LDS had urged citizens to boycott the referendum and turnout was low at 31 percent. Then interior minister Rado BOHINC vowed to continue registering the erased, and the Supreme Court subsequently ruled that the referendum was illegal.

Slovenia has a comparatively free and open press. In its 2016 annual index, Reporters Without Borders ranked Slovenia at 40th out of 180 countries in freedom of the press.

Foreign relations. The European Community (EC, later the EU) recognized the independence of both Croatia and Slovenia on January 15, 1992, with the two countries establishing diplomatic relations on February 17. (Relations with Yugoslavia were not normalized until December 8, 2000.) In February 1992 Slovenia joined the Conference on (later Organization for) Security and Cooperation in Europe (CSCE/OSCE). On May 23 Slovenia, Croatia, and Bosnia and Herzegovina were admitted to the UN.

In March 1992 Slovenia was admitted to membership of the Central European Initiative (CEI), becoming active in efforts to revive the Slovenian and Italian Adriatic ports as entrepôts for the CEI countries. In the longer term, Slovenia aspired to membership in the EC/EU, as did the other non-EU CEI states. On January 15, 1993, it became a member of the International Monetary Fund (IMF), and in May it was admitted to membership of the Council of Europe. In February 1994 Slovenia joined the Partnership for Peace program launched by NATO the previous month for former Communist and neutral states.

Slovenia contributed troops to the international peacekeeping mission in Bosnia. In March 2004 Slovenia deployed troops and equipment to Afghanistan as part of the UN-led peacekeeping operation. In August, firefighting units were also sent to Kabul, Afghanistan, to train locals.

Unresolved border disputes have strained Slovenia's postindependence relations with Croatia. The issue flared up in October 1994 when the Slovenian Assembly adopted local boundary changes that assigned territory claimed by Croatia to the Slovenian municipality of Piran. Although the Slovenian government quickly called for revision of the measure, Croatia lodged an official protest. Talks at the prime ministerial level in June 1995 were reported to have yielded agreement on "98 percent" of land and maritime border issues. However, relations cooled in December 1997 when Croatia amended its constitution, dropping Slovenes from a list of recognized ethnic minorities and raising suspicions about Zagreb's intentions.

Notwithstanding their bilateral territorial dispute, Slovenia and Croatia remained in agreement on the need to resist any revival of irredentism on the part of Italy, which had long pressed the issue of compensation for Italians whose property in Istria had been appropriated following post–World War II border changes that favored Yugoslavia. The pressure on Slovenia intensified in May 1994 with the advent of the right-wing government of Italian prime minister Silvio Berlusconi, with Rome making it clear that it would block Slovenia's EU membership aspirations until it obtained satisfaction. However, following the fall of Berlusconi in December, the new nonparty Italian government lifted the veto on March 4, 1995, enabling Slovenia to commence associate membership talks with the EU, which were assisted by Spanish mediation on the dispute with Italy. Following the resolution of most outstanding issues, Slovenia signed an association agreement with the EU in June 1996, also lodging an application for full EU membership. In the same month Slovenia became an "associate partner" of the Western European Union (WEU), seeing such status as a necessary precursor to the goal of NATO membership. Subsequently, in February 1998, Slovenia agreed to compensate 21,000 ethnic Italians for property they left behind when they fled to Italy at the end of World War II.

Relations with Croatia took a step forward after the death of Croatian president Franjo Tudjman in December 1999 and the election of a new president, Stipe Mesič, two months later. Following talks with President Kučan during a March visit to Ljubljana, Mesič described bilateral issues as "solvable with just a little stronger will on both sides." Border concerns, including Slovenian access to Piran Bay, were largely resolved in July 2001, as was a disagreement over management of the jointly owned nuclear power plant in Krško, Slovenia. Austria also expressed concern about the safety of the nuclear facility, but a more contentious issue involved Austrian calls, particularly from the right, for Slovenia to renounce the World War II–era decrees under which the partisan-led Antifascist Council for the National Liberation of Yugoslavia

(*Antifašističko Vee Narodnog Oslobodjenja Jugoslavije*—AVNOJ) expelled the German minority from Yugoslavia and confiscated German property.

At the NATO Summit Meeting in Prague, on November 21–22, 2002, Slovenia was invited to begin accession talks for NATO membership along with six other countries: Bulgaria, Estonia, Latvia, Lithuania, Romania, and Slovakia. On March 29, 2004, Slovenia became a member of NATO, and on May 1 it joined the EU. The assembly approved the proposed EU Constitution on February 2, 2005.

Once in office in December 2004, the Janša government announced its intention to maintain close ties with the United States. (Tension between the two countries over the International Criminal Court had strained what had previously been very good relations.) The administration also pursued deeper ties with Romania, actively working to aid Romania's successful quest to join the EU.

Ongoing disputes with Croatia over the border continued in 2005–2006, including the demarcation of fishing areas in the Adriatic Sea (the talks over that issue also included Italy). Additionally, the two countries maintained overlapping claims in the Bay of Piran, Slovenia's only deepwater access to the Adriatic.

In response to complaints from Slovenia and other new EU members, the European Central Bank called in February 2007 for countries such as Germany and France to remove restrictions on the migration of workers from the Central and Eastern European states. Subsequently, in April, Slovenia and Greece signed three bilateral agreements on maritime transport, coordination of oceanographic services, and tourism.

On January 1, 2008, Slovenia assumed the rotating presidency of the EU. (For further information, see 2015 *Handbook.*)

In November 2009, Slovenia signed an agreement with Russia to allow the construction of a gas pipeline into Western Europe, known as the South Stream pipeline. The agreement was the culmination of several years of negotiations and resulted in concessions for Slovenia, including a 50 percent stake in the construction of the pipeline.

By 2009 Slovenia had become the largest foreign investor in Kosovo. In February Slovenia extended its participation in the NATO-led peacekeeping mission in Kosovo for an additional year, and in July Slovenia announced the donation of $794,000 to Kosovo for infrastructure programs as part of an ongoing aid initiative. In April the Pahor government approved the continuation of the nation's participation in the NATO mission in Afghanistan. In October 2010 the government announced that it would expand the mission to include civilian instructors as part of an effort to train Afghan security forces. Also in October Iran opened its first embassy in Slovenia. Also in October two Islamic extremists, wanted in Germany, were arrested in northwestern Slovenia and extradited.

In March 2010 Pahor accepted an opposition plan to hold a referendum on the country's agreement to allow the EU to arbitrate Slovenia's border dispute with Croatia. In voting on June 6, the accord was approved by 52 percent of voters. Negotiations on Croatia's EU bid were subsequently restarted.

On February 24, 2011, the legislature enacted measures to allow the United States to send prisoners from Guantánamo Bay to Slovenia. In March, Russian president Vladimir Putin travelled to Slovenia to finalize agreement on Slovenia's participation in the South Stream pipeline. An additional 31 economic cooperation agreements were signed between Russia and Slovenia. The following month Pahor met with the leaders of Croatia and Serbia and pledged Slovenian support for EU membership for both countries. In July Slovenia recognized South Sudan as an independent nation. In December the EU parliament was increased in size from 736 to 752 members. Slovenia's delegation would rise from seven to eight in the 2014 elections.

Slovenia closed its embassies in Iran, Ireland, Finland, Portugal, and Sweden, as well as its consulate in New York City, in 2012–2013, as part of the government austerity program. Croatia and Slovenia reached a deal on March 20, 2012, that resolved the last obstacle to Croatia's July 1 accession to the EU. The two countries agreed to have the Bank for International Settlements resolve Croatia's demand for €270 million paid to 430,000 Croats whose Nova Ljubljanska Banka accounts were frozen when Yugoslavia began to collapse in 1990.

In January 2014 the Slovenian government reported that it was $15.6 million in arrears to the UN but pledged to pay its dues as quickly as possible. Meanwhile, the foreign ministry announced plans to open embassies in Tanzania and either Kuwait or Saudi Arabia. In April Slovenia and Croatia signed a series of agreements to improve security cooperation.

In February 2016 Slovenia announced the implementation of new border controls in an effort to reduce the flow of migrants across its borders, including a new registration system and the deployment of troops. Estimates were that 474,000 refugees had entered Slovenia in 2015–2016. The government sought to limit the number of new migrants to 3,200 per day. On July 6 Slovenia became a member of the European Space Agency (ESA). Slovenia was criticized by NATO for failing to spend the required 2 percent of GDP on defense; it spent less than 1 percent in 2015 and 2016.

Current issues. In early elections on December 4, 2011, the newly formed Positive Slovenia (*Pozitivna Slovenija*—PS), led by Zoran JANKOVIĆ, the popular mayor of Ljubljana, secured the most votes. When coalition talks between Janković, Pahor, and other parties failed, the president nominated Janša to form a government, despite his ongoing trial for corruption. The former prime minister crafted a coalition government that took power in February 2012. That month, international credit agencies downgraded Slovenia's debt in light of rising debt.

Janša faced mounting economic crises in 2012, while his corruption trial proceeded in the background. He introduced an austerity package that included a 7.5 percent pay cut for civil servants and raised the retirement age to 65.

The government was forced to bail out Nova Ljubljanska Banka, the country's largest bank, for €380 million in July. Slovenia's state-owned banks were saddled with bad debt incurred when the bankers lent money to a small circle of friends who wanted to buy the state-owned companies they had managed. The buyers were offered cut-rate prices to keep the businesses in Slovene hands, and they used the firms as collateral. When the businesses collapsed in the global slump of 2008, their loss wiped out the equity of many banks. In total, Slovenia's banks held some €6.8 billion in bad debt, an amount equal to one-fifth of the national economy.

In December 2012 the National Assembly adopted the budget for 2013, which aimed to reduce the budget deficit from 4.2 percent of GDP in 2012, to 2.8 percent in 2013 and 2.5 percent in 2014.

On January 8 the Corruption Prevention Commission ruled that Prime Minister Janša had "systematically and repeatedly violated the law" by failing to report more than €200,000 in assets of "unknown origin." The commission also suggested that PS leader and Ljubljana mayor Zoran JANKOVIĆ had benefitted from lucrative contracts given to firms owned by his sons. Janković resigned from PS and was replaced by Alenka BRATUŠEK, a PS legislator and former state budget director.

On January 24 the DL pulled out of the government coalition when Janša refused to resign over the corruption charges, leaving the government 42 out of 90 seats. The ministers of justice and finance, both from DL, also submitted their resignations. The SLS and DeSUS also called for Janša's exit, but remained in the now-minority government.

The National Assembly passed a vote of no confidence in Janša on February 27 and selected Bratušek as interim prime minister. Bratušek formed a government comprised of the PS, DeSUS, DL, and SD on March 14. Departing from Janša's austerity program, Bratušek pledged to promote growth and fiscal stability and repeatedly insisted that Slovenia would not need an EU or IMF bailout.

The government successfully raised $1.3 billion in a bond sale in April and another $15 billion in May, even though Moody's had downgraded it to junk status. Bratušek announced on May 9 plans to raise the value-added tax from 20 percent to 22 percent and to sell 15 state-owned companies, including Telekom Slovenje, Adria Airways, and Nova Kreditna Banka Maribor.

In May 2012 the EU granted Slovenia an additional two years to reach the 3 percent deficit ceiling. Bratušek responded with a supplemental budget bill in July that set a 4.4 percent deficit, using the additional funds for pensions, public sector wages, bank recapitalization, and other growth measures. Two constitutional amendments took effect in May, one requiring a balanced budget as of 2015 and the second amending the referendum law so that referendum requests must come from voters, not legislators. Janša and two other defendants in the Patria case were sentenced to two years in jail on June 5, 2012. Janša denounced his conviction as politically motivated.

Ahead of early elections on July 13, 2014, political neophyte Miro Cerar formed a new center-left grouping, the SMC. The SMC took advantage of voter dissatisfaction with existing parties and won 34.5 percent of the vote, the highest percentage of any party at the national level since 2000. Both the SDS and the SD saw their vote shares decline, the SDS down to 20.7 percent (–5.5 percent), and the SD down to 6 percent (–4.5 percent). The PS received only 2.9 percent of the vote and, therefore, no seats. Cerar formed a coalition government of the SMC, DeSUS, and SD in September.

In February 2015 the government announced a plan to privatize most of the banks that had been taken over by the government during the 2009–2013 financial crisis. On March 3, 2015, parliament voted 51 to 28 in favor of legalizing same-sex marriage. However, opponents of the measure quickly gathered the requisite signatures to place the issue before voters in referendum. Lawmakers voted to block the referendum on March 26, but the constitutional court ruled on October 22 that the assembly could not block the ballot initiative. In a national referendum on December 20, 63.5 percent of voters rejected legalization of same-sex marriages.

POLITICAL PARTIES

For four-and-a-half decades after World War II the only authorized political party in Yugoslavia was the **Communist Party**, which was redesignated in 1952 as the **League of Communists of Yugoslavia** (*Savez Komunista Jugoslavija*—SKJ). In 1989 noncommunist groups began to emerge in the republics, and in early 1990 the SKJ approved the introduction of a multiparty system, thereby effectively triggering its own demise. The most important initial outgrowth of liberalization was the creation of the broad electoral alliance the **Democratic Opposition of Slovenia** (*Demokratične Opozicije Slovenije*—Demos). (For more information on political parties and coalitions between 1990 and 2008, see the 2011 *Handbook.*)

Government Parties:

Modern Center Party (*Stranka Modernega Centra*—SMC). The SMC was originally formed by Miro Cerar in June 2014 as the **Party of Miro Cerar** (*Stranka Mira Cerarja*—SMC). The center-left party emphasized economic reforms in the July 2014 legislative balloting and won 36 seats. Cerar was named prime minister in August and formed a coalition government in September. Meanwhile, SMC member Milan BRGLEZ was elected president of the National Assembly on August 1. In March 2015 the party voted to change the name of the SMC to the Modern Center Party in an effort to broaden its appeal.

Leaders: Miro CERAR (Prime Minister and President of the Party), Milan BRGLEZ (President of the National Assembly and Vice President of the Party).

Slovenian Democratic Party of Pensioners (*Demokratična Stranka Upokojencev Slovenije*—DeSUS). Also known as the **Grey Panthers**, the DeSUS was a component of the leftist ZLSD until it opted to contest the November 1996 election in its own right, winning five seats and 4.3 percent of the vote. The party's decision to join the government in February 1997 was crucial in providing the coalition with a slim majority in the assembly. The DeSUS saw its vote share rise to 5.2 percent in 2000, but it won only four seats. It agreed to accept junior status in the subsequent LDS-led government. The DeSUS gained four seats in the 2004 elections. It joined the SDS-led coalition government. The DeSUS split with its government coalition partners and backed Danilo Türk in the 2007 presidential polling. However, the party continued to support the SDS-led coalition government. It secured seven seats in the 2008 assembly balloting and joined the SD-led coalition government. Party leader Karl Erjavec was appointed minister of the environment and physical planning. In 2010 Erjavec was forced to resign by Pahor, but DeSUS agreed to continue to support the government; however, it withdrew in May 2011. Minister of the Environment and Physical Planning Roko ŽARNIĆ resigned from DeSUS at that time and became an independent in order to remain in office. DeSUS secured six seats in the 2011 elections, and the party joined the SDS-led government in 2012. Erjavec was appointed a deputy prime minister and foreign minister. The party won one seat in the 2014 EU elections. DeSUS then won ten assembly seats and joined the SMC-led coalition government.

Leaders: Karl ERJAVEC (Deputy Prime Minister, Foreign Minister, and President of the Party), Franc JURŠA (Parliamentary Leader), Branko SIMONOVIČ (General Secretary).

Social Democrats (*Socialni Demokrati*—SD). The SD was known as the **United List of Social Democrats** (*Združena Lista Socialnih Demokratov*—ZLSD) until 2005. The ZLSD was originally formed prior to the December 1992 election as a United List (ZL) of groups deriving from the Communist era, winning 14 seats and joining a coalition headed by the LDS. The original components were the SDP, the **Social Democratic Union** (*Socialdemokratska Unija*—SDU), the **Workers' Party of Slovenia** (*Delavska Stranka Slovenije*—DSS), and the DeSUS. Of these, the SDR declined to join a formal merger creating the ZLSD in 1993, while the DeSUS reverted to independent status after the ZLSD left the government in January 1996. Advocating neutrality as an alternative to NATO membership (but favoring EU accession), the ZLSD won 9 lower house seats on a 9 percent vote share in the November balloting. In the October 2000 election, it won 12 percent of the vote and 11 seats, after which it agreed to join Prime Minister Drnovšek's new government. The ZLSD secured 14.2 percent of the vote and one seat in the June 2004 European parliamentary elections. In the October 2004 legislative elections, the ZLSD received 10.2 percent of the vote and ten seats. Former prime minister Anton Rop and three other LDS members of parliament left the LDS to join the SD in March 2007, making the SD the largest opposition group. Party leader Borut Pahor was expected to be the SD presidential candidate in 2007, but the party instead endorsed the independent candidate Danilo Türk, who eventually won the balloting.

The SD won the legislative balloting in 2008, and party leader Pahor was named prime minister of an SD-led coalition government. Pahor was reelected party leader at a Congress in March 2009. In protest of the party opposition to Croatian entry into the EU, SD member of the EU Parliament Aurelio JURI resigned from the party in June 2009. Following a disappointing showing in local balloting in 2010, Pahor pledged to redouble the government's efforts to revive the economy. Nonetheless, in the local balloting Peter BOSSMAN of the SD, who was born in Ghana, became the first African-born Slovene mayor when he was elected chief executive of Piran. Pahor refused calls to resign after DeSUS and *Zares* withdrew from the governing coalition. The SD secured only ten seats in the 2011 balloting. At a 2012 party congress, Igor LUKŠIČ was elected president of the SD. The SD won only one seat in EU parliamentary elections in May 2014, prompting Lukšič to resign. The SD secured six seats in subsequent assembly balloting. The party joined the SMC-led government in September 2014 and acting party leader Dejan ŽIDEN was appointed as deputy prime minister.

Leaders: Dejan ŽIDAN (Deputy Prime Minister and Acting President); Tanja FAJON, Mojca KLEVA, Bojan KONTIČ (Vice Presidents).

Other Parliamentary Parties:

Slovenian Democratic Party (*Slovenska Demokratska Stranka*—SDS). Founded in 1989 as the **Social Democratic League of Slovenia** (*Socialdemokratska Zevza Slovenije*—SDZS), one of the Demos participants, the SDS has described itself as a "social-democratic party in the traditions of European democracy and the social state." However, the party has adopted center-right policies and aligned itself with Christian Democrat parties and the **European People's Party** (EPP) in the European Parliament.

In May 1995 it absorbed the **National Democrats** (*Narodnimi Demokrati*—ND), which had separated from the **Slovenian Democratic League** (SDZ) in 1991. (For more on the history of the party, see the 2014 *Handbook.*) As part of the SP in the November 1996 balloting, the party took third place with 16 seats on a 16.1 percent vote share. It remained in opposition until formation of the SLS+SKD-led government of Andrej Bajuk in April 2000. Holding five ministerial portfolios, the SDS remained in the cabinet despite termination of the coalition agreement in July. For the October 2000 election, the party concluded a cooperation pact, **Coalition Slovenia** (*Koalicija Slovenija*), with the new NSi (below) and went on to win 14 National Assembly seats.

In September 2003 the party changed its name from the **Social Democratic Party of Slovenia** (*Socialdemokratična Stranka Slovenije*) to the Slovenian Democratic Party (*Slovenska Demokratska Stranka*) but kept the initials SDS. The change was designed to align the party with center-right groups in the European Parliament, including the EPP. In the European parliamentary elections of June 2004, the SDS secured two seats. In the October legislative elections, the SDS became the largest parliamentary group after it won the elections with 29 seats. Party leader Janez Janša was subsequently nominated as prime minister and formed a coalition government on December 3. On May 15, 2005, Janša was reelected as party president at the Eighth SDS Congress.

In June 2007 the SDS endorsed Lojze Peterle for the 2007 presidential balloting. Despite bribery allegations (see Current issues, above), Janša continued to enjoy strong backing from the SDS ahead of the 2008 legislative elections. The SDS placed second in the assembly balloting with 28 seats and became the largest opposition party. In 2009 SDS member of parliament Franc PUKŠIČ defected from the party to join the SLS.

The SDS placed second in balloting in the 2011 elections, and Janša became prime minister of a coalition government in February 2012. He lost a parliamentary vote of no confidence in March 2013, and was removed as prime minister, but was confirmed as party president at the May 2013 SDS party congress. The SDS placed first in EU balloting in May 2014, winning three seats. However, it was second in the July legislative elections with 21 seats.

Leaders: Janez JANŠA (President of the Party), Jože TANKO (Parliamentary Leader), Anja Bah ZIBERT (Secretary General).

New Slovenia–Christian People's Party (*Nova Slovenija–Krščanska Ljudska Stranka*—NSi). The NSi was established on August 4, 2000, following a split within the SLS+SKD over the issue of adopting a majoritarian electoral system for the National Assembly, as favored by then Prime Minister Bajuk. Like its predecessor, the SKD, the NSi is a conservative, Christian democratic formation supporting deregulation, privatization, a market economy, and membership in both the EU and NATO. For the October 2000 election, it concluded a cooperation agreement with the SDS and won eight seats on an 8.8 percent vote share. The NSi received the highest number of votes in the June 2004 European parliamentary elections, with 23.5 percent and two seats. The NSi won 9 percent of the vote and nine seats in the 2004 National Assembly elections. The party subsequently joined the SDS-led coalition government, and Bajuk was appointed finance minister.

Lojze Peterle, a member of the European Parliament from the NSi, was chosen as the party's presidential candidate for the 2007 balloting. He ran as an independent and was subsequently endorsed by all of the members of the governing coalition. Peterle placed second in the presidential polling. A group of conservative members of the party, led by Janez DROBNIC, defected to form the Christian Democratic Party (KDS) in August 2008. The NSi received no seats in the 2008 assembly elections. Following the balloting, Bajuk resigned. Ljudmila Novak became party president. The NSi did gain one seat in the EU parliamentary elections in June 2009. Reports in 2011 indicated that Peterle had revived the defunct **Slovenian Christian Democrats** (*Slovenski Krščanski Demokrati*—SKD). In the 2011 elections, the NSi secured four seats and subsequently became part of the SDS-led governing coalition. New party vice presidents were elected at the December 2012 party congress. The NSi joined with the SLS in an electoral alliance for the 2014 EU balloting. The two parties secured two seats. In legislative balloting in July 2014, the NSi, won five seats by itself. The NSi played a major role in the 2015 referendum that overturned the legalization of same-sex marriage in Slovenia.

Leaders: Ljudmila NOVAK (President of the Party); Alojz PETERLE (2007 presidential candidate); Aleš HOJS, Iva DIMIC (Vice Presidents).

Alliance of Social Liberal Democrats (*Zavezništvo Socialno-Liberalnih Demokratov*—ZSD). The centrist ZSD was established by former prime minister Alenka Bratušek after she was ousted as party leader of the PS in April 2014. The party was originally named the **Alliance of Alenka Bratušek** (*Zavezništvo Alenke Bratušek*—ZaAB). The majority of the party's members were former members of the PS. The ZaAB won four seats in the July 2014 parliamentary elections. The party adopted its current name in May 2016.

Leaders: Alenka BRATUŠEK (Former Prime Minister and President of the Party); Maša KOCIPER, Robert GOLOB, Peter VILFAN (Vice Presidents).

United Left (*Združena Levica*—ZL). The United Left was formed in March 2014 as an electoral alliance among three small leftist parties, the **Democratic Labour Party** (*Demokratična Stranka Dela*—DSD), the **Party for Sustainable Development of Slovenia** (*Stranka za Trajnostni Razvoj Slovenije*—TRS), and the **Initiative for Democratic Socialism** (*Iniciativa Za Demokratični Socializem*—IDS). The grouping has collective leadership. In the July 2014 legislative balloting, the IDS won six seats.

Other Parties:

Positive Slovenia (*Pozitivna Slovenija*—PS). Originally established as **Zoran Janković's List–Positive Slovenia** (*Lista Zorana Jankovića–Pozitivna Slovenija*—LZJ-PS) by Ljubljana mayor Zoran Janković in October 2011, the PS is a center-left grouping. When the PS placed first in the 2011 assembly elections, with 28 seats, Janković resigned as mayor with plans to become prime minister. When he was unable to form a coalition government, he entered and won the by-election to replace himself as mayor of Ljubljana. In January 2013 the Corruption Prevention Commission ruled that Janković had benefitted from lucrative contracts given to firms owned by his sons. Janković suspended his PS chair. The party replaced him with Alenka Bratušek. When Prime Minister Janša (SDS) lost a vote of confidence in February, Bratušek created a governing coalition consisting of the PS, DeSUS, DL, and SD on March 14. On April 25, 2014, Janković defeated Bratušek to once again become party leader. Bratušek resigned from the party and as prime minister. She subsequently formed a new political grouping, the Alliance of Alenka Bratušek (*Zavezništvo Alenke Bratušek*—ZaAB) (see ZSD, above). The PS failed to secure any seats in the 2014 EU elections, and it was heavily defeated in the July 2014 legislative elections, securing no seats.

Leaders: Zoran JANKOVIĆ (President of the Party and Founder), Melita ZUPEVIC (Vice President), Vasja BUTINA (Secretary General).

Slovenian People's Party (*Slovenska Ljudska Stranka*—SLS). The SLS is the current rubric of the party that had been named the SLS+SKD Slovenian People's Party in April 2000 upon the merger of the long-standing SLS and the Slovenian Christian Democrats (*Slovenski Krščanski Demokrati*—SKD). The 2000 merger had occurred following the decision by nine SLS ministers to leave the government. (For party history prior to 2000, see the 2013 *Handbook.*)

At the congress that formally approved the merger into the SLS+SKD in 2000, Franc ZAGOŽEN, the SLS parliamentary leader, was elected party president; his deputies included Lojze Peterle and Andrej Bajuk. The new party immediately claimed a plurality of 28 seats in the 90-seat National Assembly, and on April 28, it renewed its coalition with its former SP partner, the SDS. That agreement produced assembly approval of Bajuk as prime minister on May 3, although it took until June 7 for the legislature to approve an SLS+SKD-led cabinet. The coalition soon began unraveling, however, over the issue of whether to adopt a majoritarian electoral system. On July 25 most of the SLS—but not Bajuk and Peterle—sided with the LDS and other opposition parties in supporting retention of proportional representation. A day later, the SLS+SKD and SDS announced the end of their coalition agreement, although they agreed to remain in a caretaker government pending legislative elections in October. On August 4, Bajuk and Peterle established the New Slovenia–Christian People's Party (see NSi, above).

In the October 2000 election, the SLS+SKD won only nine seats on a 9.5 percent vote share. It subsequently agreed to accept three ministries in a reconstituted LDS-led government. In 2002 the SLS+SKD decided to readopt the SLS rubric. At a party congress in November 2003, Janez PODOBNIK was elected party president. The SLS withdrew from the LDS-led government in April 2004 over the unpopular citizenship law (see Political background, above). In the October 2004 legislative elections, the SLS secured seven seats in the assembly. It subsequently joined the SDS-led coalition government. The party announced in June 2007 that it would support Lojze Peterle in the upcoming presidential election. Bojan ŠROT was elected party president in November 2007. In August 2008 Šrot received the endorsement of the SLS executive committee and party members as president of the party following a challenge by Ales PRIMC, who accused Šrot of corruption. The SLS campaigned in a coalition with the SMS in the 2008 assembly balloting, and the grouping won five seats (all were SLS candidates). Šrot resigned as SLS leader in March. At a May 2009 party congress, Radovan ŽERJAV was elected party president. The SLS placed third in the 2010 local balloting with 9.8 percent of the vote. It also secured 32 mayoral posts, more than any other party in the elections. In the 2011 elections, the SLS gained six seats. It joined the SDS-led governing coalition in 2012 but not the PS-led coalition formed in 2013. Franc BOGOVIČ was unanimously elected party president on March 2, 2013. The SLS ran in a coalition with the NSi in EU elections in May

2014, and the alliance won two seats. However, the SLS failed to secure any seats in assembly balloting in July. In December Marko ZIDANŠEK was elected party president.

Leaders: Marko ZIDANŠEK (President); Primoz JELŠEVAR, Franc ROZMAN, Jasmina OPEC (Vice Presidents); Jakob PRESEČNIK (Parliamentary Leader).

Civic List (*Državljanska Lista*—DL). Formed by Gregor VIRANT in October 2011, the centrist DL was intially known as **Gregor Virant's Civic List** (*Državljanska lista Gregorja Viranta*—LGV). It sought to offer an alternative to existing center-right parties. In the 2011 balloting, the then LGV placed fourth with eight seats. It joined the SDS coalition government in 2012. At an April 2012 party congress, the DL adopted its current name. Party leader Gregor Virant resigned after the DL failed to win any seats in the 2014 EU elections. Bojan STARMAN was elected DL president in June 2014. The DL failed to secure any seats in the 2014 legislative balloting.

Leaders: Bojan STARMAN (President); Aleksandra MARKOVIČ, Alois SELIŠNIK (Vice Presidents).

Liberal Democracy of Slovenia (*Liberalna Demokracija Slovenije*—LDS). The LDS was formed in March 1994 as a merger of the main government formation, the **Liberal Democratic Party** (*Liberalna Demokratična Stranka*—LDS), led by Prime Minister Drnovšek, and three small groupings. (For the early history of the LDS, see the 2013 *Handbook*.)

Prime Minister Janez Drnovšek was narrowly reelected in January 1997 and subsequently established a coalition government with the SLS and the DeSUS. The April 2000 departure of the SLS led to Drnovšek's resignation, although he returned to office following the October 2000 election, the LDS having won a plurality of 34 seats. Drnovšek was elected president of the republic in 2002 and successfully nominated Anton Rop as prime minister.

The LDS participated in the 2004 EU elections in an alliance with the DeSUS, but the alliance performed poorly, securing two seats. The LDS subsequently fell to second place in the October legislative elections with 23 seats and then began to fragment.

In January 2007 Drnovšek left the LDS and did not seek reelection as president of the republic. When Rop and a number of other LDS members left in March 2007 to join the ZLSD the party's parliamentary grouping dropped from 23 to 11. Six former ZLSD parliamentary members formed the grouping **For Real** (*Zares*), while others became independents. On June 30 Katerina Kresal was elected as the LDS president, becoming the first woman to lead a Slovenian political party. In the 2007 presidential balloting, the LDS supported Mitja GASPARI, who placed third in the first round of balloting.

The LDS secured five seats in the assembly in 2008 and joined the SD-led coalition government. Kresal was appointed interior minister. The LDS campaigned strongly in support of the June 2010 referendum on the border agreement with Croatia. Following charges of corruption, Kresal resigned her cabinet post on August 10, 2011, and vowed to allow the party to conduct a confidence vote on her leadership. Despite her resignation, the LDS remained part of the SD-led coalition government. The LDS secured no seats in the 2011 parliamentary elections. Iztok PODBREGAR was elected president in March 2012, but resigned three months later, citing personal reasons. Anton ANDERLIĆ became party leader in 2013.

Leaders: Anton ANDERLIĆ (President); Anton PRESKAR, Milan RAZDEVŠEK, Debora BURIĆ, Tadeja DRENOVEC (Vice Presidents).

For Real (*Zares*). *Zares* was formed in 2007 by dissidents from the ZLSD, led by Minister of the Economy Matej Lahovnik. In 2007 **Active Slovenia** (*Aktivna Slovenia*—AS), led by Franci KEK, which won 3 percent of the vote in the 2004 balloting, merged with *Zares*. *Zares* supported Danilo Türk in the 2007 presidential balloting. *Zares* placed third in the assembly elections in September 2008 and secured nine seats. It subsequently joined the SD-led coalition government. Party founder Lahovnik resigned from the government and from the party after accusing *Zares* chair Gregor Golobič of corruption. *Zares* withdrew from the governing coalition in June 2011, and party member Pavel GANTAR announced he would resign as speaker of the assembly on September 1 as *Zares* had joined the opposition. *Zares* secured no seats in the assembly in the 2011 or 2014 balloting. Gantar was elected party chair in February 2012 but resigned after the party failed to win any seats in the 2014 EU balloting. Darja RADIĆ subsequently became acting president.

Leaders: Darja RADIĆ (Acting President); Cveta RIBARIČ LASNIK, Vito ROZEJ (Vice Presidents).

Slovenian National Party (*Slovenska Narodna Stranka*—SNS). The SNS is an extreme right-wing grouping that stands for a militarily strong and sovereign Slovenia, the family as the basic unit of society, and preservation and restoration of the country's cultural heritage. In the 2004 assembly elections, the SNS increased its representation to six seats. (For more on the history of the party, see the 2014 *Handbook.*)

Jelinčič announced his presidential candidacy in May 2007. He placed fourth in the first round of polling. In 2008, SNS Vice President Sašo PEČE led a number of members out of the SNS to form a new party, **Lipa** (Linden Tree). The SNS secured five seats in the 2008 assembly balloting. The SNS led the unsuccessful campaign against ratification of the border agreement with Croatia during the national referendum in June 2010. It also continued to oppose Croatian EU membership after Slovenia officially endorsed the neighboring country's bid in 2011. The SNS failed to secure any seats in the 2011 or the 2014 legislative balloting.

Leader: Zmago JELINČIČ (President).

Youth Party of Slovenia–European Greens (*Stranka Mladih Slovenije–Zeleni Evrope*—SMS-*Zeleni*). The SMS was organized in July 2000 by former members of youth groups at the universities of Maribor and Ljubljana. Claiming no firm ideology, but emphasizing youth-oriented issues, the party won a surprising four seats in the October 2000 National Assembly election on a vote share of 4.3 percent. It subsequently agreed to support the return of Janez Drnovšek as prime minister. The SMS did not gain any seats in the 2004 legislative election. In April 2007 party leader Darko Krajnc was chosen as the SMS candidate for the upcoming presidential elections. He placed fifth in the first round of balloting with 2.2 percent of the vote and failed to qualify to advance to the second round. The SMS joined the SLS in an electoral coalition in the 2008 balloting, but none of its candidates were elected to office. Krajnc was reelected as party leader in June 2009. Later that year the party adopted its new name, the Youth Party of Slovenia–European Greens. It secured 0.9 percent of the vote in the 2011 assembly and no seats.

Leaders: Darko KRAJNC (President), Uroš BREŽAN (Vice President), Jože VOZELJ (Secretary General).

Other parties that contested the 2011 or 2014 assembly elections included (the parties received less than 1 percent of the vote unless noted) the **Party of the Slovenian Nation** (*Stranka Slovenskega Naroda*—SSN); the **Greens of Slovenia** (*Zeleni Slovenije*—ZS); **Acacias** (*Akacije*); the **Movement for Slovenia** (*Gibanje za Slovenijo*); the **Slovenian Party of Equal Opportunities** (*Stranka Enakih Možnosti Slovenije*—SEM-Si); **Forward Slovenia** (*Naprej Slovenija*—NPS); the **Party of the Slovenian Nation** (*Stranka Slovenskega Naroda*—SSN); the **Humana Party** (*Stranka Humana*); the **Slovenian Pirate Party** (*Piratska Stranka Slovenije*—PSS), formed in 2012 and which won 1.3 percent of the vote in the 2014 assembly balloting; **I Believe** (*Verjamen*), which won one seat in the 2014 EU polling.

For more information on **Lipa** (Linden Tree), the **List for Justice and Development** (*Lista za Pravičnost in Razvoj*—LPR), **Go, Slovenia!** (*Naprez Slovenija*—NPS), and the **Christian Democratic Party** (*Krščanski Demokrati Stranka*—KDS), see the 2012 *Handbook.*

LEGISLATURE

Prior to implementation of the 1991 constitution, the Slovene Assembly (*Zbòr*) was a directly elected tricameral body consisting of a Socio-Political Chamber, a Chamber of Associated Labor, and a Chamber of Communes. On December 6, 1992, the first elections were held for a National Assembly and a portion of a National Council.

National Council (*Državni Svet*). The 40 members of the council, who serve five-year terms, are chosen by electoral colleges of local (22 seats) and functional (18 seats) interest groups. The breakdown is as follows: 4 seats for employer groups; 4 for employee groups; 4 for farmers, tradespeople, and professions; 6 for noncommercial activities; and 22 for local interests. The council is able to propose new laws, require the holding of referendums relating to legislation, call for a parliamentary inquiry, request the Constitutional Court to review the constitutionality and legality of legislative acts, and direct the National Assembly to reconsider newly passed legislation. The last election for the National Council was conducted on November 20–21, 2012.

President: Mitja BERVAR (LDS).

National Assembly (*Državni Zbor*). The 90 members of the assembly are elected for four-year terms, with 88 of the members elected in eight electoral districts by proportional representation. Lists must receive a minimum of 4 percent of the national vote to achieve representation. The remaining two seats are reserved for Hungarian and Italian ethnic minorities, with one seat going to each group and with each elected in a special nationwide electoral district. The balloting on July 13, 2014, resulted in the following seat distribution: Modern Center Party, 36; Slovenian Democratic Party, 21; Slovenian Democratic Party of Pensioners, 10; Social Democrats, 6; United Left, 6; New Slovenia–Christian People's Party, 5; Alliance of Alenka Bratušek, 4; and minority representatives, 2.

President: Milan BRGLEZ (SMC).

CABINET

[as of August 7, 2016]

Prime Minister	Miro Cerar (SMC)
Deputy Prime Ministers	Boris Koprivnikar (SMC)
	Karl Erjavec (DeSUS)
	Dejan Židan (SD)
Ministers	
Agriculture, Forestry, and Food	Dejan Židan (SD)
Culture	Anton Peršak (SDS)
Defense	Andreja Katič (SD) [f]
Economic Development and Technology	Zdravko Počivalšek (SMC)
Education, Science, and Sports	Maja Makovec Brenčič (SMC) [f]
Environment	Irena Majcen (DeSUS) [f]
Finance	Alenka Smerkolj (Acting) (SMC) [f]
Foreign Affairs	Karl Erjavec (DeSUS)
Health	Milojka Kolar (SMC) [f]
Infrastructure and Urban Planning	Peter Gašperšic (SMC)
Interior	Vesna Györkös Žnidar (SMC) [f]
Justice	Goran Klemenčič (SMC)
Labor, Family, and Social Affairs	Anja Kopač Mrak (SD) [f]
Public Administration	Boris Koprivnikar (SMC)
Without Portfolio, Responsible for Development	Alenka Smerkolj (SMC) [f]
Without Portfolio, Responsible for Relations with Slovenes Abroad	Gorazd Žmavc (DeSUS)

[f] = female

INTERGOVERNMENTAL REPRESENTATION

Ambassador to the U.S.: Božo CERAR.

U.S. Ambassador to Slovenia: Brent HARTLEY.

Permanent Representative to the UN: Andrej LOGAR.

IGO Memberships (Non-UN): CEUR, EBRD, EIB, EU, IADB, ICC, IOM, NATO, OSCE, WTO.

For Further Reference:

Fink-Hafner, Danica. "Post-Accession Politicalization of National EU Policy Coordination: The Case of Slovenia." *Public Administration.* 92, no. 1 (March 2014): 39–54.

Luthar, Oto, ed. *The Land Between: A History of Slovenia.* 2nd ed. Frankfurt am Main: Peter Lang, 2013.

Zajc, Drago. "Role of Opposition in Contemporary Parliamentary Democracies: The Case of Slovenia." *Journal of Comparative Politics.* 9, no. 1 (January 2016): 19–35.

SOLOMON ISLANDS

Political Status: Former British-administered territory; achieved internal self-government on January 2, 1976, and full independence within the Commonwealth on July 7, 1978.

Area: 10,639 sq. mi. (27,556 sq. km).

Population: 595,000 (2016E—UN); 635,000 (2016E—U.S. Census).

Major Urban Center (2014E—UN): HONIARA (73,000).

Official Language: English (Solomons Pidgin is the effective lingua franca).

Monetary Unit: Solomon Islander Dollar (market rate October 1, 2016: 7.79 dollars = $1US).

Sovereign: Queen ELIZABETH II.

Governor General: Sir Frank Ofagioro KABUI; elected by the National Parliament on June 15, 2009, and sworn in on July 7 for a five-year term, succeeding Sir Nathaniel WAENA; reelected by the National Parliament for a second five-year term on May 7, 2014.

Prime Minister: Manasseh SOGOVARE (Social Credit Party); elected by the National Parliament and assumed office on December 9, 2014, succeeding Gordon Darcy LILO (National Coalition for Reform and Advancement).

THE COUNTRY

The Solomons comprise a twin chain of 922 Pacific islands stretching nearly 900 miles in a southeasterly direction from the Papua New Guinean territory of Bougainville to the northern New Hebrides. The six largest islands are Guadalcanal (on which the capital, Honiara, is located), Choiseul, Malaita, New Georgia, San Cristobal, and Santa Isabel. Approximately 94 percent of the inhabitants are Melanesian, with smaller groups of Polynesians (3 percent), Micronesians (1.5 percent), Europeans (0.7 percent), and Chinese (0.3 percent). Anglicans are the most numerous among the largely Christian population, followed by Roman Catholics and adherents of a variety of evangelical sects. An estimated 85 percent of the population is rural, with women bearing much of the responsibility for subsistence agriculture. One woman serves in the current legislature; meanwhile, the government pledged action to improve their status and a women's party was launched in June 2010 (see Political parties, below).

More than 90 percent of the land is governed by customary landownership practices, creating, in combination with the strong influence of tribal nationalism, some barriers to recent development efforts. More than 75 percent of the workforce works in agriculture, fishing, and subsistence farming. The principal export commodities are copra, gold, timber, fish, and palm oil. Untapped resources include lead, zinc, and bauxite.

The economy has encountered severe difficulty in past years, with timber resources (the second-most important source of foreign earnings) rapidly dwindling and a period of civil unrest in 1999–2000. Gross domestic product (GDP) growth averaged 8.2 percent in 2006–2008 but plunged to 0.4 percent in 2009 with the global financial crisis and declining copra and lumber sales. Conditions improved in 2010, with GDP growth of 6.5 percent. In October 2010 the World Bank agreed to provide $3 million in aid for rural development. In May 2012 the government signed a $2 million grant agreement with the World Bank to help the Solomons identify areas of growth economic reform and protect it from the effects of climate change, and in December, the International Monetary Fund initiated a three-year extended credit facility arrangement. This arrangement was extended in March 2016 with an additional $420,000 made available for immediate disbursement. Despite a slow start to 2013, with sagging production in the agriculture and logging sectors, that year saw growth of 4 percent, which slowed slightly to 3.8 percent in 2014, 3.2 percent in 2015, and an estimated 3 percent in 2016. Inflation has fluctuated from 4.4 percent in 2014 to 4.1 percent in 2015 and an estimated 4.4 percent for 2016.

GOVERNMENT AND POLITICS

Political background. Originally named on the basis of rumors that the 16th-century Spanish explorer Alvaro de Mendana had discovered the source of the riches of King Solomon, the islands became the object of European labor "blackbirding" in the 1870s. The excesses of the indenture trade prompted Britain to declare a protectorate over the southern islands in 1893, the remaining territory being added between 1898 and 1900. Occupied by the Japanese in 1941, some of the bitterest fighting of the Pacific war occurred near Guadalcanal and in the adjacent Coral Sea during 1942–1943. After the war, a number of changes in British administration were introduced in response to a series of indigenous political and evangelical movements. The territory became internally self-governing in January 1976, and the country was administered by an elected Legislative Council, led by a chief minister who appointed his own cabinet. After lengthy constitutional discussions in London in 1977, full independence was achieved on July 7, 1978. Former chief minister Peter KENILOREA was designated prime minister.

Kenilorea was redesignated following a legislative election on August 6, 1980, but was defeated 20–17 in intraparliamentary balloting on August 31, 1981, and obliged to yield office to Solomon MAMALONI, who had served briefly as chief minister during the transition period immediately preceding independence.

Neither of the leading parties gained an absolute majority in the election of October 24, 1984. Following a 21–17 legislative vote on November 19, Kenilorea formed a coalition government that included members of his United Party and the recently organized *Solomone Agu Sogufenua,* in addition to a number of independents.

Although the opposition charged the ruling coalition with inefficiency and "inexplicable delays" in presenting a national development plan, Kenilorea survived a nonconfidence vote on September 6, 1985. However, he was obliged to resign on November 14, 1986, because of controversy surrounding the allocation of aid in the wake of a severe cyclone. The National Parliament approved Deputy Prime Minister Ezekiel ALEBUA as Kenilorea's successor on December 1.

While the opposition People's Alliance Party (PAP) obtained a plurality of only 11 legislative seats in the election of February 22, 1989, its leader, former Prime Minister Mamaloni, benefiting from crossover and independent support, was returned to office with 21 of 38 MP votes on March 28. In May the High Court ruled the 1988 appointment of Sir George LEPPING as governor general unconstitutional on the ground that he had not taken a leave of absence from a civil service position.

In a startling move on October 9, 1990, shortly before he was to face a leadership challenge at the ruling party's annual convention, Mamaloni resigned from the PAP to form a government of "national unity" that included a number of theretofore opposition parliamentarians and was designed to be broadly representative of the country's principal islands in terms of both geography and population. The action was later formalized by the launching of a Group for National Unity and Reconciliation (GNUR), which won 21 of 47 parliamentary seats in legislative balloting on May 26, 1993. However, the GNUR was unable to attract sufficient additional support to ensure the incumbent's retention of office on June 18. By a one-vote margin, the National Coalition Partners (NCP), an alliance of six anti-Mamaloni groups, elected Francis Billy HILLY, an independent who had not participated in national politics for eight years, as the new prime minister. Mamaloni immediately charged that Hilly's 24–23 victory did not meet the constitution's definition of an absolute majority as "at least one half of all the members plus one." Eventually both the governor general and the Court of Appeal ruled against the contention, although the issue was rendered moot in November, when three government ministers joined the opposition and one opposition MP joined the government, presumably giving Mamaloni the capacity to defeat Hilly on a 25–22 vote. However, a further shift in the fragile balance yielded approval of the government's budget on a 25–21 vote late in the year.

The defection of two ministers during a legislative adjournment in early October 1994 again reduced the Hilly coalition to a minority, and on October 13 Governor General Moses PITAKAKA dismissed the prime minister. A government crisis ensued, with Hilly refusing to stand down and the Court of Appeal upholding the action of the governor general, who proceeded to swear in Mamaloni on a caretaker basis on October 24. Two days later the judiciary reversed itself by agreeing with Hilly that dismissal required a legislative vote of nonconfidence, but added that the governor general was not obligated to take advice from a minority administration. As a result, Hilly resigned on October 31 and Mamaloni, buttressed by additional NCP defections, was formally confirmed as his successor by a 29–18 vote on November 7.

In the face of a growing financial crisis, Mamaloni called for an election on August 6, 1997. While it appeared after the vote that his National Unity group had won a plurality, Mamaloni was unable to command a legislative majority, and on August 27 Bartholomew ULUFA'ALU of the Solomon Islands Liberal Party (SILP) was elected as his successor.

Soon after assuming office, Ulufa'alu became embroiled in a long-standing ethnic dispute between the indigenous (Isatambu) inhabitants of Guadalcanal and those of the adjacent island of Malaita, many of whom had migrated to Honiara, an urban area that had emerged from the World War II American base at Henderson Field as the nation's capital. In early 1999 leaders of the Guadalcanal Revolutionary Army (GRA) demanded $4 million annual rent for accommodating the capital, eventually accepting $103,000 as a "temporary goodwill gesture." Hostilities continued, however, between the GRA, restyled as the Isatambu Freedom Movement (IFM), and the so-called Malaita Eagles Force (MEF), despite the formal signing of a peace accord on June 28. A second accord was concluded on August 12, while a third, cosigned by Fiji, Papua New Guinea (PNG), and Vanuatu on October 23, paved the way for a multinational peace-monitoring group that began arriving two days later.

On April 10, 2000, following a series of riots in Honiara, further peace talks were postponed, and on June 5 the MEF mounted a coup that included the kidnapping of Prime Minister Ulufa'alu, who, although himself a Malaitan, was charged with failure to resolve the conflict. Ulufa'alu was released on June 9 and resigned under pressure four days later; former finance minister Manasseh SOGAVARE succeeded him on June 30.

Another cease-fire agreement between the IFM and MEF was concluded under Australian auspices on August 3, 2000, while additional peace talks were conducted on September 7–13 on a New Zealand frigate before the conclusion on October 15 in Townsville, Queensland, of a peace agreement that included provision for Australia and New Zealand to provide peace monitors. Forces on both sides nevertheless remained reluctant to turn in their weapons, as called for in the Townsville Peace Agreement, and by the initial deadline of December 15 only about half of the anticipated weapons—and virtually none of the more modern ones—had been surrendered. Four days later parliament passed a bill granting amnesty to the militias for crimes committed during the civil uprising. On February 7, 2001, the IFM and another group, the Marau Eagles Force from east Guadalcanal, completed a peace agreement.

In August 2001 parliament was dissolved ahead of the general election. In the balloting of December 5 the PAP captured a plurality of 20 seats, and on December 17 the PAP's Sir Allan KEMAKEZA was named prime minister by the National Parliament.

In May 2005 a new rebel group, the Malaita Separatist Movement (MSM), was reported to have been launched by former members of the MEF to oppose what were perceived as injustices perpetrated by the Kemakeza government and what had become known as the Regional Assistance Mission to the Solomon Islands (RAMSI).

The turmoil intensified after the April 2006 election, with rioting erupting in Honiara upon the appointment as prime minister of Snyder RINI, who was accused of being influenced by local Chinese on behalf of Taiwan, which the Solomon Islands recognized rather than the People's Republic of China (PRC). In the wake of widespread looting of Chinese businesses, Rini resigned and was replaced on May 4 by former Prime Minister Manasseh Sogavare. Sogavare was again obliged to step down in the wake of an adverse nonconfidence vote on December 13, 2007, and was succeeded on December 30 by Dr. Derek SIKUA. RAMSI was deployed during elections on August 4, 2010, which passed relatively peacefully but set off three weeks of negotiations to gain control of the legislature. Danny Philip of the newly formed Solomon Islands Reform and Democratic Party (SIRPD) was elected on August 25, defeating Steven ABANA with 26 votes to 23. Heading a coalition known as the National Coalition for Reform and Advancement, he appointed a 24-member cabinet on August 28.

In May 2011 the governor general, Sir Frank Ofagioro KABUI, refused to swear in newly reappointed fisheries minister Jimmy LUSIBAEA, who had been convicted of assault. (For more on Lusibaea, see the 2011 *Handbook*.) Following a case brought by the opposition on October 17, 2011, the country's High Court barred Lusibaea from serving in Parliament. (In a by-election for his seat on August 1, 2012, his wife, Vika LUSIBAEA, became the second woman to be elected to National Parliament.)

On November 11, 2011, Prime Minister Philip resigned rather than face a vote of no confidence over allegations regarding the misuse of development aid from Taiwan. His former finance minister, Gordon Darcy LILO, was elected on November 17, 2011. Opposition leader Derek Sikua filed a motion of no confidence against Lilo's government one day after his election drew protests in the capital due to his close links with the former government. Several ministerial posts turned over before an ultimately unsuccessful no-confidence motion came up for vote in October 2012.

A motion of no confidence filed by Sikua triggered a reshuffle of the cabinet in October 2012 before the parliament vote. Reportedly, nine government legislators were expected to support the motion. However, most opposition members, including Sikua, did not turn up to the scheduled vote on October 26. The motion was opposed by 28 votes, with three abstentions and no supporters.

In parliamentary elections on November 19, 2014, the first since the end of the Australian peacekeeping mission, independent candidates won 32 of the total 50 seats. The newly formed Democratic Alliance Party (DAP), with 7 seats, won the most of any party, followed by the new United Democratic Party (UDP), led by Sogavare, with 5 seats. The People's Alliance Party (PAP) secured 3 seats, with the Solomon Island Party for Rural Advancement, the Kadare Party of the Solomon Islands, and the Solomon Islands People's First Party each claiming 1 of the 3 remaining seats won by parties. Parliament elected Sogavare prime minister and leader of the Solomon Islands People's Democratic Coalition (SIPDC), a governing coalition party. He was sworn in on December 9 to his third, nonconsecutive term.

Constitution and government. The independence agreement negotiated in September 1977 provided for a constitutional monarchy with the queen represented by a governor general of local nationality, who is appointed for a five-year term on the advice of parliament. Upon independence, the unicameral Legislative Assembly, which had been increased to 38 members in April 1976, became the National Parliament, with the authority to elect a prime minister from among its membership (subsequently increased to 47 and then to 50 legislators). The cabinet, which is appointed by the governor general on advice of the prime minister, is responsible to the parliament. In addition, the independence agreement called for devolution of authority to local government units, within which the traditional chiefs retain formal status. The most seriously contested issue yielded a provision that nonindigenous Solomon Islanders (mainly Gilbertese, Chinese, and European expatriates) would be granted automatic citizenship upon application within two years of independence. The judicial system includes a Court of Appeal, a High Court, magistrates' courts, and local courts whose jurisdiction encompasses cases dealing with customary land titles. Ultimate appeal, as in certain other nonrepublican Commonwealth nations, is to the Judicial Committee of the Privy Council in London.

For administrative purposes the islands are currently divided into nine provinces, each headed by a premier.

Prime Minister Hilly informed the provincial premiers in mid-1994 that he was committed to a responsible partnership between the national and provincial administrations. By contrast, three provincial premiers threatened secession in mid-1996 after the Mamaloni administration secured legislation transferring powers of the provincial assemblies to 75 local assemblies and councils. In 2001 adoption of a state-based federal system was again being considered.

The first draft of a document detailing a proposed federal system became available in mid-2009, but the review process was placed on hold in January 2010 for lack of funding, with no report of its resumption following the August election. Earlier, parliament rejected a proposal advanced by a 2009 Constituency Boundaries Commission report that 17 new constituencies be created.

The constitutional provision for freedom of expression is generally well respected. However, media outlets are restricted by criminal defamation laws. Reporters Without Borders notes that self-censorship and a lack of resources constrain free journalistic practices.

Foreign relations. The nation retains close links with Britain, which agreed in 1977 to provide some $43 million in nonrepayable financial assistance during 1978–1982. Additional aid has been obtained from Australia, New Zealand, Japan, and such multilateral sources as the Asian Development Bank. Regionally, Honiara has been a strong supporter of the South Pacific Nuclear Free Zone movement and an opponent of what former prime minister Kenilorea called French "imperialism," although he stopped short of offering material aid to independence activists on New Caledonia. Despite its antinuclear posture, the Solomons was one of the few Pacific island states to express concern about the future of the Australia, New Zealand, United States Security Treaty (ANZUS), given its own lack of defense forces.

Relations between PNG and the Solomon Islands were strained from the mid-1980s over an insurrection in PNG's province of Bougainville. In late 1990 then foreign minister Kenilorea flew to Port Moresby to discuss the provision of humanitarian aid for the rebellious province, which is closer to the Solomons than to the PNG mainland. In March 1991 the Solomons reiterated that the rebellion was an internal PNG matter—but the Namaliu government charged that the Bougainville rebels were using the Solomons as a safe haven and a conduit for arms.

In April 1992 PNG military units on two occasions crossed into Solomon territory on search-and-destroy missions. A third incursion in mid-September, during which two Solomon Islanders were killed and a third abducted, further strained relations, despite PNG acceptance of full responsibility for what its prime minister termed an "atrocious act." Subsequently, Prime Minister Mamaloni was accused of meddling in PNG internal affairs upon publication of a confidential letter to a Papuan provincial premier that seemed to support secession if PNG Prime Minister Wingti abolished the regional government system. Tension eased somewhat with a series of ministerial-level meetings in early 1993 yielding tentative agreement on rules for "hot pursuit" in border areas affected by the insurrection. Comprehensive border talks in 1996 yielded the Basic Border Agreement, signed in July 1997, which recognized Bougainville as part of PNG, endorsed cooperation in security matters, and acknowledged the rights of indigenous peoples in the border area. (A revised treaty was concluded in July 2009.)

In July 2006 Prime Minister Sogavare announced a one-year extension of the Australian-led RAMSI, which had been augmented to include personnel from 14 countries. In mid-September, however, Australia's high commissioner, Patrick Cole, was declared persona non grata in the Solomons, apparently due to criticism of the handling of an inquiry into the riots after the April election. In late September relations deteriorated further because of Sogavare's refusal to permit the extradition to Australia of his recently appointed attorney general, Julian MOTI, who had been charged with an underage sex offense in Vanuatu. Thereafter, the deportation of an Australian national accused of complicity in a plot to assassinate Sogavare contributed to a thaw, and in March 2007 the prime minister agreed to accept the credentials of a new high commissioner.

On September 5, 2007, Sogavare's police minister reiterated the government's refusal to turn Moti over to Australian authorities. Two weeks later, Sogavare called for a review of RAMSI operations. His successor, Derek Sikua, promised renewed support for RAMSI and on December 27 ordered Moti's deportation. In mid-2010 the Queensland Court of Appeals overruled a stay on charges against the former attorney general, thus clearing the way for his trial.

In September 2011 Australia announced that it would allow guest workers from the Solomon Islands, and in October granted the islands $1 million to support greater political participation by women. Meanwhile total aid from Australia increased to $68 million per year. In July 2012 Australia reaffirmed its commitment to bilateral relations, pledging $239.4 million in development assistance for 2012–2013. New Zealand also signed a Joint Commitment for Development in September 2011.

In April 2012 Australia and the Solomon Islands began preliminary talks on a timetable for withdrawing RAMSI troops. The final rotation of Australian troops withdrew in August 2013. The RAMSI mission is now focused on the training of Solomon Islands' police and first responders.

In January 2013 concerns arose over transborder crime between the Solomon Islands and PNG after there was a raid on a Solomon logging settlement.

The United States provided $250,000 in disaster relief aid following the impact of Cyclone Ita in 2014. In July 2014 the Solomon Islands opened an embassy in Cuba, the first Pacific island nation to do so. Cuba had offered some assistance to the Solomons, including free medical training.

A dispute with Fiji began in July 2014 when the Solomon Islands Civil Aviation Authority denied a request from Fiji Airways to operate extra flights to Honaira. On July 15, all flights between the two countries were suspended indefinitely. The stalemate between aviation authorities, which impacted tourism and generated calls for government intervention and resolution, dragged on until January 2015, with flights resuming on January 24.

In February 2016 the Solomon Islands and Pakistan established diplomatic relations. In May a solar energy plant, funded by New Zealand and the United Arab Emirates (UAE), began operation in the Solomon Islands. The renewable energy plant was expected to provide 7–10 percent of the country's energy. The plant was one of five scheduled to be built in the Pacific by New Zealand and the UAE.

Current issues. Ahead of the 2014 elections, the Solomon Islands introduced a biometric voting system, prompting a series of challenges. The electronic infrastructure for the new voting system posed logistical challenges, including setting up power sources for laptop computers at every polling station. Shortly after voter registration began on March 10, allegations of voter fraud began, with some candidates accused of buying identification cards off of individual voters.

A riot in May 2014 in the capital resulted in the arrest of 53 people. Reportedly, the riots began as a protest by people unsatisfied with a government response for victims of severe flooding in April. However, advocacy groups for the victims said the rioters were opportunists.

Independents won the majority of seats in legislative balloting on November 19, 2014. Former prime minister Sogavare was reelected for his third nonconsecutive term by Parliament.

Interest in bauxite mining has been rekindled, with an Australian company, Iron Mountain Mining, purchasing prospecting licenses in March, 2016. This could have significant, long-term benefit to the agriculture-based economy of the Solomon Islands.

Rising sea levels are expected to pose an increasing threat to the Solomon Islands. Five islands in the Solomon chain have disappeared since 2014. Six others are considered to be "severely eroded" by Australian engineers who examined the problem. Sea level rise in the area is estimated to be about three times the world average.

POLITICAL PARTIES

As in neighboring Papua New Guinea, party affiliations tend to be transient and based more on personality than ideology. Leaders often represent more than one movement, or transition in and out of independent status, throughout their careers. The People's Alliance Party (PAP) government formed by Prime Minister Mamaloni in 1989 was the first single-party administration since independence; in 1990, by contrast, Mamaloni withdrew from the PAP to form a "national unity" government that became the basis of the Group for National Unity and Reconciliation (GNUR). In June 1993 the five anti-Mamaloni parliamentary parties, led by Francis Billy Hilly, joined with Christian Fellowship and independent members to form a government alliance called the **National Coalition Partners** (NCP), which lost its slim legislative majority and became effectively moribund in October 1994.

The government grouping during the Sogavare administration was styled the Grand Coalition for Change, while the opposition, in early December 2007, announced formation of a **Coalition for National Unity and Rural Advancement** (CNURA), led by theretofore independent Derek Sikua, that was victorious in the December 20 balloting.

In 2001 a **Solomon Islands Alliance for Change Coalition** (SIACC) evolved from the Solomon Islands Alliance for Change (SIAC), which had contested the 1997 election and saw its leader, Bartholomew Ulufa'alu, form a government on August 30. (As a consequence of its origins and name, the group was frequently referenced simply as the SIAC.) Ulufa'alu was forced to resign in June 2000 but a year later filed a constitutional challenge to the action and the election of Prime Minister Sogavare of the People's Progressive Party (PPP). In November 2001 the High Court dismissed Ulufa'alu's case.

An effort by the Sikua administration to require the registration of political parties and control their activity, particularly during election campaigns, was defeated by parliament in April 2010, and numerous new parties were launched prior to the August poll. Following the elections, party lines proved less significant than personal choice as legislators jockeyed for power. A coalition of some seven parties, styled the **National Coalition for Reform and Advancement** (NCRA), supported Danny Philips and, subsequently, Gordon Darcy Lilo.

After the November 2014 general election failed to produce a single winning party, a ruling coalition known as the **Solomon Islands People's Democratic Coalition** (SIPDC) was formed. SIPDC was led by Prime Minister Sogavare. Independents won the majority of seats in the 2014 balloting.

Government Parties:

Democratic Alliance Party (DAP). The DAP was launched by Steve ABANA to run in the 2014 elections. It won seven seats, making it the largest single party in Parliament.

Leader: Steve Abana (Founder).

Kadere Party (KP). KP was founded by former member of parliament Peter BOYERS, in part to promote shipping and logging interests. The party won 1 seat in the 2014 elections and joined in the coalition government.

Leaders: Alfred LEGUA (President), Peter BOYERS (Founder and Former Member of Parliament).

Solomon Islands Party for Rural Advancement (SIPRA). SIPRA was launched in July 2005 by former Prime Minister Manasseh Sogavare. Sogavare had previously headed the now defunct PPP, which had been founded and led, through a number of changes, by former Prime Minister Mamaloni before his death in January 2000. SIPRA secured one seat in the 2010 legislative balloting. Gordon Darcy LILO, the former prime minister, lost his local seat in the 2014 elections, but the party as a whole 1 won seat. SIPRA formed a part of the coalition government, working with the Democratic Alliance Party (DAP), the Solomon Islands People First Party (SIPFP), and the People's Alliance Party (PAP).

Leader: Job Dudley TAUSINGA (Parliamentary Leader).

People's Alliance Party (PAP). Also called the Solomon Islands People Alliance (SIPA), the PAP was formed in late 1979 by merger of the **People's Progressive Party** (PPP), led by former chief minister Solomon Mamaloni, and the **Rural Alliance Party** (RAP), led by David KAUSIMAE. After becoming prime minister in August 1981, Mamaloni was forced into opposition after the election of October 1984 but returned to the office on March 28, 1989. He resigned from the PAP in October 1990 to head a coalition administration that included a revived PPP. In January 1992 PAP leader Kausimae announced the expulsion from the party of ten MPs who were serving in the second Mamaloni government.

Party leader Allan Kemakeza served as deputy prime minister under Sogavare until his dismissal in August 2001 for alleged mishandling of compensation funds related to the recent civil disruptions. With the PAP having achieved a plurality of 20 seats in the December parliamentary election, Kemakeza, with independent support, was elected prime minister, continuing in office until after the April 2006 election. The PAP has called for adoption of a federal republic headed by a president. In 2010 balloting, the PAP won two seats. In April 2014, ahead of October balloting, the PAP encouraged candidates to contest with registered parties, not as individuals, for national stability. PAP won 3 seats in the 2014 elections.

Leaders: Clement KENGAVA (President), Sir Allan KEMEKAZA (General Secretary).

United Democratic Party (UDP). The UDP was formed to contest the 2014 elections. Its founder, Sir Thomas Ko CHAN, unified two smaller parties, the **Solomon Islands Reform and Democratic Party (RDP)** and the **Solomon Islands Independent Democratic Party (SIRDP)** (see below), and carried 5 seats in the 2014 elections.

Solomon Islands People First Party (SIPFP). SIPFP was founded to combat corruption and to reestablish leadership principals in government. The party won 1 seat in the 2014 parliamentary elections.

Leader: Dr. Jimmie RODGERS (Acting Leader).

Other Parties:

Independent Democratic Party (IDP). The IDP was formed after the 2010 election by Snyder Rini, a former prime minister, who previously led the Association of Independent Members of Parliament (AIMP).

The AIMP had not been a party in the strict sense of the word, since it was composed of independents (some of whom were party aligned). The AIMP secured 13 seats in 2001 30 in 2006 and 2 in 2010. The party did not run in the 2014 elections.

Leader: Snyder RINI (Former Prime Minister).

Solomon Islands Liberal Party (SILP). The SILP was originally founded in 1976 by Bartholomew Ulufa'alu as the **National Democratic Party** (Nadepa). The only formal party to contest the 1976 election, Nadepa won five legislative seats. Having won four seats in 1989 (three years after redefining itself as the SILP), the party joined a number of smaller groups and independents in a parliamentary formation called the Coalition for National Unity. In the course of the 1990 realignment, Mamaloni persuaded SILP leader Ulufa'alu to resign from parliament and accept appointment as a government consultant.

Joining Ulufa'alu in the formation of the SIACC grouping in 2001 was former prime minister Francis Billy Hilly, Fred FONO, and Patteson Oti. In the December parliamentary election the SILP won 12 seats. Shortly thereafter Ulufa'alu decided to seek the prime ministership despite the party's endorsement of Oti. Oti ultimately finished second to the PAP's Kemakeza, with 13 votes, while Ulufa'alu won only 3. Although a member of the SIACC, Fono served in the Kemakeza cabinet. Ulufa'alu died on May 25, 2007. The SILP won 1 seat in the 2010 balloting. As opposition leader, Derek Sikua initiated two unsuccessful no-confidence motions against the Lilo administration in 2011 and 2012. The party did not run in the 2014 elections.

Leaders: Derek SIKUA (Former Prime Minister), Japhet WAIPORA (Former Member of Parliament).

Solomon Islands New Generation Party. The youth-focused party was founded in February 2012 to represent young people's interests, particularly in the area of education. Party membership is restricted to those between the ages of 18–40. The party won no seats in the 2014 elections.

Leader: Ishmael NORI (President).

Parties that were created for the 2014 elections, but that won no seats, include the **National Transformation Party**, led by George Edward OSIFELO; the **Solomon Islands Pan-Melanesian Congress Party**, led by Enif PETSAKIBO; the **Youth Owned Rural and Urban Party**, led by Charles KIRA; the **New Nation Party**, led by Catherine Ngalena ADIFAKA; and the **People's Progressive Party**, led by Charles DAUSEBEA.

Other minor parties include the **Autonomous Solomon Islanders Party** (ASIP), founded in January 2010; the **Direct Development Party**, founded by Dick Ha'amori and Alfred SASAKOAND; the **Twelve Pillars to Peace and Prosperity Party** (TP4), which was launched in June 2010 as the Solomons' first women's party; the **Solomon United Nationalist Party** (SUN), founded in January 2010 and led by Ramon QUITALES; and the **New Nations Solomon Islands Party**, established by Belani TEKULU. None of these parties won seats in the 2014 elections.

For more information on the **Solomon Islands Democratic Party** (SIDP), the **Solomon Islands Reform and Democratic Party** (SIRDP), **Ownership, Unity, and Responsibility** (OUR), the **Solomon Islands People's Congress Party** (SIPCP), the **Rural and Urban Political Party** (RUPP), the **Solomon Islands National Party** (NP), the **Solomon Islands United Democratic Party** (SIUDP), and the **People's Federation Party** (PFP), see the 2015 *Handbook*.

LEGISLATURE

The unicameral **National Parliament** currently consists of 50 members elected for four-year terms. The last legislative election on November 19, 2014, gave the Democratic Alliance Party 7 seats; United Democratic Party, 5; People's Alliance Party, 3; Solomon Island Party for Rural Advancement, 1; Kadare Party, 1; Solomon Islands People's First Party, 1; and independents, 32.

Speaker: Ajilon Jasper NASIU (ind.).

CABINET

[as of July 19, 2016]

Prime Minister	Manasseh Sogovare (ind.)
Deputy Prime Minister	Manasseh Maelanga (PAP)
Ministers	
Agriculture and Livestock	Duddley Kopu (UDP)
Aid Coordination and Development Planning	Danny Philip (UDP)
Aviation and Communication	Peter Shanel Agovaka (UDP)
Commerce, Industry, and Employment	Elijah Dore Muala (PAP)
Education and Human Resources	John Moffat Fugui (UDP)
Environment and Conservation	Samuel Manetoali (UDP)
Finance and Treasury	Snyder Rini (UDP)
Fisheries and Marine Resources	John Maneniaru (Kadere)
Foreign Affairs and Trade Relations	Milner Tozaka (PAP)
Forestry	Chris Laore (PAP)
Health and Medical Services	Tautai Angikimua Kaitu'u (UDP)
Home Affairs	Manasseh Maelanga (PAP)
Infrastructure and Development	Jimmy Lusibaea (PAP)
Justice and Legal Affairs	William Bradford Marau (UDP)
Lands and Housing	Moses Garu (Kadere)
Mines and Energy	David Day Pacha (Kadere)
Peace and Reconciliation	Samson Maneka (UDP)
Police and National Security	Stanley Festus Sofu (Kadere)
Provincial Government and Institutional Strengthening	David Tome (PAP)
Public Service	John Dean Kuku (UDP)
Rural Development and Indigenous Affairs	Jimson Fiau Tanangada (UDP)
Tourism and Culture	Bartholomew Parapolo (Kadere)
Women, Youth, and Sports	Freda A.B. Tuki Soriacomua (UDP) [f]
Attorney General	James Apiniaia

[f] = female

INTERGOVERNMENTAL REPRESENTATION

Ambassador to the U.S.: Colin David BECK.

U.S. Ambassador to the Solomon Islands (resident in Papua New Guinea): Catherine EBERT-GRAY.

Permanent Representative to the UN: Robert SISILO.

IGO Memberships (Non-UN): ADB, CWTH, IOM, PIF, WTO.

For Further Reference:

Dinnen, Sinclair. *Politics and State Building in Solomon Islands.* Canberra: Australian National University Press, 2011.

McCarthy, Stephen. "The Limits of Civil Society in Militarized Regimes: Evidence from the Asia–Pacific." *Australian Journal of International Affairs* 69, no. 6 (December 2015).

Wood, Terence. "The 2014 Elections in Solomon Islands: Did Anything Change? Will Anything Change?" *Devpolicyblog* (January 22, 2015). http://devpolicy.org/the-2014-elections-in-solomon-islands-did-anything-change-will-anything-change-20150122. Accessed on September 21, 2016.

SOMALIA

Somali Republic
Jamhuuriyada Soomaaliyeed

Note: In elections that were marred by violence, fraud, and corruption, Somalis began voting for the Senate and the House of the People on October 23, 2016, in balloting that ran through November 10. At the conclusion of the voting, about 10 percent of the seats had not been decided because of ongoing strife in some districts. Delays in tabulating the returns led to a postponement of presidential balloting, which was scheduled for November 30 to January 24, 2017. (The legislature indirectly elects the president.)

Political Status: Independent republic established July 1, 1960; revolutionary military regime installed October 21, 1969; one-party state proclaimed July 1, 1976; multiparty system authorized on December 25, 1990, but unimplemented prior to the assumption of power by rebel forces on January 27, 1991; national charter providing for three-year transitional national government adopted by Somali National Peace Conference July 16, 2000, in Arta, Djibouti; Transitional Federal Charter approved January 29, 2004, providing for a four-year transitional government; provisional constitution approved on August 1, 2012.

Area: 246,199 sq. mi. (637,657 sq. km), including Somaliland (68,000 sq. mi.; 176,120 sq. km).

Population: 11,079,000 (2016E—UN); 10,817,354 (2016E—U.S. Census).

Major Urban Center (2016E—UN): MOGADISHU (2,265,000, urban area).

Principal Language: Somali.

Monetary Unit: Somali Shilling. Conditions in Somalia in recent years have rendered attempts to determine a genuine national currency rate essentially futile; approximate market rate on October 1, 2016, was 579.50 shillings = $1US.

President: Hassan Sheikh MOHAMUD (Peace and Development Party); elected by the Federal Parliament on September 10, 2012, and inaugurated on September 16 for a four-year term to succeed acting President Mohamed Osman JAWARI (nonparty).

Prime Minister: Omar Abdirashid Ali SHARMARKE (nonparty); appointed prime minister by the president on December 17, 2013, and approved by the parliament on December 24, succeeding Abdiweli Sheikh AHMED (nonparty), who lost a vote of no confidence on December 6.

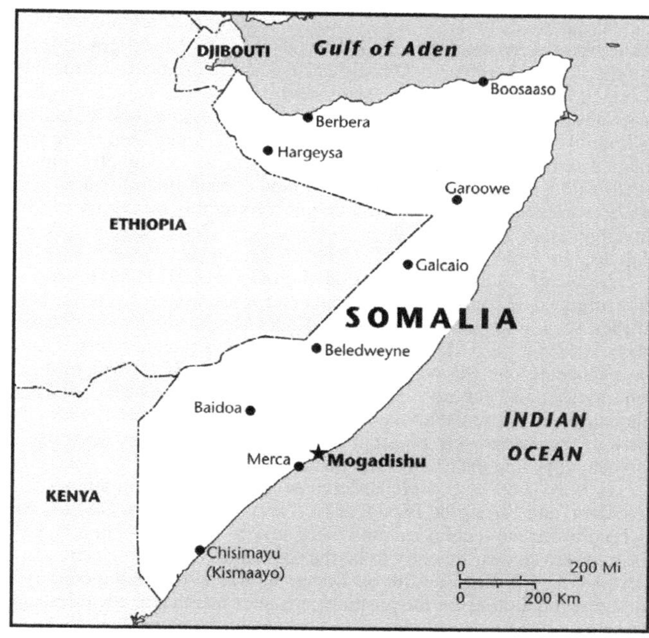

THE COUNTRY

The easternmost country in Africa, Somalia (including Somaliland) encompasses a broad band of desert and semidesert territory extending eastward along the Gulf of Aden and continuing southwestward to a point just south of the equator. The Somalis, who constitute 85 percent of the population, are a people of nomadic and pastoral traditions who share a common religion (Islam) and a common language (Somali). However, interclan rivalry has generated numerous economic and political cleavages, particularly between northern and southern groups. Nonindigenous inhabitants include Arabs, Ethiopians, Italians, Indians, and Pakistanis.

The economy is largely undeveloped, and the country remains one of the world's poorest. Agriculture accounts for more than 60 percent of economic activity, although it is compromised by irregular rainfall. The country possesses some mineral deposits that have not been commercially exploited. Although fishing, textile, and food processing industries have been established, much of the country's foreign exchange is derived from livestock and livestock-related products. In addition, Somalia has long been the world's largest producer of myrrh, an incense that is widely used in the Gulf region. Inflation, drought, inefficiency in state enterprises, bureaucratic corruption, and disruptions occasioned by civil war and interclan hostilities contributed to economic stagnation.

As momentum developed toward the resolution of the long-standing hostilities, the World Bank, European Union (EU), and United Nations (UN) relaunched some of its aid programs to Somalia in 2003. However, the resumption of conflict in the spring of 2006 prompted many aid groups to withdraw personnel and suspend assistance (see Current issues, below). GDP grew by an average of 2 percent from 2008 to 2011, partly as the result of ransoms paid by international shippers for hijacked vessels during that period (see Foreign relations, below). Most economic activity continued to be in the informal sectors of the economy or based on remittances, estimated to be $1.6 billion in 2013. However counterterrorism laws in the United States led a succession of banks to cease money transfers to Somalia in 2012–2013, severely constraining remittances. In September 2013 the EU and other international donors pledged €1.8 billion in reconstruction aid for Somalia. In October 2015 the World Bank released $144 million to Somalia to support government salaries. Annual GDP per capita in 2015 was approximately $547. That year GDP grew by about 6 percent.

GOVERNMENT AND POLITICS

Political background. Divided into British, French, and Italian sectors at the end of the 19th century, Somalia was partially reunited in 1960 when British Somaliland in the north and the Italian-administered Trust Territory in the south achieved their independence and promptly merged to form the United Republic of Somalia. Large numbers of Somalis remained in Ethiopia, Kenya, and the French Territory of the Afars and the Issas (subsequently Djibouti), and the new Somali regime announced that their inclusion in a "Greater Somalia" was a leading political objective.

The Somali Youth league (SYL) was the country's principal political party at independence and formed the republic's initial governments. During the late 1950s and early 1960s Somalia pursued a strongly irredentist policy toward Ethiopia and Kenya, relying increasingly on aid from the Soviet Union and other communist states. A change of policy occurred in 1967 with the presidential election of Abdirashid Ali SHERMARKE and his appointment of Mohamed Haji Ibrahim EGAL as prime minister.

The Egal regime was ousted by military units under the command of Maj. Gen. Mohamed SIAD BARRE on October 21, 1969, in an action that included the assassination of President Shermarke. Pledging to reduce tribalism and corruption, the new military government launched a restructuring along socialist lines of what was now termed the Somali Democratic Republic. Although briefly interrupted by antigovernment plots in 1970 and 1971, the program moved forward at a deliberate pace. In 1970 foreign banks and other foreign-controlled enterprises were nationalized, and in October 1972 local government reorganization was begun. On July 1, 1976, the Supreme Revolutionary Council (SRC) that had been established in the wake of the 1969 coup was abolished, and its powers were transferred to a newly created Somali Revolutionary Socialist Party (SRSP) of which Siad Barre was named secretary general. Civilian government was nominally reinstituted following popular approval of a new constitution on August 25, 1979, the one-party election of a People's Assembly on December 30, and the assembly's election of General Siad Barre as president on January 26, 1980.

A state of emergency was declared on October 21, 1980, following a resurgence of conflict with Ethiopia (for a discussion of earlier hostilities, see Foreign relations, below). Radio Mogadishu announced two days later that the SRC had been reconstituted. The emergency decree was rescinded on March 1, 1982, despite reports of a northern army mutiny in mid-February and sporadic border incidents that persisted thereafter. In the legislative election of December 31, 1984, 99.8 percent of the voters were reported to have cast ballots, with less than 1 percent opposing the SRSP's nominees.

In May 1986 Siad Barre suffered severe injuries in an automobile accident, and First Vice President Lt. Gen. Mohamed Ali SAMATAR served as de facto chief executive for several months. Although Siad Barre recovered sufficiently to be the sole candidate for reelection to a seven-year presidential term on December 23, 1986 (in the country's first direct balloting for the position), his poor health and advanced age generated intense speculation as to a successor. Samatar appeared to be a leading candidate, particularly after being additionally named to the new post of prime minister in January 1987. However, in the wake of a government reshuffle in December, all references to his vice presidential role ceased. Given the constitutional significance of the office in regard to succession, the change was interpreted as reflecting Siad Barre's desire to be succeeded either by a family member or an individual from his Marehan clan, to which Samatar did not belong.

During 1988 the Somali National Movement (SNM), a northwestern rebel group that had joined Ethiopian units in a cross-border assault the year before, mounted a broad offensive that eventually succeeded in driving government forces from most of the region's rural areas by mid-1989. President Siad Barre thereupon announced the appointment of a constitutional review committee charged with laying the groundwork for a multiparty system that would permit the SNM to engage in electoral activity, provided it did "not solely seek to satisfy tribal interests." Meanwhile, other clan-based groups had taken up arms, including the United Somali Congress (USC) in the center and the Somali Patriotic Movement (SPM) in the south.

On September 3, 1990, in the wake of heightened rebel activity, Prime Minister Samatar was dismissed in favor of Mohamed HAWADIE MADAR. On January 20, 1991, as USC forces converged on the capital, Umar ARTEH GHALIB, a former foreign minister who had only recently been released from house arrest, was asked to form an essentially transitional government, and six days later Siad Barre departed for exile in Kenya. (He died in Nigeria on January 2, 1995.) On January 28, one day after assuming control in Mogadishu, the USC appointed its principal financial backer, Ali MAHDI MOHAMED, to the post of interim president. Mahdi, in turn, named Arteh Ghalib to head a reconstituted administration on January 29. However, neither appointment proved acceptable to the SNM, which, after rejecting two invitations to attend "national reconciliation" meetings with its erstwhile allies, announced the secession of the former British Somaliland on May 18 (see entry Somaliland). Subsequently, Gen. Mohamed Farah AIDID was elected USC chair at the party's third congress held July 4–5, provoking a bitter dispute with President Mahdi because the two came from different Hawiye subclans. In early September, on at least 300 people were killed in a clash between the two factions in Mogadishu, while more intense fighting, which erupted in mid-November, resulted in the slaughter of at least 4,000 civilians by the end of the year, with some 100,000 having fled the city.

In early February 1992 General Aidid was dismissed as USC chair, formalizing the cleavage between the group's pro-Mahadi and anti-Mahdi factions. The action came after the announcement by UN Secretary General Boutros Boutros-Ghali of the first of a number of cease-fires, none of which proved effective. On April 24, in response to the team's recommendations, the Security Council authorized the creation of a United Nations Operation in Somalia (UNOSOM). Meanwhile, General Aidid launched a new opposition grouping called the Somali National Alliance (SNA).

On June 6, 1992, representatives of 11 Somali factions, meeting in Bahr Dar in northwest Ethiopia, agreed to support a UN-implemented cease-fire and convene a "comprehensive and joint conference" to "smooth the way" for the establishment of a provisional government in Somalia within three months. However, by late August, with reports that some 2,000 people were perishing daily from starvation, arrangements were made for the deployment of a 500-member UN peacekeeping force to guard relief supplies. In mid-September, responding to heightened evidence of famine, U.S. president George H. W. Bush ordered four warships with 2,400 marines to the Somali coast. On October 1, the UN announced that it was increasing its peacekeeping body to 1,200, despite protests from General Aidid, whose forces claimed control of two-thirds of the capital and most of southern Somalia. On November 27, Washington offered to provide 30,000 troops as part of a UN military intervention effort to thwart the theft of food aid. General Aidid thereupon reversed himself and hailed the U.S. overture as a way to "solve our political, economic, and social problems." On December 4, President Bush ordered the U.S. forces to Somalia as part of a projected multinational United Task Force (UNITAF) of some 35,000 soldiers.

Despite the breakdown of peace talks among 14 warring Somali factions in early January 1993, agreement was subsequently reached on a cease-fire and the appointment of a 7-member committee to lay the groundwork for a national reconciliation conference in mid-March. Meanwhile, the U.S. forces committed to "Operation Restore Hope" commenced a withdrawal, preparatory to handing peacekeeping operations over to a new 28,000-member UN Operation in Somalia (UNOSOM II) in early May.

Intense fighting erupted in the southern port city of Kismayu in mid-March 1993 between forces commanded by Siad Barre's son-in-law, Gen. Mohamed SAID HERSI, and Col. Ahmed UMAR JESS, an ally of General Aidid. However, at the conclusion of the conference in Addis Ababa, Ethiopia, on March 27, 1993, it was announced that agreement had been reached on a Transitional National Council for Somalia, which was given a mandate to lead the country to elections within two years.

On May 4, 1993, the UN formally assumed control of the multinational relief effort led since December by a U.S. commander. Unlike previous peacekeeping missions, however, the UN troops were provided with rules of engagement that permitted them to use offensive force to disarm Somali clans. This mandate was invoked on June 11 in retaliation against General Aidid, whose faction was accused of ambushing and killing 23 Pakistani peacekeepers on June 5. The action, which commenced with an attack by U.S. helicopter gunships on Aidid's Mogadishu compound, concluded on June 17 with a ground assault that failed to curb the general's military capability, Aidid himself evading capture. On November 16 the UN Security Council revoked its warrant for the arrest of Aidid, who nonetheless boycotted a further UN-sponsored peace conference in Addis Ababa in November.

Frustrated in its efforts to reconcile Somalia's rival factions, the UN Security Council voted on November 4, 1994, to withdraw the UNOSOM II force by March 31, 1995. In fact, the UN completed its withdrawal on March 1. Eleven days later Aidid and Mahdi concluded an agreement for joint control of the port and airport, both of which reopened on March 14. However, by mid-May the agreement appeared to be fading, each side charging the other with violating its terms, and on May 25 Aidid's sector of Mogadishu came under shelling from the north. On June 12 Aidid was formally ousted as SNA leader by a joint SNA-USC conference called by his longtime ally and fellow Habr Gedir subclansman, Osman HASAN ALI "Osman Ato," who was named the general's successor. Aidid, who refused to accept the conference action, responded by convening a meeting of representatives from a number of groups of supporters who unanimously elected him Somali "president" for a three-year term. On June 16 acting president Mahdi joined Osman Ato in condemning Aidid's "self-appointment."

In late August 1995 fighting broke out along a Green Line demarcating sectors of Mogadishu controlled by Aidid and Mahdi. The clash was apparently triggered by Aidid's efforts to confiscate weapons from civilians as part of a "rehabilitation and disarmament" drive, which followed the failure of a "reconciliation" conference launched by Osman Ato in Nairobi with the support of the Organization of the Islamic Conference (OIC). In September Aidid's forces captured the important town of Baidoa, some 90 miles northwest of the capital.

Aidid and his militiamen continued their offensive through early 1996, scoring a number of victories outside of the capital, including the capture of at least two more towns, before being slowed by the

Mahdi-allied Rahanweyn Resistance Army (RRA). Subsequently, theretofore low-level hostilities erupted into widespread fighting following the collapse of peace talks in April. Particularly intense clashes were reported in Mogadishu, where, in July, the warring factions were reported to be preparing for an all-out battle for control of the capital. However, on August 1, 1996, General Aidid died from wounds reportedly suffered one week earlier in a battle against Ato's forces in the Medina neighborhood of Mogadishu. Calling Aidid's death an opportunity to launch fresh peace negotiations, Mahdi and Ato immediately announced a cease-fire.

Optimism was quickly dampened, however, by the SNA's election of Aidid's son, Hussein Mohamed Farah AIDID, as "interim president of Somalia." At his "inauguration" on August 4, 1996, Aidid, a U.S.-educated former Marine who had returned to Somalia a year earlier, pledged to gain revenge on his father's killers and renewed fighting was subsequently reported in Mogadishu. Meanwhile, international observers had persuaded Aidid, Mahdi, and Ato to accept the establishment of a commission to prepare for reconciliation negotiations, and in Nairobi on October 15 the three agreed to begin a cease-fire, remove roadblocks between the areas under their control, and facilitate the distribution of humanitarian aid. The cease-fire proved short-lived, however, with fighting beginning anew in late October.

In mid-November 1996 representatives of 26 groups, including nearly all of the major factions (with the notable exception of Aidid's), convened in Sodere, Ethiopia, for peace talks sponsored by the Organization of African Unity (OAU, subsequently the African Union—AU). On January 3, 1997, the participants announced the creation of a 41-member National Salvation Council (NSC) under the leadership of five faction leaders (including Mahdi and Ato), as well as an 11-member National Executive Committee (NEC). The NSC was charged with organizing a national reconciliation conference (then scheduled for June 1997) at which a transitional government would be formed. For his part, Aidid rejected the NSC's entreaties to participate, reasserting that he was already the "legitimate leader of all Somalia."

Aidid actively sought to resuscitate the October 1996 accord, meeting and signing new pacts with Ato and Mahdi in Cairo, Egypt, in early and late May, respectively. In June the NSC rescheduled the proposed reconciliation conference to November; however, in October the conference was postponed indefinitely, ostensibly because of a lack of international funding. On the other hand, Egypt continued its efforts to provide an alternative to the now-stalemated Sodere plan, and in early December Aidid and leaders of other factions signed an accord in Cairo that included provisions for a "government of national union." The NSC ratified the accord in early January 1998 and scheduled a national reconciliation conference for February 15 to select a transitional president, government, and Council of Deputies. However, the conference was postponed, and, despite subsequent efforts to resuscitate the pact, Somalia remained without a national governing authority. (On March 20 Aidid had reportedly renounced his claim to the presidency and, restyling himself "co-president," had pledged to cooperate with nominal president Mahdi.)

On July 23, 1998, a conference of some 300 leaders from the northeast region of Puntland declared the establishment of an autonomous government under the presidency of Col. Abdullahi YUSUF AHMED, a longtime military and political leader (see Somali Salvation Democratic Front under Political Parties and Groups, below). Although the conference also established a 66-member House of Representatives (appointed by local leaders, essentially on a subclan basis), a charter endorsed by the house (as well as an informal council of traditional leaders) in September rejected secession for the region, calling instead for eventual establishment of a federal system in which regional governments would enjoy extensive autonomy. A transitional government of three years' duration was initially envisioned for Puntland.

On May 2, 2000, in Arta, Djibouti, Ismail Omar Guelleh, the new president of Djibouti, convened a Somali National Peace Conference (SNPC) of prominent Somali figures representing a wide range of constituencies, including religious groups, the business community, traditional elders, intellectuals, women's organizations, and clans. (The conference was endorsed by the UN, OAU, and the Inter-Governmental Authority on Development [IGAD].) On July 16 the SNPC approved a national charter providing for a three-year Transitional National Government (TNG) to be led by a Transitional National Assembly (TNA, appointed on a clan basis) and a president (elected by the TNA). The TNA convened for the first time in Arta on August 13, and on August 27 it elected Abdiqassim SALAD HASSAN, a former deputy prime minister and interior minister in the Siad Barre regime, as president. On October 2 Salad Hassan appointed Ali Khalif GALAYDH, a professor and prominent businessman, as prime minister. Galaydh announced his first ministerial appointments, carefully balanced among clans, on October 20. Although the fledgling interim central government subsequently moved to Mogadishu, its potential effectiveness remained in serious question because it had not received the endorsement of Somaliland, the regional administration established in Puntland, or most factional militia leaders. Of the prominent Somali "warlords," only Mahdi had attended the SNPC. He was subsequently appointed to the new assembly and pledged his support to the TNG.

In February 2001 Prime Minister Galaydh announced a cabinet reshuffle, with the pro-Mahdi faction of the USC formally joining the government. However, Galaydh's government, apparently being blamed by the public for the lack of progress in negotiations with the recalcitrant warlords, lost a confidence motion in the assembly by a reported vote of 141–29 on October 28. President Salad Hassan on November 12 named Hasan Abshir FARAH, a former cabinet member, to replace Galaydh. Following the successful negotiation of a power-sharing agreement with several minor warlords in late December, Farah announced a new cabinet on February 16, 2002.

In Puntland, as the conclusion neared of the three-year mandate accorded the transitional government of Yusuf Ahmed in 1998, in late June 2001, the House of Representatives and clan elders extended the government's authority for another three years. However, Puntland chief justice Yusuf Haji NUR in early July declared the extension "unconstitutional" and announced he had assumed authority as "acting president" pending new regional elections. Yusuf Ahmed rejected Nur's dictate, and fighting was reported in August between Yusuf Ahmed's forces (reportedly supported by Ethiopia) and those of Nur's (believed to have the support of the TNG and, according to charges from Yusuf Ahmed, the Islamic Union [see Political Parties and Groups, below].) With Yusuf Ahmed now "ruling" from the city of Galkacyo and Nur controlling the regional capital of Garowe, a controversial congress of clan elders opened in Garowe in late August. On November 14 the congress, deemed "illegal and destabilizing" by Yusuf Ahmed, elected Jama Ali JAMA, a former army colonel who had been imprisoned during the Siad Barre regime's tenure, as the new president of Puntland from among 12 candidates. Although Jama was inaugurated on November 19, Yusuf Ahmed's forces by May 2002 had effectively regained control of the region. The TNG subsequently continued to reference Jama as the "legitimate" president, but Yusuf Ahmed was still exercising full authority as the year ended.

On April 1, 2002, the self-described State of Southwestern Somalia, the third such breakaway administration (the others being Somaliland and Puntland) was formed. Although internal dissension was reported on the matter, the new regional government was launched under the umbrella of the Somali Reconciliation and Reconstruction Council (SRRC), a loose coalition of southern factions that had been launched in 2001 in opposition to the TNG (See Somali National Alliance under Political Parties and Groups, below, for additional information on the SRRC.) Col. Hassan Mohammed NUR "Shatigadud" of the RRA was named president of the new administration.

The warring factions resumed negotiations in October 2002 in Kenya, although Somaliland declined to attend. On July 5, 2003, the parties appeared to agree on a transitional peace plan, but Salad Hassan rejected the proposal, claiming that Prime Minister Farah had exceeded his authority by agreeing to allow too much power to remain at the regional level under the tentative agreement. On August 9 Salad Hassan dismissed Farah as prime minister, naming Osman JAMA ALI (former deputy prime minister) to the post. However, Jama Ali resigned on November 28, reportedly due to conflict with the president. He was succeeded on December 8 by Mohamed Abdi YUSUF, the deputy speaker of the TNA, which subsequently endorsed a new 37-member cabinet. Meanwhile, in Puntland, Yusuf Ahmed had initiated peace talks with rival groups in May 2003 that had yielded an agreement under which he was fully recognized as president while former opponents were named to the new Puntland cabinet.

In January 2004 several hitherto reluctant rebel and opposition groups (including the RRA) joined the peace negotiations in Kenya, and on January 29 some 42 factions and warlords signed a potentially historic comprehensive accord based on a Transitional Federal Charter (TFC) that provided for a transitional legislature that would elect a president and confirm a new transitional government. The TNA approved the settlement on February 9, and the new legislature (the Transitional Federal Parliament—TFP) was filled by clan and subclan appointees by early August.

In the third round of balloting for a national president in the TFP on October 10, 2004, Yusuf Ahmed was elected by a vote of 189–79. (Eleven candidates had contended the first round.) On November 3, the new president appointed Ali Mohammed GHEDI as prime minister, but the TFP on December 11 voted down his first proposed cabinet, apparently because a number of clans were not happy with their representation. However, an expanded and revised Transitional Federal Government (TFG) won TFP approval on January 7, 2005, all activity occurring in Kenya due to continued unsettled conditions in Somalia. Somaliland remained divorced from the new institutions, although the breakaway status of the State of Southwestern Somalia appeared resolved by Colonel Shatigadud's inclusion in the new national government.

Tensions over where the government should locate subsequently constrained the TFG's effectiveness, as did reported clan rivalries within the cabinet. Consequently, plans for the demobilization of clan militias in favor of a unified national army failed to produce significant results. Ghedi, the cabinet, and some legislators settled in Jowhar, while other legislators attempted to operate out of Mogadishu. Ghedi survived another assassination attempt during a trip to Mogadishu in November, an event that triggered a new round of fighting in the capital. At the same time it was reported that Islamic fighters were filtering into Mogadishu to support the Islamic Courts Union (ICU). Formed in 2004, the ICU was a fundamentalist movement devoted to the creation of an Islamic state in Somalia governed by sharia (Islamic religious law). Dominated by the Hawiye clan, the ICU created its own militia to protect the courts and help to enforce the courts' decisions. (For more on the ICU, see the 2013 *Handbook*.) The Ifka Halam court, led by Sheikh Hassan Dahir AWEYS, took control of Mogadishu along with other ICU fighters in June 2006 and held the city until December, when they were ousted by TNG-allied militias with the support of Ethiopian troops.

The TNG faced numerous internal challenges in addition to its struggle with the ICU. While Ghedi retained his post during a reorganization of the cabinet in February 2007, he resigned under intense pressure on October 29, 2007, for his inability to pacify the capital and for his support for Ethiopian troops stationed in Somalia. He was replaced by an interim prime minister, Salim Aliyow IBROW, on October 30. Tensions between Ibrow and the president led Yusuf Ahmed to name a new prime minister, Nur Hassan HUSSEIN "Nur Adde," on November 22. Nur Adde was confirmed by the TFP two days later. On December 2 Nur Adde named a new cabinet, but that government was dismissed and a new one formed on January 5, 2008. It was confirmed by the TFP on January 10. On June 9 a peace agreement was signed by the TNG and the main opposition (see Current issues, below). Ten ministers resigned on August 2 in protest over an effort by Nur Adde to dismiss the mayor of Mogadishu, an ally of Yusuf Ahmed. A new, smaller cabinet, with six vacancies, was named on August 3. Tensions between Nur Adde and the president led Yusuf Ahmed to attempt to dismiss the prime minister on December 14. However, the legislature voted to block the president's action, even as Ahmed tried to appoint former minister of internal affairs Mohammed Mahmud GULED as prime minister. Unable to remove Nur Adde, the president resigned on December 29 and was replaced on an interim basis by the speaker of the legislature, Sheikh Adan MADOBE.

On January 8, 2009, Abdirahman Mohamed MOHAMUD "Farole" was elected president of Puntland. Mohamud campaigned as a reformer and promised to improve security and economic development. Once in office, the new president undertook steps to improve cooperation with other powers to repress pirates in the region. The Puntland parliament ratified a new constitution on June 30 that introduced a multiparty political system.

Meanwhile, on January 30 Sheikh Sharif AHMED of the Islamist group the Alliance for the Liberation and Reconstruction of Somalia (ALRS) was elected president of the Somali TNG by the transitional assembly. During the second round of runoff balloting, Ahmed received 293 votes to 126 for Gen. Maslah Mohammed SIYAD, a son of the former dictator. Ahmed was a leader of the moderate faction of the ALRS (known as the "Djibouti wing"), so members of the TNG and the international community hoped his election would ease the Islamic insurgency in Somalia. The new president appointed as prime minister Omar Abdirashid Ali SHARMARKE, the son of former president Sharmarke and a Western-educated diplomat. His appointment was seen as an effort to gain the backing of both the Darod clan and the Somali expatriate community for the new government. Sharmarke formed a government of national unity that was approved by the TFP on February 22. The new cabinet initially met in Djibouti, then transitioned to Mogadishu before being forced to withdraw (see Current issues, below).

Following an agreement with the moderate Islamic group *Ahlu Sunnah Wal-Jamaa* (ASWJ) in March 2010, Sharmarke carried out a cabinet reshuffle in order to provide the ASWJ with cabinet positions. In addition, Adan Muhammad Nur MADOBE, former speaker of the transitional parliament, was appointed a deputy prime minister, and deputy prime minister Sharif Hassan Sheikh ADEN was elected speaker of the assembly. On September 21 Sharmarke resigned as prime minister, and Ahmed named Mohamed Abdullahi MOHAMED to replace him (see Current issues, below). Mohamed named a new cabinet on November 12, including members of the ASWJ.

The UN brokered a new political agreement in the spring of 2011 in which the terms of the president and parliament were extended and a new prime minister appointed (see Current issues, below). Consequently, on June 19, 2011, Mohamed resigned. Abdiweli Mohamed ALI was named prime minister and confirmed on June 23. He named a smaller, inclusive cabinet on July 23.

On March 28, 2012 Ahmed dismissed Deputy Prime Minister and Minister of Agriculture and Livestock, Mohamed Mohamud IBRAHIM, accusing him of corruption. He was replaced by Hussein Sheikh Mohamed HUSSEIN on May 3. With the TNG's mandate set to expire in August, a constituent assembly was created to draft a new constitution. The new basic law was approved on August 1.

A new federal parliament was established on August 20, 2012, under the guidelines of the new constitution. Members of the parliament were chosen by tribal and clan leaders and approved by a federal transition committee (see Legislature, below). Also on August 20, Ahmed left office and was succeeded on an interim basis by the speaker of the parliament, Muse Hassan ABDULLE (nonparty), who served for eight days until another interim president, Mohamed Osman JAWARI (nonparty), took over. Hassan Sheikh MOHAMUD (Peace and Development Party) subsequently won the second round of indirect presidential balloting by the parliament on September 10 (see Current issues). He appointed Abdi Farah SHIRDON (nonparty) prime minister. Shirdon named a new cabinet that was approved by the parliament on November 13. Fowsiyo Yusseuf Haji AADAN was appointed deputy prime minister and foreign minister, the first woman in Somalia to hold these positions. Shirdon lost a no-confidence vote on December 2 (see Current issues, below). Mohamud appointed Abdiweli Sheikh AHMED (nonparty) as prime minister on December 12. Ahmed was unanimously confirmed on December 21 and named a new, substantially larger cabinet on January 16, 2014.

Tensions between the president and prime minister escalated through 2014. Mohamud rejected a cabinet reshuffle by Ahmed on October 25, 2014, and the prime minister subsequently lost a vote of no confidence, 153–80, on December 6. Mohamud appointed former prime minister Sharmarke to replace Ahmed on December 17. Parliament approved his appointment on December 24. He named a new cabinet on January 12, but parliamentary opposition caused him to nominate a new government on January 27, 2016. The assembly approved the cabinet on February 9.

Constitution and government. For the decade after the October 1969 coup, supreme power was vested in the Central Committee of the SRSP, whose secretary general served as head of state and chief executive. For all practical purposes these arrangements were continued under a constitution approved in 1979, which provided additionally for a People's Assembly of 177 members, 171 of whom were nominated by the party and 6 by the president. The president was popularly elected for a seven-year term after having been nominated by the SRSP as the sole candidate. These and other provisions of the 1979 basic law were effectively suspended with the collapse of the Siad Barre regime in January 1991, following which the independent republic of Somaliland was declared in May in the northwest (see separate entry for details on the administration in Somaliland).

In part with the goal of encouraging eventual participation by the administrations already established in Somaliland and Puntland, the national charter adopted by the SNPC in July 2000 called for a federal system with strong regional governments. Pending formal establishment of such a system under a new constitution, the SNPC authorized a three-year TNG, with legislative responsibility delegated to an appointed House of Representatives. The charter also promised an independent judiciary, protection of the freedom of expression and other human rights, and support for multiparty activity. (For details of transitional institutions established through the Transitional Federal

Charter of January 2004, see Political background, above.) In March 2009 the cabinet voted to impose sharia law throughout Somalia.

A constituent assembly approved a new constitution on August 1, 2012. The new basic law created a bicameral legislature with members directly elected for four-year terms. The head of state is the president who is elected by both chambers of the legislature for a four-year term. The president is commander-in-chief of the military. The head of government is a prime minister appointed by the president and confirmed by the parliament. The judiciary consists of national and regional courts, with a constitutional court as the nation's supreme judicial body.

Administratively, the country is divided into 18 regions (including the autonomous areas of Somaliland and Puntland), which are subdivided into 70 districts, plus the city of Mogadishu.

The press is undeveloped. Few people are literate enough to read newspapers or wealthy enough to buy them. Both the ICU and the interim government have reportedly repressed independent media and have harassed and assassinated journalists. In 2011 the government launched a state-run television service, the first since 1991. In 2012, 18 journalists or media figures were killed in Somalia and 7 more in 2013. In January 2016 a controversial new media law required all reporters and journalists to register with the government and pay an annual fee. In its 2016 ranking of press freedom, Reporters Without Borders ranked Somalia 167th out of 180 countries.

Foreign relations. Although a member of the United Nations, the AU, and the Arab League, Somalia has been chiefly concerned with the problems of its own immediate area, where seasonal migrations by Somali herdsmen have long strained relations with neighboring states. (For information on Somalia's foreign relations prior to 1979, see the 2012 *Handbook.*) Although the 1979 constitution called for "the liberation of Somali territories under colonial occupation"—implicitly referencing Somali-populated areas of Kenya as well as of Ethiopia—the Somalis promised that they would not intervene militarily in support of external dissidents. Tense relations and occasional border hostilities continued, however, with Ethiopia supporting the major Somali opposition groups in guerrilla operations. In January 1986 President Siad Barre and Ethiopian leader Mengistu Haile Mariam established a joint ministerial commission to resolve the Ogaden question, but no results were achieved during the ensuing year, with Somalia condemning Ethiopia for a cross-border attack in February 1987. Following major Ethiopian reverses at the hands of Eritrean secessionists in the north, Siad Barre and Mengistu conferred during a drought conference in Djibouti in March 1988 and agreed to peace talks in Mogadishu in early April. The discussions yielded a communiqué that pledged a military "disengagement and separation," an exchange of prisoners, the reestablishment of diplomatic relations, and the joint cessation of support for opposition groups.

In early August 1996 Ethiopian forces attacked three towns in Somalia's Gedo region in an apparent attempt to squash the activities of the Islamic Union (see Political Parties and Groups, below), which had claimed credit for bombings and assassination attempts in Ethiopia as part of its campaign for the Ogaden region's independence. The offensive continued into 1997, and by early February Ethiopian troops had reportedly overrun the Islamic fighters' last base in the region. Ethiopia's military advances proved costly on the diplomatic front, however, as a number of Somalian faction leaders, most important the SNA's Aidid, condemned the "occupation" and refused to participate in the peace process launched in November 1996 in Sodere, Ethiopia. Thereafter, Aidid's efforts to revive the short-lived Nairobi accord of October 1996 were actively supported by Kenya and Egypt. The latter championed the establishment of a unified and centrally governed Somalia as opposed to an Ethiopian diplomatic advance, which one analyst labeled "divisive." Much of southern Somalia subsequently came under Ethiopian influence as the result of Ethiopian initiatives relating to its war with Eritrea in 1998–2000. The TNG in Somalia subsequently accused Ethiopia of supplying weapons to anti-TNG warlords in Somalia. Meanwhile, the activities of the Islamic Union also attracted the interest of the United States because of the latter's "war on terrorism" following the terrorist attacks in September 2001.

Many African states recognized the TFG established in late 2004 and early 2005 to govern Somalia, and the AU authorized a contingency peacekeeping force for possible deployment in Somalia. Meanwhile, the EU pledged financial and technical aid for the new administration, but the United States had developed only "informal ties" with the TFG as of mid-2005. However, responding to the risk of potential Islamic terrorist activity in the region, the U.S. government has tacitly supported the TFG in its battles against Islamist militias and was directly involved in at least one air-strike against al-Qaida targets near the Somali-Kenyan border in January 2007 (see Current issues, below). Negotiations over the proposed AU peacekeeping force continued through 2006. The UN authorized the deployment of the AU force, the African Union Mission in Somalia (AMISOM), in February 2007. Although AMISOM was designated to have up to 8,000 troops, only 2,600 peacekeepers were dispatched, mainly from Uganda and Burundi. AMISOM was initially deployed only in Mogadishu.

In April 2006 Prime Minister Ghedi gave the United States permission to patrol the waters off the coast of Somalia to suppress piracy. Reports had also previously surfaced that U.S. marines and special forces had undertaken several covert antiterrorist operations in Somalia, prompting minor rioting and protests in some cities. During 2007, the United States launched at least four airstrikes against suspected terrorist targets. More than 40 pirate attacks occurred in Somali waters during 2007 and early 2008, including an attack on a Spanish fishing boat with a crew of 26 that was captured in April 2008 and released only after a ransom of $1.2 million was paid. In response to these attacks, the UN Security Council on June 2 authorized countries that had prior agreements with the TNG to enter Somali waters to interdict or apprehend pirates, based on the existing model between the United States and Somalia. After a Ukrainian vessel carrying 33 tanks en route to Kenya was hijacked in September, Russia deployed naval forces to the region. In April Somali pirates captured a U.S. vessel, the *Maersk Alabama.* U.S. naval forces killed three pirates while rescuing the ship's captain on April 12. Meanwhile, a hostage was killed when French forces recaptured the *Tanit.* In December the EU initiated a joint naval deployment to suppress pirates in Somali waters. The mission was undertaken following a UN Security Council Resolution that granted member states expanded authority to take steps to counter piracy in the region, including pursuing pirates on land.

In November 2008 Ethiopia announced the withdrawal of all its forces from Somalia. The last Ethiopian troops departed in January 2009, but reports in June indicated that Ethiopian forces had again crossed the border. Meanwhile, on January 16 the UN Security Council authorized the deployment of a UN peacekeeping force to replace AMISOM, but no formal steps had been taken to deploy a force by the summer of 2011. By January 2009 pirates had possession of at least 14 vessels captured in Somali waters. In April international donors pledged more than $250 million in economic and security aid for the TNG.

Through 2009, piracy continued in Somali waters despite increased international naval patrols and deaths of pirates in 214 attacks and 47 hijackings. By year's end more than 100 suspected Somali pirates were in custody awaiting trial in various locations outside of Somalia.

Ethiopian forces crossed into Somalia in May 2010, during fighting that left 13 dead and dozens wounded. Reports through the year indicated that Ethiopian incursions into Somalia continued. In July *Al-Shabaab* terrorists launched a series of bomb attacks in Kampala, Uganda, that killed 76 people. The strikes were reportedly in retaliation for Uganda's participation in AMISOM. Also in July, AU leaders rejected a UN call to expand AMISOM's mandate but pledged to contribute more troops to the peacekeeping mission. AMISOM troops were subsequently increased from 5,000 to 6,300. A covert U.S. military mission on September 14 killed a leading Somali al-Qaida figure, Saleh Ali Saleh NABHAN. In response *Al-Shabaab* conducted a suicide bombing against the main AMISOM headquarters in Mogadishu.

In January 2011 the International Maritime Bureau reported that 49 ships had been hijacked by Somali pirates in 2010 and more than 1,000 foreign sailors had been taken hostage. By the end of that year, pirates held 31 vessels and more than 700 crewmen hostage.

AMISOM and progovernment forces launched a major campaign against *Al-Shabaab* in February 2011 in the southern areas of the country. More than 50 coalition troops and more than 100 insurgents were killed. In order to bolster AMISOM, Uganda deployed an additional 750 troops in 2011, and the EU provided a further €47 million to support the mission. Increased antipiracy patrols led to a series of setbacks for would-be pirates. For instance, on March 13 two Indian naval vessels captured 61 pirates from a mother ship that was used to launch raids against commercial vessels. On June 23 a U.S. pilotless drone attack killed two *Al-Shabaab* leaders in the first such strike in Somalia. Two days later, the United States pledged $45 million to Burundi and Uganda to fight *Al-Shabaab*.

On October 16, 2011, 1,600 Kenyan troops invaded Somalia as part of a coordinated effort, with Ethiopia, to suppress *Al-Shabaab* (see entry on Kenya). Also in October, African Union Mission in Somalia

(ANISOM) troops recaptured the last areas of Mogadishu held by *Al-Shabaab*. Twelve ANISOM troops were killed in the fighting. ANISOM subsequently expanded its operations into other regions of Somalia. On October 24 the UN Security Council adopted a resolution that called for member states to cooperate in efforts to suppress piracy and hostage taking in the region. Meanwhile, U.S., British, and Kenyan naval and security forces conducted a series of operations and rescue missions to free hijacked vessels off of Somalia.

On February 23, 2012, the London Summit brought together representatives from 55 countries and international groups for talks on Somalia. Participants called for greater international cooperation to suppress piracy and terrorism and for the creation of a permanent government to replace the TFG. On February 25 the UN Security Council approved the expansion of ANISOM to 17,700 troops and the integration of Kenyan forces in Somalia as part of the mission. In March South Africa established diplomatic relations with Somalia.

Kenyan and progovernment forces conducted an amphibious landing on Kismaayo on September 28, 2012. The city was the last major stronghold of *Al-Shabaab*. Allied forces quickly captured the town. In October, security officials in Puntland captured a Yemeni vessel loaded with weapons for *Al-Shabaab*. The incident led international security officials to express concerns over expanding cooperation between *Al-Shabaab* and al-Qaida in the Arabian Peninsula (AQAP). Puntland forces also freed the crew of a Panamanian vessel on December 23. The hostages had been held since 2010, the longest of any hijacked crew. Meanwhile, by the end of 2012, pirate attacks in Somali waters had fallen to a three-year low with just 36 incidents.

A failed attempt by French security forces to rescue French intelligence agent Denis ALLEX on January 11, 2013, left the hostage, two soldiers, and 17 *Al-Shabaab* fighters dead. Allex had been captured by *Al-Shabaab* in July 2009.

On January 17, 2013, the United States recognized the government of Somalia for the first time since 1991 as part of a broader international effort to bolster the legitimacy of the new government. International donors, including the United States, the UK, China, and the World Bank, pledged more than $300 million in aid for Somalia at a conference in London that ended on May 7.

In March 2013 the UN Security Council curtailed its arms embargo on Somalia, in place since 1992, to allow the government to purchase weapons and munitions. In May the UN Security Council voted to end the world body's existing political mission in Somalia, the UN Political Office for Somalia (UNPOS), and replace it with the UN Assistance Mission in Somalia (UNSOM). Whereas UNPOS focused on political reconciliation, UNSOM was tasked to aid in reconstruction. UNSOM began operations in June. In November the UN facilitated an agreement between Somalia and Kenya to begin voluntary repatriations of the more than 400,000 Somali refugees in Kenya. The accord also called for the closure of exiting refugee camps, which the Kenyan government charged had become recruiting centers for Islamic militants.

During 2013 there were only seven pirate attacks and no successful hijackings. However, on January 19, 2014, pirates were able to capture a vessel. In April 2014 the Somalia ambassador to Kenya returned to Mogadishu and launched a vigorous protest after a Somali consular officer was briefly arrested in Kenya (see entry on Kenya). Reports indicated that, by the summer of 2014, between 80,000 and 100,000 refugees had returned to Somalia from Kenya.

In April 2014 British officials pledged $16.7 million annually to support the Somali security forces. On July 11 former prime minister Sharmarke became the first Somali ambassador to the United States in more than 20 years. Meanwhile the United States announced it would nominate an ambassador to Somalia. China also announced it would reopen its embassy in Somalia after 23 years.

On May 5, 2015, John Kerry became the first U.S. secretary of state to visit Somalia. During his three-hour stay, Kerry met with Somali leaders and pledged continuing U.S. security and economic support. Somalia and India reestablished diplomatic relations in July; they had collapsed in 1991.

In October 2015 the EU provided the AU with €165 million to support the operating costs of AMISOM. In November the UN Security Council voted to authorize a new support mission for AMISOM, the UN Support Office in Somalia (UNSOS). UNSOS was tasked to provide logistical and medical support for AMISOM and the Somali national army. Also in November Michael KEATING of the United Kingdom was appointed as the new head of UNSOM and the UN secretary general's special envoy to Somalia.

Somalis expelled all Iranian diplomats on January 7, 2016, officially for undermining Somali security, but reportedly in solidarity with Saudi Arabia in its ongoing struggle with Iran in Yemen (see entry on Yemen). Saudi Arabia simultaneously pledged $50 million in aid for Somalia. In June Stephen SCHWARTZ became the first U.S. ambassador to Somali since 1991.

Current issues. The cabinet was reconstituted in February 2007 in response TFP dissatisfaction with cabinet members' attendance and work ethic. In September 2007, at a congress of opposition groups in Eritrea, a new coalition, the Alliance for the Liberation and Reconstruction of Somalia (ALRS), alternatively known as the Alliance for the Reliberation of Somalia (ARS), was created. The ALRS hoped to coordinate political and military efforts against the TNG (see Political Parties and Groups, below). Meanwhile, the TFG was hampered by infighting between President Ahmed and Prime Minister Ghedi, who were at odds over the handling of the Islamist insurgency. Ghedi resigned on October 29, 2007, following immense pressure from Ahmed and the transitional parliament. President Ahmed designated Deputy Prime Minister Salim Aliyow Ibrow as interim prime minister on October 30. (The president is required to appoint a permanent replacement within 30 days.) Nur Hassan Hussein "Nur Adde" was appointed prime minister on November 22. However, conflicts quickly emerged between Yusuf Ahmed and Nur Adde over the insurgency.

Ongoing territorial disagreements between Puntland and neighboring Somaliland continued to complicate relations in the Horn of Africa in 2007. Fighting subsequently broke out between the neighbors in early October 2007 in one of the contested cities, Sool, which itself is split between sub-clans calling for Sool's independence, or backing either Somaliland or Puntland in the dispute (see Somaliland entry).

In March 2008 renewed violence in the capital killed scores of people and prompted an estimated 20,000 to flee Mogadishu. Then in May massive food riots in Mogadishu over rising prices led to a new wave of refugees. On June 9 an 11-point peace agreement was signed between the TNG and the ALRS following negotiations sponsored by the UN. However, hard-line factions within the ALRS rejected the agreement and vowed to continue fighting until Ethiopian troops were withdrawn. The factions rejected a new round of negotiations between the TNG and the ALRS in August in Djibouti. Osman Ali Ahmed, the head of the UN's development program in Somalia, was killed by gunmen on July 6. Renewed fighting in Mogadishu in September left at least 100 dead and prompted a new wave of refugees. In addition, 30 trucks of the World Food Program were looted by hungry crowds on September 25.

Islamic fighters formed a new group, *Al-Shabaab*, in late 2008. *Al-Shabaab* opposed both the TNG and the ICU and as Ethiopian troops withdrew in 2009 was able to capture large areas of Somalia, including Baidoa, the interim site of the nominal government. In February 2009 *Al-Shabaab* forces killed 11 AMISOM troops in a battle in Mogadishu and subsequently launched a series of targeted assassinations and suicide bombings. The group claimed responsibility for a suicide bombing that killed Security Minister Omar HASHI on June 18 and a subsequent failed assassination attempt on the interior minister. Fighting forced the TNG to again withdraw from Mogadishu. By the end of July renewed fighting in and around Mogadishu was estimated to have killed 200 civilians and displaced more than 100,000. In October fighting broke out between *Al-Shabaab* and the Party of Islam (*Hizb al-Islam*). An *Al-Shabaab* suicide attack on December 3 killed 22, including 3 government ministers, at a university graduation ceremony in Mogadishu.

On January 5, 2010, the World Food Program suspended operations in southern Somalia due to violence and demands from *Al-Shabaab* that the program pay the Islamic group for security and dismiss its female staff members. From March through June, heavy fighting in Mogadishu between *Al-Shabaab* and government forces, supported by AMISOM and ASWJ fighters, left more than 100 dead and at least 1,000 wounded. Meanwhile, in combat in Kismaayo between Islamic militants and AMISOM, Sheikh Daud Ali HASAN, an *Al-Shabaab* leader, was killed. An *Al-Shabaab* attack on a hotel in Mogadishu killed 33, including 6 members of the interim assembly on August 24. Also in August Mohamed Abdi GAG declared a new autonomous republic in Hiiraan region of central Somalia.

In May 2010 President Ahmed attempted unsuccessfully to dismiss Prime Minister Sharmarke. Sharmarke subsequently resigned on September 21, citing disputes with Ahmed over a new draft constitution. Deputy Prime Minister Abdiwahid Ilmi GONJEH was appointed interim prime minister. The president appointed Mohamed Abdullahi MOHAMED on October 14, but his confirmation was stalled in the legislature due to a dispute over the manner in which his confirmation vote would be held. Mohamed was sworn in on November 1 and appointed a new cabinet the following day. Meanwhile, government troops and allied militia forces were able to recapture large portions of Mogadishu and areas near the Kenyan border in an offensive in October. The fighting created more than 60,000 new refugees.

International efforts to resolve tensions between President Ahmed and the powerful speaker of the legislature, Sharif Hassan Sheikh Aden, led to the June 9, 2011, Kampala accord. Brokered by the UN and Uganda, the deal allowed Ahmed and TFP to remain in office for an additional year in exchange for a pledge to conduct elections before August 2012. Mohamed was forced to resign, and Abdiweli Mohamed Ali was appointed prime minister on June 23. Reports indicated that Mohamed's resignation was a precondition for Aden's acceptance of the accord. Mohamed was widely perceived as the most proficient prime minister in recent history, and news of his resignation prompted demonstrations and riots in Mogadishu. Meanwhile, on June 10 the Interior and National Security Minister, Abdishakur Sheikh Hasan Farah, was assassinated by a suicide bomber.

Throughout the summer of 2011, a severe drought put an estimated 2 million people at risk of starvation. The famine was exacerbated by continued fighting, which prevented international aid groups from conducting humanitarian operations. On October 4 an *Al-Shabaab* suicide bomber killed more than 100 in Mogadishu.

By February 2012 the famine and drought had ended as the country experienced a record harvest. Following the adoption of a new constitution on August 1 and the inauguration of the new lower chamber of parliament on August 20, 22 candidates contested the indirect balloting for president. Former president Ahmed received a plurality in the first round, prompting a runoff election. He was defeated in the second round on September 10 by Hassan Sheikh Mohamud who was sworn in six days later. Meanwhile, Mohamud survived an assassination attempt on September 12.

On March 18, 2013, ten people were killed and dozens injured in a car bomb attack in Mogadishu that was described as the worst terrorist attack in the capital in more than a year. In response, General Ahmed Moallim FIQI, the director of Somalia's intelligence and security agency, resigned. In April Puntland postponed local elections scheduled for May 15. Ahmed Mohamed ISLAAN "Madobe," the leader of the pro-Kenyan Oagden Ras Kambori Brigade, was declared president of Jubaland in May 2013, following a conference of tribal elders. The Mohamud government refused to recognize Madobe. Meanwhile, rival claimants launched a series of attacks on the areas under control of Madobe's militia. In August the federal government signed a peace agreement with Jubaland that recognized the region's existing administration and called for the integration of Jubaland's militias into the federal security forces. The accord designated the region as Juba Federal State on an interim basis for a two-year transitional period.

In November 2013 reports emerged that President Mohamud had refused to accept recommendations for a cabinet reshuffle from Prime Minister Shirdon. The president subsequently asked the prime minister to resign, but he refused. Shirdon lost a vote of no confidence in December, 184 to 65. The prime minister was replaced by Abdiweli Sheikh Ahmed on December 12. In security sweeps in December more than 600 suspected militants were arrested.

On February 21, 2014, *Al-Shabaab* fighters attacked the presidential palace in Mogadishu, but all nine attackers were killed, along with five security guards, and Mohamud was unhurt. Other *Al-Shabaab* raids in April killed one member of parliament and resulted in the kidnapping of another. In June the federal government announced the creation of a three-region state in southwestern Somalia in an effort to end fighting between factions in the area. The new region, Southwest State, would include Bay, Bakool, and Lower Shabelle. On March 27 more than 700 clan leaders and officials elected Mohamed Haji ABDINUR as president of the state. In July reports indicated creation of another region, Central Somalia, in the Galgadud and Mudug regions. In October the presidents of the Somali federal government and Puntland signed a 12-point agreement that paved the way for negotiations to reintegrate the breakaway province into the federal system.

In April 2015 a 75-member regional assembly was inaugurated in Kismaayo, Jubaland. However, in June the government for South Jubaland announced it had suspended cooperation with the federal administration after the national assembly voted no confidence in the regional government. Relations were restored following negotiations overseen by UN officials. Also in June AMISOM troops, along with Somali national army forces, launched a major offensive against *Al-Shabaab* in the southern bay region. Multinational forces recaptured the town of Toorotorow, killing a reported 40 militants. On June 26, 35 AMISOM troops were killed when *Al-Shabaab* overran a military compound in Leego. The following month AMISOM and federal troops recaptured the towns of Bardera and Dinsoor, which had been under the control of *Al-Shabaab* since 2008.

On August 15, 2015, Madobe, the incumbent president of Jubaland, was reelected by the regional legislature.

Al-Shabaab fighters overran the Kenyan El Adde AMISOM base on January 15, 2016, reportedly killing 100 soldiers. Reports in January indicated that *Al-Shabaab* fighters attacked militias that had pledged allegiance to the Islamic State.

Presidential and other elections were repeatedly postponed. In August 2016 balloting for the presidency was postponed until October 30 of that year by the National Leadership Forum, composed of the president, prime minister, and regional leaders. Opposition groups and rival presidential candidates condemned the postponement, especially after reports emerged that polling might be further delayed until December. At the meeting, leaders endorsed a 30 percent minimum quota for women members in the House and Senate.

POLITICAL PARTIES AND GROUPS

From the time of its inaugural congress in June 1976 to the nominal authorization of a multiparty system in December 1990, the **Somali Revolutionary Socialist Party** (SRSP) was the country's only authorized political formation. The SRSP virtually ceased to exist with the collapse of the Siad Barre regime in January 1991, at which time a large number of additional groups, almost all of them clan-based, emerged from clandestine or insurrectionary activity. The most important of the new formations was the United Somali Congress (USC), organized in January 1989. Subsequently, in November 1993 several components of the USC helped to launch the **Somali Salvation Alliance** (SSA), a loose coalition that also included components of a number of parties, as well as the **Somali Democratic Front,** led by Ali MOHAMED HAMED; the **Somali National Democratic Union** (SNDU); and the **Somali National Union** (SNU), led by Mohamed RAJIS MOHAMED. The SSA was supportive of Ali MAHDI MOHAMED (who had become the nominal president of Somalia in 1991 following the ouster of Gen. Siad Barre) in his leadership fight with Gen. Mohamed Farah Aidid and, after 1996, General Aidid's son, Hussein Mohamed Farah Aidid. Both Aidids were supported by the Somali National Alliance (SNA, see below).

Peace and Development Party (*Xisbiga Nabadda Iyo Horumarka*—PDP). The PDP was a social democratic grouping launched in April 2011 at a congress that also elected Hassan Sheikh MOHAMUD as party chairman. The PDP is comprised mainly of members of the New Blood (*Damul Jadiid*) faction of the **Muslim Brotherhood** (*al-Islah*). In September 2012 Mohamud was elected president of Somalia by the country's new parliament.

Leaders: Hassan Sheikh MOHAMUD (President of the Republic and Party Chair), Hamza Abdi AAR (Secretary General).

Alliance for the Liberation and Restoration of Somalia (ALRS). The ALRS was a loose coalition of opposition groups formed following a congress in Asmara, Eritrea, in September 2007. The coalition was an effort by Islamic resistance groups, such as the ICU, to reach out to secular and other opposition parties. Sheikh Sharif Ahmed of the ICU was named chair of the group, while Sheikh Hassan Dahir Aweys of the ICU emerged as the main leader of the ALRS's central committee. By late 2008 the ALRS was divided into two broad camps, the moderate Djibouti faction, which sought reconciliation with the TNG, and the hard-line Asmara wing, led by Aweys, which refused to negotiate with the interim government and eventually formed the **Party of Islam** (*Hizb al-Islam*) and then merged with *Al-Shabaab* (see below). The ALRS signed a new peace accord with the TNG in October 2008. Although the agreement was rejected by the Asmara faction, the accord paved the way for the expansion of the TFP to include ALRS deputies and the election of Ahmed as the president of the TNG. The new cabinet included a number of ALRS ministers. In July 2010 Mohammad Ahmed TARZAN of the ALRS was appointed mayor of Mogadishu. President Ahmed rejected a UN plan for elections in April 2011 and instead agreed to an extension of his term until August 2012. Ahmed faced criticism within the ALRS for cooperating with Kenya and Ethiopia, two mainly Christian nations, in the campaign against

Al-Shabaab. Ahmed was defeated in the second round of indirect balloting for the Somali presidency in September 2012. Reports indicated that supporters of Ahmed were behind a letter signed by 100 parliamentarians that called for President Mohamud to resign on May 8, 2014, because of a lack of progress on security issues.

Leaders: Sheikh Sharif AHMED (Former President of the Transitional National Government and Leader of the Djibouti Faction), Sheikh Yusuf Mohammad SIYAD "Indha Adde."

United Somali Congress (USC). Organized in January 1989 by members of the Hawiye clan of central Somalia, the USC was instrumental in the ouster of President Siad Barre in 1991, and the grouping's principal financial backer, Ali Mahdi Mohamed, was shortly thereafter named interim president of the republic. However, at the party's third congress held July 4–5, Gen. Mohamed Farah Aidid was elected USC chair, provoking a bitter dispute with Mahdi and clashes between their respective factions in the autumn that produced widespread death and dislocation in Mogadishu. The USC subsequently remained split between pro-Mahdi and pro-Aidid factions referenced as the USC-SSA and USC-SNA, respectively. Further splintering occurred in June 1995 when Osman Hasan Ali "Osman Ato," a longtime ally of Aidid's, turned against the general and was named chair of a dissident USC-SNA. The USC-SNA later became the core of the Somali Reconciliation and Reconstruction Council (SRRC).

In February 2001 Muhammad Qanyarsh AFRAH, a USC leader, was named to the cabinet. However, a major USC-SSA faction, under the leadership of Musa Sudi YALLAHOW (who had challenged Mahdi for the SSA leadership in 1999) and Umar Muhammad MAHMUD "Umar Finish," continued to reject participation in the government. Further splintering occurred in December when Umar Finish and his supporters signed the proposed expanded power-sharing agreement, while Yallahow opposed the pact. Fighters loyal to Yallahow engaged TNG troops routinely throughout 2002, and his faction remained an integral part of the SRRC and joined in the launching of the breakaway autonomous administration in the southwest (see Political background, above). Some factions joined in the negotiations, which resulted in the 2004 TFC, and Osman Ato and Yallahow joined the 2004 transitional government. No longer a united front, factions of the party support different warlords, such as Ato and Yallahow, and continued to support the TNG. However, other faction leaders opposed the presidency of Yusuf Ahmed. Most of the former USC factions are united in their opposition to *Al-Shabaab* and other fundamentalist Islamic groups.

Somali National Alliance (SNA). The SNA was launched by Gen. Mohamed Farah Aidid following the leadership conflict in 1992 in the USC (see above). The SNA claimed the support of some two dozen affiliates. (For more on the early history of the SNA, see the 2014 *Handbook.*)

Following the death of General Aidid in August 1996, his son, Hussein Mohamed Farah Aidid, an American-educated former U.S. Marine, was elected "president" and SNA leader in a three-day, two-part electoral process that reportedly split the clan along generational lines. Subsequently, although there was widespread speculation that the younger Aidid would only serve as a figurehead for the SNA's militia, he immediately pursued reconciliation pacts with a number of SNA clan leaders whom his father had alienated.

In April 1997 approximately 800 SNA militants broke off from the grouping, accusing the Farah Aidid "government" of corruption and complaining that they had not been given the respect due a national army. SNA militiamen subsequently battled with forces from the RRA (below) for control of Baidoa.

Aidid, whose militia continued to control portions of Mogadishu and surrounding areas, declined to participate in the SNPC, held in Arta, Djibouti, in 2000, and rejected the resultant transitional government. In early 2001 Aidid, still referring to himself as chair of the SNA, was announced as chair of the Somali Reconciliation and Reconstruction Council (SRRC), a new grouping of some 21 southern faction leaders committed to establishing their own interim central government as an alternative to the "Arta" plan.

Other prominent SRRC members included the RRA, and a main faction of the SPM. Aidid was elected as the first SRRC chair, while Mawlid MA'ANE MAGMUD was named as the group's general secretary. However, Ma'ane Magmud, described as the leader of the Bantu community in Somalia, broke from the SRRC and endorsed the December 2001 power-sharing agreement between the TNG and several warlords and faction leaders. The SRRC subsequently continued to serve as the primary challenge to the TNG's authority, and in April 2002 it announced the formation of a breakaway state in southern Somalia. Farah Aidid supported the 2004 TFC and was appointed a deputy prime minister and the internal affairs minister in the December transitional government. Aidid's portfolio was then shifted to minister of public works and housing during the cabinet reshuffle of February 2007. In May 2007 PM Ghedi sacked him from the cabinet completely, though he maintained a parliamentary seat in the TFP and was a vocal opponent of the Ethiopian troop presence in the country. Reports in 2008 indicated that Aidid and his followers had joined the ALRS and had established a base of operations in Asmara, Eritrea. In February 2012 Aidid ally Abdi Hasan Awale QEYBDID survived a suicide bombing in Puntland.

Leader: Hussein Mohamed FARAH AIDID (Chair).

Rahanweyn Resistance Army (RRA). Assisted by troops from Ethiopia, the RRA in 1999 seized control of much of south-central Somalia (home to the Digil and Mirifle clans) and expelled Ethiopian rebel groups from the region. The RRA was a core component of the Somali Peace Alliance (SPA), established in August 1999 to promote the "rebuilding" of a central government through the initial establishment of a number of autonomous regional governments. (The SPA was led by Col. Abdullahi Yusuf Ahmed of Puntland and also included the pro-Ethiopian wing of the SNF.) In December 2000, the leader of the RRA, Col. Hassan Mohammed Nur "Shatigadud," rejected the authority of the TNG, and the RRA subsequently indicated plans to set up its own regional administration. In January 2001 the SPA appeared to have been superseded by a National Restoration Council (NRC), itself a precursor, in part at least, to the SRRC (see SNA, above). Colonel Shatigadud was elected president of the Southwestern Regional Government announced in April 2002, although some RRA members, led by Muhammad Ibrahim HABSADE and Adan Muhammad Nur MADOBE, opposed that initiative. Fierce fighting was subsequently reported between the two RRA factions. Shatigadud was appointed agriculture minister in December 2004 and changed his portfolio to finance minister in 2005, but resigned from the government in December 2007 after being appointed minister of national security. Madobe was appointed minister of justice in the transitional government and became speaker of parliament in January 2007. He briefly served as interim president of the TNG following the resignation of Ahmed in 2008 and was instrumental in the negotiations that led to the reconciliation between the government and the ALRS in January 2009. He was appointed a deputy prime minister in 2009 but lost his position in a subsequent cabinet reshuffle. The RRA was reported to be in talks with other groups for an alliance ahead of the selection of a new president in August 2012. On April 8, 2013, Shatigadud died of a heart attack. Madobe was appointed minister of commerce and industry in the cabinet in January 2014.

Leaders: Adan Muhammad Nur MADOBE (Minister of Commerce and Industry), Mohamed Ali Adeh QALINLEH.

Ahl al-Sunnah wal-Jamaa (ASWJ). The ASWJ is a moderate, Sufi Islamic group founded in 1991 in an effort to counter the growing militancy of some sects in Somalia. Over the next decade it slowly increased its authority in Galguduud Province in central Somalia with military and financial support from Ethiopia. In 2009 the ASWJ created a semiautonomous government for the region. However, in March 2010 the ASWJ agreed to support the TFG and several group leaders were appointed to the government. In September 2010 reports indicated a division within the group, with one faction advocating withdrawal from the TFG and the other pledging to continue to work with the interim government. ASWJ militias were instrumental in the campaign against *Al-Shabaab* from 2010 through 2012. However, ASWJ forces attacked Somali national forces and captured Dhuusa Mareeb, the capital of Galguduud on June 7, 2015.

Leaders: Sheikh Muhammad Sheikh HASSAN, Sheikh Omar Sheikh Muhammad FARAH.

Mujahideen Youth Movement (*Harakat al-Shabaab al-Mujahidin,* or more commonly "*Al-Shabaab*"). *Al-Shabaab* is a fundamentalist Islamic movement led by Sheikh Muktar Abdirahman GODANE, which captured large areas of Somalia in 2009 in an alliance with *Hizb al-Islam.* It also launched an increasing number of terrorist attacks in 2009 and 2010, including suicide bombings. *Al-Shabaab* was reported to have received substantial financial and military support from Saudi Arabia and has drawn a significant number of foreign fighters to

Somalia. Aden Hashi AYRO, the leader of *Al-Shabaab* and the head of al-Qaida in Somalia, was killed in U.S. air strikes on May 1, 2008. In 2010 the **Party of Islam** (*Hizb al-Islam*), formed in 2008 as an Islamic party, was absorbed into *Al-Shabaab*. (For more information on *Hizb al-Islam*, see the 2012 *Handbook*.) Former ICU and *Hizb al-Islam* leader Sheikh Hassan Dahir AWEYS became a leader in *Al-Shabaab* in 2011. Through 2013 the group suffered a number of military defeats by AMISOM and progovernment forces. In 2013 *Al-Shabaab* was estimated to have approximately 10,000 fighters and allied militiamen. On September 12 *Al-Shabaab* commander Omar HAMMAMI was killed by a rival faction of the grouping loyal to Godane. Reports indicated the killing reflected growing dissension within the group. *Al-Shabaab* militants carried out an attack on the Westgate Mall in Nairobi, Kenya, in September, killing 63 (see entry on Kenya) in retaliation for Kenya's military presence in Somalia.

On January 26, 2014, a U.S. drone attack killed Sahal ISKUDHUQ, a senior *Al-Shabaab* official.

A U.S. drone attack killed *Al-Shabaab* commander Adnan GARAAR on March 12, 2015, in the bay area. Garaar was thought to be behind the 2013 Westgate Mall attack (see entry on Kenya). On January 31, 2016, a drone strike killed Abdinur MAHDI ("Yusuf DHEEG"), reported to be *Al-Shabaab*'s chief of operations.

Leaders: Sheikh Muktar Abdirahman GODANE, Sheikh Hassan Dahir AWEYS.

Horseed. Formed in November 2012 in anticipation of presidential elections in 2014, *Horseed* is a regional grouping in Puntland. *Horseed* is the political base of former Puntland president Abdirahman Mohamed Mohamud "Farole." Mohamud was defeated in presidential balloting on January 8, 2014. Mohamud announced his intention to run for the presidency in 2016.

Leaders: Abdirahman Mohamed MOHAMUD "Farole" (Former President of Puntland), Abdisamad Ali SHIRE (Former Vice President of Puntland).

Other groupings include the **United Somali Parliamentarians,** formed in 2007 to support then prime minister Ali Mohammad Ghedi; Islamist **Unity Party** (*Midnimo*), formed in 2012 by Sheikh Umar Dahir Abdurahman MUHAMMAD; **Quality** (*Tayo)*, formed in 2012 by former prime minister Mohamed Abdullahi Mohamed; the **Democratic Party of Somalia,** formed in 2010 and led by Maslah MUHAMMAD, the son of former president Siad Barre; the **Hiil Qaran Party,** founded in 2011 and led by 2012 presidential candidate Ahmad Ismail SAMATAR; the **Daljir Party,** led by Sheikh Dahir Muhammad GELLE; and the **Somalia Green Party**.

For information on the **Southern Somali National Movement** (SSNM), see the 2014 *Handbook.*

For more information on the **Juba Valley Alliance** (JVA), the **Muslim Youth Party,** the **Somali African Muki Organization** (SAMO), the **Somali Islamic Party** (SIP), the **Unity for the Somali Republic Party** (USRP), and the **National Democratic League**, see the 2012 *Handbook.*

For more information on the **Somali National Front** (SNF), the **Somali Salvation Democratic Front** (SSDF), the **Islamic Union** (*al-Ittihad al-Islami*), the **Somali Democratic Party,** the **Somali Peace Loving Party,** the **Somali Solidarity Party** (SSP), the **Somali Unification Party,** and the **Somali Patriotic Movement** (SPM), see the 2009 *Handbook.*

LEGISLATURE

The former People's Assembly was dissolved after the overthrow of the SRSP government in January 1991. On August 13, 2000, a Transitional National Assembly (TNA) was inaugurated in accordance with the national charter adopted by the Somali National Peace Conference meeting in Arta, Djibouti. (For more information on the TNA, see the 2013 *Handbook*.)

In January 2004 most of the parties involved in the political and military conflict in Somalia agreed to a comprehensive agreement that included provision for the creation of an appointed Transitional Federal Parliament (TFP) to serve for four years, after which direct elections were to be held for a permanent legislature. The TFP, sworn in on August 29, 2004, comprised 275 deputies; each of the four major clans (Hawiye, Rahanweyn, Dir, and Darod) appointed 61 members, while 31 seats were allocated to smaller clans and subclans. On January 26, 2009, the TFP voted to expand to 550 members, including 200 deputies from the ALRS and an additional 75 members from civil society groups.

Under the terms of the constitution approved in August 2012, a new bicameral legislature, the **Federal Parliament** (*Golaha Shacabka Soomaaliya*) was created. Owing to the difficulty of conducting elections, it was agreed that the initial members of the new parliament would be selected by the clans, using the same formula that was utilized for the TFP in 2004. The constitution mandated that 30 percent of the seats in parliament were reserved for women, but only 38 women were appointed (13.8 percent) during the clan selection process.

Senate. The upper chamber has 54 members, directly elected to represent the 18 regions of the country. Elections for the Upper House were scheduled for September 25, 2016.

Speaker: (Vacant).

House of the People. The lower house has a maximum of 275 members, directly elected for four-year terms. Initially 215 members were appointed and sworn-in on August 21, 2012, with the remaining members taking office on September 10. Elections for the House were scheduled to begin September 24.

Speaker: Mohamed Osman JAWARI.

CABINET

[as of August 15, 2016]

Prime Minister	Omar Abdirashid Ali Sharmarke
Deputy Prime Minister	Mohamed Omar Arte
Ministers	
Agriculture	Ahmed Hassan Gabobe
Animals, Plants, and Pasture Care	Said Hussein Eid
Commerce and Industry	Abdullahi Mohamed Ahmed
Constitutional Affairs	Hussein Mohamed Sheikh Hussein
Defense	Abdulkadir Sheikh Ali Dini
Education	Abdikadir Abdi Hashi
Energy and Water	Mohamed Mursal Sheikh
Finance	Mohamed Ibrahim Adan
Fishing and Sea Resources	Mohamed Omar Eymoy
Foreign Affairs and International Cooperation	Abdisalan Hadliye Omar
Health	Mohamed Haiji Abdi Noor
Human Resources	Abdiweli Ibrihim Sheikh Muudeey
Information	Mohamed Abdi Hayir Maareeye
Interior and Federalism	Abdirahim Mohamed Hussein
Justice and Constitution	Abdullahi Ahmed Jama
Mineral Resources and Petroleum	Mohamed Mukhtar Ibrahim
National Security	Abdirizak Omar Mohamed
Planning	Abdirahman Yusuf Ali Aynte
Ports and Sea Transportation	Nur Farah Hirsi
Religious Affairs	Abdulkadir Sheikh Ali Baqdadi
Sports and Youth	Mohamed Abdullahi Hassan
Telecommunications and Posts	Mohamed Jama Mursal
Transport and Aviation	Ali Ahmed Jama
Women and Human Rights	Sahra Mohamed Ali Samatar [f]
Works and Reconstruction	Sala Sheikh Osman Muse

[f] = female

INTERGOVERNMENTAL REPRESENTATION

Ambassador to the U.S.: Ahmed Isse AWAD.

U.S. Ambassador to Somalia: Stephen SCHWARTZ.

Permanent Representative to the UN: Yusuf Garaad OMAR.

IGO Memberships (Non-UN): AfDB, AU, IOM, LAS, NAM, OIC.

For Further Reference:

Ferguson, James. *The World's Most Dangerous Place: Inside the Outlaw State of Somalia.* Boston: Da Capo Press, 2013.

Hansen, Stig Jarle. *Al-Shabaab in Somalia: The History and Ideology of a Militant Group.* Oxford: Oxford University Press, 2016.

Harper, Mary. *Getting Somalia Wrong?: Faith, War, and Hope in a Shattered State.* London: Zed Books, 2012.

Shay, Shaul. *Somalia in Transition since 2006.* New Brunswick, NJ: Transaction, 2014.

SOMALILAND

Republic of Somaliland
Jamhuuriyada Soomaaliland

Political Status: Former British Somaliland Protectorate; joined with (Italian) Trust Territory of Somalia on July 1, 1960, to form Somali Republic; announced secession as independent state on May 18, 1991; constitution endorsing independence and providing for multiparty activity approved by national referendum on May 31, 2001.

Area: 68,000 sq. mi. (176,120 sq. km).

Population: 4,033,691 (2015E).

Major Urban Centers (2012E): HARGEISA (850,000), Berbera (45,000).

Principal Language: Somali.

Monetary Unit: Somaliland shilling, which became Somaliland's sole legal tender on January 31, 1995, with an initial value of 100 Somali shillings = $1US. Due to the lack of international recognition of Somaliland's self-declared independent status, the exchange value of the shilling is not reported in regular currency listings. However, it reportedly has averaged 6,500 to 7,000 Somaliland shillings = $1US.

President: Ahmed Mohamed MOHAMOUD "Silanyo" (Solidarity Party); popularly elected on June 26, 2010, and sworn in for a five-year term on July 27; succeeded Dahir Riyale KAHIN (United and Democratic People's Alliance).

Vice President: Abdirahman Abdallahi ISMAIL "Saylici" (Solidarity Party); popularly elected along with the president on June 26, 2010, and sworn in for a five-term term, concurrent with that of the president, on July 27; succeeded Ahmad Yusuf YASIN (United and Democratic People's Alliance).

THE COUNTRY

The northwest portion of the Somali Republic as constituted in 1960, Somaliland extends some 400 miles eastward from Djibouti along the Gulf of Aden (see map). Most of the terrain is desert or semidesert, and it is estimated that nomadic animal-herders still constitute about one-half of the population. While sharing, as throughout Somalia, a common religion (Islam) and a common language (Somali), the people are divided into numerous clans and subclans, which contributed to the 1991 break with the south as well as subsequent difficulty in forging a wholly unified regime in the north.

Largely stable and peaceful since 1997, Somaliland has nevertheless failed to achieve international recognition for its independence as the result of concern, particularly among African leaders, that the "Balkanization" of Somalia would embolden secessionists throughout the continent. Consequently, international aid has been constrained, and the economy has depended primarily on remittances from workers abroad (an estimated $350 million in 2012). In 2012 the World Bank estimated that livestock accounted for about 30 percent of gross domestic product (GDP), with 20 percent from the wholesale and retail sectors, 8 percent from crops, and 6 percent from real estate and construction. The government has adopted a free-market orientation, including liberal investment policies. Development plans focus on

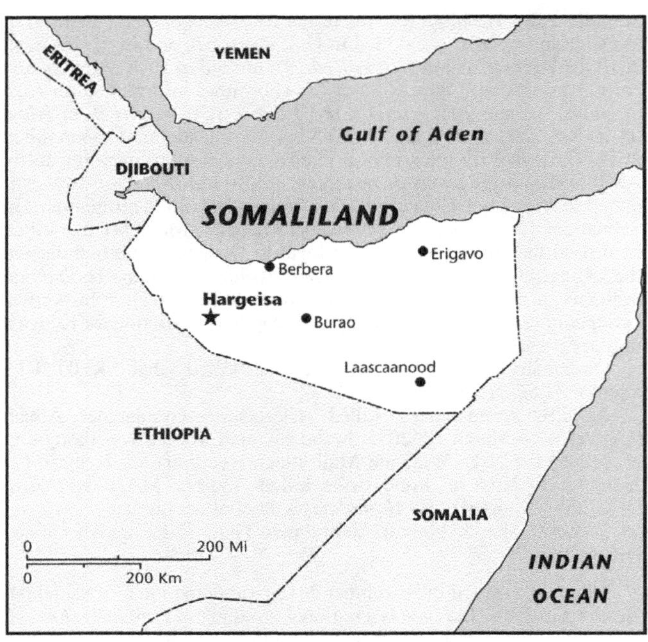

expanding the production of frankincense and myrrh, exploiting rich coastal fishing grounds, and exploring the potentially lucrative gem sector. A degree of economic progress (particularly around Hargeisa and the port of Berbera) has occurred in recent years, lending support to the contention of the government that Somaliland would best be served by remaining outside the political and economic "maelstrom" of Somalia proper. Oil companies from South Africa, Malaysia, India, and the United Kingdom were authorized by the Somaliland administration to pursue offshore oil exploration. The United States announced that it would increase its aid to Somaliland from $7 million to $25 million per year in 2010 following successful presidential elections (see Current issues, below). According to the UN, Somaliland received approximately $100 million in international aid and assistance in 2011. Somaliland's GDP was estimated to be approximately $3 billion in 2012, although the majority of economic activity remained in the unregulated informal sector. GDP per capita was approximately $510 in 2013. Remittances were estimated to account for $400 million per year. The Somaliland government budget for 2016 was $295.3 million, a 13 percent increase over the previous year. Estimates are that 29 percent of urban dwellers live in poverty, while poverty rates are 38 percent in rural regions.

GOVERNMENT AND POLITICS

Political background. A British protectorate since 1887, Somaliland was overrun by Italian forces at the outbreak of World War II but was recaptured by Britain in 1941. The protectorate was terminated on June 26, 1960, and on July 1 Somaliland joined its theretofore Italian-administered counterpart in the south to form what was styled the United Republic of Somalia, prior to its redesignation as the Somali Democratic Republic in 1969.

In 1988 the Somali National Movement (SNM), a rebel group that had joined with Ethiopian units in a cross-border assault the year before, mounted a broad-gauged offensive that succeeded in driving government forces from most of the northern region's rural areas by mid-1989. However, the government continued its heavy bombing campaign against Hargeisa and other towns, much of the northern population reportedly fleeing to Ethiopia to escape the "genocidal campaign" of the Siad Barre regime. Meanwhile, elsewhere in Somalia, other clan-based groups had taken up arms, most important among them the United Somali Congress (USC) in central regions and the Somali Patriotic Movement (SPM) in the south (see Political Parties and Groups in entry on Somalia for details).

On January 27, 1991, USC forces assumed control in Mogadishu, the Somalia capital, and appointed their principal backer, Ali Mahdi Mohamed, to the post of interim president. Ali Mahdi attempted to convene a "conference of national reconciliation" on February 28 but was rebuked by the SNM for having taken the initiative without prior consultation. A second such effort on March 14 also failed, and on May 18 the north proclaimed its independence as the Republic of Somaliland under the presidency of Abdurahman AHMED ALI "Taur." Many refugees subsequently returned to Somaliland from Ethiopia, discovering that the recent fighting, which had reportedly left 40,000 dead, had also devastated the region's infrastructure.

Ahmed Ali's control proved to be somewhat tenuous, and he did not attend a grand *shir* (gathering) of leading tribal, political, and military figures in Somaliland that met for most of February 1993 to discuss clan relations and the formalization of independence. Subsequently, a "parliamentary" meeting of the SNM Central Committee was convened to implement the *shir*'s conclusions. On May 5 the same body named Mohamed Ibrahim EGAL, a former prime minister of Somalia who had been imprisoned by the Siad Barre regime for many years, to succeed Ahmed Ali as president, with Col. Abdurahman ALI, who had been sacked as education minister in February, as vice president.

During a meeting with Gen. Mohamed Farah Aidid of the Somali National Alliance (SNA) in Ethiopia in April 1994, Ahmed Ali unexpectedly called for Somaliland to rejoin Somalia. The appeal was immediately rejected by President Egal, who branded his predecessor as a traitor and termed Somaliland's independence as "irrevocable." Egal reiterated the position in late May by rejecting inclusion in a federal state. On October 15, 1994, fighting erupted in Hargeisa airport between government forces and defecting militiamen of the Issaq subclan of Eidegalla. By late November the rebels appeared to control most of the capital, despite claims by President Egal to the contrary, and by early December about three-quarters of the city's population had reportedly fled.

In January 1995, having embarked on a build-up of arms (reportedly supplied by Albania) and with an army increased to more than 3,000 men, Egal mounted an offensive that succeeded in driving the rebels from Hargeisa. Further clashes occurred in Hargeisa airport in August 1995 and along the frontier with Djibouti three months later. On the latter occasion the government blamed the Djibouti regime for providing support to dissident Issa militiamen belonging to the United Somali Front (see Political Parties and Groups, below).

In May 1995 the SNM Central Committee, acting as an interim parliament, reelected Egal president. In July Egal appointed a ten-member constitutional drafting committee that he charged with writing a new basic charter within 12 months. However, immediately thereafter, the president employed a Sudanese constitutional consultant who, along with the president and a reportedly shrinking circle of presidential advisors, drew up a draft document that included provisions for a U.S.-style presidency. In response to Egal's proposed constitution, the Central Committee, many of whose members were described as "infuriated" by the president's actions, presented a rival draft highlighted by a parliamentary democracy. The constitutional deadlock continued through mid-1996, thus "forcing" Egal to continue governing by decree.

Concurrent with the expiration of its own charter, the advisory Council of Elders in October 1996 convened a 315-member National Communities Conference to which President Egal presented the two draft documents. In early 1997 the conference provisionally approved a new constitution (see Constitution and government, below), and on February 23 the delegates reelected Egal to a five-year term (the incumbent secured 223 votes in what observers described as remarkably "amicable" polling). In May Egal appointed a new government.

In December 1997 President Egal submitted his resignation to the legislature. He complained of a "lack of collaboration" from his government and other senior officials, but the legislators voted overwhelmingly to reject his request. A number of analysts attributed Egal's actions to his desire to fortify his position amid accusations of rampant corruption as well as to underline Somaliland's independence claims at the same time that Somalian faction leaders held unity talks in Cairo, Egypt.

Constitutional amendments were proposed by the government in mid-1999 with the goals of strengthening the role of the president and responding to opposition demands for greater judicial independence. Following a number of further revisions, the new constitution received a reported 97 percent endorsement from those voting in a national referendum on May 31, 2001. Among other things, the new basic law contained an entry affirming Somaliland's status as an independent republic. The first multiparty elections under the new constitution were initially scheduled at the local level for December 2001. However, they were subsequently postponed, and in early 2002 the legislature reportedly extended Egal's term of office (as well as that of Vice President Dahir Riyale KAHIN) until February 2003, although opponents of the administration criticized that decision and demanded that another all-inclusive conference of clan elders be held to determine the presidential status.

President Egal died on May 3, 2002, and he was succeeded on the same day by Kahin. Local elections were conducted in December 2002, with Kahin's United and Democratic People's Alliance (*Ururka Dimuqraadiga Ummadda Bahawday*—UDUB) securing a reported 41 percent of the vote, followed by the Solidarity Party (*Hisbiga Kulmiye*) with 19 percent and the Justice and Welfare Party (*Uruka Caddaalada Iyo Daryeelka*—UCID) with 11.2 percent. Those three parties consequently qualified for legal status under new constitutional provisions (see Political Parties and Groups, below, for details).

In presidential balloting on April 14, 2003, Kahin was reelected by a razor-thin margin (42.08 percent to 42.1 percent or 80 votes out of 490,000 cast) over Ahmed Mohamed MOHAMOUD ("Silanyo") of *Kulmiye.* A new "propresidential" government was announced on July 3. Silanyo initially protested the results, but following a ruling from the Constitutional Court that validated the outcome, he urged his supporters to accept the verdict. In October 2003 the government initiated a series of "antiterrorism" measures following an attack on Westerners, which Kahin blamed on illegal immigrants with connections to militant Islamic organizations. Foreigners without legal permits were expelled from the country.

In Somaliland's first national legislative balloting since its declaration of independence, the UDUB secured a plurality of 33 seats in the elections to the House of Representatives on September 25, 2005. However, following the elections, the UCID and *Kulmiye* announced a cooperation agreement that produced immediate results—the election of a member of the UCID as speaker. In the poll, there was reportedly severe tension over Somaliland's inclusion of the disputed territory of Sool along the border with Puntland. (Fighting broke out in 2004 between forces from Somaliland and Puntland.) However, the balloting was completed in Sool without violence.

Foreign observers described the 2005 elections as generally fair and free, further bolstering Somaliland's argument that it represented an oasis of developing democracy in an otherwise turbulent region and should be rewarded with international recognition. However, conflict over the election of the speaker of the House of Representatives prompted a walkout by UDUB legislators and riots outside the parliament buildings. After securing the speaker's post, the UCID/*Kulmiye* coalition presented a legislative agenda calling for, among other things, sweeping anticorruption measures and a reduction in the president's national security powers. Meanwhile, the government announced that security forces had arrested a group of heavily armed men accused of plotting assassinations and other terrorist acts. The government characterized the detainees as members of al-Qaida who had been trained in Afghanistan.

In May 2006 the House of Elders announced that it had extended its term of office until October 2010 even though elections had been scheduled for October 2006. President Kahin supported the extension, and he and the House of Elders were strongly criticized by UCID and *Kulmiye* leaders for seemingly trying to hold on to a degree of legislative authority through extraconstitutional means. In response to the rise of the Union of Islamic Courts in Somalia, a debate over the role of Islam in Somaliland's public life gained prominence in late 2006, with President Kahin announcing in October that the country would be run by Islamic law (sharia). However, specifics regarding the timing and implementation of sharia remained unknown.

Kahin's term was extended by the House of Elders in 2008 and 2009, a decision that was roundly criticized by the UCID and *Kulmiye.* Meanwhile, presidential balloting was postponed until September 2009 (see Current issues, below). Kahin rejected opposition calls to step down and appoint an interim government until the presidential balloting. In April 2009 the new Somali government (see entry on Somalia) initiated negotiations with Somaliland on mutual recognition. In September the House of Elders voted to extend Kahin's term if a date was set for presidential balloting.

After repeated delays, presidential elections were held on June 26, 2010. Silanyo defeated Kahin in the balloting with 49.6 percent of the vote, compared with 33.2 percent for the incumbent. Faisal Farah ALI "Warabe" of the UCID placed third with 17.2 percent. After his inauguration, Silanyo named a new cabinet on July 28. Silanyo also appointed new governors in seven of the country's provinces. On September 11, elections for the House of Elders were postponed until 2014. The term of the lower house was extended to 2012, while local and regional balloting was postponed for 18 months.

Silanyo reshuffled the cabinet on January 15, 2011, dismissing two ministers and moving others to new portfolios. He reorganized the government again on March 15, 2012, replacing five ministers, including the minister of finance. A major cabinet reshuffle occurred on June 25, 2013. The president appointed 19 new ministers or deputy ministers and transferred or promoted an additional seven. Silanyo conducted significant cabinet reshuffles in March and October 2015 and August 2016.

Constitution and government. The government, established in the wake of the May 1991 independence proclamation, encompassed a president and vice president, appointed by the SNM, initially for a two-year transitional period during which a constitution was to be drafted that would permit the holding of open, multiparty elections. On May 28 *Radio Hargeisa* announced that the SNM leadership had also approved the formation of a high court and a civil service, in addition to the appointment of an attorney general, an auditor general, and a Central Bank governor.

In early July 1995 President Egal announced that a ten-member constitutional drafting committee had been appointed and that a basic law for Somaliland would be forthcoming within the ensuing 12 months. Meanwhile, the SNM Central Committee continued to serve as an interim legislature and electoral body for the presidency. In early 1997 the National Communities Conference provisionally approved a constitution that provided for a bicameral legislature (see Legislature, below), an electoral system of direct universal suffrage, and the organization of political parties (although groups with "tribal" or religious affiliations were proscribed). Among the details to surface subsequently about the document were stipulations that future presidents and their spouses be both native Somalians and Muslims. In late 1998 the legislature reportedly approved the implementation of measures based on Islamic religious law.

The 1997 constitution was approved with the provision that it be presented to a national referendum within three years. A one-year extension was granted in February 2000 and a three-month extension in February 2001, with the referendum finally being held on May 31, 2001. The new basic law confirmed Somaliland's independence, strengthened the executive branch, confirmed Islam as the "national faith," provided for a free press, and endorsed multiparty elections at all levels of government through universal suffrage. In March 2008 legislation reconfigured Somaliland into 12 regions and 57 districts.

Freedom of the press was codified in the constitution approved by national referendum in 2001. However, the government still controls the media, and a number of journalists have been imprisoned for criticizing the regime. In December 2007, 24 exiled Somali reporters were ordered to leave Somaliland. From March through July 2009, more than 20 journalists were arrested and imprisoned for varying lengths of time. In January 2011 the editor of a private newspaper was sentenced for three years on criminal defamation charges. In January 2012 more than 21 journalists were arrested for disseminating "propaganda" against the government. On April 24 masked assailants attacked a Hargeisa newspaper office. It was later discovered that one of the attackers was a police officer.

Foreign relations. Refusals to attend "reconciliation" conferences in Djibouti in 1991 were defended by SNM leaders on the ground that the meetings were called to address matters of domestic concern to "Southern Somalia." However, relations between Djibouti and Somaliland had been less than cordial because of conflict between the Issa community common to both countries and the Issaq grouping in Somaliland.

Despite what was described as a "flurry of meetings" designed to promote international recognition, by mid-1995 no foreign government had complied, partly because of long-standing opposition by the Organization of African Unity (OAU, subsequently the African Union—AU) to secessionist regimes and partly because of uncertainties surrounding continued anarchic conditions in the south. Significantly, while Somaliland had agreed in 1993 to the introduction of 500 UN peacekeepers to supervise the distribution of relief supplies, it rejected any deployment of U.S. troops on the ground that its claim to autonomy would thereby be jeopardized. In May 1994 President Egal threatened to expel any UN personnel advocating reintegration into Somalia.

In mid-1995 President Egal was reported to have sent a fax message to Israeli Prime Minister Yitzhak Rabin proposing the establishment of "strategic links" between their two countries. Egal spoke of the need to counter Islamic fundamentalism in the Horn of Africa, attributed with some degree of imprecision to "the growing influence of Saudi Arabia and the pro-Islamic Yemen."

Egal's efforts to gain international support bore fruit in late 1997 as Djibouti announced that it would exchange diplomatic credentials with Somalia. Italy subsequently told Egal in early 1998 that it would support a European Union (EU) proposal to grant Somaliland "semi-diplomatic" recognition. For his part, Egal agreed to accept the offer of limited recognition for an interim period. Such concerns dominated Somaliland's foreign policy agenda through early 1999, with reports of Somaliland's enhanced international standing being balanced by continued calls from regional leaders for it to be included in a unified Somalia.

Relations with Djibouti deteriorated in 2000 when that country's leadership played a major role in the establishment of the transitional government in Somalia. However, Somaliland and Djibouti agreed to "normalize" their ties again in 2001. By that time it was clear that, in addition to opposing the notion of reunification with Somalia, Somaliland was in the midst of an ongoing territorial dispute with the Puntland autonomous region in Somalia.

Relations with Ethiopia improved in January 2002, when Ethiopia appointed an ambassador to Somaliland, and the Ethiopian government has since indicated that it may recognize Somaliland unilaterally if the AU refuses its membership bid. Reports indicated in 2008 that Somaliland and Ethiopia had increased military ties.

Intense lobbying efforts by officials from Somaliland to convince the UK government to recognize Somaliland's status as a fully independent nation continue to the present day. UK lawmakers visited Somaliland, and London agreed to help pay costs involved in the 2003 presidential poll. However, no official recognition was forthcoming, as most of the international community pressed (unsuccessfully) the Kahin administration to participate in the comprehensive Somalia peace talks. The Arab League in 2005 declined a request for membership from Somaliland, and the country's application for AU membership is still pending.

In January and July 2007 the EU sent foreign affairs delegations to discuss future cooperation between the EU and Somaliland. The EU has also pledged to support the upcoming elections in the country. Additionally, Somaliland interacts directly with the Swedish government in aid negotiations, despite the fact that Sweden has not yet granted formal recognition to the country.

In February 2008 France announced an initiative to improve ties with Somaliland by funding French language and cultural programs. In June the United Nations provided Somaliland with vehicles for its security forces and judiciary. The UN Development Program concurrently announced that it was doubling its aid to Somaliland to $7 million per year. Beginning in September 2008, Somaliland security forces launched an aggressive antipiracy campaign that resulted in the arrest of more than 100 alleged pirates by May 2009. The effort was reportedly part of the larger campaign to gain support from the West. In May 2009, following negotiations with Puntland officials, Ethiopia offered to host discussions in an effort to mediate the dispute over the Sool region. Renewed fighting in Somalia led an estimated 26,000 Somalis to flee to Somaliland by the summer of 2009.

In October 2010 Somaliland and Ethiopia agreed to increase security cooperation to suppress terrorism and piracy. Somali-backed antigovernment groups were reportedly responsible for terrorist attacks in early 2010 in Laas Anood, the capital of the Sool region.

In August 2011 the government announced that a Chinese firm would refurbish the port of Berbera and construct a refinery. In December Somaliland granted additional licenses to British and Italian and energy companies to explore for oil.

In May 2012 reports indicated that the project to rebuild Berbera was placed on hiatus after Chinese officials refused to grant Somaliland diplomatic recognition as a condition for the deal. In June the United States announced a $1 million program to promote economic development in Somaliland. This was followed by an additional $17 million economic development aid package in December.

In June 2013 Somaliland's foreign minister announced that the UN Assistance Mission in Somalia (UNSOM) would not be allowed to operate in the country. Reports indicated that the decision was based on apprehension that UNSOM would promote reunification of Somalia.

The United Kingdom city of Sheffield became the first city to recognize Somaliland as an independent country on April 7, 2014. Sheffield also called on the UK government to recognize Somaliland. In May Kenya announced it would open a diplomatic liaison office in

Hargesia, and Somaliland would open a reciprocal office in Nairobi. However, officially, Kenya continued to support a unified Somalia. In June the EU and the aid organization Oxfam launched a three-year $6.8 million program to increase fisheries capacity for both Somaliland and Puntland.

In January 2016 Somaliland officials began a widespread campaign to detain and deport Ethiopian refugees. As the Somaliland economy has improved, the country has attracted economic migrants from across the region, and the enhanced enforcement measures seemed to be an effort to dissuade additional refugees. Also in January, President Silanyo strongly condemned Iran and offered support to the Saudi-led coalition fighting in Yemen (see entry on Yemen).

Current issues. Controversy erupted in the capital after the formation in April 2007 of the Qaran Party, whose leaders challenged administration claims that the constitution requires politicians to join one of the existing three political parties to enter government. The QP leaders were arrested in July (see Political Parties and Groups, below). On October 8, 2007, the National Electoral Commission announced it was delaying upcoming presidential and local government polls, scheduled for December 2007 and April 2008. Long-standing territorial disputes between Somaliland and neighboring Puntland deepened in 2007. Puntland claimed the Bari, Nugaal, and Mudug regions as well as the Sanaag and Sool regions, which Somaliland also claimed. Sanaag declared independence from both in July 2007, renaming itself Makhir and choosing Badhan as a capital. Somaliland Defense Minister Adan Mire Mohamed was dismissed by Kahin for failing to prevent the fighting in Sanaag in April. Fighting then broke out between the neighbors in early October 2007, as Sool was rent by conflict between subclans calling for Sool's independence or backing the claims of either Somaliland, which claimed Sool due to the regions' shared history under British rule, or Puntland, which asserted its rights to the region based on common Darod clan ethnicity. By the end of October, Somaliland forces had captured Las Anod, the regional capital of Sool. The strife created an estimated 20,000 refugees. Later in the month, Somaliland levied an additional tax of 2 percent on its inhabitants, reportedly for the purpose of providing relief to displaced residents of Sool. There was renewed fighting in the region in January 2008 and again in July.

On September 29, 2008, suicide bombers attacked the presidential palace and Ethiopian embassy in Hargeisa. The attacks killed 19, including the president's secretary, and wounded more than 100. The strikes were believed to have been carried out by Islamic extremists.

On March 28, 2009, the president's term was extended through September by the House of Elders, and Kahin issued a decree setting September 27 as the date for presidential elections. Officially, continued fighting in Sool, caused the delay, but opposition parties and groups decried it and threatened to withdraw recognition of the government. Meanwhile, a new dispute arose over voter registration when the president ordered the head of an international rights group, which was overseeing a new registration drive, to leave the country. On April 6 police used force to disperse opposition-led demonstrations in Hargeisa. The government subsequently banned demonstrations in the capital until the September balloting. On July 11, 2009, negotiations resulted in an agreement between the three major parties to support presidential elections in September. The balloting was subsequently postponed until June 2010.

In the long-delayed presidential elections on June 26, 2010, Silanyo won comfortably over Kahin and Warabe in balloting that international observers described as mostly free and fair. Despite threats from extremist groups, the polling was also peaceful. After his inauguration on July 27, the new president appointed a cabinet that was smaller than any since independence. The government included a number of Western-educated technocrats. In one of its first acts, it imposed a hiring freeze to reduce the deficit. Silanyo also released a number of political prisoners and pledged not to issue emergency decrees, as his predecessor had.

A drought and a devastating famine reduced crop production in 2011. On March 23, for the first time, Somaliland naval forces captured Somali pirates. Meanwhile, the government announced on September 5 that it would expel all illegal immigrants and refugees. The announcement was criticized by human rights groups. In September the government launched a program to expand the use of the Somaliland shilling by replacing the widely used Somali shilling with the currency. The initiative was part of a larger program to increase tax revenues by reducing the informal economy. On October 8 a Somaliland court convicted seven of piracy and sentenced them to five years in prison.

In May 2012 ten opposition leaders were arrested and political demonstrations banned following the disqualification of several new political parties. In June Silyano met with the president of Somalia's interim government for discussions in Dubai. The two leaders signed a general accord that called for greater cooperation between the two governments. There were large demonstrations in support of the talks in the Mogadishu, but the meeting was criticized by officials from Puntland. Meanwhile, Turkey sponsored further negotiations in April and July 2013.

Seven political parties or groupings competed in local elections in November 2012. *Kulmiye* won the majority of the vote with 30.2 percent, followed by the newly formed Somaliland National Party (*Wadani*), 20.2 percent, and the UCID, 13 percent. Three people were killed and dozens injured in postelection violence as opposition parties protested the results. Security forces imposed a curfew in Hargeisa to contain the violence.

In January 2014 Somaliland and Somalia resumed bilateral talks in Istanbul. Somaliland security forces arrested three Somali government officials in February at the Hargeysa international airport. Somaliland officials charged the three were attempting to enter the region clandestinely, while Somalia claimed the arrestees were simply traveling through Somaliland. The three were subsequently released. Somaliland forces captured the town of Taleh in June, following incursions into the disputed regions of Sool and Sanaag.

Somaliland rejected calls from the Somali national government for new negotiations on reintegration in February 2016. National elections, scheduled for 2016, were postponed until March 2017. The delay was criticized by opposition groups and international donors. Renewed fighting broke out between Somaliland and Puntland forces in the Sanaag region in July 2016. The strife was reportedly the result of efforts by Somaliland to register voters ahead of elections in 2017.

POLITICAL PARTIES AND GROUPS

The constitution endorsed by national referendum in May 2001 provided for multiparty activity, with the restriction that parties could not be based on tribal/clan or religious affiliations. The parties were provisionally recognized but had to secure 20 percent of the vote in four of the country's six provinces in local balloting in December 2002 in order to be registered for national elections. In local balloting in 2012, *Kulmiye,* the UCID, and *Wadani*, secured the right to compete in the next round of presidential and legislative elections.

Official Parties:

Solidarity Party (*Hisbiga Kulmiye*). Also known as the **Peace, Unity, and Development Party** (*Kulmiye Nabad, Midnimo iyo Horumar*), *Kulmiye* was established in early 2002, and is led by Ahmed Mohamed Mohamoud "Silanyo," who was chair of the SNM from 1984–1990. Silanyo had resigned from the Egal government in 2001, indicating his desire to campaign for the presidency. *Kulmiye* finished second to the UDUB in the December 2002 municipal balloting, securing, according to the government, about 83,000 votes to UDUB's 198,000. Silanyo finished second in the very close vote for president in April 2003. Subsequently, when the Kahin government was criticized by world leaders for refusing to participate in the Somali peace negotiations, Silanyo announced that he supported Kahin in the matter.

Kulmiye finished second in the 2005 legislative balloting with 30.3 percent of the vote. Following the election, *Kulmiye* announced a cooperative agreement with the other "opposition" party—the UCID (below). The party has supported the efforts of the Qaran party to become a registered political party. Silanyo was chosen as the *Kulmiye* presidential candidate in the 2009 elections at a September 2008 party convention. A division in the party emerged over the selection of the vice presidential candidate, Mudane SAYLICI. The choice was deeply opposed by a faction led by Ahmed Ali ADAMI. Through the spring and summer of 2009, *Kulmiye* members and supporters held a series of demonstrations against the extension of President Kahin's term. Silanyo won in the presidential balloting of June 2010. Deputy party chair Abdirahman ABDIQADIR was removed from office at a party conference in April 2012 for criticizing Silyano. At the same conference, Muse BIHI was elected party chair. In May 2014 Party Chair Bihi announced he would challenge Silanyo for the right to represent the party in the 2015 presidential election. Silanyo subsequently announced he would not seek reelection, and Bihi emerged as the party's candidate for the 2017 balloting.

Leaders: Ahmed Mohamed MOHAMOUD "Silanyo" (President of the Republic), Muse BIHI (Chair).

Justice and Welfare Party (*Ururka Caddaalada Iyo Daryeelka*—UCID). Established as a "modern" party devoted to "good governance," the staunchly nationalist UCID was described as an outgrowth of a **Social Democratic Party** that had been previously organized within the diaspora. UCID leader Faisal Farah Ali "Warabe" was one of the founders of the SNM. In December 2002 the UCID secured the third place out of six contesting parties in the municipal elections. Warabe placed third in the 2003 presidential election with 16 percent of the vote. The UCID secured 29 percent of the vote in the 2005 legislative elections, and after announcement of a UCID/*Kulmiye* cooperation agreement, the UCID's Abdirahman Muhammad Abdullahi IRRO was elected speaker of the House of Representatives. The UCID choose Warabe as its presidential candidate at a party congress in 2009. He placed third in the June 2010 presidential polling. In June 2012 Warabe was appointed to a reconciliation commission charged to open new discussions with Somalia. Warabe announced that his party had declared "war" on Puntland. International banker Jamal Ali HUSSEIN was chosen as the party's candidate for the 2017 presidential elections.

Leaders: Faisal Farah ALI "Warabe" (Chair), Mohamed Osman FADAL (Vice Chair).

Somaliland National Party (*Wadani*). Formed in 2012 by the speaker of the House of Representatives, Abdirahman Muhammad Abdullahi Irro, *Wadani* drew supporters from the UDUB and other opposition parties. *Wadani* placed second in the local elections in November 2012. The party announced it would select its presidential candidate for the 2017 elections at a party congress to be held on October 2016.

Leader: Abdirahman Muhammad Abdullahi IRRO (Speaker of the House).

Other Parties and Groups:

United and Democratic People's Alliance (*Ururka Dimuqraadiga Ummadda Bahawday*—UDUB). Launched in June 2001 by President Egal, the UDUB was subsequently routinely referenced as the "ruling" party in Somaliland. Although some observers viewed the UDUB as primarily a personal vehicle for Egal, the party was reportedly "resuscitated" by President Kahin following Egal's death in May 2002. The party went on to dominate the December 2002 municipal elections and to achieve a plurality in the 2005 legislative balloting on a vote share of 40.7 percent. In February 2009 a party congress elected Kahin as the UDUB candidate for the upcoming presidential balloting. However, UDUB opponents of Kahin, led by Abdullahi DARAWEL, left the meeting and held a rival congress. Kahin placed second in the presidential election in 2010. The UDUB failed to qualify as one of the three official parties following the November 2012 local elections.

Leaders: Dahir Riyale KAHIN (Chair and Former President of the Republic), Ahmad Yusuf YASIN (Former Vice President of the Republic), Usman GARAD (Secretary).

Somali National Movement (SNM). The SNM was organized in London in April 1981 by an exile group that declared its commitment to the overthrow of the Mogadishu regime but did not wish to ally itself with either the United States or the Soviet Union. Deriving most of its support from Somaliland's Issaq clan, the SNM long supported greater autonomy for the area. Ideologically, however, the movement suffered from a lack of cohesion, apparently counting Marxist, pro-Western, and Islamic fundamentalist groups within its ranks. (For more information on the history of the SNM, see the 2014 *Handbook*.)

After being ousted from the Somaliland presidency in favor of Ibrahim Egal in May 1993, Abdurahman Ahmed Ali took up residence in London before surfacing in Mogadishu in August 1994 as a pro-Aidid opponent of secession. In September President Egal denounced a claim from Ahmed Ali that Ahmed Ali remained SNM chair. Thereafter, in early 1996 it was reported that Ahmed Ali was advising an anti-Egal rebel group in the Burao region.

Anti-Egal forces within the SNM accused the president of corruption in 1997 and threatened to launch a legal challenge against the composition of the National Communities Conference. However, such opposition reportedly failed to materialize. The SNM subsequently remained fractionalized concerning Egal's role and other issues, the president's critics also questioning his commitment to independence. Egal in 2001 formed his own political party (see the UDUB, above), with several other former SNM leaders following suit. The SNM ceased to function as a political entity after the 2001 referendum.

Qaran Party (QP). Founded in 2007, the party has met fierce resistance from the national government, which argues that the constitution requires that only three parties can exist in Somaliland. Despite this, the leaders of the Qaran Party announced its founding in April 2007. The three top officials in the party were then arrested by the Somaliland government on July 28, 2007, for engaging in unauthorized political activity. They were released in December 2007 and the charges against them dismissed. Efforts to gain official recognition of Qaran prior to the September 2009 presidential elections were unsuccessful. Party leader Mohammad Gabose was appointed interior minister in the 2010 government, but he resigned in March 2011, to form a new political grouping, **Ummada**.

Other minor groupings include the **Party of God** (*Hizbullah*), formed in 2012; **Rays**, led by Hasan Muhammad Ali "GAAFAADHI"; and **Haqsoor**, led by Hassan ISSE.

For information on the **United Somali Front** (USF), see the 2009 *Handbook*.

LEGISLATURE

Following Somaliland's declaration of independence in 1991, the Central Committee of the Somali National Movement (SNM) served as a nominal "provisional" legislature for several years, although its actual authority was limited due to the subclan conflict that left substantial territory outside SNM control. In May 1993 the SNM "parliament" endorsed the recommendation of a recently concluded grand *shir* (gathering) for the formal establishment of a two-chamber legislature, comprised of a House of Elders and a House of Representatives (initially to be appointed on a clan basis but ultimately to be filled by elections). The two chambers began to operate shortly thereafter, although some clan seats in the House of Representatives remained vacant until August 1994. The new constitution approved by national referendum in 2001 provided for a bicameral **Parliament.**

House of Elders (*Golaha Guurtida*). The upper house is authorized to review legislation passed by the House of Representatives and to approve legislation on its own in regard to religion, culture, and security. It comprises 82 members and a number of nonvoting honorary members. The first elections to the House of Elders were scheduled for October 2006, but in a controversial decision the current appointed membership decided in May 2006 to extend its mandate until October 2010 and then again until 2014.

Speaker: Suleiman Mohamud ADAM.

House of Representatives (*Golaha Wakiilada*). The lower house comprises 82 members directly elected via proportional representation (in six regions) for five-year terms. In the first elections for the house on September 29, 2005, the United and Democratic People's Alliance reportedly secured 33 seats; Solidarity Party, 28; and Justice and Welfare Party, 21.

Speaker: Abdirahman Muhammad Abdullahi IRRO.

CABINET

[as of August 15, 2016]

President	Ahmed Mohamed Mohamoud "Silanyo"
Vice President	Abdirahman Abdallahi Ismail "Saylici"
Ministers	
Agriculture	Muhaamad Aw Dahir Ibrahim
Civil Aviation	Mohamoud Hashi Abdi
Commerce	Mohamed Abdilahi Omer
Defense	Ahmed Haji Ali Adami
Development of Rural Areas and Environment	Shukri Ismael Bandare [f]
Education and Higher Education	Ibrahim Abdullah Habane "Abdullah Dheere"

Finance	Abdi-Aziz Samaale
Fisheries and Marine Resources	Ali Jama Farah "Bureed"
Foreign Affairs	Mohamed Bihi Yonis
Health	Yusuf Ahmad Ali
Industry	Shu'aib Muhammad Musse
Information and Culture	Abdilahi Mohamed Dahir
Interior	Yasin Mohaud Hir "Faraton"
Justice and Attorney General	Hussein Ahmed Aided
Labor and Social Welfare	Mohamud Ahmed Barre "Garaad"
Livestock	Abdi Aw Dahir
Mineral and Water Resources	Hussein Abdi Du'aale
Parliament	Aden Ahmed Warsame
Planning and Development	Saad ali Shire
Post and Telecommunication	Ali Elmi Abgal
Presidency	Hersi Ali Haji Hassan
Public Works and Housing	Abdirizak Khalif Ahmed
Religion	Sheikh Khalil Abdullahi Ahmed
Resettlement and Rehabilitation	Ahmed Abdi Kahin
Sports, Youth, and Culture	Abdullahi Farah Mayane
Water	Hussein Ahmed Abdule
Ministers of State	
Education	Ahmed Nur Faarhiye
Finance	Osman Abdilahi Sahardid
Foreign Affairs	Mohamed Rashid Sheikh Hasan
Minerals and Energy	Mohamed Faarah Ducaale
Peacebuilding	Ali Mohamed Ahmed "Sandule"
Presidential Affairs	Mohamed Musa Abees
Water	Abdisalaan Mohamed Hassan

[f] = female

INTERGOVERNMENTAL REPRESENTATION

As of February 2017, Somaliland was not a member of the UN.

IGO Memberships (Non-UN): None.

For Further Reading:

Bradbury, Mark. *Becoming Somaliland.* Bloomington: Indiana University Press, 2008.

Hoehne, Markus Virgil. *Between Somaliland and Puntland: Marginalization, Militarization, and Conflicting Political Visions.* London: Rift Valley Institute, 2015.

Richards, Rebecca. *Understanding Statebuilding: Traditional Governance and the Modern State of Somaliland.* New York: Routledge, 2016.

SOUTH AFRICA

Republic of South Africa
Republiek van Suid-Afrika

Political Status: Fully independent state since 1934; republic established May 31, 1961; Interim Constitution ratified on December 22, 1993, with effect from April 27, 1994, for a five-year term; new text signed into law on December 10, 1996, effective February 4, 1997, with certain provisions implemented gradually through 1999.

Area: 470,882 sq. mi. (1,221,037 sq. km).

Population: 54,979,200 (2016E—UN); 54,300,704 (2016E—U.S. Census).

Major Urban Centers (urban areas, 2016E—UN): PRETORIA (administrative capital, 2,125,000), Cape Town (legislative capital, 3,698,000), Bloemfontein (judicial capital, 503,000), Johannesburg (9,616,000), Durban (2,914,000), Port Elizabeth (1,186,000), Vereeniging (1,164,000). Pretoria is part of the City of Tshwane Metropolitan Municipality.

Official Languages: There are 11 official languages, of which English and Afrikaans are the languages of record.

Monetary Unit: Rand (market rate October 1, 2016: 13.72 rand = $1US).

President: Jacob Gedleyihlekisa ZUMA (African National Congress); reelected by the National Assembly on May 7, 2014, and inaugurated for his second five-year term on May 24; succeeded Kgalema Petrus MOTLANTHE (African National Congress) on May 9, 2009.

Deputy President: Cyril RAMAPHOSA (African National Congress); appointed by President Zuma on May 25, 2014, and sworn in on May 26; succeeded Kgalema Petrus MOTLANTHE (African National Congress).

THE COUNTRY

Industrially the most developed country in Africa, the Republic of South Africa is a land of rolling plateaus within a mountainous escarpment that rims its territory on the seaward side and separates the coastal cities of Cape Town and Durban from the inland centers of Johannesburg and Pretoria. The country is peopled by four separate ethnic elements as unequal in numbers as they used to be in political status. The largest and historically least favored group, comprising approximately 79 percent of the population, consists of the Xhosa, Zulu, and Sotho, who are collectively known as the Bantu. Whites comprise 9.6 percent of the population; mixed-race people, 8.9 percent; and Asians, mainly Indians living in KwaZulu-Natal Province, 2.5 percent.

Some three-fifths of the whites are "Afrikaners," who descend from the Dutch, German, and French Huguenot settlers who colonized the country beginning in the 17th century. Traditionally agrarian in their social practices and outlook, their native language is Afrikaans, a language closely related to Dutch (although many Afrikaners also speak English). Afrikaners, predominantly affiliated with the Dutch Reformed Church, were the most resolute supporters of the policy of separation of the races (apartheid). Most other whites speak English as their first language, identify with the British tradition, and are more involved in business and industry than Afrikaners, although this pattern has changed as Afrikaners have moved to urban areas.

South Africa has become a highly urbanized country, with half of the white population, a third of the blacks, and most Asians and mixed-race people (known in South Africa as "Cape Coloureds" or simply "Coloureds") residing in and around the dozen large cities and towns. The Coloureds form a distinct group. They are frequently of mixed nonwhite and Afrikaner descent, with Afrikaner-sounding last names and Afrikaans often their first language. They are concentrated in Western Cape Province. The term "Coloured," while still in general and official use, is coming under increasing criticism.

In predominantly white areas, black women are employed mainly as domestic servants and casual agricultural laborers. Men's migration to white-controlled employment sites has left women largely in charge of subsistence agriculture. Women's participation in government was long limited to minor representation by white women in national and provincial legislatures; however, women of all races were prominent in the anti-apartheid movement. The award of cabinet portfolios to women since the 2009 administration has fulfilled a pledge by former president Nelson Mandela to give women one-third of all posts at all levels. Women currently occupy 15 out of 35 cabinet-level posts. Nhlanhla NENE is South Africa's first black finance minister. Minister of Public Enterprises Lynne BROWN is the first openly gay cabinet member. Following the 2014 legislative elections, women held 163 seats in the lower house (40.8 percent) and 19 in the upper chamber (35.2 percent).

The first African country to experience the full force of the industrial revolution, South Africa now has an advanced economy and plays an important role in international economic affairs. South Africa mines diamonds, copper, asbestos, chrome, platinum, and vanadium, and is tapping recently discovered ocean reserves of oil. In 2006 South Africa led the world in gold production, producing nearly one-third of the global output. Today, South Africa is the sixth-leading producer, yielding just

over 5 percent. The country has abundant coal, which provides a large share of energy. Agriculturally, South Africa is self-sufficient (except in coffee, rice, and tea) and exports wool, maize, sugar, and fruit. Although agriculture now contributes only about 2.5 percent of the gross domestic product (GDP), it continues to employ almost 6 percent of the labor force. The manufacturing sector, spurred by the government during the apartheid era to promote industrial self-sufficiency, presently accounts for approximately 15.2 percent of GDP; mining adds another 4.9 percent. South Africa's leading trade partner is China, with 15 percent of overall trade. In 2000 South Africa concluded with the European Union (EU) a free-trade agreement, which covered some 90 percent of transactions by 2012. (For more on the economy prior to 2000, see the 2013 *Handbook*.)

In recent years, South Africa has seemed to prefer public–private partnerships to large-scale privatization. All economic sectors are required to draw up charters that commit them to black economic empowerment.

Annual GDP growth averaged 4.7 percent in 2006–2008, and inflation soared to 11.3 percent in 2008 in response to high commodity prices. The unemployment rate decreased to approximately 23 percent by mid-2008. The economy went into recession in 2009, owing in large part to the global economic downturn. GDP fell that year by 1.5 percent. International Monetary Fund (IMF) managers said South Africa weathered the global crisis without major problems or need for public stimulus. GDP growth of 3.1 percent was recorded for 2010, and the IMF commended South Africa for its "impressive economic performance in recent years" and its efforts toward improving infrastructure and educational and health services. Meanwhile, the World Bank approved a $3.75-billion loan in 2010 to develop renewable energy and help pay for work on a coal-fired plant, described as one of the largest of its kind in the world.

Another recent focus of attention has been HIV/AIDS. In 2010 South Africa was reported to have the world's largest number of HIV-positive citizens, with 6.3 million, or over 11 percent of the population. The government estimated that $88 billion would be required over the next two decades to pay for the cost of caring for AIDS patients and for prevention efforts.

In 2012 the economy struggled under flagging demand for South African exports as a result of the European debt crisis. On July 17, 2014, the South African Reserve Bank raised interest rates to 5.75 percent, and rates reached 7 percent by August 2016. GDP grew by 1.9 percent in 2013, while inflation rose by 5.7 percent and the unemployment rate remained high at 24.1 percent. A 2012 World Bank report highlighted that uneven distribution of growth in South Africa has perpetuated inequality: The top decile of the population accounted for 58 percent of the country's income, while the bottom decile accounted for just 0.5 percent. In 2014 GDP growth was 1.5 percent, while inflation was 5.8 percent, and unemployment was 25 percent. In 2015 GDP grew by 1.3 percent, inflation was 4.8 percent, and unemployment held steady. Estimates for 2016 had GDP growth at just 0.6 percent, with inflation rising to 7 percent and unemployment rising to 26 percent. The World Bank rated South Africa 73rd out of 189 countries in its ease of doing business index for 2016, placing it between Botswana and Tunisia.

GOVERNMENT AND POLITICS

Political background. The Republic of South Africa as it exists today is the result of a long and complicated process of interaction between indigenous peoples and the Dutch and British colonists who came to exploit the territory. The original Cape Colony was settled by the Dutch in the 17th century but fell into British hands as a result of the Napoleonic wars. Discontented Afrikaners, known as "Boers," the Afrikaans word for farmers, trekked northward in 1835–1837, commencing a half-century subjugation of the Zulu and other native peoples and establishing the independent republics of Transvaal and Orange Free State. Following the discovery of diamonds and gold in the late 19th century, the two Boer republics were conquered by Britain in the Anglo-Boer War of 1899–1902. In 1910 they were joined with the British colonies of the Cape and Natal (annexed in 1843) to form the Union of South Africa, which obtained full independence within the Commonwealth in 1931.

Although South Africa joined with Britain in both world wars, its British and Commonwealth attachments progressively weakened as the result of widespread anti-British sentiment and racial preoccupations. The National Party (*Nasionale Party*—NP), led by Daniel F. MALAN, came to power in 1948 with a program strongly reinforcing racial separation under white "guardianship." It proceeded to enact a body of openly discriminatory legislation that was further amplified under Hendrik F. VERWOERD (1958–1966). Segregation was strictly enforced, the already token political representation of nonwhites was progressively reduced, and overt opposition was severely repressed. Similar policies were applied in South West Africa, a former German territory occupied by South Africa in World War I and subsequently administered under a mandate from the League of Nations (see entry under Namibia).

With apartheid, the African National Congress (ANC), the largest party advocating racial partnership, went underground and began a three-decade-long armed struggle against the NP government. Much of its leadership either was imprisoned or went abroad. Many received military training in the USSR or other communist countries.

Increasing institutionalization of segregation under the Verwoerd regime led to international condemnation. External opposition was intensified by the Sharpeville incident of March 21, 1960, during which South African police fired on black demonstrators, killing 69 of them. In view of the increasingly critical stand of other Commonwealth members, South Africa formally withdrew from the grouping and declared itself a republic on May 31, 1961.

Prime Minister Verwoerd was assassinated by a deranged white man in September 1966, but his successor, Balthazar J. VORSTER, continued Verwoerd's policies, bringing to fruition the idea of dividing the blacks into separate tribal homelands, or "Bantustans." These areas, encompassing approximately 13 percent of the country's land, were ultimately intended to house upward of three-quarters of the population. However, a series of minor concessions to the blacks brought about a challenge from the right-wing, or *verkrampte* ("unenlightened" or "ultra-Conservative"), faction of the NP under the leadership of Dr. Albert HERTZOG, who formed the Reconstituted National Party (*Herstigte Nasionale Party*—HNP) to compete, with little success, in the 1970 election.

The 1974 Portuguese revolution and subsequent changes in Angola and Mozambique further isolated the South African regime. Early in 1975 the government announced a policy of "ending discrimination" within South Africa and of working for détente in external affairs. During the following year, however, the country experienced its worst outbreak of racial violence since the Sharpeville episode in 1960. The rioting, which began in Soweto, the huge black township next to Johannesburg, in mid-June, grew out of black student protests against the compulsory use of Afrikaans as a medium of instruction. Although the government announced in early July that it would begin phasing out Afrikaans at the primary and secondary school levels, the disturbances spread to townships around Pretoria and, in late August and early September, to the heart of Cape Town. Despite the unrest, the Vorster government gave no indication of abandoning its commitment to "separate development" of the races, with the official position being that the policy was not based on race but on the conviction that, within South Africa, blacks made up distinct nations to which special political and constitutional arrangements should apply. It was in accordance with this philosophy that nominal independence was granted to the territories that would become known as the black homelands: Transkei in October 1976, Bophuthatswana in December 1977, Venda in September 1979, and Ciskei in December 1981.

Rioting intensified during 1977 amid growing signs that the Vorster government felt itself under siege. Drastic new security legislation was approved, and the government instituted its most drastic crackdown in two decades, closing the leading black newspaper, arresting its editor, and banning a number of protest groups. Apparent white endorsement of these moves was revealed in a parliamentary election on November 30, in which the NP captured 134 of 165 lower house seats.

On September 20, 1978, Prime Minister Vorster announced his intention to resign for reasons of health. Nine days later he was elected by a joint session of Parliament to the essentially titular post of president, succeeding Nicolaas J. DIEDERICHS, who had died on August 21. One day earlier the NP elected Defense Minister Pieter W. BOTHA as its new leader, making him prime minister. On June 4, 1979, President Vorster also resigned after being charged with participation in a variety of clandestine propaganda activities and of giving false evidence in an effort to conceal gross irregularities in the affair. He was immediately succeeded, on an interim basis, by Senate president Marais VILJOEN, who was elected to a full term as head of state by Parliament on June 19. Despite the scandal and increasingly vocal opposition from both the HNP and remaining *verkrampte* elements within the NP, the Botha government remained in power with a marginally reduced parliamentary majority after the election of April 29, 1981, having campaigned on a 12-point platform, first advanced in 1979, that called for constitutional power-sharing among whites, Coloureds, and Asians, with full independence for the black homelands.

In a referendum conducted November 2, 1982, a Constitution Bill, providing for an executive state president and a tricameral parliament excluding blacks, was endorsed by 66 percent of white voters and was approved by the House of Assembly on September 9, 1983. After balloting for delegates to the Coloured and Indian chambers in August 1984, Prime Minister Botha was unanimously elected president by an electoral college of the majority parties in each house on September 5, and he was inaugurated in Cape Town on September 14.

Faced with mounting internal unrest and near-universal foreign condemnation, the government in April 1985 abandoned legislation outlawing sex between the races and the prohibition of multiracial political movements. These moves, while provoking an immediate backlash from right-wing extremists, were received by black and moderate white leaders as "too little, too late." Clashes between police and demonstrators increased, prompting a state of emergency in 36 black townships, the first in a quarter-century. On August 15, in a speech in Durban, President Botha rejected demands for further racial concessions, insisting that they would constitute "a road to abdication and suicide" by white South Africans.

In an address at the opening of Parliament on January 31, 1986, President Botha shocked the extreme right by declaring, "We have outgrown the outdated colonial system of paternalism, as well as the outdated concept of apartheid." In late April, he announced that a bill would be introduced terminating the hated pass laws, which required black South Africans to carry a document showing any white areas they were allowed to enter, though the legislation would not affect segregation in schools, hospitals, and residential areas. Earlier, on March 7, the partial state of emergency imposed eight months before was rescinded; however, a nationwide state of emergency was declared on June 12 to quell anticipated violence on June 16, the anniversary of the Soweto uprising.

Although the term of the House of Assembly had been extended from 1986 to 1989 to coincide with the five-year mandates of the Coloured and Indian chambers, President Botha announced in January 1987 that an early election for a new white chamber would be held on May 6. The results of the poll reflected a distinctly rightward swing by the white voters.

During the ensuing months the government continued grudgingly yielding on the substance of apartheid while severely limiting the freedom of its opponents. A variety of new press restrictions were announced in August, while the government banned the activities of numerous groups. Banned groups included labor unions; civic, educational, and youth associations; the umbrella United Democratic Front (UDF), which linked some 650 anti-apartheid organizations; and a new Committee for the Defence of Democracy (CDD), organized in Cape Town in March 1988. In September a major constitutional crisis was averted by the government's withdrawal of five bills designed to tighten residential segregation laws, upon which the two nonwhite parliamentary chambers had refused to act. Throughout the period numerous long-incarcerated regime opponents were released, while others, primarily from the "new generation" of UDF and other leaders, were arrested and convicted of treason.

On January 18, 1989, President Botha suffered a stroke, and Constitutional Development Minister J. Christiaan HEUNIS was sworn in as acting chief executive the following day. On February 2 Botha resigned as NP leader, with Education Minister Frederik W. DE KLERK being named his successor. On March 13 the party's parliamentary caucus voted unanimously that de Klerk should also become state president; Botha, however, refused to step down and on March 15 resumed the presidency, vowing to stay in office for the remainder of his term. Less than five months later Botha complained of not being advised of a proposed meeting that de Klerk and Foreign Minister Roelof Frederik "Pik" BOTHA had scheduled with Zambian president Kenneth Kaunda. Terming the proposed meeting inopportune, President Botha resigned on August 14, with de Klerk succeeding him on an acting basis the following day.

In balloting for all three legislative chambers on September 6, 1989, the NP retained its overall majority in the House of Assembly, although its share of the vote fell to less than half (48.6 percent). On September 14 de Klerk was named by the parliamentary electoral college to a regular five-year term as president. In October his administration released seven prominent ANC leaders from prison, including Walter SISULU, who had been incarcerated for 26 years.

On February 2, 1990, de Klerk lifted the bans against the main anti-apartheid organization, the African National Congress (ANC), the Pan-Africanist Congress (PAC), and the South African Communist Party (SACP), and on February 11 he freed the long-incarcerated ANC leader, Nelson Rolihlahla MANDELA. However, on April 17, two weeks before the start of talks with ANC leaders, the president flatly rejected majority rule on the ground that it would "lead to the domination and even the suppression of minorities." He also rejected a demand by right-wing whites for racially based partition of the country and proposed a system under which power would be shared by all groups and minority rights would be constitutionally guaranteed. For its part, the ANC indicated that it would not engage in full negotiations until the nearly four-year state of emergency had been rescinded and all political prisoners and exiles had been amnestied.

On June 1, 1990, the government introduced legislation to rescind the Reservation of Separate Amenities Act that had sanctioned "petty apartheid" at public locations, such as beaches, libraries, and places of entertainment.

On June 27, 1990, de Klerk stated that he was prepared to negotiate a new constitution that would eliminate all aspects of apartheid, and on August 7, one day after his second meeting with the president, Mandela announced that the ANC was suspending its 30-year armed struggle. In early October de Klerk and the leaders of the six self-governing homelands agreed to scrap the Lands Acts, and on October 15 the Separate Amenities Act was formally repealed. Subsequently, in a historic move, de Klerk asked the National Party to open its rolls to all races. On December 13 ANC President Oliver TAMBO was permitted to return from more than three decades' exile.

In January 1991 the government and the ANC agreed to convene an all-party conference on the constitutional drafting process, although Chief Mangosuthu BUTHELEZI, leader of the Zulu-based *Inkatha* Freedom Party (IFP), responded coolly, while the Communist Party of South Africa (CPSA), the PAC, and the Azanian People's Organization (Azapo) indicated that they would not participate. Meanwhile, on January 29 the ANC's Mandela and *Inkatha*'s Chief Mangosuthu Buthelezi met for the first time in 30 years to defuse the bitter rivalry that had caused the death of more than 4,000 people and had split the anti-apartheid movement. However, within two days of the leaders' reconciliation, renewed fighting had broken out between their followers.

The Lands Acts of 1913 and 1936, which reserved 87 percent of the country's land for the white minority, and the Group Areas Act, which provided for racially segregated residential areas, were abolished on

June 5, 1991. Five days later, the Population Registration Act, which mandated the classification of South Africans by race from birth, was repealed. Revocation of the Population Act left the capacity to vote (promised by the government under the new constitution) as the major remaining obstacle to black emancipation.

The first session of the Convention for a Democratic South Africa (Codesa), held December 20–21, 1991, featured a "declaration of intent" whereby constitutional proposals would require the approval of both the ANC and the government, with the latter pledging to employ its parliamentary majority to translate Codesa's decisions into law. Meanwhile, the de Klerk administration had become embroiled in an "Inkathagate" scandal stemming from evidence that the South Africa Defence Force (SADF) had been engaged over a three-year period in providing IFP members with anti-ANC military training.

On February 20, 1992, President de Klerk announced that a "whites-only" referendum would be held March 17 to renew his mandate for negotiating with anti-apartheid organizations. The projected poll was immediately denounced by white extremist groups as well as by the leftist PAC and Azapo, which had long demanded that a new basic law be approved by a broadly based constituent assembly rather than by the existing nonblack Parliament. The result of the referendum was a triumph for the president, with 68.7 percent of the participants endorsing continuation of the reform process.

The Codesa II session held May 15–16, 1992, proved unproductive, largely because the parties were unable to resolve an impasse over the size of the majority required for interim legislative approval of key constitutional provisions. On May 27 a commission headed by Richard GOLDSTONE, a respected South African jurist, issued a six-month study on the sources of internal violence. While not completely exonerating the government, the commission found no evidence of "a sinister and secret organization orchestrating political violence on a wide front." Rather, it attributed the disturbances in the townships to "the political battle between supporters of the ANC and the *Inkatha* Freedom Party." The conclusions of the commission were tested on June 17, when South African police were accused of transporting a group of Zulu speakers to Boipatong township, south of Johannesburg, where a bloody massacre ensued that claimed 45 lives. After touring Boipatong, ANC Secretary General Cyril RAMAPHOSA insisted that the slaughter was a government response to the launching of an ANC mass action campaign designed to force majority rule. While the government vehemently denied the charge, Nelson Mandela declared on June 21 that negotiations were "in tatters," and the ANC Executive Committee voted two days later to withdraw from Codesa.

ANC suspicions that the Goldstone Commission had not uncovered the whole truth about township violence were confirmed when a raid on a covert operations center of military intelligence in Pretoria yielded information that impelled President de Klerk to announce on December 19, 1992, that illegal activities by senior SADF officers were under investigation. In further reports, the commission in October 1993 found strong circumstantial evidence of security force involvement in the violence. In March 1994 it cited allegations of a conspiracy among senior police officers involving a "third force" of *agents provocateurs* tasked with anti-ANC destabilization in collaboration with the IFP.

Meanwhile, a "record of understanding" drawn up in September 1992 between the ANC and the NP had given renewed impetus to constitutional talks, which were resumed in March 1993 within what was later designated the Multi-Party Negotiating Process (MPNP). The 26 parties involved included several that had boycotted Codesa, notably the PAC and the SACP, the latter being a leading component of the Concerned South Africans Group (COSAG) of apartheid-era formations, including the IFP. The MPNP came under immediate strain as a result of the assassination on April 10 of Chris HANI, SACP general secretary and an ANC executive member. However, counsels of restraint from Mandela and others prevented the violent reaction in the black townships from getting out of control.

Negotiating breakthroughs came in May and June 1993, when most of the MPNP parties agreed that nonracial elections for a five-year transitional government of national unity would take place on April 27, 1994. Also crucial was the ANC's shift from insistence on a centralized state to acceptance of a federal structure with entrenched powers for provincial governments. The concession did not prevent the IFP and the CPSA from withdrawing from the MPNP shortly before the publication on July 26 of a draft interim constitution providing for equal citizenship rights for all races and a nine-province federal structure integrating the black homelands into the new South Africa. In September the remaining MPNP parties also reached agreement on the creation of a multiracial Transitional Executive Council (TEC), which as approved by Parliament on September 23, was to operate alongside the government in the election run-up to ensure fair play and to monitor the operations of the security forces. After the package of texts had been formally adopted by the MPNP on November 18, the TEC was installed on December 7. Finally, on December 22 Parliament ratified the Constitution of the Republic of South Africa Bill by 237 votes to 45, most of those against being CPSA members.

The problem of reconciling opponents, both white and black, to the settlement remained. In May 1993 the CPSA had joined with various right-wing Afrikaner groups to form the Afrikaner People's Front (*Afrikaner Volksfront*—AVF) under the leadership of Gen. (Ret.) Constand VILJOEN, a former head of the SADF, with the aim of achieving self-determination for Afrikaners in a separate homeland. In June tensions mounted when armed members of the Afrikaner Resistance Movement (*Afrikaner Weerstandsbeweging*—AWB), a paramilitary group led by Eugene TERRE'BLANCHE, forcibly occupied the building where MPNP talks were in progress, with no resistance from the police. In October the AVF, together with the IFP and other conservative black elements, launched the Freedom Alliance as successor to COSAG. Its constituent elements at first presented a united front against the constitutional settlement, although a January 1994 decision in favor of electoral participation by the Ciskei government (originally a Freedom Alliance member) was a serious setback.

The situation was transformed in March 1994 when the AWB and other Afrikaner paramilitaries, apparently sanctioned by the AVF, tried to protect the Bophuthatswana government of Chief Lucas MANGOPE (a Freedom Alliance member) from ANC-led protests against his decision to boycott the elections. Order was restored by speedy deployment of SADF troops, the Afrikaners being routed with 3 fatalities among at least 60 deaths overall and Mangope being removed from office by decision of the TEC on March 12. In light of this debacle and earlier divisions in the Freedom Alliance, Viljoen broke ranks with the AVF by forming the Freedom Front (*Vryheidsfront*—VF), which registered for the elections, whereas the CPSA and the other AVF formations maintained their nonparticipation stance. The split marked the effective collapse of the Freedom Alliance, as confirmed by the eleventh-hour decision of the IFP on April 19 that it too would contest the forthcoming elections, despite bloody ANC-IFP clashes near the ANC's Shell House headquarters in Johannesburg on March 28 in which over 50 IFP demonstrators had been killed.

The IFP's participation ensured that South Africa's first multiracial balloting, to be held April 26–29, 1994, would be relatively free of violence. According to the Independent Electoral Commission and numerous foreign observers, the election was in the main conducted fairly. As expected, the ANC registered an overwhelming victory in the national contest, winning 252 of 400 seats in the new National Assembly, against 82 for the NP, 43 for the IFP, 9 for the VF, and 14 for three smaller parties. In simultaneous polls for new provincial assemblies, the ANC won majorities in seven provinces, losing only Western Cape (to the NP) and KwaZulu-Natal (to the IFP).

Elected president by unanimous vote of the new assembly on May 9, 1994, Nelson Mandela was sworn in the following day. Under the terms of the constitutional settlement, the ANC's Thabo MBEKI became first deputy president and de Klerk second deputy president. The new cabinet installed on May 11 contained 19 ANC representatives, 5 from the NP, and 3 from the IFP (including Chief Buthelezi as home affairs minister). The new Senate, its members designated by the newly elected provincial assemblies, convened on May 20, with the ANC holding 60 of 90 seats.

Nelson Mandela was inaugurated as South African president on May 10, 1994. Far-right Afrikaners continued to press for political autonomy, although talks between Mandela and CPSA leader Ferdi HARTZENBERG in Pretoria on August 12 suggested that the AVF did not intend to resort to force. As for the IFP, while Chief Buthelezi had accepted cabinet membership, relations between his Zulu-based formation and Mandela's ANC remained tense. Intensifying post-election controversy was the disclosure on May 19 that on the eve of the election some 7.4 million acres of state land in KwaZulu, about a third of the ex-homeland's area, had been transferred to the control of the Zulu King Goodwill ZWELITHINI under legislation adopted by the outgoing KwaZulu Assembly and approved by President de Klerk, without the knowledge of the ANC. Although the new minister of land affairs, Derek HANEKOM (ANC), announced on June 15 that the transfer would stand, the affair angered many ANC members, who suspected that its purpose had been to entice the IFP into the electoral process.

A year after the advent of majority rule, the most serious political problem facing the government was the disaffection of the IFP and its Zulu supporters, centering on their demand for a degree of autonomy for KwaZulu-Natal. Accompanied by periodic clashes between ANC and IFP supporters, the confrontation worsened in April 1995 when IFP members withdrew from the Constituent Assembly charged with drafting a permanent constitution. Although Chief Buthelezi remained a member of the government, he asserted that his party would not accept any constitution drawn up in its absence and repeated his demand for international mediation of KwaZulu-Natal's dispute with the central authorities. ANC ministers and officials responded that a formal international role in the dispute would imply acceptance of KwaZulu-Natal's claim to separate status; they also insisted that drafting of the new constitution would proceed according to schedule, if necessary without IFP participation.

ANC-IFP relations were further aggravated by President Mandela's admission on June 1, 1995, that he had personally authorized ANC members "to shoot to kill if necessary" during bloody clashes between the ANC and IFP on March 28, 1994, near the ANC's headquarters in Johannesburg, in which over 50 IFP demonstrators had died. Amid IFP calls for his impeachment over this admission, the president sought to regain the initiative by proposing on June 14 that responsibility for the pay and perquisites of tribal chiefs should be transferred from the provincial authorities to the central government. Such a change would pose a special threat to Chief Buthelezi's power base in the KwaZulu-Natal countryside, where control of the purse strings sustained the IFP's network of support among tribal chiefs. Serious IFP-ANC clashes in August 1995 were followed on December 25 by an attack by IFP supporters on the village of Shobashobane (an ANC enclave in KwaZulu-Natal) in which at least 19 people were killed, with the security forces failing to intervene.

In sharp contrast, relations between the ANC and the white minority continued to be accommodating, with occasional rifts within the transitional government being quickly resolved. The discovery by the ANC justice minister in January 1995 that the outgoing NP government had secretly granted indemnities from prosecution to over 3,500 policemen and security officials provoked a cabinet crisis in which de Klerk claimed that he and the NP had been subjected to "insulting attack." However, the possibility of an NP withdrawal receded when de Klerk and Mandela met on January 20 and agreed that a fresh start should be made. The president also established working relations with several Afrikaner groups that had vigorously opposed black majority rule, with a disavowal of violence by General Viljoen and the VF seen as particularly helpful.

Two days after the endorsement of the new constitution in Parliament, de Klerk announced on May 10, 1996, that the NP was withdrawing from the government of national unity with effect from June 30. He cited the diminishing influence of the NP on government policy, the refusal of the ANC to include power-sharing arrangements in the new constitution, and the need for an effective opposition. Commentators considered that the decision was motivated by a desire to assert the NP's independence well in advance of legislative elections in 1999. The party subsequently also withdrew from all provincial governments except that of Western Cape, where it was in the majority. President Mandela appointed ANC members to replace the outgoing NP ministers and abolished the post of second deputy president vacated by de Klerk.

Much domestic attention subsequently focused on the initial proceedings of the Truth and Reconciliation Commission (TRC), which had been created in July 1995 to investigate human rights abuses and political crimes of the apartheid era with the aim of consigning their legacy to history. Chaired by Archbishop Desmond TUTU (head of the Anglican Church in South Africa until his retirement in June 1996), the TRC was empowered to grant judicial amnesties to people confessing to apartheid-era crimes (depending on their gravity) if it was satisfied that full disclosure had been made and that the crime in question had been politically motivated. The TRC began a scheduled two years of hearings in April 1996, its authority to grant amnesties being upheld by the Constitutional Court in July after Azapo and the families of several murdered political activists had argued that the commission's power to protect human rights violators from prosecution and civil damages denied them the opportunity to obtain justice through the courts.

Former state president de Klerk gave evidence to the TRC on August 21, 1996. He stated that the security forces had not, to his knowledge, been authorized during the period of NP government to commit human rights abuses, although he apologized for suffering caused by the apartheid system. However, Eugene DE KOCK, a former colonel in the South African police who was convicted in the same month for murder and other crimes during the apartheid era, subsequently claimed in court that members of the former NP government had had full knowledge of a systematic campaign by the police, armed forces, and covert security units against apartheid opponents. Furthermore, in testimony to the TRC in October, several former members of the police claimed that former president P. W. Botha and two former ministers, Louis LE GRANGE and Adriaan VLOK, had ordered state violence against anti-apartheid organizations in the 1980s. In May 1997 de Klerk, in a second appearance, again denied knowledge of human rights violations. He retired from politics in August, and the NP inaugurated a new leadership under Marthinus VAN SCHALKWYK, by which time the party had ended its cooperation with the TRC on the grounds of political bias.

In September 1997 the deadline for submitting petitions to the TRC passed. Among those who did not file and attempted to stave off the TRC's calls to testify were former president Botha and a number of apartheid-era judicial officials. (Botha was convicted in August 1998 for refusing to appear before the TRC, although in June 1999 his appeal was upheld on technical grounds.) The ANC was the most prominent of the organizations to apply and in its petition admitted to torture, abuse, and even executions; however, the party attempted to justify such actions as being in the name of the "dirty war" fought against apartheid.

The dominant event of 1998 was the October release of a comprehensive report from the TRC. Having reviewed evidence from some 20,000 people, the TRC described apartheid as a "crime against humanity." It also declared the government responsible for a large majority of the abuses committed between 1960 and 1994, condemning the NP regime for a broad range of atrocities that included kidnappings, torture, killings, and bombings. However, the ANC and other liberation groups as well as extreme right organizations were also held accountable for violent acts. The report caused controversy, and every major party rejected its conclusions to some degree. It cited prominent individuals from across the entire political spectrum for human rights abuses. They included P. W. Botha, Chief Buthelezi, General Viljoen, Eugène Terre'Blanche, and President Mandela's ex-wife, Winnie MADIKIZELA-MANDELA, one of the country's most popular female politicians and an ANC leader, who was implicated in a dozen violent acts, including murder. Although the activities of two of the TRC's three committees—the Reparation and Rehabilitation Committee and the Human Rights Violations Committee—drew to a close with the release of the report, the mandate of the Amnesty Committee, with over 1,000 cases yet to review, was extended by act of Parliament "until a date determined by the President."

In December 1997 President Mandela had resigned as ANC president and was succeeded, as expected, by Thabo Mbeki, who led the ANC into the June 2, 1999, national elections. The ANC emerged from the balloting with 266 National Assembly seats, one short of the two-thirds majority needed to amend the constitution, prompting party leaders to quickly negotiate a coalition with the Minority Front (MF), an Indian party that had won a single seat. On June 14 the National Assembly unanimously elected Mbeki as president, and he took the oath of office two days later. On June 17 the new president named ANC deputy leader Jacob ZUMA as deputy president and appointed a cabinet in which Chief Buthelezi retained his position as home affairs minister.

In the June 1999 balloting, the dominance of the ANC was evident not only at the national level but also in the provinces, where it retained outright majorities in seven, formed a coalition government with the IFP in KwaZulu-Natal, and won a plurality in Western Cape. In the national balloting, the Democratic Party (DP), led by Tony LEON, displaced the NP (subsequently reconstituted as the New National Party [NNP]) as the leading opposition formation, winning 38 seats (up from 7 in 1994), while the NNP managed only 28, a net loss of 54. Facing diminished prospects, in June 2000 the NNP joined the DP in forming a Democratic Alliance (DA), the expectation being that a full merger of the parties would eventually occur. The DA surprised many observers by winning 23 percent of the national vote in the December municipal elections, but policy and leadership clashes ultimately led the NNP to part ways with the DP in October 2001. In abandoning the DA for a closer relationship with the ANC, the NNP's van Schalkwyk noted that the two erstwhile antagonists no longer had significant ideological differences. Thus, at the end of 2001 the only opposition formations with more than a handful of National Assembly members were the rump DA (the DP plus the small Federal Alliance) and the United Democratic Movement.

In June 2001 public hearings opened into a December 1999 arms deal involving the purchase of surface ships, submarines, helicopters, and jet aircraft from a number of EU countries, at a cost of $5.4 billion. Despite accusations that officials had received kickbacks and engaged in other illegalities, in November the resultant report concluded that the procurement procedure had been flawed but not corrupt, although individuals who had derived "some form of benefit from the acquisition process" could be held criminally liable. The National Assembly opposition condemned the report as a whitewash. Throughout much of the following decade, the affair led to legal troubles for Jacob Zuma.

The Truth and Reconciliation Commission intended to release the final volumes of its report in 2002, but publication was delayed when the IFP went to court in opposition to conclusions that it had been responsible for major human rights violations. The final report was presented to the president in 2003. The commission granted amnesty to 1,200 people but rejected more than 5,000 other applications. After rejecting a suggestion that a special tax be imposed on companies that had profited from apartheid, Mbeki announced that those designated as victims by the TRC would each receive a single payment worth $3,800.

In 2000–2002 the Mbeki administration drew severe criticism for its failure to present a cohesive plan for fighting the HIV/AIDS crisis. Late in 2002 the government announced that it would look into making crucial antiretroviral drugs available through the public health system.

In February 2004 Mbeki signed into law the controversial Restitution of Land Rights Amendment Act, which gave the state the right to expropriate land for restitution purposes without a court order or the seller's agreement. The act applied only to land from which blacks were forcibly removed under the colonial and apartheid regimes. "Just and equitable" compensation was guaranteed to farmers whose land was expropriated. The legislation was an attempt to overcome logjams under the "willing buyer, willing seller" policy, which had been marked by disputes over fair market value of land.

In the elections to the National Assembly and the provincial councils on April 14, 2004, the ANC emerged as the dominant party, winning 279 of the 400 National Assembly seats with 69.7 percent of the vote. The ANC also took control of seven of the nine provincial assemblies and nominated premiers to head all nine provincial governments. On April 23 President Mbeki was reelected by the National Assembly for a second term. Members of the NNP and Azapo were included in the subsequent cabinet, as were six members of the SACP. On August 7 Marthinus van Schalkwyk announced the dissolution of the NNP, asked its members to join the ANC (as van Schalkwyk and some of his colleagues had, former president de Klerk being a notable exception), and agreed to contest all future elections under the ANC banner. In June former president Nelson Mandela officially retired from public life.

In June 2005 Schabir SHAIK, financial adviser to deputy president Jacob Zuma, was found guilty of two counts of corruption and one count of fraud in one of the most closely watched criminal trials since the end of apartheid. On June 15 Zuma, who the judge said was "compliant" in the malfeasance, was dismissed as deputy president. Two weeks later he was charged with two counts of bribery. However, a groundswell of popular support developed for Zuma, a key figure in the fight against apartheid. The Congress of South African Trade Unions (COSATU), the largest trade union federation in South Africa and political ally of the ANC, described the pending legal action as a "political trial" and called on President Mbeki to reinstate Zuma. At year's end, matters became further complicated when Zuma was charged with rape. In May 2006 a judge acquitted Zuma of rape charges, and within days, Zuma was reinstated as ANC deputy president.

In local elections on March 1, 2006, the ANC was unseated in Cape Town where Helen ZILLE of the DA became mayor of the only opposition-controlled city in the country. The DA cited subsequent ANC maneuvers to abolish Zille's position as further evidence of the ANC's drive for power and inability to accept electoral defeat.

Amid the ANC's June 2007 national policy conference and a huge public service strike, COSATU's general secretary, Zwelinzima VAVI, claimed Mbeki's government had marginalized not only COSATU and the SACP, but also the ANC. COSATU and the SACP became increasingly vocal critics of President Mbeki, denouncing what they said were his autocratic tendencies, conservative and pro-business economic policies, and alleged failure to address unemployment, poverty, and inequality effectively.

Mbeki's status declined after he lost the ANC chair at the party's 2008 convention (see Political Parties, below). Further, Zuma appeared to be encroaching on his position. In March Zuma declared that the ANC, rather than the government, was the main source of political power in South Africa, and in April he visited the United Kingdom, where he met with Prime Minister Gordon Brown in a manner more suggestive of a head of government than a party leader. Together, they called for a break in the Zimbabwean electoral stalemate (see article on Zimbabwe), demanding that Zimbabwean president Robert Mugabe release the election results.

The criminal case against Zuma proceeded slowly through much of 2008. Some of Zuma's ANC supporters, particularly in the party's youth wing, threatened bloodshed if he were convicted. Zuma, in turn, promised to name names if he were ever made to give evidence. Some news reports had linked President Mbeki to the arms scandal, and it was assumed that Zuma would accuse Mbeki if necessary. After numerous postponements, the case appeared to have finally collapsed on September 12, 2008, when a High Court judge ruled that the case against Zuma could not continue. The judge said that Zuma's constitutional rights had been denied because he had not been questioned before charges were brought. In a blow to Mbeki's reputation, the judge expressed suspicion that the prosecution had been politically motivated, noting that the latest round of charges against Zuma came shortly after he defeated Mbeki for the ANC presidency. The judge criticized all parties in the case and emphasized that they were eroding South Africa's reputation for electoral freedom and an independent judiciary. (Charges against Zuma were reinstated but were thrown out of court shortly before the April 2009 elections.)

After the High Court ruling, the ANC voted on September 24, 2008, to ask Mbeki to step down as president. Mbeki agreed to honor the motion when parliament named his replacement. The ANC nominated Kgalema MOTLANTHE, its deputy leader and an ally of Zuma, as caretaker president until the 2009 presidential election. Parliament ratified the choice on September 25, and Motlanthe was sworn in. Mbeki's departure prompted 11 cabinet resignations. Some resignations were a courtesy to the new president, as in the case of Trevor MANUEL, the well-respected finance minister who resigned but was reappointed. Other ministers were unwilling to serve in the new administration. The replacement of health minister Mantombazana TSHABALALA-MSIMANG, who had advocated garlic and beetroot to combat HIV, was widely praised.

President Mbeki's forced resignation angered many within the ANC. Among the ministers resigning in protest was Defense Minister Mosiuoa LEKOTA, who led a dissident group in forming a new political party to contest the spring 2009 elections. Many observers believed the new party might deny the ANC the two-thirds majority necessary to change the constitution. The ANC successfully challenged two names proposed for the new party by claiming ownership rights over each. Ultimately, the new party was granted the name Congress of the People (COPE) over the ANC's objections. In January 2011 a document from WikiLeaks suggested that Mbeki had been involved in writing a policy statement for COPE. Mbeki denied this, and the ANC declared that he was still a member in good standing.

In the run-up to the 2009 elections, the Constitutional Court confirmed an earlier High Court decision allowing South African citizens living outside the country to vote. The campaign was marked by intermittent violence, and several unions vowed to boycott the elections. Desmond Tutu initially said he would not vote but later changed his mind. Critics also objected to Zuma's appeal for support from members of his tribe, the Zulus, and his apparent willingness to distribute key positions to loyalists. They argued that tribalism and related practices were incompatible with South Africa's modern social aspirations and norms. Despite increasing poverty and persistent inequality during the period of ANC rule, Zuma remained popular with poor black voters. He also made significant efforts to court Afrikaners, addressing them as a "white tribe" implicitly superior to English-speaking (and presumably nontribal) whites. Middle-class blacks and ANC dissidents, however, increasingly gravitated toward COPE, while the DA remained the party of choice for many whites and made inroads with the Coloureds.

The ANC won the poll on April 22, 2009, with a vote share of 65.9 percent, just short of the two-thirds majority required to amend the constitution, something observers attributed to the rising profile of COPE. The ANC won 294 Assembly seats, followed by the Democratic Alliance with 67. On May 6 the National Assembly elected Zuma president. Days later, he named Kgalema Petrus MOTLANTHE as deputy president and formed a new government.

Facing an economic recession and high unemployment, the government announced in June that it would not expropriate white-owned farms, a move deemed harmful to the economy. Zuma's first two years in office were met with praise for programs to providing AIDS treatment drugs for pregnant women. But the country was plagued by intermittent strikes, including tens of thousands of government workers demanding an 8.6 percent pay raise in hospitals and schools. Zuma's administration took some measures to fight corruption, but observers noted troublesome issues remain, including a lack of transparency in government and the militarization of police.

A major cabinet reshuffle occurred on October 31, 2010; 7 ministers were dismissed, and 14 new deputy ministers were appointed, among other changes. The move was widely seen as an attempt by Zuma to cater to allies in the ANC rather than enhance the effectiveness of government. Another, albeit minor, cabinet reshuffle occurred in June 2012.

Throughout 2011 and 2012, corruption allegations provided ammunition for Zuma's critics in a deepening rift within the ANC over his bid for a second term as president (see Political Parties, below). In October 2011, under mounting pressure from the opposition to tackle corruption, Zuma fired two government ministers and suspended a police chief, all accused of corruption offenses.

On July 15, 2012, Nkosazana DLAMINI-ZUMA, South Africa's home affairs minister and the ex-wife of President Zuma, won the chair of the African Union (AU) over Gabon's incumbent Jean Ping. The vote ended months of gridlock after neither secured the required two-thirds majority at an AU summit in January.

On August 16, 2012, police opened fire on a crowd of 3,000 striking miners at the Marikana platinum mine in Lonmin, killing 34 and wounding 78 others. The police claimed they were defending themselves from a crowd armed with machetes and spears. But, the Marikana Massacre touched a political nerve as the mining sector is considered by some in the ANC to be a bastion of white control. In the week before the shooting, ten people, including two police officers, had been killed at the mine in a conflict between rival unions: The long-dominant National Union of Mineworkers (NUM), a key supporter of the ANC, was challenged by the Association of Mineworkers and Construction Union (AMCU). In the weeks that followed, the mine's operations came to a halt, and global platinum prices jumped.

A new round of labor unrest peaked in October 2012, when wildcat mine strikes spread to other sectors, eventually involving an estimated 100,000 workers. Most of the strikes were settled by late October, following a negotiated settlement with mine companies that included a series of concessions and minor wage increases. The labor strife cost South Africa an estimated $5 billion and reportedly prompted foreign firms to reconsider locating new plants in the country. Continuing labor unrest led Fitch to downgrade South Africa's credit rating in January 2013. In late June 2014 platinum mine workers ended a five-month strike, the longest and costliest in the mining industry.

In 2014 the public protector, an independent anticorruption entity, ruled that Zuma had benefited unduly from $23 million in publicly funded renovations of his homestead Nkandla in the KwaZulu-Natal. The ANC-controlled parliament responded to the so-called Nkandla scandal or "Nkandlagate" by officially clearing the president of any wrongdoing by accepting two reports that claimed the upgrades were necessary to improve security. In March 2016 the nation's highest court ruled unanimously that $8 million of the renovations were legitimate but that Zuma had violated the constitution by not repaying $16 million of the costs. In September Zuma repaid $542,000. The scandal significantly impacted the 2016 local elections (see Current issues, below).

Constitution and government. Under the Interim Constitution adopted by the outgoing Parliament on December 22, 1993, a president, named for a five-year term by the National Assembly, exercised executive power. Legislative authority was vested in a bicameral Parliament consisting of a Senate, 10 of whose 90 members were elected from each of nine regional legislatures, and a National Assembly, half of whose 400 members were elected from national and half from regional party lists. The two houses sat jointly as a Constituent Assembly, which debated and approved a permanent constitution (see below). The Interim Constitution detailed rights of citizenship, which for the first time constituted a universal bill of rights applying equally to all races, to be safeguarded by a Constitutional Court as the supreme judicial authority. In its first major ruling on June 6, 1995, the Court decided unanimously to abolish the death penalty in South Africa.

The four historic provinces (Cape, Natal, Orange Free State, and Transvaal) were replaced by nine new provinces: Eastern Cape, Eastern Transvaal (now Mpumalanga), KwaZulu-Natal, Northern Cape, Northern Transvaal (now Limpopo), North-West, Orange Free State (now Free State), Pretoria-Witwatersrand-Vereeniging (PWV, now Gauteng), and Western Cape, each with an elected legislature. Under the new provincial structure, the four "independent" and six "self-governing" black homelands created by the apartheid government were effectively abolished. (For details regarding the "independent" homelands, see 1993 *Handbook*.) Town and city councils were established as multiracial, with a group of white voters and a group of black voters each electing 30 percent of the councilors and the remainder being selected on a nonracial basis.

In November 1995, following 18 months of work by the Constituent Assembly, the first draft of the new permanent constitution was published, with the main political parties reaching agreement on a final version on May 7, 1996, shortly before the expiry of the deadline set during the transitional period. The following day the text was approved overwhelmingly by Parliament. The NP voted in favor, despite its reservations over provisions relating to labor relations, property rights, language, and education, in order to safeguard concessions already secured from the ANC. The IFP was absent for the vote, maintaining its boycott of the Constituent Assembly, from which it had withdrawn in April 1995. Ratified in its final version on December 4 by the Constitutional Court, which had previously rejected certain draft clauses, particularly in relation to the reduction of provincial powers, the new constitution was finally signed into law on December 10 by President Mandela in a ceremony in Sharpeville. The IFP, which had briefly returned to the Constituent Assembly on October 1 before withdrawing again on October 7, accepted the legitimacy of the new document.

The new constitution took effect February 4, 1997. The new basic law incorporated many essentials of the 1993 text, although it abandoned the principle that all parties with 5 percent of the vote should be represented in the cabinet. It also provided for a National Council of Provinces (NCOP) to replace the existing Senate, with the aim of enhancing the influence of the provinces on the policy of the central government—although it fell short of guaranteeing the provincial powers that the IFP had demanded. In addition, it enshrined an extensive bill of rights, one of the most liberal in the world. In the future, changes to the constitution would require the approval of at least two-thirds of the members of the National Assembly and at least six of the nine provinces represented in the National Council.

With regard to ordinary legislation, the powers exercised by the two houses vary. Bills affecting the republic as a whole are introduced in the National Assembly and, if passed, proceed to the NCOP, where the members, voting individually, may concur or may propose changes for consideration by the assembly. Bills affecting the provinces may be introduced in either house, but in the NCOP each of the nine provincial delegations has one vote. If the two chambers disagree on a provincial bill, an 18-member mediation committee (9 members from each chamber) attempts to reconcile the differences and return compromise legislation for a new vote in both houses. Failing that, the National Assembly may pass the bill with a two-thirds vote and send it on for presidential signature.

In early 1997 the legislature approved the creation of a National House of Traditional Leaders, aiming to provide a forum for the leaders of tribal groups and increasing communication between the legislature and the provinces. The new body was inaugurated on April 17. Members are named by provincial-level Houses of Traditional Leaders. In 2001 the Department of Justice and Constitutional Development, responding largely to requests from rural areas, announced that traditional leaders would be permitted to function as Commissioners of Oaths (with a function similar to that of a notary public). At the same time, the Department of Provincial and Local Government has begun the process of more clearly delineating the powers and functions of the traditional leadership.

Provincial governments are led by elected legislatures of 30 to 80 members. Each legislature elects a provincial premier, who heads an Executive Council. Beneath the provincial level are 284 municipalities, including 6 metropolitan municipalities ("megacities," incorporating surrounding townships): Cape Town, Durban Unicity, Ekurhuleni (East Rand), Johannesburg, Nelson Mandela (Port Elizabeth), and Tshwane (Pretoria). Legislatures are elected at each municipal level. In 2000 the proportion of traditional representatives on councils was raised from 10 to 20 percent. The smaller jurisdictions are represented throughout the governmental system by the South African Local Government Association (SALGA).

The 1996 constitution had an anti-defection clause prohibiting floor-crossing because it was felt that permitting representatives to change parties would interfere with the proportional electoral system. In June 2002 legislation regulated floor-crossing in national, provincial, and local government elections. Legislators wishing to change parties were required to do so within the first 15 days of the second year of a legislative term; they could form another party or merge with a party without losing their seats. The UDM and others submitted an urgent application to the Constitutional Court challenging the constitutionality of the new legislation. In October the court ruled that floor-crossing at the municipal level could proceed but indicated that the legislation for the national and provincial levels had technical deficiencies and would require redrafting. In February 2003 the constitution was amended to permit members of the National Assembly and the nine provincial legislatures to switch allegiances from one party to another, thus bringing uniformity to the three levels of government regarding defections. In January 2009 floor-crossing was again abolished by the parliament.

National Assembly and provincial elections were held on May 7, 2014. The ANC won 62 seats in parliament, while the Economic Freedom Fighters (EFF), an ANC splinter group, won 25. The Democratic Alliance (DA) won 89 seats.

Freedom of the press is guaranteed, and Reporters Without Borders ranked South Africa 39th out of 180 countries (up 3 places) in media freedom in 2016, the fourth-highest rating for an African state. The improved ranking is the result of President Zuma's veto of the Protection of State Information Bill (POSIB) on September 12, 2013. The law included penalties for revealing state secrets and classified information and would have endangered investigative journalism in the country.

Foreign relations. Although South Africa was a founding member of the United Nations, its international standing was greatly impaired as a result of the racial restrictions maintained in its own territory and, until late 1988, that of Namibia (South West Africa). In the post–World War II period its rejection of external advice and pressure resulted in an atrophy of international contacts, notably through its departure from the Commonwealth in 1961, its suspension from membership in the Economic Commission for Africa in 1963, and its withdrawal or expulsion from a number of UN Specialized Agencies. It was also denied participation in the UN General Assembly, which repeatedly condemned the policy and practice of apartheid and advocated "universally applied economic sanctions" as the only means of achieving a peaceful solution to the problem. The UN Security Council, while stopping short of economic measures, called as early as 1963 for an embargo on the sale and shipment to South Africa of military equipment and materials.

Relations with the United Nations were further aggravated by South Africa's refusal to apply economic sanctions against Rhodesia, as ordered by the Security Council in 1966, and its long-standing refusal to relinquish control over Namibia, as ordered by both the General Assembly and the Security Council. Despite its political isolation on these key issues, Pretoria refrained from quitting the world body and attempted to maintain friendly political relations and close economic ties with most Western countries. Regionally, it belonged to the Southern African Customs Union (SACU), along with Botswana, Lesotho, Swaziland, and, later, Namibia. It also cooperated closely with the Ian Smith regime in Rhodesia over economic and defense matters, assisting its neighbor in circumventing UN sanctions. However, in accordance with its policy of seeking détente with neighboring black regimes, it publicly called for a "resolution of the Rhodesian question," endorsing in 1976 the principle of black majority rule if appropriate guarantees were extended to the white minority of what became in 1980 the Republic of Zimbabwe.

For more than a decade the government mounted repeated forays into Angola in its protracted conflict with Namibian insurgents, while relations with Swaziland and Mozambique were aggravated by the presence of ANC guerrilla bases in both countries, despite the conclusion of a nonaggression pact with the former in 1982 and with the latter in May 1984.

During 1985 Western states came under increased pressure to impose sanctions on the Botha government. U.S. president Ronald Reagan had long opposed any action that would disrupt the South African economy, but faced in mid-September with a congressional threat to act on its own, he ordered a number of modest punitive actions, with the countries of the European Community (EC, subsequently the EU) following in an equally restrained manner. The principal American prohibitions focused on bank loans and the export of nuclear technology and computers, while the Europeans imposed an oil embargo, halted most arms sales, and withdrew their military attachés. In addition, substantial corporate divestment occurred, particularly by U.S. firms. None of these sanctions presented a serious challenge to South Africa, which was, however, sufficiently aggrieved to threaten an embargo on the export of strategic metals to the United States.

Pretoria's capacity to act with impunity in regard to neighboring states was amply demonstrated during 1986. On January 1 Lesotho was effectively blockaded, and three weeks later its government was overthrown by forces supportive of South African efforts to contain cross-border attacks by ANC guerrillas. Subsequently, on May 19 ANC targets in Botswana, Zambia, and Zimbabwe were subjected to bombing attacks by the South African Air Force, in addition to ground raids by units of the SADF. Additional forays were conducted against alleged ANC bases in Swaziland late in the year and in Zambia in early 1987.

During 1988 South Africa's regional posture softened dramatically. In September President Botha traveled to Mozambique for his first state visit to a black African country. "Fruitful and cordial" discussions were held with President Chissano on a variety of topics, including the supply of power from Mozambique's Cahora Bassa hydroelectric facility, the status of Mozambican workers in South Africa, and "reactivation and reinforcement" of the Nkomati agreement of March 1984, which promised mutual nonaggression between South Africa and Mozambique. Subsequently, Botha visited Zaire and Côte d'Ivoire for talks with presidents Mobuto and Houphouët-Boigny, respectively. The most important development, however, concerned the Angola–Namibia conflict. During a November meeting in Geneva, Switzerland, Pretoria accepted a U.S.-mediated agreement, previously endorsed by Angola and Cuba, for the phased withdrawal of Cuban troops from Angola, accompanied by a withdrawal of all but 1,000 South African troops from Namibia and a UN-supervised election seven months thereafter in implementation of UN Security Council Resolution 435 of 1978. A protocol finalizing the agreement was signed in Brazzaville, Congo, on December 13, followed by the formal conclusion of a tripartite peace accord at UN headquarters in New York on December 22 (see entries on Angola and Namibia for details). Not addressed by the Namibia settlement was the status of the port enclave of Walvis Bay, which, although historically South African territory, had been administered since 1977 as part of South West Africa. Discussions on the issue began in March 1991, but it was not until August 16, 1993, in a major decision of the multiparty forum convened to decide the future of South Africa, that the South African government delegation agreed under pressure from the ANC and other participants to transfer the Walvis Bay enclave to Namibia. Formal conveyance occurred at midnight on February 28, 1994.

In a setback for ANC efforts to increase Pretoria's diplomatic isolation, in September 1990 President de Klerk was received at the White House by U.S. president George H. W. Bush. A few days earlier Foreign Minister Botha had announced that South Africa was prepared to accede to the UN Nuclear Non-Proliferation Treaty (see International Atomic Energy Agency, under UN: Related Organizations) in furtherance of an effort to make the African continent a nuclear weapons–free zone.

The progress made in dismantling apartheid during 1991 yielded significant diplomatic gains for Pretoria globally and on the African continent. Most economic sanctions imposed by Western nations (save in regard to military items) were relaxed, and in April 1992, after a number of political exchanges with neighboring regimes, President de Klerk made a highly symbolic state visit to Nigeria for talks with the incumbent chair of the Organization of African Unity (OAU, subsequently the AU), Ibrahim Babangida. No less symbolic was South Africa's return to international sport.

On July 1, 1993, President de Klerk and ANC President Mandela held separate meetings in Washington with U.S. president Bill Clinton and three days later were joint recipients of Liberty Medals in Philadelphia, with President Clinton in attendance. The end of apartheid was further celebrated on October 15, when de Klerk and Mandela were jointly awarded the 1993 Nobel Peace Prize. At the same time, most UN economic sanctions against South Africa were terminated.

During 1994 South Africa gradually reentered the international community. On June 1 it rejoined the Commonwealth after a break of 33 years; two weeks later it became the 53rd member of the OAU. On June 23, following the Security Council's lifting of its long-standing arms embargo on South Africa, the suspension of Pretoria's participation in the UN General Assembly was rescinded, thus facilitating full reintegration into the world body. Two months later, South Africa joined the Southern African Development Community (SADC), and in October it signed an economic cooperation agreement with the EU.

In November 1996 the South African government announced that it was canceling its diplomatic relations with Taiwan, one of its foremost trading partners, and establishing formal relations with the People's Republic of China.

In the fall of 1998 South Africa deployed troops to help restore order in Lesotho in the fall (see entry on Lesotho). President Mandela also continued to pursue a role as Africa's most prominent peacemaker, becoming heavily involved, for example, in efforts to resolve the conflict in the Democratic Republic of the Congo. In addition, the government further exhibited the independent nature of its foreign policy by extending ties with Iraq and North Korea, despite strong objections from Washington and several EU capitals.

South Africa has emerged in recent years as an ambitious diplomatic power. Mbeki was the leading figure behind the New Partnership for Africa's Development (NEPAD) and was instrumental in brokering peace in Burundi and the Democratic Republic of the Congo, providing 3,000 troops in the two countries as part of UN peacekeeping operations and also shouldering most of the financial burden. South African companies stand out in the region with strong investment strategies. With 40 percent of sub-Saharan Africa's GDP, South Africa is the only country capable of projecting both military power and economic clout.

South Africa consistently opposed the U.S.-led war in Iraq and has promoted relations with many countries with whom the United States is at odds. Nevertheless, the United States considers South Africa an ally in its efforts to promote democracy on the continent.

Mbeki was deeply involved in efforts to resolve the 2008 political crisis in neighboring Zimbabwe (see entry on Zimbabwe).

The Zuma administration has made a strong push to enhance South Africa's international stance. U.S. secretary of state Hillary Rodham Clinton visited South Africa in August 2009 in an effort to improve bilateral relations. She also suggested that South Africa take a leading role in helping poorer African countries and work for political stability in Zimbabwe. In the same month, South Africa and India pledged stronger economic ties.

In August 2010 Zuma made a state visit to China, where he signed numerous business deals and announced that talks were in progress for South Africa to join BRIC, an economic coalition of Brazil, Russia, India, and China. South Africa formally joined the group, hereafter known as BRICS, in January 2011.

In September 2010, at the South African–European Union summit, Brussels reaffirmed the EU's commitment to a strategic partnership with South Africa, the EU's leading trade partner in Africa.

Prior to the 2011 Libyan civil war, Zuma's relations with strongman Muammar Qadhafi had been quite friendly, and his attitude to the conflict was somewhat inconsistent. In early March South Africa, a nonpermanent member of the UN Security Council, voted to impose a no-fly zone over Libya, authorizing military action, if necessary, to enforce it and to protect civilians. Zuma also telephoned Qadhafi, demanding that he stop killing civilians. On March 10 he introduced a resolution in the AU to suspend Libya's membership in that body and instructed the South African Treasury to freeze any asset transactions involving the Libyan leader. However, Zuma spoke out against regime change in Libya, and called the North Atlantic Treaty Organization (NATO) countries to use restraint. On May 30 he visited Tripoli as an AU representative in an attempt to find a diplomatic solution to the conflict.

On October 4, 2012, after several months of waiting for a visa to visit South Africa for the 80th birthday of Archbishop Desmond Tutu, the Dalai Lama withdrew his application. In response, Tutu surprised journalists with an angry tirade alleging that the South African government had caved to pressure from China.

In June 2012 South Africa was one of seven states granted waivers by the United States on oil imports from Iran. The waiver allowed South Africa to avoid U.S. sanctions targeted at countries that imported Iranian oil.

In April 2013 the Central African Republic (CAR) requested that South African peacekeeping forces be withdrawn from the country. Meanwhile, the mission grew increasingly unpopular among the South African public. Opposition figures asserted that the mission was undertaken in order to gain increased access to the CAR's mineral resources.

In May South Africa announced it would consider rebuilding a border fence in an effort to stop poaching in Kruger National Park. The original fence had been demolished in an effort to create a supranational park, the Great Limpopo Transfrontier Park, with Mozambique. However, by 2013 more than 240 rhinos were being killed annually, mainly by poachers from Mozambique (see entry on Mozambique). South Africa is home to 70 percent of the world's rhinos, and authorities were considering plans to relocate large numbers of rhinos from Kruger National Park to sanctuaries in other countries, including Australia. Demand in China and Vietnam for rhino horn continued to motivate poachers despite steep penalties for offenders. President Zuma hosted the Fifth BRICS Summit on March 27, 2013, the first time that the Summit was hosted on the African continent. South Africa was selected to host the BRICS bank's regional office for Africa, the New Development Bank.

Media outlets reported in 2014 that border guards from all three countries were accepting bribes from passport holders from Zimbabwe and Botswana to conceal their illegal stays in South Africa. Relations with Cuba remained cordial, and South Africa supported the release of three Cubans detained in the United States. On July 14 President Xi Jinping met with President Jacob Zuma in Brazil and agreed to strengthen relations.

In September 2015 the International Criminal Court (ICC) formally requested an explanation from South Africa for why Sudanese president Omar Hassan Ahmed al-Bashir was not arrested when he visited that country in June of that year. Bashir was under indictment by the ICC. Zuma subsequently announced that South Africa intended to withdraw from the ICC.

Current issues. In his state-of-the-nation speech on February 9, 2012, Zuma announced a massive public spending program: $112 billion in power generation, transport, and telecom investments and more than $50 billion to build six new power stations by 2030. While the government's stated goals included doubling the average growth rate (at the time) of 3.5 percent and creating 5 million new jobs by 2020, critics allege that wealthy ANC supporters will receive state contracts for the program in exchange for political and financial backing of Zuma.

South African Olympian and double-amputee Oscar PISTORIUS killed his girlfriend Reeva STEENKAMP at their home in Pretoria on February 14, 2013. The high-profile case, combined with the murder of 17-year-old Anene BOOYSEN in Bredasdorp on February 2, 2013, prompted renewed public attention on the problem of violence toward women and gun ownership. (South Africa has one of the highest rates of gun ownership in Africa.) Meanwhile, also in February, Zuma announced the National Development Plan, a $33 billion stimulus program designed to improve infrastructure and create 11 million jobs.

In May the AMCU refused to sign a new mining pact, and violence again flared in Lonmin. Security forces used rubber bullets to disperse protesting miners. Meanwhile, the NUM renewed a call for the nationalization of the mining sector following an announcement that the Anglo-American Platinum Corporation would lay-off some 14,000 workers. The unrest spread to farms and an estimated 1,500 agricultural workers went on strike.

Nelson Mandela was hospitalized on June 8, for a lung infection and remained in critical care for his 95th birthday on July 18. He passed away at his home on December 5.

Oscar Pistorius's trial for murder began on March 3, 2014. On May 20 Pistorius' trial was adjourned pending a mental evaluation. On June 30 Pistorius's trial resumed with no finding of mental illness. Pistorius was found guilty of culpable homicide (a far lesser charge than murder) in September and sentenced to five years in prison. His attorneys announced their intention to appeal.

The National Union of Metalworkers of South Africa (NUMSA), the largest trade union in the country and the largest affiliate of COSATU, resolved not to endorse or support any political party in the May 2014 elections. Despite the reduced support, the ANC still won a plurality of seats, followed by DA and EFF.

In early June, 200,000 metal and engineering workers from NUMSA went on strike, demanding 15 percent higher wages, just after the conclusion of the platinum workers' strike. NUMSA's archrivals in COSATU, the NUM and the National Education, Health and Allied Workers Union (Nehawu) came out in support of the strike. Standard & Poor's downgraded South Africa's sovereign credit rating to BBB on June 13.

Beginning in March 2015 and continuing through April, a wave of violent attacks on foreign nationals swept across the country, killing at least seven and displacing more than 5,000. On April 16 fighting broke out in Durban between armed South Africans and foreign nationals during a protest against the violence. The violence spread to Johannesburg on April 16, and to Pretoria and Pietermaritzburg the next day, forcing the government to deploy the military.

In October 2015 Standard and Poor's downgraded South Africa's credit rating again, and other rating agencies followed suit, because of high deficits and growing government debt. In response, Zuma replaced Finance Minister Nhlanhla NENI with David VAN ROOYEN on December 9. Neni was blamed for the downgrade as well as misuse of public funds. Weeks later, President Zuma changed his mind, switching van Rooyen to the Ministry of Cooperative Governance and Traditional Affairs and moving Pravin GORDHAN from that ministry to the finance portfolio.

On April 5, 2016, the government survived a vote of no confidence, which failed by 120 votes, amid allegations that Zuma accepted a bribe over a 2005 arms deal. In July, following an appeal that vacated his original sentence, Pistorius was sentenced to six years for the murder of his girlfriend.

The ANC suffered a significant setback in municipal elections on August 3, 2016, as the result of growing public anger over corruption scandals. The ANC won the elections, but with only 53.9 percent of the vote, 8 percentage points behind its previous total in local balloting. The ANC lost the most ground in urban voting, with Nelson Mandela Bay, Tshwane (Pretoria), and Johannesburg falling to the opposition. The Democratic Alliance came in second in the voting, with 26.9 percent, while the Economic Freedom Fighters were third, with 8.2 percent.

POLITICAL PARTIES

During most of the apartheid era South Africa's leading political party was the predominantly Afrikaner **National Party** (NP), which came to power in 1948 and steadily increased its parliamentary strength to a high of 134 (64.8 percent) of lower house seats in the November 1977 election, before falling to 94 seats (48.1 percent) in 1989.

In 2003 five new parties were represented in the assembly: the **African Independent Movement** (AIM), **African Democratic Party** (ADP), Independent Democrat (ID), **National Action** (NA), and **Peace and Justice Congress** (PJC), as the result of floor crossing.

By 2007 the Democratic Alliance (DA) was the chief opposition party, holding 50 seats while the ANC had 279 seats. By this time AIM, ADP, NA, and PJC had disappeared from the National Assembly. The 2014 elections granted Economic Freedom Fighters (EFF), an ANC splinter group, the third-largest number of seats in Parliament.

Government Parties:

African National Congress (ANC). Organized in 1912 as the **South African Native National Congress** and long recognized as South Africa's leading black formation, the ANC (as it became known in 1923) was banned from 1960 to February 1990. The organization's most charismatic figure, Nelson Mandela, was released from prison in February 1990, while its president, Oliver Tambo, was permitted to return from more than three decades' exile the following December. (Tambo died in 1993.)

On May 28–31, 1992, the ANC held a policy conference in Johannesburg, during which it celebrated its evolution from a liberation movement to a political party and replaced a 1955 commitment to comprehensive nationalization with an emphasis on a mixed economy. In January 1994, prior to its assumption of power, it did, however, announce an ambitious program to end economic apartheid by redistributing land, building more than a million low-income dwellings, assuming state control of the mining industry, and breaking up white-owned conglomerates. The draft plan, known as the Reconstruction and Development Program, drew immediate criticism from the country's business leaders and yielded a caveat from Mandela that it required "a substantial amount of additional work to be anywhere near what we want it to be."

Since April 1994, the ANC has governed in a tripartite alliance with COSATU and the South African Communist Party (SACP), whose leaders appear on ANC party lists. Among those elected on the ANC ticket in the party's landslide election victory in April 1994 was Winnie Mandela, the controversial estranged wife of the new president, whose 1991 conviction for kidnapping and being an accessory to assault did not prevent her appointment as a deputy minister in the new government. In a strengthening of radical elements in the party leadership, Winnie Mandela regained her position on the ANC executive at the 49th congress in December, when First Deputy President Thabo Mbeki succeeded the ailing Sisulu as ANC vice president, thus becoming President Mandela's heir apparent. Mrs. Mandela's dismissal from the government in March 1995, following her public assertions that it lacked radicalism, drew official endorsement from ANC bodies, although she retained strong rank-and-file support. The Mandelas' 38-year marriage ended in divorce in March 1996.

In November 1995 the ANC won 66.4 percent of the votes cast in South Africa's first democratic local elections. As expected, at the ANC's congress held December 16–20, 1997, Nelson Mandela announced his retirement from the party's top post and his chosen successor, Thabo Mbeki, was unopposed in the subsequent election for party president. Zuma, Secretary General Kgalema Motlanthe, and Treasurer General Mendi MSIMANG also ran unopposed. Winnie Mandela secured a seat on the National Executive Committee.

The ANC unsuccessfully tried to block release of the comprehensive TRC report in the fall of 1998, objecting to conclusions that the ANC had been responsible for human rights abuses and acts of terrorism against its opponents during the anti-apartheid campaign and prior to the 1994 balloting. Party officials, led by Mbeki, condemned the report as "scurrilous," but President Mandela, in a pointed departure from the views of his successor, acknowledged that some of the abuses reported by the TRC had occurred and chastised the other ANC leaders for their angry responses. Winnie Mandela was singled out in the TRC report for her alleged role in violent acts committed by the Mandela United Football Club, described as her "private army."

In the June 1999 elections, the ANC widened its parliamentary majority to 266 seats (with a 66.4 percent vote share) and retained control of seven provincial legislatures. The ANC's entrenchment as the dominant party in South African politics was helped by the splintering of opposition parties and by its ability to woo opposition legislators and career politicians with jobs and favors. The ANC has made heavy inroads among Zulus, other working-class blacks, Indians, and Coloureds. It still has not won over many white voters, who generally vote for the DA or other white liberal or right-wing parties.

At the ANC's five-yearly national policy conference on June 27–30, 2007, Mbeki warned the SACP and COSATU not to try to dictate ANC policy. The conference adopted a compromise on the succession issue. It was agreed that it was party preference but not a principle that the party leader and the president be the same person.

ANC custom makes it inappropriate for candidates to declare their interest in the party's presidential post, as one is supposed to be asked to serve. Mbeki said he would be willing to continue to serve as ANC president if asked to do so. At the same time, the COSATU and SACP leadership announced their support for Zuma, in part due to his pledge to pursue a more left-wing agenda than Mbeki should he come to power.

In 2007 many Mbeki loyalists were also ousted from ANC leadership positions, and some of them eventually left the ANC to form the COPE. Jacob Zuma was elected president of the ANC at the party's leadership convention on December 18, easily defeating Mbeki. Zuma, a populist who enjoyed the support of trade unions, the Communist Party of South Africa, and other left-wing elements of the ANC, consequently became the presumptive ANC candidate for the 2009 presidential election. His status remained compromised by corruption charges that were reinstated shortly after the convention but were dropped just before his April 2009 election as president of the republic. The party dominated the April 2009 national elections, but while retaining a large overall majority among voters, it suffered a noticeable decline in the May 2011 local elections, with its share reduced to 63.7 percent.

Throughout much of 2011 and 2012, a growing power struggle pitted Zuma against ANC Youth League President Julius MALEMA, who was quietly pushing Deputy President Kgalema Motlanthe to replace him, and others disappointed by Zuma's leadership and the abandonment of his initial promise to serve for only one term. Meanwhile, General Secretary Gwede Mantashe's candid report on the state of the party said the ANC was divided into factions supporting or opposing Zuma's reelection and by groups trying to profit from access to state resources.

By November 2012 fierce purges were underway among opponents and supporters of Zuma's reelection bid. Citing "political risk issues," Moody's Investors Services downgraded the state-owned electrical utility Eskom's rating to "negative" on November 11. Within a week, the ANC disciplinary committee had suspended Malema for five years for undermining the presidency and bringing the party into disrepute, a decision Malema tried to appeal. By the February State of Union address, Zuma was seen to have strengthened his position. However, when he gathered the party's top leaders in April to endorse Molina's suspension, three refused: Deputy President Motlanthe, Deputy General Secretary Thandi MODISE, and Treasurer Mathews Phosa. By May the power struggle encompassed not only the ranks of the party's leadership but also the security services, courts, and the state broadcasting service, where journalists were reportedly under pressure to uncover evidence of wrongdoing by Zuma's opponents. Still, other serious contenders for the presidency had emerged, including Human Settlements Minister Tokyo SEXWALE and businessman Cyril Ramaphosa. (Ramaphosa, however, was subsequently tainted by his post on the board of the mine at Lonmin, where police killed workers.)

Rather than a substantive debate on issues, the June 25–29 ANC National Policy Conference was reportedly dominated by the clash of personalities and their supporters, who reportedly threw plastic water bottles at each other. Malema's office at the ANC headquarters was also burgled and computer hard drives stolen. On June 30 a prominent ANC leader from KwaZulu-Natal was shot outside his home, a murder allegedly tied to the election controversy. Supporters of both Motlanthe and Sexwale looked to influence the choice of delegates, who would in turn elect the party leaders in the country's nine provinces. In the three largest provinces, Zuma was said to have near-total support in KwaZulu-Natal, Guateng was mostly split between Motlanthe and Sexwale, and Eastern Cape split between Zuma and Sexwale. Late in the year, Zuma was also challenged by Motlanthe for party leadership. Nevertheless, on December 19, 2012, Zuma was overwhelmingly reelected as the head of the ANC. Meanwhile, former pro-Zuma official, Malema, was expelled from the party after campaigning against the president. In January 2013 pro-Motlanthe members of the ANC executive committee were purged.

Reports in 2013 indicated a division within the party between General Secretary Gwede Manthase and deputy party president Cyril Ramaphosa. In July Limpopo premier Cassel MATHALE was recalled by the party, ostensibly for poor performance. Reports indicated that Mathale's resignation was part of Zuma's continuing purge of potential rivals within the ANC. In December 2013 NUMSA, the largest trade union in South Africa and the largest affiliate of COSATU, resolved not to endorse or support any political party, including the ANC, in the 2014 elections. In a press briefing on March 2, NUMSA declared that the ANC-led tripartite alliance was no longer capable of defending working-class interests.

ANC lost more seats after the May 2014 elections, winning just 62 percent (down from 66 percent). In response to corruption concerns, in July the ANC concluded a two-day *lekgotla* (a meeting called by government to discuss strategy planning) to refine government and parliamentary strategies. The ANC's parliamentary caucus developed a five-year program of action to strengthen parliamentary oversight of key election focus areas, especially in the area of contracts for public work. Meanwhile, Zuma appointed his 25-year-old daughter Thuthukile ZUMA chief of staff at the telecommunications and postal services department, making her the youngest head of a minister's office. The rise of rival parties DA and EFF challenged the ANC's majorities in Johannesburg and Tshwane (Pretoria), leading to a significant loss of votes for the party in the August 2016 municipal elections in which the ANC secured 53.9 percent of the vote, its lowest total since independence.

Leaders: Jacob ZUMA (President of the Republic), Cyril RAMAPHOSA (Deputy President of the Republic), Baleka MBETE (National Chair), Kgalema MOTLANTHE (Deputy ANC President), Gwede MANTASHE (Secretary General), Mathews PHOSA (Treasurer General).

South African Communist Party (SACP). The SACP was formed in 1953, following the dissolution in 1950 of the original **Communist Party of South Africa** (CPSA), which was organized in 1921 but banned by the Suppression of Communism Bill in 1950. The SACP has long cooperated closely with the ANC, to which a number of senior SACP members have been appointed. The party's former chair, Dr. Yusef DADOO, died in 1983, while its former general secretary, Moses MABHIDA, died in Maputo, Mozambique, in March 1986. A year later, following his appointment as Mabhida's successor, Joe SLOVO resigned as chief of staff of the ANC's military wing, *Umkhonto we Sizwe* (Spear of the Nation). He returned to South Africa in April 1990. The party gathered for a "relaunching"—its first public rally within South Africa in 40 years—on July 29, 1990. In a stinging opening address to the SACP's first legal congress on December 8, 1991, Slovo insisted that former Soviet president Mikhail Gorbachev had "completely lost his way" and that what was being buried in Eastern Europe was not true socialism. Subsequently, Slovo was elected party chair, with the longtime chief of *Umkhonto we Sizwe,* Chris Hani, being named his successor as general secretary. Hani was assassinated on April 10, 1993.

Part of the governing coalition, SACP members sit as ANC members in parliament, though they are identified as SACP in their cabinet biographies. A number of cabinet ministers have SACP membership.

At the SACP's national conference held in Port Elizabeth in July 2007, most of those elected to the Central Committee supported Jacob Zuma in his bid to become the next ANC president, while a number of pro-Mbeki cabinet members lost their committee posts. Several of the latter subsequently resigned from the party to protest the militant anti-Mbeki stance. Meanwhile, COSATU's president, Willie Madisha, was voted off the Central Committee for being perceived as pro-Mbeki. SACP general secretary Blade NZIMANDE warned that the party would hold an extraordinary congress to consider a break with the ANC if Zuma was not elected as the next ANC president.

The SACP refuses to publish membership information, but the party reported a large increase since 2009, when membership was believed to exceed 50,000. The Young Communist League (YCL), the youth wing of the SACP, has become an important power broker in the SACP. The 13th Congress of the SACP occurred on July 11–15, 2012.

In July 2013 the SACP endorsed new restrictions on the media, including legislation that would criminalize criticism of the president and senior political leaders. In a December press release, NUMSA declared that fundamental philosophical, ideological, and political problems exist between the organization and SACP under Nzimande's leadership. This announcement came in response to Nzimande's Political Report to the 13th SACP Congress, where he stated the intention to defeat efforts to divide the labor movement from the ANC and SACP.

The SACP Central Committee convened from May 30 to June 1, 2014, to discuss priorities for the coming five years of the fifth ANC-led administration. SACP leadership also identified serious challenges to the unity of COSATU as a concern for the ANC-led alliance.

Leaders: Blade NZIMANDE (General Secretary); Jeremy CRONIN, Solly Afrika MAPAILA (Deputy General Secretaries); Senzeni ZOKWANA (National Chair); Joyce MOLOI-MOROPA (National Treasurer).

Other Parliamentary Parties:

Democratic Alliance (DA). The DA was established in late June 2000 by the **Democratic Party** (DP), **New National Party** (NNP); and the small **Federal Alliance** (FA), which earlier in the month had agreed to present its candidates for upcoming local elections on the DP list. Formal merger of the three was delayed, however, pending passage of legislation permitting party consolidations. Initially seen as an attempt by the principal white formations to form a united front, the DA registered considerable success in the December municipal elections, taking 23 percent of the national vote and capturing Cape Town from the ANC. However, differences within the leadership resulted in the departure of the NNP from the DA in November 2001, and local defections in October 2002 delivered control of Cape Town to an ANC-NNP coalition.

Since it had been formed especially to contest the 2000 municipal elections, the DA's legal status was initially limited to the local level. Therefore, in order to constitute itself as a party at the provincial and national levels, the DA in 2001 launched an initiative in support of floor-crossing legislation, which, with the crucial support of the ANC, parliament passed in 2002. In the 2004 assembly balloting the DA emerged as the principal opposition party in the national parliament with 50 seats.

Tony Leon, leader of the DP/DA since 1994, said in November 2006 that he would not seek reelection at the 2007 party congress. At the DA's congress in March 2007, Helen Zille won 70 percent of the delegates' votes to replace Leon. Joe Seremane, the only black rival, won 6 percent of votes. In her acceptance speech, Zille criticized the ANC's "race-based politics," indicating that, like Leon, she would oppose affirmative action.

In the 2009 parliamentary elections, the DA won 67 seats in the National Assembly and 10 in the National Council of Provinces.

Throughout 2009 and 2010, the DA campaigned to have the corruption charges against President Zuma reinstated. In the July 2010 DA federal congress election, no black candidates were elected to senior positions in the party. The outcome embarrassed Zille, who vowed that in future the party would use democratic persuasion to ensure a more racially balanced ticket. The DA did well in the May 18, 2011, local elections. While failing to gain control of any major city in addition to its base in Cape Town, the party increased its share of the popular vote to 24.2 percent, as against 16.6 percent in the 2009 national election.

On October 27, 2011, the DA elected Lindiwe Mazibuko as its first black female parliamentary leader, a strategy to reach out to young black voters outside its traditional support base. Critics alleged she lacked support in black communities. In December 2012 Zille was reelected president of the DA, while Wilmot James was reelected chair.

In February 2014 Mamphela RAMPHELE, founder of the new party Agang South Africa (below), backed out of an agreement with DA to merge her party and stand as DA's presidential candidate in the 2014 general election. DA won 22 percent of the vote (89 seats) during the May general election. On July 25, 2015, the party held internal elections, and Mmusi MAIMANE was elected president.

On November 9, 2015, DA member Dianne KOHLER-BARNARD was ejected from the party after re-posting Facebook messages praising P. W. Botha. The ejection was later overturned by the party's Legal Commission.

The party came in second in the August 2016 municipal elections, with 23.9 percent of the vote, gaining control in major cities including Johannesburg and Cape Town.

Leaders: Mmusi MAIMANE (President and Leader of the Opposition); Athol TROLLIP (Chair); Ivan MEYER, Desiree VAN DER WALT (Deputies); Phumzile VAN DAMME (National Spokespersons).

Economic Freedom Fighters (EFF). After being expelled from the ANC, former African National Congress Youth League (ANCYL) president Julius Malema formed EFF in July 2013.

EFF is currently the third-largest party in parliament, having won more than 6 percent of the vote (25 seats) in the May 2014 general election and 30 seats in provincial elections, including 8 in Guateng and 6 in Limpopo. In July Malema came out in support of the NUMSA strike (see current issues) despite NUMSA's criticism of EFF for its use of militaristic jargon and organizational structure. The majority of EFF members are under the age of 50, and 49 percent are younger than 25. Malema has been accused of corruption and criticized for conspicuous material consumption.

The party came in third in the August 2016 municipal elections, with 8.1 percent of the vote, gaining particular ground on the ANC in urban areas.

Leaders: Julius MALEMA (Commander in Chief), Dali MPOFU (Chair), Mpho RAMAKATSA (National Coordinator), Floyd SHIVAMBU (Deputy President), Godrich GARDEE (Secretary General).

***Inkatha* Freedom Party** (IFP). In response to charges of tribalism, the *Inkatha,* a predominantly Zulu organization, voted at a general conference in 1990 to transform itself into a political party that would be open to all races; however, most observers felt that the organization remained primarily a vehicle for the expression of Zulu interests in KwaZulu. Chief Mangosuthu Buthelezi, the KwaZulu homeland leader from 1978 to 1994, was unanimously elected president of the IFP. The party shares many ANC positions, except what it considers are the rights and prerogatives of "traditional leaders," as well as its emphasis on individual responsibility. (For details about IFP activity prior to 2002, see the 2014 *Handbook.*)

Relations between the IFP and ANC in 2002 fell to their lowest ebb since 1994. The main arena of the quarrel between the two parties was KwaZulu-Natal, where, in late 2002, the ruling IFP ejected two ANC ministers from the provincial government and formed a partnership with the opposition Democratic Alliance. After floor crossing in 2003, the IFP held 31 assembly seats.

The IFP suffered considerable erosion of support in the 2004 general election, in which it secured 28 seats. For the first time since 1994, the IFP subsequently had no representation in the cabinet.

At the IFP's annual conference in July 2004, Ziba JIYANE was nominated from the floor, against the leadership's wishes, to run against the incumbent national chair and former provincial premier, Lionel MTSHALI, whom he defeated in a landslide victory. Rev. Musa ZONDI was nominated for the revived position of secretary general. In the 2004 elections, the party won 28 seats in the National Assembly, making it the fourth-largest party.

After floor crossing in 2005, the IFP lost an additional five assembly seats, ceding four to the newly formed Nadeco and one to the DA. (In April 2006 three IFP defectors to Nadeco returned to the IFP, whose Operation *Buyela eKhaya* [Come Back Home] encouraged defectors to return to the party.) At the IFP's annual national conference in September 2005, Zondi was elected secretary general and Zanele KAMAGWAZA-MSIBI was unanimously elected national chair, replacing Ziba Jiyane, who had defected earlier to help form Nadeco.

Ideologically, the IFP views itself as right of the ANC. It opposed the passage of legislation in 2005 to expropriate white-owned land because of its opposition to state intervention in the market. In 2007 the IFP submitted a private member's bill calling for an end to floor crossing, which it considers a betrayal of the electorate. The party's main support base is among Zulus in rural KwaZulu-Natal. However, the party seeks to project itself as a national party, and IFP parliamentarians have included non-Zulus.

In the 2009 national elections, the IFP posted its worst results in recent years, securing just 4.5 percent of the vote and 18 seats in the National Assembly, down from 28 seats in 2004. In January 2011 Zanele kaMagwaza-Msibi, former party chair, along with other party members, left to create the National Freedom Party (see below).

The party's secretary general Musa Zondi, who was considered by some to be next in line for the IFP presidency, resigned his seat in the National Assembly in a letter dated January 24, 2012. At the IFP Elective National Conference in December, attendees elected new members of the executive committee, including for a new post, deputy president. After two former members of parliament defected to the ANC in June 2013, the IFP charged that the rival party had launched a concerted campaign to lure defectors through illicit incentives. After the May 2014 general elections, IFP won only 10 seats, falling from the third-place to the fourth-place party in parliament. IFP retained its 1 seat in Gauteng but won just 9 seats in Kwazulu-Natal, down from 18 in the 2009 election. It secured 4.3 percent of the vote in the 2016 local balloting.

Leaders: Chief Mangosuthu BUTHELEZI (President), Inkosi Mzamo BUTHELEZI (Deputy President), Sibongile NKOMO (Secretary General), Themba C. MSIMANG (Deputy Secretary General).

National Freedom Party (NFP). In January 2011 former IFP chair Zanele kaMagwaza-Msibi established NFP after registering with the Independent Electoral Commission on December 13, 2010. In a press release, she characterized her break with IFP as ostracism and expulsion. The NFP received 2.4 percent of the vote in the 2011 municipal election. In the 2014 elections, NFP won six seats in parliament and six provincial seats in KwaZulu-Natal.

Leaders: Zanele kaMAGWAZA-MSIBI (President), Rammekoa Alexander Martin KEKANA (Deputy President), Nhlanhla KHUBISA (Secretary General), Muzienkosi B. GWALA (National Chair).

United Democratic Movement (UDM). The UDM was launched on September 27, 1997, by former NP secretary general Roelf MEYER and former ANC deputy minister Bantu HOLOMISA, also a former Transkei homeland leader. The new grouping, which promoted a moderate and nonracial platform, was reportedly immediately bolstered by the enrollment of a number of young, liberal NP defectors. Its first secretary general, Sifiso NKABINDE, was murdered in January 1999. Like Holomisa, Nkabinde had been expelled from the ANC.

The UDM subsequently was reported to be gaining popular support, and it competed in the 1999 assembly campaign on a pledge to narrow the gap between rich and poor without imperiling the wealth of the financial elite. The party won 14 seats on a 3.4 percent vote share. In January 2000 Meyer announced his retirement from politics, and on August 31, 2007, he joined the ANC. The second National Congress in December 2001 confirmed Holomisa as president.

The UDM is identified with Xhosa interests in Eastern Cape Province. It supported the ANC during the latter's bitter struggle with the IFP for control of the KwaZulu-Natal legislature. (For more on the defections and expulsions form the party during the 2003 floor crossing window, see the 2011 *Handbook.*)

In 2009 the party won four seats in the National Assembly, down from nine in 2004. In February 2014 the UDM announced the formation of a coalition with Mbhazima SHILOWA and his breakaway faction from the Congress of the People (COPE, below). Although UDM won just four seats in the general election, the party rebounded somewhat in provincial elections, winning four seats in Eastern Cape and displacing COPE as the third-largest party in the region. In local balloting in 2016, the party secured 0.6 percent of the vote.

Leaders: Bantu HOLOMISA (President), Bongani MSOMI (General Secretary), Zolisa LAVISA (National Chair).

Freedom Front Plus (*Vryheidsfront Plus*—VF Plus). The **Freedom Front** (*Vryheidsfront*—VF), the CPSA, and the ***Afrikaner Eenheids Beweging*** founded this group in 2004 to contest the upcoming national election as a single party.

The VF was launched by Gen. (Ret.) Constand Viljoen in March 1994 following a split in the Afrikaner People's Front (AVF) over the issue of participation in the April election, with the VF opting to register to present the case for a "white homeland." (For details on VF activity before 2008, see the 2014 *Handbook*).

Following the VF's legacy, the VF Plus seeks to protect and enhance Afrikaner rights and interests through the creation of an autonomous region. The proposed region lies between Northern Cape and Western Cape provinces. In May 2008 Pieter MULDER announced that the VF Plus had established Afrikaners as a member group in the Unrepresented Nations and Peoples Organization (UNPO), an international organization based in the Netherlands, that campaigns for the rights of minority and indigenous populations. The party has actively, and thus far successfully, opposed changing the name of South Africa's capital from Pretoria to Tshwane.

In the 2009 and 2014 elections, the party retained its four seats in the National Assembly. In the 2014 provincial elections, VF Plus retained its single seats in Free State and Guateng and gained a seat in North-West. In the 2016 local elections, the party won 0.8 percent of the vote.

Leaders: Pieter MULDER (Party Leader), Pieter GROENEWALD (Chair and Parliamentary Leader).

Congress of the People (COPE). Congress of the People was the name finally given to the group that broke away from the ANC after Thabo Mbeki's forced resignation from the presidency in September 2008. Former defense minister Mosiuoa LEKOTA formed COPE to contest the April 2009 elections. Its aim was to deny the ANC the two-thirds majority needed to change the constitution. In this, COPE was successful, returning 30 members and becoming the third-largest parliamentary party behind the ANC and the DA. COPE's manifesto presents an alternative to a race-based, one-party state under the ANC to "depoliticize the institutions of state" and expedite economic growth for "large-scale labor absorption." COPE's December 2010 conference ended in a bitter, actually physical, struggle between President Mosiuoa LEKOTA and Deputy President Mbhazima Shilowa for leadership of the party. COPE's credibility has declined greatly, and some of its parliamentarians returned to the ANC. In July 2013 there were calls to disband the Lekota-affiliated youth wing after the group's leader, Nqaba BHANGA, began negotiations with the Shilowa youth faction. After a period of rival leadership, Shilowa and six other COPE party members sought to postpone the National Conference in January 2014. Shilowa failed, and COPE reelected Lekota, who ran unopposed, leader of the party. Consequently, Shilowa led a breakaway COPE faction to join with UDM (see above) ahead of the election. In May COPE lost 27 of its previous 30 seats in parliament and won just 3 seats in provincial elections. COPE won 0.4 percent of the vote in municipal elections in 2016.

Leaders: Mosiuoa LEKOTA (President and Parliamentary Leader), William Mothipa MADISHA (Deputy President), Pakes DIKGETSI (National Chair), Lyndall SHOPE-MAFOLE (General Secretary).

African Christian Democratic Party (ACDP). The ACDP, a conservative Christian group, was organized in 1993 with the aim of representing Christians in parliament. Prior to the 1994 balloting, in which it won two seats on a 0.5 percent vote share, the ACDP also secured representation in three provincial assemblies. (For details on ACDP activity prior to 2009, see the 2014 *Handbook*.)

In the 2009 National Assembly elections, the party won three seats, down from seven in 2004. In June 2013 party leader Kenneth Meshoe resigned from parliament in order lead a fund-raising campaign for the party. The ACDP won three seats in the general election and one seat in the provincial elections in 2014. In 2016 it secured 0.4 percent of the vote in local polling.

Leaders: Rev. Kenneth MESHOE (President), Wayne M. THRING (Deputy President), Raymond TLAELI (Secretary General), Jo-Ann DOWNS (National Executive Committee Chair).

African Independent Congress (AIC). AIC is a minority party established in 2005. The party contested the 2014 general election but ran only in the Eastern Cape in the provincial elections. After winning three seats in parliament and one provincial seat, the AIC denied assertions in the media that the electoral successes were the result of voter name confusion. The national ballot listed the AIC above the ANC. In municipal balloting in 2016, the party won 1.2 percent of the vote.

Leaders: Mandla GALO (President), Andries TLOUAMMA (Deputy President), Sam NJELA (Secretary General).

Agang South Africa (Agang SA). Mamphela Ramphele founded Agang in February 2013 (see DA, above). The party held its first congress in June 2013 and won two seats in the May 2014 general election. In July 2014 Ramphele announced that she was quitting politics to return to civil society work. With no clear leadership structure, the future of the party is in doubt.

Leaders: Mike TSHISONGA (Acting President), John McCONNACHIE (Spokesperson).

Pan Africanist Congress of Azania (PAC). Formerly known as **Pan Africanist Congress**, the PAC is a militant ANC off-shoot that was banned in 1960. The PAC long sought to unite all black South Africans in a single national front. Based in Lusaka, Zambia, the PAC announced in May 1979 the establishment in the Sudan of a "June 16 Azania Institute" (named after the June 1976 Soweto uprising) to instruct displaced South African students in a variety of academic and artisan skills. Its underground affiliate, the Azanian People's Liberation Army (APLA), was relatively small, compared to the military wing of the rival ANC. The PAC's longtime leader, John Nyati POKELA, died in June 1985; its president, Zephania MOTHOPENG, was released from nine years' imprisonment in November 1988, while another leader, Jafta MASEMOLA, was released in October 1989. In September 1990 the PAC rejected a government invitation to participate in constitutional talks, branding the overture as "not serious or honest." In October the PAC joined the ANC and some 60 other groups (*Inkatha* being the most notable exception) in the attempted formation of a united Patriotic Front. However, the PAC subsequently broke with the Mandela-led formation in opposing Codesa, insisting that it would settle for nothing less than "a democratically elected constituent assembly." The PAC has abandoned its more radical programs and now concentrates on the plight of the poor and related issues.

The PAC announced in the early 1990s that it was abandoning armed struggle, thus permitting it to register for elections. The party won 1.2 percent of the vote and five assembly seats in the 1994 balloting. Following a protracted leadership struggle, Clarence MAKWETU stepped down as PAC president in December 1996 and was replaced by Rev. Mmutlanyane Stanley MOGOBA. Makwetu was expelled from the party in 1997.

Under Mogoba's leadership the PAC in 1997 evinced a conciliatory attitude toward whites, while party leaders also expressed an interest in opening a dialogue with the ANC, the PAC's longtime rival. Subsequently, in January 1999 it was announced that the APLA had been officially disbanded, and the PAC was registered to contest the June national elections, in which it won three seats on a 0.7 percent vote share. In July 2001 the PAC, responding to delays in land distribution and government housing construction, began helping thousands of homeless people occupy a wasteland near Johannesburg. The government quickly evicted them.

In the 2003 floor-crossing, Patricia de Lille left the PAC to form the ID (below), thus leaving the PAC with only two assembly seats. The PAC deputy president, Dr. Motsoko PHEKO, was elected president on June 15, replacing Mogoba, who had continued as president after the dispute over 2002 party congress results. In February 2004 Mogoba resigned from parliament to give his seat to the deputy president of the party, Themba Godi. After the April 2004 national election, the PAC again had three assembly seats. In 2006 the PAC congress elected a new president, Letlapa MPHAHLELE. At the September 2007 floor-crossing, two members left to form the **African People's Convention.** The party has since experienced severe factional infighting, with supporters of Pheko and Mphahlele each claiming to be the "real PAC." Mphahlele was elected to parliament in place of Pheko in April 2009, when the party won one seat in the assembly.

In May 2013 PAC's executive committee suspended Secretary General Narius Moloto and two other senior party officials. In response, Moloto and a group of supporters voted to expel Mphahlele, creating a new rift within PAC. At PAC's annual national conference, Alton

MPHETHI was appointed president. He subsequently entered into negotiations with EFF leader Julius Malema in December to merge the two parties. However, by March 2014 EFF representatives denied that a merger would take place before the elections. PAC won one seat in the general elections and no seats at the provincial level.

After a dispute, Luthando MBINDA was affirmed as party leader by the High Court in October 2015. PAC won 0.2 percent of the vote in the 2016 local polling.

Leaders: Luthando MBINDA (President), Sibusiso XABA (Deputy Leader), Narius MOLOTO (Secretary General).

African People's Convention (APC). The APC was founded at the September 2007 floor-crossing with the withdrawal of Themba Godi and Mofihli Dikotsi from the Pan Africanist Congress.

After the April 2009 election, Godi was the only APC member in the National Assembly. APC retained its seat after the 2014 election. In October 2015 Deputy Party President Hlabira MATHUME left the APC to form a breakaway party called the **African People's Socialist Party**. The APC won 0.2 percent of the vote in the 2016 local balloting.

Leaders: Themba GODI (President), Paseka oa MOSHWADIBA (Secretary General).

Other Parties and Groups:

United Christian Democratic Party (UCDP). The UCDP was founded by Chief Lucas Mangope, former president of the Bophuthatswana homeland. The conservative formation includes in its platform support for the authority of traditional leaders. Despite reports that Mangope considered merging the UCDP with the newly formed UDM in 1997, it contested the 1999 elections independently, winning three seats in the National Assembly on a 0.8 percent vote share. In 2004 it retained three seats, was reduced to two in 2009 and in 2014 lost both of them. The main UCDP power base is in the North West province. It won just 0.1 percent of the vote in 2016's local elections.

Leaders: Isaac Sipho MFUNDISI (President), Tediye Phillip MOERANE (Deputy President), Ipuseng Celia DITSHETELO (National Chair), Christopher Seero TSILE (Secretary General).

Azanian People's Organization (Azapo). Azapo was founded in April 1978 to carry on the work of the black consciousness movement that was banned in October 1977; however, its founders were immediately detained, and it did not hold its first congress until September 1979. Although never a mass party, it enjoyed the support of black intellectuals. Avowedly nonviolent, it adopted a hard line on the possibility of negotiating with the white government and was strongly anti-Codesa. In early 1994 Azapo declared its opposition to the forthcoming all-party election and announced that it would intensify its struggle until land had been returned to the country's blacks. Although Azapo had boycotted the 1994 balloting, it was registered for the 1999 elections, in which it won 0.2 percent of the vote and one National Assembly seat. Some Azapo members had defected to join the **Socialist Party of Azania** (SOPA), which was formed on March 21, 1998, allegedly because Azapo had abandoned its socialist principles, and its leadership was undemocratic. In January 2001 the Azapo leader, Mosibudi Mangena, was named deputy minister of education, prompting mass resignations by Azapo members who accused him of betrayal for participating in the ANC's nonsocialist and multiracial government.

In the cabinet announced after the 2004 election, Azapo leader Mangena was appointed minister of science and technology, again generating criticism that Azapo should not be in the ANC government. In the 2009 elections, the party won one seat. President Zuma did not name any Azapo members to the new government appointed in May. Mangena retired in March 2010.

In 2013 the anticipated merger between AZAPO and SOPA broke down. In the May 2014 elections, Azapo won no seats. It won 0.1 percent of the vote in the 2016 municipal elections.

Leaders: Jacob Dikobo CDE (President), Strike THOKOANE (Deputy President), Laurence MOLAI (Treasurer), Senaoane NORUKA (Secretary General), Mosibudi MANGENA (Former President).

Minority Front (MF). The MF represents the rights of Indians in South Africa; it participated without success in the 1994 balloting but won one National Assembly seat in 1999 on a vote share of 0.3 percent. It then formed an alliance with the ANC, giving the latter the 267 votes needed to amend the constitution. In 2004 the MF won two assembly seats. The MF manifesto supports increased subsidies for education and housing, job creation, improving social grants and pensions, fighting unfair implementation of affirmative action, and protecting minority rights. After Rajbansi's death in 2011, his widow, Shameen THAKUR-RAJBANSI, became the official leader in December 2013.

In the 2009 elections, the party won one assembly seat. MF won no seats in the 2014 elections.

Leader: Shameen THAKUR-RAJBANSI.

Afrikaner Resistance Movement (*Afrikaner Weerstands beweging*—AWB). Founded in 1973, the extreme right-wing AWB became the most visible of the Afrikaner paramilitary formations opposed to majority rule. In June 1993 armed AWB members invaded the Johannesburg building where constitutional talks were in progress, meeting no resistance from the police on duty. Having been convicted and fined in October for electoral violence in 1991, controversial AWB leader Eugène Terre'Blanche in November urged whites to arm themselves for "inevitable" civil war. In March 1994, however, the failure of AWB and other Afrikaner paramilitaries to preserve the Bophuthatswana regime contributed to the collapse of the broad Freedom Alliance of conservative forces. In April 1996 ten AWB members were imprisoned for their part in a bombing campaign aimed at disrupting the 1994 election.

Further arrests of AWB activists were reported in early 1997. Moreover, in June Terre'Blanche was sentenced to prison for six years for allegedly attempting to murder a black laborer. (In March 2001 he lost his final appeal and began serving his sentence.) He was released in 2004. He was also condemned by the TRC for his role in the 1993–1994 violence. In March 2008 Terre'Blanche announced that he was re-founding the movement, which had become defunct. In April 2010 Terre'Blanche was killed by Chris Mahlangu, a young black man who worked on his farm, in a dispute over unpaid wages. Steyn VAN RONGE succeeded him as party leader. The AWB has continued to recruit members and hold rallies. On August 22, 2012, Mahlangu was sentenced to life in prison. In December seven members of the AWB were arrested with weapons outside of a white-owned farm in the midst of a strike.

Leader: Steyn VAN RONGE.

Independent Democrats (ID). The ID is a defunct party that was formed during the floor-crossing window in March–April 2003 under the leadership of Patricia de Lille, a former trade unionist and a long-time member of the Pan Africanist Congress, which she left to form the ID. The party's main support area was the Cape metro area. With the motto "Back to Basics," the ID's policies were generally centrist. (For details on ID activity before 2010, see the 2014 *Handbook*.)

On August 15, 2010, the ID merged with the Democratic Alliance. De Lille left the national parliament to become a member of Helen Zille's administration in the Eastern Cape. De Lille assumed office as mayor of Cape Town on June 1, 2011 representing DA. The ID executive committee was abolished in May 2014.

Reconstituted National Party (*Herstigte Nasionale Party*—HNP). The HNP is a right-wing Calvinist party organized by Dr. Albert Hertzog following his dismissal from the government in 1968. The party, which adopted the racist doctrine that blacks are genetically inferior to whites, competed in four subsequent elections without securing parliamentary representation. Dr. Hertzog (son of original National Party founder J. B. M. Hertzog) relinquished the HNP leadership in May 1977. In March 1979 the NP-dominated Parliament, by amendment to a 1978 electoral act, refused to register the HNP as a political party, although it was permitted to contest most constituencies (none successfully) in 1981 by producing 300 signatures in support of each nomination. It secured its first parliamentary seat, previously held by the NP, in a by-election in October 1985 but was unable to retain it in 1987. Although the HNP withdrew from the AVF shortly after its formation in May 1993, it nevertheless joined the AVF in boycotting the April 1994 election.

The HNP's attempts to reach a broader constituency were reportedly hindered in 1997 by its well-publicized conflicts with other Afrikaner groups, most notably the VF. It was reported in 1998 that the HNP was hoping to contest the 1999 balloting, but it did not appear on the final list of approved parties. Longtime leader Jaap MARAIS died in August 2000 and was officially succeeded by Willem Marais at a March 2001 party congress. Marais died in 2007 and was replaced as leader by Japie Theart, who was subsequently replaced by Andries BREYTENBACH in 2011. As leader of the Boer-Afrikaner Volksraad, a group of 36,000 people, Breytenbach commenced talks with the presidency on August 9, 2014, to discuss establishing a state within South Africa.

Leaders: Andries BREYTENBACH (Chair), Simon DUVENAGE (Deputy Chair).

For more information on the **United Independent Front** (UIF) and the **New National Party** (NNP), the name adopted by the now defunct **National Party** (*Nasionale Party*—NP) at a December 1998 congress, see the 2013 *Handbook*.

LEGISLATURE

Prior to 1981 the South African **Parliament** was a bicameral body consisting of a Senate and a House of Assembly, from which blacks and Coloureds lost their previous limited indirect representation in 1959 and 1968, respectively. The Senate (consisting largely of members designated by the provincial assemblies) was abolished, effective January 1, 1981, some of its duties being assumed by a newly created President's Council of nominated members.

The 1983 document provided for a tricameral body encompassing a House of Assembly, a continuation of the former lower house; a House of Representatives, representing Coloured voters; and a House of Delegates, representing Indian voters. Each was empowered to legislate in regard to "its own" affairs, while the assent of all was required in regard to collective issues.

The interim constitution, which was in effect from April 27, 1994, to February 4, 1997, was the first to be based on the one-person–one-vote principle. It provided for a Senate of indirectly elected members and a directly elected National Assembly, both with five-year mandates. The two bodies sat jointly as the Constituent Assembly that drafted the permanent basic law, which entered into effect on February 4, 1997, and, among other things, replaced the Senate with a National Council of Provinces.

National Council of Provinces. The National Council replaced the Senate on February 6, 1997, at which time 54 permanent elected members (6 from each of the nine provinces) and 36 special delegates (4 from each province) were inaugurated. Members are elected by each provincial legislature from among its own ranks. Each delegation is headed by the provincial premier who is one of the special delegates.

Delegations are required to reflect the party makeup of the provincial legislatures. Following elections on May 7, 2014, the seat distribution was as follows: African National Congress, 60 seats; Democratic Alliance, 20; Economic Freedom Fighters, 7; *Inkatha* Freedom Party, 1; National Freedom Party, 1; and United Democratic Movement, 1.

Chair: Thandi MODISE.

National Assembly. The lower house contains 400 members, 200 of whom are elected by proportional representation from national party lists and 200 from regional lists. All serve a five-year term.

Following the election of May 7, 2014, the seat distribution was as follows: African National Congress, 249 seats; Democratic Alliance, 89; Economic Freedom Fighters, 25; *Inkatha* Freedom Party, 10; National Freedom Party, 6; United Democratic Movement, 4; Freedom Front Plus, 4; Congress of the People, 3; African Christian Democratic Party, 3; African Independent Congress, 3; Agang South Africa, 2; Pan Africanist Congress of Azania, 1; and African People's Convention, 1.

Speaker: Baleka MBETE (ANC).

CABINET

[as of July 28, 2016]

President	Jacob Gedleyihlekisa Zuma (ANC)
Deputy President	Cyril Ramaphosa (ANC)
Ministers	
Agriculture, Forestry, and Fisheries	Senzeni Zokwana (SACP)
Arts and Culture	Nkosinathi Emmanuel "Nathi" Mthethwa (ANC)
Basic Education	Matsie Angelina Motshekga (ANC) [f]
Communications	Faith Muthambi (ANC) [f]
Cooperative Governance and Traditional Affairs	David van Rooyen (ANC)
Defense and Military Veterans	Nosiviwe Noluthando Mapisa-Nqakula (ANC) [f]
Economic Development	Ebrahim Patel (ANC)
Energy	Tina Joemat-Pettersson (ANC) [f]
Environmental Affairs	Bomo Edna Molewa (ANC) [f]
Finance	Pravin Jamnadas Gordhan (ANC)
Health	Pakishe Aaron Motsoaledi (ANC)
Higher Education and Training	Blade Nzimande (SACP)
Home Affairs	Malusi Knowledge Nkanyezi Gigaba (ANC)
Human Settlements	Lindiwe Nonceba Sisulu (ANC) [f]
International Relations and Cooperation	Maite Nkoana-Mashabane (ANC) [f]
Justice and Correctional Services	Tshililo Michael Masutha (ANC)
Labor	Nelisiwe Mildred Oliphant (ANC) [f]
Mineral Resources	Mosebenzi Zwane (ANC)
Planning, Performance, Monitoring, Evaluation, and Administration	Jeffrey Thamsanqa Radebe (ANC)
Police	Nkosinathi Phiwayinkosi Thamsanqa Nhleko (ANC)
Public Enterprises	Lynne Brown (ANC) [f]
Public Service and Administration	Ngoako Ramatlhodi (ANC)
Public Works	Thembelani Thulas Nxesi (ANC)
Roads and Traffic Affairs	Charles Nqakula
Rural Development and Land Reform	Gugile Nkwinti (ANC)
Science and Technology	Grace Naledi Mandisa Pandor (ANC) [f]
Small Business Development	Lindiwe Zulu (ANC) [f]
Social Development	Bathabile Olive Dlamini (ANC) [f]
Sport and Recreation	Fikile April Mbalula (ANC)
State Security	Mbangiseni David Mahlobo (ANC)
Telecommunications and Postal Services	Siyabonga Cyprian Cwele (ANC)
Tourism	Derek Andre Hanekom (ANC)
Trade and Industry	Rob Davies (SACP)
Transport	Elizabeth Dipuo Peters (ANC) [f]
Water and Sanitation	Nomvula Paula Mokonyane (ANC) [f]
Women	Susan Shabangu (ANC) [f]

[f] = female

Note: Ministers designated as SACP are also members of the ANC.

INTERGOVERNMENTAL REPRESENTATION

Ambassador to the U.S.: Mninwa Johannes MAHLANGU.

U.S. Ambassador to South Africa: Jessye LAPENN (Chargé d'Affaires).

Permanent Representative to the UN: Kingsley MAMABOLO.

IGO Memberships (non-UN): AU, CWTH, G-20, ICC, IOM, NAM, SADC, WTO.

For Further Reference:

Deegan, Heather. *Politics South Africa.* 2nd ed. New York: Routledge, 2011.

Johnson, R. W. *How Long Will South Africa Survive: The Looming Crisis.* London: C. Hurst, 2015.

Worden, Nigel. *The Making of Modern South Africa: Conquest, Apartheid, Democracy.* Oxford: Blackwell, 1994; reprint Chichester, UK: Wiley, 2012.

SOUTH SUDAN

Republic of South Sudan
Junhuriyat Janub Al-Sudan

Political Status: Independent republic established in 2011; transitional constitution approved on July 7, 2011.

Area: 967,494 sq. mi. (2,505,813 sq. km).

Population: 12,733,000 (2016E—UN); 12,530,717 (2016E—U.S. Census).

Major Urban Centers (2015E—UN): Juba (321,000).

Official Language: English.

Monetary Unit: South Sudanese Pound (market rate October 1, 2016: 6.22 pounds = $1US). The South Sudanese pound was introduced after independence in 2011.

President and Prime Minister: Salva KIIR Mayardit (Sudan People's Liberation Movement); sworn in on July 9, 2011, following independence; previously appointed as president of the autonomous regional government of South Sudan (GOSS) on August 11, 2005, to succeed John GARANG (Sudan People's Liberation Movement), who died in a helicopter crash on July 30, 2005; reappointed on May 28, 2010, following presidential elections during April 11–15.

First Vice President: Taban DENG GAI (Sudan People's Liberation Movement in Opposition); appointed on July 25, 2016, following the dismissal of Riek MACHAR Teny Dhurgon (Sudan People's Liberation Movement in Opposition) on the same day (see Government and Politics, below.)

Second Vice President: James Wani IGGA (Sudan People's Liberation Movement); appointed as vice president by the president on August 23, 2013, and approved by the legislature the next day, following the dismissal on July 23 of Riek MACHAR Teny Dhurgon (Sudan People's Liberation Movement in Opposition); appointed as second vice president on February 11, 2016.

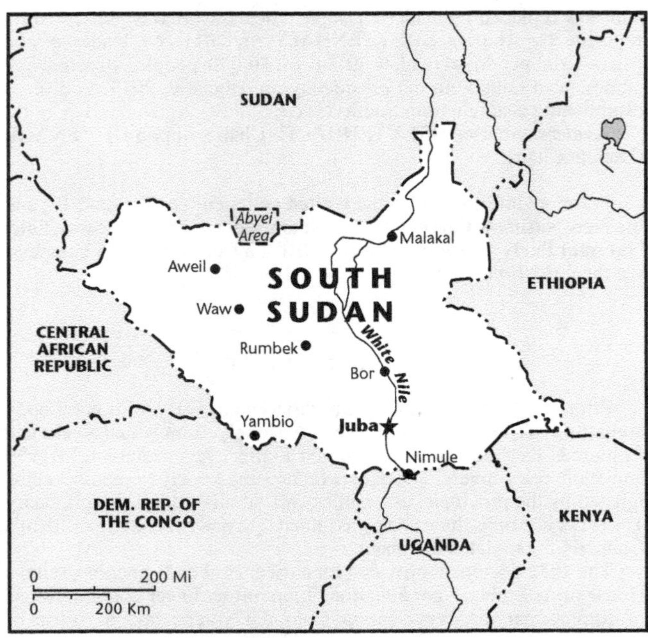

THE COUNTRY

Formerly the southern ten provinces of Sudan, South Sudan gained independence in 2011. It borders the Central African Republic, the Democratic Republic of the Congo, Ethiopia, Kenya, Sudan, and Uganda. The area traditionally marked the beginning of Africa's subtropical zone, and the White Nile flows through the country that is home to the Sudd—a wetlands area that constitutes about 15 percent of the total area of South Sudan. More than 90 percent of the population practices Christianity or traditional beliefs. The majority of the population is African, with a small Arab minority. Following elections in 2011, women secured 88 of 332 seats in the assembly (26.5 percent), and 5 of 50 seats in the upper chamber (10 percent). Women also held six cabinet positions in 2016.

South Sudan possesses significant mineral resources and produces about 600,000 barrels of oil per day. Petroleum accounts for 98 percent of government revenues; however, oil is currently exported through two pipelines that run through Sudan, forcing the GOSS to share revenues. In addition to fossil fuels, there are deposits of iron, copper, tungsten, silver, and zinc. South Sudan has extensive agricultural capabilities, producing bananas, cotton, mangos, papayas, peanuts, rice, sesame, sorghum, sugarcane, and wheat. The country is also home to 10 million to 20 million head of cattle.

Gross domestic product (GDP) growth was 6 percent in 2011, while inflation was 8.6 percent. A dispute with Sudan over export fees led South Sudan to suspend oil exports in January 2012 (see Current issues, below). The result was a significant reduction in GDP in 2012. The IMF and World Bank estimated GDP fell by 47.6 percent, while inflation rose grew by more than 45 percent. Observers complemented the government for its ability to function, with the aid of loans and grants, during this crisis. GDP was estimated to grow by 29.3 percent in 2013 with the resumption of oil shipments (see Foreign relations, below). That year, inflation was flat, while GDP per capita was $1,262. As the result of an ongoing civil war, GDP growth slowed to 2.9 percent in 2014, before becoming negative in 2015 at –0.2 percent and in 2016 at –7.8 percent. Inflation soared from 1.7 percent in 2014 to 52.8 percent in 2015 and 212.4 percent in 2016. GDP per capita declined to $246 in 2016. Oil production declined from 116,000 barrels per day to 50,000.

GOVERNMENT AND POLITICS

Political background. After a period of informal rule by Egypt, the territory that is now South Sudan was united as the Egyptian province of Equatoria in 1869. The region became part of the area controlled by Muhammad Ahmad, the MAHDI ("awaited religious leader"), following a rebellion (1881–1885) against Egyptian rule. By 1898 Anglo-Egyptian forces had reestablished control over the area. North and South Sudan were ruled as two relatively distinct colonies until after World War II. In 1946 the British endeavored unsuccessfully to merge South Sudan with Uganda. However, at the 1947 Juba Conference, North and South Sudan were combined into a single unitary state that became self-governing in 1954 and independent two years later.

Two bloody civil wars (1955–1972 and 1983–2005) were fought between the mainly African, Christian south and the Arab Muslim north. (For more details on the history of South Sudan prior to independence in 2011, see the entry on Sudan.) More than 2.5 million were killed during the conflicts and the concurrent droughts and famines. The conflicts also produced more than 4 million refugees. The Sudan People's Liberation Army (SPLA), led by Col. John GARANG, emerged as the main rebel group in the South. A peace accord, the Comprehensive Peace Agreement (CPA), was finalized in January 2005. The agreement created a system of power sharing between the national government of Sudan, led by General and President Umar Hassan Ahmad al-BASHIR of the National Congress (NC), and groups in the South, including the political arm of the SPLA, the Sudan People's Liberation Movement (SPLM). In addition, the ten southern provinces were granted autonomy, and on October 21, 2005, the GOSS was established. Garang, the SPLA's leader, was appointed the first president of South Sudan, but he died in a helicopter crash on July 30 and was succeeded by Vice President Salva KIIR Mayardit of the SPLM. Riek MACHAR Teny Dhurgon of the SPLM was appointed vice president to replace Kiir. National elections were scheduled for 2009 (these were delayed until 2010), with a referendum on independence for South Sudan planned for 2011.

In suspect elections held during April 11–15, 2010, Bashir was reelected president after the SPLM candidate Yasir ARMAN withdrew from the balloting. Meanwhile, Kiir was reelected president of the GOSS. The SPLM subsequently joined a unity government led by Bashir.

The South Sudan referendum on independence was conducted January 9–15, 2011. More than 98 percent of the voters cast ballots in favor of forming a new nation. A new, transitional constitution was subsequently drafted (see Constitution and government, below). South Sudan became independent on July 9. Kiir resigned that day as vice president to become the president of South Sudan. He named a new cabinet on August 26, which included the SPLM, the NC, the United Sudan African Party (USAP), the South Sudan Democratic Front (SSDF), and the United Democratic Salvation Front–Mainstream (UDSF-M). The government was formally approved on September 1. Also in September, the government announced plans to relocate the capital from Juba to Ramciel.

On July 23, 2013, Kiir unexpectedly dismissed the vice president and cabinet. A new cabinet was appointed July 27–31 (see Current issues, below). Another reshuffle occurred on August 4 that expanded the cabinet, and James Wani Igga, the president of the National Assembly, was named vice president on August 23.

Elections scheduled for June 2015 were postponed in February 2015 because of ongoing fighting between supporters of Kiir and those of former vice president Machar who described themselves as the Sudan People's Liberation Movement in Opposition (SPLM-O) (see Current issues, below). A peace deal was signed on August 17. The accord mandated a cease-fire and the expansion of the legislature to include supporters of Machar and other opposition groups (see Legislature, below). In addition, a 30-member transitional government was established on April 28, 2016, after months of further negotiations. Kiir remained president, while Machar was appointed first vice president and Igga became second vice president. Included in the cabinet were members of the SPLM, the SPLM-O, the SSDF, the Sudan People's Liberation Movement–Democratic Change (SPLM-DC), and two representatives of former detainees.

New fighting in July 2016 prompted Machar to flee South Sudan (see Current issues, below). On July 25 Kiir dismissed Machar as first vice president and appointed Taban DENG GAI (SPLM-O) in his place. A number of SPLM-O ministers who remained loyal to Machar were replaced with Deng Gai supporters.

Constitution and government. A transitional constitution was approved by the parliament on July 7, 2011. The new basic law was scheduled to remain in place for four years, during which time a permanent constitution was to be developed. The interim basic law provided for a bicameral legislature, consisting of both previously elected legislators and appointees. Presidential and legislative elections were scheduled for 2015. The constitution also created an independent judiciary with a Supreme Court. Opposition groups criticized the interim constitution for concentrating too much power in the hands of the president, including the authority to dismiss elected governors and to declare war without parliamentary consent.

South Sudan is divided into ten states, with 86 counties. The Kiir government sought to include the disputed Abyei region in the 2011 referendum. However, in May an estimated 5,000 Sudanese troops invaded the region (see Foreign relations, below), and the status of the area remains unresolved as of July 2012.

The transitional constitution established English as the official language but also recognized indigenous languages. The interim government pledged to maintain freedom of the press. There are a number of newspapers, including the *Juba Post* and the *Akhbar al-Yaum*. In 2016 the media watchdog group Reporters Without Borders ranked South Sudan 140th out of 180 countries in freedom of the press, a decline from 119th in 2014.

Foreign relations. In September 1993 Eritrea, Ethiopia, Kenya, and Uganda created the Intergovernmental Authority on Drought and Development (IGADD), which became the Intergovernmental Authority on Development (IGAD). IGAD endeavored to mediate the Sudanese conflict. IGAD and regional powers, including Egypt and Ethiopia, played an important role in fostering the 2005 CPA. (For more information on the civil wars and international efforts to mediate the crises prior to 2011, see the entry on Sudan.)

After South Sudan became independent in July 2011, it joined the UN and African Union (AU). Concurrently, the United States and other countries ended sanctions against South Sudan, while maintaining them against Sudan. In 2011 there were an estimated 81,000 refugees in South Sudan, mainly from Ethiopia and the Democratic Republic of the Congo.

The AU sponsored negotiations over the status of the disputed region of Abyei in Addis Ababa, Ethiopia, in June 2011. On June 20 South Sudan and Sudan signed an accord to demilitarize the area and allow a 7,000-member UN peacekeeping force (the UN Mission in the Republic of South Sudan, or UNMISS) to be deployed. Despite the presence of UNMISS and ongoing peace negotiations between Sudan and South Sudan, renewed fighting broke out in December 2011 and continued into 2012.

On January 20, 2012, Kiir announced that South Sudan would cease oil exports through Sudan because of a dispute over transit fees. South Sudanese officials claimed that the Sudanese had illegally diverted more than $815 million of oil. The suspension of production cut government revenues by 90 percent, leading to increased inflation. Meanwhile, South Sudan finalized an agreement to build a pipeline through Kenya for its energy exports.

In February 2012 South Sudan and Sudan agreed on a plan to repatriate more than 300,000 South Sudanese from the north and to finalize the demarcation of the remaining disputed border areas. However, in March, renewed fighting commenced along the border, and SPLA troops captured the oil town of Heglig. However, the South Sudanese forces withdrew under international pressure. Sudan then undertook an irregular aerial bombing campaign of South Sudan despite repeated calls from the UN and international actors to end the strikes.

In April South Sudan became the 188th member of the IMF.

On September 27, 2012, South Sudan and Sudan signed a series of agreements to resolve issues remaining from succession (see entry on Sudan). The accords paved the wave for the resumption of oil shipments in April 2013. On December 4 the East African Community rejected South Sudan's membership bid.

In January 2013 South Sudan agreed to sell oil to Israel. In March the United Kingdom announced it would expand economic and cultural cooperation with South Sudan. Amid a growing civil war (see Current issues, below), more than 100,000 refugees fled to Ethiopia. Meanwhile, the UN Security Council authorized an increase in UNMISS to 12,500 troops in January 2014. IGAD voted on March 13, 2014, to also deploy a 5,000-person peacekeeping force, the Protection and Deterrent Force (PDF). In May Norway hosted an international donors conference for South Sudan, which culminated in more than $600 million in pledges in addition to $500 million previously promised by various countries and international organizations to meet a growing food insecurity crisis caused by the fighting.

When fighting continued after an August 2015 peace deal, the UN Security Council authorized the deployment of an additional 4,000 troops and threatened to impose an arms embargo on the country. On April 15, 2016, Kiir signed the ascension treaty to join the East African Community, and South Sudan became the sixth member of the organization.

Current issues. After 21 years of civil war, the people of the southern provinces of Sudan voted in a referendum during January 9–15, 2011, to form the new nation of South Sudan. Formal independence came on July 9. After independence, there remained an estimated 100,000 internally displaced persons in South Sudan.

A renegade SPLA force, the South Sudan Democratic Movement (SSDM), led by George ATHOR signed a cease-fire agreement with the GOSS on January 5, 2011. However, new fighting broke out, and the militia group captured Fangak in Jonglei state on February 15, 2011. SPLA forces quickly recaptured the town, but more than 210 people were killed, mainly civilians. In April militias under the command of Maj. Gen. Gabriel "TANGINYE" CHAN and loyal to Khartoum launched a series of attacks in the Upper Nile state. After a counteroffensive, Tanginye surrendered on April 25, and was placed under house arrest. By November 2011 the UN estimated that more than 1,500 people had been killed in fighting in South Sudan between the government and rebel militias since independence. On December 19 Athor was killed while fighting government forces.

Ethnic clashes in Jonglei killed an estimated 3,000 civilians in January 2012. The government declared martial law and dispatched troops to end the fighting. On March 19 the SPLA and the UN launched a program to demobilize an estimated 4,000 child soldiers.

In April 2013 the government and rebel groups, including the South Sudan Liberation Army, the South Sudan Democratic Army, and South Sudan Defense Force, signed a comprehensive peace agreement. However, renewed fighting in Jonglei with other groups created an additional 23,000 refugees. In June Kiir dismissed the Minister of Cabinet Affairs Deng Alor KUOL and Finance Minister Kosti Manibe NGAL, following allegations of corruption. The next month, the president dismissed Vice President Machar and the cabinet in a reported effort to consolidate power. The firing of the vice president came amid rising tension between the two (see the SPLM under Political Parties and Groups, below). By December fighting had broken out between the two largest ethnic groups in the country: the Dinka, who supported Kiir; and the Nuer, who supported Machar. The rebel forces dubbed themselves the Sudan People's Liberation Army in Opposition (SPLA-O). On December 16, in a televised address, Kiir accused Machar and his supporters of attempting a coup following an attack on the army's headquarters in Juba. Fighting escalated in the new year, as did reports of atrocities by both sides, including mass killings. Uganda deployed military forces to support the Kiir government in December. A January cease-fire accord failed to stop the violence. By March the fighting had killed more than 10,000 and created some 740,000 refugees.

The fighting created a humanitarian crisis that the UN estimated left more than 3.7 million South Sudanese facing malnutrition or starvation by February of 2014. In May IGAD brokered a cease-fire agreement between Kiir and Machar, which called for the creation of a unity government and the drafting of a new constitution. Nonetheless, by July more than 100,000 refugees remained in ten UN emergency compounds.

From 2014 to 2016, fighting between the SPLM factions loyal to Kiir and Machar displaced more than 2.2 million South Sudanese and killed more than 50,000. The two sides agreed to a preliminary cease-fire in January 2015, and then a formal agreement was finalized in August. However, new fighting began in July, prompting Machar to flee to the Democratic Republic of the Congo and then to Sudan, where he called for an armed struggle to overthrow Kiir.

POLITICAL PARTIES AND GROUPS

The SPLM led the effort to gain independence and was the dominant political force in the postindependence government. The transitional Constitution guaranteed the right to develop new political parties.

Parties and Groupings:

Sudan People's Liberation Movement/Army (SPLM/A). Originally formed in 1983 as a Marxist-Leninist grouping, the SPLM and its military wing, the SPLA, were led by Col. John Garang until his death in 2005. Salva Kiir Mayardit succeeded Garang and was reelected president of South Sudan in 2010. (For more information on the SPLM/A prior to South Sudanese independence in 2011, see the entry on Sudan.) Yasir ARMAN became the SPLM leader in the north (SPLM-N) after independence, although the party was banned in Sudan. After independence in July 2011, Kiir was automatically appointed interim president for a four-year term. Kiir appointed an SPLM-dominated cabinet in August. Following his dismissal as vice president in July 2013, Riak Machar pledged to challenge Kiir for the presidency of South Sudan. Tensions between the two leaders led to a bloody civil war that began in December. Macher's supporters called themselves the **Sudan People's Liberation Movement in Opposition** (SPLM-O). A cease-fire accord was signed in May, followed by renewed fighting and then another peace agreement in August 2015, in which Machar was made first vice president as part of a transitional government. New fighting led to Machar's dismissal in July 2016 and his replacement as first vice president by Taban Deng Gai, who also attempted to gain control of the SPLM-O. By November 2016 the SPLM-O was estimated to have 10,000 fighters, the majority loyal to Machar.

Leaders: Salva KIIR Mayardit (President of South Sudan and Party Chair), Riak MACHAR (Former Vice President of South Sudan and SPLM-O Leader), Taban DENG GAI (First Vice President of the Republic and SPLM-O Rival Leader), Yasir ARMAN (2010 presidential candidate and SPLM-N Leader).

Sudan Peoples' Liberation Movement–Democratic Change (SPLM-DC). The SPLM-DC was originally established as the **Sudan People's Liberation Army–United** (SPLA-United), which was formed in 1993 in Nairobi, Kenya, by an anti-Garang faction of the SPLA. The SPLA-United was led by Lam Akol, who founded the SPLM-DC ahead of the 2010 legislative and presidential elections. Akol was the SPLM-DC candidate in the GOSS presidential balloting but was defeated by Kiir. (For more on the SPLA-United prior to South Sudanese independence, see the entry on Sudan.)

The SPLM-DC emerged as the main opposition party after independence and did not join the SPLM-led coalition cabinet. Nonetheless, it was estimated that more than 500 members of the party defected to the SPLM during the transition to independence. In September 2011 Sisto Olur was appointed interim secretary general of the party. Following a meeting between Akol and Kiir in Nairobi, Kenya, in October, the SPLM-DC leader pledged to cooperate with the new government. The SPLM-DC remained loyal to the government during the 2013 civil war. However, the SPLM-DC withdrew from the transitional government after Machar was dismissed as vice president in July 2016.

Leaders: Lam AKOL (Commander in Chief and 2010 presidential candidate), Sisto OLUR (Secretary General).

National Congress (NC). The NC was originally founded in 1986 as the National Islamic Front (NIF) (*al-Jabhah al-Watani al-Islami*). The NC emerged as the dominant northern Sudanese party. (For more information on the NC, see the entry on Sudan.) The southern faction of the NC agreed to participate in the SPLM-led coalition government. NC member Gen. Alison Manani MAGAYA was appointed minister of internal affairs and Agnes Kwaje LASUBA, minister of Gender, Children, and Social Welfare (Lasuba resigned in October 2011). Party chair Agnes Poni LUKUDU reportedly defected to the SPLM in July 2012. Subsequent reports indicated that the NC was largely defunct in South Sudan.

Leader: Agnes Poni LUKUDU.

United Democratic Salvation Front (UDSF). The USDF was formed by dissident members of SPLA as a moderate faction that initially promoted reconciliation between the north and south. The original leader, Riak MACHAR, left the party in 2002 and joined the SPLA. Following South Sudanese independence in July 2011, the UDSF retained a cabinet post in the Sudanese government. The southern branch of the USDF became known as the United Democratic Salvation Front–Mainstream (UDSF-M). The UDSF-M was given two cabinet posts in the government appointed by President Kiir in August 2011. In September the UDSF executive council dismissed party leader Joseph Malual DOUNG. Martin Tako Moyi was appointed as interim UDSF chair. Following the cabinet reshuffle in July 2013, the UDSF called for Kiir to step down.

Leaders: Martin Tako MOYI (Chair), Maj. Gen. (Ret.) Albino Akol AKOL (General Secretary).

United Sudan African Parties (USAP). The USAP was formed in 1987 as a coalition of seven minor parties. Initially led by Hilary LOGALI, the USAP joined the opposition National Democratic Alliance in 1994. After Logali died in 1998, he was succeeded by the current chair, Joseph Ukel Abango. Ukel was appointed minister of education in the South Sudanese postindependence government but lost his post in the July 2013 cabinet reshuffle.

Leader: Joseph UKEL Abango.

South Sudan Democratic Front (SSDF). The SSDF was formed in 2007 through the merger of the South Sudan Democratic Forum and the South Sudan United Democratic Alliance. The SSDF was a centrist organization that supported a negotiated settlement between the north and the south. Following independence, a member of the SSDF was appointed to the SPLM-led government, although reports indicated that the party portrayed itself as an opposition grouping. In July 2012 SSDF Maj. Gen. James Duit YIETCH and a number of party members defected to the SPLM/A. In July 2013 Martin Elia LOMORO was appointed minister of cabinet affairs, a position he retained in the transitional government appointed in August 2015.

Leader: Gordon BUAY.

United Democratic Front (UDF). Formed in 2003 and led by Peter Abdulrahman Sule, the UDF was a pro-independence South Sudanese party. In 2003 Sule became the only representative from South Sudan

in the Sudanese national parliament. The UDF supported the 2005 CPA and sought to unite South Sudanese parties into a single, unified opposition coalition. In November 2011 Philip Yona JAMBI was elected party chair. Former UDF member David YAUYAU launched a rebellion against the Kiir government in June 2012, before joining the SSDM (see below).
Leader: Gabriel Chanson CHANG.

South Sudan Democratic Movement (SSDM). Formed in 2010 by former SPLA Maj. General George Athor, the SSDM consists mainly of fighters from the minority Murle clan. Athor was killed on December 19, 2011, although the SSDM continued to conduct attacks against government targets in Jonglei. In January 2014 the SSDM signed a cease-fire agreement with the Kiir government.
Leader: David YAUYAU.

Other parties include the small **African National Congress**, led by George Kongor AROP, a former vice president of the national Sudanese government; the **Labour Party of South Sudan** (LPSS), led by Frederico Awi VUNI; the **Sudan African National Union** (SANU), led by Toby MADUOT; and the **Communist Party of South Sudan** (CPSS), led by Joseph Wol MODESTO.

LEGISLATURE

The **National Legislature** currently comprises the Council of States and the National Assembly. After independence, South Sudanese members of the Sudanese national legislature were automatically appointed to the parliament of the new nation.

The **Council of States** comprises 50 members, including the 20 South Sudanese former members of the Sudanese Council of States, 2 from each state, and 30 additional members appointed by the presidents.
Speaker: Joseph Bul CHAN.

The **National Assembly** is composed of 332 members, including 170 members elected in balloting for the South Sudan regional assembly during April 11–15, 2010; 96 South Sudanese members of the Sudanese assembly who were elected in concurrent balloting but who resigned after the January 2011 independence referendum; and 66 members appointed by the president. Under the terms of the August 2015 peace deal, the size of the assembly was expanded to 400, adding 68 members of the opposition. New elections were required by May 2018.
President: Anthony Lino MAKANA (SPLM).

CABINET

[as of November 1, 2016]

President	Salva Kiir Mayardit (SPLM)
First Vice President	Taban Deng Gai (SPLM-O)
Second Vice President	James Wani Igga (SPLM)
Ministers	
Agriculture and Food Security	(Vacant)
Cabinet Affairs	Martin Elia Lomoro (SSDF)
Culture, Youth, and Sports	Nadia Arop Dudi (SPLM) [f]
Defense and Veterans Affairs	Kuol Manyang Juuk (SPLM)
Energy and Dams	Dhieu Mathok Diing (SPLM-O)
Environment and Forestry	Josephine Akoon (SPLM) [f]
Federal Affairs	Richard Kebe Mulla (SPLM-O)
Finance and Planning	David Deng Athorbei (SPLM)
Foreign Affairs and International Cooperation	Deng Alor Kuol (Former Detainees)
Gender and Social Development	Awut Deng Acuil (SPLM) [f]
General Education	Deng Deng Hoc Yai (SPLM)
Health	Riek Gai Kok (SPLM)
Higher Education, Science, and Technology	Yien Oral Lam Tut (SPLM-O)
Humanitarian Affairs and Disaster Management	Hussein Mar Nyuot (SPLM-O)
Information, Communication, and Postal Service	Michael Makuei Lueth (SPLM)
Interior	Michael Chiengjiek Geay (SPLM-O)
Justice and Constitutional Affairs	Paulino Wanawilla (SPLM)
Labor, Public Service, and Human Resource Development	Gabriel Duop Lam (SPLM-O)
Land, Housing, and Urban Development	Alfred Lado Gore (SPLM-O)
Livestock and Fisheries	James Janda Duku (SPLM)
Mining	Gabriel Thokuj Deang (SPLM-O)
National Security	Obuto Mamur Mete (SPLM)
Office of the President	Mayiik Ayii Deng (SPLM)
Parliamentary Affairs	Peter Bashir Gbandi (SPLM)
Petroleum	Ezekiel Lul Gatkuoth (SPLM-O)
Roads and Bridges	Rebecca Joshua Okwaci (SPLM) [f]
Trade and Industry	Stephen Dhieu Dau (SPLM-O)
Transport	John Luk Jok (Former Detainees)
Water Resources and Irrigation	Sofia Pal Gai (SPLM-O) [f]
Wildlife Conservation and Tourism	Jemma Nunu Kumba (SPLM) [f]

[f] = female

INTERGOVERNMENTAL REPRESENTATION

Ambassador to the U.S.: Garang Diing AKUONG.

U.S. Ambassador to South Sudan: Mary Catherine PHEE.

Permanent Representative to the UN: Akuei Bona MALWAL.

IGO Memberships (Non-UN): AU, Comesa, EAC, IMF.

For Further Reference:

Johnson, Hilde. *South Sudan: The Untold Story from Independence to Civil War.* London: I. B. Taurus, 2016.
Thomas, Edward. *South Sudan: A Slow Liberation.* London: Zed Books, 2015.
Turse, Nick. *Next Time They Will Count the Dead: War and Survival in South Sudan.* Chicago: Haymarket Books, 2016.

SPAIN

Kingdom of Spain
Reino de España

Political Status: Formerly under a system of personal rule instituted in 1936; monarchy reestablished November 22, 1975, in accordance with the Law of Succession of July 26, 1947, as amended in 1969 and 1971; parliamentary monarchy confirmed by constitution effective December 29, 1978.

Area: 194,896 sq. mi. (504,782 sq. km).

Population: 46,065,000 (2016E—UN); 48,563,476 (2016E—U.S. Census). (Includes the Canary Islands, Ceuta, and Melilla.)

Major Urban Areas (2015E—UN): MADRID (6,199,000), Barcelona (5,258,000), Valencia (810,000), Seville (701,000), Zaragoza (701,000), Málaga (574,000), Murcia (463,000).

Official Languages: Spanish and regional languages (principally Basque, Catalan, Galician, and Valencian).

Monetary Unit: Euro (market rate October 1, 2016: 0.89 euro = $1US).

Monarch: FELIPE VI de Borbón y Grecia; enthroned as king on June 19, 2014, following the abdication of his father, JUAN CARLOS I de Borbón y Borbón, the previous day.

Heir to the Throne: Princess LEONOR; sworn in as heir apparent on June 19, 2014.

President of Government (Prime Minister): Mariano RAJOY Brey (Popular Party); nominated by the king on December 16, 2011, following the parliamentary election of November 20, elected by the Congress of Deputies on December 20, sworn in on December 21 for a four-year term, succeeding José Luis Rodríguez ZAPATERO (Spanish Socialist Workers' Party); remained as caretaker prime minister following legislative elections on December 20, 2015; nominated by the king on July 28, 2016, following legislative balloting on June 26, elected by the Chamber of Deputies on October 29 and sworn in on October 31.

THE COUNTRY

Occupying more than four-fifths of the Iberian peninsula (which it shares with Portugal), Spain is separated by the Pyrenees from France and the rest of Europe and includes within its national territory the Balearic Islands in the Mediterranean, the Canary Islands in the Atlantic, and small North African enclaves, including the *presidios* of Ceuta and Melilla. Continental Spain, a region of varied topography and climate, has been noted more for its beautiful landscape than for wealth of resources, but possesses valuable deposits of slate, iron, coal, and other minerals, as well as petroleum. The Spanish are a mixture of the original mainly Iberian population with later invading peoples. The population includes several cultural/linguistic groups: Castilians, Galicians, Andalusians, Catalans, and Basques (who claim distinct ethnicity). Regional feelings remain strong, particularly in the Basque and Catalan areas in the north and east, and various local languages and dialects are used in addition to the long-dominant Castilian Spanish and are increasingly taught in schools. About 94 percent of the population is Roman Catholic, although religious liberty is formally guaranteed. Women's participation in government is increasing, and several parties have adopted quota systems to ensure women have access to senior party posts. Following the 2008 elections, the national cabinet contained more women than men for the first time in the country's history. Women make up 38.6 percent of the legislature.

Spain's economy is largely driven by production of processed foods, textiles, footwear, petrochemicals, steel, automobiles, consumer goods, and electronics. Tourism contributes 10 percent of gross domestic product (GDP), and agriculture and fisheries yield less than 3 percent, though grain, vegetables, fruit, wine, olives and olive oil, sunflowers, and livestock remain important exports. Roughly 70 percent of Spain's exports go to European Union (EU) member states, and Morocco is an important trading partner. Spain's entrance into the European Community (EC, subsequently the EU) in 1986 stimulated the economy, although the country experienced recessions in the early 1990s. Spain participated in the launch of the EU's Economic Monetary Union in 1999.

Between 1999 and 2008, economic growth transformed Spain from an economy with high unemployment, public deficits, and high inflation to a modern, dynamic economy with fiscal surpluses, low inflation, a strong currency, and low interest rates. However, the construction boom and housing bubble burst, plunging Spain into one of the worst recessions in Europe. Home values dropped 31 percent between 2008 and 2012. The federal bureaucracy and the legal system discourage foreign investment, and the recent devolution of powers to the regional level has increased bureaucracy. Basque terrorism also remains a concern to potential foreign investors.

Economic conditions deteriorated significantly beginning in 2008. The combination of falling tax revenue and increased spending on fiscal stimulus measures widened Spain's budget deficit from 3.8 percent in 2008 to 9.3 percent of GDP in 2010. That year GDP fell by 0.2 percent, marking the second year of GDP contraction. In 2011 GDP grew by 0.1 percent, while inflation was 3 percent, and unemployment was a crippling 21.6 percent. GDP declined again in 2012, by 1.6 percent, inflation rose 2.4 percent, and unemployment grew to 25 percent. Unemployment for persons under age 25 exceeded 60 percent. Debt pressures led Spain to negotiate a financial rescue package from the EU and International Monetary Fund (IMF) in June 2012 (see Current issues, below).

GDP declined again in 2013, falling by 1.2 percent, while inflation expanded by 1.5 percent. Unemployment continued to climb, rising to 26.4 percent. GDP began to recover in 2014, rising 1.4 percent, and then 3.2 percent in 2015. GDP expanded by 2.6 percent in 2016. That year inflation was –0.4 percent, while unemployment declined to 19.7 percent. In 2016 the World Bank ranked Spain 33rd out of 189 in its annual report on the ease of doing business index, up from 52nd in 2014, and one place ahead of Japan (34th).

GOVERNMENT AND POLITICS

Political background. Conquered in the 8th century by North African Moors (Arabs and Berbers), who established a flourishing Islamic civilization in the south of the peninsula, Christian Spain completed its self-liberation in 1492 and went on to found a world empire that reached its apogee in the 16th century and then gradually disintegrated. Monarchical rule under the House of Bourbon continued into the 20th century, surviving the dictatorship of Miguel PRIMO de Rivera in 1923–1930 but giving way in 1931 to a multiparty republic that became increasingly subject to leftist influences. The electoral victory of a leftist Popular Front coalition in 1936 provoked a military uprising led by Gen. Francisco FRANCO Bahamonde, precipitating the three-year civil war in which the republican forces, although assisted by Soviet and other foreign volunteers, were ultimately defeated with aid from Fascist Italy and Nazi Germany. A fascist regime was then established, Franco ruling as leader (*caudillo*) and chief of state with the support of the armed forces; the Catholic Church; and commercial, financial, and landed interests.

Having preserved its neutrality throughout World War II and suffered a period of ostracism thereafter by the United Nations (UN), Spain was gradually readmitted to international society. The political structure was modified in 1947 with the adoption of a Law of Succession, which declared Spain to be a monarchy (although without a monarch), and again in 1967 by an Organic Law confirming Franco's position as chief of state, defining the structure of other government bodies, and providing for strictly limited public participation in elections to the legislature (*Cortes*). Political and administrative controls in effect since the Civil War were considerably relaxed during the early 1960s, but subsequent demands for change generated increasing instability. In December 1973

Prime Minister Luis CARRERO Blanco was assassinated by Basque separatists and was succeeded by Carlos ARIAS Navarro.

Franco became terminally ill on October 17, 1975, and on October 30 Prince JUAN CARLOS I de Borbón y Borbón, who had been designated heir to the Spanish throne, assumed the powers of provisional chief of state and head of government. Franco died on November 20, and two days later Juan Carlos was sworn in as king, in accordance with the 1947 Law of Succession.

On July 1, 1976, Arias Navarro resigned as prime minister—reportedly at the king's request—following criticism of his somewhat cautious approach to promised reform of the political system. His successor, Adolfo SUÁREZ González, moved energetically to advance the reform program, securing its approval by the National Council of the National (Francoist) Movement on October 8, by the *Cortes* on November 10, and by the public in a referendum conducted on December 15. The National Movement was abolished by cabinet decree on April 1, 1977, and on June 15 balloting took place for a new, bicameral *Cortes,* with Prime Minister Suárez's Union of the Democratic Center (*Unión de Centro Democrático*—UCD) obtaining a substantial plurality in both houses. A new constitution went into force on December 29, 1978, following overwhelming approval by the *Cortes* on October 31, endorsement in a referendum on December 6, and ratification by King Juan Carlos on December 27. Suárez was formally reappointed on April 2, 1979, a general election on March 1 having yielded no substantial party realignment within the legislature.

During 1979–1980, an increase in terrorist activity, particularly in the Basque region, gave rise to manifest uneasiness within military circles, while the Union of the Democratic Center (*Unión de Centro Democrático*; see the 2013 *Handbook* for more on the party) experienced internal dissension following the introduction of a liberal divorce bill that the Catholic Church and most right-wing elements bitterly opposed. On January 29, 1981, Suárez unexpectedly resigned. Before his designated successor had been confirmed, a group of Civil Guards, led by Lt. Col. Antonio TEJERO Molina, seized control of the Congress of Deputies chamber in an attempted coup on February 23. Due largely to the prompt intervention of King Juan Carlos, the rebellion failed, with Leopoldo CALVO Sotelo i Bustelo, the UCD secretary general, being sworn in as prime minister on February 26. However, the fissures between moderate and rightist elements within the UCD continued to deepen, with a number of new parties being spawned during late 1981 and the first half of 1982. As a result, lower house UCD representation plummeted to a mere dozen deputies at an election held October 12, when the Spanish Socialist Workers' Party (*Partido Socialista Obrero Español*—PSOE) obtained a comfortable majority (202 to 106 seats) over the Popular Alliance (*Alianza Popular*—AP), an emergent right-wing group that had previously held only a handful of seats. On December 2, PSOE leader Felipe GONZÁLEZ Márquez was inaugurated as the first left-wing head of government since the 1930s. González was sworn in for a second term on July 24, 1986, following an early election on June 22 at which the PSOE, despite marginally declining strength, retained majority control of both houses of the *Cortes.*

Throughout the 1980s, the Socialists continued to dominate as the conservative Popular Party (*Partido Popular*—PP, successor to the AP) engaged in a process of ideological self-examination and as the Communist Party reeled from events in Eastern Europe. The PSOE was rocked by a financial corruption scandal in 1992 and combined with economic problems narrowly avoided defeat in June 6, 1993 balloting due to support from the main Catalan (*Convergéncia i Unió*—CiU) and Basque nationalist (*Partido Nacionalista Vasco*—PNV) parties, which gave the minority PSOE government a 181-seat majority. The immediate price of CiU support was a government commitment to transfer 15 percent of taxes raised in Catalonia to the regional Catalan government and CiU demands for "real" autonomy for Catalonia.

To add to the government's problems, the Basque *Euzkadi ta Azkatasuna* (ETA), which had been engaged in a violent separatist campaign since the 1960s, launched a new wave of terrorist attacks in 1995, including an attempt to assassinate PP leader José María AZNAR López in a Madrid car bomb attack on April 19.

Parliamentary balloting on March 3, 1996, brought the PP to power, and its leader, Aznar, formed a minority government with external support from Basque (PNV), Catalan (CiU), and Canarian (*Coalición Canaria*—CC) regionalist parties, which won concessions that included a doubling (to 30 percent) of the proportion of income tax revenues accruing to the autonomous regions.

An increase in civilian deaths due to ETA terrorism led to a government crackdown in which the entire national committee of the political wing of the organization, the *Herri Batasuna* (HB), was placed on trial and sentenced to a minimum of seven years, although the Constitutional Court ultimately ordered their release in July 1999.

In September 1998 ETA announced a unilateral cease-fire and, having finished third in the regional elections, participated in the formation of a Basque regional government—a first for an ETA-linked group—with the PNV and the Basque Solidarity (*Eusko Alkartasuna*—EA).

In direct talks between the Aznar administration and ETA representatives, ETA continued to insist on the withdrawal of security forces from the Basque region, the release of some 450 jailed comrades (or, at the very least, their transfer to prisons in Basque Country), and an independence referendum. Citing the lack of progress toward any of its goals, ETA announced that it would end its cease-fire as of December 3 and was forced to withdraw from the Basque regional government.

At the general election of March 12, 2000, Prime Minister Aznar's PP surpassed expectations, winning an outright majority in both houses of the *Cortes,* including 183 seats in the Congress of Deputies. Reelected prime minister by the lower house on April 26, with external support from the CiU and the CC, Aznar was sworn in for a second term on April 27 at the head of a revamped and expanded cabinet. A ministerial reshuffle announced on July 9, 2002, was highlighted by the selection of Spain's first woman foreign minister, Ana PALACIO Vallelersundi, who was sworn in the following day.

On March 11, 2004, in the worst peacetime attack on Spanish civilians since the Civil War of the 1930s, a series of bombs exploded on four Madrid commuter trains, killing 191 and injuring another 1,400. The bombings had clearly been timed to affect the general election scheduled for March 14. Although the Aznar government immediately focused blame on ETA, it soon emerged that the coordinated assault had been perpetrated by militants associated with the al-Qaida terrorist network. (In 2007, 21 of 28 defendants were convicted of their roles in the bombing, most of the defendants were of North African descent.)

Prior to the March 2004 terrorist bombings in Madrid, the PP appeared on its way to a comfortable victory in the March 14 election. The Aznar government had weathered a number of difficulties, including a mishandling of the environmental crisis caused by the sinking of the Greek oil tanker *Prestige* off the coast of Galicia in November 2002. It had also overcome an 80 percent public disapproval rating of Spain's military involvement in Iraq.

Fearing adverse repercussions from the Madrid bombings, the government argued that a defeat at the polls would constitute a victory for the bombers, but by election day many Spaniards believed that the government had tried to manipulate the flow of information for political reasons, and voters displayed their anger through the ballot. On March 14 the voters gave the PSOE 42.6 percent of the vote, good for 164 seats, versus 37.6 percent and 148 seats for the PP. The rapid reversal of the PP's fortunes was generally attributed to the bombings, the government's misplaced blame, and underlying public opposition to Spain's military involvement in Iraq. With support from the IU and a handful of regional parties, the PSOE's José Luis Rodríguez ZAPATERO was confirmed as prime minister on April 16.

Some dozen seats short of a majority in the Chamber of Deputies, the Zapatero government came into office in 2004 through the support of a number of small regional parties, including the Catalan Republican Left (*Esquerra Republicana de Catalunya*—ERC), the Canarian Coalition, and the Galician Nationalist Bloc (*Bloque Nacionalista Galego*—BNG). In addition to quickly fulfilling a campaign pledge to withdraw from Iraq, Prime Minister Zapatero advanced a social agenda that included recognition of gay marriage (approved by both houses of the *Cortes* in 2005), streamlined divorce proceedings, allowed scientific research on embryonic stem cells, and reduced the role of religion in state schools. However, the policy changes provoked a backlash by conservatives, led by the Roman Catholic Church. The government maintained that advancing secular values was key to the modernization of Spain.

On December 20, 2007, Zapatero called a general election for March 9. Analysts predicted a tight race against the PP, stemming from public discontent over the ruling party's perceived leniency toward ETA and uneasiness over Spain's economic slowdown after more than a decade of expansion. High turnout, prompted in part by the March 7 assassination of PSOE councilor Isaias CARRASCO by a suspected ETA gunman, helped the PSOE secure 169 seats in the balloting with 43.6 percent of the vote, 7 short of an absolute majority, while the PP won 153 seats with 40.1 percent of the vote. Both leading parties expanded at the expense of smaller, regional parties such as the United Left and the Catalan Republican Left, which suffered a steep drop in support.

Although the PSOE was 7 short of an absolute majority, Zapatero said he had a "sufficient majority" to carry out his agenda. The PSOE shunned a formal coalition government, opting instead to negotiate with opposition parties on a case-by-case basis. His newly created cabinet, Spain's first with a female majority, included two new ministries: science and innovation as well as equality. The latter was headed by Bibiana AÍDO, who at 31 became Spain's youngest-ever cabinet minister.

Zapatero immediately turned his attention to the deteriorating economy. On April 18, 2008, the government announced a two-year, US$28.5 billion stimulus plan to support the real estate sector and small- to medium-sized businesses. In October the government raised guarantees on bank deposits and new debt and announced an $87 billion fund to buy state shares of healthy financial institutions to inject liquidity into the market. A stimulus package was directed toward job creation in the public works and automobile industries.

To cobble together enough support for the 2009 budget, Zapatero won key votes from nationalist parties in the Basque Country and Galicia with an agreement to provide the two regions with $283 million in infrastructure and research funds. However, in order to make the budget numbers work, Zapatero inserted a 1 percent growth forecast for 2009, an amount the PP called "legal fraud." Even the Economy Minister Pedro SOLBES deemed the growth forecast unrealistic.

In February 2009 Justice Minister Mariano Fernández BERMEJO resigned following a judges' strike and a scandal involving a hunting trip he took with a prominent judge. He was replaced by Francisco CAAMAÑO Domínguez.

In early April, only a year after the start of his second term, Zapatero announced a major cabinet reshuffle to boost public confidence in the PSOE, which had declined as the economic recession deepened. The PSOE was defeated in the June 7 European Parliament election, in which the PP won 42 percent of the vote compared to the PSOE's 39 percent. Analysts saw the PSEO's loss of 5 percentage points from the previous election as a reflection of the poor economy and not necessarily a lengthy move away from the party.

Zapatero reshuffled seven cabinet posts on October 20 after the introduction of unpopular austerity measures. A new minister of labor was appointed in an attempt to restart talks with trade unions following major changes to the country's labor laws in June. Zapatero put more power in the hands of popular interior minister Alfredo Perez RUBALCABA who, renowned for his success in suppressing the ETA, gained two extra portfolios in the arrangement—deputy prime minister and official government spokesperson. In cost-cutting moves, Zapatero incorporated the ministries of equality and housing into other portfolios.

In May 2010, under pressure from the EU to drive down Spain's budget deficit to the mandatory 3 percent by 2013, Zapatero pushed through the Congress of Deputies a highly unpopular austerity package (the measures passed by one vote). They included cuts to civil service salaries, a freeze on state pensions, and the abolition of the "baby bonus" for families. Civil servants held strikes in June, which disrupted schools, transit, and the postal service. In June Zapatero's labor reform legislation, designed to lower the country's 20 percent unemployment by reducing the cost of hiring and dismissing permanent employees, was passed by the Congress of Deputies solely by the PSOE as most deputies abstained from the vote.

Zapatero's 2011 austerity budget, presented in September 2010, proposed new income taxes for the wealthy and an 8 percent cut in federal spending. To gain minimal support for passage, the PSOE secured backing from the Basque National Party and the Canarian Coalition by agreeing to transfer funds and power to the Basque region and the Canary Islands.

The retirement age was raised from 65 to 67 in January 2011 as part of a broader effort to reform the pension system. On January 2 Spain introduced a nationwide smoking ban in public areas, including restaurants. In June the government enacted a 3.8 percent cut in the national budget in response to increased concern by the EU and IMF that Spain could need an economic bailout similar to those granted to Ireland, Greece, and Portugal. The IMF warned that the €150 billion debt accumulated by regional governments threatened Spain's future borrowing ability. On June 19 massive protests erupted across the country over the government's management of the economy.

In April 2011 Zapatero announced that he would not seek reelection. The following month the PSOE suffered its worst electoral defeat in decades in local and regional balloting as the PP won 11 of the 13 regions that held elections. The PSOE also lost the mayorship of Barcelona for the first time since 1979. In response, Zapatero announced snap elections scheduled for November 20, and Rubalcaba resigned in July 2011 to lead the PSOE in the November balloting, but to no avail. The PP retained its majority in the Senate and gained a majority in the Congress of Deputies. PP leader Mariano RAJOY Brey was sworn in as prime minister of a PP government on December 21.

On June 2, 2014, King Juan Carlos announced his intention to abdicate, reportedly stating that he did not "want my son to grow old waiting like Prince Charles [of the United Kingdom]." He formally relinquished the throne on June 18, and his son was enthroned as FELIPE VI the next day.

In legislative balloting on December 20, 2015, the PP secured a plurality with 123 seats, followed by the PSOE with 90. The new left-wing, antiestablishment We Can (*Podemos*) was third with 69 seats. Rajoy was nominated again to form a new coalition government, but was unable to negotiate a working majority. Instead Rajoy remained prime minister of a caretaker government.

New elections were called for June 26, 2016. The PP again emerged as the largest party, but with 137 seats, it was still short of a majority. The PSOE was second with 85 seats, and *Podemos* third with 71 seats. Rajoy remained unable to form a governing coalition; however, the PSOE agreed in October to not vote against the PP-led government, allowing the prime minister to form a minority government. The new cabinet was sworn in on November 3.

Constitution and government. The 169-article Spanish constitution of 1978, the seventh since 1812, abrogated the "fundamental principles" and organic legislation under which General Franco had ruled as chief of state (*jefe del estado*) until his death in 1975. The document defines the Spanish state as a parliamentary monarchy and guarantees a variety of basic rights, including those of speech and press, association, and collective bargaining. "Bordering provinces" and "island territories and provinces" with common characteristics and/or historic regional status may, under prescribed circumstances, form "autonomous communities," but no federation of such communities is to be permitted. Roman Catholicism was disestablished as the state religion, although authorities were directed to "keep in mind the religious beliefs of Spanish society." Torture was outlawed, the death penalty abolished, and "a more equitable distribution of regional and personal incomes" enjoined. Freedom of the press is guaranteed, and in 2016, media watchdog group Reporters Without Borders ranked Spain 34th out of 180 countries.

The powers of the king include nominating a candidate for the post of prime minister, after consulting the parties in the *Cortes;* dissolving the house and calling fresh elections if such approval is not forthcoming; serving as commander in chief of the armed forces, which are specifically recognized as guardians of the constitutional order; and calling referenda. The prime minister, who is empowered to dissolve the *Cortes* and call an election at any time, is assisted by a cabinet that is collectively responsible to the lower house.

Legislative authority is exercised by the bicameral *Cortes,* consisting of a 264-member Senate (208 directly elected territorial representatives plus 56 indirectly chosen by the assemblies of the autonomous regions and representing one senator for every million inhabitants) and a Congress of Deputies of 300–400 (currently 350) members elected on the basis of universal adult suffrage and proportional representation. Both houses serve four-year terms, barring dissolution; each can initiate legislation, although the upper house can only delay measures approved by the lower.

The judicial system is headed by a Supreme Tribunal (*Tribunal Supremo*) and includes territorial courts, provincial courts, regional courts, courts of the first instance, and municipal courts. An independent General Council of Judicial Power (*Consejo General del Poder Judicial*) oversees the judiciary.

The country is divided into 19 regions containing 50 administrative provinces, including the island provinces of Baleares, Las Palmas, and Santa Cruz de Tenerife. Although it was envisaged in 1978 that devolution to the regions would involve only a limited range of powers, such as alteration of municipal boundaries, control of health and tourism, instruction in regional languages, and the establishment of local police agencies, the tendency has been to delegate ever more functions to regional governments.

In October 1979 devolution statutes presented for the Basque and Catalan regions were overwhelmingly approved in regional referenda. In March 1980 elections for regional Legislative Assemblies were held in the Basque provinces of Alava, Guipúzcoa, and Vizcaya, and in the Catalan provinces of Barcelona, Gerona, Lérida, and Tarragona. Similar elections were held in Galicia in October 1981 and in Andalucía in May 1982. By February 1983 autonomy statutes had been approved for the (then) remaining 13 regions, with balloting in each being conducted in May. In 1994 the African enclaves of Ceuta and Melilla were also accorded the status of autonomous regions, bringing the total to 19. A referendum in Catalonia in 2006 on a proposal already approved by the Spanish parliament endorsed even greater autonomy for Catalonia, giving the regional parliament more powers on taxation and judicial affairs.

Known as one of the most decentralized countries in Europe, Spain has struggled to respect regional allegiances while fulfilling the essential obligations of the central government. Spain's electoral system of proportional representation is structured around provincial constituencies and is partly responsible for regional parties gaining more seats in parliament than parties that compete nationwide.

The presidents of government of the autonomous regions are elected by the regional legislatures.

Autonomous Region	*President of Government [as of November 30, 2016]*
Andalucía	Susana Díaz Pacheco (PSOE) [f]
Aragón	Javier Lambán (PSOE)
Asturias	Javier Fernández Fernández (PSOE)
Baleares (Balearic Islands)	Francina Armengol (PSOE) [f]
Canarias (Canary Islands)	Fernando Clavijo (CC)
Cantábria	Miguel Ángel Revilla Roiz (PRC)
Castilla y León	Juan Vicente Herrera Campo (PP)
Castilla–La Mancha	Mariá Dolores de Cospedal Garcia (PP) [f]
Catalunya (Catalonia)	Carles Puigemont I Casamajo (CiU)
Ceuta	Juan Jesús Vivas Lara (PP)
Euzkadi/País Vasco (Basque Country)	Iñigo Urkullu (PNV)
Extremadura	Guillermo Fernández Vara (PSOE)
Galicia	Alberto Núñez Feijóo (PP)
Madrid	Cristina Cifuentes Cuencas (pp) [f]
Melilla	Juan José Imbroda Ortiz (PP)
Murcia	Pedro Antonio Sanchez López (PP)
Navarra	Uxue Barkos (*Geroa Bai*) [f]
La Rioja	José Ignacio Ceniceros González (PP)
Valencia	Joaquin Francisco Puig Ferrer (PSOE)

[f] = female

Foreign relations. Neutral in both world wars, Spain sided with the anti-communist powers after World War II but under Franco was prevented by certain democratic governments from becoming a member of the North Atlantic Treaty Organization (NATO), the EC (subsequently the EU), and other Western organizations. It was, however, admitted to the UN in 1955 and, in due course, to all of the latter's specialized agencies. The 1970s and early 1980s saw a strengthening of relations with Portugal, France, and West Germany. There also was a reduction of tension with Britain over Gibraltar (see entry on United Kingdom: Related Territories), which resulted in reopening of the border in early 1985 and a British commitment to talks from which the sovereignty question was not excluded. Relations with the United States remained cordial following the conclusion in 1970 of an Agreement of Friendship and Cooperation to replace the original U.S.–Spanish defense agreement of 1953. Following the restoration of democracy in 1975–1976, Spain was admitted to the Council of Europe in 1977 and to NATO in 1982, with membership in the EC following on January 1, 1986.

In February 1976 Spain yielded control of its North African territory of Spanish (Western) Sahara to Morocco and Mauritania. The action was taken despite strong protests by Algeria and the passage of a resolution by the UN General Assembly's Committee on Trust and Non-Self-Governing Territories in December 1975 that called for a UN-sponsored plebiscite to permit the Saharans to exercise their right to self-determination. Formerly cordial relations with the Saharan representative group Polisario (see entry on Morocco) were broken and its envoys expelled following a late 1985 Polisario attack on two Spanish vessels off the coast near Mauritania.

In May 1986 voters endorsed NATO membership, but on condition that Spain remain outside the alliance's command structure, ban nuclear weapons from Spanish territory, and reduce the number of U.S. forces in Spain. Subsequent negotiations yielded an agreement in principle on January 15, 1988, whereby the United States would, within three years, withdraw from the Torrejón facility outside Madrid and transfer its 72 F-16 jet fighters to a new base in Italy. The accord, as finalized at UN headquarters in September, contained no provision for continued military or economic assistance to Spain, while permitting U.S. military activity at a number of bases, including naval operations at Rota (near Cadiz). Most importantly, it allowed both sides to maintain their positions on nuclear arms, Spain reaffirming its opposition to the presence of such weapons but agreeing not to ask for compliance by inspection of U.S. vessels. In September 1990 González defied Spanish public opinion by contributing three warships to the buildup of allied forces in response to Iraq's August invasion of Kuwait. In the early 1990s, Spain signed a series of agreements that placed some of its forces under NATO's operational control.

A perennial obstacle to Spain's participation in NATO exercises was its refusal to join in any military activity that appeared to endorse British rule in Gibraltar. Full participation in NATO came on the heels of the installation of a conservative government in May 1996. A number of administrative accommodations regarding control of Gibraltar were achieved in 2000.

The Spanish Parliament overwhelmingly approved the EC's Maastricht Treaty in October–November 1992. Subsequently, Spain, together with Portugal, secured agreement on the creation of a "cohesion fund" for the four poorer members, including itself. Spain was also due to benefit from a similar fund established under the European Economic Area (EEA) agreement signed between the EC and five countries of the European Free Trade Association in March 1993.

In 2003 Zapatero won continued EU structural and cohesion funds for Spain in the EU's 2007–2013 budget, following concerns that it would lose EU funds as a result of the increase in membership in the EU. In February 2005 Spanish voters overwhelmingly endorsed the proposed EU constitution, which had the support of both the PSOE and the PP.

A frequent source of tension in Spain's external relations has been the activities of its 18,000-vessel fishing fleet (the EU's largest), whose crews combined a determination to protect home waters with a desire to exploit distant fishing grounds, often in alleged contravention of conservation and other international agreements. (See the 2013 *Handbook* and the entry on Canada for details.) In December Spain's endorsement of the admission of three new EU members was only granted after it had secured additional fishing access to Irish and UK waters.

In early 2003, despite wide public opposition, the Aznar government dispatched Spanish forces to aid in peacekeeping and humanitarian efforts in Iraq following the U.S.-led ouster of Saddam Hussein's regime. A pledge by PSOE candidate Zapatero to withdraw Spanish troops from Iraq contributed to the March 2004 Socialist victory at the polls. By late May all 1,300 troops had returned home, beginning three years of frosty relations between Spain and the United States.

More tension with the United States arose in November 2005, when EADS-CASA, the Spanish subsidiary of the European aerospace consortium, began negotiating the sale of military aircraft to the Venezuelan government of Hugo Chávez. In June 2006 the United States officially blocked the sale because the planes in question contained U.S. technology.

In June 2006 the United Kingdom, Gibraltar, and Spain concluded talks in Córdoba, Spain, concerning several issues affecting the Rock and the Campo de Gibraltar, removing many of the restrictions imposed by Spain. The agreement allowed improved traffic flow at the frontier, direct flights between Gibraltar Airport and Madrid-Baraja, and recognition of the "350" telephone code. In March 2007 talks resumed in Córdoba with an agenda that included work on cooperation on environmental issues, financial services and tax issues, judicial and law enforcement cooperation, education, maritime communications, and Schengen visa issues.

In June 2007 U.S. secretary of state Condoleezza Rice visited Spain. While the trip was billed as an opportunity to improve bilateral relations, Rice expressed displeasure that Spanish foreign minister Miguel Angel MORANTIS would not visit with Cuban dissident groups during his April 2007 visit to Cuba, arguing that Spain's willingness to engage Castro would not aid democratization in Cuba. Spain has a policy of "constructive engagement" with Cuba, following a 2007 agreement that improved relations by aiding Cuban businesses and social programs in exchange for human rights reforms and the release of political prisoners. Spain supported Castro's decision to hand over power to his brother, Raúl, saying the move would advance political reforms. In June 2008 Spain urged an easing of international sanctions against Cuba because of progress made in reforms.

In July 2008 Spain's Senate approved the EU's Lisbon Treaty after Irish voters rejected it.

Faced with its own troubles with separatist movements, Spain in February 2008 became one of the few European countries not to recognize Kosovo's declaration of independence from Serbia. The government faced considerable domestic criticism over its deployment of nearly 600 troops in the NATO peacekeeping operation in Kosovo.

Upon winning a second term, Zapatero said he would seek a "new chapter" in relations with the United States based on "mutual respect." The election of Barack Obama to the U.S. presidency in November 2008 brought renewed commitments in Spanish support for U.S. military operations. In December Spain lifted a 3,000-troop ceiling on the number of soldiers that may be deployed overseas, thereby clearing the way for a troop increase in Afghanistan, and in February 2009 expressed a willingness to accept detainees from the U.S. military camp at Guantanamo on a case-by-case basis.

Angered at not being invited to a European meeting on the global financial crisis in October 2008, Zapatero lobbied heavily to attend a Group of 20 summit in Washington in November on the grounds that, as the world's eighth largest economy, Spain deserved a seat at the table. Spain eventually prevailed when France ceded one of its two seats. Subsequently, Zapatero called for a permanent seat at the Group of 20, while analysts saw the incident as an effort to enlarge Spain's international standing.

In December 2008 Spain and Morocco sought to patch up lingering resentments over the 2007 visit of Spanish King Juan Carlos and Queen Sofia to Ceuta and Melilla by hosting a bilateral summit in Madrid during which Spain pledged $730 million to finance "projects of common interest" in Morocco with the aim of strengthening the two countries' economic ties (see Related territories, below). Zapatero and Moroccan Prime Minister Abbas El Fassi reportedly also discussed construction of a tunnel under the Straits of Gibraltar.

To advance Spanish business prospects, Spanish king Juan Carlos visited Libyan president Muammar Gadhafi in early 2009 to finalize an investment pact that would boost Spanish oil and construction interests there. In March Spain hosted Russian president Dmitry Medvedev and signed an energy agreement that allows Spanish oil companies to help develop Russia's vast Shtokman gas field and to partake in joint energy sector projects with Russia around the globe.

Revelations in January 2009 that Gibraltan authorities were extending into Spanish territorial waters by reclaiming land for building projects aroused the PP, which threatened to seek a European Commission investigation into the matter and demanded Zapatero oppose an official visit to Gibraltar in March by Britain's Princess Anne. In July foreign minister Miguel Moratinos went to Gibraltar to sign agreements on judicial, environmental, security, and customs measures, while the PP argued that the visit validated the territory as a sovereign state.

In February 2009 Spain signed a comprehensive security agreement with Algeria on antiterrorism intelligence, training, and technology cooperation. In June a similar accord was struck with Morocco.

Spain angered NATO allies with an unexpected decision to withdraw all peacekeeping forces from Kosovo by the autumn of 2009, saying that postwar operations there no longer needed outside support. U.S. officials complained that Spain made its decision without coordinating with other NATO members. Analysts believe that Spain withdrew to avoid appearing to endorse the precedent of Kosovar independence.

In response to growing tensions with foreign governments, the Congress of Deputies in June 2009 voted to restrict the ability of Spanish judges to investigate crimes against humanity around the world to cases only involving Spanish citizens. Spain had first used the principle of "universal jurisdiction" in an unsuccessful attempt to extradite Chilean dictator Augustus Pinochet in 1998. The Spanish judge in that case, Baltasar GARZÓN Real, also invoked the principle in May 2009 against six former White House officials who he alleged provided the legal cover for torture at the U.S. prison at Guantanamo, and to investigate a deadly Israeli incursion into Gaza in 2002. At the time of the lower house vote, the Spanish High Court was investigating 13 crimes against humanity around the world involving both Spanish and non-Spanish victims.

In January 2010 Spain assumed the six-month rotating EU presidency, a tenure that was marred by the European debt crisis and the Greek financial bailout. Zapatero led a successful effort to require public disclosure of stress tests on banks, and he concluded the signing of a free trade agreement between the EU and Central America. Efforts to normalize relations between the EU and Cuba were resisted by a number of EU nations, including France, Sweden, and the Czech Republic, which argued that the 1996 EU "common position" on the Caribbean island be preceded by democratic reforms.

In July 2010 Spain's foreign minister, Miguel Moratinos, supported by the Catholic Church, negotiated the release of 52 Cuban political prisoners and arranged their asylum in Spain. In October Spain called on Venezuela to examine evidence that several suspected ETA members, who had been arrested in Spain, had received weapons training in the South American country. Spain requested "concrete action" against ETA member Arturo Cubillas Fontan, who had been given a senior post in the administration of Venezuelan president Hugo Chavez in 2005. The Venezuelan government insisted it had no ties with ETA.

Also in 2010, tensions flared between Spain and Great Britain over Gibraltar. In June Spain refused to allow the British air force to use airspace over Gibraltar for military exercises, and in October Gibraltar asked the British Royal Navy to intercede because of a growing number of face-offs with Spanish naval and police boats in Gibraltar's waters. In October Spain agreed to resume talks with the UK over the future of the British enclave.

In October 2010 Argentine judge Mariá Servini announced that her court would begin investigating the atrocities committed during the Franco era since the 1977 amnesty law in Spain prevented prosecution for crimes during the period. On December 10 Spain expelled two Russian diplomats following charges of espionage. Russia retaliated by expelling two Spanish diplomats on December 24. In October 2011 Spain announced that it would participate in the NATO missile defense shield, despite opposition from Russia.

After Argentina took control of 51 percent of the Spanish oil company Repsol's South American operations in April 2012, Spain imposed restrictions on the import of biodiesel from Argentina. (Repsol later filed suit against Argentina for a loss of $10.5 billion.) The legislature approved a treaty with the Philippines in May 2012, whereby Filipinos working in Spain would be eligible for social security benefits. As a result of Spain's growing budget deficit, the government canceled development aid for Central and South America in May, and in November appealed to its former colonies to expand trade. Spain agreed to host four U.S. missile-interceptors in October.

Gibraltar dropped 70 concrete blocks into the sea to create an artificial reef in August 2013, but failed to alert Spain. Madrid protested the development, saying it impeded Spanish fishing rights, and increased border checks. The United Kingdom filed a protest with the European Commission (EC), saying the Spanish move impeded the flow of goods and people. The ambassadors of Latvia and Lithuania were summoned by the Spanish foreign minister following comments from both that seemed to indicate support for independence for Catalonia (see below, and Current issues, below). In November the EC rejected the British protest over enhanced border checks. A Spanish warship entered Gibraltarian waters in February 2014 and disrupted a military exercise, prompting another protest from the United Kingdom.

In May 2014 King Juan Carlos conducted a state visit to Tunisia, his first since that country's 2011 revolution. During the visit, the two countries signed more than 20 economic cooperation agreements. In June, Spain and Mexico signed a series of accords to improve trade and economic collaboration. Ahead of an unauthorized, nonbinding referendum on Catalonian independence in November 2014 (see Current issues, below), German chancellor Angela Merkel expressed support for the Spanish government's opposition to the measure.

A Russian fishing trawler sank off of the coast of the Canary Islands in April 2015, spilling more than 1,400 tons of fuel. The spill harmed beaches and wildlife, and had a devastating impact on tourism on the islands.

As part of an EU immigration deal in 2015, Spain agreed to take 15,000 refugees. Meanwhile, Spain was able to dramatically reduce the flow of migrants seeking to enter the EU through Ceuta and Melilla as well as across the Mediterranean through enhanced border controls and coastal patrols. For instance, the number of migrants entering Spain via the Canary Islands fell from 31,600 in 2006 to 275 in 2014, although the number increased to 874 in 2015.

Current issues. By 2008 Spain's immigrant population, largely from South America, Eastern Europe, and North Africa, had swelled to nearly 5 million people, or 10 percent of the population. At the height of the economic boom in 2005 Zapatero approved an amnesty that legalized some 600,000 illegal immigrants, to the dismay of EU leaders seeking greater immigration controls in the border-free block. The Zapatero administration announced plans to allow immigrants to vote in local elections. When the economy entered a severe downturn in 2009, the Zapatero government offered financial incentives for unemployed immigrants to return to their home countries, halted a program to recruit immigrants from abroad, and enacted harsher penalties on illegal immigration. As a result, the number of immigrants arriving on Spanish shores dropped by 40 percent between 2008 and 2010. The Spanish government reported that the number of immigrants in 2009 dropped to less than one-tenth of that of the previous year, and that the number of illegal immigrants dropped by half.

Since the rise of Islamic terrorism, public tolerance for violent Basque separatists has waned considerably, although the issue of nationhood for the Basque County remains unresolved. The Zapatero administration sought a conciliatory approach with ETA, brokering a peace deal in March 2006, which collapsed 15 months later when a faction of ETA detonated a bomb at the Madrid airport. In response, the government arrested ETA leaders and initiated efforts to ban political parties that are suspected fronts (see Illegal Groups, below).

In June 2006 voters in Catalonia overwhelmingly approved a referendum giving their region greater autonomy, including retention of a higher percentage of tax collections and greater authority over judicial appointments, immigration, licensing, and mass transportation. It also recognized Catalan as the "preferential" language over Castilian Spanish and acknowledged that Catalonia considers itself a distinct nation. Prime Minister Zapatero supported the Catalan referendum and said other regions were free to propose their own such referenda.

Voters in Andalusia acted on Zapatero's comment and in February 2007 overwhelmingly approved a referendum that expanded that region's autonomy, especially in the area of fiscal management. However, an effort by the Basque Nationalist Party (*Partido Nacionalista Vasco*—PNV/*Euzko Alderdi Jeltzalea*—EAJ) to hold a referendum on self-determination was blocked by the central government in October 2007 on grounds that it was unconstitutional. The referendum also sought approval for a negotiated peace accord with ETA.

In October 2007 the government passed the controversial Law of Historical Memory to wipe out remaining monuments to Franco's dictatorship and compensate the families of victims of the regime and the Spanish Civil War. Conservative parties, which in some cases had not explicitly renounced the fascist era, argued that the law was socially divisive and did not address the suffering inflicted by leftist Republican forces on Catholics and other groups. The Catholic Church, which opposed the law, won a concession to keep memorials of fascist-era symbols on church property so long as there were "artistic–religious" reasons to keep them. The Spanish parliament in 2008 approved decrees under the historical memory law that compensated victims' families, cleared victims' names, and extended Spanish citizenship to the children and grandchildren of Spaniards who fled the country during the civil war. Approximately 150,000 Mexicans were expected to qualify for citizenship under the new provision.

Basque regional elections on March 1, 2009, terminated the three-decade-old reign of the Basque Nationalist Party, which failed to gain an absolute majority and was thereby defeated in a governing agreement led by the PSE-EE, a PSOE affiliate. Analysts saw the results as a blow to the radical left and a sign that voters valued Zapatero's efforts, however unsuccessful, toward a negotiated peace. However, the PSOE's success was tempered by an upset in Galicia, where the PP ousted the PSOE-led coalition in a vote of 39 for the PP and 24 for the PSOE in the 75-seat regional assembly. Analysts blamed voter discontent with the coalition on the PSOE's response to the severe economic recession, although clashes over requirements that the regional language, Galician, be taught in schools also featured prominently in the election.

In July 2009 the Zapatero administration approved a new financing mechanism for the regions, following two years of tense negotiations that were heavily promoted by the autonomous government of Catalonia. The agreement allows regional governments to keep more tax revenue without reducing net transfers to poorer regions in Spain. Critics complained that the result significantly increased the central government's contribution to the system by about 1 percent of GDP.

In a major blow to regional demands for autonomy, the Constitutional Court in June 2010 struck down or changed more than a dozen articles in Catalonia's autonomy statute, including preferential use of Catalan over Spanish. Significantly, the court declared that use of the word "nation" to describe the region had "no legal value."

The national elections on November 20, swept the PSOE out of power. The PP increased its majority in the Senate and won an absolute majority in the lower chamber. Party leader Rajoy was sworn in as prime minister of a PP government in December.

In February 2012 the finance minister announced that Spain's budget deficit for 2011 was 8.5 percent of GDP, far above estimations by the former PSOE government. Credit firms again downgraded Spain's debt. The government instituted a new round of austerity measures, including the elimination of public-sector jobs, reducing severance packages, providing benefits to part-time workers, and incentives for firms hiring people under age 30. The measures were met with widespread protests and strikes. In regional elections in March 2012, the PP increased its seats in Andalusia but failed to gain a majority. The PSOE was able to form a coalition government for the region. Meanwhile, the PSOE won balloting in Asturias.

In June, following contentious negotiations, the EU and IMF agreed to provide Spain up to €100 billion to shore up its financial sector and to create an independent agency to monitor government finances. Unlike the bailout packages given to Greece or Ireland, these funds would go straight to the banks, not the government. In July the EU-IMF released the first €30 billion of the deal after Spain agreed to limit its deficit in 2012 to 6.3 percent of GDP. However, depositors transferred €74.2 billion from Spanish banks to foreign banks that month—4.7 percent of holdings—amid fears that Spain would withdraw from the eurozone. Spain also agreed to establish a bad bank, the Fund for Orderly Bank Restructuring, to absorb €50 billion in toxic assets from the financial sector.

The government unveiled its 2013 budget in September, which included €40 billion in government spending cuts and a value-added tax rate increase from 18 to 21 percent. The government also acknowledged an unexpected 5 percent increase in benefit costs due to the high unemployment rate. The budget included a deficit of 4.5 percent of GDP. Proposed €1 billion cuts to education led parents to pull their children out of school in protest on October 18. Nearly 80 percent of the national student body was absent.

Regional leaders used the dire financial situation to press for independence. When Prime Minister Rajoy rejected his request for increased tax authority, the president of Catalonia, Artur MAS (CiU) called snap regional elections for November 25. Some 1.5 million Catalans had staged a rally for independence in Barcelona on September 11, angry that they paid more taxes to Madrid than they received in benefits. Meanwhile Andalusia, Castilla-La Mancha, Catalonia, Murcia, and Valencia regions requested a total of €14.5 billion from the central government's €18 billion regional rescue fund.

Pro-independence parties won regional elections in Basque country on October 21. The moderate Basque Nationalist Party (PNV) took 27 seats, followed by the new coalition Basque Country Assembly (*Euskal Herria Bildu*) with 21. The PSOE placed third, with 16 seats. Also on October 21, the ruling PP won a majority (41 of 75 seats) in Galicia, while a new nationalist group, the Galician Left Alternative, won 9 seats.

In November the European Commission released €37 billion to four Spanish banks, conditioned on their closing offices and laying off thousands of employees to cut costs. Industry analysts warned that the banks might need up to €60 billion to recapitalize. Meanwhile, separatist parties won 71 of the 135 seats in elections to Catalonia's regional parliament on November 25. On January 23 Catalonia's parliament passed a motion stating that Catalonia is a sovereign entity. Yet six days later, Catalonia's leaders asked Madrid for €9.1 billion in regional development funds.

Also in January, Prime Minister Rajoy and the ruling PP became embroiled in a corruption scandal that undermined public confidence in the government. Luis BÁRCENAS, who had resigned as PP treasurer in 2009 amid bribery charges, was discovered to have €22 million in Swiss bank accounts. Facing jail time, Bárcenas disclosed that he had presided over an elaborate kickback scheme whereby PP leaders, including Rajoy, had received regular cash payments from Spanish businessmen for more than 20 years. The news left voters disgusted and disillusioned and prompted calls for improved oversight of political contributions. A February poll showed that 96 percent of Spaniards believed most politicians are corrupt.

Corruption also sapped public support for the monarchy. King Juan Carlos continued to suffer the fallout from his lavish April 2012 African safari, which became public knowledge when he broke his hip and had to be flown home. Cash-strapped Spaniards had little sympathy for the king, and his staff staged an unprecedented strike in March 2013. Inaki Urdangarin, the king's son-in-law, stood accused of taking €6 million from regional governments in return for organizing sports and tourism events. In April, the PSOE introduced a motion requesting information on the king's finances, especially how public funds were spent. Many Spaniards called for Juan Carlos to abdicate in favor of his son.

The government announced plans in March to help residents fight evictions when they fall behind on their mortgage payments. To raise additional cash, the government decided on March 28, 2013, to sell part of its stake in the European Aeronautic Defense and Space Company for €400 million. Meanwhile, employees of Iberia airways called off their strike when the company agreed to lay off 3,141 workers instead of 4,500 and to reduce planned pay cuts.

In May Rajoy moved to rein in excessive spending of regional governments by lowering their deficit targets from 1.7 percent of GDP to 1.2 percent. However, compliance with the 2012 target varied widely. PP-run regions, such as Castille-La Mancha went from 7.9 percent in 2011 to 1.5 percent in 2012, while CiU-dominant Catalonia registered 2 percent and PSOE-run Andalusia at 1.7 for 2012. Regional leaders complained, resulting in individual targets for each region. In late May the EU granted Spain two additional years to meet the 3 percent deficit target.

In July 28, 2013, a commuter train derailed in Galicia, injuring nearly 200 passengers and killing 79. It was the worst train accident in over 40 years. The driver was arrested as records indicated he was traveling at more than twice the posted speed limit and talking on the phone as he approached a sharp curve. In December the government approved new restrictions on abortion, limiting the procedure to cases involving rape, risks to the physical or mental risk of the mother, or when the fetus was not viable.

As part of its broader effort to privatize state-owned businesses, in February 2014 the government sold a 7.5 percent stake in Bankia, with plans to sell an additional 18 percent (out of its total of 68 percent ownership). Also in February the legislature approved a bill to narrow the scope of universal jurisdiction so that only Spanish citizens or foreign residents of Spain were subject. On February 7 the civil code was amended to grant Spanish citizenship to Sephardic Jews whose ancestors were expelled during the Inquisition.

On March 22, 2014, anti-austerity protests turned violent in Madrid. Nineteen people were arrested and more than 50 police officers injured in demonstrations by more than 50,000, mostly young people. On March 25 the Constitutional court rejected a measure by the Catalonian legislature declaring sovereignty for the region and calling for a referendum on independence on November 9. In response, Catalonian president Artur MAS declared his intent to proceed with the vote as a non-binding referendum.

The Bank of Spain reported in April 2014 that the economy grew by 0.4 percent and predicted that Spain's 2014 growth would be 1.2 percent. Meanwhile, tourism was reported to have reached a record high in 2013, with more than 60 million visitors to the country that year. The number of tourists in the first months of 2014 was up 9.1 percent. Improving economic conditions prompted the yield on Spain's 10-year bonds to fall below 3 percent for the first time since 2005 in May. The government was able to raise €5 billion by issuing a new type of inflation-linked bond. The government also announced a €6.3 billion stimulus package, including a reduction in the corporate tax rate from 30 to 25 percent. Meanwhile, all three major international credit agencies upgraded Spain's debt.

Although the Spanish government declared the measure illegal and pledged to not abide by its results, Catalonians voted in the November 9 referendum for independence by a margin of 80.8 in favor. However, turnout was low at 41.6 percent.

On July 1, 2015, a controversial new measure, the Citizen Security Law, went into effect. The bill instituted new restrictions on accessing websites that endorse terrorism, on public protests, and on recording or distributing unauthorized pictures of police or security officials. The law prompted widespread protests and lawsuits.

In early elections in September 2015, Catalonians elected a slate of pro-independence parties. In November the regional legislature enacted legislation to begin the process of "the creation of an independent Catalan state" on a vote of 72–63. Rajoy pledged to block any moves toward independence. In November the EU warned Spain that it would miss the Union's 3 percent target deficit, with a deficit of 4.7 percent. In December the constitutional court annulled the November measure on Catalan independence.

Princess Cristina, the sister of the king, went on trial for tax evasion related to business deals by her husband in 2015. She became the first member of the royal family to stand trial since the restoration of the monarchy. The king stripped her and her husband of all titles in June 2015. The trial began in January 2016 and concluded in June. A verdict was expected by March 2017.

Pro-independence president Mas of Catalonia resigned on January 9, 2016, after failing to gain the support of a majority of the regional parliament. The legislature elected Carles PUIGDEMONT (CiU) president on January 10.

POLITICAL PARTIES

The only authorized political formation during most of the Franco era was the Spanish Falange (*Falange Española Tradicionalista y de las Juntas de Ofensiva Nacional-Sindicalista*—FET y JONS), subsequently referred to as "The National Movement." In January 1975, prior to Franco's death, a law permitting the establishment of noncommunist and nonseparatist "political associations" went into effect, and during the next two years a large number of parties, both legal and illegal, proceeded to organize. In March 1976 the **Democratic Coordination** (*Coordinación Democrática*—CD) was launched as a unified front embracing all strands of the opposition, from communists to liberal monarchists.

Following a December 1976 referendum on political reform and the subsequent enactment of legislation simplifying the registration of political parties, the CD broke up. Most of its moderate members joined with a number of non-CD parties in establishing the **Union of the Democratic Center** (UCD), which won the June 1977 election and controlled the government for the ensuing five years. Following a disastrous showing against the PSOE in the October 1982 election, the UCD leadership voted in February 1983 to dissolve the party. By then what was to become the Popular Party had emerged as the main conservative alternative to the PSOE. Although 92.8 percent of the 1996 congressional vote was shared by just five parties (with no other party securing even 1 percent), the development of a straight two-party system was qualified by a diversity of regional parties and continuing support for left-wing groups. There are presently more than 2,000 registered national, regional, and local parties.

Government Party:

Popular Party (*Partido Popular*—PP). The PP was known until January 1989 as the **Popular Alliance** (*Alianza Popular*—AP), which emerged in 1976 as a right-wing challenger to the Union of the Democratic Center (UCD). Following the UCD victory in 1977, most AP deputies in late 1978 joined with representatives of a number of other rightist parties in an alliance that contested the 1979 election as the **Democratic Coalition** (*Coalición Democrática*—CD), winning nine lower house seats. Despite its Francoist image, the AP opposed the 1981 coup attempt. Prior to the 1982 poll, the UCD national executive, by a narrow margin, rejected a proposal to form an alliance with the AP, although a constituent group, the **Popular Democratic Party** (*Partido Demócrata Popular*—PDP), formerly the **Christian Democracy** (*Democracia Cristiana*—DC), elected to do so. In the October voting the AP/PDP coalition, benefiting from the effective demise of the UCD, garnered 106 congressional seats, thus becoming the second-ranked group in the lower house. Although pro-NATO, the AP urged a boycott of the March 1986 referendum on the NATO membership issue in an effort to undermine the González government.

The AP contested the June 1986 election as part of the **Popular Coalition** (*Coalición Popular*—CP), which included the PDP and secured 105 congressional seats. Describing the outcome as "unsatisfactory," the PDP (with 21 deputies and 11 senators) broke with the Coalition upon convening of the new *Cortes* on July 15, while four members of the AP also defected in opposition to Manuel FRAGA Iribarne's CP/AP leadership. Further disintegration of the CP at the regional level prompted Fraga's resignation as AP president on December 2, 1986. Antonio HERNÁNDEZ Mancha was named AP president (and leader of what remained of the CP) in February 1987.

At a party congress held January 20–22, 1989, the formation undertook a number of moves, including the change of name, to reorient itself toward the center as a moderate conservative alternative to the PSOE. In the same year, it absorbed the **Liberal Party** (*Partido Liberal*—PL), which nevertheless elected to retain its legal identity. The PP also has, from time to time, had local and regional pacts with a variety of other parties.

The PP retained its second-ranked standing in the October 1989 poll (albeit with a gain of only 1 lower house seat, for a total of 106) and, on December 17, won an absolute majority in the Galician Parliament. Recently reinstated party chief Fraga was thereupon installed as regional president, being succeeded as PP leader by José María Aznar.

The party was able to mount an impressive opposition threat in the run-up to the June 1993 parliamentary balloting, in which it won 141 congressional and 107 senatorial seats on a vote share of 34.8 percent, less than four points behind the PSOE. Having overtaken the PSOE in the June 1994 European Parliament balloting, the PP solidified its standing as the largest party in the March 1996 national balloting, winning 156 seats and 38.9 percent of the vote, enabling Aznar to form a minority government supported by three regionalist groupings: **Catalonia's Convergence and Union** (CiU), the Canarian Coalition (CC, below), and the Basque Nationalist Party (PNV, below).

At a party congress in January 1999, Aznar's handpicked candidate, Javier ARENAS Bocanegra, was chosen to succeed Francisco ÁLVAREZ-CASCOS as secretary general. Bocanegra's ascendancy reportedly underlined the prime minister's professed desire to foster the image of a more centrist PP as well as his increasing control over the party.

In March 2000 the PP won 183 seats on an unexpectedly high vote share of 46.6 percent, but the PP's quest for a third term in office failed in March 2004, when its results fell to 37.6 percent and 148 seats. In September 2003 Aznar announced that Deputy Prime Minister Mariano Rajoy would lead the PP in the next election.

After the PP's surprise loss in the 2004 elections following terrorist attacks in March, the PP became the lead opposition party, shifting further to the right. In the 2008 elections, Rajoy led a campaign against Zapatero that centered on tax cuts, a tough stance on terrorism with no engagement with ETA, tough immigration laws, and the promotion of "family values" as a counterweight to the PSOE's radical social policies.

In June 2008 María Dolores de Cospedal became the first woman general secretary of the party, replacing Ángel ACEBES Paniagua. The move was seen as a way to renew leadership. Rajoy was reelected with 84 percent of the vote at a party congress in November, which did little to mask emerging fractures within the party and with PP allies. A long-standing partner in Navarre, the UPN, split from the PP in October.

The PP was beset by a series of corruption scandals and political infighting in 2009. Several top Madrid officials accused PP rivals of using a regional government agency to spy on them during an internal battle for power within the party. A judge in the Gürtel case subsequently charged 37 members of the PP with corruption related to a network that allegedly ran building permits and lucrative contracts in Madrid. The highest-ranking officials implicated were the PP's national treasurer, Luis Bárcenas, and the president of Valencia's regional government, Francisco CAMPS. Rajoy reacted by accusing state prosecutors of acting in concert with the PSOE to smear the party's name and influence regional elections. Despite the scandal, regional elections on March 1 in Rajoy's home region of Galicia handed the PP a victory, while the June 7 European parliamentary elections resulted in the party's first victory in European elections.

In July 2009 Bárcenas quit his post as Valencia's president as his case came before the Supreme Court. In August, the Supreme Court dropped bribery charges against Camps and two other Valancian party members. Meanwhile, the PP secretary general María Dolores De Cospedal accused the government of using law enforcement to spy on PP members. In November Rajoy announced he would strengthen his party's ethics code in reaction to the corruption scandal and called for those found guilty to feel the "full weight of the law." In April Bárcenas resigned as treasurer of the party following the public release of a large dossier on him in the corruption investigation. In spite of the PP's corruption problems, polls consistently showed it to be more popular than the PSOE.

The PP swept regional and municipal balloting in May 2011, securing 37 percent of the vote and winning 11 of 13 regional presidencies while securing majorities in 3,317 of 8,078 councils. Prior to balloting, in January, former general secretary and deputy prime minister Francisco Álvarez-Cascos left the PP to form the **Forum Asturias** (*Foro Asturias*—FAC). In November the PP swept national elections, and Rajoy became prime minister. In December 2013 dissident members of the PP formed the rightwing **Voice** (Vox). The PP was first in the May 2014 EU parliamentary balloting with 26.1 percent of the vote and 16 seats, a decline of 8 seats from the previous EU elections. The party was hurt by a long-running corruption scandal over alleged kick-backs and bribes in exchange for public contracts. The scandal forced health minister Ana MATO Adrover to resign on November 26, 2014. In regional balloting on May 24, 2015, the PP secured 27 percent of the vote, down from 33 percent in 2011.

The PP secured 28.7 percent of the vote in the December 2015 congressional balloting, and 123 seats. In the June 2016 polling, it won 33 percent of the vote and 137 seats. Rajoy remained prime minister of a minority government after the 2016 balloting.

Leaders: Mariano RAJOY Brey (Prime Minister and President of the Party), José María AZNAR López (Honorary President), María Dolores DE COSPEDAL (Secretary General), Soraya Sáenz DE SANTAMARÍA (Deputy Prime Minister).

Other National Parties:

Spanish Socialist Workers' Party (*Partido Socialista Obrero Español*—PSOE). Founded in 1879 and a member of the Socialist International, the PSOE, under the young and dynamic Felipe González Márquez, held its first legal congress in 44 years in December 1976, and in 1979, the PSOE became the second-strongest party in the *Cortes,* winning 121 seats in the Congress of Deputies and 68 seats in the Senate at the election of March 1 in conjunction with a regional ally, the **Party of Socialists of Catalonia.** In April 1978 the **Popular Socialist Party** (*Partido Socialista Popular*—PSP), which had contested the 1977 election as part of the **Socialist Union** (*Unidad Socialista*—US), formally merged with the PSOE.

At a centennial congress in May 1979, González unexpectedly stepped down as party leader after a majority of delegates refused to abandon a doctrinal commitment to Marxism. His control was reestablished during a special congress in late September, the hard-liners being defeated by a vote of more than ten to one. In the 1982 election, the PSOE/PSC won an absolute majority in both the Congress and Senate, González being invested as prime minister on December 2. In the following year, the PSOE absorbed the centrist **Democratic Action Party** (*Partido de Acción Democrática*—PAD). Subsequently, the PSOE experienced internal strain as a result of the government's pro-NATO posture, which ran counter to the party's long-standing rejection of participation in any military alliance. The issue was resolved in favor of qualified NATO membership by the March 1986 referendum, held shortly after the PSOE government had taken Spain into the EC.

The PSOE held power with a reduced majority in 1986. Its retention of only 175 lower house seats in the 1989 balloting was blamed, in part, on the emergence in September of a dissident internal faction, **Socialist Democracy** (*Democracia Socialista*—DS), and the subsequent defection of party members to the IU (see below). Thereafter, the PSOE's standing was adversely affected by a series of financial scandals involving prominent party figures, although at an early election in June 1993, the party retained a narrow plurality of 159 seats, sufficient for González to form a minority government with regional party support.

Continuing financial and security scandals led to the defeat of the PSOE in the election of March 1996, which left it with 141 seats in the lower house on a vote share of 35.5 percent. González declined to run for reelection as PSOE general secretary in 1997 and was succeeded by Joaquín ALMUNIA Amann.

In 1999–2000, the PSOE suffered a series of setbacks. On May 14, 1999, Josep BORRELL Fontelles, the party's candidate for prime minister in the next election, withdrew because of a financial scandal involving two former associates. Ten days later, the man who had served as the PSOE's president for more than 20 years, Ramón

RUBIAL Cavia, died. On June 13, at local and regional elections, the PSOE saw its vote share increase, largely at the expense of the IU, but succeeded in gaining control of only one regional government, in Asturias. In the May 2000 national balloting, the party and its affiliates lost ground to the PP, losing 16 of their 141 seats in the lower house and prompting its prime ministerial candidate, Almunia, to immediately resign from the leadership.

Almunia's successor as secretary general, José Luis Rodríguez Zapatero, was elected by a party conference on July 23, 2000, narrowly defeating José BONO Martínez, the heavily favored president of Castilla–La Mancha. Rodríguez Zapatero, whose supporters compared him to the UK's Tony Blair, soon made wholesale changes in the party's hierarchy in the interest of "modernization" and a "New Way" (*Nueva Via*).

In July 2001 the **Democratic Party of the New Left** (*Partido Democrático de la Nueva Izquierda*—PDNI), which had been organized in 1996 by former members of the United Left, principally Cristina ALMEIDA and Diego LÓPEZ Garrido, merged with the PSOE. The PDNI had been allied with the PSOE in recent elections.

In the general election of March 2004, the PSOE won an unexpected victory, taking 42.6 percent of the vote and 164 seats (including those won by regional affiliates). With the support of the IU and several small regional parties allowing the party a majority, Zapatero was confirmed as prime minister in April. The PSOE then reversed some of the reforms implemented by the Anzar government, countering a strengthened role for private education and focusing primarily on social, as opposed to economic, concerns.

Since forming the government in 2004, the PSOE has decreased in popularity, due in part to its response to the Basque problem. The PSOE publicly condemned the arrest of the Batasuna party members in October 2007 (see Current issues, above) and endorsed engagement with ETA, in contrast to the opposition PP position. The PSOE also supports increased autonomy for Spain's regions.

At a congress on October 21, 2007, Juan Fernando López Aguilar was named the new PSOE general secretary, succeeding Prime Minister Zapatero with 93 percent of delegates' votes.

The PSOE performed better than expected in the March 9, 2008, election, winning the largest majority in both legislative houses and slightly boosting its membership. In the Congress of Deputies, the number of seats increased from 164 to 169 and in the Senate increased from 100 to 101. However, the PSOE's minority status meant the small regional parties would continue to hold the balance of power. At the July party convention, Zapatero won the position of secretary general a second time with 98.5 percent of the vote.

The 2008 elections led to significant policy shifts in the party. Among them was a renunciation of negotiations with ETA following the murder of a PSOE local politician two days prior to the poll as well as muted support for further concessions on regional autonomy, particularly concerning the Basque Country.

However, the PSOE refused to back down on its liberal social policies after drawing ire from leaders of the Catholic Church, which joined hands with the PP to condemn the PSOE for policies that legalized same-sex marriage, instituted fast-track divorce, and introduced a new civics course for students as an alternative to religious studies. The party's policies stoked deep divisions within Spain. Particularly controversial was a plan to ease restrictions on abortions that the PSOE introduced in early 2009, which the Vatican denounced on a state visit to Spain in February.

Opposition to the PSOE's sweeping social policies was compounded by the onset of the severe economic recession, which battered the party's popularity in public polls and in the June 7, 2009, European Parliament election.

Ironically, the PSOE's victory in regional elections in the Basque Country on March 1 served to further isolate the party in parliament. The Basque Nationalist Party, a crucial legislative ally, said it would no longer support Zapatero's government after it lost governing power in the Basque parliament. However, a regional financing agreement passed in July helped shore up support among Catalan nationalist parties for an autumn debate over the 2010 budget, which was expected to be especially contentious. An unexpected agreement was reached in November when the Basque National Party and Canarian Coalition lent the PSOE enough support to ensure passage of the 2010 budget. However, in 2010 the Zapatero government faced close votes on a series of economic reforms that, had they failed, would have precipitated a vote of no confidence and potentially an early election. As a result of the reforms, PSOE popularity plunged among an electorate largely unwilling to accept deep cuts to social services.

The PSOE secured only 28 percent of the vote in regional and local balloting in May 2011, winning majorities in 1,860 of 8,078 municipal councils. Deputy Prime Minister and Interior Minister Alfredo Pérez Rubalcaba subsequently resigned his government posts after he was chosen at a party primary to lead the PSOE in the November national elections, which the party lost to the PP.

In addition to the PSC, regional parties affiliated with the PSOE include the Basque Socialist Party–Basque Left (see PSE-EE, below), the Party of Galician Socialists (see PSdeG, below), the **Madrid Socialist Federation** (*Federación Socialista Madrileña*—FSM), the **Socialist Party of Navarra** (*Partido Socialista de Navarra*—PSN), and the **Socialist Party of the Valencian Country** (*Partido Socialista del País Valenciano*—PSPV).

The PSOE placed second in the 2014 EU balloting, but lost 9 seats on a voteshare of 23 percent. In response to the poor showing, Rubalcaba resigned and was replaced by Pedro Sánchez on July 26. In the December 2015 lower chamber polling, the PSOE won 22 percent of the vote and 90 seats. Sánchez refused to join in a coalition government with the first-place PP, prompting new elections in June 2016 in which the party secured 22.6 percent of the vote and 85 seats. Sánchez continued to refuse to enter into coalition talks with the PP despite growing public pressure and support within the PSOE for a unity government. Sánchez resigned as party leader on October 1, and from his legislative seat on October 29. Javier FERNÁNDEZ Fernández was appointed on October 1 to lead a party committee to oversee the PSOE until formal elections for new leaders were held.

Leader: Javier FERNÁNDEZ Fernández (Acting President).

United We Can (*Unidos Podemos*). Formed May 2016 to contest legislative balloting on June 26, the coalition brought together We Can (*Podemos*), the United Left (*Izquierda Unida*—IU), and EQUO (*Partido Equo*). In the June polling, it won 21.2 percent of the vote and 71 seats.

Leader: Pablo IGLESIAS.

We Can (*Podemos*). Formed in January 2014 by Pablo Iglesias, an academic and media commentator, the left-wing *Podemos* was an anti-establishment grouping. The party shocked the political establishment in the EU elections when it placed fourth with 8 percent of the vote, securing five seats. The party placed third in the 2015 congressional balloting with 20.7 percent of the vote and 65 seats.

Leader: Pablo IGLESIAS.

United Left (*Izquierda Unida*—IU). The IU was formed in April 1986 as an anti-NATO electoral coalition that principally included the Spanish Communist Party (PCE, below), the **Republican Left** (*Izquierda Republicana*—IR), the **Socialist Action Party** (*Partido de Acción Socialista*—Pasoc), the **Progressive Federation** (*Federación Progresista*—FP), the left-wing liberal **Carlist Party** (*Partido Carlista*—PC), and the libertarian **Humanist Party** (*Partido Humanista*—PH). It won a total of seven congressional seats at the June 1986 election. (For more information on the history of the party, see the 2014 *Handbook.*)

In 2007 the communist-led IU supported the PSOE-sponsored Law of Historical Memory, condemning the Franco regime, which had executed many of its political forebears. The IU was also the only parliamentary party to vote against the deployment of an additional 52 Spanish troops to Afghanistan in September. In November, IU leader Gaspar LLAMAZARES Trigo won reelection with 62 percent of the vote under a pledge to form a coalition of all "forces of the left," including the **Green Confederation** (*Confederación de Los Verdes*) and nationalist groups. His rival, Marga SANZ, was backed by a PCE faction whose criticism of Llamazares led Llamazares supporters to oust three PCE members from the executive board in December. The ousting included PCE leader Francisco Frutose and was meant to unify the party going into the 2008 election. However, continued infighting was partially to blame for the IU's dismal performance in the March 9, 2008, election, in which the IU lost one-quarter of its voters to the PSOE and two of the party's five seats in Congress.

Afterward, Llamazares announced he would not be standing for reelection in November, complaining of a "bipartisan tsunami" that was limiting political diversity. The IU's ninth party convention met in November and elected a new national committee but failed to agree on a new leader. Still stinging from losses in the March election, it approved a document stating that the IU must change because "it has reached the end of a political era" and "needs to return a sense of credibility and urgency to its leftist, anti-capitalist, alternative and transformational agenda." In December the party settled on a PCE leader, Cayo Lara Moyo, as general coordinator of the IU in a vote of 55 percent. Lara threatened to call a general strike if the PSOE did not change its response to the economic crisis by doing more to support workers.

In April 2009 the IU's only remaining city mayor left her post to become part of the PSOE government in Andalusia. However, the IU kept its two seats in the European Parliament following the June 7 election.

Other closely linked organizations include the **Ezker Batua** (EB—also translated as **United Left**) in Basque Country and Navarre, the **United Left of the Balearic Islands** (*Esquerra Unida de los Illes Balears*—EU), the **United Left of Valencia** (*Esquerra Unida del País Valenciá*—EUPV), and the Catalan **United and Alternative Left** (*Esquerra Unida i Alternativa*—EUiA). The IU has frequently formed coalitions with other small parties to contest regional elections. In the May 2011 regional and local polling the IU secured 6.3 percent of the vote and majorities on 58 municipal councils. The IU placed fourth and secured 11 seats in the 2011 Congress of Deputies balloting. In the May 2014 EU polling, the IU led an electoral coalition, the **Plural Left** (*La Izquierda Plural*—IP). The coalition won six seats, four of which were secured by the IU.

Leaders: Cayo LARA Moyo (General Coordinator), Ramón LUQUE (Parliamentary Group Coordinator), Montserrat MUÑOZ DE DIEGO (Institutional Relations).

Spanish Communist Party (*Partido Comunista de España*—PCE). Founded in 1920 but soon banned, the PCE was legalized in April 1977, following the release from detention in December 1976 of its secretary general, Santiago CARRILLO Solares. On April 19–23, 1977, in Madrid, it held its first legal congress in 45 years, while on May 13 the PCE's most celebrated figure, Dolores IBÁRRURI Gómez "La Pasionaria," returned to Spain after 38 years in exile. The PCE and its regional ally, the **Unified Socialist Party of Catalonia** (*Partit Socialista Unificat de Catalunya*—PSUC), secured 20 seats in the Congress of Deputies and 12 seats in the Senate in the June 1977 election. In March 1979, with Ibarruri having declined to seek legislative reelection for reasons of health and age, it placed three additional deputies in the lower house but lost all of its upper house seats. In the context of sharp differences between pro-Soviet and "Eurocommunist" factions, its congressional representation declined sharply in 1982 to only four members, with the result that Carrillo, the only survivor of the Civil War still to lead a major party, was forced to step down in November. Carrillo's influence was eroded still further by the decision of new party leaders, who favored nonalignment, to adopt internal reforms and work for a "convergence of progressive forces" with other leftist groups, both elective and nonelective; in April 1985, Carrillo and 18 supporters were expelled following an emergency national congress in March, subsequently forming the **Spanish Workers' Party–Communist Unity** (*Partido de los Trabajadores de España–Unidad Comunista*—PTE-UC), which joined the PSOE in February 1991.

Immediately prior to the 1986 election a pro-Soviet splinter group, the **Spanish Communist Workers' Party** (*Partido Comunista Obrero Español*—PCOE), led by Enrique LISTER, voted to disband and rejoin the PCE. A second pro-Soviet splinter, the **Communist Party of the Peoples of Spain** (*Partido Comunista de los Pueblos de España*—PCPE), rejoined the party at a congress of unity in January 1989. The PCPE, led by Ignacio GALLEGO, had broken from the party in 1984 because of the "politico-ideological degeneration . . . which introduced Eurocommunism."

At a party congress in December 1998, the PCE elected Francisco FRUTOS as its new secretary general. In 2007 the PCE sought to build collaboration between European leftists to counter the influence of new center-right formations such as the Sarkozy government in France (see entry on France). The PCE is the largest member organization of the IU.

In November 2009 José Luis CENTELLA became the new leader of the PCE, and he struck a more moderate tone than his predecessor. In May 2010 Centella met with Cuban president Raul Castro in Havana to boost ties between the countries' communist parties. Through 2012 the PCE was a leading force in organizing protests against the government's austerity measures.

Leader: José Luis CENTELLA Gómez (Secretary General).

EQUO (*Partido Equo*). EQUO is comprised of 35 green parties and individuals, including 13 parties from the Green Confederation. EQUO was established as a political movement in 2011 and as a party in 2012. Members include Green organizations from all parts of Spain. The Greens joined the IU-led electoral coalition for the 2014 EU elections, and the Podemos-led coalition for the 2016 balloting.

Cospokespersons: Juan López DE URALDE, Reyes MONTIEL.

Citizens–Party of the Citizenry (*Ciudadanos–Partido de la Ciudadanía*—C's) C's, a center-left grouping opposed to Catalonian independence, secured two seats in EU parliamentary elections in 2014. In 2015 it won 40 seats in the Chamber and 3 in the Senate. In the following year's elections, the party secured 32 Chamber seats, but won no additional Senate posts.

Leader: Albert RIVERA.

The Greens (*Los Verdes*). Long a somewhat disparate movement of pacifists, feminists, and ecologists, the **Spanish Green Party** (*Partido Verde Español*—PVE) was established in June 1984. In the 1986 election the **Green Alternative** (*Alternativa Verde*) list fared poorly, and the Greens made little headway thereafter until a congress held at Grenada in 1993 resulted in formation of a **Green Confederation** (*Confederación de Los Verdes*) was established in 1993, following the collapse of the PVE. At its peak, the Confederation consisted of 16 national and regional parties, including the **Initiative for Catalonia–Greens** (below). It was part of the United Left coalition in the 2011 parliamentary elections. In May 2012, 13 of the 16 parties joined the new EQUO movement, and the European Greens Council canceled the Confederation's membership.

Union, Progress and Democracy (*Unión Progreso y Democracia*—UPyD). Founded in 2007, the UPyD is a liberal, progressive party that advocates expanded federalism, including restoring central control over education and health care. It tried to garner support as a centrist alternative to both the PP and PSOE. The UPyD secured five seats in the 2011 lower chamber balloting. As corruption allegations damaged PP and PSOE in 2013, UPyD emerged as the third national party. In the 2014 EU balloting, the UPyD, placed fifth with 6.5 percent of the vote, and won four seats. The party only received 0.6 percent of the vote in 2015, and 0.2 percent in 2016, and no seats in either election. Gorka MANEIRO became party leader in April 2016.

Leader: Gorka MANEIRO.

Spain has a long history of right-wing formations, many of them descendants of the Franco-era **Spanish Falange**. Reduced to little more than a shadow of its former significance, the Falange joined with a number of other neo-fascist groups in forming a National Union (*Unión Nacional*) that secured one legislative seat in 1979. It appeared to have been largely superseded by the formation in October 1984 of a new right-wing grouping, the Spanish Integration Committees (*Juntas Españolas de Integración*), which in 1993 was absorbed by the **National Front** (*Frente Nacional*—FN). Formation of the far-right FN was announced in October 1986 by Blas PIÑAR López, former secretary general of the New Force (*Fuerza Nueva*), which had been dissolved in 1982. Many of the FN's supporters participated in the **Alliance for National Unity** (*Alianza por la Unidad Nacional*—AUN), with little impact in the 1996 election. With its leader, Ricardo SAENZ de Ynestrillas, in prison for attempted murder, the AUN did not contest the 2000 national election. In the 1996 national election the rump Falange, which had split into "Authentic" and "Independent" wings, secured less than 0.1 percent of the vote. In 2000 a new four-party far-right electoral alliance, **Spain 2000** (*España 2000*), suffered a similar fate. The four constituent groups in the alliance were the **National Democracy** (*Democracia Nacional*—DN) of Francisco PEREZ Corrales, the **National Workers' Party** (*Partido Nacional de los Trabajadores*—PNT), the **Republican Social Movement** (*Movimiento Social Republicano*—MSR), and the **Spanish Social Apex** (*Vértice Social Español*—VSE). In late 2005 National Democracy, the Falange, and **Spanish Alternative** (*Alternativa Española*) began negotiations to form a new electoral coalition in anticipation of municipal elections in 2007 and general elections in 2008. The Spanish Alternative won 0.1 percent of the vote in the June 7, 2009, European Parliament election. Falange's symbol, the arrow and yoke, was banned in Spain under the Law of Historical Memory (see Current issues, above). Falange ran candidates but failed to win any seats in the March 9, 2008, election. The **Spanish Traditionalist Phalanx of the Assemblies of the**

National Syndicalist Offensive (*Falange Española Tradicionalista y de las Juntas de Ofensiva Nacional Sindicalista*—FE JONS), secured 0.1 percent of the vote in the 2014 EU balloting.

Leader: Roberto PICO Sanabria.

Regional Parties:

There are hundreds of regional parties in addition to the local affiliates of the PP, PSOE, and IU/PCE. Grouped by alphabetical order of region, the parties discussed below are represented in the *Cortes* or regional assemblies.

Andalusian Party (*Partido Andalucista*—PA). Known until 1984 as the Andalusian Socialist Party (*Partido Socialista de Andalucía*—PSA), the PA won 1 seat in the Congress of Deputies in 2000 and none in 2004. At the regional level, the PA won 5 of 109 seats in the Andalusian elections in 2000 and 2004. The PA collaborated with a previously unknown grouping, Andalusian Platform (*Plataforma Andaluces*) to push for separate elections for Andalusia, emphasizing its distinct sense of nationhood.

PA returns for regional elections held May 27, 2007, were as follows: Almería, 4.3 percent; Cádiz, 9.1 percent; Córdoba, 6.5 percent; Granada, 3.1 percent; Huelva, 7.3 percent; Jaén, 4.6 percent; Málaga, 4.8 percent; Sevilla, 8 percent.

After its loss of 5 seats in the March 9, 2008, regional election, the party failed to enter the regional parliament for the first time in its history. In the May 2011 regional and local balloting, the party secured 470 seats and majorities on 11 councils. A leadership shuffle at the 2012 party congress installed Antonio Jesús Ruiz to reorient the PA. The party won 0.3 percent of the vote in the 2014 EU balloting as part of the **Coalition for Europe** (*Coalición por Europa*—CpE).

Leader: Antonio Jesús RUIZ (Secretary General).

Aragonese Party (*Partido Aragonés*—PAR). Called the **Aragonese Regionalist Party** (*Partido Aragonés Regionalista*—PAR) until February 1990, the PAR is a center-right grouping that retains its predecessor's initials. Although the party did not contest the 1996 national congressional election in its own right, it won three Senate seats on the strength of an alliance with the PP. In the May 2003 regional election it won eight seats and then joined a governing coalition as junior partner to the PSOE, as it had in 1999. In the 2004 national election it failed to win any seats but continued to hold one designated Senate seat.

On September 19, 2007, the PAR National Committee elected Alfredo Boné Pueyo as secretary general, succeeding Juan Carlos TRILLO Baigorri. An Executive Commission meeting on November 30 finalized candidate lists for the 2008 general elections.

In the March 9, 2008, election the PAR failed to win any seats, registering 0.4 percent of the vote for Congress. In 2009 PAR president José Ángel Biel was reportedly behind a controversial project to build a casino resort complex in Aragon. PAR won 992 seats and majorities on 147 councils in local balloting in May 2011.

Leaders: José Ángel BIEL Rivera (President), Arturo López ALIAGA (Secretary General).

Aragonese Junta (*Chunta Aragonesista*—ChA). The ChA won five seats in the regional *Cortes* in 1999 and nine in the 2003 election, after which it joined the PSOE in forming a government. Nationally, it won one seat in the 2000 and 2004 congressional polls.

ChA regional vote shares on May 27, 2007, were as follows: Huesca, 8.2 percent; Teruel, 5.6 percent; Zaragoza, 9.4 percent. In the March 9, 2008, national election, the party won no seats, registering 0.2 percent of the vote for Congress. The ChA secured 184 seats on councils in the 2011 local elections.

Leaders: José Luis SORO (President), Juan MARTIN (General Secretary).

PSM–Nationalist Union of Majorca (PSM–*Entesa Nacionalista de Mallorca*—PSM-EN). The PSM-EN traces its origins to 1976, when the **Socialist Party of the Islands** (*Partit Socialist de les Illes*—PSI) was established. In December 1977 the party changed its name to the **Socialist Party of Majorca** (*Partit Socialista de Mallorca*—PSM), to which the **Nationalist Left** (*Esquerra Nacionalista*—EN) was added in 1984. Between then and 1990, when the PSM-EN restyled itself as the **PSM–Majorca Nationalists** (*PSM–Nacionalistes de Mallorca*), the party contested regional, national, and European elections in a number of alliances with other left-oriented formations. In November 1998 the organization assumed its current name.

Following the June 1999 regional election the PSOE negotiated an anti-PP governing alliance that was joined by the PSM-EN, which had won 5 of the 59 legislative seats. In May 2003 the PSM-EN retained 4 seats, but the PP returned to power. Nationally, the party contested the March 2004 lower house elections as part of a coalition, the **Balearic Islands Progressives** (*Progressistes per les Illes Balears*—PIB), that also included the IU-affiliated United Left of the Balearic Islands (EU), the regional Greens, and the Catalan Republican Left (ERC, below).

Initiatives in 2007 included motions to protect Mediterranean coral and ensure protections for minority languages under the European Charter for Regional and Minority Languages, first passed in 1992. The PSM-EN received 6.8 percent of votes in Illes Balears during the May 2007 regional elections. It gained four seats in the 2011 regional parliament balloting and has one seat in the Spanish Senate.

Leaders: Joana Llüisa MASCARÓ Melià (President), Gabriel BARCELÓ Milta (General Secretary).

Amaiur. A leftist Basque separatist grouping that was formed in September 2011, *Amaiur* brought together a range of smaller Basque parties and supporters who were dissatisfied with the Basque Nationalist Party. In the 2011 national elections, *Amaiur* outpolled the Basque Nationalist Party and secured three seats in the Senate and seven in the Congress of Deputies.

Leader: Iñaki ANTIGÜEDAD.

Aralar. Named for a Basque mountain range, *Aralar* is a recent leftist-nationalist splinter from the now-outlawed *Batasuna* (below). Advocating nonviolence, the party won four seats in the Navarre legislature in May 2003 and one in the Basque regional election in April 2005. For the 2004 national election *Aralar* joined with the Basque Nationalist Party (PNV), the Basque Solidarity (EA), and another nationalist Basque party, **Batzarro,** in the **Navarre Yes** (*Naffaroa Bai*—Na-Bai) coalition, which won one seat in the Chamber of Deputies.

Aralar received 6.2 percent of votes in Vizvaya in the 2007 regional elections. In May 2008 party members and Basque separatist lawmakers helped pass a motion in the regional parliament accusing the Spanish government of complicity in police torture of a suspected ETA member. The group also voiced support for Kosovo's declaration of independence in February 2008. In September 2008 *Aralar* joined the Basque Nationalist Party to continue pressing for a referendum on Basque self-determination, despite a block by the Constitutional Court.

During the Basque regional elections on March 1, 2009, *Aralar* boosted its seats in the regional parliament from one to four, winning 6 percent of the vote. Its success was taken as a sign that voters had rejected more extremist parties. Following the election, *Aralar* asserted that it would only consider working with *Batasuna* if it used "exclusively political means" to try to achieve its goals. Because their activities allegedly occurred prior to the 1999 ban on *Batasuna,* in September 2010 *Aralar* publicly supported 20 of its members who were on trial for having links to ETA. In October *Aralar* called on ETA to impose a "permanent, unilateral, and verifiable" cease-fire in exchange for the government's transfer of ETA prisoners to jails in the Basque Country. *Aralar* secured 42 seats on local councils in the 2011 municipal balloting.

Leader: Patxi ZABALETA (General Coordinator).

Basque Country Assembly (*Euskal Herria Bildu—EH Bildu*). Also known as **Basque Country Unite,** the grouping is a coalition of pro-independence, left-wing forces, placed second in the October 21, 2012, regional parliamentary election, winning 21 seats. Founded in June 2012, *EH Bildu* unites *Aralar*, Basque Solidarity, Alternatiba, and *Batasuna,* the political wing of the ETA. The new coalition grew out of ETA's decision to end violence. Laura Mintegi, a University of Basque Country professor and *EH Bildu*'s candidate for the regional presidency, won praise for publically insisting on the need to acknowledge all victims of separatist violence in the region. The party formed the **Peoples Decide** coalition with the **Galician Nationalist Bloc** (see below), and it won one seat in the 2014 EU elections. It secured two seats in the chamber in the 2015 and 2016 polling.

Leader: Pella URIZAR.

Basque Nationalist Party (*Partido Nacionalista Vasco*—PNV/ *Euzko Alderdi Jeltzalea*—EAJ). A moderate party that has campaigned for Basque autonomy since 1895, the PNV obtained a plurality in the 1980 Basque election and formed a regional government headed by Carlos GARAICOETXEA Urizza. After the 1984 regional election a dispute regarding devolution of power to individual Basque provinces led to Garaicoetxea's replacement as premier and party leader by José Antonio ARDANZA in January 1985, with the PNV eventually concluding a legislative pact with the PSOE's local affiliate, the Basque Socialist Party (see PSE-EE, below), while Garaicoetxea joined Basque Solidarity (EA, below). (For more on the history of the party, see the 2014 *Handbook*).

In balloting for the Basque regional legislature in October 1998, the PNV led all the parties, but its lack of a majority led it to form a coalition government with We the Basque Citizens (EH, the restyled political arm of the ETA) and the EA. In January–February 2000, following a renewal of ETA violence, the PNV ended its alliance with the EH. In the national election of March 2000 the PNV picked up 2 seats in the Congress of Deputies, for a total of 7, while at an early regional election on May 13, 2001, it registered its biggest success in a quarter-century, winning 33 seats (a gain of 6) on a 43 percent vote share.

Having retained seven seats in the March 2004 election, the PNV entered the April 2005 regional election seeking support for the "Plan Ibarretxe," a proposal for increased autonomy that had been put forward by PNV leader and Euzkadi President Juan José Ibarretxe. The plan, which included establishment of a union with French Basque areas as well as Basque representation in the EU, had been described by Prime Minister Zapatero as secessionist and unconstitutional and then rejected by the *Cortes* earlier in the year. At the polls, the PNV lost four seats, and Ibarretxe managed to retain the presidency by only one vote when the regional legislature met in June. The PNV received 38.8 percent of votes in the province of Vizcaya during the 2007 regional elections. The PNV's moderate president, Josu Jon IMAZ, later resigned, citing the growing influence of separatists. He was replaced in November 2007 by Iñigo Uukullu, who condemned ETA violence but nonetheless announced he would meet with all the political forces in the Basque region, including the banned *Batasuna.* The power shift prompted the party to call for a referendum on self-determination, a move swiftly rejected by Prime Minister Zapatero, to preempt further PP criticism of his line on the Basque question.

In July 2008 the party's efforts to conduct the referendum in October 2008 were suspended by a Spanish court pending a review of its legality. The referendum was to be part of a "new model," announced by the PNV earlier in the year, for political relations between Basque Country and the federal government based on the "free accession of its nations."

In the March 9, 2008, election the PNV won 27 percent of the vote in the Basque region, granting the party six seats in the Congress. However, voter turnout was a low 35 percent in the region, owing to a call by separatists to boycott the election to protest "oppression" by the Spanish state. In October the PNV secured $114 million from the PSOE for research and development projects in the region in exchange for supporting the 2009 budget.

On March 1, 2009, the PNV captured 38 percent of the vote in regional elections, winning 30 seats, but was 8 short of an absolute majority. In the following days party leader and Euzkadi President Juan José Ibarretxe scrambled to maintain control by attempting to cobble together support from minority parties and offering a "stability agreement" with the PSE-EE. The PSE-EE instead formed a governing agreement with the PP, forcing the PNV to enter opposition status for the first time since 1980. In May Ibarretxe announced he would be retiring from politics.

In November 2009, in an unexpected accord following the tense March regional elections, the Zapatero government passed its 2010 budget with support from the PNV and in return agreed to strengthen the Basque region's fiscal autonomy.

In September 2010 the PNV struck a deal to support the 2011 budget in exchange for $700 million to generate employment in the region. In October the PNV traded support of upcoming measures to alleviate the economic crisis for 32 concessions for the Basque region. The concessions had been outlined in the 1979 Basque autonomy ruling, the Gernika Statute, but had been stalled by successive governments. Additionally, the PSOE agreed to send $157 million in investment money to the region as part of the coalition arrangement. The party won 882 seats and majorities on 59 municipal councils in local balloting in 2011, and 5 Congress seats. PNV prevailed in the October 21, 2012, regional parliamentary election, winning 27 seats. Party leader Iñigo Urkullu Renteria was elected regional president on December 13, 2012. Andoni Ortuzar was elected PNV president on January 12, 2013. The PNV was part of the CpE coalition in the 2014 EU balloting.

The PNV won six Senate seats in 2015, and five in 2016, for a total of six. The party won six seats in the lower chamber in 2015, and five in 2016.

Leaders: Andoni ORTUZAR (Party President), Iñigo URKULLU Renteria (Basque President), Juan José IBARRETXE Markuartu (Former Basque President), Belén GREAVES (Secretary), Josu ERKOREKA (Parliamentary Spokesperson).

Basque Socialist Party–Basque Left (*Partido Socialista de Euzkadi–Euzkadiko Ezkerra*—PSE-EE). The PSE-EE was formed in March 1993 by merger of the PSOE-affiliated Basque Socialist Party, led by Ramón JÁUREGUI, and the smaller, more radical Basque Left, led by Juan María BANDRÉS and Jon LARRINAGA. In the May 2001 regional election the PSE-EE finished third, winning 13 of 75 seats, a relatively weak performance that contributed to the resignation of the party's secretary general, Nicolás REDONDO Terreros, in December. In the balloting of April 2005 the party finished second, with 18 seats. Despite the support of the PP, the new PSE-EE leader, Paxti López, lost the contest for regional president to the incumbent, the PNV's Ibarretxe, by one vote. The PSE-EE took a 23 percent vote share during the 2007 regional poll in the Vizcaya province.

The PSE-EE performed well in the March 9, 2008, election, capturing 38 percent of the vote in the Basque region. In April 2008 ETA set off a bomb in front of the group's offices in Bilbao, injuring seven police officers and causing extensive property damage.

In October 2007 a Spanish High Court opened proceedings against PSE-EE leaders Patxi López and Rodolfo ARES, as well as Ibarretxe of the Basque Nationalist Party, under charges that they conducted meetings with *Batasuna* after the group's cease-fire was announced to discuss the political future of the Basque Country.

Basque regional elections on March 1, 2009, handed the PSE-EE/PSOE 25 seats, an increase of 18. The PSE's success catapulted López to the premiership after nearly a month of tense negotiations with nonnationalist parties. On March 30 the PSE-EE and the PP, which held 13 seats, announced a coalition agreement. On May 5 López was elected as the first nonnationalist president of the Basque parliament with the support of the PP and the sole representative of the UPyD party. Upon taking office, López announced his "priority task" was to fight ETA. He said he would also halt a program that made Basque the main language in schools. ETA responded by announcing that the López government would be its "priority target" (see ETA, below).

In January 2010 the Supreme Court dismissed the case against López and other officials, writing that "meeting contacts in not a crime." In November it was reported that the PSE-EE held talks with *Batasuna* to discuss the nationalist party's strategy of pursuing its goals by exclusively political means. The meeting was noteworthy because the PSE-EE had repeatedly denied it had contacts with the outlawed group. The party tumbled to third place in the October 21, 2012, regional elections with 16 seats, down from 25. Lopez lost the regional presidency as well. Idoia Mendia was elected secretary general of the party on September 16, 2014.

Leaders: Jesus EGUIGUREN (President), Idoia MENDIA (Secretary General).

Basque Solidarity (*Eusko Alkartasuna*—EA). The EA was formed in September 1986 as the **Basque Patriots** (*Eusko Abertzaleak*) by a group of PNV dissidents, subsequently joined by former Basque premier Carlos Garaicoetxea Urriza. A left-wing nationalist group opposed to political violence, it currently holds one seat in the national Chamber of Deputies. It contested the 1996 election in alliance with the now-defunct **Basque Left** (*Euskal Ezkerra*—EuE), which had separated from the *Euskadiko Ezkerra* (also translated as Basque Left) in 1993.

In late 1998 the EA agreed to participate in the formation of a Basque regional coalition government with the PNV and EH, and in the May 2001 and April 2005 elections it remained allied with the PNV. The party received 5.4 percent of votes during Basque local elections in 2007. In the March 1, 2009, regional election, the EA won 3.6 percent of the vote, taking one seat. In September 2010 the EA and *Batasuna* presented a roadmap for peace that called on ETA to declare a "permanent cease-fire under international verification," among other measures. The EA joined with the small grouping, *Alternatiba,* to form the electoral alliance **Join Together** (*Bildu*) for the 2011 regional and local balloting. *Bildu* secured 1,138 seats on local councils.

Leader: Pello URIZAR Karetxe (President).

Create (*Sortu*). In February 2011 *Batasuna* (see below) attempted to launch a new political grouping, **Create** (*Sortu*), to compete in regional and local balloting in May. However, in March the Supreme Court ruled that *Sortu* could not be registered as a party. Instead, *Batasuna* leaders established the **Basque Country Assembly** (see above). Following the electoral success of EH Bildu, *Batasuna* announced its dissolution on January 3, 2013. Meanwhile, the Constitutional Court ruled on June 20, 2012, that Sortu was separate from the ETA and thus legal. Sortu held its founding congress in February 2013. Members elected Hasier Arraiz as president, and Arnaldo Otegi as general secretary. Since 2009 Otegi has been serving a 10-year jail sentence for trying to re-establish *Batasuna* in 2009.

Leaders: Hasier ARRAIZ (President), Arnaldo OTEGI (General Secretary).

Unity (*Batasuna*). *Batasuna* descends from the United People (*Herri Batasuna*—HB), which was founded in 1978. Linked with the political wing of the terrorist ETA, the Marxist HB coalition had limited success in regional elections throughout the 1980s and in the 1993 national election won two congressional seats and one senatorial seat. However, the party has persistently faced government censure. (See the entry in the 2010 *Handbook* for details.) On December 1, 1997, the entire 23-member National Committee was convicted of supporting terrorism, and members were sentenced to at least seven years in prison. In 1999 the Constitutional Court threw out the convictions.

In the 1998 regional elections, the HB joined a leftist coalition, or platform, styled **We the Basque Citizens** (*Euskal Herritarrok*—EH) and finished third with 14 seats. It participated in a regional coalition government with the PNV and EA, although an ETA decision to end its 14-month cease-fire led directly to EH's ouster from the coalition. On June 23, 2001, the EH joined in forming the unified *Batasuna* party.

Amid an upsurge in ETA attacks, on April 30, 2002, police detained 11 *Batasuna* members suspected of channeling funds to ETA or laundering "taxes" collected by ETA. In August a judge suspended the organization's activities for three years and ordered its offices closed, citing its relationship with ETA. In the same month the national legislature supported a government request that the Supreme Court ban *Batasuna* altogether, and on March 17, 2003, the court concurred. The ban, which extended to the HB and EH designations, was the first of its kind since the Franco era. Subsequent efforts by *Batasuna* members to register other organizations, most prominently an *Autodeterminaziorako Bilgunea* (AuB) coalition, were rejected.

In May 2003 the United States added *Batasuna* to its list of terrorist organizations, and the United Kingdom followed suit in June. In November 2004 *Batasuna* called for peaceful dialogue among all sides to end the decades of violence, but a Spanish court extended the ban on party activity for two more years in January 2006. On March 22, 2006, ETA announced a permanent cease-fire, and the Zapatero government began direct negotiations with ETA. However, in December 2006 the truce was broken by an ETA attack at Barajas, the Madrid airport, revealing splinters within ETA that undermined *Batasuna*'s leverage.

In October 2007 Spanish police arrested 22 senior *Batasuna* members, nearly the entire leadership, in a raid on an important meeting that government officials believed was held to transfer power to a new cadre of leaders.

In late August 2008 *Batasuna* leader Arnaldo Otegi, who was reportedly instrumental in brokering the 2006 peace negotiation with ETA, was released from jail after serving a 15-month sentence for glorifying terrorism. After his release Otegi served as the group's de facto spokesperson and called for renewed peace talks. A series of bomb attacks that month by ETA prompted *Batasuna* to call the violence an "obstacle" to the Basque independence movement and to begin promoting a clean list of candidates with no criminal records for the regional elections in March 2009.

In January 2009 Spanish authorities carried out raids on two new entities, Askatasuna and 3DM (Democracy 3,000,000) for suspected links to *Batasuna* and later banned the groups from participating in the March regional election.

The Supreme Court in mid-May banned the *Iniciativa Internacionalista II* from taking part in the June 7 European Parliament election on the grounds that it was a front for *Batasuna.* However, weeks later the Constitutional Court reversed the decision because of insufficient evidence. Otegi then endorsed the group, and *Iniciativa* won 1.1 percent of the vote but failed to take a seat.

In June the European Court of Human Rights upheld the Spanish court's ban on *Batasuna* on the grounds that it was a front for ETA. In November it rejected an appeal, effectively closing all avenues for the party to resume its political presence. In March 2010 Spain's High Court sentenced Otegi to two years for "glorifying terrorism" for comments he made at a 2005 rally. In 2010 *Batasuna* sought to salvage its political standing in advance of the 2011 regional elections by signing an agreement in June with the small left-leaning nationalist party Eusko Alkartasuna to use peaceful and democratic means to achieve Basque independence. Interior Minister Alfredo PÉREZ Rubalcaba rejected the move, saying the agreement would have little effect on ETA's renouncing violence. Subsequently, *Batasuna* toughened its stance by calling for ETA to unconditionally abandon its armed struggle. Reports in 2013 indicated that members of *Batasuna* had launched a new political grouping, led by Hasier Arraiz BARBADILLO as president, and Otegi as secretary general.

Canarian Coalition (*Coalición Canaria*—CC). The CC was formed prior to the 1993 general election as a regional alliance that included the **Canarian Independent Groupings** (*Agrupaciones Independientes de Canarias*—AIC); the socialist **Canarian Initiative** (*Iniciativa Canaria*—ICAN); and the left-wing **Mazorca Assembly** (*Asamblea Majorera*—AM). Also initially part of the alliance were the **Canarian Nationalist Party** (*Partido Nacionalista Canario*—PNC) and the **Canarian Independent Center** (*Centro Canario Independiente*—CCI), predecessor of the current **Canarian Nationalist Center** (*Centro Canario Nacionalista*—CCN). More recently, the CC was joined by the **Lanzarote Nationalist Party** (*Partido Nacionalista de Lanzarote*—PNL).

The AIC, consisting principally of the **Tenerife Independents Group** (*Agrupación Tinerfeña de Independientes*—ATI) and the **Las Palmas Independent Group** (*Agrupación Palmera de Independientes*—API), had captured one congressional seat in the 1989 general election and was subsequently the only non-PSOE party to support Prime Minister González's reelection; in the 1991 regional balloting it took second place behind the PSOE in the Canaries, and the AIC nominee, ATI leader Manuel HERMOSO Rojas, secured the island presidency.

In September 1994 the CC-led regional government lost its narrow majority when the PNC withdrew from the coalition. The coalition won a plurality of 21 regional assembly seats in 1995, so Hermoso remained in office. Its four national deputies, reelected in 1996, backed the formation of a PP government in exchange for various concessions. The CC won 25 seats in the June 1999 Canarian election and continued to rule, with PP support. In the May 2000 national balloting, the coalition won four Chamber and five Senate seats.

Following the May 2003 regional election, in which the CC won a plurality of 22 seats, the CC and the PP formed a coalition government. Nationally, the CC won 3 lower house seats in 2004 and then voted to approve the PSOE's Zapatero as prime minister. During the 2007 regional elections, the CC ran a joint ballot with a former ally, the previously unknown Canarian Nationalist Party (*Partido Nacionalista Canario*—PNC), with whom it championed Canarian identity, taking 9.5 percent of votes in Las Palmas and 37.7 percent in Santa Cruz de Tenerife.

In the March 9, 2008, election the CC-PNC won 17.5 percent of the vote for the Congress in the region, taking two seats in the lower house and one in the Senate. In January 2009 the CC was reportedly debating whether to give the federal government control over underage migrants, hundreds of whom have arrived on the island in recent years on boats from sub-Saharan Africa. The debate was significant because it represented an unusual decision to cede regional authority to the central government. In November 2009 the Zapatero administration passed its 2010 budget with support from the CC and agreed to earmark additional budget commitments to the Canary Islands. Again in October 2010, Zapatero won the much-needed support of the CC to pass its 2011 budget. In local balloting in 2011 the CC secured 391 seats on local councils. The CC secured 2 seats in the 2011 lower house elections. The coalition condemned the 1.2 percent of GDP deficit limit for 2013 set by Prime Minister Rajoy, asking for 2 percent instead. In June 2012 the CC elected Paulino Riveror to a fourth term as president. The CC was part of the CpE coalition in the 2014 EU balloting.

The CC-PNC alliance won two seats in the 2016 Senate elections, and one seat in the Congress.

Leader: Claudina MORALES.

Party of Independents from Lanzarote (*Partido de Independientes de Lanzarote*—PIL). Based on the Canarian island of

Lanzarote, the PIL held one seat in the previous Spanish Senate. In March 2001, having been sentenced to a three-year prison term for bribery, Dimas MARTÍN Martín, the PIL president and senator, announced his resignation from both posts. In 2003 the PIL won three seats in the regional legislature as part of the **Canarian Nationalist Federation** (*Federación Nacionalista Canaria*—FNC). The PIL received a 1.8 percent vote share during the 2007 local elections in Las Palmas.

In May 2009 police arrested Dimas Martín and several members of the PIL on charges of operating a corruption ring in Lanzarote. Martín was sentenced to eight years in prison for embezzlement and social security fraud. Martín's son Fabian Martín Martín was elected party president in 2010. Infighting led to the expulsion of popular Arrecife mayor Emilia PERDOMO in late 2012. The elder Martín was granted work release in May 2013.

Leaders: Fabian MARTÍN Martín (President), Dimas MARTÍN Martín (Founder).

Cantabrian Regionalist Party (*Partido Regionalista Cántabro*—PRC). The PRC is a moderate conservative party that won 6 seats out of 39 in the 1995 and 1999 Cantabrian regional assembly elections.

Following the 2003 election, at which it won 8 seats, the PRC held the balance of power and negotiated formation of a governing coalition with the PSOE. In 2007 the PRC received 21.5 percent of votes in Cantabria's local balloting. A PP/PRC/PSOE coalition government was installed in Cantábria following the 2007 regional elections. In 2010 the PRC threatened to pull out of the coalition if the Cantabrian government did not reverse its decision to cancel work on a high-speed rail line. In the 2011 local elections, the PRC won 322 seats on municipal councils.

Leader: Miguel Ángel REVILLA Roiz (President of the Cantabria Government).

León People's Union (*Unión del Pueblo Leónes*—UPL). The UPL won 3 seats in the *Cortes* of Castilla y León in 1999 and 2003. The party continues to support autonomous status for the León region, where it received 10.7 percent of votes during the 2007 regional elections. The UPL secured 135 seats on local councils in the May 2011 municipal balloting. Infighting led to calls for new leadership in late 2013.

Leader: Pedro ÁNGEL Gallego (President).

Catalan Republican Left (*Esquerra Republicana de Catalunya*—ERC). Founded in 1931, the ERC was one of two Catalan republican parties, the other being the Democratic Spanish Republican Action (*Acció Republicana Democrática Española*—ARDE), granted legal recognition in August 1977. In July 1991 the Catalan radical separatist Free Land (*Terre Lliure*) announced that it was dissolving, with its members being accepted into the ERC. In December 1991 the ERC abandoned its call for federalism, appealing instead for Catalan independence.

In the 2004 national election, the ERC won eight seats in the Congress of Deputies, seven more than it had previously held. (For more information on the party prior to 2004, see the 2014 *Handbook*.) For the Senate it campaigned as part of the PSC-led Catalan Accord for Progress (ECP; see under the PSC, below). No individual regional returns for 2007 were registered with the electoral records of the Interior Ministry. In the March 9, 2008, election the ERC sustained further losses and dropped from five seats in Congress to three. The losses prompted president Joan Puigcercós to announce his intent to resign from his post in the Catalan regional government to devote his efforts full time to party building.

In December 2008 the ERC in concert with the CiU voted against Zapatero's 2009 budget because it did not provide sufficient funding for the Catalan region under the 2006 autonomy statute. In November the ERC joined forces with the IU to press for revisions to the Law of Historical Memory that would declare null and void all sentences issued under Franco, a step that would potentially open the state up to compensation claims by victims and their families. In December ERC congress member Joan TARDÀ provoked outrage when he ended a speech at festivities marking the 30th anniversary of the Spanish constitution by declaring "death to the Bourbon," a reference to the royal dynasty of King Juan Carlos.

A new regional financing deal was finally passed in July 2009. It allowed Catalonia to retain a greater share of its tax revenue, rather than collect and redistribute it to poorer regions, effectively boosting regional coffers by $5 billion. In the May 2011 local elections the ERC won 1,399 seats on municipal councils. In national elections, the ERC won 3 Congress of Deputies seats. The party share rose from 11 to 21 seats in the regional parliamentary election of November 26, 2012. Leaders agreed to support the CiU independence referendum but not join the CIU minority government. The ERC joined two other Catalonian parties, the **Catalan New Left**, and ***Catalunya Si,*** to create the **Left for the Right to Decide** coalition for the 2014 EU balloting. The alliance won 2 seats in that balloting. In the 2015 chamber balloting, the party won 8 seats, and 9 in 2016. The alliance secured 8 Senate seats in 2015, and 12 in 2016.

Leader: Gabriel RUFIÁN (President).

Convergence and Union (*Convergéncia i Unió*—CiU). The center-left CiU was formed in November 1978 as a coalition of the **Democratic Convergence of Catalonia** (*Convergéncia Democrática de Catalunya*—CDC) and the **Democratic Union of Catalonia** (*Unió Democrática de Catalunya*—UDC). In its first federal elections (1979) the CiU elected eight deputies and one senator. In the first elections to the Parliament of Catalonia in 1980, the CiU won 43 seats, allowing CDC president Jordi Pujol i Soley to be elected President of Catalonia. The CiU won a majority of seats in the Catalan legislative election of March 1992, and at the national level the CiU secured 17 congressional and 14 senatorial seats in June 1993, after which it gave qualified support to the PSOE minority government. Having initially made greater tax transfers to Catalonia its quid pro quo for supporting the PSOE government, the CiU in February 1994 lodged a demand for full Catalan autonomy and moved into opposition in mid-1995.

The CiU lost seats but retained power in the November 1995 Catalan election, not winning an absolute majority for the first time since 1984. The 16 lower house seats it secured in the March 1996 national balloting enabled it to extract tax and other concessions in return for backing the new PP government. It retained a slim plurality in the October 1999 Catalan election and at the May 2000 national election won 8 Senate and 15 congressional seats.

In the regional election of November 2003 the CiU won a plurality of seats but surrendered the government to a coalition led by the PSC (below) and ERC. Nationally, the party won four directly elected Senate seats and ten Chamber seats in March 2004. For the European Parliament election of June 2004 the CiU joined the PNV, the BNG (below), and others in the **Galeuca** (for Galician, Euskadi, and Catalonia) coalition. In the 2007 local elections the CiU took 22.3 percent of votes in Barcelona; 33.2 percent in Girona; 32.8 percent in Lleida; and 31.2 percent in Tarragona, underscoring its position as a favored party for nationally minded Catalonian voters.

In December 2007 the CiU faction in the Senate led a veto of the government's 2008 budget under claims that the spending proposals did not provide the amount of funding called for under the Catalan charter that was approved the previous year.

In the March 9, 2008, election the CiU gained the third highest number of votes, or 21 percent of the electorate, in Catalonia and boosted its number of deputies in Congress by 1 to a total of 11. The party was considered a key potential coalition partner for Zapatero, a situation that deepened in 2009 when he lost needed support from the Basque Nationalist Party after an upset in Basque regional elections on March 1. Shortly after the vote, CiU president Artur MAS warned Zapatero that the CiU would not be a "lifeboat" for him in Madrid.

In May 2010 the CiU abstained from voting on Zapatero's economic austerity measures (see Current Issues, above), and in August the party reversed its prior support of Spanish troops in Afghanistan, following the shooting deaths of three Spanish soldiers. The CiU won the November 28 regional elections in Catalonia, taking 62 seats. Party leader Artur MAS i Gavarró was elected president of the region.

In local and regional balloting in May 2011 the CiU placed fourth in the balloting, securing 58 out of 135 seats in the Catalonia regional assembly and 3,862 seats on municipal councils. In the November 2011 national elections, the CiU placed third and secured 9 Senate seats and 16 Chamber seats. It dropped from 62 to 50 seats in the November 25, 2012, regional election, but remained the largest party in the local legislature. Mas planned to use his election mandate to call a referendum on independence, but his lower-than-expected vote complicated that strategy. The CiU was part of the CpE in the 2014 EU balloting, winning one of the alliance's seats.

The CIU split apart in June 2015 after the UDC refused to endorse the CDC's independence campaign. The CDC won four seats in the Senate and eight in the Chamber in 2016, before dissolving to be reformed as the **Catalan European Democratic Party** (*Partit Demòcrata Europeu Català—PDECAT*) in July 2016.

Initiative for Catalonia–Greens (*Iniciativa per Catalunya–Verds*—IC-V). Initially an alliance headed by the PCE-affiliated Unified Socialist Party of Catalonia (PSUC), the IC was established in 1987 and became, in effect, the Catalonian branch of the United Left. Other initial participants in the IC were the **Party of Communists of Catalonia** (*Partit dels Communistes de Catalunya*—PCC) and the **Accord of Left Nationalists** (*Entesa Nacionalistas d'Esquerra*—ENE). In 1990 the grouping evolved into a party that then became increasingly close to the Catalan branch of the Greens (*Els Verds*—EV), and together they won 11 seats in the November 1995 regional election. The coalition was formalized as the IC-V in 1998. In the 1999 regional election it won only 3 seats while cooperating with the PSOE-affiliated Party of Socialists of Catalonia (PSC). Nationally, the IC-V won 2 seats in the Congress at the March 2000 election.

In 2003 the IC-V and the allied EUiA (see the IU, above) won nine seats in the regional legislature. In the 2004 national balloting, the IC-V/EUiA won two seats. As participants in a coalition ballot with the EUiA again in 2007, the IC-V added candidates from the obscure EPM party to its candidate lists. The IC-V–EUiA–EPM list took 10.5 percent of votes in Barcelona; 7 percent in Girona; 4.1 percent in Lleida; and 4.4 percent in Tarragona.

The party has since favored various redistribution schemes and advocated the legalization and regulation of prostitution. With the introduction of the Law of Historical Memory, the IC-V organized a conference at the Frankfurt Fair with its German counterparts to identify best practices for acknowledging dark chapters in the history of their respective countries.

In 2008 the party advocated for immigrant rights by taking a stand against government policies to expand the amount of time illegal immigrants could be held in detention. IC-V also supported giving immigrants the right to vote in local elections. In July 2010 the IC-V successfully won a vote in the Catalonian parliament banning bullfighting, which was seen by some analysts as a nationalist response to the June Constitutional Court ruling that overturned aspects of Catalonia's self-rule charter. In the May 2011 balloting the IC-V secured 398 seats on local councils. IC-V was part of the IU-led electoral coalition for the 2104 EU elections. The IC-V won one of the coalition's six EU seats.

Leaders: Joan SAURA Laporta (President), Joan HERRERA Torres (Secretary General).

Socialist Party of Catalonia (*Partit dels Socialistes de Catalunya*—PSC). The regional affiliate of the PSOE, the PSC dates from the late 1970s, when several like-minded leftist parties merged. At the national level, it remains a major contributor to the PSOE's success. In March 2004 it won 18 seats in the lower house. In addition it won 8 in the Senate as part of the **Catalan Accord for Progress** (*Entesa Catalana de Progrés*—ECP), an alliance forged with the ERC, the IC-V, and the United and Alternative Left (EUiA; see under the IU, above).

The PSC performed strongly in 2007 regional elections, taking a 33.6 percent vote share in Barcelona; 25.6 percent in Girona; 31.1 percent in Lleida; and 30.2 in Tarragona. (For more on the electoral history of the PSC prior to 2007, see the 2012 *Handbook.*) In the March 9, 2008, elections it again performed well and was responsible for four of the five additional seats won by the PSOE, thereby outperforming its regional rival, the ERC. With 25 of the PSOE's 169 seats in Congress, it brought a strong Catalonian voice to the government. In September 2010 Catalan premier José MONTILLA announced that regional elections would be held on November 28 against the backdrop of widespread anger in Catalonia over a June Constitutional Court ruling that overturned aspects of the region's self-rule (see Current Issues, above). The PSC's popularity eroded after the court ruling because the CiU and other opposition forces criticized Montilla for not more strongly opposing the court's decision. The PSC's opposition to the 2014 independence referendum was reported to have cost the party significant public support.

Leaders: Isidre MOLAS i Barllori (President), Pere NAVARRO Morea (First Secretary).

Galician Left Alternative (*Alternativa Galega de Esquerda*—AGE). A left-wing, nationalist coalition of former BNG parties formed in September 2012, AGE won nine seats in the October 21, 2012, regional parliamentary election. Member parties include regional branches of the United Left, EQUO, and Galician Ecosocialist Space, as well as the ANOVA-Nationalist Brotherhood. Led by BNG founder Xosé Manuel Beiras, AGE is modeled after the Greek Syriza coalition.

Leaders: Xosé Manuel BEIRAS, Yolanda DÍAZ.

Galician Nationalist Bloc (*Bloque Nacionalista Galego*—BNG). Founded in 1983, the BNG is a left-wing group that came in third in the 1989 regional election, winning 5 seats out of 75. In the October 1993 balloting in Galicia it more than doubled its vote (to 18.7 percent) and won 13 seats out of 75. In late 1991 it had been joined by the **Galician National Party** (*Partido Nacionalista Galego*—PNG), which had split from the (now defunct) **Galician Coalition** (*Coalición Galega*—CG) in 1986. In 2000 the BNG won 3 seats in the national lower house, 1 less than in 2000. In the regional election of June 19, 2005, it won 13 seats, 4 fewer than in 2001, but sufficient to form a coalition government with the PSOE-affiliated PSdeG (below), thereby ousting the PP from power for the first time in a quarter-century. In the 2007 local balloting the BNG received 19.3 percent of votes in A Coruña; 16.5 percent in Lugo; 18.8 percent in Ourense; and 20.3 percent in Pontevedra. Following the coalition's defeat to the PP in regional elections in March 2009 (see Current events, above), party leader Anxo QUINTANA González resigned and said he had failed to create a "coalition culture" with the PSdeG. In the May 2011 balloting the BNG secured 590 seats on local councils and majorities in 11 municipalities, and it won 2 seats in the Chamber elections that year. The coalition split in January 2012, with founder Xosé Manuel BEIRAS launching the Galician Left Alternative. BNG dropped from 12 seats to seven in the October 21, 2012, regional parliamentary election, prompting national spokesperson Guillerme Vázquez Vázquez to resign. The party joined the Peoples Decide coalition for the 2014 EU elections. The BNG won just 0.2 percent of the vote in the 2016 Chamber of Deputies balloting, and no seats.

Leader: Xavier VENCE (National Spokesperson).

Party of Galician Socialists (*Partido dos Socialistas de Galicia*—PSdeG). As the regional affiliate of the PSOE, in June 2005 the PSdeG won 25 seats in the Galician election, 8 more than in 2001. It then formed a coalition with the Galician Nationalist Bloc that ousted the PP from power for the first time in a quarter-century. In regional elections in March 2009, the coalition was defeated by the PP. The secretary general of the PSdeG, Emilio PÉREZ Touriño, subsequently resigned from party leadership. In April Manuel Vázquez Fernández was elected to the post in an extraordinary party congress. The party dropped from 25 seats to 18 in the October 21, 2012, regional parliamentary election.

Leader: Manuel "Pachi" VÁZQUEZ Fernández (Secretary General of the Party).

Navarrese People's Union (*Unión del Pueblo Navarro*—UPN). A conservative grouping allied with the PP and firmly opposed to the Basque nationalist goal of reincorporating Navarra in Euzkadi, the UPN was formed in 1979 and governed the province from 1991 to 1995, when it went into opposition (although remaining the largest party). In the June 1999 election it won 22 of the 50 legislative seats and recaptured the presidency. It increased its representation by 1 in 2003 and then in 2004 won 2 seats in the national lower house. Although it failed to achieve a majority in the 2007 regional elections, the UPN continued to govern Navarra in minority status.

Inconclusive results in the May 2007 parliament election in Navarra resulted in a protracted struggle for power between the UPN and the PSOE's Socialist Party of Navarra, the latter of which gave up the effort after ending negotiations to form a governing coalition with Nafarroa Bai, whose members include former *Batasuna* members. As part of the power-sharing arrangement, UPN president Miguel Sanz was reelected to the regional premiership August 13 as four Socialists resigned and others abstained from the vote.

In October 2008 the UPN ended its 17-year alliance with the PP following a conflict concerning the UPN's autonomy to direct its members' votes on the 2009 federal budget. The PP announced it would begin establishing a party presence in Navarra and invited UPN politicians to join the PP.

In June 2009 the UPN joined hands with the PP and other conservative forces to vocally oppose a PSOE-led abortion reform bill.

In 2011 the UPN secured 322 seats on local councils and gained majorities in 25 municipalities. Also, in the balloting party leader Yolanda Barcina Angulo was elected president of Navarra.

Leaders: Yolanda BARCINA Angulo (President of Navarra and Party President), Miguel SANZ Sesma (Former President of Navarra), Oscar ARIZCUREN (Secretary General).

Rioja Party (*Partido Riojano*—PR). A center-left formation in Spain's main wine-growing area, the PR won one seat in the 1993 general election and two in the 1995 regional contest. Although subsequently unsuccessful at the national level, it retained its regional seats in 1999 and 2003. In the regional poll of May 2007 it received 6.5 percent of votes, while in 2011 it secured 56 seats on local councils and majorities in six municipalities.

Leaders: Miguel GONZÁLEZ de Legarra (President), Gomez Miguel IJALBA (Secretary General).

Asturian Forum (*Foro Asturias*—FAC). This is a center-right grouping established in 2011 by dissidents from the PP led by former party leader Francisco Álvarez-Cascos, who had lost the primary to lead the PP in regional elections in May 2011. Álvarez-Cascos won the balloting as president of Asturias, and the FAC secured 16 seats in the regional assembly and 158 seats on local councils. The FAC secured 1 seat in the lower house in national elections in 2011. It secured only 0.2 percent of the vote in the 2014 EU elections.

Leaders: Francisco ÁLVAREZ-CASCOS (President), Mariá Teresa ALONSO (Secretary General).

In 2011 the newly formed Basque grouping, **Yes to the Future** (*Geroa Bai*), and the Valencian leftist **Compromise Coalition** (*Coalició Compromís*) each won one seat in the lower chamber in national elections.

For information on the **The Rebirth and Union of Spain** (*Partido Renacimiento y Unión de España—PRUNE*), and the **Convergence of Navarran Democrats** (*Convergencia de Demócratas Navarros*—CDN), see the 2012 *Handbook*. For more information on the **Majorcan Union** (*Unió Mallorquina*—UM), and the **Valencia Entesa** (*Entesa pel País Valenciá*), see the 2010 *Handbook*.

Illegal Groups:

Basque Homeland and Liberty (*Euzkadi ta Azkatasuna*—ETA). Founded in 1959, ETA has long engaged in a violent separatist campaign directed primarily at police and government targets, although, in recent years, journalists and anti-ETA civilians have increasingly been targeted as well. By 2001 the number of deaths attributed to ETA attacks approached 800.

In 1978 ETA's political wing was indirectly involved in formation of the United People (HB; see Unity, below). More recently, the HB was the driving force behind the We the Basque Citizens (*Euskal Herritarrok*—EH) coalition, which contested the 1998 regional election. The EH participated in the resultant governing alliance until the end of a unilateral ETA cease-fire (September 1998–December 1999) that led to the EH's expulsion. In June 2001 elements of the EH established a unified party, Unity. In its more than three decades of operations ETA has demonstrated considerable resiliency despite the arrests or deaths of numerous leaders. In September 2000 French authorities captured the reputed ETA chief, Ignacio GRACIA Arregui (also known as Iñaki de RENTERÍA), for whom a French arrest warrant had been issued in 1987. The French also arrested the suspected ETA military commander, Francisco Xabier GARCÍA Gaztelu, in February 2001 and the alleged head of logistics, Asier OIARZABAL Txapartogi, in September 2001. In September 2002 senior leaders Juan Antonio OLARRA Guridi and Ainhoa MUGIKA Goni were arrested in Bordeaux, France, while in December Ibón FERNÁNDEZ Iradi and half a dozen other ETA leaders were arrested near Bayonne. Fernández Iradi escaped from custody two days later but was recaptured by the French in December 2003. By then, increased French-Spanish cooperation against ETA was severely hampering the organization's activities, with nearly four dozen suspected operatives having been arrested in October–November 2003 alone. Key suspects arrested in April 2004 included Félix Alberto LÓPEZ de la Calle, a military commander, and Félix Ignacio ESPARZA Luri, a logistics chief; in December alleged political leader Mikel ALBIZU Iriarte and Soledad IPARRAGUIRRE Genetxea, a suspected military commander, were also captured. In response to overtures from the Zapatero government for peace talks, ETA offered a partial truce in June 2005, involving a commitment not to attack elected officials, an offer that was deemed as insufficient by the government to begin talks. On March 22, 2006, the group announced a permanent cease-fire. The Zapatero government began to directly negotiate with the group. Unfortunately, the group itself was splintered and a part of it took responsibility for the bombing of a parking structure in the Madrid airport in December 2006. The cease-fire was officially called off by ETA in June 2007, following the attack of the previous year. In September the ETA released a statement blaming the breakup of the peace accord on the government's failure to set the "minimum conditions" for a negotiated solution and vowed to "open all its fronts" to further the creation of a Basque state.

In the aftermath of the failed peace process, ETA announced its intentions to replace would-be moderates who had been open to negotiations, implementing a stricter hierarchy of control over related groups to ensure sufficient militancy. This was confirmed by the dismissal of Rafael DÍEZ Usabiaga, who in October 2007 was replaced as secretary general of the ETA-affiliated Union of Patriotic Workers (*Langile Abertzale Sozialista*—LAB) by Ainhoa ETXAIDE Amorrortu, who represents ETA's radical wing.

In 2008 Spanish authorities made a series of arrests of prominent ETA suspects and shut down several active cells. Nevetheless, the group's violent campaign continued into the summer tourist season with a series of bomb attacks on seaside resorts.

In late July Spanish authorities reportedly stepped up security measures in the Basque region after issuing an unusual warning that a huge attack by ETA would take place. In an effort to enhance secrecy and prevent more arrests, ETA leaders reportedly removed members in prison from the group's national committee and appointed a new set of leaders and sent them underground.

In August 2008 the release of ETA member De Juana CHAOS, who served 20 years of a 3,000-year sentence for a bomb blast that killed 25 people, provoked considerable public outrage. Further attacks in northern Spain later in the month were found to be staged from France, where ETA members had apparently reorganized their logistical base. Prosecutors launched more arrests and indictments on ETA supporters into the fall, including 24 people who were charged in October with extorting money from businesses in the Basque region in the form of a "revolutionary tax." The suspected military chief of ETA was arrested in southwestern France in November, delivering what Zapatero described as a "decisive blow" against the organization.

ETA was reportedly responsible for the December killing of a businessman whose construction company had been working on a high-speed rail project in the Basque Country. In January 2009 ETA marked its 50th anniversary by vowing to continue fighting for Basque independence and warning that it would target Spanish media outlets and those involved in the construction of the rail line.

In advance of the March 1, 2009, regional elections in Basque Country, ETA issued a statement calling the elections "anti-democratic" because of bans of two far-left independence parties and urged voters to support those parties. ETA reportedly set off a bomb in front of the PSOE headquarters in the Basque Country in late February, causing extensive damage but no injuries. Nevertheless, election results demonstrated ETA's waning support in the region, according to analysts. The number of spoilt ballot papers, a common sign of ETA's support within the population, dropped by a third from previous polls to about 10 percent of the vote. Furthermore, *Aralar*, a new leftist independence party that is against violence, boosted its number of seats in the regional parliament from one to four. At the end of March police arrested eight members of an ETA-affiliated youth group, following the group's alleged planned attacks on the high-speed rail line project.

The election of the new Basque Country premier, Paxi López of the PSE-EE, in May ushered in a tougher stance against ETA activity. Efforts were directed at minimizing the legitimacy of a separate Basque state, including removal of pro-independence posters and other material from public buildings and the refusal to give permits to pro-ETA demonstrators. ETA stepped up attacks over the summer, which resulted in the death of a police investigator of ETA, nearly three dozen injuries in a Civil Guard barracks attack in the northern city of Burgos, and the deaths of two police officers on the resort island of Mallorca. A second explosion on Mallorca in August at a restaurant, in which no one was harmed, called into question government claims that ETA had been seriously weakened by the surge in arrests.

As of July 2009, there were nearly 1,000 ETA members jailed in Spain and France. ETA has been blamed for 828 deaths in its campaign for independence.

In 2010 the government refused to resume peace talks unless ETA agreed to an unconditional and permanent end to its armed struggle. In March the interior ministry sought legislative measures that would give it the ability to ban any separatist party that had not purposefully condemned ETA violence. An ETA-declared cease-fire in September was roundly rejected by government officials and opposition parties because it did not explicitly call for ETA to surrender weapons, renounce violence permanently, and halt other illegal activities such as extortion.

In October 2011 the ETA renounced the use of force and called for negotiations with the Spanish and French governments. In February 2014 the ETA began to decommission its weaponry. In November 2015 ETA political leader Mikel Albizu Iriarte, along with two others, was arrested by French and Spanish security forces in a joint operation in Ascain, a French town near the border with Spain.

Communist Party of the Basque Lands (*Partido Comunista de las Tierras Vascas*—PCTV/*Euskal Herrialdeetako Alderi Komunista*—EHAK). The PCTV/EHAK was established by former members of *Batasuna* after that party was banned in March 2003. In late 2008 the court ordered the liquidation of all PCTV assets and froze its bank accounts, and the PCTV was not allowed to enter the 2009. (For more information, see the 2013 *Handbook*.)

LEGISLATURE

Traditionally designated as the *Cortes* (Courts), the Spanish legislature was revived by General Franco in 1942 as a unicameral body with strictly limited powers and officially named *Las Cortes Españolas*. Initially, it had no directly elected members, but provision was made in 1967 for the election of 198 "family representatives." The essentially corporative character of the body was retained in 1971, when several new categories of indirectly elected and appointed members were added.

In November 1976 the *Cortes* approved a long-debated Political Reform Bill, which, calling for a largely elected bicameral assembly, secured overwhelming public endorsement in a referendum held on December 15. The new **Cortes Generales,** consisting of a Senate and a Congress of Deputies, held its inaugural session in July 1977. Both houses serve four-year terms, subject to dissolution.

Senate (*Senado*). The upper house currently has 266 members, of whom 208 were directly elected in 2011: 4 from each of the 47 mainland provinces; 6 from Santa Cruz de Tenerife (3 from Tenerife and 1 each from La Gomera, La Palma, and Hierro); 5 from the Balearic Islands (3 from Mallorca and 1 each from Menorca and Ibiza-Formentera); 5 from Las Palmas (3 from Gran Canaria and 1 each from Fuerteventura and Lanzarote); and 2 each from the North African enclaves of Ceuta and Melilla. The remaining 56 members are designated at varying times (depending on regional elections) by 17 autonomous regional legislatures (Ceuta and Melilla being excluded). Each designates at least 1 senator, with the more populous regions entitled to an additional senator for each million inhabitants. The current distribution is Andalucía, 9; Aragón, 2; Asturias, 2; Balearic Islands, 2; Basque Country, 3; Canary Islands, 3; Cantábria, 1; Castilla y León, 3; Castilla–La Mancha, 2; Catalonia, 8; Extremadura, 2; Galicia, 3; Madrid, 7; Murcia, 2; Navarra, 1; La Rioja, 1; and Valencia, 5.

The overall party distribution after the elections of June 26, 2016, was as follows (the number of seats won in the most recent balloting in parentheses): Popular Party, 151 (130); Spanish Socialist Workers' Party, 63 (43); United We Can, 23 (16); Catalan Republican Left, 12 (10); Basque Nationalist Party, 6 (5); Democratic Convergence of Catalonia, 4 (2); Citizens 3, (0); Canarian Coalition, 2 (1); Basque Country Unite, 1 (0); and Gomera Socialist Group, 1 (1).

Speaker: Pío GARCÍA-ESCUDERO Márquez.

Congress of Deputies (*Congreso de los Diputados*). The lower house currently consists of 350 deputies elected on block lists by proportional representation. Each province is entitled to a minimum of 3 deputies, with 1 deputy each from the African enclaves of Ceuta and Melilla.

The balloting on June 26, 2016, produced the following seat distribution: Popular Party, 137 seats; Spanish Socialist Workers' Party, 85; United We Can, 71; Citizens, 32; Catalan Republican Left, 9; Democratic Convergence of Catalonia, 8; Basque Nationalist Party, 5; Basque Country Unite, 2; and Canarian Coalition, 1.

President: Ana PASTOR (PP).

CABINET

[as of November 30, 2016]

Prime Minister	Mariano Rajoy
Deputy Prime Minister	Soraya Sáenz de Santamaría [f]
Ministers	
Agriculture and Fisheries, Food, and Environmental Affairs	Isabel García Tejerina [f]
Defense	María Dolores de Cospedal [f]
Economic Affairs, Industry, and Competition	Luis de Guindos Jurado
Education, Culture, and Sport	Íñigo Méndez de Vigo y Montojo
Energy, Tourism, and the Digital Agenda	Álvaro Nadal Belda
Finance and Public Administration	Cristóbal Montoro Romero
Foreign Affairs and Cooperation	Alfonso Dastis Quecedo
Government Spokesperson	Íñigo Méndez de Vigo y Montojo
Health, Equality, and Social Policy	Dolors Montserrat [f]
Interior	Juan Ignacio Zoido
Justice	Rafael Catalá Polo
Labor and Social Security	Fátima Báñez [f]
Presidency	Soraya Sáenz de Santamaría [f]
Public Works	Íñigo de la Serna

[f] = female

INTERGOVERNMENTAL REPRESENTATION

Ambassador to the U.S.: Ramón GIL-CASARES SATRÚSTEGU.

U.S. Ambassador to Spain: Krishna R. URS (Chargé d'Affaires).

Permanent Representative to the UN: Román OYARZUN Marchesi.

IGO Memberships (Non-UN): ADB, AfDB, CEUR, EBRD, EIB, EU, ICC, IEA, IOM, NATO, OECD, OSCE, WTO.

For Further Reference:

Balfour, Sebastian. *The Politics of Contemporary Spain.* New York: Routledge, 2005.

Encarnación, Omar G. *Democracy without Justice in Spain: The Politics of Forgetting.* Philadelphia: University of Pennsylvania Press, 2014.

Tusell, Javier. *Spain: From Dictatorship to Democracy.* Translated by Rosemary Clark. Malden, MA: Blackwell, 2011.

RELATED TERRITORIES

Virtually nothing remains of Spain's former colonial empire, the bulk of which was lost with the independence of the American colonies in the early 19th century. Cuba, Puerto Rico, and the Philippines were acquired by the United States in 1898. More recently, the West African territories of Río Muni and Fernando Pó became independent in 1968 as the state of Equatorial Guinea; Ifní was ceded to Morocco in 1969; and the Western (Spanish) Sahara was divided between Morocco and Mauritania in February 1976 (the latter subsequently renouncing its claim on August 5, 1979). Thereafter, the only remaining European possessions in the African continent were the small Spanish enclaves discussed below.

Places of Sovereignty in North Africa (*Plazas de Soberanía del Norte de Africa*). These Spanish outposts on the Mediterranean coast of Morocco, dating from the 15th century, encompass the two enclaves of Ceuta and Melilla, officially referred to as *presidios,* or garrison towns, and three "Minor Places" (*Plazas Menores*): the tiny, volcanic Chafarinas and Alhucemas islands, and Peñón de Vélez de la Gomera, an arid garrison spot on the north Moroccan coast. Ceuta, with an area of 7.6 square miles (19.7 sq. km) and a population of 70,400 (2007E), and Melilla, with an area of 4.8 square miles (12.5 sq. km) and a population of 67,700 (2007E), are considered parts of metropolitan Spain, and before being accorded the status of autonomous regions in September 1994, they were organized as municipalities of the provinces of Cádiz and Málaga, respectively. The Minor Places, with military garrisons of about one hundred each, are under the jurisdiction of Málaga. (For information on areas prior to 1991, see the 2012 *Handbook.*)

During a state visit to Morocco in July 1991 by King Juan Carlos, the Spanish and Moroccan prime ministers signed a friendship treaty (the first between Spain and an Arab country) providing in particular for the peaceful settlement of disputes between the two countries. Madrid had long felt that any attempt to alter the status of the enclaves would be interpreted by Rabat as an "annexation" of "occupied territory." Thus, it had branded as "unconstitutional" a unilateral pronouncement by Melilla's mayor in early 1993 that the city was an "autonomous community" within Spain. On September 2, 1994, however, the Spanish government approved statutes of autonomy, effective from March 13, 1995, that upgraded the status of the enclaves by authorizing the replacement of their local councils by 25-member assemblies, to which an executive and president would be responsible. The Moroccan government responded by launching a major diplomatic offensive against Spanish possession of the enclaves. In 1998 Spanish officials refused a Moroccan invitation to take part in a panel discussion on granting residents of the enclaves dual citizenship.

In the elections of June 13, 1999, the recently formed Independent Liberal Group (*Grupo Independiente Liberal*—GIL), led by a mainland mayor, Jesús GIL, won pluralities in the 25-seat assemblies of both Ceuta and Melilla, but in both jurisdictions anti-GIL coalitions prevailed in forming governments. (See the 2010 *Handbook* for details.)

Tensions with Morocco flared again in July 2002 when Moroccan police set up camp on the offshore islet of Perejil (also known as Tourah or Leila), five miles west of Ceuta, ostensibly to combat smuggling and drug trafficking. In response, Spain dispatched members of its armed forces to Perejil. In an effort to mediate the dispute, then U.S. Secretary of State Colin Powell proposed that the islet be returned to its pre-July status. Both Spain and Morocco agreed, although Morocco subsequently voiced objection to the presence of a Spanish naval vessel near another islet, Nekor. On July 30 Morocco's King Mohamed VI reasserted his country's claims to Ceuta, Melilla, and the offshore islands and stated that Spain should end its "occupation."

The balloting on May 25, 2003, was more definitive. In Ceuta the PP won an overwhelming majority, taking 19 seats; the second-place **Ceuta Democratic Union** (*Unión Demócrata Ceutí*—UDCE), a Muslim formation led by Muhammad MUHAMMAD Ali, won 3, while the PSOE and PDSC each won 1. In Melilla, Imbroda Ortiz's UPM took 15 seats, followed by the CpM with 7 and the PSOE with 3. In 2004, as in 2000, all six representatives elected to the *Cortes Generales* from the enclaves ran as PP candidates or chose to sit with the PP parliamentary group.

On September 29, 2005, five Africans were shot to death and dozens of others were injured when hundreds of individuals tried to scale the fence separating Morocco from Ceuta. The fatal shots reportedly came from the Moroccan side of the border. On the same day Madrid announced that it would deploy some 500 troops to Melilla and Ceuta in an effort to prevent such attempts, which had claimed nine lives in the preceding two months. The incidents led directly to a decision by 60 African and European countries to meet in Rabat, Morocco, in July 2006, in an effort to formulate a strategy that would stem the flow of illegal immigrants into EU countries.

In regional elections in May 2007, the PP retained its absolute majorities in Ceuta and Melilla.

In August a series of protests in Melilla concerning alleged mistreatment of Moroccans by Spanish police shut down the border for days and triggered supply problems. The protestors claimed that police were preventing Moroccans, particularly pregnant women, from crossing the border to prevent births that would lead to Spanish citizenship. Morocco temporarily recalled its ambassador to Spain in protest of the first official visit to Ceuta and Melilla in November 2007 by Spain's King Juan Carlos and Queen Sofia.

In the March 9, 2008, national election the PP won the seats representing Ceuta and Melilla in the congress and senate. In a July visit to Morocco, Zapatero was reportedly pressed by his Moroccan counterpart, Abbas El Fassi, about the return of Ceuta and Melilla to Moroccan sovereignty.

After the storming of a border fence by a large group of African migrants in June 2008, Spain's Defense Minister Carme Chacón announced she would station 100 extra troops in Ceuta and 250 extra in Melilla. However, the additional troops failed to quell violence in subsequent incidents. In November about 200 African migrants in Melilla stormed the border in a series of clashes with security forces. In January 2009 troops in Melilla opened fire on a group of about 80 migrants, killing one man, who were attempting to cross illegally, prompting calls by human rights groups for an investigation. Meanwhile, a stampede at a border crossing near Ceuta in May resulted in the deaths of two women and brought attention to the high amount of trade, including contraband business, between the two sides.

In May 2010 Spain reaffirmed the "absolute Spanishness" of Ceuta and Melilla following Moroccan demands for new talks over the status of the territory. In August mounting tension over a number of incidents involving harsh treatment of Moroccan nationals by Spanish police led to a flurry of diplomatic contacts between both countries' high officials, including their kings. When PP leader Mariano Rajoy attended anniversary festivities in Melilla to mark the city's incorporation into Spain, Moroccan politicians became enraged. Moroccan prime minister Abbas el Fassi sent a letter of protest to Rajoy, calling his visit "an attack on the dignity and national feelings of Moroccans."

Regional elections in May 2011 gave the PP 18 of 25 seats in Ceuta and 15 of 25 in Melilla.

In May 2012 joint Spanish–Moroccan police posts were established in Tangiers and Algeciras to improve cooperation between the two states in counternarcotics efforts and human trafficking.

Spain's foreign minister José Manuel García-Margallo warned Morocco in April 2013 not to raise the issue of Ceuta and Melilla, while Moroccan deputy foreign minister Youssef Amrani complained of illegal immigrants trying to scale the fence around Melilla. "If we let them climb the border fence and enter Spain, we fail to honor our commitments to the European Union," he said. "But if we prevent them from doing so, we will be accused of committing human rights violations." On March 18 more than 500 migrants broke through a border fence and crossed into Melilla. On May 28 another 400 stormed across the border. By month's end, more than 10,000 migrants were housed in Melilla in temporary facilities. In response, Spain's interior minister called for €2.3 million in border security enhancements.

Police in March 2015 reported they had arrested two men and broken up a terrorist cell in Ceuta that was plotting attacks in Spain. The **Gomera Socialist Group** (*Agrupación Socialista Gomera*—ASG), a left-wing grouping that was formed in 2015 by defectors from the PSOE, won one Senate seat in the 2016 national legislative elections.

SRI LANKA

Democratic Socialist Republic of Sri Lanka
Sri Lanka Prajatantrika Samajawadi Janarajaya (Sinhala)
Llankais Sananayaka Socialisak Kutiyarasa (Tamil)

Political Status: Independent since February 4, 1948; present constitution adopted on August 6, 1978, effective September 7.

Area: 25,332 sq. mi. (65,610 sq. km).

Population: 20,811,000 (2016E—UN); 22,235,000 (2016E—U.S. Census).

Major Urban Centers (2014E—UN): SRI JAYEWARDENEPURA (Kotte, administrative capital, 128,000), Colombo (Kolamba, commercial capital, 650,000).

Official Languages: Sinhala, Tamil. English is recognized as a link language.

Monetary Unit: Sri Lankan Rupee (market rate October 1, 2016: 146.67 rupees = $1US).

President: Maithripala SIRISENA (New Democratic Front); elected president on January 8, 2015, and sworn in January 9 for a six-year term, succeeding Mahinda RAJAPAKSE (United People's Freedom Alliance).

Prime Minister: Ranil WICKREMASINGHE (United National Party); designated by the president and sworn in on January 9, 2015, succeeding Disanayaka Mudiyanselage JAYARATNE (United People's Freedom Alliance).

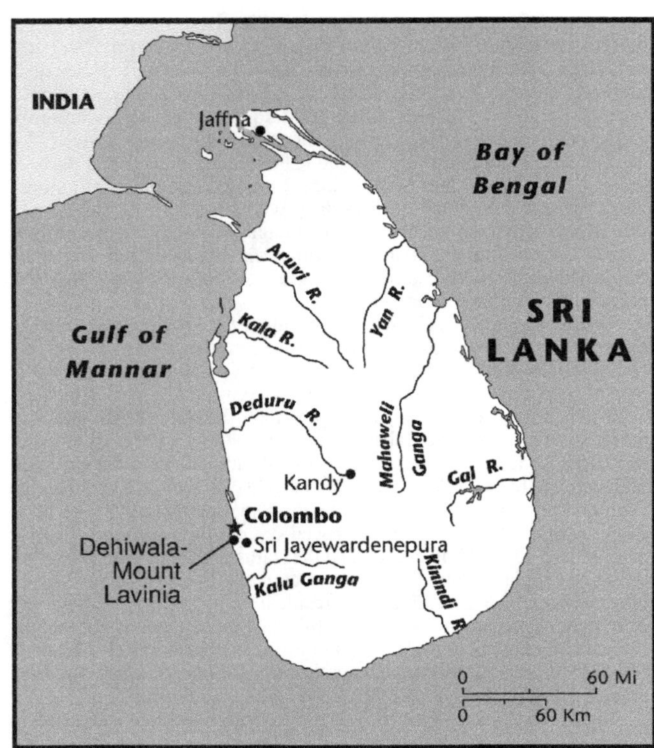

THE COUNTRY

The insular location of Sri Lanka (formerly Ceylon) off the coast of southeast India has not prevented the development of an ethnic and religious diversity comparable to that of other parts of southern Asia. Approximately 74 percent of the people are of Sinhalese extraction, descended from Aryan stock of northern India, while 18 percent are Tamil, akin to the Dravidian population of southern India, and 7 percent are Moors; small minority groups include Europeans, Burghers (Eurasians), and Veddah aborigines. Roughly 70 percent of the inhabitants are Buddhist, while about 8 percent are Hindu, 7 percent Christian, and 7 percent Muslim.

The country's major ethnic problem has long centered on the Tamil population, which is divided into two groups: "Ceylon Tamils," whose ancestors have lived in Sri Lanka for many generations, and "Indian Tamils," whose forebears were brought to the island late in the 19th century as plantation laborers. The former, numbering nearly 2 million, predominate in the north and constitute about 40 percent of the population in the east. The latter, numbering about 900,000, are concentrated on the central tea plantations and were not been prominently involved in the Tamil *eelam* (homeland) movement.

Women constitute 33 percent of the active labor force. Even though they have occupied both the presidency and the prime ministership, they make up only 5.8 percent of the parliament (13 of 225 seats) following the 2015 elections.

Sri Lanka ranks with Kenya as the world's leading exporter of tea; other traditional exports include rubber, coconuts, and coconut products, with cinnamon being a leader among the specialized export crops promoted by a government-sponsored diversification program.

In the early 1980s Sri Lanka possessed one of Asia's most promising economies. However, falling commodity prices, drought, Sinhalese militancy in the south (1987–1989), and widespread Tamil unrest in the north and east (since 1983) have held back growth. The complex, at times fratricidal, maelstrom of violence left more than 100,000 dead, with some 1 million displaced during the Tamil conflict. It also has contributed to infrastructure decay (particularly in the Tamil areas). Gross domestic product (GDP) growth averaged 5.2 percent between 2000 and 2008. Inflation averaged 11.9 percent, and unemployment was 7.5 percent.

In late December 2004 the Indian Ocean tsunami disaster, killed more than 35,000 Sri Lankans, displaced hundreds of thousands, and caused an estimated $1 billion in damage.

High inflation led the government to impose price controls on rice in April 2008; however, inflation continued to spike, rising to 28.2 percent in June, before moderating. Despite the global economic slowdown, Sri Lanka recorded more than $850 million in foreign investment in 2009, a record for the country. In 2010 the International Monetary Fund (IMF) extended a $2.6 billion loan to the country. GDP grew by an average of 8.1 percent in 2010 and 2011. In 2012 GDP grew by 6.3 percent, inflation was 7.4 percent, and unemployment 4.9 percent. The following year, GDP rose by 7.3 percent, while inflation moderated slight to 6.9 percent, and unemployment declined to 4 percent. GDP per capita was $3,161. Foreign direct investment in Sri Lanka was expected to exceed $2.5 billion in 2014, an increase of more than 50 percent over the previous year. In 2015 GDP grew by 5.2 percent and then 5 percent in 2016. Inflation dropped to 0.9 percent in 2015, and then rose to 3.4 percent the following year. Unemployment increased to 4 percent in 2015, and remained approximately the same in 2016. GDP per capita in 2016 was $3,990. In its annual report on the ease of doing business index in 2016, the World Bank ranked Sri Lanka 110th out of 189 countries.

GOVERNMENT AND POLITICS

Political background. After nearly four and a half centuries of foreign domination, beginning with the arrival of the Portuguese in 1505, followed by the Dutch (1658–1815) and the British (1815–1948), Sri Lanka (then Ceylon) became an independent state within the Commonwealth on February 4, 1948. Since the country's first parliamentary election in 1947, political power has oscillated between the moderate and generally pro-Western United National Party (UNP) and the Sri Lanka Freedom Party (SLFP), which has emphasized Buddhism, nationalism, "democratic socialism," and nonalignment in international affairs. Until 1956 the country was governed by the UNP, led successively by D. S. SENANAYAKE, his son Dudley SENANAYAKE, and Sir John KOTELAWALA. The SLFP, led by S. W. R. D. BANDARANAIKE, came to power in the 1956 election with an aggressively Sinhalese program reflecting the emergence of a nationalist, Sinhala-educated professional class, but a series of disorders culminated in the prime minister's assassination in 1959. The UNP formed a shaky minority government following the March 1960 general election but was unable to withstand a no-confidence vote shortly thereafter.

In July 1960 the SLFP, under the leadership of Sirimavo R. D. BANDARANAIKE, wife of the former prime minister, won a near-majority in the legislature and organized an all-SLFP government. Ceylonese policy under her leadership acquired an increasingly anti-Western character, accompanied by allegations of rightist plots and attempted coups. The UNP, however, regained a leading position in the 1965 election and organized a coalition government under the premiership of Dudley Senanayake. Subsequently, political power shifted back to the SLFP under Mrs. Bandaranaike, the UNP winning a bare 17 seats in a house of 157 members in 1970.

Sri Lanka's democratic tradition received a serious setback in 1971 when a radical Sinhalese group with Maoist underpinnings, the People's Liberation Front (*Janatha Vimukthi Peramuna*—JVP), attempted unsuccessfully to overthrow the government at the cost of an estimated 20,000 deaths.

An extremely bitter election campaign culminated in July 1977 in an unprecedented victory for the UNP, which, led by J. R. JAYEWARDENE, obtained 142 of the 168 legislative seats. SLFP representation plummeted from 91 to 8. Following adoption by the National State Assembly of a constitutional amendment providing for a French-style executive system, Jayewardene assumed the presidency in February 1978 and named Ranasinghe PREMADASA prime minister.

Having secured passage of a constitutional revision permitting the president to call an election after a minimum of four years in office, Jayewardene was reelected for a second six-year term in October 1982 (effective from February 1983). In November, by a near-unanimous vote, the Parliament endorsed a government proposal that its own term be extended by six years to August 1989, subject to approval in a popular referendum. In December, the measure was approved with 54.7 percent of the vote. In July 1983 the killing of 13 soldiers near the northern city of Jaffna set off a wave of anti-Tamil rioting. Over 400 people, mainly Tamils, died in the disturbances. In addition to proscribing three leftist parties, President Jayewardene secured passage of a constitutional amendment banning all separatist activity and requiring MPs to take loyalty oaths. The 16 MPs of the Tamil United Liberation Front (TULF) responded by withdrawing from Parliament and were subsequently declared to have forfeited their seats.

Indian prime minister Indira Gandhi sent an envoy to mediate between the Jayewardene government and the Tamil militants; however, most opposition leaders boycotted projected multiparty talks in October 1983. It was not until late December that the president agreed to invite the TULF to attend, without preconditions, a roundtable conference scheduled for January 1984. A series of "amity talks" ensued, with Tamil representatives advancing, as a minimal demand, the creation of an autonomous regional council encompassing the northern and eastern regions of the country. At midyear Jayewardene countered with a proposal for a second legislative chamber consisting of district representatives plus spokespersons for special interests. The overture was quickly rejected by the TULF.

During 1985 the level of violence intensified. Four of five exile groups based in Madras (now Chennai), India, announced in mid-April that they had formed a coalition to facilitate "armed revolutionary struggle for national independence." Meanwhile, the new Indian prime minister, Rajiv Gandhi, retreated somewhat from the overtly pro-Tamil posture of his recently assassinated mother. He declared his opposition to any attempt by the Tamils to establish an autonomous regime in Sri Lanka but sponsored a series of ultimately inconclusive talks between the rebels and Sri Lankan officials in Thimphu, Bhutan.

In December 1986 the government cut off essential northern services. Two months later, it mounted a major offensive against the rebels that recaptured most of the Jaffna peninsula by late May. The Indian government, under strong domestic pressure to take action on the insurgents' behalf, responded by airlifting humanitarian supplies to the north in early June, which drew a sharp diplomatic protest from Colombo. Subsequently, high-level discussions between the two governments produced an India–Sri Lanka Accord (ISLA) that brought Indian troops to Sri Lanka in support of a cease-fire and the establishment by an elected provincial council of an integrated northeastern government. On July 30 the day after conclusion of the ISLA, a 3,000-man Indian Peacekeeping Force (IPKF) arrived in Jaffna to assist in disarming the Tamils. However, the IPKF found itself in a major confrontation with the Liberation Tigers of Tamil Eelam (LTTE), the largest of the guerrilla groups. While the IPKF, augmented to a force of some 30,000, eventually gained control of much of the contested area, heavy fighting resumed in October. The LTTE rebuffed an Indian call to surrender during a unilateral cease-fire in late November, and by early 1988, IPKF troop strength had risen to 70,000.

In the south, the extremist JVP experienced a resurgence because of its insistence that the ISLA conceded too much ultimate power to the Tamil minority. From mid-1987 the JVP engaged in a widespread assassination campaign against political figures and on August 18 almost succeeded in killing President Jayawardene in a grenade attack in the Parliament building. The government nonetheless proceeded to enact legislation that provided for elected provincial councils patterned after the Indian state legislatures.

The UNP swept a series of provincial council elections in non-Tamil areas during April and June 1988. With the SLFP refusing to participate because of alleged UNP concessions to the northern rebels, most of the remaining seats were won by the recently organized United Socialist Alliance (USA) which, although a leftist formation, had supported the mid-1987 pact with India. On September 8 Jayawardene signed a proclamation merging the Northern and Eastern Provinces. However, both the LTTE and the TULF declared a boycott of the subsequent provincial council election. Consequently, the Eelam People's Revolutionary Liberation Front (EPRLF) and the Eelam National Democratic Liberation Front (ENDLF) filled the council seats from the north without an election, while in the east the EPRLF and the Sri Lanka Muslim Congress (SLMC) each won 17 seats, compared to 1 for the UNP, in November.

In December 1988 Prime Minister Premadasa was elected to succeed the aging President Jayawardene, barely avoiding the necessity of a runoff by capturing 50.4 percent of the vote; Mrs. Bandaranaike received 44.9 percent, while USA candidate Ossie ABEYGUNASEKERA ran a distant third, with 4.6 percent. Parliament was immediately dissolved, and in the resultant legislative election in February 1989 the UNP won 125 of 225 seats. The SLFP, benefiting from the introduction of proportional representation, won 67 seats.

In March 1989 Premadasa selected former finance minister Dingiri Banda WIJETUNGE as prime minister. A month later he offered amnesty to Tamil guerrillas in the north and JVP militants in the south if they would renounce violence and join the political process. As an inducement he offered them 29 of the UNP's legislative seats. Although the LTTE agreed to negotiations, the JVP responded with a fresh wave of bombings and killings. The subsequent average daily death toll of 35–40 led to the June reimposition of a nationwide state of emergency.

In an apparent effort to neutralize one of the JVP's most popular positions, Premadasa, never a supporter of the 1987 accord with New Delhi, requested in mid-1989 that the Indian troops in Sri Lanka (then estimated at 50,000) leave immediately. An international crisis loomed over the issue until an agreement was reached in September for complete withdrawal by the end of the year. Fighting among Tamil groups broke out again, however, and the new Indian government announced in December that the deadline would be extended into 1990.

Meanwhile, bombings and assassinations continued in the south despite the killing of all known JVP leaders during an intensified anti-insurgency campaign that apparently included the use of shadowy "death squads."

India completed its withdrawal from Sri Lanka on March 24, 1990, leaving the LTTE in virtual control of the northern region. Three weeks earlier, the North-East Provincial Council had approved a resolution proclaiming the area to be an independent state of Eelam. The action was repudiated by New Delhi and seen as a "last gesture" by the council's chief minister, Annamalai Varatharaja PERUMAL, who, with numerous EPRLF associates, subsequently sought refuge in South India from the advancing LTTE.

In June 1990 President Premadasa agreed to dissolve the North-East Provincial Council and hold fresh elections, but the LTTE launched a new wave of insurgent activity and the elections were indefinitely postponed. In mid-1992 the government mounted a new offensive in the north that produced widely divergent casualty estimates. The LTTE responded in August–November with a series of assassinations and terrorist attacks on both military and civilian targets. In April 1993 opposition leader Lalith ATHULATHMUDALI of the Democratic United National Front (DUNF, subsequently the United Lalith Front) was killed by an LTTE suicide attack, as was President Premadasa on May 1. Prime Minister Wijetunge, who immediately succeeded Premadasa on an acting basis, was elected by parliament on May 7 to serve the balance of his predecessor's term, with Ranil WICKREMESINGHE filling the prime ministerial vacancy.

In the parliamentary election of August 1994, an SLFP-led People's Alliance (PA), in coalition with the SLMC, won 112 of 225 seats and obtained sufficient support from minor groups to provide a solid majority for PA leader Chandrika Bandaranaike KUMARATUNGA, who became the third member of her family to serve as prime minister. Concurrently, most mainstream Tamil parliamentarians extended their support to the new administration.

In October 1994 the UNP presidential candidate, Gamini DISSANAYAKE, and a number of his associates were assassinated in a suicide bomb attack at an election rally in Colombo. The UNP named as Gamini's replacement his widow, Srima DISSANAYAKE, who failed to prevent Kumaratunga from winning with a record-setting 62.2 percent of the vote. Following her inauguration in November, the new president not only reappointed her mother, Sirimavo Bandaranaike, to her former post as prime minister but also pledged to abolish the executive presidency by July 1995—a pledge she proved unable to keep.

In December 1994 President Kumaratunga announced that a government proposal for a cease-fire had been accepted by the LTTE, and talks aimed at ending the conflict opened in Jaffna in January 1995. The talks collapsed in April with a resumption of attacks by the rebels. Tiring of the search for a negotiated solution, in October the government launched a major military offensive, code-named *Rivirasa*

(Sunshine), aimed at capturing the rebel stronghold of Jaffna. Government forces encountered fierce LTTE resistance and terrorist counteractions. Nevertheless, in December the city of Jaffna finally came under government control.

In January 1996 the financial center of Colombo was devastated by a huge LTTE truck bomb, killing over 90 people and injuring more than 1,400. With heavy fighting continuing, the government declared an extended nationwide emergency that secured parliamentary approval in April despite opposition objections, and a week later the military launched operation *Rivirasa* II to capture the areas around the city of Jaffna. On May 17 the government claimed that its forces were in control of the whole of the Jaffna peninsula, but its assertions that the LTTE had been effectively destroyed as a fighting force were disproved in mid-July when Tamil guerrillas overran the army garrison in Mullaittivu, southeast of Jaffna, inflicting the heaviest defeat on government forces since 1993. The military responded by launching another offensive in the north, during which an estimated 200,000 refugees fled.

In April 1997 Sri Lanka's two leading political parties agreed to a pact, brokered by the United Kingdom, to end the civil war. In May the military launched operation *Jaya Sikuru* (Victory Assured) in an effort to establish a stable overland supply route to Jaffna. (For more on the operation, see the 2013 *Handbook.*) Efforts by the government to restore normalcy to the Jaffna region included holding local elections in January 1998. Most of the leading Tamil parties participated despite threats from the LTTE, which the government had formally outlawed in response to the bombing of the country's most sacred Buddhist site, the Temple of Tooth in Kandy. Thereafter the LTTE undertook a bombing and assassination campaign to eliminate key leaders of the TULF and other government-supportive parties. In August the government again declared a nationwide state of emergency, thereby permitting it, under the constitution, to cancel elections scheduled for late August in five provinces.

In January 1999 the PA won a majority in the North-Western Provincial Council election, wresting control from the UNP. Two days later the Supreme Court censured President Kumaratunga for having illegally postponed the August 1998 elections; polling in the five provinces, held in April, saw the PA uniformly finish ahead of the UNP, which had previously controlled four of the five councils. In June the voters in Southern Province also went to the polls, with the PA again besting the UNP. The 1999 local elections had, however, collectively confirmed the JVP as the country's third most influential party.

In October 1999 President Kumaratunga called an early presidential election with a year left in her term. A suicide bombing three days before the balloting killed 26 individuals and wounded many others, including the president, who won reelection with 51.1 percent of the vote and was sworn in for a second term. She again named her mother as prime minister.

In early November 1999 the LTTE had initiated its latest military campaign, "Unceasing Waves III," which within five days had cost the government ten towns, including, once again, Mankulam. The offensive constituted the most sustained operation ever by the insurgents. In April 2000 the LTTE forced some 17,000 government troops to retreat northward from the strategic causeway at Elephant Pass, severing the army's land connection to the south. On May 3 President Kumaratunga invoked, for the first time in the country's history, the Public Security Ordinance, which placed the country on a war footing. She also banned strikes and political demonstrations and imposed strict media censorship. Although the LTTE moved to within several kilometers of Jaffna city and also launched an assault in the east, around Batticaloa, the offensive stalled in June.

In February 2000 the government had confirmed that Norway was prepared to act as a mediator in direct talks with the LTTE. The Tamil Tigers insisted, however, on several preconditions, principally that government forces be withdrawn from the north and east and restricted to barracks during the discussions. The government refused. Meanwhile, the resurgent JVP questioned Norway's neutrality and demonstrated against its involvement in the peace process. Staunch Sinhalese Buddhists, including hundreds of monks, also were taking to the streets, demanding that the government achieve a military victory over the separatists and accusing Norway of giving LTTE leaders a safe haven.

In August 2000 the government introduced a long-delayed, controversial constitutional reform bill in Parliament that had already been rejected by the UNP and all the main Tamil parties. The bill's provisions included devolving powers to seven elected provincial councils and establishing an interim appointed council for a North-East region, with the final status of the latter jurisdiction dependent on whether the multiethnic population in the east approved a future referendum on union with the north. The government quickly acknowledged, however, that it could not marshal the needed two-thirds parliamentary majority to pass the 31-chapter bill and therefore withdrew it. Ten days later President Kumaratunga dissolved Parliament in preparation for a general election.

Octogenarian Prime Minister Bandaranaike resigned for health reasons on August 10, 2000, and was replaced by the minister for public administration and home affairs, Ratnasiri WICKREMANAYAKE. The retired prime minister died shortly after casting her ballot in the general election of October 10, which saw the PA capture 107 seats in the 225-member Parliament. Six seats short of a majority, the PA quickly negotiated a coalition with the National Unity Alliance (an affiliate of the PA-supportive SLMC), the Tamil-based Eelam People's Democratic Party (EPDP), and an independent deputy, which permitted Prime Minister Wickremanayake to remain in office.

On November 27, 2000, the LTTE leader, Velupillai PRABHAKARAN, reversed his stance and called for unconditional peace talks. In December the LTTE initiated a month-long unilateral cease-fire but the government rejected the overture. Despite cease-fire extensions into April 2001, as well as the efforts of Norwegian negotiator Erik Solheim, at midyear the two sides appeared no closer to peace negotiations.

On June 20, 2001, President Kumaratunga dismissed SLMC leader Rauff HAKEEM from the cabinet, leading Hakeem and 6 other MPs from the SLMC to defect to the opposition. The loss cost the PA-led coalition its parliamentary majority and left the president's administration subject to a vote of no confidence. On July 10 the president suspended Parliament until September to avoid that consequence, and then on September 5 the PA announced a formal agreement with the JVP that restored the government majority's to 119 parliamentary seats. Although the JVP remained outside the reshuffled cabinet, it won a number of policy concessions, including an end to further moves toward Tamil autonomy, a halt to privatizations, a major reduction in the size of the cabinet, and loan relief for farmers. The pact was severely criticized by the TULF and other Tamil parties and ultimately served only to postpone the government's collapse.

On October 10, 2001, 13 PA legislators, including S. B. DISSANAYAKE, secretary general of the president's own SLFP, defected to the opposition. With a no-confidence motion looming, Kumaratunga dissolved Parliament and called a general election for December 5, only 14 months after the previous election. This latest setback also brought to an end the president's effort to hold a referendum on a new constitution, which had been scheduled for mid-October. Meanwhile, in a daring raid on July 24 an LTTE assault team had attacked the country's principal international airport and an adjoining military air base, causing an estimated $400 million in damages. Although all 13 LTTE assailants were killed, the attack constituted a major blow to the administration and also harmed an ailing economy.

With much of the public having turned against President Kumaratunga's increasingly hard-line stance toward the LTTE, the UNP surged ahead during a violence-plagued campaign, and in the December 2001 parliamentary election it captured a plurality of 109 seats, compared to the PA's 77. As a consequence, Prime Minister Wickremanayake handed in his resignation, and Kumaratunga was forced to turn to her longtime foe, the UNP's Wickremesinghe, to form a new cabinet. The UNP leader quickly established a majority coalition, dubbed the United National Front (UNF), with the SLMC, which had won 5 seats, and also secured the external support of the TULF-led Tamil National Alliance (TNA). The bulk of the new cabinet was sworn in on December 12, with most remaining appointments then being made in February 2002. The president was forced to surrender the defense and finance portfolios she had held in the preceding cabinet.

Although the LTTE had launched a series of attacks to coincide with induction of the Wickremesinghe cabinet, it declared a unilateral cease-fire from December 24. The government reciprocated, reiterating, over the president's objections, its intention to open negotiations with the LTTE. Wide public relief, if not unanimous acclaim, greeted the announcement on February 22, 2002, of an indefinite cease-fire. The first direct government-LTTE talks in seven years were launched on September 16–18 in Thailand under Norwegian sponsorship, with the principals quickly reaching agreement on formation of a joint committee on security and a joint task force on reconstruction. An estimated 65,000 people had been killed since the beginning of the Tamil conflict.

Through early February 2003 four additional negotiating sessions were held at various locations, but on April 21 the LTTE announced its withdrawal from further talks, citing the government's unwillingness to put establishment of an interim administration for Tamil areas at the top of the agenda. It also complained of too little progress on reconstruction and rehabilitation. Meanwhile, President Kumaratunga continued to assert that Prime Minister Wickremesinghe was conceding too much to the LTTE; she insisted that a political settlement should be concluded only after the LTTE disarmed—a proposition that the LTTE labeled as "suicidal." She further insisted that the LTTE disband the Black Tigers squad of suicide bombers and fulfill its pledge to end the induction of child soldiers.

On November 4, 2003, during a visit by Prime Minister Wickremesinghe to Washington, President Kumaratunga suspended Parliament for two weeks and dismissed three key ministers, taking over the defense, interior, and mass communications portfolios herself. In response to the resultant governmental crisis, on November 14 Norway withdrew from its role as mediator of the peace process, although it left its Sri Lanka Monitoring Mission in place to continue supervising the cease-fire.

In January 2004 the SLFP and the JVP concluded an alliance, and on February 7 Kumaratunga dissolved Parliament and called an election for April 2. The multiparty United People's Freedom Alliance (UPFA, successor to the PA) won 105 seats to 82 for the UNP, and on April 6 the popular SLFP parliamentary leader, Mahinda RAJAPAKSE, was sworn in as prime minister. Although the UPFA remained 8 seats short of a parliamentary majority, Rajapakse won the external support of the newly organized Buddhist National Heritage Party (*Jathika Hela Urumaya*—JHU), which had won an unexpected 9 seats. It took the UPFA government until September 10, 2004, to cement a legislative majority, by bringing in an erstwhile UNP ally, the Ceylon Workers' Congress (CWC). Earlier, an MP from the SLMC had defected to the government, and in late October three additional members of the SLMC joined the government as noncabinet ministers.

The coalition government lost its legislative majority on June 15, 2005, when the JVP withdrew in opposition to the inclusion of Tamil separatist organizations in the distribution of international aid following the 2004 Indian Ocean tsunami. In a further blow to the UPFA, Foreign Minister Lakshman KADIRGAMAR, the government's senior ethnic Tamil, was assassinated by an unidentified gunman on August 12, 2005. The Supreme Court ruled on August 26, 2005, that President Kumaratunga's second term would expire in December 2005—not a year later to compensate for the year lost by the early election of December 1999. With the incumbent prohibited from seeking a third term, the presidential election was contested by Prime Minister Rajapakse, the UNP's Ranil Wickremesinghe, and 11 other minor candidates, several of whom withdrew at the last minute. Rajapakse had won the endorsement of the JVP and JHU by agreeing to support a unitary state rather than broad provincial or regional autonomy, to end privatization of state-run companies, and to renegotiate the terms of the cease-fire with the LTTE. On November 17 Rajapakse won 50.3 percent of the vote versus 48.4 percent for Wickremesinghe, who almost certainly lost because of a low voter turnout among Tamils following an expression of "disinterest" in the outcome by the LTTE and its political partner, the TNA. Sworn in as president on November 19, Rajapakse named Ratnasiri Wickremanayake as prime minister.

The JVP's external support remained vital to the Rajapakse administration until late January 2007, when 18 UNP legislators crossed the aisle. In the interim, the CWC and the Up-Country People's Front (UCPF) had joined the government. On January 28 President Rajapakse announced a greatly expanded cabinet, which included 10 new UNP ministers as well as the leader of the SLMC. Two days later, the JHU agreed to accept its first cabinet post. In December, however, the SLMC withdrew because of what it considered lack of progress on Muslim issues.

In balloting for the Eastern Province regional council in May 2008, the Tamil People's Liberation Party (*Tamileela Makkal Viduthalai Pulikal*—TMVP), a progovernment Tamil group that is part of the UPFA, won 20 of the council's 37 seats. The government claimed the victory was a rejection of the LTTE and a mandate for its policies.

In January 2009 government forces captured most of the remaining LTTE strongholds and forced the rebels into a remote region of the northeast. In February 2009, the UPFA swept provincial elections in the North-Western and Central provinces. The UPFA continued its electoral success in April when it won elections for the Western Province. Government forces defeated the last significant LTTE units in May 2009 and killed Prabhakaran, effectively ending the organized Tamil insurgency (see Current issues, below).

Ahead of parliamentary balloting scheduled for 2010, the UNP relaunched its electoral alliance, the United National Front (UNF), including the SLMC and a dozen smaller parties. In November General Sarath FONSEKA, the military commander who had led the forces that defeated the LTTE, announced his resignation. Fonseka subsequently launched a campaign ahead of presidential elections, which had been called for 22 months early (see Current issues, below). In the balloting on January 26, 2010, Rajapakse was reelected with 57.9 percent of the vote, and Fonseka placed second with 40.2 percent. There were 20 other candidates, none of whom received more than 1 percent of the vote. After the election Fonseka emerged as the leader of the new opposition grouping, the Democratic National Alliance (DNA).

In legislative elections on April 8, the UPFA won a significant victory, increasing its number of seats in the 225-member parliament to 144, six votes short of the two-thirds majority necessary to amend the constitution. The UNF secured 60 seats; the TNA, 14, and the DNA, 7. Disanayaka Mudiyanselage JAYARATNE was appointed prime minister of a new UPFA government on April 22. On November 22, Rajapakse appointed a reshuffled and enlarged 58-member cabinet.

On March 17, 2011, the ruling coalition won local balloting, securing a majority of 205 of the 234 municipal councils. In local elections, from October 8–23, the UPFA won 21 of 23 councils. In September 2012, the UPFA won majorities in provincial three councils where elections were held, securing 63 of 114 contested seats. In January 2013 Rajapakse reshuffled and expanded the cabinet. In August a new ministry for law and order was created from the ministry of defense. In November a ministry of special projects was established.

Former health minister Maithripala SIRISENA temporarily defected from the SLFP to lead the opposition New Democratic Front—NDF (*Nava Prajathantravadi Peramuna*) in presidential balloting on January 8, 2015. Sirisena won with 51.3 percent of the vote, and Rajapakse received 47.6 percent. Sirisena was sworn in on January 9. Former prime minister Wickremesinghe was reappointed to his old post. He named a reshuffled, expanded cabinet on March 22 that included the pro-Sirisena members of the SLFP.

On August 17, 2015, assembly elections were held in which the UNP-led United National Front for Good Governance—UNFGG (*Eksath Yahapalana Jathika Peramuna*), a revised version of the UNF, won 106 seats, while the UPFA secured 95. Although short of a majority, the UNP secured support from the Sirisena wing of the SLFP to form a working coalition. Wickremesinghe was reappointed on August 21 to lead a unity government led by the UNP, but including members of the SLFP and smaller parties.

Constitution and government. In May 1972, under the country's second constitution since independence, Ceylon was redesignated the Republic of Sri Lanka. Under the present constitution (adopted August 16, 1978, as a codification and enlargement of a series of constitutional amendments approved October 20, 1977), the name was further changed to Democratic Socialist Republic of Sri Lanka, and a British-style parliamentary structure was abandoned in favor of a "Gaullist" presidential-parliamentary system. The most visible feature of the present system is the concentration of powers in a "strong" president who serves a renewable five-year term (a September 2010 constitutional amendment removed a two-term limit on the presidency, but the limitation was restored through a constitutional amendment in April 2015 that also reduced the term of office to five years from six; see Current issues, below). The president appoints a prime minister and, in consultation with the latter, other senior administrative officials, the only restriction being that all ministers and deputy ministers must hold legislative seats. Should Parliament reject an appropriations bill or approve a no-confidence motion, the president may appoint a new government.

The legislative term is five years, subject to presidential dissolution. A constitutional amendment passed in August 1983 requires all members of parliament to take an oath of loyalty to the unified state of Sri Lanka and bans all activity advocating "the division of the state."

Judges of the Supreme Court and the Court of Appeal are appointed by the president. Courts of first instance include a High Court, which tries criminal cases, and district courts. A presidentially appointed parliamentary commissioner for administration (ombudsman) investigates complaints of wrongdoing by public officials.

In September 2001 parliament passed legislation authorizing creation of a Constitutional Council that has as part of its mandate naming independent commissions with responsibilities over police, the judiciary, public servants, and elections.

Prior to 1988 the country was divided into nine provinces, each with an appointed governor and elected Development Council. In November 1987 a constitutional amendment provided for the election of substantially more autonomous provincial councils, each headed by a chief minister. The amendment also authorized the president to merge the Northern and Eastern Provinces, a long-sought objective of their Tamil inhabitants. President Jayawardene implemented the change in September 1988. A North-East provincial government was temporarily installed, but the continuing civil strife rendered the merger moot by the early 1990s. (In October 2006 the Supreme Court ruled the merger unconstitutional.) Further devolutionary measures, approved in January 1988, called for a network of district councils (*pradeshiya sabhas*) throughout the country. Municipalities have urban or town councils, while rural areas are administered by elected village councils.

The 1978 constitution guarantees free speech and publication, but these and other rights are "subject to such restrictions as may be presented by law." "Restrictions" have been enforced to maintain racial and religious harmony, national security, and public order and welfare. As a consequence, varying degrees of censorship and other forms of media control prevail. In particular, the government periodically banned news coverage of military operations against the Tamil Tigers. In February 2009 the British Broadcasting Service stopped providing news stories to the Sri Lankan national broadcasting service because of continuing censorship. In 2011 Sri Lanka refused entry to Frank La Rue, a UN envoy tasked to promote freedom of expression. In 2016 Reporters Without Borders ranked Sri Lanka 141th out of 180 countries in press freedom (see Current issues, below).

Foreign relations. Sri Lanka has long maintained a nonaligned position in world politics despite its membership in the Commonwealth and a mutual defense agreement that grants the United Kingdom the right to maintain naval and air bases, as well as land forces, on its territory. While the Jayawardene government stressed Sri Lanka's economic similarity and cultural affinity with Southeast Asia, the country's application for admission to the Association of Southeast Asian Nations (ASEAN) was rejected in 1982 on geographical grounds. The action helped to precipitate the 1985 launching of the South Asian Association for Regional Cooperation (SAARC), of which Sri Lanka was a founding member.

The island state's major foreign policy problems since independence have involved relations with India. Conflicting claims to Kachchativu Island in the Palk Strait, which separates the two countries, were resolved in 1974; India yielded its claim, and Sri Lanka agreed to permit Indian fishermen and pilgrims easy access to the island. The Palk Strait accord was supplemented in 1976 by a general agreement on maritime economic zones. At the end of 1998 New Delhi and Colombo signed a trade agreement designed to phase out most tariffs and to facilitate trade, investment, and development.

Much more explosive has been the situation involving Sri Lanka's Tamil dissidents, who have strong ties to some 50 million Tamils in southern India. As ethnic violence on the island escalated, relations between Colombo and New Delhi became strained, largely because of the use of Indian territory as a refuge and staging area by Tamil guerrilla groups. By 1986 local authorities in the Indian state of Tamil Nadu were becoming increasingly disenchanted with the LTTE presence, and the rebels transferred most of their operations to Sri Lanka's Jaffna area. In addition, New Delhi and Colombo concluded a treaty in mid-1987 under which Indian troops attempted a peacekeeping role in Sri Lanka, although the accord ultimately became a political liability for both governments, and the troops were withdrawn in March 1990 (see Political background). In 1995 the Indian government again attempted to come to its neighbor's aid by setting up the equivalent of a naval quarantine around Sri Lanka's northern coast, thereby depriving the rebels of easy access to supply bases in Tamil Nadu. Since then, Indian support has been less direct. The breakdown of the cease-fire in 2006–2007 generated renewed interest on the part of many Sri Lankans, including many Tamils, for Indian mediation.

In 1997 the United States announced that it had added the LTTE to its list of terrorist organizations. The European Union (EU) did likewise in May 2006, which prompted the LTTE to demand the removal of the European members of the five-country, 57-person Sri Lanka Monitoring Mission (SLMM), which had been established in 2002 to assist with the cease-fire.

In 2007 Brazil announced that it was reopening its mission to Sri Lanka after a 40-year absence. The move was a reflection of increasing commercial ties between the two countries.

In April 2008 Sri Lanka signed six new commercial agreements with Iran, including an arrangement whereby Iran pledged $1.9 billion in loans and grants to increase Sri Lanka's energy output. Through the year, the government continued to reject calls for the establishment of a UN human rights office in the country.

A continuing government offensive in 2009 was condemned by a number of foreign governments, including the United States, members of the EU, and India. International offers to mediate the conflict were rebuffed by both the government and the LTTE, which refused to lay down its weapons as a precondition to negotiations.

The government expelled UNICEF official James Elder on September 6, 2009, after he criticized the government's management of Tamil internment camps. In October India offered Sri Lanka $100 million to resettle displaced Tamils. The next month, 21 Tamils, including French LTTE leader Nadaraja MATINTHIRAN, were convicted in Paris of illegally providing funds to the LTTE. In addition, the Tamil Coordinating Committee in France (CCTF) was designated a terrorist group and ordered dissolved.

In February 2010 the EU suspended Sri Lanka's participation in a preferential economic program because of what the body described as the government's "failure" to abide by basic human rights standards. In February 2011, 25 Indian vessels and 136 crewmen were arrested by Sri Lankan naval forces for illegally fishing in Sri Lankan waters. The ships and crewmembers were released two days later following the intervention of the Indian government. Reports that the Sri Lankan navy killed two Indian fishermen prompted an accord between the two countries that pledged no force would be used against fishing vessels.

In January 2012 India's foreign minister visited Sri Lanka for the first time since November 2010. Bilateral agreements on transportation, communications, and education were signed during the visit. In August, Sri Lanka and Swaziland signed a series of economic cooperation accords. Meanwhile, as part of a broader effort to expand its diplomatic influence, Sri Lanka announced that it would open diplomatic relations with 13 nations in the Caribbean and Latin America (the country had formal ties with 20 of the region's 33 countries).

On September 3–4, 2012, 150 Sri Lankan Christian pilgrims were attacked in Tamil Nadu state in India by pro-Tamil activists. Sri Lanka evacuated the pilgrims amidst rising tensions with India. China, Japan, and India increased foreign aid to an estimated $1.4 billion for 2012, with $920 million from China alone.

India cancelled annual security talks with Sri Lanka in March 2013. Also in March, the government negotiated a $510 million, 40-year, infrastructure loan from Japan. In July the United States threatened to reduce development aid to Sri Lanka by 20 percent over concerns about human rights. Sri Lanka launched negotiations with China and Japan on free trade agreements in 2013.

Concerns over media freedom and human rights led to considerable controversy over the decision of the commonwealth heads of state to meet in Sri Lanka in November 2013. The government issued a series of assurances that journalists would have complete freedom to cover the sessions. Nonetheless, several commonwealth leaders, including Prime Minister Stephen Harper of Canada, boycotted the meeting.

Following negotiations in January 2014, 160 Sri Lankan and 236 Indian fishermen were released after being detained for operating in the other country's territorial waters. In order to avoid future incidents, the two countries agreed to establish a joint committee on fishing. In March the UN Human Rights Council (UNHRC) voted to launch an investigation into potential human rights abuses by both sides in Sri Lanka's lengthy civil war. The government rejected the investigation and promised not to cooperate with the UNHRC. In September the government announced it would sign an extradition treaty with Russia in what was reported to be a sign of increasingly close ties between the two countries.

Following his election, President Sirisena made a state visit to India in February 2015 in an effort to enhance relations between the two nations after ties deteriorated under his predecessor. While in India, the president signed new cooperation agreements on security, trade, and energy. Tensions over Indian fishing in Sri Lankan territorial waters remained high. In May Sri Lanka rejected a proposal to allow Indians to fish in the country's maritime territory for 65 days a year.

During a visit by Pakistani prime minister Nawaz Sharif in January 2016, eight economic and security agreements were signed, including a deal whereby Sri Lanka would purchase eight JF-17 fighter aircraft from Pakistan; India objected to the purchase. In May the IMF announced a $1.5 billion loan to Sri Lanka (see Current issues, below).

Current issues. In May 2006 Swedish negotiator Ulf Henricsson asserted that the four-year-old cease-fire between the government and the LTTE had become a "low-intensity war," and by August 21, when the SLMM withdrew from Jaffna and Trincomalee to Colombo, no objective observer could characterize what was happening—ground assaults, sea battles, air strikes, suicide bombings—as anything remotely resembling a cease-fire. LTTE and government representatives met in Geneva, Switzerland, on February 22–23, 2006, to discuss the escalation in cease-fire violations, but a second round of talks scheduled for April 24–25 was canceled because the Sri Lankan navy had denied sea access to eastern LTTE leaders. In early August both sides accused the other of responsibility for the latest atrocity in the conflict: the execution in Muttur of 17 Tamils who were working for the French aid agency Action Against Hunger (*Action Contre le Faim*). Later in the month, an air strike by government forces killed some 60 Tamil schoolgirls, while in mid-October an LTTE suicide bomber attacked a military convoy and killed nearly 100 people. A further effort on October 28–29 to restart peace talks concluded without an agreement. Also in October, President Rajapakse and the UNP's Wickremesinghe signed a memorandum of understanding that called for cooperation on a range of issues, including the LTTE, electoral reform, and good governance. The agreement proved to be short-lived after 18 UNP legislators defected to the government in January 2007.

The Tamil conflict continued unabated into 2007. In March the LTTE used at least one light aircraft to launch its first-ever bombing run (against an airport), but the Sri Lankan Army was gradually gaining ground. In July the army claimed to have full control of the east and was pressing ahead in the north. At the same time, reports continued to surface about what Human Rights Watch termed "shocking abuses" of human rights by the military.

The government ended a 2002 cease-fire and launched a major offensive against the LTTE in January 2008. By November, 172 security forces had been killed and 1,122 wounded, and losses among the LTTE were reported to be close to 2,000 killed or wounded. Meanwhile, on April 6 the minister for highway and road development was killed by a suicide bomber affiliated with LTTE near Colombo. The attack also killed 12 others and wounded more than 100. Three weeks later, another suicide bomber killed 24 and injured 40 on a bus in Colombo; subsequent attacks continued through the spring and summer. In June security forces began the forced mass relocation of Tamils living in Colombo. At least 370 ethnic Tamils were removed by security forces before a court order halted the deportations. The renewed fighting left an estimated 300,000 civilians displaced and at least 250,000 trapped in the combat zone. Meanwhile, the UN reported that at least 6,000 civilians had been killed and 14,000 wounded since the offensive began. Also in June, heavy monsoons killed at least 20 and displaced more than 350,000.

In May 2009 government forces captured the last remaining LTTE stronghold in the Mullaitavu district. On May 19 government forces announced that Prabhakaran; his son and heir, Charles Anthony; and other senior LTTE leaders were killed in the final fighting. Even after the formal defeat of the LTTE, sporadic attacks continued against government figures and facilities by Tamil separatist groups. Also in May, the government revealed a plan to resettle up to 80 percent of the 260,000 Tamils held in refugee camps by the end of the year and announced that it would fully implement the Thirteenth Amendment to the country's constitution, which devolves political power to local and regional governments.

In October 2009 the government reported that it had resettled more than 130,000 of the estimated 260,000 displaced Tamils. Meanwhile, the EU and the U.S. State Department accused the Sri Lankan government of numerous human rights violations against civilians during the final campaign against the LTTE. The government rejected the accusations. After the defeat of the LTTE, Rajapakse called for early presidential elections to capitalize on his popularity.

Rajapakse easily won reelection as president in January 2010, defeating opposition candidate and former general Sarath Fonseka, who placed second in the polling. Fonseka was supported by the major opposition parties, including the TNA, the UNP, and the People's Liberation Front (JVP). Fonseka was subsequently arrested on February 8 as part of a sweep that included the arrests of more than 40 people on charges of conspiracy and treason. Most of those detained were members of the military. The arrests prompted widespread protests. Although still in detention and awaiting trial, Fonseka was elected a member of parliament in April. The president's brother Chamal RAJAPAKSE, was subsequently elected speaker of the parliament, while another brother, Basil RAJAPAKSE, was appointed minister of economic development.

In May the government lifted about half of the state of emergency restrictions that had been in place for 27 years because of the LTTE insurgency. Demonstrations against the UN prompted the world body to close its main office in Sri Lanka in July. Protestors objected to the creation of a UN panel to investigate abuses against Tamil civilians in 2009. Also in July additional charges of embezzlement and illegal arms trafficking were filed against Fonseka. He was convicted in September of engaging in political activities while still a member of the military and sentenced to three years in prison. (In January 2011 the Supreme Court rejected an appeal by Fonseka.)

The UN issued a report on April 25, 2011, that criticized both sides for civilian deaths during the civil war, but the Sri Lankan Army was blamed for the majority of casualties. The report recommended an investigation of war crimes. The Sri Lankan government rejected the findings. On May 30 the police fired on striking workers in Colombo, wounding more than 250. The incident prompted the resignation of the head of the national police, Gen. Mahinda Balasuriya. On August 25 Rajapakse ended the state of emergency that had been in place off and on since the start of the civil war. The measures gave security forces wide powers of arrest and detention.

On January 22, 2012, the government expelled 161 foreign Muslim clerics who were accused of promoting radical Islam. In March the UN Human Rights Council (UNHRC) passed a resolution calling for Sri Lanka to launch an independent investigation of human rights violations during the civil war. On May 21 Fonseka was released after pledging not to seek political office for seven years. In September the main camp for displaced Tamils was closed, following the release of the remaining 1,160 persons.

In March 2013 reports indicated that a new Sinhalese grouping, the Buddhist Strength Force (*Bodu Bala Sena*—BBS), had carried out a number of attacks on Christians and Muslims.

In June 2013 police closed the offices of two internet news sites and arrested nine journalists after charging that the media outlets presented "false and malicious reports." The government subsequently dismissed concerns expressed by the United States and the European Union over intimidation of the media. Security forces opened fire on protestors on August 1, killing 6 and injuring 50 during a peaceful demonstration against water pollution in Weliweriya. Local elections were held on September 21, 2013, in the war-torn Northern Province for the first time in 25 years. The TNA won 30 of 38 seats on the region's provincial council.

Buddhists attacked two Christian churches in Hikkaduwa on January 12, 2014. Security officials later arrested 24 individuals for their roles in the violence. In March, prominent human rights activist Jeyakumari BALENDRAN was arrested and charged with harboring a criminal. Opponents of the regime decried the arrest as retaliation for Balendran's campaign to highlight those who disappeared during the civil war. Two other dissidents were subsequently detained when they launched an investigation into Balendran's arrest.

In April security forces killed three men who they charged were endeavoring to relaunch the LTTE in Nedunkerni. In June, DNA tests linked Sampath VIDANAPATHIRANA, an SLFP member and the head of the local government in Tangalle, to the murder of a British tourist and the concurrent gang rape of the victim's girlfriend in 2011.

In March 2015 newly elected president Maithripala Sirisena announced the formation of a national committee to investigate allegations of war crimes during the country's civil war. On April 28 parliament, on a vote of 215–1, with 1 abstention, ratified the 19th amendment, which, in effect, overturned the 18th amendment of 2010. The new amendment restored the two-term limit for the presidency and established a five-year term of office, previously a six-year term. A constitutional court was reestablished and the powers of the presidency were reduced. Henceforth, the president was required to consult with the prime minister on cabinet nominations, and the authority to dissolve parliament was constrained. Sirisena had campaigned on pledges to limit presidential power.

The 2017 budget, approved in December 2016, raised taxes, including a hike in the VAT from 11 percent to 15 percent. The tax increases were an effort to reduce the government deficit from 6.7 percent of GDP to 5.4 percent, with an eventual target of 3.5 percent in 2020, in line with conditions of a $1.5 billion IMF loan. There were also increases on medical taxes and utilities, and the government initiated a privatization plan, including the sale of the national airline.

POLITICAL PARTIES AND GROUPS

Government Parties:

United National Front—UNF (*Eksath Jathika Peramuna*). Formed in October 2009, the UNF was a revival of an electoral alliance launched in 2001. Led by the UNP, the UNF included the SLMC, the mainly **Tamil Democratic People's Front** (DPF) and a dozen smaller parties. The UNF backed opposition candidate Fonseka in the January 2010 presidential balloting. In the April 2010 parliamentary balloting, the UNF placed second with 29.3 percent of the vote and 60 seats in the 225-member parliament. The constituent parties did not campaign as a coalition in the 2011, 2012, or 2013 local and regional balloting. Ahead of the January 2015 presidential elections, members of the front campaigned under the banner of the **New Democratic Front**—NDF (*Nava Prajathantravadi Peramuna*) to support the candidacy of Maithripala Sirisena of the SLFP. Sirisena won the balloting with 52.3 percent of the vote. For the August 2015 parliamentary polling, the UNF was reconstituted as the **United National Front for Good Governance**—UNFGG (*Eksath Yahapalana Jathika Peramuna*), led by Wickremesinghe and the UNP. The grouping was first, with 45.7 percent of the vote and 106 seats. Wickremesinghe was subsequently appointed prime minister of a coalition government.

Leader: Ranil WICKREMESINGHE (Prime Minister).

United National Party—UNP (*Ekshat Jathika Pakshaya*). A democratic-socialist party founded in 1946, the UNP advocates a moderate line and the avoidance of a narrowly "communal" posture. Having survived virtual annihilation as a legislative force in 1970, the party swept 142 of 168 assembly seats in 1977 and remained in power by subsequent extension of the parliamentary term to 1989. It won 125 of 225 seats in the 1989 election. From 1978 until 1989 the UNP's Junius R. Jayewardene served as executive president of Sri Lanka.

The UNP finished second in 1994 with 94 of 225 seats, including 7 won by members of the CWC, who ran on the UNP ticket but subsequently announced that they would sit as progovernment independents. The party's initial choice as 1994 presidential candidate, Gamini Dissanayake, was assassinated less than three weeks before the November election, in which his widow, Srima, won 35.9 percent of the vote as his replacement. In the first half of 1999 the UNP uniformly finished second to the PA in elections for seven provincial councils, despite having won majorities in five of them in the previous provincial elections.

In November 1999 five members of parliament and two dozen or so other elected officials announced their break from the UNP leadership over the party's lack of support for constitutional reform. The MPs indicated that they would remain within the party but function independently. They also threatened a judicial challenge if the leadership formally expelled them, which it did. Two of the five were named to President Kumaratunga's cabinet as "special assignment" ministers.

UNP presidential candidate Ranil Wickremesinghe finished second in December 1999, with 42.6 percent of the vote. In the October 2000 parliamentary election the UNP won 89 seats on a 40 percent vote share. Three UNP dissidents received cabinet portfolios in the subsequent Wickremanayake government.

In the run-up to the December 2001 election, Wickremesinghe negotiated electoral alliances with the Sri Lanka Muslim Congress (SLMC), the recently formed four-party Tamil National Alliance (TNA, below), and the CWC. With the UNP having won 109 seats and 46 percent of the vote, Wickremesinghe formed a governing coalition with the SLMC, also brought the CWC leader into the cabinet, and obtained external support from the TNA.

In April 2004 the UNP and the CWC, running together as the **United National Front** (UNF), won 37.8 percent of the vote and 82 seats (74 claimed by the UNP). In November 2005 former prime minister Wickremesinghe once again lost the presidency, this time by only 2 percent of the vote.

In 2006 several MPs defect to the UPFA. At the same time, some party members voiced dissatisfaction with Wickremesinghe's continuing leadership. In January 2007 the UNP saw another 18 MPs, led by former deputy leader Karu JAYASURIYA, cross the aisle, with 10 being named to the cabinet and the others assuming lesser ministerial posts. Jayisuriya subsequently indicated that he intended to form a **Democratic Group** party. In 2008 the leader of the UNP's women's wing, Chandra WANNIARACHCHI, led an estimated 500 members of the UNP in a mass defection to the SLFP. Regional UNP leaders increasingly criticized party leaders and called for a reorganization to make the grouping more competitive. In July 2009 a court issued an order preventing the UNP from expelling party members that joined the UPFA government. Wickremesinghe declined to run for the presidency in 2010. He instead called on the party to support Fonseka. In September 2010 the UNP expelled six senior members for supporting an amendment to abolish the presidential term limit. In the March 2011 local elections, the UNP secured majorities in only nine councils, and it won one council in the October balloting.

Reports in July 2013 indicated a rift within the party between stalwarts and a faction led by Sajith PREMADASA. In 2014 a number of UNP members resigned over what they described as corruption within the party.

Leaders: Ranil WICKREMESINGHE (Prime Minister), Kabir HASHIM (General Secretary).

Sri Lanka Muslim Congress (SLMC). Formed in 1980, the SLMC declared itself a political party at a conference convened in 1986 to represent Muslim interests in the negotiations for a political settlement of the Tamil question. (For more on the early history of the party, see the 2014 *Handbook*.)

Party founder Mohamed H. M. ASHRAFF died in September 2000 in a helicopter crash. His widow, Ferial, was named to the cabinet, announced after the October election, as was her party coleader, Rauff Hakeem. Hakeem soon supplanted Ashraff within the SLMC, although she became the NUA leader.

In June 2001 President Kumaratunga removed Hakeem from the cabinet, at which time he and six other SLMC members of parliament abandoned the government, thereby costing it its legislative majority. Ashraff initially resigned her cabinet post but continued her support for the government. She resumed her ministerial position in early July, leaving the SLMC/NUA asunder. Following the December 2001 election, in which the SLMC won five seats, Hakeem negotiated a coalition agreement with the UNP and joined the new cabinet. Ashraff's NUA had remained with the PA. Subsequent efforts to resolve their differences did not succeed. In 2002–2003, the party splintered further, largely over the perception of a faction led by A. L. M. Athaullah that the UNP government was favoring the LTTE at the expense of eastern Muslims (see NC, above).

For the April 2004 general election, the SLMC ran independently, capturing five parliamentary seats. In May one SLMC MP defected to the UPFA, and three others did likewise in October, for which the three were named noncabinet ministers responsible for rehabilitation and development in three Tamil districts. The SLMC leadership attempted to expel the three but was overruled by the Supreme Court.

The SLMC supported the UNP's Ranil Wickremesinghe in the 2005 presidential contest. In 2006, however, it announced that it would extend issue-based support to the government, and in January 2007 Hakeem brought the SLMC back into the government, only to withdraw on December 12 because of insufficient progress on Muslim-related issues. In 2008 a faction of the party, led by M. Lalith GUNARATNE, announced that they would support the government at the local and regional level and rejected Hakeem's call for noncooperation. In 2009 several leading SLMC figures were reported to have left the party and joined the NC. The SLMC broke with other parties in the UNF and supported the constitutional amendment that abolished presidential term limits. In local balloting in March 2011, the SLMC gained majorities in just 4 out of 234 councils. It won a majority in 1 additional council in October.

In September 2012 the SLMC agreed to join with the UFPA to establish a coalition government for the Eastern Province.

The SLMC defected from the UPFA-led government in December 2014 and supported Sirisena for the presidency in 2015, and then campaigned as part of the UNFGG in that year's parliamentary elections. The party did campaign separately from the UNFGG in two districts, winning one.

Leaders: Rauff HAKEEM (Minister of Justice), Basheer Cego DAWOOD (Chair), Hasan ALI (General Secretary).

Tamil Progressive Alliance (TPF). The TPF was a Tamil electoral alliance formed in June 2015 by the **Democratic People's**

Front (DPF), the **National Union of Workers** (NUW), and the Up-Country People's Front (UCPF, below).

Leader: Mano GANESAN.

Up-Country People's Front (UCPF). Representing Indian Tamil plantation workers, the UCPF was organized as an alternative to the CWC by former CWC member P. Chandrasekaran, who was elected to parliament as an independent in 1994 but aligned with the PA. (For more on the history of the party, see the 2014 *Handbook.*) The UCPF backed the UNP's Wickremesinghe for president in 2005 but shifted its support to the Rajapakse government in 2006. The party's leader has proposed the direct participation of India in settling the Tamil question, a call that Chandrasekaran repeated in 2008. The UCPF backed the UPFA in the 2010 legislative elections. It campaigned independently in the 2011 local balloting and 2013 and 2014 provincial balloting but participated in governing coalitions with the UPFA.

Leaders: Velusami RADHAKRISHNAN.

Democratic National Alliance (DNA). Formed in February 2010, the DNA was created by the JVP in an effort to bring together opposition parties to defeat the UPFA legislative balloting in April 2010. The DNA also served as a political vehicle for former general and opposition leader Fonseka, who was elected as a member of parliament. The JVP placed fourth in the balloting with 5.5 percent of the vote and 7 seats in the parliament. In 2013 Fonseka formed a new political grouping, the **Democratic Party** (DP) but continued to be affiliated with the DNA. The DP joined the UNFGG in February 2016, and Fonseka was given a cabinet post in the UNP-led government.

Leaders: Sarath FONSEKA, Vijitha HERATH (General Secretary).

National Heritage Party (*Jathika Hela Urumaya*—JHU). Launched in March 2004 with a platform that called for protecting Buddhism as the state religion, rooting out government corruption, and rejecting concessions to the Tamil Tigers, the JHU grew out of the strongly nationalist **Sinhalese Heritage** (*Sihala Urumaya*—SU). The SU was established in April 2000 on a similar platform that opposed concessions to Tamil militants, including any movement toward a federal state. In the October 2000 election the party won only one national list seat. An intraparty dispute over who should occupy the parliamentary seat led the SU president, S. L. GUNESEKARA, to resign and form the **Sinhala National Front** (*Sinhala Jathika Sangamaya*—SJS). In December 2001 the SU won under 0.6 percent of the vote and no seats in Parliament.

In the April 2004 election, the Buddhist JHU won an unexpected nine seats with 6 percent of the vote, after which it gave its external support to Prime Minister Rajapakse. Differences subsequently surfaced over whether the organization should abandon any future electoral role. The JHU supported Rajapakse in the 2005 presidential election. The JHU agreed to accept its first-ever cabinet post in January 2007.

In June 2008 the JHU announced a boycott of the All Party Representative Committee (APRC), a group formed to promote dialogue among the country's political parties. The JHU returned to the talks in August. The JHU was highly critical of international efforts to mediate the Tamil insurgency, and the party organized a series of protests outside of Western embassies in 2009 and petitioned for the UN to investigate human rights violations by the United States. The JHU campaigned with as part of the UPFA in the 2010 legislative elections and joined the subsequent government. At a 2011 party congress the JHU called for the government to undertake sterner measures to combat terrorism. In May 2013 a former JHU official committed suicide through self-immolation following his expulsion from the party.

Leaders: Katapola AMARAKITHTHI Thera (Chair), Patali Champika RANAWAKA (Minister of Technology and Research), Omalpe SOBHITHA (Secretary General).

Other parties in the UNF or the UNFGG include the **National Development Front** and the **Sri Lanka Freedom Party** (Mahajana Wing).

United People's Freedom Alliance (UPFA). The UPFA coalition was formed for the April 2004 parliamentary election primarily by the Sri Lanka Freedom Party (SLFP, below) and the People's Liberation Front (JVP, below). The UPFA was an expansion of the **People's Alliance** (PA; *Bahejana Nidasa Pakshaya*), formed as an SLFP-dominated coalition prior to the 1993 provincial elections. A number of the PA parties, but not the SLFP, had theretofore operated under the banner of the opposition United Socialist Alliance (USA), formed by Chandrika Kumaratunga in 1988 on the basis of her Sri Lanka People's Party (SLMP). In the 1993 elections the PA defeated the United National Party (UNP) in Western Province (including Colombo) while limiting the ruling party's majorities elsewhere. In August 1994 a broader coalition formed with the SLMC produced, with the support of minor parties, a parliamentary majority of one seat.

In the first half of 1999, the PA claimed victories in all seven provincial council elections, winning clear majorities in two, exactly half the seats in two others, and pluralities in three. In the October 10, 2000, parliamentary election the PA won 45 percent of the vote and 107 seats, 6 short of a majority, although President Kumaratunga quickly picked up sufficient support from the National Unity Alliance (NUA), the Tamil Eelam People's Democratic Party (EPDP), and an independent to form a governing coalition. In the December 2001 election the PA won only 37 percent of the national vote and 77 parliamentary seats.

Formation of the UPFA was announced in January 2004 by the SLFP and the JVP. On February 3 the National Liberation People's Party (DVJP), the NUA, the People's United Front (MEP), and the Sri Lanka People's Party (SLMP) announced their participation, as did the Lanka Equal Society Party (LSSP) and the Sri Lanka Communist Party (SLCP) two weeks later.

The participation of the JVP, which won 39 of the alliance's 105 seats, propelled the UPFA to 45.6 percent of the vote and a near-majority in the April 2004 parliamentary election. In July the UPFA also won victories in all six provinces that held elections. Sharp differences between the staunchly leftist JVP and other alliance parties persisted, however, especially over the terms of peace negotiations with the LTTE. In August President Kumaratunga resigned as alliance leader, reportedly because of differences with the JVP.

In June 2005 the JVP withdrew from the government, although it continued to provide external support. By late January 2007, however, President Rajapakse had brought several additional parties, including the Ceylon Workers' Congress (CWC) and the SLMC, plus defectors from the UNP, into the governing coalition and was therefore no longer dependent on JVP support. (For information on the defunct **Socialist People's Alliance** [SPA], see the 2012 *Handbook.*)

In July 2013 a UNP member of parliament and six other party officials defected to the UPFA. Also in July, Wasantha KUMARA, the UPFA member and chair of the Yatiyantota provincial council, was arrested on bribery charges. The UPFA won majorities on provincial councils of North-Western Province and Central Province in voting in September 2013.

In elections in March 2014, the UPFA retained majorities on the provincial councils in the Southern and Western Provinces. Prior to the 2015 presidential elections, health minister Maithripala SIRISENA (SLFP) announced he would run as the opposition candidate for the NDF. Sirisena defeated Rajapakse, and then led the UPFA in the August 2015 balloting in which the coalition won 95 seats. The SLFP then joined the UNP-led government, but not all members of the UPFA supported the unity cabinet.

Leaders: Maithripala SIRISENA (President of the Republic), Susil PREMAJAYANTHA (Secretary General).

Sri Lanka Freedom Party—SLFP (*Sri Lanka Nidahas Pakshaya*). Founded in 1951 and a leading advocate of republican status prior to adoption of the 1972 constitution, the SLFP initially advocated a neutralist foreign policy and the progressive nationalization of industry. Although winning a clear majority of seats in the House of Representatives in the election of 1970, it governed in coalition with the *Lanka Sama Samaja* and communist parties until September 1975. Its legislative representation plummeted from 90 seats to 8 in the election of July 1977.

In October 1980 former prime minister Sirimavo Bandaranaike was deprived of her civil rights for a seven-year period for alleged corruption while in office. She nevertheless remained active in party affairs, causing a split between her supporters and those of the nominal president, Maithripala SENANAYAKE. Mrs. Bandaranaike's rights were restored by means of a presidential "free pardon" issued on January 1, 1986, and she immediately launched a campaign for early general elections. In August the SLFP joined with some 20 groups, as well as prominent Buddhist leaders, in establishing the Movement for the Defense of the Nation (MDN) to oppose government policy that "conceded too much" on the Tamil question.

The party boycotted the 1988 provincial council elections but provided the main challenge to the United National Party (UNP) in subsequent presidential and legislative balloting. Mrs. Bandaranaike won nearly 45 percent of the December presidential vote, while the SLFP secured 67 parliamentary seats in February 1989.

In October 1993 Anura Bandaranaike, the former prime minister's son and theretofore leader of the opposition, withdrew from the party amid reports of a family power struggle, and subsequently joined the first Wickremesinghe administration. His departure opened the way for Mrs. Bandaranaike's younger daughter, Chandrika Kumaratunga, to assume a leading role in the SLFP-led PA and to become prime minister after the PA's electoral victory in August 1994. (Anura rejoined the SLFP prior to the December 2001 election.)

In October 2001 the SLFP general secretary, S. B. Dissanayake, was among the 13 PA defectors to the opposition, which precipitated the dissolution of Parliament. Following the PA's election loss in December, former prime minister Ratnasiri Wickremanayake, under pressure, resigned as leader of the opposition. In December 2004 Dissanayake was sentenced to two years in prison for defaming Supreme Court judges while he was SLFP general secretary.

In June 2006 President Rajapakse was elected party president, replacing former president Kumaratunga, who was resident in the United Kingdom. A year later, former foreign minister Mangala SAMARAWEERA, who had been removed from the cabinet in January 2007 after voicing policy differences with the president, announced formation of a breakaway **Sri Lanka Freedom Party–Mahagana** (SLFP-M), which quickly formed an alliance with the UNP.

In June 2008 it was reported that as many as 1,000 former members of the UNP and the JVP had defected and joined the SLFP. The SLFP led the UPFA coalition to 15 consecutive local and regional electoral victories from 2007 to 2009, through campaigns that emphasized the government's success in suppressing the LTTE. Two JVA leaders, Johnston FERNANDO and Indika BANDARANAYAKE, defected to the UPFA and were appointed to government posts in December 2009. In 2010 the **National Unity Alliance** (NUA) merged with the SLFP. (For more on the grouping, please see the 2012 *Handbook*.)

Rajapakse was reelected president in January 2010, and the UPFA received 60.3 percent of the vote in the April parliamentary balloting. The UPFA placed first in local balloting on March 17, 2011, securing 1,839 out of 3,036 seats in the local councils. It also won the second round of local elections in October with 51.9 percent of the vote.

In June 2013 the SLFP announced it supported amendments to the Thirteenth Amendment that critics argued would dilute the power of provincial councils. In August 2014 the party pledged to increase the number of women candidates in future elections. Maithripala SIRISENA was elected president of Sri Lanka in January 2015, and then party leader in March. The party joined the UNP-led government that month, and remained part of the coalition after the August parliamentary balloting, even though it had campaigned against in the UNP-led alliance in the polling. Reports have indicated a growing rift between the Sirisena and Rajapakse wings of the party.

Leaders: Maithripala SIRISENA (President of the Republic and of the Party), Mahinda RAJAPAKSE (Former President), Chandrika Bandaranaike KUMARATUNGA (Patron), Ratnasiri WICKREMANAYAKE (Former Prime Minister).

National Congress (NC). The NC, initially called the National Muslim Congress, was formed in 2004 by A. L. M. Athaullah, who had previously been a leader in the SLMC and a noncabinet minister under Prime Minister Wickremesinghe. In 2003, having criticized the government for favoring the LTTE and not addressing the needs of the eastern Muslim community, Athaullah and S. SUBAIRDEEN broke away from the SLMC and established the Ashraff Congress. In February 2004 Athaullah left the Ashraff Congress and allied himself with the UPFA, joining the cabinet under Prime Minister Rajapakse. The party adopted its present name in September 2005. Shortly thereafter, some of its original members, dissatisfied with the UPFA government, returned to the SLMC. However, reports in 2009 indicated that a number of SLMC members continued to defect to the NC. The NC was part of the UPFA in the 2010 legislative elections and party leader Athaullah was given a cabinet post in the subsequent UPFA government.

Leader: Ahamed Lebbe Marikkan ATHAULLAH (Minister of Local Government and Provincial Councils).

National Liberation People's Party (*Desha Vimukthi Janatha Pakshaya*—DVJP). Active nationally since 1988, the DVJP is a leftist group often linked to the SLCP, SLMP, and LSSP. The DVJP was one of the founding members of the SPA.

Leader: Ven Galagama DHAMMARANSI (Chair).

People's United Front (*Mahajana Eksath Peramuna*—MEP). The MEP, a left-wing party formed in 1956, was formerly allied with the JVP. Strongly Sinhalese and Buddhist, it long advocated the nationalization of foreign estates. In April 1999 it captured three legislative seats in Western Province and subsequently backed President Kumaratunga's reelection. Although it later protested against the government's proposed constitutional changes, the MEP joined the PA for the October 2000 general election. Its president was named transport minister in the reshuffled Wickremanayake cabinet.

In 2004 the MEP won two seats in the legislative balloting, and Dinesh Gunawardena was appointed to the Rajapakse cabinet, a status he retained under Prime Minister Wickremanayake. The MEP campaigned for the UPFA during regional balloting in 2008. However, it joined the JHU in boycotting all-party talks during the summer of 2008. The MEP was part of the UPFA in the 2010 parliamentary elections, and Gunawardena was given a cabinet post in the subsequent government. The MEP participated with the UPFA in provincial elections in 2012.

Leaders: Dinesh GUNAWARDENA (President of the Party and Minister of Water Supply and Drainage), Piyasena DISSANAYAKE (General Secretary).

Sri Lanka Communist Party—SLCP (*Sri Lankavay Komiyunist Pakshaya*). Founded in 1943, Sri Lanka's official Communist party consistently urged the nationalization of all banks, estates, and factories and the use of national languages rather than English. Initially, differences within the party membership prevented it from taking a clear position on Sino-Soviet relations, but subsequent trends yielded a strongly pro-Soviet posture. During 1976 the SLCP proposed a United Socialist Front with what it called the "centralized Left" in the SLFP. The initiative resulted in the formation in April 1977 of the United Left Front (ULF), comprising the SLCP, the LSSP, and the now-defunct People's Democratic Party (PDP); however, the ULF obtained no national state assembly seats in the July election. Briefly banned in 1983, the SLCP joined the SLFP in forming the USA in 1988 and then the PA in 1993. Longtime party leader Pieter KEUNEMAN died in 1997.

In May 2004, following the UPFA's victory at the polls, the SLCP secretary general, D. E. W. Gunasekera, was named minister for constitutional reforms. The SLCP helped create the SPA in 2006 and ran with the coalition in regional polling that year. It campaigned as part of the UPFA in 2010, and won two seats. Gunasekera was appointed to a cabinet post in the UPFA-led government and given another portfolio after the cabinet was reshuffled in 2010. Through 2013 the SLCP attempted to block efforts by the JVP to join the Communist International. The SLCP campaigned as part of the UPFA in the 2013 and 2014 provincial balloting.

Leaders: D. E. W. GUNASEKERA (Secretary General of the Party and Minister of Human Resources), Raja COLLURE.

Sri Lanka People's Party (*Sri Lanka Mahajana Pakshaya*—SLMP). The socialist SLMP was formed in 1984 by Vijaya KUMARATUNGA, a popular film star, and his wife, Chandrika Kumaratunga, who had left the SLMP because of policy differences and the leadership style of her brother, Anura Bandaranaike. Vijaya was assassinated in February 1988, apparently as part of a campaign by the JVP (below) to suppress support of the 1987 India–Sri Lanka Accord. After several years abroad, Chandrika returned to Sri Lanka, organized the USA, and ultimately assumed leadership of the SLFP.

The party's general secretary and USA presidential candidate in 1988, Ossie Abeygunasekera, was among those killed in the October 1994 bomb attack that also took the life of UNP presidential nominee Gamini Dissanayake. The SLMP participated in regional balloting in 2008 as part of the SPA. The SLMP was part of the UPFA in the 2010 parliamentary balloting, the 2011 local polling, as well as the 2012, 2013, and 2014 provincial elections.

Leader: Ranjith NAWARATNE (General Secretary).

Tamil People's Liberation Party (*Tamileela Makkal Viduthalai Pulikal*—TMVP). Formation of the TMVP was announced in October 2004 by Colonel Karuna, the former LTTE eastern commander who broke with the LTTE in March 2004 and quickly saw his forces, numbering some 6,000, bear the brunt of an LTTE offensive. Later in October, Karuna and the leaders of the long-dormant ENDLF announced formation of the TIVM front "to achieve the cherished rights and the reasonable aspirations" of Sri Lanka's Tamils. Since then, the Karuna breakaway group has continued to engage in open hostilities with the LTTE, amid indications that it was cooperating with the Sri Lankan military. In 2007 Karuna announced that the TMVP was prepared to enter parliamentary politics. The TMVP campaigned as part of the UPFA in provincial balloting in 2008 and won 20 of 37 seats in the Eastern regional council elections. Karuna was appointed minister of national reconciliation and integration in March 2009. In 2009 it was reported that many TMVP members had defected to join the SLFP. The TMVP contested local balloting in 2011 and 2012 with the UPFA. In September 2012 TMVP leader Sivanesathurai Chandrakanthan "Pillayan" was appointed as a presidential advisor.

Leaders: Sivanesathurai CHANDRAKANTHAN "Pillayan," P. PRASHANTHAN (General Secretary).

Ceylon Workers' Congress (CWC). Formed as part of the labor union movement in 1939, the CWC is a Tamil group that participated in formation of the Tamil United Liberation Front (TULF, below) in 1976. It regards itself as the main spokesperson for the Indian Tamils who work primarily as laborers on centrally located tea plantations. It has attempted to prevent their forging links with the Tamil insurgents in the north and east.

In 1994 the CWC elected seven members of parliament on the UNP list, but they subsequently withdrew to sit as a group of progovernment independents. In the April 1999 provincial elections, the party campaigned under the banner of the National Union of Workers (NUW) because of a legal dispute over use of the party symbol. In three provinces the NUW's support was sufficient to give the PA a working legislative majority.

The CWC's longtime president, Sauvmiamoothy THONDAMAN, died in 1999. He was succeeded as minister of livestock development and estate infrastructure by his grandson Arumugam.

In late August 2000 five MPs broke from the CWC over a leadership dispute and announced their support for the UNP. In September 2001 the party severed its ties to the PA and then negotiated an electoral pact with the UNP, but not before the original dissidents rejoined the PA as the Ceylon Workers' Alliance. Following the December 2001 election, Thondaman joined the new UNP-led cabinet.

In 2004 the CWC ran as the UNP's partner in the United National Front (UNF), winning eight parliamentary seats. Following the election, the CWC was courted by the UPFA, which needed eight seats to claim a majority. In early June the CWC leadership rejected joining the minority government, but in early September it offered its "unconditional full support," thereby giving the UPFA a parliamentary majority and earning a cabinet post. Less than a year later, however, in February 2005 the CWC threatened to resign from the government, which it accused of neglecting the needs of its Tamil constituency. Differences were patched up late in the month and the CWC remained in the government, but in October the party announced that it would support the UNP's Wickremesinghe for the presidency.

In August 2006 the CWC rejoined the government, which it had supported in the March 2006 local elections. It left again in August 2007 but returned in October. In regional balloting through the summer of 2008, the CWC did poorly and failed to win seats in previously secure districts. In April 2009 public officials in the CWC agreed to donate one month's salary to relief efforts among Tamils displaced by fighting between the government and the LTTE. The CWC remained part of the UPFA-led government after the 2010 legislative elections. Meanwhile, CWC member of parliament V. S. RADHAKRISHNAN left the party to join the Up-Country People's Front (UCPF), which was also a member of the UPFA. The CWC ran as part of the UPFA coalition in local balloting in March 2011 but joined a coalition with the UCPF and the small Democratic People's Front (DPF) for provincial balloting in July 2012.

Reports in February 2013 indicated that the Plantation Trade Union Federation had begun to attract members of the CWC. The CWC did not campaign as part of the UPFA in provincial balloting in 2014.

Leaders: Muthu SIVALINGAM, Arumugam THONDAMAN (General Secretary).

Lanka Equal Society Party (*Lanka Sama Samaja Pakshaya*—LSSP). Established in 1935 as a Trotskyite formation named the Ceylon Equal Society Party, the LSSP first entered into a coalition with Mrs. Bandaranaike's SLFP in 1964. The party, which went into opposition in September 1975, lost all 19 of its legislative seats as a component of the ULF in the election of July 1977. Subsequently, it joined the SLMP and the SLCP in supporting measures to negotiate a settlement with Tamil activists.

In 1994 Vasudeva Nanayakkara rejoined the party. A presidential candidate in 1982, the outspoken Nanayakkara formed a new group during his hiatus from the LSSP. In 1999 he was expelled from party membership for crossing to the parliamentary opposition, thereby technically depriving the PA of its one-vote majority. Nanayakkara ran as the candidate of the Left and Democratic Alliance in the presidential balloting of December 1999.

In February 2004, despite some initial objections to the SLFP-JVP alliance, the LSSP decided to join the UPFA for the April parliamentary election and party leader de Mel won the LSSP's lone seat in Parliament. Shortly after the election, longtime LSSP Secretary Batty WEERAKOON resigned. LSSP member and constitutional advisor to the government, Jayampathy WICKRAMARATNE, resigned in protest over what he described as a lack of commitment on the part of the SLFP-led government on Tamil issues. The LSSP participated in regional elections in 2008 as a member of the SPA. It was part of the UPFA in the 2010 legislative elections, the 2011 local balloting, and the 2012 provincial polling. In May 2013 the LSSP joined the opposition in opposing a UPFA-sponsored increased in electricity process. In June 2014 the LSSP joined other UPFA parties in rejecting a UN human rights investigation.

Leader: Wimalasiri de MEL (Secretary to the Central Committee).

Liberal Party (LP). The LP began as the Council for Liberal Democracy, founded in 1981 by UNP member Chanaka AMARATUNGA, who ultimately formed the LP in 1987. It won two Western Province council seats in 1988 and ran on the SLFP ticket in 1989. In August 1996 Amaratunga, who had helped draft the revolutionary constitutional amendments favored by the Kumaratunga administration, died in an automobile accident.

The LP won no provincial council seats in 1999 despite offering candidates in six provinces. Its current leader ran for president in December 1999 but attracted little support, and in December 2001 and April 2004 the LP won only a handful of votes. Party leader Rajiva Wijesinha was appointed secretary general of the peace group, the Secretariat for Coordinating the Peace Process (SCOPP) in 2007. He was replaced by Kamal Nissanka, who was elected general secretary at a party congress. The LP received less than 1 percent of the vote in the 2010 legislative elections. Although the LP campaigned with the UPFA in 2015, it did unsuccessfully contest some seats independently.

Leaders: Kamal NISSANKA (General Secretary), Swarma AMARATUNGA (Honorary President).

Other Parliamentary Parties:

Tamil National Alliance (TNA). The TNA was established on October 18, 2001, by Tamil parties in preparation for the December general election, in which it ran under the symbol of the TULF, the "rising sun." The TNA, strongly supportive of a negotiated settlement with the Tamil Tigers (LTTE, below), soon concluded an electoral pact with the opposition UNP and went on to win 15 parliamentary seats on a vote share of 3.9 percent. Following the election, it extended its external support to the United National Front government.

In the April 2004 election, the TNA appeared on the ballot under the house symbol of the **Sri Lanka Tamil Government Party** (*Ilankai Tamil Arasu Kachchi*—ITAK), an original component of the TULF that had been revived because of a split in the TULF. For the first time the TNA explicitly served as the proxy of the LTTE, winning 22 seats in the north and east.

In November 2005 the LTTE and TNA indicated their "disinterest" in the outcome of the presidential election, which probably contributed to a low voter turnout in Tamil areas and a resultant loss for UNP candidate Wickremesinghe. The TNA officially boycotted regional balloting in 2008 to protest the manner in which district lines were drawn. Between 2005 and 2008 three TNA legislators were killed in attacks. In February 2009 the TNA was invited to rejoin all-party negotiations. After the defeat of the LTTE in 2009, the TNA launched an initiative to develop closer ties with India and seek that country's assistance in protecting the Tamil minority. In March 2010 the TNA renounced its longtime goal of an independent Tamil homeland. In the April parliamentary balloting, the TNA placed third with 14 seats in the legislature.

Following its victory in provincial balloting in September 2013, TNA official C. V. VIGNESWARAN was named chief minister of Northern Province.

The TNA supported Sirisena for the presidency in 2015. In that year's parliamentary balloting, the grouping won 4.6 percent of the vote and 16 seats. In September TNA leader Rajavarothiyam SAMPANTHAN became the leader of the opposition, the first Tamil to hold that position.

Leaders: Rajavarothiyam SAMPANTHAN (Parliamentary Leader), Mavai S. SENATHIRAJAH (ITAK).

Tamil United Liberation Front—TULF (*Tamil Vimuktasi Peramuna*). The TULF was initially organized as the Tamil Liberation Front (*Tamil Vimukthi Peramuna*—TVP) in 1976 by a number of Tamil groups, including the CWC, the All Ceylon Tamil Congress (ACTC), the ITAK, the National Liberation Front (*Jatika Vimukthi Peramuna*—JVP), and the Muslim United Front.

Despite pressure from militants, the TULF maintained an essentially moderate posture, engaging in talks with the government and supporting the 1987 India–Sri Lanka Accord. (For more on the history of the TULF, see the 2014 *Handbook.*) Under pressure from the LTTE, the TULF boycotted the North-East Provincial Council balloting of November 1988; however, it won ten seats in the February 1989 parliamentary poll, its candidates reportedly having been supported by other proaccord Tamil groups. The TULF secretary general, Appapillai AMIRTHALINGAM, was killed and the party president seriously wounded in a July 1989 attack attributed by some reports to a "rogue cell" of the LTTE.

The TULF won five seats in Parliament in the 1994 election, after which it agreed to support the PA. In January 1998 the TULF won a majority of seats on the Jaffna Municipal Council, but in March the party president was quoted as saying that his organization would step aside in favor of the LTTE if the PA and the UNP would reopen talks with the group and accept it as the legitimate representative of the Tamils. In May the newly elected TULF mayor of Jaffna, Sarojini YOGESWARAN, was assassinated by a group claiming allegiance to the LTTE. Four months later her successor, Ponnuthurai SIVAPALAN, was also killed, and in December a party secretary, Ponnathurai MATHIMUGARAJAH, was assassinated at a public rally. The well-respected party vice president, Neelan TIRUCHELVAM, was killed by an LTTE suicide bomber in July 1999.

Because of intraparty differences, the TULF did not officially endorse a presidential candidate in December 1999. In October 2000 it won five seats in Parliament. In 2001 it was a prime mover in forming the TNA.

Technically, the TULF did not contest the April 2004 parliamentary election because of a leadership dispute that remained in the courts. The TNA-supportive wing of the party, led by R. Sampanthan, backed the LTTE as the sole representative of the Tamil people, while the other wing refused to accept the LTTE's contention. The latter wing, led by V. Anandasangaree, offered a slate of independent candidates but won no seats.

In December 2005 party leader and TNA legislator Joseph PARARAJASINGHAM was assassinated. The government blamed the LTTE; the LTTE blamed government-backed paramilitaries. In January 2006 the Anandasangaree wing, the anti-LTTE faction of the Eelam People's Revolutionary Liberation Front (EPRLF, below), and the People's Liberation Organization of Tamil Eelam (PLOTE, below) formed a new Tamil electoral alliance, the Tamil Democratic National Alliance, to compete in regional elections. However, reports in 2009 indicated that Anandasangaree had reconciled with the mainline TULF leaders.

Leaders: Veerasingham ANANDASANGAREE, Rajavarothiyam SAMPANTHAN.

Eelam People's Revolutionary Liberation Front (EPRLF). Founded in 1980, the EPRLF conducted guerrilla activity in Tamil areas in the first half of the 1980s before being decimated by a full-scale LTTE offensive in late 1986. In the wake of the 1987 accord that brought Indian troops to the region, the EPRLF was rebuilt, with New Delhi's support, to serve as a vehicle for the assumption by moderate Tamils of local political autonomy. (For more on the history of the party, see the 2014 *Handbook.*)

The party failed to win control of any of the local bodies in the January 1998 Jaffna balloting. A year later former party chief and North-East chief minister Annamalai Varatharaja Perumal returned from exile, reportedly to rebuild the EPRLF, but in January 2000 he was expelled by the party's central committee for "antiparty" activities. Two months earlier he had stated that he no longer considered Tamil independence realistic. Perumal and his dissident supporters contested the October 2000 elections on independent district lists while voicing support for the PA at the national level.

In June 2003 the leader of Perumal's faction, Thambirajah SUBATHIRAN, was assassinated, apparently by the LTTE. The party remained divided through 2004, with the wing loyal to Suresh Premachandran (Suresh Faction) and continuing its participation with the TNA. The Perumal faction, led by T. Sritharan, backed the presidential candidacy of Prime Minister Rajapakse in 2005. In 2008, a faction of the EPRLF joined with the TULF in the Tamil Democratic National Alliance. The grouping, led by G. SRITHARAN, declared its intention to elect a Tamil as the chief minister of the regional council. In June 2009 EPRLF fighters engaged in a series of gun battles in Jaffna with LTTE guerillas, which left an estimated 75 dead and scores wounded. Reports indicated that a large number of EPRLF members surrendered and subsequently joined the LTTE. The EPRLF won 2 of the TNA's 14 seats in the 2010 parliamentary elections. In 2011 the party opposed the inclusion of the EPRLF—Pathmanabha faction as part of the TNA for future balloting.

Faction Leaders: Suresh K. PREMACHANDRAN (Suresh Faction), Thirunavakkarasu SRITHARAN (Pathmanabha Faction).

Tamil Eelam Liberation Organization (TELO). The TELO resulted from the merger, in Madras, India, in 1984, of a preexisting group of the same name with the Eelam Revolutionary Organization (EROS; see under EDF, below) and the Eelam People's Revolutionary Front (EPRF). The organization was reported to have been "virtually eliminated" in battles with the LTTE in 1986, with its principal leader, Mohan Sri SABARATNAM, among the estimated 300 casualties.

In the January 1998 balloting, the TELO won control of only one village council. In the 2000 and 2004 national elections the party won three seats in parliament. In 2007 and 2008 a number of TELO regional officials were attacked or killed by the LTTE, which rejected TELO's political accommodation with establishment parties. In some local elections in 2009, TELO candidates campaigned jointly with the UPFA. TELO campaigned as part of the TNA in the 2010 legislative balloting and secured 2 of the alliance's 14 seats. A breakaway faction of the TELO registered as the **Tamil National Liberation Alliance** (TNLA) in 2010. In 2013 TELO leader Selvam ADAIKALANATHAN reportedly undertook a hunger strike to protest continuing ethnic inequality in Sri Lanka.

Leaders: Selvam ADAIKALANATHAN (President), Indrakumar PRASANNA (General Secretary).

Sri Lanka Tamil Government Party (*Ilankai Tamil Arasu Kachchi*—ITAK) Organized in the 1940s, the ITAK, also known as the Federal Party, was revived in 2004. It had not directly competed in a national election since 1970. In the 2004 balloting, it secured 5 seats as part of the TNA. In the 2010 elections, it won 8 of the TNA's 14 seats. In local balloting in 2011, ITAK won 17 seats on municipal councils. In 2013 ITAK threatened to withdraw from the TNA over the division of responsibilities within the grouping. In September 2014 Mavai Senathirajah was elected ITAK leader at a party congress.

Leader: Mavai SENATHIRAJAH (Chair).

Eelam People's Democratic Party (EPDP). The EPDP was formed in the late 1980s by Douglas Devananda, a founding member of the EROS (see EDF, below) in the 1970s and of the EPRLF (below) in the 1980s. Having abandoned armed conflict, Devananda joined the political mainstream following the India–Sri Lanka Accord.

In the 1994 legislative election, EPDP members won nine "independent" seats from Jaffna, while in January 1998, defying LTTE threats and the deaths of at least two of its candidates, the party claimed victories in a majority of the 17 local council elections in the region. Nadarajah ATAPUTHARAJAH, an influential EPDP MP and editor of a widely read Tamil weekly, was assassinated in 1999.

The party backed President Kumaratunga's reelection in December 1999. Following the October 2000 general election, in which the party won four seats, it agreed to support the PA government. Its leader was awarded a cabinet post. In December 2001 the EPDP won two parliamentary seats on a vote share of 0.8 percent. In April 2004 it won only 0.3 percent and one seat. Devananda was then named to the Rajapakse cabinet, and he continues to serve under Prime Minister Wikremanayake. A close aide, Maha KANAPATHIPILLAI, was assassinated in July 2006. In 2008 Tharmalingam ELANGAKUMARAN, a regional EPDP leader, was arrested on criminal charges, including kidnapping and murder, and the party's office in Chenkaladi was reportedly closed by authorities. In 2009 the EPDP campaigned against the UPFA in local balloting in Jaffna and Vavuniya. But the EPDP campaigned as part of the UPFA in the 2010 parliamentary elections, winning three seats, and joined the subsequent UPFA government. The EPDP campaigned as part of the UPFA coalition in the March 2011 municipal balloting and the 2012 provincial elections. The EPDP also announced in July 2013 it would participate within the UPFA in polling in September in the Northern Province. In February 2014 Kandasamy KAMALENDRAN, an EPDP member and the opposition leader on the Northern Provincial Council was expelled from the party after he was arrested in connection with the murder of a political rival.

The party won one seat in the August 2015 parliamentary balloting with 0.3 percent of the vote.

Leader: Douglas DEVANANDA (General Secretary of the Party).

People's Liberation Front (*Janatha Vimukthi Peramuna*—JVP). The Sinhalese JVP (not to be confused with the Tamil National Liberation Front—JVP, under TULF, above) was formed as a legal Maoist party in the mid-1960s. It led an attempt to overthrow the government in 1971. The front regained legal status in 1977 and emerged as the third-ranked party in Colombo as the result of local elections in 1979. It was again proscribed after the July 1983 riots, reemerging in 1987 as a major threat to the government through a campaign of killing and terror in the south directed at government targets and Sinhalese supporters of the India–Sri Lanka Accord. In an attempt to win the JVP over to conventional politics, the government again legalized the party in 1988, but JVP leaders renounced the offer and remained underground.

The JVP subsequently expanded its guerrilla campaign in the south, apparently operating through a military wing called the Patriotic People's Movement (*Deshapriya Janatha Viyaparaya*—DJV). Having disrupted provincial, presidential, and legislative elections in 1988 and early 1989, the front again rejected government overtures in September 1989. Subsequently, JVP founder and leader Rohana WIJEWEERA, General Secretary Upatissa GAANAYAKE, and other senior JVP members were killed by security forces under questionable circumstances. In all, the armed struggle in the south may have cost 50,000 lives or more.

Having disavowed violence in the mid-1990s, the JVP gathered strength late in the decade as a "third force" in opposition to the PA and the UNP, sometimes releasing joint statements with other leftist formations. In 1999 it presented candidates for all seven provincial council elections, capturing at least one seat at each. In Western and Southern Provinces, where neither the PA nor the UNP secured a majority, the JVP held the balance of power, although JVP leaders stated that they had no intention of entering either provincial government. Its December 1999 presidential candidate, Nandana GUNATHILAKE, finished third, with 4.1 percent of the vote, having campaigned on a platform that included abolition of the executive presidency and rejection of World Bank and IMF prescriptions for economic reform. In October 2000, the party won 6 percent of the vote and ten seats in parliament.

In September 2001 the JVP's Gunathilake and President Kumaratunga signed a 28-point agreement that guaranteed the JVP's support to the PA government, in return for which the JVP obtained key policy concessions. Parliament was nevertheless dissolved in October, and in the December election the JVP picked up an additional 6 seats on a 9 percent vote share. In 2004 the JVP was credited with 39 of the UPFA's seats. Despite participating in the Rajapakse cabinet, the JVP continued to press its own agenda, including an end to privatization, noncooperation with World Bank and IMF economic prescriptions, and opposition to broad autonomy for Tamil areas.

Despite having left the Rajapakse government in June 2005, the JVP lent its support to Rajapakse's presidential candidacy later in the year in return for his commitment to key elements of the JVP's agenda, including renegotiation of the cease-fire agreement with the LTTE. The JVP nevertheless remained outside the subsequent Wickremanayake government and reconfirmed its decision in July 2006, when it rebuffed overtures from the UPFA and demanded the expulsion of the Sri Lanka Monitoring Mission.

In 2008 the JVP called for a boycott of Indian goods and declared that reducing Indian influence in Sri Lanka would henceforth be one of the planks in its party platform. It was reported that a large number of JVP stalwarts defected from the party to the SLFP. In April 2009 the JVP experienced its worst electoral defeat, losing regional balloting in its political base in the Western Provincial Council elections. Its representation dropped from 23 to 3 seats. Several senior party members defected to the UPFA to protest the JVA's endorsement of Fonseka as a presidential candidate in January 2010 (see UPFA, above). Reports in 2011 indicated a continuing split within the party. In February 2014 Anura DISSANAYAKA was elected chair of the JVP at a national convention.

Leaders: Anura DISSANAYAKA (Chair), M. Tilvin SILVA (General Secretary).

Other National or Sinhalese Parties:

All Ceylon Tamil Congress—ACTC (*Akila Ilankai* Tamil Congress). Organized in 1944 and generally regarded as the founder of the movement for Tamil statehood, the ACTC participated in formation of the TULF in 1976 but subsequently reregistered as a separate party.

On January 5, 2000, its leader, Kumar PONNAMBALAM, was assassinated. An anti-LTTE group calling itself the National Front Against Tigers later claimed responsibility. The party won one seat in the 2000 and 2004 parliament elections but failed to gain any seats in the 2010 balloting. Reports in 2013 indicated that the ACTC would not participate with the TNA in future balloting. In the 2015 parliamentary balloting, the party led the **Tamil National People's Front,** which won 0.2 percent of the vote and no seats.

Leaders: Gajendrakumar PONNAMBALAM (General Secretary), Kumar PONNAMBALAM.

Muslim National Alliance (MNA). The MNA was established in May 2005 by three parties: the **Democratic Unity Alliance** (DUA); **the Sri Lanka Muslim Kachchi** (SLMK), led by Abdul RASOOL; and the **United Muslim People's Alliance** (UMPA), led by Nizar MOULANA. The alliance backed the UNP's Wickremesinghe. In October 2005, however, it switched its allegiance to Prime Minister Rajapakse of the UPFA. Other organizations joining the MNA included the Ashraff Congress (see NC, above) and the **Muslim United Liberation Front** (MULF). The MNA received less than 0.01 percent of the vote in the 2010 parliamentary elections.

Leader: Hafiz Nazeer AHAMED.

Sri Lanka Progressive Front (SLPF). The SLPF, which was formed in the late 1980s by former SLFP leader Ariya BULEGODA, won one seat in the 1994 balloting for Parliament. Its 1994 presidential candidate, Nihal Galappathy, won only 0.3 percent of the vote; Galappathy later joined the JVP. The SLPF failed to secure provincial council representation in balloting in 1999. Bulegoda died in April 2004. The party's 2005 presidential candidate, Nelson PERERA, withdrew in favor of Prime Minister Rajapakse. In the 2000, 2001, 2004, and 2010 general elections, it failed to gain any seats.

Leader: Rohan JAYATUNGA (Secretary).

Among other parties that contested the 2010 election (none obtained more than 0.2 percent of the vote) were the **Ceylon Democratic Unity Alliance** (CDUA), led by S. SATHASIVAM; the **Jathika Sangwardhena Peramuna** (JSP), led by 2005 presidential candidate Achala Ashoka SURAWEERA; the **National People's Party** (NPP), led by Mudhitha KARUNAMANI; the **Ruhuna Janatha Party** (RJP), led by Aruna SOYZA; the **Socialist Equality Party** (SEP), led by 2005 presidential candidate Wije DIAS; the **Sri Lanka National Front** (SLNF), led by Piyasena DISSANAYAKE; and the **United Socialist Party** (USP), led by 2005 presidential candidate, Siritunga JAYASURIYA.

For more information on the **New Equal Society Party** (*Nawa Sama Samaja Pakshaya*—NSSP) and the **Sons of the Soil Party** (*Sinhalaye Mahasammatha Bhoomiputra Pakshaya*—SMBP), see the 2011 *Handbook.* For information on the **National Freedom Front** (NFF), see the 2015 *Handbook.*

Other Tamil Parties and Groups:

Liberation Tigers of Tamil Eelam (LTTE). Founded in 1972 as the Tamil New Tigers, the LTTE is the largest and most hard-line of the militant Tamil groups. It has proposed a socialist Tamil homeland, although ideology has recently been overshadowed by military considerations. In 1985 the Tigers joined the EPRLF, EROS (see under EDF, below), and TELO in an antigovernment coalition, the Eelam National Liberation Front (ENLF), to fight for a separate Tamil state. However, the LTTE was soon engaged in a bloody campaign against some of its former allies, assuming effective control of much of northern Sri Lanka, especially the Jaffna peninsula. The Tigers also conducted extensive guerrilla activity against the Indian troops brought into the region as peacekeepers under the 1987 accord between Colombo and New Delhi. The LTTE boycotted and partially sabotaged the provincial elections in November 1988 and the presidential elections in December.

In 1989 the LTTE agreed to peace negotiations with the government, announced a temporary cease-fire, and vowed to renounce violence if the other militant Tamil groups did likewise. It also launched the People's Front of Liberation Tigers (PFLT) as a "democratic socialist" political party. However, fighting was reported at year's end between the LTTE and the EPRLF, the Tigers' primary opposition in the struggle for Tamil dominance. Completion of the Indian withdrawal in March 1990 left the LTTE in virtual control in the north. Amid periodic hostilities and an ongoing LTTE terrorist campaign against civilian targets, various peace initiatives in the 1990s failed to yield a durable settlement. The government consistently rejected LTTE demands for third-party mediation of the conflict.

In January 1998, in response to the bombing of the country's holiest Buddhist shrine in Kandy, the government officially banned the LTTE. In November the High Court ruled that party members could be tried in absentia on charges related to the January 1996 Colombo financial center bombing that killed nearly 100 and injured another 1,400. Near the end of the year, for the second time since 1995, the LTTE reportedly responded to a revolt in its ranks with a crackdown against dissident troops.

A major LTTE offensive begun in November 1999 continued into 2000, reversing many of the losses suffered in the preceding 18 months and threatening government control of Jaffna. Meanwhile, a series of LTTE-sponsored assassinations and suicide bombings continued unabated. The targets included leaders of the government-supportive Tamil parties as well as President Kumaratunga, who narrowly escaped assassination in December 1999. In the two years following the January 1998 local elections in the north, the LTTE killed at least 25 councilors.

In March–April 2000 the LTTE appeared to be inching closer to talks with the government, with Norway to serve as mediator, although the Kumaratunga administration steadfastly rejected an LTTE demand that government forces be confined to barracks during any such negotiations. A breakthrough finally occurred in the wake of the December 2001 parliamentary election, and in February 2002 the LTTE and the new UNP-led government concluded an indefinite cease-fire agreement, with formal negotiations then opening in September. In April 2003, after four additional rounds of negotiations, the LTTE called a halt to the peace process, citing lack of progress with regard to autonomy, rehabilitation, and reconstruction.

On October 31, 2003, the LTTE published its proposal for an Interim Self-Governing Authority (ISGA) for the northeast. The plan called for Tamils to exert complete control over the region for five years, after which an election would be held.

The most significant challenge to the LTTE leadership of Velupillai Prabhakaran was launched in March 2004 by the commander of forces in the east, Colonel Karuna, who led an estimated 6,000 troops (out of the LTTE's total of 15,000) in a revolt against northern domination. The rebellion was largely suppressed in April, however, and Karuna went underground. In October he announced formation of the Tamil People's Liberation Party (TMVP, below). By early 2005 his forces were again challenging the LTTE, which accused the Sri Lanka Army and Karuna of cooperating in a "secret war" against the LTTE.

The LTTE and the Rajapakse government met in February 2006 in Switzerland to discuss increasingly frequent cease-fire violations, but the severity of the clashes continued to escalate. Talks scheduled for April were canceled, and in May the EU labeled the LTTE a terrorist organization, threatening its main fund-raising activities. (In 2007 the United States, France, and the United Kingdom all arrested LTTE representatives for criminal fund-raising.) An attempt to renew peace talks in October 2006 proved unsuccessful. In December the LTTE's chief negotiator, Anton BALASINGHAM, died in London of cancer.

On March 26, 2007, the LTTE, using one or two light aircraft, conducted its first air attack, but the additional capability did nothing to halt the Sri Lankan army's progress. By mid-July the army had claimed control in the east and continued on the offensive in the north. On November 2 the LTTE's political leader, S. P. THAMISELVAN, was killed in an air attack.

A new government offensive begun in January 2008 reduced the amount of territory under the control of LTTE from about 15,000 square kilometers to 4,000 square kilometers. However, Prabhakaran pledged not to negotiate with the government but to continue LTTE's armed struggle. Into 2009, government forces continued to advance, and Prabhakaran and other senior LTTE leaders were killed in fighting in May as the last rebel stronghold was captured by security forces. Although organized military resistance ceased, an estimated 5,000–7,000 fighters continued to wage a guerilla campaign against the government and progovernment Tamil groups. Selvarasa Pathmanathan was named as Prabhakaran's replacement in July by the LTTE's central committee, but the new leader was captured by authorities on August 5. In 2011 joint efforts were launched by Germany, the Netherlands, and Switzerland to suppress illegal fund-raising for the LTTE. A 2012 investigation by the United States reported that the LTTE used charitable organizations and humanitarian groups to illegally raise funds. The United States subsequently kept the LTTE on its list of international terrorist groups. Reports in 2013 indicated that the LTTE had trained terrorist groups in India.

In May 2014 reports emerged that three suspected LTTE members had been arrested in Malaysia and extradited to Sri Lanka, despite two of them having been granted refugee status by the UN High Commissioner for Refugees.

An EU court in October 2014 annulled the Union's 2006 designation of the LTTE as a terrorist organization, and ordered sanctions on the organization to be removed.

Leader: Selvarasa PATHMANATHAN.

Eelam National Democratic Liberation Front (ENDLF). Initially a strong ally of the EPRLF and a supporter of the India–Sri Lanka Accord of 1987, the ENDLF filled 13 uncontested seats from the north in the creation of the North-East Provincial Council in November 1988. Since the withdrawal of Indian troops from Sri Lanka, the ENDLF has operated primarily in India. In October 2004, however, it announced formation of the **Tamil Eelam United Liberation Front** (*Tamileela Iykkiya Viduthalai Munnani*—TIVM) with the TMVP, the new party of ex-LTTE commander Karuna. In 2008 ENDLF leader G. Gnanasekaran called for military intervention by India to end the conflict between the government and the LTTE and to protect the Tamil minority. In August 2011 the Sri Lankan government deregistered the ENDLF as a political party.

Leaders: G. GNANASEKARAN, Parathan RAJAN (TIVM Co-leader), R. RAJARATTINAM (General Secretary).

Eelavar Democratic Front (EDF). The EDF emerged in 1988 from reorganization of the Eelam Revolutionary Organization of Students (EROS, but also known as the Eelam Revolutionary Organization), which had been organized in London in the mid-1970s. Although not legally registered, the EDF presented a slate of independent candidates (with the reported tacit approval of the LTTE) in the February 1989 parliamentary balloting, securing 13 seats and becoming the third largest legislative block. EDF representatives boycotted subsequent parliamentary sessions, calling for repudiation of the 1987 India–Sri Lanka Accord, immediate withdrawal of Indian troops, and the release of all Tamil prisoners. Two of its parliamentary members resigned their seats in early 1990, while the remaining 11 followed suit in July, saying they did "not want to be dormant spectators who witness the torment of our people." The EDF did not present a slate of candidates for the 2004 general election.

In mid-2007 the EROS reemerged as the **Eelam Revolutionary Organization** under the leadership of Nesan Shankar Raji (son of an original EROS founder), who described the revived EROS as a democratic Tamil front committed to a federal secular state. The EDF participated in regional and local balloting in 2008, but its candidates faced attacks and intimidation from other Tamil groups, and two were killed. The EDF failed to gain any seats in local and regional balloting in 2012. Reports in 2014 indicated the EDF would campaign with the UPFA in future balloting.

Leaders: Nesan Shankar RAJI (Nesan THIRUNESAN), Rajanathan PRABAHARAN (Secretary General).

People's Liberation Organization of Tamil Eelam (PLOTE). The PLOTE was the most important of the separatist groups not involved in the May 1985 coalition (see LTTE, above). Attempts were made on the lives of a number of its leaders in Madras in March 1985, apparently by the LTTE, which severely curtailed PLOTE rebel activity in 1986. PLOTE General Secretary Uma WAHESWARAN, who along with other PLOTE members had been implicated in an attempted coup in the Maldives in late 1988, was reportedly assassinated in Colombo in July 1989.

Since 1988 the PLOTE's political wing has been the **Democratic People's Liberation Front** (DPLF), which won three parliamentary seats in 1994 and extended its support to the PA (even though the leader of a progovernment faction, N. S. K. Uma PRAKASH, had been assassinated early in the year). The DPLF's vice president, Karavai KANDASAMY, was assassinated in December 1994.

The DPLF contested the January 1998 local elections in Jaffna, but it won control only of two urban and two village councils. The PLOTE, running under its own banner, had even less success, achieving no majorities. In September 1999 the PLOTE military commander, Thasan MANIKKADASAN, and a deputy were killed by a suspected LTTE suicide bomber. The party backed President Kumaratunga's reelection two months later.

In the December 2001 general election, the DPLF won under 0.2 percent of the vote but one seat in parliament. It failed to hold the seat in 2004. In 2008 it joined with other Tamil parties to form the Tamil Democratic National Alliance in regional balloting. In June 2009 the PLOTE joined discussions with the TNA in developing a common platform on Tamil issues. In the April 2010 parliamentary elections, the DPLF received 0.08 percent of the vote. In 2011 the DPLF requested that the government implement programs to reintegrate former youth fighters into civil society. In 2012 the DPLF rejected a TNA coalition offer. Reports in 2013 indicated that PLOTE would join the TNA. The DPLF failed to gain any seats in provincial balloting in the Northern Province in 2013.

Leaders: Dharmalingam SIDDHARTHAN (President), S. SATHANANTHAN (DPLF).

LEGISLATURE

Under the 1978 constitution the National State Assembly was redesignated as the **Parliament.** In December 1982 the life of the existing parliament was extended by referendum for an additional six years to August 1989 (although dissolution was decreed on December 20, 1988). The current 225-member body serves a six-year term, subject to dissolution.

In the early election of August 17, 2015, 196 members were chosen by proportional representation at the district level, while 29 members were elected on the basis of nationwide vote totals. Following the balloting, United National Front won 106 seats (93 district proportional seats, and 13 national seats); the United People's Freedom Alliance, 95 (83, 12); Tamil National Alliance, 16 (14, 2); People's Liberation Front, 6 (4, 2); Sri Lanka Muslim Congress, 1 (1, 0); and Eelam People's Democratic Party, 1 (1, 0).

Speaker: Karu JAYASURIYA (UNP).

CABINET

[as of October 10, 2016]

Prime Minister	Ranil Wickremasinghe (UNP)
Ministers	
Agriculture	Duminda Dissanayake (SLFP)
Buddha Sasana	Wijayadasa Rajapaksa (UNP)
Christian Religious Affairs	John Amarathunga (UNP)
City Planning and Water Supply	Rauff Hakeem (SLMC)
Defense	Maithripala Sirisena (UNF)
Development Strategies and Internal Trade	Malik Samarawickrema (UNP)
Disaster Management	Anura Priyadharshana Yapa (SLFP)
Education	Akila Viraj Kariyawasam (UNP)
Environment and Natural Resources	Maithripala Sirisena (UNF)
Finance and Planning	Ravi Karunanayake (UNP)
Fisheries and Aquatic Resources Development	Mahinda Amaraweera (SLFP)
Foreign Affairs	Mangala Samaraweera (UNP)
Foreign Employment Promotion and Welfare	Thalatha Atukorala (UNP) [f]
Health	Rajitha Senaratne (UNP)
Higher Education and Highways	Lakshman Kiriella (UNP)
Hill Country New Villages, Infrastructure, and Community Development	U. Palani Digambaram (NUW)
Hindu Religious Affairs	D. M. Swaminathan (UNP)
Home Affairs	Vajira Abeywardena (UNP)
Housing and Construction	Sajith Premadasa (UNP)
Indigenous Medicine	Rajitha Senaratne (UNP)
Industry and Commerce	Rishad Bathiudeen (ACMC)
Internal Affairs, Wayamba Development, and Cultural Affairs	Seneviratne Bandara Navinne (UNP)
Irrigation and Water Management	Vijith Wijayamuni de Soysa (SLFP)
Justice and Law Reforms	Wijayadasa Rajapaksa (UNP)
Labor and Trade Union Relations	W. D. J. Seneviratne (SLFP)
Land and Land Development	John Amarathunga (UNP)
Law and Order	Sagala Ratnayake (UNP)
Local Government and Provincial Councils	Faiszer Musthapha (SLFP)
Megapolis and Western Development	Patali Champika Ranawaka (JHU)
Muslim Religious Affairs	Mohamed Hashim Abdul Haleem (UNP)
National Coexistence Dialogue and Official Languages	Mano Ganesan (UNP)
National Policies and Economic Affairs	Ranil Wickremashinghe (UNP)
Nutrition	Rajitha Senarathne (UNP)
Parliamentary Reforms and Media	Gayantha Karunathilaka (UNP)
Petroleum and Petroleum Resource Development	Chandima Weerakkody (SLFP)
Plantation Industries	Navin Dissanayake (UNP)
Ports and Shipping	Arjuna Ranatunga (UNP)
Postal Services	Mohamed Hashim Abdul Haleem (UNP)
Power and Energy	Ranjith Siyambalapitiya (SLFP)
Primary Industries	Daya Gamage (UNP)
Public Administration and Management	R. M. Ranjith Madduma Bandara (UNP)
Public Enterprises Development	Kabir Hasheem (UNP)
Regional Development	Sarath Fonseka (DNA)
Rehabilitation and Prison Reforms	D. M. Swaminathan (UNP)
Resettlement and Disaster Relief Services	D. M. Swaminathan (UNP)
Rural Economy	Pelisge Harrison (UNP)
Science, Technology, and Research	Susil Premajayantha (SLFP)
Skills Development and Vocational Training	Mahinda Samarasinghe (SLFP)
Social Empowerment and Welfare	S. B. Dissanayake (SLFP)
Southern Development	Sagala Ratnayake (UNP)
Special Projects	Sarath Amunugama (SLFP)
Sports and Public Recreation	Dayasiri Jayasekara (SLFP)
Sustainable Development and Wildlife	Gamini Jayawickrema Perera (UNP)
Telecommunications and Digital Infrastructure	Harin Fernando (UNP)
Tourism Development	John Amarathunga (UNP)
Transport and Civil Aviation	Nimal Siripala De Silva (SLFP)
Women and Child Affairs	Chandrani Bandara Jayasinghe (UNP) [f]

[f] = female

INTERGOVERNMENTAL REPRESENTATION

Ambassador to the U.S.: Prasad KARIYAWASAM.

U.S. Ambassador to Sri Lanka: Atul KESHAP.

Permanent Representative to the UN: Amrith Rohan PERERA.

IGO Memberships (Non-UN): ADB, CWTH, IOM, NAM, SAARC, WTO.

For Further Reference:

Hashim, Ahmed S. *When Counterinsurgency Wins: Sri Lanka's Defeat of the Tamil Tigers*. Philadelphia: University of Pennsylvania Press, 2013.

Kukreja, Sunil, ed. *State, Society, and Minorities in South and Southeast Asia*. Lanham, MD: Lexington Books, 2015.

Rasaratnam, Madurika. *Tamils and the Nation: India and Sri Lanka Compared.* Oxford: Oxford University Press, 2016.

SUDAN

Republic of the Sudan
Jumhuriyat al-Sudan

Political Status: Independent republic established in 1956; revolutionary military regime instituted in 1969; one-party system established in 1971; constitution of May 8, 1973, suspended following military coup of April 6, 1985; military regime reinstituted on June 30, 1989; ruling military council dissolved and nominal civilian government reinstated on October 16, 1993; nonparty presidential and legislative elections held on March 6–17, 1996; new constitution providing for limited multiparty system ratified on June 30, 1998; peace agreement signed between the government of Sudan and the Sudanese People's Liberation Movement on January 9, 2005, ending a civil war between the north and the south; six-year power-sharing period initiated on July 9, 2005, with the signing of an interim constitution; peace agreement signed on October 14, 2006, between the government of Sudan and the Eastern Front, effectively ending the rebellion by eastern rebel groups; succession of South Sudan, following referendum, on July 9, 2011.

Area: 718,722 sq. mi. (1,861,484 sq. km).

Population: 41,176,000 (2016E—UN); 36,729,501 (2016E—U.S. Census).

Major Urban Centers (2014E—UN): KHARTOUM (2,090,000), Omdurman (2,970,000), Khartoum Bahri (1,623,000), Port Sudan (474,000), Wad Medani (425,000), Kassala (419,000), Gedaref (338,000).

Official Language: Arabic.

Monetary Unit: Sudanese Pound (market rate October 1, 2016: 6.22 pounds = $1US). The Sudanese pound was introduced in 2007 to replace the dinar, the official currency since 1992, at a rate of 1 pound = 100 dinars.

President and Prime Minister: Umar Hassan Ahmad al-BASHIR (National Congress); installed as chair of the Revolutionary Command Council for National Salvation (RCC) following the overthrow of the government of Prime Minister Sadiq al-MAHDI (Umma Party) on June 30, 1989, succeeding the former chair of the Supreme Council, Ahmad al-MIRGHANI (Democratic Unionist Party); assumed title of prime minister upon formation of government of July 9, 1989; named president by the RCC on October 16, 1993; elected to a five-year term as president in nonparty multicandidate balloting on March 6–17, 1996, and inaugurated on April 1; formed new government on April 21, 1996; reelected on December 13–20, 2000, and inaugurated for a second five-year presidential term on February 13, 2001; formed new government on February 23, 2001; reelected April 11–15, 2010, and inaugurated for a third five-year term on May 27; formed new government on June 15; reelected on April 13–16, 2015, and inaugurated on June 2 for a fourth five-year term; formed a new government on June 6.

First Vice President: Lt. Gen. Bakri Hassan SALIH (National Congress); appointed on December 8, 2013, to succeed Ali Uthman Muhammad TAHA (National Congress) who resigned on December 7; reappointed on June 6, 2015, following elections on April 13–16.

Second Vice President: Hasbo Mohamed ABDULRAHMAN (National Congress); appointed on December 8, 2013, to succeed Al-Hadj Adam YOUSSEF (National Congress) who resigned on December 7; reappointed on June 6, 2015, following elections on April 13–16.

THE COUNTRY

One of the largest countries in Africa, Sudan shares its borders with seven neighboring states as well as the Red Sea and forms part of the transitional zone between the continent's largely desert north and its densely forested, subtropical south. The White Nile flows north for almost 2,500 miles, from the Ugandan border, past the river's union with the Blue Nile near Khartoum, to Egypt above Aswan. Approximately 90 percent of the population is Arab and/or Muslim. The geographic, ethnic, and religious cleavages have yielded political discord marked by prolonged periods of southern rebellion.

Women continue to be underrepresented in the economic and political spheres. However, women are guaranteed a minimum of 30 percent of the seats in the assembly through a separate electoral list. Following the 2015 elections, women held 130 of 426 seats in the assembly (30.5 percent) and 19 of 54 seats in the council (35.2 percent).

The economy is predominantly agricultural, although only a small part of the arable land is cultivated. Cotton is the most important cash crop, followed by gum arabic, of which Sudan produces four-fifths of the world supply. Other crops include sesame seeds, peanuts, castor beans, sorghum, wheat, and sugarcane. The country has major livestock-producing potential, and large numbers of camels and sheep are raised for export. Industry is largely limited to the processing of agricultural products and the manufacture of light consumer goods.

Sudan was plagued in the 1980s and 1990s by persistent drought, starvation, and civil war. By 1999, it was estimated that as many as 1.5 million Sudanese had died in the previous 16 years as the result of famine and war, while more than 2 million were in danger of starving as a result of drought. (For more information, see the 2012 *Handbook.*)

Economic distress resulted in more than $15 billion of external debt. Foreign aid decreased sharply in the 1990s due to Khartoum's human rights abuses and its failure to democratize. (For information on relations with the International Monetary Fund [IMF] in the 1990s, see the 2013 *Handbook.*)

The fighting in Darfur compounded the instability, starting in early 2003, with an estimated 113,000 villagers fleeing to Chad by January 2004 and a death toll leading U.S. officials to declare the killing genocide (see Current issues, below).

On January 8, 2007, as part of the Comprehensive Peace Agreement (CPA) mandate, the Central Bank of Sudan (CBS) introduced its new currency, the Sudanese pound, valued at US$2 = S£1. The pound replaced the dinar, which was seen, especially in the south, as a symbol of Islamization and Arabization. In 2010, gross domestic product (GDP) growth was 5.1 percent as international fuel prices declined. Rising food costs kept inflation high at 12.9 percent. The economy continued to be hampered by ongoing conflict, with 14.9 percent of the population unemployed and 40 percent below the poverty line in 2010. After the independence of South Sudan, the new country secured control over approximately 75 percent of the nation's oil production but agreed to pay fees to Sudan for the transshipment of oil through pipelines to the Red Sea. In 2011 the country plunged into recession. GDP declined 1.9 percent that year and fell by 4.4 percent the next as South Sudan stopped oil transshipments (see Foreign relations, below). Inflation rose by 18.1 percent in 2011 (see Current issues, below), and then doubled to 35.6 percent in 2012. Unemployment was 12 percent in 2011 and 10.8 percent in 2012. In February 2012 the government announced that new oil discoveries would allow Sudan to increase production from 115,000 barrels per day to 180,000. In 2013 GDP rose by 3.9 percent, while inflation remained high at 36.5 percent, and unemployment increased to 15.2 percent. GDP expanded by 3.3 percent in 2014, 3.5 percent in 2015 and 3.7 percent in 2016. That year, inflation was 13 percent, while unemployment was 20.6 percent. GDP per capita

was $2,367. The IMF estimated that Sudan's external debt had risen to $45.1 billion in 2016, of which a massive 80 percent was in arrears.

GOVERNMENT AND POLITICS

Political background. Historically known as the land of Kush, Sudan was conquered and unified by Egypt in 1820–1821. Under the leadership of Muhammad Ahmad, the MAHDI ("awaited religious leader"), opposition to Egyptian administration broke into open revolt in 1881; the insurrection had succeeded by 1885, and the Mahdist state controlled the region until its reconquest by an Anglo-Egyptian force in 1896–1898. Thereafter, Sudan was governed by an Anglo-Egyptian condominium, becoming self-governing in 1954 and fully independent on January 1, 1956, under a transitional constitution that provided for a democratic parliamentary regime. A civilian government, led successively by Ismail al-AZHARI and Abdallah KHALIL, was overthrown in November 1958 by Lt. Gen. Ibrahim ABBUD, whose military regime was itself dislodged following protest demonstrations in October and November 1964. The restored constitutional regime, headed in turn by Sir al-Khatim KHALIFA, Muhammad Ahmad MAHGUB, and Dr. Sadiq al-MAHDI (a descendant of the 19th-century religious leader), was weakened both by political party instability and by revolt in the southern provinces.

Beginning in 1955 as a protest against Arab-Muslim domination, the southern insurgency rapidly assumed the proportions of a civil war. Led by the *Anyanya* (scorpion) movement under the command of Joseph LAGU, the revolt prompted military reprisals and the flight of thousands of refugees to neighboring countries. While moderate southern parties continued to seek regional autonomy within the framework of a united Sudan, exile groups worked for complete independence, and a so-called Provisional Government of Southern Sudan was established in January 1967 under the leadership of Agrev JADEN, a prominent exile leader.

The stability of the new Mahgub government was interrupted in May 1969 by a military coup organized by a group of nationalist, left-wing officers led by Col. Jafar Muhammad NUMAYRI. In response to Numayri's ten-man Revolutionary Council, a former chief justice, Abu-Bakr AWADALLA, formed a civilian administration of communists and extreme leftists. Revolutionary activity continued, however, including successive communist attempts in 1969 and 1971 to overthrow the Numayri regime. The latter effort succeeded for three days, after which Numayri regained power with Egyptian and Libyan help and instituted reprisals that included the execution of Abd al-Khaliq MAHGUB, the Communist Party's secretary general.

Subsequent to a temporary constitution in August 1971, Numayri was elected to the presidency in September. A month later, in an effort to consolidate his position, Numayri dissolved the Revolutionary Council and established the Sudanese Socialist Union (SSU) as the only recognized political party. Of equal significance was the ratification in April 1973 of a negotiated settlement that temporarily brought the southern rebellion to an end. The terms of the agreement, which provided for an autonomous Southern Sudan, were included in a new national constitution that became effective May 8, 1973. In November the Southern Region voted for a Regional People's Assembly, while the first national election under the new basic law took place in May 1974 for a 250-member National People's Assembly.

In September 1975 rebel army personnel led by a paratroop officer, Lt. Col. Hassan Husayn USMAN, seized the government radio station in Omdurman in an attempted coup. President Numayri subsequently blamed Libya for instigating the uprising, which was quickly suppressed. The attack had been preceded by an army mutiny in Akobo on the Ethiopian border in March and was followed by an uprising in Khartoum in July 1976 that reportedly claimed 300 lives. At a news conference in London on August 4, former prime minister Mahdi, on behalf of the outlawed Sudanese National Front (SNF), a coalition of former centrist and rightist parties that had been organized in late 1969, accepted responsibility for having organized the July rebellion but denied that it had involved foreign mercenaries. President Numayri attempted to accommodate the dissidents. In July 1977 a number of SNF leaders, including Dr. Mahdi, returned from abroad and were immediately appointed to the Central Committee of the SSU. A year later the Rev. Philip Abbas GHABUSH, titular president of the SNF, expressed his conviction that the government was committed to the building of "a genuine democracy in Sudan" and ordered the dissolution of both the internal and external wings of the Front.

In early 1980 the north was divided into five new regions to provide for more effective local self-government, and in October 1981 the president dissolved the National Assembly and the Southern Regional Assembly to decentralize legislative power to new regional bodies. He appointed Gen. Gasmallah Abdallah RASSA, a southern Muslim, as interim president of the Southern Region's High Executive Council (HEC) in place of Abel ALIER, who continued as second vice president of the republic. Immediately thereafter a plan was advanced to divide the south into three regions based on the historic provinces of Bahr al-Ghazal, Equatoria, and Upper Nile.

The projected redivision of the south yielded three regional blocs: a "unity" group led by Vice President Alier of the numerically dominant Dinka tribe, who branded the scheme a repudiation of the 1973 agreement; a "divisionist" group led by former rebel commander Joseph Lagu of the Wahdi tribe of eastern Equatoria; and a "compromise" group, led by Clement MBORO and Samuel ARU Bol, which styled itself "Change Two" (C2) after an earlier "Wind for Change Alliance" that had opposed Alier's election to the HEC presidency. None of the three obtained a majority in an April 1982 election to the Southern Regional Assembly, and on June 23 a divisionist, Joseph James TOMBURA, was designated by the assembly as regional president with C2 backing (the alliance being styled "C3"). Six days later President Numayri named General Lagu to succeed Alier as second vice president of the republic. Earlier, on April 11, Maj. Gen. Umar Muhammad al-TAYYIB (who had been designated third vice president in October 1981) was named to the first vice presidency in succession to Lt. Gen. Abd al-Majid Hamid KHALIL, who had been dismissed on January 25.

As expected, President Numayri was nominated for a third term by an SSU congress in February 1983 and reelected by a national plebiscite held April 15–26. In June 1983 the tripartite division of the south was formally implemented, with both the HEC and the southern assembly being abolished.

In the face of renewed rebellion in the south and rapidly deteriorating economic conditions, which prompted food riots and the launching of a general strike in Khartoum, a group of army officers, led by Gen. Abd al-Rahman SIWAR al-DAHAB, seized power on April 6, 1985, while the president was returning from the United States. Numayri's ouster was attributed in part to opposition by southerners and some urban northerners and to the adoption of Islamic religious law (sharia) in September 1983.

On April 9, 1985, after inconclusive discussions between a civilian National Alliance for the Salvation of the Country (NASC), General Siwar al-Dahab formed a 14-member Transitional Military Council (TMC), with himself as chair and Gen. Taq al-Din Abdallah FADUL as his deputy. After further consultation with NASC leaders, Dr. al-Gizouli DAFALLAH, who had played a prominent role in organizing the pre-coup demonstrations, was named head of an interim Council of Ministers on April 22. On May 25 a seven-member southern cabinet that included representatives of the three historic areas (henceforth to be known as "administrative regions") was appointed. Concurrently, the Sudanese People's Liberation Army (SPLA), which had become the primary rebel force in the south under the leadership of Col. John GARANG, resumed antigovernment military activity.

Under Numayri, the size and composition of the unicameral National People's Assembly changed several times; the assembly elected in 1974 was the only one to complete its full constitutional term of four years. All existing legislative bodies were dissolved by the TMC in April 1985. Adhering to its promise to hold a national election within a year, the TMC sponsored legislative balloting April 1–12, 1986, despite continued insurgent activity that precluded polling in 41 southern districts. The new body, serving as both a Constituent and Legislative Assembly, convened on April 26 but disagreed on the composition of a Supreme (Presidential) Council and the designation of a prime minister until May 6, with a coalition government being formed under former prime minister Mahdi of the Umma Party (UP) on May 15. The UP's principal partner was the Democratic Unionist Party (DUP), which had finished second in the assembly balloting. Although several southern parties were awarded cabinet posts, most "African bloc" deputies boycotted assembly activity because of alleged lack of representation and unsatisfactory progress towards repealing sharia.

The Council of Ministers was dissolved on May 13, 1987, primarily because of a split within the DUP that weakened the government's capacity to implement policy. A new government was formed on June 3 with little change in personnel. On August 22, while cooperating with the UP, the DUP formally withdrew from the coalition because of a dispute over an appointment to the Supreme Council. Eight months later the DUP rejected a proposal by Mahdi to form a more broadly based administration that would include the opposition National Islamic Front (NIF). Undaunted, the prime minister resigned on April 16, 1988, to make way for a government of "national reconciliation." Reappointed on April 27, he issued an appeal for all of the parties to join in a proposed national constitutional conference to decide the role of Islam in a future state structure. Mahdi formed a new administration that included the DUP and NIF on May 14. In July 1988 the DUP joined the fundamentalists in calling for a legislative vote on the introduction of sharia prior to the constitutional conference. On September 19, following the government's introduction of a sharia-based penal code, the southern deputies withdrew from the assembly. In mid-November, purportedly with the prime minister's approval, DUP representatives met with SPLA leader Garang in the Ethiopian capital of Addis Ababa to negotiate a peace treaty that entailed abandoning sharia legislation, lifting the state of emergency, and convening of a national constitutional conference. However, rioting subsequently broke out in Khartoum, and on December 20, in the wake of a reported coup attempt and suspension of parliamentary debate on policy toward the south, Prime Minister Mahdi declared another state of emergency. On December 28 the DUP withdrew from the government in response to Mahdi's failure to recognize the agreement with the SPLA, the DUP ministerial posts being refilled by NIF representatives. On February 27, 1989, after another cabinet reshuffle in which the DUP did not participate, Mahdi threatened to resign if the army refused him the latitude to negotiate peace with the rebels. On March 5 some 48 parties and trade unions indicated their general acceptance of the November peace accord, and on March 22 a new governing coalition was announced composed of the UP, the DUP, and representatives of the unions and southern parties, with the NIF in opposition.

In May 1989, complaining that Khartoum had "done absolutely nothing" to advance peace, Col. Garang announced a cease-fire in the south. A month later he met with northern representatives in Addis Ababa for peace talks mediated by former U.S. president Jimmy Carter. Shortly thereafter, Khartoum agreed to implement the November 1988 accords and schedule a September constitutional conference. The plan was nullified on June 30, when the Madhi regime was overthrown by a military coup led by Brig. Gen. Umar Hassan Ahmad al-BASHIR, who assumed the chair of a Revolution Command Council for National Salvation (RCC) and ultimately rejected the November 1988 treaty. The RCC immediately suspended the constitution, dissolved the Constituent Assembly, imposed emergency rule, and freed military leaders arrested on June 18 for allegedly plotting an earlier coup. Claiming that factionalism and corruption had led to economic malaise and an ineffective war effort, the military regime banned all political parties and arrested senior government and party leaders. On July 9 Bashir assumed the additional office of prime minister, heading a 21-member cabinet composed primarily of career bureaucrats drawn from the NIF and supporters of former president Numayri.

Despite claims that "peace through negotiation" was its first priority, the new government rejected the November 1988 treaty, suggesting instead that the sharia issue be decided by national referendum. However, the SPLA, which sought suspension of sharia while negotiations continued, resumed military activities in October.

A major cabinet reshuffle on April 10, 1990, was viewed as a consolidation of Islamic fundamentalist influence, and on April 24, a total of 31 army and police officers were executed in the wake of an alleged coup attempt the day before. Another reshuffle in January 1991 was followed by the introduction of a nine-state federal system (see Constitution and government, below), and on March 22 a new sharia-based penal code was instituted in the six northern states, prompting a strong protest from the SPLA.

On February 13, 1992, Prime Minister Bashir announced the appointment of a 300-member Transitional National Assembly, which met for the first time on February 24. Included in the assembly were all members of the RCC; a number of RCC advisors; all cabinet ministers and state governors; and representatives of the army, trade unions, and former political parties. The prime minister decreed that the assembly would sit for an indeterminate period, pending the selection of a permanent body as the final step of the new pyramidal legislative structure envisioned by the government.

In the wake of heavy fighting between his supporters and several SPLA breakaway factions in the south, Garang announced a unilateral cease-fire in late March 1993 in the conflict with government troops. Khartoum endorsed the cease-fire several days later, and peace talks with Garang representatives resumed in Abuja in late April. The government also initiated parallel negotiations in Nairobi, Kenya, with the SPLA dissidents, who had recently coalesced as the SPLA-United. However, both sets of talks were subsequently suspended when fighting between government forces and Garang's SPLA faction resumed near the Ugandan border by midyear.

On July 8, 1993, Prime Minister Bashir announced a cabinet reshuffle that was described as an "overt increase in NIF involvement." Subsequently, in a surprise, albeit essentially cosmetic, return to civilian control, the RCC dissolved itself on October 16 after declaring Bashir president and granting him wide authority to direct a transitional government. Bashir announced his administration's commitment to an undefined democratization program that would lead to national elections by the end of 1995. Nevertheless, the new cabinet, announced on October 30, appeared to further solidify NIF control and support the opposition's charges that the military-fundamentalist alliance had no true intention of loosening its stranglehold on political power.

In September 1993 the Inter-Governmental Authority on Drought and Development (IGADD, later the Inter-Governmental Authority on Development—IGAD), composed of representatives from Ethiopia, Eritrea, Kenya, and Uganda was established to mediate the Sudanese conflict. However, the talks ended in deadlock in late 1994 after the two sides had "adopted irreconcilable positions on southern self-determination and the relationship between state and religion."

On March 27, 1995, Bashir announced a unilateral two-month cease-fire to facilitate another peace initiative launched by former U.S. president Jimmy Carter. While the leading southern factions cautiously supported the truce, no progress was reported in resolving the conflict, despite a two-month extension of the cease-fire on May 25.

Widespread rioting broke out in several locations, including Khartoum and Port Sudan, in September 1995, bolstering observations of a weakened northern regime. The outbreaks, which appeared to be spontaneous, involved both student protesters and conservative elements angered by low salaries and food shortages. Further violence erupted in Khartoum in early January 1996 between police and Muslim fundamentalists calling for conversion of the country's Christians and animists to Islam.

In January 1996 the regime announced that elections would be held in March for president and a new 400-member National Assembly. However, that balloting (conducted March 6–17) was boycotted by nearly all the major opposition groups, most of whom had coalesced under the banner of the National Democratic Alliance (NDA). Because political parties remained banned, candidates campaigned as independents. Most of the 275 elected assembly members were selected during the balloting, although in October President Bashir appointed eight legislators from constituencies in the south, where the civil war made voting impossible. When the assembly convened on April 1, the elected legislators were joined by 125 legislators who had been selected in January by representatives of local and state councils and numerous professional associations. Some 40 independent candidates contested the presidential balloting, and Bashir was elected to a five-year term on the strength of a reported 75.7 percent share of the vote. He was sworn in on April 1, and on the same day the new assembly convened and unanimously elected the NIF's Hassan Abdallah al-TURABI (long considered the dominant political leader in the country) as its president. On April 21 Bashir appointed a new cabinet, which excluded the signatories of a recent peace accord, the SPLA-United and the Southern Sudan Independence Movement (SSIM).

In January 1997 a major rebel offensive was reportedly launched by a more cohesive and potent NDA. In April the regime reached another agreement with the SSIM, the SPLA-United, and four SPLA breakaway groups, calling for suspension of sharia in the south and southern autonomy. With both the government and the SPLA claiming military success, IGAD proposed a "framework of principles" for a resumption of peace talks in July aimed to secure a self-determination plebiscite in the south. However, negotiations were quickly suspended until April 1998 and fighting continued.

Elections were held for ten southern gubernatorial posts in November 1997, and on December 1 the SSIM's Riak MACHAR was named head of a new Southern States' Coordination Council (SSCC) and given a four-year mandate to govern the south pending a decision on its permanent political status. However, the exercise was widely viewed as futile, considering Col. Garang's depiction of the SSCC as a "sham."

A plane crash on February 12, 1998, killed First Vice President Maj. Gen. al-Zubayr Muhammad SALIH (one of the president's oldest and most trusted associates) and a number of other government officials. On March 8 Bashir finally settled on Ali Uthman Muhammad TAHA, considered second in authority in the NIF, to succeed Salih. In addition, the NIF had an enhanced presence in the extensively reshuffled cabinet, which also included dissident Umma members and representatives of southern rebels who had aligned with Khartoum.

In the face of heavy international pressure for political reform, the assembly, on March 28, 1998, approved the government's proposed new constitution, which authorized the legalization of political associations. The new basic law was endorsed by a reported 96.7 percent "yes" vote in a national referendum in late May and signed into law by President Bashir on June 30, 1998. On November 23 the assembly approved the Political Association Act, which established legal governance of party activity and registration of parties from January 1999.

As conflict rapidly escalated between Bashir and Turabi, Turabi proposed a series of constitutional amendments in November 1999 to curb Bashir's power. Bashir responded by announcing a three-month state of emergency and dissolving the National Assembly on December 12, 1999 (effective December 13). Bashir's declaration occurred a mere 48 hours prior to the scheduled National Assembly vote regarding Turabi's proposed amendments. The cabinet responded by formally issuing its resignation on January 1, 2000. Bashir appointed a new cabinet on January 25, retaining his backers in some ministry posts. The power struggle continued, however, because Turabi, while holding no official position, remained secretary general of the National Congress (NC), the successor to the NIF. Meanwhile, the government also was buffeted in February by the departure of Machar and his supporters due to the perceived failure of Bashir to implement the 1997 accord.

On March 12, 2000, the cabinet extended the state of emergency until the end of the year. Bashir consolidated power by removing Turabi as secretary general of the NC and replacing him with Ibrahim Ahmed OMAR. As part of an overall effort to enhance his regime's image, President Bashir announced an amnesty for his opponents in June 2000.

Despite seemingly positive negotiations between the government and the UP (see UP under Political Parties and Groups, below), the UP led an opposition boycott of assembly and presidential elections on December 13–23, 2000. Consequently, the NC secured 355 of the 360 contested assembly seats, while Bashir was elected to a second five-year term with a reported 86.5 percent of the vote. (After returning from 14 years in exile in May 1999, former president Numayri, as the candidate of the Popular Working Forces Alliance, finished second with 9.6 percent of the vote in the presidential poll.) DUP dissidents were included in the new cabinet named on February 23, 2001, as were UP dissidents in the reshuffle of August 19, 2002. Two DUP dissidents were also among those named to the cabinet in a reshuffle on November 30, 2002.

The political climate deteriorated when the state of emergency was again extended in January 2001, and Turabi and several of his associates were arrested in February after Turabi's Popular National Congress (PNC) had signed an accord with the SPLA to "resist" the government. (Most of the PNC members were released by presidential order in October, but Turabi remained under house arrest until October 2003. He was rearrested on March 31, 2004, along with ten military officers and seven PNC members for what government officials said was a plot to stage a coup. Some reports claimed that those arrested had links to rebels in the western province of Darfur [see below and Current issues]. Turabi was released on June 30, 2005, when Bashir announced the release of all political detainees.)

Meanwhile, a historic accord was signed in Kenya on July 20, 2002, by representatives of the government and the SPLM. The agreement envisioned the establishment of a joint, six-year transitional administration for the south to be followed by a self-determination referendum in the region.

Although elections were scheduled to occur in 2004, continued conflict between north and south and an unwillingness to relinquish power by the Bashir regime impeded the electoral process. The government and the SPLM signed a Comprehensive Peace Agreement (CPA) on January 9, 2005, in Nairobi, bringing to an end the 21-year war in the south. The CPA led to a new 30-member power-sharing cabinet on September 22, 2005. Fifteen posts went to the NC, 9 to the SPLM, and 6 to northern and southern opposition groups. On October 21 the first cabinet of the Government of South Sudan (GOSS) was appointed. The 22-member southern unity cabinet included 16 seats designated for the SPLM, 3 for the NC, and 3 for other south Sudan opposition groups. The peace agreement between north and south called for elections in 2009 and a referendum on the south in 2011. Meanwhile, the 450-member "national unity" assembly, which Bashir appointed by decree, convened for the first time on August 31, 2005, and members were selected according to a power-sharing quota.

Conflict between the leadership of the SPLM and the NC resulted in a cabinet reshuffle in October 2007, with a number of new appointments. Under the CPA, the SPLM was authorized to keep its army in the south but agreed to withdraw from the east, while the regime agreed to withdraw its troops from the south by July 2007. Despite Bashir's insistence that 85 percent of troops had withdrawn from the region, in late August 2007, observers charged that 10,000 northern troops remained in the south, largely concentrated around the oil installations. In December the two parties reached an agreement that allowed the SPLM members to rejoin the cabinet.

There were minor cabinet reshuffles in February and May 2008. In September a more substantial rearrangement accompanied the dismissal of Pagan AMUM of the SPLM, who had been minister of cabinet affairs, following Amum's highly public criticism of the government and the NC.

On February 17, 2009, the government and JEM signed a preliminary agreement on several areas of cooperation and an eventual ceasefire. The accord was brokered by the UN, AU, Arab League, and Qatar. In March Bashir was indicted by the ICC for his role in Sudan's ethnic conflict (see Current issues, below). Following the expulsion of international aid groups in response to Bashir's indictment (see Foreign relations, below), JEM suspended further talks with the government.

Ahead of presidential elections in April 2010, the SPLM nominated Yasir ARMAN, the vice president of South Sudan, as its candidate. However, Arman withdrew in March, expressing concerns over the potential for fraud (see Current issues, below). With no other significant opposition, Bashir was reelected with 68.2 percent of the vote in April 11–15 balloting, which international observers cited for fraud and irregularities (see Current issues, below). In concurrent presidential balloting in the south, incumbent president Salva KIIR Mayardit (SPLM) won with 93 percent of the vote. The SPLM and other opposition parties also boycotted national legislative elections in most of the north. Consequently, the NC won a commanding 312 seats in the assembly polling April 11–15. The SPLM secured 99 seats, and no other party gained more than 4 seats. Bashir formed a new government in June that included the NC, SPLM, the UP, and the United Democratic Salvation Front (UDSF).

Under the terms of the comprehensive peace agreement, from January 9 to 15, 2011, a referendum was held on independence for South Sudan. Results showed that 98.8 percent voted in favor of independence. Following the vote, most of the SPLM ministers resigned from the government. On April 11 the assembly revoked the membership of legislators from the south. The removal of the SPLM deputies gave the NC near-total control of the assembly. When South Sudan achieved formal independence on July 9 (see entry on South Sudan), the remaining SPLM cabinet members resigned. On September 13 Bashir appointed Al-Hadj Adam YOUSSEF of the NC as vice president to replace Kiir, who resigned on July 9 to become the president of South Sudan. On December 10 Bashir appointed a government of national unity that included members of the opposition.

The cabinet was reshuffled on July 8, 2012. The minister of religion guidance and endowments was killed in a plane crash on August 19. He was replaced by Fatih Taj-al-Sir ABDALLAH in January 2013. On December 8, the cabinet was again reshuffled and Lt. Gen. Bakri Hassan Salih (NC) was appointed first vice president, while Hasbo Mohamed Abdulrahman was named second vice president. Both were close allies of the president.

Most opposition groups boycotted national elections on April 13–16, 2015. Bashir was overwhelmingly reelected with 94 percent of the vote; his closest opponent received only 1.4 percent of the ballots. In concurrent legislative balloting, the NC also won a huge victory with 323 seats. The second-largest party, the Democratic Unionist Party–Original (DUP-Original), secured 25 seats. Election observers described the voting as peaceful but marred by the opposition boycott, low turnout, and some irregularities. Bashir was inaugurated for his fourth term on June 2, and he named a largely reshuffled cabinet four days later.

Constitution and government. The 1973 constitution provided for a strong presidential form of government. Nominated by the Sudanese Socialist Union for a six-year term, the president appointed all other executive officials and served as supreme commander of the People's Armed Forces. Legislative authority was vested in the National People's Assembly, a unicameral body that was partially elected and partially appointed.

The Southern Sudan Regional Constitution, abrogated by the June 1983 redivision, provided for a single autonomous region governed, in nonreserved areas, by the president of a High Executive Council (cabinet) responsible to a Regional People's Assembly. Each of the three subsequent regions in the south, like the five in the north, was administered by a centrally appointed governor, acting on the advice of a local People's Assembly. In a move that intensified southern dissent, President Numayri announced in June 1984 the incorporation into the north of a new province (Wahdah), encompassing territory theretofore part of the Upper Nile region, where oil reserves had been discovered.

Upon assuming power in 1985, the Transitional Military Committee (TMC) suspended the 1973 basic law, dissolved the central and regional assemblies, appointed a cabinet composed largely of civilians, and assigned military personnel to replace regional governors and their ministers. An interim constitution was approved by the TMC in October 1985. Assembly members chosen in April 1986 were mandated to draft a new basic law, although many southern districts were unrepresented because of rebel activity. The assembly's charge to act as a constituent body ceased with the call in April 1988 to convene a national constitutional conference.

In January 1987 the government announced the formation of a new Administrative Council for the South, comprising representatives of six southern political parties and the governors of each of the three previously established regions. The council, although formally empowered with only "transitional" authority, was repudiated by both the "unity" and "divisionist" groups. Subsequently, following the signing of a pro-pluralism "Transitional Charter" on January 10, 1988, to serve as an interim basic law, the council was suspended, and the administration of the southern provinces was assigned to the regional governors.

During negotiations between the Mahdi regime and southern rebels in early June 1989, an agreement was reached to open a constitutional conference in September. However, the Bashir junta rejected the June agreement and suspended the Transitional Charter. Subsequently, a national "political orientation" conference, held on April 29–May 2, 1991, in Khartoum, endorsed the establishment of a pyramidal governmental structure involving the direct popular election of local councils followed by the successive indirect election of provincial, state, and national lawmaking bodies. On February 13, 1992, Prime Minister Bashir appointed a 300-member Transitional National Assembly, and he was named president on October 16, 1993, by the RCC, which then dissolved itself. Elections were held on March 6–17, 1996, to a new National Assembly, with concurrent nonparty balloting for president.

On February 5, 1991, the RCC announced the establishment of a new federal system comprising nine states—six (Central, Darfur, Eastern, Khartoum, Kordofan, and Northern) in the north and three (Bahr al-Ghazal, Equatoria, and Upper Nile) in the south. The states, each administered by a federally appointed governor, deputy governor, and cabinet of ministers, were given responsibility for local administration and some tax collection, although control over most major sectors remained with the central government. In early February 1994 President Bashir announced that the number of states had been increased from 9 to 26, new governors being appointed later in the month. A Southern States Coordination Council was named in December 1997 to govern the south pending final determination of the region's status, but authority of the new body remained severely compromised by the opposition of the main rebel group, the SPLA. In 2006 the state of West Kurdufan was merged with two others, reducing the number of states to 25. The 10 states of South Sudan became independent on July 9, 2011 (see Current issues, below), leaving the 15 northern states to constitute Sudan.

On March 22, 1991, a new penal code based on sharia went into effect in the north, the government announcing that the issue would be "open" in regard to the south, pending the outcome of peace negotiations. The new constitution, which went into effect on June 30, 1998, annulled most previous decrees by the Bashir regime, thereby permitting the reintroduction of a multiparty system. The new basic law described Islam as "the religion of the majority," while noting the "considerable number of Christians and animists" in the country and guaranteeing freedom of religion. The controversial issue of sharia, particularly as it might apply to the south, was skirted, the constitution stating only that the "religion, customs, and consensus of the Nation shall be the sources of legislation."

Following the peace agreement reached on January 9, 2005, between the government and the SPLM, an interim constitution was signed on July 9, 2005, allowing for power sharing during a six-year transitional period. (For more information, see the 2014 *Handbook.*)

In July 2007 the UN Security Council passed a resolution that included provisions for a joint AU–UN peacekeeping mission. Despite Khartoum's formal acceptance of the resolution, controversy over the size, troop competence, source countries, and command structure of the force delayed full deployment into 2008, while conflict continued unabated. However, in a gesture of cooperation, the government rescinded the old, "Islamist" currency, the dinar, in favor of the new Sudanese pound (see Current issues, below). The AU–UN mandate of operations in Sudan was scheduled to expire in June 2008, but the ongoing conflict resulted in extensions of operations through 2011.

In July 2009 the Permanent Court of Arbitration in the Netherlands granted control over most of the disputed oil-rich region of Abyei to the national government in Khartoum. The ruling was a defeat for the SPLM, which argued that the area should be part of the region included in the South's 2011 independence referendum.

On August 12, 2003, President Bashir issued a decree ending press censorship. Despite an increase in daily papers and online press, state media maintained control and censorship was evident. In 2008 it was reported that the government had quietly reinstituted media censorship. Following violent anti-regime demonstrations in September 2013, the government suspended publication of a number of newspapers and endeavored to block the broadcasts of satellite news channels. In its 2016 report on press freedom, Reporters Without Borders ranked Sudan a dismal 174th out of 180 countries.

Foreign relations. During much of the Cold War Sudan pursued a policy of nonalignment, modified in practice by changing international circumstances, while focusing its attention on regional matters. Prior to the 1974 coup in Ethiopia, relations with that country were especially cordial due to the prominent role Ethiopian Emperor Haile Selassie had played in bringing about a settlement in the initial southern rebellion. However, Addis Ababa later accused Khartoum of providing covert support to Eritrean rebels, while Sudanese leaders charged that SPLA camps were flourishing in Ethiopia with the approval of the Mengistu regime. Not surprisingly, relations between the two countries improved dramatically following the May 1991 rebel victory in Ethiopia; the presumed SPLA contingents were forced back into Sudan by Ethiopian troops and the Bashir regime became a vocal supporter of the new leadership in Addis Ababa. By contrast, the secular administration in Eritrea charged in early 1994 that Sudan was fomenting fundamentalist antigovernment activity in the new nation of Eritrea, and in December it severed relations with Khartoum. After a period of improved relations, recent tension arose over border demarcation disputes between Sudan, Ethiopia, and Eritrea, where Sudanese troops are occupying Ethiopian lands to the north. Relations have since improved, as the Eritrean government played a significant role in mediating a peace agreement between Khartoum and eastern rebel groups (see Current issues, below).

Soon after taking power in 1969, Prime Minister Numayri forged close ties with Egyptian president Gamal Abdel Nasser within a federation scheme encompassing Sudan, Egypt, and the newly established Libyan regime of Col. Muammar Qadhafi. Although failing to promote integration, the federation yielded joint Egyptian-Libyan military support for Numayri in defeating the communist insurgency of June 1971. However, Numayri was reluctant to join a second unity scheme—the abortive 1972 Federation of Arab Republics—because of Libyan-inspired conspiracies and opposition from the non-Arab peoples of southern Sudan. President Sadat's own estrangement from Qadhafi during 1973 led to the signing of a Sudanese-Egyptian agreement on political and economic coordination in February 1974. In subsequent years Sadat pledged to support Numayri against continued Libyan attempts at subversion, and Sudan followed Egypt into close alignment with the United States. While rejecting the Egyptian-Israeli peace treaty of 1979, Sudan was one of the few Arab states that did not break diplomatically with Cairo. Egypt's main strategic interest in Sudan focuses on water supplied from the Nile River via Sudan, which is currently governed by a 1959 treaty granting Egypt generous access to the Nile. Cairo supports the Comprehensive Peace Agreement CPA (see Current issues, below) but remains ambivalent towards the prospect of southern autonomy, which would require renegotiation of the water treaty.

In October 1988 Prime Minister Mahdi, reportedly desperate for arms, signed a unity proposal with Col. Qadhafi that was denounced by the DUP and in January 1989 labeled "inappropriate" by the United States following reports that Libyan forces had used chemical weapons in attacks on SPLA forces. Concurrently, Washington, whose nonintervention policy had drawn criticism from international aid groups, announced its intention to supply aid directly to drought victims in areas under SPLA control rather than through allegedly corrupt government channels. Four months later Washington cut off all nonfamine relief support because of Khartoum's failure to service its foreign debt, lack of democratic commitment, and human rights record. Later in the year relations with the United States deteriorated even further when Sudan refused to join the UN coalition against Iraq, a decision that also cost Sudan financial support from Saudi Arabia and Egypt. In addition, many Arab states subsequently expressed concern over the growing influence of Islamic fundamentalism under the Bashir regime. However, Iran, anxious to support the fundamentalist cause, funded Sudanese economic and, according to some reports, military aid.

In August 1994 authorities in Khartoum seized terrorist Ilich Ramírez Sanchez (also known as "Carlos"), who was flown to Paris for trial on charges stemming from a 1983 attack in the French capital. In return, France was reported to have persuaded the Central African Republic (CAR) to provide Sudanese military transit through CAR territory. In addition, Khartoum sought French assistance in restoring its relations with the United States following unexpectedly low aid grants from Iran.

Meanwhile, relations with other neighboring states deteriorated sharply. In September 1994 Egypt was accused of moving troops into Sudan's northern Halaib region, and relations deteriorated further in mid-1995 after President Mubarak had intimated that the NIF might have been involved in the failed attempt on his life in Addis Ababa on June 26. In the south, Uganda canceled a 1990 agreement providing for a military monitoring team on its side of their border, and in April 1995 it broke relations because of the alleged bombing of a Ugandan village by Sudanese government forces; however, relations were restored in mid-June as the result of talks between presidents Bashir and Museveni that were brokered by Malawian president Bakili Muluzi.

By late 1995 Sudan had come under widespread criticism for its alleged sponsorship of international terrorism, including possible involvement in the Mubarak assassination attempt. On December 19 foreign ministers of states belonging to the Organization of African Unity (OAU, subsequently the African Union—AU), met in Addis Ababa and called on Khartoum to extradite three Egyptians wanted for questioning in the Mubarak affair. On January 31, 1996, the UN Security Council instituted sanctions and adopted a unanimous resolution to the same effect. Earlier, as an expression of its displeasure, Ethiopia had ordered a reduction in Sudan's embassy staff to four, the closure of a Sudanese consulate, and a ban on nongovernmental organizations linked to the Sudanese regime.

In 1997 and early 1998, Eritrea, Ethiopia, and Uganda cooperated to restrict the spread of militant fundamentalism in the Horn of Africa, further straining relations with Sudan, which accused the other governments of supporting the SPLM and NDA. (Relations with Ethiopia subsequently improved, however, in conjunction with the outbreak of hostilities between that nation and Eritrea, which Khartoum charged was still backing Sudanese rebels.) Meanwhile, South African president Nelson MANDELA played a prominent role in efforts to bring the Bashir regime and its opponents together for peace talks under the aegis of IGAD.

In November 1997 Washington accused the Bashir government of supporting international terrorism and human rights abuses and imposed economic sanctions against Sudan. The friction that arose between the United States and Sudan after a meeting between U.S. secretary of state Madeleine Albright, Col. Garang, and other NDA leaders in Uganda subsequently intensified when U.S. missiles destroyed a pharmaceutical plant in Khartoum on August 20, 1998, in response to bombings of the U.S. embassies in Kenya and Tanzania on August 7. Despite inconclusive evidence, Washington claimed the Sudanese facility had been producing nerve gas for the "terrorist network" of militant Islamic fundamentalist Osama bin Laden. The government in Khartoum, which had expelled bin Laden from the country in 1996 under U.S. pressure, strongly denied the U.S. accusations.

In 1999 and 2000 Sudan reestablished diplomatic relations with the United Kingdom, Kuwait, Ethiopia, Eritrea, Egypt, and Tunisia, and later requested that the UN Security Council lift the 1996 sanctions. The Security Council unanimously approved the request in September 2001.

Throughout 2004 and early 2005, the international response to human rights abuses in Darfur materialized slowly (see Current issues, below). In April 2005 the UN Security Council voted to refer 51 Sudanese—many of them said to be high-ranking NIF officials—for International Criminal Court (ICC) prosecution for crimes against humanity in Darfur. That same month, Western countries pledged $4.5 billion in urgent food aid for southerners displaced by the civil war. In response to food shortages, the Arab Authority for Agriculture and the Abu Dhabi Fund for Development in 2008 worked in conjunction with the Sudanese government to develop a large-scale agricultural program to mitigate food insecurity in Sudan by providing 28,000 hectares of free land for crop production.

In response to continuing attacks on Uganda by the Lord's Resistance Army (LRA) from bases in Sudan, the newly installed Government of South Sudan signed a security protocol with Uganda in October 2005 calling for joint efforts to suppress the LRA. Recent reports indicate that despite a December 1999 accord, violence continued to occur as the LRA accused Sudanese troops of attacks by their forces on the Congo border, preventing peace meetings.

Relations with Chad worsened in 2005 as Chadian rebels launched a series of attacks from bases in Sudan. By December 2005 Chadian president Idriss Déby described the two countries as being in a state of "belligerency." In April 2007 Chad severed diplomatic ties with Sudan after a rebel movement springing from Darfur attacked N'Djamena (see entry on Chad). Through 2008 rebel activity by both Chadian rebels and Darfur rebels continued on the Sudan–Darfur frontier. On March 13, 2008, the two governments signed a nonaggression accord in Dakar, Senegal, but the rebels dismissed the accord and continued armed activity.

As an economic and military partner, China has been Sudan's closest ally and has done the most to protect the regime from UN sanctions. China is Sudan's largest trade partner and the largest investor in Sudan's oil industry, with almost 68 percent of Sudan's total export portfolio and 60 percent of Sudan's oil exports accounted for by trade with China since 2004. China has also supplied the Sudanese government with small arms, anti-personnel mines, howitzers, tanks, helicopters, and ammunition, in addition to constructing three arms factories in Sudan, despite a UN-sanctioned arms embargo on the region. The government also ordered new fighter jets from China in late 2005.

In 2006 China placed limited pressure on Khartoum to relieve international criticism before the 2008 Beijing Olympic Games. China voted in favor of the October 2006 resolution for a UN force in Darfur. Nonetheless, China continued its strong bilateral ties with Sudan. The October revelation that a hijacked freighter bound for South Sudan was carrying tanks and other weaponry with Kenyan licenses strained relations between Khartoum and Nairobi.

U.S. president George W. Bush authorized the transfer of vehicles and equipment for UNAMID in January 2009. In March Sudan expelled 13 international aid agencies in retaliation for the ICC indictment of Bashir (see Current issues, below). The agencies were allowed to return in June. Unidentified aerial forces attacked a Sudanese weapons convoy en route to Egypt. The attack was reportedly conducted by Israeli forces to prevent the arms and munitions from being smuggled into Gaza. Sudan and Chad signed an agreement to normalize relations on May 3, following negotiations brokered by Qatar and Libya. However, the accord failed within weeks, and reports indicated that the JEM was establishing new bases in Chad for operations against the government in Khartoum. Meanwhile, reports throughout the year indicated that the Bashir government was buying an increasing number of arms and munitions from Iran. An international effort to convince firms to divest from Sudan secured a growing number of companies in 2009. In October the United States renewed sanctions against the Bashir regime because of the Sudanese government's actions in Darfur, and it offered new incentives to Sudan for resolving the Darfur conflict. In October reports indicated that the Ugandan guerilla group, the Lord's Resistance Army, had established new bases in Darfur (see the entry on Uganda).

In February 2010 the presidents of Sudan and Chad held a new round of negotiations in an effort to revive the failed 2009 accord between the two countries. The two presidents agreed to stop supporting rebel groups.

Most foreign leaders and dignitaries boycotted Bashir's inauguration in May 2010. In July the ICC issued a new arrest warrant for Bashir on charges of genocide in Darfur. However, the AU announced its members should not arrest the Sudanese president. In July Bashir attended the Community of Sahel and Saharan States in Chad and then travelled to Kenya in August in defiance of the ICC warrants.

In September 2010 the Lord's Resistance Army conducted two attacks in the CAR from bases in Sudan, killing 16. The group also carried out a series of attacks on Sudanese villages, killing 15 and injuring more than 20.

On June 20, 2011, the governments of Sudan and South Sudan signed an agreement in Addis Ababa, Ethiopia, under the auspices of the AU, to demilitarize the border area around the contested town of Abyei (see Current issues, below). As part of the accord, Ethiopia agreed to deploy a 4,200-member peacekeeping force. The deployment was endorsed by the UN Security Council through Resolution 1990 on June 27.

Sudanese and Chinese officials signed a new agreement in June 2011 to allow Chinese firms to develop oil and gas fields in the country. In August Sudan recognized the new transitional government of Libya. Following continued fighting between Sudanese and South Sudanese forces in December, the UN Security Council adopted a resolution calling for both countries to demilitarize their joint border.

Fighting in Sudan in 2012 created a new wave of refugees with more than 100,000 fleeing to South Sudan and another 30,000 to Ethiopia in what reports described as a new round of ethnic cleansing. In February 2012 the northern branch of the SPLM released 29 Chinese construction workers who had been detained during fighting with government forces.

On September 27, 2012, the leaders of Sudan and South Sudan signed nine bilateral agreements to cover a range of issues remaining from the South's secession. The accords covered citizenship matters, the exchange of prisoners and reparation of refugees, the creation of a demilitarized border and, most significantly, the resumption of oil shipments from the South. Border crossings were reopened in October.

On October 24, 2012, Israeli launched an air attack that destroyed a weapons factory in Khartoum. Israel charged that the facility was operated by Iran to produce weapons for Palestinians in the Gaza Strip.

In February 2013 reports emerged that insurgents from Mali established bases in Darfur, following French-led military operations in Mali. Meanwhile, disputes over implementation of the 2012 agreements continued and led to a series of bilateral meetings between Bashir and Kiir under the auspices of the AU. Troops were finally withdrawn from the border regions in March 2013, and oil shipments from South Sudan resumed in April. However, in June Khartoum threatened to shut off the pipelines, asserting that Juba was supporting rebel groups in the north. Shipments continued following mediation by the AU and China.

In September 2013 an estimated 2,500 South Sudanese were transported from the White Nile State to South Sudan. The refugees had been stranded in the area when South Sudan became independent. The following month, the AU adopted a resolution calling on the ICC to grant immunity to sitting heads of state and defer cases against Bashir and Uhuru Kenyata, the president of Kenya (see the entry on Kenya).

Saudi Arabia and the United Arab Emirates imposed financial sanctions on Sudan for its continued support for the Muslim Brotherhood in April 2014. Reports in June indicated that Sudan had ended its opposition to the Ethiopian Nile dam project (see the entry on Ethiopia). In August a U.S. court in New York ruled that Sudan and Iraq were liable for $8 billion in compensation to be paid to the survivors and relatives of victims of the 1998 African embassy bombings.

The ICC suspended its investigation in Darfur in December 2014, citing a lack of cooperation from both the UN and the Sudanese government. On March 9, 2015, the ICC ruled that Sudan had consistently refused to cooperate with the court and referred that case back to the UN Security Council. In June Bashir flew to Johannesburg, South Africa, to attend an AU meeting. A South Africa Court issued a warrant for his arrest to comply with the existing ICC warrants; however, the government refused to take action.

In June 2016 reports indicated that Sudan had begun to implement economic reforms that would allow it to join the World Trade Organization (WTO). Meanwhile, the WTO was expected to take action on Sudan's application in July 2017. Also in June 2016 the ICC's chief prosecutor for Darfur excoriated the UN Security Council for failing to enforce ICC warrants for Bashir. In October the presidents of Sudan and Egypt signed a strategic partnership agreement designed to improve trade between the two countries and enhance social and culture exchanges. In November Sudan announced it had severed military ties with North Korea following negotiations with South Korea over enhanced bilateral economic cooperation.

Current issues. A bloody struggle in the western region of Darfur erupted in February 2003 following years of tribal clashes. Escalation occurred when the Darfur Liberation Front claimed in February 2003 to have seized control of Gulu, and government forces were sent to retake the village in early March. The conflict, fueled by the scarcity of water and grazing land, became an increasingly fierce rivalry between Arab tribesmen who raised cattle and needed the land, and black African farmers who relied on the water. The fighting intensified in 2004, as black Africans accused the government in Khartoum of using the mounted, Arab *Janjaweed* militias, sometimes accompanied by fighters in Sudanese military uniforms, to force people from their land. The insurgent groups—the Sudan Liberation Movement/Army (SLM/A) and the Justice and Equality Movement (JEM)—claimed that the government had neglected the impoverished areas for years.

In 2004 human rights workers charged that the government had used the *Janjaweed* to implement a policy resembling ethnic cleansing. Peace talks began in mid-July, as demanded by U.S. secretary of state Colin Powell, but soon dissolved when Khartoum rejected the rebels' conditions, including a time frame for disarming the militias. On July 29 the UN Security Council threatened to enact punitive measures short of sanctions. In response, 100,000 people reportedly protested against a Security Council resolution in Khartoum, prompting rebel groups and government authorities to agree to meet in Nigeria for peace talks starting on August 23, 2004. However, the talks had broken down completely by August 8. The government refused to agree to stop aerial bombardment in Darfur and to disarm the *Janjaweed* militias, and the rebel groups refused to move into AU-designated confinement sites, arguing they would be too vulnerable to government attack. Powell declared on September 10 that the United States considered the killing, rape, and destruction in Darfur to be genocide and asked for urgent action by the Security Council.

On November 9, 2004, the government agreed to ban military flights over Darfur and signed two deals with the rebels after two weeks of talks in Nigeria. However, no agreement was reached on a long-term resolution to the fighting, and violence resumed within weeks. On March 23, 2005, the Security Council unanimously approved a resolution calling for 10,000 peacekeepers for Darfur and southern Sudan. However, resistance from the Sudanese government to a UN mission led to the continuation of the AU mission in Sudan. In May 2005 NATO agreed to assist the AU-led mission in Darfur with transport and other logistical aid, and Rwanda and Nigeria sent peacekeeping forces into Darfur in July. The AU force eventually numbered some 7,000. By September estimates of those killed in the conflict ranged from 70,000 to 300,000, and 2 to 3 million people were believed to have been displaced.

On another unsettling front, a tense military situation in eastern Sudan in the states of Kassala and the Red Sea Hills began to escalate in 2005 led by a group called the Eastern Front. This group came out of an alliance between the Beja Congress and the Rashaida Free Lions, which had also long complained about the government ignoring them. The conflict was widely resolved in late 2006 with aid from the Eritrean government, which mediated talks that led to the signing of the Eastern

Sudan Peace Agreement (ESPA) on October 14, 2006. The agreement granted the eastern states more representation in the national government and established the Eastern Sudan Reconstruction and Development Fund.

On July 10, 2005, Bashir ended the national state of emergency in all but three of Sudan's provinces: Darfur, Kasala, and Red Sea Hills. Bashir also ordered the release of hundreds of political prisoners, including Turabi. The SLM/A subsequently launched a new offensive in Darfur, and the AU initiated a new round of peace talks between the government and the SLM/A and the JEM in Abuja, Nigeria. The AU developed a comprehensive peace plan, which the Sudanese government accepted on April 30, 2006. On May 5, 2006, the Darfur Peace Agreement was created as a result of the peace talks in Abuja, Nigeria. The document was signed by a faction of the SLM/A as well as the Government of National Unity (GNU), which was the result of the 2005 CPA, but the primary rebel forces, a large faction of the SLM/A and JEM, did not sign the agreement. The plan called for the disarmament of the *Janjaweed* militias, elections within three years, and the provision of $500 million for the establishment and operation of an autonomous regional authority. Meanwhile, Sudan rejected a proposal from UN secretary general Kofi Annan in April 2006 to replace the AU mission with a more expansive UN-led operation.

Unfortunately, the April 2006 peace agreement heightened tensions in Darfur, as rival rebel groups clashed and the government stepped up military offensives against the SLA/A and JEM. On October 20, 2006, the Sudanese government threw out the UN special envoy Jan Pronk, accusing him of undermining Sudan's armed forces and of trying to force the government to accept an August 2006 Security Council Resolution calling for 20,000 UN peacekeeping troops in Darfur. In December 2006 a proposal presented at the AU's Joint Ceasefire Commission in Addis Ababa called for a beefed up AU mission that would include only African troops with support staff of other nationalities. Bashir initially agreed in principle to the plan, but negotiation regarding details, such as the force's size, purpose, and command structure, were all subject to controversy, allowing the Sudanese government to stall the process.

In January 2007 Bill Richardson, governor of the U.S. state of New Mexico, brokered a short-lived 60-day cease-fire agreement between the government and the main rebel groups, including the JEM and the SLA/A. In February 2007 the ICC formally accused two Sudanese of war crimes and crimes against humanity during the Darfur crisis, the first potential prosecutions since the UN Security Council referred cases to the ICC in April 2005. Formal indictments were made by June 2008, when arrest warrants issued on May 2, 2007, were pending against Ali Kushayb and Ahmad Haroun. In the same month, chief ICC prosecutor Luis Moreno-Ocampo complained of noncooperation with the ICC by the Sudanese government; ICC investigations found "no trace of Sudanese proceedings in relation to crimes in Darfur during the last three years. The Government itself has clarified that there were none." The ICC presented an application for the arrest of President Bashir for war crimes on July 14, 2008, but over two-thirds of council members were in favor of deferring the decision to arrest Bashir for one year. Nations such as China, Libya, and South Africa, as well as members of the Sudanese government and the AU, fear that Bashir's arrest would damage any progress made during the peace process. The Arab League has recommended that Sudan surrender the two Sudanese already indicted, and create a domestic court for judicial proceedings related to Darfur under the supervision of international bodies.

In 2007 the conflict was exacerbated by floods and resulting epidemics. A Security Council resolution passed in July 2007 authorized special envoys with the maximum authorized strength of approximately 26,000 military troops and police forces. The Sudanese government announced its formal acceptance of the plan, which outlines a joint AU–UN mission, with the majority of troops to come from African countries with logistical support from other UN member countries. Disagreement with the Sudanese government over the makeup of the mission slowed the implementation, with UN claims that many of the African troops that volunteered to take part in the mission did not meet UN peacekeeping standards in terms of training and equipment and needed to be supplemented with troops from other parts of the world. The government of Sudan and some AU leaders resisted this and argued that the African troops were capable of carrying out the UN mandate. Rebel leaders, government representatives, and international ministers and mediators prepared for peace talks in Tripoli, Libya. Talks began on October 27, 2007, and quickly collapsed. As of April 30, 2008, the AU and the UN had deployed 7,393 troops, 128 observers, and 1,716 police. The African Union/United Nations Hybrid Operation in Darfur (UNAMID) forces primarily come from Nigeria, Rwanda, South Africa, and Senegal.

By late 2007 the conflict in Darfur was attracting so much attention that the SPLM withdrew from the National Legislature, arguing that the concerns of south Sudan were being ignored. The SPLM withdrawal, announced by the party's secretary general, Pagan Amum, threatened to reignite the civil war between north and south Sudan. Peace between north and south was threatened by border disputes, which dictate oil revenue allocations between the two regions, and southern complaints that the NC did not adhere to the terms of the CPA. As a result of the SPLM withdrawal, Bashir reorganized the cabinet in December 2007 to appease the opposition.

In September 2008 the *New York Times* reported that an estimated 2.5 million people had been uprooted by the conflict in Darfur and that at least 200,000 had died. In October the government arrested the leader of a progovernment militia in Darfur, Ali Muhammad Ali ABD-AL-RAHMAN (Ali KUSHAYB), whom the ICC had indicted for war crimes. Although the government placed Kushayb in custody, it refused to turn him over to the ICC, and reports were that his arrest was a preventative measure designed to forestall his arrest by peacekeeping forces.

The ICC indicted Bashir on war crimes and crimes against humanity on March 4, 2009, and issued an international warrant for his arrest. The warrant was the first by the ICC for a sitting head of state. The government rejected the warrant and accused the court of "colonialism." In addition, African and Arab states refused calls to arrest Bashir, who openly made trips to Eritrea and Saudi Arabia and attended the Arab League Summit in Qatar. In April the National Election Commission announced that balloting would be held in February 2010 with 75 percent of the posts chosen by national balloting and the remaining 25 percent selected by state legislatures in indirect elections. The following month, fighting left at least 20 government soldiers and 40 JEM rebels dead in Darfur. Renewed fighting in South Sudan in June killed more than 1,000 and created more than 135,000 displaced persons. The strife originated in long-standing disputes among tribes over water rights and cattle-grazing areas. Opposition groups criticized the government census in August, arguing that the population count underestimated the inhabitants of southern Sudan.

In January 2010 Bashir resigned from the military, as required by the constitution, to run for the presidency. Preelection violence reportedly killed more than 1,000 between January and April. Concerns over voter registration and potential fraud led opposition parties and international observers to request a delay in presidential and assembly polling scheduled for April. When the government refused to postpone the balloting, the SPLM, the UP, and other major opposition groups withdrew from the presidential elections and boycotted the assembly polling in the north. Nonetheless, the SPLM agreed to abide by the results of the balloting in exchange for assurances that the January independence referendum would take place as planned. In balloting that ran April 11–15, Bashir was reelected president, and the NC secured an overwhelming majority in the assembly. In balloting for president of the GOSS, Kiir was reelected, defeating Lam AKOL of the Sudan People's Liberation Army–Democratic Change (see Political Parties and Groups, below). In May Kiir appointed a new cabinet for the GOSS. Fighting in May in Darfur killed more than 600 and created a new wave of displaced persons. In July the JEM signed an accord with UNICEF to prohibit the use of child soldiers and remove underage fighters from areas of conflict.

The long-anticipated referendum on southern independence was conducted during January 9–15, 2011. Voters in the south overwhelmingly endorsed independence, with 98.8 percent of the vote in favor of separation from Sudan. Turnout was 97.6 percent. On February 21 Bashir announced that he would not seek reelection in 2015.

In May 2011 Sudanese forces attacked the disputed town of Abyei, killing more than 800 and creating an estimated 90,000 refugees. The oil-rich area was claimed by both Sudan and South Sudan. Under the CPA the region was supposed to conduct a referendum on independence, and reports indicated that the attack was an effort to ethnically cleanse the area. The AU mediated a settlement to demilitarize the region and deploy Ethiopian peacekeepers in June. Also in May, under the auspices of the UN, the Arab League, and the AU, a peace agreement for Darfur was signed in Doha. The accord called for the creation of a new regional government for the area. In September 2011 a number of political parties were suspended because their leaders had South Sudanese citizenship. In November 2011 the Sudan Revolutionary

Front (SRF) was formed to unify the armed Sudanese opposition. The SRF united JEM, the northern branches of the SPLM/A (see Political Parties and Groups, below), and other smaller rebel groups. SRF forces secured a series of victories against Sudanese security forces in South Kordofan and the Blue Nile states in late 2011 and 2012.

In January 2012 South Sudan cut off the flow of oil to the north after charging that the north illicitly diverted more than $815 million in revenues due to Juba. This resulted in a 75 percent loss of revenue for the Bashir government (see entry on South Sudan). By July the government had to cut popular subsidies on food, consumer goods, and fuel, leading to widespread protests. In addition, inflation rose to more than 30 percent.

On February 8, 2012, the Darfur Regional Authority was created. The new body was tasked to implement the Doha peace accord. Nonetheless, renewed fighting in the region created an estimated 70,000 internal refugees by May 2012. Meanwhile, after Sudanese air attacks on South Sudan, SPLA forces captured the oil town of Heglig in April (they subsequently withdrew under international pressure).

The ICC issued an arrest warrant for Defense Minister Lt. Gen. Abdel-Rahim HUSSEIN, on March 1, 2012, indicting him on 20 charges of crimes against humanity and 21 charges of war crimes for his actions in Darfur in 2003 and 2004.

Sudan approved a smoking ban in interior public places such as schools and hospitals in September 2012. Tribal fighting in South Kordofan killed more than 200 during the winter of 2012–2013. Human rights groups criticized a government offensive in the Nuba mountains in the region, which left hundreds of civilians dead and prompted new allegations of war crimes against the regime.

In January 2013 the government and JEM signed a new peace framework that recommitted the group to the 2011 Doha agreement. Meanwhile, on January 5 the SRF and other opposition groups signed the New Dawn Charter, which pledged collaboration against the Bashir regime. In March Bashir stated in two published interviews that he would not seek reelection. On April 1 Bashir announced a general amnesty for all political prisoners. Opposition groups were skeptical that the regime would release all detainees. Eleven military officers were convicted in April of plotting a coup in November 2012. Also in April a donor conference pledged $3.65 billion for the reconstruction of Darfur, following the signing of a comprehensive peace treaty between JEM and the government. In May, the paramount chief of the Abyei region, Koul Deng KUOL, was assassinated while travelling in a UN convoy. Opposition figures accused the Bashir regime of orchestrating the killing.

Major flooding in Sudan in August 2013 killed more than 50 people and left more than 200,000 homeless. The floods also significantly damaged roads and other infrastructure. In September the government announced a series of economic reforms, including the elimination of fuel subsidies. The rise in fuel prices prompted widespread protests (see Political Parties and Groups, below). When security forces endeavored to suppress the demonstrations, an estimated 50–100 protestors were killed, while at least 700 were detained.

Sudan ordered the International Committee of the Red Crescent to suspend activities in February 2014 without providing a rationale for the decision. In April Bashir announced the release of hundreds of political prisoners and the easing of some restrictions on political parties and the press. The president also invited political parties to join together in a national dialogue, a call that was rejected by most opposition groupings. Through the summer of 2014, renewed fighting in Darfur was estimated to have created an additional 300,000 refugees. Opposition groups charged that the government's newly created paramilitary Rapid Support Forces (RSF) were thinly disguised *Janjaweed* militias. Meanwhile, reports indicated that the SRF had secured a series of military victories against regimes forces in Kordofan.

The government reported in January 2015 that its forces had recaptured territory in Darfur, held by rebel forces, including the SPLM-N. Also in January the international medical assistance group, Doctors Without Borders (*Médecins Sans Frontières*), announced its withdrawal from areas of conflict in Sudan due to lack of cooperation, along with overt obstructions, by the government. In February Human Rights Watch released a report that charged Sudanese government forces with widespread rape and other human rights violations during the capture of Tabit in November 2014.

Bashir launched a new "national dialogue" on October 10, 2015, with rebel and opposition groups and repeated offers of a new ceasefire and amnesty. However, the talks were boycotted by the principal rebel and opposition groups, including the SRF.

An October 2016 Amnesty International report accused the Sudanese government of using chemical weapons in more than 30 separate instances in Darfur. The report was based on interviews, video and photographic evidence, and satellite data but was strongly denied by the Bashir regime.

POLITICAL PARTIES AND GROUPS

Following the 1969 coup, all political parties, except the Sudanese Communist Party (SCP), were outlawed. After the failure of the SCP coup in July 1971, the party was driven underground and its leaders were arrested. The following October, President Numayri attempted to supplant the existing parties by launching the Sudanese Socialist Union, modeled after the Arab Socialist Union of Egypt, the country's only recognized political group until its suspension by the TMC in April 1985. In 1986 the Union of Sudan African Parties (USAP) was formed, with six parties representing the south of Sudan and the Nuba mountain region and won 36 seats in the assembly in 1986. The USAP was a founding member of the **National Democratic Alliance** (NDA), a loose antigovernment coalition. More than 40 parties were reported to have participated in the post-Numayri balloting of April 1986, although only the Umma (People's) Party (UP), Democratic Unionist Party (DUP), and National Islamic Front (NIF) obtained substantial legislative representation. The NDA called for a boycott of the March 1996 presidential and general elections. A joint NDA military command was established in October 1996 under the direction of the SPLM's Col. John Garang. (For more on the NDA, see the 2012 and 2014 *Handbooks.*)

In January 2007 the National Assembly passed the controversial Political Parties Bill, which allowed for the suspension or dissolution of any political party that the government deems to be carrying out activities contrary to the terms of the CPA, including preventing parties from participating in elections. The bill also prevents any member of security forces or government from joining any political party with the exception of President Bashir and Vice President Kiir, who are both military commanders, until the end of the CPA's transitional period. Following the announcement that elections would be held in February 2010, the government registered 37 new parties, bringing the number of official parties in Sudan to 72, a figure that grew to 76 by 2014. In 2014, opposition parties announced a new grouping, the **National Consensus Front** (NCF), in an effort to unify ahead of elections scheduled for 2015. However, the opposition boycotted the 2015 balloting. At the time of that polling, there were 82 registered parties in Sudan but only 42 competed in the elections.

Government and Legislative Parties:

National Congress (NC). The NC is a partial successor to the **National Islamic Front** (*al-Jabhah al-Watani al-Islami*—NIF), which was organized prior to the April 1986 balloting by the leader of the fundamentalist Muslim Brotherhood, Dr. Hassan Abdallah al-Turabi, who as attorney general had been largely responsible for the harsh enforcement of sharia law under the Numayri government. (For more on the history of the party, see the 2014 *Handbook.*) As it became more and more identified with fundamentalism, the Bashir government appointed numerous NIF adherents to key government posts, most observers agreeing that the Front had become a de facto government party. NIF/Muslim Brotherhood supporters also were reported to be directing the Islamic "security groups," which had assumed growing authority since 1990.

Turabi, one of the world's leading Islamic fundamentalist theoreticians, was routinely described as the country's most powerful political figure. A follower of Iran's late Ayatollah Khomeini, he called for the creation of Islamic regimes in all Arab nations, a position that concerned several nearby states (particularly Egypt) and major Western capitals. The NIF's "number two," Ali Uthman Muhammad Taha, was named foreign minister in February 1995 and first vice president in early 1998.

It was reported in 1996 that Turabi had directed that the NIF be renamed the National Congress (NC), to reflect a broader umbrella political organization open to all citizens, and to act as a quasi-institutional governing body. Subsequent news reports appeared to use the two names interchangeably, with the NIF rubric predominating. In January 1999 it was announced that a National Congress had been officially registered as a political party, while reports in March indicated similar status had been accorded to a National Islamic Front Party. It was not immediately clear what relationship, if any, the two groupings had to each other or the traditional NIF. Meanwhile, reports (officially denied) surfaced of friction between Turabi and party reformists as well as between Turabi and Sudanese President Bashir, who was named chair of the recently established NIF advisory council. Tensions between Turabi and Bashir resulted in the removal of Turabi as general secretary in May. Turabi subsequently formed a new party, the Popular (People's) National Congress (PNC, below), and Bashir's supporters formally used the NC rubric in the December 2000 elections.

The party held a general congress in October 2009 to determine candidates ahead of the 2010 elections. Although the ICC had indicted Bashir for his role in the country's genocide, he was the NC presidential candidate. Bashir was reelected president in April 2010. In addition, the NC won 312 seats in the assembly and dominated a unity government formed by Bashir in June and a new cabinet named in December. After Bashir announced that he would not seek reelection in 2015, reports indicated growing factionalism within the NC as possible successors jockeyed for influence.

Led by NC South Sudan chair Agnes Poni LUKUDU, the party's main leaders in the South defected to the SPLM in July 2012. Reports subsequently indicated that the NC was defunct in South Sudan.

After Bashir underwent surgery in November 2012, reports indicated that the president had been treated for throat cancer. The reports stirred speculation that Bashir might step down before scheduled presidential elections in 2015.

Following protests against the elimination of fuel subsidies in September 2013, 31 senior members of the NCP sent a petition to Bashir criticizing the government's response to the demonstrations. Several of the signatories were expelled from the NC in November, including former presidential advisor Salah al-Din ATABANI, who subsequently announced the formation of a new political grouping, the **Reform Now Movement**.

Bashir was reelected president in April 2015, while in concurrent polling the NC won 323 seats in the assembly.

Leaders: Umar Hassan Ahmad al-BASHIR (President of the Republic and Chair of the Party's *Shura* [Council]), Ibrahim Ahmed OMAR (Secretary General), Lt. Gen. Bakr Bakri Hassan SALIH and Hasbo Mohamed ABDULRAHMAN (Vice Presidents of the Republic).

Islamic Umma Party (*Hizb al-Ummah al-Islamiyah*—IUP). This small party split off from the mainstream Umma (People's) Party (UP, below) in 1985. In applying for recognition in early 1999, the IUP announced it would advocate sharia as the sole source of law while promoting "Mahdist" ideology and a nonaligned foreign policy. The IUP was officially registered in April 1999 and convened its first general congress with delegates from all parts of Sudan the same month. The IUP backed the NC in the 2010 and 2015 balloting.

Leader: Wali al-Din al-Hadi al-MAHDI.

Umma (People's) Party (*Hizb al-Ummah*—UP). A moderate right-of-center formation, the UP has long been led by former prime minister Mahdi. Founded in 1945, UP receives its strongest support from Ansar Muslims of the White Nile and western Darfur and Kordofan provinces. It obtained a plurality of 100 seats at the 1986 assembly balloting. Members traditionally advocated the repeal of sharia law and were wary of NIF fundamentalism. Despite a historically pro-Libyan, anti-Egyptian posture, the party cultivated good relations with Western countries based, in part, on Mahdi's personal ties to Britain.

Prime Minister Mahdi and Idriss al-Banna were arrested shortly after the military coup in June 1989 (the latter being sentenced to 40 years in jail for corruption; Mahdi was released from prison and placed under house arrest in January 1990), amid rumors that the UP was considering some form of cooperation with the new regime. In light of growing fundamentalist influence within the Bashir government, the UP announced an alliance with the SPLM (see Other Groups, below) dedicated to overthrowing the government; ending the civil war; and reintroducing multiparty, secular democracy. The southern liaison notwithstanding, the UP membership was reported to be deeply divided following Mahdi's release from house arrest in May 1991. With southern groups tending more and more to support independence for their region, the UP in early 1994 was described as "open" on the question. Mahdi was rearrested in June 1994 on charges of plotting against the government and again in May 1995 for a three-month period. He was reportedly invited by the Bashir regime to join the new government formed in April 1996 but declined and eventually fled to Asmara, Eritrea, in December.

The UP was one of the first groups to seek recognition in early 1999, the pro-negotiation faction having apparently gained ascendancy. For his part, Mahdi in November concluded an agreement with Bashir known as the "Call of the Homeland Accord," which proposed a new, pluralistic constitution for Sudan and a four-year transitional period that would conclude with a self-determination referendum for the south. Consequently, in March 2000 Mahdi announced that the UP had withdrawn from the NDA, which he criticized for refusing to negotiate with the government, and directed the Umma militia to honor a cease-fire. Mahdi returned to the Sudan in November after four years of exile in Egypt, but the UP nonetheless boycotted the December legislative and presidential elections, arguing that the balloting should be postponed pending comprehensive "national reconciliation." The UP also declined Bashir's invitation to join the cabinet in February 2001, again on the premise that a "bilateral" agreement was not appropriate while other opposition groups remained in conflict with the government. Subsequent to leaving the NDA in 2000, the Umma Party split into several factions: the **Umma Reform and Renewal** faction, led by Mubarak al-FADIL al-Mahdi, a cousin of former prime minister al-Mahdi; the **Umma General Leadership** faction, also known as the **Umma National Party**, led by Dr. al-Sadiq al-Hadi al-MAHDI, another cousin of al-Mahdi; and the **Federal Umma Party**, led by Ahmed Babiker NAHAR. The Reform and Renewal splinter faction accepted ministerial posts in August 2002 and in the 2005 unity government. The party officially favors the deployment of a hybrid AU-UN peacekeeping force in Darfur. The party remains active but outside of the unity government. It complains that the CPA served to solidify the NC's hold on power, leaving little room for northern opposition parties to contest Bashir's power. Fadil was arrested in July 2007, together with 27 other opposition leaders, and was charged with plotting to overthrow the government, although he was subsequently released. In 2009 several prominent UP members defected to the newly formed SPLM-DC. In July the UP and the JEM signed an agreement of principles, which was criticized by the government and NC.

The UP National faction initially nominated former prime minister al-Mahdi as its presidential candidate in 2010, but the party withdrew from the presidential and legislative elections to protest alleged electoral irregularities. Nonetheless, al-Mahdi placed fifth in the polling, albeit with less than 1 percent of the vote. The faction also secured one seat in the assembly. Fadil of the Reform and Renewal faction received less than 1 percent of the vote in presidential balloting, and his grouping gained two seats in the assembly, despite participation in the boycott. The Federal faction secured three seats, and its leader, Nahar, was appointed to a cabinet position in the subsequent government.

In August 2011 the UP signed a memorandum of understanding with the government of South Sudan as part of an effort to foster political reconciliation. Both the Umma National faction and the Umma Reform and Renewal grouping received posts in the 2011 unity government.

The Umma National faction endorsed the series of agreements with South Sudan in 2012 and 2013. In May 2014 al-Mahdi was arrested on charges of sedition but released the following month. He then went into exile. In August al-Mahdi's daughter, Mariam al-MAHDI, a deputy party leader, was arrested and held for a month, though no charges were filed against her. Also in August, the Umma National faction signed an accord with the SRF in Paris. The Paris Declaration called for an end to conflict and the restoration of democracy.

The Umma factions were among the few parties that participated in the 2015 assembly balloting, although the National wing officially boycotted the polling. The Federal faction won seven seats; the Collective Leadership wing, six; the Reform and Renewal grouping, five; the United Umma, four; and the National faction, three.

Leaders: Dr. Sadiq al-MAHDI (Former Prime Minister and 2010 presidential candidate), Idris al-BANNA, Mubarak Abdullah al-MAHDI, Mubarak al-FADIL al-Mahdi (Umma Reform and Renewal Party Leader and 2010 presidential candidate), Sarrah NAGDALLA, Umar Nur al-DAIM (Secretary General), Ahmed Babiker NAHAR (Federal Umma Party Leader).

Democratic Unionist Party (*al-Hizb al-Ittihadi al-Dimuqrati*—DUP). The right-of-center DUP draws its principal strength from the Khatmiya Muslims of northern and eastern Sudan and is one of the parties that comprised the NDA. Based on its second-place showing at the 1986 poll, the DUP was the UP's junior partner in subsequent government coalitions, although internal divisions prevented the formulation of a clearly defined outlook. The faction led by party chair

Usman al-Mirghani included pro-Egyptian traditionalists once linked to the Numayri regime, who were reluctant to repeal sharia until an alternative code was formulated. Younger members, on the other hand, urged that the party abandon its "semi-feudal" orientation and become a secular, centrist formation capable of attracting nationwide support. In early 1986, the DUP reunited with an offshoot group, the **Democratic People's Party** (DPP), and subsequently appeared to have absorbed the small **National Unionist Party** (NUP), which had drawn most of its support from the Khartoum business community. (For more information on the history of the DUP, see the 2013 *Handbook.*)

Despite significant divisions, the DUP was described by *Middle East International* in early 1994 as still officially opposed to independence for the South and "not adverse to some form of Islamic state" for Sudan. The latter issue apparently had contributed to the defection in 1993 of the DUP faction led by former deputy prime minister Sharif Zein al-Abidin al-HINDI, who advocated the separation of church and state despite his position as a religious leader. A possible change in the DUP's stance toward fundamentalism and Southern secession may have been signaled by the party's participation in subsequent NDA summits.

DUP Chair Mirghani described the guidelines adopted in late 1998 for legalization of parties as too restrictive, and his supporters did not submit a request for registration, although a splinter group reportedly sought recognition under the DUP rubric. Ahmad al-Mirghani returned from exile in November 2001, but Usman al-Mirghani, who had been elected chair of the NDA in September 2000, remained outside the country. Meanwhile, a DUP splinter faction, calling itself the DUP-General Secretariat, had accepted cabinet posts in the government in February 2001 and in the 2005 unity government. The mainstream DUP has since refused to take part in the unity government. Deputy secretary-general of the party Ali Mahmoud Hassanein was arrested in July 2007 at gunpoint with 27 other opposition politicians and charged with plotting to overthrow the government. The General Secretariat splinter faction, represented by Sharif Zein al-Abidin al-Hindi until his death in 2006, is now led by the former minister of industry, Jalal Yusuf Mohammed DIGAIR. The General Secretariat DUP continued to take part in the GNU government, in contrast to the Mirghani faction. Chair Mirghani's faction requested official representation in the cabinet but was rejected by the SPLM. The DUP suffered from a number of defections in 2008 and 2009. The Mirghani faction began to call itself the DUP-Original in 2010.

The DUP factions declined to join the opposition boycott of the 2010 elections. Hatim al-SIR was the DUP-Original's candidate in the presidential balloting. He received 1.9 percent of the vote, and the DUP-Original secured one seat in the assembly. Another faction, calling itself simply the DUP, secured four seats. The DUP-Original and the DUP refused to participate in the NC-led government of national unity after the balloting. In October the DUP reportedly attempted to launch a new opposition coalition, the Broad National Front. The DUP and the DUP-Original both received ministries in the 2011 unity government. In 2013 the DUP signed a partnership agreement with the NC.

The DUP-Original won 25 seats in the 2015 assembly elections, while the DUP secured 15 seats.

Leaders: Usman al-MIRGHANI (Symbolic Chair), Dr. Ahmad al-Sayid HAMAD (Former DDP Leader), Ali Ahmed al-SAYYED, Ali Mahmoud HASSANEIN.

A number of small and regional parties won seats in the 2015 balloting, including the **National Freedom and Justice Party,** which won four seats; the **Freedom and Justice Party,** three seats; the **Federal Truth Party**, led by 2015 presidential candidate Fadl al-Sayed SHUAIB, who placed second with 1.4 percent of the vote, while his party secured two assembly seats; and the **National Bond Party** which earned two seats.

The following parties won one seat in the assembly voting **I, the Sudan** (*Ana al-Sudan*), led by Al-Hadi Mohamed KUKU; the **Constitution Party**; the **National Reform Party**, led by Tagwa Siddiq al-TAHIR; the **Popular Forces for Rights and Democracy Movement**; the **People's Movement Party**; the **Center Party for Justice and Development**; the **General Federation of North and South Funj**; and the **Black Free Party**.

Regional Interests, Opposition Parties, and Rebel Groups:

Sudan People's Liberation Movement/Army (SPLM/A). The SPLM and its military wing, the Sudanese People's Liberation Army (SPLA), were formed in 1983 by Col. John Garang, who was an officer in the Sudanese army. Sent by the Numayri administration to negotiate with mutinous soldiers in the southern garrisons, Col. Garang joined the mutineers, and under his leadership, the SPLA became the dominant southern rebel force. The SPLM and SPLA were supported by Libya prior to Numayri's ouster, when Tripoli endorsed the new regime in Khartoum. The SPLA called a cease-fire immediately following the coup but thereafter initiated military action against the Khartoum government after failing to win concessions on the southern question. Relying on an estimated 20,000–25,000 troops, the SPLA subsequently gained control of most of the nonurban south; sporadic negotiations with various northern representatives yielded several temporary cease-fires but no permanent solution to the conflict.

In 1986 the SPLM downplayed its Marxist-Leninist policies and supported a unified Sudan in which the south would be granted a larger voice in national affairs and a greater share of the nation's economic development programs. However, secessionist groups and SPLM's leaders in 1992 reportedly endorsed a division of Sudan into two autonomous, yet confederated, states, with the south operating under secular law and the north under sharia.

In August 1991 the SPLM was severely splintered when a group of second-tier leaders headquartered in the eastern town of Nasir announced their intention to wrest SPLA control from Garang, whom they accused of perpetrating a "dictatorial reign of terror." Longstanding tribal animosity also contributed to a split in the SPLA, where support for Nasir came primarily from the Nuer ethnic group, which has had a stormy relationship with Garang's Dinka supporters since the creation of the SPLA. Several months of fighting between the two factions left thousands dead, with Garang's supporters charging the dissidents with the "massacre" of Dinka civilians in January 1992. Although a temporary reconciliation between the SPLA factions was achieved at the Abuja peace talks with the government in June, sporadic fighting resumed later in the summer.

In September 1992 William Nyuon BANY conducted negotiations with the splinter group on behalf of Garang but defected to form his own faction, which in April 1993 coalesced with other anti-Garang groups as the SPLA-United (below). In early 1994 negotiations between the SPLA and the SPLA-United yielded a tentative cease-fire agreement, in which Garang reportedly agreed to support southern self-determination. Despite the possible reunification of southern forces, there was ongoing friction between Garang and the SPLA-United's Riak Machar.

In April 1994 some 500 delegates attended the first SPLA-SPLM conference since 1983. The conference was reportedly called to shore up Garang's authority in the face of competition from the SPLA-United. The SPLM leader was put in charge of the joint military command announced by the NDA in October 1996, after the SPLA-United and Machar's SSIM signed a peace accord with the Bashir government.

In late 2004 rumors of a "revolt" against Garang by secessionist SPLA officers who wanted Salva Kiir Mayardit to replace Garang as head of the SPLA surfaced, but Kiir feared a repeat of the 1991 uprising against Garang. On July 30, 2005, Garang died in a helicopter crash, an event that ignited rioting that led to the death of more than 100 people. He was succeeded as SPLM leader by his deputy Kiir. Kiir appointed Machar as vice president of the Government of Southern Sudan in August 2005.

Factions of the Southern Sudan Defense Force (SSDF) signed the Juba Declaration in 2006 in collaboration with the SPLA, but a splinter group of the SSDF still remains loyal to Gordon KONG and rejects the Juba Declaration and the CPA.

Throughout 2009 the SPLM endeavored to unite southern opposition groups under a single grouping in order to contest the 2010 elections. This effort was complicated by the emergence of a new rival party, the **Sudan People's Liberation Movement–Democratic Change** (SPLM-DC) (see the SPLA-United, below). The SPLM nominated Yasir Arman as its presidential candidate but boycotted the elections. Arman's name had already been printed on the ballots, and he received 21.7 percent of the vote in spite of the boycott. The SPLM also refused to participate in assembly balloting in the northern provinces but still secured 99 seats in the legislature and joined the subsequent NC-led unity government. Kiir was reelected president of the GOSS, defeating Akom in balloting concurrent with the national elections. Kiir was sworn in on May 21.

The SPLM led the campaign for a "yes" vote in the January 2011 referendum on independence for South Sudan. After the referendum passed with 98.8 percent of the vote, several SPLM members of the government resigned. The remainder left office after formal independence on July 9. Kiir became president of the new country and named an SPLM cabinet.

For information on the SPLM after South Sudan's independence, please see the entry on South Sudan. The northern faction of the SPLM, the **Sudan People's Liberation Movement–North** (SPLM-N) was outlawed by Bashir in October 2011. SPLM-N chair Arman was banned from Sudan.

AU-sponsored peace negotiations brought the SPLM-N and the government together in Addis Ababa beginning in April 2013, although little progress was reported. In March 2014 Arman and other SPLM-N leaders were convicted in absentia and sentenced to death for their roles in anti-regime violence. Fighting between government forces and the SPLM-N intensified in early 2015, with both sides claiming territorial gains.

Leaders: Yasir ARMAN (2010 presidential candidate and SPLM-N Chair), Abdel Aziz Adam el-HILU (SPLM-N Deputy Chair).

Sudan People's Liberation Army–United (SPLA-United). The formation of the SPLA-United was announced in early April 1993 in Nairobi, Kenya, by SPLA dissidents who opposed the "one-man rule" of longtime SPLA leader John Garang. Included in the grouping was the Nasir faction (see SPLM, above); William Nyuon Bany's self-styled **Forces of Unity**; the so-called **Kerubino Group**, formed in February by Kerubino Kwanyin BOL; and several other dissidents who had escaped from a Garang prison in the fall of 1992.

Early in 1994 the SPLA-United faced heavy domestic and international pressure to reconcile with the SPLA, as fighting resulted in civilian casualties and exacerbated famine conditions in the south. Simultaneously, the SPLA-United's independence advocates gained widespread support. In 1995 the Nasir faction split from SPLA-United, where Riak Machar formed the Southern Sudan Independence Movement (SSIM). Concurrently, Nyuon Bany was expelled from the SPLA-United after being accused of collaboration with Khartoum, despite reports in 1996 of alliances with the north and Nyuon Bany resuming a pro-Garang posture within the SSIM. In April 1997 the SPLA-United and the SSIM signed an agreement with the government endorsing the preservation of Sudan's "known boundaries," thus relinquishing their drive for independence.

The SPLA-United, under Lam Akol, subsequently gained strength through a merger with the SSDF led by Machar. As a result, Machar was named head of the new Southern States Coordination Council (SSCC; see Political background, above). However, Machar later pulled out of the government, accusing President Bashir of failing to consult with him regarding governmental appointments. Machar subsequently became the USDF leader. Meanwhile, Akol served in Bashir's cabinet until August 2002, when he was dismissed for announcing that he intended to leave the NC and form a new party. By that time, Machar and his supporters had reintegrated into the SPLA and presented a unified front during peace negotiations. SPLA leader Akol was subsequently appointed foreign minister in the 2005 government of national unity. In October 2007 the SPLM, the political wing of the SPLA, withdrew from the National Legislature, demanding that the NC abide by the terms of the CPA and Akol be removed from government due to questionable loyalties, as Akol was developing closer ties with the NC. Bashir removed Akol from his position as foreign minister and appointed SPLM member Deng Alor Kol in his place. By December 2007 SPLM legislature members were reappointed to their posts. In June 2009 Akol formed a new grouping, the SPLM-DC, to challenge the SPLM in the 2010 balloting. Akol was defeated by Kiir by an overwhelming margin in the April presidential elections. The SPLM-DC gained two seats in the National Assembly. (For information on the grouping after South Sudan's independence on July 9, 2011, see the entry on South Sudan.)

Meanwhile, the Sudan People's Liberation Army–North (SPLA-N) joined the rebel alliance, the Sudanese Revolutionary Front (Front), and continued to fight Sudanese forces in South Kordofan, Blue Nile, and Darfur. (For more information on the grouping, see the entry on South Sudan.)

Leaders: Lam AKOL (Commander in Chief), Deng ALOR Kol (Spokesperson), Pagan AMUM (Secretary General), Abdel Aziz Adam el-HILU (SPLA-N Commander).

United Democratic Salvation Front (UDSF). The UDSF is an outgrowth of the SSIM and was composed of southern Sudanese political figures and dissidents from the SPLA under the leadership of Riak Machar. The UDSF included representatives of rebel groups who had signed the 1997 peace accord with the government in Khartoum and was seen as a progovernment grouping that advocated a peaceful resolution of the North–South conflict. By 1999 the UDSF was fully operational, and in January 2000 Machar resigned as chair; he rejoined the SPLA in 2002. He was replaced by Elijah HON at a party congress. In September 2001, the party's general secretary, Ibrahim al-TAWIL, led a large group of UDSF members in a defection to the NC. In October 2001, in an effort to unify the party, new leadership elections were conducted, and Eng Joseph MALWAL was chosen chair. In March 2003 the UDSF signed a cooperation agreement with the NC and was subsequently included in successive cabinets, including the 2005 unity government. At a party congress in April 2009, the UDSF elected Gabriel Changson CHANG as its new leader. The UDSF supported Bashir in the 2010 presidential balloting and gained one cabinet post in the subsequent unity government. The USDF retained its cabinet post after the withdrawal of the SPLM cabinet members and the independence of South Sudan in July 2011 but lost the post in the December 2011 cabinet reshuffle. The UDSF subsequently emerged as a predominantly South Sudanese grouping (see entry on South Sudan).

Leaders: Gabriel Changson CHANG (Chair), Maj. Gen. (Ret.) Albino AKOL (General Secretary).

Popular (People's) National Congress (*al-Mutamar al-Shabi*—PNC). The PNC, also known as the **Popular Congress Party**, is an Islamic fundamentalist organization that was formed by the Turabi faction of the NIF/NC. Turabi had earlier accused President Bashir of betraying the NC's Islamist tenets. Thus, Turabi claimed he was merely adding "Popular" to the original party's name and expelling members who had produced the crisis. Nevertheless, the PNC officially registered as a distinct party in July 2000. Turabi described the PNC as a "comprehensive *shura* organization," which indicated it would be outside the government. The PNC has few policy differences with the NC.

Turabi and several of his PNC supporters were arrested in February 2001 (see Current issues, above). Turabi was released in October 2003 and rearrested on March 31, 2004. The registrar of political parties issued a decree on April 1, 2004, to suspend the PNC's activities, following Turabi's arrest. Turabi was released as part of the general amnesty issued by Bashir in July 2005. Turabi has since refused to take part in the unity government and called for a popular uprising against the ruling party. He was arrested in January 2009 after he called on Bashir to surrender himself to the ICC. Turabi was released in March.

The PNC did not join the opposition boycott of the 2010 presidential and assembly elections. Abdullah Deng NHIAL was the presidential candidate of the PNC. He placed third in the balloting with 3.9 percent of the vote. The PNC secured four seats in the assembly and refused to join the NC-led unity government in June 2010. Meanwhile, Turabi was arrested again in May after his newspaper published an article that was critical of Sudan's foreign policy. Turabi was arrested on January 17, 2011, for criticizing the rising prices of food and commodities. He was released nine days later. In July 2012, the leader of the PNC's central committee, Kamal OMAR, was arrested. In 2012 the offices of the PNC party newspaper were raided and the publication suspended. The PNC was one of the signatories of the 2013 New Dawn opposition agreement. In July 2014 members of the PNC were expelled from parliament during a debate on electoral reform, which they argued was designed to bolster the NCP.

The PNC boycotted the 2015 national elections.

Leaders: Hassan Abdallah al-TURABI, Ali al-Hajj MUHAMMAD (Secretary-General).

Sudanese Communist Party (*al-Hizb al-Shuyui al-Sudani*—SCP). Founded in 1944 and a leading force in the struggle for independence, the SCP was banned under the Abbud regime and supported the 1969 Numayri coup, becoming thereafter the sole legal party until the abortive 1971 uprising, when it was again outlawed. During the 1970s the SCP was persecuted by the Numayri government with a series of quick trials that resulted in several executions of SCP members. The SCP resurfaced in the mid-1980s and campaigned as a recognized party in 1986, calling for opposition to Islamic fundamentalism; repeal of sharia; and the adoption of a secular, democratic constitution. It won three seats in the 1986 elections. The party displayed no interest in joining the government coalition in 1988 but accepted one cabinet portfolio in March 1989. Secretary General Muhammad Ibrahim NUGUD Mansur was arrested following the June 1989 coup, and in September four more party members were detained for alleged involvement in an antigovernment protest. Nugud was released from prison in February 1990 but was placed under house arrest until May 1991, at which time he was freed under what the government described as a blanket amnesty for all remaining political detainees. The SCP, operating primarily from exile, subsequently remained active in the anti-NIF opposition; with some NDA members complaining in late 1992 that the SCP's influence continued at a higher level than was warranted in view of communism's worldwide decline. The party leadership was reportedly critical in late 1998 and early 1999 of the closer ties apparently being established by UP leader Sadiq al-Mahdi with the NIF government. The SCP currently plays only a marginal role in national politics and opposes the secession of South Sudan from the federation. Nugud was the SCP's candidate in the 2010 presidential elections, but he received less than 1 percent of the vote. After the January 2011 referendum on South Sudan independence, the SCP called for an end to violence in the region. Nugud died in London on March 22, 2012, at age 82. The SCP was one of the parties of the New Dawn accord in 2013. In June 2014 the government banned the publication of the party's newspaper.

The SCP boycotted the 2015 national elections.

Leader: Muhammad Mukhtar Al-KHATIB.

Sudan Liberation Movement/Army (SLM/A). This group is a successor of sorts to the Darfur Liberation Front, a rebel group organized to combat repressive conditions in Darfur. The SLM/A was the main force for the 2003 Darfur based rebellion against the Sudanese government. The rebels split into two groups in 2004, as the SLM/A vehemently opposed Khalil Ibrahim, a radical opponent of Khartoum (see JEM, below). The SLM/A claimed to represent the region's black African farmers, who were angry over alleged government support for Arab militias. One faction of the SLM/A, known as the *Mani Arkoi* and led by Minni Minawi, was a nongovernment group that signed the AU-backed 2006 Darfur peace accord, but the main SLM/A body, led by party chair Abdallah Wahid Mohamed Ahmad Nur, rejected the agreement. After the signing in 2006, the SLM/A split further, with some factions joining the National Redemption Front and others joining with the JEM to form the Alliance of Revolutionary Force of West Sudan (ARFWS), though the ARFWS unification quickly ended after its formation in 2006. In August 2009 six factions of the SLM agreed to a unity accord ahead of the 2010 elections, although one group, led by Khamis Abdullah ABAKR, refused to reconcile.

In February 2010 new fighting broke out between the SLM/A and government forces. Reports indicated that more than 200 civilians had been killed and more than 10,000 had been displaced. In July an estimated 400 SLM/A fighters agreed to cease fighting as part of a UN initiative to reintegrate rebels into civil society. A new round of fighting broke out in June 2012, although the SLM/A officially endorsed a peaceful regime change. The SLM/A was one of the groups that formed the SRF in 2012. The SLM/A subsequently joined other SRF forces in a series of attacks on government areas. Reports in 2014 indicated a split in the Minni MINAWAI faction of the SLM, after Miniwai agreed to talks with the government.

Leaders: Abdallah Wahid Mohamed Ahmad NUR (Chair), Mustafa TIRAB (General Secretary), Minni MINAWAI (Leader of the *Mani Arkoi* faction).

Justice and Equality Movement (JEM). The JEM was founded in 2002 and commenced operations in 2003 after its split from the SLM in mid-2004. This split further complicated peace negotiations with Khartoum, with each of the groups at odds with the others based on tribal rivalries. It is reportedly supported by Islamists close to Hassan Abdallah al-Turabi. Many JEM adherents reside in the Sudanese–Chad frontier region and the JEM also reportedly has the support of the Chadian government. In May 2006 the JEM refused to sign the AU-supported Darfur peace plan and helped create the **National Redemption Front** (NRF). The NRF was a short-lived coalition of rebel groups operating in Darfur and included the **Sudan Federal Democratic Alliance** (SFDA). (For more on the SFDA, see the 2012 *Handbook.*)

The JEM supported the effort by the ICC to arrest President Bashir for genocide, along with the SPLM. The JEM attacked a Chinese oil-field on October 23, 2007, and kidnapped five Chinese workers with the intent of driving out foreign ownership. On May 10, 2008, the JEM carried out an attack on the Omdurman capital region of Sudan, demonstrating to the people of Darfur that the Sudanese government was potentially vulnerable to rebel reprisals. Meanwhile Bahar Idriss Abu GARDA, who was under indictment by the ICC for crimes against humanity, broke with the JEM and founded a new opposition grouping, the **United Resistance Front.** JEM signed a new cease-fire agreement with the government in February 2010. However, fighting between government forces and JEM groups continued through 2010.

In September 2011 JEM fighters rescued group leader Khalil Ibrahim Mohamed, who had been placed under house arrest in Tripoli by the Libyan government. Mohamed was subsequently killed in an air strike on December 22. Meanwhile, JEM was one of the founding groups of the SRF.

JEM led the effort to create the New Dawn Charter in January 2013. JEM and the government finalized a comprehensive peace accord in April. However, a breakaway faction of the group, the **Justice and Equality Movement–Sudan** (JEM-Sudan), continued military operations against the regime. Meanwhile in August 2014, mainline JEM fighters began to be integrated into the Sudanese military.

JEM boycotted the 2015 national elections.

Leader: Jiril IBRAHIM.

Sudan Alliances Forces (SAF). The SAF is a rebel group operating in eastern Sudan, reportedly from bases in Ethiopia and Eritrea. In late 1996 it was described as a participant in the NDA, although its fighters were not believed to be under the direct command of the SPLA's Col. Garang. The SAF currently engages in anti-fundamentalist activities from their offices outside of the Sudan, primarily in Poland. More than 40 fighters and 60 civilians were killed in combat between the SAF and SPLA in April and May 2009. In 2011 the SAF launched a new campaign in the Blue Nile state, forcing the evacuation of 1,400 civilians. In 2012 the group was estimated to have 500 fighters.

Leader: Brig. Gen. Abd al-Aziz Khalid OSMAN.

The small grouping, the **Muslim Brothers**, led by Sheikh Sadiq Abdallah Abd al-MAJID, secured one seat in the assembly in the 2010 legislative elections.

For information on the **Eastern Front** and the **East Democratic Party** (EDP), see the 2012 *Handbook.*

Other Groups:

Other groups that have applied for, or been granted, recognition prior to the 2010 balloting include the **Alliance for People's Working Forces,** led by Kamal al-Din Muhammad ABDULLAH and former president Numayri; **Party of God** (*Hizb Allah* or *Hezbollah*), led by Sulayman Hasan KHALIL; **Future Party** (*Hizb al-Mustaqbal*), led by Abd al-Mutal Abd al-RAHMAN; **Islamic–Christian Solidarity,** launched under the leadership of Hatim Abdullah al-Zaki HUSAYN on a platform of religious harmony and increased attention to social problems; the **Islamic Path Party,** led by Hasab al-RASUL; the **Islamic Revival Movement,** led by Siddiq al-Haj al-SIDDIQ; the **Islamic Socialist Party,** led by Sabah al-MUSBAN; the **Liberalization Party;** the **Moderate Trend Party,** led by Mahmud JINA; the **National Popular Front,** led by Umar Hasan SHALABI and devoted to pan-Arab and pan-Islamic unity; the **National Salvation Party;** the **New Forces Association,** led by Abd al-Rahman Ismail KIBAYDAH; the **Popular Masses' Alliance,** founded by Faysal Muhammad HUSAYN in support of policies designed to assist the poor; the **Socialist Popular Party,** led by Sayyid Khalifah Idris HABANI; the **Sudanese Central Movement,** led by Muhammad Abu al-Qasim Haji HAMAD; the **Sudan Federal Party,** launched by Ahmed DIRAIGE (a leader of the Fur ethnic group) in support of a federal system; the **Sudan Green Party,** led by Zakaraia Bashir IMAN; the **Sudanese Initiative Party,** led by Jafar KARAR; the **Union of Sudan African Parties** (USAP), led by Joseph UKELLO; the **Sudan Labor Party,** led by James ANDERIA; the **South Sudan Democratic Front** (SSDF), led by Gordon BUAY; the **Covenant Democratic Party,** under Benjamin OCHAN; the **Sudanese National Alliance,** led by Abdel-Aziz KHALID; the **New National Democratic Party,** led by Munir Sheikh el-Din JALLAB; the **Sudanese Socialist Democratic Union,** under Fatima ABDEL-MAHMOOD; and the **United Democratic Front,** led by Peter Abdrhaman SULE. In February 2006 the **National Democratic Party** (NDP) was formed by a merger of several small groupings with leftist or nationalist orientations. On March 10, 2007, the **Socialist Union Party,** under the leadership of Fatimah Abd-al-MAHMOUD, was formed.

For more information on the now-defunct **National Movement for Reform and Development in Darfur** (NMRD), see the 2008 *Handbook*. For information on the **Sudanese National Party** (*al-Hizb al-Watani al-Sudani*—SNP), see the 2009 *Handbook*. For further details on the **Baath Party**—BP (*Hizb al-Baath al-Sudan*), see the 2011 *Handbook*.

LEGISLATURE

The **National Legislature** currently comprises the Council of States and the National Assembly.

The **Council of States** comprises 54 members, 3 from each state who are indirectly elected by state legislatures. There are also 2 nonvoting observer councilors from the disputed Abyei territory. Members serve five-year terms. The most recent elections to the council were held on June 1, 2015.

Speaker: Omer Suleiman ADAM (NC).

The **National Assembly** is composed of 426 members who are elected for five-year terms. In the most recent balloting, held on April 13–16, 2015, the National Congress won 323 seats; Democratic Unionist Party–Original 25; Democratic Unionist Party, 15; Federal Umma Party, 7; Umma Collective Leadership party, 6; Umma Reform and Renewal Party, 5; United Umma Party, 4; Umma National Party, 3; National Freedom and Justice Party, 4; Freedom and Justice Party, 3; Federal Truth Party, 2; National Bond Party, 2; Constitution Party, 1; National Reform Party, 1; Popular Forces for Rights and Democracy Movement, 1; People's Movement Party, 1; Center Party for Justice and Development, 1; General Federation of North and South Funj, 1; *Ana al-Sudan*, 1; Black Free Party, 1; Independents, 19.

President: Ibrahim Ahmed OMER (NC).

CABINET

[as of October 25, 2016]

President and Prime Minister	Umar Hassan Ahmad al-Bashir (NC)
First Vice President	Lt. Gen. Bakri Hassan Salih (NC)
Second Vice President	Hasbo Mohamed Abdulrahman (NC)
Ministers	
Agriculture and Irrigation	Ibrahim Adam Ahmed al-Dekhairi (NC)
Animal Resources	Musa Tibin Musa
Antiquities, Tourism, and Wildlife	Mohammed Abu Zaid Mustafa (NC)
Cabinet Affairs/Council of Ministers	Ahmed Sa'ad Omer Khidir (DUP)
Communications and Science	Tahani Abdullah Attiya (NC) [f]
Culture	Al-Tayeb Hassan Badawi (NC)
Defense	Lt. Gen. (Ret.) Awad Mohamed Ahmed Ibn Auf (NC)
Education	Su'ad Abdel Razik Mohamed Saeed (NC) [f]
Environment, Forestry, and Physical Development	Hassan Abdel Gadir Hilal (DUP)
Federal Government	Faisal Hassan Ibrahim (NC)
Finance and Economic Planning	Badr Al-Din Mahmoud Abbas (NC)
Foreign Affairs	Ibrahim Ghandour (NC)
Foreign Trade	Osman Omer Al-Sharef (DUP)
Guidance and Endowments	Al-Fatih Taj al-Sir Abdullah (NC)
Health	Bahar Idris Abu Garda (LJM)
Higher Education and Scientific Research	Sumaya Mohamed Ahmed Abu Kashawa [f]
Human Resources Development	Al-Sadiq Al-Hadi Abdul-Rahman al-Mahdi (NC)
Industry	Mohammed Yousif Ali Yousif (NC)
Information	Ahmed Bilal Osman (NC)
Interior	Lt. Gen. Ismat Abdul-Rahman Zain Al-Abdin (NC)
International Cooperation	Al-Fatich Ali Sidiq (NC)
Investment	Modathir Abdelghani Abdul-Rahman (NC)
Justice	Awad al-Hassan al-Nur (NC)
Labor and Administrative Reform	Ahmed Babikir Nahar (Umma)
Minerals	Ahmed Mohamed Sadiq Al-Karouri (NC)
Petroleum	Mohamed Zayed Awad (NC)
Presidency	(Vacant)
Roads and Bridges	Makkawi Mohammed Awad
Trade	Mansour Yousif al-Ajab (NC)
Water Resources and Electricity	Muataz Musa Abdalla Salim (NC)
Welfare and Social Development	Mashair Ahmed al-Amin al-Dawalab (NC) [f]
Youth and Sports	Haider Galokoma (NC)

[f] = female

INTERGOVERNMENTAL REPRESENTATION

Ambassador to the U.S.: Maowia Osman KHALID.

U.S. Ambassador to Sudan: Steven KOUTSIS (Chargé d'Affaires).

Permanent Representative to the UN: Omer Dahab Fadl MOHAMED.

IGO Memberships (Non-UN): AfDB, AU, Comesa, IOM, LAS, NAM, OIC.

For Further Reference:

Crockett, Richard. *Sudan: Darfur and the Failure of an African State.* New Haven, CT: Yale University Press, 2010.

Idirs, Amir. *Conflict and Politics of Identity in Sudan.* New York: Palgrave Macmillan, 2005.

Salomon, Noah. *For Love of the Prophet: An Ethnography of Sudan's Islamic State.* Princeton, NJ: Princeton University Press, 2016.

SURINAME

Republic of Suriname
Republiek Suriname

Political Status: Former Netherlands dependency; granted internal autonomy on December 29, 1954, and complete independence on November 25, 1975; constitution of November 21, 1975, suspended on August 15, 1980, following military coup of February 25; present constitution approved by referendum of September 30, 1987.

Area: 63,036 sq. mi. (163,265 sq. km).

Population: 548,000 (2016E—UN); 585,824 (2016E—U.S. Census).

Major Urban Center (2014E—UN): PARAMARIBO (234,000).

Official Language: Linguistically, Suriname is exceptionally diverse. The official language is Dutch, but English, Hindi, Javanese, Chinese, and Sranan Tongo (*Taki-Taki*), a Creole lingua franca, are widely spoken, while Spanish has been adopted as a working language to facilitate communication with Latin American neighbors. In the interior, a number of indigenous languages are also spoken.

Monetary Unit: Surinamese Dollar (market rate October 1, 2016: 7.71 dollars = $1US).

President: Désiré "Dési" BOUTERSE (National Democratic Party); elected by the National Assembly on July 19, 2010, and inaugurated on

August 12 for a five-year term, succeeding Ronald "Runaldo" VENETIAAN (Suriname National Party); reelected by the National Assembly on July 16, 2015, for a second five year-term on August 12.

Vice President and Chair of the Council of Ministers: Ashwin ADHIN (National Democratic Party); elected by the National Assembly on July 16, 2015, and inaugurated on August 12 for a term concurrent with that of the president, succeeding Robert AMEERALI (ind.).

THE COUNTRY

Formerly known as Dutch Guiana, Suriname lies on the north-central coast of South America and is bordered by Guyana on the west, French Guiana on the east, and Brazil on the south. Because of the early importation of slave labor from Africa and contract labor from Asia, its society is one of the most ethnically varied in the world. The largest groups are Hindustanis (39 percent) and Creoles (31 percent), followed by Javanese (15 percent), Chinese (10 percent), black Africans, Amerindians, and various European minorities. The World Bank estimates women constituted 37.3 percent of the labor force as of 2012. Twelve percent of the current legislators are women.

The greater part of the land area is covered with virgin forest, although the coastal region is both flat and fertile. The tropical climate yields a wide range of agricultural products that include rice, various fruits, sugar, and coffee. Suriname ranks among the world's leading producers of alumina and bauxite that, together with aluminum, account for nearly 80 percent of the country's exports; however, the Australian-based BHP-Billiton, reportedly the world's largest bauxite mining company, announced in late 2008 that it would discontinue mining activities in Suriname by 2010 because of exhaustion of deposits at its three principal mines. Gold is increasingly becoming of economic importance.

Although long enjoying a higher standard of living than many of its neighbors, the country has experienced economic difficulty since 1980, due largely to reduced world demand for bauxite and the suspension of Dutch and U.S. aid in reaction to a wave of official killings in December 1982. Some aid programs resumed in 1988 but were subsequently stopped in 1993 because of unacceptable economic policies according to the International Monetary Fund (IMF).

Bolstered by increased gold production in recent years, Suriname was less affected than other countries by the global economic crisis. Annual gross domestic product (GDP) growth averaged 4.1 percent in 2009–2011, owing to "buoyant activity" in the mineral sector, according to the IMF. In January 2011 the authorities devalued the Surinamese dollar by 20 percent; at the same time, fuel taxes increased by 40 percent. Subsequently, inflation rose to 18.6 percent. Nevertheless, the IMF noted a favorable economic outlook for Suriname due to robust commodity prices and increased investment in the mineral and energy sectors and in infrastructure, which continued into 2012 as inflation dropped to 5 percent. Suriname's economy also saw a boost in foreign investment in its natural resource development, namely mining and oil. GDP grew by 4.5 percent in 2013 and 1.8 percent in 2014, when inflation was 3.4 percent. GDP growth slowed to 0.1 percent in 2015, and then declined by 2 percent in 2016. Inflation was 8.7 percent in 2015 and 2016. Unemployment surged from 6.9 percent in 2015 to 36.8 percent in 2016. The World Bank ranked Suriname 156th out of 189 countries in its annual ease of conducting business survey in 2016, one of the worst rankings in North and South America.

GOVERNMENT AND POLITICS

Political background. First acquired by the Netherlands from Great Britain in 1667 in exchange for Manhattan Island, the territory now known as Suriname passed among Britain, France, and the Netherlands several times before Dutch authority was formally confirmed by the Congress of Vienna in 1815. It remained a dependency of the Netherlands until enactment of a Statute of the Realm in December 1954 that provided the country with a parliamentary form of government and the right of local constitutional revision, thereby according it full equality with the Netherlands and the Netherlands Antilles.

A substantial portion of Suriname's Hindustani population, which accounted for the bulk of the country's skilled labor force, opposed independence, fearing economic and political repression by the Creole-dominated government of Henck ARRON, who had become prime minister in 1973. More than 40,000 Surinamese, most of them Hindustanis, subsequently emigrated, the majority settling in the Netherlands, creating social and economic problems there, while leaving Suriname with gaps in commerce, medicine, and teaching. Because of the émigré problem, provisions guaranteeing certain Hindustani rights were incorporated into the independence constitution of 1975.

Prime Minister Arron was reconfirmed following a parliamentary election in October 1977 but was ousted in an armed rebellion of 300 noncommissioned officers on February 25, 1980, following government refusal to sanction trade union activity within the armed forces. On March 15 the leaders of the revolt, organized as a National Military Council (NMC), designated the politically moderate Dr. Henk CHIN A Sen as prime minister while permitting the essentially titular president, Dr. Johan H. E. FERRIER, to retain his office. On August 15 the constitution was suspended, with Ferrier dismissed and Chin named as his acting successor while continuing as prime minister. On December 3 Chin was confirmed as president, and the office of prime minister was abolished.

During 1981 differences arose between President Chin, who had called for a return to democratic rule, and Lt. Col. (formerly Sgt. Maj.) Dési BOUTERSE, who had emerged as the strongman of the NMC. As a result, Chin resigned on February 4, 1982, being replaced four days later, on an acting basis, by Lachmipersad F. RAMDAT-MISIER. In the wake of an unsuccessful uprising by right-wing military elements on March 10–11, martial law was declared, while in apparent response to foreign pressure, a new government headed by Henry N. NEYHORST in the reactivated post of prime minister was announced on March 31. Following the reported discovery of a new antigovernment conspiracy on December 8, Neyhorst also resigned, and the NMC ordered the execution of 15 leaders of a political group called the Association for Democratic Action, claiming that they had scheduled a coup for Christmas day. On February 26, 1983, Dr. Errol ALIBUX of the leftist Progressive Workers' and Farm Laborers' Union (PALU) was chosen to head a new cabinet dominated by PALU members. Austerity measures provoked a strike in December by bauxite workers, who were joined by electricity workers in early January 1984. The action forced the revocation of retroactive increases in income taxes, and on January 8 Colonel Bouterse announced the dismissal of the Alibux government. On February 3 an interim administration led by former Arron aide Willem "Wim" UDENHOUT was sworn in, pending "the formation of new democratic institutions." In December, the government announced a

27-month program for a "return to democracy" that included the establishment, on January 1, 1985, of an appointive 31-member National Assembly charged with the drafting of a new constitution.

On August 2, 1985, the Assembly formally designated Colonel Bouterse as "head of government," while reconfirming Ramdat-Misier as acting president. In early September it was announced that the Assembly had appointed a commission, structured on an essentially corporative basis (including representatives of the major unions and the Association of Surinamese Manufacturers), to draft a new basic law. Subsequently, a number of party leaders accepted an invitation from Colonel Bouterse to join the NMC in forming a Supreme Council (*Topberaad*) that would serve as the country's highest political organ. The new body approved the installation of a government headed by Pretaapnarain RADHAKISHUN on July 17, 1986, following the resignation of Prime Minister Udenhout on June 23. Radhakishun was in turn succeeded by Jules Albert WIJDENBOSCH on February 13, 1987.

Despite an earlier announcement that a general election would not be held until March 1988, Colonel Bouterse stated on March 31, 1987, that the balloting would be advanced to independence day, November 25, 1987, preceded by a September 30 referendum on the new constitution. The election yielded a landslide victory for the Front for Democracy and Development (FDO), a coalition of the three leading opposition parties, with Bouterse's recently organized National Democratic Party (NDP) winning only 3 of 51 legislative seats. On January 12, 1988, the new Assembly unanimously elected former agriculture minister Ramsewak SHANKAR to a five-year term as president, with former prime minister Arron designated as vice president and prime minister. Bouterse, however, remained commander in chief of the army and, because of a lack of constitutional specificity in regard to both the membership and functions of a revamped Military Council and a nonelective Council of State, appeared to have lost little capacity for the exercise of decisive political influence.

Of more immediate concern was the continued activity of a rebel Surinamese Liberation Army (SLA), led by former Bouterse aide Ronnie BRUNSWIJK, which had severely disrupted bauxite mining in the eastern region before a government counteroffensive that had driven it back to the border with French Guiana. In June 1988 the government reversed its long-standing position and announced that it would begin talks with the rebels, which did not commence until late October. Following a number of clashes between elements of the "Jungle Commando" and government militia units, the National Assembly approved an amnesty for the rebels on June 1, 1989, and ratified a formal agreement for terminating the conflict on August 8.

The four-year rebellion took a surprising turn on June 18, 1990, when Brunswijk appeared in Cayenne, French Guiana, stating that he had tired of the struggle and wished to seek asylum in the Netherlands. He then departed for Paris, leadership of the rebel group seemingly having been assumed by his deputy, Johan "Castro" WALLY. However, it soon appeared that the action had been a ruse to facilitate what proved to be unproductive talks with Dutch officials, followed by Brunswijk's return to Suriname in July.

Discussions between army and rebel representatives in October and November culminated in a request by Colonel Bouterse that the government withdraw several arrest warrants dating from the period of military rule. Bouterse was angered by the president's failure to offer assistance during a period of detention by Dutch authorities while on a European trip, and on December 22 the colonel resigned as military commander. His successor, Cdr. Iwan GRAANOOGST, mounted a Christmas Eve coup, which yielded Bouterse's reinstatement following the December 30 replacement, on an acting basis, of President Shankar by Johannes Samuel KRAAG and of Vice President and Prime Minister Arron by former prime minister Wijdenbosch.

In legislative balloting on May 25, 1991, what was now termed the New Front for Democracy and Development (NFDD) won 30 of 51 seats, while the army-backed NDP increased its representation from 3 seats to 10. After a lengthy impasse, during which no candidate was able to secure a presidential majority, a special United People's Assembly was convened (see Constitution and government, below) that on September 7 elected NFDD nominee Ronald "Runaldo" R. VENETIAAN as the new head of state; ten days later a cabinet headed by the vice president and prime minister, Jules R. AJODHIA, was announced.

On March 25, 1992, the National Assembly approved a number of constitutional amendments, including abolition of the political role of the army, which would thenceforth be limited to national defense and combating "organized subversion." On May 5 Brunswijk's SLA and another leading guerrilla group, the Amerindian *Tucayana Amazonicas*, agreed to suspend hostilities, and on August 8 signed a revised peace treaty with the government that included revival of the 1989 amnesty. Under the accord, members of the rebel groups would be permitted to join the police force for the interior, while the government was to give the region priority in economic development and social welfare programs.

On November 20, 1992, Colonel Bouterse, buffeted by reports that he had become the country's richest man by corrupt means, again resigned as army commander. However, on October 4, 1993, he returned to the limelight as leader of a mass demonstration in Paramaribo against government-mandated austerity measures and by mid-1995 appeared poised to reenter politics as NDP leader.

In an inconclusive general election on May 23, 1996, a four-party New Front (NF) coalition led by President Venetiaan's Suriname National Party (NPS) won 24 seats, contrasted with the NDP's second-place showing of 16. Thereafter, a series of failed efforts by Venetiaan to forge a majority with smaller parties prompted defections from the NF (see Political Parties, below) that yielded a bloc of 28 legislators supporting the NDP. However, the NDP's augmented strength fell short of the two-thirds needed to elect a president. A new United People's Assembly was therefore convened, which on September 5 named NDP Vice Chair Wijdenbosch to the presidency on a 437–407 vote. While Bouterse's party returned to power, the former dictator was himself barred from office at the insistence of the NDP's allies. Pretaapnarian "Pretaap" RADHAKISHUN, who had first served as cabinet head a decade earlier, became vice president and prime minister.

Through late 1997 and early 1998, a number of party realignments and defections took place, but the government succeeded in securing the support of 26 of the 51 legislators by late March.

On May 28, 1999, President Wijdenbosch dismissed his entire cabinet in the wake of an economic collapse that had triggered widespread popular demonstrations. On June 1 the National Assembly voted to remove the president from office, but he refused to comply on the grounds that such action required a two-thirds majority. Six weeks later, on July 16, a Dutch court sentenced Bouterse in absentia to 11 years' imprisonment and a \$2.18 million fine for participating in smuggling drugs into the Netherlands between 1989 and 1997.

Before the election of May 25, 2000, Wijdenbosch left the NDP to form a group called the Democratic National Platform 2000. However, the new formation ran a poor third behind Venetiaan's New Front, which captured 47 percent of the vote, and an NDP-led Millennium Combination, which secured 15 percent. After lengthy interparty discussions, Venetiaan succeeded in securing a new mandate on August 4 and assumed office on August 12, with Ajodhia returning as vice president and prime minister.

In inconclusive balloting on May 25, 2005, the New Front lost a third of its National Assembly representation and failed to secure a necessary two-thirds majority for Venetiaan's reelection in two legislative ballots in July. Subsequently, the party concluded an alliance with the A-Combination, a recently formed Maroon-based coalition that yielded a third term for Venetiaan in a United People's Assembly poll on August 3.

Bouterse's Mega Combination secured 23 assembly seats in balloting on May 25, 2010, and with the support of Ronnie Brunswijk's A-Combination and the People's Alliance for Progress, obtained the two-thirds required for legislative designation of the former dictator as president.

The finance minister was replaced on June 10, 2011, and a subsequent major cabinet reshuffle occurred in May 2012 following the National Assembly's passage of the Amnesty Law. Three cabinet ministers were replaced in June and July 2013. Bouterse conducted a minor reshuffle in April 2014 following the departure of the *Pertjaja Luhur* from the coalition.

In legislative balloting on May 25, 2015, the NDP won a majority with 26 seats. Bouterse was unanimously reelected president by the legislature on July 14, and was sworn in on August 12. The president formed a coalition government that retained two ministers from the previous cabinet.

Constitution and government. In the immediate wake of the 1990 coup, Commander Graanoogst promised an early return to civilian rule, a pledge that yielded the election of May 25, 1991. The 1987 constitution, under which the polling took place, sets forth a complex system of government within which the intended distribution of power is by no means clearly defined. A 51-member National Assembly, elected for a five-year term, selects a president and vice president for terms of the same duration; however, the action must be by a two-thirds majority, lacking which the choice is made by a simple majority of a United People's Assembly (*Vereinigde Volksvergadering*), comprising the National Assembly members plus 289 local and regional councilors. The selection must be deferred until 30 days after the election to accommodate any disputed legislative contests. The president serves as chair of a nonelective State Council whose composition is "regulated by law" and whose purpose is to advise the government on public policy, ensuring that its actions are in conformity with the basic law; the president also chairs a Security Council, which is empowered to assume governmental authority in the event of "war, state of siege, or exceptional circumstances to be determined by law." The cabinet of ministers, on the other hand, is chaired by the vice president in a role equivalent to that of a prime minister serving under a "strong" president.

The Assembly may amend the constitution by a two-thirds majority or, lacking such a majority, by convening the equivalent of a presidential assembly. For electoral purposes the country is divided into ten districts.

In early 1992 the Assembly began debate on a variety of constitutional amendments, only one of which, a ban on political activity by the army, was subsequently approved. Other proposed changes would have limited the State Council to a purely advisory role, with no capacity to veto government decisions, and given the president the power of legislative dissolution, while permitting a two-thirds majority of the assembly to dismiss the president. In August 2012 the Senate Committee on Constitutional Reform issued a questionnaire to individuals, organizations, and institutions within Suriname to gather feedback at a hearing on possible revisions to the Constitution of 1987. The questionnaire addressed issues such as problems with the current constitution, individual freedoms, elections, and function of the branches of government.

Though freedom of expression is generally respected, libel remains a criminal offense and journalists practice self-censorship on sensitive issues. Suriname ranked 22nd on the Reporters Without Borders annual press freedom index in 2016.

Foreign relations. Before the 1980 coup, Suriname's foreign relations turned on two main issues: long-standing border disputes with neighboring Guyana and French Guiana and the status of development assistance from the Netherlands. The border disputes resulted from Guyana's claim to a 6,000-square-mile tract reputedly rich in bauxite deposits and from France's claim to a 780-square-mile tract believed to contain deposits of gold; neither controversy has yet been resolved, although Suriname and Guyana agreed in mid-1995 to open negotiations on their dispute within the framework of a joint commission.

Foreign policy uncertainty followed the first Arron overthrow, though a leftward thrust, led by the Bouterse faction and the NMC's pro-Cuban posture, emerged, prompting an increased flow of Surinamese to the Netherlands and the recall of the Dutch ambassador in March 1982. The subsequent withdrawal of Dutch aid (which had been the principal source of Suriname's relatively high standard of living) dealt a severe blow to the country's economy. In early 1983 it appeared that the fiscal shortfall might be alleviated by commitments from Cuba and Libya. However, on June 1, coincident with reports that the administration of U.S. president Ronald Reagan had considered a Central Intelligence Agency (CIA) plan to infiltrate and destabilize the self-proclaimed "socialist" regime, a substantial military and trade agreement was concluded with Brazil. Two weeks later, amid Dutch reports that Brazil had threatened to invade Suriname if efforts were not taken to curb Cuban influence, Colonel Bouterse announced that Sgt. Maj. Badressein SITAL, one of the most pro-Cuban members of the NMC, had been dismissed from both his Council and ministerial positions. In mid-October Bouterse visited the United States and later in the month asked Cuba to withdraw its ambassador and sharply reduce its remaining diplomatic staff in Paramaribo.

In early 1984 the regime lodged official protests with the French and Netherlands governments over their alleged complicity in an invasion plot, and in March 1985 Suriname threatened to take the Netherlands to the International Court of Justice (ICJ) for discontinuance of its aid program under the 1975 independence accord. The latter pronouncement came in the wake of an adverse UN Human Rights Commission report on the 1982 killings. On the other hand, an announcement by the government that it would proceed with ICJ action appeared to be rendered moot by The Hague's positive response in 1988 to the balloting of the previous November. Subsequently, at the conclusion of a three-day visit to the Hague by President Venetiaan in June 1992, the Netherlands and Suriname signed a cooperation treaty that formally ended their lengthy estrangement, although Dutch financial assistance was again suspended in mid-1993 (see The Country, above). A member of the UN and other international and regional organizations, Suriname was admitted to the Caricom in February 1995.

In September 1997 the Netherlands requested that Interpol issue an international warrant for the arrest and extradition of Dési Bouterse on drug-trafficking and money laundering charges. Bouterse went on trial in absentia in a Dutch court in March 1999 and four months later was convicted of the charge against him. Development aid from the Netherlands was again suspended in June 1999 before being resumed in early 2001, partly in response to the positive reaction of the Netherlands to the 2000 elections. Relations improved further in September 2001 when the Netherlands formally apologized for the practice of slavery in Dutch Guiana.

A new dispute with Guyana erupted in 2000 over an offshore oil concession by Guyana in disputed territory. The two countries filed claims with the UN in 2004, and in September 2007 the tribunal issued a ruling in favor of Guyana. (For more, see the 2013 *Handbook.*)

In early 2007 Suriname concluded an agreement allowing Venezuelan nationals to fish in its waters, if all of the catches were delivered to Paramaribo. However, the Surinamese government cited payment concerns in taking no immediate action to join PetroCaribe, under which Venezuela supplies oil and its byproducts to Caribbean countries on preferential terms.

Just one foreign head of state, Guyana's president Bharrat Jagdeo, attended Bouterse's 2010 inauguration. Relations with the Netherlands worsened under Bouterse, with a Dutch spokesperson declaring that contacts would be restricted to "functional necessities."

Following the passage of the Amnesty Law in 2012 (see Current issues, below), the Netherlands immediately withdrew its ambassador, and the Inter-American Court of Human Rights, the UN High Commissioner for Human Rights, and the European Union (EU) spoke out against the perceived interference with justice.

Ties with China strengthened. China is the second largest aid provider to Suriname. In 2011 illegal and legal Chinese immigrants reportedly constituted 10 percent of the population.

In November 2012 Suriname announced there were no plans to name an ambassador to The Hague, and the following month said there would be no rush to approve the reappointment of the Dutch ambassador. In March 2013 Suriname appointed its first ambassador to Turkey as part of an effort to strengthen economic ties between the two countries. An open skies agreement with the United States signed in July paved way for an increased economic relationship between the two countries.

Tensions mounted in December 2013, when Guyana granted permission for a geological survey in the disputed territory. Subsequently, Suriname circulated a map marking the area as Suriname territory ahead of a June 2014 conference on mining, prompting Guyanese representatives to withdraw from the summit.

President Bouterse's son Dino, the head of Suriname's antiterrorism unit, plead guilty in U.S. court in August 2014 to charges that he attempted to offer the Lebanese terrorist group Hezbollah a base in Suriname. He had been extradited from Panama to the United States on drug- and weapons-trafficking charges in April 2013. In October 2014 Surinam restored full diplomatic relations with the Netherlands.

Current issues. Following the election, Bouterse accepted "political responsibility" for the 1982 killings but insisted that he had not been personally involved. He stated that he would not intervene in the ongoing military trial, known as the December 8 trial, which reconvened on October 15 and then was postponed until November 19, but he subsequently appointed one of his codefendants as ambassador to France.

On April 4, 2012, the National Assembly passed a controversial piece of legislation designed to grant amnesty to the suspects of the 1982 political killings of opponents of the then military regime, which was led by current President Bouterse. A pro-Bouterse majority in parliament passed the Amnesty Law weeks before the verdict was to be delivered in the December 8 trial. Prompted by internal opposition to the law, Bouterse dismissed eight ministers in a May 5 cabinet reshuffle. When the trial resumed on April 13, the defense called for the trial to be ended and for the lawsuit to be dismissed in light of the Amnesty Law. On May 11 the presiding judge, Cynthia Valstein-Motnor, suspended the trial in order to allow the constitutionality of the Amnesty Law to be examined by the Constitutional Court, which, though created in the 1987 Constitution, was never established. Although due to restart on December 12, the trial was further postponed while prosecutors awaited a ruling from the Constitutional Court. In January 2013 the International Commission of Journalists issued a statement voicing concern for the trial's delay.

Cracks in the leading coalition came to light when AC leader Ronnie Brunswijk, whose support helped Bouterse win in 2010, announced at a rap concert in April 2013 that he plans to run for president in 2015. A Bouterse spokesperson shortly thereafter announced that Bouterse plans to seek a second term.

June and July 2013 saw three ministers replaced, part of an effort to root out corruption, nepotism, and to depoliticize the ministry of education. In April 2014 Bouterse ejected the *Pertjajah Luhur* from the Mega Combination, accusing the party of "blackmail politics." With the loss of the six *Pertjajah Luhur* seats, the Mega Combination was reduced to a bare majority of one seat.

Family members of the December 8 victims announced they would pursue the stalled case in the Inter-American Court of Human Rights in April 2014. In early May Bouterse appealed to the Hague over his 1999 conviction in absentia for drug smuggling, arguing that a key witness had given false testimony (see the NDP in Political Parties, below). Later that month, Bouterse asked Suriname's Supreme Court to review the same conviction by the Hague court. Bouterse's annulment campaign began as the president told legislators that his administration will launch a battle against corruption in government, and he ordered an investigation of all government departments.

Following his reelection as president in July 2015, Bouterse announced significant spending cuts and reductions in the number of public servants. In an effort to bring the government's budget deficit down to 6 percent of GPD in order to qualify for additional IMF assistance, the cabinet approved a value added tax to be implemented in 2018. However, the government refused to phase out costly subsidies for electricity and fuel.

POLITICAL PARTIES

Government Groups:

National Democratic Party (*Nationale Democratische Partij*—NDP). The NDP was formed before the 1987 election as a political vehicle for the supporters of Colonel Bouterse. As such, it succeeded the February 25 Movement, styled *Stanvaste* ("Steadfast") in Dutch, which had been characterized as a "movement, not a party" at its launching in 1984. Contrary to expectations, the NDP secured only three Assembly seats in 1987. The party's representation rose to 12 in 1991 and to 16 in May 1996.

Tension emerged in early 1999 between the rank-and-file of the NDP, described as supporters of Bouterse, and supporters of President Wijdenbosch. The president dismissed Bouterse as a presidential adviser in early April, Wijdenbosch subsequently forming the DNP 2000 (see under VVV, below).

An international arrest warrant was issued by a court in the Netherlands for Bouterse in 1997 on charges involving his alleged involvement in the smuggling of cocaine from Suriname to Europe. In June 2000 the Netherlands' court sentenced Bouterse in absentia to 11 years in prison in the case; however, Bouterse remained free in Suriname under protection of the Surinamese constitution, which prohibits extradition of nationals. Meanwhile, prosecutors in the Netherlands in 2000 also attempted to pursue a case against Bouterse in connection with the execution of 15 political opponents in Suriname in 1982. The Netherlands High Court dismissed the charges in September 2001 on the ground that Netherlands had no jurisdiction in the case. (See Current issues, above, for the case in Suriname.)

For the 2000 campaign, the NDP served as the core component of an alliance styled the Millennium Combination (*Millenium Combatie*) that included the KTPI (below) and the DA'91 (below). Running alone in 2005, the NDP was legislative runner-up with 15 seats.

Bouterse relinquished the NDP chairmanship when he became president in 2010, saying that the two posts were incompatible; however, he resumed the post in March 2012. The NDP won 45.5 percent of the vote in the May 2015 parliamentary balloting, securing a majority of 26 seats. It was the first time in Suriname history that a single party had won a majority in the National Assembly. Bouterse was reelected to the presidency in July, and formed a coalition government after his inauguration in August.

Leaders: Lt. Col. Désiré "Dési" BOUTERSE (Chairman and President of the Republic), Ricardo PANKA (Mega Combination Faction Leader).

Government-Supportive Groups:

Progressive Workers' and Farmers' Union (*Progressieve Arbeiders en Landbouwers Unie*—PALU). The only trade union to have retained a public role after many labor leaders were killed in December 1982, the left-wing PALU dominated the Alibux cabinet but was not represented in subsequent administrations. It won 4 Assembly seats from "war zone" constituencies in 1987, none in 1991 or 1996, and 1 in 2000. It joined the Mega Combination in 2010. In early 2014 vice chair Henk RAMNANDANLAL said the party may not continue cooperation with the Mega Combination for the 2015 elections, noting that the majority of the party does not support a merge with the NDP. It won one seat in the 2015 balloting with 0.7 percent of the vote.

Leaders: Jim K. HOK (Chair), Henk RAMNANDANLAL (Vice Chair).

Party for Democracy and Development in Unity (*Partij Voor Democratie en Ontwikkeling Eenheid*—DOE). The DOE was formed in 1999. In 2001 party chair Carl Breeveld took his anticorruption campaign to Radio Nederland in Suriname, where he urged adoption of the country's draft anticorruption law, the first version of which had been introduced into parliament in 2008. The DOE secured one legislative seat in 2010. In August 2014 the DOE declared intentions to contest the 2015 elections. In the May 2015 election, the DOE secured one legislative seat. It was also given a position in the NDP-led government that took office in August.

Leaders: Carl BREEVELD (Chair), Joany LANSDORF-WATKIN (Vice President), Paul BRANDON (Secretary).

A-Combination (*A-Combinatie*—AC or A-Com). The AC was formed before the 2005 election as an alliance that included the **General Liberation and Development Party** (*Algemene Bevrijdings en Ontwikkelings Partij*—ABOP), led by former SLA leader Ronnie Brunswijk, and the **Brotherhood and Unity in Politics** (*Broederschap en Eenheid in Politiek*—BEP), led by Caprino Allendy. Celsius Waterberg assumed BEP leadership in September 2012.

An alliance with the NF in mid-2005 yielded the majority supporting Venetiaan's retention of the presidency, while its support of Bouterse in 2010 was crucial to legislative endorsement of the former dictator.

In April 2013 Burnswijk announced his intent to run for president in 2015. The BEP left the AC and joined the V7. The alliance was joined by the Party of National Unity and Solidarity (*Kerukunan Tulodo Pranatan Inggil*—KTPI, see below).

The alliance won five seats and 11.2 percent of the vote in the May 2015 elections.

Leader: Ronnie BRUNSWIJK (ABOP Chair).

Party of National Unity and Solidarity (*Kerukunan Tulodo Pranatan Inggil*—KTPI). Formerly known as the **Indonesian Peasants' Party** (*Kaum-Tani Persuatan Indonesia*), the KTPI is a small, predominantly Javanese rural party founded in 1947. It joined the National Party Alliance before the 1977 election but withdrew in December 1978. As a participant in the New Front, it won seven seats in 1991 and five in 1996 before withdrawing to enter the Wijdenbosch government. It contested the 2000 balloting as part of the Millennium Coalition and joined the Mega Combination in 2010. It initially joined the V7 for the 2015 balloting, but defected to the A-Combination.

Leader: Willy SOEMITA.

Democratic National Platform 2000 (*Democratisch Nationaal Platform 2000*—DNP 2000). The DNP 2000 was launched by Jules Wijdenbosch following his break with Colonel Bouterse in 1999. Closely affiliated with the group for the 2000 elections were D21 (below) and the **Democratic Party** (*Democratische Partij*—DP), led by Frank PLAYFAIR. For the 1996 election the DP had joined the HPP (below) in forming the Alliance.

In the 2000 balloting, the DNP 2000 list won three National Assembly seats, one of which was taken up by Playfair.

Leaders: Jules Albert WIJDENBOSCH, Liakat Ali Errol ALIBUX.

Grassroots Party for Renewal and Democracy (*Basispartij voor Vernieuwing en Democratie*—BVD). Initially called the **Movement for Freedom and Democracy** (*Beweging voor Vriheid en Democratie*—BVD), the BVD is a Hindu party formed by a group of VHP dissidents in 1996. The movement participated in formation of the Wijdenbosch government in September and was subsequently registered as a party under its current name. Its former chair, Motilal MUNGRA, was dismissed as finance minister in August 1997 after accusing the president of extravagant expenditure, although the party retained its other cabinet posts. The BVD's Pretaapnarain RADHAKISHUN served as vice president and prime minister from 1996 until 2000. He died shortly after leaving office.

In the 2000 election, the BVD won 3.2 percent of the National Assembly vote but no seats.

In June 2010 the party ended its alliance with the PVF (below) as the latter was going to be focusing more on agriculture and the BVD "had other plans."

Leaders: Dilip SARDJOE (Chair), Dr. Tjanrikapersad "Tjan" GOBARDHAN.

Other Legislative Groups:

V7 Coalition, formed by Chandrikapersad SANTOKHI in 2015, comprised of seven parties. Four of those parties (all below) came from New Front for Democracy and Development (*Nieuw Front voor Democratie en Ontwikkeling*—NF, below): the Suriname National Party (*Nationale Partij Suriname*—NPS), Progressive Reform Party (*Vooruitstrevende Hervormde Partij*—VHP); Suriname Labor Party (*Surinaamse Partij van de Arbeid*—SPA), and the Full Confidence Party (*Pertjajah Luhur*—PL). The other three members were the Democratic ALTERNATIVE '91 (*Democratisch Alternatief '91*—DA'91), the **Brotherhood and Unity in Politics** (*Broederschap en Eenheid in Politiek*—BEP), led by Celsius WATERBERG, and the Party of National Unity and Solidarity (KTPI, above). (The KTPI withdrew before the elections and joined the A-Combination.) The V7 won 18 seats in the National Assembly with 37.3 percent of the vote. The coalition fell apart following the defection of several members to the NDP in support of Bouterse's election as president. In addition, the BEP withdrew in August.

Leader: Chandrikapersad SANTOKHI.

New Front for Democracy and Development (*Nieuw Front voor Democratie en Ontwikkeling*—NF). Initially a three-member coalition of traditional ethnic parties (NPS, VHP, SPA, below) styled the **Front for Democracy and Development** (*Front noor Democratie en Ontwikkeling*—FDO), the NF, augmented by the KTPI, gained 30 of 51 National Assembly seats in 1991, as contrasted with 40 won by the FDO in 1987. Its representation dropped to 24 after the election of May 23, 1996, and was reduced thereafter as a result of KTPI withdrawal and defections by VHP members in support of the Wijdenbosch presidency. The New Front recovered its majority in the May 2000 elections, the *Pertjajah Luhur* having joined the coalition to once again bring its membership to four parties. The *Pertjajah Luhur* left the NF ahead of the 2010 election, when the NF won 14 seats.

Leaders: Ronald "Runaldo" VENETIAAN (Former President of the Republic), Ruth WIJDENBOSCH.

Suriname National Party (*Nationale Partij Suriname*—NPS). A Creole grouping founded in 1946, the NPS was the leading advocate of independence from the Netherlands and the core party of the National Party Alliance before the 1980 coup. Its leader served as president from 1991 to 1996 and was returned to the office in 2000, when the NPS won 14 of the NF's 33 National Assembly seats, and again in 2005, despite reduction of the NF to a plurality of 23 seats. Gregory Allan Rusland succeeded Venetiaan as chair in June 2012. At a party congress in August, the NPS approved continuation of partnerships with the NF parties.

Leaders: Gregory Allan RUSLAND (Chair), Ruth WIJDENBOSCH (Vice Chair), Ronald "Runaldo" VENETIAAN (Former President of the Republic).

Progressive Reform Party (*Vooruitstrevende Hervormde Partij*—VHP). Initially called the United Reform Party (*Verenigde Hervormings Partij*—VHP), and long the leading Hindu party, the left-of-center VHP originally opposed independence because of anticipated repression by the Creole-dominated Alliance. The VHP's legislative representation of 16 seats in 1987 dropped to 9 in 1991, all of which were retained in 1996 before the defection of a group styled the Movement for Freedom and Democracy. Cahndrikapersad Santokhi, who became chair in 2011, noted that the VHP is not committed to the NF in 2015, but the VHP recommitted to the NF in 2014.

Leader: Cahndrikapersad SANTOKHI (Chair).

Suriname Labor Party (*Surinaamse Partij van de Arbeid*—SPA). The SPA is a social democratic formation affiliated with the Centrale 47 trade union. It withdrew as a member of the New Front in July 2005 but subsequently returned, with its leader, Sigfried Gilds, being named minister of trade and industry. Gilds resigned his ministerial post in January 2006 after being accused of complicity in a money-laundering operation and was convicted and sentenced to 12 months in jail in early 2009. Meanwhile, the party named a new chair, Guno Castelen, a former Port Management director who was asked to step down for reasons described as "political considerations."

Leader: Guno CASTELEN (Chair).

Full Confidence Party (*Pertjajah Luhur*—PL). A splinter from *Pendawa Lima* (below), the *Pertjajah Luhur* joined the New Front before the 2000 legislative balloting. Its leader, Paul SOMOHARDJO, was president of the National Assembly during the Venetiaan presidency. The party opted not to continue with the New Front for the 2010 balloting and went on to win six seats as part of the VVV, putting its support behind the Mega Combination. However, in April 2014, *Pertjajah Luhur* was ejected from the combination as Bouterse and others accused the party of "blackmail politics." Members of the PL defected to the NDP in August 2015.

Leader: Paul SOMOHARDJO.

Democratic ALTERNATIVE '91 (*Democratisch Alternatief '91*—DA'91). The DA'91 was launched before the 1991 election by Gerard BRUNINGS, an airline executive who urged a constitutional amendment precluding political activity by both labor and the military. At its inception the formation was a coalition of Brunings's **Alternative Forum** (*Alternatief Forum*—AF), which is now led by Ricardo (Rick) Otto van RAVENSWAAY; the Bushnegro Unity Party (*Bosneger Eenheids Partij*—BEP, see under AC, above), and two groups that withdrew before the 1996 election: the *Pendawa Lima* and the HPP (both below). The coalition won nine legislative seats in 1991, four in 1996, and two in 2000. Party leader Djagendre RAMICHELAWAN died in 2010.

Other Parties:

Alternative-1 (A-1). The A-1 was formed before the 2005 balloting as a coalition that included the two groups immediately below, as well as DA'91 (above), which left to join the V7 coalition for the 2015 general election. A-1 secured three seats in the 2005 poll.

Democrats of the 21st Century (*Democraten van de 21ste Eeuw*—D21). Organized in 1986, D21 was affiliated with DNP 2000 for the 2000 poll. In 2010 party leader Soewarto Moestadja was given a ministry post.

Leader: Soewarto MOESTADJA.

Political Wing of the Federation of Farmers and Farm Workers (*Politieke Vleugel van de Federatie van Agrariërs en Landarbeiders*—PVF, or Political Wing of the FAL). The PVF was organized in the late 1990s to advance the agenda of the FAL trade union, which opposed the Wijdenbosch government. In the 2000 National Assembly election it won two seats.

Leaders: Soedichand JAIRAM (Chair), Jiwan SITAL.

Prior to the 2010 election, two additional minor groups joined A-1: the **Amazone Party of Suriname** (APS), led by Kenneth VAN GENDEREN; and **Trepunt 2000** (T-2000), led by Arti JESSURUN.

Reformed Progressive Party (*Hernieuwde Progressieve Partij*—HPP). Formerly a member of the DA'91, the HPP is a predominantly

Hindu social democratic formation that split from the VHP in 1975 and later participated in the pre-1980 National Party Alliance. For the 1996 election it joined the Democratic Party in forming The Alliance (*De Alliantie*), which secured three National Assembly seats. Also subsequently associated with the Alliance was the Christian democratic **Progressive People's Party of Suriname** (*Progressieve Surinaamse Volkspartij*—PSV) of W. WONG Loi Sing. In 2000 the HPP and the PSV registered separately.

Leader: Prim RAMTAHALSING (Chair).

Pendawa Lima. A predominantly Javanese party dating from 1975, the *Pendawa Lima* ("Five Sons of King Pandu") joined DA'91 in 1991, thereafter winning four parliamentary seats in its own right in 1996. Before the 2000 legislative poll, the *Pendawa Lima* split into two factions, with theretofore *Pendawa Lima* Chair Paul Somohardjo leading his faction into the New Front and subsequent government as the *Pertjajah Luhur.* (Both the rump *Pendawa Lima* and *Pertjajah Luhur* use the abbreviation "PL," causing confusion in some news reports.) Associated with *Pendawa Lima* in recent elections has been the **Progressive Bosneger Party** (PBP), led by Armand KANAPE. In January 2010 the party ended its alliance with the A1 due to differences with the PVF. Party leader Raymond Sapoen holds a ministry post.

Leader: Raymond SAPOEN.

Other parties include the **National Party for Leadership and Development** (*Nationale Partij voor Leiderschap en Ontwikkeling*—NPLO), led by Oesman WANGSABESARIE; the **National Reform Party** (*Nationale Hervormings Partij*—NHP), led by Kenneth MOENNE; the **New Choice** (*Naya Kadam*—NK), led by Waldo RAMDIHAL; the **Party for Progression, Justice, and Perseverance** (PPRS), led by Renee KAIMAN; the **Progressive Political Party** (PPP), led by Surinder MUNGRA; **Seeka**, led by Paul ABENA; **New Suriname** (*Nieuw Suriname*—NS), led by Radjen Nanan PANDAY; and the **Union of Progressive Surinamers** (UPS), led by Sheoradj PANDAY.

Exile Group:

In January 1983 a Movement for the Liberation of Suriname was formed by exiles in the Netherlands under the leadership of former president Chin and former deputy prime minister André HAAKMAT. However, the Dutch government refused to recognize the group as a government in exile, and both subsequently declared their support for the Surinamese Liberation Army (see SLA, below).

Guerrilla Groups:

Surinamese Liberation Army (SLA). The largely *bosneger* SLA was formed in early 1986 by former army private Ronnie Brunswijk with the avowed aim of overthrowing Colonel Bouterse and "[restoring] the constitutional state" through free elections. The government charged Surinamese émigrés in the Netherlands with supporting the SLA, whose approximately 2,000 members launched a guerrilla campaign in the country's eastern and southern regions that appeared to have been largely contained by mid-1987. In the wake of the November election, the SLA's "Jungle Commando" was reported to have declared an unconditional truce, effective January 1, 1988. Sporadic conflict, interspersed by talks with government and army representatives, nonetheless continued, before the conclusion of a preliminary peace accord in a ceremony attended by Bouterse and Brunswijk on March 26, 1991, which was followed by a suspension of hostilities on May 5 and the conclusion of a formal peace treaty on August 1, 1992. The General Liberation and Development Party, led by Brunswijk, competed unsuccessfully in the 1996 and 2000 elections. Brunswijk was sentenced in absentia to eight years in prison by a court in the Netherlands in April 1999 following his conviction on charges of cocaine trafficking. He now heads the ABOP (under AC, above), the present status of the SLA being unclear.

Other guerrilla formations have included the **Union for Liberation and Democracy,** a radical derivative of the SLA led by Kofi AJONGPONG; the Saramaccaner *bosneger* **Angula** movement, led by Carlos MAASSI; the **Mandela Bushnegro Liberation Movement,** led by Leendert ADAMS "Biko"; the Amerindian **Tucayana Amazonica,** led by Alex JUBITANA and Thomas SABAJO, which participated in the 1992 peace accords; and the previously unknown **Suriname Liberation Front,** led by Cornelius MAISI, which was routed by the army after a hostage seizure at a hydroelectric facility south of Paramaribo in March 1994.

LEGISLATURE

The former unicameral Parliament (*Staten*) was abolished on August 15, 1980. A constituent National Assembly (*Volksvergadering*) of 31 nominated members was established on January 1, 1985, as part of the government's "return to democracy" program. Balloting for the successor **National Assembly** (*Nationale Assemblee*) occurred on November 25, 1987, and, in the wake of the 1990 coup, on May 25, 1991. In the most recent election for 51 members on May 24, 2015, the seat distribution was as follows: National Democratic Party, 26 seats; V7 Coalition, 18; A-Combination, 5; Party for Democracy and Development in Unity, 1; and Progressive Workers' and Farmers' Union, 1.

President: Jennifer GEERLINGS-SIMONS (NDP).

CABINET

[as of October 12, 2016]

Chair	Ashwin Adhin (NDP)
Ministers	
Agriculture, Livestock, and Fisheries	Soeresh Algoe (NDP)
Defense	Brig. Gen. Ronni Benschop (NDP)
Education Science and Culture	Robert Peneux (NDP)
Finance	Gillmore Hoefdraad (NDP)
Foreign Affairs	Niermala Badrising (NDP) [f]
Internal Affairs	Mike Noersalim
Justice and Police	Jennifer Van Dijk-Silos (NDP) [f]
Labor, Technological Development, and the Environment	Steven Relyveld (NDP)
Natural Resources	Regillio Dodson (DOE)
Planning, Land, and Forest Management	Steven Relyveld (NDP)
Public Health	Patrick Pengel (NDP)
Public Works	Siegfried Wolff (NDP)
Regional Development	André Dikan (BEP)
Social Affairs and Public Housing	Sieglien Burleson (NDP) [f]
Trade and Industry	Sieglien Burleson (NDP) [f]
Transport, Communication, and Tourism	Andy Rusland (NDP)
Sport and Youth Affairs	Faizal Abdoelgafoer (NDP)

[f] = female

INTERGOVERNMENTAL REPRESENTATION

Ambassador to the U.S.: Sylvana Elvira SIMSON (Chargé d'Affaires).

U.S. Ambassador to Suriname: Edwin Richard NOLAN.

Permanent Representative to the UN: Henry L. MACDONALD.

IGO Memberships (Non-UN): CARICOM, IADB, ICC, NAM, OAS, OIC, WTO.

For Further Reference:

Goslinga, Cornelis. *A Short History of the Netherlands Antilles and Suriname.* The Hague, Netherlands: Martinus Nijhoff, 1979.

Hoefte, Rosemarijn. *Suriname in the Long Twentieth Century: Domination, Contestation, Globalization.* New York: Palgrave Macmillan, 2013.

Singh, Chairtram. "Suriname and the Limits of Consociationalism." *Journal of Third World Studies.* 31, no. 1 (2014).

SWAZILAND

Kingdom of Swaziland

Political Status: Independent monarchy within the Commonwealth since September 6, 1968.

Area: 6,703 sq. mi. (17,363 sq. km).

Population: 1,304,000 (2016E—UN); 1,451,428 (2016E—U.S. Census).

Major Urban Centers (2010E—UN): MBABANE (administrative capital, 76,000), Lobamba (royal and legislative capital, 10,000), Manzini (110,000).

Official Languages: English, siSwati.

Monetary Unit: Lilangeni (official rate October 1, 2016: 13.72 emalangeni = $1US). The lilangeni is at par with the South African rand.

Sovereign: King MSWATI III; installed on April 25, 1986, succeeding (as Head of State) Queen Regent Ntombi THWALA.

Prime Minister: Barnabas Sibusiso DLAMINI; appointed by the king on October 16, 2008, and sworn in on October 23 to succeed Absalom Themba DLAMINI; reappointed by the king on October 28, 2013, following legislative elections on September 28. (Barnabas Sibusiso Dlamini had also held the post of prime minister in 1996–2003.)

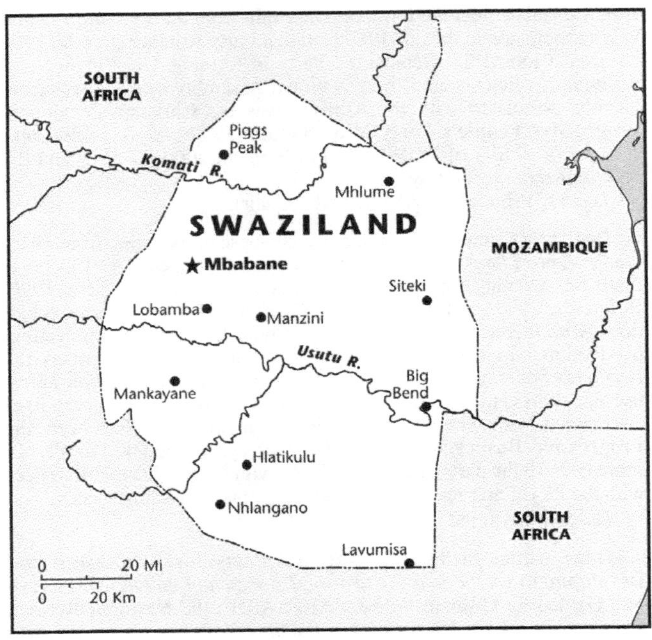

THE COUNTRY

Bordered on the north, west, and south by South Africa and on the east by Mozambique, Swaziland is the smallest of the three former British High Commission territories in southern Africa. The country comprises a mountainous western region (Highveld), a middle region of moderate altitude (Middleveld), an eastern lowland area (Lowveld), and the so-called Lubombo plateau on the eastern border. About 97 percent of the population is Swazi African, the remainder being of European and Eurafrican (mixed) stock. English is an official language, but siSwati (akin to Zulu) prevails among the indigenous population; Afrikaans is common among the Europeans, many of whom are of South African origin. Christianity is the religion of approximately half the people; there are a few Muslims, the remainder adhering to traditional beliefs. Women constitute about 37 percent of the workforce; female participation in government, with the exception of the former queen regent, has been minimal, although some women recently have been elected to the National Assembly (four in the 2013 balloting) and appointed to the cabinet. Overall, the influence of Swaziland's traditional culture (dominated by tribal chiefs) remains high, thereby compromising women's rights.

The economy is quite diversified given the country's small land area and population, although its composition, particularly in the mining sector, has changed. Production of iron ore, which had accounted for 25 percent of export earnings in 1967, virtually ceased by the end of the 1970s, while asbestos reserves, after 40 years of extraction, also approached depletion. Coal mining, on the other hand, underwent rapid development, while other minerals, such as tin, barites, and silica, were found in commercially exploitable quantities. Under normal conditions, water supplies are sufficient not only to support agriculture, which yields sugar (the main cash crop), forest products, and livestock, but also to provide a potential hydroelectric power base.

Growth of 3.5 percent was achieved in 2002, mainly due to expansion of the textile industry, which took advantage of reduced U.S. tariffs and quotas designed to assist developing African nations. However, the economy subsequently continued to suffer from high unemployment, persistent poverty, localized food shortages, and according to some international donors, irresponsible spending on the part of the royal family, said to control as much as 60 percent of the economy. In addition, Swaziland faced one of the highest rates of HIV/AIDS infection in the world; UN officials estimated in 2004 that 25–40 percent of adults were infected. After many years of seeming failure to implement a plan to combat the pandemic, the government in 2004 declared a national emergency regarding the issue and solicited international assistance in trying to halt the spread of the disease.

Little progress was subsequently made in reducing poverty, according to the International Monetary Fund (IMF), which cited a prolonged drought and factory closings that contributed to Swaziland's 30–40 percent unemployment rate. The IMF urged the government to reduce its budget deficit and increase privatization in order to attract investors. As the economic downturn spread across the globe, gross domestic product (GDP) growth registered an annual average of 1.2 percent in 2009–2010, far short of the 3.6 percent the IMF deemed necessary to prevent worsening poverty, said to affect as much as 70 percent of the population. In 2011 the IMF reported that the country was facing a "severe fiscal crisis," due to a sharp decline in revenue from the South African Customs Union (SACU), an unbudgeted 4.5 percent salary increase for civil servants and politicians, and spending "overruns" on defense. Among other things, the government was advised to slash 7,000 public-sector jobs and otherwise significantly reduce spending, measures that appeared increasingly difficult to enact in light of subsequent public protests. Although the economy contracted in 2011, a SACU "windfall" of $818 million in 2012 at least temporarily eased the fiscal crisis. Real GDP growth was estimated at 2.8 percent in 2013, the IMF again calling for "comprehensive structural reforms" to promote the private sector and encourage the return of foreign investment. GDP grew by 2.5 percent in 2014, 1.7 percent in 2015, and 0.5 percent in 2016. Inflation was 6.7 percent in 2016, while GDP per capita was $2,611. In its annual survey on the ease of conducting business, the World Bank rated Swaziland 105th out of 189 countries, behind Antigua and Barbuda (104th) and ahead of the Bahamas (106th).

GOVERNMENT AND POLITICS

Political background. Swaziland came under British control in the mid-19th century when a Swazi ruler requested protection from his people's traditional enemies, the Zulu. Kept intact when the Union of South Africa was formed in 1910, the territory was subsequently administered under native rulers by the British high commissioner for South Africa. Preparations for independence began after World War II and culminated in the promulgation of internal self-government in 1967 and the achievement of full independence within the Commonwealth in 1968 under King SOBHUZA II, who subsequently exercised firm control of the country's political institutions. In the wake of small gains by the semi-radical Ngwane National Liberation Congress (NNLC) in a 1972 parliamentary election and frustration of his attempts to have an opposition legislator deported, the king in April 1973 repealed the constitution, abolished the legislature, introduced a detention act, and banned all opposition political activity.

On August 21, 1982, King Sobhuza died, having technically reigned from the age of one in 1899, although he had not been formally enthroned until 1921 and had not been recognized as paramount ruler by the British until 1966. He was succeeded as head of state by Queen Mother Dzeliwe SHONGWE, authorized to act as regent until a successor king was designated and reached maturity.

The naming of Prince Bhekimpi DLAMINI to succeed Prince Mabandla Fred DLAMINI as prime minister in March 1983 seemed to mark the ascendancy of conservative elements within the royal house. In August Queen Regent Dzeliwe was ousted from power, reportedly because she differed over the interpretation of her role with traditionalists within the *Liqoqo,* historically an advisory council of royal family members that had been elevated to the status of Supreme Council of State shortly before King Sobhuza's death. Queen Regent Dzeliwe was replaced by Ntombi THWALA, the mother of Prince MAKHOSETIVE, who was named successor to the former sovereign on August 10. Two months later, however, Prince Mfanasibili DLAMINI and Dr. George MSIBI, who were prominently involved in the palace coup that installed Queen Regent Ntombi, were dismissed from the *Liqoqo.*

On April 25, 1986, two years earlier than originally planned, Prince Makhosetive assumed the title of King MSWATI III in an apparent effort to halt the power struggle that had followed his father's death. The 19-year-old king, the world's youngest monarch, moved quickly to consolidate his control, temporarily disbanding the *Liqoqo* and appointing Prince Sotsha DLAMINI, a relatively obscure former police official, as prime minister on October 6.

After authorizing the arrest in May 1987 of 12 people allegedly involved in the palace intrigue of recent years, the king dissolved Parliament in September, one year early. Assembly elections were held in November, and the government was extensively reorganized at the end of the month. Although the king's bold action at the outset of his reign surprised some observers, most Swazis appeared to support his exercise of monarchical prerogative as a means of preserving stability.

The king formally assumed full executive authority at age 21 on April 19, 1989. Three months later he dismissed Prince Sotsha as prime minister, replacing him with Obed Mfanyana DLAMINI. The new prime minister was the founder and former secretary general of the Swaziland Federation of Trade Unions (SFTU), a background that appeared to strengthen the government's capacity to deal with a growing number of labor disputes.

On October 9, 1992, one month before the expiration of Parliament's term, the king dissolved Parliament and declared that, with the assistance of his cabinet (which would be restyled a Council of Ministers and act as a caretaker government), he would rule by decree until the adoption of a new constitution and the holding of elections. Balloting scheduled for November was postponed until 1993 to allow for the redefinition of constituencies and compilation of a voters' register. The monarch's action followed his approval of a draft charter that called for retention of the monarchy and the revival of multipartyism (banned in 1973 by King Sobhuza II).

Fearing a conservative backlash if the reform movement outpaced the prerogatives of the royal court and powerful traditional chiefs, the constitutional commission subsequently recommended that decisions regarding political parties be deferred. Consequently, candidates for the House of Assembly elections on September 18 and October 11, 1993, competed on a nonparty basis; nonetheless, the polling marked the first time that legislators had been popularly elected and royal family members had been prohibited from participating. Underscoring the change, Prime Minister Dlamini and all but three cabinet ministers lost their seats. As a result, on October 25 King Mswati named Andreas FAKUDZE as interim prime minister with responsibility for all 16 ministries. Ten days later the king appointed Prince Jameson Mblini DLAMINI, a conservative, to succeed Fakudze. Traditionalists hailed the monarch's choice, although the government named by Prince Jameson on November 10 included several reformists.

A follow-up round to the 1993 balloting was held on October 2, 1994, with voters selecting secretaries for the country's 55 regions (*Inkundla*). The new officials were described as links between legislators and their constituents, as well as coordinators of development activities in their areas.

The SFTU called a general strike (the most comprehensive in recent years) on March 13–14, 1995, to secure acceptance of a variety of demands, including the reinstatement of summarily dismissed state employees. The action was called off after the government appointed a select committee to consider the grievances. Subsequently, the SFTU called for another strike on July 17, which was called off after the House of Assembly imposed severe penalties for work stoppages. In mid-August the Senate endorsed a statement by King Mswati that Swazis did not want multiparty politics. Three months later, a well-attended opposition conference rejected the royal assessment in that matter.

On January 22–29, 1996, the SFTU organized a widely observed general strike, which was abandoned only after the king ordered the strikers back to work, threatening "to go to war" if necessary to end the action. Although some observers described the SFTU as "tarnished" by its capitulation to the monarch's threat, on February 16, three days before a scheduled resumption of the strike, King Mswati promised to reform the constitution and consider lifting the political party ban. Subsequently, the union suspended plans for renewed action; however, prodemocracy rallies continued.

On May 8, 1996, the king dismissed Prime Minister Dlamini, promising "concrete democratic changes." Subsequently, the king named Deputy Prime Minister Sishayi NXUMALO as acting prime minister, but Nxumalo immediately asserted that the Swazi people were not ready for political parties, which he described as ill-suited for the "close-knit, non-ethnic, traditional society." Nevertheless, on July 26 the king announced the creation of a 29-member Constitutional Reform Commission (CRC) with responsibility for drafting a new constitution. Concurrently, he named former finance minister and IMF executive director Barnabas Sibusiso DLAMINI as the new prime minister. The cabinet was reshuffled on November 13, the king pledging emphasis on economic development and the pursuit of foreign investment and trade.

In an apparent effort to quell increasingly vocal calls for reform from prodemocracy activists, the king abruptly dissolved the House of Assembly in August 1998. Observers attributed the low voter turnout in the October assembly elections to voter apathy and the prodemocracy forces' call for an electoral boycott. On November 13 the king reappointed Dlamini as prime minister, and on November 20 a new government was sworn in.

On May 31, 2003, the king dissolved the assembly and appointed a special council to act as a caretaker government until new elections were held. Following the September–October legislative polls, which were boycotted by most of the major opposition groups, the king appointed Absalom Themba DLAMINI as prime minister on November 14.

Unprecedented protests were reported in the run-up to the September 2008 assembly elections, as thousands demonstrated for the legalization of political parties. Commonwealth election observers stated that they could not declare the results of the legislative poll credible because political parties were denied participation and the power of Parliament remained severely restricted. Following the elections, the first since the promulgation of a new constitution in 2006 (see Constitution and government, below), the king named Barnabas Sibusiso Dlamini to return to the premiership, which he had held in 1996–2003. Dlamini named a new government on October 24.

Suppression of political activists heightened in 2010 with the arrests of several union leaders and other prodemocracy demonstrators.

Attention in early 2011 turned to the country's severe financial crisis, as the finance minister ordered drastic budget cuts in February after warning that there might not be enough money to pay public employees. Despite the shortage of funds, the government stood firm on its plans to complete construction of a new airport—described as a pet project of the king and a "white elephant" by critics, who claimed the project already was over budget and, at nine years and counting, well behind schedule. Tensions heightened as economic conditions worsened, culminating in a mass protest in late March that led to the government agreeing to a 10 percent cut in ministers' salaries. In April thousands of teachers, students, and doctors, among others, rallied in protest against cuts to social spending and, perhaps inspired by popular uprisings elsewhere on the continent, to show their dissatisfaction with the monarchy. Police detained about 100 people, including journalists and labor leaders, in what was described as the largest security mobilization in Swaziland in decades. As pressure mounted on the political front, the government also faced a dire economic situation, prompting the king to issue an international plea for loans to prevent the country's total fiscal collapse. Both the IMF and the World Bank refused to provide short-term assistance, but in early August South Africa agreed to a tentative $355 million bailout conditioned on political and economic reforms, including the promotion of democracy, human rights, and good governance. Among other things, human rights advocates alleged that security forces had abused detainees in Swaziland by using torture and unjustified use of lethal force. Clashes broke out again in September 2011 between police and protesters in several cities as the government refused to accept a petition from civic groups calling for the introduction of multipartyism and reform of the judiciary.

Following the legislative replenishments of September–October 2013, the king reappointed Prime Minister Barnabas Sibusiso Dlamini on October 28, 2013, and a new cabinet was inaugurated on November 4. A minor cabinet reshuffle was conducted on October 7, 2016.

Constitution and government. For some years after independence, King Sobhuza II was reported to have been working on a revised Western-style constitution. However, in March 1977 he announced that he had abandoned the effort in favor of a form of traditional government (based on tribal councils [*Tinkhundla*]), which was formally introduced in October 1978. Under the *Tinkhundla* electoral system, polling was held without political campaigns or electoral rolls for an 80-member electoral college charged with naming four-fifths of a 50-member House of Assembly, which in turn named half of a 20-member Senate. Ten members of each were designated by the monarch, who also named the prime minister and other cabinet officials.

On February 14, 1992, a royal constitutional commission appointed by the king in late 1991 presented a draft charter for a multiparty electoral system, which was given preliminary approval by the monarch in October. The proposal called for a two-stage balloting process beginning with polling in the *Tinkhundla* for local representatives from among candidates chosen by the chiefs. In the second round of the secret balloting, the leading vote-getters from the first round were to compete for berths in an expanded House of Assembly and Senate of 55 and 20 members, respectively (the monarch having the right to appoint 10 additional members to each). The plan served as a partial blueprint for the 1993 and 1998 polls.

A Constitutional Reform Committee (CRC) formed in 1996 proceeded haltingly. In January 2001 a draft constitution report from the CRC was criticized by the opposition and human rights groups as a "doctored document" and "not a truly representative report because group submissions were denied." The long-awaited new draft constitution was presented to the king in November 2003, but he did not sign it into law until July 26, 2005, after ordering the legislature to amend sections regarding religion and taxing the royal family. The new constitution promulgated on February 8, 2006, contained no specific language to legalize political parties and stipulated that candidates for election must run as individuals. Though the constitution included a bill of rights guaranteeing limited freedoms, the king retained ultimate authority, including appointment of the prime minister and the cabinet.

The judiciary, whose members are appointed by the king, encompasses a High Court, a Court of Appeal, and district courts. There are also 17 Swazi courts for tribal and customary issues. Swaziland is divided for administrative purposes into four districts, each headed by a commissioner appointed by the central government. There are partially elected town boards and councils (five each) and two fully elected municipal councils.

The government severely restricts press freedom, even though it is constitutionally guaranteed. Most major media outlets are state controlled (there is only one independent newspaper), and no criticism is permitted of the government or the king, who is included in the list of "Predators of Press Freedom" issued by Reporters Without Borders (RWB). In a case that attracted wide international condemnation, two journalists were sentenced to two years in prison in 2014 on charges of contempt of court in regard to articles they had published that reflected poorly on the judiciary. RWB ranked Swaziland 153rd out of 180 countries in freedom of the press in 2016.

Foreign relations. Swaziland is a member of the United Nations (UN), the Commonwealth, and the African Union (AU, formerly the Organization of African Unity—OAU). It maintains close relations with South Africa as a result of geographic proximity, administrative tradition, and economic dependency (more than 80 percent of the kingdom's imports are from South Africa, and a substantial portion of its national income consists of remittances from Swazis employed in the neighboring state). Despite its ties to South Africa, Swaziland established diplomatic relations with Mozambique during 1976, prompted by a need to facilitate the movement of goods through Mozambique's port of Maputo. (A security accord was concluded between the two countries in mid-1984.)

Despite OAU strictures, Swaziland concluded a secret nonaggression pact with Pretoria in 1982 and subsequently strove to contain African National Congress (ANC) activity within its territory. However, a series of major raids on purported ANC strongholds in Swaziland by South African security forces in 1986–1987 led to vehement protests by the Swazi government.

In September 1989 it was reported that Swaziland and South Africa had agreed on a border adjustment that would bring the largely Swazi-populated South African homeland of KaNgwane within the kingdom. However, no date was given for the formal transfer. (In 1994 KaNgwane was reintegrated into Transvaal in northern South Africa; Swaziland has continued to lay claim to the territory.)

In late 1997 relations between Swaziland and Mozambique were strained after it was reported that a Swazi prince leading a committee studying their shared border had asserted that Swazi territory legally encompassed all of Mozambique's Maputo Province. (The claim was dismissed by Maputo, which declared that it had never been formally contacted by Swaziland.)

Taiwan currently contributes $200 million per year in aid to Swaziland, one of Taiwan's few "allies" in Africa.

In June 2014 the United States terminated its preferential trade arrangements with Swaziland due to the lack of progress in Swaziland regarding democratization and the protection of human rights, notably freedom of expression.

In July 2016 Taiwan signed an agreement with Swaziland to help improve the country's health care system and reduce the prevalence of HIV/AIDS. In 2016 Swaziland had the world's highest HIV/AIDS infection rate, with 27.2 percent of the population infected. One result was that an estimated 15 percent of the population was made up of children who had been orphaned by HIV/AIDS.

Current issues. Negotiations with the IMF collapsed in mid-2012 over the government's disinterest in severe austerity measures, which many analysts concluded would have the immediate effect of further inflaming popular resentment. New strikes and protests in July–September again prompted harsh responses from authorities.

In October 2012 the assembly passed a nonconfidence motion against the government in the wake of questions about a recent contract for the nation's sole telephone provider. However, Prime Minister Dlamini, stating he served at the pleasure of the king, refused to resign, and a potential constitutional crisis arose when the king declined to dissolve the government. The assembly subsequently reversed the nonconfidence motion, thereby easing the immediate impasse, but not before it had become clear that legislative prerogatives still remained severely constrained. Most opposition groups subsequently joined organizations representing teachers, other public employees, students, and trade unions in calling for a boycott of the November local elections.

Protests over the extent of the king's authority continued in the first half of 2013, and opposition forces again supported a boycott of the September balloting for the House of Assembly, calling the poll "pointless." Although the balloting was peaceful, international observers strongly lamented the fact that political parties were still barred from formally presenting candidates. The international community also criticized the government's crackdown in the first half of 2014 on prodemocracy activists, some of whom faced "terrorism" charges for speeches advocating reform and for displaying banners referencing banned organizations.

The minister of labor and social security ordered all labor unions to cease operations in October 2014.

In April 2015 Chief Justice Michael RAMODIBEDI was charged with corruption but refused to surrender to police, instead barricading himself in his house for 37 days. He then fled to Lesotho rather than face a disciplinary hearing. On June 18 the king formally dismissed Ramodibedi from his position.

The budget for 2016–2017 had a deficit of 16.1 percent of GDP, prompting concerns about long-term fiscal sustainability. The high spending led donors such as the United States to threaten to withhold aid to Swaziland. (The United States provided about $1 million assistance in 2016.)

POLITICAL GROUPS

During 1994 a number of groups, including Pudemo (below), joined with human rights and other groups to form a Confederation for Full Democracy in Swaziland (CFDS). (See the 2013 *Handbook* for additional information on the CFDS.) In early 1996 the CFDS appeared to have been superseded by the Swaziland Democratic Alliance (SDA), a coalition that included Pudemo; the Swaziland Federation of Trade Unions (SFTU), an 80,000 member grouping then led by Jan SITHOLE; and representatives of the Institute for Democracy and Leadership (Ideal), led by Dr. Jerry GULE. Organized to "try to force change," the SDA led a march on the prime minister's office and parliamentary building, although only a few activists participated. In early 1999 the SDA was bolstered by the addition of the NNLC (below) to its ranks, and in April the NNLC's Obed Mfanyan Dlamini (a former prime minister) was elected, along with Pudemo's Jerry Nxumalo and Sithole, to lead the reorganized alliance. However, in 2003 Obed Dlamini was elected to the assembly, even though other SDA members had called for a boycott of the elections. The conflict appeared to signal the collapse of the SDA.

Despite analysts' speculation about the freedom of association clause in the revised constitution allowing for the legal registration of political parties, in 2007 King Mswati declared that political parties remained banned. That pronouncement was reiterated in 2008 by the elections commissioner, and political parties were not allowed to participate in the September assembly elections.

The **Swaziland United Democratic Front** (SUDF) was launched in 2008 by Pudemo, trade unions, church groups, student activists, and other civic organizations. The SUDF, whose national coordinator is Wandile DLUDLU, served a prominent role in the 2011–2014 protests calling for economic and political reform. Most opposition groups called for a boycott of the September 2013 legislative poll, but former SFTU leader Sithole, now described as a leader of the **Swaziland Democratic Party** (Swadepa), was elected to the assembly after changing course and deciding to pursue reform "from within."

People's United Democratic Movement (PUDM or Pudemo). Initial reports about Pudemo surfaced in 1989 when the government accused the group of illegally circulating political pamphlets. In mid-1990 it was reported that after a period of inactivity, the group had resumed actively campaigning for electoral reform and an end to corruption. In January 1996 Pudemo threatened to make the country "ungovernable" if the monarch failed to adopt a multiparty democratic system of government. Underscoring its more militant stance, Pudemo subsequently replaced President Kislon SHONGWE, who was described as "uncombative," and Secretary General Dominic MNGOMEZULU with Mario Masuku and Bonginkhosi DLAMINI, respectively. Masuku was named to the constitutional review commission established in May but later resigned on the ground that it had become apparent that the king had no intention of lifting the political party ban. In November 2000 Pudemo was among the forces of opposition to join the general strike called by the SFTU, during which Masuku was arrested along with other opposition leaders. Masuku was acquitted of sedition charges in August 2002.

In 2005 the king accused 13 Pudemo members of firebombing homes and offices of government officials; all were subsequently released. The government cracked down on a Pudemo rally in March 2006, arresting several party members, including Masuku (who was released the same day), and Bonginkhosi Dlamini (who was charged with high treason before being released later). In August members of the party's youth wing, the Swaziland Youth Congress (Swayoco), were routed by police as the prodemocracy group marched near the capital.

In 2008 Pudemo called the assembly elections "a sham" and vowed to continue to press for political reforms. Party leader Masuku was charged in November under the country's new Suppression of Terrorism Act (STA) and was temporarily sent to a maximum security prison. His arrest came in the wake of the prime minister's announcement that four political groups, including Pudemo and Swayoco, had been deemed to be terrorist organizations and were therefore banned.

In May 2010 a leader of Swayoco died in police custody after his arrest at a May Day rally. Several other youth leaders were detained following a series of bombings in June. Participation in a prodemocracy rally in September resulted in the temporary detention of Masuku and party vice president Sikhumbuzo Phakathi.

In February 2011 the king refused an initiative suggested by Pudemo that would have led to opening a dialogue between the government and prodemocracy groups. Pudemo was at the forefront of protests that broke out later in the spring and continued sporadically into the fall of 2012. Pudemo, insisting it eschewed violence in favor of peaceful dialogue, joined other opposition groups in calling for a boycott of the November 2012 local elections and the 2013 assembly poll.

Pudemo's secretary general Mlungisi MAKHANYA and six other Pudemo members were arrested in April 2014 on sedition charges that reportedly included wearing T-shirts with the Pudemo logo on them. The following month, Masuku and Swayoco's secretary general Maxwell Dlamini were also arrested on STA charges in connection with speeches they had made at a May Day workers' rally. Pudemo subsequently sought to have the terrorism charges dismissed through, among other things, an appeal to the High Court to declare the STA unconstitutional. Masuku was released in July 2015.

Leaders: Mario MASUKU (President), Jerry NXUMALO, Maxwell DLAMINI (Secretary General of Swayoco), Mlungisi MAKHANYA (Secretary General of Pudemo).

Ngwane National Liberatory Congress (NNLC). The NNLC was at the forefront of opposition activities in the 1970s but thereafter was reported to have become temporarily moribund. At a meeting of the resuscitated body in December 1998, former prime minister Obed Mfanyana Dlamini was elected president of the congress, and in April 1999 he reportedly agreed to enter into the SDA (see Political Groups introductory text, above). In the 2003 legislative elections, Dlamini was elected to the assembly after campaigning as a nonpartisan. In 2005 NNLC member Jimmy HLOPHE, also running as an unaffiliated individual, won an assembly seat in a special election following the death of a member of the assembly. Earlier in 2005, requests to the high court by the NNLC and Pudemo to be involved in the constitutional review process were denied because, according to the judge, "in terms of the law they are nonexistent." The NNLC was among several political groups that protested the 2008 assembly elections.

In 2009 Obed Dlamini was appointed to the *Liquoqo* (the king's advisory council), his acceptance of the post generating strong criticism within the NLCC. In early 2012 the NLCC argued that Swaziland would become a "failed state" without democratic reforms.

Leaders: Alvit DLAMINI (President), Obed Mfanyana DLAMINI (Former Prime Minister), Thamsanqa HLATSHWAYO (Secretary General).

African United Democratic Party (AUDP). References to the AUDP first appeared in 2006 in reports that it was taking its fight for registration to the courts. It was subsequently reported that the high court had ordered the government to register the AUDP in accordance with the revised constitution's freedom of association clause. However, King Mswati soon after confirmed that political parties remained illegal. The AUDP as of mid-2014 continued to be active in efforts to compel establishment of a multiparty system.

Leaders: Stanley MAUNDZISA (President), Sibusiso DLAMINI (Secretary General).

Swaziland National Progressive Party (SNPP). This party was referenced in 2000 as being affiliated with the SDA. In 2009 the SNPP condemned the prime minister's "attitude" following his remarks that those who were critical of the king's remarks at the opening session of Parliament could be charged with sedition. In supporting a teachers' strike in August 2012, the SNPP argued that the *Tinkhundla* system had failed the country and that cabinet ministers were self-serving.

Leader: Magadeyiwile MDLULI (President).

Swaziland Solidarity Network (SSN). Based in South Africa and led by a South African, Solly Mapaila, the SSN is a "pressure group" that has been critical of the Swaziland regime's alleged efforts to squelch prodemocracy activity. In October 1997 Mapaila, who was himself banned from Swaziland for allegedly fomenting unrest, accused the monarch of maintaining a list of ANC officials it sought to ban from entering the country. The SSN launched a campaign in 2000 calling for the international community to "isolate" Swaziland until political reforms were enacted. It renewed its calls for international action in 2005, citing the king's reported extravagant spending while most of the population lived in extreme poverty.

In 2008 the SSN backed the election boycott organized by Pudemo. Following the election, the SSN was among four political groups listed as "terrorist organizations" and banned by the prime minister of Swaziland. The SSN's response was that it was impossible for the Swazi government to ban the group because it is based in South Africa.

In June 2010 the SSN asserted that Swazi security forces were behind a spate of recent bombings and were using the attacks to cover up alleged illegal raids and arbitrary detentions of political activists.

Leaders: Solly MAPAILA (Chair), Lucky LUKHELE (Spokesperson).

***Imbokodvo* National Movement** (INM). The *Imbokodvo* ("Grindstone") grouping dominated the political scene during the late 1960s and was the only political group permitted to function openly after 1973. The leadership of the party became vacant following the dismissal of Prince Mabandla Dlamini as prime minister in March 1983. Two royalist groups, formed as "cultural organizations" in 1996, were the *Sive Siyinqaba*, an offshoot of the INM led by Isaac SHABANGU and Zibuse SIMELANE, and the *Sibahle Sinje*, led by former assembly speaker Marwick KHUMALO. In 2000 the *Sive Siyinqaba* called on the king to lift the ban on political parties, while the *Sibahle Sinje* continued to back the no-party system. Khumalo, a member of the assembly, was described in 2012 as secretary general of a joint *Sive Siyinqaba–Sibahle Sinje*, which sent representatives to meetings of opposition groups promoting multipartyism, although *Sive Siyinqaba–Sibahle Sinje* argued that monarchical authority should be preserved. Khumalo was described as increasingly critical of the government in 2013–2014.

Communist Party of Swaziland (CPS). The CPS was launched in 2011 with the assistance of the South African Communist Party. CPS officials applauded recent reform activity on the part of Pudemo, Swayoco, and the SSN but called for an "intensified struggle." In addition to its antimonarchical stance, the CPS also opposed recent IMF demands as harmful to workers. The CPS, led by Secretary General Kenneth KUNENE, called for a boycott of the September 2013 assembly poll, several of its members reportedly having been arrested in connection with recent protest demonstrations.

Other political groups are the **Inhlava Party**, founded in 2006 by Mfomfo NKHAMBULE; the **Ngwane Socialist Revolutionary Party**, led by Thomas Vabula MAGAGULA; and the **National Congress for Democratic Change** (Nacodec), a breakaway from Pudemo. A group known as the **Swaziland People's Liberation Army** (*Umbane*), whose leadership remained "faceless," was reported in 2009 to be receiving financial backing and training for its members from the Sudan People's Liberation Army. The group was subsequently declared a terrorist organization by Swaziland's prime minister.

LEGISLATURE

On October 9, 1992, King Mswati dissolved the bicameral **Parliament** (*Libandla*) in preparation for new elections scheduled to follow the adoption of a new multiparty constitution in 1993. However, further deliberation on the draft charter was suspended, and the subsequent elections have been held on a nonparty basis.

Senate. The Senate is composed of 30 members (20 chosen by the monarch plus 10 elected via majoritarian vote by the House of Assembly), whose term of office is five years. The most recent balloting in the House of Assembly for the 10 elected members was held on October 23, 2013, and the king's appointments were announced on October 30.

President: Chief Gelane ZWANE.

House of Assembly. Enlarged by 15 seats following the 1992 elections, the assembly consists of 55 popularly elected members (1 for each electoral district), 10 monarchial appointees, and the speaker, who can be elected by the assembly from outside its membership and serve in an ex officio (nonvoting) capacity. (If popularly elected to the assembly, the speaker may vote but only to break a tie vote among the other members.) The term of office is five years, subject to dissolution by the king. Political parties are not permitted to participate in assembly elections, and all candidates run officially as independents. The most recent balloting for the 55 elected members was held on September 20, 2013, and the king's appointments were announced on October 5.

Speaker: Themba MSIBI.

CABINET

[as of November 18, 2016]

Prime Minister	Barnabas Sibusiso Dlamini
Deputy Prime Minister	Paul Dlamini
Ministers	
Agriculture	Moses Vilakati
Commerce, Industry, and Trade	Jabulani Mabuza
Economic Planning and Development	Prince Hlangusemphi
Education and Training	Phineas Magagula
Finance	Martin Dlamini
Foreign Affairs and International Cooperation	Chief Mgwagwa Gamedze
Health	Sibongile Ndlela-Simelane [f]
Home Affairs	Princess Tsandzile [f]
Housing and Urban Development	Phiwayinkosi Mabuza
Information, Communications, and Technology	Dumisani C. Ndlangamandla
Justice and Constitutional Affairs	Edgar Hillary
Labor and Social Security	Winnie Magagula [f]
Natural Resources and Energy	Jabulile Mashwama [f]
Public Service	Owen Nxumalo
Public Works and Transport	Pastor Lindiwe Gwebu [f]
Sports, Culture, and Youth Affairs	David Ngcamphalala
Tinkhundla Administration and Development	Mduduzi Dlamini
Tourism and Environmental Affairs	Christopher Gamedze

[f] = female

INTERGOVERNMENTAL REPRESENTATION

Ambassador to the U.S.: Abednego Mandla NTSHANGASE.

U.S. Ambassador to Swaziland: Lisa J. PETERSON.

Permanent Representative to the UN: Zwelethu MNISI.

IGO Memberships (Non-UN): AfDB, AU, Comesa, CWTH, IOM, NAM, SADC, WTO.

For Further Reference:

Crush, Jonathan. *The Struggle for Swazi Labor, 1890–1920.* Montreal: McGill-Queen's University Press, 1987.

Gillis, D. Hugh. *The Kingdom of Swaziland.* Westport, CT: Praeger, 1999.

Rose, Laurel. *The Politics of Harmony: Land Dispute Strategies in Swaziland.* Cambridge: Cambridge University Press, 1992.

SWEDEN

Kingdom of Sweden
Konungariket Sverige

Political Status: Constitutional monarchy established on June 6, 1809; under revised constitution effective January 1, 1975.

Area: 173,731 sq. mi. (449,964 sq. km).

Population: 9,852,000 (2016E—UN); 9,880,604 (2016E—U.S. Census).

Major Urban Centers (2015E—Government): STOCKHOLM (923,516), Göteborg (548,190), Malmö (322,574), Uppsala (210,126).

Official Language: Swedish.

Monetary Unit: Krona (official rate October 1, 2016: 8.57 kronor = $1US).

Sovereign: King CARL XVI GUSTAF; succeeded to the throne September 19, 1973, following the death of his grandfather, King GUSTAF VI ADOLF.

Heir Apparent: Crown Princess VICTORIA Ingrid Alice Désirée, daughter of the king.

Prime Minister: Stefan LÖFVEN (Social Democrats); elected by the *Riksdag* on October 2, 2014, to succeed Fredrik REINFELDT (Moderate Party), following the legislative elections of September 14; formed minority government on October 3, 2014.

THE COUNTRY

Situated on the Baltic side of the Scandinavian Peninsula and projecting north of the Arctic Circle, Sweden is the largest and most populous of the Scandinavian countries. The indigenous population, about 70 percent of which belongs (at least nominally) to the Evangelical Lutheran Church, is generally homogeneous except for some 400,000 Finns spread over the country and a Sámi (Lapp) minority in the north. In addition, there are more than 1 million resident aliens who have arrived since World War II. Early on, the resident aliens came mainly from Finland and Mediterranean countries such as Greece, Turkey, and Yugoslavia. However, following Sweden's accession to the European Union (EU) in 1995, people from various EU countries have also immigrated to Sweden. In addition, Sweden has granted permanent residency to an increasing number of asylum-seeking refugees from Africa and Asia, including a large group from Iraq. Immigration has become an important political issue recently, in part in regard to the Muslim population (currently estimated at approximately 500,000).

In 2007 approximately 78 percent of women ages 25–64 were in the labor force, compared with close to 85 percent of men. Women won 44 percent of the seats in the *Riksdag* in 2014, making it one of the most gender-balanced parliaments in the world. Women are equally well represented in the cabinet.

Sweden is almost self-sufficient in foodstuffs, although only 7 percent of the land is cultivated and agriculture and fishing contribute only 2 percent of GDP. The country's wealth of resources has enabled it to assume an important position among the world's industrial nations. A major producer and exporter of wood, paper products, and iron ore, Sweden also is a leading manufacturer of vehicles, pharmaceuticals, chemicals, and telecom equipment. The growing creative sector (including design, music, fashion, and gastronomy) also contributes to a healthy export income. Leading trading partners include Germany, Norway, and Denmark.

Despite socialist leadership throughout most of the post–World War II period, the private sector accounts for 80 percent of Sweden's output, although approximately 30 percent of jobs are in the public sector. The government provides generous benefits in education (universities are free), health care, and "social protection," and as a result, an estimated 44 percent of the average worker's labor costs are deducted in taxes.

The government decided in late 1997 that Sweden would not participate, despite meeting the economic prerequisites, in launching the EU's Economic and Monetary Union (EMU). Although the possibility of eventual membership remained open, Swedish voters again rejected adoption of the euro in a 2003 referendum.

Sweden's economy was hit hard by the global financial crisis in 2008, as exports weakened and investment declined significantly. In late 2008 the center-right government that had been elected in 2006 approved a $2.4-billion cut in income taxes, $205 billion in aid to banks, and a three-year stimulus package, which included assistance to local municipalities and infrastructure development. GDP contracted by 5 percent in 2009, but rapidly rising export demand (particularly from Germany and Asia) subsequently underpinned a remarkably swift economic recovery. Growth rates of 5.9 percent and 4.0 percent were achieved in 2010 and 2011, respectively, but the economy weakened significantly (only 0.9 percent growth) in 2012 as a result of the conclusion of domestic stimulus measures and a decline in demand for Swedish exports from stagnant European economies. Improvement to 1.6 percent growth was recorded in 2013, although unemployment remained troublesome at 8.0 percent. GDP expanded by 2.3 percent in 2014, 4.1 percent in 2015, and 3.7 in 2016. That year inflation was 1.1 percent, while unemployment declined to 6.9 percent, and GDP per capita was $51,136. Like the other Nordic countries, Sweden consistently ranks high in the World Bank's annual ease of conducting business survey, rating 8th, between the United States (7th) and Norway (9th), out of 189 nations in 2016.

GOVERNMENT AND POLITICS

Political background. A major European power in the 17th century, Sweden later declined in relative importance but nevertheless retained a significant regional position, including linkage with Norway in a union under the Swedish crown from 1814 to 1905. (Finland was a part of Sweden from the Middle Ages until 1809, when the two countries peacefully separated.) Neutrality in both world wars in the first half of the 20th century enabled Sweden to concentrate on its industrial development and the perfection of a welfare state under the auspices of the Social Democratic Labor Party (*Socialdemokratiska Arbetareparti*—SdAP, currently widely referenced as the Social Democrats), which was in power almost continuously from 1932, either alone or in coalition with other parties.

In the *Riksdag* election of 1968 the Social Democrats won an absolute majority for the first time in 22 years under Tage ERLANDER, who had led the party and the country since 1946. Erlander was succeeded as party chair and prime minister by Olof PALME in October 1969. Although diminished support for the Social Democrats was reflected in the parliamentary elections of 1970 and 1973, the party maintained control until September 1976, when voters, disturbed by a climate of increasing labor unrest and inflation as well as declining economic growth, awarded a combined majority of 180 legislative seats to the Center Party (*Centerpartiet*), the Moderate Coalition Party (*Moderata Samlingspartiet*—MSP, currently referenced as the Moderates), and the Liberal People's Party (*Folkpartiet Liberalerna*—FpL, currently widely referenced as the Liberal Party or the Liberals). On October 8 a coalition government was formed under Center Party leader Thorbjörn FÄLLDIN. However, policy differences between the antinuclear Center Party and the pronuclear Moderates and FpL forced the government to resign in October 1978, providing the opportunity for Ola ULLSTEN to form a minority FpL government.

Following the election of September 16, 1979, a center-right coalition with a one-seat majority was formed by the Center Party, Moderates, and FpL, with the Center Party's Fälldin returning to the premiership. However, the Moderates withdrew from the coalition on May 4, 1981, in a dispute over tax reform, although they tacitly agreed to support the remaining two-party government to avoid an early election and the likely return to power by the Social Democrats. Fälldin continued in office until the election of September 19, 1982, in which the Social Democrats obtained a three-seat plurality over nonsocialists, permitting Olaf Palme to return as head of a Social Democrats' minority administration supported in Parliament by the Left Party–Communists (*Vänsterpartiet-Kommunisterna*—VpK). Although the center-right FpL gained substantially at the balloting of September 15, 1985, the Palme government remained in power with the support of the VpK.

On February 28, 1986, Prime Minister Palme was assassinated in Stockholm by an unidentified gunman, the first postwar West European head of government to be killed while in office. (A drug addict was convicted of the crime in 1989, but he was subsequently freed by an appellate court.) Deputy Prime Minister Ingvar CARLSSON immediately assumed interim control of the government and was confirmed as Palme's official successor on March 12. The Social Democrats retained their dominant position in the election of September 18, 1988, with the conservative parties losing ground and the Green Ecology Party (*Miljöpartiet de Gröna*—MjP, widely referenced as the Greens) entering the *Riksdag* for the first time with 20 seats.

Prime Minister Carlsson resigned on February 15, 1990, after losing a key vote on an economic austerity plan that would have placed upper-middle-income taxpayers in a 72 percent bracket while freezing both prices and wages through 1991. However, he was returned to office 11 days later after accepting a substantially watered-down tax schedule that left most of the country's budgetary problems unresolved. As a result, the Social Democrats fell to a total of 138 seats out of 349 at triennial legislative balloting on September 15, 1991. Meanwhile, the aggregate strength of the four traditional "bourgeois" parties—the Center Party, Moderates, Liberals, and Christian Democratic Community Party (*Kristdemokratiska Samhällspartiet*—KdS)—rose to 170 seats, due mainly to gains by the Moderates and the Christian Democrats. While the Left Party (*Vänsterpartiet*, formerly the VpK) lost ground and the Greens disappeared from the *Riksdag,* the populist New Democracy (*Ny Demokrati*—NyD) party won a startling 25 seats in its first parliamentary race. The result was the installation of a four-party center-right administration under the Moderates' Carl BILDT that was 5 seats short of an assured parliamentary majority and therefore dependent on the NyD's external support.

Faced with the country's worst postwar economic crisis, Prime Minister Bildt and opposition Social Democratic leader Carlsson on September 20, 1992, concluded an unprecedented economic pact that called for tax increases and major public spending cuts over five years. However, the new cooperative spirit was damaged in November, when the Social Democrats declined to support specific austerity measures, obliging the Swedish authorities to allow the krona to float and thereby to depreciate by 9 percent. Further welfare spending cuts mandated by the 1993–1994 budget ended the already frayed consensus.

Through 1993 the government relied on the NyD in critical parliamentary decisions, but in late March 1994 the NyD withdrew its support following the resignation the previous month of its leader, Count Ian WACHMEISTER. In campaigning for the fall legislative election, the ruling coalition derived some benefit from a modest economic upturn, but continuing high unemployment and uncertainty about the future of the welfare state gave the opposition Social Democrats powerful ammunition. Overhanging the campaign was the issue of Sweden's projected membership in the EU from January 1995, on which negotiations had been successfully concluded on March 1.

The outcome of the legislative balloting on September 18, 1994 (prior to which the legislative term of office had been extended permanently to four years), was a decisive swing to the left. The Social Democrats and the ex-communist Left Party both gained ground sharply, and the left-oriented Greens reentered the *Riksdag* after a three-year absence. Of the outgoing coalition parties, the Moderates held their vote, but the other three lost seats, while the NyD disappeared from parliament altogether. Having rejected the Liberals' offer of a majority center-left coalition, the Social Democrats proceeded to form a minority one-party government headed by Carlsson, with qualified pledges of external support from the Left Party and the Greens.

Attention subsequently turned to the EU referendum set for November 13, 1994, with the pro-accession center-right parties, Social Democratic leadership, and business community countering a lively anti-EU coalition of the Left Party, the Greens, and many rank-and-file Social Democrats. The result, in a turnout of 82.4 percent, was a 52.2 to 46.9 percent vote in favor of accession.

On August 18, 1995, Prime Minister Carlsson unexpectedly announced that he would retire in March 1996, more than two years before the expiration of his government's mandate. Finance Minister Göran PERSSON was elected as chair of the ruling party on March 15, 1996, and he was sworn in as prime minister on March 17 to head a substantially reshuffled cabinet.

In the general election of September 20, 1998, the Social Democratic legislative representation fell from 161 to 131 seats, with the Moderates finishing second with 82 seats. The decline by the Social Democrats was largely seen as a result of voter dissatisfaction with the government's fiscally conservative policies and willingness to make cuts in the welfare system. Once again relying on the qualified support of the Left Party and the Greens to avoid a legislative nonconfidence vote, Persson announced a reshuffled Social Democratic minority government on October 6.

The Social Democrats improved to 144 seats in the September 15, 2002, legislative election. Running on a platform of tax cuts, including abolition of wealth and real estate taxes, the Moderates won only 55 seats, many Swedes having apparently concluded that the party's policies would endanger social benefits. Meanwhile, the Liberals made surprising gains, analysts attributing the increase, at least in part, to the party's call for a language test for citizenship. Persson immediately ruled out giving government positions to either the Left Party or the Green Party because those parties opposed adoption of the euro. However, the Left Party joined the Moderates in providing parliamentary support for the Social Democrats to form a minority government again under Persson.

On September 10, 2003, Foreign Minister Anna LINDH, a key proponent in the pro-euro campaign, was assassinated in a Stockholm department store. On September 14 Swedish voters rejected adoption of the euro by 56 percent to 42 percent, despite the measure's strong backing by Prime Minister Persson.

In the September 17, 2006, parliamentary election, the Social Democrats won a plurality of 130 seats but lost power to the Alliance for Sweden (*Allians för Sverige*), whose member parties (the Moderates, Center Party, Liberals, and Christian Democrats) won a combined 178 seats. The chair of the Moderates, Fredrik REINFELDT, who was endorsed by all parties in the Alliance, was appointed prime minister on October 5. His new center-right coalition government named on October 6 included the four Alliance parties.

Tax cuts became a cornerstone of the governing coalition despite socialist concerns that the tax base supporting the welfare state would be eroded and thereby create a greater divide between rich and poor. In order to pay down the public debt as well as to encourage foreign investment, the Alliance also embarked on a widespread effort to privatize state-owned assets by selling shares in some 50 publicly owned companies.

Following the influx of thousands of refugees from Iraq, the government in 2007 tightened its immigration policies, ruling that, in the case of asylum seekers from Afghanistan, Iraq, and Somalia, Sweden could legally deport immigrants unless it was proved that they would be threatened if they returned home. Additionally, the *Riksdag* approved legislation denying publicly funded health care to illegal immigrants. At the same time, relations with the global Muslim community were deeply strained by the publication in 2007 of a controversial cartoon by Swedish artist Lars VILKS depicting the prophet Mohammed. (Vilks claimed he meant to test the boundaries of speech and press freedoms in Sweden, not provoke Muslims.) Meanwhile, several Swedish newspapers republished the cartoon as a show of solidarity with Vilks and a defense of "Scandinavian values of openness."

Amid mounting concerns over potential terrorist attacks, the *Riksdag* in June 2008 narrowly passed one of the most comprehensive—and divisive—government surveillance laws in Europe. The law, effective January 1, 2009, authorized the defense department to scan all cross-border phone calls, e-mails, and faxes without a court order. The new security measures provoked outrage from the youth wings of the governing coalition parties as well as from journalists, who were not exempt from possible surveillance. The public backlash prompted the *Riksdag,* spurred by the Alliance, to adopt amendments in September providing for judicial oversight of the electronic surveillance. Meanwhile, though Sweden's military budget was cut significantly, the government dropped plans to disband several military units in the wake of security concerns related to Russia's military attacks in Georgia.

In March 2009 the government announced a major restructuring of the military starting in 2010. The plan provided for an end to the century-old practice of universal conscription in favor of a professional volunteer army as well as an increase in the number of Swedish troops by 50 percent, to 50,000. The Social Democrats criticized the plan, saying they didn't believe the military could meet its goals by voluntary conscription.

Prime Minister Reinfeldt formed a new minority government (comprising the four Alliance parties) on October 5, 2010, following the September 19 *Riksdag* balloting in which the Alliance parties won a plurality of 173 seats, followed by the Red-Green coalition (the Social Democrats, Left Party, and Greens) with 156 seats. For the first time in its history, the right-wing, anti-immigration Sweden Democrats won representation in parliament with 20 seats.

Prime Minister Reinfeldt announced his resignation immediately following the September 14, 2014, *Riksdag* election in which the Social Democrats led all parties with 113 seats and combined with the other center-left parties to secure a total of 159 seats, compared to 141 seats for the Alliance of Swedes. Social Democratic leader Stefan

LÖFVEN was inaugurated as prime minister on October 3 as head of a minority government that also included the Greens (see Current issues, below).

On May 9, 2016, Deputy Prime Minister Åsa ROMSON (Greens) resigned (see Political Parties, below). She was replaced by Isabella LÖFVEN (Greens) on May 25 as part of a minor cabinet reshuffle.

Constitution and government. The present Swedish constitution retains the general form of the old governmental structure, but the king is now a figurehead (formerly, as nominal head of government, he appointed the prime minister and served as commander in chief of the armed forces). In 1979 the *Riksdag* took final action on making women eligible for succession; thus the present king's daughter, VICTORIA, born in 1977, has become the heir apparent.

The chief executive officer (the prime minister) is nominated by the speaker of the *Riksdag* and confirmed by the whole house. The prime minister appoints the other members of the cabinet, which functions as a policy-drafting body. Routine administration is carried out largely by independent administrative boards (*centrala ämbetsverk*). Legislative authority is vested in the *Riksdag,* which has been a unicameral body since 1971. The judicial system is headed by the Supreme Court (*Högsta Domstolen*) and includes 6 courts of appeal (*hovrätt*) and 100 district courts (*tingsrätt*). There is a parallel system of administrative courts, while the *Riksdag* appoints four *justitieombudsmen* to maintain general oversight of both legislative and executive actions. Any proposed amendment of the constitution must be approved by the *Riksdag* in successive legislative terms, requiring that a general election occur between the first approval and the second.

Sweden is administratively divided into 21 counties (including Stockholm) with appointed governors and elected councils and into 290 urban and rural communes with elected councils. The 20,000-strong Sámi (Lapp) community in the north has its own local assembly.

Under legislation approved in 1996, the Evangelical Lutheran Church was effectively disestablished as the Church of Sweden on January 1, 2000, terminating a legal and financial relationship between church and state that dated from the 16th century.

Under Sweden's Mass Media Act, which was implemented in January 1977, principles of noninterference dating to the mid-1700s and embodied in the Freedom of the Press Act of 1949 were extended to all media. Sweden is currently listed by Reporters Without Borders as one of the top countries in regard to press freedom. It was 8th out of 180 countries in 2016.

Foreign relations. Sweden has not participated in any war nor fully joined any military alliance since 1814, although its neutrality is backed by an impressive defense system. Unlike Denmark, Iceland, and Norway, Sweden declined to enter the North Atlantic Treaty Organization (NATO) in 1949. However, it is a strong supporter of nonmilitary international cooperation, participating in the United Nations and all its related agencies. In 1975 Sweden became the first industrial nation to meet a standard set by the Organization for Economic Cooperation and Development (OECD), allocating a full 1 percent of its GNP to aid for developing countries. Sweden also attaches importance to regional cooperation through the Nordic Council, while in 1960 it was a founding member of the European Free Trade Association (EFTA), although its membership in that body ceased upon its accession to the EU in 1995.

Stockholm's traditionally good relations with Moscow were strained during the 1980s and early 1990s by numerous incidents involving Soviet submarines in Swedish waters and intrusions of Russian planes into the country's airspace. However, during an official visit to Moscow by Prime Minister Carl Bildt in February 1993, the long-standing controversy appeared to end when the Russians for the first time formally admitted to violations of Swedish territorial waters.

Citing the end of the Cold War and the need to improve its economy by means of increased trade, Sweden applied for membership in the European Community (EC, subsequently the EU) on July 1, 1991. To pave the way, Sweden became a signatory of the European Economic Area (EEA) treaty between the EC and certain EFTA countries on May 2, 1992. Sweden also placed emphasis on post-Soviet regional cooperation, becoming a founding member of the ten-nation Council of the Baltic Sea States in March 1992 and of the Barents Euro-Arctic Council (comprising the five Nordic countries and Russia) in January 1993. Two months later Sweden modified its tradition of neutrality by agreeing to join a NATO military maneuver in August, and in May 1994, Sweden enrolled in NATO's Partnership for Peace program for the neutral and former communist states of Europe and the ex-USSR. Following referendum approval in November 1994 and *Riksdag* endorsement (by a vote of 278–36) in December, Sweden acceded to the EU on January 1, 1995.

Sweden became involved in Afghanistan in 2002 as a member of the International Security Assistance Force (ISAF), focusing primarily on humanitarian support. Meanwhile, following the U.S. invasion of Iraq in 2003, thousands of Iraqi refugees immigrated to Sweden, and Sweden adopted a prominent role in efforts to rebuild Iraq.

In 2008 Sweden also deployed personnel to the NATO peacekeeping mission in Kosovo. In May 2008 Denmark, Finland, Iceland, Norway, and Sweden met to discuss greater Nordic cooperation on defense matters, specifically agreements on a joint response to emergencies, as well as cooperation in defense procurement and coast guard activities. Tensions heightened between Sweden and Russia in the wake of the latter's military intervention in Georgia in August. Among other things, Sweden suspended all military cooperation with Russia (the two countries periodically had conducted joint military maneuvers). In 2009 Sweden negotiated with NATO, Norway, and Finland to collaborate on a Nordic air control operation (which Baltic states could later join) as a defense measure for the participating nations. New Swedish prime minister Stefan Löfven said in October 2014 that his minority government would not pursue full NATO membership even though some observers had previously suggested that the country's defense readiness had deteriorated. On October 30 the Löfven government formally recognized the Palestinian State, prompting Israel to recall its ambassador to Sweden and cancel a visit by that country's foreign minister.

In April 2015 Sweden's foreign minister issued an apology to Saudi Arabia after she referred to the kingdom as a "dictatorship" that violated human rights.

In June 2016 Sweden was elected for a two-year term on the UN Security Council, beginning in 2017.

Current issues. Nearly a week of riots in May 2013 in several suburbs of Stockholm heavily populated by immigrants severely jolted the nation and raised questions over the efficacy of immigrant absorption policies, previously heralded as a progressive model for the rest of the world. Some observers cited festering antipolice sentiment among young immigrants facing high unemployment and perceived racism as a contributing factor. It was also noted that several decades of curtailment of previous "cradle-to-grave" social welfare benefits had resulted in rising income inequities.

Immigration concerns contributed to the surprising third-place finish (49 seats) by the Sweden Democrats in the September 2014 *Riksdag* election. Observers also attributed the decline of the Moderates (84 seats) to a growing perception among voters that the probusiness reforms of the past eight years had perhaps gone a bit too far. Immediately following the election, Social Democratic leader Stefan Löfven announced that he would not invite the Left Party into his proposed new government, reportedly in the hope of recruiting the Center Party and/or the Liberals to participate. That plan failed, however, and Löfven's minority coalition with the Greens was approved (by a vote of 132–49) only because the Alliance for Sweden parties abstained. Acknowledging the vulnerability of his government, Löfven, a welder and former labor leader who had never been a legislator or cabinet member, promised a centrist approach that would somehow permit legislative approval of his proposed budget, absent which the government could quickly collapse.

On December 3, 2014, Parliament rejected Löfven's proposed budget after his coalition partners, the Greens, voted against the measure. The prime minister threatened to call early elections but was able to secure a cross-party agreement with the opposition on the budget on December 27.

In April 2015 Löfven reached an agreement with opposition parties to support a $111.9 million increase in defense spending and closer relations with NATO. In December Sweden permitted NATO to undertake surveillance flights over its territory. Sweden imposed enhanced border controls in November after a record 122,000 asylum seekers entered the country over the previous year. By 2015 Sweden had more refugees per capita than any other EU member.

POLITICAL PARTIES

In advance of the 2006 general election the Moderate Party, Center Party, Liberal People's Party, and Christian Democratic Party formed the **Alliance for Sweden** (*Allians för Sverige*). The parties in the coalition fielded their own candidates for the *Riksdag* but backed a single candidate, Fredrik Reinfeldt of the Moderates, for prime minister. After securing a slight majority (178 of 349 seats) among them in the legislative poll, the four parties served in the subsequent Reinfeldt-led center-right government. The Alliance won a plurality (173 seats) in the September 2010 *Riksdag* poll, which was also contested by the center-left **Red-Green** coalition of the Social Democrats, Left Party, and Greens (156 seats among the three parties). Reinfeldt subsequently formed a minority government of the four Alliance parties, and the Red-Green coalition dissolved. The Alliance parties fell to a total of 141 seats in the September 2014 legislative poll (compared to a total of 159 seats for the center-left parties) and subsequently moved into opposition to the new government led by the Social Democrats.

Government Parties:

Social Democrats (*Socialdemokraterma*). The Social Democrats is currently the most widely used rubric for the party also referenced as the **Social Democratic Labor Party** (*Socialdemokratiska Arbetareparti*—SdAP) or the **Social Democratic Party**. Formed in the 1880s and long a dominant force in Swedish politics, the party has a "pragmatic" socialist outlook. During more than four decades of virtually uninterrupted power from 1932, it refrained from nationalizing major industries but gradually increased government economic planning and control over the business sector. When the party's representation in the *Riksdag* dropped to 152 seats in 1976, the Social Democrats were forced, despite their sizable plurality, to move into opposition. The party regained control of the government in 1982 and retained it in 1985.

There were few, if any, changes in party ideology and practice following the assassination of Prime Minister Olof Palme in 1986 and the accession of his deputy, Ingvar Carlsson, to the prime ministership. Although the Social Democrats continued their government control following the 1988 elections with the aid of the VpK (see Left Party, below), the party was again forced into opposition in the legislative poll of September 1991, when its seat tally fell from 156 to 138. The party staged a comeback in 1994, winning 161 seats and 45.3 percent of the vote.

Carlsson's surprise announcement in August 1995 of his impending departure as party leader and prime minister, combined with rapid public disenchantment with the EU, yielded a dramatic slump in support for the Social Democrats to only 28.1 percent in the September European Parliament balloting, when three of the seven Social Democrats who were elected were critical of EU membership. The leadership mantle subsequently passed to the finance minister, Göran Persson, who secured the party position on March 15, 1996, two days before he was appointed prime minister.

Persson led the party to a strong showing in the September 2002 general elections, with the Social Democrats winning 144 seats (up from 131 seats in 1998). The party was later thrown into confusion by the assassination of Foreign Minister Anna Lindh, who had been considered by many to be the natural successor to Prime Minister Persson.

While the party officially was in favor of the EMU in 2004, several prominent party members, including Margot WALLSTRÖM, vice president of the European Commission, openly declared that they were against adoption of the euro.

Despite the healthy state of the Swedish economy, the Social Democrats lost control of the parliament to the center-right Alliance for Sweden in the 2006 election, though the Social Democrats won the most seats (130) of any single party. Following the election, Göran Persson stepped down as party leader, and former deputy premier Mona SAHLIN was elected party chair, becoming the first woman to hold that position in the party.

The Social Democrats objected to but took few steps to stop the subsequent efforts of the Alliance for Sweden to pare back the social welfare system and privatize state-owned assets. In October 2008 Sahlin announced the formation of the Red-Green (*De Rödgröna*) coalition between the Social Democrats and the Greens. Sahlin pointedly excluded the former communist Left Party from the initial alliance, prompting criticism from trade unions and other sectors of the Social Democrats. Consequently, Sahlin reopened negotiations with the Left Party, and by December key differences over economic policy had been resolved, with all sides agreeing to a common economic proposal. The proposal included the Left Party's dropping its opposition to the maintenance of a state budget surplus and a spending ceiling.

The Social Democrats fell to 112 seats in the 2010 *Riksdag* poll, barely maintaining the party's position as the leading legislative grouping, and the Alliance for Sweden retained its legislative majority. In the wake of the party's worst electoral performance in nearly 100 years, Sahlin relinquished her party leadership post at a special party congress in March 2011. New party leader Hakan JUHOLT vowed to restore left-wing policies, including ending child poverty, cutting youth unemployment, and reviewing the privatization of the energy and rail sectors.

Prominent labor union leader Stefan Löfven was elected party president in January 2012 following Juholt's resignation. The party's popularity subsequently rose, according to public opinion polls, as Löfven called for the easing of government austerity measures. Löfven became prime minister as head of a minority Social Democrats/Greens government following the September 2014 *Riksdag* election in which the Social Democrats led all parties with 113 seats on a 31 percent vote share.

Lena Rådström BAASTAD was elected secretary general in August 2016 after her predecessor, Carin JÄMTIN, resigned to devote herself to her position as member of parliament.

Leaders: Stefan LÖFVEN (Chair and Prime Minister), Tomas ENEROTH (Parliamentary Leader), Lena Rådström BAASTAD (Secretary General).

Green Party (*Miljöpartiet de Gröna*—MjG). Established in 1981, the Greens (as the party is most commonly referenced) benefited in the 1988 election from an upsurge of popular interest in environmental issues. The party advocated tax reduction for low-income wage earners, increased charges for energy use, and heightened penalties for pollution by commercial establishments and motor vehicle operators. It also called for the phasing out of nuclear-generated electricity and curtailment of highway construction. The party's parliamentary representation plummeted from 20 seats in 1988 to none in 1991 but recovered to 18 seats in 1994. The Greens opposed EU membership, which was approved in the November 1994 referendum.

The party declined to 16 seats in the 1998 general election but agreed to continue to support the minority government of the Social Democrats on confidence motions. The Greens participated in negotiations with center-right parties after the election before deciding to renew its agreement with the Social Democrats. In the 2006 election the Greens won 19 *Riksdag* seats, but the party improved to 25 seats (third best) in the 2010 *Riksdag* poll as part of the Red-Green coalition led by the Social Democrats. The Greens subsequently resisted reported overtures from the Alliance for Sweden to participate in the new government.

Promoting a "non-growth" policy in order to protect the environment, the Greens retained their 25 seats in the 2014 legislative poll (on a vote share of 6.9 percent) and subsequently joined the Social Democrats in the new minority government.

Instead of leaders, the party has two spokespersons—by party rule one man and one woman. Greens co-leader Åsa ROMSON resigned her party post and her position as deputy prime minister in October 2014 and was succeeded by Isabella LÖVIN.

Leaders: Gustav FRIDOLIN, Isabella LÖVIN (Spokespersons); Maria FERM (Parliamentary Leader); Anders WALLNER (Secretary General).

Other Legislative Parties:

Moderate Party (*Moderate Partiet*—MP). This party was known as the **Conservative Party** before the 1968 election, after which it adopted the rubric **Moderate Coalition Party** (*Moderata Samlingspartiet*—MSP). However, it was subsequently widely referenced simply as the Moderate Party; the name was formally adopted in 2007. The party currently refers to itself as the Moderates (*Moderaterna*), a usage (rather than initials) that is widely employed in the media and government circles as well.

The party was originally organized as a vehicle for the financial and business communities and advocated tax cuts and reduced governmental interference in the economy. It favored a robust defense policy and strongly supported Sweden's accession to the EU. The MSP joined a center-left coalition government in 1976 but withdrew in 1981 after disagreeing with a tax reform plan. Its *Riksdag* representation dropped from 86 seats in 1982 to 66 in 1988 but rose again to 80 in 1991, when it formed a center-right coalition with the FpL, Center Party, and the Christian Democrats under the premiership of MSP leader Carl Bildt. The MSP retained 80 seats in the 1994 national balloting, but an overall electoral swing to the left returned the party to opposition. The MSP was unable to improve its position substantially in the September 1998 *Riksdag* election (82 seats), thwarting Bildt's determined campaign to return to the prime ministership. Bildt, a prominent EU/UN negotiator in Yugoslavia since 1995, resigned as party chair in mid-1999 and was succeeded by Bo LUNDGREN, a former minister of finance.

After the party declined to 55 seats in the 2002 general election, Lundgren announced his resignation as party chair. Fredrik Reinfeldt replaced him in October 2003 and subsequently spearheaded the formation of the four-party Alliance for Sweden (see introductory text, above).

In a bid to capture the middle ground of Swedish politics prior to the 2006 election, the party dropped its call for radical tax cuts, instead emphasizing support for public services. It won 97 of the Alliance for Sweden's 178 seats. Following Reinfeldt's installation as prime minister, the Moderate-led Alliance embarked on a plan to liberalize the economy through the privatization of state-owned assets and reform of the welfare system, including a reduction in employers' social security contributions, restrictions on access to unemployment and sick benefits, and efforts to boost employment.

The Reinfeldt administration was widely praised for its handling of the effects on Sweden of the global financial crisis of 2008–2009, and the Moderates improved to 107 seats in the 2010 *Riksdag* balloting. However, the party declined to 84 seats (on a vote share of 23.3 percent) in the September 2014 poll, following which Reinfeldt announced he would step down as leader of the Moderates in the spring of 2015. Anna Kinberg BATRA was elected party chair on January 10, 2015.

Leaders: Anna Kinberg BATRA (Chair), Fredrik REINFELDT (Former Prime Minister), Jessica POLFJÄRD (Parliamentary Leader), Tomas TOBÉ (Secretary General).

Liberals (*Liberalerna*). Originally formed as a parliamentary group in 1895, the first ***Folkpartiet*** merged with the **Liberal Coalition Party** in 1900. The two split in 1923 over alcohol issues and reunited in 1934. (The grouping has since usually been referred to simply as the Liberal Party or the Liberals.) The party draws support from rural free-church movements as well as from professionals and intellectuals. Favoring socially progressive policies that also strive to acknowledge individual responsibility, the Liberals sought the cooperation of the Center Party (below) on many issues, promoting "knowledge, work, and security." The Liberals lost half of their parliamentary representation in the 1982 general election, and in July 1984 former prime minister Ola Ullsten resigned as chair "to make way for more dynamic influences."

In the September 1985 balloting, the party gained 30 additional *Riksdag* seats for a total of 51, but its representation fell in the next two ballots. The party changed its name to the **Liberal People's Party** (*Folkpartiet Liberalerna*—FpL) in 1990. The party entered a four-party center-right coalition in 1991.

After another electoral setback in 1994 (26 seats), the Liberals reverted to opposition status, with Bengt WESTERBERG standing down as party chair. He was succeeded by Lars LEIJONBORG. In June 1996 the FpL announced its relaunch as a "bourgeois left" party emphasizing the fight against unemployment and ethnic separation. The party fell to 17 seats in the September 1998 general election but made dramatic gains in the 2002 election, winning 48 seats in the *Riksdag.*

The FpL secured 28 of the Alliance for Sweden's 178 seats in the 2006 *Riksdag* poll. Leijonborg subsequently stepped down as party chair; he was succeeded by Jan Björkland, who was also named education minister in the subsequent four-party Alliance government. Under Björkland's leadership, the FpL moved toward what was described as conservative liberalism, taking tougher positions on crime, school, and discipline and strengthening its antidrugs stance. The party secured 24 of the Alliance's 173 seats in the 2010 *Riksdag* balloting and 19 of the Alliance's 141 seats on a vote share of 5.4 percent in the 2014 poll. The FpL subsequently indicated it had no interest in joining the new government led by the Social Democrats.

In November 2015 the party changed its name to the **Liberals** (*Liberalerna*).

Leaders: Jan BJÖRKLUND (Chair), Erik ULLENHAG (Parliamentary Leader), Maria ARNHOLM (Secretary General).

Center Party (*Centerpartiet*). Farmers' representatives first began breaking away from other parties to promote rural rights in 1910, and in 1922 they formally launched the **Agrarian Party** (the precursor to the Center Party). In return for agricultural subsidies, the party began to support the Social Democrats in the 1930s, occasionally serving as a junior partner in coalition with the Social Democrats. Since adopting its present name in 1958, the Center Party, campaigning for decentralization of government and industry and for reduced impact of government on the lives of individuals, has developed nationwide strength, including support from the larger urban centers. Opposition to nuclear power became another major party stance in the 1970s.

A major advance to 86 seats in the 1976 election enabled the Center Party to head a center-right coalition until 1978 under Thorbjörn Fälldin, who returned to the premiership in 1979 despite his party's 22-seat decline in that year's election. In opposition after a further slump to 56 seats in 1982, the Center Party continued to lose ground in 1985 (43 seats).

At a congress in June 1986, Karin SÖDER was elected as party leader to succeed Fälldin, who had resigned from the post six months earlier because of his party's poor showing in the 1985 election. However, Söder (Sweden's first female party leader) was forced to step down in March 1987 for health reasons. The party's fortunes continued to decline in 1988 (42 seats) and 1991 (31 seats). In the September 1994 election, the Center Party was reduced to 27 seats (on a vote share of 7.7 percent) and again went into opposition.

Party chair Olof JOHANSSON resigned in April 1998, and he was succeeded in June by Lennart DALÉUS, a staunch opponent of nuclear power who had led the party's successful 1980 referendum on decommissioning nuclear plants. Daléus promptly announced that the party would no longer cooperate with the Social Democrats and also voiced reservations about the Moderates. He hoped to be part of a centrist government following the September 1998 general election, but the Center Party fell to 18 seats. Daléus was replaced as party leader by Maud Olofsson in 2001.

The Center Party won 22 seats in the 2002 general election, and it secured 29 of the Alliance for Sweden's 178 seats in the 2006 *Riksdag* poll. With pressure mounting from coalition partners, Olofsson, serving as deputy prime minister and minister of enterprise and energy, convinced the Center Party in February 2009 to reverse its long-standing position against nuclear power.

The Center Party declined to 23 seats in the 2010 *Riksdag* balloting. Annie Lööf, 28, was elected party chair on September 23, 2011, and six days later she was named minister for enterprise, saying she wanted the party to focus on green issues and the underprivileged. After securing 22 seats (on a vote share of 6.1 percent) in the September 2014 *Riksdag* poll, the Center Party rebuffed overtures to join the new government led by the Social Democrats.

Leaders: Annie LÖÖF (Chair), Maud OLOFSSON, Anders W. JONSSON (Parliamentary Leader), Michael ARTHURSSON (Secretary General).

Christian Democrats (*Kristdemokraterna*—Kd). Also referenced as the **Christian Democratic Party**, this group was formed in 1964 as the **Christian Democratic Coalition** (*Kristen Demokratisk Samling*—KDS) to promote Christian values in politics. The group claimed a membership of more than 25,000 but for two decades was unable to gain *Riksdag* representation, although it secured a growing number of local and state seats. In September 1984 it entered into an electoral pact with the Center Party, thereby securing its first legislative seat in 1985 despite a marginal 2.6 percent vote share.

The KDS adopted the name **Christian Democratic Community Party** (*Kristdemokratiska Samhällspartiet*—KdS) in 1987. Excluded completely from representation in 1988, the KdS won 26 legislative seats in 1991 and joined a center-right coalition. Reduced to 15 seats in the 1994 balloting, the KdS went into opposition. In 1996 the party adopted the rubric of the Christian Democratic Party, widely referenced simply as the Christian Democrats (Kd). Opposing adoption of the euro and stressing "cleaner politics," the Christian Democrats ran the most successful campaign in the party's history for the general election of September 1998, winning 42 seats (a gain of 27).

Göran Hägglund was elected party leader on April 3, 2004, succeeding Alf SVENSSON, who had been Sweden's longest-serving party leader with 31 years in the post. In the 2006 legislative election Christian Democrats secured 24 of the Alliance for Sweden's 178 seats. Distancing his party from the growing popularity of the right-wing Sweden Democrats, Hägglund in 2008 accused the Sweden Democrats of being xenophobic and spreading Nazi ideology.

In April 2009 the Christian Democrats, reflecting their rural base, were the only party in parliament to dissent on a bill that legalized same-sex marriage. The Christian Democrats won 19 seats in the

2010 *Riksdag* poll and 16 seats (on a vote share of 5.6 percent) in the 2014 election.

Ebba BUSCH THOR was elected party chair in April 2015.

Leaders: Ebba BUSCH THOR (Chair), Jakob FORSSMED (Vice Chair), Acko Ankarberg JOHANSSON (Secretary General).

Left Party (*Vänsterpartiet*). Originally formed in 1917 as the **Left Social Democratic Party** (*Vänster Socialdemokratiska Partiet*—VSdP), the party was renamed the **Communist Party** (*Kommunistiska Partiet*—KP) in 1921 and the **Left Party–Communists** (*Vänsterpartiet-Kommunisterna*—VpK) in 1967. In May 1990 the party adopted its present name.

Long before the decline of communism in Eastern Europe, the party pursued a "revisionist," or "Eurocommunist," policy based on distinctive Swedish conditions. This posture provoked considerable dissent within the party before the withdrawal of a pro-Moscow faction in early 1977. Following the 1982 election, the party agreed to support a new government of the Social Democrats, and the Vpk's voting strength became crucial following the declining fortunes of the Social Democrats in 1985 and 1988. Having won 16 seats in the 1991 general election, the Left Party went into full opposition to the new center-right coalition government. In the 1994 balloting the party achieved its best result since 1948, winning 22 seats.

Having unsuccessfully opposed Sweden's accession to the EU, the Left Party nearly doubled its parliamentary representation in the September 1998 elections, winning 43 seats, its best showing since its formation. The party's legislative support subsequently remained crucial in the continuation of the minority government of the Social Democrats.

Gudrun Schyman was leader of the Left Party between 1993 and 2003, promoting feminism as well as socialism. Lars OHLY replaced Schyman in a party election on February 20, 2004. Ohly's election highlighted a division between modernist and traditional wings of the party, with Ohly, a former railroad worker, representing the traditionalist wing. The party faced a possible split in January 2005, largely caused by Ohly's insistence (subsequently retracted) on calling himself a communist. Meanwhile, Schyman helped to form the new Feminist Initiative (below).

After the Left Party's representation fell to 22 seats in the 2006 general election, efforts to modernize the party and address its communist past failed following an unsuccessful challenge to Ohly's leadership in June 2008 by Staffan NORBERG. In December the Left Party entered into the Red-Green coalition with the Social Democrats and the Greens (see Social Democrats, above, for details).

In the wake of the global economic recession, the Left Party in 2009 advocated an increase in state ownership and control of Swedish banks, including the proposed launch of a new state-owned investment bank.

Prior to the 2010 *Riksdag* balloting, the Left Party announced it would formally join a cabinet for the first time if the Red-Green coalition won a legislative majority. However, the Red-Greens fell short in that quest, securing 156 of 349 seats (19 seats for the Left Party).

Ohly resigned as party chair in January 2012, and he was succeeded by Jonas Sjöstedt, a member of the *Riksdag* and former labor union leader.

In response to the riots near Stockholm in May 2013, Left Party leaders accused the government of having contributed to an erosion of social services, which had left the immigrant population segregated, "stigmatized," and bereft of opportunities for future advancement.

In the run-up to the September 2014 *Rickdag* balloting, the Left Party strongly criticized the center-right government's policy of encouraging private equity firms to participate in operating public schools and hospitals for profit. The Left Party secured 21 legislative seats (on a vote share of 5.7 percent), but it was not invited by the Social Democrats to join the new government (see Current issues, below). Although Sjöstedt called that decision "a big mistake," the Left Party was still considered likely to provide key legislative support as needed to the minority government installed in October.

Leaders: Jonas SJÖSTEDT (Chair), Hans LINDE (Parliamentary Leader), Aron ETZLER (Secretary).

Sweden Democrats (*Sverigedemokraterna*—Sd). A far-right, nationalist party that was established in 1988, the Sweden Democrats (considered by some to have links to neo-Nazi ideology) won 2.9 percent of the vote in the 2006 *Rikstag* election. The party platform included encouraging higher birthrates, stopping the development of a "multicultural society," promoting a robust national defense, and advocating harsher prison sentences. At the annual congress in May 2008, the Sweden Democrats called for an end to the special status rights of Sámi herders. However, the Sweden Democrats gained the most attention for the party's extreme anti-immigration stance, which called for a reduction in legal immigration by 90 percent. The party's harshest rhetoric was aimed at Muslims, party leader Jimmie Åkesson describing the growth of the Muslim population as Sweden's "biggest foreign threat since World War II."

In the 2010 *Riksdag* poll, the party entered the legislature for the first time with 20 seats (more than the Christian Democrats or the Left Party) on a vote share of 5.7 percent, sending a shockwave through the nation's political landscape. Although some analysts predicted that the Sweden Democrats might play a kingmaker's role in the formation of the next government, all of the other legislative parties denounced the platform of the Sweden Democrats and announced they would not work with that party.

In 2011 it was reported that the Sweden Democrats had adopted a more progressive stance on gay rights and had dropped its opposition to foreign adoptions and its support for the death penalty.

In mid-2013 the Sweden Democrats blamed the recent rioting in Stockholm's suburbs (see Current issues, above) on the government's "irresponsible" liberal immigration policies. The Sweden Democrats won their first-ever seats (two) in the May 2014 balloting for the European Parliament and, apparently drawing support from the Moderates in regard to immigration, zoomed to a third-place finish (49 seats on a vote share of 12.9 percent) in the September 2014 *Riksdag* poll. Although all the other legislative parties refused to consider inviting the Sweden Democrats to join a new government, Åkesson said the traditional parties "will have to deal with us sometime." The Sweden Democrats subsequently voted against the minority government installed in October and threatened to align with the Alliance of Swedes in the crucial upcoming budget deliberations.

In January 2015 Richard JOMSHOF was elected party secretary.

Leaders: Jimmie ÅKESSON (Leader), Mattias KARLSSON (Parliamentary Leader), Richard JOMSHOF (Secretary General).

Other Parties That Contested the 2014 Legislative Elections:

Feminist Initiative (*Feministiskt Initiativ*—FI). The FI was established in 2005, by, among others, former Left Party leader Gudrun Schyman, Ebba WITT-BRATTSTRÖM, and Stina SUNDBERG. (Witt-Brattström later became a vocal critic of the party, saying it was too far to the left and thus excluded some women.) The FI, which won approximately 0.7 percent of the vote in the 2006 election, aimed to achieve economic and social justice for women and eliminate societal complacency regarding violence against women. The FI subsequently decided to function as a feminist organization rather than a political party in order to accept state grant money for gender equality projects. (Swedish law prohibits political parties from receiving state grants.) However, in early 2008 the FI announced that it would reestablish itself as a political party to field candidates in upcoming local and general elections. The party won 2 percent of the vote in the June 2009 European Parliamentary election on a campaign that called for abortion to be a human right. Although the party won only 0.4 percent of the vote in the 2010 *Riksdag* election, it improved dramatically to 5.3 percent (good for one seat) in the May 2014 balloting for the European Parliament. The FI secured 3.1 percent of the vote in the 2014 *Riksdag* poll (making it the largest nonparliamentary party) and also earned a number of seats in the concurrent local elections.

Leaders: Gundrun SCHYMAN (Chair); Stina SVENSSON, Sissela Nordling BLANCO, Carl EMANUELSSON (Spokespersons).

Pirate Party (*Piratpartiet*—Pp). The Pp was founded by Rickard FALKVINGE in early 2006 to advocate for an open-information society in relation to the popular Internet-based file-sharing site Pirate Bay, which had recently been shut down by the government on charges of copyright infringement because it offered free downloads of films and music. Despite a rapidly growing membership, the Pp gained only 0.6 percent of the vote in the 2006 *Riksdag* election. The party's program mainly focused on fundamental reforms of copyright and patent laws and ensuring that citizens' rights to privacy were respected. Hence, it was a vocal opponent of the country's new far-reaching surveillance law, which permitted the government to identify people downloading material from the Internet.

The party won 7 percent of the vote and one of Sweden's 18 seats in the European Parliamentary election in June 2009, its support coming largely from males under age 30.

The Pirates secured only 0.6 percent of the vote in the 2010 *Riksdag* balloting. Meanwhile, the party announced plans to launch an Internet service provider that would not store the Internet addresses of its users and would thereby thwart government efforts to gain access to that information.

In January 2011 party founder Falkvinge announced that he was stepping down as leader to focus on promoting the party internationally. Party deputy Anna Troberg took over at the helm. The Pirates secured 0.4 percent of the *Riksdag* vote in 2014. Magnus ANDERSSON was elected party leader in 2015.

Leader: Magnus ANDERSSON (Chair).

Swedish Pensioners' Interest Party (*Sveriges Pensionärers Intresseparti*—SPI). Founded in 1987, the SPI seeks to secure higher social and financial status for retired people. Although it has never had a significant electoral impact nationally, the party remains active at the regional level.

Leaders: Pelle HÖGLUND, Leif EKSTRÖM.

Some 24 other small parties participated in the 2010 *Riksdag* election, none securing more than 0.1 percent of the vote.

LEGISLATURE

The unicameral ***Riksdag*** consists of 349 members serving four-year terms. (Prior to the 1994 election, the term length was three years.) Of the total, 310 are elected by proportional representation in a closed party-list system in 29 constituencies (2–34 seats each, depending on population). To gain representation a party must secure at least 4 percent of the nationwide vote or 12 percent of the vote within a constituency. The remaining 39 members are selected from a national pool designed to give absolute proportionality (based on the national vote) to all parties receiving at least 4 percent of the nationwide vote.

Following the most recent election on September 14, 2014, the seat distribution was as follows: Social Democrats, 113; Moderate Party, 84; Sweden Democrats, 49; Green Party, 25; Center Party, 22; Left Party, 21; Liberal People's Party, 19; and Christian Democrats, 16.

Speaker: Urban AHLIN.

CABINET

[as of October 3, 2014]

Prime Minister	Stefan Löfven (SD)
Deputy Prime Minister	Isabella Lövin (MjG) [f]
Ministers	
Children, the Elderly, and Gender Equality	Åsa Regnér (SD) [f]
Climate and the Environment	Karolina Skog (MjG) [f]
Culture and Democracy	Alice Bah Kuhnke (MjG) [f]
Defense	Peter Hultqvist (SD)
Education	Gustav Fridolin (MjG)
Employment	Ylva Johansson (SD) [f]
Energy	Ibrahim Baylan (SD)
Enterprise and Innovation	Mikael Damberg (SD)
Finance	Magdalena Andersson (SD) [f]
Financial Markets and Consumer Affairs	Per Bolund (MjG)
Foreign Affairs	Margot Wallström (SD) [f]
Higher Education and Research	Helene Hellmark Knutsson (SD) [f]
Home Affairs	Anders Ygeman (SD)
Housing and Urban Development	Peter Eriksson (MjP)
Infrastructure	Anna Johansson (SD) [f]
International Development Cooperation	Isabella Lövin (MjG) [f]
Justice and Migration	Morgan Johansson (SD)
Public Administration	Ardalan Shekarabi (SD)
Public Health, Health Care, and Sports	Gabriel Wikström (SD)
Rural Affairs	Sven-Erik Bucht (SD)
Social Security	Annika Strandhäll (SD) [f]
Strategy, Future Issues, and Nordic Cooperation	Kristina Persson (SD) [f]
Upper Secondary School and Adult Education and Training	Anna Ekström (SD) [f]

[f] = female

INTERGOVERNMENTAL REPRESENTATION

Ambassador to the U.S.: Björn Olof LYRVALL.

U.S. Ambassador to Sweden: David E. LINDWALL (Chargé d'Affaires).

Permanent Representative to the UN: Olof SKOOG.

IGO Memberships (Non-UN): ADB, AfDB, CEUR, EBRD, EIB, EU, IADB, IEA, ICC, IOM, OECD, OSCE, WTO.

For Further Reference:

Olsen, Gregg. *The Politics of the Welfare State: Canada, Sweden, and the United States.* Oxford: Oxford University Press, 2002.

Sejersted, Francis. *The Age of Social Democracy: Norway and Sweden in the Twentieth Century.* Princeton, NJ: Princeton University Press, 2011.

Steinmo, Sven. *The Evolution of Modern States: Sweden, Japan, and the United States.* Cambridge: Cambridge University Press, 2010.

SWITZERLAND

Swiss Confederation
Schweizerische Eidgenossenschaft (German)
Confédération Suisse (French)
Confederazione Svizzera (Italian)
Confederaziun Svizra (Romansch)

Note: In the annual election on December 7, 2016, Vice President Doris Leuthard (Christian Democratic People's Party) was elected president of the confederation with 188 of 207 votes. She previously served as president in 2010, and was scheduled to be inaugurated for her new term on January 1, 2017. The next balloting is scheduled for December 7, 2017.

Political Status: Neutral confederation since 1291; equivalent of federal system embodied in constitution of May 29, 1874; current constitution, revising and reforming that of 1874, adopted April 18, 1999, effective January 1, 2000.

Area: 15,943 sq. mi. (41,293 sq. km).

Population: 8,380,000 (2016E—UN); 8,179,294 (2016E—U.S. Census); 8,327,100 (2015E—Government). (After having conducted a standard full census every ten years since 1850, Switzerland in 2010 adopted a new system under which a census is completed each year using advanced methods of data collection and evaluation that rely on cantonal and communal population registers as well as a survey of approximately 5 percent of the population annually.)

Major Urban Centers (metropolitan area, 2015E—UN): BERN (358,000), Zürich (1,246,000), Geneva (558,000), Basel (508,000), Lausanne (353,000).

Official Languages: German, French, Italian. Romansch is recognized as a national language but without full official status.

Monetary Unit: Swiss Franc (market rate October 1, 2016: 0.97 franc = $1 US).

President of the Confederation and Chair of the Federal Council: Johann SCHNEIDER-AMMANN (FDP.The Liberals); elected on

December 9, 2015, and inaugurated on January 1, 2016, for a one-year term to succeed Simonetta SOMMARUGA (Social Democratic Party).

Vice President of the Confederation: Doris LEUTHARD (Christian Democratic People's Party); elected on December 9, 2015, and inaugurated on January 1, 2016, for a one-year term to succeed Johann SCHNEIDER-AMMANN (FDP.The Liberals).

THE COUNTRY

Situated in the mountainous heart of Western Europe, Switzerland has traditionally set an example of peaceful coexistence among different indigenous ethnic and cultural groups, although a post–World War II increase in the country's nonnative population has been somewhat less than harmonious. The well-educated, politically sophisticated Swiss generally speak one of four languages: German (63.7 percent), French (20.4 percent), Italian (6.5 percent), and Romansch (0.5 percent). Roman Catholics account for 42 percent of the population, Protestants 33 percent, and Muslims 4 percent, while 11 percent claim no religious affiliation. The influx of foreign workers has ebbed in recent years, although they constitute 25 percent of the population, one of the highest rates in Europe. Women made up 45.6 percent of the employed labor force in 2016.

Switzerland is one of the world's richer countries, registering GDP per capita of more than $75,000 in 2015. The country's durable goods output is largely based on the production of precision-engineered items, pharmaceuticals, and special quality products that are not readily mass produced. The industrial sector as a whole contributes 28 percent of GDP, compared to only 1 percent for agriculture. (Raising livestock is the principal agricultural activity; the chief crops are wheat and potatoes.) Tourism and insurance are other major contributors to the economy, as is international banking, which has been under intense scrutiny for decades because of Switzerland's long-standing tradition of bank secrecy and consequential status as one of the world's biggest offshore tax havens. The country relies heavily on external transactions; foreign exchange earned from exports of goods and services, mostly to the European Union (EU), constitutes more than a third of the total national income.

GDP contracted by 1.9 percent in 2009 as the result of the global recession, but modest growth returned in 2010. In August 2011 the central bank cut interest rates in an effort to weaken the Swiss franc, after declaring that the currency was "massively overvalued" against the dollar and the euro. A month later the Swiss National Bank announced that the Swiss franc would not be permitted to appreciate any further than 1.2 Swiss francs = 1 euro, the eurozone debt crisis having continued to encourage investor flight into the perceived safety of the franc. The Swiss economy has performed better than most of the other European countries recently (2 percent growth in 2013, in conjunction with unemployment of 3.2 percent and negligible inflation), and harsh austerity measures have been avoided. However, the banking sector has continued to receive intense international attention (see Current issues, below). In 2014 GDP grew by 2 percent, while inflation was –0.01 percent. For 2015 GDP growth declined slightly, to 0.8 percent, but was estimated to be 1.2 percent for 2016, while inflation that year was –0.4 percent and unemployment, 3.6 percent.

GOVERNMENT AND POLITICS

Political background. The origins of the Swiss Confederation date back to 1291, when the cantons of Uri, Schwyz, and Unterwalden signed an "eternal alliance" against the Hapsburgs. The league continued to expand until 1648, when it became formally independent of the Holy Roman Empire at the Peace of Westphalia. Following French conquest and reorganization during the Napoleonic era, Switzerland's boundaries were fixed by the Congress of Vienna in 1815, when Switzerland's perpetual neutrality was guaranteed by the principal European powers. The constitution adopted in 1874, superseding one from 1848, increased the powers conferred on the central government by the cantons.

For nearly five decades beginning in 1959, Switzerland was governed at the national level by a four-party coalition of the Social Democratic Party of Switzerland (*Sozialdemokratische Partei der Schweiz*—SPS), the Christian Democratic People's Party (*Christlich Demokratische Volkspartei*—CVP), the Radical Democratic Party of Switzerland (*Freisinnig-Demokratische Partei der Schweiz*—FDP),

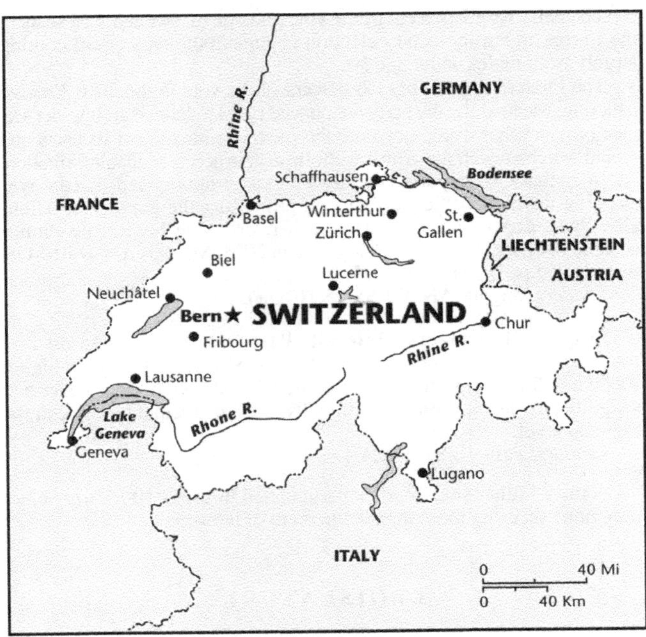

and the Swiss People's Party (*Schweizerische Volkspartei*—SVP). Until 2004 each party participated in the confederal executive body (the Federal Council), according to what was dubbed the "Magic Formula" (*Zauberformei*): two seats apiece for the SPS, the CVP, and the FDP, and one for the right-wing SVP.

However diverse the philosophical makeup of the Federal Council, it remained until 1984 a male bastion, with no female members. (Women had won the right to vote in federal elections in 1971, but it took a 1990 ruling by the Federal Supreme Court to end male-only voting in the half-canton of Appenzell-Innerrhoden, the last European jurisdiction to extend suffrage to women.) In October 1984, following a heated national debate, the bicameral Federal Assembly approved the FDP's nomination of Elisabeth KOPP, mayor of the Zürich suburb of Zumikon, as the first female member of the Federal Council. In so doing, the assembly appeared to have ensured that the position of nominal head of state would eventually fall to Kopp (due to the system of presidential rotation). However, she resigned her council post in December 1988 when critics argued that she had improperly advised her husband about a government investigation into a financial company of which he was a board member.

In August 1991 Switzerland observed the 700th anniversary of the signing of its initial federal charter—the oldest such document known to exist—with minimal fanfare. In the October federal election the FDP, which had overtaken the SPS as the plurality party in 1983, again finished first but by a reduced margin of only three seats over the second-place SPS.

In May 1992 the government announced that it would apply for membership in the European Community (EC, subsequently the EU). Earlier that month Bern had signed a treaty providing for the creation of the European Economic Area (EEA) between the EC and the looser European Free Trade Association (EFTA), of which Switzerland was a founding member. The EEA treaty generated considerable public debate, culminating in a December 1992 referendum in Switzerland in which 50.3 percent of those voting (and 16 of 23 cantons) rejected ratification, despite having been urged to vote in favor by three of the four government parties, the centrist opposition parties, employers, trade unions, and the powerful banking sector. Opposing the measure were the most conservative government party (the SVP) and an uneasy coalition of ecologists and rightists. The voter turnout of 78.3 percent was the highest for any referendum since 1947; analysis showed that German and Italian speakers were decisively against the EEA, whereas the French-speaking Swiss voted overwhelmingly in favor.

In 1994 the government came under strong pressure to adopt tougher policies on immigration and crime. Swiss voters had already endorsed referendum proposals restricting immigration and making political asylum more difficult to obtain. In March the National Council voted to give the police increased powers to search and detain foreigners who lacked appropriate identification. The following month the government was embarrassed by an Amnesty International report asserting that some Swiss police officers were using unwarranted force against persons in custody, especially foreigners. As a result, government legislation that criminalized racial discrimination and racist propaganda was approved by referendum in September. More indicative of the popular mood, however, was a December referendum in which 73 percent of those voting endorsed tougher action against drug dealers and illegal immigrants.

The issue of proposed accession to the EU dominated the October 1995 federal lower house election, but the result was far from conclusive. The pro-EU Social Democrats achieved their best result ever (54 seats), mainly in the urban areas of Zürich, Basel, and Geneva. However, rural voters favored the strongly anti-EU SVP, which won 29 seats. The question of EU accession was subsequently deferred as both parties wished to preserve the ruling four-party coalition.

On January 1, 1999, Ruth DREIFUSS of the SPS became the first woman to hold the presidency of the confederation, while the most notable development at the national election in October was the rise of the SVP, which finished neck and neck with the SPS in total votes and moved into second place with 44 seats in the National Council.

In the National Council election of October 19, 2003, the SVP surpassed the SPS as the plurality party, winning 55 seats to 52 for the SPS, 36 for the FDP, and 28 for the CVP. As a consequence, the SVP, having threatened to go into opposition, successfully argued for a second seat on the Federal Council, with the CVP dropping to one, effective January 1, 2004. At that time the SVP's charismatic leader, Christoph BLOCHER, joined the Federal Council as councilor for justice and police.

Reflecting a rise in nationalistic, conservative sentiment, the SVP made further gains at the National Council poll on October 21, 2007, winning 29 percent of the vote and 62 seats, 19 more than the SPS. Nevertheless, the SPS, the CVP, and The Greens (*Die Grunë*) marshaled sufficient votes to replace the controversial Blocher on the Federal Council with the more moderate SVP parliamentarian Eveline WIDMER-SCHLUMPF. The SVP thereupon overturned Switzerland's four-party coalition formula, declaring that it would act as an opposition party. Consequently, in mid-2008 the SVP expelled Widmer-Schlumpf for accepting appointment to the Federal Council without the party's support. Widmer-Schlumpf and another expelled SVP member, the centrist Samuel SCHMID, subsequently formed the Conservative Democratic Party (*Bürgerlich-Demokratische Partei*—BDP). However, the SVP rejoined the government in January 2009 when party member Ueli MAURER was installed in the Federal Council as successor to Schmid, who, under pressure, had announced his resignation as defense councilor in November.

The SVP remained the largest party in the balloting for the National Council on October 23, 2011, although its vote total and representation declined. The five-party SVP-SPS-CVP-FDP-BDP coalition subsequently remained intact, as it did after the October 18, 2015, balloting when the SVP placed first with 65 seats. The SVP's historic legislative victory allowed it to gain a second seat on the Federal Council, displacing the BDP, which nevertheless, remained part of the governing coalition. There was a minor cabinet reshuffle following the election.

Constitution and government. The 1874 constitution was revised by referendum on April 18, 1999, and a new constitution was put into legal force on January 1, 2000. The changes were primarily aimed at modernizing and updating the 1874 charter, which had been altered 140 times since it was written. The new constitution was approved by 59 percent of the vote; however, only 35 percent of eligible voters participated in the referendum. In addition to modernizing the document's language, the new constitution included provisions pertaining to labor rights and equal opportunity for people with disabilities.

Switzerland is (despite the retention of "confederation" in its official name in the 2000 constitution) a federal republic of 23 cantons, 3 of which are subdivided into half-cantons. The cantons retain autonomy over a range of local concerns but lack the right to nullify national legislation. Responsibility for the latter is vested in a bicameral parliament, the Federal Assembly, both houses of which (the Council of States and the National Council) have equal authority. Legislation passed by the two chambers may not be vetoed by the executive nor reviewed by the judiciary. In addition to normal legislative processes, the Swiss constitution provides for the use of initiatives to amend the constitution and referendums to ratify or reject federal legislation. To go forward, the two require petitions bearing 100,000 and 50,000 signatures, respectively.

Executive authority is exercised on a collegial basis by the Federal Council, whose seven members are elected by the entire Federal Assembly. Each December the assembly elects two of the seven to serve for the following year as president of the confederation (in effect head of state) and vice president of the Federal Council (equivalent to deputy head of state). The president has limited prerogatives and serves as a first among equals. Although the Federal Council is responsible to the legislature, the council has increasingly become a nonpolitical body of experts from the leading political parties. Its members are usually reelected as long as they are willing to serve. A federal chancellor, elected by the Federal Assembly for a four-year term, heads the administrative arm of the Federal Council.

The Swiss judicial system functions primarily at the cantonal level; the only regular federal court is the Federal Supreme Court, which has the authority to review cantonal court decisions involving federal law. (Sublevels of the Supreme Court include a Federal Administrative Court, a Federal Patent Court, and a Federal Criminal Court.) Each canton has civil and criminal courts, a Court of Appeal, and a Court of Cassation.

Local government exists on two basic levels: the cantons and the approximately 3,000 communes (municipalities). In some of the larger cantons the communes are grouped into districts, which are headed by commissioners. There are two basic governing organs at the cantonal and communal levels—a unicameral legislature and, much like the federal system, a collegial executive. In five cantons and half-cantons (as well as in numerous smaller units) the entire voting population functions as the legislature, while in the others the legislature is elected. As at the federal level, initiatives and referendums may be used to propose, amend, or annul legislation within a canton.

After 30 years of separatist strife in the largely French-speaking, Roman Catholic region of Jura, Swiss voters approved cantonal status for most of the area in 1978. The creation of the 23rd canton, the first to be formed since 1815, was approved by over 82 percent of those voting in the national referendum. Jura's full membership in the confederation took effect on January 1, 1979. Southern Jura, predominantly Protestant and German-speaking, remained part of the Bern canton. The small German-speaking district of Laufental, having been cut off geographically from Bern by the creation of the Jura canton, voted on September 26, 1993, to be transferred from the Bern canton to the half-canton of Basel-Land.

In a constitutional referendum in March 1996, 76.1 percent of voters supported official recognition of Romansch, the 2,000-year-old language used, in five dialects, by approximately 50,000 inhabitants of the eastern canton of Graübunden (or Grisons). The measure enhanced the "national" status accorded by a 1938 referendum, obliging federal authorities to provide services to Romansch speakers in their own language. However, it did not grant Romansch the same "official" status given to German, French, and Italian; the law requires that all federal documents be issued in the three fully official languages.

The Swiss press is privately owned and free from governmental influence, although editors are accustomed to using discretion in handling national security information. In 2016 Reporters Without Borders rated Switzerland as seventh in the world out of 180 countries in freedom of the press.

Canton and Capital	*Area (sq. mi.)*	*Population (2014E)*
Aargau/Argovie (Aarau)	542	645,300
Appenzell		
Ausserrhoden (Herisau)	94	54,100
Innerrhoden (Appenzell)	66	15,900
Basel/Bâle		
Basel-Land (Liestal)	165	281,300
Basel-Stadt (Basel)	14	196,600
Bern/Berne (Bern)	2,336	1,009,400
Fribourg (Fribourg)	645	303,400
Genève/Geneva (Genève)	109	477,400
Glarus (Glarus)	264	39,800
Graübunden/Grisons (Chur)	2,744	195,900
Jura (Delémont)	323	72,400
Luzern/Lucerne (Luzern)	576	394,600
Neuchâtel (Neuchâtel)	308	177,300

St. Gallen/St. Gall (St. Gallen)	778	495,800
Schaffhausen/Schaffhouse (Schaffhausen)	115	79,400
Schwyz (Schwyz)	351	152,800
Solothurn/Soleure (Solothurn)	305	263,700
Thurgau/Thurgovie (Frauenfeld)	391	263,700
Ticino/Tessin (Bellinzona)	1,085	350,400
Unterwalden		
Nidwalden (Stans)	106	42,100
Obwalden (Sarnen)	189	36,800
Uri (Altdorf)	416	36,000
Valais (Sion)	2,018	331,800
Vaud (Lausanne)	1,243	761,400
Zug/Zoug (Zug)	92	120,100
Zürich (Zürich)	667	1,446,400

Foreign relations. Swiss foreign policy has historically stressed neutrality and scrupulous avoidance of membership in military alliances. In the interest of maintaining that neutrality, Switzerland chose to remain outside the United Nations through the Cold War era, although it was accredited as a permanent observer to the organization. It also adhered to the statute of the International Court of Justice and belonged to many UN specialized agencies. In addition, foreign policy subsequently remained influenced by the principle of "solidarity," which holds that a neutral state is morally obligated to undertake social, economic, and humanitarian activities contributing to world peace and prosperity. Partly for this reason, Switzerland subsequently agreed to convert assorted debts owed by various developing nations into grants.

In 1984 both the National Council and the Council of States approved a government proposal that the country apply for UN membership; however, voters overwhelmingly rejected such action in a referendum in 1986. In contrast, in 1992 the electorate readily approved joining the IMF and World Bank.

In the aftermath of the December 1992 referendum that rejected participation in the EEA (see Political background, above), Swiss policy concentrated on limiting the negative effects of remaining outside that economic area. The government's strategy received a boost in May 1995 when Liechtenstein acceded to the EEA while retaining its 70-year-old economic and monetary union with Switzerland. As a result, Swiss exporters with outlets in Liechtenstein could benefit from the tariff concessions available under the EEA. The Swiss federal government also continued its legislative program to bring Swiss law into line with EEA/EU practice, although it was hindered by voters' rejection of attempts to ease existing restrictions on foreign ownership of property in Switzerland in a June 1995 referendum.

There were signs in 1995–1996 of a softening in Switzerland's stance of armed neutrality. In June 1996 Flavio COTTI became the first Swiss foreign minister to address a meeting of the North Atlantic Treaty Organization (NATO); the Swiss government appointed a military attaché to an observer role in NATO soon thereafter. Despite opposition from conservative parties, in October the government announced plans to enter the NATO Partnership for Peace (PfP) program, while stressing that it had no intention of joining NATO itself. The government also pledged that it would abide by the June 1994 referendum decision precluding any armed participation in PfP peacekeeping exercises, although since December 1995 Switzerland had permitted NATO to fly over its territory and use its railways to supply peacekeeping operations in Bosnia.

The international image of Switzerland as a bastion of banking probity and humanitarian values was damaged, particularly in the United States and Israel, when new developments began to emerge in 1995 in the 50-year-old dispute over the assets of World War II Holocaust victims. The controversy centered on allegations that Swiss banks had knowingly accepted gold that had either been looted from the central banks of occupied countries or plundered from victims of the Holocaust by German Nazis. (U.S. officials argued that Germany had relied heavily on the sale of the gold to prolong its war effort.) Holocaust survivors and their heirs demanded a new investigation into the thousands of long-dormant Swiss bank accounts that they suspected contained assets of Nazi victims.

The Swiss commercial banks initially assumed an extremely conservative position on the inquiries, concentrating solely on dormant accounts for which complete documentation was available. By late 1997 they had identified some 16,000 such accounts, valued at about $54 million. It was agreed that the unclaimed money would be released through an independent panel; the banks also contributed to a government-sponsored voluntary fund of some $200 million that had been established to assist needy elderly survivors of the Holocaust. However, those measures failed to address the central question of looted gold, and pressure intensified on behalf of the plaintiffs in class-action suits against the banks.

In early 1998 an independent Swiss commission reported that some $450 million in Nazi gold had been received in Switzerland during the war, about 80 percent having been handled by the Swiss Central Bank and the remainder by private banks. (It was estimated that the gold was valued at about $4 billion in 1998, without interest.) Another commission concluded shortly thereafter that officials of the Central Bank had been aware that some of the gold had come from the Central Banks of countries overrun by the Germans. Jewish organizations demanded a settlement, without which a number of U.S. states threatened to discontinue their substantial dealings with Swiss financial institutions.

In April 1998 the three major Swiss commercial banks reversed themselves and announced they would pursue a "global settlement" of the claims, and a figure of $1.25 billion was reached in August. Most of the money was to be used to compensate victims (or their families) of the Holocaust for whom specific claims could not be documented—the so-called "rough justice" approach. The Swiss Central Bank notably refused to participate in the settlement, as the government argued that none of its actions as a neutral state during the war had been improper. That position partly reflected the sentiment of a growing segment of the population, which lashed out against the intense international scrutiny. (In November 1998 a government commission reported that the Holocaust debate had drawn attention to a degree of "latent Swiss anti-Semitism," creating "a political crisis concerning Switzerland's self-image.")

After four years of negotiations, Switzerland completed a trade agreement with the EU in 1998, and a national referendum endorsed the measure in May 2000. Swiss banks subsequently faced intensified international scrutiny on several fronts beyond that of Nazi gold: for their role in providing services for apartheid South Africa during the international embargo; for their reluctance to disclose and freeze the money held by former Zairian president Mobutu Sese Seko; for their alleged involvement in money laundering by organized crime syndicates in Russia; and for "serious shortcomings" (according to a September 2000 report by the Federal Banking Commission) in accepting an estimated $500 million in deposits from Nigerian dictator Sani Abacha and his family. Meanwhile, in February 2001 the government identified the names on 21,000 accounts considered likely to have been owned by Holocaust victims between 1933 and 1945. Some 100,000 claims were expected to be filed for the dormant accounts.

In a referendum held in June 2001, Swiss voters narrowly approved (by 50.9 percent) permitting armed Swiss troops to participate in international peacekeeping missions. The vote also authorized training with NATO forces, although opponents of the proposal argued that Switzerland's traditional neutrality would be jeopardized. The government subsequently maintained its stance in favor of eventual accession to the EU, although in March 2001, 76.7 percent of voters rejected a referendum proposal to immediately apply for membership. However, the Swiss public finally endorsed UN membership in a March 2002 referendum with a yes vote of 54.1 percent, and Switzerland joined the UN in September.

Concerns about the influx of foreigners into Switzerland subsequently took on increasing political significance because many Swiss feared the loss of what they viewed as their unique culture. In November 2002, by the thin margin of 0.2 percent, voters defeated a measure (offered by the SVP) to restrict the country's asylum laws. However, in September 2004 provisions that would have made it easier for foreigners to become Swiss citizens were defeated.

In a referendum held in June 2005, 54.6 percent of voters supported joining the Schengen agreement, which provided for closer security cooperation with the EU and allowed persons from other Schengen countries (most of Europe) to enter Switzerland without passports. It also permitted signatory countries to share information, such as whether an asylum seeker has sought refuge in more than one country. (Switzerland became the 25th country to join the Schengen zone in December 2008.)

In another referendum, held in September 2005, 56 percent of voters approved a government-sponsored proposal to allow citizens of the ten new EU member states to live and work in Switzerland, provided they had jobs and were able to support themselves. Meanwhile, under an accord that had gone into force in July after 15 years of negotiations, Swiss banks agreed to withhold taxes on accounts belonging to depositors from EU and other countries. (In 2006 the new system yielded more than $500 million in tax revenue, three-quarters of which was handed over to EU countries whose residents held Swiss bank accounts.) However, Swiss-EU relations soured somewhat after the EU complained in December 2005 that low corporate tax rates in Switzerland violated the terms of their trade agreement.

U.S. objections to Switzerland's bank policies resurfaced in 2008, when the U.S. Internal Revenue Service sued Swiss banking giant UBS for helping wealthy American account holders evade taxes. In February 2009 UBS admitted to helping U.S. taxpayers hide their accounts, and in August the bank agreed to provide the U.S. government with the names and account information for some 4,450 bank customers. The bank also agreed to pay $780 million in fines and penalties. In January 2010, however, the Swiss Federal Administrative Court ruled that lifting banking secrecy was illegal, necessitating ratification of the 2009 agreement by the Federal Assembly in June. Meanwhile, in September 2009, after completing a dozen bilateral double-taxation agreements to improve transparency and information exchange, Switzerland had been removed from the "grey list" of tax havens published by the Organization for Economic Cooperation and Development (OECD). Relations with the EU and Germany remained strained, however, over Switzerland's retention of generous corporate tax breaks. In October 2013 the Swiss government signed the OECD convention regarding the sharing of tax information.

On May 27, 2015, Switzerland signed an agreement with the EU ending the special secrecy that EU residents had enjoyed from Swiss banks. Beginning in 2018, Switzerland and the EU countries will automatically exchange information on the financial accounts of each other's residents.

Current issues. In January 2013 Wegelin & Company, Switzerland's oldest private bank, pled guilty in a U.S. court to abetting tax evasion on the part of scores of U.S. citizens in 2002–2010. The bank agreed to pay $74 million in fines and restitution and subsequently went out of business. International pressure subsequently continued to mount on other Swiss banks, and in May the Federal Council announced support for a sweeping plan to permit banks to release information on foreign clients to aid in U.S. investigations into possible tax evasion by U.S. nationals. However, the National Council rejected the proposal in June as a broad spectrum of legislators expressed concern that the collapse of secrecy would put Swiss banks at a disadvantage versus other offshore havens not yet subject to greater transparency.

In July 2013 it was announced that UBS had reached a $700 million agreement to settle civil claims from a U.S. regulatory agency related to mortgage-backed securities the bank had packaged and sold during 2004–2007. The U.S. officials had sued USB and a number of other banks in 2011, claiming that they had misrepresented the quality of the mortgages, thereby contributing to the massive financial losses suffered worldwide from the collapse of the "housing bubble." *Credit Suisse* (Switzerland's second largest bank) reached an $885 million settlement regarding similar claims in March 2014. Attention subsequently turned to the criminal case that had been filed against *Credit Suisse* by the U.S. Department of Justice, which charged the bank with having helped more than 20,000 U.S. citizens to avoid their tax obligations over several decades. In a landmark disposition, the bank pled guilty in May to one felony count of conspiracy to aid tax evasion and agreed to pay $2.6 billion in fines and restitution. However, the bank was not required to release the names of the individual clients involved in the illegal activity, while other possible penalties were waived by U.S. officials so as to avoid "collateral damage" among the bank's clients and customers. In other activity in the first half of 2014, Swiss voters narrowly endorsed a proposal to impose strict quotas on immigration from EU countries, despite opposition to the measure from the Swiss government and business sector. The EU strongly objected to the quotas and implied that retaliatory measures could be expected.

In a referendum on February 28, 2016, voters rejected a proposal to deport noncitizens who were convicted of minor crimes, on a vote of 58.9 percent to 41.1 percent. A referendum that called for the establishment of a basic monthly income of $1,650 for all adults, and lesser amounts for children, was also defeated in a vote on June 5 by a margin of 76.9 percent to 23.1 percent.

POLITICAL PARTIES

The Swiss political scene was long characterized by a multiplicity of political parties; however, from 1959, it was dominated by a four-party coalition of the Swiss People's Party (SVP), the Social Democratic Party (SPS), the Radical Democratic Party (FDP), and the Christian Democratic People's Party (CVP) that controlled the majority of seats in both houses of the Federal Assembly. The SVP's December 2007 decision to move into opposition occasioned the creation of a new government party, the Conservative Democratic Party (BDP), founded by moderate former SVP members. In January 2009 the SVP returned to what thereby became a five-party government, which continued intact following the 2011 and 2015 legislative elections.

Government Parties:

Swiss People's Party (*Schweizerische Volkspartei*—SVP/*Union Démocratique du Centre*—UDC/*Unione Democratica di Centro*—UDC/*Partida Populara Svizra*—PPS). Formed in 1971 by a merger of the former **Farmers', Artisans', and Citizens' Party** (BGB) with the **Democratic Party,** the SVP is a populist, right-wing party holding strong agrarian and socially conservative positions. Traditionally based in German-speaking cantons, it advocates a robust national defense as well as the protection of agriculture and small industry.

The SVP was the only government party to oppose the unsuccessful EEA accord in 1992. It increased its electoral support in 1995 to 14.9 percent, yielding 29 lower house seats (a gain of 4 over 1991), and improved to 44 seats in the 1999 poll, at which it secured approximately the same number of votes nationwide as the SPS (51 seats). The SVP's capture of 26.6 percent of the vote in 2003, largely in French-speaking Switzerland, for a plurality (55) of lower house seats led the governing coalition to grant the SVP a second seat on the Federal Council.

During the 2007 campaign, Christoph Blocher, a billionaire chemicals magnate serving as the nation's justice councilor, led the party's controversial calls to crack down on crimes committed by foreigners and prohibit the construction of minarets at Muslim places of worship. The SVP won 29 percent of the 2007 vote, more than any party since 1919, and 62 seats in the National Council, confirming it as Switzerland's strongest party. In an unprecedented move, Blocher's critics nominated Eveline Widmer-Schlumpf, a moderate SVP legislator, to run for the seat on the Federal Council theretofore held by Blocher. When she won, the SVP parliamentary group voted to exclude her and Samuel Schmid (the other SVP member of the Federal Council) from the party and threatened to act as an opposition party. Widmer-Schlumpf and Schmid subsequently affiliated with a new SVP spinoff, the BDP (see below).

Opinion polls showed waning support for the SVP after its formal move to the opposition in 2008. Among other things, business owners who had traditionally been SVP supporters criticized Blocher's call for capping executive pay at troubled Swiss banks *Crédit Suisse* and UBS and opposed SVP-backed efforts to curb the free movement of workers from EU countries. The party's return to the government in 2009, with former SVP leader Ueli Maurer replacing Schmid as defense minister, was seen as a victory for SVP moderates.

After 20 years of steady growth, the SVP's vote percentage fell to 26.6 percent in the 2011 elections, although it retained its plurality status (54 seats). Once again, the SVP had campaigned on a heavily anti-immigrant platform, party officials decrying, among other things, what they perceived as the "Islamization" of the country.

The party scored a spectacular win in the 2015 elections, securing 65 seats in the National Council and 5 seats on the Council of States.

In January 2016, soon after the 2015 federal election, Blocher announced that he would not stand for reelection. In April Albert RÖSTI was elected party president.

Leaders: Albert RÖSTI (President); Adrian AMSTUTZ (Vice President of the Party and Leader of Parliamentary Group); Celine AMAUDRUZ, Oskar FREYSINGER, Thomas AESCHI, Oskar FREYSINGER (Vice Presidents); Gabriel LUECHINGER (General Secretary), Christophe BLOCHER (Former Leader).

Social Democratic Party (*Sozialdemokratische Partei der Schweiz*—SPS/*Parti Socialiste Suisse*—PS/*Partito Socialista Svizzero*—PS/*Partida Socialdemocrata da la Svizra*—PS). Frequently referenced as the Socialist Party (SP/PS), the SPS, which was organized in 1888, is the most left-leaning governing party; it advocates direct federal taxation, a degree of state intervention in the economy, and accession to the EU. The party adopted an essentially reformist social democratic program in 1982, and it also was subsequently influenced by the ecologist and feminist movements. In 1984 it came close to withdrawing from the government after its coalition partners rejected Christine BRUNNER for the Federal Council. Subsequently, SPS member Ruth Dreifuss joined the council in 1993, and she became the first woman to hold the presidency of the federation in 1999.

Since 1992 the former ***Partito Socialista Unitario*** (PSU), now led by Manuele BERTOLI, has operated as an autonomous section of the national party, the ***Partito Socialista,*** *Sezione Ticinese del PSS*, in the Italian-speaking canton of Ticino.

In the 2007 lower house election, the SPS won 43 seats, a loss of 9 seats from 2003, though it remained the second largest party in the chamber, behind the SVP. In 2010 the SPS was seen as having moved somewhat farther to the left after it presented a new manifesto calling for capitalism to be "transcended" and replaced by the "democratization" of the economy. The party secured 46 seats in the National Council in the 2011 election on a vote share of 18.7 percent. In the 2015 elections, the party secured 43 seats in the National Council and 12 in the Council of States.

Leaders: Christian LEVRAT (President); Marina Carobbio GUSCETTI, Barbara GYSI, Géraldine SAVARY, Beat JANS (Vice Presidents); Roger NORDMANN (Leader of Parliamentary Group); Flavia WASSERFALLEN, Leyla GÜL (Co-Secretary Generals).

FDP.The Liberals (*FDP.Die Liberalen*—FDP/*PLR.Les Libéraux-Radicaux*—PLR/*PLR.I Liberali*—PLR/*PLD.Ils Liberals*—PLD). The FDP.The Liberals was founded on February 28, 2009, upon the merger of the **Radical Democratic Party** (*Freisinnig-Demokratische Partei der Schweiz*—FDP/*Parti Radical-Démocratique Suisse*—PRD/*Partito Liberale-radicale Svizzero*—PLR/*Partida Liberaldemocrata Svizra*—PLD) and the **Liberal Party** (*Liberale Partei der Schweiz*—LPS/*Parti Libéral Suisse*—PLS/*Partito Liberale Svizzero*—PLS/*Partida Liberal-conservativa Svizra*—PLC). Leader of the historic movement that gave rise to the federated state, the FDP (also known as the Free Democrats) was liberal in outlook and advocated free-market policies and closer ties with the EU. The LPS was led by Pierre WEISS and had a political base among Protestants in the French-speaking part of the country. The FDP and LPS formed a legislative coalition (called the Radical and Liberal Union) in 2005 to strengthen their united front in parliament.

The FDP lost ground in 2007, winning 31 seats (15.8 percent of the vote) in the lower house, down from 36 in 2003, and 12 in the upper house, down from 14. As a result, the party formally brought the Liberals into its ranks in an effort to increase popular support, in the process adding the Liberals' 4 lower house seats to the FDP total. The center-right FDP.The Liberals finished third in the balloting for the National Council in 2011 on a vote share of 15.1 percent. Analysts attributed the party's modest decline to its perceived association with the banking sector, which had been under intense public scrutiny for several years.

In the 2015 elections, the party came in third with 33 seats in the National Council, and second in the Council of States with 13 seats. On April 16, 2016, at a party conference, Petra GOSSI replaced Philipp MÜLLER as party president.

Leaders: Petra GOSSI (President); Andrea CARONI, Philippe NANTERMOD, Christian LÜSCHER, Christian VITTA, Christian WASSERFALLEN (Vice Presidents); Charles-Jean RICHARD (Leader of Parliamentary Group); Samuel LANZ (General Secretary).

Christian Democratic People's Party (*Christlichdemokratische Volkspartei*—CVP/*Parti Démocrate-Chrétien*—PDC/*Partito Popolare Democratico*—PPD/*Partida Cristiandemocratica*—PCD). The CVP is a successor to the **Swiss Conservative Party,** formed in 1912 by elements long opposed to the centralization of national power; the party adopted its current name in 1970. Appealing primarily to Catholics, the party traditionally advocated cantonal control over religious education and supported taxes on alcohol and tobacco, while opposing direct taxation by the federal government. As its Catholic base subsequently dwindled, the CVP gained strength in Protestant areas by promoting less-conservative social policies and defining itself as a centrist party.

The CVP's lower-house representation declined gradually beginning in 1979, falling to a low of 28 seats in 2003 on a vote share of 14.4 percent. As a result, the CVP lost 1 of its 2 seats on the Federal Council to the SVP. In 2007 the party showed increased strength, winning 31 seats in the lower house, but its seat total declined to 28 in 2011 (on a vote share of 12.3 percent). In 2015 the party won 27 seats in the National Council elections, and 13 seats in the Council of States.

Leaders: Christophe DARBELLAY (President); Ida GLANZMANN-HUNKELER, Dominique DE BUMAN (Vice Presidents); Doris LEUTHARD (Vice President of the Confederation); Tim FREY (Secretary General).

Conservative Democratic Party (*Bürgerlich-Demokratische Partei*—BDP/*Parti Bourgeois Démocratique*—PBD/*Partito Borghese Democratico*—PBD/*Partida Burgais Democratica*—PBD). The BDP was founded on November 1, 2008, by former members of the SVP, including Eveline Widmer-Schlumpf and Samuel Schmid, "moderates" who had recently clashed with SVP hard-liners. Both politicians had been elected to the National Council in 2007 under the SVP banner but had been subsequently expelled from the party after they opposed the reelection of SVP firebrand Christoph Blocher to the Federal Council. The BDP at its formation held one seat in the upper house, five seats in the lower house, and two positions (Widmer-Schlumpf and Schmid) in the Federal Council. However, Schmid resigned from the Federal Council shortly thereafter.

Unlike the SVP, the BDP supports closer ties with the EU. However, it echoes the SVP in strictly defending Switzerland's neutrality.

The centrist BDP secured nine seats in the National Council in the 2011 poll on a vote share of 5.4 percent. Meanwhile, Samuel Schmid was reported to have formed a new, small party called the **Social Liberal Movement** (*Sozial-Liberale Bewegung*—SLB/*Mouvement Social-Libérale*—MSL/*Movimento Social-Liberale*—MSL).

The BPD won seven seats in the 2015 National Council elections, and one in the Council of States. The party lost its seat in the Federal Council, but remained part of the governing coalition.

Leaders: Martin LANDOLT (President); Lorenz HESS, Barbara JANOM (Vice Presidents); Hansjörg HASSLER (Parliamentary Leader); Nina SOSSO (Secretary General).

Other Parliamentary Parties:

The Greens–Green Party of Switzerland (*Grüne–Grüne Partei der Schweiz/Les Verts–Parti Écologiste Suisse*—PES/*I Verdi–Partito Ecologista Svizzero/La Verda–Partida Ecologica Svizra*). The Swiss Federation of Green/Ecology Parties was founded in May 1983 by nine groupings, including two that had gained representation at the cantonal level in Zürich and Luzern the previous month and one that had gained a seat in the National Council in 1979. The federation obtained 3 National Council seats in 1983, 9 in 1987, and 14 in 1991. The party adopted its current name in 1993. Its National Council representation fell to 9 seats in 1995 when it received only 5 percent of the vote. The party sustained both its vote share and number of seats in the 1999 lower house elections, in which it worked jointly with the **Green Alliance** (*Grünes Bündnis/Alliance Verte*), an ecologist/feminist group, which subsequently merged with The Greens. The party increased its seat share in the lower house to 13 in 2003 and 20 in 2007, but its percentage of the vote declined to 8.4 percent (good for only 15 seats) in what was considered a "surprising setback" in the 2011 poll. The party won 11 seats in the National Council in 2015, and 2 seats in the Council of States.

Leaders: Regula RYTZ (President); Gerhard ANDREY, Bastien GIROD, Gina REUTSCHI, Luca MAGGI, Lisa MAZZONE (Vice Presidents); Balthasar GLÄTTLI (Leader of Parliamentary Group); Regula TSCHANZ (Secretary General).

Green Liberal Party (*Grünliberale Partei Schweiz*—GLP/*Parti Vert-Libéral*—PVL/*Partito Verde-Liberale*—PVL/*Partida Verda-Liberala*—PVL). A centrist party, the GLP was founded on July 19, 2007, by four canton-level green parties; it called for measures to combat climate change and other threats to the environment, while otherwise maintaining a free-market, probusiness platform. In its first electoral test, the GLP won 3 seats in the National Council and 1 in the Council of State in the 2007 balloting. The party capitalized on growing antinuclear sentiment to improve sharply to 12 seats (on a vote share of 5.4 percent) in the National Council in the 2011 balloting, but only 7 in the 2015 elections.

Leaders: Martin BÄUMLE (President); Kathrin BERTSCHY, Isabelle CHEVALLEY (Vice Presidents); Tiana Angelina MOSER (Parliamentary Leader); Michael KÖPFLI (General Secretary).

Evangelical People's Party (*Evangelische Volkspartei der Schweiz*—EVP/*Parti Evangélique Suisse*—PEV/*Partito Evangelico Svizzero*—PEV/*Partida Evangelica de la Svizra*—PEV). Established in 1919, the EVP is committed to a program that advocates conservative Protestant positions on abortion and other social issues while adopting a more centrist approach to economic policy and supporting center-left goals on environmental protection and immigration. It retained its two seats in the National Council in the 2015 balloting on a vote share of 1.9 percent.

Leaders: Heiner STUDER (President of the Party), Joel BLUNIER (Secretary General).

Ticino League (*Lega dei Ticinesi—Lega*). The Ticino League, founded in 1991, is a right-wing formation that advocates greater autonomy for Ticino. It won two lower house seats in the 1991 balloting, after which it formed a parliamentary group with the Swiss Democrats. It secured one National Council seat in 1995, two in 1999, one in 2003 and 2007, and two in 2011 (on a vote share of 0.8 percent).

Giuliano BIGNASCA, the founder and primary financial backer of the Ticino League, died in March 2013. The following month the party won a vote share of 36 percent and three of seven seats in polling for the Lugano city council. In the 2015 National Council elections, the party won two seats.

Leaders: Lorenzo QUADRI, Norman GOBBI (Secretary).

Citizens Movement of Geneva (*Mouvement Citoyens Genevois*—MCG). Founded in 2005, the right-wing MCG subsequently urged that restrictions be placed on the number of French commuters, estimated at 60,000, allowed to work in Geneva. The MCG argued that more jobs could be filled by Swiss nationals. After improving to 17 of 100 seats on the Grand Council of Geneva in the 2009 elections, the MCG secured its first seat (on 0.4 percent of the vote) in the National Council in the 2011 balloting. The MCG won 20 of the 100 seats in the Geneva Grand Council in the October 2013 local elections, and Mauro POGGIA (the party's representative in the National Council) was subsequently elected as the MCG's first member of the executive body of Geneva's cantonal government. Poggia's seat in the National Council was subsequently assumed by MCG president Roger Golay, a trade union leader. The party retained one seat in the National Council elections of 2015.

Leaders: Roger GOLAY (President of the Party), Eric STAUFFER (Founder), Mauro POGGIA.

Swiss Labor Party (*Partei der Arbeit der Schweiz*—PdA/*Parti Suisse du Travail–Parti Ouvrier et Populaire*—PST-POP/*Partito Svizzero del Lavoro*—PdL/*Partida Svizra de la Lavur*—PSdL). Organized in 1921 as the **Swiss Communist Party**, outlawed in 1940, and reorganized under its present name in 1944, the urban-based PdA long maintained a pro-Moscow position. The party removed all references to "communism" and "democratic centralism" from its statutes in September 1991 and the following month increased its representation in the National Council from one to three seats. It retained those seats in the 1995 balloting, after which its deputies affiliated with the Social Democratic parliamentary group.

In the 1999 lower house elections, the PdA gained 0.9 percent of the vote and won two seats, which it kept in 2003 with 0.7 percent of the vote. The PdA secured one lower house seat in 2007 but failed to gain representation in 2011 with a vote share of 0.5 percent. The party regained its seat in the National Council in 2015.

Leader: Norberto CRIVELLI (President).

Other Parties That Contested the 2015 Legislative Elections:

Christian Social Party (*Christlich-Soziale Partei*—CSP/*Parti Chrétien-Social*—PCS/*Partito Cristiano Sociale*—PCS/*Partida Cristian-Sociala*—PCS). A small center-left party, the CSP contested several National Council elections without success until it was able to secure one seat in 1995. It held one seat until the 2015 elections.

Leaders: Marius ACHERMANN (President), Beat BLOCH (Vice President), Karl VOGLER (Former Member of the National Council), Marlies SCHAFER-JUNGO (General Secretary).

Federal Democratic Union (*Eidgenössisch-Demokratische Union*—EDU/*Union Démocratique Fédérale*—UDF/*Unione Democratica Federale*—UDF/*Uniun Democrata Federala*—UDF). The EDU is a fundamentalist Protestant, anti-immigration party founded in 1975. After holding at least one seat in the National Council since 1991, the EDU failed to secure representation in 2015.

Leaders: Hans MOSER (President), Roland HALDIMANN (Vice President), Andreas BRÖNNIMANN, Christian WABER (Secretary General).

Freedom Party of Switzerland (*Freiheits-Partei der Schweiz*—FPS/*Parti Suisse de la Liberté*—PSL/*Partito Svizzero della Libertà*—PSL/*Partida Svizra da la Libertad*—PSL). Launched in 1985 as the **Swiss Automobile Party** (*Schweizer Auto-Partei*), a motorists' pressure group based in German-speaking Switzerland, the right-wing Freedom Party adopted its present name in 1994 but is still widely referred to as *Die Auto-Partei*. Its representation at the federal level peaked at eight National Council seats in 1991 after it had added an anti-immigration component to its manifesto. It fell back to seven seats in 1995 on a 4 percent vote share. Since 1999 its vote share has been under 1 percent. The party failed to gain any seats in the 2015 elections.

Leaders: Jürg SCHERRER (President), Frank KARLI (Vice President), Ursula WALTHER (Secretary).

Swiss Democrats (*Schweizer Demokraten*—SD/*Démocrates Suisses*—DS/*Democratici Svizzeri*—DS/*Democrats Svizers*—DS). The far-right SD emerged in 1961 as the National Action against Foreign Infiltration of People and Homeland (*National Aktion gegen Überfremdung von Volk und Heimat/Action Nationale contre l'Emprise et la Surpopulation Etrangéres*) and as of 1977 was known as the National Action for People and Homeland (*National Aktion für Volk und Heimat*—NA/*Action National*—AN). The group adopted its present name prior to the 1991 elections. It subsequently sought to reduce the number of resident foreign workers as well as the number of naturalizations. The party secured five seats in the National Council in 1991, but its share of the vote declined thereafter. It won three seats in 1995 and then only one in 1999 and 2003. The SD lost that seat in 2007 as former supporters apparently voted for the SVP. The SD again failed to gain representation in the 2011 balloting, at which it garnered 0.2 percent of the vote. The party failed to gain any seats in the 2015 elections.

Leader: Bernhard HESS (President).

Swiss Pirate Party (*Piratenpartei Schweiz*—PPS/*Parti Pirate Suisse*—PPS/*Partito Pirata Svizzero*—PPS/*Partida da Pirats Svizra*—PPS). Based on the Swedish Pirate Party, the PPS was founded on July 12, 2009, by advocates of freedom of information; among other things, it has called for the elimination of patents and copyrights, perceived as a barrier to public access to information. The PPS secured 8.9 percent of the vote in local elections in Berlin in September 2011 but failed to gain representation in the October balloting for the National Council on a 0.48 percent vote share. The party failed to gain any seats in the 2015 elections.

Leaders: Guillaume SAOULI, Stefan THONI (Presidents); Denis SIMONET (Founding President).

LEGISLATURE

The bicameral **Federal Assembly** (*Bundesversammlung/Assemblée Fédérale/Assemblea Federale*) consists of a Council of States and a National Council.

Council of States (*Ständerat/Conseil des Etats/Consiglio degli Stati*). The upper house consists of 46 members, 2 elected from each of the 20 cantons and 1 from each of the 6 half-cantons. Although election methods vary among the cantons, most of the elections are held on a two-round (if necessary) majoritarian basis. Following the elections of October 18–December 9, 2015, the Christian Democratic People's Party held 13 seats; FDP.The Liberals, 13; Social Democratic Party, 12; Swiss People's Party, 5; The Greens–Green Party of Switzerland, 1; Conservative Democratic Party, 1; and independent, 1.

President: Raphael COMTE (FDP.The Liberals).

National Council (*Nationalrat/Conseil National/Consiglio Nazionale*). The lower house consists of 200 members elected for four-year terms by direct popular vote within each canton or half-canton, for the most part on a proportional representation basis, which varies among cantons. Seats are allocated to the cantons and half-cantons based on population. The Zurich canton has 34 seats, while the six half-cantons have only 1 seat each. (Majoritarian balloting is used in the six half-cantons.) The seat distribution resulting from balloting on October 18, 2015, was as follows: the Swiss People's Party, 65; Social Democratic Party, 43; FDP.The Liberals, 33; Christian Democratic People's Party, 27; The Greens–Green Party of Switzerland, 11; Green Liberal Party, 7; Conservative Democratic Party, 7; Evangelical People's Party, 2;

Ticino League, 2; Citizens' Movement of Geneva, 1; Swiss Party of Labor, 1; and independents, 1.

President: Christa MARKWALDER (FDP.The Liberals).

FEDERAL COUNCIL

[as of September 20, 2016]

President	Johann Schneider-Ammann (FDP.The Liberals)
Vice President	Doris Leuthard (CVP) [f]
Department Heads	
Defense, Civil Protection, and Sports	Guy Parmelin (SVP)
Economic Affairs, Education, and Research	Johann Schneider-Ammann (FDP.The Liberals)
Environment, Transportation, Communications, and Energy	Doris Leuthard (CVP) [f]
Finance	Ueli Maurer (SVP)
Foreign Affairs	Didier Burkhalter (FDP.The Liberals)
Home Affairs	Alain Berset (SPS)
Justice and Police	Simonetta Sommaruga (SPS) [f]
Federal Chancellor	Corina Casanova (CVP) [f]

[f] = female

INTERGOVERNMENTAL REPRESENTATION

Ambassador to the U.S.: Martin Werner DAHINDEN.

U.S. Ambassador to Switzerland: Tara Feret ERATH (Chargé d'Affaires).

Permanent Representative to the UN: Juerg LAUBER.

IGO Memberships (Non-UN): ADB, AfDB, CEUR, EBRD, EFTA, IADB, IEA, ICC, IOM, OECD.

For Further Reference:

Church, Clive H. *The Politics and Government of Switzerland, 2004 Edition*. New York: Palgrave Macmillan, 2004.

Church, Clive H., and Randolph C. Head. *A Concise History of Switzerland.* Cambridge: Cambridge University Press, 2013.

Kriesi, Hans Peter. *The Politics of Switzerland: Continuity and Change in a Consensus Democracy.* Cambridge: Cambridge University Press, 2008.

SYRIA

Syrian Arab Republic
al-Jumhuriyah al-Arabiyah al-Suriyah

Political Status: Republic proclaimed in 1941; became independent on April 17, 1946; under military regime since March 8, 1963.

Area: 71,586 sq. mi. (185,408 sq. km).

Population: 18,564,000 (2016E—UN); 17,185,170 (2016E—U.S. Census).

Major Urban Centers (2016E—UN, including suburbs): DAMASCUS (2,586,000), Aleppo (3,641,000), Homs (1,695,000), Hamah (1,297,000).

Official Language: Arabic.

Monetary Unit: Syrian Pound (official rate October 1, 2016: 214.05 pounds = $1US). The Syrian pound, formerly pegged to the U.S. dollar, has been pegged to a basket of currencies since 2007.

President: Lt. Gen. (Dr.) Bashar al-ASSAD (Ba'ath Party); sworn in July 17, 2000, May 27, 2007, and July 16, 2014.

Vice Presidents: Farouk al-SHARAA (Ba'ath Party), appointed by President Assad February 11, 2006; and Najah al-ATTAR (ind.), appointed by the president March 23, 2006. Both were reappointed July 18, 2014.

Prime Minister: Imad Mohammad Deeb KHAMIS (Ba'ath Party); appointed by President Assad on June 22, 2016, and sworn in on July 3, to succeed Wael Nader AL-HALAQI (Ba'ath Party), following legislative elections on April 13.

THE COUNTRY

The Syrian Arab Republic is flanked by Turkey on the north; the Mediterranean Sea, Lebanon, and Israel on the west; Jordan on the south; and Iraq on the east. Its terrain is distinguished by the Anti-Lebanon and Alawite mountains running parallel to the Mediterranean, the Jabal al-Druze Mountains in the south, and a semidesert plateau in the southeast, while the economically important Euphrates River Valley traverses the country from north to southeast. Ninety percent of the population is Arab; the most important minorities are Kurds, Armenians, and Turks. The Kurdish population, numbering 300,000, has faced discrimination in a variety of forms since the Ba'ath Party came to power in 1963.

Islam is professed by 87 percent of the people, most of whom belong to the Sunni sect, which dominated the region for some 1,400 years prior to the assumption of power in 1970 by Hafiz al-ASSAD, an Alawite. About 13.5 percent of the population is Alawite, a Shiite offshoot that also draws on some Christian traditions and is viewed as "non-Muslim" by many Sunnis. Alawites have dominated governmental affairs under the regimes of Hafiz al-Assad and, more recently, his son, Bashar al-Assad. Arabic is the official language, but French and English are often spoken in government and business circles. Women have achieved a larger role in government and politics than in many other regional states. In 2016 the cabinet had three women, and one of two vice presidents was female. After legislative balloting in April 2016, women held 33 seats in the legislature (13.2 percent of the 250 seats), and a woman was elected speaker of the Assembly.

Syria is one of the few Arab countries with adequate arable land. One-fifth of the workforce is engaged in agriculture (more than half of the women work as unpaid family workers on rural estates). However, a lack of proper irrigation facilities makes agricultural production dependent on variations in rainfall. An agrarian reform law, promulgated in 1958 and modified in 1963, limits the size of individual holdings. Wheat, barley, and cotton are the principal crops, and Syria is one of the world's leading producers of olive oil. Major Syrian industries, the most important of which are food processing, tobacco, and textiles, are nationalized.

After more than three years of civil war, Syria's gross domestic product (GDP) contracted significantly. Though the conflict has obscured key economic data, in May 2014, the International Monetary Fund (IMF) estimated that Syria's real GDP has shrunk 40 percent since the war began. In addition, the Syrian stock market has lost most of its worth, and the local currency lost more than 60 percent of its prewar value. Agriculture output has dropped drastically, while tourism and direct investment have dried up almost completely. As the crisis in Syria entered its fourth year, an IMF report estimated that wartime losses to the economy have totaled more than $144 billion. With 2014 oil production at only 4 percent of its prewar high, Syria's oil minister revealed that the country's oil and gas industries have forfeited $21.4 billion. By 2016 production had increased slightly from its low in October 2014.

GOVERNMENT AND POLITICS

Political background. Seat of the Umayyad Empire in early Islamic times before conquest by the Mongols in 1400, Syria was absorbed by the Ottoman Turks in 1517 and became a French-mandated territory under the League of Nations in 1920. A republican government, formed under wartime conditions in 1941, secured the evacuation of French forces in April 1945 and declared the country fully independent on April 17, 1946. Political development was subsequently marked by alternating weak parliamentary governments and

unstable military regimes. Syria merged with Egypt on February 1, 1958, to form the United Arab Republic but seceded on September 29, 1961, to reestablish the independent Syrian Arab Republic.

On March 8, 1963, the Ba'ath Arab Socialist Party assumed power through a military-backed coup. Gen. Amin al-HAFIZ became the dominant figure until February 1966 when a second coup led by Maj. Gen. Salah al-JADID resulted in the flight of Hafiz and the installation of Nur al-Din al-ATASSI as president. With Jadid's backing, the Atassi government survived war with Israel and the loss of the Golan Heights in 1967. Crises within the Ba'ath Party precipitated by philosophical differences culminated in a coup led by Lt. Gen. Hafiz al-ASSAD in 1970. Assad became president and was subsequently elected secretary general of the party. The regime established a legislature, and in 1973, held the first national elections. The National Progressive Front (NPF), consisting of the Ba'ath Party and its allies, won an overwhelming majority of seats in the People's Assembly. By 1981, all the seats were distributed among NPF members.

The Alawite background of Assad and some of his top associates triggered opposition among the country's predominantly urban Sunni majority, which experienced economic adversity as a result of the regime's socialist policies. The opposition turned into a rebellion led by the Muslim Brotherhood (see Political Parties, below) after Syria's 1976 intervention on the Maronite side in the Lebanese civil war. The struggle reached its climax in February 1982 in the northern city of Hama in a three-week uprising, which was suppressed with great bloodshed. By 1983 the seven-year insurgency had been decisively crushed, along with the Muslim Brotherhood's stated aim of establishing a fundamentalist Islamic state. (For information about the presidency of Hafiz Assad from 1983 to 1999, see the 2011 *Handbook*.)

After nearly 30 years in power, President Assad died on June 10, 2000. Vice President Abd al-Kalim KHADDAM assumed the position of acting president, although it was immediately apparent that careful plans had been laid for the swift succession of the deceased president's son, Bashar al-Assad. The international community had high hopes for the new president, a Western-trained ophthalmologist. Early in his regime, during what some called the Damascus Spring, Bashar Assad advocated greater media freedom, the release of hundreds of political prisoners, and a more active civil society. However, the emergency law, which was enacted when the Ba'ath Party came to power in 1963, retained a ban on political opposition. The only reforms allowed to flourish were in the economic sector, which experienced an influx of private investment, particularly in Damascus. Nevertheless, the government remained hamstrung by Syria's national security challenges, war in Iraq, anti-Syrian ferment in Lebanon, and worsening relations with the United States. By 2003, with reform efforts foundering and relations with the United States turning sour, President Assad appointed Muhammad Naji al-UTRI as prime minister. In 2007 President Assad was endorsed for a second seven-year term, with a "yes" vote of 97.6 percent.

Bashar Assad was confident that Syria was immune from the type of sociopolitical discontent affecting significant portions of the Middle East during the Arab Spring of 2011. However, when what began in February of that year as tepid street protests evolved into large-scale demonstrations by a multifaceted opposition movement, Assad alternated between ruthless, bloody suppression of dissent and a placating, rhetorical approach offering an array of what his critics described as disingenuous reforms.

In an effort to quell antigovernment protests, President Assad accepted the resignation of his entire cabinet on March 29, 2011. Assad announced on April 3 that he had appointed a new prime minister, Adel SAFAR. Legislation approved in July seemed to usher in a new political era, as it allowed for the licensing of new political parties as long as they were secular and respected "the rule of law."

Throughout 2011 Syria's opposition coordinated its activities by attending meetings in Istanbul to discuss strategy. These meetings spurred the formation of Local Coordination Committees, loose coalitions of grassroots activists intent upon coordinating scattered pockets of antigovernment sentiment. The Committees, in turn, spawned the Syrian National Council (SNC). The Council—founded by a diverse set of secularists, Islamists, and Kurds—was intent upon bringing democratic pluralism to Syria. In October the SNC called for Assad's resignation and declared itself a government-in-exile. It also established a quasi-unified military—the Free Syrian Army (FSA) led by former Syrian Army colonel Riad al-ASAAD. By late 2012 the SNC's legitimacy as a unified opposition group was challenged by a new group, the National Coalition for Syrian Revolution and Opposition Forces (see Political Parties, below).

As fighting between the FSA and government forces intensified in 2011, the Arab League met in Cairo to force a ceasefire. Assad agreed to abide by the league's peace plan, but his forces kept up their attacks on opposition militias. In response, the League voted to suspend Syria's membership. At two Friends of Syria summits held in February and April 2012, member countries pressed for sanctions on Syria's leadership. In addition, the Assad regime was criticized by Human Rights Watch (HWR) as the perpetrator of crimes against humanity for relentless shelling of the city of Homs and the torture of civilians and political prisoners. Human Rights Watch (HRW) urged the UN Security Council to refer Syria to the International Criminal Court.

During 2012 the FSA and Syrian forces clashed throughout the country. In all cases, the government forces held a superior advantage, from access to heavy munitions to a monopoly over airpower. In the midst of violence and instability, Syria managed to hold parliamentary elections, though many newly licensed opposition groups boycotted.

The Assad regime experienced many defections from the military and government in 2012, the most significant defection being that of Prime Minister Riad HIJAB, who had been in office only two months. In July, a bomb targeting the heart of the regime's power in Damascus killed three top-level defense officials, including the defense minister.

The war intensified in 2013 as many cities experienced extended sieges. Though it appeared in February that the rebels had gained tactical advantage over the Syrian army, infighting between rebel militias erased their advantage: by July, the tide of war had turned to Assad's favor. Analysts speculated that, with support from his allies Russia, Iran, and Hezbollah, it appeared that Assad was capable of fending off the challenge to his rule.

Reports also indicated the opposition had become increasingly fractious, beset by ideological and religious differences. The FSA had only moderate influence on the plethora of militias such as the Nusra Front (*Jabhat al-Nusra*) that were financed by private donors. Led by Abu Muhammad al-JOULANI, Nusra was in regular contact with the head of al-Qaida in Pakistan, Ayman al-ZAWAHRI. Western intelligence noted that another al-Qaida affiliate—al-Qaida in Iraq and the Levant (*al-Shams*), or ISIS—became increasingly active in Syria during 2013. Foreign fighters from as far away as the United States were drawn to Syria as ZAWAHIRI declared a *fatwa* against Alawites. Despite this evidence that the rebels were becoming more radical and sectarian,

Western countries continued to train those groups it vetted for ties to hard-line Islamists. In addition, Saudi Arabia, Qatar, and Turkey continued to provide weapons and cash to certain groups. However, by September 2013 it became clear rebels groups were killing each other either for ideological reasons—many hard-line Salafi groups viewed secular fighters as corrupt "sinners"—or to control spoils of conquest such as food and oil. ISIS was especially ruthless against other rebels, even members of Nusra.

The specter of chemical weapons cast a long shadow over Iraq in 2013. The UN reported the use of sarin gas near Damascus, Homs, and Aleppo in April and May. The Assad regime blamed rebels, but the rebels implicated the regime. Meanwhile, U.S. president Barack Obama threatened military intervention if Assad used chemical weapons. On August 21, 2013, gas attacks in Ghouta—a suburb of Damascus—claimed hundreds of victims overnight. In what was verified as the deadliest lethal gas attack since the 1980s, an estimated 1,400 people died from exposure to sarin gas delivered by rocket fire. Western leaders condemned the attack, promising dire consequences. Syria denied involvement and again blamed the opposition.

Knowing that the U.S. Congress was poised to give President Obama authorization to intervene militarily in Syria, Russian president Vladimir Putin proposed a plan whereby the United States would forgo military action against Syria if the Assad regime would place its chemical arsenal—estimated to be more than 1,000 tons—under international control for destruction. Russia and the United States reached an agreement on September 14 requiring Syria to enumerate its chemical weapons, transfer them to a UN-sponsored disposal team, and sign the Chemical Weapons Convention. The UNSC passed a resolution in late September backing the U.S.–Russian agreement, though it did not include punitive consequences for noncompliance.

Assad was reelected on June 3, 2014 (see Current issues, below). In legislative balloting on April 13, 2016, the NPF-led coalition won 200 seats, while the remaining 50 seats were won by pro-presidential independents. Assad appointed former electricity minister Imad Mohammad Deeb KHAMIS as prime minister on June 22. Khamis and a reshuffled cabinet were sworn in on July 3.

Constitution and government. According to the 1973 constitution, which succeeded the provisional constitutions of 1964 and 1969, Syria is a socialist popular democracy. Nominated by the legislature upon proposal by the Regional Command of the Ba'ath Party, the president, who must be a Muslim, is elected by popular referendum for a seven-year term. The chief executive wields substantial power, appointing the prime minister and other cabinet members, military personnel, and civil servants; he also serves as military commander in chief. Legislative authority is vested in the People's Assembly (*Majlis al-Shaab*), which is directly elected for a four-year term. Only members of the Ba'ath Party, or independents approved by the government, are allowed to run for an assembly seat. The judicial system, based on a blend of French, Ottoman, and Islamic legal traditions, is headed by the Court of Cassation and includes courts of appeal, summary courts, courts of first instance, and specialized courts for military and religious issues. Constitutional amendments may be proposed by the president but must secure the approval of two-thirds of the assembly.

For administrative purposes, Syria is divided into 13 provinces and the city of Damascus, which is treated as a separate entity. Each of the provinces is headed by a centrally appointed governor who acts in conjunction with a partially elected provincial council.

Government agencies or licensed political, religious, labor, and professional organizations issue most publications. The government controls broadcasting through the Syrian Arab Republic Broadcasting Service. In its 2016 index of freedom of the press, Reporters Without Borders ranked Syria 177th out of 180 countries. The same organization ranked Syria as the deadliest country for journalists in 2012. Once antigovernment protests began in March 2011, press access to Syria was extensively curtailed. The UN Human Rights Council (UNHRC) reported that many members of the press have been detained and harassed by Syrian officials. In response to street protests, in August 2011 the Syrian cabinet passed a new law, Legislative Decree No. 108, which criminalized all public forms of political dissent.

In February 2012 constitutional changes struck the provision that ensconced the Ba'ath party's political dominance. However, in parliamentary elections held in May 2012, the Ba'ath party and its affiliates in the National Progressive Front (NPF) continued their stranglehold on the government. In March 2014 the assembly passed legislation allowing multiple candidates to run for president. However, the law excluded many potential candidates by requiring ten consecutive years of habitation in the country prior to the election, a requirement disqualifying all expatriates and members of the opposition-in-exile.

Foreign relations. Syrian foreign policy priorities are rooted in the fundamental objective of regime survival and center on four issues: Lebanon, the Arab–Israeli conflict, Syria's place in the Arab world, and relations with the United States.

Lebanon has been a problem and an opportunity for Syria since the emergence of the two independent states in the mid-1940s. France carved Lebanon out of Ottoman Syria to create a state containing a small Christian majority. From the standpoint of successive Syrian governments dating back some 50 years, a real "red line" issue is the specter of Lebanon falling altogether out of Syria's orbit and becoming a national security threat to the Damascus regime. (For a discussion of Syria's relations with Lebanon from 1975–2000, see the 2013 *Handbook*.)

In 2004 Syria tried to strengthen its position in Lebanon by compelling the Lebanese parliament to adopt a constitutional amendment extending the term of President Emile Lahoud. However, the move fueled Lebanese resentment and drew international condemnation. The UN Security Council (UNSC) passed Resolution 1559, calling for the withdrawal of Syrian military and intelligence personnel and free elections in Lebanon. Rafiq al-Hariri, the former prime minister, was assassinated on February 14, 2005, prompting intense international pressure and massive Lebanese protests against Syria since Damascus topped the list of suspects. Syrian military forces withdrew from Lebanon in April 2005, and Lebanese elections in June produced a majority in parliament supportive of ending Syrian suzerainty. In 2008 Syria signed a formal agreement that for the first time recognized Lebanon's sovereignty, and the country established an embassy in Beirut.

Syria's hard-line policy toward Israel dates back to the first Arab-Israeli war in 1948. At the war's end, Syria alone among the Arab participants was in possession of land allotted to the Jewish state in the UN partition plan. Successive Syrian governments have employed anti-Zionist policies—including wars in 1967, 1973, and 1982—as an essential element of legitimacy within the country. Syrians have traditionally found the dispossession of the Palestinians, the occupation of the Golan Heights, and the willingness of other Arab states to make formal peace with Israel unacceptable and unjust. Yet Syrian policy has not been one of unremitting hostility toward Israel. Since 1974, Damascus has ensured that the cease-fire in the Golan Heights has remained in effect, and since the mid-1990s Syria has indicated its desire for conditional peace with Israel, provided the Israelis withdraw from the Golan Heights up to the boundary that separated Syrian and Israeli forces on the eve of war in 1967.

Since becoming president, Bashar al-Assad has publicly stated a willingness to resume negotiations with Israel, but Syria's alliance with Iran, its support of Hezbollah, and its sheltering of Hamas leaders have made both Israel and the United States skeptical of Syrian motives. Indeed, Syria's arms conduit to Hezbollah was an important factor in the July–August 2006 war between Israel and Hezbollah (see entry on Israel).

Realizing the image and reality of an Arab-nationalist leadership role has traditionally been a Syrian foreign policy objective with important domestic political implications. The Ba'ath Party founded the notion of pan-Arabism—a political philosophy that sought the unification of Arabs in a common cause. However, by the late 1970s, Syria had begun to recognize that the Arab nationalist movement had run its course. Indeed, Syria's decision to support Iran during the Iran–Iraq war placed it at odds with the entire Arab world, but the schism was mended by Iraq's 1990 invasion of Kuwait. The Iran–Syria alliance is vital to both parties and has taken on added significance in the wake of the 2006 summer war between Hezbollah and Israel. Hezbollah's ability to fight Israel and avoid defeat gave the Shiite organization a heroic image in the Sunni Arab streets, alarming the leaders of Egypt, Jordan, and Saudi Arabia. In their eyes, Syria had become Iran's junior partner and Tehran's tool to penetrate the Levant.

Syria's decisions to participate in the coalition that ousted Iraq from Kuwait and to join in the Arab-Israeli peace process launched at the 1991 Madrid Conference helped reconcile Damascus with Cairo and strengthened its relationship with Saudi Arabia, whose financial assistance was essential. At the same time, the Palestine Liberation Organization's (PLO) closeness to Iraq under Hussein and its decision to seek a separate peace with Israel only hardened the long-standing enmity between Assad and PLO chair Yasir Arafat and convinced Assad to pursue a peace process of his own.

In 1998 Turkey threatened to counter Syrian support of Kurdish nationalists by invading Syria. However, the two countries eventually found common ground on Kurdish separatism and overcame their differences over Euphrates River water and the Turkish province of Hatay, which Syria claimed.

(For information about U.S.–Syrian relations from 1990–2008, see the 2011 *Handbook*.) The Obama administration began to engage Syria diplomatically in 2009, and some analysts suggested that efforts by Assad to reorganize the Syrian government were attempts to improve relations with the United States. However, the United States announced renewed sanctions against Syria in May, with President Obama declaring that Syria was a serious threat to his country.

In 2010 Syria's foreign relations improved on a number of fronts. In March Saudi Arabia extended development loans to help Syria finance infrastructure. Although Washington had rebuked Syria for sending long-range missiles to Hezbollah, the Obama administration eased exports of American telecommunications equipment to private U.S. firms working on projects in Syria. In addition, President Obama appointed Stephen Ford as the first U.S. ambassador to Syria since 2005.

In 2011 Syria's foreign relationships were significantly affected by the public uprising against President Assad. Violent crackdown on protests resulted in U.S. sanctions against Syrian officials. In August President Obama called on Assad to step down—stopping short, however, of suggesting military intervention. The United States supported UN attempts to stop Syrian violence, but unrelenting bloodshed prompted the Obama administration to recall Ambassador Ford and close its embassy. Intelligence community observers reported in 2012 that the United States was covertly supporting certain elements of the Syrian opposition movement. Meanwhile, the United States criticized Russia over its relationship with Syria when reports surfaced that Russia was shipping attack helicopters to Damascus. In light of statements made by an Assad regime official in August 2012 that the country's chemical weapons would be used in case of an external attack (the first-ever admission that Syria possessed such weapons), President Obama warned that the U.S. military would interpret the movement of such weapons as a provocation.

Despite reservations about al-Qaida affiliated groups operating within the rebel fold, the Obama administration increased financial aid to the rebels and started to provide some weapons and munitions in September 2013. However, when U.S. materiel provided to FSA troops was stolen by the Islamic Front in November 2013 (see Current issues, below), President Obama suspended nonlethal aid to the opposition. In March 2014 Ambassador Ford, whose role had been reduced to special envoy to the exiled Syrian opposition, resigned and was replaced by Daniel Rubenstein. The same month the United States ordered Syria to close its meager diplomatic mission in Washington.

Russia and China scuttled all UN attempts to condemn the Syrian government through 2013. In March 2011 a peace plan offered by the UN's special envoy to Syria—former UN secretary general Kofi Annan—authorized the deployment of UN observers to implement a ceasefire. The deployment could not stop the violence, but did bring about Annan's resignation. He was replaced by former Algerian foreign minister Lakhdar Brahimi. Intent upon implementing a ceasefire of his own, Brahimi tried to halt the violence in October 2012, but neither the government nor the rebels adhered to his plan. The UNHRC warned Syrian rebel groups that they would be prosecuted for crimes against humanity along with Assad if they were found guilty of atrocities in their prosecution of the war. Concerned about human costs in the conflict, the UN appealed to member states in 2013 to raise $5 billion in humanitarian aid for the estimated 6 million Syrians affected by the war.

EU officials announced an arms embargo against Syria in late 2011, and banned the importation of Syrian oil into Europe—Syria's biggest market. Anti-Assad groups requested North Atlantic Treaty Organization (NATO) intervention against the Assad regime, asking Alliance members to implement a no-fly zone over the country. However, NATO members ruled out such an action. After the Syrian army was accused of committing a massacre in the city of Houla, many European Union (EU) states suspended diplomatic relations with Syria. In 2013 the EU also increased sanctions against the Assad regime and stepped up nonlethal support to the opposition.

Relations between Syria and Turkey began to deteriorate in 2011 and continued through 2014. At the outset of the uprising against Assad, Turkish prime minister Recep Erdoğan declared that Assad should not be forced from power. The Turks pressed Assad to enact political reforms and to avoid bloodshed at all costs. However, Turkish troops were forced to guard their border repeatedly from 2011 through 2014, as the Syrian army besieged towns along the divide between the two countries. Turkey increased sanctions on Syria, and trade between the two countries slowed to a trickle. Istanbul also allowed Syrian exile groups to use Turkey as a base.

Turkish–Syrian relations were put to a severe test in June 2012, when Syrian air defense shot down a Turkish jet that had strayed into Syria's airspace. In response to a rocket that hit Turkish territory in October, the Turkish artillery shelled positions inside Syria for a week, an act representing the first direct military intervention in Syria during the crisis. Both Syria and Turkey eventually closed their airspace to one another. In October 2013 Turkey shelled Islamist rebel positions inside Syria in response to cross-border mortar fire into Turkish towns. Turkey shot down a Syrian jet in March 2014, causing strong words from Damascus and Ankara: Assad accused Turkey of siding with terrorists, while Erdogan declared that Syria was at war with his country.

By February 2012 all six of the Gulf Cooperation Council (GCC) member states had recalled their diplomats and had expelled their Syrian counterparts. The Saudis and Qataris increased both financial and military aid to Syrian rebels, often indiscriminately. Acting with Turkey, the Gulf States attempted to coordinate the opposition's military operation by forming and arming a Supreme Military Council consisting of many allied rebel militias.

By successfully negotiating for the destruction of Syria's chemical weapons program, in the eyes of many analysts, Russia became the preeminent actor in Syria's foreign relations from late 2013 through 2014. Though rhetorically committed to a political solution for Syria's civil war, Moscow increased its supply of weapons, machinery, fighter aircraft, aerial drones, and artillery to Syria—even in the weeks leading up to the unsuccessful Geneva II peace talks in January and February 2014 (see Current issues, below).

In response to the hundreds of thousands of Syrians crossing over their border in 2011 and 2012, some Lebanese politicians called upon Arab leaders to force Assad to stop his violent crackdown. However, Beirut's official stance on Syria was neutrality: In both UN and Arab League votes condemning the Assad regime, Lebanon either voted not to criticize its neighbor or abstained from voting. However, Lebanon's growing sectarian divide helped fuel conflict in Syria, as Shia Hezbollah militia members loyal to Assad and Sunni Salafi fighters loyal to the opposition fought inside Syria. In May 2013 Hezbollah declared it had joined an all-out battle to defeat anti-Assad forces, a move that increased the ranks of Sunni radicals drawn to fight in Syria. In 2014 rebels from Nusra, as well as from ISIS, were successful in penetrating the Lebanese border and engaging in extended battles with the Lebanese Forces near Arsal (see entry on Lebanon).

Observers noted that Israel's natural preference vis-à-vis the crisis in Syria was to deal with Assad rather than a possible al-Qaida influenced successor regime. However, reacting to intelligence that Iranian weapons were being shipped to Hezbollah via Syria, the Israeli air force bombed five Syrian targets in 2013. After several instances of cross-border fire from Syria into Israel's territory near the Golan Heights during 2014, in which Israeli citizens and military personnel were wounded, the Israeli air force hit both regime and rebel targets inside Syrian territory.

In November 2011 Jordan's King Abdullah II called on Assad to resign, becoming the first Arab leader to do so. In retaliation, Assad loyalists attacked the Jordanian embassy in Damascus. In 2012 military units from Syria and Jordan exchanged gunfire near the Jordanian border. In response, officials in Amman started providing greater support for Syrian rebels, and requested U.S. weaponry to bolster Jordan's border defenses. Jordanian warplanes hit rebels that breached Jordan's border in April 2014, showing the monarchy's resolve to protect its territory from the type of spillover experienced by Syria's other neighbors Iraq, Turkey, and Lebanon.

In July 2011 Iranian president Mahmoud AHMADINEJAD strongly urged Assad to embrace the Syrian opposition. Rhetorical stances aside, Iran provided diplomatic cover for Syria in the Organization of Islamic Cooperation (OIC), which sought to expel Syria in August 2012. In addition, Western and Israeli intelligence officers reported in 2012 that Tehran was providing Syria with war materiel, personnel, intelligence, and funding. In September 2012 Iran confirmed that members of the Revolutionary Guards elite Quds Force were helping the Assad regime as "counselors." Tehran's continued support for the Assad regime led the Syrian opposition to demand Iran's exclusion from the Geneva II peace talks, a demand granted by the UN.

As the war in Syria escalated, Iraq became concerned about refugee inflows: Border troops were reinforced and crossings into Syria randomly closed to limit immigration and maintain security. In 2013 Iraqi officials admitted that some parts of western Iraq bordering Syria were out of Baghdad's control and were increasingly dominated by ISIS (see entry on Iraq).

The United States and Russia negotiated a limited cease-fire on February 26, 2016, following UN Security Resolution 2268, which called for all sides to stop fighting (see Current issues, below). However, combat continued and the cease-fire was abandoned in July. A second major cease-fire agreement between Russia and the United States that began on September 10 was designed to allow the UN to deliver humanitarian aid. As with the first cessation of hostilities, fighting continued and the cease-fire was abandoned on September 20.

Current issues. Though the destruction of Syria's chemical weapons took longer than planned, the international agency charged with the task, the Organization for the Prohibition of Chemical Weapons (OPCW) was lauded for its efforts. However, evidence presented by the OPCW indicated that bombs containing chlorine were used in Hama province during April 2014. A subsequent UN report blamed the Syrian government for using chlorine gas bombs, an allegation denied in Damascus. The Assad regime was also criticized by the UNHRC, HRW, and many Western governments for the use of barrel bombs, crude, unguided munitions that produce extensive and indiscriminate harm to civilian populations. Attempts to pass a UNSC resolution implicating the regime for war crimes and crimes against humanity, and referring its actions to the International Criminal Court (ICC) for investigation, were stymied by China and Russia. Opposition militias were also identified as possible war crimes perpetrators for their use of indiscriminate mortar attacks, car bombs, and torture.

The ongoing civil war continued to affect every aspect of Syrian life in 2014. Though world leaders attempted to fashion peace at the Geneva II talks, it was not forthcoming. Meeting in Córdoba, Spain, prior to attending the Geneva conference, rebels sought an interim government without Assad. In Geneva, Assad's representatives rejected that notion, suggesting that the first step to solving Syria's crisis was eradication of "terrorism." In the meantime, government forces continued their sieges of Homs and Aleppo, where residents had been reduced to eating leaves and stray animals. In May rebels in Homs agreed to a truce whereby they agreed to leave permanently: Their evacuation from what was known as "the capital of the revolution" was a symbolic victory for the regime.

Assad's forces enjoyed modest success in the first half of 2014 for two reasons: continued monopoly over air power and rebel infighting caused—primarily—by ISIS. Though some rebel militias also employed siege tactics, it was often rival rebel forces they were trying to drive out. In June 2014 ISIS took control of the al-Omar oil field at Deir al-Zor from al-Nusra forces that had held it for months. Observers noted that ISIS, or the Islamic State as it preferred to be called, was primarily concerned with acquiring territory, whether the territory was held by Assad loyalists or antigovernment rebels. Meanwhile, other rebel groups expressed outrage at the tactics of ISIS, and formed coalitions—such as the Islamic Front and Mujahedeen Army—to oppose it. Even the Islamic Front turned on more moderate rebel forces, as its members attacked FSA storage depots and caused the demotion of FSA senior commander General Salim IDRIS. Nusra, with the backing of al-Qaida's Zawahiri, decided in February 2014 to declare war on the Islamic State. In April Zawahiri called on ISIS to quit the fight in Syria, only to be rebuffed by ISIS leader Abu Bakr BAGHDADI, who declared the area his forces occupied in Iraq and Syria a new Islamic caliphate, with him as its emir.

Non-jihadi rebels, despite attempts at consolidation in 2014 (at one point 30 rebel groups joined forces under one banner) were unable to confront ISIS effectively, as the latter group had U.S.-made military equipment, cash, a steady stream of foreign fighters, and significant economic resources (oil, gas, and wheat fields). The FSA experienced an exodus of top commanders disillusioned with the lack of substantial support from both Western and Gulf State sponsors.

In the midst of war and a serious humanitarian crisis, Syria conducted a presidential election in June 2014. President Assad easily defeated two challengers by capturing almost 89 percent of the votes cast by the 74 percent of eligible voters who turned out. Some of the opposition chose to boycott the election, Syrians in rebel-held territory ignored it, and Western leaders described it as a farce. However, the scope of Syria's continuing humanitarian crisis could not be ignored: By September 2014 the UN reported the war had produced more than 3 million refugees—most of whom sought shelter in Lebanon, Jordan, and Turkey. In addition, more than 6.5 million Syrians were internally displaced, and more than 191,000 had been killed since the war began. Providing aid to the estimated 50 percent of the population that needed it was hampered by Syria's refusal to accept convoys through its border with Turkey.

After President Assad was inaugurated in late June, ISIS—after enjoying significant territorial gains in Iraq—ramped up its operations in Syria. In the largest rebel engagement with government forces since the start of the conflict, ISIS captured the Shaar gas fields in Homs province and, in August, took the Tabqa military airport in Raqaa province—from which it obtained portable antiaircraft missiles. By September 2014 ISIS had laid siege to the Kurdish region of northern Syria along the Turkish border, at first drawing in hundreds of foreign Kurdish militiamen, then causing an estimated 130,000 refugees to seek asylum in Turkey.

After ISIS released video on the Internet showing its beheading of two American reporters in August 2014, President Obama announced an American-led mission to destroy ISIS as a military organization. After already authorizing U.S. bombing missions in support of Iraqi forces battling ISIS in Anbar province, Obama indicated that the United States would strike ISIS targets in Syria as necessary. In late August the United States began surveillance flights over Syria, paving the way for U.S.-led coalition airstrikes that began in late September. Among the initial focal points for the aerial attacks was the mainly Kurdish city of Kobanî, near the Turkish border, which was under siege by ISIS. By January 2015 Kurdish fighters had lifted the siege.

Through the early months of 2015, opposition forces made gains throughout the country. Moderate opposition fighters captured Idlib in March, while ISIS seized Palmyra in May. ISIS then began a concerted campaign to destroy ancient monuments in the city. In September Russia intervened militarily first through airstrikes, and then the deployment of a reported 4,000 to 5,000 ground troops. Russian and Iranian support turned the tide against both the moderate opposition and ISIS, as airstrikes were carried out against both groups. Government forces retook Homs from the rebels in December.

In March 2016 Russian-backed government forces recaptured Palmyra. Russia then announced the withdrawal of most of its ground forces, but maintained an airbase at Khmeimim and a naval port at Tartus, and continued airstrikes. In August Turkey deployed ground troops inside Syria in an offensive against both ISIS and Kurdish forces.

In October 2016 UN investigators accused the Assad regime of using chemical weapons on civilians during an attack in Idlib in March 2015, even though the world body had reported in June 2014 that the country's chemical weapons stockpile had been removed or destroyed.

The siege of Aleppo, the last major Syrian city controlled by moderate rebels, produced a new wave of approximately 20,000 to 50,000 internal refugees, as civilians fled advancing government forces in November 2016. By the end of that month government forces were poised to retake the city. Meanwhile, the UN estimated that there were 6 million internally displaced persons in Syria, and almost 5 million external refugees. The majority of Syrian refugees, some 2.7 million, were in Turkey.

POLITICAL PARTIES

Since the 1970s, Syria has been a single-party state. Though theoretically committed to pluralism, the Arab Ba'ath Socialist party has dominated politics since the assent of its most dominant leader, Hafiz al-Assad. However, in July 2011 the country adopted legislation allowing new political parties to form—ostensibly in opposition to the Ba'ath party. Though a dozen new groups have gained official party status, many more have preferred to remain unlicensed. Most true opposition parties and coalitions do not even operate in Syria, while many domestic entities recognized by the Assad regime as legitimate opposition parties are widely believed to be part of a pseudo-opposition fabricated by Assad loyalists. Opposition groups boycotted the June 2014 presidential elections and the April 2016 legislative balloting.

Government Parties:

National Progressive Front—NPF (*al-Jabha al-Wataniyyah at-Taqaddumiyyah*). In 1972 President Hafiz al-Assad formed the NPF, a coalition of parties that has always been heavily dominated by the Syrian Ba'ath. Following the death of Hafiz al-Assad in 2000, the other NPF components joined the Ba'ath in endorsing his son, Bashar, as his presidential successor. Bashar al-Assad was elected that year.

Subsequently, some previously outlawed parties were allowed to join the NPF as long as membership was not based on ethnicity or religion, including the Syrian Social Nationalist Party (below), which had been banned since 1955. Assad was reelected in 2007 for a second seven-year term, and for a third term in June 2014. Minor parties that make up the remainder of the NPF are the **Arab Socialist Union Party**, **Arab Socialist Party**, **Syrian Communist Party**, **Union Socialist Party**, and **Union Socialist Democratic Party**.

Leader: Bashar al-ASSAD (Chair).

Ba'ath Party. The Ba'ath Party enjoyed de facto dominance of the Syrian political system since 1963, its long tenure partly attributable to its influence among the military. Formally known as the **Ba'ath (Renaissance) Arab Socialist Party** (*Hizb al-Ba'ath al-Arabi al-Ishtiraki*), the Ba'ath Party is the Syrian branch of an international political movement that began in 1940. The contemporary party dates from a 1953 merger of the **Arab Resurrectionist Party**, founded in 1947 by Michel Aflak and Salah al-Din Bitar, and the **Syrian Socialist Party**, founded in 1950 by Akram al-Hawrani. The Ba'ath Party philosophy stresses socialist ownership of the principal means of production, redistribution of agricultural land, secular political unity of the Arab world, and opposition to imperialism.

At the Ba'ath Party's 2005 congress, younger members were elected to key committee positions, reflecting efforts by President Bashar al-Assad to give the party a more youthful look. Nevertheless, in terms of policy direction there was little substantive change from the party's core principles. Assad's regime resorted to more repressive measures after the 2005 Congress, leading to a consolidation of power before the 2007 elections. Nevertheless, the party has been challenged by violence and independent politicians calling for democratic change.

As President Assad turned to violent suppression of antigovernment demonstrations in 2011, 230 party members resigned. By 2013, however, some defectors estimated that half of Ba'ath's members were dissatisfied with party leadership and were contemplating resignation. In July the party chose 16 new leaders to replace the existing leadership. One of the deposed leaders was Vice President Farouk al-SHARAA, who was retained as vice president despite losing his position in the party. The speaker of the People's Assembly, Jihad al-LAHAM, and Prime Minister Wael AL-HALAQI were among the new slate of leaders.

Leaders: Bashar al-ASSAD (President of the Republic, Secretary General of the Party, and Chair of the NPF), Jihad al-LAHAM, Wael Nader al-HALAQI.

Syrian Social Nationalist Party—SSNP (*al-Hizb al-Suri al-Qawmi al-Ijtimai*). Formally banned in the 1970s, the SSNP supports creation of "Greater Syria" and has a wing in Lebanon. In 2005 the SSNP was legalized and became the first official non-Arab, non-socialist political grouping. The party secured two seats in the 2007 elections. The party is led by regime stalwart and former minister of national reconciliation Ali HAIDAR. The SSNP and the National Committee for the Unity of Syrian Communists–People's Will Party—PWP (*Hizb Iradat Al-Sha'ab*, below) combined forces to form the **Popular Front for Change and Liberation**—PFCL (*al-Jabha aš-š'abiyya li'l-taghayyir wa'l-taḥrīr*) in 2011. Haidar chose to run for parliament in May 2012 under the banner of the PFCL, and won that seat. The party left the PFCL coalition in 2014 to support Assad's reelection. An estimated 6,000- to 8,000-strong militia from the SSNP has fought alongside government forces in the country's ongoing civil war. Party leader Ali Haidar retained a cabinet post in the July 2016 government.

Leader: Ali HAIDAR.

Opposition Groups:

The Arab Revolutionary Workers' Party (*Hizb Al-'Amal Al-Thawriy Al-'Arabi*). This socialist party has been active in the National Democratic Rally, while still participating in the Damascus Declaration for Democratic National Change (see below). Party leader Maher Abdul-Hafiz HAJJAR was one of three candidates on the ballot for the June 2014 presidential election, though he and candidate Hassan Abdullah al-Nouri only garnered 11 percent of the vote.

Leaders: Maher Abdul-Hafiz HAJJAR (Secretary General), Tariq Abu al-HASSAN (Chair).

The Assyrian Democratic Organization (ADO). The largest Assyrian political organization in Syria, this party counts primarily Christians as members. It was a founding member of the Damascus Declaration, and as a party in exile, the ADO was also a founding member of the SNC in 2011. Party leader Gabriel Moushe GAWRIEH brought the party into the National Coalition for Syrian Revolution and Opposition Forces (NC, below) in December 2012. A year later, Gawrieh was briefly detained by government security officials in the town of Qamishli.

Leader: Gabriel Moushe GAWRIEH (President).

Communist Labor Party (*Hizb Al-'Amal Al-Shuyu'iy*). As a far left opposition party, the Communist Labor Party has been in a plethora of coalitions simultaneously: the National Democratic Assembly, the Marxist Left Assembly, and the National Coordination Body for Democratic Change.

Leader: Fateh JAMOUS (Secretary General).

Democratic Arab Socialist Union (*Al-Ittihad Al-Ishtiraki Al-'Arabi Al-Dimuqratiy*—DASU). Though this party was originally established in 1964, it drifted toward an oppositional role in June 2011, when it helped found the National Coordination Body for Democratic Change. Party leader Hassan Abdul AZIM became the general coordinator for that coalition, yet the DASU officially parted way with the National Coordination Body in 2012.

Leader: Hassan Abdul AZIM (Secretary General).

Democratic Socialist Arab Ba'ath Party (*Hizb Al-Ba'ath Al-Dimuqratiy Al-'Arabi al-Ishtiraki*). A splinter group from the ruling Ba'ath party, this group has been in existence since 1970. In light of the 2011 uprising against President Assad, the party joined the National Coordination Body for Democratic Change.

Syrian Democratic People's Party (*Hizb Al-Sha'ab Al-Dimuqratiy Al-Suri*). This is an opposition party that is a member of both the National Democratic Assembly and the SNC. The party opposed the Damascus Declaration and allied itself loosely with other opposition groups in the banned opposition alliance, the **Democratic National Gathering** (DNG). A leading figure in the party, Georges SABRA, was arrested in June 2011 for the third time in three years and was held by Syrian security services until September 19, 2011. Sabra was the first leader of the SNC.

Leaders: Giath Uyoun al-SOUD (Secretary General), Riad al-TURK (Founder).

Kurdish Democratic Union Party (*Partiya Yekitiya Demokrat*—PYD). A spin-off from the Turkistan Workers' Party outlawed by the Turkish government, this Syrian branch has not been well received by Damascus either. In 2011 the party chose not to join the largest Kurdish opposition block, the Kurdish National Council, instead opting for the smaller grouping in the Kurdish Patriotic Movement. Saleh Muslim MOHAMMED has led this party since 2010 and was reconfirmed as chair in 2012. In November 2013 the PYD announced it had formed a provisional government serving the Kurdish regions in northern Syria.

Leaders: Saleh Muslim MOHAMMED (Chair), Asiyah ABDULLAH (Cochair).

Kurdish Democratic Party in Syria (*Partiya Dimoqrata Kurd Li Suriya*). This party helped found the Kurdish National Council in October 2011 and is closely allied with Kurdish movements outside of Syria—most notably, the Kurdish Democratic Party in Iraq. Observers agree that the Kurdish Democratic Party in Syria is the strongest of Syria's Kurdish parties. Party leader Abdulhakim BASHAR was elected vice president of the National Coalition, representing that group at the Geneva II peace conference in 2014.

Leader: Abdulhakim BASHAR (Secretary General).

Kurdish Future Movement (*Sepela Peseroja Kurd li Suri*). Founded by Mashaal TAMMO in 2005, this group allied in 2011 with the smaller Yekiti and Azadi Kurdish parties to join the SNC. Tammo was assassinated in late 2011, with loyalists blaming either the Syrian government or members of the Kurdish Democratic Union Party for his death. Since Tammo's murder, internal leadership battles have weakened the Movement.

Leaders: Rezan Bahri SHAYKHMUS (Chair), Jangidar MUHAMMAD (Rival Chair).

National Committee for the Unity of Syrian Communists–People's Will Party—PWP (*Hizb Iradat Al-Sha'ab*). This party is a splinter from one branch of the Syrian Communist Party (a member of the ruling NPF) and is led by Qadri JAMIL. In 2011 the party allied with Ali Haidar's branch of the Syrian Social Nationalist Party to form the Popular Front for Change and Liberation, which changed its name to People's Will Party. Though it has not received official status as a party, Jamil decided to take his group into the larger Coalition of Peaceful Change Forces. In June 2012 Jamil was appointed deputy prime minister for economic affairs while the party won two seats in that year's legislative balloting. In the 2014 presidential polling, Maher Adb al-Hafiz HAJJAR claimed to represent the PWP. However, the party disavowed Hajjar, who instead ran as an independent and won 3.2 percent of the vote.

Leader: Qadri JAMIL (Chair).

National Development Party. Licensed by the Syrian government in 2012, observers question whether this secular party calling for a modern, democratic Syria is a true voice of opposition or merely a façade constructed by the Assad regime. Party leader Zaher Saadaldine announced the party's intention to field candidates in the May 2012 parliamentary elections but later joined a boycott against the polling.

Leaders: Zaher SAADALDINE (Founder), Mohammed SAMAAN (Spokesperson).

National Youth for Justice and Development. Though some observers have questioned whether this officially licensed party is a legitimate opposition party, it did run candidates in the 2012 parliamentary elections. However, it denounced the polling as fraudulent and asked the Supreme Constitutional Court to void the results. The party was not invited to take part in 2012's national reconciliation dialogue. Party president Berwyn Ibrahim is the only female political party leader in Syria.

Leader: Berwyn IBRAHIM (Secretary General).

Other newly licensed parties include **Syria the Homeland Party,** led by Ghatfan Hammoud and Majd Niazi; **Together for a Free and Democratic Syria,** represented by Munther Bader Halloum and Munther Khaddam; **National Democratic Solidarity Party,** led by Selim Al-Kharrat; **National Initiative Party; Syrian National Youth Party; Democratic Vanguard; Arab Democratic Solidarity Party; Partisans Party;** and **Democratic Party.**

Reform Party of Syria—RPS (*Hizb al-Islah al-Suri*). The RPS is a U.S.-based opposition party formed in 2001. It is opposes the Ba'ath ideology of the Syrian government. In September 2011 the RPS criticized the administration of U.S. president Barack Obama for holding talks with the Syrian American Council, known supporters of the Muslim Brotherhood in Syria. The RPS suggested that the Obama administration was giving tacit support for the Brotherhood's aspirations to turn Syria into an "Islamic state instead of a democracy."

Leaders: Marc HUSSEIN (Cofounder), Farid GHADRY (Cofounder and Former President).

Muslim Brotherhood (*al-Ikhwan*). Founded in the 1940s, the Brotherhood is a Sunni Islamist movement that took part in parliamentary elections in its early history, winning 10 seats in 1961. The Brotherhood was banned by the Ba'ath Party after the 1963 coup, and since then it has maintained an active underground campaign against the Ba'ath Party and its leadership. It was charged, inter alia, with the massacres in Aleppo and Latakia in 1979 as well as the killing of a number of Soviet technicians and military advisers in 1980. In February 1982 it instigated an open insurrection in Hama that government troops quelled after three weeks of intense fighting that resulted in the devastation of one-fourth of the city and the deaths of more than ten thousand. Brotherhood members were among political prisoners released in 2000 with the advent of the so-called Damascus Spring. At the same time, the Brotherhood remained illegal, membership was punishable by death, and its leadership remained in exile.

Under Ali Sadr al-Din al-BAYANUNI, the Brotherhood intermittently negotiated with the Syrian government, stopped insisting on the right to use violence, no longer called for the introduction of sharia, and claimed to support a democratic system of government. It played a key role in drafting the Damascus Declaration. In 2005 the Brotherhood formed the National Salvation Front with other Syrian opposition members, but broke with the group in 2009.

In 2010 the Brotherhood elected a new secretary general, Riyadh al-SHAQFA, a leading figure in the group's military wing during the 1980s. Analysts believed the vote indicated the party's move toward a more aggressive stance against the Assad regime. In August al-Shaqfa announced that the Brotherhood's "truce" with the Assad regime had ended. In April 2011 the Brotherhood lent its rhetorical support to the antigovernment protestors and called upon all Syrians to unite for freedom. In addition, it helped establish the SNC, and in 2012 Brotherhood members held more than a quarter of the Council seats. In 2013 the Brotherhood started distributing a newspaper, *al-Ahed*, in areas occupied by rebel groups, and it became closely aligned with a coalition of antigovernment militias known as Shields of the Revolution. In early 2014 the Brotherhood launched a new party, **Promise** (*Waad*). Sponsored by Turkey's ruling AKP, *Waad* is an attempt to distance the Brotherhood in Syria from the deposed Egyptian Brotherhood. The new party is led by Mohammad Hikmat WALID and Mohammad Zuhair KHATIB.

Leaders: Mohammad Riyadh al-SHAQFA (Secretary General), Mohammad Farouk TAYFOUR (Deputy Secretary General), Hatem al-TABSHI (Shura Council President).

Islamic Liberation Party—ILP (*Hizb al-Tahrir al-Islami*). The ILP advocates the political and religious union of the entire Arab world. Hundreds of ILP members were reportedly detained by security forces in late 1999 and early 2000 in connection with a crackdown that coincided with fighting between Islamist militants and the Lebanese army in northern Lebanon. The ILP also strongly criticized the resumption of peace talks between Syria and Israel. Many of the ILP detainees were reportedly released in November 2000 under an amnesty issued by president Bashar al-Assad. In 2003 five ILP members were sentenced to prison terms ranging from eight to ten years. In July 2009 the ILP caused a stir in the United States when it held a conference in Chicago on the fall of capitalism and the rise of Islam.

Leader: Mohammad JABER.

Coalitions:

Damascus Declaration for Democratic National Change (DDDNC). Reformers had hoped Bashar al-Assad's pledge to promote greater openness during the Damascus Spring would translate into the formation of new parties. When it became apparent the promise of openness had been abandoned, the Damascus Declaration, signed by members of the opposition in October 2005, called for a nonviolent democratic overhaul of the Syrian government. In December 2007 coalition members met to elect the leadership of the group's National Council. Forty attendees were subsequently arrested, although most were released. In October 2008, 12 activists, including Secretary General Riad SEIF and chair of the National Council Fida al-HAWRANI, were found guilty of "weakening national feeling" and "spreading false news" and sentenced to 30 months in prison. Seif was released and left the Declaration. In 2011 the Declaration's members helped found the SNC (see below). The DDDNC organized a late 2012 meeting in Damascus that featured critics of the Assad regime calling for the president to step down.

Leaders: Samir NASHAR (Secretariat General President), Anas al-ABDEH (Secretariat General Member).

Syrian National Council—SNC (*al-Majlis al-Watani as-Suri*). Operating in exile with headquarters in Turkey, the SNC was one of the largest political groups opposing the Assad regime. However, its leadership has been in constant flux, and critics note its effectiveness has been weakened by internal discord. Several subfactions exist within the SNC, and two of the most important are the Revolutionary Movement—represented by Hozan IBRAHIM—and the Bloc of Liberal Independents—led by former SNC chairman Burhan GHALIOUN. During 2012 both statements issued at the Friends of Syria conference and the actions of heads of state showed that the SNC's legitimacy as a government in exile was highly suspect. Though many SNC members were also members in the National Coalition, the SNC decided against participation in the Geneva II peace talks in 2014.

National Coordination Body for Democratic Change. The goal of this loose coalition of unarmed opposition groups and parties—including the PYD—is to provide the impetus for a new constitution, a democratic electoral system, the release of political prisoners, and—eventually—the prosecution of those responsible for Syria's political violence. However, members of the group decided not to attend the two Friends of Syria conferences held during 2012. The Assad regime has treated members of this coalition as part of the so-called tolerated opposition. However, the regime did not allow the group to publish its plan for a "political solution" to the Syrian crisis in 2014.

Leaders: Hassan Abdul AZIM (Chair), Haytham MANNA (Deputy Chair).

National Bloc. This coalition has featured a fluid and unstable membership list. In June 2012 the Bloc met in Rome and split into two factions: One was christened the Union of Democratic Coordination, and was led by Ahmad Ramadan; the other faction did not name itself but picked Radwan ZIADEH as its leader. An influential female leader, Basma Qodmani, left the Bloc in July 2012.

Leaders: Ahmad RAMADAN, Mutie al-BUTEIN, Tawfik DUNIA.

Kurdish National Council in Syria (KNC). Another coalition operating in exile, this group was founded during late 2011 and is based in Iraq. At its high point in 2012, it attracted 11 Kurdish parties to its ranks, including groups formerly allied with the Kurdish Democratic Front.

Leaders: Abdul-Hakim BASHAR (Chair), Khair al-Dien MURAD (Head of Foreign Relations).

National Coalition for Syrian Revolution and Opposition Forces—The National Coalition (NC). The Syrian Nation Council, facing criticism that its exile status and unstable leadership made it difficult to attract international support, was convinced to join with activists and fighters based inside Syria in the National Coalition for Syrian Revolution and Opposition Forces—an organization cobbled together at a November 2012 conference in Qatar. The new grouping is known as the National Coalition, and in addition to the members of the Syrian National Council, it includes representatives from local coordinating committees, Syrian human rights groups, academics, and citizens' groups. The first leader was Moaz al-KHATIB, a well-known cleric. At the fourth Friends of Syria conference in December 2012, the NC was formally recognized as the legitimate representative of the Syrian people, though non-attendees—notably, Russia and China—did not. The NC went forward with installing a shadow government with a prime minister and a military command, though its effect on governance and the prosecution of the war within Syria was minimal. Its effectiveness was not helped by internecine squabbles, such as when the group elected as shadow Prime Minister Ghassan HITTO, a favorite of the Syrian Muslim Brotherhood, and the Coalition's military command leader, General Salim Idris, refused to recognize him. In 2014 the NC elected Hadi al-BAHRA for a six-month term as president while accepting the resignation of the second vice president, Suhair ATASSI. In March 2016 Anas al-ABDAH was elected president.

Leaders: Anas al-ABDAH (President), Mouaffaq NYRABIA (Vice President).

LEGISLATURE

The **People's Assembly** (*Majlis al-Shaab*) is a directly elected, unicameral body presently consisting of 250 members serving four-year terms. In elections held on April 13, 2016, the NPF (which comprises the Syrian Ba'ath Party and six small parties) won 200 seats, and independents won 50 seats.

Speaker: Hadiyeh Khalaf ABBAS (Ba'ath Party).

CABINET

[as of November 30, 2016]

Prime Minister	Imad Mohammad Deeb Khamis
Deputy Prime Ministers	Gen. Fahd Jassem al-Freij Walid Muallem

Ministers

Administrative Development	Hassan al-Nouri
Agriculture and Agrarian Reform	Ahmad al-Qadri
Communications and Technology	Ali al-Zafir
Culture	Mohamed al-Ahmad
Defense	Gen. Fahd Jassem al-Freij
Economy and Foreign Trade	Adib Mayyaleh
Education	Hazwan al-Waz
Electricity	Mohammad Zuhair Kharboutli
Finance	Maamoun Hamdan
Foreign Affairs and Expatriates	Walid al-Moallem
Health	Nizar Wehbe Yazigi
Higher Education	Atef Naddaf
Industry	Ahmad al-Hamo
Information	Mohamed Ramez Tourjuman
Interior	Lt. Gen. Mohammad Ibrahim al-Shaar
Internal Trade and Consumer Protection	Abdullah al-Gharbi
Justice	Najem Hamad al-Ahmad
Labor and Social Affairs	Rima al-Qadiri [f]
Local Administration	Hussein Makhlouf
Petroleum and Mineral Resources	Ali Ghanem
Presidential Affairs	Mansour Fadlallah Azzam
Public Works	Hussein Arnous
Religious Trusts	Mohammad Abdelsattar al-Sayed
Tourism	Bishr Riyad al-Yazigi
Transport	Ali Hamoud
Water Resources and Irrigation	Nabil al-Hasan

Ministers of State

National Reconciliation	Ali Haidar (SSNP)
Without Portfolio	Abdullah Abdullah Wafiqa Hosni [f] Rafea abu Saad Salwa Abdullah [f]

[f] = female

Note: Unless noted, members of the cabinet belong to the Ba'ath Party.

INTERGOVERNMENTAL REPRESENTATION

Ambassador to the U.S.: (Vacant).

U.S. Special Envoy to Syria (located in Istanbul, Turkey): Michael RATNEY.

Permanent Representative to the UN: Bashar JA'AFARI.

IGO Memberships (Non-UN): NAM, OIC, LAS.

For Further Reference:

Glass, Charles. *Syria Burning: A Short History of a Catastrophe.* London: Verso Books, 2016.

McHugo, John. *Syria: A Recent History.* London: Saqi Books, 2014.

Phillips, Christopher. *The Battle for Syria: International Rivalry in the New Middle East.* New Haven, CT: Yale University Press, 2016.

TAJIKISTAN

Republic of Tajikistan
Jumhurii Tojikiston

Political Status: Designated autonomous republic within the Uzbek Soviet Socialist Republic on October 27, 1924; became constituent republic of the Union of Soviet Socialist Republics (USSR) on October 16, 1929; declared independence as Republic of Tajikistan on September 9, 1991; current constitution adopted by referendum on November 6, 1994.

Area: 55,250 sq. mi. (143,100 sq. km).

Population: 8,670,000 (2016E—UN); 8,330,946 (2016E—U.S. Census).

Major Urban Centers (2015E—UN): DUSHANBE (822,000), Khujand (172,700).

Official Language: Tajik. Although the 1994 constitution accords Russian the status of a language of interethnic communication, a law passed in October 2009 requires all official government communication to be conducted in Tajik and states that all citizens should have a working knowledge of the language. Use of other languages in daily communication has not, however, been proscribed.

Monetary Unit: Somoni (official rate October 1, 2016: 7.87 somoni = $1US).

President: Emomali RAHMON (Imomali RAKHMONOV; People's Democratic Party of Tajikistan); designated by the Supreme Soviet on November 19, 1992, upon the resignation of Akbarsho ISKANDAROV (Islamic Renaissance Party); reelected by popular vote on November 6, 1994, and inaugurated for a five-year term on November 16; reelected for a seven-year term on November 6, 1999; reelected on November 6, 2006; reelected on November 6, 2013.

Prime Minister: Kohir RASULZODA (People's Democratic Party of Tajikistan); appointed by the president on November 25, 2013, to succeed Oqil OQILOV (Akil AKILOV, originally identified with Communist Party of Tajikistan), who was dismissed along with the cabinet on November 18, 2013, following presidential elections on November 6.

THE COUNTRY

Mountainous Tajikistan is bordered by Kyrgyzstan on the north, China on the east, Afghanistan on the south, and Uzbekistan on the west. Approximately 80 percent of the population is Tajik, 15 percent Uzbek, and only 1 percent Russian, as a consequence of a significant exodus of minorities in the 1990s. The dominant religion is Sunni Islam. Women make up about 44 percent of the active labor force, as well as 19 percent of the lower house and 14.7 percent of the upper house in parliament.

Although less than 10 percent of Tajikistan is arable, ample water supplies have helped make its farmland very productive, the leading crops being cotton, grains, vegetables, and fruits. The agricultural sector as a whole employs half of the workforce, and accounts for 21.4 percent of gross domestic product (GDP). The industrial sector employs 12.8 percent of the active labor force but contributed 21.7 percent of GDP in 2011. Fueled by the country's extensive hydroelectric capacity, industry remains concentrated in such energy-intensive ventures as ore extraction and refining. Aluminum, by far the most important industrial product, is the leading national export, followed by hydroelectricity and cotton. Other mineral resources include gold, silver, and uranium. Leading manufactures include clothing and textiles, processed foods, and carpets. Turkey is the country's largest export partner at 30.5 percent, and China is the largest import partner at 42.3 percent of total.

Tajikistan was severely impacted by the 2009 international financial crisis with a GDP growth rate of 7.9 percent in 2008, falling to 3.9 percent in 2009. A key factor in the slower growth rate was a drop in remittances from the millions of Tajiks working abroad, mainly in Russia. (Remittances typically amount to 30–40 percent of GDP.) Lower export earnings for cotton and aluminum also contributed to the slower expansion. The country recovered by 2010 with a GDP growth rate of 6.5 percent. In 2012 GDP grew by 7.5 percent, while it increased by 7.4 percent the next year. In 2013 inflation was 5 percent. GDP expanded by 6.7 percent in 2014, and 3 percent in 2015 and 2016. Inflation in 2016 was 9.2 percent. GDP per capita was $721 in 2016. For 2016 the World Bank ranked Tajikistan 132nd out of 189 countries in its annual ease of doing business index, a rise from 143rd in 2014.

GOVERNMENT AND POLITICS

Political background. Most of the Tajik lands were conquered by Russia in the 1880s and 1890s. Popular uprisings in the wake of the 1917 Bolshevik Revolution were not completely suppressed until 1921. In 1924 the region was made an autonomous republic within the Uzbek Soviet Socialist Republic and in 1929 a constituent republic of the USSR.

On February 11, 1990, rioting erupted in Dushanbe when demonstrators, initially responding to reports that Armenian refugees were to be settled there, began calling for democratic reforms. A resultant state of emergency led to the suppression of the demonstrations, in part by Soviet soldiers. On August 25, with nationalism on the rise, a sovereignty declaration was issued asserting the precedence of the republic's constitution and laws over those of the USSR, and on November 30 the republic's legislature, the Supreme Soviet, voted to replace its chair with a president as head of state.

On August 25, 1991, in the wake of the failed Moscow coup against USSR president Mikhail Gorbachev, the Supreme Soviet ordered the nationalization of the assets of the Communist Party of the Soviet Union (CPSU) within the republic. On August 29 the Communist Party of Tajikistan (CPT) voted to withdraw from the CPSU, while the words "Soviet Socialist" were dropped from the republic's name. At the same time, anticommunist opposition groups, principally the Islamic Renaissance Party (IRP), the secular and pro-Western Democratic Party of Tajikistan (DPT), and the nationalist *Rastokhez* (Rebirth) movement, continued to organize demonstrations against the government.

On September 1, 1991, after losing a nonconfidence vote, the CPT's Qahhor MAHKAMOV (Kakhar MAKHKAMOV) resigned the presidency in favor of the Supreme Soviet chair, Kadreddin ASLONOV. On September 9 the legislature declared the independence of the Republic of Tajikistan, and on September 22 Acting President Aslonov issued a decree banning all CPT activities, despite the fact that the party had redesignated itself as the Tajik Socialist Party (TSP) the day before. On September 23 the ban was reversed and Aslonov resigned, being succeeded by former CPT first secretary Rakhman NABIYEV.

Nabiyev immediately imposed a state of emergency, but he lifted it on October 2, 1991. Opposition demonstrations continued, and on October 6 Nabiyev submitted his resignation, ostensibly to permit all candidates an opportunity to campaign on equal footing for a presidential election. On November 24, despite his reputation as a hard-line conservative, Nabiyev drew a 58 percent vote share in a field of seven candidates. Significantly, his closest competitor, Davlat KHUDONAZAROV of the DPT, received backing from the IRP, thus sealing an Islamic-prodemocracy opposition alliance that was to become a crucial factor in the unfolding civil conflict, which was based more on ethnic and regional differences than on ideology. In January 1992 Nabiyev named Akbar MIRZOYEV prime minister.

In March 1992 Maksud IKRAMOV, a prominent DPT member and chair of the Executive Committee (mayor) of Dushanbe, was arrested and charged with bribery. Coupled with an earlier dismissal of a minister from the Gorno-Badakhshan Autonomous Region, the action triggered widespread antiregime protests. Led by the IRP, the DPT, *Rastokhez,* and *Lali Badakhshan* (Badakhshan Ruby Movement, a nationalist formation organized by the Pamiri ethnic group of Gorno-Badakhshan), the demonstrators called for dissolution of the Supreme Soviet and the adoption of a new constitution. In late April, with the unrest continuing and the local army commander having indicated that his troops would not intervene, President Nabiyev organized a series of progovernment rallies in the capital, many of the demonstrators being communists from the southern Kulyab and northern Leninabad regions. In addition, Nabiyev secured legislative approval for a six-month period of direct presidential rule, including a suspension of civil liberties.

On April 22, 1992, the hard-line Safarali KENJAYEV resigned as chair of the Supreme Soviet. His reinstatement on May 3 triggered a fresh wave of protests, including a demonstration by upward of 100,000 persons on May 5. On May 10 security forces killed a reported 20 individuals gathered in front of the National Security Committee headquarters, where negotiations were taking place between government and opposition representatives. The next day, following intervention by the Muslim spiritual leader Kazi Ali Akbar TURAJONZODA of the IRP, Vice President Narzullo DUSTOV and a number of other hard-line officials resigned, and agreement was reached on a power-sharing arrangement whereby the opposition DPT and IRP would be awarded 8 of 24 cabinet posts. It was also agreed that an interim representative Assembly (*Majlis*) would be established, pending multiparty election of a permanent successor. However, the local soviets in Leninabad and Kulyab refused to accept the accord. Fighting between supporters and opponents of the agreement broke out in Kulyab and soon spread to the adjacent region of Kurgan-Tyube, where in August clashes between progovernment Kulyabi militiamen and Islamic-prodemocracy oppositionists reportedly cost hundreds of lives.

On August 30, 1992, Prime Minister Mirzoyev resigned and was succeeded on an interim basis by his deputy, Jamshed KARIMOV, while on September 7 President Nabiyev was forced to resign by opposition elements that had seized him during a melee in the Dushanbe airport. On September 24 Nabiyev's acting successor, Supreme Soviet chair Akbarsho ISKANDAROV, named Abdumalik ABDULLOJONOV to replace Karimov as the acting head of a coalition administration. Nevertheless, the conflict continued to intensify, with the new government losing effective control of Kulyab and Kurgan-Tyube to Nabiyev supporters led by Sangak SAFAROV. In early October former Supreme Soviet chair Kenjayev, who had organized a pro-Nabiyev Popular Front, tried to seize control of the capital from Islamic-prodemocracy forces. On November 19 Supreme Soviet chair Iskandarov stepped down in favor of Emomali RAHMON, leader of the pro-Nabiyev forces in Kulyab. Concurrent with Iskandarov's departure, the presidential system was abolished in favor of a parliamentary system, with the chair of the legislature again serving as head of state. Prime Minister Abdullojonov remained in office, but the cabinet was stripped of opposition appointees. On December 10, after a two-month blockade of the capital led by Kenjayev's militias, troops loyal to the successor government regained control of Dushanbe from Islamic-prodemocracy forces, most of which were eventually driven into the Afghan border region.

On April 3, 1993, the DPT's Maksud Ikramov was for the second time dismissed as mayor of Dushanbe, after having been reinstated to the position in late 1992. On April 11 former president Nabiyev died of an apparent heart attack, and on April 27 the Russian Supreme Soviet voted to send a peacekeeping force to Tajikistan to join contingents from Kazakhstan, Kyrgyzstan, and Uzbekistan that had been dispatched by the Commonwealth of Independent States (CIS). Two months later, on June 21, the Supreme Court banned the four leading opposition groups—the IRP, DPT, *Rastokhez,* and *Lali Badakhshan*—for engaging in assassination, kidnapping, and rebellion. By that time, the government had regained control over most of the country, and many opposition leaders, including the IRP's Turajonzoda, had gone into exile. The conflict nonetheless continued in the border region, with the Islamic forces reportedly receiving support from Afghan guerrillas.

Prime Minister Abdullojonov resigned in December 1993, at least in part because of the country's economic decline, and was succeeded by his deputy, Abdujalil SAMADOV. Subsequently, peace talks with opposition leaders were initiated in Moscow, despite the assassination in March 1994 of Deputy Prime Minister Mayonsho NAZARSHOYEV, who had been named to head the government delegation. The talks yielded an agreement to cooperate on aid to refugees and to seek national reconciliation through "political measures alone," but clashes continued to occur in areas along the Afghan frontier. Further UN-sponsored talks in Tehran, Iran, resulted in the signature of a cease-fire accord in September, seemingly without the government making any major concessions to the opposition. The cease-fire did little to reduce hostilities, however, with another deputy prime minister, Munavvarsho NASIRYEV, being killed by a land mine on the day of its notional implementation, October 20. Meanwhile, in July the Supreme Soviet had approved a draft constitution that was to be submitted to a popular referendum in conjunction with the first direct election of a state president, who would have expanded executive powers under the new constitution.

Held on November 6, 1994, the constitutional referendum and presidential election were boycotted by the Islamic opposition and the DPT, although some secular opposition parties backed the candidacy of former prime minister Abdullojonov. According to the official results, over 90 percent of the voters endorsed the constitution. In the presidential election the incumbent, Rahmon, received 58 percent of the votes cast, against some 35 percent for Abdullojonov, who complained of vote-rigging. On December 2, having been nominated by the president and endorsed by the legislature, Jamshed Karimov returned as prime minister to preside over a government that continued to be dominated by current or former communists.

Elections to the new 181-member Supreme Assembly, held in February–March 1995, were boycotted by most of the opposition parties, Islamic and secular. A majority of the winning candidates had no overt party allegiance, although about a third were declared communists.

Despite the presence since December 1994 of a small UN observer mission charged with monitoring the supposed cease-fire, fighting continued unabated between government and opposition forces. In a major flare-up in Gorno-Badakhshan in April 1995, hundreds died as government and CIS forces advanced on units of the Afghanistan-based IRP armed wing operating in alliance with Badakhshan separatists. By mid-year some 25,000 CIS peacekeeping troops were deployed in Tajikistan, the majority of them Russian.

Further peace talks took place in Kabul, Afghanistan, in May 1995 between President Rahmon and the IRP leader, Sayed Abdullo NURI, but no substantive progress was made on the opposition's demand for the legalization of all political parties, press freedom, release of political prisoners, amnesty for rebel leaders, and full autonomy for Gorno-Badakhshan. In June–July 1995 the government succeeded in bringing about a split in the DPT, with one faction accepting official registration and the other remaining in full opposition. During the latter part of 1995, notwithstanding an extension of the notional cease-fire, the civil war continued in the south and along the Afghan border.

An escalation of the conflict at the beginning of 1996 impelled President Rahmon to carry out a government reorganization in early February, with Karimov being replaced as prime minister by Yakhyo AZIMOV and with Mahmadsaid UBAIDULLOEV being dismissed as first deputy prime minister. The changes were reportedly made in response to demands by two rebel military leaders who had occupied the southern and western towns of Kurgan-Tyube and Tursunzade; troops loyal to one of the rebels, Col. Makhmud KHUDOBERDIYEV, an ethnic Uzbek from Leninabad, had briefly threatened the capital. Thereafter, fighting intensified in the central Garm and Tavil Dara areas.

The fall of Kabul to Taliban forces in September 1996 provided a spur to further peace efforts, and new negotiations between the government and the opposition were launched in October. At a meeting in Afghanistan on December 10–11, President Rahmon and the IRP's

Nuri agreed to another cease-fire and to open formal peace talks in Moscow later in the month. Despite violations, the cease-fire appeared to contain the fighting, and on December 23 Rahmon and Nuri signed accords in the Russian capital providing for the establishment of a transitional National Reconciliation Commission (NRC), to be headed by a representative of the IRP-led United Tajik Opposition (UTO). The NRC would assume responsibility for overseeing reform of electoral laws and the reintegration of the opposition into normal life. Under the accords, opposition representatives were to be introduced into the structures of executive power, including central and local government and law enforcement agencies, in proportion to the representation of the parties on the NRC, taking regional balance into account. The commission would cease its work after the convocation of a new parliament and the formation of its ruling bodies.

Early in 1997 the secular National Revival movement, which had been organized in July 1996 by former prime ministers Abdullojonov, Karimov, and Samadov, staged protests against its exclusion from the peace process. At the same time, further negotiations between the government and the UTO were being overshadowed by kidnappings and battles among warlords and rogue military officers, most prominently Colonel Khudoberdiyev, who for a time controlled much of southern Tajikistan and again threatened the capital before being repulsed by government troops. Nevertheless, the cease-fire between the UTO and the government, which controlled little more than the capital region, continued to hold. When an assassination attempt on the life of President Rahmon failed in April, the UTO joined world capitals in condemning the attack.

On June 27, 1997, Rahmon and UTO leader Nuri signed a peace agreement in Moscow, officially ending the five-year civil war. The agreement provided for the eventual legalization of the UTO parties, the return of refugees and Afghan-based opposition forces, the integration of the latter within the regular army, and the granting to the UTO of 30 percent of government posts. The signatories also agreed that the NRC would have 26 members, 13 from the government and 13 from the UTO. Implementation of the peace was by no means assured, however, and in January 1998 the UTO briefly quit the NRC, citing government delays in meeting the terms of the agreement. Under pressure from the UTO, President Rahmon named five UTO members to his cabinet in February. In March he added as deputy prime minister the UTO's recently repatriated Ali Akbar Turajonzoda, who, however, failed to win formal parliamentary approval until November even though the position, which had previously carried supervisory responsibilities involving the economy, defense, and the interior, had been redefined to cover only economic and trade relations with CIS countries.

Sporadic fighting continued to break out throughout 1998. The combatants included troops loyal to the government, renegade field commands, UTO contingents (sometimes against each other), and unaffiliated militias. The most serious incident occurred in the northern city of Khujand (formerly Leninabad) on November 4–7, when forces under Colonel Khudoberdiyev staged a rebellion that claimed an estimated 300 lives and injured another 650 before being put down. Among those implicated in the rebellion were former prime minister Abdullojonov; his brother, Abdughani ABDULLOJONOV, who had previously served as mayor of Khujand; and a former vice president, Narzullo Dustov.

In the second half of 1999, progress accelerated toward fulfilling the terms of the 1997 peace accords. In June Nuri and President Rahmon had agreed to emphasize constitutional reform while continuing to decommission UTO forces, to integrate UTO troops into national military and security units, and to pursue the 30 percent target for UTO staffing of government positions. In early August Nuri announced that the military goals had been accomplished, which, under the terms of the June agreement, led the Supreme Court on August 12 to reinstate the four political groups that had been banned in 1993. In September 71.8 percent of those voting in a national referendum approved constitutional amendments that affected more than two dozen articles, included provisions permitting sectarian political parties, creating a bicameral parliament, and lengthening the presidential term to seven years. With the notable exception of President Rahmon's People's Democratic Party of Tajikistan (PDPT) and the IRP, most political parties had campaigned against the revisions, arguing that they would increase the current president's authority over legislation, regional administration, and the courts, and that the new upper house would slow down legislation and exacerbate regional tensions.

In October 1999 the UTO suspended its participation in the NRC and announced that it would boycott the November 6 presidential election, primarily because the Central Commission for Elections and Referendums had disqualified opposition candidates (technically, for having failed to obtain sufficient signatures to get their names on the ballot). Hours before the voting began, the UTO canceled the boycott, Nuri having received assurances from Rahmon regarding the conduct of upcoming parliamentary elections. With Rahmon's only opponent on the ballot, Davlat USMON of the IRP, having denounced the presidential contest as a sham, Rahmon secured 97 percent of the vote, and on November 16 he took the oath of office for another term. On November 23 Yakhyo Azimov and his cabinet resigned, as constitutionally mandated. The president named Oqil OQILOV (Akil AKILOV) as the new prime minister on December 20 and continued to make cabinet changes well into the new year.

With several of the smaller opposition parties having been declared ineligible, an election for the new lower house, the Assembly of Representatives, took place in February–March 2000. Amid accusations of campaign and voting irregularities, the PDPT and supporting parties captured more than two-thirds of the 63 seats. The Communists won only 13, and the IRP, 2. On March 23 indirect elections were held for the majority of the seats in the new upper house, the National Assembly, which was also expected to support President Rahmon's agenda.

In the next four years, amid numerous ministerial changes, President Rahmon consolidated his power, in part through passage in June 2003 of a referendum that removed a constitutional proscription against his seeking reelection in 2006. Similarly, the dominance of the PDPT was confirmed by the legislative elections of February–March 2005, which saw the opposition win only two seats in the National Assembly and six in the Assembly of Representatives. The Organization for Security and Cooperation in Europe (OSCE) described the elections as seriously flawed.

On November 6, 2006, President Rahmon won reelection with 79 percent of the vote against token opponents in a contest that was again criticized by objective international observers, as was the lower house election held on February 28, 2010 (with reballoting for one undecided seat occurring on March 14). Once again, the PDPT won overwhelmingly, taking 54 seats, while two government-supportive parties added another 4. The CPT and the IRP, with 2 seats each, were the only successful opposition parties. A minor cabinet reshuffle was undertaken on March 10, 2010. Another minor cabinet reorganization took place on January 4, 2012.

With the main opposition parties boycotting the November 6, 2013, presidential election, President Rahmon carried 83.6 percent of the vote, winning a constitutionally limited fourth seven-year term. He dismissed the prime minister and cabinet on November 18. Kohir Rasulzoda was appointed prime minister on November 25, while a largely new cabinet was sworn in on November 30.

On March 1, 2015, elections were held for the Assembly of Representatives. The PDPT continued its electoral dominance, winning 51 seats. The balloting was criticized by opposition groups and international observers from the OSCE, who claimed that the "election campaign took place in a controlled environment, amid arrests of opposition politicians, candidates, and election officials."

In December 2015 Rahmon was granted the title "Leader of the Nation" by the legislature and granted additional powers, as well as broad immunity. A May 2016 constitutional referendum removed presidential term limits, lowered the minimum age to run for the presidency (see Political Parties, below), and banned faith-based political parties. The referendum was passed with 96.6 percent of the vote, although observers from the OSCE were not allowed to monitor the voting.

Constitution and government. The last of the ex-Soviet Central Asian republics to do so, Tajikistan adopted a post-Soviet constitution by referendum on November 6, 1994. It defines Tajikistan as a democratic, secular, and unitary state, and the people as the sole source of state power. Amendments approved by referendum in September 1999 included a provision permitting formation of sectarian political parties. In all, the referendum authorized changes to 27 articles of the basic law. Another referendum, passed on June 22, 2003, made 56 mostly minor changes (which voters had to accept or reject as a single package), with the most controversial provision being removal of a one-term limit for the presidency.

The 1999 revisions also replaced the unicameral legislature with a bicameral Supreme Assembly encompassing a National Assembly of indirectly elected and appointed members (plus former presidents of the republic) and an Assembly of Representatives, the latter directly elected from a combination of single-seat districts and national party lists. Parliamentarians serve five-year terms. The powers of the

National Assembly, which must meet at least twice a year, include redefining territorial divisions and considering laws proposed by the lower house. The Assembly of Representatives, meeting in continuous session, is authorized to independently adopt the state budget and can override an upper house rejection of legislation with a two-thirds vote. The Supreme Assembly can override presidential vetoes of legislation with a two-thirds vote. Passage of constitutional amendments requires a two-thirds vote of both bodies and a three-fourths vote in the event of a presidential veto.

The president, described as the head of the executive branch and commander in chief, is now directly elected for a seven-year term, with no limits on the number of terms. His powers include appointing the prime minister and other ministers, as well as judges and other senior state and regional administrators, subject to legislative endorsement. He can also initiate referendums. The system of judicial authority is headed by a Constitutional Court and includes a Supreme Court, a Supreme Economic Court, and a Military Court.

Administratively, Tajikistan currently comprises the capital city of Dushanbe, the centrally administered Region of Republican Subordination (Nohiyahoi Tobei Jumhurii, formerly Karotegin), and three other regions (*viloyatho*): in the north, Sughd (formerly Leninabad); in the southwest, Khatlon, established in 1992 by the merger of the Kulyab (Kŭlob) and Kurgan-Tyube (Qŭrghonteppa) regions; and in the east, the Gorno-Badakhshan Autonomous Region (Badakhshoni Kŭhí Viloyati Avtonomii), which the 1994 constitution specifically defines as "an integral and indivisible part of Tajikistan." Regions, districts, and towns elect local assemblies that are chaired by presidential appointees, subject to the approval of the respective assemblies.

Press freedom is constrained in Tajikistan. The government controls most of the press and broadcast media. In 2016 Reporters Without Borders ranked the country 150th, down from 115th in 2014, out of 180 countries as the government increased media repression ahead of elections in 2015.

Foreign relations. On December 21, 1991, Tajikistan became a charter member of the post-Soviet CIS. By early 1992 it had established diplomatic relations with a number of foreign countries, including the United States, and had been admitted to the Conference on (later Organization for) Security and Cooperation in Europe (CSCE/OSCE). It joined the United Nations in March 1992, the IMF in April 1993, and the World Bank in June 1993. As a predominantly Muslim country, Tajikistan also became a member of the Organization of the Islamic Conference. In February 2002 it formally joined NATO's Partnership for Peace program.

In March 1998 Tajikistan was admitted as a candidate member to the Central Asian Economic Union—renamed the Central Asian Economic Community in July 1998 and then the Central Asian Cooperation Organization (CACO) in February 2002—which had been established four years earlier by Kazakhstan, Kyrgyzstan, and Uzbekistan. In April 1998 a Tajik application to join Russia, Belarus, Kazakhstan, and Kyrgyzstan in the CIS Customs Union was approved, and formal entry occurred in February 1999. In 2005 the CACO merged into the Eurasian Economic Community (Belarus, Kazakhstan, Kyrgyzstan, Russia, Tajikistan, and Uzbekistan).

Relations with Moscow have remained close since independence. From 1993 until the mission's end in September 2000, Russia provided the bulk of troops for the CIS peacekeeping operation, which also included contingents from Kazakhstan, Kyrgyzstan, and Uzbekistan. Primarily to deter infiltration across the Afghan and Kyrgyz borders by such extremist groups as the Islamic Movement of Uzbekistan (IMU), Russian troops remain in Tajikistan. In June 2004, after lengthy negotiations, the Rahmon government granted Russia permission to establish a permanent military base for its troops and also agreed to permit unlimited Russian use of the Soviet-built space surveillance center in Nurek, one of the world's most sophisticated facilities for tracking satellites. In return, Russia reportedly agreed to forgo some $300 million in debt payments, to be offset by partial ownership of a hydroelectric power facility.

Postindependence relations between Tajikistan and Uzbekistan have been complicated by persecution of ethnic Tajiks in Uzbekistan and by nationalist resentment in Tajikistan over the prominence of ethnic Uzbeks in the state hierarchy. Although not espoused by the government, territorial claims by Tajik nationalists on Uzbek cities, including Samarkand and Bukhara, have also caused strains. In late 1998 President Rahmon accused the Uzbek government of complicity in the failed November revolt in Khujand. Captured rebels later claimed that members of the Uzbek special forces had helped train them, but Uzbek president Islam Karimov denied any involvement and subsequently accused Tajik officials of drug-trafficking.

Despite such tempestuous exchanges, in January 1999 Tajik prime minister Azimov met with President Karimov in Tashkent to discuss trade and economic cooperation. (Tajikistan remains dependent on Uzbekistan for almost all overland traffic.) Three months later the presidents of both countries joined their counterparts from Kazakhstan and Kyrgyzstan in signing a mutual security agreement intended to combat terrorism, Islamic extremism, and related threats. In June 2000 Tajikistan and Uzbekistan reached agreement on a protocol for delimiting their common border and signed a treaty of friendship.

Beginning in 1994 Tajikistan met regularly with the other members of the so-called Shanghai Five—China, Kazakhstan, Kyrgyzstan, and Russia—which focused their attention primarily on matters of regional stability and security. In 2001 Uzbekistan joined the grouping, which renamed itself the Shanghai Cooperation Organization (SCO); a formal SCO charter was signed in 2002 and a Secretariat was inaugurated in January 2004. Islamic militancy in Afghanistan and elsewhere in the region has been of particular concern.

Even before the October 2001 launch of U.S.-led strikes against al-Qaida and Afghanistan's Taliban regime, Tajikistan aided the anti-Taliban Northern Alliance, which was dominated by ethnic Tajiks. Special forces from the Ministry of the Interior were subsequently reported to be directly assisting the Northern Alliance in its march toward Kabul, and Tajikistan permitted several of its air bases to be used by the United States and its allies in the campaign. In January 2002, apparently rewarding the Rahmon government for its cooperation, the United States lifted a 1993 restriction on the transfer of military equipment to Tajikistan.

In December 2003 Tajikistan joined China, Iran, Pakistan, Turkmenistan, and Uzbekistan in pledging to respect post-Taliban Afghanistan's sovereignty and to remain aloof from its internal affairs. In August 2007 President Rahmon and his Afghan counterpart, Hamid Karzai, inaugurated a bridge over the Pyranzh River. In July 2009 the presidents of Russia and Tajikistan attended the launching of Sangutdin-1 Hydropower Plant in Tajikistan, a joint venture in which Russia is the main shareholder.

Meanwhile Uzbekistan significantly reduced natural gas exports to Kyrgyzstan and Tajikistan in mid-June 2009 as the two countries fell into arrears on their energy payments, and in November Uzbekistan announced it intended to withdraw from the regional electrical grid because of differences over transit tariffs with Tajikistan, which imports electricity from Turkmenistan via Uzbekistan. Tajikistan responded by threatening to withhold water, which it claimed, would be needed to generate additional domestic hydroelectricity. Uzbekistan proceeded to stop transit of rail freight except for a two-week period in May 2010, when relief supplies were needed to overcome severe flooding in the south.

In July 2011 the United States announced that it would construct a $10 million center to train Tajik security forces and counternarcotics officials. Tajikistan and China pledged greater bilateral cooperation on border security in August. In September Russia limited fuel exports to Tajikistan after Rahmon refused a request to allow additional Russian troops to be deployed along the Afghan–Tajik border. In November tension further increased when Russia deported 300 ethnic Tajiks. Meanwhile, Tajikistan agreed to accept a Russian proposal for a free trade area with the other CIS states in October. Also in October, Tajikistan and Belarus finalized a series of bilateral economic cooperation agreements.

In October 2012 Tajikistan granted a 30-year extension on the lease of Russian bases. Also in April, Uzbekistan suspended gas shipments to Tajikistan in a dispute over the Tajik construction of a hydroelectric plant that Uzbek officials claimed would cut water supplies to that country. Shipments resumed after two weeks under a short-term contract.

In January 2013 Tajikistan and Kyrgyzstan announced the delineation of 567 km of their 970 km joint border with plans to complete demarcation by the end of the year. In March Tajikistan was accepted as a full member of the World Trade Organization. In April the World Bank announced a $14.85 million grant to support agriculture in Tajikistan. In October Tajikistan and Afghanistan signed agreements to cooperate on strengthening their economic ties and land mine removal.

On January 11, 2014, Tajik and Kyrgyz border guards fired on each other. Both countries deployed additional troops to the region but withdrew the forces after negotiations on January 28. The governments of Tajikistan and Belarus signed ten agreements in May designed to foster cooperation on cultural issues, ranging from their respective Olympic teams to university research. In June Tajikistan and Pakistan finalized an agreement for the former to export 1,000 megawatts of electricity to the latter. The arrangement was part of a larger $1.6 billion project funded by the World Bank and the Islamic Development Bank, through which Tajikistan would also provide 300 megawatts of electricity to Afghanistan. The government announced in October that China had pledged to invest $6 billion in the country over a three-year period.

Current issues. During 2009 and 2010 government forces continued to face militant opposition from two sources in the east: the IMU and former UTO commanders who oppose the Rahmon regime. In August 2009 a three-month campaign against IMU-linked militants concluded. Among those killed in the operation in the Tavil Dara Valley were Nemat AZIZOV and Mirzo ZIYOYEV, the latter a former minister of emergency situations and civil defense as well as a former UTO field commander. According to some reports, Ziyoyev had been facilitating the movement of IMU militants back and forth across the Afghan border, but some observers saw him as an assassination target because of his connections to other Rahmon opponents.

In September 2010 an ambush in the Rasht Valley killed 28 Tajik soldiers, part of a contingent that had been dispatched to the region following an August prison break by 25 inmates from a national security facility. All 25 had been convicted of links to the IMU, but the ambush was apparently engineered by opposition commanders, whose numbers include Sokh ISKANDAROV, Loudon DAVLAT, Abdullo RAHIMOV (aka Mullo Abdullo). A fourth commander, Mirzokhudzha AKHMADOV, reportedly surrendered in mid-October in return for amnesty.

On April 15, 2011, the insurgent leader Mullo Abdullo and 16 fighters were killed by Tajik security forces during a government offensive in the Rasht Valley. In August parliament approved legislation that placed significant restrictions on religious freedom, including a ban on youth under the age of 18 attending mosques. On August 2 First Deputy Prime Minister Asadullo GHULOMOV died in office; he was replaced by Matlubkhon DAVLATOV on January 4, 2012.

In May 2012 the government stopped exports of coal as part of a program to increase domestic use of the fuel. In July, following the assassination of a security official in Gorno-Badakhshan, Tajik security forces launched an offensive against a rebel group led by former warlord Tolib AYOMBEKOV. Twelve government troops and 30 insurgents were killed in the fighting.

In May 2013 following the launch of the New Tajikistan Party, party leader Zaid SAIDOV was arrested. Saidov was subsequently convicted of a variety of crimes in September and sentenced to 20 years in prison in what opposition groups described as a politically motivated conviction. In November three earthquakes struck, destroying more than 100 homes and damaging more than 250 others. The earthquakes ranged from 4.0 to 6.2 on the Richter scale.

In November 2013 President Rahmon solidified his presidency with a fourth seven-year term, winning 83.6 percent of the electorate. The election was widely seen as corrupt by the international community with the U.S. Department of State citing "a lack of pluralism and genuine choice." The president appointed Kohir Rasulzoda (PDPT) as prime minister on November 25 and named a replacement for Sherali KHAYRULLOYEV, who had been defense minister for 18 years.

Economic sanctions on Russia led to a 20 percent decline in remittances from Tajik workers in that country in 2014 and 2015.

Attacks on government buildings in Dushanbe on September 4–5, 2015, were blamed on an alleged coup attempt led by Abduhalim NAZARZODA, a deputy defense minister. The fighting in the capital killed 26, while Nazarzoda and 10 supporters were killed on September 16 by government forces outside of Dushanbe. The government subsequently accused the IRP of supporting the attacks, and arrested 13 members of the party (see Political Parties, below).

POLITICAL PARTIES

For most of the first decade after independence, political parties did not play a significant role in governance, although the Communist Party of Tajikistan (CPT) continued to be influential in the Supreme Assembly, and, as the 1990s drew to a close, President Rahmon's People's Democratic Party of Tajikistan (PDPT) became increasingly important.

In the wake of the June 1997 peace agreement that ended the civil war, Tajik politics was dominated by efforts to reintegrate the United Tajik Opposition (UTO) into government and the military. Established in Afghanistan in 1993 as the Islamic Revival Movement and renamed in 1996, the UTO included most opposition paramilitary organizations and four groups banned in 1993: the Islamic Rebirth Party (IRP), whose chair, Sayed Abdullo Nuri, served as principal negotiator in peace talks with the government; the Democratic Party of Tajikistan (the so-called Almaty wing of the DPT, following a party rupture in 1995); and two social organizations, the *Lali Badakhshan* and the *Rastokhez* movements. The *Lali Badakhshan,* led by Atobek AMIRBEK, had been formed in the late 1980s as a nationalist movement of the Pamiri people, who belong to the Ismaili Muslim sect and who demanded full autonomy for Gorno-Badakhshan. *Rastokhez* (Rebirth Movement) had been founded in 1990 as a nationalist/religious organization advocating the revival of Tajik culture and traditions. As a result of the 1996–1997 accords, the UTO and the government were equally represented on the National Reconciliation Commission (NRC). The IRP, DPT (Almaty), *Lali Badakhshan,* and *Rastokhez* had their legal standing restored in 1999. (For more on political parties in 1999 and 2000, see the 2014 *Handbook.*)

Meanwhile, the government had begun closing political parties on technical grounds, including the **People's Unity Party** (PUP), the **Agrarian Party,** and the **Party of Justice.** (See the 2012 *Handbook* for more information.)

In April 2004 looking toward the 2005 elections, the IRP, the SDPT, and the Socialist Party of Tajikistan (SPT) agreed to cooperate in a loose **For Fair and Transparent Elections** alliance, which the DPT then joined in August. Given that a party must be formally registered for at least a year to contest an election, the only other parties eligible for the February 2005 balloting were the president's PDPT and the CPT. Two additional parties were registered in November 2005, bringing the total number of officially recognized parties to eight.

Presidential Party:

People's Democratic Party of Tajikistan—PDPT (*Hizb-i-Khalq-i-Demokrati Tojikiston*). Formed in 1993 as the **People's Party of Tajikistan** (PPT) by a group of northern business interests centered in Khujand, the PDPT includes in its membership many former Soviet-era Communists, including President Rahmon. Formally registered in December 1994, the PPT emerged from the 1995 Supreme Assembly election with only a handful of seats, but its representation subsequently swelled to about 90 with the addition of members who had run without declaring affiliations. The party adopted its present name in 1997.

President Rahmon officially joined the PDPT in March 1998 and was elected chair at a party congress in April. Described by a spokesperson at the time as a party of pragmatists and technocrats, the PDPT significantly expanded its base of support throughout the country as a result of the president's membership. In the election for the new lower house of the Supreme Assembly in February–March 2000, the PDPT won 15 of 22 party list seats on a 65 percent first-round vote share. In 2005 it won 52 of the lower house's 63 seats.

At the party's tenth congress, held in December 2009, most of the top leadership was replaced. In the subsequent lower house election, the PDPT won 54 seats. In assembly balloting on February 28, 2010, the PDPT won 54 seats. In August 2011 the PDPT launched an initiative to increase cooperation with the Communist Party of China.

President Rahmon also chairs the Central Council of a closely associated social movement, the **Movement for National Unity and Revival of Tajikistan** (frequently shortened to the National Unity Movement), which was established in 1997. Rahmon was reelected president in 2013. In the March 2015 Assembly elections, the party won 65.4 percent of the vote and 51 seats.

A constitutional amendment passed in May 2016 that lowered the minimum age for the presidency from 35 to 30, allowing the president's eldest son Rustam EMONALI, age 33, to run for the office in the near future.

Leaders: Emomali RAHMON (President of the Republic and Chair of the Party), Safar SAFAROV (First Deputy Chair).

Other Parliamentary Parties:

Agrarian Party of Tajikistan—APT (*Hizbi Agrarii Tojikiston*). The APT was formed in September 2005 and officially registered two months later. (An earlier Agrarian Party was permanently suspended in 1999.) In January 2006 the APT chair, Amir Qoraqulov, denied that his party intended to form a coalition with the PDPT before the November 2006 presidential election, in which he won 5.2 percent of the vote.

Some opponents have asserted that the APT is a product of government efforts to split the opposition vote.

In 2010 the APT won two seats in the lower house, one on the basis of capturing 5.1 percent of the proportional vote. Tolibbek BUKHORIYEV was the party's candidate in the 2013 presidential balloting. He received 4.6 percent of the vote.

In the March 2015 Assembly of Representatives balloting, the APT won 11.7 percent of the vote and five seats.

Leaders: Amir QORAQULOV (Amirkul KARAKULOV, Chair), Rustum LATIPOV.

Communist Party of Tajikistan—CPT (*Hizb-i-Kommunisti Tojikiston*). Primarily based in the northern industrial region of Sughd (previously Leninabad) and in other areas of high ethnic Uzbek or Russian population, the CPT was the only registered party prior to the Tajik declaration of independence. In September 1991 it was banned by the Aslonov government, one day after it had decided to reorganize as the Tajik Socialist Party (TSP). The ban was immediately overturned but reimposed in October. Again functioning legally under its original name, the CPT regained its status as the dominant political group with the outlawing of its principal opponents in June 1993. In the February–March 1995 legislative balloting, at least a third of the elected candidates were acknowledged CPT members. It continued to advocate collective ownership and revival of a Soviet-based union of republics.

Claiming that a presidential victory by a Communist candidate would anger Russia, the CPT unexpectedly supported President Rahmon for reelection in 1999. It nevertheless remained within the opposition Consultative Council of Political Parties. The CPT won five party list seats, on a 20.6 percent vote share, in the Assembly of Representatives in the 2000 legislative election. In 2005 it won a total of four seats in the lower house. In 2006 its presidential candidate, Ismoil TALBAKOV, won 5.2 percent of the vote.

The February 2010 lower house election resulted in a loss of two seats. It won 7 percent of the party list vote. Ismoil Talbakov was the CPT presidential candidate in 2013, securing 5 percent of the vote. The party won one seat in the Assembly in March 2015, with 2.2 percent of the vote.

Leaders: Shodi SHABDOLOV (Chair), Ismoil TALBAKOV (2013 presidential candidate and Deputy Chair).

Party of Economic Reforms (PER). Formation of the government-supportive PER was announced in September 2005, and it was officially registered in November. It was initially accused of attempting to split the opposition vote. In 2006 the party's chair, Olimjon BOBOEV, ran for president and finished second, with 6.2 percent of the vote. In 2009 he was named minister of transport and communication by the president.

In the February 2010 election, the PER won two seats, one of them on the basis of taking 5 percent of the party list vote. PER candidate Olimjon BOBOYEV won 3.9 percent in the 2013 presidential balloting.

The PER won 7.5 percent of the vote in March 2015, and three seats in the Assembly.

Leaders: Mahmadsharif NOZIMOV, Sharofiddin SIROJOV.

Socialist Party of Tajikistan—SPT (*Hizb-i-Sotsialisti Tojikiston*). The SPT was organized in 1996 by former Supreme Soviet chair and Popular Front leader Safarali Kenjayev. In November 1998 the party reportedly expelled former vice president Narzullo Dustov for his alleged participation, earlier in the month, in the abortive revolt in the north. (Dustov went into exile.) Kenjayev, who had been serving as the head of the Supreme Assembly's Committee on Legislation and Human Rights, was murdered by unknown gunmen in March 1999.

The SPT advocates economic and social pluralism, decentralization of power, and secularism. It supported President Rahmon for reelection in November 1999 and won only 1.2 percent of the party list vote in the subsequent lower house election.

In August 2004 Mirhusayn NAZRIYEV was reelected chair, although he was opposed by members of a splinter group led by Abduhalim GHAFFOROV. In December, with both factions claiming to control the party, the Supreme Court ruled in Ghafforov's favor. In November 2006 Ghafforov won 2.8 percent of the presidential vote. In February 2010 the SPT finished last among the eight parties competing for lower house seats, winning only 0.5 percent of the proportional vote. Ghafforov campaigned unsuccessfully in a by-election in November 2011. Ghafforov was the party's 2013 presidential candidate, winning 1.5 percent of the vote.

In the March 2015 Assembly election, the party secured 5.5 percent of the vote and one seat.

Leader: Abduhalim GHAFFOROV (Chair).

Democratic Party of Tajikistan—DPT (*Hizbi Demokratii Tojikisto*). Drawing its support largely from Gorno-Badakhshan, the strongly anticommunist DPT was launched in 1990 on a platform that called for Tajik sovereignty within a framework of confederal states. It was formally outlawed in June 1993.

Divisions between moderate and hard-line DPT factions led to an open split in June 1995, when Shodmon YUSUF was ousted from the leadership but refused to recognize the election of Jumaboy NIYAZOV as his successor. Claiming to be the authentic DPT leader, Yusuf approved terms with the government under which his faction was relegalized in July as the DPT, although it was thereafter often referenced as the DPT (Tehran Platform) to distinguish it from Niyazov's DPT (Almaty Platform). The latter entered into an opposition alliance with the IRP and functioned as part of the UTO. The peace agreement of June 1997 provided for the eventual legalization of the outlawed faction, and Niyazov was later named to the NRC's political committee.

Closely associated with the DPT during the civil war was the Coordinating Center for the Democratic Forces of Tajikistan, led by Otakhon LATIFI until his return from exile in 1997. The head of the NRC legal committee, Latifi was assassinated in September 1998.

At its third congress in July 1999 the DPT (Tehran) replaced Yusuf with Azam AFZALI and in September nominated a former presidential defense adviser, Zafar IKROMOV, as its candidate for the presidential election in November. When Ikromov withdrew, citing the election commission's failure to issue the papers needed to obtain the 145,000 signatures required for a place on the ballot, the party nominated in his stead Sulton Quvvatov. Along with two other opposition candidates, Quvvatov announced in early October that he would boycott the balloting because his campaign workers were being harassed and the news media were not providing impartial campaign coverage. The boycott became moot when the election commission disqualified Quvvatov because he had not met the deadline for obtaining the requisite signatures.

Meanwhile, in accordance with the June 1997 peace accords, the DPT (Almaty) had been legalized by the Supreme Court in August 1999, although the Ministry of Justice refused to register it because of a prohibition against two parties having similar names. At its fifth congress in late September the Almaty group replaced Jumaboy Niyazov with Mahmadruzi Iskandarov. Subsequently, the Supreme Court recognized the DPT (Almaty) as the official DPT, permitting its registration in time to contest the 2000 parliamentary election. With the DPT (Tehran) officially disbanded, Afzali and Quvvatov formed the Progress Party (below).

Iskandarov was detained by Russian authorities in December 2004 at the request of the Tajik government, which accused him of terrorism and corruption. Shortly after his April 2005 release, he was abducted and delivered to Tajikistan, where in October he was convicted of terrorism, attempted murder, embezzlement, and weapons possession. He was sentenced to 23 years in prison.

In 2006 a *Watan* (Motherland) faction within the party was organized under the leadership of Masud Sobirov. In August Sobirov's supporters held an extraordinary congress that elected him party chair. Despite claims from the Iskandarov wing that the congress had been illegal, the Justice Department recognized Sobirov as DPT leader. Subsequently, however, a party congress ousted Sobirov for inadequate performance, including a failure to get the party's presidential candidate, Tabvardi ZIYOYEV, on the November ballot. In January 2007 Acting Chair Saidjaffar ISMONOV, who had previously belonged to the PDPT and then the unregistered Party of Progressive Youth of Tajikistan, was confirmed as Sobirov's successor. Reconciliation efforts have not succeeded, with the result that the DPT remains split into three wings headed by Iskandarov, Ismonov, and Sobirov. The government continues to recognize the Sobirov wing as the official DPT. In the 2010 lower house election, it won only 1 percent of the party list vote. Ismonov ran as the DPT candidate in the 2013 presidential election, again securing 1 percent of the vote.

In the March 2015 Assembly voting, the DPT won 1.7 percent of the vote and one seat in the legislature.

Leaders: Masud SOBIROV (Chair of Registered DPT), Saidjaffar ISMONOV (Chair of Ismonov Wing), Mahmadruzi ISKANDAROV (Chair of Iskandarov Wing, in prison), Rahmatullo VALIYEV (Deputy Chair of Iskandarov Wing).

Other Registered Parties:

Social Democratic Party of Tajikistan—SDPT (*Hizbi Sotsial-Demokratii Tojikiston*). The SDPT traces its origins to the **Party of Justice and Development** (*Adolat va Taraqqiyot*), formation of which was announced in 1998 by Rahmatullo Zoirov. Initially registered in February 1999, the party subsequently added "Social Democratic Party" to its name, but shortly thereafter the Ministry of Justice indicated that it intended to seek the party's closure for violating a proscription against membership by servicemen, law enforcement personnel, and judiciary staff. As a result, its registration was annulled. Zoirov subsequently served President Rahmon as senior adviser on legal policy from 2001 until resigning in 2003. Meanwhile, in December 2002 Zoirov had succeeded in registering the current SDPT. In 2005 he was a leading critic of how the legislative elections were conducted.

In November 2005 a deputy chair of the party, Hurinisso GHAFFORZODA, resigned from the SDPT to establish a social movement aimed at reviving cultural values. In the same month, Zoirov called for the opposition to name a joint candidate for the 2006 presidential election. When that effort failed, the SDPT chose not to contest the election. Earlier in the year, Zoirov accused the government of holding over 1,000 political prisoners, to which the regime warned him that he could face criminal charges unless he presented proof.

In the February 2010 lower house election the SDPT won only 0.8 percent of the party list vote. In December 2011 Zoirov was reelected party leader. In addition, reports indicated that party would change its name to the **National Social Democratic Party of Tajikistan.** The party boycotted the 2013 presidential polling. In the 2015 polling, it won 0.5 percent of the vote, but no seats in the Assembly.

Leader: Rahmatullo ZOIROV (Chair).

Unregistered Parties:

Islamic Rebirth Party—IRP (*Hizb-i-Nahzati Islom,* also translated into English as the Islamic Renaissance Party and the Islamic Revival Party). A rural-based grouping founded in June 1990, the IRP has indicated that its long-term objective is the conversion of Tajikistan into an Islamic republic, although it has rejected the label "fundamentalist." It supported the DPT's Davlat Khudonazarov for the presidency in 1991 but was banned in June 1993.

During 1992–1996 the armed Defense of the Fatherland wing of the IRP engaged in hostilities against government and CIS forces, drawing support from Tajiks who had fled to Afghanistan, from pro-Tajik Afghan mujahidin, and possibly from the Afghan government. Following the June 1997 peace agreement, the IRP remained at the center of the UTO.

Re-legalized in August 1999, the IRP elected UTO leader Sayed Abdullo Nuri as chair and, in the interest of national unity, gave grudging support to the September constitutional referendum despite objections to particular provisions. For the November presidential election the IRP designated as its candidate Davlat Usmon, minister of economics and foreign economic relations. Usmon subsequently decided to boycott the election, but his name remained on the ballot and he won 2 percent of the vote.

Party and UTO deputy chair Ali Akbar Turajonzoda reportedly resigned both positions in October 1999 after being expelled from the IRP because he had broken party regulations and had described President Rahmon as worthy of reelection.

In the first-round legislative election of February 2000, the IRP won two party list seats on a 7.3 percent vote share. In September 2003 the party's fourth conference reelected Chair Nuri, who consistently denied the existence of any IRP connections to militant Islamic groups, particularly the Islamic Movement of Uzbekistan (IMU). Nuri also charged the government with persecuting the IRP in the guise of cracking down on another regional Islamic group, the *Hizb-ut-Tahrir.*

In May 2003 IRP deputy chair Shamsiddin SHAMSIDDINOV was arrested and subsequently charged with murder, forming an armed group, and other crimes dating back to the civil war. In January 2004 he was sentenced to a lengthy term in prison, where he died of natural causes in January 2008.

In the 2005 legislative elections the IRP again won two seats. Nuri died in 2006 and was succeeded by his deputy chair, Muhiddin Kabiri. The party refused to nominate a candidate for the 2006 presidential election. Kabiri was reelected party chair in September 2007.

In the February 2010 lower house election the IRP retained its two party-list seats by winning 8.2 percent of the proportional vote. It remains the only officially recognized Islamic party in Central Asia. In July 2012 Sabzali MAMADRIZOYEV, a member of the IRP presidium, was murdered.

Oinikhol BOBONAZAROVA, a female lawyer and human rights activist backed by IRP, failed to secure the 210,000 signatures needed to have her name on the 2013 presidential election ballot. Bobonzarova was widely seen as the only legitimate potential challenge for the election. Instead, the IRP boycotted the 2013 election. The party participated in the 2015 Assembly balloting, winning 1.6 percent of the vote and no seats.

In August 2015 the party was deregistered for not having enough members. Following a reported coup in September, 13 members of the IRP were arrested and the grouping was declared to be a terrorist organization. The IRP vehemently denied any involvement in the September attacks.

Leaders: Muhiddin KABIRI (Chair), Muhammadali HAIT (Deputy Chair), Hikmotulla SAYFULLOZODA, Sayidumar HUSAYNI.

Progress Party (*Taraqqiyot,* also translated into English as the Development Party). *Taraqqiyot* held its founding congress in the capital in May 2001. Committed to protecting the political rights of all citizens without regard to ethnicity, religion, language, or gender, the party has repeatedly tried to register without success. Virtually all of its initial membership had previously belonged to the disbanded DPT (Tehran). One of its founders, Sulton Quvvatov, was a former chair of the state tax committee and a prospective candidate for president in 1999 (see the DPT, above). Another founder, Azam Afzali, stated that the party would offer "constructive opposition" to the government. (For more on the history of the party, see the 2012 *Handbook.*) In July 2004 the SDPT offered to reserve places for *Taraqqiyot* members, including Quvvatov, on its party list for the 2005 legislative elections. In June 2005 party leader Rustam Fayziyev was given a six-year prison sentence for insulting the president and stirring up ethnic hatred. Quvvatov died of natural causes on November 14, 2011.

Leaders: Rustam FAYZIYEV (Chair, in prison), Shodikhon KENJAYEV.

In March 2008 the Ministry of Justice, for the sixth time, rejected the registration application of the progovernment **Union Party** (*Vahdat*), led by Hikmatullo SAIDOV. In February 2012 Izzat AMON announced the formation of the **Taijkistan Youth Party.**

Banned Organizations:

Two banned Islamic organizations, the ***Hizb-ut-Tahrir*** and the **Islamic Movement of Uzbekistan** (IMU), have been active in Tajikistan. The IMU, now also known as the **Islamic Party of Turkestan,** has claimed responsibility for or been linked to numerous terrorist incidents in the Central Asian region and beyond, and both Kyrgyzstan and Uzbekistan have asserted that the group has operated from bases in Tajikistan, a charge that the government has denied. Reports in 2014 indicated continued fighting between the IMU and government security forces. Members of the transnational *Hizb-ut-Tahrir* have been tried and sentenced to prison in Tajikistan, although the organization has not been as militant as the IMU. Umarali QUVATOV, the leader of the banned opposition movement **Group 24,** was shot dead in Istanbul on March 5, 2015. He had been fighting extradition by Tajikistan, and media accounts in Turkey blamed the assassination on Tajik agents.

LEGISLATURE

The 1994 constitution established a 181-member unicameral **Supreme Assembly** (*Majlisi Oli*). Constitutional amendments passed by referendum in September 1999 reconstituted the body as a bicameral legislature, all of whose members serve five-year terms.

National Assembly (*Majlisi Milli*). The upper chamber encompasses 25 indirectly elected members, 8 presidential appointees, and former presidents of the republic (currently one, Qahhor Mahkamov). The elected members are chosen by secret ballot of regional legislators in each of five equally weighted electoral districts: the country's four regions and Dushanbe. The most recent election was held March 27, 2015.

Speaker: Mahmadsaid UBAIDULLOEV.

Assembly of Representatives (*Majlisi Namoyandagon*). The lower chamber encompasses 63 members: 41 deputies directly elected on a majority basis from single-seat districts, and 22 divided proportionally among eligible parties receiving at least 5 percent of the national vote. Following the most recent election of March 1, 2015, the People's Democratic Party of Tajikistan held 51 seats (35 constituency, 16 proportional); Agrarian Party of Tajikistan, 5 (2, 3); Party of Economic Reforms, 3 (1, 2); Communist Party of Tajikistan, 2 (2, 0); Democratic Party, 1 (1, 0); and Socialist Party, 1 (0, 1).

Speaker: Shukurjon ZUHUROV.

CABINET

[as of November 15, 2016]

Prime Minister	Kohir Rasulzoda
First Deputy Prime Minister	Davlatali Saidov
Deputy Prime Ministers	Marhabo Jabbarova [f] Murodali Alimardonov Azim Ibrohim
Ministers	
Agriculture and Nature Protection	Qosim Qosimov
Culture	Shamsiddin Orumbekov
Defense	Col. Gen. Mirzo Sherali
Economic Development and Trade	Rahimzoda Sharif
Education	Nuriddin Saidov
Energy and Industry	Usmonali Usmonov
Finance	Abdusalom Kurbonov
Foreign Affairs	Sirojiddin Aslov
Health	Nustratullo Salimov
Industry and New Technologies	Shaykat Boboev
Internal Affairs	Ramazon Rakhimov
Justice	Rustam Mengliyev
Labor, Migration, and Public Employment	Sumangul Taghoeva [f]
Transport	Khayrullo Asoyev
State Committee Chairs	
Investment and Management of State Property	Qosim Qodiri
Land Management and Geodesy	Mahmadtoir Zokirov
National Security	Lt. Gen. Saimumin Yatimov
Women and Family Affairs	Maghfirat Khidirova [f]

[f] = female

INTERGOVERNMENTAL REPRESENTATION

Ambassador to the U.S.: Farhod SALIM.

U.S. Ambassador to Tajikistan: Elisabeth MILLARD.

Permanent Representative to the UN: Mahmadamin MAHMADAMINOV.

IGO Memberships (Non-UN): ADB, CIS, EBRD, ICC, IOM, OIC, OSCE, SCO, WTO.

For Further Reference:

Heathershaw, John. *Post-Conflict Tajikistan: The Politics of Peacebuilding and the Emergence of Legitimate Order.* New York: Routledge, 2009.

Olcott, Martha Brill. *Tajikistan's Difficult Development Path.* Washington, DC: Carnegie Endowment for International Peace, 2012.

Tunçer-Kilavuz, Idil. *Power, Networks, and Violent Conflict in Central Asia: A Comparison of Tajikistan and Uzbekistan.* New York: Routledge, 2014.

TANZANIA

United Republic of Tanzania
Jamhuri ya Muungano wa Tanzania

Political Status: Independent member of the Commonwealth; established in its present form on April 26, 1964, through union of the Republic of Tanganyika (independent 1961) and the People's Republic of Zanzibar (independent 1963); one-party constitution adopted April 25, 1977; multiparty system legalized June 17, 1992.

Area: 364,898 sq. mi. (945,087 sq. km), encompassing Tanganyika, 363,948 sq. mi. (942,626 sq. km) and Zanzibar, 950 sq. mi. (2,461 sq. km), the latter including Pemba, 350 sq. mi. (906 sq. km).

Population: 55,156,000 (including Zanzibar, 2016E—UN); 52,482,726 (2016E—U.S. Census).

Major Urban Centers (2015E—UN): DAR ES SALAAM (5,116,000), Mwanza (838,000), Zanzibar (569,000), Arusha (444,000), Mbeya (444,000), Morogoro (341,000), Dodoma (228,000). The deadline for the transfer of government operations to a new capital in Dodoma has been extended numerous times. Although the National Assembly now sits in Dodoma, it remains uncertain when, or even if, full governmental relocation will occur.

Official Languages: English, Swahili.

Monetary Unit: Tanzanian Shilling (official rate October 1, 2016: 2,182.00 shillings = $1US).

President: John MAGUFULI (Revolutionary Party of Tanzania); elected on October 25, 2015, and sworn in a for a five-year term on November 5, succeeding Jakaya KIKWETE (Revolutionary Party of Tanzania).

Vice President: Samia SULUHU (Revolutionary Party of Tanzania); elected concurrently with the president on October 25, 2015, and sworn in on November 5, succeeding Mohamed Gharib BILAL (Revolutionary Party of Tanzania).

Prime Minister: Kassim MAJALIWA (Revolutionary Party of Tanzania); appointed by the president and confirmed by the National Assembly on November 19, 2015, and sworn in on November 20, in succession to Mizengo PINDA (Revolutionary Party of Tanzania).

President of Zanzibar: Ali Mohamed SHEIN (Revolutionary Party of Tanzania); elected on October 31, 2010, and sworn in on November 3, succeeding Amani Abeid KARUME (Revolutionary Party of Tanzania); reelected on March 20, 2016, after the results of the disputed election in Zanzibar on October 25, 2015, were dismissed (see Government and Politics, below).

THE COUNTRY

The United Republic of Tanzania combines the large territory of Tanganyika on the East African mainland and the two islands of Zanzibar and Pemba off the East African coast. Tanzania's people are overwhelmingly African (primarily Bantu) stock, but there are significant Asian (largely Indian and Pakistani), European, and Arab minorities. In addition to the indigenous tribal languages, Swahili (Kiunguja is the Zanzibari form) serves as a lingua franca, while English and Arabic are also spoken. About 35 percent of the population on the mainland is Christian, 30 percent is Muslim, and the remainder adheres to traditional religious beliefs. Over 90 percent of the population on Zanzibar is Muslim, with Christian and traditional belief minorities. Women comprise nearly 50 percent of the labor force, with responsibility for over 70 percent of subsistence activities; Tanzanian women have a relatively high level of literacy and are represented in most levels of government and party affairs. After the 2015 elections, women held 136 of the 372 seats in the assembly (36.6 percent of the seats).

The economy is primarily agricultural. The most important crops on the mainland are coffee, cotton, and sisal, which collectively account for approximately two-fifths of the country's exports. The economies of Zanzibar and Pemba are based on cloves and coconut products. In

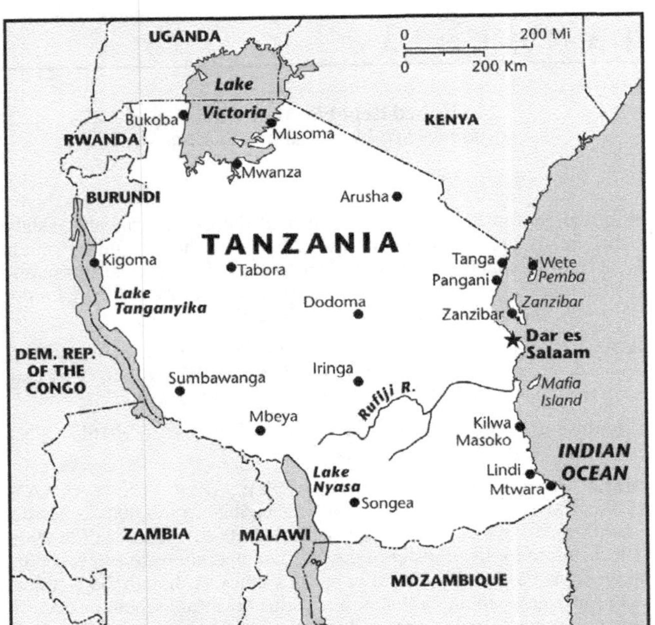

2006 Tanzania became Africa's third leading producer of gold. In addition, several international mining companies have recently begun exploration for uranium in several sites.

In April 2000 the International Monetary Fund (IMF) and World Bank agreed to support a comprehensive debt relief package for Tanzania, encouraged by reduction in the size of the public sector and greater influence of the free market. (See the 2011 *Handbook* for information on the economy prior to 2000.) Gross domestic product (GDP) growth averaged about 6.8 percent annually between 2000 and 2008, based on expansion in the manufacturing, mining, and construction sectors. Tanzania was also one of the countries approved for debt relief through the World Bank's Heavily Indebted Poor Country (HIPC) initiative. Growth was helped by a series of economic reforms, including privatization initiatives and anticorruption measures. The World Bank also committed $2.3 billion in 2006 in economic development assistance over a three-year period, and Japan canceled Tanzania's $580 million debt in 2007.

In 2008 the Millennium Challenge Account pledged $698 million to Tanzania for economic development. However, the global economic crisis that began in 2008 prompted the government to initiate a $1.3 billion stimulus package. The government's deficit rose to 13.3 percent of GDP in 2009. Meanwhile, foreign aid continued to contribute about 4 percent of the country's total GDP, and in August 2009 the EU announced more than $550 million in economic assistance for Tanzania. The IMF provided another $350 million. However, the UK reduced its aid for governmental budget support in 2008 and 2009 in response to the failure of the Tanzanian government to carry out agreed-upon reforms. In 2010 GDP grew at 6.5 percent, while inflation rose to 10.4 percent, and foreign aid accounted for 10 percent of GDP. Rising gold and commodity prices, combined with a new wave of foreign investment, helped spur the economy. In 2011 the United Kingdom cut its budgetary support to Tanzania by 30 percent, citing lack of progress in improving the business environment.

Despite the impacts of ongoing power shortages and the global economic situation, GDP grew by 6.4 percent in 2012 and 6.9 percent the next year. The government cut spending and tightened fiscal policy to curb rising inflation—caused by higher oil import prices and high food costs following a drought in the Horn of Africa—which reached 19 percent in late 2011 and declined to around 9 percent in 2013. In May 2013 Brazil announced it would cancel Tanzania's $237 million debt. In 2013 GDP rose by 7.3 percent, while inflation increased by 7.9 percent. GDP grew by 7.2 percent in both 2014 and 2015. In 2016 GDP growth slowed slightly to 7.1 percent, and inflation was 4.5 percent. GDP per capita was $1,071. Although Tanzania was ranked the second-best place to conduct business in Africa in 2007 by the World Bank, the country fell to tenth place on the continent, or 134th overall out of 185 countries in 2013, before declining to 145th out of 189 nations in 2014 and then rising to 139th in 2016.

GOVERNMENT AND POLITICS

Political background. The former British-ruled territories of Tanganyika and Zanzibar developed along separate lines until their union in 1964. Tanganyika, occupied by Germany in 1884, became a British-administered mandate under the League of Nations and continued under British administration as a United Nations trust territory after World War II. Led by Julius K. NYERERE of the Tanganyika African National Union (TANU), it became independent within the Commonwealth in 1961 and adopted a republican form of government with Nyerere as president in 1962.

Zanzibar and Pemba, British protectorates since 1890, became independent in 1963 as a constitutional monarchy within the Commonwealth. However, little more than a month after independence, the Arab-dominated government of Sultan Seyyid Jamshid bin Abdullah bin KHALIFA was overthrown by African nationalists, who established a People's Republic with Sheikh Abeid Amani KARUME of the Afro-Shirazi Party (ASP) as president.

Following overtures by Nyerere, the two countries combined on April 26, 1964, to form the United Republic of Tanganyika and Zanzibar, renamed the United Republic of Tanzania later in the same year. Nyerere became president of the unified state, and in September 1965 he was overwhelmingly confirmed in that position by popular vote in both sections of the country. Karume, in addition to becoming first vice president of Tanzania, continued to head the quasi-independent Zanzibar administration until April 1972, when he was assassinated. Nyerere thereupon appointed Aboud JUMBE to succeed Karume as first vice president and as leader of the ASP.

On February 5, 1977, TANU and the ASP merged to form the Revolutionary Party of Tanzania (*Chama Cha Mapinduzu*—CCM); subsequently, a new constitution was adopted on April 25, according the CCM a "dominant" role in the Tanzanian governmental system. On November 5, 1980, Prime Minister Edward SOKOINE announced his retirement for reasons of health, and two days later the president named Cleopa David MSUYA as Sokoine's successor. Sokoine returned as prime minister on February 24, 1983, but was killed in an automobile accident on April 12, 1984; he was succeeded 12 days later by Salim Ahmed SALIM. Earlier, on January 27, Vice President Jumbe had submitted his resignation in the wake of mounting secessionist agitation on Zanzibar, Ali Hassan MWINYI having been named his replacement on January 30.

Carrying out a pledge made in early 1984 to step down as head of state upon the expiration of his existing term, Nyerere withdrew from contention at the 1985 CCM congress in favor of Vice President Mwinyi, who was overwhelmingly nominated as the sole candidate for the October presidential balloting. Because of a constitutional prohibition against Zanzibaris occupying both presidential and prime ministerial offices, Prime Minister Salim was replaced following the October 27 poll by Justice Minister Joseph S. WARIOBA, who also assumed the post of first vice president; concurrently, Idris Abdul WAKIL, who had been elected president of Zanzibar on October 13, became second vice president, while Salim was named deputy prime minister and minister of defense.

Mwinyi's elevation to the presidency and his encouragement of private enterprise appeared to stem secessionist sentiment on Zanzibar. However, discord attributed to a variety of economic, religious, and political motives broke out again in late 1987. An apparent power struggle developed between Wakil and supporters of Chief Minister Seif Sharif HAMAD, a leader from the northern island of Pemba (where 90 percent of the islands' cloves are produced), after Hamad was dropped from the CCM Central Committee. On January 23, 1988, Wakil, claiming that dissidents were plotting a coup, suspended the Zanzibari government; three days later he announced a new administration in which Hamad was replaced by Omar Ali JUMA. In May Hamad and six of his supporters were expelled from the CCM for alleged "anti-party" activity. Observers reported a continued "undercurrent of rebellion" on the islands, however, and Hamad was arrested in May 1989 on charges of organizing illegal meetings, the government also accusing his supporters of forming a political group, *Bismallah* ("In the name of God"), dedicated to "breaking the union."

Mwinyi consolidated his authority during 1990; in March he ousted hard-line socialist cabinet members who opposed his economic policies, and, following Nyerere's retirement on August 17, he was elected CCM chair. On October 28 the president won reelection for a second five-year term, and on November 8 he named John S. MALECELA first vice president and prime minister, replacing Warioba. Meanwhile, on October 21 Salmin AMOUR had been elected president of Zanzibar and second vice president of the republic after Wakil had declined to seek reelection to the posts.

On June 17, 1992, President Mwinyi signed a bill legalizing opposition parties, following approval by the National Assembly and the Zanzibar House of Representatives, along with endorsement by the CCM. On July 1 the CCM became the first group to be officially registered under the new law, and by the end of August, 12 of the reportedly 35 parties that had requested application forms had been granted provisional registration.

In late 1992 the government scheduled multiparty elections, beginning with municipal and local balloting in 1993 and concluding with national elections in 1994–1995. Subsequently, the Civic United Front (CUF), a prominent opposition grouping, and four smaller parties threatened to boycott the polling, saying that the delays favored the CCM and calling instead for the convening of a constitutional conference before any elections were held.

In February 1993 Zanzibari membership in the Organization of the Islamic Conference (OIC) was categorized as "unconstitutional" and "separatist" by a Tanzanian parliamentary commission. (The membership was reportedly withdrawn in August 1993, although uncertainty on the question continued [see Membership in OIC].) The affair highlighted continued debate within the government over the two regions' respective roles, as well as a growing schism between Christians and Muslims, which was further evidenced by the anti-Muslim rhetoric of the increasingly popular Democratic Party leader, Rev. Christopher MTIKILA, and the militant activities of the Council for the Dissemination of the Koran in Tanzania (*Balukta*).

In April 1993, at the first balloting since the introduction of multipartyism, the CCM, aided by a CUF boycott, easily won two Zanzibari municipal by-elections. However, fiscal problems, coupled with the Muslim fundamentalist issue, continued to bedevil the ruling party. By late 1994, with less than a year remaining before the next presidential poll, its leadership had fallen into disarray, with former president Nyerere criticizing President Mwinyi as a political weakling and attacking Prime Minister Malecela and CCM secretary general Horace KOLIMBA as "hooligans" who should resign their positions. The immediate upshot was an extraordinary event: a total ministerial boycott of a cabinet meeting called by the president. Mwinyi responded on December 4 by dissolving the National Assembly, and on December 5 he named a new government headed by former prime minister Cleopa Msuya. Meanwhile, the assembly, two days before the dissolution, had approved a constitutional amendment that created a furor on Zanzibar by specifying that henceforth the island president would no longer become a union vice president unless specifically elected as the president's running mate.

In preparation for the first nationwide multiparty elections, the CCM in July 1995 elected Minister of Science Benjamin William MKAPA as its presidential nominee, President Mwinyi being ineligible for a third term. The balloting of October 29 featured more than 1,300 legislative candidates, with nine opposition parties announcing that they would form a postelectoral coalition if it would give them a parliamentary majority. However, in results that were hotly disputed, Mkapa was credited with winning 61.8 percent of the valid presidential votes, while the CCM garnered 186 of 232 elective assembly seats. Earlier, in even more contentious Zanzibari balloting on October 22, the National Electoral Commission (NEC) had announced that President Amour had been reelected on a 52 percent vote share, with the CCM having been awarded 26 of 50 elective seats in the Zanzibar House of Representatives. Mkapa subsequently named former agriculture minister Frederick Tluway SUMAYE to head a new cabinet, which contained a majority of relatively young newcomers and excluded nearly all former ministers who had been tinged by charges of corruption.

Of 13 opposition parties that contested the 1995 election, only 4 obtained legislative representation. Their disappointing capture of only 24 percent of the seats on a near 40 percent share of the vote was attributed by many to the majority electoral system and by some to widespread electoral fraud, particularly in the Zanzibari balloting, in which the opposition's Seif Hamad was widely believed to have attracted more than the 48 percent vote share officially credited to him in the presidential poll.

Mkapa's economic and political reform efforts in 1996 drew broad praise. Such advances were overshadowed, however, by the political stalemate in Zanzibar where the CUF continued to boycott the legislature in protest over the CCM's alleged rigging of the 1995 elections. In addition, the government's anticorruption campaign was tarnished by the resignation of several ministers in late 1996 and early 1997 following bribery and abuse of power investigations, which also prompted a cabinet reshuffle in February 1997.

In January 1998 Commonwealth mediators introduced a seven-point plan to ease the tension in Zanzibar. However, both sides rejected the accord. In March the Commonwealth released another proposal that was subsequently reported to have been positively received by the CCM and CUF negotiators. The government continued its crackdown on alleged CUF militants in early 1999, but an agreement was finally signed by the CCM and the CUF providing for the return of the CUF to the National Assembly, the award of two additional assembly seats to the CUF, and the creation of an independent electoral commission to oversee the elections scheduled for October 2000. Each side subsequently charged the other with foot-dragging in implementing some provisions of the accord, and tension remained substantial on the island, exacerbated by the death in October 1999 of former president Nyerere, whose considerable domestic and international prestige and influence had been credited with holding the shaky union together. Attention in early 2000 focused on the attempt by Zanzibari president Amour to have the constitution amended to permit him to run for a third term. After reportedly "tumultuous" debate, the CCM rejected the appeal from Amour, who had been widely criticized on Zanzibar for hard-line tactics, including the arrest of prominent CUF members on treason charges (see CUF under Political Parties, below).

Balloting for the National Assembly and Zanzibar's House of Representatives, as well as for the presidencies of Tanzania and Zanzibar was held on October 29, 2000. However, reruns were required in 16 island constituencies on November 5 because of ballot problems in the initial poll. The CUF and many other opposition parties boycotted the reruns, arguing that new voting should have been ordered in all island constituencies. (See the 2012 *Handbook* for more information on the unrest and increasing tensions over Muslim fundamentalism that followed.) Final results showed President Mkapa securing a second five-year term with 71.7 percent of the vote against a fractured opposition. In addition, the CCM maintained its stranglehold on the assembly and a comfortable majority in the House of Representatives. Meanwhile, the CCM's Amani Abeid KARUME, the son of the first president of independent Zanzibar, was declared winner of the Zanzibari presidential poll with 67 percent of the vote. On November 23 President Mkapa reappointed Sumaye to head a reshuffled CCM cabinet.

The CCM candidate, Foreign Minister Jakaya KIKWETE, easily won the December 2005 presidential election in Tanzania with more than 80 percent of the vote, while the CCM increased its majority in the National Assembly. Edward LOWASSA was appointed prime minister on December 29, and a CCM cabinet was approved by the assembly on January 6, 2006. In October Kikwete conducted a major cabinet reshuffle in which ten ministers and eight deputy ministers changed positions.

In 2007 Foreign Minister Dr. Asha-Rose MIGERO was appointed as the UN's first deputy secretary general. She was succeeded as foreign minister by Bernard MEMBE.

On February 7, 2008, Lowassa resigned as prime minister following revelation of corruption charges linked to a scandal over illicit payments to an energy company. Nine other ministers were sacked as the president attempted to restore confidence in the government. Lowassa was replaced by the minister of state in the prime minister's office Mizengo PINDA, who was confirmed by the assembly on February 8. A new cabinet was approved on February 12. In response to the global economic crisis and in anticipation of legislative and presidential elections in 2010, the CCM government endeavored to enact broad economic reforms in 2009 in an effort to improve the economy (see Current issues, below). In June 2009 the UN announced that it would help conduct the 2010 balloting by providing technical assistance, monitors, and $23 million in support.

In balloting on October 31, 2010, Kikwete was reelected president, defeating six other candidates, including Willibrod Peter SLAA of Chadema, who placed second (see Current issues, below). Meanwhile national vice president Ali Mohamed SHEIN of the CCM was elected president of Zanzibar in concurrent polling. In concurrent legislative balloting, the CCM secured 185 seats, followed by Chadema with 28, and the CUF with 18. No other party gained more than 5 seats. In voting for the Zanzibar assembly, the CCM secured 28 seats, and the CUF,

22. The CUF subsequently agreed to join the CCM in a coalition government for Zanzibar.

On November 16, 2010, CCM member Anna Semamba MAKINDA was elected as the first female speaker of the Tanzanian assembly. Pinda was reappointed prime minister of Tanzania and sworn in on November 17. A reshuffled cabinet was named on November 24. Meanwhile, on November 18 Shein appointed a sixteen member coalition cabinet for Zanzibar which included ministers from the CCM and the CUF. Meanwhile in response to continuing government anticorruption efforts, a group of international donors who had withheld aid announced in November that they would release more than $700 million in assistance.

In April 2012 Kikwete conducted a major cabinet reshuffle following the publication of an audit that reported fraud and corruption in several ministries, including Energy and Minerals, which the president divided into two separate portfolios. Finance Minister William MGIMWA died of natural causes on January 1, 2014. His successor was named during a cabinet reshuffle on January 19 (see Current issues, below).

Former prime minister Lowassa was the frontrunner to be the CCM's candidate for the 2015 presidential election. However, Works Minister John MAGUFULI won the nomination. Lowassa then defected to Chadema (see Political Parties, below) to run as the candidate for a four-party opposition coalition, the Union for a People's Constitution (*Umoja wa Katiba ya Wananchi—Ukawa*), consisting of Chadema, the CUF, the National League for Democracy (NLD), and National Convention for Constitution and Reform–Mageuzi (NCCR-Mageuzi). In polling on October 25, 2015, Magufuli was elected president with 58.5 percent of the vote. Lowassa placed second with 40 percent of the vote. In concurrent legislative balloting, the CCM retained its majority with 253 seats. Lowassa and opposition leaders challenged the results of the balloting, but the high court dismissed their suit. Kassim MAJALIWA (CCM) was named prime minister on November 19, of a mostly reshuffled cabinet that included six ministers from the previous government. The new government launched a broad anticorruption campaign, combined with a range of austerity initiatives.

Balloting in Zanzibar on October 25, 2015, was marred by a variety of factors (see Current issues, below) and the results subsequently nullified. New voting took place on March 20, 2016, but was boycotted by the opposition CUF. In the new elections, Shein was reelected president with 91.4 percent of the vote, while the CCM secured 81 of the 85 seats in the Zanzibar legislature.

Constitution and government. An "interim" document of 1965 was replaced on April 25, 1977, by a "permanent" constitution, although the system of government was essentially unaltered. A number of amendments were adopted prior to the 1985 election; significantly, however, Tanzania remained a one-party state, with controlling influence exercised by the CCM at both national and regional levels. Legislation authorizing multiparty activity was approved in 1992 (see Political background, above).

The president is elected by universal suffrage for no more than two five-year terms. Since 1995 the vice president has also been elected as part of a national president/vice president ticket. (Previously Tanzania had two vice presidents: the president of Zanzibar [who served as first vice president if the president was from the mainland] and a presidentially appointed prime minister. The December 1994 constitutional amendment ending the automatic designation of the Zanzibar president as one of the two vice presidents left the insular region without mandated representation at the national executive level.) The prime minister is currently appointed by the president subject to confirmation by the National Assembly. Cabinet ministers are also appointed by the president.

The National Assembly, more than four-fifths of whose members are at present directly elected, sits for a five-year term, subject to presidential dissolution (in which case the president himself must stand for reelection). The judicial system on the mainland is headed by a High Court and includes local and district courts. In August 1979 a Tanzanian Court of Appeal was established to assume, inter alia, the functions of the East African Court of Appeal, which had ceased to exist with the collapse of the East African Community in 1977. All judges are appointed by the president.

Tanzania's 26 administrative regions (21 on the mainland, 3 on Zanzibar, and 2 on Pemba) are each headed by a regional commissioner appointed by the central government. Below the regional level there are 114 municipalities, town councils, and, in rural locations, area or district councils.

On October 13, 1979, a new constitution for Zanzibar was promulgated by its Revolutionary Council after having been approved by the CCM. Under the new system, designed to provide for "more democracy" without contravening the union constitution of Tanzania, the president of Zanzibar is directly elected for a five-year term and held to a maximum of two successive terms. There is also a largely elected House of Representatives endowed with the legislative authority previously exercised by the Revolutionary Council. The latter, however, has been retained as a "high executive council" of cabinet status, with members appointed by the president.

In 2000 the Thirteenth Amendment was ratified by a two-thirds majority in the National Assembly. The measure expanded presidential prerogatives to include the appointment of ten members to the National Assembly and permitted election of the president by a plurality instead of a majority of voters. The amendment also increased the percentage of seats reserved for women from 15 percent to 20 percent. In April 2002 the Zanzibari House of Representatives approved constitutional amendments that called for restructuring the national electoral commission to include opposition representation. In 2004 the Revolutionary Council on Zanzibar announced plans for a new flag, national anthem, and identity cards for the island.

In February 2005 the Fourteenth Amendment was ratified by the assembly. The measure had a number of provisions, including a section that allowed the prime minister to act as president in the absence of the president and vice president. It also loosened the rules about electoral campaigning.

In June 2009 the government announced plans to overturn laws that forbade dual citizenship and enact a new measure that would allow Tanzanians living abroad to retain, or regain, citizenship and participate in elections.

In a referendum in Zanzibar on July 31, 2010, voters approved a constitutional amendment which would allow political parties to form coalition governments by a margin of 66.4 percent in favor and 33.6 opposed.

There are few formal media restrictions in Tanzania. In 2006 Reporters Without Borders declared that Tanzania had the freest press in East Africa. In 2013 the group ranked Tanzania 70th out of 179 countries in freedom of the press (a decline from 36 the previous year, following reports of increased harassment of reporters and the murder of two prominent journalists). In 2016 Tanzania was ranked 71st out of 180 countries.

Foreign relations. Tanzania belongs to the United Nations and most of its Specialized Agencies, the Commonwealth, and the African Union. In addition, it participated with Kenya and Uganda in the East African Community (EAC) until the organization was dissolved in mid-1977. Under President Nyerere's leadership, Tanzania pursued a policy of international nonalignment and of vigorous opposition to colonialism and racial discrimination, particularly in southern Africa, maintaining no relations with Pretoria and strongly supporting the effort of the Front-Line States to avoid South African trade routes. In addition, declaring South African destabilization efforts in nearby states to be a direct threat to Tanzania, the government in 1987 sent troops to Mozambique to assist Maputo in the fight against Renamo rebels. (The troops were withdrawn in December 1988, in part, reportedly, because of the cost of their maintenance.) Tanzania also gave asylum to political refugees from African countries, and various liberation groups were headquartered in Dar es Salaam.

Relations with Britain were severed from 1965 to 1968 to protest London's Rhodesian policy. Meanwhile relations with the United States were strained from the 1960s through the 1980s due to Tanzanian disagreement with U.S. policies on Africa.

Long-standing friction with Uganda escalated into overt military conflict in late 1978 (see entry on Uganda). After a six-month campaign that involved the deployment of some 40,000 Tanzanian troops, the forces of Ugandan president Idi Amin were decisively defeated, Amin fleeing to Libya. Subsequently, under an agreement signed with the government of Godfrey Binaisa, approximately 20,000 Tanzanians remained in the country to man security points pending the training of a new Ugandan army. During 1980 Kenya and Sudan were among the regional states expressing concern over the continuing presence in Uganda of the Tanzanian troops, the last of which were finally withdrawn in May–June 1981. (In 2007 Uganda paid Tanzania $67 million to retire debts that remained from the 1978 conflict.)

Relations with Kenya improved measurably upon the conclusion of a November 1983 accord among the two and Uganda on the distribution of EAC assets and liabilities. The border between Tanzania and

Kenya, originally closed in 1977 to "punish" Kenya for allegedly dominating Tanzania's economy, was reopened, and the two countries reached agreement on a series of technical cooperation issues. Rapprochement was further enhanced in December, when the three former EAC members exchanged high commissioners in an effort "to facilitate expansion and consolidation in economic matters." (See Foreign relations in entry on Kenya for information regarding the recent reactivation of the EAC.)

In September 1995 Prime Minister Msuya appealed to the UN High Commissioner for Refugees (UNHCR) to aid in the repatriation of more than 800,000 Burundian and Rwandan refugees living in border area camps. In January 1996 the Tanzanian Army turned back an estimated 17,000 Rwandan Hutu refugees fleeing violence in Burundi; however, three days later the government reversed itself and reopened its border. In February relations between Tanzania and Burundi were enhanced by an agreement on border security and refugee repatriation; however, in March, as fighting in Burundi spilled over Tanzania's border, Dar es Salaam rejected the appointment of a Burundian ambassador for the second time.

Conditions deteriorated significantly toward the end of 1996 when large numbers of Hutu refugees crossed Burundi from Zaire (where Tutsis had destroyed Hutu camps and assumed control of the eastern part of the country) into Tanzania. Burundi's President Pierre Buyoya accused Tanzania of supporting Hutu "rebels" and criticized former Tanzanian president Nyerere for spearheading the regional economic sanctions against Burundi. (For more on the normalization of relations between the countries and the repatriation of refugees, see the 2012 or an earlier *Handbook*.) By February 2004 Tanzania had returned all identifiable Rwandan refugees; according to UN estimates, 20,000 remained in Tanzania illegally.

On August 7, 1998, 11 Tanzanians had been killed in Dar es Salaam when alleged militant Islamic fundamentalists set off simultaneous bomb blasts at U.S. embassies in Tanzania and Kenya. (For further details, see entries on Kenya and Saudi Arabia, the latter containing a section on Osama bin Laden, whose terrorist network was suspected by U.S. officials of complicity in the bombings.)

The European Union (EU) provided $1.9 million in aid to support the 2001 peace accord between the government and the CUF and $14.82 million to assist Burundian refugees. Collaterally, relations between Tanzania and the United Kingdom (UK) improved significantly in the 1990s. The UK agreed in 2003 to provide assistance for Tanzania's refugee repatriation efforts, and in 2005 the UK announced that Tanzania would be the first African country to benefit from an initiative to write off the debt of poorer countries. Later in 2005, however, a diplomatic row occurred between the two countries when Tanzania unilaterally ended a $143.5 million water privatization project funded jointly by Britain and the World Bank. The Tanzanian government charged that the foreign companies involved in the project were not fulfilling their obligations.

In 2006 the United States granted Tanzania funds for an anticorruption campaign and a malaria suppression initiative on the heels of increasing its security assistance for counterterrorism efforts and launching a program to train personnel from the Bank of Tanzania to interdict financing of terrorist groups.

Reports surfaced in 2007 that China had delivered a number of shipments of arms and weapons to Tanzania, provoking criticism from the assembly over the secret nature of the transactions. The revelations coincided with a scandal in which a British arms firm was discovered to have paid $12 million to Tanzanian figures to secure the sale of a radar system to the country. (The firm BAE was forced to pay the Tanzanian government $47 million in 2011 in fines and fees because of the scandal.) On more positive notes, the UK in 2007 announced that it would provide $530 million over a ten-year period to finance improvements in Tanzania's educational system, and Switzerland granted Tanzania $15.5 million for poverty-reduction programs.

In March 2008 Tanzania commanded the 1,500 AU troops (750 of whom were Tanzanian) who deployed in the Comoros during a sovereignty dispute between the leader of Anjouan Island and the central government (see entry on Comoros). Tanzania also pledged to contribute troops to the UN peacekeeping mission in Darfur but strongly condemned the International Criminal Court's issuance of charges of genocide against Sudanese leader Umar Al-Bashir (see entry on Sudan). In September Tanzania announced that it would grant citizenship to up to 76,000 Burundian refugees, many of whom had been in the country since 1972. More than 60,000 Burundians were repatriated between 2007 and 2008. The government subsequently announced the closure of most of the camps for the Burundians and threatened forcible repatriation for the remaining 36,000 refugees. In addition, an estimated 89,000 Congolese refugees remained in Tanzania in 2008. In October Foreign Minister Bernard Membe announced the government intended to seek membership in the OIC. The initiative was met with criticism from the opposition and Christian groups within Tanzania. No action was taken, although the government of Zanzibar subsequently sought permission to join the OIC on its own.

The government announced in March 2009 that it would increase efforts to reduce illegal fishing off its coastline and in its waters in Lake Victoria. Tanzania also joined a multilateral effort with South Africa, Kenya, and Mozambique to patrol waters for poachers of fisheries in the Indian Ocean. In November members of the EAC signed an agreement to create a common market in the region.

On April 16, 2010, the government announced that it would grant citizenship to the remaining Burundian refugees in Tanzania. In May Tanzania, Ethiopia, Kenya, Rwanda, and Uganda, signed an accord which altered previous water-sharing agreements among the nations of the Nile River basin. The new accord was expected to create a more equitable distribution of water resources in the region. The EAC common market was formally launched on July 1.

Kikwete was one of five African presidents to participate in a joint mediation initiative in January 2011 to resolve the political crisis in Côte d'Ivoire (see entry on Côte d'Ivoire). In April the government opened new areas offshore for drilling exploration following oil discoveries in the region by British Petroleum. In May the prime ministers of Tanzania and India signed a series of agreements on counterterrorism cooperation and the suppression of piracy. India also agreed to provide Tanzania with a $180 million line of credit to support infrastructure projects. The following month the United States announced it would provide $70 million to Tanzania to enhance agricultural production. In October Malawi requested African Union (AU) arbitration in a border dispute with Tanzania over disputed maritime boundaries on Lake Malawi (Lake Nyasa). The next month both nations agreed to new negotiations over the disputed areas.

In January 2013 Tanzania announced it would contribute troops to a UN peacekeeping force to be deployed to the Democratic Republic of the Congo (DRC). Kikwete and Chinese president Xi Jingping signed 16 economic cooperation agreements worth $800 million during the latter's state visit to Tanzania in March. The next month Malawi withdrew from maritime negotiations with Tanzania. Then in June, Malawi protested a Tanzanian decision to allow passenger ships to travel in the disputed areas of Lake Malawi.

International donors pledged $559 million to Tanzania to support the government's budget in 2014, up from $495 million the previous year. In June Tanzania announced it would train more than 1,000 Somali soldiers in an effort to improve Somalia's security forces. The United Kingdom extended a $24.5 million grant to Tanzania in July to enhance that government's tax collection efforts. Also in July, Tanzania became the first country to ratify an EAC proposal to create a monetary union.

In September 2015 the World Bank announced an $80 million credit to support economic development in Tanzania.

Following disputed elections on Zanzibar in March 2016 (see Current issues, below), the United States suspended $473 million in aid. However, in August Tanzania and the United States signed a $407 million economic assistance agreement. Meanwhile, in July Tanzania announced it would not sign a trade accord between the East African Community and the European Union (EU) because of the UK referendum on withdrawal from the EU (see entry on the United Kingdom).

Current issues. A series of corruption scandals dominated headlines in 2012. In March, after an annual report from the controller and auditor general blasted a handful of cabinet ministers for corruption and financial laxity, Kabwe launched a petition that threatened a vote of no confidence in the government, eventually gathering signatures from dozens of MPs across party lines. The parliamentary caucus of the CCM demanded the resignation of eight cabinet ministers in response. In May Kikwete announced a cabinet reshuffling, replacing six ministers and transferring two.

After years of rising calls for a new constitution from civil society and opposition parties, Kikwete named on April 6 a 30-member team to recommend constitutional changes over a period of 18 months. Despite initial objections from opposition parties to Kikwete appointing the team's members, the media and public were reportedly supportive of the eventual nominees, which included politicians, academics, lawyers, and activists in different political parties from the mainland and Zanzibar. In May, however, Chadema's John MNYIKA called for a new constitution. He alleged that the ruling party was drafting the revisions behind closed doors.

The country's total estimated natural gas reserves nearly tripled following new finds in May and June 2012 off Tanzania's coast. In August an assessment from the Economist Intelligence Unit predicted the dominance of Kikwete and the CCM would assure stability in the run-up to the October 2015 elections. In October two people died and dozens were injured, including a security officer, during proseparatist rioting in Zanzibar.

In May 2013 riots broke out following a general strike called to protest continuing economic inequality. At least nine protesters were killed and scores arrested in the violence. In reaction the government announced a series of major economic development projects estimated to be worth $500 million. Also in 2013 a wave of attacks against Christians on Zanzibar heightened concerns over the potential of Islamic extremism on the island. In June a new draft constitution was publicized by the constitutional review committee. Proposals included greater protections for civil liberties and the creation of separate regional governments for Tanzania and Zanzibar, with a union government. The new basic document was scheduled to be vetted through local and regional councils before its final ratification by a planned constitutional congress in 2014. Two British female volunteer aid workers were attacked with acid in Zanzibar on August 7. The attack highlighted concerns over Islamic extremism in Zanzibar and prompted the arrest of radical cleric Sheikh Issa PONDA over "incitement" of violence. In November three Chinese nationals were arrested, and 797 elephant tusks were seized during antipoaching raids.

In December 2013 four cabinet ministers were sacked after an investigation charged that security officers and game wardens had murdered 13 civilians and engaged in other crimes, including rape, during antipoaching operations. The dismissals prompted a cabinet reshuffle in January 2014, the announcement in May of the deployment of an additional 900 game wardens, and the creation of an independent wildlife agency. From 2009–2013, the elephant population in Tanzania declined by 25,000.

In September 2014 the constitutional assembly reported that it had suspended deliberations and would resume after general elections scheduled for 2015. Although the delegates had agreed on a range of measures, including a requirement that presidential candidates receive an absolute majority of the vote, the participants were deadlocked over proposals to restructure the federal government to include separate, more-powerful regional governments for Zanzibar and the mainland, along with a smaller, less influential union parliament. Opponents of the draft constitution formed the *Ukawa* grouping. *Ukawa* boycotted a session of the assembly during the summer of 2014. A draft constitution was finalized in October. *Ukawa* threatened to boycott a referendum on a new constitution, leading the president to indefinitely postpone the vote.

A major scandal led to the resignations of the energy and minerals minister, the housing and human settlements minister, and the attorney general between December 2014 and January 2015. More than $122 million that had been earmarked for energy contracts were instead transferred to offshore and private accounts. Five other senior officials were charged with corruption as Kikwete named new ministers in January. International donors withheld more than $449 million in aid in response to the scandal.

The Zanzibar elections commission annulled presidential and legislative elections in Zanzibar on October 25, 2015, citing "gross irregularities" such as voter intimidation and ballot rigging. New voting was scheduled for March 20. However, the CUF called for a boycott of the new polling, asserting that it had actually won the original election. Incumbent president Shein won the new balloting, and the CCM secured a commanding majority in the legislature.

POLITICAL PARTIES

Constitutional amendments in 1992 allowed the formation of political parties other than the CCM. The first multiparty elections were held in 1995. In February 2003 opposition parties formed an electoral coalition to oppose the CCM in presidential and legislative balloting in October 2005. The coalition chose Bob Nyanga MAKANI of Chadema as its chair. The alliance failed to present a unified candidate list for the 2005 legislative balloting and could not unite behind a single candidate in the mainland presidential polling.

Four opposition parties (CUF, TLP, Chadema, and NCCR-Mageuzi) signed an agreement in May 2007 to support a single candidate in the 2010 elections and field joint electoral lists. In December a similar agreement was concluded among five smaller parties, the CCD, the National League for Democracy (NLD), the Progressive Party of Tanzania (PPT-*Maendeleo*), *Sauti Ya Umma* (SAU), and *Demokrasia Makini* (*Makini*). The grouping adopted the Patriotic Front Parties (PFP) designation.

In June 2009, 12 opposition parties in Zanzibar formed an electoral alliance ahead of the 2010 balloting and agreed to support a single candidate in the island's presidential balloting. The parties included the African Progressive Party of Tanzania (APPT-*Maendeleo*), Chadema, *Jahazi Asilia*, NCCR-Mageuzi, *Makini,* NLD, NRA, SAU, TLP, Tadea, UMD, and United People's Democratic Party (UPDP). The grouping was named the **Zanzibar Opposition Alliance**.

Four opposition parties, Chadema, the CUF, the NLD, and NCCR-Mageuzi, formed the **Union for a People's Constitution** (*Umoja wa Katiba ya Wananchi—Ukawa*) ahead of the October 2015 national elections.

Government Party:

Revolutionary Party of Tanzania (*Chama Cha Mapinduzi*—CCM). The CCM was formally launched on February 5, 1977, two weeks after a merger was authorized by a joint conference of the **Tanganyika African National Union** (TANU) and the **Afro-Shirazi Party** (ASP) of Zanzibar. During the January conference, President Nyerere had asserted that the new organization would be supreme" over the governments of both mainland Tanzania and Zanzibar. Subsequently, a National Executive Committee (NEC) was named by a process of hierarchical (indirect) election, with the NEC, in turn, appointing a smaller Central Committee, headed by President Nyerere.

Founded in 1954, TANU was instrumental in winning Tanganyika's independence from Britain in 1961. It served after independence as the nation's leading policymaking forum, nominating the president and candidates for election to the National Assembly. Its program, as set forth in the 1967 Arusha Declaration and other pronouncements, called for the development of a democratic, socialist, one-party state.

The ASP, organized in 1956–1957 by Sheikh Abeid Amani Karume, had played a minor role in Zanzibari politics until the coup of 1964. Subsequently, it became the dominant party in Zanzibar and the leading force in the Zanzibar Revolutionary Council. Communist and Cuban models influenced its explicitly socialist program.

In July 1995 Benjamin William Mkapa, then minister of science, education, and technology, defeated two opponents in intraparty balloting for designation as the CCM presidential nominee, and he won 61.8 percent of the vote in the October–November general election. (For more information on the history of the party, see the 2014 *Handbook*.) Underlining his commitment to a reform-minded agenda, Mkapa named only one senior CCM party official to his technocrat-dominated cabinet. Although observers praised the new president's early initiatives, a split emerged within the party between Mkapa's supporters and old guard members aligned with former first vice president and prime minister Malecela and former party secretary general Horace Kolimba.

At party balloting on June 22, 1996, Mkapa easily captured the party chair and, bringing his reform efforts to bear on the CCM, began to replace old guard members with his supporters. In February 1997 Horace Kolimba publicly denounced the new team of CCM leaders for their lack of "vision" (a charge that was promptly seconded by the CCM's Pius MSEKWA, speaker of the assembly). Furthermore, Kolimba accused the party of abandoning its "socialist" origins. The intraparty flap and public relations imbroglio arising from Kolimba's statements quickly dissipated in March after Kolimba died of a heart attack while defending his position to party officials. At a party congress in 1997, Mkapa was reelected to the party's top post by acclamation; meanwhile, Mkapa's continued efforts to infuse fresh blood into the CCM resulted in the election of a number of new faces to top posts. On the other hand, John Malecela's retention of the vice chair was described by observers as a reminder of the continued influence (albeit waning) of the party's old guard.

In 1998 the CCM experienced further intraparty tension when, after minimal consultation, Mkapa appointed a three-member CCM team to meet with Commonwealth officials in charge of the negotiations to end the Zanzibar stalemate. Several powerful CCM leaders were subsequently reported to be considering forming a breakaway group in reaction to the CCM-CUF agreement of early 1999. However, as the October 2000 national elections approached, the CCM exhibited greater unity and discipline. A March 2000 special congress rejected an intense effort by controversial Zanzibar president Amour to have the constitution amended to permit him to run for a third term. The CCM also subsequently agreed to delay further consideration of proposed constitutional amendments that had been condemned by opposition groups on both the mainland and Zanzibar.

At a June 2000 CCM congress, President Mkapa was selected without opposition to run for a second term in the October poll. Concurrently, Amani Abeid Karume, a longtime member of the Zanzibari cabinet, was chosen as the CCM candidate for president of Zanzibar from among four candidates, including one supported by Amour. Karume was widely viewed as a strong candidate for the post based on his anticorruption image and the fact that he was the son of Abeid Amani Karume, the first president of independent Zanzibar.

Mkapa was reelected party chair at the 2002 CCM party convention. At a party congress in May, Foreign Minister Jakaya Kikwete was chosen as the party's candidate for the mainland presidency. At a party congress in June 2006, Kikwete was elected party chair. In 2007 four senior CCM figures were suspended from the party for alleged misuse of funds, while five regional officials were removed for disobeying party regulations. The disciplinary actions were reported to be part of a larger program by the CCM to improve its national reputation prior to elections in 2010. Kikwete replaced Philip MANGULA with Yusuf MAKAMBA as the CCM secretary general at the party's November 2007 congress. Makamba was a close ally of the president and his choice was reported to be part of a larger effort by Kikwete to consolidate control of the party.

In June two CUF members of Parliament defected to the CCM. In August former APPT-*Maendeleo* presidential candidate Ana SENKORO joined the CCM along with a large number of members of the small party. Former Zanzibar chief minister Dr. Mohamed Gharib BILAL was chosen as Kikwete's vice presidential running mate for the 2010 presidential balloting.

Prior to the 2010 national elections, reports indicated a growing divide within the CCM between an anti-corruption wing, led by then house speaker Samwel SITTA and a status quo or "old guard" faction led by former prime minister Edward LOWASSA. In the October balloting, Kikwete was reelected president of the republic, while vice president Ali Mohamed SHEIN was elected president of Zanzibar. The CCM also secured a majority in the assembly and elected Anna Semamba MAKINDA as the nation's first woman speaker.

In June 2011 Lowassa and other senior CCM officials were forced to resign from the party's national executive committee because of the 2008 arms scandal, reportedly as part of an effort to bolster the image of the CCM prior to new elections in 2015. Other reports indicated that the dismissals were the result of intraparty strife. Lowassa retained the support of most of the CCM's youth wing and used young supporters to pressure CCM leaders. In August Kikwete suspended an ally, Energy and Minerals Permanent Secretary David JAIRO, a month after CCM MP Beatrice MATUMBO SHELLUKINDO read aloud in Parliament a letter from Jairo soliciting money to ensure the smooth passage of the ministries' budgets. Shellukindo later reported receiving death threats. Observers described the rift in the CCM as increasingly bitter, while Kikwete, taking frequent trips abroad, remained aloof.

The CCM's elections to determine party leadership at a variety of local, regional, and national levels were scattered throughout 2012 in advance of the party's presidential nomination for the 2015 elections. The main contenders were Lowassa and Sitta, along with Bernard Membe, Works Minister John MAGUFULI, and Asha-Rose MIGIRO. Under new rules instituted by Kikwete, district leaders—rather than regional leaders—will make up a greater proportion of NEC delegates, a change that was intended to empower grassroots supporters but that some observers said could open the door to widespread vote buying. In November 2012 Abdulrahman KINANA became secretary general of the party.

The CCM joined the Socialist International in February 2013. More than 30 candidates announced their intention to seek the party's nomination for the presidency in 2015. The leading candidates included former prime ministers Lowassa and Frederick Tluway Sumaye, along with Membe, Migiro, and Magufuli. Magufuli was chosen as the party's candidate through a system of primaries that culminated in a vote by the CCM executive committee. Lowassa left the party and joined Chadema. Magufuli won the presidential election in October 2015 with 58.5 percent of the vote. The CCM also dominated the federal House elections, securing 55 percent of the vote and 253 seats. Shein was reelected president of Zanzibar following new polling in March 2016, while the party won 81 seats.

Leaders: John MAGUFULI (President of the Republic and Chair), Jakaya KIKWETE (Former President of the Republic), Benjamin William MKAPA (Former President of the Republic), Philip MANGULA (Vice Chair, Mainland), Ali Hassan MWINYI (Former President of the Republic), Ali Mohamed SHEIN (President of Zanzibar), Samia SULUHU (Vice President of the Republic), Kassim MAJALIWA (Prime Minister), Job NDUGAI (Speaker of the National Assembly), Salim Ahmed SALIM (Member of the Executive Committee and Former Secretary General of the Organization of African Unity), Abdulrahman KINANA (Secretary General).

Opposition Parties:

Civic United Front (CUF). Also referenced as the **People's Party** (*Chama Cha Wananchi*—CCW), the CUF was founded in late 1991 by former NCCR-Mageuzi leader James MAPALALA, a lawyer who had also been instrumental in the February 1990 establishment of the Civil and Legal Rights Movement. Mapalala was reportedly arrested following the creation of the CUF, which was then deemed to be an illegal formation.

As in the case of other opposition groups, the CUF has been wracked by internal dissent; party chair Mapalala went so far in 1994 as to institute court action against his deputy, Seif Sharif Hamad, and Secretary General Shaaban MLOO. Although Hamad was officially declared runner-up to Salmin Amour in Zanzibar's 1995 presidential race, many observers felt he was the actual victor. Labeling the Amour government "illegal," the CUF refused to assume its Zanzibar parliamentary seats and accused the government of falsely arresting its members. Thereafter, despite a ban on its activities, CUF-directed unrest spread, with observers attributing incidents of arson and harassment to the group.

The split between the CUF's mainland and island wings widened dramatically in early 1997 when the former passed a resolution recognizing Amour's Zanzibar government. Intraparty dissension continued to plague the CUF throughout the year, and, in December, 14 members were arrested for their alleged roles in a coup plot in Zanzibar. In early 1998 further arrests of CUF dissidents were reported.

In May 1998 Mapalala broke with the CUF, announcing that he had formed a new group, the Justice and Development Party (below). Meanwhile, at Commonwealth-brokered negotiations with the Amour administration, CUF islanders agreed to participate in legislative proceedings, abandoning the position that Amour had to be removed prior to the representatives being seated.

The trial of the 18 CUF members (including four members of the House of Representatives) arrested in 1997–1998 formally opened in February 1999, the charge against them having been upgraded to treason, which carried a mandatory death sentence upon conviction. Proceedings were subsequently postponed until January 2000, when another short session resulted in further delay until at least August. Meanwhile, domestic and international human rights groups criticized the prolonged imprisonment of the defendants, whom Amnesty International described as "prisoners of conscience," and the apparent political nature of the charges.

At a general congress in early June 2000, Hamad was once again selected as the CUF candidate for president of Zanzibar in the balloting scheduled for October. The CUF candidate for president of Tanzania, Ibrahim LIPUMBA, finished second in the 2000 poll with 16.3 percent of the vote, while Hamad was credited with 33 percent of the vote in the controversial balloting for president of Zanzibar. Meanwhile, all of the 16 seats the CUF secured in the 2000 balloting for the Zanzibar House of Representatives came from CUF strongholds on Pemba. In the 2005 elections, Hamad was again the CUF's candidate for the presidency of Zanzibar. Hamad was defeated in controversial balloting in which he received 46.1 percent of the vote. (Only 32,000 votes separated Hamad from the winning candidate.)

In the legislative balloting in Zanzibar, the CUF increased its seats in the house to 19. Lipumba was also the CUF candidate for president of Tanzania in 2005, but he was again defeated, securing only 11.7 percent of the vote. The CUF remained the largest opposition party with 30 seats in the Tanzanian assembly.

In 2007 the CUF led efforts to create an electoral coalition of opposition parties ahead of the 2010 elections. The CUF undertook a boycott of the Zanzibar assembly in April 2008 in an effort to force the ruling CCM to create a unity government on the islands. After refusing to accept the results of the 2005 presidential balloting on Zanzibar, the CUF finally agreed in May 2008 to accept Amani Abeid Karume of the

CCM as the legitimate leader of Zanzibar. Meanwhile, negotiations between the CUF and the CCM on a power-sharing arrangement in Zanzibar broke down during the summer.

The party's three top leaders, including Hamad, Lipumba, and Machano Khamis ALI, were reelected to their posts at a CUF congress in February 2009. Former CUF member of parliament and CUF deputy secretary general Wilfred LWAKATERE defected to Chadema in June, along with several hundred of his supporters after he lost his leadership position.

Lipumba placed third in balloting for president of Tanzania in October 2010, while Hamad placed second in polling for president of Zanzibar. In the direct legislative elections, the CUF increased its seats in the Zanzibar assembly to 22, but lost one seat in the national parliament to bring its total to 18. In September 2011, during a by-election, a CUF candidate was charged with election violations, accusations the party claimed were politically motivated.

In June 2013 the CUF organized a demonstration in Dar es Salaam against both rising crime and incidents of police brutality. Meanwhile, senior CUF leaders called on party members to support the proposed constitution. At a July 2014 party conference, Hamad and Lipumba were both reelected to their respective posts. In September, Hamad announced his intention to seek the party's nomination for the 2015 presidential election. In August 2015 Lipumba resigned.

The CUF was part of the *Ukawa* coalition and backed Edward LOWASSA in the 2015 presidential elections. The party received 8.6 percent of the vote in the concurrent legislative balloting and 42 seats. The CUF boycotted the rerun polling on Zanzibar in March 2016. In August Lipumba and ten other CUF members were temporarily suspended from the party after reportedly disrupting a meeting to choose new party leaders.

Leaders: Seif Sharif HAMAD (1995, 2000, 2005, and 2010 presidential candidate of Zanzibar and General Secretary), Ibrahim LIPUMBA (1995, 2000, 2005, and 2010 presidential candidate of Tanzania), Machano Khamis ALI (Vice Chair).

Party for Democracy and Progress (*Chama Cha Demokrasia na Maendeleo*—Chadema). Chadema was launched in 1993 by former finance minister Edwin I. M. Mtei. It was awarded three elected assembly seats in 1995. (For more information on the history of the party, see the 2015 *Handbook*.)

Chadema supported the CUF candidate in the 2000 presidential poll; in concurrent legislative balloting the party improved its representation to four of the elected seats. The Chadema vice presidential candidate in the 2005 mainland elections died on October 27, 2005, causing a postponement of the balloting until December 14. The party's presidential candidate, Freeman MBOWE, placed third with 5.9 percent of the vote. Chadema secured five of the elected seats in the legislative polls. Chadema refused to participate in the CUF-led parliamentary boycott in Zanzibar, but it joined the CUF in an electoral coalition ahead of the 2010 balloting.

In 2009 a number of CUF members defected to Chadema and were rewarded with leadership posts within the party. Deputy Secretary General of Chadema Zitto Kabwe launched a campaign to take the party's top leadership post away from Mbowe in party elections scheduled for the fall. Chadema was instrumental in the formation of the Zanzibar Opposition Alliance in preparation for the 2010 elections. After losing a party primary in 2010, Chadema member Charles MWERA defected to the CUF, along with a number of other party members. Chadema secretary general Willibrod Peter SLAA was the party's 2010 presidential nominee. He placed second in the balloting. In legislative elections, Chadema dramatically increased its seats in the parliament to 28, overtaking the CUF as the largest opposition party. In August 2011 a by-election was postponed following a court challenge by Chadema that other candidates had violated election laws.

To many observers, the victory of Chadema candidate Joshua NASSARI in the April 1, 2012, Arumeru East by-election, seen as a key opener for the 2015 polls, signaled that the party could challenge the CCM's continued dominance and end its era of landslide victories. Following the election, some 300 young men, many armed, invaded a nearby gated estate that Nassari had identified for redistribution. On April 27 Ally BANANGA, who had been a member of CCM's National Central Committees, defected to the Chadema.

Beginning in February 2013, Chadema led a boycott of an assembly committee's investigation into misconduct by members of the assembly. On June 16 a bomb attack killed four at a Chadema rally in Arusha. Chadema officials claimed the attack was directed at party members who had defected from the CCM. Mbowe was briefly detained by security forces in September 2014 over what were reported to be "inflammatory" comments at a party congress. At the same congress, Mbowe and Slaa were reelected.

Former CCM prime minister Edward LOWASSA joined the party in 2015 and became the *Ukawa* candidate in that year's presidential balloting. He placed second with 40 percent of the vote. In the 2016 parliamentary balloting, the party secured 31.8 percent of the vote and 70 seats.

Leaders: Freeman MBOWE (2005 presidential candidate and Chair), Edward LOWASSA (2015 presidential candidate), Edwin I. M. MTEI (2000 presidential candidate), Willibrod Peter SLAA (Secretary General and 2010 presidential candidate).

National Convention for Constitution and Reform–Mageuzi (NCCR-Mageuzi). The NCCR-Mageuzi was formed in the first half of 1991 as an outgrowth of the Steering Committee for a Transition Towards a Multiparty System, a broad-based organization comprising leading business owners and lawyers as well as political dissidents and student activists. Its initial chair, Abdallah Said FUNDIKIRA, and vice chair, James K. Mapalala, subsequently formed splinter organizations (below), although their successors vowed to keep the committee at the forefront of the "multiparty debate" and to push for its legalization. The party was again split in 1994 when Secretary General Prince Mahinja BAGENDA and several of his supporters withdrew to form the National Convention for Constitution and Reform–*Asili* (the Swahili word for "original").

In April 1995 Augustine Lyatonga MREMA, who had been dismissed as minister of labor and youth development in February for "indiscipline" and who withdrew from the CCM a month later, was selected as the NCCR-Mageuzi's standard-bearer for the presidential election in October. Mrema was credited with 27.8 percent of the vote, while his party captured only 16 assembly seats.

In May 1997 Mabere MARANDO, the NCCR-Mageuzi's secretary general, and Masumbuko LAMWAI, a NCCR-Mageuzi parliamentarian and former CCM member, attempted to oust Mrema, who had accused Marando of acting in complicity with the CCM. During the subsequent legal and political infighting, the Central Committee reportedly aligned behind Marando and his supporters and the National Executive Committee with Mrema. The reportedly irreconcilable nature of the split was underscored by the unwillingness of the two factions (styled the NCCR-Mrema and NCCR-Marando) to cooperate on by-election campaigns, thus, according to observers, costing the group winnable legislative seats. Furthermore, in October both factions sent representatives to an opposition summit.

After sustained legal and political infighting between the two camps, in April 1999 Mrema announced that he was leaving the NCCR-Mageuzi to join the TLP (see below). Lamwai subsequently rejoined the CCM. The NCCR-Mageuzi won only one elected seat in the 2000 legislative poll, while its proposed presidential candidate, Edith LUSINA, was precluded from running for failure to secure sufficient advance signatures of support.

In the 2005 presidential election, four parties, including the FORD, NRA, UMD, and UPDP, agreed to support the NCCR-Mageuzi candidate, Sengondo Mvungi. The NCCR-Mageuzi failed to gain any seats in the assembly. In 2007 the NCCR-Mageuzi became part of the CUF-led opposition electoral coalition. In September 2008 Mvungi was injured when violence erupted at a NCCR-Mageuzi rally. The NCCR-Mageuzi blamed the incident on pro-CCM youths. The NCCR-Mageuzi led the opposition to the government initiative to join the OIC in 2008–2009 (see Foreign relations, above).

Hashim Spunda RUNGWE was the party's 2010 candidate in the presidential balloting. He placed fifth in the voting with less than one percent of the votes. The NCCR-Mageuzi secured four seats in the national parliament in concurrent legislative elections. Ambar Haji KHAMIS was the NCCR-Mageuzi candidate in the Zanzibar presidential balloting. He also received less than 1 percent of the vote and the party did not gain any seats in the Zanzibar assembly. In by-election voting for the representative for the Igunga district, the NCCR-Mageuzi endeavored unsuccessfully to convince opposition parties to support a single candidate.

The party joined a Chadema-led boycott of an investigation into parliamentary misconduct in 2013, arguing that the inquiry was politically motivated. Party leader James MBATIA dismissed reports in September 2014 that he would campaign for the union presidency in 2015, asserting that he instead would stand for parliament.

The party was part of the *Ukawa* opposition alliance and backed Edward Lowassa for the presidency in October 2015. It won 1.5 percent of the vote in the concurrent House balloting, earning one seat.

Leaders: James MBATIA (Chair), Hashim Spunda RUNGWE (2010 presidential candidate), Sengondo MVUNGI (2005 presidential candidate), Hussein Mwaiseje POLISYA (Secretary General).

Alliance for Change and Transparency (ACT). The ACT was formed in 2014. It obtained one seat in the federal House when former CCM member of parliament Zito KABWE joined the grouping in 2015. Its 2015 presidential candidate, Anna Elisha MGHWIRA, placed third in that year's elections with 0.7 percent of the vote. The party won 2.2 percent of the vote in concurrent House balloting and one seat.

Leaders: Zito KABWE, Anna Elisha MGHWIRA (Chair and 2015 presidential candidate), Juma SAANANI (Secretary General).

Other Parties That Contested the 2015 Elections:

United Democratic Party (UDP). The UDP's John Cheyo ran fourth in the 1995 presidential race, with a 3.9 percent vote share; in the assembly balloting the party ran fifth, winning three elective seats. In 1997 the UDP added a fifth seat when Cheyo scored an upset victory in a by-election contest. Cheyo secured 4.2 percent of the vote in the 2000 presidential poll. The UDP was a member of the opposition electoral coalition in the 2005 balloting and supported the CUF candidate in the presidential election. The party secured one seat in the assembly. In 2007 Cheyo emerged as one of the most vocal critics of government corruption. In June 2009 Cheyo was temporarily ejected from Parliament for his conduct during a debate on the government's response to pollution. Yahmi Nassoro DOVUTWA was the UDP presidential candidate in the 2010 elections. He placed sixth with less than 1 percent of the vote. The UDP did retain one seat in the assembly balloting. The UDP won just 0.09 percent of the vote in 2015 and no seats.

Leaders: John CHEYO (Chair and 1995 and 2000 presidential candidate), Yahmi Nassoro DOVUTWA (2010 presidential candidate), Isaac CHEYO (Acting Secretary General).

Tanzania Democratic Alliance Party (Tadea). The previously London-based Tadea was founded by Oscar Salathiel KAMBONA, a former TANU secretary general and Nyerere cabinet member who went into voluntary exile in 1967 after government authorities alleged he had been involved in a coup plot. Kambona was also one of the founders of the Tanzania Democratic Front (TDF), formed in London by a number of exile opposition groups to promote the introduction of a multiparty system. Tadea was registered in Tanzania in 1993. In 1996 Tadea was buffeted by allegations that its officials had misused publicly funded campaign finances.

The party joined the opposition alliance to contest the 2005 elections and supported the CUF mainland presidential candidate. In the October 2010 presidential elections in Zanzibar, Tadea secretary general Juma Ali KHATIB was the party's candidate. He placed fifth with less than 1 percent of the vote. Tadea competed unsuccessfully in a by-election for Bububu in September 2012. In August 2014 Tadea's central committee expelled party leader John D. LIFA-CHIPAKA, replacing him with Joackim MWINGIRA.

The party only won 0.09 percent of the vote in the federal House elections in 2015, but it secured one seat in the Zanzibar House in 2016.

Leaders: Joackim MWINGIRA (Acting Chair), John D. LIFA-CHIPAKA, Juma Ali KHATIB (Secretary General and 2010 presidential candidate).

Tanzania Labour Party (TLP). This small party's profile grew significantly in 1999 when the leading opposition figure Augustine Mrema and over 1,000 of his followers joined after leaving the NCCR-Mageuzi. Mrema won 7 percent of the vote in the 2000 presidential poll, while the TLP secured three seats in concurrent assembly elections. The TLP opposed the opposition coalition formed for the October 2005 election and decided to contest the balloting independently. Its candidate, Mrema, placed fourth with less than 1 percent of the vote, and the TLP secured one seat in the assembly. In 2007 the TLP agreed to participate in the CUF-led electoral coalition. In October a court stripped TLP parliamentary deputy Phares KABUYE of his seat because he had defamed his rival in the 2005 balloting. In 2008 many TLP members reportedly defected to other parties. The party nominated Muttamwega Bhatt Mgaywa as its presidential candidate for Tanzania in 2010. He received less than 1 percent of the vote. On July 10, 2011, the party's central committee voted to suspend Deputy Secretary General Rajabu TAO after he allegedly submitted wrongful personal information about TLP candidates to the National Electoral Commission. The month before, Tao had alleged that Mrema had misappropriated party funds.

In 2013 Mrema was accused of corruption by fellow parliamentarians who sought to remove him from the chairmanship of the Local Authority Accounts Committee. The TLP joined a boycott of the constitutional assembly in August 2014. It won just 0.1 percent of the vote in the 2015 House balloting and no seats. Its presidential candidate, Machmillan Elifatio LYIMO, secured just 0.05 percent of the vote.

Leaders: Augustine MREMA (Chair and 2000 and 2005 presidential candidate), Muttamwega Bhatt MGAYWA (2010 presidential candidate).

Union for Multiparty Democracy (UMD). The UMD was organized in late 1991 by Abdallah Said Fundikira, a well-known Tanzanian businessman, and others who had previously been involved in the NCCR. They proposed that a national conference be held to draft a new Tanzanian constitution that would permit multiparty activity. In addition, the UMD suggested that the union between the mainland and the islands of Zanzibar and Pemba be reevaluated. Following the formation of the UMD, Fundikira was arrested and released on bail after being charged with establishing an illegal organization. The UMD was nonetheless registered in 1993. The UMD supported the NCCR-Mageuzi candidate in the 2005 presidential elections and failed to gain any seats in the assembly. The UMD did not gain any seats in the 2010 legislative balloting. Reports in 2011 indicated that the party had become limited to a small number of areas, and in the 2015 House balloting, it won just 0.01 percent of the vote.

Leaders: Chief Abdallah Said FUNDIKIRA (President of the Party and 1995 presidential candidate), Stephen M. KIBUGA (Vice President), Hussein Hassan YAHAYA (Secretary General).

National Reconstruction Alliance (NRA). Former industries and trade minister Kigoma Ali MALIMA resigned from the CCM on July 16 to become the NRA's 1995 presidential candidate; however, he died unexpectedly on August 5. The NRA joined the electoral coalition that supported the NCCR-Mageuzi candidate in the 2005 elections. After being denied a permit for a demonstration in August 2008 in Zanzibar, the NRA filed a lawsuit against security forces. In presidential balloting on Zanzibar, the NRA candidate, Haji Khamis HAJI, placed fourth with less than one percent of the vote. The party won only 0.01 percent of the vote in the 2015 legislative elections.

Leaders: Rashid MTUTA (Chair), Maoud RATUU (Secretary General), Haji Khamis HAJI (2010 presidential candidate).

Justice and Development Party (*Chama cha Haki na Usitawi*—Chausta). Chausta was launched in Zanzibar in May 1998 by former CUF leader James Mapalala. According to Mapalala, the new party was founded on the principle of development of the "individual." The party was officially recognized in late 2001. In August 2008 CCM youth disrupted a Chausta rally in Zanzibar. Chausta failed to win any seats in the 2010 legislative balloting and lost several by-elections in 2011 and 2014. It secured just 0.06 percent of the vote in the 2015 legislative elections.

Leaders: James MAPALALA (Chair), Joseph MKOMAGU (Secretary General).

Democratic Party (*Chama Cha Demokrasi*—CCD). The CCD was formed in late 1991 in anticipation of the introduction of a multiparty system. The CCD is sometimes referred to as the DP. Soon thereafter, the party was thrust into the national limelight by the August 1992 conviction of its leader, Christopher Mtikila, on charges of illegal assembly. The High Court subsequently dismissed the charges against Mtikila, whose nationalistic rhetoric had made him increasingly popular. However, in January 1993 Mtikila was arrested on charges of having fomented sedition and rioting by a speech in which he had accused the government of having "sold [Tanzania] to Arabs and Gabacholics [Asians]," urged Indo-Pakistanis, Arabs, Somalians, and Zanzibaris to emigrate, and warned that blood would flow if the alleged favoritism to foreigners continued. He was rearrested a number of times thereafter on a variety of charges, including the leadership of illegal demonstrations.

In 1997 Mtikila ran as a Chadema candidate in a legislative by-election, thus casting uncertainty on the future of the CCD, which had been unable to secure official recognition because of its unwillingness to accept Zanzibar as a legitimate part of the country. The CCD's candidate in the 2005 presidential election was Mtikila, who placed sixth in the balloting.

In 2008 the CCD joined with four other opposition parties in the Patriotic Front Parties coalition. The party did not gain any seats in the 2010 legislative elections. The CCD boycotted sessions of the constitutional assembly in 2014. It won 0.1 percent of the vote in the 2015 House polling.

Leaders: Christopher MTIKILA (Chair and 2005 presidential candidate), Natanga NYAGAWA (Secretary General).

Other parties that contested the 2010 or 2015 elections (none received more than 1 percent of the vote) included the **African Progressive Party of Tanzania** (APPT-*Maendeleo*), formed in 2003 and led by Peter Kuga MZIRAY (Chair and 2010 presidential candidate); ***Jahazi Asilia***, led by Abuu Juma AMOUR (Chair) and 2010 Zanzibar presidential candidate Kassim Bakar ALIY; the ***Demokrasia Makini*** (*Makini*), formed in 2001 and led by Godfrey HICHEKA and Georgia MTIKILA; and the ***Sauti Ya Umma*** (SAU), formed in 2005 and led by Paulo KYARA (2005 presidential candidate and Chair).

Other parties that participated in the 2010 or 2015 balloting included the **National League for Democracy** (NLD), led by Emmanuel MAKAIDI; the **United People's Democratic Party** (UPDP), led by Fahmi Nassoro DOVUTWA; the **Party of Associations** (*Chama Cha Kijamii*—CCK), led by Constantine AKITANDA; the **Movement for Economic Change** (MEC); and the **Association of Farmer's Party** (*Chama Cha Wakulima*—AFP), formed in 2009, led by Soud Said SOUD (Chair and 2010 Zanzibar presidential candidate) and which won one seat in the Zanzibar House in 2015.

For information on the **Forum for Restoration of Democracy** (FORD), the **Patriotic Front Parties** (PFP), the **Zanzibar Organization,** the **Party of Society** (*Chama Cha Jamii*—CCJ), and the banned **Council for the Dissemination of the Koran in Tanzania** (*Balukta*), see the 2010 *Handbook.* See the 2015 *Handbook* for information on the **Association for the Awakening and Propagation of Islam in Zanzibar** (*Jumuiya ya Uamsho na Mihadhara ya Kiislamu Zanzibar—Uamsho*).

LEGISLATURE

The Tanzania **National Assembly** (*Bunge*), also referenced as the Union Parliament, has a five-year mandate, barring dissolution. The current assembly totals 384 members, including 264 members directly elected in single-member constituencies. The constitution requires that women hold 20 percent of the assembly seats, an increase of 5 percent with the elections in 2000. Following every general election, parties in the assembly must nominate (according to the seats they hold) a number of women to fill any remaining seats of the 20 percent allotted them. The Zanzibar House of Representatives elects 5 of its members to the assembly, and the Tanzanian attorney general is entitled to a legislative seat. Another revision made in 2000 allows the president to appoint 10 members. At the most recent balloting of October 25, 2015, the Revolutionary Party of Tanzania secured 253 seats (189 of the directly elected seats, and 64 seats reserved for women); Party for Democracy and Progress, 70 (34, 36); Civic United Front, 42 (32, 10); National Convention for Constitution and Reform–Mageuzi, 1 (1, 0); and Alliance for Change and Transparency, 1 (1, 0).

Speaker: Job NDUGAI (CCM).

The Zanzibar **House of Representatives** is a 82-member body encompassing 50 elected members, 10 presidential nominees, 20 members representing women and selected organizations, the attorney general (ex officio), and the speaker if elected from outside the House. At the rerun balloting of March 20, 2016, the Revolutionary Party of Tanzania won 47 of the elected seats; Alliance for Democratic Change, 1; Tanzania Democratic Alliance Party, 1; and Association of Farmer's Party, 1.

Speaker: Zubeir Ali MAULID (CCM).

CABINET

[as of September 15, 2016]

President	John Magufuli
Vice President	Samia Suluhu [f]
President of Zanzibar	Ali Mohamed Shein
Prime Minister	Kassim Majaliwa
Ministers of State in the President's Office	
Good Governance	George Simbachawene
Regional Administration and Local Government	Angellah Kairuki [f]
Minister of State in the Vice President's Office	
Union Affairs and Environment	January Makamba
Minister of State in the Prime Minister's Office	
Parliamentary Affairs, Labor, Employment, and Youth and the Disabled	Jenista Mhagama [f]
Ministers	
Agriculture, Livestock, and Fisheries	Charles Tizeba
Defense and National Service	Hussein Mwinyi
Education, Science, and Vocational Training	Joyce Ndalichako [f]
Energy and Mineral Resources	Sospeter Muhongo
Finance and Economic Affairs	Philip Mpango
Foreign Affairs and International Cooperation	Augustine Mahiga
Health and Welfare Development	Ummy Mwalimu [f]
Home Affairs	Mwigulu Nchemba
Industries and Trade	Charles Mwijage
Information, Culture, and Sport	Nape Nnauye
Justice and Constitutional Affairs	Harrison Mwakyembe
Lands, Housing, and Human Settlement	William Lukuvi
Tourism	Jumanne Maghembe
Water and Irrigation	Gerson Lwenge
Works	Makame Mbarawa

[f] = female

INTERGOVERNMENTAL REPRESENTATION

Ambassador to the U.S.: Wilson MASILINGI.

U.S. Ambassador to Tanzania: Virginia BLASER (Chargé d'Affaires).

Permanent Representative to the UN: Tuvako N. MANONGI.

IGO Memberships (Non-UN): AfDB, AU, Comesa, CWTH, ICC, IOM, NAM, SADC, WTO.

For Further Reference:

Aminzade, Ronald. *Race, Nation, and Citizenship in Postcolonial Africa: The Case of Tanzania.* Cambridge: Cambridge University Press, 2013.

Brennen, James R. *Taifa: Making Nation and Race in Urban Tanzania.* Athens: Ohio University Press, 2012.

Maddox, Gregory H., and James L. Giblin, eds. *In Search of a Nation: Histories of Authority and Dissidence in Tanzania.* Athens: Ohio University Press, 2006,

THAILAND

Kingdom of Thailand
Prathet Thai

Note: Considerable variation occurs in the English transliteration of Thai names. Where possible, Thai sources have been relied on, but these also present variations.

Political Status: Independent monarchy functioning under a constitution approved by popular referendum on August 19, 2007, validated by the Constitutional Drafting Assembly on August 21, and promulgated on August 24. The constitution was suspended following a military coup on May 22, 2014, but replaced by a new constitution approved by referendum on August 7, 2016; executive and legislative authority is still vested in the National Council for Peace and Order (NCPO) until the new constitution takes effect and a general election is held in late 2017.

Area: 198,455 sq. mi. (514,000 sq. km).

Population: 68,147,000 (2016E—UN); 68,200,824 (2016E—U.S. Census).

Major Urban Center (2016E—UN): BANGKOK (metropolitan area, 9,444,000).

Official Language: Thai.

Monetary Unit: Thai Baht (market rate October 1, 2016: 34.59 baht = $1US).

Sovereign: King Maha VAJIRALONGKORN (King RAMA X); ascended the throne December 1, 2016, in succession to his father King BHUMIBOL Adulyadej (King RAMA IX), who died on October 13.
Heir Apparent: Dipangkorn RASMIJOTI.

Prime Minister: PRAYUTH Chan-ocha; appointed by the king on May 26, 2014, to succeed Acting Prime Minister Niwatthamrong BOONSONGPAISAN (For Thais Party) following a military coup on May 22.

THE COUNTRY

The Kingdom of Thailand (known historically as Siam) is located in the heart of mainland Southeast Asia. Its immediate neighbors are Myanmar (Burma) in the west, Laos in the north and northeast, Cambodia in the southeast, and Malaysia in the deep south. Thailand is a tropical country of varied mountainous and lowland terrain. About 75 percent of its population is Thai; another 14 percent are ethnic Chinese, mostly urban residents prominent in commerce, banking, and manufacturing. Other minorities are of Malaysian, Indian, Khmer, and Vietnamese descent. Theravada Buddhism is professed by about 95 percent of the population, but religious freedom prevails and a number of other religions claim adherents. Women constitute approximately 51 percent of the labor force, primarily in agriculture; female participation in government, while increasing somewhat in recent years, remains low. Following the most recent elections in 2008 and 2011, women constituted 15.4 percent of the Senate and 15.8 percent of the House of Representatives, respectively. Yingluck SHINAWATRA became the first woman prime minister of Thailand in 2011.

Like most countries in Southeast Asia, Thailand is predominantly rural, with over 40 percent of its people still engaged in agriculture. Bulk and processed foodstuffs, especially rice, and other agricultural products, such as rubber, account for the majority of export earnings, but the growth of industrial output since the mid-1980s has raised earnings from manufactured goods that range from garments and electrical appliances to information technology items and vehicle components. Tourism is also a significant earner. The country's mineral resources include cassiterite (tin ore), tungsten, antimony, coal, iron, lead, manganese, molybdenum, and gemstones. Thailand's primary trade partners are Japan, China, the United States, the European Union, and the ASEAN region.

In 1999 gross domestic product (GDP) growth was 4.4 percent, rising to 6.1 percent by 2004. (For more on the economy prior to 1999, see the 2012 *Handbook.*) The Indian Ocean tsunami of December 2004—which according to official reports killed more than 100,000 people, left another 700,000 homeless, and caused $4.4 billion in property and infrastructure damage—combined with a drought, a weaker electronics market, and political unrest in the southern provinces reduced growth to 4.5 percent in 2005. Uncertainty following a military takeover in 2006, public demonstrations around the 2008 change of government, and the subsequent international financial crisis also depressed the growth rate, which was a recessionary—2.3 percent in 2009. In 2010 the IMF reported that GDP grew by 7.8 percent, but only by 0.1 percent in 2011, before rising by 6.4 percent in 2012 and 2.3 percent in 2013. That year inflation rose by 2.2 percent, and the official unemployment rate was 0.7 percent. GDP per capita in 2013 was $5,674. The May 2014 coup (see Current issues, below) led to a 0.6 percent fall in GDP for the months of May through July. However, the economy began to grow by the end of July, helped by a massive $75 billion infrastructure program launched by the military government. The Thai economy slowly regained strength and achieved GDP growth of 2.8 percent in 2015 after the coup. In the first half of 2016, the Thai economy continued its recovery and was projected to reach 3.2 percent growth in 2016. Inflation was projected at 0.9 percent in 2016, and unemployment at 0.8 percent. GDP per capita that year was $5,393. In its annual ease of doing business index in 2016, the World Bank ranked Thailand 49th out of 189 countries, a sharp decline from 18th in 2013 when it had a higher rating than that of more economically developed nations such as Canada (19th) or Germany (21st).

GOVERNMENT AND POLITICS

Political background. Historical records indicate that the Thai people migrated to present-day Thailand from China's Yunnan Province about a thousand years ago. By the 14th century the seat of authority was established in Ayutthaya. Toward the end of the 18th century, Burmese armies conquered the kingdom but were eventually driven out by Rama I, who founded the present ruling dynasty and moved the capital south to Bangkok in 1782. Upon the conquest of Burma by the British in 1826, Rama III began the process of accommodating European colonial powers by negotiating a treaty of amity and commerce with Britain. Subsequent monarchs, Rama IV and V, by a combination of diplomacy and governmental modernization, avoided colonization by European powers in the 19th and early 20th century, the only Southeast Asian country to do so.

Thailand was ruled as an absolute monarchy until 1932, when a group of military and civilian officials led by Col. (later Field Mar.) Luang PIBULSONGGRAM (PIBUL Songgram) and Pridi PHANOMYONG seized power in the first of a series of military coups. The Pibulsonggram dictatorship sided with the Japanese in World War II, but the anti-Japanese *Seri Thai* (Free Thai) movement, led by Pridi and Seni PRAMOJ, paved the way for reconciliation with the Allied powers at the war's end. Pridi dominated the first postwar government but was discredited and fled to China in 1947. Pibulsonggram ruled for the following decade, until overthrown by Field Marshal Sarit THANARAT, who in turn was succeeded in 1963 by Field Marshal Thanom KITTIKACHORN with the support of Gen. Prapas CHARUSATHIRA, the army commander and national strongman.

Following promptings from the throne, the military regime in June 1968 promulgated a new constitution restoring limited parliamentary government. In the resultant 1969 election the Democrat Party (DP), led by Seni Pramoj, won all seats in the major urban centers of Bangkok and Chon Buri, but the government, through its vehicle the United Thai People's Party (UTPP), mustered sufficient strength elsewhere to retain control. The Thanom government in November 1971 dissolved the legislature, suspended the constitution, and banned all political parties except the government-sponsored Revolutionary Party. In October 1973, however, as a result of widespread student demonstrations and disapproval of the king, the Thanom government fell, and the rector of Thammasat University, SANYA Dharmasakti (Thammasak), was appointed prime minister. A period of civilian democratic rule, led successively by Sanya, Seni Promoj, and KUKRIT Pramoj, lasted until October 1976, when Adm. SANGAD Chaloryu reasserted military control. He was succeeded by Gen. KRIANGSAK Chamanan in 1977, and then Gen. PREM Tinsulanond in 1980.

In 1988 a period of civilian-led constitutionalism began. Leaders such as Maj. Gen. CHATCHAI Choonhavan and Gen. CHAOVALIT Yongchaiyut resigned their military commissions, joined political parties, and led civilian-dominated multi-party coalition governments. Subsequently, civilian party leaders, including the DP's CHUAN Leekpai and BANHARN Silpa-Archa of the *Chart Thai* (Thai Nation), emerged to win the prime minister's post by means of constitutional elections. (For details of the period 1970–2000, see the 2010 *Handbook.*)

A landmark election took place in January 2001, in which the *Thai Rak Thai* (Thais Love Thais) party, emerged into prominence by winning 248 seats in a 500-seat House of Representatives. Its founder, THAKSIN Shinawatra, who had amassed a fortune in the telecommunications industry and served as a minister in previous civilian governments, negotiated a coalition with the New Aspiration Party (NAP) and *Chart Thai* enabling him to claim the office of prime minister.

Prime Minister Thaksin's popularity in rural Thailand, coupled with a well-managed response to the December 2004 tsunami disaster, carried Thaksin to a further election victory in February 2005. *Thai Rak Thai* won a commanding 377 House seats, permitting Thaksin to form a one-party government. The opposition DP won only 96 seats.

During the following year, opposition to the prime minister's policies and alleged authoritarianism grew, especially among middle-class and upper-class political elites in Bangkok, where in February 2006 an anti-Thaksin rally drew an estimated 100,000 protesters to Royal Plaza. A direct precipitant had been the tax-free sale by Thaksin's family of its 49 percent stake in the Shin Corporation, a telecommunications company, for $1.9 billion. Immediately after the anti-Thaksin rally, leaders from some 40 nongovernmental organizations and other groups announced formation of a People's Alliance for Democracy (PAD), which demanded Thaksin's resignation and a return to political reform. The PAD brought together a broad cross-section of predominantly urban interest groups, including nongovernmental organizations, academics, students, organized labor, businesses, and advocates for the poor. The PAD campaign, in addition to demanding Thaksin's resignation, hoped to rekindle the political reform movement that had brought down the government of Suchinda KRAPRAYOON in 1992. Critics of the PAD alleged, however, that it was covertly manipulated by the military and the Bangkok elite to derail the rural reforms proposed by the *Thai Rak Thai.*

Responding to the growing crisis of confidence in his administration, on February 26 Thaksin dissolved the House of Representatives and called an election for April 2. Opposition leaders Abhisit VEJJAJIVA of the DP, former prime minister Banharn Silpa-Archa of *Chart Thai,* and Sanan KACHORNPRASART of *Mahachon* (Public Party) announced that they would boycott the election. Although Thaksin's party won 61 percent of the valid votes, 38 percent of voters abstained and about 12 percent of ballots were deliberately spoiled by voters. Consequently, on April 5 Thaksin announced that he was "taking some time off" and named Deputy Prime Minister Chitchai WANNASATHIT to act in his stead.

On April 25, 2006, in a nationwide address, King Bhumibol asked the nation's highest courts to resolve the country's "political mess." By that time, lawsuits had been filed requesting nullification of the April 2 results, and on May 8 the Constitutional Court did so by an 8–6 vote, primarily on technical grounds that voters' right to a secret ballot had been compromised by the positioning of voting booths and that the Electoral Commission had not allowed sufficient time between the late February dissolution of the sitting House of Representatives and the election date. The court by a 9–5 decision further ordered that new elections be held. On May 23 Thaksin reassumed his post, now as caretaker prime minister, and near the end of the month the Election Commission and the cabinet set October 15 as the new election date. As the election campaign intensified, Thaksin's opponents claimed he was corrupt, arrogant, favored cronies in his numerous cabinet shuffles, surrounded himself with "yes men," tried to manage the government as if he were CEO of a private business, and used his political power to curtail media critics.

In addition, the army commander-in-chief, Gen. Sonthi BOONYARATGLIN, a Muslim, objected to the Thaksin government's heavy-handed crackdown on the Muslim insurgency in the south. In January 2004 the government had declared martial law in the three Muslim-majority southern provinces in response to escalating attacks that targeted not only authorities but also school teachers, civil servants, and Buddhist monks. On April 30 a coordinated series of attacks against 11 police bases was met with a lethal response from the police and military, leaving over 100 Muslims dead, 30 of them killed during the storming of a mosque. An official inquiry concluded that excessive force had been used. In October another deadly encounter ended with nearly 80 of some 1,300 detainees suffocating or dying of heat stroke while being transported in overcrowded trucks.

Although Thaksin established a National Reconciliation Commission (NRC) in March 2005 to formulate "peace-building" proposals for the south, in mid-July the cabinet approved an Emergency Powers Act that was promulgated by executive decree. The act, which was passed by both houses of the National Assembly in August, granted Thaksin authority to conduct wiretaps, ban media, conduct searches and detain suspects without warrants, censor news, and ban publications. In January 2006, with the death toll in the south having passed 1,000, Amnesty International accused the government and military of using arbitrary detentions, excessive force, and torture. In June the NRC, headed by former prime minister Anand PANYARACHUN, reported that the underlying issues could not be resolved militarily. Instead, it recommended that indigenous Malay be adopted as a "working language" in the south, that the application of Islamic law be permitted in some situations, that a dialog be opened with militants, that a Fund for Healing and Reconciliation be created, and that mechanisms be established to allow greater local input in cultural and governmental matters.

On September 19, 2006, the Thai military, led by General Sonthi, seized power in a bloodless coup. (For more information, see the 2014 *Handbook.*) On September 20 King Bhumibol appointed General Sonthi head of a Council for Democratic Reform in order "to create peace in the country" while the political impasse was resolved. Sonthi promised to install a civilian government and hold legislative elections under a new constitution by the end of the year. The coup leaders subsequently reconstituted the Council of Democratic Reform as the Council of National Security to advise the interim government. Surayud CHULANONT, a retired general, was named interim prime minister of Thailand by royal decree on October 1. Surayud named a new cabinet, which was sworn in on October 9. The new cabinet enlisted a majority of civilian experts and notables; only three ministers were serving military officers, although others had reserve rank or were retired.

Following the April 2006 election, the Election Commission had recommended to the attorney general that five parties—*Thai Rak Thai,* the DP, and three minor formations—be dissolved for violating the constitution and the Political Party Act. Allegations included that *Thai Rak Thai* had bankrolled small parties to offer token competition, thereby illegally circumventing a requirement that a candidate in an uncontested race had to receive at least 20 percent of the vote to claim the seat. The DP was charged with paying bribes to elicit accusations that *Thai Rak Thai* had committed electoral fraud. The cases were heard by the Constitutional Tribunal, which ruled against *Thai Rak Thai* on May 28, 2007, dissolving the party and excluding 111 of its executives, including Thaksin, from political office for five years. The DP was cleared of electoral fraud, but the other three parties were also dissolved. In June corruption charges were brought against Thaksin and his wife, and many of their bank accounts were frozen.

With regard to the southern insurgency, the Thaksin government's harsh measures had been moderated in October 2006 by General Surayud, who apologized for his predecessor's wrongs, freed a number of detainees, and urged Thai security officials to engage with the Muslim subjects. Nevertheless, the insurgency escalated, signaled by intimidation, arson, assassinations, beheadings, and ambushes of security forces. The government responded by reinforcing several local paramilitary formations, including the Ranger Force (*Thahan Phran*), the Volunteer Defense Corps (*Or Sor*), and the Village Defense Volunteers (*Chor Ror Bor*). Queen SIRIKIT sponsored a new Village Protection Force (*Or Ror Bor*). These militia were poorly trained and equipped, reported to be of dubious effectiveness save as reassurance to local Buddhists, and were allegedly implicated in extortion, beatings, and extrajudicial executions. Meanwhile, a mid-2007 report by Human Rights Watch put the number of deaths at the hands of the insurgents at 2,500, many of them victims of indiscriminate bombings and gruesome assaults. (For more information, see the 2013 *Handbook.*)

With a new constitution having been approved in a referendum on August 19, 2007 (see Constitution and government, below), and with Sonthi, having retired from the military, being named deputy prime minister for security affairs in October, the interim government scheduled fresh elections for a reconstituted, 480-member House of Representatives. The December 2007 legislative election gave a plurality to the People Power Party (*Pak Palang Prachachon*—PPP), which was widely seen as the successor to *Thai Rak Thai.* A dozen seats short of a majority, SAMAK Sundaravej, the new leader of the PPP, invited five of the other six parties that had won seats in the House of Representatives to join in a coalition government. The new government, with Samak as prime minster, was sworn in on February 6, 2008. The DP took up the role of opposition in the House.

Subsequently, 11 members of the PPP accused of vote-buying lost their House seats and four PPP ministers were obliged to resign, two for electoral fraud, one because he allegedly insulted the king, and one because he made an unconstitutional agreement with Cambodia over a disputed temple at their common border (see Foreign relations, below). These events, compounded by Thaksin's brief return and subsequent flight to London, and the conviction (subsequently overturned) of his wife, KHUNYING Potjaman, for corruption, undermined the PPP's credibility and fuelled the PAD's protests.

The PAD also opposed Prime Minister Samak's alleged intent to amend the constitution to restore the 111 *Thai Rak Thai* executives to political eligibility, to forestall ongoing legal challenges to the PPP's existence, and to pardon Thaksin and his wife. The protests escalated in June and culminated in mass demonstrations and the occupation of the prime minister's office grounds in August. On September 2, 2008, Samak declared a state of emergency, empowering the military and police to ban gatherings of more than five people; to prevent media reporting that "causes panic, instigates violence, or affects stability"; and to hold suspects for up to 30 days without charge. The PAD persisted with demonstrations, in which one person was killed, and the Federation of State Enterprises, encompassing more than 40 labor unions, approved strikes that would cut off power and water to government buildings and disrupt public transportation and telecommunications. PAD demonstrations in August had already closed three airports in southern Thailand, stranding thousands of tourists.

On September 9, 2008, the Constitutional Court ordered Samak's resignation, having found him guilty of a conflict of interest for taking money for participating in two chef shows on commercial television. Deputy Prime Minister Somchai WONGSAWAT, a brother-in-law of former prime minister Thaksin, became acting prime minister on September 9, was elected prime minister in his own right by the House on September 17, and was endorsed by the king on September 18. He presented his cabinet list to the king on September 24, whereupon it was approved. The PAD threatened not to accept the new government, which was dominated by many of the same PPP figures as the previous Samak-led government, but Somchai, having complied with the constitution and received a parliamentary majority and royal assent, vowed to carry on. Violent demonstrations erupted on October 9 and were broken up by the police at the cost of several deaths and numerous injuries among the protesters.

On October 20, 2008, at the request of Prime Minister Somchai, the House set up a 120-member assembly to redraft the constitution, but the opposition DP boycotted the session and the speaker of the Senate, 40 senators, and several academics spoke out against the redrafting project, which stalled. The PAD called new demonstrations, and on November 25 its followers occupied Bangkok's recently opened Suvarnabhumi International Airport, stopping all flights and stranding 7,000 passengers for a week. The Civil Court issued an injunction and Somchai declared a limited state of emergency, but the riot police did not move against the demonstrators. The crisis ended on December 2 when the Constitutional Court dissolved the PPP, *Chart Thai,* and Neutral Democratic parties and banned Somchai from holding office. Deputy Prime Minister Chaovarat CHANWEERAKUL took over as acting prime minister. Democrat Party leader Abhisit commanded only 165 votes from his own party but attracted five other parties to form a coalition government that was sworn in on December 22. Among those rallying to Abhisit were former PPP legislators who established the Friends of Newin Group within the Proud Thais Party.

Elections for the House were conducted on July 3, 2011. The For Thais Party (*Phak Phuea Thai*—PPT), the successor to the PPP, led by Thaksin's sister, Yingluck Shinawatra, secured an absolute majority in the balloting, with 265 seats. Yingluck was elected prime minister by the house on August 5. She subsequently formed a six-party coalition government on August 10, which included the PPT, Thai Nation Development Party (TNDP), Thais United National Development Party (TUNDP), *Phalang Chon* (PC), the Great People's Party (*Phak Mahachon—Mahachon*), and the New Democracy Party (NDP).

The king approved a cabinet reshuffle in January 2012. The new government included the PPT, the TNDP, the PC, and a number of independents. Several of the new appointees were longtime supporters of Thaksin. The cabinet was reshuffled in October 2012 and again on June 30, 2013.

Balloting in early elections on February 2, 2014, was invalidated by the constitutional court on March 21, 2014 (see Current issues, below). Yingluck was removed from office by the court on May 7, and an interim government put in place under former deputy prime minister Niwatthamrong Boonsongpaisan (PPT). On May 22 a military coup removed Niwatthamrong, who was replaced by the commander-in-chief of the Thai Army, General PRAYUTH Chan-ocha (see Current issues, below).

Following the 2014 military coup, the constitution was suspended. Thailand then adopted an interim constitution that allocated supreme authority to the military-led National Council for Peace and Order (NCPO). The NCPO appointed a 220-member unicameral legislature, the National Legislative Assembly (NLA). None of the appointed members of the NLA was formally affiliated with a political party. The NLA was approved by the king on July 31. A draft constitution was rejected, but a second draft was completed by a new 21-member committee on January 29, 2016.

On August 7, 2016, Thai voters approved the new constitution in a referendum on a vote of 61.4 percent in favor and 38.6 percent opposed. The new constitution assigned significant power to the military and granted full amnesty toward the junta members (see Constitution and government, below). Many opposition groups boycotted the balloting.

King Bhumibol died on October 13, 2016. Crown Prince Maha VAJIRALONGKORN ascended to the throne on December 1, with his formal coronation expected the following year.

Constitution and government. Thailand is a highly centralized constitutional monarchy whose governments in the modern era have been led by a prime minister and cabinet. Since 1932 the king has exercised little direct power but remains a popular symbol of national unity and identity and has played a pivotal indirect role in times of political crisis. He is advised by a Privy Council of his own appointees.

Since 1932 Thailand has had 18 constitutions, each reflecting the locus of political power of the day. An interim constitution approved by the monarch after the 1991 coup assigned a virtually unlimited "supervisory" role to the military-led National Peacekeeping Council (NPC). A new draft constitution was subsequently endorsed by the NPC-appointed National Legislative Assembly and, after being scrutinized by an assembly-appointed review committee, was declared in effect on December 9, 1991. Bicameralism was restored, with the House of Representatives being elected but the Senate remaining appointed.

On September 14, 1996, a joint session of the two legislative houses called for the election of an assembly to draft a new constitution. The assembly's new "open government" charter elicited intense debate and drew considerable opposition, for the most part from entrenched political groups. However, in view of large public demonstrations in support of the proposal, the new basic law was approved by the National Assembly (the collective term for the House and the Senate) on September 27, 1997. Changes included the expansion of the House of Representatives to 500 members, 400 to be elected on a single-member constituency basis and 100 by proportional representation from party lists. Other provisions called for the direct election of senators; guarantees regarding human rights, freedom of the press, and the right to assembly; and establishment of increased accountability on the part of officials, "with greater governmental transparency" overall. Senatorial powers include removal of ministers, members of the House, and justices.

The 1997 constitution was set aside by the military junta and an interim charter imposed by decree on September 27, 2006. Empowered by this charter, the junta appointed a 2,000-person National Assembly, which in turn appointed 200 candidates for a Constitution Assembly, which then selected a Constitution Drafting Committee of 25. The junta chose an additional 10 members for the committee, which set about drafting a new constitution according to guidelines set out by the junta.

The draft constitution was submitted to the public in a constitutional referendum, Thailand's first, on August 19, 2007. The junta encouraged officials at all levels to advocate approval but outlawed campaigning against the draft constitution. The turnout was 57 percent and the approval rate was 58 percent, both lower than expected by the junta. The Constitution Drafting Assembly endorsed the outcome on August 20, 2007, and the constitution came into force on August 24, after obtaining the king's assent.

The thrust of the new constitution was to reduce the influence of populist political parties (such as the *Thai Rak Thai*) over the selection of legislators and to restrict the powers of the prime minister. Major changes from the 1997 constitution included the appointment rather than election of senators and a reduction in their number from 200 to 150, and the adoption of an electoral system for the House of Representatives of 400 single-member constituencies plus 80 selected by proportional representation. As before, the king was to appoint the political leader commanding a majority in the House to serve as prime minister, who in turn was to nominate the ministers and other members of the cabinet, subject to approval by the House. But the role of the prime minister was to be circumscribed by new provisions, including a two-term restriction, a reduction in the number of legislators necessary to launch a no-confidence debate, and a prohibition against a prime minister's leading a caretaker administration after the legislature was dissolved—all directed at preventing the alleged abuses of the Thaksin regime. Controversial provisions included the granting of amnesty to members of the junta that staged the 2006 coup, articles forbidding legislators from overseeing the work of bureaucrats or the military, and the designation of the military as the protector of the monarchy and constitution. However, passages protecting human rights and civil liberties remained as extensive in the new constitution as in its predecessor, and the practice of electing local government officials down to the subdistrict level was reaffirmed. The 2007 constitution prescribed no fundamental changes to the judiciary or the local administrative system.

The 2016 constitution reestablished a bicameral legislature, but allowed the military to appoint all 250 senators to the upper house. The size of the Senate would shrink to 200 seats after five years. The lower chamber, the House, would be comprised of 500 members directly elected for four-year terms. The newly recreated Senate was assigned a role in the selection of the prime minister, who would be elected by a joint session of the legislature for a five-year period. The prime minister is approved by the monarch. Members of government are forbidden to also be members of the legislature.

The Thai judicial system is patterned after European models. The Supreme Court, whose justices are appointed by the king, is the final court of appeal in both civil and criminal cases; an intermediate Court of Appeals hears appeals from courts of first instance located throughout the country. The constitutionality of parliamentary acts, royal decrees, and draft legislation falls under the purview of a Constitutional Court, which may also rule on the appointment and removal of public officials and political party issues.

Administratively, the country is divided into 76 provinces, including Bangkok. Provincial governors are appointed by the minister of the interior, except for Bangkok, where the governor (often referred to as the mayor) is elected. Provincial subdivisions include districts (*amphoe*), communes (*tambons*), and villages (*mubans*). The larger towns are governed by elected municipal councils. Legislation passed in March 2000 authorizes direct election of municipal mayors and most local administrators.

Freedom of the press is curtailed in Thailand. In its 2016 index of media freedom, Reporters Without Borders ranked Thailand 136th out of 180 countries, dropping by six places since 2014.

Foreign relations. One of the few Southeast Asian governments to depart from a neutralist posture, Thailand was firmly aligned with the United States and other Western powers after World War II and signed onto the Southeast Asia Collective Defense Treaty, which established the Southeast Asia Treaty Organization (SEATO) in Bangkok in 1954. From 1952 to 1972 Thailand received almost $1.2 billion in U.S. military aid, more than twice the value of U.S. economic assistance. The Thanom government approved the use of Thai air bases for U.S. military operations in Laos and South Vietnam, and the American buildup totaled 48,000 personnel in Thailand at its peak in 1969. The U.S. withdrawal from South Vietnam led to a corresponding reduction in Thailand, and by mid-1976, all remaining U.S. military installations were closed down. SEATO was declared inactive in 1977 and its Bangkok headquarters closed.

Various UN bodies functioning in East and Southeast Asia maintain headquarters in Bangkok, and Thailand has played a leading role in the establishment of several regional organizations, such as the Association of Southeast Asian Nations (ASEAN), of which Thailand became a charter member in 1967. More recently, Thailand has been active in the ASEAN Free Trade Agreement (AFTA), ASEAN Regional Forum (ARF), ASEAN Plus Three talks, the Asia-Pacific Economic Cooperation (APEC), and the East Asian Summit process begun in 2004. Thailand is second only to Singapore in its pursuit of free trade agreements with governments as diverse as New Zealand, Australia, China, the United States, India, and Bahrain. In 1999 Thailand dispatched some 1,500 troops as part of the international peacekeeping force sent to East Timor (now Timor-Leste) following the territory's independence vote in August and served as co-commander with Australia; from 2006 to the present Thailand has deployed a police team to the UN Integrated Mission in Timor-Leste.

Relations with Cambodia have traditionally been antagonistic, although Thailand joined with other ASEAN nations in recognizing the Pol Pot regime in mid-1975 and in calling for "the immediate withdrawal of all foreign troops" following the Vietnamese invasion of December 1978. While tacitly aiding *Khmer Rouge* forces in their opposition to the Vietnamese-backed regime of Heng Samrin, Thailand encouraged the noncommunist Khmer resistance to form a united front, an effort that contributed toward the organization of the Coalition Government of Democratic Kampuchea in June 1982.

As many as 250,000 Cambodians crowded into refugee camps in eastern Thailand during the Pol Pot era and the ensuing occupation by Vietnamese forces, and as late as 1998 the region continued to be a haven for those fleeing fighting between the Cambodian military and remaining *Khmer Rouge* guerrillas. Periodically, however, charges that Thailand provided sanctuary to fleeing *Khmer Rouge* strained relations with a number of countries, including the United States. Concern that arms might end up in guerrilla hands led Washington to terminate military aid and training under its 1995 Foreign Operations Act. Angered by the American action, Thailand joined Indonesia and Malaysia in opposing a request for the stationing of a "rapid response" flotilla of U.S. military supply ships in the Gulf of Thailand. Relations improved when Thailand received strong U.S. support in 1998 for its economic reforms.

In mid-2008 Thai–Cambodian relations soured over a dispute regarding ownership of land adjacent to the Preah Vihear temple. The International Court of Justice in 1962 had awarded this temple to Cambodia, but the status of surrounding land remained unresolved. Cambodia subsequently applied to register the temple and grounds with UNESCO as a World Heritage Site under Cambodian trusteeship. Thailand's minister of foreign affairs, NOPPADON Pattama, initially endorsed the application, but the Constitutional Court found that he had exceeded his authority and he was forced to resign. When UNESCO granted registration, in July 2008 Thailand moved troops onto the disputed land, and Cambodia reciprocated. In mid-October the armed confrontation erupted into a series of sporadic fire fights that left seven soldiers dead. Tension-reducing talks between the foreign ministers of Thailand and Cambodia were disrupted when Thaksin visited Phnom Penh in November 2009 at the invitation of Prime Minister Hun Sen, provoking Thailand to recall its ambassador to Cambodia and issue an extradition request. Cambodia in turn withdrew its ambassador to Thailand and rejected the extradition request, labeling it "politically motivated." In November 2010 the chief of the Thai–Cambodian Joint Border Commission VASIN Teeravechyan resigned amid criticism by the People's Alliance for Democracy that he was not pursuing Thailand's claim with sufficient vigor.

A history of uneven relations with neighboring Laos reached a low point in late 1987, when fighting broke out over disputed border territory. Bangkok subsequently adopted a conciliatory economic policy that facilitated a mutual troop withdrawal from border areas in March 1991. Five months later a border security and cooperation agreement provided for the repatriation of some 60,000 Laotian refugees from Thailand over a three-year period. More than 8,000 remained in 2008. In June Thai authorities repatriated 837 Hmong refugees, prompting concern by the UN High Commissioner for Refugees (UNHCR) that they would be persecuted by the Lao authorities.

Following an initiative by Prime Minister Chatchai Choonhavan in 1988 to turn Indochina "from a battleground into a market place," Thai policy toward Hanoi softened. In February 1993 Thai officials met in Hanoi with representatives of Cambodia, Laos, and Vietnam to chart a new framework of cooperation for developing the resources of the lower Mekong River. Subsequently, talks were also initiated with Laos,

Myanmar, and China on development of the upper Mekong, which led to completion in April 2000 of a treaty governing navigation on the waterway.

In March 1996 Banharn Silpa-Archa became the first Thai prime minister in 16 years to visit Myanmar, with whose military leaders a border trade agreement was signed, while in 1998 the UN agreed to help protect some 100,000 Mon, Kayin (Karen), and other ethnic refugees from Myanmar who had taken refuge on the Thai side of the border. In March 1999 Myanmar's head of state, Than Shwe, joined Prime Minister Chuan for discussions on narcotics control and border tensions, but the cordiality ended in October when Thai authorities freed five dissidents who had taken 89 hostages at the Myanmar embassy in Bangkok the preceding day. Myanmar's military leaders immediately closed the Thai–Myanmar border. Bangkok, in turn, threatened to expel hundreds of thousands of illegal migrant workers from Myanmar. The border remained closed until late November. A second hostage incident occurred in January 2000 when members of an ethnic-minority militia called God's Army occupied a hospital in Ratchaburi, near the border, taking some 700 hostages. In contrast to the October incident, the Thai forces stormed the hospital on January 25, freed all the hostages, and killed all ten rebels, some, according to eyewitnesses, by summary execution, earning Yangon's approbation.

In February 2001 Thai troops engaged Myanmar forces that had reportedly pursued members of the Shan State Army across the border. The encounter led to a series of bilateral meetings, in which the two governments agreed not only to work toward resolution of remaining border issues but also jointly to fight drug production and smuggling. Nevertheless, difficulties continued into 2002, with the border being closed from May until early October. In February 2003 Thaksin again traveled to Myanmar in furtherance of improved relations, and in July he announced that all dissidents from Myanmar would be moved to refugee camps near the border, of which nine had been established. The Thai government's preferred policy was voluntary repatriation, but continued political strife, ethnic warfare, and noncooperation by the authorities in Myanmar precluded this solution. In 2007 Thailand, with the help of the UNHCR, negotiated the removal of approximately 4,000 refugees, the majority from Myanmar, to third countries, led by the United States, and issued identity cards to up to 140,000 others, enabling them to work legally outside their camps. Thailand joined its ASEAN partners in urging the Myanmar junta to consult with the democratic opposition and take steps to resolve Myanmar's domestic disputes peacefully. In October Prime Minister Surayud proposed to UN special envoy Ibrahim Gambari that the UN organize regional talks including ASEAN, China, and India to address the crisis in Myanmar. Surayud also postponed the visit to Bangkok by Myanmar's new prime minister, Gen. Thein Sein. Relations improved in 2009 with Energy Minister WANNARAT Charnnukul's announcement on August 4 of a Thai-financed project to develop an offshore natural gas field in Myanmar's waters and import 300 million cubic feet of gas per day from Myanmar starting in 2013.

In January 1998 Malaysia took a stand against the Muslim separatists of southern Thailand when it quietly arrested several alleged Muslim insurgents from a faction of the Pattani United Liberation Organization (PULO) and returned them for trial in Bangkok. Malaysia, which is predominantly Muslim, had previously been a sanctuary for the separatists, who want independence for the 2.5 million Muslims residing in Thailand's southern provinces. The change in policy was seen as evidence of a new cooperativeness at a time when both countries faced the Asian Financial Crisis. In 1997 Thailand and Malaysia established a Joint Commission on Bilateral Cooperation to facilitate border control and enhance confidence and security-building measures. In 2004 they set up a Committee on Joint Development Strategy, and by 2007 they had implemented Joint Working Groups on Education, Employment, and Entrepreneurship tasked with raising standards of living of depressed communities on both sides of the border.

Even after the September 2001 al-Qaida attacks on the United States, and despite growing Islamic militancy in Thailand's southern provinces, Thai authorities routinely discounted the possible involvement of the Indonesia-based *Jemaah Islamiah* (JI) and al-Qaida in sporadic bombings and attacks against police stations. In June 2003, however, alleged JI members were among those arrested in connection with a plot to blow up two tourist resorts and the Bangkok embassies of Australia, Germany, Singapore, the United Kingdom, and the United States. Citing the urgency of the situation, in August 2003 the government bypassed the National Assembly and issued two antiterrorism laws by decree. In the same month the U.S. Central Intelligence Agency assisted Thai authorities in capturing Riduan Isamuddin (a.k.a. Hambali), an alleged JI leader with ties to al-Qaida.

Thailand has a warm relationship with China, exemplified by a plan jointly announced by their prime ministers in 2005 to develop a "strategic partnership" in a host of areas, including trade, security, and science and technology. China's cordial Olympics diplomacy and improved relations between Beijing and Taipei further reassured Bangkok, and bilateral trade grew to make China Thailand's second largest supplier of imports. But local producers remained skeptical of the growth of cheap goods allowed into the local market by the China–Thailand Free Trade Agreement of 2004 and a China–ASEAN agreement including Thailand that came into effect on January 1, 2010.

Relations with the U.S. administration of President George W. Bush were close. Thailand assisted in the U.S.-led invasion of Iraq, although its 440 medical and engineering personnel were withdrawn in August 2004. In 2003 the U.S. government designated Thailand a "major non-NATO ally." The U.S. government in 2006 and 2007 publicly urged the Thai military junta to lift martial law and restore democracy. Washington withheld over $35 million in economic aid, mainly for military training and assistance programs, but imposed no other sanctions, and continued programs related to development, democracy promotion, disaster assistance, counterterrorism, counternarcotics, human trafficking, and refugee assistance valued at $34 million. Full diplomatic, economic, and military relations were restored in 2008, and Secretary of State Hillary Clinton on July 23, 2009, reiterated the Barack Obama administration's commitment to work closely with Thailand on national, regional, and global issues. State Department reports in 2010 identified Thailand as a transit country for drug smuggling and human trafficking. Nevertheless, on May 13 Thailand was elected by the UN General Assembly to a three-year term on the Human Rights Council and on September 30 announced its candidacy for a seat on the UN Security Council.

The two governments began free trade agreement negotiations in 2004, but the talks stalled in mid-2006 over Bangkok's reluctance to grant legal protection to U.S. pharmaceutical companies and "national treatment" to U.S. multinational firms. The military coup of 2006 led to U.S. suspension of the talks. Despite officials-level consultations in June 2008 and March 2009, formal negotiations have not resumed.

In April 2011 renewed fighting between Thai and Cambodian soldiers in a disputed border region near the Preah Vihear temple killed 16 and wounded a score of others. Some 40,000 Thais and 20,000 Cambodians were displaced. A truce on April 30 ended the strife, followed by a more comprehensive cease-fire agreement on May 9. Meanwhile, Cambodia petitioned the International Court of Justice (ICJ) to revise its 1962 ruling on the disputed area.

On April 5, 2012, Thailand and Cambodia agreed to begin demining operations in the disputed area around Preah Vihear. Following major flooding in Myanmar in August 2012, Thailand pledged financial and humanitarian assistance to Myanmar.

In January 2013, under pressure from China, Thailand announced that it would "invite" leaders of the banned Chinese religious group, the Falun Gong, to leave the country. Thailand and Mozambique finalized an agreement in February to ease restrictions on the import of minerals to Thailand. Thailand and the European Union (EU) initiated talks on a free trade agreement in March. Following more than 20 years of negotiations, Thailand and India signed an extradition treaty in May. In July, during a visit by Myanmar's President Thein Sein, three economic agreements were signed between Thailand and Myanmar. In November the ICJ ruled that most of the area around Preah Vihear belonged to Cambodia.

Countries, including the United States and Australia, reduced ties with Thailand in the aftermath of the May 2014 military coup. Other countries, such as Canada, France, and the United Kingdom, condemned the coup. A smaller number of regional states, including China, Myanmar, and Vietnam, expressed support for the military government. Also following the coup, an estimated 200,000 Cambodian workers left Thailand after the new government began to tighten laws regulating migrant workers.

In May 2015 the Thai government initiated a crackdown on human trafficking to reduce the estimated 5,000–8,000 migrants who were illegally transported to Thailand from Myanmar and Malaysia each month.

Thailand continued to defer to China on a range of areas in an effort to maintain positive trade relations. Reports indicated that the Thai government deported two political activists to China in November 2015 at the request of the Chinese government.

In July 2016 Thailand lost a bid to secure a nonpermanent seat on the UN Security Council. (The seat instead went to Kazakhstan.) Thailand received the fewest votes of the seven countries seeking one of the five seats, and reports indicated that the military coup was a major consideration in the voting patterns of UN members. On October 10 Iranian president Hassan Rouhani visited Thailand and conducted bilateral trade talks to increase trade between the two countries.

Current issues. On October 22, 2008, the Constitutional Court found former prime minister Thaksin guilty of corruption in a land deal case, sentenced him to two years imprisonment, and issued a warrant for his arrest. The government revoked his Thai passport in April 2009, but Thaksin continued his travels on Montenegrin and Nicaraguan passports. Meanwhile, he continued to reject the Abhisit government's validity and to incite his followers by video broadcasts and by "tweets" through the social networking and blogging service Twitter. On March 31, 20,000 of his followers under the banner of the United Front of Democracy Against Dictatorship (UDD), also known as the Democratic Alliance Against Dictatorship (DAAD), and colloquially as the Red Shirts, forced the cancellation of a cabinet meeting in Bangkok. Further demonstrations took place on April 8 against Gen. Prem Tinsulanand, the king's chief privy counselor, and on April 11 when 10,000 protesters forced the cancellation of an ASEAN summit in Pattaya and obliged the government to fly visiting international leaders to safety by helicopter from their hotel venue. Pro-Thaksin supporters staged a major demonstration in September 2009 at which Thaksin spoke by videolink, and in November Thaksin visited neighboring Cambodia, further encouraging his supporters and angering the government.

In April 2010 the ongoing confrontation between the Abhisit government (the Yellow Shirts) and the antigovernment United Front for Democracy against Dictatorship (UDD, or Red Shirts), allegedly incited and financed from exile by Thaksin, escalated. A military and police attempt on April 10–11 to dislodge the red shirts from their encampment in central Bangkok was repulsed with a loss of 25 lives and injuries to an estimated 850. A second attempt by the authorities ended in success on May 19, with the surrender of UDD leaders, including JATUPORN Prompam and NATTHAWUT Saikua. The authorities dismantled barricades and dispersed the protesters but at a cost of another 39 dead and 279 wounded, considerable property damage, and a diminution of foreign tourism.

In February 2011 seven leaders of the UDD were released as part of a reconciliation initiative. In August former prime minister Thaksin's sister, Yingluck Shinawatra, was elected prime minister of a coalition government following the July balloting, in which the PPT gained an absolute majority in the house. The coalition gave the Yingluck government the support of 300 members of the house. Meanwhile, throughout the campaign and her early period in office, Yingluck denied reports that her government was a front for Thaksin to reassert political power and influence.

Renewed fighting in the four southernmost provinces in August and September 2011 between Muslim insurgents and government security forces killed 53 and wounded more than 75. Widespread flooding inundated two-thirds of the country during the summer monsoon season. The floods killed more than 600 Thais and affected more than 3 million. Damage from the flooding was estimated to exceed $8 billion, in what many Thai officials described as the worst natural disaster in the nation's history. There was widespread domestic criticism of the Yingluck cabinet's response to the flooding, especially the government's initial refusal of foreign aid. In October Doctors Without Borders announced it was suspending operations in the country after continued interference in its efforts to treat undocumented Burmese workers in Thailand. In December, the government restored Thaksin's passport. However, the former prime minister was disqualified from a royal amnesty, meaning Thaksin still faced arrest if he returned to Thailand.

In February Thai police arrested three Iranians in Bangkok for planning an attack on the Israeli embassy. Also in February, the cabinet approved the formation of a new constitutional assembly to draft a new basic law for the country. In June the House of Representatives postponed controversial legislation on an amnesty for those involved in political fighting between 2005 and 2010. Meanwhile, the Supreme Court rejected a petition to declare the PPT illegal because of its efforts to revise the constitution. (Drafters of the petition argued that the PPT sought to weaken or even abolish the monarchy.) However, the court also issued a stay on previously approved legislation to create the new constitutional assembly.

Yingluck easily survived a no-confidence vote on November 28, 2012, 308–159. The motion followed a contentious debate over a rice subsidy program in which the government paid farmers over-market prices for rice. Opposition parties alleged the program was rife with widespread corruption. In June 2013 the government announced it would reduce the subsidies by 20 percent after the program lost $4.4 billion when the government was unable to resell the rice to other governments. One result was that India and Vietnam surpassed Thailand as the leading international rice exporters.

On January 1, 2013, a new measure went into effect, setting the national minimum wage at 300 baht per day (approximately $9.55). The measure was highly popular among unions but opposed by business groups, which argued it would prompt companies to relocate outside of Thailand (for instance, Cambodia's daily minimum wage was $2.03). On March 24 a fire at a Karin refugee camp in Mae Hong Song province killed 37, injured 115, and temporarily left 2,300 without shelter. In July the Supreme Court ruled that a PPT bid to revise the constitution would require a referendum but that the legislature could adopt amendments without a national vote.

Antigovernment protests erupted through November and December 2013 against Prime Minister Yingluck and her attempt to pardon her brother, former Prime Minister Thaksin, of accusations of corruption through a broad amnesty bill. The bill passed the House on November 1 on a vote of 310–0 (the opposition boycotted the vote), but it was defeated in the Senate 141–0 on November 12. Prime Minister Shinawatra survived a no-confidence vote on November 27, only to dissolve the parliament on December 9 in an attempt to quell continuing protests, which drew up to 150,000 people in Bangkok. Demonstrators called for the dismissal of the Yingluck government and its replacement by an appointed "people's council." New elections were held on February 2, 2014, but were boycotted by the DP. Protests and demonstrations prevented the balloting from being finished in one day, and the Constitutional Court on March 21 annulled the balloting for that reason.

On May 7 the Constitutional Court dismissed Yingluck, asserting that her 2011 transfer of the secretary general of the Thai National Security Council was unconstitutional. (The replacement was a brother of the former wife of Thaksin.) Yingluck was also indicted on corruption charges the following day. An interim government was appointed, but on May 20 the military declared martial law and deployed troops to strategic areas around the country. Two days of negotiations among the military, PPT, and DP failed to resolve the growing crisis. On May 22 the military deposed the civilian government and announced the formation of a National Committee for Peace and Order (NCPO), chaired by Gen. Prayuth Chan-ocha and comprised of other senior officers from the armed services and police. Prayuth was subsequently confirmed by the king as head of government. Prayuth composed a government on August 31, 2014, largely made of military officers.

The military regime suppressed opposition groups and dissent. From 2014 through 2016 more than 1,300 people were detained or arrested for subversion or antigovernment activities. More than 600 of those detained were tried by military courts. In 2016 more than 120 political activists, former politicians, and opposition figures were arrested for criticizing the NCPO's draft constitution. On August 17, 2015, a bomb was detonated in Bangkok, killing 20 and injuring 125. Two suspects were arrested, but their motive in the attack remained unclear. The government asserted the attack was directed against the military government, and might have involved as many as 20 in the planning and conduct of the strike.

In October 2016 a specialized corruption court was established in an effort to speed prosecutions of both public and private misconduct. In November the government announced $514 million in financial aid to rice farmers to subsidize prices.

POLITICAL PARTIES

For the quarter-century preceding the 2001 election, Thailand's civilian governments typically featured shifting multiparty coalitions, with no single party being able to emerge from national elections holding a legislative majority. (For details on the political parties in coalition governments prior to 2001, see the 2010 *Handbook.*) Since 2001 three broad political groupings have maneuvered for power. The first was represented by the populist *Thai Rak Thai,* succeeded in 2007 by the People Power Party (PPP), which drew its support from poorer rural districts in the northeast. The second were urban civilian elites based in Bangkok, Songkhla, and other urban centers and in the southern Muslim provinces, who supported the Democrat Party. The third, a loose grouping of military officers, government officials, monarchist civilians, and business interests in central Thailand, was manifested by the *Chart Thai* party. Each was riven by factions. Numerous smaller parties formed around strong personalities or local interests, often originating in breakaway factions of the three main parties.

In the election of April 2006, 28 parties were eligible, although many had minuscule memberships or existed primarily on paper; 18 ran in at least one district and 8 presented party lists for proportional seats. But the election was boycotted by the principal opposition parties, the Democrat Party (DP), *Chart Thai,* and *Mahachon.*

The Constitutional Court's banning of *Thai Rak Thai* in May 2007, and the exclusion of Thaksin and 111 party executives from political office or party leadership for five years, altered the political landscape. The DP emerged by default as the country's largest and most popular party. But *Thai Rak Thai* members and followers regrouped in the previously minor People Power Party (PPP) and reinvigorated it to the point where it overtook the DP as the country's most popular party. The PPP was reported to be financed by Thaksin from exile, and its leader, Samak Sundaravej, declared his intention to continue Thaksin's populist policies. In the election held December 23, 2007, only seven parties gained House seats out of 66 registered, the others failing either to win any of the 400 constituency seats or to reach the 5 percent threshold for one of the 80 proportional seats. The PPP led all parties, followed by the DP. On December 2, 2008, however, the Constitutional Court dissolved the PPP, the *Chart Thai,* and the Neutral Democratic Party for vote-buying in the 2007 election, which brought a six-party coalition, led by Abhisit and the DP, to power.

Former Government Parties:

For Thais Party (*Phak Puea Thai*—PPT). The PPT emerged in September 20, 2008, set up by 80 PPP members of the house who deserted the party ahead of its ban in December by the Constitutional Court. Its leaders included Apiwan WIRIYACHAI, former vice president of the house; Chalerm YOOBAMRUNG, former health minister and PPP leader; and Mingkwan SAENGSUWAN, formerly a minister of industry. Declining to endorse Abhisit as the new prime minister, the PPT in December called for an all-party national unity government to be led by Sanoh Thienthong of the Royalist People's Party. When that failed, the PPT called for the dissolution of the house and endorsed Pracha Promnok as a candidate for prime minister in a possible new government, but without success. Nevertheless, the January 2009 by-election victories in five constituencies and shifting party alliances enabled the PPT's strength in the house to grow to 189 out of 480 seats. In November 2010 executive board members Witthaya BURANASIRI and Surapong TOWICHAKCHAIKUL resigned amid speculation that the Constitutional Court might dissolve the PPT. The PPT won 265 seats in the 2011 house elections, and Yingluck Shinawatra was elected prime minister by the house. In local balloting in 2012, the PPT lost seats in several strongholds with reports indicating that the losses were the result of voter displeasure over the government's handling of the 2011 floods. In October 2012 Yongyuth WICHAIDIT resigned as both party leader and deputy prime minister after being implicated in a corruption scandal. He was replaced by then-Transport Minister Jarupong RUANGSUWAN. Following the May 2014 coup, Yingluck was detained by security forces for three days. Other party leaders were also detained. Jarupong fled into hiding in the northeast of Thailand and resigned as party leader. He reportedly formed an anti-coup grouping, the Free Thais for Human Rights and Democracy.

Yingluck Shinawatra was retroactively impeached in January 2015. She was also charged with criminal negligence over the 2012 rice subsidy scheme and fined $1.4 billion. The party led the opposition to the 2016 constitution.

Leaders: Yingluck SHINAWATRA (Former Prime Minister), Phumtham WECHAYACHAI (Secretary General).

Thai Nation Development Party—TNDP (*Chart Thai Pattana*). The TNDP was founded on April 18, 2008, and became the new political home for members of the *Chart Thai* Party when the latter was dissolved in December 2008. The TNDP joined the Abhisit-led coalition and was awarded a deputy prime ministership; the tourism and sports, and energy ministries; and the deputy transport portfolio. The party had 25 seats in the house in 2010 and won 19 in the 2011 balloting. It joined the PPT-led coalition government following the balloting. Following a succession of cabinet reshuffles, the TNDP held two ministries in August 2013, while Yukol LIMLAEMTHONG had been appointed deputy prime minister. Following the 2014 coup, Yukol and other party officials were briefly detained.

Leaders: Yukol LIMLAEMTHONG (Former Deputy Prime Minister), Wannarat CHANNUKUL.

Thais United National Development Party—TUNDP (*Ruam Jai Thai Chart Pattana*). The party arose from the formation of *Ruam Jai Thai* (variously translated as United Hearts Thai and Thais United), which was announced in late June 2007 by leaders including Pradit Phataraprasit. Although prohibited from active involvement because of his former standing in *Thai Rak Thai,* Somkid JATUSRIPITAK, a former deputy prime minister, was a key figure behind the organization.

In September 2007 *Ruam Jai Thai* leaders announced a merger with the *Chart Pattana* (National Development) group, led by Suwat LIPTAPANLOP, who, like Somkid, was prohibited from direct politicking. A possible merger with the *Pracharaj* and *Matchima* parties and the Bangkok 50 and *Saman Chan* groups was explored but was not consummated. The December 2007 election found the *Ruam Jai Thai* in sixth place, with nine seats. The party then joined the PPP-led coalition government and was awarded the positions of deputy finance minister and minister of energy. Following the fall of the Somchai government in December 2008, the TUNDP rallied to Abhisit's coalition, and the party's leader, Wannarat Channukul, was made minister for energy, and its secretary general was awarded the deputy finance portfolio in the new cabinet. In 2011 the party merged with **For the Motherland** (*Puea Pan Din*—PPD). The PPD emerged in September 2007 in the context of an ultimately unsuccessful merger effort by *Matchima, Pracharaj,* and other post–*Thai Rak Thai* groups. (For more information on the PPD, see the 2011 *Handbook.*)

The TUNDP secured seven seats in the house in the 2011 elections, and Wannarat Channukul was appointed minister of industry in the PPT-led cabinet but left the government following the January 2012 cabinet reshuffle. Theera WONGSAMUT was elected party leader in March 2013.

Leaders: Theera WONGSAMUT (Party Leader), Pradit PHATARAPRASIT (Secretary General).

Phalang Chon (PC). The pro-Thaksin, regional *Phalang Chon* party was formed in 2011 by former tourism minister Sonthaya KUNPLOME. The party gained seven seats in the 2011 balloting, all from Chonburi Province, its home base. The PC joined the Yingluck coalition government in 2011.

Leaders: Chao MANEEWONG, Sonthaya KHUNPLUEM.

Two other small parties joined the governing coalition: the **Great People's Party** (*Phak Mahachon—Mahachon*), a small grouping that was originally formed in 1998, which won one seat in the 2011 balloting; and the **New Democracy Party** (NDP), led by Surathin PIJARN, which also secured one seat in the 2011 elections.

Opposition Parties:

Democrat Party—DP (*Pak Prachatipat*). Organized in 1946, the DP is Thailand's oldest party. Traditionally a strong defender of the monarchy, it has derived much of its support from officials and urban professionals. It considers itself a left-of-center party but emerged as a right-of-center party as the popularity of Thaksin and the *Thai Rak Thai* shifted the political spectrum to the left. The fourth-ranked party in March 1992, it moved up to second with 86 seats in 1995 and similarly ranked with 123 seats in 1996.

In August 2000 the Constitutional Court convicted DP Secretary General Sanan Kachornprasart of having falsified an assets declaration and banned him from politics for five years. In the January 2001 election the party gained seats for a total of 128, but was far outdistanced by *Thai Rak Thai.* With former prime minister Chuan Leekpai having stepped aside as party leader, the April 2003 DP congress chose longtime party stalwart Banyat Bantadtan as leader. With his party having won only 96 seats in the February 2006 election, Banyat stepped down in favor of a younger leader, Abhisit Vejjajiva, who was unanimously confirmed as party leader in March.

After the banning of rival *Thai Rak Thai,* the DP emerged as the most popular party among Bangkok residents polled in November 2007, attracting 48 percent approval. Popular support was strongest in the capital's middle-class constituencies and in the conservative southern districts of the country. In the December election the DP again came in second to *Thai Rak Thai's* successor, the PPP, with 165 seats, and chose to sit in opposition and form a shadow cabinet rather than join the coalition government led by the PPP. In December 2008 the DP formed the core of a coalition government led by Abhisit and took 15 of the 24 cabinet posts. It won seven seats in the January 11, 2009, by-elections and, with defections from other parties, commanded 172 seats in the House. On April 5, 2010, the Electoral Commission made a preliminary finding that the Democrat Party had received 258 million baht illegally in 2005 and recommended the party be dissolved and its executives banned from politics for five years, but the finding was overturned on appeal. The June 2010 appointment of Chaiwut BANNAWAT as industry minister and other personnel changes brought the number of DP members in the cabinet to 17 out of 24. On November 11 Abhisit announced that he would reappoint the party's secretary general Suthep THAUGSUBAN, recently elected to the House in a by-election, as deputy prime minister. Following the defeat of the DP in the legislative elections in July 2011, Abhisit resigned as DP leader. However, he was reelected as DP chair on August 6.

In March 2013 the governor of Bangkok, DP member Sukhumbhand PARIBATRA, was reelected in a fierce campaign in which polls and pundits predicted his PPT opponent would win. In November Suthep and five other DP representatives resigned from the House to lead protests against the Yingluck government. Suthep subsequently was reported to have formed a new opposition grouping, the People's Democratic Reform Committee, to coordinate antigovernment activities. On December 8 all the DP representatives in the House resigned. Also in December Abhisit was indicted for his role in the 2010 Red Shirt crackdown.

Abhisit opposed the 2016 constitution, although other party leaders endorsed the new basic law.

Leaders: Abhisit VEJJAJIVA (Leader), Korn CHATIKAVANIJ (Deputy Leader), Chuan LEEKPAI (Chief Adviser), Banyat BANTADTAN (Deputy Chief Adviser), Suthep CHALERMCHAI SRI-ON (Secretary General).

Proud Thais Party—PTP (*Bhum Jai Thai*). Also called the **Thai Pride Party,** the PTP is an offshoot of the Neutral Democratic Party (below), which was dissolved by the Constitutional Court in December 2008. The PTP was founded on November 5, 2008, and on December 15 its members in the House joined with Abhisit's Democrat Party to form the current ruling coalition government. Characterized as a populist party, it shares many values with the rural populist parties spawned by Thaksin. (The NDP had entered into a coalition with the PPP in 2008.) With over 40 seats in the House, it viewed itself as a possible alternative to the currently dominant Democrats. It is divided by factions, including the Friends of Newin group (a fluid subcaucus led by banned politician Newin CHIDCHOB who is identified by media commentators as the PTP's de facto leader), a smaller *Matchimathipatai* group, and the *Spra-at Klinpratoom* splinter. The PTP's House strength in 2010 stood at 32, and its members held the portfolios of commerce, interior, and transport in the Abhisit cabinet. In the July 2011 balloting, the party secured 34 seats in the house. In September 2012 Anuthin CHANWEERAKUL was elected PTP leader, succeeding his father, Chaovarat CHANWEERAKUL.

Leaders: Anuthin CHANWEERAKUL (Leader), Saksayam CHIDCHOB (General Secretary).

Love Thailand Party (*Phak Rak Prathet Thai*—Rak Thailand). A protest party established by Chuwit KAMOLVISIT in 2011, Rak Thailand campaigned against political corruption. It secured four seats in the 2011 house balloting.

Leader: Chuwit KAMOLVISIT.

Motherland Party—MP (*Matubhum*). The MP's parent party, the **Citizen's Party** (*Rassadorn,* also translatable as Party of the People), was registered in 1986 by a largely military group whose leader, Gen. Tienchai SIRISAMPHAN, had played a prominent role in the countercoup of September 1985. *Rassadorn* disbanded after failing to win any House seats in the November 1996 election, but in February 1999 it was reregistered by Vatana ASAVAHAME, one of the *Prachakorn Thai* rebels who had defied the party leadership by supporting the Chuan administration. Nine more of the rebels subsequently joined *Rassadorn. Rassadorn* won only two House seats in January 2001. In July 2004 the party adopted the name ***Mahachon*** (Public Party—PP) after having been joined by former DP leader Sanan Kachornprasart and his followers.

In 2007 *Mahachon* claimed over two million members, mainly in the rural region centered on Nonthaburi district, but was weakened when Sanan and several other leaders decided to join *Chart Thai* and it won no seats in the December 2007 election. The party was revived under the *Rassadorn* label in February 2009 by Man Pattanotai, a former minister of information and communications technology in the Samak and Somchai governments. Its ranks included defectors from PPD and the DP. Its three House members generally aligned with the governing coalition, while remaining formally independent. In June 2009 the *Rassadorn* leaders formally changed the party's name to *Matubhum.* The party secured two seats in the 2011 house balloting. Despite being in the opposition, the MP's members of the House voted with the government in the November 2012 no-confidence vote.

Leaders: Man PATTANOTAI, Somsak WIWATANANT.

The small ***Rak Santi*** **Party** (RSP), led by Thawin SURACHETPONG, also secured one seat in the 2011 balloting.

Other Parties:

Social Action Party—SAP (*Kit Sangkhom*). A 1974 offshoot of the DP, the SAP is somewhat more conservative and free enterprise oriented than the parent group. It was the leading party in the 1983 balloting and served as the core of the Prem government coalition prior to the emergence of internal fissures, which prompted the resignation of longtime party leader Kukrit Pramoj in late 1985 and necessitated the legislative dissolution of May 1986. It was runner-up to the *Chart Thai* in 1988. Kukrit returned to the party leadership in August 1990. The party won 31 legislative seats in March 1992 and joined the Suchinda government in April; however, it left the promilitary alignment in June. It secured 22 seats in the September 1992 poll. Although it was a participant in the ensuing Chuan coalition, its leader, Montri PONGPANIT, was not offered a cabinet portfolio because of allegations that he had become "unusually rich."

The party went into opposition in September 1993, subsequently joining the Chaovalit coalition after the 1996 election, after which it held 20 seats, down from 22 in 1995. Kukrit Pramoj died in October 1996, and two years later Montri announced that he was stepping down as formal party leader, in part as a gesture of responsibility for a scandal that had cost the party its health portfolio.

In July 1999 the SAP withdrew from the governing coalition as a result of a dispute between Deputy Prime Minister Suwit Khunkitti and Rakkiat SUKTHANA over the party's cabinet seats. In March 2000 Suwit resigned his party leadership post, and in August he led a mass defection to *Thai Rak Thai.* (He later became leader of the new PPD.) With Rakkiat having joined *Seri Tham,* Montri having died in June, and Suwit having defected, the SAP's political life appeared limited, and it won one seat in the January 2001 house election. Nevertheless, under new leadership, the party registered for the December 2007 general election, but it did not win any seat. In mid-2008, however, Suwit left the PPP as a consequence of an intraparty dispute and returned to the SAP. The change of government in December 2008 and the by-election in January 2009 then offered the SAP a chance to revive by shifting its allegiance to the DP and joining Abhisit's coalition government, in which Suwit was awarded the portfolio of natural resources and environment. The SAP did not gain any seats in the 2011 house balloting.

Leaders: Suwit KHUNKITTI, Thongphlu DIPHRAI.

Thai Citizens (*Prachakorn Thai*—PT). *Prachakorn Thai* was launched prior to the 1979 election by the promilitary and charismatic populist Samak Sundaravej and displaced the Democrat Party to won a majority in Bangkok. From 1983 to 1986 it participated in a quadripartite governing coalition with the DP, the SAP, and the now-defunct **National Democracy Party** (*Chart Prachathipatai*), and in 1990 it entered the reshuffled Chatchai coalition.

Although the party won only three House seats in the 1992 election, it took 18 in 1995 and 18 again in 1996. Twelve of its MPs joined the governing coalition formed by Prime Minister Chuan in late 1997, for which they were expelled from the party. The Constitutional Court ruled the dismissal unconstitutional but the rebels declined to return to the PT. Nine subsequently joined the revived *Rassadorn,* two joined *Chart Pattana,* and one joined *Seri Tham.*

Samak won the Bangkok gubernatorial election in 2000, but the party failed to win any House seats in the elections of 2001, 2005, or 2006. In 2007 Samak moved to become leader of the PPP, leaving PT leadership to his brother Sumit. Despite putting up nearly 200 candidates in the December election, the party won no seats; nor did it secure representation in the 2011 house elections.

Leaders: Sumit SUNDARAVEJ (President), Somboon WESASUNTHORNTHAEP (Secretary General).

Referendum Party (*Prachamati* Party—PP). Established September 25, 2007, the PP was considered close to *Matchimathipataya.* Its leader proposed that General Sonthi be named prime minister following the December election. Although the party fielded nearly 300 candidates, the PP was unsuccessful in capturing any House seats. It did not secure representations in the 2011 house balloting.

Leaders: Pramuan RUCHANASEREE (Leader), Withun NAEWPHANICH (Secretary General).

New Politics Party—NPP (*Karn Muang Mai*). The NPP was formally registered on June 2, 2009. An offshoot of the urban progovernment People's Alliance for Democracy (PAD), it contested the 2011 election to offset the popularity of the rural parties and movements mobilized by Thaksin's populist appeal. Labor leader Somsak KOSAISUUK was chosen as the NPP's inaugural leader. The NPP did not gain any seats in the 2011 house elections. A split emerged in the party afterward, with a faction led by Sondhi LIMTHONGKUL defecting from the NPP.

Leaders: Somsak KOSAISUUK, Suriyasai KATASILA (Secretary General).

For information on the **New Alternative**—NA (*Thang Luak Mai*), see the 2012 *Handbook.* For information on the **Royalist People's Party**—RPP (*Pracharaj*), see the 2013 *Handbook.*

Parties Dissolved in 2007:

Thais Love Thais (*Thai Rak Thai*—TRT). Thaksin Shinawatra, a leading figure in the telecommunications industry and a former leader of *Palang Dharma,* announced formation of *Thai Rak Thai* in July 1998. His platform included popular reforms such as debt relief for farmers and measures to promote business expansion. He was successful in recruiting senior members from the country's other parties, all vulnerable to factionalism. In the January 2001 election *Thai Rak Thai* won 248 seats, permitting Thaksin to claim the prime minister's office.

A series of mergers followed. In July 2001 *Thai Rak Thai* absorbed *Seri Tham* (also known as the Liberal Democratic Party); in March 2002 the **New Aspiration Party**—NAP (*Pak Kwam Hwang Mai*) disbanded, and its members joined Thai Rak Thai; and in August 2004 *Chart Pattana* (National Development Party) followed. (For more information on the NAP, see the 2011 *Handbook.*)

Internally, *Thai Rak Thai* was dominated by various faction leaders loyal to Thaksin, including Sudarat KEYURAPHAN and Suriya JUNGRUNGREANGKIT. When his party was banned and 111 former senior party members were prohibited from direct involvement in party politics for five years after the military takeover in September 2006, Thaksin left Thailand and lived in exile thereafter, although he remained active in supporting the PPP (below) and other populist parties to which his followers transferred, and the Red Shirt movement. (For further details on *Thai Rak Thai* and the other banned political parties discussed below, see the 2010 *Handbook.*)

Other parties forced to dissolve in May 2007 for having committed electoral fraud were the **Pattana Chart Thai,** the **Progressive Democratic Party,** and the **Thai Ground Party.**

Parties Dissolved in 2008:

People Power Party (*Pak Palang Prachachon*—PPP). Previously a minor party established in 1998, the PPP attracted former members of the populist-welfare *Thai Rak Thai* (see above) after the latter was banned in 2007. The PPP, set up in August 2007, was led by veteran politician Samak Sundaravej, a former DP member and *Prachakorn Thai* founder. Notable new members included Wichienchot SUKCHOTRAT, a former member of the National Counter-Corruption Commission; former ambassador PHITTAYA PUKKAMAL; and Wikran SUPHAMONGKOL, nephew of former foreign minister Kantathi SUPHAMONGKOL. Support was strongest in the poorer constituencies of the capital and in the north and northeast of the country, where former prime minister Thaksin enjoyed his greatest popularity.

The PPP was the clear winner of the December 2007 election, taking 199 out of 400 constituency seats and 34 out of 80 proportional seats. Eight seats short of clear majority in the House of Representatives, the PPP negotiated a coalition with five other parties, for a total of 316 seats, enabling it to form a government. The new cabinet, led by PPP leader Samak, was sworn in on February 6, 2008, with the PPP taking two-thirds of the 36 portfolios. Three of the female ministers were wives of banned executives of the disbanded *Thai Rak Thai.*

In July 2008 the Constitutional Court found Public Health Minister Chaiya SASOMSUP guilty of electoral reporting irregularities, ruled that Foreign Minister Noppadon Pattarna had violated the constitution in an agreement with Cambodia, and found House Speaker Yongyuth TIYAPAIRAT guilty of vote-buying, obliging all three to resign. Large public demonstrations against Samak's government erupted in Bangkok in mid-2008, led by the People's Alliance for Democracy, which had agitated successfully against Thaksin's government in 2006. PPP was dissolved on December 2, 2008, by the Constitutional Court for vote-buying in the 2007 election and its leader and executives banned from holding office for five years.

Leaders: Samak SUNDARAVEJ (Party Leader and Former Prime Minister), Somchai WONGSAWAT (Former Prime Minister), Chalerm YOOBAMRUNG (Deputy Leader), Suraphong SUEBWONGLEE (Secretary General).

Thai Nation (*Chart Thai*—CT). *Chart Thai* was regarded as the principal heir of the Thanom military regime's **United Thai People's Party** (UTPP). In 1983 it merged with the **Siam Democratic Party** (*Prachatipat Siam*), a rightist monarchist group dating from 1981. (For more on the history of the party, see the 2014 *Handbook.*)

In the December 2006 election, *Chart Thai* emerged as the third strongest party, winning 34 seats, and subsequently agreed to join the six-party coalition led by the newly formed PPP and won several cabinet posts. But on December 2, 2008, the Constitutional Court upheld indictments by the Electoral Commission and the attorney general that *Chart Thai* be disbanded for electoral fraud during the 2007 election.

Leaders: Banharn SILPA-ARCHA (Leader), Somsak PRISANAN-ANTHAKUL (Deputy Leader), Sanan KACHORNPRASART (Chief Adviser), Wirai WIRIYAKIJJA, Praphat BHOTHASUTHON (Secretary General).

For more information on the **Neutral Democratic Party**—NDP (*Matchimathipataya*), see the 2014 *Handbook.*

Insurgent Groups:

The insurgency dates back to 1960 with the formation of the **Barisan Revolusi Nasional** (BRN). This movement, based in *pondoks* or Islamic schools, produced three wings, the **BRN Ulema** to rally and coordinate Islamic clergymen, the **BRN Coordinate Group** to conduct agitation and sabotage, and the **BRN Congress**, a military formation. A recently formed BRN youth wing **Pemud** and associated "small commando groups" known as the ***Runda Kumpulan Kecil*** (RKK) have been implicated in many attacks against civilians as well as the military since 2004, including August 2008 bombs in Sungai Kolok that killed two and a beheading of a local official in early September. In March 2013 the government opened a new round of negotiations with the BRN in Kuala Lumpur, Malaysia.

In parallel, the small **Pattani United Liberation Organization** (PULO), a secular organization, has fought since 1968 for an independent Islamic state carved from several southern provinces having Muslim majorities. In 1995 a "New PULO" militant splinter emerged. Also allegedly involved in carrying out escalating attacks against officials, teachers, and Buddhist leaders were the ***Pattani Islamic Mujaheddin*** **Movement** (*Gerakan Mujaheddin Islam Pattani*) and the **Patani Freedom Fighters** (*Pejuang Kemerdekaan Patani*). Connections to the international al-Qaida terrorist network and to *Jemaah Islamiah* have been alleged, particularly on the part of the ***Jemaah Salafi,*** founded in 1999 by Muhammad Haji JAEMING (Abdul Fatah) upon his return from training in a mujahidin camp in Afghanistan, but few substantial links have been verified. No group claimed responsibility for the rising tempo of attacks experienced in 2006 and 2007, and analysts believe they were carried out by decentralized territorial and mobile cells loosely inspired and supported by a loose network of secessionists and militant Muslim religious leaders. The widely varying locations, tactics, and weapons of the assaults suggest the absence of a central command despite the efforts since 1997 of an umbrella group, **Bersatu** (United), to coordinate the initiatives of the various antigovernment groups and movements.

LEGISLATURE

The 1991 basic law restored bicameralism in the form of a **National Assembly** (*Ratha Sapha*) encompassing an appointed Senate and an elected House of Representatives. The 1997 constitution provided for a directly elected Senate of 200 members not affiliated with political parties serving six-year terms. The House expanded to 500 seats in the January 2001 election, four-fifths directly elected from single-member constituencies and, for the first time, one-fifth chosen on a proportional basis from parties obtaining at least 5 percent of the national vote. Under the new constitution of August 2007, the legislature was to retain its two-chamber structure, but the number and method of selection of legislators were altered as described below.

Senate (*Woothi Sapha*). The first election to the new Senate was held March 4, 2000, with the successful candidates being a mix of unaffiliated political neophytes, reformers, and established figures. The Election Commission quickly disqualified 78 victors for vote-buying, fraud, and campaign offenses. All but 2 were, however, allowed to compete in a second round of balloting on April 29 for the vacated seats. Meanwhile, the term of the predecessor Senate had expired on March 21, and the Constitutional Court had ruled that the new body could not convene without the full complement of 200 senators. Sixty-six were elected on April 29, eight in a third round on June 4, three in a fourth round on July 9, and the final senator in a fifth round on July 22. The new Senate convened on August 1.

The election of April 19, 2006, was once again conducted amid numerous charges that some candidates circumvented proscriptions against campaigning or were too closely connected to political parties. By late July, 180 of the 200 potential senators had been endorsed by the Election Commission, but the commission ceased to function when its three remaining members were convicted of malfeasance and forced to resign. Meanwhile, the previous Senate continued to serve in an interim capacity until suspended by the military coup of September 19, 2006.

The 2007 constitution prescribed a Senate of 150 nonpartisan members. Seventy-six senators, one from each province, were to be directly elected. A Senate Selection Committee of seven officials and judges chaired by the president of the Constitutional Court was to select the remaining 74 senators from among nominees of professional, academic, public sector, and private sector associations. The last Senate elections were held on March 2, 2008. Seventy-four senators were appointed on February 14, 2008, by a seven-member committee headed by the chief of the Constitutional Court. The Senate was dissolved following the military coup of May 2014.

Speaker: Nikom WAIRATPANIJ.

House of Representatives (*Sapha Poothan Rassadorn*). The House of Representatives is composed of 500 seats, 375 members elected from 157 multi-seat constituencies and 125 elected on a proportional party-list basis; members serve four-year terms. The election on July 3, 2011, yielded the following results: For Thais Party, 265 (204 constituency and 61 party list); Democrat Party, 159 (115, 44); Proud Thais Party, 34 (29, 5); Thai Nation Development Party, 19 (15, 4); Thais United National Development Party, 7 (5, 2); *Phalang Chon*, 7 (6, 1); Love Thailand Party, 4 (0, 4); Motherland Partu, 2 (1, 1); Great People's Party, 1 (0, 1); New Democracy, 1 (0, 1); and *Rak Santi*, 1 (0, 1).

House elections on February 2, 2014, were annulled, and the chamber remains dissolved.

Speaker: Somsak KIATSURANONT.

CABINET

[as of December 6, 2016]

Prime Minister	Gen. Prayuth Chan-ocha
Deputy Prime Ministers	Gen. Prawit Wongsuwan Gen. Tanasak Patimapragorn Prajin Juntong Wissanu Krea-ngam Narong Pipatanasai Somkid Jatusripitak
Ministers	
Agriculture and Cooperatives	Gen. Chatchai Sarikalya
Commerce	Apiradi Tantraporn [f]
Culture	Vira Rojpochanarat
Defense	Gen. Prawit Wongsuwan
Deputy Head of National Council for Peace and Order	Gen. Prawit Wongsuwan
Education	Gen. Dapong Ratanasuwan
Energy	Gen. Anantaporn Kanjanarat
Finance	Apisak Tantivorawong
Foreign Affairs	Don Pramudwinai
Industry	Atchaka Sibunruang [f]
Information and Communications Technology	Uttama Savanayana
Interior	Gen. Anupong Paochinda
Justice and Attorney General	Gen. Paiboon Koomchaya
Labor	Gen. Sirichai Distakul
Natural Resources and Environment	Gen. Surasak Karnjanarat
Office of the Prime Minister	Mom Luang [f]
Public Health	Piyasakol Sakolsatayadorn
Science and Technology	Pichet Durongkaveroj
Social Development and Human Security	Adul Sangsingkeo
Spokesperson	Col. Winthai Suvaree
Tourism and Sports	Kobkarn Wattanavrangkul [f]
Transport	Arkhom Termpittayapaisith

[f] = female

Note: All are members of the National Council for Peace and Order.

INTERGOVERNMENTAL REPRESENTATION

Ambassador to the U.S.: Pisan MANAWAPAT.

U.S. Ambassador to Thailand: Glyn T. DAVIES.

Permanent Representative to the UN: Virachai PLASAI.

IGO Memberships (Non-UN): ADB, APEC, ASEAN, IOM, NAM, WTO.

For Further Reference:

Chaloemtoarana, Thak. *Thailand: The Politics of Despotic Paternalism.* Ithaca, NY: Cornell University Press, 2007.

Doner, Richard. *The Politics of Uneven Development: Thailand's Economic Growth in Comparative Perspective.* Cambridge: Cambridge University Press, 2009.

Marshall, Andrew MacGregor. *A Kingdom in Crisis: Thailand's Struggle for Democracy in the Twenty-first Century.* London: Zed Books, 2014.

TIMOR-LESTE (EAST TIMOR)

Democratic Republic of Timor-Leste
República Democrática de Timor-Leste

Political Status: Independent republic established May 20, 2002; constitution approved by Constituent Assembly on March 22, 2002.

Area: 5,641 sq. mi. (14,609 sq. km).

Population: 1,211,000 (2016E—UN); 1,261,072 (2016E—U.S. Census).

Major Urban Center (2014E—UN): DILI (228,000).

Official Languages: Portuguese, Tetum. A majority of Timorese are fluent in Bahasa Indonesia (a form of Malay); both it and English are "working languages."

Monetary Unit: U.S. Dollar (see U.S. entry for principal exchange rates).

President: José Maria VASCONCELOS (popularly known as Taur Matan RUAK); elected by popular vote on April 16, 2012, and sworn in for a five-year term on May 20, succeeding José RAMOS-HORTA.

Prime Minister: Rui Maria DE ARAÚJO (Revolutionary Front for an Independent East Timor); appointed by the president on February 10, 2015, following the resignation of Xanana GUSMÃO (National Congress of East Timorese Reconstruction).

THE COUNTRY

Timor-Leste occupies the eastern half of the tropical island of Timor, near the eastern end of the Indonesian archipelago, plus the small islands of Ataúro (Pulo Cambing) and Jaco (Pulo Jako) as well as Oecussi (Ocussi Ambeno), an enclave on the northern coast of Indonesian West Timor. As a result of the 1859 division of the island by Portugal and the Netherlands, Timor-Leste shares its only land border with Indonesia. The nearest overseas neighbor is Australia to the south across the Timor Sea. The Timorese population is primarily of Malay and Papuan descent. About three-quarters spoke Bahasa Indonesia in 2000, but this proportion declined after the end of Indonesian rule. Less than one-quarter are fluent in Portuguese and one-fifth in English. Commonly spoken is Tetum, an Austronesian language that incorporated elements of Portuguese over the centuries. The vast majority of the population is Roman Catholic, with small Protestant, Muslim, Hindu, and Buddhist minorities. Equality of the sexes is guaranteed under the 2002 constitution. Twenty-five women won election to the current 65-member National Parliament, and 7 were appointed to the extended cabinet.

The leading occupations continue to be subsistence agriculture and fishing, which in 2012 accounted for 64 percent of employment and 26 percent of GDP. Principal crops include coffee (by far the leading export), grains, cassava, spices, coconut, vanilla, and tropical fruits. Small-scale manufacturing, accounting for 18 percent of GDP and 10 percent of employment, involves construction and the production of processed coffee, handicrafts, cloth, and a limited range of other consumables. Services, led by public administration, accounted for 57 percent of non-oil GDP and 26 percent of employment in 2012.

In 1999 violence perpetrated mainly by anti-independence militias, covertly supported by the Indonesian army, destroyed much of the country's infrastructure and precipitated refugee flows that together produced a 35 percent economic contraction in the first year of independence. Economic growth fluctuated thereafter, peaking at 12.7 percent in 2009, reflecting receipts of overseas aid, loans, and a multidonor UN Trust Fund for infrastructure and construction projects. Growth eased to 10 percent in 2012, and the International Monetary Fund (IMF) projected a growth rate of 9.0 percent in 2014 and 8.8 percent in 2015. Although per-capita income rose steadily in 2012, approximately two-fifths of Timorese remained below the poverty line, and one-fifth was unemployed. Much of the population had only limited access to education and basic infrastructure. Adult literacy was under 60 percent; only three-fifths of the population had safe drinking water, only one-fourth had electricity, the under 5 mortality rate was 57 per 1,000 live births, and the country ranked 128th (out of 187) on the 2013 Human Development Index.

Prospects for growth and development rest on tapping extensive offshore hydrocarbon reserves. Revenues from oil and gas exports and royalties, supplemented by export earnings from coffee, gold, manganese, and marble, generated a brief surplus in both external trade and the domestic budget, but the surpluses turned into deficits in 2013. The government's Petroleum Fund, in which oil and gas revenues are lodged, and which is invested in sovereign and European Union (EU) bonds and securities, reached $16.6 billion in June 2014. Timor-Leste's principal export partners in 2012 were Singapore, United States, Germany, Japan, and Malaysia, and main sources of imports were Finland, Indonesia, Malaysia, Singapore, and China.

GDP grew by 5.5 percent in 2014, and then 4.3 percent, while inflation was 0.8 percent and 0.6 percent, respectively. The IMF estimated that GDP expanded by 5 percent in 2016, while inflation was 1.5 percent, and GDP per capita was $1,768. In its 2016 survey on the ease of conducting business, the World Bank ranked Timor-Leste 173rd out of 189 countries.

GOVERNMENT AND POLITICS

Political background. Even though the bulk of the Indonesian archipelago came under Dutch control in the 17th century, the eastern end of the island of Timor and the enclave of Oecussi were claimed by Portugal, whose traders first arrived there in the early 1500s. In 1859 the Netherlands and Portugal delineated the border between West and East Timor (although the resulting treaty was not ratified until 1904), and East Timor continued to be governed from Macao until reorganized as a separate colony in 1896. A local rebellion in 1910–1912 was repressed.

Following harsh Japanese occupation during World War II, East Timor returned to Portuguese control. Although Indonesia won independence from the Netherlands in 1949, a parallel struggle in East Timor failed. After a coup in Lisbon in 1974, the new democratic government of Portugal offered to conduct a referendum on the future of East Timor, designated an overseas territory since 1951. Although some organizations favored a continued relationship with Portugal or a gradual process of separation, by 1975 all the leading parties but one were advocating independence. Violence escalated, however, over what form of independent government should be established. On November 28 the left-wing Revolutionary Front for an Independent East Timor (*Frente Revolucionário do Timor-Leste Independente*—Fretilin) declared a "Democratic Republic," but this move was opposed by a number of anticommunist parties, including the Timorese Democratic Union (*União Democrática Timorense*—UDT) and the Timorese Democratic People's Association (*Associação Popular Democrática de Timor*—Apodeti). On December 7 Indonesian forces, with a tacit U.S. and Australian acquiescence, invaded to forestall an alleged communist takeover and restore order, ultimately driving Fretilin from the capital. Indonesia formally annexed East Timor on July 17, 1976, but Portugal and the United Nations refused to recognize the action.

The initial years of Indonesian rule were marked by political repression and a severe humanitarian crisis that saw an estimated 100,000 East Timorese succumb to starvation or what some observers characterized as genocidal violence by Indonesian forces intent on suppressing the Fretilin-led opposition. On November 12, 1991, Indonesian troops fired on demonstrators who had assembled in a Dili cemetery for the funeral of a student killed by the police two weeks earlier. More than 200 persons were shot or subsequently arrested and executed, and others beaten or tortured, provoking worldwide condemnation and a suspension of U.S. military training aid. The following November Fretilin's leader, Xanana GUSMÃO (born José Alexandre Gusmão), was captured and later sentenced to life imprisonment. But resistance by Fretilin's military wing, the *Forças Armadas de Libertação Nacional de Timor-Leste* (Falintil), continued in the mountains.

Sporadic clashes between protesters and Indonesian security forces punctuated the next three years and became international news when in October 1996 two prominent Timorese pro-independence campaigners were awarded the Nobel Peace Prize. In its citation for Bishop Carlos Felipe XIMENES BELO (Roman Catholic prelate of East Timor) and José RAMOS-HORTA (a former journalist and leader of Fretilin campaigning in exile against Indonesian rule), the Norwegian Nobel committee accused the Suharto government of "systematically oppressing the people" of East Timor and also referred to estimates that under Indonesian occupation "one third of the population of East Timor have lost their lives due to starvation, epidemics, war, and terror." Fact-finding visits and critical reports by a U.S. human rights expert and a UN envoy followed.

In April 1998, 200 delegates of the All-Inclusive Intra-East Timorese Dialogue (AIETD) convened in Portugal and formed the National Council of Timorese Resistance (*Conselho Nacional de Resistência Timorense*—CNRT) to better coordinate the efforts of pro-independence groups such as the UDT and Fretilin. Xanana Gusmão and Ramos-Horta were named president and vice president, respectively, of the CNRT political committee.

Massive demonstrations in Jakarta led to President Sukarno's resignation in 1989 and the decision by his successor President Habibie to consider eventual independence for East Timor. Meeting in New York on May 5, 1999, the Portuguese and Indonesian foreign ministers agreed to hold a referendum on East Timor independence, and this agreement was endorsed by the UN Security Council, which set up the UN Assessment Mission in East Timor (UNAMET) to conduct the ballot. Pro-independence advocates warned that elements in the army were giving clandestine support to pro-integrationist militias, most prominently the Red and White Iron (*Besi Merah Putih*—BMP) and the Thorn (*Aitarak*). The referendum was held on August 30, with UNAMET reporting a 98.6 percent voter turnout, in which 78.5 percent favored independence and 21.5 percent favored autonomy within Indonesia. Pro-Indonesian militia leaders rejected the outcome and took to the streets in violent assaults on UN workers and journalists as well as East Timorese. The Indonesian military failed to intervene, and in subsequent days attacks, murders, and arson were reported throughout the territory, and 450,000 Timorese fled their homes.

On September 9, 1999, responding to international pressure by regional leaders meeting at the APEC summit in Auckland, New Zealand, and later by the UN Security Council, President Habibie agreed to allow a peacekeeping presence in East Timor, and on September 15 the UN Security Council unanimously approved formation of the International Force East Timor (INTERFET). Led by some 4,500 Australians and commanded by Maj. Gen. Peter Cosgrove, 8,000 peacekeepers from 30 countries began deploying on September 20. Seven days later, with most of the Indonesian armed forces having withdrawn, INTERFET formally assumed control and despite sporadic clashes with militia fighters moved into the hinterlands to restore order.

On October 19, 1999, Indonesia's supreme legislature, the People's Consultative Assembly, ratified the referendum results and revoked its 1976 integration decree, and three days later Gusmão flew into Dili, receiving a hero's welcome. On October 25, the UN Security Council was able to replace INTERFET with the United Nations Transitional Administration in East Timor (UNTAET), a multipurpose body including not only troops and police but also civilian specialists. Led by Special Representative Sergio Vieira de Mello, the UNTAET was assigned the task of administering East Timor during the transition to independence.

On December 1 José Ramos-Horta ended his 24-year exile, and on December 11 Vieira de Mello convened a 15-member advisory National Consultative Council (NCC), which included integrationists as well as CNRT representatives and UNTAET members.

On July 12, 2000, the NCC approved formation of a transitional government comprising João CARRASCALÃO, president of the UDT; Marí ALKATIRI of Fretilin; Fr. Filomeno JACOB; Mariano LOPES, head of the Public Service Commission; and four UNTAET members. Ramos-Horta joined as foreign minister on October 19.

On August 30, 2001, East Timor democratically elected the 88 members of a Constituent Assembly to supersede the ETNC and begin drafting a constitution. Fretilin dominated the election, winning 55 seats; the Democratic Party (*Partido Democrático*—PD) followed with 7 seats; the Social Democratic Party (*Partido Social Democrata*—PSD), 6; and the Timorese Social Democratic Association (*Associacão Social-Democrata Timorense*—ASDT), 6. As a result, Fretilin's secretary general, Marí Alkatiri, who had spent many years in African exile, was named chief minister of an interim East Timor Council of Ministers that included Fretilin, the PD, and a number of independents. Meanwhile, a UNTAET-sponsored court in Dili continued investigating militia-related crimes.

In January 2002 the Constituent Assembly voted to convert itself into a National Parliament and to adopt the constitution, both achieved on March 22. On April 14 Gusmão, who had severed his ties to Fretilin after the 1999 referendum, was elected to the presidency as an independent, capturing 82 percent of the vote against the token opposition of the ASDT's Francisco Xavier do AMARAL. Gusmão was inaugurated for a five-year term on May 20 in conjunction with the formal establishment of the Democratic Republic of Timor-Leste. On the same day Fretilin's Alkatiri was sworn in as Timor-Leste's first prime minister.

Independence Day also marked the end of the UNTAET mission, which was succeeded by a United Nations Mission of Support in East Timor (UNMISET), whose mission was to enhance political stability, provide interim law enforcement while assisting the development of a domestic police service, and help maintain external security. UNMISET was replaced in May 2005 by a scaled-down UN Office in Timor-Leste (UNOTIL), subsequently recast in 2006 as the United Nations Integrated Mission in Timor-Leste (UNMIT).

On April 28, 2006, demonstrations in the capital supporting soldiers who had been dismissed from the army turned violent, precipitating two months of sporadic gang violence as well as clashes between elements of the police and armed forces that left nearly 40 people dead. The roots of the civil disorder can be traced to early February, when some 400 soldiers of the Timorese army (Falintil–*Forças de Defesa de Timor-Leste*—F-FDTL), led by Lt. Gastão SINHALA, left their barracks to protest alleged discrimination. The disgruntled troops from western districts of the country (*Loromonu*), whose numbers grew to about 600 later in the month, complained of favoritism toward the majority easterners (*Lorosae*), who had been more prominent and numerous in Falintil. The F-FDTL rebels were joined early in May by Maj. Alfredo REINADO and a contingent of military police. On May 24 Foreign Minister Ramos-Horta requested international aid, and the first of some 2,500 Australian, New Zealand, Malaysian, and Portuguese troops and police began arriving to restore a semblance of order to Dili and its environs. At the urging of the new government, the UN Security Council in August 2006 set up the UN Integrated Mission in Timor (UNMIT) to succeed UNOTIL and committed it to a two-year deployment, which was later extended. On May 29, 2006, President Gusmão convened the Council of State. And the next day he declared a 30-day state of emergency and, as commander in chief, assumed control of the F-FDTL and the Timorese police (*Policia Nacional de Timor-Leste*—PNTL), superseding the authority of Minister of the Interior Rogério LOBATO (Fretilin) and Secretary of State for National Defense Roque Félix RODRIGUES. Both cabinet members resigned on June 1, after which Ramos-Horta was assigned the defense portfolio in addition to his duties as foreign minister. Alkatiri and Lobato were charged with arming civilian supporters and inciting them to eliminate Alkatiri's opponents; charges against Alkatiri were dismissed in February 2007, but Lobato was convicted in March 2007 and given a prison sentence of seven and a half years.

On June 26, 2006, Prime Minister Alkatiri resigned under pressure brought to bear by supporters of the dismissed soldiers, the parliamentary opposition, and President Gusmão. Gusmão named José Ramos-Horta prime minister, and a reshuffled cabinet was sworn in on July 14.

In a role reversal Ramos-Horta was elected president for a five-year term in a two-way runoff on May 9, 2007, with 69.1 percent of votes. Gusmão, having chosen not to seek a second term as president, had assumed the leadership of a newly formed opposition party, the National Congress for Timorese Reconstruction (*Congresso Nacional de Reconstrução do Timor*—CNRT). His party won only 18 of 65 seats in the June 30 poll but was able to form a governing coalition, dubbed the Alliance of the Parliamentary Majority (*Aliança com Maioria Parlamentar*—AMP), with three other parties. Weeks of wrangling followed, with Fretilin failing in its attempts to form an alternative coalition. President Ramos-Horta appointed Gusmão as prime minister on August 6, and he assumed office two days later. In 2010 his coalition cabinet after adjustments included one CNRT leader holding two portfolios, three PSD ministers, one ASDT minister, a Fretilin Reform Group vice minister and six independents.

On February 11, 2008, rebels attempted to assassinate President Ramos-Horta, severely wounding him, and fired shots at Prime Minister Gusmão's motorcade. The rebels' leader, Reinado, was killed by Ramos-Horta's guards. Parliament declared a state of emergency, Australia dispatched 350 additional troops and police, and order was restored. On April 29 Reinado's second in command, Gastão SALSINHA, and 12 followers surrendered to the government, joining 15 others who had previously surrendered. Indonesia in May 2008 apprehended and turned over four rebels who had fled to West Timor. In all, 23 persons were sentenced to prison for terms ranging from 9 to 16 years.

Urban gang violence, which peaked in 2006, was also brought under control. Parliament, encouraged by a peace-building project sponsored by Oxfam, Concern, Action Asia, Yayasan Hak, and NGO Forum, in July 2008 passed a law to register and regulate "martial arts groups" (the core of many gangs) and in August 2008 brokered a "peace pact" between the two leading gangs, 7–7 and FSHT.

Corruption in government remained an obstacle to investment, as Timor-Leste declined from 123rd to 143rd in the Transparency International Index during the period 2006–2012 and Fretilin leaders accused the prime minister of awarding government contracts to political associates and family members. The government appointed Timor-Leste's first anticorruption commissioner, Aderito de Jesus SOARES, in February 2010 and in the following three years, he investigated more than 150 cases of corruption among elected and appointed officials. By 2013 Timor-Leste moved up to 119th on the corruption index, suggesting modest effectiveness of remedial measures. Reporters Without Borders noted that Timor-Leste's standing improved from 94th in 2010 to 77th in 2014.

Reforms in 2010–2012 included the launch of a Civil Service Commission, a National Development Bank, a National Liberation Combatants (veterans) Consultative Council, and a Chamber of Commerce and Industry.

The presidential election of 2012 began in March with 12 candidates. Tuar Matan Ruak (ind.) and Francisco GOMES (Aileba People's Liberty Party) proceeded to the runoff in April. Ruak won with 61.23 percent of the popular vote. The National Parliament election of July 7 was contested by 21 political parties, of which 4 secured seats: CNRT, Fretilin, PD, and Reform Front (*Frenti*-Mudança), whereupon CNRT formed a coalition government with PD and Reform Front, leaving Fretilin again in opposition. President Taur Matan Ruak swore in the new government on August 8, with Xanana Gusmão of CNRT again as prime minister. The cabinet included 55 members, including 31 CNRT leaders, 13 PD members, 5 Reform Front members, and 6 independents.

The U.S. State Department described the elections as "free and fair" but noted persistent human rights violations such as abuse of power by the police, an inefficient judiciary depriving citizens of expeditious trials, poor prison conditions, and social violence against women and children.

Gusmão resigned on February 6, 2015 (see Political Parties, below). After consultations with the outgoing prime minister, the president nominated Rui Maria DE ARAÚJO (Fretilin) to form a unity government on February 10. De Araújo's unity government was sworn in six days later with Gusmão as the planning and strategic investment minister. The government included Fretilin, CNRT, and PD.

Constitution and government. The constitution drafted by the Constituent Assembly and approved in its final form on March 22, 2002, after a period of popular consultation, provides for freedom of speech and of the press, freedom of religion, the right of *habeas corpus,* and freedom of association (except that "armed, military or paramilitary associations, including organizations of a racist or xenophobic nature or that promote terrorism, shall be prohibited"). The chief executive, a popularly elected president serving a once-renewable five-year term, plays a largely ceremonial role. In the event no presidential candidate receives a majority on a first ballot, the constitution mandates a runoff between the top two contenders. Most executive power resides with the prime minister, who is appointed by the president but must command a parliamentary majority. The prime minister selects the members of the cabinet, who are then appointed by the president.

Prior to the 2007 election, the National Parliament altered the electoral law to reduce the number of representatives from 88 to 65, chosen by a mixed single-member constituency and party list electoral system. The National Parliament, which has a five-year term, may be dissolved prematurely and new elections held, but not within six months of the next scheduled election or within six months of the end of a presidential term. Among its powers, the legislature may amend the constitution by a two-thirds vote. The 2002 constitution also provides for a Council of State, an advisory body chaired by the president and encompassing all past presidents, the current prime minister and speaker of the National Parliament, five citizens selected by the legislature, and five designated by the president.

The independent judiciary is headed by a Supreme Court of Justice with authority to rule on the constitutionality of statutes and referenda and to certify "the regularity and validity of the acts of the electoral process." There is also a High Administrative, Tax, and Audit Court and provision for Military Courts. Below the national level, Timor-Leste is divided into 13 administrative districts. The constitution recognizes the enclave of Oecussi as meriting a "special administrative policy and economic regime." In 2009 the Indonesian-imposed law code was replaced by a civil law code based on the Portuguese system, and the criminal law code was likewise altered in 2011.

Freedom House in 2013 rated Timor-Leste only "partly free" and below average on civil liberties, while Reporters Without Borders in 2016 ranked the country 99th in press freedoms out of 180 countries surveyed, a decline from 77th in 2014.

Foreign relations. Timor-Leste became the 191st member of the United Nations General Assembly on September 27, 2002, and subsequently joined a number of international organizations (see list below). It has participated in the ASEAN Regional Forum, a regional security consultative body, since 2005, and as an observer to both ASEAN and the Melanesian Spearhead Group, both of which it aspires to join. After the outbreak of violence in 2006, Timor-Leste's security was underpinned by the United Nations Integrated Mission in Timor-Leste (UNMIT) and an International Stabilization Force of Australian and New Zealand troops. Reflecting an improved security situation, the UN Police command UNPOL transferred its functions to the PNTL, the National Police of Timor-Leste in 2011. UNMIT's mandate expired on December 31, 2012, and by mid-2014 only a small number of foreign military and policy personnel remained for training and liaison.

Even before independence, Timor-Leste's leaders favored close relations with its immediate neighbors, Australia and Indonesia. The Australian delegation to the independence festivities was led by Prime Minister John Howard, who joined President Gusmão in signing a Timor Sea Treaty that granted Timor-Leste 90 percent of revenue from a Joint Petroleum Development Area (JPDA). However, the neighbors remained at odds over delineation of their maritime boundary and eligibility for royalties from further oil exploitation development rights. Consequently, in 2003 Dili sought to revise the provision of the treaty that would give Timor-Leste only 20 percent of the larger Greater Sunrise field, which lies outside the JPDA in what Australia considers its territory, and was estimated to contain gas valued at $50 billion. Dili also wanted to redraw the maritime boundary with Australia in accordance with the Law of the Sea midpoint principle, but the Howard government argued for retaining the border as delineated by a 1972 agreement with Indonesia based on the continental shelf principle. Boundary talks, occasionally turbulent, led in January 2006 to the Treaty on Certain Maritime Arrangements in the Timor Sea (CMATS Treaty), ratified in February 2007, whereby final determination of the boundary was to be postponed for 50 years but Timor-Leste was to receive 50 percent of Greater Sunrise revenues in the interim.

Australia remains Timor-Leste's principal security and trading partner as well as a source of aid and foreign investment. In February 2002 Timor-Leste and Australia signed two Memorandums of Understanding (MOUs) on combating illegal immigration and people smuggling, followed in August 2003 by an MOU on Cooperation to Combat International Terrorism. The two governments also signed an MOU in October 2006 on security arrangements within the JPDA. Australia funds and staffs training programs for the Timorese armed forces and police under its Defense Cooperation Program and Timor-Leste Police Development Program (TLPDP). Canberra in 2003 granted Timorese products duty-free access to the domestic market. Nevertheless, Australian prime minister Julia Gillard's proposal in July 2010 to set up and fund a regional refugee processing center in Timor-Leste provoked controversy; while President Ramos-Horta and Prime Minister Gusmão expressed initial interest, the National Parliament and the Fretilin party opposed the scheme, and it died in early 2011. On July 25, 2011, Timor Air, connecting Dili with Darwin, made its inaugural flight. In February 2012 Prime Minister Xanana Gusmão visited Canberra to meet his counterpart, Prime Minister Julia Gillard, and in May, Governor General Quentin Bryce and Minister for Veterans Affairs Warren Snowdon joined the celebrations of 10 years of independence in Dili. Defense Minister Stephen Smith visited in April 2013 to discuss security cooperation.

In May 2002, in a gesture of reconciliation, Indonesian president Megawati Sukarnoputri attended the independence ceremonies in Dili, prompting President Gusmão to announce that decades of repression and violence under Indonesian rule were to be relegated to "history and the past." In July Timor-Leste and Indonesia signed a joint communiqué establishing diplomatic relations, and in April 2005, during a visit by Indonesian president Susilo Bambang Yudhoyono, the two governments signed an agreement to begin demarcation of their 268 kilometer common border.

Relations with Indonesia were shadowed by the issue of justice for the victims of the militia violence of 1999. Indonesia refused to extradite persons indicted by East Timor's Serious Crimes Unit, and in Jakarta, a handful of civilian and military figures convicted of crimes against humanity by an Indonesian Ad Hoc Human Rights Court were acquitted on appeal.

However the Indonesia Timor-Leste Joint Commission on Truth and Friendship, which reported in July 2008, found the Indonesian government, military, and police responsible for murder, rape, torture, and forced displacement of Timorese in 1999. The Indonesian president expressed "deep regret," and he and the president of Timor-Leste pledged to forgo further recriminations or prosecutions in order to lay a foundation for future harmonious relations, a pledge that was renewed in August 2009 on the tenth anniversary of the independence referendum. (For further details on the indictments, trails, and reports relating to the 1999 violence, see the 2013 *Handbook*.) In 2012 President Susilo Bambang Yudhoyono attended the tenth anniversary ceremonies of East Timor's independence and renewed his support of East Timor's bid to join ASEAN. Consultations in Jakarta by Prime Minister Gusmão and President Taur Matan Ruak in March and June 2013, respectively, resulted in settlement of a disputed border segment (Delumi–Memo), establishment of three joint border-crossing posts, a visa exemption agreement for diplomatic and service officials, and establishment of a joint security and defense committee. Yudhoyono paid a return visit in August 2014.

China emerged as a leading benefactor, having been among the first to recognize the new state in 2002. In 2007 China was financing the construction of the presidential palace and a hospital, building barracks and providing uniforms for the armed forces, deploying police and medical aid personnel, training civil servants and farmers, and giving scholarships to students and officials to visit China. PetroChina won a contract to conduct a seismic survey and has expressed interest in developing offshore oil fields. In August 2008 President Ramos-Horta visited Beijing, where he was received by China's president, Hu Jintao, and in 2009 officials indicated that Timor-Leste would be purchasing two oil-fired power plants. In June 2010 Timor-Leste took command of two Jaco-class patrol boats purchased from China, which also trained 36 Timorese sailors to operate the vessels to counter fish poaching estimated to cost Timor-Leste $36 million annually. Wang Zhizen, vice-chair of the Chinese People's Political Consultative Conference National Committee, visited Dili in May 2012 to consult with officials and join the celebration of East Timor's 10th anniversary of independence.

The United States signed an agreement in 2009 for the U.S. Army to train Timor-Leste's marines alongside Indonesia's marines. A U.S.–Timor-Leste naval exercise Cooperation Afloat Readiness And Training (CARAT) in February 2014 was followed in June by the Pacific Partnership exercise, which brought U.S. navy ships, along with those of Australia, New Zealand, and Japan, to Dili to conduct disaster relief exercises. U.S. aid, totaling more than $168 million in 2006–2012, focused on technical assistance to government prosecutors, legal aid institutions, media and journalists, civil society bodies, and security and health care. Guided by Timor-Leste's Strategic Development Plan 2013–2030, the U.S. Agency for International Development initiated a five-year Country Development Cooperation Strategy (2013–2018) valued at $73.2 million focusing on good governance, health, education, and economic growth. Australia pledged A$96.6 million for the year 2014–2015 for good governance, agricultural production, clean water, mobile health clinics, classroom construction, and road rehabilitation. New Zealand allocated NZ$7 million annually through 2015 for mentoring of small businesses, upgrading of security and justice institutions, notably through the Community Policing Program, and childhood education.

The Asian Development Bank (ADB) approved a loan of $76.2 million for Timor-Leste in March 2016 for road construction and improvement. The ADB then approved in June a separate $325 million partnership agreement to diversify the country's economy over a four-year period. In August Timor-Leste and Cambodia finalized three agreements to improve economic cooperation between the two countries.

Current issues. In April 2013 Timor-Leste appealed to the Permanent Court of Arbitration to declare the 2006 agreement (*Certain Maritime Arrangements in the Timor Sea*) regarding sharing of revenues from the Timor Sea oil and gas joint development zone (*Greater Sunrise*) invalid on grounds of espionage by Australia during the negotiations and claimed a larger share of the revenues. In December 2013 the Australian Security Intelligence Organization seized documents from Timor-Leste's lawyer relating to the claims, whereupon Timor-Leste instituted proceedings against Australia in the International Court of Justice (ICJ) to regain the documents. The ICJ in March 2014 upheld Australia's right to the documents but required they be sealed pending the outcome of the arbitration case and that Australian espionage be terminated.

The 2014–2015 budget of $1.5 billion was approved by the National Parliament on January 24, 2014; it gave priority to rural infrastructure, food security, human capital development, public security, and good governance.

The Media Law, passed in May 2014, was criticized by opposition parties and international civil liberties groups as violating Timor-Leste's constitution and the International Covenant on Civil and Political Rights, and in August was declared unconstitutional by the Court of Appeal. A proposal introduced in mid-2014 to create an Ambeno-Oecusse Special Administrative Region to be called the Social Market and Special Economy Zone (ZEEMS in Portuguese) with regulatory, taxing, and land expropriation powers attracted United Nations Development Program backing but also criticism from local nongovernmental organizations, whose members objected that the public had not been consulted.

On October 23, 2015, the Timor-Leste parliament approved a measure to remove all foreign prosecutors, justices, and legal advisors after seven judicial rulings favored the ConocoPhillips energy company in cases over the firm's tax liabilities. The foreign legal staff had been invited to Timor-Leste to help establish the nation's judiciary. Opposition groups asserted that the expulsions would undermine the independence and efficiency of the judiciary.

POLITICAL PARTIES

Timor-Leste's oldest parties date from 1974, when local elites banded together to promote or resist movement toward independence. After the December 1975 Indonesian invasion, opposition to Indonesian annexation was led by the leftist Revolutionary Front for an Independent East Timor (Fretilin) and its military wing, Falintil. The anti-independence parties, such as the Timorese Democratic Union (UDT), accommodated the Indonesian authorities but later became disillusioned and opposed the occupation. In April 1998 Fretilin agreed to join other surviving parties in forming an umbrella National Council of Timorese Resistance (*Conselho Nacional de Resistência Timorense*—CNRT). The end of the Indonesian occupation in 1999 saw a proliferation of new parties, most of them small, personality based, and short-lived. In preparation for Timor-Leste's first election in August 2001, 16 parties registered candidate lists, and 12 won at least 1 seat in the Constituent Assembly. In the June 2007 parliamentary election 14 parties registered, but only 7 won seats, the rest failing to reach the threshold of 3 percent of the popular vote. Fretilin won the most seats, 21, but the next 3 finishers formed a coalition government, the Alliance of the Parliamentary Majority (*Aliança com Maioria Parlamentar*—AMP), under Xanana Gusmão, the leader of the National Congress for the Reconstruction of East Timor (CNRT), leaving Fretilin in opposition. In the July 2012 Parliamentary election, CNRT won 30 seats, followed by Fretilin with 25, PD 8, and Reform Front 2; no other party reached the threshold necessary to secure a seat.

Governing Coalition Parties:

National Congress for Reconstruction of Timor (*Congresso Nacional de Reconstrução do Timor*—CNRT). The CNRT is an indirect descendant of the National Council for Reconstruction of Timor (*Conselho Nacional de Resistência Timorense*—CNRT) that functioned as an umbrella body for resistance to Indonesian rule. Established in 1998, it lapsed following the country's independence. The current CNRT, with a modified name but same acronym, coalesced in early 2007 from elements dissatisfied with the existing political parties. It is centrist, moderate, and pragmatic in its ideology. Its organization is based on prominent personalities rather than a formal branch structure. Outgoing president Xanana Gusmão assumed leadership of the party in March 2007 and attracted many of his followers and supporters in the electorate. The party polled well in the June 2007 parliamentary election but did not succeed in gaining a majority, winning only 24 percent of the vote and 18 seats, placing second behind Fretilin, which won 21. As neither party could command a majority, in July Gusmão negotiated an agreement with the Timorese Social Democratic Association–Social Democratic Party alliance and the Democratic Party to forge a parliamentary majority. On August 6 Ramos-Horta requested that the CNRT form a government, appointing party president as prime minister. In government, CNRT has pursued an ambitious national development plan, funded by substantial withdrawals from the Petroleum Fund. No party won the majority seats in the 2012 election; CNRT led with 36.7 percent, negotiated a coalition with two other parties, PD and Reform Front, formed a new government, and took 31 cabinet posts.

On February 6, 2015, Gusmão announced his resignation as prime minister, reportedly asserting that the country needed a new generation of leaders. The CRNT remained part of the unity government formed on February 16, with Gusmão as minister of planning and strategic investment and party members in eight other portfolios.

Leaders: Xanana GUSMÃO (President), Deonisio da Costa Babo SOARES (Secretary General).

Revolutionary Front for an Independent East Timor (*Frente Revolucionário do Timor-Leste Independente*—Fretilin). Founded in 1974 with a commitment to East Timorese independence from Portugal, the leftist Fretilin emerged from the Timorese Social Democratic Association (ASDT, below). It mounted an insurrection in 1975 and then declared formation of a Democratic Republic of East Timor on November 28. In December, however, it was forced from the capital by Indonesian forces.

Fretilin and its military wing, the Armed Forces of National Liberation of East Timor (*Forças Armadas de Libertação Nacional de Timor-Leste*—Falintil), led by Xanana Gusmão, continued to resist Indonesian annexation for more than two decades. In November 1992 Gusmão was captured by Indonesian forces, and in May 1993 he was sentenced to life in prison (subsequently reduced to 20 years, and then in 1999 to house arrest).

In the context of the UN intervention that followed the August 1999 independence referendum, Fretilin accepted a role in a UN-sponsored National Consultative Council (NCC). In July 2000 Fretilin's secretary general, Marí Alkatiri, joined a transitional government. Meanwhile, Gusmão had resigned from Fretilin after the 1999 referendum.

In the Constituent Assembly election of August 2001, Fretilin emerged with 57.3 percent of the popular vote and 55 of 88 seats, leading to Alkatiri's selection as chief minister in the second interim government and, ultimately, his assumption of the prime ministership at independence.

The April–July 2006 crisis strengthened a dissident group that sought Alkatiri's removal as party leader. In May his position was challenged at a party congress by José Luís Guterres, Timor-Leste's ambassador to the UN and the United States, who withdrew when Alkatiri engineered a change from secret ballot to a show of hands. On June 25 the Fretilin leadership backed his continuing as prime minister, but he stepped down the following day. He was replaced as president of the party by Francisco Guterres, while José Luís Guterres accepted the post of foreign minister in the Ramos-Horta cabinet. In 2007 José Luís Guterres's rebellious Fretilin *Grupo Mudança* (Fretilin Reform Group) supported the CNRT in the parliamentary election and its leader was subsequently named vice prime minister, provoking the mainstream leadership to expel the Reform Group members. In March 2009 prominent member Ana Maria Pessoa Pereira da SILVA PINTO was named prosecutor-general by the CNRT-led government and resigned her Fretilin membership, leaving Fretilin with 21 seats. In the 2012 election, Fretilin finished second with 29.9 percent of the vote and 25 seats, whereupon it continued as the sole opposition in Parliament. Its leader ran unsuccessfully for president in March 2012.

After negotiations in February 2015, Fretilin agreed to become part of a unity government with the CNRT and the PD. Former health minister and party member, Rui Maria DE ARAÚJO, was appointed prime minister of the new cabinet, and the party assumed four cabinet posts.

Leaders: Rui Maria DE ARAÚJO (Prime Minister); Francisco "Lu'Olo" GUTERRES (President), Jose dos REIS (Secretary General).

Democratic Party (*Partido Democrático/Parta Demokrat*—PD). Organized in June 2001 in preparation for the August Constituent Assembly election, the centrist PD advocates participatory democracy, an independent judiciary, and a market economy with selective intervention by the government. The PD is influenced by student and youth movement activists and former resistance figures. Based on an 8.7 percent vote share in the balloting, in 2001 it was awarded seven assembly seats. In the June 2007 legislative election, the PD won 11 percent of the vote and eight seats. Its leader, Fernando LASAMA de Araujo, who ran unsuccessfully for the presidency, and ten other PD members were awarded cabinet portfolios.

In March 2012 Araujo ran again for the presidency but came in fourth in the first round with 17.7 percent of the vote. In the parliamentary elections of 2012, the PD won 8 seats (10.3 percent of the vote) and entered a coalition with its ally CNRT, thereby being awarded 13 cabinet posts. The party remained part of the new unity government formed in February 2015, with two cabinet posts.

Arajua died at age 52 on June 2, 2015.

Leader: Mariano Assanami Sabino LOPEZ.

Parliamentary Opposition Party:

Reform Front (*Frenti-Mudança*). From 2006 to 2011, this party was called Fretilin-Mudança (**Revolutionary Front for an Independent East Timor—Change**) to signal its leaders' disillusionment with the failure of the radical Fretilin leadership to adapt to the needs of a modernizing and pluralistic East Timor. As a faction in 2006, they tried to reform Fretilin from within. José Luis GUTERRES, formerly East Timor's UN ambassador, led a movement at the party congress to replace Marí Alkatiri as secretary-general but was outmaneuvered, and the faction members subsequently left Fretilin.

In the 2007 presidential election, Fretilin-Mudança activists supported José Ramos-Horta's candidature, and in the parliamentary election, they supported CNRT. José Luis Guterres was appointed vice-prime minister in the AMP government after the elections.

The group renamed itself Fretlin-Mudança (dropping the *i* for independent) to distinguish itself from the original Fretilin in order to register as a new political party for the 2012 elections. The Court of Appeal found the new name too similar to that of Fretilin and refused to approve it. A July 2011 resubmission with the new name Frenti-Mudança (Reform Front) was approved, although the party flag had to be changed to distinguish it from Fretilin's. Reform Front won two seats in the 2012 elections and was invited into the CNRT-led coalition government. It was awarded five cabinet posts, with Guterres appointed minister of foreign affairs. The party was not part of the unity government formed in February 2015, refusing to participate with Fretilin.

Leaders: José Luis GUTERRES (President), Jorge da Conceição TEME (Secretary General).

Other Parties That Contested the 2012 Elections:

Timorese Social Democratic Association (*Associação Social-Democrata Timorense*—ASDT). The current ASDT was formed in 2001 by one of the earliest Fretilin leaders, Francisco Xavier do Amaral, as a third-way Fretilin offshoot positioned between the parent party and more conservative elements. In 1974, Nicolau dos Reis LOBATO, Xavier do Amaral, José Ramos-Horta, and others had established the original ASDT, which was soon superseded by Fretilin. During Indonesian rule, Xavier do Amaral had resided in Jakarta, and he initially returned to East Timor as a proautonomy integrationist. He has also been associated with a more radical Fretilin offshoot, the CPD–RDTL.

In the 2001 Constituent Assembly election, the ASDT won 7.8 percent of the vote and six seats. Its leader Xavier do Amaral contested the 2002 and 2007 presidential elections without success.

Prior to the June 2007 parliamentary election, the ASDT negotiated an agreement with the PSD (below) to cooperate in supporting each other's electoral campaign initiatives. The ASDT–PSD won 15.7 percent of the popular vote and 11 parliamentary seats, subsequently joining the CNRT and the PD in forming a coalition government.

Xavier do Amaral died on March 6, 2012 at age 74. The party won 1.8 percent of the vote in 2012 and no seats but was awarded one ministerial post in the current cabinet.

Leaders: Joao Andre CORREIAL (President), Vicente dos SANTOS (Secretary General).

Social Democratic Party (*Partido Social Democrata*—PSD). Founded in September 2000 as a centrist alternative to Fretilin and the Timorese Democratic Union (UDT, below), the PSD advocates consensus and formation of a national unity government. Its platform stresses social justice, better health care, participatory democracy, and Timor-Leste's membership in ASEAN. It would abolish the death penalty and establish a Timorese currency. In the 2001 election, it won 8.1 percent of the vote and six seats.

In 2007 its presidential candidate, Lúcia LOBATO, won 8.9 percent of the vote, for fifth place. In the run-up to the June 2007 legislative election, the PSD formed an electoral alliance with the ASDT that won 11 seats and then joined in establishing the governing coalition, gaining 3 cabinet posts. PSD won 2.2 percent of the vote in 2012.

Leaders: Zacarias de COSTA (President), Marito MAGNO (Secretary General).

Timorese Nationalist Party (*Partido Nacionalista Timorense—PNT*). Established in 1999 as a post-autonomy party, PNT was at one time a member of Fretilin, but its leader Abilio ARAUJO was expelled because of business links with the Suharto family of Indonesia. In the 2001 Constituent Assembly election, it won 2.2 percent of the votes and won 2.4 percent of the votes in the 2007 parliamentary election but no seats. PNT then joined a loose alliance with PDRT, PDC, PST, UDT, and PMD under the name **Democratic Progressive League** (*Liga Democratica Progressiva*—LDP).

Republic of Timor-Leste Party (*Partido Democrática Republica de Timor-Leste*—PDRT). The PDRT is supported by voters in the western districts of Timor-Leste and by those who sympathized with the 594 Group comprised of dissenting soldiers led by Maj. Alfredo Reinado. PDRT won 1.9 percent of the popular vote in the 2007 election. In the 2012 election, PDRT entered into a coalition with the PLPA (below) but won no seats.

Aileba People's Liberty Party (*Partido Liberta Povo Aileba*—PLPA). The PLPA was founded in December 2009 and was officially registered in 2010. *Aileba* means carriers of wood and connotes itinerate peddlers. The party champions the rural poor and calls for better roads and access to clean water, schools, and health facilities in the rural districts. PLPA won 0.9 percent of the parliamentary vote and no seats in the 2012 election; its leader Francisco GOMES contested the presidential election but failed to make the runoff.

Leaders: Francisco GOMES (President), Gabriel FERNANDES (General Secretary).

Republican Party (*Partidu Repub likanu*—PR). The PR was established in December 2005 by a leading academic and member of the Council of State, Joao Mariano Saldanha, who remains the party president. The party platform advocates popular democratic participation and emphasizes security, employment, education, health, and decentralization. Reflecting its promotion of gender equality and minority rights, the PR would establish a Ministry of Gender and Minority Affairs and wants to refocus the armed forces on peacekeeping. The party advocates making Tetum the primary official language.

The PR won 1.1 percent of the popular vote in the 2007 election and slumped to only 0.9 percent in the 2012 election.

Leaders: Joao Mariano SALDANHA (President), Belarmino F. NEVES (Secretary General).

Christian Democratic Party (*Partido Democrata Cristão/Partai Demokrasi Kristen*—PDC/PDK). The PDC was founded in 1998 in Portugal and in August 2000 in Dili as a largely Catholic party with links to churches in Australia and Portugal and to the Indonesian Christian Democratic Party. The PDC was briefly allied with the **Christian Democratic Union of Timor** (*União Democrata-Cristão de Timor*—UDC). Considered somewhat more left-leaning than the UDC, it attracted both Protestants and Catholics. In the 2001 election it won 1.9 percent of the vote and two Constituent Assembly seats, whereas the UDC won one seat on a 0.6 percent vote share. In 2006 the UDC and the PDC merged under the PDC title.

The PDC advocates Christian values, social justice, and a multilateral foreign policy free from great-power domination. In the June 2007 parliamentary election the PDC won 1 percent of the popular vote. The PDC president, António XIMENES, studied theology in Indonesia and directed the National Commission for Study on the Future of East Timor. PDC won 0.2 percent of the vote in 2012.

Leaders: António XIMENES (President), Julio PEREIRA (Secretary General).

Socialist Party of Timor (*Partido Socialista de Timor*—PST). The PST, a Fretilin splinter, leans toward Marxist-Leninism and has a small base of support among students and labor. In August 2001 it won one legislative seat on a 1.7 percent vote share but in 2007, gained no seat with 1 percent of the vote. Avelino Coelho da Silva, the party's secretary general, was named secretary of state for energy policy in the Gusmão government. In the July 2012 election, PST won 2.4 percent of votes and no seat, but the president of the party was appointed by Prime Minister Gusmão as the secretary of state for the Council Ministers of the 2012 government.

Leaders: Avelino Coelho da SILVA (President), Pedro SARMENTO (Secretary General).

Timorese Democratic Union (*União Democrática Timorense*—UDT). The conservative UDT was established in 1974 as a predominantly Catholic, anticommunist formation that was initially open to federation with Portugal. Having opted for independence, the UDT was briefly allied with Fretilin, but the two were on opposite sides of the civil war that saw Fretilin's declaration of a republic in November 1975 and the subsequent invasion by erstwhile UDT ally Indonesia.

The UDT operated primarily from exile in Portugal and Australia during the period of Indonesian rule, although it again allied itself with Fretilin in 1986. It was revived in 1997 and participated in the CNRT, the NCC, and the transitional government of October 2000 before competing in the August 2001 Constituent Assembly balloting. In the election it won 2.3 percent of the vote, for two seats.

In the 2007 election, UDT obtained 0.9 percent of the popular vote and in the 2012 election gained 1.1 percent. The former leader of the party and East Timor ambassador to the Republic of Korea João Viegas CARRASCALÃO died in February 2012.

Leaders: Gilman EXPOSTO (President), Cipriano J. da Costa GONCALVES (Secretary General).

National Unity Party (*Partidu Unidade Nacional*—PUN). Founded in 2006, the PUN is a Christian democratic party committed to moral and family values, basic human needs, democracy, and human rights.

In the June 2007 parliamentary election, the PUN won three seats. Fernanda Borges was the parliamentary group leader and chaired the Parliamentary Committee on Constitutional Issues, Justice, Public Administration, Local Power and Government Legislation. In the 2012 election, PUN won no seats in national parliament with 0.7 percent of the vote.

Leaders: Fernanda Mesquita BORGES (President), Maria F. de DEUS (Secretary General).

Democratic Alliance (*Aliança Democratica*—AD). The AD was formed by the Association of Timorese Heroes (KOTA, below) and the **People's Party of Timor** (PPT) as a joint electoral front for the 2007 legislative elections. The grouping secured two seats. In the 2012 election, it received only 0.6 percent votes.

Association of Timorese Heroes (*Klibur Oan Timor Asuwain*—KOTA). Also known as the **Sons of the Mountain Warriors**, the KOTA was established in 1974 by Leão Pedro dos Reis Amaral and the late José MARTINS. The KOTA descended from the Popular Association of Monarchists of Timor (*Associação Popular Monarquia de Timor*—APMT), which represented traditional royalty. In 1975 the KOTA joined the UDT (above) and Apodeti in actively opposing Fretilin's efforts to establish a leftist government and for a time backed the Indonesian intervention. Reemerging in the late 1990s, the KOTA backed independence, joined the CNRT, and participated in the 2001 Constituent Assembly election, in which it won 2.1 percent of the vote and two seats.

Prior to the 2007 legislative election, KOTA formed a coalition with the People's Party of Timor (PPT), called the Democratic Alliance (DA, above).

Leaders: Manuel TILMAN (President), Maria Angela Freitas da SILVA (Secretary General).

National Democratic Unity of Timorese Resistance (*Unidade Nacional Democrática da Resistência Timorense*—Undertim). Undertim split from Fretilin in early 2005 and launched itself as a new party on August 30, 2005. Its leader was a prominent resistance fighter with Falintil for 20 years. The party platform stresses better housing, health, environment, and social security. It advocates compulsory military service, traditional justice in villages, and active engagement with Australia and Indonesia.

Undertim won two seats in the June 2007 election but gained no seat in the 2012 election, winning only 1.5 percent of the vote.

Leaders: Cornelio GAMA (President), Francisco Guterres MANUBUY (Secretary General).

National Development Party (*Partido Desenvolvimento Nacional*—PDN). Founded by a former secretary-general of PSD, Fernando Dias GUSMÃO, PDN was established on May 30, 2009. Gusmão was elected to the Constituent Assembly in 2001 and reelected to the National Parliament in 2007 as a PSD representative but left the party and resigned from the parliament in 2009 because of disenchantment with PSD's failure to implement its election policy promises.

In the July 2012 election, PND won 2 percent of the vote.

Leader: Lucas SOARES (Secretary General).

Enrich the National Unity of the Sons of Timor Party (*Partidu Kmanek Haburas Unidade Nasional Timor Oan*—Khunto). Khunto is a new party that was granted legal registration on June 22, 2011. Khunto won 3 percent of the votes in the 2012 election.

Leaders: Armanda Berta dos SANTOS (President), Antonio Verdial de SOUSA (Secretary General).

Liberal Democratic Party (*Partido Democrático Liberal*—PDL). The PDL originated as the Liberal Party (*Partai Liberal*), which was registered in 2001 and contested the Constituent Assembly elections in that year. Although the party consistently ran last in the voting, its 1.1 percent of the vote entitled it to one seat in the Assembly and also in the First National Parliament. In the 2012 election, PDL won 0.5 percent of the vote but no seat.

Leaders: Marito de ARAÚJO (President), Gaspar de ARAÚJO (Secretary General).

Timorese Democratic Party (*Partido Timorense Democratico*—PTD). The PTD, founded in 2011, contested the 2012 election but only won 0.5 percent of the vote.

Leader: Alianca da Conceicao ARAÚJO (President).

Popular Development Party (*Partido Desenvolvimento Popular*—PDP). This minor party won 0.4 percent of the vote in the 2012 parliamentary election.

Leaders: Antonio SOARES (President), Calistro das NEVES (Secretary General).

Millennium Democratic Party/East Timor National Republican Party (*Partidu Milénium Demokrátik*—PMD; *Partido Republika Nacional Timor Leste*—Parentil). PMD was founded in 2004 by pro-independence activist Herrmenegildo "Kupa" LOPES and former members of the PSD. The party was registered in December 2005. PMD, a center party, calls for reconciliation and democracy. In the 2012 election, PMD formed a coalition with East Timor National Republican Party (*Partido Republika Nacional Timor Leste*—Parentil) called the Proclaimed Block, which won 0.7 percent of the parliamentary vote.

Leaders: Arlindo Francisco MARÇAL (President), Hermenegildo LOPES (Secretary General).

Timorese Popular Monarchy Association Party (*Associação Popular Monarquia Timorense*—APMT). This new party contested elections for the first time in 2012 and won only 0.8 percent of the vote.

Leaders: Pedro da Costa RAMALHO (President), Cesar Augusto dos Santos CARLOS (Secretary General).

LEGISLATURE

An 88-member Constituent Assembly (*Assembleia Constituinte*) was elected on August 30, 2001, superseding a 36-member interim body, the East Timor National Council, which had been appointed by UN administrators in October 2000. In 2002 the assembly was reconstituted as the **National Parliament** (*Parlamento Nacional*) and now comprises 65 members elected for a five-year term on a proportional basis.

In the July 7, 2012, election, the National Congress for Timorese Reconstruction won 30 seats; Revolutionary Front for an Independent East Timor, 25 seats; Democratic Party, 8; and Reform Front, 2.

Speaker: Adérito Hugo DA COSTA (CNRT).

CABINET

[as of November 15, 2016]

Prime Minister	Rui Maria de Araújo (Fretilin)
Ministers of State	
Economic Affairs	Estanislau da Silva (Fretilin)
Presidency and Council of Ministers	Agio Pereira (CNRT)
Social Affairs	(Vacant)
State Administration and Justice	Dionísio Babo-Soares (CNRT)
Ministers	
Agriculture and Fisheries	Estanislau da Silva (Fretilin)
Commerce, Industry and Environment	António da Conceição (PD)
Defense and Security	Cirilo José Cristovão (CNRT)
Education	(Vacant)
Finance	Santina Cardoso (ind.) [f]
Foreign Affairs	Hernâni Coelho (Fretilin)
Health	Maria do Céu Sarmento (CNRT) [f]
Interior	Longuinhos Monteiro (ind.)
Justice	Ivo Valente (CNRT)
Petroleum and Mineral Resources	Alfredo Pires (CNRT)
Planning and Strategic Investment	Xanana Gusmão (CNRT)
Public Works	Gastão Francisco de Sousa (PD)
Social Solidarity	Isabel Amaral Guterres (ind.) [f]
State Administration	Dionísio Babo-Soares (CNRT)
Tourism	Francisco Kalbuadi Lay (CNRT)

[f] = female

INTERGOVERNMENTAL REPRESENTATION

Ambassador to the U.S.: Domingos Sarmento ALVES.

U.S. Ambassador to Timor-Leste: Karen Clark STANTON.

Permanent Representative to the UN: Maria Helena Lopes de Jesus PIRES.

IGO Memberships (Non-UN): ADB, ICC, IOM, NAM.

For Further Reference:

Molnar, Anrea Katalin. *Timor Leste: Politics, History, and Culture.* New York: Routledge, 2010.

Shepherd, Christopher. *Development and Environmental Politics Unmasked: Authority, Participation, and Equity in East Timor.* New York: Routledge, 2014.

Stanley, Elizabeth. *Torture, Truth, and Justice: The Case of Timor-Leste.* New York: Routledge, 2009.

TOGO

Republic of Togo
République Togolaise

Political Status: Independent republic since 1960; personal military rule imposed in 1967; one-party state established November 29, 1969; Third Republic proclaimed on January 13, 1980, under constitution adopted in referendum of December 30, 1979; constitution suspended by a National Conference on July 16, 1991; multiparty constitution adopted by popular referendum on September 27, 1992.

Area: 21,622 sq. mi. (56,000 sq. km).

Population: 7,497,000 (2016E—UN); 7,756,937 (2016E—U.S. Census).

Major Urban Center (2015E—UN): LOMÉ (956,000).

Official Language: French.

Monetary Unit: CFA Franc (official rate October 1, 2016: 592.38 francs = $1US). The CFA franc, previously pegged to the French franc, is now permanently pegged to the euro at 655.93 CFA francs = 1 euro.

President: Faure Essozimna GNASSINGBÉ (Union for the Republic, originally elected from the Rally of the Togolese People); elected on April 24, 2005, and inaugurated on May 4 following an extended constitutional crisis triggered by the death on February 5 of his father, Gen. Gnassingbé EYADÉMA (Rally of the Togolese People), who had been president since 1967; reelected on March 4, 2010, and inaugurated for a second term on May 3; elected for a third term on April 25, 2015, and inaugurated on May 4.

Prime Minister: Sélom Komi KLASSOU (Union for the Republic); appointed by the president in April 2015, and sworn in on June 10; to succeed Kwesi AHOOMEY-ZUNU (Pan-African Patriotic Convergence), who resigned on May 22, 2015.

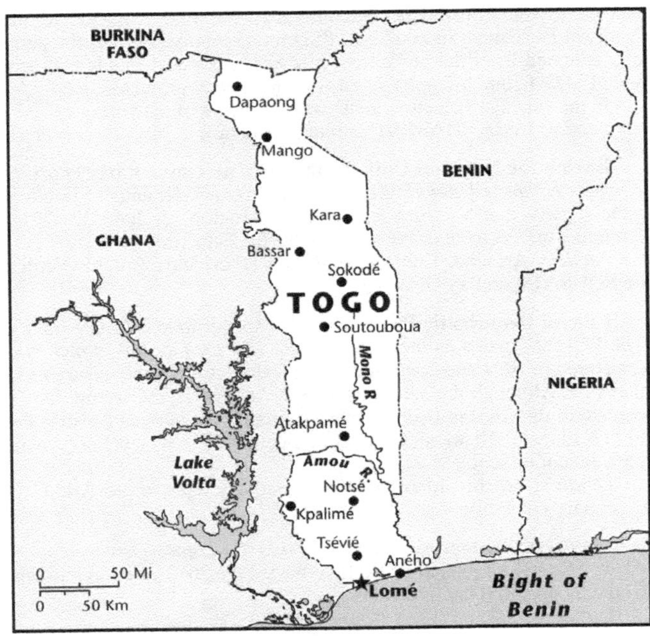

THE COUNTRY

Wedged between Ghana and Benin on Africa's Guinea Coast, the small Republic of Togo extends inland from a 31-mile coastline for a distance of 360 miles. Eighteen major tribal groups are located in its hilly, hot, and humid territory, the best known being the culturally dominant Ewe in the south, whose traditional homeland extends into Ghana; the Mina, another southern people; and the Kabiyé in the north, who staff most of the country's small army. Although French has been accorded official status, most people use indigenous languages; Ewe is predominant in the south and Twi in the north. About 51 percent of the population practice indigenous and animist religions; 29 percent are Christians (mainly Roman Catholicism); and 20 percent are Muslims. Somewhat more than half of adult women are in the work force, predominantly in the agricultural and trading sectors, but are generally underrepresented in the government and legislature. In the 2013 elections, women secured 14 seats in the assembly, or 15.4 percent of the total. In 2016 the Inter-Parliamentary Union ranked Togo at 105th out of 181 countries with only 17.6 percent (16 of 91 seats) of seats held by women in the legislature. In 2016 there were four women in the cabinet.

The economy depends primarily on subsistence agriculture, the three most important crops being cocoa, coffee, and cotton. Phosphate is the leading export, and oil refining, steel fabrication, and cement production are assuming increasing industrial importance. Smuggling has long been a source of contention with Ghana; as much as a third of Togo's cocoa exports originates in the neighboring state and are smuggled into Togo in exchange for luxury items that are much cheaper than in other parts of Africa.

GDP grew by an average of 2 percent from 2002 to 2008, and increased to 4 to 6.1 percent 2010 to 2015, fueled by increased agricultural output and expanded phosphate production. (For information on the Togolese economy prior to 2002, see the 2012 *Handbook.*) The government's fiscal status was also improved by better tax collection procedures. However, most international donors continued to withhold assistance due to the Eyadéma regime's poor human rights record and failure to implement democratic reform. In 2004 the EU resumed aid after Togo met 22 preconditions, and in September 2005, the IMF followed suit. In April 2006 the World Bank included Togo among 11 countries that qualified for debt relief under the Heavily Indebted Poor Countries (HIPC) initiative.

Following the 2007 legislative elections, which were judged fair by international observers, Togo was granted additional economic aid. In 2008 the EU pledged an additional $190 million over a five-year period, while the World Bank agreed to write-off the arrears owed by Togo on past loans, some $135 million, and the Paris Club of creditor nations forgave $347 million in debt. In addition, the African Development Bank (AfDB) canceled 99 percent of Togo's $23.5 million debt to the institution. In November the IMF announced that Togo qualified for the HIPC program, which would allow the country to write off $2.2 billion in external debt if it completed the terms of the program. Togo's GDP grew by 4 percent in 2010, while inflation grew at 3.2 percent. In December 2010 the Paris Club agreed to cancel $203 million of Togo's debt, while the IMF and World Bank provided an additional $1.8 billion to Togo as part of the HIPC initiative (a reduction of 82 percent of Togo's foreign debt). Meanwhile, France eliminated $143 million of Togo's debt in May 2011, while Italy, Sweden, and Switzerland canceled an additional $84 million in debt in June. In 2014 GDP grew by 5.9 percent. That year inflation increased by 3 percent, and GDP per capita rose to $700. In 2015 GDP grew by 5.5 percent with inflation at 1.8 percent and GDP per capita of $643. Human Development Indicators remain low, ranging from 0.4 to 0.484 (162nd out of 181) in the world. In 2016 the World Bank ranked Togo 150th out of 189 countries for ease of doing business.

GOVERNMENT AND POLITICS

Political background. The present Republic of Togo is the eastern section of the former German Protectorate of Togoland, which became a League of Nations mandate after World War I and was divided into separate zones of British and French administration. After World War II, France and Britain continued to administer the eastern and western sections, respectively, as United Nations trust territories. Following a UN-supervised plebiscite, Western (British) Togoland became part of the new state of Ghana on the latter's accession to independence in 1957. Eastern (French) Togoland, which became a French-sponsored autonomous republic in 1956, achieved complete independence in an agreement with France and the United Nations on April 27, 1960.

Sylvanus OLYMPIO, leader of the predominantly Ewe party then known as the Togolese Unity Committee (CUT), became the country's first chief executive. Olympio's somewhat dictatorial rule, coupled with his alienation of the army by the imposition of an austerity program, contributed to his assassination in 1963. Nicolas GRUNITZKY, Olympio's chief political rival, succeeded him as president and attempted to govern on a multiparty basis with northern support. Grunitzky failed, however, to establish firm control and was deposed in 1967 by (then) Maj. Etienne EYADÉMA, a northerner who was chief of staff of the armed forces. Acting in the name of a National Reconciliation Committee (NRC), Eyadéma suspended the constitution, outlawed political activity, and instituted direct military rule. Later the same year, he dissolved the NRC and declared himself president. The Rally of the Togolese People (RPT), a regime-supportive party, was established in 1969 and, in that year and in 1971, made pro forma attempts (which were described as overruled by the "popular will") to return the nation to civilian rule.

A constitution drafted in 1969 was accepted by a reported 98 percent of the registered electorate on December 30, 1979, in balloting at which General Eyadéma (whose first name had been "Africanized" to Gnassingbé in 1974) stood as the sole candidate for a seven-year term as president. Concurrently, a unicameral general assembly was constituted on the basis of a single list of candidates presented by the RPT.

In September 1986 the government reported that it had rebuffed a coup attempt allegedly fomented in Ghana and Burkina Faso by supporters of the exiled sons of former president Olympio. However, some external critics suggested that the seriousness of the coup attempt may have been overstated by the Eyadéma regime to shift attention away from earlier reports of torture and illegal detention of political prisoners. On December 21, President Eyadéma was unopposed in election to a further seven-year term.

In early October 1990 the imposition of lengthy jail terms on two opposition figures for alleged antigovernment activity ignited a series of protests and strikes. On October 10 President Eyadéma responded by telling a RPT Central Committee meeting that the country's "apprenticeship in democracy" was complete and preparations should be made for a multiparty system. However, the establishment of a constitutional commission and scheduling of a referendum for late 1991 failed to appease government critics, with violent protests continuing into 1991.

In March 1991 ten opposition groups formed a Front of Associations for Renewal (FAR) under the leadership of Yawovi AGBOYIBO, and four days later, after a meeting with FAR representatives, the president agreed to accelerate reforms. In mid-April he authorized the legalization of opposition parties and pledged to hold multiparty elections within a year. Nevertheless, violent demonstrations continued, fueled by the discovery of the bodies of 30 slain protestors in a Lomé lagoon. Subsequently, in the course of negotiations with opposition leaders, Eyadéma agreed to transfer power to a prime minister to be elected by a National Conference on Togo's Future, which convened in Lomé on July 8. On July 16 the opposition-dominated conference declared its sovereignty, dissolved the National Assembly, abrogated the 1980 constitution, and stripped Eyadéma of all but ceremonial powers, thus prompting a government and army withdrawal from the proceedings. On July 23 the government rejoined the conference, and, at its close on August 28, the president publicly accepted most of its findings, including a diminished presidency, the election of Joseph Kokou KOFFIGOH as prime minister, and the replacement of the RPT-dominated National Assembly with an interim High Council of the Republic (HCR). However, Eyadéma's military supporters continued to reject both the conference's sovereignty claims and the new government, in particular Koffigoh's assumption of the defense ministry. Subsequently, military coup attempts on October 1 and 8 ended only after public appeals from Eyadéma that the troops return to their barracks.

In mid-October 1991 the HCR, under pressure from newly enfranchised party leaders to establish control of the government, formally ousted Eyadéma, and on November 26 the council banned the RPT on the eve of a party congress. The following day rebel troops surrounded Koffigoh's residence, and on December 2 the troops announced that they had "reclaimed" strategic points throughout Togo and had called on Eyadéma to name a new prime minister and dissolve the HCR. On December 3 Koffigoh was seized by the rebel soldiers and brought to Eyadéma, whereupon the prime minister announced his "surrender" and agreed to Eyadéma's request that he form a national unity government, assignments to which were announced on December 30.

On January 29, 1992, the government issued a revised electoral calendar that called for a constitutional referendum and municipal balloting in early April, a legislative poll in late May, and a presidential election in June. The schedule was subsequently abandoned because of widespread violence, including the May 5 wounding of opposition leader Gilchrist OLYMPIO, son of the former president, in an attack for which Capt. Ernest GNASSINGBÉ, the president's son, was implicated two months later. On August 13 negotiations between a presidential delegation and representatives of eight opposition parties on resumption of the transitional process were suspended, and on August 23 the government, citing ongoing unrest, canceled a constitutional referendum. Meanwhile, following extensive talks between the president and prime minister, at which the latter reportedly agreed to a number of concessions reversing earlier limitations on the president's power, the transition period, scheduled to expire on August 28, was extended to December 31.

On September 27, 1992, a new constitution was endorsed in a referendum by 99.1 percent of the voters. Concurrently, a new electoral calendar was released, which called for balloting to take place between October and December. However, the democratization process was halted on October 22 with seizure of the National Assembly building by pro-Eyadéma troops, who demanded the release of frozen RPT funds in return for the release of 40 legislative hostages. The crisis was resolved the following day when the HCR agreed to release the funds; however, Koffigoh declared the HCR's action invalid because it was performed under duress, while Eyadéma, who had supported earlier efforts to free the funds, called for sanctions against the intruders. Unappeased by the government's response, the opposition organized a general strike on October 26 to protest the military's action.

On November 11, 1992, Eyadéma, rejected as "unconstitutional" Koffigoh's dismissal of two propresidential cabinet ministers, one of whom had reportedly threatened to have the prime minister arrested. The United States responded on November 13 with suspension of $19 million in aid payments. Three days later Togolese unions, acting in concert with the Democratic Opposition Collective (COD-2), launched a general strike, which they warned would continue until the government agreed to the formation of a politically neutral security force, a new government, free and fair elections, prosecution of the troops implicated in the October National Assembly incident, and international monitoring of the transitional period. Meanwhile, Koffigoh's repeated compromises with Eyadéma appeared to have cost him the support of the COD-2, whose leaders, in early January 1993, refused to meet with him.

On January 13, 1993, Eyadéma dismissed Koffigoh, claiming that the transitional government's mandate had ended on December 31, 1992. However, five days later, in an action that the HCR described as "unconstitutional," he reappointed Koffigoh to his post. Tensions were further heightened on January 25 when security forces killed at least 20 people. Nationwide clashes between prodemocracy and government forces were subsequently reported, and at the end of the month, amid reports of rampaging soldiers and an imminent civil war, 300,000 Togolese fled to Benin and Ghana.

Negotiations opened on February 11, 1993, in Colmar, France, with representatives of the president, the government, the HCR, and the opposition in attendance; however, Eyadéma's delegation soon withdrew because of the opposition's demand for political neutralization of the armed forces. Three days later, following negotiations between the president and prime minister, during which the former reportedly pledged to keep troops loyal to him in their barracks, Koffigoh was named to head a "crisis government" dominated by presidential loyalists. The HCR rejected the legality of the new administration, calling it the product of a "constitutional coup d'état."

On March 25, 1993, Eyadéma's top military aide was among a number of military personnel reportedly killed when the president's residence came under attack from raiders who fled into Ghana. Olympio, who was accused of planning the attack, countered by charging that the incident was part of a purge of army dissidents. Lending credence to his argument, over 140 former Eyadéma troops were reported to have fled Togo by early April, claiming that a presidentially sanctioned ethnic cleansing campaign was under way. An election timetable was subsequently released, which called for new presidential and legislative balloting. However, most of the opposition boycotted the long-deferred presidential poll of August 25 at which Eyadéma was credited with reelection amid increasing evidence that he had regained most of his pre-1991 powers.

In late September 1993 the COD-2 threatened to boycott legislative elections then scheduled for December unless the government agreed to provide access to state-controlled media, redefine voting constituencies, and increase the number of poll watchers. The balloting was further postponed until February following renewed fighting near Eyadéma's residence on January 5, 1994, which left more than 60 dead.

The multiparty poll, which was finally mounted on February 6 and 20, 1994, was marred by violence, with RPT militants accused of attacking opposition candidates. International observers nonetheless endorsed the results, which included a majority of 43 seats for the opposition Patriotic Front (FP) and 35 for the RPT. Subsequently, however, the Supreme Court, responding to petitions filed by the RPT, vacated 3 seats won by the opposition. Therefore, the FP's overall lead was imperiled, pending by-elections, which, having initially been scheduled for May, were deferred. Criticizing the Court's action, the FP's leading components (the Action Committee for Renewal—CAR and the Togolese Union for Democracy—UTD) threatened to boycott the National Assembly; however, the coalition's unanimity was sorely tested on April 22, when the president, in apparent violation of an earlier agreement, rejected CAR leader Yawovi Agboyibo as the FP's prime minister designate in favor of the UTD's Edem KODJO.

In mid-1994 a RPT characterization of the FP as a "facade of a coalition" seemed increasingly apt, as the CAR resisted UTD entreaties to join Kodjo's government. Earlier, on May 20, the CAR, which unlike the UTD had carried through on a legislative boycott, announced that it was abandoning the action, explaining that the regime's failure to mount by-elections by the legally mandated date of May 15 was tantamount to a confession that "conditions for legality, transparency, and security" had not been met. In December the CAR once again withdrew from the assembly, but in April 1995 President Eyadéma and Agboyibo reached an agreement on electoral reform, which called for equal representation for government and opposition parliamentary groups on all electoral commissions. As a result, the CAR rejoined the assembly in August; however, an alliance of RPT and UTD parliamentarians defeated the reform bill in February 1996.

Already strained relations between President Eyadéma and Prime Minister Kodjo deteriorated sharply in May 1996 when the Supreme Court supported Eyadéma's assertion that he alone controlled the appointment of senior administrative officials. For his part, Kodjo reportedly accused the president of establishing a "parallel government." Subsequently, following the RPT's capture of three assembly seats (and consequently a narrow legislative majority) in early August by-election balloting, Kodjo resigned on August 19, citing his desire to avoid the "legal war," which he described as likely to arise from the lack of an "obvious majority." The following day Eyadéma appointed Planning and Territorial Development Minister Kwassi KLUTSE as Kodjo's successor, and on August 27 the new prime minister announced the formation of a new government.

On December 3, 1996, the National Assembly voted to adopt a RPT-drafted document delineating the responsibilities of a new Constitutional Court. The poll was boycotted by the CAR, which had unsuccessfully sought to broaden the court's powers to include mediation of electoral disputes. (The new body was inaugurated in March 1997.) Thereafter, in September, the opposition boycotted an assembly vote on a new electoral code after attempts to persuade the legislature to include provisions for an independent electoral body were rebuffed. The code, approved unanimously by the pro-presidential legislators, provided for a nine-member commission (four from the pro-presidential forces and four from the opposition, in addition to an appointed chair).

Following presidential balloting on June 21, 1998, President Eyadéma was credited with a vote share of 52 percent and Gilchrist Olympio of the Union of Forces of Change (UFC) with 34 percent. The remainder of the tally was shared by four other candidates, led by Yawovi Agboyibo with 9.6 percent. However, the polling process was widely criticized by both domestic and international observers. Furthermore, two days after the polling, the chairperson of the electoral commission, Awa NANA, resigned, claiming that her efforts to prepare provisional electoral results had been blocked by "unidentified" individuals widely believed to be presidential supporters. Subsequently, the opposition, led by Olympio, who claimed that he had actually won the election with a 59 percent vote share, refused the president's offer to join a unity government and organized a number of demonstrations and work stoppages. Amid reports of mounting violence, on August 19 Prime Minister Klutse resigned; however, the president reappointed Klutse the following day, and on September 1 Klutse named a government that included a number of new members but no prominent opposition leaders.

In December 1998 government and opposition leaders announced that they had made progress in their efforts to organize a dialogue. Thereafter, however, the preparations ground to a halt as the two sides proved unable to agree on a venue for the proposed talks. Subsequently, in early 1999 the opposition announced its intention to boycott legislative polling then scheduled for early March. The Eyadéma administration rejected calls to delay the balloting until after interparty talks and proceeded with electoral preparations, albeit delaying the start of polling for two weeks.

Following legislative balloting on March 21, 1999, and two subsequent by-elections, the RPT, facing only limited competition from independent candidates and two minor parties, was credited with having won 79 of the 81 seats. On April 17 Klutse dissolved his government and offered his resignation, although he agreed to continue thereafter on a caretaker basis. On May 22 the president appointed Eugene Koffi ADOBOLI, a former official of the United Nations Conference on Trade and Development, as Klutse's successor. Facing continuing criticism for his inability to improve the economic condition, however, Adoboli resigned on August 25, 2000, one day after a vote of no-confidence against his government in the legislature. The president named Agbéyomé Messan KODJO of the RPT as Adoboli's successor on August 29.

Relations between the government and the opposition remained severely strained in late 2001 and the first half of 2002. Particularly galling to the opposition was an amendment to the electoral code approved by the assembly in February 2002 that required future presidential candidates to have resided in Togo for 12 consecutive months. Critics described the new law as designed to prevent another presidential run by the UFC's Gilchrist Olympio, who remained outside the country. The opposition parties also strongly objected to the government's offer of only five seats on the proposed 20-member electoral commission. In view of the impasse on that membership, the government in May appointed a committee of judges to oversee legislative elections which had already been twice postponed.

On June 27, 2002, President Eyadéma appointed Koffi SAMA of the RPT to replace Prime Minister Kodjo. (Kodjo was subsequently expelled from the RPT for criticizing the president; he later went into exile.) Sama was sworn in on June 30, and he announced his cabinet on July 5.

The RPT dominated the October 27, 2002, assembly balloting (72 of 81 seats), in part due to a boycott by most opposition parties. Sama was reappointed as prime minister on November 13. In December the RPT-controlled assembly approved a constitutional revision that removed the limit on the number of presidential terms for one person, thereby permitting Eyadéma to seek another term in the election scheduled for 2003. The assembly also lowered the eligibility age for presidential candidates from 45 to 35, a measure apparently designed to permit the eventual succession of Eyadéma's son, Faure Essozimna GNASSINGBÉ, who was only 37 years old at the time. Moreover, the basic law was changed to require presidential candidates to have resided in Togo for one year prior to the election. That provision prevented Gilchrist Olympio, who had been in exile in France, from contesting the election; he urged supporters to vote for Emmanuel BOB-AKITANI, the vice president of the UFC.

In the presidential poll of June 1, 2003, Eyadéma was credited with 58 percent of the vote, followed by Bob-Akitani (34 percent), and four minor candidates. Prime Minister Sama and his cabinet resigned on June 23, but the president reappointed Sama on July 1. On July 29 Sama formed a new cabinet that included a few members of minor opposition parties and, notably, Faure Gnassingbé.

President Eyadéma died of a heart attack on February 5, 2005. His son, Faure Gnassingbé, backed by the military and Sama, was immediately named interim president, although the constitution required the speaker of the assembly to fill a presidential vacancy. Because the current speaker, Fambaré NATCHABA, was out of the country at the time, the assembly, on February 6, elected Gnassingbé to replace Natchaba as speaker, and Gnassingbé was sworn in as president the following day to serve until the end of his father's term in 2008. The assembly also rescinded the constitutional provision that new presidential elections be held within 60 days in case of a vacancy. However, in the wake of intense domestic and international criticism, the assembly, on February 21, voted to reverse its decisions (see Foreign relations, below). Gnassingbé resigned as speaker and interim president on February 25 and was succeeded in both positions by Abbas BONFOH (hitherto the deputy speaker) pending new elections. In highly controversial balloting on April 24, Gnassingbé was credited with 60 percent of the vote and runner-up Bob-Akitani with 38.25 percent. The opposition and international observers described the election as fraudulent. The outcome triggered a new wave of violence and the flight of more than 30,000 people to neighboring countries.

After the Constitutional Court validated the results on May 3, Gnassingbé was sworn in on May 4. On June 9 the president appointed Edem Kodjo of the Pan-African Patriotic Convergence (*Convergence Patriotique Panafricaine*—CPP) as prime minister in an attempt to reach out to opposition groups. Kodjo's new cabinet, formed on June 20, comprised mostly members of the RPT, although several small opposition parties agreed to join. Efforts to form a broader unity government were initially rebuffed by the major opposition parties. However, in July nine of the leading political parties signed a Comprehensive Political Accord, which established the framework for future elections. Provisions included the creation of an independent national electoral commission and the preparation of new voter rolls (to be used in conjunction with new identification cards). The UFC initially rejected the accord but later reversed itself after the government pledged to reform the nation's security forces. The UN reported that more than 500 people were killed in post-election violence, while property damage was estimated at $7 million. Turmoil continued throughout the summer, despite Gnassingbé's pledge to support new legislative elections if reconciliation could be achieved with the opposition. Gnassingbé undertook a range of actions to mollify the opposition, including the November 2005 release of 460 political prisoners.

As an outgrowth of the new pact, President Gnassingbé appointed opposition leader Agboyibo of the CAR as prime minister on September 16, 2006. Four days later, Agboyibo took office as head of a national unity government that included 16 new ministers. The RPT and its allies retained the majority of the ministries, but 16 posts were held by the opposition or independents, including members of the CAR, CPP, the Democratic Convention of African People, the Socialist Renewal Pact, and the Party for Democracy and Renewal.

The EU provided $18.7 million to support legislative balloting in 2007, while France pledged an additional $4.1 million. The elections were initially set for June but were postponed several times because of delays in voter registration and cost overruns. In legislative balloting on October 14, 2007, the governing RPT won 50 seats, followed by the UFC with 27 seats and the CAR with 4 seats. Foreign observers certified the elections as free and fair, but the opposition challenged the balloting. On October 20 the constitutional court rejected the challenges and certified the results in which the RPT won a reduced majority. In November Gnassingbé met with exiled opposition leader Olympio in an unsuccessful effort to convince the UFC leader to have his party participate in the subsequent government. Agboyibo resigned on November 13 and Komlan MALLY of the RPT was appointed prime minister on December 3. He named a cabinet composed of the RPT, with representation from some minor parties, including the Democratic Convention of African People (*Convention Démocratique des Peuples Africains*—CDPA) and independents. Both the UFC and the CAR refused to participate in the government.

In April 2008 Gnassingbé launched a series of public meetings as part of a national truth and reconciliation process to heal lingering divisions. On September 5 Mally resigned following tensions with the president, who accused the prime minister of being ineffective. Mally was replaced two days later by Gilbert HOUNGBO, a political independent and former diplomat. Houngbo named a new cabinet on September 15 that was dominated by the RPT and did not include any members of the UFC or CAR. The size of the cabinet was increased from 22 to 26, and Mally was retained as minister of state for health. However, as part of the consolidation of power, the president's half-brother, Kpatcha, was not reappointed as minister of defense. Kpatcha was subsequently arrested for allegedly planning a coup (see Current issues, below).

Gnassingbé launched the Permanent Committee on Dialogue and Consultation (*Le Comité Permanent de Dialogue et de Concertation*—CPDC) in February 2009. The CPDC included the country's main political parties and served as a standing forum to develop consensus on issues such as elections, the constitution, and media rules. However, the CAR and the UFC initially boycotted the body. In June the CPDC allocated seats for the national electoral commission in preparation for the 2010 presidential balloting. The president replaced the minister of primary and secondary education in March and created a new post, minister of state for water resources and village water, in May to oversee internationally funded improvements to the nation's water system.

In presidential balloting on March 4, Gnassingbé was reelected with 60.9 percent of the vote, defeating six other candidates. Jean-Pierre FABRÉ of the UFC placed second in the balloting with 33.9 percent of the vote. On April 16, 2009, the president's half-brother Kpatcha GNASSINGBÉ and a number of military and civilian officials were arrested for planning a coup. Five people were killed in fighting between security forces and the rebels. Gnassingbé reshuffled several senior positions within the armed forces in response in an effort to shore up his support among the security forces. Kpatcha's supporters argued that his arrest was an effort by the president to remove a political rival ahead of the 2010 presidential election. Houngbo was reappointed prime minister on May 7. The RPT and the UFC signed an agreement that on May 27 that paved the way for the creation of a coalition unity government (see Current issues, below). The new cabinet, including seven UFC ministers, was sworn in on May 28. In June Togo abolished the death penalty.

Gnassingbé was reelected president in balloting on March 4, 2010. Opposition parties challenged the results, but their complaints were dismissed by the Constitutional Court, which affirmed the outcome on March 18. The RPT and the UFC subsequently formed a unity government in May, and Houngbo was reappointed prime minister. As a precondition for UFC involvement in the new government, the RPT agreed to support redrawing legislative districts and a new census. Floods in October left 21 dead and more than 80,000 displaced in the East and South of the country. Meanwhile a new 100-megawatt power plant that was funded by foreign donors opened in October and was expected to meet Togo's energy needs and allow the country to export electricity to neighboring states.

In March 2011 Gnassingbé conducted a minor cabinet reshuffle. In September Togo's Truth and Reconciliation Commission began hearings for 250 victims of political and sectarian violence as part of a national reconciliation effort.

In April 2012 Gnassingbé dissolved the RPT to form a new grouping, the Union for the Republic (*Union pour la République*—UNIR) with himself as party president (see RPT, below). On July 11 Houngbo and the cabinet resigned (see Current issues, below). Former commerce minister Kwesi AHOOMEY-ZUNU (CPP) was appointed prime minister on July 19, and a new cabinet, including opposition UFC figures, was sworn in on July 31.

Ahead of the 2013 Assembly elections, opposition groups decried legislation that expanded the Assembly from 81 to 91 seats as an effort by the ruling UNIR to increase its majority. Opposition groups also denounced the negotiations between the government and opposition groups, leading to the postponement of balloting from the original date of July 21 to July 25. In the polling, the UNIR won 62 seats, followed by the newly formed Let's Save Togo (*Collectif Sauvons le Togo*—CST) with 19, the Rainbow Alliance (*Coalition Arc-en-Ciel*—CAEC) with 6, and the UFC, 3. Opposition groups protested the results, alleging widespread fraud and voter intimidation. However the constitutional court confirmed the UNIR victory on August 12. Meanwhile opposition groups called for changes to the electoral law to transition to a system of proportional voting and the redrawing of districts because the opposition collectively received more votes than the UNIR in the balloting. The UNIR won 41.3 percent of the vote to the CST, 34.5 percent; CAEC, 11.2 percent; and UFC, 5.3 percent.

Thousands demonstrated unsuccessfully on November 21 and 28, 2014, in favor of changing the constitution to bar a third term for President Gnassingbé. Gnassingbé was reelected for a third term on April 25, 2015, with 58.8 percent of the vote. Following the balloting, Prime Minister Ahoomey-Zunu stepped down, and a new government was formed by Sélom Komi KLASSOU (UNIR) on June 28.

Constitution and government. The 1979 constitution provided for a highly centralized system of government headed by a strong executive presiding over a cabinet of his own selection and empowered to dissolve a single-chambered National Assembly after consulting the Political Bureau of the RPT. It detailed a judicial system headed by a Supreme Court that included a Court of Appeal and courts of the first and second instance, with special courts for administrative, labor, and internal security matters.

On July 16, 1991, the National Conference on Togo's Future abrogated the 1979 basic law, transferred all but ceremonial presidential powers to a prime minister, and dissolved the legislature, with assignment of its powers to a High Council of the Republic (HCR), pending the promulgation of a new constitution and the holding of multiparty elections.

A draft constitution accepted by the HCR on July 2, 1992, called for a semi-presidential system with the head of state elected to a once-renewable five-year term and a prime minister chosen by the president from a parliamentary majority and responsible to the legislature, which would also have a five-year mandate. Other projected institutions included a High Court of Justice and a Supreme Court, in addition to a Constitutional Court, an Accounts Court, and an Economic and Social Council. On September 27 the new basic charter was approved by 99.1 percent of the participants in a referendum. In March 1997 a seven-member Constitutional Court was appointed to serve a seven-year term.

The country is divided for administrative purposes into five provinces, which are subdivided into 30 prefectures that were formerly administered by presidentially appointed chiefs and "special delegations" (councils) but are now subject to prefectural and municipal elections on the basis of direct universal suffrage.

For many years the media were almost exclusively government controlled. In early 2000 a new press bill further limited press freedom and made "defamation of the government" an offense subject to a prison sentence. A second repressive law was passed in 2002 and allowed fines of up to $7,500 and sentences of five years in prison for defaming the president and lesser penalties for defamation of other officials. However, many of the new measures were repealed in August 2004 as part of Togo's effort to restart international aid. In 2014 Reporters Without Borders ranked Togo 76th out of 180 countries in freedom of the press, up from 83rd in 2013 but dropped it back to 88th in 2015 because of new laws that criminalize certain journalistic behaviors such as the publication of "false news" or distributing literature that might cause a "breach of peace." The new laws superseded the 2004 media code.

Foreign relations. Togo's foreign policy has long been based on nonalignment, although historical links have provided a foundation for continued financial and political support from the West. Bowing to pressure from the Arab bloc, diplomatic relations with Israel were severed from 1973 to 1987.

Although one of the smallest and poorest of the African states, Togo has played a leading role in efforts to promote regional cooperation and served as the host nation for negotiation of the Lomé conventions between the European Community (EC) and developing African, Caribbean, and Pacific (ACP) countries. It worked closely with Nigeria in organizing the Economic Community of West African States (ECOWAS) in May 1975 and, having assumed observer status earlier with the francophone West African Economic Community (CEAO), joined the CEAO states in a Non-Aggression and Defense Aid Agreement (ANAD) in 1979. Its major regional dispute concerns the status of Western Togoland, which was incorporated into Ghana in 1957. A clandestine "National Liberation Movement of Western Togoland" has been active in supporting Togo's claim to the 75-mile-wide strip of territory and has called for a new UN plebiscite on the issue. There have been numerous incidents along the Ghanaian border, and the Eyadéma and Rawlings regimes regularly accused each other of destabilization efforts, including the "harboring" of political opponents. Heated exchanges occurred with Ghana and, to a lesser degree, Burkina Faso, following the reported coup attempt in Togo in September 1986. However, Eyadéma avoided charging Accra and Ouagadougou with direct involvement in the plot, and relations were largely normalized by mid-1987, with Lomé calling for help from regional organizations to keep further enmity from developing. In December 1991 the Koffigoh administration announced that a comprehensive cooperation agreement had been reached with Ghana.

Togo's foreign affairs in 1992 and early 1993 were determined in great part by its domestic political turmoil. In early November 1992 both Benin and Ghana reported deaths of their nationals in border incidents involving Togolese security forces, although their complaints were relatively low-key in apparent support of the transitional government. On November 13 a deteriorating political situation led the United States to suspend all but humanitarian aid payments. Thereafter, in late January 1993, a French and German mediation effort was cut short when 20 prodemocracy demonstrators were killed by government forces outside the negotiation site. In mid-February France, citing the death of the demonstrators and lack of progress toward democracy, announced restrictions on aid payments. France's decision came only weeks after its former president, Valéry Giscard D'Estaing, had written a controversial letter in support of Eyadéma.

Meanwhile, relations between Togo and Ghana continued to worsen. In March 1993 rebels who had attacked the Eyadéma compound retreated into Ghana, setting off an exchange of accusations between the two capitals. In early January 1994 Togo and Ghana were described as "close to war" after Lóme once again accused Accra of aiding alleged anti-Eyadéma insurgents in an attack on the president's residence. For its part, Ghana described the unrest in Togo as "the consequence of the government's refusal to establish a credible democratic process" and called on Lomé to resist always accusing Ghana "whenever there is an armed attack or political crisis." Such charges notwithstanding, relations between the two improved dramatically by midyear; on November 16 diplomatic ties were formally restored, and in December Eyadéma ordered the reopening of their shared border. Lomé's relations with Paris improved when France agreed to reschedule and forgive Togolese debt in May 1995.

In August 1998 the Togolese government reported that troops based near Lomé had been attacked by opposition-affiliated "terrorists" based in Ghana; however, the opposition countered that the fighters were actually government provocateurs who had attacked the headquarters and homes of UFC members. Collaterally, the incident proved to be a showcase for improved relations between Accra and Lomé (the two nations' presidents having signed cooperation agreements in Accra earlier in the year) because Ghana deployed forces to carry out a joint operation with Togolese troops pursuing the alleged "aggressors." However, conflicts over property rights were reported in 1999 along the border between Togo and Ghana, and in March 2001 Togo closed the border without explanation. The border was reopened and relations between the two sides improved dramatically with the election of John Kufuor as president of Ghana.

In 1998 Eyadéma helped mediate the conflict in Guinea-Bissau. Togolese troops also joined the international peacekeeping mission in Guinea-Bissau, and Eyadéma played a role in efforts to end the conflicts in Liberia and Sierra Leone. In addition, Togolese troops participated in the ECOWAS mission in Liberia and the UN mission in Sierra Leone. In light of Togo's importance to regional peacekeeping operations, the United States initiated joint training exercises with the Togolese military in April 2002.

Faure Gnassingbé's takeover in February 2005, following the death of his father, prompted regional organizations such as ECOWAS and the African Union (AU) to condemn the Togolese military for what was perceived as a coup. On February 9 the International Organization of the Francophonie suspended Togo's membership. On February 20 ECOWAS imposed a range of sanctions on Togo, including suspension of the country's membership, a travel ban on Togolese officials, and an arms embargo.

France was the first country to accept Faure Gnassingbé's controversial victory in the 2005 presidential election. In February 2006 Gnassingbé traveled to China to promote increased economic interaction between the two countries. (In 2005 trade between Togo and China was worth more than $500 million.)

Togo, Benin, and Nigeria entered into a pact in February 2007 to promote peace and economic development in the region. Subsequently, Togo, Ghana, and the UN signed a tripartite agreement in April to facilitate the voluntary return of Togolese refugees, many of whom had been in Ghana since the early 1990s. In June a cooperation framework was signed between Togo and Angola in an effort to overcome tensions that have lingered from Togo's past support of the Angolan rebel movement UNITA.

In December 2007 Togo and the United Arab Emirates established full relations as part of a broader effort by Togo to improve trade and political relations with countries in the Middle East. In January 2008 Togo announced that it would contribute 800 soldiers to the AU-led peacekeeping force in Darfur. In addition, in September, Togo and Belgium resumed diplomatic ties.

Togo and France signed a new defense accord in March 2009. Following meetings between Gnassingbé and German chancellor Angela Merkel in June, the Togolese president proclaimed a "new start" in relations between Togo and its former colonial power. Togo and Ghana launched an initiative in August to reduce cross-border crime, including joint border patrols. Also in August, the two governments signed an agreement in Accra whereby Ghana agreed to provide technical assistance during the 2010 elections. In December Togo expelled a French diplomat who was accused of interfering in national politics by supporting an opposition presidential candidate in upcoming presidential elections. France retaliated by expelling a Togolese diplomat.

During the Africa Cup of Nations, Angolan separatists attacked a convoy with the Togolese national soccer team and killed three, on January 8, 2010. Togo subsequently withdrew its team from the tournament. Fighting in Ghana in May prompted at least 3,500 refugees to flee into Togo. In November China granted Togo $25 million and offered technical assistance to improve the government's Internet and Web capabilities.

After clashes between rival tribes in northern Togo, Ghanaian authorities reported that more than 360 refugees had fled across the border in September 2011. Also in September, Togo recognized the transitional government of Libya. On October 24 Togo was elected for a two-year term on the UN Security Council.

In April 2012 Togolese and Nigerian officials held negotiations to speed the trials of 85 Nigerians under arrest in Togo. Reports were that as many as 800 Nigerians were in custody for various offenses in Togo, and the Nigerian government had expressed concern over the slow pace of judicial proceedings. In July Togo and Sri Lanka agreed to establish diplomatic relations. In September India offered a $100 million incentive package to begin extracting rock phosphate from Togo for export as fertilizer. Togo and Sri Lanka established diplomatic relations in 2012.

In January 2013 Togo agreed to contribute troops to the AU-led military force fighting Islamist militants in Mali. Reports in 2013 indicated that Togo had increasingly become a route for the transshipment of illegal ivory, rhino horns, and animal skins. For instance, in July 2013 officials in Hong Kong intercepted more than two tons of illicit elephant tusks worth an estimated $2.5 million.

In January 2014 Togolese officials seized 3.8 tons of ivory in port containers headed to Vietnam. Ghana announced plans in September to open negotiations with Nigeria, Togo, and Benin to define maritime boundaries in order to avoid disagreements in the future regarding gas and oil concessions. In October 2014 Togo and Benin complained that the Ghana Civil Aviation Authority (GCAA), which manages the airspace of the two countries, was not remitting revenue from air navigation charges. The Agency for Aerial Navigation Safety in Africa and

Madagascar based in Senegal offered to manage Togo's airspace and pay revenue.

In 2015 President Gnassingbé pledged cooperation with Nigeria and regional neighbors to reduce the risks of piracy, oil theft, and drug trafficking along the shores of West Africa, which were collectively estimated to cost the region over $7 billion per year. In May 2016 Gnassingbé met with Chinese president Xi Jinping to enhance bilateral cooperation and prepare for the Forum on China-Africa Cooperation (FOCAC), which met in December 2015.

In August 2016 Germany and Togo reached an agreement to reduce unemployment in the African country and improve relations between the two states. Togo made efforts to strengthen ties with Israel in 2016, including creating a Lomé-Jerusalem Alliance with support from Netanyahu. Togo is hosting the First Annual Africa–Israel Security Summit in 2017 to address security issues shared between the regions.

Current issues. In March 2011 demonstrations against a new law restricting public protests resulted in 53 arrests and more than 50 injuries after security forces intervened. Protestors denounced the new measure, which instituted mandatory prison sentences for those involved in public protests that resulted in violence or property damage and that required government permission for demonstrations. On June 16 Gnassingbé replaced Health Minister Komlan Mally with Charles Condji AGBA after widespread strikes by health care workers over pay and working conditions. In September Kpatcha Gnassingbé and 32 others were sentenced to various prison terms for their role in the failed 2009 coup. In July Togo released the results of its first census in more than 29 years. The census revealed that the population had doubled since 1981.

Following widespread protests, Houngbo and the government resigned on July 18, 2012. Reports indicated Gnassingbé replaced the increasingly unpopular prime minister in an effort to reduce public discontent ahead of local and parliamentary elections, which were postponed until 2013.

In September 2014 nine newly appointed members of Togo's Constitutional Court took the oath of office. President Gnassingbé appointed three of the members, and a majority in parliament elected the other six, all of whom serve for a seven-year term. In October the Togolese weekly council of ministers' meeting decided to reorganize the Togolese Armed Forces (FAT) in preparation for the presidential election scheduled for 2015. Changes include the creation of the Presidential Election Security Force (FOSEL). The meeting also appointed Lieutenant-Colonel Massina YOTROFÉÏ as the new director of the National Gendarmerie.

Deadly protests occurred on November 6, 2015, over the forced relocation of villagers from an area slated to become a national preserve. The violence broke out when police attempted to disperse the protestors with teargas, but the demonstrators responded by throwing rocks, and five were killed. President Gnassingbé restored order by suspending the 179,000 hectare preserve that would have displaced 38 villages. The initial plan was supported by the UN Development Program. On August 29, 2016, officials from Togo slaughtered more than 11,500 chickens in an effort to eradicate the H5N1 bird flu outbreak. No human cases of the virus were reported.

POLITICAL PARTIES

Political parties were banned after the 1967 coup. Two years later, the official Rally of the Togolese People (RTP) was organized as the sole legitimate political party. However, in 1991, the RPT's 24-year-old monopoly was reversed, and opposition activities were coordinated by a **Front of Associations for Renewal** (*Front des Associations pour le Renouvellement*—FAR). In May the FAR was superseded by a Democratic Opposition Collective (*Collectif de l'Opposition Démocratique*—COD), which in turn gave way to the **National Council for the Safeguard of Democracy** (*Conseil National pour la Sauvegarde de la Démocratie*—CNSD) in late December. In July 1992 the CNSD was succeeded by a revived Democratic Opposition Collective (COD-2). In early 1993 the COD-2 appeared to split into two wings: a "moderate" faction aligned under the banner of the Patriotic Front (FP, below) and a "radical" component, the Union of Forces of Change (see UFC, below). (For more on political parties prior to 2002, see the 2012 *Handbook.*)

In early 2002 a group of opposition parties formed The Front, which subsequently participated in the October launching of the **Coalition of Democratic Forces** (*Coalition des Forces Démocrates*—CFD) with other groups, including the Pan-African Patriotic Convergence and the UFC. The CFD sought to present a single candidate for the June 2003 election but ultimately boycotted that balloting due to perceived unwillingness on the part of the administration to permit full electoral participation by the opposition. Prior to the 2005 presidential election, six opposition parties agreed to support the candidacy of Bob-Akitani, including the UFC, the PDR, the **Action Committee for Renewal** (*Comité d'Action pour le Renouveau*—CAR), the **Democratic Convention of African People** (*Convention Démocratique des Peuples Africains*—CDPA), and the **Alliance of Democrats for Integrated Development** (*Alliance des Démocrates pour le Développement Intégré*—ADDI).

Ahead of presidential elections in March 2010, a new opposition coalition, the **Republican Front for Change in Power** (*Front Républicain pour l' Alternance et le Changement*—FRAC) was formed to support the candidacy of Jean-Pierre Fabré. The FRAC included the UFC, the ADDI, the **Socialist Renewal Pact** (*Pacte Socialiste pour le Renouveau*—PSR), the **Alliance** (*L'Alliance*), and **Sursaut Togo.**

In 2012 the **Union for the Republic** (*Union pour la République*—UNIR) was formed from the RPT as the main vehicle for Gnassingbé. Meanwhile opposition groups coalesced around two new coalitions, Let's Save Togo (*Collectif Sauvons le Togo*—CST) and the Rainbow Alliance (*Coalition Arc-en-Ciel*—CAEC).

Government Parties:

Union for the Republic (*Union pour la République*—UNIR). Initially formed as the **Rally of the Togolese People** (*Rassemblement du Peuple Togolais*—RPT), under President Eyadéma, the RPT was Togo's sole legal party until its constitutional mandate was abrogated by the National Conference in July 1991. In February 1994 the RPT captured 33 of the 57 seats decided in the first round of assembly balloting; however, the party subsequently fell short of an overall majority by winning only 2 second-round seats. The RPT's three victories in legislative by-election balloting in August 1996 left the party in control of 38 of 57 seats. It also claimed the vote of former interim prime minister Koffigoh and two former opposition legislators who held seats as independents. In November the RPT absorbed the **Union for Justice and Democracy** (*Union pour la Justice et la Démocratie*—UJD), a small grouping that controlled 2 assembly seats. At the RPT's congress on January 9–11, 1997, the party continued its recent swing back toward a hard-line posture and away from the pro-reform, youth movement that had characterized a 1994 congress. Evidencing the sea change were the appointments to the Central Committee of a number of old guard stalwarts. In November the party was bolstered by the addition of another minor party, the **Movement for Social Democracy and Tolerance.** The RPT captured 79 seats in the 1999 assembly balloting and 72 in 2002.

Following the death of President Eyadéma in February 2005, his son, Faure Gnassingbé, was elected RPT president. At the party's ninth congress in December 2006, Gnassingbé was reelected as RPT leader and Solitoki Esso was selected as secretary general. In the 2007 legislative elections the RPT secured 39.4 percent of the vote and 50 seats in the National Assembly.

Following the arrest of Kpatcha Gnassingbé after an alleged coup in April 2009, reports indicated divisions within the RPT along ethnic lines (Faure's mother was Ewe, from southern Togo, and Kpatcha's mother was Kabye, from the north). Nonetheless, president Gnassingbé was the RPT candidate in the 2010 balloting and easily won reelection with 60.9 percent of the vote. The RPT formed a new unity government in May.

At a RPT congress on April 14, 2012, the party voted to reconstitute itself as the Union for the Republic. Gnassingbé was elected party leader of the new formation. The UNIR won a supermajority in the 2013 Assembly balloting, granting it the ability to amend the constitution at will. In preparation for the presidential election planned for 2015, on October 2014 a Togolese delegation appointed former state prosecutor Robert Baoubadi Bakaï to the National Independent Electoral Commission (Céni) to represent UNIR. Gnassingbé was nominated for a third term by his party on February 25, 2015, and he won the April 25 balloting with 58.8 percent of the vote with a voter turnout of 60.9 percent.

Leaders: Faure Essozimna GNASSINGBÉ (President of the Republic and the Party), Koffi SAMA (Former Prime Minister), Solitoki ESSO (Secretary General).

Opposition Parties:

Union of Forces of Change (*Union des Forces du Changement*—UFC). The UFC coalition is led by Gilchrist OLYMPIO, who has long been linked to the MTD (below). In July 1993 the Eyadéma government issued an arrest warrant that linked Olympio to an attack on the president's residence in March, and in early August, the UFC leader, who had been calling for a new electoral register, was disqualified from presidential polling for refusing to return to Togo for a medical checkup. Subsequently, the UFC spearheaded a successful boycott of the balloting by its (then) COD-2 partners; however its calls for a boycott of Assembly balloting in February 1994 were ignored. In December 1997 UFC Secretary General Jean-Pierre FABRÉ was arrested and briefly detained after he sought to investigate the alleged murder of opposition activists by government security forces.

Although officially declared the runner-up in June 1998 presidential balloting, Olympio, who had been blocked from entering Togo from his base in Ghana during the closing days of the campaign, claimed that he had received 59 percent of the vote, not the 34 percent with which he had been credited. Subsequently the UFC was at the forefront of the antigovernment actions that followed the polling, and in August UFC headquarters were attacked by unknown assailants. Although remaining critical of the French government's previous support of the Eyadéma regime, the UFC followed President Jacques Chirac's call for reconciliation and joined talks with the government in July 1999 along with the CAR and UTD.

The UFC helped form the antiregime CFD in 2002 but withdrew from the group in 2003. Olympio returned to contest the presidential election in 2003 but failed to meet the residency requirements. BOB-AKITANI ran as his proxy and placed second in the balloting. Bob-Akitani also finished second in the disputed April 2005 presidential poll. In September 2005 UFC member Gabriel Sassouvi DOSSEH-ANYROH was dismissed from the party after he accepted a cabinet post in the Gnassingbé government. The UFC subsequently declined to participate in the 2006 unity government, but party member Amah GNASSINGBÉ agreed to serve as a minister of state on a "personal basis," not as a representative of the party.

In the 2007 legislative elections, the UFC placed second with 37 percent of the vote and 27 seats. At the UFC's 2008 congress, Olympio was unanimously reelected president of the party and chosen as the UFC's 2010 presidential candidate. Jean-Pierre Fabré was reelected secretary general and Patrick Lawson was selected as first vice president. The UFC subsequently launched discussions with other opposition parties in an effort to rally them behind Olympio in the 2010 presidential balloting. Prior to the elections, Olympio was barred from campaigning by the electoral commission, reportedly for health reasons. Fabré became the UFC presidential candidate and the UFC formed the FRAC electoral coalition. Fabré placed second in the balloting but rejected the results. The UFC subsequently agreed to join the RPT-led government. Tensions between Fabré and Olympio over participation in the government prompted Fabré to withdraw from the UFC. Kokou AHOLOU was elected to replace Fabré as UFC general secretary on October 1. Also in October 2010 Fabré launched a new political party, the National Alliance for Change (*Alliance Nationale pour le Changement*—ANC) (see below). Several UFC ministers remained in the new government named in July 2012. The UFC unsuccessfully filed suit in 2013, challenging the results of the July Assembly balloting. On September 17, 2014, the National Assembly held an extraordinary session to establish the 17-member National Independent Electoral Commission (Céni). Three meetings were necessary in order to determine whether UFC, which has been participating in the current government, should be considered part of the opposition when designating representatives on the Commission for the party. Ultimately, the UFC received one of the five opposition slots. The UFC only won three seats in the July 25, 2013, elections.

Leaders: Gilchrist OLYMPIO (Party President and 1998 presidential candidate), Kokou AHOLOU (Secretary General), Emmanuel BOB-AKITANI (2005 presidential candidate and Honorary President of the Party), Alexander AKAKPO (First Vice President).

Togolese Movement for Democracy (*Mouvement Togolais pour la Démocratie*—MTD). Prior to the legalization of political parties in April 1991, the MTD was a Paris-based organization. It disclaimed any responsibility for a series of bomb attacks in 1985 while charging that the Eyadéma regime had "unleashed a wave of repression" in their wake. In mid-1986 MTD Assistant Secretary General Paulin LOSSOU fled France in the face of a decision by authorities to expel him to Argentina for his "partisan struggle" against the Eyadéma regime. Several reported MTD members were imprisoned in 1986 for distributing anti-Eyadéma pamphlets, but all of their sentences were commuted by 1987.

The government accused the MTD of complicity in the September 1986 coup attempt, insisting that it planned to install Gilchrist Olympio, exiled son of the former chief executive, as president. Olympio, who was sentenced to death in absentia for his alleged role in the plot, described the charges as "preposterous," suggesting that internal dissent had generated the unrest. Olympio returned to Lomé on July 6, 1991, under an April 12 general amnesty, to participate in the National Conference. Although claiming no interest in avenging his father's death, Olympio described the existing regime as lacking "legitimacy." Subsequently, *Africa Confidential* cited his influence in Joseph Kokou Koffigoh's capture of the prime ministerial post.

In May 1992 Olympio was critically wounded in an assassination attempt that took the lives of four others, including MTD leader Eliot OHN. Following his return from rehabilitation in Europe, Olympio emerged as the opposition's most prominent spokesperson, and in early 1993 he reportedly suggested that ECOWAS establish a presence in Togo to counter the reemergence of pro-Eyadéma military factions as well as help facilitate the transitional process.

Leader: Gilchrist OLYMPIO (Party Leader).

Party of the Togolese (*Parti des Togolais*). Alberto Olympio launched the party in April 2014. In October 2014 Olympio announced plans to challenge Gnassingbé in the presidential election scheduled for 2015.

Leader: Alberto OLYMPIO.

Rainbow Alliance (*Coalition Arc-en-Ciel*—CAEC). The Rainbow Alliance was an opposition grouping formed in 2013 by the **Action Committee for Renewal** (*Comité d'Action pour le Renouveau*—CAR), the **Democratic Convention of African People** (*Convention Démocratique des Peuples Africains*—CDPA), and a number of small parties, including the **Union for Democracy and Solidarity–Togo** (*Union pour la Démocratie et la Solidarité–Togo*—UDS–Togo), the **Citizen Movement for Democracy and Development** (*Citoyen pour la Démocratie et le Développement*—MCD), and the **Democratic Pan-African Party** (*Parti Démocratique Panafricain*—PDP), whose presidential candidate, Bassabi KAGBARA, received less than 1 percent of the vote in the 2010 polling. The Alliance secured six seats in the 2013 Assembly balloting. In September 2014 the Alliance received one of the five opposition slots on the 17-member National Independent Electoral Commission (Céni). The Alliance and Let's Save Togo (below) announced in October that the two parties had not ruled out backing a single candidate in 2015. Both parties backed a constitutional amendment imposing a two-term presidential limit. Although the national assembly rejected the reform bill on June 30, the parties insist they will keep fighting to get the bill passed. The bill could bar Gnassingbé from running again. The CAEC only won six seats in the July 25, 2013, elections.

Leaders: Brigitte Kafui ADJAMAGBO-JOHNSON (2010 presidential candidate), Dodji APÉVON.

Action Committee for Renewal (*Comité d'Action pour le Renouveau*—CAR). The CAR was one of the leaders, along with the UTD, below, in the formation in October 1992 by "moderate" COD-2 parties of the **Patriotic Front** (*Front Patriotique*—FP), which sought to maintain links with the government despite the objection of other coalition partners. The FP boycotted presidential balloting in August 1993. However, dismissing calls from the more militant UFC for a second boycott, the FP split from its ally and participated in the February 1994 legislative balloting. The CAR captured 36 seats (2 of which were subsequently vacated); however, despite an earlier pledge, President Eyadéma refused to appoint Yawovi Agboyibo, the CAR's leader and presidential candidate, prime minister.

At a mid-March 1994 meeting, the FP, attempting to dispel rumors that dissension would render the coalition unable to assume a governing role, issued a communiqué demanding the right to form a cabinet. On March 26 the group agreed that the next prime minister would be a CAR member, and two days later it nominated Agboyibo as its choice for the post. Consequently, on April 22 the CAR denounced the appointment of the UTD's Edem Kodjo as prime minister as a "blatant and inadmissible violation" of the March agreement, called on Kodjo to "reconsider" his position, and declared that it would not participate in a UTD-led government, thereby effectively ending the Front's existence. Nevertheless, the following day Kodjo insisted that the FP was still viable and that he controlled a parliamentary majority (albeit a tenuous one in light of a Supreme Court ruling that had invalidated three FP electoral victories).

The CAR boycotted assembly by-election balloting in August 1996, thus conceding the loss of two more seats. Meanwhile, party officials complained that they had been the victim of a RPT-orchestrated "smear campaign." In October the party's legislative seat total dropped to 32 after a deputy defected to the RPT. (Earlier, two other CAR legislators had quit the party, switching their allegiances to the Eyadéma camp.)

The CAR reportedly organized a number of antigovernment demonstrations beginning in late 1996 and continuing through 1997. Furthermore, the group spearheaded concurrent legislative boycotts. In November 1997 Agboyibo, whom *Africa Confidential* described as seeming to "seek outright confrontation with the government," was attacked after attending a function at the U.S. embassy.

Following presidential elections in June 1998, Agboyibo reportedly asserted that the UFC's Olympio was the true top vote-getter. For his part, Agboyibo finished third in the balloting with 9 percent of the tally. The CAR joined the opposition boycott of the 1999 balloting. Agboyibo was found guilty of defamation charges in August 2001. Although a court of appeal nullified a six-month sentence against him in January 2002, he was held on additional conspiracy charges. In mid-March the president ordered his release for the "sake of national reconciliation." Agboyibo ran for the presidency in 2003 and placed third with 5.2 percent of the vote. In the 2005 presidential election, CAR supported the candidacy of Bob-Akitani. Agboyibo was appointed prime minister in September 2006, but resigned in November 2007, following legislative balloting in which the CAR received 8.2 percent of the vote and four seats in the National Assembly.

Agboyibo resigned as party president in October 2008 and was replaced by CAR Secretary General Dodji Apévon. Agboyibo was CAR's 2010 presidential candidate. He placed third in the balloting with 3 percent of the vote. In March 2011 Apévon began to participate in a series of regular meetings between President Gnassingbé and opposition leaders. Apévon called for the formation of a unified opposition bloc ahead of elections scheduled for October 2012. He was later instrumental in the creation of the Rainbow Alliance. In October 2014 Yao DATE, a civil society activist close to CAR, was named first rapporteur on the 17-member National Independent Electoral Commission (Céni).

Leaders: Dodji APÉVON (President), Gahoun EGBOR (First Vice President), Yawovi AGBOYIBO (Former Prime Minister).

Democratic Convention of African People (*Convention Démocratique des Peuples Africains*—CDPA). In December 1989 CDPA members Godwin TETE and Kuevi AKUE were arrested for distributing antigovernment leaflets. Their sentencing in October 1990 led to violent protests, which in turn were followed by the government's decision to move toward a multiparty system. The CDPA was legalized in 1991.

In September 1992 the house of CDPA leader Nguessan Ouattara was bombed during a wave of political assassination attempts allegedly orchestrated by Eyadéma supporters. In 1993 the CDPA initiated the formation of the **Pan-African Social Democrats' Group** (*Groupe des Démocrates Sociaux Panafricains*—GDSP).

In August 1997 the CDPA's founder and secretary general, Léopold GNININVI, returned from a four-year, self-imposed exile, and in presidential elections in June 1998, he captured less than 1 percent of the vote.

The CDPA joined the boycott of the 2002 legislative elections and was one of the founding parties of both the CFD and The Front. In 2003 CDPA General Secretary Léopold Gnininvi registered to run in the presidential election, but he subsequently withdrew from the race. The CDPA joined the coalition that supported Bob-Akitani's candidacy in the 2005 presidential elections. The CDPA subsequently joined the unity governments in 2006 and 2007. In the 2007 legislative balloting, the CDPA placed fifth with 1.6 percent of the vote but no seats in the Assembly. The CDPA was part of the new government formed in 2008. However, opposition to participation in the coalition government led a number of members to publically quit the CDPA in 2008. Brigitte Kafui ADJAMAGBO-JOHNSON was the party's presidential candidate in the 2010 balloting and the nation's first woman presidential contender. She placed fifth with less than 1 percent of the vote.

In September 2014 the CDPA received one of three seats reserved for political parties not represented in the National Assembly on the 17-member National Independent Electoral Commission (Céni). CDPA held its party convention in celebration of the party's 24th anniversary on October 5.

Leaders: Nguessan OUATTARA, Léopold GNININVI (Secretary General and 1998 and 2003 presidential candidate), Brigitte Kafui ADJAMAGBO-JOHNSON (2010 presidential candidate), Emmanuel GU-KONU (First Secretary).

Let's Save Togo (*Collectif Sauvons le Togo*—CST). The CST was an opposition coalition formed in 2013 to contest that year's Assembly elections. The CST included: the **National Alliance for Change** (*Alliance Nationale pour le Changement*); **Socialist Renewal Pact** (*Pacte Socialiste pour le Renouveau*—PSR); **Alliance of Democrats for Integrated Development** (*Alliance des Démocrates pour le Développement Intégré*—ADDI), led by Nagbandja KAMPATIBE; **Organization to Build a United Togo** (*Organisation pour Bâtir ans l'Union un Togo Solidaire*—OBUTS), led by former prime minister Agbéyomé KODJO, who secured less than 1 percent of the vote in the 2010 presidential balloting as the candidate for the coalition; and **Workers' Party** (*Parti des Travailleurs*—PT), led by Claude AMENGAVI. The CST secured 19 seats in the 2013 Assembly balloting, becoming the largest opposition party in the legislature.

CST and the Rainbow Alliance (see above) announced in October that the two parties had not ruled out backing a single candidate in 2015. The CST won 19 seats in the July 2013 elections, making it the largest party after UNIR.

Leaders: Ata Messan Zeus AJAVON, Gérard ADJA.

National Alliance for Change (*Alliance Nationale pour le Changement*—ANC). The ANC was formed in October 2010 by Jean-Pierre FABRÉ and dissidents from the UFC. In November 2011 Fabré and eight other ANC members were removed from the legislature by the constitutional court, which ruled that they were ineligible to serve because they had been elected from the UFC. Fabré was arrested in March 2013, along with more than 30 others, following opposition demonstrations. In September 2014 the ANC received three of the five opposition slots (in partnership with ADDI) on the 17-member National Independent Electoral Commission (Céni). On October 12 the ANC nominated Fabré to represent the party in the presidential election scheduled for 2015. Fabré secured 35.2 percent of the vote in the April 2015 presidential elections and protested the results, which were upheld in court.

Leader: Jean-Pierre FABRÉ (2015 presidential candidate).

Socialist Renewal Pact (*Pacte Socialiste pour le Renouveau*—PSR). The PSR's 2003 presidential candidate placed fourth with 2.3 percent of the vote. The PSR was part of the six-party coalition that endorsed Bob-Akitani in the 2005 presidential polling. PSR leader Tchessa ABI broke with other opposition parties and joined the cabinet in June 2005. The PSR also participated in the 2006 unity government. The party did not gain any seats in the 2007 balloting and was not invited to join the 2008 government. The PSR joined the opposition coalition FRAC to support the UFC's Fabré in the 2010 presidential elections. The party sought to create a broad opposition front ahead of the October 2012 balloting.

In September 2014 the PSR received one of three seats reserved for political parties not represented in the National Assembly on the 17-member National Independent Electoral Commission (Céni).

Leader: Tchessa ABI (Party Leader).

Other Parties That Contested Recent Elections:

Pan-African Patriotic Convergence (*Convergence Patriotique Panafricaine*—CPP). The CPP was formed in August 1999 with the formal merger of the **Togolese Union for Democracy** (*Union Togolaise pour la Démocratie*—UTD); the **Party of Democrats for Unity** (*Parti des Démocrates pour l'Unité*—PDU); the **Democratic Union for Solidarity** (*Union Démocratique pour la Solidarité*—UDS); and the **African Party for Democracy** (*Parti Africain pour la Démocratie*—PAD).

On April 22, 1994, UTD leader and former secretary general of the Organization of African Unity, Edem Kodjo, was chosen by the president to head a new government. Kodjo subsequently led the negotiations to form the CPP. (For more on the history of the UTD, see the 2013 *Handbook*.)

The CPP was among the main opposition groups that continued talks with the government in 2000 and 2001 and was subsequently active in the formation of the independent electoral commission and the CFD. CPP leader Kodjo was named prime minister in June 2005. He was replaced in September 2006 but was appointed minister of state in charge of the office of the presidency in the subsequent unity government. The CPP was given two other posts in the cabinet. In the 2007 balloting for the National Assembly, the CPP placed fourth with 1.9 percent of the voting, but no seats. At the CPP's 2009 congress, Kodjo initiated a reorganization of the party leadership. Kodjo also announced that he would soon retire from politics and not be a presidential candidate in 2010. In July Kwesi AHOOMEY-ZUNU was appointed prime minister. The CPP failed to secure any seats in the 2013 Assembly balloting.

Leaders: Kwesi AHOOMEY-ZUNU (Prime Minister), Edem KODJO (President of the Party and Former Prime Minister), Jean-Lucien Savide TOVÉ (First Vice President), Cornelius AIDAM.

Other parties that remained active or participated in the 2007 balloting included the **Togolese Alliance for Democracy** (*Alliance Togolaise pour la Démocratie*—ATD), led by Adani Ifé ATAKPAMEVI, who was an independent presidential candidate in 1993; the centrist **Alliance of Democrats for the Republic** (*Alliance des Démocrates pour la République*—ADR), which contested successive legislative elections beginning in August 1996; **Party of Action for Democracy** (*Parti d'Action pour la Démocratie*—PAD), led by Francis EKOH; **Party for Democracy and Renewal** (*Parti pour la Démocratie et le Renouvellement*—PDR), led by Zarifou AYEWA (who joined the cabinet in June 2005 and was appointed a minister of state in the 2006 unity cabinet, but not subsequent governments) and which received in September 2014 one of three seats reserved for political parties not represented in the National Assembly on the 17-member National Independent Electoral Commission (Céni); the hard-line Marxist-Leninist **Pan-African Socialist Party** (*Parti Socialiste Panafricain*—PSPA), led by Francis AGBOBLI; **National Front** (*Front National*—FN), led by Amela AMELA VI; **Movement of Republican Centrists** (*Mouvement des Républicains Centristes*—MRC), led by Kabou Gssokoyo ABASS; **Party for Renewal and Redemption**, whose leader, Nicholas LAWSON, won 1 percent of the vote in the 2005 presidential poll and less than 1 percent in the 2010 presidential balloting; and **Party for Renewal and Social Progress** (*Parti pour le Renouveau et le Progrès Social*—PRPS), led by Agbessi MAWOU. In 2005 the **Initiative and Development Party** was formed by Adanu Kokou KPOTUI as the country's 63rd registered party.

Other newer parties include the **Union for Democracy and Solidarity–Togo** (*Union pour la Démocratie et la Solidarité–Togo*—UDS–Togo), led by Antoine FOLLY. Other new parties that contested the 2007 balloting but failed to secure seats were **The Nest** (*Le Nid*), **New Popular Dynamic** (*Nouvelle Dynamique Populaire*), and **Regrouping of the Live Forces of Youth for Change** (*Regroupement des Forces Vives de la Jeunesse pour le Changement*). Among the parties formed since the 2007 balloting was **The Alliance** (*L'Alliance*), led by former National Assembly speaker and RPT official Dahuku PERE and a member of the 2010 opposition coalition, FRAC; **Sursaut Togo**, formed in 2010 by Kofi YAMGNANE; **Action Bloc for Change**, formed in July 2011 by Thomas Kokou NSOUKPOÉ; and **Mission for the Emergence of Togo in Memory of Eyadema** (METOME), established by Badjo RAGOUTANTI-TIBA in April 2012.

For more information on the now-defunct **Coordination of Political Parties of the Constructive Opposition** (*Coordination des Partis de L'Opposition Constructive*—CPOC), see the 2008 *Handbook*. For information on the **Coordination of New Forces** (*Coordination des Forces Nouvelles*—CFN), see the 2010 *Handbook*.

For information on the **Rally for Support for Democracy and Development** (*Rassemblement pour le Soutien pour la Démocratie et le Développement*—RSDD), see the 2012 *Handbook*.

LEGISLATURE

On July 16, 1991, the National Conference dissolved the existing National Assembly and subsequently transferred its powers to a High Council of the Republic (*Haut Conseil de la République*—HCR) for a transition period leading to multiparty elections. In early 1993 the HCR, already involved in a constitutional debate with the president over his efforts to reverse the prime minister's dismissal of two cabinet members, once again found itself in conflict with Eyadéma, who, in response to criticism of his dismissal and then reconfirmation of the prime minister, argued that the HCR's mandate had expired along with the transition period. Subsequently, after numerous postponements, Togo's first multiparty balloting took place over two rounds on February 6 and 20, 1994.

National Assembly (*Assemblée Nationale*). The National Assembly is composed of 91 members directly elected for five-year terms. In the most recent balloting on July 25, 2013, the Union for the Republic secured 62 seats; Let's Save Togo, 19; Rainbow Alliance, 6; Union of Forces of Change, 3; and independents, 1.

President: Sélom Komi KLASSOU (UNIR).

CABINET

[as of August 26, 2016]

Prime Minister	Sélom Komi Klassou (UNIR)
Minister of State	
Secretary of State	Nakpah Polo [f]
Ministers	
Agriculture, Livestock, and Water Resources	Col. Ouro-Koura Agadazi (ind.)
Basic Development, Handicrafts, Youth, and Youth Employment	Victoire Sidémého Tomégah-Dogbé (UNIR) [f]
Budget (Ministry of Economy and Finance)	Sani Yaya
Civil Service, Labor, and Administrative Reform	Gilbert Bawara (UNIR)
Commerce, Industry, Promotion of the Private Sector, and Tourism	Bernadette Essossimna Légzim-Balouki (UNIR) [f]
Communication, Culture, Sports, and Civic Education	Guy Madjé Lorenzo (UNIR)
Development Planning (Ministry of Economy and Finance)	Kossi Assimaïdou
Environment and Forest Resources	André Johnson (UFC)
Foreign Affairs, Cooperation, and African Integration	Robert Dussey (UNIR)
Health and Social Protection	Moustapha Mijiyawa
Higher Education and Research	Octave Nicoué Broohm (CPP)
Infrastructure and Transport	Ninsao Gnofam (UNIR)
Justice, Relations with the Institutions of the Republic, and Human Rights	Pius Agbétomé
Mines and Energy	Dèdèriwè Abli-Bidamon (UNIR)
Post and the Digital Economy	Cina Lawson (UNIR) [f]
Presidency	Batienne Kpabre-Sylli
Primary and Secondary Education and Professional Training	Komi Paalamwé Tchakpélé
Prime Minister	Elliott Ohin
Security and Civil Protection	Col. Damehane Yark (ind.)
Social Action, Promotion of Women, and Literacy	Tchabinandi Kolani Yentcharé [f]
Technical Education and Professional Training	Georges Aïdam (UNIR)
Territorial Administration, Decentralization, and Local Authorities	Payadowa Boukpéssi (UNIR)
Urban Affairs, Housing, and the Built Environment	Fiatuwo Kwadjo Sessenou (UNIR)

[f] = female

INTERGOVERNMENTAL REPRESENTATION

Ambassador to the U.S.: Yokoudema KADOKALIH (Chargé d'Affaires).

U.S. Ambassador to Togo: David R. GILMOUR.

Permanent Representative to the UN: Kokou KPAYEDO.

IGO Memberships (Non-UN): AfDB, AU, ECOWAS, IOM, NAM, OIC, WTO.

For Further Reference:

Cogneau, Denis, and Alexander Moradi. "Borders That Divide: Education and Religion in Ghana and Togo since Colonial Times." *The Journal of Economic History* 74, no. 03 (2014): 694–729.

Tobolka, Radim. "Togo: Legislative Elections of July 2013." *Electoral Studies* 35 (2014): 389–394.

U.S. Department of State. *Togo: 2015 Human Rights Report.* Washington, DC: State Department, 2016.

TONGA

Kingdom of Tonga
Fakatu'i 'o Tonga

Political Status: Constitutional monarchy; independent within the Commonwealth since June 4, 1970.

Area: 289 sq. mi. (748 sq. km).

Population: 107,000 (2016E—UN); 106,513 (2016E—U.S. Census).

Major Urban Center (2014E—UN): NUKU'ALOFA (25,000).

Official Languages: Tongan, English.

Monetary Unit: Pa'anga (official rate October 1, 2016: 2.17 pa'anga = $1US).

Head of State: King TUPOU VI; succeeded to the throne following the death of his father, King SIAOSI (GEORGE) TUPOU V, on March 18, 2012.

Crown Prince (Heir to the Throne): TUPOUTOU'A 'ULUKALALA (eldest son of the king).

Prime Minister: 'Akilisi POHIVA; appointed (upon the recommendation of the Legislative Assembly) by the king on December 30, 2014, to succeed Lord TU'IVAKANO following the legislative elections of November 27.

THE COUNTRY

Located south of Samoa in the Pacific Ocean, Tonga (also known as the Friendly Islands) embraces some 200 islands that run north and south in two almost parallel chains. Only 45 of the islands are inhabited, the largest being Tongatapu, which is the seat of the capital and the residence of almost two-thirds of the country's population. Tongans (mainly Polynesian with a Melanesian mixture) constitute 98 percent of the population, while Europeans and other Pacific islanders make up the remainder. The majority of the population is Christian, approximately 60 percent belonging to the Free Wesleyan Church of Tonga. The official female labor force participation rate is less than 14 percent, due in part to child-rearing demands in a society with an average of five children per family. As of mid-2014, there was one woman in the cabinet; by virtue of that position, she also served as an appointed member (the sole female) in the Legislative Assembly.

Primarily an agricultural country, Tonga produces coconuts and copra, bananas, vanilla, yams, taro, sweet potatoes, squash, pumpkins, and tropical fruits. Pigs and poultry are raised, while beef cattle (traditionally bred by Europeans) have assumed importance, thus reducing dependence on beef imports. Government-sponsored diversification efforts have focused on fishing and cultivation of specialty crops, including kava and mozuku (a type of edible seaweed). With the exception of some coconut-processing plants, no significant industries exist, although exploration for oil and seabed minerals has begun recently. (Tonga in 2014 became one of the first countries in the world to codify regulations regarding seabed mining in an attempt to balance commercial interests with environmental concerns.) Donor aid accounts for 60 percent of the national budget, and remittances from Tongans abroad (estimated at more than 50,000) also provide "economic lifelines" in light of limited job opportunities in Tonga proper. Vast marine resources remain largely untapped in part due to the country's remoteness, while the tourism sector is still in its nascent stage.

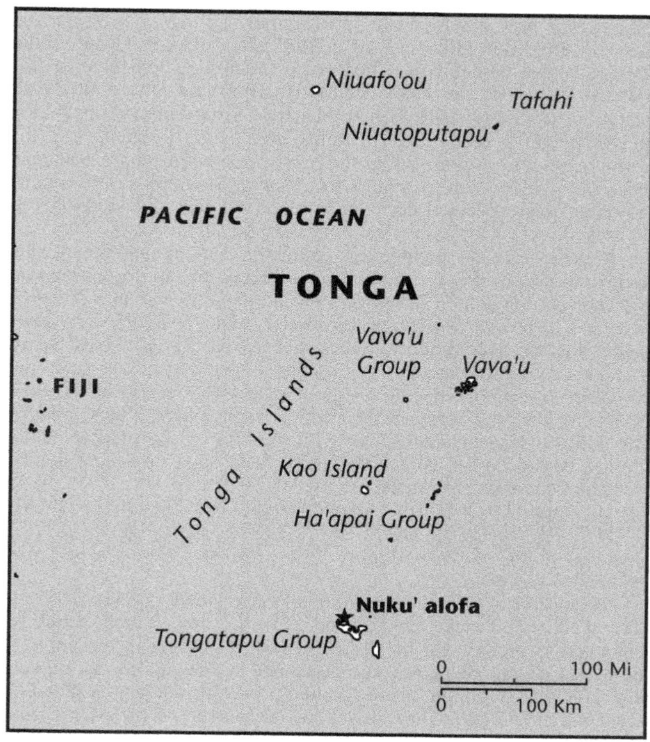

The economy was negatively affected by prodemocracy riots in November 2006 that virtually destroyed the capital, Nuku'alofa. Subsequently declines in remittances and exports (associated with the global financial crisis) combined with a massive tsunami in September 2009 and a cyclone in February 2010 to dampen growth.

In October 2010 the World Bank pledged $50 million in grants over the next four years to promote recovery, stating that Tonga was at a "high risk of debt distress" and could not afford new borrowing. International institutions subsequently urged the government to assess incompetence (or perhaps even fraud) in state-owned enterprises and to combat money laundering. The reconstruction, financed by China, of the business section of Nuku'alofa contributed to gross domestic product (GDP) growth of about 2.9 percent in fiscal year 2010–2011, although that rate fell to 0.8 percent in fiscal year 2011–2012 and 0.3 percent in 2012–2013. The International Monetary Fund (IMF) in 2013 called upon the government to broaden the tax base to permit greater spending on infrastructure development, with the goal of encouraging foreign investment.

Cyclone Ian caused an estimated $93 million in damage in the northern Ha'apai island group in January 2014, destroying nearly 1,000 homes and compromising the tourism sector. The World Bank and other donors subsequently pledged substantial aid for reconstruction.

GDP grew by 2 percent in 2014, 2.6 percent in 2015, and 2.8 percent in 2016. That year, inflation was –0.3 percent, while GDP per capita was $3,967.

GOVERNMENT AND POLITICS

Political background. Christianized by European missionaries in the early 19th century, Tonga became a unified kingdom in 1845. British protection began in 1900 with the conclusion of a treaty of friendship and alliance whereby a British consul assumed control of the islands' financial and foreign affairs. New treaties with the United Kingdom in 1958 and 1968 gave Tonga full internal self-government in addition to limited control over its external relations, with full independence within the Commonwealth occurring on June 4, 1970.

While not organized as formal parties, two major groupings emerged in the 1980s: a prodemocracy movement headed by 'Akilisi POHIVA that criticized the islands' maldistribution of wealth and called for more responsible and efficient government and a conservative group primarily concerned with economic development and the creation of new employment opportunities. Pohiva was discharged from an education ministry post in 1985 after announcing in a radio broadcast that assemblymen had voted themselves 400 percent pay increases. Prior to the 1987 election (in which he successfully contested an assembly seat), Pohiva launched a hard-hitting opposition newsletter, *Ko'e Kele'a,* and instituted a suit for reinstatement to his former cabinet position. While the basic issue had become academic because of his assembly status, the Tongan Supreme Court handed down an unprecedented decision in mid-1988 awarding damages to Pohiva plus costs for unfair dismissal and a denial of free speech.

In June 1989 the commoner (popularly elected) members of the Legislative Assembly for the first time forced rejection of a proposed government budget. In February 1990 the country mounted its most intensely contested legislative election to date, with 55 candidates vying for the 9 commoners' seats and 23 for the 9 nobles' seats. Pohiva's formation captured a majority of the commoner seats but remained a minority overall as the conservatives strengthened their control of the seats reserved for election by the nobles. Subsequently, the political ferment intensified, with the king of the predominantly Protestant country accusing both Pohiva and Tonga's Roman Catholic bishop of communist sympathies.

On August 21, 1991, the younger brother of King TAUFA'ANAU TUPOU IV, Prince Fatafehi TU'IPELEHAKE, stepped down after 26 years as prime minister. Deputy Prime Minister Baron VAEA was named his successor.

In November 1992 the prodemocracy movement organized a four-day public conference to indicate how the constitution could be amended to provide for greater popular participation in the political process. However, the government declined to participate in the conference, prevented foreign invitees from entering the country to attend its sessions, and refused to broadcast news of the event on the grounds that it was not officially sponsored. Nonetheless, the movement appeared to grow, as evidenced by its capture of six of nine popularly elected seats in the 1993 legislative balloting and formation of the Tonga Democratic Party (TDP) under the auspices of the Friendly Islands Human Rights and Democracy Movement (FIHRDM, see under Democratic Party of the Friendly Islands [DPFI] under Political Parties, below) in August 1994. Prodemocracy candidates retained a majority of commoner seats at the January 1996 poll. Although Pohiva and the Human Rights and Democracy Movement in Tonga (HRDMT, a successor to the TDP) expected to increase the representation of prodemocracy advocates in the March 1999 commoner balloting, only five were elected.

Crown Prince TUPOUTO'A was thought to have been the leading candidate to succeed Prime Minister Vaea upon the latter's retirement in early 2000, but he was passed over in favor of the king's youngest son, Prince 'ULUKALALA Lavaka Ata. The January 3, 2000, appointment was followed by a cabinet expansion and reorganization on January 25, 2001. In late September 2001 two cabinet ministers were forced to resign after being linked to the loss of millions in investments from the Tonga Trust Fund, into which income from the questionable sale of Tongan passports in 1983–1991 had been deposited.

In the legislative election of March 7, 2002, the HRDMT won seven of the nine popularly elected seats despite a controversy involving its recent publication in the *Times of Tonga* of a letter, possibly forged, that accused the king of holding $350 million in secret offshore accounts. In the election of March 16–17, 2005, eight of the nine victorious commoners were HRDMT members. In an unprecedented move following the poll, King Taufa'ahau named two commoners to an expanded 16-member cabinet, one of whom, Feleti "Fred" SEVELE, became the first commoner to serve as prime minister.

Following his death on September 10, 2006, King Taufa'anau was succeeded by his son, Crown Prince Tupouto'a, who assumed the title King SIAOSI "George" TUPOU V. However, the new king's coronation was postponed when, on November 16, 2006, a renewed prodemocracy demonstration quickly turned into a riot that destroyed some 80 percent of the capital's business district. By the end of the month, order had been restored with the help of 150 Australian and New Zealand troops and a pledge by the government of a new election in 2008, with the proviso that a majority of legislators would be selected by popular vote. However, Prime Minister Sevele announced in mid-2007 that the constitutional changes could not be enacted in time for the 2008 election but would be in place prior to another poll in 2010.

In the election of April 23–24, 2008, commoner representation under the FIHRDM banner was reduced to six seats, although Pohiva's endorsement by 11,290 voters was more than that of any other candidate. King Tupou V was finally coronated on August 1, 2008, having eagerly supported the diminution of his executive responsibilities as part of the country's democratization plans.

On April 15, 2010, a bill was passed that reduced the size of the Legislative Assembly to 26 members, of whom a majority of 17 would be popularly elected, while 9 would continue to be allocated to noble representatives. At the ensuing election of November 25, the FIHRDM-sponsored DPFI won 12 of the commoner seats, while independents won 5. The success of the DPFI was welcomed as an important step in the nation's democratization program, but reformers were surprised when the independents on December 21 joined the 9 nobles to elect Lord TU'IVAKANO as prime minister by a vote of 14–12 over Pohiva, who thereby lost the chance to become the first commoner prime minister. Analysts attributed the elevation of Lord Tu'ivakano to the post to concern among independent legislators that a "party-based" government might prove divisive. The new cabinet inaugurated on January 14, 2011, included two members of the DPFI but not Pohiva (see DPFI under Political Parties for details).

Lord Tu'ivakano, a former speaker and cabinet minister, pledged in early 2011 to focus on economic recovery, particularly in regard to agriculture and fishing and other private-sector development. In March his administration finally lifted the state of emergency that had given the police broad authority since the 2006 riots. At midyear, King Tupou initiated the "next stage" of reform by appointing an interim attorney general and interim lord chancellor, the latter being authorized to oversee the judiciary pending installation of a planned Judicial Appointments and Disciplinary Board. (See Constitution and government, below, for subsequent developments.)

King Tupou V died of natural causes on March 18, 2012. He was succeeded by his brother, former prime minister 'Ulukalala Lavaka Ata, who had been designated as heir to the throne in 2008. The new monarch assumed the title King TUPOU VI.

In the elections for the assembly on November 27, 2014, the DPFI won 9 of the 17 people's representatives' seats, with the other 8 seats going to independents. (Nine seats reserved for nobles were also elected by the nobles on the same day.) One of the independent people's representatives subsequently announced his alignment with the DPFI, giving the DPFI control of 10 seats. After extended negotiations with the remaining independents, DPFI leader Pohiva on December 30 was elected as the country's first "commoner" prime minister by a vote of 15–11 in the assembly. Concurrently, incumbent prime minister Lord Tu'ivakano was elected as the assembly's new speaker. On December 31 the king formally appointed Pohiva's proposed cabinet, which included six members of the DPFI, five independents, and one noble.

Constitution and government. Tonga is a hereditary constitutional monarchy whose constitution dates back to 1875. The executive branch has traditionally been headed by the Privy Council, including the king and a cabinet encompassing a prime minister, a deputy prime minister, other ministers, and the governors of the Ha'apai and Vava'u island groups. Prior to constitutional change in 2010, the unicameral Legislative Assembly included an equal number of elected hereditary nobles' and people's representatives, plus the cabinet members sitting ex officio. It is now composed of 26 elected members (17 people's representatives and 9 nobles). The prime minister, appointed by the king from among the members of the assembly upon the recommendation of the assembly, may appoint up to four cabinet members from outside the legislature. Upon inauguration, those cabinet members become members of the assembly with full voting privileges except on no-confidence motions.

The judicial system is composed of a Supreme Court, magistrates' courts, and a Land Court. Ultimate judicial appeal is to the king, who appoints all judges. The 2010 constitutional revisions provided for an attorney general and a lord chancellor (appointed by the king) to assist in fostering legal transparency and independence of the judiciary. In September 2014 the assembly approved legislation that would (if signed by the king) replace the lord chancellor with a chief justice and establish a Judicial Services Commission (appointed by the minister of justice with the approval of the full cabinet) to make judicial recommendations to the king, thereby providing the government with increased influence in such matters.

Tonga is administratively divided into several groups of islands, the most important of which are the Tongatapu group, the Ha'apai group, and the Vava'u group. The governors of Ha'apai and Vava'u are appointed by the king on the advice of the prime minister.

Conditions regarding freedom of the press in Tonga are generally considered satisfactory, although several instances of government pressure on publishing enterprises have been reported recently.

Foreign relations. In 1900 Tonga and the United Kingdom signed a Treaty of Friendship and Protection, which provided for British control over financial and external affairs. Tonga became a member of the Commonwealth upon independence in 1970 and subsequently joined a number of UN-related organizations, including the Food and Agriculture Organization (FAO), the World Health Organization (WHO), and the United Nations Educational, Scientific, and Cultural Organization (UNESCO). It was admitted to the IMF in September 1985.

Relations with the United States were initially formalized in an 1888 treaty, which was largely revoked by Tongan authorities in 1920. A successor Treaty of Amity, Commerce, and Navigation was concluded during ceremonies marking the king's 70th birthday in July 1988. The most important component of the new accord was a provision guaranteeing transit of U.S. military vessels—including nuclear-armed craft—in the Tongan archipelago. The action was seen as underscoring a "tilt toward Washington" by a government that had failed to join a majority of its neighbors in ratifying the 1985 South Pacific Nuclear Free Zone Treaty (Treaty of Rarotonga).

Earlier, in October 1986, Tonga had served as the venue for the completion of negotiations that, after 25 months, yielded agreement on a tuna treaty between the United States and members of the South Pacific Forum (subsequently the Pacific Islands Forum) Fisheries Agency. The accord permitted access by the U.S. tuna fleet to nearly 8 million square miles of prime fishing grounds over a five-year period. Tonga became the final signatory to the pact in June 1989.

In late 1998 relations with Taiwan ended after the kingdom had switched recognition to the People's Republic of China, which had promised to extend both trade and aid. Tonga became the 188th member of the United Nations in September 1999.

In January 2008 a Nationality Act, approved in June 2007, came into effect. The act sanctioned dual citizenship for nonresident Tongans who had lost their native citizenship by being naturalized elsewhere.

In 2010 Prime Minister Sevele announced the deployment of 275 soldiers to Afghanistan under an agreement with Britain, which was to cover all first-year costs. (The Tongan contingent was subsequently gradually reduced to 50 marines, whose mission ended in early 2014.)

Tonga has been embroiled in a long-standing dispute with Fiji regarding sovereignty over the uninhabited Minerva Reefs, located some 900 miles north of New Zealand. The dispute intensified in mid-2011 when forces from the two countries reportedly squared off (without violence) near the reefs following the alleged destruction of a Tongan navigation beacon. Tensions with Fiji were also exacerbated by Tonga's apparent accommodation of Fijian oppositionists.

On February 24, 2016, Tonga became the 187th member of the International Labor Organization (ILO) despite not having any approved trade unions.

Current issues. Following the death of King Tupou V at the age of 63 in March 2012, domestic and international observers appeared unanimous in their praise for his role in Tonga's recent democratization process. Reformers called upon new King Tupou VI, described as deeply religious and conservative, to pursue further democratic changes, noting that the monarchy still retained broad appointment powers and the authority to veto legislation. The king's extensive political experience, including service as prime minister 2000–2006, was expected to be of use in addressing the nation's economic woes as well as ongoing political friction. One manifestation of the latter was the tabling (under the direction of opposition leader Pohiva) of a nonconfidence motion against the government in June. Although it initially appeared that the motion would succeed, a vote was delayed because of a lack of clarity in the new constitution on how to proceed. Subsequently a cabinet reorganization in early July and other developments served to rearrange the Assembly sufficiently to permit the government to survive by a margin of 13–11 when the vote was finally taken on October 8. Lawmakers in 2013 turned their attention to reform proposals aimed at, among other things, enhancing women's rights (only men are allowed to own land, and domestic violence has been a long-standing problem) and combating corruption. In January 2015 *Fale Alea* speaker Lord Tu'ivakano agreed to allow parliamentary committees to elect their chairs instead of appointing them.

Cyclone Winston struck Tonga on February 16 and 19, 2016, with winds in excess of 103 miles per hour (165 km per hour). The storm destroyed more than 230 houses and caused extensive damage to crops and livestock.

POLITICAL PARTIES

Traditionally there were no political parties in Tonga, the initial equivalent of such a formation (see DPFI, below) being an outgrowth of the Pro-Democracy Movement that sponsored the conference on democracy in November 1992.

Legislative Parties:

Democratic Party of the Friendly Islands (DPFI). The DPFI was launched prior to the November 2010 election by the Friendly Islands Human Rights and Democracy Movement (FIHRDM), which had been styled the Human Rights and Democracy Movement in Tonga (HRDMT) from 1998 to 2005. Earlier, the HRDMT had been known as the **People's Party** (PP), which had initially been launched in August 1994 as the **Tonga Democratic Party** (TDP) by opposition MP 'Akilisi Pohiva.

Supporters of the HRDMT captured five of the nine commoner seats in the March 1999 balloting, disappointing prodemocracy activists, who had hoped to capture at least seven (and possibly all nine) and thereby generate momentum for the petition to the king to make all assembly seats subject to election by universal suffrage. In August 2001 the government turned down the HRDMT's application for registration as an incorporated society.

In the March 2002 legislative election, the HRDMT won seven seats. Subsequently, Pohiva was one of several persons charged with publication of a letter that accused the king of secreting some $350 million in offshore bank accounts; verdicts of acquittal were issued in May 2003. However, Pohiva was among those temporarily detained in early 2007 for perceived involvement in the riot of the preceding November (see Political background, above).

Following constitutional revision to provide commoners with a majority of legislative seats, the DPFI won 12 of the 17 commoner seats in the November 2010 assembly poll. Although Pohiva's supporters expected that he would consequently become prime minister, the five independent legislators voted with the nine nobles to deny him the post. Pohiva initially indicated that he would accept the health portfolio in the cabinet proposed by the new prime minister, Lord Tu'ivakana, but Pohiva ultimately rejected the post, arguing that the DPFI should receive more than the two cabinet positions being offered and objecting to Lord Tu'ivakana's decision to offer posts to nonlegislators. On the other hand, 'Isileli PULU, previously described as Pohiva's "right-hand man," accepted the tourism portfolio (arguing it was best for reformers to "get started" in the new system), and another DPFI member, 'Uliti UATA, accepted the health portfolio. Pulu and Uata were among three ministers who resigned in late June 2012 in support of the no-confidence motion against the government (see Current issues, above).

Significant tensions developed within the DPFI in the first half of 2014 regarding the nomination of the party's candidates for the November legislative elections. Several current DPFI legislators, including Deputy Leader Sitiveni HALAPUA, were left off the candidate lists, and they subsequently announced plans to run for reelection as independents. Halapua had reportedly urged the party to adopt a more collaborative approach with other political groups than espoused by Pohiva.

The DPFI won nine seats in the 2014 elections, and an independent member of parliament subsequently joined the grouping. Pohiva was appointed prime minister in December.

Leader: 'Akilisi POHIVA (Prime Minister and General Secretary).

Other Parties That Contested the 2010 Legislative Elections:

People's Democratic Party (PDP). The PDP was formed on April 15, 2005, by a group of HRDMT defectors with the announced goal of pursuing reform more aggressively than the parent group. On July 13 it became Tonga's first officially registered party. Although none of the PDP members had won a seat in the March 2005 legislative balloting, one of the party's founders, William Clive Edwards, won a by-election in 2006. After securing two seats in the 2008 assembly poll, the PDP was unsuccessful in 2010. However, Edwards was named to the January 2011 cabinet and remained in the government until 2014.

Leaders: Sione Teisina FUKO (President), William Clive EDWARDS (Minister of Justice), Semisi TAPUELUELU (Secretary).

Sustainable Development of the Land Party (*Paati Langafonua Tu'uola*—PLT). The PLT, calling for a moderate approach to political reform, was launched in August 2007 to recruit candidates for the Legislative Assembly, two of whom were elected in 2008. The party won no seats in 2010. In the run-up to the November 2014 elections, the PLT called for greater emphasis on tourism, aided by infrastructure improvements.

Leaders: Sione FONUA (President), Kamipeli TOFA (Secretary).

Tongan Democratic Labor Party (TDLP). The TDLP was organized by members of the Public Servants Association, who objected to a proposed amendment to Tonga's Public Service Act that would require government employees to resign before registering as electoral candidates. The TDLP ran a distant fourth with a 0.4 percent vote share in the 2010 assembly poll.

Leader: Mele AMANAKI (PSA General Secretary).

LEGISLATURE

Prior to 2010 constitutional revision, the unicameral **Legislative Assembly** (*Fale Alea*) consisted, apart from the speaker, of nine nobles selected by the hereditary nobles of Tonga, nine people's representatives (commoners) elected by universal suffrage in single-round plurality voting, and the Privy Council, encompassing the king and his ministers. Under the 2010 changes, the number of people's representatives was increased to 17. The king appoints the speaker (upon the recommendation of the assembly) from among the members of the legislature. Any members of the cabinet who are not elected legislators become members of the assembly upon their inauguration to the cabinet. They may vote on all matters except confidence motions. The king can dissolve the assembly and call for new elections at any time, but no-confidence motions cannot be entertained in the assembly until 18 months have passed since the last election. In the most recent election of November 27, 2014, the Democratic Party of the Friendly Islands won 9 of the commoner seats, and independents won 8.

Speaker: Lord TU'IVAKANO.

CABINET

[as of November 20, 2016]

Prime Minister	'Akilisi Pohiva (DPFI)
Deputy Prime Minister	Siaosi Sovaleni (ind.)
Ministers	
Agriculture, Food, Fisheries, and Forestry	Semisi Fakahau (DPFI)
Commerce, and Labor	Pohiva Tui'onetoa (DPFI)
Defense	Lord Ma'afu (Noble)
Education and Training	'Akilisi Pohiva (DPFI)
Environment and Climate Change	Siaosi Sovaleni (ind.)
Finance and National Planning	'Aisake Valu Eke (DPFI)
Foreign Affairs and Trade	'Akilisi Pohiva (DPFI)
Health	Saia Piukala (ind.)
Information and Communications	Siaosi Sovaleni (ind.)
Infrastructure	Semisi Sika (DPFI)
Internal Affairs	Penisimani Fifita
Justice	Sione Vuna Fa'otusia (DPFI)
Lands and Survey	Lord Ma'afu (Noble)
Police, Prisons, and Fire Services	Pohiva Tui'onetoa (DPFI)
Public Enterprises	Poasi Tei (ind.)
Revenue and Customs	Tevita Lavemaau (DPFI)
Attorney General	'Aminiasi Kefu (Acting)
Lord Chancellor	Albert Harison Waalkans (Acting)

INTERGOVERNMENTAL REPRESENTATION

Ambassador to the U.S. and Permanent Representative to the UN: Mahe 'Uli'uli Sandhurst TUPOUNIUA.

U.S. Ambassador to Tonga (resident in Fiji): Judith Beth CEFKIN.

IGO Memberships (Non-UN): ADB, CWTH, PIF, WTO.

For Further Reference:

Besnier, Niko. *On the Edge of the Global: Modern Anxieties in a Pacific Island Nation.* Stanford, CA: Stanford University Press, 2011.

Latukefu, Sione. *Church and State in Tonga: The Wesleyan Methodist Missionaries and Political Development, 1822–1875.* Brisbane: University of Queensland Press, 2014.

Wood-Ellem, Elizabeth. *Queen Salote of Tonga: The Story of an Era, 1900–1965.* Auckland: Auckland University Press, 1999.

TRINIDAD AND TOBAGO

Republic of Trinidad and Tobago

Political Status: Independent member of the Commonwealth since August 31, 1962; republican constitution adopted August 1, 1976.

Area: 1,980 sq. mi. (5,128 sq. km), of which Trinidad encompasses 1,864 sq. mi. (4,828 sq. km) and Tobago 116 sq. mi. (300 sq. km).

Population: 1,365,000 (2016E—UN); 1,220,479 (2016E—U.S. Census).

Major Urban Center (2014E—UN): PORT-OF-SPAIN (34,000).

Official Language: English. On September 1, 2005, the government announced that Spanish would be adopted as an official language by 2020 to permit Trinidadians to compete more effectively in regional markets.

Monetary Unit: Trinidadian Dollar (market rate October 1, 2016: 6.71 dollars = $1US).

President: Anthony Thomas Aquinas CARMONA; elected by Parliament to a five-year term on February 15, 2013, and inaugurated on March 18, succeeding Dr. George Maxwell (Max) RICHARDS.

Prime Minister: Keith ROWLEY (United National Congress); appointed by the president on September 9, 2015, succeeding Kamla PERSAD-BISSESSAR (United National Congress).

THE COUNTRY

The English-speaking state of Trinidad and Tobago, a pair of scenic tropical islands off the northern coast of South America, forms the southern extremity of the island chain known as the Lesser Antilles. Trinidad is the larger and more highly developed of the two islands, accounting for nearly 95 percent of the country's area and population and by far the greater part of its national wealth. Approximately 43 percent of the population are descendants of African slaves, while another 40 percent are descendants of East Indian indentured laborers brought in during the 19th century. Most of the former are presently concentrated in urban areas, while most of the latter are active as independent farmers. People of mixed ancestry, together with a few Europeans and Chinese, make up the rest of Trinidad's inhabitants, while Tobago's population is largely of African extraction. Roman Catholicism predominates, but Hinduism, Protestant Christianity, and Islam are also practiced. The Inter-Parliamentary Union ranked Trinidad and Tobago 42nd out of 181 countries for female representation in parliament with 31 percent (13 of the 42 seats in the lower house and 10 of 31 seats in the upper house) held by women. Eight of 13 cabinet members were held by women in 2016.

The economy depends heavily on refined petroleum and related products derived from both domestically extracted and imported crude oil. Although domestic reserves were thought to be approaching exhaustion in the late 1960s, natural gas and oil deposits subsequently discovered off Trinidad's southeast coast gave new impetus to the refining and petrochemical industries, which now account for more than 90 percent of export earnings. Tourism is of growing importance, while agriculture plays a relatively minor role in the islands' economy. In late

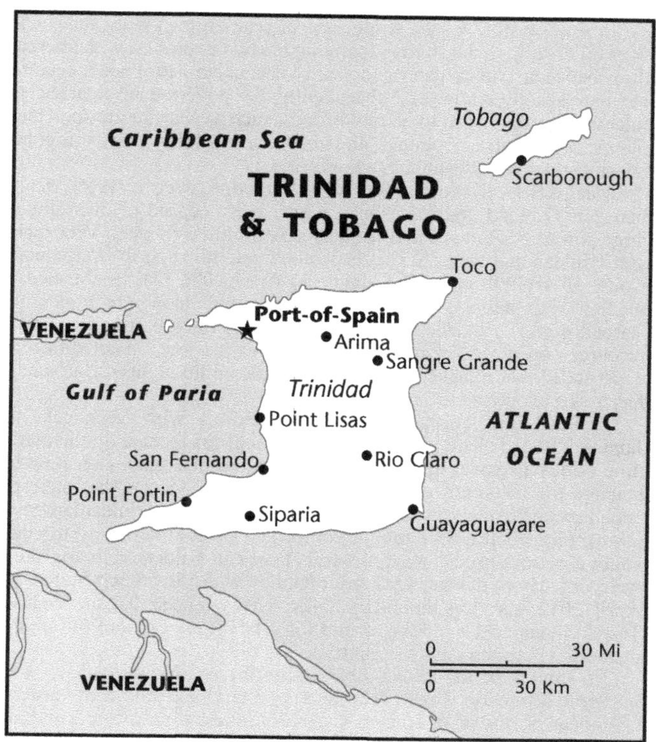

2007 the government closed down its long-standing, but increasingly unprofitable, sugar industry in favor of a more balanced agricultural sector geared to domestic consumption.

A boom fueled by soaring oil prices in the 1970s was followed by a bust in 1982, and real gross domestic product (GDP) declined by 30 percent over the next decade. Marginal recovery registered from 1991 to 1998. Spurred by sales of recently discovered natural gas, growth averaged 9.3 percent per year in 2003–2007 but saw a sharp recession by 4.4 percent in 2009 with the global financial crisis. Near stagnation over the following three years gave way to growth of 2 percent in 2013, reflecting the development of non-energy sectors. Growth increased to 2.5 percent in 2014 with the conclusion of maintenance-related suspensions in the energy sector. Unemployment was 5.5 percent and inflation, 4 percent. In 2015 the GDP growth rate shrunk to 1.1 percent with an inflation rate of 4.7 percent. The World Bank ranked Trinidad and Tobago 88th out of 181 countries for ease of doing business in 2016, down from 85 in 2015, mainly based on issues with building contracts, property registration, taxes, and trade.

GOVERNMENT AND POLITICS

Political background. Discovered by Columbus and ruled by Spain for varying periods, Trinidad and Tobago became British possessions during the Napoleonic wars and merged in 1888 to form a single Crown Colony. Political and social consciousness developed rapidly during the 1930s, when the trade union movement and socialism began to emerge as major influences. The People's National Movement (PNM), the country's first solidly based political party, was founded in 1956 by Dr. Eric WILLIAMS and controlled the government without interruption for the next 30 years. Following participation in the short-lived, British-sponsored Federation of the West Indies from 1958 to 1962, Trinidad and Tobago was granted full independence within the Commonwealth on August 31, 1962.

After an initial period of tranquility, "black power" demonstrations broke out, resulting in the declaration of a state of emergency in April 1970 and later to an attempted coup by elements of the military. Subsequent political instability included a fresh wave of labor unrest that triggered a state of emergency in October 1971.

In October 1973 Prime Minister Williams announced his intention to retire from politics, but he reversed himself two months later until steps had been taken to implement a republican constitution. In the legislative election of September 13, 1976, the PNM won 24 of the 36 House seats. Williams died unexpectedly on March 29, 1981, and was succeeded as prime minister and party leader by George M. CHAMBERS, who led the PNM to a 26–10 victory in parliamentary balloting on November 9.

Severe economic decline and the formation for the first time of a solid coalition of opposition groups—the National Alliance for Reconstruction (NAR)—led to reversal in 1986 of the PNM's theretofore uninterrupted control of the government, with the NAR winning 33 of 36 House seats in balloting on December 15, and Arthur N. R. ROBINSON succeeding Chambers as prime minister. The Robinson government proved no more successful in coping with fiscal adversity than its predecessor. In April 1989 a group of dissidents under the leadership of Basdeo PANDAY, who had been expelled from the NAR seven months earlier, organized the United National Congress (UNC), which secured a stunning by-election victory over both the NAR and PNM on May 1. An attempted coup by members of a militant, Black Muslim sect, the *Jamaat-al-Muslimeen,* on July 27, 1990, further embarrassed the administration. The rebels occupied Trinidad's state-run TV station and its legislative building, taking a number of hostages (including the prime minister) before agreeing to surrender on August 1.

In a forceful repudiation of Robinson's austerity program, the PNM, under Patrick MANNING, won 21 house seats on December 16, 1991; only the ousted prime minister and Tobago's other representative survived the PNM landslide.

During 1995, both leading parties were overtaken by scandals that included indecent assault charges against the leader of the opposition, a storm over demotion of the PNM foreign minister, brief confinement of the speaker of the House of Representatives to house arrest, and suggestions that the police were operating a "death squad." In an effort to regain the political initiative, Prime Minister Manning called an early election for November 6, 1995, in which the PNM and the opposition UNC both won 17 seats. After the UNC formed a "partnership agreement" with the NAR, Panday was sworn on November 9 in as the country's first prime minister of Indian descent. Subsequently, on February 14, 1997, Robinson was elected president of the republic in a 46–18 vote in Parliament.

The UNC secured a slim majority of 19 lower house seats in the election of December 11, 2000. However, the defection of three ministers in October 2001 forced a premature dissolution and the scheduling of a new election on December 10. The results of the polling were inconclusive (the UNC and the PNM won 18 seats each, on vote shares of 49.9 and 46.5 percent, respectively), and both Panday and Manning claimed a right to form the new cabinet. On December 17 they reportedly agreed to let the president choose who should be the next prime minister. However, when Robinson named Manning on December 24, Panday protested and declared the agreement void, claiming the president was "biased." Although Manning announced his cabinet over the next few days, Panday rejected the post of "Leader of the Opposition." Meanwhile his party refused to participate in the election of a speaker of the House of Representatives, which could not therefore formally convene, forcing an extended political stalemate.

On March 14, 2002, President Robinson requested that his term (expiring on March 18) be extended temporarily "in national interest," as Parliament remained unable to elect a successor. Despite Panday's protests, Manning approved the extension. On April 7, 2002, Robinson, on the advice of Manning, suspended the Parliament following yet another failed attempt to convene the House on April 5. Manning's subsequent attempt to convene the house in August also failed.

In a new election on October 7, 2002, the PNM secured a majority of 20 house seats and Prime Minister Manning was reappointed two days later. He was reelected to a third term on November 7, 2007, when the PNM gained 26 house seats by defeating a UNC-led party alliance. Manning called for a premature election on May 24, 2010, which the People's Partnership (PP) coalition, led by the UNC's new leader, Kamla PERSAD-BISSESSAR, won 29–12. There was speculation that Prime Minister Manning called for a snap election because he hoped to block the formation of precisely the opposition alliance (see PP, below) that led to his party's defeat. However, the global recession, several local financial scandals, and a soaring crime rate led voters to favor the UNC.

Accusations of unethical and illegal behavior of government ministers led Prime Minister Kamla PERSAD-BISSESSAR to reshuffle the cabinet in June 2011. Confronted with the exceptionally high crime rate, Prime Minister Persad-Bissessar imposed a state of emergency from August 21 through December 5. In an effort to ease tensions within the ruling coalition, Persad-Bissessar reorganized the cabinet to include two new Congress of the People (COP) appointments in June 2012.

Upon the expiration of President Max RICHARD's term, Parliament elected UNC nominee Anthony CARMONA on February 15, 2013. He was inaugurated on March 18. In September Prime Minister Persad-Bissessar conducted a cabinet reshuffle—the third in as many years.

In late March 2014 unrelated misconduct incidents caused two cabinet members to leave the administration, at which time Persad-Bissessar assumed the People and Social Development portfolio. Persad-Bissessar reshuffled the cabinet on February 2, 2015. Notably, the attorney general, Anand RAMLOGAN, was replaced by Garvin NICHOLAS after evidence surfaced that Ramlogan asked the police to withdraw witness statements he made in a defamation case against opposition leader Keith ROWLEY (PNM).

In legislative balloting on September 7, 2015, the PNM won 23 seats, followed by the PP, a coalition of the UNC, COP, and the Tobago Organization of the People (TOP), with 18. PNM leader Rowley was named prime minister and sworn in on September 9.

Constitution and government. Under the 1976 constitution, Trinidad and Tobago became a republic, with a president (elected by a majority of both houses of Parliament) replacing the former governor general. The functions of the head of state remain limited, executive authority being exercised by a prime minister and cabinet appointed from among the members of the legislature. Parliament consists of an appointed Senate, a majority of whose members are proposed by the prime minister, and a House of Representatives elected by universal adult suffrage. The judicial system is headed by a Supreme Court, which consists of a High Court and a Court of Appeal, while district courts function at the local level. There is also an Industrial Court and a Tax Appeal Board, both serving as superior courts of record. Judges are appointed by the president on the advice of the prime minister. In a waning anomaly among former British dependencies, Trinidad retains the right of ultimate appeal to the Judicial Committee of the UK Privy Council. The provision is designed to afford litigants access to a completely disinterested final court.

Rural administration is carried out on the basis of 9 counties on Trinidad, which are subdivided into 29 electoral wards, plus 1 ward for all of Tobago. Four municipalities (Port-of-Spain, San Fernando, Arima, and Point Fortin) have elected mayors and city councils.

After three years of debate, the House of Representatives in September 1980 approved a bill establishing a 15-member House of Assembly for Tobago with primarily consultative responsibilities. In January 1987 Tobago was granted full internal self-government, its House being given control of revenue collection, economic planning, and provision of services. In November 1996, a constitutional amendment was passed that enhanced the constitutional status of Tobago by creating an Executive Council to oversee its day-to-day affairs.

Press freedom is constitutionally guaranteed. Although there is legislation in place protecting freedom of information, the government has attracted criticism for trying to limit the categories of public information addressed by law. Reporters Without Borders ranked it 43rd of 180 countries on the 2014 Press Freedom Index. The ranking increased to 41st in 2015 but fell back to 44th in 2016. The 2014 Libel and Defamation Act allowed for "malicious defamatory libel known to be false" to be punishable by up to two years in prison and fines.

Foreign relations. In 1967 Trinidad and Tobago, which joined the United Nations at independence, became the first Commonwealth country to be admitted to the Organization of American States (OAS). Its anticolonial but democratic and pro-Western foreign policy is oriented chiefly toward the Western Hemisphere and includes active participation in such regional organizations as the Caribbean Community and Common Market (Caricom). Since 1983, however, a number of disputes with fellow Caricom members over trade restrictions have tended to hinder regional cooperation. Trinidad and Tobago's objections to the U.S.-led invasion of Grenada in October 1983 also cooled relations with a number of Eastern Caribbean states, most notably Barbados, and strained traditionally cordial relations with the United States, with Prime Minister Chambers criticizing what he perceived as U.S. president Ronald Reagan's attempt to "militarize" the region. However, efforts have since been initiated to lower the government's profile both on trade and foreign policy issues. Relations with the People's Republic of China and the Soviet Union were established in 1974, while a broad trade agreement signed in August 1984 with China was hailed as a "major leap forward in China's relations with the Commonwealth Caribbean."

In August 1997 a long-simmering dispute erupted with Venezuela over oil drilling in the straits separating the two countries, with altercations between Trinidadian riggers and Venezuelan patrol boats becoming increasingly common. Subsequently, the government signaled its intention to supply gas to nearby islands, such as Martinique and Guadalupe, via undersea pipelines, and in 2003 a feasibility study was commissioned for a 1,800-mile line to Florida.

Meanwhile, friction arose with Barbados over a 1990 treaty between Trinidad and Venezuela, which was accused of awarding a large part of Barbados's and Guyana's maritime territory to Venezuela and Trinidad and Tobago. The dispute led to a ruling by the Permanent Court of Arbitration in The Hague in April 2006 that established a median line halfway between the exclusive economic zones of Barbados and Trinidad but allowed Barbados to exploit hydrocarbon resources up to 150 nautical miles beyond the line. Meanwhile the court stated that it lacked jurisdiction to rule on the right of Barbadian fishermen to operate in Trinidadian waters.

Trinidad and Tobago entered negotiations with Venezuela in January 2012 to share oil and natural gas deposits located on the maritime border between the two countries. Initial discussions on how to manage the resources were suspended in 2007, and another attempt ended inconclusively in 2010. Meanwhile, when the Trinidadian government awarded a $5.7 billion contract to a Saudi company to construct a petrochemical plant, several American bidders claiming they were unfairly bypassed, straining relations with the United States. In April 2012 maritime boundary talks with Grenada began because Trinidad launched a bidding round for offshore blocks that fall along the border between the two countries.

In recent years the Trinidad-based Caribbean Court of Justice (CCJ) has gained traction. Created in 2001 by the Organization of Eastern Caribbean States (OECS) as a Caribbean alternative to the London-based Privy Council, the CCJ is currently only used by three OECS states. Parliament did not approve a 2006 constitutional amendment to adopt the CCJ. The Persad-Bissessar administration maintains that, in light of the country's high crime rate, which more than doubled between 2001 and 2011, and the struggling economy, full membership with the CCJ is not a priority.

At a Caricom summit in February 2013, Prime Minister Persad-Bissessar proposed the creation of a regional security center based in Trinidad. The December 2013 discovery of 732 pounds of cocaine in a fruit juice shipment from Trinidad to the United States raised concerns over the islands' maritime security.

In January 2014 Trinidad and Tobago established diplomatic relations with Kazakhstan. During a visit to Beijing by Persad-Bissessar in February 2014, Trinidad and Tobago opened an embassy in China, acquired a long-range missile for maritime defense, and tightened bilateral relations.

On February 24, 2015, Prime Minister Persad-Bissessar and Venezuela's President Nicolas Maduro signed bilateral treaties on energy exploration near the Manakin-Cocuina field and on economic cooperation. Maduro announced that Venezuela will begin trading oil for cement, gasoline, air-conditioners, and consumer goods immediately following the signing.

In June 2, 2015, three banks (First Citizens Bank, Intercommercial Bank, and Republic Bank) were implicated in the Fédération Internationale de Football Association (FIFA) corruption. Jack WARNER (Independent Liberal Party—ILP), a former minister of national security, former football official, and then-member of parliament, threatened to release an "avalanche" of secrets that would implicate the government in the FIFA corruption, including information on FIFA officials influencing the 2010 elections (see Political Parties, below). Warner was arrested along with 13 others on corruption charges in 2015.

Current issues. The parliament elected President Anthony Carmona on February 15, 2013, and he assumed office in March.

For the third time since March 2012, the PNM filed a no-confidence motion against the government in May 2013. The opposition presented several e-mails purportedly from high-level officials that allegedly demonstrated attempts by the Persad-Bissessar administration to undermine the judiciary and the media. The administration denounced the documents as fabrications, and the motion failed.

An oil spill in mid-December 2013 on an offshore drilling site owned by the company Petrotrin severely impacted the ecology of the southern coastal area and resulted in an 80 percent decrease in catches by local fishermen. In January 2014 the Environmental Management Authority fined Petrotrin $3.2 million for 11 spills and for failing to follow reporting procedure. As the fishing industry suffered in the wake of the disaster, fishermen began holding protests, using their boats to disrupt seismic tests for new drilling sites.

On October 15, 2014, *Jamaat-Al-Muslimeen* leader, Yasin Abu BAKR (Lennox Philip), was arrested when he landed in Jamaica. Bakr was released but arrested in Trinidad on July 21, 2015, in connection with the 2014 murder of a former senator Dana SEETAHAL (independent). He was released without being charged after three days.

On August 28, 2015, officials in Port-of-Spain broke ground on a $60 million distribution center that will bring 250 jobs to Trinidad. However, the IMF warned that Trinidad needed to dramatically adjust its fuel subsidy program in June 2016 to see continued economic growth. An IMF report found that fuel subsidies in Trinidad and Tobago equaled almost 2.3 percent of GDP.

POLITICAL PARTIES

Government Coalition:

People's National Movement (PNM). Organized in 1956 by historian-politician Eric Williams, the PNM was the first genuinely modern party in the country's history and owed much of its success to its early formation, its founder's gift for leadership, and its comparatively high degree of organization. Although its support is predominantly African, its progressive and internationalist programs have been distinguished by their emphasis on national unity irrespective of ethnic origin. Following Williams' death on March 29, 1981, George M. Chambers was elected party leader.

After three decades of uninterrupted rule, the PNM was forced into opposition in December 1986, when it won only 3 of 36 lower house seats. Following the defeat, Chambers resigned as party leader and retired from politics (he died on November 5, 1997). Patrick Manning led the party comeback in December 1991, when it captured 21 legislative seats. In 1995 the PNM secured a vote share of 48.8 percent (an increase of 3.7 percent from 1991) but tied in seats with the UNC, which was able to form a ruling coalition with the NAR. The PNM won 16 seats in legislative polling in December 2000, and 8 seats in the Tobago House of Assembly polling in January 2001. The party increased its representation to 18 in the December 2001 legislative polling, resulting in an extended stalemate with the UNC. In new balloting on October 7, 2002, the PNM secured a majority of 20 seats. It increased its majority to 26 of an enlarged house of 41 members in November 2007, and retained its 8 Tobago Assembly seats in balloting on January 19, 2009.

Its lower-house representation dropped to 12 at the premature general election of May 24, 2010. Three days later, Manning resigned as PNM leader in favor of Keith ROWLEY. In May 2011 former prime minister Manning was dismissed from parliament after being found guilty of contempt of parliament by the parliament's Privileges Committee, after he made serious accusations about actions taken by Prime Minister Persad-Bissessar.

In May 2013 the PNM filed its third no-confidence motion against the Persad-Bissessar administration, which, in July threatened Rowley with a defamation lawsuit.

Rowley set internal elections for May 19, 2014, for the first time replacing the party delegate system with a one-man, one-vote system. Rowley won with a decisive margin over his challenger, Pennelope BECKLES-ROBINSON.

The PNM won 23 seats in the September 2015 House elections, and Rowley became prime minister on September 9.

Leaders: Keith ROWLEY (Prime Minister), Orville LONDON (Deputy Political Leader for Tobago), Franklin KHAN (Chair), Ashton FORD (General Secretary).

Opposition Parties:

People's Partnership (PP). The PP was formed prior to the May 2010 election as a grouping of the parties below. Fissures emerged in early 2012, as a leading figure from the COP defected to the UNC in March and the Movement for Social Justice (MSJ, below) left the coalition in June. The PP won 18 seats in the September 2015 House elections, transitioning to the opposition. Former prime minister Kamla PERSAD-BISSESSAR was appointed the leader of the opposition by the president on September 21, 2015.

Leader: Kamla PERSAD-BISSESSAR (Former Prime Minister and Leader of the Opposition).

United National Congress (UNC). The UNC was formally launched on April 30, 1989, by the members of Club '88 (see under NAR, below) who had been formally expelled from the NAR in October 1988 after having campaigned against Prime Minister Robinson's style of leadership. The new group drew much of its support from former ULF members opposed to Robinson's IMF-mandated austerity policies. The UNC defeated both the NAR and the PNM in a local council by-election on May 1, 1989, but did not seek appointment as the official opposition until September 1990.

Although the UNC was unable to secure a plurality of seats in the 1995 balloting (it and the PNM winning 17 each), Party Leader Basdeo Panday formed a government on the basis of a "partnership agreement" with the NAR. The UNC won 19 seats in the December 2000 poll.

Relations between Prime Minister Panday and Ramesh MAHARAJ, the attorney general and UNC deputy leader, had long been strained. In early October 2001 Panday dismissed his rebellious colleagues, who promptly entered into an "alliance" with the opposition PNM. Subsequently, Maharaj claimed that his faction controlled the UNC and would place candidates in all 36 constituencies in the forthcoming election. Although Panday briefly registered a new formation—the United National Party (UNP)—in case the courts allowed the Maharaj faction to use the UNC rubric, both the Elections and Boundaries Commission and the High Court ruled in November in favor of Panday, prompting the Maharaj faction to leave the party to form a group styled Team National Unity (TNU), which won only 2.5 percent of votes in the December 2001 poll. Maharaj subsequently returned to the UNC.

The early legislative poll of December 10, 2001, yielded a stalemate with the PNM; in the subsequent balloting of October 7, 2002, UNC representation dropped to 16.

Charges of corruption against Panday while heading the UNC administration led to his brief imprisonment in mid-2005, and in October he moved from the post of party leader to that of chair, albeit with no apparent loss of party control. His successor as party leader, Winston DOOKERAN, resigned in September 2006 to form a new party, the Congress of the People (COP, below).

For the 2007 election, the UNC was restyled the United National Congress–Alliance (UNC-A) as the leading component of a coalition that included the NAR and the NDP (below).

In February 2009 Deputy Leader Jack WARNER and (then) Chief Whip Ramesh Maharaj threatened to leave the UNC if Panday did not endorse internal leadership elections. A month later, Maharaj was fired as chief whip by Panday.

In January 2010 Kamla Persad-Bissessar became leader of the opposition after defeating Panday as leader of the UNC in December 2009. In the May 2010 elections, Persad-Bissessar led the PP coalition, with the UNC as its core component, to victory over the PNM with 29 seats.

Three party figures defected in 2013, including former minister of security Jack WARNER, who resigned amid a fraud inquiry and subsequently formed the Independent Liberal Party (ILJ, below). The UNC won 17 of the PP's 18 seats in the 2015 legislative balloting.

Leaders: Kamla PERSAD-BISSESSAR (Former Prime Minister and Party Leader); Surujrattan RAMBACHAN, Marlene COUDRAY and Roodal MOONILAL (Deputy Party Leaders); David TANCOO (General Secretary).

Congress of the People (COP). The COP was launched on September 10, 2006, by former UNC party leader Winston Dookeran, who had been threatened with expulsion from the UNC on the basis of claims that he was maintaining a parallel political organization.

In March 2012 San Fernando Mayor Marlene COUDRAY defected from the COP to join the UNC, sparking outrage within the COP. Citing a need for younger party leadership, Dookeran refused calls to stand as leader in June 2014, instead endorsing Carolyn SEEPERSAD-BACHAN. In internal balloting later that month, however, leader Prakash RAMADHAR was reelected by a narrow margin. The COP won 1 of the PP's 18 seats in the 2015 House elections.

Leaders: Prakash RAMADHAR (Party Leader), Anirudh MAHABIR (Acting Political Leader).

Tobago Organization of the People (TOP). The TOP is the result of a split within the Democratic Action Congress in 2008. It was launched as a coalition member of the PP prior to the Tobago poll of January 19, 2009, in which it won four seats. The party did

not win any seats as part of the PP coalition in the 2015 polling, securing just 0.2 percent of the vote.
Leader: Ashworth JACK (Party Leader).

National Joint Action Committee (NJAC). The NJAC was organized in 1969 by Geddes GRANGER as a political extension of the black power movement. Granger played a leading role in the black power disturbances of 1970 and was under detention from October 1971 to June 1972 before changing his name to Makandal Daaga. The group contested elections in 1981, when it secured 3.3 percent of the popular vote, and in 1986, when it won 1.5 percent. Although a member of the PP, the NJAC elected none of its own members in May 2010 and has historically been more active in local politics. It won 0.8 percent of the vote in the 2015 legislative elections.
Leaders: Makandal DAAGA (Political Leader), Aiyegoro OME (President).

Independent Liberal Party (ILP). The ILP was launched in July 2013 by former international football official Jack WARNER, who left the UNC in April after he was accused of embezzlement during his tenure at an international football organization. In a by-election for his vacated parliamentary seat, Warner won a decisive victory with 69 percent of the vote. After an investigation into allegations of fraud against Warner launched in January 2014, the party founder did not seek leadership nomination. Lyndira OUDIT assumed leadership on June 9. Warner resigned in September 2015 after the ILP failed to secure any seats in the general elections. Rekha RAMJIT assumed the leadership after serving as the chair and then defeating Simeon MAHABIR in the party elections
Leader: Rekha RAMJIT.

Other Parties:

National Alliance for Reconstruction (NAR). The NAR was launched in 1984 as a coalition of the **United Labour Front** (ULF), the **Democratic Action Congress** (DAC), and the **Tapia House Movement** (THM); all had participated in the 1981 campaign as members of the Trinidad and Tobago National Alliance (TTNA). In September 1985 the **Organization for National Reconstruction** (ONR) joined the new formation, which reorganized as a unified party in February 1986. (For more on the history of the four parties that formed the NAR, see the 2011 edition of the *Handbook.*)

The NAR's success in coalescing behind former PNM associate (and one-time heir apparent) of Prime Minister Williams, Arthur N. R. Robinson, and his ability to attract support from diverse ethnic and labor groups were considered major factors in the group's stunning victory in the December 1986 balloting. However, by early 1988 the alliance had encountered severe internal stress, culminating in the expulsion of a number of ULF dissidents led by Basdeo Panday, who had formed an anti-Robinson intraparty formation known as **Club '88** ("Club" being an acronym for Caucus for Love, Unity, and Brotherhood). In April 1989 the Club '88 group reorganized as a separate party, the UNC. (For more on the history of the party, see the 2015 *Handbook.*)

In October 1999 the NAR National Council named former party chair Anthony SMART as interim leader after "vacating of the post" by Nizam MOHAMMED, who insisted he had been dismissed and was subsequently reinstated. The NAR won one seat in the 2000 legislative election and four seats in the January 2001 Tobago House of Assembly poll. The party won no House of Representatives seats in 2001, 2002, or 2007. Carson CHARLES was reelected party leader on October 23, 2006.

During 2006 the NAR joined with a number of smaller parties in a series of shifting alliances. On April 20 a merger with the **Movement for National Development** (MND) and **Democratic Party of Trinidad and Tobago** was announced, which, without reference to the MND but with the addition of the DNA (below), was subsequently styled the Democratic National Alliance. However, the DNA withdrew on June 9, while in July the grouping was restyled the National Democratic Alliance. The alliance subsequently fell apart after the 2007 election.
Leader: Carson CHARLES (Political Leader).

Movement for Social Justice (MSJ). The MSJ, founded in 2009, is closely aligned with the country's trade unions. It withdrew from the PP in June 2012.
Leader: David ABDULAH.

National Vision Party (NVP). The NVP was formed in early 1994 by Yasin Abu Bakr, leader of the unsuccessful 1990 coup by the *Jamaat-al-Muslimeen.* It contested the 2010 election as the **New National Vision**, winning a vote share of 0.3 percent. In the 2015 balloting, the party won 0.1 percent of the vote.
Leader: Fuad Abu BAKR.

Other parties that competed in the 2015 general elections (none received more than 0.3 percent of the vote) included **Tobago Forwards, Platform of Truth, Democratic Development Party, The New Voice,** and **Youth Empowerment Party.**

For more information on the **Democratic Action Congress** (DAC) and **Democratic National Assembly** (DNA), see the 2015 *Handbook.*

LEGISLATURE

The national **Parliament** is a bicameral body consisting of an appointed Senate and an elected House of Representatives following the Westminster model of government inherited from the British; Tobago has a unicameral **House of Assembly.**

Senate. The upper chamber consists of 31 members appointed by the president for a maximum term of five years: 16 are named on the advice of the prime minister; 6 on the advice of the leader of the opposition; and 9 at the president's discretion from religious, economic, and social groups.
President: Christine KANGALOO.

House of Representatives. The lower chamber currently has 41 members directly elected for five-year terms, subject to dissolution. In the September 7, 2015, elections, the People's National Movement won 23 seats, and People's Partnership, 18 seats (United National Congress, 17; and Congress of the People, 1).
Speaker: Bridgid Annisette GEORGE.

Tobago House of Assembly. Tobago's legislature consists of 15 members, 12 directly elected and 3 named by the majority party; its term is four years. In the January 21, 2013, election, the People's National Movement won all 12 elected seats.
Chief Secretary: Orville LONDON.

CABINET

[as of September 15, 2016]

Prime Minister	Keith Rowley
Ministers	
Agriculture, Land, and Fisheries	Clarence Rambharat
Attorney General	Faris Al-Rawi
Community Development, Culture, and the Arts	Nyan Gadsby-Dolly [f]
Education	Anthony Garcia
Energy and Energy Affairs	Nicole Olivierre [f]
Finance	Colm Imbert
Foreign Affairs	Dennis Moses
Health	Terrence Deyalsingh
Housing and Urban Development	Randall Mitchell
Labor and Small and Micro-Enterprise Development	Jennifer Baptiste-Primus [f]
National Security	Maj. Gen. (Ret.) Edmund Dillon
Office of the Attorney General	Stuart Young
Office of the Prime Minister	Ayanna Webster Roy [f]
Planning and Sustainable Development	Camille Robinson-Regis [f]
Public Administration and Communications	Maxie Cuffie
Public Utilities	Brig. Gen. (Ret.) Ancil Antoine
Rural Development and Local Government	Franklin Khan
Social Development and Family Services	Cherrie-Ann Crichlow-Cockburn [f]
Sport	Darryl Smith
Tourism	Shamfa Cudjoe [f]
Trade and Industry	Paula Gopee-Scoon [f]
Works and Infrastructure	Fitzgerald Hinds

[f] = female

INTERGOVERNMENTAL REPRESENTATION

Ambassador to the U.S.: Brig. Gen. (Ret.) Anthony PHILLIPS-SPENCER.

U.S. Ambassador to Trinidad and Tobago: John W. McINTYRE (Chargé d'Affaires).

Permanent Representative to the UN: Pennelope BECKLES.

IGO Memberships (Non-UN): Caricom, CWTH, IADB, ICC, IOM, NAM, OAS, WTO.

For Further Reference:

Boomert, Arie. *The Indigenous Peoples of Trinidad and Tobago: From the First Settlers until Today*. Havertown, PA: Casemate Publishers, 2016.

Home, Robert, and Hilary Lim, eds. *Demystifying the Mystery of Capital: Land Tenure and Poverty in Africa and the Caribbean.* New York: Routledge, 2013.

Singh, Sandra. "Women in Local Government Elections in Trinidad and Tobago 1946–2013." *Commonwealth Journal of Local Governance* 0, no. 16–17 (2015).

TUNISIA

Republic of Tunisia
al-Jumhuriyah al-Tunisiyah

Political Status: Independent state since 1956; republic proclaimed July 25, 1957; under one-party dominant, presidential regime; interim government formed following civil unrest that resulted in the ouster of the president on January 14, 2011.

Area: 63,170 sq. mi. (163,610 sq. km).

Population: 11,375,000 (2016E—UN); 11,134,588 (2016E—U.S. Census).

Major Urban Centers (2015E—UN): TUNIS (1,993,000), Sfax (Safaqis, 714,000).

Official Language: Arabic; French is widely spoken as a second language.

Monetary Unit: Tunisian Dinar (market rate October 1, 2016: 2.20 dinars = $1US).

President: Beji Caid ESSEBSI (*Nidaa Tounes*); elected in runoff balloting on December 21, 2014, and sworn in for a five-year term on December 31, to succeed Moncef MARZOUKI (Congress for the Republic).

Prime Minister: Youssef CHAHED (*Nidaa Tounes*); appointed by the president on August 1, 2016, to succeed Habib ESSID (nonparty), who resigned that day following the loss of a confidence vote on July 30. (See Politics and government, below.)

THE COUNTRY

Situated midway along the North African littoral between Algeria and Libya, Tunisia looks north and eastward into the Mediterranean and southward toward the Sahara. Along with Algeria and Morocco, it forms the Amazigh-influenced (often referred to as Berber) part of North Africa known as the "Maghreb" (West) to distinguish it from other Middle Eastern countries, which are sometimes referred to as the "Mashreq" (East). Tunisia's terrain, well wooded and fertile in the north, gradually flattens into a coastal plain adapted to stock-raising and olive culture, and becomes semiarid in the south. The population is almost exclusively of Arab and Amazigh stock and speaks Tunisian Arabic (except for a small Amazigh-speaking minority). The majority of Tunisians are Sunni Muslims. Although most members of the former French community departed after Tunisia gained independence in 1956, French remains a widespread second language, and small French, Italian, Jewish, and Maltese minorities remain. Women, who constitute approximately 31 percent of the paid labor force, were the focus of relatively progressive national policies on equal rights, educational access for girls, and family planning. However, women have faced increasing repression since the 2011 Jasmine Revolution.

About one-quarter of the working population is engaged in agriculture, which provides about 13 percent of GNP; the main products are wheat, barley, olive oil, wine, and fruits. Petroleum has been a leading export, although there is also mining of phosphates, iron ore, lead, and zinc. Industry has expanded to more than 30 percent of GDP, with steel, textiles, and chemicals firmly established. Most development is concentrated in coastal areas, where tourism is the largest source of income; however, poverty is widespread in the subsistence farming and mining towns of the south. (See the 2013 *Handbook* for more information on the economy from the 1970s to 2000s.)

Strong performance in the energy sector in particular, as well as in agriculture, manufacturing, and services, contributed to average annual growth of 6 percent in 2005–2007, though unemployment remained at about 14 percent. The International Monetary Fund (IMF) commended Tunisia for adopting banking reform measures and praised the country's efforts toward liberalizing trade and combating money laundering and the financing of terrorism. Despite the global economic recession, annual GDP growth of 3 percent was forecast for 2009, owing in large part to Tunisia's lower import costs and a fully implemented free-trade agreement with the European Union (EU). The economy continued to perform well in 2010, with annual GDP growth of 3.8 percent.

A state of uncertainty prevailed for most of 2011 following the ouster of the president in January. In May funding commitments of $500 million each were secured from the World Bank and the African Development Bank (AfDB), while the EU agreed to provide $367 million over three years. The economy was estimated to have contracted by 1.8 percent in 2011 on the heels of a 30 percent drop in tourism receipts and 25 percent decrease in foreign direct investment. Unemployment reached 19 percent (and youth unemployment hit 42 percent). Rapid credit growth was accompanied by a rise in headline inflation (from an average of 3.5 percent in 2011 to 5.7 percent by spring 2012).

Faced with an ailing economy, in 2012 the Tunisian government worked to steady its cash reserves and prop up its currency The IMF, which was working on a technical assistance program to strengthen bank regulation in Tunisia, predicted a gradual recovery. In 2012 GDP grew by 3.6 percent, while inflation was 5.6 percent, and unemployment, 17.6 percent. GDP per capita that year was $4,214.

Authorities were reportedly struggling to track down assets linked to the former regime's top officials, including foreign real estate, yachts, and bank accounts worth billions of dollars. By late August 2012, according to the *Financial Times,* officials had seized 550 buildings, 300 companies, 367 bank accounts, 48 boats, 223 cars, and 83 horses from Ben Ali's associates. Meanwhile officials began selling off hundreds of millions of dollars' worth of holdings in the automotive, telecommunications, construction, and financial sectors. In April 2013 officials were able to recover $28.8 million from a Lebanese bank account owned by the former president's wife. Meanwhile the IMF agreed to provide a $1.75 billion stability loan to Tunisia.

In 2013 GDP grew by 2.7 percent, while inflation was 6 percent and unemployment 16.7 percent. GDP expanded by 2.3 percent in 2014, 0.8 percent in 2015, and 2 percent in 2016. In 2016 inflation was 4 percent, while unemployment fell to 14 percent and GDP per capita was $3,919.

GOVERNMENT AND POLITICS

Political background. As the seat of the Carthaginian Empire destroyed by Rome in 146 B.C., Tunisia was successively conquered by Romans, Arabs, and Turks before being occupied by France in 1881 and becoming a French protectorate under a line of native rulers (*beys*) in 1883. Pressure for political reforms began after World War I and in 1934 resulted in establishment of the nationalist Neo-Destour (New Constitution) Party, which spearheaded the drive for independence under the leadership of Habib BOURGUIBA. Nationalist aspirations were further stimulated by World War II, and an initial breakdown in independence negotiations led to the outbreak of guerrilla warfare against the French in 1952. Internal autonomy was conceded by France on June 3, 1955, and on March 20, 1956, the protectorate was terminated, with the country gaining full independence.

A national constituent assembly controlled by the Neo-Destour Party voted on July 25, 1957, to abolish the monarchy and establish a

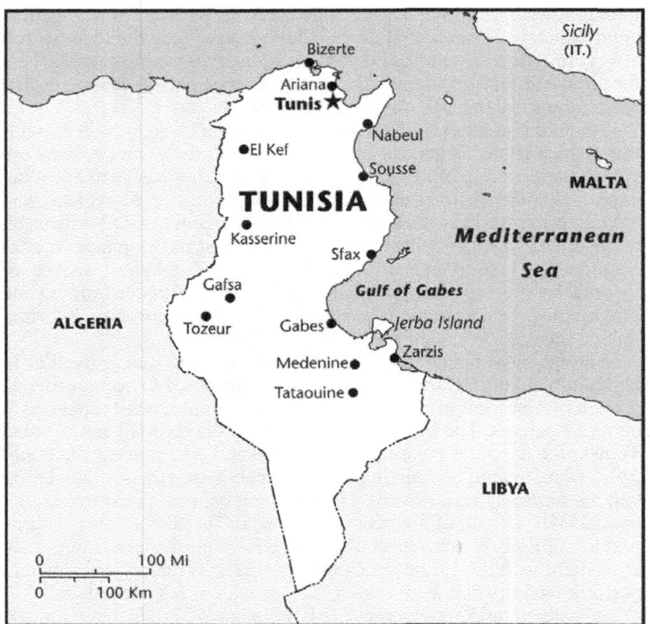

republic with Bourguiba as president. A new constitution was adopted on June 1, 1959, while Bourguiba's leadership and that of the party were overwhelmingly confirmed in presidential and legislative elections in 1959 and 1964.

Bourguiba was reelected in 1969, but his failing health precipitated a struggle for succession to the presidency. One-time front-runner Bahi LADGHAM, prime minister and secretary general of the party, was apparently too successful. The attention he received as chair of the Arab Superior Commission on Jordan and as effective executive during the president's absences led to a falling-out with an eventually rejuvenated Bourguiba; he was dismissed in 1970 and replaced by Hedi NOUIRA. President Bourguiba encountered an additional challenge from Ahmed MESTIRI, interior minister and leader of the liberal wing of the party. The liberals succeeded in forcing democratization of the party structure during the eighth party congress in October 1971, but Bourguiba subsequently reasserted his control over the party apparatus. Mestiri was expelled from the party in January 1972 and from his seat in the National Assembly in May 1973, while Bourguiba was named president for life on November 2, 1974.

In February 1980 Prime Minister Nouira suffered a stroke, and on April 24 Mohamed MZALI, the acting prime minister, was asked to form a new government. Mzali was reappointed following a general election on November 1, 1981, in which three additional parties were allowed to participate, although none secured legislative representation. Bourguiba dismissed Mzali on July 8, 1986, replacing him with Rachid SFAR, theretofore finance minister.

Gen. Zine El-Abidine BEN ALI was named to succeed Sfar on October 2, 1987, reportedly because of presidential displeasure at recent personnel decisions. Five weeks later, after a panel of doctors had declared the aged president medically unfit, Bourguiba was forced to step down in favor of Ben Ali, who designated Hedi BACCOUCHE as his prime ministerial successor.

Although widely termed a "bloodless coup," the ouster of Bourguiba and succession of Ben Ali were in accord with relevant provisions of the Tunisian constitution. Moreover, the takeover was generally welcomed by Tunisians, who had become increasingly disturbed by Bourguiba's erratic behavior and mounting government repression of the press, trade unions, legal opposition parties, and other sources of dissent, including the growing Islamic fundamentalist movement. (Following his deposition, Bourguiba retired from public view. He died at age 97 in 2000.)

Upon assuming office the Ben Ali government announced its commitment to domestic pluralism and launched a series of wide-ranging political and economic liberalization measures, which included the legalization of some political parties, the loosening of media restrictions, and the pardoning of more than 8,000 detainees, many of them fundamentalists. Additionally, in late 1988, the new regime negotiated a "national pact" regarding the country's political, economic, and social future with a number of political and labor groups. However, the Islamic Tendency Movement (*Mouvement de la Tendance Islamique*—MTI) refused to sign the accord, foreshadowing a steady deterioration in relations between the fundamentalists and the government.

Presidential and legislative elections, originally scheduled for 1991, were moved up to April 2, 1989, Ben Ali declaring they would serve as an indication of the public's satisfaction with the recent changes. No one challenged the popular Ben Ali in the presidential poll, but the legal opposition parties and fundamentalist independent candidates contested the House of Representatives balloting, albeit without success.

On September 27, 1989, Ben Ali dismissed Baccouche and named former Justice Minister Hamed KAROUI as prime minister. The change was reportedly precipitated by disagreement over economic policy, Baccouche having voiced concern over the "social effects" of the government's austerity program. Shortly thereafter, the government announced the formation of a "higher council" to oversee implementation of the national pact, although several opposition parties and MTI followers, now operating as the Renaissance Party (*Hizb al-Nahda*—generally referenced as *Nahda*) boycotted the council's meetings. Charging that the democratic process was in reality being "blocked" by the government, the opposition also refused to contest municipal elections in June 1990 or national by-elections in October 1991. Apparently in response to criticism that the government's enthusiasm for democratization had waned as its antifundamentalist fervor had surged, electoral law changes were adopted in late 1993 to ensure opposition parties of some legislative representation in the upcoming general election. Nevertheless, the Democratic Constitutional Assembly (RCD), officially credited with nearly 98 percent of the vote, won all 144 seats for which it was eligible in the balloting for a 163-member House on March 20, 1994. On the same date, Ben Ali was reelected without challenge, two potential independent candidates being stricken from the ballot by their failure to receive the required endorsement of at least 30 national legislators or municipal council presidents.

The RCD won control of all 257 municipal councils in local elections on May 21, 1995. While opposition candidates (standing in 47 municipalities) won only 6 of 4,090 seats, it was the first time since independence that the opposition had gained any such representation at all.

Ben Ali was reelected to a third full presidential term (then the constitutional limit) in balloting on October 24, 1999, securing more than 99 percent of the vote against two candidates presented by small opposition parties. Meanwhile, the RCD again secured all the seats for which it was eligible (148) in the concurrent legislative poll. Two days after being sworn in for his new term, President Ben Ali appointed Mohamed GHANNOUCHI, theretofore the minister for international cooperation and foreign investment, as the new prime minister.

Constitutional revision in 2002 removed the limit on the number of presidential terms, thereby permitting Ben Ali on October 24, 2004, to seek a fourth term, which he won with 95 percent of the vote against three other minor candidates. On the same date the RCD won all 152 seats contested on a district basis for an expanded assembly. Ghannouchi, who was retained as prime minister, headed a new government formed on November 10.

In the municipal election of May 8, 2005, to renew 264 councils comprising 4,366 seats, the RDC garnered 93.9 percent of the vote, while 4 opposition parties and 1 independent won representation with 6.1 percent of the vote. Three opposition groups whose candidates were barred from running boycotted the election. The RDC also dominated the new House of Advisers, which was established in balloting of July 3, 2005, in accordance with provisions adopted in the 2002 constitutional revision. The cabinet was reshuffled on August 17, 2005; January 25 and September 3, 2007; and August 29, 2008. One minister was replaced on October 10, 2009.

Ben Ali and the RCD swept the elections on October 25, 2009. Ben Ali secured 89.4 percent of the vote, defeating three other candidates, the closest challenger being Mohamed BOUCHIHA of the Popular Union Party (*Parti de l'Unité Populaire*—PUP) with 5 percent of the vote. The RCD won all 161 seats for which it was eligible in the enlarged, 214-member House of Representatives. Ben Ali was sworn in on November 12 and reshuffled the cabinet on January 14, 2010, retaining Ghannouchi as prime minister. In municipal elections in May the RCD won 75 percent of seats. The Progressive Democratic Assembly (*Rassemblement Démocratique Progressiste*—RDP) boycotted the elections.

In June the MR and the FDTL formed the Alliance for Citizenship and Equality, with what were described as two "nascent" groups—the Patriotic and Democratic Labor Party and the Reform and Development Movement—seeking a dialogue on a "transition to democracy," with little further explanation. In August Amnesty International warned that an amendment to Tunisia's penal code was designed to further silence government critics and human rights activists. The amendment provides for imprisonment of up to 20 years, with a minimum sentence of five years, for those who contact foreign organizations "in order to harm Tunisia's vital interests." Further changes to the cabinet were made on October 14 and on December 29. Tensions heightened in the repressive environment, and in December, after a street vendor named Bouazizi set himself on fire in protest against his treatment by the police, demonstrators took to the streets for ten days in the town of Sidi Bouzid. Because of constraints on the media, little support emerged from other parts of the country. However, once news of the self- immolation appeared on the social media, protests spread to Tunis.

President Ben Ali visited Bouazizi in the hospital and promised reforms. Following Bouazizi's death on January 5, 2011, protests increased significantly, lawyers went on strike, and students and members of trade unions and political groups began demonstrating. The protests quickly spread across the country, focused on rising unemployment and inflation, government corruption and repression, and demands that Ben Ali leave. The president deployed the police to quell the protests after the army refused to fire on protesters—resulting in the dismissal of the army chief—but violence escalated, and scores of demonstrators were killed in what by then was termed the Jasmine Revolution. President Ben Ali attempted to mollify demonstrators by dismissing the interior minister on January 12, 2011, and promising elections. On January 14 he dissolved the entire government, declared a state of emergency, and called for early legislative elections. Later that day, however, Ben Ali handed over presidential authority to Prime Minister Ghannouchi and fled with his family to Saudi Arabia after having been refused entry into France. The following day, the president of the House of Representatives, Fouad Mbazaâ, ascended to the interim presidency by appointment of the Constitutional Council, and two days later Ghannouchi, as interim prime minister, named a caretaker unity government that included opposition leaders along with cabinet members from the RCD regime. The powerful General Union of Tunisian Workers (*Union Générale des Travailleurs Tunisiens*—UGTT), which had initially refused to recognize the interim government, shifted its stance and supported Ghannouchi.

On January 17 Prime Minister Ghannouchi named a government of national unity, retaining several members of the previous regime and opposition leaders from the Renewal Movement (*Harakat Ettajdid/ Mouvement de la Rénovation*—MR), the Progressive Democratic Assembly (*Rassemblement Démocratique Progressiste*—RDP), and the Democratic Forum for Labor and Liberties (*Le Forum Démocratique pour le Travail et les Libertés*—FDTL). The following day, several ministers from the former opposition resigned in protest against RCD ministers having been retained in the cabinet. On January 19 the remaining RCD ministers and the prime minister resigned from the party. The foreign affairs minister resigned on January 27, and a further reshuffle of 20 ministers followed. On February 13, the newly appointed foreign affairs minister resigned. He was replaced on February 21. The interior minister subsequently suspended the RCD and announced that the state of emergency would remain in place indefinitely. During the protests it was reported that nearly 150 protesters had died and 94 had been wounded. Later in the month the justice minister announced that Tunisia had issued an international arrest warrant against Ben Ali and several members of his family for allegedly stealing large sums of money from the government, among other charges.

Faced with continued violent protests, a police force crippled by mass desertions, a judiciary weakened by its ties to the former regime, and increasing political uncertainty, Ghannouchi resigned on February 27, 2011, and was immediately replaced by Beji Caid ESSEBSI, 84, who had held several ministerial posts over the years. Five more ministers, who had been aligned with Ben Ali, resigned the same day. Meanwhile, the president of the newly formed Higher Political Reform Commission (HPRC), Yadh BEN ACHOUR, who had been appointed by former interim prime minister Ghannouchi, announced that the constitutional deadline for holding new presidential elections within 60 days of Ben Ali's departure could not be met. On March 3 interim president Mbazaâ said he would remain in office until July 24, the date set for the election of a constituent assembly, which would draft a new constitution. Shortly thereafter, Mbazaâ appointed a new interim government, this time with no members from the previous regime, reaffirming his commitment to "break with the past," lifting restrictions on the media, and releasing political prisoners. He also accused Ben Ali of high treason during the civil unrest. At the same time, the newly appointed interior minister, responding to a key demand of the protesters, announced the dissolution of the secret police and the state security system.

On March 7 Essebsi named a new interim cabinet, which did not include any members with ties to the previous regime. On March 9 the former ruling RCD was abolished by court order. In the meantime, political groups were reorganizing, and new ones were forming as the interim government lifted the ban on political parties. Notably, Islamic fundamentalist *Nahda* party leader Rachid GHANOUCHI (no relation to the former prime minister), returned to Tunisia after 20 years in exile, and his party was subsequently legalized. However, other Islamist parties and religious groups were denied legal party status. The independent electoral commission set a new date of July 24 for the constituent assembly election to allow adequate time for preparation of electoral rolls and other organizational matters. The interior minister resigned on March 28 and was immediately replaced.

In April 2011 Tunisia requested the extradition of Ben Ali from Saudi Arabia to face dozens of charges, including voluntary manslaughter, drug trafficking, and conspiring against the state. Ben Ali was alleged to have ordered air strikes against Kasserine in the days before he fled the country. More than 350 property deeds of Ben Ali were confiscated, along with other assets. Meanwhile, a judge remanded to custody former RCD secretary general Abderrahmin ZOUARI on charges that he had misappropriated public funds and abused his position of power within the party. On April 15 hundreds of demonstrators protested outside the Saudi embassy in Tunis, demanding Ben Ali's extradition. As tensions and political debates continued to escalate, resulting in more clashes between demonstrators and the police and the arrest of hundreds of protesters, the interim prime minister imposed a night-time curfew in May, though it was soon lifted. In June Ben Ali and his wife Leila TRABELSI were convicted in absentia of embezzling state funds and unlawful possession of jewelry and artifacts, sentenced to 35 years each in prison, and fined $65 million. The following month Ben Ali was convicted in absentia of smuggling guns, drugs, and other artifacts and sentenced to more than 15 years in prison and fined $72,000. On June 8 the interim government accepted a recommendation from the electoral commission to postpone the election from July 24 to October 23. Meanwhile, the slow pace of reforms and reports that Ben Ali loyalists still had significant political influence fomented further civil unrest. More violent clashes with the police were reported in July, as well as Internet censorship and police beating of journalists. "The optimism and euphoria of January's revolution has given way to dread," *Africa Research Bulletin* reported. In early August, with the investigation of the previous regime still ongoing, the interim government seized 234 luxury cars that had belonged to Ben Ali's friends and relatives. In mid-August hundreds in Tunis protested the release of several former ministers facing corruption charges and called for judicial reforms, though the judiciary claimed it had been independent since Ben Ali's ouster. In September the main parties agreed that the assembly would draw up a new constitution under which presidential and legislative elections would be held by October 2012. As the October 2011 constituent assembly election neared, at least 50 new parties were reportedly formed ahead of the poll.

Hamadi JEBALI (*Nahda*) was named prime minister on December 14, 2011 (see Current issues, below). He resigned on February 19, 2013, after failing to form a government (see Current issues, below). Ali LAARAYEDH (*Nahda*) was named prime minister three days later and formed a *Nahda*-dominated coalition government on March 8. On February 6, 2013, prominent left-wing secular figure Chokri Belaïd was assassinated. Secular figure Mohamed Brahmi was then assassinated on July 25. The murders triggered public outrage and intensified anti-government protests (see Current issues, below. Laarayedh resigned on January 9, and Jomaa was appointed to succeed him on January 29.

In parliamentary balloting on October 26, 2014, Tunis Calls (*Nidaa Tounes*) won a plurality with 85 seats, followed by *Nahda* with 69. Presidential elections were held on November 23. Among more than 25 candidates, interim president Marzouki received 33 percent of the vote, while Essebsi received 39 percent. Essebsi won the December runoff with 55.7 percent of the vote, and he assumed office on December 31.

After months of negotiations, Habib ESSID (ind.) formed a coalition government led by *Nidaa Tounes*. He was sworn in on February 6,

2015. Essid lost a confidence vote on July 30, 2016. Youssef CHAHED (*Nidaa Tounes*) was named to succeed Essid on August 1. He formed a coalition government on August 20, again led by *Nidaa Tounes* but including *Nahda,* among other parties. The legislature approved the cabinet on August 27.

Constitution and government. The constitution of June 1, 1959, endowed the Tunisian Republic with a presidential system backed by the dominant position of the (then) Neo-Destour Party. The president was given exceptionally broad powers, including the right to designate the prime minister and to rule by decree during legislative adjournments. In addition, the incumbent was granted life tenure under a 1975 amendment to the basic law. In the wake of President Bourguiba's ouster in 1987, the life presidency was abolished, the chief executive being limited to no more than three five-year terms.

A new constitution approved in a referendum on May 26, 2002, and promulgated on June 2, made provisions for an upper house, the House of Advisers; removed presidential term limits; and raised the age limit for a presidential candidate to 75 (from 70). The succession procedure was also altered, the president of the House of Representatives being designated to serve as head of state for 45–60 days, pending a new election, at which he could not present himself as a candidate. Other changes included reduction of the role of prime minister from leader of the government to "coordinator" of ministerial activities. Further constitutional amendments affecting the electoral code and expanding eligibility criteria for presidential candidates were promulgated on April 13, 2008. Following the civil unrest in January 2011, which resulted in the president's ouster, a state of emergency was declared. On January 17 the prime minister formed a Higher Political Reform Commission (HPRC) to oversee constitutional reform. On February 9 the legislature granted the prime minister broad authority to issue laws by decree.

The legislature was a unicameral body until 2005, with only a House of Representatives.

The House of Representatives (styled the National Assembly until 1981 and also referenced as the Chamber of Deputies) is elected by universal suffrage for a five-year term. Under Bourguiba it had limited authority and in practice was wholly dominated by the ruling party. Constitutional changes approved in July 1988 contained measures designed to expand the House's control and influence, although their impact has been minimal. The upper House of Advisers was seated after balloting on July 3, 2005. It comprises 126 members, 85 of whom are directly elected and 41 appointed by the president, all serving six-year terms, with half of the seats renewed every three years. Consultative bodies at the national level include a Social and Economic Council and a Higher Islamic Council. The judicial system is headed by a Court of Cassation and includes 3 courts of appeal, 13 courts of first instance, and 51 cantonal courts. Judges are appointed by the president.

Tunisia is administratively divided into 23 provinces, each headed by a governor appointed by the president. The governors are assisted by appointed government councils and 264 elected municipal councils.

In October 2012 the government refused opposition and media calls for a broad guarantee of freedom of the press in the draft constitution. Reporters Without Borders ranked Tunisia 96th out of 180 countries in 2016, up from 138th in 2013.

In January 2014 the transitional National Constituent Assembly adopted the new constitution, concluding a process launched in October 2011.

Foreign relations. Tunisia assumed a nonaligned posture at independence, establishing relations with both Eastern and Western countries, although placing particular emphasis on its relations with the West and with Arab governments. It became a member of the United Nations in 1956 and is active in all the UN-related agencies. It joined the Arab League in 1958 but boycotted its meetings from 1958 to 1961 and again in 1966 as a result of disagreements with the more "revolutionary" Arab states. As a signal of its support for peace negotiations (particularly the 1993 accord between Israel and the Palestine Liberation Organization), Tunisia exchanged low-level economic representatives with Israel in October 1994 in what was considered a possible precursor to eventual establishment of full diplomatic relations. However, Tunisia recalled those representatives from Israel in 1997 as part of the broad Arab protest over a perceived intransigence on the part of the Netanyahu administration in Israel.

Beginning in 1979, a series of agreements were signed with Algeria, culminating in a March 1983 "Maghreb Fraternity and Co-Operation Treaty," to which Mauritania acceded the following December. Relations with Libya, though reestablished in 1982 after a 1980 rupture over seizure of a southern town by alleged Libyan-trained insurgents, continued to be difficult. President Bourguiba's visit to Washington in June 1985 led to a mass expulsion of Tunisian workers from Libya, as well as reported Libyan incursions into Tunisia and efforts to destabilize its government. After suspending relations with Tripoli in September 1986, Tunis resumed relations a year later following a pledge by Libya to reimburse the expelled workers. Further economic and social agreements, including provisions for the free movement of people and goods between the two countries, were announced in 1988 as Tunisia stepped up its call for regional cooperation and unity, the latter bearing fruit with the formation of the Arab Maghreb Union in February 1989 (see article under Intergovernmental Organizations). Also in 1988, relations were reestablished with Egypt after an eight-year lapse.

The Iraqi invasion of Kuwait in August 1990 appeared to precipitate a change in Tunisia's theretofore unwavering pro-Western orientation. Although critical of the Iraqi occupation, Tunis strongly condemned the subsequent deployment of U.S. troops in Saudi Arabia and the allied bombing of Iraq in early 1991. However, security forces clamped down on large-scale pro-Iraqi demonstrations during the Gulf war, apparently out of concern that the situation might be exploited by Islamic fundamentalists.

President Ben Ali welcomed the antifundamentalist stance adopted by the Algerian military in early 1992, and Tunis was subsequently in the forefront of efforts among North African capitals to coordinate an "antiterrorist" campaign against Muslim militants. In October 1991 Tunisia recalled its ambassador from Sudan, charging Khartoum with fomenting fundamentalist unrest and providing sanctuary and financial support for groups intent on overthrowing the Tunisian government.

The EU, the focus of an estimated 80 percent of Tunisia's trade, and signed an association agreement with Tunis in 1995 that provided for the progressive reduction of tariffs (and elimination of many by 2008).

In 2006 Defense Secretary Donald Rumsfeld, on a visit to Tunis, discussed strengthening military ties with Tunisia while at the same time encouraging greater political reform. The United States provided $11 million to Tunisia for military training in 2006.

In October 2006 Tunisia closed its embassy in Doha, Qatar, after Qatar-based *Al Jazeera* television broadcast an interview with Moncef MARZOUKI, leader of the banned Congress for the Republic and former head of the Tunisian Human Rights League, in which he criticized the government and the lack of freedom in Tunisia.

In 2009 Tunisia, unlike many countries, agreed to the return of ten Tunisian detainees being held at the U.S. military prison in Guantánamo Bay, Cuba. In May Tunisia asked the United States to turn over two men who were being held on suspicion of being Islamist militants, both of whom had been convicted in absentia in Tunisian courts.

Following the Jasmine Revolution in Tunisia in January 2011, Western governments expressed concern over the violence but generally refrained from taking sides. In February thousands of Tunisian refugees fled to the Italian island of Lampedusa in the hope of gaining entry to the EU. Ultimately, the United States called on the interim prime minister to carry out democratic reforms, and French president Nicholas Sarkozy backed the protest movement as well, after denying Ben Ali refuge.

On February 24, 2012, Tunis hosted the Friends of Syria conference, which was attended by representatives from more than 70 countries and international organizations. The conference resulted in agreements to tighten sanctions and travel bans against Syrian president Bashir Assad and his senior aides and pledges of food and medicine for displaced Syrians. In November Libya announced it would provide $131 million in economic aid to Tunisia.

In March security forces and insurgents fought a series of battles along the border with Libya. In June the two countries announced a series of measures designed to improve border security. Meanwhile, a report found that 70 percent of the Tunisian workers who had fled Libya during that country's civil war had returned. In July eight Tunisian soldiers were killed along the border between Tunisia and Algeria. The Tunisian government blamed insurgents based in Algeria for the attacks.

France's interior minister Bernard Cazeneuve visited Tunisia on November 10, 2014, to pledge support in stopping French and Tunisian citizens from traveling to fight in Syria and Iraq. By late 2014 more than 2,400 Tunisians had traveled to fight with the extremist group in Syria, the most of any country. Meanwhile hundreds of French citizens made the journey, more than any other European country.

In late November Tunisian authorities and aid agencies prepared for additional floods of refugees from Libya despite growing public hostility to the influx ahead of presidential elections. A working group of Tunisian regional and central authorities, local civil society organizations, UN agencies and international NGOs drafted a crisis plan to ensure space for refugees in the event of the security situation deteriorating rapidly.

Tunisia's most-wanted terrorist, al-Qaida commander Seifallah Ben HASSINE (Abu AYADH), was killed in Libya in a U.S. airstrike in June 2015. In response to reports of large numbers of Tunisians travelling to Libya to fight in that country's civil war, Tunisia began implementing new border security measures, including vehicle barriers and increased surveillance in February 2016. Some estimates were that as many as 7,000 Tunisians were fighting in Libya. Also in February the United Kingdom announced the deployment of troops to train Tunisian border patrol guards.

Current issues. In the October 23, 2011, election, which saw a turnout of about 52 percent, the *Nahda* party obtained around 40 percent of the vote and won 89 seats, making it by far the biggest single party. Of the 217 assembly seats, 42 went to women, thanks in part to a provision requiring parties to present an equal number of male and female candidates. The strictly proportional system ensured that at least 19 parties and 8 independent lists won representation, most often a single seat.

After the sweeping *Nahda* victory, party leader Rachid Ghanouchi called for cooperation with the other main parties, promising a new model of government that would fuse an Islamic character with the ideals of liberal democracy and repeating the party's campaign promise not to ban alcohol or impose a dress code on Western tourists.

On November 21 a three-party coalition pact was established between *Nahda,* the Democratic Forum for Labor and Liberties (FDTL), and the Congress for the Republic (CPR), confirming the deal to hold presidential and legislative elections under a new constitution in late 2012 or early 2013. The parties also agreed that Hamadi JEBALI, *Nahda*'s secretary general, would take over as prime minister in December and Moncef Marzouki of the CPR would succeed interim president Fouad Mbazaâ. On November 22 the Constituent Assembly held its inaugural session.

Throughout much of the following year, as parties struggled with defections and shifting alliances, the deep rivalries between secularists and ultraconservative Salafi Islamists were increasingly evident. On March 28, 2012, groups of liberal artists and Salafis both staged marches on Avenue Bourguiba, the central thoroughfare where the protests that had launched the Arab Spring began. Clashes ensued, with the ultraconservatives reportedly assaulting their rivals. The government subsequently announced a ban on marches there, but demonstrations continued. On April 5 the police first used teargas and batons on crowds after a group of unemployed demonstrators challenged the ban. Some liberal members of the assembly were reportedly beaten by police. Meanwhile, a string of confrontations between the dean of Tunis' Manouba University and Salafist student groups and their supporters, who demanded a prayer room and the right for female students to wear veils, occupied much of the national attention, feeding claims that the *Nahda*-dominated government was unwilling to confront ultraconservative Islamists. In May Salafis burned police stations and bars in several towns. The police arrested 15 people, but moderates argued it was an all too rare response. Critics also took issue with a $1,500 fine levied against a TV executive for showing *Persepolis,* a film that offends some Muslims by depicting God, as well as the lack of investigative follow-up into attacks on the station and the executive's home.

In June 2012 Ben Ali was sentenced to life in prison for the killing of protesters, but Saudi Arabia refused to extradite him.

On August 13, 2012, thousands of women marched in Tunis to protest a provision in the new draft of the constitution that describes women as "complementary to men." On September 14 Salafist Islamic militants attacked the U.S. embassy in Tunis. Security forces killed 4 of the militants and injured 40. However, sections of the embassy were burned or looted. The protest was in response to a U.S. film that was critical of Islam. Also in September the Ministry of Culture filed a series of lawsuits against Salafist groups that had disrupted cultural events and festivals. Violent protests led by the Tunisian General Labor Union in Siliana in December prompted the government to negotiate a truce that included pledges to spur job creation. These and other protests in December injured more than 250 protestors and 72 police officers.

On February 6, 2013, opposition leader Chokri BELAÏD (Democratic Patriots' Movement) was assassinated by three masked gunmen, creating a political crisis that resulted in the resignation of Prime Minister Jebali 13 days later. Most Tunisians blamed Salafist militants, and opposition leaders accused the government of not taking strong action to curb the extremists. A new government under Ali Laarayedh was installed in March and included a large number of independents. Also in March Kamel KEDHKADH, identified as one of Belaïd's assassins, was arrested in Algeria and extradited to Tunisia. Protests and demonstrations against the *Nahda*-led government continued through the summer and prompted the government to agree to new elections. Opposition leaders formally requested a UN inquiry into the murder, alleging that the government could not be trusted to investigate the crime. On July 25 opposition figure Mohamed BRAHMI was assassinated, leading to renewed protests and strikes. Meanwhile the growing crisis led the interim assembly to suspend its work in August after 60 deputies began a boycott of the body.

Amid the antigovernment protests, the brutal murders of several Tunisian soldiers increased public outrage. Nahda condemned the killings; however, the opposition accused the ruling party of failing to rein in radical Islamists. In December the Islamist-led government agreed to step down from power. Jomaa's name was one of six put forward for the post by the parties involved in negotiations on December 14. Laarayedh resigned after a two-month political standoff. Jomaa assumed office in January 2014 and announced his cabinet on January 26, 2014.

Campaigning in the presidential race began on November 1. Kalthoum KANNOU contested the elections as an independent. She was the only woman among 27 contestants, and the first ever to seek an office higher than that of parliamentarian.

On March 18, 2015, three Islamic State–affiliated gunmen attacked the Bardo National Museum in Tunis, killing 22, including a number of foreign tourists, and wounding more than 50. It was the deadliest terrorist attack in the country since 2002. Two of the attackers were killed during the raid. Security forces killed nine suspected terrorists in a strike on March 28, while the following day more than 20,000 Tunisians marched in Tunis against terrorism and Islamic extremism. On June 26 a gunman with alleged ties to the Islamic State attacked a luxury hotel in the resort town of Port El Kantaoui, killing 38 tourists, 30 of whom were citizens of the United Kingdom. The attack prompted the deployment of more than 1,000 additional security forces in key tourist areas, but when combined with the Bardo massacre, delivered a significant blow to Tunisia's lucrative tourist sector. An estimated 3,000 UK tourists were advised by their government to leave Tunisia in the aftermath of the attacks. In July a 30-day state of emergency was declared while security forces undertook a broad offensive against suspected terrorists, including arrests and military action.

Massive protests against unemployment swept the country in January 2016. Estimates were that unemployment was 15.3 percent by January 2016, with youth unemployment as high as 40 percent. The unrest led to a three-week curfew, which ended in February.

POLITICAL PARTIES

Although not constitutionally mandated, Tunisia was effectively a one-party state from the time the **Tunisian Communist Party** (PCT) was banned in January 1963 until its return to legal status in July 1981. (For more on the subsequent legalization of other historically significant parties, see the 2012 *Handbook.*)

Following the civil unrest, referred to as the Jasmine Revolution, that began in early 2011, the ruling government party (RCD) was suspended by the interim government on February 6, and on March 9 a court in Tunis ordered the party's dissolution. The interim government also removed the ban on political parties, and by midyear more than 50 parties and 100 political associations had been formed. More than 80, including 3 religious groups, were denied authorization.

By mid-2012 observers highlighted a persistent imbalance between the organizational clout and cohesion of the well-organized *Nahda* party and the smaller, fractured secular parties as a challenge to the development of Tunisia's political sphere. The governing coalition, which controlled 138 of the interim assembly's 217 seats, was also said to be a fragile "marriage of convenience" that was marked by mutual suspicions and showing signs of strain. Further tensions were highlighted by the July 27 resignation of Finance Minister Hussein Dimassi, reportedly over his feelings that a proposed compensation plan for political prisoners of the former regime, mostly Islamists from *Nahda,* was a reckless vote-buying tactic. Meanwhile, an effort by some secular parties to unite into a grand coalition proved short-lived, and a changing roster of small, shifting alliances predominated despite the many small parties that share similar ideologies and political incentives to join forces but nonetheless remain outside of coalitions. On August 14 the head of the drafting committee announced the new constitution would not be adopted by February 2013, which was seen as another hitch in the country's transition.

Tunisia's interim assembly finished work on a new constitution in January 2014 and voted to approve it in February. Parliamentary elections took place on October 26 without any significant security incidents, and observers reported no major polling violations. Presidential elections were held on November 23, with runoffs in December. A *Nidaa Tounes*-led coalition was formed thereafter, and another formed in August 2016 after the prime minister lost a no-confidence vote (see Political background, above).

Tunis Calls (*Nidaa Tounes/Appel de la Tunisie*). Formed in the summer of 2012 by Beji Caid Essebsi, the modernist, centrist, secular *Nidaa Tounes* party includes business professionals, intellectuals, trade unionists, and politicians from the old regime. In January 2013 *Nidaa Tounes* and four other parties, including *Hizb al-Joumhouri* (below), ***al-Massar,*** the **Patriotic and Democratic Labor Party** (PTPD), and the **Socialist Party** (PS), joined to form **Union for Tunisia** (*Ittihad min ajal Tunis*—UPT). On March 9, 2013, Faouzi ELLOUMI, a member of the party's executive committee, made controversial statements on a popular talk show about his party's willingness to include former-RCD party members. Sound bites of the statements went viral, causing *Nidaa Tounes* party leaders to deny publicly accusations that the party was simply an extension of Ben Ali's RCD. Detractors of the *Nidaa Tounes* party accused the group of lacking a substantive political program and existing merely as a vehicle to get Essebsi elected president. On July 28, 2013, the Popular Front (below) and UPT formed the **National Salvation Front.** *Hizb al-Joumhouri* withdrew from the UPT coalition in December 2013. In June 2014 Nidaa Tounes left the UPT.

After winning a plurality of seats in the October 2014 parliamentary elections, the party resisted forming a coalition with Islamists parties. Instead, following balloting, the party was working to form a collection of smaller parties to garner the necessary 109-seat majority and name a prime minister. Many members of the Tunisia's principal labor union, Tunisian General Labor Union (UGTT), and the national employers' union, *Union Tunisienne de l'Industrie, du Commerce et de l'Artisanat* (UTICA) supported *Nidaa Tounes* in the elections. Nidaa Tounes ran on an explicitly anti-Islamist platform, winning 86 of the 217 seats with 49.4 percent of the vote). Essebsi won runoff balloting for the presidency in December 2014. A *Nidaa Tounes*-led government was appointed in February 2015.

Reports in January 2016 indicated a split in the party, with as many as 16 legislators resigning and defecting to opposition parties. In August 2016 Youssef CHAHED was appointed prime minister of a coalition government.

Leader: Beji Caid ESSEBSI (President of the Republic), Youssef CHAHED (Prime Minister).

Renaissance Party (*Hizb al-Nahda/Parti de la Renaissance*—PR or *Nahda*). Also known as the **Renaissance Movement** (*Harakat al-Nahda/Mouvement de la Renaissance*), *Nahda* was formed as the **Islamic Tendency Movement** (*Mouvement de la Tendance Islamique*—MTI) in early 1981 by a group of Islamic fundamentalists inspired by the 1979 Iranian revolution. Charged with fomenting disturbances, many MTI adherents were jailed during a series of subsequent crackdowns by the Bourguiba government. However, the MTI insisted that it opposed violence or other "revolutionary activity," and the Ben Ali government pardoned most of those incarcerated, including the movement's leader, Rachid Ghanouchi, shortly after assuming power. The new regime also initiated talks that it said were designed to provide moderate MTI forces with a legitimate means of political expression in order to undercut support for the movement's radical elements. As an outgrowth of that process, the MTI adopted its new name in early 1989; however, the government subsequently denied legal status to *Nahda,* ostensibly on the grounds that it remained religion based. Undaunted, the group quickly established itself as the government's primary opposition, its "independent" candidates collecting about 13 percent of the total popular vote (including as much as 30 percent of the vote in some urban areas) in 1989 legislative balloting.

Nahda boycotted higher council negotiations and municipal elections in 1990, Ghanouchi remaining in exile to protest the lack of legal recognition for the formation and the continued "harassment" of its sympathizers. Friction intensified late in the year following the arrest of three groups of what security forces described as armed extremists plotting to overthrow the government. Although the government alleged that some of those arrested had *Nahda* links, the party leadership strongly denied the charge, accusing the regime of conducting a propaganda campaign aimed at discrediting the fundamentalist movement in order to prevent it from assuming its rightful political role.

On October 15, 1991, the government announced that it had uncovered a fundamentalist plot to assassinate President Ben Ali and other government officials in order to "create a constitutional vacuum." However, *Nahda* leaders again denied any connection to violent anti-government activity, reiterating their commitment to "peaceful methods" of protest and stressing that their vision for the "Islamization" of Tunisia was "compatible" with democracy and a pluralistic society. The disclaimers notwithstanding, the government flatly labeled *Nahda* "a terrorist organization" and intensified the campaign to "silence" it. Thousands of suspected *Nahda* sympathizers were detained, many later claiming that they had been tortured or otherwise abused in prison (a charge supported by Amnesty International). At a widely publicized trial in mid-1992, about 170 *Nahda* adherents were convicted of sedition. A number were sentenced to life imprisonment, including Ghanouchi and several other leaders who were tried in absentia. The government subsequently issued an international arrest warrant for Ghanouchi, who was living in London, but in mid-1993, the United Kingdom granted him political asylum. In 1994 Ghanouchi dismissed the recent Tunisian presidential and legislative elections as "a joke." Despite the "banned and fragmented" status of *Nahda,* Ghanouchi was described in 1996 as still the only possible "serious challenger" to Ben Ali. A number of *Nahda* adherents were released in November 1999 from long prison terms. In March 2001 Ghanouchi, in conjunction with **Democratic Socialist Movement** (*Mouvement des Démocrates Socialistes*—MDS) leader Mohamed Mouada, proposed establishment by *Nahda* and the legal opposition parties of a National Democratic Front to challenge the RCD, suggesting to some observers that *Nahda* hoped to return to mainstream political activity. However, *Nahda* remained relatively quiescent during the 2004 election campaign.

In March 2006 the government released 1,600 prisoners on the 50th anniversary of Tunisia's independence. Among those released were reportedly many political prisoners who had been jailed for 10 years because they were members of *Nahda.* Further, in November President Ben Ali, marking his 19th year at the helm, pardoned 55 Islamists, all said to be members of *Nahda,* including leaders Habib ELLOUZE and Mohamed AKROUT, both of whom had received life sentences in 1992. In November 2008 Ben Ali pardoned and released another 21 PR members, some of whom had been serving life sentences. A former PR leader, Sadek CHOUROU was arrested in 2008 on charges of maintaining an outlawed organization. In 2009, an appeals court upheld his one-year prison sentence and subsequently extended it by one year to cover time the court said he should have served in the 1990s. Chourou was released in October 2010. In December several Islamists were sentenced for trying to revive *Nahda* by holding meetings and trying to raise funds. Two were sent to jail for six months; others were convicted in absentia or given suspended sentences.

Party leader Ghanouchi (no relation to the former prime minister), who had been in exile in the United Kingdom for 20 years, returned to Tunisia on January 30, 2011, following the ouster of President Ben Ali and the interim government's decision to lift the ban on all political parties. *Nahda,* which Ghanouchi likened to Turkey's ruling Justice and Development Party (adhering to Islamist values in a secular state), was legalized on March 1.

Well-funded and the best-organized party, *Nahda* utilized its strong grassroots in the poorest areas during the run-up to the 2011 balloting for the assembly. Some of the support for *Nahda* was attributed to its credibility for opposing the former regime. It was also seen by supporters as more socially responsible and less likely to be corrupted.

During the campaign, the prospect of a strong *Nahda* showing divided the country, with women's groups and secularists mounting demonstrations against Islamist rule and a series of dramatic advertisements that suggested an Islamist win would scare off tourists and see women's rights curtailed.

On March 27, 2012, leaders announced the new constitution would not cite Islamic law as a source of legislation, a rejection of demands from ultraconservatives for an Islamic state. Some observers considered it a step toward delivering on the party's campaign promises not to overturn the secular order. Later, party officials complained of pressure from Salafist rivals to embrace more conservative positions. *Nahda* secured 89 seats in the assembly.

On February 22, 2013, Ali Laarayedh was appointed prime minister of a *Nahda*-led coalition government. Reports in 2013 indicated growing divisions within the party between moderates who sought negotiations and accommodations with the secular opposition and hard-liners, led by Ghanouchi. The party failed to win a plurality of votes in legislative balloting in October 2014, obtaining 69 seats with 36.2 percent of the vote. *Nahda* did not field a candidate for the presidential elections in November. The party joined the *Nidaa Tounes*–led government in August 2016 and received two portfolios in the cabinet.

Leaders: Rachid GHANOUCHI (Party President), Ali LAARAYEDH (Former Prime Minister), Noureddine BHIRI, Samir DILOU.

Free Patriotic Union (*al-Ittihad al-Watani al-Hurr/Union Patriotique Libre*—UPL). In October 2011 millionaire and former exile Slim RIAHI formed the secular party as a counterweight to Islamist factions. UPL won just one seat in the October 2011 elections. On March 7, 2013, UPL announced the creation of a new centrist party of socialist-liberal orientation that would include seven other minor parties: the **Third Alternative Party**, the **Modern Left Party**, the **Citizenship Movement**, the **Tunisian Liberal Party**, the **Social-Democratic Alternative**, the **Citizenship and Justice Party**, and the **Path of Will Party**. In the October 2014 balloting, UPL won 16 seats with 3.8 percent. The party was part of the February 2015 coalition government, but not the new cabinet formed in August 2016.

Leader: Slim RIAHI.

Popular Front (*Front Populaire/Front Populaire pour la Réalisation des Objectifs de la Revolution*). Formed in October 2012, the Popular Front began as a leftwing coalition of 11 parties with a total of six seats in the National Constituent Assembly. The **Party of Tunisian Communist Workers** (*Parti des Ouvriers Communistes Tunisiens*—POCT), a formerly unrecognized splinter of the former PCT, is a member of the coalition and secured three seats in the assembly in 2011. POCT founder Hamma HAMMANI leads the coalition. The assassinations of three coalition members in 2013, Shukri BELEID, Mohammad BRAHMI, and Mohamed BELMOFTI, contributed to popular discontent with the Islamist-led governments installed after 2011. In addition, about a dozen members of the security forces had been killed in battles with extremists and bombings between 2011 and 2014. On July 28, 2013, the Popular Front and UPT formed the **National Salvation Front**. By 2014 the coalition had reduced to nine members, including Marxist and Nasserist parties, pan-Arab populists and others. In the legislative elections in October, the Popular Front won 15 seats (3.2 percent of the vote).

Leader: Hamma HAMMAMI.

Tunisian Aspiration (*Afek Tounes*). *Afek Tounes* is a center-left party that was close to the PDP before the PDP merged into *Hizb al-Joumhouri*. Founded in 2011, the party is close to the business community and the pro-business regime of Ben Ali. The party secured four seats in the assembly after October 2011 balloting. On April 9, 2012, *Afek Tounes* joined with the PDP and the Tunisian Republican Party to form the Republican Party (*al-Joumhouri*) (see below). However, the partnership between *al-Joumhouri* and *Afek Tounes* ended in August 2013. On September 28, 2013, party members elected Yassine Brahim president of the revived party. *Afek Tounes* won eight seats in the October 2014 balloting 2.4 percent of the vote. It joined the coalition governments in February 2015 and August 2016, and secured two cabinet posts in the latter one.

Leader: Yassine BRAHIM.

Congress for the Republic (*al-Mottamar/Le Congrès Pour la République*—CPR). Formed by activist Moncef Marzouki in July 2001, the political party was established to try to help create a democratic republic. Marzouki, who faced a year in prison for belonging to another illegal organization, lived in self-imposed exile in France for five years, returning to Tunisia in 2006 to encourage Tunisians to engage in peaceful demonstrations for human rights. Soon thereafter, Marzouki was charged with "incitement to civil disobedience." He returned to Tunisia from exile in France days after Ben Ali fled in January. The CPR has a history of past cooperation with *Nahda.* Some 40 members of the opposition in the assembly cast blank ballots to protest Marzouki's election as Tunisia's interim president, a position his critics said was largely powerless and meant to distract from the reality of Islamist control. The party subsequently showed signs of strain, with some members accusing Marzouki of putting his own ambition before the interests of the party. Twelve CPR representatives in the assembly seceded from the CPR and formed a new party on May 17, the **Independent Democratic Congress**, whose leaders include Abderraouf AYADI and Slim BOUKHDHIR.

The CPR secured 29 seats in the assembly. Reports in March 2013 indicated that CPR Secretary General Mohamed ABBOU had resigned and was forming a new party. He was replaced by Imed DAÏMI. CPR secured three cabinet posts in the coalition government announced in March. Although many CPR representatives within the Constituent Assembly have defected to other parties since the 2011 elections, in the October 2014 elections the party won 4 seats with 0.9 percent of the vote. Marzouki was defeated in his bid for reelection in runoff balloting in December 2015.

Leaders: Moncef MARZOUKI (Former Acting President of the Republic), Imed DAÏMI (Interim Secretary General).

People's Movement (*Mouvement du Peuple*). Formed in April 2011, the party has undergone a series of mergers and splits. Mohammad Brahmi was party leader when he was assassinated. The party has been a member of the Popular Front; however, in the October 2014 elections, the won three seats of its own with 0.8 percent of the vote, separate and apart from those won by the Popular Front coalition.

Leader: Zouhair MAGHZAOUI.

Democratic Current (*Attayar/Courant Démocrate*). Former secretary general of CPR Mohamed ABBOU founded the party in 2013. Several party members formerly belonged to CPR. In the October 2014 elections it won three seats of its own with 0.7 percent of the vote.

Leader: Mohamed Abbou (Secretary General).

Current of Love or **Mahabba Current** (*Tayar al-Mahabba/ Courant de l'Amour*), known before 2013 as **Popular Petition for Freedom, Justice, and Development** (*Pétition Populaire Pour la Liberté*—Popular Petition). Formed in March 2011 by Mohamed Hechim Hamdi, a London-based TV station owner, Current of Love offered an ambiguous platform, and analysts said some of its campaign promises, including free health care for the elderly, were unrealistic. While the party came in third in the assembly elections, Hamdi postponed his return to Tunisia after an anticorruption commission published a letter he wrote in December 2009 to Ben Ali offering to produce television programs highlighting the country's "democratic developments." The Popular Petition secured 26 seats in the assembly in 2011. After several announcements declaring his intention to quit politics, Hamdi announced on May 22, 2013, the creation of his new party, the Current of Love. Current of Love won 2 seats with 0.6 percent of the vote in the October 2014 elections.

Leader: Mohamed Hechim HAMDI.

National Constitutional Initiative (*Initiative Nationale Destourienne Tunisie/al-Moubadara*). Founded by Kamal Morjane, formerly a defense minister and foreign minister in Ben Ali's regime, the party secured five seats in the assembly in 2011. Like **The Homeland Party** (*Parti de la Patrie*/Al Watan Party)—founded in 2011 by Mohammed JEGHAM and Ahmed FRIAA, both interior ministers in the former regime—The Initiative absorbed members of the banned RCD. On July 31, 2014, six parties merged to form the **Tunisian National Destourian** (Constitutional) **Initiative** (PINDT): the **Party of Freedom for Justice and Development;** the **Party of Independence,** the **Party of Tomorrow's Tunisia,** and the **Party of Third Path.** In the 2014 legislative elections, the Initiative won three seats with 0.6 percent of the vote.

Leaders: Kamal MORJANE (President); Mohamed Jegham, Mohamed Ayachi AJROUDI (Vice Presidents).

Democratic Forum for Labor and Liberties (*Le Forum Démocratique pour le Travail et les Libertés—Ettakatol* or FDTL). Legalized in 2002, the FDTL had been active as an opposition group since it was organized in 1994. Its platform endorsed a commitment to "defending freedom, democracy, and social justice," among other things.

After the party failed to prevent passage of a constitutional amendment allowing Ben Ali to seek a fourth term in 2004, it called for a boycott of the 2004 elections and urged opposition parties to work toward cohesion. The FDTL was barred by the government from participating in the 2005 municipal elections, along with the RDP and the MR. The three groups had formed a loose alliance called the **Democratic Coalition for Citizenship,** which the government said did not abide by electoral regulations.

One of the party's leaders, Mustafa Ben Jafaar (formerly of MDS), who was highly critical of the 2008 constitutional amendment affecting presidential candidates, in June 2009 announced his bid for the presidency in the October general elections. However, he was ineligible to run under the new law that required a candidate to have been president of a party for two consecutive years. The party failed to win seats in the 2009 parliamentary elections.

In 2010 the party joined with the MR and two small groups in the prodemocracy **Alliance for Citizenship and Equality.**

Following the ouster of President Ben Ali in January 2011, Ben Jafaar was tapped as health minister in the interim government, but he quit in protest at the inclusion of RCD members in the cabinet.

In the run-up to the balloting on October 23, 2011, the party positioned itself as a challenger to the PDP (see below). The party secured 20 seats in the assembly. But, party leaders have been clear that the decision to join the governing "troika" was based on political expediency rather than ideological compatibility, and discontent has driven some defections from the party. In November 2011 Ben Jafaar was elected president of the Constituent Assembly. The FDTL received two ministries in the March 2013 coalition government. Between 2013 and 2014 the party lost many supporters and several members defected to other parties as Tunisians became increasingly dissatisfied with the Islamist government. The party won no seats in the 2014 legislative elections.

Leader: Mustafa BEN JAFAAR (Secretary General, 2009 presidential candidate, and President of the Constituent Assembly).

Progressive Democratic Party (*Parti Démocrate Progressiste*—PDP). The PDP had been established as the **Progressive Socialist Assembly** (*Rassemblement Socialiste Progressiste*—RSP) by a number of Marxist groups in 1983. The pan-Arabist RSP was tolerated by the Bourguiba government until mid-1986. It formed a **Democratic Alliance** with the PCT and planned to field candidates for the 1986 balloting. However, the coalition boycotted the election after the government disqualified some of its candidates and sentenced 14 of its members to six-month jail terms for belonging to an illegal organization. The party was officially recognized in September 1988. The RSP did not secure any of the legislative seats reserved for opposition parties in 1994 or 1999, and it called for a boycott of the municipal elections of May 2000. The RSP changed its name to the **Progressive Democratic Assembly** (*Rassemblement Démocratique Progressiste*—RDP) in July 2001 in an effort to "broaden its ideological base." The RDP reportedly included many Marxists as well as moderate Islamists and liberals.

RDP Secretary General Ahmed Chebbi was blocked from contesting the 2004 presidential election because of a recent decree by President Ben Ali that candidates could be presented only by parties with legislative representation. The RDP consequently called for a boycott of the presidential balloting and withdrew its candidates from the legislative poll.

In 2006 May ELJERIBI was elected secretary general, replacing Chebbi, who had held the post for 23 years. Eljeribi became the first woman to head a political party in Tunisia. In 2007 Eljeribi went on a month-long hunger strike to protest alleged harassment against the party, specifically the party's newspaper, *al-Mawkif.* Two other party members, including Rachid KHECHANA, the paper's editor, began hunger strikes in April 2008 for the same reason.

Though the party had nominated Chebbi in early 2008 to be its 2009 presidential candidate, he was subsequently deemed ineligible under the new law that permitted only elected party leaders who had held the post for two consecutive years to contest presidential elections. The party failed to win seats in the 2009 parliamentary elections and subsequently boycotted the 2010 municipal elections.

Chebbi served in Tunisia's caretaker government after the revolution. Ahead of the 2011 Constituent Assembly elections, the RSP changed its name again and rebranded itself as a liberal party with a strong market orientation that would be a counterweight to *Nahda*, waging verbal attacks against its rival in the press. The party secured 16 seats in the assembly. On April 9, 2012, the PDP dissolved when it merged with *Hizb al-Joumhouri* (see below).

Leader: Ahmed Néjib CHEBBI.

Republican Party (*Hizb al-Joumhouri*). Founded on April 9, 2012, as a merger among PDP, *Afek Tounes*, and the **Tunisian Republican Party;** *Afek Tounes* left the group in August 2013. *Hizb al-Joumhouri* has taken a less dismissive approach toward Nahda based on the understanding that political Islam has become part of the Tunisian landscape and is not necessarily a threat. *Hizb al-Joumhouri* and UPT formed a coalition in January 2013. However, the party withdrew from the UPT coalition in December 2013. *Hizb al-Joumhouri* won one seat with 0.2 percent of the vote in the 2014 elections. It joined the *Nidaa Tounes*–led government in August 2016 and secured one cabinet post.

Leader: Maya JRIBI (Secretary General).

Other parties that won seats in the 2014 legislative elections included the **Democratic Alliance** (*Alliance Démocratique*), 1; *Rad el Etebar* 1; *Lamjed Jerid,* 1; **Salvation National Front** (*al-Jibha al-Waṭanīya lil-Inqādh*), 1; **Democratic Socialist Movement** (*Mouvement des Démocrates Socialistes*—MDS), 1; **Voice of the Peasants** (*Parti Voix des Agriculteurs*), 1; and **Call Tunisians Abroad,** 1.

Other parties that contested the 2011 elections included the **Democratic Modernist Pole** (*Pôle Démocratique Moderniste*—PDM), **People's Progressive Unionist Movement** (MPPU), **Maghrebin Liberal Party, Equity and Equality Party, Progressive Struggle Party, Neo Destour Party, Democratic Social Nation Party, Cultural Unionist Nation Party, Free Patriotic Union,** and **Democratic Patriots' Movement.** (See the 2014 *Handbook* for more details.)

LEGISLATURE

Note: On February 8 and 9, 2011, in accordance with the constitution, both chambers of the legislature invested then interim president Fouad Mbazaâ with the authority to rule by decree. Subsequently Mbazaâ dissolved both houses of the parliament. On November 22, 2011, a unicameral National Constituent Assembly replaced it as the transitional parliamentary body. On December 12, 2011, the National Constituent Assembly elected Moncef Marzouki as interim president. As of parliamentary elections on October 26, 2014, the Assembly of the Representatives of the People replaced the transitional National Constituent Assembly.

House of Representatives (*Majlis al-Nuwab/Chambre des Députés*). (For the results of the most recent prerevolution balloting, see the 2012 *Handbook.*) On October 25, 2009, elections were held for an enlarged 214-member Chamber of Deputies. The body was dissolved in 2011.

President: Sahbi KAROUI.

House of Advisers (*Majlis al-Mustasharin*). (For the results of recent prerevolution balloting, see the 2012 *Handbook.*) The body was dissolved in 2011.

National Constituent Assembly (*Assemblée Nationale Constituante*). The transitional Constituent Assembly of the transitional government came in to power in the balloting of October 23, 2011.

Speaker: Mustapha Ben JAFAAR.

Assembly of the Representatives of the People. In parliamentary elections held on October 26, 2014, turnout was about 66 percent. The distribution of the 217 seats was as follows: *Nidaa Tounes* Party, 86 seats; *Nahda,* 69; Free Patriotic Union, 16; Popular Front, 15; *Afek Tounes,* 8; Congress for the Republic, 4; People's Movement, 3; Democratic Current, 3; National Constitutional Initiative, 3; Mahabba Current, 2; Democratic Alliance, 1; *Rad el Etebar,* 1; *Lamjed Jerid,* 1; *Al Joumhouri,* 1; Salvation National Front, 1; Movement of Social Democrats, 1; Voice of the Peasants, 1; and Call Tunisians Abroad, 1. The constitution of February 2014 authorizes parliament to select the prime minister, who shares power with the president.

Speaker: Mohamed ENNACEUR (*Nidaa Tounes*).

CABINET

[as of November 15, 2016]

Prime Minister	Youssef Chahed (*Nidaa Tounes*)
Ministers	
Agriculture, Fisheries, and Water Resources	Samir Taïeb (*al-Massar*)
Civil Service and Governance	Abid Briki (ind.)
Communications Technologies and Digital Economy	Anouar Maârouf (ind.)
Constitutional Bodies, Civil Society, and Human Rights	Mehdi Ben Gharbia (Democratic Alliance)
Culture	Mohamed el Abidine (ind.)
Development, Investment, and International Cooperation	Fadhel Abdelkefi (ind.)

Economy and Finance	Lamia Zribi (ind.) [f]
Education	Néji Jalloul (*Nidaa Tounes*)
Employment and Vocational Training	Imed Hammami (*Nahda*)
Energy, Mining, and Renewable Energy	Héla Cheikhrouhou (ind.) [f]
Equipment, Housing, and Regional Planning	Mohamed Salah Arfaoui (ind.)
Foreign Affairs	Khemaies Jhinaoui (ind.)
Health	Samira Merai Friaa (*Afek Tounes*) [f]
Higher Education and Scientific Research	Slim Khalbous (ind.)
Industry and Trade	Zied Ladhari (*Nahda*)
Interior	Hédi Majdoub (ind.)
Justice	Ghazi Jeribi (ind.)
Local Affairs and Environment	Riadh Mouakhar (*Afek Tounes*)
National Defense	Farhat Hochani (ind.)
Prime Minister's Office, in Charge of Relations with Parliament	Iyed Dahmani (*Hizb al-Joumhouri*)
Religious Affairs	Ghazi Jeribi (ind.) (Acting)
Social Affairs	Mohamed Trabelsi (ind.)
Tourism and Handicrafts	Selma Elloumi Rekik (*Nidaa Tounes*) [f]
Transport	Anis Ghedira (*Nidaa Tounes*)
Women, Family and Children	Naziha Laabidi (ind.) [f]
Youth and Sports	Majdouline Cherni (ind.) [f]

[f] = female

INTERGOVERNMENTAL REPRESENTATION

Ambassador to the U.S.: Fayçal GOUIA.

U.S. Ambassador to Tunisia: Daniel RUBINSTEIN.

Permanent Representative to the UN: Mohamed Khaled KHIARI.

IGO Memberships (Non-UN): AfDB, AU, IOM, LAS, NAM, OIC, WTO.

For Further Reference:

Alexander, Christopher. *Tunisia: From Stability to Revolution in the Maghreb.* 2nd ed. New York: Routledge, 2016.

King, Stephen J. *Liberalization against Democracy: The Local Politics of Economic Reform in Tunisia.* Bloomington: University of Indiana Press, 2003.

Willis, Michael. *Politics and Power in the Maghreb: Algeria, Tunisia, and Morocco from Independence to the Arab Spring.* Oxford: Oxford University Press, 2014.

TURKEY

Republic of Turkey
Türkiye Cumhuriyeti

Political Status: Independent republic established in 1923; parliamentary democracy since 1946, save for military interregna from May 1960 to October 1961 and September 1980 to November 1983; present constitution approved by referendum of November 7, 1982.

Area: 300,948 sq. mi. (779,452 sq. km).

Population: 79,622,000 (2016E—UN); 80,274,604 (2016E—U.S. Census).

Major Urban Centers (2016E—UN): ANKARA (4,852,000), İstanbul (14,365,000), İzmir (3,090,000), Bursa (1,974,000), Adana (1,879,000), Gaziantep (1,567,000), Konya (1,226,000).

Official Language: Turkish. A 1982 law banning the use of the Kurdish language was rescinded in early 1991.

Monetary Unit: Turkish Lira (*Türk Lirası*—TL) (market rate October 1, 2016: 3.00 Turkish New Liras = $1US).

President of the Republic: Recep Tayyip ERDOĞAN (Justice and Development Party); elected in presidential elections on August 10, 2014, and inaugurated on August 28, succeeding Abdullah GÜL (Justice and Development Party).

Prime Minister: Binali YILDIRIM (Justice and Development Party); appointed by the president and sworn in on May 24, 2016, succeeding Ahmet DAVUTOĞLU (Justice and Development Party), who resigned that day.

THE COUNTRY

Guardian of the narrow straits between the Mediterranean and Black seas, present-day Turkey occupies the compact land mass of the Anatolian Peninsula together with the partially European city of İstanbul and its Thracian hinterland. The country, which borders on Greece, Bulgaria, Georgia, Armenia, the Nakhichevan Autonomous Republic of Azerbaijan, Iran, Iraq, and Syria, has a varied topography and is subject to extreme variation in climate. It supports a largely Turkish population (approximately 75 percent in terms of language) but has a substantial Kurdish minority of approximately 14 million, plus such smaller groups as Arabs, Circassians, Greeks, Armenians, Georgians, Lazes, and Jews. Some 99 percent of the populace, including both Turks and Kurds, are Muslim (the majority are Sunni). Islam remains a strong influence despite the secular emphasis of government policy since the 1920s.

Women constitute approximately 30 percent of the official labor force according to 2016 World Bank data, with large numbers serving as unpaid workers on family farms. While only 10 percent of the urban labor force is female, there is extensive participation by upper-income women in such professions as medicine, law, banking, and education, with the government being headed by a female prime minister from 1993 to 1995. In the November 2015 parliamentary election, women secured 82 seats, or 14.9 percent of the total.

Turkey is traditionally an agricultural country, with about 30 percent of the population still engaged in agricultural pursuits. Grain (most importantly wheat), tobacco, cotton, nuts, fruits, and olive oil are the chief agricultural products; sheep and cattle are raised on the Anatolian plateau, and the country ranks among the leading producers of mohair. Natural resources include chrome, copper, iron ore, manganese, bauxite, borax, and petroleum. The most important industries are textiles, iron and steel, sugar, food processing, cement, paper, and fertilizer. State economic enterprises (SEEs) account for more than 60 percent of fixed investment, although substantial privatization has been implemented.

After suffering a financial crisis in late February 2001, a "rescue package" from the International Monetary Fund (IMF) aided a rebound, and the Turkish economy averaged growth of 4.7 percent in 2000–2008, while inflation averaged 24.9 percent (although the average inflation between 2004 and 2008 was 9.1 percent following a currency conversion). The economic stabilization was in large part due to banking reforms, privatization, and debt reduction.

In April 2006 parliament approved a long-sought social security reform bill, raising the retirement age to 65 and including measures to deter abuse. The 2009 global economic crisis impacted the Turkish economy, sharply decreasing exports, and causing GDP to decline by 4.8 percent. The following year, GDP rebounded with 9.2 percent growth, mainly due to rising exports to the European Union (EU), which carried over to support growth of 8.5 percent in 2011. In 2012 GDP growth fell to 2.6 percent, and grew by 3.4 percent in 2013, the same year the IMF encouraged implementation of policies to reduce external vulnerabilities. GDP grew by 2.9 percent in 2014 and 3.8 percent in 2015. The IMF estimated that GDP expanded by 3.8 percent in 2016, while inflation was 9.8 percent and unemployment was 10.8 percent. GDP per capita was $9,562. In its 2016 ease of doing business survey, the World Bank ranked Turkey 55th out of 189 countries.

GOVERNMENT AND POLITICS

Political background. Present-day Turkey is the surviving core of a vast empire created by Ottoman rule in late medieval and early

modern times. After a period of expansion during the 15th and 16th centuries in which Ottoman domination was extended over much of central Europe, the Balkans, the Middle East, and North Africa, the empire underwent a lengthy period of contraction and fragmentation, finally dissolving in the aftermath of a disastrous alliance with Germany in World War I.

A secular nationalist republic was proclaimed on October 29, 1923, by Mustafa Kemal ATATÜRK, who launched a reform program under which Turkey abandoned much of its Ottoman and Islamic heritage. Its major components included secularization (separation of religion and state), establishment of state control of the economy, and creation of a new Turkish national identity. Following his death in 1938, Atatürk's Republican People's Party (*Cumhuriyet Halk Partisi*—CHP) continued as the only legally recognized party under his close associate, İsmet İNÖNÜ. One-party domination was not seriously contested until after World War II, when the opposition Democratic Party (*Demokrat Parti*—DP) was established by Celal BAYAR, Adnan MENDERES, and others.

Winning the country's first free election in 1950, the DP ruled Turkey for the next decade, only to be ousted in 1960 by a military coup led by Gen. Cemal GÜRSEL. The military justified the coup as a response to alleged corruption within the DP and the growing authoritarian attitudes of its leaders. Many of those so charged, including President Bayar and Prime Minister Menderes, were tried by martial courts and found guilty of violating the constitution, after which Bayar was imprisoned and Menderes and two of his ministers were executed.

Civilian government was restored under a new constitution in 1961, with Gürsel remaining as president until he suffered a stroke, and was replaced by Gen. Cevdet SUNAY in 1966. The 1961 basic law established a series of checks and balances to offset a concentration of power in the executive and prompted a diffusion of parliamentary seats among several parties. A series of coalition governments, most of them led by İnönü, functioned until 1965, when a partial reincarnation of the DP, Süleyman DEMİREL's Justice Party (*Adalet Partisi*—AP), won a sweeping legislative mandate.

Following its 1965 victory, the Demirel regime became the target of popular discontent. Although surviving the election of 1969, it was subsequently caught between left-wing agitation and military insistence on the maintenance of public order, a critical issue because of mounting economic and social unrest and the growth of political terrorism. The crisis came to a head in 1971 with an ultimatum from the military that resulted in Demirel's resignation and the formation of a "nonparty" government by Nihat ERİM. The new government amended the 1961 constitution, declared martial law in eleven provinces, arrested dissident elements, and outlawed the left-wing Turkish Workers Party (*Türkiye İşçi Partisi*—TİP) and the moderate Islamist National Order Party (*Millî Nizam Partisi*—MNP). The period immediately after the fall of the Erim government in 1972 witnessed another "nonparty" administration under Ferit MELEN and the selection of a new president, Adm. (Ret.) Fahri KORUTÜRK. Political instability was heightened further by an inconclusive election in 1973 and by both foreign and domestic policy problems stemming from a rapidly deteriorating economy, substantial urban population growth, and renewed conflict on Cyprus, which led to a Turkish invasion of the island in the summer of 1974.

Bülent ECEVİT was appointed prime minister in January 1974, heading a coalition of his own moderately progressive CHP and the smaller, more religious National Salvation Party (*Millî Selâmet Partisi*—MSP). Despite securing widespread domestic acclaim for the Cyprus action and for his insistence that the island be formally divided into Greek and Turkish federal regions, Ecevit was opposed by Deputy Prime Minister Necmettin ERBAKAN, who called for outright annexation of the Turkish sector and, along with his MSP colleagues, resigned, precipitating Ecevit's own resignation in September. After both Ecevit and former prime minister Demirel failed to form new governments, Sadi IRMAK, an independent, was designated prime minister on November 17, heading an essentially nonparliamentary cabinet. Following a defeat in the National Assembly only twelve days later, Irmak also was forced to resign, although he remained in office in a caretaker capacity until Demirel succeeded in forming a Nationalist Front coalition government on April 12, 1975.

At an early general election on June 5, 1977, no party succeeded in gaining a lower house majority, and the Demirel government fell on July 13. Following Ecevit's inability to organize a majority coalition, Demirel returned as head of a tripartite administration that failed to survive a vote of confidence on December 31. Ecevit then returned to his former position, organizing a minority government.

Widespread civil and political unrest throughout 1978 prompted a declaration of martial law in 13 provinces on December 25. The security situation deteriorated further during 1979, and, faced with a number of ministerial defections, Prime Minister Ecevit was obliged to step down again on October 16, with Demirel returning as head of an AP minority government on November 12.

Divided by rising foreign debt and increasing domestic terrorism, the National Assembly failed to elect a president to succeed Fahri Korutürk, despite casting over 100 ballots. Senate president İhsan Sabri ÇAĞLAYANGİL assumed the office on an acting basis at the expiration of Korutürk's seven-year term on April 6. On August 29 Gen. Kenan EVREN, chief of the General Staff, publicly criticized the assembly for its failure both to elect a new president and to promulgate more drastic security legislation, and on September 12 he mounted a coup on behalf of a five-man National Security Council (NSC) that suspended the constitution, dissolved the assembly, proclaimed martial law in all of the country's 67 provinces, and on September 21 designated a military-civilian cabinet under Adm. (Ret.) Bülent ULUSU. The junta banned all existing political parties, detaining many of their leaders, including Ecevit and Demirel; imposed strict censorship; and arrested upwards of 40,000 persons on political charges.

In a national referendum on November 7, 1982, Turkish voters overwhelmingly approved a new constitution, under which General Evren was formally designated as president of the Republic for a seven-year term. One year later, on November 6, 1983, the recently established Motherland Party (*Anavatan Partisi*—ANAP) of former deputy prime minister Turgut ÖZAL won a majority of seats in a newly constituted unicameral Grand National Assembly. Following the election, General Evren's four colleagues on the NSC resigned their military commands, continuing as members of a Presidential Council upon dissolution of the NSC on December 6. On December 7 Özal was asked to form a government and assumed office as prime minister on December 13.

Turkish voters rebuked Prime Minister Özal on March 26, 1989, when ANAP candidates ran a poor third overall, securing only 22 percent of the vote and losing control of the three largest cities. Özal refused, however, to call for new legislative balloting and, despite a plunge in personal popularity to 28 percent, utilized his assembly majority on October 31 to secure the presidency in succession to Evren. Following his inauguration at a parliamentary ceremony on November 9 that was boycotted by opposition members, Özal announced his choice of Assembly Speaker Yıldırım AKBULUT as the new prime minister.

Motherland's standing in the opinion polls slipped to a minuscule 14 percent in the wake of a political crisis that erupted in April 1991 over the somewhat heavy-handed installation of the president's wife, Semra Özal, as chair of the ruling party's İstanbul branch. Both Özals declared their neutrality in a leadership contest at a party congress in mid-June, but they were viewed as the principal architects of an unprecedented challenge to Prime Minister Akbulut, who was defeated for reelection as chair by former foreign minister Mesut YILMAZ.

Yılmaz called for an early election on October 20, 1991, "to refresh the people's confidence" in his government. The outcome, however, was a defeat for the ruling party, with former prime minister Demirel, now leader of the right-of-center True Path Party (*Doğru Yol Partisi*—DYP), negotiating a coalition with the left-of-center Social Democratic People's Party (*Sosyal Demokrat Halkçı Parti*—SHP) and returning to office for the seventh time on November 21, with the SHP's Erdal İNÖNÜ as his deputy.

Demirel's broad-based administration, which brought together the heirs of Turkey's two oldest and most prominent political traditions (the CHP and the DP), claimed greater popularity—50 percent voter support and more than 60 percent backing in the polls—than any government in recent decades. Thus encouraged, Demirel and İnönü launched an ambitious program to counter the problems of rampant inflation, Kurdish insurgency, and obstacles to full democratization.

On April 17, 1993, President Özal died of a heart attack, and on May 16 the Grand National Assembly elected Prime Minister Demirel head of state. The DYP's search for a new chair ended on June 13, when Tansu ÇİLLER, an economics professor, defeated two other candidates at an extraordinary party congress. On July 5 a new DYP-SHP coalition government, committed to a program of further democratization, secularization, and privatization, was accorded a vote of confidence by the assembly, and Çiller became Turkey's first female prime minister.

A major offensive against guerrillas of the Kurdistan Workers' Party (*Partîya Karkerên Kurdistan*—PKK) in northern Iraq was launched on March 20, 1995. Six weeks later the government announced that the operation had been a success and that all of its units had returned to Turkey. The popularity of the action was demonstrated in local elections on June 4, when the ruling DYP took 22 of 36 mayoralties on a 39 percent share of the vote. However, on September 20 a revived CHP, which had become the DYP's junior coalition partner after absorbing the SHP in February, withdrew its support, forcing the resignation of the Çiller government. (The SHP has since left the CHP.)

On October 2, 1995, Çiller announced the formation of a DYP minority administration that drew unlikely backing from the far-right Nationalist Action Party (*Milliyetçi Hareket Partisi*—MHP) and the center-left Democratic Left Party (*Demokratik Sol Parti*—DSP). However, the prime minister was opposed within the DYP by former National Assembly speaker Hüsamettin CİNDORUK, who resigned on October 1 and was one of ten deputies expelled from the party on October 16, one day after Çiller's defeat on a confidence motion. On October 31 President Demirel appointed Çiller to head a DYP-CHP interim government pending a premature election in December.

At the December 24, 1995, balloting the pro-Islamic Welfare Party (*Refah Partisi*—RP) emerged as the legislative leader, although its 158 seats fell far short of the 276 needed for an overall majority. Eventually, on February 28, 1996, agreement was reached on a center-right coalition that would permit the ANAP's Yılmaz to serve as prime minister until January 1, 1997, with Çiller occupying the post for the ensuing two years and Yılmaz returning for the balance of the parliamentary term, assuming no dissolution.

Formally launched on March 12, 1996, the ANAP-DYP coalition collapsed at the end of May amid renewed personal animosity between Yılmaz and Çiller over the former's unwillingness to back the DYP leader against corruption charges related to her recent premiership. The DYP then opted to become the junior partner in an alternative coalition headed by RP leader Necmettin ERBAKAN, who on June 28 became Turkey's first avowedly Islamist prime minister since the creation of the secular republic in 1923. Under the coalition agreement, Çiller was slated to take over as head of government in January 1998. However, on February 28, 1997, the military members of the National Security Council (*Milli Güvenlik Kurulu*—MGK) presented the civilian members of the council with a memorandum, reportedly expressing their concern that Erbakan's tolerance for rising religious activism would seriously threaten the country's secular tradition. Erbakan resigned on June 18, 1997, seemingly paving way for the leadership of his coalition partner, Çiller. However, on June 20 President Demirel bypassed Çiller, whose DYP had been weakened by steady defections, and selected the ANAP's Yılmaz to return as the next prime minister. A new coalition composed of the ANAP, the DSP, and the new center-right Democratic Turkey Party (*Demokrat Türkiye Partisi*—DTP) was approved by Demirel on June 30, and Yılmaz and his cabinet were sworn in on the following day.

The new coalition government in July 1997 proposed an eight-year compulsory education plan that included the closure of Islamic secondary schools, prompting weeks of right-wing and militant Islamic demonstrations.

The Yılmaz government collapsed on November 25, 1998, when he lost a vote of confidence in the Grand National Assembly following accusations of corruption against members of his cabinet. President Demirel asked Bülent Ecevit to form a new government on December 2, thereby abandoning the long-standing tradition of designating the leader of the largest party in the legislature as prime minister. (Such action would have put Recai KUTAN's moderate Islamist Virtue Party [*Fazilet Partisi*—FP] in power, an option opposed by the military.) When Ecevit proved unable to form a government, Demirel turned to an independent, Yalım EREZ, who also failed when former prime minister Çiller rejected his proposal that her DYP be part of a new coalition. After Erez abandoned his initiative on January 6, 1999, President Demirel again invited Ecevit to form the government. This time Ecevit succeeded in forming a minority cabinet made up of the DSP and independents; the DYP and ANAP agreed to provide external support.

Ecevit's cabinet survived a crisis that erupted in mid-March 1999, when the FP threatened to topple the government and joined forces with disgruntled members of parliament from various political parties who were not nominated for reelection. In balloting on April 18, 1999, Ecevit's DSP received 22 percent of the votes and became the largest party in the assembly, with 136 seats. On May 28 Ecevit announced the formation of a coalition cabinet comprising the DSP, MHP, and ANAP. Meanwhile, on May 16 Ahmet Necdet SEZER, chief justice of the Constitutional Court, was sworn in as the new president, following the legislature's rejection of President Demirel's request for constitutional revision that would have permitted him a second term.

In October 2001 the Grand National Assembly approved several constitutional amendments aimed at easing Turkey's path into the EU. The changes provided greater protection for political freedom and civil leaders, including protection for the Kurdish minority. Moreover, the number of civilians on the National Security Council was increased from five to nine, with the military continuing to hold five seats.

In January 2002 the Constitutional Court banned Justice and Development (AKP) leader Recep Tayyip ERDOĞAN from running for the legislature because of alleged seditious activities and ordered his removal from party leadership. In July Prime Minister Ecevit was forced to call early elections to the Grand National Assembly in the wake of the DSP-led coalition having lost its majority due to resignations. Subsequently, the DSP won only 1.2 percent of the vote and no seats in the November 3 election, as the AKP gained control with 34.3 percent of the vote and 363 seats. The CHP won 19.4 percent of the vote and 178 seats.

With Erdoğan prohibited from holding a seat in the assembly, the AKP's deputy leader, Abdullah GÜL, was appointed prime minister, though Erdoğan reportedly acted as de facto prime minister. Meanwhile, the AKP majority adopted constitutional changes that allowed Erdoğan to run for parliament, and in a March 9, 2003, by-election, Erdoğan won. Five days later he was appointed prime minister.

Also in March 2003 Turkey's Constitutional Court banned the People's Democracy Party (HADEP) from politics as a result of its alleged support for the PKK. In addition, 46 party members were individually banned from politics for five years. In September 2003 the PKK announced that it was ending its five-year cease-fire with the Turkish government. In a September 2004 offensive, the largest in five years, government troops killed 11 Kurdish rebels in the southeast province of Hakkari. The government blamed Kurdish rebels for a series of bombings in August and September.

The AKP boasted a strong showing in local elections on March 28, 2004, winning 42 percent of the vote, well ahead of the second-place CHP with 18 percent. Parliament adopted further reforms aimed at promoting Turkey's accession to the EU, including measures allowing broadcasting and education in Kurdish. Another law, enacted after an override of President Sezer's veto, allowed peaceful advocacy of an independent Kurdish state.

In early March 2006 tensions between Islamic and secular forces were evident in President Sezer's veto of the government's nominee for central bank governor, BÜYÜKDENİZ, speculated to have been nominated because of his religious convictions.

The killing of a Catholic priest in Trabzon in February 2006 preceded a series of killings of Christians, including three Protestants in the eastern city of Malatya on April 18. These were followed by the killing of Hrant Dink, an ethnic Armenian journalist, in January 2007 in

Istanbul, which sparked demonstrations over democratization and protection of minorities.

Prime Minister Erdoğan's nomination of Foreign Minister Gül as the AKP candidate for the May 2007 presidential election prompted widespread anxiety among secular elites and the military, who claimed that Gül's Islamist leanings made him unfit for office in Turkey's secular system. The military issued a memorandum publicly opposing Gül's candidacy and asserting that the military could not remain indifferent to the threat of an Islamist takeover. On April 27 and May 5 opposition parties boycotted presidential election votes, and Gül withdrew as a candidate. Meanwhile, the Constitutional Court ruled that a quorum of two thirds, or 367 members, was necessary for a legal presidential election. Erdoğan called for early general elections on July 22, a measure parliament unanimously approved. The assembly voted to amend the constitution to allow for direct popular election of the president, but the measure was vetoed by President Sezer. Two subsequent attempts on behalf of parliament to amend the constitution were vetoed by Sezer.

In the July 2007 early elections, the AKP secured a stunning victory with 46.7 percent of votes and 341 seats, after campaigning on economic growth, proposed constitutional amendments aimed at democratic reforms, and progress toward EU accession. The AKP enjoyed unprecedented electoral support in Kurdish regions as a result of reforms that promoted minority rights. The CHP and the MHP won 98 and 71 seats, respectively. Several smaller parties managed to circumvent the threshold and achieve small representation via coalitions or independent candidacies. Following the strong showing of the AKP, Gül, again nominated by Erdoğan, received 339 votes in parliament on August 28 to become president of the republic.

Meanwhile, the AKP, with the support of the Motherland Party (*Anavatan Partisi*—ANAP), in mid-2007 passed a law reducing from 120 to 45 the number of days required for holding a referendum on the AKP's amendment package, which was vehemently opposed by the military. On October 21, 69 percent of voters approved the constitutional amendments providing for the direct election of the president, reducing the presidential term from seven years to five, allowing the president to stand for a second term, and reducing the parliamentary quorum to 184 members.

Earlier in 2008, 33 people were arrested for their alleged participation in an organization accused of destabilizing the country through assassinations and bombings attributed to Islamist or Kurdish terrorists. Named after the mythical birthplace of the Turkish nation, "Ergenekon" reportedly intended to maximize polarization, wreak havoc in Turkish society and, thus, precipitate a military coup. Those arrested included the leader of the Workers' Party, Doğu Perinçek; the former rector of the University of Istanbul; and the chief editor of the secularist daily *Cumhuriyet*. The discovery of "Ergenekon" operations by the state prosecutor reinforced allegations of planned military coups in 2003 and 2004. On July 1, 2008, a new round of arrests included three retired generals; the chair of the Ankara Chamber of Commerce, and the Ankara bureau chief of the secularist *Cumhuriyet* daily. Further arrests followed throughout 2008 and into 2009. Concern grew among some observers over the possible use of the Ergenekon investigation as a tool against government opposition.

Controversy over the role of Islam in public life continued after the election, as in June 2008 the Constitutional Court annulled a constitutional amendment lifting a ban on women wearing headscarves on university campuses. A parliamentary majority, led by the AKP and the MHP, had supported a constitutional amendment to lift the ban. Subsequently, secular parties, fearing the Islamist leanings of the AKP, called for the party to be disbanded. In July the Constitutional Court ruled against the banning of the AKP, though it found the party guilty of "antisecularist activities."

Following the poor performance of the AKP in the March 2009 municipal elections, in which the AKP lost several key cities, Erdoğan reshuffled the cabinet on May 1. His appointments included his long-time foreign policy adviser Ahmet DAVUTOĞLU as foreign minister. Davutoğlu's appointment was seen by observers as a move toward enhancing Turkey's relations with the Middle East, among other things. In October, after years of declining electoral success, the ANAP merged with the DP (see Political Parties, below).

On March 22 the AKP introduced a range of constitutional amendments designed to strengthen the powers of the government in relation to Turkey's traditionally secular institutions, including the military and the judiciary. The AKP failed to secure the needed two-thirds majority in the Parliament to adopt the amendments, forcing Erdoğan to present the measures in a national referendum. On July 7 the Constitutional Court rejected two of the amendments, but allowed 26 others to be put forward in a referendum on September 12. The constitutional changes were approved with 58 percent in favor (see Constitution and government, below). All of the major opposition parties opposed the amendments.

In legislative balloting on June 12, 2011, the AKP won a reduced majority in the 550-member assembly, with 327 seats. The majority fell short of the two-thirds needed to revise the constitution. On June 29 Erdoğan was reappointed prime minister of a reshuffled, smaller cabinet.

Erdoğan orchestrated a cabinet reshuffle in January 2013, replacing four ministers with close allies of the administration. A significant cabinet reshuffle occurred in December 2013 following a sweeping corruption probe. After a posting significant victory in the municipal elections of March 2014, the AKP reinforced its dominance in the presidential elections of August 10, 2014, in which Erdoğan was elected president. Ahmet Davutoğlu became the prime minister and reorganized the cabinet.

In parliamentary elections on June 7, 2015, the AKP failed to secure an overall majority of seats for the first time since 2002. It won 258 seats, followed by the CHP with 132, and the MHP and the People's Democratic Party (*Halkların Demokratik Partisi*—HDP) with 80 seats each. Davutoğlu remained prime minister as coalition talks among opposition groups failed to produce a new government, and on November 1, 2015, early elections were held. The AKP won a majority with 317 seats, and Davutoğlu was reappointed prime minister.

On May 5, 2016, Davutoğlu resigned as AKP leader and prime minister. Binali YILDIRIM, a close ally of Erdoğan, was confirmed as prime minister on May 24. Davutoğlu's resignation was reportedly the result of rising conflict with Erdoğan over the president's efforts to strengthen the powers of his office. A reshuffled government was named the same day. Erdoğan used a failed July coup attempt to launch a broad campaign to suppress dissent and target opposition groups (see Current issues, below).

Constitution and government. The 1982 constitution provided for a unicameral 400-member Grand National Assembly elected for a five-year term (the membership being increased to 450 in 1987 and 550 in 1995). The president, elected by the assembly for a five-year term, renewable once, is empowered to appoint and dismiss the prime minister and other cabinet members; to dissolve the assembly and call for a new election, assuming the concurrence of two-thirds of the deputies or if faced with a government crisis of more than 30 days' duration; to declare a state of emergency, during which the government may rule by decree; and to appoint a variety of leading government officials, including senior judges and the governor of the Central Bank. Political parties may be formed if they are not based on class or ethnicity, linked to trade unions, or committed to communism, fascism, or religious fundamentalism. Strikes that exceed 60 days' duration are subject to compulsory arbitration.

In 2003 the constitution was amended to change the membership and rules of operation of the country's National Security Council (*Milli Güvenlik Kurulu*-MGK), which has served as one of the most important levers for the control of Turkish politics by the military. The amendments reduced the number of council seats reserved for the military. For the first time in its history, the MGK had a civilian majority and a civilian secretary general.

Further amendments approved in 2007 provide for the direct election of the president every four years, reducing the presidential term from seven years to five, and allowing the president to stand for a second term (see Current issues, below). Amendments enacted in 2010 reduced the authority of the military to intervene in civilian affairs and made it easier for military officers to be charged by civilian authorities. The number of Constitutional Court justices was increased and Parliament was given greater control over the selection of judges. The measures also expanded civil liberties and made it more difficult to suspend political parties.

The Turkish judicial system is headed by a Court of Cassation (*Yargıtay*), which is the court of final appeal. Other judicial bodies include an administrative tribunal styled the Council of State (*Danıştay*), a Constitutional Court (*Anayasa Mahkemesi*), a Court of Accounts (*Sayıştay*), various military courts, and 12 state security courts.

The country is presently divided into 82 provinces, which are further divided into subprovinces and districts. Mayors and municipal councils have long been popularly elected, save during the period 1980–1984.

After decades of censorship, freedom of the press was largely restored in the first half of the 1990s. On July 21, 1997, the Council of Ministers accepted a draft granting amnesty to imprisoned journalists. Under current law, however, journalists still face prosecution and imprisonment for reporting on issues deemed sensitive by the government. Article 301 of the Turkish Penal Code, which punishes those who "publicly denigrate Turkishness or the Republic of Turkey," has been repeatedly invoked to allow persecution of journalists and intellectuals who express opinions contrary to official Turkish views on a number of political issues, such as the Armenian question. Hrant DİNK and Orhan PAMUK were targeted based on the code.

Concerns were raised in April 2008 over apparent government involvement in efforts to promote concentration of media ownership. Financial support of state banks to progovernment entrepreneurs to facilitate the purchase of the Sabah media group was seen as an overt government attempt to strengthen its grip over media.

The government's long-standing feud with the country's biggest media conglomerate, Dogan Media Group (*Doğan Medya Grubu*), attracted international attention following the levying of a $500 million tax fine against the group in February 2009. In October 2010 Turkey opened access to the Website *YouTube* for the first time since 2008 but banned it again in November. A report by the EU indicated that Turkey continued to block more Websites than any other European country. In 2014 the media watchdog group Reporters Without Borders ranked Turkey 154th out of 180 countries in terms of freedom of the press, and called the country "the world's biggest prison for journalists," estimating some 50 media professionals to be imprisoned. Reports of journalists being targeted by police with violence and arbitrary arrest during the Gezi Park protests in 2013 drew international criticism. Ahead of the March 2014 municipal elections, the government imposed an Internet ban on the social media sites Twitter and YouTube. In 2016 Reporters Without Borders ranked Turkey 151th out of 180 countries for press freedom. Since the July 2016 failed coup attempt, recent news sources have reported that more than 130 broadcast stations and newspapers had been shuttered by the government (see Current issues, below).

Foreign relations. Neutral until the closing months of World War II, Turkey entered that conflict in time to become a founding member of the United Nations and has since joined all of the latter's affiliated agencies. Concern for the protection of its independence, primarily against possible Soviet threats, made Turkey a firm ally of the Western powers, with one of the largest standing armies in the non-Communist world. Largely on U.S. initiative, Turkey was admitted to the North Atlantic Treaty Organization (NATO) in 1952 and in 1955 became a founding member of the Baghdad Treaty Organization, later the Central Treaty Organization (CENTO), which was officially disbanded in September 1979, following the Iranian and Pakistani withdrawals.

Relations with a number of Western governments stagnated in the 1960s, partly because of tensions over Cyprus. The dispute, with the fate of the Turkish Cypriot community at its center, became critical upon the island's attainment of independence in 1960 and nearly led to war with Greece in 1967. The 1974 Greek junta coup resulted in the temporary ouster of Cypriot president Makarios, and the subsequent Turkish invasion on July 20 yielded Turkish occupation of the northern third of the island. (For details, see the entries on Cyprus and Cyprus: Turkish Sector.)

Relations with the United States, strained by a congressional ban on military aid following the Cyprus incursion, were further undermined by a Turkish decision in July 1975 to repudiate a 1969 defense cooperation agreement and force the closure of 25 U.S. military installations. However, a new accord concluded in March 1976 called for reopening of the bases under Turkish control and substantially increased American military assistance. The U.S. arms embargo was finally lifted in September 1978, with the stipulation that Turkey continue to seek a negotiated resolution of the Cyprus issue.

While the Turkish government under Evren and Özal consistently affirmed its support of NATO and its desire to gain full entry to the EC (having been an associate member of the European Economic Community since 1964), relations with Western Europe deteriorated in the wake of the 1980 coup because of alleged human rights violations.

Ankara submitted a formal membership request to the EC, and in December 1989 the commission had laid down a number of stringent conditions for admission to the community, including an improved human rights record, progress toward improved relations with Greece, and less dependence on agricultural employment. Because of these concerns, Turkey remained outside the EU upon the latter's inception in November 1993, although, in an action viewed as linked to its EC bid, it had become an associate member of the Western European Union in 1992.

On March 6, 1995, Turkey and the EU agreed to a customs union, which entered into force on January 1, 1996. However, in July 1997 the EU Commission excluded Turkey from first-round enlargement negotiations scheduled for early 1998. Moreover, the commission recommended Cyprus for full membership, a decision that Turkey saw as controversial given the lack of a settlement of the Cyprus question. In light of improving Turkish–Greek relations, a December 1999 EU summit finally accepted Turkey as an official candidate for membership.

Apart from Cyprus, the principal dispute between Greece and Turkey has centered on territorial rights in the Aegean. In late 1984 Ankara rejected a proposal by Prime Minister Papandreou to assign Greek forces on Limnos to NATO, invoking a long-standing contention that militarization of the island was forbidden under the 1923 Treaty of Lausanne. The controversy revived in early 1989 with Turkey refusing to recognize insular sea and airspace limits greater than six miles on the premise that to do otherwise would convert the area into a "Greek lake." The dispute intensified in September 1994, with Greece declaring that it would formally extend its jurisdiction to 12 nautical miles upon entry into force of the UN Convention on the Law of the Sea on November 16. Turkey warned that the move would be considered an "act of aggression," and on October 30 Athens announced that it would defer expansion. On June 8, 1995, the Turkish Parliament approved a declaration that an extension of Greek territorial waters in the Aegean to 12 miles would comprise a *casus belli* for Turkey, further straining bilateral relations with Greece.

Another territorial issue was addressed when Turkey concluded an agreement with Iraq in October 1984 that permitted the security forces of each government to pursue "subversive groups" (interpreted primarily as Kurdish rebels) up to a distance of five kilometers on either side of the border and to engage in follow-up operations for five days without prior notification.

However, the Turkish government strongly supported UN-endorsed sanctions against Iraq in the wake of its invasion of Kuwait in August 1990. Turkey moved quickly to shut down Iraqi oil pipelines by banning ships from loading crude at offshore terminals. In September the legislature granted the administration special authority to dispatch troops to the Gulf and to allow foreign forces to be stationed on Turkish soil for non-NATO purposes (importantly, the stationing of F-111 fighter bombers at İncirlik air base to monitor the UN-sanctioned Iraqi no-fly zone north of the 36th parallel).

Turkey's attention refocused on maritime issues in 1994 as Ankara angered Moscow by seeking to impose restrictions on shipping through the Bosporus, despite the 1936 Montreux treaty, which provided complete freedom of transit through both the Bosporus and Dardanelles during peacetime. Turkey insisted that the new regulations were prompted only by technical considerations that had not existed at the time of the treaty's adoption.

During the 1992 conflict in Bosnia and Herzegovina, both the Bosnians and Turkish citizens of Bosnian descent appealed for action to oppose Serbian advances in Muslim areas; however, Atatürk's secularist heirs were reluctant to move in a manner that might be seen as religiously inspired. Urging limited military intervention, Turkey launched a pro-Bosnian campaign in various international venues, including the UN, the Conference on (subsequently the Organization for) Security and Cooperation in Europe (CSCE/OSCE), NATO, the Council of Europe, and the OIC.

Turkey commenced its own military action on March 20, 1995, targeting the Kurds in northern Iraq, provoking condemnation from West European governments. On April 10 the EU foreign ministers called on Ankara to withdraw troops "without delay." On April 26 the Parliamentary Assembly of the Council of Europe approved a resolution calling for suspension of Turkey's membership if it did not leave Iraq by late June. The Turkish government reacted angrily to an April 12 announcement that political exiles had established a Kurdish "parliament in exile" in the Netherlands. A renewed cross-border offensive was launched by some 30,000 troops on July 5–10. (See the 2013 *Handbook* for more on Kurdish relations in the mid-1990s.)

A major diplomatic dispute erupted in 1998 over Syria's alleged sheltering of PKK rebels, with Ankara warning Damascus in October of possible military action. The crisis was also colored by Syria's concern over the recent rapprochement between Turkey and Israel. Following intense mediation by several Arab leaders from the region, Syria subsequently agreed that it would not allow the PKK to set up "military, logistical, or financial bases" on Syrian territory. Collaterally, PKK leader Abdullah ÖCALAN was forced to leave Syrian-controlled territory in Lebanon. Öcalan moved to Russia, which, under insistent Turkish pressure, also refused him asylum. He then entered Italy, prompting a row between Rome and Ankara. Italy rejected Turkey's extradition request on the grounds that it could not send a detainee to a country that permitted the death penalty, but attempted to negotiate Öcalan's transfer to Germany, where he also faced terrorism charges. However, Germany, apparently fearing violence between its own Turkish and Kurdish minorities, declined to file an extradition request. Consequently, Öcalan was released from detention in Italy in mid-December. In mid-February 1999 Öcalan was arrested shortly after he left the home of the Greek ambassador in Nairobi, Kenya. Despite the renewed animosity surrounding Öcalan's arrest, Turkish-Greek relations thawed noticeably in late 1999 when Greece lifted its veto on EU financial aid earmarked to Turkey and agreed to a European Council decision that gave Turkey the status of a candidate state for EU membership. In early 2000 the two countries agreed to establish a joint commission to "reduce military tensions" in the Aegean and to pursue cooperation in several other areas.

In 2003 Turkey's relationship with the United States faced a major challenge with Turkey's refusal to allow U.S. troops to use Turkish territory as a staging area for the invasion of Iraq in March 2003. Relations with the United States cooled because the Turkish government felt that Washington was indifferent to Kurdish terrorist activity in Turkey and northern Iraq. Indeed, in November 2004 Turkish newspapers published unconfirmed reports that the Turkish government had formulated a plan to move 20,000 Turkish troops into northern Iraq to prevent Kurds from taking complete control of Kirkuk. On January 26, 2005, a senior Turkish army general said bluntly that the Turkish military was prepared to intervene if clashes erupted in northern Iraq or if Iraqi Kurds attempted to form an independent state.

Iran and Turkey signed a security agreement on July 30, 2004, to place rebels opposed to either government on each government's list of terrorist organizations.

Relations with Russia were strained by Turkey's ongoing efforts to control the passage of oil tankers through the Bosporus straits. Turkey has maintained that the increased number of oil tankers represented an environmental threat to its coastline and waterways and has imposed tighter regulations on passage, which Russia said added greatly to transit time and thus to costs. In August 2004 Turkey also proposed, and offered to help fund, construction of pipelines to reduce waterborne traffic. Apart from the issue of the Bosporus strait, however, Turkish relations with Russia have been generally good.

Turkey's relations with the EU reached a peak on December 17, 2004, when the European Council agreed to define October 3, 2005, as the starting date of EU–Turkey accession negotiations. However, accession to the EU by the Republic of Cyprus, and the political confusion caused by popular rejection of the European Constitution, downgraded Turkish membership on the EU agenda. Negotiations followed a rather slow pace in 2005, while the reform drive that had pleasantly surprised EU entities between 1999 and 2004 seemed to have been exhausted. In 2005 and 2006, however, European officials charged Turkey's government with backtracking on some reforms and slowing implementation of others. External observers, along with some Turks, voiced concern about the growing tensions between Islamic and secular forces inside Turkey. This was complicated by the opposition of Germany and France, two of the most influential EU member states, whose political leaders objected to full EU membership for Turkey and suggested a "privileged partnership" status instead. EU representatives in recent years have cited Turkey's failure to open air and sea connections with the Republic of Cyprus as a major hurdle to membership.

Iraq resurfaced as a contentious issue between Turkey and the United States in July 2006, when Turkey again called on the United States to crack down on Kurdish rebels in northern Iraq and made veiled threats to attack rebel bases if action was not taken.

Turkey's reputation in parts of the Middle East was enhanced when it offered in May 2008 to moderate peace negotiations between Syria and Israel, the dispute over the Golan Heights considered by Turkey easier to resolve than the dispute between the Israelis and the Palestinians. In addition, a September meeting in New York between President Gül and Iraqi president Jalal Talabani further improved relations between Turkey and Iraq. A visit by Mahmoud Ahmadinejad in August, the first such visit by an Iranian president in 12 years, was seen as paving the way toward improved relations between the two countries.

The fighting between Russia and Georgia in August 2008 over the latter's sovereignty underlined the complexity of Turkish policy toward the Caucasus. As Georgia's strongest regional strategic partner, Turkey's cooperation with Georgia has focused on the construction of oil and natural gas pipelines that circumvent Russia. However, with Russia as Turkey's second biggest trade partner, bilateral relations have significantly improved in recent years. Turkey thus condemned violation of Georgia's territorial integrity and the continuation of hostilities, while at the same time Ankara tried to avoid heightened tensions with Russia by refraining from joining NATO'S most outspoken critics. In an effort to balance its Russian interests, Turkey invoked the 1936 Montreux Treaty to prohibit the immediate passage of U.S. war vessels through the Turkish straits to the Black Sea. Interestingly, a significant part of Turkey's Caucasian diaspora, which had mobilized Turkish public opinion against Russia during the Chechnya crisis, justified Russia's military intervention in 2008 by objecting to Georgia's move to restore its sovereignty over the breakaway provinces of Abkhazia and South Ossetia.

The Georgian crisis provided an opening to Armenia, which had closed its borders with Turkey in 1993 during the Armenian–Azeri war in Nagorno Karabagh. Armenia was included in Turkey's new "Caucasus Alliance" initiative, and in September President Gül accepted, despite vehement objections from the opposition, an invitation from Armenian president Serzh Sarkisyan to visit Erivan. A subsequent meeting of the foreign ministers of Turkey, Armenia, and Azerbaijan in New York raised hopes for resolution of the Nagorno Karabagh question.

Turkish–Israeli relations suffered a serious diplomatic crisis in January 2009 when Prime Minister Erdoğan quarreled with Israeli president Shimon Peres during a discussion at the annual meeting of the World Economic Forum at Davos, Switzerland. Erdoğan lashed out against Israel's Gaza operations and abandoned the forum. He was welcomed in Istanbul by jubilant crowds, who approved of his anti-Israeli stance.

The visit of U.S. president Barack Obama to Turkey in May 2009 was seen as a big boost for Turkish foreign policy, as Obama aimed to restore relations with Turkey and further promote U.S. relations with the Islamic world. Shortly before his arrival, President Obama had reiterated support for Turkey's accession to the EU, causing a clash with French president Nicolas Sarkozy, a vocal opponent of Turkey's full EU membership. While Obama's visit helped improve the image of the United States in Turkey, it failed to produce solutions for a series of long-lasting disputes, including over Armenia and the status of Kurds in northern Iraq. In April 2009 Turkey and Armenia signed a "road map" for rapprochement between the two countries. The result was a historic accord, signed on October 10, 2009, establishing diplomatic relations between the two countries for the first time. The agreement also called for reopening the Turkish–Armenian border, which has been closed since 1993, and paved the way for resolution of the century-old dispute regarding the deaths of many Armenians in the final days of the Ottoman Empire through the creation of a joint committee of historians which would review Armenia's claims of genocide.

Turkey and China signed series of trade agreements worth more than $1.1 billion in January 2010. Also in January, the European Court of Human Rights released a report claiming that, of its signatories, Turkey was the single greatest violator of the European Convention of Human Rights during the period from 1960 to 2000. In February the European Parliament called on Turkey to withdraw its troops from Cyprus and engage in reunification negotiations over the island in order to accelerate EU membership discussions. The Erdoğan government rejected the call. Membership negotiations over eight areas of EU membership were suspended by the EU as a result of Turkey's unwillingness negotiate over Cyprus. Concurrently, EU member Cyprus announced it would prevent new negotiations with Turkey over EU membership in five additional areas.

In March 2010 Turkey withdrew its ambassador from the United States after the U.S. House of Representatives adopted a resolution recognizing Turkey's actions against Armenians in the early 1900s as genocide. The Swedish legislature passed a similar measure, prompting Turkey to also recall its ambassador from Sweden. Erdoğan threatened to expel an estimated 100,000 illegal Armenian immigrants if foreign governments continued to enact comparable resolutions.

On April 22 Armenia suspended ratification of the accord with Turkey, accusing the Turkish government of imposing additional conditions in exchange for approval of the agreement. Meanwhile, also in April Gül hosted the leaders of Bosnia and Serbia in negotiations that resulted in the Istanbul Declaration, an agreement to settle a number of border and economic issues between the two countries. In June Turkey, Jordan, Lebanon, and Syria agreed to create a free trade zone by strengthening existing bilateral economic agreements.

During a raid on a convoy delivering aid to the Gaza Strip, eight Turkish activists were killed by Israeli security forces on May 31, 2010. Turkey recalled its ambassador in protest. On October 12 the assembly adopted a resolution to permit Turkish military forces to launch attacks into Northern Iraq to suppress the PKK.

On January 27, 2011, the European Court of Human Rights reported that Turkey had more human rights violations than any of the other 47 signatories to the European Convention on Human Rights. More than 10,000 Syrian refugees crossed into Turkey by the summer of 2011, fleeing growing strife in the country.

On February 18, 2011, the Erdoğan government strongly condemned U.S. ambassador Francis Ricciardone for criticizing restrictions on the Turkish press and the arrest of journalists. Tensions between Turkey and Israel also eroded U.S.–Turkish relations. In September 2011 Turkey expelled the Israeli ambassador and other senior diplomats and recalled its ambassador. It also suspended defense contracts with Israel for new weaponry. On September 12 Erdoğan announced publicly that he believed the May 2010 Israeli raid was "cause for war." Also in September, Erdoğan condemned a joint Israeli–Greek Cypriot exploratory drilling venture off Cyprus (see entry on Cyprus).

Progress on EU membership slowed in 2011 as the Erdoğan government delayed implementation of reforms needed to join the organization.

Erdoğan conducted a diplomatic tour of Egypt, Libya, and Tunisia in September 2011 as part of a broader effort to increase Turkish influence in the Mediterranean, during which Erdoğan reaffirmed Turkish support for Palestinian statehood. That same month, Turkey and the United States signed an agreement to deploy U.S. radar units as part of the NATO-backed missile defense system for Europe. In December, Erdoğan apologized for the deaths of 35 Kurdish youths who were killed in northern Iraq during a Turkish air strike. On December 22 Turkey recalled its ambassador and suspended bilateral relations with France after the French National Assembly voted to criminalize Armenian Genocide denial.

In February 2012 Turkish aircraft bombed suspected PKK bases in Northern Iraq, prompting condemnation from the Iraqi government. Turkey and Turkmenistan signed a number of bilateral economic agreements in March. In May, despite Baghdad's protests, Turkey negotiated a deal to import oil from the Kurdish region of Iraq.

On June 22, 2012, Syria shot down a Turkish plane that Damascus claimed had strayed into Syrian airspace. Ankara insisted that the plane was in Turkish airspace when it was attacked. Turkey condemned the downing and called for consultations with NATO. Relations with Syria soured further in October 2012, when Turkish civilians were killed by Syrian mortar fire along the border of the two countries. The incident prompted Turkish forces to fire into Syria for four days and deploy additional troops to the region.

In March 2013 Israeli prime minister Benjamin Netanyahu apologized to Erdoğan for the 2010 flotilla raid. Subsequently meetings were held to normalize ties between the two countries, but they stalled in June.

Turkish involvement with the Syrian crisis deepened in 2013. On May 11 two car bombs killed 53 people in Reyhanli, near the Syrian border. Turkish officials arrested nine suspects with alleged links to the Assad regime. The incident heightened tensions toward Turkey's Syrian refugee population, which by October numbered more than 600,000, according to Turkish estimates. In August Erdoğan emerged as a vocal supporter of military intervention in Syria when President Obama weighed U.S. involvement (see the entry on the United States). Turkish military actions along the border increased in the autumn.

German Chancellor Angela Merkel sharply criticized the Turkish government's handling of antigovernment protests in June 2013 (see Current issues, below), causing further postponement of EU ascension talks that were slated to resume that month. In October it was announced negotiations would resume in November after a three-year hiatus.

In September 2013 Turkey announced plans to purchase a missile defense system from a Chinese company under U.S. sanctions for violating the North Korea, Iran, and Syria Nonproliferation Act, raising objections from the United States.

In March 2014 Turkish forces shot down a Syrian military plane for violating Turkish air space near the border town of Kasab. The Turkish government reported in June that the number of Syrian refugees in Turkey had exceeded one million.

On June 11, 2014, militants from the group the Islamic State of Iraq and Syria (ISIS) seized the Turkish consulate in Mosul, Iraq, taking 49 hostages. The previous day, 32 Turkish truck drivers had been captured in Mosul, who were released in early July. Throughout the summer months, Turkey remained hesitant to take action against ISIS, balancing its concerns over the new force with its interests against Assad in Syria and the Kurdish question. The consulate hostages were released after negotiations on September 20, which, it was later revealed, involved an exchange for two Turkish-held British ISIS fighters.

The Syrian refugee crisis deepened late in September when increased activity in a Kurdish-dominated region of Syria drove an estimated 150,000 refugees to cross the border in a single week. After significant deliberation, Turkey's parliament voted to approve military operations in Iraq and Syria on October 2, signaling a step toward joining the U.S.-led campaign against ISIS. In July 2015 Turkey granted the United States and its coalition allies permission to use Incirlik Air Base to launch air strikes on ISIS targets in Syria. In February 2016 Saudi aircraft also began using the facility for raids.

Turkey repeatedly claimed that Russian aircraft violated Turkish airspace during Russia's military intervention in Syria. In October 2015 Turkish fighters shot down a Russian drone that entered Turkish airspace, and the following month a Russian aircraft was shot down. Both nations increased military deployments in the region, and Turkey increased military cooperation with Ukraine in 2016.

By the end of 2016 an estimated 2.7 million refugees had crossed into Turkey because of the Syrian conflict. Meanwhile, in August Turkey deployed ground forces against both ISIS and Kurdish fighters in northern Syria. In August 2016 Turkey and Russia undertook a series of reciprocal measures to improve relations, including renewed military cooperation in several areas.

A deal was struck in March 2016 between the EU and Turkey to halt the influx of Syrian refugees into Europe. According to news sources, the EU agreed to provide Turkey with €3 billion in economic aid and visa-free travel to Turkish citizens, and to reinvigorate talks on Turkey's EU candidacy. In the aftermath of the failed July 2016 coup attempt and President Erdoğan's continued crackdown on the opposition, the prospects of the agreement had diminished (see Current issues, below). In November 2016 the EU Parliament adopted a nonbinding measure to freeze EU membership talks with Turkey. In response, Turkey threatened to cease any efforts to prevent refugees from crossing into the EU.

Current issues. Security forces arrested more than 60 people suspected of ties to the PKK in raids across the country on January 21, 2010. The following day, nationwide raids resulted in the detention of 120 people believed to have ties with al-Qaida. On February 22 police arrested 49 current and retired senior military officers for involvement in an alleged coup. Eventually more than 196 were charged in the plot, known as "Sledgehammer." Government critics charged that the arrests were part of a government effort to reduce the independence of the military. In March General Saldiray BERK was arrested and charged with being the leader of the Ergenekon movement.

In response to actions by security forces against suspected PKK members, the organization ended a unilateral cease-fire on June 1 (see Political Parties, below, for further developments). As attacks on government and security personnel escalated through the summer, Turkish commandos launched raids into neighboring Iraq.

Major opposition figures and senior military and political officials boycotted the Republic Day, October 29, 2010, after Erdoğan announced that his wife would attend the ceremonies wearing a traditional headscarf. On December 16 trials began for the 196 military officers charged in the alleged Sledgehammer plot.

The AKP won legislative elections in June 2011. During the balloting, a number of smaller parties had their candidates campaign as independents, reducing the number of groupings that formally participated from 27 to 15. In the balloting independent candidate Erol DORA became the first Christian to be elected to the assembly since 1960.

In March 2012 a controversial new education law ended prohibitions on attendance at single-sex Islamic schools by youths under 15. The new measure prompted widespread protests by secular groups. Also in March, two more former generals were arrested in connection with the Sledgehammer plot. Twenty-nine former military officers were arrested in April for their roles in the 1997 coup. In June, the high court decreed that President Gül could stand for reelection. Gül had been elected for a seven-year term to end in 2014, but constitutional changes in 2007 reduced the term of the president to five years.

In March 2013 jailed PKK leader Abdullah Öcalan called for a cease-fire and urged the withdrawal of Kurdish rebel fighters from Turkey. On April 25 the PKK announced that all forces would be withdrawn from the country by May 8, a step Ankara considered necessary for the progression of peace talks.

On May 28, 2013, a demonstration broke out against the demolition and redevelopment of Gezi Park, a public park in central Istanbul. The eviction of activists occupying the park by police on May 31 triggered a large-scale reaction with thousands taking to the streets of Istanbul and solidarity protests breaking out in some 80 towns and cities across Turkey. Over the following week, the actions widened to represent general antigovernment sentiment. Clashes with police left at least 5 dead and some 8,000 injured. In October a new political party registered as the Gezi Party.

The PKK halted its withdrawal in September, claiming the Turkish government had failed to take steps toward "democratization and the resolution of the Kurdish problem," though the cease-fire remained in place. On September 30, 2013, Erdoğan unveiled a broad set of a reforms billed as the "democratization package." Though several measures addressed Kurdish rights—including allowing Kurdish language to be taught in private schools and decriminalizing characters found in the Kurdish but not Turkish alphabet—the PKK said the package was insufficient. Other reforms included the scaling back of the head scarf ban and the opportunity for the parliament to debate the 10 percent electoral threshold.

Some 52 people, including the sons of three cabinet ministers, were detained early on December 17, 2013, amid allegations of corruption as part of a graft probe. Some observers suggested the move was indicative of a rift within the ruling party between Erdoğan and exiled preacher Fethullah GÜLEN, leader of an Islamist movement that was an uneasy partner in the AKP's rise to power, with followers amid the top ranks of the judiciary and police. In response, the government carried out a purge of police forces and the judiciary branch, dismissing and reassigning a number of key figures over the following months.

With antigovernment sentiment running high in the wake of the December scandal, several cities seemed poised to topple AKP leadership in the March 2014 municipal elections. On March 21 the government banned the website Twitter, a microblogging site that had been very popular during the previous year's demonstrations, and less than a week later imposed a similar ban on YouTube. Despite the apparent rising popularity of opposition figures, notably the CHP's Istanbul mayoral candidate Mustafa SARIGÜL, the AKP enjoyed a sweeping victory of 45.5 percent of votes nationwide, a result widely interpreted as a vote of confidence in Erdoğan's leadership.

Following months of speculation, Prime Minister Erdoğan announced on July 1 that he would be a candidate in the country's first direct presidential election. Candidates needed to be nominated by 20 members of parliament in order to contest, a threshold the smaller parties were unable to meet. Ekmeleddin Mehmet İHSANOĞLU contested as the joint candidate for the CHP and MHP, while Selahattin DEMIRTAŞ represented the HDP. Erdoğan won 51.65 percent of the vote in the first round of balloting on August 10, 2014, thus precluding the second round of voting. Erdoğan resigned from AKP leadership on August 27 and was inaugurated on August 28. The following day, Ahmet Davutoğlu was sworn in and formed a government. Erdoğan's election represents a shift in the presidency from being a largely symbolic office to one with greater political power.

On July 15, 2016, units of the Turkish military launched a failed attempt to overthrow the Erdoğan government. Approximately 300 people were killed, and more than 2,000 injured. The government blamed Fethullah GÜLEN, a Muslim cleric in exile in the United States, for instigating the coup. In the aftermath of the failed takeover, pro-Erdoğan security forces arrested more than 40,000, including soldiers, judges, police officers, teachers, and other state employees. Media outlets were closed and approximately 125,000 state employees were sacked or suspended. Independent media sources and opposition groups accused the government of using the coup to carry out a broad purge of the military and civil service.

POLITICAL PARTIES

Turkey's multiparty system developed gradually out of the monopoly originally exercised by the historic Republican People's Party (*Cumhuriyet Halk Partisi*—CHP), which ruled the country without serious competition until 1950 and which, under Bülent Ecevit, was most recently in power from January 1978 to October 1979. The **Democratic Party** (*Demokrat Parti*—DP) of Celal Bayar and Adnan Menderes, founded by CHP dissidents in 1946, came to power in 1950 and maintained control for the next decade but was outlawed following the military coup of May 27, 1960, with many of its members subsequently entering the conservative **Justice Party** (*Adalet Partisi*—AP). Other formations included an Islamic group, the **National Salvation Party** (*Millî Selâmet Partisi*—MSP), the ultra-rightist Nationalist Action Party (*Milliyetçi Hareket Partisi*—MHP); and the leftist **Turkish Labor Party** (*Türkiye İşçi Partisi*—TİP). All party activity was banned by the National Security Council on September 12, 1980, while the parties themselves were formally dissolved and their assets liquidated on October 16, 1981. In July 1992 the government lifted bans on all of the parties.

Government Party:

Justice and Development Party (*Adalet ve Kalkınma Partisi*—AKP). The AKP was launched in August 2001 by the reformist wing of the FP (see SP, below) as a moderate religious, center-right formation. Out of the former parliamentarians from the FP and other parties, 53 later joined the AKP, making it the second-largest opposition party in the assembly (after the DYP).

In January 2002 the electoral commission ruled that AKP president Recep Tayyip Erdoğan was ineligible to run for office due to his imprisonment in 1999 on charges of having "incited hatred on religious grounds." In the November 2002 elections, the AKP won 34.3 percent of the vote and 363 legislative seats. Erdoğan's ineligibility was overturned when parliament approved a change to the constitution that allowed Erdoğan to run in a by-election in March 2003. A few days later, he was named prime minister.

The elections of July 22, 2007, gave Erdoğan the chance to shift the party toward the center. More than 150 members of parliament from the party's Islamist wing were removed from AKP candidate lists. The new party lists included prominent liberal secularists, academics, and young professionals. The crushing electoral victory, in which the party improved its margin of victory by more than 12 percent over the previous election, yielded 341 seats. (This seat share was less than in 2002 due to the electoral system but, nevertheless, consolidated the party's political dominance.)

On March 14, 2007, the chief prosecutor of the Court of Cassation sought to shut down the AKP because of the party's alleged antisecular activities. However, a ruling by the Constitutional Court in 2008 upheld the party's viability. The AKP suffered a blow in July 2008 when one of its most prominent members, former minister and member of parliament Abdülatif ŞENER, resigned and formed the **Turkey's Party** (*Türkiye Partisi*—TP) in 2009.

In municipal elections in March 2009, the AKP garnered 38.8 percent of the vote and 492 municipal seats. AKP candidates were elected in the country's biggest cities, İstanbul and Ankara. However, the results were perceived as less than satisfactory compared to the AKP's performance in the 2007 parliamentary elections.

In legislative balloting in June 2011 the AKP received 49.8 percent of the vote and secured 327 seats. Erdoğan was reappointed as prime minister. He was reelected AKP chair at the September 30, 2012, congress, his third and final term as party leader.

Widespread protests in mid-2013 seemed to articulate dissatisfaction across the country with AKP leadership, and December corruption allegations led Erdoğan to dimiss key members of his cabinet in a reshuffle. However, municipal elections in March 2014 seemingly reinforced AKP political dominance, winning about 45.5 percent of the vote (an improvement over its 2009 victory), and retaining leadership of İstanbul and Ankara. In May the party voted to retain its three-term limit, indicating that Erdoğan was preparing for a presidential run. He declared his candidacy on July 1. Erdoğan won the country's first direct presidential election on August 10. At an extraordinary congress on August 27, Erdoğan handed party leadership over to former foreign minister Ahmet Davutoğlu, which was confirmed by a largely ceremonial vote.

The AKP lost its majority in the June 2015 assembly balloting when it won 40.1 percent of the vote and 258 seats. In the November 2015 parliamentary elections, AKP received 49.5 percent of the vote and won 317 seats. Davutoğlu resigned in May 2016 and was replaced as prime minister and party chair by Erdoğan ally Binali YILDIRIM.

Leaders: Recep Tayyip ERDOĞAN (President of the Republic), Binali YILDIRIM (Prime Minister and Chair of the Party), Abdulhamit GÜL (Secretary General).

Opposition Parties:

Republican People's Party (*Cumhuriyet Halk Partisi*—CHP). The CHP is a left-of-center party founded in 1923 by Kemal Atatürk. It was dissolved in 1981 and reactivated in 1992 by 21 MPs who resigned from the **Social Democratic People's Party** (*Sosyal Demokrat Halkçı Parti*—SHP) to reclaim the group's historic legacy. The CHP absorbed the SHP on February 18, 1995.

A member of the Socialist International, the SHP was formed in November 1985 by merger of the **Populist Party** (*Halkçı Parti*—HP), a center-left formation that secured 117 seats in the 1983 Grand National Assembly election; and the **Social Democratic Party** (*Sosyal Demokrat Parti*—SODEP), which was not permitted to offer candidates for the 1983 balloting. A leftist grouping that drew much of its support from former members of the CHP, SODEP had participated in the 1984 local elections, winning 10 provincial capitals. The SHP was runner-up to ANAP in November 1987, winning 99 assembly seats despite the defection in December 1986 of 20 of its deputies, most of whom joined the DSP. Its parliamentary representation was reduced to 82 upon formation of the People's Labor Party, whose candidates were, nevertheless, entered on SHP lists for the 1991 campaign. Subsequently, 18 of those so elected withdrew from the SHP, reducing its representation to 70.

On September 20, 1995, former CHP chair Deniz BAYKAL, who had been succeeded by the SHP's Hikmet CETİN at the time of the February merger, was reelected to his earlier post. Immediately thereafter he withdrew the party from the government coalition, thereby forcing Tansu Çiller's resignation as prime minister. In the resultant December election the CHP fell back to 49 seats on a 10.7 percent vote share. Baykal's CHP gave outside support to the Yılmaz-led ANAP-DSP-DTP coalition government of June 1998. However, amid accusations of corruption against various ministers, the CHP's call for a vote of no confidence against the Yılmaz cabinet brought the coalition down in November 1998. The CHP failed to surpass the 10 percent threshold in the April 18, 1999, elections, securing only 8.5 percent of the vote, therefore left out of the assembly. Baykal resigned from his chair's post on April 22. The CHP elected famous journalist and former tourism minister Altan ÖYMEN as its new leader on May 23; however, Baykal regained the post at an extraordinary congress in October 2000. The CHP's ranks were strengthened in 2002 by defections from the DSP.

In the November 2002 elections, the CHP won 19.3 percent of the vote and 178 legislative seats, becoming the main opposition party. In October 2004 the **New Turkey Party** (*Yeni Türkiye Partisi*—YTP) merged with the CHP. (The YTP had been formed in July 2002 by former DSP cabinet ministers, including Ismail Cem, among others.)

In January 2005 Baykal's presidency was challenged at a highly explosive CHP party congress by Mustafa Sarigül, the popular mayor of the İstanbul district of Şişli, who eventually lost his bid but vowed to continue his opposition. A few pro-Sarigül legislators left the party following the congress to join the SHP (see below). By mid-2005 rifts had developed within the party, resulting in the resignations of numerous dissidents. The losses were reflected in the decline in the CHP's legislative seats, down to 154 by mid-2005.

The CHP spearheaded secularist reaction against the candidacy of Abdullah Gül, culminating in several large "Republican Demonstrations" in spring 2007. The party was accused of abandoning its leftist identity and identifying itself with the military establishment. On June 8, 2007, the **Party of Liberty and Change** (*Hürriyet ve Değişim Partisi*—HÜRPARTI) decided to merge into the CHP, though its leader Yaşar OKUYAN declared that he would not be a CHP candidate.

On the eve of the 2007 parliamentary elections, the party struck an alliance with the Democratic Left Party (*Demokratik Sol Parti*—DSP, below), and 13 members of that party ran under the CHP ticket. The party received 20.9 percent of the vote and 112 seats, which dropped to 99 when the 13 members withdrew from the CHP parliamentary group. In the aftermath of the elections, observers and party rank-and-file members expressed concerns about the CHP's future under Baykal's leadership.

The CHP continued its opposition by appealing to the Constitutional Court against AKP parliamentary decisions, such as the proposed constitutional amendment to allow women to wear headscarves in universities. CHP's identification with the most radical elements of the bureaucracy was revealed in its fierce opposition to the "Ergenekon" investigations, which it saw as an AKP ploy to rout political opponents.

In the March 2009 municipal elections, the CHP won 23.12 percent of the vote and the municipality of Izmir. At a party convention in May, Kemal KILIÇDAROĞLU was elected chair of the CHP. In May 2010 the short-lived **Democratic Left People's Party** (*Demokratik Sol Halk Partisi*—DSHP) voted to merge with the CHP (the DSHP had formed in November 2009). In legislative elections in June 2011 the CHP secured 26 percent of the vote and 135 seats. In July 2012, Kılıçdaroğlu was reelected party president.

In September Prime Minister Erdoğan accused the CHP of being behind the mass antigovernment protests that swept the country in June 2013. Şişli mayor Sarıgül rejoined the CHP in November 2013 after an eight-year suspension and, in December, was named the party's İstanbul mayoral candidate for the March 2014 municipal elections. Despite some polls showing that Sarıgül was the third most popular politician in the country, after Erdoğan and Gül, the party did not make any significant gains in the elections, winning 27.8 percent of votes. Following the defeat, the CHP fielded a joint candidate with the MHP. Former head of the Organization of Islamic Cooperation Ekmeleddin Mehmet İhsanoğlu was selected in June. Dissenting CHP members attempted to nominate their own candidate, Emine Ülker TARHAN, but she refused to stand. İhsanoğlu failed to gain the necessary support to defeat Erdoğan in the August 10 balloting, winning 38.6 percent of the vote. The CHP received 25 percent of the vote and 132 seats in the June assembly polling. In the November 2015 parliamentary elections, the CHP secured 25.3 percent of the vote and won 134 seats.

Leaders: Kemal KILIÇDAROĞLU (President), Veli AĞBABA (Deputy Chair).

Nationalist Action Party (*Milliyetçi Hareket Partisi*—MHP). Until 1969 the ultranationalist MHP was known as the **Republican Peasant Nation Party** (*Cumhuriyetçi Köylü Millet Partisi*—CKMP), formed in 1948 by conservative dissidents from the old Democratic Party. Dissolved in 1953, the grouping reformed in 1954, merging with the **Turkish Villager Party** in 1961 and sustaining the secession of the **Nation Party** in 1962.

The MHP dissolved following the 1980 military coup; in 1983 its sympathizers regrouped as the **Conservative Party** (*Muhafazakar Parti*—MP), which then was renamed the **Nationalist Labor Party** (*Milliyetçi Çalişma Partisi*—MCP) in 1985. (The MHP rubric was reassumed in 1992.) The MHP's extremist youth wing, members of which were known as the Grey Wolves (*Bozkurtlar*), remained proscribed, although similar activities were reportedly carried out under semi-official youth clubs. Holding 17 legislative seats as of September 1995, the MHP's 8.2 percent vote share on December 24 was short of the 10 percent required for continued representation. However, it subsequently acquired 2 seats from defections.

Historic MHP leader Alparslan TÜRKEŞ died in 1997. Following the election of Devlet Bahçeli as the new MHP president, members close to Türkeş's son and wife left the party to form the ATP and UBP.

The MHP won 18 percent of votes in the election of April 1999, gaining 129 assembly seats. The MHP suffered a major electoral blow in November 2002, when it received only 8.3 percent of the vote and no legislative seats. Although Devlet Bahçeli initially announced he would step down from his leadership position after the election, he ran for and won the party's presidency again in October 2003.

The party benefited from rising nationalist sentiment, which was bolstered by the Iraq crisis and deteriorating EU–Turkey relations. In the 2007 parliamentary elections, the party won 14.3 percent of the vote and 71 seats.

The MHP supported the constitutional amendment proposed by the AKP to allow women to wear headscarves in universities, a concession made to the ruling party despite the MHP's continued nationalist stance, notably in the country's disputes with Armenia and Cyprus. The MHP and CHP vehemently objected to President Gül's unofficial visit to Armenia in September 2008. In the 2009 municipal elections, the MHP won 16 percent of the vote. This was perceived as a success, although hardly an indicator of the party's ability to become a major political contender. At a party congress in 2009, Bahçeli was reelected MHP president.

In May 2011 prior to national elections, a scandal involving alleged sex videos prompted the resignation of six senior MHP figures. In the assembly balloting, the MHP received 13 percent and 53 seats. In September, security forces arrested 36 MHP members. Defeating nine other candidates, Bahçeli remained party president in internal elections in November 2012.

After a poor showing in the March 2014 municipal elections, winning 15.2 percent of the vote, the MHP fielded a presidential candidate with the CHP for the presidential elections on August 10. Despite the unified support base Ekmeleddin İshanoğlu failed to win the presidency. The MHP won 16.3 percent of the vote and 80 seats in the June assembly elections. In that year's November parliamentary elections, the MHP received 11.9 percent of the vote and won 40 seats.

Leaders: Devlet BAHÇELI (President), İsmet BÜYÜKATMAN (Secretary General).

People's Democratic Party (*Halkların Demokratik Partisi*—HDP). The HDP was launched in October 2012 from the **People's Democratic Congress** (*Halklarin Demokratik Kongresi*—HDK) alliance, a grouping of some 20 socialist parties that contested the 2011 elections together with the BDP. The HDP aims to make itself representative of minorities across the country, allocating a 10 percent quota for LGBT individuals and a 50 percent quota for women. The party gained significant footing in October 2013 when four deputies of the BDP defected to join the HDP. The BDP and HDP contested the March 2014 municipal elections in parallel, with BDP candidates running in Kurdish-dominated regions while HDP candidates contested in the rest of the country, winning 1.9 percent. Subsequently, on April 28 the BDP joined the HDP. Former BDP leader Selahattin Demirtaş contested the presidential election, winning 9.8 percent of the vote.

The HDP secured 80 seats with 13.1 percent of the vote in June 2015. In the November parliamentary elections, the party received 10.8 percent of the votes and 59 seats. In November 2016 the government arrested several leaders of HDP, including the cochairs of the party, as part of its ongoing crackdown on the opposition. According to news sources, leaders of HDP declared that, in response to the arrests, the party would no longer participate in the parliament.

Leaders: Figen YÜKSEKDAĞ, Selahattin DEMIRTAS (Cochairs).

Other Parties:

Democratic Left Party (*Demokratik Sol Parti*—DSP). Formation of the DSP, a center-left populist formation, was announced in March 1984 by Rahşan Ecevit, the wife of former prime minister Bülent Ecevit, who was barred from political activity prior to the constitutional referendum of September 1987. In the October 1991 election, the party attracted sufficient social democratic support to weaken the SHP, although it won only 7 seats. It recovered in the December 1995 balloting, winning 76 legislative seats with 14.6 percent of the vote. The DSP became a junior partner in a Mesut Yılmaz–led coalition government, which also included the DTP (below), on June 30, 1998. After the Yılmaz–led coalition government collapsed in November 1998, Ecevit formed on January 12, 1999, a minority government that ruled the country until the early elections of April 18. The DSP became the largest party in that balloting with 22 percent of the votes and 136 seats. Ecevit subsequently formed a DSP-MHP-ANAP coalition cabinet.

In 2002 rifts within the party led some prominent members to resign to form the YTP. The DSP suffered a major electoral defeat in November 2002, winning no legislative seats. Bülent Ecevit resigned as party leader. Zeki Sezer, a former cabinet minister, was elected at the party's congress in July 2004.

The DSP struck an electoral alliance with the CHP on May 18, 2005. Thirteen DSP parliamentarians, including Sezer, were elected on the CHP ticket in the 2007 balloting. These members withdrew from the CHP during the first legislative session to form an independent DSP parliamentary group.

On May 18, 2009, Masum Türker defeated Sezer to become party president. In the March 2009 municipal elections, the DP garnered 2.78 percent of the vote. Ahead of the September 2010 referendum, a number of DSP members resigned to protest their party's opposition to the proposed constitutional changes. In the June 2011 national balloting the DSP received 0.3 percent of the vote. The party only received 0.07 percent of the vote in the November 2015 elections.

Leaders: Masum TÜRKER (President), Hasan ERÇELEBİ (Secretary General).

Peace and Democracy Party (*Barış ve Demokrasi Partisi*—BDP). Formed in 2008, the BDP emerged as the successor party to the **Democratic Society Party** (*Demokratik Toplum Partisi*—DTP). Formerly known as the **Democratic People's Party** (*Demokratik Halk Partisi*—DEHAP), the DTP was launched in January 1999 by former members of the **People's Democracy Party** (*Halkin Demokrasi Partisi*—HADEP), the pro-Kurdish DTP (not to be confused with the Democratic Turkey Party [DTP]), which was initiated by former legislators Leyla ZANA, Orhan DOĞAN, Hatip DİCLE, and Selim SADAK, who had joined the Democracy Party (*Demokrasi Partisi*—DEP) in 1994. The Turkish Grand National Assembly lifted the parliamentary immunity of these four Kurdish politicians, and they were arrested and jailed from 1994–2005. Based on concerns that the DEHAP would be banned by the Constitutional Court, the DTP was launched reportedly as a preemptive "successor" on November 9, 2005. Since then, all DEHAP mayors, members, and leaders have entered the DTP. While the DEHAP decided to dissolve itself in December 2005, the Constitutional Court continued to consider banning the party and started to address the case on July 13, 2006.

In an attempt to circumvent the 10 percent electoral threshold, which had prevented it from securing legislative representation in the past, the DTP decided to abstain from the July 22, 2007, elections and support party members who would formally resign their membership to run as independent candidates. Subsequently, 22 of these candidates were elected, and 20 of them formed the DTP parliamentary group in the first parliamentary session. The presence of DTP parliamentarians presented an opportunity to reconsider Turkey's Kurdish question.

On November 16, 2007, the chief prosecutor of the Court of Cassation sought to close the DTP because it was "a focal point of activities aiming to damage the independence of the state and the indivisible integrity of its territory and nation." As the DTP failed to draw a clear line between itself and the PKK, a rift developed between PKK sympathizers and social-democrats, who opposed terrorism. The party succeeded in restoring its electoral strength in southeastern and eastern Turkey in the March 2009 municipal elections.

On December 11 the Constitutional Court voted to ban the DTP because of its links to the PKK. The parliamentary deputies, and most members, of the DTP joined the BDP. However, 35 senior DTP officials were banned from politics for five years. In addition, some 80 members of the party were arrested,

In February 2010 Selahattin Demirtaş was elected leader of the BDP. In September Demirtaş was convicted of illegal propaganda on behalf of the PKK and sentenced to 10 months in prison. At the behest of the PKK's jailed leader Abdullah Öcalan, the BDP aligned with some 20 socialist parties to contest the June 2011 elections, winning 36 seats and allying under the HDK banner. After running in parallel with the HDP in the March 2014 municipal elections (and winning 4.18 percent of the vote), the BDP voted and joined the HDP in April 2014.

Leaders: Selahattin DEMIRTAŞ, Gülten KIŞANAK (Cochairs).

Great Unity Party (*Buyük Birlik Partisi*—BBP). A nationalist Islamic grouping, the BBP was launched in 1993 by a member of dissident MCP parliamentarians prior to the reactivation of the MHP in 1992. The party, whose members are known as "Turkish-Islamic Idealists" (*Türk-Islam ülkücüleri*), returned 13 deputies on the ANAP ticket in the 1995 election but subsequently opted for separate parliamentary status. The BBP won only 1.5 percent of the votes in the general election of April 1999. In November 2002 the party received 1.1 percent of the vote and no legislative seats.

The party did not present candidates in the 2007 parliamentary elections, though its leader, Muhsin YAZICIOĞLU, ran and won as an independent. On March 25, 2009, Yazıcıoğlu was killed in a helicopter crash; party president Yalçın Topçu was elected as his successor.

In the 2009 municipal elections, the BBP won 2.2 percent of the vote. Members of the BBP were abroad the Gaza-bound convoy of ships that was attacked by Israeli forces in May 2010 (see Foreign affairs, above). In balloting in June 2011 the BPP secured 0.8 percent of the vote. The next month, Mustafa DESTICI was elected party leader. The BBP secured 0.5 percent of the vote in the November 2015 polling.

Leader: Mustafa DESTICI.

Liberty and Solidarity Party (*Özgurlük ve Dayanışma Partisi*—ÖDP). Backed by many leftist intellectuals, feminists, and human rights activists, the ÖDP was launched after the December 1995 election as a broad alliance of various socialist factions together with elements of the once powerful Dev-Yol movement (see Extremist Groups, below). Some of the socialist groups, notably the **United Socialist Party** (*Birleşik Sosyalist Parti*—BSP), had contested the balloting as part of the HADEP bloc. The BSP had been formed as a merger of various socialist factions, including the **Socialist Unity Party** (*Sosyalist Birlik Partisi*—SBP), itself founded in February 1991 (and represented in the 1991–1995 assembly) as in large part successor to the **United Communist Party of Turkey** (*Türkiye Birleşik Komünist Partisi*—TBKP), led by Haydar KUTLU and Nihat SARGIN.

The TBKP had been formed in 1988 by a merger of the **Communist Party of Turkey** (*Türkiye Komünist Partisi*—TKP, separate from the TKP, below, led by Erkan BAŞ) and the **Turkish Workers Party** (*Türkiye İşçi Partisi*—TİP). Proscribed since 1925, the pro-Soviet TKP had long maintained its headquarters in Eastern Europe. Although remaining illegal, its activities within Turkey revived in 1983. The TİP, whose longtime leader, Behice BORAN, died in October 1987, had been formally dissolved in 1971 and again in 1980 but had endorsed the merger with TKP at a congress held on the first anniversary of Boran's death. Prior to the November 1987 election, the TKP and TİP general secretaries, Kutlu and Sargin, respectively, had returned to Turkey but had been promptly arrested and imprisoned.

With the Constitutional Court confirming a ban on the TBKP in early 1990, former TBKP elements were prominent in the new ÖDP. The ÖDP fared poorly in the April 1999 elections, gaining less than 1 percent of the votes. Several constituent groups reportedly left the ÖDP in 2002. In November 2002 the party won 0.3 percent of the vote and no legislative seats.

In the July 22, 2007, elections, the party won 0.2 percent of the vote. However, ÖDP leader Ufuk URAS, in order to avoid the electoral threshold requirement, ran as an independent, was elected a representative for Istanbul and was then reinstated in the party presidency. With parliamentary representation, the ÖDP became known as a substantial social-democratic opposition party.

Growing discord between the party's liberal and socialist wings led to the resignation of Uras from the party and the formation of a new leftist liberal group. On June 22, 2009, Alper Taş was elected party president.

In the 2009 municipal elections, the ÖDP garnered 0.2 percent of the vote. The TİP reportedly reformed as a separate party in February 2010. ÖDP candidates ran as independents in the 2011 balloting but failed to secure any seats. In March 2012 the ÖDP led protests against Turkey's inclusion as part of NATO's missile defense system.

Leader: Alper TAŞ.

Democrat Party (*Demokrat Parti*—DP). Also known as the **True Path Party** (*Doğru Yol Partisi*—DYP), the center-right party was organized as a successor to the **Grand Turkey Party** (*Büyük Türkiye Partisi*—BTP), which was banned shortly after its formation in May 1983 because of links to the former Justice Party of Süleyman Demirel. Though permitted to participate in the local elections of March 1984, it won control in none of the provincial capitals. By early 1987, augmented by assemblymen of the recently dissolved **Citizen Party** (*Vatandaş Partisi*—VP), it had become the third-ranked party in the Grand National Assembly. The DYP remained in third place by winning 59 seats in the November 1987 balloting and became the plurality party, with 178 seats, in October 1991. In November it formed a coalition government under Demirel with the SHP. A second DYP-SHP government was formed by the new DYP leader, Tansu Çiller, following Demirel's assumption of the presidency in May 1993. A new coalition was formed with the CHP in March 1995, following the latter's temporary absorption of the SHP. However, a CHP leadership change in September led to the party's withdrawal and the collapse of the Çiller government.

The DYP placed second in the December 1995 election (with 19.2 percent of the vote), eventually forming a coalition government with ANAP on March 12, 1996, that featured a "rotating" leadership. However, animosity between the DYP and ANAP leaders quickly resurfaced, with Çiller calling Prime Minister Mesut Yılmaz a "sleaze ball" and withdrawing the DYP's support for the coalition in late May. Overcoming its previous antipathy toward the RP, the DYP the following month entered a new coalition as junior partner of the Islamist party, with Çiller becoming deputy premier and foreign minister, pending a scheduled resumption of the premiership at the beginning of 1998. By mid-January 1997 a parliamentary inquiry had cleared the DYP leader of all corruption charges relating to her tenure as premier. After the DYP-RP coalition collapsed in June 1997, the DYP remained in the opposition during the Yılmaz-led ANAP-DSP-DTP coalition. After the November 1998 collapse of the Yılmaz government, the DYP then gave outside support to Bülent Ecevit's minority government. In the April 1999 elections, the DYP secured only 12 percent of the votes and 85 seats.

The DYP experienced a major electoral defeat in November 2002, receiving 9.5 percent of the vote and no legislative seats, prompting Tansu Çiller's resignation. With defections from other parties, the party had, by mid-2005, four legislative seats. In the run-up to the 2007 parliamentary elections, party leader Mehmet AĞAR announced an electoral alliance with the ANAP. Ağar and ANAP president Erkan Mumcu named their joint party the Democrat Party (*Demokrat Parti*—DP). However, the ANAP withdrew from the alliance after barely a month, and the DP ran in the elections on its own. The DP subsequently received 5.4 percent of the vote, 4.1 percent less than in the 2002 elections. This result led Ağar to resign from the presidency of the party and call for an extraordinary congress to elect a new leader.

The party maintained the rubric of the DP and in 2008 elected Süleyman SOYLU as president. Nonetheless, the party did not seem to attract significant political support. On May 16, 2009, the veteran politician Hüsamettin Cindoruk was elected party president. In the 2009 municipal elections, the DP won 3.7 percent of the vote. In October the ANAP merged with the DP. (For more information on the ANAP, see the 2009 *Handbook.*) Namik Kemal Zeybek was elected party leader at a DP congress on January 15, 2011. In balloting for the national assembly on June 12 the DP won 0.7 percent of the vote. At a DP congress in May 2012, Gültekin UYSAL was elected party leader. DP influence further waned in the March 2014 municipal elections, in which it won 0.4 percent of the vote. In the November 2015 balloting, the party won 0.1 percent of the vote.

Leader: Gültekin UYSAL (President).

Party of the People's Rise (*Halkin Yükselişi Partisi*—HYP). The centrist HYP was established in February 2005 by Yaşar Nuri ÖZTÜRK, a former scholar of Islamic theology who became popular because of his "reformist" and modernist interpretations of religion. Öztürk is a former CHP legislator who left his party in April 2004 to protest Deniz Baykal's leadership style. In the 2007 parliamentary elections, the HYP collected 0.5 percent of the vote. At a November 2009 party conference, Ragıp Önder GÜNAY was elected president of the HYP. HYP candidates ran as independents in the 2011 assembly elections but failed to gain any seats.

Leader: Ragıp Önder GÜNAY (President).

Communist Party of Turkey (*Türkiye Komünist Partisi*—TKP). The TKP was launched in November 2001 as a merger of the **Party for Socialist Power** (*Sosyalist Iktidar Partisi*—SIP) and the **Communist Party** (*Komünist Partisi*—KP). The SIP was a continuation of the banned **Party of Socialist Turkey** (*Sosyalist Türkiye Partisi*—STP). The hard-line Marxist-Leninist SIP contested the 1995 election under the HADEP rubric. It secured less than 1 percent of the vote in 1999. The TKP was formed in July 2000 by former SIP members. In November 2002 the party won 0.2 percent of the vote and no legislative seats.

During 2007 legislative balloting, the party won 0.2 percent of the vote, while in the 2009 municipal elections, the BTP received 0.2 percent of the vote and in the June 2011 assembly polling, 0.2 percent of the vote. In the November 2015 polling, the party received 0.1 percent of the vote.

Leader: Erkan BAŞ (President).

Felicity Party (*Saadet Partisi*—SP). The SP was formed in July 2001 by the traditionalist core of the **Virtue Party** (*Fazilet Partisi*—FP), which had been shut down by the constitutional court in June. The Virtue Party had been launched in February 1998, days before a constitutional court decision banned the Islamic-oriented Welfare Party, which was in the coalition government until June 18, 1997, on charges of undermining the secular foundations of the Turkish Republic.

The **Welfare Party** (*Refah Partisi*—RP) had been organized in 1983 by former members of the Islamic fundamentalist MSP. It participated in the 1984 local elections, winning one provincial capital. It failed to secure assembly representation in 1987.

Having absorbed Aydın MENDERES' faction of the Democrat Party (DP), the RP attained a plurality in the December 1995 election with 21.4 percent of the vote, but at that stage was unable to recruit allies for a government. However, the speedy collapse of an alternative administration brought the RP to office for the first time in June 1996, heading a coalition with the DYP. Under intense pressure from the military and secular political establishment, Prime Minister Necmettin ERBAKAN resigned on June 18, 1997, and the RP-DYP coalition failed. On February 22, 1998, the Constitutional Court banned the RP and barred some of its founders, including Erbakan, from political activity for five years. On March 6, 2002, Erbakan was sentenced to two years and four months in jail because he had embezzled more than $3 million from the fund of the banned RP. After several appeals, his sentence was converted to house arrest due to his ailing health.

Some 135 parliamentarians of the proscribed Welfare Party joined the FP, making it the main opposition party in the parliament. Although FP leaders denied their party was a successor to the RP, Turkey's secularists did not find the denial credible. The FP assumed the role of the main opposition party to both the Yılmaz-led ANAP-DSP-DTP coalition government that ended in November 1998 and to the Ecevit-led minority DSP government that was installed in January 1999. Although some analysts initially saw the FP as a likely winner of the general elections in April, the party secured only 15 percent of the votes and 111 seats. Recai Kutan was narrowly reelected as FP chair at the party congress in May 2000, fending off a challenge from a "reformist" wing led by Recep Tayyip Erdoğan (former mayor of Istanbul) and Abdullah Gül, which then broke away to launch its own formation, the Justice and Development Party (*Adalet ve Kalkınma Partisi*—AKP, above) in

August 2001, following the banning of the FP in June. Further weakened by legislative defections and a marked shift of popular support to the AKP, FP received an electoral setback in November 2002, winning only 2.5 percent of the vote and no legislative seats. In 2007 the party failed to provide a credible Islamist alternative to the ruling AKP and won just 2.34 percent of the vote.

On August 19, 2008, President Gül pardoned Erbakan and lifted his house detention. While AKP officials defended the decision on humanitarian grounds, secularists again became concerned about links between the AKP leadership and Islamists.

In the 2009 municipal elections, the SP garnered 5.2 percent of the vote. In October 2010 the SP elected the 84-year-old Erbakan as party president once again. Erbakan died on February 27, 2011. He was replaced by Mustafa Kamalak. The FP secured 1.3 percent of the vote in the 2011 national elections.

In January 2012 Kamalak visited Syria as part of an unofficial effort to maintain relations between the two countries. The FP won 2 percent of the vote in the municipal elections of March 2014. However, it only won 0.7 percent of the vote in the November 2015 balloting.

Leaders: Mustafa KAMALAK (President), Tacettin ÇETİNKAYA (Secretary General).

Young Party (*Genç Parti*—GP). A populist, nationalist party, the GP was founded in 2002 by the controversial magnate Cem UZAN, who took control of the tiny **Rebirth Party** (*Yeniden Doğuş Partisi*—YDP), renaming it about two months before the November 2002 elections. His family controlled the substantial Uzan Holding, which counted a bank (İmar Bankası), a media group (Star), and Telsim, Turkey's second biggest mobile phone operator, among its assets. In the November 4, 2002, elections, the GP won 7.3 percent of the vote but secured no seats due to the 10 percent electoral threshold. Meanwhile, corruption and fraud charges against the Uzan family culminated in a lawsuit against Uzan by Motorola and Nokia, which accused him of defaulting on more than $2.5 billion worth of loans they had provided to Telsim. İmar Bankası was taken over by Turkish banking regulatory authorities, amid family complaints that the government was persecuting their businesses to neutralize Cem Uzan's political popularity. While Uzan's father, Kemal Uzan, and brother, Hakan Uzan, escaped abroad to avoid arrest, Cem Uzan remained in Turkey because he had no personal involvement in corruption and fraud activities. The GP maintained its overtly populist and nationalist stance in the 2007 election campaign and won 3.03 percent of the vote.

On September 9, 2008, Uzan was convicted of insulting Prime Minister Erdoğan in a speech he gave in 2003. He was ordered by the court to enter an "anger management program." Uzan fled to France following new charges of fraud and forgery. He was sentenced in absentia to 23 years in prison in April 2010. GP candidates ran as independents in the 2011 legislative balloting but failed to gain any seats. Uzan was reportedly in Jordan in 2012.

Leader: Cem UZAN (President).

Workers' Party (*İşçi Partisi*—IP). The Maoist-inspired IP, founded in 1992, is the successor of the **Socialist Party** (*Sosyalist Parti*—SP), which was launched in February 1988 as the first overtly socialist formation since the 1980 coup. The party called for Turkey's withdrawal from NATO and nationalization of the economy. The SP was deregistered by order of the Constitutional Court in June 1992, the IP securing less than 0.5 percent of the vote in 1995. Since 2000 the IP, self-described as "national leftist," has garnered public attention due to its staunchly nationalist and anti-EU stance.

In November 2002 the party received 0.5 percent of the vote and no legislative seats. In 2007 it received 0.4 percent of the vote. On March 21, 2008, Doğu Perinçek was arrested in connection with the "Ergenekon" investigation. In the 2009 municipal elections, the IP garnered 0.3 percent of the vote. In August 2010 Perinçek led a large protest over what he described as the government's arrest and detention of secularists in Istanbul. In balloting in June 2011 the party's candidates ran as independents and did not secure any seats in the assembly.

Leader: Doğu PERİNÇEK.

Other minor parties that participated in the 2011 or 2015 elections were the **Turkey's Party** (*Türkiye Partisi*—TP), led by former AKP minister Abdülatif Şener; the **Labor Party** (*Emek Partisi*—EMEP), led by Selma GÜRKAN; the **Liberal Democrat Party** (*Liberal Demokrat Parti*—LDP), a free market grouping led by Cem TOKER; **Independent Turkey Party** (*Bağımsız Türkiye Partisi*—BTP), led by Haydar BAŞ; and the **People's Voice Party** (*Halkın Sesi Partisi*—HAS Party), led by Numan KURTULMUŞ. (For more on the **Social-Democrat People's Party** [*Sosyaldemokrat Halk Partisi*], see the 2012 *Handbook.*) Minor parties that participated in November 2015 Parliamentary elections but did not win seats included the **Patriotic Party** (*Vatan Partisi*), the **People's Liberation Party** (*Halkın Kurtuluş Partisi*), and the **True Path Party** (*Doğru Yol Partisi*).

Extremist Groups:

Pre-1980 extremist and terrorist groups included the leftist **Revolutionary Path** (*Devrimci Yol*—Dev-Yol) and its more radical offshoot, the **Revolutionary Left** (Dev-Sol). (For more information on the Dev-Sol, see the 2009 *Handbook.*) Both derived from the **Revolutionary Youth** (*Dev Genç*), which operated in the late 1960s and early 1970s. Some of its members also joined the far leftist **Turkish People's Salvation Army** (*Türkiye Halk Kurtuluş Ordusu*—THKO). Other groups were the **Turkish People's Liberation Party Front** (*Türkiye Halk Kurtuluş Partisi–Cephesi*—THKP-C), the **Turkish Workers' and Peasants' Liberation Army** (*Türkiye İşçi Köylü Kurtuluş Ordusu*—TİKKO, below), and the **Kurdistan Workers' Party** (PKK, below). Armenian guerrilla groupings include the **Secret Army for the Liberation of Armenia** (ASALA), including a so-called Orly Group; the **Justice Commandos for the Armenian Genocide;** the **Pierre Gulmian Commando;** the **Levon Ekmekçiyan Suicide Commando;** and the **Armenian Revolutionary Army.** The activities of many of these groups have subsided, notable exceptions being Dev-Sol and the PKK.

See the 2012 *Handbook* for more on the extreme left groupings, the **Communist Party of Turkey-Marxist Leninist** (*Türkiye Komünist Partisi–Marksist-Leninist*—TKP-ML) and its armed wing, the **Turkish Workers' and Peasants' Liberation Army** (*Türkiye İşçi Köylü Kurtuluş Ordusu*—TİKKO), and the **Communist Labor Party of Turkey–Leninist** (*Türkiye Komünist Emek Partisi–Leninist*—TKEP-L).

Kurdistan Workers' Party (*Partîya Karkerên Kurdistan*—PKK). Founded in 1978, the PKK, under the leadership of Abdullah (Apo) Öcalan, was for a long time based principally in Lebanon's Bekaa Valley and northern Iraq. In southeast Anatolia, where it continues to maintain a presence, the party's 1992 call for a general uprising on March 21, the Kurdish New Year (Nevruz), was generally unheeded. Subsequently, a unilateral cease-fire declared by Öcalan under pressure from northern Iraq Kurdish leaders proved short-lived, and PKK terrorism re-escalated. In late July 1994 Turkish warplanes reportedly completely destroyed a PKK base in northern Iraq, and in mid-August a London court convicted three separatists of a number of attacks on Turkish property in the United Kingdom. Öcalan thereupon reiterated his call for a cease-fire as a prelude to the adoption of constitutional reforms that would acknowledge the "Kurdish identity." The government again failed to respond and in September charged the PKK with responsibility for the killing of a number of Turkish teachers in the southeastern province of Tunceli. Government military offensives against the Kurdish insurgents in 1995–1996 were combined with efforts to eradicate the PKK party organization.

Through 1997 and 1998, extensive Turkish military operations seriously undermined the PKK's ground forces. On April 13, 1998, the PKK's second-highest ranking commander, Şemdin SAKIK, who had left the organization a month earlier, was captured in northern Iraq by Turkish security forces. A more significant blow to the organization came with the arrest of party chair Öcalan by Turkish commandos in Nairobi, Kenya (see Foreign relations, above), in February 1999. The commander of the PKK's armed wing, the People's Liberation Army of Kurdistan (ARGK), Cemil BAYIK, had reportedly threatened Turkish authorities and foreign tourists on March 15, claiming that the whole of Anatolia "is now a battlefield." Some sources also reported a leadership struggle between Bayik and Abdullah Öcalan's brother, Osman ÖCALAN.

From February to July 1999 Kurdish militants engaged in various attacks, including suicide bombings, in response to their leader's arrest. A State Security Court accused Öcalan of being responsible for 30,000 deaths between 1984 and 1999. He was found guilty of treason and sentenced to death on June 29. During his defense, Öcalan argued that he could "stop the war" if the Turkish state would let him "work for peace" and spare his life. He apologized for the "sufferings PKK's actions may have caused," claiming that the "armed struggle had fulfilled its aims" and that the PKK would now "work for a democratic Turkey, where Kurds will enjoy cultural and linguistic rights." On

August 2 Öcalan called on his organization to stop fighting and leave Turkish territory starting September 1. The PKK's "Presidential Council" quickly announced that it would follow its leader's commands, and during the PKK's congress in February 2000, it was announced that the party's political and armed wings would merge into a front organization called the People's Democratic Union of Kurdistan. Some analysts argued that the decision was in line with the PKK's decision to stop its armed struggle and seek Kurdish political and cultural rights within the framework of Turkey's integration with the European Union.

In 2001 a small group of renegade PKK members launched the Kurdistan Workers' Party–Revolutionary Line Fighters (*Partîya Karkarên Kurdistan–Devrimci Çizgi Savaşçıları*—PKK-DÇS) with the expressed aim to continue the armed struggle. In April 2002 the PKK decided to dissolve itself (announcing it had fulfilled its "historical mission") to launch a new organization called the Kurdistan Freedom and Democracy Congress (*Kongreya Azadî û Demokrasiya Kurdistan*—KADEK). The KADEK claimed to be against armed struggle, to have rejected fighting for an independent Kurdish homeland, and to have espoused a "political" line to press for cultural and linguistic rights for Turkey's Kurds as "full and equal members under a democratic and united Turkey." However, in May the EU announced it still considered the PKK a "terrorist organization." The Turkish government continued to claim that the PKK's transformation into KADEK was a "tactical ploy."

In September 2003 KADEK was restyled as the Peoples' Congress of Kurdistan (*Kongra Gelê Kurdistan*—Kongra-Gel). Several high-level defections occurred in the ranks, including that of Osman Öcalan, who reportedly joined a splinter group, the Democratic Solution Party of Kurdistan (*Partiya Welatparêzên Demokratên Kurdistan*—PWDK) that was established in April 2004. In June 2004 Kongra-Gel announced that the cease-fire declared by Abdullah Öcalan in September 1999 was not respected by the Republic of Turkey and that they would return to "legitimate armed defense" to counter military operations against their "units." In April 2005 it was announced that PKK was reconstituted and the new formation was styled as the PKK–Kongra-Gel. Since the announcement, numerous sporadic clashes have been reported between the Turkish security forces and PKK–Kongra-Gel's armed wing, People's Defense Forces (*Hezen Parastina Gel*—HPG).

Since March 2005 a hitherto unknown group called "Kurdistan Freedom Falcons" (*Teyrêbazên Azadiya Kurdistan*—TAK) has taken responsibility for numerous car bomb explosions and other urban terrorist acts. Although some press reports claimed that TAK was one among many breakaway wings of PKK–Kongra-Gel, the organization quickly denounced any links with the group.

In 2007 there was a considerable rise in PKK activity and government operations in eastern and southeastern Turkey; on May 22 a suicide bomb in Ankara killed seven people, including the bomber, who was thought to be linked to the PKK. On October 22, a Turkish military patrol was ambushed near Dağlıca by some 200 PKK militants. Twelve Turkish soldiers were killed, 16 were wounded, and 8 were taken hostage by PKK insurgents. A DTP committee negotiated their release on November 4. However, the released soldiers were prosecuted following their return to Turkey because of their failure to obey orders. The Dağlıca incident was the largest PKK military attack on Turkish territory in many years, shocking the Turkish public.

Following reports of rifts within the PKK, Turkish forces invaded northern Iraq on February 21, 2008, attacking a PKK outpost and headquarters. Turkish troops withdrew eight days later. In July two bombs exploded in the Istanbul suburb of Gungören, killing 17 people and wounding more than 100. While the authorities accused the PKK of having been behind the attack, the evidence apparently was inconclusive. Investigation of the "Ergenekon" affair also led to speculation about possible links between the PKK and "Ergenekon."

In May 2009 in a newspaper interview, Murat Karayilan indicated the PKK had changed and was pursuing the promotion of Kurdish rights in Turkey without aiming to disrupt the unitary Turkish state. Further, he declared his readiness for armistice and dialogue with Turkey. Karayilan stressed that the solution he envisioned did not necessarily entail a federation, but greater local autonomy in accordance with a reform of the local authorities' law.

After negotiations with the government, the PKK declared a new unilateral cease-fire in August 2010 and pledged to maintain the truce through national elections scheduled in June 2011. In November the TAK claimed responsibility for a bombing in Istanbul that wounded more than 30. The TAK asserted that it would not join the PKK cease-fire. Meanwhile, in October 151 people, including 12 mayors, were arrested on suspicion of ties with the PKK.

On February 28, 2011, the PKK ended its unilateral truce after the government rejected a proposal to end the 10 percent threshold required for parties to gain seats in the assembly. In April an additional 35 political figures with suspected ties to the PKK were detained. In November, Turkish security forces killed a PKK hijacker during an aborted ferry takeover.

In January 2012 more than 30 suspected PKK members were arrested in a security sweep in Turkey. In May, Ankara accused Syria of providing bases and military support for the PKK. In March 2013 imprisoned Kurdish leader Öcalan called for a cease-fire and the withdrawal of the PKK from Turkey. However, the withdrawal was halted in September (see Current issues, above).

With the advancement of ISIS into northern Iraq beginning in June 2014 and into the territory recognized as Kurdistan by Syrian, Iraqi, and Turkish Kurds, the PKK became one of the principle counteroffensive forces. Despite American classification of the PKK as a "terrorist organization," the PKK and the United States joined forces in operations to rescue members of the Yazidi sect besieged by ISIS in northern Iraq in August 2014. The advancement of ISIS put Turkey's government in a predicament, as it weighed its wariness of ISIS with its desire not to legitimize the PKK.

After the failed 2016 coup, the government intensified its campaign against the PKK. In response the PKK initiated a series of attacks on government facilities and police targets.

Leaders: Abdullah ÖCALAN (Honorary President), Zübeyir AYDAR (President), Murat KARAYILAN (Chair of the Executive Council).

Party of God (*Hizbullah*). *Hizbullah,* a militant Islamist Sunni group unrelated to the Lebanon-based Shiite *Hezbollah*, was active in southeast Anatolia in the early 1990s, when it launched a campaign of violence against PKK militants and pro-Kurdish lawyers, intellectuals, and human rights activists. On January 17, 2000, Hüseyin VELİOĞLU, reportedly a leader of the **Party of God** was killed and two of his associates were arrested in a shoot-out with police in İstanbul. Some unconfirmed press reports claimed that the group members were tolerated if not encouraged by the state security forces, which allegedly explained the fact that none of its members was caught until the shoot-out. During the months of January and February 2000, police arrested over 400 alleged members of *Hizbullah,* some reportedly civil servants. State security forces also found several safe-houses of the group, where they reportedly recovered mutilated bodies of dozens of victims, including famous moderate Islamic feminist Gonca KURİŞ, who was kidnapped in July 1998. In February 2012, 24 members of *Hizbullah* were convicted of terrorism charges.

Following the arrest of PKK leader Abdullah Öcalan in February 1999, a shadowy far-right group, **Turkish Avenger Brigade** (*Türk İntikam Tugayı*—TİT), issued death threats against pro-Kurdish activists and politicians and claimed responsibility for attacks on various HADEP buildings. Some unconfirmed reports suggest that the group is merely a facade for occasional "agent-provocateur" activities allegedly linked to factions within the Turkish security forces. Similar activities resurfaced with the rise of nationalist sentiment after 2004. On June 13, 2007, in a shanty house in the Istanbul neighborhood of Ümraniye, police discovered large quantities of explosives, hand grenades, and other ammunition, which were allegedly intended for use in terrorist attacks against minorities and liberal Turks. The discovery marked the unraveling of the "Ergenekon" affair. The subsequent investigation sought links with the aforementioned attacks.

For information on the **Unity** (*Tevhid*), see the 2012 *Handbook.*

LEGISLATURE

The 1982 constitution replaced the former bicameral legislature with a unicameral 550-member **Turkish Grand National Assembly** (*Türkiye Büyük Millet Meclisi*) elected for a five-year term on a proportional basis (10 percent threshold).

Following the election in November 2015, the seat distribution was as follows: Justice and Development Party, 317 seats; Republican People's Party, 134; People's Democratic Party, 59; and Nationalist Action Party, 40.

Speaker: Ismail KAHRAMAN (AKP).

CABINET

[as of November 1, 2016]

Prime Minister	Binali Yildirim
Deputy Prime Ministers	Nurettin Canikli Mehmet Simsek Yildirim Tugrul Turkes Veysi Kaynak Numan Kurtulmuş
Ministers	
Agriculture, Food, and Animal Husbandry	Faruk Çelik
Culture and Tourism	Nabi Avcı
Customs and Trade	Bülent Tüfenkci
Development	Lütfi Elvan
Economy	Nihat Zeybekci
Energy and Natural Resources	Berat Albayrak
Environment and Urban Planning	Mehmet Özhaseki
European Union Affairs	Ömer Çelik
Family and Social Policy	Fatma Betül Sayan-Kaya [f]
Finance	Naci Ağbal
Foreign Affairs	Mevlüt Çavuşoğlu
Forestry and Water Works	Veysel Eroğlu
Health	Recep Akdağ
Industry, Science and Technology	Faruk Özlü
Interior	Süleyman Soylu
Justice	Bekir Bozdağ
Labor and Social Security	Mehmet Müezzinoğlu
National Defense	Fikri Işık
National Education	İsmet Yılmaz
Transport	Ahmet Arslan
Youth and Sports	Akif Çağatay Kılıç

[f] = female

Note: All ministers are members of the Justice and Development Party (AKP).

INTERGOVERNMENTAL REPRESENTATION

Ambassador to the U.S.: Serdar KILIÇ.

U.S. Ambassador to Turkey: John BASS.

Permanent Representative to the UN: Feridun SINIRLIOĞLU.

IGO Memberships (Non-UN): ADB, AfDB, CEUR, EBRD, G-20, IEA, IOM, NATO, OECD, OIC, OSCE, WTO.

For Further Reference:

Genç, Kaya. *Under the Shadow: Rage and Revolution in Modern Turkey.* London: I. B. Tauris, 2016.

Polat, Necati. *Regime Change in Contemporary Turkey: Politics, Rights, Mimesis.* Edinburgh: Edinburgh University Press, 2016.

White, Jenny. *Muslim Nationalism and the New Turks.* Princeton, NJ: Princeton University Press, 2014.

TURKMENISTAN

Republic of Turkmenistan
Tiurkmenostan Respublikasy

Political Status: Declared independence as Republic of Turkmenistan on October 27, 1991; new constitution adopted May 18, 1992; present constitution adopted September 26, 2008. First emerged as a political entity when the Turkmenian districts of the former Bukhara and Khorezm republics were added to the autonomous Turkistan Soviet Socialist Republic within the Russian Soviet Federative Socialist Republic on October 27, 1924; became a constituent republic of the Union of Soviet Socialist Republics (USSR) on May 12, 1925.

Area: 188,456 sq. mi. (488,100 sq. km).

Population: 5,439,000 (2016E—UN); 5,291,317 (2016E—U.S. Census).

Major Urban Center (2015E—UN): ASHGABAT (Ashkhabad, 746,000.)

Official Language: Turkmen.

Monetary Unit: Manat (market rate October 1, 2016: 3.50 new manats = $1US).

President and Prime Minister: Gurbanguly BERDIMUHAMMEDOV (Democratic Party of Turkmenistan); elevated from deputy prime minister to acting president and prime minister on December 21, 2006, following the death of Gen. Saparmurad Atayevich NIYAZOV (Saparmyrat NYYAZOW; Democratic Party of Turkmenistan); reelected on February 12, 2012, for a second five-year term.

THE COUNTRY

The southernmost republic of the former Soviet Union, Turkmenistan is bordered on the northwest by Kazakhstan, on the north and northeast by Uzbekistan, on the southeast by Afghanistan, on the south by Iran, and on the west by the Caspian Sea. The Kara Kum (Garagum) Desert occupies about 80 percent of the land area. Ethnic Turkmens, who are predominantly Sunni Muslims, account for approximately 77 percent of the population, followed by Uzbeks (9 percent), Russians (7 percent), and Kazakhs (2 percent). Turkmenistan is the most ethnically homogeneous of the five independent Central Asian republics to emerge out of the former Soviet Union in 1991, the other four being Kazakhstan, Kyrgyzstan, Tajikistan, and Uzbekistan. Women hold 25.8 percent of the seats in the current Assembly (32 seats).

Industry, which contributes about 50 percent of the gross domestic product (GDP) and employs about 12 percent of the active labor force, is dominated by hydrocarbons. According to current estimates, Turkmenistan has the fourth largest reserve of natural gas in the world—8 trillion cubic meters, or more than 4 percent of the world's total gas reserves. Natural gas accounts for over half of the export earnings, with petrochemicals and other oil products adding another 30 percent. In recent years, the country has been trying to diversify its economy so that it relies less on exports of crude oil and gas and more on domestically refined hydrocarbon products, such as gasoline and bitumen, as well as agricultural products such as cotton.

Agriculture employs about 29 percent of workers, but its share of GDP is much smaller, approximately 8 percent, and is declining. About half of the population lives in rural areas. A principal component of the country's irrigation network is a 500-mile Karakum canal that carries water from the Amu-Darya (Oxus) River, a major tributary of the Aral Sea. That diversion has contributed to an ecological catastrophe, the Aral Sea having lost 75 percent of its surface area and 90 percent of its water volume since the canal's completion in 1967. This has devastated fish stocks and created major public health hazards as newly dried-out saline seabeds have become contaminated with pesticides and fertilizer runoffs. Only about 4 percent of the country is arable land, and half of that is planted with cotton. Apart from cotton, the country's other main crop is wheat, while in the livestock sector, it specializes in cattle meat, cow milk, and poultry production.

The breakup of the Soviet Union caused a dramatic decline in Turkmenistan's GDP in the mid-1990s, coupled with hyperinflation. However, growth has been constant since then due largely to the extensive development of its oil and natural gas resources. For example, oil exports in 2014 were estimated at $23.5 billion, which amounts to 50 percent of the country's total GDP of $47.7 billion for that year. By the early 2010s, the economy was expanding at around 10 percent a year, in large part because the government was developing trade relationships with countries in all directions, in particular with China but also Japan, South Korea, Iran, and even Europe and the United States. Trade with Russia, however, was stagnating, mainly due to the tense political relationship between the two nations. While foreign investment has grown steadily in recent years, corruption and the extremely tight grip the government maintains over the economy remain a disincentive to investors. Turkmenistan was ranked 168th out of 177 countries in

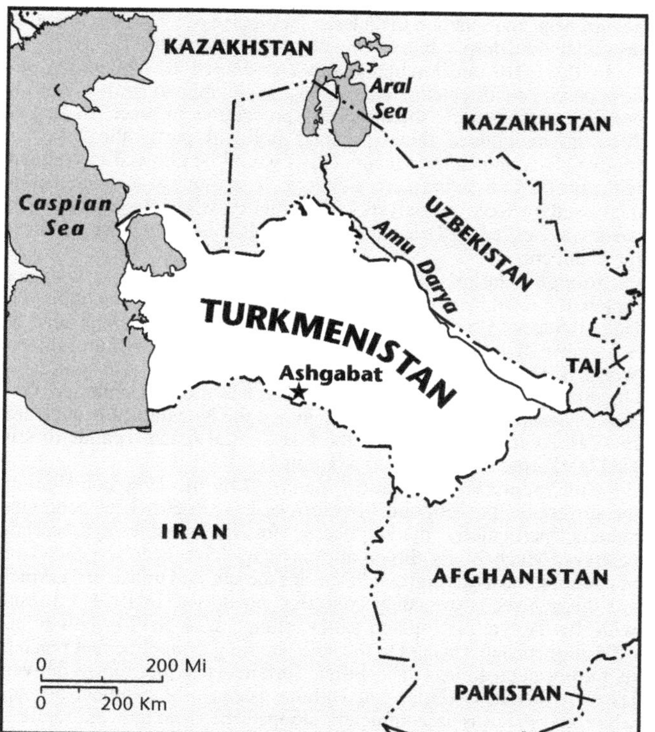

Transparency International's 2013 Corruption Perceptions Index. Turkmenistan is currently both a net exporter, with oil and gas being its leading export commodities, and a net creditor.

Average life expectancy in Turkmenistan is 64 years, and the median age is 26.4 years, while only 7.2 percent of the population is Internet users. The share of the population in employment is 62 percent, with the labor force participation rate 76.5 percent for males and 46.7 percent for females. GDP grew by 10.3 percent in 2014, 9 percent in 2015, and 9.2 percent in 2016. Inflation was 6.6 percent in 2016, while GDP per capita was $8,673.

GOVERNMENT AND POLITICS

Political background. Historic Turkestan occupied a vast area extending from the Caspian Sea in the west to the border of China in the east, and from the Aral Sea watershed in the north to Persia (Iran) and Afghanistan in the south. In 1924 what had been an autonomous republic of the Russian Soviet Federative Socialist Republic was split into (western) Turkmen and (eastern) Uzbek components, both of which became constituent republics of the USSR in 1925.

Following republican elections on January 7, 1990, Saparmurad NIYAZOV, the first secretary of the Turkmen Communist Party (TCP), was named chair of the Supreme Soviet (head of state). On August 23 the Supreme Soviet issued a declaration of Turkmenistan's "independent statehood," on the basis of which the adjectives "Soviet" and "Socialist" were dropped from the republic's official name and the Turkmen constitution and laws were assigned precedence over those of the Soviet Union. In a somewhat unusual move, the declaration identified Turkmenistan as a nuclear and chemical weapons–free zone. On October 27 Niyazov was unopposed in direct elections to the new post of executive president.

In August 1991 with democratic activists reportedly being arrested for alleging that Niyazov had supported the failed hard-liners' coup in Moscow against USSR president Mikhail Gorbachev, the president broke with the leaders of most fellow republics by not dismantling the Communist Party. Nevertheless, a referendum on independence was conducted on October 26 that yielded a 93.5 percent affirmative vote, and an implementing declaration was issued by the Supreme Soviet the following day. On December 16 the TCP was formally dissolved and immediately succeeded by the Democratic Party of Turkmenistan (DPT), which abandoned the Marxist-Leninist precepts of its predecessor while maintaining an absolute grip on power.

The Supreme Soviet approved a new constitution on May 18, 1992, and on June 26 Niyazov was reinvested as president after an election five days earlier in which he was again the sole candidate. On January 15, 1994, a reported 99.5 percent of voters favored exempting the president from having to stand for an additional term, while in elections to the lower house of the new legislature, held on December 11, only 1 of 50 seats was contested, with most of the returned candidates being DPT nominees.

During his tenure President Niyazov kept absolute control of Turkmenistan. He adopted the title *Turkmenbashi* (Leader of the Turkmen People), and the epithet "the Great" was routinely appended to his name in government press releases. He also took on the mantle of cultural protector, banning, for example, car radios, ballet, and opera. He developed a cult of personality around himself, ordering that the months of the year and days of the week be renamed in honor of famous Turkmen, including his mother and himself. His own books, called the *Ruhnama,* were used as historical texts, while his suppression of Islamic holy texts such as the Koran and hadith led Islamists to view him as a blasphemer. From 1991 to 2001 Niyazov implemented a massive urban renewal project in the capital, Ashgabat, which led to large-scale demolition of houses using forced evictions. Some of the evicted received neither financial compensation nor a new home.

The first evidence of popular unrest came in July 1995 when demonstrators in Ashgabat called for new presidential elections and an end to economic hardship and shortages. Authorities swiftly removed the demonstrators, and a number of political opponents subsequently were detained in prisons or psychiatric facilities.

In early November 2001 it was reported that the government had issued an arrest warrant for Boris SHIKHMURADOV, a former Western-oriented foreign minister who had most recently served as ambassador to China and was then in Russia. In addition to denying allegations that he had appropriated $25 million in state property, chiefly aircraft and armaments, and then sold them, Shikhmuradov responded by announcing that he was forming an opposition group, subsequently identified as the People's Democratic Movement of Turkmenistan (PDMT), to help depose Niyazov.

On November 25, 2002, gunmen fired on a presidential motorcade. Niyazov, who was uninjured, immediately attributed the attack to a number of former government officials who had aligned with Shikhmuradov, including former deputy prime minister Hudayberdi ORAZOW (Khudaiberdy ORAZOV) and the recently resigned ambassador to Turkey, Nurmuhammet HANAMOW (Nurmukhammed KHANAMOV), who subsequently emerged as a leader of the exiled opposition. A month later Shikhmuradov, who had secretly returned to Turkmenistan, announced on an opposition Website that he intended to surrender to authorities in an effort to prevent further persecution of government opponents. The Assembly election of December 19, 2004, with runoff balloting on January 9, 2005, was once again conducted without international monitoring. All candidates were members of the DPT.

On December 21, 2006, President Niyazov died unexpectedly. Although the constitution specified that the speaker of the Assembly, Ovezgeldi ATAYEV, should serve as acting president pending the election of a successor, Atayev was relieved of his duties and charged with an unrelated criminal offense. (In February 2007 he was convicted of driving a prospective daughter-in-law to suicide.) As a result, the cabinet elevated Deputy Prime Minister Gurbanguly BERDIMUHAMMEDOV to the presidency. The following day, Akja NURBERDIYEWA was appointed acting speaker of the Assembly.

In an extraordinary session on December 26, 2006, the People's Council called a presidential election for February 2007 and amended the constitution, which had previously prohibited an acting president from seeking election to the presidency. The People's Council also endorsed Berdimuhammedov and five other presidential candidates, all from the DPT. In the February 11 election Berdimuhammedov was credited with 89 percent of the vote, and he was inaugurated on February 14.

Following constitutional reforms that expanded the size of the *Mejlis,* new elections were held on December 14 and 28, 2008, a year earlier than required by the constitution. All 125 members elected to the Assembly were members of the DPT or pro-presidential independents. The balloting marked the first time that foreign monitors were present as observers, although international groups criticized the elections for irregularities and because no opposition parties contested the elections. In 2008 the new government initiated limited economic reforms, including the redenomination of the currency, reductions in state subsidies, and new incentives for foreign investment.

In elections held on December 15, 2013, the governing Democratic Party of Turkmenistan won 47 seats, the recently created Party of Industrialists and Entrepreneurs won 14, trade unions won 33, women's groups 16, youth organizations 8, and citizens' groups 7. An observer mission from the Commonwealth of Independent States concluded that the elections were free, orderly, and competitive, but human rights campaigners dismissed them as a token gesture, noting that genuine opposition leaders are all in jail or in exile. Observers from the Organization for Security and Cooperation in Europe said that some improvements were made in the legal framework for elections but that choice was limited. The Turkmen government noted that, apart from Turkmen, there are also ethnic Russians, Kazakhs, and Uzbeks represented in the parliament.

A cabinet reshuffle occurred in July and August 2015. Another reshuffle occurred on January 8, 2016. In February 2016 Deputy Prime Minister Palwan TAGANOV was dismissed amid accusations of corruption. He was replaced by Batyr ATDAYEV.

Constitution and government. The 1992 constitution featured a popularly elected strong president (head both of state and of government as well as commander-in-chief) whose powers include issuing laws, save those amending the constitution or revising the criminal code. Up until 2003, the country's highest representative body, the People's Council (*Khalk Maslakhaty*), typically met once a year with a mandate that included consideration of basic economic, social, and political policy; constitutional changes; ratification of intergovernmental treaties; and declarations of war and peace. The smaller Assembly (*Mejlis*) was chiefly responsible for enacting ordinary legislation. At the initiative of the president, in August 2003 the People's Council was restructured as a "fourth branch" of government, a "permanently functioning supreme representative body of popular government having the powers of supreme state authority and government." The body's membership was expanded to 2,507, encompassing executive, judicial, and legislative members as well as representatives of regional, local, civic, labor, party, and other groups.

In September 2008 the People's Council unanimously approved a new constitution touted as a step toward democracy and the free market. The document guarantees the right to free expression and the right to "receive information unless it represents a state secret or any other secret protected by law." Changes from its predecessor include an endorsement of market economic principles. A strong presidency is retained, but an expanded Assembly may censure the president and amend the constitution, and it was given most of the powers of the People's Council, which was abolished.

The country is divided into five administrative regions, or *velayaty* (Akhal, Balkan, Dashkhovuz, Lebap, and Mary), which are subdivided into districts (*etraps*), towns, and urban settlements.

All media, including the Internet, are strictly controlled by the government. Reporters Without Borders ranked Turkmenistan as 178th out of 180 countries in 2016. The report laments that Turkmenistan is "subjected to little pressure from the international community for the simple reason that they are rich in oil and gas deposits." A law adopted in 2013 to promote media pluralism "is a complete fiction," it says, because the totalitarian regime still controls all of the media and "independent journalists can only operate clandestinely, reporting for news media outside the city." Niyazov's successor, Gurbanguly Berdimuhammedov, had formerly been Niyazov's personal dentist before rapidly ascending the political ladder in the late 1990s. As health minister, he had implemented Niyazov's plan to close most of the country's medical facilities. After Niyazov died, he distanced himself from Niyazov's cult of personality and initially showed signs that he intended to reverse some of Niyazov's more draconian policies. He opened up the economy to greater foreign investment and called for educational and social reforms as well as restoring the pension benefits that Niyazov had withdrawn from 100,000 elderly people. To reassure Russia and Western Europe, he stated that Turkmenistan would honor all existing natural gas contracts. Rather than condemn the fundamentally undemocratic process by which Berdimuhammedov assumed the presidency, the United States and other Western countries chose to view the new president's pronouncements as positive steps that merited support (particularly given the potential for improved access to Turkmenistan's hydrocarbons). Berdimuhammedov has, however, continued his predecessor's practice of dismissing cabinet ministers, typically for "grave shortcomings" in their work, on a regular basis. When the Turkmen athletes failed to win any medals in the 2012 London Olympics, the president fired the sports minister. In October 2012 the authorities arrested a former minister, Geldymyrat NURMUHAMMEDOV, after he openly criticized the government, and sent him to undergo six months of forced treatment for drug addiction, despite him having no history of drug use.

In May 2010 Berdimuhammedov encouraged the registration of a new party and directed the assembly leadership to draft a law on political parties to put the necessary procedures in place. In August 2012 he announced that a second political party, the Party of Industrialists and Entrepreneurs (PIE) would be allowed to compete with the DPT in subsequent elections. The move was immediately dismissed by Western analysts of the country, who noted that the new party was headed by Orazmammed MAMMEDOV, a close friend of the president.

Foreign relations. By early 1992 Turkmenistan had established diplomatic relations with a number of foreign countries, including the United States. On March 2 it joined the United Nations and on September 22 was admitted to the International Monetary Fund and the World Bank. As a predominantly Muslim country, it also joined the Organization of the Islamic Conference. It has attended summits of the Turkic-speaking states and in 1995 joined the Nonaligned Movement. In 1994 Turkmenistan became the first Central Asian republic to join NATO's Partnership for Peace program.

With "permanent neutrality" mandated by the 1992 constitution, the government's geopolitical priorities have focused on economic matters, particularly market access for its massive hydrocarbon reserves. Much of its diplomatic energies have been expended on negotiating the terms and conditions for the sale and transit of Turkmen gas through the surrounding countries' territories. In 1994 a dispute with Russia over pricing and barter arrangements led Moscow to cut off Turkmenistan's access to the sole natural gas pipeline that reached its European customers. Thereafter, Turkmenistan interrupted deliveries to Armenia, Georgia, and Ukraine because of payment arrears, while in 1997 Russia completely stopped the flow into the regional pipeline in retaliation for Turkmenistan's decision to dissolve the financially troubled joint venture the two countries had set up to export Turkmen gas.

In December 1997 President Niyazov and the new Iranian president Mohammad Khatami inaugurated a 125-mile-long pipeline carrying comparatively small quantities of natural gas to Iran. A second pipeline was completed in 2010. An October 2000 visit by Ukraine president Leonid Kuchma resolved differences over payments arrears and future gas deliveries between those two countries. In 2006 Turkmenistan resolved a dispute with Russia over gas prices when Gazprom agreed to pay 54 percent more for Turkmen gas.

On the global security front, Turkmenistan became an increasingly significant actor due to its proximity to unstable countries and regions. In late 1996, the government took a more conciliatory line than neighboring republics toward the overthrow of the Afghan government by the Taliban militia, in part because the Islamic group had reportedly approved plans for a gas pipeline to Pakistan. Following the September 2001 al-Qaida attacks on the United States and the consequent U.S.-led invasion of Afghanistan, Turkmenistan opened land and air corridors for the delivery of humanitarian aid to the Afghan people, and Niyazov indicated his support for a UN-led effort against international terrorism. He denied U.S. forces access to military facilities, however, citing his country's commitment to neutrality, but he was not averse to accepting U.S. military aid for training and equipment. The overthrow of the Taliban led to a May 2002 agreement with Pakistan and the interim Afghan government to conduct a new feasibility study for the pipeline project, which was approved in December 2002 at an initial projected cost of $2 billion to $3 billion.

In April 2006, during a visit to China, President Niyazov and Chinese officials approved a framework agreement for a natural gas pipeline to China via Uzbekistan and Kazakhstan. In December 2009 the presidents of the four countries met to inaugurate the recently completed 1,139-mile (1,833-km) pipeline from Turkmenistan's Saman-Depe field. The new pipeline is due to reach its full capacity of 40 billion cubic meters by 2015, although China has already indicated it needs 60 billion cubic meters. China has come to eclipse Russia as Turkmenistan's top trading partner. In 1992, Turkmen–China trade amounted to a mere $4.5 million—by 2013, it was $10 billion. Turkmenistan has, in addition, expressed interest in a possible Trans-Caspian gas pipeline called TANAP that would transit Azerbaijan and Georgia and then terminate in Turkey, thereby bypassing Russia and providing a new route to European customers. This project is also supported by the European Union (EU), which hopes that some of the Turkmen gas can ultimately be transported to its markets through the construction of another pipeline or pipelines that will link up to

TANAP. Previously, Turkmenistan relied heavily on Russia's natural gas giant, Gazprom, to distribute its gas, but President Berdimuhammedov has been keen to reduce this dependence. Another regional issue involves national claims to the Caspian Sea, which borders Azerbaijan, Iran, Kazakhstan, Russia, and Turkmenistan. Russia, Azerbaijan, and Kazakhstan have negotiated bilateral agreements dividing the seabed into territorial sectors, but Iran and Turkmenistan have argued for a more comprehensive approach. A joint task force continues to meet, but the basic issue remains unresolved and is a source of regional tension. In November 2004 President Niyazov met with Uzbek president Islam Karimov in Bukhara, Uzbekistan, where they signed a declaration of friendship and pledged closer cooperation in trade and a variety of other areas.

Relations between Turkmenistan and Russia deteriorated in 2009 following an explosion in one of the pipelines carrying Turkmen gas to Europe. The Turkmenistan government blamed Gazprom for the accident. In addition, Turkmenistan's agreement to supply China with 40 billion cubic meters of gas each year further alienated Moscow. Relations between the EU and Turkmenistan were normalized in April 2009, following years of strain over the country's human rights record. Concurrently, the EU Parliament approved a new trade agreement with Turkmenistan.

In May 2011 a British energy auditor reported that Turkmenistan had the world's second-largest gas field, South Yolotan, which holds 14 trillion to 21 trillion cubic meters and is bigger than the state of Luxembourg in size. The range of actual or potential customers for these gas supplies continues to broaden and now includes Afghanistan, India, Iran, Malaysia, Pakistan, South Korea, and eastern and western Europe. In July 2011 Turkmenistan opened its first offshore gas production plant at Kiyanli in the Caspian Sea. In September 2013 production began at an onshore gas field, Galkynysh, with the goal being for it to produce 30 billion cubic meters by the end of 2014.

In May 2015 Turkmenistan and Kazakhstan ratified an agreement to demarcate their maritime border along the Caspian Sea.

In June 2016 Russia announced it would provide weapons, training, and financial assistance to Turkmenistan amid growing concerns over the spread of the Afghan insurgency and the emergence of the Islamic State in Afghanistan (see entry on Afghanistan). Pakistan opened an embassy in Turkmenistan's capital, Ashgabat, on November 16 in a sign of growing ties between the two countries.

Current issues. By September 2014 the economy was continuing to register strong economic growth on the back of its hydrocarbon sector while enjoying relatively low inflation and unemployment and a modest budget surplus. Goods exports for 2013 were $19.9 billion, of which hydrocarbons comprised $18.7 billion, while goods imports were $14.6 billion. The government continues to focus its efforts on concluding contracts with foreign energy companies—including from China, the United States, and the United Kingdom—to further develop and diversify its hydrocarbon sector. In June 2014 Turkmenistan concluded two deals with South Korean firms to build two gas-to-liquid plants for $4 billion, and in August 2014 it signed a $1.7 billion deal with Turkish and Japanese investors to construct a gasoline production plant by April 2018. The government is also interested in building up its road and rail transportation infrastructure. For instance, it completed its part of a Kazakhstan–Turkmenistan–Iran rail link in August 2014. And it is collaborating with neighboring Uzbekistan to build a rail link with Iran, through which Uzbek and Turkmen cotton can be exported to Iran and the Middle East.

The president has been trying to develop a Caspian-based tourism industry too by building a new resort city, Awaza, at a cost of $2 billion. Turkmenistan's record on political freedom and human rights continues to be heavily criticized. According to Human Rights Watch, the government is one of the most repressive in the world. It imprisons political opponents and keeps their families in the dark about their whereabouts, refuses to allow journalists and human rights defenders to work openly, and imposes arbitrary travel bans on political activists and their relatives. There is no indication that the country is moving toward a genuinely pluralist political system despite the president having allowed a second party to form. Religion remains tightly controlled by the state, with all religious groups obliged to register to gain legal status, and the government continues to imprison Jehovah's Witnesses, who refuse to do military service on religious conscience grounds. In 2014 it permitted 650 of its Muslim citizens to travel to Mecca, Saudi Arabia, for the Hajj pilgrimage, only one-seventh of the quota allocated to it by the Saudi authorities, which regulate the Hajj pilgrim numbers to prevent potentially lethal overcrowding. It can take Turkmen Muslims up to 11 years to be approved to travel to Mecca after putting one's name on the waiting list, religious freedom advocacy group Forum 18 has noted.

President Berdimuhammedov appears to be replacing the late President Niyazov's personality cult with one of his own. He is now known as "Arkadag" meaning "protector." His portrait features ubiquitously in schools, universities, hospitals, aircrafts, newspapers, and markets. He is praised endlessly by the state-controlled media, and he has built a grandiose new presidential palace, abandoning the one Niyazov built. In the February 2012 presidential elections, while seven other candidates were permitted to compete against him, news reports described them as token challengers drawn from government ministries and state enterprises. Several of them even praised Berdimuhammedov, and the president won reelection overwhelmingly, taking 97 percent of the vote. The Organization for Security and Cooperation in Europe (OSCE) refused to send election monitors on account of the conditions in the country, while the Russian head of an election observer mission from the Commonwealth of Independent States praised the ballot. A good illustration of his iron grip of the media was seen in April 2013 when he fell off his horse while competing in a horse race that appeared clearly choreographed to have him win. The thousands of spectators present observed the fall moments after he crossed the finish line. However, the state-owned national broadcaster edited out the episode and made no reference to it in their extensive coverage of the event. Later, police checked computers, tablets, and mobile phones of departing passengers at airports to prevent footage of the fall being smuggled out.

Turkmenistan is also a major source country for men and women who are subjected to forced labor and prostitution, according to the U.S. State Department. Many are trafficked to Turkey, with some women subjected to forced prostitution and both men and women subjected to forced labor on construction sites, in textile sweatshops, and as domestic servants. The government has not made a serious effort to address the problem, nor is it trying to tackle the major overcrowding in Turkmen prisons, the report found. In September 2012 the country held the first-ever naval war games in its history, with warships and fighter jets staging attacks on an oil tanker in the Caspian Sea, maneuvers that were observed by the president. Most of the country's arms have been bought from Russia.

In September 2016 a constitutional provision that set the maximum age for presidents at 70 was removed in order to allow Berdimuhammedov to seek reelection. In October the government announced that presidential elections would be held in February 2017. In a November by-election, Serdar BERDIMUHAMMEDOV, the son of the president, was elected to parliament in what reports indicated was a signal that he was being prepared to be his father's successor.

POLITICAL PARTIES

The Turkmen political system is dominated by the Democratic Party of Turkmenistan (DPT). A **National Movement "Revival"** (*Galkynysh*), chaired by the president, is a government-sponsored association of various associations and the DPT. Most political opponents currently operate from exile in Russia, Scandinavia, and Eastern Europe.

Government Party:

Democratic Party of Turkmenistan (DPT). The DPT is the successor to the **Turkmen Communist Party,** which was dissolved on December 16, 1991, after its 25th congress had admitted to "mistakes" during seven decades of Soviet rule. The DPT describes itself as the country's "mother party" and has been virtually unchallenged as the leading political force in the country. President Berdimuhammedov was elected chair of the party in August 2007. In the December 2008 elections to the expanded Assembly, all seats were claimed by DPT candidates or party-approved independents. Akja NURBERDIYEWA was reelected speaker of the chamber. In the December 2013 elections (the first multiparty ballot in the country's history), the DPT won 47 seats in the 125 Mejlis. In January 2014 Nurberdiyewa was reelected speaker, while Gurbanguly BAYRAMOVA was elected deputy speaker.

Leader: Kasymguly Babaev.

Government-Sanctioned Party:

Party of Industrialists and Entrepreneurs (PIE). This party was established in August 2012 after President Berdimuhammedov announced that a new party would be allowed to compete against his ruling DPT. The independence of the PIE immediately came under suspicion, with one news report noting that the party was inaugurated by a panel seated under a wall-sized picture of the president and that little was known about the new party's leader. It has since been reported that the leader is a close friend of President Berdimuhammedov. The PIE gained its first seat in parliament in June 2013 when its leader Orazmammed MAMMEDOV won a by-election in the eastern province of Lebap. It won 14 seats in the December 2013 elections.

Leader: Orazmammed MAMMEDOV.

Unregistered Parties:

Unity (*Agzybirlik*). Originally formed in 1989 as a cultural and environmental forum, *Agzybirlik* was banned in 1990 and one of its founders, Shiraly NURMYRADOV, imprisoned, ostensibly for fraud. Released in 1992, Nurmyradov then relocated to Moscow. The party advocates adoption of a multiparty democracy.

In February 2000 another leader, Nurberdy NURMAMEDOV, was sentenced to five years in prison, reportedly for hooliganism and intent to murder. He was released in January 2001 and attempted to run for president in 2007, but he was denied a place on the ballot. Nurmamedov remains the only significant opposition leader still living in Turkmenistan, but he remains under house arrest.

Leader: Nurberdy NURMAMEDOV.

Exile opposition groups have included the Vienna-based **Republican Party of Turkmenistan** (RPT), chaired by Nurmuhammet Hanamow, a former ambassador to Turkey, which was expressly forbidden from campaigning in the 2008 Assembly elections; the **United Democratic Opposition of Turkmenistan** (UDOT), led by former foreign minister Avde Kuliev until his death in Oslo in April 2007; and the **People's Democratic Movement of Turkmenistan** (PDMT, also identified as the National Democratic Movement of Turkmenistan), founded by former foreign minister Boris Shikhmuradov. Shikhmuradov and Hanamow were both accused of involvement in an alleged November 2002 assassination attempt against President Niyazov, and Shikhmuradov is serving a life sentence.

In October 2003 four opposition groups, all in exile, announced formation of a **Union of Democratic Forces of Turkmenistan** (UDFT). Founding members were the RPT; the UDOT; the **Socio-Political Movement *Watan*** (Motherland), now led by Hudayberdi ORAZOW (Khudaiberdy ORAZOV); and the **Socio-Political Movement "Revival,"** led by Nazar SUYUNOV. Earlier, in June 2002, various opposition formations had convened in Vienna, Austria, and had organized a "Roundtable of the Turkmen Democratic Opposition"; participants included *Agzybirlik,* the **Communist Party of Turkmenistan,** the **National Patriotic Movement of Turkmenistan,** the PDMT, Shirali NURMURADOV's **Popular Social Movement "Mertebe"** (Dignity), the **Social Democratic Party,** Turkmen communities from Russia and elsewhere, and a veterans' group.

Following President Niyazov's death, the RPT and *Watan* formed a **Democratic Coalition of Turkmenistan,** which nominated *Watan*'s Orazow as its 2007 presidential candidate. Orazow was not allowed on the ballot. Farid TUKHBATULLIN, who lives in exile in Austria, is the head of the Turkmen Initiative for Human Rights, one of the most prominent human rights groups in Turkmenistan.

LEGISLATURE

Assembly (*Mejlis*). The *Mejlis* consists of 125 members elected for five-year terms from single-seat constituencies. Members of the Mejlis may not concurrently serve as government ministers. The Supreme Soviet elected on January 7, 1990, became the *Mejlis* as of May 19, 1992. Elections were held on December 14, 2008, with run-off balloting on December 28 for districts in which no candidate had received more than 50 percent of the vote. All 287 candidates, including the 125 members elected to the *Mejlis,* were either members of the Democratic Party of Turkmenistan or independents who ran with state backing. In the December 15, 2013, elections, there were 283 candidates.

Chair: Akja NURBERDIYEWA.

CABINET

[as of November 24, 2016]

President	Gurbanguly Berdimuhammedov
Deputy Chair (Office of the President)	Shamuhammet Durdylyev
	Baymyrat Hojamuhammedov
	Rashid Meredov
	Satylk Satlykov
	Gulshat Mamedova [f]
	Batyr Ereshov
	Yesenmyrat Orazgeldyew
	Batyr Atdayev
	Annageldy Yazmuradov
Ministers	
Agriculture and Water Resources	Nursahet Sapardurdyyew
Communications	Bayramgeldi Ovezov
Construction	Tchary Atayev
Culture and the Media	Annageldi Garadzhaev
Defense	Lt. Gen. Yaylim Berdiyev
Economics and Development	Batyr Bazarov
Education	Purli Agamyradov [f]
Energy	Davranmamed Rejepov
Environmental Protection and Natural Resources	Babageldi Annabayramow
Finance	Muhammetguly Mukhammedov
Foreign Affairs	Rashid Meredov
Healthcare and Pharmaceutical Industry	Nurmuhammet Amannepesov
Industry	Dowran Nursahedow
Interior	Iskander Mulikov
Justice	Begmurat Muhammedov
Labor and Social Protection	Seyidmammad Akhmammadow
Municipal Services	Mammetniyaz Nurmammedov
National Security	Col. Dovrangeldy Bairamov
Oil, Gas, and Mineral Resources	Myratgeldi Meredov
Railways	Bajram Annameredov
Road Transport	Maksat Aydogdyev
Textile Industry	Tachmammet Gurbanmammedov
Trade and Foreign Economic Relations	Dovran Orazmyradov

[f] = female

INTERGOVERNMENTAL REPRESENTATION

Ambassador to the U.S.: Meret Bairamovich ORAZOV.

U.S. Ambassador to Turkmenistan: Allan Phillip MUSTARD.

Permanent Representative to the UN: Aksoltan T. ATAYEVA.

IGO Memberships (Non-UN): ADB, CIS, EBRD, IDB, NAM, OIC, OSCE.

For Further Reference:

Edgar, Adrienne Lynn. *Tribal Nation: The Making of Soviet Turkmenistan.* Princeton, NJ: Princeton University Press, 2004.

Peyrouse, Sebastien. *Turkmenistan: Strategies of Power, Dilemmas of Development.* New York: M. E. Sharpe, 2012.

Rashid, Ahmed. *The Resurgence of Central Asia: Islam or Nationalism.* London: Zed Books, 1994.

TUVALU

Constitutional Monarchy of Tuvalu
Fakavae Aliki-Malo i Tuvalu

Political Status: Former British dependency; independent with "special membership" in the Commonwealth since October 1, 1978.

Land Area: 10 sq. mi. (26 sq. km).

Resident Population: 10,000 (2016E—UN); 10,959 (2016E—U.S. Census).

Major Urban Center (2014E)—UN: VAIAKU (Funafuti, 6,000).

Official Language: English (Tuvaluan is widely spoken).

Monetary Unit: Australian dollar (market rate October 1, 2016: 1.30 dollar = $1US). The Tuvaluan dollar, introduced in 1977, is used largely for numismatic purposes (market rate November 1, 2013: 1.06 dollar = $1US).

Sovereign: Queen ELIZABETH II.

Governor General: Iakopa ITALELI; sworn in on April 15, 2009, to succeed Rev. Filoimea TELITO.

Prime Minister: Enele SOPOAGA; elected by Parliament on August 4, 2013, succeeding Willy TELAVI, following a vote of no confidence on August 2; reelected on April 9, 2015, following legislative elections on March 31.

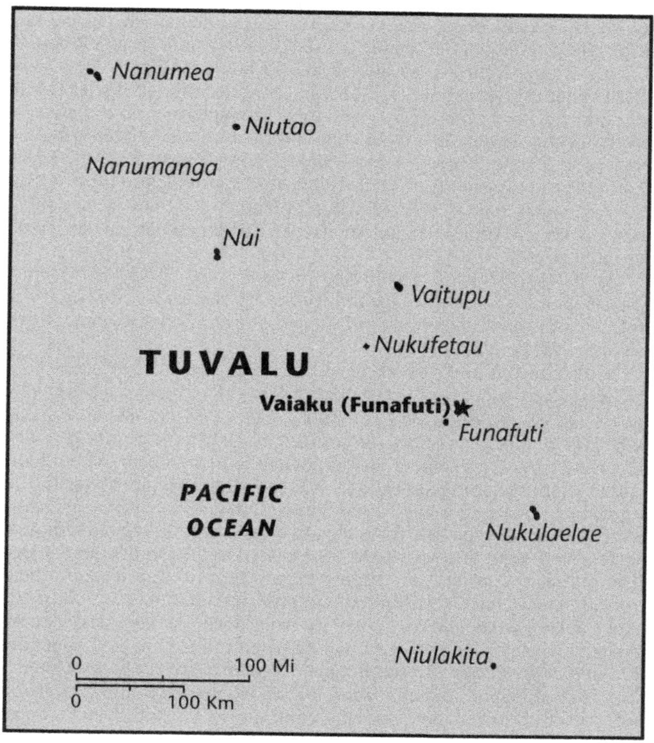

THE COUNTRY

Formerly known as the Ellice Islands in the Gilbert group, Tuvalu consists of nine atolls stretching over an area of 500,000 square miles north of Fiji in the western Pacific. Only eight of the islands are considered inhabited for electoral purposes; activity on the ninth is confined to a copra plantation. With a total land area of 10 square miles, Tuvalu is one of the world's smallest countries, although its population density is the highest among South Pacific island nations and some 35 percent of its population is estimated to live beneath the poverty line. Its inhabitants are predominantly Polynesian and Protestant Christian. The soil is poor, with crops subject to variable rainfall, frequent cyclones, and increasing salinization. As a consequence, agricultural activity is confined largely to the coco palm and its derivatives, yielding a dependency on imported food. Women constitute 30 percent of the paid labor force, concentrated almost entirely in the service sector; female participation in politics and government has traditionally been minimal, although a woman entered the Paeniu cabinet in 1989.

Only about a third of Tuvaluans are formally employed, and the primary employer is the government. Much of the islands' revenue is derived from service-based industries and from remittances by Tuvaluans working abroad, primarily as merchant seamen or as phosphate miners on Nauru and Kiribati's Banaba Island. Since 1987, approximately one-third of the operating expenses have been covered by donations from foreign governments. In November 1999 a California-based firm agreed to pay Tuvalu $50 million over the ensuing decade for use of the country's Internet suffix ".tv," which would be licensed to Web address customers as an alternative to ".com." The global depression brought a short period of significant economy growth to an end in 2009, when Tuvalu experienced a 1.7 percent decline. Between 2008 and 2012, remittances from workers abroad, mainly seafarers, dropped by more than 50 percent. The World Bank in November 2013 approved a new support plan for Tuvalu to rebuild from the crisis and fund social services. In 2014 GDP grew by 1.2 percent, with inflation of 2.7 percent.

GOVERNMENT AND POLITICS

Political background. Proclaimed a protectorate with the Gilbert Islands (now independent Kiribati) in 1892 and formally annexed by Britain in 1915–1916, when the Gilbert and Ellice Islands Colony was established, the Ellice Islands were separated on October 1, 1975, and renamed Tuvalu. Independence on October 1, 1978, occurred only five months after the acquisition of full internal self-government, former chief minister Toalipi LAUTI becoming prime minister and Sir Fiatau Penitala TEO being designated Crown representative. On September 17, 1981, nine days after the country's first general election since independence, a 5–7 parliamentary vote replaced Lauti with Dr. Tomasi PUAPUA. Lauti's defeat was blamed largely on his controversial decision in 1979 to invest most of the government's capital with a California business that promised assistance in obtaining a $5 million development loan; the money, plus interest, was reported to have been returned by mid-1984.

Dr. Puapua remained in office as head of a largely unchanged administration after the election of September 12, 1985. He stepped down in favor of Bikenibeu PAENIU because of the loss of parliamentary seats by two cabinet members in the election of September 27, 1989.

Following legislative balloting on September 2, 1993, parliament found itself in a 6–6 tie between those who wished to retain Prime Minister Paeniu and supporters of his predecessor. A new election was held on November 25. Puapua chose not to present himself as a candidate; Kamuta LATASI, a parliamentary backbencher and former private secretary to Governor General Toalipi Lauti, was chosen over Paeniu on a 7–5 vote. Latasi lost a nonconfidence vote by 7 to 5 on December 17, 1996, and was succeeded by Paeniu on December 23.

Following a campaign of exceptional bitterness, new balloting for parliament on March 26, 1998, returned Paeniu to his seat. Paeniu was reappointed for a new term as prime minister on April 8. However, he lost a vote of confidence by 7–4 on April 14, 1999, and the parliament on April 27 selected Ionatana IONATANA as his successor.

Prime Minister Ionatana died unexpectedly on December 8, 2000, and was succeeded by Deputy Prime Minister Lagitupu TUILIMU, in an acting capacity. On February 23, 2001, parliament elected Faimalaga LUKA as his successor. He was sworn in at the head of a reshuffled cabinet the following day.

On December 13, 2001, the parliament elected Koloa TALAKE, a former minister of finance, as head of government. The previous week, Prime Minister Luka had lost a no-confidence motion when four legislators, including Talake, crossed the aisle to support the motion. (Named governor general on September 9, 2003, Luka retired in April 2005 and died on August 19.)

In balloting for an expanded 15-seat parliament on July 25, 2002, Talake, three other government ministers, and the speaker of parliament all lost their seats. On August 2 Saufatu SOPOANGA defeated the other candidate for prime minister, Amasone KILEI, by a vote of 8–7 and named a completely new cabinet. Sopoanga lost a no-confidence vote (8–6) on August 25, 2004, and delayed the naming of a successor by resigning his legislative seat, thus forcing a by-election. Reelected on October 7, Sopoanga was named deputy prime minister by Maatia TOAFA following his election as the new prime minister on October 11.

On August 14, 2006, Prime Minister Toafa was succeeded by Apisai IELEMIA following a general election on August 3, in which 8 of the 15 incumbent legislators lost their seats. Ielemia yielded to Toafa after the election of September 29, 2010. After only three months in office, Prime Minister Maatia Toafa lost a confidence motion in Parliament on December 21, 2010, by one vote after Willy TELAVI, the minister for home affairs, withdrew his support from the government. Telavi was elected as the new prime minister on December 24 and subsequently named a new cabinet. On August 5, 2013, Enele SOPOAGA was sworn in after Telavi lost a confidence motion (see Current issues, below). A by-election in January led to the unseating of house speaker Otinielu Tauteleimalae TAUSI when parliament reconvened in March.

In delayed legislative balloting on March 31, 2015 (see Current issues, below), 12 of 15 incumbents were reelected. Sopoaga was reelected prime minister on April 4, and a reshuffled government was sworn in the next day.

Constitution and government. The 1978 constitution (a substantially revised version of a preindependence document adopted three years earlier) provides for a governor general of Tuvaluan citizenship who serves a four-year term (or until age 65) and a prime minister who is elected by a unicameral parliament of 15 members. Should the office of prime minister become vacant with parliament unable to agree on a successor, the governor general may, at his discretion, name a chief executive or call for legislative dissolution. The government collectively reports to parliament, whose normal term is four years. The judiciary consists of a High Court, which is empowered to hear appeals from courts of criminal and civil jurisdiction on each of the eight inhabited islands as well as from local magistrates' courts. Appeals from the High Court may be taken to the Court of Appeal in Fiji and, as last resort, to the Judicial Committee of the Privy Council in London. Island councils (most of whose members are reportedly wary of centralized government) continue to be dominant in local administration.

In accordance with the results of a 1986 public poll that rejected republican status, the government announced that the link with the Crown would be retained, although constitutional changes would be introduced that would limit the governor general to a largely ceremonial role. However, the High Court in August 2003 ruled that the governor general retained the power to convene parliament in the face of a government effort to delay recall as a means of continuing in office. In early 2005 Prime Minister Toafa reopened the republican issue, declaring, over the apparent objection of his deputy, former prime minister Sopoanga, that he planned to hold a referendum on replacing Queen Elizabeth II with a president as head of state. Action in the matter was delayed, however, until April 2008, at which time a low turnout (22 percent) of the electorate rejected the change by a 2–1 majority.

Freedom of speech is constitutionally guaranteed, and the government generally respects freedom of the press. A semipublic company, the Tuvalu Media Corporation runs the country's only television and radio stations and also publishes a biweekly newspaper. Although external groups have criticized the company for failing to cover human rights issues, there have been no allegations of censorship.

Foreign relations. Upon independence Tuvalu elected to join Nauru as a "special member" of the Commonwealth, having the right to participate in all Commonwealth affairs except heads of government meetings. It was admitted to the United Nations as the world body's 189th member on September 5, 2000. At the regional level it participates in the Pacific Islands Forum (PIF) and the Pacific Community. Most contacts with other states are through representatives accredited to Fiji or New Zealand, although in 1984 formal relations, backdated to 1979, were established with former colonial partner Kiribati.

In 1979 Tuvalu and the United States signed a treaty of friendship (ratified in June 1983) that included provision for consultation in the areas of defense and marine resources, with Washington acknowledging Tuvalu's sovereignty over four islands (Funafuti, Nukufetau, Nukulaelae, and Niulakita) originally claimed by the U.S. Congress in the so-called Guano Act of 1856.

In February 1986 Tuvalu, which had signed the antinuclear Treaty of Rarotonga in 1985, refused to sanction a "goodwill visit" by a French warship as a means of protesting continued nuclear testing in French Polynesia.

In December 1998 Prime Minister Paeniu visited Taiwan, whose battle with China for diplomatic support in the South Pacific had recently intensified. Taiwanese officials pledged development aid for Tuvalu's fishing industry. Taiwan is the only country in the world to maintain a resident ambassador in Tuvalu.

In March 2005 Tuvalu and Kiribati sought assistance from the PIF for wage arrears and repatriation of some 1,000 of their nationals who had been working for a decade as laborers in Nauru's phosphate mines.

In early 2008 Tuvalu became the 11th PIF member to ratify the Pacific Island Countries Trade Agreement (PICTA), which seeks the gradual reduction of import duties among participants. On June 24, 2010, Tuvalu became the 187th member of the International Monetary Fund.

On May 26, 2011, Tuvalu signed a communiqué with the Baltic nation Estonia establishing formal diplomatic relations, and in October, Russia and Tuvalu did the same. In March 2012, a month after the severing of diplomatic relations with Georgia, Tuvalu established ties with Georgia's rebel Abkhazia government. Tuvalu revoked its recognition of Abkhazia in March 2014 when it reestablished ties with Georgia.

In July 2012 Tuvalu was criticized by the United States for reflagging Iranian oil tankers, violating sanctions that were put in place to try to curb Iran's nuclear program. Tuvalu agreed to deregister the ships in August.

Tuvalu established diplomatic relations with Guyana in September 2012 and, the following year in July, did the same with Cyprus. In March 2013 Tuvalu opened its first embassy in Taipei, Taiwan.

At a PIF meeting in September 2013, Tuvalu and the other 14 member states committed to taking radical steps toward reduction of greenhouse gas emissions, part of an initiative presented later to the UN General Assembly to mark a "new wave of climate leadership."

In February 2015 Tuvalu enacted the Seabeds Minerals Act to ensure the sustainable development of overseas mineral resources. With the new law Tuvalu joined the Cook Islands, Fiji, and Tonga as part of a regional effort to ensure sustainable mining.

Current issues. Recent estimates suggest Tuvalu's land areas will be severely flooded within the next 15 to 20 years and will be submerged by the end of the century. Overtures to New Zealand and Australia about possible resettlement have produced mixed responses for the endangered island nation. Meanwhile Tuvalu adopted an ambitious $20 million plan to replace its imported fossil fuels with renewable solar energy and wind power by the year 2020. Tuvalu declared a state of emergency in 2011 when a year-long drought nearly exhausted the country's drinking water. New Zealand and Australia led the international charge, sending desalinization plants and emergency water tanks. Water donations alleviated the crisis by mid-November. In August 2013 Tuvalu signed a $4.2 million agreement with the United Nations Development Program toward sustaining fisheries and disaster risk management.

As opposition lawmakers prepared to table a no-confidence motion against Prime Minister Telavi's administration in July 2013, Speaker Kamuta Latasi blocked the action by suspending the house to await a by-election to fill a recently emptied seat. Controversy deepened when Governor General Iakopa ITALELI ordered Telavi's resignation; Telavi in turn wrote to Queen Elizabeth to inform her that he was dismissing Italeli. Ultimately on August 2 parliament voted 8–4 against Telavi. Enele Sopoaga was elected on August 4. He and his new cabinet took office on August 5.

In a by-election in January 2014, former house speaker Otinielu Tauteleimalae Tausi won the vacant seat and threw his support behind Sopoaga, who then claimed a two-thirds majority in the house. When parliament reconvened on March 5, Latasi was ousted as speaker and Tausi resumed the post.

Cyclone Pam caused widespread destruction on March 10–11, affecting 45 percent of the population, causing $10 million in damage and forcing the postponement of legislative elections. In September the World Bank provided a grant of $3 million to assist with recovery efforts.

POLITICAL PARTIES

Political affairs in Tuvalu are grounded in family ties and personalities, not ideology. In late 1992 it was reported that a group called the **Tuvalu United Party** (*Tama i Fulu a Tuvalu*) had been organized by Prime Minister Paeniu and his deputy, Dr. Alesana Kleis SELUKA, but the party has played no part in recent elections. While there have not been any political parties since, the 15 independent members who are elected to parliament do form loose coalitions consisting of government and opposition.

LEGISLATURE

Known prior to independence as the House of Assembly, the unicameral **Parliament** (*Palamente o Tuvalu*) consists of 15 members: 2 each from seven islands and 1 from the least populous inhabited island. The legislative term, subject to dissolution, is four years. In legislative balloting held on March 31, 2015, three new members were among the 15 legislators elected.

Speaker: Otinielu Tauteleimalae TAUSI.

CABINET

[as of November 15, 2016]

Prime Minister	Enele Sopoaga
Deputy Prime Minister	Maatia Toafa
Ministers	
Communication, Transport, and Public Utilities	Monise Laafai
Education, Youth, and Sports	Fauoa Maani
Finance and Economic Development	Maatia Toafa
Foreign Affairs	Taukelina Finikaso
Health	Satini Tulaga Manuella
Home Affairs and Rural Development	Namoliki Neemia
Natural Resources and Public Works	Elisala Pita
Public Utilities and Infrastructure	Enele Sopoaga
Trade, Tourism, Environment, and Labor	Taukelina Finikaso

INTERGOVERNMENTAL REPRESENTATION

Ambassador to the U.S. and Permanent Representative to the UN: Aunese Makoi SIMATI.

U.S. Ambassador to Tuvalu (resident in Fiji): Judith Beth CEFKIN.

IGO Memberships (Non-UN): ADB, CWTH, IOM, PIF.

For Further Reference:

Besnier, Niko. *Gossip and the Everyday Production of Politics.* Honolulu: University of Hawaii Press, 2009.

MacDonald, Barrie. *Cinderallas of the Empire: Towards a History of Kiribati and Tuvalu.* Suva, Fiji: University of the South Pacific, 2001.

McQuarrie, Peter. *Strategic Atolls: Tuvalu and the Second World War.* Canterbury, New Zealand: University of Canterbury, 1994.

UGANDA

Republic of Uganda

Political Status: Independent member of the Commonwealth since October 9, 1962; republican constitution adopted on September 8, 1967; personal military rule (instituted on January 25, 1971) overthrown with establishment of provisional government on April 11, 1979; military regime installed on January 29, 1986; present constitution adopted on September 22, 1995, with effect from October 8; amended by public referendum on July 28, 2005, to provide for multiparty system.

Area: 93,104 sq. mi. (241,139 sq. km).

Population: 40,323 (2016E—UN); 38,319,241 (2016E—U.S. Census).

Major Urban Center (2016E, urban area—UN): KAMPALA (2,012,000).

Official Language: English (Swahili and Luganda are widely used).

Monetary Unit: Ugandan Shilling (market rate October 1, 2016: 3,390.00 Ugandan shillings = $1US).

President: Lt. Gen. Yoweri Kaguta MUSEVENI (National Resistance Movement); sworn in on January 29, 1986, following the overthrow of Lt. Gen. Tito OKELLO Lutwa on January 27; popularly elected on May 9, 1996, and inaugurated for a five-year term on May 12; reelected for another five-year term on March 12, 2001; reelected in multiparty balloting on February 23, 2006, and inaugurated for another five-year term on May 12; reelected in multiparty balloting on February 18, 2011, and sworn in for another five-year term on May 12; reelected on February 18, 2016, and inaugurated for another five-year term on May 12.

Vice President: Edward Kiwanika SSEKANDI (National Resistance Movement); appointed by the president on May 24, 2011, succeeding Gilbert Balibaseka BUKENYA (National Resistance Movement); reappointed and sworn in on June 22, 2016.

Prime Minister: Ruhakana RUGUNDA (National Resistance Movement); appointed by the president on September 18, 2014, succeeding Amama MBABAZI (National Resistance Movement); reappointed on June 6, 2016.

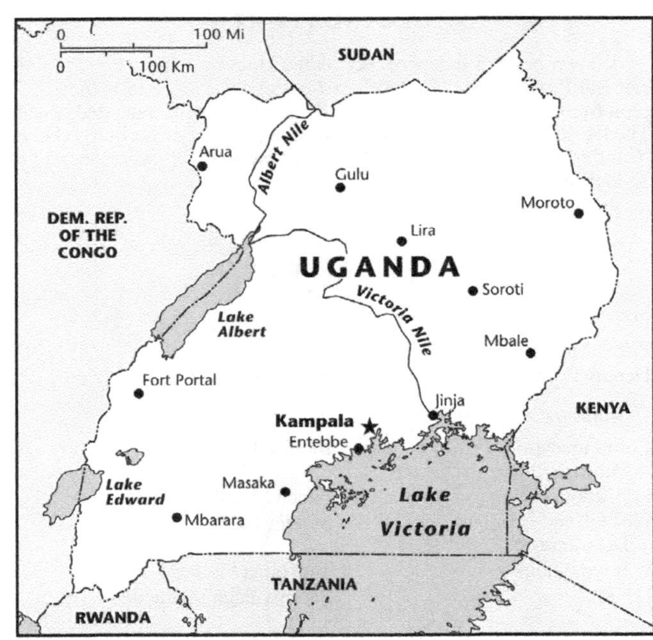

THE COUNTRY

Landlocked Uganda, located in east-central Africa, is bounded on the east by Kenya, on the south by Tanzania and Rwanda, on the west by the Democratic Republic of the Congo (DRC), and on the north by Sudan. The country is known for its lakes (among them Lake Victoria, the source of the White Nile) and its mountains, the most celebrated of which are the Mountains of the Moon (the Ruwenzori), lying on the border with the DRC. The population embraces a number of African tribal groups, including the Baganda, Banyankore, Basoga, and Iteso. For many decades a substantial Asian (primarily Indian) minority engaged in shopkeeping, industry, and other professions. In 1972, however, the Idi Amin government decreed the expulsion of all noncitizen Asians as part of a plan to put Uganda's economy in the hands of nationals, and at present only a scattering of Asians still reside in the country. Approximately 60 percent of the population is Christian and another 15 percent is Muslim, with the remainder adhering to traditional African beliefs. Women are primarily responsible for subsistence agriculture. The government is considered progressive regarding women's rights, with seats in the current parliament being reserved for women. Following the 2016 balloting, women held 143 seats in Parliament, or 33.5 percent. Women held 10 cabinet portfolios in 2016. One-third of the seats in local councils must, by law, also go to women.

Agriculture, forestry, and fishing contribute about one-third of Uganda's gross domestic product (GDP); industry, which is growing in importance, accounts for about 21 percent of GDP. Services account for the remainder. Coffee is the principal crop (Uganda is one of Africa's leading producers), followed by cotton, tea, peanuts, and tobacco.

In May 2000 the IMF and World Bank announced that Uganda had qualified for $2 billion in debt service relief over the next 20 years based on the government's adherence to its comprehensive reform program and continued economic progress. (For information on Uganda's economy prior to 2000, see the 2012 *Handbook*.) By mid-2005 GDP growth of 5.4 percent was offset by one of the highest population growth rates in the world and widespread poverty. Subsequently, the IMF in 2006 cited poverty reduction as the foremost economic issue for Uganda, and it urged reforms to curb corruption. Unhappy with alleged corruption in government spending and the country's slow progress toward democratization, the UK, traditionally Uganda's biggest donor, and three other donor countries canceled millions of dollars in aid to Kampala.

Oil was discovered in Uganda in 2009, though production plans were stalled by government claims that it was owed $434 million in capital gains tax by one of the interested oil companies (see Foreign relations, below). The economy was spared the worst effects of the global economic downturn, according to the IMF, and annual GDP growth averaged 6 percent in 2009–2011, owing in large part to increased investment. Fund managers advised Ugandan authorities to boost non-oil revenue, since anticipated oil revenue will last only a limited number of years. In 2011 severe food and water shortages due to drought affected 36 of 112 districts, particularly in the east. In 2012, Britain announced increased aid of $638 million through 2015 (see Foreign relations, below). GDP grew by 6.7 percent in 2011 and 2.6 percent in 2012. GDP grew by 6 percent in 2013. Inflation that year was 5.4 percent, a significant decline from 14.1 percent in the previous year. GDP expanded by 3.9 percent in 2014, 4.9 percent in 2015, and an estimated 5.6 percent in 2016. That year inflation was 4.8 percent, while GDP per capita was $695. The World Bank ranked Uganda as 122nd out of 189 countries in its 2016 ease of doing business index, an improvement from 132nd in 2014.

GOVERNMENT AND POLITICS

Political background. Uganda became a British protectorate in 1894–1896 and began its progress toward statehood after World War II, achieving internal self-government on March 1, 1962, and full independence within the Commonwealth on October 9, 1962. A problem involving Buganda and three other traditional kingdoms was temporarily resolved by granting the kingdoms semiautonomous rule within a federal system. The arrangement enabled Buganda's representatives to participate in the national government, and the king (*kabaka*) of Buganda, Sir Edward Frederick MUTESA II, was elected president of Uganda on October 9, 1963. The issue of national unity versus Bugandan particularism led Prime Minister Apollo Milton OBOTE, leader of the Uganda

People's Congress (UPC) and an advocate of centralism, to depose the president and vice president in February 1966. A constitution eliminating Buganda's autonomous status was ratified in April 1966 by the National Assembly, which consisted mainly of UPC members. Failing in an effort to mobilize effective resistance to the new government, the *kabaka* fled the country in May, and a new republican constitution, adopted in September 1967, eliminated the special status of Buganda and the other kingdoms. Earlier, on April 15, 1966, Obote had been designated president by the National Assembly for a five-year term. In December 1969 he banned all opposition parties and established a one-party state with a socialist program known as the Common Man's Charter.

On January 25, 1971, Maj. Gen. Idi AMIN Dada, commander in chief of the army and air force, mounted a successful coup that deposed Obote while the president was abroad at a Commonwealth meeting. In addition to continuing the ban on opposition political activity, Amin suspended parts of the constitution, dissolved the National Assembly, and secured his own installation as president of the republic.

Following an invasion by Tanzanian troops and exile forces organized as the Uganda National Liberation Army (UNLA), the Amin regime, which had drawn worldwide condemnation for atrocities against perceived opponents, was effectively overthrown with the fall of Kampala April 10–11, 1979, with Amin fleeing to Libya. Concurrently, the National Consultative Council (NCC) of the Uganda National Liberation Front (UNLF) designated Professor Yusuf K. LULE, former vice chancellor of Makerere University, as president of the republic and head of a provisional government. On June 20 the NCC announced that Godfrey Lukongwa BINAISA, a former attorney general under President Obote, had been named to succeed Lule in both capacities.

After a series of disagreements with both the NCC and the UNLF's Military Commission, Binaisa was relieved of his authority on May 12, 1980. (Binaisa died at age 90 in 2010.) On May 18 the chair of the Military Commission, Paulo MUWANGA, announced that a three-member Presidential Commission had been established to exercise executive power through a cabinet of ministers on advice of its military counterpart, pending a national election later in the year.

Former president Obote returned from Tanzania on May 27, 1980, and in mid-June agreement was reached between party and UNLF representatives on four groups that would be permitted to participate in the presidential/legislative campaign. Following balloting December 10–11, the UPC declared that it had secured a majority in the National Assembly, thus assuring Obote's reinvestiture as chief executive. Although the runner-up Democratic Party (DP) denounced the results as fraudulent, most victorious DP candidates took their legislative seats. The Uganda Patriotic Movement (UPM), led by former president Lule and his former defense minister, Yoweri MUSEVENI, refused to accept the one seat it had won. After shedding the party apparatus, Lule and Museveni formed a National Resistance Movement (NRM) and initiated a guerrilla campaign against Obote through the affiliated National Resistance Army (NRA).

During the next five years, while the UNLA achieved some success in repulsing the rebels, the NRA continued to hold the agriculturally important "Luwero triangle" north of Kampala, as well as its traditional strongholds in the Banyankore-dominated southwest. During the same period, many army actions against civilians were reported, including the harassment, wounding, or killing of DP members; by mid-1985, more than 200,000 were estimated to have died, either from army "excesses" or official counterinsurgency efforts.

On July 27, 1985, in a self-proclaimed attempt to "stop the killing," Brig. Basilio Olara OKELLO led a senior officers' coup against Obote, who had lost much international support and was again forced into exile. Two days later the constitution was suspended, and Obote's army chief of staff, Lt. Gen. Tito OKELLO Lutwa, was sworn in as chair of a ruling Military Council. On August 6 General Okello called for all guerrilla groups, including former Amin soldiers, to join his army, while naming Paulo Muwanga, who had served as Obote's vice president, as prime minister and DP leader Paul SSEMOGERERE as minister of the interior. Unlike most other resistance leaders, Museveni, the dominant NRM figure following Lule's death in January 1985, did not accede to Okello's call for "unity," citing continued abuses by army personnel who routinely failed to defer to Okello. In contrast, the NRA had a reputation for being well disciplined, relatively free of tribal rivalries, and far less brutal toward civilians.

By September 1985, when the first of a series of Kenyan- and Tanzanian-mediated peace talks began in Dar es Salaam, NRA forces had taken control of a number of strategic towns and supply routes, while another Obote associate, Abraham WALIGO, replaced Muwanga as prime minister. In November Museveni announced that "in order to provide services pending an agreement with the regime in Kampala," an "interim administration" was being established in rebel-held areas. A peace pact signed in Nairobi on December 17 gave Museveni the vice chair of the Military Council while providing for the dissolution of all existing armed units and the recruitment, under external supervision, of a new, fully representative force. However, the accord did not take effect. After failing to attend "celebrations" scheduled for January 4, 1986, Museveni, citing continuing human-rights abuses, launched a drive on Kampala, which culminated in the overthrow of the six-month-old Okello regime on January 27. Two days later, while NRA forces consolidated their control, Museveni was sworn in as president, thereafter appointing a cabinet that included as prime minister Dr. Samson KISEKKA, formerly the NRM's external spokesperson. In an attempt to prevent further civil war, Museveni also named representatives of other major political groups to his government. However, some UNLA units that had not disbanded fled to the north and the east, where they and other rebel groups continued to resist the NRA.

In mid-1986 Museveni absolved his immediate predecessor, General Okello, of atrocities committed by troops under his command. No such tender was made to former presidents Amin and Obote, with Museveni calling for their repatriation from exile in Saudi Arabia and Zambia, respectively, to face charges by a special commission of inquiry established to review the "slaughter" of Bantu southerners by their Nilotic followers. (Obote died in Zambia in October 2005.)

In February 1988 Museveni named three deputy prime ministers, including DP leader Ssemogerere, to assist the ailing Kisekka. In addition, the cabinet was reshuffled to include more representatives from the north and east, where rebel activity continued to impede national reconciliation. An even more drastic reshuffle was ordered in April 1989 coincident with conversion of the theretofore appointive National Resistance Council (see Constitution and government, below) into a largely elective body. Six months later the council voted to extend the government's interim mandate (originally limited by President Museveni to four years) to January 1995. The action was justified by the minister of justice on the grounds that the country lacked the "essential political machinery and the logistics for the evolution of a democratic and a permanent stable government."

On January 22, 1991, Museveni appointed Kisekka to the new, largely ceremonial position of vice president, with George Cosmas ADYEBO, a 43-year-old economist, named prime minister. The government subsequently conducted a "final sweep" against rebel forces in the north and east, and in July Kampala reported that its troops had decimated the rebel forces, killing 1,500 insurgents between March and July (many, Amnesty International charged, after perfunctory military trials) and absorbing many others into the NRA. In August the government described the remaining rebels, predominantly from Joseph KONY's Uganda Democratic Christian Army, as "thugs" who had been reduced to raiding villages for food and whose earlier atrocities prevented their reintegration.

In January 1993 Museveni, who continued to reject domestic and international calls for the immediate introduction of multipartyism on the grounds that it would exacerbate religious and ethnic cleavages, announced plans for nonparty elections by the end of 1994. In February the NRC passed a constituent assembly bill that called for the delay of multiparty politics until at least the year 2000 (see Constitution and government, below).

Earlier, in what was described by critics as political repayment to the Baganda people for supporting the NRA struggle in the early 1980s, Museveni had begun negotiating with Baganda to restore its monarch. Consequently, on July 31, 1993, the son of Mutesa II, Ronald Muwenda MUTEBI, was crowned *kabaka,* an event described as a purely "ceremonial" action. Collaterally, pro forma recognition was granted to the coronation of Patrick David Matthew Olimi KABOYO II as monarch of the smaller Toro kingdom. (Kaboyo died on September 13, 1995 and was succeeded by his three-year-old son, Oyo Nyimba Kabamba IGURU IV.) On June 11, 1994, the oldest of Uganda's historic kingdoms was restored, with the crowning of Solon Iguri GAFABUSA I as king of the Bunyoro tribe. (The crowning of John BARIGYE as monarch of Uganda's Ankore kingdom was indefinitely delayed because of disputes within the clan leadership.) Meanwhile, on February 11, 1996, Henry Wako MULOKI, the Basoga's traditional leader, was reinstalled as *kyabazinga* (king) at a ceremony attended by Museveni.

On March 28, 1994, nonparty balloting was held to fill the 214-seat Constituent Assembly. As anticipated, NRM-affiliated candidates captured the majority of the seats (114), although the president's actual assembly supporters were reported as numbering only 93. In December the government announced that nonparty general elections would be held by late 1995; however, they were deferred until April–May 1996. Meanwhile, the Constituent Assembly on September 22 approved a new basic law that continued the ban on political campaigning and provided that the NRC would remain in existence for another five years. Upon promulgation of the document on October 8, the constituent body was dissolved.

At Uganda's first presidential balloting on May 9, 1996, President Museveni captured 74.2 percent of the vote, easily outpolling his two competitors, the DP's Ssemogerere (23.7 percent) and an Islamic candidate, Mohamed MAYANJA Kibirige (2.1 percent). Although Museveni controlled the media and local councils administering the polling, international observers described the polling as "fair. Thereafter, in "no-party" legislative polling staged between June 6 and 27, NRM candidates secured or were appointed to 271 of the 276 available posts. On July 6 Museveni named an enlarged cabinet that included only NRM members.

In early 1998 Museveni named his half-brother, Gen. Salim SALEH, as defense minister, a post held theretofore by the president himself. The appointment of Saleh, who had been credited with coordinating the government's highly successful offensives against its various rebel opponents in mid-1997, underscored Museveni's apparent dedication to a total rout of the Lord's Resistance Army (LRA—see Political Parties and Groups, below), whose call for a cease-fire in July had been rejected. (Saleh resigned in December after allegations of corrupt financial dealings were made against him.)

In May 1998 Museveni reshuffled the government and, following the retirement of Prime Minister Musoke, on April 6, 1999, the president named Apolo NSIBAMBI to head a substantially altered cabinet. In a referendum on June 29, 2000, 90 percent of the voters endorsed continuance of the no-party system.

On March 12, 2001, President Museveni was reelected to another five-year term, securing 69 percent of the vote compared to 28 percent for his nearest rival, Kizza BESIGYE, Museveni's former doctor and former military ally. Subsequently, the NRM retained its stronghold on the parliament in elections held on June 26. Although a dozen sitting cabinet members lost their legislative seats, most of them were defeated by other Museveni supporters. Following the elections, Museveni reappointed Prime Minister Nsibambi to head a significantly altered cabinet, which was sworn in on July 24. A constitutional referendum on July 28, 2005 (see Constitution and government, below), allowed for the registration of political parties, among other things, in advance of presidential and parliamentary elections on February 23, 2006. In the multiparty presidential election, Museveni defeated four challengers by garnering 59.3 percent of the vote. His nearest rival, Kizza Besigye, running as the Forum for Democratic Change (FDC) candidate, received 37.4 percent. The Democratic Party's John SSEBAANA Kizito won 1.6 percent, and the Uganda People's Congress (UPC) candidate, Miria OBOTE, widow of the former president, won less than 1 percent. In concurrent parliamentary elections, the NRM retained power, while five opposition parties also won representation. A reshuffled and enlarged cabinet, again led by Prime Minister Apolo Nsibambi, was sworn in on June 2, 2006.

The cabinet was reshuffled on February 16, 2009. In addition to naming 25 ministers, the new government appointed 44 ministers of state, including President Museveni's wife, Janet, as minister of state for the Karamoja region.

Former foreign minister and UN diplomat Olara Otunnu returned to Uganda in August 2009 after 23 years, most recently from exile in Zambia, to seek the presidential nomination of the UPC for the 2011 election. Despite a long career as an advocate for children's rights and international peace, Otunnu received what was described as a mixed reception by his party stemming from his role in Okello's military government in 1985. Museveni easily won a fourth consecutive term in the February 18, 2011, election, this time with 68.4 percent of the vote to Besigye's diminished 26 percent, while the DP's Norbert MAO finished a very distant third with 1.9 percent, and Otunnu was fourth with 1.6 percent. Four other candidates each received less than 1 percent. The NRM kept its stronghold in concurrent parliamentary elections, and all five parties previously represented retained small numbers of seats. Opposition leaders, including five presidential contenders, claimed the results were fraudulent because of alleged bribery, ballot stuffing, and harassment, and the European Union (EU) cited problems with the election as well. The government postponed local and mayoral elections from February 23 to March 14 after the electoral commission announced it had found evidence of fraud and subsequently dismissed 20 of its officials accused of participating in vote rigging. The minister of state for ethics and integrity resigned on March 15. He was one of nine ministers who had been suspended for contesting parliamentary elections as an independent in violation of a court ruling. Museveni was sworn in on May 12, and on May 24 he replaced both the vice president and the prime minister. Edward Kiwanika SSEKANDI was named vice president, and former security minister Amana MBABAZI was tapped as prime minister. The extensively reshuffled cabinet appointed on May 27 included 42 ministers of state and 10 women, and the president's wife was named to a ministerial post. Former vice president Gilbert Balibaseka BUKENYA, who had been appointed by the president on June 6, 2003, faced corruption charges in court on May 30.

The minister of foreign affairs, Sam KUTESA, was suspended on October 14, 2011, following allegations of corruption (see Current Issues, below). The cabinet was reshuffled on August 15, 2012, following the resignation of several ministers, and Kutesa was reinstated to his portfolio.

The first deputy prime minister, Eriya KATEGAYA, died on March 2, 2013. He was replaced during a broad cabinet reshuffle in May, in which the second and third deputy prime ministers were promoted.

After rumors surfaced in 2014 that Prime Minister Mbabazi planned to challenge Museveni for the NRM presidential nomination (see Political Parties and Groups, below), the president replaced him on September 18 with Ruhakana RUGUNDA. In March 2015 there was a major cabinet reshuffle, with a minor reshuffle in November.

In general elections on February 18, 2016, Museveni was reelected with 60.8 percent of the vote, defeating the FDC's Besigye and six other candidates. In legislative balloting, the NRM increased its majority to 293 seats, followed by the FDC with 36. The European Union, the United States, and the Commonwealth all criticized the conduct of the elections. Rugunda was reappointed prime minister of a largely new cabinet on June 6.

Constitution and government. The 1962 constitution was suspended by Prime Minister Obote in February 1966. A successor instrument adopted in April 1966 terminated the federal system but was itself replaced in September 1967 by a republican constitution that established a president as head of state, chief executive, and commander in chief of the armed forces. While he did not formally revoke the 1967 constitution when he came to power, President Amin in February 1971 assumed judicial as well as executive and legislative powers. Subsequently, though martial law was never declared, military tribunals tried both civil and criminal cases and authorized numerous public executions. With but minor modification, the 1967 constitution was reinstated by the UNLF as the basis of post-military government in 1980; it was suspended by the Military Council in mid-1985 and remained inoperative thereafter.

On February 1, 1986, while in the process of organizing an interim government dominated by members of his NRM, President Museveni announced the formation of a National Resistance Council (NRC) to serve as an appointive surrogate for the former National Assembly. The NRC was converted into a largely elective body of 278 members in February 1989.

In early 1993 a 15-member commission, appointed by President Museveni in February 1989, released a report proposing the delay of multipartyism for seven years, during which time a largely elected Constituent Assembly would draft a new constitution. (Representatives of special interest groups, including the NRA, NRC, women, youths, and unions, were subsequently added to the 214-member parliament elected in March 1994.) However, the charter that emerged in September 1995 was promulgated without submission to a promised referendum. More importantly, it continued the ban on partisan activity (save behind closed party doors). In the wake of intense criticism from U.S. and British authorities, regime opponents sought to have the ban rescinded but were told that such action could be initiated only by the legislature elected under the constitution as adopted. The "no-party" system was subsequently endorsed by national referendum in June 2000.

In January 2004 the government initiated negotiations with opposition parties on the transition to multiparty politics and the future system of government. Six months later a court ruling invalidated (on a technicality) the 2000 referendum. Subsequently, as pressure for a multiparty system continued, parliament voted in May 2005 in favor of a national referendum on a multiparty political system, abolishing the two-term limit on the presidency, and granting the president the authority to dissolve parliament in case of a constitutional crisis. In balloting of July 28, 2005, the amendments were approved by 92.4 percent of voters.

Local government has assumed a variety of forms since 1971, the Amin and Lule governments both having reorganized the provincial and district systems. Currently, under initiatives adopted by the Museveni administration, local affairs are handled by several tiers of elected "resistance councils" ranging from village to regional levels. In August 2006 parliament approved 11 new districts, creating more seats for women (99) in advance of the August 28 elections for women district representatives.

On August 25, 2010, the Constitutional Court struck down Uganda's sedition law, ruling that it infringed on the right to freedom of speech guaranteed in Uganda's constitution. In 2016 Reporters Without Borders ranked Uganda 102nd out of 180 countries in freedom of the press, a significant rise from 139 in 2012.

Foreign relations. From independence, Uganda based its foreign policy on anticolonialism, retaining moderate Western support from its consistently nonaligned posture. However, reacting to criticism by the Amin regime of U.S. policies in Vietnam, Cambodia, and the Middle East, Washington terminated its economic assistance program in mid-1973 and subsequently closed its embassy because of public threats against officials and other Americans residing in the country. Three years later, in an event of major international import, Israeli commandos raided the Entebbe airport during the night of July 3–4, 1976, to secure the release of passengers of an Air France airliner that had been hijacked over Greece by Palestinian Arab guerrillas and flown to Uganda via Libya. Denying allegations that he had cooperated with the hijackers, Amin protested Israel's action and accused Kenya of aiding in its implementation.

Tensions with both Kenya and Tanzania resulted not only in the collapse of the tripartite East African Community (EAC) in June 1977 but ultimately in the Tanzanian military intervention of early 1979 (see Political background, above). The latter action came in the wake of an ill-conceived incursion into northern Tanzania in October 1978 by Ugandan troops, with effective Tanzanian withdrawal from Uganda not occurring until mid-1981 due to retraining requirements of the post-Amin Ugandan army. The two neighbors were critically involved in discussions between the short-lived Okello regime and the NRA, Kenyan president Daniel arap Moi being credited with brokering the December peace agreement between Okello and Museveni. Following Museveni's takeover in January 1986, both governments were quick to recognize the new regime, as was the United States. Nevertheless, relations with Kenya were subsequently strained by a series of border incidents, mutual accusations over the harboring of political dissidents, and Nairobi's displeasure at Ugandan links with Libya, particularly as manifested in an April 1989 trade accord. During a summit of the Ugandan, Kenyan, and Tanzanian presidents in Nairobi on November 22, 1991, the three declared an interest in reactivating cooperation efforts and appointed a three-member commission to draft an agreement.

Kampala concluded a security accord with Sudan in mid-1987 but subsequently charged that Khartoum was still aiding anti-Museveni rebel forces. Border tension intensified following the June 1989 coup in Sudan, precipitating the signing of another mutual nonaggression pact in April 1990, which provided for a Sudanese monitoring team on the Ugandan side of their border after Khartoum had accused Kampala of aiding the southern Sudanese rebels. Meanwhile, the Museveni administration accused former president Obote of training soldiers in Zambia, intimating that Lusaka was turning a blind eye to the activity.

Unrest in the Sudan and Zaire/Democratic Republic of the Congo (DRC) has dominated Uganda's regional relations since the early 1990s. In October 1992 Kampala warned its northern neighbor that it would mount an "appropriate response" against Sudanese troops crossing the border in pursuit of rebels, and in January 1993 it expressed its concern that a Sudanese plot to launch an Islamic fundamentalist movement in Uganda was under way. Meanwhile, the approximately 20,000 Sudanese refugees within Uganda's borders were joined by thousands of Zaireans fleeing unrest in their country.

In October 1994 Uganda canceled the 1990 agreement with its northern neighbor and ordered Sudan to withdraw its monitoring group, accusing it of activity incompatible with its mandate. In April 1995 Kampala severed relations with Khartoum, alleging improper activity by Sudanese diplomatic personnel and the sponsorship of a cross-border rebel attack on April 20. A subsequent agreement failed to bring an end to the border hostilities, with at least a limited number of Ugandan units operating in support of Sudanese rebels and the NRA conducting raids on Ugandan rebel bases inside Sudan.

Relations were restored with Kenya in January 1996 following a border summit between the two countries' leaders. The discussions also yielded mutual pledges to revive the dormant EAC. However, the continuing fragile nature of Ugandan–Kenyan ties was subsequently underlined by Nairobi's charge that the Museveni regime was supporting Kenyan rebels.

Meanwhile, rebel-related activities along their shared border continued to buffet Ugandan–Sudanese relations in 1996, but on September 9 diplomatic representatives from the two countries signed an agreement in Khartoum that reestablished ties. In December 1999 President Museveni signed an agreement with Sudanese authorities calling for mutual elimination of support for rebel movements, but in mid-2000 Museveni complained that Sudan was not living up to its end of the bargain. Relations between Sudan and Uganda appeared to improve in 2001, as Sudan reportedly permitted Ugandan forces to conduct military action in Sudan against rebels in the LRA. However, Uganda continued to accuse Sudan of helping the LRA, and rebel attacks—some targeting aid workers—continued.

Regional observers described Uganda as playing a crucial role in Laurent Kabila's ouster of the Mobutu government in Zaire (subsequently the DRC) in 1997. Kampala denied actively supporting Kabila, although admitting that its troops had crossed the border in pursuit of Ugandan rebels. Clashes occurred in August 1999 and the spring of 2000 between previously allied Ugandan and Rwandan troops in Kisangani in north-central DRC. A UN-sponsored disengagement agreement in June 2000 brought relative peace to the area, although tensions between Ugandan and Rwandan military forces remained high. Negotiations between senior levels of the two governments under British auspices in November 2001 failed to resolve the underlying strains between the two countries.

In July 2003 a tripartite agreement was signed among Uganda, Rwanda, and the office of the UN High Commissioner on Refugees, providing for the voluntary repatriation of some 26,000 Rwandans in refugee camps in western Uganda. In February 2004 the two countries signed a bilateral agreement to strengthen cooperation in several fields. Yet Uganda still accused Rwanda of aiding the rebel People's Redemption Army (PRA), said to operate in eastern Congo and West Nile. Uganda claimed the PRA was the armed wing of the new opposition group FDC and its exiled leader, retired colonel Kizza Besigye. The FDC claimed to know nothing of the PRA and accused the government of inventing the connection to discredit the FDC. Both Uganda and Rwanda were accused of meddling in the Ituri Province of the DRC, arming rebels there in exchange for minerals. Museveni and Rwandan president Paul Kagame tried to defuse the situation. In May 2005 three Ugandan soldiers were tried for spying against Rwanda, and months later, as tensions eased, Uganda and Rwanda signed an extradition treaty to crack down on criminals crossing the borders. Meanwhile, Uganda denied UN claims that it was trading weapons for minerals with the DRC.

Tensions in the region continued into 2006 following reports that Uganda had acknowledged issuing forged passports to Hutu rebels from Rwanda. The two countries subsequently began discussions to resolve the matter. Meanwhile, Uganda asked the UN to expel the DRC for allegedly harboring rebels intent on destabilizing Uganda. Upgrades to Uganda's airstrip at its borders with the DRC and Sudan raised concerns in those countries, but Ugandan authorities said the improvements were made to prepare for the November 2007 Commonwealth summit in Kampala. Some observers said the upgrades were designed to preempt surveillance flights out of the DRC and Sudan. On a more positive note, Kenya and Uganda reached an agreement to help curb illegal arms trafficking across their shared border, and in 2007 Rwanda and Uganda undertook the first steps toward demarcating disputed areas along their border.

China in 2006 boosted its arms sales to Uganda from $2.5 million to a contract for $1.5 billion over the next five years and agreed to provide training to the Ugandan military. Uganda also bought $4 million worth of weapons from Iran in 2007 for its "anti-insurgency" operation in the north.

In March 2007, in a move observers said was designed to strengthen relations with the United States, Uganda sent 1,600 peacekeeping troops to Somalia to help protect the interim government there and bolster U.S. efforts to prevent suspected al-Qaida terrorists from establishing a foothold there.

In 2008 a dispute between Uganda and the DRC over an oil-rich island in Lake Albert was resolved in Uganda's favor. The dispute dated to a violent confrontation between Congolese and Ugandan forces in 2007. Another territorial dispute, this one involving Kenya, over an island on Lake Victoria was set to be resolved by a panel of experts in Britain. Uganda has maintained ownership of Migingo Island, a source for deep-water fish, and has had troops stationed there since 2004. When Uganda began charging residency fees to Kenyans, tensions heightened, leading to bilateral negotiations and an agreement in 2009 to have the panel resolve the issue. However, in May 2009 Kenya asked the UN to intervene in the dispute.

For the first time since 2003, the presidents of Uganda and the DRC met face-to-face in March 2009 following the discovery of oil in the region, amounting to 1 billion barrels, to discuss regional security and disputes over land.

In December 2009 the UN Security Council condemned the increasing attacks by the LRA across the region and for the first time called on all UN missions in the region to coordinate strategies and activities against the rebels in order to better protect civilians. The LRA was reported to have abducted nearly 1,000 children in the past year. The Security Council also reiterated its demand that the rebels surrender and disarm.

In May 2010 Uganda was among five Nile River basin countries that signed what was described as an historic agreement providing for equitable water-sharing among the signatories. In June, Uganda, as a nonpermanent member of the UN Security Council, voted to support a fourth round of sanctions on Iran prompted by its nuclear development program.

Also in May 2010 U.S. president Barack Obama signed into law the LRA Disarmament and Northern Uganda Recovery Act, which gave the administration the authority to coordinate a strategy to help Uganda, among other countries, disarm the LRA rebels. Critics said the strategy lacked details in its overall aims of protecting civilians and apprehending LRA leader Kony and his commanders or removing them from the battlefield.

In September 2010 the Ugandan army rejected LRA rebels' calls for renewed talks, saying they were waiting for Kony to sign a final peace agreement. In October the DRC, Central African Republic (CAR), and Sudan agreed to form a joint military force with Uganda to fight the rebels. The LRA was reported to be based in southern Darfur in late 2010.

On November 28, 2010, President Museveni traveled to Somalia—one of very few heads of state to travel to the dangerous region—to discuss security issues with President Sheikh Sharif Sheik Ahmed and other officials. Uganda and Burundi were the only countries providing troops for the AU peacekeeping force in Somalia.

In October 2011 the United States announced it was deploying 100 special operations forces to Uganda to help suppress the LRA and train Ugandan security forces. A short, highly critical film about the LRA, dubbed *Kony 2012*, became a viral Internet hit after its release in March 2012, with more than 90 million viewers. The film was credited with raising international awareness of the crimes of the LRA and prompted a U.S. Senate resolution supporting the deployment of U.S. special operations to Uganda.

The Irish company Tullow Energy finalized an oil production agreement with Uganda in March 2012. Estimates were that oil production would be worth up to $2 billion annually to Uganda. Meanwhile, in May Uganda agreed to increase its troop strength in Somalia by 2,000 troops, to a total of 8,000, in response to a request by the AU. In September a UN report accused Uganda of providing support for the M23 militants in the Democratic Republic of the Congo, including the transfer of weapons and the direct involvement of Ugandan troops alongside M23 fighters. In December the EU suspended approximately $300 million in aid, citing corruption (see Current issues, below).

In May 2013 Uganda was deemed to have been in breach of the East African Community (EAC) Treaty for denying entry to a Kenyan citizen in 2011. Also in May, Uganda signed a trade treaty with Sri Lanka and became a signatory to the 2008 Convention on Cluster Munitions, which banned cluster bombs. In April Uganda suspended military operations in the CAR against the LRA following a coup.

In April 2013 the UK's Commercial Court affirmed a Ugandan court's decision that Heritage Oil owed the Ugandan government $434 million in taxes as a result of that company's sale of oil rights to Tullow Energy. In December 2013 Uganda deployed troops to support the government in South Sudan (see entry on South Sudan). By the end of 2013, more than 317,000 refugees had fled into Tanzania to escape regional conflicts in South Sudan, Somalia, and the DRC. The influx overwhelmed humanitarian relief systems in the country.

Human rights groups, international organizations, and various countries condemned the February 2014 enactment of a new anti-homosexuality measure (see Current issues, below). The World Bank suspended a $90 million loan to Tanzania, while the United States, the Netherlands, Norway, and Sweden suspended all or some of their development aid. Washington also canceled a joint military exercise. However, both the United States and the United Kingdom pledged to continue medical aid, including $55 million from the UK and $32 million from the United States to fight malaria. In March the United States deployed four aircraft and 150 special operations forces to the region to hunt the LRA.

In May 2015 Uganda announced it would repatriate approximately 1,350 Kenyan refugees who had fled political violence in that country in 2007–2008. The return of the refugees would be under the auspices of the UN High Commissioner for Refugees.

Fighting in South Sudan led to a wave of refugees, estimated at 110,000, who fled into Uganda in 2016. In May 2016 Uganda cut military and security ties with North Korea, ending arms purchases and not renewing a North Korea training program for the Ugandan military. Uganda signed new economic cooperation accords with South Korea when that country's president, Park Geun-hye, visited Uganda in May.

Current issues. The plight of the Baganda people and the restoration of their kingdom became key issues as Ugandans' attention turned to the next presidential poll, scheduled for February 18, 2011. With the approaching elections, analysts said President Museveni aimed to cause a rift between Ronald Mutebi, the *kabaka* of the Baganda, and the Baganda people, an effort that began in 2009, when the government shut down the pro-Baganda radio station after the September riots, leaving the kingdom without an instrument to mobilize people against government policies. The government wanted to keep the radio station closed until after the election, observers said, to prevent the Baganda people from hearing about a controversial policy in which the government bought land from absentee landlords and gave it to Banyankore villagers.

In early 2010 four minor parties formed an electoral coalition, styled as Change 2011, and five opposition parties formed the Inter-Party Cooperation (IPC), an electoral coalition committed to backing a single presidential candidate and fielding joint candidates in parliamentary and local elections. The component parties—the UPC, Justice Forum (Justice, Education, Economy, Morality, African Unity—JEEMA), Conservative Party (CP), Social Democratic Party (SDP) and FDC—also agreed to form a coalition government if they were successful. The Democratic Party (DP), meanwhile, declined to join the IPC, saying its objectives were not clear. The DP's new president, Norbert Mao, overcame rifts in the party and became its flag bearer in March, while another party member, Samuel LUBEGA, chose to run as an independent. Meanwhile, former foreign minister and UN diplomat Olara Otunnu, who had returned to Uganda after 23 years, began to position himself in the political arena. Otunnu, the recipient of several major international awards for his work in advocating for children's rights and world peace, had had a role in the 1985 military government before leaving the country, but observers said once he returned he was the most well-known UPC member and garnered much media attention. Otunnu took over the helm of the party, despite detractors in the UPC who still had concerns about his role in the 1985 military government.

In 2012 Otunnu was summoned by police for the third time for allegedly using "sectarian language" in radio broadcasts in which he alleged that President Museveni's troops had fomented war in northern Uganda; Otunnu refused to submit to questioning. Earlier in the month, during a rally of supporters, FDC leader Besigye was flogged by police and members of the country's notorious Kiboko—described as a "ragtag paramilitary"—wielding canes and led by Juma SEMAKULA. A number of opposition parties subsequently formed their own youth squads to counter Kiboko attacks. Meanwhile, that same month, the government established a registry and agreed to compensate some 10,000 people in northern Uganda who had been maimed by LRA rebels over the past two decades.

As politics continued to be the focus of attention, in July 2010 a former prominent member of the FDC, Beti Olive KAMYA, gained political registration for the Uganda Federal Alliance (UFA), which she had formed as a civil society in 2009 to promote a campaign to educate the Baganda people about their political rights.

A terrorist attack rocked Kampala on July 11, 2010, when suspected members of al-Shabbab killed 76 civilians while they were watching a television broadcast of the World Cup finals. In August 2010 the cohesion of the opposition broke down when the UPC withdrew from the IPC, citing "irreconcilable reasons." A rift had reportedly developed over how to proceed with the IPC's battle against the electoral commission, as the UPC opposed participation in any activities organized by the commission in preparation for the 2011 polls. UPC leader Otunnu subsequently became the flag bearer for his party, promising a new constitution if elected, and offering assurances to the Baganda people that there would be no restrictions on their movement. The day after the UPC's withdrawal, the IPC announced that its leader, Kizza Besigye of the FDC, would be the coalition's presidential candidate, as analysts had predicted. His nomination was said to have been conditioned on his signing an agreement to grant Baganda federal status and return its land if he was elected.

Though Musevni was unopposed in his bid to be the NRM's flag bearer, the party vote reportedly was marked by violence and fraud in some parts of the country. The 2011 presidential poll, with seven candidates lined up to challenge Museveni, was predicted to be a test of the Baganda Kingdom's willingness to break with the current regime and support the opposition. Besigye, the IPC candidate, meanwhile, had the support of coalition members who championed Baganda interests.

In a landmark legal victory for Otunnu and others who had been arrested in the past months, the Constitutional Court on August 25, 2010, struck down the sedition law and said that the warrant against Otunnu had been unlawfully issued. Journalists hailed the ruling, which allowed them to freely criticize the government. The government immediately announced it would appeal the ruling. That same month the UN refugee agency called on Uganda to halt the forcible deportation of hundreds of Rwandans from refugee camps in the southwest of the country, saying the refugees did not feel safe returning to their homeland. The government said the deportations targeted illegal immigrants.

In September 2010 Uganda charged 32 people, including 4 Ugandans, as alleged masterminds, in connection with the July terrorist attack. All were charged with 76 counts of murder, 10 counts of attempted murder, and committing acts of terrorism.

In a ruling hailed by the United States and others as a sign of judicial independence, the Constitutional Court on October 12, 2010, unanimously voted to dismiss the treason case against Kizza Besigye and ten others on grounds that the state had violated his constitutional rights by having him stand trial in a military court and a civilian high court at the same time. The ruling effectively protected Besigye from further prosecution ahead of the 2011 election. Besigye, for his part, called for the resignations of the chief prosecutor and the attorney general. Days before official campaigning began in November, the president announced the reopening of a Baganda radio station that the government had shut down in 2009, a move widely regarded as one of appeasement ahead of the elections. In December the government approved a huge supplementary budget, including $162 million for the president's office, the defense ministry, the police force, and the state house.

In early January 2011 police investigations of Otunnu and Besigye were reported, and DP members Annet NAMWANGA and her husband, journalist and former exile Lawrence KIWANUKA, were detained by the army for their alleged connection to a terrorist plot. Authorities said they had thwarted a grenade attack on a military base in Kampala.

Prior to the presidential and parliamentary elections in February 2011, the Constitutional Court ruled that it was illegal for independent members of parliament to contest the election on a party ticket and for members affiliated with a party to run as independents. The ruling called for independent members to vacate their seats before being nominated to stand in the election. Subsequently, 77 legislators whose term was due to expire in May left their seats and were forced to repay the salary they had received since their nominations in November 2010. The Supreme Court immediately granted an interim stay of the ruling. The day before the presidential election, the president signed a new law authorizing the tapping of phones and other communications equipment for security purposes. On the eve of the election, weeks after civil unrest had had a major impact in Egypt and Tunisia, Uganda's communication commissioner ordered mobile phone operators to block text messages with words referring to Egypt, dictator, and guns, among others. President Museveni made it clear there would be no revolution such as the one occurring in Egypt, in Uganda.

Following Museveni's overwhelming reelection, outcry over the fairness of the poll came not only from the opposition but also from election monitors. African Union (AU) observers said there was "an urgent need" to reform the electoral laws before the next election, and EU observers cited the use of state resources to turn the polling in Museveni's favor. According to the Inter-Parliamentary Union (IPU), a Ugandan nongovernmental organization reported "groups of people with sacks of money openly handing it out." *Africa Confidential* reported after the election that the government remained "unapologetic" about its use of party and state finances. Besigye, who claimed the polling was "fundamentally flawed," and five other presidential challengers alleged widespread bribery and vote rigging. Notwithstanding these allegations, some analysts pointed to the opposition's failure to unite ahead of the polls. The DP's Mao, the UPC's Otunnu, and Besigye called for peaceful protests. On March 9 demonstrators who gathered in Kampala to denounce the alleged fraud were dispersed by police firing shots into the air and using tear gas. Ten people were arrested. Unrest continued to mount, resulting in a series of Walk-to-Work protests in April against the escalating food and fuel prices. Besigye was arrested on the first day of the protests, April 11, for the fourth time in two weeks, though the walks attracted party leaders, members of parliament, and others who walked alongside "ordinary Ugandans" said to have been priced out of the transport system. Three days later Besigye was wounded by a rubber bullet, and as protests spread to other areas, there were reports of police brutality and the government halting live broadcasts of events. On April 18 opposition members who tried to walk from their homes in Kampala had their way blocked, and several party officials and local council leaders were arrested. Meanwhile, Besigye and Otunnu were charged with inciting violence. Mao was remanded to prison until May 2 after he refused to apply for bail. Among those said to be key to initiating the protests was a civil society coalition called Action for Change, run by political activists in Baganda. In response to the spreading protests, the government banned the social networks Facebook and Twitter.

President Museveni's inauguration on May 12, 2011, was spoiled somewhat by a simultaneous "people's inauguration" organized by Besigye, who had returned that morning from his medical treatment in Kenya for injuries he had sustained during protests the previous month. The opposition leader, who was subsequently placed under house arrest, agreed to conditional talks with the government but vowed to continue the prodemocracy protests. President Museveni accused the opposition of wanting to overthrow the government. On May 18 the president reshuffled the top army officers, reportedly removing the army chief because of his "born-again" Christian beliefs. A new government, composed largely of NRM loyalists, was sworn in on June 6 following the recent dismissal of the former vice president and the appointment of a new prime minister.

Domestic tensions remained high following the earlier protests, in which at least 300 people reportedly were arrested, 100 were wounded, and 9 people died. On June 9, 2011, police broke up a demonstration in Kampala organized by what was described as a new "pressure group," Free Uganda Now, comprising UPC, DP, and SDP members. In August police fired tear gas on thousands of demonstrators who had gathered in a show of support for Besigye one day after a court dismissed charges against Besigye stemming from his role in earlier protests.

Foreign minister Kutesa and two other government officials were voluntarily suspended on October 12, 2012, following charges that they accepted $22.6 million in bribes from foreign oil companies. Investigations by Ugandan and British police later proved the charges were false, and Kutesa was restored to office. Meanwhile, Tarsis KABWEGYERE, Museveni's choice to be the new minister of gender, labor, and social affairs after a cabinet reshuffle on August 15, was rejected by parliament on August 28.

Gay rights continue to be a significant issue in Uganda, where harassment and intimidation against homosexuals is common. Homosexuality remains illegal and same-sex marriage was banned in 2005. In 2009 legislation that would have imposed capital punishment for those repeatedly convicted of homosexuality was defeated after Western governments and international organizations threatened to suspend aid if the measure was enacted. However, in 2012 a similar measure was reintroduced and remained awaiting action in August 2013. On September 13 British Producer David CECIL was arrested for staging *The River and the Mountain,* a play about a young Ugandan who discloses the fact that he is gay to his family and colleagues. Cecil was released on bail four days later.

In December 2012 an internal auditor's report found that officials in the prime minister's office had misappropriated $13.4 million in foreign aid. Donors began to suspend assistance in response to the scandal. Uganda subsequently began refunding $4.2 million in aid to countries including Denmark, Norway, and Ireland.

Reports in May 2013 revealed that 11 senior military officers had been arrested and another 30 placed under surveillance for antigovernment activities, while Gen. (Ret.) David SEJUSA went into exile. From London, Sejusa announced his intention to overthrow Museveni. The auditor general reported in September that government officials had lost or illegally diverted more than $100 million in the 2012–2013 fiscal year. In November Kampala mayor Ssalongo Erias LUKWAGO (DP) was removed from office following a vote by the city council for "abuse of office." Critics of the removal asserted the NRM majority on the council removed Lukwago because he was an outspoken critic of the president.

A sweeping indecency act was signed into law on February 18, 2014. The legislation increased restrictions on pornography and forbade women from wearing revealing clothing, including miniskirts. On February 24 a new anti-homosexuality measure was enacted. The legislation required Ugandans to report homosexual activity and authorized life imprisonment for "aggravated homosexuality." On August 1 the constitutional court annulled the law because of a flaw in the manner in which it was enacted. President Museveni subsequently announced he would not reintroduce anti-homosexuality legislation because of the threat of international economic boycotts.

On March 30, 2015, Joan KAGEZI, the interim assistant director for public prosecutions, was assassinated by two assailants while driving. Kagezi was leading prosecutorial efforts in the trial of 13 suspected *Al-Shabaab* militants.

After Museveni was reelected on February 18, 2016, there were widespread demonstrations and riots which prompted the deployment of military and security forces. In the violence, 2 were killed and more than 20 injured.

Reports in 2016 indicated that defense spending was on track to rise above $460 million, up from $260 million in 2010.

POLITICAL PARTIES AND GROUPS

In 1986 President Museveni ordered the suspension of political party activity pending the adoption of a new constitution, although several parties were allowed to maintain offices and small staffs. The 1989 elections were conducted on a "nonparty" basis, even though members of at least four parties (the CP, the DP, UPC, and the **Uganda Patriotic Movement** [UPM]) ran for office with their affiliations obvious to voters. Several others, principally political wings of military groups that had been absorbed by the NRA, had by then been effectively dissolved. (For more on party history, see the 2014 *Handbook*.)

A referendum was held on June 28, 2005, on legalizing political parties. Originally, the referendum questions of a multiparty versus a no-party system and the extension of presidential term limits were to appear on the same ballot. A "yes" vote for multiparty activity would have also meant a "yes" for term-limit extensions. In a remarkable show of independence in June 2005, parliament voted to allow citizens to vote on each issue separately. Both amendments were approved by voters, though opposition groups—styled the G6 (the FDC, UPC, DP, CP, JEEMA, and the **Free Movement**)—boycotted the referendum, and turnout was low (officially 47 percent, though reports from exit polls put turnout at about 20 percent). Multiparty presidential and parliamentary elections were held for the first time in 20 years in February 2006. The UPC and the DP subsequently withdrew from the G6.

In August 2006 a dozen parties and groups reportedly merged to form The Parties Platform (TPP), chaired by Emmanuel TUMUSIIME, to present a united front to try to gain power. The groups opposed a proposal by President Museveni that only the parties that held seats in parliament could participate in drafting a code of conduct for interparty cooperation. The parties of the TPP were: the **Forum for Integrity in Leadership**; the **National Unity Party**; the National Peasants Party; the Farmers Party of Uganda; the Movement for Democratic Change; the National Unity, Reconciliation, and Development Party; the **Uganda People's Party**; the **Movement of Volunteers and Mobilizers**; the **Liberal Democratic Transparency**; the **People's United Movement**; the National Convention for Democracy; and the Uganda Patriotic Movement.

Ahead of the 2011 presidential elections, an electoral coalition of minor parties called Change 2011 included the People's Development Party, **National Coalition for Democracy**, National Peasants Party, and Movement of Volunteers and Mobilizers. Another coalition, the Inter-Party Cooperation, which included JEEMA, CP, SDP, and FDC, backed coalition leader and FDC president Kizza Besigye for president.

Ahead of the 2016 presidential elections, the CP, DP, and JEEMA formed the Go Forward coalition to support the candidacy of former prime minister Amama Mbabazi (see below).

Dominant Government Party:

National Resistance Movement (NRM). The NRM was formed following the controversial 1980 election by former president Yusuf K. Lule and Yoweri Museveni, the former directing the political wing from exile in London and the latter leading internal guerrilla activity through the National Resistance Army (NRA). Upon his assumption of the presidency in January 1986, Museveni declared that the NRM was a "clear-headed movement" dedicated to the restoration of democracy in Uganda. Despite the ineffectiveness of subsequent membership drives, Museveni on several occasions suggested that the NRM could become the centerpiece of a one-party or limited-party state in which wide-ranging political expression would be permitted but ethnic and religious sectarianism avoided.

In a dramatic turnaround, however, Museveni sponsored the motion in parliament in 2005 for a national referendum on a multiparty system versus a no-party system. Museveni championed multiparty political activity, observers said, to appease Western donors by assuring them of his intention to move toward a more democratic society. In addition, the multiparty ballot question was paired with a provision that would eliminate the two-term limit on the presidency, thus virtually assuring Museveni of a third five-year term.

In 2008 rifts were reported within the party between those who backed Museveni for another term and those who pressed for finding a successor, in addition to tensions resulting from Museveni's tightened control over the party. In September some 500 disaffected members of the FDC reportedly joined the NRM.

In advance of the 2011 general elections, in which Museveni said he would seek a fourth term, the NRM dominated local by-elections in 2009, winning in areas traditionally dominated by the opposition. The party, as expected, endorsed Museveni for the 2011 presidential bid, but the process was marred by irregularities and violence in some districts in the country. The party subsequently introduced biometric data registration to help eliminate fraud. Some 500 defectors, mainly from the UPC, reportedly joined the NRM late in 2010.

In a by-election in September 2012, 19-year-old Proscovia Alengot OROMAIT of the NRM was elected as the youngest member of parliament in the history of Uganda. Meanwhile, reports indicated a growing faction of the NRM supported the parliamentary speaker, Rebecca KADAGA, as the party's presidential candidate in 2016, although Museveni endeavored to garner support for his son, Brig. Kainerugaba MUHOOZI as his successor. Reports indicated little support for Muhoozi.

Reports in August 2013 indicated a growing number of defections from the NRM to the FDC. In September 2014 Museveni announced he would seek another term in 2016, sparking additional party infighting. Reports emerged that Prime Minister Amama MBABAZI intended to challenge Museveni for the party's nomination. Museveni dismissed Mbabazi as prime minister on September 18, and the former head of government was briefly arrested on July 9, 2015.

Mbabazi ran for the presidency as the candidate for the **Go Forward** coalition. He placed third with 1.4 percent of the vote in the February 18, 2016, balloting, while Museveni was easily reelected with 60.8 percent of the vote. Meanwhile, the NRM increased its majority in Parliament to 293 seats.

Leaders: Lt. Gen. Yoweri MUSEVENI (President of the Republic and Chair of the Party), Moses KIGONGO (Vice Chair), Rebecca KADAGA (Speaker of the Parliament), Dorothy HYUHA (Deputy Secretary General), Ruhakana RUGUNDA (Prime Minister).

Other Legislative Parties:

Uganda People's Congress (UPC). The largely Protestant UPC was formed in 1960 with a stated commitment to "African socialism." It served as the ruling party under former president Apollo Milton Obote from independence until 1971 and again from late 1980 to 1985. Despite the inclusion of several UPC adherents in the initial Museveni administration, friction persisted between the government and Obote loyalists, particularly hardliners who launched splinters, such as the UPF, in response to the pro-Museveni posture of their former colleagues.

In February 1991 the **October 9 Movement,** an Obote-led UPC faction named after the date of Ugandan independence, was reportedly operating from a Nairobi-subsidized "training camp" along the Ugandan border in Kenya. Obote's chief of staff was identified as Lt. Col. John OGORE; also listed as movement leaders were Peter OTAI, former commander of the **Uganda People's Army** (UPA), and Peter OWILI, known as "the butcher of Nile Mansions" for the brutal interrogation methods he employed during Obote's presidency.

Despite living in exile in Zambia, Obote continued to control the UPC, and in June 1996 he ordered Assistant Secretary General Cecilia OGWAL not to participate in parliamentary elections. However, Ogwal, who had been credited with maintaining party unity after Obote's departure, defied his edict and captured a seat. Consequently, Obote dismissed her and named James RWANYARARE party spokesperson and chair of the UPC's Presidential Policy Commission (i.e., de facto party leader). For her part, Ogwal rejected Obote's authority to intervene and announced the formation of her own "task force," an act one observer described as an intraparty "coup" attempt. Her underfinanced splinter group was subsequently described as unlikely to challenge Rwanyarare, although she remained a controversial figure in the party. In 2005 Obote dismissed Rwanyarare and dissolved the Presidential Policy Commission, replacing it with a Constitutional Steering Committee. Ultimately, a court ordered the party to sort out its differences following the death of Obote in October 2005. The former president's widow, Miria Kalule Obote, was elected party leader in November 2005. She placed last in 2006 presidential balloting with less than 1 percent of the vote. (She was the first woman presidential candidate in Uganda and the first woman to lead a major political party.)

In January 2008 one faction within the party expressed its dissatisfaction with Miria Obote, but she refused to relinquish the presidency. Party veteran Joseph OTHIENO was vying to become party president in late 2009, as were numerous others, including former secretary general Peter Walubiri. Meanwhile, following an amendment to the party's constitution that reduces the president's term from seven years to five, Miria Obote said that she was ready to retire. In a subsequent move seen as Obote's way of ensuring that her son succeeded her, Obote reshuffled the party leadership in June 2009, replacing Walubiri and installing her son, Jimmy Akena, as vice chair. However, Akena's rein was short-lived, as in August 2009 former UN diplomat Olara Otunnu, a longtime critic of Museveni, returned to Uganda after an absence of 23 years. His return split the party, as opponents believed he had betrayed Obote and the UPC by siding with the 1985 coup plotters and subsequently accepting the post of foreign minister. Miria Obote fired at least one party official who met Otunnu upon his arrival at the airport. However, Otunnu's supporters prevailed, and he was elected party president on February 18, 2010.

Despite having initially agreed to join the IPC electoral alliance in advance of the 2011 general election, the UPC ultimately decided to field its own presidential and legislative candidates. Otunnu was tapped as the party's flag bearer and campaigned for sovereignty for the Baganda Kingdom and a federal system of government. He won a major legal victory in August when the Constitutional Court struck down the country's sedition law, nullifying the warrant against Otunnu, which the court ruled had been unlawfully issued. The ruling removed restrictions on freedom of expression, an important victory for Otunnu, who repeatedly took to the airwaves to criticize Museveni.

In October 2010 Apollo Milton Obote was posthumously awarded the country's independence medal on Independence Day.

In the 2011 presidential election Otunnu finished fourth with 1.6 percent of the vote. The party secured ten seats in concurrent parliamentary elections. In midyear, infighting escalated between Akena and Otunnu over claims by Akena that Otunnu was trying to suspend him.

In May 2012 eight UPC members of parliament sued Otunna over the president's unwillingness to call a special party congress to discuss fissures within the UPC. In March 2014, the UPC branch in Mt. Elgon declared itself independent of the national party and rejected the presidency of Otunnu.

The UPC supported Amama Mbabazi in the 2016 presidential contest as part of the Go Forward coalition. Mbabazi placed third. In legislative balloting, the party won 6 seats.

Leaders: Olara A. OTUNNU (Chair and 2011 presidential candidate), Miria Kalule OBOTE (2006 presidential candidate), Jimmy AKENA, Joseph BBOSA (Vice President), Akhbar Adoko NEKYON, Patrick MWONDHA (Treasurer), Chris OPOKA, John ODIT (Secretary General).

Democratic Party (DP). An advocate of centralization and a mixed economy, the DP draws on a solid Roman Catholic base and enjoys widespread support in southern Uganda. Officially, it ran second to the UPC in the post-Amin balloting of December 1980, winning 51 of 126 legislative seats, although the results were strongly challenged. The DP subsequently was weakened by defections to the UPC and sporadic harassment, killing, or detention of its leadership by the Obote government. While DP president Paul Ssemogerere joined the Okello cabinet, most DP leaders supported Museveni's NRA in continued guerrilla fighting. Several members of the DP executive committee were included in Museveni's first cabinet, and, despite reports of some deterioration in DP–NRM relations, Ssemogerere was named second deputy prime minister and foreign minister in February 1988; he retained both posts in the cabinet reorganization of July 1991.

In mid-1992 Ssemogerere was the reported leader of a cabinet revolt against Museveni's request for extension of the ban on political party activities; however, in May 1993 he advised party activists to curtail operations in the face of a presidential decree banning theretofore implicitly acceptable activities. In June 1995 the DP leader resigned as second deputy prime minister and minister of public service to position himself for the forthcoming presidential campaign.

In early 1996 the DP and the UPC forged an unofficial alliance, the Inter-Party Coalition (IPC), on the premise that in return for its support of DP candidates in the 1996 elections the UPC would be the opposition's standard-bearer at the next national elections. Subsequently, a number of UPC leaders made campaign appearances with Ssemogerere; however, following the DP leader's overwhelming electoral defeat, the UPC's Obote reportedly denied the coalition's existence. Collaterally, observers speculated that the alliance had cost Ssemogerere the votes of the Baganda people, who had been oppressed by Obote's regime and continued to resent him. Although Ssemogerere described the presidential polling as "rigged" in favor of the incumbent and subsequently boycotted the June legislative balloting, suggestions that the party would go into opposition were greeted with skepticism by observers, who cited the DP's history of participation in NRM governments. Subsequent to the June 2000 referendum (which the DP boycotted) on political party activity, Ssemogerere announced his intention to resign the party presidency, but he stayed on until his retirement in 2005. Factions within the party clashed in advance of the 2005 constitutional referendum but reportedly reunited a month later. John Ssebaana Kizito was elected party leader in November 2005, ending Ssemogerere's 25-year reign, and faction leader Hajji Ali Sserunjogi was elected vice president. Ssebaana finished third behind Museveni in the 2006 presidential election with 1.58 percent of the vote.

Dissension in the party was reported in 2007, resulting in the formation of a breakaway group, the Social Democratic Party (see Other Groups, below), and the demotion of Secretary General Lulume Bayiga to deputy secretary general. Subsequently, Bayiga served as acting secretary general until August 2008, when the party elected Mathias Nsubuga to fill the post. In September party vice president Hajji Ali Sserunjogi and chair Joseph Mukiibi were suspended because of their refusal to accept the appointment of Nsubuga. The two men disputed their suspension. Meanwhile, the party rejected joining the IPC electoral coalition that ultimately included the FDC and several other parties for the 2011 poll, as some DP members backed a regional party leader, Norbert Mao, to be the party's flag bearer. Mao was elected party chair at a conference in February 2010 that was boycotted by a faction led by Mukiibi and Lulume.

Mao, a former member of parliament, was among those who had tried to resolve the conflict between the government and the LRA by lobbying for a general amnesty.

In the 2011 presidential election Mao was third, with just 1.9 percent of the vote. Samuel Lubega, who had hoped for the party nod, ran for president as an independent and finished eighth with 0.4 percent. In concurrent parliamentary elections the party secured 12 seats. In September 2012 Nsubuga reportedly angered members of the party by declaring that he would support Rebecca KADAGA of the NRM in the next presidential election. In August 2013 the DP rejected a proposal to field a single opposition presidential candidate for the 2016 balloting. In July 2014 Mao was hospitalized for a month with pneumonia.

The DP joined the Go Forward coalition in the 2016 presidential election. The party won 15 seats in the concurrent legislative elections.

Leaders: Norbert MAO (Party President and 2011 presidential candidate), John KAWANGA, Issa KIKUNGWE, Hajji Beswale KEZAALA, John SSEBAANA Kizito (2006 presidential candidate), Joseph MUKIIBI, Lulume BAYIGA, Mathias NSUBUGA (Secretary General).

Forum for Democratic Change (FDC). This opposition group was formed in July 2004 by a merger of the **Reform Agenda**, the **Parliamentary Advocacy Forum**, and the **National Democratic Forum**. The FDC's leader in exile, retired colonel Kizza Besigye, had challenged Museveni in the 2001 presidential election. Several opposition members of parliament previously affiliated with the UPC and DP reportedly joined the new group, which declared its intentions of becoming "a strong, democratic, mass organization."

Besigye returned from the United States in 2005 in order to participate in 2006 elections and drew large crowds at a number of rallies in areas that traditionally had supported Museveni. In what observers said was an attempt to prevent Besigye from challenging Museveni in the 2006 elections, Besigye was arrested in Kampala for allegedly supporting the rebel PRA based in the DRC and charged with treason. He was also charged with rape in connection with a 1997 case but was cleared of that charge in March 2006. Earlier, the FDC nominated him as the group's presidential candidate, and Besigye was freed on bail a month ahead of the 2006 presidential election. He came in a distant second to

Museveni. Besigye subsequently was offered a seat in parliament by a newly elected delegate who reportedly calculated that the FDC leader would wield more power as leader of the opposition. However, Besigye turned down the offer.

In 2007 Besigye said he would step down as party leader in 2010 in advance of party preparations for the 2011 elections. Regan OKUMU, a member of parliament, soon declared his intention to contest the party presidency. A rift reportedly developed in the party in July 2008 during a meeting to determine a successor to Sulaiman KIGGUNDU, the party's national chair who had died a month earlier. John Butime was named acting national chair. In February 2009, however, Besigye defeated former army commander Gregory Mugisha MUNTU to retain leadership of the party. In April the FDC challenged the country's electoral commission, seeking to delay local by-elections with legal challenges accusing the commission of being unable to conduct fair elections.

In 2009 more than 100 NRM members defected to the FDC.

Ahead of the 2011 presidential election, in early 2010 the FDC was one of four parties that joined the electoral alliance known as the IPC, and Besigye was voted its flag bearer with the stipulation that he agree to sovereignty for the Baganda Kingdom. During the course of the campaign, he was beaten by security forces and the paramilitary Kiboko.

In October 2010 Besigye's treason trial was dismissed by the Constitutional Court, a ruling hailed as a sign of judicial independence and effectively protected him from further prosecution ahead of the 2011 election.

In the 2011 parliamentary poll the party won 34 seats. Following the concurrent presidential election, which Besigye claimed was rife with fraud after finishing a distant second, he organized a series of protests in April and was arrested several times. Injuries resulting from rubber bullets fired by the police during one of the protests resulted in his seeking medical treatment in Kenya. Upon his return, coinciding with the inauguration of President Musaveni in May, he participated in additional protests. In July Besigye announced that he would not run for the presidency in 2016, nor would he seek reelection as party president after his second term expires in 2014. In August charges against Besigye related to the protests were dismissed. In October 2012 he was arrested for holding a banned rally. In November Besigye resigned, and Maj. Gen. (Ret.) Mugisha MUNTU was elected party leader. In February 2014 rifts were reported in the party over Muntu's dismissal of Nathan Nandala MAFABI as the FDC's parliamentary leader and his replacement by Wafula OGUTTU. Besigye was arrested and released on July 9, 2015, without explanation or charges, and then briefly detained again on October 15.

Besigye was again the party's presidential candidate in the February 2016 balloting after the FDC withdrew from the Go Forward coalition over disagreements on how to choose a unified presidential candidate. Besigye was arrested both before and immediately after the polling. The FDC champion placed second with 35.4 percent of the vote. In concurrent legislative balloting, the FDC won 36 seats. Besigye was arrested on May 11 during a mock presidential inauguration. He remained in custody until July 1.

Leaders: Mugisha MUNTU (Party Leader), Dr. Kizza BESIGYE (2001, 2006, 2011, and 2016 presidential candidate), Salaami MUSUMBA (Vice President), Alice ALASO (Secretary General).

Other Groups:

Justice Forum (Justice, Education, Economy, Morality, African Unity—JEEMA). The JEEMA was formed in October 1996 by Mohamed Mayanja Kibirige, who secured only 2.1 percent of the vote in the 1996 presidential election, to rally support for his candidacy in the 2001 presidential election. (Mayanja received just 1 percent of the vote in 2001.) In 2004 the group, which reportedly seeks a democratic, federal system of government, rejected a merger with the FDC.

Mayanja initially announced he would seek the presidency in 2006 but later withdrew.

JEEMA joined the IPC electoral coalition in advance of the 2011 general election. In June 2010 party leader Mayanja stepped down to make way for "a new breed of leaders." Nonetheless, he was elected party chair, with the presidency going to Asuman Basalirwa.

In the 2011 legislative election the party retained its seat. In 2013 JEEMA called for a constitutional amendment calling for the parliamentary speaker and deputy speaker to resign their seats after being elected and become ex officio members. In 2014 JEEMA dropped its long-standing call for presidential term limits.

JEEMA was part of the Go Forward coalition in the 2016 presidential elections. It failed to secure representation in the concurrent legislative balloting.

Leaders: Mohamed MAYANJA Kibirige (Chair and 1996 and 2001 presidential candidate), Asuman BASALIRWA (President), Diana OGWAL (Vice President), Yahya SSEREMBA (Spokesperson), Hussein KYANJO (Secretary General).

Conservative Party—CP. The CP is a small formation whose first leader was prime minister of Baganda in 1964–1966 and who participated in the Okello and Museveni governments. CP has adopted to some extent the positions of the **Baganda Royalist Movement,** which has long sought restoration of the traditional Kingdom of Baganda.

In early 2005 rival factions divided the group, and a lengthy dispute over leadership ensued until May, when Mayanja Nkangi, on one side, reconciled with Yusufu Nsubuga Nsombu and John Ken Lukyamuzi on the other. Lukyamuzi, who supported the DP's Ssemogerere in the 1996 presidential election over Museveni, initially supported the FDC's Besigye in 2006, then said he would run for president but did not appear on the ballot. Lukyamuzi was forced to leave parliament in 2006 for allegedly breaking the law by failing to disclose his wealth. (Lukyamuzi petitioned the High Court to review the case.) Subsequently, a dispute over his leadership of the party remained unresolved. In 2008 Lukyamuzi continued to lead one faction of the party, while Nkangi claimed leadership of the "mainstream" CP faction. According to the inspector general for government (IGG), however, Lukyamuzi was ineligible for any leadership post for five years because of his earlier failure to reveal his assets.

In May 2008 the CP and other opposition parties called for electoral reforms, including banning representation of the army in parliament and establishing an impartial and independent electoral commission.

In 2010 the CP joined the IPC electoral coalition ahead of the 2011 presidential poll.

The party retained its single seat in the 2011 parliamentary election. In August 2012 Daniel Walyemera MASUMBA was elected president of the party. In 2013 the CP initiated coalition discussions with other opposition parties.

The party failed to win any seats in the 2016 parliamentary elections.

Leaders: Daniel Walyemera MASUMBA (President), Mubiru ALI (Vice President), Mukasa HUSSEIN (Secretary General).

Uganda Federal Alliance (UFA). Established as a civil society in May 2009 by former FPC member Beti Olive Kamya, the group was registered as a political party in July 2010, three months after the electoral commission challenged the registration over ghost names on its party lists. At the time, UFA leaders claimed they were a civil society, not a political party, and therefore could not be deregistered by the electoral commission.

Kamya, a member of parliament, had formed the group to lobby for political rights for the people of the Buganda Kingdom. As the UFA's flag bearer in the 2011 election, Kamya—the only woman seeking the presidency—campaigned for a federal system of government, as well as a national public health plan, education reforms, and a guaranteed minimum wage.

In the 2011 presidential election Kamya won 0.7 percent of the vote, finishing fifth. In March 2012 the UFA threatened to sue the electoral commission, claiming the body did not do enough to allow Ugandans living outside the country to vote.

In July 2016 Kamya was appointed minister of the Kampala City Authority in the NRM government.

Leaders: Beti Olive KAMYA (President and 2011 presidential candidate), Aniba BONIFANS (Vice President), E. P. N. MAYEKU-MALESI (National Chair), Kavuma KAGGWA (Publicity Chair), Maj. Acikule NOAH.

Progressive Alliance Party (PAP). Established in April 2005 by Bernard KIBIRIGE, a former aide to Brig. Henry TUMUKUNDE, who was dismissed from his post as Uganda's military intelligence chief, the PAP has had a divisive history. (For more, see the 2014 or 2015 *Handbook*.) In April 2014 the high court approved a recommendation from the electoral commission to deregister ten small parties, including the PAP, for inactivity.

Leaders: David PULKOL (President), Dr. Kaddu MULINDWA (Interim Chair).

Other groups include the **Freedom Movement,** part of the so-called G6 group of opposition parties; **Forces for Change,** a splinter opposition group formed in March 2005 by Nasser Ntege SSEBAGALA and David Pulkol (who later joined the PAP); the **National Peasants Party,** led by Erias WAMALA; the **Republican Women and Youth Party,** led by Stella NAMBUYA; the **People's Independent Party,** led by Yahaya KAMULEGEYA and Amin SSENTONGO; **Movement for Democratic Change,** led by Paulsen KITIMBO; the **National People's Organization,** led by Abdu JAGWE; the **National Convention for Democracy,** led by Haji Jingo KAAYA; the **Farmers Party of Uganda,** led by Mudde Bombakka NSKIO; the **National Unity, Reconciliation, and Development Party,** led by Joseph NYANZI; and the **People's Progressive Party,** established in 2004 and led by Jaberi Bidandi SSALI, the party's 2011 presidential candidate; and the **People's Development Party,** whose leader, Dr. Abed BWANIKA, secured 0.6 percent of the vote in the 2011 presidential election. In November 2007 the **Social Democratic Party** (SDP) was formed by a group of dissidents from the DP, including Henry LUBOWA and Michael MABIKKE.

Guerrilla Groups:

Lord's Resistance Army (LRA). The LRA first emerged in the late 1980s as Lakwena Part Two, a small, predominantly Acholi successor group to the Holy Spirit Movement that had been led by "voodoo priestess" Alice LAKWENA from 1986 until her flight to Kenya in 1987 (Lakwena died in 2007). Under the leadership of Joseph Kony, the anti-NRA rebels remained active in northern Uganda, and in early 1991 the militants reportedly began referring to themselves as the Uganda Democratic Christian Army. Following inconclusive negotiations with government representatives in early 1994, Kony and his supporters launched a new offensive under their current name, claiming they were fighting "a holy war against foreign occupation" and seeking to install a government guided by the biblical Ten Commandments.

LRA bases in Sudan came under sustained attack by Sudanese rebel forces and the Ugandan Army beginning in April 1997, and in July LRA commanders reportedly called for a cease-fire. (For more information on the history of the LRA prior to 1996, see the 2012 *Handbook.*) Subsequently, in the second half of 1997 Kony led his fighters in a series of cross-border raids, although the LRA had been forced to break into much smaller fighting cells than its usual 150–200 member units. Despite heavy casualties, according to government officials, the LRA continued to replenish its ranks by abducting teenage Ugandans and forcing them to march to Sudan for training and indoctrination.

In late 1998 a group of LRA dissidents led by Ronald Otim KOMAKECH reportedly split from the group following a dispute over the LRA's alleged targeting of civilians; subsequently, Komakech formed the **LRA–Democratic** and allied the splinter with the **Uganda National Rescue Front** (UNRF, below). The level of LRA activities actually increased after a December 1999 treaty between Sudan and Uganda ostensibly designed to end support for guerrilla groups. LRA activity subsided in 2000–2001, largely due to behind-the-scenes negotiations mediated by the U.S.-based Carter Center in Atlanta, which tried to initiate talks with LRA leader Kony and his backers, the Sudanese government. In February 2001, however, LRA rebels attacked a northern Ugandan town and abducted 40 people. In March Ugandan wildlife authorities suspended game-viewing activities in parts of the northwestern Murchison Falls National Park following an alleged LRA ambush in which at least 10 people were killed. In 2004 gains made by the Ugandan People's Defense Force (UPDF) against the rebels seemed to compel the LRA to seek a cease-fire. By mid-2005, however, talks had not made significant progress. Meanwhile, evidence of cooperation between Sudanese and Ugandan troops against the LRA raised hopes that combined pressure might force Kony's group into meaningful negotiations. In 2005 the ICC issued arrest warrants for Kony and other LRA leaders. Subsequently, the LRA leaders ensconced themselves in forested areas of the DRC and intermittently engaged in negotiations toward a permanent truce with the Ugandan government in 2006 and 2007.

Kony was reported to have executed his one-time deputy, Vincent Otti, in October 2007. Alfred James OBITA took over as leader of the LRA's negotiation team after David MATSANGA was dismissed in April 2008. Subsequently, it was reported that Matsanga had returned to replace Obita, whom Kony had dismissed. On August 4 the government granted amnesty to Obita and several other LRA and ADF rebels (see Current issues, above). Two of Kony's top commanders, Okot ODHIAMBO (whom Kony was reported to have killed in 2008) and Dominic ONGWEN, reportedly were wounded in December when their hideout was attacked by a joint military operation from which Kony escaped. Subsequently, other unconfirmed reports surfaced that Odhiambo had defected from the Kony camp in 2009 and was requesting amnesty, and that Ongwen had moved from the DRC to South Sudan. Another top commander, Thomas KWOYELO, was said to have been captured on March 3, 2009. Also in 2010, the United States adopted a law aimed at developing a strategy to help disarm the LRA rebels and apprehend Kony.

Attacks continued as the LRA reportedly moved through the DRC, the CAR, and Sudan. In late 2010 and early 2011 the LRA was reported to be based in southern Darfur. On May 12, 2012, Ugandan security forces captured Caesar ACHELLAM, a senior LRA leader. Meanwhile, the United States offered a $5 million reward for the capture of Kony and other top LRA leaders. As a result of continued international efforts, by 2014, estimates were that the LRA had declined to approximately 220 fighters, including approximately 160 Ugandans. In April 2014 Charles OKELLO, a senior LRA commander, was captured by Ugandan troops in the CAR.

In January 2015 Ongwen surrendered to AU forces in the CAR and was turned over to the International Criminal Court for trial.

Leaders: Joseph KONY, Oti LAGONY, Willy ORYEM, Yusuf ADEK.

Allied Democratic Forces (ADF). The ADF is reportedly composed of remnants of the late Amon BAZIRA's National Movement for the Liberation of Uganda, and Islamic militant fighters, styled the *Salaaf Tabliqs,* allegedly funded by the Sudanese government. ADF activity was first reported in 1995, but the group did not achieve prominence until 1997 when its numbers were reportedly swollen by the addition of former Zairean government forces and Rwandan Hutu *Inter-hamwé* fighters.

A government offensive in mid-1997 decimated the ADF's fighting strength and drove a majority of its fighters deep into the mountains of the Democratic Republic of the Congo (DRC). However, ADF militants were allegedly responsible for grenade attacks in Kampala in early 1998, and thereafter the ADF launched a series of attacks that claimed dozens of civilian lives. In February 1999 the ADF was accused of orchestrating a deadly bomb attack in Kampala. A number of ADF militants were killed in subsequent government raids, while the ADF was accused of killing both civilians and soldiers in several incidents throughout the rest of the year. In April 2000 the Ugandan government pulled out 2,000 soldiers from eastern DRC, claiming that the threat of cross-border ADF incursions was greatly reduced. Ugandan authorities in July arrested 28 ADF recruits accused of undertaking bomb attacks that have killed 67 people and injured 262 others since 1997. The ADF had resorted to urban terrorism after its ground insurgency was defeated in the mountains straddling Uganda's western border with the DRC. Some ADF rebel leaders and fighters allegedly were trained in terrorist Osama bin Laden's Afghan camps, and in December 2001 the United States listed the ADF as a terrorist organization. Clashes between Ugandan forces and ADF rebels continued into 2006, with security forces arresting and killing many suspected ADF members in the western forests of Uganda. The militants reportedly were fleeing the DRC following fighting between the Congolese army and UN peacekeeping forces. In 2007 the ADF's second in command, Balaya ISIKO, was killed in fighting with DRC soldiers. The ADF in western Uganda reportedly had been defeated by the Ugandan army.

In 2008 it was reported that the ADF was seeking peace talks with the Ugandan government. News reports said that the group had not been active in recent years. However, in July the Ugandan army claimed the ADF was regrouping and recruiting in the DRC. In 2009 the group's leader, Jamir Mukulu, was reported as saying he was ready to resume fighting if the Ugandan government did not commit to a peace process.

In July 2010 President Museveni appealed to ADF "remnants" in eastern Congo to give up their rebellion and return to Uganda. Meanwhile, Uganda increased its troops along the western border to counter possible further ADF attacks. In 2012 reports indicated that a new rebel grouping, the Revolutionary Forces for the Liberation of Uganda (RFLU), sought an alliance with the ADF. In 2013 Uganda launched a program to return child soldiers of the ADF to their villages. In August 2014 nine ADF members were charged with terrorism for past activities.

ADF leader Mukulu was captured, along with five other ADF members, by Tanzanian security forces and extradited to Uganda in July 2016. Reports indicated that Musa BALUKU was appointed the new leader of the group.

Leaders: Jamir MUKULU, Yusuf KABANDA, Musa BALUKU.

For information on other guerrilla groups that have largely been inactive in recent years, see the 2009 *Handbook.*

LEGISLATURE

The former National Assembly was dissolved following the July 1985 coup. Balloting for a new, formally recognized **Parliament** was held on a "no-party" basis in June 1996. (For more information on the legislature prior to 2011, see the 2012 *Handbook.*) In multiparty balloting on February 18, 2016 (the third following the 2005 constitutional revision), 289 seats were directly elected on a constituency basis; 112 additional district seats are reserved for women, and another 25 seats are reserved for representatives of youth, workers, and disabled persons and the Uganda People's Defense Force; 13 seats are filled on an ex-officio basis by cabinet ministers appointed by the president, and the number may vary according to the president's wishes. The seat distribution was as follows: National Resistance Movement, 293 (199 constituency, 84 district women, 10 indirectly chosen); independents, 66 (44, 17, 5 indirectly chosen); Forum for Democratic Change, 36 (29, 7); Democratic Party, 15 (13, 2); Uganda People's Congress, 6 (4, 2); and Uganda People's Defense Forces, 10.

Speaker: Rebecca KADAGA (NRM).

CABINET

[as of September 15, 2016]

Prime Minister	Ruhakana Rugunda
First Deputy Prime Minister	Gen. Moses Ali
Second Deputy Prime Minister	Kirunda Kivejinja
Office of the President	Esther Mbulakubuza Mbayo [f]
Prime Minister's Office	Mary Karooro Okurut [f]
Ministers	
Agriculture, Animal Husbandry, and Fisheries	Vincent Bamulangaki Ssempijja
Attorney General	William Byaruhanga
Communications and Information Technology	Frank Tumwebaze
Defense and Veterans Affairs	Adolf Mwesige
East African Affairs	Kirunda Kivejinja
Education and Sports	Janet Kataha Museveni [f]
Energy and Mineral Development	Irene Muloni [f]
Finance, Planning, and Economic Development	Matia Kasaija
Foreign Affairs	Sam Kutesa
Gender, Labor, and Social Affairs	Janet Mukwaya [f]
Government Chief Whip	Ruth Sentamu Nankabirwa [f]
Health	Jane Ruth Aceng [f]
Internal Affairs	Gen. Jeje Odongo
Justice and Constitutional Affairs	Maj. Gen. Kahinda Otafiire
Kampala City Authority	Betty Kamya (UFA) [f]
Karamoja Affairs	John Byabagambi
Lands, Housing, and Urban Development	Betty Amongi [f]
Local Government	Tom Butane
Public Works	Wilson Muruli Mukasa
Relief and Disaster Preparedness	Hilary Onek
Science, Technology, and Innovation	Elioda Tumwesigye
Security	Lt. Gen. (Ret.) Henry Tumukunde
Tourism and Wildlife	Ephraim Kamuntu
Trade and Industry	Amelia Kyambadde [f]
Water and Environment	Sam Cheptoris
Without Portfolio	Abdul Nadduli
Works and Transport	Monica Azuba Ntege [f]

[f] = female

INTERGOVERNMENTAL REPRESENTATION

Ambassador to the U.S.: Oliver WONEKHA.

U.S. Ambassador to Uganda: Deborah R. MALAC.

Permanent Representative to the UN: Richard NDUHUURA.

IGO Memberships (Non-UN): AfDB, AU, Comesa, CWTH, IOM, NAM, OIC, WTO.

For Further Reference:

Mutibwa, Phares. *Uganda since Independence: A Story of Unfulfilled Hopes*. London: C. Hurst & Co., 1992.

Mwakikagile, Godfrey. *Uganda: A Nation in Transition, Post-Colonial Analysis.* Trenton, NJ: New Africa Press, 2012.

Tripp, Aili Mari. *Museveni's Uganda: Paradoxes of Power in a Hybrid Regime.* Boulder, CO: Lynne Rienner, 2010.

UKRAINE

Ukrayina

Political Status: Formerly the Ukrainian Soviet Socialist Republic, a constituent republic of the Union of Soviet Socialist Republics; declared independence on August 24, 1991; new constitution adopted on June 28, 1996.

Area: 233,090 sq. mi. (603,700 sq. km). (Includes Crimea [approximately 10,000 sq. mi. or 26,000 sq. km], which was annexed by Russia in March 2014 but was still formally recognized by the Ukrainian government and much of the international community as part of Ukraine.)

Population: 44,624,000 (2016E—UN); 44,209,733 (2016E—U.S. Census). (Includes Crimea, whose population has been estimated recently at 2,300,000.)

Major Urban Centers (2013E—UN): KIEV (KYÏV, 2,803,716), Dnepropetrovsk (Dnipropètrovsk, 987,621), Donetsk (Donèc'k, 944,552), Kharkov (Charkiv, 1,431,461), Lviv (L'viv, 723,605), Odessa (Odèsa, 997,189).

Official Language: Ukrainian (replaced Russian in 1990). Following independence in 1991, the Council for Language Policy and the National Orthography Commission began working to restore syntax, style, and other aspects of Ukrainian to what they were before the 1930s, when Moscow ordered Ukrainian to be made more uniform with Russian. As proposed by the generally pro-Russian Ukrainian government installed in 2010, Ukrainian regions with Russian populations of more than 10 percent were authorized as of August 2012 to give official language status to Russian in addition to Ukrainian. Eight regions had reportedly done so by the end of the month. The status of Russian was an important issue in the political upheaval of the first half of 2014 and subsequently remained a subject of political negotiations, particularly in regard to pro-Russian eastern regions under separatist control.

Monetary Unit: Hryvna (official rate October 1, 2016: 25.94 hryvnas = $1US).

President: Petro POROSHENKO (elected as an independent, subsequently Petro Poroshenko Bloc); popularly elected in first-round balloting on May 25, 2014, and inaugurated on June 7. (Oleksandr TURCHYNOV [Fatherland], the speaker of the Supreme Council, had been named acting president by the Supreme Council on February 23, 2014, after the Supreme Council had voted to dismiss President Viktor YANUKOVYCH

[Party of Regions] the previous day. [Yanukovych, who fled the country, continued to claim he was the rightful president, although by the fall there was little international support for that assertion.])

Prime Minister: Volodymyr GROYSMAN (Petro Poroshenko Bloc); appointed on April 14, 2016, to succeed Arseniy YATSENYUK (initially Fatherland, subsequently People's Front), who resigned that day. (See Government and Politics, below).

THE COUNTRY

The third largest and second most populous of the former Soviet republics, Ukraine is bordered on the north by Belarus, on the east by Russia, on the south by the Black Sea and the Sea of Azov, and on the west by Moldova, Romania, Hungary, Slovakia, and Poland. The population is approximately 78 percent Ukrainian and 18 percent Russian, with no other group greater than 1 percent. The ethnic Russian population is located primarily in eastern and southern Ukraine, where there is significant sentiment in favor of the reestablishment of greater economic, political, and military integration with Russia. The population in western Ukraine is described in general as supportive of the country's orientation toward Western Europe. Most Ukrainians profess Eastern Orthodoxy, although there is a sizable Roman Catholic community and smaller numbers of Muslims and Jews. (This information, and most subsequent information in this section, is presented as if Crimea is still a part of Ukraine, despite the annexation of Crimea by Russia in March 2014.)

The black-earth steppe of the south, one of the world's most productive farming regions, provided about one-quarter of the foodstuffs for the former Union of Soviet Socialist Republics (USSR). Agriculture currently accounts for about 12 percent of GDP and 15 percent of employment. The leading crop is wheat (Ukraine is one of the world's top grain producers), followed by sugar beets, potatoes, and a wide variety of other vegetables and fruits. Natural resources, including iron, coal, bauxite, zinc, oil, and natural gas, have long supported a broad range of manufacturing activity, including metallurgy, machine building, and chemical production, which accounted for nearly a third of the Soviet Union's industrial output. Industry now contributes about 40 percent of Ukrainian GDP, primarily from mining and metallurgy, and employs some 25 percent of the labor force. Steel is the country's leading export.

The demise of the Soviet system yielded a 50 percent contraction in economic output in Ukraine in 1990–1994, accompanied by inflation that spiraled to more than 4,700 percent in 1993 before falling to 890 percent in 1994 and to under 100 percent in 1995. GDP also contracted from 1995 to 1997, albeit at a lower rate each year. A modest recovery appeared possible for 1998 until the economy was rocked by the Russian financial collapse of August, which constrained trade between the two countries and prompted a significant outflow of capital.

In 2000 the economy expanded for the first time since independence, achieving 6 percent growth. The International Monetary Fund (IMF), which had encouraged stabilization and liberalization measures, attributed the advance to exchange rate depreciation, unexpected economic resilience in Russia (Ukraine's principal trading partner), and an improved world market for Ukraine's exports, led by metals. However, virtually all the large Soviet-era state enterprises remained in government hands, while privatization and other market-oriented reforms continued to meet opposition from a Communist-Socialist-Agrarian parliamentary bloc. On the right, politically well-connected entrepreneurs, the so-called oligarchs, also opposed many reform efforts, particularly in the energy sector, where the oligarchs benefited from a lack of transparency and informal barter arrangements among consumers, sellers, and suppliers.

GDP rose by more than 9 percent annually in 2001–2004, led by growth in the industrial sector and strong domestic consumer demand. However, Ukraine remained heavily dependent on imported energy products, particularly from Russia.

Upon taking office in early 2005, President Yushchenko pledged to pursue free-market policies and to investigate the some 3,000 nontransparent privatizations that had been completed during the Kuchma administration. Foreign investors initially welcomed the market orientation brought on by the so-called Orange Revolution but were described as "unnerved" by the subsequent political turmoil. On a more positive note for supporters of proposed Ukrainian membership in the

European Union (EU) and the World Trade Organization (WTO), the United States in December 2005 formally recognized Ukraine as a market economy, with the EU following suit in February 2006.

The Ukrainian economy was hit extremely hard by the global financial crisis that erupted in late 2008. In November the IMF approved $16.4 billion in emergency lending over the next two years to help stabilize the financial system, although conditions attached to the lending proved domestically controversial. Declines of more than 50 percent in the metal and chemical industries contributed to a shocking 15 percent drop in GDP for 2009, with unemployment climbing to more than 9 percent and annual inflation reaching 22 percent.

In August 2010 the IMF approved a new 29-month, $15.1 billion loan agreement, while the World Bank in September agreed to additional support for the financial sector, particularly the recapitalization of Ukrainian banks. The government also implemented a new tax code late in the year, although some 40 percent of business reportedly remained in the "shadow economy" and Ukraine continued to decline in corruption rankings. Increased demand for steel and other exports contributed to growth of 4.1 percent and 5.2 percent for 2010 and 2011, respectively, while inflation declined to 4.6 percent and unemployment fell to 7.9 percent by the end of 2011. Real GDP growth fell dramatically to 0.2 percent in 2012 due to severe drought (which compromised the wheat harvest) and deteriorating trade conditions (including a reduction in global demand for steel). However, significant longer-term improvement was projected as the result of a major new oilfield discovery in the east in July 2013 and the recent signing of a $10 billion agreement with Royal Dutch Shell for exploitation of the nation's massive shale gas reserves.

Real GDP fell by 0.3 percent in 2013, and the recession deepened significantly in the first half of 2014 in the wake of antigovernment demonstrations that culminated in the ouster of President Yanukovych and installation of a new pro-European government. In April 2014 the IMF approved a two-year $17 billion loan to help Ukraine avoid default after Russian support was withdrawn. In return, the Ukrainian government pledged to combat corruption, trim the bloated bureaucracy, permit the Ukrainian currency to float downwards, and simplify the regulatory environment and otherwise improve the business climate. Economic contraction was projected for 2014, exacerbated by continued conflict in pro-Russian separatist areas in the east (see Current issues, below). GDP fell by 6.6 percent in 2014 and 9.9 percent in 2015. The economy began to recover in 2016 with GDP rising by 1.5 percent. Inflation that year was 15 percent, a marked decline from 48.7 percent the previous year. Unemployment in 2016 was 9.2 percent, while GDP per capita was $1,965, down from $3,095 in 2014. The World Bank ranked Ukraine 83rd out of 189 countries in its annual ease of doing business survey in 2016.

GOVERNMENT AND POLITICS

Political background. Under Polish rule in the 16th century, Ukraine experienced a brief period of independence in the 17th century before coming under Russian control in the 18th century. Ukraine again proclaimed independence following the overthrow of the Russian tsarist regime in 1917, with the region becoming a battlefield of conflicting forces that eventually yielded a Red Army victory and Ukraine's incorporation into the USSR as a constituent republic in 1922.

On July 16, 1990, the Ukrainian Supreme Soviet, under pressure from nationalist opposition forces, issued a sovereignty declaration that asserted the "indivisibility of the republic's power on its territory," its "independence and equality in external relations," and its right to countermand the utilization of its citizens for military service beyond its boundaries. In an equivocal vein, however, it failed to claim a right of secession from the Soviet Union and explicitly provided for dual Soviet and Ukrainian citizenship. The less than clear-cut nature of the declaration prompted widespread nationalist demonstrations, led primarily by student activists. On October 23 the chair of the council of ministers, Vitaliy A. MASOL, responded by submitting his resignation; he was succeeded by Vitold FOKIN.

Ukraine endorsed Soviet president Mikhail Gorbachev's union proposal in April 1991 but, in the wake of the subsequent failed hard-line coup against Gorbachev in Moscow, issued a formal declaration of independence on August 24. On August 31 the chair of the Ukrainian Supreme Soviet, Leonid KRAVCHUK, suspended the activities of the Communist Party of Ukraine (*Komunistychna Partiya Ukrainy*—KPU), and on September 4 the leader of the KPU legislative bloc announced that the group would disband. On December 1, in a vote held simultaneously with Kravchuk's reconfirmation in direct presidential balloting, Ukrainians overwhelmingly endorsed the August independence declaration. On December 8 the republic joined Belarus and Russia in announcing the demise of the Soviet Union, and on December 21 Ukraine became a founding member of the Commonwealth of Independent States (CIS).

Fokin, who had continued as prime minister upon reorganization of the council of ministers in May 1991, survived a confidence vote on July 1, 1992, following a decision to raise food prices, but he was forced to step down on September 30 amid uncertainty over the direction and pace of the republic's economic reform program. He was succeeded on an acting basis by First Deputy Prime Minister Valentin SIMONENKO, who yielded the office on October 27 to Leonid D. KUCHMA, the "technocrat" director of the former Soviet Union's largest arms production complex.

Increasingly battered by conservative parliamentarians opposed to his economic reform efforts, Prime Minister Kuchma submitted his resignation for the fifth time in as many months on September 9, 1993, with the Supreme Council (as the Supreme Soviet had been renamed) finally voting acceptance of the resignation on September 21. Kuchma's deputy, Yukhym ZVYAHILSKIY, was named acting prime minister, although President Kravchuk assumed direct control of the government by decree on September 27. (Three days earlier the Supreme Council had averted a constitutional crisis by agreeing that parliamentary and presidential elections would be held in the first half of 1994.)

In an apparent overture to his pro-Russian critics, President Kravchuk, on June 16, 1994, appointed Vitaliy Masol to return to the prime ministership. In first-round presidential balloting on June 26, Kravchuk won 37.7 percent of the vote, as contrasted with 31.3 percent for former prime minister Kuchma. However, at the runoff on July 10, Kravchuk lost to his opponent, 45.1 percent to 52.1 percent. Critical factors in Kuchma's success were the endorsement of his candidacy by the revived KPU and support for him in the eastern industrialized areas with a heavy ethnic Russian population. At his inauguration on July 19 the new head of state promised gradual electoral reform and closer ties to Russia. Prime Minister Masol resigned in March 1995, reportedly over economic policy differences with President Kuchma, who was seeking more active reform. Masol was replaced by Col. Gen. Yevhen MARCHUK, theretofore a deputy premier and state security chair.

The 292–4 parliamentary passage on April 4, 1995, of a motion of nonconfidence backed by both Communist conservatives and reformers precipitated a major political crisis. President Kuchma reappointed Prime Minister Marchuk on April 8 and proposed strengthening the powers of the presidency pending the adoption of a new constitution (see Constitution and government, below). The Supreme Council's failure to ratify the changes on May 30 caused the president to threaten to call a referendum, whereupon the legislature, cognizant of the wide public support for the changes, on June 15 acceded to an interim "constitutional treaty" that granted most of the new powers sought by Kuchma. Conflict over economic reform nevertheless simmered between the legislature and the president, with Kuchma's determined pursuit of a market economy generating strains not only between the president and the KPU-led bloc but also within the mainly centrist political groups that provided the president's core support.

Prime Minister Marchuk was dismissed by President Kuchma on May 27, 1996, ostensibly for shortcomings in the conduct of economic policy, and was replaced by the first deputy prime minister, Pavlo LAZARENKO. Following the adoption in June of a new constitution that permanently extended presidential authority, Kuchma reshuffled the cabinet in October and again in February 1997 in an attempt to combat corruption, stabilize the financial system, and press on with economic reforms. In June 1997 Prime Minister Lazarenko was replaced on an acting basis by First Deputy Prime Minister Vasyl DURDYNETS, ostensibly because of Lazarenko's failing health. However, Lazarenko had faced serious allegations of corruption and antireform sentiment, and his ouster had reportedly been ordered by Kuchma. In July the legislature approved Kuchma's nomination of Valeriy PUSTOVOYTENKO, minister of cabinet affairs and a member of the People's Democratic Party of Ukraine (*Narodno-Demokratychna Partiya Ukrainy*—NDPU), as the new permanent prime minister.

In late 1997 a new electoral law was adopted to increase the role of political parties in legislative elections by providing for half the legislators to be selected from party lists in nationwide balloting. New Supreme Council balloting was conducted under the revised system for the first time on March 29, 1998. Thanks to a strong performance in the proportional poll, the KDU improved its representation substantially. However, the KDU-led left-wing opposition was still unable to achieve a majority, with many of the independent candidates elected in the single-member districts representing business interests supportive of President Kuchma's economic reform efforts. Consequently, Prime Minister Pustovoytenko remained in office following the election, although the cabinet was extensively reshuffled in early 1999.

Thirteen candidates contested the presidential election of October 31, 1999, including Kuchma, KPU leader Petro SYMONENKO, Oleksandr MOROZ of the Socialist Party of Ukraine (*Sotsialtstychna Partiya Ukrainy*—SPU), and former prime minister Yevhen Marchuk, who was backed by a number of smaller parties. (Moroz, Marchuk, and two other candidates had agreed in August that they would unite behind one of their number before the election, but Marchuk's selection as the consensus candidate on October 25 immediately led Moroz to assert that he would nevertheless remain in the race. A third member of the "Kaniv Four," Oleksandr TKACHENKO, chair of the Supreme Council and leader of the Peasants' Party of Ukraine [*Selyanska Partiya Ukrainy*—SelPU], withdrew in favor of Symonenko, not Marchuk.) The first round of presidential balloting ended with Kuchma claiming 36.5 percent of the vote, necessitating a November 14 runoff against the second-place Symonenko, who had won 22.2 percent. With third-place finisher Moroz and the other leftist candidates having thrown their support to Symonenko for the second round, Kuchma wielded his presidential prerogatives in an effort to secure the victory. On November 3 he dismissed the governors of three regions that had supported either Moroz or Symonenko, and on November 10 he named Marchuk head of the National Security and Defense Council in a bid to gain the 8.1 percent support Marchuk had received as fifth-place finisher in the first round. In the runoff election Kuchma was credited with 57.7 percent of the vote. The Parliamentary Assembly of the Council of Europe and the Organization for Security and Cooperation in Europe (OSCE) were among the observer organizations citing flaws in the conduct of the second round.

Following President Kuchma's inauguration for a second term on November 30, 1999, the cabinet resigned, as required by the constitution. Kuchma quickly renominated the incumbent prime minister, but on December 14 the Supreme Council rejected Pushtovoytenko by a vote of 206–44. Two days later Kuchma nominated reformist Viktor YUSHCHENKO, the nonparty chair of the National Bank of Ukraine, who was confirmed and sworn in on December 22. The new prime minister came into office pledging a reform program that included "open" privatization, lower inflation, a balanced budget, cuts in the size of the government bureaucracy, payment of remaining wage and pension arrears, and restructuring of the agricultural sector. (President Kuchma had proposed converting the country's 10,000 collective farms into cooperatives and joint stock companies.) Subsequent cabinet changes included the appointment by Kuchma of three new deputy prime ministers, including Yulia TYMOSHENKO, a leader of the Fatherland

(*Batkivshchnyna*) party and a former energy industry executive, who assumed responsibility for fuel and energy policy in January 2000.

On January 13, 2000, former president Kravchuk announced formation of a government-supportive parliamentary majority by 11 center-right factions, including his own Social Democratic Party of Ukraine (United) (*Sotsial-Demokratychna Partiya Ukrainy [Obyednana]*—SDPU[O]) and a number of independent deputies. The new Supreme Council majority immediately attempted to remove the SelPU's Tkachenko as parliamentary chair, but obstruction from the left initially prevented a vote. Convening in a nearby exhibition hall, the 239-member majority voted Tkachenko out of office on January 21, and on February 1 it elected in his place Ivan PLYUSHCH, who had previously served in the same capacity. The leftist opposition continued to meet in the Supreme Council chamber despite lacking a quorum, but a week later a group of majority deputies forced its way into the building. By February 15 the leftist opposition effort had lost its momentum, and regular parliamentary sessions resumed shortly thereafter.

Despite her earlier background in the energy sector, Deputy Prime Minister Tymoshenko vowed in 2000 to fight the sector's oligarchs and to end graft, insisting, for example, that electricity contracts specify transparent cash settlements instead of the barter arrangements that had left the industry open to profiteering and abuse. However, by mid-2000 Tymoshenko was drawing fire from President Kuchma, who was particularly critical of a natural gas deal Tymoshenko had initialed with Turkmenistan to reduce reliance on Russia's Gazprom, to which several of Ukraine's oligarchs had connections.

On November 28, 2000, SPU leader Moroz released to the public audiotapes implicating President Kuchma and others in a plot to "get rid of" independent journalist and presidential critic Heorhiy GONGADZE, who had gone missing in mid-September and whose headless body had been recovered near Kiev in early November. Kuchma, supported by the prosecutor general's office, insisted that the relevant recordings were fabrications, although participants in other conversations on the tapes attested to their authenticity. In response to the scandal, an anti-Kuchma National Salvation Forum (NSF) was organized in February 2001, including as a member former deputy prime minister Tymoshenko, who had been dismissed by Kuchma in January after being formally charged with corruption while head of Unified Energy Systems of Ukraine in 1996–1997.

Tymoshenko characterized her January 2001 removal from office as a reprisal carried out by Kuchma on behalf of "criminal clans of oligarchs." For its part, the prosecutor general's office justified Tymoshenko's detention in February–March by citing new evidence that she had paid nearly $80 million in bribes to former prime minister Lazarenko while he was in office. (Lazarenko, his immunity from prosecution having been lifted by the Supreme Council in 1999, also continued to face numerous charges [ranging from accepting bribes to ordering contract killings] in Ukraine.) Moreover, in June 2000 he was convicted in Switzerland of money laundering during his earlier tenure as governor of Dnepropetrovsk. Lazarenko, not to be outdone, charged in 2000 that Kuchma and his aides had themselves embezzled and laundered hundreds of millions of dollars, including proceeds from IMF loans that were used to purchase high-yielding Ukrainian debt.

In early 2001 a philosophically incongruous coalition, ranging from Oleksandr Moroz's Socialist Party to the fascist Ukrainian National Assembly (*Ukrainska Natsionalna Asambleya*—UNA), continued to stage a series of militant "Ukraine Without Kuchma" rallies. Meanwhile, the NSF, led by Moroz, Tymoshenko (who had quickly donned the mantle of an anticorruption, proreform antagonist), and others, also pressed for President Kuchma's resignation or removal from office. In addition, there were indications that the loyalty of Ukraine's oligarchs, who had been among Kuchma's strongest supporters, might also be wavering. As a further complication, Kuchma and Prime Minister Yushchenko were not always in agreement, although they jointly condemned the NSF in a February 2001 statement that was also signed by Supreme Council Chair Ivan Plyushch.

The new center-right parliamentary majority having already dissipated, the country's oligarchs in early 2001 demanded formation of a new government that would better represent their interests. (The oligarchs' "fiefdoms" were being threatened by Prime Minister Yushchenko's reform policies.) From the opposite side of the political spectrum, the Communists and other leftists joined the oligarchic parties in calling for the market-oriented, centrist Yushchenko to be replaced. After Yushchenko lost a no-confidence vote in the Supreme Council, 263–69, he submitted his resignation on April 27, and a day later President Kuchma dismissed the cabinet, which remained in office in a caretaker capacity. On May 29 the Supreme Council confirmed Anatoliy KINAKH, a former first deputy prime minister, as Yushchenko's successor. Kuchma announced the final appointments to a revamped cabinet on July 10.

In the context of ongoing efforts by a frequently fractious opposition to force President Kuchma's resignation or to impeach him, Ukrainians elected a new Supreme Council on March 30, 2002. Former prime minister Yushchenko's "Our Ukraine" Bloc (*Blok Viktora Yushchenka "Nasha Ukraina"*—NU) finished with a plurality of 110 seats, followed by the pro-Kuchma "For a United Ukraine!" Electoral Bloc (*Vyborchiy Blok "Za Yedinu Ukrainu!"*—ZYU) with 101, and the KPU with 66. The NU and the KPU were joined by the Yulia Tymoshenko Bloc (*Blok Yuliyi Tymoshenko*—BYT) and the SPU as the principal opposition formations, which, despite their ideological differences, pledged to renew a joint effort to force Kuchma from office.

On November 16, 2002, President Kuchma nominated Viktor YANUKOVYCH, the governor of the Donetsk *oblast* (province) and leader of the recently formed pro-Russian Party of Regions (*Partiya Rehioniv*—PR), to be the new prime minister. The appointment was confirmed with 234 votes in the Supreme Council on November 21.

In October 2002 a senior judge opened a criminal investigation into alleged corruption and abuse of power on the part of the Kuchma administration. Although the Supreme Court subsequently ordered the investigation suspended, anti-Kuchma demonstrations were held in major cities in 2003 and 2004, the opposition claiming that inappropriate force was used by security forces to quell the protests. Consequently, Kuchma in early 2004 announced that he would not seek reelection, despite having been authorized to run by the Constitutional Court. The three major presidential contenders thereby became Prime Minister Yanukovych (Kuchma's preference as a successor), former prime minister Yushchenko, and Oleksandr Moroz of the SPU. The presidential campaign subsequently became one the world's most closely watched political developments, one major focus of attention being the apparent poisoning of reformist candidate Yushchenko, who nearly died as a consequence of what was initially described as an unknown illness. (He later claimed that he had been poisoned during a meeting in September with leaders of the Ukrainian security forces.) Tests subsequently appeared to verify that Yushchenko was suffering from dioxin poisoning, which among other things, had left his face severely disfigured. For many observers, the before and after photos of Yushchenko seemed to encapsulate the essence of the presidential contest—a corrupt, perhaps criminal, entrenched administration (represented by Prime Minister Yanukovych, President Kuchma's handpicked candidate as his potential successor) versus a rising tide of reformists determined to shake off the last vestiges of a communist past. Of course, such analysis was simplistic at best, as Yanukovych enjoyed substantial genuine support in industrialized areas of eastern and southern Ukraine, where much of the population spoke Russian and continued to prefer strong ties with Russia. He also appeared generally content with the economic role of the nation's oligarchs. Meanwhile, Yushchenko campaigned on a pro-Western platform that called, among other things, for Ukraine's eventual membership in the EU and North Atlantic Treaty Organization (NATO). Underscoring Ukraine's long-standing geographic schism, Yushchenko's support was strongest in central and western areas of the country.

The first round of presidential balloting on October 31, 2004, produced a close race between Yanukovych (40.2 percent of the vote) and Yushchenko (39 percent), with observers reporting numerous violations of fair election practices. The government announced that Yanukovych won the November 21 runoff balloting with 49.5 percent of the vote, compared to 46.3 percent for Yushchenko, prompting protest demonstrations in major Ukrainian cities as well as an international outcry over perceived fraud on the government's part. The Supreme Council refused to ratify Yanukovych's victory and ordered a second runoff for December 26, at which Yushchenko, now the leader of an Orange Revolution (so named after his main campaign color) achieved a clear victory with 52 percent of the vote. Yanukovych initially refused to accept the results, but, in the face of intense international pressure, he resigned as prime minister on December 31, paving the way for Yushchenko's inauguration on January 23, 2005. The following day Yushchenko named Yulia Tymoshenko, his main Orange Revolution partner, as prime minister. Her appointment was confirmed on February 4 via 457 votes in the Supreme Council. Prime Minister Tymoshenko's new cabinet contained a number of "Our Ukraine" ministers as well as representatives of the SPU and the Party of Industrialists and Entrepreneurs of Ukraine; the legislators from the KPU provided the main opposition to her appointments. The new administration promised immediate reform in many areas, most notably in regard to combating corruption. Consequently, a number of investigations were reportedly launched into the recent spate of privatizations, which some observers had characterized as members of its Kuchma/Yanukovych administration having "looted" public resources.

In March 2005 the government relaunched the criminal investigation into the Gongadze case, President Yushchenko charging that the previous administration had covered up the facts in the matter. However momentum toward uncovering the details of the previous privatizations (another reform goal) was subsequently reported to have slowed. It appeared that enthusiasm for the review of the privatizations had waned in part due to concern expressed by foreign investors, who reportedly feared that their interests might be compromised by such scrutiny. Consequently, the government announced new guidelines designed to convince investors that property rights would henceforth be protected.

Reform efforts also subsequently appeared to be compromised by the growing friction between President Yushchenko and Prime Minister Tymoshenko. In April 2005, faced with gasoline prices that had soared by 30 percent, Tymoshenko imposed mandatory price caps. Perhaps in protest, Russian oil suppliers (responsible for 80 percent of Ukraine's oil needs) subsequently cut back on their distribution to Ukraine, causing significant shortages and consumer angst. Consequently, Yushchenko ordered that the price caps be removed, arguing that they ran counter to his administration's commitment to a market economy. Analysts thereafter noted additional problems, including personal rivalries, that were constraining the ability of the disparate elements behind the Orange Revolution to enact change. Overall, the lack of effective action was seen as eroding the government's credibility both domestically and internationally only six months after the new administration had been installed amid much optimism.

Mutual allegations of corruption from the supporters of Yushchenko and Tymoshenko contributed to Tymoshenko's dismissal as prime minister on September 8, 2005.

Tymoshenko immediately announced that she and her supporters were crossing over to the opposition. On September 9 Yushchenko nominated Yuriy YEKHANUROV, the governor of the Dnepropetrovsk region and a member of the NU, to be the next prime minister. However, the appointment was able to muster only an insufficient 223 votes of support in the Supreme Council on September 20, forcing Yushchenko to offer significant concessions to Yanukovych in order to get support from the PR, which subsequently agreed to endorse Yekhanurov, who was confirmed with 289 votes on September 23. The new cabinet announced on September 27–28 was dominated by the NU, although a number of posts were filled by nonparty technocrats.

In early January 2006 Russia reduced the flow of natural gas to Ukraine in the wake of several months of conflict over prices. An agreement was reached a few days later that permitted a resumption of full deliveries, but opponents of the accord claimed that Ukraine was being forced to double its payments as a punishment for the Orange Revolution. Popular discontent also was exacerbated by the lack of progress in the Gongadze case. (The trial of three police officers charged with involvement in the journalist's death was initially adjourned for the judge to assess if state secrets were involved, and trial proceedings continued slowly. The three officers were convicted in March 2008, although critics of the investigation charged that the masterminds of the crime remained at large.)

The Supreme Council on January 10, 2006, passed a motion of no confidence against the Yekhanurov government. However, the government remained in place pending balloting for a new Supreme Council, which, under recent constitutional revision, would be empowered to appoint most of the new cabinet.

The March 26, 2006, legislative balloting produced a surprising plurality for the PR, with the BYT and NU, which had been unable to forge an electoral coalition, splitting the Orange Revolution vote. Several attempts by the NU and BYT to form a coalition government foundered over the ensuing months, as did the PR's attempts to find enough partners to achieve a legislative majority. Conditions reached a critical point by July, with President Yushchenko facing the choice of calling for new elections or accepting an arrangement with his former arch-rival Yanukovych. Finally, on August 3 Yushchenko agreed to nominate Yanukovych to lead a new government dominated by the PR but also including members of the SPU, NU, and KPU. The proposed government was approved the following day with 271 votes in the Supreme Council. However, friction between Yushchenko and Yanukovych contributed to the resignation of four NU ministers in October and the NU's concurrent decision to officially move into opposition.

Conflict between President Yushchenko and Prime Minister Yanukovych subsequently continued unremittingly. In addition to disagreement on foreign policy (Yanukovych remaining much more oriented toward Russia than Yushchenko), the uncomfortable cohabitation was strained by the prime minister's effort (in conjunction with the PR-dominated Supreme Council) to wrest control of the foreign and defense ministries from the president's control. Various legislative and court maneuvers resulted in a standoff, and after the NU and the BYT had announced their joint opposition to Yanukovych's anticrisis coalition in February 2007, mass demonstrations by supporters of both camps rocked the capital at the end of March.

Charging Yanukovych with "unconstitutional behavior" in regard to the alleged solicitation of floor crossing by NU legislators in order to maintain a legislative majority for the government, Yushchenko in April 2007 ordered that new legislative elections be held in late June. However, the Supreme Council continued to meet in defiance of Yushchenko's dissolution decree and refused to allocate funds for new elections. With government essentially paralyzed, 169 NU and BYT legislators resigned in June, providing the basis for Yushchenko to issue another dissolution decree on the grounds that the legislature no longer had two-thirds of its seats filled (a constitutional requirement for its continuation). Although many of the legal issues remained unresolved, a compromise was reached between the PR and the NU/BYT in late May for new legislative elections on September 30. Interestingly, the campaign focused less on international issues such as relations with Russia and NATO and more on domestic affairs. Among other things, all three leading electoral blocs (the PR, BYT, and Yushchenko's Our Ukraine–People's Self-Defense [*Nasha Ukraina–Narodna Samooborona*—NU-NS]) made what independent analysts considered unrealistic campaign pledges regarding financial assistance to the working class.

The September 30, 2007, Supreme Council balloting again revealed a deeply divided electorate, as the PR secured a plurality, but the BYT and NU-NS combined for a slim majority. After extensive negotiations between the BYT and the NU-NS, Yulia Tymoshenko returned to the premiership on December 18 after being approved by the Supreme Council by the barest possible majority (226 votes in the 450-member council).

Considering the history of bickering between Yushchenko and Tymoshenko, it was not surprising that the Orange Revolution "redux" of late 2007 failed to usher in a period of political calm. Continued disputes with Russia also roiled the political waters in the first half of 2008, as did Yushchenko's insistence that the April NATO summit approve a membership action plan for Ukraine. (Large PR-led demonstrations against the NATO initiative were conducted in several cities.) Although Tymoshenko was perceived as less vehemently anti-Russian than Yushchenko in regard to Russia's actions in Georgia in August, most independent observers concluded that the schism between the two leaders was primarily personal, not ideological. Their mutual antipathy continued to dominate political affairs, and on September 3 ministers and legislators from the NU-NS announced that they were withdrawing their support for the coalition government led by Tymoshenko. When Tymoshenko and the BYT were subsequently unable to entice the NU-NS back into the coalition, the speaker of the Supreme Council on September 15 declared that the government had formally collapsed. Negotiations toward a new coalition government subsequently failed, and on October 8 President Yushchenko ordered the dissolution of the Supreme Council and announced that new legislative balloting would be held on December 7. However, under pressure from Tymoshenko, the Supreme Council challenged the dissolution decree and refused to approve funds for the elections, which Yushchenko subsequently postponed. On December 9 it was announced that a new majority coalition had been formed in the Supreme Council by the BYT, some 40 of the legislators from the NU-NS, and the Lytvyn Bloc, whose leader, Volodymyr LYTVYN, was elected speaker of the council with 244 votes, signaling that the coalition enjoyed sufficient legislative support to preclude immediate snap elections.

In April 2009 the Supreme Council, which had recently forced the dismissal of Foreign Minister Volodymyr OHRYZKO (one of President Yushchenko's two cabinet appointees), called for early presidential elections to be held on October 25. However, Yushchenko challenged that initiative, and in May the Constitutional Court declared the legislative resolution invalid. The first round of the next presidential balloting was therefore scheduled for January 2010. (An attempt by Yanukovych and Tymoshenko to forge a BYT–PR coalition had collapsed at midyear over the long-standing issue of the division of authority between the president and the prime minister [see BYT, below, for additional information].)

In a remarkable reversal of fortune, former prime minister Viktor Yanukovych of the PR finished first in the first round of presidential balloting on January 17, 2010, with 35 percent of the vote. Prime Minister Tymoshenko finished second with 25 percent of the vote, while incumbent president Yushchenko secured only 5 percent. Yanukovych defeated Tymoshenko in the runoff on February 7 by a vote of 49 percent to 45.5 percent ("Against All Candidates" was also a voting option). Although international observers characterized the poll as generally fair (despite a "bitter" campaign), Tymoshenko alleged fraud and initially refused to resign the premiership as requested by Yanukovych in order for him to install a new government. However, in early March the Lytvyn Block withdrew from the BYT-led government, and Tymoshenko resigned after losing a confidence motion in the Supreme Council. On March 10 Yanukovych named the PR's Mykola AZAROV to head a "Stability and Reforms" government comprising members of the PR (supported legislatively by the KPU), the Lytvyn Block, and independents, Yanukovych having convinced the legislature to loosen regulations regarding the formation of coalition governments (see Constitution and government, below). A dozen renegade legislators from the BYT and NU-NS provided support for the new government.

Analysts described Azarov, a Russian-born former finance minister who had headed the tax administration under President Kuchma, as a "stern figure" who would focus primarily on economic recovery, leaving domestic and international political affairs to Yanukovych. In that regard, although Yanukovych pledged to pursue "equal relations" with Russia and the West, his initial pro-Moscow orientation quickly became clear. Perhaps most noteworthy was the signing in April of a lease extension under which Russia was given the right to base its Black Sea Fleet at Sevastopol until 2042 (the current lease had been scheduled to expire in 2017). Among other things, the extension effectively ended further consideration of Ukraine's possible accession to NATO, which forbids members to host military forces from non-NATO countries. Ukraine and Russia also announced new arrangements for the delivery of Russian natural gas as Russian president Dmitri Medvedev expressed his joy at "finally" having a "worthy Ukrainian partner."

Although his economic reforms were endorsed by the international community, Yanukovych was criticized domestically for his adoption of a Russian-style "managed democracy," under which the executive branch dominated. In the view of the opposition, the government's increasingly authoritarian bent was evidenced by increased pressure on journalists, growing influence of politics within the judiciary, and constraints imposed on small parties in advance of the October 31 elections for mayoralties and provincial and municipal legislatures. (Western observers called those polls, in which the PR led all contenders by a wide margin, as a step backwards for democratization.) Many analysts also characterized the reopening of the bribery case (closed in 2005) against Tymoshenko and the arrest of several members of her recent government as politically motivated. Finally, prosecutors concluded their investigation into the Gongadze case by saying that the murder had been ordered solely by then interior minister Yury KRAVCHENKO, who himself had died mysteriously in March 2005 (authorities had ruled the death a suicide). The ruling appeared to close the case (except for the ongoing prosecution of the alleged hit man—Oleksiy PUKACH), and skeptics noted that it might preclude any action against officials from that era who are still alive. (In a surprising development, the prosecutor general's office in the first half of 2011 announced that former president Kuchma was being charged with "exceeding his authority" in the case, with the inference that he might have played an at least indirect role in the events leading up to Gongadze's murder. However, the case against Kuchma was dropped in December after the Constitutional Court ruled that the evidence against him had been illegally obtained through secret audio recordings. Subsequently Pukach was convicted in January 2013 and sentenced to life in prison.)

Former prime minister Tymoshenko was formally charged in December 2010 with abuse of power while in office. That charge involved the use of so-called carbon credits to pay state pensions. Additional charges were placed against her in April 2011 in regard to the 2009 gas contract signed with Russia. Investigations and trials involving former officials from Tymoshenko's government were also launched, and Tymoshenko gained widespread international support for her claim that the prosecutions were politically motivated. The EU was particularly critical of the administration's approach, characterizing it as a "contravention" of EU standards and suggesting that Tymoshenko's conviction might prove a hindrance to the proposed negotiation of an EU-Ukrainian trade deal.

Domestic critics of the government described the "political" trials of 2011 as part of a broader repression of democratic expression that had also affected journalists and numerous civic organizations. Several demonstrations also broke out to protest the spending cuts and other retrenchment (including pension reform) enacted by the Yanukovych administration at the request of the IMF.

In October 2011 Tymoshenko was sentenced to seven years in prison following her conviction for abuse of power in connection with the 2009 gas contract with Russia. The conviction and sentencing set off a firestorm of protest among her domestic supporters and the international community. Nonetheless, the verdict and sentence were subsequently upheld in the courts, and President Yanukuvych brushed aside calls for him to issue a pardon. In fact, prosecutors in April 2012 filed new charges of tax evasion against Tymoshenko, whose supporters alleged that she was being mistreated in prison. The issue damaged Ukraine's relationship with the EU (see Foreign relations, below) and dominated the run-up to the October 2012 legislative poll, in which the PR faced strong competition from Tymoshenko's Fatherland and two surging groups—the right-wing Freedom (*Svoboda*) party and Vitali Klitschko's Ukrainian Democratic Alliance for Reform (UDAR).

The PR was credited with securing a plurality of 185 seats in the October 28, 2012, balloting for the Supreme Council, although voters also provided significant support for the opposition, which organized demonstrations in early November to protest alleged fraud surrounding the poll. Prime Minister Azarov was reappointed in December as head of another PR-led government that enjoyed the legislative support of the KPU (32 seats) and independents.

In an apparent response to heavy pressure from Russia, President Yanukovych in late November 2013 announced that Ukraine was not prepared to sign an association agreement and other accords designed to deepen Ukraine's economic ties to the EU. The decision triggered massive protests in Kiev by pro-EU demonstrators led by the major opposition parties. Russia, encouraging Ukraine to join the Russian customs union with Belarus and Kazakhstan, subsequently approved $17 billion in loans and sharply reduced the price of Russian gas exports to Ukraine.

With the conflict between protestors and police having intensified, Prime Minister Azarov resigned on January 28, 2014. When negotiations with opposition leaders ultimately failed to resolve the situation, the Supreme Council on February 22 voted to dismiss Yanukovych from the presidency, which was assumed in an acting capacity by Oleksandr TURCHYNOV, who had just been elected as the council's new speaker. With Yanukovych having fled the country, the Supreme Council on February 27 approved a new cabinet headed by Arseniy YATSENYUK, a Fatherland leader who had been prominent in the recent so-called Euromaidan demonstrations.

In first-round presidential elections on May 25, 2014, Petro POROSHENKO, running as an independent but backed by the UDAR and others, was elected with 54.7 percent of the vote. Problems within the government coalition prompted Poroshenko to dissolve the Supreme Council on August 25, and early elections were scheduled for October 26.

In elections for the Supreme Council on October 26, 2014, the pro-presidential Petro Poroshenko Bloc (*Blok Petra Poroshenka*—BPP) won a plurality with 132 seats, followed by Yatsenyuk's grouping, the People's Front (PF), with 82; Self-Reliance (*Samopomich*), 33; pro-Russian Opposition Bloc, 29; Radical Party of Oleh Lyashko (Radical Party), 22; Fatherland, 19; independents, 96; and 10 seats to minor parties. Elections were not held for 12 seats in Crimea, which was annexed by Russia the previous March, or for 15 seats in the Donetsk and Luhansk Regions, parts of which were under the control of pro-Russian separatists.

After extended negotiations, the five major pro-Western parties (the BPP, PF, Self-Reliance, Radical Party, and Fatherland) reached agreement on a coalition government on November 21, 2014. The Supreme Council on November 27 endorsed incumbent prime minister Yatsenyuk to head the new government, and on December 2 approved Yatsenyuk's proposed cabinet, which included members of all five parties. Yatsenyuk pledged that the administration would pursue further integration with the European Union and eventual membership in NATO, while continuing to combat Russian "aggression" in eastern Ukraine.

On September 1, 2015, the Radical Party withdrew from the government to protest legislation that granted greater autonomy to regional governments and temporary self-rule to Donetsk and Luhansk. Fatherland withdrew from the coalition on February 17, 2016. In response Yatsenyuk resigned on April 14 and was replaced by

Volodymyr GROYSMAN (BPP) as the leader of a new coalition government, led by the BPP and the PF.

Political background (Crimea). In 1954 the Soviet leadership under Nikita Khrushchev transferred the Crimean autonomous republic from Russian to Ukrainian administration, despite Crimea's largely ethnic Russian population. Subsequent moves to "rehabilitate" the original Crimean Tatars, who had been transported to Central Asia during World War II because of alleged collaboration with the Germans, yielded the return of some 250,000 Tatars to Crimea by the early 1990s. (It has been recently estimated that there are 1 million ethnic Russians, 600,000 Ukrainians, and 300,000 Tatars in Crimea.)

The status of Crimea became intertwined with postindependence political developments when the aspiration of the majority ethnic Russian population for union with Russia generated strains in Moscow-Kiev relations (see Foreign relations, below). Also complicating matters was disaffection among the peninsula's original Tatar inhabitants. Another source of friction was the long-running dispute over the ownership of the ex-Soviet Black Sea fleet based in the Crimean port of Sevastopol. In February 1992 Ukraine refused a Russian request for the retrocession of Crimea on the grounds that the CIS agreement included a commitment to accept existing borders, to which the Russian *Duma* responded in May by declaring the 1954 transfer of Crimea to Ukraine unconstitutional and void. The *Duma*'s action was in support of a declaration of independence from Ukraine by the Crimean Supreme Soviet, which the Crimeans repealed after the Ukrainians had voted to annul its content by an overwhelming margin. Subsequently, the Ukrainian foreign ministry issued a statement declaring that "the status of the Crimea is an internal Ukrainian matter which cannot be the subject of negotiation with another state."

In June 1992 an agreement in principle between President Kravchuk of Ukraine and President Boris Yeltsin of Russia provided for the Black Sea fleet of more than 800 ships, including auxiliary vessels, to be divided equally between the two countries. Differences nevertheless persisted, accompanied by periodic incidents involving naval personnel in Sevastopol and by nationalist opposition to compromise in the Ukrainian and Russian parliaments.

The election of Yuriy MESHKOV, leader of the secessionist Republican Movement of Crimea (*Republikanskve Dvizheniya Kryma*—RDK), as Crimean president on January 31, 1994, was seen in Kiev as a threat to the country's territorial integrity. On May 19 the Crimean legislature voted to restore its proindependence constitution of May 1992, with Sevastopol declaring in August that it had "Russian legal status." The Ukrainian Supreme Council consequently adopted legislation designed to curb Crimea's autonomy, enacting a measure in November providing for the automatic invalidation of any Crimean legislation in conflict with Ukrainian law. In March 1995, moreover, the Kiev legislature annulled Crimea's constitution and effectively abolished the Crimean presidency, with Ukrainian president Kuchma assuming direct control over the region from April 1. Meshkov denounced these actions as unconstitutional, although plans to hold a referendum on the separatist 1992 basic law were canceled at the end of May. In June 1995 Presidents Kuchma and Yeltsin reached a further accord, with Russia agreeing to buy part of the Ukrainian half of the Black Sea fleet, thus increasing its share to 81 percent. (Both sides retained naval bases in Sevastopol.)

Kuchma rescinded his direct rule over Crimea in August 1995, while still asserting that candidates for the Crimean premiership had to be approved by him. In February 1996 the appointment of Arkady DEMYDENKO as Crimean prime minister was so confirmed.

In May 1997 Russian president Yeltsin made a state visit to Ukraine to sign a 10-year friendship treaty and to resolve remaining differences over the Black Sea fleet. By virtue of a 20-year lease, the fleet was to be based primarily in Sevastopol. Both the Russian and Ukrainian navies were to use Streletskaya Bay, but the rest of the Black Sea would be used exclusively by Ukraine. Russia also would recognize Crimea and the city of Sevastopol as Ukrainian territory. In addition, the agreement would settle questions about Ukraine's bilateral debts and its claims on ships the Russians "inherited" upon the dissolution of the Soviet Union. (In February 1999 the Russian *Duma* ratified the treaty, which formally recognized, for the first time, Ukraine's sovereignty within its current borders.)

On June 3, 1997, Ukrainian president Kuchma approved the dismissal of Crimean prime minister Demydenko after the Crimean parliament had voted three times to sack Demydenko. Kuchma subsequently approved the appointment of Anatoli FRANCHUK, Kuchma's ally and a former Crimean premier (1994–1995), as Crimean prime minister; Franchuk's cabinet was approved by the Crimean parliament on June 19.

Elections to the Crimean Supreme Council were conducted on March 29, 1998, in conjunction with the balloting for the Ukrainian Supreme Council. Left-wing parties advanced in the Crimean Supreme Council, which elected Leonid HRACH of the Communist Party of Crimea (*Kommunisticheskaya Partiya Kryma*—KPK) as its new speaker. However, in an apparent reflection of the balance of power maintained at the national level, Kuchma named Serhiy KUNITSYN, the leader of the centrist factions in the Crimean Supreme Council, as the new Crimean prime minister on May 19. Subsequently, in January 1999, a new constitution was adopted for Crimea, which, among other things, was granted substantial budgetary authority.

Tensions between factions loyal to Hrach and Kunitsyn subsequently continued to play out, with Hrach repeatedly working through the legislature for Kunitsyn's dismissal. In September 2000 President Kuchma commented that he saw no need for the removal of Kunitsyn given the current balance of powers in the province, but on July 18, 2001, the Crimean legislature voted to dismiss Kunitsyn, who stepped down five days later. Kuchma then named Valeriy HORBATOV as Kunitsyn's successor. However, Kunitsyn returned to the Crimean prime minister's post in April 2002 following the March Crimean legislative elections, which were reportedly marred by numerous irregularities. (Horbatov had been elected to the Ukrainian Supreme Court.)

Tension between Crimea and the national government continued to simmer into 2004, as the Russian nationalists who dominated Crimea pressed for designation of Russian as an official language and for stronger military and political links with Russia. In the wake of the Orange Revolution at the national level in late 2004 and early 2005, Kunitsyn resigned as Crimean prime minister in April 2005, being described as the last major leader of the Kuchma era to leave office. He was succeeded by Anatoliy MATVIYENKO, a close associate of Ukrainian Prime Minister Tymoshenko and a member of the BYT. However, Matviyenko also fell victim to national politics a few months later when Tymoshenko and President Yushchenko became estranged. Anatoliy BURDYUHOV, a member of the NU, was named in September to replace Matviyenko as head of a Crimean government that included a number of bankers (including Burdyuhov) and increased representation for the Crimean Tatars.

Prior to the March 26, 2006, balloting for the Crimean Supreme Council, the region was described as still polarized along ethnic lines and suffering economic malaise. Not surprisingly, considering the fact that ethnic Russians constituted 60 percent of the Crimean population, the pro-Russian For Yanukovych Bloc won a strong plurality of 44 seats in the new council. With President Yushchenko's endorsement, Viktor PLAKYDA was selected in June as the new Crimean prime minister. Plakyda, the former director of the Crimean energy company, announced his intention to focus on economic development. However, political discord continued to dominate regional events as evidenced by major anti-NATO protests that forced cancellation of planned Ukrainian–U.S. military exercises in June as well as by ongoing calls from members of the Russian *Duma* for the reannexation of Crimea by Russia.

International attention focused on Crimea in August 2008 following the military conflict between Russia and Georgia over South Ossetia, observers wondering if the Russian hard line might also soon extend to Crimea. However, Russian leaders, at least at the national level, continued to disavow any interest in regaining sovereignty over Crimea. Meanwhile, the Crimean Supreme Council in mid-September endorsed Russia's recognition of the independence of South Ossetia and Abkhazia.

Leaders of the Crimean Tatars in 2010 criticized the pro-Russian leanings of new Ukrainian president Yanukovych, particularly in regard to the new lease arrangement for the Russian Black Sea Fleet (see Current issues, below).

Crimean prime minister Plakyda resigned in March 2010, and he was succeeded by Vasyl DZHARTY, a former Ukrainian minister of the environment and natural resources who was described as having an open mind concerning Tatar legal efforts to reclaim land and property confiscated during World War II. When Dzharty died in August 2011, he was succeeded by Anatoliy MOHYLIOV, who as chief of police in Crimea from 2007 to 2010 had overseen a crackdown on Tatar protest demonstrations.

In the wake of antigovernment protests in early 2014 that eventually forced the ouster of the Yanukovych administration, pro-Russian demonstrations broke out in Crimea in late February. Local "self-defense forces" took control of Crimea's Supreme Soviet building, apparently with the support of Russia, which claimed that "fascist" elements of the new government in Kiev posed a threat to Russian speakers in Crimea and throughout the rest of Ukraine. The Crimean

Supreme Soviet on February 27 voted to dismiss Prime Minister Mohyliov and his government, and Sergei AKSYONOV succeeded Mohyliov in an acting capacity, while Aleksei CHALY, a Russian citizen, was named the new government leader in Sevastopol. In early March the Crimean Supreme Council formally requested Russian assistance, and soldiers believed to be Russian (initially denied by Russia) took up positions at several key locations (including the airport) in Crimea, prompting a massive international outcry. On March 6 the Crimean Supreme Count called for the peninsula's return to Russian sovereignty, and a referendum on March 16 endorsed the proposal with a reported 96.8 percent yes vote. Russian president Vladimir Putin on March 18 signed a treaty with Aksyonov, Chaly, and Vladimir KONSTANTINOV (the speaker of the Crimean Supreme Council) under which Crimea and Sevastopol were to be incorporated into Russia. Treaty ratification was accomplished within three days by the Russian parliament, which also approved constitutional amendments providing for a new Crimean Federal District comprising the Republic of Crimea and the Federal City of Sevastopol.

The essentially bloodless annexation by Russia of Crimea was condemned as illegal by the Ukrainian government as well as the West, which imposed a series of economic sanctions against Russia in protest. However, there was little talk of any military confrontation in the matter, and Russian de facto control was easily cemented through, among other things, the introduction of the Russian ruble as the currency in Crimea, gradual implementation of Russian laws, and the conferring of Russian citizenship on the Crimean population. New legislatures were elected in Crimea and Sevastopol as part of Russia's nationwide regional and local elections on September 14, with Putin's United Russia reportedly garnering more than 70 percent of the vote in Crimea. Tatar leaders called for a boycott of that balloting as part of their overall opposition to the Russian takeover.

Constitution and government. In mid-1990 the Council of Ministers was restructured as a Western-style cabinet headed by a prime minister. Coincident with Leonid Kravchuk's formal reinstallation as Ukrainian head of state on December 5, 1991, his title changed from chair of the Supreme Soviet to president of the republic. The draft of a new constitution published in October 1993 called for retention of most of the existing governmental structure, providing for a 450-seat Supreme Council and a Council of Ministers guided by a president directly elected for a five-year term.

Under the terms of a June 1995 interim "constitutional treaty," a Constitutional Commission completed work on the draft of a new constitution in March 1996. Despite some opposition to stronger presidential authority at the expense of the legislature, the Supreme Council in June adopted the new text. Among other things, it granted significant new powers to the president, including the right to name the prime minister (with the concurrence of a parliamentary majority) and other officials, and recognized the right to own private property. In addition, the new basic law provided for the establishment of a National Security and Defense Council and for the holding of parliamentary and presidential elections in March 1998 and October 1999, respectively. It also specified that parliamentary deputies could not simultaneously hold government appointments. The parliament in September 1997 approved a mixed voting system for the Supreme Council, designating that half of the council members be directly elected from single-seat constituencies, with the remaining 225 seats being apportioned to parties that received at least 4 percent of all ballots cast in separate nationwide balloting.

In an April 2000 referendum voters overwhelmingly approved four Kuchma proposals that, if enacted, would have cut the number of legislative deputies from 450 to 300, added an appointive upper chamber to parliament to represent regional interests, limited legislators' immunity from prosecution, and given the president authority to dismiss the parliament if it went more than a month without a working majority or if it failed to pass the annual budget within three months of submission. Kuchma lobbied for the measures as a means of furthering "the systematic and efficient work of the legislature," whereas the majority of the Supreme Council saw the referendum as Kuchma's attempt to diminish the council's authority and to install a presidential system of government. In January 2001 the Supreme Council instead passed a bill adopting a strictly proportional party-list system for the next general election, with parties having to achieve 4 percent of the vote to obtain representation. The bill obviously favored the larger parties and factions and could have dramatically altered the balance of power in the Supreme Council. However, Kuchma promptly vetoed the electoral bill.

In August 2002 President Kuchma announced formation of a constitutional commission to study reforms in the hope of eliminating the administrative impasses that had characterized governance since independence. Among other things, he again called for establishment of a bicameral legislature. However, his lack of a legislative majority precluded progress.

A number of constitutional revisions were negotiated as part of the resolution of the presidential crisis of late 2004. Under the changes (which went into effect on January 1, 2006), significant authority previously exercised by the president was transferred to the Supreme Council. Although the president retained the formal right to nominate the prime minister, the Supreme Council acquired de facto control of the post. The Supreme Council was also given authority over all cabinet appointments except for the defense and foreign affairs portfolios, which remained under the president's purview. In addition, the Supreme Council was authorized to dismiss the prime minister and cabinet members. The basic law revisions also decreed that all 450 members of the Supreme Council would henceforth be elected by proportional voting.

In the midst of ongoing conflict between the president and the prime minister, the Supreme Council in December 2006 adopted additional legislation designed to further undercut presidential prerogatives. However, President Yushchenko refused to sign the new legislation, asking for a review by the Constitutional Court. The issue of the division of authority between the president and the prime minister/legislature subsequently remained contentious, although legislation was approved in May 2008 confirming that the foreign affairs and defense ministers were presidential nominees. Yushchenko presented his proposals for constitutional revision to the Supreme Council in March 2009, based on recommendations from the National Constitutional Council he had established in late 2007. However, little attention was given to his proposals (including creation of a bicameral legislature and codification of substantial presidential authority) because of his diminished legislative clout.

Prior to trying to form a new government in March 2010, President Yanukovych successfully lobbied the Supreme Council to approve amendments to the laws regarding the formation of government coalitions. Previously, factions in the legislature were required to vote as blocs in regard to proposed governments. However, the revisions permitted individual legislators to vote for a coalition on their own, the change permitting Yanukovych to get legislative endorsement for the new government with the help of defectors from opposition parties.

In October 2010, at the urging of the Yanukovych administration, the Constitutional Court voided the constitutional changes (approved in 2004 and implemented in 2006) under which the Supreme Council had been given responsibility for most cabinet appointments and other previously presidential prerogatives. Under the 2010 changes, only the prime minister required legislative approval, not the other cabinet members. Electoral law revision in 2011 returned elections for the Supreme Council to a mixed proportional/majoritarian system.

A Supreme Court was installed in January 1997; there is also a Constitutional Court with members appointed by the president, legislature, and the bar association. In addition, the 2005 Code of Administrative Procedure provided for an additional court system headed by a High Administrative Court to deal with a variety of issues, including election-related cases.

Reacting to months of anti-administration protests, the Supreme Council on February 21, 2014, readopted the constitutional amendments regarding cabinet authority that had been implemented in 2006 but overturned in 2010. Consequently, the Supreme Council now must approve all cabinet members, all of whom are nominated by the prime minister except for the ministers of defense and foreign affairs, who are nominated by the president. The president also formally nominates the prime minister, but he must propose the candidate chosen by the majority legislative coalition.

Ukraine is still technically divided into 24 provinces (*oblasts*), with Crimea administered as an autonomous republic and the metropolitan areas of Kiev and Sevastopol having special administrative status. However, de facto control of Crimea (including Sevastopol) passed to Russia in March 2014. Local self-government functions in Ukraine in divisions and subdivisions.

Freedom of speech is guaranteed in the Ukrainian constitution, but prior to liberalization following the Orange Revolution, opposition publications were frequently subjected to official harassment and libel suits brought by government officials. Collaterally, domestic and international advocates for freedom of expression criticized the Ukrainian government for inadequately investigating the disappearance and murder of independent journalist Heorhiy Gongadze in 2000. The Parliamentary Assembly of the Council of Europe, for one, cited "intimidation, repeated aggressions, and murders" directed against journalists.

The Kuchma administration passed legislation in 2004 allowing the government to monitor Internet publications and e-mails, an initiative critics claimed was aimed at popular opposition Websites. The hard line toward media freedom was perceived as partially responsible for the popular antigovernment sentiment that propelled the Orange Revolution in late December 2004, after which the Yushchenko administration pledged quick liberalization in favor of a Western-style media policy. The media were subsequently generally perceived as operating freely in regard to criticizing government officials. However, growing concern was subsequently voiced in regard to increased pressure on journalists by the Yanukovych administration. In 2016 Reporters Without Borders ranked Ukraine 107th out of 180 countries in its annual survey on media freedom.

At least six journalists were killed in the first three quarters of 2014, and many others were attacked and/or detained, particularly in connection to the military conflict in the eastern part of Ukraine. The "constant violation of press freedom" also included restrictions on Russian media in western Ukraine.

Foreign relations. Although at the time not an independent country, Ukraine, like Byelorussia (now Belarus), was accorded founding membership in the UN in 1945 as a gesture to the USSR, which feared the world body would have an anti-Soviet bias. Theretofore not a member of the IMF or World Bank, independent Ukraine was admitted to both institutions in September 1992; earlier, it had become a member of the Conference on (subsequently Organization for) Security and Cooperation in Europe (CSCE/OSCE) following the demise of the Soviet Union and the creation of the CIS in December 1991.

Ukrainian leaders insisted following independence that they wished the country to become nuclear free, even though a substantial proportion of the former USSR's nuclear arsenal was located in Ukraine. Although Ukraine was a signatory of the 1992 Lisbon Protocol to the 1991 Strategic Arms Reduction Treaty (START I), which designated Russia as the sole nuclear power in the CIS, implementation was delayed by difficulties over the terms demanded by the Ukrainian government and the Ukrainian nationalist opposition. Not until November 1993 did the Ukrainian Supreme Council conditionally ratify START I, while indicating that it was not prepared to endorse the Nuclear Non-Proliferation Treaty (NPT) without substantial Western security guarantees, financial assistance for weapons dismantling, and compensation for nuclear devices transferred to Russia for destruction. The conditional ratification and statement of terms yielded speedy progress in January 1994 on a tripartite agreement, whereby the United States would provide assistance for the dismantling of nuclear weapons by Ukraine, with warheads being shipped to Russia for destruction. Eventually, Ukraine would also receive about $1 billion, via Russia, from the sale of reprocessed uranium from the warheads. In accordance with the agreement, Ukraine began shipping warheads to Russia in early March, and in December Ukraine formally acceded to the NPT, following parliamentary ratification the previous month. (On June 1, 1996, President Kuchma announced that Ukraine had completed the process of nuclear disarmament by transferring the last of its warheads to Russia.)

Ukraine acceded to NATO's Partnership for Peace program in February 1994, and in June it signed a partnership and cooperation agreement with the EU. An important aspect of the latter accord was the provision of EU aid for closure of the remaining nuclear reactors in Chernobyl, site of the world's worst nuclear accident in 1986. Having been formally admitted to the Council of Europe in November 1995, Ukraine became a full member of the Central European Initiative (CEI) in May 1996 and was granted observer status within the Nonaligned Movement in September. In September 1997 Ukraine tentatively agreed to a plan by which it would join the Central European Free Trade Agreement (CEFTA, see Foreign relations in the entry on Poland), though no firm timetable was announced. (Ukraine had not joined by late 2014.) A new EU economic cooperation agreement with Ukraine took effect on March 1, 1998, committing each to increased trade and investment. Ukraine concurrently indicated that it eventually intended to apply for full EU membership.

As one of the largest recipients of U.S. foreign aid, Ukraine bowed to the pressure from the United States and Israel in March 1998 and declined to sell turbines for Russia to use in nuclear reactors destined for Iran. The agreement on commercial nuclear technology removed an impediment to improved relations with Washington at a time of sharply increased contacts between Ukraine and NATO officials. Despite the prospect of reprisals by Russia, which asked Kiev not to cancel the turbine contract, Ukraine tried to maintain the momentum it had gained in July 1997 when it had signed a cooperation charter with NATO. The agreement, reportedly modeled on the Russia–NATO Founding Act of May 1997, established a special relationship (short of membership) that included the exchange of military missions and the establishment of a NATO–Ukraine Commission, through which Ukraine could consult with NATO if it came under an external threat. In March 1998, clarifying its neutrality and its relationship with the Western alliance, Kiev said it did not rule out joining NATO in the future if membership would not jeopardize its relationship with neighbors, particularly Russia. President Kuchma also endorsed the expansion of NATO in March 1999 (again contrary to Moscow's wishes), although he condemned the subsequent NATO military campaign in the former Yugoslavia.

In June 1997 the presidents of Ukraine and Romania signed a treaty, subsequently approved by their respective parliaments, confirming existing borders and protecting the rights of national minorities. Meanwhile, the informal "Union of Three" alliance of Georgia, Ukraine, and Azerbaijan became identified through the abbreviation GUAM when Moldova joined the group in October. Earlier, in the fall of 1996, those former Soviet bloc nations had begun to strengthen their economic and political relationships based on a common pro-Western orientation, suspicion of Russia, and the prospects of collaborating on the exploitation of Azerbaijan's Caspian oil reserves. GUAM expanded to the GUUAM upon the accession of Uzbekistan in April 1999. (In May 2005 Uzbekistan withdrew from the grouping, which in May 2006 changed its name to the GUAM Organization for Democracy and Economic Development.)

Having received grant and loan pledges valued in the billions of dollars from the European Bank for Reconstruction and Development (EBRD) and other multilateral agencies as well as individual countries, Ukraine officially shut down the last operating nuclear reactor in Chernobyl on December 15, 2000. The financial and technical assistance was targeted for a range of projects, including construction of a more permanent sarcophagus around the highly radioactive reactor that was destroyed by the 1986 explosion. Other priorities included building replacement power facilities, upgrading safety at remaining nuclear plants, and aiding the local population.

A decade after the demise of the Soviet Union, delineation of Ukraine's borders with Moldova and Romania remained somewhat problematic. A treaty concluded with Moldova in 1999 provided the basis for border demarcation that began in late 2003. Meanwhile, negotiations with Romania continued over areas encompassing various arms of the Danube, the adjacent delta, the Black Sea continental shelf, and the minuscule Zmiyiny (Serpent) Island in potentially oil- and gas-rich waters in the Black Sea. (The question of Serpent Island and maritime delimitation in the Black Sea was submitted in 2004 to the International Court of Justice, which in February 2009 issued a ruling that awarded partial control to both countries but appeared to favor Romania by declining to classify the islet as qualifying for maritime demarcation.) Romania has long claimed Northern Bukovina and Southern Bessarabia, which it ceded to the Soviet Union in 1940, and fervent Romanian nationalists remained committed to incorporating the two areas into a Greater Romania.

Ukraine's foreign policy under President Kuchma was driven by two seemingly contradictory goals: to maintain friendly relations with Russia on the one hand and to open the door to Europe with a possible view to membership in the EU on the other. In reference to the former, in 2003 Kuchma was elected as chair of the CIS, becoming the first non-Russian to hold the post. In addition, treaties were signed in 2003 delineating the land boundary between Russia and Ukraine as well as resolving the status of the Sea of Azov as joint territorial waters. At the same time, the Kuchma administration sought to counterbalance its close relations with Russia through a policy of engagement with the United States and the EU. In pursuit of this opening to the West, Kuchma sent 1,650 troops to serve in Iraq in 2003, even though the Supreme Council had approved a motion condemning the U.S.-led intervention there. (The troops were withdrawn in 2005.)

The victory of Viktor Yushchenko in the controversial 2004 presidential race put a strain on Ukraine's relations with Russia, as Russian president Vladimir Putin had openly supported Yushchenko's main opponent, Viktor Yanukovych. However, Yushchenko's first foreign visit after his inauguration was to Moscow, where he pledged continued close relations. At the same time, Yushchenko intensified Ukraine's efforts to join the EU and endorsed eventual membership in NATO.

In what was seen as at least a symbolically significant initiative, the EU in November 2005 sent 70 police and customs personnel to help combat smuggling along the Ukrainian–Moldovan border. The EU also recognized Ukraine as having a market economy in February 2006, an important step toward additional integration. However, the EU clearly remained skeptical of further membership expansion and as of late

2007 was offering Ukraine only enhanced economic cooperation, with accession remaining off the negotiating table for the immediate future. By that time it was also apparent that possible NATO membership had also receded from both Ukraine's and NATO's immediate concerns. Significantly, public opinion in Ukraine reportedly opposed NATO accession, particularly in view of Russia's strong objection to such an initiative. Russia was also distressed over the passage by Ukraine's Supreme Council in mid-2007 of legislation needed to proceed with Ukraine's WTO membership request. Analysts agreed that Moscow preferred that Ukraine not join the WTO unless Russia also gained admission; however, Ukraine acceded to the WTO in May 2008, Ukrainian officials indicating that they expected the WTO membership to enhance the country's EU membership prospects.

In late March 2008 the United States and Ukraine reached agreement on "strategic priorities" and additional trade cooperation. U.S. president Bush also urged the April NATO summit to approve a Membership Action Plan (MAP) for both Ukraine and Georgia despite Russia's continued strong objections. Although no MAPs were approved (primarily due to opposition from France and Germany), the summit appeared to endorse eventual memberships for Ukraine and Georgia. In the opinion of most analysts, the NATO issue contributed to Russia's intensifying hard line regarding regional security issues, culminating in the Georgian–Russian military conflict in August. Arguing that Crimea could be the next focus for Russia (despite Russia's insistence that it did not challenge Ukraine's current borders), President Yushchenko immediately called for Ukraine's accelerated integration into "Euro-Atlantic structures."

An acrimonious dispute erupted with Russia in January 2009 over the delivery of natural gas to Ukraine as well as the transshipment of gas through Ukraine to EU countries, several of which suffered shortages before resolution was achieved. Although the EU was critical of Ukrainian leaders (as well as those in Russia) in the matter, it nevertheless included Ukraine among the six post-Soviet countries invited in May to participate in the EU's Eastern Partnership. Subsequently, in June U.S. vice president Joseph Biden during a visit to Ukraine affirmed the U.S. administration's continued support for Ukraine's eventual NATO membership, despite recent U.S. efforts to improve U.S. relations with Russia. For his part, Russian president Medvedev in August accused Ukrainian president Yushchenko of pursuing "anti-Russian policies" and urged Yushchenko's defeat in the upcoming presidential poll. Following his election in early 2010, President Yanukovych initially appeared to steer Ukrainian foreign policy on a pro-Russian course that essentially precluded NATO accession. However, Yanukovych also pledged to continue to pursue further integration with the EU, and his relationship with Russian leaders was subsequently viewed as complicated. Among other things, Russian prime minister Putin objected to the prosecution of former Ukrainian prime minister Tymoshenko in regard to a ten-year Russian-Ukrainian gas contract signed in 2009. Putin in 2011 encouraged Ukraine to join the customs and trade union recently established by Belarus, Kazakhstan, and Russia. Yanukovych deflected consideration of such a move, analysts noting that Ukraine's full participation in the new union might interfere with further Ukrainian integration with the EU. (Putin had reportedly offered Ukraine a massive reduction in gas prices in return for Ukraine's commitment to the union.)

In the second half of 2011 the EU postponed completion of a significant trade and association agreement with Ukraine out of concern over Tymoshenko's arrest and conviction. Although the accord was ultimately initialed in March 2012, final approval remained suspended at least until the Eastern Partnership summit scheduled for November 2013, while Ukraine addressed EU concerns regarding "selective justice" and electoral deficiencies. Yanukovych's last-minute decision not to sign the EU accord triggered protests that culminated in his ouster in February 2014. The United States and EU subsequently pledged financial assistance to the new pro-Western government, while mulling over the possibility of supplying it with military equipment and armaments to assist in the conflict with Russian-supported separatists in eastern Ukraine. The EU association and trade agreement was approved at midyear, although the implementation of some provisions was delayed until at least 2016 due to Russian concerns.

The IMF approved a $17.5 billion loan to Ukraine in March 2015 as part of a $40 billion international assistance package that included the restructuring of the country's billion external debt. In August a restructuring accord was finalized, in which 20 percent of the country's $18.9 billion debt was written-off, along with a four-year suspension on debt payments.

A new 13-point peace agreement was finalized in Minsk on February 12, following negotiations among the Trilateral Contact Group consisting of representatives from Ukraine, Russia, and the OSCE. However, despite the call for an immediate cease-fire in the Minsk II accord, fighting continued.

On December 16, 2015, the government enacted a trade embargo on Crimea. Two days later Ukraine declared a moratorium on its $3.5 billion debt repayment to Russia. The government claimed repaying the debt would run counter to the March billion bailout given to Ukraine by the IMF. The government noted that Moscow was required to agree to the restructuring program that had been accepted by commercial creditors in order for payments to resume. This program included a 20 percent write-down and an extension of payments. Subsequently, Moscow declared it would sue Ukraine.

Current issues. The OSCE argued that "democratic progress" appeared to have been reversed in the October 2012 legislative elections, citing the abuse of power and excessive role of money in general and extensive irregularities in the counting of the votes in the single-member constituencies in particular. The EU subsequently reaffirmed that the "erosion of democracy" was jeopardizing further integration with Ukraine.

The mass protest demonstrations that erupted in Kiev in late November 2013 were initially aimed at convincing President Yanukovych to reverse his recent decision not to proceed with the long-awaited EU association and trade accords. (The protesters coalesced at Kiev's Independence Square, which thereby led to references to the "Maidan" or "Euromaidan" movement ["maidan" is Ukrainian for square].) Calls also quickly arose for the dismissal of the Azarov cabinet, particularly after police cracked down on the theretofore peaceful demonstrations. The conflict became more violent in January 2014 as new antiprotest legislation was adopted by the Supreme Council, and activists were attacked by unidentified young men (possibly working for the government). After the first fatalities occurred on January 22, President Yanukovych met with the three best-known politicians associated with the demonstrations (Arseniy Yatsenyuk of Fatherland, Vitali Klitschko of UDAR, and Oleh Tyahnybok of Freedom) and reportedly offered Yatsenyuk the opportunity to lead a new cabinet in return for the end to the demonstrations. However, it was eventually concluded that the protesters, having established a tent city in the barricaded square, would no longer accept any outcome other than Yanukovych's removal.

Prime Minister Azarov's departure in late January 2014 led to a brief "truce," but the tipping point was reached in mid-February when protests spread to a number of cities and reports circulated that the administration was planning to call in the army to quell the unrest. With Euromaidan activists having taken control of a number of governmental buildings, the Supreme Council on February 22 voted to "dismiss" Yanukovych, although his supporters strongly disputed the constitutionality of his ouster. The Supreme Council also freed Tymoshenko, who gave an emotional speech to the Euromaidan crowd that evening, and adopted constitutional revision to limit presidential authority. Attesting to the power of the anti-Yanukovych movement, the proposed Yatsenyuk-led cabinet was informally presented to the demonstrators in the square prior to its formal installation.

Russia objected vehemently to Yanukovych's ouster, pointing out that he had been democratically elected and that voters would have had a chance to elect a new president in 2015. Following the suspension of Russian financial aid, Prime Minister Yatsenyuk identified the threat of default as his administration's most immediate priority and warned Ukrainians that severe fiscal pain was in the offing. Meanwhile, claiming that the rights of Russian-speaking Ukrainians were being threatened by far-right Euromaidan components, Russia stunned the West in March by annexing Crimea (see Political background on Crimea, above) and by providing support for pro-Russian separatists in the eastern *oblasts* of Donetsk and Luhansk. Russian president Vladimir Putin also urged the new Ukrainian government to remain "militarily neutral", that is, to forgo NATO membership.

Petro Poroshenko, elected president of Ukraine in first-round balloting in May 2014, was a prominent business "magnate" who had been an enthusiastic Euromaidan supporter. The new president pledged to pursue economic reform based on European standards and to keep Ukraine "unified," a reference to the eastern rebels, whose "trust" Poroshenko said he hoped to gain. (Referendums held in May in the self-proclaimed "People's Republics" of Donetsk and Luhansk overwhelmingly supported "self-rule.") However, conflict in the east subsequently intensified, and the downing (purportedly by a rebel missile) of a Malaysian airliner in July attracted broad international scrutiny.

By September an estimated 3,000 people had died and perhaps as many as 1 million had been displaced in the wake of a series of offensives by the Ukrainian military and counter-offensives on the part of the rebels. (Putin ultimately acknowledged that Russian soldiers were operating in eastern Ukraine but said they were there as "volunteers.") A tentative cease-fire dampened the fighting, and the Ukrainian government offered three years of "special status" to the separatist regions while a permanent political settlement was negotiated, known as the Minsk I.

The September cease-fire was essentially over by November as Russia increased military aid to the separatists. Analysts predicted that the increased intervention was designed to create a land corridor from Russia to Crimea. In contravention of the September cease-fire, elections were held in Donetsk and Luhansk on November 2. Aleksandr ZAKHARCHENKO was reelected president of the self-proclaimed Donetsk's People's Republic with 79 percent of the vote, and Igor PLOTNITSKY was reelected president of the self-proclaimed Luhansk People's Republic with 63 percent of the vote. The balloting was condemned by Western governments, and the OSCE refused to send an observer team to monitor the elections.

By 2016 fighting in the separatist regions had killed more than 8,000 and injured more than 19,000. Conflict also created 1.2 million internally displaced persons and another 765,000 external refugees.

POLITICAL PARTIES

As of early 2001 there were 110 officially registered parties in Ukraine. In January 2001 a reported 11 parties and 30 civic groups joined the **Ukrainian Right-Wing** (*Ukrainska Pravytsya*) alliance as a step toward consolidation of anti-Kuchma forces on the right. It was largely superseded, however, by formation in February of the **National Salvation Front** (NSF), which was organized as a "citizens' initiative," primarily by supporters of Yulia Tymoshenko. The NSF had as its goals coordinating activities with the "Ukraine Without Kuchma" movement, advancing a center-right legislative agenda, and marshaling diplomatic support for its anti-Kuchma stance. At the same time, other elements on the center-right coalesced around former prime minister Viktor Yushchenko, and in July they announced formation of an electoral bloc, "Our Ukraine" ("*Nasha* Ukraina"—NU).

In July 2001 the NSF formed an electoral committee that Tymoshenko indicated was prepared to engage in "peaceful coexistence or cooperation" with Yushchenko, but Yushchenko ultimately rejected any alliance with Tymoshenko. In early November the NSF was renamed the **Yulia Tymoshenko Bloc** (*Blok Yuliyi Tymoshenko*—BYT). Parties in the BYT initially included Fatherland, USDP, UNP *"Sobor,"* and URP. Meanwhile, in October the pro-Kuchma forces had established the third principal electoral bloc, **"For a United Ukraine!"** (*Vyborchiy Blok "Za Yedinu Ukrainu!"*—ZYU), which was chaired by Volodymyr Lytvyn, head of presidential administration. The parties in the ZYU included the APU, NDPU, PPPU, PR, and TU. (The ZYU finished second in the 2002 legislative balloting with 102 seats.) Forces on the left continued to be led by the Communist Party of Ukraine (KPU) and the Socialist Party of Ukraine (SPU).

Twenty-eight parties competed independently in the March 2006 legislative balloting, while another 50 parties participated in 17 electoral blocs, including a revamped NU and a slightly modified BYT. Under recent changes in the electoral law, parties were required to have been registered for at least one year to participate in the elections. Twenty-one parties or blocs presented candidates in the 2007 legislative poll, and 21 parties contested the proportional component of the 2012 elections, many small parties having opted to have their members included on a larger party's official slate. (Under electoral law changes approved in 2011, bloc lists, which had previously referenced multiple parties, were no longer permitted.) Twenty-nine parties or blocs participated in the 2016 balloting.

Legislative Parties:

Petro Poroshenko Bloc (*Blok Petra Poroshenka*—BPP). The pro-presidential BPP had its roots in the Solidarity (*Solidarnist*) parliamentary grouping of Petro Poroshenko formed in 2000. The BPP itself was established in August 2014 to provide a parliamentary party for Poroshenko, who had been elected president in June of that year. In the October 2014 balloting, the BPP became the largest party in parliament, with 132 seats and 21.8 percent of the vote. Approximately one-third of the BPP's seats were won by candidates from the Ukrainian Democratic Alliance for Reform (UDAR, below), led by former world heavyweight boxing champion Vitaliy KLITSCHKO. The UDAR formally merged with the BPP in August 2015. Klitschko became BPP leader with the merger, but resigned his party position in May 2016 in order to remain mayor of Kiev after a new law was enacted forbidding party leaders from holding state office. Meanwhile, Volodymyr GROYSMAN became prime minister in April 2016.

Leaders: Petro POROSHENKO (President of the Republic), Volodymyr GROYSMAN (Prime Minister).

Ukrainian Democratic Alliance for Reform (UDAR). Headed by world heavyweight boxing champion Vitaliy KLITSCHKO (*Udar* translates as "Punch"), UDAR is an outgrowth of political support that coalesced around Klitschko for local elections in Kiev from 2006–2008. Klitschko's backers at the local level during that time included *Pora*, the RiP, *Rukh*, the USDP, and the small European Capital party, which changed its name to the New Country party in 2009 before formally adopting the UDAR rubric in April 2010. The center-right UDAR performed well in the 2010 Kiev municipal poll and, based on Klitschko's immense popularity, surged in national public opinion polls in the run-up to the October 2012 legislative balloting, for which it campaigned on a pro-Western, anticorruption platform. Although a degree of cooperation was reported between UDAR and Fatherland regarding single-member constituencies, friction between the two surfaced shortly before the balloting regarding final candidate selections. UDAR consequently declined to sign a proposed preelection coalition agreement with Fatherland and Freedom, the two other leading opposition parties. UDAR won 40 seats in the 2012 poll, including 34 on a vote share of 14 percent in the proportional poll, propelling the party and Klitschko into the forefront of national political affairs.

Klitschko, who had earlier indicated his intention to run for president in 2015, was one of the most visible of the opposition politicians at the forefront of the Euromaidan demonstrations that led to the ouster of President Yanukovych in early 2014. Although the UDAR did not accept positions in the new Fatherland-led cabinet, it initially provided important legislative support for the administration.

Deciding to run instead for the mayorship of Kiev, Klitschko supported Petro Poroshenko (then an independent) in the May 2014 presidential election. After helping to force early legislative elections by withdrawing its support from the government in July, the UDAR participated in the Petro Poroshenko Bloc (*Blok Petra Poroshenka*—BPP, above) for the October balloting for the Supreme Council. The BPP, led by Yuriy LUTSENKO, called for anticorruption measures, pursuit of EU membership, and negotiations with separatists in the east with the goal of the preservation of the nation's "territorial integrity."

Party of Regions (*Partiya Rehioniv*—PR). The PR held its initial congress in March 2001 as the culmination of a process that began with the signing of a merger agreement by five centrist parties in July 2000. Connected to Donetsk financial and industrial interests, the nascent PR quickly formed a new parliamentary faction, Regions of Ukraine.

Of the PR's five founding organizations, the **Labor Party of Ukraine** (*Partiya Pratsi Ukrainy*—PPU) dated from late 1992, when it was organized by elements descended from Soviet-era official unions. Led by Valentyn LANDYK, the PPU participated in the 1998 general elections in the "Together" electoral alliance with the LPU (below). The **Party of Regional Revival of Ukraine** (*Partiya Rehionalnoho Vidrodzhennya Ukrainy*—PRVU), which won 0.9 percent of the proportional vote in the 1998 legislative election, was led by Donetsk's mayor, Volodymyr RYBAK, and Yukhym ZVYAHILSKIY. The other three founding parties were the recently formed **Party "For a Beautiful Ukraine"** (*Partiya "Za Krasyvu Ukrainu"*—PZKU), led by Leonid CHERNOVETSKIY; the **All-Ukrainian Party of Pensioners** (*Vseukrainskoi Partiya Pensioneriv*—VPP), led by Andriy KAPUSTA and Hennadiy SAMOFALOV; and the **Party of Solidarity of Ukraine** (*Partiya Solidarnosti Ukrainy*—PSU), formed in July 2000 by the Solidarity (*Solidarnist*) parliamentary faction under Petro Poroshenko.

In November 2000 the emerging grouping had adopted the unwieldy designation Party of Regional Revival "Labor Solidarity of Ukraine" (*Partiya Rehionalnoho Vidrodzhennya "Trudova Solidarnist Ukrainy"*). At the time, it was considered pro-Kuchma, while claiming to represent the interests of the regions within a unified state. At the March founding congress, Mykola Azarov, the chair of the State Tax Administration, was elected chair of the party, although he was quoted as saying he saw the position as temporary. Poroshenko, who had reportedly sought the chair's position, continued to lead the separate Solidarity faction in the

Supreme Council and ultimately established the Solidarity Party. With the next legislative election in sight, Azarov resigned as PR leader in January 2002 to avoid charges of conflict of interest.

The PR was a principal forum for Viktor Yanukovych in the 2004 presidential elections. It was assisted in the 2006 legislative balloting by financial support from billionaire tycoon Rinat AKHMETOV, who was elected on the PR's list, along with a number of his business associates. Western campaign consultants also contributed to the PR's success (a plurality of 186 seats on a vote share of 32.1 percent). The PR advocated "strong ties" to the EU but opposed NATO membership. Yanukovych also pledged to pursue official language status for Russian and improvements in relations with Russia in general.

Yanukovych was named prime minister in the cabinet installed in August 2006, but the PR was forced into opposition status following the September 2007 legislative elections (despite having won a plurality of 175 seats on a vote share of 34.4 percent). The PR organized several mass protests in Kiev in April 2009 to protest government policies, particularly interaction with the IMF.

After withdrawing from a proposed grand coalition with the BYT in June 2009 (see Fatherland, below), Yanukovych, considered Russia's preferred candidate, and the PR called for increased wages and pension benefits (despite strong IMF objections) in his successful 2010 presidential bid, in which he finished first in the first round with 35.3 percent of the vote and won the runoff with 49 percent of the vote. Following his victory, Yanukovych turned over leadership of the PR to Mykola Azarov, who was named prime minister in March. The PR was credited with 36 percent of the nationwide vote in the October local elections.

In 2012 **Strong Ukraine** (*Sylna Ukrayina*—SU), a centrist, middle-class party merged with the PR. The SU was previously known as the **Ukrainian Labor Party,** also referenced as the Working (*Trudova*) Party, which was launched in September 1999 by Mykhaylo SYROTA, a member of the legislature who had been instrumental in the adoption of the new Ukrainian Constitution in 1996. (That party should not be confused with the historical Labor Party of Ukraine, which was a founding member of the PR, or with Working Ukraine, below, with which Syrota had briefly been associated.) The Ukrainian Labor Party participated in the Lytvyn Bloc (see People's Party, below) in the 2007 legislative elections, securing 7 of that bloc's 20 seats. Syrota died in a car accident in August 2008. His son, Dmytro SYROTA, was subsequently elected as the SU's new leader.

Serhiy Tihipko, former leader of Working Ukraine, joined the Ukrainian Labor Party in 2009 and was elected party leader at the November congress, at which the SU rubric was adopted. Tihipko finished third in the first round of presidential balloting in January 2010 with 13.1 percent of the vote. He was reportedly offered the post of prime minister by Yulia Tymoshenko in return for his support in her bid in the presidential runoff, but he declined to endorse her. Tihipko was subsequently named deputy prime minister for the economy in the new PR-led cabinet, after which the SU merged with the PR. (The party was reestablished in 2014, see below.)

The PR, campaigning on a platform of stability and emphasizing its government record, secured 30 percent of the proportional component of the 2012 legislative elections. Official PR candidates secured 185 seats overall, and most of the officially independent successful candidates ultimately joined the PR parliamentary faction.

A number of PR legislators left the party's Supreme Council faction in February 2014 during the chaotic events that led to the ouster of President Yanukovych, and the party subsequently strongly condemned the actions of his administration and formally separated from Yanukovych, Azarov, and other former leaders. PR candidate Mykhailo Dobkin finished sixth in the May 2014 presidential poll with 3 percent of the vote, while Serhiy Tihipko, running officially as an independent, finished fifth with 5.2 percent. Although the PR opted not to present its own candidates in the October legislative elections, a number of current and former PR members were included on the slate of the new **Opposition Bloc** (OB), led by former deputy prime minister Yuriy BOYKO. Meanwhile, the SU reemerged as a formal party for the poll under Tihipko's leadership.

OB candidates won 9.4 percent of the total votes, securing 29 seats in the 2014 balloting.

Leaders: Boris KOLESNIKOW (Executive Secretary), Mykhailo DOBKIN (2014 presidential candidate), Oleksandr YEFREMOV (Parliamentary Leader), Volodymyr RYBAK (Former Speaker of the Supreme Council).

Fatherland (*Batkivshchyna*). The social-democratic Fatherland (also sometimes translated as Motherland) was established as a Supreme Council faction in March 1999 by Yulia Tymoshenko and other members of the All-Ukrainian Association *Hromada* (below) who objected to the parent party's support for Pavlo Lazarenko. Ironically, Tymoshenko had once been a close associate of Lazarenko, who had encouraged her to enter politics. Initially numbering about two dozen deputies, the Fatherland faction soon surpassed *Hromada,* which ultimately fell below the 14 adherents needed for official faction status.

In late December 1999 President Kuchma named Tymoshenko to the new Yushchenko cabinet as deputy prime minister for fuel and energy, but by mid-2000 she was already drawing criticism from Kuchma for her handling of the sector. Despite continuing support from the prime minister, she was dismissed from her cabinet post by Kuchma on January 19, 2001, four days after being formally charged with gas smuggling, tax evasion, and document forgery while head of Unified Energy Systems of Ukraine in 1996–1997.

In late 2001 Fatherland absorbed Stepan Khmara's **Ukrainian Conservative Republican Party** (*Ukrainska Konservatyvna Respublikanska Partiya*—UKRP). Intensely anti-Communist and anti-Russian, the UKRP had been formed in June 1992 by a radical wing of the URP (below) led by Khmara. (For additional information on the UKRP, see Fatherland in the 2007 *Handbook.*)

Tymoshenko's supporters were instrumental in formation of the National Salvation Front (NSF) in 2001 and its successor, the Yulia Tymoshenko Bloc (*Blok Yuliyi Tymoshenko*—BYT) in 2002 (see introductory text, above, for additional information on the NSF and BYT [the latter of which won 22 seats in the 2002 legislative election]).

For the 2006 elections (at which it secured 129 seats on a vote share of 22.3 percent), the BYT comprised Fatherland, the USDP (see Ukraine-Forward!, below), and remnants of the **Ukrainian People's Party Assembly** (*Ukrainskoho Narodnoho Partiya "Sobor"*—UNP *"Sobor."*) The UNP *"Sobor,"* an anti-Kuchma party formed in 1999, had split in 2005 after a party congress voted to align with the BYT. (See *"Sobor,"* below, for additional information.)

The BYT was also aided in 2006 by the inclusion of Levko LUKYANENKO and his supporters from the URP (below), who had been left without affiliation following a split in the URP. The BYT campaigned on a platform of support for integration with Western Europe and opposition to the recently completed natural gas deal with Russia. Tymoshenko also maintained a populist stance that promised increased welfare spending and wide-ranging corruption investigations.

Having in 2006 declared its uncompromising opposition to the Yanukovych government and having subsequently aligned itself with the NU, the BYT finished second in the September 2007 legislative balloting. For that election the BYT also included the **Reforms and Order Party** (*Reformy I Poryadok Partiya*—RiP). The previously pro-Kuchma RiP had secured 3.1 percent of the national proportional vote in the 1998 legislative poll after negotiations for its inclusion in the Forward, Ukraine! alliance with the PKNS and UKhDP (see URP, below) had fallen through. In December 2000 it joined Hennadiy Udovenko's *Rukh* and the KUN in announcing formation of a center-right electoral bloc, which supported economic reform and greater integration of Ukraine with Western Europe. The RiP participated in the NU for the 2002 legislative poll but formed an alliance called the **Civil Political Bloc** (*Pora*—PRP) with the reformist It Is Time (*Pora*) Party for the 2006 legislative poll, winning 1.5 percent of the vote.

The BYT was credited with winning 155 seats in the 2007 legislative poll (165 for Fatherland, 9 for the RiP, 8 for the USDP, and 33 for "unaffiliated" candidates who ran on the BYT list). Following the election, the BYT formed a coalition government with the NU-NS that included Tymoshenko as prime minister, although friction between her and President Yushchenko subsequently continued to dominate the political scene. Meanwhile RiP leader Viktor PYNZENYK, a noted economist who had been named finance minister in the December 2007 government, resigned the post in early 2009, saying policy initiatives were being held "hostage to politics."

In the first half of 2009, the BYT appeared close to reaching a coalition agreement with the PR, the primary opposition party led by former prime minister Viktor Yanukovych. According to various reports, the proposed accord called for the groups to cooperate within parliament to amend the constitution to authorize parliament to elect the president (currently elected by popular vote), with Yanukovych slated to fill that position, while Tymoshenko would continue as prime minister (with expanded powers). However, the proposed grand coalition collapsed in June when Yanukovych abruptly withdrew his support.

In October 2009 the BYT unanimously nominated Tymoshenko as its candidate for the January 2010 presidential election. She subsequently pledged, if elected, to pursue warmer relations with Russia (while also supporting additional cooperation with the EU) and to combat corruption (in part through judicial reform).

Tymoshenko finished second in the first round of presidential balloting in January 2010 with 25 percent of the vote and lost the subsequent runoff with 46 percent of the vote. Following the collapse of her government coalition in March, she became the leading voice of the opposition to new PR-led government and a key member of the new Committee to Protect Ukraine, formed in May to protest the pro-Russian policies of President Yanukovych. Prominent author Dmytro PAVLYCHKO was named coordinator of the new committee, which in addition to Fatherland and the RiP, included elements of the NU-NS, and the right-wing, nonparliamentary All-Ukrainian Union Freedom.

Tymoshenko and a number of former ministers from her government were arrested in 2011 in a crackdown the government attributed to its anticorruption campaign and Tymoshenko's supporters to a political lynching (see Current issues, above). The BYT components and other opposition parties subsequently formed a Committee to Resist Dictatorship, which served as the foundation of cooperation for the 2012 legislative poll. Due to electoral law changes that had banned bloc formation for those elections, Tymoshenko allies were all presented on the Fatherland list. Included on the United Opposition Fatherland list were members of the RiP, the Popular Movement of Ukraine (*Rukh*, below), the People's Self-Defense Party (below), the **Front for Change, the Civic Platform, For Ukraine,** and the **Social Christian Party.**

The Front for Change, Civic Platform, and For Ukraine, were outgrowths of the NU-NS (see NSNU, below). The Front for Change was formed by Arseny Yatsenyuk, a former speaker of the Supreme Council, following the splintering of the NU-NS in late 2008. Yatsenyuk subsequently attracted significant support in public opinion polls by criticizing the prevalence of personal politics among the country's leading figures. Although he had initially professed a middle-of-the-road approach to Ukraine's main issues, Yatsenyuk, reportedly enjoying support among the oligarchs, campaigned for the presidency in 2010 on a platform that opposed NATO and EU membership. He won 7 percent of the first-round vote. Following the poll, the Front for Change declined to join the new-PR led government.

The Civic Platform was formed (following the NU-NS breakup) by former defense minister Anatoliy HRYTSENKO, who won 1.2 percent of the vote in the first round of the 2010 presidential election. (The European Party of Ukraine [*Evropeyska Partiya Ukraini*—EPU], another component of the NU-NS, merged into the Civic Platform in mid-2011.)

For Ukraine, led by Byacheslav KRYLENKO, is a successor to the Party of Social Protection. The Social Christian Party was established in 2004 under the leadership of singer Oksana BILOZIR (a supporter of Viktor Yushchenko); the party secured 0.1 percent of the vote in the 2006 legislative elections. For the 2007 poll, it formed the Christian Bloc with the **All-Ukrainian Political Party of Ecology and Social Protection.**

The Fatherland list won 25.6 percent of the vote in the proportional component of the 2012 poll, good for 62 seats. For some of the single-member constituencies Fatherland cooperated with both the UDAR and Freedom, and those three parties formed a united front to protest what they claimed to be massive fraud in the counting of votes, particularly in the single-member constituencies.

Tymoshenko, having been sentenced to seven years in prison following her conviction in October 2011 on a charge of abuse of power, was barred from contesting the 2012 legislative election. In January 2013 she was named as a suspect (along with Pavlo Lazarenko) in the case of the murder of a national legislator in 1996. She also continued to face tax evasion charges, although all proceedings against her were postponed due to her health issues.

In June 2013 it was announced that the RiP, *Rukh,* and the Front for Change had all formally merged into Fatherland, with Yatsenyuk being elected chair of the party. Fatherland subsequently called on all opposition parties to coalesce behind a single presidential candidate for 2015.

Tymoshenko was released from prison in February 2014 in connection with the Euromaidan demonstrations, during which Yatsenyuk served as one of the most visible proponents of the anti-Yanukovych initiative. Yatsenyuk was named head of the post-Yanukovych government, which included a number of other ministers from Fatherland. However, a leadership dispute between Yatsenyuk and Tymoshenko, who finished second in the May presidential balloting with 12.8 percent of the vote and was listed first on Fatherland's slate of candidates for the October legislative poll, prompted Yatsenyuk and other Fatherland members to form a new party (see PF, below). Meanwhile, Anatoliy Hrytsenko finished fourth (5.5 percent of the vote) as the Civic Platform candidate in the May presidential election.

In the 2014 council elections, the party secured 5.7 percent of the vote and 19 seats. It was part of the subsequent BPP-led government, but left the coalition in February 2016.

Leaders: Yulia TYMOSHENKO (Leader and 2015 presidential candidate), Sergei SOBOLEV (Parliamentary Leader).

Popular Movement of Ukraine (*Narodnyi Rukh Ukrainy—Rukh,* or NRU). *Rukh* was organized in September 1989 as the Popular Movement of the Ukraine for Restructuring (*NRU za Perebudovu*). From the outset the grouping advocated Ukrainian independence, causing its critics among the anti-Communist groups to charge it with being more nationalist than democratic. Its founding chair, the writer Ivan DRACH, appealed to his colleagues to rally behind President Kravchuk after the latter's break with the KPU. Another leader, Vyacheslav CHORNOVIL, who had secured a 25 percent vote share as the grouping's presidential candidate in 1991, insisted that *Rukh* should continue in opposition. Thereafter, the grouping remained deeply divided in regard to the president, although it agreed to fill two important positions (first deputy prime minister and economics minister) in the Kuchma administration. Having been formally registered as a party in 1993, *Rukh,* campaigning on a platform of market reform and opposition to CIS membership, won 20 seats in the 1994 legislative elections. The party called for Ukraine's integration into NATO and the EU and for other democratic and reformist parties to unite against the left.

Rukh was the second leading party in the 1998 legislative poll, being credited with about 10 percent of the vote in the nationwide proportional balloting. However, it continued to suffer from what one analyst described as a "crisis in direction," occasioned more by personality differences than policy disputes. In January 1999 Chornovil was ousted as chair in favor of Yuriy Kostenko, a former cabinet minister. Chornovil and his supporters subsequently formed a new parliamentary faction called the Popular *Rukh* of Ukraine-1, or *Rukh*-1. Chornovil died in a car accident in March, and Hennadiy UDOVENKO, a former foreign minister, was named acting chair of the new faction.

Kostenko and Udovenko both ran for president in 1999; the former, technically on the ballot as an independent, won 2.2 percent of the vote, and the latter took 1.2 percent. Following a court challenge over the use of the party name, the two factions were registered separately in January 2000, with Udovenko's party assuming the NRU designation and the Kostenko group taking the name Ukrainian Popular Movement (*Ukrainskyi Narodnyi Rukh—Rukh,* or UNR).

In November 2000, looking ahead to the next legislative election, Udovenko's NRU announced an electoral alliance with the Congress of Ukrainian Nationalists (KUN, below) and the RiP (see Fatherland, above). In early 2001 it appeared that the two *Rukh* parties could well be allies for the next Supreme Council balloting and might even reunite beforehand. However, although both joined the Yushchenko bloc, they failed to resolve their differences before the March 2002 election. Afterward, both branches continued to express an interest in reuniting. In 2004 Udovenko was replaced as head of his faction by Borys TARASYUK, while Kostenko and his supporters formed the UNP (below). Both branches participated in the NU-NS for the 2007 legislative balloting. After participating in the Fatherland list for 2012 legislative poll, Tarasyuk and his *Rukh* component formally merged with Fatherland in June 2013.

People's Self-Defense Party. This grouping is an outgrowth of **Forward, Ukraine!,** which had initially been formed for the 1998 legislative poll by the **Centrist Christian Popular Union Party** (*Partiya Khrystiyansko Noradniy Soyuz*—PKNS) and the **Christian Democratic Party of Ukraine** (*Khrystiyansko Demokratychnya Partiya Ukrainy*—KhDPU). The alliance secured 1.7 percent of the vote in that election. Forward, Ukraine! subsequently registered as a party in its own right and participated in the NU in the 2002 legislative poll. In 2003 the PKNS and KhDPU formed the **Christian Democratic Union** (*Khrystiyansko Demokratychnya Soyuz*—KDS) with the All Ukrainian Union of Christians. The KDS was reportedly a member of the NU bloc for the 2006 legislative poll, although Forward, Ukraine! was listed as competing on its own in that poll, securing 0.02 percent of the vote.

Yuriy Lutsenko, who was dismissed under pressure from the PR as interior minister in December 2006 and subsequently became an adviser to President Yushchenko, later established a civic movement called People's Self-Defense that included Forward, Ukraine! and the KDS. That movement formed an important component of the NU-NS in the 2007 legislative balloting, in which Forward, Ukraine! secured 4 of the NU-NS's 72 seats and the KDS secured 2. Lutsenko subsequently served as interior minister in the Tymoshenko cabinet from 2007–2010.

In February 2010 a Forward, Ukraine! congress voted to change the party's name to the People's Self-Defense Party, with Lutsenko as its leader. Lutsenko was arrested in December 2010 on embezzlement charges, his supporters characterizing the case as an element of a politically motivated campaign by the Yanukovych administration against Tymoshenko and her former ministers.

In February 2012 Lutsenko was convicted and sentenced to four years in prison, the verdict prompting broad criticism from the international community for its political overtones. He was pardoned by President Yanukovych in April 2013, and shortly thereafter, he launched a new opposition movement called the Third Republic. Meanwhile, the status of the People's Self-Defense Party remained unclear; the party's merger into Fatherland had been announced by Lutsenko in December 2011, but no formal action was subsequently reported in that regard by a party congress. In September 2014 it was reported that Lutsenko was a leader of the new Petro Poroshenko bloc (see UDAR, above).

People's Front (PF). Formed in mid-2014 under the leadership of prime minister and former Fatherland chair Arseniy Yatsenyuk and other former Fatherland members, the PF campaigned for the October legislative poll on a platform that called for heavy defense spending to combat "the foreign enemy" (i.e., Russia) in eastern Ukraine and for development of "European social standards." In the October 2014 council elections, the party received 22.1 percent of the vote and 82 seats. It was part of the pro-Western governments formed in 2014 and 2016.

Leaders: Arseniy YATSENYUK (Prime Minister and Chair of the Political Council), Oleksandr TURCHYNOV (Former Speaker of the Supreme Council).

Freedom (*Svoboda*). A successor to the right-wing **Social-National Party of Ukraine,** Freedom is led by Oleh Tyahnybok, who has been described as having no serious rivals in the right flank. (Its strongest critics characterize Freedom as racist and anti-Semitic.) The party secured less than 1 percent of the vote in the 2006 and 2007 national legislative balloting but, promising to preserve the Ukrainian language and culture, had a greater impact in subsequent local elections, while Tyahnybok secured 1.4 percent of the vote in the first round of presidential balloting in January 2010.

Having softened its rhetoric, Freedom soared to 10.5 percent of the vote in the proportional component of the October 2012 legislative poll (good for 25 seats). It also captured 12 seats in the single-member constituencies, having cooperated with the Fatherland list in some of those races.

Tyahnybok and other Freedom adherents were prominent in the Euromaidan protests of early 2014, prompting criticism from Russia and pro-Russian Ukrainians that "fascist elements" were involved in the anti-Yanukovych movement. Freedom accepted several cabinet posts in the subsequent Fatherland-led government. Tyahnybok finished tenth in the May presidential poll with 1.2 percent of the vote.

In the 2014 elections, the party secured 4.7 percent of the vote and six seats.

Leaders: Oleh TYAHNYBOK (Leader and Parliamentary Leader), Andry MOKHNYK (Deputy Leader).

Radical Party of Oleh Lyashko. This party is an outgrowth of the **Ukrainian Radical-Democratic Party** that was formed in September 2010 under the leadership of Vladislav TELIPKO. Oleh LYASHKO, who had been elected to the Supreme Council on the BYT lists in 2006 and 2007 but had been expelled from the BYT faction in October 2010 for his perceived cooperation with the PR-led government, subsequently joined the party, which in August 2011 adopted its current rubric and elected the flamboyant Lyashko as its leader. Lyashko was reelected to the Supreme Council in 2012, and campaigning on a populist platform, he surprised observers with a third-place finish (on a vote share of 8.3 percent) in the May 2014 presidential election.

The party won 7.4 percent of the vote in the 2014 balloting, and 22 seats. It subsequently joined the pro-Western government, but withdrew in September 2014 to protest increased autonomy for the separatist regions.

Leaders: Oleh LYASHKO, Viacheslav SHAPOSHNIK.

Self-Reliance (*Samopomich*). Formed in mid-2014 by Andriy Sadovyi (the mayor of Lviv, Ukraine's second-largest city) and a number of young activists who had participated in the Euromaidan movement, Self-Reliance campaigned for the October legislative poll on an anticorruption platform that also promised decentralization and a reduction in the size of local government bureaucracies. In keeping with the party's reform orientation, veteran politicians were not permitted on its candidate list. The party won 33 seats in the October 2014 parliamentary elections, and joined the pro-Western government.

Leaders: Andriy SADOVYI (Mayor of Lviv), Hanna HOPKO.

Right Sector. Having gained attention (some say notoriety) as a paramilitary group during the Euromaidan movement in early 2014 and as a strident opponent of pro-Russian separatists in eastern Ukraine, Right Sector subsequently became a formal political party. Its leader, Dmytro Yarosh, finished 11th in the May 2014 presidential poll with 0.7 percent of the vote. The party won one seat in the 2014 parliamentary polling.

Leader: Dmytro YAROSH.

Other parties that secured representation in the 2014 elections included (all won one seat each): **Strong Ukraine** (*Sylna Ukrayina*—SU), a party which was reformed in 2014 by Serhiy TIHIPKO, formerly of the PR; **Zastup,** which was established in 2011 and led by Vira ULIANCHENKO; and **Voila,** formed in 2010.

Other Parties Contesting Both the Proportional and Majoritarian Components of the 2012 or 2014 Legislative Elections:

Communist Party of Ukraine (*Komunistychna Partiya Ukrainy*—KPU). Formerly Ukraine's ruling party, the KPU was banned in August 1991 but was allowed to reregister in October 1993 (without regaining party property of the Soviet era); Petro Symonenko was elected party leader. Standing on a traditional platform of anticapitalism and antinationalism, the KPU secured a plurality of seats in the 1994 legislative balloting and subsequently served as the core of the parliamentary opposition to the economic restructuring efforts of President Kuchma.

The KPU's plurality rose in the 1998 legislative poll, the party performing particularly well in the nationwide proportional balloting, winning about 25 percent of the votes. First Secretary Symonenko finished second in the 1999 presidential poll, winning 22.2 percent of the initial vote and 38.8 percent in a runoff against the incumbent. KPU demands of the subsequent Yushchenko government included severance of ties to NATO, designation of Russian as an official language, commitment to a socialist economy, and central planning for state enterprises.

In 2000 it was reported that the KPU had split into two factions. The first was led by Symonenko and remained decidedly antimarket, anti-American, and pro-Russian. The second adopted the name **Communist Party of Ukraine (Reformed);** its leader was reported to be Mikhail SAVENKO, a "progressive socialist" who was a member of the Working Ukraine faction in the Supreme Council.

At the March 2002 election the KPU took 66 seats, 59 of them on the basis of winning 20 percent of the proportional vote. It secured 21 seats in 2006 on a vote share of 3.7 percent and 27 seats in 2007 on a vote share of 5.4 percent. (The KPU [Reformed] won 0.3 percent of the vote in 2007.) The KPU continued its anti-NATO campaign in 2008.

In late 2009 Symonenko was named as the candidate of a KPU-led Bloc of Left and Center-Left Forces for the January 2010 presidential elections. Other groups in the bloc included the **Justice Party,** the SDPU, and the **Union of Left Forces.** Symonenko won 3.5 percent of the vote in the first round of balloting. The KPU subsequently supported the new PR-led government.

The KPU improved dramatically to 13.2 percent of the proportional vote in the 2012 legislative elections, good for 32 seats; none of its candidates won in the single-member constituencies, however. Symonenko announced after the balloting that the KPU would not necessarily support the PR in the future, but most KPU legislators voted with the government throughout the next year. The KPU also strongly backed President Yanukovych during the Euromaidan demonstrations of early 2014. Symonenko finished ninth in the May presidential poll with 1.5 percent of the vote. In the October legislative elections, the party won 3.9 percent of the vote and no seats.

Leader: Petro SYMONENKO (First Secretary, Parliamentary Leader, and 2010 and 2014 presidential candidate).

United Center. This grouping was formed following the breakup of the NU-NS in late 2008 by former chief of staff Viktor Baloga, reportedly as an official successor to the **Party of Private Property,** which had not presented candidates in the 2007 legislative poll. As the result of defections from the NU-NS, United Center claimed control of six legislative seats as of mid-2010. Baloga joined the PR-led government in November 2010, and the United Center legislators generally supported the government in subsequent legislative votes. Running on its own, the United Center secured three seats in the voting for single-member constituencies in the October 2012 elections. The party did not compete at a national level in the 2014 balloting, and lost the few single constituency seats it contested.

Leaders: Viktor BALOGA (Leader), Ihor KRIL.

Union Party (*Partiya Soyuz*). Essentially a Crimean grouping that advocates creation of a union of Ukraine, Belarus, and Russia, this party secured 0.7 percent of the vote in the 1998 national proportional poll. In 2002 it ran as part of a Russian Bloc that also included the **For a United Russia Party** and the **Russo-Ukrainian Union Party.** In 2005 it formed the For Union Bloc with the **Socialist Ukraine Party,** the **Homeland Party,** and the **Slavic Party.** The bloc secured 0.2 percent of the vote in the 2006 legislative poll.

For the 2007 poll, the Union Party participated in the Election Bloc of Political Parties Kuchma (led by Oleksandr VOLKOV) with the **Center Party** (led by Viktor HOLOVKO). The Union Party, which holds seats in the Supreme Council of Crimea and in municipal bodies in Crimea, won one seat in the balloting for single-member constituencies in the 2012 national legislative balloting.

Leader: Lev MYRYMSKY.

People's Union "Our Ukraine" (*Narodni Soyus "Nasha Ukraina"*—NSNU). The right-of-center NSNU was formed in early 2005 by supporters of President Yushchenko to, among other things, contest the 2006 legislative elections. It was considered to be a successor to "Our Ukraine" (*"Nasha Ukraina"*—NU), the electoral bloc that had been formed in 2001 to support Yushchenko's successful presidential campaign. Among the groups signing the 2001 NU accord were *Rukh*, the KUN, PKNS, RiP, LPU, Solidarity, the Republican Christian Party (RKP), and the **Youth Party of Ukraine.** Reports indicated that some 25 components of "Our Ukraine" participated in the launching of the NSNU. Described by some as the "next party of power," the NSNU nevertheless failed to attract a number of major Yushchenko allies.

Meeting in Kiev in March 2005, some 6,000 delegates to the NSNU's founding congress elected a 120-member Council and an Executive Committee. Deputy Prime Minister Roman BEZMERTNY was elected as head of the Council, while Yuriy YEKHANUROV was named head of the Executive Committee and Yushchenko was named as the party's honorary chair. The NSNU's 21-member presidium included 5 cabinet members.

Like its predecessor, the NSNU advocated market-driven economics and accelerated integration with Europe. It was initially reported that the NSNU planned to contest the 2006 elections in alliance with the BYT and the APU (see NP, above), but the NSNU ultimately served as the core component of the "Our Ukraine" bloc, which did not include the BYT or APU. The new bloc, which included the NSNU, *Rukh,* PPPU, KUN, KDS, and URP *"Sobor,"* finished third in the 2006 legislative election, securing 81 seats on a vote share of 14 percent.

Some members of the NSNU components joined the new cabinet that was installed in early August 2006, but most of them resigned as the NSNU formally went into opposition in October. The NSNU subsequently formed a pact with the BYT to coordinate their legislative activities.

For the 2007 poll, the NSNU served as the core component of the Our Ukraine–People's Self-Defense (*Nasha Ukraina–Narodna Samooborona*—NU-NS) bloc, which included *Rukh*, the UNP, URP "Sobor," Forward, Ukraine!, KDS, and *Pora*. Other components were the **European Party of Ukraine** (*Evropeyska Partiya Ukraini*—EPU), which was organized in 2006 under the leadership of Mykola KATERYNCHAK, and the **Party of Motherland Defenders** (*Partiya Zakhisnikiv Vitchizni*—PZV), led by Yuri KARMAZIN. Some NU-NS members subsequently lobbied for the members of the electoral bloc to merge into a single party, but the initiative failed to gain momentum. The NU-NS secured 14.2 percent of the 2007 vote, good for 72 seats (NSNU, 29; *Rukh,* 6; UNP, 6; Forward, Ukraine!, 4; EPU, 2; URP "Sobor," 2; KDS, 2; *Pora*, 1; PZV, 1; and 19 unaffiliated). Yuschenko subsequently negotiated a coalition agreement with BYT.

The NU-NS splintered in late 2008 when a majority of its legislators agreed to support the new BYT-led government despite objections from Yushchenko, whose relationship with Prime Minister Tymoshenko had deteriorated sharply. Some 17 NU-NS deputies, led by parliamentary leader Byacheslav Kyrylenko formed their own For Ukraine faction in parliament to support Yushchenko, while Arsensy Yatsenyuk (sacked in December as speaker of the Supreme Council) subsequently formed the Front for Change, former defense minister Anatoliy Hrytsenko launched a Civic Platform, and former chief of staff Viktor Baloga established the United Center. Although their groups initially remained nongovernmental organizations rather than parties, Yatsenyuk and Hrytsenko ran as candidates for the January 2010 presidential elections (see Front for Change and Civic Platform under Fatherland, above). Meanwhile, Yushchenko, reduced to single-digit support in public opinion polls, registered as an independent candidate in his reelection bid, although he was endorsed by the NSNU, which was described as "bankrupt" following the withdrawal of business-sector financial support for the president. Yushchenko secured only 5.5 percent of the vote in the first round of balloting in January 2010. A group of NU-NS deputies subsequently offered key legislative support to the new PR-led government. The NU-NS in 2011 announced that NU-NS deputies who cooperated with the government would be excluded from the NU-NS legislation faction.

Several key NU-NS splinters participated in the Fatherland list for the October 2012 elections to the Supreme Council, and the NU list (including members of the NSNU, UNP, and KUN) won only 1.1 percent of the proportional vote, with Yushchenko leading the list of candidates. In addition, none of the NU's 25 candidates was successful in the constituency balloting. It was reported in March 2013 that "Our Ukraine" had dissolved itself, although some members continued party operations. The grouping did not compete in the 2014 legislative elections.

Ukrainian People's Party (*Ukrainska Narodna Partiya*—UNP). The UNP was formed in 2004 by Yuriy Kostenko and other members of the UNR faction of *Rukh.* The UNP reportedly won several mayoral races in the 2006 local elections.

In advance of the 2006 legislative elections, the UNP participated with other center-right parties in the launching of an electoral bloc called the Ukrainian National Bloc of Kostenko and Plyushch, which won 1.9 percent of the 2006 vote. (The bloc supported the UNP's Kostenko and parliamentarian Ivan Plyushch. Other components of the bloc included the Party of Free Peasants and Entrepreneurs of Ukraine.) The UNP secured 6 of the NU-NS's 72 seats in the 2007 legislative elections. Kostenko, who had won 2.2 percent of the presidential vote in 1999, secured only 0.2 percent of the vote in the first round of the presidential poll in 2010. After the UNP competed on the NU list in the 2012 legislative elections, there were reports that the UNP had been reabsorbed into *Rukh*. The party contested eight seats in the 2014 balloting but lost all of them.

Leader: Yuriy KOSTENKO (Leader).

Congress of Ukrainian Nationalists (*Konhres Ukrainskykh Natsionalistiv*—KUN). The KUN was founded in October 1992 as an electoral front of the émigré Organization of Ukrainian Nationalists (*Orhanizatsiya Ukrainskykh Natsionalistiv*—OUN), which had led the struggle against Soviet communism before being finally suppressed internally in the 1950s. In 1994 elements of the original OUN opposed to the formation of the KUN reestablished the OUN as a separate civic association.

Advocating Ukraine's exit from the CIS but divided between procapitalists and those favoring a state economic role, the KUN won five seats in the 1994 balloting, although its leader was prevented from standing in a Lviv constituency. The KUN participated in the National Front alliance with the Ukrainian Republican Party and Ukrainian Conservative Republican Party in the 1998 legislative poll. The KUN participated in the "Our Ukraine" bloc for the 2006 legislative poll but decided not to participate in the 2007 balloting. In 2012 its membership was represented on the NU list. In the 2014 balloting, the party only received 0.05 percent of the vote.

Leader: Steven BRATSIUN.

People's Party (*Narodna Partiya*—NP). The NP is the rubric adopted in 2005 by the former **Agrarian Party of Ukraine** (*Ahrarna Partiya Ukrainy*—APU), which was established in 1996 to support farmers and which secured 3.7 percent of the proportional vote in the 1998 legislative balloting, just missing the 4 percent threshold necessary to be allocated proportional seats. The APU supported President Kuchma's reelection in the October–November 1999 balloting.

The APU was renamed the People's Agrarian Party of Ukraine in 2004, with Volodymyr Lytvyn, the speaker of the Supreme Council, becoming its leader. The NP rubric was adopted in 2005.

For the 2006 legislative balloting, the NP served as the core component of the Lytvyn Bloc, which also included the **Peasant Democratic Party,** and the small **Party of All-Ukrainian Union of the Left Justice.** The bloc secured 2.4 percent of the vote in 2006 and failed to gain representation. However, the Lytvyn Bloc, performing well in rural areas and small towns in central Ukraine, won 20 seats on a vote share of 4 percent in the 2007 elections, when its primary components were the NP and the Ukrainian Labor Party (see under PR, above).

Lytvyn, the leader of the bloc, was again elected speaker of the Supreme Council in December 2008 as part of the formation of a new BYT-led coalition government, announcing he hoped to serve as a peacemaker in the nation's frayed political affairs. In declaring his candidacy for the January 2010 presidential election, Lytvyn lobbied for support from disgruntled former SPU members. After Lytvyn secured 2.4 percent of the vote in the first round of presidential balloting in January 2010, the Lytvyn Bloc defected from the Tymoshenko coalition, prompting its collapse in early March. The Lytvyn Bloc subsequently joined the new PR-led government.

After an initial plan for the NP's merger into the PR failed to materialize, the NP competed independently in the single-member constituencies in the October 2012 legislative poll, winning two seats.

Leaders: Volodymyr LYTVYN (Leader and Former Speaker of the Supreme Council), Kateryna VASHCHUK.

All-Ukrainian Association Community (*Vseukrainske Obyednannya Hromada*). Founded in September 1997, *Hromada* elected former prime minister Pavlo Lazarenko as its first chair and joined the KPU and other leftist groups in blocking many initiatives proposed by the Kuchma/Pustovoytenko administration. The party's legislative stance appeared less founded in ideology than in Lazarenko's enmity toward Kuchma, who had insisted on Lazarenko's ouster as prime minister in the wake of corruption allegations. *Hromada* was credited with about 5 percent of the nationwide proportional vote in the 1998 legislative poll.

In December 1998 Lazarenko was arrested at the border by Swiss authorities on money laundering charges; he was subsequently released on bail of $2.6 million. Lazarenko left Ukraine for the United States in February 1999 after the Supreme Council had removed his immunity from prosecution and Ukrainian prosecutors had begun preparations to charge him with embezzlement and other malfeasance. The scandal surrounding Lazarenko split *Hromada,* with his supporters nominating him as the party's 1999 presidential candidate despite the corruption charges, while Lazarenko's opponents coalesced in a breakaway faction called Fatherland (above) under the leadership of Yulia Tymoshenko.

Lazarenko pleaded guilty to Swiss charges in June 2000. He received an 18-month sentence in absentia, and authorities confiscated $6.6 million from his accounts for return to Ukraine. In August 2006 Lazarenko was convicted of money laundering and other offences by a U.S. court and sentenced to nine years in prison.

Supporters of Lazarenko formed the Lazarenko Bloc for the 2006 legislative elections. In addition to *Hromada,* the bloc included the SDPU (below) and the **Social Democratic Union** (*Sotsial Demokratychnyy Soyuz*—SDS). The Lazarenko Bloc secured 0.3 percent of the vote in 2006. When the election commission refused to register Lazarenko as a candidate for the 2007 legislative elections, the Lazarenko Bloc refused to participate in that poll.

Hromada, running on its own, won 0.1 percent of the vote in the proportional component of the October 2012 legislative poll, Lazarenko again being barred from the party's candidate list. Lazarenko was released from U.S. prison in November and immediately applied for a U.S. residency permit, so he would not have to return to Ukraine, where charges against him remained outstanding.

Leader: Pavlo LAZARENKO (Former Prime Minister).

Liberal Party of Ukraine (*Liberalna Partiya Ukrainy*—LPU). Largely based in Donetsk, the LPU was formed in 1991 by Volodymyr SHCHERBAN, who subsequently served as the governor of the Sumy *oblast,* and Yevhen SHCHERBAN, who was assassinated in 1996. The LPU contested the 1998 legislative poll in the Together alliance with the Labor Party of Ukraine; the alliance won 1.9 percent of the national proportional vote.

In January 2005 Shcherban left office, and he subsequently reportedly fled Ukraine after an arrest warrant was issued charging him with corruption. (The former governor insisted the charges were politically motivated.) As a result of Shcherban's status, the LPU was not permitted to participate in the NU for the 2006 legislative poll. Running on its own, the LPU won only 0.04 percent of the vote. After boycotting the 2007 poll, the LPU secured 0.1 percent of the vote in the proportional component of the 2012 balloting. The LPU received only 0.02 percent of the vote.

Leader: Petro TSYHANKO (President).

Ukrainian National Assembly (*Ukrainska Natsionalna Asambleya*—UNA). Following its formation in the early 1990s, the UNA (also referenced as the UNA–Ukrainian People's Self-Defense—UNA-UNSO) pursued what was widely perceived as a neo-Nazi stance that emphasized Ukrainian nationalism and intense opposition to Russian policies, particularly in regard to ongoing Russian influence in areas such as Crimea. The party won three legislative seats in 1994, none in 1998, and one in 2002 (when it supported Viktor Yushchenko and the Orange Revolution). After securing no legislative seats in 2006 and not participating in the 2007 poll, the UNA-UNSO list won 0.08 percent of the vote in the proportional component of the 2012 balloting.

Leader: Yuriy SHUKHEVYCH.

Socialist Party of Ukraine (*Sotsialtstychna Partiya Ukrainy*—SPU). Although organized in 1991 by the former leader of the Communist legislative majority, the SPU was described as "not so much a successor to the Communist Party, as a party of economic populism." As such, it urged retention of a major state role in the economy while favoring priority for workers in privatization. It won 15 parliamentary seats in 1994 and attracted a further 12 independent deputies into its parliamentary group. In early 1996 two SPU deputies, Nataliya Vitrenko and Volodymyr Marchenko, were expelled from the party for criticizing the leadership for deviating from socialist ideals; they subsequently formed the PSP (below).

The SPU and the Peasants' Party of Ukraine (SelPU, below) formed an electoral bloc called For Truth, for the People, for Ukraine for the 1998 legislative poll, the alliance being credited with about 8 percent of the national proportional vote. SPU Chair Oleksandr Moroz, a former chair of the Supreme Council, finished third in the 1999 presidential election, taking 11.3 percent of the vote.

In November 2000 Moroz released secret tape recordings implicating President Kuchma in the disappearance of an independent journalist and then helped form the Ukraine Without Kuchma movement and the National Salvation Forum. At the March 2002 election, the SPU won 22 seats, 20 of them on the basis of a 6.9 percent share of the proportional vote.

The SPU joined the cabinet named in January 2005, and after winning 33 seats on a vote share of 5.7 percent in the March 2006 legislative poll, the party was initially perceived as a potential partner in a coalition government that would have included the NU and the BYT. However, Moroz switched allegiance to the PR, after which he was elected speaker of the Supreme Council, and the SPU joined the new PR-led cabinet. The SPU suffered a dramatic reversal (reflecting dissatisfaction among party members over Moroz's 2006 defection from the Orange Revolution) in the September 2007 balloting, securing only 2.9 percent of the votes and thereby losing all representation. Moroz, who had finished third in the three previous presidential elections, won only 0.4 percent of the vote as the SPU candidate in the first round of presidential balloting in January 2010. He was replaced as SPU leader in April 2012, and the SPU fell to 0.5 percent of the vote in the October legislative poll, the party's effort to merge with a number of other small leftist parties having been blocked by the government.

Leader: Petro USTENKO.

Other parties that ran unsuccessfully in both components of the 2012 or 2014 legislative poll included: the **Russian Bloc** (0.3 percent of the vote in the 2012 proportional component), led by Olexandr SVISTUNOV; **New Politics** (0.1 percent in 2012), recently formed under the leadership of former PR legislator Volodymyr SEMYNOZHENKO; the **Ukrainian Party Green Planet** (0.4 percent in 2012); the **Party of Pensioners of Ukraine** (0.6 percent); the **Greens** (0.3 percent); the **Party of the Greens of Ukraine** (0.4 percent in 2012 and 0.3 percent in 2014), led by Denys MOSKAL; **Ukraine of the Future** (0.2 percent in 2012 and 0.08 percent in 2014), a liberal grouping led by Sviatoslav OLIYNK; the **People's Labor Union of Ukraine** (0.1

percent); **Power of the People** (0.1 percent in 2014); and the **Political Union "Native Fatherland"** (0.2 percent).

Other Parties That Contested the 2007 Legislative Elections:

Ukrainian Republican Party "Assembly" (*Ukrainska Respublnkanska Partiya "Sobor"*—URP *"Sobor"*). The center-right URP *"Sobor"* was formed in December 2005 by former UNP *"Sobor"* leader Anatoliy MATVIYENKO and disaffected members of the Ukrainian Republican Party. The party participated in the NU-NS for the 2007 legislative balloting and unsuccessfully presented a small number of candidates in the single-member constituencies in 2012.

Leader: Pavlo ZHEBRIVSKY.

Progressive Socialist Party (*Prohresyvna Sotsialistychna Partiya*—PSP). Formed in 1996 by legislators recently expelled from the SPU, the PSP, considered the most radical of the country's leftist groupings, secured 4 percent of the national proportional vote in the 1998 legislative poll. Labeling herself a true Marxist, the party's 1999 presidential candidate, Nataliya Vitrenko, finished fourth in the balloting, with 11 percent of the vote.

For the 2002 election Vitrenko organized the Nataliya Vitrenko Bloc (*Blok Nataliyi Vitrenko*), which included the PSP and the **Party of Educators of Ukraine** (*Partiya Osvityan Ukrainy*—POU). The bloc won 3.2 percent of the proportional vote but no seats.

The PSP participated in the 2006 legislative poll in a People's Opposition Bloc of Nataliya Vitrenko (*Blok Nataliyi Vitrenko Narodna Opoziciya*) with the **Rus'-Ukrainian Union Party** (*Partiya Rus'ko-Ukrainsky Soyus*—RUS). The extremely pro-Russian and anti-American grouping opposed Ukraine's proposed membership in NATO, the EU, and the WTO and called for a new union of Belarus, Russia, and Ukraine. It won 2.9 percent of the vote, narrowly missing the threshold required to gain representation. Running on its own, the PSP won 1.3 percent of the vote in the September 2007 balloting. It did not participate in the 2012 poll.

Leaders: Nataliya VITRENKO, Volodymyr MARCHENKO.

Party of National Economic Development (*Partiya Natsionalno Ekonomichnoho Rozvytku Ukrainy*—PNERU). Led by banker Volodymyr Matviyenko, the PNERU won one seat in the 2002 legislative balloting but fell to a 0.2 percent vote share in the 2006 poll and 0.1 percent in 2007. It did not participate in the 2012 poll.

Leader: Volodymyr MATVIYENKO.

Election Bloc of Lyndmyla Suprun–Ukrainian Regional Activists. This grouping was formed for the 2007 legislative poll by the **People's Democratic Party** (led by Lyudmyla SUPRUN), the **Democratic Party of Ukraine** (led by Serhiy KOZACHENKO and Anna ANTONYEVA), and the **Republican Christian Party** (led by Volodymyr POROVSKY and Mykhaylo POROVSKY). (The People's Democratic Party and the Democratic Party had participated in the 2006 elections in a People's Democratic Party Bloc that also included the **Christian and Democratic Party** [led by the mayor of Kiev, Leonid CHERNOVETSKY].) The 2006 bloc secured 0.5 percent of the vote, and the 2007 bloc won 0.3 percent. As the candidate of the People's Democratic Party, Suprun secured 0.2 percent of the vote in the first round of presidential balloting in January 2010. Her party presented candidates unsuccessfully in the single-member constituencies in 2012.

Leader: Lyudmyla SUPRUN.

Party of Free Democrats. This center-right grouping was formerly known as *Yabluko* (Apple), which was formed in December 1999 to support Ukraine's capitalists and the middle class. A corresponding faction of about 14 deputies (the minimum required for recognition) formed within the Supreme Council. At the 2002 legislative election, however, *Yabluko* won only 1.2 percent of the proportional vote and no seats. The party's leader, Mykhaylo Brodskiy, announced in 2005 that *Yabluko* was merging with the BYT. However, *Yabluko* was revived in early 2007 following a rift between Brodskiy and Yulia Tymoshenko. The party adopted its new rubric in March; it secured 0.2 percent of the vote in the September legislative poll. Brodskiy won 0.1 percent of the vote as the party's candidate in the first round of presidential balloting in January 2010. The party competed (unsuccessfully) for only one seat in the single-member constituencies in the 2012 legislative election.

Leaders: Viktor CHAIKA, Mykhaylo BRODSKIY.

Party of Industrialists and Entrepreneurs of Ukraine (*Partiya Promislovtsiv i Pidpryyemtsiv Ukrainy*—PPPU). The PPPU was established by Prime Minister Anatoliy KINAKH in late November 2001. Previously the head of the Ukrainian Union of Industrialists and Entrepreneurs, Kinakh was elected to lead the new party at its February 2002 congress. The party's probusiness platform called for measures such as a significant reduction in the value-added tax and the adoption of policies favoring investment and the development of high-tech, export-oriented industry. Kinakh was named deputy prime minister in the January 2005 cabinet.

The PPPU participated in President Yushchenko's "Our Ukraine" (NU) bloc in the March 2006 legislative poll. However, Kinakh was named economics minister in the PR-led cabinet in March 2007, and most of the PPPU legislators concurrently switched allegiance to the PR's anticrisis coalition. (They were subsequently expelled from the NU.) Kinakh was elected to the Supreme Council in 2007 on the list of the PR, to which the PPPU had thrown its support.

Leaders: Lyudmyla DENYSYUK (Leader), Anatoliy KINAKH (Former Prime Minister).

Other parties and blocs that participated unsuccessfully in the 2007 legislative elections included the Agrarians Bloc Agrarian Ukraine, which included the **Ukrainian Peasant Democratic Party** (led by Valeriy VOSHCHEVSKIY); and the **All-Ukrainian Party of People's Trust,** which under the leadership of Andriy AZAROV, had secured 0.1 percent of the vote in the 2006 balloting.

Other Parties and Blocs That Contested the 2006 Legislative Elections:

Social Democratic Party of Ukraine (United) (*Sotsial-Demokratychna Partiya Ukrainy [Obyednana]*—SDPU[O]). Launched in 1990 by the minority leftist faction of the Ukrainian Social Democratic Movement (*Sotsial-Demokratychna Dvizheniya Ukrainy*—SDDU), the SDPU(O) was committed to democratic socialism in the tradition of the Second International, as exemplified by the prewar Ukrainian Social Democratic Workers' Party. The party's failure to win representation in the 1994 legislative poll strengthened those within it, favoring reunion with what was by then the SDPU.

Although the party included critics and prominent rivals of Kuchma, officials of the Kuchma government were also members. The SDPU(O) attempted a merger with the SDPU (below) late in 1997, but the negotiations failed. However, the SDPU(O) displayed surprising strength in the 1998 legislative election, attaining the required threshold of 4 percent to be allocated seats in the nationwide proportional voting. At the March 2002 election, the SPDU(O) won 6.3 percent of the proportional vote and 24 seats.

The SPDU(O) served as the core component of the Not Right Bloc (*Bloc Ne Tak)* that was formed in December 2005 by parties opposed to the Orange Revolution and Ukraine's proposed membership in Western organizations such as NATO and the EU. Other parties in the bloc (which won 1 percent of the vote in the 2006 legislative poll) included the **All-Ukrainian Political Union Women for the Future** (*Vseukrainske Politychne Obyednannya Zhinky za Majbutnie*—ZM), which had won 2.1 percent of the proportional vote in the 2002 legislative elections under the leadership of Valentyna DOVZHENKO; the small, centrist **Republican Party of Ukraine,** which had been launched in early 2005 by Yuriy Boyko, a former head of the state gas company; and the **All-Ukrainian Union Center.**

The SPDU(O)'s Mykhaylo PAPIEV was named minister for labor and social policy in the August 2006 PR-led cabinet, and party Deputy Chair Nestor SHUFRYCH was appointed minister of emergency situations in December. Viktor MEDVEDCHUK, the SPDU(O) chair since 1998 and the head of the administration of President Kuchma in 2002–2005, resigned as party leader in July 2007. The new leaders subsequently announced that the SPDU(O) would not participate in the September legislative elections, describing them as unconstitutional. However, the party informally supported the PR in the balloting. The SPDU(O) presented (unsuccessfully) one candidate in a single-member constituency in the 2012 legislative poll.

Leaders: Yuriy ZAHORODNIY (Chair), Ihor SHURMA (Deputy Chair).

Peasants' Party of Ukraine (*Selyanska Partiya Ukrainy*—SelPU). Organized in January 1992 as the rural counterpart of the SPU, the SelPU was committed to land collectivization and opposed to rapid economic reform. By virtue of its strong support in the Soviet-era rural bureaucracy, it won 19 seats in the 1994 legislative balloting and subsequently attracted 31 independent deputies into its parliamentary group. Following the 1998 legislative poll (in which the SelPU competed in alliance with the SPU), Chair Oleksandr TKACHENKO, a strong opponent of IMF-requested economic reform, was elected chair of the Supreme Council. However, in early 2000 he was voted out in what was dubbed a "velvet revolution," by a pro-Kuchma majority. Since 2002 Tkachenko has been included on the KPU electoral list for national legislative balloting. The SelPU secured 0.3 percent of the vote in the 2006 legislative poll but did not participate in the 2007 or 2012 balloting.

Social Democratic Party of Ukraine (*Sotsial-Demokratychna Partiya Ukrainy*—SDPU). The SDPU was formed as the SDP by the majority moderate faction of the Ukrainian Social Democratic Movement, which split at its inaugural congress in May 1990. Likened to the German SPD, the party urged a complete break with Marxism but attracted only sparse support, winning two seats in 1994. In February 1995 the SDPU was reregistered following a merger with the Human Rights Party and, according to reports, the Ukrainian Party of Justice, although the latter contested the 1998 election as part of the Working Ukraine alliance. The SDPU received only 0.3 percent of the proportional vote in the 1998 legislative election. In the 2002 campaign it renewed its claim to being the only truly social democratic party in Ukraine, but it again attracted negligible vote support.

For information on other parties and blocs that presented candidates in the 2006 legislative elections, see the 2012 *Handbook*.

Other Parties:

Ukraine-Forward! This party is a successor, at least in part, to the **Ukrainian Social Democratic Party** (*Ukrainska Sotsial-Demokratychna Partiya*—USDP), which was established in November 1998 by former justice minister Vasyl ONOPENKO, previously the leader of the Social Democratic Party of Ukraine (United). Onopenko finished eighth in the 1999 presidential election, with 0.5 percent of the vote. The USDP ran as part of BYT in the 2002, 2006, and 2011 legislative elections, securing 8 of the BYT's 155 seats in the latter poll.

In December 2011 BYT legislator Natalia Korolevska was elected leader of the USDP, considered a probusiness party. However, Korolevska was expelled from the BYT legislative faction in March 2012, faction leaders arguing that she had cooperated, against faction directives, in several instances with the Yanukovych administration. Two other USDP deputies withdrew from the BYT faction to protest her dismissal. Subsequently, the USDP changed its name to Ukraine-Forward!, positioned itself as between the opposition and the administration, and ran on its own in the 2012 legislative poll, securing 1.6 percent of the vote in the proportional component. Korolevska was named minister of social policy in the December 2012 cabinet, although it was not clear if the full party endorsed that decision.

Leaders: Natalia KOROLEVSKA, Andriy SHEVCHENKO.

It Is Time (*Pora*). The reformist *Pora* was formed in 2005 by members of youth organizations that had supported the Orange Revolution. It participated unsuccessfully in an electoral bloc with the RiP in the 2006 legislative elections before gaining one seat in the 2007 balloting as part of the NU-NS. It did not participate in the 2012 legislative elections.

Leader: Vladyslav KASKIV.

Liberal-Democratic Party of Ukraine (*Liberalno-Demokratychna Partiya Ukrainy*—LDPU). The LDPU was founded in Kiev in November 1990 on the premise that "socialism is incompatible with humanism and democracy." Its centrist orientation sharply distinguished it from the right-wing Russian Liberal Democratic Party. In the December 1991 presidential election the LDPU backed the candidacy of Volodymyr HRYNYOV. The LDPU participated in the European Choice electoral alliance with the USDP for the 1998 legislative balloting. The party was refused permission to participate in the 2006 legislative poll for technical reasons. It did not participate in the 2007 legislative elections but presented one candidate in a single-member constituency in 2012.

Leader: Andriy KOVAL.

Ukrainian Republican Party (*Ukrainska Respublikanska Partiya*—URP). The URP was launched during a congress of the Ukrainian Helsinki Union in April 1990, becoming Ukraine's first modern non-Communist party to receive official recognition. Its stated aim was the creation of a "parliamentary republic . . . [with] guaranteed freedom of activity."

In 1992 Mykhaylo HORYN, a cofounder of *Rukh*, joined the URP and was instrumental in organizing the Congress of National Democratic Forces (*Kongres Natsionalno–Demokratychnykh Syl*—KNDS), a coalition of some 20 organizations dedicated to working for national unity under President Kravchuk. The KNDS was credited with winning an aggregate of some 25 seats in the 1994 balloting, although the URP, weakened by the exit of a radical faction that became the Ukrainian Conservative Republican Party (UKRP, see Fatherland, above), won only 11 of those seats, one of its defeated candidates being Horyn. (He subsequently helped form the Republican Christian Party.) The URP led an unsuccessful effort to impeach President Kuchma in September 1997, accusing him of compromising the nation's sovereignty through the Black Sea treaty with Russia.

The URP contested the 1998 legislative election in a National Front (*Natsionalnyi Front*) alliance with the KUN (above) and the UKRP; however, the front won only 2.7 percent of the national proportional voting and therefore no proportional seats. The URP joined several other right-wing parties in supporting the 1999 presidential candidacy of former Security Service chief and prime minister Yevhen Marchuk, who won 8.1 percent of the vote, for fifth place in the October election.

In late 2001 the URP absorbed Oleksandr SERHIYENKO's **Ukrainian Christian Democratic Party** (*Ukrainska Khrystiyansko-Demokratychna Partiya*—UKhDP). Based in the Uniate Catholic population of Galicia, the UKhDP had been organized in April 1990 as the outgrowth of a Ukrainian Christian Democratic Front, formed in 1989. Its founders hoped to emulate the success of Bavaria's Christian Social Union before encountering a number of internal controversies that led in 1992 to the withdrawal of a moderate faction to form the Christian Democratic Party of Ukraine (*Khrystiyansko-Demokratychna Partiya Ukrainy*—KhDPU).

At an extraordinary session in October 2005, the URP split into two camps. One faction under the leadership of Levko Lukyanenko retained the URP rubric, while a larger faction formed the URP *"Sobor"* (above). The rump URP was left without legal standing for the 2006 legislative poll. Consequently, Lukyanenko and several supporters were elected to the Supreme Council as part of the BYT. Following the elections, Lukyanenko launched the **URP-Lukyanenko,** which presented several unsuccessful candidates in the single-member constituencies in the 2012 legislative poll.

Leader: Levko LUKYANENKO.

Working Ukraine (*Trudova Ukraina*—TU). Working Ukraine (frequently translated into English as Labor Ukraine) was organized in March 1999 as a parliamentary faction. A 1998 electoral bloc of the same name, encompassing the **Ukrainian Party of Justice** (*Ukrainska Partiya Spravedlyvosti*—UPS) and the **Civil Congress of Ukraine** (*Hromadyanskiy Kongres Ukrainy*—HKU), had won 3 percent of the national proportional vote and one seat, held by the UPS's Andriy DERKACH, who joined the new faction.

Established as a party in June 1999, the TU was initially led by Mykhaylo SYROTA, who was subsequently associated with the Solidarity parliamentary faction. By that time, TU leadership had passed to former economic minister Serhiy Tihipko, a prominent banker. As of February 2001 the party's parliamentary faction comprised 48 deputies, second only to that of the KPU. Having called for formation of a coalition government, the TU subsequently campaigned to unseat Prime Minister Yushchenko.

One of the TU's stalwarts was Viktor PINCHUK, a son-in-law of former President Kuchma and representative of the powerful Dnepropetrovsk clan. The TU participated in the For a United Ukraine electoral bloc in 2002.

Tihipko, who managed the 2004 presidential campaign of the PR's Viktor Yanukovych, resigned as the TU leader in 2005. The party ran on its own in the 2006 legislative balloting but garnered only 0.1 percent of the vote. In August 2007 TU leaders announced plans for the party's merger into the PR. Tihipko subsequently became the leader and 2010 presidential candidate of the SU (see PR, above).

Oleksandr PABAT secured 0.1 percent of the vote in the first round of presidential balloting in January 2010 as the candidate of the **People's Salvation Army.**

Regional Parties:

There are a number of active Crimean parties in addition to Crimean branches of many Ukrainian parties. The **Communist Party of Crimea** (*Kommunisticheskaya Partiya Kryma*—KPK), led by Leonid Hrach, was banned in 1991 but was permitted to reregister in 1993. The **National Movement of the Crimean Tatars** (*Natsionalyi Dvizheniya Krymskikh Tatar*—NDKT), led by Vashtiy ABDURAYIMOV, is the oldest of the Crimean Tatar groups, dating from the 1960s and formally established in April 1987. The **National Party** (*Milli Firka*—MF) is a radical Tatar group founded in August 1993 and named after the party that attempted to set up an independent Crimean Tatar republic in 1917–1918. The **Organization of the Crimean Tatar National Movement** (*Organizatsiya Krymskotatarskogo Natsionalnogo Dvizheniya*—OKND), the largest of the Crimean Tatar parties, urges exclusive jurisdiction for the Crimean parliament. The business-oriented **Party for the Economic Revival of Crimea** (*Partiya Ekonomicheskogo Vozrozhdeniya Kryma*—PEVK), which won one seat in the Ukrainian Supreme Council in 1994, has been led by Vladimir SHEVIOV (Volodymyr SHEVYOV). The secessionist **Republican Movement of Crimea** (*Republikanskoe Dvizheniya Kryma*—RDK) is led by Yuriy Meshkov, who was elected president of Crimea in January 1994. The **Russian Party of the Crimea** (*Russkoi Partiya Kryma*—RPK) was founded under the leadership of Sergei SHUVAINIKOV in September 1993 as a radical splinter of the RDK. The **For Yanukovych Bloc** was organized in Crimea in 2005 by supporters of former prime minister Viktor Yanukovych, while the **Kunitsyn Bloc** was launched by supporters of former Crimean prime minister Serhiy Kunitsyn. The former won 44 seats on a 33 percent vote share in the March 2006 balloting for the Crimean Supreme Council, while the latter secured 10 seats on a 7.6 percent vote share. The KPK finished fourth in the balloting with 9 seats. Reports in 2008 described the **Russian Bloc**, led by Vladimir TYUNIN, as the most powerful party in Crimea. Among other things, Tyunin called for Crimea to become part of Russia. (The above information primarily references the political landscape prior to Russia's March 2014 annexation of Crimea.)

Other regional or ethnically based groups include the **Democratic Movement of the Donbas** (*Demokraticheskoe Dvizheniya Donbassa*—DDD); the **Union for Democratic Reforms** (*Obiednannia Demokratychnykh Peretvoren*—ODP), formed under the leadership of Serhiy USTYCH in December 1993 by former Soviet officials in the Transcarpathia region of western Ukraine; and the **Subcarpathian Republican Party** (SRP), which was established in 1992 to press for Transcarpathian autonomy. In 2008 the **Congress of the Carpathian Rusyns** called for creation of an ethnic Rusyn (or Ruthenian) state.

LEGISLATURE

Supreme Council (*Verkhovna Rada*). Formerly styled the Supreme Soviet, Ukraine's legislature is a unicameral body of 450 members. Under constitutional changes that went into effect in January 2006, all 450 members were selected in 2007 via proportional representation from a single nationwide constituency. The threshold to secure representation was 3 percent (reduced in 2006 from 4 percent); the term of office was four years. However constitutional amendments in early 2011 extended the term of the current legislature from four to five years and permanently fixed the term of office at five years. Later in the year, electoral law changes reintroduced a mixed proportional/single-member constituencies system (250 deputies elected via party-list proportional balloting in one nationwide constituency [5 percent threshold to gain representation] and 250 deputies elected via majoritarian [first-past-the-post] voting in single-member districts for which party and independent candidates were permitted). In addition, the formation of blocs (a previous fixture of the electoral landscape) was prohibited.

Following the balloting on October 26, 2014, the seats were distributed as follows: Petro Poroshenko Bloc, 132 (63 in the nationwide proportional balloting, and 69 from single-member constituencies); People's Front, 82 (64, 18); Self-Reliance Party, 33 (32, 1); Opposition Bloc, 29 (27, 2); Radical Party of Oleh Lyashko, 22 (22, 0); Fatherland, 19 (17, 2); Freedom, 6 (0, 6); Strong Ukraine, 1 (0, 1); Zastup, 1 (0, 1); Right Sector, 1 (0, 1); Viola, 1 (0, 1); and 96 independents. (Elections were not held for 12 seats in Crimea, annexed by Russia the previous March, or for 15 seats in the Donetsk and Luhansk Regions, parts of which were under the control of pro-Russian separatists.)

Speaker: Volodymyr GROYSMAN (BPP).

CABINET

[as of December 8, 2016]

Prime Minister	Volodymyr Groysman (BPP)
First Vice Prime Minister	Stepan Kubiv (ind.)
Vice Prime Minsters	Pavlo Rozenko (UDAR)
	Vyacheslav Kyrylenko (People's Front)
	Volodymyr Kistion (ind.)
	Hennadii Zubko (ind.)
Vice Prime Minister (European and Euro-Atlantic Integration)	Ivanna Klympush-Tsintsadze (ind.) [f]
Ministers	
Agrarian Policy and Food	Taras Kutovyi (Freedom)
Cabinet of Ministers	Olexandr Saienko (Fatherland)
Culture	Yevhen Nyschuk (ind.)
Defense	Stepan Poltorak
Ecology and Natural Resources	Ostap Semerak (Fatherland)
Economic Development and Trade	Stepan Kubiv (ind.)
Education and Science	Lilia Hrynevych (People's Front) [f]
Energy and the Coal Industry	Ihor Nasalyk (ind.)
Finance	Olexandr Danyliuk
Foreign Affairs	Pavlo Klimkin (ind.)
Healthcare	Uliana Nadia Suprun (Acting) [f]
Infrastructure	Volodymyr Omelyan (Fatherland)
Information Policy	Yurii Stets (BPP)
Internal Affairs	Arsen Avakov (People's Front)
Justice	Pavlo Petrenko (People's Front)
Regional Development, Construction, Housing, and Communal Services	Hennadii Zubko (ind.)
Social Policy	Andrii Reva (People's Front)
Temporary Occupied Territories and Internally Displaced Persons	Vadym Chernysh (ind.)
Youth and Sports	Ihor Xhdanov (ind.)

[f] = female

INTERGOVERNMENTAL REPRESENTATION

Ambassador to the U.S.: Valeriy CHALY.

U.S. Ambassador to Ukraine: Geoffrey PYATT.

Permanent Representative to the UN: Yuriy SERGEYEV.

IGO Memberships (Non-UN): CEUR, CIS, EBRD, IOM, OSCE, WTO.

For Further Reference:

Aslund, Anders. *Ukraine: What Went Wrong and How to Fix It.* Washington, DC: Peterson Institute for International Economics, 2015.

Plokhy, Serhii. *The Gates of Europe: A History of Ukraine.* New York: Basic Books, 2015.

Sakwa, Richard. *Frontline Ukraine: Crisis in the Borderlands.* London: I. B. Tauris, 2016.

Wilson, Andrew. *Ukraine Crisis: What It Means for the West.* New Haven, CT: Yale University Press, 2014.

UNITED ARAB EMIRATES

al-Imarat al-Arabiyah al-Muttahidah

Political Status: Federation of six former Trucial States (Abu Dhabi, Ajman, Dubai, Fujairah, Sharjah, and Umm al-Qaiwain) established December 2, 1971; the seventh, Ras al-Khaimah, joined on February 10, 1972.

Area: 32,278 sq. mi. (83,600 sq. km).

Population: 9,267,000 (2016E—UN); 5,927,482 (2016E—U.S. Census). Comprises seven sovereign emirates: Dubai (2,504,000, 2016E), Sharjah (1,332,000, 2016E), Abu Dhabi (1,179,000, 2016E), Ajman (323,000, 2015E), Ras al-Khaimah (300,000, 2016E), Fujairah (203,000, 2014E), and Umm al-Qaiwain (73,000, 2016E). United Nations figures include noncitizens, who in 2015 constituted approximately 85 percent of the population.

Major Urban Center (2016E—UN): ABU DHABI (1,179,000).

Official Language: Arabic.

Monetary Unit: Emirati Dirham (market rate October 1, 2016: 3.67 dirhams = $1US).

Supreme Council: Composed of the rulers of the seven emirates (in order by dates of accession): Sheikh Sultan ibn Muhammad al-QASIMI (Sharjah, 1972), Sheikh Hamad ibn Muhammad al-SHARQI (Fujairah, 1974), Sheikh Saud ibn Rashid al-MUALLA (Umm al-Qaiwain, 1981), Sheikh Humayd ibn Rashid al-NUAYMI (Ajman, 1981), Sheikh Khalifa ibn Zayed al-NAHYAN (Abu Dhabi, 2004), Sheikh Muhammad ibn Rashid al-MAKTUM (Dubai, 2006), and Sheikh Saud ibn Saqr al-QASIMI (Ras al-Khaimah, 2010).

President: Sheikh Khalifa ibn Zayed al-NAHYAN (Ruler of Abu Dhabi); elected by the Supreme Council on November 3, 2004, to a five-year term, succeeding his father, Sheikh Zayed ibn Sultan al-NAHYAN, who died on November 2; reelected by the Supreme Council for a second five-year term on November 3, 2009; confirmed for another term on November 3, 2014..

Vice President and Prime Minister: Sheikh Muhammad ibn Rashid al-MAKTUM (Ruler of Dubai); named vice president and prime minister by the Supreme Council on January 5, 2006, succeeding his older brother, Sheikh Maktum ibn Rashid al-MAKTUM, who died on January 4.

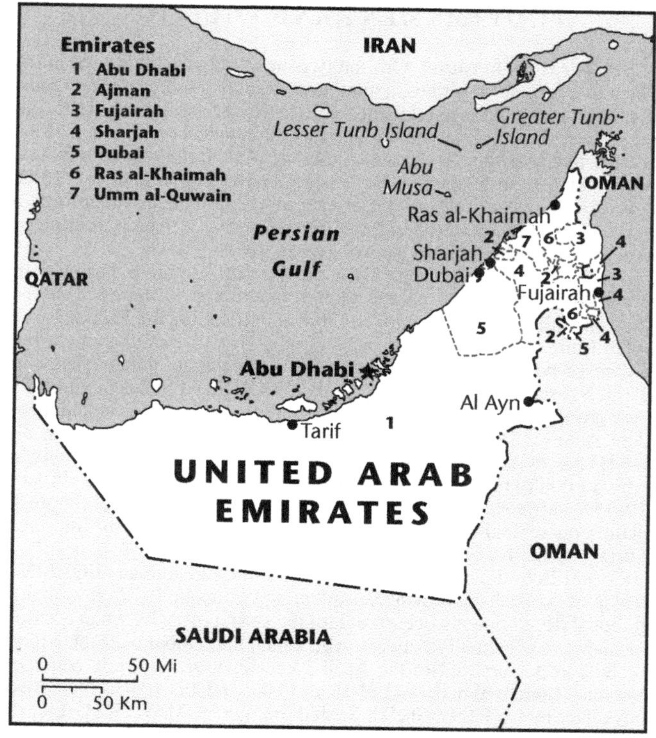

THE COUNTRY

Formerly known as the Trucial States because of truces concluded with Britain in the 19th century, the United Arab Emirates (UAE) extends some 400 miles along the Persian Gulf from the southeastern end of the Qatar peninsula to the Gulf of Oman. (UAE territory separates Oman's governorate of Musandram, which overlooks the Strait of Hormuz, from the rest of Oman.) The UAE encompasses a barren, relatively flat territory characterized by extreme temperatures and sparse rainfall. The majority of the indigenous population is Arab and adheres to Islam (80 percent Sunni); there are also significant numbers of Iranians, Indians, Pakistanis, Baluchis, and descendants of former African slaves among the noncitizen population. (Some 100,000 descendants of immigrants are currently considered "stateless," despite having been born in the UAE.) Most UAE citizens are employed by the government, and they enjoy broad social benefits such as subsidized housing and free health care and education. Tribal alliances contribute to long-standing support for the ruling families. The UAE has one of the most open societies in the Gulf region in terms of welcoming its huge foreign population and vast numbers of tourists without strictly enforcing many of its social and religious laws among either group. Also, the UAE encourages women to participate in in the labor force and in public life in general. Although Arabic is the official language, English is commonly used in schools and among the diverse population; Farsi, Urdu, and Hindi are also spoken.

Traditionally, the area was dependent upon trading, fishing, and pearling. However, the discovery in 1958 of major oil reserves in Abu Dhabi and, subsequently, of smaller deposits in Dubai and Sharjah dramatically altered the economy. Oil wealth led to rapid infrastructural modernization, advances in education and health services, and a construction boom requiring a massive inflow of foreign labor. New industrial cities established at Jebel Ali in Dubai and Ruwais in Abu Dhabi gave rise to shipyards, cement factories, and other manufacturing sites. However, during the 1980s the UAE experienced a slowdown in economic growth because of reduced export revenues. As a result, the government moved to streamline the petroleum industry, which continued to account for 70 percent of government income, and began to develop the marketing, refining, and petrochemical aspects of the oil trade.

Oil reserves are estimated at more than 95 billion barrels, approximately 8 percent of the world's total; approximately 90 percent of the UAE's known deposits are located in Abu Dhabi. The UAE government controls 60 percent of the energy sector, although it has permitted partial foreign ownership, thereby maintaining links with Western companies that have provided important ongoing infrastructure support. Moreover, the nation has firmly established itself as the region's leading trading center, partly on the strength of the Jebel Ali Free Trade Zone, where more than 350 companies operate. Dubai, in particular, has been effectively promoted as the region's trading and financial investment and services hub, and as a major tourist destination.

The international financial crisis that developed in the second half of 2008 affected the UAE significantly, particularly in Dubai, where the recent rapid expansion of real estate prices and related construction ground to a halt. Real GDP in the UAE declined by more than 4 percent in 2009 as Dubai grappled with severe debt problems and oil receipts plummeted. Thanks to a major restructuring of Dubai's debt in 2010 and stimulus spending (including bank recapitalization and approval of funds for a massive new airport and other infrastructure improvements in Dubai) by the federal government, growth began to recover in 2010 and reached 4.3 percent in 2012 and 5.2 percent in 2013. Concurrently, the UAE regained its reputation as a safe haven for investors concerned about turmoil related to the Arab Spring elsewhere in the region. Other contributing expansionary factors included (in 2012) higher oil prices, additional hydrocarbon production, increased tourism, and (in 2013) rapidly rising real estate prices. GDP growth dropped from 3.6 percent to –3.2 percent from 2014 to 2015, in large part as a result of a marked fall in the price of oil in the world market. The IMF estimated that GDP expanded by 3.2 percent, while inflation grew by 2.3 percent, and GDP per capita was $39,786.

GOVERNMENT AND POLITICS

Political background. Originally controlling an area known in the West as a refuge for pirates, a number of sheikhs in the eastern Persian Gulf first entered into agreements with the British in the early 19th century. After the failure of the initial treaty agreements of 1820 and 1835, a Perpetual Maritime Truce was signed in 1853. Relations with Britain were further strengthened by an Exclusive Agreement of 1892, whereby the sheikhs agreed not to enter into diplomatic or other foreign relations with countries other than Britain. In return, Britain guaranteed defense of the sheikhdoms against aggression by sea.

The treaty arrangements with the United Kingdom lasted until 1968, when the British announced their intention to withdraw from the Persian Gulf by 1971. An early attempt at unification, the Federation of Arab Emirates, was initiated in 1968 with British encouragement but collapsed when Bahrain and Qatar declared separate independence in 1971. Subsequently, the leaders of six of the Trucial States organized a new grouping, the UAE, which was formally constituted as an independent state on December 2, 1971, with Sheikh Zayed ibn Sultan al-NAHYAN of Abu Dhabi as president. The emirate of Ras al-Khaimah, which initially rejected membership, acceded to the UAE on February 10, 1972, after receiving assurances that the UAE would not relinquish claims on several islands in the Gulf recently occupied by Iran (see Foreign relations, below).

Apart from the death of Sheikh Khalid ibn Muhammad al-QASIMI (ruler of Sharjah) following an attempted coup in 1972, few major political developments occurred until the spring of 1979, when a series of disputes, principally between Abu Dhabi and Dubai over the extent of federal powers, led to the April 25 resignation of Prime Minister Sheikh Maktum ibn Rashid al-MAKTUM and his replacement five days later by his father, Sheikh Rashid ibn Said al-MAKTUM, ruler of Dubai, who also retained his position as vice president. In 1981 the emir of Ajman, Sheikh Rashid ibn Humayd al-NUAYMI, and the emir of Umm al-Qaiwain, Sheikh Ahmad ibn Rashid al-MUALLA, both of whom had ruled for more than 50 years, died and were succeeded by their sons, Sheikh Humayd ibn Rashid al-NUAYMI and Sheikh Rashid ibn Ahmad al-MUALLA, respectively.

On June 17, 1987, Sheikh Abd al-Aziz al-QASIMI seized power in Sharjah, accusing his brother, Sheikh Sultan ibn Muhammad al-QASIMI, of fiscal mismanagement. On July 20 Sheikh Muhammad was reinstated by the Supreme Council, which decreed that Sheikh Abd al-Aziz should thenceforth hold the title of crown prince and deputy ruler; however, Sheikh Abd al-Aziz was stripped of his title on February 4, 1990.

Following the death of Sheikh Rashid ibn Said al-Maktum on October 7, 1990, his son, Sheikh Maktum ibn Rashid, was named vice president. He also returned to his former position as prime minister.

In 1991 the UAE suffered a major blow to its international prestige by the midyear collapse of the Luxembourg-chartered Bank of Credit and Commerce International (BCCI), 77 percent of whose shares were owned by President Zayed and a group of financial associates. Ultimately, it was revealed that Sheikh Zayed had provided at least $1 billion to shore up the troubled institution since 1989. (For additional information, see the 2005–2006 *Handbook*.) A plan was approved in December 1995 under which BCCI creditors would be reimbursed $1.8 billion by the bank's major shareholders, observers estimating the paybacks would cover 20 to 40 percent of most deposits. The BCCI was formally liquidated by the UAE Central Bank in February 1996. (As of 2003 $5.7 billion had been authorized in paybacks to BCCI creditors, total claims by some 80,000 depositors having been estimated at $9 billion. The case, unprecedented in scope in British courts, went to trial in 2004, but liquidators dropped their case in 2005 in a move that shocked financial observers.)

The UAE cabinet submitted its resignation on March 17, 1997, and Sheikh Maktum was asked to form a new government, which was announced on March 25. The reshuffle, the first significant government change since 1990, was promoted as infusing "young blood" in the UAE policymaking process, although several important ministries remained in the hands of incumbents.

The president and vice president were reelected by the Supreme Council on December 2, 2001. The first cabinet reshuffle since 1997 took place on November 1, 2004; among the new cabinet members was the first female minister, a move in line with a stated government policy to involve more women in decision making. Sheikh Zayed, who had decreed the cabinet reshuffle, died on November 2; he was succeeded as president of the UAE and ruler of Abu Dhabi by his son, Sheikh Khalifa ibn Zayed al-NAHYAN.

In 2005 President Khalifa announced plans to hold limited elections as part of a package of political reforms. He proposed allowing half of the 40 members of the Federal National Council (FNC) to be elected by citizens appointed to electoral colleges in each emirate. The remaining 20 members of the FNC would continue to be appointed by the rulers of the 7 emirates (see Constitution and government, below).

Following the death of 62-year-old Sheikh Maktum on January 4, 2006, his younger brother, Defense Minister Sheikh Muhammad ibn Rashid al-MAKTUM, was named vice president and prime minister by the Supreme Council on January 5. He also succeeded his brother as ruler of Dubai.

Domestic attention in 2006 focused on the limited elections on December 16–20 for 20 members of the legislature. The elections were considered only a modest political reform since the rulers of the seven emirates chose those who could vote as members of an electoral college, and the actual number of electors was less than 7,000.

The global financial crisis that began in 2008 had major negative effects on the UAE, particularly in Dubai, where real estate prices fell by more than 30 percent and construction of many projects was suspended. The federal government initially provided $33 billion to prop up banks in all seven emirates and then in February 2009 approved an additional $10 billion bailout for the financial sector in Dubai. However, Dubai World, the investment and management company that oversees much of the Dubai government's massive business interests, roiled international financial markets again in November by announcing plans to suspend payments on $23.5 billion of its debt for at least six months. However, Abu Dhabi in December agreed to an additional $10 billion bailout, which convinced the global financial community that Dubai was not headed for a catastrophic default. Meanwhile, intense debt-restructuring negotiations continued, and in May 2010, seven leading creditors agreed to extend repayments on $14.4 billion of Dubai's debt over five to eight years at reduced interest rates. Nearly all the other creditors accepted new terms in September in a comprehensive restructuring plan that also called for Dubai World and affiliated bodies to sell some of their assets.

Sheikh Saqr ibn Muhammad al-QASIMI, who had ruled Ras al-Khaimah since seizing power from his brother in 1948, died on October 27, 2010, at the age of 92. He was succeeded by his son, Sheikh Saud ibn Saqr al-QASIMI, who had for a number of years been responsible for most governmental responsibilities in the emirate due to his father's advanced age. Sheikh Saud's half-brother, Sheikh Khalid ibn Saqr al-QASIMI, initially challenged the succession, announcing that he deserved consideration as the next emir despite having been deposed as crown prince in a 2003 family dispute. However, the UAE Supreme Council immediately endorsed Sheikh Saud's claim, and Sheikh Khalid reportedly left the country after security forces were deployed near his house.

In March 2011 some 100 UAE reformers petitioned the government to install a genuine parliamentary democracy with a fully elected legislature empowered to make law. With an apparent eye on developments in Egypt and Tunisia, the UAE government adopted a hard line, arresting five reformers. The federal government also announced a $1.5 billion investment program for its poorer northern emirates, mindful that economic disparities were playing a major role in the Arab Spring uprisings.

The number of UAE citizens eligible to vote in the electoral colleges was increased to nearly 130,000 for the September 2011 balloting for the Federal National Council, which was described as a "small nod" toward prodemocracy sentiment. Nonetheless, the UAE remained poorly rated in the annual Freedom House Freedom in the World ratings from 2012–2016, earning scores of 6 all five years in a scale from 1–7, with the least free states scoring at the upper end of the scale.

Constitution and government. The institutions of the UAE were superimposed upon the existing political structures of the member states, which generally maintained their monarchical character. (Effective power within the federation remains in the hands of senior members of the ruling families of the seven emirates, led by Abu Dhabi, by far the most oil-rich emirate, and, to a lesser extent, Dubai, a major business center.) Under the federal constitution adopted in 1971 (designated an "interim" basic law until 1996), the rulers of the constituent states are members of the Supreme Council, which elects a president and vice president for five-year terms. Supreme Council decrees require the approval of the rulers of Abu Dhabi and Dubai and at least three other emirates. The president appoints a prime minister and a cabinet, and there is a consultative Federal National Council (FNC).

In July 1976 the FNC, following a failure to reach agreement on a new constitutional draft, voted to extend the life of the existing constitution for another five years beyond December 2. Further extensions were voted at five-year intervals thereafter until 1996, when the Supreme Council (May 20) and the FNC (June 18) approved an amendment removing "interim" from the language in the constitution, thereby effectively making it a permanent document.

In 2006 indirect elections were authorized for 20 of the 40 members of the FNC, all of whom were previously appointed by the rulers of the constituent emirates. Eight of the total FNC seats were reserved for women. Constitutional amendment in late 2008 empowered the FNC, previously confined to domestic affairs, to make recommendations on international matters as well.

Judicial functions have traditionally been performed by local courts applying Islamic law (sharia) and by individual decisions rendered by the ruling families. In June 1978 the president signed a law establishing four Primary Federal Tribunals (in Abu Dhabi, Ajman, Fujairah, and Sharjah) to handle disputes between individuals and the federation, with appeal to the federal Supreme Court (five judges appointed by the Supreme Council). However, a later decree of February 1994 specified that a variety of crimes (including murder, theft, adultery, and juvenile and drug-related offenses) would be tried in Islamic, rather than civil, courts.

The basic administrative divisions are the constituent states, each of which retains local control over mineral rights, taxation, and police protection. Abu Dhabi effectively controls the UAE's 65,000-member federal army.

While the constitution of the UAE guarantees freedom of the press, the government closely monitors Arabic-language media, which is widely self-censored; the English-language media receive much less scrutiny. Meanwhile, journalism watchdogs have strongly criticized the UAE government recently for blocking politically charged Websites and otherwise filtering Internet use. Bloggers and users of other social media have been among those subjected to a sustained government crackdown that began in 2011 and continued as of the fall of 2014, the government in December 2012 having enacted a new cybercrime law that critics argued was designed to suppress freedom of expression among netizens. Reporters Without Borders ranks the UAE as 119th out of 180 countries in its 2016 world press freedom index and characterizes the government as a potential "enemy of the Internet."

Foreign relations. The UAE is a member of the United Nations, the Arab League, the Organization of the Petroleum Exporting Countries (OPEC), and various regional groupings. Relations have been cordial with most countries, including the United States, although there have been territorial disputes with Iran, Oman, Qatar, and Saudi Arabia.

In 1971 Iran occupied Abu Musa, a small island in the Persian Gulf, and laid claim to the Greater and Lesser Tunbs, two uninhabited but potentially strategically important islands. Soon after, an agreement was reached between Tehran and the emir of Sharjah that provided for joint administration of Abu Musa and the sharing of revenue from offshore oil wells. However, no accord was reached regarding the Tunbs (claimed by Ras al-Khaimah). Following the establishment of diplomatic relations between Iran and the UAE in 1972, the issue remained relatively dormant before flaring up in 1992 (see below).

A dispute with Saudi Arabia and Oman concerned portions of Abu Dhabi, including the potentially oil-rich Buraimi Oasis, located at the juncture of the three states. Under the terms of an agreement reached in 1974, six villages of the oasis were awarded to Abu Dhabi and two to Oman; Saudi Arabia, in return for renouncing its claim, was granted a land corridor coterminous with the existing Abu Dhabi–Qatar border to the Persian Gulf port of Khor al-Adad. (The border demarcation issue resurfaced in September 1992 in the form of a clash between Saudi Arabian and Qatari forces [see entry on Qatar, Foreign relations]. In June 2002 Oman and the UAE implemented an agreement to demarcate their border.)

In early 1981 the UAE joined with five neighbors—Bahrain, Kuwait, Oman, Qatar, and Saudi Arabia—in establishing the Cooperative Council of the Arab Gulf States (more commonly known as the Gulf Cooperation Council—GCC) to coordinate members' policies on security and stability in the area. Concern over the subsequent Iran–Iraq war led the UAE to participate in the GCC's annual Peninsula Shield joint military maneuvers. Although the hazards of the regional conflict did not preclude an increase in trade with Tehran, the UAE and the other GCC states became increasingly aware of their vulnerability to the potentially destabilizing effects of an Iranian-inspired Islamic revolution. Subsequently, in the wake of oilfield bombings by the Gulf combatants, including one by unidentified aircraft that killed eight people and destroyed two of five platforms in Abu Dhabi, the UAE took steps to purchase advance-warning systems from Britain, France, and the United States.

The UAE reacted nervously to Iraq's occupation of Kuwait on August 2, 1990, because the UAE, like Kuwait, had been charged by Baghdad with overproduction of oil. On August 19, having joined with other GCC governments in calling for Iraq's withdrawal from Kuwait, the UAE agreed to the deployment of foreign military units on its soil. It also cooperated with coalition forces during the confrontation that concluded with Iraq's defeat in February 1991. In April it was reported that the UAE had contributed nearly $3 billion to U.S. Gulf War costs.

With Iraqi belligerence still appearing to present a challenge to regional security, the Gulf states subsequently attempted to improve relations with Iran, and the UAE in July 1991 named its first ambassador to Tehran since the latter's 1979 revolution. However, in early 1992 Iran reignited the long-dormant Gulf dispute between the two nations by expelling some 700 UAE nationals from Abu Musa and seizing complete control of the island. After the GCC demanded in September that Iran repudiate its "annexation" of Abu Musa, Tehran reasserted its claim of sovereignty over the island as well as over the Greater and Lesser Tunbs, vowing that UAE forces would have to cross a "sea of blood" to retake the territory. Although the UAE subsequently sought international mediation of the dispute, Iran rejected the proposal, and tension between the countries continued.

In July 1994 the UAE became the fourth GCC country to conclude a military cooperation pact with the United States. The agreement, which provided for joint military exercises and the stationing of a U.S. naval task force on UAE territory, was reportedly signed because of the UAE's perceived vulnerability to attack by Iran or Iraq.

As did its GCC neighbors, the UAE expressed concern in the 1990s over the security implications of growing Islamist militancy in North Africa and the Middle East. In March 2000 the UAE, as part of an ambitious defense program, signed a contract with the U.S.-based Lockheed Martin Corporation worth $6.4 billion for 80 F-16 fighters, having previously concluded a deal in 1998 for $3.5 billion for French planes. Concurrently, the UAE announced plans to spearhead an $8 billion regional gas network in conjunction with other GCC members as well as Western energy companies. As a first stage of the 25-year project, Abu Dhabi negotiated a $3.5 billion agreement to develop gas fields in Qatar and ship gas from there, initially to the other emirates and Gulf states, such as Oman, and eventually to India and Pakistan. The project, the first such cross-border arrangement in GCC history, was considered an important element in establishing the UAE as the hub of a regional "energy security" network. At the same time, however, it brought increasing pressure from the international community on the UAE to establish procedures to ensure greater transparency and accountability in its financial sector. The UAE's banking system and financial practices were further criticized after the September 2001 attacks in the United States when it became evident that close associates of Osama bin Laden had used the country's banks to transfer and receive money from several of the hijackers. Promising reform, the UAE in January 2002 adopted a series of policy changes to monitor banking practices and financial transactions and instituted new penalties to combat money laundering. The UAE also agreed to cooperate closely with the George W. Bush administration's war on terrorism. Among other measures, the UAE severed diplomatic relations with the Taliban administration in Afghanistan after it refused to hand over bin Laden for prosecution in the West.

In March 2003 the UAE president offered a vague plan for Iraqi president Saddam Hussein's permanent exile, defying the Arab League stance on noninterference in the internal affairs of a neighboring country. After the U.S. invasion and occupation of Iraq, the UAE, whose embassy in Baghdad had reopened in 2000, was among the first countries to send relief shipments to Iraq.

In 2004 the commander of U.S. Central Command described U.S.–UAE military cooperation as among the strongest in the region. France's defense minister expressed similar sentiments, while the United Kingdom in 2005 announced its commitment to developing military and industrial cooperation with the UAE.

In 2006 the U.S. State Department set up offices in Dubai to enhance its ability to monitor Iran. Other countries initiated similar efforts, given Dubai's proximity to Iran and its popularity with

Iranian businesspeople and tourists. As international concern regarding Iran's nuclear program increased, the UAE sought to balance its extensive commercial interests with Iran with its strong political ties to the United States.

DP World, a subsidiary of Dubai World, created a major political controversy in 2006 when it sought to manage terminal operations at six U.S. ports. The company sold its interests in the ports after what the *New York Times* described as "an unrelenting bipartisan attack" in the U.S. Congress over security concerns.

In April 2008 French president Nicolas Sarkozy visited the UAE, where he signed a deal to establish a permanent French military base in Abu Dhabi. On the same occasion, France and the UAE also signed a memorandum of understanding on cooperation in civil nuclear power projects. The UAE signed a similar nuclear deal with the United Kingdom in June 2008, while a nuclear cooperation pact was approved in January 2009 with the United States under which the UAE forswore uranium enrichment and plutonium reprocessing. The U.S. administration of President Barack Obama accepted a plan in June for the UAE to buy fuel and materials for its nuclear power plants from the United States. The UAE subsequently signed a $20 billion agreement for a South Korean consortium to build four such plants, with the first scheduled to become operational in 2017.

In May 2009 the UAE announced that it would not participate in a proposed GCC monetary union, thereby appearing to doom the union's prospects.

International concern arose following the assassination of a Palestinian militant visiting Dubai in January 2010. Police in Dubai accused Israel's spy agency, Mossad, of the assassination and said many of the 26 attackers had used fake or stolen passports from European countries. Dubai authorities objected to Israel's actions and launched their own investigations into the passport situation.

The UAE continued in 2010 to voice its concern over Iran's nuclear program and Iran's support for militant Shiite groups in the Middle East. In May 2011 the UAE government reportedly agreed to hire an American-led mercenary force of some 800 soldiers (mostly from Latin America) to provide additional security against the possibility of conflict with Iran or unrest among the Shiite population in the UAE.

In March 2011, following the outbreak of the Arab Spring in North Africa, the UAE along with Saudi Arabia deployed troops to Bahrain to support the Sunni-dominated government in Bahrain against Shiite protesters. Shiite–Sunni tensions also apparently contributed to renewed diplomatic conflict with Iran over the disputed Gulf islands when Iranian president Mahmoud Ahmadinejad visited Abu Musa in April 2012 and the Iranian military pledged a military response if its sovereignty claim was threatened.

In June 2012 the UAE announced the launching of a new pipeline from the offshore oil fields of Dubai to Fujairah, thereby opening up 50 percent of UAE oil production to transshipment directly from the Gulf of Oman and avoiding the Strait of Hormuz, which could be blocked by Iran in case of conflict. Concurrent regional concerns for the UAE included the fighting in Syria (the UAE supported the opposition forces there and accused President Bashar al-Assad's government of "crimes against the Syrian people") and the ascendancy of to political dominance in Egypt of the Muslim Brotherhood, which the UAE accused of "exporting revolution."

In July 2013 the UAE expressed satisfaction over the ouster of Egyptian president Morsi and pledged $3 billion in aid to the new interim Egyptian administration. Meanwhile, still with a wary eye on Iran, the UAE agreed to buy 26 more U.S. F-16 warplanes (for $5 billion) as well as recently developed U.S. air-to-ground missiles.

In March 2014 the UAE joined Saudi Arabia and Bahrain in withdrawing their ambassadors from Qatar, perceived as supporting, at least to a certain degree, the Muslim Brotherhood. Although a GCC agreement subsequently appeared to paper over those tensions, the UAE remained a leading opponent of "political Islam" in the region.

In what represented a marginal improvement in the relationship between the UAE and Israel, in November 2015 the Jewish state announced plans to open a mission to the Abu Dhabi–based International Renewable Energy Agency. The mission will be Israel's first in the UAE.

In 2015 the UAE joined the Saudi-led coalition against Houthi rebels in Yemen (see entry on Yemen). The UAE announced in June 2016 that it was ending its participation in the coalition.

Current issues. Human Rights Watch accused the government of "an unprecedented crackdown on peaceful dissent in 2012–2013." In the eyes of some analysts, the government's approach appeared unnecessarily heavy-handed, considering the fact that the Arab Spring had prompted little response from within the UAE population, which was benefiting from the nation's renewed economic vigor. Nevertheless, nearly 70 defendants, including members of *al-Islah,* were convicted in July 2013 and sentenced to up to 15 years in jail after a mass trial on various security charges. Included were professors, lawyers, and other prominent members of society who argued that they were promoting reform (and, for some, a "more Islamic government"), not overthrow. Thirty more defendants (20 from Egypt and 10 from the UAE) were given jail terms in January 2014 on charges related to the alleged formation of a local branch of the Muslim Brotherhood, while the government continued to display what one *New York Times* correspondent characterized as "extreme sensitivity" to perceived criticism in social media. In an initiative that apparently reflected the administration's intense concern over Islamist militancy in the region, new legislation was adopted at midyear requiring compulsory military service for males between the ages of 18 and 30.

In an effort to temper criticism of the UAE's insular political system, Prime Minister Muhammad ibn Rashid al-Maktum added two new cabinet positions for happiness and tolerance, and appointed women to both positions in a February 2016 reshuffle.

POLITICAL GROUPS

There are no political parties in the UAE.

Al-Islah (Reform). First organized in the 1970s, the Islamist *al-Islah* society was informally tolerated by the UAE government for several decades, and the organization gained influence in, among other areas, educational and judicial associations. However, the government adopted a more cautious approach toward *al-Islah* following the 2001 terrorist attacks in the United States. In the wake of the recent Arab Spring uprisings in the region, a number of *al-Islah* members were among the petitioners calling in early 2011 for democratization in the UAE. The government responded with a crackdown that included the dissolution of *al-Islah*'s elected governing board and the replacement of *al-Islah* members in various associations with government appointees. In addition, in December a group of *al-Islah* members had their UAE nationality revoked over what the government described as matters of national security.

Sheikh Sultan ibn Kayed al-QASSIMI, described as the chair of *al-Islah,* was briefly detained in April 2012, and more members of the group were arrested later in the year and in 2013, the government reportedly viewing *al-Islah* as a proxy in the UAE for the Muslim Brotherhood, whose recent rise to power in Egypt had generated concern in the Gulf sheikdoms. Leaders of *al-Islah,* claiming the support of 20,000 followers in the UAE, denied formal links with the Muslim Brotherhood. Many of those tried in mid-2013 (see Current issues, above) were members of *al-Islah,* the defendants (backed by international human rights organizations) claiming their rights had been severely abused during detention.

LEGISLATURE

Federal National Council (*Majlis al-Watani al-Itihadi*). The UAE's consultative body currently consists of 40 delegates (8 each from Abu Dhabi and Dubai, 6 each from Sharjah and Ras al-Khaimah, and 4 each from Ajman, Fujairah, and Umm al-Qaiwain). Twenty are appointed by the rulers of the constituent states, and 20 are elected by electoral colleges (established in 2006) appointed by the rulers. The first elections were held in three rounds December 16–20, 2006, for 20 seats (one-half of the members in each emirate). The 20 elected and 20 appointed delegates were sworn in on February 12, 2007, for a two-year term. However, their term was extended to four years in late 2008, with the term of office being permanently set at four years for subsequent elections. The most recent election for the 20 elected delegates was held in September 2015. That balloting was punctuated by the election of Amal al-Qubaisi as the body's first female speaker.

Speaker: Amal al-QUBAISI.

CABINET

[as of September 1, 2016]

Prime Minister	Sheikh Muhammad ibn Rashid al-Maktum
Deputy Prime Ministers	Lt. Gen. Sheikh Saif ibn Zayed al-Nahyan
	Sheikh Mansur ibn Zayed al-Nahyan
Ministers	
Cabinet Affairs and the Future	Mohammed Abdullah al-Gergawi
Climate Change and Environment	Thani ibn Ahmed al-Zeyoudi
Community Development	Najla bint Mohammad al-Awar [f]
Culture and Knowledge Development	Nahyan ibn Mubarak al-Nahyan
Defense	Sheikh Muhammad ibn Rashid al-Maktum
Development and International Cooperation	Sheikha Lubna bint Khalid al-Qasimi [f]
Economy	Sultan Said al-Mansuri
Education	Hussain ibn Ibrahim al-Hammadi
Energy	Suhail Muhammad al-Mazrui
Federal National Council Affairs	Noura bint Mohammed al-Kaabi [f]
Finance	Sheikh Hamdan ibn Rashid al-Maktum
Foreign Affairs and International Cooperation	Sheikh Abdallah ibn Zayed al-Nayhan
Foreign Trade	Sheikha Lubna bint Khalid al-Qasami [f]
Health and Prevention	Abdul Rahman Muhammad ibn Nasir al-Owais
Higher Education and Scientific Research	Hamdan ibn Mubarak al-Nahyan
Human Resources and Emiratisation	Saqr ibn Ghubash Saeed Ghubash
Infrastructure Development	Abdullah Bilhaif al-Nuaimi
Interior	Sheikh Saif ibn Zayed al-Nahyan
Justice	Sultan ibn Said al-Badi
Labor	Saqr Ghabbash
Presidential Affairs	Sheikh Mansur ibn Zayed al-Nahyan
Social Affairs	Mariam al-Roomi [f]
Ministers of State	
Defense Affairs	Mohammed ibn Ahmad al-Bawardi
Federal National Council Affairs	Anwar Muhammad Gargash
Financial Affairs	Ubayd Humaid al-Tayir
Foreign Affairs	Anwar Muhammad Gargash
	Abdullah Ghubash
Happiness	Ohud bint Khalfan al-Roumi [f]
Higher Education	Ahmad ibn Abdullah Humaid Belhoul al-Falasi
International Cooperation	Reem bint Ebrahim al-Hashimy [f]
Public Education	Jameela bint Salem al-Muhairi [f]
Tolerance	Lubna bint Khalid al-Qasimi [f]
Without Portfolio	Rashid ibn Ahmad bin Fahad
Without Portfolio	Reem Ibrahim al-Hashimi [f]
Without Portfolio	Sultan al-Jabir
Without Portfolio	Maitha Salim al-Shamsi [f]
Youth	Shamma bint Suhail Feris al-Mazrui [f]
Secretary General of the Cabinet	Abdulla Mohammed al-Basti

[f] = female

INTERGOVERNMENTAL REPRESENTATION

Ambassador to the U.S.: Yousef Mana Saeed al-OTAIBA.

U.S. Ambassador to the United Arab Emirates: Barbara A. LEAF.

Permanent Representative to the UN: Lana Zaki NUSSEIBEH.

IGO Memberships (Non-UN): GCC, NAM, OIC, OPEC, WTO.

For Further Reference:

Krane, Jim. *City of Gold: Dubai and the Dream of Capitalism*. New York: Picador, 2010.

Morton, Michael Quentin. *Keepers of the Golden Shore: A History of the United Arab Emirates*. New York: Reaktion Books, 2016.

Soffan, Linda Usra. *The Women of the United Arab Emirates*. New York: Routledge, 2016.

Zahlan, Rosemarie Said. *The Origins of the United Arab Emirates: A Political and Social History of the Trucial States*. New York: Palgrave Macmillan, 1978.

UNITED KINGDOM

United Kingdom of Great Britain and Northern Ireland

Political Status: Constitutional monarchy, under democratic parliamentary regime.

Area: 94,249 sq. mi. (244,104 sq. km), embracing England and Wales, 58,382 sq. mi. (151,209 sq. km); Scotland, 30,415 sq. mi. (78,775 sq. km); Northern Ireland, 5,452 sq. mi. (14,120 sq. km).

Population: 65,111,000 (2016E—UN); 64,430,428 (2016E—Census)

Major Urban Centers (2015E): *England:* LONDON (urban area, 10,313,000), Birmingham (1,101,000), Liverpool (466,000), Leeds (475,000), Sheffield (518,000), Bristol (536,000), Manchester (514,000); *Wales:* CARDIFF (335,000); *Scotland:* EDINBURGH (459,000), Glasgow (590,000); *Northern Ireland:* BELFAST (281,000).

Principal Language: English (Scottish and Irish forms of Gaelic are spoken in portions of Scotland and Northern Ireland, respectively, while Welsh is spoken in northern and central Wales).

Monetary Unit: Pound Sterling (market rate October 1, 2016: 0.77 pound = $1US).

Sovereign: Queen ELIZABETH II; proclaimed queen on February 6, 1952; crowned June 2, 1953.

Heir Apparent: CHARLES Philip Arthur George; invested as Prince of Wales on July 1, 1969.

Prime Minister: Theresa MAY (Conservative Party); appointed by the queen on July 13, 2016, to succeed David William Donald CAMERON (Conservative Party), who announced his resignation following the approval on June 23 of a referendum on the United Kingdom's withdrawal from the European Union. (See Government and Politics, below).

THE COUNTRY

The United Kingdom of Great Britain and Northern Ireland (UK) occupies the major portion of the British Isles, the largest island group off the European coast. The individual identity of its separate regions, each with distinctive ethnic and linguistic characteristics, is reflected in the complex governmental structure of the country as a whole. England, the heart of the nation, accounts for over half the total area and 83 percent of the total population. Wales, conquered in the Middle Ages, has its own capital, Cardiff, and a national language, Welsh, with which some 30 percent of the population have familiarity. Scotland, ruled as a separate kingdom until 1707, has long had its own legal and educational systems; its capital is Edinburgh. Conquered by the English in the Middle Ages, Ireland became part of the UK in 1800 but in 1921 was partitioned into Northern Ireland, whose Protestant majority opted for retention of British status, and the predominantly Catholic Irish Republic. Varieties of the Gaelic language are spoken in both Scotland

and Northern Ireland. There are two established churches, the Church of England (Episcopalian or Anglican), with some 1.5 million active members, and the Church of Scotland (Presbyterian), with some 700,000 members. Nonestablished religions include Roman Catholicism, Islam, and Methodism. At the 2011 census, 59.3 percent of the population identified themselves as Christians, while 25.1 percent reported no religious affiliation. Apart from a legal prohibition on the monarch (who is head of the Church of England) or the heir to the throne becoming a Roman Catholic, religious freedom prevails.

In 2010 women comprised 50.8 percent of the paid (including part-time) workforce, concentrated in the retail, clerical, and human services sectors. Following the election of May 2015, women held 192 of the 650 seats in the House of Commons (29.6 percent). Women also occupied 204 of the 799 seats in the House of Lords (25.6 percent) and held 14 ministries in the new government. Theresa MAY became the second woman prime minister in UK history in July 2016.

Great Britain was the seat of the industrial revolution of the 18th century, and most of its urbanized and highly skilled population is engaged in manufacturing and service industries, mainly transport, commerce, and finance, with agriculture accounting for only 1 percent of GDP and employment. Machinery, basic manufactures, and agricultural products constitute the bulk of British imports. Machinery and transport equipment, basic manufactures, chemicals, and mineral fuels are the chief exports. Germany, the United States, and Japan rank as the leading trading partners.

The "British economic miracle" foundered in the wake of the stock market crash of October 1989. (For more on the British economy prior to 1989, see the 2014 *Handbook.*) Initially, the government sought recovery by increasing liquidity, but a rapid inflationary surge forced it to apply interest rates at record highs. In October 1990 the pound sterling was placed in the broad band of the European Community (EC) exchange rate mechanism (ERM), which in effect pegged it to the deutsche mark. By then, the economy had entered its deepest and longest recession since the 1930s, aggravated by similar difficulties in other industrial economies. In 1991–1992 overall output dropped by 3.6 percent and unemployment, having fallen to a ten-year low of 5.9 percent in 1989, rose to 10.5 percent by late 1992. In September 1992 massive speculation against the pound sterling forced its withdrawal from the ERM and, in effect, a 20 percent devaluation.

Clear signs of a rebound appeared in 1993, and by April 1994 the GDP had regained its pre-slump (1990) peak. The recovery continued in 1995–1997, with annual GDP growth averaging about 3 percent. A global slowdown held expansion to 2.2 percent in 1998 and 2 percent in 1999, although growth in the last three quarters of the latter year returned to an annualized rate of about 3 percent and helped vault the UK over France and into fourth place among the world's largest economies. Moreover, unemployment stood at only 4 percent, the lowest rate in a quarter of a century, while retail inflation remained below the target of 2.5 percent. GDP growth in 2000–2004 ranged between 2 percent and 3.2 percent annually.

In its 2005 report, the IMF praised the UK for a "remarkable performance" over the past decade, marked by sustained growth, low inflation, and steadily low unemployment. However, GDP growth for 2005 fell to 1.9 percent (the lowest in 13 years) and continued to fall as the global economic crisis spread. After contracting 4.4 percent in 2009, GDP increased by 1.7 percent in 2010, 1.1 percent in 2011, and just 0.3 percent in 2012. Unemployment rose, from 7.5 percent in 2009 to 7.9 percent in 2010, and then 8.1 percent in 2011, before falling to 7.9 percent in 2012. The new Conservative-led government elected in 2010 announced plans to restore confidence in the economy with a front-loaded proposal to cut spending and raise taxes, with the intention of balancing the budget by 2017. Instead, the UK entered its first double-dip recession (defined as consecutive quarterly drops in GDP before the economy has recovered from the latest recession) since 1975. GDP grew by 2.1 percent in 2013, while inflation increased by 2.6, and unemployment decreased to 7.6 percent. Growth continued in 2014 and 2015, with GDP rising by 2.9 percent and 2.3 percent, respectively. Inflation fell to 0.1 percent in 2015, and unemployment that year was 5.4 percent. Economic uncertainty following a referendum endorsing the withdrawal of the UK from the EU in June 2016 slowed growth in 2016 (see Government and Politics, below). GDP expanded by 1.9 percent in 2016. That year inflation was 0.8 percent, while unemployment continued to fall to 5 percent with the country essentially at full employment. GDP per capita in 2013 was $39,567. The World Bank ranked the United Kingdom as 6th out of 189 countries in its annual ease of doing business index in 2016, behind only Denmark (3rd) among EU members.

GOVERNMENT AND POLITICS

Political background. After reaching its apogee of global influence in the closing decades of the Victorian era, the UK endured the strains of the two world wars with its political institutions unimpaired but with sharp reductions in its relative economic strength and military power. The steady erosion of the British imperial position after World War II was only partially offset by the concurrent development and expansion of the Commonwealth, a grouping that continued to reflect an underlying British philosophy but whose center of gravity shifted to newly developed and developing nations. Despite continuing differences on many issues, the three traditional parties—Conservative, Labour, and Liberal (now the Liberal Democrats)—have in some respects drawn closer together.

The Labour Party, after winning the postwar elections of 1945 and 1950 under the leadership of Clement R. ATTLEE, went into opposition for 13 years while the Conservative Party governed under prime ministers Winston CHURCHILL (1951–1955), Anthony EDEN (1955–1957), Harold MACMILLAN (1957–1963), and Alec DOUGLAS-HOME (1963–1964). A Conservative defeat in the general election of October 1964 returned Labour to power under Harold WILSON. At the election of June 1970 the tide swung back to the Conservatives, who under Edward HEATH obtained a 30-seat majority in the House of Commons. In February 1974 the Conservatives outpolled Labour but fell 3 seats short of a plurality, Wilson returning to head the first minority government since 1929. A second election eight months later gave Labour an overall majority of 3 seats. In April 1976 Wilson unexpectedly resigned and was succeeded as prime minister by Foreign Secretary James CALLAGHAN, who saw Labour's fortunes plummet in the 1978–1979 "winter of discontent" that featured damaging public sector strikes.

In May 1979 the Conservatives obtained 339 seats (a majority of 44) in the House of Commons, enabling Margaret THATCHER to become the first female prime minister in British (and European) history. Benefiting from popular response to her handling of the Falkland Islands War (see Foreign relations, below), the Conservatives surged to a 144-seat majority at the election of June 1983. They retained control of the Commons with a somewhat diminished but still comfortable majority of 102 in June 1987, Thatcher becoming the first prime minister in modern British history to win three consecutive terms.

Following the introduction of a widely disliked community charge ("poll tax") in April 1990, the Conservatives' popularity took a downward turn that was only briefly reversed by public appreciation of Thatcher's firmness in response to the Persian Gulf conflict precipitated by Iraq's invasion of Kuwait in August. Amid a damaging series of by-election defeats for the Conservatives, a sense of crisis was generated by the resignation on November 1 of the deputy prime minister, Geoffrey HOWE, over the prime minister's lack of support for enhanced British participation in the EC. On November 13 the former defense secretary, Michael HESELTINE, reversing an earlier pledge, challenged Thatcher for the party leadership, and at an intraparty poll on November 20 he won sufficient backing to deny the prime minister a first-round victory. Two days later Thatcher announced her intention to resign. In the second-round ballot on November 27 Chancellor of the Exchequer John MAJOR defeated both Heseltine and Foreign Secretary Douglas HURD. Having abandoned the poll tax and moderated other aspects of "Thatcherite" policies that had enjoyed his keen support theretofore, Major led the Conservatives to a fourth successive election victory on April 9, 1992, despite economic recession and negative forecasts from opinion pollsters. Although Labour made significant gains, the Conservatives retained a working majority of 336 seats in the 651-member House of Commons.

The Danish referendum vote in June 1992 against the Maastricht Treaty on greater EC economic and political union caused divisions to surface within the Conservative Party between pro-EC and anti-EC factions, the latter being dubbed "Eurosceptics." Because of the government's modest majority, anti-EC Conservative MPs were able to mount protracted resistance to parliamentary ratification of the Maastricht Treaty until after reversal of the Danish negative vote in May 1993 (see Foreign relations, below).

The opposition Labour Party displayed its own internal fissures over the EC. However, its main task was to revitalize its leadership following the resignation of Neil KINNOCK, who had suffered defeat in two successive general elections. Elected leader in July 1992, John SMITH maintained Kinnock's moderate, pro-EC stance while initiating reviews of Labour's social and constitutional policies. A rapid Labour rise in the opinion polls in late 1992 was assisted by a series of major government reverses and blunders, amid a European currency crisis that forced the pound sterling out of the EC's ERM.

The withdrawal from the ERM represented a traumatic collapse of government economic policy. In March 1993 Chancellor of the Exchequer Norman LAMONT presented a "budget for jobs" and claimed that the recession was over, but a spiraling budget deficit obliged him to introduce tax increases effective in 1994, some in breach of Conservative election pledges. Major later sought to recover the initiative by launching a "back to basics" campaign, stressing traditional Conservative values on education, law and order, and other matters.

The issuance of the joint UK–Irish Downing Street Declaration on Northern Ireland in December 1993 yielded some political credit to Major (and led eventually to the historic cease-fire announcement by the Irish Republican Army [IRA] on August 31, 1994—see Northern Ireland entry). Conservative fortunes nevertheless continued their decline, and in June 1994 the party lost 16 of its 34 seats in the European Parliament. The clear victor in the balloting was the Labour Party, under the interim leadership of Margaret BECKETT following the sudden death of Smith on May 12. Subsequent Labour leadership elections, for the first time involving all individual party members, resulted in 41-year-old Tony BLAIR emerging an easy winner on July 22. Seeking to appeal to "middle England," Blair accelerated the modernization of Labour policies and structures.

Rocked by scandals, including the press revelation that certain Conservative MPs had accepted "cash for questions" (payment from outside interests for tabling parliamentary questions to ministers), the government continued to face bitter opposition from some of its own backbenchers. On November 28, 1994, eight Conservative Eurosceptics rebelled against a financing bill for the EU that the government had made an issue of confidence. The EU issue, the "sleaze factor" resulting from an unremitting flow of sex and financial scandals, and other divisions contributed to all-time low opinion-poll ratings for the Conservatives, who in local elections on May 4, 1995, suffered the party's heaviest postwar defeat.

Amid renewed speculation about his future, Prime Minister Major on June 22, 1995, announced his formal resignation from the party leadership, forcing critics to "put up or shut up" regarding his reelection. All but one cabinet minister declared support for the prime minister, the exception being John REDWOOD, who resigned as secretary for Wales in order to challenge Major on a strongly Eurosceptic platform. Major emerged the comfortable first-round victor on July 4.

Local elections in May 1996 dropped the Conservatives to third place, behind Labour and the Liberal Democrats, in terms of total local councilors. With allegations of improper financial conduct on the part of Conservative members of Parliament (including junior ministers) being supported by the Nolan Commission on Standards in Public Life, and with time running out on the five-year legislative term, the prime minister on March 17, 1997, asked for a dissolution of Parliament. The election held on May 1 resulted in one of the worst defeats for any governing party in the last century, as the Conservatives won only 165 seats, its losing candidates including 7 cabinet members. Labour swept to power by securing 418 seats on the strength of 44.4 percent of the vote. In keeping with his "centrist" stance, Blair named a mix of "old hands" and "New Labour modernizers" to the new cabinet appointed on May 7. Following the election, former prime minister Major announced his resignation as Conservative leader, with Eurosceptic William HAGUE defeating the pro-EU Kenneth Clarke in the subsequent contest to lead the party.

Carrying through on one of Labour's most prominent campaign pledges, the Blair government quickly pursued decisions in Wales and Scotland regarding devolution of regional authority. In a referendum on September 11, 1997, 74 percent of the voters in Scotland approved the proposed creation of a Scottish Parliament, while on September 18 a plan for establishment of a Welsh National Assembly was endorsed by 50.3 percent of the voters in Wales. (Elections for the two bodies—the first Scottish legislature since 1707 and the first ever in Wales—were held on May 6, 1999, with Labour emerging as the plurality party in both. The Scottish Parliament and Welsh National Assembly both held opening ceremonies on July 1, with Queen Elizabeth II in attendance in Edinburgh.)

The long process of negotiation and accommodation in Northern Ireland, which included the direct involvement of both British and Irish governments, led to the signing on April 10, 1998, of a multiparty peace accord, the Belfast (Good Friday) Agreement, followed on June 25 by the election of a Northern Ireland Assembly. Devolution of powers from London to the assembly and a power-sharing executive occurred on December 2, 1999.

In 1998–1999 the government issued white papers, or commission reports, addressing the future makeup of local government, various proportional representation schemes, campaign finance reform, freedom of information, and social service reform. At the same time, however, the Blair government downplayed any commitments that might entail substantial increases in spending or taxation, while encroaching even further on traditional Conservative territory by promoting "family values," social responsibility, citizenship, and a hard line on street crime. The "New Labour" program also attacked "something for nothing" welfare policies and proposed pension reform, despite considerable opposition from Labour traditionalists.

One of the most contentious issues during the early years of the Blair administration was if and when to adopt the EU's euro as a replacement for the pound sterling. Although the Blair government consistently supported eventual entry into the EMU, widespread public opposition forced the administration to review its strategy and adjust its timetable.

A lingering dispute over the disarming of the paramilitary IRA led London to reimpose direct rule in Northern Ireland on February 11, 2000. On May 30 power was again devolved, the IRA having agreed, earlier in the month, to put its arsenals under international supervision. Little progress was made in the following 16 months, despite repeated negotiating efforts by Prime Minister Blair, Irish Prime Minister Ahern, and others, as paramilitary arms decommissioning, police reform, and withdrawal of British forces continued to be at issue. On August 10, 2001, and again on September 22, London briefly suspended the assembly as a technical maneuver to avoid calling a new election. The devolved government was given new life by the IRA's October 23 announcement that it had begun decommissioning to "save the peace process," but revelations of IRA spying ultimately led London to reimpose direct rule from October 15, 2002 (see Northern Ireland entry for details).

The issues of immigration and political asylum also came to the fore in the late 1990s and early 2000s. With the Conservative Party calling for tough measures to discourage "economic migrants" posing as political refugees, Home Secretary Jack Straw in March 2000 called for a complete reexamination of the 1951 UN Convention on the Status of Refugees. An Immigration and Asylum Bill, passed in November 1999 with effect from April 1, 2000, instituted a voucher system instead of cash payments to asylum seekers and also authorized their dispersal around the country, over the objections of many local authorities.

At an early election called by Prime Minister Blair for June 7, 2001, Labour was overwhelmingly returned to office with 412 seats in the House of Commons (6 fewer than in 1997). A reshuffled cabinet was announced on June 8, and on the same day Conservative leader Hague stepped down despite modest gains by his party in simultaneous local elections. (Hague was succeeded in 2001 by Iain DUNCAN SMITH and in 2003 by Michael HOWARD. See section on the Conservative Party under Political Parties for details.)

In the wake of the September 11, 2001, terrorist attacks in the United States, the Blair government stood as the most steadfast supporter of the George W. Bush administration's October decision to launch military attacks against the al-Qaida network and the Taliban regime in Afghanistan. Earlier, Blair had called for tighter domestic security and had initiated steps to freeze assets of suspected terrorist organizations, monitor bank transactions, and introduce fast-track extradition. On December 14 an Anti-Terrorism, Crime, and Security Bill was enacted, although the Conservative majority in the House of Lords had exacted a number of tempering concessions beforehand.

At the poll of May 5, 2005, Labour, for the first time, registered its third consecutive victory in the House of Commons, albeit with a substantially reduced majority of 355 seats. Prime Minister Blair conducted a minor cabinet reshuffle on the following day.

The terrorist threat became a British reality in July 2005 with a series of London subway bombings in which 56 persons died and a subsequent second, albeit failed, series of attacks in three subway trains and a bus. The newly returned Blair government adopted a number of antiterrorist measures, including a catalog of offenses for which foreign militants could be deported. In September the government introduced new antiterrorism legislation calling, among other things, for an extension of the time a suspect could be held without charges being filed from 14 to 90 days. The following month a number of foreign-based Islamic groups were banned from operating in the UK on the government's assertion that they had ties to al-Qaida. These antiterrorism measures appeared to gain acceptance among the population and most political parties, but the more stringent initiatives fueled a growing debate over the extent to which civil rights and liberties should be curtailed in the name of national security.

Attention in early 2006 focused on the ongoing slide of the Labour Party (buffeted by a series of scandals and policy disputes) and the collateral emergence of the new Conservative leader, David CAMERON, as a dynamic actor on the political stage. Both appeared to contribute to the "meltdown" of Labour at the partial local elections in early May, as the government party suffered a third-place finish in vote percentage. Particularly costly (apparently) for Labour was the revelation that several wealthy businessmen who had secretly lent money to the party's 2005 campaign had been nominated by Blair for peerages, status that automatically includes appointment to the House of Lords. Popular discontent was also reported concerning the perceived lax enforcement of deportation laws for foreigners being released from prisons. Although Blair reportedly faced growing criticism from Labour backbenchers, his cabinet reshuffle (the biggest of his tenure) on May 5, 2006, (the day after an extremely poor performance by Labour in partial local elections) indicated his intention to pursue with vigor additional reform in areas such as education, energy, pensions, and health. At the same time, Blair pledged that he would resign the premiership in sufficient time to let Gordon BROWN (his presumed successor) establish himself as prime minister prior to the general election due by 2010. (In early September Blair announced that he would hand over the premiership within a year.) Meanwhile, Brown (the chancellor of the exchequer and an architect with Blair of "New Labour") began to speak out on a variety of issues outside the purview of his office, prompting some observers to suggest the Blair-Brown relationship was in effect an "undeclared shared premiership." For his part, Cameron focused on a determined effort to move the Conservatives toward the center on many topics in order to sustain the party's electoral momentum for, among other things, the elections scheduled for the spring of 2007 in Scotland and Wales.

By July 2006 public satisfaction with the way the government was running the country and with Blair as prime minister had dropped below 25 percent. An August report from the Home Office drew further attention to the simmering issue of immigration, reporting that almost 50,000 work applications from East Europeans had been approved in the second quarter of the year and that since 2004, when a number of East European countries had joined the EU, 427,000 Eastern Europeans had registered for work in the UK. Meanwhile, some cabinet ministers remained in open disagreement with Blair over his muted response to Israeli bombings in the Israeli–Lebanon war and his refusal to distance himself from Washington's pro-Israeli posture. On September 16, 8 junior aides resigned to protest Blair's refusal to set a definite date for his resignation, and an open letter from 17 Labour MPs called for Blair to step down. On the following day, Blair announced that he would leave within a year. However, Blair continued to be dogged by the "cash for peerages" scandal, in which the Labour Party received large loans from individuals later nominated for peerages. (Such loans, unlike direct donations, are not subject to strict public reporting requirements.) The suspicions of a quid pro quo got so close to Blair that he became the first prime minister interviewed by police in a criminal investigation. (In the end no one was charged with a criminal offense.) Blair also alienated members of the Labour Party in December 2006 when he urged that Britain's nuclear arms program be extended with a new generation of submarines. The March 2007 vote on the matter in the House of Commons produced the largest Labour Party rebellion since the Iraq war began; the measure passed only because of support from Conservatives.

The balloting for the Scottish Parliament on May 3, 2007, was most noteworthy for the advancement of the Scottish National Party (SNP) to a plurality status with 47 of 129 seats, compared to 46 for Labour. The SNP subsequently formed a minority government in Scotland, but the party's lack of a legislative majority was expected to preclude further movement (at least for the immediate future) toward its goal of full independence for Scotland. Meanwhile, Labour and *Plaid Cymru,* a Welsh nationalist party, formed a coalition government in Wales following the May elections to the Welsh National Assembly. Among other things, the coalition negotiations had apparently produced a pledge from Labour to support a referendum on *Plaid Cymru*'s call for the assembly to be given additional legislative authority.

After further losses by Labour and gains by Conservatives in May 3, 2007, local balloting and Labour's loss of plurality party status in the Scottish Parliament to the SNP on the same day, Prime Minister Blair announced on May 10 he would step down as party leader and prime minister before the end of June. When no viable challenge to the long anticipated leadership transfer to Gordon Brown emerged, Brown accepted the position as Labour leader on June 24 and as prime minister on June 27.

Confidence in Brown's leadership waned throughout his first year in office. The depth of the financial crisis, apparent since July 2007, led the government to nationalize Northern Rock bank in February 2008, after Brown failed to find a private-sector solution to the bank's impending failure. Further complicating matters for Brown, the government was able to secure only a 28-vote margin to stave off a Conservative Party attempt to force a public inquiry into decisions leading up to the invasion of Iraq, with 12 Labour backbenchers defecting from the government's position that such an inquiry should wait until the operations had ended. In June 2008 a vote on the government's bill to extend the maximum period terrorism suspects could be held without charge from 28 to 42 days (which was whittled back from the 90-day period Blair had proposed in 2005 and on which Blair had suffered his first defeat by parliament) passed by a mere 9-vote margin, supplied by 9 members of the Democratic Unionist Party as 36 Labour backbenchers defected.

Prime Minister Brown's leadership regarding the rescue of financial institutions in the fall of 2008 was generally well received by the public, and the double-digit lead the Conservatives had earlier held over Labour in opinion polls was cut to single digits. However, in May 2009 a major scandal erupted in the House of Commons involving expense account abuses. Although legislators from other parties were also cited, Labour appeared to suffer the greatest fallout from the scandal, especially since cabinet members and other Labour leaders were involved. The speaker of the House of Commons, Michael MARTIN (originally elected on the Labour ticket), announced his resignation from the speaker's post (effective June 21) after being harshly criticized for his handling of the issue. In addition, two Labour peers were suspended from the House of Lords (the first suspensions in 350 years), and two others were rebuked for allegedly seeking money in return for adding amendments to proposed legislation. Meanwhile, the harsh realities of the ongoing effects of the economic crisis had become apparent. The country's creditworthiness was downgraded, and government debt reportedly breached the level of 40 percent GDP, which Labour for many years had set as the maximum acceptable level. Consequently, Labour fell to third place in both the local elections and balloting for the European Parliament, held concurrently on June 4.

In an apparent attempt to counter anticipated challenges to his premiership, Brown reshuffled the cabinet on June 5, 2009. However, the government subsequently faced criticism on several policy fronts. In August the SNP government in Scotland returned a convicted Lockerbie bomber to Libya on compassionate grounds (the prisoner had been diagnosed with terminal cancer). Opposition parties and other critics charged that the Labour government in Westminster had been complicit in the decision and had bargained, in conjunction with the SNP, for oil and gas concessions from Libya (Brown denied that any deal had been made).

Despite polls showing that more than two-thirds of the public favored an early withdrawal of UK troops from Afghanistan, Brown declared in November 2009 that his government would not bow to the popular mood on the subject. Attention also focused on the Iraqi War Inquiry, some of whose opening witnesses in November questioned the bona fides of the intelligence on which the decision to participate in the U.S.-led invasion had been based. Others questioned the legitimacy (but not the legality) of the decision, given the lack of support from the UK populace and much of the international community. Former prime minister Blair testified in January 2010 and Brown in March.

Having never been in a strong enough position in public opinion polls to call for early elections, Brown did not seek dissolution of the House of Commons until April 2010 (the last possible moment since a new poll was constitutionally mandated by May). The month-long campaign focused on charges that 13 years of Labour government had gone too far in expanding the scope and role of the national government, infringed on too many civil liberties, and, in the end, been associated with the worst financial crisis since the depression of the 1930s. In balloting for the House of Commons on May 6, 2010, the Conservatives won 306 seats to Labour's 258 (neither major party securing an outright majority). In the early days after the election, Brown floated the idea of joining forces in government with the Liberal Democrats, but when this idea gained no traction, he resigned as Labour leader and prime minister on May 11. The same day the queen asked Conservative leader Cameron to form a government, which he did by announcing that the Conservatives and Liberal Democrats, which won 57 seats, would come together in the country's first coalition government since World War II, with Nick CLEGG of the Liberal Democrats as deputy prime minister.

In the balloting for the Scottish parliament on May 5, 2011, the SNP won an outright majority with 69 of the 129 seats. Alex SALMOND, first minister and leader of the SNP, vowed to pursue Scottish independence from the UK and to hold a referendum on Scottish secession. In Wales the May 5 balloting resulted in a substantial loss for *Plaid Cymru,* which led the Labour Party to form a one-party minority administration.

A minor cabinet reshuffle was undertaken between October 2013 and February 2014. A major government reshuffle occurred in July, ahead of a referendum on Scottish independence (see Current issues, below).

In the 2015 electoral campaign, Cameron pledged to hold a referendum on a UK exit (a British exit or "Brexit") from the EU if elected. The planned referendum was both a concession to Euroscepticism and an incentive for the EU to grant greater autonomy to the UK. Cameron, most of his cabinet, and the majority of Conservative members of parliament did not support a UK withdrawal. The Conservatives also emphasized their economic record in the election campaign as unemployment fell below 6 percent. Cameron pledged that if returned as prime minister, he would not seek a third term in 2020. In the balloting on May 7, 2015, the Conservatives won a majority with 330 seats, while Labour was second with 232, and the SNP third with 56. The Liberal Democrats were fourth with 8 seats, a loss of 49. Cameron was reappointed prime minister, and named a Conservative cabinet.

Cameron conducted a series of negotiations with the EU and gained some concessions (see Foreign relations, below). In the Brexit referendum on June 23, 2016, voters endorsed leaving the EU, 51.9 percent to 48.1 percent. Cameron, who had campaigned in favor of EU membership, announced his resignation after the vote, and home secretary Theresa MAY was chosen as the party's new leader and prime minister. She took office on July 13, and named a reshuffled cabinet over the next week. May announced her intention to invoke Article 50 of the EU charter, which would launch a two-year window for Brexit by March 2017.

Constitution and government. The UK is a constitutional monarchy that functions without a written constitution on the basis of statutes, common law, and long-standing but flexible traditions and usages, subject since 1973 to EC/EU membership and thus acceptance of the primacy of EC/EU law. Executive power is wielded on behalf of the sovereign by a cabinet of ministers drawn from the majority party in the House of Commons and, to a lesser degree, from the House of Lords. The prime minister is the leader of the majority party in the House of Commons and depends upon it for support. There is also a historically important Privy Council of government members and some 300 other individuals drawn from public life. Although superseded in importance by the cabinet, it retains an advisory role in some policy areas and continues to issue "orders in council," either under authority of the monarch, who presides over its meetings, or as authorized by Parliament. The Privy Council also reviews legislation passed by Crown dependencies (the Channel Islands and the Isle of Man).

Elected by universal adult suffrage, the House of Commons has become the main repository of legislative and sole repository of financial authority. The House of Lords retains the power to review, amend, or delay for a year legislation other than financial bills and takes a more leisurely overview of legislation, sometimes acting as a brake on the House of Commons. The lower house, which has a maximum term of five years, may be dissolved by the sovereign on recommendation of the prime minister if the latter's policies should encounter severe resistance or if the incumbent feels that new elections would increase the ruling party's majority.

Under legislation approved by the House of Lords 221–81, with Conservatives abstaining, on October 26, 1999, Labour's 1997 campaign pledge to end hereditary membership in the upper house moved forward. The bill, which received royal assent on November 11, authorized formation of an interim upper chamber to include among its members 92 hereditary peers. Meanwhile, the Wakeham Royal Commission appointed in October 1998 continued to draft proposals for a permanently restructured upper body. The final report, issued on January 20, 2000, proposed a chamber of 550 mostly appointed members but with a minority of 65, 87, or 195 to be elected through regional proportional representation. Law Lords (Lords of Appeal in Ordinary), lifetime appointees who have traditionally constituted the kingdom's highest court of appeal, would retain their seats. The existing 26 seats held by archbishops and bishops would be supplemented by 5 seats for representatives of non-Christian religions. Other life peers would be gradually phased out and replaced by a combination of appointed and elected members.

Following the developments of 2000–2002, the Blair administration called for abolition of the post of Lord Chancellor, the establishment of a Supreme Court, and, in the wake of devolution, absorption of the offices for Scotland and Wales by a department of constitutional affairs. Thus, in a mid-2003 cabinet reshuffle, the secretaries of state for Scotland and Wales, while retained, were assigned secondary status, with Lord FALCONER of Thoroton named secretary of state for constitutional affairs and invested as Lord Chancellor "for the transitional period."

In March 2004 the House of Lords referred the Constitutional Reform Bill to a special select committee, while the government abandoned plans for a bill to abolish the 92 seats held by remaining hereditary peers.

A year later, on March 25, 2005, royal assent was given to a revised Constitutional Reform Bill that provided for a Supreme Court separate from the House of Lords and, without abandoning the office itself, transferred the legislative functions of the Lord Chancellor to the Lord Speaker and the judicial functions to a President of the Courts for England and Wales.

In March 2007 the parliament took a series of free votes (no party obligation) on preferences for an elected House of Lords. Majorities in the House of Commons supported both an 80 and 100 percent elected composition. A majority in the House of Lords supported a wholly appointed body. Justice Secretary Jack STRAW announced in July that work on "fundamental" reform would continue. However, decisive action appeared unlikely before the next general election.

Apart from the newly established Supreme Court, which was inaugurated on October 1, 2009, the judicial system of England and Wales centers on a High Court of Justice for civil cases, with three divisions (Chancery, Family, and Queen's Bench); a Crown Court for criminal cases; and a Court of Appeal, with civil and criminal divisions. Scotland has its own High Court of Justiciary (criminal) and Court of Session (civil), both including appeal courts, while Northern Ireland has a separate Supreme Court of Judicature, comprising a (civil) High Court of Justice, a (criminal) Crown Court, and a Court of Appeal. In relevant cases, UK citizens and groups have the right of appeal against national legal rulings to the European Court of Human Rights in Strasbourg, France.

Local government in England traditionally encompassed a two-tier structure of county and district (or borough or city) councils, but in recent years dozens of unitary authorities have been established. The traditional structure largely survives in 34 counties and more than 200 district councils, although some of the counties have seen unitary authorities established within their geographical boundaries. Under legislation enacted in 1994, Wales and Scotland, formerly with two tiers, moved on April 1, 1996, to a unitary system, with 22 and 32 elected councils, respectively. Northern Ireland has 26 district councils.

Since 1986, when the Greater London Council was abolished, the capital has been governed through 32 boroughs, each with its own elected council, and the Corporation of the City of London, its unique status reflecting its commercial rather than residential character. Additionally, at a referendum held on May 7, 1998, Londoners overwhelmingly approved direct election of a mayor and establishment of a 25-member London Assembly. The first mayoral and assembly elections were held in May 2000. (Subsequent mayoral and assembly elections were held in June 2004 and May 2008.)

The viability of the UK as a political entity has been a matter of major concern for three decades. The most intractable problem has been that of deep-rooted conflict in Northern Ireland between the majority Protestants, most of whom remain committed to the union with Great Britain, and a Catholic minority, substantial elements of which have long sought union with the Republic of Ireland. A multiparty peace accord, the Belfast (Good Friday) Agreement of April 10, 1998, was approved in Northern Ireland by referendum on May 22, with a new Northern Ireland Assembly being elected on June 25. Devolution of authority from London to the assembly and a Northern Ireland Executive occurred on December 2, 1999, although differences over the decommissioning of weapons held by the IRA resulted in reimposition of direct rule from February 11 to May 30, 2000. Upon devolution, the secretary of state for Northern Ireland retained authority in "excepted and reserved" areas, including law, criminal justice, and foreign affairs. Direct rule was again imposed for 24 hours in August and September 2001, and then for an indefinite period on October 15, 2002. In October 2006 talks involving the British government, the government of the Republic of Ireland, and all major parties in Northern Ireland produced the St. Andrews Agreement, which prompted new elections in Northern Ireland on March 7, 2007, and the restoration of the Northern Ireland Assembly on May 8 (see entry on United Kingdom: Northern Ireland).

Although not characterized by the violence endemic in the Irish question, a powerful separatist movement has also developed in Scotland. Alarmed by the growing influence of the SNP, which won a third of the Scottish votes in the October 1974 general election, the Labour leadership, in a 1975 government paper, proposed the establishment of elected assemblies for both Scotland and Wales. Despite Conservative criticism that the departure would prove costly and contain "the danger of a break-up of Britain," pertinent legislation was completed in mid-1978. In March 1979, however, referendums yielded rejection of devolution in Wales and approval by an insufficient majority in Scotland. Successive Conservative administrations subsequently ruled out the creation of regional assemblies, although in March 1993 the government, in what was officially described as the first major review of the England-Scotland relationship since 1707, introduced measures to give the 72 Scottish MPs a larger role in decision making.

Immediately after taking power in May 1997, the new Labour government set out plans for new Scottish and Welsh devolution referendums. On September 11 the Scottish electorate voted by a substantial majority for an elected Parliament, and on September 18 Welsh voters approved creation of a National Assembly. Under the Government of Wales Act and the Scotland Act, both passed by the UK Parliament following the referendums, elections for the two new bodies were held on May 6, 1999, with formal transfer of devolved powers occurring on July 1. Although the UK Parliament retains ultimate authority to legislate on all matters, it will not routinely do so in devolved sectors, which include education, health, culture, local government, housing, transportation, and the environment. The Scottish Parliament cannot propose independence from the union, nor can it legislate in reserved areas, which include defense and treaty obligations. Because Wales has a closer legal association with England, the Welsh assembly has a more limited scope than the Scottish Parliament, with no authority to pass primary legislation governing, for example, the legal system or taxation. Both Scotland and Wales, like Northern Ireland, continue to be represented in the UK Parliament and in the Westminster cabinet. With regard to England, the Blair administration indicated its willingness to go beyond establishing the RDAs and the London Authority (mayor plus assembly) and to devolve powers from the UK government to English regional bodies as the demand arises.

Following the 1997 election, the Labour government began to examine proportional representation for use in British elections. The 1999 balloting for the new Scottish and Welsh legislatures utilized, for the first time, a combination system in which each voter cast two ballots, one for a constituency representative elected under the traditional "first-past-the-post" basis and the second for a party list from which "top-up" seats were allocated, thereby assuring that the makeup of the legislatures would better reflect each party's overall vote share. A proportional scheme was also introduced for the European Parliament elections held in June 1999. However, many members of the UK House of Commons, including a substantial number of Labour MPs, have not expressed enthusiasm for converting to a basically proportional system for the House, as proposed in the report of the Jenkins Commission on electoral reform in October 1998. In March 2008 Justice Secretary Jack Straw proposed consultation on whether the centuries-old "first- past-the-post" electoral system should be replaced by an "alternative vote" system, which would allow voters to express a first and second preference for candidates running in a constituency. Straw's proposal also asked whether voting should be designated a civic duty, thereby making voting mandatory, and whether elections should be conducted over a two-day weekend. A May 2011 referendum rejected the alternative-vote electoral system.

On October 28, 2011, all 15 Commonwealth countries approved a change to the rules of succession to abolish primogeniture and create equality between the sexes. Queen ELIZABETH II gave royal assent to the Succession to the Crown Bill on April 25, 2013. The change meant that the first child of the Duke and Duchess of Cambridge would assume the throne, regardless of sex. (Prince GEORGE of Cambridge was born on July 22, 2013.) In addition, marriage to a Roman Catholic will no longer remove an individual from the order of succession, although the monarch still must be a Protestant.

Freedom combined with responsibility represents the British ideal in the handling of news and opinion. The press, while privately owned and free from censorship, is subject to strict libel laws and is often made aware of government preferences with regard to the handling of news reports. Reporters Without Borders ranked the United Kingdom 33rd of 180 countries in its 2014 Index of Press Freedom.

In late 1989, faced with the prospect of parliamentary action to curb the excesses of the more sensationalist papers, publishers adopted an ethics code that limited intrusion into private lives, offered the objects of press stories reasonable opportunity for reply, provided for appropriately prominent retraction of errors in reporting, precluded payments to known criminals, and barred irrelevant references to race, color, and religion. In 1997 the Press Complaints Commission announced a revised code of conduct that widened the definition of privacy for individuals, prohibited "persistent pursuit" by photojournalists, and offered additional protections for children. A communications bill, which was first published in May 2002, replaced five regulatory bodies for the press, television, and radio with a single Office of Communications. A unanimous ruling in October 2006 by the Law Lords (Britain's highest court) tightened the provisions under which the press can be sued for libel. In July 2011 Prime Minister Cameron established a public inquiry to investigate ongoing allegations that reporters for the Rupert Murdoch–owned *News of the World* tabloid had hacked private phone calls and voice mails of a variety of public figures. Led by Lord Justice (Brian) Levenson, the inquiry has led to the arrest of *News* staff for hacking and bribing public officials. In October 2013 eight former employees of *News of the World* went to trial on allegations of hacking voice mails and bribery of public officials. Meanwhile, in March 2013 the three major political parties announced the creation of a new press regulatory body answerable to the queen, not parliament. Reporters Without Borders ranked the UK 38th of 180 countries, due in part to antiterrorism legislation that allowed authorities to order journalists to produce unpublished source material "in the interests of justice." The ranking marked a decline from 19th in 2010.

Foreign relations. Reluctantly abandoning its age-long tradition of "splendid isolation," the UK became a key member of the Allied coalitions in both world wars and has remained a leader in the Western group of nations, as well as one of the world's nuclear-armed powers. Postwar British governments have sought to retain close economic and military ties with the United States while maintaining an independent British position on most international issues. Britain has continued to play an important role in the United Nations and in collective security arrangements, such as the North Atlantic Treaty Organization (NATO), although after 1957 Britain's withdrawal of most military forces from the Far East and the Persian Gulf substantially diminished its weight in the global balance of power.

The UK's participation in the work of such institutions as the IMF, the General Agreement on Tariffs and Trade/World Trade Organization

(GATT/WTO), and the Organization for Economic Cooperation and Development (OECD) reflects its continued central position in international financial and economic affairs as well as its commitment to assist in the growth of less-developed countries. (Similar concerns have also become a focus of the Commonwealth, which was formally established in 1931.) Unwilling to participate in the creation of the original three EC components (the European Economic Community [EEC], European Coal and Steel Community [ECSC], and European Atomic Energy Community [Euratom]), it took the lead in establishing the European Free Trade Association (EFTA) in 1960. Subsequently, Conservative and moderate Labour leaders began to urge British entry into the EC despite anticipated problems for the UK and other Commonwealth members. France, however, vetoed the British application for admission in 1963 on the grounds that the country remained too closely tied to the United States and the Commonwealth to justify close association with the continental nations. With the abandonment of French objections after President de Gaulle's resignation in 1969, a bill sanctioning entry was approved by the House of Commons in October 1971, and Britain was formally admitted to the EC on January 1, 1973. In a referendum held in June 1975, continued membership of the EC was endorsed by a two-thirds majority of participating voters, but enthusiasm for the European venture remained low in Britain over the subsequent two decades.

In late 1979 the Thatcher government won worldwide plaudits for its resolution of the seven-year Rhodesian civil war through a lengthy process of negotiation that culminated in independence under black majority rule in April 1980 (see the entry on Zimbabwe). In September 1981 Belize (formerly British Honduras) secured independence, as did Antigua and Barbuda in November. These were the latest territories to benefit from Britain's post-1957 imperial disengagement, which had seen 18 former possessions, protectorates, and colonies becoming independent during the 1960s, 10 in the 1970s, and 2 (including Zimbabwe) in 1980. Subsequently, St. Kitts and Nevis achieved independence in 1983, followed by Brunei in 1984.

The Falkland Islands War that erupted in April 1982 followed nearly two decades of sporadic negotiations between Britain and Argentina in a fruitless effort to resolve a dispute that had commenced in the late 18th century (see Falkland Islands under Related Territories, below). Following the Argentine defeat, the UN General Assembly renewed appeals for a negotiated solution to the sovereignty issue, and since 1984 the UN Committee on Decolonization has routinely passed Argentine-sponsored resolutions asking London to reopen negotiations on the matter. Two days of high-level talks in Madrid, Spain, in February 1990 produced a compromise settlement of conflicting claims to fishing rights and an agreement to restore a seven-year rupture in diplomatic relations, but the sovereignty issue remains unresolved.

In September 1984 Britain and China agreed that the latter would regain possession of Hong Kong in 1997, although the Conservative government continued to rebuff Spanish appeals for the reversion of Gibraltar, given manifest opposition to such a move by its inhabitants (see Special Administrative Region in China entry for information on Hong Kong, and Gibraltar under Related Territories, below).

While the Thatcher government had reservations about U.S. military intervention in Grenada in 1983, its generally close foreign policy alignment with Washington was demonstrated by endorsement of the U.S. bombing of Libya in 1986, as contrasted with the prevailing view of other EC countries. UK–U.S. cooperation was also a key factor during the Gulf crisis of 1990–1991, with British forces participating in the U.S.-led coalition that expelled Iraq from Kuwait.

In December 1991 the Major government was successful in negotiating various UK opt-outs from the EC's Maastricht Treaty on European union, notably from its commitment to a single European currency and from its jobs-imperiling social policy chapter. However, not until July 23, 1993, did the government obtain final parliamentary authority for its opt-out policy. This followed a stinging attack on the treaty by former prime minister Margaret Thatcher in the House of Lords, who cast her first vote in 34 years against her party's leadership, and came about only after Major had gained the reluctant support of his Conservative opponents in the House of Commons by making the decision a confidence motion. On July 30 a British court rejected the last legal challenge to the treaty, and on August 2 instruments of UK ratification were deposited in Rome.

In October 1997 the new Labour administration signaled a slightly more pro-European position by announcing that Britain would consider joining the EU's Economic and Monetary Union (EMU), but not immediately. Earlier, in May, the incoming foreign secretary had confirmed a Labour commitment to accept the social charter of the EU. In November 1998 the queen gave her assent to legislation that incorporated into British law the 1950 European Convention on Human Rights, with effect from October 2, 2000.

During 1992 UK diplomacy became increasingly preoccupied with the conflict in former Yugoslavia. Although some 3,400 British troops were committed to the UN humanitarian effort by 1994, the government firmly opposed any direct military intervention by external powers and backed both the UN arms embargo and the Vance-Owen diplomatic effort to obtain a negotiated settlement. Following major escalation of the Bosnian crisis in March 1995, London's policy underwent a significant shift. In addition to raising its troop contingent in the former Yugoslavia to 10,000, Britain agreed to contribute an additional 7,000 soldiers to a new NATO-led rapid reaction force charged with providing "enhanced protection" to the UN peacekeeping force. Subsequently, the British government was party to a NATO decision to step up air strikes around the Bosnian capital with the twin aims of relieving pressure on its inhabitants and of forcing Bosnian Serb acceptance of the latest peace plan. Britain gave its full support to the Dayton Accords of December 1995, which brought the conflict to a swift close. British troops remained part of the continuing UN peace force.

The Blair and Brown governments consistently supported the second U.S.-led incursion into Iraq, often at their political peril. A number of Blair's key aides resigned over the issue, including parliamentary leader Robin COOK in March 2003 and International Development Secretary Claire SHORT two months later. Even greater damage came from the fallout after the apparent suicide on July 13, 2003, of David KELLY, a ministry of defense weapons expert, who had been the source for alleged reports that Downing Street had "sexed up" a 2002 dossier on Iraqi weapons of mass destruction.

In 2009 Prime Minister Brown declared that some 9,000 UK troops would remain in Afghanistan, forming the second-largest contingent (behind that of the United States). In response to public discontent, in 2011 Prime Minister Cameron revealed plans to begin slowly drawing down the number of UK troops, but it would maintain its presence in Afghanistan with 9,000 troops until 2015. Cameron moved up the departure date to late 2014 following a meeting with U.S. president Barack Obama in March 2012. Prince Harry began a second deployment to Afghanistan on September 7.

In April 2004 Blair announced that he would call for a referendum on Britain's commitment to the EU after the next election. However, in June 2005 he said that the government would not proceed with a referendum bill, given the rejection of the EU constitution by the French and Dutch electorates. In mid-2006 the administration indicated that it might approve certain revisions in EU institutions on a "piece-by-piece" basis without a referendum. In December 2007 Prime Minister Brown signed the EU's Lisbon Treaty, which contains 96 percent of the language of the erstwhile EU constitution. The treaty, which amends rather than replaces previous EU treaties and would take effect no earlier than 2014, includes protocols and vetoes to protect UK interests in regard to security, foreign affairs, and social policy. The UK Parliament ratified the treaty in June 2008.

In November 2011 Prime Minister Cameron and French president Nicolas Sarkozy signed a treaty and agreed to strengthen cooperation and coordination between the two countries in areas of defense. In February, Cameron and Sarkozy announced a £500 billion contract to build a "next generation" nuclear power station. Cooperation between the two countries was set to last for 50 years, but following Sarkozy's reelection defeat in May, the new French defense minister, Jean-Yves Le Drian, announced Paris wanted to open the bilateral agreement to other countries.

The UK joined the United States and France in enforcing a no-fly zone in Libya and in the protection of Libyan citizens during the Libyan uprising of 2011.

Cameron positioned himself as the face of opposition to increasing the EU's regulatory powers. He withdrew from talks about the EU fiscal pact in 2011 and declined to join the European Stability Mechanism in 2012. Eurosceptic Conservatives called for a referendum on EU membership in October 2011. The motion was rejected 483–111, including 81 Tory defectors, making it the biggest defeat Cameron had faced to date (see Current issues, below).

The UK held the rotating presidency of the G-8 in 2013, and Cameron hosted the annual leaders' summit in Northern Ireland in June. Cameron set three priorities for his term: advancing trade, ensuring tax compliance, and promoting greater transparency. In December 2013 the United Kingdom and China signed a historic film treaty which would exempt British companies from Beijing's quota system limiting theaters to showing a maximum of 34 non-domestic movies per year.

Following an outbreak of the Ebola virus in West Africa in 2014 (see entries on Guinea, Liberia, and Sierra Leone), the UK government implemented enhanced screening for infected persons at airports, and pledged £125 million in aid to combat the disease. In addition, 750 UK military personnel were deployed to the region, along with equipment and hundreds of medical personnel and volunteers.

In April 2014 President Michael D. Higgins became the first Irish head of state to pay an official visit to the United Kingdom. Also in April, the United Kingdom ratified the UN Arms Trade Treaty (see entry on UN).

On September 26, 2014, Parliament approved an authorization to allow the United Kingdom to participate in U.S.-led airstrikes against the Islamic State of Iraq and Syria (ISIS) in Iraq (see entries on Iraq and Syria). The United Kingdom had deployed aircraft to Cyprus in August in anticipation of the strikes, which began on September 30.

In January 2015 the United States announced the closure of three U.S. military facilities in the United Kingdom, which would reduce the number of U.S. military personnel there from 8,000 to 6,000. Tensions with Russia escalated substantially as fighter aircraft were scrambled in response to Russian military airplanes flying close to UK airspace in repeated incidents from May 2015 through September 2016.

During a state visit by Chinese president Xi Jinping in November 2015, more than $30 billion in economic and investment agreements were signed. Cameron faced criticism for not raising controversial issues such as human rights during the Chinese leader's visit. Parliament authorized airstrikes on ISIS targets in Syria on December 2, 2015, and UK military aircraft immediately began attacks as part of the U.S.-led coalition.

Cameron finalized a deal with his fellow EU leaders in February 2016 that granted the UK concessions in a number of areas, including the ability to implement restrictions on social welfare benefits for new immigrants. Cameron also gained an exemption for the UK from pursuing "ever closer union." With the agreement, the prime minister set June 23 as the date for the Brexit referendum (see Current issues, below).

Current issues. The Conservative Party won 258 seats in the May 10, 2010, general elections but fell short of the 326 needed for a majority. David Cameron was appointed prime minister on May 11 and formed a coalition with the Liberal Democrats, which had 57 seats. The governing agreement (officially published on May 20) called for immediately addressing the budget deficit, finding a middle ground on immigration, creating a common policy regarding adoption of the euro, revising the manner in which UK parliamentary elections are conducted, resetting pension provisions, granting more local control over public education, and restoring civil liberties.

The government moved quickly on its budget proposals by announcing plans to cut overall spending by nearly 20 percent, including 7.5 percent cuts in defense. The most severe tax increase in the government's package was a change in the value-added tax (VAT) from 17.5 to 20 percent. The only spending that was held safe was for health and international development assistance. In a reversal of the Conservative Party's campaign pledge, the withdrawal of the popular child benefit from middle-class families paying the 40 percent tax rate was included in the first round of announced cuts. Although labor union leaders promised a strong opposition to the cut, public reaction was muted.

Strains emerged in the governing coalition as the economic outlook took a turn for the worse. Cameron's austerity measures were called into question after it was revealed that the UK economy was not improving. The 2011–2012 budget included spending cuts and tax hikes and few measures to stimulate economic growth. Labour repeatedly insisted that the government needed to introduce some form of stimulus package to create jobs and growth.

Despite poor economic performance and some growing concerns over the government's continued austerity measures, the Conservatives fared well in the local elections on May 5, 2011, with overall gains in local council seats, and emerged as the winning party in the balloting. The opposition Labour Party also fared well, winning control of 57 local councils. The Liberal Democrats, in contrast, appeared to bear the brunt of voter frustrations and saw their vote share drop to its lowest level in 30 years. In a double defeat for the Liberal Democrats, the UK overwhelmingly voted against switching to the alternative-vote method of election in the referendum held on May 5 (67.9 percent of the voters voted against the proposal). Support for the Liberal Democrats had also fallen amid a controversial vote for raising university tuition (the party had campaigned against such an increase) and several other policy U-turns made by the party.

Meanwhile, the SNP gained an outright majority of seats in the May 5 balloting for the devolved Scottish parliament, in part driven by a poor performance by the Liberal Democrats. Under the leadership of Alex Salmond, first minister in the Scottish parliament, much of the party's previous administration was left intact. Salmond immediately announced his intention to work toward securing additional financial powers for the Scotland bill, already under consideration by the House of Commons, and pledged to hold a referendum on Scottish secession in the autumn of 2014. In light of the SNP's new majority, Cameron's government vowed to keep the UK intact while promising not to stop the referendum from occurring. The UK government also announced that it would consider changes in the Scotland Bill that would increase the borrowing power of Scotland.

Concurrent elections to the Welsh parliament produced Labour government that controlled exactly half of the seats (30 out of 60). Two months earlier, a referendum in Wales on whether to give the Welsh parliament the power to pass laws in the 20 devolved policy areas was approved by a strong majority (63.5 percent) of the voters.

Cameron was put under fire again in August 2011 after the worst riots in 25 years broke out in London and subsequently spread to over 20 cities and towns while he was out of the country on holiday. The riots endured over several days and caused large-scale damage, while the police forces were restrained from engaging the rioters. The riots were quelled only after Cameron returned to the country and police activities increased. More than 3,000 people were arrested for looting, arson, and other offenses. In an intense questioning session in the House of Commons about the riots, Cameron reaffirmed his commitment to cut 16,000 police officers from the payroll.

On November 29 Chancellor of the Exchequer Osborne presented a gloomy budget update to the House of Commons. Unemployment stood at 8.1 percent, a 17-year high. He conceded that the government would not be able to eliminate the deficit by 2015, as promised, and more austerity measures were needed. Specifically, he imposed a 1 percent cap on pay raises for public-sector wages in 2012 and 2013, wages that had already been frozen in 2010–2011. With inflation running at 4.5 percent, this meant a cut in wages. He also raised the retirement age of civil servants from 60 for women and 65 for men to 68 for both. The next day, more than 2 million public workers staged a one-day strike, the largest since the 1970s.

The coalition also split over EU policy. In late 2011 leaders of the EU tried to hammer out a treaty that would enshrine fiscal discipline among all of its members. Greece, Ireland, and Portugal had already received financial bailouts to save them from bankruptcy, and German chancellor Angela Merkel and French president Sarkozy argued for a mechanism that would prevent countries from spending themselves into insolvency. Meeting in Brussels on December 8–9, the leaders of EU member states agreed to rewrite the Lisbon Treaty, the de facto EU constitution. Prime Minister Cameron shocked observers by vetoing the move when other members refused to make concessions to the London financial community. "For the first time since Britain joined the European Community in 1973," observed the *Guardian* newspaper, "a treaty that goes to the heart of how the EU works will be struck without a British signature."

A key part of Cameron's objection related to the proposed introduction of an EU financial transaction fee, known as a Tobin tax. He wanted veto power over any plan to transfer financial regulatory power from individual countries to the EU, insisted the European Banking Authority should remain in London, and opposed a regulation requiring that all euro-denominated transactions take place in countries that use the euro—which the UK does not.

Deputy Prime Minister Clegg insisted that the UK should sign the new treaty, arguing that Europe "can only address these problems by pulling together." Cameron appeared convinced by Clegg's plea and reversed his opposition regarding enforcement. His U-turn angered Tory Eurosceptics.

Presenting the 2012–2013 budget to the House of Commons on March 21, 2012, Osborne conceded that the government would not be able to eliminate the deficit before 2016–2017 and declared the overriding necessity of protecting the UK's AAA credit rating. His proposed budget predicted a deficit of 7.6 percent of projected GDP (nearly double the EU ceiling) and anticipated unemployment peaking at 8.7 percent in 2012 before falling to 6.3 percent by 2016–2017.

The electoral reform proposals stalled admit party politics. The alternative-vote system was rejected in an April 2011 referendum. The proposal to reduce the size of the House of Commons to 600 floundered on disputes over redistricting. On August 6 Clegg denounced the

Conservatives for backing out of a promise to reform the House of Lords into an elected body.

The UK put on two enormous celebrations in 2012. Queen Elizabeth II celebrated 60 years on the throne, and London played host to the 2012 Olympic Games. A series of jubilee events put the royal family on display to the world, while "Team GB" placed third in the medal count at the Olympics. The Olympic Committee suffered a major public relations setback in the final days before the Opening Ceremonies, when the security contractor announced that it could not provide enough staff; the government called on the armed forces to fill the gap. That news, as well as concerns over transportation bottlenecks, may have scared off some tourists, as many venues wound up with empty seats. The last-minute cost overruns and unsold tickets added to the $14 billion price tag for the Games, which Cameron insisted would be recouped in four years.

On September 4, 2012, Cameron reshuffled almost his entire cabinet. Environment secretary Caroline Spelman was sacked, along with Welsh secretary Cheryl Gillan and Sir George Young, leader of the Commons. The changes undermined Cameron's promise to improve diversity within the Conservative Party and to have one-third of government posts be held by women by 2015. Two of the five women in the cabinet lost jobs altogether, and Baroness Sayeeda Warsi, a Muslim and the only nonwhite cabinet member, was moved to a nonvoting cabinet post. Only one of the 19 men in the cabinet was removed completely.

The British economy contracted in 2012, to a point that it was smaller than when Cameron took office in 2010. Wages dropped 5.5 percent between 2010 and 2012, when adjusted for inflation. GDP grew only 0.3 percent in 2012, and unemployment registered at 8.0 percent. As the economy continued to languish, Moody's downgraded the UK's AAA credit rating in February 2013. The 2013–2014 budget, announced in March 2013, predicted a deficit of 7 percent of GDP, far above the EU 3 percent ceiling.

In a speech delivered on January 23, 2013, Cameron reversed earlier statements by publicly committing to holding a referendum on continuing British participation in the EU before the end of 2017. Tory backbenchers warned they would vote against continued EU membership unless London was allowed to opt out of the fiscal ceiling, transaction tax, and other unpopular measures. Public opinion, according to a May 2013 poll, favored exit 43 percent to 37 percent. Labour and the Liberal Democrats have expressed interest in the referendum but argued for boosting the domestic economy first. Cameron had long resisted the idea of a referendum but changed course in a move calculated to tame the surging UKIP. However, his shift might have instead validated their demand.

Cameron delivered a major speech on immigration reform on March 25, announcing new regulations and screenings to prevent new arrivals from immediately accessing the country's extensive social safety net. Conservatives feared an influx of immigration from Romania and Bulgaria when the countries acceded to the EU's Schengen Area in January 2014.

The UKIP and Greens fielded a record number of candidates in local elections on May 2, and both increased their representation. With 36 councils up for grabs, Labour took 29 percent of the vote, followed by the Conservatives (25 percent), UKIP (23 percent), and Liberal Democrats (14 percent). The balloting provided further evidence of the declining popular support for the junior government party. Going into the September Liberal Democrat annual conference, Clegg's popularity had sunk to 8 percent, and he faced many calls for his resignation.

On May 22, 2013, Pvt. Lee Rigby was walking near the Royal Artillery headquarters in London when a car jumped the curb and rammed into him. Two men jumped out of the car and hacked Rigby to death with knives and machetes while shouting Islamist slogans. Cameron labeled the horrific incident an act of terrorism, prompting fears of more attacks against soldiers recently returned from Afghanistan. The two attackers were subsequently convicted of murder and sentenced to life in prison.

The House of Commons dealt Cameron his worst defeat to date on August 29, 2013, when members refused to authorize military strikes against Syria, 285–272. Still smarting from poor intelligence that led Great Britain into war against Saddam Hussein in 2003, the parliament regarded intelligence reports about Syria warily. Miliband extracted a range of concessions from Cameron before the vote, but even the Labour leader's support for the bill was not enough for its passage.

In July 2013 Parliament legalized same-sex marriage in England and Wales. The government divested itself of 62 percent (worth $5.3 billion) of ownership of the Royal Mail in October in the largest privatization in decades. That same month, the government announced plans to construct a new twin nuclear reactor in Somerset.

GDP grew by 1.8 percent in 2013, the fastest rate of expansion since 2007. The government forecast GDP to expand by 2.4 percent in 2014. Meanwhile, unemployment fell to 7.1 percent in the final quarter of 2013, before dropping to 6 percent in October 2014, its lowest level since 2008.

In January 2014 a bill authorizing a referendum on EU membership was defeated in the House of Lords. In May 2014 Parliament enacted a controversial new law designed to tighten immigration policies. Among its provisions was a measure that allowed the home secretary to strip naturalized citizenship in cases where a person's actions were "prejudicial to national interests." Meanwhile, a report found that immigration to the United Kingdom had increased from 177,000 in 2012 to 212,000 in 2013.

The coalition government's 2014–2015 budget forecast a reduction in the deficit from 6.6 percent of GDP in 2014 to 5.5 percent in 2015. The budget also raised the national minimum wage to $10.33, with lower rates for teens and apprentices.

As the September Scottish independence referendum approached, *Plaid Cymru* called for a greater devolution of powers to Wales to match those exercised by Scotland and Northern Ireland. Party leader Leanne Wood also has demanded a role for Wales in any constitutional amendments that arise from the Scottish referendum. Prior to the referendum, the Chancellor of the Exchequer warned that Scotland would not be able to retain the pound, while EU officials cast doubts on Scotland's ability to quickly gain membership in the organization. Meanwhile, a succession of major corporations, including the Royal Bank of Scotland announced they would relocate operations to England should Scotland become independent. Cameron conducted a major cabinet reshuffle in July as part of an effort to appeal to Scots. Nonetheless, polls on the eve of the referendum showed a closely divided electorate, prompting Cameron to pledge greater devolution of powers if Scots voted to remain part of the United Kingdom. In the September 18 referendum, Scots rejected independence on a vote of 55.3 opposed to 44.7 percent in favor with a record turnout of 84.6 percent.

On November 17, 2014, the general synod of the Church of England approved the consecration of women bishops. (Alison WHITE and Rachel TREWEEK were consecrated in March 2015, becoming the first female bishops in the Church of England.) In December Wales was granted greater autonomy on taxes and revenues.

The government approved the construction of what would be the world's largest wind farm in February 2015. Located in the North Sea off of the coast of Yorkshire, the $8 billion project would have 400 turbines and would be capable of providing 2.5 percent of the UK's electrical needs. In March the government approved the largest increase in the minimum wage since 2008, raising the wage from £6.50 to £6.70.

In local elections in May 2015, the Conservatives won control of 163 councils with 5,521 seats. Labour was second with 74 councils and 2,278 seats, while the Liberal Democrats were third with 4 councils and 658 seats. The UKIP won control of 1 council and 202 seats. The Scottish Parliament approved a measure in June 2015 that lowered the voting age to 16 for local elections and balloting for Scotland's legislature.

A report in August 2015 found that a record 330,000 people had immigrated to the UK over the past year, and that a record 2 million foreign workers were in the country. The report also found that one in eight UK residents, or 8.3 million people, had been born abroad. In November 2015 the government announced that it would raise various taxes by £56 billion over the next five years in order to reduce the deficit.

In February 2016 Cameron set June 23 as the date for the Brexit referendum, and he freed his cabinet to campaign according to their conscience. The Brexit campaign was highly divisive. Although most polls consistently put the "no" vote in the lead, a "yes" to Brexit won with 51.9 percent of the vote. Cameron resigned and was replaced by Theresa May, who began preparations to negotiate the UK withdrawal.

POLITICAL PARTIES

Government Party:

Conservative Party. Although in opposition during 1945–1951, 1964–1970, 1974–1979, and since 1997, the Conservative Party (formally the **Conservative and Unionist Party,** informally the Tory Party) dominated British politics through much of the 20th century, drawing support from business, the middle class, farmers, and a segment of the working class.

In February 1975 Margaret Thatcher, former secretary of state for education and science, was elected party leader, succeeding Edward Heath, under whom the Conservatives had lost three of the previous four elections. Following the party's return to power in May 1979, a rift developed between moderate members (derogatively styled "wets") and those supporting Thatcher's stringent monetary and economic policies; through the 1980s prominent wets were gradually dropped from the government, while others came to terms with "Thatcherism." The party's successful 1983 campaign manifesto called for, among other things, tough laws to curb illegal strikes and privatization of state-owned industry. The emphasis for the June 1987 election was on continued "positive reform" in such areas as fiscal management, control of inflation, greater financial independence for individuals, and improved health care.

Deepening divisions over European policy led in November 1990 to a leadership challenge by former cabinet minister Michael Heseltine, who obtained enough first-round votes to force Thatcher's resignation. But the succession went to the chancellor of the exchequer, John Major, who was regarded as the "Thatcherite" among the three second-round contenders but who quickly jettisoned his predecessor's more controversial policies. The Conservatives fought the April 1992 election on a platform of further privatization (including British Rail and the coal mines), financial accountability in the National Health Service, and freedom of choice in the state education sector. On a vote share of 41.9 percent, the party won its fourth consecutive term, taking 336 (out of 651) seats in the House of Commons, 40 fewer than in 1987.

Postelection difficulties caused a massive slump in the Conservatives' public standing, as evidenced by unprecedented local electoral trouncings in 1993–1994 and the concurrent loss in by-elections of several "safe" Conservative parliamentary seats to the Liberal Democrats. In June 1994 the party also fared badly in European Parliament balloting, falling from 34 to 18 seats (out of 87). Increasing intraparty criticism led Prime Minister Major to place his leadership on the line in June 1995. Reelected the following month with the support of 218 of the 329 Conservative MPs, he proceeded to elevate Heseltine to "number two" status in the Conservative hierarchy.

Additional by-election losses and several defections were followed by another rout in local elections in May 1996, even in the party's southern heartland. By the end of 1996, the government was perilously close to minority status in the House of Commons and reliant on the tactical support of Ulster Unionists to survive until the May 1997 election, at which Conservatives captured only 165 seats. The defeat was so extensive that Major resigned as party leader.

After three rounds of balloting, William Hague, former Welsh secretary, defeated former chancellor of the exchequer and EU advocate Kenneth Clarke to become (at 36) the youngest Conservative leader of the century. The EU issue flared up again later in the year when Clarke, Heseltine, and others objected to the decision by party leaders to maintain opposition to the EU's proposed single currency. Following through on a Hague commitment, in January 1998 the parliamentary delegation approved new procedures for selecting the party leader and challenging the incumbent. Under the new rules all party members, not just MPs, were empowered to vote for the leader.

At the annual party conference in October 1998, Hague reiterated his opposition to a single European currency, citing in support the results of a recently concluded referendum of party members. In February 1999 Heseltine, Clarke, and former prime minister Heath all voiced support for Prime Minister Blair's "national changeover plan" and later joined the cross-party "Britain in Europe" movement.

On December 2, 1998, Hague dismissed the party's leader in the upper house, Viscount CRANBORNE, for failing to consult with him before approving the so-called Cranborne compromise with Labour over the hereditary membership of an interim upper house of Parliament (pending full reform of the House of Lords) and over passage of a proportional representation scheme for the European Parliament elections in June 1999. Subsequently, Hague's apparent willingness to accept proportional representation for some elected bodies as well as an end to hereditary voting rights in a new upper chamber drew fire from hard-line Conservatives, as did his initial support for a statement by (then) deputy leader Peter LILLEY in April 1999 that "the free market has only a limited role in improving public services like health, education, and welfare." The right interpreted the statement as further evidence of a retreat from Thatcherism.

As expected, the party fared poorly at the May 6, 1999, elections for the new Scottish Parliament and Welsh National Assembly, although it registered significant gains in simultaneous nationwide local elections. Conservatives took only 18 seats (all of them "top-up") in the 129-member Scottish legislature and 9 (8 "top-up") in the 60-member Welsh Assembly, but, following up on modest gains made locally in 1998, the party displaced the Liberal Democrats as the second largest party at the local level. A month later Conservatives outpolled Labourites in balloting for the European Parliament, winning 36 seats, more than reversing the party's losses in 1994. The trend continued in 2000, when a March by-election victory gave the party its first directly elected seat in the Scottish Parliament, with further gains recorded in May's local council elections.

In October 1999 Hague, in a retreat from an earlier attempt to delineate a "caring" conservatism, had outlined a "common sense revolution" that marked a clear return to Thatcherism. Over the next six months Hague elaborated on his call for tax cuts; repeated his "sterling guarantee" that the party would not adopt the euro during the next Parliament; took a strong Eurosceptic stance, including support for a proposal that the founding Treaty of Rome be renegotiated to permit members to opt out of EU policies unrelated to trade; accused the Labour administration of being soft on criminals, including sexual offenders; and opposed initiatives on homosexual rights. By mid-2000 the party's standing in public opinion polls had risen dramatically. Prior to the turnaround, many observers had expected Hague's leadership to be challenged by Michael PORTILLO, a former defense secretary under John Major who had returned to the House of Commons with a November 1999 by-election win. Hague, showing new confidence, nevertheless awarded Portillo the key role of shadow chancellor of the exchequer in February 2000.

Despite successes in local council elections, the Conservatives failed to make gains against Labour at the election of June 2001, winning 166 seats and 32.7 percent of the vote in England, Scotland, and Wales. As a consequence, Hague resigned on June 8. Although Portillo was initially regarded as his likely successor, the acrimonious leadership contest ultimately narrowed to a choice between Eurosceptic Iain Duncan SMITH and Kenneth Clarke, with Smith winning a clear victory on September 13. However, dissatisfaction subsequently arose over Duncan Smith's quiet and perceived unsure leadership, and he was forced to resign on October 29, 2003, after losing a vote of confidence among Conservative MPs. He was succeeded by Michael HOWARD on November 6. Howard himself resigned following the Conservative defeat in May 2005, although the Conservatives had improved their seat total to 197 on a vote share of 32.3 percent.

David Cameron, a youthful (39-year-old) "modernizer," was elected chair of the party in December 2005 by a two-to-one margin of party member votes over David DAVIS. Cameron immediately pledged to move the Conservatives toward the center for upcoming elections, promising a "more compassionate party" that would present a much larger percentage of female candidates (only four of the party's current MPs were women) and minority candidates. The new leader also emphasized environmental issues, called upon businesses to address "social concerns," and announced that it would undermine the party's credibility to pledge tax cuts during the next general election considering the national budget situation. Although the party's right wing reportedly objected to many of Cameron's centrist policies, the immediate results of the shift to the center included resounding success for the Conservatives in the May 2006 local elections (40 percent of the vote) and continued improvement in the party's position in public opinion polls. The Conservatives also secured 40 percent of the vote in the May 2007 local balloting and improved its representation by three seats in the London Assembly in May 2008 balloting. In the London balloting its mayoral candidate, Boris JOHNSON, defeated two-term incumbent and Labour candidate Ken Livingstone.

The Conservatives gained majority control of 26 of 27 county councils on a vote share of 38 percent in the June 2009 local elections. The party also won 25 of 69 seats in simultaneous balloting for the European Parliament on a vote share of 27.7 percent. A few weeks later Conservative MP John BERCOW was elected speaker of the House of Commons.

The Conservatives were the leading party in the May 2010 elections for the House of Commons, capturing 306 seats (20 short of a majority) on a vote share of 36.1 percent. Cameron subsequently formed a coalition government with the Liberal Democrats. The party lost 405 councilors in the May 2012 elections, while Labour picked up 823.

Lord STRATHCLYDE abruptly resigned as party leader in the House of Lords in January. After 25 years in the Lords he was reportedly weary of Liberal Democratic peers defecting to Labour on a number of issues.

The Conservatives won 1,116 council seats in the May 2013 local elections, down 335. In the May 2014 local balloting, the Conservatives won 1,364 seats, losing 236. In concurrent balloting for the EU parliament, the Conservatives secured 19 seats, third behind the UKIP and Labour. In an effort to broaden the appeal of the party prior to the Scottish independence referendum, there were a number of leadership changes within the party. Lord HILL OF OAREFORD, the party leader in the House of Lords became an EU commissioner in July. Meanwhile, Sir George YOUNG, the chief government whip, stepped down.

The Conservatives won a majority of 331 seats with 36.8 percent of the vote in the May 2015 parliamentary elections, and Cameron was reappointed prime minister. In November the party was rocked by a "bullying and sleaze" scandal in its youth wing following the suicide of a young conservative activist. Revelations over the scandal led to the resignations of several party officials.

Following the June 2016 Brexit referendum, Cameron resigned and was succeeded by Theresa MAY as party leader and prime minister.

Leaders: Theresa MAY (Prime Minister and Leader of the Party), Philip HAMMOND (Chancellor of the Exchequer), Baroness EVANS OF BOWES PARK (Party Leader in the House of Lords), Patrick MCLOUGHLIN (Chair).

Other UK Parliamentary Parties:

Labour Party. An evolutionary socialist party in basic doctrine and tradition, the Labour Party (founded in 1900) has moved to the center over the past decade but continues to reflect the often conflicting views of trade unions, doctrinaire socialists, and intellectuals, while seeking to broaden its appeal to the middle class and white-collar and managerial personnel. The trade unions traditionally constituted the basis of the party's organized political strength and provided the bulk of its income, although their influence over policy formulation and candidate selection has been reduced in recent years.

After periods of prewar minority government and participation in the wartime coalition, Labour won a large parliamentary majority in 1945 under Clement Attlee and between then and 1951 proceeded to create a comprehensive welfare state, while nationalizing some of the "commanding heights" of the economy. (For more on the history of the party, see the 2014 *Handbook.*) Defeated by the Conservatives in the May 1979 balloting, Labour swung to the left and also changed its leadership selection procedure. Designated party leader in November 1980 under the old system of election by Labour MPs, Michael FOOT, a revered representative of Labour's "old left," presided over changes that in 1981 established an electoral college of affiliated trade unions, Labour MPs, and local constituency parties for selection of the party leader and deputy leader. This change, and a mainstream antipathy to the EC, caused a small number of right-wing, pro-EC MPs to break away in March 1981 and form the Social Democratic Party (see under Liberal Democrat Party, below). Foot fought the June 1983 election on a platform of withdrawal from the EC, unilateral nuclear disarmament, and socialist economic policies. Overwhelmingly defeated, he resigned the Labour leadership and was succeeded in October 1983 by Neil Kinnock. A disciple of Foot, Kinnock contested the June 1987 election on broadly the same policies as in 1983 and also suffered defeat. Thereafter, he initiated a radical policy review, which eventually resulted in Labour's dropping its hostility to the EC and to Britain's nuclear deterrent, while supporting market economics (subject to regulation). Kinnock continued Foot's policy of expelling Trotskyites of the "Militant Tendency."

Kinnock suffered a further election defeat in April 1992, although Labour's tally of 271 seats and a 34.4 percent vote share represented a significant gain over the 1987 results. He thereupon resigned and was succeeded by John Smith, a moderate who continued the "modernizing" thrust, notably by forcing through "one member, one vote" arrangements for the selection of Labour candidates and leaders. Smith led Labour to major advances in local balloting in 1993 and 1994 but died on May 12, 1994. He was succeeded in July, under the new voting arrangements, by another "modernizing" lawyer, Tony Blair. In the interim, Labour had won a major victory in the June European Parliament elections, taking 62 of the 87 UK seats with a 42.7 percent vote share, while the "Blair factor" boosted the party's electoral resurgence in subsequent parliamentary by-elections and in local balloting in May 1995. In a symbolic change to Labour's constitution, a special party conference on April 29 agreed to drop its celebrated "clause 4" commitment to "the common ownership of the means of production, distribution and exchange" in favor of a general assertion of democratic socialist aims and values. The trend toward "modernization" of the party continued with efforts to further reduce the role of union bloc votes. Moreover, Blair moved the party to the center by co-opting Conservative issues—a strategy often compared to that used by Democratic president Bill Clinton against the Republicans in the United States.

Labour's huge victory in the May 1997 balloting for the House of Commons (418 seats) included the election of 101 female Labour MPs, the party having purposefully presented "women only" lists in a number of safe constituencies. Following his accession to the prime ministership, Blair continued to promote "New Labour" in such areas as budget constraint and welfare reform while pressing ahead with promised initiatives on devolution of regional power in Wales and Scotland. Labour's "pro-yes" campaigns on the devolution referenda were conducted in alliance with the Liberal Democrats as well as *Plaid Cymru* in Wales and the Scottish National Party in Scotland.

In May 1998 the party's National Executive Committee (NEC) approved tightened procedures for vetting of parliamentary candidates, the main intention being to weed out those who had voted contrary to party policy or were otherwise deemed unsuitable. Six months later the NEC banned its members from leaking committee discussions and began requiring them to inform the Labour press office before making public comments on NEC matters. The measures offered opponents a further opportunity to label the Blairites as autocratic, as had a decision early in the year to expel two Labour members of the European Parliament, in part for attacking proposed welfare reforms and the leadership's control of the European Parliament candidate list.

Although failing to win a majority in either the new Scottish Parliament or the Welsh National Assembly, Labour emerged from the May 6, 1999, elections as the plurality party in both, taking 56 of 129 seats in Scotland and 28 of 60 in Wales. It entered into a coalition agreement on May 13 with the Scottish Liberal Democrats but in Wales chose to form a minority government under UK Secretary of State for Wales Alun MICHAEL. In a heated battle, Michael, relying on Prime Minister Blair's support, had defeated Rhodri MORGAN for leadership of Welsh Labour three months earlier. A year later, however, on February 9, 2000, Michael resigned as Welsh first minister shortly before the assembly passed a no-confidence motion, 31–27, largely because of his failure to distance himself from London. On February 15 the assembly confirmed Morgan as his successor. (The title of the office was subsequently changed to first secretary.)

At the European Parliament balloting of June 1999 Labour suffered its first major defeat since Blair's assumption of power, taking only 28 percent of the vote and 29 seats, a loss of 33. The defeat was largely explained by voters' opposition to Labour's pro-euro policy.

On February 20, 2000, Blair's preferred candidate for the new London mayoralty, former minister of health Frank DOBSON, won a narrow victory in a party electoral college, defeating leftist MP Ken LIVINGSTONE. The latter won 60 percent support from London party members and 72 percent from labor unions and societies, but Dobson prevailed on the strength of 86 percent support from the third, equally weighted electoral college bloc: Labor MPs, members of the European Parliament, and candidates for the Greater London Authority (GLA). To the chagrin of the party hierarchy, Livingstone ran as an independent and won the election on May 4. Despite Labour's previous strength in the capital, the party won only 9 seats on the 25-member GLA, equaling the Conservative total. In a further setback on May 4, Labour lost control of 16 of the 73 local councils it had previously held.

At the same time, intraparty disputes continued to surface over Prime Minister Blair's "command and control" managerial style (dubbed "control freakery" by opponents), his reliance on a small circle of advisers that critics dubbed "Tony's cronies," and his centrist "New Labour" programs. Peter KILFOYLE, who had resigned as under secretary of state for defense in January 2000, announced in February that he was forming a "heartlands group" of Labour MPs committed to the party's core supporters and traditional, left-of-center policies. Blair nevertheless remained firmly in control of Labour, which handily won the June 2001 House of Commons election, capturing 412 seats on a slightly reduced vote share of 42 percent.

The May 2005 poll was won by Labour with a Commons majority (55 percent) reduced for a number of reasons, including widespread disagreement over constitutional revision, Britain's role in the EU, and Blair's support of the U.S. position in Iraq. The prime minister subsequently faced growing criticism from left-wing backbenchers opposed to his ongoing reformist agenda. Following Labour's dismal performance in the May 2006 local elections (third place with only 26 percent of the vote), calls intensified for Blair to determine a timetable for his resignation in favor of Gordon Brown (the chancellor of the exchequer). At summer's end, Blair announced that he would step aside within a year. Eight months later, on the heels of another setback for Labour in the May 2007 local elections as well as in the Welsh Assembly and Scottish Parliament elections the same day, Blair said he would resign as party leader and prime minister by the end of June. By mid-May it was clear Gordon Brown would be the only leadership candidate with the required nomination support among MPs. Brown accepted the leader position unopposed at a party conference in Manchester on June 24. The same conference elected Harriet Harman as deputy leader over five others, including the odds-makers' preconference favorite and presumed Blair favorite, Alan JOHNSON. Brown was sworn in as prime minister on June 27.

The party subsequently found itself in the political doldrums. It lost a series of by-elections in early 2008, some in what had been strongly pro-Labour constituencies. The party was generally able to hold its own in the May 2008 London Assembly elections. However, its mayoralty candidate (Ken Livingstone, a two-term incumbent who had been expelled from the party in 2002 for his renegade run in 2000, only to be reinstated in the run-up to the 2004 mayoralty balloting) lost his reelection bid. By summer Labour's support had declined to 24 percent in public opinion polls, and it continued to fare poorly in by-elections. Plotting among Labour backbenchers to depose Brown as party leader subsequently became increasingly public, but the prime minister's standing rebounded in the wake of the support he received, at home and abroad, for his handling of the financial credit crisis.

Public discussion of removing Brown arose again in mid-2009 in the wake of a major scandal in the House of Commons over dubious expense account payments to MPs and the poor performance by Labour in the simultaneous balloting in June for local councils and the European Parliament. (Labour finished third in the local elections in the popular vote and won just 178 of the more than 2,300 seats on the councils, losing more than 60 percent of the seats it had previously held. The party also finished third in the European Parliament elections with 15.7 percent of the vote, good for only 13 seats [down from 22.6 percent of the vote and 19 seats in 2004].) Brown also faced the resignation of several cabinet ministers and outright revolt among some Labour members, although his leadership position remained intact at the September party conference.

The party was unable to overcome the decline in public favor before the May 2010 general election. Labour won just 29 percent of the vote in the House of Commons (its second-worst showing since rising to the status of one of two major British parties in the 1920s) and secured 258 seats. Five days after the election Brown resigned his premiership and his position as leader of the party. He was succeeded as leader on an interim basis by Harriet Harman until the party could hold an election. Four nominations for the leadership position were entered in late May, and, after a summer of maneuvering, Ed Miliband, a minister in Brown's former cabinet, emerged the winner in the final tally by edging out his brother, David MILIBAND (also a cabinet minister under Brown), by one percentage point in the fourth round of balloting.

Labour performed very well in the May 2012 council elections, taking 38 percent nationally compared to 31 percent for the Conservatives.

Labour picked up an additional 291 council seats in the May 2013 local elections. In the following year's local balloting, the party gained 324 additional seats. In concurrent EU polling, Labour was first with 24 seats.

The party lost the May 2015 parliamentary elections, securing 30.5 percent of the vote and 232 seats. Miliband resigned in May, and Labour's deputy leader Harriet HARMAN became interim chair. Jeremy CORBYN, a leading figure of the extreme left wing of the party, won a four-person contest to replace Miliband in September. Corbyn's selection to lead the party exposed a divide between the moderate and leftist wings of the party as centrists resigned leadership positions in the party. An ardent antiwar activist and opponent of nuclear weapons, Corbyn was forced to allow Labour members of parliament a free vote over the December 2015 authorization to use military force in Syria in the face of a revolt over his efforts to oppose the measure.

Corbyn survived a leadership challenge in September 2016 following a June no-confidence vote by Labour Party parliamentarians, 172–40. Corbyn went on to win the general party leadership election with 61.8 percent of the vote to Owen SMITH's 38.2 percent.

Leaders: Jeremy CORBYN (Party Leader), Tom WATSON (Deputy Leader), Baroness SMITH of BASILDON (Shadow Leader in the House of Lords), Iain McNicol (Secretary General).

Co-operative Party. Founded in 1917, the Co-operative Party operates largely through some 200 affiliated cooperative societies throughout Britain. Under a 1927 agreement with the Labour Party, it cosponsors candidates at local, national, and European elections, and has 27 Labour Co-ops currently in Westminster.

Leaders: Gareth THOMAS (Chair), Karin CHRISTIANSEN (General Secretary).

Liberal Democrats. A federal organization of largely autonomous English, Welsh, and Scottish parties, the Liberal Democrats (also referenced as the **Liberal Democratic Party**) formed by merger of the Liberal and Social Democratic parties, as approved at conferences of the two groups on January 23 and 31, 1988, respectively. Initially called the **Social and Liberal Democratic Party** (SLDP), it adopted the shorter name in October 1989.

Reduced to a minority position by the rise of Labour after World War I, the Liberal Party (founded in 1859) continued to uphold the traditional values of European liberalism and sought, without notable success, to attract dissident elements in both of the main parties by its nonsocialist and reformist principles. Despite having won only 13 seats in the election of October 1974, the party played a crucial role in 1977–1978 by entering into a parliamentary accord with Labour, thus, for the first time in nearly 50 years, permitting a major party to continue in office by means of third-party support. In September 1982 the party voted to form an electoral alliance with the **Social Democratic Party** (SDP), which yielded an aggregate of 23 parliamentary seats in the 1983 election and 27 in 1987.

The SDP had been formally organized on March 26, 1981, by the "gang of four" right-wing Labour dissidents (Roy JENKINS, Dr. David OWEN, William RODGERS, and Shirley WILLIAMS), who strongly objected to the party's swing to unilateralist and anti-European positions. However, after a series of by-election successes in 1981–1982, the SDP lost impetus. Objecting to the proposed merger with the Liberals after the 1987 election, Owen resigned from the SDP leadership in August 1987 and in February 1988 announced the formation of a "new" SDP, which was ultimately dissolved in June 1990. Meanwhile, in July 1988 the merged Liberal Democrats had elected Paddy ASHDOWN as its leader.

At the April 1992 election the Liberal Democrats won 20 seats, which rose to 25 as a result of subsequent by-election victories. The May 1995 and May 1996 local elections saw the Liberal Democrats overtake the Conservatives as the second party (after Labour) in local government, its greatest strength being mainly in the south and west of England. In the May 1997 general election the party increased its representation to 46 seats, adding another with a by-election win in November. Having announced that it would cooperate with the new government, it subsequently agreed to participate in a special cabinet committee established by Prime Minister Blair for regular consultation in areas of "mutual interest."

In May 1999 the party finished fourth in balloting for the new Scottish and Welsh legislatures, but its 17 seats in the Scottish Parliament enabled it to emerge as the junior partner in a coalition administration in Scotland with Labour. As part of the agreement, David STEEL, former leader of the Liberal Democrats, was chosen to be speaker of the Scottish Parliament. In the May local council elections, Conservative gains dropped the Liberal Democrats back to third place in terms of total local seats.

On August 9, 1999, Charles KENNEDY was elected party leader, Ashdown having announced in January that he would step down following the June European Parliament elections. Under a proportional representation system, the Liberal Democrats saw their European Parliament seat total rise to ten, eight more than in 1994, despite a reduced vote share.

In March 2000 the party threatened to stop cooperating with the government if Labour reneged on its campaign pledge to pursue adoption of proportional voting for the House of Commons. The party also remained firmly committed to the EU and adoption of the euro.

In October 2000 the Liberal Democrats joined Labour in forming a coalition government in Wales. At the June 2001 election for the House of Commons, the party gained 6 seats, for a total of 52, although in local elections it lost the 2 local councils it had controlled. At the 2005 poll, the party gained 10 lower house seats for a total of 62 on a vote share of 22.1 percent.

Kennedy resigned as chair on January 7, 2006, after acknowledging an ongoing struggle with alcoholism. Walter Menzies ("Ming") CAMPBELL, a former Olympic sprinter and Scottish MP, became interim leader the same day and won the March 2 leadership contest in a three-way race. The Liberal Democrats subsequently remained opposed to British participation in the war in Iraq and expressed concern about the effect on civil rights of recent antiterrorism initiatives. The Liberal Democrats moved into second place (on a 27 percent vote share) behind the Conservatives in the May 2006 local elections.

Campbell resigned as party leader on October 15, 2007, after it became clear that new Prime Minister Brown did not intend to call for early elections. By that time, the Liberal Democrats were experiencing a decline in popularity polls, and party members had publicly expressed worries that Campbell's advanced age would be a detriment in leading the party into an election that was still two years away. Vincent Cable served as interim leader until Nick Clegg was elected as the party's new leader in December in a closely contested contest with Chris HUHNE.

The party suffered a setback in the May 2008 London Assembly elections, winning just 11.4 percent of the vote and three seats (a loss of two). Its candidate for mayor finished a distant third, with 9.6 percent of the first-preference votes. Although the party finished second in the June 2009 local elections with 28 percent of the vote, its seat total declined as it lost seats to the Conservatives. In concurrent balloting for the European Parliament, the Liberal Democrats finished fourth with 13.7 percent of the vote and 11 seats (down 1 from 2004).

The Liberal Democrats won 57 seats in the May 2010 elections for the House of Commons on 23 percent of the vote. The party subsequently joined a new coalition government (which included five Liberal Democrats) led by the Conservatives' David Cameron. The party lost 336 councilors in the May 2012 elections, dropping below 3,000 councilors for the first time in its history.

Energy secretary Chris Huhne was forced to resign on February 2, 2010, following allegations that he had conspired to have his wife take responsibility for a speeding ticket. The first cabinet minister to resign due to a criminal charge since 1721, Huhne was sentenced to eight months in prison in March 2013.

The party won 352 council seats in the May 2013 local elections, a loss of 124 seats.

Two factions emerged at the annual party conference in September. One faction, led by Clegg, wants to continue the alliance with the Conservatives for the 2015 parliamentary election and beyond. The other faction, led by Business, Innovations, and Skills Minister Vince CABLE, argued that the party should distance itself from the Tories prior to balloting in 2015.

A party committee suspended former Liberal Democrat chief executive Lord RENNARD after he refused to apologize to four women who accused him of sexual harassment. The episode exacerbated tensions within the party, with leading supporters of Rennard calling for his reinstatement. Reports characterized the scandal as the worst faced by the party since its creation.

In local balloting in May 2014, the Liberal Democrats lost 310 seats, falling to 427. Meanwhile, in EU polling, the party lost ten seats, securing only one. Following these losses there was an abortive attempt to replaced Clegg with Cable. The leader of the effort, Lord OAKESHOTT subsequently resigned from the party.

The party lost heavily in the May 2015 parliamentary balloting, winning just 7.9 percent of the vote and eight seats. Clegg resigned as leader of the party in July and was replaced by Tim FARRON.

Leaders: Tim FARRON (Leader of the Party), Lord NEWBY (Party Leader in the House of Lords), Baroness BRINTON (President).

Scottish National Party (SNP). Founded in 1934, the SNP advocates Scottish independence within the EU. At the 1979 election it lost 9 of its 11 seats in the House of Commons and since then has managed to win no more than 6. The SNP aligned with Labour and the Liberal Democrats in support of a "yes" vote in the September 1997 referendum on creation of a Scottish Parliament. (For more on the history of the party, see the 2014 *Handbook.*)

At the party's annual conference in September 1999 party leader Alex Salmond predicted that Scotland would be independent by 2007, and in March 2000 the SNP put forward an independence referendum plan that it would pursue if it won the next Scottish election. Four months later Salmond announced that he would resign as SNP leader in September, at which time the party elected John SWINNEY, his deputy, to succeed him. Swinney had been challenged on the left by Alex NEIL.

At the June 2001 UK general election the SNP retained 5 of the 6 seats it had previously held. Amid criticism for ineffective election leadership and arguably disappointing results, Swinney resigned in June 2004. Salmond returned as leader following his election on September 3. The SNP returned to a representation of 6 in the House of Commons in 2005 on a vote share of 17.7 percent of the votes cast in Scotland, and the SNP became the largest party in the 129-seat Scottish Parliament when it won 47 seats in the May 3, 2007, balloting for that body. Salmond was elected first minister of Scotland on May 16 and was sworn in as leader of a minority government the next day.

The SNP retained its six seats in the House of Commons in 2010, securing 19.9 percent of the vote in Scottish constituencies. As 2010 drew to a close, Salmond continued to encourage the UK Parliament to make provisions for a referendum on possible additional devolution of powers to the Scottish Parliament, possibly even independence for Scotland. In the May 2011 elections the SNP gained its first ever majority in the Scottish parliament, prompting Salmond to schedule a referendum on Scottish independence for September 18, 2014. In October 2012 the SNP voted 394–365 to end its traditional opposition to an independent Scotland joining NATO.

After Scots voted to remain part of the United Kingdom in the September 18, 2014, referendum, Salmond resigned as first minister of Scotland and did not seek reelection as SNP leader. Nicola STURGEON was declared the sole candidate for leader of SNP, and succeeded Alex Salmond as SNP leader and first minister in November. Sturgeon pledged not to call another referendum on Scottish independence unless polls indicated public support at more than 60 percent.

In the May 2015 parliamentary elections, the SNP won 4.7 percent of the vote, but won 56 of the 59 Scottish seats. The victory came at the expense of the Labour Party, which was decimated in Scotland. In balloting for the Scottish Parliament in May 2016, the SNP lost its majority, winning 63 seats with 46.5 percent of the vote. Sturgeon formed a minority SNP government.

After the Brexit referendum, Sturgeon issued new calls for a referendum on Scottish independence.

Leaders: Nicola STURGEON (Party Leader and First Minister of Scotland), Angus ROBERTSON (Deputy Leader).

Plaid Cymru (literally, "Party of Wales," usually referred to by its Welsh name, or informally as the **Welsh Nationalist Party**). Founded in 1925, *Plaid Cymru* sought full self-government for Wales as a democratic socialist republic. In May 1987 it entered into a parliamentary alliance with the SNP to work for constitutional, economic, and social reform in both regions. It elected four MPs in 1992, when it gained 8.9 percent of the Welsh vote (partly through an alliance in six constituencies with the Welsh Green Party). In 1997 the party retained the four seats, and it joined the Labour Party and the Liberal Democrats in urging passage of the September referendum regarding establishment of a Welsh regional assembly.

Plaid Cymru finished second to Labour in balloting for the Welsh National Assembly on May 6, 1999, taking a 28.4 percent first-vote share and winning a total of 17 seats (9 constituency, 8 "top-up"). Labour subsequently backed the party's nominee as speaker of the new legislature, Lord Dafydd ELIS-THOMAS. In June 1999 *Plaid Cymru* won 2 seats in the European Parliament.

In May 2000, citing health reasons, the party's president, Dafydd WIGLEY, resigned. Ieuan Wyn Jones handily won election as his successor on August 3, and at the party's September annual conference he set 2003 as the target date for supplanting Labour as the foremost party in the Welsh National Assembly. At the June 2001 election for the House of Commons, *Plaid Cymru* retained its four seats. Three months later, at its annual conference, the party formally ended its demand for Welsh independence.

At the May 1, 2003, assembly election the *Plaid Cymru* lost 5 of its 17 seats and barely kept its position as the official opposition. Jones resigned as president and assembly leader within a week of the election. Folk singer and politician Dafydd IWAN was subsequently elected party president, with Jones winning reelection as assembly leader. *Plaid Cymru*'s representation in the House of Commons dropped to 3 in 2005 on a vote share of 12.6 percent of the votes in Wales. Jones subsequently warned party members at the *Plaid Cymru* annual conference that internal squabbling was compromising electoral effectiveness.

In the May 3, 2007, balloting for the Welsh assembly, *Plaid Cymru* improved by 3 seats to a total of 15. The party joined Labour in a coalition government that was installed on May 25, after negotiations had prompted a commitment from Labour to hold a referendum on *Plaid Cymru*'s proposal for additional law-making powers to be given to the assembly.

The party retained its three seats in the UK parliamentary balloting in May 2010 with an 11.3 percent vote share across Welsh constituencies.

A month later, Iwan announced he would resign as president; he was succeeded by Jill Evans, who won the position in a June party vote. In June 2013 Jones resigned and was replaced by Leanne Wood. The UK government held a referendum on March 4, 2011, asking whether to increase the Welsh assembly's law-making powers on 20 devolved areas, including health and education. Some 63.5 percent of voters favored the motion. In 2013 the position of party president was abolished.

In the 2014 EU elections, former party president Evans won the grouping's sole seat. *Plaid Cymru* won 0.6 percent of the vote in the May 2015 parliamentary elections and 3 seats. In the May 2016 Welsh assembly balloting, the party was second with 12 seats.

Leaders: Leanne WOOD (Party Leader), Dafydd Trystan DAVIES (Chair), Dwyfor MEIRIONNYDD (UK Parliamentary Leader).

Green Party of England and Wales. Organized in 1973 as the Ecology Party, the Greens adopted their present name in 1985. (The semiautonomous Welsh branch is the **Welsh Green Party** [*Plaid Werdd Cym*].) The party addresses human rights issues in addition to problems affecting the environment.

The Greens have consistently polled less than 1 percent of the vote for the House of Commons. In June 1999, however, the Greens won two seats in the European Parliament on a 6.3 percent vote share. In November 1999 Lord BEAUMONT of Whitley, a life peer in the House of Lords, resigned from the Liberal Democrats and joined the Greens as their sole member in the UK Parliament. The party secured no lower house seats on a 1 percent vote share in 2005, and the death of Lord Beaumont in April 2008 meant the party went unrepresented in either chamber of parliament between 2008 and 2010. However, the party retained its two seats in the London Assembly in 2008 and its two seats (on a vote share of 8.6 percent) in the European Parliament in 2009. Also in 2008, the party switched from a collective leadership to a single leader, Caroline LUCAS. In the 2010 UK general election, Lucas became the first Green candidate to gain a seat in the UK parliament.

The Greens won 22 seats in the May 2013 local elections, adding 5 new constituencies. The Greens did even better in the 2014 local balloting, winning 38 seats. In concurrent EU elections, the party secured 3 seats.

In the May 2015 balloting, the Greens won 3.8 percent of the vote and one seat. The party's 1.1 million votes were the most it had ever received. Nonetheless, party leader Natalie BENNETT did not seek reelection as chair of the Greens. Instead, former leader Lucas and Jonathan BARTLEY were elected as cochairs of the party in September 2016.

Leaders: Caroline LUCAS and Jonathan BARTLEY (Cochairs); Amelia WOMACK (Deputy Leader).

UK Independence Party (UKIP). The UKIP was created in 1993 by Alan SKED and members of the Anti-Federalist League (founded 1991) to oppose what it saw as the surrender of British sovereignty implicit in the terms of the EU's Maastricht Treaty; the party urged withdrawal from the EU and warned of the dangers posed by unrestricted immigration. It failed to win any parliamentary seats in 1997 but won 7 percent of the vote and 3 seats in the European Parliament balloting in June 1999. It fared even better in the European poll of June 2004, winning 12 of 75 seats in a third-place showing. Two members of the UKIP were elected to the London Assembly in 2004, but they subsequently defected to Veritas, a new party dedicated to the restoration of probity in public life, which had been founded in January 2005 by the UKIP's most celebrated MP, former talk show host Robert KILROY-SILK. Following the dissolution of Veritas, the two members of the assembly formed their own **One London** party. (They lost their seats in the assembly in 2008.)

In January 2007 three Conservative Party members of the House of Lords defected to the UKIP and thus gave the party its first parliamentary representation. The party claimed one seat in the House of Commons in April 2008 when Conservative member Bob SPINK declared his membership in the UKIP.

The UKIP recorded its best-ever electoral showing by finishing second (behind only the Conservatives) in the June 2009 balloting for the European Parliament, winning 13 seats on a vote share of 16.5 percent. However, the members of the European Parliament (MEPs) have missed one-third of the votes in Strasbourg. In November Lord Pearson (Malcom Pearson) was elected as the new party leader, succeeding Nigel FARAGE, who had stepped down as party leader to concentrate on his membership in the European Parliament. Subsequently, Lord Pearson offered to keep the UKIP out of the general election due in 2010 if the Conservatives would pledge in writing that, if elected, they would hold a national referendum on the EU's Lisbon Treaty. However, Conservative leader David Cameron rejected the offer.

The UKIP vigorously contested the May 2010 general election, fielding 572 candidates for the House of Commons, and recorded its best performance to date with 3.1 percent of the vote. In the process, party leader Lord Pearson did an about-face on his challenge to the Conservatives by campaigning on behalf of some of their candidates. He resigned his UKIP position in the summer, saying he was not cut out for party politics. Nigel Farage won a three-way contest for the leadership post on November 5.

The UKIP surged in popularity in 2013, and the party won 147 local council seats in May. In a huge public gaffe, MEP Godfrey BLOOM referred to a group of women's activists as "sluts" during the party's annual conference. He was forced to quit the party's delegation in the European Parliament. Farage blasted Bloom for "destroying UKIP's national conference."

In 2014 the party continued to gain popularity, winning 161 seats in local balloting and placing first in concurrent EU polling with 24 seats. Two Conservative MPs defected to the UKIP, triggering by-elections. One, Douglas CARSWELL, subsequently won a by-election in October, becoming the first elected UKIP MP.

The UKIP received 12.7 percent of the vote in the May 2015 elections. However, it only secured Carswell's seat. Farage was third in his district, and after the Brexit referendum, Farage announced his resignation on July 4. Diane JAMES was chosen to succeed him but resigned after little more than two weeks in office. Farage returned as acting leader on October 18, and was then replaced by Paul NUTTALL on November 28.

Leaders: Paul NUTTALL (Leader), Peter WHITTLE (Deputy Leader).

Note: For information on the Democratic Unionist Party, *Sinn Féin*, the Social Democratic and Labour Party, and the Alliance Party of Northern Ireland (all represented in the UK House of Commons), see Political Parties and Groups in the entry on United Kingdom: Northern Ireland.

Nonparliamentary Parties:

British National Party (BNP). The BNP was founded in 1982 by a breakaway faction of the fascist National Front (NF) and advocates on behalf of "Native British" under attack from immigrants. In early 2006 BNP leader Nick Griffin was acquitted of charges of inciting racial hatred related to a speech he gave at a party conference in 2004 in which he reportedly made strongly anti-Muslim remarks. In the 2005 general election the BNP's 119 candidates secured 0.7 percent of the nationwide vote, up from 0.5 percent in 2001. The BNP doubled its seats in the local elections held in May 2006, performing well in the white working-class areas of east London, and held its own in the May 2007 local elections. The BNP claimed its first seat on the London Assembly when it won 5.4 percent of the party-list voting in the May 2008 balloting. In June 2009 the party won its first seats above the local level, securing two seats on 6.2 percent of the nationwide vote for the European Parliament. The Equality and Human Rights Commission sued the party in 2009 for violating race relation laws for its "Whites only" membership, employment, and services policies. The party dropped the rule because it could not afford a legal battle, but the EHRC says the policy continues in practice. Although the party fielded 338 candidates in the 2010 general election, no BNP candidate received as much as 15 percent of the vote in any constituency. It lost its seat on the London Assembly in the 2012 election. Andrew BRONS, one of two BNP MEPs, resigned from the party in late 2012, citing personal disagreements with Griffin. The BNP lost one of two seats it contested in local balloting in May 2014, while the party lost both its EU seats in concurrent elections. In response to the party's poor performance, Griffin resigned in July and was replaced on an acting basis by Adam Walker.

Leader: Adam WALKER (Acting Chair).

Respect Party. Respect was launched in January 2004 by MP George Galloway, who had been expelled from the Labour Party in October 2003 after being found guilty of inciting UK troops in Iraq to disobey orders. Galloway, running as the candidate of **Respect–The Unity Coalition,** was reelected in 2005 by a constituency heavily populated by immigrants.

The party allows its members to hold memberships in other parties, most notably, until late 2007, the Socialist Workers Party. A schism emerged over Galloway's charge that the party was too disorganized to be effective, which drew the countercharge that he was willing to sacrifice principle for election. In the May 2008 London Assembly elections, the two factions ran on different lists, and both received less than 2.5 percent of the vote. Galloway decided to contest the 2010 balloting for the House of Commons in a new constituency, with another Respect member standing in his former constituency. Both candidates finished third in their respective contests. Galloway won a March 29, 2012, parliamentary by-election in Bradford Wells, a northern England constituency long regarded as a Labour stronghold. The party ran 12 candidates in the May 3, 2012, council elections, winning 5 seats.

Salma YAQOOB, the party's highly visible chair, resigned in September 2012 due to conflict with Galloway that was sparked by his comments about sexual assault charges levied against Julian Assage. The party lost both its seats on local councils that were contested in the 2014 elections. The party received only ten votes in the 2015 balloting.

Leader: George GALLOWAY (Founder).

The 2010 and 2015 general elections were contested by more than 100 parties, with only 10 receiving 0.5 percent or more of the nationwide vote and with many parties fielding a candidate in but a single constituency. Covering the full political spectrum, the small parties highlighted below are among those recently active.

On the left, the **Socialist Labour Party** (SLP) was launched in 1996 by miners' union leader Arthur SCARGILL to protest the perceived rightward drift of the Labour Party. The more militant **Socialist Workers' Party** (SWP), dating from 1950, has recently withdrawn its traditional support for Labour and until recently formed part of Respect–The Unity Coalition (see Respect Party, above). Earlier, the SWP had formed an electoral coalition (the London Socialist Alliance) with the **Communist Party of Britain** (CPB) to support maverick Ken Livingstone's successful campaign for the capital's mayoralty in 2000. In 1997 the **Militant Labour** (ML, originally the Militant Tendency within the Labour Party) founded the Trotskyite **Socialist Party** (SP), led by Peter TAAFFE. An ML minority, led by the group's founder, Ted GRANT, remained within Labour as the Socialist Appeal, while the ML's Scottish branch, led by Tommy SHERIDAN, helped form a Scottish Socialist Alliance that, in turn, in 1998 established the autonomous **Scottish Socialist Party** (SSP), which is led jointly by Colin FOX and Frances CURRAN. In 1999 the SSP took one seat (won by Sheridan) in the new Scottish Parliament, and increased its numbers to six in the 2003 Scottish Parliament elections. However, it won no seats in 2007. The **Scottish Green Party** (SGP), led by Clir Martha WARDROP (co-conveners), also won one seat in 1999, increased its representation to six in 2003, but fell back to two seats following the 2007 balloting. It currently has two members in the Scottish Parliament and 14 councilors. The **Socialist Party of Great Britain** (SPGB), a non-Leninist Marxist group founded in 1904, continues to maintain branches throughout the country but did not have a candidate in the 2005 or the 2010 UK general elections. Prior to the 2010 election, Dave NELLIST and Bob CROW organized the **Trade Unionist and Socialist Coalition** (TUSC), comprised of the SWP, SP, **Solidarity: Scotland's Socialist Movement**, and **Socialist Resistance.** TUSC also ran candidates in local elections in 2011 and 2012, receiving an average of 6.2 percent of the vote in 2012.

On the extreme left, the CPB, currently led by Robert GRIFFITHS, split in 1988 from the historical **Communist Party of Great Britain** (CPGB) to protest the CPGB's conversion to Eurocommunism. The CPGB was founded in 1920, briefly enjoyed parliamentary representation, and was influential in the trade union movement. However, it is now defunct, most of its remaining membership having reorganized in 1992 as the moderate **Democratic Left** (DL). The DL presented itself as an association rather than a party and so did not contest elections. In 1999, under the leadership of Nina TEMPLE, the DL membership voted to reorganize as the nondoctrinaire New Times Network. Other CPBG remnants include the Marxist-Leninist **New Communist Party** (NCP), formed by dissidents in 1977, and the **Communist Party of Scotland** (CPS). (Although the CPGB continues to pursue a reforging of the original CPGB, it is not officially registered as a party. Neither is the NCP or CPS.) The **Workers' Revolutionary Party** (WRP) has also undergone extensive splintering; the faction that has retained the WRP name is led by Sheila TORRANCE. A WRP offshoot includes the Trotskyite **Socialist Equality Party** (SEP, formerly the International Communist Party), which is led by Christopher Howard MARSDEN and serves as the British branch of the International Committee of the Fourth International. Other small groups include the Trotskyite **Alliance for Workers' Liberty** (AWL), led by Cathy NUGENT; the **Revolutionary Communist Group** (RCG); and the **Revolutionary Communist Party of Great Britain** (Marxist-Leninist), led by Chris COLEMAN.

On the extreme right, the **National Front** (NF), a fascist grouping founded in 1967, won a number of local council seats in the 1970s but largely disintegrated thereafter. Most of the NF defected in 1982 to what is now the BNP (above). In 1995 most remaining NF members regrouped under Ian ANDERSON as the **National Democrats** (ND). Under the leadership of Thomas HOLMES, the rump NF contested 17 constituencies in 2010. Founded in 1990 as the **Third Way** and registered in 2006 as the **National Liberal Party–the Third Way,** the party has roots in the NF but denounced national socialism in favor of worker participation in industry, adoption of Swiss-style democratic reforms, immigration restrictions, withdrawal from the EU and other multilateral groups, and an ecological agenda. The party is currently led by Daniel KERR. Extremist groups include the violent **Combat 18**.

Other formations include the **Christian People's Alliance** (CPA), launched in May 1999 as a Christian Democratic party and chaired by Alan CRAIG; the **Liberal Party** (currently led by Rob WHEWAY), which was formed by those who opposed the conversion of the historic party into what became the Liberal Democrats; ***Mebyon Kernow*** (literally, "Sons of Cornwall"), a Cornish separatist group formed in 1951 and currently led by Dick COLE; the **Islamic Party of Britain,** founded in 1989 and led by David Musa PIDCOCK; and the **Legalize Cannabis Alliance** (LCA), which voted in 2006 to deregister and continue as a pressure group. In addition, the anti-euro Democracy Movement, a self-described "non-party movement" led by Robin BIRLEY, was organized in 1999 as successor to the Referendum Movement, which began in 1994 as the Referendum Party of the late James GOLDSMITH. A new anti-EU grouping, **An Independence from Europe,** formed in 2013, secured 1.7 percent of the vote in the 2014 EU balloting.

Among the numerous British fringe groups are the **Natural Law Party** (NLP), founded in 1992 by practitioners of Transcendental Meditation and led by Dr. Geoffrey CLEMENTS (the NLP is no longer registered as a party); the **Official Monster Raving Loony Party,** led by Alan (Howling Laud) HOPE since the 1999 suicide of the party's founder, former rock singer (Screaming Lord) David SUTCH; and the **Make Politicians History Party** (led by Ronnie CARROLL), a successor to the individualist Rainbow Dream Ticket Party, which advocated abolishing Parliament and instituting government by home-based electronic referenda (the party voluntarily deregistered in 2009).

LEGISLATURE

The **Parliament** serves as legislative authority for the entire UK. Meeting in Westminster (London) with the queen as its titular head, until November 1999 it consisted of a partly hereditary, partly appointed House of Lords and an elected House of Commons (the real locus of power). Under the House of Lords Act 1999 the membership of the upper house was restructured (see below).

Following voter approval at separate devolutionary referendums held in Scotland and Wales in 1997, the UK Parliament passed legislation in 1998 that authorized creation of a Scottish Parliament and a Welsh National Assembly. Elections for both legislatures were held for the first time on May 6, 1999. Creation of a New Northern Ireland Assembly was approved by referendum on May 22, 1998, with the initial election occurring a month later, on June 25 (see the Northern Ireland entry). All three of the new legislative bodies are elected for four-year terms under a proportional representation system that combines single-member constituencies and "top-up" seats drawn from party lists.

House of Lords. Before reforms were instituted in 1999, the House of Lords had 1,330 members, of whom 751 were hereditary peers, either by succession or of first creation. The remaining members included the 2 archbishops and 24 other senior bishops of the Church of England, serving and retired Lords of Appeal in Ordinary (who constituted the nation's highest body of civil and criminal appeal), and other life peers. Only about 200 to 300 members of the House of Lords attended sessions with any degree of regularity. The House of Lords Act 1999 abolished the hereditary component and replaced it on an interim basis, pending more comprehensive reform, by 92 ex-hereditary members: 75 elected by all the hereditaries according to a predetermined party ratio, 15 house officers elected by the full membership, and 2 appointed royal office holders (the Earl Marshall and the Lord Great Chamberlain). The 75 peers elected on October 29 on a party basis comprised 42 Conservatives, 28 "crossbenchers" (independents), 3 Liberal Democrats, and 2 Labour members. The collateral election of house officers added 9 Conservatives, 2 Labour peers, 2 Liberal Democrats, and 2 crossbenchers.

Following the reforms, the full interim chamber had 670 members. The subsequent naming of new life peers—most of them Labour supporters, in an effort by the government to achieve political parity—plus the naming in April 2001 of 15 independent "people's peers" by an appointments commission, brought the total to 715 as of July 31, 2001. As of December 2016, the total current and qualified members was 809: Conservative Party, 256 seats; Labour Party, 204; "crossbenchers," 180; Liberal Democrats, 103; Democratic Unionist Party, 3; United Kingdom Independence Party, 3; Ulster Unionist Party, 2; Independent Labour, 2; Green Party, 1; Independent Social Democrat, 1; Independent Ulster Unionist, 1; *Plaid Cymru,* 1; archbishops and bishops, 26; and independents, 26. Thirty-six were on leave of absence or disqualified as senior members of the judiciary or the European Parliament.

On June 28, 2006, the House of Lords for the first time elected its own leader as part of broader governmental changes proposed by the prime minister in 2003. The new Lord Speaker, who may serve a maximum of two five-year terms, assumed (effective July 4) the leadership role previously exercised by the Lord Chancellor (the prime minister's appointee and a member of the cabinet). Baroness Hayman of the Labour Party was elected as the first Lord Speaker, and, following the custom of the speaker of the House of Commons, she subsequently withdrew her party affiliation. The current incumbent, Baron Norman FOWLER, of the Conservative Party, assumed the speakership on September 1, 2016.

Lord Speaker: Baron FOWLER.

House of Commons. Following the general election of May 7, 2015, the House of Commons consisted of 650 members directly elected from single-member constituencies for terms of five years, subject to earlier dissolution. The strength of the parties was as follows: Conservative Party, 330 seats; Labour Party, 232; Scottish National Party, 50; Liberal Democrats, 8; Democratic Unionist Party, 8; *Sinn Féin,* 4 (seats not taken); *Plaid Cymru,* 3; Social Democratic and Labour Party, 3; Ulster Unionist Party, 2; UK Independence Party, 1; Green Party of England and Wales, 1; independent, 1; and speaker (running as "The Speaker Seeking Reelection"), 1. (According to long-standing convention, the speaker serves without party affiliation and votes only in case of a tie vote. The current speaker was initially elected to the House of Commons on the Conservative ticket in 2005.)

Speaker: John BERCOW.

Scottish Parliament. Party strength in the 129-member Parliament after the May 5, 2016, election was as follows: Scottish National Party, 63 seats; Conservative Party, 31; Labour Party, 24; Scottish Green Party, 6; and Liberal Democrats, 5.

Presiding Officer: Ken MACINTOSH.

Welsh National Assembly (*Cynulliad Cenedlaethol Cymru*). Party strength in the 60-member National Assembly after the May 5, 2016, election was as follows: Labour Party, 29 seats; *Plaid Cymru,* 12; Conservative Party, 11; UK Independence Party, 7; and Liberal Democrats, 1.

Presiding Officer: Elin JONES (*Plaid Cymru*).

CABINET

[as of October 25, 2016]

Prime Minister and First Lord of the Treasury	Theresa May [f]
Secretaries of State	
Business, Energy, and Industrial Strategy	Greg Clark
Communities and Local Government	Sajid Javid
Culture, Media, and Sport	Karen Bradley [f]
Defense	Michael Fallon
Education	Justine Greening [f]
Energy and Climate Change	Edward Davey (LD)
Environment, Food, and Rural Affairs	Andrea Leadsom [f]
Foreign and Commonwealth Affairs	Boris Johnson
Health	Jeremy Hunt
Home Department	Amber Rudd [f]
International Development	Priti Patel [f]
International Trade	Liam Fox
Justice	Liz Truss [f]
Leaving the European Union	David Davis
Northern Ireland	James Brokenshire
Scotland	David Mundell
Transport	Chris Grayling
Wales	Alun Cairns
Work and Pensions	Damian Green
Chancellor of the Duchy of Lancaster	Patrick McLoughlin
Chancellor of the Exchequer	Philip Hammond
Leader of the House of Lords and Lord Privy Seal	Baroness Evans of Bowes Park [f]
Lord Chancellor	Chris Grayling
Lord President of the Council and Leader of the House of Commons	David Lidington

[f] = female

Note: All of the above are members of the Conservative Party unless noted.

INTERGOVERNMENTAL REPRESENTATION

Ambassador to the U.S.: Kim DARROCH.

U.S. Ambassador to the UK: Matthew BARZUN.

Permanent Representative to the UN: Lewis LUKENS (Chargé d'Affaires *ad interim).*

IGO Memberships (Non-UN): ADB, AfDB, CEUR, CWTH, EBRD, EIB, EU, G-8, G-20, IADB, IEA, ICC, IOM, NATO, OECD, OSCE, WTO.

For Further Reference:

Clegg, Nick. *Politics: Between the Extremes.* London: Bodley Head, 2016.

Deacon, Russell. *Devolution in the United Kingdom.* 2nd ed. Edinburgh: Edinburgh University Press, 2012.

Glencross, Andrew. *Why the UK Voted for Brexit: David Cameron's Great Miscalculation.* New York: Palgrave Macmillan, 2016.

Heyward, Andrew. *Essentials of UK Politics.* New York: Palgrave Macmillan, 2008.

RELATED TERRITORIES

All major, and many minor, territories of the former British Empire achieved full independence during the last century, and most are now members of the Commonwealth, a voluntary association of states held together primarily by a common political and constitutional heritage and, in most cases, use of the English language (see "The Commonwealth" in Intergovernmental Organizations section). In conventional usage, the term Commonwealth also includes the territories and dependencies of the UK and other Commonwealth member countries. As of 2006 the UK retained a measure of responsibility, direct or indirect, for 3 Crown dependencies, 11 inhabited territories, 2 essentially uninhabited territories, and the so-called Sovereign Base Areas on Cyprus.

In September 1998, following up on a commitment made at the Dependent Territories Association conference in London the preceding February, the Blair government announced that it intended to introduce legislation that would supersede the 1981 British Nationality Act, which had excluded most colonial residents from British citizenship, and restore their "right of abode" in the UK, which had been revoked in 1962. The dependencies would be restyled British overseas territories. A white paper issued in March 1999 reaffirmed the government's intentions, although the government added that the Caribbean colonies would be required to introduce various criminal justice reforms—for example, abolishing the death penalty and decriminalizing consensual homosexual relations—before attaining the new status. Implementing legislation was passed in 2002, with British citizenship being conferred on citizens of all British overseas territories (except the Sovereign Base Areas, below) from May 21.

Several of the Overseas Territories and Crown Dependencies were hit hard by the 2008 global financial crisis, prompting the UK's chancellor of the exchequer, Alistair DARLING, to commission a report on their need to improve standards of financial regulation and to find new methods for raising tax revenue. The report called upon UK related territories to put their government finances on firmer footing through more diversified tax systems, including the possible introduction of taxes on income, profits, capital gains, and sales. The report also called on territories with significant financial sectors to provide more help in tracking financial crimes. In May 2013 Prime Minister Cameron wrote the leaders of the Crown Dependencies, asking for their help in setting a new global standard for tax information exchanges and knocking "down the walls of company secrecy."

The 2016 Brexit referendum created new uncertainty among the UK's overseas territories, and prompted most to express their support for a negotiated withdrawal that would allow the United Kingdom to retain its economic access to EU markets and allow for easy travel by EU citizens.

Crown Dependencies:

Though closely related to Great Britain both historically and geographically, the Channel Islands and the Isle of Man are distinct from the UK and are under the jurisdiction of the sovereign rather than the state.

Channel Islands. Located in the English Channel off the northwest coast of France, the Channel Islands have been attached to the English Crown since the Norman Conquest in 1066. The nine islands have a total area of 75 square miles (198 sq. km) and a population (2016E) of 165,000. The two largest and most important are Jersey and Guernsey, each of which has its own parliament (the States) but is linked to the Crown through a representative who bears the title lieutenant governor and serves as commander in chief. While the Channel Islands control their own domestic affairs, defense policy and most foreign relations are administered from London. St. Helier on Jersey and St. Peter Port on Guernsey are the principal towns. Because of their mild climate and insular location, the islands are popular tourist resorts, and their low tax rate has attracted many permanent residents from the UK.

The government of Jersey is based in the "Assembly of the States," a 53-member elected body composed of 29 deputies, 12 constables (heads of parishes), and 12 senators, not counting 3 nonvoting ex officio members (attorney general, solicitor general, dean of Jersey) plus the lieutenant governor and a bailiff, who presides over the legislature. Deputies and constables serve three-year terms; senators serve six-year terms, with elections for half their number held triennially.

November 2005 marked a major change in Jersey's governmental structure. Under the States of Jersey Law 2005, the previous committee system of governance was replaced by a ten-member cabinet-style system headed by a chief minister. The other nine ministers are nominated by the chief minister from among the membership of the Assembly of the States, which then elects each minister individually. The authority of the lieutenant governor to veto resolutions of the states was abolished, and "orders in council," issued by the Privy Council in London, were henceforth to be referred to the States for review. On December 5 Sen. Frank WALKER was elected chief minister by a vote of 38–14 over Senator SYVRET.

Following Walker's election, the government launched two public consultations in 2007. Jersey residents were surveyed for their views on civil unions for homosexual and heterosexual couples, and also registered their preferences for alternative strategies to provide public services to an aging population in the face of a shrinking workforce.

Elections for senators were held October 15, 2008, with the balloting for deputies following on November 26. All winning senatorial candidates ran as independents, although three parties had candidates on the ballot: the **Jersey Democratic Alliance** (JDA), **Time 4 Change,** and **Jersey 2020.** The Centre Party, which had fielded senatorial candidates in 2005, changed its name to the **Jersey Conservative Party** (JCP) in 2007 but presented no candidates in 2008. Three JDA candidates won election as deputies, with the remaining 26 deputy seats being filled by independents. On December 9, 2008, Terry LE SUEUR, formerly a senator and theretofore deputy chief minister, was elected chief minister, 36 to 17, over senator Alan BRECKON. On the policy front, in October 2009 the assembly approved legislation to legalize civil partnerships, and the Law on Civil Partnerships came into effect on July 12, 2011.

The most recent senatorial election was October 19, 2011, and on November 14 Ian GORST defeated incumbent Sir Philip Bailhache, 27 to 24, to become chief minister. The Jersey Electoral Commission is in the process of formulating ways to restructure the assemblies, most likely to reduce the number of members to streamline operations.

The Organization for Economic Cooperation and Development commended Gorst in July 2013 for his government's efforts to increase tax transparency.

Guernsey is governed through its "States of Deliberation," which comprises 45 people's deputies elected from multi- or single-member districts every four years, 2 representatives from Alderney, 2 ex officio members (attorney general and solicitor general), and a bailiff. Prior to the election of April 21, 2004, the States had included 10 local (parish) representatives, but those seats were eliminated as part of a governmental reform process that also saw, from May 1, 2004, adoption of a ministerial administration. At that time, 43 separate committees were abolished in favor of a Policy Council, comprising a chief minister and 10 other ministers elected from and by the members of the States; 10 departments, each headed by a minister; and 5 "specialist" committees. The first Privy Council resigned en masse in February 2007 after revelations of an alleged rigged bidding process for a hospital construction project.

Peter HARWOOD was elected chief minister of Guernsey, 27 to 20, on May 1, 2012. A retired lawyer, Harwood entered the April 18 States election as a political novice, emphasizing that he would be "free of previous political baggage." He has prioritized improving the island's tax transparency requirements.

The small islands of Alderney, Sark, Herm, Jethou, Brecqhou, and Lihou are usually classified as dependencies of the Bailiwick of Guernsey, although Alderney and Sark have their own legislatures: the States of Alderney, encompassing a president and 10 deputies serving four-year terms (half elected every other year), and the Sark Court of Chief Pleas, comprising 40 hereditary "tenants" (landowners) and 12 deputies elected for three-year terms. Anticipating the need to dismantle the island's feudal political system in order to comply with the European Convention on Human Rights, voters in October 2006 approved the creation of a Chief Pleas Assembly, to comprise 28 elected and 2 ex officio members. The Chief Pleas approved the new law in February 2008, and elections were scheduled for the following December, pending approval from the British Privy Council. The election of 28 councilors (from 57 candidates) was held December 10, after which the councilors voted to assign themselves initial two- or four-year terms in order to permit the subsequent election of half the members every two years for staggered four-year terms.

Although the Channel Islands are not legally part of the EU, certain EU directives are deemed to apply to them, notably those relating to tariffs and agricultural policy. In February 1995 the Sark Court of Chief Pleas rejected the incorporation of relevant parts of the EU's Maastricht Treaty into Sark law. In November 1999, however, the court voted to rescind a 1611 law that had restricted property inheritance to men. In December the UK Privy Council approved the change, thereby preventing a future challenge in the European Court of Human Rights.

In November 1998 a report presented by the UK Home Office recommended that the Channel Islands and the Isle of Man, which between them have registered some 90,000 offshore businesses, require such operations to provide greater details about their ownership and activities. The report also proposed that the dependencies take additional steps to prevent money laundering and other financial offenses. The June 2000 decision of the OECD to include the Channel Islands and the Isle of Man among 35 international jurisdictions with harmful tax and investment regimes led the islands' administrations to assert that reform would be pointless unless other, larger jurisdictions, such as Switzerland and Luxembourg, also participated. In early August, however, the islands pledged to cooperate with OECD efforts to eliminate tax crimes perpetrated by offshore corporations, and in February 2002 they were removed from the blacklist.

In a February 2000 ruling with major implications for a number of UK institutions, the European Court of Human Rights determined that a Guernsey flower grower had been denied a fair trial when he appealed a planning decision denying him use of a packing shed as a residence. The original appeal had involved the bailiff of Guernsey, who held executive and legislative as well as judicial responsibilities, thereby calling into question his impartiality, according to the court. The decision increased the likelihood of future challenges against, for example, the UK's lord chancellor, particularly in cases based on policies that the chancellor helps administer.

In December 2007 an amendment to the Reform Law granting 16-year-olds the right to vote received Royal Sanction and was implemented ahead of the April 23, 2008, general election with all 45 members standing as nonpartisans. Guernsey's "Zero-10" tax strategy was also implemented in 2008, with income tax on company profits eliminated. The strategy singled out a minority of banking activities for a uniform 10 percent tax. However, the tax had to be modified in 2012 to make it EU compliant.

In March 2014 Jonathan LE TOCQ (independent) was elected chief minister of Guernsey.

Lieutenant Governor and Commander in Chief of Jersey: John McCOLL.

Bailiff of Jersey and President of the Assembly of the States: William BAILHACHE.

Chief Minister of Jersey: Ian GORST.

Lieutenant Governor and Commander in Chief of the Bailiwick of Guernsey and Its Dependencies: Ian CORDER.

Bailiff of Guernsey and President of the States of Deliberation: Richard COLLAS.

Chief Minister of Guernsey: Jonathan LE TOCQ.

Isle of Man. Located in the Irish Sea midway between Northern Ireland and northern England, the Isle of Man has been historically connected to Great Britain for over 700 years but remains politically distinct. It has an area of 227 square miles (588 sq. km) and an estimated population of 88,000 (2016E). The principal town is Douglas, and most income is derived from offshore banking and business services.

The island's self-governing institutions include the High Court of Tynwald (the world's oldest parliament in continuous existence), encompassing a president elected by the court, the Legislative Council, and the House of Keys, which is a 24-member body popularly elected for a five-year term. The Legislative Council includes a president, the lord bishop of Sodor and Man, a nonvoting attorney general, and eight others named by the House of Keys. The British monarch serves as head of state ("Lord of Man") and is represented by a lieutenant governor, who historically functioned as head of government and presided over an Executive Council. In 1986, however, the office of chief minister was created, and in 1990 a Council of Ministers replaced the Executive Council. Concurrently, the president of the Tynwald assumed many of the responsibilities of the lieutenant governor, who nevertheless still reserves important constitutional powers, including the authority to dissolve the House of Keys. The chief minister, elected by the legislature, nominates the other ministers.

The island levies its own taxes and has a special relationship with the EU, falling within the EU customs territory but remaining fiscally independent of it. In August 2000 the Manx administration joined the Channel Islands in agreeing to work with the OECD on tax harmonization, improved financial transparency, and information exchange.

At the election of November 22, 2001, independents won 19 seats in the House of Keys. Candidates affiliated with the **Alliance for Progressive Government** (APG), an identifiable political group but not an official party, won 3 seats, and the **Manx Labour Party** (MLP) won 2. The nationalist **Mec Vannin** (Sons of Mannin), which dates from 1962 and advocates republican independence, boycotts elections.

Following the 2001 polling the incumbent chief minister, Donald GELLING, was unanimously reelected to the post, but he stepped down a year later and was succeeded by Richard CORKHILL. In December 2004 Corkhill resigned because of a financial scandal, and on December 14 Gelling was returned as chief minister. James Anthony (Tony) Brown was elected chief minister on December 14, 2006, resigning, as required by law, his position of speaker of the house. Stephen Rodan was subsequently elected speaker. The November 23, 2008, balloting for the House of Keys resulted in the election of 21 independent members (1 affiliated with the APG), with the Liberal Vannin Party (LVP, founded in 2006) winning 2 seats and the MLP 1. Following elections on September 29, 2011, Allan BELL was elected chief minister. In August 2014 the Isle of Man and Northern Ireland signed a trade accord to encourage investment and tourism in both regions.

In the 2016 September elections for the House of Keys, independents again won the majority of seats, with 21. The Sons of Mannin won 4. Five women were elected (21 percent of the total), a record for the island.

Lieutenant Governor: Adam WOOD.

President of the Tynwald: Stephen Charles RODAN.

Speaker of the House of Keys: Juan Paul WATTERSON.

Chief Minister: Howard QUAYLE.

Inhabited Overseas Territories:

The territories described below remain directly subordinate to the UK, although a number of them enjoy almost complete autonomy in internal affairs. The term "colony" or "crown colony," a historical relic without contemporary legal import, is often still used in reference to these jurisdictions.

Anguilla. One of the most northern of the Caribbean's Leeward Islands (see the Antigua and Barbuda map), Anguilla has a land area of 35 square miles (91 sq. km), exclusive of Sombrero's 2 square miles (5 sq. km), and a resident population (2016E) of 15,000. There is no capital city as such, apart from a centrally located sector known as The Valley. The main industries are tourism, offshore banking and finance, and construction. Overseas remittances from Anguillans living abroad are a substantial source of island revenue.

Anguilla was first settled by the British in 1632 and became part of the Territory of the Leeward Islands in 1956. Following establishment of the Associated State of St. Kitts-Nevis-Anguilla in early 1967, the Anguillans repudiated government from Basseterre, St. Kitts, and a British commissioner was installed following a landing by British security forces in March 1969. The island was subsequently placed under the direct administration of Britain, while a separate constitution that was enacted in February 1976 gave the resident commissioner (subsequently governor) authority over foreign affairs, defense, civil service, and internal security. Other executive functions are undertaken on the advice of an Executive Council that, in accordance with a 1982 constitution (amended in 1990), consists of a chief minister; three additional ministers; and the deputy governor and attorney general, ex officio. Legislative authority, save in respect of the governor's reserve powers, is the responsibility of a House of Assembly encompassing a speaker; seven elected members; two nominated members; and the deputy governor and attorney general, ex officio. An act of December 1980 formally confirmed the dependent status of the territory, which also includes the neighboring island of Sombrero.

Ronald WEBSTER, then leader of the People's Progressive Party, headed Anguilla's government after the separation from St. Kitts-Nevis in 1967 until 1977, when he was replaced by Emile GUMBS, then leader of what became the **Anguilla National Alliance** (ANA). Webster returned to power in 1980 as leader of the **Anguilla United Party** (AUP) but in 1984 was again replaced by Gumbs, who remained chief minister following the 1989 election until his retirement in February 1994 (by which time he was Sir Emile). Meanwhile, Webster had founded what became the **Anguilla Democratic Party** (ADP) but had reverted to the AUP for the 1989 election; subsequently, he formed the **Anguillans for Good Government** (AGG) party.

The March 1994 election failed to produce a clear winner, with the ANA (led by Eric REID), the ADP (led by Victor BANKS), and the AUP (led by Hubert HUGHES) each winning two seats; an independent, one; and Webster's new party, none. The outcome was an AUP-ADP coalition under the chief ministership of the AUP leader. At the election of March 4, 1999, the ANA, led by Osbourne FLEMING, captured three house seats, but with the ADP and the AUP again winning two seats each, a renewal of the AUP-ADP coalition permitted Hughes to claim a second term as chief minister. Earlier, Hughes had stated that he hoped to move Anguilla closer to full internal self-government, citing Bermuda as a model and commenting that the present constitution placed ministers in "positions without power."

Within months of the election, a constitutional deadlock developed, Victor Banks having resigned as finance minister over Hughes's managerial style and his failure to consult the ADP. Banks then realigned his ADP with the ANA, and together they began a boycott of the house, leaving it without a quorum. Having failed to convince the High Court that the speaker of the house, a member of the ADP, should be forced to convene the legislature, in January 2000 Hughes asked the governor to call a new election. Held on March 3, the balloting returned all the incumbents to office, but with the **Anguilla United Front** (AUF) alliance of the ANA and the ADP controlling four seats; the AUP, two; and a former ADP member, now an independent, the seventh. On March 6 Osbourne Fleming assumed office as chief minister, with Banks again in charge of finance and economic development as well as investment and commerce.

At the election of February 21, 2005, the AUF retained its four seats; the **Anguilla National Strategic Alliance,** led by opposition leader Edison BAIRD, secured two; and Hubert Hughes's **Anguilla United Movement** (AUM) won one. Also competing in the election was the **Anguillan Progressive Party** (APP), led by Brent DAVIS.

Anguilla's process for constitutional review and reform, consistent with the 1999 white paper on overseas territories, was jump-started in 2006 with the appointment of a Constitutional and Electoral Reform Commission. The commission presented its report in August of that same year. Negotiations with UK officials over proposed constitutional changes, scheduled for July 2007, were delayed by Chief Minister Fleming in order to extend the period for public consultation. The government issued a press release on July 17, 2007, stating that Anguilla planned to seek "full internal self government" status from the UK.

On April 21, 2009, Alistair Harrison assumed the governorship from Andrew GEORGE, who retired. In a May address Harrison said he considered financial regulation of the off-shore financial industry his top priority. Of particular concern was Anguilla's inclusion on the OECD's so-called grey list of countries that have stated their intention to comply with rules for sharing tax information but have not yet done so.

In the February 15, 2010, balloting for the seven elected members of the assembly, the AUM won four seats, the AUF won two, and the APP won one, despite a vote distribution which had the AUF ahead of the AUM 39 to 33 percent. The next day the AUM's Hughes was sworn in as chief minister, named his cabinet, and announced the government would concentrate on restoring the economy. Anguilla's GDP decreased by 6.7 percent in 2012, and 0.9 percent in 2013, mainly because of a continuing decline in tourism.

In elections on April 22, 2015, the AUF won six seats, and the remaining seat was won by an independent. Victor BANKS (AUF) was appointed chief minister the day after the election.

Governor: Christina SCOTT.

Chief Minister: Victor BANKS.

Bermuda. Named after Juan de Bermudez, a Spanish sailor who reached the islands in the early 1500s, Bermuda remained uninhabited for a century. Settled by the British and then established as a Crown colony in 1684, it consists of 150 islands and islets in the western Atlantic. It has a total land area of 21 square miles (53 sq. km) and a population (2016E) of 62,000, concentrated on some 20 islands. Blacks make up approximately 60 percent of the total population. The capital is Hamilton, with a population of about 10,000 (2014E). The main economic activities are offshore business services (principally insurance and reinsurance), tourism, and light manufacturing. Over 10,500 international companies are registered, but only about 300 maintain a physical presence. Customs duties constitute the principal source of government revenue.

Under a constitution approved in mid-1967 (amended, in certain particulars, in 1979), Bermuda was granted a system of internal self-government whereby the Crown-appointed governor, advised by a Governor's Council, exercises responsibility for external affairs, defense, internal security, and police. The governor appoints as premier the majority leader in the lower chamber of the Parliament, the House of Assembly, which is popularly elected for a five-year term. (Formerly consisting of 40 members from 2-member constituencies, the representation was reduced to 36 single-member constituencies prior to the 2003 election.) The 11 members of the upper house, the Senate, are appointed by the governor, including 5 on recommendation of the premier and 3 on recommendation of the leader of the opposition.

The first general election under the new constitution, held in May 1968 against a background of black rioting, resulted in a decisive victory for the moderately right-wing, multiracial **United Bermuda Party** (UBP), whose leader, Sir Henry TUCKER, became the colony's first premier. The left-wing **Progressive Labour Party** (PLP), mainly black in membership, had campaigned for independence and an end to British rule, and its unexpectedly poor showing was generally interpreted as a popular endorsement of the existing constitutional arrangements.

At the election of October 5, 1993, the UBP (led since 1981 by Sir John SWAN) returned 22 members to the House of Assembly against 18 for the PLP (led by Frederick WADE), while the **National Liberal Party** (NLP; led by Gilbert DARRELL) lost the seat it had won in 1989. In February 1994, following an announcement that U.S. and UK forces would vacate Bermuda in 1995, the new legislature voted 20–18 in favor of holding a referendum on independence. The consultation eventually took place on August 16, 1995, with traditional party lines being partially reversed in that Sir John and some other UBP leaders (although not the party as such) urged a "yes" vote and the pro-independence PLP advocated abstention. Of a 58.8 percent turnout, 73.6 percent of the voters opposed independence, whereupon Sir John resigned from the premiership and UBP leadership and was replaced by Finance Minister David SAUL. The new premier moved to heal divisions within the UBP remaining from the bruising independence referendum and a subsequent conflict in the summer of 1996 over approval of a franchise license for a fast food chain. Three members who had rebelled against party leadership on both issues were returned to cabinet portfolios in January 1997, although the moves were insufficient to save the premier. On March 27 Saul was replaced by Pamela GORDON, the new leader of the UBP. Earlier, in December 1996, Jennifer SMITH had been elected leader of the PLP following the death of Frederick Wade.

Premier Gordon's decision to reshuffle her cabinet in May 1998 failed to prevent a dramatic victory by the PLP at the election of November 9. The PLP won for the first time, capturing 26 house seats versus 14 for the UBP, which had been in power for three decades. The victory was even more remarkable in that the winning party had run only 34 candidates for the 40 seats. Jennifer Smith was sworn in as premier on November 10 and shortly thereafter named a cabinet of 12 additional ministers, all but 1 black.

At the election of July 24, 2003, the PLP won 22 House seats and the UBP 14. Although reinstalled as premier, Smith had drawn criticism for an alleged "arrogant and secretive" leadership style and was forced to step down on July 28 in favor of Alex SCOTT.

In December 2004 the issue of independence was reopened by Prime Minister Scott, who announced the establishment of a Bermuda Independence Commission (BIC) that was instructed to hold public hearings on the subject in early 2005. While the current government favored independence, a July 2007 opinion poll indicated that 63 percent of Bermudans opposed it, with 25 percent in favor and 12 percent undecided.

At an October 2006 PLP delegate conference Dr. Ewart BROWN was elected party chair by a 107–76 vote over Scott. Brown was subsequently sworn in as premier on October 30. UBP leader Wayne FURBERT stepped down on March 31, 2007, and was replaced by Michael DUNKLEY on April 2 by a unanimous vote.

The Brown government's health minister resigned from the cabinet in February 2007 amid the opening of a criminal investigation into his business activities. In June the police arrested the former minister under theft and corruption charges. A new heath minister was sworn in on June 12.

At the election of December 18, 2007, in a replay of the previous balloting, the PLP won 22 House seats and the UBP 14. New UBP leader Michael Dunkley failed to win reelection from his constituency, leaving the party in disarray. Sir Richard Gozney was named governor in December in succession to Sir John VEREKER.

Ewart Brown's premiership subsequently continued to prove contentious with all parties, including his own. His standing among the public and his own party plummeted in 2009 when he accepted four Chinese Uighur detainees released from Guantánamo, telling neither his own cabinet ministers nor the British foreign office. Brown survived a motion of no confidence, but members of his own party took to the streets in protest, and polls showed his approval rating among the public was at an historic low. Brown resigned his premiership and his seat in the assembly in October 2010. The PLP elected Deputy Premier Paula Cox as Brown's successor.

In regularly scheduled elections on December 12, 2012, Cox and the PLP lost to the One Bermuda Alliance (OBA), 17 seats to 19. OBA formed in 2011 from the merger of the UBP and the short-lived Bermuda Democratic Alliance. The OBA's Craig CANNONIER was named premier. In May 2014 Cannonier resigned and was succeeded by Michael H. DUNKLEY (OBA). John James RANKIN (CMG) was appointed governor of Bermuda on September 19, 2016.

Governor: John James RANKIN.

Premier: Michael H. DUNKLEY.

British Indian Ocean Territory. At the time of its establishment in 1965 the British Indian Ocean Territory consisted of the Chagos Archipelago, which previously was a dependency of Mauritius, and the islands of Aldabra, Farquhar, and Desroches, which had traditionally been administered from the Seychelles (see the Mauritius map). The territory was created to make defense facilities available to the British and U.S. governments and was legally construed as being uninhabited, although in 1967–1973 some 1,800 Chagos Islanders (Ilois) were relocated from Diego Garcia in the Chagos group to make way for the construction of U.S. air and naval installations. Upon the granting of independence to the Seychelles in June 1976, arrangements were made for the reversion of Aldabra, Farquhar, and Desroches, the territory thenceforth to consist only of the Chagos Archipelago, with its administration taken over by the Foreign and Commonwealth Office. The total land area of the archipelago, stretching over some 21,000 square miles (54,400 sq. km) of the central Indian Ocean, is 20 square miles (52 sq. km). Presently the only inhabitants are some 2,000 members of the British and U.S. military and another 1,500 civilian personnel (mainly Filipinos and Sri Lankans) providing services for the Diego Garcia naval facility.

On March 3, 1999, the UK High Court ruled that the Chagos Refugee Group, led by Louis Olivier BANCOULT, could challenge the legality of the Ilois removal. The majority of the Ilois had settled in Mauritius, from where they have long pressed unsuccessful compensation claims. Appearing in the High Court in 2000, the claimants' counselor successfully argued that the 1971 Immigration Ordinance, which barred permanent residence in the archipelago, should be overturned, in part because it violated the European Convention on Human Rights. In 2004, however, the UK Privy Council issued orders in council that again placed visits to the islands under immigration control. On May 11, 2006, the High Court overruled the orders, calling the removal of the Chagossians "repugnant" and opening the possibility of their return. In late June the UK government indicated that it would appeal the decision. Meanwhile, in late March 102 islanders had set sail from Mauritius for a 12-day visit to the archipelago, the first such excursion permitted by the UK in more than three decades.

Under the joint usage agreements between the UK and the United States, the archipelago will be ceded to Mauritius when it is no longer needed for defense purposes.

The UK government began its appeal on February 5, 2007, of the High Court's 2006 decision overturning the removal order. In March Mauritian president Sir Anerood Jugnauth revealed that Mauritius was prepared to withdraw from the Commonwealth in order to bring the UK before the International Court of Justice (IJC) on behalf of the Chagossians. On May 23, 2007, the court of appeal upheld the previous decision and ordered the UK government to pay the Chagossians' legal fees and allow resettlement of all but Diego Garcia. The government appealed the decision to the House of Lords, and in October 2008 the lower court ruling was overturned, thereby barring the return of the Chagossians and removing any obligation for the UK government to pay further compensation.

On April 1, 2010, the British government established the Chagos Marine Reserve, a "fully no-take" marine reserve that banned commercial fishing. Environmental groups welcomed the declaration until diplomatic cables released by WikiLeaks in 2011 suggested the UK government added the no-fishing requirement to prevent the Chagossians from resettling the islands. Greenpeace, among others, condemned this policy as a "huge violation" of Chagossian rights. In March 2014 the UK government commissioned a team of experts to prepare a report on the feasibility of resettling Chagossians on the islands.

In 2016, after a decades-long legal battle, the UK restated that it would not allow the Chagossians to return to the islands.

Commissioner: Peter HAYES (resident in United Kingdom).

Administrator: Tom MOODY (resident in United Kingdom).

British Virgin Islands. A Caribbean group of 46 northern Leeward Islands located some 60 miles east of Puerto Rico, the British Virgin Islands have a total area of 59 square miles (153 sq. km) and a population (2016E) of 31,000. Tourism and international business are the main industries, with the latter reportedly accounting for 90 percent of government revenue. The largest island, Tortola, is the site of the chief town and port of entry, Road Town (population 13,000 in 2014). The administration is headed by a governor. Representative institutions include a 15-member Legislative Council (13 elected members serving four-year terms; the attorney general, ex officio; and a speaker) and a 6-member Executive Council appointed and chaired by the governor. A chief minister is chosen from the legislature by the governor.

At the election of September 1986 the **Virgin Islands Party** (VIP), led by H. Lavity STOUTT, won five of nine Council seats, ousting the administration headed by independent member Cyril B. ROMNEY, who had been involved with a company undergoing investigation for money laundering. In March 1988 the deputy chief minister, Omar HODGE, was dismissed for attempting to delay the issuance of a report charging him with bribery; the following year he formed the **Independent People's Movement** (IPM). Stoutt remained in office following the balloting of November 2, 1990, at which the VIP won six seats; the IPM, one; and independents, two. The **United Party** (UP), led by Conrad MADURO, lost the two seats it had held since 1986.

In early 1994 a proposal by a UK constitutional review commission to expand the Legislative Council to 13 elective seats by adding four "at-large" members drew criticism from several islands parties. Chief Minister Stoutt led the attack on the plan, but to no avail. Balloting on February 20, 1995, for the 13 legislators yielded 6 seats for the VIP, 2 for the UP, 2 for Hodge's new **Concerned Citizen's Movement** (CCM), and 3 for independents. One of the independents sided with the VIP in return for a ministerial post, enabling Stoutt to begin a fifth successive term as chief minister. However, Stoutt died unexpectedly on May 16 and was succeeded by Deputy Chief Minister Ralph O'Neal. The opposition—numbering five members—received an unexpected boost when two supporters of the government temporarily switched sides in April 1997, coming close to bringing the government down. By June, however, the failure to unseat the government and dissatisfaction with the leadership of the UP's Maduro led three of the five opposition members to rebel, and in December 1997 Maduro was replaced as leader of the opposition by the leader of the CCM, Walwyn BREWLEY.

The VIP claimed a narrow election victory in balloting on May 17, 1999, winning seven seats in the Legislative Council to five for the recently formed **National Democratic Party** (NDP) and one for the CCM. Both the CCM and the UP took less than 10 percent of the total constituency and at-large votes, many of their previous supporters having switched allegiance to the NDP, led by Orlando SMITH.

At the election of June 16, 2003, the NDP won eight seats and the VIP five, permitting Smith to head the new government.

The Smith government won unanimous approval from the Legislative Council for its proposed draft of a new constitution in May 2007. The UK Privy Council ratified the bill and the new constitution came into force on June 15, 2007. Among the new powers of the British Virgin Islands government was the creation of a national security council.

The VIP regained control of the government in balloting on August 20, 2007, winning in a landslide with ten seats to two for the NDP, while the remaining elective seat went to an independent. Voter turnout was 66 percent. Ralph O'Neal headed the new government as First Premier under the new constitution (formerly the position was titled Chief Minister).

Power shifted in the November 7, 2011, election, as the NDP won 9 seats, VIP 4, and PPA none. NDP party chair Orlando SMITH was sworn in as premier following a campaign in which he pledged to protect the tourism and offshore financial services sectors while improving health care, education, and other services for residents. In August 2014 John DUNCAN was sworn in as the new governor of the territory.

In balloting on June 8, 2015, the NDP secured 52.5 percent of the vote and 11 seats, followed by the VIP, with 39 percent and 2 seats. Smith was reappointed premier.

Governor: John DUNCAN.

Premier: Orlando SMITH.

Cayman Islands. Located in the Caribbean, northwest of Jamaica, the Cayman Islands (Grand Cayman, Little Cayman, and Cayman Brac) cover 100 square miles (259 sq. km) and have a population (2016E) of 61,000. George Town, on Grand Cayman, is the capital. The traditional occupations of seafaring and turtle and shark fishing have largely been superseded by tourism and other services. The islands have become one of the world's half-dozen largest offshore banking centers as well as a corporate tax haven. As of December 2016, 179 operating banks and trust companies, more than 10,000 mutual funds, and some 860 insurance companies were registered, and as of December 2015, almost 90,000 other companies were registered. In mid-1999 the territory became the first government to request certification under the newly introduced UN Offshore Initiative. Accordingly, the UN Global Programme against Money Laundering had agreed to review the islands' banking and financial systems.

Discovered by Columbus in the early 1500s, the essentially uninhabited Caymans passed from Spain to England in 1670. Governed from Jamaica from the 1860s until 1959 and then briefly a part of the Federation of the West Indies, the islands were placed in 1962 under a British administrator (later governor), who chairs an Executive Council of 8 other members, including 3 ex officio and 5 chosen by and from among the Legislative Assembly. The latter body initially consisted of a speaker, 3 ex officio members, and 12 elected members. At balloting for an enlarged assembly on November 18, 1992, a National Team of government critics won 12 of the elective 15 seats, the remaining 3 going to independents. The outcome rendered uncertain a plan to introduce ministerial government, as the National Team had campaigned against it. However, after deliberations involving the governor and London, a ministerial system was introduced under a constitutional revision implemented in February 1994. Thus, the 5 elected members of the Executive Council now have ministerial responsibilities.

At a general election on November 22, 1996, the National Team secured nine seats, while two recently formed groupings, the **Democratic Alliance** and **Team Cayman,** took two and one, respectively, with independents winning three. In 1997 W. McKeeva Bush, now of the **United Democratic Party** (UDP), was ousted from the Executive Council following allegations that a bank of which he was a director had approved more than $1 billion in fraudulent loans.

In June 2000 George Town expressed astonishment at the decision of the international Financial Action Task Force (FATF) to place the Caymans on its list of 15 jurisdictions considered noncooperative with efforts to combat money laundering. In addition to having repeatedly asked the FATF to visit the Caymans, the government had recently been praised by the UK's Foreign and Commonwealth Office for its regulatory and enforcement efforts. In June 2001 Cayman Islands was delisted.

At the election held on May 11, 2005, after a six-month postponement because of damage from Hurricane Ivan in September 2004, the **People's Progressive Movement** (PPM), led by Kurt TIBBETTS, won 9 of the 15 elective seats, while the UDP won 5 and an independent, 1.

Following more than two years of discussion, a referendum on a new constitution was held alongside the general election in May 2009, at which the draft constitution received 63 percent support. Meanwhile, the UDP won nine seats, the PPM five, and independents one in the general election.

Newly elected assembly members were sworn in on Mary 27, 2009, with Bush returning to the post of Leader of Government Business. Throughout the remainder of the year the Bush administration struggled to deal with the deeply troubling government debt crisis and a much-threatened financial sector. He secured a $277 million loan from the UK government and pledged to cut spending, but Bush resisted calls from the UK to impose new taxes, claiming that they would negatively alter the islands' unique economic base. The new constitution entered into force on November 6, and Bush was sworn in as premier, the territory's first, the same day. As part of overall efforts to comply with international financial standards established by the OECD, the Bush administration over the next year negotiated bilateral agreements with a number of countries regarding the exchange of tax information.

In February 2011 Kurt Tibbets stepped down as leader of the PPM and was replaced as party leader and leader of the opposition by Alden McLaughlin. The Islands held a nonbinding referendum on July 18, 2012, on whether to adopt single-mandate constituencies. Although 64 percent of voters favored the change, turnout was so low that Bush proclaimed the results an indirect victory for the "no" side.

Bush was arrested in December 2012 and charged with corruption and mismanagement. Governor Duncan TAYLOR appointed Deputy Premier Juliana O'Connor-Connolly as interim premier. In parliamentary elections on May 22, 2013, the PPM won 9 of 18 seats; the UDP took only 3. Incoming Premier Alden MCLAUGHLIN (PPM) pledged to implement automatic exchanges of tax information regarding the islands' thriving financial sector. Helen KILPATRICK was appointed governor in September 2013. Bush's trial began in September 2014, but a jury acquitted him of all charges the following month.

Governor: Helen KILPATRICK.

Premier: Alden MCLAUGHLIN.

Falkland Islands. Situated some 480 miles northeast of Cape Horn in the South Atlantic (see Argentina map), the Falkland Islands currently encompasses the East and West Falklands in addition to some 200 smaller islands; the South Georgia and the South Sandwich islands ceased to be governed as dependencies of the Falklands in 1985. The total area is 4,700 square miles (12,173 sq. km), and the resident population, almost entirely of British extraction, was estimated at 3,000 (2016E), excluding military personnel and civilian employees of a British military base, who numbered 1,350 in 2013; most inhabitants live in the capital, Stanley, on East Falkland Island. The economy, traditionally dependent on wool production, has diversified in recent years, with fishing licenses now being the main source of revenue. Tourism has also increased in importance.

Under a constitution introduced in 1985 (replacing one dating from 1977), the governor is assisted by a Legislative Council that includes eight members elected on a nonpartisan basis (most recently on November 17, 2005) and by an Executive Council, three of whose members are selected by and from the elected legislators. In addition, both bodies have two ex officio members and a chief executive and a financial secretary, who are responsible to the governor. The attorney general and the commander of British forces may also attend Executive Council sessions.

The territory is the object of a long-standing dispute between Britain and Argentina, which calls it the Malvinas Islands (*Islas Malvinas*). Argentina's claim to sovereignty is based primarily on purchase of the islands by Spain from France in 1766; Britain claims sovereignty on the basis of a 1771 treaty, although uninterrupted possession commenced only in 1833. The Argentine claim has won some support in the UN General Assembly, and the two governments engaged in a lengthy series of inconclusive talks on the future disposition of the territory prior to the Argentine invasion of April 2, 1982, and the eventual reassertion of British control ten weeks later (see the entry on Argentina). The issue is complicated by evidence that significant oil and gas deposits may lie beneath the islands' territorial waters. In addition, Britain has taken the position that any solution must respect the wishes of the inhabitants. Thus, the current constitution refers explicitly to the islanders' right of self-determination.

In the wake of the 1982 war, Britain imposed a 150-mile protective zone, to which it added a 200-mile economic zone, effective February 1, 1987, although only a 150-mile radius was subsequently policed, principally to protect Falklands fisheries. As part of the 1990 Madrid agreement that led to the resumption of diplomatic relations with Argentina, Britain maintained its claim to a 200-mile economic zone but conceded that Argentine ships and planes could approach within 50 and 75 miles, respectively, of the islands without prior permission. In a further concession to Buenos Aires, London agreed in November 1990 to convert its 200-mile zone (exclusive of overlap with Argentina's own 200-mile limit) into an Anglo-Argentine cooperation area from which fishing fleets from other countries would be excluded.

In 1992 President Carlos Menem of Argentina pursued a dual policy of behind-the-scenes diplomacy and public assertions of the inevitability of Argentinean sovereignty over the Falklands. In November the first direct meeting between islanders' representatives and an Argentinean minister since 1982 took place in London. A major issue was Argentina's policy of reducing the cost of its fishing licenses in an attempt to lure foreign fleets into Argentinean waters and thus to deprive the Falklands government of its main source of revenue. In legislative elections on October 14, 1993, the eight elective seats were contested by 25 candidates, all independents, with those elected all rejecting unnecessary contact with Argentina until its sovereignty claim was dropped.

After the new Argentinean constitution promulgated in August 1994 repeated the claim to the islands, the UK government announced that the full 200-mile Falklands' economic zone would be policed even where it overlapped with the Argentinean zone. Talks in London in October at the foreign minister level made little progress on possible joint oil exploration in Falklands waters and other issues, while the collateral confirmation by President Menem that Argentina was prepared to pay substantial individual compensation to islanders in exchange for sovereignty did nothing to improve relations.

In October 1996 the Falklands administration issued oil exploration licenses to 13 companies, refusing only one application, from a consortium with Argentinean involvement. In a significant departure from previous policy, President Menem on December 30 suggested that sovereignty over the islands might be shared. His suggestion was immediately rejected by the UK government and by the Falkland Islands administration.

In April 1998 the UK announced that oil exploration of the Falklands coast had started, while in Argentina legislators introduced a bill to impose sanctions on commercial companies that failed to obtain Argentinean permission before operating in Falkland waters. The following October President Menem paid the first official visit to the UK by an Argentinean leader in nearly 40 years. Topics covered in a meeting with Prime Minister Blair included Falklands relations, while a subsequent letter from Menem to the islanders called for reconciliation "to heal old wounds." With secret talks reportedly under way on the territory's status, in January 1999 Buenos Aires offered to put in abeyance its sovereignty claim if the UK, in a largely symbolic gesture, would permit Argentinean flags to fly at selected locations, including the graveyard for its service-members killed during the Falklands war. Two months later Prince Charles visited both the Falklands and Argentina, where he laid a wreath at a monument to casualties of the conflict, as President Menem had done in England during his 1998 visit.

In May 1999 an Argentinean ministerial delegation met in London with members of the Falklands Legislative Council. Discussion topics included fishing and air connections. In the latter regard, in March Chile had announced a halt to Falklands flights—the only such contact between the islands and South America—to protest the continuing detention in London of former president Augusto Pinochet, pending resolution of a Spanish extradition warrant for human rights abuses during his reign. In July Buenos Aires and London agreed to permit air travel between Argentina and the islands, and Chile resumed flights with stopovers in Argentina.

In early 2004 Argentina granted its flagship airline two routes between Buenos Aires and Stanley. However, the islanders rejected the prospect of regularly scheduled flights from Argentina, and the recently installed Néstor Kirchner regime responded by denying permission for Chilean planes to fly through Argentine air space. Meanwhile, the Falkland economy, which had expanded 13-fold in the two decades after the war, was increasingly imperiled by a decline in sales of fishing licenses that was attributed to collapse in stocks of the previously abundant Ilex squid.

Relations between the UK and Argentina soured further in 2006 as President Kirchner, backed by the UN Special Committee on Decolonization and the Organization of American States, repeated his call for London to reopen negotiations on the territory's future status. Kirchner also indicated that he was considering taking a more hard-line approach on the issues of fishing rights and oil exploration. Upon his wife's investment in the presidency in 2007 (see the entry on Argentina), Cristina Fernández de Kirchner maintained Argentina's right to the islands. For its part, the British government reiterated that it had no intention to negotiate sovereignty in the absence of evidence that the islanders themselves sought a change.

A new constitution was announced for the islands in November 2008, effective January 1, 2009. In order to enhance internal self-government, the governor was required by the new constitution to abide by the advice of the Executive Council on most domestic policies. However, the governor retained veto power with respect to external, defense, and justice policies as well as when the governor deems the advice of the council to be contrary to the "the interests of good government." The new constitution also tightened rules for the acquisition of Falkland "status" (and thereby voting rights), installed the chief executive as head of the civil service, established a public accounts committee and a complaints commissioner in order to enhance transparency, and adopted provisions of the European Convention on Human Rights. The UK government emphasized that the constitutional revisions did not change the UK's commitment to the islands, nor the status of the islands as an overseas territory, nor the Falklanders' right to self-determination.

A new UK–Argentina dispute arose in February 2010 when UK-based oil company Rockhopper Exploration announced the discovery of a field, Sea Lion, believed to hold 320 million barrels of oil near the Falklands. The Argentinean government subsequently announced it would require permits for ships travelling through its waters and asked the UN to intervene. As U.S. and UK-based firms announced plans to buy stakes in Sea Lion, Argentina vowed to sue to prevent them from developing the field, and the capital city passed a law barring ships flying the British flag from using any of its ports. In a referendum on the political status of the islands held on March 10–11, 2013, 99.7 percent of voters indicated they preferred to remain an Overseas Territory of the United Kingdom. With a 92 percent turnout, only three valid no votes were recorded. Colin ROBERTS was appointed governor of the islands in April 2014.

Governor: Colin ROBERTS.

Chief Executive: Barry ROWLAND.

Gibraltar. The territory of Gibraltar, a rocky promontory at the western mouth of the Mediterranean, was captured by the British in 1704 and ceded by Spain to the UK by the Treaty of Utrecht in 1713. It has an area of 2.1 square miles (5.5 sq. km), and its population numbers 32,000 (2016E). The economy was long dependent on expenditures in support of its air and naval facilities; in recent years, however, tourism and financial services have grown in importance, and special status within the EC/EU has permitted it to transship foreign goods without payment of such duties as VATs. Financial services currently constitute about one-fifth of the economy, significantly more than UK defense expenditures.

British authority is represented by a governor. Substantial self-government was introduced in 1964 and further extended in 1969 by a new constitution that provided for a House of Assembly of 15 elected and 2 ex officio members (the attorney general and the financial and development secretary), plus a speaker appointed by the governor. Of the elected members, no more than 8 can represent the same party. The executive Gibraltar Council, chaired by the governor, has 4 additional ex officio members and 4 other members, including a chief minister, drawn from the elected members of the House of Assembly. The governor names as chief minister the majority leader in the assembly.

Gibraltar has been the subject of a lengthy dispute between Britain and Spain, which has pressed in the UN and elsewhere for "decolonization" of the territory and has impeded access to it by land and air. A referendum conducted by the British in 1967 showed an overwhelming preference for continuation of British rule, but Spain rejected the results and declared the referendum invalid. Spain's position was subsequently upheld by the UN General Assembly, which called in December 1968 for the ending of British administration by October 1, 1969. A month after promulgation of the 1969 constitution, which guarantees that the Gibraltarians will never have to accept Spanish rule unless the majority so desires, Spain closed its land frontier. In January 1978 Spain agreed to the restoration of telephone links to the city, but the border was not fully reopened until February 1985, following an agreement in November 1984 to provide equality of rights for Spaniards in Gibraltar and Gibraltarians in Spain; Britain also agreed to enter into discussions on the sovereignty issue.

At the election of March 1988 the **Gibraltar Socialist Labour Party** (GSLP) won the permissible maximum of eight legislative seats, its leader, Joe BOSSANO, becoming chief minister. Upon assuming office Bossano declared that most of the residents opposed the 1984 accord with Spain. Earlier, in December 1987, the assembly had rejected a UK-Spanish agreement on cooperative administration of the territory's airport. Quite apart from the impact of exclusive British control on the sovereignty issue, Spain has argued that the isthmus to the mainland, on which the airport is located, was not covered by the 1713 treaty.

The GSLP was again victorious at the election of January 16, 1992, retaining its majority with a vote share of 73 percent; the **Gibraltar Social Democrats** (GSD), led by Peter Caruana, won seven seats and the **Gibraltar National Party** (GNP), led by Dr. Joseph GARCIA, none. Following the election, Bossano insisted that his party's campaign for greater autonomy from Britain was not anti-Spanish, but rather "a clear expression of the desire for self-determination." Declining tourism and rising unemployment in 1993 caused further strains, with Bossano accusing Britain of neglecting Gibraltar's interests at the EU level.

The December 1994 round of UK–Spanish foreign ministers' talks on Gibraltar was snagged by heightened Spanish vigilance and consequential delays at the border crossing. Part of the Spanish concern was that Gibraltarians were increasingly supplementing traditional cigarette smuggling operations with drug trafficking and money laundering. In July 1995 UK pressure led the government to table a bill designed to stop money laundering and to bring Gibraltar's offshore banking into line with British and EU standards. Meanwhile, Chief Minister Bossano maintained his refusal to participate in the UK–Spanish talks, calling instead for direct discussions with Madrid on self-determination for Gibraltar.

A more flexible stance by the center-right GSD, which held that negotiations could proceed on any issue other than sovereignty, won the support of 48 percent of voters in a general election on May 16, 1996, with the GSLP slumping to 39 percent. The GSD secured eight assembly seats against seven for the GSLP, with the GNP again failing to win representation despite taking 13 percent of the vote. GSD leader Peter Caruana was sworn in as chief minister, pledging to participate in UK-Spanish talks.

In April 1998, in a shift of strategy, Madrid offered to open bilateral talks with Chief Minister Caruana regarding its recent proposal that Britain and Spain share sovereignty during a transitional period, with Gibraltar ultimately to achieve self-governing status under Spain—a proposal that Caruana and the Blair government dismissed. Later in the year both sides demonstrated a willingness to improve cooperation with regard to overflights of Spanish territory by Royal Air Force and NATO aircraft as well as the use and development of Gibraltar's airport. In 1999, however, a continuing dispute over fishing rights off Gibraltar for Spanish trawlers led Spanish customs officials to enforce strict, time-consuming border controls in retaliation. In October Caruana labeled bilateral talks on sovereignty between London and Madrid as "inappropriate and unacceptable." Instead, he proposed a "two flags, three voices" approach—the third voice being Gibraltar—which Spain has rejected.

In January 2000 Caruana surprised the opposition by calling an election for February 10, three months ahead of schedule. At the balloting his GSD increased its vote share to 58 percent and again claimed eight seats in the House of Assembly. An alliance of Bossano's GSLP and Joseph Garcia's small **Gibraltar Liberal Party** (successor to the GNP) won the other seven elective seats.

Two months later, on April 19, 2000, Spain and Britain announced that they had resolved differences over the territory's administrative status. Madrid's refusal to accept Gibraltar as a "competent authority" had delayed a range of EU business and economic initiatives. Spain agreed to recognize the validity of various documents issued by Gibraltar, including passports and identity cards. Britain agreed to act as a "postal box," relaying communications to and from Spain, which could thereby continue to avoid direct contact with the Gibraltar government. In addition, the agreement cleared the way for Britain to accede to parts of the EU's Schengen agreement on frontier controls, and it opened the way for Gibraltar-based financial corporations to compete throughout the EU. Chief Minister Caruana responded to the announcement of the agreement by saying, "Spain, Britain, and Gibraltar have all preserved their interests; there are no winners and no losers."

For the first time since December 1997, ministerial talks between Spain and the UK resumed on July 26, 2001, and by early 2002 it was clear that the two sides were moving closer toward a joint sovereignty arrangement. However, the prospect of any such arrangement was greeted with scorn by Caruana and generated, over the ensuing months, massive demonstrations by Gibraltarians.

Madrid and London nonetheless pressed ahead and by mid-2002 had reached agreement on joint rule, though differing as to its duration. The UK clearly viewed it as more than "transitional." In addition, Britain insisted that its military bases remain under its control. Caruana, meanwhile, refused to participate in the talks, save as an equal partner. Subsequently, on November 7 Gibraltar mounted a referendum in which 98.9 percent of the participants voted against shared sovereignty. In the November 28, 2003, general election, Caruana's Gibraltar Social Democrats retained its eight seats, while the GSLP-Liberal alliance again won seven.

After winning a challenge before the European Court of Human Rights to Gibraltar's exclusion from participating in elections to the European Parliament as part of the UK, Gibraltarians cast EU ballots for the first time in 2004 (as part of the South West England constituency). The UK's Conservative Party secured 69.5 percent of the vote in Gibraltar, reflecting dissatisfaction with the Labour government's joint sovereignty proposal as well as the significant attention (including an appearance by Conservative leader Michael Howard) voters in Gibraltar had received from the Conservatives.

In October 2004 Spain agreed, for the first time, to give Gibraltar a seat at the negotiating table, which led to the first three-party discussion in December. On February 10, 2005, the first session of a Trilateral Forum, with an open agenda, met in Málaga, Spain. Issues considered by the forum have included the airport and benefits for Spanish workers, but sovereignty has remained off the table.

On November 30, 2006, a referendum approved the new constitution, which was implemented on January 2, 2007. The updated constitution aimed to "modernize" relations with Britain, emphasize self-determination, and strengthen local autonomy, notably by increasing the number of legislative seats to 17, with the House of Assembly renamed the Gibraltar Parliament. The governor's veto powers were curtailed and those of the British foreign secretary were eliminated.

An August 12 collision between a Danish tanker, *Torm Gertrude,* and *New Flame,* a bulk carrier, prompted official complaints that Spanish beaches were being polluted. The Gibraltar government rejected these claims, but the incident emphasized the importance of coordination on maritime safety between the two neighbors.

In elections held October 11, 2007, the Gibraltar Social Democrats received 49 percent of votes; the Gibraltar Socialist Labour Party-Liberal coalition, 45 percent; the **Progressive Democratic Party,** 4 percent; the Parental Support Group, 1 percent; and the **New Gibraltar Democracy Party,** 1 percent. Turnout was 84.1 percent. (The **Progressive Democratic Party** [PDP] was launched in 2006, touting itself as a "positive alternative" for voters dissatisfied with the two major parties.) Caruana remained chief minister, with 10 seats in the Gibraltar Parliament, while the GSLP-Liberal alliance claimed 7.

Voters from Gibraltar showed their continued support for the UK Conservative Party by giving it 53.3 percent of the vote in the June 2009 balloting for the European Parliament. No other party received as much as 20 percent.

The general elections of December 8, 2011, dealt a loss to Caruana and the GSD, as the GSLP/LIB coalition took 48.9 percent of the vote and 10 seats. The GSD, which had governed the region since 1996, was awarded the remaining 7 seats. GSLP's Fabián PICARDO, who had become head of the party in April, was appointed chief minister on December 9.

Spain and Gibraltar became embroiled in a fishing rights dispute in early 2012, with skirmishes involving the British Royal Navy and Spanish police. Verbal conflict increased in August 2013, when Gibraltar dropped 70 concrete blocks into the sea to create an artificial reef but failed to alert Spain. Madrid stepped up border checks in response, prompting London to file a protest with the European Commission, saying the Spanish move impeded the flow of goods and people. Sir James DUTTON was appointed governor of Gibraltar in December. In February 2014 a Spanish naval vessel interrupted a British military exercise in Gibraltarian waters, prompting a formal protest by London.

In parliamentary elections on November 26, 2015, the GSLP/LIB coalition won an overwhelming victory with 68.4 percent of the vote and ten seats. The GSD won 31.6 percent of the vote and seven seats. Following Brexit, the Gibraltar government announced that it would remain part of the UK, despite overtures from Spain that reunification would allow the area to remain part of the EU.

Governor and Commander in Chief: Lt. Gen. Ed DAVIS.

Chief Minister: Fabián PICARDO.

Montserrat. A West Indian dependency in the Leeward Island group (see the Antigua and Barbuda map) with an area of 39.4 square miles (102 sq. km), Montserrat had a population (1996E) of 10,500 prior to large-scale evacuation (see below), which reduced the total to 4,482 in the 2001 census before recovering to an estimated 5,000 in 2010, and it remained unchanging in 2016. Its principal sources of income are tourism, offshore business services, and export of machinery and transport equipment. Ministerial government was introduced in 1960, the territory currently being administered by an Executive Council comprising the chief minister, three additional elected ministers, and two ex officio members (attorney general and financial secretary) under the presidency of the London-appointed governor. The Legislative Council is composed of nine elected members plus the same two ex officio members. Elections are normally held every five years.

In August 1987 John OSBORNE of the **People's Liberation Movement** (PLM) was installed for a third five-year term as chief minister. In August 1989 a dispute arose between Osborne and Gov. Christopher TURNER over the latter's alleged failure to inform elected officials of police raids on banks suspected of illicit financial transactions. In late November, with most banking licenses having been canceled, the Organization of Eastern Caribbean States issued a statement condemning as "absolutely repugnant" an announcement by the UK Foreign and Commonwealth Office (FCO) that a proposed new constitution would transfer responsibility for offshore banking regulation to the governor. In return for Osborne's acceptance of the controversial change, the new basic law as implemented in February 1990 recognized Montserrat's right to self-determination and withdrew certain legislative powers formerly held by the governor.

Osborne's PLM retained only one seat in the balloting of October 8, 1991, after which a new administration was formed by the **National Progressive Party** (NPP), led by Reuben MEADE, who had accused the Osborne administration of corruption and mismanagement. Efforts by the new Legislative Council to reestablish Montserrat as an offshore banking center failed. On February 2, 1993, after an investigation by Scotland Yard, Osborne and Noel TUITT, an associate, were cleared of the corruption charges, and in March 1994 Tuitt joined the NPP government following Meade's dismissal of David BRANDT as deputy chief minister. A partial eruption of long-dormant Chance's Peak volcano on July 19, 1995, precipitated the evacuation of some 5,000 people from their homes by late August. Further disruption was caused by a hurricane and tropical storm in September.

The eruptions continued intermittently in 1996, by the end of which the entire population of the southern part of the island, including the capital, Plymouth, had been evacuated; 800 were admitted to Britain under a special exemption from normally strict immigration rules, and the rest were housed in temporary accommodation in the north, where the second town, St. Peter's, became the de facto capital. With the island administration and the UK overseas aid program disputing how emergency aid grants should be used, the NPP retained only one seat in an election that was held on November 11 even though residents had fled four southern election districts. Two seats were won by the **Movement for National Reconstruction** (MNR), two by John Osborne's new **People's Progressive Alliance** (PPA), and two by independents. The outcome was an MNR-PPA coalition, MNR leader Bertrand OSBORNE being sworn in as chief minister on November 13.

In June 1997 the Soufrière Hills volcano erupted, claiming at least 19 lives and obliterating the capital. By the end of the year, only 3,400 of the original population were still on the island (with 500 living in temporary shelters), the remainder having either migrated to the UK or relocated to adjacent islands. The destruction slowed economic activity to a near standstill. As aid packages were caught up in London's governmental transition in May–June 1997 and the island administration was coping with abandoning the capital, simmering discontent grew among the islanders. On August 21, 1997, after four days of continuous demonstrations and protest, Chief Minister Osborne resigned and was replaced by independent David Brandt, who received the support of the MNR and NPP. Almost immediately, the new chief minister created conflict with London, alleging that aid packages for reconstruction and personal assistance, especially for off-island relocation, were insufficient to meet the emergency and that British policy was directed at depopulating the island. The criticism led London's secretary of state for international development to assert that the island was asking for "mad money" and "golden elephants next." A November 27, 1997, report by a Commons select committee placed blame for delays and maladministration on all parties, leading to a rationalization of the aid process and a gradual cooling of tensions.

On February 14, 1998, Robin Cook became the first FCO secretary to visit Montserrat. In May the UK government announced that all Montserratians who had not resettled elsewhere would be allowed to reside in Britain, while in June a draft development plan for the northern part of the island was announced. Despite continuing periodic volcanic activity and additional damage caused by Hurricane Georges in September, residents and businesses gradually began returning to the island's central zone. In 1999 the Blair administration announced that it would pay relocation travel costs for most Montserratians who wished to return to the island from Britain or Caribbean relocation sites. At the same time, the island administration moved forward with a proposal to build a new capital at Little Bay, on the northwestern coast, a project expected to take at least ten years to complete.

With the devastation in the south having made the parliamentary constituency system unworkable, in 2000 the government introduced legislation to facilitate adoption of a nine-member, at-large system for the 2001 election. By mid-2000 the resident population numbered about 5,000.

The collapse of Chief Minister Brandt's coalition in February 2001 precipitated an early election. At balloting on April 2 John Osborne's **New People's Liberation Movement** (NPLM) won seven of the nine seats in the Legislative Council, permitting him to reclaim the title of chief minister a decade after his last term in office. The NPP won the other two council seats.

Three parties and four independents contested the May 2006 legislative election. Although Rosalind CASSELL-SEALY's recently formed **Movement for Change and Prosperity** (MCAP) won four of the nine seats, Osborne's NPLM, which won three, formed a coalition administration with independent David BRANDT and Lowell LEWIS, the head of the **Montserrat Democratic Party** (MDP) and the leading vote-getter. Lewis stated after the election that the government's priorities would be the economy, housing, use of natural resources, and discussions with London about development projects, including a safe harbor and marina at Little Bay that would attract more visitors.

In June 2009 Chief Minister Lewis removed two cabinet ministers and called an election for September 8, two years earlier than required. The balloting produced a six-seat majority for the MCAP, and its leader, Reuben Meade, was sworn in as chief minister on September 9. The three remaining seats were won by independents, including Lewis.

After multiple rounds of talks with Montserratian and British officials, a new constitution came into force on September 27, 2011. The document grants the island more autonomy in international relations and strengthens human rights. Meade was sworn in as Montserrat's first premier on September 27, 2011. In balloting on September 11, 2014, the newly established **People's Democratic Movement** (PDM) won seven of the nine council seats. The remaining two were won by the MCAP. Donaldson ROMEO of the PDM was sworn in as premier on September 12. Elizabeth CARRIERE was appointed governor on August 5, 2015.

Governor: Elizabeth CARRIERE.

Premier: Donaldson ROMEO.

Pitcairn Islands. Isolated in the eastern South Pacific and known primarily because of its settlement in 1790 by the *Bounty* mutineers, Pitcairn has been a British possession since 1838. Jurisdictionally encompassing the adjacent uninhabited islands of Ducie, Henderson, and Oeno, the dependency has a total area of 1.75 square miles (4.53 sq. km) and a declining population, which in 2014 totaled 49 persons. The only established community is Adamstown. The largest island of the group, Henderson, is a UNESCO World Heritage Site and wildlife sanctuary.

The British high commissioner to New Zealand serves as governor. Locally, the island is administered by an Island Council that also has judicial responsibilities. It consists of ten members: an elected island mayor, who serves a three-year term; the chair of the council, ex officio; four directly elected members; one member indirectly selected by the chair and the elected members; two members nominated by the governor, including the island secretary; and a commissioner, who serves as liaison, linking the mayor, council, and governor. All but the mayor and secretary serve one-year terms. The offices of mayor and council chair were established in 1999, prior to which the duties of both were performed by an island magistrate.

The main sources of income are sales of fruits, vegetables, and souvenirs to passing ships and online sales of honey, soaps, stamps, collectible coins, handicrafts, as well as *Bounty*-related souvenirs. Pitcairn has also begun licensing its Internet designation, "pn," an international abbreviation for "telephone." At present, the territory is accessible only by ship; the closest airport is in Mangareva, French Polynesia, some 310 miles away. The UK Department for International Development (DFID) has funded repairs to infrastructure and provision of limited television and Internet service, as well as telephone connections for each household.

In mid-2004 a scandal that had simmered for more than a decade erupted with charges of child rape, incest, and indecent assault against seven men, including the island mayor, Steve CHRISTIAN. Upon Christian's conviction in October, the Island Council designated his sister, Brenda CHRISTIAN, as interim mayor. On December 15 the islanders elected Jay WARREN, a former council chair and the only one of the seven to be acquitted, as her successor. In December 2007 Mike Warren defeated Jay Warren in a three-person mayoralty election.

Discussions in September 2009 produced an agreement between the UK government and the Pitcairn Council to establish the Pitcairn Constitutional Order 2010 as of March 2010. The new constitution included provisions to ensure protection of fundamental rights, obligated the governor to consult with the council before making laws, and clarified the independent role of Pitcairn courts. Elections to the island council were held on December 24, 2011. Councilors do not have party affiliations. DFID funded programs to reduce the sexual exploitation of children on Pitcairn in its 2011–2015 work plan. In balloting on November 12, 2013, Shawn CHRISTIAN was elected mayor.

Governor: Jonathan SINCLAIR.

Island Mayor: Shawn CHRISTIAN.

St. Helena. St. Helena and its dependencies, Ascension Island and the Tristan da Cunha island group, occupy widely scattered positions in the South Atlantic between the west coast of Africa and the southern tip of South America. St. Helena, the seat of government, has an area of 47 square miles (122 sq. km) and a population (2016E) of 4,000. Its principal settlement is Jamestown. The economy currently depends on budgetary aid from the UK and on the sale of fishing licenses; small quantities of coffee are exported. Remittances from abroad also provide income, and a fish freezing facility has been established. With the final residence of the French Emperor Napoleon having been developed into a museum, St. Helena has potential as a tourist destination, but it remains largely inaccessible, with no airport or safe anchorage for small vessels.

Under a 1989 constitution the territory's governor presides over an Executive Council that includes 5 committee chairs drawn from the 12 elected members of the Legislative Council, who serve four-year terms; both councils also include, as ex officio members, the government secretary, attorney general, and financial secretary. The governor, represented by island administrators, holds executive and legislative powers for the dependencies.

Issues of immigration to the UK and citizenship in the mother country, along with local resentment over decisions by Gov. David SMALLMAN, led to disturbances in April 1997 over the governor's choice of a different social services committee chair than the nominee of the legislators. The approach of the July 9 Legislative Council elections also underscored the relatively limited power of the council compared to the reserve powers of the governor. Smallman retired in 1999.

The November 1999 breakdown of the island's only regularly scheduled cargo and passenger ship led to panic buying by Saints (as the islanders call themselves) concerned about running out of basic provisions. Although interim shipping arrangements were soon made, the temporary halt in the *St. Helena*'s bimonthly visits raised renewed concerns about the territory's isolation and led islanders to call for construction of an airport that would promote what has been termed "big earner" tourism. (Initial plans called for construction of an airport by 2010, but the UK government put the schedule on hold in light of the global recession of 2008–2009. However, in July 2010 the new British government announced it was overturning the previous Labour government's decision and committing £100 million for the project.)

In mid-2008 Gov. Andrew GURR proposed a new draft constitution for St. Helena, Ascension Island, and Tristan da Cunha that would, among other things, eliminate references to Ascension Island and Tristan da Cunha as dependencies of St. Helena, expand the authority of restructured elected councils on the islands, and incorporate a bill of rights. The new basic law was endorsed by the Legislative Council, submitted to the Queen, and came into force on September 1, 2009.

General elections were held on November 4, leading to the election of 12 nonpartisan councilors. Funding for an airport was secured in late 2011; when the facility is finished it is expected to transform the local economy (delays in construction led to the postponement of the airport's opening until February 2016).

Twelve nonpartisan councilors were elected in the July 17, 2013, general elections. All candidates came from a single constituency; in 2009 six councilors were selected from each of two constituencies. Lisa PHILLIPS became governor of the territory on April 26, 2016.

Governor: Lisa PHILLIPS.

Speaker of the Legislative Council: Margaret Anne Catherine HOPKINS.

Ascension Island. Encompassing an area of 34 square miles (88 sq. km) and with a 2010 population (excluding Royal Air Force personnel) of about 680, Ascension Island was annexed to St. Helena in 1922 and is presently the site of a major sea-turtle hatching ground, a BBC relay station, and a U.S. space-tracking station. During the Cold War it served as a signals intelligence base, and during the 1982 Falklands war it was a transit point for UK aircraft and ships. In March 1990 an Ariane telemetry reception station became operational under an agreement with the European Space Agency.

In mid-2000 a government study warned that the island's social structure was in danger of collapse without private sector development that could then fund such common services as education and health care. Otherwise, the island could become a "single-person's work-camp," with severe consequences not only for the permanent residents but also for the St. Helena citizens who earn their living there.

The first island government was introduced in April 2001, and an Island Council, chaired by the St. Helena governor, met for the first time in November 2002. Seven members are elected on a nonpartisan basis; two others (the attorney general and the director of financial services) serve ex officio. The governor later dissolved that council and called new elections in 2005. Claiming they were being used as bit players in a nonexistent democracy, six of the seven council members resigned in January 2007. The administrator announced in October 2010 that he was scheduling another election for February 2011, previously election attempts having failed because too few candidates were presented. Elections were held on February 25, 2011, with seven nominated candidates. Five of the candidates were subsequently elected and sworn in as councilors. New balloting was held on September 1, 2016, with six candidates seeking the five seats.

Administrator: Marc HOLLAND.

Tristan da Cunha. Annexed to St. Helena in 1938, Tristan da Cunha has an area of 38 square miles (98 sq. km), with a population in 2016 of 265 following the census that year. The dependency also includes the uninhabited islands of Inaccessible and Nightingale as well as Gough, a UNESCO World Heritage Site and residence of a South African meteorological team. The main island's entire population was evacuated because of a volcanic eruption in 1961 but was returned in 1963. Under the original 1985 constitution, the island administrator is advised by an Island Council of 11 members, with 8 elected for three-year terms (most recently in April 2010) and 3 appointed. The 2009 constitution reasserted the advisory role of the Island Council. In balloting on March 9, 2016, eight council members were elected, and three appointed.

Administrator: Alex MITHAM.

Chief Islander: Ian LAVARELLO.

Turks and Caicos Islands. The Turks and Caicos Islands, a southeastward extension of the Bahamas, consist of 30 small cays (8 inhabited) with a total area of 166 square miles (430 sq. km) and a population (2016E) of 35,000. The capital is Cockburn Town on Grand Turk. The principal industries are tourism, offshore banking and finance, and fishing. As of 1997, some 14,600 offshore businesses were registered in the islands.

Linked to Britain since 1766, the Turks and Caicos became a Crown colony in 1962 following Jamaica's independence. A constitution adopted in 1976 provided for a governor and an Executive Council comprising a chief minister, 5 additional ministers chosen by the governor from among elected legislators, and 3 ex officio members (governor, attorney general, chief secretary). A 20-member Legislative Council comprises 13 elected members, the 3 ex officio members of the Executive Council, 3 members appointed by the governor, and a speaker.

The former chief minister, Norman B. SAUNDERS, was obliged to resign after his arrest on drug-trafficking charges in Miami, Florida, in March 1985, Deputy Chief Minister Nathaniel J. S. FRANCIS being elected as his successor on March 28. Francis was also forced to resign following the issuance of a commission of inquiry report on arson, corruption, and related matters. The British government decided on July 25, 1986, to suspend the constitution and impose direct rule under the governor, with assistance from a four-member advisory council. Subsequently, a three-member constitutional commission was appointed to draft revisions in the basic law to inhibit corruption and patronage and promote "fair and effective administration."

At an election marking the islands' return to constitutional rule on March 3, 1988, the **People's Democratic Movement** (PDM), previously in opposition, won 11 of the 13 elective Legislative Council seats; by contrast, at the poll of April 3, 1991, the PDM (led by Derek TAYLOR) lost 6 seats to the **Progressive National Party** (PNP), whose total of 8 permitted Charles Washington MISICK to form a new government. In an election on January 31, 1995, Taylor and the PDM regained power, winning 8 seats against 4 for the PNP and 1 for Saunders standing as an independent, while the recently formed **United Democratic Party** (UDP), led by Wendal SWANN, failed to secure representation.

Resentment remaining from the 1986 constitutional suspension, objections to the reserve powers of the governor, and alleged British indifference to the islands found a focus in hostility to Gov. Martin BOURKE in April 1996. Among other things, he was charged with favoring one island (Providenciales, the center of the booming tourist industry) over the others in development. In addition, he caused concern by alleging both police corruption and a steady flow of drugs through the island chain. A petition for his removal from the island administration to the Foreign and Commonwealth Office was rejected in April 1996 after consultations with the islands, but in September, when his term expired, he was not reappointed.

At the election of April 24, 2003, the PDM secured seven of the elective seats on the Legislative Council, while the PNP took six. The PNP challenged the results in two closely fought constituencies and won both at by-elections on August 7. As a result, Taylor was obliged to resign in favor of Michael Misick.

A constitutional review process begun in 1999 concluded in 2006 with the adoption of a new constitution providing increased internal autonomy. The new document entered into force on August 9, at which time Misick was sworn in as the first premier of Turks and Caicos. The new constitution provides for a governor appointed by HM Queen Elizabeth II, a House of Assembly with 15 elective seats, and 6 seats appointed by the governor, including a speaker and attorney general. The cabinet consists of the governor, the premier, 6 other ministers, and the attorney general.

At the election of February 9, 2007, the PNP won a decisive majority by securing 13 of the elective seats on the Legislative Council, while the PDM, then led by Floyd SEYMOUR, took only 2.

In July 2008 (a month before leaving office), Gov. Richard TAUWHARE announced that a commission of inquiry had been launched to investigate allegations of government corruption in the islands. Premier Misick described the UK House of Commons report that had spurred the inquiry as "unbalanced" and based on false accusations.

By March 2009 the UK government had raised the possibility of temporarily suspending self-government in the islands and transferring governmental powers to the recently appointed governor, George WETHERELL. The inquiry commission subsequently reported that there were strong indications of "political immorality and immaturity and of general administrative incompetence," prompting Misick to resign his premiership. Galmo WILLIAMS was sworn in as premier on March 24. Misick sought to combat the charges in British courts, but by early summer he had exhausted his appeals. On August 14, 2009, under instructions from the UK Foreign Office, the governor imposed direct rule, which he said could last two years. Meanwhile, criminal investigation in the corruption charges against Misick and four of his cabinet ministers continued.

In June 2010 Douglas PARNELL was reelected as leader of the PDM. In August a PNP convention chose Clayton GREENE, a former speaker of the legislature, as the party's new leader. Although new elections had initially been scheduled for July 2011, the UK government in September 2010 postponed the balloting (and the return of local rule) indefinitely. PDM and PNP leaders strongly criticized the postponement, while also calling on the UK to increase funding to combat the recent upsurge in violent crime on the islands.

Shortly before leaving office in September 2011, Wetherell announced that the Commission of Inquiry report on possible corruption was recommending a criminal investigation by the police or others into the loan and land swap dealings of Misick. At his swearing-in ceremony on September 19 the newly appointed governor Ric Todd promised that elections would be held the following year. Interpol issued an arrest warrant for Misick, who asserted his innocence and moved to Brazil.

British direct rule ended with parliamentary elections held on November 9, 2012. The PNP won eight seats to the PDM's seven. Rufus EWING of the PNP was sworn in as premier on November 12. GDP declined by an average of 2.7 percent per year from 2009 to 2013. However, the gradual recovery of the tourist sector was expected to lead to an increase in GDP of 3.3 percent in 2014. Elections were scheduled for December 15, 2016.

Governor: John FREEMAN.

Premier: Rufus EWING.

Uninhabited Overseas Territories:

South Georgia and the South Sandwich Islands. South Georgia is an island of 1,387 square miles (3,592 sq. km) situated approximately 800 miles east-southeast of the Falklands; it was inhabited only by a British Antarctic Survey team at the time of brief occupation by Argentine forces in April 1982. The South Sandwich Islands lie about 470 miles southeast of South Georgia and were uninhabited until occupied by a group of alleged Argentine scientists in December 1976, who were forced to leave in June 1982. Formerly considered dependencies of the Falklands, the islands were given separate status in October 1985. The governor of the Falkland Islands also serves, ex officio, as territorial commissioner.

In 1993 concern over unregulated fishing led London to impose a 200-mile maritime zone and to increase efforts to manage the territory's fisheries, with particular emphasis on Patagonian toothfish, icefish, krill, and crab. On September 18, 1998, London announced that the 15-member military presence on South Georgia would be withdrawn in 2000, with territorial security to be assumed by troops stationed in the Falkland Islands.

In March 2004, in recognition of management practices that had been introduced to maintain sustainability, the South Georgia toothfish fishery became the first southern ocean fishery to be certified by the independent Marine Stewardship Council. Increased eco-tourism has brought more traffic to the islands in recent years, with indigenous species providing the greatest attractions. As ground-nesting birds have come under attack by a growing rodent population, the South Georgia Heritage Trust announced a plan to eradicate the rodents in 2011. In 2013 a reindeer eradication program began to protect the vegetation and avian residents.

Commissioner: Colin ROBERTS.

British Antarctic Territory. Formerly the southern portion of the Falkland Islands Dependencies, the British Antarctic Territory was separately established in 1962. Encompassing that portion of Antarctica between 20 degrees and 80 degrees west longitude, it includes the South Shetland and South Orkney Islands as well as the Antarctic Peninsula. Sovereignty over the greater portion of the territory is disputed by Great Britain, Argentina, and Chile, and its legal status remains in suspense in conformity with the Antarctic Treaty of December 1, 1959. Until June 30, 1989, the responsible British authority was a high commissioner, who served as governor of the Falkland Islands; on July 1 the administration was moved to the Foreign and Commonwealth Office, London, the head of the South Atlantic and Antarctic Department being designated commissioner. The British Antarctic Survey team, based year-round at Halley and Rothera stations, numbers roughly 40 to 50 in winter and 150 in summer, when stations at Fossil Bluff on Alexander Island and Signy in the South Orkneys are also manned. A number of other countries also maintain research facilities in the territory.

As of 2007 Britain planned to submit to the UN claims to areas of the Antarctic seabed, believed to be rich in energy reserves, based on UK sovereignty over the territory. Chile and Argentina could register competing petitions for rights to the seabed. Critics argued that the claims would undermine the 1959 Antarctic Treaty. In 2012 the UK announced that the southern area of the territory, some 169,000 square miles (437 square km) would henceforth be known as Queen Elizabeth Land.

Commissioner: Peter HAYES (resident in the United Kingdom).

Sovereign Base Areas:

Akrotiri and Dhekelia. Under the 1960 Treaty of Establishment, which recognized Cyprus as an independent republic, the UK retained sovereignty over two Sovereign Base Areas (SBAs). Akrotiri (Western Sovereign Base Area) and Dhekelia (Eastern Sovereign Base Area) are to remain sovereign British territory "until the Government of the United Kingdom, in view of changes in their military requirements, at any time decide to divest themselves of the sovereignty or effective control over the SBAs or any part thereof." Although the SBA boundaries were drawn to exclude civilian population centers, the separation of the island into predominantly ethnic Greek and ethnic Turkish sectors in the mid-1970s led to a influx of civilians, and approximately 7,000 Cypriots now live within the SBAs. The UK resident population, military and civilian, numbers some 7,800. The UK Ministry of Defense owns approximately 20 percent of the 98 square miles (254 sq. km) that constitute the SBAs, as does the Crown, with the balance being privately held. Most of the private land is farmed.

Reporting to the Ministry of Defense rather than the Foreign and Commonwealth Office, the SBA administration, headquartered in Episkopi, is led by the commander of the British Forces Cyprus, who has executive and legislative powers comparable to those of a governor in a civilian overseas territory. Assisting the administrator are a chief officer, an attorney general, an administrative secretary, and two area officers. A Court of the Sovereign Base Areas adjudicates nonmilitary offenses.

Administrator: Maj. Gen. Richard J. CRIPWELL.

UNITED KINGDOM: NORTHERN IRELAND

Political Status: Autonomous province of the United Kingdom under separate parliamentary regime established in 1921 but suspended March 30, 1972; coalition executive formed January 1, 1974; direct rule reimposed May 28, 1974; consultative Northern Ireland Assembly elected October 20, 1982, but dissolved by United Kingdom June 19, 1986; devolution of limited self-rule to (new) Northern Ireland Assembly and multiparty power-sharing Northern Ireland Executive effected December 2, 1999; direct rule reimposed February 11–May 30, 2000, for one day on August 11, 2001, for one day on September 22, 2001, and from October 15, 2002, until the return of limited self-rule upon the convening of a new assembly and election of a new executive on May 8, 2007, in accordance with the St. Andrews Agreement of October 2006.

Area: 5,452 sq. mi. (14,120 sq. km).

Population: (Included in Ireland).

Major Urban Center (2015E—UN): BELFAST (605,000).

Official Language: English.

Monetary Unit: Pound Sterling (market rate October 1, 2016: 0.77 pound = $1US).

First Minister: Arlene FOSTER (Democratic Unionist Party); was appointed by the Northern Ireland Assembly on January 11, 2016, succeeding Peter ROBINSON (Democratic Unionist Party), who resigned on January 11, 2016; elected on May 12, 2016.

Deputy First Minister: Martin McGUINNESS (*Sinn Féin*); elected by the Northern Ireland Assembly on May 8, 2007; reelected June 5, 2008, and again on May 5, 2011, on a joint ticket with First Minister Peter Robinson; reappointed on joint ticket with the first minister on January 11, 2016; reelected on May 12, 2016.

United Kingdom Secretary of State for Northern Ireland: James BROKENSHIRE (Conservative Party); appointed on July 11, 2016, by UK Prime Minister Theresa May (Conservative Party), succeeding Theresa VILLIERS (Conservative Party).

THE COUNTRY

Geographically an integral part of Ireland, the six northern Irish counties (collectively known as "Ulster," although excluding three counties of the historic province of that name) are politically included within the UK for reasons rooted in the ethnic and religious divisions introduced into Ireland by English and Scottish settlement in the 17th century. As a result of this colonization effort, the long-established

Roman Catholic population of the northern counties came to be heavily outnumbered by Protestants, who assumed a dominant political, social, and economic position and insisted on continued association of the territory with the UK when the rest of Ireland became independent after World War I. Although a minority, Roman Catholics are strongly represented throughout Northern Ireland and constitute a rising proportion of the total population (40.3 percent according to the 2001 UK census, compared to 45.6 percent Protestant). Catholic complaints of discrimination, especially in regard to the allocation of housing and jobs and to limitation of the franchise in local elections, were the immediate cause of the serious disturbances that commenced in Northern Ireland during 1968–1969.

Despite recurring political violence, foreign investors have been drawn to Ulster by lucrative financial incentives and its proximity to the European market. After sharing in the UK recession of the early 1990s, Northern Ireland experienced an economic upturn in 1993. The signing of the multiparty Good Friday Agreement in April 1998 served as another spur to growth.

Northern Ireland's primary trading partners are Great Britain and the rest of the European Union. For 2010–2011, sales to Great Britain represented 46 percent of total sales, while France, Germany, and the Netherlands comprised 58.6 percent of sales to the rest of the EU. In addition to clothing and textiles, food and beverages, and machinery, growth industries include pharmaceuticals, software, telecommunications, and electronics. The creative media sector, which includes television, radio, film, animation, and computer games, is growing, and efforts are being made to locate and train workers with appropriate skillsets.

Women made up 45.6 percent of the active labor force in 2007, and the ratio of male/female hourly wage rates was virtually at parity. Women hold 20 of 108 seats in the Northern Ireland Assembly, 3 of 13 cabinet posts, 4 of the 18 seats at Westminster, and 21 percent of local councilor–elected posts.

Gross value added (GVA) per capita (the UK measure of economic prosperity) is only 79 percent of the UK as a whole. Meanwhile, unemployment, which had improved steadily over the past decade to 4 percent in 2007, rose steadily to 8 percent in 2011 as the effects of the global financial crisis took hold. GDP for the region declined by 0.8 percent in 2012, before rising by 0.2 percent in 2013. The unemployment rate was 7.5 percent for 2013, slightly lower than the overall UK rate. GDP grew by 1.4 percent in 2015, and was estimated to expand by 0.9 percent in 2016. In 2016 unemployment fell to 5.6 percent.

GOVERNMENT AND POLITICS

Political background. Governed as an integral part of Ireland, and therefore of the UK, throughout the 19th and early 20th centuries, Northern Ireland acquired autonomous status in 1921 as part of a general readjustment necessitated by the success of the Irish independence movement in the rest of Ireland. The Government of Ireland Act of 1920 provided for a division of Ireland as a whole into separate northern and southern sections, each with its own legislature. Enshrined in the December 1921 Anglo-Irish treaty, this arrangement was reluctantly accepted by the Irish nationalist authorities in Dublin but embraced in Northern Ireland as the best available means of continuing as an integral part of the UK. The new government of Northern Ireland was dominated from the beginning by the pro-British, Protestant interests controlling the Ulster Unionist Party (UUP), with militant elements becoming known as "loyalists." Ties with Britain were sedulously maintained, for both religious and historic reasons and because of accompanying economic benefits, including social services and agricultural subsidies. Opposition Catholic sentiment in favor of union with the Irish Republic represented a continuing but long-subdued source of tension.

Catholic-led "civil rights" demonstrations against political and social discrimination erupted in 1968, evoking counterdemonstrations by Protestant extremists and leading to increasingly serious disorders, particularly in Londonderry (known to Catholics as Derry). In November 1968 the government of Terence O'NEILL proposed a number of reform measures that failed to halt the disturbances and yielded an erosion of support for the prime minister within his own government and party. Parliament was accordingly dissolved, with a new election in February 1969 producing the usual unionist majority but failing to resolve an internal UUP conflict. In April mounting disorder and acts of sabotage led the Northern Ireland government to request that British army units be assigned to guard key installations. Although O'Neill persuaded the UUP to accept the principle of universal adult franchise at the next local government elections, he resigned as party leader on April 28 and as prime minister three days later. His successor in both offices, Maj. James D. CHICHESTER-CLARK, an advocate of moderate reform, was chosen by a 17–16 vote of the UUP over Brian FAULKNER, an opponent of the O'Neill reform program. The government promptly announced an amnesty for all persons involved in the recent disturbances and received a unanimous vote of confidence on May 7.

After renewed rioting in Belfast, Londonderry, and elsewhere during the first half of August 1969, Chichester-Clark agreed on August 19 that all security forces in Northern Ireland would be placed under British command; that Britain would assume ultimate responsibility for public order; and that steps would be taken to ensure equal treatment of all citizens in Northern Ireland in regard to voting rights, housing, and other issues. The subsequent deployment of regular British soldiers in the province was at first welcomed by the Catholic population as affording protection from Protestant incursions into their localities. However, under the influence of the Provisional Irish Republican Army (Provisional IRA or the "Provos"), many Catholics quickly came to see the British troops as an occupying force, and their alienation increased as the result of the internment without trial of several hundred Catholics in August 1971. Growing polarization was highlighted by the formation in 1971 of the ultra-loyalist Democratic Unionist Party (DUP) by a hard-line faction of the UUP led by Dr. Ian PAISLEY.

The situation turned sharply worse on "Bloody Sunday," January 30, 1972, when a prohibited Catholic civil-rights march in Londonderry was infiltrated by hooligan elements, and 14 unarmed civilians died as the result of clashes with British troops. A wave of violence and hysteria followed. Unable to act in agreement with the Belfast regime of Prime Minister Brian Faulkner, who had succeeded Chichester-Clark in March 1971, British Prime Minister Edward Heath announced that he would reimpose direct rule. The Northern Ireland Parliament was prorogued rather than dissolved, and William (subsequently Viscount) WHITELAW was designated to exercise necessary authority through the newly created office of secretary of state for Northern Ireland. With the backing of the three leading British parties, these changes were quickly approved by the British Parliament and became effective, initially for a period of one year, on March 30, 1972. The 1972 death toll from political violence reached 478, the highest annual total during the post-1969 "Troubles."

A plebiscite on the future of Northern Ireland was held on March 8, 1973, but was boycotted by the Catholic parties. An unimpressive 57.4 percent of the electorate voted for Ulster's remaining within the UK, while 0.6 percent voted for union with the Republic of Ireland and the remainder abstained. The British government subsequently organized the election on June 28 of a Northern Ireland Assembly of 80 members to serve a four-year term. This step was formalized on July 18 by passage of a parliamentary bill permitting the devolution of powers to the assembly and an executive, and on November 27 Brian Faulkner was named chief of an executive-designate that included representatives of both Protestant and Catholic factions.

In a meeting in Sunningdale, England on December 6–9, 1973, that was attended by members of the Irish and UK governments as well as the executive-designate of Northern Ireland, agreement was reached on the establishment of a tripartite Council of Ireland to oversee changes in the relationship between the northern and southern Irish governments. On January 1, 1974, direct rule was terminated. While the (mainly Catholic) Social Democratic and Labour Party (SDLP) endorsed the agreement, the bulk of the Unionist Party rejected it, forcing Faulkner's resignation as party leader on January 7 and as chief executive on May 28, in the wake of which direct rule was again imposed.

In July 1974 the UK Parliament passed the Northern Ireland Act of 1974, which authorized the election of a Constitutional Convention. At balloting on May 1, 1975, the United Ulster Unionist Coalition (UUUC), a grouping of largely "anti-Sunningdale" parties, won 45 of 78 convention seats. On September 8 the UUUC convention members voted 37–1 against the participation of republicans in a future Northern Ireland cabinet, and on November 20 the convention concluded its sitting with a formal report that embraced only UUUC proposals. The convention was reconvened on February 3, 1976, in the hope of reaching agreement with the SDLP and other opposition parties, but it registered no further progress and was dissolved a month later.

The UUUC was itself dissolved on May 4, 1977, following the failure of a general strike called by its more intransigent loyalist components, acting in concert with the Ulster Workers' Council (UWC) and the Ulster Defense Association (UDA), the largest of the Protestant paramilitary groups. With the level of violence having declined, Secretary of State for Northern Ireland Roy MASON proposed in late

November that a new attempt be made to restore local rule. The effort was abandoned, however, because of intensified violence in the first quarter of 1978, which prompted the House of Commons in late June to extend the period of direct rule for another year. In the absence of a political settlement, the order was renewed annually thereafter.

Following the failure of another attempt at constitutional talks in early 1980 and a further escalation of violence, seven republican inmates of the Maze prison near Belfast began a hunger strike on October 27 in support of a demand for "political" status. While the strike was called off on December 18 following government promises of improvement in prison conditions, the action was widely publicized and was renewed in March 1981, with ten prisoners ultimately dying, including Bobby SANDS and Kieran DOHERTY, who had won election to, respectively, the UK and Irish parliaments shortly before their deaths. The most significant diplomatic development of the year was a meeting in London on November 6 at which UK prime minister Margaret Thatcher and Irish prime minister Garret FitzGerald agreed to set up an Anglo-Irish Intergovernmental Council (AIIC) to meet on a periodic basis to discuss matters of common concern.

In early 1982 the Thatcher government secured parliamentary approval for the gradual reintroduction of home rule under a scheme dubbed "rolling devolution." The initiative assumed substantive form with balloting on October 20 for a new 78-member Northern Ireland Assembly. For the first time the Provisional *Sinn Féin* (the political wing of the Provisional IRA) participated in the process, obtaining five seats. The poll was accompanied, however, by an upsurge of terrorist activity, with both the Provisional *Sinn Féin* and the SDLP boycotting the assembly session that convened on November 11 to formulate devolution recommendations.

During a meeting in Hillsborough Castle, Northern Ireland, on November 15, 1985, Prime Ministers Thatcher and FitzGerald concluded an Anglo-Irish Agreement that established an Intergovernmental Conference (IGC) within the context of the AIIC to deal on a regular basis with political and security issues affecting the troubled region. Subsequently, in reaction to unionist maneuvering, the small nonsectarian Alliance Party joined *Sinn Féin* and the SDLP in boycotting the Northern Ireland Assembly, while the 15 unionist MPs resigned their seats in the UK House of Commons to force by-elections as a form of referendum on the Hillsborough accord. (One unionist seat fell to the SDLP.) On June 19, 1986, the UK government dissolved the assembly, which had become little more than an anti-accord forum for unionists. The dissolution, which signaled the failure of London's seventh major peace initiative in 14 years, did not, however, abolish the body, leaving open the possibility of future electoral replenishment.

In February 1989 agreement was reached on the functions and membership of another joint undertaking provided for in the Anglo-Irish accord: a British–Irish Inter-Parliamentary Body of 25 MPs from each country, including minority party representatives. The first meeting of the new group opened in London on February 26, 1990, but two seats reserved for unionist parliamentarians remained vacant because of their continued opposition to the 1985 accord.

In March 1991 continued tension in the province was momentarily eased by the announcement of agreement on new talks in three "strands": first, discussions between the Northern Ireland "constitutional" parties, focusing on devolution and power sharing, chaired by Secretary of State Peter BROOKE; second, "North-South" talks between the Northern Ireland parties and the UK and Irish governments; and third, "East-West" talks between London and Dublin on replacing the 1985 Anglo-Irish Agreement. Any agreement reached under the talks would be put to referendums in both Northern Ireland and the Republic of Ireland.

Although preliminary first-strand talks opened on schedule on April 30, 1991, the so-called Brooke initiative quickly ran into procedural and political obstacles. Not until June 17 was it possible for full first-strand discussions to begin in Belfast, marking the first formal inter-party talks in Northern Ireland in 16 years. However, it became apparent that Brooke had overestimated the willingness of the parties to seek common ground, with the unionist parties remaining resolutely opposed to any formula that appeared to give Dublin a role in Northern Ireland's affairs.

A July 1991 breakdown in the talks was followed by an escalation of sectarian violence, and by January 1992 the number of British troops assigned to the province had risen to 11,500. The conflict nonetheless continued, with the number of killings attributed to Protestant paramilitary groups, principally the Ulster Volunteer Force (UVF) and the Ulster Freedom Fighters (UFF), reportedly approaching those perpetrated by the IRA.

The talks were formally suspended by Brooke on January 27, 1992, pending the outcome of the UK election on April 9. In that contest the 17 Northern Ireland constituencies returned 13 Unionists, while the SDLP increased its representation in the House of Commons to 4 by gaining the West Belfast seat held since 1983 by the *Sinn Féin* president, Gerard (Gerry) ADAMS. In the postelection reshuffle Brooke was replaced as Northern Ireland secretary by Sir Patrick MAYHEW, who on April 17 announced his intention to resume the talks.

On June 30, 1992, representatives of the four leading Ulster formations met in London with an Irish government delegation, the first time since Ireland became independent in 1921 that hard-line unionists had met with Irish officials. On July 1 the participants agreed to undertake sustained negotiations on the North-South relationship, but deadlock soon emerged, in part over the Republic of Ireland's continuing constitutional claim to the whole of Ulster. The talks formally concluded without agreement in early November, whereupon meetings of the IGC resumed. Meanwhile, sectarian violence continued unabated. On August 10, 1992, the UK government announced the banning of the loyalist UDA, bringing the number of proscribed organizations in Northern Ireland to ten.

The advent of a *Fianna Fáil*/Labour coalition government in the Republic of Ireland in January 1993 heralded a more accommodating line by Dublin, and despite continuing IRA bombings in England, the quest for a negotiated settlement appeared to gain momentum. During April and May 1993, SDLP leader John HUME held a series of meetings with *Sinn Féin* leader Adams in what was characterized by Hume as an effort to bring about "a total cessation of all violence." On May 27 Irish President Mary Robinson conferred in London with Queen Elizabeth II in the first such meeting between the two countries' heads of state. Most significantly, on December 15, 1993, Prime Ministers John Major and Albert Reynolds issued their Downing Street Declaration. Aiming to bring about the end of hostilities in the province, the declaration acknowledged that "the people of the island of Ireland" might wish to opt for unification but reiterated that "it would be wrong to attempt to impose a united Ireland in the absence of the freely given consent of the majority of the people of Northern Ireland." The declaration thereby raised the possibility that Dublin would take steps to delete its constitutional claim to the North; it also stated that if IRA violence were brought to "a permanent end," *Sinn Féin* could expect to participate in all-party talks. Reaction to the new document was decidedly cool among the unionists, while *Sinn Féin* declined to give an immediate response, preferring instead to call for "clarifications."

The 25-year-old logjam in Northern Ireland appeared to be broken by an IRA announcement on August 31, 1994, that from midnight that day "there will be a complete cessation of military operations" by all IRA units. Noting that "an opportunity to secure a just and lasting settlement has been created," the statement called for "inclusive negotiations." Received with great rejoicing in Northern Ireland, especially among Catholics, the IRA announcement prompted London to take the position that if the cease-fire proved to be a permanent renunciation of violence, *Sinn Féin* would be invited to participate in future negotiations. In Dublin Prime Minister Reynolds took speedier action, receiving Adams on September 5 to discuss the convening of a "forum of peace and reconciliation." Unionist spokespersons, however, described the cease-fire as a public relations ploy and demanded that the IRA surrender its weapons and explosives prior to meaningful talks. On October 13 the three main loyalist paramilitary organizations also declared a cessation of hostilities but made it clear that they would not surrender their weapons until the IRA had done so.

The position of *Sinn Féin,* however, was that arms decommissioning should be dealt with at the talks rather than before and should be part of a complete "demilitarization" of Northern Ireland, including the withdrawal of British troops. This basic impasse persisted, despite the progressive upgrading of the UK government's contacts with *Sinn Féin.* The first public talks between the two sides took place in December 1994 in Belfast, while Adams and Secretary of State Mayhew finally met on May 24, 1995, on the margins of a Washington conference aimed at promoting investment in Northern Ireland.

Meanwhile, the UK and the Irish government, now headed by Prime Minister John Bruton, continued to clarify their positions. A joint "framework document" issued on February 22, 1995, envisaged the creation of a North-South council with "executive, harmonizing or consultative functions" and the restoration of self-government to Northern Ireland under a power-sharing formula. The document also recorded the Irish government's pledge to introduce a constitutional amendment deleting any territorial claim to Northern Ireland, while the UK government would propose constitutional legislation enshrining its commitment to uphold the democratic wish of the Northern majority. Reactions to the document were predictable: conditional approval from Adams, who noted that "its ethos is for one Ireland," but strong condemnation from unionist leaders, with Paisley of the DUP describing it as "Ulster's death warrant."

In early July 1995 violence resurged in conjunction with the annual "marching season," during which Protestant fraternal orders hold upward of 3,000 marches, some through Catholic neighborhoods, chiefly to mark the July 1690 defeat of the Catholic King James II by the Protestant William of Orange at the Battle of the Boyne. Amid fears that the peace process was losing momentum, on July 24 the UK and Irish prime ministers issued a three-part plan under which the disarmament of paramilitary groups would be supervised by an international commission, a target date would be set for the opening of all-party talks, and early release dates would be set for some of the 1,000 republican and loyalist paramilitaries currently serving prison sentences. The timing of decommissioning remained a sticking point, however, with London continuing to insist on paramilitary disarmament as a precondition for all-party discussions. While attempting to persuade London to modify its stance, the Dublin government went ahead with its "forum of peace and reconciliation," in which *Sinn Féin,* the SDLP, and a large number of others (but not the main unionist parties) set out their positions on the issue and the constitutional future. In September the UUP elected a new leader, David TRIMBLE, who had come to prominence in July by defying a police blockade and leading an Orange Order march through the Catholic neighborhood of Drumcree, near Portadown.

Intensive UK–Irish negotiations in October–November 1995 attempted to confront the decommissioning issue and thereby prepare the way for multiparty negotiations. As a result, on December 15 an international commission headed by former U.S. senator George Mitchell began to address the disarmament question, while a tentative date of February 1996 was set for opening interparty talks. In January 1996 the Mitchell panel proposed that all parties adhere to six principles, including the renunciation of political violence and a commitment to eventual, full decommissioning under international supervision.

Blaming what it labeled British intransigence, the IRA abruptly ended its cease-fire on February 2, when a massive bomb exploded in London, killing two men and causing damage later estimated at up to $300 million. The bombing appeared to catch even *Sinn Féin* off guard, casting doubt on the extent of its influence over the IRA. Security measures in Northern Ireland, which had been relaxed, were rapidly stepped up, and on February 28 both governments demanded an immediate and unequivocal restoration of the cease-fire, pending which *Sinn Féin* would be excluded from talks.

After individual discussions with Northern Ireland parties started in March (the uninvited *Sinn Féin* representatives being turned away), the UK government enacted legislation authorizing election of a consultative Northern Ireland Forum for Political Dialogue. Balloting took place on May 30, returning 90 members from 18 constituencies and a further 20 members from the 10 parties securing the largest shares of the popular vote. Although *Sinn Féin* participated in the election, winning 17 seats on a larger-than-expected vote share, it remained aloof from the forum. Moreover, the SDLP, with 21 seats, soon withdrew, preferring to concentrate on direct talks. Thus, the forum was left to the two main unionist parties, the UUP (30 seats) and the DUP (24 seats), and to various smaller groupings. The latter included the Ulster Democratic Party (UDP) and the Progressive Unionist Party (PUP), which were described as "close to the thinking of" the leading loyalist paramilitaries, the UDA and the UVF, respectively.

With the forum effectively sidelined by the absence of the nationalist parties, attention turned to the multiparty negotiations, which opened on June 10, 1996, in Stormont Castle, the seat of the direct-rule administration. Both governments and all of the main parties except *Sinn Féin,* whose leaders were again turned away, took part, although the proceedings were initially stalled by unionist objections to the proposal that former senator Mitchell be the chair. In July the traditional Protestant marches again provoked sectarian altercations, while the IRA and a splinter, the Continuity Army Council, or Continuity IRA, continued their attacks into the autumn and beyond. In October the UUP and the SDLP finally agreed on a full agenda for the Stormont negotiations, while in November the SDLP and *Sinn Féin* requested, among other things, a guarantee that *Sinn Féin* would be admitted to the talks if the IRA declared another cease-fire. Britain and Ireland disagreed, however, on the precise terms for *Sinn Féin*'s participation.

Talks resumed in January 1997 but were suspended in March to await the UK election of May 1, in which the UUP took 10 of Northern Ireland's 18 seats in the House of Commons, followed by the SDLP with 3, and the DUP and *Sinn Féin* with 2 each. Under Prime Minister Tony Blair the new UK Labour government moved swiftly to place Northern Ireland high on the political agenda, with Dr. Marjorie "Mo" MOWLAM assuming office as secretary of state for Northern Ireland. Despite another round of hostilities associated with the Protestant marching season, on July 19 the IRA announced a resumption of the August 1994 cease-fire, opening the way for *Sinn Féin* to join the multiparty talks when they began again in mid-September. Although *Sinn Féin* had explicitly endorsed the six Mitchell principles, which also included a commitment to abide by the terms of any negotiated peace settlement, the unionists, objecting to *Sinn Féin*'s presence, boycotted the opening session. In late September, however, in a precedent-shattering shift of policy that drew the wrath of hard-line loyalists, the UUP's Trimble agreed to rejoin the talks despite *Sinn Féin*'s presence. Thus, representatives of eight parties—the UUP, SDLP, *Sinn Féin,* UDP, PUP, the Alliance Party of Northern Ireland (APNI), the Northern Ireland Women's Coalition, and the Labour Coalition—gathered in Stormont in October, the principal absentee being Paisley's DUP. In tandem, an Independent International Commission on Decommissioning (IICD), chaired by a retired Canadian general, John de Chastelain, broached the disarmament issue.

In October 1997 Tony Blair met with Gerry Adams, the first such meeting between a UK prime minister and *Sinn Féin* in more than 70 years, while in November the new Irish prime minister, Bertie Ahern, conferred with the UUP's Trimble. Despite such confidence-building steps, little progress was achieved before the Christmas break, during which the leader of the paramilitary Loyalist Volunteer Force (LVF), Billy WRIGHT, was murdered inside the Maze prison by members of the Irish National Liberation Army (INLA). Retaliations ensued, and on January 9, in a spectacular political gambit, Secretary Mowlam met in the Maze with loyalist prisoners and earned their support for continued peace discussions.

Although provocations by paramilitaries on both sides continued, Prime Ministers Blair and Ahern issued a brief framework for peace titled "Propositions on Heads of Agreement" on January 12, 1998. The outline proposed "balanced" constitutional change by both the UK and Ireland; establishment of a directly elected Northern Ireland legislature and a North-South ministerial body; formation of British–Irish "intergovernmental machinery"; and adoption of "practical and effective measures" concerning such issues as prisoners, security, and decommissioning. The constitutional changes put forward by the prime ministers included excision of the Irish Republic's territorial claim to Northern Ireland, coupled with revision of British constitutional legislation dealing with the UK's authority over affairs in the North. *Sinn Féin* initially evinced little enthusiasm for the proposal, which fell significantly short of the party's long-standing demand for reunification with the South, while unionists expressed concern that creation of a North-South organ would in fact pave the way for reunification.

Early in 1998 the UDP and *Sinn Féin* were separately suspended from the multiparty talks because of cease-fire violations committed by their paramilitary associates, the UFF and the IRA, respectively, but in March both parties were readmitted to Stormont. On March 25 Mitchell set a 15-day deadline for the two governments and the eight participating parties to achieve a final peace plan, which was concluded on April 10 (a day late) following a marathon negotiating session. The Belfast Agreement, which quickly became better known as the Good Friday Agreement, called for the following: (Strand One) creation of a Northern Ireland Assembly with full authority to legislate "in devolved areas," an Executive Committee (Northern Ireland Executive) of ministers drawn from the legislature and headed by a first minister and a deputy first minister, a consultative Civic Forum of community and business leaders, and a continuing role for the secretary of state for Northern Ireland in matters not devolved to the new institutions; (Strand Two) creation of a North-South Ministerial Council; and (Strand Three) establishment of a British-Irish Council with representatives from Ireland and all the British isles, including devolved institutions in Scotland and Wales. In addition to requiring removal from Ireland's constitution of the claim to Northern Ireland, the agreement mandated adherence to human rights and equal opportunity, full decommissioning by May 2000, normalization of security arrangements in Northern Ireland (including the withdrawal of the roughly 17,500 British troops), and formation of an independent commission to review policing procedures. Finally, an assessment of the criminal justice system was to include "an accelerated programme for the release of prisoners" affiliated with those organizations maintaining a "complete and unequivocal" cease-fire. Accompanying the Good Friday Agreement was a new British–Irish Agreement, superseding the 1985 Anglo-Irish Agreement and committing London and Dublin to carrying through on the peace arrangements.

With an island-wide referendum—the first such vote since partition—scheduled for May 22, supporters and opponents of the Good Friday Agreement quickly began campaigning. In April David Trimble convinced the UUP as a whole to back the agreement despite vehement opposition from six of his party's ten MPs, the DUP, the small United Kingdom Unionist Party (UKUP), and the fraternal Orange Order. Meeting in Dublin on May 10, a special *Sinn Féin* conference also endorsed the agreement and authorized members to sit in the proposed Northern Ireland Assembly. In the end, the referendum passed with a 71 percent affirmative vote in the North, on a turnout of 81 percent. Balloting for the new 108-member assembly took place on June 25, with 16 parties offering candidates. The UUP obtained a plurality of 28 seats, followed by the SDLP with 24, the DUP with 20, and *Sinn Féin* with 18. In all, opposition unionists claimed 28 seats, just short of the number that would have enabled them to tie up legislation. (See Constitution and government, below, for a discussion of rules governing passage of measures requiring "cross-community support.")

On July 1, 1998, the new Northern Ireland Assembly elected the UUP's Trimble as first minister and the SDLP's Seamus MALLON as deputy first minister, John Hume having declined the latter nomination. Already, however, a major stumbling block to full formation of the power-sharing Executive Committee, and thus to devolution, had emerged. Whereas Trimble demanded that the IRA begin decommissioning its arms before he would allow *Sinn Féin* to take up any ministerial positions, Gerry Adams argued that the Good Friday Agreement contained no such stipulation.

Once again, the Protestant marching season brought with it a series of violent incidents, including the torching of ten Catholic churches on July 2–3, 1998. Following a ruling by an independent Parades Commission that the traditional Orange Order parade in Drumcree would not be allowed to pass through a Catholic neighborhood, more than 5,000 Orangemen protested at the barricades. A month later, on August 15, in the worst carnage since the "Troubles" began, a car bomb exploded in Omagh, killing 29 and injuring more than 200 others. A recently formed IRA splinter, the "Real IRA," claimed responsibility for the attack, which even the INLA and the Continuity IRA condemned. The bombing provoked Prime Ministers Blair and Ahern to introduce in their respective legislatures antiterrorism measures that Ahern characterized as "extremely draconian." Both parliaments passed similar bills in early September.

On September 10, 1998, for the first time, Trimble and Adams met privately in Stormont, but they made no progress on the decommissioning dispute. Trimble, responding to the announcement on October 16 that he and John Hume had won the Nobel Peace Prize for their efforts, expressed the hope that the decision had not been "premature." On October 31 the negotiators missed the deadline set by the Good Friday Agreement for creation of the "shadow" (predevolution) Executive Committee and the North-South Ministerial Council. The stalemate appeared broken on December 18 with the announcement in Stormont of a further agreement covering formation of ten government departments and six cross-border bodies, the principal goal being British transfer of authority to the Northern Ireland Assembly and Executive Committee in February 1999. The new agreement provided for the UUP and the SDLP to head three departments each, with *Sinn Féin* and the DUP being responsible for two each. Ministerial nominations would await progress on disarmament. Although the LVF on the same day became the first paramilitary group to turn in some of its weapons, the IRA refused to reciprocate, calling the LVF action a "stunt."

In January 1999 Trimble set February 15 as the date for inaugurating the Executive Committee, while Secretary of State Mowlam established March 10 as the date for transferring powers to the assembly. However, neither deadline was met. On February 16 the assembly voted 77–26 in favor of the December power-sharing accord and also approved creation of the Civic Forum, the North-South Ministerial Council, the British-Irish Council, and the cross-border bodies. Nevertheless, the decommissioning issue remained unresolved, even after the UUP and *Sinn Féin* held their first party-to-party session the following day. Despite personal efforts by Prime Ministers Blair and Ahern, Secretary of State Mowlam announced on March 9 that she was postponing devolution again, until April 2, Good Friday.

Although all the principal paramilitary groups continued to adhere to cease-fires (despite a notable increase since late 1998 in the number of "punishment beatings" inflicted by gangs against members of their own communities), a prominent nationalist civil rights lawyer, Rosemary NELSON, was killed by a car bomb on March 15, 1999. The apparent perpetrator, the recently organized loyalist Red Hand Defenders (RHD), was quickly added by Secretary of State Mowlam to the list of banned organizations, as was another new loyalist paramilitary group, the Orange Volunteers (OV). At the end of March, Blair and Ahern made another attempt to resolve the decommissioning impasse. They proposed in the Hillsborough Declaration that the UUP, SDLP, *Sinn Féin,* and DUP nominate their members of the Executive Committee and that within one month, in a "collective act of reconciliation," the paramilitaries voluntarily "put beyond use" various arms. Upon IICD certification of the decommissioning, the assembly could confirm the nominees to the Executive Committee. The "changed security situation" would also permit "further moves on normalisation and demilitarisation." On April 13, however, *Sinn Féin* rejected the declaration, reiterating that all parties should adhere to the letter of the Good Friday Agreement, which specified only that decommissioning occur by May 2000. On April 20 Ahern and Blair met in London with UUP, SDLP, and *Sinn Féin* leaders, to no avail. In mid-May London and Dublin set a new deadline of June 30 for formation of the Executive Committee, but further attempts by Blair and Ahern to broker an agreement proved fruitless. On July 14 Trimble reaffirmed that the UUP would not sit with *Sinn Féin* in a devolved government until decommissioning had begun, prompting Deputy First Minister-elect Mallon to resign on July 15 and Blair to announce that devolution would be further postponed.

Through August 1999, unionists and *Sinn Féin* verbally skirmished over whether the IRA had broken its cease-fire. Meanwhile, former U.S. senator Mitchell had agreed to chair a review of the peace process that opened on September 6 in Belfast and moved on October 12 to London, where the newly appointed secretary of state for Northern Ireland, Peter MANDELSON, insisted that the negotiators had no alternative but to meet the terms of the Good Friday Agreement. "There is no Plan B," he asserted. "It's that or nothing." An effort by both the UUP and *Sinn Féin* to temper their rhetoric prompted Mitchell to extend negotiations beyond an October 23 deadline, and in early November he held meetings with U.S. president Clinton as well as the British and Irish prime ministers. Shortly thereafter, *Sinn Féin* reported that the IRA was prepared to establish contact with General de Chastelain. On November 15–16, in a sequence of carefully worded, coordinated statements, Mitchell, Trimble, and Adams separately endorsed the continuance of devolution and decommissioning. On November 17 the IRA confirmed that, following establishment of the institutions outlined in the Good Friday Agreement, it would name a representative to "enter into discussions" with de Chastelain. In a secret ballot on November 27, 58 percent of the UUP's governing council backed Trimble's cautious acceptance of the IRA initiative. Thus, the UUP gave up its demand that decommissioning had to begin before it would sit with *Sinn Féin* on the power-sharing Northern Ireland Executive.

On November 29, 1999, the Northern Ireland Assembly approved ten nominees to serve in the executive under Trimble and Mallon. The latter had been reaffirmed as deputy first minister by a 71–28 vote of the assembly, thereby negating his July resignation through a legally questionable maneuver that was challenged by the DUP and other hardliners. (The stratagem circumvented having to jointly reelect Mallon and First Minister Trimble, who probably would not have secured the necessary 30 unionist votes.) On December 1 the UK Parliament authorized devolution, and on December 2 London formally transferred power to the assembly and the executive; however, the cabinet convened minus the two DUP ministers, who refused to sit with the two *Sinn Féin* ministers. On the same day, Dublin formally promulgated the constitutional changes that ended the Irish Republic's claims to the North, and on December 2–3 IRA representatives met for the first time with General de Chastelain. On December 13 the North-South Ministerial Council held its inaugural meeting, and on December 17 representatives of Ireland, the UK, the Channel Islands, the Isle of Man, and the devolved governments of Northern Ireland, Scotland, and Wales gathered in London for the first session of the Council of the Isles.

The IRA's subsequent failure to begin disarming led the UK government to reimpose direct rule on February 11, 2000. In a last-minute effort to salvage the power-sharing government, the IRA had told General de Chastelain that it was prepared to address putting its arms and explosives "beyond use," but the offer came too late to forestall the reimposition. In response, on February 15 the IRA suspended further contacts with de Chastelain.

While attending talks in Washington in mid-March 2000, Trimble indicated that he might consider reinstituting the power-sharing government prior to any actual arms decommissioning by the IRA. The statement catalyzed his opponents within the UUP, and at a March 25 session of the party's governing council he faced a leadership challenge by the Rev. Martin SMYTH. Although Trimble managed to win 57 percent of the council vote, Smyth's supporters, including the influential hard-liner Jeffrey DONALDSON, succeeded in linking restoration of the government to a highly charged symbolic issue: retaining the name of the territory's controversial police agency, the Royal Ulster Constabulary (RUC). On September 9, 1999, Chris Patten, a former UK governor of Hong Kong, had released a report on RUC reform that proposed, among a list of 175 recommendations, changing the force's name to the Police Service of Northern Ireland (PSNI). Unionists had immediately denounced the proposal as well as suggestions that the police oath and insignia be revised to remove all association with the UK. (*Sinn Féin* had responded to the report by repeating its long-held position that the RUC should be abolished.)

Despite a series of diplomatic meetings and public negotiations, little substantive progress on resolving the armaments impasse occurred until May 6, 2000, when the IRA announced that it would accept international inspection of its arms stockpiles and would "completely and verifiably" put its weapons beyond use. As inspectors it nominated Martti Ahtisaari, former president of Finland, and Cyril Ramaphosa, former secretary general of South Africa's ruling party, the African National Congress. London and Dublin quickly proposed that power-sharing be resumed on May 22, but on May 18 Trimble, fearing defeat, postponed a crucial meeting of the UUP governing council. In an effort to defuse the RUC issue, Secretary of State Mandelson agreed to amend pending legislation on RUC reform, adding, for example, mention of the RUC to the legal description of the police service. On May 27, by a vote of 459–403, Trimble again prevailed over the UUP hard-liners, despite the opposition of Deputy Leader John TAYLOR, who viewed Mandelson's concessions as inadequate.

On May 30, 2000, London returned authority to the Northern Ireland Assembly and Executive. In early June Mandelson made additional concessions to garner republican support for the RUC reform legislation, but he left the name-change issue unresolved. At the same time, the new home rule government faced differences over other symbolic issues—principally, the refusal of the *Sinn Féin* ministers to fly the Union Jack over their offices.

On June 25 the IRA stated that it had reopened discussions with de Chastelain's IICD, and on June 26 arms monitors Ahtisaari and Ramaphosa reported that they had conducted their first inspections of IRA stockpiles. In further fulfillment of the Good Friday Agreement, authorities by late July had released more than 425 paramilitary prisoners, loyalist and republican alike, from prison, although Johnny ADAIR, a former leader of the UFF, was returned to prison on August 22 following renewed feuding between loyalist paramilitary groups in July–August. Responding to the outbreak of violence, Secretary of State Mandelson ordered British troops onto the streets of Belfast.

On October 28, 2000, First Minister Trimble overcame another challenge to his leadership when the UUP governing council rejected a hard-line proposal that the party withdraw from the government if the IRA failed to actively begin disarmament by November 30. Trimble instead proposed that he prohibit the executive's two *Sinn Féin* ministers from participating in official North-South meetings until the IRA actively engaged with the IICD. Trimble's decision drew immediate criticism not only from Gerry Adams, but also from Deputy First Minister Mallon. Meanwhile, in the last week of October weapons inspectors Ahtisaari and Ramaphosa conducted their second inspection of IRA stockpiles, as a result of which they described the IRA as "serious about the peace process."

During the first half of 2001 no significant progress was made in resolving three linked issues: IRA decommissioning, as demanded by the unionists; departure of the UK military, as demanded by the republicans; and reform of the RUC, as demanded by both (though with seemingly irreconcilable goals). Renewed negotiating efforts by Prime Ministers Blair and Ahern failed, leading First Minister Trimble to announce in May 2001 that he would resign his office on July 1, in the absence of concrete action by the IRA.

As predicted by Trimble himself, hard-liners made notable gains in the general election of June 7, 2001. Whereas his UUP lost 3 of its 9 seats in the UK House of Commons (having already lost 1 to the DUP at a September 2000 by-election) and 31 of its 185 local council seats, Ian Paisley's DUP gained 2 seats in the House of Commons, for a total of 5, and 40 additional council seats, for a total of 131. The SDLP held steady, retaining its 3 parliamentary seats and losing only 3 of its 120 local council seats, while *Sinn Féin* saw its membership in the House of Commons rise from 2 to 4 and its local council representation increase from 74 to 108.

With a backdrop of renewed sectarian rioting, centered on a Roman Catholic school in a predominantly Protestant area of Belfast, Trimble, as he had threatened, resigned on July 1, 2001. His action automatically vacated the office of deputy first minister. A diplomatic scramble ensued as Ireland and the UK attempted to reinvigorate the peace process before six weeks had passed, after which a new first minister had to be elected, a Northern Ireland Assembly election called, or direct rule reimposed. On August 6 the IICD released a statement confirming that the IRA had accepted a method for putting its weapons "completely and verifiably" beyond use, but in the absence of a timetable and at least a minimal surrender of weapons, the unionists dismissed the agreement as inadequate. Nevertheless, believing that a breakthrough might be near, London decided to exploit a legal loophole and reset the six-week clock by imposing direct rule for a single day beginning at midnight on August 11. The move by Secretary of State for Northern Ireland John REID angered the IRA, however, and it withdrew from its agreement with the IICD. The situation was further complicated by the arrest in Colombia of three alleged IRA members who, according to Colombian authorities, had been assisting the principal leftist guerrilla organization, the Colombia Revolutionary Armed Forces (*Fuerzas Armadas Revolucionarias de Colombia*—FARC). (Gerry Adams subsequently denied accusations that at least one of the men was acting as a *Sinn Féin* representative.) Meanwhile, the sectarian violence in Belfast again worsened, leading Reid to announce on October 12 that the government no longer recognized the cease-fires with the UDA/UFF and the LVF.

Facing increasing international pressure following the September 11, 2001, attacks by Islamic terrorists in the United States, the IRA stated on September 20 that it would renew and accelerate its talks with the IICD. Collaterally, London heralded a breakthrough based on the decisions of the SDLP and then the UUP and DUP (but not *Sinn Féin*) to participate in the formation of a cross-community Northern Ireland Policing Board as part of a new Police Implementation Plan. (The RUC was formally renamed the PSNI on November 4.) Citing these positive developments, on September 21, with the second six-week period about to expire, London announced another direct-rule interregnum that began at midnight on September 22 and concluded 24 hours later.

On October 18, 2001, the UUP and DUP ministers withdrew from the executive after the assembly had rejected a unionist demand that the two *Sinn Féin* ministers be excluded. Shortly thereafter, Adams and his deputy, Martin McGUINNESS, for the first time explicitly called on the IRA to begin disarming, and on October 23 both the IRA and the IICD released statements announcing that a quantity of arms had in fact been decommissioned. In response, Trimble announced that the UUP would return to the executive and that he would seek reelection as first minister.

At the assembly's first vote on November 2, two members of the UUP voted against Trimble, leaving him one vote short of the necessary unionist majority, despite unanimous nationalist support. On November 6 he achieved the necessary margin when the assembly allowed three members of the Alliance Party to temporarily redesignate themselves as unionists. However, the DUP was incensed by the maneuver, which led to scuffles outside the assembly.

An additional IRA decommissioning occurred in April 2002, but continuing sectarian violence in Belfast prompted Trimble, in early July, to threaten the withdrawal of the UUP from the assembly if authorities did not take corrective measures. Although he accused the IRA of fomenting the rioting, loyalist paramilitaries appeared to be equally culpable. The annual marching season once again led to repeated clashes, and in late July London vowed to stiffen its response to security violations. A week earlier, on July 16, the IRA had issued an unprecedented public apology to the families of its innocent victims.

On October 4, 2002, the *Sinn Féin* offices in Stormont were raided by authorities investigating alleged IRA spying, and two days later Denis DONALDSON, a *Sinn Féin* administrator, was arrested and charged with possessing some 1,200 documents of potential use to paramilitaries. The unionists immediately demanded the resignations or dismissal of the *Sinn Féin* ministers. On October 15, in an effort to forestall the collapse of the peace process, London reimposed direct rule for the fourth time.

Despite the continuation of direct rule, elections to the suspended Northern Ireland Assembly were held on November 26, 2003. The results suggested that resumption of the peace process might prove impossible. For the Protestants, Ian Paisley's DUP, which strongly opposed the 1998 Good Friday Agreement, displaced Trimble's UUP to become the largest party, with 30 seats. For the Catholics, in a similar reversal of the 1998 results, *Sinn Féin* won 24 seats, as opposed to the SDLP's 18.

Despite the 2003 electoral results, multiparty talks were resumed on February 3, 2004, with the DUP and *Sinn Féin* communicating through intermediaries. Subsequently, UK prime minister Blair and Irish prime minister Ahern held a series of meetings that yielded no consensus on power-sharing, while in December Paisley announced a hardening of the DUP position by insisting on photographic evidence of IRA arms decommissioning.

In early 2005 the peace process reached a new point of collapse with the IRA being blamed for an armed attack on Belfast's Northern Bank in December 2004 and thereafter withdrawing its offer to decommission. On April 7 *Sinn Féin* leader Adams drew no response in urging the IRA to abandon its "armed struggle," while an appeal by Blair and Ahern for the IRA to end "all paramilitary and criminal activity" was equally unproductive until late July when, in a potentially historic development, the IRA pledged to lay down its arms and oppose British rule in the future only through peaceful political involvement. Specifically, the IRA announced that it had "formally ordered an end to the armed campaign" and would pursue a "purely political and democratic program through exclusively peaceful means." Promises were also made that the IRA's massive stockpiles of arms (reportedly buried in bunkers throughout Northern Ireland) would be quickly dismantled.

The May 5, 2005, local elections reinforced the shifts in unionist and nationalist party success. The DUP gained more than 50 additional councilors; *Sinn Féin* improved by 18; the UUP dropped by 39 to fall behind the DUP in number of unionist councilors region-wide; and the SDLP dropped by 16 seats to fall behind *Sinn Féin* in number of nationalist councilors. However, a single party gained majority control in only 2 of 18 councils (the DUP in Ballymena and Castlereagh).

Prime Minister Blair labeled the IRA announcement a step of "unparalleled magnitude," and in August 2005 the UK indicated that it would cut its troop level (then 10,000) in Northern Ireland in half by 2007 in view of the improved security outlook. In addition, in September General de Chastelain said the IICD was satisfied with the decommissioning of the IRA weapons. However, DUP leader Paisley condemned the UK response as "premature," calling for the "dissolution" of the IRA. He and other Protestant leaders also accused the British and Irish governments of "disregarding" loyalist concerns. Consequently, the DUP continued to refuse to meet directly with *Sinn Féin* when Blair and Ahern relaunched negotiations toward another power-sharing government.

In February 2006 the Independent Monitoring Commission (IMC), established by the UK and Ireland in 2004 to monitor armed groups in Northern Ireland, concluded that the IRA was no longer "engaged in terrorism," while Protestant militants had been responsible for more than 20 killings in the fall of 2005. Encouraged by the IRA's "progress," Blair and Ahern subsequently appeared to focus on pressuring the DUP to adopt a more positive negotiating role. In April the two prime ministers declared a deadline of November 24 for the assembly parties to agree on formation of a new executive, without which a "new way to govern" Northern Ireland would be pursued. Analysts suggested that the deadline posed a "veiled threat" to the DUP, as it implied that the alternative to a power-sharing government could be greater control by the Irish Republic. Adams welcomed the announcement, and in May he proposed that Paisley be named as first minister of the proposed new government. However, the offer was emphatically rejected by Paisley (described as *Sinn Féin*'s "most intractable foe"), and little progress was reported through the summer, despite the establishment of a multiparty Preparation for Government Committee and the reconvening of the Northern Ireland Assembly (see Legislature, below).

Prime Minister Blair and Ahern managed to organize "last ditch" negotiations that brought the two chief protagonists (Ian Paisley of the DUP and Gerry Adams of *Sinn Féin*) and leaders of other parties together for a series of meetings in St. Andrews, Scotland, on October 11–13, 2006. Tentative agreement was reached for the restoration of self-rule the following spring, assuming that final details were successfully negotiated for the proposed power-sharing arrangements. In addition, final approval was required from *Sinn Féin* regarding the acceptance of and support for the police force and the criminal justice system. (Theretofore, *Sinn Féin* supporters had refused to recognize the authority of the PSNI, which the nationalists believed was dominated by the unionists.)

Although neither the DUP nor *Sinn Féin* expressly endorsed the St. Andrews Agreement by the November 10, 2006, deadline, the British and Irish governments deemed the parties' statements of intent to be sufficient to continue. Consequently, on November 22 Westminster approved the enabling legislation required for the agreement to go into effect. Two days later, the Northern Ireland Assembly that had been elected in 2003 met to receive nominations from the DUP and *Sinn Féin* (expected to finish first and second, respectively, in the upcoming assembly balloting) for the two principal executive positions. Adams nominated *Sinn Féin*'s Martin McGuinness for deputy prime minister, but Paisley deferred acceptance of the post of first minister pending *Sinn Féin*'s formal agreement to participate in the police force and criminal justice system. After a *Sinn Féin* conference on January 28, 2007, Blair and Ahern announced on January 30 that new assembly elections would be held as planned.

In the assembly balloting on March 7, 2007, DUP increased its seat representation from 30 to 36, while *Sinn Féin* advanced from 24 to 28. Paisley and Adams met on March 26 and agreed upon the nominations of Paisley and McGuinness to head the new executive. Those appointments were approved when the new assembly convened on May 8, as were the remaining cabinet appointments. (Under the unique system in Northern Ireland whereby cabinet posts are assigned according to assembly representation, DUP was accorded 5 of the 12 cabinet posts; *Sinn Féin,* 4; the UUP, 2; and the SDLP, 1.)

Despite widespread concerns over the potential stability of the new government, it survived without major incident throughout 2007. Symbolic of the cooperative working relationship between Paisley and McGuinness was their joint visit to the United States in December, at which time President George W. Bush congratulated all parties in the decades-long dispute for having apparently put violence behind them in favor of a "more hopeful chapter."

A leading indicator that Ian Paisley's time as first minister may have been nearing its end came with his January 2008 resignation as leader of the Free Presbyterian Church. He also announced on March 4 that he would resign as DUP party leader. Although his age (82) and recent resignation of his son from a junior ministerial position likely weighed in his decision, the main impetus appeared to be dissatisfaction among church and party leaders with Paisley's facilitation of the peace process and cooperation with McGuinness.

On April 14, 2008, Peter Robinson, theretofore deputy leader of DUP, was elected unopposed as Paisley's successor as DUP leader. Cooperation between DUP and *Sinn Féin* was expected to diminish under Robinson's leadership, and, when Paisley officially vacated the office of first prime minister on May 31, interparty tensions reemerged. *Sinn Féin* initially threatened to prevent Robinson from replacing Paisley as first minister by refusing to renominate McGuinness on the joint ticket unless DUP took action on the issues of policing, justice, and the Irish Language Act. However, negotiations led by UK prime minister Gordon Brown, as well as officials from the U.S. and Irish governments, succeeded in getting *Sinn Féin* to lift its threat. On June 5 Robinson was elected as first minister and McGuinness was reelected as deputy first minister. However, three months of stalemate followed, as *Sinn Féin* blocked all efforts for the executive to meet on other business until DUP agreed to a date for transferring policing and justice powers to local ministers. Progress in that regard was achieved in October when Paul GOGGINS, minister of state in the UK Northern Ireland office, clarified that the transfer of the related responsibilities to the Northern Ireland Assembly would not include access to sensitive national security information, such as secret files on IRA informers. Consequently, the assembly in November met for the first time since June and forged a compromise to create a justice ministry. The plan called for the justice minister to be chosen from outside the ranks of DUP or *Sinn Féin,* although both parties would have a veto over the appointment. (It was believed that a member of the Alliance Party was likely to be named to the post.)

No firm timetable was set for inauguration of the Department of Justice, and throughout 2009 progress toward a final agreement was slow. On the republican side, some opponents of the transfer resorted to violence. The Real IRA claimed responsibility for the March 2009 murder of two British soldiers, the first such murders in the province since 1997. Two days later, members of the Continuity IRA (CIRA) claimed responsibility for the murder of a police constable in Amagh. On a more positive note, three unionist paramilitary groups (the UVF, RHC, and UDA) voluntarily decommissioned their weapons in June. On the unionist side, the strength of DUP's resolve to see the process through came into doubt on the heels of two political developments. In the June balloting for the European Parliament, the newly formed Traditional Unionist Voice (TUV), created by a DUP dissident, cut substantially into DUP's vote support while running on a platform objecting to joining in a government in which participation by *Sinn Féin* was mandated. Unionist voters also appeared upset over revelations of unseemly personal expense charges to the public by DUP leaders (see DUP under Political Parties and Groups, below). Even an October pledge of £800 million by UK prime minister Brown to fund Northern Ireland's takeover of policing and justice functions left DUP unmoved.

In early January 2010 DUP leader Robinson found himself in deep personal political difficulty as the media published scandalous details of alleged sexual and financial improprieties on the part of his wife, Iris Robinson. On January 9 Iris Robinson was expelled from DUP for financial misconduct, and, with speculation swirling that the first minister had been aware of his wife's alleged fiscal misdeeds, Peter Robinson took three weeks' leave from his formal duties on January 11. Arlene FOSTER (DUP minister for enterprise, trade, and investment) stepped in as interim replacement under an arrangement whereby Robinson would continue to lead negotiations over the unresolved policing and justice issue and Foster would oversee day-to-day matters. Robinson returned to office on February 3, and the next day *Sinn Féin* and DUP announced they had reached agreement on the creation of the Department of Justice. On March 9 the assembly endorsed the proposal by a vote of 88–17, with only the UUP in dissent. In accordance with the agreement, the new department was established on April 12, and, as long expected, David FORD, leader of the nonsectarian APNI, was installed as minister. Ominously, less than a half hour after the transfer of powers, a bomb exploded at the Northern Ireland headquarters of the British M15 security forces, with the Real IRA claiming responsibility.

The year-long anticipation of a sharp decline in DUP's political standing proved ill-founded, at least as recorded in the May 5, 2010, balloting for the UK House of Commons. DUP held on to eight of its nine seats and outpolled the upstart TUV by better than a six-to-one margin. The one loss was noteworthy, however, inasmuch as DUP leader Peter Robinson was defeated in his reelection bid for the UK parliamentary seat he had held for 31 years. His poor electoral showing immediately provoked questions about whether he should remain as party leader and first minister. These questions were pushed aside in short order; five days after the election DUP unanimously endorsed his continuing service in both positions.

Just over a month after his election to the UK premiership in May 2010, David Cameron presented the long-awaited report on the 12-year investigation into the 1972 Bloody Sunday killings. The report found that all those shot by British soldiers were unarmed and that the shootings were both unjustified and unjustifiable. New Northern Ireland justice minister Ford was left with the responsibility to decide whether to prosecute any of the soldiers involved.

Terrorist incidents increased in 2010 compared with the previous year. Some observers attributed this escalation of violent activities to the province's poor economic condition, as Northern Ireland was targeted for stringent cuts by the UK government's austerity measures in the midst of an already faltering economy. Against this backdrop, a climate of peace and negotiation characterized the province's official politics. In response to the murder of a Catholic constable in the Police Service of Northern Ireland (PSNI) in April 2001, McGuiness called for nationalists to inform on the attackers. This call marked a reversal in the position of McGuiness on the issue, who had previously declined to call for nationalists to provide information on dissident republicans. Around the same time, the power-sharing executive of Northern Ireland successfully completed the entire four-year term. The National Assembly was dissolved in March, and with no noticeably controversial issues on the agenda, the parties embarked on an electoral campaign described by commentators as uneventful. Voting behavior was expected to fall along sectarian lines, and the balloting on May 5 resulted in few changes to the composition of the National Assembly. DUP gained two seats, while *Sinn Féin* and the APNI each gained one. The UUP and the SDLP each lost two seats, while the Green Party maintained its one seat. Of note in an otherwise unremarkable election was the success of the upstart TUV in its attempt to capture a seat in the assembly. Robinson and McGuinness were reelected as first minister and deputy minister, respectively, shortly after the election on May 12, and David Ford of the APNI was reinstated as minister of policing and justice. The new cabinet was a mix of new and old faces among the five parties, with *Sinn Féin* now heading the ministries of Agriculture, Education, and Culture, the UUP heading the Department of Regional Development, and the APNI heading the Department of Employment and Learning. Minor cabinet reshuffles occurred in June 2013 and September 2014.

Robinson and most of the DUP cabinet members stepped down on September 10, 2015, over suspected IRA activity in the August 12 murder of Kevin McGUIGAN, a former IRA fighter (see Current issues, below). Robinson stopped short of a full resignation and instead appointed finance minister Arlene Foster (DUP) as acting first minister while the other cabinet posts remained open through a series of resignations and reappointments. After failing to convince the UK government to suspend the assembly, Robinson and the DUP ministers returned to their posts on October 20. Meanwhile, the UUP left the government in protest on September 1 over the suspected renewal of IRA activity.

Robinson, who had suffered a heart attack in May 2015, announced on November 19 of that year that he would resign as party leader and first minister. When his resignation took effect on January 11, 2016, Foster became first minister of a caretaker government.

The DUP again won 38 seats in assembly balloting on May 5, 2016, followed by *Sinn Féin* with 28, and the UUP with 16, among others. On May 12 Foster and McGuiness were reelected to their respective posts.

Constitution and government. The Government of Ireland Act of 1920 gave Northern Ireland its own government and a Parliament empowered to act on all matters except those of "imperial concern" (e.g., finance, defense, foreign affairs) or requiring specialized technical input. The royal authority was vested in a governor appointed by the Crown and advised by ministers responsible to Parliament; in practice, the leader of the majority party was invariably designated as prime minister. Parliament consisted of a 52-member House of Commons, directly elected from single-member constituencies, and a Senate, whose 26 members (except for 2 serving ex officio) were elected by the House of Commons under a proportional representation system. Voting for local government bodies was subject to a property qualification that excluded an estimated 200,000 adults, including a disproportionate number of minority Catholics. The effective disenfranchisement of a substantial portion of the Catholic population precipitated the original disturbances in 1968–1969.

Until 1998 British efforts to bring about agreement on a form of coalition government acceptable to both Protestants and Catholics failed to bear fruit. The Northern Ireland Constitution Act of 1973 abolished the office of governor and provided for a regional assembly and executive; however, the executive functioned only in 1974, and the assembly and its successor in 1973–1974 and 1982–1986. A Constitutional Convention in 1975–1976 failed to produce agreement, and the only major constitutional developments for more than a decade thereafter involved the extension of a consultative role to the Irish government by means of various bilateral accords. Accordingly, direct rule, in effect since 1972 (save for January–May 1974), continued through the UK secretary of state for Northern Ireland. Under direct rule local government encompassed 26 elected city, district, and borough councils with very limited responsibilities for refuse collection, street cleaning, recreational facilities, environmental health, and consumer protection.

Following completion of the Belfast Agreement of April 10, 1998 (familiarly called the Good Friday Agreement but also referenced in some official documents as the Multi-Party Agreement), and pending approval of the agreement by referendum on May 22, the British Parliament passed legislation authorizing election of a New Northern Ireland Assembly, the term "New" being dropped upon formal devolution of authority to the body. Elected on June 25, the legislature comprised 108 members from 18 constituencies.

Under the terms of the Good Friday Agreement and the Northern Ireland Act of 1998, which Parliament passed in November 1998 and which repealed the Government of Ireland Act of 1920, assembly members individually defined themselves as a "designated unionist," a "designated nationalist," or "other." Decisions requiring "cross-community support"—for example, standing orders, budget allocations, and election of the assembly chair—required either majority approval, including support from a majority of both nationalists and unionists, or assent by a weighted majority of 60 percent, with affirmative votes from at least 40 percent of unionists and 40 percent of nationalists. To further protect the minority, the cross-community provision could be triggered on any other matter if 30 or more assembly members presented a "petition of concern."

Assembly members were to be elected for five-year terms, subject to early dissolution by a vote of two-thirds of the entire membership. Devolved legislative authority extended to such areas as agriculture, economic development, tourism, and education, while "excepted and reserved matters" remaining in the hands of the UK Northern Ireland secretary included international relations, defense, security, criminal justice, taxation, regulation of financial services, national insurance, and regulation of broadcast and telecommunication services. Under devolution, executive authority resided in an Executive Committee of ministers chosen from the leading assembly parties in proportion to their membership in the body. The assembly selected a first minister and a deputy first minister, who stood for election jointly and were required to secure majority support from both nationalists and unionists. In addition to heading the executive, which might have up to ten additional members, the two leaders jointly nominated ministers and junior ministers to two principal intergovernmental bodies, the North-South Ministerial Council and the British-Irish Council (also known as the Council of the Isles), both of which were established under treaties concluded by the UK and Ireland on March 8, 1999.

The North-South Ministerial Council had as its mandate bringing together "those with executive responsibilities in Northern Ireland and the Irish Government, to develop consultation, co-operation, and action within the island of Ireland," on both an island-wide and a cross-border basis. Decisions required agreement by both sides. The British–Irish Council, which was to meet at the summit level twice a year and in other formats "on a regular basis," included representatives from Scotland, Wales, the Channel Islands, and the Isle of Man in addition to Great Britain, Northern Ireland, and Ireland, the purpose being "to promote the harmonious and mutually beneficial development of the totality of relationships among the peoples of these islands." Two additional treaties signed on March 8 authorized formation of various implementing bodies and of a British–Irish Intergovernmental Conference, the latter replacing the Anglo-Irish Intergovernmental Council and the Intergovernmental Conference of 1985.

Northern Ireland is represented in the UK House of Commons, currently with 18 seats (increased from 17 in 1997). It also has 3 seats in the European Parliament.

The UK government reimposed direct rule on Northern Ireland on October 15, 2002. However, limited self-rule was restored on May 8, 2007 (see Political background, above).

Northern Ireland's press, radio, and television are organized along the same lines as in Great Britain.

Current issues. A new round of sectarian conflict began when the Belfast City Council voted on December 3, 2012, to stop flying the Union flag over city hall on a daily basis, as it had since 1906. Instead, it would be raised only on 17 significant days. Council members from *Sinn Féin*, the SDLP, and the APNI backed the measure. Outraged loyalists began nightly protests that grew in size and lasted through February. As tensions escalated, bricks, gasoline bombs, rubber bullets, and water cannons were used. Dozens of police were injured and more than 200 protestors arrested as the violence spread to other cities. Business leaders complained that the violence had ruined the Christmas shopping season and cost them £15 million in lost sales.

Prime Minister David Cameron hosted the G-8 summit in Enniskillen on June 17–18, 2013. Leaders cited the event as a sign of increased stability in the region. Others suggested it was a way for London to emphasize that Northern Ireland is undeniably part of the United Kingdom, given the secessionist tendencies in Scotland. Shortly before the summit, Westminster announced an economic pact that would create enterprise zones in Northern Ireland, £20 million to develop an aerospace industry, housing and to rid Belfast of the "peace walls" dividing Protestant and Catholic neighborhoods.

Northern Ireland's political leaders watched Scotland's independence referendum very closely (see entry on the United Kingdom). Deputy First Minister Martin McGuinness stated that he planned to introduce a motion on independence during the next session of the NI Assembly, possibly by 2016. First Minister Robinson called on all Unionist parties to combine into one party to defend the UK from separatism. Meanwhile, in August 2013 Robinson withdrew his support for a proposal to convert Maze Prison in Belfast into an international conflict resolution center. In December all-party negotiations on parades and flags, led by former U.S. diplomat Richard Haass, collapsed after the UUP and APNI withdrew their support for a preliminary proposal.

On April 30, 2014, Gerry Adams was arrested and held for four days of questioning over the 1972 murder of alleged IRA informant Jean McCONVILLE. *Sinn Féin* denounced the arrest as politically motivated and designed to discredit the party ahead of local and EU balloting in May.

On December 14, 2014, the main political parties agreed to a range of reforms, including the creation of new bodies to manage ongoing controversies over unsolved murders from the "Troubles." The accord, dubbed the Stormont Agreement, also committed the government to balancing the budget in 2015 and enacting welfare reform in exchange for £2 billion from the UK government to offset any spending cuts. One contentious issue the agreement did not resolve was that of parades.

On August 11, 2015, former IRA gunman Kevin McGuigan was murdered, allegedly as part of an intra-IRA rivalry. Unionist parties charged that the murder demonstrated that the IRA had resumed or continued its activities and sparked a government crisis.

POLITICAL PARTIES AND GROUPS

Parties Represented in the Cabinet:

Democratic Unionist Party (DUP). The DUP was founded in 1971 by a hard-line loyalist faction of the UUP, attracting working-class Protestant support for its strongly anti-Catholic, anti-Dublin position. It was consistently the runner-up to the parent party, winning 21 seats in the 1982 assembly election and 3 UK House of Commons seats in June 1983, all of the latter being retained in 1987. The party was represented at the 1988 Duisburg talks by Deputy Leader Peter Robinson, who urged the creation of an alternative to the 1985 Anglo-Irish accord.

A growing schism between the DUP's older and younger members was, in part, responsible for the party leader's decision in May 1990 to agree to political negotiations. The older faction, led by Ian Paisley, had long adhered to a "no negotiation" policy, while the more youthful faction, exemplified by Robinson, advocated the creation of a political and religious dialogue. At the same time, the party mainstream was moving from an "integrationalist" to a "devolutionist" posture that favored a provincial government with relatively strong legislative and executive powers.

The DUP retained its three Westminster seats in the UK balloting of April 1992, after which the failure of yet another round of constitutional talks left the party's internal divisions unresolved. In the forum elections of May 1996 the party fell into third place, with 19 percent of the vote, and in the May 1997 UK election it lost the constituency of Mid Ulster to *Sinn Féin.*

The DUP strongly opposed *Sinn Féin*'s presence at the Stormont negotiations of 1997–1998 and refused to participate. It campaigned against the Good Friday Agreement and won 20 of the 28 seats captured by unionist oppositionists at the June Northern Ireland Assembly election. Allotted two portfolios in the Northern Ireland Executive, the DUP adopted obstructionist tactics to protest *Sinn Féin*'s presence in the body.

In a September 2000 by-election for a seat in the UK House of Commons, the DUP captured the district from the UUP, prompting Paisley to declare that First Minister Trimble "is finished, absolutely finished." In the UK general election of June 2001 the DUP won 5 seats, a gain of 2. In simultaneous local balloting the party added 40 council seats, for a total of 131.

In the Northern Ireland Assembly balloting of November 2003, the DUP outpolled the UUP for a plurality of 30 seats. The DUP also won 1 of 3 Northern Ireland seats in the June 2004 elections to the European Parliament. In the House of Commons election of May 2005, the DUP increased its representation from 5 to 9, securing 33.7 percent of the vote in Northern Ireland and consolidating its status as the dominant unionist party with a similar advance in the simultaneous local elections. The DUP remained the plurality party in the March 7, 2007, balloting for the Northern Ireland Assembly, securing 36 seats on a 30.1 percent share of first-round votes. As the largest party, the DUP was able to nominate Paisley for the position of first minister in the subsequent coalition government with *Sinn Féin.* The power-sharing coalition and Paisley's overtly friendly relationship with Deputy First Minister McGuinness subsequently created strains in party ranks. Amid controversies over power sharing and his son's property dealings, Paisley announced in March 2008 that he would resign as party leader at the end of May. His longtime adviser and confidant, Peter Robinson, won election to the party leader post in April, assumed the leadership position on May 31, and was elected first minister on June 5.

Although Robinson's subsequent approach to the DUP's power-sharing arrangements with *Sinn Féin* was less friendly and less accommodating than Paisley's, hard-line unionist elements still remained skeptical, thereby creating a possible source of a permanent fracture within the party. In addition, Robinson found himself in political trouble over reports in April 2009 that he, his wife, and other DUP members were "double dipping" on salaries and claiming large expense reimbursements. (Robinson and his wife, each of whom held positions as representatives in both the UK Parliament and the Northern Ireland Assembly, reportedly were paid more than one-half million pounds in annual salaries and expenses.)

The DUP's vote share fell to 18.1 percent in the June 2009 elections to the European Parliament, down dramatically from 32 percent in 2004. In what was initially thought to be an ominous sign for the DUP's long-term political standing, most of the defecting voters appeared to turn to the TUV (below), a new hard-line unionist alternative. Nevertheless, the DUP held onto 8 of its 9 seats in the May 6, 2010, UK parliamentary balloting. The one lost seat was the one previously held by Peter Robinson, with the loss being attributed to his personal difficulties more so than DUP shortcomings. (See Political background, above, for information on the issues surrounding Robinson and also on his retention of both his party leadership post and his position as first minister of Northern Ireland.) The other noteworthy change came as a result of former leader Ian Paisley deciding not to seek reelection. He was succeeded by his son (Ian Paisley Jr.), who won handily, and in June Ian Paisley Sr. was named to a peerage in the UK House of Lords. In the May 2011 National Assembly elections the DUP won 38 seats, an increase of 2, with 30.6 percent of first-preference votes.

In local balloting on May 22, 2014, the DUP won 130 seats, down from 145. In concurrent elections for the EU parliament, the party secured one seat. Ian Paisley Sr. died of natural causes on September 12.

Robinson resigned as party leader on December 17, 2015, and Arlene FOSTER was elected to replace him. When he also stepped down as first minister on January 11, 2016, she also replaced him in that post. In legislative balloting in May 2016, the DUP won 29.2 percent of the first preference votes, maintaining its 38 seats.

Leaders: Arlene FOSTER (First Minister of Northern Ireland and Party Leader), Nigel DODDS (Deputy Leader), Maurice MORROW (Chair).

Sinn Féin. The island-wide *Sinn Féin* (see also Ireland: Political Parties) serves as the legal political wing of the outlawed IRA (see Former and Current Republican Paramilitary Groups, below). In addition to advocating improved living and working conditions for its primarily Catholic, working-class constituency, throughout the 1970s and 1980s it consistently called for the disbanding of British security forces, the withdrawal of Britain from Northern Ireland's government, and the negotiation of a political settlement through an all-Ireland constitutional conference.

Its president, Gerard (Gerry) Adams, was *Sinn Féin*'s only successful candidate in the 1987 UK general election, but, as in 1983, he refused to occupy his seat in the Commons. In early 1988 the SDLP (below) attempted to forge ties with *Sinn Féin,* but its interest waned in April when *Sinn Féin* refused to "repeal its commitment to limited guerrilla warfare." A second attempt at linkage was broken off in September following the resumption of IRA bombings in downtown Belfast.

Responding to comments made by UK Secretary of State Peter Brooke, in April 1990 Adams said that the IRA might be persuaded to cease terrorist activities if London established a dialogue with *Sinn Féin.* However, *Sinn Féin*'s continued refusal to renounce IRA violence led to its exclusion from the April 1991 talks. In April 1992 Adams lost his Westminster parliamentary seat to the SDLP.

The IRA cease-fire declaration of August 31, 1994, yielded enhanced international stature and negotiating prominence for Adams and other *Sinn Féin* leaders. However, the IRA renewed hostilities in February 1996 while continuing to press for unconditional talks. Though successful in both the 1996 Forum elections (winning 15 percent of the vote) and in the May 1997 UK general elections (winning two seats), the party still chose to remain aloof from either political process. Renewal of the IRA cease-fire in July 1997 and *Sinn Féin*'s affirmation of its commitment to the six Mitchell principles, including full decommissioning and rejection of political violence, enabled Adams to join the Stormont multiparty peace talks in September. In response, a hardline faction left the party and formed the 32 County Sovereignty Committee (below).

At a special party session convened in Dublin on May 10, 1998, and attended by a number of furloughed nationalist inmates from prisons in Northern Ireland and Britain, Adams won overwhelming endorsement of the Good Friday peace plan and permission for *Sinn Féin* members to take up seats in the new Northern Ireland Assembly. In balloting for the assembly in June, the party won 18 seats, sufficient for it to claim 2 positions on the governing Executive Committee upon devolution.

In June 2000 Cathal CRUMLEY became the first member of *Sinn Féin* to be elected mayor of a Northern city, Londonderry, since partition. Earlier in the year the UK government had introduced a bill in the House of Commons that would permit a member of any UK legislature, including the Northern Ireland Assembly, to hold simultaneously a legislative seat in the Republic of Ireland. The Disqualifications Bill, which passed Parliament on November 30, was widely regarded as a "sweetener" for *Sinn Féin* as it permitted the party's assembly members, particularly Gerry Adams, to seek election to the *Dáil.*

In the UK general election of June 2001, *Sinn Féin* doubled its representation in the House of Commons, to 4 seats. It also made gains locally, adding 34 council seats to the 74 it had previously held.

On October 4, 2002, the *Sinn Féin* offices in Stormont were raided by authorities investigating IRA spying, and two days later Denis Donaldson, the party's office administrator, was arrested and charged with possessing some 1,200 documents of potential use to paramilitaries. The revelations ultimately contributed to London's reimposition of direct rule on October 15. (The case took a surreal turn in December 2005 when the charges against Donaldson were dropped and Donaldson acknowledged that he had in fact been a British agent for 20 years.)

The party won 24 seats in the Northern Ireland Assembly election of November 2003.

In August 2004 Adams, in an effort to counter the DUP's objection to revival of the peace talks, called publicly for the disbanding of the IRA as a paramilitary force.

Sinn Féin gained one of Northern Ireland's three seats in the 2004 European Parliament elections and secured five seats (including one by Adams) in the May 2005 UK House of Commons balloting on a share of 24.3 percent of the votes in Northern Ireland. Shortly thereafter, Adams intensified his call for the renunciation of violence, and the IRA subsequently announced its historic pledge to disarm. (Adams has never acknowledged having played a leadership role in the IRA, although many observers have ascribed such status to him.)

In January 2007 *Sinn Féin* formally endorsed the provisions for police services in the St. Andrews Agreement of the previous November, thereby permitting plans for new assembly elections to proceed in March. *Sinn Féin* won 28 seats (finishing second to the DUP) in that balloting on a 26.2 percent share of first-preference votes. The party also retained its 1 seat from Northern Ireland in the June 2009 European Parliament elections with a first-place vote total of 26.3 percent and remained the leading nationalist party in the May 2010 balloting for the UK House of Commons. In the May 2011 National Assembly elections *Sinn Féin* increased its seat share by 1, bringing the total number of seats under the party's control to 29 with 26.9 percent of first-preference votes. This time the party's representatives did not include Adams, who had resigned his seat in the National Assembly in order to contest, and ultimately win, a parliamentary seat in the Republic of Ireland. In November 2013 Liam ADAMS, the brother of the *Sinn Féin* leader, was sentenced to 16 years in prison for sexually abusing his daughter.

Sinn Féin won 105 seats in Northern Ireland's local balloting in May 2014, down 10 seats from the previous election. It also secured one EU seat in concurrent polling.

In assembly polling in May 2016, the party won 24 percent of the vote and 28 seats.

Leaders: Gerard (Gerry) ADAMS (President), Martin McGUINNESS (Deputy First Minister of Ireland), Declan KEARNEY (Chair), MaryLou McDONALD (Vice President), Dawn DOYLE (General Secretary).

Other Parties That Won Seats in the 2016 Assembly Elections:

Ulster Unionist Party (UUP). The UUP, historically Northern Ireland's dominant party, was split by the 1973 Sunningdale Agreement, the anti-Sunningdale majority becoming known as the **Official Unionist Party** (OUP). The formation of a "joint working party" between the OUP and the DUP (above) was announced in August 1985 to protect "Ulster's interests within the UK." Throughout 1986 the working party attempted to disrupt local government in protest of the Anglo-Irish Agreement of 1985. By contrast, joint OUP-DUP publications in 1987 called for all Northern Ireland parties to negotiate an alternative to the 1985 accord in a spirit of "friendship, cooperation, and consultation." In addition, the OUP, DUP, and the now-defunct Ulster Popular Unionist Party (UPUP) of James KILFEDDER agreed to present only one unionist candidate from each constituency in the 1987 House of Commons elections, at which they retained 13 of 14 seats. The OUP continued to issue conciliatory statements during 1988, but the party's demand that the Anglo-Irish accord be rescinded before any substantive negotiations could take place between unionists and republicans helped derail initiatives advanced at a meeting of the OUP, DUP, Alliance Party, and Social Democratic and Labour Party (SDLP, below) in October in Duisburg, West Germany.

In May 1990 OUP leaders softened their position, reportedly agreeing to tripartite talks between the province's parties and the British and Irish governments in return for "de facto" (temporary) suspension of the bilateral pact. Subsequently, in April 1991, OUP and DUP representatives attended the opening of the Ulster talks as joint unionist negotiators despite the incompatibility of the DUP's "devolutionist" position and the OUP's "integrationalist" call for increased linkage between Ulster and Britain. The Official Unionists won 9 of the 17 Northern Ireland seats in the UK election of April 1992, by which time they had officially adopted the UUP designation to signify continuity with the historic party.

Having held the party leadership since 1979, James MOLYNEAUX stood down in August 1995 and was succeeded by David Trimble, a leading UUP critic of the concessions being made to Dublin in the peace process. Two years later, in a remarkable turnaround, Trimble agreed to sit at the same negotiating table as *Sinn Féin,* and on April 10, 1998, UUP representatives signed the multiparty Good Friday Agreement. Fighting off intraparty opponents, including 6 of the party's 10 members of Parliament, Trimble secured UUP approval of the peace plan, and in the June 25 election the party won a plurality of 28 seats in the 108-seat Northern Ireland Assembly. On July 1 the assembly elected Trimble first minister of the Executive Committee, and in October 1998 he shared the Nobel Peace Prize with the SDLP's John Hume.

On October 9, 1998, a faction within the UUP formed Union First in opposition to the Good Friday Agreement and the presence of *Sinn Féin* in the government. Thereafter, criticism of Trimble continued to grow. Resentment over what hard-line unionists viewed as ill-advised concessions to *Sinn Féin* culminated in a March 25, 2000, challenge to his leadership by the Rev. Martin Smyth. Although the party's governing Ulster Unionist Council (UUC) gave Trimble 57 percent of the vote, Union First's Jeffrey Donaldson and Deputy Leader John Taylor were both considered to be likely future challengers. On May 27, having threatened to resign in the event of a negative vote, Trimble gained only 53 percent endorsement of the UUC (459–403) to accept the IRA's offer to permit international monitoring of its arms stockpiles.

On October 28, 2000, the UUC reconvened to consider a Donaldson proposal that the UUP withdraw from the government unless the IRA began decommissioning by November 30. Trimble countered by asserting that, as first minister, he would not authorize the government's two IRA ministers to participate in official North-South meetings until the IRA actively engaged with General de Chastelain's IICD. Trimble again won the council's support, 445–374.

Trimble resigned as first minister effective July 1, 2001. A month earlier the UUP had seen its support at the polls decline, costing it 3 of its 9 seats in the UK House of Commons and 31 of its 185 local council seats. Trimble was reelected first minister on November 6, 2001, although he had failed to obtain the needed majority of nationalist votes four days earlier when two UUP members, Peter WEIR and Pauline ARMITAGE, voted against him. Weir was subsequently expelled from the party and joined the DUP in April 2002; Armitage's membership was suspended.

The UUP lost its plurality to the DUP in the Northern Ireland Assembly election of November 26, 2003, and in late December Trimble's most severe intraparty critic, Jeffrey Donaldson, announced that he was quitting the UPP and aligning himself with the DUP. The UUP member of the European Parliament, Jim NICHOLSON, retained his seat in the 2004 balloting for that body, as the UUP came in third in votes (behind the DUP and *Sinn Féin*). At the UK general election of May 5, 2005, the UUP lost four of its five seats in the House of Commons, including the one held by Trimble, on a share of only 17.7 percent of the votes in Northern Ireland. The UUP also declined in the concurrent local elections, and Trimble, who had apparently suffered from the voters' perception that he and the UUP had been "too soft" regarding *Sinn Féin* and the IRA, promptly resigned as party leader. He was succeeded on June 24 by Reg Empey. While Trimble officially remained a UUP member of the suspended Northern Ireland Assembly through 2007, he was named as a member of the House of Lords in April 2006 and sat on that body as a crossbencher. In April 2007 Trimble announced he had joined the Conservative Party.

The UUP won 18 seats in the March 2007 elections for the Northern Ireland Assembly on a 14.9 percent share of first-preference votes. With 9 fewer seats than it had won in 2003, the UUP fell from second to third largest party in the assembly. Throughout 2008 UUP and UK Conservative Party leaders held discussions on reestablishing their once strong relationship, with an eye toward the UUP regaining lost support and the Conservatives broadening their geographical appeal. In November the parties announced an agreement to field candidates jointly for the June 2009 European Parliament elections and the 2010 balloting for the UK Parliament under the rubric of the **Ulster Conservative and Unionists–New Force.** The alliance finished third with 17 percent of the vote in the European Parliament poll, with the UUP incumbent retaining his seat. Prior to the May 2010 balloting for the UK House of Commons the UUP's one incumbent in that body left the party. He won as an independent, while none of the official UUP candidates was successful. In the May 2011 National Assembly elections the UUP held onto 16 of its seats with 13.2 percent of first-preference votes. In 2013 UUP members Basil McCREA and John McCALLISTER resigned to form a new grouping, **NI21** (McCallister resigned from NI21 in July 2014).

In the May 2014 local balloting, the UUP increased its representation by 11, securing a total of 88 seats. It also won one seat in EU elections. The UUP withdrew from the government in September 2015 in protest over possible renewed IRA activity. In assembly elections in May 2016, the party won 33 seats with 12.6 percent of the vote.

Leaders: Mike NESBITT (Party Leader), May STEELE (President), Lord EMPEY (Chair).

Social Democratic and Labour Party—SDLP (*Páirtí Sóisialta Daonlathach an Lucht Oibre*). Founded in 1970 and a member of the Socialist International, the SDLP is a largely Catholic, left-of-center party that has championed the reunification of Ireland by popular consent, with Catholics being accorded full political and social rights in the interim. Its longtime leader, Gerard FITT, participated in the post-Sunningdale Faulkner government and subsequently became the only non-unionist to hold a seat in the UK House of Commons. Fitt resigned as party leader in November 1979 after the SDLP constituency representatives and executive had rejected the government's working paper for the 1980 constitutional conference on devolution. The SDLP won 14 assembly seats in 1982 but joined *Sinn Féin* in boycotting sessions. It won 3 UK House of Commons seats in 1987 on a platform that attacked the Thatcher government on employment, housing, education, and agricultural policies.

In addition to supporting the 1985 Anglo-Irish Agreement and resultant UK-Irish cooperation on Northern Ireland, the party became an enthusiastic participant in the 1991 Brooke initiative and its successor talks. Seeking a framework for peace, in April and May 1993 SDLP leader John Hume undertook an unprecedented series of meetings with *Sinn Féin* leader Gerry Adams and subsequently helped negotiate the 1994 IRA cease-fire.

The SDLP had mixed results at the polls during the 1990s, picking up 1 seat in the 1992 UK general election but returning just 3 MPs in 1997. A year earlier it had won a somewhat disappointing 21 seats in balloting for the Northern Ireland Forum. A strong supporter of the 1998 Good Friday Agreement, the party carried 24 seats, second to the UUP, in the subsequent election for the Northern Ireland Assembly. The party's deputy leader, Seamus Mallon, was elected deputy first minister of the Executive Committee, the position having been turned down by the overtaxed Hume, who served in the European Parliament as well as the UK House of Commons.

Hume received the 1998 Nobel Peace Prize, not only for his contribution to the Good Friday Agreement, but also for having been, over several decades, "the clearest and most consistent of Northern Ireland's political leaders" in the search for peace. In August 2000 Hume announced that he intended to resign his assembly seat but would retain his other positions. On September 17, 2001, however, he indicated that he would step down as party leader, and a day later Mallon made a similar announcement. At a November party conference Mark Durkan was named to replace Hume. Hume retired from public life in February 2004.

In balloting for the European Parliament in June 2004, the SDLP failed to win any of Northern Ireland's 3 seats. At the May 2005 balloting for the UK House of Commons, the SDLP retained its 3 seats with 17.5 percent of the votes in Northern Ireland. The party finished fourth in the March 7, 2007, elections for the Northern Ireland Assembly, securing 16 seats on a 15.2 percent share of first-preference votes. It also came in fourth (only 1 percent behind the UUP/Conservative alliance that won the third and final seat) in the June 2009 balloting for the European Parliament. Mark DURKAN stood down as party chair in September 2009, and Margaret Ritchie was elected as the first female leader of a major Northern Ireland party. The party retained its 3 seats in the May 2010 UK parliamentary election. In the May 2011 National Assembly elections the SDLP lost 2 of its previously held seats for a new total of 14, winning 14.5 percent of first-preference votes. The SDLP won 66 seats in local elections in 2014. Colum EASTWOOD was elected party leader in November 2015. The party won 12 assembly seats in the May 2016 elections with 12 percent of the vote.

Leaders: Colum EASTWOOD (Party Leader), Ronan McCAY (Chair).

Alliance Party of Northern Ireland (APNI). A nonsectarian and nondoctrinaire group founded in 1970 in reaction to growing civil strife, the Alliance Party, like the SDLP, participated in the post-Sunningdale Faulkner government. It won ten assembly seats in 1982 and was the only non-unionist party to participate in that body's subsequent proceedings. For lack of alternative proposals, the party in 1987 announced continued support of the 1985 Anglo-Irish Agreement, although it called for the additional enactment of a bill of rights for Northern Ireland. It has achieved occasional success in local elections but has never won a seat in the UK House of Commons.

The Alliance was one of the four Ulster parties represented at talks between unionists and republicans in Duisburg, West Germany, in October 1988. Alliance officials attended the opening of the interparty Ulster talks on April 30, 1991, and, although sympathetic to the unionist position, indicated that they would support the SDLP.

Party leader Dr. John ALDERDICE was nominated to the House of Lords in 1996, giving the Alliance representation in the UK Parliament for the first time. It backed the Good Friday Agreement of 1998 but won only six seats at the subsequent assembly election, a performance that led Lord Alderdice to resign the party leadership. UK Secretary of State for Northern Ireland Mo Mowlam immediately named him as initial presiding officer of the assembly.

Party Leader Sean NEESON announced on September 6, 2001, his decision to step down in favor of "a fresh face," with David Ford then being elected in October as his successor. A month later, in a maneuver designed to secure David Trimble's reelection as first minister and thereby avert a collapse of the power-sharing government, Ford and two other Alliance assembly members temporarily redesignated themselves as unionists. As a result, Trimble was able to secure a bare majority of unionist votes, permitting his return to office.

The party retained its existing six seats at the 2003 assembly election, improving to 7 seats in 2007. The party's nonsectarian standing proved instrumental to Ford becoming the cross-community consensus candidate to head the newly created Department of Justice in April 2010. One month later, the party won its first-ever seat in the UK House of Commons when its candidate defeated DUP leader Peter Robinson. In the May 2011 National Assembly elections the party increased its seat share to seven, with 7.7 percent of first-preference votes, and Ford was reconfirmed as the head of the Department of Justice. The APNI won 32 seats in local polling in May 2014.

The APNI won 7 percent of the vote and 8 seats in the May 2016 legislative balloting. In October Naomi LONG was elected party leader.

Leaders: Naomi LONG (Party Leader), Anna LO (President), Duncan MORROW (Chair).

Green Party in Northern Ireland (GPNI). A left-leaning branch of the Irish Green Party, the GPNI emphasizes environmental concerns and an integrationist perspective on the governance of Northern Ireland. In the 1998 assembly balloting the party placed last in first-preference votes, and in the 2003 assembly balloting its first-preference support was only 0.4 percent of the total votes. After the party won only three local council positions in 2005, a party conference on December 4, 2006, chose to replace its constitution by taking on the status of a regional grouping with direct association with the Irish Green Party and enhanced ties to green parties in Scotland, England, and Wales. The GPNI won one seat in the May 2011 National Assembly elections, with 0.9 percent of first-preference votes. The party won four seats in the 2014 local elections. The party gained a second assembly seat in the May 2016 elections with 2.7 percent of the vote.

Leaders: Steven AGNEW (Party Leader), John HARDY (Chair).

Traditional Unionist Voice (TUV). The TUV was established in October 2007 by James (Jim) Allister, who had been elected to the European Parliament on the DUP ticket in 2004. Allister had resigned from the DUP in March 2007 in disagreement over the DUP's willingness to accept the requirement that *Sinn Féin* be included in a power-sharing arrangement. The TUV holds essentially the same positions as the DUP with regard to strong bonds with the UK and traditional family values. However, the TUV more stridently opposed putting police powers under the control of the Northern Ireland Assembly. It also completely rejects any form of devolution arrangement that requires a unionist and republican coalition. (The TUV does not formally oppose the possible formation of such a coalition but argues that it should not be mandated.)

Allister lost his seat in the European Parliament in the June 2009 balloting, as the TUV finished fifth with 13.5 percent of the vote and thereby did not qualify for any seats. However, the party appeared ready to continue to press its policy principles, having attracted many disaffected UUP voters. Allister subsequently stated his intention to contest the new UK House of Commons elections (2010) and Northern Ireland Assembly balloting (2011) as a candidate in the unionist stronghold of North Antrim, Ian Paisley's constituency. He was unsuccessful in the former, finishing a distant second (with 17 percent of the vote) to Ian Paisley Jr. (46 percent), but successful in the latter, winning the North Antrim seat with 10 percent of first-preference votes. The party increased its number of local councilors from 3 to 13 in the 2014 polling. In the 2016 assembly elections, the party won 1 seat with 3.4 percent of the vote.

Leaders: James "Jim" ALLISTER (Leader), William ROSS (President), Ivor McCONNELL (Chair).

People Before Profit Alliance (PBPA). The PBPA is a socialist party that participates as an all-Ireland party (see entry on Ireland). The PBPA was founded in October 2005 to promote union workers' rights and to oppose privatizing public lands. The party met with success in the 2016 election, taking two seats in the Northern Ireland Assembly with 2 percent of the vote. The PBPA operates under a collective leadership.

Other Parties That Contested the 2016 Assembly Elections:

Progressive Unionist Party (PUP). The PUP emerged out of the loyalist paramilitaries, in this case the Ulster Volunteer Force (UVF). The PUP's former leader, David ERVINE, served in the UVF and was imprisoned for five years for possession of explosives. The party is distinctive in that, while it is part of the unionist camp, it also champions working-class causes without regard to sect, and the party leader speaks openly of parallels in policy to British Labour. With a definition of unionism based more on the idea of citizenship than on religion, the party has appeared the most flexible in the unionist camp. It signed the 1998 Good Friday Agreement and won two seats in the June Northern Ireland Assembly election, one of which was lost in 2003.

In the wake of the renunciation of violence by the IRA in 2005, Ervine came under increasing pressure to facilitate similar action on the part of the UVF (below). Meanwhile, in May 2006 Ervine formed a controversial alliance with the UUP in the assembly in an attempt to secure an executive position for unionist forces. However, the assembly speaker ruled that the maneuver violated assembly rules.

Ervine died unexpectedly in early January 2007. He was succeeded as party leader by Dawn PURVIS, who also was chosen to defend (successfully) Ervine's assembly seat in the March 2007 balloting for the Northern Ireland Assembly. Purvis resigned in June 2010 after the UVF was linked to a murder, despite its previous commitments to decommission its weapons. She said she could not lead a party that maintained relations with the UVF. Brian Ervine, brother of the late David Ervien, took over as party leader until the October 2011 party conference elected Billy Hutchinson.

In November 2013 security forces announced that a ceasefire with the UVF had ended after the organization was blamed for shooting a 15-year-old. In May 2014 balloting, the PUP won four local seats, a gain of three from the previous elections. The party won 0.9 percent of the vote in the 2016 assembly elections and no seats.

Leader: Billy HUTCHINSON (Party Leader).

Northern Ireland Conservatives (NI Conservatives). This grouping is the Northern Ireland branch of the UK Conservative Party. Its branch affiliation previously was with the UUP, which sat with the Conservatives in Westminster until disagreement over the 1973 Sunningdale Agreement split the UUP and severed the UUP's bond with the UK Conservatives. The Conservatives NI fielded candidates in the 1998, 2003, and 2007 Northern Ireland Assembly elections, its best showing being in 2007, when it won 0.5 percent of the first-preference votes. In July 2008 UK Conservative Party leader David Cameron announced exploratory talks that could lead to recementing relations with the UUP. Among other things, Cameron promised to include a UUP MP in a ministerial post in a future Conservative government in Westminster. The Conservatives NI formed an electoral alliance with the UUP later in the year. On June 14, 2012, the party relaunched as NI Conservatives a "fresh, pro-Union, center-right party, which is proudly and distinctly Northern Irish." In its new form, the party is fully part of the UK Conservative Party but responsible on devolved issues. The party secured just 0.4 percent of the vote in local balloting in 2014 and no seats. The party also won 0.4 percent of the vote in the 2016 assembly elections.

Leader: Alan DUNLOP (Chair).

Other registered parties that fielded candidates in the 2016 assembly elections without success included the **UK Independence Party** (UKIP), led by Paul NUTTALL; the **Workers' Party,** led by Michael DONNELLY; the **Socialist Party; Procapitalism,** led by Charles SMYTH; the **Northern Ireland Labour Party,** led by Kathryn JOHNSTON; and the **British National Party,** led by Nick Griffin.

Other Parties and Groups:

32 County Sovereignty Movement (32 CMA). This *Sinn Féin* splinter was formed in September 1997 as the 32 County Sovereignty Committee by ardent nationalists opposed to Gerry Adams's decision to support the Mitchell principles and join the multiparty negotiations in Stormont. One of its organizers, Bernadette SANDS-McKEVITT, is the sister of Bobby Sands, a leader of the Maze prison hunger strikes who died in 1981. The Movement is believed to be affiliated with the paramilitary Real IRA (below), which claimed responsibility for the August 1998 Omagh bombing. In June 2000 the Movement condemned the IRA's decision to permit international inspections of its arms stockpiles as "the first stop in a decommissioning surrender process." The U.S. State Department, describing the 32 CMA as an "alias" for the Real IRA, has designated the 32 CMA as a terrorist organization.

Leader: Francie MACKEY.

Numerous parties based in the Republic of Ireland also have branches in Northern Ireland. (See the entry on Ireland for information on those parties.)

For information on the following deregistered parties—the **United Kingdom Unionist Party** (UKUP), the **Northern Ireland Unionist Party** (NIUP), and the **Ulster Democratic Party** (UDP)—see the 2013 *Handbook.* For more information on the **United Unionist Assembly Party** (UUAP) and the **Northern Ireland Women's Coalition** (NIWC), see the 2014 *Handbook.*

Former and Current Republican Paramilitary Groups:

Irish Republican Army (IRA). In the late 1960s arguments escalated between the dominant socialist faction in the Republican Clubs, as the (illegal) Northern Ireland section of *Sinn Féin* was then known, and traditional nationalist elements wanting to organize an armed defense of Catholic areas under attack from police and Protestant gangs. The dispute led to the creation in 1969 of a breakaway "Provisional" Army Council that set about rebuilding the IRA, which had withered away since its last terrorist campaign in 1956–1962. The "Provisional" IRA, supported by the "Provisional" *Sinn Féin,* quickly became a large and effective guerrilla organization, defining its aims as British withdrawal from Northern Ireland and the reunification of Ireland as a socialist republic. (Although in frequent use into the 1990s, the term "Provisional" had become redundant in the early 1980s, when the "Official" rump of the *Sinn Féin* became the Workers' Party—see the discussion of *Sinn Féin* in the Republic of Ireland entry.)

Especially active in 1971–1976, when it carried out more than 5,000 bombings, a similar number of armed robberies, and more than 15,000 shootings, resulting in many hundreds of security-force and civilian deaths, the IRA was banned under the 1978 Emergency Provisions Act. It continued its activities in Northern Ireland, Britain, and sometimes continental Europe almost without interruption until 1994.

On August 31, 1994, following secret contacts with the British government, the IRA instituted a cease-fire with the aim of making it possible for *Sinn Féin,* which after 1981 had developed a strong electoral following, to take part in negotiations with the British and Irish governments and with regional parties. With *Sinn Féin* remaining marginalized by demands from most parties and the government that the IRA surrender its weapons, the IRA resumed its military activities in February 1996 by exploding a massive bomb in the financial district of London.

The cease-fire was renewed on July 19, 1997, which opened the way for *Sinn Féin* to join the peace negotiations in Stormont two months later. The IRA gave qualified support to the Good Friday Agreement of April 1998 but at the time refused to link decommissioning of its arms to formation of a devolved government for Northern Ireland, as demanded by the plurality UUP. In December 1998 senior IRA leaders elected a seven-member Army Council headed by hard-liner Brian KEENAN, reinforcing the possibility that the cease-fire might be rescinded were *Sinn Féin* to be excluded from the Northern Ireland Executive.

The IRA's continuing refusal to begin disarming before the inauguration of the power-sharing executive delayed devolution until December 2, 1999, shortly after the IRA had indicated that it was willing to discuss disarmament with Gen. John de Chastelain of the IICD. Nevertheless, no tangible progress was made in the following two months. On February 11, 2000, the IRA offered, in the words of a report from de Chastelain, "to consider how to put arms and explosives beyond use," but the proposal was too late to prevent London's reimposition of direct rule. On May 6, however, the IRA announced that it would accept international monitoring of its arsenals and would "completely and verifiably" put its weapons beyond use. The breakthrough and a subsequent positive UUP response led London, on May 30, to return authority to the Northern Ireland Assembly and Executive. On June 25 the IRA stated that it had reopened discussions with de Chastelain's IICD, and on June 26 arms inspectors reported that they had completed their first visits to IRA caches. Another inspection occurred in May 2001, although the IRA still refused to consider a firm timetable for decommissioning. In early August the IICD announced an agreement on how decommissioning might proceed, but a week later the IRA rescinded its approval because of the August 11 suspension of the power-sharing government. In mid-September it agreed once again to move forward on discussions with the IICD, and on October 23 the IRA announced its first confirmed decommissioning of weapons. An additional, larger decommissioning occurred in April 2002, and on July 16 the IRA issued its first public apology to the families of its innocent victims.

In October 2002 the discovery of alleged IRA spying in official offices in Stormont led to demands from UK Prime Minister Blair, among others, that the IRA reject violence and fully commit itself to peace. The reimposition of direct rule from London on October 15 led the IRA, two weeks later, to discontinue talks with the IICD.

The IRA's alleged involvement in the December 2004 robbery of Belfast's Northern Bank yielded a breakdown in what had appeared to be a promising outcome for the lengthy peace talks. However, momentum returned in mid-2005 when the IRA, following the encouragement of *Sinn Féin* leader Gerry Adams, renounced the use of violence and vowed to disarm. There have been few reports of IRA activity recently in the wake of cross-community political progress (see Political background, above). The Independent Monitoring Commission (IMC), a group organized by the UK and Irish governments to evaluate paramilitary activities, reported in September 2008 that the IRA leadership and terrorist structure were no longer operational and thus no longer posed a security threat.

In November 2016 Donal ÓCOISDEALBHA of Dublin was arrested and pleaded guilty to being a member of the IRA after Irish police discovered explosives and bomb-making devices ahead of a visit by Prince Charles in May.

Irish National Liberation Army (INLA). Formed in 1975 by dissident members of the "Official" IRA after that group had adopted a policy of nonviolence, the INLA was banned in 1979 after assassinating a close associate of Margaret Thatcher. A number of INLA members joined the Maze hunger strikes of 1980–1981. Other members of the INLA and its political front, the **Irish Republican Socialist Party** (see Ireland: Political Parties), were killed in internal feuds, in disputes with the IRA, or in attacks allegedly related to the involvement in the drug trade of the INLA itself and a splinter group, the **Irish People's Liberation Organization** (IPLO). The INLA declared a cease-fire on August 22, 1998, in the wake of the Omagh bombing, and reaffirmed it in early August 1999. In March 2000 the INLA stated that it had delivered to the principal loyalist paramilitary groups, the UDA and UVF, a paper on maintaining the cease-fire even in the face of political impasse. The INLA announced in 2010 that it had decommissioned its weapons.

Continuity IRA (CIRA). Adamantly opposed to the peace process, including the IRA cease-fire announced in 1994, the CIRA (also referenced as the Continuity Army Council—CAC) in 1996 claimed responsibility for a number of attacks in Northern Ireland. Some reports characterized the CIRA as an armed wing of the Republican *Sinn Féin* (RSF) party (see Ireland: Political Parties), although the RSF denied any such linkage. Although itself responsible for bombings and killings, the CIRA condemned the August 1998 Omagh bombing as an unjustified "slaughter of the innocents." Believed to number at that time only about 30, the group may have attracted additional members following the cease-fire declared by the Real IRA (below) in September 1998. The CIRA remained the only republican group not to have declared a cease-fire, and in the first seven months of 2000 it claimed responsibility for a number of bombings in Northern Ireland and England. Some antiterrorism agencies suspected, however, that other groups, particularly the Real IRA, may have been using the CIRA as a cover name. In March 2009 the CIRA, declared a terrorist organization by the United States, claimed responsibility for the murder of a Catholic PSNI officer. Tommy CROSSAN, a former CIRA commander was shot and killed by an unknown assailant in Belfast on April 18, 2014.

Real IRA. Apparently organized in October 1997 in opposition to the renewed IRA cease-fire and *Sinn Féin*'s participation in the Stormont peace talks, the Real IRA probably numbered no more than 100 to 150 members. It was believed in some quarters to be serving as the military wing of the 32 County Sovereignty Movement, whose leaders have denied any connection.

In June 1998 reports surfaced that the Real IRA, the Continuity IRA, and the INLA had held a summit in Dundalk, Ireland, and may have agreed to unify their forces. Following the August Omagh bombing, however, the Continuity IRA and the INLA distanced themselves from the attack, for which the Real IRA claimed responsibility. On August 18, three days after the car bombing, the Real IRA announced a "complete cessation of all military activity." On September 8, reportedly after its leaders received personal visits from the IRA, it declared a "permanent" cease-fire, although it was implicated in subsequent bombings, including a number in England. In May 2000 it warned that it was preparing a renewed bombing campaign. Two months later the Real IRA was implicated in a failed effort to smuggle a shipment of explosives and weapons from Croatia, and in September it was branded as the probable perpetrator of two attacks on security bases in the North. In March 2001 authorities implicated the Real IRA in a car-bomb explosion outside the West London offices of the British Broadcasting Corporation (BBC). Other bombings in May and August were also attributed to the Real IRA. In May 2002 three Real IRA members pleaded guilty to conspiracy and other charges and received 30-year sentences.

Michael McKevitt, the leader of the Real IRA, was convicted in 2003 of the charge of heading a terrorist organization; he was sentenced to a 20-year prison term. (The verdict was handed down by a nonjury Special Criminal Court authorized to adjudicate terrorism cases following the 1998 Omagh bombing.) In March 2009 the Real IRA claimed responsibility for the murder of two UK soldiers, apparently in the hope of forestalling the policing and justice negotiations (see Political background, above). The group also claimed responsibility for the detonation of a bomb at British security headquarters in Northern Ireland within 30 minutes of the opening of the new Department of Justice. In 2013 a splinter group, the **New Irish Republican Army** (NIRA) began operations and claimed responsibility in October 2013 for the shooting deaths of two men that the organization claimed were dangers to the "community." On October 29 the NIRA mailed a letter bomb to Northern Ireland Secretary Theresa VILLIERS. In May 2016 McKevitt was released from prison after completing his sentence.

Leader: Michael McKEVITT.

Former and Current Loyalist Paramilitary Groups:

Ulster Defense Association (UDA). Formed in 1971 by the amalgamation of loyalist paramilitary groups, mainly in greater Belfast and Londonderry, the UDA was initially a mass-membership organization involved in street protests and rallies, including the political strike and accompanying intimidation that brought down the power-sharing administration in 1974. It became increasingly involved in sectarian violence, using such cover names as **Ulster Freedom Fighters** (UFF) and "Ulster Young Militants" to claim responsibility for several hundred killings, the vast majority being noncombatant Catholics. From the mid-1970s the UDA also became deeply enmeshed in racketeering in Northern Ireland, while in the late 1980s it obtained significant material support from the apartheid regime in South Africa.

The UFF was banned in 1973, but the UDA remained legal until 1992, when it was proscribed after a British Army intelligence agent operating in the UDA high command was convicted of conspiracy to murder. The case highlighted allegations that the loyalist paramilitaries had benefited extensively from collusion with members of the police, the army, and the intelligence services. In the interim, the UDA had established a political front, the **Ulster Democratic Party** (UDP), which remained legal.

In 1991 the UDA/UFF joined the Ulster Volunteer Force and the Red Hand Commando (below) in forming a Combined Loyalist Military Command (CLMC) to coordinate paramilitary activities. The CLMC declared a brief cease-fire in 1991 and then an indefinite cease-fire (subsequently violated) in October 1994, four months after the IRA had done so. In October 1997 conflict within the CLMC broke into the open, and the UDA announced its withdrawal, leading to reports that the joint command had disbanded. Within days sporadic intraloyalist violence was reported, without, however, threatening the cease-fire.

Cease-fire violations attributed to the UFF led to suspension of the UDP from the Stormont peace talks in January–March 1998, but on April 25 the UDA announced its support for the Good Friday Agreement. It may now number only several hundred members, although it claimed the support of as many as 40,000 at its peak in the 1970s. In September 1999 UFF leader Johnny Adair was released from prison in accordance with the peace agreement, having served 4 years of his 16-year term for terrorism.

On June 20, 2000, members of the UFF threatened to break its cease-fire, "reserving the right" to defend Protestant homes in the context of "ethnic cleansing" and "intimidation" perpetrated by nationalists. Three days later, however, it retracted its warning. Two months later, Adair's early release was suspended in the context of violent clashes between the UFF/UDA and the UVF/PUP in Belfast. Altercations continued for several more months. On December 15 the UDA, the UVF, and the Red Hand Commando agreed to a truce.

On October 12, 2001, responding to a renewed wave of violence and rioting, Secretary of State for Northern Ireland John Reid declared an end to the government's cease-fire with the UDA/UFF. Adair, having completed his sentence, was released from prison on May 15, 2002.

The UDA formally renounced violence and disbanded its armed units in November 2007 and in 2009 announced the decommissioning of its weapons.

Ulster Volunteer Force (UVF). The UVF was founded in 1966 and was quickly banned after allegedly killing two Catholics. It was restored to legal status in 1974 to encourage it to become involved in politics through the **Volunteer Political Party** (later reconstituted as the Progressive Unionist Party—PUP, above). Banned again after several murders in October 1975, the UVF conducted a protracted campaign of sectarian assassinations designed to put pressure on the IRA to halt its activities, the most active UVF units being based in Belfast, Armagh, and Tyrone.

In general, the UVF held to the CLMC cease-fire of 1994, despite differences with the UDA that reportedly led to the UVF's expulsion from Londonderry in November 1997. A splinter group, the Loyalist Volunteer Force (below), left the UVF in 1996, and infighting between the two persisted. In January 2000 a UVF commander, Richard JAMESON, was assassinated, with suspicion immediately falling on the LVF. The parent group may now number a few hundred members, compared to 1,500 in the 1970s.

In July and August 2000 a renewed feud with the UFF for control of loyalist territory (and possibly drug trafficking) in Belfast resulted in the redeployment of UK troops in the capital. In December 2000 the UVF joined the UDA and the Red Hand Commando in a truce.

The UK government charged that the UVF was significantly involved with "loyalist riots" that broke out in Belfast in September 2005, and the UVF was also blamed for several murders in connection with its ongoing feud with the LVF. Consequently, the UK signaled that it no longer considered the UVF to be honoring the cease-fire. In mid-2006 the UVF was pressured to disband (as the LVF had), but it refused to "clarify" its stance. Although the UVF announced in 2009 that it would decommission its arms, the Independent Monitoring Commission linked the group to the shooting of a loyalist in June 2010.

Red Hand Commando (RHC). Formed in 1972 and proscribed since 1973, the small RHC was frequently linked to the UVF, with some reports describing it as nothing more than a cover name for the larger group. The RHC agreed to the December 2000 truce between the UVF and the UDA. In 2009 the RHC joined the UVF and UDA in agreeing to the decommissioning of their weapons.

Loyalist Volunteer Force (LVF). Apparently dating from about 1994, the LVF formed within the UVF around the leadership of Billy

Wright, who opposed the 1994 cease-fire and any concessions to nationalists. The LVF withdrew from the UVF in 1996 and was banned a year later. On December 27, 1997, Wright was murdered in Maze prison by INLA inmates, after which the LVF was implicated in a number of apparently retaliatory sectarian killings. (Collaterally, unconfirmed reports suggested that the group was permitting UFF paramilitaries to use the LVF name as a cover.)

The LVF declared a unilateral cease-fire on May 15, 1998, but also urged a "no" vote at the May 22 referendum on the Good Friday Agreement. Three months later it called for an "absolute, utter" end to terrorism and made its cease-fire permanent, thereby qualifying its incarcerated members for early release under the peace accord. On December 18, 1998, the LVF became the first paramilitary organization to decommission some of its weapons, a gesture that the IRA labeled a "stunt."

In November 2005 it was reported that the LVF had disbanded after directing its members to discontinue all operations. The decision was described as a "direct response" to the IRA's recent decision to decommission its arms.

Orange Volunteers (OV). Reviving the name of a major loyalist paramilitary group of the 1970s, the Orange Volunteers emerged in 1998 in opposition to the Good Friday Agreement and the cease-fires declared by other loyalist organizations. It subsequently conducted a small number of sectarian attacks. Its membership, apparently numbering no more than a few dozen individuals disaffected from the UDA/UFF and the LVF, may have overlapped that of the Red Hand Defenders (below). In 2000 both groups were added to the U.S. government's annual list of organizations suspected of terrorism.

Red Hand Defenders (RHD). Like the OV, the RHD was formed in 1998 by loyalist rejectionists. In March 1999 it claimed responsibility for the car bombing that killed prominent lawyer Rosemary Nelson. Two days later, Frankie CURRY, a reputed RHD member, was killed in what some officials characterized as an ongoing conflict between loyalist groups engaged in organized crime. The RHD blamed the UVF for Curry's death but denied that he was a member. In January 2002, following the shooting of a postal worker, the RHD indicated that it was disbanding at the request of the UFF, but another shooting in April was attributed to the group. Some analysts argued that the RHD was a cover name for the UDA/UFF. In September 2014 the RHD reportedly sent warnings that it would attack Catholic schools in Belfast.

LEGISLATURE

The former bicameral Northern Ireland Parliament was replaced by a unicameral Northern Ireland Assembly under the Northern Ireland Constitution Act of July 1973. The assembly and a Northern Ireland Executive functioned in 1973–1974, while a 1982 act of Parliament led to the election of another assembly, initially with consultative powers, in November 1982. With its tasks unfulfilled, the assembly was dissolved in June 1986, although subject to legislative provision that it could be reactivated. On May 30, 1996, provincial elections were held for a 110-member Northern Ireland Forum for Political Dialogue, a nonlegislative body designed to provide a platform for discussion and to assist in choosing delegates to the coming peace talks.

A 108-member body, initially termed the New Northern Ireland Assembly, was elected for a five-year term on June 25, 1998, but was suspended upon the reintroduction of direct rule on October 15, 2002. New assembly balloting was conducted on November 25, 2003, although the body remained under suspension.

The assembly convened "without power" on May 15, 2006, for the first time in three-and-a-half years as part of the revived effort to resolve the governmental impasse, and assembly committees continued to meet throughout the summer. The St. Andrews Agreement of November 2006 provided for the return of self-rule to Northern Ireland, and balloting was held for a **Northern Ireland Assembly** on March 7, 2007. The most recent balloting occurred on May 5, 2016, resulting in the following distribution of seats: the Democratic Unionist Party, 38 seats; *Sinn Féin,* 28; Ulster Unionist Party, 16; Social Democratic and Labour Party, 12; Alliance Party of Northern Ireland, 8; Green Party in Northern Ireland, 2; People before Profit Alliance, 2; Traditional Unionist Voice, 1; and independents, 1. (The 108 members of the assembly [6 from each of 18 constituencies] are elected via universal suffrage under a single-transferable vote system for five-year terms, subject to dissolution.)

Speaker: Robin NEWTON (DUP).

CABINET

[as of September 15, 2016]

First Minister	Arlene Foster (DUP) [f]
Deputy First Minister	Martin McGuinness (SF)
Ministers	
Agriculture, Environment, and Rural Development	Michelle McIlveen (DUP) [f]
Communities	Paul Givan (DUP)
Economy	Simon Hamilton (DUP)
Education	Peter Weir (DUP)
Finance	Máirtín Ó Muilleoir (SF)
Health	Michelle O'Neill (SF) [f]
Infrastructure	Chris Hazzard (SF)
Justice	Claire Sugden (ind.) [f]

[f] = female

For Further Reference:

Cochrane, Feargal. *Northern Ireland: The Reluctant Peace.* New Haven, CT: Yale University Press, 2013.

Laforest, Guy, and André Lecours, eds. *The Parliaments of Autonomous Nations*. Montreal: McGill-Queen's University Press, 2016.

McCulloch, Allison. *Power-sharing and Political Stability in Deeply Divided Societies*. London: Routledge, 2014.

UNITED STATES

United States of America

Political Status: Independence declared on July 4, 1776; federal republic established under constitution adopted on March 4, 1789.

Area: 3,732,396 sq. mi. (9,666,532 sq. km); includes gross area (land and water) of the 50 states, excluding Puerto Rico and other territories. These totals are somewhat higher than earlier ones because of a 1990 change in the method of calculating interior waters.

Population: 324,119,000 (2016E—UN); 323,995,528 (2016E—U.S. Census). Does not include the U.S. Territories.

Major Urban Centers:

City Proper	*Population (2015E)*	*Metro Area (2015E)*
WASHINGTON, D.C.	672,228	6,097,684
New York, N.Y.	8,550,405	20,182,305
Los Angeles, Calif.	3,971,883	13,340,068
Chicago, Ill.	2,720,546	9,551,031
Houston, Texas	2,296,224	6,656,947
Philadelphia, Pa.	1,567,442	6,069,875
Phoenix, Ariz.	1,563,025	4,574,531
San Antonio, Texas	1,469,845	2,384,075
San Diego, Calif.	1,394,928	3,299,521
Dallas, Texas	1,300,092	4,707,151
San Jose, Calif.	1,026,908	1,976,836
Austin, Texas	931,830	2,000,860
Jacksonville, Fla.	868,031	1,449,481
Indianapolis, Ind.	864,816	1,988,817
San Francisco, Calif.	853,173	4,656,132
Columbus, Ohio	850,106	2,021,632
Fort Worth, Texas	833,319	2,395,645
Charlotte, N.C.	827,097	2,426,363
Seattle, Wash.	684,451	3,733,580
Denver, Colo.	682,545	2,814,330

El Paso, Texas	681,124	838,972
Detroit, Mich.	677,116	4,302,043
Boston, Mass.	667,137	4,774,321
Memphis, Tenn.	655,770	1,344,127
Nashville, Tenn.	654,610	1,830,345
Portland, Ore.	632,309	2,389,228

Principal Language: English. In the 2010 census approximately 80.1 percent spoke only English; 12.2 percent Spanish; 7.7 percent other.

Monetary Unit: Dollar (selected market rates October 1, 2016: $1US = 3.26 Brazilian real, 6.67 Chinese yuan renminbi, 0.89 euro, 66.61 Indian rupee, 101.35 Japanese yen, 19.39 Mexican peso, 62.88 Russian ruble, 13.72 South African rand, 0.77 UK pound).

President: Donald J. TRUMP (Republican Party); elected on November 8, 2016, and inaugurated on January 20, 2017, for a four-year term, succeeding Barack H. OBAMA (Democratic Party).

Vice President: Mike PENCE (Republican Party); elected on November 8, 2016, and inaugurated on January 20, 2017, for a term concurrent with that of the president, succeeding Joseph R. BIDEN Jr. (Democratic Party).

THE COUNTRY

First among the nations of the world in economic output, the United States ranks third in area (behind Russia and Canada) and also third in population (after China and India). Canada and Mexico are the country's only contiguous neighbors. Most of U.S. territory ranges across the North American continent in a broad band that encompasses the Atlantic seaboard; the Appalachian Mountains; the Ohio, Mississippi, and Missouri river valleys; the Great Plains; the Rocky Mountains; the deserts of the Southwest; and the narrow, fertile coastland adjoining the Pacific. Further contrasts are found in the two noncontiguous states: Alaska, in northwestern North America, where the climate ranges from severe winters and short growing seasons in the north to equable temperatures in the south; and Hawaii, in the mid-Pacific, where trade winds produce a narrow temperature range but extreme variations in rainfall.

Regional diversity is also found in economic conditions. Industrial production is located mainly in the coastal areas and in those interior urban centers with good transportation connections, as in the Great Lakes region. Agricultural products come primarily from the far western, plains, midwestern, and southeastern states. The median household income varies considerably from state to state, with a national median of $55,775 in 2016, a 3.8 percent increase from the previous year.

The nation's ethnic diversity is a product of large-scale voluntary and involuntary immigration, much of which took place before 1920. According to Census Bureau estimates, the population in 2015 was 77.1 percent white, 13.3 percent black, 5.6 percent Asian, 1.2 percent American Indian and native Alaskan, and 0.2 percent Pacific Islander or native Hawaiian. In addition, Hispanic Americans (a nonexclusive category) constituted 17.6 percent in 2013, up from 16.3 percent in 2010, and up from 12.5 percent in 2000 (thereby becoming the country's largest minority group).

In 2009, 83.1 percent of adults identified themselves as religious, of whom Protestants constituted 51.3 percent; Roman Catholics, 23.9 percent; Jews, 1.7 percent; and Orthodox Christians, 0.6 percent. Although English is the principal language, Spanish is the preferred tongue of sizable minorities in New York City (largely migrants from Puerto Rico), in Florida (primarily Caribbean expatriates), and in the Southwest and California (mainly from Mexico and Central America). Other languages are spoken among foreign-born and first-generation Americans.

In 2012 women constituted 53 percent of the labor force and were concentrated in management, professional, sales, and office occupations. Women earned approximately 84 percent of the median male wage. As a result of the November 2016 national election, female representation in the incoming 115th Congress climbed to a record 21 seats in the Senate and 83 seats in the U.S. House of Representatives. Women governors led six states following the 2016 balloting.

Owing to a historic transfer of population from farm to city (now seemingly at an end, with migration to rural areas fluctuating close to a reversal in 1990–2000), only a small proportion of the population is engaged in agriculture, which nevertheless yields a substantial proportion of U.S. exports. As of 2011 agriculture employed 1.2 percent of the population. By contrast, 19.2 percent of the labor force was engaged in mining, manufacturing, and construction and 79.6 percent in service activities. Of increasing importance to the administration of the nation's Social Security system is the aging of the population; the percentage of those age 65 and older rose from approximately 4 percent in 1900 to 13.5 percent in 2011.

The United States has experienced long-term economic growth throughout most of its history, with marked short-term fluctuations in recent years. During 1960–2005 the real per capita rise in GDP averaged 3.7 percent. December 2000 marked the 127th consecutive month of economic expansion, the longest period of peacetime growth in U.S. history. Federal budget surpluses were recorded from 1998 through 2001, but government spending went into deficit thereafter.

Due to the Federal Reserve Bank's lowering interest rates and collateral government tax cuts, annual growth averaged about 3 percent reported for 2002–2005, and cooled slightly to average 2.1 percent in 2006–2007. A significant decline of 1.9 percent was registered in 2008 following the dramatic downturn in the housing market and the stock market and the collapse of several large financial institutions (see Political Background, below). The government responded with varying public and private capital injections that dramatically increased the deficit and national debt.

GDP decreased by 3 percent in 2009 as a result of declines in investments and exports, but recovered to grow by 2.4 percent in 2010 and 1.8 percent in 2011, according to the IMF. Inflation almost doubled from 1.6 percent in 2010 to 3.1 percent the next year, while unemployment declined from 9.6 percent to 9 percent. Gross government debt rose from 98.6 percent of GDP to 102.9 percent over those two years. In 2013 GDP growth of 1.5 percent was charted, with inflation of 1.5 percent. Unemployment was 7.4 percent—dipping below 8 percent for the first time since the financial crisis. Despite a lag in growth early in the year owing in part to a harsh winter, an ailing housing market, and slow external demand, growth improved in 2014, rising to 2.4 percent. That year, inflation fell to 1.6 percent, and unemployment fell further to 6.2 percent. GDP expanded by 2.4 percent in 2015 and 2016. In 2016 inflation fell to 0.1 percent, while unemployment was 4.9 percent.

GOVERNMENT AND POLITICS

Political background. Beginning as a group of 13 British colonies along the Atlantic seaboard, the "United States of America" declared themselves independent on July 4, 1776, gained recognition as a sovereign state at the close of the Revolutionary War in 1783, and in 1787 adopted a federal constitution that became effective on March 4, 1789. George WASHINGTON took office as the first president of the United States on April 30. Westward expansion, colonization, judicious purchase, and annexation during the ensuing 100 years found the nation by 1890 in full possession of the continental territories that now make up the 48 contiguous states. Alaska, purchased from Russia in 1867, and Hawaii, annexed in 1898, became the 49th and 50th states, respectively, in 1959.

The constitutional foundation of the Union has been severely threatened only by the Civil War of 1861–1865, in which the separate confederacy established by 11 southern states was defeated and reintegrated into the Federal Union by military force. The U.S. political climate has been characterized by the alternating rule of the Republican and Democratic parties since the Civil War, which initiated a period of industrial expansion that continued without major interruptions through World War I before being temporarily checked by the Great Depression of the early 1930s.

The modern era of administrative centralization and massive federal efforts to solve economic and social problems began in 1933 with the inauguration of Democratic president Franklin D. ROOSEVELT. The onset of direct U.S. involvement in World War II on December 7, 1941, brought further governmental expansion. Following the defeat of the Axis powers, efforts supporting European reconstruction and attempting to meet the challenge posed by the rise of the Soviet Union as a world power dominated the administration of Harry S. TRUMAN, the Democratic vice president who succeeded Roosevelt upon his death on April 12, 1945, and was elected in 1948 to a full four-year term. Newly armed with atomic weapons, the United States abandoned its traditional isolation to become a founding member of the United Nations (UN) and the leader of a worldwide coalition directed against the efforts of the Soviet Union and, after 1949, the People's Republic of China, to expand their influence along the periphery of the communist world. A series of East-West confrontations over Iran, Greece, and Berlin culminated in the Korean War of 1950–1953, in which U.S. forces were committed to large-scale military action under the flag of the UN.

Dwight D. EISENHOWER, a Republican elected president in 1952 and 1956, achieved a negotiated settlement in Korea and some relaxation of tensions with the Soviet Union, but efforts to solve such basic East-West problems as the division of Germany proved unavailing. Whereas Eisenhower's attempts to restrict the role of the federal government met only limited success, his eight-year incumbency witnessed a resumption of progress toward legal equality of the races—after a lapse of 80 years—pursuant to the 1954 Supreme Court decision declaring segregation in public schools unconstitutional. An economic recession developed toward the end of Eisenhower's second term, which also saw the beginning of a substantial depletion of U.S. gold reserves. In spite of a resurgent economy, balance-of-payments problems persisted throughout the succeeding Democratic administrations of presidents John F. KENNEDY (1961–1963) and Lyndon B. JOHNSON (1963–1969).

The assassinations of President Kennedy in 1963 and civil rights advocate Martin Luther KING Jr. and Sen. Robert F. KENNEDY in 1968 provided the most dramatic evidence of a deteriorating domestic climate. To counter sharpening racial and social antagonisms and growing violence on the part of disaffected groups and individuals, Congress, at President Johnson's urging, passed laws promoting equal rights in housing, education, and voter registration and establishing programs to further equal job opportunities, urban renewal, and improved education for the disadvantaged. These efforts were in part offset by the negative domestic consequences of U.S. involvement in the Vietnam War, which had begun with limited economic and military aid to the French in the 1950s but by the mid-1960s had become direct and massive. Disagreement over Vietnam was also largely responsible for halting a trend toward improved U.S.–Soviet relations that had followed the Cuban missile crisis of 1962 and had led in 1963 to the signing of a limited nuclear test-ban treaty. Moved by increasing public criticism of the government's Vietnam policy, President Johnson on March 31, 1968, announced the cessation of bombing in most of North Vietnam as a step toward direct negotiations to end the war, and preliminary peace talks with the North Vietnamese began in Paris on May 13.

Richard M. NIXON, vice president during the Eisenhower administration, won the election on November 5, 1968, in a three-way race against Democratic nominee and Vice President Hubert H. HUMPHREY and former Alabama governor George C. WALLACE, a dissident Democrat who ran under the segregationist American Independent Party. Nixon took 43.4 percent of the national popular vote, the lowest of any victorious candidate since 1912, while Humphrey secured 42.7 percent and Wallace, 13.5 percent, the largest total for a third-party candidate since 1924.

As president, Nixon embarked on a vigorous foreign policy campaign while selectively limiting the nation's external commitments in Southeast Asia and elsewhere. Domestically the Nixon administration became increasingly alarmed at the growing antiwar movement and reports of radical extremist activity, and in April 1970 it initiated a program of surveillance of militant left-wing groups and individuals. In May the president's decision to order Vietnamese-based U.S. troops into action in Cambodia provoked an antiwar demonstration at Kent State University, in the course of which the Ohio National Guard killed four students. Final agreement on a peace treaty in Vietnam was not obtained until January 27, 1973 (see Foreign relations, below), by which time the "youth rebellion" that had characterized the late 1960s was in pronounced decline.

Nixon was reelected in a landslide victory over antiwar Democrat senator George S. McGOVERN of South Dakota on November 7, 1972. Winning a record-breaking 60.7 percent of the popular vote, Nixon swept all major electoral units except Massachusetts and the District of Columbia, although the Democrats easily retained control of both houses of Congress. Within a year, however, the fortunes of Republican executive leaders were quickly reversed. On October 10, 1973, Spiro T. AGNEW resigned as vice president after pleading no contest to having falsified a federal income-tax return. He was succeeded on December 6 by longtime Michigan representative Gerald R. FORD, the first vice president to be chosen, under the 25th Amendment of the Constitution, by presidential nomination and congressional confirmation. On March 1, 1974, seven former White House and presidential campaign aides were charged with conspiracy in an attempted cover-up of the Watergate scandal (involving a break-in at Democratic National Committee headquarters at their Washington, D.C., building on June 17, 1972), while President Nixon, because of the same scandal, became on August 9 the first U.S. chief executive to tender his resignation. Vice President Ford, who succeeded Nixon on the same day, thus became the first U.S. president never to have participated in a national election.

In the election of November 2, 1976, the Democratic candidate, former Georgia governor Jimmy CARTER, defeated President Ford by a bare majority (50.6 percent) of the popular vote. Ford thus became the first incumbent since 1932 to fail in a bid for a second term. Carter also became a one-term president on November 4, 1980, as his Republican opponent, Ronald REAGAN, swept all but six states and the District of Columbia with a popular vote margin of 10 percent and a near ten-to-one margin in the Electoral College. In congressional balloting the Republicans ended the Democrats' 28-year control of the Senate and registered substantial gains in the House of Representatives, the two bodies for the first time since 1916 being controlled by different parties.

The 1980 outcome was hailed as a "mandate for change" unparalleled since the Roosevelt landslide of 1932. Accordingly, President Reagan moved quickly to address the nation's economic problems by a combination of across-the-board fiscal retrenchment and massive tax cuts. Only the military establishment received significant additional funding to redress the perception of a widening gap between U.S. and Soviet tactical and strategic capabilities. Part of the so-billed New Federalism involved sharply curtailed aid to the states, passing to state governments responsibility for social programs that had long been funded directly from Washington, D.C. While most liberals decried the new administration's commitment to economic "realism," the country made significant progress in lowering interest rates and slowing inflation.

Despite the onset of a severe economic recession that the administration sought to counter with a series of "hard-line" fiscal and monetary policies, the midterm elections of November 2, 1982, yielded no significant alteration in the domestic balance of power. The Democrats increased their majority in the House of Representatives by 26 seats to 269–166. However, Republican control of the Senate remained unchanged at 54–46.

On November 6, 1984, President Reagan won reelection by the second-largest electoral college margin (97.6 percent) in U.S. history, nearly equaling the record of 98.5 percent set by President Roosevelt in 1936. His Democratic opponent, Walter F. MONDALE, won only in his home state of Minnesota and in the District of Columbia. The Republicans also retained control of the Senate (53–47), while the Democrats retained control of the House with a reduced majority of 253–182.

Over the 18 months following Reagan's second inauguration on January 21, 1985, the administration followed on campaign promises regarding taxes with sweeping changes that ultimately emerged as the Tax Reform Act of 1986, marked by a reduction in the number of tax brackets and a lowering of the top rate, with families at or below the poverty line freed of any obligation. The package was to be paid for, in part, by the elimination of many deductions and loopholes, with little measurable gain for individuals in the middle-income range. During the same period, while inflation and unemployment remained at moderate levels, the nation recorded massive trade deficits, despite steady erosion in the value of the U.S. dollar, which declined by more than 20 percent in trade-weighted terms from December 1984 to March 1986. As a result the Reagan administration, steadfastly maintaining its commitment to free trade, called for measures to counter what it perceived as a "protectionist upsurge" on the part of many of its trading partners.

In the nonpresidential balloting of November 4, 1986, the Democrats increased their margin in the House to 258–177 while regaining control of the Senate, 55–45. At the state level they suffered a net loss of 8 governorships, retaining a bare majority of 26.

On November 8, 1988, Republican George H. W. BUSH became the first sitting vice president since Martin Van Buren in 1836 to win the presidency, defeating his Democratic opponent Michael S. DUKAKIS by securing 54 percent of the popular vote and 79 percent of the Electoral College vote. The Democrats marginally increased their control of the House (260–175), with no change in the composition of the Senate and a net gain of 1 gubernatorial office over the 27 held immediately before the election.

Following the midterm balloting of November 6, 1990, the Democrats held 267 House seats (a net gain of 8 over the preelection distribution) and 56 Senate seats (a net gain of 1), while retaining a total of 28 governorships (a net loss of 1). One House seat in 1990 was won by Bernard SANDERS, an independent Vermont socialist, and the remaining 167 by the Republicans, who retained 44 Senate seats and 20 governorships, with 2 of the state houses being filled by independents. In the presidential poll of November 3, 1992, Arkansas governor William (Bill) CLINTON denied Bush reelection, winning 43 percent of the popular and 69 percent of the electoral college votes, contrasted with 38 percent and 31 percent, respectively, for the incumbent. Business owner H. Ross PEROT, running as an independent, secured no electoral college support despite capturing 19 percent of the popular vote (the best showing by a third candidate since 1912). In congressional balloting the Democrats retained control of the Senate by an unchanged majority of 57; they also retained control of the House of Representatives by a reduced majority of 259 seats, 175 being won by Republicans and Sanders retaining his seat from Vermont. At the state level the Republicans gained a single governorship from the Democrats, the resultant distribution being 27–21–2. A record number of voters (more than 104 million) cast ballots in 1992, although the 55.9 percent turnout of those eligible fell short of the 60.8 percent reported in 1968.

Five days after Clinton's inauguration on January 20, 1993, the president named his wife, Hillary Rodham CLINTON, to head a task force on health care reform, for which he campaigned vigorously in the months that followed. The president's proposals were challenged as administratively burdensome and far too costly. Other legislative matters included a struggle (ultimately successful on November 30, 1993) to secure passage of the so-called Brady bill, requiring a waiting period for the purchase of a handgun, and a bitterly contested budget and deficit reduction plan that secured final approval on August 6.

By early 1994 the president's agenda was becoming increasingly hostage to the Whitewater scandal, involving a failed property venture in which the Clintons had a substantial interest. At the president's request, a special prosecutor was appointed on January 20, 1994, to investigate the affair, which also became the subject of congressional hearings. To add to the administration's troubles, Paula JONES, a former Arkansas state employee, filed a sexual harassment suit against President Clinton on May 6. Despite such distractions, the president in late August finally secured congressional approval for his centerpiece crime bill, approving (but not authorizing) expenditure of $30 billion over six years on anticrime measures and banning certain categories of assault weapons.

The midterm election of November 8, 1994, yielded disastrous setbacks for the Democrats, who lost control of the Senate for the first time since 1986 by a margin of 52–48 and, far more unexpectedly, of the House for the first time since 1954 by a margin of 230–204, with Sanders again returning as an independent. Astonishingly, no Republican incumbent at either the gubernatorial or congressional levels was defeated. The day after the November poll, Alabama senator Richard C. SHELBY switched his allegiance from Democrat to Republican. Far more embarrassing to the Democrats was the defection of Colorado senator Ben Nighthorse CAMPBELL, a Native American, on March 3, 1995, leaving the Republicans with an upper house majority of 54.

A chastened President Clinton accepted responsibility for the congressional defeat and called for a "partnership" between the executive and legislative branches of government. The appeal drew a guardedly favorable response from Republican Senate leader Robert J. (Bob) DOLE, while the more flamboyant incoming House speaker, Newt GINGRICH, indicated that cooperation with the president would take second place to implementation of a ten-point "Contract with America," which called for, among other items, a balanced-budget amendment to the Constitution, a presidential line-item veto of budget legislation, welfare reform, and the introduction of congressional term limits. The balanced-budget and term-limits amendments subsequently were defeated, while nine other proposals were approved in the House and pending in the Senate. (On May 27 the Supreme Court ruled that action by the states to impose term limits on federal legislators was unconstitutional.)

In the aftermath of the country's worst domestic bombing attack, the destruction of a federal office complex in Oklahoma City on April 19, Congress approved several administration proposals designed to inhibit and punish terrorist attacks on U.S. property or personnel at home and abroad.

Buffeted by continuing legal problems but buoyed by public opinion polls that showed Clinton leading Republican challenger Dole by as much as 20 points, the president accepted renomination by the Democrats and went on to defeat Dole on November 5, 1996, by a popular vote margin of 49–41 percent, with third-party candidate Perot winning 8 percent. In the Electoral College the race was substantially more unbalanced; Clinton secured 379 of the 538 votes, whereas Dole won 159. Despite the president's victory, the Republicans retained control of both houses of Congress by substantial margins (55 of 100 Senate and 227 of 435 House seats). The biennial congressional balloting of November 3, 1998, yielded an unchanged Senate division, but the Democrats scored an upset by gaining 5 seats in the House despite the president's mounting personal difficulties and conventional wisdom regarding midterm elections.

On December 19, 1998, President Clinton became the second U.S. president (after Andrew Johnson in 1868) to be impeached by the House of Representatives. The principal charges against him were perjury in testimony before a grand jury regarding a sexual relationship with a former White House intern, Monica LEWINSKY, and obstruction of justice in seeking false testimony from Lewinsky in the sexual harassment case brought by Paula Jones. On February 12, 1999, Clinton was acquitted, the Senate having failed to register the two-thirds majority needed for conviction on largely party-line votes of 45–55 and 50–50, with 10 Republicans defecting on the first count and 5 on the second.

In the presidential election of November 7, 2000, exit polls that initially gave Florida to the Democratic nominee, Vice President Al GORE, changed to favor Texas governor George W. BUSH (son of the 41st president), and then suggested a race "too close to call." Subsequently, a recount of 45,000 disputed ballots was halted by Florida's secretary of state, resumed by order of the state supreme court, suspended by the U.S. Supreme Court, and then effectively terminated by the Court on December 12. Bush won the Florida contest by only 537 votes of 6 million cast. As a result Bush was declared the victor by an Electoral College count of 271–266, although he trailed Gore in the popular count. Meanwhile the Senate was evenly split (50–50) for the first time in 120 years, while the Republican House majority fell to its narrowest since 1954: 221 against 212 for the Democrats, with 2 independents. On June 6, 2001, however, the Democrats assumed control of the Senate following a decision by Republican Sen. James JEFFORDS of Vermont to sit as an independent and vote with Democrats on most matters. Tihs marked the first time in U.S. history that the balance of power in a house of Congress shifted because of a midterm change in party allegiance.

On the morning of September 11, 2001, the United States suffered the most devastating terrorist attack in its history when two hijacked commercial airliners were deliberately flown into the upper floors of the World Trade Center's twin 110-story towers in New York City. The towers collapsed shortly after impact, destroying neighboring buildings as well, killing some 2,800 people. Meanwhile hijackers steered a third airliner into one side of the Pentagon, the headquarters of the U.S.

Department of Defense, near Washington, D.C., costing an additional 184 lives. A fourth hijacked flight crashed in rural Pennsylvania, killing the 44 passengers and crew, some of whom, having been alerted by mobile phone to the fate of the other three aircraft, had attempted to overpower the hijackers. In response to the terrorist assaults, the White House ordered all civilian flights in U.S. airspace grounded and temporarily closed the country's borders.

Attention immediately focused on the al-Qaida terrorist network of Osama bin Laden, and within days the government confirmed that all 19 hijackers had connections to al-Qaida. The Bush administration subsequently demanded that the Taliban regime in Afghanistan, which had afforded safe harbor to bin Laden, hand him over and eliminate his terrorist training camps. The Taliban refused. On October 7 aerial forces from the United States and the United Kingdom, supported on the ground by the opposition Northern Alliance, launched a military assault to unseat the Taliban, capture or kill bin Laden, and destroy the al-Qaida bases. The Taliban succumbed in December, and late in the month an interim government was established in Kabul (see the entry on Afghanistan). Military action against pockets of al-Qaida and Taliban resistance continued as the U.S. government contemplated additional steps in what it characterized as a worldwide "war on terrorism."

In late October 2001 the U.S. Congress passed the USA PATRIOT Act, a cornerstone of the Bush administration's domestic response to the terrorism threat. The act expanded the government's authority to wiretap, conduct Internet surveillance, combat money laundering, and detain foreign nationals. Additional legislation strengthened airport security, while an executive order of November 13 authorized secret military tribunals for foreign nationals. By the end of the year 1,200 individuals were being detained in connection with the September 11 events, and the government had begun "voluntary" questioning of 5,000 noncitizens.

The U.S. economy, already in a slump, also suffered significant damage from the September 11 attacks, which the hijackers, most of them Saudi nationals, had aimed at the heart of the U.S. financial and business district. The New York Stock Exchange experienced a massive, but temporary, sell-off upon reopening on September 17, consumer confidence flagged, unemployment rose, and the U.S. airline industry registered losses that threatened bankruptcy as business and tourist travel declined precipitously. The government acted quickly to shore up the airlines, supplement defense appropriations, provide tens of billions of dollars for homeland security and for relief and recovery efforts in New York City, and stimulate the economy. One consequence was a swift end to the brief era of budget surpluses recorded during the final years of the Clinton administration.

In the midterm elections of November 5, 2002, the Republican Party recaptured control of the U.S. Senate by a 51–48 margin (Senator Jeffords remained an independent) and added 6 seats in the House, its majority rising to 229. On November 25 President Bush signed legislation creating a cabinet-level Department of Homeland Security and then named Tom RIDGE, then director of the White House Office of Homeland Security, as its head. Two days later he approved the establishment of an independent ten-member commission to investigate intelligence failures leading up to the attacks of September 11, 2001.

In his State of the Union address on January 29, 2002, President Bush grouped Iraq, Iran, and North Korea in an "axis of evil" intent on developing weapons of mass destruction (WMD) and, in the case of Tehran and Baghdad, supporting international terrorism. In October Congress authorized President Bush to take preemptive military action against Iraq if all other means failed to deter the Saddam Hussein regime from an alleged buildup of WMD. Given the Bush administration's view that Hussein had not adequately complied with UN Security Council Resolution 1441 of November 8, 2002, to begin disarming, U.S. forces launched an attack (code-named Operation Iraqi Freedom) on March 20, 2003. On May 1 Bush announced that combat operations had ended, despite resistance that took on an increasingly complex character in the following three years (see the entry on Iraq).

In the 2004 presidential election, President Bush won a second term with 286 Electoral College votes on a popular vote share of 50.7 percent, versus 252 Electoral College votes for his Democratic opponent, Sen. John KERRY of Massachusetts. In the congressional poll Republicans secured a majority in both chambers (55–44 in the Senate and 232–202 in the House of Representatives). Following the election, the Republicans held 29 governorships versus the Democrats' 21. Bush subsequently won congressional approval for the creation of an overarching director of the nation's 15 spy agencies, tapping former UN ambassador John D. NEGROPONTE for the post.

In late 2005 a controversy erupted over President Bush's authorization that allowed the National Security Agency (NSA) to conduct eavesdropping on telecommunications between U.S. citizens and foreign nationals. The administration argued that the monitoring was key to prosecuting the war on terror, was within the president's authority as commander in chief, and had been authorized by a congressional resolution to use "all necessary and appropriate force" in response to the September 2001 terror attacks. Critics of the policy, including the Republican chair of the Senate Judiciary Committee, Arlen SPECTER of Pennsylvania, countered that it violated the 1978 Foreign Intelligence Surveillance Act (FISA) and had not been authorized by Congress. (In August 2007 Congress passed the FISA Amendment Act, clarifying the FISA court's oversight responsibility with respect to domestic and foreign eavesdropping.)

Throughout 2006 the war in Iraq continued to dominate domestic politics. The rapid U.S. military ouster of Saddam Hussein and the dismantling of his Sunni regime had been followed by several years of unremitting sectarian violence, mostly between Shiite and Sunni factions, as well as attacks from diverse sources—remnants of the prior regime, militias loyal to Islamic clerics and tribal leaders, Iraqi nationalists, al-Qaida recruits, and foreign nationals—against U.S. military forces and their newly trained Iraqi counterparts.

In the November 2006 midterm elections, Democrats won control of the House of Representatives by a margin of 31 seats (233–202) and, somewhat unexpectedly, of the Senate, where a 49–49 tie was broken by two pro-Democratic independents. Following the polling, the Democrats also held 28 of 50 governorships, effectively reversing the Republican Party's gains in 2004. At the start of the 110th Congress in January 2007, Democrat Nancy PELOSI of California, a severe critic of the Bush administration, was elected Speaker of the House, becoming the first woman to hold that position.

Economic problems mounted in the second half of 2007, with spiraling energy costs; a record trade deficit; increased foreclosures in the housing market, accompanied by a wave of major financial institutions losing unprecedented amounts of money as fallout from a subprime mortgage-lending crisis; and a drop in the value of the dollar to its lowest level in 25 years. The housing market declined further in 2008 as house prices fell dramatically and foreclosures mounted. This trend was exacerbated by a tightening of credit as banks reported huge losses linked to the mortgage-backed securities. Several large investment firms went bankrupt or were taken over, and unemployment reached a five-year high of 5.8 percent for the year. Congress approved a revised version of a Bush administration proposal for a $700 billion emergency bailout to buy up "toxic" mortgage assets and stabilize the economy in response to the most serious crisis since the Great Depression. The Treasury Department announced plans to invest up to $250 billion into nine of the largest U.S. banks, a measure designed to help ease the credit crunch.

Insurgent attacks in Iraq declined significantly in 2007 and 2008 as a result of the U.S. troop "surge," which had been initiated in February 2007. The United States began withdrawing the additional troops in 2008, though many U.S. politicians complained that the Iraqi government had failed to meet many of the benchmarks that had been established.

Beginning in mid-2007, the 2008 presidential campaign dominated the political scene. Early in the contest, Hillary Clinton, the junior senator from New York, and Barack Obama, the junior senator from Illinois, became the Democratic Party front-runners. Obama, 47, claimed victory on June 3, 2008, becoming the first African-American to win the nomination of either major party. Meanwhile, Republican senator John McCain of Arizona, a prisoner of war during the Vietnam War, overcame a wave of Republican opposition to immigration legislation he sponsored in 2007 and emerged from a large field of primary contenders to claim victory as the party's nominee on March 4. McCain surprised political pundits and the public at large with his subsequent selection of Alaska governor Sarah PALIN as his running mate. Palin, a virtual unknown outside of her home state, appeared to energize the Republican Party with her conservative values. McCain's campaign focused on government reforms, national security, and the economy. Obama named a veteran legislator, Senator Joseph BIDEN of Delaware as his running mate. Obama, campaigning on a broad platform of change, pledged to withdraw all troops from Iraq within 16 months of taking office and to raise taxes on wealthier citizens and reduce taxes for the middle class. Meanwhile, a surge in violence along the Pakistan–Afghanistan border prompted both U.S. presidential candidates to support military efforts to oust Taliban supporters of al-Qaida in the region.

In the general elections on November 4, 2008, Obama was elected president with 365 electoral college votes and 52 percent of the popular vote, defeating McCain, who received 173 electoral votes and 46 percent of the popular vote. Democrats substantially increased their standing in Congress.

After his January 2009 inauguration, President Obama called for the closure of the controversial Guantánamo Bay prison camp and overseas secret prisons set up by Bush for suspected terrorists. The closure of the Guantánamo prison was deferred when Congress refused to fund it due to fears that some of the detainees, who could not be tried because the evidence provided in their cases could compromise covert agents, were nevertheless deemed too dangerous to be released or transferred to U.S. prisons. Obama was able to convince several allies to take a number of the prisoners. The first detainee from the camp to be transferred to U.S. soil, Tanzanian national Ahmed Ghailani, was tried in New York City on charges involving the bombing of U.S. embassies in Africa and convicted of conspiracy on November 17, 2011.

The new administration responded to the worsening economic recession, the deepest since the 1930s, in February 2009 with the American Recovery and Reinvestment bill, a stimulus package to temper the growing unemployment rate. Obama signed the $789 billion measure into law on February 17. Subsequently, the Treasury made significant investments to aid American International Group (AIG) and General Motors and Chrysler.

Obama called on Congress to pass legislation before the end of 2009 extending health insurance to almost all Americans, almost 50 million of whom had no coverage, barring private insurers from refusing coverage to individuals with "preexisting conditions," and creating a new, government-sponsored health insurance plan that consumers could choose instead of private insurance. The proposal sparked a contentious debate between Democratic supporters and Republican opponents. Independents and conservatives criticized the plan's impact on the ballooning budget deficit, which was projected to expand by a trillion dollars in addition to existing debt from 2010 to 2019 if the plan was passed.

Democrats in Congress pushed through the final version of the health care reform package in March 2010 with near unanimous opposition from Republicans and a minority of conservative Democrats. The Patient Protection and Affordable Care Act and the Health Care and Education Reconciliation Act were designed to be implemented in stages, the most far-reaching of measures, which mandated that all Americans obtain health insurance through reforms in the private insurance market, or pay a penalty, to begin taking effect in 2014.

On April 20, 2010, a British Petroleum deep-water oil-drilling rig in the Gulf of Mexico caught fire and sank, spilling for 86 days, and prompting Obama to announce new environmental safeguards for oil and gas exploration.

In June Obama accepted the resignation of Gen. Stanley McCHRYSTAL after the four-star general and commander of forces in Afghanistan made disparaging remarks about the president and top aides in a magazine article. McChrystal was replaced by Gen. David PETRAEUS, who previously commanded forces in Iraq. In other staff changes, bank executive William DALEY became Obama's chief of staff after Rahm EMANUEL resigned and ran successfully for mayor of Chicago.

The 2010 midterm elections on November 2 were a Republican landslide in the U.S. House. Republicans gained 66 seats, bringing the GOP ranks to 242. In the U.S. Senate the GOP took 6 additional seats, bringing its total to 47, thereby slimming the Democratic majority to 3 seats. The election was widely viewed as a referendum on the still ailing economy. The 2010 midterms were the electoral debut of Tea Party candidates in the GOP, whose populist message railed against spending, particularly on social services and economic stimulus, and against health care reform. Tea Party candidates defeated a number of high-profile GOP-endorsed candidates in primary elections, and went on to win 3 Senate seats and as many as 60 GOP seats in the House. Tea Party successes in Congress and in state races increased pressure on Republicans to move farther to the right. Republicans brought their total of governorships to 29, compared with 20 for the Democrats, along with 1 independent. Republican John BOEHNER of Ohio was elected speaker of the House of Representatives on January 5, 2011.

By 2011 the GOP controlled 28 state legislatures, the Democrats, 15, with 6 divided between the two parties (Nebraska's legislature is non-partisan), offering Republicans additional power in redistricting political boundaries prior to the 2012 elections.

The lame-duck 111th Congress managed to pass three major measures after the elections: (1) Senate ratification of the U.S.–Russian START treaty (see Foreign relations, below), (2) an extension of Bush-era tax cuts and unemployment benefits, and (3) the repeal of the "Don't Ask, Don't Tell" policy prohibiting homosexuals from serving in the military.

Mitt ROMNEY won the Republican presidential nomination for the 2012 election and named Wisconsin House member Paul RYAN, a leading fiscal conservative, as his running mate. Obama, unopposed, won Democratic nomination. The national campaign was highly negative as outside interest groups (commonly known as "super PACs," with no limits on their ability to raise and spend funds) combined with the major parties to spend more than $6 billion on national, state, and local polling. While Democrats painted Romney an archconservative who favored the rich, the Romney campaign criticized the president's handling of the economy and health care reform.

On November 6, 2012, Obama was reelected with 50.6 percent of the vote and 332 electoral votes to Romney's 47.8 percent and 206 electoral votes. In concurrent congressional balloting, Democrats gained two seats in the Senate, to bring their total to 55, including two independents who caucus with the party, while Republicans were reduced to 45 seats. The GOP maintained a majority in the House with 233 seats to 201 Democrats. Republicans gained one additional governorship, North Carolina, in the 2012 balloting, bringing their total to 30, compared with 20 held by Democrats.

After six years in office, Attorney General Eric Holder announced his resignation on September 25, 2014. The administration nominated Loretta LYNCH for the post, and she was confirmed in April 2015.

The Republican Party made significant gains in the midterm elections of November 2014, gaining a majority in the Senate of 54 seats, and reinforcing its power in the House of Representatives, gaining 12 seats for a total of 244 seats. Meanwhile, Democrats retained 44 seats in the Senate, plus two independents who caucus with the party, and 184 House seats. The GOP also emerged the winner in state elections, winning 31 governorships, compared with 17 for the Democrats.

Secretary of Defense Chuck HAGEL resigned on February 17, 2015, and was replaced by Ash CARTER, who was confirmed by the Senate on a vote of 93–5. With Republican control of Congress, Obama increasingly turned to the use of executive orders to achieve his policy objectives (see Current issues, below). Facing growing opposition from Republicans in the House, Boehner resigned on October 29 and was replaced by former vice-presidential candidate Paul Ryan.

After an unusually bitter and divisive series of primaries and caucuses, billionaire tycoon Donald J. TRUMP defeated 16 other Republicans and won the 2016 GOP presidential nomination. Trump chose Indiana governor Mike PENCE as his running mate. Former first lady and secretary of state Hillary CLINTON defeated Vermont senator Bernie SANDERS for the Democratic nomination amid allegations that party officials undertook various steps to ensure Clinton won the contest (see Political Parties, below). Clinton picked Virginia senator Tim KAINE as her running mate.

The general election proved even more contentious than the primaries as Trump embraced a populist message but made controversial comments about women and Muslims. Trump also faced questions over his refusal to release his tax returns, which is a customary practice for presidential candidates. Clinton was dogged by a controversy over her use of a private e-mail server, instead of her government e-mail, while secretary of state. There were also concerns over contributions and the operations of the Clinton Foundation, a charitable organization formed after former president Bill Clinton left office. These matters tended to overshadow any discussion of policies or issues during the campaign.

Although polls consistently put Clinton in the lead, Trump won the election, winning 30 states and securing 306 of 538 Electoral College votes, although Clinton won the popular vote, 48.1 percent to 46 percent. Republicans maintained majorities in Congress, with 52 seats in the Senate to 48 for the Democrats (including two independents who caucus with the Democrats), and 241 House seats to 194 seats for the Democrats. In the elections, Republicans gained two governorships to bring their total to 31, with 18 for the Democrats, and 1 independent. Republicans also increased the number of state legislatures under their control to 32, with 13 controlled by Democrats and 5 with power split between the two parties.

Constitution and government. The Constitution of the United States, drafted by a Constitutional Convention in Philadelphia in 1787 and declared in effect on March 4, 1789, established a republic in which extensive powers are reserved to the states, currently 50 in number, that compose the Federal Union. The system has three distinctive characteristics. First, powers are divided among three federal branches—legislative, executive, and judicial—and between the federal and state governments, themselves each divided into three branches. Second, the power of each of the four elements of the federal government (the presidency, the Senate, the House of Representatives, and the federal judiciary) is limited by being shared with one or more of the other elements. Third, the different procedures by which the president, senators, and members of the House of Representatives are elected make each responsible to a different constituency.

Federal executive power is vested in a president who serves for a four-year term and, by the 22nd Amendment (ratified in 1951), is limited to two terms of office. The president and vice president are formally designated by the Electoral College, composed of electors from each state and the District of Columbia. Selected by popular vote in numbers equal to the total congressional representation to which the various states are entitled, the electors are pledged to vote for their political parties' candidates and customarily do so. Presidents are advised by, and discharge most of their functions through, executive departments headed by officers whom they appoint but who must have Senate approval. Presidents may, if they desire, use these officers collectively as a cabinet having advisory functions. In addition, presidents serve as commanders in chief, issuing orders to the military through the secretary of defense and the Joint Chiefs of Staff of the Army, Navy, Air Force, and Marine Corps, who also serve the chief executive collectively as an advisory body.

Legislative power is vested in the bicameral Congress: The Senate has two members from each state chosen by popular vote for six-year terms, with renewal by thirds every two years; the House of Representatives, elected by popular vote every two years, has a membership based on population, although each state is entitled to at least one representative. The two houses are further differentiated by their responsibilities: For example, money bills must originate in the House, whereas the advice and consent of the Senate is required for ratification of treaties and appointment of top government officials such as cabinet members. In practice no major legislative or financial bill is considered by either chamber until it has been reported by, or discharged from, one of many standing committees. By custom the parties share seats on the committees on a basis roughly proportional to their legislative strength. Within the parties preference in committee assignments has traditionally been accorded on the basis of seniority (continuous service in the house concerned), although departures from this rule are becoming more common. The Senate (but not the House) permits "unlimited debate," a procedure under which a determined minority may, by filibustering, bring all legislative action to a halt unless three-fifths of the full chamber elects to close debate. Failing this, a bill objectionable to the minority will eventually be withdrawn by the leadership. A presidential veto may be overridden by separate two-thirds votes of the two houses.

Congress has created the General Accountability Office (formerly the General Accounting Office) to provide legislative control over public funds and has established 66 agencies, boards, and commissions—collectively known as independent agencies—to perform specified administrative functions.

The federal judiciary is headed by a nine-member Supreme Court and includes courts of appeal, district courts, and various special courts, all created by Congress. Federal judges are appointed by the president, contingent upon approval by the Senate, and serve during good behavior. Federal jurisdiction is limited, applying most importantly to cases in law and equity arising under the Constitution, to U.S. laws and treaties, and to controversies arising between two or more states or between citizens of different states. Jury trial is prescribed for all federal crimes except those involving impeachment, which is voted by the House and adjudicated by the Senate.

In early July 2005 Supreme Court Justice Sandra Day O'CONNOR, the Court's first female justice, announced her retirement, providing President Bush with his first opportunity to influence the Court's direction. To replace O'Connor, who in recent years had been a prominent swing vote on a range of conservative-versus-liberal issues, including abortion rights, Bush selected a conservative, John ROBERTS, who was a judge on the Court of Appeals for the District of Columbia Circuit. As Senate and media investigations into Roberts's background were getting under way, the court's chief justice, William REHNQUIST, died on September 3, with Bush then nominating Roberts to succeed Rehnquist. Roberts was quickly confirmed by the Senate and sworn in on September 29. Bush's new pick to succeed O'Connor was more controversial. Samuel ALITO's opposition to abortion and his support for expanding presidential powers while serving as a judge on the Third Circuit Court of Appeals sparked considerable opposition, but not enough to block Senate confirmation. Alito was sworn in on January 31, 2006.

After Justice David SOUTER, a centrist on the Court, announced his retirement in April 2009, President Obama selected Sonia SOTOMAYOR, a judge of Puerto Rican descent on the Court of Appeals for the Second Circuit. Though some critics objected to earlier comments that she had made alluding to what she had termed the superior judicial insights of a "wise Latina woman," the Senate confirmed Sotomayor's appointment. She was sworn in on August 6, becoming the first Hispanic justice to serve on the Supreme Court. In April 2010 Supreme Court Justice John Paul STEVENS announced his retirement, leading to the August appointment of then solicitor general Elena KAGAN, who brought female representation on the court to an unprecedented three seats.

The federal Constitution and the institutions of the federal government serve generally as models for those of the states. Each state government is made up of a popularly elected governor and legislature (all but one bicameral) and an independent judiciary. The District of Columbia, as the seat of the national government, was traditionally administered under the direct authority of Congress; however, in May 1974 District voters approved a charter giving them the right to elect a mayor and city council, both of which took office on January 1, 1975. Earlier, under the 23rd Amendment to the Constitution (ratified in 1961), District residents had won the right to participate in presidential elections, and in 1970 they were authorized by Congress to send a nonvoting delegate to the House of Representatives. An amendment to give the District full congressional voting rights was approved by both houses of Congress in 1978 but not ratified by the requisite 38 of the 50 state legislatures.

In practice, the broad powers of the federal government, its more effective use of the taxing power, and the existence of many problems transcending the capacity of individual states have tended to make for a strongly centralized system of government. Local self-government is a well-established tradition, based generally on English models, with approximately 87,500 municipalities, townships, counties, or other substate entities. Education is a locally administered, federally subsidized function.

Freedom of the press is constitutionally guaranteed, and the media are broad based and multifaceted. Several media outlets, including newspapers such as the *New York Times* or the *Wall Street Journal* and broadcasters such as the Cable News Network (CNN), have international markets. The press and broadcasting media are privately owned and enjoy editorial freedom within the bounds of state libel laws. There is no legal ban on the ownership of broadcasting facilities by the press. The Federal Communications Commission (FCC) has, however, been under some pressure to deny relicensing under potentially monopolistic circumstances. In its 2014 report on freedom of the press, the media watchdog group Reporters Without Borders ranked the United States 41st out of 180 countries, a fall from 30th in 2014 owing in part to the government's crackdown on whistleblowers, including the secret seizure of phone records from the Associated Press.

State and Capital	*Area (sq.mi.)*	*Population (2016E)*
Alabama (Montgomery)	51,705	4,863,300
Alaska (Juneau)	591,004	741,894
Arizona (Phoenix)	114,000	6,931,071
Arkansas (Little Rock)	53,187	2,988,248
California (Sacramento)	158,706	39,250,017
Colorado (Denver)	104,091	5,540,545
Connecticut (Hartford)	5,018	3,576,452
Delaware (Dover)	2,045	952,065
Florida (Tallahassee)	58,664	20,612,439
Georgia (Atlanta)	58,910	10,310,371
Hawaii (Honolulu)	6,471	1,428,557
Idaho (Boise)	83,564	1,683,140
Illinois (Springfield)	56,345	12,801,539
Indiana (Indianapolis)	36,185	6,633,053
Iowa (Des Moines)	56,275	3,134,693
Kansas (Topeka)	82,277	2,907,289
Kentucky (Frankfort)	40,410	4,436,974
Louisiana (Baton Rouge)	47,752	4,681,666
Maine (Augusta)	33,265	1,331,479

Maryland (Annapolis)	10,460	6,016,447
Massachusetts (Boston)	8,284	6,811,779
Michigan (Lansing)	58,527	9,928,300
Minnesota (St. Paul)	84,402	5,519,952
Mississippi (Jackson)	47,689	2,988,726
Missouri (Jefferson City)	69,697	6,093,000
Montana (Helena)	147,046	1,042,520
Nebraska (Lincoln)	77,355	1,907,116
Nevada (Carson City)	110,561	2,940,058
New Hampshire (Concord)	9,279	1,334,795
New Jersey (Trenton)	7,787	8,944,469
New Mexico (Santa Fe)	121,593	2,081,015
New York (Albany)	49,108	19,745,289
North Carolina (Raleigh)	52,669	10,146,788
North Dakota (Bismarck)	70,702	757,952
Ohio (Columbus)	41,330	11,614,373
Oklahoma (Oklahoma City)	69,956	3,923,561
Oregon (Salem)	97,073	4,093,465
Pennsylvania (Harrisburg)	45,308	12,784,227
Rhode Island (Providence)	1,212	1,056,426
South Carolina (Columbia)	31,113	4,961,119
South Dakota (Pierre)	77,116	865,454
Tennessee (Nashville)	42,144	6,651,194
Texas (Austin)	266,807	27,863,596
Utah (Salt Lake City)	84,899	3,051,217
Vermont (Montpelier)	9,614	624,594
Virginia (Richmond)	40,767	8,411,808
Washington (Olympia)	68,139	7,288,000
West Virginia (Charleston)	24,232	1,831,102
Wisconsin (Madison)	56,153	5,778,708
Wyoming (Cheyenne)	97,809	585,501
Federal District		
District of Columbia	69	681,170

Foreign relations. U.S. relations with the world at large have evolved subject to the changing conditions created by the growth of the country and its international influence. An initial policy of noninvolvement in foreign affairs, which received its classical expression in President Washington's warning against "entangling alliances," gradually gave way to one of active participation in the concerns of international community. At the same time, the nation has evolved from a supporter of revolutionary movements directed against the old monarchical system into a predominantly conservative influence, with a broad commitment to the support of traditional democratic values.

U.S. policy in the Western Hemisphere, the area of most historical concern, continues to reflect the preoccupations that inspired the Monroe Doctrine (of President James Monroe) of 1823, in which the United States declared its opposition to European political involvement and further colonization in the Americas and in effect established a political guardianship over the states of Latin America. Since World War II this responsibility has become largely multilateral through such bodies as the UN and the Organization of American States (OAS), and direct U.S. intervention in Latin American affairs has typically been limited to instances in which a Central American or Caribbean country appeared in immediate danger of falling into chaos or under leftist control.

Overseas expansion during the late 19th and early 20th centuries resulted in the acquisition of American Samoa, Hawaii, and, following the Spanish–American War of 1898, the Philippines, Puerto Rico, and Guam; in addition, the United States secured a favored position in Cuba in 1902–1903, obtained exclusive rights in the Panama Canal Zone in 1903, and acquired the U.S. Virgin Islands by purchase in 1917. The country did not, however, become a colonial power in the European sense and was among the first to adopt a policy of promoting the political evolution of its dependent territories along lines desired by their inhabitants. In accordance with this policy, the Philippines became independent in 1946; Puerto Rico became a commonwealth freely associated with the United States in 1952; Hawaii became a state of the Union in 1959; measures of self-government have been introduced in the Virgin Islands, Guam, and American Samoa; and the Canal Zone was transferred to Panama on October 1, 1979, although the United States retained effective control of 40 percent of the area through 1999. Certain Japanese territories occupied during World War II were provisionally retained for strategic reasons, with those historically of Japanese sovereignty, the Bonin and Ryukyu islands, being returned in 1968 and 1972, respectively. The greater part of Micronesia (held by Japan as a League of Nations mandate after World War I) became, by agreement with the UN, the U.S. Trust Territory of the Pacific. In 1986, following the conclusion of a series of compacts of association with the Commonwealth of the Northern Mariana Islands, the Federated States of Micronesia (FSM), the Republic of the Marshall Islands, and the Republic of Palau (Belau), the UN Trusteeship Council indicated that it would be appropriate to terminate the trusteeship. All were eventually approved by the UN Security Council by October 1, 1994.

Globally, U.S. participation in the defeat of the Central Powers in World War I was followed by a period of renewed isolation and attempted neutrality, which, however, was ultimately made untenable by the challenge of the Axis powers in World War II. Having played a leading role in the defeat of the Axis, the United States joined with its allies in assuming responsibility for the creation of a postwar order within the framework of the UN. However, the subsequent divergence of Soviet and Western political aims, and the resultant limitations on the effectiveness of the UN as an instrument for maintaining peace and security, impelled the United States during the late 1940s and 1950s to take the lead in creating a network of special mutual security arrangements that were ultimately to involve commitments to more than four dozen foreign governments. Some of these commitments, as in the North Atlantic Treaty Organization (NATO), the Australia, New Zealand, United States (ANZUS) Security Treaty Pact, and the Inter-American Treaty of Reciprocal Assistance (Rio Pact), are multilateral in character; others involve defense obligations toward particular governments, such as those with Thailand, the Philippines, and the Republic of Korea.

The United States also exercised leadership in international economic and financial relations through its cosponsorship of the International Monetary Fund (IMF) and World Bank, its promotion of trade liberalization efforts, and its contributions to postwar relief and rehabilitation, European economic recovery, and the economic progress of less-developed countries. Much of this activity, like parallel efforts put forward in social, legal, and cultural fields, has been carried on through the UN and its related agencies.

The United States has pursued international agreements on measures for the control and limitation of strategic armaments. Agreements and bilateral talks with the Soviet Union on disarmament stretched from 1969 under Nixon into the Reagan administration nearly 20 years later through, for instance, the strategic arms limitation treaties (SALT I and SALT II), the strategic arms reduction talks (START), and the intermediate-range nuclear forces (INF) negotiations. (See below and the 2010 *Handbook* for more details.)

U.S. military forces, operating under a UN mandate, actively opposed Communist-sponsored aggression in the Korean War of 1950–1953. Other U.S. forces, together with those of a number of allied powers, assisted the government of South Vietnam in combating the insurgent movement that was actively supported by North Vietnamese forces for nearly two decades. By 1965 this assistance had become a major U.S. military effort, which continued after the initiation of peace talks in 1968. The lengthy discussions, involving U.S. secretary of state Henry A. KISSINGER and North Vietnamese diplomat Le Duc Tho as the most active participants, resulted in the conclusion of a four-way peace agreement on January 27, 1973, that called for the withdrawal of all remaining U.S. military forces from Vietnam, the repatriation of American prisoners of war, and the institution of political talks between South Vietnam and its domestic (Viet Cong) adversaries. The U.S. withdrawal was followed, however, by a breakdown in talks, renewed military operations in late 1974, and the collapse of the South Vietnamese government on April 30, 1975.

In a move of major international significance, the United States and the People's Republic of China announced on December 15, 1978, that they would establish diplomatic relations as of January 1, 1979. The United States met all three of China's long-sought conditions: severance of U.S. diplomatic relations with Taipei, withdrawal of U.S. troops from Taiwan, and abrogation of the Republic of China defense treaty. However the United States indicated that it would maintain economic, cultural, and other unofficial relations with Taiwan.

In the Middle East, Secretary Kissinger embarked on an eight-month-long exercise in "shuttle diplomacy" following the Arab–Israeli "October War" of 1973. U.S. economic interests were, for the first time, directly undermined as a result of an Arab embargo instituted in October 1973 on all oil shipments to the United States and the Netherlands, and on some shipments to other Western European states. The embargo was terminated by all but two of the producing nations, Libya and Syria, in March 1974, following the resumption of full-scale diplomatic relations (severed since 1967) between the United States and Egypt. Kissinger brokered an Israeli–Egyptian disengagement agreement in January 1974 and a second in September 1975. Meanwhile Kissinger brought about a limited Golan Heights disengagement between Israel and Syria in May 1974, followed a month later by a renewal of diplomatic relations between the United States and Syria (also suspended since 1967). In September 1978 President Carter, hosting a Camp David summit, was instrumental in negotiating accords that led to the signing of a peace treaty between Egypt and Israel in Washington, D.C., on March 26, 1979.

Despite a recognized danger to U.S. diplomatic personnel, the Carter administration permitted the deposed shah of Iran to enter the United States in October 1979 for medical treatment. On November 4 militants stormed and occupied the U.S. embassy compound in Tehran, taking 66 hostages. Iranian leader Ayatollah Khomeini announced on November 17 that female and black hostages would be released because they had experienced "the oppression of American society." Thirteen hostages were released; the militants demanded the return of the shah in exchange for the remaining 53. Although condemnations of the seizure were forthcoming from the UN Security Council, the General Assembly, and the World Court, neither their nor personal pleas by international diplomats were at first heeded by the Islamic Republic's leadership, which vilified the United States as "the great Satan." President Carter aborted a rescue mission by a U.S. commando force in April 1980 after early mishaps. Eventually, however, negotiations that commenced on the eve of the 1980 U.S. election culminated in the freeing of the hostages on Reagan's presidential inauguration day (January 20, 1981).

The Reagan administration viewed the conclusion of the 1988 INF treaty as the result of consistent (and largely successful) pressure on U.S. European allies to maintain a high level of military preparedness as compared with the Soviet Union. In the Middle East the Reagan administration attempted to negotiate a mutual withdrawal of Israeli and Syrian forces from Lebanon in the wake of the Israeli invasion of June 1982 and the subsequent evacuation of Palestinian Liberation Organization (PLO) forces from Beirut, for which the U.S. government provided truce supervision assistance. In 1987, despite the risk of a major confrontation with Iran, the Reagan administration mounted a significant naval presence in the Persian Gulf to protect oil tankers from seaborne mines and other threats stemming from the Iran-Iraq conflict. In Asia, the United States provided substantial military assistance to Pakistan and Thailand in response to Soviet intervention in Afghanistan and communist operations in Cambodia, respectively, while strongly supporting the post-Marcos regime in the Philippines. In the Caribbean, the United States provided the bulk of the forces that participated in the 1983 postcoup intervention in Grenada, and it welcomed the 1986 ouster of Haitian dictator François Duvalier. In Central America, the Reagan administration attempted to contain Soviet-Cuban involvement in Nicaragua and to help the Salvadoran government defeat leftist guerrilla forces. Overall, in keeping with a 1980 campaign pledge, President Reagan sought to restructure both the military and civilian components of the nation's foreign aid program so as to reward "America's friends," whatever their domestic policies, in an implicit repudiation of his predecessor's somewhat selective use of aid in support of global human-rights objectives.

Seven months after the nullification of Panama's May 1989 presidential balloting, Gen. Manuel Noriega assumed sweeping powers to deal with what was termed "a state of war" with the United States. On December 20 the George H. W. Bush administration intervened militarily. (For more, see the 2013 *Handbook.*)

In 1990 the Bush administration became preoccupied with the international crisis generated by Iraq's seizure of Kuwait on August 2 and the remarkable prodemocracy upheaval in Eastern Europe that had been triggered by Gorbachev's reforms in the Soviet Union. Five days after the fall of Kuwait, the United States announced the deployment of ground units and aircraft to defend Saudi Arabia, and on November 29 the UN Security Council approved the use of "all necessary means" if Iraq did not withdraw from Kuwait by January 15, 1991. On January 12 the U.S. Congress authorized military action against Iraq, and on January 16 "Operation Desert Storm" began, yielding the liberation of Kuwait on February 26–27 by a U.S.-led multinational force.

Four decades of superpower confrontation formally ended on November 21, 1990, with the adoption of a treaty reducing conventional forces in Europe at a Paris summit of the Conference on Security and Cooperation in Europe (CSCE). Agreement eight months later on final details of the long-sought START paved the way for signing by Bush and Gorbachev at a Moscow summit on July 30–31, 1991. Under the accord, 50 percent of the Soviet and 35 percent of the U.S. ballistic missile warheads were slated for destruction.

Following the Gulf War, President Bush identified resolution of the Arab-Israeli dispute as the top priority of his administration. In pursuit of this objective, Secretary of State James BAKER painstakingly negotiated a conference involving Israel, Syria, Lebanon, and a joint Jordanian-Palestinian delegation, convened in Madrid, Spain, in October 1991 under the joint auspices of the United States and Soviet Union. Additional bilateral and multilateral talks were held over the ensuing months, with no substantive results.

Following the failed Moscow coup of August 1991, the United States welcomed the achievement of independence by the Baltic states, and in December, after the legal collapse of the Soviet Union, Congress moved to recognize Ukraine, followed later by recognition of the remaining former Soviet republics as well as the former Yugoslavian republics of Croatia, Slovenia, and Bosnia and Herzegovina. President Bush and Russia's Boris Yeltsin signed an unprecedented extension of the 1991 START accord during their first formal summit on June 16–17. Under START II, each nation would be limited to 3,000–3,500 long-range weapons (down from 11,000–12,000 on the eve of START I), while all land-based multiple warhead missiles would be banned. Another summit highlight was an agreement on reciprocal most-favored-nation trade status.

On November 24, 1992, the United States completed its military withdrawal from the Philippines (see the entry on Philippines), ending a presence that had existed since 1898, save for three years during World War II. Ten days later, in an operation termed "Restore Hope," President Bush ordered the dispatch of 28,000 U.S. soldiers to Somalia to ensure the safe delivery of international relief supplies to the country's starving population (see the entry on Somalia).

Trade issues occupied center stage during the waning months of the Bush administration. The North American Free Trade Agreement (NAFTA), which had been concluded on August 12, 1992, by the United States, Canada, and Mexico after 14 months of negotiation, was formally signed on December 17. It secured U.S. legislative approval in November 1993 and came into force on January 1, 1994.

The foreign policy highlight of Clinton's first year was the formal signing at the White House on September 13, 1993, of a historic agreement between Israel and the PLO on Palestinian self-rule in Jericho and the Gaza Strip (see the entries on Israel and PLO following the country listings). Other 1993–1994 concerns included a deteriorating situation in Somalia, where 18 U.S. soldiers were killed in October 1993, due in large part to the refusal by Defense Secretary Les ASPIN to provide more tanks and armored vehicles. Aspin subsequently admitted his mistake, and on December 15, President Clinton announced Aspin's resignation. On February 3, 1994, William J. PERRY was sworn in as the new defense secretary. By March 31, 1994, all but a small number of U.S. troops were withdrawn from Somalia.

In the face of a somewhat wavering posture regarding events in Bosnia and Herzegovina, the Clinton administration in early 1994 issued a new set of guidelines for peacekeeping and related activities that would preclude U.S. military involvement short of a clear threat to international security, a major natural disaster, or a gross violation of human rights. From February 1994 the launching of UN-approved NATO air strikes against Serbian positions in Bosnia eased U.S. – European differences on how to respond to the conflict in former Yugoslavia, where deployment of U.S. ground troops continued to be confined to the UN/CSCE observer contingent in Macedonia. Thereafter, the genocidal Rwandan crisis that erupted in April elicited a substantial U.S. humanitarian effort in neighboring countries and the dispatch of 200 U.S. troops to help run Kigali airport, although participation in UN peacekeeping was ruled out. These measures, however, failed to prevent widespread bloodshed.

On June 2, 1994, the Clinton administration called for international economic sanctions against North Korea to force disclosure of that country's nuclear weapons capacity (see the entry on Democratic People's Republic of Korea); following the death of North Korean leader Kim Il Sung on July 8, a U.S.–North Korean agreement signed on August 12 met some of the concerns of the international community.

In July 1994 U.S. Middle East diplomacy registered a major success when President Clinton on July 25 supervised the White House signing of a peace declaration between King Hussein of Jordan and Prime Minister Rabin of Israel.

During 1994 the Clinton administration worked to implement a 1993 agreement providing for departure of the military junta and the return of exiled President Jean-Bertrand Aristide in Haiti. On September 19 an advance contingent of 20,000 troops landed on Haitian soil under a UN mandate to oust the incumbent regime. On October 13 junta leader Gen. Raoul Cédras left aboard a U.S. flight to Panama, and on October 15 Aristide returned to Haiti (see the entry on Haiti). Meanwhile, large numbers of Haitian "boat people" had been picked up and transported to the U.S. Guantánamo Bay Naval Base in Cuba, with Cuban refugees (in a change of policy) being accorded like treatment as of August 19. In another policy shift on May 2, 1995, the United States agreed to admit Cuban, but not Haitian, detainees remaining at Guantánamo, with all subsequent refugees being returned to their homeland. Meanwhile, the U.S. Senate on December 1, 1994, ratified the 1993 GATT accord establishing the World Trade Organization (WTO).

In 1996 the Clinton administration, which for some time had indicated its displeasure with UN secretary general Boutros Boutros-Ghali, vetoed his reelection by the Security Council. At issue was Boutros-Ghali's alleged failure to reform the world body, in response to which Congress continued to withhold dues of more than $1 billion. On December 13 a lengthy confrontation with France over Boutros-Ghali's successor ended with the selection of Kofi Annan, a Ghanaian and longtime UN civil servant who had earned high marks for directing peacekeeping operations in Bosnia.

On October 26, 1997, Jiang Zemin began a nine-day state visit to the United States, the first by a Chinese head of state since 1985, with President Clinton reciprocating in June 1998. Shortly thereafter, Clinton failed to win "fast track" trade authority, a practice precluding Congress from partial amendment of trade legislation, even though it had been extended to every other president since 1974 (and would be granted to Clinton's successor, George W. Bush, in August 2002).

In 1998 President Clinton ordered cruise missile attacks on Afghanistan and Sudan in response to the August 7 terrorist bombings of U.S. embassies in Kenya and Tanzania. He also ordered air strikes against Iraq in mid-December after Baghdad had failed to honor a November 14 pledge to resume full cooperation with UN weapons inspectors.

On March 24, 1999, following a year of escalating ethnic fighting between the Kosovo Liberation Army (KLA), a group of ethnic Albanians, and Serb and Yugoslav security forces, U.S.-led NATO air strikes began. At the same time, Clinton pledged that no U.S. ground troops would be sent to Kosovo. By June, however, Clinton said he would send as many as 7,000 ground troops to assist NATO in peacekeeping operations.

In April 1999 relations with China were sorely tested by the NATO bombing of the Chinese embassy in Belgrade, Yugoslavia, which the United States attributed to a mapping error. In August the Senate, by a 51–48 vote, refused to ratify the Comprehensive (nuclear) Test Ban Treaty (CTBT).

Talks began in Geneva in April 2000 on a START III accord, following Russian ratification of START II, while the House on May 24 approved the China trade bill, thus paving the way for Chinese admission to the WTO. On August 22 President Clinton signed a controversial measure providing upward of $1.3 billion to aid Colombia's war on drug traffickers. On October 12, 17 U.S. sailors were killed and 37 wounded in a terrorist attack on the USS *Cole,* a destroyer docked in Aden, Yemen.

Before leaving office on January 20, 2001, President Clinton, voicing reservations, signed a treaty to establish an International Criminal Court (ICC) to succeed the ad hoc international war-crimes tribunals in The Hague (an action for which the succeeding Bush administration promptly withdrew support). Concurrently, Senator Helms, the Senate's leading critic of UN financing, agreed to the release of $582 million in back dues to the world body under a deal providing for reduction of the U.S. share in the annual $1.1 billion administrative budget to 22 percent (down from 25 percent) and of its contribution to the peacekeeping budget to 26 percent (down from 31 percent) by 2004.

The second war in the Persian Gulf, launched by President George W. Bush on March 20, 2003, proved far more divisive and much more costly than the first. While the United States expressed regret that the UN Security Council would not issue a resolution specifically authorizing military action against Iraq, it insisted that Resolution 1441 provided sufficient authority. However, the chief UN weapons inspector, Hans Blix, had, on March 7, given a decidedly mixed assessment of Iraq's compliance with the 2002 resolution, and at midyear an administration spokesperson conceded that the President Bush had relied on "incomplete and possibly inaccurate" intelligence in having declared in his January State of the Union address that Saddam Hussein had attempted to secure uranium from Africa. Subsequent evidence that Iraq apparently possessed no WMDs at the outset of hostilities damaged the credibility of the administration. By early 2005 more than a dozen countries participating in the U.S.-led military coalition had decided to pull out or reduce their forces in Iraq, with more following in 2006 and 2007.

In November 2007 Arab leaders, including Syria's foreign minister, accepted an invitation by the United States to attend a broadly inclusive Middle East peace summit. Although the summit issued a statement of "joint understanding," further progress proved unobtainable after the collapse of a five-month-old cease-fire in Gaza in November 2008 and renewed border fighting between Israel and the Palestinians.

Tension heightened between the United States and Russia in August 2008, after Russia invaded the former Soviet state of Georgia in response to that country's deployment of troops in South Ossetia. The United States and the EU called for a halt to fighting, and NATO deployed ships to the Black Sea carrying U.S.-supplied humanitarian aid to Georgia. NATO suspended interaction with Russia in alliance bodies.

In October 2008 the United States removed North Korea from its list of states that sponsor terrorism, citing North Korea's recent agreement on measures to verify its nuclear program. In November President Bush, in his final days in office, called Libyan leader Col. Muammar Abu Minyar al-Qadhafi, marking the first conversation ever between the Libyan leader and a U.S. president. However, the August 2009 release from a Scottish prison of a terminally ill, convicted perpetrator of the 1988 Lockerbie attack, and his hero's welcome home in Libya prompted a souring of U.S.–Libyan relations.

In October 2009 the Norwegian Nobel committee awarded president Obama the Nobel Peace Prize, just 263 days after taking office.

Obama's Afghan strategy was hampered by a resurgence of Taliban attacks, weakening resolve by allied forces to engage in combat missions, and dwindling confidence in Afghan president Karzai. In January 2010 Obama committed to sending 30,000 additional U.S. troops to Afghanistan, raising the total there to nearly 100,000, as part of a strategy to stabilize the country and train Afghan security forces in preparation for a U.S. exit. In November NATO and U.S. officials agreed to hand security over to Afghan forces by the end of 2014, with some allied forces remaining beyond that date. Obama declared an end to the American combat mission on August 31, 2010, in Iraq, leaving some 50,000 troops to "advise and assist" Iraqi security forces.

In March 2009 the administration unveiled the "Af-Pak" strategy to treat the border region as part of a single theater, linking stability in Afghanistan with the disruption of militant "safe havens" within tribal areas of Pakistan, part of a new policy to counter Taliban and al-Qaida forces. To gain Pakistan's support the U.S. approved a $7.5 billion aid package to Pakistan in October, tripling non-military aid to the country. A failed car bombing on March 1, 2010, in Times Square, New York, was linked to the Pakistani Taliban.

After Iran rejected an offer to have uranium shipped out of the country for enrichment, the Obama administration in June 2010 led efforts at the United Nations Security Council to impose a fourth round of sanctions on Iran. Meanwhile, Obama resolved to sign the Strategic Arms Reduction Treaty (START) with Russia by the end of the year, despite stiff resistance from Senate Republicans. In late November NATO members and Russia agreed to set up a "working group" on a missile defense system that would protect Europe and North America through mobile and sea-based radars and interceptors. However, tensions over missile defense continued, and in 2011 Russia threatened to target U.S. antimissile bases in Europe.

The group WikiLeaks released more than 200,000 internal and classified state department and military documents at the end of 2010. Allegedly obtained from a U.S. soldier, the releases exposed diplomatic and military activities, intelligence reports and assessments, and correspondence between U.S. officials.

The Obama administration endeavored to maintain a delicate balance during the Arab Spring movements that swept through North

Africa and the Middle East beginning in January 2011. The popular uprisings toppled regimes in Egypt and Tunisia and threatened other U.S. allies such as Morocco and Bahrain. The United States publicly backed the spread of democracy, although concerns were raised over instability in the region and the potential for the spread of Islamic extremism.

The Obama administration deployed U.S. military forces to support an international coalition that intervened in Libya in March 2011 in order to enforce the UN no-fly zone over the country, which was in the midst of a civil war. The United States and other powers conducted air and cruise missile attacks against the regime of Libyan leader Muammar Qadhafi, who was overthrown and eventually killed by rebels on October 20, 2011. Obama faced domestic criticism for deploying the U.S. military in combat operations without congressional authorization.

Al-Qaida leader Osama bin Laden was killed by U.S. special operations forces on May 2, 2011, during a raid on his compound in Abottabad, Pakistan. The discovery that bin Laden had lived near one of Pakistan's main military academies reinforced U.S. concerns over Islamabad's commitment to suppress al-Qaida and the Taliban. Tensions between the two countries were exacerbated by U.S. drone attacks on suspected terrorist targets in Pakistan. In July 2011 the Obama administration suspended $800 million in military aid to Pakistan.

Negotiations over a continued U.S. military presence in Iraq broke down in October 2011. Consequently, all U.S. forces withdrew from Iraq in December. During 2012 an increase in attacks on NATO troops by Afghan security forces (known as "blue-on-green" attacks) prompted U.S. military leaders to suspend joint operations with their Afghan counterparts in September. Meanwhile, through 2012 the Obama administration continued to attack suspected Taliban and al Qaeda leaders in Pakistan, Yemen, and Somalia with aerial drone strikes. Growing civilian and military casualties from the drone attacks prompted Pakistan to suspend NATO convoy routes for six months from January to July 2012 (see entry on Pakistan).

In November 2011 Hillary Clinton became the first U.S. secretary of state to visit Myanmar since 1955. U.S. sanctions were relaxed following significant political reforms in the country (see entry on Myanmar). A free trade agreement with South Korea was ratified by the U.S Senate in October 2011 and went into effect in March 2012.

Throughout 2012 the Obama administration pressed for increased economic sanctions against Iran in an effort to pressure Tehran into abandoning its nuclear weapons program. The United States also attempted, less successfully, to increase pressure on the Syrian regime to end an ongoing civil war. However, efforts to foster international sanctions or other measures were frustrated at the UN by China and Russia (see entry on Syria).

On September 11, 2012, militants attacked the U.S. consulate in Benghazi, Libya. Ambassador Chris Stevens and three other Americans were killed in the attack. The Obama administration initially asserted that the incident was caused by anti-U.S. sentiment over a film that lampooned Islam. The administration was criticized for its response when intelligence revealed that the attack was likely a preplanned terrorist attack (see Current issues, below).

Among the files released by Edward SNOWDEN in the May 2013 NSA leak (see below) was documentation of a U.S. surveillance program targeting EU offices as well as 38 embassies of U.S. allies including France, Japan, India, and more. The revelations surfaced in late June and early July and stirred anger from longtime allies in Europe and Asia, generating calls from the European Parliament to veto data-sharing agreements with the United States.

The affair proved particularly stressful for U.S.-Russian relations when Snowden, who initially fled to Hong Kong, flew to the Moscow airport to avoid an extradition request filed by the United States in late June. Russia granted Snowden's request for temporary asylum on August 1, rejecting repeated requests from U.S. authorities. Already strained by the ongoing conflict in Syria, relations further deteriorated as the United States threatened to withdraw from upcoming high-profile summits, including the September G-20 in St. Petersburg.

An unspecified threat in early August caused the State Department to close 21 U.S. embassies across the Middle East and North Africa, some for up to a week.

On August 21, 2013, a poison gas attack was reported to have taken place in Syria, almost exactly one year after President Obama warned that the use of chemical or biological weapons by the Assad regime was a "red line." Obama on September 1 announced that he would seek congressional approval for a "limited" military strike on Syria. On October 9 Russian Foreign Minister Sergey Lavrov proposed a negotiated compromise that Damascus could turn over its chemical weapons stockpiles to avoid a military strike. Obama subsequently changed course, and talks between U.S. and Russian officials begun in Geneva on September 12 yielded agreements for disarmament framework and, on September 26, a UN Security Council resolution.

Amid months of turmoil in Ukraine due to rising pro-Russian separatist sentiment, Obama on November 12, 2014, pledged to "stand with Ukraine" days before Russia annexed Crimea. The following month, accusing Russian President Putin of failing to cooperate on the Ukraine crisis, the United States imposed sanctions on Russian companies considered part of Putin's inner circle.

In late May Taliban-held prisoner of war Sgt. Bowe BERGDAHL was released in exchange for the release of five Guantánamo Bay prisoners, a controversial exchange brokered with the aid of Qatar.

Meanwhile, the expansion of the so-called Islamic State of Iraq and Syria (ISIS) into Iraq in June prompted Obama on to announce on June 19 plans to send 300 military advisors to Iraq to help secure the Sunni government and protect the U.S. embassy in Baghdad. The situation escalated over ensuing months, with the United States beginning targeted airstrikes on August 8 to prevent ISIS militants from advancing into Erbil, Iraq, the capital of the Kurdistan regional government. On August 19 ISIS released a video responding to the airstrikes showing the beheading of American journalist James FOLEY. On September 2 another video was released depicting the killing of a second American hostage, Steven SOTLOFF, and on November 16 a third video showing the murder of hostage Peter KASSIG. At a NATO summit in Wales in September, Obama recruited the support of nine allies to suppress the rise of ISIS. The U.S-led coalition began air strikes on ISIS positions in Syria in September.

Meanwhile, later in September, Ukrainian president Petro Poroshenko visited Washington, D.C., and appealed to Congress for help combatting pro-Russian separatists.

On November 7, 2014, President Obama authorized 1,500 troops to go to Iraq to train Iraqi and Kurdish forces fighting ISIS militants. In December Obama announced that the United States would begin to restore relations with Cuba (see entry on Cuba).

In March 2015, following requests from Afghan president Ashraf Ghani and growing strife, Obama announced that the United States would maintain 9,800 troops in Afghanistan through at least 2016 despite earlier pledges to further reduce the number of U.S. service personnel in the country. Hackers accessed the personal data of more than 4 million U.S. government workers in June. The Obama administration asserted that China was behind the breach. Following negotiations between Iran and the P5+1 (the five permanent member of the UN Security Council—the United States, China, France Russia, and the United Kingdom, plus Germany), an agreement was finalized in July. The accord eliminated most economic sanctions on Iran in return for the suspension of the country's uranium enrichment program for a ten-year period (see entry on Iran).

The United States deployed 50 special operations forces to Syria to fight ISIS in September 2015.

The United States and ten other countries finalized the Trans-Pacific Partnership (TPP), a broad free trade agreement, in October 2015. The TPP was signed on February 4, 2016. Also in February, the United States and Russia agreed on a cease-fire in Syria; however, the agreement quickly broke down. A second cease-fire later in the year also had limited success.

In April 2016 the number of U.S. special operations forces in Syria was increased to 250 in April 2016. By the end of 2016, there were an estimated 5,400 U.S. troops in Iraq training the Iraqi military and fighting against ISIS.

During the 2016 U.S. presidential elections, revelations emerged that foreign hackers had accessed and released negative information about Democratic candidate Hillary Clinton and her campaign. Most sources blamed Russian hackers for the attacks, while some reports suggested the direct involvement of the Russian government.

Current issues. The White House announced several staff changes in early 2011: Gene SPERLING, an adviser to Treasury Secretary Geithner, succeeded Larry SUMMERS as chair of the National Economic Council; General Electric executive Jeff IMMELT took the helm of a new jobs and competitive council; and Biden assistant James "Jay" CARNEY replaced Robert GIBBS as press secretary. Later in the year retiring Defense Secretary Robert GATES was replaced by CIA director Leon PANETTA, who was, in turn, succeeded by General Petraeus.

Differences between congressional Republicans, who emphasized spending cuts to reduce the deficit, and Democrats, who supported tax increases to cut spending created a stalemate over an increase to the federal debt ceiling. A last-minute compromise averted a government shutdown in August 2011. The deal included the creation of a bipartisan supercommittee charged with forging a deal to obtain $1.5 trillion in deficit reductions over a ten-year period. Meanwhile, in response to concerns over the ability of the United States to address its growing debt and deficit, the credit agency Standard & Poor's downgraded the creditworthiness of Treasury bonds for the first time since the initial rating in 1917. By August the U.S. debt reached $14.58 trillion, or more than 100 percent of the nation's $14.53 trillion GDP, while the federal deficit was 8.7 percent of GDP in 2011, down from 8.9 percent the year before. On November 21 the committee reported that it was unable to reach an agreement.

White House chief of staff Daley resigned on January 27, 2012, and was replaced by Jacob J. LEW. Voters in North Carolina approved a state constitutional amendment on May 8 banning same-sex marriage. The next day, Obama became the first U.S. president to endorse same-sex marriage.

On June 5, 2012, Wisconsin governor Scott WALKER became the first incumbent to win a gubernatorial recall election in U.S. history. He received 53 percent of the vote. Democrats sought to turn Walker out of office after he oversaw an effort that reduced collective bargaining rights in the state. Commerce secretary John BRYSON resigned on June 21 following two car accidents and a period of medical leave. He was replaced by his deputy on an acting basis.

In a major reversal of U.S. immigration policy, on June 15, 2012, Obama issued an executive order that halted the deportations of illegal immigrants under the age of 30 and allowed them to defer deportment and apply for work permits under certain conditions. The measure was harshly criticized by Republicans who argued it was an attempt by the president to bolster his share of the Latino vote ahead of the November balloting.

Meanwhile, on June 28, 2012, a divided Supreme Court upheld the major provisions of Obama's health care reform but granted states the option of whether or not to participate in the program's expanded Medicaid initiative. On the same day, attorney general Eric HOLDER became the first cabinet member to be held in contempt of Congress in response to his refusal to turn over documents related to the "Fast and Furious" scandal (a controversial program that supplied Mexican drug cartels with U.S. weapons in an effort to track the flow of the arms). Concurrently, the Obama administration exerted executive privilege to avoid the release of additional information.

Through the summer of 2012 the United States experienced its worst drought in 55 years, affecting 29 states. On July 20, 2012, a gunman killed 12 and injured 58 at a cinema in Aurora, Colorado. Both Obama and Romney temporarily suspended their political campaigns, but the mass shooting did not prompt renewed debate over the country's gun laws.

In national balloting on November 6, 2012, Obama was reelected, while Democrats expanded their majority in the Senate, and Republicans kept control of the House. In the polling, Tammy BALDWIN of Wisconsin became the first openly gay person elected to the Senate. In state ballot initiatives, voters in Maine, Maryland, and Washington endorsed same-sex marriage, while Washington and Colorado voted to decriminalize the possession of small amounts of marijuana. Oklahomans passed a measure to eliminate affirmative action.

In the midst of continuing congressional investigations into the death of ambassador Chris Stevens in Benghazi, General Petraeus resigned on November 9 after it was revealed that he had engaged in an extramarital affair.

On December 14, 2012, a gunman entered an elementary school in Newtown, Connecticut, and killed 20 children and 6 adults. Following the shooting, President Obama sought a ban on assault weapons. The measure was abandoned in March 2013 when it didn't secure the necessary 60 votes in the Senate.

A tense fiscal debate between Democrats and Republicans ended in the late hours of December 31, when the House voted 257–167 in support of the American Taxpayer Relief Act, on the eve of automatic tax increases and large spending cuts known as the "fiscal cliff." The bill, which had passed the Senate with overwhelming support less than a day earlier, raised taxes on high-earning Americans, the first tax hike in two decades.

Barack Obama was inaugurated for his second term on January 21, 2013.

On April 15 two bombs exploded near the finish line of the Boston Marathon, killing 3 and injuring more than 140 people. A three-day manhunt ensued for Chechen immigrant brothers Tamerlan and Dzhokhar Tsarnaev. Tamerlan was killed in a shoot-out by police. Dzhokhar, a naturalized U.S. citizen, was arrested on April 19 and later charged with using weapons of mass destruction.

Revelations that the U.S. Internal Revenue Service (IRS) disproportionately evaluated conservative groups associated with the Tea Party movement led to the resignation of acting IRS director Steve MILLER in May.

In response to an article published in the UK's *Guardian* newspaper the day before, the U.S. federal government confirmed on June 6 two separate surveillance operations: a seven-year program collecting and monitoring phone records within the United States and an overseas Internet surveillance effort that began six years earlier, known as Prism. Officials defended the classified programs, saying they were known to Congress and helped to thwart more than 50 potential terrorist events. Former CIA employee Edward Snowden, whose subsequent flight to Moscow strained U.S–Russian relations (see Foreign relations, above), was revealed to be responsible for the leaks, part of a massive disclosure of some 50,000 documents. Domestic and international fallout from the leaks continued as fresh details were released through the summer and fall.

In two landmark rulings handed down on June 26, 2013, the Supreme Court ruled that same-sex married couples were entitled to federal benefits and struck down a key section of the 1965 Voting Rights Act.

Because lawmakers in Congress were unable to reach agreement on a new budget in September, a partial government shutdown began on October 1. The Democratic-led Senate and Republican-led House failed to negotiate the key point of contention—a GOP demand that federal government funding come on the condition of a one-year delay in the implementation of health care reforms.

The political crisis deepened as the looming debt ceiling threatened to cause the country to default on public debt. After weeks of bitter negotiations, on October 17 Congress passed a bill ending the shutdown, raising the debt ceiling until February 7, 2014, and authorizing current spending levels through January 15. Following passage by the House, the Senate on February 12 passed a bill to approve increased borrowing levels through March 2015 with support from Republicans and Democrats. The passage of the legislation was seen as a blow to Tea Party Republicans.

In a landmark ruling in late June, a federal appeals court struck down Utah's ban on same-sex marriages, becoming the first federal appeals court to do so. Meanwhile, a federal judge ruled against Indiana's same-sex marriage ban. Days later, on June 30 the Supreme Court struck a blow to the Affordable Care Act, ruling in favor of the store chain Hobby Lobby, which argued that the law's mandate that insurance cover contraception violates the owner's religious liberty.

An unarmed black teenager was fatally shot by police in Ferguson, Missouri on August 9, sparking weeks of demonstrations and unrest. One week later Governor Jay NIXON issued a state of emergency and set a curfew.

On September 19 a veteran of the Iraq War armed with a knife hopped the fence of the White House and entered the building. Amid concerns over the president's security, Secret Service director Julia PIERSON faced a congressional hearing and subsequently resigned, following disclosure of several security breaches.

While the outbreak of the Ebola virus raged in several West African countries, the first diagnosis of the Ebola virus in the United States in late September prompted widespread fears. In response, Obama appointed Ron KLAIN Ebola response director.

Running a campaign deeply critical of the Obama administration, particularly focused on the Affordable Care Act, the Republican Party soared to victory in the November 4, 2014, midterm elections. Within the GOP, traditional party candidates had regained several posts from the Tea Party wing. The election was among the most expensive in the country's history, with campaign spending by parties and super PACs estimated to be more than $3.5 billion, yet voter turnout rates were the lowest since the Second World War. The GOP gained control of the Senate and increased its majority in the House, reducing the Democratic total to 184 seats.

Obama issued an executive order on November 20, 2014, which granted temporary residence rights, including the ability to work legally, to approximately 4 million undocumented immigrants.

"Black Lives Matter," a loose network of activists and concerned citizens, organized protests following a series of deaths of African

Americans by police officers or in police custody in 2015 and 2016. Some of the demonstration turned violent and led to riots. The protests focused attention on the use of deadly force and led some police forces to implement new training procedures and increase the use of body cameras by officers to record interactions with the public and suspected criminals.

Nine African Americans were killed in a church in a shooting in Charleston, South Carolina, on June 17, 2015. The gunman, Dylann ROOF, targeted the parishioners in an effort to exacerbate racial tensions. In response to the shooting, a number of state and local governments stopped displaying the Confederate battle flag, and some monuments to Confederate generals and leaders were removed.

In a landmark 5–4 ruling on June 26, 2015, the Supreme Court in the case *Obergefell v. Hodges* legalized same-sex marriage in the United States.

On December 2, 2015, a radicalized Muslim couple killed 14 people at a disability center in San Bernardino, California. The attack heightened concerns about lone-wolf style terrorist attacks in the United States while also reinvigorating debate over gun control.

On January 15, 2016, the Obama administration suspended the issuance of new coal mine permits on public lands.

U.S. Supreme Court associate justice Antonin SCALIA died on February 13, 2016. Obama named Merrick GARLAND on March 16 to replace Scalia, but the Republican-led Senate refused to act on the nomination in an unprecedented action. Republicans argued that the next president should be the one to choose Scalia's replacement. In June a divided Supreme Court let stand a lower court ruling that blocked Obama's 2014 executive order shielding some illegal immigrants from deportation.

On June 11, 2016, a gunman, Omar MATEEN, with self-proclaimed allegiance to ISIS, attacked a gay nightclub in Orlando, Florida, killing 49 and wounding 53. On July 7 five Dallas police officers were shot and killed during a Black Lives Matter protest by a gunman who deliberately targeted the officers in revenge for the past deaths of African Americans by police.

POLITICAL PARTIES

Although the U.S. Constitution makes no provision for political parties, the existence of two (or occasionally three) major parties at the national level has been a feature of the U.S. political system almost since its inception. The present-day Democratic Party traces its origins back to the Democratic-Republican Party led by Thomas JEFFERSON during George Washington's administration, whereas the contemporary Republican Party, though not formally constituted until the 1850s, regards itself as the lineal descendant of the Federalist Party led by Alexander Hamilton during the same period.

The two-party system has been perpetuated by tradition, by the practical effect of single-member constituencies as well as a single executive, and by the status accorded to the second main party as the recognized opposition in legislative bodies. The major parties do not, however, constitute disciplined doctrinal groups. Each is a coalition of autonomous state parties—themselves coalitions of county and city parties—that come together chiefly in presidential election years to formulate a general policy statement, or platform, and to nominate candidates for president and vice president. Control of funds and patronage is largely in the hands of state and local party units, a factor that weakens party discipline in Congress. Policy leadership is similarly diffuse, both parties searching for support from as many interest groups as possible and tending to operate by consensus.

For at least a quarter of a century, popular identification with the two major parties was remarkably stable. From 1960 to 1984, according to surveys by the University of Michigan, between 40 and 46 percent of the voters considered themselves Democrats, whereas 22 to 29 percent identified with the Republicans. During the same period, 23 to 35 percent viewed themselves as independents (the higher figure occurring in the mid-1970s, when younger voters tended to dissociate themselves from partisan politics). In a subsequent poll conducted in early 1995, 37 percent of respondents called themselves independents, 30 percent Republicans, and 29 percent Democrats, with nearly 60 percent of voting-age individuals voicing their preference for a tripartite system.

Since 1932 the rate of voter participation has averaged 55.7 percent in presidential elections, ranging from a low of 49.0 percent for Bill Clinton in 1996 to a high of 64 percent for Barack Obama in 2008 (turnout was 57.5 percent in 2012). The turnout in nonpresidential years has been substantially lower, averaging between 30 and 40 percent. Turnout levels dipped to a 72-year low of 36.4 percent in the 2014 mid-term elections, down from 40.9 percent in 2010. In the 2016 balloting, the turnout rate was 55.4 percent.

Congressional Parties:

Republican Party. Known informally as the "Grand Old Party" (GOP), the present-day Republican Party was founded as an antislavery party in the 1850s and includes Abraham LINCOLN, Theodore ROOSEVELT, Dwight D. Eisenhower, Richard Nixon, and Ronald Reagan among its past presidents. Generally more conservative in outlook than the Democratic Party, the Republican Party traditionally drew its strength from the smaller cities and from suburban and rural areas, especially in the Midwest and parts of New England. In recent years Republicans have tended to advocate welfare and tax reforms, including a simplified tax system and revenue-sharing to relieve the burden of local property taxes; the achievement of a "workable balance between a growing economy and environmental protection"; and military preparedness sufficient to preclude the nation's becoming a "second-class power." The party's base has shifted primarily to the South and West.

Following a hard-fought campaign, with results not clear until December 12, the party's presidential candidate in 2000, George W. Bush, secured a bare majority of electoral votes. The Senate was split 50–50, while the Republicans retained control of the House with a reduced majority of 221 seats. In June 2001 the Republicans lost control of the Senate when Jeffords of Vermont became an independent, but they regained it in the November 2002 election and held it for the ensuing four years.

Charged with violating Texas campaign laws, House Majority Leader Tom DeLAY stepped down in January 2006 and was replaced by John Boehner on February 2. In the presidential primary campaign, which began in early 2007, the following Republican candidates sought the party's nomination, in addition to McCain: Michael D. (Mike) Huckabee; Mitt Romney; Fred THOMPSON, former senator from Tennessee; Duncan HUNTER, congressman from California; Ron PAUL, congressman from Texas; and Rudolph Giuliani. Mitt Romney was the most serious challenger to McCain until the latter's campaign surged ahead in mid-2008.

In the 2008 elections Republican representation declined by 21 House seats and 8 Senate seats. In the presidential election, Senator John McCain received 173 electoral votes and 45.7 percent of the popular vote as the Republican nominee. After Sen. Arlen Specter's defection to the Democratic Party in 2009, the Republicans lost the ability to filibuster in the Senate.

The GOP faced its greatest internal challenge in the form of a populist revolt from the "Tea Party." The movement opposed federal spending initiatives, including so-called "pork barrel" riders on legislation that drove money home to districts. Loosely organized by chapters, the Tea Party toppled a number of GOP favorites in the 2010 primary, including Utah's long-standing incumbent Senator Robert BENNETT. In Delaware, Tea Party candidate Christine O'DONNELL, who defeated the GOP's preferred Senate candidate in the primary, former governor Michael CASTLE, rankled voters with revelations of financial troubles and a well-publicized admission that she had once "dabbled into witchcraft," while Sharron ANGLE, running against Democratic senator Harry Reid in Nevada, raised concerns because of her unorthodox views that the Department of Education should be eliminated, the United States should withdraw from the United Nations, and a disbelief that the U.S. Constitution mandates the separation of church and state. Both were defeated in November.

Historic gains in the House gave the GOP a strong majority in that chamber, while the Republicans also increased their seats in the Senate and made sizable gains at the state and local levels. The new House speaker, John BOEHNER, vowed to cut government spending, reduce the size of government, and repeal the health care reforms. There were eight major contenders for the Republican Party's presidential nomination for the 2012 election: Texas governor Rick Perry, former Massachusetts governor Mitt Romney, Texas representative and former Libertarian presidential candidate Ron Paul, Minnesota representative and congressional Tea Party leader Michele Bachmann, former pizza chain executive Herman Cain, former house speaker Newt Gingrich, former Pennsylvania senator Rick Santorum, and former Utah governor and ambassador to China Jon Huntsman. Romney quickly emerged as the frontrunner, but many conservatives and Tea Party activists opposed his nomination. Several candidates were able to challenge Romney, including Santorum who won the Iowa Caucus, and Gingrich, but Romney's funding advantages eroded the field, and the former governor had a commanding delegate lead by March. Romney lost the general election to incumbent president Obama on November 6, 2012. Republicans did maintain control of the House of Representatives and took control of the legislature in Arkansas for the first time since Reconstruction. The GOP also gained control of the state senates in Alaska and Wisconsin but lost their majorities in both houses in Minnesota and Maine and in at least one chamber in Colorado, New Hampshire, New York, and Oregon.

In a May 2013 special election the GOP retained the South Carolina House seat vacated by Tim SCOTT, who was appointed to the state's vacant Senate seat in January, when former governor Rick SANFORD, who had resigned as chair of the Republican Governors Association in 2009 amid scandal, defeated Democrat Elizabeth COLBERT BUSCH.

The rise of the Tea Party element within the Republican Party stalled ahead of the 2014 midterm elections, as traditional Republican candidates defeated Tea Party candidates in primary elections around the country, accounting for the surge in GOP primary spending to $46 million, up from $33 million the previous cycle. However, Tea Party candidates did make some gains, including defeating House Majority Leader Eric CANTOR, who announced his resignation from his post in mid-June, thereby sparking an internal competition to reshuffle party leadership. Kevin McCARTHY assumed the post on August 1. Subsequently, the GOP made significant gains in the 2014 mid-term elections, increasing its House majority to 244 seats and regaining control of the Senate for the first time since 2007. In the contest for Louisiana's open Senate seat, Republican Bill CASSIDY split the conservative vote with Tea Party candidate Rob MANESS, winning 42 percent and 14 percent respectively. Cassidy went on to win a December runoff election against Democrat incumbent Mary LANDRIEU. The week following the election, the party overwhelmingly voted Senate Minority Leader Mitch McCONNELL to serve as Senate majority leader upon the convening of the new Congress in January 2015.

Seventeen candidates vied for the 2016 Republican presidential nomination. Among the leading candidates were billionaire Donald J. TRUMP, Senators Ted CRUZ (Texas) and Marco RUBIO (Florida), Governors John KASICH (Ohio) and Chris CHRISTY (New Jersey), former governor Jed BUSH (Florida), and neurosurgeon Ben CARSON. Despite his political inexperience, Trump gained the nomination in a highly bitter contest that prompted some Republicans to declare themselves "Never Trumpers" and refuse to support the GOP candidate.

Trump's populist campaign emphasized his status as a candidate outside of the political mainstream. He won the election by securing states such as Wisconsin and Michigan, which had not voted Republican in a presidential election since 1984 and 1988, respectively. Republicans maintained majorities in both the House, 241 seats, and Senate, 52 seats. The GOP also made minor gains at the state level.

As part of his transition, Trump named party chair Reince PRIEBUS as the White House chief of staff. Deputy Chair Ronna ROMNEY McDANIEL, the niece of Mitt Romney, was named to succeed Priebus as party chair.

Leaders: Donald J. TRUMP (President), Mike PENCE (Vice President), Paul RYAN (Speaker of the House), Mitch McCONNELL (Senate Majority Leader), Ronna ROMNEY McDANIEL (Party Chair), Mitt ROMNEY (2012 presidential candidate and Former Governor of Massachusetts), Reince PRIEBUS (Former National Chair).

Democratic Party. Originally known as the **Democratic-Republican Party**, the Democratic Party counts Thomas Jefferson, Andrew JACKSON, Woodrow WILSON, Franklin D. Roosevelt, John F. Kennedy, Lyndon B. Johnson, and Bill Clinton among its past presidents. Its basis has traditionally been an unstable coalition of conservative politicians in the southeastern states, more liberal political leaders in the urban centers of the Northeast and the West Coast, and populists in some towns and rural areas of the Midwest. The party was weakened in 1968 by the conservative secessionist movement of southern Democrats led by George C. Wallace and the challenge to established leadership and policies put forward by senators Eugene J. McCarthy and Robert F. Kennedy, both of whom had sought the presidential nomination ultimately captured by Hubert H. Humphrey. The party was further divided by the nomination of Sen. George S. McGovern, a strong critic of the Vietnam policies of both presidents Johnson and Nixon, as Democratic presidential candidate in 1972.

The party benefited from the circumstances surrounding the resignations of Vice President Spiro Agnew in 1973 and of President Nixon in 1974, scored impressive victories in both the House and Senate in 1974, recaptured the presidency under Jimmy Carter in 1976, and maintained substantial congressional majorities in 1978. In 1980 it retained control of the House by a reduced majority while losing the Senate and suffering a decisive rejection of President Carter's bid for reelection. The party's strength in Congress was largely unchanged in 1984, despite the Reagan presidential landslide, and in 1986 it regained control of the Senate; it retained control of both houses, despite the defeat of its presidential candidate, Michael Dukakis, in 1988. Led by Clinton of Arkansas, the Democrats regained the White House in 1992 while preserving their congressional majorities, but, in a startling reversal, the party lost control of both houses in 1994. Although unable to regain control in 1996 or 1998, the Democrats countered expectations by registering marginal recovery in 1998. Denied the presidency in 2000, despite a popular majority for Vice President Al Gore, the party drew even with the Republicans in the Senate, whereas a ten-seat gain in the House was insufficient to win control. In June 2001 the Democrats assumed control of the Senate with the support of Sen. James Jeffords of Vermont, who had left the Republican Party to sit as an independent.

The disappointing results of the November 2002 balloting, in which the party was unable to win either house of Congress, were attributed by many observers to the Democrats' inability to present clear policy alternatives to the Republican agenda. Following the election, Richard A. GEPHARDT of Missouri, the House minority leader, resigned his post and was succeeded by Nancy Pelosi of California, the first woman to head either party in Congress.

In 2004 the party was even less successful than in 2000, failing to gain the White House for its standard-bearer, Sen. John Kerry of Massachusetts, and losing further ground in both the Senate and House.

On February 12, 2005, the party elected former Vermont governor Howard Dean as its national chair.

The lengthy presidential primary campaign got under way following the midterm elections in November 2006, with candidates stumping in earnest by early 2007. Those vying for the party's nomination, in addition to Hillary Rodham Clinton, Barack Obama, and Joseph Biden, were Christopher DODD, senator from Connecticut; Mike GRAVEL, former senator from Alaska; Dennis KUCINICH, congressman from Ohio; Bill RICHARDSON, governor of New Mexico; and Tom VILSACK, former governor of Iowa. Senator Clinton's early lead tapered into 2008, until she conceded the closely fought race four days after Obama won the party's nomination on June 3.

The Democratic Party's presidential nominee, Barack Obama, secured 365 Electoral College votes and 52.9 percent of the popular vote in November 2008 to become the first presidential candidate since Carter to receive more than a 50 percent vote share.

The Democrats captured significant majorities in the Senate and the House in the 2008 elections but initially fell 2 seats short of the 60-seat powerful majority in the upper house. On April 30, 2009, Republican Arlen Specter of Pennsylvania switched to the Democratic Party, and on June 30 the Minnesota Supreme Court upheld the decision of a lower court to recognize the narrow victory of Democrat Al FRANKEN over Republican incumbent Norm COLEMAN, ending the Republicans' ability to filibuster to defeat legislation. Following Massachusetts senator Edward M. KENNEDY's August 25 death, Republican Scott BROWN was elected, reducing the party's majority to 59 seats.

In June 2010 West Virginia senator Robert BYRD, the longest serving member of Congress in history and a Democratic leader, died in office. In the November midterm elections, the Democrats lost more than 60 House seats in the biggest shift in power since 1948. After losing the majority, disgruntled House Democrats reportedly sought a change in leadership, although Hoyer's stated refusal to run against Pelosi secured her victory in caucus elections on November 17 in a 150–43 vote. In December 2010 the House censured long-serving Democratic representative Charles RANGEL of New York for financial misconduct in filing inaccurate tax papers and other improprieties.

In May 2012 the trial of former Democratic senator and 2004 vice-presidential candidate John Edwards on six counts of campaign fraud ended in a mistrial.

Obama faced no formal opposition in his bid for the Democratic presidential nomination in 2012. However, significant percentages of voters in southern states, including Arkansas, Kentucky, and North Carolina, voted "uncommitted" rather than endorse the president. An intricate and comprehensive "get-out-the-vote" effort generated a large turnout among the party's base. Obama won the balloting, while Democrats gained two seats in the Senate, although the GOP maintained control of the House of Representatives. Results at the state level were mixed, as Democrats gained control of state legislatures in Minnesota and Maine but lost both houses in Arkansas. Democrats gained a supermajority in the California legislature.

In a May 2013 special election to fill a vacant South Carolina House seat, Democrat Elizabeth Colbert Busch lost to GOP candidate former governor Mark SANFORD.

The Democrats suffered significant losses in the November 2014 midterm elections, losing an additional 12 seats in the House and losing control of the Senate.

Hillary Rodham Clinton was the early frontrunner to secure the 2016 Democratic presidential nomination. She faced far-left Vermont senator Bernie SANDERS and former Maryland governor Martin O'MALLEY. Three other candidates withdrew before the primaries commenced. Sanders espoused an economic populist message that resonated with the left wing of the party, but Clinton was able to secure the nomination. In July Donna BRAZILE became acting chair of the Democratic National Committee after her predecessor, Debbie WASSERMAN SCHULTZ, was forced to resign over allegations that she had inappropriately aided the Clinton campaign during the primaries. Tom PEREZ was elected chair in February 2017.

Clinton lost the presidential contest to Republican Donald J. Trump, securing 232 Electoral College votes to Trump's 306. She did win the popular vote, 48.1 percent to 46 percent. Democrats gained two seats in the Senate, and six in the House, but were disappointed in their efforts to retake control of either chamber.

Leaders: Barack H. OBAMA (Former President), Joseph R. BIDEN Jr. (Former Vice President), Hillary Rodham CLINTON (2016 presidential candidate), Charles "Chuck" SCHUMER (Senate Minority Leader), Nancy PELOSI (House Minority Leader), Tom PEREZ (National Chair).

Other Parties:

Although third parties have occasionally influenced the outcome of presidential balloting, the Republican Party in 1860 was the only such party in U.S. history to win a national election and subsequently establish itself as a major political organization. The third parties having the greatest impact have typically been those formed as largely personal vehicles by prominent Republicans or Democrats who have been denied nomination by their regular parties, such as Theodore Roosevelt's **Progressive ("Bull Moose") Party** of 1912 and the **American Independent Party** organized to support the 1968 candidacy of George C. Wallace.

The only nonparty candidates in recent history to attract significant public attention were former Democratic senator Eugene J. McCARTHY, who secured 751,728 votes (0.9 percent of the total) in 1976; former Republican representative John B. ANDERSON, who polled 5,719,722 (6.6 percent) in 1980; and Texas entrepreneur H. Ross PEROT, who won 19,237,247 (19 percent) in 1992 and whose substantial support gave rise to subsequent attempts to establish a credible third party before his **Reform Party**'s far less impressive showing of 8 percent in 1996. Thereafter, despite a 1998 Minnesota victory for the party's gubernatorial candidate, former professional wrestler Jesse VENTURA, the party declined further, winning only 0.4 percent of the vote in 2000 under longtime Republican conservative Patrick J. BUCHANAN. In a marginally more impressive showing, **Green Party** nominee Ralph NADER obtained 2.7 percent of the vote, whereas the **Natural Law Party** candidate, Harry BROWNE, secured 0.4 percent. Nader ran as an independent in 2004, winning only 0.3 percent of the vote, and in 2008.

Third-party candidates in 2016 were **Libertarian Party** (LP) nominee Gary JOHNSON, a former Republican governor of New Mexico; Green Party nominee Jill STEIN; **Constitution Party** (CP) nominee Darrell Lane CASTLE; and David Evan McMULLIN who ran as an independent.

Other minor parties, none of national significance in recent elections, have included the **Alaskan Independence Party** (AKIP), led by Lynette CLARK; the **America's Party** (formally **America's Independent Party**); the **American Nazi Party** (ANP), led by Rocky SUHAYDA; the **Communist Party of the United States of America** (CPUSA), led by Sam WEBB; the **Concerned Citizens** (CC), Connecticut affiliate of the **Constitution Party**, led by Jim CLYMER; the **Conservative Party** (CP), led by Sam A. GALLO and based in Louisiana with affiliates in 21 other states; the Rhode Island–based **Cool Moose Party,** led by Robert J. HEALEY Sr.; the **Corrective Action Party** (CAP), led by Bernard PALICKI; the **Democratic Socialists of America** (DSA), which is a member of the Socialist International and led by Maria SVART; the **Expansionist Party of the United States** (XP), which seeks expansion of the United States into an eventual world union, led by L. Craig SCHOONMAKER; the **Independent Party** (IP); the **Independent American Party** (IAP), led by Kelly GNEITING; **Justice Party** (JP); the Latino **La Raza Unida** (People United) **Party** (LRUP); the **Liberal Party** (L); the **Liberty Union Party** (LU) of Vermont; the **Light Party,** led by Da VID; the **Mountain Party** (MP) of West Virginia; the **National Democratic Policy Committee** (NDPC), which has supported dissident Democrat, Lyndon LAROCHE, as a presidential candidate; the white supremacist **National Patriot Party** (NPP), which was formally launched in April 1994, mainly by former supporters of Perot; the now-defunct **National Unity Party** (NUP), which in 1984 endorsed John Anderson for a second presidential bid; the **New Federalist Party** (NFP), organized in 1975 "to promote the principles of George Washington and the Federalist founders of this nation"; the **Pacific Party** (PP); the **Pansexual Peace Party** (PPP); the feminist and socialist **Peace and Freedom Party** (PFP), based in California; **Politicians Are Crooks** (PAC); the now-defunct **Populist Party of America** (PPA), an outgrowth of the middle-class "America First" movement of the 1930s; the **Progressive Party** (PR); the Marxist **Progressive Labor Party** (PLP); the **Right to Life Party** (RLP), based in New York; the **Social Democrats USA** (SDUSA), a member of the Socialist International; the **Socialist Labor Party** (SLP); the **Timesizing.com Party** (TCP), based in Massachusetts; the **United States Pacifist Party** (USPP); the **Vermont Grassroots Party** (VGP); the **Veterans Industrial Party** (VIP), led by Ernest Lee EASTON; the **Working Families Party** (WFP); and the **World Socialist Party of the United States** (WSPUS).

LEGISLATURE

Legislative power is vested by the Constitution in the bicameral **Congress of the United States.** Both houses are chosen by direct popular election; one-third of the Senate and the entire House of Representatives are elected every two years. Congresses are numbered consecutively, with a new Congress meeting every second year. The last election (for the 114th Congress, beginning on January 3, 2015) was held on November 4, 2014.

Senate. The upper chamber consists of 100 members—2 from each state—elected on a statewide basis for six-year terms. Following the most recent balloting on November 8, 2016, the Republicans controlled 52 seats and the Democrats controlled 48 (including 2 independents).

President: Mike PENCE (Vice President of the United States).
President Pro Tempore: Orrin HATCH.

House of Representatives. The lower house consists of 435 voting representatives, with each state entitled to at least 1 representative and the actual number from each state being apportioned periodically on the basis of population. The size and shape of congressional districts are determined by the states themselves; however, the Supreme Court has ruled that such districts must be "substantially equal" in population and must be redefined when they fail to meet this requirement. Resident commissioners from the District of Columbia, Guam, Puerto Rico, and the Virgin Islands were traditionally nonvoting delegates; however, in January 1993, over unanimous Republican opposition, they were given the right to vote in the body's Committee of the Whole, though not in the (usually pro forma) final passage of legislation. The right was revoked by the new Republican majority in January 1995; Democrats restored the privilege when they retook House control following the 2006 elections. In 2009 the resident commissioner of the Northern Marianas joined the ranks of nonvoting delegates, bringing their total to six, all of whom were Democrats or pledged to caucus with the Democrats. In the most recent elections on

November 8, 2016, Republicans won 241 seats and the Democrats won 194.

Speaker: Paul RYAN.

CABINET

[as of March 9, 2017]

President	Donald J. Trump
Vice President	Mike Pence
Secretaries	
Agriculture (Nominated)	Sonny Perdue
Commerce	Wilbur Ross, Jr.
Defense	James Mattis
Education	Betsy DeVos [f]
Energy	Rick Perry
Health and Human Services	Tom Price
Homeland Security	John Kelly
Housing and Urban Development	Ben Carson
Interior	Ryan Zinke
Justice	Jeff Sessions
Labor (Nominated)	R. Alexander Acosta
State	Rex Tillerson
Transportation	Elaine Chao [f]
Treasury	Steven Mnuchin
Veteran's Affairs	David J. Shulkin
Cabinet-Level Aides	
Administrator, Environmental Protection Agency	Scott Pruitt
Administrator, Small Business Administration	Linda McMahon [f]
Chief, Council of Economic Advisers	(Vacant)
Director, Central Intelligence Agency	Mike Pompeo
Director, National Intelligence	Dan Coats
Director, Office of Management and Budget	Mick Mulvaney
United States Trade Representative	Robert Lighthizer
White House Chief of Staff	Reince Priebus

[f] = female

Note: All of the above are members of the Republican Party.

INTERGOVERNMENTAL REPRESENTATION

The various U.S. ambassadors to foreign governments, as well as the various foreign ambassadors accredited to the United States, are given at the end of the relevant country entries.

Permanent Representative to the UN: Nikki HALEY.

IGO Memberships (Non-UN): ADB, AfDB, APEC, EBRD, G-8, G-20, IADB, IEA, IOM, NATO, OAS, OECD, OSCE, WTO.

For Further Reference:

Brattebo, Douglas, Tom Lansford, and Jack Covarrubias, eds. *A Transformation in American National Politics: The 2012 Presidential Election.* Akron, OH: University of Akron Press, 2016.

Noll, Mark A. *God and Race in American Politics: A Short History.* Princeton, NJ: Princeton University Press, 2008.

Reichard, Gary W. *Deadlock and Disillusionment: American Politics since 1968.* Malden, MA: Wiley/Blackwell, 2016.

Zelozer, Julian, ed. *The American Congress: The Building of Democracy.* New York: Houghton Mifflin, 2004.

RELATED TERRITORIES

The United States never acquired a colonial empire of significant proportions. Among its principal former overseas dependencies, the Philippines became independent in 1946, Puerto Rico acquired the status of a commonwealth in free association with the United States in 1952, and Hawaii became the 50th state of the Union in 1959. In addition to Puerto Rico, the United States now exercises sovereignty in the Virgin Islands, Guam, American Samoa, the Commonwealth of the Northern Mariana Islands, and an assortment of smaller Pacific and Caribbean islands, including the Midway Islands and Navassa. On January 6, 2009, President George W. Bush established the Pacific Remote Islands Marine National Monument, which encompasses Johnston, Palmyra and Wake atolls; Howland, Baker, and Jarvis islands; and Kingman Reef—a total of 86,888 square miles (225,040 sq. km). The Department of the Interior supervises the monument, the components of which are all national wildlife refuges.

Numerous other small insular territories have historically been claimed by the United States, including Christmas Island in the Indian Ocean, which passed from British to Australian administration in 1958. Quita Sueño, Roncador, Serrana, and Serranilla, a group of uninhabited islets in the western Caribbean, were turned over to Colombia under a 1972 treaty that the U.S. Senate failed to ratify until 1981 because of conflicting claims by Nicaragua.

Under the so-called Guano Act of 1856, the United States claimed jurisdiction over 58 Pacific islands ostensibly discovered by American citizens and presumed to contain extractable resources, principally phosphate. In 1979 the United States concluded a treaty with the newly independent state of Tuvalu whereby it renounced all claims under the act to the four southernmost of the country's nine islands. The following September the U.S. government concluded a similar treaty with Kiribati under which, in addition to surrendering Canton (subsequently Kanton) and Enderbury (theretofore under joint British and American administration), the United States relinquished claims to the eight Phoenix Islands, the five Southern Line Islands, and Christmas (subsequently Kiritimati) Island in the Northern Line group. In June 1980 a treaty was concluded with New Zealand whereby U.S. claims to four islands in the northern Cook group were also abandoned. The treaties were ratified by the U.S. Congress in 1983 over strong conservative opposition.

Until October 1, 1979, the United States held administrative responsibility for the Panama Canal Zone (see Panama: Panama Canal Zone), while U.S. administration of the Trust Territory of the Pacific Islands was effectively terminated with the independence of Palau on October 1, 1994. (For a discussion of the Trust Territory, see the 1993 *Handbook.*)

Major Caribbean Jurisdictions:

Puerto Rico. Situated in the Caribbean between the island of Hispaniola in the west and the Virgin Islands in the east, the Commonwealth of Puerto Rico is composed of the large island of Puerto Rico together with Vieques, Culebra, and many smaller islands. Its area is 3,515 square miles (9,103 sq. km). In 2016 the population of Puerto Rico was estimated at 3,681,000 (99 percent Hispanic). Despite a falling birth rate, population density remains among the highest in the world, amounting in 2016 to 1,080 persons per square mile (415 per sq. km). San Juan, with an estimated population of 2,463,000 in 2015, is the capital and principal city. Spanish blood and culture are dominant, with an admixture of Native American, African, and other immigrant stock, largely from Western Europe and the United States. Most Puerto Ricans are Spanish-speaking and Roman Catholic, although religious freedom prevails. Both English and Spanish served as official languages from 1902 to 1991, when a bill was approved requiring that all government proceedings take place in Spanish, with official bilingualism being reestablished in 1993. The economy, traditionally based on sugar, tobacco, and rum, advanced dramatically after 1948 under a self-help program known as Operation Bootstrap that stressed diversification and the use of incentives to promote industrialization through private investment, both local and foreign. Subsequently, industry surpassed agriculture as a source of income. Despite marked economic and social gains, however, the commonwealth has been burdened by high public debt and a high unemployment rate that has consistently been in the double digits (14.2 percent in 2012). Reflecting a significant maldistribution of wealth, 45.6 percent of the population was listed in 2011 as below the poverty line.

Ceded by Spain to the United States under the 1898 Treaty of Paris, Puerto Rico was subsequently governed as an unincorporated U.S. territory. The inhabitants were granted U.S. citizenship in 1917, obtaining in 1947 the right to elect a chief executive. The present commonwealth status, approved by plebiscite in 1951, entered into effect on July 25, 1952; under its terms, Puerto Rico now exercises approximately the same control over its internal affairs as do the 50 states, but residents, though U.S. citizens, do not vote in U.S. presidential elections and are represented in the U.S. Congress only by an elected resident commissioner in the House of Representatives. The resident commissioner has voting privileges in House committees (except for the House's Committee of the Whole) but not on the House floor. In November 1997 the Puerto Rican Supreme Court recognized the existence of Puerto Rican, in addition to U.S., citizenship. Federal taxes do not apply in Puerto Rico except by mutual consent (for example, Social Security taxes). The commonwealth constitution, modeled on that of the United States but incorporating many social and political innovations, provides for a governor and a bicameral Legislative Assembly (consisting of a 27-seat Senate and a 51-seat House of Representatives) elected by universal suffrage for four-year terms. An appointed Supreme Court heads the independent judiciary.

Puerto Rican politics was dominated from 1940 through 1968 by the **Popular Democratic Party** (*Partido Popular Democrático*—PPD) of Governor Luis MUÑOZ Marín, the principal architect of Operation Bootstrap and of the commonwealth relationship with the United States. While demands for Puerto Rican independence declined sharply after 1952, a substantial movement favoring statehood continued under the leadership of Luis A. FERRÉ and others. In a 1967 plebiscite 60.4 percent opted for continued commonwealth status, 39 percent for statehood, and 0.6 percent for independence. Following shifts in party alignments in advance of the 1968 election, Ferré was elected governor as head of the pro-statehood **New Progressive Party** (*Partido Nuevo Progresista*—PNP). Four years later the PPD, under Rafael HERNÁNDEZ Colón, regained the governorship, while the PNP, under San Juan mayor Carlos ROMERO Barceló, returned to power in 1976. Romero served until January 1985, when Hernández Colón began the first of two additional terms. The PNP's Pedro ROSSELLÓ was elected governor in 1992 and reelected in 1996.

The anti-statehood PPD secured an upset victory at the election of November 7, 2000, sweeping the governorship, both legislative houses, and most city halls. Its standard-bearer, Sila María CALDERÓN, who on January 7, 2001, became the commonwealth's first female governor, obtained 49 percent of the vote. The pro-statehood PNP candidate, Carlos PESQUERA, won 46 percent, with Rubén BERRÍOS Martínez of the **Puerto Rican Independence Party** (*Partido Independentista Puertoriqueño*—PIP) finishing a distant third.

A disputed gubernatorial poll in 2004 generated a recount that lasted two months, followed by a bitter court battle. The PPD's Aníbal ACEVEDO-VILÁ was declared the winner over former president Pedro Rosselló by 3,500 votes out of 2 million cast. In the Senate and House races, however, the pro-statehood forces secured majorities.

In 2008 Acevedo-Vilá sought another term despite a federal indictment against him on corruption charges, which he insisted were politically motivated. Though acquitted in early 2009, the charges contributed to his defeat in the November poll by the PNP's Luis FORTUÑO, theretofore Puerto Rico's representative (resident commissioner) in the U.S. Congress, who captured 52.8 percent of the vote. Acevedo-Vilá won 41.3 percent, followed by Rogelio FIGUEROA of the **Puerto Rico for Puerto Ricans Party** (*Partido Puertoriqueños por Puerto Rico*—PPR) with 2.8 percent and the PIP's Edwin IRIZARRY Mora with 2 percent. The PNP also won overwhelming majorities in both houses of the Legislative Assembly. (See below for information on the 2012 elections.)

A small but frequently violent independence movement became active in the 1920s, when the radical Nationalist Party was formed by Pedro ALBIZU Campos. On November 1, 1950, a group of *nacionalistas* attempted to assassinate President Harry S. Truman, while on March 1, 1954, another group wounded five U.S. members of Congress on the floor of the House of Representatives. (In 1979 President Jimmy Carter commuted the sentences of the four Puerto Ricans still serving sentences for the two attacks, despite Governor Romero Barceló's strong objection.) Currently, the separatist movement is directed by the PIP and the Marxist **Puerto Rican Socialist Party** (*Partido Socialista Puertoriqueño*—PSP), which collectively have won no more than a combined 6 percent of the vote in recent elections. The most militant organization advocating independence was the **Armed Forces for National Liberation** (*Fuerzas Armadas de Liberación Nacional*—FALN), which engaged in terrorist activities in New York City as well as in San Juan from the mid-1970s to the mid-1980s. In late 1979 three other terrorist groups—the **Volunteers of the Puerto Rican Revolution,** the **Boricua Popular Army** (*Ejército Popular Boricua,* also known as the *Macheteros*), and the **Armed Forces of Popular Resistance**—claimed joint responsibility for an attack on a busload of U.S. military personnel that killed two and left ten injured. In 2000 President Bill Clinton offered clemency to 16 FALN members who had been convicted of terrorist acts more than two decades earlier. A month later, 11 of the prisoners were released, despite a 311–41 House vote that condemned the president's action. The FALN leader, Carlos Alberto TORRES, having served nearly 30 years in prison, was released in July 2010.

In September 1978 the UN Decolonization Committee endorsed a Cuban resolution that labeled Puerto Rico a colony of the United States and called for a transfer of power before any referendum on statehood. On December 13, 1998, in a nonbinding referendum, 50.8 percent of Puerto Ricans voted for no change in status, while 46.5 percent favored statehood, and 2.5 percent, independence. (See below for information on the 2012 referendum.)

The status of the island of Vieques, two-thirds of which had long been used as a bombing range by the U.S. Navy, came to a head after the killing of a civilian security guard during a bombing run in April 1999. Numerous protests erupted in the ensuing months.

On June 14, 2001, President Bush announced that all exercises on Vieques would end by May 2003, but Vieques residents on July 29 voted by a 2–1 margin for immediate closure of the naval facility. The U.S. Congress insisted that the range was needed for war on terrorism related tests, but the PIP threatened to mount a general strike. Accordingly, the navy withdrew on May 1, 2003, turning about 14,500 acres over to the U.S. Fish and Wildlife Service. Since then, with oversight from the Environmental Protection Agency, contract workers have been clearing the site of unexploded munitions. Some 7,000 of the island's more than 9,000 residents have filed claims for illnesses from pollutants released during the period of live-fire exercises.

In June 2011 Barack Obama became the first U.S. president since John F. Kennedy in 1961 to make an official visit to Puerto Rico. A two-part nonbinding referendum on November 6, 2012, asked voters if they wanted to change the current Commonwealth status and which of three alternatives (statehood, sovereign free association [informally referenced as "enhanced commonwealth," which would provide greater autonomy], or independence) they preferred. According to initial results, 54 percent answered yes to the first question, while in response to the second question 61 percent endorsed statehood, 33 percent sovereign free association, and 5 percent independence. Consequently, a request for statehood was expected to be forwarded to the U.S. Congress. In concurrent balloting, Alejandro GARCÍA Padilla, the candidate of the PPD, was elected governor by a narrow margin over Fortuño, a statehood advocate. Following his election, García Padilla said that a constituent assembly should be convened to prepare another plebiscite on the statehood matter for 2014.

Some observers suggested that Fortuño's defeat reflected the recent increase in violent crime and ongoing economic difficulties. Though Fortuño's austerity program was credited with a return to financial stability following four years of economic contraction, it was unpopular among many Puerto Ricans. Meanwhile, the PPD secured strong majorities in Puerto Rico's Senate and House of Representatives in the November 6 poll as well as a majority of mayoralties. Garcia Padilla was sworn in on January 2, 2013.

In May 2013 Resident Commissioner Pedro PIERLUISI introduced legislation in Congress that would allow Puerto Rico to seek statehood, beginning with a referendum. The Obama administration allocated $2.5 million in the 2014 budget to go toward resolution of Puerto Rico's status. In February 2014 Senator Martin HEINRICH of New Mexico introduced a companion measure in the Senate.

Meanwhile, Governor García Padilla in early February announced that he planned to overhaul the tax system and balance the budget, months after a debt crisis shut Puerto Rico out of the bond market. In August 2015 Puerto Rico failed to make a $58 million debt payment. A June 2016 measure approved by the U.S. Congress appointed a federal oversight board to restructure Puerto Rico's debt.

García Padilla did not seek reelection in November 2016, and the balloting was won by Ricardo ROSSELLÓ of the pro-statehood PNP with 41.8 percent of the vote to the PPD's David BERNIER's 38.9 percent.

Governor: Ricardo (Ricky) ROSSELLÓ Nevares.

Resident Commissioner (member of the U.S. House of Representatives): Jenniffer GONZÁLEZ-COLÓN.

Virgin Islands. Situated 40 miles east of Puerto Rico and just west and south of the British Virgin Islands, the U.S. Virgin Islands (formerly known as the Danish West Indies) include the large islands of St. Croix, St. Thomas, and St. John, and about 50 smaller islands. The total area, including water surfaces, is 132 square miles (342 sq. km); the population was estimated at 106,000 in 2016. The capital, Charlotte Amalie on St. Thomas, is the sole substantial town. Two-thirds of the people are of African origin, and approximately one-quarter are of Puerto Rican descent. English is the principal language, although Spanish is widely spoken. The people are highly religious, with most being either Baptist or Roman Catholic.

Purchased by the United States from Denmark in 1917, the Virgin Islands, an unincorporated territory, were initially administered by the U.S. Navy and then, from 1931 to 1971, by the Department of the Interior. Residents were made U.S. citizens in 1927 and were granted a considerable measure of self-government in the Revised Organic Act of 1954, which authorized the creation of an elected 15-member Senate. Under a New Organic Act of 1968, executive authority was vested in a governor and a lieutenant governor, both of whom since 1970 have been popularly elected. Since 1973 the territory has sent one nonvoting delegate to the U.S. House of Representatives. (The delegate can vote in House committees but not on the House floor.) Elected governors were Melvin EVANS (to 1975), a Republican; Cyril KING (1975–1978) of the **Independent Citizens' Movement** (ICM), who died in office; Juan F. LUIS (1978–1987), also of the ICM; and Alexander FARRELLY (1987–1995), a Democrat.

In a referendum held October 11, 1993, 90 percent of those voting favored continued or enhanced U.S. territorial status, while the options of full integration with the United States and independence each attracted about 5 percent. The 27.4 percent turnout fell short of the required 50 percent plus one to validate the outcome.

In November 1994 Dr. Roy SCHNEIDER, a Republican standing as an independent, was elected governor, defeating the former lieutenant governor, Derek HODGE, a Democrat. In November 1998 retired university professor Charles TURNBULL, a Democrat, defeated Schneider, criticized for overspending. Turnbull won reelection on November 5, 2002, and a fellow Democrat, John de JONGH Jr., succeeded him in a runoff poll on November 21, 2006.

On June 12, 2007, voters chose 30 delegates for a constitutional convention. (Voters rejected previous constitutional efforts in 1964, 1971, 1979, and 1981.) After two years of often-contentious negotiations, the convention forwarded a draft proposal to Governor de Jongh in late May 2009. However, the governor refused to submit the proposal to U.S. president Barack Obama and the U.S. Congress for consideration on the grounds that some of its provisions were outside the framework of the U.S. constitution and thereby unacceptable. Among other things, the proposal failed to recognize the supremacy of the U.S. constitution and offered extra rights (including property tax exemptions) to "native" Virgin Islanders.

On November 2, 2010, Governor de Jongh easily won reelection. Following the November 6, 2012, elections, the Democrats held 10 seats in the Senate; independents, 4; and the ICM, 1.

With de Jongh prohibited from seeking another term by term limits, Delegate Donna CHRISTENSEN beat out five other candidates to secure the Democratic nomination in August 2014 ahead of the gubernatorial elections. In balloting on November 4, Christensen won 38 percent of the vote, compared with 47.5 percent for her opponent, independent Kenneth MAPP. As neither secured the necessary 50 percent, the election was due to proceed to a runoff on November 18, which was won by Mapp with 63.9 percent of the vote to Christensen's 35.9 percent. Democrat Stacey PLASKETT beat Republican Vince DANET in the race for delegate to the U.S. House.

Governor: Kenneth MAPP.

Delegate to the U.S. House of Representatives: Stacey PLASKETT.

Major Pacific Jurisdictions:

American Samoa. Located in the South Pacific just east of the independent state of Samoa, American Samoa includes the six Samoan islands (Annuu, Ofu, Olosega, Rose, Tau, Tutuila) annexed by the United States pursuant to a treaty with Great Britain and Germany in 1899, and also the privately owned Swain's Island (currently with 4–30 inhabitants, at various times), 200 miles to the north and west, which was annexed in 1925. The land area of 77 square miles (199 sq. km) is inhabited by a population almost entirely of Polynesian ancestry that more than doubled from 27,159 at the 1970 census to 57,291 at the 2000 census but fell to 55,519 at the 2010 census. In 2016 the population was estimated at 56,000. Fagatogo village, on Tutuila's Pago Pago Harbor, is the administrative capital. The social structure is based on the same *matai* (family chief) system that prevails in neighboring Samoa. Although educational levels are comparatively high, subsistence farming and fishing remain the predominant way of life. U.S. government spending, fish canning, and tourism are the main sources of income, and the government is the territory's single largest employer. About one-third of all high school graduates leave Samoa for the U.S. mainland.

Constitutionally, American Samoa is an unincorporated territory. Indigenous inhabitants are nationals but not U.S. citizens and therefore cannot vote in U.S. presidential elections. Administered until 1951 by the U.S. Navy and then by the Department of the Interior, the territory held its first gubernatorial elections in November 1977. Its bicameral legislature (*Fono*) consists of an 18-member Senate chosen by clan chiefs and subchiefs, and a popularly elected, nonpartisan, 20-member House of Representatives, exclusive of a nonvoting member from Swain's Island. The judiciary consists of five district courts and a High Court, although a Court of Appeals in San Francisco ruled that the U.S. District Court for Hawaii has jurisdiction over federal crimes committed in American Samoa. Appointed district governors head the territory's three political districts.

Between January 1981 and January 1997 the Republican Peter Tali COLEMAN and the Democrat A. P. LUTALI alternated four-year terms as governor. In 1996 Coleman, in poor health, chose not to run again, while Lutali placed third in the first round of nonpartisan voting on November 5. Lutali's lieutenant governor, Tauese P. F. SUNIA, emerged victorious in the November 19 runoff. He was reelected in 2000. Lieutenant Governor TOGIOLA T. A. Tulafono became governor following Sunia's death in March 2003 and was reelected to full terms in 2004 and 2008.

In December 2006 a Future Political Status Study Commission recommended continuation of the island's "unorganized and unincorporated" status, enactment of legislation to strengthen the *matai* system and prevent further alienation of communal land, and the imposition of new restrictions on the entry and residence of aliens. However, in June 2010 a constitutional convention called for greater autonomy from the federal government. The proposed 34 changes to American Samoa's constitution were put before the voters on November 2 despite objections from many that they were faced with an up-or-down, all-or-nothing ballot question. The package lost by a 70 percent to 30 percent vote.

Governor Togiola in the first half of 2012 again called for the territory to explore options for greater autonomy. Traditional chiefs argued that the 2010 referendum had settled the matter. Togiola also suggested a referendum be held on his proposal that members of the Senate (currently selected by the chiefs) be chosen through direct popular election in the future.

Six candidates contested the first round of gubernatorial balloting on November 6, 2012, Togiola being precluded by term limits from seeking reelection. LOLO Matalasi Moliga, an independent who had recently resigned as president of the Development Bank of American Samoa to run for the post, and Lieutenant Governor FAOA Aitofele Sunia, a Democrat, proceeded to a November 20 runoff. Lolo won with 52.9 percent of votes and took office on January 3, 2013. In a concurrent referendum, voters rejected by a near two to one majority a proposed constitutional amendment that would authorize the *Fono* to override a governor's veto instead of the U.S. secretary of the interior, who is currently so empowered.

Lolo was reelected in November 2016 with 60.2 percent of the vote to Faoa's 35.8 percent.

Governor: LOLO Matalasi Moliga.

Delegate to the U.S. House of Representatives: Amata RADEWAGEN.

Guam. The unincorporated U.S. territory of Guam is geographically the southernmost and largest of the Mariana Islands in the west-central Pacific. Its area of 209 square miles (541 sq. km) supports a population estimated at 172,000 in 2016, inclusive of U.S. service members and their dependents. The capital, Hagåtña (formerly Agaña), has a civilian population of about 1,430 in 2014. The islanders, predominantly of Chamorro (Micronesian) stock and Roman Catholic faith, have a high level of education, with a literacy rate of more than 90 percent. The economy depends largely on military spending and tourism (over 1 million arrivals a year, mostly from Japan and South Korea).

Acquired from Spain by the 1898 Treaty of Paris, the island is the responsibility of the U.S. Department of the Interior. Guamanians were made U.S. citizens by an Organic Act of 1950; although they do not vote in U.S. presidential elections, they have since 1973 sent a delegate to the U.S. House of Representatives. (The delegate has voting rights in House committees but not on the House floor.) Under the Guam Elective Governor Act of 1968, since November 1970 the governor and lieutenant governor have been popularly elected for four-year terms. The legislature, reelected every two years, was reduced from 21 to 15 members in 1998. A Federal District Court heads the judicial system. Local government in 19 municipalities is headed by elected district commissioners.

In 1982 voters, by a three-to-one margin, expressed a preference for a commonwealth rather than statehood, and in an August 8, 1987, referendum, approved 10 of 12 articles of a Commonwealth Act; on November 7 the remaining articles, providing for the recognition of indigenous Chamorro rights and local control of immigration (both bitterly opposed by non-Chamorros) were also approved. In 1992 the end of protracted talks between Guam's Commission on Self-Determination and a Bush administration task force achieved a "qualified agreement" on a commonwealth bill. Although endorsed by Democratic presidential candidate Bill Clinton at the party's 1992 convention, the measure was not introduced in the U.S. Senate until November 1997; by then, President Clinton, under pressure because of congressional unwillingness to sanction a Chamorro-only franchise, or line-item veto power over federal legislation, had reversed himself, and the measure did not pass.

Early elected governors were Republican Carlos G. CAMACHO (to January 1975), Democrat Ricardo J. BORDALLO (1975–1979 and 1983–1987), Republican Paul McDonald CALVO (1979–1983), and Republican Joseph F. ADA (1987–1995). In 1987 Bordallo was convicted for influence peddling; although he secured partial suspension of his prison sentence in October 1988, he committed suicide in 1990, immediately before he was to serve out the remainder of the sentence.

On November 8, 1994, Democrat Carl GUTIERREZ defeated Tommy TANAKA, the Republican nominee, by a comfortable 54.6 percent majority; concurrently, the Democrats also bucked a national trend by retaining legislative control with a slightly reduced majority of 13–8. In 1996, on the other hand, Republicans regained legislative control for the first time since 1980 by a razor-thin margin of 11–10. In a comeback effort, former governor Ada failed to turn back Gutierrez's reelection on November 3, 1998, even though the Republicans surged to a 12–3 majority in the downsized legislature.

In the November 5, 2002, election Republican Felix CAMACHO won the governorship over Democrat Robert UNDERWOOD, taking 55.2 percent of the vote. In the legislative election, Democrats won 9 seats, while Republicans took the other 6. There was no shift in the legislative balance at the next election, held November 2, 2004, but on November 7, 2006, the Republicans won an 8-to-7 majority. Collaterally, Camacho won reelection by again defeating Underwood, but the margin of victory was narrow, 50.3 percent to 48.0 percent. The Democrats regained their legislative majority by securing 10 of the 15 seats on November 4, 2008.

Term limits precluded Governor Camacho from seeking reelection in November 2010. Republican nominee Eddie B. CALVO won a narrow victory over former governor Gutierrez. Meanwhile Democrats maintained a legislative advantage, winning nine seats.

A significant improvement in Guam's economy is expected as the result of a decision reached in 2006 for the eventual relocation of many U.S. servicemen and their dependents from the Japanese island of Okinawa to Guam and other Pacific territories. Initially, it was estimated that some 8,600 servicemen and perhaps as many at 9,000 of their dependents would be moved to Guam. However, as negotiations regarding the final parameters (including the start date) of the initiative continued in the fall of 2012, it was reported that the number of servicemen moving to Guam would be reduced to about 5,000, some on a rotational basis that would reduce the number of dependents to about 1,300.

In balloting on November 6, 2012, the Democrats retained their 9–6 advantage in the legislature, while Madeleine BORDALLO, a Democrat, was reelected as delegate to the U.S. House of Representative. Calvo was reelected with a significant majority of 64 percent of the vote in elections on November 4, 2014, beating out his Democratic opponent, Carl Gutierrez.

Bordallo was reelected in November 2016,

Governor: Eddie B. CALVO.

Delegate to the U.S. House of Representatives: Madeleine BORDALLO.

Commonwealth of the Northern Mariana Islands (CNMI). Located north of the Caroline Islands and west of the Marshalls in the western Pacific, the Marianas (excluding Guam) constitute an archipelago of 16 islands with a land area of 184 square miles (477 sq. km). The estimated population of 55,000 in 2016 resides on six islands, including Saipan (the administrative center), Tinian, and Rota. Classed as Micronesian, the people are largely Roman Catholic.

In 1972 a Marianas Political Status Commission initiated negotiations with Washington that resulted in the 1975 signing of a covenant to establish a Commonwealth of the Northern Mariana Islands in political union with the United States. The covenant was approved by the U.S. Senate on February 24, 1976, and signed by President Gerald Ford on March 24. In January 1978 a government consisting of the commonwealth's first governor, Democrat Carlos S. CAMACHO, and a Northern Marianas Commonwealth Legislature was established. The bicameral legislature encompasses a 9-member Senate elected for staggered four-year terms and a 20-member (formerly 14-member) House of Representatives elected biennially. Under U.S. and local law, the commonwealth ceased to be a component of the Trust Territory of the Pacific Islands on November 3, 1986, with its residents becoming U.S. citizens on the same day. (According to a census report, the percentage holding U.S. citizenship had dropped to 50.3 in 2008.) The change in status under international law came with formal removal from trusteeship by vote of the UN Security Council on December 22, 1990. Since 2009 the commonwealth has been represented in the U.S. House of Representatives by a delegate who has voting rights in House committees but not the House floor.

Governor Camacho was succeeded by Republican Pedro Pangelinan ("Teno") TENORIO (1982–1990), who was in turn followed by another Republican, Lorenzo (Larry) I. De Leon GUERRERO. Governor Guerrero lost a reelection bid in 1993 to his Democratic opponent, Froilan C. ("Lang") TENORIO, although the Republicans retained majorities in both legislative houses. In the election of November 1997 Tenorio and Lt. Gov. Jesus C. BORJA ran on separate tickets (the latter technically as an independent), thus splitting the Democratic vote and enabling former Republican governor Pedro Tenorio to win with 45.6 percent of the vote. A subsequent judicial challenge to his victory on the basis of a two-term limit adopted in 1986 was rejected on the grounds that the change could not be applied retroactively.

In the election of November 3, 2001, Juan BABAUTA, a Republican, captured the governor's office with 42.8 percent of the vote, defeating Benigno R. Fitial of the **Covenant Party** (CP, recently formed by Fitial), the Democrat Borja, and Froilan Tenorio, now of the **Reform Party.** Republicans also retained control of both legislative chambers.

A four-way gubernatorial race on November 5, 2005, pitted Governor Babauta against Speaker of the House Fitial, Froilan Tenorio, and independent Heinz HOFSCHNEIDER. The contest was so close, however, that the outcome remained unclear until more than 1,200 absentee ballots were counted two weeks later. In the end, Fitial won by 99 votes over Hofschneider. In simultaneous legislative balloting, no party won a majority in either house. In the Senate, the CP and the Republicans each held three seats, the Democrats, two, and one independent; in the House, the CP and the Republicans each won seven seats, followed by the Democrats and independents with two each.

In contrast, Republicans dominated the November 3, 2007, election for an expanded House, winning 12 of the 20 seats. The CP won 4; the Democrats, 1; and independents, 3. Of the 3 Senate seats up for election, a member of the CP, a Democrat running as an independent, and an independent each won.

In early 2009 former chief justice Jose S. DELA CRUZ predicted likely bankruptcy for the commonwealth if changes were not made in a land alienation rule that discourages foreign investment.

The assessment came in the wake of a sharp decline in tourism (expected to continue because of the exclusion of Chinese and Russians from the federal visa waiver process) and U.S. congressional approval of measures to federalize labor and immigration controls that would severely affect the status of "guest workers." The "federalization" transition was subsequently postponed at least until the end of 2014.

Governor Fitial was reelected to another five-year term in runoff balloting on November 23, 2009, in which Hofschneider, the Republican candidate, lost by 370 votes despite having narrowly led the first round. In December 2010 Fitial announced the planned merger of the CP and the Republican Party (his original party), but leaders of both parties objected, and the initiative was dropped. After Fitial rejoined the Republican Party in early 2012, he continued to face criticism in the CNMI House of Representatives from members of the CP and so-called Independent Republicans. The anti-Fitial bloc in September tabled a 16-count impeachment resolution accusing Fitial of corruption and neglect of duty in regard to, among other things, recent government contracts. The impeachment resolution was defeated by a 10–9 October House vote.

Twelve independents, four Republicans, and four CP members were elected to the House in balloting on November 6, 2012, while two independents and one Republican were elected in the partial Senate replenishment. Sixteen of the House members were described as anti-Fitial, and his opponents vowed to introduce another impeachment motion soon, although Fitial argued that they would be better off focusing on economic problems. Meanwhile, Gregorio SABLAN, an independent who caucuses with the Democrats, was reelected as the CNMI delegate to the U.S. House of Representatives with 80 percent of the vote. He pledged to ask the federal government to investigate possible corruption in the CNMI and endorsed proposed immigration reform that would permit foreign workers, many who have arrived without legal status, to remain in the Commonwealth under new visa protocols, as requested by business leaders and CNMI officials.

On February 11, 2013, the House impeached Fitial for charges of corruption and failure to perform duties. The governor resigned on February 20, before the impeachment proceedings were considered in the Senate, and lieutenant governor Eloy INOS took office. Inos was elected governor with a decisive victory in November 2014, and was succeeded by Ralph Torres upon his death on December 28, 2015. Sablan was reelected in November 2016.

Governor: Ralph TORRES.

Delegate to the U.S. House of Representatives: Gregorio SABLAN.

Pacific Remote Islands Marine National Monument:

Johnston Atoll. Encompassing Johnston, Sand, North, and East islands, Johnston Atoll lies about 700 miles southwest of Hawaii. The islands have a combined area of about 1.0 square mile (2.7 sq. km), most of which was engineered by dredging and filling. The population of Johnston Island was 1,387 (primarily government personnel) in 1994; the other islands are officially uninhabited. Annexed in 1858, the atoll was under the joint administration of the U.S. Defense and Interior departments after World War II and continues to be managed by the U.S. Air Force.

During 1990 a number of island governments, including those of American Samoa, the Marshall Islands, and the Northern Marianas, complained to the federal government of the incineration of dangerous chemicals (including nerve gas) and armaments on Johnston Island, arguing that there was a danger of the jet stream carrying pollutants not only to their shores but "around the world." Subsequently, during an October summit meeting with Pacific leaders in Hawaii, President George H. W. Bush indicated that the Defense Department would proceed with disposal of the materials already on the island but had no plans to continue the practice thereafter. In early 1999 the U.S. Army announced that its Johnston Island Atoll Chemical Disposal System (JACADS) would be closed. It was subsequently reported that the destruction of chemical weapons on Johnson had been completed in 2004, and the U.S. Environmental Protection Agency in 2009 certified that the facility had been properly cleaned and closed. (Since 1926 the U.S. Fish and Wildlife Service has been responsible for the area as a wildlife refuge, but it remains closed to the public.)

Palmyra Atoll. A group of about 50 islets situated on a horseshoe-shaped reef about 1,000 miles south of Honolulu, Palmyra became a U.S. territory upon the annexation of Hawaii in 1898. It was placed under civil administration of the Interior Department by the Hawaii Statehood Act of 1959. Privately owned by the Fullard-Leo family of Hawaii from 1922, the atoll, covering 4 square miles (10.44 sq. km), was occupied during World War II by the U.S. Navy, which built an airstrip subsequently used by the U.S. Air Force until 1961. In early 2000 the U.S.-based Nature Conservancy announced that it had launched a $37 million fund-raising campaign to buy the atoll, which is home to 20 bird species and has five times as many coral species as the Florida Keys. The sale, concluded in November 2000, led to the construction of a $1.5 million wildlife research station.

Wake Atoll. Consisting of three islets with a combined area of 3 square miles (7.8 sq. km) with no indigenous population, Wake Atoll lies roughly midway between Hawaii and Guam. It was formally claimed by the United States in 1900.

Although Wake falls under the jurisdiction of the Department of the Interior, activities have long been administered by the U.S. military. An air and naval station was established before World War II, during which Wake was occupied by Japanese forces. It is also the site of a U.S. Missile Defense Agency facility. In August 2006 the remaining military personnel, numbering fewer than 200, were evacuated in advance of one of the central Pacific's most powerful storms, Typhoon Ioke, which caused an estimated $88 million in damage on the island. Subsequently, upwards of 100 people, mainly civilian contractors, were engaged in restoring services. The airfield remains available for emergency landings by civilian as well as military aircraft.

Howland, Baker, and Jarvis Islands. Uninhabited, with a combined land area of about 3.8 square miles (9.84 sq. km), Howland, Baker, and Jarvis are widely scattered islands situated more than 1,300 miles south of Honolulu. Claimed by the United States in 1936, all three were designated national wildlife refuges in 1974, and in late 2007 the U.S. Fish and Wildlife Service announced the availability of a number of conservation plans for their management over the next 15 years.

In May 1999 President Teburoro Tito of Kiribati claimed that the three islands were geographically part of Kiribati and should come under its jurisdiction; there has been no indication, however, that Washington was prepared to consider the claim.

Kingman Reef. The uninhabited Kingman Reef, surrounding a lagoon 932 miles southwest of Honolulu, has no permanent land. It was annexed in 1922 and subsequently administered by the Department of the Navy. Characterized by the Scripps Institution of Oceanography in early 2008 as "one of the planet's most pristine coral reefs," Kingman has been a national wildlife refuge since 2001.

Other Insular Possessions:

Midway Islands. Consisting of Eastern and Sand islands (not to be confused with Johnston Atoll's Sand Island, above), the Midway Islands have a combined area of 2 square miles (5.2 sq. km). Located at the northwestern end of the Hawaiian chain, the Midway Islands were annexed in 1867 and are best known as the site of a major U.S. naval victory against Japan in 1942. Administered by the Department of the Navy until 1996, Midway was then taken over by the Department of the Interior. The largely military population of about 2,500 (1994) was withdrawn.

On June 15, 2006, President George W. Bush turned a 200,000 square mile tract of ocean including the Midway Islands into the world's largest marine sanctuary, the Northwestern Hawaiian Islands Marine National Monument. Renamed the Papahanaumokuakea Marine National Monument in March 2007, it is home to approximately 7,000 wildlife species, a number of which are endangered by plastic debris and lead paint flakes from former military buildings, prompting extensive cleanup operations scheduled for completion by 2017.

Navassa. Situated between Jamaica and Haiti and claimed by the United States in 1916, Navassa is a small island of 2 square miles (5 sq. km) that served as the site of a lighthouse maintained by the U.S. Coast Guard until 1996. In July 1981 six U.S. Marines were temporarily deployed on Navassa to thwart a semi-official attempt by Haitians to lay claim to the island. The island is currently administered by the Department of the Interior.

URUGUAY

Oriental Republic of Uruguay
República Oriental del Uruguay

Political Status: Independent state proclaimed in 1825; republic established in 1830; presidential-congressional system reinstated on March 1, 1985, supplanting military-controlled civilian government in power since February 1973.

Area: 68,037 sq. mi. (176,215 sq. km).

Population: 3,444,000 (2016E—UN); 3,351,016 (2016E—U.S. Census).

Major Urban Center (2016E—UN): MONTEVIDEO (1,716,000, urban area).

Official Language: Spanish.

Monetary Unit: Uruguayan Peso (market rate October 1, 2016: 28.47 pesos = $1US).

President: Tabaré Ramón VÁZQUEZ Rosas (Progressive Encounter–Broad Front); elected in run-off balloting on November 30, 2014, and inaugurated on March 1, 2015, for a five-year term, succeeding José Alberto MUJICA Cordano (Progressive Encounter–Broad Front); named a new government on March 1, 2015.

Vice President: Raúl Fernando SENDIC Rodríguez (Progressive Encounter–Broad Front); elected on November 30, 2014, and inaugurated on March 1, 2015, for a term concurrent with that of the president, succeeding Danilo ASTORI (Progressive Encounter–Broad Front).

THE COUNTRY

Second smallest of South American countries, Uruguay has historically been among the best performers in terms of education, per capita income, and social welfare. Its official designation as the Oriental (Eastern) Republic of Uruguay derives from its position on the eastern bank of the Uruguay River, which forms its frontier with Argentina and opens into the great estuary of the Rio de la Plata, on which both Montevideo and the Argentine capital of Buenos Aires are situated. From its 120-mile Atlantic coastline, Uruguay's rolling grasslands gently climb to the Brazilian boundary in the northeast. More than half of the population, which is almost entirely of Spanish and Italian origins, is concentrated in Montevideo, the only large city. While Uruguay was once a popular destination for immigrants, the flow of people has reversed. An estimated one-fifth of the population lives abroad, mostly in Europe or the United States. According to the World Bank, 56 percent of women are in the labor force. Currently, 16 women serve in the legislature (16.2 percent of the total seats).

Although cattle-raising and sheep-raising were the traditional basis of the economy, crop farming has increased in recent years, and a sizable industrial complex (primarily food processing) has developed around the capital. Textiles, meat, wool, and leather goods are currently the leading exports, while industrial promotion and foreign investment laws instituted in the early 1980s encouraged production of electrical equipment and minerals.

Gross domestic product (GDP) growth averaged 3.2 percent annually throughout the 1990s but the economy entered a protracted recession from 1999 through 2002, contracting by 3.9 percent annually through the period. Economic recovery and a resumption of growth led to a significant expansion of 5.7 percent annually from 2003 to 2008. GDP fell to 2.4 percent in 2009, though overall, the country was among the few able to avoid a recession during the global economic downturn, according to the International Monetary Fund (IMF), due to recent financial system reforms, robust growth in exports, and lower poverty rates. High GDP growth of 8.9 percent in 2010 slowed to 5.7 percent in 2011 and fell further in 2012 to 3.8 percent, a decline reflecting weaker external demand, which the IMF nonetheless praised as a "sustainable pace." Growth of 4.4 percent in 2013 gave way to 3.3 percent in 2014, when inflation was 8.9 percent and unemployment 6.5 percent. GDP expanded by 2.8 percent in 2015 and 2.9 percent the following year. In 2016 inflation rose by 7.5 percent, while unemployment was 7 percent and GDP per capita was $17,340. The World Bank ranked Uruguay 92nd out of 189 countries in its 2016 survey on the ease of conducting business, far behind other regional states such as Chile (48th) or Peru (50th), but ahead of Paraguay (100th) and Brazil (116th).

GOVERNMENT AND POLITICS

Political background. Before the 20th century Uruguay's history was largely determined by the buffer-like position that made it an object of contention between the colonial powers Spain and Portugal and, later, between Argentina and Brazil. Uruguay proclaimed its independence in 1825 and was recognized by its two neighboring countries in 1828, but both continued to play a role in the internal struggles of Uruguay's Colorado and Blanco parties following the proclamation of a republic in 1830. The foundations of modern Uruguay were laid during the presidency of José BATLLE y Ordóñez, who took office under the Colorado banner in 1903 and initiated the extensive welfare program and governmental participation in the economy for which the nation was subsequently noted. Batlle y Ordóñez and the Colorado Party were also identified with a method of government characterized by a presidential board, or council, employed from 1917 to 1933 and again from 1951 to 1967. The Colorados, who had controlled the government continuously from 1865, were finally ousted in the election of 1958 but were returned to power in 1966, when voters also approved a constitutional amendment returning the country to a one-person presidency.

The first of the presidents under the new arrangement, Oscar Diego GESTIDO (Colorado), took office in March 1967 but died nine months later and was succeeded by Vice President Jorge PACHECO Areco (Colorado). Faced with a growing economic crisis, rising unrest among workers and students, and increasing activity by *Tupamaro* guerrillas, both presidents sought to enforce economic austerity and resorted to emergency security measures. Economic and political instability continued after the election of Juan María BORDABERRY Arocena (Colorado) in November 1971, and worsening circumstances culminated in military intervention on February 8, 1973. Under the direction of Gen. César Augusto MARTÍNEZ, José PÉREZ Caldas, and Esteban CRISTI, the military presented a 19-point program that emphasized economic reform, reducing corruption by officials, and greater military participation in political life. President Bordaberry accepted the program on February 13, with governmental reorganization commencing almost immediately. A National Security Council was created to oversee the administration, Congress was dissolved and replaced by a Council of State, and municipal and local councils were supplanted by appointed bodies. Opposition to the increasing influence of the military was met by coercion: a general strike by the National Confederation of Workers (*Confederación Nacional de Trabajadores*—CNT) resulted in the group's proscription, while several opposition political leaders were placed in temporary detention during July and August. The National University of Montevideo was closed in October, and the Communist-led *Frente Amplio,* in addition to numerous minor leftist groups, was banned in December. Subsequently, as many as 400,000 Uruguayans were reported to have fled the country.

In early 1976 President Bordaberry, whose constitutional term was due to expire, butted heads with the military because he wished to remain indefinitely in office as head of a corporativist state within which normal political activity would be prohibited. The military, on the other hand, preferred a Brazilian-style "limited democracy," with the traditional parties gradually reentering the political process over the ensuing decade. On June 12 the military view prevailed: Bordaberry was deposed, and Vice President Alberto DEMICHELLI was named as his interim successor. On July 14 a newly constituted Council of the Nation (incorporating the Council of State, the three heads of the armed services, and other high-ranking officers) designated Dr. Aparicio MÉNDEZ Manfredini as president for a five-year term commencing September 1.

In August 1977 the government announced that President Méndez had accepted a recommendation by the military leadership that a general election be held in 1981, although only the Colorado and National (Blanco) parties would be permitted to participate. Subsequently, it was reported that a new constitution would be promulgated in 1980, while all parties would be permitted to resume their normal functions by 1986.

The proposed basic law, which would have given the military effective veto power within a context of "restricted democracy," was rejected by more than 57 percent of those participating in a referendum held November 30, 1980. The government promptly accepted the decision while announcing that efforts toward "democratic institutionalization" would continue "on the basis of the current regime."

Following designation by the Council of the Nation, the recently retired army commander, Lt. Gen. Gregorio Conrado ALVAREZ Armellino, assumed office on September 1, 1981, as "transition" president for a term scheduled to end upon reversion to civilian rule in March 1985. Fourteen months later, on November 28, 1982, a nationwide election was held to select delegates to conventions of three legally recognized groups, the Colorado and Blanco parties and the Civic Union, whose leaders were to participate in the drafting of a constitution to be presented to the voters in November 1984. The balloting, in which antimilitary candidates outpolled their promilitary counterparts within each party by almost five to one, was followed by a series of talks between the regime and the parties, which broke down in July 1983 over the extent of military power under the new basic law. The impasse yielded a period of instability through mid-1984, with escalating public protests (including Chilean-style "banging of the pots"), increased press censorship, and arrests of dissidents (most prominently the respected Blanco leader, Wilson FERREIRA Aldunate, upon his return from exile on June 16). Government statements that adherence to the declared electoral timetable (which called for balloting on November 25) would be "conditional" upon the cooperation of the civilian parties yielded further protests, while deteriorating economic conditions prompted a series of work stoppages.

After talks resumed in July 1984 between the army and a multiparty grouping (*Multipartidaria*) consisting of the legal parties (excluding the Blancos, who had quit the group in protest at the imprisonment of their leader) and a number of formations that were still nominally illegal, an agreement was reached on August 3 confirming the November 25 election date and establishing a transitional advisory role for the military until late 1985. The signing of the pact was followed by a relaxation of press censorship and the legalization of a number of additional parties that, in concert with the Communist Party of Uruguay (*Partido Comunista*—PCU), which remained outlawed at the time, reactivated the 1971 Broad Front (*Frente Amplio*—FA) coalition (see Political Parties, below).

Despite the Blanco Party's condemnation of the August 1984 agreement as an "acceptance of dictatorship," the party rejoined the *Multipartidaria* after the group had initiated talks with business and union leaders on a peaceful transition to civilian rule. However, because of the continued proscription of both the Blanco leader and *Frente Amplio*'s Gen. Liber SEREGNI, the Colorado candidate, Julio María SANGUINETTI Cairolo, enjoyed a considerable advantage in the presidential race, gaining a 38.6 percent vote share at the November balloting while his party won a slim plurality in both houses. The new Congress convened on February 15, 1985, followed by Sanguinetti's inauguration on March 1. To avoid public embarrassment at the swearing-in ceremony (the president-elect having indicated an aversion to accepting the presidential sash from a military ruler), President Alvarez had resigned on February 12, Supreme Court President Rafael ADDIEGO Bruno being named his interim replacement. In further attempts to remove the legacy of the military regime, the Sanguinetti government, with broad support from the public and opposition parties, released all political prisoners, including former *Tupamaro* guerrillas, and permitted the return of an estimated 20,000 exiles. Subsequently, a 1986 decision to declare an amnesty for military members charged with human rights abuses generated strong dissent, although Uruguayan voters failed to reverse the action in a referendum conducted in April 1989.

While the Blanco right-wing candidate, Luis Alberto LACALLE Herrera, won the presidency in November 1989, the party's inability to win more than a plurality of legislative seats necessitated the formation of a National Agreement (*Coincidencia Nacional*) with the Colorados under which the latter were assigned four portfolios (later three) in the government that took office on March 1, 1990. Lacalle terminated the de facto coalition in the course of a cabinet reshuffle in January 1993, albeit with two right-wing Colorados being retained until mid-May 1994.

The election of November 27, 1994, returned Sanguinetti Cairolo to the presidency, but in the legislature the vote share was split nearly three ways by the Colorado, Blanco, and recently launched Progressive Encounter (*Encuentro Progresista*—EP) groupings. Earlier, in a plebiscite conducted on August 28, a number of reforms that had been expected to pass easily (including a measure that would have sanctioned "ticket-splitting") were overwhelmingly rejected. Given the Colorados's narrow legislative plurality, President Sanguinetti emulated his predecessor in organizing a coalition government with 6 of 13 cabinet posts awarded to members of three other parties: 4 from the Blancos and 1 each from two nonlegislative groups, the Civic Union (*Unión Cívica*—UC) and the People's Government Party (*Partido por el Gobierno del Pueblo*—PGP) (see Political Parties, below).

In the election of October 31, 1999, the left-wing Progressive Encounter–Broad Front (EP-FA) captured pluralities in both legislative chambers. In a presidential runoff on November 28, however, the EP-FA candidate, Tabaré Ramón VÁZQUEZ Rosas, saw his first-round lead of 38.5 percent overcome by the Colorado candidate, Jorge BATLLE Ibáñez, who had also received Blanco's backing following the third-place finish of Lacalle Herrera in the initial balloting. Installed as Sanguinetti's successor on March 1, 2000, President Batlle named a coalition cabinet of Colorados and Blancos.

In late October 2002, with Uruguay in the throes of a serious economic crisis, the five Blanco ministers announced their intention to resign, and on November 3 a party convention supported the decision, although the Blancos, despite some dissent, indicated that they would continue to work with the government in the legislature.

In presidential balloting on October 31, 2004, the EP-FA's Tabaré Vázquez Rosas secured 51.7 percent of the vote to become the first left-wing chief executive in Uruguay's history. The Blanco's Jorge LARRAÑAGA was a distant second with 35 percent of the vote; 6 other challengers garnered no more than 11 percent each. In the concurrent parliamentary election, the EP-FA won 53 of the 99 seats in the Chamber of Representatives and 17 of 30 seats in the senate, ending 170 years of control by the Blanco and Colorado parties. In a constitutional referendum the same day, 62.8 percent of voters approved an amendment providing for public ownership of the water supply and sanitation services, the provision describing them as "fundamental human rights."

President Vázquez was inaugurated on March 1, 2005, and appointed the country's first leftist cabinet on March 2.

Former president Bordaberry was arrested in 2006 in connection with the assassination of two lawmakers in Buenos Aires, after a judge ruled that alleged killings outside Uruguay were not covered under the country's amnesty laws. Due to ill health, Bordaberry was allowed to serve his prison term under house arrest. In 2008 Bordaberry was charged in connections with the murder of two opposition members and the disappearance of nine others.

The cabinet was reshuffled on March 1, 2008, when President Vázquez replaced six ministers in advance of the 2009 presidential elections. Ministers with leading roles in political parties were removed to ensure that government work was not interrupted by party activities.

In the run-up to the 2009 general election, a rift developed in the governing coalition as President Vázquez denounced an EP-FA dissenter's attempt to seek a constitutional amendment to allow presidential reelection. (For more information, see the 2011 *Handbook.*) Vázquez, who said he would not seek reelection, supported Danilo ASTORI, his former finance minister from the more conservative wing of the coalition in the primaries. The nomination went to the EP-FA's José Alberto MUJICA Cordano, a former National Liberation Movement *(Movimiento de Liberación Nacional*—MLN) guerilla leader who had spent 14 years in prison. In recent years, Mujica, an MPP (Movement of Popular Participation, below) senator, adopted the moderate policies of the coalition. Subsequently, Astori agreed to be Mujica's running mate. Mujica's main challengers were former president Luis Alberto Lacalle of Blanco and Pedro Bordaberry, son of the former president, of the Colorado party. In parliamentary balloting on October 25, the EP-FA retained its majority in both houses. Two measures in concurrent referenda failed; one would have repealed a general amnesty for military and law enforcement officials involved in human rights abuses during the dictatorship between 1973 and 1985. A week ahead of the election the Supreme Court voted unanimously in ruling the amnesty law unconstitutional. The referendum, which 47 percent of voters approved, would have annulled the law that was confirmed in a 1989 plebiscite. The other measure defeated in 2009 was one that would have allowed absentee ballots.

Neither Mujica nor Lacalle won a majority in first-round balloting on October 25, 2009, forcing a runoff on November 29, in which Mujica secured 52.4 percent of the vote to Lacalle's 43.5 percent. Though voting is compulsory in Uruguay, turnout of only 89 percent was recorded.

On February 10, 2010, the Supreme Court sentenced former president Bordaberry to 30 years in prison for his role in the 1973 military coup.

When members of the new parliament took their seats on February 15, 2010, it marked the first time in Uruguay's history that both chambers were presided over by women (only temporarily, since control of the senate was handed over to Vice President Astori upon his March 1 inauguration). President Mujica, pledging to maintain the moderate-left ideology of the preceding administration, was inaugurated on March 1, 2010, and named a new government on March 2 that included four members of the MPP.

In what Vice President Astori deemed a "wake-up call" for the EP-FA, the Blanco Party dominated the May 9, 2010, municipal elections, winning 12 of 19 departments. In August 2010, the navy commander resigned after his nephew was indicted in a corruption scandal that involved selling military procurements for personal gain. The government announced in early 2011 that it would move 1,000 soldiers into the ranks of the national police to bolster public security efforts; this move was prompted by public perception that the country had grown more dangerous.

Former president Vázquez led the EP-FA ticket for the October 2014 presidential elections, contending against the Colorado Party's Pedro Bordaberry and the Blanco's Luis LACALLE POU, the son of the former president. Vázquez won 49.5 percent of the vote in the first round of balloting on October 26, followed by Lacalle Pou, with 31.9 percent, and five other candidates. Vázquez and Lacalle Pou advanced to runoff polling on November 30, which the former president won with 56.6 percent of the vote. The EP-FA secured a majority in the chamber with 50 seats, while it won 15 seats in the Senate. Vázquez named a mostly new government on March 1, 2016, retaining four ministers from the previous cabinet.

Constitution and government. The present governmental structure is modeled after that of the 1967 constitution. Executive power is vested in the president who appoints the cabinet, while legislative authority is lodged in a bicameral General Assembly. Both the president and the legislature were elected, before 1996, through a complex system of electoral lists that allowed political parties to present multiple candidates, with the leading candidates within each of the leading lists being declared the victors. However, on December 8, 1996, voters narrowly approved a constitutional amendment that provided for internal party elections for presidential candidates. Under the change, a runoff between the two leading candidates is required if one does not win 40 percent of the vote with a 10 percent lead over the runner-up. The judicial system includes justices of the peace, courts of first instance, courts of appeal, and a Supreme Court. Subnationally Uruguay is divided into 19 departments, which were returned to administration by elected officials in November 1984.

In accordance with "Institutional Act No. 19" (the August 1984 agreement between the Alvarez regime and the *Multipartidaria*), the army, navy, and air force commanders participate in an advisory National Security Council (*Consejo Nacional de Seguridad*), which also includes the president, the vice president, and the defense, foreign, and interior ministers. The council's actions are subject to the approval of the General Assembly. Other provisions of the act require the president to appoint military commanders from a list presented by the armed forces, limit the scope of military justice to crimes committed by members of the armed forces, and preclude the declaration of a state of siege without congressional approval.

Freedom of expression is constitutionally guaranteed, and there are few violations of press freedom. In the 2016 Press Freedom Index, Reporters Without Borders ranked Uruguay 20th of 180 countries.

On October 31, 2004, a constitutional amendment, approved in a national referendum, provided for public ownership of the water supply and sanitation services, describing them as "fundamental human rights."

Foreign relations. A member of the United Nations, the Organization of American States (OAS), the Latin American Free Trade Association, Mercosur, and other Western Hemisphere organizations, Uruguay has been a consistent supporter of international and inter-American cooperation and of nonintervention in the affairs of other countries. Not surprisingly, the former military government maintained particularly cordial relations with neighboring rightist regimes, while vehemently denying accusations of human rights violations by a number of international bodies. As a result, military and economic aid was substantially reduced under U.S. president Jimmy Carter. Although marginal increases were permitted during the Ronald Reagan's first administration, a campaign led by the exiled Ferreira Aldunate tended to isolate the Méndez and Alvarez regimes internationally, while the January 1984 accession of Raúl Alfonsín in Argentina substantially inhibited relations with Buenos Aires.

Before his initial assumption of office, President Sanguinetti met with Alfonsín and other regional leaders. His inauguration, attended by 500 representatives of more than 70 countries, featured a carefully staged but largely unproductive meeting between U.S. Secretary of State George Shultz and Nicaraguan President Daniel Ortega. Diplomatic relations with Cuba, broken in 1974 at the request of the OAS, were restored in late 1985, while in an effort to stimulate economic revitalization, trade accords were negotiated with Argentina, Brazil, Mexico, Paraguay, and the Soviet Union. During a 1988 regional summit with Presidents Alfonsín of Argentina and Sarney of Brazil, President Sanguinetti pledged his government's accession to protocols of economic integration adopted by the neighboring states in December 1986; after reaffirmation of the pledge in November 1989, on May 22, 1991, the Uruguayan senate unanimously approved entry into what had become known as the Southern Cone Common Market (*Mercado Común del Cono Sur*—Mercosur). By early 2000, however, Uruguay had joined Paraguay in complaining of "creeping bilateralization" of Mercosur decision-making, with the smaller partners being pressured to accept agreements reached between Argentina and Brazil. As a result, a number of concessions were made for the minor participants.

Relations with Argentina have been strained since early 2006 because of the construction of two pulp mills by Spanish and Finnish firms in Uruguay across the Uruguay River from Gualeguaychú, Argentina. In July the International Court of Justice (ICJ) rejected Argentina's request to suspend construction. Meanwhile, President Vázquez filed a complaint to the ICJ over roadblocks erected by Argentinian environmental protesters to block tourists bound for Uruguay's coast. The Spanish company abandoned its plan to build on the Uruguay River, instead building on the River Plate. The Finnish mill was completed in 2007. Movement toward concessions in 2007 was disrupted when in early 2008 Argentine environmentalists, supported by the Entre Rios provincial government, pledged biweekly traffic blocks. Tensions eased in July when the Argentine and Uruguayan foreign ministers agreed to establish a binational commission to study the environmental impact, but protests continued. Consequently, Uruguay vetoed the nomination of former Argentine president Nestor Kirchner as president of the Union of South American Nations (UNASUR).

In 2009, as part of a move to demonstrate close relations, Uruguay provided vital support to Venezuela in its efforts to launch its first satellite in cooperation with the Chinese government. In August, Uruguay, along with six other South American nations, contributed to the founding of *Banco del Sur* (Bank of the South), a development bank intended to rival the power of U.S. banks in the region.

On April 20, 2010, the ICJ handed down a final ruling on the paper-mill dispute between Argentina and Uruguay, ruling that Uruguay had breached its procedural obligations but not its substantive obligations under a previous treaty signed by the two countries. An Argentine federal tribunal ruled in June that the roadblock would be lifted. In July the two countries agreed to joint environmental monitoring for the mills and in November signed a technical agreement that guaranteed joint supervision and monitoring of environmental and water quality of the river by the two countries' scientists.

At a meeting of Mercosur heads of state in December 2010, member countries signed agreements to standardize national policies on trade, immigration, and investment.

Brazil's president, Dilma Rousseff, visited Uruguay on an official state visit in May 2011. Rousseff signaled that Brazil would move to enroll Uruguay as a strategic partner. The two sides also signed eight accords that spelled out deepening connections in exchanging energy and technology as well as bilateral efforts to improve education and health care. In August Mujica signed more bilateral treaties with his Argentine counterpart, Cristina Fernández, demonstrating the warming relations between the two countries, and a transnational passenger rail line that had been out of service for three decades was restarted.

In September 2011 Uruguay announced plans to open an embassy in Hanoi, Vietnam. Uruguay also sought deeper bilateral relations with Iran and China. Signifying a radical shift in Uruguay's financial standing over the past decade, the head of the Central Bank's Economic Advisory said in November that Uruguay had become a net creditor to the IMF.

In December 2011 Uruguay sponsored a proposal to ban vessels under the flag of the Falkland Islands from docking in ports of Mercosur countries, signifying Mujica's commitment to regional diplomatic solidarity. The measure was adopted as the debate between Argentina and the United Kingdom over the long-disputed territory resurfaced. The ban chiefly affects fishing vessels from the Falklands, though it also inconveniences British ships bound for the islands that stop off in the port of Montevideo. Several Spanish shipping associations took issue with the ban as their vessels are under the Falklands flag.

Relations with Argentina inflamed in April 2013 when Mujica, accidentally speaking in front of a live microphone, insulted Argentine president Fernández, calling her worse than her predecessor and late husband.

Inaction within Mercosur relating to the June 2012 suspension of Paraguay led Uruguayan leaders to seek independent bilateral trade relations. In May Mujica visited China to strengthen ties, and in June Vice President Astori moved to create links, in hopes of eventual integration, with the Pacific Alliance trade bloc (including Mexico, Colombia, Chile, and Peru).

On March 20, 2014, President Mujica announced that he had agreed to accept six prisoners from Guantánamo Bay detention camp for "human rights reasons." He said they would be treated as refugees and would be welcome to work and live with their families.

Argentina's attempts to lower its own trade deficit contributed to worsening relations with Uruguay. After banning its exporters from using Uruguayan ports because Uruguay was not compliant with Mercosur shipping accords in November 2013, Argentinian import barriers became stricter in the first part of 2014, causing Uruguayan exports to Argentina to fall by 14.6 percent compared to the previous year and sparking concerns about implications for Uruguay's economy. In July Mujica said that Mercosur was "not working," because of competing visions of how the trade bloc should function.

In December 2015 Uruguay and Brazil finalized a free trade agreement on automobiles. During a 12-day trade mission to China in October 2016, Vázquez announced that the two countries would begin negotiations on a free trade agreement.

Current issues. The EP-FA moved to dismantle the amnesty law in 2011. The effort received more fuel with a second Supreme Court decision ruling the law unconstitutional in November 2010 and a trial in the Inter-American Court of Human Rights (IACHR) on charges brought by María Macarena GELMAN García against Uruguay for the death of her mother, dissident María Claudia García Iruretagoyena de Gelman. The IACHR ruled in March that the government of Uruguay should open an investigation into the deaths of the plaintiff's mother and pay her $180,000 as compensation. In April the senate narrowly voted (by 16–15) to repeal several articles of the amnesty law. Opposition legislators slammed the vote as having no respect for the will of the people as embodied in the two previous referenda votes. Mujica opposed the annulment of the law—which the more left-wing constituents of his coalition favored on the grounds that the choice of the country had already been made in the referenda—while simultaneously saying that he would not veto it if it passed through the legislature. However after 14 hours of debate in May, those in favor of repealing the law were unable to secure a majority, and it continued to remain in effect.

Concerned with the concentration of rural land among few owners, Mujica pushed for high taxes on large landowners in 2011. Despite a rift with Vice President Astori, who believed the tax should be based instead on farm profitability, the measure passed in November. In February 2013 the Supreme Court struck down the tax as unconstitutional and redundant, prompting the administration to introduce a revised version of the law in April.

In a May 2012 interview with an Argentinean newspaper, Uruguay's first lady, Senator Lucía TOPOLANKSY, called for the military to be "loyal" to the ruling FA coalition, sparking friction between the armed forces and the administration. The administration's uneasy relationship with the military branch was aggravated later in the month when the commander of the navy resigned, at Mujica's urging, over his links to the 2010 corruption scandal that prompted his predecessor's departure.

Mujica unveiled a controversial new security plan in June 2012 calling for the "regulated and controlled legalization of marijuana." The proposal suggests combating drug-related violence by creating a state-run industry in which the government controls the importation, production, sale, and distribution of the drug. Other regional leaders have discussed legalization as a method of tackling narcotics-related violence throughout Central and South America, but the United States strongly opposes the strategy. The bill was introduced to the Chamber of Representatives in November 2012 and, after 13 hours of debate, was approved in July 2013 with the support of all 50 FA members in the 96-member body. The measure, expected to pass the Senate, prompted a warning from the International Narcotics Control Board that the law would "be in complete contravention to the provisions of the international drug treaties to which Uruguay is party."

In October 2012 the Senate approved a FA-supported bill to legalize abortion, 17–14, after it was approved 50–49 in the lower house in September. The Blanco and Colorado Parties opposed the bill. Several lawmakers on both sides of the debate allowed substitutes to vote in their places because they were unwilling to support their party line. Antiabortionists called for a referendum; however, in consultation balloting in June 2013, the measure received support of 9 percent of the electorate, short of the 25 percent needed to authorize a referendum.

The lower house approved a bill legalizing the cultivation, distribution, and consumption of marijuana in August 2013. It was approved by the Senate on December 11 and signed into law by Mujica on December 24. The unprecedented legalization of marijuana drew heavy criticism from abroad, including from the United Nations Office on Drugs and Crime. In May 2014 Mujica signed legislation establishing a market for legal marijuana and setting regulations for its cultivation and sale. Two months later, the president announced that "practical difficulties" would delay the start of legal sales until 2015.

Voters defeated a constitutional amendment to lower the age of criminal responsibility from 18 to 16 on October 26, 2014, with 53.2 percent opposed and 46.8 percent in favor (see the Colorado Party, below).

In July 2016 the government announced that pharmacies would be able to sell marijuana, but only 50 out of the 1,200 eligible facilities actually registered to offer the drug. Instead reports indicated that many pharmacists asserted that the sale of marijuana was medically "irresponsible," while others were afraid of increased robberies.

POLITICAL PARTIES

In 2004 the leftists, for the first time, won majorities in both the presidential and congressional balloting. Their representation remained virtually unchanged after the 2014 elections.

Presidential Coalition:

Progressive Encounter–Broad Front (*Encuentro Progresista–Frente Amplio*—EP-FA). Encompassing a number of left-wing groups, plus a group of Blanco dissidents, the EP was launched before the 1994 election. While running third in the November poll, the alliance was only marginally eclipsed by the second-place Blancos, thus effectively terminating Uruguay's traditional two-party system. Tabaré Vázquez, the popular former mayor of Montevideo who had been the EAP standard-bearer in 1994, easily won the EP's 1999 presidential nomination, securing 82 percent of the votes in the April primary. Although winning a plurality of 38.5 percent in October 1999, he was defeated in second-round balloting by Colorado-Blanco nominee Jorge Batlle Ibáñez. However, in 2004 Vázquez won the presidency with slightly more than 50 percent of the first-round vote.

Originally a Communist-led formation of 11 members that included the Uruguayan Socialist Party (*Partido Socialista del Uruguay*—PSU), Christian Democratic Party (*Partido Demócrata Cristiano*—PDC), and Oriental Revolutionary Movement (*Movimiento Revolucionario Oriental*—MRO), the FA contested the 1971 election but was subsequently proscribed by the military regime. Its presidential candidate, retired general Líber Seregni, was imprisoned and stripped of his military rank. Seregni was released in March 1984 but was banned from political activity. In the 1984 balloting, Front candidate Juan CROTTOGINI won 20.4 percent of the vote, while the coalition won 21 Chamber seats (almost as many as the Blancos) and 6 senate seats with the new support of some Colorado and Blanco dissenters. In early 1985 a split developed between the group's Marxist and social democratic legislators over the degree of support to be given to the Sanguinetti administration, although in May the president, in a gesture to the Front, decreed that Seregni's military rank be restored. Subsequently a noncommunist "Lista 99" faction joined with elements of the PDC and PSU in a "Triple Alliance" that contested elections in student and labor organizations, winning the leadership of the leading student federation in July.

Throughout 1986 the Front was solidly opposed to the military amnesty program, joining the call for a plebiscite to decide the issue, although it initially rejected a membership bid by the like-minded MLN (see under MPP, below). Meanwhile the **"Lista 99"** group became increasingly identified as the **People's Government Party** (PGP), which, before the 1989 balloting, joined the PDC and Civic Union in a coalition styled the New Space (*Nuevo Espacio*) (below), with the MLN subsequently becoming a Front member.

By 1992 the Socialists had displaced the long-dominant Communists as the leading component of the Front, but the Socialists failed to control the group's plenum, with the highly popular mayor of Montevideo, Vázquez, threatening in late 1993 to withdraw from the 1994 presidential race if internal party elections were not held; however, in March 1994 Vázquez was proclaimed the group's standard-bearer for the presidential campaign.

On February 5, 1996, Seregni resigned as FA president because of irreconcilable differences over electoral reform (primarily in regard to Seregni's willingness to endorse second-round presidential balloting in return for abolition of the *ley de lemas*). In late 1996, following the interim leadership of a 12-member executive, Tabaré Vázquez was elected Seregni's successor; however, he resigned in September 1997 because of opposition to his support of the privatization of a Montevideo hotel complex. Seregni died on July 31, 2004.

At the time of the 2004 election, the EP-FA (sometimes referenced as EP-FA-NM [*Nueva Mayoría*]) encompassed the groups listed below. The New Space Party (*Nuevo Espacio*) joined the EP-FA following the election, and the 26th of March Movement (*Movimiento 26 de Marzo*—M26M) withdrew in mid-2008. Despite President Vázquez's endorsement of Danilo Astori in the 2009 primary elections the party's nomination was won by former MLN rebel leader and senator José Mujica, who was supported by the party's former guerrilla and communist factions. Mujica earned the endorsement of Argentine president Cristina Fernández. Argentine Peronism movement leaders also campaigned for Mujica, who won the presidency in second-round balloting on November 29, 2009.

The coalition began to strain before May 2010 regional elections, when several of the parties vied for seats in races across the country; the Communist Party of Uruguay (*Partido Comunista*—PCU), PSU, and MPP fought for the mayorship of Montevideo, which the EP-FA ultimately won. In some races support for the coalition declined by as much as 10 percent compared to previous years.

Former president Vázquez of the PSU and coalition leaders signaled in early 2011 that he would be the EP-FA's presidential candidate in 2014. The coalition faced questions about its future election prospects after it went ahead with a plan to repeal the country's long-standing military amnesty law, even though the electorate had twice voted in referenda to keep the law. Using a large sum of political capital in early 2011, the legislative leaders enforced coalition discipline to get the repeal measures passed through the lower house and did the same in the senate, though the bills failed in the upper chamber. The leader of the coalition's Current Thought-Action and Freedom (CAP-L), Eleuterio FERNÁNDEZ Huidobro, resigned his senate seat in protest against the coalition's push to repeal the amnesty law in 2011. He was replaced by an EP-FA alternate but was appointed by Mujica in July to become Uruguay's defense minister.

By July 2011 Mujica appeared to be indecisive. The PCU voiced anger over the lack of pressure from the president to move on redistributing wealth to deal with Uruguay's income gap, while the more centrist Liber Seregni Front (FLS, below) and PSU pushed for policies to preserve economic stability. In August elements of the coalition, including Mujica's MPP, were working on introducing legislation that would limit foreign ownership of Uruguayan land, a quarter of which was found to be in the hands of interests from abroad in 2011. Mónica XAVIER of the PSU emerged victorious in a four-way contest for the FA presidency in May 2012. Land reform policy continued to be divisive within the coalition, with Vice President Astori heading the moderate FA faction that opposed Mujica's land tax. Renewed divisions emerged in early 2013 when Astori described inflation as the country's greatest challenge, a claim immediately dismissed by Mujica. In February Mujica announced that he would not modify his socially progressive economic policies despite internal tensions.

Former president Vázquez confirmed his candidacy in August 2013 for the 2014 presidential election. In a primarily election held on June 1, 2014, Vázquez defeated Senator Constanza MOREIRA for the FA nomination, winning 83.5 percent of the vote. He selected Raúl Fernando SENDIC Rodríguez as his running mate, widely seen as a symbol of renewal within the party. Vázquez won the 2014 election in runoff balloting, while the party secured 50 seats in the chamber and 15 in the Senate.

Leaders: Tabaré Ramón VÁZQUEZ Rosas (President of the Republic); José Alberto MUJICA Cordano (Former President of the Republic); Mónica XAVIER (President of the Coalition); Ivonne PASSADA, Rafael MICHELINI, and Juan CASTILLO (Vice Presidents).

Liber Seregni Front (*Frente Liber Seregni*—FLS). The center-left coalition, named after the FA founder, the FLS was founded in August 2009 ahead of the October general elections by vice-presidential candidate Danilo Astori of the Uruguayan Assembly (Asamblea Uruguay—AU), as well as the leaders of New Space (*Nuevo Espacio*—NE) and the Progressive Alliance (*Alianza Progresista*—AP). As moderates in the coalition, the FLS in 2011 pushed the EP-FA to adopt strategies that would bolster economic stability and investment in education and infrastructure. In July 2012 Astori clashed with Mujica over their positions on the admittance of Venezuela to Mercosur. Astori nominated FA president member Mónica Xavier to be Vázquez's running mate in June 2014, but she was not selected. In the 2014 senate elections, the FLS won three of the coalition's seats.

Leader: Danilo ASTORI (Vice President of the Republic and Party Leader).

New Space (*Nuevo Espacio*—NE). The NE was founded following a struggle within the *Frente Amplio* nominees for the 1989 presidential balloting. The Marxist wing wished to renominate General Seregni as the coalition's sole candidate, while social democrats within the party supported PGP leader Hugo BATALLA, or, alternatively, both contenders under an electoral law provision permitting multiple nominees. The PGP and PDC withdrew from the *Frente Amplio* in March 1989, subsequently joining the Civic Union in launching *Nuevo Espacio* as a tripartite formation with Batalla as its standard-bearer.

Prior to the 1994 balloting, the PGP's Batalla agreed to campaign as a vice-presidential contender on a ticket with Sanguinetti, the Colorados' presidential candidate. The PDC joined the Progressive Encounter, and the Civic Union withdrew to campaign separately, with a rump group of PGP members remaining within a reorganized *Nuevo Espacio,* which came fourth in the presidential race. After the 2004 election the party decided to join the EP-FA and was accepted in November 2005. It joined the FLS in 2009.

Leaders: Rafael MICHELINI (President), Jorge POZZI (Deputy), Héctor PÉREZ Piera (Former President).

Uruguayan Assembly (Asamblea Uruguay—AU), Founded in 1994 by then senator Danilo Astori, the social democratic AU developed a reputation for pragmatism in developing successful legislation supported by ideologically diverse parties. The AU's Carlos Baráibar was elected president of the Chamber of Representatives in 1997.

Leaders: Danilo ASTORI (Vice President of the Republic and President of the Party), Carlos BARÁIBAR (Senator and Former President of the Chamber of Deputies).

Progressive Alliance (*Alianza Progresista*—AP). This social-democratic party was founded in 1999 by Rodolfo NIN Novoa and subsequently joined the EP-FA and the FLS.

Leader: Rodolfo NIN Novoa (Former Vice President).

Uruguayan Socialist Party (*Partido Socialista del Uruguay*—PSU). Founded in 1910, the PSU has participated in the *Frente Amplio* since its inception in 1971. The PSU fell into a period of uncertainty when President Tabare Vazquez resigned from his own party while still in office in protest over the platform to legalize abortion. Following the EP-FA's presidential win in 2009, PSU members were named to two cabinet posts. In 2011 the party began a reelection campaign for former President Vázquez, whose reform plan included nine points to alter the coalition's ideological foundation. The PSU won 2 of the Front's 15 senate seats in 2014.

Leaders: Reinaldo GARGANO (President), Yerú PARDIÑAS (Secretary General).

Movement of Popular Participation (*Movimiento de Participación Popular*—MPP). Commonly referred to as the Tupamaros (after Túpac Amaru, an 18th-century Inca chief who was burned at the stake by the Spaniards), the MPP is an outgrowth of the **National Liberation Movement** *(Movimiento de Liberación Nacional*—MLN), a longtime clandestine guerrilla group that used violence and charges of political corruption in an attempt to radically alter Uruguayan society. Its last recorded clash with the police was in Montevideo in April 1974; six years later, in 1980 MLN founder Raúl SENDIC Antonaccio was sentenced to 45 years' imprisonment after having been held without trial since 1972. Many Tupamaros were among the hundreds who returned to Uruguay at the end of 1984, while the core of the group, including Sendic, was released when all political prisoners were freed in March 1985. At the MLN's first legal convention in December 1985, an estimated 1,500 delegates established a 33-member central committee and endorsed the abandonment of armed struggle in favor of nonviolent electoral politics. Its bid to join the *Frente Amplio* was rebuffed in 1986, reportedly due to PDC objection, but approved before the 1989 poll. The MLN was a leading opponent of the government's controversial military amnesty program. Sendic died in Paris in April 1989, reportedly from a neurological condition occasioned by his years of imprisonment. The Movement campaigned as a Front member during the ensuing electoral campaign.

In 1991 relations with other Front members reportedly cooled, with the MLN's Eleuterio FERNÁNDEZ calling for General Seregni's resignation and an internal election to determine "who are the real leaders of the Uruguayan Left."

MPP candidates attracted nearly one-third of the EP-FA votes in the 2004 balloting. In 2009 MPP leader José Mujica won the presidential primary for the EP-FA, and Astori, who had the support of President Vázquez, agreed to be his running mate. Mujica quit the MPP after the primary election so as not to be tied to a particular group within the coalition. Following the selection of Vázquez as the FA presidential candidate in 2014, Mujica nominated MPP leader Lucía TOPOLANSKY to complete the ticket, but she was passed over for MLN founder Raúl Sendic, son of the late MLN leader. The MPP secured six of the Front's senate seats in 2014.

Leaders: Lucía TOPOLANSKY Saavedra (President), Edison Eduardo BONOMI Varela (Party Co-founder and Interior Minister).

Christian Democratic Party (*Partido Demócrata Cristiano*—PDC). Currently left-democratic in orientation, the PDC was founded in 1962 by dissidents from the predecessor of the current Civic Union. Banned at the time of the primary balloting in November 1982, the PDC operated negatively as a "fourth party" by calling on its followers for blank ballots, 84,000 of which were cast. The ban was lifted in August 1984. Before joining the *Nuevo Espacio* in 1989 the PDC operated as the "moderate" tendency within the *Frente Amplio.* It participated in forming the Progressive Encounter before the 1994 poll. The party is a member of the Christian Democratic International. At an October 2006 party convention, the PDC confirmed its complete support for the government of President Vázquez. A new executive committee was elected on December 16, 2013.

Leader: Matías RODRÍGUEZ (Secretary General).

Additional EP-FA components that secured cabinet posts in the Mujica administration were the **Artiguist Source** (*Vertiente Artiguista*—VA), led by Daoiz URIARTE; **Current Thought and Action–Freedom** (*La Corriente de Acción y Pensamiento–Libertad*—CAP-L), led by Eleuterio FERNÁNDEZ Huidobro; and **Communist Party of Uruguay** (*Partido Comunista*—PCU), led by Eduardo LORIER.

Other parties in the EP-FA in 2004 were the **Blanco Popular and Progressive Movement** (*Movimiento Blanco Popular y Progresista*—MBPP); **Left Front of Liberation** (*Frente Izquierda de Liberación*—Fidel); **Leftist Current** (*Corriente de Izquierda*—CI); **Nationalist Action Movement** (*Movimiento de Acción Nacionalista*—MAN); **Party for the Victory of the People** (*Partido por la Victoria del Pueblo*—PVP); **Pregon Group** (*Grupo Pregón*—GP); and **26th of March Movement** (*Movimiento 26 de Marzo*—M26M), which announced its departure from the EP-FA in March 2008, citing ideological differences.

Other Legislative Parties:

Colorado Party (*Partido Colorado*—PC). Founded in 1836 and in power continuously from 1865 to 1958, the urban-based PC emphasized liberal and progressive principles, social welfare, government participation in the economy, and inter-American cooperation.

For some years the party's leading faction, as heir to the policies of former president José Batlle y Ordóñez, was the *Unidad y Reforma,* led by a longtime opponent of the military establishment, Jorge Batlle Ibáñez. However, the group was formally headed by Dr. Julio María Sanguinetti because of the personal proscription of Batlle Ibáñez under the military regime. *Unidad y Reforma* obtained 45 percent of the vote in the November 1982 election and successfully advanced Sanguinetti as its presidential candidate in 1984. Other factions included the promilitary *Unión Colorado Batllista* (*pachequista*) group led by former president Jorge Pacheco Areco, who ran as a minority presidential candidate in 1984; the *Libertad y Cambio,* led by former vice president Enrique Tarigo; and the antimilitary *Batllismo Radical* and *Corriente Batllista Independiente.*

In 1986 the party strongly endorsed the military amnesty urged by President Sanguinetti, while continuing to promote coalition efforts with elements of the Blanco Party. Runner-up in the 1989 balloting, the PC was awarded four portfolios in the Lacalle administration of March 1990, an alliance that effectively ended in January 1993, although two Colorado ministers retained their portfolios until May 1994.

By 1992 *Unidad y Reforma* had split into two components, the *Batllismo Unido* (subsequently *Batllismo Radical*), headed by Batlle Ibáñez, and the *Foro Batllista,* led by Sanguinetti. Also active were the *Unión Colorado Batllista* and *Cruzada 94,* led by Pablo MILLOR. Batlle Ibáñez captured 54 percent of the votes within the PC's presidential primary in April 1999, earning the nomination over Luis HIERRO López (45 percent), who had the support of President Sanguinetti. Batlle won the November runoff against the *Frente Amplio*'s Tabaré Vásquez and took office as president in March 2000.

The party placed third in the 2004 presidential poll with only 10.3 percent of the vote, while losing two-thirds of its congressional representation. A call for renewal began after the PC's poor showing, which in 2007 crystallized into a new faction calling itself *Vamos Uruguay* under the leadership of Juan Pedro BORDABERRY Herrán. At the PC's national convention in September 2009, Bordaberry, son of former president Bordaberry, became the Colorado presidential candidate for the October 2009 general elections. At the same meeting it was also decided that two former presidents, Julio María Sanguinetti and Jorge Batlle, would not participate in the National Executive Committee, breaking a forty-year tradition.

Pedro Bordaberry won 17 percent of the vote and placed third in the 2009 presidential election. The party won 17 seats in the Chamber of Representatives and 5 seats in the senate in concurrent legislative elections. The party saw a resurgence of support during the 2010 regional elections.

In early 2011 the PC and the PN presented a unified front of opposition to the EP-FA–driven attempt to dismantle the country's long-standing amnesty law, which eventually failed. With rising youth criminality becoming a political issue, the party in August 2011 began collecting signatures to hold a plebiscite during the 2014 general election on lowering the age of sentencing from 18 to 16 years.

In August 2013 the PC and PN took steps toward creating an alliance to compete in the 2015 Montevideo municipal elections. Pedro Bordaberry announced his candidacy for president in November 2013 and won the party's nomination in a primary election in June 2014. He was third in the first round of presidential balloting in the October election with 13.3 percent of the vote. The PC won 13 chamber seats and 4 Senate seats in the concurrent legislative polling.

Leaders: Max SAPOLINSKI (Secretary General), Juan Pedro BORDABERRY Herrán (2009 and 2014 presidential candidate), Guillermo STIRLING (2004 presidential candidate).

National Party (*Partido Nacional*—PN). Commonly known as the **White Party** (*Partido Blanco—Blanco*), the PN traditionally represented conservative, rural, and clerical elements but is now largely progressive in outlook. The *Partido Nacional* won the elections of 1958 and 1962, subsequently failing to win either the presidency or a legislative plurality until November 1989. Its longtime principal grouping, the centrist *Por la Patria,* was led, before his death in March 1988, by Wilson Ferreira Aldunate, who was in exile at the time of the 1982 balloting. His absence did not prevent the *ferreiristas* from obtaining 70 percent of the party vote in 1982; other anti-military factions in 1982 included the *Consejo Nacional Herrerista (Herrismo),* heir to a grouping formed in 1954 by Luis Alberto de Herrera, and the conservative *Divisa Blanca,* led by Eduardo Pons Etcheverry.

Ferreira returned to Uruguay in June 1984 and was promptly arrested, along with his son, Juan Raúl, who had led an exile opposition group known as the Uruguayan Democratic Convergence. After officially rejecting the August "Institutional Act No. 19" and refusing to participate in the election campaign, the main faction, at Ferreira's urging, offered Alberto Zumarán as its presidential candidate. Zumarán won 32.9 percent of the vote, while the Blancos obtained 35 seats in the Chamber of Deputies and 11 senate seats. Released from prison five days after the November poll, Ferreira was elected party president in February 1985. Although he initially criticized the reported "deal" between the military and the Colorados to thwart the initiation of human rights trials, he vowed to "let the president govern" and supported the military amnesty program in 1986. The issue split the party, however, as the left-leaning *Movimiento Nacional de Rocha* faction, led by Carlos Julio Pereyra, called for a referendum to defeat the measure. The smaller, right-leaning *Divisa Blanca* not only supported the amnesty but also reportedly urged coalition with the Colorados.

Both Pereyra and Zumarán presented themselves as Blanco candidates in the 1989 presidential poll, which was won by Luis Alberto de Herrera's grandson, Luis Alberto Lacalle, with Gonzalo Aguirre Ramírez of the *Renovación y Victoria* faction as his running mate. The coalition forged by Lacalle with the Colorados was effectively terminated as the result of a midterm cabinet reshuffle in January 1993, with the last two Colorado ministers resigning in May. At the 1994 poll, four Blancos presented themselves as presidential candidates: Aguirre Ramírez, party chair Carlos Julio Pereyra, former interior minister Juan Andrés Ramírez (favored by President Lacalle), and state power utility head Alberto Volonté.

Lacalle, the candidate of the party's right-wing, secured the Blanco nomination for the 1999 presidential election by winning 49 percent of the votes in the April primary, but he ran third in the first-round poll of October 31. To prevent a possible victory by the Left, the Blancos threw their support in the runoff of November 28 to the Colorado's Batlle Ibáñez, who then formed a coalition government in which the Colorados participated until withdrawing in November 2002.

In 2003 Cristina MAESO, leader of a *Basta y Vamos* ("Enough–Let's Go") faction, became the first woman to contend (albeit unsuccessfully) for a major party's presidential nomination.

The party ran second in the 2004 presidential race with a 36.9 percent vote share, while increasing its lower house representation from 22 to 34.

The Blancos unified behind Luis Alberto Lacalle de Herrera as its 2009 presidential candidate. He finished second in the October balloting, with 29.1 percent of the vote. The Blancos won 9 seats in the senate and 30 in the Chamber of Representatives. The party was the recipient of strong voter support in the 2010 regional elections, particularly in rural areas.

In early 2011 the PN and the PC presented a unified front of opposition to the EP-FA–driven attempt to dismantle the country's long-standing amnesty law, which eventually failed. In June Lacalle resigned as president of the party, calling on the PN to renew and reform itself in order to take on the EP-FA. He signaled that the party would look to taking up a more centrist position in Uruguay's political spectrum and reaching out to a broader segment of the population.

The PN led the opposition of the legalization of abortion in 2012 (see Current issues, above). In May 2013 the party selected Luis LACALLE POU, the son of the former president Lacalle, as 2014 presidential candidate, which he secured in June 2014 primary balloting. Lacalle Pou was second in the presidential election with 43.4 percent of the vote in the runoff. The PN won 32 chamber seats and 10 Senate seats.

Leaders: Luis Alberto HÉBER Fontana (President), Luis LACALLE POU (2014 presidential candidate), Gustavo PENADÉS (Secretary General), Luis Alberto LACALLE Herrera (Former President of the Republic and 1999 and 2009 presidential candidate), Gonzalo AGUIRRE Ramírez (Former Vice President of the Republic and leader of *Renovación y Victoria*).

Independent Party (*Partido Independiente*—PI). The small centrist PI was formed in 2003 and won a single seat in the Chamber of Representatives in the 2004 general election. The PI chose Pablo Andrés Mieres Gomez as its 2009 presidential candidate. He placed fourth with 2.5 percent of the vote. Concurrently, the party won two seats in the Chamber of Representatives. Mieres was also the party's candidate for the presidency in 2014. He won 3.2 percent of the vote, while the PI secured three seats in the chamber and one in the Senate.

Leaders: Pablo Andrés MIERES Gomez (President of the Party and 2009 and 2014 presidential candidate), Iván POSADA (2009 vice-presidential candidate).

Popular Assembly (*Asamblea Popular*—AP). The left-wing AP was formed in 2006. In the 2009 presidential election, José Raúl RODRIGUEZ da Silva finished fifth with 0.7 percent of the vote. The AP remained active through 2011 at the local-advocacy level, organizing marches for trade unions and to further human rights goals. The AP won one chamber seat in 2014, while its presidential candidate, Gonzalo ABELLA, secured 1.2 percent of the vote.

Leaders: Gonzalo ABELLA (2014 presidential candidate), José Raúl RODRIGUEZ da Silva (2009 presidential candidate), Helios SARTHOU.

Other Parties:

Anti-Imperialist Unitary Commissions (*Comisiones Unitarias Antiimperialistas*—COMUNA). COMUNA was formed is 2008 through the unification of the Oriental Revolutionary Movement (*Movimiento Revolucionario Oriental*—MRO) and various defectors from the FA coalition. The MRO is a pro-Cuban former guerrilla group that participated in the FA's launching in 1971. It made headlines (and embarrassed other Front groups) in late 1991 by characterizing a follower who had been arrested for robbery as a "social fighter." It was expelled from the FA in 1993 after some of its leaders had urged a return to "armed revolutionary struggle for Latin America."

Leader: Mario ROSSI Garretano (Founder and President of the Party).

Other parties that contested the 2014 elections included the **Ecologist Radical Intransigent Party** (*Partido Ecologista Radical Intransigente*—PERI), formed in 2013 and led by 2014 presidential candidate César VEGA, and the **Worker's Party** (*Partido de los Trabajadores*—PT), led by Rafael FERNÁNDEZ. Neither won any seats in the balloting.

For information on the **Civic Union** (*Unión Cívica*—UC) party, see the 2010 edition of the *Handbook.*

LEGISLATURE

The bicameral Congress (*Congreso*), dissolved in June 1973 and replaced under the military regime with an appointive Council of

State, reconvened for the first time in 12 years on February 15, 1985, following the election of November 25, 1984. The two houses, now styled collectively as the **General Assembly** (*Asamblea General*), are elected simultaneously on a proportional basis, both for five-year terms.

Chamber of Senators (*Cámara de Senadores* o *Senado*). The upper house consists of 30 elected members and one ex-officio member (the vice president). Following the October 26, 2014, election, the seat distribution was as follows: Progressive Encounter–Broad Front, 15 seats; National (Blanco) Party, 10; Colorado Party, 4; and Independent Party, 1.

President: Raúl Fernando SENDIC Rodríguez.

Chamber of Representatives (*Cámara de Representantes*). The lower house comprises 99 members. Following the election of October 26, 2014, the seat distribution was as follows: the Progressive Encounter–Broad Front, 50; National (Blanco) Party, 32; Colorado Party, 13; Independent Party, 3; and Popular Assembly, 1.

President: Gerardo AMARILLA.

CABINET

[as of October 5, 2016]

President	Tabaré Ramón Vásquez Rosas (EP-FA)
Vice President	Raúl Fernando Sendic Rodríguez (EP-FA)
Ministers	
Agriculture, Livestock, and Fisheries	Tabaré Aguerre (ind.)
Economy and Finance	Danilo Astori (FLS)
Education and Culture	María Julia Muñoz (EP-FA) [f]
Foreign Affairs	Rodolfo Nin Novoa (EP-FA)
Housing, Territorial Planning, and Environment	Eneida de León (MPP) [f]
Industry, Energy, and Mining	Carolina Cosse (MPP) [f]
Interior	Eduardo Bonomi (MPP)
Labor and Social Welfare	Ernesto Murro (EP-FA)
National Defense	Jorge Menendez (PSU)
Public Health	Jorge Basso (PSU)
Social Development	Marina Arismendi (PCU) [f]
Tourism and Sport	Liliam Kechichián (Progressive Alliance) [f]
Transport and Public Works	Victor Rossi (EP-FA)

[f] = female

INTERGOVERNMENTAL REPRESENTATION

Ambassador to the U.S.: Carlos GIANELLI Derois.

U.S. Ambassador to Uruguay: Kelly KEIDERLING.

Permanent Representative to the UN: Elbio ROSSELLI.

IGO Memberships (Non-UN): IADB, ICC, IOM, Mercosur, OAS, WTO.

For Further Reference:

Churchill, Lindsey. *Becoming the Tupamaros: Solidarity and Transnational Revolutionaries in Uruguay and the United States.* Nashville, TN: Vanderbilt University Press, 2014.

Johnson, Niki. "Keeping Men in, Shutting Women Out: Gender Biases in Candidate Selection Processes in Uruguay." *Government & Opposition* 51, no. 3 (July 2016): 393–415.

Zucco, Cesar. "Legislative Coalitions in Presidential Systems: The Case of Uruguay." *Latin American Politics & Society* 55, no. 1 (Spring 2013): 96–118.

UZBEKISTAN

Republic of Uzbekistan
Ozbekiston Respublikasi

Political Status: Eastern portion of Turkistan Soviet Socialist Republic detached on October 27, 1924, to form Uzbek Soviet Socialist Republic within the Russian Soviet Federative Socialist Republic (RSFSR); became constituent republic of the Union of Soviet Socialist Republics (USSR) on May 12, 1925; declared independence as Republic of Uzbekistan on August 31, 1991; present constitution adopted on December 8, 1992.

Area: 172,740 sq. mi. (447,400 sq. km).

Population: 30,300,000 (2016E—UN); 29,473,614 (2016E—U.S. Census).

Major Urban Centers (2015E—UN): TASHKENT (2,251,000), Namangan (521,000), Andijan (402,000), Samarkand (364,000).

Official Language: Uzbek. Russian remains the principal everyday language.

Monetary Unit: Uzbekistani som (market rate October 1, 2016: 3,009.95 som = $1US).

President (Acting): Shavkat MIRZIYOYEV (MIRZIYAYEV) (National Revival Democratic Party); elected as acting president by the Supreme Assembly on September 8, 2016, to succeed acting president and speaker of the Senate Nigmatilla YULDASHEV (National Revival Democratic Party), who had assumed the presidency following the death of Islam A. KARIMOV (Liberal Democratic Party) on September 2.

Prime Minister: Shavkat MIRZIYOYEV (MIRZIYAYEV) (National Revival Democratic Party); appointed by the president and confirmed by the Supreme Assembly on December 11, 2003, succeeding Otkir SULTONOV; reconfirmed on January 28, 2005, and on January 27, 2010; reconfirmed on January 23, 2015.

THE COUNTRY

The Central Asian state of Uzbekistan—the region's most populous—is bordered on the north and west by Kazakhstan, on the northeast by Kyrgyzstan, on the southeast by Tajikistan, and on the south, save for a short frontier with Afghanistan, by Turkmenistan. The national territory also includes several small exclaves in Kyrgyzstan, the largest being the town of Sokh. The principal ethnic groups are Turkic-speaking Uzbeks (approximately 76 percent); Russians (6 percent); Tajiks (5 percent), Kazakhs (4 percent), and Tatars (2 percent). The vast majority of citizens are Sunni Muslims, but there is also a small Shiite population; Eastern Orthodoxy predominates among the Russians. Women make up slightly less than half of the workforce and constitute 16 percent of the current lower house (24 seats) and 17 percent of the current upper house (17 seats).

Crops include cotton (Uzbekistan's top export), rice, wheat, tobacco, sugarcane, and a wide variety of vegetables and fruits. The agricultural sector contributes 19.1 percent of gross domestic product (GDP) and employs 25.9 percent of workers. Uzbekistan has the fourth-largest gold reserves in the world, but its top industrial exports are cars and refined cooper. Other extractable resources include oil, coal, uranium, molybdenum, tungsten, zinc, and natural gas. As a whole, industry accounts for 32.2 percent of GDP. A growing source of income has been remittances and other transfers (7 percent of GDP in 2012) from some of the 5.5 million Uzbek citizens working abroad. (For information on the economy prior to 2000, see the 2012 *Handbook.*)

Government figures, which are historically unreliable and difficult to verify, reflected an average GDP growth of 7.5 percent between 2002 and 2012, while inflation has decreased from 45 percent in 2002 to 15 percent in 2012. Inflation in 2013 was 14 percent, and GDP increased 8 percent, while unemployment remained steady from the previous five years at 11 percent. GDP expanded by 8.1 percent in 2014, 8 percent in 2015, and 5 percent in 2016. Inflation in 2016 was 8.6 percent, while

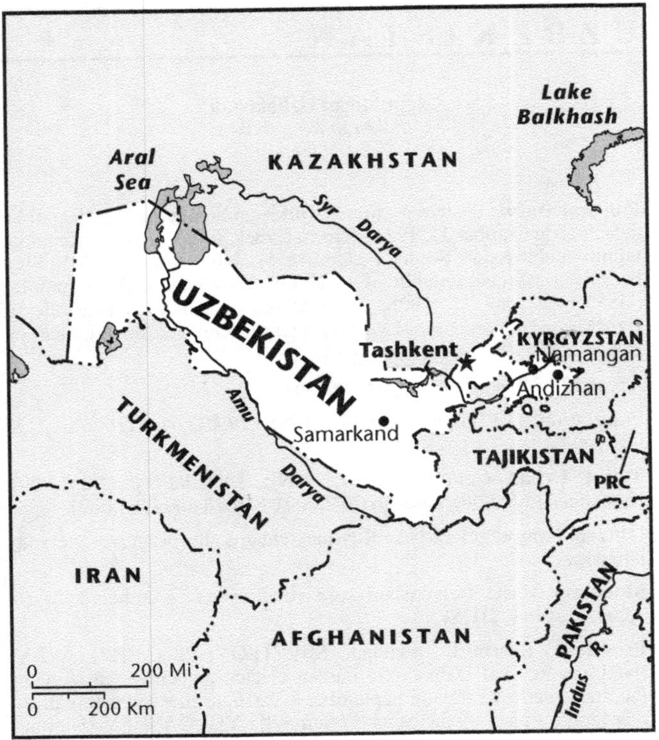

GDP per capita was $8,550. In its 2016 ease of doing business index, the World Bank ranked Uzbekistan 87th out of 189 countries, an increase from 146th in 2014. The uptick is mostly a result of Uzbekistan making it easier to start a business within the country. However, the country continues to lag far behind neighboring states such as Kazakhstan (41st) or Kyrgyzstan (67th) because of endemic corruption.

GOVERNMENT AND POLITICS

Political background. Astride the ancient caravan routes to the Orient, Uzbekistan is one of the world's oldest civilized regions. In the 14th century what is now its second city, Samarkand, served as the hub of Tamerlane's vast empire. In the 19th century, after a lengthy period of decay, much of its territory was conquered by Russia. In 1920 it became part of the Turkistan Soviet Socialist Republic within the Russian Soviet Federative Socialist Republic. Separated from Turkmenia in 1924, Uzbekistan entered the USSR as a constituent republic in 1925. In 1929 its eastern Tajik region was detached and also accorded the status of a Soviet republic.

On March 24, 1990, at the opening of a recently elected Uzbek Supreme Soviet, Islam A. KARIMOV was elected by secret ballot to the new post of Supreme Soviet president. The following November, as part of a government reorganization, the chair of the Council of Ministers, Shakhrulla MIRSAIDOV, was named vice president. In August 1991, in the wake of a failed Moscow coup against USSR president Mikhail Gorbachev, President Karimov resigned from the Politburo of the Communist Party of the Soviet Union, and the property of the Uzbek Communist Party (UCP) was nationalized. On August 28 Uzbekistan assumed control of all union enterprises within its territory and declared its intention to conduct its own foreign policy. Three days later the Supreme Soviet issued a declaration of independence and announced a change of name to Republic of Uzbekistan. In November the UCP was replaced by the People's Democratic Party of Uzbekistan (PDP), and on December 29 independence was endorsed, by a 98.2 percent vote, in a popular referendum. In a parallel poll, Karimov, as the PDP candidate, won confirmation as president with an 86 percent share of the vote, as contrasted with the 12 percent garnered by Muhammad SALIH of the opposition Freedom (*Erk*) grouping. Following the poll, Abdulhashim MUTALOV of the PDP was named independent Uzbekistan's first prime minister. A month later, the vice presidency was abolished.

Although the 1992 constitution enshrined a commitment to multiparty democracy, Uzbekistan remained effectively a one-party state under the PDP. Genuine opposition parties, such as the nationalist Unity (*Birlik*) movement and the more moderate *Erk*, experienced systematic harassment leading to outright proscription, while the authorities encouraged the formation of new parties broadly supportive of the government.

Elections to a new 250-member legislature, held in three rounds in December 1994 and January 1995, were contested by two parties, the PDP and the government-aligned Progress of the Fatherland, with the PDP winning a large majority of the seats claimed by party nominees. In a March referendum President Karimov further consolidated power by securing what most observers regarded as an implausible 99.6 percent endorsement for a three-year extension of his existing five-year term, due to expire at the end of 1996. In December the Supreme Assembly confirmed Otkir SULTONOV as prime minister in succession to the demoted Mutalov, who three months later was dismissed from the cabinet altogether. Meanwhile, critics of the regime, including former vice president Mirsaidov, continued to accuse the government of authoritarianism and one-party rule.

In November–December 1997 an outbreak of violence in Namangan precipitated a government crackdown against alleged Islamic activists, and between May 1998 and January 1999 several dozen were convicted of terrorism and anticonstitutional acts. A series of at least six bomb blasts shook Tashkent on February 16, 1999, killing 15 and injuring more than 120. Hundreds of Islamic activists and government critics were arrested in succeeding weeks. Between June and August more than two dozen individuals were sentenced to death or lengthy prison terms on related charges that included attempted assassination of the president. Most of those arrested in the wake of the bombings were subsequently released, after months in detention.

For the Supreme Assembly elections of December 1999 *Birlik* and *Erk* were denied registration. The PDP again won more seats than any of its competitor parties, but its predominance was challenged by the National Democratic Party "Self-Sacrificers" (*Fidokorlar*), formation of which had been announced, with President Karimov's imprimatur, in December 1998. In January 2000 Karimov easily won reelection as president, capturing 92 percent of the vote against the PDP's token candidate, Abdulkhafiz JALOLOV, who stated on election day that he, too, had cast his ballot for the incumbent.

In a January 27, 2002, referendum a reported 92 percent of those voting approved extending the presidential term to seven years, while 94 percent endorsed introducing a bicameral legislature, as had been proposed by President Karimov in May 2000. The Supreme Assembly subsequently passed implementing legislation, effective from the next legislative election. In December 2003 the Supreme Assembly confirmed President Karimov's selection of Shavkat MIRZIYOYEV, governor of Samarkand and an agricultural specialist, as successor to Prime Minister Sultonov, who was retained as a deputy prime minister.

On March 28–April 1, 2004, a series of explosions in Bukhara and Tashkent claimed nearly 50 lives, the majority of them suspected terrorists. On July 30 three coordinated suicide bombings occurred outside the U.S. and Israeli embassies and at the prosecutor general's office. A then unknown group called the Jihad Islamic Group (JIG), a splinter from the Islamic Movement of Uzbekistan (IMU), claimed responsibility for the attacks. Dozens of individuals were ultimately tried, convicted, and sentenced to between 3 and 18 years in prison for the spring incidents.

In the first election for the new 120-seat Legislative Chamber, held on December 26, 2004, with runoff balloting on January 9, 2005, the recently organized Liberal Democratic Party of Uzbekistan (LDP) won a plurality of seats, ahead of the PDP and *Fidokorlar.* Elected members of the new Senate were chosen indirectly by regional bodies on January 17–20.

On May 13–14, 2005, the eastern city of Andijan erupted in mass protest against civil rights abuses and widespread poverty. In response, troops reportedly fired indiscriminately into crowds of mostly unarmed civilians numbering in the low thousands. The government, which put the death toll at 187, blamed the unrest on terrorists and Islamic extremists associated with the IMU and another banned organization, the *Hizb-ut-Tahrir.* Human rights groups put the death toll at 500–750 and charged that many had been massacred in the streets. Hundreds fled across the Kyrgyz border. Tashkent refused to allow an independent inquiry, as called for by the UN and others, leading the European Union

(EU) to impose sanctions that included banning the import of arms or equipment that could be used in state repression.

President Karimov easily won reelection on December 23, 2007. Two of the other three presidential candidates on the ballot represented government-supportive parties, while the third, Akmal SAIDOV, nominated by a citizens' initiative group, was a legal scholar, member of the Legislative Chamber, and former ambassador. The Organization for Security and Cooperation in Europe (OSCE) determined that the elections failed to meet international standards, but the Russian-led Commonwealth of Independent States (CIS) called the vote legitimate.

In the two-stage Legislative Chamber election held December 27, 2009, and January 10, 2010, once again only progovernment parties were permitted to offer candidates. The LDP won a leading 53 of the 150 seats in the expanded lower house, followed by the PDP with 32, the new *Milliy Tiklanish* Democratic Party with 31, and the Justice (*Adolat*) Social Democratic Party of Uzbekistan with 19. Fifteen reserved seats were indirectly filled by the Ecological Movement of Uzbekistan (EMU). In March 2010 the cabinet was shuffled under the continuing leadership of Prime Minister Mirziyoyev. Between December 2010 and November 2011, three ministers were replaced. Another minor cabinet reshuffle took place in January 2012 when several new ministers were appointed and the number of deputy prime ministers was reduced from seven to six. In August Deputy Prime Minister Abdulla ORIPOV was dismissed (see Current issues, below). In September Health Minister Adham Ilkhamovich IKROMOV was promoted to replace Oripov. In February 2013 two ministers were replaced.

Parliamentary elections were held on December 21, 2014, with runoff balloting on January 5, 2015. The LDP lost 1 seat for a total of 52; the MTDP won 36; the PDP, 27; and *Adolat,* 20. Fifteen seats were reserved for the EMU. The balloting was criticized by international observers for a lack of choice among the four pro-presidential parties. On January 23 Mirziyoev was reelected prime minister by the legislature.

Karimov was reelected president on March 29, 2015, with 90.4 percent of the vote. However, he died in office on September 2, 2016. The speaker of the Senate was immediately appointed acting president until the legislature met and voted Mirziyoyev as interim president on September 8, pending new elections.

Constitution and government. The 1992 constitution describes Uzbekistan as a democratic presidential republic in which "there may be no official state ideology or religion." Freedom of thought and conscience and respect for human rights are guaranteed, although a 1998 law set stringent requirements governing the reregistration and activities of religious groups, which are prohibited from engaging in sectarian social movements, missionary work, proselytizing, most forms of religious education, and publication of religious materials deemed extreme, chauvinistic, or separatist. Formal press censorship ended in 2002, but the government continues to dominate the media and exert overwhelming pressure on nongovernment outlets. (In 2008 the International Crisis Group concluded that there were "strong indications" that Uzbek security forces murdered a journalist who had written extensively about torture in Uzbek prisons.) In 2016 Reporters Without Borders ranked Uzbekistan 166th out of 180 countries in freedom of the press.

The popularly elected head of state may serve no more than two consecutive terms, a restriction that the current president circumvented in 2007 by arguing that the 2002 referendum on extending his term reset the clock. The president wields broad authority that includes initiating legislation, and serving as commander in chief. Constitutional reforms in 2011 granted the assembly the power to nominate the prime minister (the prime minister can also be removed through a no-confidence vote) and reduced the term of the president from seven to five years. The bicameral Supreme Assembly comprises a directly elected Legislative Chamber and a Senate that is largely chosen by and from among regional and local councils but also includes presidential appointees. The Senate has authority to approve certain government officials (e.g., ambassadors and Supreme Court justices) as well as limited powers to delay or block bills passed by the Legislative Chamber.

At its highest level the independent judiciary includes a Constitutional Court, a Supreme Court, and a High Economic Court. Administratively, Uzbekistan encompasses 12 regions (*wiloyatlar*), the autonomous republic of Karakalpakstan (Qoraqalpoghiston), and the capital city (Tashkent). Subdivisions include more than 160 districts and over 110 cities and towns. The president appoints regional governors (*khokims*) as well as lower court judges.

Foreign relations. On December 21, 1991, Uzbekistan became a sovereign member of the CIS. By early 1992 it had established diplomatic relations with a number of Western countries, including the United States. In March it was admitted to the United Nations and in September became a member of the International Monetary Fund and the World Bank. It joined the Conference on (later Organization for) Security and Cooperation in Europe (CSCE/OSCE) in 1992 and subscribed to the North Atlantic Treaty Organization (NATO)-sponsored Partnership for Peace program in July 1994. In June 1996 Tashkent signed a partnership and cooperation agreement with the EU.

The Uzbek government has maintained close relations with Russia. A March 1994 economic integration agreement led in July 1995 to the signing of 15 detailed accords covering economic and military cooperation. During a visit by President Karimov to Russia in May 1998, he and President Boris Yeltsin agreed to coordinate their efforts to control the spread of fundamentalism, with President Imomali Rakhmonov of Tajikistan concurring. In October Yeltsin paid a return visit to Uzbekistan, at which time the two chiefs of state promised mutual aid in the case of an attack on either country, presumably by Afghanistan's Taliban or its allies. In 2006 Uzbekistan joined the Collective Security Treaty Organization (CSTO), seven years after having announced its withdrawal from the predecessor Collective Security Treaty (CST).

In January 1994 Uzbekistan joined with Kazakhstan and Kyrgyzstan to form the Central Asian Economic Union (CAEU), reconfigured as the Central Asian Cooperation Organization (CACO) in 2002, which was absorbed into the Eurasian Economic Community (EurAsEc) in 2006. In November 2008, the Uzbek government confirmed its withdrawal from EurAsEc and intentions to pursue closer relations with non-Eurasian countries.

In June 2001 Uzbekistan joined China, Kazakhstan, Kyrgyzstan, Russia, and Tajikistan in establishing the Shanghai Cooperation Organization (SCO). The principal mandate of the SCO is to ensure regional stability, with a particular focus on containing Islamic militancy. The SCO has also played an increasingly important role in determining oil and natural gas production development and diversification throughout the region. The organizations tenth annual summit convened in Tashkent on June 11, 2010.

Uzbekistan's overriding concern with Islamic militancy can be traced to the Afghan civil war of the 1990s, when the Uzbek government, despite its denials, was widely reported to be providing weapons and financial assistance to the anti-Taliban militia led in the north by Gen. Abdul Rashid Dostam, an ethnic Uzbek. In July 1999, as a member of the "Six-Plus-Two" contact group on Afghanistan, Uzbekistan hosted UN-sponsored peace talks between the Taliban and its principal opponents, producing no significant results. In late 2001, following the September terrorist attacks on the United States, the Karimov government agreed to support the United States and its allies in their effort to oust the Taliban.

In April 2000 the presidents of Kazakhstan, Kyrgyzstan, Tajikistan, and Uzbekistan signed a mutual security agreement providing for joint action against terrorism, political and religious extremism, organized crime, and other threats.

In January 1998 Presidents Karimov of Uzbekistan and Rakhmonov of Tajikistan signed several bilateral agreements covering, among other things, the resolution of debt issues and joint antidrug activities. The meeting also apparently indicated Karimov's grudging acceptance of proposed Islamist participation in the Tajik government. Later in the year, however, relations grew heated when Rakhmonov asserted that Uzbekistan had allowed leaders of a failed revolt in northern Tajikistan to enter the country and that Uzbekistan aimed "to take the whole of Tajikistan under its control." Shortly thereafter, captured rebels reportedly admitted that members of the Uzbek special forces had helped train them. In addition to denying the allegations, Karimov later accused Tajik officials of involvement in drug trafficking. In August 1999, in an effort to root out ethnic Uzbek militants, government aircraft bombed camps across the Tajik border. Some of the bombs hit Tajik villages, provoking an outcry from Dushanbe. In June 2000, however, Uzbekistan and Tajikistan signed a friendship treaty and agreed to demarcate their border, although the alleged persecution of ethnic Tajiks in Uzbekistan and claims by Tajik nationalists to Uzbek territory continue to cause strains.

In August 1999 fundamentalists associated with the IMU seized hostages in southern Kyrgyzstan. Uzbekistan joined Russia and Kazakhstan in providing military assistance to the Kyrgyz government, which negotiated the release of the final hostages in October. In 2000 Uzbekistan unilaterally began mining its borders with Tajikistan and

Kyrgyzstan as part of its efforts to stop incursions by militants and to halt the flow of illegal drugs. Tashkent announced the removal of the mines in 2004. A terrorist bombing along the Uzbek–Kyrgyz border in May 2009 and Kyrgyzstan's agreement to host a second Russian military base, potentially located near its border with Uzbekistan, further complicated the relationship, as did the flight in June 2010 of some 400,000 ethnic Uzbek refugees across the border from southern Kyrgyzstan, where they and their property had been subjected to unrestrained violence by elements of the Kyrgyz community. By the end of the month, however, civil order had been restored and many Uzbeks were returning.

Water rights have long been a source of regional disputes. Tensions over water supplies erupted in a demonstration in July 1997 on the Kazakh-Uzbek border when Tashkent decided to reduce the amount of water flowing through its territory to southern Kazakhstan. Meanwhile, Kyrgyzstan debated how much to begin charging Uzbekistan and Kazakhstan for water from Kyrgyz reservoirs. In September the three nations agreed with Turkmenistan and Tajikistan to set up a fund to try to save the Aral Sea by alleviating the damage caused by overuse of the Amu-Darya and Syr-Darya rivers for irrigation. More recently, in March 2008 the Uzbek government held an international conference on the Aral Sea crisis, as the volume of the sea had dropped to a tenth of its 1977 levels.

The U.S.-led "war on terrorism" provided the Karimov regime with an opportunity to exploit its strategic location. In October 2001 Karimov granted U.S. forces access to the former Soviet air base in Khanabad—the largest such facility in Central Asia—as part of a "qualitatively new relationship" with the United States. Although the initial announcement indicated that the base would be used for launching search and rescue missions and for funneling humanitarian aid to the Afghani people, Khanabad was soon being used for offensive staging by U.S. and NATO forces. In March 2002 Karimov met with President Bush at the White House, and Karimov and U.S. secretary of state Colin Powell signed five cooperation agreements, one of which stated that the United States would "regard with grave concern any external threat" to Uzbekistan. U.S. operations in Afghanistan aimed at defeating the Taliban were also directed at IMU elements present in Afghanistan and elsewhere in the region. For its part, Uzbekistan promised to move forward with its political and economic transformation. In July 2005, however, hard U.S. criticism of the events in Andijan may have contributed to Tashkent's demand that U.S. forces vacate the Khanabad base. The United States completed its withdrawal on November 21.

In February 2009 the Uzbek government agreed to allow U.S. supplies transit through Uzbek territory from Russia and Kazakhstan to NATO forces in Afghanistan. Gen. David Petraeus, then the head of the U.S. military's Central Command, visited Uzbekistan in mid-August 2009 and signed a military cooperation agreement with the government. In December Uzbekistan and the United States finalized an accord to increase technology cooperation between the two countries. Meanwhile, in October 2011 the United States ended a limited arms embargo on Uzbekistan that had been put in place to protest the nation's human rights record.

In April 2011, during a visit to China, Karimov signed a series of investment agreements. On October 18 Russia proposed a free trade agreement with other CIS states, but Uzbekistan, along with Azerbaijan and Turkmenistan, asked for additional time before accepting the offer. In November Uzbekistan and Kyrgyzstan finalized an agreement for the former to supply electricity to the latter.

In March 2012 Uzbekistan and the United States signed an agreement to allow U.S. military air and land shipments to cross the country on their way to Afghanistan. The initiative was designed to reduce U.S. dependency on Pakistan as a supply route for forces in Afghanistan (see entry on Pakistan). On April 1 Uzbekistan suspended gas shipments to Tajikistan in response to the Tajik construction of a hydroelectric plant on the Amu Darya River. Uzbek officials claimed the facility would seriously limit the water flow into their country. Shipment was resumed after two weeks under a temporary contract following pledges by Tajikistan to reenter into negotiations on the issue. In February 2013 Uzbekistan and China finalized a range of agreements on the transfer and sale of plants and agricultural products beginning as series of agreements throughout 2013 leading to an end-of-the-year agreement to expand cooperation along political, economic, and cultural lines. In April Uzbekistan and Russia signed new investment and immigration accords during a visit by Karimov to Moscow. The U.S. State Department gave Uzbekistan its lowest rating in combating human trafficking and child labor in June 2013. In December the Senate ratified the entry of Uzbekistan into CIS, making them the ninth member to enter into this free trade zone.

In March 2014 Uzbekistan signed an agreement to create a transport corridor with Turkmenistan, Iran, and Oman. In July Kazakhstan announced intentions of joining the World Trade Organization.

Border incidents in January 2013 between Uzbekistan and Kyrgyzstan led to reciprocal temporary blockades against ethnic enclaves in each country. Both nations pledged a joint investigation into the episodes. Beginning in early 2014 Kyrgyzstan and Uzbekistan formalized a series of discussions to finish delimiting their common border. While most of their 1,378 kilometers of common border have been set, 350 kilometers have remained a point of contention due to four Uzbek enclaves in Kyrgyzstan and one Kyrgyz enclave in Uzbekistan. Relations between the two states cooled in April, however, due to the stoppage of gas supplies into Kyrgyzstan over a contract dispute.

Uzbekistan and NATO announced in February 2016 a series of measures to enhance cooperation. In November Uzbekistan assumed the rotating presidency of the Organization of Islamic Cooperation.

Current issues. Energy and water disputes continue to complicate regional relationships. Uzbekistan significantly reduced its export of natural gas to Kyrgyzstan and Tajikistan in mid-June 2009 as the two countries fell into arrears on their energy payments, and in November it announced it intended to withdraw from the regional electrical grid because of differences over transit tariffs with Tajikistan, which imports electricity from Turkmenistan via Uzbekistan. Tajikistan responded by threatening to withhold water. Uzbekistan proceeded to stop transit of rail freight. In contrast, in December 2009 the presidents of Uzbekistan, Turkmenistan, Kazakhstan, and China met to inaugurate a recently completed 1,139-mile (1,833-km) Turkmenistan–China natural gas pipeline that passes through Uzbekistan and Kazakhstan.

In March 2012 Karimov announced that legislative elections would be held in December 2014. The government launched a major privatization initiative in May. The program sought to sell off 500 state enterprises over a two-year period. In July Karimov approved an increase to the salaries of local and regional government employees as part of an effort to reduce graft and corruption. In response to international pressure, the government banned the use of child labor in cotton harvests in August.

In September 2012 two major telecommunications scandals prompted the dismissal of Deputy Prime Minister Abdulla Oripov. The first involved the telecommunications giant Uzdunrobita, which had its license revoked for tax evasions, leaving 40 percent of Uzbek mobile phone owners without service. Courts subsequently ordered the confiscation of the company's $700 million in assets in what independent media outlets described as a "shakedown." Meanwhile, Western reports alleged that a Nordic telecommunications company had been forced to improperly pay $320 million to obtain licenses to operate in Uzbekistan.

In August 2013 Uzbekistan and Kazakhstan signed a strategic partnership covering political, economic, and environmental areas. Most important to the agreement is the inclusion of a fair system of water management within the region.

In 2014 President Karimov proposed changes to the constitution that would transfer some presidential powers to the legislative and executive branches. Karimov, in office since 1989, has held an iron grip on the reins of government; however, questions have recently arisen over who might succeed President Karimov, who is 76. Some speculation has focused on his daughter, Gulnara KARIMOVA (recently in disfavor and under investigation for corruption), while other reports indicated the successor may be Prime Minister MIRZIYOEV, First Deputy Prime Minister Rustam AZIMOV, or National Security Service chief Rustam INOYATOV.

Reports emerged in January 2015 that the government had required as many as 1 million civil servants, including teachers and police officers, to help harvest cotton in the previous year in an effort to bolster exports.

Karimov's death on September 2, 2016, created a power struggle that was reportedly won by Prime Minister Mirziyoyev, who appeared set to win presidential elections scheduled for December.

POLITICAL PARTIES

The political system was dominated by President Karimov, who traditionally made all important decisions for the state. Karimov was initially the head of the People's Democratic Party of Uzbekistan (PDP), successor to the Soviet-era Uzbek Communist Party; however, in a bid for the appearance of a multiparty system, he formed the Liberal Democratic Party of Uzbekistan in 2003 and then became its leader. Although authorities permitted a small number of other parties to form, the government routinely bans true opposition parties. All five of the progovernment parties and organizations discussed below were established with President Karimov's participation or approval. (For more on political parties prior to 2004, see the 2012 *Handbook.*)

Progovernment Parties and Organizations:

Liberal Democratic Party of Uzbekistan—LDP (*Ozbekiston Liberal-Demokratik Partiyasi*—OzLiDeP). Aiming to attract businesses, entrepreneurs, and industrial workers, the LDP held its founding congress in November 2003, a month after receiving the imprimatur of President Karimov. The only new party to have been registered since the 1999 Supreme Assembly election, the LDP contested the December 2004–January 2005 balloting for the new lower house of the Supreme Assembly, finishing first, with 41 seats. The party's original chair, Qobiljon TOSHMATOV, resigned in May 2004, ostensibly for health reasons, although some reports indicated that he had earned President Karimov's displeasure at a session of the Supreme Assembly. The LDP held its fifth congress in November 2009. In the Legislative Chamber election of December 2009–January 2010 the party won a leading 53 seats. Reports in 2012 indicated a significant increase in efforts to expand local LDP chapters. Despite a 2012 spat between the LDP and the PDP and a 2010 commitment by Karimov to strengthen the legislative branch, all major decisions continued to be made by the president. In the December 2014–January 2015 Chamber balloting, the party won 52 seats. Karimov was reelected president in March 2015.

Karimov died on September 2, 2016. On September 16 prime minister and acting president Shavkat MIRZIYOYEV changed parties to run as the LDP candidate in the next presidential elections.

Leaders: Shavkat MIRZIYOYEV (Acting President of the Republic and Prime Minister), Muhammadyusuf TESHABOYEV (Chair), Baxtiyor YOQUBOV (Leader in the Legislative Chamber).

People's Democratic Party of Uzbekistan—PDP (*Ozbekiston Xalq Demokratik Partiyasi*). The PDP was organized in November 1991 as successor to the former Uzbek Communist Party, whose activities had been suspended in August. Officially committed to promarket reform and multi-party democracy, the PDP has nevertheless backed the Karimov government's cautious line on both fronts. In June 1996 President Karimov resigned as party chair and PDP member. His successor, Abdulkhafiz Jalolov, contested the January 2000 presidential race, with Karimov's approval, but won only 4.2 percent of the vote and subsequently retired from politics. A month earlier the PDP had won 48 Supreme Assembly seats, down from the 69 it had claimed in the balloting of December 1994–January 1995.

In the December 2004–January 2005 election for the new lower house the PDP won 28 seats, with another 8 being captured by party members who had been nominated by independent citizens' groups. In December 2007 the party's presidential candidate, Asliddin Rustamov, finished second, with 3.3 percent of the vote. In the 2009–2010 Legislative Chamber election the PDP won 32 seats.

Reports in 2011 indicated that a number of PDP members had defected to join a new grouping, the Social Democratic Party of Workers and Farmers.

In April 2013 at a party congress, Hotamjon KETMONOV became party chair. The party won 27 seats in the 2014–2015 Chamber elections. Ketmonov was the party's 2015 presidential candidate, and he received 2.9 percent of the vote.

Leaders: Hotamjon KETMONOV (Central Committee Chair, First Secretary, and 2015 presidential candidate), Asliddin RUSTAMOV (2007 presidential candidate), Latifjon GULOMOV (Leader in the Legislative Chamber).

National Revival Democratic Party (*Milliy Tiklanish Demokratik Partiyasi*—MTDP). The MTDP was formed in June 2008 by the merger of the **National Democratic Party "Self-Sacrificers"** (*Fidokorlar*) and the **National Revival Party** (*Milli Tiklanish Partiyasi*—MTP).

Established at a congress in December 1998, *Fidokorlar* (sometimes translated as "Patriots") was created in response to President Karimov's call a month earlier for a new party of uncorrupted, more youthful, future leaders. *Fidokorlar* won 34 seats in the December 1999 national election, and in January 2000 President Karimov was reelected under the party's banner. In April 2000 *Fidokorlar* and **Progress of the Fatherland** (*Vatan Tarrakiyeti*—VT) announced a merger, with the new group retaining *Fidokorlar* as its name. The VT, founded in 1992, was a promarket party broadly supportive of the Karimov government. In the 2004–2005 national election *Fidokorlar* won 18 seats, not counting 1 won by a party member nominated by an independent group of citizens.

The MTP, based in the Uzbek artistic and intellectual community, was founded in June 1995. It won 10 Supreme Assembly seats in 1999 and 11 in 2004–2005. The party chair, Xurshid DOSTMUHAMMAD, was nominated for the presidency in 2007, but he was kept off the ballot after failing to obtain the required number of supporting signatures (5 percent of the electorate).

The MTDP, which held its second congress in November 2009, won 31 seats in the subsequent Legislative Chamber election. In May 2013 Sarvar OTAMURADOV was elected party chair.

The party secured 36 seats in the 2014–2015 legislative balloting. Akmal SAIDOV was the MTDP presidential candidate in 2015, and he was second with 3.1 percent of the vote. MTDP prime minister Shavkat MIRZIYOYEV became acting president after Karimov's death, but switched parties to the LDP.

Leaders: Sarvar OTAMURADOV (Chair), Ulegbek MUHAMMADIYEV (Leader in the Legislative Chamber).

Justice Social Democratic Party of Uzbekistan (*Adolat Sotsialdemokratik Partiyasi*). *Adolat* was relaunched in February 1995 as a progovernment grouping, having in a previous incarnation been a grouping of Muslim dissidents that was banned shortly after its formation in 1992. Adopting a left-of-center economic and social program, the new party claimed the support of some 50 deputies in the new Supreme Assembly and subsequently obtained official registration. It won 11 Supreme Assembly seats in 1999 and 8 in the 2004–2005 election, not counting 2 seats claimed by party members nominated by independent citizens' groups.

In 2007 the party's leader at the time, Dilorom Tashmukhamedova, became the first woman to stand for president in Uzbekistan. She finished third in the December 2007 presidential election, capturing 3 percent of the vote, and is the current speaker of the lower house, in which *Adolat* holds 19 seats. Narimon UMAROV, chair of the State Committee for Nature Protection, was elected party leader in June 2013. The party won 20 seats in the legislative elections that began in December 2015. Umarov was the *Adolat* presidential candidate in March 2015, and he won 2 percent of the vote.

Leaders: Narimon UMAROV (Chair of the Party's Political Council), Dilorom TASHMUKHAMEDOVA (Speaker of the Legislative Chamber).

Ecological Movement of Uzbekistan—EMU (*Ozbekiston Ekologik Harakati*). Formed in August 2008 and sponsored by the government, the EMU focuses on environmental and public health issues. Aslan MAVLYANOV, the director of the Institute of Hydrology and Geological Engineering under the State Committee on Geology, initially led the group, whose members are primarily scientists and medical professionals. Under a law passed in December 2008, the EMU now holds 15 reserved seats in the Legislative Chamber. The EMU led the 2012 opposition to the proposed Tajik hydroelectric plant on the Amu Darya River and opposition in 2013 to a Tajik aluminum plant.

Leader: Boriy ALIXONOV (Chair).

Unregistered Groups:

***Birlik* Popular Movement Party** (*"Birlik" Xalq Harakati Partiyasi*). The *Birlik* Party, which held its founding congress in August 2003, traces its origin to the **Popular Movement of Uzbekistan "Unity"** (*Ozbekiston "Birlik" Xalq Harakati—Birlik*), a nationalist and secular formation launched in 1988 on a platform that urged secession from the Soviet Union. Presumed to be the strongest of the opposition groups (although weakened by the formation of *Erk*, below), it was not permitted to contest the presidential balloting of December 1991 and was banned by the Supreme Assembly for "antigovernment activities" the following year. Most of its principal leaders were subjected to beatings, imprisonment, and other forms of harassment by the Karimov regime.

Having failed to obtain reregistration as a party, *Birlik* did not contest the 1994–1995 election and held a congress in exile in Moscow in July 1995. Since again being denied party status in 1999, *Birlik* has continued as a nongovernmental social movement. Hoping to finally achieve recognition as a party, in 2003 *Birlik* members organized the *Birlik* Party, which was equally unsuccessful in its effort to register. The organization has close ties to the *Ezgulik* human rights society headed by Vasila INOYATOVA. However, while *Ezgulik* condemned the EU's decision in 2007 to ease sanctions against the Uzbek government, *Birlik* leadership supported the EU's move. *Birlik* leaders also asked the EU to demand their party be allowed to participate in the 2009 parliamentary elections. On November 21, 2010, party leader Abdurahim PULAT (Abdurakhim PULATOV) died in exile in the United States. Vasila Inoyatova was denied entry into Kyrgyzstan in 2014.

Leaders: Vasila INOYATOVA (Secretary General), Pulat AHUNOV (Deputy Chair).

Freedom Democratic Party of Uzbekistan (*Ozbekiston "Erk" Demokratik Partiyasi*). *Erk* was organized in April 1990 by a group of *Birlik* dissidents who called for economic and political autonomy for Uzbekistan within a Soviet federation. Its chair, Muhammad Salih, a prominent poet, was a distant runner-up to the Islam Karimov, then representing the PDP, in the 1991 presidential poll and in July 1992 resigned from the legislature (and left the country) after being denied an opportunity to speak. At a joint meeting the same month, *Erk* and *Birlik* representatives committed themselves to common action against the Karimov regime.

In October 1993 *Erk* failed to meet a deadline for reregistration as a party because it had no address, its offices having been declared a fire risk. A brother of the *Erk* chair was reported in August 1995 to have been jailed for five years for activism in the Association of Young Democrats of Turkistan, an *Erk* affiliate.

Karimov accused Salih of being behind the February 1999 bombings in Tashkent, despite an absence of convincing evidence. Salih was convicted of terrorism in November 2000 and sentenced, in absentia, to 15 years in prison.

Erk was permitted to hold its first party congress in ten years in October 2003, but it remained unregistered. An internal dispute saw a number of party members, led by Samad MUROV, argue for replacement of the party leadership—an effort that Secretary General Otanazar Oripov characterized in February 2004 as a government effort to undermine the party. In May 2006 a National Salvation Committee, newly established among exiles in Kyrgyzstan, proposed Salih as a presidential candidate for 2007. In June 2012 the second congress of *Erk* was held in Prague and reelected Salih as its leader. Reports in October 2012 indicated that several *Erk* members had been detained.

Leaders: Muhammad SALIH (SOLIH, SOLIKH; also known as Salay MADAMINOV) (Chair, in exile), Polat OXUNOV (Deputy Chair), Otanazar ORIPOV (Secretary General).

Free Peasants' Party (*Ozod Dehqonlar*—OD). At its founding congress in December 2003, the OD called for agricultural reform and limitations on presidential powers. The party failed to achieve legal status in 2004, and in September 2008 held a meeting in Tashkent to discuss economic issues. Among those invited were four human rights activists from the Jizakh region, who were detained at a Tashkent hotel by antiterrorism officials but released after a few hours. Other rights activists saw the arrests as an attempt to intimidate the organizers.

In April 2005 the OD announced formation of an opposition coalition called **Sunshine Uzbekistan** (*Serquyosh Ozbekistonim*). The Sunshine Coalition, as it is also known, is headed by Sanjar UMAROV, who in March 2006 was given a ten-year prison sentence for theft. After visiting him in July 2008, family members sent a letter to President Karimov pleading for his release, citing health concerns. Another of the group's leaders and sister to the general secretary, Nodira HIDOYATOVA, received a ten-year sentence but was released in May 2006. Umarov was finally released in November 2009, after which he left for the United States. In July 2012 party leader Nigora Hidoyatova fled Uzbekistan claiming she was about to be arrested.

Leader: Nigora HIDOYATOVA (Nigara KHIDOYATOVA).

Solidarity (*Birdamlik*). *Birdamlik* is an opposition movement led from the United States and committed to nonviolent change. In March 2007 it attempted to stage small protests in Tashkent, but these were disrupted by the authorities. It later called for a peaceful demonstration on the anniversary of the 2005 Andijan protest. Its leader, Bahodyr CHORIEV, has stated that *Birdamlik* hopes to unify all democratic Uzbek opposition parties. He was expelled from Uzbekistan in December 2009, only two months after having returned from abroad. An attempt to hold a constituent assembly in November was canceled when the government prevented delegates from attending. Three *Birdamlik* leaders were arrested in June 2012 for leading anti-Kyrgyz protests and only released after paying fines. The 71-year-old father of opposition leader Choriev was arrested and sentenced to five and a half years for the rape of a 19-year-old female in August 2013 only to be released in January 2014. Reports indicate that the initial charges were politically motivated.

Leaders: Bahodyr CHORIEV, Dilorom SHAKO.

Banned Groups:

Islamic Movement of Uzbekistan (IMU). The militant IMU, which has also been known since 2001 as the **Islamic Party of Turkestan,** advocates creation of an Islamic republic under religious law. Some of its members may have participated in the Justice (*Adolat*) Movement that was banned in 1992, but the IMU itself did not emerge until 1999. In May 2000 a U.S. State Department report labeled it as one of the world's most dangerous terrorist organizations and alleged that it had been behind the February 1999 Tashkent bombings and an August–October hostage situation in Kyrgyzstan. Later reports indicated that at least some members were moving from bases in Tajikistan to Afghanistan, where many of its members were apparently trained at al-Qaida camps.

In August 2000 two IMU incursions from across the Tajik border occurred. Operations against the 100 or so militants continued into September. Two months later the Supreme Court found IMU leaders Tahir YOLDASH (Tohir YOLDOSHEV) and Juma NAMANGONIY guilty, in absentia, of terrorism and imposed death sentences. In November 2001 Namangoniy was killed in Afghanistan, where IMU forces suffered heavy losses as allies of the Taliban. Policy differences within the IMU over whether to focus on opposing the Karimov regime or expanding its support for Islamic militancy throughout Central Asia and elsewhere apparently led to formation in 2002 of the Islamic Jihad Union (below). In May 2005 the Uzbek government assigned blame for the Andijan unrest to the IMU and *Hizb-ut-Tahrir* (below).

In January 2008 Yoldash, in a video, declared jihad on the Pakistani government and its security forces. In July Pakistan premier Yousaf Raza Gillani asserted that the IMU was behind a spike in violence in his nation's tribal areas. In September 2009 Pakistan stated that the 5,000 IMU operatives in the country's tribal areas constituted the area's largest foreign militant group. In August 2010 the IMU confirmed that Yoldash had been killed in August 2009 by a U.S. drone attack in Pakistan's northwest. Six suspected IMU militants were killed in a U.S. drone strike in July 2012 in Pakistan. In June 2013 Afghan officials asserted that IMU militants were increasingly active in the country and fighting alongside Taliban forces.

Videos emerged in March 2015 in which IMU fighters pledged their loyalty to the Islamic State (IS), and reports indicated joint IMU–IS attacks in Afghanistan against the Taliban. However, another faction of the group affirmed its loyalty to the Taliban in June 2016.

Leader: Usman ODIL.

Islamic Jihad Union—IJU (*Ittehad-e-Jihad Islamic;* aka Jihad Islamic Group—JIG). Believed to have been established in March 2002 by the most militant faction of the IMU after the IMU was severely weakened by the U.S.-led war in Afghanistan, the IJU claimed responsibility for a series of terrorist acts in Uzbekistan in March–July 2004. The organization also took responsibility for a foiled terrorist plot against the U.S. military base in Ramstein, Germany, in September 2007 and for two terrorist attacks in May 2009, one taking place at a post along the Uzbek–Kyrgyz border, and another in Andijan. The IJU claims to have hundreds of members operating in Europe. In April 2012 an Uzbek citizen was arrested in Philadelphia in the United States for supporting the IJU. Reports in April 2013 revealed that U.S. law enforcement officials were investigating links between the IJU and Tamerlan and Dzhokhar Tsarnaev, two brothers who carried out the Boston Marathon bombing (see entry on the United States).

For more on the banned ***Hizb ut-Tahrir*** (Liberation Party), see the 2012 *Handbook.*

LEGISLATURE

The Supreme Assembly (*Oliy Majlis*) was initially established as a unicameral legislature of 250 directly elected members. Constitutional revisions passed by referendum in February 2002 called for the establishment of a bicameral Supreme Assembly encompassing a Senate and a Legislative Chamber, with the members of both serving five-year terms. A law passed in December 2008 disqualifies independent candidates from contesting seats in the Legislative Chamber.

Senate (*Senati*). The Senate comprises 100 members: 16 presidential appointees in addition to 84 representatives (6 from each of the country's 12 regions, 6 from the capital, and 6 from the Karakalpakstan autonomous republic), chosen by and from among regional "representative bodies of state power. The initial presidential appointees included several cabinet members, judges, academics, heads of civil organizations, and industrialists. Elected members were most recently chosen on a nonpartisan basis on January 13–14, 2015.

Speaker: Nigmatilla YULDASHEV (MTDP).

Legislative Chamber (*Konunchilik Palatasi*). The lower chamber comprises 150 members, 135 directly elected and 15 chosen to represent the Ecological Movement of Uzbekistan. The most recent election was held December 21, 2014, with runoff balloting on January 4, 2015, produced the following results: Liberal Democratic Party of Uzbekistan, 52 seats; People's Democratic Party of Uzbekistan, 36; *Milliy Tiklanish* Democratic Party, 27; and Justice (*Adolat*) Social Democratic Party of Uzbekistan, 20,

Speaker: Nuriddinjon ISMAILOV.

CABINET

[as of August 7, 2016]

Prime Minister	Shavkat Mirziyoyev
First Deputy Prime Minister	Rustam Azimov
Deputy Prime Ministers	
Chair of the Women's Committee	Elmira Basitkhanova [f]
Chair State Committee for Architecture and Construction	Batir Zakirov
Culture, Education, Healthcare, and Social Security	Adham Ilkhamovich Ikromov
Industrial Sector	Ulugbek Rozukulov
Marine Geology, Fuel and Energy, and Chemical, Petrochemical, and Metallurgical Industries	Gulomjon Ibragimov
Ministers	
Agriculture and Water Resources	Shukhrat Teshayev
Culture and Sports	Bakhodir Akhmedov
Defense	Kabul Berdiyev
Economics	Galina Saidova [f]
Emergency Situations	Tursinkhon Khudayberganov
Finance	Rustam Azimov
Foreign Affairs	Abdulaziz Kamilov
Foreign Economic Relations, Investments, and Trade	Elyor Ganiev
Higher and Secondary Specialized Education	Alisher Vakhobov
Information Technology and Communications	Khurshid Mirzohidov
Internal Affairs	Maj. Gen. Adkham Ahmedbaev
Justice	Muzraf Ikramov
Labor and Social Protection	Aziz Abdukhakimov
Public Education	Inoyatov Ilyasovich
Public Health	Anvar Alimov
Secretary, National Security Council	Murod Atayev
Chairs of State Committees	
Customs	Zokhid Dusanov
Demonopolization and Development of Competition	Davron Khidoyatov
Geology and Mineral Resources	Ilkhomboy Turamuratov
Land Resources, Geodesy, Cartography, and Real Estate	Saidqul Arabov
Statistics	Botir Turaev
Taxes	Botir Parpiyev

[f] = female

INTERGOVERNMENTAL REPRESENTATION

Ambassador to the U.S.: Bakhtiyar GULYAMOV.

U.S. Ambassador to Uzbekistan: Pamela L. SPRATLEN.

Permanent Representative to the UN: Muzaffar A. MADRAHIMOV.

IGO Memberships (Non-UN): ADB, CIS, EAPC, EBRD, ECO, OIC, OSCE, PfP, SCO.

For Further Reference:

Adams, Laura. *The Spectacular State: Culture and National in Uzbekistan.* Durham, NC: Duke University Press, 2010.

Khalid, Adeeb. *Making Uzbekistan: Nation, Empire, and Revolution in the Early USSR.* Ithaca, NY: Cornell University Press, 2015.

Tunçer-Kilavuz, Idil. *Power, Networks and Violent Conflict in Central Asia: A Comparison of Tajikistan and Uzbekistan.* New York: Routledge, 2014.

VANUATU

Republic of Vanuatu
République de Vanuatu (French)
Ripablik blong Vanuatu (Bislama)

Political Status: Formerly the New Hebrides; became the Anglo-French Condominium of the New Hebrides in 1906; present name adopted upon becoming an independent member of the Commonwealth on July 30, 1980.

Area: 4,647 sq. mi. (12,035 sq. km).

Population: 271,000 (2016E—UN); 266,937 (2016E—U.S. Census).

Major Urban Center (2014E—UN): VILA (Port Vila, 53,000).

Official Languages: English, French, and Bislama. The latter, a pidgin dialect, is recognized constitutionally as the "national language," and efforts are currently under way to accord it equal status with English and French as a medium of instruction. Vanuatu has the highest density of languages per capita in the world, with an estimated 138 languages, or slightly less than 1 per 2,000 inhabitants.

Monetary Unit: Vatu (official rate October 1, 2016: 107.11 vatu = $1US).

President: Baldwin LONSDALE (ind.); elected by the electoral college on September 22, 2014, and inaugurated on the same day for a five-year term, succeeding Iolu Johnson ABIL (Party of Our Land), whose term of office had expired on September 2. (Philip BOEDORO, the speaker of Parliament, served as acting president from September 2 to September 22.)

Prime Minister: Charlot SALWAI (Reunification Movement for Change); elected on February 11, 2016, to replace Sato KILMAN (People's Progress Party).

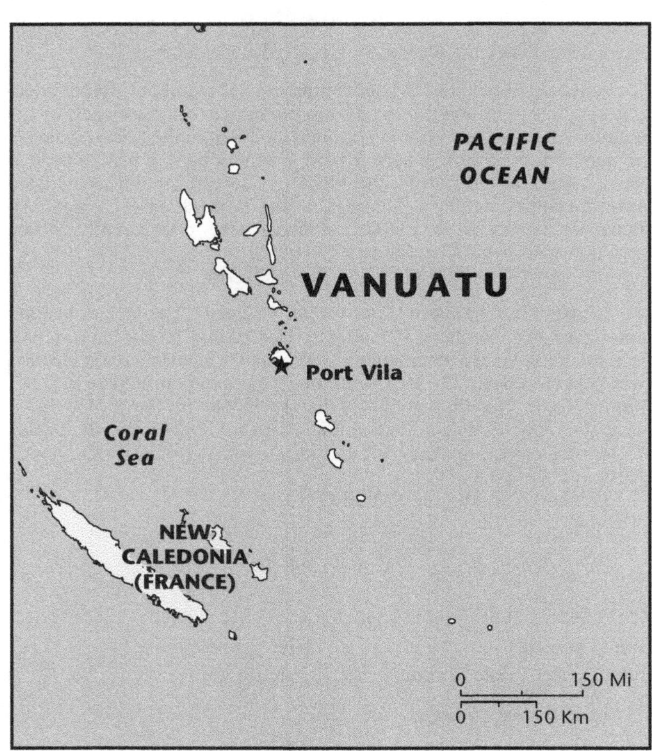

THE COUNTRY

An 800-mile-long archipelago of some 80 islands, Vanuatu is situated in the western Pacific southeast of the Solomon Islands and northeast of New Caledonia. The larger islands of the group are Espiritu Santo, Malekula, Tanna, Ambrym, Pentecost, Erromanga, Aoba, Epi, and Efaté, on which the capital, Vila, is located. Over 90 percent of the inhabitants are indigenous Melanesians; the remainder encompasses small groups of French, English, Vietnamese, Chinese, and other Pacific islanders. Approximately 85 percent are Christian, Presbyterians constituting the largest single denomination, followed by Roman Catholics and Anglicans. Approximately three-quarters of adult women have been described as "economically active," most of them in agricultural pursuits; female participation in government, on either the village or national level, is minimal.

The bulk of the population is engaged in some form of agriculture. Coconuts, taro, and yams are grown for subsistence purposes, with copra, kava, timber, cocoa, and beef constituting the principal exports. In 1981 a national airline was established, while maritime legislation was enacted to promote Vanuatu as "a flag of convenience." The country also emerged as an offshore financial center. Approximately 500 companies (including more than 50 banks as of 2016, according to the U.S. Federal Reserve) incorporated in Port Vila still yield close to $1.5 million annually in revenue. Foreign investors are not permitted to own land but can invest, and the lack of individual and corporate income taxes makes the island nation an attractive investment location.

In June 2000 Vanuatu was threatened with economic sanctions by the Organization for Economic Cooperation and Development (OECD) for "harmful" policies related to its offshore financial services. Although the government pledged its cooperation in fighting money laundering and other financial crimes, in 2001 it insisted that it had the right to set its own tax policies and would not share information about nonnational accounts with foreign tax authorities. Further action regarding Vanuatu's international tax status produced a dispute with Australian authorities in early 2008.

Vanuatu has remained one of six Pacific island countries on the OECD list of money-laundering venues.

Although Vanuatu was formally characterized by the United Nations as a "least developed country," tourism, forestry projects, and the discovery of promising mineral deposits, including gold and manganese, offer potential for long-term economic growth. From 1990 to 1999, the annual real change in GNP averaged 2.5 percent. Improvements early in the next decade yielded an annual average of 6.4 percent for 2004–2008. The economic progress led the UN to announce in July 2006 that Vanuatu would likely qualify for "developing country" status by 2013, a change rejected by the Edward NATAPEI administration in mid-2009, since it would entail a reduction in foreign aid. Current projections are that the country will lose status in 2017. Growth slowed to 3.5 percent in 2009 and, in the face of challenging economic times worldwide, averaged 2 percent through 2012. In 2013 GDP rose by 2.3 percent while inflation reached 1.3 percent. In 2014 GDP shrunk by 0.8 percent, while unemployment settled at 1 percent. In 2015 growth resumed at 4.5 percent, although inflation kept pace at 3.3 percent. Estimates for 2016 show 4 percent GDP growth and a drop in inflation to 2.4 percent. Estimated unemployment for 2016 is 10.6 percent.

GOVERNMENT AND POLITICS

Political background. Settled during the first half of the 19th century by a variety of British and French nationals, including a sizable contingent of missionaries, the New Hebrides subsequently became the scene of extensive labor recruitment by plantation owners in Fiji and Queensland. Following a series of unsuccessful efforts to stem the frequently inhumane practice of "blackbirding," Britain and France established a Joint Naval Commission in 1886 to safeguard order in the archipelago. Two decades later, faced with competition by German interests, the two governments agreed to form a cumbersome but reasonably serviceable condominium structure that entailed dual instruments of administration at all levels, including two police forces, two resident commissioners, and two local commissioners in each of the territory's four districts.

A 42-member Representative Assembly (replacing an Advisory Council established in 1957) convened for the first time in November 1976 but immediately became embroiled in controversy as to whether 13 members not elected by universal suffrage (4 representing tribal chiefs and 9 representing economic interests) should be required to declare party allegiance. Condemning what they termed the "present unworkable system of government," the 21 representatives of the Party of Our Land (*Vanua'aku Pati*—VP) boycotted the second assembly session in February 1977, prompting the colonial administrators to call a new election, the results of which were voided because of another VP boycott.

In the assembly election of November 14, 1979, the VP won 26 of 39 seats, and on November 29 party leader Fr. Walter Hadye LINI was designated as chief minister. Earlier, the colonial powers had agreed to independence in 1980, a constitution having been drafted in September and approved in a series of notes between London and Paris in October.

The attainment of independence on July 30, 1980, was clouded by secessionist movements on a number of islands, most importantly Espiritu Santo, whose principal town had been seized, with indirect support from the local French community, by the cultist *Na-Griamel* movement under the leadership of Jimmy Tupou Patuntun STEVENS. The Vanuatu flag was, however, raised on Santo on July 30 by an emissary of the Lini government in the presence of a contingent of British and French troops that was withdrawn on August 18 upon the arrival of a Papua New Guinean force backed by central government police. Most of the insurgents subsequently surrendered, and Stevens was sentenced on November 21 to a prison term of 14.5 years (ultimately serving 11, before being released because of poor health). The aftermath of the revolt continued well into 1981, with over 700 eventually convicted of related crimes. Stevens's trial had revealed that the insurgency was supported by both the former French resident commissioner (subsequently declared *persona non grata* by the Lini government) and the Phoenix Foundation, a right-wing group based in Carson City, Nevada. By late 1981 the security situation had improved substantially, and all of the imprisoned rebels except Stevens and his principal lieutenant, Timothy WELLES, were released.

The Lini government was returned to office in the islands' first postindependence election on November 2, 1983. Three months later, following his conviction on a charge of nonpayment of a road tax, President George Ati SOKOMANU resigned. Despite voicing his frustration with Father Lini and offering to lead a new "national unity" government as prime minister, Sokomanu was reappointed to his former post by the electoral college on March 8.

Lini was returned to office in the balloting of November 30, 1987, with the VP's vote share falling for the first time below 50 percent, while the opposition Union of Moderate Parties (*Union blong Moderet Pati*—UMP) increased its showing to 42 percent, compared with 33 percent in 1983.

Following the 1987 election a leadership dispute erupted between Lini and party ideologue Barak SOPE Ma'au Tamate, who mounted an unsuccessful bid for the prime minister position and was subsequently charged with instigating a major riot in Vila on May 16, 1988. In the wake of the disturbance, Sope was dismissed from the cabinet, stripped of his long-time post as party secretary general, and, along with four associates, expelled from the party after endorsing a no-confidence motion against the administration. On July 25 the "Gang of Five" was also ousted from Parliament under a 1983 Vacation of Seats Act that precluded alteration of party affiliation by members. In response to the action, 18 members of the opposition UMP initiated a legislative boycott and on July 27 were also expelled for violating a parliamentary ban on three consecutive absences. Ironically, the Vanuatu Court of Appeal on October 21 ruled the 1983 act unconstitutional and reinstated the Sope parliamentarians (who had regrouped as the Melanesian Progressive Party—MPP) while upholding the ouster of the UMP members.

Five days after by-elections on December 13, 1988, for the vacated UMP seats, which neither the UMP nor the MPP contested, President Sokomanu attempted to dissolve Parliament and name an "interim" government headed by Sope. Lini reacted by arresting Sope and his "ministers," with the Supreme Court ruling on December 19 that the president's action had been unconstitutional because it had not been undertaken with the support of two-thirds of the legislators and the advice of the prime minister. On January 12, 1989, Sokomanu was dismissed from office for "gross misconduct," and on January 30 Health Minister Fred TIMAKATA was designated by the electoral college as his successor. Subsequently, Sokomanu was convicted of incitement to mutiny and sentenced to a six-year prison term, while Sope and UMP leader Maxime CARLOT received five-year sentences for seditious conspiracy and treason. The sentences were dismissed in April by an appeals tribunal of jurists from Tonga, Papua New Guinea, and Vanuatu, although the convictions were allowed to stand.

In the wake of severe criticism from key party leaders for dismissing dissident party members and numerous other purges of government personnel (the prime minister at one point was reported to be holding more than 50 portfolios), Lini was replaced by General Secretary Donald KALPOKAS as VP president at a special party congress on August 7, 1991. On September 6, after President Timakata had denied a request that Parliament be dissolved, Lini was also ousted as prime minister, with Kalpokas designated his successor. Lini and a number of supporters thereupon organized the National Unity Party (NUP), which, by splitting the traditional VP vote in the election of December 2, gave a plurality to the francophone UMP. On December 16, in an action he characterized as stemming from a "pact with the devil," the UMP's CARLOT (the honorific "Korman" subsequently being added to his name) formed a governing coalition with the NUP and a small regional formation, *Fren Melanesia.*

Initially withdrawing to the status of a parliamentary backbencher, Lini precipitated a government crisis in mid-1993 by reportedly demanding appointment as deputy prime minister and minister of justice. Rebuffed in the matter, Lini and five legislative colleagues withdrew their support for the government, thereby causing a rupture with a progovernment NUP faction led by Sethy John REGENVANU, which subsequently reorganized as the People's Democratic Party (PDP). The ensuing reduction in Carlot Korman's parliamentary majority to 24 of 46 seats made it impossible to reach the two-thirds majority in the electoral college needed to elect a new president at the expiration of the incumbent Timakata's term on January 31, 1994. It was not until March 2 that a compromise government nominee, Jean-Marie LEYE Lenelgau, was able to secure election through a decision by the VP, which held 9 legislative seats, to support his candidacy. As a result of its action the VP was expelled from the opposition coalition, with Barak Sope succeeding the VP's Kalpokas as leader of the opposition.

In September 1994, as the result of a Decentralisation Act approved four months earlier, the country's 11 local government councils were abolished to pave the way for elected bodies in six newly defined provinces. For the ensuing provincial council balloting of November 15, the opposition consisted, on the one hand, of Lini's NUP and, on the other, of a Unity Front (UF) coalition encompassing the VP, the MPP, the Tan Union, and a relegalized *Na-Griamel* under the leadership of its founder's son, Frankie STEVENS (although the younger Stevens was also serving as the leader of government business in Parliament). The result was a three-way split, with the UMP, NUP, and UF winning two provinces each, although the UF secured an overall plurality of 41 seats, as contrasted with 34 and 20 for the UMP and NUP, respectively.

In the general election of November 30, 1995, Kalpokas's UF secured a plurality of 20 legislative seats, while Carlot's UMP won 17 and Lini's NUP, 9. Meanwhile, a deep intra-UMP split had developed between Carlot and the party president, Serge VOHOR, with the UF seeking an alliance both with the Vohor faction and with the NUP. Intense negotiation then ensued, with Vohor eventually concluding a pact with the NUP that yielded his installation as Carlot's successor on December 24.

In early February 1996 a number of Carlot's supporters joined the UF in a motion of no confidence in Vohor, whose resignation averted the need for a vote and permitted Carlot to form a new government in coalition with the UF. The dispute between Carlot and Vohor intensified in March, with Vohor convening a UMP congress (on his home island of Santo) at which Carlot and his supporters were expelled from the party. Two months later, anti-Vohor faction leader Amos ANDENG called for a retaliatory congress (in Carlot's home village of Erakor) that declared the action of the Santo meeting invalid and named Carlot to succeed Vohor as UMP president.

In mid-1996 the Carlot administration was rocked by the issuance of an ombudsman's report charging that the country faced bankruptcy because of an alleged scam involving issuance of letters of guarantee signed by Carlot and his finance minister, Barak Sope. While denying any wrongdoing, the prime minister shuffled his cabinet on August 5, reassigning Sope to the Ministry of Commerce and Trade. Having refused to accept the demotion, Sope was dismissed from the government on August 12. Concurrently, Carlot cited the MPP leader for "disloyalty" in withdrawing his party from the UF in favor of a new alliance with the Tan Union and *Fren Melanesia,* styled the MTF. The government coalition thus being effectively reduced to his UMP faction and the VP rump of the UF, Carlot succumbed to a no-confidence vote on September 30 and was immediately succeeded by party rival Vohor, who named Sope as his deputy.

On October 12, 1996, while Vohor was visiting French Polynesia, striking members of the paramilitary Vanuatu Mobile Force (VMF) abducted President Leye and flew him to the northern island of Malekula for talks at gunpoint with Acting Prime Minister Sope, who promised that payment would be forthcoming to the VMF for long overdue arrears of $980,000. Thirteen days later Sope and three MTF ministerial colleagues were sacked in a cabinet shakeup that brought the VP into the government as a coalition partner of Vohor's UMP faction and the NUP. In late May 1997 Vohor and Carlot reconciled, with Carlot and his UMP-Natora faction joining Vohor's UMP group, Sope's MPP, and the NUP in a new government coalition, the VP's Kalpokas again becoming leader of a one-party opposition. Friction between Carlot and Vohor resurfaced, with the former filing a no-confidence motion in November against the prime minister. President Leye immediately dissolved the legislature and ordered new elections, which, following a January 1998 Court of Appeal ruling upholding his decision, were held on March 6. The balloting produced no significant alteration in the party makeup of the Parliament, and after intense negotiations the VP and the NUP, long-time rivals, agreed to form the next government. On March 30 the VP's Kalpokas returned as prime minister.

On October 19, 1998, Kalpokas dismissed his deputy, Lini, and expelled his NUP from the ruling coalition because of the party's participation in drafting a no-confidence motion. Kalpokas then formed a new alliance with a faction of the UMP headed by Willie JIMMY and the John Frum Movement (JFM).

Nearly two dozen candidates competed in the 1999 presidential race. No one received the required support in the first round of balloting of the electoral college in mid-March. Following negotiations, Fr. John Bernard BANI, an Anglican minister and Kalpokas ally, was elected on March 25 with the reported support of all parties except the NUP, even though he had received only two votes on the first ballot.

The government lost its parliamentary majority in by-elections in August 1999 and, facing the loss of a no-confidence vote, Kalpokas resigned on November 25. MPP leader Barak Sope was immediately elected his successor, appointing a coalition administration that included members of the JFM, the NUP, the UMP, the Vanuatu Republican Party (VRP), and *Fren Melanesia Pati* (FMP).

Divisions within the UMP, including the departure in early 2001 of Willie Jimmy's faction, were followed in late March by Serge Vohor's decision to withdraw what was left of the UMP from the government and side with the VP, now headed by Edward Natapei, leader of the opposition. Without UMP support, Prime Minister Sope could no longer command a parliamentary majority, but he failed to convince President Bani to dissolve Parliament and schedule a new general election. In early April, Parliament Speaker Paul Ren TARI of the NUP refused to permit legislative debate on a no-confidence motion filed by the opposition, which turned to the courts for redress. With the country's chief justice having threatened to cite Tari for contempt if he failed to let debate proceed, the no-confidence motion passed 27–18 on April 13, immediately after which Natapei was elected prime minister at the head of a VP-UMP coalition.

In the parliamentary election of May 2, 2002, Natapei's VP secured 14 seats and its coalition partner, the UMP, won 15, thereby ensuring the reelection of Natapei as prime minister when the new Parliament convened on June 3. His tenure ended with an inconclusive election on July 6, 2004, that yielded the third designation of the UMP's Serge Vohor on July 29. Vohor subsequently became embroiled in a dispute over his decision in early November to establish diplomatic relations with Taiwan, and his government fell on December 11, followed by the election of Ham LINI as head of a nine-party coalition administration.

In the election of September 2, 2008, the VP won a plurality of 11 seats, and Natapei was again designated to lead a coalition government that included Lini as his deputy prior to a reshuffle in November 2009 in which the ministers from the NUP and VPR were dropped from the cabinet and members of the opposition, including Sato KILMAN, theretofore the leader of the opposition, were added.

In mid-2009 Maxime Carlot Korman abandoned his post as deputy opposition leader to support the Natapei administration, while Natapei's deputy, Ham Lini, expelled the parliamentary speaker, George WELLS, from the NUP for alleged involvement in negotiations to topple the coalition government. Subsequently, Carlot Korman replaced Wells as speaker but was obliged to return the office to his predecessor in January 2010. In December 2010 the Natapei government lost a vote of no confidence, resulting in his dismissal as prime minister. Parliament immediately elected Deputy Prime Minister Sato Kilman as the next prime minister; he defeated former prime minister Vohor by a vote of 29–23. Kilman's tenure ended with a no-confidence motion on April 24, 2011, passed 26–25. Parliament subsequently elected Serge Vohor to a fourth term as prime minister, though his term was voided by a May 13 Court of Appeals ruling that by winning half of parliamentary votes, Vohor had failed to secure the constitutionally mandated clear majority.

The office thus returned to its previous holder, Sato Kilman. Shortly thereafter, however, the Chief Justice of Vanuatu voided Kilman's initial 2010 election on the grounds that it was not conducted by the appropriate secret balloting prescribed by the Constitution, and Edward Natapei was appointed to head an interim government. On June 26, 2011, Kilman was elected for technically his first term as prime minister defeating Vohor with 29 votes to 23.

Legislative elections were held on October 30, 2012, and after three weeks, Kilman negotiated a ruling coalition. He resigned in March 2013, and Moana Carcasses Kalosil of the Vanuatu Green Party (VGP) was elected on March 23. Following a confidence vote on May 15, 2014, Joe Natuman of the VP became prime minister and appointed a new cabinet. Baldwin Lonsdale was elected and inaugurated president on September 22, 2014.

In legislative balloting on January 22, 2016, the VP, UMP, and Land and Justice Party (*Graon mo Jastis Pati*—GJP) each won 6 of the 52 seats, and the remaining seats were distributed among 15 other parties (see Current issues, below). On February 11 Charlot SALWAI of the Reunification Movement for Change—RMC (*Namangi Aute*) was elected prime minister of a ten-party coalition government, led by the VP.

Constitution and government. Under the independence constitution, Vanuatu's head of state is a largely titular president designated for a five-year term by an electoral college consisting of all members of the Parliament and the presidents of the six provincial councils. Executive power is vested in a prime minister elected by secret legislative ballot; both the prime minister and other ministers (whom the prime minister appoints) must hold legislative seats. Members of the unicameral Parliament are elected from multimember constituencies through a partially proportional system intended "to ensure fair representation of different political groups and opinions." The legislative term is four years, subject to dissolution. There is also a National Council of Chiefs, whose members are designated by peers sitting in District Councils of Chiefs. The National Council is empowered to make recommendations to the government and Parliament on matters relating to indigenous custom and language. A national ombudsman is appointed by the president after consultation with the prime minister, party leaders, the president of the National Council of Chiefs, and others. The judicial system is headed by a four-member Supreme Court, the chief justice being named by the president after consultation with the prime minister and the leader of the opposition; of the other three justices, one is nominated by the speaker of Parliament, one by the president of the National Council of Chiefs, and one by the six council presidents. A Court of Appeal is constituted by two or more Supreme Court justices sitting together. Parliament is authorized to establish village and island courts, as deemed appropriate.

President Kalkot MATASKELEKELE wrote a formal letter to Prime Minister Lini in June 2006 repeating a recommendation he had made earlier that Vanuatu adopt a republican system of government with a popularly elected president who would be the head of state and the head of government with the power to appoint a cabinet whose members would not necessarily be members of Parliament. Lini responded by acknowledging that the country needed to engage in a review of the national constitution but stopped short of endorsing a presidential system.

The six provinces created in 1994 bear names that are acronyms of those of their principal islands. Stretching roughly from north to south they are Torba (Torres, Banks), Sama (Espiritu Santo, Malo), Penama (Pentecost, Ambae, Maéwo), Malampa (Malakula, Ambrym, Paama), Shefa (Shepherds, Epi, Efaté), and Tafea (Tanna, Anatom, Futuna, Erromango, Aniwa).

Freedom of speech is constitutionally protected, and the government generally respects freedom of the press. There is one government-owned newspaper, in addition to several privately owned ones. Vanuatu has just one television station.

Foreign relations. Although Vanuatu was not admitted to the United Nations until the fall of 1981, it became, at independence, a member both of the Commonwealth and the *Agence de Coopération Culturelle et Technique,* an organization established in 1969 to promote cultural and technical cooperation within the French-speaking world. Regionally, it is a member of the Pacific Community and the Pacific Islands Forum (PIF), which increased Vanuatu's support for greater regional and international labor mobility, especially in regard to greater access to Australia and New Zealand labor markets for its citizens. In 1984 both the Asian Development Bank and the Economic and Social Commission for Asia and the Pacific established regional headquarters in Port Vila. Diplomatic relations were established with the Soviet Union in July 1986 and with the United States the following October, although Vanuatu maintains no embassies abroad, save for the appointment in late 2007 of an ambassador to the European Union in Brussels as part of an effort to secure enhanced development aid. In addition, Vanuatu established a diplomatic office in Fiji, which opened on March 29, 2011.

Under the francophone UMP, Vanuatu's prior policy of supporting liberation struggles and actively attacking remaining pockets of colonialism in the Pacific subsided, particularly with regard to the French territory of New Caledonia. (For information about Vanuatu and the South Pacific Nuclear-Free Zone, see the 2013 *Handbook.*) Nevertheless, Vanuatu still disputes two islands, Matthew and Hunter, near New Caledonia, with France.

Vanuatu is a member of the Melanesian Spearhead Group (MSG), a South Pacific island regional bloc that includes Fiji, Papua New Guinea, and the Solomon Islands, formed in 1986 to promote economic development and sustainable growth, good government, preservation of Melanesian cultures, and regional cooperation and security among members, and in the 1990s was a force supporting decolonization movements in New Caledonia.

Prime Minister Vohor announced on November 3, 2004, that Vanuatu established relations with Taiwan, asserting intentions to maintain existing relations with the People's Republic of China (a position to which the PRC took immediate exception). Vohor's own cabinet voted twice against the action, and upon his ouster, all agreements made by Vohor with Taiwan were repealed by the new government. Subsequently, Prime Ministers Lini and Natapei lauded Beijing's one-China policy in meetings with PRC officials in 2005 and 2010, respectively.

In early 2008 Vanuatu completed domestic requirements for inclusion in the Pacific Island Countries Trade Agreement (PICTA).

Vanuatu has recently sought to formally restart talks for accession to the World Trade Organization (WTO). Talks had been suspended in 2001, in part over Vanuatu's unwillingness to expose its retail, telecommunications, and services sectors to rapid liberalization. In furtherance of its independence in trade policy, Vanuatu continued to withhold negotiation on WTO entry until April 2009, when discussions resumed after most of its concerns had apparently been resolved. The WTO welcomed Vanuatu as a new member on October 26, 2011. Parliament passed the legislation, and President Abil signed on in June 2012.

The Kilman administration announced in May 2011 that it was formally recognizing Abkhazia, a disputed region within Georgia that claims to be a sovereign state, becoming one of six countries to do so. In May 2013 Georgian media reported that the island nation had revoked its recognition of Abkhazia. Georgian media reported an agreement on diplomatic and consular relations was established in July 2013. In April 2014 Vanuatu formalized diplomatic relations with Tblisi.

Tensions escalated between Vanuatu and Australia after a senior advisor to Prime Minister Kilman was arrested in May 2012 at Sydney Airport for his part in an international tax scam. In response to what the administration interpreted as international humiliation, Vanuatu's foreign office expelled 12 Australian Federal Police (AFP) officers, who had been stationed in Port Vila as part of Australia's policing expansion through the Pacific region. Following talks in early 2013, Vanuatu in February agreed on the return of AFP officers.

In May 2016 Vanuatu agreed to follow international standards regulating the automatic exchange of financial account information in an effort to further curb tax evasion, money laundering, and potential financing of terrorism.

Current issues. More than 70 candidates, including Kilman, were left off the initial ballot list for the October 30, 2012, election because of outstanding government debts. Nearly 350 candidates from over 30 parties, a record high, contested. Sixteen parties secured representation. No single group secured more than 10 seats (the VP, with 8, won the largest presence). Kilman, uniting his PPP with groupings, including the NUP and VGP, scraped together the 29 votes needed to confirm him for a second term on November 21. His administration immediately faced a no-confidence motion and a lawsuit charging Kilman's ineligibility due to outstanding debt (dismissed by the Supreme Court in late January). By mid-March parliamentary opposition had reportedly gathered 33 supporters for a no-confidence motion. Kilman resigned on March 21 to avoid the motion. Moana Carcasses Kalosil of the VGP was elected with 34 votes on March 23 and appointed his cabinet the same day.

In mid-February 2014 the opposition had reportedly garnered the necessary support for a successful no-confidence motion, including six defectors from the Carcasses government. The prime minister reshuffled the cabinet on February 26 to include four new opposition members and regained the support of the defectors, staving off the confidence vote scheduled for February 27.

Controversy over the funding of a new airport project and accusations that the government was selling diplomatic passports in 2013 helped the opposition gather 35 votes to oust Carcasses in a May 15, 2014, confidence vote. The VP's Joe Natuman was elected prime minister that day and reshuffled the cabinet.

For almost three weeks after the conclusion of President Abil's term on September 2, the presidency remained vacant, as 13 candidates vied for the position. On September 22, after eight rounds of voting, independent Baldwin Lonsdale won 46 votes of the total 58 votes, winning the presidency. He was inaugurated the same day.

In one of the worst natural disasters in the country's history, on March 3, 2015, Tropical Cyclone Pam struck Vanuatu and other island nations in the region, causing an estimated $240 million in damage (approximately one-third of annual GDP).

On October 15, 2015, half of Kilman's government, including his deputy prime minister, Moana CARCASSES Kalosii, was sacked following a bribery scandal. Fourteen ministers and legislators were imprisoned. This led to the dissolution of the government and new elections on January 22, 2016. Following the elections, Kilman's government fell as the result of a vote of no confidence. Charlot Salwai was elected to replace him on February 11.

POLITICAL PARTIES

Government Parties:

Reunification Movement for Change—RMC (*Namangi Aute*). The RMC secured three seats in the October 2012 balloting. Two RMC members joined the Carcasses cabinet in 2014, helping the prime minister to avert a no confidence vote, but failed to secure the administration in May 2014. Nonetheless, one minister retained his seat in the Natuman cabinet named that month. Charlot SALWAI was elected prime minister following the January 2016 parliamentary elections, when the party won three seats.

Leader: Charlot SALWAI (Prime Minister).

Party of Our Land (*Vanua'aku Pati*—VP). Long at the forefront of the drive for independence and the return of indigenous lands, the VP was formed in 1972 as the **New Hebrides National Party.** Its boycott of a Representative Assembly election in 1977 led to cancellation of the results. It won 26 of 46 legislative seats in November 1987, a reduction, proportionally, from 24 of 39 in 1983. In December 1987 Secretary General Barak Sope challenged Fr. Walter Lini for the party leadership but was defeated by a near 2–1 vote. Sope was expelled from Parliament on July 25, 1988, for reportedly instigating a riot in Vila in mid-May. He and four other former VP members announced the formation of a rival Melanesian Progressive Party (MPP, below), whose members refused to accept court-sanctioned legislative reinstatement on October 21. In early 1989 Sope was convicted of sedition. The VP won all of the 5 vacant seats filled by special elections in 1989 because of boycotts by the MPP and UMP.

The VP split as a result of the 1991 ouster of its longtime leader, Father Lini, who subsequently formed the NUP. Prior to the November 1994 provincial elections the party joined the MPP and the Tan Union in a coalition called the **Unity Front** (UF), which won a plurality of 20 seats in the general election of November 1995 but became effectively moribund upon withdrawal of the MPP and Tan Union in August 1996.

The VP returned to government in October 1996, moved into opposition in May 1997, and in March 1998 joined with the NUP in forming an administration that lasted until November 1999. Shortly thereafter, Donald Kalpokas was replaced as party leader by Edward Natapei, who became prime minister in April 2001 and retained the post after the May 2002 election, in which the party won 14 seats. Natapei was forced to resign after the election of June 2004, in which the VP was reduced to 8 seats, but became Lini's deputy prime minister in July 2007. He returned as prime minister in September 2008. A leadership struggle in early 2010 led to the suspension of Natapei's rival, Harry IAUKO. In 2010 Natapei lost a vote of no confidence. In June 2011 he was named the leader of the opposition in a coalition with the UMP. With 8 seats, the VP was the biggest vote-getter in October 2012 balloting, however initial attempts to form a ruling coalition failed and the VP was relegated to the opposition. Following Kilman's March 2013 resignation, the VP supported a VGP-led government. In May 2014, the VP supported a successful motion of no confidence in Prime Minister Carcasses. On May 15 Joe Natuman was elected prime minister and took over party leadership after Natapei's death in July 2015. Natuman remained in office until he lost a no-confidence vote on June 11, 2015. The VP held six seats after the January 2016 elections, and Natuman was designated deputy prime minister.

Leaders: Joe NATUMAN (Deputy Prime Minister and Party Leader), Sela MOLISA (Secretary General), Iolu ABIL (Former President of the Republic).

Melanesian Progressive Party (MPP). The MPP was organized by Barak Sope and four other VP members after the former VP secretary general had been expelled from the party in mid-1988. In April 1989 ousted President George Sokomanu formally joined the new group after he, Sope, and two others had been released from prison by reversal of their sedition convictions.

During 1989 both the **Vanuatu Independent Alliance Party** (VIAP) and the **National Democratic Party** (NDP) merged with the MPP. The VIAP was a Santo-based group formed in June 1982 by two dismissed VP ministers, Thomas Reuben SERU and George WOREK; for the 1983 campaign it adopted a platform based on "free enterprise capitalism and anticommunism," losing all three of its existing parliamentary seats. The NDP, formed in late 1986 under former Lini government minister John NAUPA, was critical of the administration's handling of the economy and emphasized good relations with Britain and France.

Following Prime Minister Sope's ouster in April 2001, it appeared likely that the MPP and the other leading opposition party, the NUP, would establish a coalition. Instead, an MPP faction led by Sato Kilman split off (see PPP, below) in August. The MPP won only three seats in the 2002 election and an equal number in 2004. It declined further to one seat in 2008. In 2011 Witeu SOPE, the younger brother of party President Barak Sope, defected from the party and joined the **Vanuatu Labor Party**. It won two seats in the October 2012 election. Though initially joining Kilman's coalition, the MPP threw its support behind Carcasses in March 2013. Party leader Esmon SAIMON was appointed to the VGP-led cabinet and retained his position after Joe Natuman became prime minister in May 2014. The party won one seat in the 2016 elections.

Leaders: Esmon SAIMON (Leader of Parliament), Barak SOPE (Former Prime Minister).

Land and Justice Party (*Graon mo Jastis Pati*—GJP). The GJP, created in November 2010 by former independent MP Ralph REGENVANU, is centered on the ideas of land and justice, and it represents what it calls "four legs": the church, chiefs, women, and youth. In October 2012 balloting, the GJP won four seats. Attempts to form a ruling coalition with the VP and the UMP failed in November. The GJP joined the ruling government formed under Carcasses in March 2013 and joined the Natuman government in May 2014. The party won six seats in the January 2016 elections, tying with the VP and joining them in the VP-led cabinet.

Leaders: Ralph REGENVANU (Party President and Founder, Minister for Lands and Natural Resouces), Anthea TOKA (Secretary).

National Unity Party (NUP). The NUP was organized by Fr. Walter Lini following his ouster as VP president on August 7, 1991, and his defeat on a parliamentary no-confidence motion on September 6. Third-ranked with nine seats, after the 1995 election, the NUP reentered the government as the UMP's junior partner. Excluded from the Carlot government of February 1996, the NUP returned as a participant in the second Vohor administration in late October 1996, although Lini did not enter the cabinet until succeeding his estranged sister, Hilda LINI, as justice minister in November.

Prior to his dismissal in October 1998, Walter Lini served as Prime Minister Kalpokas's deputy in a VP-NUP coalition. He died on February 21, 1999. Ten months later the NUP was a leading participant in formation of Barak Sope's five-party government. In the 2002 parliamentary election, the NUP declined from 11 to 8 seats, but it rebounded to 10 seats in July 2004, with Lini's brother, Ham, forming a coalition government on December 11. It retained the eight seats but lost its plurality to the VP in the September 2008 poll. A participant in the subsequent Natapei administration, it was obliged to go into opposition by the cabinet reshuffle of November 2009. The UNP returned to government with the election of Sato Kilman as prime minister in June 2011. Kilman named Ham Lini as deputy prime minister and appointed two other NUP members to the cabinet. The NUP won three seats in October 2013 balloting. A party split subsequently emerged as Ham Lini signed an agreement to join Kilman's alliance, while party vice president Mokin STEVENS penned an agreement with the VP and the UMP. Ham Lini's support proved critical to the VP-led ouster of Carcasses in May 2014, and Lini became deputy prime minister under Joe Natuman. The party won four seats in the scandal-induced January 2016 elections, but Lini was not among them. However, Lini was given a cabinet post in the VP-dominated government.

Leaders: Ham LINI (Party President and Minister for Climate Change), Mokin STEVENS (Vice President), James BULE (Secretary General).

Vanuatu Green Party (VGP). Vincent Boulekone and Paul Telukluk organized the Vanuatu Greens, sometimes called the Green Confederation, after leaving the UMP (see below) in early 2001. Boulekone had previously helped found the Tan Union, also a splinter from the UMP, before the December 1988 election but subsequently rejoined the parent party. His 2001 departure coincided with that of Willie Jimmy and was generally regarded as reflecting leadership rather than ideological differences with the UMP's Serge Vohor faction. The Greens won three parliamentary seats in May 2002; the seats were retained in 2004 by a **Green Confederation** (GC) that included the VGP and the **Vanuatu Green Alliance** (VGA). The Greens lost one seat in the 2008 balloting, but the VGP joined the government with Moana Carcasses's appointment to cabinet. In 2011, the VGP entered into an alliance with Prime Minister Sato Kilman's PPP. In October 2012 balloting, the VGP secured three seats. The party initially joined the coalition led by Kilman following the elections. Following Kilman's March 2013 resignation, Carcasses made a successful bid for prime minister. Carcasses was ousted by a no-confidence vote in May 2014. He served as deputy prime minister in the second Kilman government until its fall in January 2016, receiving a four-year prison term for his role in the scandal. The party went on to win two seats in the January elections.

Leaders: John TERRY (Secretary General), Daniel TOARA (Health Minister).

Union of Moderate Parties (*Union des Partis Moderés*—UPM/ *Union blong Moderet Pati*—UMP). The UMP is the successor to the **New Hebrides Federal Party,** which was organized in early 1979 as an alliance of predominantly pro-French groups, including Jimmy Tupou Patuntun Stevens's *Na-Griamel.* Following the deportation of two Federal Party MPs to New Caledonia in 1982 for involvement in the Santo rebellion, the non-secessionist elements of the party regrouped under the present label, winning 12 seats in 1983 and 19 seats in 1987. Party leader Vincent Boulekone was ousted from Parliament in 1986 for missing meetings but was reinstated by the Supreme Court. Following the 1987 balloting; Boulekone was replaced by Carlot.

On July 27, 1988, 18 UMP members walking out in protest of Barak Sope's expulsion were dismissed from Parliament; the party refused to re-contest the seats in by-elections on December 13. Carlot was among those convicted of sedition after having been named deputy prime minister in the abortive Sope government of December 18. The **Tan Union,** a now-defunct breakaway UMP faction headed by Boulekone, became the official opposition upon winning six legislative seats.

Following the December 1991 election, in which it won a plurality of 19 seats, the UMP joined with Lini's NUP to form a coalition government under Carlot. Most of the Lini group went into opposition in mid-1993. A new UMP–NUP coalition was concluded after the November 1995 balloting, although the UMP was by then divided into factions led by Carlot and Vohor. Carlot left the UMP in early 1998 to launch the VRP, and the party was further split by the decision of a faction led by Willie Jimmy to support the VP-led Kalpokas government in October. Vohor and Jimmy, rivals for the party leadership, reached a short-lived accommodation at a November 2000 party congress, but in early 2001, Jimmy announced his resignation from the UMP. Meanwhile, Vohor's decision to leave the Barak Sope government led to the no-confidence motion that ended Sope's tenure in April 2001, with Vohor then being appointed deputy prime minister in the Natapei VP–UMP administration. The UMP won a plurality of 15 seats at the May 2002 parliamentary election, 7 of which were lost in July 2004. Seven of the remaining seats were retained in September 2008.

Vohor was temporarily elected prime minister in 2011, but the election was later voided by the courts. He was confirmed as party president in a party congress in February 2012.

In the October 2012 elections, the UMP won five seats and subsequently, unsuccessfully, attempted to form a ruling coalition with the VP and the GJP. The party's representation was reduced to four with the defection of Silas YATAN to the VGP. Three party members were appointed to the Carcasses cabinet in March 2013. The appointment of an additional UMP minister helped save the Carcasses government from a no-confidence vote in February 2014, but when Carcasses failed to defeat another motion in May, the UMP and VGP joined the opposition, Vohor becoming deputy leader of the antigovernment faction. The party weathered the bribery scandal of 2015, winning six seats in the January 2016 elections. Vohor, however, did not because he was one of the ministers convicted of receiving bribes and received a three-year prison sentence.

Leader: Jack NORRIS (Minister of Sports and Youth).

***Na-Griamel* Movement.** *Na-Griamel* (NAG) was founded by Jimmy Tupou Patuntun Stevens, whose secessionist rebellion on Espiritu Santo was crushed in 1980. Stevens was released from 11 years' imprisonment in August 1991 and died on February 28, 1994, the leadership of *Na-Griamel* passing to his son, Frankie. Elected to Parliament in 1991, the younger Stevens served briefly as deputy opposition leader before defecting to the government in early 1994. *Na-Griamel* was permitted to reopen its headquarters for the first time in 14 years the following August. Despite the ambiguous role of its leader, *Na-Griamel* participated in the UF for the 1994 provincial poll before formally rejoining the government in February 1995. It secured one legislative seat in 1995, and none thereafter until 2008, when it again captured one seat. In October 2011 *Na-Griamel* signed a solidarity agreement with the VGP. In October 2012 balloting *Na-Griamel* won three seats, repeating that victory in the 2016 parliamentary elections.

Leaders: Moli Abel NAKO (Leader), Simon OMAWA (Member of Parliament). The previous leader, Havo MOLISALE, died on February 23, 2016.

Parliamentary Parties:

People's Progressive Party (PPP). Formation of the PPP was announced in August 2001 by Sato Kilman, previously a faction leader of the MPP. Kilman indicated that the party's focus would be on development of agriculture, commerce, communications, and tourism. The party won four parliamentary seats in 2004 and participated in the Lini government until forced out in mid-2007 because of alleged involvement in a financial scandal. Its legislative representation was unchanged in 2008. In 2009 the PPP again joined the government when Kilman defected from the opposition and was appointed deputy prime minister in Edward Natapei's VP-led coalition government. In 2011 Kilman replaced Natapei as prime minister. In October 2012 balloting, the PPP secured six seats and Kilman negotiated a ruling coalition, thereby confirming his continued leadership. Strong opposition immediately challenged the tenuous coalition, and in March 2013, facing a no-confidence motion, Kilman resigned as prime minister. Subsequently, one PPP parliamentarian, David TOSUL, was appointed to the Carcasses cabinet. The PPP joined the VP in ousting the Carcasses government with a no confidence vote in May 2014 and subsequently joined the government. Kilman was heavily criticized for his handling of the 2015 bribery scandal; as a result, the party lost five seats in the January 2016 elections, winning only three, while Kilman was replaced as prime minister.

Leaders: Sato KILMAN (Former Prime Minister and President of the Party), Dunstan HILTON (Vice President), Willie LOP (Secretary General).

Natatok Indigenous People's Democratic Party (NIPDP). Launched in July 2011, the NIPDP is a modern formation of a 1979 political group led by Efate leaders. The party secured two seats in October 2013 elections. Under the Carcasses government formed in March 2013, one NIPDP member held a cabinet post. The party held one seat in the January 2016 elections.

Leaders: Alfred CARLOT, Alickson VIRA (Member of Parliament).

Iauko (Eagle) Group (IG). Founded by VP defector Harry IAUKO ahead of the October 2012 elections, the new grouping secured three seats in the balloting. The party's presence was reduced to two with Iauko's sudden death in December, but his son, Pascal Sebastien IAUKO, filled the seat in a by-election held in May 2013. The party won four seats in the January 2016 elections.

Leaders: Pascal Sebastien IAUKO, North TANNA.

Vanuatu Labour Party (VLP). A trade-union grouping launched in 1986, the VLP captured one parliamentary seat in 2008. In early 2011, after the eventually voided election of Serge Vohor as prime minister, the VLP joined the government when VLP president and MP, Joshua Kalsakau, was named deputy prime minister. The VLP unsuccessfully contested the 2012 elections, but won a single seat in the January 2016 elections.

Leader: Joshua KALSAKAU (President).

Other parties that secured one seat in the 2016 parliamentary elections include the **Peoples Service Party** (PSP); the **Leader's Party of Vanuatu** (LPV), led by Jotham NAPAT; the **Vanuatu National Development Party** (VNDP), led by Christophe EMELEE; the **Vanuatu Presidential Party** (VPP), formed by Louis KALNPEL; and the **Fren Melanesian Party** (FMP).

Other Parties and Groups:

Vanuatu Republican Party (VRP) (*Ripablikan Pati blong Vanuatu*). The formation of the VRP was announced in January 1998 by Carlot, who had previously led a UMP faction opposed to Prime Minister Vohor. The VRP won three seats at the May 2002 legislative election, four in 2004. A split within the party emerged in June 2009, when Carlot crossed the aisle to support the government, thereby relinquishing his position as deputy leader of the opposition. However, most VRP legislators eventually endorsed the action by Carlot, who thereafter served as speaker of Parliament until his party returned to opposition in the cabinet reshuffle of November 2009. Carlot returned to the office of speaker in December 2010, when Natapei was defeated as prime minister following a vote of no confidence. In April 2011 the VRP saw a major split within the party, resulting in the defection of four MPs from the VRP to other parties in Parliament. Carlot defected from the party ahead of the October 2012 balloting, launching the **Vanuatu Democratic Party** (VDP). The VRP won one seat in October 2012, but it lost it in the January 2016 elections. Jean-Yves CHABOD, a former vice president, was imprisoned for his role in the 2015–2016 scandal.

Leaders: Maxime CARLOT Korman (President), Jossie MASMAS (Secretary General).

Vanuatu Labour Party (VLP). A trade-union grouping launched in 1986, the VLP captured one parliamentary seat in 2008. In early 2011, after the eventually voided election of Serge Vohor as prime minister, the VLP joined the government when VLP president and MP, Joshua Kalsakau, was named deputy prime minister. The VLP unsuccessfully contested the 2012 elections, but won a single seat in the January 2016 elections.

Leader: Joshua KALSAKAU (President).

A record 36 parties contested the 2016 elections, including the **Vanuatu Democratic Party** (VDP), the **Vanuatu National Party** (VNP), the **Vanuatu Progressive Development Party** (VPDP), the **Vanuatu Progressive Republican Farmers' Party**, the **Vanuatu Liberal Democratic Party** (VLDP), and the **People's Action Party** (*Parti de L'Action Populaire*—PAP). For more on parties that participated in the 2012 balloting and earlier elections, see the 2013 *Handbook*.

LEGISLATURE

The Vanuatu **Parliament** is a unicameral body currently consisting of 52 members elected for four-year terms, subject to dissolution. Balloting was most recently held on January 22, 2016, with results as follows: Party of Our Land, 6 seats; Union of Moderate Parties, 6; Land and Justice Party, 6; National Unity Party, 4; Iauko Group, 4; Reunification Movement for Change, 3; *Na-Griamel* Movement, 3; Greens Confederation, 2; Vanuatu National Development Party, 2; People's Progress Party, 1; Vanuatu Presidential Party, 1; Melanesian Progressive Party, 1; Natatok Indigenous People's Democratic Party, 1; People's Service Party, 1; Fren Melanesian Party, 1; Vanuatu Labor Party, 1; Leader's Party of Vanuatu, 1; and independents, 8.

Speaker: Esmon SAIMON (MPP).

CABINET

[as of September 15, 2016]

Prime Minister	Charlot Salwai (RMC)
Deputy Prime Minister	Joe Natuman (VP)
Ministers	
Agriculture, Forestry, and Fisheries	Matai Seremaia (ind.)
Climate Change	Ham Lini (NUP)
Education	Jean-Pierre Nirua (ind.)
Finance and Economic Management	Gaetan Pikioune (*Na-Griamel*)
Foreign Affairs, External Trade, and Telecommunications	Bruno Leingkone (NUP)
Health	Daniel Toara (GC)
Internal Affairs and Labor	Alfred Maoh (GJP)
Justice	Ronald Warsal (VP)
Lands and Natural Resources	Ralph Regenvanu (GJP)
Public Utilities and Infrastructure	Jotham Napat (VP)
Sports and Youth	Jack Norris (UMP)
Tourism, Commerce, Trade, and Ni Vanuatu Business	Joe Natuman (VP)

INTERGOVERNMENTAL REPRESENTATION

Ambassador to the U.S.: Vanuatu does not maintain an embassy in Washington.

U.S. Ambassador to Vanuatu (resident in Papua New Guinea): Catherine EBERT-GREY.

Permanent Representative to the UN: Odo TEVI.

IGO Memberships (Non-UN): ADB, CWTH, NAM, PIF.

For Further Reference:

Crowley, Terry. *Beach-La-Mar to Bislama: The Emergence of a National Language in Vanuatu.* Oxford: Clarendon Press, 1990.

Forsythe, Miranda. *A Bird That Flies with Two Wings: The Kastom and State Justice Systems in Vanuatu.* Canberra: Australian National University Press, 2011.

Miles, William F. S. *Bridging Mental Boundaries in a Postcolonial Microcosm: Identity and Development in Vanuatu.* Honolulu: University of Hawaii Press, 1998.

VATICAN CITY STATE

Stato della Città del Vaticano

Political Status: Independent sovereign state, under papal temporal government; international status governed by the Lateran Treaty with Italy of February 11, 1929; constitution of June 7, 1929, superseded by a New Fundamental Law signed by the pope on November 26, 2000, with effect from February 22, 2001.

Area: 0.17 sq. mi. (0.44 sq. km).

Population: 800 (2016E—Vatican). Four hundred and fifty one of these have Vatican citizenship; the rest are lay workers, most of them Italian citizens, who live outside the Vatican.

Official Language: Latin (Italian is the working language).

Monetary Unit: Euro (market rate October 1, 2016: 0.89 euro = $1US). On December 29, 2000, the Vatican and Italy signed an agreement permitting Vatican adoption of the euro, authorization having already been granted in principle by the European Union. Since introduction of euro notes and coins in 2002, the Vatican has been permitted to mint its own euro coins, which are issued in small quantities for collectors, as was true of Vatican lire.

Sovereign (Supreme Pontiff): Pope FRANCIS (Jorge Mario BERGOGLIO); elected to a life term by the College of Cardinals on March 13, 2013, and invested as pope on March 19, succeeding Pope BENEDICT XVI (Josef RATZINGER), who resigned on February 28, 2013.

Secretary of State of the Roman Curia and Papal Representative in the Civil Government of the Vatican City State: Cardinal Pietro PAROLIN; appointed by Pope Francis on August 31, 2013, and took office on October 15, succeeding Cardinal Tarcisio BERTONE, who resigned on June 3, 2013.

Secretary for Relations with States: Archbishop Paul Richard GALLAGHER; appointed by Pope Francis on November 8, 2016, succeeding Cardinal Dominique François Joseph MAMBERTI.

President of the Pontifical Commission for the Vatican City State and President of the Governatorate of the Vatican City State: Cardinal Giuseppe BERTELLO; appointed by Pope Benedict XVI on October 1, 2011, succeeding Cardinal Giovanni LAJOLO.

THE COUNTRY

An enclave surrounding the Basilica of Saint Peter and including 13 other buildings in and around the city of Rome, the Vatican City State, the smallest independent entity in the world, derives its principal importance from its function as the world headquarters of the Roman Catholic Church and official residence of its head, the pope. The central administration of the church is customarily referred to as the Holy See (*Santa Sede*), or more informally as the Vatican. The Vatican City State is the territorial base from which the leadership of the church exercises its religious and ecclesiastical responsibilities for a worldwide Catholic population of more than 1.2 billion people and over 400,000 Catholic priests. The city state's population, predominantly of Italian and Swiss extraction, is limited mainly to Vatican officials and resident employees and their families. Italian is the language of common use, although Latin is employed in the official acts of the Holy See.

The inherent separation of the Vatican City State (as the physical "nation" of the Vatican) and the Holy See (which is the government of that state) is also found in Vatican finances. The Holy See's income is based on contributions from Roman Catholic congregations around the world ("Peter's Pence") and substantial investments in real estate, bonds, and securities. The Vatican City State generates income through facility admission fees as well as the sale of postage stamps, publications, and souvenirs. Neither the Holy See nor the Vatican City State imposes taxes, customs, or excise duties; regulates the import or export of monetary instruments; or otherwise receives funds based on financial levies on its workforce or visitors. The Administration of the Patrimony of the Apostolic See (*Amministrazione del Patrimonio della Sede Apostolica*) manages the holdings of both the Holy See and the Vatican City State, while the Institute for Religious Works (*Istituto per le Opere di Religione* [IOR], also known as the Vatican Bank) acts as a bank for monies held by affiliated religious orders. The Vatican's financial status long remained confidential and hence the object of intense speculation, until a 1979 announcement revealed that the church's operations would be $20 million in deficit for that year.

Strong investment performance buoyed Vatican finances in the 1990s, but the weakening dollar contributed to the return of deficits in most of the early 2000s, exceeding $14 million in 2007. (Although the euro is its official currency, the Holy See has substantial investments in U.S. dollars and receives generous contributions from the church in the United States.) The global financial crisis, a corresponding decline in donations, and a major overhaul of the Vatican's telecommunications infrastructure were blamed for deficits of $1.28 million in 2008 and $5.1 million in 2009. Vatican finances bounced back in 2010, registering a surplus of $14.5 million, but they were back in the red by $19 million in 2011, one of the worst budget deficits in years. In 2012 the Vatican had a small surplus of $2.8 million; however, worldwide donations declined.

For the first time in its history, the IOR published an annual report in October 2013, in which it revealed that favorable trading had boosted profit from $25.6 million in 2011 to $117 million in 2012, of which some $60.4 million was transferred to the Vatican. In July 2014 a subsequent annual report issued by the IOR noted a dramatic reduction in net profit for 2013 at $3.9 million, the result of "extraordinary expenses, losses related to propriety investments in externally managed investment funds committed to in 2012 and early 2013, and the fluctuation in the value of the IOR's gold reserves."

GOVERNMENT AND POLITICS

Political background. Italy's recognition of the Vatican City State in the Lateran Treaty of 1929 terminated a bitter political controversy that had persisted since the unification of Italy in 1860–1870. Before that time the popes had exercised political sovereignty over the city of Rome and substantial portions of the Italian peninsula, where they ruled as territorial sovereigns in addition to performing spiritual and administrative functions as heads of the Catholic Church. The absorption of virtually all territorial holdings by the new Italian state and the failure of Pope PIUS IX to accept the legitimacy of the compensation offered by the Italian Parliament left the Holy See in an anomalous position that was finally regularized after a lapse of two generations. In addition to the Lateran Treaty, by which Italy recognized the independence and sovereignty of the Vatican City State, a concordat was concluded that regulated the position of the church within Italy, while a financial convention compensated the Holy See for its earlier losses. The status of the Vatican City State as established by the Lateran Treaty has since been recognized, formally or tacitly, by a great majority of the world's governments.

Pope Paul VI (Giovanni Battista MONTINI), who had been elected on June 21, 1963, died on August 6, 1978, and was succeeded on August 26 by Pope JOHN PAUL I (Albino LUCIANI), who in turn succumbed on September 28 after the shortest pontificate since that of

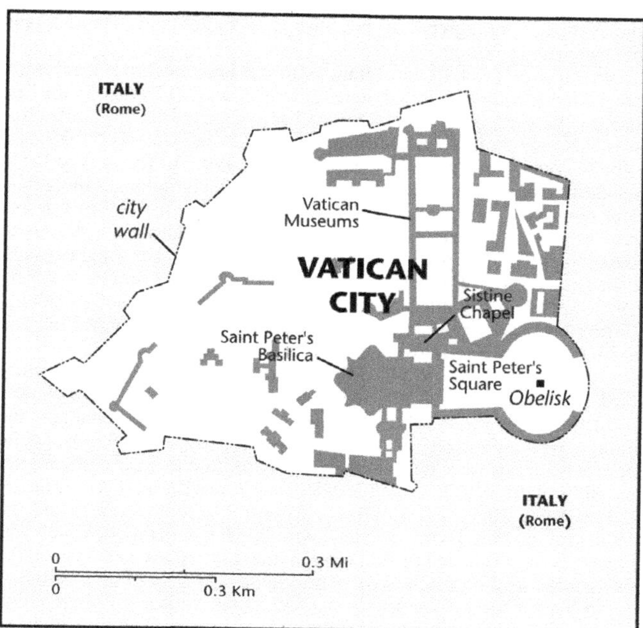

Pope LEO XII in 1605. His successor, Cardinal Karol WOJTYŁA, archbishop of Kraków, Poland, who assumed the title Pope JOHN PAUL II, became pope on October 16, 1978, the first non-Italian to be elected since Pope ADRIAN VI in 1522.

The papal term of John Paul II was one of the longest and most significant in modern history. Among other things, he was the most widely traveled pope of any era, and he commanded worldwide veneration, even as he moved the church away from the liberal direction of the Second Vatican Council, opened in 1962 during the papacy of Pope JOHN XXIII. Following John Paul II's death on April 2, 2005, he was succeeded on April 19 by Cardinal Josef RATZINGER, who became Pope BENEDICT XVI. Ratzinger, a close confidant of John Paul II, had served since 1981 as head of the Congregation for the Doctrine of the Faith (once known as the Holy Office of the Inquisition), the Vatican office responsible for maintaining orthodox doctrine throughout the Roman Catholic communion.

Since 2001 the Vatican has struggled to deal with the repercussions of a major scandal in the United States and elsewhere involving child sexual abuse by clergy. On November 21, 2001, John Paul II voiced an apology to the victims, and in January 2002 the Vatican issued new procedures for handling alleged abuse, including trying accused clergy in secret ecclesiastical courts but without precluding civil and criminal action by secular authorities. In subsequent statements John Paul II called pedophilia "grievously evil" and, during a summit of all U.S. cardinals in Rome in April, both a crime and an "appalling sin." Individual dioceses, generally responsible for their own finances, faced millions of dollars in settlements to victims. The Vatican's immunity from U.S. prosecution, under the Foreign Sovereign Immunity Act, was challenged in June 2006, when a U.S. district judge ruled that a lawsuit brought against the Vatican for allowing a priest who was a known child molester to be transferred from city to city could proceed.

Pope Benedict XVI was initially perceived as showing ambivalence in this matter, a view perpetuated by a meeting early in his rule with Cardinal Bernard Francis Law, former archbishop of Boston, who had been forced to resign because of his lack of action against pedophile priests. However, in May 2006 Benedict asked the Rev. Marcial Maciel Degollado, founder of the conservative Legionaries of Christ and the target of multiple molestation charges, to leave the ministry for a life of "prayer and penitence." In 2012 the Vatican launched an investigation into seven Legion priests over allegations of sexual abuse of minors dating back decades. It also defrocked a Roman Catholic monk who had sexually abused boys at an abbey and school in London. In 2008 Benedict met with victims of abuse during his American visit in April and on World Youth Day in July in Sydney, Australia. During his U.S. trip, he met with President George W. Bush and addressed the UN, stressing the need for religious freedom.

In his January 2006 first encyclical, viewed as an inclusive and conciliatory message, Pope Benedict XVI affirmed the importance of charity and love, including sexual intimacy, as fundamental expressions of Christian faith. During his first year in office, however, Benedict XVI mostly lived up to his reputation for conservatism in doctrinal matters, continuing his predecessor's affirmation of traditional teachings on such matters as papal primacy and infallibility, the exclusion of women from the priesthood (while at the same time acknowledging that the church has long marginalized and discriminated against women), and opposition to birth control and gay marriage.

On July 7, 2009, Benedict issued a third encyclical, *Caritas in Veritate* (Charity in Truth), the first encyclical on social teaching in 20 years, issued in part as a response to the economic crisis that had gripped the world for the last year. Perhaps the most controversial suggestion was its call for reforming the United Nations into a stronger institution that could protect the vulnerable nations of the developing world as well as regulate the world economic system while recognizing national sovereignty. In addition to issuing apologies for the abuses, in July 2010, the Vatican released a revision of the 2001 norms dealing with clerical sexual abuse, which streamlined the procedures dealing with accusations of abusive priests and extended the statute of limitations to 20 years after the victim's 18th birthday.

From the first month of his pontificate, Pope Benedict XVI spoke out forcefully against a proposed measure to legalize gay marriage in Spain, urging Catholics to work and vote against it. In 2012 Benedict was critical of the failure of the European Union (EU) to mention Europe's Christian roots in the proposed EU constitution.

On February 28, 2013, Benedict became the first pope since 1415 to resign (see Current issues, below). Cardinal Jorge Mario BERGOGLIO, the archbishop of Buenos Aires, was elected on March 13 to succeed Benedict. The new pope was the first from the Western Hemisphere and the first Jesuit. He became Francis I on March 19, 2013.

During his initial round of appointments, Pope Francis I selected many newcomers to the government and created several new structures in an effort to democratize the Church. On April 13, 2013, he established an eight-member advisory council that included cardinals with substantial reformist credentials. During his first two years, Francis appointed new leaders to many of his senior offices, including Cardinal Pietro PAROLIN as secretary of state, Monsignor Paolo BORGIA as assessor for general affairs, and Archbishop P. Fernando Vérgez ALZAGA as secretary general.

Constitution and government. On November 26, 2000, Pope John Paul II signed a new constitution intended to "harmonize in a legal manner" various governmental changes that had been introduced since promulgation of the preceding basic law on June 7, 1929. As in the past, the Vatican City State retains the form of an absolute monarchy. Supreme legislative, executive, and judicial power is vested in the pope in his capacity as bishop of Rome; the pope, who is elected for life, serves concurrently as supreme pontiff of the Universal Church, primate of Italy, archbishop and metropolitan of the Province of Rome, and sovereign of the Vatican City State. Assisting the pope in the exercise of his varied responsibilities are the members of two major organs, the College of Cardinals and the Roman Curia (*Curia Romana*).

Members of the College of Cardinals, who numbered 216 as of February 15, 2016, are named by the pope and serve as his chief advisers and coadjutors during his lifetime; upon the pope's death, those under the age of 80, of which there were 98 as of February 15, 2016, meet to elect his successor, which is their right as titular clergymen in the city of Rome. The meeting of the college to elect a pope is still referred to as a conclave from the Latin *cum clave* (with a key), which refers to the locked room where the cardinals meet. Reforms instituted by John Paul II in February 22, 1996, in an "Apostolic Constitution" entitled *Universi Dominici Gregis,* ended the practice of detaining the electors in a locked room until a result emerged, although strict secrecy of the voting process has been maintained. Also, prior to 1996 a candidate for pope (usually a cardinal but not necessarily even a bishop) required a majority of two-thirds (or two-thirds plus one, depending on the number of electors). However, the 1996 reforms authorized election by a simple majority in the event of a protracted deadlock. The 1996 revisions also eliminated the options of election by universal acclamation or by delegation to an electoral subcommittee. On June 11, 2007, Benedict XVI modified the election procedures established in *Universi Dominici Gregis,* phasing out the possibility of election by simple majority even in the case of a protracted deadlock. Future elections under any circumstances will require a two-thirds majority. While the papacy is vacant, the full college (meeting in General Congregation) or subcommittees (Particular Congregations) may deal with the ordinary government of the church and of the Vatican City State as well as with any emergency matters arising, with the strict exception of matters that would otherwise be reserved to the authority of the pope.

Apart from conclaves, the full college meets infrequently. A number of cardinals also hold positions on the various bodies that constitute the Curia, which serves as the church's central administrative organ. Political responsibilities have devolved primarily to the Secretariat of State, which in 1988 was divided into two sections, one dealing with general affairs and the other addressing relations with states. A secretary of state heads the Secretariat. The Pontifical Commission, headed by the President of the Pontifical Commission (essentially functioning as the "mayor" of Vatican City), oversees civil administration of the Vatican and works closely with the Secretariat. The President of that commission is concurrently the President of the Governorate of Vatican City State and is therefore sometimes informally referenced as the Vatican's "governor."

The Vatican City State has its own security force (the Swiss Guard), postal service, coinage, utilities, department store, communication system, and local tribunal with a right of appeal to higher ecclesiastical courts. A papal edict issued in July 1995 set out "rules of conduct" for all Vatican employees, requiring them, on pain of automatic sanctions (including dismissal), to observe Catholic moral doctrines "even in the private sphere" and not to associate with organizations whose "goals are incompatible" with those of the church.

Foreign relations. The Holy See, which is a sovereign entity, is the ecclesiastical jurisdiction of the Catholic Church that holds Vatican City State as sovereign territory and maintains all international relations for the enclave. Diplomatic relations are centered primarily on the Holy See's international status as seat of the Catholic Church, set in the context of its position as a sovereign entity. Its activities as a sovereign state continue to be governed by the Lateran Treaty and related agreements with the Italian government, which enable it to enter into international agreements and bilateral diplomatic relations in its own right. Diplomatic linkages now total well over 100, supplemented by unofficial representation in other countries. Additionally, the Holy See maintains permanent observer status at the United Nations, with, as of July 2004, all rights of full membership except that of voting. It is also a full member of certain specialist agencies at the UN, and it participates in the Organization for Security and Cooperation in Europe (OSCE).

The Vatican's close relations with Italy were threatened in the 1980s by the revelation of links between the IOR, otherwise known as the Vatican Bank, and Italy's Banco Ambrosiano, which collapsed in August 1982. The Vatican and the Italian government subsequently appointed a joint commission to investigate the matter, and in May 1984 the IOR agreed "in recognition of moral involvement," but without admission of culpability, to pay 109 creditor banks up to $250 million of a $406 million settlement against Banco Ambrosiano's successor institution.

Earlier, in February 1984, negotiations were concluded on a new Italian–Vatican concordat. Provisions included the abandonment of Roman Catholicism as Italy's state religion and of mandated religious instruction in public schools, although secular authorities would continue to accord automatic recognition to church marriages and full freedom to Catholic schools.

John Paul II exemplified a concerted effort to use the papal position to improve relations, not only with non-Catholic Christian entities but also with some non-Christians. The historic breach with Protestant Christendom, dating to the 16th century, was partly overcome in 1982, when the Vatican established full diplomatic relations with the United Kingdom and with the Lutheran countries of Denmark, Norway, and Sweden.

In contrast, major differences with the Orthodox Christian hierarchy continued to affect the Vatican's relations with a number of countries. In 1992 the Orthodox Church severely criticized Rome for seeking converts in "Orthodox" territory, as signified by Pope John Paul II's 1991 creation of new dioceses in the former Soviet Union. The ecumenical patriarch, Bartholomew I (representing 15 churches, with 170 million adherents), made a first official visit to the Vatican in June 1995, while a trip by John Paul II to Romania in May 1999 marked the first visit in 1,000 years by a Roman Catholic pope to a country having an Orthodox majority. It was followed in May 2001 by a first visit to Greece, where the pope met with Archbishop Christodoulos of the Greek Orthodox Church. At that time John Paul II apologized for the sacking of Constantinople in 1204. The pope subsequently undertook groundbreaking visits to Ukraine (June 2001), Kazakhstan and Armenia (September 2001), and Azerbaijan and Bulgaria (May 2002). Benedict XVI continued John Paul II's outreach to the Orthodox Church by visiting with Bartholomew I during Benedict's trip to Turkey (November 2007). In December 2009 Russian president Dmitry Medvediv visited the Vatican and agreed to establish full diplomatic relations and exchange ambassadors.

In January 1984 formal relations at the ambassadorial level were reestablished with the United States after a lapse of 117 years. In the first meeting between a pope and a Soviet head of state, Mikhail Gorbachev was accorded a private audience at the Vatican in December 1989, and official contacts were established in March 1990. Earlier, in July 1989, relations had been reestablished with Poland after a rupture of more than four decades. Further reflecting the tide of change in Eastern Europe, relations were reestablished with Hungary in February 1990, with Czechoslovakia in April, and with Romania in May. The Vatican established relations with most of the other former Soviet republics during 1992. Speedy recognition was extended to the predominantly Catholic former Yugoslav republics of Croatia and Slovenia in January 1992 and to Muslim-dominated Bosnia and Herzegovina in August.

In addition, relations with Mexico (broken in 1861) were normalized in September 1992, following the deletion of anticlerical clauses from the country's 1917 constitution. As a result of the changes, the church was authorized to own property and operate schools, while priests and nuns were enfranchised and permitted to wear clerical garb in public. John Paul II visited Mexico four times during his pontificate (1979, 1990, 1993, and 1999). On August 21, 2009, Bolivia and the Vatican signed the Treaty of Inter-Institutional Cooperation, which was meant to improve relations between the two states and reflect the important role the church plays in providing social services in Bolivia.

In September 1993 a senior member of the Vatican's Congregation for the Oriental Churches became the highest-ranking Catholic official to visit China since the Communist takeover in 1949. Ostensibly responding to an invitation to attend China's National Athletic Games, the emissary reportedly met with government officials amid indications of a possible end to the lengthy estrangement. Further discussions took place between 1996 and 1998, but the Vatican's continuing recognition of the Taiwanese government prevented normalization with Beijing. The Vatican has long been troubled by the existence of the Chinese Catholic Patriotic Association (CCPA), a Catholic organization that observers view as a creation of the Beijing government. Although the CCPA claims that it wants to maintain a "religious connection" with the Vatican, it rejects the pope's power to govern the Chinese Church, saying that the Vatican's assertion of authority in China amounts to political interference. In a letter to the Chinese people dated May 27, 2007, Benedict XVI objected to the ordination of bishops without the approval of the Vatican while maintaining that the Vatican had no desire to meddle in Chinese politics. Tensions with Beijing increased again in 2012 when the Vatican excommunicated a Chinese bishop ordained without papal approval.

In February 2000 John Paul II became the first pope to visit Egypt, and a month later he made the first papal pilgrimage to the Holy Land since 1964, visiting Jordan and Israel. In Palestinian-controlled Bethlehem, he recognized the Palestinians' "natural right to a homeland." In May 2009, Pope Benedict undertook an 11-day trip to Jordan, the Palestinian territories, and Israel, with the aim of building better relations with Muslims and Jews, defending the rights of Christians living in the Holy Land, and encouraging peace between Israel and its neighbors. He reiterated the Vatican's position that both Israelis and Palestinians have a right to their own states, and he also stressed that members of all three religions are children of Abraham and should show mutual respect for each other. At the request of Israeli Prime Minister Benjamin Netanyahu, Benedict affirmed Israel's right to exist in view of Iran's hostility.

In January 1998 John Paul II made a highly publicized trip to Cuba. In addition to calling upon the government to introduce pluralism, he criticized the long-standing U.S. economic sanctions against Fidel Castro's regime as "unjust and ethically unacceptable." During his 2012 visit to the country, Pope Benedict XVI urged the Cuban government to introduce economic and political reforms, called for an end to Cuba's isolation, and criticized the U.S. trade embargo against Cuba.

On March 12, 2000, Pope John Paul II delivered a far-reaching but nonspecific apology for sins committed by Catholics, the church's "children," over the two preceding millennia. Without mentioning the Crusades, the Inquisition, or the Holocaust, church leaders cited such offenses as intolerance and discrimination against women, minorities, indigenous peoples, Jews, and the poor. The apology, an "act of repentance," according to the Vatican, came two years after release of a long-awaited report from the Vatican on the role of the church during the Nazi era.

Pope Benedict XVI was largely unsuccessful in improving Jewish-Catholic relations, despite the dramatic change in the church's attitude toward Jews, who have gone from being called "perfidious" in the old Good Friday service to being referred to as "our elder brothers" by John

Paul II. As Cardinal Ratzinger, Benedict XVI had played an important role in articulating a new theological position for the church toward Jews and other non-Catholics. However, he was criticized by Jewish leaders when he failed to explicitly condemn anti-Semitism during a May 2006 visit to the Nazi death camp Auschwitz-Birkenau in Poland. (See the 2011 *Handbook* for background on the relationship between the Vatican and Israel.)

In 2009, there was another temporary setback in Catholic–Jewish relations. Benedict lifted a ban on four bishops of the Society of St. Pius X, a schismatic group that does not recognize the Second Vatican Council. Unbeknownst to the pope, one of the bishops, Richard Williamson, had denied the mass murder of the Jews during World War II, which strained the relationship between the Chief Rabbinate of Israel and the Vatican. Subsequently, the pope denounced Holocaust deniers and wrote a letter of apology.

In March 2009 Pope Benedict visited Cameroon and Angola, discussing peace, reconciliation, democracy, and human rights. Particularly noteworthy was his meeting in Luanda on women, where he lamented the adverse conditions to which women have been subjected and affirmed their right to "equal dignity." Far more controversial was his comment that acquired immune deficiency syndrome (AIDS) "cannot be overcome by the distribution of prophylactics." This assertion provoked the Belgian parliament to "condemn the unacceptable statements of the pope." The Vatican deplored the condemnation and maintained that it was an attempt to intimidate the pope from teaching the church's doctrine. The pope appeared to reverse this stance in November 2010, when he declared that the use of condoms is permissible as a means to prevent the spread of AIDS. He did not, however, change the church's prohibition of birth control, enshrined in *Humanae Vitae*, the encyclical of PAUL VI, which condemned artificial means of birth control.

In June 2010 Vatican officials criticized the government for raiding the headquarters of the Roman Catholic Church in Belgium while investigating the church after the bishop of Bruges resigned in April for allegedly sexually abusing a child 25 years before. There were two shocking government reports on sexual abuse in Ireland and numerous allegations in Germany, Switzerland, Austria, and the Netherlands. The scandals caused five bishops to resign. The Vatican suffered a setback when the U.S. Supreme Court refused to hear a Vatican appeal claiming that, as a sovereign nation, it is immune from prosecution.

In September 2010, Benedict visited the United Kingdom, his fourth international trip that year after visiting Cyprus, Malta, and the Czech Republic. He again apologized four times for the Church's failure to have dealt more forcefully in the past with the problems of sexual abuse. In a major speech to the British people, he addressed the role of religion in modern, secular societies, urging it as a moral compass for making decisions that affect the common good.

Although the Vatican normalized diplomatic ties with the predominantly Muslim nation of Malaysia in July 2011, papal relations with Islam were volatile during Benedict XVI's tenure, after his speech at the University of Regensburg on September 13, 2006, in which he quoted a 14th-century Byzantine emperor who claimed that Islam was "evil and inhuman." Continued fallout from the speech threatened to sour Benedict XVI's visit to Turkey in November 2006, but he was warmly greeted by the Turkish prime minister at the airport and received favorable coverage on Turkish television.

Pope Benedict's visit to Beirut in September 2012 was marred by unrelated demonstrations against an anti-Islamic film. The protests left one dead and scores injured.

In March 2013, during a meeting with Pope Francis, Argentine president Cristina Fernández de Kirchner asked the pontiff to help initiate bilateral discussions with the United Kingdom over the status of the Falkland Islands.

In an effort to curb money laundering, the Vatican Bank closed accounts for foreign diplomats in October 2013 after reports emerged that Iranian, Iraqi, and Indonesian officials were using the bank to move large sums of cash.

A delegation from the Vatican sat before the United Nations Committee on the Rights of the Child (UNCRC) in January 2014 to discuss the handling of child sexual abuse cases. On February 5 the UNCRC called for the removal of suspected child abusers from their posts and to hold officials accountable for concealing such crimes. Francis met with U.S. president Barack Obama for the first time on March 27. The Vatican came under further fire from the UN in May 2014 when the Committee Against Torture called on the church to impose "meaningful sanctions" against those who fail to deal with abuse allegations and rejected the Vatican's claim that it exercises control only over the city state, not Catholic priests and bishops around the world.

Francis promoted the Oslo peace process between Israel and the Palestinian Authority to include hosting Israeli president Shimon Peres and Palestinian president Mahmoud Abbas in 2014 at the Vatican for "peace prayers."

Francis was instrumental in the restoration of diplomatic relations between the United States and Cuba (see entry on Cuba). The Pope hosted secret discussions at the Vatican in 2015 between the two parties as well as personally corresponding with U.S. president Barack Obama and Cuban president Raul Castro. In June 2015 Francis conducted the first papal visit to Bosnia Herzegovina in almost 20 years.

Current issues. On May 1, 2011, before the biggest crowd since his investiture, Pope Benedict presided over a mass celebrating the life of John Paul II and beatified him, making him an object of public veneration.

Far less positive was an assessment of the Vatican's role in dealing with the sexual abuse scandal in Ireland, historically one of the world's most predominantly Catholic societies. A scathing criticism of the Vatican's behavior in allegedly covering up child abuse by priests, issued in July 2011 by Prime Minister Enda Kenny, won widespread popular acclaim, but it prompted the Vatican to recall its ambassador. In September 2011 two U.S. advocacy groups asked the International Criminal Court in The Hague to investigate Pope Benedict XVI and three cardinals for alleged crimes against humanity by sheltering Roman Catholic clergy who were guilty of sexually abusing children.

In December 2010, after the IOR came under investigation for money laundering, the Vatican issued norms to comply with European Union banking transparency standards. The new law was required under a 2009 monetary agreement with the EU, which allowed the Vatican to adopt the euro as its currency. In April 2012 the bank's board dismissed president of the IOR, Ettore Gotti Tedeschi, because of poor job performance, erratic behavior, and chronic absence from board meetings. In June the director of the famously secretive bank met with a few dozen journalists to highlight the bank's serious efforts at fighting money laundering and to stress its internal and external financial controls.

The dismissal of Tedeschi happened amid a growing scandal—dubbed "Vatileaks" by the Italian press—over leaked Vatican documents, which involved periodic releases of correspondence that laid bare discord within the Holy See, including internal allegations of cronyism and corruption. The IOR board suggested that Tedeschi might have himself leaked some of the documents. A few days after Tedeschi's ouster, Pope Benedict's butler, Paolo GABRIELE was arrested for allegedly leaking the pope's confidential correspondence.

One of the most prominent clashes involved Archbishop Carlo Maria Viganò, the second-ranking official in the part of the Curia that administers Vatican City. In letters to the pope and Vatican Secretary of State Cardinal Tarcisio Bertone, Viganò claimed he had made enemies within the Curia and beyond after ferreting out corruption and financial misconduct. He requested permission to continue cleaning up the Holy See's financial affairs but was instead removed from his post and, in August 2011, named the papal nuncio, or ambassador, to the United States. A Vatican spokesman insisted the appointment of Viganò was, contrary to press reports, "proof of unquestionable respect and trust."

In April 2012 the Vatican appointed Joseph TOBIN, an American bishop, to rein in the largest and most influential group of Catholic nuns in the United States because the group had "serious doctrinal problems." The Leadership Conference of Women Religious, in the Vatican's assessment, had challenged church teaching on homosexuality and the male-only priesthood. The sisters were also scolded for making public statements that contradicted the bishops. Six weeks later, the 21 national board members of the group announced their rejection of the Vatican's judgment and their intention to send their president and executive director to Rome to open a dialogue with Vatican officials. On October 6, a Vatican court convicted former papal butler Gabriele of theft and leaking confidential documents.

Citing age and poor health, Pope Benedict stunned Catholics with his decision to resign in February 2013. Benedict continued to live in the Vatican and was granted the title "pope emeritus." His successor, Jorge Mario Bergoglio, chose the papal name Francis, in honor of St. Francis of Assisi. The new pontiff's humility and personal warmth contrasted significantly with the reserved and "aloof" Benedict. Once in office, Francis undertook a number of steps to reduce tensions within and outside of the Church, including directing Church leaders to "act decisively" against abusive priests.

In late August 2013 Francis ousted Cardinal Tarcisio BERTONE, seen by many as a source of corruption within the Church, as secretary of state, replacing him with Cardinal Pietro PAROLIN, who was officially appointed on October 15. Francis pushed for greater transparency in Vatican finances in 2014, naming a new oversight commission on January 15.

Pope Francis restructured the Vatican's financial system on February 24, 2014, calling for a review in light of the church's "mission to evangelize, with particular concern for the most needy," and creating a Secretariat of the Economy, a new position, which was filled by George PELL. Francis canonized John Paul II and John XXIII at a ceremony on April 27. The pope replaced all four members of the Vatican's Financial Information Authority in early June and, in July, named Jean-Baptiste de FRANSSU, a French businessman, to head the Vatican Bank. As part of creating a more open and transparent financial environment, the Vatican Bank entered into an agreement in June 2014 with the United State Treasury for the purpose of exchanging information, addressing corruption, and fighting money laundering. One of the most significant actions taken by this body has been the termination of customers who are not "Catholic institutions, clerics, employees, or former employees of the Vatican with salary and pension accounts, as well as embassies and diplomats accredited to the Holy See," resulting in a 25 percent reduction in customers as of September 2015.

The pope's populism has changed the balance in the Church's position on poverty, social justice, and the environment. Francis has professed his Jesuit principles and used public messaging to confront the conditions of poverty, including consultations in 2013 with Chancellor Angela Merkel regarding management of the Eurozone Crisis and calls for a "sustainable solution" to the European migration crisis. Francis also published an encyclical (doctrine publication) in 2015 on the need for humans to reduce their consumer appetites.

THE ROMAN CURIA

[as of February 15, 2016]

Secretariat of State

Delegate for Pontifical Representations	Archbishop Jan Romeo Pawłowski
Official of the Secretariat of State	Archbishop Marco Dino Brogi
Secretary of State	Cardinal Pietro Parolin
Secretariat for Communications, Prefect	Monsignor Dario Edoardo Viganò
Secretariat for the Economy, Prefect	Cardinal George Pell
Secretary for Relations with States	Archbishop Paul Richard Gallagher
Substitute for General Affairs	Archbishop Giovanni Angelo Becciu

Governorate of Vatican City State

President	Cardinal Giuseppe Bertello
Secretary General	Bishop P. Fernando Végez Alzaga
Deputy Secretary General	(Vacant)
Emeritus President	Cardinal Giovanni Lajolo

Note: In addition to the bodies noted below, which have political and administrative functions relating to the Vatican as a state, there are numerous other bodies within the Curia with mainly ecclesiastical, theological, ecumenical, disciplinary, cultural, or pastoral functions, including congregations, tribunals, councils, commissions, and committees. The major bodies are referred to as dicasteries of the Roman Curia.

INTERGOVERNMENTAL REPRESENTATION

Apostolic Nuncio to the U.S.: Christophe PIERRE.

U.S. Ambassador to the Holy See: Louis L. BONO (Chargé d'Affaires).

Permanent Observer to the UN: Archbishop Bernardito AUZA.

IGO Memberships (Non-UN): IOM, ITSO, ITUC, OSCE.

For Further Reference:

Posner, Gerald. *God's Bankers: A History of Money and Power at the Vatican.* New York: Simon and Schuster, 2015.

Reese, Thomas. *Inside the Vatican.* Cambridge, MA: Harvard University Press, 1996.

Thavis, John. *The Vatican Diaries: A Behind-the-Scenes Look at the Power, Personalities, and Politics at the Heart of the Catholic Church.* New York: Viking, 2013.

VENEZUELA

Bolivarian Republic of Venezuela
República Bolivariana de Venezuela

Political Status: Independence originally proclaimed in 1821 as part of Gran Colombia; independent republic established in 1830; federal constitutional system restored in 1958. Current constitution approved by referendum on December 15, 1999.

Area: 358,850 sq. mi. (916,445 sq. km).

Population: 31,519,000 (2016E—UN); 29,680,303 (2016E—U.S. Census).

Major Urban Centers (2016E—UN): CARACAS (2,923,000), Maracaibo (2,229,000), Valencia (1,757,000), Maracay (1,186,000), Barquisimeto (1,044,000).

Official Language: Spanish.

Monetary Unit: Bolívar (market rate October 1, 2016: 9.99 bolívares fuertes = $1US). [Note: devalued February 2013.]

President: Nicolás MADURO (United Socialist Party of Venezuela); inaugurated on April 19, 2013, for a five-year term, following the death of Lt. Col. (Ret.) Hugo Rafael CHÁVEZ Frías (United Socialist Party of Venezuela) on March 5, 2013.

Executive Vice President: Aristóbulo ISTÚRIZ Almeida (United Socialist Party of Venezuela); appointed by the president on January 6, 2016, to succeed Jorge ARREAZA (United Socialist Party of Venezuela).

THE COUNTRY

Situated on the northern coast of South America between Colombia, Brazil, and Guyana, the Republic of Venezuela is made up of alternating mountainous and lowland territory drained, for the most part, by the Orinoco River and its tributaries. Two-thirds or more of the rapidly growing population, most of it concentrated in coastal and northern areas, is of mixed descent, the remainder being Caucasian, Negro, and Amerindian. Roman Catholicism is the dominant faith, but other religions are tolerated. Women constitute about one-third of the paid labor force, concentrated in the clerical and service sectors. After the December 2015 elections, women held 24 seats (14. 4 percent) in the assembly.

One of the world's leading oil producers, Venezuela has one of the highest per capita incomes in Latin America: $14,415 in 2013. Oil exports generate 96 percent of all export revenue. Oil revenues have spurred a dramatic increase in government spending, which in turn has resulted in a somewhat more equitable distribution of wealth. However, Venezuela's energy market is in decline, with oil production declining 27 percent from 2005 to 2013 despite having the world's largest oil reserves. The poverty rate fell from 49 percent in 2002 to 29 percent by 2011. Evidence indicates that these gains are slated to reverse going into 2014.

The industrial sector, which includes iron and natural gas, employs about one-fourth of the labor force and contributes 37 percent of gross domestic product (GDP). By contrast, agriculture now accounts for only 4 percent of GDP; rice, corn, and beans are the principal subsistence crops, while coffee and cocoa are exported, along with some sugar, bananas, and cotton. Under government sponsorship Venezuela has been attempting to regain its historic position as a major stock-raising country, while diversification has become the keynote of economic planning, in part to reduce a dependence on oil sales.

In January 2010 the government devalued the Venezuelan bolívar, setting one exchange rate for imported goods and a lower one for essential goods, such as staple foods, which are heavily subsidized. The devaluation, intended to make Venezuelan exports more competitive abroad, threatened to stimulate further inflation and rampant black market currency trading. Growth contracted significantly, reportedly making Venezuela the region's worst performer in 2010. Annual GDP of about 4 percent in 2011 rebounded to 5.5 percent in 2012 but dropped to 1.3 percent in 2013, and then declined by 3.9 percent in 2014. Unemployment averaged 8 percent between 2009 and 2013, rising to 9.4 in 2014. Inflation continued to be an issue at 21 percent in 2012 but significantly increasing to 62 percent in 2014, and then to 121.7 percent in

2015. GDP fell again in 2015, declining by 5.7 percent, and then contracting by 8 percent in 2016. In 2016 inflation soared to 481.5 percent, while unemployment climbed to 17.4 percent as many analysts and observers described the economy as imploding. Venezuela is ranked 186st out of 189 in the World Bank's 2016 ease of doing business index. The average ranking for Latin America is 100th.

GOVERNMENT AND POLITICS

Political background. Homeland of Simón BOLIVAR, "the Liberator," Venezuela achieved independence from Spain in 1821 and became a separate republic in 1830. A history of political instability and lengthy periods of authoritarian rule culminated in the dictatorships of Gen. Juan Vicente GÓMEZ from 1908 to 1935 and Gen. Marcos PÉREZ Jiménez from 1952 to 1958, the interim being punctuated by unsuccessful attempts to establish democratic government. The ouster of Pérez Jiménez by a military-backed popular movement in January 1958 prepared the way for subsequent elected regimes.

The return to democratic rule was marked by the December 1958 election of Rómulo BETANCOURT, leader of the Democratic Action (AD) party and of the non-Communist Left in Latin America. Venezuela made considerable economic and political progress under the successive AD administrations of Betancourt (1959–1964) and Raúl LEONI (1964–1969), with Cuban-supported subversive efforts being successfully resisted. The election and inauguration of Dr. Rafael CALDERA Rodríguez of the Social Christian Party (COPEI) in 1969 further institutionalized the peaceful transfer of power. As the first Christian Democratic president in Venezuela and the second in Latin America (following Eduardo Frei Montalva of Chile), Caldera adhered to an independent pro-Western policy while seeking to "normalize" Venezuelan political life through such measures as legal recognition of the Communist Party, appeals to leftist guerrilla forces to lay down their arms, and the broadening of diplomatic contacts with both Communist and non-Communist regimes.

Venezuela's politics were dominated by its two leading parties during the administrations of the AD's Carlos Andrés PÉREZ (1974–1979), Luis HERRERA Campíns of COPEI (1979–1984), and Jaime LUSINCHI of AD (1984–1989). (See the entry in the 2010 *Handbook* for details.)

Although economic conditions steadily worsened under Lusinchi, the AD retained the presidency in the election of December 4, 1988, as Carlos Pérez became the first Venezuelan president to be elected for a second term; the AD, on the other hand, lost its congressional majorities, winning only 23 of 49 elective seats in the Senate and 97 of 201 seats in the Chamber of Deputies. (For more on Pérez's "economic shock program" and the riots it precipitated, see the 2012 *Handbook*.)

On February 4, 1992, the president escaped assassination during an abortive coup by junior officers, including a prominent paratrooper named Hugo CHÁVEZ, which included an attack on his official residence. On June 11 COPEI's two representatives resigned from the "National Unity" government they had joined only three months before, and on June 29, in accepting the resignations of 11 cabinet members, Pérez implemented a previously announced plan to slash cabinet-rank personnel by two-thirds. Despite a second major coup attempt on November 27, state and local elections were held on December 6, in which the AD lost further ground.

In March 1993 the attorney general applied to the Supreme Court for a ruling as to whether President Pérez should be charged with the embezzlement of $17 million in state funds that the chief executive said had been expended for secret security and defense purposes, but that opponents insisted had been diverted to campaign and other nonofficial uses. After the court responded in the affirmative, the Senate on May 21 suspended the president, who was constitutionally succeeded, on an interim basis, by the Senate president, Octavio LEPAGE, on May 22. On June 5 the Congress named a highly respected, pro-AD independent, Sen. Ramón José VELASQUEZ, to complete the final eight months of the Pérez presidency.

On December 5, 1993, former president Caldera, who had been expelled from COPEI in June for refusing to support its presidential candidate, Oswaldo ALVAREZ Paz, was elected to a second term as the nominee of a recently organized, 17-party National Convergence (CN) coalition. Although credited with only 30.5 percent of the vote, he was but one contender in a record field of 18.

On June 24, 1994, in the face of continued economic and political problems that had sparked rumors of a possible coup, President Caldera adopted wide-ranging powers that included a suspension of six constitutional guarantees, five of which were restored by Congress on July 21. Among the financial difficulties was a liquidity crisis that resulted in 13 banks being brought under state control by mid-August.

Although no respite from the recession was evident, President Caldera suspended his remaining emergency powers on July 6, 1995, promulgating instead a financial emergency law that authorized him to intervene in the economy without having to abrogate constitutional rights.

Considerable social unrest preceded the accord finally concluded with the IMF in April 1996, which called for accelerated privatization and flotation of the bolívar. Thereafter, on May 30, the Supreme Court handed down a guilty verdict against former president Pérez, who was, however, released from 28 months of detention on September 19 and then returned to the political arena by campaigning successfully for his old Senate seat in November 1998.

On December 8, 1998, the February 1992 coup leader, Hugo Chávez Frías, gained an impressive victory in presidential balloting over Henrique SALAS Römer, the nominee of both traditional rival parties, with former beauty queen Irene SÁEZ a distant third. Following his election, Chávez pledged to pursue constitutional revision to lay "the foundations of a new republic," and at a Constituent Assembly poll on July 25, 1999, candidates from his Patriotic Pole coalition won 121 of 128 contested seats.

The assembly created a "judicial emergency commission" to restructure the nation's court system on August 19, 1999, and on August 30 stripped the opposition-controlled Congress of its remaining powers. The Assembly then drafted a new basic law (see below), which was approved by 71.2 percent of the participants in a December 15 referendum.

At its concluding session on January 30, 2000, the Constituent Assembly named its president, Chávez's political mentor Luis MIQUILENA, to head a transitional National Legislative Commission, pending the election of a National Assembly on May 28. However, the balloting was subsequently postponed for technical reasons until July 30, when President Chávez was elected to a new six-year term and his Fifth Republic Movement (*Movimiento Quinta República*—MVR) and its allies won a majority of the 165 seats in the new National Assembly.

In November 2000 Chávez secured legislative approval of an enabling law granting him decree powers for a year. Further enhancing his power was voter approval of rigid labor controls in a December 3 referendum. Having already alienated organized labor, Chávez exacerbated a growing rift with the military leadership in February 2001 by naming a longtime associate, José Vicente RANGEL, as Venezuela's first civilian minister of defense. In June, in an effort to consolidate his support among leftists and the poor, he authorized formation at the neighborhood level of Bolivarian Circles (*Círculos Bolivarianos*) committed to advancement of the "Bolivarian revolution."

On November 13, 2001, using his decree powers, President Chávez promulgated 49 laws involving economic, financial, infrastructural, and social policies. The most controversial measures permitted expropriation of underutilized farmland, in the name of an "agrarian revolution," and required that joint hydrocarbon ventures include majority government participation. Oil royalties were also increased. In response, the Venezuelan Federation of Chambers of Commerce and Industry (*Federación Venezolana de Cámaras y Asociaciones de Comercio y Producción—Fedecámaras*), supported by the country's largest labor union group, the Venezuelan Workers' Confederation (*Confederación de Trabajadores de Venezuela*—CTV), announced that it would mount a nationwide one-day strike in December.

In March 2002 managerial staff of the state petroleum company, *Petróleos de Venezuela* (PDVSA), with support from the industry's union, the *Federación de Trabajadores Petroleros* (*Fedepetrol*), began a job action, which was followed on April 9 by a general strike organized by the CTV and *Fedecámaras*. Two days later, with 150,000 anti-Chávez protesters massed outside the presidential palace, more than a dozen demonstrators were killed by gunfire from, apparently, members of the Bolivarian Circles.

On April 12, 2002, senior military officers, led by Gen. Luis RINCON, the armed forces commander, announced that Chávez had resigned, although it quickly became apparent that a coup had been mounted against him. With Chávez in custody, the military named Pedro CARMONA, president of *Fedecámaras,* as provisional president. Acting by decree, Carmona attempted to dissolve the National Assembly and the Supreme Court and to suspend the constitution, but wide popular support for the government takeover failed to materialize as advocates of democracy joined Chávez loyalists in the streets. Carmona subsequently resigned, and on April 13 the National Assembly elevated Vice President Diosdado CABELLO to the presidency. Cabello, in turn, returned the presidency to Chávez on April 14. (In 2009 Cabello was serving as the Chávez government's minister of public works.)

In late 2002 and early 2003 major business and labor sectors staged a general strike over several months that crippled the economy, severely reducing oil production. In the end, the strike's proponents were forced to call off their action in the face of rising public anger.

In 2003 the opposition was confident that it could remove Chávez by means of a popular referendum, campaigning for which was launched on November 21. The recall ballot on August 26, 2004, was endorsed by only 40.7 percent of the participating voters. The president and his allies were further strengthened on October 31 by winning 20 of 23 state governorships (15 of which had been held by *antichavistas*), as well as the mayoralty of Caracas. The leading opposition parties boycotted the December 4, 2005, legislative balloting, resulting in a 75 percent abstention rate and an assembly with almost no opposition representation.

The administration advanced proposals for a constitutional change that permitted Chávez to run, successfully, for a third term on December 3, 2006. The opposition united behind a single candidate, endorsing Zulia state governor Manuel ROSALES under the New Time (*Un Nuevo Tiempo*—UNT) banner. Chávez defeated Rosales by a 62–37 percent margin in voting that was internationally judged to be free and fair. No other candidate received more than 0.04 percent of the vote. On January 8, 2007, just before his inauguration, Chávez replaced nearly every minister in his cabinet and named a new vice president, former National Electoral Council president Jorge RODRÍGUEZ. Another cabinet reshuffle occurred on January 3–4, 2008, with the naming of a new vice president, retired Col. Ramón CARRIZALEZ, and nine new ministers.

In 2007 Chávez began to take Venezuela in a markedly more radical direction toward "21st Century Socialism," as the National Assembly approved a second "enabling law" allowing him to rule by decree for 18 months. Though he suffered a setback with the December constitutional referendum proposing central control over states and municipalities, the president pushed through a host of reforms by other means, including decrees and laws that easily passed the assembly.

Ostensibly to increase "participatory democracy," Chávez moved to bolster the funding of thousands of "community councils," citizen groups accountable to the presidency that take on functions formally under the purview of local governments. An April 9, 2008, decree started the process of consolidation of 126 regional or municipal police forces into a single national force. Chávez also removed authority from Venezuela's central bank, placing monetary policy under presidential control.

The president's 18-month decree authority expired on July 31, 2008. On that day, Chávez issued 26 decrees, including a restoration of the "Geometry of Power" proposal for central control over states and municipalities, which had been defeated in the December 2007 referendum. Another decree increased the state's ability to regulate the production, distribution, import, and export of food.

Following President Chávez's victory in a February 2009 constitutional referendum to abolish term limits (see Constitution and government, below), he reshuffled the cabinet, consolidating some ministries and giving Vice President Carrizalez the additional portfolio of defense minister.

In September 2009 Chávez restructured the Council of Ministers, giving six cabinet ministers the additional title of "vice president" with responsibility for broader policy issues. Vice President Carrizalez assumed the title of first vice president.

Several ministers resigned on January 24, 2010. Following the resignation of Vice President Carrizalez on January 25, Agriculture Minister Elías JUAU Milano was named to replace him on January 26. More cabinet changes were made in February, April, May, June, July, and October.

In the National Assembly elections held on September 26, 2010, the PSUV secured the most seats but failed to retain its two-thirds majority.

Since 2009 the Chávez government has moved forward with plans to nationalize key sectors, including banking, energy and hydrocarbon, and gold. The expropriations, along with the arrests of some wealthy businessmen, resulted in a significant decline in foreign investment. The economy slid into a recession, which continued through the first half of 2010 and was compounded by a severe drought. Adding to the tension was the nation's spiraling homicide rate, as more than 16,000 suspected murders were recorded for the year. Analysts said Venezuela's persistent economic inequality, insufficient national police force, and increasingly politicized judicial system were hampering the government's ability to improve security.

Attention in 2010 turned to the National Assembly elections, the first held under a new law passed in 2009, which observers said favored the major parties and their candidates. Another law adopted around the same time allowed the election commission to redraw electoral districts at any time. In 2010 the districts were drawn to give more representation to states that were pro-Chávez, and the percentage of seats filled by proportional representation was reduced. The opposition Democratic Unity Table (*Mesa de la Unidad Democrática*—MUD) coalition, consisting of several dozen national and regional parties with diverse ideologies, nevertheless managed to win 65 seats, while the PSUV and its allies won 98, short of a two-thirds majority by 12 seats.

Virtually all significant legislation enacted since January 2011 has been by decree of President Chávez. Among the laws he issued are those that gave the government the rights to take over all "idle and underused land and buildings" and impose a profit tax on oil sales over $40 per barrel.

In June Chávez flew to Cuba for emergency surgery to treat a "pelvic abscess." He remained in Cuba for several weeks, undergoing additional surgery and chemotherapy. He returned to Venezuela in October and declared himself cured of cancer. However, rumors abounded that Chávez's cancer had spread and was more virulent than had previously been reported.

On November 1, 2011, Chávez announced the nationalization of a subsidiary of the UK-owned agricultural company Vestey Group, following failed talks between the government and the company over compensation. Meanwhile, the government introduced price controls on many basic goods in order to curb the 27 percent annual inflation rate. On November 11 Juan Carlos Fernandez, Chile's consul in Venezuela, was abducted while leaving a Caracas hotel. During a two-hour hostage ordeal, Fernandez reportedly suffered a gunshot wound before he was released. One week later Chávez announced that the government was deploying up to 3,650 troops in Caracas and surrounding areas to bolster police forces in their fight against violent crime.

On January 6, 2012, Chávez appointed General Henry Rangel SILVA, whom the U.S. government had formerly accused of being a drug kingpin, as the new defense minister, prompting speculation that Chávez was trying to shore up support within the military.

In a sign of the most energized and unified opposition in years, a group of parties held a joint primary on February 12 for voters to decide on a MUD unity candidate to oppose Chávez in the October 7 general elections. The 39-year-old former Miranda governor Henrique CAPRILES, of the Justice First party, won the primary by a decisive margin. However, he faced long odds in the general election, given Chávez's control over the entire state apparatus to promote his campaign and a massive increase in government spending on social programs to attract voters during the run-up to the election. Capriles touted his administrative successes as governor, vowing to continue the fight against poverty, but with better management skills.

Many voters were said to be anxious about losing their jobs or government benefits if they voted for Capriles, especially after the introduction of a new electronic voting system that some feared might be used by the government to track who voted against the president.

Chávez easily won reelection on October 7, securing 55.1 percent of the vote to Capriles's 44.2 percent, although Capriles took more votes from than any past Chávez challenger. Three days later, Chávez selected Foreign Minister Nicolás MADURO to be his vice president.

Gubernatorial elections were held on December 16, with the ruling PSUV winning 20 or 23 races. Capriles held onto his seat, defeating former vice president Elías Jaua Milano.

Chávez vowed to take Venezuela farther down the road of "21st century socialism," but his health began to rapidly deteriorate. He returned to Cuba for additional surgeries in November and December and announced on December 8 that his cancer had returned. He also addressed the people of Venezuela on television, instructing them to "elect Nicolás Maduro as president of the republic." Chávez was too ill to be inaugurated on January 10, 2013, prompting speculation over who was actually running the country. Chávez returned to Venezuela on February 18 and passed away on March 5 at age 58. Maduro won election to formally succeed Chávez and was inaugurated on April 19, 2013 (see Current Issues, below). Maduro was granted the power to rule by decree for a year by the assembly on November 19, 2013.

The assembly again granted the president the power to rule by decree for one year on March 15, 2015. In assembly balloting on December 6, 2015, the MUD coalition won an overwhelming victory with 109 seats, while the PSUV and its allies secured 55 seats. MUD and the three indigenous representatives thus constituted a supermajority, but the PSUV challenged the results of four seats.

Maduro appointed Aristóbulo ISTÚRIZ Almeida (PSUV) as executive vice president on January 6, 2016, and moved incumbent Jorge ARREAZA (PSUV) to vice president for social development as part of a broader cabinet reshuffle. Also in January, Maduro issued a decree permitting him to rule by decree for 60 days in response to the nation's economic collapse (see Current issues, below). Although challenged by the assembly, he periodically reissued the decree through 2016. Additional cabinet reshuffles occurred in August and October.

Constitution and government. Under its constitution of January 23, 1961, Venezuela was designated a federal republic. It now encompasses 23 states (the newest, Vargas, created with effect from January 1, 1999), a Federal District, and 72 Federal Dependencies (islands in the Antilles). Executive power was vested in a president who was elected by universal suffrage for a five-year term and until mid-1992 (when a one-term ban was imposed on all future incumbents) could be reelected after a ten-year interval. The legislative body (Congress of the Republic) consisted of a Senate and a Chamber of Deputies, both elected by universal suffrage for five-year terms concurrent with that of the president. The states were administered by popularly elected governors; had their own elected, unicameral legislative assemblies; and were divided into county-type districts with popularly elected mayors and municipal councils.

Among the numerous changes introduced by the 1999 basic law, the presidential term was extended to six years with the possibility of one immediate renewal; executive authority vis-à-vis the economy was substantially enhanced; the bicameral legislature was abandoned in favor of a unicameral National Assembly; public administration was drastically reorganized; oil production was to remain vested in the state; the rights of indigenous peoples were affirmed; and the country was renamed *República Bolivariana de Venezuela* in honor of the independence hero.

In May 2004 the Supreme Court was enlarged from 20 to 32 members.

In October 2008 constitutional reforms were approved that allow the president to appoint officials, popularly referred to as "viceroys," empowered to carry out most of the functions of elected mayors and governors. On February 15, 2009, a referendum to remove the two-term limit on the president, mayors, governors, and National Assembly members was approved by a vote of 54.9 percent.

The Venezuelan media transmits a broad range of political views, and private media remain occasionally critical of the government, but threats to revoke broadcast licenses have resulted in widespread self-censorship. The Radio and Television Social Responsibility Act prohibits any programming viewed as an incitement to antistate violence and requires broadcasters to air government material for up to 70 hours a week.

In August 2009 the government closed 32 radio stations and 2 regional television stations, nearly all of them opposition-leaning, claiming that they were broadcasting illegally. Reporters Without Borders ranked Venezuela 139th out of 180 countries in its 2016 Index of Press Freedom, citing arbitrary closures of media outlets and at least 500 violations of the right to information since 2013.

Foreign relations. A member of the United Nations and its related agencies, the Organization of Petroleum Exporting Countries (OPEC), the Organization of American States (OAS), the Latin American Integration Association, the Union of South American Nations (UNASUR), and other hemispheric organizations, Venezuela was traditionally aligned with the West in both inter-American and world affairs. During the presidencies of Betancourt and Leoni, it was subjected by the Cuban regime of Fidel Castro to repeated propaganda attacks and armed incursions. Although it consequently took a particularly harsh line toward Cuba, it was equally critical of right-wing dictatorships in the Americas and for some years refused to maintain diplomatic relations with governments formed as a result of military coups. This policy was modified during the 1960s by the establishment of diplomatic relations with Argentina, Panama, and Peru as well as with Czechoslovakia, Hungary, the Soviet Union, and other Communist countries, while in December 1974, despite earlier differences, a normalization of relations with Cuba was announced.

A long-standing territorial claim to the section of Guyana west of the Essequibo River has caused intermittent friction with that country, Venezuela declining in June 1982 to renew a 12-year moratorium on unilateral action in the dispute and subsequently refusing to sanction submission of the controversy to the International Court of Justice. In September 1999 the issue was revived by the Venezuelan foreign minister, who rejected the century-old award to the former UK dependency.

A Venezuelan claim to tiny Bird Island (*Isla de Aves*) to the west of Dominica has periodically strained relations with its Caribbean neighbors. While the island, on which Venezuela is reportedly constructing a scientific station, is of little intrinsic importance, the Organization of Eastern Caribbean States (OECS) has expressed concern that it might serve as the basis of a claim by Caracas to a 200-mile-wide exclusive economic zone.

For more than three decades Caracas has been engaged in a dispute with Colombia regarding sovereignty over the Gulf of Venezuela (Gulf of Guajira). Other disagreements have arisen over the smuggling of foodstuffs, drug trafficking, and alleged attacks by Colombia's guerrilla and paramilitary groups on the Venezuelan National Guard and Venezuelan citizens. Over the years the two countries have concluded a number of agreements aimed at combating drug traffickers, but an "open border" has made interdiction of drug shipments difficult.

The Chávez government's ties with the United States have deteriorated steadily, with some of the first problems brought about by an August 2000 visit by President Chávez to Iraq (the first by a head of state since the first Gulf war), a visit to Caracas by Fidel Castro in late October, the conclusion of a military cooperation treaty with Russia in May 2001, and subsequent criticism of the U.S. bombing of Afghanistan as "fighting terror with terror." Relations deteriorated following the failed April 2002 coup attempt, which, it is widely believed, occurred with strong U.S. backing and support.

In December 2004 Chávez embarked on a tour of countries viewed as potential buyers of Venezuelan oil, including the People's Republic of China. Earlier, Venezuela concluded an agreement with Cuba to supply Havana with cut-rate oil in return for a medical assistance program valued at over $750 million. Venezuela has been Cuba's closest ally during the 2000s, with President Chávez the only foreign leader routinely granted audiences with the Castro brothers. Out of the Cuba–Venezuela relationship sprang the Bolivarian Alliance for the Americas (ALBA), an organization of left-leaning Latin American and Caribbean nations that Chávez proposed as an alternative to the proposed Free Trade Area of the Americas.

A major rupture in Colombian–Venezuelan relations followed Colombian security forces' abduction from Caracas of Rodrigo Granda, a Colombian citizen considered to be the "foreign minister" of Colombia's largest guerrilla group, the Revolutionary Armed Forces of Colombia (FARC), in early 2005. Tensions heightened as top Colombian officials, including Defense Minister Juan Manuel Santos, accused Venezuela of harboring and assisting Colombian guerrillas on Venezuelan territory. For his part, Chávez continued to be an ardent critic of "Plan Colombia" and other U.S. programs in the Andes. Venezuela also objected to Colombia's decision to grant asylum to Pedro Carmona, the business leader briefly named to Venezuela's presidency during the abortive April 2002 coup.

Venezuela's relations with Peru soured in 2006, when Chávez openly endorsed Peruvian presidential candidate Ollanta Humala. Humala did not win, in part because opponents, including the eventual victor, Alán García, portrayed him as a Chávez puppet. Relations between Chávez and García remained rocky.

A similar election-year dynamic that year damaged relations between Venezuela and Mexico, with Chávez and Mexican president

Vicente Fox engaging in a series of bitter verbal exchanges. Relations with Fox's successor, Felipe Calderón, improved somewhat, and Venezuela sent an ambassador to Mexico City in September 2007.

In August and September 2007 relations with Colombia appeared to improve as President Uribe invited Chávez to facilitate possible peace and prisoner-exchange dialogues with the FARC. However, relations broke down after Uribe abruptly "fired" Chávez from this role on November 22. The two leaders engaged in months of name-calling.

South America's worst security crisis in decades was triggered by a March 1, 2008, Colombian raid into Ecuadorian territory that killed Raúl Reyes, one of the FARC's most senior leaders. In response to what he viewed as a serious violation of Ecuador's sovereignty, Chávez warned Colombia that he would respond to a similar operation in Venezuela with fighter jets, and ordered his military to deploy ten tank battalions—about 9,000 troops—to Venezuela's border with Colombia. The threat of hostilities was defused by a March 7 meeting of the region's leaders in Santo Domingo, at which the leaders agreed to reinstate their ambassadors.

Tensions remained very high, however, as files recovered from Reyes's computer appeared to indicate that guerrilla leaders and key Venezuelan government officials had been discussing the possibility of material support for the FARC's cause. While Venezuela denied any wrongdoing and challenged the files' authenticity, Chávez's Colombia rhetoric toned down substantially over the following months. On June 8 Chávez surprised nearly all observers by publicly calling on the FARC to release all of their hostages and to abandon the armed struggle. Tensions with Colombia did not flare up again for the remainder of 2008.

On September 11, 2008, after Bolivia expelled its U.S. ambassador, Venezuela declared U.S. ambassador Patrick Duddy *persona non grata* in an act of "solidarity." The U.S. government responded by expelling Ambassador Bernardo Álvarez HERRERA. A few days later, the U.S. Treasury Department added Ramón RODRÍGUEZ CHACÍN, who had just vacated his post as Venezuela's interior minister, to its list of major international narcotrafficking figures, citing indications of links to Colombia's FARC that appeared on recovered guerrilla computers.

The U.S. government has placed a series of sanctions on Venezuela for failing to cooperate on initiatives against drugs and terrorism, and for violating religious freedom, making it impossible for Caracas to receive U.S. aid or to purchase weapons with U.S.-made components. In October 2008 the Venezuelan government expelled two researchers for Human Rights Watch from the country. The move prompted a sharp rebuke from the European Parliament.

President Chávez sought warmer relations with countries that are generally cool to the United States. A 2008 visit to China resulted in a host of new investment agreements, including increased Chinese access to Venezuelan oil. Ties with Russia have warmed significantly. Venezuela is one of a very few countries to recognize the breakaway Georgian regions of Abkhazia and South Ossetia. Venezuela has made many arms purchases from Russia, including a fleet of tanks and help from the Medvedev government in establishing a nuclear energy program.

President Chávez offered more conciliatory language to incoming U.S. president Barack Obama in early 2009. The two presidents exchanged cordial public greetings at the April Summit of the Americas in Trinidad and Tobago. In June the two countries reinstated their ambassadors.

Venezuela's relations with Peru deteriorated in April 2009, when the government of Alán García granted asylum to President Chávez's chief political rival, former presidential opponent Manuel Rosales. Venezuelan authorities had ordered Rosales's arrest on corruption charges.

President Chávez and Colombian president Uribe met in January 2009, pledging greater economic cooperation. In April Chávez, speaking at a joint press conference with Uribe, again called on the FARC guerrillas to negotiate and plan to disband.

In mid-July, when the Colombian media revealed that Bogotá would allow U.S. military personnel to use bases on Colombian soil, Chávez responded by freezing relations with Colombia. The Uribe government parried by revealing that it had recovered several Swedish-made rocket launchers from the FARC that had originated in Venezuela. Chávez recalled his ambassador and announced plans to cut annual trade with Colombia and to expropriate Colombian businesses in Venezuela. Tensions increased following the U.S.-Colombia defense agreement signing on October 30, as Chávez instructed the Venezuelan military to "prepare for war" with Colombia.

Chávez cultivated closer ties with Iran during a visit to Tehran in April 2009, when he became one of the first foreign leaders to visit following President Ahmadinejad's crackdown on protests against alleged electoral fraud. The leaders discussed sales of Venezuelan uranium for Iran's nuclear program. Chávez's September visit to Iran was part of a so-called "rogue states" tour that included Libya, Syria, Algeria, Turkmenistan, and Belarus, among others.

In July 2010 Colombia's ambassador to the OAS formally accused Venezuela of sheltering 1,500 Colombian guerrillas. President Chávez severed relations and ordered a military alert. However, the incoming Colombian president, Juan Manuel Santos, declared his willingness to resolve the conflict. On August 10, three days after his inauguration, Santos met with Chávez, and the two leaders agreed to restore full relations.

On September 9, 2011, the U.S. government named four officials close to President Chávez in its drug "kingpin" list and imposed sanctions against Venezuela, including freezing assets and prohibiting U.S. citizens from conducting business deals in Venezuela.

On January 8, 2012, the United States ordered the expulsion of Livia Acosta NOGUERA, Venezuela's consul general in Miami, following accusations that she had discussed the possibility of orchestrating cyber-attacks against the U.S. government while serving in Venezuela's embassy in Mexico City. On January 16 Venezuela announced that it was withdrawing its remaining diplomatic and consular officials from Miami.

On June 13, 2012, Chávez confirmed that Venezuela was building unmanned aerial drones in cooperation with China, Russia, and Iran.

The Netherlands concluded a trade agreement with Venezuela in June 2013 that will provide greater economic cooperation between the two countries. Venezuela is the closest neighbor of Aruba, Curaçao, and St. Maarten in the Dutch Caribbean.

The March 8, 2013, funeral for Chávez provided an opportunity for heads of state to signal their continued interest in Venezuela. Some 33 heads of state attended, including Cuba's Raúl Castro and Iran's Ahmadinejad. The United States sent a token delegation, especially after then-Vice President Maduro suggested that Washington had infected Chávez with the fatal cancer and on March 5 expelled two U.S. diplomats for allegedly encouraging the Venezuelan military to overthrow the Chávez government. On March 11 the United States expelled two Venezuelan diplomats. Three additional U.S. diplomats were expelled in September 2013 and an additional three in February 2014. The U.S. retaliated in each case with expulsions of its own.

Maduro visited Beijing in September 2013, signaling increasingly closer ties with China. Chinese president Xi Jinping and Maduro agreed on a $5 billion line of credit and signed 12 cooperation agreements on energy, education, agriculture, and construction. The deal also included $1.4 billion to further develop Venezuelan oil production capacity. Venezuela pulled out of the OAS's human rights court on September 11, 2013, with Maduro arguing that the court is "a tool to protect U.S. geopolitical interests" to "harass progressive governments."

Venezuela and Russia signed agreements on risk and disaster management as well as police services on October 29, 2013. This came a day after two Russian strategic Tu-160 long-range bombers landed in Caracas as part of the two states increasing levels of engagement.

In January 2014 Venezuela reopened its embassy in Paraguay, 18 months after closing it in retaliation for the impeachment of Chávez ally and former Paraguayan president Fernando Lugo. Chinese president Xi Jinping visited in July 2014. The two states signed a $4 billion line of credit and $690 development loan for gold and cooper exploration.

In March 2015 the United States imposed economic and travel sanctions on seven senior Venezuelan officials. Also in March, Maduro accused the United States of supporting a purported coup in February (see Current issues, below). On March 16 a World Bank panel ordered Venezuela to pay $46 million to the U.S. shipping firm Tidewater for the seizure of 11 of its vessels in 2009.

Maduro issued broad claims over extensive maritime areas reported to contain vast oil deposits in May 2015. The president also escalated territorial claims against Guyana, asserting that Venezuela had sovereignty over almost two-thirds of the country (see entry on Guyana). In August Venezuela and Colombia recalled their respective ambassadors and closed border crossing after three Venezuelan soldiers were wounded in an exchange of gunfire along the border.

In September 2016 Venezuela was blocked from assuming the rotating presidency of MERCOSUR over the country's human rights record and violations of trade agreements.

Current issues. The Venezuelan constitution specifies that presidential elections had to be held within 30 days of Chávez's death. Maduro became acting president and appointed Jorge ARREAZA as acting vice president. Arreaza was minister for science and technology as well as Chávez's son-in-law. He had been the family spokesperson during the president's long illness. On April 14 Maduro narrowly defeated Capriles for the presidency, 50.6 percent to 49.1 percent. While Chávez beat

Capriles by 1.6 million votes in 2012, Maduro's margin was less than 250,000. When Capriles demanded a recount, Maduro initially agreed then reversed himself, sparking protests from both sides. When opposition legislators refused to acknowledge Maduro's victory, Cabello, the speaker of the National Assembly, refused to let them speak and seized their paychecks, sparking fistfights. The Supreme Court later fined Capriles for challenging the results.

As he struggled to consolidate his legitimacy, Maduro lashed out at critics at home and abroad. When the United States, Chile, and Peru declined to recognize Maduro's election, he denounced U.S. president Barack Obama as the "grand chief of devils." Peru's foreign minister Rafael Roncagliolo urged him to adopt a "climate of dialogue, tolerance, and mutual respect," but Maduro called the advice "the mistake of his life." The president also accused several Colombian political leaders of trying to assassinate him. The PSUV is reportedly fracturing, with Cabello leading the anti-Maduro camp.

Meanwhile the economy rapidly declined. The government had spent 40 percent more than in took in in 2012, and Maduro devaluated the currency twice in early 2013 as inflation passed 30 percent. Shortages, including food, increased throughout the year. In September power failures caused blackouts in 70 percent of the country. Maduro accused the United States of supporting plots to sabotage the power grid and expelled three diplomats, including the chargé d'affaires, in October. He also requested special powers to rule by decree in order to "fight against corruption and the economic war declared by the bourgeoisie against the people."

Protests and clashes between the opposition and progovernment movements broke out in early 2014 with opposition leader Leopoldo LOPEZ imprisoned on February 19, 2014. The protest movement that started as an isolated student demonstration had spread across the country and multiplied into the tens of thousands. By the end of February, several hundred demonstrators had been hurt or imprisoned and at least 18 were left dead. Venezuela broke diplomatic ties with Panama on March 6, 2014, and threatened to default on $1 billion owed in retaliation for Panama calling on the OAS to look into the crisis. A second opposition leader was jailed on March 20, 2014. San Cristobal mayor Daniel Ceballos was jailed after attending a meeting of opposition mayors held in Caracas.

By the end of March, the protests killed at least 30 and cost an estimated $10 billion to the economy. On April 1 the government ordered the army into San Cristobal to break up the protests. In May, after the United States froze the assets and restricted the travel of Venezuelan leaders accused of human rights violations, Maduro expelled three U.S. diplomats, accusing them of conspiring to assassinate him. However, he offered no proof of this claim.

Protests continued as of October 2014; however, the movement peaked in February and has steadily declined since. The Venezuelan Observatory of Social Conflict identified 6,369 protests and more than 40 deaths within the country in the first six months of the year.

Former Venezuelan president Ramon Jose VELASQUEZ died at the age of 97 on June 25, 2014.

On February 12, 2015, Maduro claimed that a planned coup had been disrupted. Opposition figures, including Caracas mayor Antonio LEDEZMA, were arrested.

Falling oil prices and gross financial mismanagement led to an economic collapse in the country. Between 2014 and 2017, GDP contracted by more than 17 percent, inflation soared to more than 450 percent, and unemployment was expected to top 25 percent by the end of 2017. Basic goods and services were increasingly unavailable, and repeated increases in the minimum wage failed to keep pace with inflation.

In June 2016 opposition groups began a drive to recall Maduro, whose approval ratings had fallen to 20 percent. In September the country's election commission rejected the recall petition, asserting voter fraud. In October Maduro postponed regional elections in a reported bid to prevent opposition parties from gaining control of provincial and local governments. Meanwhile, the election commission ordered an end to a new recall effort against the president.

POLITICAL PARTIES

It is a sign of Chávez's profound influence that even after his death, Venezuela's political party system can be divided into in two broad categories: pro-Chávez and anti-Chávez. The United Socialist Party of Venezuela (*Partido Socialista Unido de Venezuela*—PSUV) has dominated the political scene for over a dozen years, and it has created alliances with like-minded smaller parties ahead of elections. These include the Patriotic Pole (*Polo Patriótica*—PP) in 2000, the **Block for Change** (*Bloque para el Cambio*) in 2005, the **Patriotic Alliance** (*Alianza Patriótica*) in 2008, and the Great Patriotic Pole (*Gran Polo Patriótica*—GPP) for the 2012 and 2013 presidential elections. The anti-Chávez camp is led by the Democratic Unity Table (*Mesa de la Unidad Democrática*—MUD). Eleven parties formed MUD in June 2009 and by the 2010 election that number had grown to more than 50 groups.

Presidential Party:

United Socialist Party of Venezuela (*Partido Socialista Unido de Venezuela*—PSUV). Before the 2000 election, a Patriotic Pole (*Polo Patriótica*—PP) of 14 pro-Chávez parties included the MVR and MAS (below). A year later, the MAS withdrew, leaving the MVR as the coalition's only major component. For the 2005 poll, the pro-Chávez group reorganized as the Block for Change (*Bloque para el Cambio*).

Following his 2006 reelection victory, President Chávez pressured all government-supportive parties to form a single party instead of, in his words, "an alphabet soup that is fooling the people." Instead of a ruling coalition of 21 groups as before, the president declared that all of his supporters must join the new party and cease to exist as independent entities, or be considered political adversaries. The PSUV held its inaugural congress on January 12, 2008, and became the dominant pro-Chávez force. Three coalition members—For Social Democracy (*Podemos*), Fatherland for All (PPT), and the Communist Party of Venezuela (PCV)—remained independent, but allied, parties. The still-forming PSUV united with smaller progovernment parties to compete in the 2008 municipal and state elections as the Patriotic Alliance (*Alianza Patriótica*), a designation that by 2009 was no longer used.

In May 2010 the party conducted primary votes in which roughly 2.5 million members (more than one-third of the party's registered membership) chose nominees for the 110 National Assembly seats elected by district. It was reportedly the largest intraparty election in Venezuelan history. Party leaders, including President Chávez, selected the state-based candidates for the seats elected by proportional representation. Meanwhile, some leading *chavistas* complained about the degree of control exercised by the government over the party.

The PSUV won 95 seats in the September 26 legislative election with 46 percent of the vote. Its three allied parties (PCV, COPEI, and the indigenous Foundation for Training, Integration, and Dignity) each took a single seat, giving the PSUV control over 98 of 165 seats, 12 short of a majority.

Going into the October 7, 2012, presidential election, the PSUV anchored a new alliance, the **Great Patriotic Pole** (*Gran Polo Patriótica*—GPP) formed exclusively to support Chávez's reelection. Chávez easily won with 55.1 percent of the vote, although he was too ill to take the oath of office in January.

Following the death of President Chávez in March 2013, Nicolás MADURO replaced him as president of the country and the PSUV. The party reportedly fractured in late 2013 into a Maduro faction and one loyal to Diosdado CABELLO, the president of the National Assembly. Maduro announced plans to reactivate the GPP for upcoming elections. The PSUV-led coalition secured 40.9 percent of the vote in the December 2015 balloting, and 55 seats.

Leaders: Nicolás MADURO (President of the Republic), Diosdado CABELLO (First Vice President of the Party), Hugo CHÁVEZ (Eternal President).

Fifth Republic Movement (*Movimiento Quinta República*—MVR). The MVR was launched in July 1997 by presidential aspirant Hugo Chávez Frías, who had previously been associated with the outlawed Revolutionary Bolivarian Movement–200 (*Movimiento Bolivariano Revolucionario–200*—MBR-200), an intensely nationalist formation composed largely of former military figures opposed to the alleged corruption and social disparity occasioned by government economic policies. Chávez, having been arrested following the February 1992 revolt and then released from prison in March 1994 as part of a conciliatory gesture by President Caldera toward the military, had indicated that the MBR-200 would be converted into a political formation. In 2002 the MVR saw some Chávez opponents leave to form the **Solidarity Party** and the **Revolutionary Transparency Party** (TR).

For the 2005 legislative poll, all MVR candidates were designated by the party's "National Tactical Command," with nearly a quarter of sitting members of the National Assembly deemed insufficiently loyal to be given an opportunity for reelection. MVR announced its decision to merge with PSUV in 2007, completing its merger on October 20, 2007.

Unity of Electoral Victors (*Unidad de Vencedores Electorales—*UVE). The UVE, founded in 2005, was one of several pro-Chávez parties competing within the Block for Change coalition. The group appeared to be indistinguishable from the MVR, even using the same logo; critics alleged it was part of a strategy to increase the progovernment bloc's majority by adding to the proportional representation. The group won four National Assembly seats in the 2005 legislative elections; immediately afterward, however, its deputies joined the MVR and later PSUV in 2007.

People's Electoral Movement (*Movimiento Electoral del Pueblo—*MEP). The MEP was founded in 1967 by a left-wing faction of the Democratic Action (AD, below) that disagreed with the party's choice of a presidential candidate for the 1968 election. It won three lower house seats in 1978, none thereafter. In 1987 the party selected Edmundo CHIRINOS, rector of the Central University of Venezuela, as its 1988 presidential nominee, who, in addition to being supported by the Communist Party, received the endorsement of the Independent Moral Movement (*Movimiento Moral Independiente—*MMI), a small left-wing group formed in 1986. Based on nationwide polling results, the MEP was granted one seat in the Chamber of Deputies after the November 1998 election. In 2005 the MEP won one National Assembly seat. That legislator joined the PSUV, with the MEP later dissolving into PSUV in 2007.

Leader: Wilmer NOLASCO (Secretary General).

Venezuelan Popular Unity (*Unidad Popular Venezolana—*UPV). The UPV was founded in February 2004 as a "radical and ruthless" pro-Chávez leftist party. It won one seat in the December 2005 National Assembly election. In 2007 its leader, Lina RON, indicated that the party would accept President Chávez's dictate that supporting parties unite as the PSUV, given that Chávez is "the messiah God sent to save the people." Ron died suddenly in 2011 at age 51.

Several other parties and groups in the pro-Chávez coalition with no legislative representation joined the PSUV as well. They include the **Independent Solidarity Movement** (*Movimiento Solidaridad Independente—*MSI or SI), organized in early 1997 to support the interests of the middle class and led by Paciano PADRON and Luis EDUARDO Ortega; the **Union Party** (*Partido Unión—*PN), launched in May 2001 as a social democratic alternative to the AD and COPEI by Lt. Col. (Ret.) Francisco ARIAS Cárdenas; the Agriculturalist **Action** (*Acción Agropecuaria—*AA), led by Hiram GAVIRIA and Gustavo BASTIDAS; the **Emergent People** (*Gente Emergente—*GE), founded in 1991 in opposition to the "irresponsible power elite" and led by Fernando ALVAREZ Paz and Lazaro CALAZÁN; the **Independents for the National Community** (*Independientes por la Comunidad Nacional—*IPCN), which was organized by Antonio GONZÁLEZ to foster community development; the **Moral Force** (Fuerza Moral—FM), formed in 1998 by Hernán GRÜBER Odreman, a former rear admiral who participated in the abortive coup of November 1992 and was appointed governor of the Federal District by Chávez in January 1999; and the **New Democratic Regime** (*Nuevo Régimen Democrático—*NRD), which was launched in 1997 by Guillermo GARCÍA Ponce, Manuel ISIDRO Molina, and Pedro MIRANDA. In addition, by 1998 an **Independence Movement** *(Movimiento Independencia—*MI), headed by J. A. COVA Sosa, had evolved from The Notables (*Grupo Notables*), a group of well-known public figures who had supported the 1992 coup attempts. One of The Notables was José Vicente Rangel, the 1983 presidential candidate of the **New Alternative** (*Nuevo Alternative—*NA), a coalition that had included, among other groups, the pro-Moscow faction of the MIR (see Movement to Socialism [*Movimiento al Socialismo—*MAS], below).

Pro-Government Parties in the National Assembly:

Communist Party of Venezuela (*Partido Comunista de Venezuela—*PCV). Founded in 1931, the PCV was proscribed in 1962 but relegalized in 1969 following its renunciation of the use of force. The party lost its three seats in the assembly after endorsing the 1988 presidential candidacy of the MEP's Edmundo Chirinos. In 1997 it expelled its only MP, Ricardo GUTIÉRREZ, who subsequently became a leader of *Podemos*.

The PCV won eight National Assembly seats in 2005; all but three deputies subsequently defected to the PSUV. The party joined in an electoral alliance with the PSUV for the 2015 legislative elections and won two seats. Jerónimo CARRERA, president of the party, died on April 29, 2013, at the age of 90.

Leaders: Pedro EUSSE (Secretary), Oscar FIGUERA (Secretary General).

National Indian Council of Venezuela (*Consejo Nacional Indio de Venezuela—*CONIVE). Founded in 1989 to defend indigenous rights, this pro-Chávez party won all three National Assembly seats reserved for indigenous communities in the 2000 elections and won two of three seats in the 2005 elections. Both CONIVE deputies later joined the PSUV. The party contested the 2010 National Assembly elections in alliance with the PSUV and received one seat.

Leaders: Noeli POCATERRA, Raúl TEMPO (Executive Secretary).

Fatherland for All (*Patria para Todos—*PPT). The leftist revolutionary PPT was organized in late 1997 by a dissident faction of *La Causa Radical* (below). In December 2005 it won 11 seats in the National Assembly. While it was a member of the Patriotic Alliance in the 2008 local elections, the PPT's remaining five deputies declined to join the PSUV. In early 2010 Henri FALCON, the governor of Lara state, defected from the PSUV to join PPT. The PPT leadership subsequently announced it would not join in coalition with PSUV for the 2010 legislative elections, in light of the president's drift toward authoritarian rule. The party won two assembly seats in 2010 but was not part of either electoral alliance.

Leader: Rafael UZCÁTEGUI (Secretary General).

For Social Democracy (*Por la Democracia Social—Podemos*). The center-left *Podemos* was formed in November 2002, primarily by former members of MAS (below) who remained loyal to President Chávez. In 2005, it finished a distant second to the MVR in the National Assembly election, winning 15 seats. Though it lost some deputies to the PSUV, its six remaining legislators resisted joining the new party. Former party president Ramon MARTINEZ received asylum in Peru in January 2010 in the wake of corruption charges against him in Venezuela. *Podemos* won two seats as part of the MUD coalition in the 2010 legislative elections. In June 2012 a faction led by Secretary General Ismael GARCÍA broke away to help establish the **Advanced Progressive** party. The remaining party left MUD and affiliated with GPP.

Leaders: Didalco BOLIVAR (President), Baudillo REINOSO (Vice President).

Opposition Parties in the National Assembly:

Democratic Unity Table (*Mesa de la Unidad Democrática—*MUD). The **National Unity** (*Unidad Nacional—*UN) was the principal opposition coalition participating in the November 2008 regional elections. It was formed with the signing of an agreement in January 2008 by the leaders of 11 member parties. Several more parties joined in February. The coalition won five states and four of the five Caracas mayors' offices.

On June 8, 2009, all of the same major opposition parties—plus *Podemos* (above), the only coalition member with legislative representation—came together to form the MUD. The coalition included a total of 50 major and minor parties. Despite some infighting, the coalition assembled a common slate of candidates to challenge the PSUV in the September 2010 legislative elections, with one main opposition candidate in most districts. The grouping won 65 seats on a 48 percent vote share, compared with the PSUV's 46 percent vote share and 98 seats. The vote distribution was attributed to the way the districts were defined for the polling.

In the 2012 presidential contest, the MUD backed Henrique Capriles, who won 44 percent of the vote to Chávez's 54 percent. Capriles ran for president again in April 2013, following the death of Chávez, winning 49.1 percent to Maduro's 50.6 percent. Capriles' demands for a recount were rejected by the National Election Council.

Hard-line coalition members undertook a series of organized protests from February to May 2014 in an effort called *La Salida* or The Exit in order to pressure the administration of Maduro. Suffering internal divisions, Executive Secretary Ramon GUILLERMO Aveldo resigned in July 2014, leading to the selection of Jesus "Chuo" TORREALBA in an effort to save the coalition from fracture. The coalition won 56.2 percent of the vote in the 2015 assembly balloting and 109 seats.

Leader: Jesus "Chuo" TORREALBA (Executive Secretary).

Justice First (*Primero Justicia—*PJ). The PJ traces its origins to a civil association formed in 1992 by a Supreme Court justice, Alirio ABREU Burelli, to promote legal reform. It was constituted as a political party in 2000 and went on to win five seats from the state of Miranda in the National Assembly election. It was the second largest vote getter of the 44 parties in the coalition that supported Manuel Rosales's failed 2006 opposition presidential bid.

The PJ won 33 seats as part of the MUD coalition in the 2015 assembly elections. Henrique CAPRILES Radonski, governor of Miranda, was the opposition presidential candidate in 2012 and 2013, finishing second both times.

Leaders: Julio BORGES (National Coordinator), Henrique CAPRILES Radonski (2012, 2013 Presidential Candidate).

A New Time (*Un Nuevo Tiempo*—UNT). The Zulia-based UNT movement was founded in 1999 by regional dissidents from the Democratic Action Party. Manuel Rosales, an outspoken Chávez opponent from a social-democratic background, was a longtime member of Democratic Action.

In 2006 a coalition of 44 opposition groups, including all of Venezuela's dominant pre-1998 political parties, joined behind the UNT standard to support one presidential candidate, Rosales, to challenge Chávez. Subsequently, the UNT ceased to play a formal leadership role in the opposition, as the coalition's member parties remained autonomous. The **Democratic Left** (*Izquierda Democrática*—ID), a group of former communists opposing what they perceived as Chávez's lack of commitment to democracy, folded their membership into the UNT in 2007. As a single party, UNT was the largest of several opposition parties participating in the 2008 municipal and gubernatorial elections under the National Unity banner.

In April 2009 Rosales, then the mayor of Maracaibo, went into exile in Peru to avoid arrest on corruption charges he claimed were politically motivated.

The UNT won 18 seats as part of the MUD coalition in the 2015 legislative elections. UNT joined the worldwide association Socialist International in February 2013.

Leaders: Omar BARBOZA (President), Manuel ROSALES, Enrique OCHOA.

Democratic Action (*Acción Democrática*—AD). Founded in 1937, the AD was forced underground by the Pérez Jiménez dictatorship but regained legality in 1958 and held power for ten years thereafter. An advocate of rapid economic development, welfare policies, and Western values, it won an overwhelming victory in 1973, capturing the presidency and both houses of Congress. Although it lost the presidency in 1978, it remained the largest party in the Senate and tied the Social Christians for representation in the Chamber of Deputies. In 1983 it regained the presidency and won majorities in both houses of Congress. By 1987, with its popularity waning because of continued economic crisis, the AD was deeply divided in the selection of its candidate for the 1988 presidential poll, former interior minister Octavio LEPAGE Barretto. Handpicked by President Lusinchi as his successor, he was ultimately defeated in party electoral college balloting by former president Carlos Andrés Pérez, who, following his election on December 4, returned to office on February 2, 1989.

The party suffered a major setback in state and municipal balloting in December 1992, and its candidate finished second with 23.6 percent of the vote in the presidential poll of December 1993, although it won pluralities in both houses of Congress on the latter occasion.

In November 1998 presidential hopeful Luis ALFARO Ucero was expelled by the party but nevertheless pursued his quest as an independent supported by an assortment of small parties, including the URD (Democratic Republican Union, below). The AD, which had retained both its congressional pluralities earlier in the month, backed the PRVZL's Salas Römer (Project Venezuela, below) in the December presidential race. Alfaro Ucero received 0.4 percent of the vote for a fourth-place finish.

AD/ABP ("Bravo People" Alliance, below) candidate Antonio LEDEZMA defeated his PSUV opponent in the November 2008 elections for the mayoralty of Caracas. Shortly afterward, President Chávez moved to strip the mayor's office of most of its powers.

The AD won 25 seats as part of the MUD coalition in the 2015 legislative elections.

Leaders: Isabel CARMONA de Serra (President), Henry RAMOS Allup (Secretary General).

Popular Will (*Voluntad Popular*—VP). Founded by Leopold LÓPEZ in 2004 as a movement against government infringement on individual freedoms and human rights, the VP won 14 seats as part of the MUD coalition in the 2015 legislative elections.

Leader: Leopoldo LÓPEZ (National Coordinator).

Movement to Socialism (*Movimiento al Socialismo*—MAS). Originating as a radical left-wing group that split from the PCV in 1971, the MAS subsequently adopted a "Eurocommunist" posture and became the dominant legislative party of the left by capturing 2 Senate and 11 Chamber seats in 1978. It supported José Vicente Rangel for the presidency in 1978 but, with the exception of a small group of dissidents, was deeply opposed to his 1983 bid as leader of the left-wing New Alternative coalition. Having responded positively to the mid-1981 appeal from AD leader Carlos Andrés Pérez for a "synchronization of the opposition," it appeared to be adopting a democratic-socialist rather than a rigidly Marxist orientation. In late 1987 the majority, anti-Moscow faction of the Movement of the Revolutionary Left (*Movimiento de Izquierda Revolucionaria*—MIR), led by Moisés MOLEIRO, was reported to have merged with the MAS. (The MIR, which was founded by radical students in 1960, engaged in urban terrorism from 1961 to 1964 and thereafter conducted guerrilla operations from a rural base. Legalized in 1973, it won 4 Chamber seats in 1978 before splitting into two factions, the smaller being a pro- Moscow group led by party founder and 1978 presidential candidate Américo MARTIN.)

In March 1996 the MAS formed an alliance with the anti-Caldera legislative bloc, while insisting, somewhat inconsistently, that by so doing it was asserting its independence rather than going into opposition. Teodoro Petkoff resigned from the MAS in July 1998 over its decision to support Chávez.

The party began distancing itself from the government coalition in May 2001 in the wake of reports that the president was considering a declaration of emergency that would permit him to rule by decree. Five months later Chávez stated that the MAS was "no longer an ally of the Bolivarian revolution" and called on it to leave the coalition. In late November a dissident group formed *Podemos*.

The MAS joined the MUD coalition ahead of the 2010 assembly elections but did not win any seats.

Leaders: Felipe MUJICA (Secretary General), Maria VERDEAL (Vice President), Segundo MELENDEZ (President).

The **Progressive Movement of Venezuela** (*Movimiento Progresista de Venezuela*—MPV) won four seats as part of the MUD coalition in the 2015 legislative elections, as did the **The Radical Cause** (*La Causa Radical*—*Causa R*), a far-left group existent in Bolívar state since the 1980s.

Parties receiving two seats each in the National Assembly in the 2015 legislative elections as part of MUD included **Project Venezuela** (*Proyecto Venezuela*—PRYZL), a center-right party based in Carabobo state; the **"Bravo People" Alliance** (*Alianza Bravo Pueblo*—ABP); the **Progressive Advance** (*Avanzada Progresista*—AP); **Come Venezuela** (Vente Venezuela—VV); and **Clear Accounts** (*Cuentas Claras*), a center-progressive party based in Carabobo state.

Other parties in the MUD coalition include **Democracy Renovated** (*Democracia Renovadora*—DR), led by José Gregorio GARCÍA Urquiola; **Liberal Power** (Fuerza Liberal—FL), led by President Haydée DEUTSCH; **Venezuela Vision** (*Visión Venezuela*—VV), led by Omar ÁVILA; the **Platform for Social Encounter** (*Plataforma de Encuentro Social*—PES), founded in 2008 by Globovisión television host Augusto URIBE; **Only One People** (*Un Solo Pueblo*—USP), founded in 2002 and led by Director General Enrique ARTEAGA; **Independent Solidarity** (*Solidaridad Independiente*—SI), led by Juan de Dios RIVAS Velásquez; the **Republican Movement** (*Movimiento Republicano*—MR), led by President Carlos PADILLA; **Red Flag** (*Bandera Roja*—BR), led by Gabriel PUERTA Aponte.

Other Parties:

For information on the **Humanist Popular Front** (*Frente Popular Humanista*—FPH), a faction in the 2005–2010 National Assembly; the **New Revolutionary Way** (*Nuevo Camino Revolucionario*—NCR); the **Venezuelan Ecological Movement** (*Movimiento Ecológico Venezolano*—MOVEV); the **Democratic Republican Union** (*Unión Republicana Democrática*—URD); and the **Social Christian Party** (*Comité de Organización Política Electoral Independiente*—COPEI), see the 2013 *Handbook*.

Armed Groups:

The Pebble (*La Piedrita*). This small, far-left, Caracas-based group launched a series of tear-gas attacks on the offices of opposition political parties, media outlets and the Catholic Church in 2008 and 2009. Its leader, Valentín Santana, gained notoriety for threatening to kill the head of the RCTV network that lost its broadcast license in 2007.

Though the roughly 50-member group claims to be ardently pro-Chávez, the president asked the attorney-general's office to arrest Santana in February 2009. He remained a fugitive in late 2013.

Leader: Valentín SANTANA.

Bolivarian Liberation Forces (*Fuerzas Bolivarianas de Liberación*—FBL). This group, which has operated sporadically in Colombian border zones since the early 2000s, is believed to work closely with Colombia's FARC guerrillas. It has allegedly killed members of the security forces, prompting President Chávez to order the dissolution of the group, which claims to support him. In May 2013 it released a video on YouTube threatening any group that opposed the election of President Maduro.

Leader: Eleazar JUÁREZ (National Coordinator).

LEGISLATURE

Under the former constitution, the Venezuelan legislature was a bicameral Congress of the Republic (*Congreso de la República*) consisting of a 46-member Senate (*Senado*) and a 189-member Chamber of Deputies (*Cámara de Diputados*), both with additional nominated members to compensate for party underrepresentation. The Congress was effectively superseded by the Constitutional Assembly elected on July 25, 1999, and was formally dissolved on January 4, 2000. On January 30 the assembly delegated its legislative powers to a 21-member National Legislative Commission that served until the National Assembly election of July 30.

National Assembly (*Asamblea Nacional*). The current legislature is a unicameral body of 167 members, including 3 representing indigenous peoples. An August 2008 electoral reform law increased, from 60 to 70 percent, the number of deputies elected directly, with the number chosen by proportional representation dropping from 40 to 30 percent.

In the most recent elections on December 6, 2015, the Democratic Unity Table won 109 seats; United Socialist Party of Venezuela and its allies, 55 seats; and indigenous representatives, 3.

President: Henry RAMOS Allup.

CABINET

[as of October 15, 2016]

President	Nicolás Maduro
Executive Vice President	Aristóbulo ISTÚRIZ Almeida
Vice President for Economy and Finance	Miguel Pérez Abad
Vice President for Planning and Knowledge	Ricardo José Menéndez Prieto
Vice President for Political Sovereignty	Delcy Eloína Rodríguez Gómez [f]
Vice President for Social Development and Missions	Jorge Arreaza Monserrat
Vice President for Territorial Development	Ricardo Molina Peñaloza
Ministers	
Agriculture and Lands	Wilmar Castro Soteldo
Banking and Finance	Rodolfo Medina del Río
Communes and Social Movements	Erika Farías Peña [f]
Communications and Information	Ernesto Villegas
Culture	Freddy Alfred Nazaret Ñañez Contreras
Defense	Gen. Vladimir Padrino López
Education	Rodulfo Humberto Pérez Hernández
Electricity	Maj. Gen. Luis Motta Dominguez
Food	Brig. Gen. Rodolfo Clemente Marco Torres
Foreign Relations	Delcy Eloína Rodríguez Gómez [f]
Health	Luisana Melo Solórzano [f]
Higher Education, Science, and Technology	Jorge Alberto Arreaza Montserrat
Housing and Habitats	Manuel Quevedo Fernández
Indigenous Peoples	Aloha Nuñez [f]
Industry and Trade	Carlos Faría Tortosa
Internal Relations, Justice, and Peace	Maj. Gen. Néstor Reverol Torres
Labor	Oswaldo Emilio Vera Rojas
Penitentiary Services	María Iris Varela Rangel [f]
Petroleum and Mining	Eulogio Del Pino Diaz
Planning	Ricardo José Menéndez Prieto
President's Office	Carmen Melendez [f]
Tourism	Marleny Josefina Contreras Hernández [f]
Transformation of Caracas	Ernesto Villegas Poljak
Transportation, Air, and Water	Maj. Gen. Giuseppe Yoffreda Yorio
Transportation and Public Works	Ricardo Molina Peñaloza
Water and Ecosocialism	Ernesto Jose Paiva Salas
Women's Affairs and Gender Equality	Blanca Eekhout [f]
Youth and Sports	Mervin Enrique Maldonado Urdaneta

[f] = female

INTERGOVERNMENTAL REPRESENTATION

Ambassador to the U.S.: Maximilien SANCHEZ Arvelaiz (Chargé d'Affaires).

U.S. Ambassador to Venezuela: Lee McCLENNY (Chargé d'Affaires).

Permanent Representative to the UN: Rafael RAMÍREZ Carreño.

IGO Memberships (Non-UN): IADB, ICC, IOM, Mercosur, NAM, OAS, OPEC, CO, WTO.

For Further Reference:

Corrales, Javier, and Michael Penfold. *Dragon in the Tropics: The Legacy of Hugo Chávez.* 2nd ed. Washington, DC: Brookings Institution Press, 2015.

Jaskoski, Maiah, Arturo C. Sotomayor, and Harold A. Trinkunas, eds. *American Crossings: Border Politics in the Western Hemisphere.* Baltimore, MD: Johns Hopkins University Press, 2015.

Lean, Sharon. *Civil Society and Electoral Accountability in Latin America.* New York: Palgrave Macmillan, 2012.

Ponniah, Thomas, and Jonathan Eastwood, eds. *The Revolution in Venezuela: Social and Political change under Chávez.* Cambridge, MA: Rockefeller Center, 2011.

VIETNAM

Socialist Republic of Vietnam
Cộng Hòa Xã Hội Chủ Nghĩa Việt Nam

Political Status: Communist republic originally proclaimed September 2, 1945; Democratic Republic of Vietnam established in the north on July 21, 1954; Republic of Vietnam established in the south on October 26, 1955; Socialist Republic of Vietnam proclaimed on July 2, 1976, following surrender of the southern government on April 30, 1975; present constitution adopted on April 15, 1992.

Area: 128,402 sq. mi. (332,561 sq. km).

Population: 94,444,000 (2016E—UN); 95,261,021 (2016E—U.S. Census).

Major Urban Centers (2016E—UN): HANOI (3,790,000), Ho Chi Minh City (formerly Saigon, 7,498,000), Can Tho (1,242,000), Haiphong (1,110,000).

Official Language: Vietnamese.

Monetary Unit: Dông (market rate October 1, 2016: 22,295.50 dông = $1US).

President: Gen. TRAN DAI QUANG; elected by the National Assembly on April 2, 2016, succeeding TRUONG TAN SANG.

Vice President: DANG THI NGOC THINH; elected by the National Assembly on April 8, 2016, succeeding NGUYEN THI DOANT.

Prime Minister: NGUYEN XUAN PHUC; elected by the National Assembly on April 7, 2016, succeeding NGUYEN Tan Dung.

General Secretary of the Vietnamese Communist Party: NGUYEN PHU TRONG; appointed by the Central Committee on January 19, 2011, succeeding NONG DUC MANH; reelected on January 26, 2016.

THE COUNTRY

A tropical land of varied climate and topography, Vietnam extends for roughly 1,000 miles along the eastern face of the Indochina Peninsula between the deltas of its two great rivers, the Red River in the north and the Mekong in the south. To the east, the country borders on the Gulf of Tonkin and the South China Sea; in the west, the mountains of the Annamite Chain separate it from Cambodia and Laos. A second mountainous region in the north serves as a partial barrier between Vietnam and China, which historically exercised great influence in Vietnam and provided its name, "Land of the South."

The Vietnamese population is of mixed ethnic stock and includes numerous highland tribes as well as Chinese, Khmer, and other non-Vietnamese peoples. The Viet (Kinh) constitute some 86 percent of the population. Although religion is not encouraged by the state, most Vietnamese are nominally Buddhist—there is a state-sponsored Buddhist Church of Vietnam—or Taoist, with a significant Roman Catholic minority (approximately 7 percent of the total population), particularly in the south. Vietnamese is the national language, while French was long the preferred second language. Women constitute 49 percent of the active labor force, but their participation in party and governmental affairs has traditionally been much less. Women hold 132, or 26.7 percent, of the seats in the current National Assembly. The current vice president and speaker of the assembly are both women.

Northern Vietnam was traditionally a food-deficient area, dependent on supplementary rice and other provisions from the south. It developed a considerable industrial economy, however, based on substantial resources of anthracite coal, chromite, iron, phosphate, tin, and other minerals. About 54 percent of the country's employed labor force works in the agricultural sector, which contributes about 21 percent of GDP, compared to 41.1 percent for industry and 38 percent for services. Manufacturing and mining account for about 15 percent of the workforce. As of 2012, crude oil constituted Vietnam's leading export, followed by marine products (mainly frozen seafood), footwear, and electronic goods and components. Wood and wood products, rubber, coffee, and coal have steadily increased in importance. In 2012 Vietnam was the world's largest exporter of rice.

Decentralization of economic planning yielded only marginal overall growth, however, and in 1986 Vietnam enacted a political and economic "renovation" (*Đổi Mới*) program, reportedly modeled after the Soviet Union's perestroika. (For an overview of the economy prior to the 1980s, see the 2011 *Handbook.*) Radical reforms included fiscal and monetary austerity, a shift away from public sector control of the economy, and an opening of markets to international trade. As a result, the average annual GDP growth rate was about 9 percent for 1992–1997.

GDP grew by 6.8 percent in 2010 and 5.9 percent the following year. In 2011 inflation more than doubled to 18.7 percent. GDP rose by 5 percent in 2012 and 2013, while inflation declined to 9.1 percent in 2012 and 7 percent in 2013. The GDP rose to 6.7 percent in 2015 while inflation declined to 0.6 percent that year. GDP expanded by 6.3 percent in 2016, with inflation at 1.3 percent and unemployment 2.4 percent. GDP per capita for 2013 was $1,910, and it rose to $2,111 by 2016. In its 2016 annual report on the ease of doing business, the World Bank ranked Vietnam 82nd out of 189 countries.

GOVERNMENT AND POLITICS

Political background. Vietnam's three historic regions—Tonkin in the north, Annam in the center, and Cochin-China in the south—came under French control in 1862–1884 and were later joined with Cambodia and Laos to form the French-ruled Indochinese Union, more commonly called French Indochina. The Japanese, who occupied Indochina in World War II, permitted the establishment on September 2, 1945, of the Democratic Republic of Vietnam (DRV) under HO CHI MINH, the Communist leader of the nationalist resistance movement then known as the Vietminh (*Việt Nam Độc Lập Đồng Minh Hộội,* or Vietnamese Independence League). Although the French on their return to Indochina accorded provisional recognition to the DRV, subsequent negotiations broke down, and in December 1946 the Vietminh initiated military action against French forces.

While fighting with the Vietminh continued, the French in 1949 recognized BAO DAI, former emperor of Annam, as head of state of an independent Vietnam within the French Union. Treaties conceding full Vietnamese independence in association with France were initialed in Paris on June 4, 1954; in practice, however, the jurisdiction of the Bao Dai government was limited to South Vietnam as a consequence of the military successes of the Vietminh, the major defeat suffered by French forces at Dien Bien Phu in May 1954, and the armistice and related agreements concluded in Geneva, Switzerland, July 20–21, 1954. The Geneva accord provided for a temporary division of Vietnam near the 17th parallel into two separately administered zones—Communist in the north and non-Communist in the south—pending an internationally supervised election to be held in 1956. These arrangements were rejected, however, by the Bao Dai government and by the republican regime that succeeded it in South Vietnam in 1955. Vietnam thus remained divided between a northern zone administered by the Communist-ruled DRV and a southern zone administered by the anti-Communist government of the Republic of Vietnam.

Within North Vietnam, a new constitution promulgated in 1960 consolidated the powers of the central government, and elections in 1960 and 1964 reaffirmed the preeminence of Ho Chi Minh, who continued as president of the DRV and chair of the Vietnam Workers' Party (VWP), successor in 1954 to the Indochinese Communist Party (ICP). Ho Chi Minh died in 1969, his party position remaining unfilled in deference to his memory. The political leadership passed to LE DUAN, who had been named first secretary of the VWP nine years earlier.

Communist-led subversive and terrorist activity against the government of South Vietnam resumed in the late 1950s by Vietcong (Vietnamese Communist) resistance elements in a continuation of the earlier anti-French offensive, now supported and directed from the north. Within the south, these operations were sponsored from 1960 onward by a Communist-controlled political organization called the National Front for the Liberation of South Vietnam, or simply the National Liberation Front (NLF). Despite the initiation of U.S. advisory assistance to South Vietnamese military forces in 1954, guerrilla operations by Vietcong and regular North Vietnamese units proved increasingly disruptive.

In 1961 the growth of the Communist-supported insurgency forced NGO DINH DIEM (who had assumed the South Vietnamese presidency following the ouster of Bao Dai in 1955) to assume emergency powers. Popular resentment of his increasingly repressive regime led, however, to his death in a coup d'état that was secretly supported by the United States and directed by Gen. DUONG VAN MINH ("Big Minh") on November 1, 1963. A period of unstable military rule followed. Leadership was held successively by General Minh (to January 1964), Gen. NGUYEN KHANH (to February 1965), and Gen. NGUYEN VAN THIEU, who assumed the functions of head of state in June 1965. The powerful post of prime minister went to Air Marshal NGUYEN CAO KY. By then, concerned that the south was facing military defeat, the United States had begun air operations against selected military targets in the north and was ordering large contingents of its ground forces into action in the south.

In response to U.S. pressure, a new constitution was promulgated on April 1, 1967. Thieu and Ky were elected president and vice president, respectively, on September 3.

On January 31, 1968, a holiday marking the Vietnamese lunar new year (*Tết Nguyên Đán*), Communist forces launched an audacious offensive throughout the south, including in Saigon and other urban centers. Although viewed by most historians as unsuccessful in strictly military terms, the Tet offensive had deep political consequences. In the United States it served to crystallize growing antiwar sentiment and contributed to the decision of U.S. president Lyndon Johnson not to seek reelection. On March 31 Johnson announced a cessation of bombing in all but the southern area of North Vietnam, adjacent to the demilitarized zone straddling the 17th parallel. The action proved more successful than a number of earlier bombing halts in paving the way for peace talks. Preliminary discussions between U.S. and North Vietnamese representatives were initiated in Paris on May 13, while expanded talks began in Paris on January 18, 1969. It was not until September 1972, however, following major U.S. troop withdrawals and the failure of another major Communist offensive, that Hanoi agreed to drop its insistence on imposing a Communist regime in the south and accepted a 1971 U.S. proposal for a temporary cease-fire.

A peace agreement was concluded on January 27, 1973, on the basis of extensive private discussions between U.S. secretary of state Henry Kissinger and DRV negotiator LE DUC THO. (Although the two were jointly awarded the Nobel Peace Prize in October 1973, Le Duc Tho declined the award, stating that peace had not yet been achieved.) The agreement provided for a withdrawal of all remaining U.S. forces and for political talks between the South Vietnamese and the Vietcong aimed at the establishment of a National Council of National Reconciliation and Concord (NCNRC). The Saigon government and the Provisional Revolutionary Government of South Vietnam failed, however, to reach agreement on the council's composition.

Despite North Vietnam's formal support of the peace accord, it was estimated that as of May 1974 some 210,000 North Vietnamese troops were fighting in the south, as compared to 160,000 at the time of the 1972 cease-fire. A new Communist offensive, launched in late 1974, resulted in the loss of Phuoc Long Province, 70 miles north of Saigon, in early January 1975. By late March, in the wake of a near total collapse of discipline within the South Vietnamese army, the cities of Hué and Da Nang had fallen. On April 21, as the Communist forces neared Saigon, President Thieu announced his resignation, and Vice President TRAN VAN HUONG was sworn in as his successor. Huong himself resigned on April 28 in favor of Gen. Duong Van Minh, who called for a cease-fire and immediate negotiations with representatives of the North Vietnamese and the NLF's military wing, the People's Liberation Armed Forces (PLAF). The appeal was rejected, and on April 30 Communist forces entered Saigon, and the South Vietnamese government surrendered.

On June 6, 1975, the Provisional Revolutionary Government under the nominal presidency of HUYNH TAN PHAT was invested as the government of South Vietnam, although real power was exercised by PHAM HUNG, fourth-ranked member of the VWP Politburo and secretary of the party's South Vietnamese Committee. On April 25, 1976, a reunified Vietnam held an election for an enlarged National Assembly, which on July 2 proclaimed the Socialist Republic of Vietnam. On the same day it named TON DUC THANG, the incumbent president of North Vietnam, as head of state, and it appointed two vice presidents: NGUYEN LUONG BANG, theretofore vice president of the DRV, and NGUYEN HUU THO, leader of the southern NLF. PHAM VAN DONG, previously the DRV premier, was designated to head a cabinet composed largely of former North Vietnamese ministers, with the addition of six South Vietnamese. On December 20 the VWP concluded a congress in Hanoi by changing its name to the Vietnamese Communist Party (VCP) and adopting a series of guidelines designed to realize the nation's "socialist goals."

Under a revised constitution, a new National Assembly was elected on April 26, 1981, and a five-member collective presidency (Council of State) designated on July 4. The second-ranked member of the VCP Politburo, TRUONG CHINH, was named council chair (thus becoming nominal head of state). The third-ranked Pham Van Dong continued as chair of the Council of Ministers.

Longtime party leader Le Duan died in July 1986. The VCP Central Committee named Truong Chinh as his successor. However, in a remarkable change of leadership at the Sixth VCP Congress in December, NGUYEN VAN LINH was named general secretary, with Chinh, Dong, and Tho being among those retired from the Politburo. A major governmental reorganization followed. In June 1987 Gen. VO CHI CONG succeeded Chinh as chair of the Council of State, and Hung replaced Dong as chair of the Council of Ministers. Following Hung's death in March 1988, Sr. Gen. VO VAN KIET, theretofore a deputy chair of the Council of Ministers, was named acting chair. In an unprecedented contest in June, the nominee of the party's Central Committee, DO MUOI, was forced to stand against Vo Van Kiet for election as permanent chair, winning the office by only 64 percent of the National Assembly vote.

Another major restructuring of the party leadership occurred at the Seventh VCP Congress in June 1991, when 7 of 12 Politburo members were dropped and Do Muoi succeeded Nguyen Van Linh as general secretary. The party shake-up was paralleled by sweeping government changes when the Eighth National Assembly met for an unusually lengthy 9th session in July and August. A new Council of State was named (albeit with Vo Chi Cong continuing as chair), as well as a new Council of Ministers under Vo Van Kiet. The legislature also initiated debate on a new constitution, the draft of which was completed at the body's 10th session in December and approved at the 11th session in April 1992. In September the National Assembly named Sr. Gen. LE DUC ANH and NGUYEN THI BINH to the newly created posts of president and vice president, respectively, while reappointing Vo Van Kiet as head of government, with the new title of prime minister.

In September 1997 the National Assembly chose TRAN DUC LUONG and PHAN VAN KHAI to succeed Le Duc Anh and Vo Van Kiet as president and prime minister, respectively. In December the VCP Central Committee elected the decidedly more conservative Lt. Gen. LE KHA PHIEU as general secretary in place of Do Muoi.

Meeting at its Ninth Party Congress, the VCP on April 22, 2001, replaced Le Kha Phieu with economic reformer NONG DUC MANH, a member of the northern Tay ethnic minority and theretofore chair of the National Assembly. No major changes in the government occurred until a new cabinet was installed on August 8, 2002, during the opening session of the expanded, 498-seat National Assembly, which had been elected on May 19. President Luong and Prime Minister Khai were reelected on July 24 and 25, respectively, by the legislature, which chose TRUONG MY HOA as vice president.

The Tenth Congress of the VCP, held April 18–25, 2006, marked the departure from the party leadership of President Tran Duc Luong and Prime Minister Phan Van Khai. On June 27, as expected, the National Assembly elected NGUYEN MINH TRIET as president (to complete the remaining year in Tran's term) and confirmed NGUYEN TAN DUNG as prime minister. Following the National Assembly election of May 20, 2007, the legislature reelected the president and prime minister on July 24 and 25, respectively.

In October 2009 nine individuals were sentenced to between 2 and 6 years in prison for engaging in activities deemed harmful to national security—in this case, hanging prodemocracy banners, passing out leaflets, writing articles critical of the government, and posting similar material on the Internet. All were accused of participating in Bloc 8406, a prodemocracy group founded in 2006 (see Opposition Movements, under Political Parties, below). Another prominent dissident, LE CONG DINH, a prodemocracy and human rights lawyer, had been arrested in June 2009 on charges of colluding with other dissidents and foreigners to subvert the government. He and three other activists were convicted of subversion in January 2010 and sentenced to 4 to 16 years in prison.

At the 11th Congress of the VCP from January 12 to 19, 2011, NGUYEN PHU TRONG was elected party chair, and TRUONG TAN SANG was selected as president. Following the assembly election of May 22, the legislature formally elected Sang president on July 25. Dung was reappointed as prime minister by the president on July 25 and reelected by the assembly the following day.

Gen. TRAN DAI QUANG was nominated to be president at the VCP's 12th party congress on January 20–28, 2016. He was formally elected to the office by the National Assembly on April 2. DANG THI NGOC THINH was elected vice president the next day, and NGUYEN XUAN PHUC was named the new prime minister on April 7, along with a new cabinet. Following assembly elections on May 22, the president and vice president were reelected for full terms on July 25, and the prime minister was reelected the following day.

Constitution and government. Upon reunification in 1976, the DRV constitution of January 1, 1960, was put into effect throughout the country pending adoption of a new basic law that on December 18, 1980, received unanimous legislative approval. The 1980 document defined the Socialist Republic as a "state of proletarian dictatorship" advancing toward socialism, and identified the Communist Party as "the only force leading the state and society." A unicameral National Assembly, the highest organ of state authority, was mandated to elect a Council of State as the state's collective presidency; administrative functions were to be directed by a Council of Ministers, appointed by and responsible to the assembly.

Under the 1992 constitution the Council of State was abolished in favor of a president who is elected by and from within the assembly. The chief executive nominates a vice president, a prime minister, a chief justice of the Supreme Court, and a head of the Supreme People's Inspectorate, all of whom must be approved by the assembly. The party continues to define overall state policy but no longer conducts its day-to-day implementation. In 2001 the National Assembly approved 24 constitutional amendments, including recognition of private enterprise as a legitimate economic sector. Another change permits the National Assembly to consider no-confidence motions against government leaders.

Vietnam adopted a new constitution in November 2013 that further cements the role of the ruling Communist Party as the de facto sole organized party of the state. The 2013 constitution makes no significant changes from the previous document.

The judicial system is headed by the Supreme People's Court and the procurator general of the Supreme People's Organ of Control. People's Courts, Military Tribunals, and People's Organs of Control operate at the local level. Economic courts to adjudicate business disputes were authorized in 1993, while the country's first comprehensive civil code entered into effect in 1996.

All communications media are controlled and operated by the government, the Communist Party, or subordinate organizations. A 2006 Decree on Cultural and Information Activities requires prepublication review of articles and sets fines for using anonymous sources, defaming unspecified "national heroes," distributing "reactionary ideology," and revealing "party secrets, state secrets, military secrets, and economic secrets." Internet access is closely monitored, and postings deemed adverse to state interests may also result in prosecution. In 2016 Reporters Without Borders ranked Vietnam 175th out of 180 in terms of freedom of the press.

For administrative purposes the country is divided into 59 provinces and 5 centrally administered municipalities (Can Tho, Da Nang, Haiphong, Hanoi, and Ho Chi Minh City); subdivisions include districts, towns, and provincial capitals. Each administrative unit elects a People's Council, which then selects a People's Committee to serve as an executive.

Foreign relations. Prior to reunification, North Vietnamese external policy combined traditional Vietnamese nationalism with Communist ideology and tactics. Relations with most other Communist nations were close, and aid from the People's Republic of China, the Soviet Union, and Eastern Europe was essential to both the DRV's industrial development and its military campaigns in the south. Consequently, the DRV avoided commitments to either side in the Sino-Soviet dispute.

An application submitted by North Vietnam in 1975 to join the UN was blocked by U.S. action in the Security Council, as was a second application submitted on behalf of the newly unified state in 1976. In May 1977 the United States withdrew its objection after Hanoi agreed to provide additional information on the fate of missing U.S. servicemen, and the socialist republic was admitted to the world body in September.

The DRV had long been involved in the internal affairs of both Laos and Cambodia (Kampuchea), where it supported insurgent movements, partly as a means of keeping open its supply routes to South Vietnam. Following reunification, Hanoi concluded a number of mutual cooperation agreements with Laos that some observers viewed as leaving that country little more than a province of Vietnam. Collaterally, relations with the *Khmer Rouge*–led government of Democratic Kampuchea deteriorated sharply, resulting in numerous military encounters along the two countries' common frontier and a severance of diplomatic relations in December 1977. The clashes escalated through 1978 and prompted a Vietnamese invasion of its neighbor at the end of the year. In January 1979 Phnom Penh fell to the Vietnamese, supported by a small force of dissident Khmers, and a pro-Vietnamese People's Republic of Kampuchea was proclaimed under Heng Samrin, a former member of the Kampuchean General Staff. Some 200,000 Vietnamese troops remained in the country.

Chinese forces invaded northern Vietnam on February 17, 1979, and occupied a number of border towns, suffering heavy casualties before withdrawing in mid-March. The incursion was described by Beijing as a "limited operation" designed to "teach Hanoi a lesson" after failure to resolve a number of long-standing disputes—primarily, the validity of late-19th-century border agreements between France and the Chinese empire, jurisdiction over territorial waters in the Gulf of Tonkin, and sovereignty over the Paracel and Spratly islands in the South China Sea. The last island group (also claimed in whole or in part by Brunei, Malaysia, Philippines, and Taiwan) was considered particularly important because of its strategic location astride shipping lanes and the possibility (subsequently confirmed) of oil and gas reserves in its vicinity. Peace talks undertaken by Hanoi and Beijing in April 1979 were broken off by the Chinese in March 1980. Intermittent border conflicts continued thereafter.

In January 1989 Hanoi dispatched a delegation to Beijing for the first high-level discussions between the two governments in eight years. On September 26, 1989, Vietnam announced that it had withdrawn all its troops from Cambodia, a claim disputed by China. In November 1991 high-level talks resulted in normalization of Vietnam-China relations after a 20-year estrangement, although it was not until October 1993 that the two countries agreed to negotiations aimed at resolving their various territorial disputes.

Following the Communist collapse in Eastern Europe and the 1991 dissolution of the Soviet Union (on which Vietnam had remained heavily dependent for economic assistance), regional relations with Japan, South Korea, Thailand, Brunei, and Malaysia improved. In 1992 Australia and Japan formally renewed aid to Vietnam. Relations also improved with the United States, which eased its long-standing trade embargo. In December U.S. President George H. W. Bush authorized U.S. companies to initiate commercial relations with Vietnam. Less than two years later, in February 1994, U.S. president Bill Clinton announced an end to the 19-year U.S. economic embargo in view of "significant and tangible results" in the search for American servicemen missing in action.

In 1995 there were more than 46,000 Vietnamese expatriates in numerous detention camps, from Thailand to Hong Kong. In mid-March representatives of 30 countries met in Geneva and agreed that 40,000 "boat people" in Hong Kong and Southeast Asia would be returned by early 1996, triggering riots by detainees in Hong Kong, Malaysia, and the Philippines. An aid program sponsored by the European Union assisted some 50,000 returnees before concluding in 1999.

Declaring that it was time to "bind up our own wounds," U.S. president Clinton extended full diplomatic recognition to Vietnam on July 11, 1995. (In November 2000 Clinton became the first U.S. president to visit the unified Vietnam, and in June 2007 Nguyen Minh Triet became the first president of the socialist republic to visit the United States.) Vietnam's admission to the Association of Southeast Asian Nations (ASEAN) was formalized a month later. In 1996 Vietnam officially applied to join the Asia-Pacific Economic Cooperation (APEC) forum, to which it was formally admitted in 1998.

In October 1998 Vietnam and China announced their intention to resolve land and Gulf of Tonkin boundary disputes by the year 2000. The two signed a land border treaty on December 30, 1999, and a maritime agreement in December 2000, although the latter did not resolve the Spratly and Paracel disputes. (Actual demarcation of the land border was finally concluded in 2008.) On November 4, 2002, China and the ten ASEAN members signed a voluntary Declaration on the Conduct of Parties in the South China Sea that, while not a formal code of conduct, pledged to seek nonviolent solutions to the competing territorial claims.

In December 1998 South Korean president Kim Dae Jung apologized for sending some 300,000 troops to supplement U.S. forces during the Vietnam War. Prime Minister Khai, noting that Vietnam required neither an apology nor reparations, called instead for a "progressive and future-oriented bilateral relationship."

In September 2000 Vietnam and Russia reached agreement on settling Soviet-era debts, with Hanoi pledging to repay $1.7 billion over 23 years, mostly through business concessions. In February 2001 Russian president Vladimir Putin became the first Russian head of state to visit Vietnam.

Vietnam's accession to the World Trade Organization (WTO) was given the highest priority by the Communist government. In May 2006 Vietnam overcame the last major hurdle: completing a new bilateral trade and investment agreement with the United States. In addition to opening up Vietnam's banking, securities, and insurance markets to foreign companies, the pact also ended U.S. quotas on the importation of Vietnamese garments, cut Vietnamese tariffs, and cleared the way for foreigners to participate in wholesale and retail trade. On November 7 the WTO voted to admit Vietnam, which ratified the accession protocol on November 28. On January 10, 2007, Vietnam officially became a member.

On October 31, 2010, the prime ministers of Vietnam and Japan signed an agreement to construct two nuclear reactors in Ninh Thuan province. Also in October, Vietnam demanded the release of a fishing vessel and its crew after Chinese naval units detained the fishermen in the disputed waters of the Paracel Islands.

In February 2011 Thailand announced the closure of the last refugee center for Montagnards who fled Vietnam. On May 26 an incident between a Chinese naval vessel and a Vietnamese survey ship highlighted tensions over the disputed Spratly and Paracel Islands. There were large protests outside the Chinese embassy in Hanoi, and the Vietnamese navy conducted drills in the area of the disputed islands. In June Vietnam and the United States initiated joint programs to remove or destroy unexploded ordnance from the Vietnam conflict and to restore areas damaged by the defoliant Agent Orange. In October Vietnam and India signed a number of economic agreements in an effort to boost trade between the two countries. The following month, Russia agreed to provide an $8 billion loan to construct nuclear power plants.

Twenty-one Vietnamese fishermen were detained by Chinese naval forces for operating in Chinese-claimed waters near the Paracel Islands in March 2012. They were released the following month. In June the Vietnamese legislature enacted a law reaffirming the country's sovereignty over the Paracel and Spratly Islands. The measure was condemned by China. Meanwhile, Vietnam protested a Chinese call for proposals from foreign oil companies for exploratory drilling in the disputed waters.

Following a visit to Vietnam by Russia's defense minister, 2013 reports indicated that Moscow sought a new lease for a naval base at Cam Ranh Bay. Also in March, Japan announced it would provide $2 billion in development assistance to Vietnam. Furthermore, in August Japan and Vietnam agreed to increase law enforcement cooperation, including training and police intelligence collaboration. Meanwhile, in 2013 Vietnam made substantial progress on free trade treaties with the EU and South Korea. Also in 2013, The United States and Vietnam signed an accord to jointly develop civil nuclear energy and India provided a $100 million line of credit to the state for military purchases.

In January 2014 Vietnam and Russia signed contracts worth $4.5 billion for military hardware. The timing of the agreement coincided with the delivery of the first of six NATO designated Kilo-class, Russian-built submarines agreed on in 2009. In May the World Bank signed a deal for $390 million to fight poverty.

In October 2014 the United States partially suspended its arms embargo on Vietnam, in place since 1975. In June 2015 the United States offered Vietnam $18 million to offset the purchase of two coastal patrol vessels.

On May 23, 2016, the United States fully lifted its embargo on military sales to Vietnam. The World Bank provided Vietnam with $371 million in July 2016 to fund projects to enhance economic competiveness, mitigate climate change, and improve sewerage systems.

Current issues. On March 30, 2012, nine executives of Vietnam's largest shipbuilding corporation, including chair PHAN THANH BINH, were convicted of fraud and mismanagement after the company accumulated debts of more than $4.5 billion and defaulted on a $600 million loan payment. Binh was an ally of Prime Minister Dung. In August another Dung ally, banking mogul NGUYEN DUC KIEN, was arrested for financial mismanagement of the country's largest bank. The arrests and uncertainty over the economy led to a dramatic $4 billion stock market decline and inflation spike, prompting calls for further economic reforms.

In January 2013, 14 dissidents were convicted of sedition for online posts and blogs and sentenced to between 3 and 13 years in prison. The government also contended that they belonged to the exile group the Vietnam Reform Party (see Political Parties, below).

Beginning in March 2013, the government allowed citizens to post comments and suggestions in an online forum on a draft constitution. The initiative was an effort to demonstrate more openness, but reports indicated that those who posted highly critical commentaries or who advocated for radical changes faced fines and harassment. A committee to draft a new constitution began work in August with a goal of submitting recommendations in October. In May the finance minister was replaced, reportedly as part of an effort to accelerate economic growth.

The years 2013 and 2014 saw an increase in tensions between Vietnam and China over the disputed Paracel Islands after a January 2013 announcement claiming oil and fishing rights in large areas of the South China Sea claimed by five other states—including Vietnam. Vietnam's claim in March 2013 that their fishing vessels were fired on by Chinese patrol vessels was followed in May by reports of Chinese vessels intentionally ramming Vietnamese vessels. One Vietnamese boat was sunk while attempting to block the movement of a Chinese $1 billion drilling rig into the area. While China and Vietnam have agreed to negotiate a settlement over the dispute, Vietnam further inflamed tension by signing an agreement granting India access to oil exploration blocks in the disputed territory in October 2014. India also agreed to a $100 million line of credit for Vietnam to bolster its naval capacity as well as "enhanced training" with the Vietnamese military.

The government in June 2015 dramatically reduced commercial regulations in more than 100 areas in an effort to increase foreign investment. The reforms were described as the most significant since 1990. In January 2016 Vietnamese submarines began patrolling disputed maritime waters in the South China Sea.

POLITICAL PARTIES

The Communist party apparatus of North Vietnam operated for many years as the **Vietnam Workers' Party**—VWP (*Đảng Lao Động Việt Nam*). The VWP was formed in 1954 as successor to the Indochinese Communist Party (founded in 1930 and ostensibly dissolved in 1954) and was the controlling party of **North Vietnam's National Fatherland Front** (NFF). In South Vietnam, the core of the Provisional Revolutionary Government formed in 1969 was the **National Front for the Liberation of South Vietnam** (*Mặt Trận Giải Phóng Miền Nam Việt Nam,* or the National Liberation Front—NLF), which had been organized in 1960 by some 20 groups opposed to the policies of President Diem.

In 1976 representatives of the NFF, NLF, and other organizations met in Hanoi to organize an all-inclusive **Vietnam Fatherland Front**—VFF (*Mặt Trận Tổ Quốc Việt Nam*), formally launched during a congress in Ho Chi Minh City January 31–February 4, 1977. In addition to the Vietnamese Communist Party (VCP), the front includes various trade union, peasants', women's, youth, and other mass organizations. Under electoral law approved by the National Assembly in 1980, the VFF nominates candidates in all constituencies in consultation with local groups.

Leading Party:

Vietnamese Communist Party—VCP (*Đảng Cộng Sản Việt Nam*). The VCP is structured on traditional Communist party lines. A party Congress meets at five-year intervals to select a Central Committee, a Politburo that functions as the executive body, and an administrative Secretariat. The ruling party's present name was adopted by the VWP at its Fourth Congress in 1976. In 1996 the Eighth Party Congress created a five-member Standing Board to replace the larger Secretariat, but the Secretariat was reinstituted at the Ninth Party Congress in 2001.

At a party plenum in June 1997 the Central Committee chose Phan Van Khai to replace Vo Van Kiet as prime minister (pending assembly approval) and voted to limit local officials to two five-year terms (the appointments were previously for life). The committee members were unable, however, to decide on a replacement for President Le Duc Anh, who, along with Vo Van Kiet, had been left off the candidate list for the National Assembly elections due in July. Subsequently, the Committee gave the nod to Tran Duc Luong, and in September its choices were approved by the National Assembly.

In December 1997 the Central Committee elected Lt. Gen. Le Kha Phieu as the party's new general secretary, replacing Do Muoi, who joined Le Duc Ahn and Vo Van Kiet in resigning from the Politburo. All three were subsequently named advisers to the VCP Central Committee.

In January 1999 the party expelled TRAN DO, a retired general and a Central Committee member, for advocating open elections and freedom of expression. His subsequent request to publish a newspaper was denied. He died in August 2002.

The Ninth Party Congress was held April 19–22, 2001. Reportedly, the outgoing Politburo had recommended a second term for General Secretary Le Kha Phieu but was resisted by the Central Committee, which settled on the chair of the National Assembly, Nong Duc Manh.

Meeting April 18–25, 2006, the 1,176 delegates to the Tenth Party Congress elected a 160-member Central Committee (plus 21 alternate members), a Politburo of 14, and an 8-member Secretariat. Although Nong Duc Manh stayed on as general secretary, President Tran Duc Luong, Prime Minister Phan Van Khai, and National Assembly Chair NGUYEN VAN AN all retired from the leadership, signaling their imminent departure from government.

At the 11th Party Congress from January 12 to 19, 2011, the 1,400 delegates elected Nguyen Phu Trong to replace Manh, who retired, and

Truong Tan Sang as president. The Congress approved an expanded Central Committee with 175 members. The Committee subsequently elected the 14 members of the Politburo, including Tong Thi Phong, only the second woman elected to the body. The Secretariat was enlarged to ten members. In May 2012 the central committee began a series of meetings on constitutional reforms designed to privatize the public sector and reduce corruption in government and industry.

In 2013 reports emerged that LE HEIU DANG, a dissident member of the party who left the VCP along with others in opposition to the movement of the VCP away from its traditional values however, Le Heiu Dang died of natural causes in January 2014.

At the 12th VCP congress in January 2016, reformist prime minister Nguyen Tan Dung challenged conservative rival Nguyen Phu Trong in the latter's reelection bid as general secretary of the party. After brief infighting, Nguyen Tan Dung withdrew from the race and rejected an offer for a position on the central committee. Nguyen Phu Trong was reelected on January 27.

General Secretary: NGUYEN PHU TRONG.

Other Members of Politburo: LE HONG ANH, LE THANH HAI (Chair, Ho Chi Minh City People's Committee), TRAN DAI QUANG (State President), NGUYEN THI KIM NGAN (Chair, National Assembly), NGUYEN XUAN PHUC (Prime Minister), PHAM QUANG NGHI (Chair, Hanoi People's Committee), Gen. NGO XUAN LICH (Minister of National Defense), PHAM MINH CHINH (Head of Central Organization Department), TONG THI PHONG (Deputy Chairwoman of the National Assembly), TO LAM (Deputy Minister of Public Security), VUONG DINH HUE (Deputy Prime Minister) TRAN QUOC VUONG (Chair, Inspectorate Commission), DINH THE HUYNH (Chief of the Committee for Propaganda and Education), PHA BINH MINH (Deputy Prime Minister and Minister of Foreign Affairs), TRUONG THI MAI (Chair, National Assembly Committee on Social Issues), TRUONG HOA BINH (Deputy Prime Minister), NGUYEN VAN BINH (Governor, State Bank), VO VAN THUONG (Deputy Secretary of Ho Chi Minh City Party Committee), DINH LA THANG (Minister of Transportation), HOANG TRUNG HAI (Deputy Prime Minister), NGUYEN THIEN NHAN (Chair of Central Committee of the Vietnamese Fatherland Front).

Secretariat: NGUYEN PHU TRONG, DINH THE HUYNH, TRAN QUOC VUONG, PHAM MINH CHINH, VO VAN THUONG, TRUONG THI MAI, LUONG CUONG, NGUYEN VAN BE, NGUYEN HOA BINH.

Opposition Movements:

The government actively suppresses prodemocracy movements and rigorously prosecutes their most outspoken proponents. On April 8, 2006, a total of 118 prodemocracy supporters signed a "Manifesto 2006 on Freedom and Democracy for Vietnam," which gave birth to the **Bloc 8406.** Signers included PHAN VAN LOI and Nguyen Van Ly, the Catholic priest who was imprisoned in March 2007 for distributing material deemed antigovernment by the state. In 2006 a dissident **Democratic Party of Vietnam**—DPV (*Đảng Dân Chủ Việt Nam*), named after an earlier party that had been disbanded in 1988, was founded by HOANG MINH CHINH, who died in 2008. Activists associated with the DPV have also been prosecuted by the government. DPV vice secretary NGAI NGUYEN met with U.S. president Obama in March 2012.

Expatriate Vietnamese in the United States, Europe, and elsewhere have established numerous political groups, many of which claim insurgent or other support within Vietnam. Examples include the **Vietnam Populist Party** (*Đảng Vì Dân*—DVD, also known as the For the People Party) is based in Houston, Texas, and the international **Vietnam Reform Party** (*Việt Nam Canh Tân Cách Mạng Đảng—Việt Tân*), chaired by DO HOANG DIEM. The *Việt Tân* dates from 2004, when it succeeded the National United Front for the Freedom of Vietnam (NUFLV).

LEGISLATURE

The present **National Assembly** (*Quốc Hội*) is a unicameral body of 500 members serving five-year terms. For the most recent election of May 22, 2016, the Fatherland Front approved 870 candidates, including 97 nonparty candidates and 11 described as self-nominated. The Vietnam Communist Party won 475 seats, with nonparty candidates winning 21. Four seats were left vacant since no candidate received the required 50 percent of the vote.

Chair: NGUYEN Thi Kim Ngan.

CABINET

[as of October 24, 2016]

Prime Minister	Nguyen Xuan Phuc
Deputy Prime Ministers	Truong Hoa Binh
	Pham Binh Minh
	Vu Duc Dam
	Vuong Dinh Hue
	Trinh Dinh Dung
Ministers	
Agriculture and Rural Development	Nguyen Xuan Cuong
Construction	Pham Hong Ha
Culture, Sports, and Tourism	Nguyen Ngoc Thien
Education and Training	Phung Xuan Nha
Finance	Dinh Tien Dung
Foreign Affairs	Pham Binh Minh
Industry and Trade	Tran Tuan Anh
Information and Communication	Truong Minh Tuan
Internal Affairs	Le Vinh Tan
Justice	Le Thanh Long
Labor, War Invalids, and Social Welfare	Dao Ngoc Dung
National Defense	Gen. Ngo Xuan Lich
Natural Resources and Environment	Tran Hong Ha
Planning and Investment	Nguyen Chi Dung
Public Health	Nguyen Thi Kim Tien [f]
Public Security	To Lam
Science and Technology	Chu Ngoc Anh
Transport	Truong Quang Nghia
Chair, Committee of Ethnic Minorities	Do Van Chien
Chair, Government Office	Mai Tien Dung
Governor, State Bank	Le Minh Hung
Inspector General	Phan Van Sau

[f] = female

INTERGOVERNMENTAL REPRESENTATION

Ambassador to the U.S.: PHAM Quang Vinh.

U.S. Ambassador to Vietnam: Theodore G. OSIUS II.

Permanent Representative to the UN: NGUYEN Phuong Nga.

IGO Memberships (Non-UN): ADB, APEC, ASEAN, IOM, NAM, WTO.

For Further Reference:

Hayton, Bill. *Vietnam: Rising Dragon.* New Haven, CT: Yale University Press, 2011.

London, Jonathan D., ed. *Politics in Contemporary Vietnam: Party, State, and Authority Relations.* New York: Palgrave Macmillan, 2014.

Womack, Brantly. *China and Vietnam: The Politics of Asymmetry.* Cambridge: Cambridge University Press, 2006.

YEMEN

Republic of Yemen
al-Jumhuriyah al-Yamaniyah

Political Status: Independent Islamic Arab republic established by the merger of the former Yemen Arab Republic (North Yemen) and the People's Democratic Republic of Yemen (South Yemen) on May 22, 1990.

Area: 205,355 sq. mi. (531,869 sq. km), encompassing 75,290 sq. mi. (130,065 sq. km) of the former Yemen Arab Republic and 195,000 sq. mi. (336,869 sq. km) of the former People's Democratic Republic of Yemen.

Population: 27,478,000 (2016E—UN); 27,392,779 (2016E—U.S. Census).

Major Urban Center (2016E—UN, urban agglomeration): SANA (3,094,000).

Official Language: Arabic.

Monetary Unit: Yemeni Rial (market rate October 1, 2016: 250.10 rials = $1US).

President: Abd Rabbo Mansour HADI (General People's Congress); elected to an interim two-year term on February 21, 2012, to succeed Ali Abdullah SALIH (General People's Congress); resigned on January 22, 2015, amid political unrest; rescinded his resignation after escaping house arrest.

Vice President: Ali Mohsen al-AHMAR (General People's Congress); appointed by the president on April 3, 2016, and sworn in on the next day.

Prime Minister: Ahmed Obeid bin DAGHR (General People's Congress); appointed by the president on April 3, 2016, to succeed Khalid BAHAH, and sworn in the following day.

THE COUNTRY

Located at the southern corner of the Arabian Peninsula, where the Red Sea meets the Gulf of Aden, the Republic of Yemen shares a lengthy northern border with Saudi Arabia and a narrow eastern border with Oman (formally demarcated in 1992). Hot, semidesert terrain separates the Red Sea and Gulf coasts from a mountainous interior. The people are predominantly Arab and are divided into two Muslim religious communities: the Zaidi of the Shiite sect in the north and east and the Shaffii community of the Sunni sect in the south and southwest. Tribal influences remain strong, often taking priority over formal governmental activity outside of urban areas. The annual population growth rate was an estimated 2.3 percent between 2010 and 2015, and the fertility rate was 5.3 children per woman. A third of Yemen's workforce is unemployed, and more than 40 percent of the population survives on under $2 a day.

As a result of topographical extremes, Yemeni farmers produce a variety of crops, including cotton (the leading export), grains, fruits, coffee, tobacco, and *qat* (a mild narcotic leaf, which is chewed daily by an estimated 90 percent of the northern population and is estimated to account for nearly 50 percent of gross domestic product [GDP]). However, the crops do not adequately feed the population.

Yemen is marked by conservative religious views that have limited women's participation in civil affairs. However, these viewpoints have waxed and waned in accordance with political and social developments. In the former Yemen Arab Republic, purdah (the seclusion of women) precluded public life for women; by contrast, the Marxist government of the former People's Democratic Republic of Yemen emphasized women's rights. Prior to the August 1990 Iraqi invasion of Kuwait, a labor shortage created by the exodus of more than a million Yemeni men to work outside the country increased women's responsibility in subsistence agriculture. The latest constitution granted women suffrage, but observers subsequently cited a turn to conservative Islam that led, inter alia, to the legalization of polygamy and the adoption of conservative Muslim dress by women in the previously more liberal south. In recent years, Yemen has made progress in construction, transportation, and trade in the non-oil sector, facilitated by privatization laws, a bank reform plan, and the establishment of an anticorruption

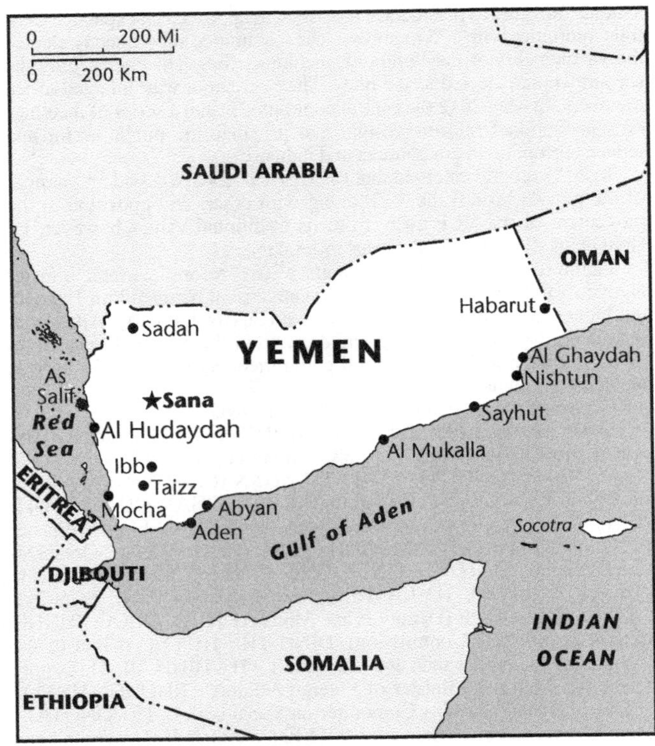

authority. Nevertheless, millions of dollars in international aid have been withheld because of little progress in rooting out corruption.

In the spring of 2011 protests against President Ali Abdullah SALIH and the political stalemate that ensued brought Yemen's economy to the brink of collapse, as the country faced shortages of fuel, food, water, electricity, and security. GDP plummeted as crises and shortages cost the economy approximately $5 billion. Of special concern was the availability and cost of water, which increased by up to 1,000 percent. Adding further injury to a bleak economic picture, oil production has diminished since 2011 as saboteurs continued to blow up pipelines and damage production facilities.

Civil discord significantly diminished after President Hadi took office in February 2012, but security remained elusive. As a result the economy continued to contract, albeit at a slower rate than 2011. The International Monetary Fund (IMF) concluded that Yemen's 2012 GDP declined by 0.09 percent, while inflation was 17.1 percent. The IMF approved an emergency loan of $94 million to Yemen in 2012, and Saudi Arabia donated $2 billion worth of fuel. Officials reported that attacks on the country's oil production infrastructure cost Yemen more than $4 billion in revenue in 2012 alone. IMF economists reported modest GDP growth in 2013 of 4.4 percent, though inflation remained high at 11.1 percent. In 2014 GDP increased by 5.1 percent, while inflation decreased to 10.4 percent. After 13 years of negotiations, Yemen gained admittance to the World Trade Organization in December 2013. However, the country still required loans and grants from many of its neighbors in order to provide basic services. GDP growth plummeted by 28.1 percent amid the intrastate conflict fracturing the country in 2015, and it was projected to decline a further 4.2 percent in 2016.

GOVERNMENT AND POLITICS

Political background. ***Yemen Arab Republic (YAR).*** Former site of the Kingdom of Sheba and an early center of Near Eastern civilization, the territory subsequently known as North Yemen fell under the rule of the Ottoman Turks in the 16th century. The withdrawal of Turkish forces in 1918 made it possible for Imam YAHYA Muhammad Hamid al-Din, the traditional ruler of the Said religious community, to gain political supremacy. The imamate persisted until September 1962 when a series of uprisings against the absolute regime of the imams culminated in the installation of a group of army officers under Col. (later Field Marshal) Abdullah al-SALAL. Modern governmental institutions were established with the adoption of a new constitution in late 1970 and the election of the Consultative Council in early 1971—which later morphed into the Presidential Council. On July 17, 1978, the four-member Presidential Council appointed Maj. Ali Abdullah Salih president of the republic, while Abd al-Aziz Abd al-GHANI remained prime minister.

Salih's early presidency was tested by continuing conflicts between republican and traditional groups, and the incursion in early 1979 of South Yemeni forces who were joined by the rebel leftist National Democratic Front (NDF). A mediation agreement brokered by the Arab League brought about a cease-fire and the withdrawal of southern troops. Unification talks between Sana and Aden began soon after. (See Republic of Yemen, below, for information on negotiations leading to unification with the People's Democratic Republic of Yemen and political developments from 1990 to the present.)

People's Democratic Republic of Yemen (PDRY). British control of South Yemen began with the occupation of Aden in 1839 and gradually extended into what came to be known as the Western and Eastern Protectorates. Aden was ruled as part of British India until 1937, when it became a separate Crown colony. On November 30, 1967, Britain handed the territory over to the area's strongest political organization, the left-wing Nationalist Front (NF). The country rapidly emerged as a center of left-wing revolutionary nationalist agitation in South Arabia, and the country's name was changed in December 1970 to the People's Democratic Republic of Yemen. Procommunist factions subsequently held power through 1978, when the NF was reorganized and retained political control as the Yemeni Socialist Party (YSP). In February 1986 the YSP Central Committee named Ali Salim al-BEIDH as its secretary general.

Republic of Yemen. In the fall of 1981 unification talks between North Yemen's President Ali Salih and his South Yemen counterpart, Ali Nasir MUHAMMAD, culminated in an agreement signed in Aden on December 2 to establish a Yemen Council that would promote political, economic, and social integration. On December 1, 1989, a draft joint constitution called for an integrated multiparty state headed by the five-member Presidential Council. The new basic law was implemented on May 22, 1990, after ratification by the constituent states' respective parliaments. Newly promoted General Salih assumed the presidency of the Republic of Yemen, and the PDRY's al-Beidh was named vice president for what was initially proclaimed a 30-month transitional term.

The first general elections on April 27, 1993, handed Salih's General People's Congress (GPC) a majority; it formed a coalition with the conservative Yemeni Congregation for Reform (*Islah*) and the YSP, and the parties shared seats on the new Presidential Council. In February 1994 sporadic fighting between military units representing the north and south broke into a full-fledged war, as Salih declared a state of emergency on May 5. On May 21 al-Beidh announced the South's succession from the union and the formation of an independent Democratic Republic of Yemen, although no international recognition was forthcoming. Northern forces secured control of Aden on July 7, effectively ending the short-lived succession.

In September 1994 the House of Representatives elected Salih to a new five-year presidential term, and in October Salih appointed Maj. Gen. Abd Rabbo Mansour HADI as vice president and named former YAR prime minister Abd al-Aziz Abd al-Ghani as prime minister of the first postwar government. Peaceful parliamentary elections held in April 1997 were broadly viewed as an important step toward improving Yemen's image as a stable country genuinely committed to democracy. Among other things, the participation of women as candidates and voters earned praise from the West.

In the country's first direct presidential election on September 23, 1999, Salih won 96.3 percent of the vote, though only one challenger was sanctioned under controversial electoral regulations. Subsequently, a national referendum on February 20, 2001, extended the presidential term from five to seven years, extended the legislature's term from four to six years, and enlarged the Shura Council (see Constitution and government, below).

In legislative elections on April 27, 2003, the GPC significantly increased its majority, winning 238 seats in comparison to the YSP's 7 and *Islah*'s 46. Some accusations of vote fraud surfaced, and polling-day violence resulted in 3 dead and 15 injured. Thereafter, a major cabinet reshuffle included the creation of a new ministry of human rights, headed by a woman.

In 2005 President Salih announced that he would not seek reelection in 2006, claiming he would turn leadership over to "young blood." A major cabinet reshuffle on February 11, 2006, replaced 16 members, resulting in a cabinet in which all ministers were members of the GPC. Despite his earlier pledge, Salih ultimately registered as a presidential candidate in 2006 and in September was reelected to a third term with 77.2 percent of the vote. Next among the president's challengers was Faisal bin SHAMLAN, a former oil minister and nominee of the Joint Meeting Parties (JMP), a coalition of oppositional parties (see Political Parties and Groups, below). Salih was sworn in for a seven-year term on September 27. The following year President Salih appointed Ali Muhammad MUJAWAR of the GPC as prime minister. Mujawar named a new cabinet on April 4 and was sworn in along with the new government on April 7, 2007.

The country's first election of provincial governors in May 2008—whereby governors were indirectly elected by members of the municipal councils—resulted in the GPC winning the governorship of Sana and 16 other provinces, while independents were elected in three provinces. The opposition JMP boycotted the election and called for direct, public voting in future polls. Progress toward electoral reform appeared to advance in August when the JMP agreed to proposed amendments to Yemen's electoral law. The amendments called for reducing the presidential term from seven years to five, shortening legislative terms from six years to four, reserving 15 percent of seats in both chambers of the legislature for women, and establishing a 15-member electoral commission. Opposition groups objected to the proposed formulation of the electoral commission, pressing for representation from more political parties and criticizing the GPC for trying to dominate the commission. Ultimately, the GPC agreed to include opposition party representatives in the electoral commission.

JMP members secured a pledge from President Salih in February 2009 that he would help push through more electoral reforms and ensure fair elections. An agreement was reached between the GPC and the JMP, and parliament approved postponing the House of Representatives elections for two years until April 2011 so electoral reforms could be implemented. The postponement appeased the opposition's concerns about vote rigging. After lengthy delay, in July 2010 the GPC and JMP agreed to start a multiparty "national dialogue" to discuss political and electoral reform. However, substantive progress on proposed reform was not forthcoming, and the government realized that the time to implement new election mechanisms for April 2011 polling had past. In January 2011 the House passed an amendment reducing the president's term from seven to five years but allowing for more than two successive terms. Opposition MPs feared that the amendment would be used by President Salih to strengthen his hold on power.

Public discontent with the new electoral amendments, antigovernment sentiment fueled by public uprisings against autocratic regimes in Tunisia and Egypt, adverse public reaction to the arrest of prominent female political activist Tawakul KARMAN (who would go on to win the Nobel Peace Prize in October 2011), and the continuation of sectional tensions in the North and South combined to spawn countrywide protests against President Salih's leadership beginning in January 2011. In February, the protestors demanded the president's resignation, and tens of thousands of people flooded the streets to protest—first in Sana and then across the country—with the protests growing in size and intensity as well as becoming increasingly violent. Eventually, secessionists in the South joined the antigovernment uprising, and in the North, antigovernment demonstrations suggested the Houthis—Zaidi Shiites with ties to Iran—had joined the revolt as well.

Fearful of a deepening crisis, Yemen's opposition parties demanded the president leave office by the end of 2011, but Salih refused. Meanwhile, some GPC members resigned from the party due to the regime's "excessive" violence against protestors. When Houthi militiamen took de facto control of Saada governorate in March 2011, it was obvious Salih's governing authority had been severely compromised. In response, diplomats from the Gulf Cooperation Council (GCC) countries presented President Salih with a power-sharing plan to end the political stalemate. Salih rejected the GCC Initiative, even as more southern territory was liberated from government control by militias affiliated with al-Qaida in the Arabian Peninsula (AQAP).

Even prior to the political crisis that began in 2011, Yemen's security situation had been deteriorating rapidly, with some observers suggesting that the country was on the verge of becoming a failed state. As one source has noted, Yemen has not enjoyed a monopoly over force within its borders. The southern secessionist movement (*Hirak*), restless Houthi rebels, and a growing al-Qaida threat detracted from Yemen's ability to develop its few natural resources. Groundwater supplies are insufficient for the demands of a growing population, and scientists warned that Sana could be the first world capital to run out of water. In addition, the country suffered from one of the highest malnutrition rates in the world, with an estimated one-third of the population experiencing chronic hunger.

Security concerns in northern Yemen can be traced to 2008, when hostilities between government forces and Houthi rebels escalated, resulting in the deaths of several Houthi militiamen. The conflict, which dates to a 2004 uprising by popular Shiite cleric Husain al-HUTHI and his Organization of Believing Youth (*al-Shabab al-Mumin*), has taken hundreds of lives in clashes with the Yemeni army and has displaced nearly 350,000 people. The government renewed its offensive against the Houthis in August 2009 after President Salih accused Iran of aiding the rebels. For their part, the Houthis blamed Saudi Arabia for supporting the Yemeni army. As fighting pressed against Yemen's northern border, the Saudis positioned ground troops along the frontier and launched air strikes targeting Houthi strongholds in Yemen.

The Houthis announced in 2012 that they would not participate in the National Dialogue Conference (NDC) mandated by the GCC Initiative, nor would they disband their militias. Throughout 2012 sporadic violence occurred between the rebels and government forces. However, observers noted that conflict in the north had taken on a sectarian dimension as more and more skirmishes involved Sunni Salafi groups—many supported politically by *Islah* party leaders—taking up arms against Shia Houthis.

Another security concern has been the growing separatist movement in the southern provinces that has spawned street demonstrations, political confrontations, and calls for independence. By 2009 the situation in South Yemen had deteriorated to the point that journalists were banned from the region. Meanwhile, Nasir al-WAHISHI, the leader of AQAP, declared his group's support for the uprising. In restless southeast Yemen, a surging AQAP kept the region embroiled in conflict. However, when U.S. drones killed top AQAP target Anwar al-AWLAKI in October 2011, the rebels were temporarily sidelined.

Even after President Salih stepped down in February 2012, the Ansar al-Sharia Brigade of al-Qaida succeeded in taking and temporarily holding a few towns in the southeast of the country, though the Yemeni army reasserted control of the region in short order. However, al-Qaida struck back with a car bomb at a military parade in Sana that killed more than 100 recruits and injured hundreds. In May 2012 the army began a concentrated effort to drive AQAP out of the major towns in Abyan province, and by June they had pushed the militants back into the countryside.

Salih's departure in February 2012 promoted Abd Rabbo Mansour Hadi to the presidency, the office to which he was duly elected by national referendum in March. Hadi's interim presidency was tasked with assembling a unity government equally representing the GPC and the JMP (see Political Parties and Groups, below). The GCC Initiative granted Salih immunity from future prosecution but only if he refrained from political activity in Yemen. Hadi's term was limited to two years, during which time new electoral laws were to be passed, the national dialogue held, and a new constitution written.

Despite the agreement he signed when vacating the presidency, Salih continued to be a force in Yemeni politics. A chorus of criticism arose from the general population regarding the immunity deal the former president received, with many voices calling for his arrest and prosecution. Though Salih was not named explicitly, the UN passed a resolution in June 2012 condemning all actors who sought to undermine Yemen's political transition.

Three issues loomed large in Yemen during 2013: political reconciliation, erosion of national unity, and continued threats from AQAP. The primary vehicle for reconciling Yemen's competing political and regional factions, the NDC, began in March 2013. A gathering of 565 representatives from established parties, coalitions, and public interests met for ten months to resolve differences and set the stage for the drafting of a new constitution. However, differences were hard to overcome. A primary fissure was the issue of southern separatism, and many key actors from *Hirak* choose not to attend the conference. In August the Yemeni government issued a blanket apology to southerners (and Houthis) for Salih's military campaigns against them. The apology failed to sway many people that the Hadi administration sought genuine reconciliation or meaningful change. Even a plan to create six subnational states in a federal system that would shift significant autonomy away from Sana failed to attract sufficient interest from delegates opposed to the status quo. By the fall of 2013 many of the southern representatives had suspended participation in the dialogue.

The extent to which national unity could exist in Yemen—as envisioned by central government leadership—appeared to lose all credibility in 2013. In south Yemen, secessionist sentiment was strong, and observers questioned whether Sana continued to exercise real authority there. In the north, Houthis were in de facto control of Saada and surrounding territory, while Salafi militias openly challenged Houthi rebels throughout the region.

Though President Hadi successfully reorganized military leadership to lessen the influence of Salih-era appointees, the steepest challenge facing security forces in Yemen continued to be AQAP. Hundreds of military officers and staff members were assassinated in 2012 and 2013. Targeted killing of al-Qaida fighters and leaders carried out by the Yemeni military, U.S. drones, and Saudi fighter pilots also resulted in hundreds of al-Qaida deaths.

With growing Iranian military support, Houthi rebels advanced on the capital in September 2014. Prime Minister Mohammed Salem BASINDWA (GPC) resigned in order to facilitate a power-sharing agreement with the Houthis that was signed on September 21. On November 1 a cease-fire agreement was signed between the Houthis and the government. Khaled BAHAH (non-party) was named prime minister on November 9, and a new government was approved by the legislature on December 18.

The Houthis rejected a draft constitution designed to end the civil war in January 2015 and renewed attacks on the capital. Hadi, Bahah, and his cabinet resigned on January 22. However, Hadi was able to escape the Houthis and announced that the resignations were void. In March Bahah and other cabinet members were released and most went into exile in Saudi Arabia. On April 13 Bahah was appointed vice president by Hadi as Saudi Arabia led a coalition to intervene in Yemen to fight the Houthis (see Foreign relations, below).

On April 3, 2016, as UN-mediated peace talks began, Hadi dismissed Bahah and appointed Gen. Ali Mohsen al-AHMAR as vice president and Ahmed Obeid bin DAGHR as prime minister. The GPC was among ten major Yemeni political parties supporting Hadi's new government. The Hadi government withdrew from the talks in July 2016 after a GPC–Houthi deal to create a ten-member interim council to govern Yemen. Peace talks were suspended in August 2016.

Constitution and government. The 1990 constitution of the Republic of Yemen stipulated that the Islamic legal code (sharia) was "one source" of Yemeni law (the wording was later changed to "the source"). A legislative branch was established, including the 301-member popularly elected House of Representatives, which was given the power to appoint the five-member Presidential Council that selected from its members a chair and vice chair, who effectively served as the republic's president and vice president. Additionally, the transitional government appointed a commission to redraw the boundaries of local provinces, some of which tribal chiefs had ruled as virtual fiefdoms.

In the aftermath of the civil war, the House of Representatives in September 1994 revised the basic law, providing for an elected chief executive, limited to two five-year terms, with broadened powers, including the right to name the vice president and prime minister.

In 1997 President Salih established the 59-member Consultative Council, an advisory body. In a 2001 constitutional referendum, the council was replaced with the new Shura Council, whose 111 presidentially appointed members had limited decision-making responsibilities. The referendum also extended the presidential term of office to seven years. On April 27, 2008, the country's local authorities law was amended to allow members of municipal councils in each province to indirectly elect all 20 provincial governors, who had previously been appointed by the president.

As stipulated in the power-sharing agreement signed by former president Salih and members of the GPC and JMP in November 2011, Yemen was required to revise its electoral laws to accommodate pluralistic politics as well as construct and ratify a new constitution. At the conclusion of the NDC in early 2014, President Hadi appointed 17 members to the Constitutional Drafting Committee. Criticism arose when leaders of the YSP, *Islah,* and independent "youth" movements realized they had been left out of the process. The committee was given one year to produce a final draft constitution, though Hadi signaled its work might take longer.

Press freedom in Yemen underwent considerable liberalization following unification in 1990, resulting in a blossoming of newspapers and other periodicals. However, censorship was re-imposed at the outbreak of the 1994 civil war: harassment and prosecution of journalists is a common occurrence. The Committee to Protect Journalists (CPJ) reported that the Yemeni High Judicial Court had established a "special press court" to handle media and publishing offenses and in 2010 noted that the court had been used to punish views critical of the government. In light of secessionist activity in the south during 2011, media freedom was further curtailed by the Salih government. Under the Hadi regime, press freedoms continued to ebb. In 2014 the CPJ objected to Yemen's expulsion of two U.S. print journalists and a crew from the al-Jazeera television network. Reporters Without Borders ranked Yemen 167th out of 180 countries in its 2014 World Press Freedom Index. Yemen was ranked 168th and 170th in the 2015 and 2016 iterations of that index.

Foreign relations. The Republic of Yemen's foreign policy agenda was dominated throughout the second half of 1990 and early 1991 by Iraq's incursion into Kuwait. (For information regarding foreign relations of the YAR and PDRY, see the 2011 *Handbook.*) Yemen was the sole

Arab UN Security Council member to vote against the resolution to use "all necessary means to uphold and implement" the council's earlier resolutions concerning Iraq. Instead, Yemen called for a peaceful, Arab-negotiated settlement. Consequently, in January 1991 the United States announced it would withhold aid promised to Yemen; the Gulf states also withheld aid. Tension between Yemen and Saudi Arabia was described as being at an all-time high in mid-1992, their border conflict having taken on greater significance in view of new oil discoveries in the region.

During the 1994 civil war the United States endorsed unity, and thereby the northern cause, and pressured Arab countries to forgo plans to recognize the Republic of South Yemen, thereby hastening the secessionist regime's collapse. Saudi Arabia's "quiet" financial and military support for the southern forces exacerbated tension with Sana, and sporadic clashes were reported in late 1994 between Saudi and Yemeni troops in the contested border region.

Yemen became the focus of intense international attention in 2000 following the bombing of the destroyer USS *Cole* while it was refueling in Aden harbor on October 12. Five years later, a Yemeni court jailed four people in the bombing, considered by the United States to have been an al-Qaida attack. Relations with Washington improved following the al-Qaida attacks on the United States in September 2001, with Salih announcing that his government would cooperate with the subsequent U.S.-led global "war on terrorism." With several hundred suspected al-Qaida members jailed as of March 2005, the United States praised the government's crackdown on terrorists. At the same time, analysts suggested that Salih faced a difficult job balancing cooperation with the United States and growing public sentiment critical of Israel and its supporters in Washington. Relations with the United States were strained in 2007–2008 following Yemen's refusal to honor a U.S. request to extradite Jamal al-BADAWI, the al-Qaida operative who had organized the attack on the *Cole*.

In 2006 members of the GCC agreed to help bolster Yemen's economy in order to secure membership in the group. In December 2008, Yemen was admitted to four GCC bodies, and in March 2009, it was admitted to the GCC's Chambers of Commerce. As of 2014, Yemen had not been granted full council membership.

In May 2009 U.S. officials held talks with their Yemeni counterparts regarding cooperation in the U.S. war against terrorism. Earlier in the year Yemen rejected a U.S. bid to send Yemeni detainees held at the U.S. military prison at Guantánamo Bay, Cuba, to a rehabilitation program in Saudi Arabia. The Yemeni government said it would take the men—who comprise the largest group of prisoners in Guantánamo—after building its own rehabilitation center. In July 2010 the United States and Yemen revisited the issue, and although no formal agreement was reached, the first Yemeni detainee was released.

A failed suicide bomb on Christmas Day 2009 aboard a U.S. airliner en route from Amsterdam to Detroit, Michigan, provoked renewed U.S. interest in Yemen's security situation. The "underwear bomber," Nigerian national Umar Farouk Abdulmutallab, allegedly attended an AQAP camp and plotted the attack with operatives there. At the time, U.S. counterterrorism officials ranked Yemen as one of their top concerns, following only Afghanistan and Pakistan.

The United Kingdom hosted an international summit in late January 2010 on combating Islamic radicalization in Yemen. Participants pledged to support Yemen in fighting al-Qaida, and in February a donor conference was held in Riyadh. In October the world witnessed the ability of AQAP to plan international terror operations from within Yemen, as aviation authorities discovered explosives hidden in the cargo of two U.S.-bound airplanes. The material found on the planes was the same as found on Umar Abdulmutallab in December 2009. Security officials in the Middle East, Europe, and the U.S. accused the American-born Muslim cleric Anwar al-Awlaki of instigating the failed bombing.

As Yemen's domestic political crisis of 2011 unfolded, one of the key actors in Yemen's foreign relations orbit changed course. Saudi Arabia's long-held preference for keeping Yemen weak was certainly realized by the political stalemate in Sana. However, as central authority weakened and both the Houthis and al-Qaida extended their influence, the Saudis lost faith in the Salih regime's ability to tamp down threats to the kingdom. As a result, the Saudis put their full backing behind GCC diplomatic initiatives and cut off money transfers to Yemeni elites.

When President Hadi took office in 2012, his first trip abroad was to Saudi Arabia, where he met with King Abdullah to discuss security issues. Later in the year, the Saudis were forced to close their consulate in Aden when a Saudi diplomat was kidnapped by AQAP gunmen. A Friends of Yemen Conference held in Riyadh the same year elicited pledges of more than $4 billion, with $3.25 billion coming from the Saudis. (In October, China, France, Russia, the UK, and the United States pledged an additional $2.5 billion.) In 2013 Saudi Arabia increased its Fund for Development commitment—aimed at increasing productive capacity in Yemen—by $275 million. At the same time, however, the kingdom embarked upon a deportation program that affected 20,000 Yemenis and prompted demonstrations at the Saudi embassy in Sana. In an unrelated incident, a Saudi diplomat was assassinated in Yemen's capital, an act attributed to either AQAP or Houthi rebels. Throughout 2012 and 2013, Saudi fighter planes continued to aid U.S.-led missions against AQAP targets in south Yemen.

In 2014 the Saudis increased the deportation rate of Yemenis living in the kingdom illegally. By some accounts, 600,000 Yeminis were expelled, and Yemen's economy was deprived of an estimated $3 billion in remittances. Meanwhile, Riyadh's concern over both the Houthis and the influence of *Islah*'s Muslim Brotherhood-based ideology led it to place both groups on its official list of terrorist organizations.

Throughout 2011 the United States helped Yemen confront the threat posed by an unrestrained AQAP. Though at first the U.S. voiced unconditional support for Yemen's counterterrorism effort, Washington withheld promised transfer payments in order to put diplomatic pressure on Salih to step down. However, unilateral U.S. airstrikes against AQAP targets using drone aircraft intensified in 2011 and 2012. With the departure of Salih and the election of Hadi as president in 2012, the United States approved $112 million in new military aid to Yemen.

With the help of both Yemeni and Saudi Arabian security agents, the United States was able to foil an AQAP plot to blow up American airliners in May 2012. In addition, close cooperation between the United States and Yemen in eliminating AQAP militants paved the way for President Obama's meeting with President Hadi when the Yemeni president visited the UN in 2012. However, Yemenis reacting to an anti-Muslim film produced in the United States by an Egyptian expatriate attempted to attack the American embassy in Sana on September 12, 2012, drawing condemnation from Washington.

Due to August 2013 intelligence reports indicating specific al-Qaida threats against Western interests, the United States, Germany, United Kingdom, and France closed their embassies in Sana for more than a week. In response to these growing threats, the United States provided Yemen $350 million in aid during 2013. In 2014 the U.S. State Department named the *al-Rashad* party secretary general, Abdallwahab al-Homaiqani, and an AQAP field leader, Shawki Ali Ahmed AL-BADANI, to its list of specially designated global terrorists. Specific security threats also forced the United States to close its embassy in Sana to the public from early May through June 2014.

Iran is a constant worry for Yemen because it supports the Shiite Houthis. Western intelligence reports in 2011 indicated that the Quds Force, an elite branch of Iran's Islamic Revolutionary Guards Corps, were actively supplying arms and materiel to the Houthi rebels. In July 2012 President Hadi rebuked Iran for "meddling" in Yemeni domestic affairs, his public denouncement coming days after the government discovered an Iranian "spy ring" operating in Northern Yemen.

Yemeni–Iranian relations hit a low when boats carrying Iranian weapons bound for the Houthi militia were detained on Yemen's southern coast, and President Hadi openly criticized Tehran. Hadi also accused the Iranians of aiding the southern secessionist movement *Hirak*. Yemeni officials also blamed Iran for fomenting secessionist activity in the south by encouraging Hezbollah to assist *Hirak* by coordinating its communication. (Intelligence sources believe Hezbollah gives support to the Houthis as well.) In 2013 and 2014 two Iranian diplomats were victims of assassination, acts that increased tension between Sana and Tehran.

Yemen officials announced in 2014 that the country entered into contracts with China for building several power plants and developing ports. Meanwhile, the UN High Commissioner for Refugees reported that up to 15,000 immigrants from Ethiopia and Somalia—most seeking jobs in Saudi Arabia—enter Yemen each month, though most end up staying in the country and increasing the ongoing humanitarian crisis caused by shortages of food, water, and medical care.

The civil war in Yemen became a proxy conflict between Iran and Saudi Arabia. As Iran increased military support for the Houthis, Saudi Arabia led a coalition of Sunni states in an intervention that began with airstrikes in March 2015, and included a naval blockade of the country, and then the deployment of ground forces. The United States and United Kingdom provided military backing for the Saudi coalition, which was able to recapture Sana and roll back many of the gains of the Houthi.

In April 2016 the UN initiated peace talks between the Hadi government and the Houthis. However, the negotiations were suspended in August.

Current issues. During 2014 Yemen continued to grapple with the contentious issues of national unity, domestic security, and a growing humanitarian crisis caused by economic stagnation and lack of resources. Though the NDC brought together stakeholders from across Yemen's political spectrum, it was plagued by disagreements. Despite the establishment of a $350 million Southern Victims' Fund underwritten by Qatar, representatives from southern Yemen attended sessions only sporadically—if at all. However, both Houthi and GPC representatives were, at times, reluctant to participate as well, the former because of security concerns (two representatives were assassinated during the process) and the latter due to demands that GPC president Salih be prosecuted for his actions while in office during the 2011 antigovernment protests.

Southern representatives were most unhappy with plans for a federal system of governance that would create six states or subregions—four in the north and two in the south. The southern city of Aden would retain autonomy under the plan, and Sana would remain the national capital. Even after the final NDC political realignment accord was signed in January, tens of thousands of southerners advocating succession and commemorating the 1994 civil war marched in the streets of Aden. Such demonstration of public sentiment led observers to question whether implementation of the NDC plan can take place.

In addition to the federal reorganization plan, the final accords reached by the NDC also extended the terms of all members of the legislature until at least December 2015 and kept President Hadi in office until at least January 2015. Hadi was also tasked with overseeing the construction of a new constitution, reforming electoral law and restructuring the composition of the Shura Council to make it more inclusive. In order to ensure compliance with the NDC directives, the UN Security Council passed Resolution 2140 warning political "spoilers" not to interfere with the culmination of Yemen's political transition. However, critics pointed out that many obstacles stand in the way of bringing the transition to a satisfactory conclusion.

Observers speculated that finalizing the transition would also require an improvement in Yemen's security environment. In late 2013, and throughout 2014, AQAP continued fighting in the Abyan, Shabwa, and Hadramawt provinces, clashing often there with government troops. It also carried out bold attacks near the seat of national authority, such as the December 2013 raid on the Yemeni Defense Ministry in Sana that claimed 52 lives. In January an AQAP team overran a prison in Sana, freeing 29 prisoners with ties to al-Qaida.

The Houthi militias gained more territory in fighting against Salafist militias and government troops during 2014, until they controlled the cities of Dammaj and Omran, large swaths of Amran province, and camped within six miles of Sana. Though President Hadi tried to revitalize his government by shuffling cabinet ministers in March 2014, the result did not help resolve any of the country's pressing domestic security threats.

The Yemeni civil war created a power vacuum that was exploited by AQAP, which launched a growing number of attacks in 2014 and 2015. On June 12, 2015, AQAP leader Nasser al-WUHAYSHI was killed by a U.S. airstrike. The civil war displaced more than 3.1 million Yemenis by 2016, with an estimated 10,000 killed and 37,000 wounded.

POLITICAL PARTIES AND GROUPS

Under the imams, parties in North Yemen were banned, political alignments determined largely by tribal and religious loyalties. The successor Republic of Yemen legalized some 70 groups and in April 1993 allowed multiparty elections that gave rise to opposition politics.

In 2006, in advance of presidential elections scheduled for September, six opposition groups formed a coalition known as the Joint Gathering or the **Joint Meeting Parties** (JMP). The six groups were the **Yemen Socialist Party** (YSP), *Islah, Ba'ath,* the Nasserite Unionist People's Party (NUPP), the **Union of Popular Forces** (UPF), and *al-Haqq.* (The *Ba'ath* later withdrew from the JMP following disputes on a number of policies.) The JMP's nominee for president was former oil minister Faisal bin Shamlan, the main challenger to Salih. (For information about the National Council of Opposition Forces [NCOP], see the 2011 *Handbook.*)

In 2008–2009 the JMP, chaired by Hasan Muhammad ZAYD of *al-Haqq,* was instrumental in pressing for fair elections. The coalition had threatened to boycott the elections if they were held as originally scheduled, claiming vote rigging ahead of the poll. The 2009 legislative elections were postponed first until 2011 and then indefinitely as a result of the political stalemate that resulted from protests against the Salih regime. The JMP sought to direct the zeal of public discontent toward the Salih government but drew criticism from various youth movement leaders who claimed that JMP coalition members were co-opting "their revolution" for crass political ends.

Government Party:

General People's Congress—GPC (*al-Mutamar al-Shabi al-Am*). Encompassing 700 elected and 300 appointed members, the GPC was founded in 1982 in the YAR. Longtime YAR president Ali Abdallah Salih relinquished his position as secretary general of the GPC upon assuming the presidency of the Republic of Yemen in May 1990; however, the group continued as one of the parties (along with the YSP, below) responsible for guiding the new republic through the transitional period culminating in the 1993 legislative election.

The GPC won a plurality—123 seats—in the April 1993 House of Representatives balloting, its support coming primarily from northern tribal areas. Although a coalition government with the YSP was announced on May 30, the two leading parties grew increasingly estranged prior to the onset of the 1994 civil war. Following that conflict, the GPC announced the formation of a new government in coalition with *Islah* (see below). At its fifth congress, held in 1995, the GPC reelected all incumbent party leaders, including Salih as chair.

The GPC, aided by a YSP boycott, won a majority of 187 seats in the April 1997 House balloting, and *Islah* joined the opposition. In the balloting of April 2003 the GPC won 238 seats. *Islah* negotiated, though ultimately unsuccessfully, to avoid splitting the antigovernment vote.

President Salih was reelected party president in 2005 and nominated as the party's 2006 presidential candidate. Following Salih's reelection in September coupled with the party's success in concurrent local elections, the GPC solidified its dominant position. Its stronghold was further enhanced in May 2008 when the party dominated elections for provincial governors, and six party members were named to a reshuffled cabinet.

In 2009–2010 the GPC struggled to govern the country in the face of growing criticism of its handling of deepening civil unrest. Demonstrations in April by opposition parties called for an end to "repressive policies," and "arbitrary arrests" increased in southern towns as the economy worsened. U.S. military operations aimed at al-Qaida targets sparked another wave of protests in June over perceived violation of Yemeni sovereignty.

As a result of antigovernment protests in 2011, nine GPC House of Representatives members resigned over concerns that the government response to street protests was too violent. President Salih formally dismissed the all-GPC cabinet in March, reducing it to a caretaker role until a new slate of ministers could be appointed at an unspecified future date. In April some former GPC ministers and MPs formed their own political grouping—the Justice and Development Bloc.

As the country's political crisis intensified in 2011, the party oversaw multiple negotiations with JMP members aimed at achieving a settlement that would transfer power to a broader base of Yemeni political actors once President Salih was persuaded to resign the presidency. After Salih was forced to leave the country in June after an attack on his life, Vice President Hadi became the lead voice articulating GPC preferences and negotiating the details of a future unity government.

In August 2011 former GPC prime minister and acting speaker of the Shura Council Abd al-Aziz Abd al-Ghani succumbed to injuries he sustained in the June attempt to assassinate President Salih. The same month party assistant secretary general Sultan al-BARAKANI implicated *Islah* party member Hamid al-AHMAR as the main suspect in that attack, though the government never charged him. In April 2012, after having stepped down as president, Salih resigned from the chairmanship of the GPC, relinquishing the position to Abdel Karim al-Iryani. In 2013 Salih reinserted himself into the GPC's leadership by retaking the position of chair and in that capacity led the GPC's delegation in the NDC. However, many GPC members voiced resentment of Salih's continued involvement with the party, especially in light of threats by the UN Security Council to sanction the former president. In 2014 President Hadi challenged Salih by closing two media outlets controlled by him then laying siege to the Salih Mosque that the former president had used to launch political movements designed to consolidate his power base. Amid the chaos of intrastate conflict, the GPC participated in UN-sponsored peace talks with the Houthis. The process broke down in August 2016.

Leaders: Ali Abdullah SALIH (Former President of the Republic), Abd Rabbo Mansour HADI (President of the Republic and Secretary General), Abd al-Qadir Abd al-Rahman BAJAMMAL (Assistant Secretary General), Sultan al-BARAKANI (Assistant Secretary General).

Other Legislative Parties:

Yemeni Congregation for Reform (*al-Tajammu al-Yamani lil-Islah*). Also referenced as the **Yemeni *Islah* Party** (YIP), *Islah* was launched in September 1990 under the leadership of influential

Northern tribal leader Sheikh Abdallah ibn Husayn al-AHMAR, formerly a consistent opponent of unification. The party subsequently campaigned against the 1990 constitution in alliance with several other groups advocating strict adherence to sharia. (For details on the party from 1993 to 2003, see the 2012 *Handbook.*)

In the elections of April 27, 2003, *Islah* garnered 46 seats, and al-Ahmar was reelected as speaker of the House of Representatives. In 2005 some in the party reportedly agreed to allow women to participate in elections, which would presumably strengthen party results, though there was no official pronouncement on the subject. (In 2009 there were reportedly female members on the *Islah* Shura Council, among them the president of Women Journalists Without Chains, Tawakul KARMAN.)

In 2005 Yemen asked the United States to remove Abd al-Maguid-ZINDANI, the chair of the *Islah* governing council, from its list of suspected terrorists. The United States had previously accused al-Zindani of working with Osama bin Laden. Party leader Sheikh al-Ahmar, who heads former president Salih's tribe, said he personally supported Salih's 2006 reelection bid, though his preference was "not binding" on the party. The party, as part of the JMP coalition, officially supported Faisal bin SHAMLAN in the election.

In February 2007 the party replaced al-Zindani as its spiritual leader but urged the government to continue to press Washington to remove al-Zindani's name from its list of suspected financiers of terrorism. In March al-Ahmar was reelected party president, and al-Zindani was named to the party's supreme panel. Muhammad Ali al-Yadoumi, formerly vice chair of the party, was named chair in January 2008 to succeed Sheikh al-Ahmar, who died in December 2007.

In May 2009 a regional party leader indicated his intent to form a new southern "reform" movement, and as civil unrest deepened, the party became increasingly critical of the governing GPC. In December *Islah* secretary general Abd al-Wahab Ali al-UNSI accused the GPC of fomenting unrest in the country with "extremist policies" so it could act as mediator and thereby cement power.

In January 2011 *Islah* leaders and MPs rejected proposed amendments to the constitution that would have allowed President Salih to stay in office indefinitely. The same month Salih criticized the opposition parties—and *Islah* in particular—for threatening to boycott the April parliamentary elections—elections that did not take place as scheduled.

Taking a cue from the spontaneous antigovernment street protests of 2011, *Islah*—working in concert with its JMP partners—promoted "Day of Rage" rallies on Fridays. However, the youth movement organizers of the popular protests accused the established opposition parties of hijacking the youths' revolutionary goals.

In June 2011 *Islah* MP Ali ASHSHAL accused President Salih of exaggerating the threats to national security posed by domestic al-Qaida elements in order to remain in power. At the same time, armed tribesmen loyal to *Islah* were engaged in conflict with Yemeni security forces north of Sana. Later in July the party accused the Salih government of attempting to assassinate *Islah* president Mohammed YADOUMI.

As a JMP member, *Islah* became part of the national reconciliation government assembled by Prime Minister Basindwa in compliance with the GCC Initiative. During 2012 *Islah* took a hard line against the Houthi rebellion, and some of its members in Aden clashed with members of *Hirak*. In June 2013 *Islah* MPs suspended their party's participation in the House due to conflicts with GPC MPs over governing procedures established by the power-sharing agreement.

Islah-backed militias became embroiled in fighting with Houthi militias throughout 2014 and in most instances suffered humiliating defeat. Bad fortune on the battlefield weakened *Islah*'s position in the Yemeni opposition. Despite being the second-largest party in Yemen, *Islah* sent signals to both its allies and opponents that cast doubt on its role in future governments. For instance, *Islah* leaders first suggested a rapprochement with the GPC as a bulwark against Houthi insurgency and then publicly pondered whether the party should withdraw altogether from the transitional government. In April 2016, after *Islah* voiced its support for Saudi military intervention against Houthi rebel forces in Yemen, the Houthis kidnapped several members of the party and attacked the home of party chair Yadoumi.

Leaders: Muhammad Ali al-YADOUMI (Chair), Sheikh Abd al-Wahhabi Ali al-ANSI (Secretary General).

Yemeni Socialist Party—YSP (*al-Hizb al-Ishtiraki al-Yamani*). (For information about the YSP prior to 1993, see the 2011 *Handbook.*) The YSP won 56 seats in the April 1993 House of Representatives election, and party leaders announced a potential merger with the GPC. However, with substantial opposition to the plan having reportedly been voiced within the YSP's 33-member Politburo, no progress toward the union ensued, and the YSP on its own was allocated 9 cabinet seats in the government formed in May.

Personal animosity between YSP secretary general Ali Salim al-Beidh and Yemeni president Salih was considered an important element in the subsequent North-South confrontation, which culminated in the 1994 civil war. However, al-Beidh and his supporters attributed the friction to the inability of security forces to protect YSP members. An estimated 150 YSP members were assassinated between May 1990 and early 1994.

Following the collapse of the YSP-led People's Democratic Republic of Yemen (PDRY) in July 1994, the party appeared to be in disarray. Al-Beidh announced from exile that he was "retiring from politics," although some of the other secessionist leaders who had fled the country pledged to pursue their goal of an independent South. Meanwhile, in September the YSP rump in Yemen elected a new Politburo comprising 13 Southerners and 10 Northerners. Aware that a significant portion of the YSP had opposed the ill-fated independence movement, President Salih announced that the reorganized party would be allowed to keep its legal status. However, he declared al-Beidh and 15 other separatist leaders to be beyond reconciliation and subject to arrest for treason should they return to Yemen. Subsequently, when the GPC/YIP coalition government was formed in October, the YSP announced it was assuming the role of "leading opposition party." The party subsequently continued to challenge the GPC's stranglehold on power, and the YSP strongly opposed the 2001 constitutional amendments that lengthened the presidential and legislative terms of office.

In 2003 Salih reconciled with al-Beidh and pardoned YSP members who had been sentenced to death. The party secured eight seats in the 2003 elections. In a move toward further cooperation, YSP leaders began talks with the GPC in 2005 to bridge the gap between them.

In July 2008 the party's MPs boycotted the legislative session to protest proposed constitutional amendments recommended by the president. YSP leaders said the amendments did not address the release of political prisoners, among other issues. The same month the YSP's agreement to enter into a national dialogue with the GPC raised the possibility of eventual YSP appointments to prominent government positions.

In March 2011 Abu Bakr BATHEEB, the party's assistant secretary general, urged ratification of the GCC Initiative. As a JMP member, in 2012 the YSP joined the reconciliation government as partners with the GPC. That year, the YSP advocated a national apology to the people of the former PDRY, calling for the reinstatement of former security officers and the repatriation of seized property. However, YSP leader Yassin NUMAN issued steady criticism of the Southern Movement, accusing *Hirak* of trying to undermine the achievements of the YSP in the region. Perhaps in response to his strong rhetoric, gunmen made an attempt on Numan's life in late August 2012.

In 2013 Numan escaped yet another attempt on his life, despite the fact that his party sided with Southern Movement leaders against NDC proposals to create a six-state federal system. Both the Southern Movement and the YSP suggested a two-state proposal that was quickly dismissed by the NDC. Since 2013 the party has faced progressively greater threats. In an April 2016 interview, the party's leader in parliament, Aydarus al-NAQUIB, noted that the "bombings and assassinations in Aden and other liberated areas are part of an ongoing dirty war" against the Houthis.

Leaders: Yassin Said NUMAN (Former Speaker of the House of Representatives and Secretary General), Yahya Abu ASBU (Deputy Secretary General), Abu Bakr BATHEEB (Assistant Secretary General), Aydarus al-NAQUIB (Parliamentary Leader).

Arab Socialist *Ba'ath* Party—ASBP (*Hizb al-Ba'ath al-Arabi al-Ishtiraki*). The Yemen branch of this secularist pan-Arab party fielded seven successful candidates in the April 1993 legislative elections, and party member Mujahid Abu SHAWARIB was subsequently named a deputy prime minister in the cabinet formed in May. However, *Ba'ath* leaders announced that the party would sit in opposition, with Abu Shawarib serving essentially as an independent rather than a *Ba'ath* representative. The grouping secured two seats in the 1997 house elections and two seats in the 2003 elections. In 2006 the party announced its support for President Salih in the presidential election. In December 2009 *Ba'ath* president Abd al-Wahhab MAHMUD became president of the JMP.

The party condemned the January 2011 arrest and detention of party member Naif al-QANIS, a leader in the JMP. In August al-Qanis spoke on behalf of the JMP when he criticized the GCC Initiative provision granting Salih immunity from future criminal prosecution. ASBP members were instrumental in organizing protests calling for the former president to be charged for the deaths of civilians during the 2011–2012 uprising. Al-Qanis noted that the GCC agreement granted immunity only if Salih disengaged from Yemeni politics permanently—a condition the former president has never fulfilled.

Leaders: Abdullah al-AHMAR (Assistant Secretary General), Muhammad Al-ZUBAIRY (Secretary General and JMP President), Abd al-Wahhab MAHMUD, Dr. Qasim SALAM.

Nasserite Unionist People's Party—NUPP (*al-Tanthim al-Wahdawi al-Shabi al-Nasri*). Formed in 1989 and the largest of the nation's Nasserite groupings, the NUPP won one seat in the 1993 legislative balloting, three in 1997, and three in 2003. The party is a member of the opposition coalition JMP, and in 2009 party leader Abdul Malik al-Makhlafi was named a member of the national committee in charge of implementing the terms of the cease-fire with Houthi rebels in Saada Province (see Current Issues above).

In July 2010 an exiled Nasserite leader, Abdel-Raqib AL-QERSHI, was shot by an unknown gunman when he returned to Yemen following an amnesty offer by President Salih. Al-Qershi had fled the country in 1978 to escape the death penalty for his alleged involvement in an armed rebellion to topple the Salih government. In 2012 party leader Mohammed al-Sabri advocated for a national committee that would investigate the Salih regime's crimes, a step that party members considered crucial for true reconciliation to occur. The party continued its support for the Hadi government amid the civil war.

Leaders: Mohammed al-SABRI, Abdul Malik al-MAKHLAFI, Sultan al-ATWANI (Secretary General).

Other Parties and Groups:

Truth Party (*al-Haqq*). Founded by Islamic religious scholars in late 1991, *al-Haqq* won two seats in the 1993 parliamentary balloting. Although *al-Haqq* had no successful candidates in the 1997 elections, party leader Ibrahim al-WAZIR was named minister of justice in the new GPC-led cabinet formed in May. He was replaced after the 2003 reshuffle. Sheikh Ahmad ibn Ali SHAMI, the secretary general of *al-Haqq,* was named minister of religious guidance in the May 1998 reshuffle, although he left the post in September. The government has accused the group of backing the rebellion of cleric and former Truth leader Husayn al-Houthi. In December 2009 Truth Party secretary general Hasan Muhammad Zayd stepped down as president of the JMP.

In February 2010 *al-Haqq* rejected the Yemeni government conditions to end the Houthi conflict in Saada Province. In July Zayd warned that a new war with Saudi Arabia might result because of an alleged Saudi attack on a mosque in the province.

In April 2011 Zayd described the role of antigovernment street protesters as purely revolutionary in nature and concluded that the youth movement should not have a role in Yemini politics, a statement that angered many of the youth protest organizers and deepened the divide between them and the political parties. In July Zayd was prevented by Yemeni intelligence services from boarding a flight to Saudi Arabia for the alleged offense of being a "spy for Iran." His brief detention drew condemnation from human rights organizations, as well as calls from JMP members that further harassment of opposition figures would not be tolerated. In March 2012 the party's Executive Committee announced the dismissal of Zayd from the secretary general post for allegedly conducting party business without consulting the Committee, though later he was reinstated. In January 2013 the party conducted the first General Conference in its history in preparation for the National Dialogue. The head of the party's Shura Council, Ibrahim al-WAZIR, narrowly escaped an assassination attempt in 2014. The party supported the Houthis in the Yemeni civil war.

Leaders: Hasan Muhammad ZAYD (Secretary General), Muhammad ibn Muhammad al-MANSUR (Vice President), Ibrahim al-WAZIR, Sheikh Ahmad ibn Ali SHAMI.

League of the Sons of Yemen (*Rabibat Abna al-Yaman*—RAY). Founded in 1990 to represent tribal interests in the South, the league campaigned against the proposed constitution for the new republic because it did not stipulate sharia as the only source of Yemeni law. The party offered 92 candidates in the 1993 general elections, none of whom were successful. League leader Abdul Rahman al-JAFARI, born in Yemen but a citizen of Saudi Arabia, was named vice president of the breakaway Democratic Republic of Yemen in 1994. Following the separatists' defeat, al-Jafari moved to London, where he served as chair of the Yemeni National Opposition Front. Al-Jafari maintained that he was also still the leader of the League of the Sons of Yemen, but members remaining in Yemen had voted to dismiss him from his post. A small league rump participated in the 1997 elections without success.

The League's Executive Committee in March 2000 called for national reconciliation through dialogue with the Salih government and subsequently suspended its antigovernment activities. Al-Jafari announced in 2006 that he would return to Yemen to support Salih's reelection bid. Speaking on Al-Jazeera in June 2009, al-Jafari called for a two-council parliament that would better represent regional interests and advocated improved training of army and security forces.

In terms of his party's vision of a political settlement that would end the stalemate of 2011, Mohsen Mohammad Bin Fareed, secretary general of the party, noted that in 2008 his party put forth a proposal that Yemen be divided into five states, with Sana as the political capital and Aden as the trading capital. Throughout the year he continued to advocate for a political solution that would preserve Yemen in a united but decentralized manner—even by allowing significant sovereignty for the separatist elements in South Yemen. Though RAY had little influence at the NDC sessions, its prior suggestion of a federalized government structure was adopted by the conference. The party opposed the Houthis in the civil war.

Leaders: Abdul Rahman al-JAFARI, Mohsen Mohammad Bin FAREED (Secretary General).

Other parties include the **Liberation Party;** the **Democratic Nasserite Party,** led by 2006 presidential candidate Yasin Abdu SAID; the **Liberation Front Party,** established in South Yemen in the 1970s by Abdul Fattah ISMAIL; the **National Social Party,** led by Abd al-Azziz al-BUKIR; the **Popular Liberation Unity Party;** and the **Popular Unity Party.**

The so-called **Southern Movement** (*Hirak*) is a loose coalition of at least seven identifiable separatist groups located in the south of the country: **Higher National Forum for the Independence of the South; Higher National Council for the Liberation of the South,** led by Hasan Baoum and Mohammed Salih TAMMAH; **Movement of the Southern Peaceful Struggle,** led by Salah al-SHANFARA and Nasser al-KHUBBAJI; **Union of the Southern Youth,** led by Fadi Hasan BAOUM; **National Forum for the Southern Peaceful Struggle,** led by Salih Yahya SAID; **Council for Leading the Peaceful Revolution,** led by Tariq al-FADHLI; and **Council of the Peaceful Movement to Liberate the South,** established in 2010 as an umbrella organization for all Southern opposition groups, and led by Hasan BAOUM and Tariq al-FADHLI.

The **Aden-Abyan Islamic Army** claimed responsibility for the December 1998 kidnapping of 16 Westerners in Southern Yemen. Zein al-Abidine al-MIHDAR, described as one of the leaders of the group, reportedly called for strikes against U.S. installations and an end to U.S. "aggression" against Iraq. Mihdar and several others went on trial in April 1999. (For information on the group's activities from 1999 to 2008, see the 2011 *Handbook.*)

In 2009 the government arrested ten members of the Aden-Abyan Islamic Army for alleged jihadist activities. However, the government later ordered the release of a number of Army members on the recommendation of clerics, who said the fighters had repented their extremist views. In April 2010 three members of the Army were arrested, accused of killing two policemen and blowing up an official's vehicle in the southern province of Abyan.

New Parties:

Al-Rashad Union Party. Also known as the **Yemeni Rashad Union,** this party was formed in March 2012 with the intention of uniting Yemen's Salafis in one party, jointly calling for implementation of sharia law while also rejecting Western democracy. Rashad differentiated itself from *Islah*—Yemen's dominant Islamist party—by excluding women from political life. Despite its theme of unification, many Salafi groups have rejected Rashad. The party sent seven representatives to the NDC in 2013.

Leaders: Mohamed Al-BAIDANI (Cofounder), Abdallwahab Al-HOMAIQANI (Secretary General).

Nation Party (*Hizb al-Umma*). Founded by a former leader of *al-Haqq*, Mohammed MUFTAH, *Umma* is closely associated with the political goals espoused by the Houthis of North Yemen, with some observers speculating that the party has been influenced by Tehran. *Umma* called for a boycott of the February 2012 presidential election won by the CGP's Hadi. In February 2014, *Umma* was granted official status by the Yemeni government.

Leader: Mohammed MUFTAH (Founder).

Justice and Building Party (*Hizb al Horriya wal-Tanmiya*). Formed in early 2012 by former GPC members, this party has attracted disaffected members of the 2011 revolution—specifically women and young men who identify as part of the "revolutionary youth."
Leader: Mohammed ABULAHOUM (President).

The Justice and Development Bloc. Originally formed by estranged GPC members, this group came together shortly after the uprising against former president Salih began in 2011.
Leaders: Mohamed Abdulelah al-KADI (Founding Member), Abdulaziz JUBARI (Party Spokesman).

Future Democratic Party (*Hizb al-Mustaqbal al-Dimuqrati*). Billed as a nonideological party, FDP has attracted former GPC members, revolutionary youth, and women—the latter group representing 35 percent of party membership.
Leaders: Saleh Al-JALAAE (Secretary General), Ammar MOHAMMED, Nabeel ABDULLA.

Arab Spring Party. The first Yemeni party established and led exclusively by a woman, the Arab Spring has attracted many members of the revolutionary youth.
Leaders: Amal Lutf al-THAWR (Founder and Chair), Alawi al-HUTAMI.

National Solidarity Party. This party was founded by Sheikh Hussein al-Ahmar, who also serves as party chair. Al-Ahmar's wealth garnered influence when NDC seats were being distributed in March 2013, as the party earned 31 seats at the Dialogue sessions.

Other new parties include **Free Yemen Party,** led by Awsan Mohammed AQLAN; ***al-Watan* Party,** formed by members of the Civic Coalition of Revolutionary Youth and led by cofounder Husam al-SHARJABI; the **Youth Justice and Development Party;** the **Social Peace Party,** led by Mohammed al-BASHIRI; the **Youth National Democratic Development Party;** the **Peace and Development Party;** the **Dialogue and National Initiative Party;** and the **Freedom and Justice Party.**

LEGISLATURE

Shura Council (*Mali's al-Shura*). The largely advisory Shura Council was established in accordance with constitutional amendments approved in a national referendum on February 20, 2001. The president appointed all 111 members of the advisory body, including some from the opposition, on April 28.
Speaker: Abdul-Rahman OTHMAN.

The transitional **House of Representatives** (*Mali's al-Nowak*) is a 301-member body installed in 1990 to include the 159 members of the former YAR Consultative Assembly, the 111 members of the former PDRY Supreme People's Council, and 31 people named by the government to represent opposition groups. On April 17, 1993, the house was directly elected by universal suffrage. A national referendum on February 20, 2001, approved a constitutional amendment increasing the legislative term of office from four to six years.

Following the most recent elections, on April 27, 2003, the seats were distributed as follows: the General People's Congress, 238 seats; Yemeni *Islah* Party, 46; Yemeni Socialist Party, 8; Nasserite Unionist People's Party, 3; Arab Socialist *Ba'ath* Party, 2; independents, 4.

Elections originally scheduled for 2009 were postponed until April 2011, and then postponed indefinitely (see Government and Politics, above).
Speaker: Yahya Ali al-RAEE.

CABINET

[As of November 20, 2016]

Prime Minister	Ahmed Obaid bin Daghr (GPC)
Deputy Prime Ministers	Abd al-Aziz Ahmad Jubari
	Abd al-Malik Abd al-Jalil al-Mikhlafi
	Husayn Muhammad Arab
Ministers	
Agriculture and Irrigation	Ahmad al-Maysari
Civil Service and Social Security	Abd al-Aziz Ahmad Jubari
Culture	Marwan Ahmad Damaj
Defense	Mahmud Ahmad al-Subayhi (GPC)
Education	Abd al-Latif al-Hakami
Electricity	Abdallah Muhsin al-Akwa
Endowments and Religious Guidance	Ahmad Zubayan Atiyah
Expatriate Affairs	Alawi Bafaqih
Finance	Ahmad Ubayd al-Fadhli
Fisheries and Marine Resources	Fahad Salim Kafayin
Foreign Affairs	Abd al-Malik Abd al-Jalil al-Mikhlafi
Higher Education and Scientific Research	Husayn Abd al-Rahman Basalma
Human Rights	Izz al-Din al-Ashabi
Industry and Trade	Muhammad al-Saadi
Information	Muamar Mutahir al-Iryani
Interior	Husayn Muhammad Arab
Justice	Khalid Bajunayd
Labor and Social Affairs	Samira Ubayd [f]
Legal Affairs	Nihal al-Awlaqi
Local Administration	Abd al-Raqib al-Aswadi
Oil and Mineral Resources	Saif Muhsin Aboud Al Sharif (GPC)
Planning and International Cooperation	Muhammad al-Maytami
Public Health and Population	Nasir Ba'um
Public Works and Roads	Wahi Taha Aman
Technical Education and Vocational Training	Abdallah Salim Lamlas
Telecommunications and Information Technology	Lutfi Basharif Basharif
Tourism	Muhammad Abd al-Majid Qubati
Transportation	Murad al-Halimi
Water and Environment	Izzi Shuraym
Youth and Sport	Nayef Al Bakri
Ministers of State	
Minister of State	Hani Ben Brik
Minister of State	Abd al-Rab Salih al-Salami
Minister of State for the Capital of Sanaa	Abd al-Ghani Jamil
Minister of State for the Implementation of the National Dialogue	Yasir Abdallah al-Raini

[f] = female

INTERGOVERNMENTAL REPRESENTATION

Ambassador to the U.S.: Ahmed bin MUBARAK.

U.S. Ambassador to Yemen: Matthew H. TUELLER.

Permanent Representative to the UN: Khaled Hussein Mohamed ALYEMANY.

IGO Memberships (Non-UN): IOM, NAM, OIC.

For Further Reference:

Clark, Victoria. *Yemen: Dancing on the Heads of Snakes*. New Haven, CT: Yale University Press, 2010.
Johnsen, Gregory D. *The Last Refuge: Yemen, al-Qaeda, and America's War in Arabia*. New York: W. W. Norton, 2012.
Macintosh-Smith, Tim. *Yemen: The Unknown Arabia*. New York: Overlook Press, 2014.

ZAMBIA

Republic of Zambia

Political Status: Independent republic within the Commonwealth since October 24, 1964; under one-party, presidential-parliamentary system from 1972 to adoption of multiparty constitution on August 29, 1991.

Area: 290,584 sq. mi. (752,614 sq. km).

Population: 16,717,000 (2016E—UN); 14,546,961 (2016E—U.S. Census).

Major Urban Center (2016E—UN): LUSAKA (2,285,000, metropolitan area).

Official Language: English.

Monetary Unit: Kwacha (official rate October 1, 2016: 10.05 kwachas = $1US). On January 1, 2013, the Zambian kwacha was revalued, with 1 new kwacha equal to 1,000 of the old kwachas.

President: Edgar LUNGU (Patriotic Front); elected on January 20, 2015, and sworn in on January 25 to succeed Guy SCOTT (Patriotic Front), the former vice president, who became acting president after the death of Michael SATA (Patriotic Front) on October 28, 2014 (see Government and politics, below); reelected on August 11, 2016, and sworn in for a full five-year term on September 13.

Vice President: Inonge WINA (Patriotic Front); elected concurrently with the president on August 11, 2016, and sworn in for a five-year term on September 13, succeeding Guy SCOTT (Patriotic Party), who had been elevated to the presidency following the death of Michael SATA (Patriotic Front) on October 28, 2014.

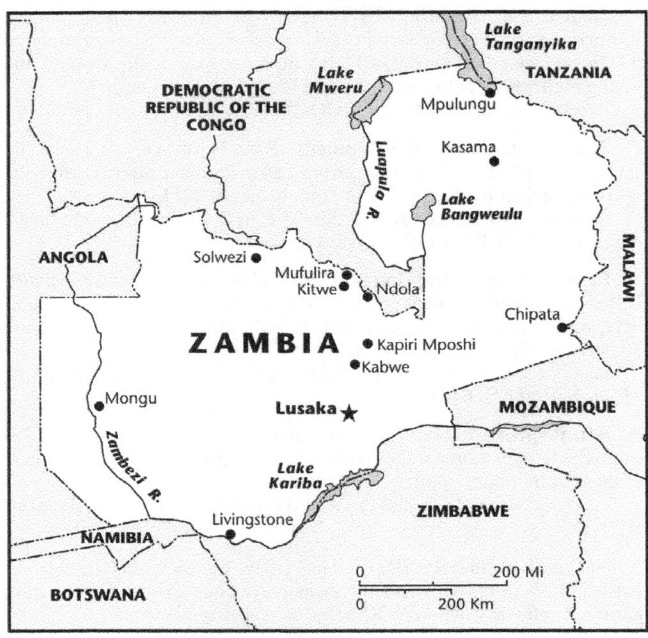

THE COUNTRY

Landlocked Zambia, the former British protectorate of Northern Rhodesia, is bordered by the Democratic Republic of the Congo, Tanzania, and Malawi on the north and east, and by Angola, Namibia, Zimbabwe, and Mozambique on the west and south. Its terrain consists primarily of a high plateau with abundant forests and grasslands. The watershed between the Congo and Zambezi river systems crosses the northern part of the country. The bulk of the population belongs to various Bantu tribes, the most influential being the Bemba in the north and the Lozi, an offshoot of the Zulu, in the southwest. (Tribal influences remain highly influential in political affairs.) Nonindigenous groups include a small number of whites (mainly British and South African), Asians, and persons of mixed descent concentrated in the Copperbelt in the north. Nearly three-quarters of native Zambians are nominally Christian, almost equally divided between Catholics and Protestants; the remainder adheres to traditional African beliefs. The official language is English, but Afrikaans and more than 70 local languages and dialects are spoken. Women comprise approximately one-third of the labor force, not including unpaid agricultural workers. Although a number of women involved in the independence struggle achieved positions of influence in the former ruling party, female representation is minimal in politics. Following the 2016 elections, women held 30 of 167 seats in the Assembly (18 percent). Meanwhile, in 2015 Inonge WINA became the country's first woman vice president.

Zambia is one of the world's largest producers of copper and cobalt. The former accounts for 75 percent of export earnings, but Zambia's share of the world copper market has declined significantly in the wake of a nearly 80 percent decline in production, attributed in large part to mismanagement of state-owned mines. Zinc, coal, cement, lime, sulfur, and magnetite are among other minerals being extracted. Agriculture employs two-thirds of the labor force, with maize, peanuts, tobacco, and cotton constituting the chief commercial crops. Because of a booming copper industry, Zambia, until the early 1970s, enjoyed one of Africa's highest standards of living, with rapid development of schools, hospitals, and highways. However, a subsequent decline in copper prices yielded infrastructural decay, rising unemployment within the rapidly growing and highly urbanized population, a foreign exchange shortage, an external debt of more than $6 billion, and the erosion of social services. Although the government had exercised budgetary restraint and relaxed its control of the economy in accordance with International Monetary Fund (IMF) strictures dating to the mid-1970s, rioting over price increases in late 1986 prompted Lusaka to abandon austerity measures and break with the IMF. However, economic reform measures were reinstated in 1998, paving the way for renewal of relations with international lenders and donors. In 1992 the Chiluba government launched a privatization program; however, market reform was subsequently seen as having failed to help the nation's poor (an estimated 83 percent of the population). Funds for education and health remained severely constrained at a time when about one-fifth of the population was believed to be HIV-positive. The IMF and World Bank continued to approve loans (Western aid accounted for one-half of the government's budget), and Zambia was included on the list of countries eligible for the international community's new debt-relief program. However, donors expressed concern over the apparent pervasive nature of corruption in government affairs at all levels. Among other things, the economic distress contributed to the emergence of a degree of political instability that was unusual by Zambian standards.

Severe drought in 2002 caused a decline in agricultural production that left 25 percent of the population temporarily dependent on food aid. Collaterally, the pace of economic reform slowed, prompting the temporary suspension of IMF and World Bank assistance. However, real gross domestic product (GDP) growth averaged 4.8 percent a year in 2004 and 2005, in part due to soaring copper prices and the investment of $1 billion by mining companies. In addition, the Group of Eight in 2005 canceled Zambia's $2.5 billion debt. GDP growth of 6 percent was reported for 2006, bolstered by expansion in the mining sector and a recovery in agricultural production. Zambia also qualified for $3.8 billion in debt relief from the IMF. Meanwhile, the Zambian administration's program for combating HIV/AIDS, including free drugs, resulted in significantly reduced death rates in its first two years and was hailed internationally as a success.

In 2008–2009 annual GDP growth averaged 5.8 percent. Owing in large part to the global economic crisis, demand for copper fell dramatically, mining companies cut thousands of jobs, and inflation increased to 15.2 percent as food costs soared. Subsequently, mining companies successfully lobbied for the abolishment of the windfall tax of 47 percent that had been approved at the height of the copper boom. On a positive note, in May the IMF approved $330 million in financial aid to help Zambia's economic recovery.

The economy began to recover in 2010, with annual growth of 7 percent continuing in 2011 due to resurgence in the mining industry and the agriculture sector. The IMF urged the government to restore the windfall mining tax in order to pay for social and public investment. Meanwhile, fund managers commended the Zambian authorities for raising electricity tariffs to recover costs and attract more private investment. A rail line linking Zambia and Malawi that was completed in 2010 after more than 30 years was hailed as a boost to trade. In June 2011 the IMF approved the final installment of $29.3 million in a three-year loan program. Significant increases in copper and cobalt revenues continued to bolster the economy. Growth remained high in 2012, but in 2013, GDP expanded by only 6 percent, nearly 2 percentage points below projections. The IMF recommended reforms to promote inclusive growth, including improving access to financial services and boosting agriculture. GDP grew by 5 percent in 2014, while inflation was 7.8 percent. GDP expanded by 3.7 percent in 2015 and then 3.4 percent in 2016. That year, inflation soared to 22.5 percent. In its 2016 ease of doing business index, the World Bank ranked Zambia 97th out of 189 countries, down from 83rd in 2014.

GOVERNMENT AND POLITICS

Political background. Declared a British sphere of influence in 1888, Northern Rhodesia was administered jointly with Southern Rhodesia until 1923–1924, when it became a separate British protectorate. From 1953 to 1963, it was linked with Southern Rhodesia and Nyasaland (now Malawi) in the Federation of Rhodesia and Nyasaland, which was dissolved at the end of 1963 in recognition of the unwillingness of the black majority populations in Northern Rhodesia and Nyasaland to continue under the political and economic domination of white-ruled Southern Rhodesia. A drive for Northern Rhodesia's complete independence, led by Harry NKUMBULA and Kenneth D. KAUNDA, concluded on October 24, 1964, when the territory became an independent republic within the Commonwealth under the name of Zambia (after the Zambezi River). Kaunda, as leader of the majority United National Independence Party (UNIP), became head of the new state; Nkumbula, whose African National Congress (ANC) had trailed in the preindependence election of January 1964, became leader of the opposition. The political predominance of Kaunda and his party was strengthened in the general election of December 1968, Kaunda winning a second five-year term as president and the UNIP again capturing an overwhelming legislative majority. In December 1972 Kaunda promulgated a law banning all parties except the UNIP and introduced what was termed "one-party participatory democracy." In December 1978 he was reelected for a fourth term following disqualification of Nkumbula and former vice president Simon M. KAPWEPWE.

On August 27, 1983, the president dissolved the National Assembly to pave the way for an October 27 election, in which, as sole presidential candidate, he garnered 93 percent of the vote and was returned to office for a fifth five-year term. Two years later Kaunda transferred both the prime minister and the UNIP secretary general to diplomatic posts; Defense Minister Alexander Grey ZULU was chosen to head the party, while Prime Minister Nalumino MUNDIA was replaced by Minister of Education and Culture Kebby MUSOKOTWANE.

Following a UNIP restructuring that was generally interpreted as enhancing his personal control of both party and government, Kaunda, again the sole candidate, was elected for a sixth presidential term on October 26, 1988, with a reported 96 percent "yes" vote. On the other hand, eight cabinet members were defeated in assembly elections held the same day, apparently reflecting increased opposition to government policy. Shortly after the election, Kaunda reshuffled the cabinet, and on March 15, 1989, he named Gen. Malimba MASHEKE to replace the young and popular Musokotwane as prime minister; the subsequent posting of Musokotwane to a diplomatic mission lent credence to the view that he had become a political threat to Kaunda.

In early 1990 the regime rejected a number of proposals for liberalization of the Zambian political system. However, by midyear the government had grudgingly agreed to implement reforms in an attempt to appease increasingly vociferous critics, particularly among the trade and business communities. In the wake of a coup attempt in June and price riots in July, Kaunda agreed to a voter registration drive and the freeing of a number of political prisoners. In September, following a series of major prodemocracy rallies, the president announced plans for multiparty elections by October 1991. On December 4 the National Assembly legalized the formation of political parties, and on December 30 the Zambian Congress of Trade Unions (ZCTU) aligned itself with the leading opposition group, the Movement for Multiparty Democracy (MMD).

In 1991 the regime's practices, including strict control of the media, drew MMD condemnation and led to violent clashes between MMD and UNIP supporters. Nevertheless, on August 2 the National Assembly approved a new multiparty constitution, and, following its formal signing on August 29, the president dissolved the legislature and allowed the state of emergency decree to lapse for the first time since independence. On October 31, in balloting supervised by former U.S. president Jimmy Carter and representatives of the Commonwealth and the Organization of African Unity (OAU, subsequently the African Union—AU), the MMD's Frederick CHILUBA won 74 percent of the presidential vote and the movement's candidates captured 125 of 150 assembly seats.

The MMD secured a vast majority of the 1,190 local council seats contested on November 30, 1992; however, the ruling party's victories were tainted by a lack of competition in approximately 400 councils, coupled with voter apathy (less than 10 percent of eligible voters reportedly having participated). Observers attributed the apparent growing disenchantment among voters to the effects of a severe economic austerity program compounded by the perception of unmitigated governmental corruption.

On March 4, 1993, the administration's prestige was further damaged when Chiluba declared an indefinite state of emergency and 25 UNIP members, including three of former president Kaunda's sons, were arrested on charges relating to an alleged coup plot. On March 9 the president shortened the detention without trial period from 28 to 7 days, apparently seeking to combat domestic and international charges that his administration had overreacted to reports about the alleged plot, and on May 25 the state of emergency was lifted.

In August 1993, 15 prominent MMD officials resigned from the government and National Assembly because of the Chiluba administration's alleged unwillingness to investigate corruption and drug trafficking charges against powerful cabinet ministers; the MMD defectors, citing a "critical national crisis of leadership and governance," launched the National Party (NP). Chiluba dismissed the resignations as the "teething problems" of democratic reform; however, in December international aid donors meeting in Paris voted to withhold aid payments until Lusaka investigated the allegations, and on January 6, 1994, the ZCTU called on the Chiluba administration to dissolve the government. Consequently, on January 11, 1994, Chiluba reshuffled his cabinet, claiming to have ousted tainted ministers, and in March the World Bank agreed to release suspended aid payments despite opposition protestations that the president had shielded corrupt ministers while dismissing two who had sought to expose malfeasance.

On July 3, 1994, Vice President Levy MWANAWASA resigned, citing alleged irresponsibility and greed among his colleagues. On the following day Chiluba named Brig. Gen. Godfrey MIYANDA, theretofore a minister without portfolio, to replace Mwanawasa.

In October 1994 former president Kaunda officially announced that he would end his retirement to campaign for early presidential elections, saying "there is a crisis in Zambia... I have accepted the call to come back." In February 1995 Kaunda, who had been under surveillance since August 1994 because of allegations that his return was being financed by foreign backers, was charged with attempting to hold an illegal political party meeting. Meanwhile, the MMD sought to block his presidential eligibility by pressing for a constitutional amendment that would disqualify anyone not born in Zambia of Zambian-born parents (Kaunda's parents having been born in Malawi). Such an amendment, as well as a second amendment disqualifying any person who had already been twice elected president, were included in a draft document issued on June 16. The proposed charter was released despite the objections of an independent constitutional review commission, which had declared the amendments "rubbish" and accused the MMD of having bribed its authors.

On May 16, 1996, the National Assembly approved the Constitution of Zambia Amendment Act 1996, and 12 days later the president sanctioned the measure, thus officially banning Kaunda from future elections. Subsequent opposition efforts to have the constitutional changes suspended and the upcoming balloting held in accordance with the 1991 document were dismissed in September by the president and High Court, respectively. On the other hand, in an effort to dampen mounting opposition charges that electoral preparations were being "rigged," Chiluba agreed to provide opposition representatives with equal access to the media and oversight of vote tabulation. On October 19 Chiluba dissolved the assembly and announced that presidential and legislative elections would be held on November 18. (The opposition's subsequent charge that the government's mandate would expire on October 31 and that any of its actions thereafter would be illegal was dismissed by the regime as "immature.") On October 23 Kaunda announced that the UNIP would boycott the November elections to protest the constitutional changes and the government's alleged manipulation of the voter registration drive.

As anticipated, President Chiluba and the MMD secured landslide victories in polling on November 18, 1996, with the former capturing 69.5 percent of the vote and his party 131 of the 150 seats contested. Their victories were marred, however, by alleged electoral irregularities and by what one observer described as a "revolt of MMD voters" in high-profile contests won by independents and opposition candidates. Thereafter, amid widespread opposition calls for a campaign of civil disobedience to force the government to hold fresh elections, Chiluba put the military on alert on November 28. On December 2 Chiluba named a new cabinet that was described as "tribalist" because of the preponderance of members from the Northern and Luapula regions (Chiluba is from the latter).

Tensions remained high in Lusaka throughout the first half of 1997 as the Chiluba administration, now reportedly under the direction of MMD hard-liners, was sharply denounced by both domestic and international observers for introducing legislation that would strictly regulate both the media and nongovernmental organizations. (In March the latter law went into effect, but in April the government suspended the controversial Press Council Bill.) In early August antigovernment demonstrations in Lusaka turned into rioting, and at an illegal opposition rally on August 23, Kaunda and Roger CHONGWE, leader of the Liberal Progressive Front, were shot and wounded in what Kaunda described as an assassination attempt.

On October 28, 1997, a group of junior military officers led by Capt. Steven LUNGU (also known as Captain Solo) took over a government radio station and declared that they had established a "National Redemption Council" and were prepared to overthrow the government. Within hours the reportedly drunken rebels were overpowered by forces loyal to the president; nevertheless, the government declared a state of emergency, and in the following weeks, more than 80 mid-level officers and dozens of opposition members were detained, with a number of others reportedly fleeing the country amid reports that those arrested were being tortured.

On December 2, 1997, Chiluba demoted his vice president, Brig. Gen. Godfrey Miyanda, to the education ministry and named as his replacement Lt. Gen. Christon TEMBO. Furthermore, Chiluba drastically reshuffled both the government and the military leadership.

In late April 2001 a fractured MMD congress agreed to seek constitutional revision to permit President Chiluba to run for a third term, prompting massive protest demonstrations and significant external condemnation. Under heavy pressure, Chiluba finally declared he would not seek reelection. However, on May 4 he dissolved the cabinet, permitting him to appoint a new government on May 6 that pointedly did not include theretofore Vice President Tembo and some 11 other MMD members who had opposed the third-term initiative. Former vice president Mwanawasa became the surprise MMD candidate in the December 27, 2001, presidential balloting, securing, according to official results, a narrow victory (28.7 percent to 26.8 percent) over the second-place finisher, Anderson K. MAZOKA of the United Party for National Development (UPND). However, opposition parties charged that the balloting had been rigged and demanded a court review. (The Supreme Court launched a review of the charges but closed the case in November 2004.) Meanwhile, the MMD was also credited with pluralities in the concurrent assembly and municipal elections, the UPND easily outdistancing the other contenders to secure its position as the dominant opposition grouping. Not surprisingly, considering the electoral challenge, no opposition parties were represented in the cabinet appointed by Mwanawasa on January 7, 2002. However, Mwanawasa appointed members of the UNIP and the Forum for Democracy and Development (FDD) to junior cabinet positions in a May 28, 2003, reshuffle. He also named Nevers MUMBA, a prominent pastor and leader of the National Citizens' Coalition (NCC), as vice president. Mumba was in turn succeeded by Lupando MWAPE of the MDD on October 4, 2004, and by 2005 it was reported that the non-MDD cabinet members had been replaced by MDD stalwarts.

On April 5, 2006, the assembly adopted a controversial electoral reform bill establishing the president's authority to set election dates and requiring only a plurality in a single-round election to decide presidential balloting, among other provisions (see Current issues, below). The bill was promulgated on May 19, and on July 26 President Mwanawasa dissolved Parliament and called for early tripartite elections on September 28, 2006. President Mwanawasa won reelection with a plurality of 43 percent of the vote, defeating main challengers Michael SATA of the Patriot Front (PF) with 29 percent, and Hakainde HICHILEMA of the United Democratic Alliance (UDA) with 25 percent. Two other candidates, including former vice president Godfrey Miyanda, received less than 2 percent of the vote. In legislative balloting the MMD remained the largest parliamentary party with 73 seats, though it lacked a clear majority without the 8 presidentially appointed members. The opposition PF, however, made a stunning comeback with 43 seats (it had won 1 seat in 2001). The newly formed United Democratic Alliance (see Political Parties, below) secured 26 seats. On October 9 the president named Rupiah BANDA of the UNIP as vice president to replace Mwape, who lost his seat in the parliamentary elections. Banda and the new cabinet were sworn in on October 10. Three cabinet ministers were replaced in early 2007.

President Mwanawasa died at age 59 on August 19, 2008, following complications of a stroke weeks earlier. A by-election to choose a successor to serve the remaining three years of Mwanawasa's term was held on October 30. The acting president, Vice President Rupiah Banda (MDD), secured 40.1 percent of the vote, narrowly defeating Michael Sata of the PF, who garnered 38.1 percent. The remaining challengers, Hakainde Hichilema (UPND) and Godfrey Miyanda of the Heritage Party (HP), trailed far behind.

On November 14, 2008, President Banda appointed Legal Affairs Minister George Kunda as vice president, while still allowing Kunda to retain his cabinet post. Banda reshuffled the cabinet the same day.

A minor cabinet reshuffle was announced on March 24, 2009. The communications and transport minister, Dora SILIYA, resigned on April 21, 2009, after she was accused of wrongdoing for allegedly ignoring advice from the attorney general in a contract matter. An appeals court subsequently cleared Siliya of the charges, and on June 17 she was reappointed as education minister in a minor cabinet reshuffle. In August 2009 former president Chiluba was acquitted on corruption charges. (He had been convicted by a London court in 2007 of stealing $46 million in public funds from Zambia.) His wife, who had been sentenced in March 2009 to 42 months in prison, was released on bail and later rearrested for allegedly having received money and property stolen by her husband when he was in office. Both Chiluba and his wife protested the charges.

The cabinet was reshuffled on January 5, 2010, and in May, a UNIP member was appointed to the post of minister of home affairs. Three ministers were reshuffled on September 28.

The minister for works and supply was replaced on February 24, 2011. On September 20 concurrent presidential, parliamentary, and local elections were held (see Current issues). On September 22 violence erupted in several areas in the country's north because of delayed publication of the final results. The next day official results showed Sata had won 42.2 percent to Banda's 35.6 percent. Voter turnout was 53.75 percent. Sata was inaugurated on September 23 and unveiled his new cabinet on September 29. Significantly, Sata appointed Guy SCOTT as his vice president; Scott was the only white man besides South Africa's P. W. Botha to reach the level of vice president in a modern, democratically elected African government. In December Sata named a number of MMD members to the cabinet as deputy ministers.

Sata died while seeking treatment in London on October 28, 2014. Scott became acting vice president until an election could be scheduled. Scott was ineligible to run for president because his parents were not born in Zambia. In November Edgar LUNGU was named as the PF candidate to serve out the remainder of Sata's term (see Political Parties, below).

In the presidential by-election on January 20, 2015, Lungu won with 48.3 percent of the vote, followed by Hichilema of the UPND, with 46.7 percent, and nine other candidates, none of whom received more than 1 percent of the vote. Lungu was inaugurated on January 25.

National elections were held on August 11, 2016. Lungu was reelected with 50.4 percent of the vote, followed again by Hichilema with 47.6, and seven other candidates. In concurrent legislative balloting, the PF won 80 seats, followed by the UPND with 58, and the MMD with 3, while independents won 14. Lungu named a reshuffled cabinet on September 14 that included two members of the MMD.

Constitution and government. Zambia's 1964 constitution was superseded by the adoption at a UNIP conference in August 1973 of a constitution of the "second republic" that reaffirmed the introduction in 1972 of a one-party system and further provided for the sharing of authority between the party and traditional organs of government. To further emphasize the role of the UNIP, its secretary general (rather than the prime minister) was designated the nation's second-ranking official.

On August 2, 1991, the National Assembly adopted a new constitution that provided for multiparty elections, a two-tiered parliament, abandonment of the post of prime minister in favor of a revived vice presidency, and a presidentially appointed cabinet. In 1993 President Chiluba named a 22-member commission to revise the 1991 document. Draft amendments, released in June 1995 in expectation of a constituent assembly and national referendum, were approved by the National Assembly on May 16, 1996, and by President Chiluba on May 28. The Constitution of Zambia Amendment Act 1996 limits participation in presidential polling to Zambian-born citizens whose parents were also born in Zambia, and it disqualifies traditional chiefs and anyone who has lived abroad during the previous 20 years. The chief executive is limited to two five-year terms.

The judiciary embraces a Supreme Court, a High Court, and various local courts. Administratively, the country is divided into nine provinces, including the city of Lusaka and its environs, which are subdivided into 55 districts.

Sata promised to introduce a new constitution within 90 days of assuming office in 2011. Sata appointed a technical committee to draft a new charter with submissions from the public. The committee began its work on December 2011, but the draft constitution was not approved. In January 2016 constitutional amendments were approved (see Current issues, below), which included requirements that presidents secure more than 50 percent of the vote or face runoff balloting and that members of parliament have a high school certificate. The amendments also established a constitutional court.

Zambia has a relatively free press, and in 2016, Reporters Without Borders ranked the country 114th out of 180 in media freedom, a dramatic decline from 93rd in 2014.

Foreign relations. While pursuing a generally nonaligned foreign policy (an 18-year coolness with Britain having been ended by a Kaunda state visit to London in 1983), Zambia consistently opposed racial discrimination in southern Africa and provided sanctuary for numerous exile groups engaged in guerrilla operations against white-controlled territories. Prior to the constitutional changes in South Africa, Zambia's prestige among Front-Line States was pronounced. In the wake of treaties concluded by Angola and Mozambique with South Africa, Lusaka became the headquarters of the African National Congress (ANC), making it a target for bomb attacks in May 1986 by South Africa forces, which also crossed the border on a "reconnaissance mission" in April 1987 that left several persons dead. Kaunda assumed the chair of the Front-Line grouping in early 1985, vowing to promote increased mutual support among member governments. In 1986 he denounced the United States and the United Kingdom for "conspiring" to support the South African government, warning they would share responsibility for the impending anti-apartheid "explosion." Zambia was also in the forefront of a regional plan to lessen reliance on South African trade routes that included rehabilitation of the Benguela Railway in Angola and the Tanzania-Zambia (Tanzam) link to Dar es Salaam. In other regional affairs, troops were at times deployed in border clashes with Malawi and Zaire, the latter agreeing in 1986 to a joint review and demarcation of disputed territory that yielded a settlement in 1989. (Disputes continued to erupt in 2005 at the border of the renamed Democratic Republic of the Congo, reportedly notorious for illegal crossings and smuggling.) In November 1989 a joint security commission was established with Mozambique in an attempt to thwart cross-border guerrilla activity.

Since its ascension to power in October 1991, the Chiluba government's foreign policy agenda was topped by relations with international creditors. In late 1991 the government negotiated a release of the aid allocations suspended in September when the Kaunda regime had allowed debt repayment and austerity programs to lapse. The government's decision to sever diplomatic ties with Iran and Iraq for their alleged financing of coup plotters against Chiluba was described in *Africa Confidential* as owing more to "fundamentalist Christian and anti-Muslim" tendencies within the administration than to substantive evidence of foreign involvement. Furthermore, the Chiluba government experienced slow progress in establishing relations with regional neighbors, many of whom were Kaunda supporters and had expressed distrust of the new administration's criticism of the ANC as well as of its links to South African commercial interests.

The Zambian assembly's approval of a controversial constitutional amendment bill in May 1996 provoked widespread disapproval from Zambia's Western donors, and in June a number of them suspended aid payments. Regionally, however, the Southern African Development Community (SADC) was described by observers as having adopted a "passive" position after the Chiluba government rebuffed its initial intervention efforts, and South Africa, the only SADC member considered powerful enough to influence Lusaka, refused to assume a leadership role.

Aid donors remained unwilling to restart payments through the first half of 1997; however, in July the suspension was partially lifted. Negotiations on further relaxation of payment restrictions were postponed after Lusaka imposed a state of emergency from October until March 1998. In May 1998 the World Bank agreed to a new aid package contingent on Lusaka enacting economic and political reforms; in particular, the bank pressed the government to speed privatization efforts and improve its human rights record.

Zambian–Angolan relations deteriorated in early 1999 as Luanda threatened military action against Zambia if Lusaka continued its alleged support for Angolan rebels. Thereafter, in a thinly veiled reference to Luanda, the Chiluba administration blamed "external forces" for a series of bombings in Lusaka. Later agreements between Luanda and Lusaka appeared to ease the tension, however, although a large Angolan refugee population subsequently continued to create difficulties for the Zambian government, as did an influx of refugees from fighting in the Democratic Republic of the Congo (formerly Zaire). A joint UN–Zambian program to repatriate Angolan refugees subsequently had substantial success, although there continued to be sporadic raids by Congolese rebels into Zambia. In response, the government increased border patrols.

In November 2004 the Zambian military launched a series of training exercises overseen by French military experts. The operations were part of a larger regional initiative through which France hoped to promote military cooperation among Tanzania, Zambia, and Zimbabwe that could lead, among other things, to joint regional humanitarian operations.

The final repatriation of some 34,500 Angola refugees was reported to be under way in 2005, though many were still living in camps in remote areas of Zambia in 2006.

Zambian opposition leader and 2006 PF presidential candidate Michael Sata was refused entry into Malawi in March 2007, reportedly on suspicion that he intended to help former Malawi president Elson Bakili Muluzi reorganize his former ruling United Democratic Front party. Sata denied the allegations. In June the Zambian government began revoking the refugee status of some 6,000 Rwandans who fled their war-torn country in the mid-1990s. Another 10,000 refugees from the Democratic Republic of the Congo also were urged to leave.

Chinese companies stepped up their investments in copper mining in Zambia in 2007, signing multimillion-dollar deals in exchange for significant tax concessions from the government. However, tension existed in relations at the popular level. In February workers at a Chinese-based company planned a large demonstration against China's president, resulting in his visit being canceled.

In 2008 Russia stepped up its economic interest in Zambia as three firms engaged in talks with President Mwanawasa over the possibility of investing $2 billion in Zambian mining projects. If successful, according to news accounts, this would amount to the country's single largest direct investment by a foreign entity.

Cordial relations with Malawi were marked in 2010 by cooperation meetings between the two countries' foreign ministers. China and Zambia agreed to "elevate" their bilateral relationship after a meeting in Beijing. Michael Sata rose to fame in 2006 on a tide of strong anti-Chinese rhetoric. But his tone has since softened, reportedly after the Chinese Embassy encouraged some companies to donate to the PF's 2011 campaign.

In August 2012 Zambia and Mozambique finalized a border demarcation project that clarified a number of disputed areas. The agreement was designed to improve border security and decrease the illegal movement of Zambians into Mozambique.

In April 2013 Zambia and Angola signed a defense cooperation agreement, following three years of negotiations. The accord called for increased intelligence cooperation and joint military maneuvers. In August, more than 1,000 workers from the Tanzania–Zambia Railway Authority were dismissed following a strike that stopped the flow of valuable minerals, including copper and magnesium.

Zambia, Malawi, and Mozambique signed a memorandum of understanding in early September 2014 for an environmental feasibility study to be completed before April 2015 on the Nsanje Inland Port before phase two of the project can begin. The port opened in October 2010 with funding from the African Development Bank, World Bank, European Union, and Government of Japan, but it has never been operational. The port will link the Shire and Zambezi Rivers, providing access for Malawi to Mozambican ports on the Indian Ocean. Angola and Zambia signed several agreements on September 25, 2014, on public safety and police issues in terms of cross-border crimes, the situation of the national prisoners, poaching, drug trafficking, and smuggling.

In March 2016 Zambia ratified the Minamata Convention on Mercury. In July Zambia withdrew recognition of the self-proclaimed Saharan Arab Democratic Republic (see entry on Morocco).

Current issues. In a move that was seen as potentially affecting the 2011 elections, the National Constitutional Conference in late June 2010 released another draft constitution, this one providing for a majoritarian system for electing a president—a system that had been rejected by the MMD in 2006. Meanwhile, Banda found himself facing criticism not only from the opposition but also from within the MMD. Much of the opposition focused on the president's ties to Chiluba, who, despite his earlier acquittal, was widely regarded as having stolen state funds. Opposition members claimed Banda's alliance with Chiluba effectively put a halt to anticorruption efforts. Dissension over the role of Chinese companies and workers escalated in October following an incident in which Chinese mine managers shot and wounded Zambian workers who were protesting against the conditions at a mine. Local residents have been concerned about loss of jobs to the immigrants following Chinese investment of more than $1 billion in the country. Presidential hopeful Michael Sata was said by observers to be courting the thousands of jobless youths in mining towns, where some 80 percent of voters lived. Late in the year three new political parties emerged as a platform from which their leaders launched presidential bids (see Other Parties and Groups under Political Parties, below).

Violence broke out in January 2011 when protesters and police clashed in a town west of the capital as the demonstrators demanded restoration of an agreement granting "half-independence" to the western province formerly known as the Barotseland. Sata, for his part, vowed to restore the Barotseland agreement of 1964 if elected. Meanwhile, the opposition was riven by fighting between the PF and the UPND, which failed to agree on supporting a single presidential candidate. In midyear Banda was spending significant amounts of money not included in the 2011 budget on roads and other infrastructure and in the poorest areas, which traditionally were strongholds of Sata and the PF. The death in June of former president Chiluba was seen as a blow to the Banda campaign, which was already marred by power struggles that resulted in the defections to the PF of several high-profile party members. It was not until July 28 that Banda announced the official date of September 20 for concurrent presidential, parliamentary, and local balloting, thus allowing only about 50 days of campaigning. In August the drawn-out process of writing a new constitution came to a halt after the new draft failed to win parliamentary approval. Observers cited the proposed majoritarian system for electing a president as among the key reasons for its demise.

In the run-up to the election, Banda was widely expected to be able to swing the vote. The MMD borrowed heavily to finance its campaign, which featured entertainers, lollipops, and thousands of free bicycles. Michael Sata ran on an anticorruption platform. The registration of 1.2 million new voters—overwhelmingly young and struggling—was believed to have played a significant role in the outcome. The participation of some 9,000 observers deployed by the Civil Society Election Coalition to monitor polls across the country played another. Analysts say the fact that Sata is Catholic, while Banda had fallen out with the Roman Catholic Church, also contributed. Sata defeated Banda in the balloting, and the PF won a plurality in the Assembly.

After the election, Sata set out to make good on campaign pledges to root out the massive corruption he alleged was going on under his predecessor and promised he would reinstate anticorruption measures that Banda's government had dismantled. He ordered police to confiscate the MMD's elections materials, including thousands of bicycles, until they could prove ownership and show they had paid taxes on them.

On March 14, 2012, the MMD was stripped of its legal status for failing to pay registration fees over the last two decades, an amount totaling roughly $70,000. The move was widely seen as engineered by Sata as a means to intimidate the MMD, and opposition officials complained of "an assault on democracy." In solidarity with the MMD, the UPND threatened to withdraw its 29 legislators from the parliament. On March 15, the MMD won a decision from the High Court to stay the cancelation of its registration.

On March 29, 2012, the BBC reported that the Barotse royal household and other Barotse leaders were demanding independence, accusing the government of ignoring a deal that granted the region semiautonomy. Government officials reportedly labeled the demand for independence "treason," even though Sata had initially claimed he would restore the agreement.

In September 2012 the government conducted a successful bond auction worth $750 million. The auction for the ten-year bonds demonstrated continued investor confidence in Zambia and provided funds for infrastructure and economic development programs. Meanwhile, Sata ended popular subsidies for fuel and corn in response to pressure from the World Bank.

In March 2013 the Assembly removed former president Banda's immunity from prosecution. Banda was subsequently arrested on corruption charges related to an oil arrangement with Nigeria. He was released on bail after his initial incarceration. Critics accused the government of targeting opposition leaders for arrest and intimidation. His trial was repeatedly delayed.

Concerns about Sata's health began mounting in Zambia when he traveled to Israel for medical treatment in June 2014 and then withdrew from the public eye. Sata visited New York in September to speak to the UN but canceled his appearance. Public speculation about Sata's poor health led to Vice President Scott declaring publicly that Sata was well. Meanwhile, the UN 2013 Hunger Report published the same month found that levels of undernourishment and malnourishment in Zambia are highest in Africa and second highest in the world.

A new draft constitution was finalized in 2014, but Sata's death prevented action on the document. Incoming president Lungu proposed amending the constitution through a two-stage process. The so-called "non-controversial" measures, including changes that required candidates to secure an absolute majority before being elected president and that allowed Zambians to hold dual citizenship, were approved by the legislature and implemented prior to the August 2016 general elections. The more contentious measures, including changes to the bill of rights, were put before voters in a constitutional referendum concurrent with national balloting. Voters approved the amendments by a margin of 71.1 percent to 28.9 percent. However, passage required a turnout rate of 50 percent. Because only 44.4 percent of voters participated in the referendum, its results were nullified.

POLITICAL PARTIES

In December 1972 the United National Independence Party (UNIP) became the country's only legal political party. During the late 1980s reformists called for a multiparty system, with President Kaunda repeatedly dismissing the idea as unworkable because of "too many tribal conflicts." However, in September 1990 he bowed to mounting pressure and agreed to termination of the UNIP monopoly. Three months later, the president signed a National Assembly bill legalizing the formation of political parties, and in August 1991 a multiparty constitution was adopted. Thereafter, on October 31 the UNIP, the Movement for Multiparty Democracy (MMD), and 12 smaller parties participated in the first multiparty balloting since 1968.

Several parties formed electoral alliances in advance of the 2006 presidential and parliamentary elections. The United Party for National Development (UPND), UNIP, and Forum for Democracy and Development (FDD) formed the United Democratic Alliance (UDA). A coalition of smaller parties, styled the National Democratic Focus (NDF), included the Zambia Republican Party (ZRP), Zadeco, and the Zambia Direct Democracy Movement (ZDDM).

Government Party:

Patriotic Front—PF. The PF was formed in 2001 by disgruntled former MMD members, including Michael Sata, who resigned as MMD (below) secretary general in September to protest what he described as the irregular method of selection of Levy Mwanawasa as the MMD's standard-bearer. Sata was credited with 3.4 percent of the vote in the 2001 presidential poll.

In 2005 Sata, a staunch critic of President Mwanawasa, was charged with alleged espionage for supporting striking mine workers, and in 2006 Sata and party secretary general Guy Scott were charged with defaming the president after Sata allegedly leaked a letter written by President Mwanawasa. Sata claimed the letter was a forgery and a "trap."

Sata's supporters engaged in violent protests when initial reports of his 2006 presidential victory were determined to be wrong. Riots occurred mainly in the Copperbelt, where Sata was regarded as a hero because of his battle for the rights of miners. Sata made headlines during the campaign by saying that if elected he would expel Chinese investors from the mining industry in Zambia and would promote ties with Taiwan, angering Chinese officials. In December 2006 Sata was arrested on charges of "false declaration of assets" in connection with documents he had filed in his election bid. The charges were dropped a few days later.

In 2008 the Supreme Court nullified three of the PF's parliamentary seats following a ruling that the seats had not been won fairly. In the run-up to the 2008 presidential by-election, a rift in the party developed in May after Sata dismissed some 20 party members who had attended a government-sponsored conference on proposed revisions to the constitution, which the PF officially opposed. The disaffected PF members were said to have joined the camp of Peter MACHUNGWA, a former minister in the Chiluba government, who had rejoined the PF in 2006. Presidential candidate Sata ruled out a proposed electoral alliance with the UPND to back the candidacy of Hakainde Hichilema, saying the PF was strong enough to win on its own. Two days before the October 30 by-election, 300 members of the PF reportedly resigned to join the MMD.

However, in advance of the 2011 elections, the PF and the UPND in 2009 agreed to an electoral alliance to challenge the MMD.

In February 2009 Secretary General Edward MUMBI resigned from the party in the wake of what he called "weird allegations" against him leveled by Sata. Following the 2008 elections, Sata had accused Mumbi of accepting a bribe to derail the PF's presidential campaign. Mumbi, for his part, said Sata failed to provide donated resources to rural areas to ensure PF success in the election, and he blamed Sata for the party's loss.

In advance of the 2011 elections, party members were pressing for Sata to be their presidential candidate, despite the PF's alliance with the UPND. Meanwhile, Mumbi accused the party of being connected to the "red card" campaign (see Current Issues, above), but party officials denied it. The party secured 60 seats in the 2011 balloting, and Sata won the presidency. He chose Guy SCOTT, a well-known moderate within the party, as his vice president. Scott was barred from succeeding Sata since he was not born in Zambia, leading observers to speculate that the president chose Scott so he could ensure that the vice-president did not emerge as a future political rival. The party's secretary general Wynter KABIMBA, one of Sata's closest confidants, is reportedly working to build a base in the party, seeking to take over its leadership in 2016. Opposition parties accused Kabimba of attempting to create a one-party state after he launched an aggressive campaign to lure opposition lawmakers to the PF. In 2013 rumors of President Sata's poor health sparked a leadership rivalry between then Defense Minister Geoffrey MWAMBA and then Justice Minister Wynter Kabimba. The power struggle escalated, and on August 28, 2014, Sata removed Kabimba as justice minister and expelled him from the party. PF won three of the five September 11, 2014, by-elections.

Since the death of Sata on October 28, 2014, divisions within the party over succession have developed between two factions. On November 3 Scott dismissed Lungu as secretary general but then reinstated him following riots. On November 14 the PF central committee endorsed Edgar LUNGU as presidential candidate for the party. However, Scott declared that only the party general conference can make such an endorsement. Scott was subsequently suspended as the PF leader on November 21, and Lungu won the January 2015 presidential election and was reelected during general elections in August 2016. In that balloting, the PF won 42 percent of the vote and 80 seats in the assembly.

Leaders: Edgar LUNGU (President of the Republic and President of the Party), Inonge WINA (Vice President of the Republic), Guy SCOTT (Former Acting President of the Republic), Given LUBINDA (Spokesperson).

Other Legislative Parties:

Movement for Multiparty Democracy—MMD. Formed in mid-1990 as a loose alliance of anti-UNIP groups in support of a voter registration drive, the MMD applied for legal party status immediately following legislative approval of a multiparty system in December. Among other things, the group issued a manifesto declaring its commitment to a free-market economy.

In June 1991 the MMD denounced a proposed draft constitution on the grounds that it would advance an excessively powerful presidency; the party threatened to boycott upcoming elections if it were adopted. Consequently, President Kaunda met in July with MMD leaders to forge a compromise document. Meanwhile, violent clashes between MMD and UNIP supporters continued, and in September the MMD complained that limiting the campaign period to two months favored the incumbents. Nevertheless, in the October 31 balloting Frederick Chiluba of the MMD defeated Kaunda's bid for reelection, with the MMD also winning an overwhelming majority of National Assembly seats. Subsequently, in sparsely attended balloting in late November 1992, the party captured nearly 75 percent of 1,190 local council seats.

In early 1993 a growing interparty chasm was reported between those members urging faster governmental reform and a second, reportedly more influential faction, which was concerned less with reform and more with "strengthening the political and financial interests of the... commercial class." Founding member and party chair Arthur Wina was one of 14 prominent MMD officials who withdrew from the grouping in August to protest the dismissal of cabinet ministers identified as having exposed corruption and drug trafficking by their colleagues. Thereafter, more members left the party as its popularity plummeted amid allegations that top officials were sheltered from the effects of the government's economic austerity program. On the other hand, in November 1993 Enoch Kavindele, leader of the **United Democratic Party** (UDP), dissolved his party and joined the MMD, claiming that he and Chiluba shared similar development strategies.

Internal friction, based in part on tribal differences as well as the personal ambition of various MMD leaders, was reported throughout the rest of the 1990s, although the party retained solid political control at both the national and local levels. Fractionalization reached its apex in early 2000 when it became apparent that President Chiluba's supporters were intent on constitutional revision that would permit him a third term. Some 400 delegates walked out of the MMD congress in Lusaka at the end of April to protest the initiative; however, the remaining delegates dutifully endorsed Chiluba as the MMD candidate in the upcoming presidential race, calling for a national referendum on the proposed constitutional change. In the wake of massive protest demonstrations, Chiluba several days later announced he had decided not to seek a third term, but at the same time more than 20 senior members of the MMD (including some 11 cabinet members) were expelled from the party, some of them subsequently helping to form new opposition parties.

In August 2001 Levy Mwanawasa, a prominent attorney and former vice president of the republic, was selected as the new MMD standard-bearer. Critics initially described Mwanawasa as Chiluba's hand-picked successor, but tension was apparent between the two MMD leaders following Mwanawasa's controversial victory in the national balloting, the new president, among other things, reportedly rejecting Chiluba's suggestions for cabinet appointments. In 2002 Chiluba was forced to resign as party president, resulting in Mwanawasa becoming acting president. According to some reports, Mwanawasa subsequently was unanimously elected as party president on the understanding that he would not prosecute Chiluba. After thousands of protesters demanded that Parliament lift Chiluba's immunity, the president made the same request. Following Chiluba's arrest on corruption charges in 2003, his supporters defected from the MMD and formed the PUDD (below).

The National Citizens' Coalition (NCC), sometimes referred to as the National Christian Coalition, merged with the MDD after the MDD's leader, prominent pastor Nevers Mumba, was appointed vice president in 2003. (Mumba had run for the presidency in 2001 but had received only 2.2 percent of the vote.) In October 2004 Mumba was dismissed as vice president following his comments accusing opposition parties of taking funds from foreign sources. He was forced to leave the party in 2005 after he reportedly accused President Mwanawasa and his wife of using government money to buy party convention votes, and subsequently supported opposition candidate Michael Sata of the PF in the 2006 presidential election.

Although Mwanawasa won the party leadership by a landslide in 2005, providing him a mandate to seek a second term as president of the republic in 2006, rifts in the party were reported among rivals who campaigned against him. Following Mwanawasa's decisive victory in 2006, the party appeared to rally behind Mwanawasa and the reforms he proposed.

Former ZRP Secretary General Sylvia MASEBO, then minister of local government and housing, defected to the MMD in June 2006.

Rifts in the party reappeared in 2008 as Mwanawasa lay ill in a Paris hospital. While some in the party suggested that a search for a successor begin, the idea was soundly rejected by others. The party had no vice president to tap as a successor to Mwanawasa (the party congress having canceled an election for the seat in the wake of reports of alleged vote-buying by candidates). Additionally, some of the party's other possible contenders, specifically Michael Mabenga and Katele Kalumba, the latter a finance minister under former President Chiluba, were tainted by allegations of corruption. The party was also divided over the selection of a presidential candidate, as 19 members sought to be the standard-bearer. Ultimately, Vice President Rupiah Banda, a former member of the UNIP, who, MMD leaders claimed, had joined the MMD "a long time ago," was chosen on September 5 as the party's presidential nominee over six others, including Finance Minister Ngandu Magande.

Despite President Banda's weak victory over the PF's Michael Sata in the October 2008 by-election, in June 2009 the party endorsed Banda for reelection in the 2011 poll. Banda pledged to strengthen the party in advance of the elections; however, corruption and infighting marked events in 2010. National Secretary Kalumba was convicted, along with two others, of corruption and sentenced to five years in prison, and former defense minister George Mpombo and former finance minister Magande were forced to resign after their alleged "outbursts" against President Banda. Magande subsequently formed a new party, the National Movement for Progress (NMP). Ahead of the 2011 presidential election, Banda, under pressure from his sons, fired his longtime friend and ally, Vernon MWAANGA, as his campaign manager after Mwaanga nominated two people for party posts in opposition to the two nominees Banda preferred. The firing of Mwaanga, the defection to the PF of several high-ranking party members in protest against Mwaanga's sacking, and the death in June of former president Chiluba were seen as considerable blows to Banda's reelection effort. Within party circles Henry and James Banda, the president's sons, received much of the blame for their father's defeat in the 2011 elections. Following the balloting, several MMD deputies in the Assembly defected to the PF, prompting a wave of by-elections. On May 25, 2012, Nevers MUMBA was elected the fourth president of the party.

In 2014 senior members of the party rebelled against Mumba, including two vice presidents, Brian CHITUWO and Michael KAINGU. In April 2014 members called for Rubiah BANDA, former president of the republic and party leader, to be reinstated. In the by-elections on September 11, 2014, MMD took the Kasenengwa seat, losing the four others.

Mumba declared his candidacy for the 2015 presidential by-election, but the MMD executive committee endorsed former president Banda and attempted to expel Mumba. Mumba appealed to the Supreme Court, which ruled in his favor. He then expelled several leading figures in the party who had opposed him. The infighting split the party into three groups. One faction supported the PF's Lungu, while another backed Hichilema of the UPND, and the third endorsed Mumba, who was fourth in the January 20, 2015, balloting with just 0.9 percent of the vote.

The party's troubles spilled over into the 2016 general elections, when the party did not have a formal candidate for the presidential election and won only 2.7 percent of the vote in the assembly balloting and three seats. Two members of the MMD were given cabinet posts in the subsequent PF government.

Leaders: Nevers Sekwila MUMBA (President), Kabinga PANDE (National Chair), Muhabi LUNGI (National Secretary).

United Party for National Development—UPND. Described as representing the interests of urbanized Zambians, the UPND was launched on December 1998 under the leadership of business leader Anderson Mazoka, who had recently left the MMD. The party quickly became a major opposition grouping, winning four of the six legislative by-elections it had contested as of mid-2000. Mazoka, running with the support of the National Party, secured an official 26.8 percent of the vote in the 2001 presidential balloting, although his supporters charged he had actually won the election and challenged the results in court. Meanwhile, the UPND easily became the leading opposition party by securing 49 seats in the concurrent legislative balloting.

Following Mazoka's death in 2006, a rift developed in the party, with members from the Southern Province backing Mazoka's widow as successor while party officials approached ZCTU president Leonard HIKAUMBA over the party's acting president, Sakwiba SIKOTA. After the party's divisive and chaotic convention in July, in which Lusaka businessman (and Mazoka protégé) Hakainde Hichilema was elected president, Sikota resigned (along with party vice president Robert SICHINGA and secretary general Logan SHEMENA), and he subsequently formed the United Liberal Party (ULP). Sikota blamed "tribalism and violence" for the party's election upheaval, though the election was declared fair by the Foundation for Democratic Process (FODEP). Sikota's departure reportedly left the party in disarray, with party vice president for economic and political affairs Patrick Chisanga trying to mend fences. Following Hichilema's failed bid for the presidency in 2006, the UDA faced a rift with FDD leader Edith Nawakwi over whether Hichilmena would automatically be the UDA's candidate for the next presidential election in 2011.

The UPND was unsuccessful in persuading the PF's Michael Sata to participate in an electoral alliance with the UPND and back Hichilema in the 2008 by-election. Meanwhile, Hichilema caused a rift in the party as a result of his trip to China in May to sign a cooperation agreement with the Chinese Communist Party, since China was seen as being a key supporter of the MMD government.

In 2009 the UPND called on parliament to repeal a public procurement act adopted a year earlier and replace it with one that had stronger anti-corruption measures. Though the UPND and the PF had agreed to an electoral alliance to challenge the MMD in the 2011 presidential election, rifts developed in 2010 over who should be the standard-bearer, with Hichilema unwilling to give ground to the PF's Sata and declaring himself a candidate. Further, some 250 members were said to have defected to the MMD.

In March 2011 it was reported that the UPND had entered into an alliance with the small APC (below). Ahead of the September election, Hichilema pledged to create more jobs, invest in education, and uphold the public trust. He placed third in the balloting with 18.4 percent of the vote. In 2013 Hichilema was charged with a series of crimes, including corruption and unlawful assembly.

In February 2013 the UPND expelled Assembly deputy Greyford MONDE after he became deputy agriculture minister in the PF-led government. UPND won all four seats in the local government by-elections held in the four districts of Southern Province on August 19, 2014. In the September 11, 2014, by-elections, UPND won the Solwezi Central seat, losing the four others.

Hichilema was the party's candidate in the 2015 presidential by-election. He was second with 46.7 percent of the vote. Hichilema again represented the UPND in the 2016 balloting, placing second with 47.6 percent of the vote. The party won 41.7 percent of the vote in the assembly polling, securing 58 seats and becoming the largest opposition faction.

Leaders: Hakainde HICHILEMA (President of the Party and 2006, 2008, 2011, 2015, and 2016 presidential candidate), Geoffrey Bwalya MWAMBA (Vice President), Charles KAKOMA (Spokesperson), Winston CHIBWE (Secretary General).

Forum for Democracy and Development—FDD. Reportedly enjoying support among students and other urban dwellers, the FDD was launched in 2001 by former MMD members opposed to efforts by President Chiluba to run for a third term. Party founders included Lt. Gen. Christon Tembo, who had been dismissed as vice president of the republic by Chiluba in May. Tembo finished third in the 2001 presidential balloting, securing 13 percent of the vote according to the official results. The FDD expelled four members in 2003 after they accepted cabinet posts in the MMD-led government. Several other FDD members subsequently left the party and joined the MMD. Former finance minister Edith Nawakwi was elected party president in 2005.

The FDD did not participate in the 2008 by-election, and in March 2009 Tembo died.

In 2010 party vice president Chifumu Bandu was chair of the country's National Constitutional Commission when it released its draft charter for public review. In March the party chastised Nawakwi for her repeated verbal attacks against President Banda, stating that they were her personal views and not those of the party. Nawakwi was the party's 2011 presidential candidate. She received less than 1 percent of the vote. The party secured one seat in the 2011 elections. In September 2014 FDD rejected the Electoral Commission of Zambia's decision to transmit the Kansenegwa and Vubwi by-election results electronically. The party called the pilot project suspicious.

Nawakwi was third in the 2015 presidential by-election, with 0.9 percent of the vote, and third in 2016, with 0.7 percent. The party won

2.2 percent of the vote in the 2016 parliamentary elections and one seat.

Leaders: Edith NAWAKWI (Party President and 2011, 2015, and 2016 presidential candidate), Chifumu BANDA (Vice President), Levy NGOMA (Youth Chair).

Other Parties That Contested the 2015 or 2016 Elections:

United National Independence Party—UNIP. The UNIP was formed as a result of the 1958 withdrawal of Kenneth D. Kaunda, Simon M. Kapwepwe, and others from the preindependence African National Congress (ANC), led by Harry Nkumbula. The UNIP was banned by the British in March 1959, reconstituted the following October, and ruled Zambia from independence until October 1991.

On May 29, 1990, in announcing that the National Council had approved the holding of a referendum on multipartyism, President Kaunda stated that it would be "stupid" for the party not to explain to the public that approval of such a system would be equivalent to "courting national disaster." Nevertheless, at the 25th meeting of the UNIP National Council on September 24, 1990, Kaunda announced that referendum plans would be canceled and a multiparty constitution adopted prior to the 1991 poll.

At an extraordinary party congress held August 6–7, 1991, Kaunda faced a leadership challenge from businessman Enoch Kavindele; however, under pressure from party stalwarts, Kavindele withdrew his bid, and Kaunda won unanimous reelection as party president. Thereafter, in nationwide balloting on October 31, both Kaunda and the UNIP suffered resounding defeats, the former capturing only 24 percent of the presidential vote and the latter being limited to 26 assembly seats. In the wake of his electoral defeat, Kaunda resigned as party leader on January 6, 1992, but reversed himself four months later.

Fueled by the defection of a number of party members to Kavindele's newly formed United Democratic Party (UDP) and the UNIP's poor showing in local elections in November 1992, speculation mounted in early 1993 that Kebby Musoktwane, who had been elected party president at an extraordinary congress on October 1, would be supplanted by Maj. Wezi Kaunda, head of the UNIP's military wing and son of the former president. However, Wezi Kaunda, along with his two brothers, Tilyenji Kaunda and Panji KAUNDA, were among approximately 25 people, including 7 UNIP central committee members, arrested in March 1993 on charges stemming from an alleged coup plot. For its part, the party denied charges that it had planned to overthrow the Chiluba administration, with Musoktwane insisting that he had aided the government in exposing the plot.

In June 1993 former president Kaunda resigned from the party, citing a desire to become "father" to all Zambians and complaining that he had been denied a pension by the Chiluba government. In March 1994 approximately 85 members of the now defunct UDP rejoined the UNIP. (Prior to its dissolution in late 1993 UDP membership had been dominated by UNIP defectors.) In June 1994 the UNIP was instrumental in the formation of the **Zambia Opposition Front** (Zofro), an opposition umbrella organization that included the **Independent Democratic Front** (IDF), led by Mike KAIRA; the **Labour Party** (LP), led by Chipeza MUFUNE; the National **Democratic Alliance** (NDA), led by Yonam PHIRI (the NDA was reportedly deregistered in 1998); the **National Party for Democracy** (NPD), led by Tenthani MWANZA; and the **Zambia Progressive** Party (ZPP).

Although Kaunda's decision in May 1995 to return to political life was coolly received by Musoktwane and his youthful supporters, the former president encountered little difficulty in being reelected to the UNIP presidency on June 28. Kaunda continued to enjoy broad party support throughout 1995 and the first half of 1996 despite intensive government efforts to discredit him. However, in June 1996 former party secretary general Benjamin Mibenge called for an extraordinary UNIP congress to elect a new leader, asserting, according to *Africa Confidential,* that it was time to break "the myth that Dr. Kaunda can forever lead the party." Meanwhile, the government arrested seven people (including Kaunda) with ties to the UNIP, charging them with complicity in a wave of bombings and bomb threats allegedly masterminded by a terrorist group called *Black Mamba,* Kaunda's nickname during Zambia's independence drive.

In early October 1996 Zofro announced it would back single candidates in the upcoming legislative balloting. Meanwhile, Kaunda declared his intention of running for president again despite the recent controversial amendment that appeared to have disqualified him. However, later in the month the UNIP announced plans to boycott the legislative balloting, citing what it described as the "mismanagement" of the voter registration drive and charging the government with manipulating the constitution. Furthermore, Kaunda asserted that the continued imprisonment of six prominent party members on treason charges had undermined the UNIP's electoral preparations. The charges were dropped on November 1. (Charges against Kaunda had been dismissed earlier.)

In April 1997 a simmering intraparty rivalry between Kaunda's supporters and members opposed to his continued domination exploded into public view as the two groups clashed at a UNIP function. Internecine concerns were subsequently overshadowed, however, by violent encounters between the UNIP and supporters of the Chiluba government. In June the UNIP and its opposition allies called for foreign intervention to ease the political and social "crisis" gripping Lusaka. Two months later Kaunda accused the government of attempting to assassinate him and Roger Chongwe, leader of the **Liberal Progressive Front** (LPF), a small party allied with the UNIP.

In January 1998 Kaunda was indicted by the government for his alleged role in the October 1997 coup attempt. The UNIP president was held under house arrest until June 1, when the government, under intense international pressure, dropped the charges. In June Kaunda said he would retire from the UNIP, although he agreed to serve as party president on an acting basis until his successor was elected. Subsequently, members of the UNIP's youth wing were reported to have rallied behind the succession ambitions of Wezi Kaunda. However, Wezi died in November 1999 after being attacked by gunmen in his driveway.

Kaunda officially retired from the UNIP presidency at the beginning of an extraordinary congress in Ndola in May 2000. He was succeeded by Francis NKHOMA, a former central bank governor, although severe factionalization was subsequently still reported in the party, particularly in regard to the new president's positive comments about potential cooperation with the MMD, of which he had been a member from 1990 to 1994. Tilyenji Kaunda was elected to the UNIP presidency in April 2001 and won almost 10 percent of the votes in the December presidential election. In 2003 the UNIP announced it would cooperate with the ruling MMD, and UNIP legislators were appointed to junior cabinet posts. Following President Mwanawasa's reelection in 2006, he appointed former UNIP representative in Europe and former cabinet minister Rupiah Banda as vice president of the republic.

The party claimed in September 2008 that Vice President Rupiah Banda had never officially resigned from the UNIP, even though Banda was on the ballot as the MMD's candidate for president. However, Kaunda threw his support behind Banda's candidacy because, observers said, he felt Banda would be more sympathetic to the UNIP than would Sata. In mid-October the party officially announced its endorsement of Banda's candidacy.

In April 2009 the UNIP and the UPND condemned the PF's plans for a protest demonstration against job losses in the Copperbelt, arguing that the demonstration would not resolve the issue, and that it was not necessary to blame the government when the global economic downturn was the cause. Secretary General Alfred Banda resigned from the party in 2009 in a dispute regarding the UNIP's not having held a national congress.

In 2010 some 100 members defected to the PF. Meanwhile, party leader Kaunda announced that he would seek the presidency in the 2011 poll and subsequently secured the party's nomination. He placed fifth in the balloting with less than 1 percent of the vote, while the UNIP secured 28 seats in the Assembly. Although UNIP lost the Mangango region by-elections in August 2014, party officials insisted the party was still active and vital.

Kaunda was fifth in the 2015 presidential by-election, with 0.6 percent of the vote, and seventh in the 2016 polling, with 0.2 percent. In the 2016 legislative polling, the UNIP secured 0.2 percent of the vote and no seats.

Leaders: Tilyenji KAUNDA (President and 2001 and 2011 presidential candidate), Njekwa ANAMELA (Vice Chair), Jemima BANDA (Secretary General).

Other parties that unsuccessfully contested the 2015 or 2016 balloting (none received more than 1 percent of the vote in either presidential or legislative balloting) included the **Rainbow Party**, formed in 2014 and led by 2016 presidential candidate Wynter KABIMBA; the **United Democratic**

Front; the **Golden Progressive Party**; the **Radical Revolutionary Party**; the **Green Party of Zambia**; and the **United Progressive Party.**

Other Parties and Groups:

Zambia Republican Party—ZRP. The formation of the ZRP was announced in February 2001 as a merger of the **Zambia Alliance for Progress** (ZAP), the **Republican Party** (RP), and the small **National Republican Party** (NRP).

The RP, with support centered in the Copperbelt, had been founded in mid-2000 by wealthy businessman Ben MWILA and a number of his supporters following their expulsion from the MMD. (Mwila had incurred the wrath of other MMD leaders by indicating a desire to run for president of the republic while a possible third term for President Chiluba was still under consideration.)

Both Mwila and Dean MUNGOMBA of the ZAP announced their presidential ambitions prior to the creation of the ZRP, and friction quickly materialized between the two. Consequently, Mungomba announced that he and his supporters were withdrawing from the ZRP to resume ZAP activity, although a number of former ZAP members remained in the new grouping.

Mwila was officially credited with 4.84 percent of the vote as the ZRP candidate in the 2001 presidential poll. Among other things, the ZRP platform called for increased privatization of state-run enterprises and the extension of agricultural subsidies.

In June 2006 a faction that included about 15 members, led by Party Secretary General Shirley Masebo, defected to the MMD.

Reports in 2011 indicated that Mwila ran unsuccessfully as an independent in that year's Assembly balloting.

Leaders: Benjamin Yorum MWILA (President and 2001 presidential candidate), Ben KAPITA (Chair).

Zambia Direct Democracy Movement—ZDDM. The ZDDM joined the NDF in 2006. In 2008 party leader Edwin Sakala urged a government of national unity prior to the October 30 by-election.

The party turned its focus in 2010 to fighting poverty and disease and began its own "white card" campaign to promote national progress.

Party leader Edwin Sakala withdrew from the national presidential race in August 2011. The ZDDM received less than 1 percent of the vote in the 2011 Assembly balloting. In September 2014 ZDDM prepared to join the PF-sponsored Development Bank of Zambia (DBZ) money demonstration despite remaining in strong opposition to the ruling party.

Leaders: Edwin SAKALA (Chair), Maurice CHOONGO (Spokesperson).

Heritage Party—HP. The HP was formed in 2001 by Brig. Gen. Godfrey Miyanda, a former MMD stalwart and former vice president of the republic, who had left the ruling party in the dispute over a proposed third term for President Chiluba. He rejected pressure to join with the FDD; subsequently, some FDD and MDD members reportedly defected to the HP in 2001. Miyanda secured 8 percent of the vote in the 2001 presidential balloting, according to official results, and the party gained 4 seats in the legislative balloting. In 2006 the HP and the AC entered into an alliance in which the AC agreed not present a presidential candidate and to support the candidate put forth by the HP. Also, candidates in parliamentary and local elections in 2006 ran under the HP banner, according to the agreement between the HP and the AC.

Miyanda was tapped as the party's flag bearer for the 2011 presidential election. He received 0.2 percent of the vote, while the HP secured just 0.02 percent of the vote in concurrent legislative polling. In August 2014 Sata's government rejected Miyanda's request that Sata's cabinet be impeached for not constituting a medical board to examine Sata amid persistent rumors of the president's poor health.

Leader: Brig. Gen. Godfrey MIYANDA (Former Vice President of the Republic and 2001, 2006, 2008, and 2011 presidential candidate).

All People's Congress—APC. Formed in 2005, the APC's stated goal was to "set the Zambian political life on a new course for the future," striving for economic progress and social justice. The APC briefly joined the NDF in March 2006 but subsequently withdrew over reported tribal differences. Some reports said that APC leader Ken NGONDO was expelled from the NDF.

Ngondo, a businessman and former member of parliament, finished last in the 2006 presidential balloting with less than 1 percent of the vote.

The APC backed Rupiah Banda in the 2008 presidential election. Party leader Ngondo died in November 2010.

In 2011 the APC failed to secure any seats in the Assembly balloting.

Leaders: Nason MSONI (President), Maggy NGONA.

New Generation Party—NGP. Former FDD youth leader Humphrey SIULAPWA formed the NGP in 2003 to address issues of youth, in particular. Siulapwa registered as a presidential candidate in 2006 but subsequently withdrew because of the high entry fee required. The party fielded parliamentary candidates in 2006 but failed to win any seats.

The NGP endorsed Banda in the 2008 and 2011 elections. It received less than 1 percent of the vote in the 2011 legislative balloting.

Leader: Humphrey SIULAPWA.

Other parties participating in the 2011 elections were the **Citizens Democratic Party** (CDP); **Zambians for Empowerment and Development** (ZED), led by Frederick MUTESA, who received 0.1 percent of the vote in the presidential balloting; the **National Revolution Party** (NRP), headed by Cosmo MUMBA, formerly of the NGP, and Kelly WALUBITA; the **United Party for Democracy and Development** (UPDD), formed by dissidents from the UPND and led by Felix SENKA; the **Federal Democratic Party**; the **New Generation Party**, led by Cosmo MUMBA; and the **Zambia Conservative Party** (ZCP), led by Joseph CHIPILI and Peter SIMPEMBA. For information on **United Liberal Party** (ULP) and **Alliance for Democracy and Development** (ADD), see the 2014 *Handbook*.

Three parties or groupings that formed ahead of the 2011 elections and provided platforms for their leaders to run for president were: the **National Restoration Party** (NAREP), founded in March 2010 by Elias CHIPIMO Jr. with the goal of providing quality services to all Zambians; and the **National Movement for Progress** (NMP), founded in September 2010 by former finance minister Ngandu Magande, a fierce critic of Banda, after Magande was expelled from the MMD. The **Mega Combination** *(Mega Combinate*—MC) was launched prior to the 2010 election as a four-party coalition supportive of Désiré BOUTERSE's bid for the presidency.

Minor parties include the **Common Cause Democracy** (CCD), led by James MTONGA; the **New Congress Party** (NCP), led by Cosmas MWALE and Secretary General John CHIBOMA; the **Progressive Parties Alliance** (PPA), led by Paul BANDA; the **United Nationalist Party** (UNP), led by Achim NGOSA; the **United Poor People of Zambia Freedom Party** (UPPZFP), led by Alex MULIOKELA; and the **People's Democratic Party** (PDP), formed in 2013 and led by George MPOMBO.

For more information on the **United Democratic Alliance** (UDA), which participated in the 2006 and 2008 elections but is now defunct, see the 2013 *Handbook*. Also see the 2013 *Handbook* for more details on the defunct **National Democratic Focus** (NDF), an alliance of smaller parties, initially referenced as the **National Democratic Front** and formed prior to the 2006 presidential election. For information on the **Barotse Patriotic Front** (BPF), the **Agenda for Change** (AC), and the **National Leadership for Development** (NLD), see the 2015 *Handbook*.

LEGISLATURE

The current **National Assembly** is a unicameral body consisting of 150 elected members, six presidentially appointed members, and the speaker, who is elected by the members of the assembly from outside their membership. The term of office is five years. Prior to the 1991 election, candidates were required to be members of the United National Independence Party (UNIP) and endorsed by that party's Central Committee. Following the most recent elections on August 11, 2016, the seat distribution was as follows: Patriotic Front, 80 seats; United Party for National Development, 58; Movement for Multiparty Democracy, 3; Forum for Democracy and Development, 1; and independents, 14.

Speaker: Patrick MATIBINI.

CABINET

[as of October 25, 2016]

President	Edgar Lungu
Vice President	Inonge Wina [f]
Ministers	
Agriculture and Livestock	Dora Siliya [f]
Chiefs and Traditional Affairs	Lawrence John Sichalwe

Commerce, Trade, and Industry	Margaret Mwanakatwe [f]
Communication and Transport	Brian Mushimba
Community Development and Mother and Child Health	Emerine Kabanshi [f]
Defense	Davis Chama
Energy	David Mabumba
Finance and National Planning	Felix Mutati (MMD)
Foreign Affairs	Harry Kalaba
Gender	Victoria Kalima [f]
General Education	Dennis Musuku Wachinga
Health	Chitalu Chilufya
Higher Education	Nkandu Luo [f]
Home Affairs	Steven Kampyongo
Information and Broadcasting	Chishimba Kambwili
Justice	Given Lubinda
Labor and Social Security	Joyce Nonde-Simukoko [f]
Lands	Jean Kapata [f]
Livestock and Fisheries	Micheal Zondani Katambo
Local Government and Housing	Vincent Mwale (MMD)
Mines, Energy, and Water Development	Christopher Yaluma
National Development Planning	Lucky Mulusa
Sport and Youth	Moses Mawere
Tourism and the Arts	Charles Romel Banda
Works and Supply	Ronald Kaoma Chitotela

[f] = female

Note: All of the above are members of the Patriotic Front unless noted.

INTERGOVERNMENTAL REPRESENTATION

Ambassador to the U.S.: Palan MULONDA.

U.S. Ambassador to Zambia: Eric SCHULTZ.

Permanent Representative to the UN: Mwaba Patricia KASESE-BOTA.

IGO Memberships (Non-UN): AfDB, AU, Comesa, CWTH, IOM, NAM, SADC, WTO.

For Further Reference:

Baldwin, Kate. *The Paradox of Traditional Chiefs in Democratic Africa.* Cambridge: Cambridge University Press, 2015.

Posner, Daniel N. *Institutions and Ethnic Politics in Africa.* Cambridge: Cambridge University Press, 2005.

Sardanis, Andrew. *Zambia: The First 50 Years.* London: I. B. Taurus, 2014.

ZIMBABWE

Political Status: Became self-governing British Colony of Southern Rhodesia in October 1923; unilaterally declared independence November 11, 1965; white-dominated republican regime proclaimed March 2, 1970; biracial executive established on basis of transitional government agreement of March 3, 1978; returned to interim British rule on basis of cease-fire agreement signed December 21, 1979; achieved de jure independence as Republic of Zimbabwe on April 18, 1980; new constitution approved by referendum on March 16, 2013, and adopted on May 22.

Area: 150,803 sq. mi. (390,580 sq. km).

Population: 15,967,000 (2016E—UN); 14,546,961 (2016E—U.S. Census).

Major Urban Center (2016E—UN): HARARE (formerly Salisbury, 1,511,000).

Official Language: English (Shona and Sindebele are the principal African languages).

Monetary Unit: U.S. Dollar (see U.S. article for principal exchange rates). Although the Zimbabwe dollar had an official exchange rate, the currency was suspended in 2009 because of hyperinflation, and the currency was demonetised in September 2015 (see Current issues, below). By 2015 Zimbabwean dollars were officially worth about 35 quadrillion to $1. The South African rand, the Botswana pula, the U.S. dollar, the Indian rupee, Japanese yen, Australian dollar, the Chinese yuan, and the British pound are now commonly used.

President: Robert Gabriel MUGABE (Zimbabwe African National Union–Patriotic Front); sworn in as prime minister on April 18, 1980, following legislative election of February 14 and 27–29; reconfirmed following election of June 30 and July 1–2, 1985; elected president by parliament on December 30, 1987, and inaugurated for an anticipated six-year term on December 31, succeeding the former head of state, Rev. Canaan Sodindo BANANA; reelected for a six-year term, following constitutional revision, by popular vote March 28–30, 1990; reelected for another six-year term March 16–17, 1996; reelected for another six-year term March 9–11, 2002; reelected in a disputed runoff on June 27, 2008, and sworn in for a five-year term on June 29; reelected in disputed balloting on July 31, 2013, and sworn in for another five-year term on August 22.

Vice President: Emmerson MNANGAGWA (Zimbabwe African National Union–Patriotic Front); appointed on December 10, 2015, to succeed Joyce MUJURU (Zimbabwe African National Union–Patriotic Front), who resigned on December 9.

Vice President: Phelekzela MPHOKO (Zimbabwe African National Union–Patriotic Front); appointed on December 10, 2014, to succeed John Landa NKOMO (Zimbabwe African National Union–Patriotic Front), who died on January 17, 2013.

THE COUNTRY

Bordered by Botswana, Zambia, Mozambique, and South Africa, Zimbabwe occupies the fertile plateaus and mountain ranges between southeastern Africa's Zambezi and Limpopo rivers. The population includes approximately 11.5 million Africans, mainly Bantu in origin; some 200,000 Europeans; and smaller groups of Asians and people of mixed race. The Africans may be classified into two multitribal groupings, the Shona (about 82 percent) in the north, and the Ndebele, concentrated in the southern area of Matabeleland. Shona-Ndebele rivalry dates to the 19th century and has contributed to a pronounced north-south cleavage. The majority of the European population is Protestant, although there is a substantial Catholic minority. The Africans include both Christians and followers of traditional religions; the Asians are a mixture of Hindus and Muslims.

In 1982 a Legal Age of Majority Act significantly enhanced the legal status of women (including the right of personal choice in selecting a marital partner, the right to own property outright, and the ability to enter into business contracts); it has, however, been unevenly utilized because of its conflict with traditional law. In 2008 about 47.5 percent of the paid labor force was estimated to be female; black women are responsible for most subsistence agriculture (cash-crop production had been undertaken mainly by some 4,500 white farmers who at one time owned more than 70 percent of the arable land); white and Asian women are concentrated in the clerical and service sectors. In the 2013 legislative balloting, women secured 85 of 270 seats (31.5 percent), including 60 reserved for women.

Zimbabwe was endowed with natural resources that historically yielded a relatively advanced economy oriented toward foreign trade. Zimbabwe exported maize and other food crops to shortage-plagued neighbors. Despite international trade sanctions on Zimbabwe (then Rhodesia), its economy prospered for much of the 1970s because of continued access to trade routes through South Africa, which became the conduit for up to 90 percent of Rhodesian imports and exports. The lifting of sanctions at the end of 1979 further stimulated the economy, although budget deficits and inflation persisted. In addition, unemployment was aggravated by a growing pool of workers seeking better jobs because of rapid educational advances by blacks.

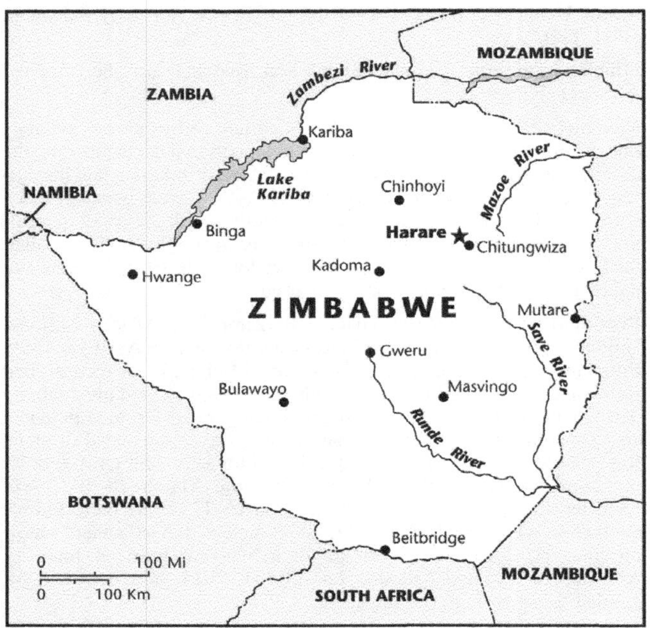

Zimbabwe has suffered from severe deterioration of economic, social, and political conditions, in large part due to the government's controversial land redistribution program (see Political background, below). The government has also been buffeted by allegations of corruption and broad mismanagement of the economy, marked by a bloated and inefficient civil service, massive budget deficits, and, at times, a soaring inflation rate. Severe poverty has remained widespread. Conditions steadily worsened from 2005 to 2007. During that period, inflation and infant mortality rates were estimated to be among the highest in the world, and millions of people were said to be suffering from food shortages. The government introduced emergency reforms, issuing new currency and seizing cash from citizens and businesses in an effort to curtail black-market trade.

In mid-2007 price controls were introduced to help regulate the market. Inflation was reported to be 100,000 percent. The International Monetary Fund (IMF) expressed "deep concern over the deteriorating economic and social conditions" and Zimbabwe's $129 million in arrears to the fund's poverty reduction program. The fund subsequently tabled its review to consider restoring Zimbabwe's voting rights.

In 2008 as the nation's reserve bank printed excess money without restraint to bankroll government spending, Zimbabwe was reported to have among the world's highest rates of inflation and debt-to-GDP ratio. GDP contracted by 14 percent, according to the IMF. Contributing to deteriorating conditions were severe food shortages and a cholera epidemic that killed more than 4,000 people. Also in 2008 the government enacted legislation which mandated that 51 percent of all businesses be owned by indigenous Zimbabweans in a policy known as "indigenization." The measure was unevenly applied to foreign firms, but it severely constrained foreign investment (see Current issues, below).

The government began to control hyperinflation in January 2009 when it abandoned the domestic currency in favor of the U.S. dollar and the South African rand. Following the establishment of the unity government in February, inflation contracted to nominal rates, and the food shortage eased. Bilateral development aid remained frozen due to donor concerns over economic mismanagement and human rights violations. However, in August and September the IMF released $500 million in reserves to Zimbabwe, marking the nation's first loan from an international financial institution in nearly a decade. An annual GDP growth of 9 percent was recorded in 2010, but the nation's external debt remained high and unemployment was estimated at 95 percent. On a positive note, the IMF restored Zimbabwe's voting rights and began the process of removing the freeze on the nation's general reserve account.

Due to the impact of drought on agricultural production, GDP growth was 10.6 percent in 2012. Inflation that year was 3.7 percent, and GDP per capita was $961. The IMF noted the government had a mixed record of success at implementing past reforms, and, while mining revenues are high, investment "appears hampered by uncertainties related to the indigenization policy and the political process." The IMF also noted significant risks ahead from political instability. GDP growth slowed to 3.9 percent in 2014, and the 1.5 percent in 2015, before rising to 2.7 percent in 2016. Meanwhile, inflation fell to –1.3 percent in 2016, and per capita GDP rose to $1,082. In its 2016 annual report on the ease of doing business, the World Bank ranked Zimbabwe 156th out of 189 countries.

GOVERNMENT AND POLITICS

Political background. Originally developed and administered by the British South Africa Company, Southern Rhodesia became an internally self-governing British colony in 1923 under a system that concentrated political power in the hands of its white minority. In 1953 it joined with Northern Rhodesia (now Zambia) and Nyasaland (now Malawi) in the Federation of Rhodesia and Nyasaland. However, Southern Rhodesia reverted to separate status in 1963 when the federation was dissolved and Northern Rhodesia and Nyasaland prepared to claim their independence. A new constitution granted to Southern Rhodesia by Britain in December 1961 contained various provisions for the benefit of the African population, including a right of limited representation in the Legislative Assembly. However, the measure failed to resolve a sharpening conflict between African demands for full political equality based on the principle of "one-person, one-vote" and white Rhodesian demands for permanent white control.

In view of the refusal of Britain to agree to independence on terms that would exclude majority rule, the colonial government under Prime Minister Ian D. SMITH on November 11, 1965, issued a Unilateral Declaration of Independence purporting to make Rhodesia an independent state within the Commonwealth. Britain repudiated the action, declared the colony to be in a state of rebellion, and invoked financial and economic sanctions; however, it refused to use force against the Smith regime.

Rhodesia approved a new constitution on June 20, 1969, declaring itself a republic; subsequently, Britain suspended formal ties with the separatist regime.

On December 8, 1974, an agreement was concluded in Lusaka, Zambia, by Bishop Abel MUZOREWA of the African National Council (ANC), Joshua NKOMO of the Zimbabwe African People's Union (ZAPU), Ndabaningi SITHOLE of the Zimbabwe African National Union (ZANU), and James CHIKEREMA of the Front for the Liberation of Zimbabwe (Frolizi), whereby the latter three, representing groups that had been declared illegal within Rhodesia, would join an enlarged ANC executive under Bishop Muzorewa's presidency for a period of four months to prepare for negotiations with the Smith regime aimed at transferring power to the majority. Three days later Prime Minister Smith announced that, upon the receipt of assurances that insurgents within Rhodesia would observe a cease-fire, all black political prisoners would be released and a constitutional conference would be held without preconditions. On December 15, however, Smith again reiterated his government's opposition to the principle of majority rule.

In March 1975 Sithole, who had returned to Salisbury in December, was arrested by Rhodesian authorities on charges of plotting to assassinate his rivals in order to assume the ANC leadership. He was released a month later, following the intervention of Prime Minister Balthazar Johannes Vorster of South Africa. On December 1, 1975, Nkomo and Prime Minister Smith concluded a series of meetings by signing a declaration of intention to negotiate a settlement of the Rhodesian issue, but the agreement was repudiated by external ANC leader Bishop Muzorewa (then resident in Zambia) and by ZANU leader Sithole.

Early 1976 witnessed an intensification of guerrilla activity by Mozambique-based insurgents under the leadership of former ZANU secretary general Robert MUGABE, and a breakdown in the talks between Nkomo and Smith on March 19. In September Smith announced that he had accepted a comprehensive package tendered by U.S. secretary of state Henry Kissinger, calling for a biracial interim government and the establishment of majority rule within two years. Britain responded to the Kissinger–Smith accord by convening a conference in Geneva between a white delegation led by Smith and a black delegation that included Nkomo, Mugabe, Muzorewa, and Sithole. However, the conference failed to yield a settlement, with the black leaders rejecting the essentials of the

Kissinger plan by calling for an immediate transfer to majority rule and the replacement of the all-white Rhodesian army by contingents of the nationalist guerrilla forces.

In September 1976 Mugabe called for a unified military command of all guerrilla forces, and on October 9 he announced the formation of a Patriotic Front (PF) linking ZANU and ZAPU units. Sithole and Muzorewa continued to assume a relatively moderate posture during 1977, engaging in sporadic negotiations with the Smith regime, while Nkomo and Mugabe constituted the core of a more radical external leadership. During 1977 a number of British proposals were advanced in hopes of resolving the impasse on interim rule. Prime Minister Smith resumed discussions with Muzorewa and Sithole based on a revision of the earlier Kissinger package.

Despite the opposition of the PF to these talks, an agreement was reached on March 3, 1978, by Smith, Muzorewa, Sithole, and Mashona Chief Jeremiah S. CHIRAU of the Zimbabwe United People's Organization (ZUPO) to form a transitional government that would lead to black rule by the end of the year. Accordingly, an Executive Council comprising the four was established on March 21, while a multiracial Ministerial Council to replace the existing cabinet was designated on April 12. On May 16 the Executive Council released preliminary details of a new constitution that would feature a titular president elected by parliament sitting as an electoral college. The projected national election was postponed in early November until April 1979, following the failure of a renewed effort to convene an all-party conference.

A new constitution was approved by the assembly on January 20, 1979, and endorsed by 84 percent of the white voters in a referendum on January 30. A lower-house election was held on April 10 and 17–20 for 20 white and 72 black members, respectively, in which the UANC won 51 seats in the face of a boycott by the PF parties. Following a Senate election on May 23, Josiah GUMEDE of the UANC was elected president of Zimbabwe/Rhodesia, and on May 29 he requested Bishop Muzorewa to accept appointment as prime minister.

Following renewed guerrilla activity by PF forces in mid-1979, talks between representatives of the Muzorewa government and the Patriotic Front commenced on September 10 and ran for 14 weeks. These discussions yielded a constitutional agreement, an interim administration agreement, and a cease-fire agreement on December 5 that called for Britain to reassume full administrative authority for an interim period, during which a new and carefully monitored election would be held as a prelude to the granting of legal independence. In December the terms of the agreement were approved by parliament, and Lord SOAMES was appointed colonial governor, with Sir Anthony DUFF as his deputy. On December 12 Lord Soames arrived in Salisbury, where he was welcomed by members of the former government of Zimbabwe/Rhodesia, who, one day earlier, had approved a parliamentary bill terminating the Unilateral Declaration of Independence and transferring authority to the British administration.

White and common roll elections were held in February 1980, the Rhodesian Front winning all 20 white seats and Mugabe's ZANU-PF winning a substantial overall majority in the House of Assembly. Accordingly, Mugabe was asked by Lord Soames on March 4 to form a cabinet that included 16 members of ZANU-PF, 4 members of Nkomo's Patriotic Front–ZAPU, and 2 members of the RF. The new government was installed during independence day ceremonies on April 18 following the inauguration of Rev. Canaan Sodindo BANANA, a Mugabe supporter, as president of the republic.

The period immediately after independence was characterized by persistent conflict between armed forces of ZANU-PF and PF-ZAPU (units of Mugabe's Zimbabwe African National Liberation Army [ZANLA] and Nkomo's Zimbabwe People's Revolutionary Army [ZIPRA], respectively). To some extent the difficulties were rooted in ethnic loyalties, with most ZANLA personnel having been recruited from the northern Shona group, while ZIPRA had recruited primarily from the Ndebele people of Matabeleland. The government announced in November 1981 that a merger of the two guerrilla organizations and the former Rhodesian security force into a 50,000-man Zimbabwean national army had been completed. However, personal animosity between Mugabe and Nkomo continued, threatening the viability of the coalition regime. On February 17, 1982, Nkomo and three other ZAPU government members were dismissed from the cabinet, Nkomo declaring that his group should thenceforth be construed as an opposition party. From 1982 to 1987, Mugabe's infamous Fifth Brigade, trained in North Korea, led a terror campaign called "Gukurahundi" to intimidate dissident Ndebeles in Matabeleland and the Midlands, resulting in thousands of deaths, burning of villages, and other atrocities.

After a series of postponements, the first postindependence legislative elections were held in mid-1985. Smith's party, renamed the Conservative Alliance of Zimbabwe (CAZ), rallied to regain 15 of the 20 white seats on June 27, while in common roll balloting held July 1–4, Mugabe's ZANU-PF won all but 1 of the non-Matabeleland constituencies, raising its assembly strength to 64 as contrasted with ZAPU's 15. Although the results fell short of the mandate desired by Mugabe for introduction of a one-party state, ZAPU members, including Nkomo, responded to overtures for merger talks, which eventually yielded an agreement on December 22, 1987, whereby the two parties would merge, with Nkomo becoming one of two ZANU-PF vice presidents. Three months earlier, following expiration of a constitutionally mandated seven-year entrenchment, the white seats in both houses of parliament had been vacated and refilled on a "non-constituency" basis by the assembly. On December 31 Mugabe, having secured unanimous assembly endorsement the day before, was sworn in as executive president; concurrently, Simon MUZENDA was inaugurated as vice president, with the post of prime minister being eliminated. On August 2, 1990, 21 of 26 ZANU-PF Politburo members voted against Mugabe's appeal for a constitutional amendment to institutionalize the one-party system that was now in place on a de facto basis.

The Senate was abolished prior to the balloting of March 28–30, 1990, in which Mugabe won 78 percent of the presidential vote and ZANU-PF swept all but four seats in the House of Assembly. Following the election, a second vice presidency was established by constitutional amendment, with Nkomo being named to the post.

On May 1, 1993, the government released a list of 70 farms, encompassing approximately 470,000 acres, which it planned to purchase for redistribution under authority of the 1992 Land Acquisition Act. Subsequently, the powerful Commercial Farmers' Union (CFU), representing approximately 4,000 white farmers, denounced the government for violating its pledge to buy only "derelict and underutilized" properties. Following the revelation in early 1994 that a majority of the parcels appropriated under the act had been granted on cheap leases to senior government officials and civil servants, Mugabe suspended that specific program in April.

At presidential balloting held March 16–17, 1996, President Mugabe captured a third term. The president's victory was tarnished, however, by the withdrawal of his only two competitors, Sithole and Muzorewa, during the week prior to balloting. Both men complained of being harassed by government security forces, and they charged that the electoral system unfairly favored the incumbent. Furthermore, voter turnout was reported to have been only 32 percent. Thus, even with an official 92 percent vote share (Sithole's and Muzorewa's names remained on the ballot, and both garnered votes), Mugabe was rumored to have secured only 28.5 percent of the potential vote, far from the mandate for which he had campaigned.

A possible settlement appeared in the making in early 1999 concerning the incendiary question of land redistribution. According to the plan, the Zimbabwean government was to buy land from the dominant white farmers for use by black farmers, while the international community was to provide substantial aid for the development of infrastructure related to agriculture. However, the government's true intentions remained obscure as President Mugabe continued to threaten to expropriate the white farms, and donor countries demanded significant economic reform on the part of the administration before releasing the promised financial assistance. Consequently, Mugabe attempted to secure authority to seize white farms through proposed constitutional revision. The amendment proposed by the government would have made Mugabe president for life, given him the power to dissolve parliament, and endorsed the administration's land redistribution program. In January 2000 Mugabe added a further proposal requiring Britain to pay compensation for all land that the government acquired compulsorily for resettlement. Underscoring growing internal discontent, 55 percent of those voting in a national referendum held on February 12–13, 2000, rejected the proposed changes in the basic law.

When the February 2000 national referendum rejected the measure, blacks, many from influential war veterans' groups, began expropriating land. Collaterally, the administration, according to a rising chorus of domestic and international critics, launched a campaign of intimidation against opposition parties and dissidents. Opposition forces had coalesced in 1999 as the Movement for Democratic Change (MDC), which lobbied strongly against the constitutional revision. In April 2000 parliament passed a constitutional amendment that incorporated the land clause that Mugabe had inserted into the draft constitution in January 2000. The clause allowed the regime to forcibly acquire land without paying compensation, which was made the responsibility of the British government. The Supreme Court's ruling in November 2000 that the land invasions were illegal was ignored.

ZANU-PF barely withstood an electoral challenge from the MDC in flawed assembly balloting held June 24–25, 2000, securing 62 of the 120 elective seats. The assembly in January 2002 approved the Public Order and Security Act banning public gatherings without police approval to undercut the MDC challenge to Mugabe in the March presidential poll. Mugabe won another term in that election, defeating Morgan TSVANGIRAI of the MDC, 56 percent to 42 percent. The MDC rejected the results as fraudulent. (A court rejected the charge of voter fraud in 2006.)

Zimbabwe's worsening economic situation was accelerated by Mugabe's land redistribution. The lack of expertise among black farmers who had received land and the disinterest of many of those who had acquired large commercial farms combined with drought conditions and the lack of government-subsidized inputs to undermine food security. The government allegedly used food to buy votes in the March 31, 2005, assembly elections, in which ZANU-PF won 78 seats, which, coupled with its 30 appointive seats, gave the president's party a two-thirds majority. The MDC won 41 seats, and 1 seat went to an independent candidate. In the first polling for the newly reestablished Senate seats on November 26, 2005, the ZANU-PF won 43 seats and the MDC won 7. The election was boycotted by the Tsvangirai faction of the MDC, the larger of the two factions into which the MDC had split in October 2005 (see Political Parties, below).

Further exacerbating the declining economic and social conditions, the government in May 2005 launched Operation Murambatsvina ("drive out rubbish") purportedly to rid urban areas of informal market traders and shantytowns. As a result, 700,000 people were displaced. The MDC charged that the program was meant to punish the urban dwellers who voted in March against the ZANU-PF. Critics claimed that by dispersing urban dwellers, the government reduced the possibility of an uprising and drove people back to rural areas in the aftermath of the economic collapse precipitated by the land redistribution program. With inflation escalating out of control in 2007, Mugabe ordered all shops and businesses to cut their prices by half and deployed troops to monitor compliance. By the end of July, some 8,500 shop owners and executives had been arrested, and shortages linked to the price-cut directive further encouraged black market demand.

In the parliamentary elections of March 29, 2008, the MDC became the largest party in the House of Assembly with 99 of 207 seats. The ZANU-PF retained its standing as the largest party in the Senate with 30 seats. In concurrent presidential balloting both Mugabe and Tsvangirai claimed victory, despite each having secured less than a clear majority. Results were not published by the constitutional deadline of April 19 for holding a runoff, as the electoral commission reported it was investigating irregularities. In official results announced on May 2, neither Mugabe nor Tsvangirai had secured the 50 percent threshold to avoid a runoff. Violence ensued, with Tsvangirai claiming some 86 MDC supporters were killed and 200,000 displaced ahead of the runoff set for June 27. Tsvangirai subsequently withdrew from the runoff, citing the violence and voting irregularities. The poll proceeded, and Mugabe was declared the winner; he was sworn in on June 29. Elections to fill 3 seats in the assembly were held concurrent with the runoff, resulting in the MDC having an edge with 100 seats while the ZANU-PF secured 99. The MDC-M, the faction headed by Arthur MUTAMBARA, won 10 seats.

On July 18, 2008, Mugabe signed an agreement with Tsvangirai and Mutambara to prepare for unity talks. The agreement stipulated that all parties refrain from convening parliament or establishing a government outside of the talks. However, on August 19 Mugabe announced that he would convene parliament, which opened its first session on August 25, some six months after the election. Yielding to international pressure, Mugabe agreed to talks with the MDC and the MDC-M mediated by South African president Thabo Mbeki. On September 15 all three groups signed the Global Political Agreement, which provided for Mugabe to remain president and tapped Tsvangirai as prime minister. Disputes over the allocation of ministerial authority remained unresolved until January 27, 2009. Tsvangirai was sworn in as prime minister on February 11. A new government was formed on February 13 with the ZANU-PF holding 15 ministerial posts and the MDC and MDC-M together holding a total of 16. The ministry of home affairs was jointly held by a ZANU-PF member and an MDC member. The deputy agriculture minister, Roy BENNETT, a senior aide to the prime minister, was arrested on February 13 and charged with treason, a charge later altered to inciting insurgency. Bennett was released on March 12 but was blocked from taking office. One of the two vice presidents, Joseph MSIKA, died on August 6. John NKOMO of the ZANU-PF was sworn in on December 14 to succeed him.

In a cabinet reshuffle on June 23, 2010, all seven posts affected went to members of Prime Minister Tsvangirai's MDC-T faction. A ministry for national healing and reconciliation was established in December.

Negotiations on political reforms broke down in July 2011 when no agreement was reached on a road map for elections. The suspicious death in August 2011 of Ret. Gen. Solomon MUJURU, leader of an influential ZANU-PF faction who had been seen by many as a likely successor to Mugabe, strengthened Mugabe's position in the party. Many analysts, as well as some MDC leaders, accused the ZANU-PF of killing Mujuru, who was the husband of Vice President Joyce Mujuru. By November the level of violence was reportedly so intense that many observers believed that the power-sharing deal was in jeopardy. On a positive note for the country's economy, international diamond regulators agreed to let Zimbabwe trade some $2 billion in diamonds. The country had been under sanctions since 2009 as the result of noncompliance with the Kimberley Process, which certifies that the source of rough diamonds is free from conflict.

Minor cabinet changes were made in January, August, and September 2011. Vice President Nkomo died on January 17, 2013, but was not replaced.

A new constitution was approved in a national referendum on March 16, 2013, with 94.5 percent of the vote. Both the ZANU-PF and the MDC supported the new basic law, which was also approved overwhelmingly by parliament (see Current issues, below). It came into force on May 22. Mugabe called for national elections on July 31 to implement the terms of the new constitution (see Current issues, below). In the balloting, Mugabe was reelected, while the ZANU-PF won a commanding majority in the legislature. Opposition groups denounced the results and unsuccessfully challenged the outcome in court. Mugabe named a ZANU-PF cabinet on September 10.

Vice President Mujuru was dismissed on December 9, 2014, along with seven cabinet ministers accused of loyalty to her during an internal ZANU-PF struggle. Mujuru was accused of plotting to overthrow Mugabe (see Political Parties, below). She was replaced by Emmerson MNANGAGWA (ZANU-PF) on December 10, while Phelekzela MPHOKO (ZANU-PF) was named to the dormant second vice presidential post the same day. A cabinet reshuffle was conducted the following day.

A cabinet reshuffle occurred on September 11, 2015, which increased the number of supporters in the government of Mnangagwa in a sign that the vice president was being groomed as a possible successor to Mugabe.

Constitution and government. The constitution that issued in 1979 was amended numerous times (see the 2013 *Handbook*). The Global Political Agreement accepted by ZANU-PF and the two MDC formations on September 15, 2008, called for a transitional power-sharing government with executive power divided between the president and prime minister. The agreement required the inclusive government to prepare a new draft constitution within 18 months to be voted on in a national referendum. The process of constitutional reform began in April 2009 with the formation of the Constitutional Parliamentary Committee. Referendums were postponed repeatedly and finally conducted on March 16, 2013.

The 2013 constitution reduced the term of the president from six to five years, renewable once (although the restrictions did not apply to incumbent President Mugabe). The basic law abolished the office of prime minister and gave the president the power to appoint the cabinet. The legislature is bicameral, with an 80-member Senate and 210-member National Assembly, both elected for five-year terms (see Legislature, below). The new constitution devolved powers to the provinces and established an independent electoral commission, as well as a peace and reconciliation commission. The measure also forbade legal challenges to the seizure of white-owned land. The existing Supreme Court was replaced by a Constitutional Court, while the judicial system has both general and appellate divisions, and includes magistrate courts at the local level.

The country is divided into ten provinces: West, Central, and East in Mashonaland; North and South in Matabeleland; Midlands; Manicaland; Masvingo; Harare; and Bulawayo (though the latter two are cities, they have provincial status). Each is headed by a centrally appointed provincial governor and serves, additionally, as an electoral district for senate elections. Local government is conducted through town, district, and rural councils.

Zimbabwe has a lengthy record of limiting press freedom. On March 15, 2002, Mugabe signed a law that made it a crime for journalists to practice without a government-approved license. Foreign journalists have been jailed. Following the formation of the unity government, press freedom improved. A new independent newspaper was published in June 2010, marking the end of the progovernment newspaper's seven-year monopoly. The 2013 constitution guaranteed freedom of the press. In 2016 Reporters Without Borders ranked Zimbabwe 124th out of 180 countries in freedom of the press.

Foreign relations. Zimbabwe became a member of the Commonwealth upon achieving de jure independence in April 1980; it was admitted to the OAU (subsequently the African Union—AU) the following July and to the UN in August. In January 1983 it was elected to a seat on the UN Security Council, where its representatives assumed a distinctly anti-American posture. The strain in relations with the United States culminated in 1986 with Washington's withdrawal of all aid in response to strongly worded attacks from Harare on U.S. policy regarding South Africa. Despite (then) Prime Minister Mugabe's refusal to apologize for the verbal onslaughts, the aid was resumed in August 1988.

In regional affairs, Harare occupied a leading position among the front-line states bordering South Africa, concluding a mutual security pact with Mozambique in late 1980 and hosting several meetings of the Southern African Development Coordination Conference (now the SADC). (For more on Zimbabwe's support for Mozambique's anti-insurgency campaign, see an earlier *Handbook*.)

The Zimbabwean government initially declined, for the sake of its own domestic "reconciliation," to provide bases for black nationalist attacks on South Africa. However, the anti-apartheid African National Congress (ANC) continued to operate from Zimbabwean territory, its cross-border attacks yielding retaliatory incursions by South African troops into Zimbabwe.

In February 1997 Zimbabwe and South Africa signed a defense agreement; however, their ties were subsequently strained by what Harare asserted were unfair South African trade practices and Pretoria's crackdown on illegal Zimbabwean immigrants. In February 1998 Zimbabwe, South Africa, and Namibia signed an extradition treaty.

In mid-1998 President Mugabe dispatched troops to the Democratic Republic of the Congo (DRC) to shore up the presidency of Laurent Kabila, from whose administration Harare reportedly sought mining concessions. At the peak of the conflict, an estimated 12,000 Zimbabwean troops were in the DRC, President Mugabe also strongly endorsing the succession of Joseph Kabila to the DRC presidency after the death of Laurent Kabila in early 2001. The support from Zimbabwe was considered crucial to the lasting power of the DRC administration, although the economic drain on scarce Zimbabwean resources contributed to growing anti-Mugabe sentiment. The last contingent of Zimbabwean troops left the DRC in November 2002.

In December 2003 the Commonwealth Heads of Government Meeting in Nigeria suspended Zimbabwe, citing continued human rights violations. Zimbabwe responded by withdrawing from the organization.

In 2005 Zimbabwe was reelected to the UN Human Rights Commission, drawing sharp criticism from Western countries, among others, which cited Zimbabwe's appalling human rights record.

Most Western donors froze development aid and imposed an arms embargo after Mugabe enacted his controversial land redistribution program. Zimbabwe increasingly turned to South Africa and China for financial aid as economic conditions worsened. South Africa loaned $470 million to bail Zimbabwe out of IMF and humanitarian crises in 2005, and China signed a $1.3 billion energy deal with the Mugabe government in 2006.

In 2007 China halted aid to Zimbabwe, citing the impact of hyperinflation on investment.

The disputed 2008 reelection of President Mugabe drew harsh rebukes from the international community. Botswana, Kenya, Sierra Leone, and Zambia called for punitive action against Mugabe, but the AU ultimately pressed for power-sharing talks. SADC pressure was instrumental in gaining MDC leader Morgan Tsvangirai's consent to form a government of national unity in February 2009.

The United States and the European Union (EU) kept "targeted" sanctions in place after the installation of the new government, citing continued violations of the rule of law. Prime Minister Tsvangirai traveled to Europe and North America in June 2009, meeting with U.S. president Barack Obama and other leaders but failing to persuade them to restart nonhumanitarian aid. EU officials refused to consider renewing aid in the absence of full implementation of the Global Political Agreement.

In February 2011 the EU extended its sanctions against Zimbabwe for another year over concerns of political violence (see Current issues, below). In March China agreed to $700 million in loans to Zimbabwe aimed at protecting Chinese companies from the indigenization program.

In December 2012 Zimbabwean troops were deployed along the border with Mozambique after incursions were reported by Mozambican rebel groups (see entry on Mozambique).

In March 2013 the EU suspended some sanctions as a reward for the successful conduct of a constitutional referendum. In June, South Africa announced it would provide $100 million to conduct national elections in July. When Zimbabwe refused to allow Western election observers to monitor polling in July, the EU, United States, and other international bodies rebuffed calls to lift remaining sanctions (including those that had been suspended). Following the balloting, the United States and other Western powers were critical of the government's oversight of the elections.

In February 2014 the EU suspended many of the remaining restrictive measures, with the exception of the arms embargo and those targeting Mugabe, his spouse, and Zimbabwe Defence Industries (ZDI). Australia likewise lifted some bans, but maintained restrictions against the first family, security service chiefs, and ZDI. Meanwhile, economic deals with China to improve infrastructure provided some financial relief as a part of Mugabe's "Look East" policy. Mugabe took over as chair of the SADC in August and is set to chair the African Union (AU) from early 2015.

In February 2015 the EU announced that it was resuming direct aid to Zimbabwe with a €234 million grant, although it renewed targeted sanctions on Mugabe and members of his inner circle. Following a state visit by Chinese president Xi Jinping in December, it was announced that China was writing off $40 million of Zimbabwe's external debt.

Current issues. Throughout 2011 and 2012 ZANU-PF stepped up attacks and intimidation against the MDC, including the reported arrest, assault, or murder of MDC officials.

Throughout the fall the failures of the Indigenization and Economic Empowerment Act became increasingly clear: Minister of Economic Development Tapiwa MASHAKADA warned the act made it impossible to attract investment into the country; economic consultant John ROBERTSON went so far as to suggest it was part of a ZANU-PF scheme to derail the economic recovery in order to prevent the MDC from benefiting politically.

The inquest into the death of General Solomon Mujuru closed on February 6, 2012, without turning up hard evidence of foul play, despite ongoing speculation. The court denied the family's request to exhume his body for examination by a forensics expert.

On February 19 Mugabe reaffirmed that he would call elections in 2012. Tsvangirai launched spirited rallies, somewhat dampening criticism of his party for giving in to Mugabe's call for elections.

In May 2012 a visit from UN human rights commissioner Navi PILLAY proved to be a public debacle. She had been invited by Justice Minister Patrick Chinamasa, who at the last minute switched the venue for her appearance without giving adequate notice to anyone but ZANU-PF members. But the tactic backfired when Pillay showed up at the original venue instead and then held a press conference in which she stated that without reform the disasters of the 2008 election would be repeated.

In early August 2012 ZANU-PF's Politburo began meeting to consider the draft constitution drawn up by a select committee. The public expectation was that any changes would be minor and the resulting draft would be ready for a plebiscite by late fall. Instead the party's revisions, announced in late August, constituted a radical rewrite that stripped away virtually all progressive measures included in the draft, removing checks and balances and dramatically tightening the powers of the president and his party over the government. In response, Welshman NCUB E said he was "astonished at the sheer scale of disrespect, contempt and audacity exhibited." For instance, the new draft allowed the president to designate his successor, subject to approval by parliament, if he left office before the completion of his term. Nonetheless, the MDC officially supported the new basic law, which reduced the president's term of office and limited the chief executive to two terms (although the term limit applied to the next president, not Mugabe). There were other limitations on executive power, including restrictions on the ability of the president to issue decrees, declare emergency rule, or dissolve parliament. The draft constitution also contained a bill of rights and permitted dual citizenship. The constitution was approved by referendum in March 2013 and came into force in May.

Meanwhile, in January 2013 the head of the nation's human rights commission, Reginald AUSTIN, resigned in protest over the body's lack of independence and dearth of resources. Opposition groups bitterly decried Mugabe's decision in May to hold elections on July 31, 2013, arguing that there was not enough time to organize campaigns and that promised reforms to the electoral system had not been enacted. In addition, while Mugabe permitted election observers from the AU and neighboring states, he forbade monitors from the EU or other international bodies. Mugabe asserted that he was responding to a constitutional court decision calling for balloting when the parliament's term ended in June.

In the balloting, Mugabe secured 61 percent of the vote and defeated three other candidates. Tsvangirai placed second with 34.9 percent of the vote. In legislative balloting, ZANU-PF won 160 seats, followed by the MDC with 49, in the Assembly. In the Senate, ZANU-PF secured 37 seats to 21 for the MDC and 2 for the MDC-M. Reports indicated a number of problems with the balloting, and opposition groups challenged the outcome. For instance, in ZANU-PF strongholds the number of eligible voters on the rolls often outnumbered the population. On August 20 the high court rejected opposition challenges to the results.

Throughout 2014 the government struggled to pay wages and provide basic services amid persistent economic crisis. In February Mugabe turned 90. Meanwhile, speculation increased that Mugabe was grooming his wife to succeed him. In August ZANU-PF nominated Grace MUGABE leader of the party's women's league. She also assumed a place on the party's central committee. On September 24, 46 non-state Zimbabwean actors formed the National Transitional Justice Working Group (NTJWG). The working group was established to provide the interface between transitional justice stakeholders and the official transitional justice processes in Zimbabwe.

In June 2015 the central bank announced that the Zimbabwean dollar was going to be phased out in favor of the U.S. dollar, while a group of currencies, including the UK pound and the South African rand, were commonly used. Bank accounts with balances up to 175 quadrillion Zimbabwean dollars were exchanged for $5, while those with more than 175 quadrillion were exchanged at a rate of 35 quadrillion to $1. The phase-out reportedly cost the government about $10 million.

In December 2015 the government announced it would delay salary payments to civil servants, sparking strikes and other protests.

A shortage of dollars in May 2016 prompted the government to begin printing new dollar notes, which it claimed were equal to the U.S. dollar. The new currency was backed by $200 million in support from the African Export-Import Bank but was widely criticized throughout Zimbabwe. A widespread drought prompted the government to appeal for $1.6 billion in emergency food relief in November.

POLITICAL PARTIES

At a convention of the Zimbabwe Congress of Trade Unions (ZCTU) in Harare in late February 1999, the ZCTU announced that it had coalesced with the anti-regime civic organization, the National Constitutional Assembly (NCA), as well as 30 other civic groups and a number of human rights, trade, and student organizations to form a political movement dedicated to pressuring the Mugabe government to enact economic, electoral, and constitutional reforms. Morgan Tsvangirai and Gibson Sibanda, leaders of both the ZCTU and the new coalition, had emerged in 1998 as point men for the anti-Mugabe forces. The NCA subsequently served as a major force in the creation of the nation's first and only effective opposition party, the Movement for Democratic Change (below).

By 2000 the MDC had emerged as the chief opposition party to Mugabe's ZANU-PF. Both ZANU-PF and the MDC are divided into factions, with alliances shifting as the inclusive government formulates policy and all sides prepare for Mugabe's eventual departure from power. ZAPU was revived as an independent party in 2009 (see below).

Governing Parties:

Zimbabwe African National Union–Patriotic Front (ZANU-PF). ZANU was formed in 1963 as a result of a split in the Zimbabwe African People's Union (ZAPU), an African nationalist group formed in 1961 under the leadership of Joshua Nkomo. Nkomo had in 1957 revived the dormant ANC, which was banned in 1959. He then was elected from exile as the president of a new National Democratic Party, which was declared illegal in 1961, leading to the formation and quick banning of ZAPU. ZANU, led by Ndabaningi Sithole and Robert Mugabe, was also declared illegal in 1964, and both ZANU and ZAPU initiated guerrilla activity against the Rhodesian government announced in November 1965.

In December 1974 ZANU President Sithole agreed to participate (along with ZAPU) in the enlargement of the African National Council to serve as the primary organization for negotiating with the Smith government (see Political background, above). However, Mugabe opposed such discussions and went into exile in Mozambique, from where he contested Sithole's dominance in ZANU. By late 1976 Mugabe was widely recognized as ZANU's leader, and he concluded a tactical (Patriotic Front—PF) agreement with Joshua Nkomo of ZAPU, although a minority of the ZANU membership apparently remained loyal to Sithole. The PF alliance broke down prior to the 1980 assembly election, Nkomo's group campaigning as PF-ZAPU and Mugabe's as ZANU-PF. Both parties participated in the government formed at independence, although ZANU-PF predominated with 16 of 22 ministerial appointments.

At ZANU-PF's third ordinary congress held in December 1989, the Politburo was enlarged from 15 to 26 members, the Central Committee was expanded from 90 to 150 members, a national chair was created, and ZAPU was formally incorporated into the party (despite rejection of its demands for a sole vice presidency filled by Nkomo and an expunging of the group's Marxist-Leninist tenets). Further, the party's socialist orientation was redefined to emphasize the Zimbabwean historical, cultural, and social experience. Ultimately, on June 22, 1991, the party agreed to delete all references to Marxism, Leninism, and scientific socialism from its constitution.

At a party congress in December 1995, Mugabe loyalists blocked efforts to open a party-wide dialogue on the question of presidential succession. The ruling party's preference for centralized power was upheld in December 1997; the Central Committee urged the president to forge ahead with plans to seize white-owned properties, in defiance of international donors and ZANU-PF moderates. Despite the schisms within ZANU-PF, Mugabe was reelected without opposition as party president in 1999. Subsequently, in controversial balloting, ZANU-PF retained a narrow majority in the assembly in June 2000, and Mugabe was reelected to another term as president in March 2002.

With the rise of factionalism within ZANU-PF, party solidarity began to disintegrate in 2004. Five party officials were arrested on espionage charges (three of the officials were later convicted of spying for South Africa), and a purge of the party targeted members who had been involved in the Tsholotsho meeting on November 18, 2004, and who opposed Mugabe's choice of Joyce Mujuru as vice president of the republic. Mujuru was appointed in December 2004 over house speaker Emmerson Mnangagwa, regarded by many as the president's likely successor until the political fallout from the failed palace coup attempt to make Mnangagwa the replacement for the late Simon Muzenda.

In December 2006 Mugabe declared at the ZANU-PF congress that only "God" could remove him from office, though a constitutional amendment would be required for an extension of his term. The Mujuru and Mnangagwa factions refused to support the motion, and no vote was taken on the resolution. The Mujuru and Mnangagwa factions united for a brief time to oppose Mugabe's attempt to remain in power.

The ZANU-PF Central Committee decided on March 30, 2007, that Mugabe would be the party's only presidential candidate and backed a proposal for parliamentary elections, which were not due until 2010, to be held concurrently with the presidential election in 2008. The Mnangagwa faction supported Mugabe, but the Mujuru faction (headed by Mujuru's husband Solomon Mujuru, a retired army general) backed former ZANU-PF member Simba MAKONI, who ran as an independent after being expelled from the party by Mugabe. The subsequent mysterious death of her husband was believed to have weakened Mujuru's alliances.

The party's internal battle over succession intensified after it lost exclusive control of Zimbabwe's government in 2009. The Mujuru faction appeared to have jockeyed successfully for the upper hand, as Joyce Mujuru was nominated by a majority of provinces to remain senior vice president of the party and of the republic. John Nkomo, loyal to the Mnangagwa faction, was elected vice president to succeed Joseph Msika, who died in August 2009. At the ZANU-PF national congress in December, Mugabe was reelected party president. At the ZANU-PF congress in December 16–18, 2010, Mugabe was tapped as the party's flagbearer for national presidential elections, which had tentatively been set for 2011 but were ultimately put off. Through 2011–2012 the party was said to be increasingly consumed by factionalism and roiled by the release from WikiLeaks of unredacted U.S. diplomatic cables that exposed ZANU-PF sources who had talked freely with American officials. In advance of the party's December 2011 congress, Chairman Simon Khaya MOYO also complained of a situation in which government had come to be "above the party," a dynamic he said he would be reversed.

Mugabe was reelected president in 2013, and the ZANU-PF won a majority in both houses of the legislature. Subsequent party infighting over the speaker's position highlighted the continuing division of the ZANU-PF between the Mnangagwa and Mujuru factions. Pro-Mnangagwa member Jacob MUDENDA was elected speaker on September 2013.

Mujuru appeared to consolidate her position in the ZANU-PF ahead of the December 2013 national conference. Her supporters secured nine of ten provincial chair positions. However, Mugabe deferred the expected reshuffle until the December 2014 congress. In the wake of Mugabe's recent call for all politburo and central committee cadres to seek reelection in December, reports suggested that Mujuru's position in the party would be challenged. The persistent power struggles in the party have distracted from the economic issues plaguing the country. ZANU PF's Zimbabwe Agenda for Sustainable Socio-Economic Transformation (ZimAsset) has squeezed the beleaguered tax base while securing only limited fiscal relief and generating resentment.

On December 9, 2014, Mujuru and her supporters in the cabinet were forced to resign by Mugabe, who accused them of plotting to overthrow his regime. Mujuru and her loyalists were purged from the party in April 2015. Reports indicated Mujuru was working to create a new political party, **People First** (PF).

Leaders: Robert Gabriel MUGABE (President of the Republic and President of the Party), Emmerson MNANGAGWA, Simon Khaya MOYO (National Chair), Didymus MUTASA (Secretary).

Movement for Democratic Change (MDC). Launched in September 1999, the MDC was an outgrowth of the ZCTU/NCA (see Political Parties introductory text, above), its core components including workers, students, middle-class intellectuals, civil rights activists, and white corporate executives opposed to the perceived corruption of the ZANU-PF government as well as its management of the economy. Many of the MDC adherents were former members of the Forum Party of Zimbabwe, which had been established in 1993 under the leadership of Enoch DUMBUTSHENA (a retired chief justice) and David Coltart. (See 1999 *Handbook* for details on the Forum Party.)

In a rapid rise, the MDC secured 57 of 120 elected seats in the 2000 assembly balloting. MDC leaders claimed fraud on the part of the government in some 37 of the 62 seats secured by the ZANU-PF. The MDC was the first opposition party to have broad inter-ethnic appeal and challenge the ruling party for every elected seat. Party leader Morgan Tsvangirai narrowly lost to President Mugabe in the controversial 2002 presidential election. On February 25, 2002, days before the presidential election in March, Tsvangirai was charged with treason for allegedly plotting to assassinate President Mugabe. He was acquitted in October 2004 but in the following month was charged with treason in connection with his call in 2003 for street protests to remove Mugabe. The government withdrew the treason charge in August 2005 without giving reasons.

In October 2005 the MDC split, leaving the lawful leadership of the party in question. Tsvangirai maintained he was still in charge of the party despite dissidents claiming he had been expelled. Prior to the November 2005 senate election, the MDC was deeply divided over whether to participate. Arthur Mutambara led the faction (MDC-M) that contested the election. Tsvangirai's faction, MCD-T, opposed participation, while a faction led by party secretary general Welshman Ncube planned to field candidates. Subsequently, 26 members who had been expelled by Tsvangirai stood for election, with only 7 winning Senate seats.

At the MDC-T party congress in March 2006, Tsvangirai was reelected president.

Ncube's faction appointed former MDC vice president Gibson Sibanda as acting president. The Ncube group held a congress in February 2006 and elected former student activist Arthur Mutambara as party president and Sibanda as vice president, with Ncube retaining the post of secretary general. The following month, however, Mutambara said it was wrong for MDC members to have contested the Senate elections, and he urged those who were elected to resign. Further, he proposed reconciling with Tsvangirai's faction, and in July the leaders of both factions vowed to work together to unseat the ZANU-PF.

After the torture and beatings of MDC members, including Tsvangirai, in Harare on March 11, 2007, the factions agreed in April to contest the 2008 elections as a coalition. It was agreed that Tsvangirai would be the coalition's president and Mutambara its vice president and that the factions would respect each other's autonomy and equality. Nevertheless, at a May 19 meeting, Tsvangirai tried to install Thokozani Khupe, his deputy, as second vice president and demanded that a panel of 30 from each faction select parliamentary candidates. In July the Mutambara faction announced it would field its own candidates in 2008.

Meanwhile, Simba Makoni, the former ZANU-PF member who had announced his candidacy as an independent in the 2008 presidential election, received the backing of Mutambara. Ahead of the elections, violence against the MDC increased, resulting in Tsvangirai's seeking shelter in the Dutch embassy in Harare. Ultimately, the MDC won the most seats (by one) in the assembly, despite weakening party alliances and alleged intimidation by the ZANU-PF.

Following the signing of the Global Political Agreement (GPA) on September 15, 2008, by Mugabe, Tsvangirai, and Mutambara, many MDC leaders, including government ministers, faced trial on what were widely deemed to be politically motivated charges. Six months after establishment of the unity government, many rank-and-file MDC-T members, frustrated at what they perceived as bad faith on the part of the ZANU-PF and continued use of repressive measures against the MDC, advocated the party's withdrawal from the coalition. In October 2009 Tsvangirai announced his faction was suspending its participation in the government and would boycott cabinet meetings, but he reversed his stance three weeks later.

Numerous MDC members, including parliamentarians and cabinet ministers, continued to be harassed and arrested. The home of Finance Minister and party secretary general Tendai BITI was bombed, and his office was attacked.

Tensions heightened between MDC factions in 2011, as Welshman Ncube, elected president of the MDC-M faction at its January congress, announced that he would assume the deputy prime minister's post, but Mutambara refused to stand down. In February Mutambara declared Ncube expelled from the party. While the case went to court, Mutambara retained his government post. The Tsvangirai faction was involved in violent clashes with supporters of competing provincial leaders ahead of the MDC-T's April congress in Bulawayo. Most of the national party leaders were reelected, including Tsvangirai, who was unopposed in his leadership bid.

By the spring of 2012 MDC secretary general Tendai Biti, whose performance as finance minister earned him a degree of credibility at both the domestic and international levels, was "seen as the natural successor to the more pedestrian, gaffe-prone Morgan Tsvangirai," according to *Africa Confidential*.

Reports indicated that the continuing rivalry between Tsvangirai and Ncube contributed to the MDC's poor showing in the 2013 balloting. In those elections, Tsvangirai placed second in the presidential contest with 34.9 percent of the vote, while Ncube, as the candidate of the MDC-M, was third with 2.7 percent. Speculation emerged after the balloting that Tsvangirai would step down as leader of the MDC.

MDC internal power struggles continued to distract from addressing the economic crisis in 2014. The opposition has been unable to formulate an economic plan behind which the country is willing to rally. For the first time since 2007, the MDC suggested that mass protest was a real option, despite ZANU-PF's past success in crushing protests. In April the MDC suspended Tsvangirai, accusing him of a failure of leadership. That same month, Tsvangirai announced the expulsion of Biti from the party. Tsvangirai gave a statement in July promising to resign his leadership if defeated at the party congress scheduled for late October. Legal battles over the constitutionality of decisions and control over party assets continued into October. Meanwhile, two breakaway MDC factions, one led by Tendai Biti (called MDC-T Renewal) and the other led by Welshman Ncube formed a coalition called **Coalition of Democrats Agreement** (*Code*) with two Zanu PF splinter groups, one led by Simba Makoni (Mavambo/Dawn/Kusile) and the other by Dumiso DABENGWA (ZAPU).

Tsvangirai requested the removal of 21 MDC members of parliament after they declared their intention to leave the party and form a new grouping, the **United Movement for Democratic Change** (UMDC), under Biti. The renegade MDC members were expelled from the assembly on March 17, 2015.

Leaders: Morgan TSVANGIRAI (President of the MDC-T faction and Former Prime Minister), Thokozani KHUPE (Vice President), Roy BENNETT (Treasurer); Welshman NCUBE (President of the MDC-M and Former Deputy Prime Minister), Arthur MUTAMBARA (MDC-M), Nelson CHAMISA, Tendai BITI (MDC-T Secretary General).

Other Parties That Contested Recent Elections:

Zimbabwe African National Union–Ndonga (ZANU-Ndonga). Led by Ndabaningi Sithole from its formation ahead of the 1980 election until his death in December 2000, the ZANU-Ndonga's main electoral base has been the small ethnic group the Ndau, who are concentrated in Chipinge in Manicaland Province.

Its sole parliamentary representative for Chipinge, who had been elected in 1985 and reelected in 1990, was killed in an automobile accident in October 1994, but Sithole recaptured the seat in a by-election held December 19–20. In the 1995 election, the Chipinge constituency was divided into two electoral districts. Sithole was elected to represent Chipinge South and Wilson Khumbula, to represent Chipinge North. ZANU-Ndonga was the only opposition party to be represented in the 1995 parliament, the other opposition seat held by independent Margaret Dongo.

In October 1995 Sithole was charged with participation in a plot to assassinate President Mugabe. Sithole, who had been released on bail, announced his candidacy in the 1996 presidential election but later withdrew from the race in March 1996, charging that security forces were harassing his supporters. In late 1997 he was found guilty of treason and sentenced to two years in prison. Sithole died in December 2000, his appeal of his 1997 sentence never having been heard.

In the June 2000 election, Wilson Khumbula won the only house seat secured by ZANU-Ndonga. He received 1 percent of the vote in the 2002 presidential election. In March 2005 Khumbula lost the seat and the party failed for the first time since 1985 to have any representative in the House of Assembly. The party sought representation in the November 2005 senate election but secured only 1.8 percent of the votes.

Khumbula supported Simba Makoni in the 2008 presidential election. Semwayo supported the MDC's Tsvangirai in the 2013 presidential election. It did not win any seats in concurrent parliamentary balloting.

Led by Khumbula, the party reunited with the ZANU-PF in March 2015, but elements of ZANU-Ndonga refused to support the merger.

Leaders: Gondai Paul VUTUZA (President of the Party), Reketayi SEMWAYO (National Chair), Wilson KHUMBULA (2002 presidential candidate).

Zimbabwe African People's Union–Federal Party (ZAPU-FP). In 2002 this Matabeleland-based breakaway party from Agrippa Madhlela's ZAPU party (below) was led by Paul SIWELA. The party supported federalism and full regional autonomy for Matabeleland. Siwela ran without ZAPU's endorsement in the 2002 presidential race after the party decided not to contest the 2002 presidential election, instead supporting the candidacy of the MDC's Morgan Tsvangirai.

ZAPU-FP contested the 2005 Senate election, securing just 0.03 percent of the vote.

In September 2007 the MDC and the ZAPU-FP agreed to form an alliance ahead of the 2008 elections, resulting in Siwela's expulsion from ZAPU-FP. Siwela subsequently formed a new party, the Federal Democratic Union (FDU), which became inactive and subsequently defunct after failing to win any seats in the 2008 legislative election.

Leader: Sikhumbuzo DUBE (Acting President).

Zimbabwe African People's Union (ZAPU). The new incarnation of ZAPU constitutes a reconfiguration of Zimbabwe's oldest political party. Originally led by Joshua Nkomo, ZAPU was formed in 1961 and played a leading role in the popular struggle against colonial rule in Rhodesia. The party and its Zimbabwe People's Revolutionary Army (ZIPRA) drew their strength primarily from the Ndebele people of Matabeleland and the Midlands. Conflict between ZAPU and ZANU intensified after independence was achieved, culminating in the Gukurahundi massacres perpetrated by ZANU-PF forces that claimed the lives of thousands of Ndebele civilians in the mid-1980s. In part to put a stop to these clashes, ZAPU agreed to the unity accord of December 22, 1987, whereby its party infrastructure was absorbed into that of ZANU-PF. Former ZIPRA fighters and ZAPU members retained a separate and subordinate party identity.

In December 2008 a national conference of ZAPU members declared that the party was pulling out of the unity accord, asserting that ZANU-PF had violated the spirit of the agreement and reneged on its commitments. Former ZANU-PF politburo member Dumiso Dabengwa was named the party's interim chairperson. A preliminary ZAPU party congress in Bulawayo on May 16, 2009, attended by more than 1,000 delegates, ratified the withdrawal. The party's ranks swelled as thousands defected from ZANU-PF in Matabeleland and other parts of the country. President Mugabe dismissed the new formation as an illegitimate endeavor by "rogue" elements within the ruling party; in response, Dabengwa claimed that ZAPU remained the nation's authentic liberation movement.

The ZAPU used the constitutional outreach process to campaign for devolution of power into five regions, including Matabeleland, and proportional representation in parliamentary elections, vowing to reject any final document that omitted these two planks. Dabengwa accused the MDC of aping the corrupt practices of ZANU-PF now that it shares government power, suggesting that the difference between the two top parties had become minimal. At the ZAPU national congress in Bulawayo in August 2010, Dabengwa was elected president on a slate of new leaders.

In March 2011 Dabengwa distanced himself from the Matabeleland secessionists (see Matabeleland Liberation Front, below), affirming that ZAPU is a nationalist party. In July a serious rift developed when Cyril NDEBELE, a former speaker of parliament who had headed ZAPU's Council of Elders, claimed the presidency of the party. Joining him was Canciwell NZIRAMASANGA, who had been interim deputy chairperson until he was defeated at the party congress by Emilia Mukaratirwa. Ndebele and Nziramasanga accused Dabengwa of running the party despotically and fanning ethnic tensions, and they vowed to create a parallel national structure for the breakaway faction.

Dabengwa was the ZAPU candidate in the 2013 presidential elections. He received 0.7 percent of the vote. The party did not secure any seats in parliament in the concurrent legislative balloting.

In October 2014 Dumiso Dabengwa and Simba Makoni (Mavambo/Dawn/Kusile) grouped with Tendai Biti (called MDC-T Renewal) and Welshman Ncube to form a coalition called **Coalition of Democrats Agreement** (*Code*). ZAPU formally became a member of *Code* in October 2016.

Leaders: Dumiso DABENGWA (President of the Party), Emilia MUKARATIRWA (Vice President), Ralph MGUNI (Secretary General).

Additional parties that participated in the 2008 or 2013 elections include, among others: the **Zimbabwe Youth in Alliance** (ZIYA), led by Chawaona KANOTI and Moses MUTYASIRA; **Zimbabwe Progressive People's Democratic Party** (ZPPDP), formed in 2007 by Tafirenyika MUDUANHU; **Zimbabwe Development Party** (ZDP), led by former ZANU-PF member Kisinoti MUKWAZHE and Rev. Everisto CHIKANGA (Mukwazhe was the party's 2013 presidential candidate, but withdrew prior to the balloting); **Peace Action Is Freedom for All,** led by Abel NDLOVU; **Voice of the People/Vox Populi** (VP), formed in 2006 by Moreprecision MUZADZI with the support of Zimbabweans living in regions such as Botswana and South Africa; **ZURD,** led by Madechiwe COLLIAS; **Patriotic Union of Matabeleland** (PUMA), established in 2006 by Leonard NKOLA, a former member of ZANU-PF, to unify Matabeleland and seek autonomy for the region; **Christian Democratic Party** (CDP), formed by William GWATA in 2008; **Freedom Front,** formed in 2013 by Cosmas MPONDA; **Alliance Khumbula Ekhaya** (AKE), launched in 2013; the **FreeZim Congress;** the **People's Democratic Union;** and the **Mavambo/Kusile/Dawn,** founded by Simba MAKONI. None receive more than 1 percent of the vote in the 2013 balloting.

Other Parties:

Democratic Party (DP). Launched by Zimbabwe Unity Movement (ZUM) expellees (including Emmanuel MAGOCHE) in 1991, the DP held its inaugural congress in September 1992. DP President Wurayayi

Zembe had been a leading member of the NCA committee, which included parties aligned to the NCA that embraced the cause for a new democratic constitution. At the annual general meeting of the NCA held in Harare, Zembe was nominated to the NCA chair but withdrew from the race. Lovemore MADHUKU was reelected after the NCA's constitution had been amended to allow for a third term.

The DP has claimed resource constraints have prevented the party from having held any congresses. The party has boycotted all elections since 1995 on the grounds that a new democratic constitution is necessary before free and fair elections can be held. The DP blasted the formation of a constitutional committee in parliament in April 2009, declaring the process illegitimate and proposing an inclusive constitutional conference facilitated by the UN, AU, and SADC. On April 30, 2009, Zembe was arrested outside the office of the national government in Harare and reportedly forced to stand at gunpoint under a water tap for 15 minutes before being released. The DP opposed the 2013 constitution.

Leader: Wurayayi ZEMBE.

Zimbabwe People's Party (ZPP). The ZPP was formed in August 2007, claiming to stand for "genuine democracy" and calling on Zimbabweans to fight poverty. There was some speculation that the ZPP was sponsored by Zimbabwe's Central Intelligence Organization to split the opposition vote in the 2008 elections, but the interim party president, Justin Chiota, denied the rumors.

In August 2008 Chiota, who was excluded from participation in elections for reportedly submitting his nomination papers past the deadline, voiced strong opposition to the March elections. The Supreme Court later ruled that the decision to exclude him from the first round of presidential balloting was invalid. Chiota's subsequent bid to overturn the presidential election was rejected by the high court. Chiota also argued that power-sharing talks between the MDC and ZANU-PF were unconstitutional. On November 22, 2011, Chiota killed his estranged wife and then committed suicide. Subsequently, the party reportedly went defunct.

Leader: Justin CHIOTA.

Matabeleland Liberation Front (or Mthwakazi Liberation Front—MLF). Launched in Bulawayo in December 2010 by a group of Zimbabwean exiles in South Africa, the members' mission was to advocate for regional power while organizing for the liberation, autonomy, or secession of Matabeleland.

Party leaders Paul Siwela, formerly of the defunct Federal Democratic Union (FDU), John Gazi, and Charles Thomas were arrested in March 2011 after distributing pamphlets calling for Zimbabweans to join the Arab Spring and demanding the dissolution of the Mugabe regime. All three were charged with treason. Gazi and Thomas were bailed out with funds from the MDC's Ncube faction. Siwela was released after 90 days in solitary confinement and banned from participating in political activity. In April four party leaders handed in a petition to the Zimbabwean embassy in South Africa demanding the secession of Matabeleland and the Midlands provinces. They also burned Zimbabwe flags to underscore their demands.

In November 2011 Siwela claimed that security forces stormed and searched his house. MLF boycotted the 2013 national elections.

Leaders: Paul SIWELA, John GAZI, Charles THOMAS.

Other parties include the **Zimbabwe People's Democratic Party** (ZPDP), led by Isabel MADANGURE, who died in 2011 (she was one of the first women to form a political party in the 1980s); the **Zimbabwe Integrated Party** (ZIP), formed in 2008 by Fanuel ZIMIDZI (a separate entity from Heneri Dzinotyiwei's ZIP, which joined the MDC on June 28, 2006); the **United Democratic People's Constitution** (UDPC), formed in February 2008 by Tasunungurwa MHURUVENGWE; and the **Zimbabwe National Congress** (ZNC), formed in 2009 by Ibbo MANDAZA and Kudzai MBUDZI.

For more information on other small parties, see the 2009 *Handbook.* For information on the **Multi-People's Democratic Party** (MPDP), see the 2013 *Handbook.*

LEGISLATURE

Zimbabwe has had seven legislatures since 1980. The first two were bicameral. (For details, see the 1989 *Handbook.*) In February 1990 the upper house (Senate) was abolished, the legislature thereupon becoming a unicameral body, the House of Assembly. A bicameral legislature was reinstituted in 2005, following a constitutional amendment approved by the house on August 30 to establish a Senate. The Constitutional Amendments No. 18, which was passed unanimously by the house on September 18, 2007, and the Senate on September 26, and No. 19, approved by both chambers on February 5, 2009, provided for changes in the number of house and Senate members (see Constitution and government, above). Under the provisions of the 2013 constitution, the lower house was renamed the National Assembly.

Senate. The Senate comprises 80 members. All serve five-year terms. As of 2013, 62 members are directly elected (6 from each of the 8 provinces and the two municipalities, and two to represent the disabled community). The remaining members are the 2 heads of the Council of Chiefs, and 16 traditional chiefs.

In the most recent balloting on July 31, 2013, the seat distribution was as follows: the Zimbabwe African National Union–Patriotic Front, 37; Movement for Democratic Change, 21; and Movement for Democratic Change–Mutambara, 2.

President: Edna MADZONGWE.

National Assembly. There are 210 members in the Assembly all of them directly elected.

Following the most recent balloting on July 31, 2013, the seat distribution was as follows: the Zimbabwe African National Union–Patriotic Front, 160; Movement for Democratic Change, 49; and independent, 1.

Speaker: Jacob MUDENDA.

CABINET

[as of November 11, 2016]

President	Robert Gabriel Mugabe
Vice Presidents	Emmerson Mnangagwa
	Phelekzela Mphoko
Ministers	
Agriculture, Mechanization, and Irrigation Development	Joseph Made
Defense	Sydney Sekeramayi
Energy and Power Development	Samuel Undenge
Environment, Water, and Climate	Oppah Muchinguri [f]
Finance	Patrick Chinamasa
Foreign Affairs	Simbarashe Mumbengegwi
Health and Child Welfare	David Parirenyatwa
Higher and Tertiary Education, Science, and Technology Development	Jonathan Moyo
Home Affairs	Ignatius Chombo
Industry and Commerce	Mike Bimha
Information Communication Technology and Postal and Courier Services	Supa Mandiwanzira
Justice, Legal Affairs, and Parliamentary Affairs	Emmerson Mnangagwa
Lands and Land Resettlement	Douglas Mombeshora
Local Government, Public Works, and National Housing	Saviour Kasukuwere
Macro-economic Planning and Investment Promotion	Obert Mpofu
Media, Information, and Broadcasting Services	Chris Mushohwe
Mines	Walter Chidhakwa
Primary and Secondary Education	Lazarus Dokora
Public Service, Labor, and Social Welfare	Prisca Mupfumira [f]
Rural Development and National Heritage	Abednico Ncube
Small and Medium Enterprise Development	Sithembiso Nyoni [f]
Sports, Arts, and Culture	Makhosini Hlongwane
State Security	Kembo Mohadi
Tourism	Walter Mzembi

Transport and Infrastructural Development	Joram Gumbo
Welfare Services for War Veterans	Col. (Ret.) Tshinga Dube
Women's Affairs, Gender, and Community Development	Nyasha Chikwinya [f]
Youth Development, Indigenization, and Empowerment	Patrick Zhuwao
Ministers of State	
Education and Vocational Training	Josiah Hungwe
Presidential Affairs	Flora Buka [f]
Senior Minister of State	Simon Khaya-Moyo
Vice President's Office	Clifford Sibanda
Vice President's Office	Tabetha Kanengoni-Malinga [f]

[f] = female

Note: All of the above are members of the Zimbabwe African National Union–Patriotic Front.

INTERGOVERNMENTAL REPRESENTATION

Ambassador to the U.S.: Ammon MACHINGAMBI.

U.S. Ambassador to Zimbabwe: Harry K. THOMAS.

Permanent Representative to the UN: Frederick Musiiwa Makamure SHAVA.

IGO Memberships (Non-UN): AfDB, AU, Comesa, IOM, NAM, SADC, WTO.

For Further Reference:

Bratton, Michael. *Power Politics in Zimbabwe.* Boulder, CO: Lynne Rienner, 2015.

Meredith, Martin. *Mugabe: Power, Plunder, and the Struggle for Zimbabwe's Future.* New York: PublicAffairs, 2007.

Rutherford, Blair. *Farm Labor Struggles in Zimbabwe: The Ground of Politics.* Bloomington: Indiana University Press, 2016.

PALESTINIAN AUTHORITY/PALESTINE LIBERATION ORGANIZATION

Political Status: Declaration of Principles establishing a "Palestinian authority" to assume partial governmental responsibility in Gaza and portions of the West Bank signed by Yasir Arafat (chair of the Palestine Liberation Organization) and Israeli prime minister Yitzhak Rabin on September 13, 1993; agreement reached on May 4, 1994, between Arafat and Rabin for formal launching of the withdrawal of Israeli troops from certain occupied territories and inauguration of the first Palestinian Authority (PA, or Palestinian National Authority [PNA]) on July 5; extension of limited Palestinian self-rule to additional territory approved in Israeli–Palestinian accord on September 24, 1995; elected civilian government inaugurated February–May 1996 to govern most of Gaza and portions of the West Bank; mixed presidential–prime ministerial system adopted for Palestinian self-rule areas on March 10, 2003; Israeli settlements in Gaza dismantled and all Israeli forces withdrawn unilaterally from Gaza in August–September 2005; control of Gaza taken over in June 2007 by the Islamic Resistance Movement (Hamas), with the PNA retaining control of Palestinian self-rule territory in the West Bank; government of national unity (covering Gaza and Palestinian self-rule territory in the West Bank) installed on June 2, 2014, following the reconciliation agreement on April 23 between Hamas and *Fatah*/Palestine Liberation Organization (theretofore the major political force behind the PNA).

Population: 4,797,000 (2016E—UN); 4,760,979 (West Bank: 2,839,777; Gaza: 1,921,202) (2016E—U.S. Census).

President: Mahmoud ABBAS (*Fatah*/Palestine Liberation Organization); directly elected on January 9, 2005, and inaugurated for a four-year term on January 15 to succeed Yasir ARAFAT (*Fatah*/Palestine Liberation Organization), who had died on November 11, 2004. (President Abbas's term has been subsequently extended indefinitely [most recently as part of the Hamas/*Fatah* reconciliation agreement of 2014] pending new elections, which had not been held as of the end of 2016.)

Prime Minister: Rami HAMDALLAH (nonparty); appointed by the president on June 2, 2013, to succeed Salam Khaled Abdallah FAYYAD, who had been serving in a caretaker capacity since his resignation was accepted on April 13; formed government on June 6, 2013; reappointed by the president on August 13, 2013; formed government (identical to the previous government) on September 19, 2013; inaugurated on June 2, 2014, as head of the new national unity government established under the *Fatah*/Hamas reconciliation agreement announced in April. (Ismail HANIYEH [Islamic Resistance Movement—Hamas] had been dismissed [along with his entire cabinet] by President Abbas on June 14, 2007, but had refused to accept the dismissal. Haniyeh served as head of Hamas's de facto government from that time until he resigned immediately prior to the inauguration of the national unity government on June 2, 2014.)

GEOGRAPHIC COMPONENTS

Gaza Strip. The Gaza Strip (routinely referenced as simply Gaza) consists of the part of the former League of Nations' Mandate for Palestine contiguous with the Sinai Peninsula that was still held by Egyptian forces at the time of the February 1949 armistice with Israel. Encompassing some 140 square miles (363 sq. km), the territory was never annexed by Egypt and was subsequently not legally recognized as part of any state. In the wake of the 1967 Arab–Israeli war, nearly half of its population of 356,100 (1971E) was living in refugee camps, according to the United Nations (UN) Relief and Works Agency for Palestinian Refugees in the Near East (UNRWA). The population was estimated by Palestinian officials to be 934,000 prior to a census conducted in late 1997, the results of which indicated an increase to about 1,022,000. (The population in Gaza was estimated at 1,760,000 in 2013. Approximately 1.2 million were categorized as refugees.)

Most of Gaza was turned over to Palestinian administration under the Israeli-Palestinian accord of May 4, 1994 (see Political background, below), with Israel retaining authority over Jewish settlements in the territory and responsibility for external defense. On February 20, 2005, the Israeli cabinet by a vote of 17 to 5 endorsed a plan for unilateral disengagement from Gaza to begin on August 15 of that year. The plan required the dismantling of all Israeli settlements in the Gaza Strip, the evacuation of 8,000 Jewish settlers, and the closure of Israeli military bases. The withdrawal was completed on September 12, marking the end of 38 years of Israeli rule over the territory. However, Israel retained offshore maritime control as well as control of airspace over Gaza.

As of early 2014, it was reported that more than 80 percent of the people in Gaza were dependent on government aid, while the territory also faced massive unemployment and major energy and water shortages. The Israeli offensive in Gaza of July and August left more than 2,100 Palestinians dead (including many children and other civilians) and displaced more than 100,000 in the midst of widespread infrastructure devastation.

Estimates were that the economic costs of the conflict in Gaza to the Palestinians were $1.7 billion and that it would not be until 2018 that the economy recovered to 2014 levels. In 2016 the World Bank estimated that unemployment in Gaza was 42 percent, with youth unemployment rates at 58 percent. GDP growth was estimated to be about 3.5 percent for 2015 and 2016.

West Bank. Surrounded on three sides by Israel and bounded on the east by the Jordan River and the Dead Sea, the West Bank encompasses what was the Jordanian portion of the former League of Nations' Mandate for Palestine between 1948 and 1967. It has an area of 2,270 sq. mi. The Palestinian population in the West Bank (including East Jerusalem) was estimated at 2,676,000 in 2013, while the Jewish settler population (including East Jerusalem) had grown to an estimated 500,000.

The West Bank was occupied by Israel following the 1967 Arab-Israeli war. In July 1988 King Hussein of Jordan announced that his government would abandon its claims to the West Bank and would respect the wishes of Palestinians to establish their own independent state in the territory.

Under the Israeli–Palestinian accord of May 4, 1994 (an extension of the September 13, 1993, Oslo Agreement [see Political background, below]), the West Bank enclave of Jericho was turned over to Palestinian administration on May 13. Palestinian control was extended to six more West Bank towns (Bethlehem, Jenin, Nablus, Qalqilya,

Ramallah, and Tulkarm) in late 1995 as the result of the second major "self-rule" accord, signed on September 28, 1995. Concurrently, civic authority in more than 450 villages in the West Bank was also turned over to the Palestinians, although Israeli forces remained responsible for security in those areas. In January 1997 Israeli troops withdrew from all but about 20 percent of the West Bank town of Hebron. In addition, an agreement was announced for additional redeployment of Israeli troops from other West Bank areas in three stages over the next 18 months.

It was generally expected in 1997 that the withdrawals would occur relatively quickly from most of the villages already under Palestinian civic authority, with as yet ill-defined redeployment from the rural areas in the West Bank to follow. However, none of the withdrawals had occurred by March 1998, as negotiations between Palestinian representatives and the Israeli government collapsed. A new series of withdrawals was authorized by the Wye agreement of October 1998, but only the first of those stages was implemented. The subsequent "effective state of war" between the Palestinians and Israelis precluded further resolution as Israeli forces occupied many of the areas previously turned over to Palestinian control.

In June 2002 Israel began constructing a barrier to separate the West Bank from Israel. The Israeli government stated that the construction of the barrier was necessary to prevent the flow of Palestinian suicide bombers from the West Bank. The route of the barrier was subsequently mired in controversy, given that it did not completely follow the 1949 Israeli–Jordanian armistice line, also known as the Green Line, and that it encircled Palestinian communities close to the Israel–West Bank border. The barrier also diverged from the Green Line in places to incorporate large Jewish settlements in East Jerusalem and the West Bank and left some Palestinian population centers on the Israeli side of the barrier. The Israeli government subsequently approved a new route after the Israeli Supreme Court ruled that the previous route would have been disruptive to the lives of Palestinians put on the Israeli side of the barrier. As a result, the new route ran closer to Israel's boundary with the West Bank, although it still included more than 6 percent of West Bank land on the Israeli side of the barrier. Concomitant with Israeli disengagement from the Gaza Strip in August–September 2005, Israeli forces were also redeployed from some areas in the northern West Bank, including the Israeli settlements of Ganim, Kadim, Sa-Nur, and Homesh.

The World Bank estimated that GDP grew in the West bank at approximately 3.5 percent in 2015 and 2016. In 2016 unemployment was 27 percent. In 2015 and 2016 Israel did increase the number of work permits for Palestinians.

GOVERNMENT AND POLITICS

Political background. (For information on developments prior to November 1988, see the section on the Palestine Liberation Organization [PLO], below.) Upon convocation of the 19th session of the PLO's Palestine National Council (PNC) in Algiers in mid-November 1988, it appeared that a majority within the PLO and among Palestinians in the occupied territories favored "land for peace" negotiations with Israel. On November 15 PLO chair Yasir ARAFAT, with the endorsement of the PNC, declared the establishment of an independent Palestinian state encompassing the West Bank and Gaza, with the Arab sector of Jerusalem as its capital, based on the UN "two-state" proposal that had been rejected by the Arab world in 1947. The PLO Executive Committee was authorized to direct the affairs of the new state pending the establishment of a provisional government.

In conjunction with the 1988 independence declaration, the PNC adopted a new political program that included endorsement of the UN resolutions that implicitly acknowledged Israel's right to exist. The PNC also called for UN supervision of the occupied territories pending final resolution of the conflict through a UN-sponsored international conference. Although Israel had rejected the statehood declaration and the new PLO peace initiative in advance, many countries (more than 110 as of April 1989) subsequently recognized the newly proclaimed entity. The onrush of diplomatic activity following the PNC session included a speech by Arafat in December to the UN General Assembly, which convened in Geneva for the occasion because of the U.S. refusal to grant the PLO chair a visa to speak in New York. A short time later, after a 13-year lapse, the United States agreed to direct talks with the PLO, Washington announcing it was satisfied that Arafat had "without ambiguity" renounced terrorism and recognized Israel's right to exist.

On April 2, 1989, the PLO's Central Council unanimously elected Arafat president of the self-proclaimed Palestinian state and designated Faruk QADDUMI as foreign minister of the still essentially symbolic government. Israel remained adamantly opposed to direct contact with the PLO, however, proposing instead that Palestinians end their intifada (uprising) in return for the opportunity to elect non-PLO representatives to peace talks.

During the rest of 1989 and early 1990, the PLO appeared to make several significant concessions, despite growing frustration among Palestinians and the Arab world in general over a perceived lack of Israeli reciprocity. Of particular note was Arafat's "conditional" acceptance in February 1990 of a U.S. plan for direct Palestinian–Israeli peace talks, theretofore opposed by the PLO in favor of a long-discussed international peace conference. However, the Israeli government, unwilling to accept even indirect PLO involvement, rejected the U.S. proposal, thus further undercutting the PLO moderates. By June the impasse had worsened, in part because of PLO protests over the growing immigration to Israel of Soviet Jews, many of whom settled in the West Bank. Moreover, Washington decided to discontinue its talks with the PLO because of a lack of PLO disciplinary action against those claiming responsibility for an attempted commando attack in Tel Aviv.

Subsequently, the PLO leadership and a growing proportion of its constituency gravitated to the hard-line, anti-Western position being advocated by Iraqi president Saddam Hussein, a stance that created serious problems for the PLO following Iraq's invasion and occupation of Kuwait in August 1990. Despite anti-Iraq resolutions approved by the majority of Arab League members, Arafat and other prominent PLO leaders openly supported President Hussein throughout the Gulf crisis. As a result, Saudi Arabia and the other Gulf states suspended their financial aid to the PLO (estimated at about $100 million annually), while Western sympathy for the Palestinian cause eroded. Following the defeat of Iraqi forces by the U.S.-led coalition in March 1991, the PLO was left, in the words of a *Christian Science Monitor* correspondent, "hamstrung by political isolation and empty coffers." Consequently, the 20th PNC session in Algiers in late September agreed to a joint Palestinian–Jordanian negotiating team with no official link to the PLO for the multilateral peace talks inaugurated in Madrid, Spain, in October.

As the peace talks moved into early 1992, Arafat and his *Fatah* component of the PLO faced growing criticism that concessions had produced little in return, and fundamentalist groups such as the Islamic Resistance Movement (Hamas) benefited from mainstream PLO defections in the West Bank and Gaza. Consequently, it was widely believed that Arafat would face yet another strong challenge at the PLO's Central Council meeting scheduled for April. However, circumstances changed after the PLO leader's plane crashed in a sandstorm in the Libyan desert on April 7, with Arafat being unaccounted for, and widely presumed dead, for 15 hours. Panic reportedly overcame many of his associates as they faced the possible disintegration of a leaderless organization. Thus, when Arafat was found to be alive, a tumultuous celebration spread throughout the Palestinian population, reconfirming his preeminence. As a result, even though the succession issue remained a deep concern, Arafat's policies, including continued participation in the peace talks, were endorsed with little opposition when the Central Council finally convened in May. Negotiations were put on hold, however, until the Israeli election in June, after which PLO leaders cautiously welcomed the victory of the Israel Labor Party as enhancing the peace process.

Although peace talks resumed in August 1992, they failed to generate any immediate progress, and criticism of Arafat's approach again intensified. In September the PLO's Democratic Front for the Liberation of Palestine (DFLP) and Popular Front for the Liberation of Palestine (PFLP), Hamas (not a PLO member), and a number of other non-PLO groups established a coalition in Damascus to oppose any further negotiations with Israel.

Israel's expulsion of some 400 Palestinians from the occupied territories to Lebanon in late December 1992 further clouded the situation, the PLO condemning the deportations and ordering Palestinian representatives to suspend their participation in the peace negotiations. Even after the talks resumed in mid-1993, they quickly appeared deadlocked, and rancorous debate was reported within the PLO leadership on how to proceed. By that time, with Hamas's influence in the occupied territories continuing to grow, onlookers were describing the PLO and its aging chair as "fading into oblivion" and "collapsing." However, those writing off Arafat were unaware that PLO and Israeli representatives had been meeting secretly for nearly eight months in Oslo, Norway, and other

European capitals to discuss mutual recognition and the beginning of Palestinian self-rule in the occupied territories. Although initial reports of the discussions in late August were met with widespread incredulity, an exchange of letters on September 9 between Arafat and Israeli prime minister Yitzhak Rabin confirmed that the peace process had indeed taken a hopeful turn. For his part, Arafat wrote that the PLO recognized "the right of the State of Israel to exist in peace and security" and described PLO Charter statements to the contrary to be "inoperative and no longer valid." The chair also declared that the PLO renounced the "use of terrorism and other acts of violence." In return, Rabin's short letter confirmed that Israel had "decided to recognize the PLO as the representative of the Palestinian people and commence negotiations with the PLO within the Middle East peace process."

For all practical purposes the initial round of direct PLO–Israeli negotiations had already been completed, and the mutual recognition letters were quickly followed by unofficial but extensive reports of a draft Declaration of Principles regarding Palestinian autonomy. The PLO Executive Committee endorsed the draft document on September 10, 1993, and the stage was set for a dramatic ceremony on September 13 in Washington, D.C., that concluded with the signing of the declaration by Arafat and Rabin. The Declaration of Principles authorized a "Palestinian authority" to assume governmental responsibility in what was projected to be a gradually expanding area of the occupied territories from which Israeli troops were to withdraw. Among other things, the accord proposed the establishment of an interim Palestinian government in Gaza and the West Bank town of Jericho and committed Israel and the PLO to negotiating a permanent settlement on all of the occupied territories within five years. However, mention of the agreement was rarely made without immediate reference to the many obstacles in its path, including strong opposition from Israel's *Likud* Party and, on the Palestinian side, from Hamas, the DFLP, and the PFLP. There was also widespread concern that militant activity could sabotage the peace agreement. In addition, many details remained to be resolved before the Declaration of Principles could be transformed into a genuine self-rule agreement. Finally, there still appeared to be a wide, and possibly unbridgeable, gulf between the Israeli and PLO positions on the future of Jerusalem, the status of Palestinian refugees, and whether a completely independent Palestinian state would ultimately be created. Nevertheless, the remarkable image, flashed via television to a transfixed world, of Arafat and Rabin shaking hands at the Washington ceremony seemed to persuade even the most skeptical observers that a historic corner had been turned. For the PLO chair, the agreement represented an extraordinary personal triumph, his enhanced status being reflected by a private session with U.S. president Bill Clinton after the signing ceremony and by a meeting the next day with UN secretary general Boutros Boutros-Ghali.

International donors quickly expressed their enthusiasm for the September 1993 agreement by pledging $2.4 billion to promote economic development in Gaza/Jericho over the next five years. Shortly thereafter, the PLO's Central Committee approved the accord by a reported vote of 63–8. However, the declaration's projection that Israeli troops would begin their withdrawal by mid-December 1993 proved unrealistic, and extended negotiations were required on issues such as the size of the Jericho enclave and the control of border crossings.

Amid growing international concern that the peace plan could unravel, negotiations resumed in April 1994, and, at a May 4 ceremony in Cairo, Arafat and Rabin signed a final agreement formally launching Israeli troop withdrawal and inaugurating limited Palestinian self-rule. The Israeli pullout, and concurrent assumption of police authority by PLO forces, was completed in Jericho on May 13 and in most of Gaza on May 18. (Israeli troops remained stationed in buffer zones around 19 Jewish settlements in Gaza.)

The 1994 accord provided for all government responsibilities in Gaza/Jericho (except, significantly, for external security and foreign affairs) to be turned over to the "Palestinian authority" for a five-year interim period. Negotiations were to begin immediately on the second stage of Israeli redeployment, under which additional West Bank territory was to be turned over to Palestinian control, while a final accord on the permanent status of the occupied territories was to be completed no later than May 1999.

On May 28, 1994, Arafat announced the first appointments to the Palestinian National Authority (PNA), with himself as chair of the cabinet-like body. (The PLO leader subsequently routinely referred to himself as "president" of the PNA. However, the title and, indeed, the Palestinian insistence on including "National" in the PNA's name were not sanctioned by the Israeli government, which remained officially opposed to the eventual creation of a Palestinian state. Meanwhile, the media was split on the matter, with some referencing the PNA and others the Palestinian Authority [PA].) With most PLO offices in Tunis having been closed, Arafat entered Gaza on July 1, setting foot on "Palestinian soil" for the first time in 25 years. It was initially assumed that the PNA's headquarters would be in Jericho, where the PNA, which had already held several preliminary sessions, was formally sworn in before Arafat on July 5. However, Arafat and most government officials subsequently settled in Gaza City. Internal security initially proved to be less of a concern than anticipated within the autonomous areas, and the PNA focused primarily on efforts to revive the region's severe economic distress. The World Bank, designated to manage the disbursement of the aid pledged by international donors the previous fall, announced plans to distribute about $1.2 billion over the next three years, primarily for infrastructure projects. On the Palestinian side, coordination of such assistance fell to a recently established Palestinian Economic Council for Development and Reconstruction (PECDAR).

In late August 1994 Israeli officials announced they were turning educational responsibilities for Palestinian areas in the West Bank over to the PNA as the beginning of an "early empowerment" program. The PNA was also scheduled to assume authority throughout the West Bank (save for the Jewish settlements) soon in four additional areas—health, social welfare, taxation, and tourism. On the political front, the PNA proposed that elections to a Palestinian Council be held in December. However, no consensus had been reached by September either between the PLO and Israel or among Palestinians themselves on the type, size, constituency, or mandate of the new legislative body.

Pessimism over the future of the self-rule plan deepened in the fall of 1994 as security matters distracted attention from political and economic discussions. Under heavy pressure from Israel, the PNA authorized the detention of several hundred members of Hamas after that grouping had claimed responsibility for a gun and grenade attack in Jerusalem on October 9. Ten days later a Hamas suicide bomber blew up a bus in Tel Aviv, killing 22 people and prompting Israel to close its borders with the West Bank and Gaza and implement other new security measures. In addition, Palestinian police arrested nearly 200 members of the militant group Islamic Jihad (*al-Jihad al-Islami*) after it claimed responsibility for a bombing in Gaza in early November that left three Israeli soldiers dead. The tension culminated on November 18 in the killing of 13 people as Palestinian police exchanged gunfire with Hamas and Islamic Jihad demonstrators in Gaza, some observers suggesting that the Palestinians were on the brink of a civil war. Further complicating matters for the PLO/PNA, a meeting of the PLO Executive Committee called by Arafat in November failed to achieve a quorum when dissidents refused to attend. Among other things, the PLO chair had hoped that the committee would formally rescind the sections in the organization's National Covenant that called for the destruction of Israel.

Another Islamic Jihad suicide bombing on January 22, 1995, killed more than 20 people in the Israeli town of Netanya. Israel responded by suspending negotiations with the PNA until stronger measures were taken to prevent such attacks from the West Bank and Gaza. Consequently, Arafat authorized the creation of special military courts in February to deal with "issues of state security" and thereby permit a crackdown on militants. While the action appeared to appease Israel, it was criticized by human rights activists and non-PLO Palestinian organizations. As a result, facing yet another test of his leadership, Arafat called for a PLO Executive Committee meeting, the absence of the proposed covenant change from the agenda apparently facilitating the achievement of a quorum. Despite intense scrutiny from the Executive Committee, which was seen as attempting to recover some of the influence it had lost to the PNA, the PLO chair emerged from the meeting with a mandate to pursue negotiations with Israel.

Following a further intensification in April 1995 of the PNA campaign against "terrorists," peace talks regained momentum, and 100-member negotiating teams from each side sequestered themselves in the Egyptian resort of Taba for several months. Finally, after six consecutive days of direct negotiations between Arafat and Israeli foreign affairs minister Shimon Peres, agreement was reached on September 24, 1995, on the next phase of Israeli troop redeployment and the extension of Palestinian self-rule to much of the West Bank. Israeli troops were to start withdrawing immediately from certain towns and villages in the West Bank, with the PNA assuming control therein. Temporary joint responsibility was arranged for rural areas, while Israeli troops were to continue to guard the numerous Jewish settlements in the West Bank and Gaza. Upon completion of the Israeli redeployment, elections were to be held, under international supervision, to a new Palestinian Council. Provision was also made for a 25-member "executive authority," whose head would be elected in separate balloting. It was estimated that self-rule would initially be extended to about 30 percent of the West Bank, with additional territory (up to a 70 percent total) to be ceded following the proposed Palestinian elections. In support of the accord, Israel pledged a three-stage release of thousands of Palestinian prisoners, while the PLO agreed to revoke the anti-Israeli articles in its covenant within two years.

The Israeli–Palestinian Interim Agreement on the West Bank and Gaza (informally referred to as "Oslo II") was signed by Arafat and Prime Minister Rabin at another White House ceremony on September 28, 1995, the attendees including King Hussein of Jordan and President Hosni Mubarak of Egypt. Israel and the PLO agreed that Israeli troops would begin to withdraw from six more West Bank towns immediately while negotiations continued on the contentious issue of the town of Hebron, home to a small but highly vocal group of ultrareligious Jewish settlers. The agreement also envisioned the turning over of authority to Palestinians in more than 450 additional villages in the West Bank, followed by Israeli withdrawal from most other rural areas. Although many details of the latter withdrawal were left unspecified, it was agreed that it would be conducted in three stages—6 months, 12 months, and 18 months after the election of the Palestinian Council, which was designated to succeed the PNA as the primary Palestinian governmental body. It was estimated that the council would be responsible for more than 70 percent of the West Bank following the proposed Israeli withdrawal, with Israel maintaining control of the Jewish settlements and its numerous military installations in the West Bank.

Although "less mesmerizing" than its 1993 predecessor, the 1995 signing was considered just as consequential since the 400-page accord delineated in "intricate detail" most of the substantive aspects of the Israeli-Palestinian "divorce." On the other hand, very contentious issues remained to be resolved, including the rights of several million Palestinian refugees in countries such as Jordan, Lebanon, and Syria, many of whom hoped to return "home" to the West Bank and Israel. Talks were scheduled to begin in May 1996 on that question as well as the future status of Jerusalem, the eastern portion of which Palestinians claimed as their "capital." Difficult negotiations were also forecast regarding the estimated 140,000 Jewish settlers in Gaza and the West Bank, many of whom vowed never to leave the region to which, in their opinion, "Greater Israel" had a biblically ordained right. A final agreement on these and all other outstanding issues was due no later than May 1999, at which point the Palestinian Council was scheduled to turn over authority to whatever new governmental organs had been established. It was by no means clear what the final borders of the Palestinian "entity" would be or, for that matter, what official form of government it would assume. Although Israeli officials maintained their formal opposition to an independent Palestine, Arafat described the 1995 agreement as leading to "an era in which the Palestinian people will live free and sovereign in their country." However, in a decision that was to have major repercussions, the Israeli and PLO negotiators postponed further discussions of the contentious issue of the proposed withdrawal of Israeli troops from Hebron.

Despite concerns that the assassination of Israeli Prime Minister Rabin in November 1995 would interfere with the implementation of the recent agreement, Israeli withdrawals from the six additional towns proceeded even more quickly than expected and were completed by December 30, 1995. Consequently, with the formal encouragement of the PLO Executive Committee, Arafat subsequently attempted to convince Hamas and theretofore "rejectionist" PLO factions to participate in the upcoming Palestinian elections. Although those discussions initially appeared promising, Hamas and a number of major PLO components (most notably the DFLP and the PFLP) ultimately urged their supporters to boycott the balloting on the grounds that electoral regulations were skewed in favor of Arafat's *Fatah* at the expense of smaller formations. Nevertheless, the elections on January 20, 1996, for the Palestinian Council and separate balloting for the head (or "president") of the council's "executive authority" were still viewed as a major milestone in the self-rule process. Only one person (Samihah Yusuf al-Qubbaj KHALIL, an opponent of the Oslo peace agreements) challenged Arafat for the latter post. The PLO chair garnered 87.1 percent of the votes in balloting that was widely construed (in conjunction with *Fatah*'s success in the legislative poll) as confirming strong support for him personally and majority endorsement of his peace policies. Arafat was inaugurated in his new position in ceremonies in Gaza City on February 12, 1996, and on May 9 he announced the formation of a new cabinet, technically the "executive authority" of the Palestinian Council but widely referenced as the "new" PNA, which continued the semantic PNA/PA controversy. The government won a vote of confidence in the Palestinian Legislative Council (PLC, as the new body had widely become known) by 50–24 on July 27.

Militant opposition to the Oslo accords moved even further to the forefront of concerns in late February and early March 1996 when bomb attacks left some 60 Israelis dead in Jerusalem and Tel Aviv. Temporary closure of the borders of the self-rule areas by Israeli forces generated pressure upon Arafat from within the Palestinian population, while the additional security issues were seen as a substantial political problem for Israeli prime minister Shimon Peres, facing an early election in May. Arafat implemented several measures apparently designed to help Peres, including the arrest of a number of militants from Hamas and other groups and the banning of some six Palestinian "militias." In addition, the PLO chair convened the 21st session of the PNC (now reported as comprising 669 members) in Gaza City on April 22–24 to consider formal revision of the National Covenant to reflect recent understanding of the issue. The PNC session, the first to be held on "Palestinian" soil since 1966, agreed by a vote of 504–54 that all clauses in the covenant that contradicted recent PLO pledges were to be annulled. In general, the changes would recognize Israel's right to exist and renounce "terrorism and other acts of violence" on the part of the PLO. Final language on the revisions was to be included in a new charter, which the PNC directed the Central Council to draft.

The "final talks" on Palestinian autonomy officially opened on May 5, 1996, but substantive negotiations were postponed until the Israeli election of May 29. Following the surprising *Likud* victory in that balloting, resulting to some extent from security concerns within the Israeli populace arising from the recent bomb attacks, progress slowed on the Palestinian front. No agreement was quickly forthcoming regarding Hebron, which became the focus of Israeli right-wing attention, and the planned three-stage withdrawal of Israeli troops from rural areas in the West Bank was not implemented. Israeli–PLO talks resumed in late July, but no progress ensued, even after face-to-face discussions between Arafat and new Israeli prime minister Benjamin Netanyahu in early September. International concern that the autonomy plan was deteriorating and growing criticism from moderate Arab states also seemingly failed to move the Netanyahu government (a tenuous coalition that included several ultraconservative groupings). Rising pressure finally erupted in fighting between Palestinians and Israelis in late September. U.S. president Bill Clinton quickly summoned Arafat, Netanyahu, and Jordan's King Hussein to Washington for a "crisis summit," which appeared to reduce tensions, albeit without any apparent resolution of the underlying issues, particularly the status of Hebron, described as a "powder keg" that seemingly had assumed a psychological importance well out of proportion to its intrinsic significance.

As Netanyahu continued to resist redeployment of Israeli troops from Hebron throughout the rest of 1996, Arafat warned of the risk of the spontaneous resumption of the intifada. Finally, under apparent heavy U.S. pressure, Netanyahu accepted an agreement in early January 1997 that essentially reaffirmed the provisions of Oslo II. Among other things, the new accord (approved by the PLO Executive Committee on January 15) provided for Palestinian control to be extended to about 80 percent of Hebron, with Israeli withdrawal from additional rural West Bank areas to occur in stages from March 1997 through mid-1998. Assuming satisfactory progress on that front (not a certainty considering differing Israeli and Palestinian views on how much territory would ultimately be ceded to Palestinian rule), final talks were to be conducted on the still highly charged issues of the status of Palestinian refugees throughout the region, the nature of permanent governmental structures for the Palestinian "entity," and disposition of sovereignty claims to East Jerusalem.

Chair Arafat convened a "national dialogue" meeting in February 1997 in an effort to involve the formerly dissident PLO factions as well as non-PLO Palestinian groups in adopting a consensus on Palestinian proposals should final status talks be launched with Israel. However, Arafat's "national unity" conference in August appeared primarily aimed not at negotiations but rather at portraying solidarity in the face of perceived Israeli intransigence. The presence of Hamas and Islamic Jihad at the session lent weight to Arafat's assertions that military resistance (including resumption of the intifada) was a growing possibility. Meanwhile, the PNA itself had come under heavy domestic and international criticism, one corruption commission suggesting that more than $300 million in aid had been mishandled. The PLC demanded in late 1997 that President Arafat replace the cabinet with a new government comprising experts in their various fields rather than political appointees. It also called upon him to address allegations that Palestinian police and security forces had been responsible for widespread human rights abuses.

In February 1998 the PLO Executive Committee deferred a final decision on the proposed new PLO charter, eliciting Israeli concern that the 1996 action by the PNC remained insufficient as far as guaranteeing Israel's security was concerned. In addition, when agreement could not be reached on the extent of the next Israeli withdrawal, the Israeli government approved highly controversial Jewish settlement construction in East Jerusalem. Meanwhile, attention within the PLO focused on the question of a successor to Arafat, whose health was believed to be in decline.

In July 1998 Israeli and Palestinian negotiators met for the first time in over a year, and in October Netanyahu traveled to the United States to meet with Arafat and Clinton at the Wye Plantation in Maryland. After ten days of reportedly "tortuous" negotiations (capped off by a surprise visit from ailing King Hussein of Jordan), Netanyahu and Arafat signed an agreement on October 23 that proposed a three-month timetable for the next withdrawals of Israeli forces from the West Bank. It was envisaged that negotiations would then begin regarding the third (and last) withdrawal phase and the other outstanding issues.

In addition to the geographic expansion of Palestinian autonomy, Israel also agreed in the 1998 Wye accords to release a number of Palestinian prisoners, permit the opening of the Gaza airport, and proceed with the establishment of a transit corridor for Palestinians from the West Bank to Gaza. For their part, Palestinian leaders pledged expanded security measures and additional repudiation of the anti-Israeli sections of the PLO Covenant. The first redeployment (centered around the northern West Bank town of Jenin) occurred on November 20, and international donors, signaling support for the resumption of progress, subsequently pledged some $3 billion in additional aid for development in the autonomous areas. However, Netanyahu faced significant opposition within his cabinet over the accord and appeared to place numerous barriers in the way of further implementation by, among other things, authorizing the expansion of Jewish settlements in the West Bank and demanding that Palestinian officials adopt a comprehensive weapons collection program, refrain from anti-Israeli "incitement," and drop their plans to unilaterally declare statehood on May 4, 1999. Clinton visited Israel and the self-rule territories on December 12–15 in an effort to reinvigorate the Wye plan, attending the session of the PNC in Gaza that endorsed the requested Covenant changes. However, the Netanyahu coalition finally collapsed in the ensuing days, and further implementation of the Wye provisions was suspended pending new Israeli national elections (later scheduled for May 1999).

Following his inauguration in July 1999, new Israeli prime minister Ehud Barak called for a comprehensive peace settlement with the Palestinians, Syria, and Lebanon within 15 months. On September 4 he and Arafat signed an agreement in Sharm al-Shaikh in Egypt that provided for the "reactivation" of the 1998 Wye accord via the immediate transfer to Palestinian control of additional territory in the West Bank and the release of some Palestinians under Israeli arrest in return for the Palestinian leadership's "zero tolerance" of terrorism. So-called final status negotiations were subsequently launched on the very difficult issues of Jewish settlements in the occupied territories, the eventual status of Jerusalem (which both sides envisioned as their capital), and the future of some 3.6 million Palestinian refugees seeking a return to Israel. Little progress was achieved by the spring of 2000, however, except for some redeployment of Israeli forces in the West Bank (bringing about 43 percent of the West Bank under complete or partial Palestinian control). In April, Barak appeared to accept the eventual creation of "an independent Palestinian entity" (he avoided using the word "state") comprising Gaza and 60–70 percent of the West Bank. However, he indicated a "majority" of the Jewish settlers in the disputed areas would remain under Israeli sovereignty. Hopes for a resolution declined further in May when sporadic violence broke out in Gaza and the West Bank, fueled by Palestinian anger over the lack of progress in negotiations.

Faced with a collapsing coalition in Israel, Barak attended a "make-or-break" summit with Arafat and U.S. president Clinton at Camp David in July 2000. Although agreement appeared close on several issues, the summit ended unsuccessfully when common ground could not be found regarding the status of Jerusalem and sovereignty over holy sites there, notably Temple Mount (*Haram al-Sharif*), a sacred location for both Jews and Muslims. (Clinton criticized Arafat for being unwilling to make the "difficult decisions" required to conclude a pact.)

Serious rioting on the part of Palestinians erupted in late September 2000 following a visit by hard-line *Likud* leader Ariel Sharon to Temple Mount that was viewed as unnecessarily "provocative" by many observers. Although Barak subsequently indicated a willingness to endorse the establishment of two separate "entities" in Jerusalem, negotiations collapsed in October in the face of the "second intifada" and heavy reprisals by the Israeli military that included the use of assault helicopter and rocket attacks. By the end of December more than 350 people had been killed and 10,000 injured in the violence. In addition, Israel had banned Palestinian workers from entering Israel and had imposed other economic sanctions such as the withholding of tax payments to the PNA.

At the end of 2000 President Clinton, attempting to cap his eight-year tenure with a "last hurrah" Middle East breakthrough, proposed a settlement under which all of Gaza and some 95 percent of the West Bank would be placed under Palestinian control, although some West Bank settlements would remain Israeli. The proposed accord also reportedly called for Palestinian sovereignty over certain areas of East Jerusalem, the return of a "small number" of Palestinian refugees, and a "mutual accommodation" regarding Temple Mount. Barak reportedly approved the compromise, but Arafat in early 2001 raised a number of objections, particularly in regard to the refugee issue. (The Palestinian position—that all refugees and their descendants be permitted to return to Israel—had been rejected as an impossibility by most Western capitals and, of course, Israel, on the grounds that the Jewish Israeli electorate would be overwhelmed politically by the returnees.)

Barak's defeat by hard-liner Sharon in the February 2001 special prime ministerial balloting in Israel appeared to doom prospects for any settlement soon of the Palestinian questions, particularly in view of the fact that President George W. Bush's new administration in Washington had announced it did not consider itself in any way bound by the "parameters" endorsed by Clinton. For his part, Sharon pledged that Jerusalem would remain "whole and unified" under Israeli sovereignty and that no Jewish settlements would be dismantled. Consequently, the rest of the year was marked by escalating violence that included numerous suicide bombings by Palestinian militants and massive retaliation by Israel in the form of missile attacks and tank incursions. However, late in the year President Bush expressed his support for the eventual establishment of a Palestinian state and called for the withdrawal of Israeli forces from the areas previously under Palestinian control. Peace advocates also saw a glimmer of hope when Arafat, whose compound was besieged by Israeli troops, subsequently called upon all Palestinian groups to honor a cease-fire and indicated "flexibility" on the refugee question. However, suicide bombings continued unabated in early 2002, and Israel in April launched an offensive of unprecedented scale that left it in control of most West Bank towns. When that initiative failed to restrain the suicide bombers, the Sharon government announced at midyear that it would begin to construct a "security fence" around the West Bank. Positions subsequently remained hardened as Sharon called Arafat an "enemy" and demanded a change in the Palestinian leadership.

Meanwhile, criticism in Palestinian circles of Arafat's government continued, although it was muted somewhat by an apparent desire within the Palestinian community to present a unified front in the face of renewed Palestinian-Israeli violence. In response to the discontent, in the spring of 2002 Arafat, whose compound in Ramallah had been under siege by Israeli forces for months as part of the broad Israeli incursion, reportedly admitted "errors" in peace negotiations as well as in the administration of the PNA, and he promised significant reform efforts. He also subsequently pledged to conduct new presidential and legislative elections when Israeli forces were withdrawn from areas previously under Palestinian control. However, concerned over the number of suicide bombings and other attacks on Israeli citizens, President Bush called for the "removal" of Arafat, portraying the Palestinian leader as unable or unwilling to combat terrorism. (Many analysts had concluded by that time that Arafat had little control over the attacks being claimed by Hamas and Islamic Jihad.)

Arafat trimmed his cabinet on June 9, 2002, although he was unable to convince the rejectionist groups (notably Hamas, Islamic Jihad, the PFLP, and the DFLP) to participate in the new government. Arafat also subsequently promised reform in social sectors and indicated support for the eventual establishment of the post of prime minister, who would theoretically assume some of the authority heretofore exercised by Arafat.

In late 2002 Arafat declared that new elections would be postponed indefinitely due to Israel's continued occupation of territory formerly under Palestinian control. However, under heavy international pressure, Arafat in early 2003 formally endorsed the proposed installation of a Palestinian prime minister. The PLC on March 10 officially established the new position, although power-sharing arrangements vis-à-vis the president were left vague. (Among other things, Arafat retained control over peace negotiations with Israel.) Mahmoud ABBAS was nominated to the premiership, and his new cabinet was installed on April 29. Abbas promised to combat corruption, disarm militants, and pursue additional reform in Palestinian institutions. However, it quickly became clear that Abbas and Arafat were locked in a power struggle, and Abbas resigned on September 6. He was succeeded on September 10 by Ahmad QURAY, the speaker of the PLC.

At the end of April 2003 the Middle East Quartet (the European Union [EU], Russia, the UN, and the United States) presented a "road map" toward the eventual establishment of an "independent, democratic, and viable" Palestinian state. The first steps would be an immediate and unconditional cease-fire and a freeze on new Israeli settlements. The plan also envisioned completion of a new Palestinian constitution, in the hope that Palestinian elections could be held by the end of the year. The major component of the second phase of the road map would be the convening of an international conference that would, among other things, help determine provisional borders for the new state. Final negotiations were slated for completion by the end of 2005, assuming Palestinian institutions had been "stabilized" and Palestinian security forces had proven adequate in combating attacks against Israel. Israeli prime minister Sharon offered qualified support for the road map, as did the Israeli *Knesset,* although the latter insisted that it be made clear that Palestinian refugees would not be guaranteed the right to return to their former homes in Israel.

In the wake of renewed heavy violence, the *Knesset* in September 2003 endorsed the potential expulsion from the Palestinian territories of Arafat, whom Sharon and Bush blamed for the ongoing stalemate. Significantly, in February 2004 Sharon announced that he intended to order the unilateral disengagement of Israel from the Gaza Strip in light of the lack of progress regarding the road map.

Apparently in response to the growing reform tide, Arafat in mid-2004 once again acknowledged that he had "made mistakes," indicating that he was prepared to lead a renewed negotiation initiative. However, by that time it was clear that his health had failed to a point of unlikely recovery, and attention mostly focused on ensuring a smooth transition to the new PNA and PLO leaderships.

In July 2004 Prime Minister Quray threatened to resign unless the PLC granted him greater authority, particularly in regard to security. His request was partially granted, and the issue became mostly moot when Arafat died of an unknown illness at a hospital near Paris on November 11. (The French inquiry into Arafat's death was reopened in 2012 after Arafat's widow claimed that a radioactive toxin was discovered on his clothes that had been returned to her. However, in December 2013 the French authorities ruled that Arafat had died of a "generalized infection.") Mahmoud Abbas was quickly named to replace Arafat as chair of the PLO executive committee, while PLC speaker Ruhi FATTUH assumed presidential authority on an acting basis.

With Hamas and Islamic Jihad boycotting the presidential balloting on January 9, 2005, on the grounds that their involvement would have implied acceptance of the 1993 Oslo accords, Abbas won the presidency with 62 percent of the vote. His nearest rival (20 percent) was Moustafa BARGHOUTI, a secular independent associated with neither the PLO nor Hamas. Abbas was sworn in on January 15, and he invited Quray to form a new government. The international community welcomed the installation of a new Palestinian regime, and President Bush called Abbas "a man of courage."

Despite its boycott of the January 2005 presidential balloting, Hamas competed in the municipal elections held in the Palestinian territories in December 2004–January 2005. Hamas performed strongly, underscoring the growing disenchantment among Palestinians with *Fatah*'s governance.

In February 2005 President Abbas appointed a new cabinet consisting mainly of technocrats, again under the leadership of Quray. The appointments were seen as an effort to reduce the influence of the *Fatah* "old guard" that had been closely aligned with Yasir Arafat. Meanwhile, Ariel Sharon pushed ahead with his plan to evacuate the Jewish settlements in Gaza and to disengage militarily from the territory, overcoming opposition from within his own governing coalition. The disengagement from Gaza was achieved in August–September. Although Sharon and Abbas subsequently agreed on a cease-fire and Hamas itself declared a period of "calm," violence continued throughout 2005 as little progress was made in negotiations. Sporadic conflict also broke out between Palestinian security forces and Islamist militants. President Abbas visited President Bush twice in 2005, but Abbas's positive international stature did not have much impact on Palestinian dissatisfaction with political and economic conditions.

Hamas, which had again showed electoral strength in additional municipal elections in May and September 2005, scored a stunning victory in balloting for the PLC on January 25, 2006, securing 74 of 132 seats, compared to 45 seats for *Fatah.* Ismail HANIYEH of Hamas was inaugurated on March 29 to lead a new government that included only Hamas members and several independents, *Fatah* having declined to join the cabinet.

The United States and European states greeted the formation of the Hamas-led cabinet by suspending financial aid to the PNA and demanding that Hamas pledge to cease violence and recognize the state of Israel. Israel also halted the transfer of customs tax revenues to the PNA, causing severe economic distress for a large part of the Palestinian population, especially those employed by the PNA.

In May 2006 three people were killed when armed supporters of Hamas clashed with Abbas loyalists in Gaza. The fighting escalated over the next few weeks as Hamas deployed a militia of some 3,000 fighters to Gaza. However, Hamas subsequently withdrew its "implementation force" from Gaza to calm tensions. Shortly thereafter, Abbas called on Hamas to endorse a national accord that had been drawn up by prisoners detained in Israel, including *Fatah* leader Marwan BARGHOUTI. The plan called for acceptance of the pre-1967 boundaries for a Palestinian state (with Jerusalem as its capital), the establishment of a national unity government to include Hamas and *Fatah*, and PLO negotiations with Israel toward a two-state solution. Furthermore, Abbas issued an ultimatum to Hamas to recognize Israel or else he would call for a referendum on the proposed accord. Hamas consented to many of the articles of the document, with the notable exception of negotiations that would lead to the recognition of Israel. However, any potential for a peace initiative was squashed after two Israeli soldiers were killed and another was kidnapped by Palestinian militants who had tunneled under the border from Gaza. While rival Palestinian factions still called for a government of national unity, Abbas tabled further negotiations on the subject because of the "sensitivity" of the most recent event. Meanwhile, Hamas demanded that Israel fully withdraw from the occupied territories, turn over tax revenues owed to the Palestinians, and immediately release all Palestinian ministers and lawmakers (including the speaker of the PLC) arrested in the months following the June abduction of the Israeli soldier.

Some analysts perceived a softening of Hamas's stance regarding potential recognition, or at least "acceptance," of the Israeli state during national unity negotiations between *Fatah* and Hamas in September 2006. Hamas also implied it might consider a "long-term truce" with Israel. However, Ehud Olmert (who had become prime minister of Israel in the wake of Ariel Sharon's stroke in January) subsequently authorized additional construction of Jewish settlements in the West Bank. Israel also maintained its economic blockade of Gaza and initiated several military offensives into Gaza in response to rocket attacks into Israel. Meanwhile, Palestinian workers went on strike in September to demand back wages, the Hamas-led government responding that it was being crippled by Israel's refusal to release tax revenues. Hamas also charged *Fatah* with promoting the demonstrations.

Israel withdrew its forces from Gaza in early November 2006, and a cease-fire was announced at the end of the month between Israel and most of the militant Palestinian groups. (Significantly, Islamic Jihad did not accept the agreement.) Olmert also urged "dialogue" that would lead to "an independent and viable Palestinian State," while Arab nations and Iran agreed to contribute financially to the PNA.

Factional Hamas–*Fatah* fighting intensified in December 2006, and President Abbas threatened to call early elections unless a national unity government could be established. Nevertheless, the factional violence continued in January 2007, spreading from Gaza into several major cities in the West Bank.

President Abbas on February 8, 2007, signed an agreement with the Hamas leadership for a new "national unity" government. Among other things, the new coalition pledged to pursue a settlement with Israel based on a 2002 "land-for-peace" proposal from King Abdullah of Saudi Arabia that had recently been reendorsed by the Arab League. Consequently, Haniyeh and his cabinet resigned on February 15, although Abbas immediately reappointed Haniyeh to form a new government. On March 17 the PLC approved the new cabinet (which included ten ministers from Hamas, six from *Fatah*, three from recently formed smaller groups, one from the DFLP, and five independents) by a vote of 83–3. However, Israel, still vehemently opposed to any negotiations with Hamas, called the new PNA a "step backwards" and continued its hard-line approach by arresting Hamas leaders and supporters in the West Bank.

Severe factional infighting broke out again between *Fatah* and Hamas in May 2007 in Gaza, and in June Hamas took over complete control of Gaza. President Abbas on June 14 dissolved the PNA in light of what he called the "military coup" in Gaza and declared a one-month state of emergency. On June 17 Abbas appointed a new "emergency" government headed by Salam FAYYAD, theretofore the PNA's finance minister. The emergency cabinet resigned on July 13, but most of its members were included in the "caretaker" or "transitional" government appointed the following day. However, Haniyeh disputed the legitimacy of Abbas's actions, arguing that a new government required approval of the PLC. Consequently, Haniyeh continued to lead a five-member cabinet in Gaza that he described as the legitimate Palestinian government.

Western donors immediately resumed aid to Abbas's PNA following the installation of the emergency government in the West Bank in June 2007. Also with the goal of supporting Abbas in his conflict with Hamas, Israel subsequently released tax revenues to the PNA and called for renewed peace talks. At the same time, Israel continued its daily attacks on what it called rocket-launching sites in Gaza.

In October 2007, as part of ongoing talks on the "fundamental issues," Israeli prime minister Olmert indicated that Israel might consider a division of Jerusalem as part of a potential final peace settlement. That and other initiatives were discussed at a U.S.-led peace conference in Annapolis, Maryland, at which Olmert and Abbas agreed to resume formal negotiations with the goal of reaching agreement within a year. However, Hamas called Abbas a "traitor" for participating in the conference, while Olmert faced significant opposition in Israel for his perceived concessions to the Palestinians.

Deadly conflict continued in Gaza in late 2007 and early 2008 between Hamas and *Fatah* and between Hamas supporters and Israeli security forces. In mid-January 2008 Israel, responding to rocket attacks from Gaza into Israel, launched a major incursion into Gaza and closed Gaza's borders. Palestinians destroyed a border fence into Egypt later in the month, permitting them to rush into Egypt to buy much-needed fuel, food, medical supplies, and other necessities constrained by the Israeli blockade.

A suicide bombing in Israel in early February 2008 (the first in more than a year) prompted another Israeli air strike in Gaza, and tit-for-tat violence intensified into the summer. Israel and Hamas finally announced a cease-fire in June, with Israel agreeing to ease its controversial blockade. Meanwhile, President Abbas called for a "national dialogue" between *Fatah* and Hamas with the goal of new national elections. (In the opinion of many analysts, the initiative reflected an acknowledgment that Hamas had solidified its control in Gaza by, among other things, replacing judges and prosecutors with Hamas supporters and by expanding the Hamas network of social services and business connections.) Nevertheless, *Fatah*–Hamas discord continued, and the prospects for a comprehensive settlement with Israel before the end of the year dimmed in the face of political chaos in Israel. Meanwhile, Haniyeh expanded the Hamas cabinet in Gaza at midyear, while the PLO Central Committee in November announced that it had elected Abbas as president of the State of Palestine, reflecting concern over how executive authority would be exercised when Abbas's term as PNA president reached its scheduled conclusion on January 8, 2009.

Hamas formally declared the six-month cease-fire with Israel ended as of December 19, 2008, arguing that Israel had not lived up to its agreements regarding the truce, which Hamas reportedly had also sporadically violated. (Hamas argued that Israeli had reneged on its pledge to lift the economic blockade on Gaza and had contravened the accord through the arrest of Hamas members in the West Bank.) After Hamas rocket attacks from Gaza into Israel intensified, Israel on December 27 launched a series of massive air strikes (Operation Cast Lead) against suspected Hamas security compounds in Gaza. In the face of additional rocket and mortar attacks into southern Israel, Israeli ground forces entered Gaza on January 3, 2009, to at least neutralize, if not topple, Hamas through "all-out war" if necessary. More than 1,500 Palestinians were killed (including some 900 civilians) during the offensive, which also destroyed or damaged 21,000 houses and otherwise decimated the infrastructure in Gaza before Israel declared a cease-fire on January 17. Hamas, which had continued to fire rockets and mortars into Israel during the conflict, declared its own unilateral cease-fire the same day, although it reserved the right to resume military activity unless Israeli troops were withdrawn quickly.

Most Arab states strongly condemned the late 2008–early 2009 Israeli offensive in Gaza (Egyptian president Hosni Mubarak characterized it as "savage aggression"), and most Western capitals expressed concern over the intensity of the Israeli campaign. A UN report later in the year criticized both sides in the conflict, citing the ongoing Hamas rocket attacks. However, the report's strongest language was reserved for the Israeli military, accused of a "disproportionate attack" that leveled "collective punishment" against civilians. The UN called for further investigation of possible war crimes, including Israel's alleged use of white phosphorous against mostly civilian targets and the alleged execution of Palestinian civilians. Israel, which rejected the report as biased, accused Hamas of having used civilians as human shields. Human rights groups also charged Hamas with arresting, torturing, and in some cases, executing alleged Palestinian "collaborators" following the conflict.

Meanwhile, on January 9, 2009, President Abbas announced that he was extending his term for another year, claiming that the Palestinian Basic Law authorized him to do so in order to "align" new presidential elections with the PLC balloting due in January 2012. However, Hamas disputed that interpretation, declaring that the speaker of the PLC was legally authorized to assume the position of acting president until new elections were held. (Although its stance had no de facto influence, Hamas continued to recognize PLC speaker Abdel Aziz DUWAIK as the acting president of the PNA until the national unity government was installed in 2014 [see below].)

In early March 2009 international donors pledged some $4.5 billion to assist in reconstruction in Gaza over the next two years, although delivery of the aid was subsequently compromised by donor insistence that it not be used to prop up Hamas. The international community also called for Hamas and *Fatah* to negotiate a resolution to their political stalemate.

Prime Minister Fayyad announced the resignation of his transitional cabinet on March 9, 2009, in anticipation of the formation of a Hamas-*Fatah* national unity government. However, when negotiations in that regard collapsed, President Abbas on May 19 appointed a new government (again led by Fayyad) that included a number of independents, several members of *Fatah*, and one member each from the DFLP, PFLP, and the Palestinian Democratic Union (PDU). Meanwhile, discussions between the Abbas administration and Israel toward resumption of formal peace talks foundered when newly installed Israeli prime minister Benjamin Netanyahu, despite some conciliatory rhetoric, resisted heavy U.S. pressure to halt the construction of Jewish settlements in East Jerusalem and the West Bank.

After new U.S. president Barack Obama in June described the stateless status of Palestinians as "intolerable," Netanyahu endorsed the proposed "two-state" solution to the impasse, although the conditions he attached on Palestinian sovereignty appeared to doom prospects immediately. Frustrated by the lack of progress, President Abbas, in scheduling new presidential elections for January 2010, announced that he might not run for reelection. For its part, Hamas did not endorse the proposed election schedule, and in December the balloting was postponed indefinitely, the terms of Abbas and the legislators being extended until new elections were held.

In March 2010 President Abbas agreed to so-called proximity talks with Israel under U.S. mediation, the PLO having endorsed the initiative. However, Israel shortly thereafter announced it had approved new settlement construction in East Jerusalem and the West Bank, delaying the new talks until early May. At that time, Palestinian negotiators indicated that direct talks could take place only if Israel imposed a freeze on all construction, the ten-month "restriction" announced by Netanyahu in November 2009 having done little to alleviate Palestinian concerns.

In late May 2010 Israeli commandos intercepted (in international waters) the six-ship Gaza Freedom Flotilla, which was attempting to deliver what organizers characterized as purely humanitarian supplies to Gaza. Nine activists were killed in the attack, which the international community widely condemned. (A subsequent UN report accused Israel of "an unacceptable level of brutality," but Israeli officials claimed their forces had been fired upon first.)

U.S. secretary of state Hillary Clinton hosted face-to-face talks between Abbas and Netanyahu in early September 2010, but Israeli settlement construction resumed apace later in the month, scuttling prospects for further meaningful negotiations. Later in the year Abbas asked the UN Security Council to consider declaring the construction of Jewish settlements in the West Bank illegal. Fourteen members of the council voted "yes" on the request in February 2011, but the United States vetoed the resolution. Meanwhile, the Arab League endorsed Abbas's decision to suspend talks with Israel until a settlement freeze was imposed.

Prime Minister Fayyad and his cabinet resigned on February 14, 2011, in the wake of anti-administration demonstrations, but Fayyad was reappointed the same day. In late April representatives from Hamas and *Fatah* announced that agreement had been reached for their reconciliation. The accord, signed on May 4 in Cairo by Abbas and Hamas leader Khalid MISHAL, called for the formation of a transitional unity government pending new balloting for the PLC and installation of a permanent government. Abbas described the agreement as ending "four black years," while Mishal said Hamas would "pay any price" to achieve unity. Not surprisingly, Israeli prime minister Netanyahu denounced the agreement, reaffirming his country's continued opposition to any peace negotiations involving Hamas.

Subsequently, Fayyad's proposed continuation as prime minister proved to be a sticking point in implementing the 2011 reconciliation agreement. With negotiations on the proposed national unification government sputtering, President Abbas, on May 16, 2012, reappointed Fayyad to head another West Bank government that included members of *Fatah*, the DFLP, and the PDU, as well as independents. On September 2 Prime Minister Haniyeh announced a reshuffle of the Hamas cabinet in Gaza.

Prime Minister Fayyad resigned on April 13, 2013, but he remained in a caretaker capacity until Rami HAMDALLAH succeeded him on June 6. Questions over authority within Hamdallah's administration prompted him to offer his own resignation only two weeks later, but he was subsequently again asked by President Abbas to form a government, which was installed on September 19.

In the wake of the April 2014 reconciliation agreement between *Fatah* and Hamas (see Current issues, below), Hamdallah was named to head the national unity government that was installed on June 2 (Haniyeh currently disbanded the Hamas cabinet in Gaza.) Hamdallah in early October convened what was promoted as an historic meeting in Gaza of the government of what Palestinians were now referencing as the "State of Palestine," but friction reportedly continued between Hamas and *Fatah* on many issues.

The International Criminal Court (ICC) began an investigation in January 2015 into Israel's actions during the Gaza conflict. In April 2015 the PNA formally joined the ICC. Despite opposition from Israel, the government of Palestine and the Vatican concluded a treaty in June in which the Holy See agreed to recognize the state of Palestine. The accord went into force in January 2016.

A minor cabinet reshuffle was announced in July 2015 in an effort to expand the unity government to include more factions. However, Hamas rejected the new ministers, prompting a new reshuffle in December.

Palestine became the 118th member of the Court of Arbitration at The Hague in March 2016.

Current issues. In October 2011 President Abbas attracted significant international attention by formally requesting UN recognition of Palestinian statehood and full UN membership for Palestine. However, the Security Council's admissions committee subsequently reported that no more than 8 of the council's 15 members appeared ready to endorse the proposal, which therefore was not presented to the full council. (Even if the accession request had received the required nine votes in the council, the United States had promised to veto it.)

President Abbas and Hamas leader Mishal met again in November 2011 and announced that presidential and legislative elections would be held in May 2012, assuming successful negotiation of the proposed national unity government. In that regard, the two leaders in February 2012 tentatively agreed that Abbas himself would head a new government of "independent technocrats" who would oversee preparations for the elections while also addressing the dire economic conditions in Gaza. However, agreement on the ministerial appointments proved elusive, prompting Abbas in May to reappoint the Fayyad-led government to attend to the administration of affairs in the West Bank.

Meanwhile, a UN report argued that Gaza might not be "a livable place" by 2020 without immediate attention to rampant unemployment and an increasing shortage of classrooms, hospital beds, food, water, and basic services. Hamas prime minister Haniyeh called upon his new cabinet (installed in September) to concentrate on such problems, adding that he still preferred the eventual appointment of a joint *Fatah*–Hamas government. By that time, many Palestinians appeared to blame the split between the two factions for the lack of economic progress. Among other things, demonstrators in September conducted a week-long protest, primarily directed at Prime Minister Fayyad, over rising prices and other hardships in the West Bank. In a possibly related vein, voter antipathy was apparent in the October 21 local elections, the first Palestinian election of any kind since 2006. (Hamas boycotted the elections, and no polls were held in Gaza.)

In early November 2012 Israel, claiming it was responding to a surge in rocket attacks into southern Israel, initiated an air assault (Operation "Pillar of Defense") on numerous targets inside Gaza, prompting Hamas and other militant groups to launch hundreds of retaliatory rockets. Israeli forces appeared poised to begin a ground campaign as well, but a cease-fire was brokered by Egypt and the United States eight days after the outbreak of hostilities. Despite massive infrastructure damage and the death of more than 160 Palestinians, Hamas declared a "victory of resistance."

In late November 2012 the United Nations General Assembly overwhelmingly voted to upgrade Palestine's UN status to "nonmember observer state" ("state" being the key word). Among other things, the change gave Palestinians access to various UN-affiliated bodies, such as the ICC (where Palestinians could press claims against Israel). Based on the UN's decision, President Abbas in January 2013 directed Palestinian diplomats to start to refer to themselves as representing the State of Palestine rather than the PNA and announced that passports and other official documents would henceforth bear the stamp of the State of Palestine. References to Abbas as president of the State of Palestine also increased, although nations (such as the United States and most EU members) that had not formally recognized Palestine continued to use the PNA rubric.

Jewish settlement activity in the West Bank ramped up in early 2013, apparently contributing to further warming in relations between Hamas and *Fatah*. Among other things, Hamas was given permission to conduct rallies in the West Bank, while similar privilege was granted to *Fatah* in Gaza.

The resignation in April 2013 of Prime Minister Fayyad, whose government had received broad international praise for its competence, was attributed, at least in part, to an ongoing power struggle between the PNA and *Fatah*'s old guard. Some observers predicted that the resignation might facilitate formation of a unity government between Abbas and Hamas (which had strongly criticized Fayyad for being aligned too closely with the United States). However, Hamas remained opposed to peace negotiations with Israel, prospects for which had reportedly been gaining background momentum under the leadership of U.S. secretary of state John Kerry. Meanwhile, new prime minister Hamdallah, the president of a West Bank university, announced that his government would continue to pursue the policies espoused by Abbas.

Although public opinion polls indicated that neither the Palestinian nor the Israeli populations held out much hope for success, direct talks between Palestinian and Israeli officials resumed in mid-August 2013 without preconditions (i.e., no freeze on Jewish settlement activity or agreement regarding the pre-1967 borders as a starting basis). Intensive negotiations continued for the rest of the year and the first part of 2014, although sporadic rocket attacks from Gaza continued to prompt Israeli retaliatory strikes and Israel infuriated the PNA by authorizing additional expansion of Jewish settlements in the West Bank. With the peace talks faltering, Israel in late March 2014 failed to meet the deadline for the fourth in a series of prisoner releases that had been agreed upon the previous year. In apparent response, President Abbas in early April signed papers for Palestinian participation in some 15 international conventions that theoretically could be used to appeal for international condemnation of various Israeli activities.

Fatah and Hamas surprised observers on April 23, 2014, by announcing that another national reconciliation agreement had been reached that envisioned the installation of a unity government covering the West Bank and Gaza to prepare for new presidential and legislative elections. Israeli Prime Minister Netanyahu immediately suspended the peace talks with the PNA, saying that the PNA would have to choose between Israel and Hamas as a negotiating party. For its part, the United States announced it would "work" with the Palestinian government inaugurated in June, noting that most of the cabinet members were technocrats without official affiliation with either *Fatah* or Hamas.

Three Jewish teenagers from a West Bank settlement were kidnapped in early June 2014, and Israel blamed Hamas for the abductions. (Abbas condemned the kidnappings and pledged PNA cooperation in the investigation of the matter.) Israeli security forces subsequently arrested some 350 Palestinians in the West Bank, and attacks from and into Gaza increased when the bodies of the three teenagers were found late in the month.

Israel launched Operation Protective Edge against Gaza on July 8, 2014, starting with thousands of air strikes followed by a full-scale ground invasion. Targets included a number of tunnels Israel accused Hamas of having built under the border into Israel as well as the homes of high-level Hamas leaders. Hamas resisted the invasion fiercely (among other things, it launched an estimated 4,500 rockets into Israel), and more than 2,100 Palestinians and some 72 Israelis (mostly soldiers) died before a cease-fire was concluded on August 26. As with previous Israeli–Hamas conflicts, much of the international community expressed concern over the disproportional aspect of the Palestinian casualties and the heavy damage inflicted on Gazan homes, hospitals, and schools. Israel defended its actions as all geared toward elimination of a "terrorist network."

In early October 2014 President Abbas asked the UN General Assembly to approve a timetable for an end to the Israeli "occupation" of the West Bank. Meanwhile, an international conference pledged $5.4 billion for reconstruction in Gaza and for financial support of the PNA in Gaza and the West Bank. Significantly, Sweden late in the month became the first country to formally recognize the State of Palestine while a member of the EU. At that point, 135 countries had extended such diplomatic recognition to Palestine.

Saint Lucia extended recognition to Palestine in September 2015. The following month a new wave of violence broke out. Alternatively known as the "Intifada of the Individuals" or the "Knife Intifada," tensions between Palestinians and Israel over the Temple Mount led to a series of individual attacks by Palestinians on Israelis (see entry on Israel). By the end of 2016, 38 Israelis, 3 foreigners, including 2 U.S. citizens and an Eritrean, and 235 Palestinians had been killed, including 31 Israeli civilians. (The number of Palestinian civilians killed was disputed, with Israel claiming 10 and Palestinian authorities asserting the figure as 162.) In addition, 558 Israelis were wounded, along with 3,917 Palestinians. More than 7,900 Palestinians were detained. The attacks prompted new border closures and additional work restrictions on Palestinians, hurting the already fragile economy.

The cabinet set October 8, 2016, as the date for local elections, but the balloting was postponed until 2017. Hamas agreed to the polling and announced that it would participate.

POLITICAL PARTIES AND GROUPS

Palestine Liberation Organization (PLO). Establishment of the PLO was authorized on January 17, 1964, during an Arab summit held in Cairo, Egypt. Largely through the efforts of Ahmad SHUQAIRI, the Palestinian representative to the Arab League, an assembly of Palestinians met in East Jerusalem the following May 28–June 2 to draft a National Covenant and General Principles of a Fundamental Law, the latter subsequently serving as the constitutional basis of a government-in-exile. Under the Fundamental Law, the assembly became a 315-member Palestinian National Council (PNC) comprised primarily of representatives of the leading *fedayeen* (guerrilla) groups, various Palestinian mass movements and trade unions, and Palestinian communities throughout the Arab world. An Executive Committee was established as the PLO's administrative organ, while an intermediate Central Council (initially of 21 members but eventually of 100) was created in 1973 to exercise legislative/executive responsibilities on behalf of the PNC between PNC sessions.

In its original form, the PLO was a quasi-governmental entity designed to act independently of the various Arab states in support of Palestinian interests. Its subordinate organs oversaw a variety of political, cultural, and fiscal activities as well as a Military Department, under which a Palestine Liberation Army (PLA) was established as a conventional military force of recruits stationed in Egypt, Iraq, and Syria.

In the wake of the 1967 Arab–Israeli war, the direction of the PLO underwent a significant transformation. Shuqairi resigned as chair of the Executive Committee and was replaced in December 1967 by Yahia HAMMUDA, who was in turn succeeded in February 1969 by Yasir Arafat, leader of *Fatah* (below). At that time the PNC adopted a posture more favorable to guerrilla activities against Israel, insisted upon greater independence from Arab governments, and for the first time called for the establishment of a Palestinian state in which Muslims, Christians, and Jews would have equal rights. In effect, the PLO thus tacitly accepted a Jewish presence in Palestine, although it remained committed to the eradication of any Zionist state in the area.

In 1970–1971 the PLO and the *fedayeen* groups were expelled from Jordan, and Lebanon became their principal base of operations. Fearing that Jordan might negotiate on behalf of Palestinians from the occupied territories following the Israeli victory in the October 1973 war, the PLO in June 1974 formally adopted a proposal that called for the creation of a "national authority" in the West Bank and Gaza as a first step toward the "liberation" of historical Palestine. This tacit recognition of Israel produced a major split among the PLO's already ideologically diverse components, and on July 29 a leftist "rejection front" was formed in opposition to any partial settlement in the Middle East.

In December 1976 the PLO Central Council voiced support for establishment of an "independent state" in the West Bank and Gaza, which was widely interpreted as again implying acceptance of Israel's permanent existence. Shortly thereafter, contacts were established between the PLO and the Israeli left.

On September 1, 1982, immediately after the PLO withdrawal from West Beirut (see the entry on Lebanon), U.S. president Ronald Reagan proposed the creation of a Palestinian "entity" in the West Bank and Gaza, to be linked with Jordan under King Hussein. The idea was bitterly attacked by pro-Syrian radicals during a PNC meeting in Algiers in February 1983, with the PNC ultimately calling for a "confederation" between Jordan and an independent Palestinian state, thus endorsing an Arab League resolution of five months earlier that implicitly entailed recognition of Israel. Over radical objections, the Algiers meeting also sanctioned a dialogue with "progressive and democratic" elements within Israel, i.e., those favoring peace with the PLO.

PLO chair Arafat met for three days in early April 1983 with King Hussein without reaching agreement on a number of key issues, including the structure of a possible confederation, representation of Palestinians in peace negotiations with Israel, and the proposed removal of PLO headquarters to Amman. Soon after, amid evidence of growing restiveness among Palestinian guerrillas in eastern Lebanon, the PLO Executive Committee met in Tunis to consider means of "surmounting the obstacles" that had emerged in the discussions with Hussein.

In mid-May 1983 Arafat returned to Lebanon for the first time since the 1982 Beirut exodus to counter what had escalated into a dissident rebellion led by Musa Awad (also known as Abu Akram) of the Libyan-backed Popular Front for the Liberation of Palestine–General Command (PFLP-GC), a splinter of the larger PFLP. In late June Arafat convened a *Fatah* meeting in Damascus to deal with the mutineers' insistence that he abandon his flirtation with the Reagan peace plan and give greater priority to military confrontation with Israel.

On June 24, 1983, Syrian president Hafiz al-Assad ordered Arafat's expulsion from Syria after the PLO leader had accused Assad of fomenting the PFLP-GC rebellion. A month later Arafat ousted two senior commanders whose promotions had caused tension within the ranks of the guerrillas in Lebanon's Bekaa Valley. The PLO infighting nonetheless continued, and in early November one of Arafat's two remaining Lebanese strongholds north of Tripoli fell to the insurgents. Late in the month the PLO leader agreed to withdraw from an increasingly untenable position within the city itself, exiting from Lebanon (for the second time) on December 20 in a Greek ferry escorted by French naval vessels.

Arafat strengthened and formalized his ties with Jordan's King Hussein in an accord signed in February 1985. The agreement, described as "a framework for common action towards reaching a peaceful and just settlement to the Palestine question," called for total withdrawal by Israel from the territories it had occupied in 1967 in exchange for comprehensive peace; the right of self-determination for the Palestinians within the context of a West Bank/Gaza/Jordan confederation; resolution of the Palestinian refugee problem in accordance with UN resolutions; and peace negotiations under the auspices of an international conference that would include the five permanent members of the UN Security Council and representatives of the PLO, the latter being part of a joint Jordanian–Palestinian delegation.

In reaction to the February 1985 pact with Jordan, six PLO-affiliated organizations formed a Palestine National Salvation Front (PNSF) in Damascus to oppose Arafat's policies. Differences over peace initiatives also erupted during a November meeting in Baghdad of the PNC's Central Council. Disagreement turned mainly on whether to accept UN Security Council Resolutions 242 and 338, which called for Israeli withdrawal from the occupied territories and peaceful settlement of the Palestine dispute in a manner that would imply recognition of Israel. Shortly thereafter, Arafat attempted to reinforce his image as "peacemaker" with a declaration denouncing terrorism. His "Cairo Declaration" was issued after lengthy discussions with Egyptian president Hosni

Mubarak on ways to speed up peace negotiations. Citing a 1974 PLO decision "to condemn all outside operations and all forms of terrorism," Arafat promised to take "all punitive measures against violators" and stated that "the PLO denounces and condemns all terrorist acts, whether those involving countries or by persons or groups, against unarmed innocent civilians in any place."

The PLO sustained a major setback at the hands of Shiite Amal forces that besieged two Palestinian refugee camps in Lebanon during May and June 1985. An extraordinary session of the Arab League Council called for an end to the siege, which was accomplished by Syrian mediation in mid-June.

By early 1986 it had become apparent that the Jordanian–PLO accord had stalled over Arafat's refusal, despite strong pressure from King Hussein and other Arab moderates, to endorse UN Resolutions 242 and 338 as the basis of a solution to the Palestinian issue. Among the PLO's objections were references to Palestinians as refugees and a failure to grant them the right of self-determination. On the latter ground, Arafat rejected a secret U.S. tender of seats for the PLO at a proposed international Middle East peace conference. In February Hussein announced that the peace effort had collapsed and encouraged West Bank and Gaza Palestinians to select new leaders. He underscored the attack on Arafat during ensuing months by proposing an internationally financed, $1.3 billion development plan for the West Bank, which he hoped would win the approval of its "silent majority." The PLO denounced the plan, while describing Israeli efforts to appoint Arab mayors in the West Bank as attempts to perpetuate Israeli occupation. The rupture culminated in Hussein's ordering the closure of *Fatah*'s Jordanian offices in July.

King Hussein's overture elicited little support from the West Bank Palestinians, and by late 1986 it was evident that Arafat still commanded the support of his most important constituency. Rather than undercutting Arafat's position, Hussein's challenge paved the way for unification talks between *Fatah* and other PLO factions that had opposed the accord from the outset. Following initial opposition from the PNSF in August, the reunification drive gained momentum in early 1987 with indications that Georges Habash of the PFLP (the PNSF's largest component) might join leaders of the DFLP and other groups in trying to rescue the PLO from its debilitating fractionalization. Support was also received from PLO factions in Lebanon that had recently coalesced under *Fatah* leadership to withstand renewed attacks by Amal forces. Indeed, Syria's inability to stem the mass return of heavily armed *Fatah* guerrillas to Lebanon was viewed as a major contribution to Arafat's resurgence within the PLO. Meanwhile, King Hussein also attempted to mend relations with the PLO by announcing that the Jordanian–PLO fund for West Bank and Gaza Palestinians, suspended at the time of the February 1986 breach, would be reactivated. Subsequently, the fund was bolstered by new pledges totaling $14.5 million from Saudi Arabia and Kuwait.

Although hard-line factions continued to call for Arafat's ouster, the PLO leader's more militant posture opened the way for convening the long-delayed 18th session of the PNC (its membership reportedly having been expanded to 426) in Algiers on April 20–26, 1987. Confounding critics who had long predicted his political demise, Arafat emerged from the meeting with his PLO chair intact, thanks in part to a declared willingness to share the leadership with representatives of non-*Fatah* factions. Thus, although several Syrian-based formations boycotted the Algiers meeting, Arafat's appearance at its conclusion arm-in-arm with former rivals Habash of the PFLP and Nayif Hawatmeh of the DFLP symbolized the success of the unity campaign.

During the last half of 1987 there were reports of secret meetings between the PLO and left-wing Israeli politicians to forge an agreement based on a cessation of hostilities, a halt to Israeli settlement in Gaza and the West Bank, and mutual recognition by the PLO and Israel. However, nothing of substance was achieved, and by November it appeared that interest in the issue had waned, as evidenced by the far greater attention given to the Iran–Iraq war at an Arab League summit in November.

The Palestinian question returned to the forefront of Arab concern in December 1987 with the outbreak of violence in the occupied territories. Although the disturbances were believed to have started spontaneously, the PLO, by mobilizing grassroots structures it had nurtured throughout the 1980s, helped to fuel their transformation into an ongoing intifada (uprising).

In an apparent effort to heighten PLO visibility, Arafat demanded in March 1988 that the PLO be accorded full representation (rather than participation in a joint Jordanian-Palestinian delegation) at any Middle Eastern peace conference. However, the prospects for such a conference dimmed in April when the PLO's military leader, Khalil al-WAZIR (also known as Abu JIHAD), was killed, apparently by an Israeli assassination team. Whatever the motive for the killing, its most immediate impact was to enhance PLO solidarity and provide the impetus for a dramatic "reconciliation" between Arafat and Syrian president Assad. However, that rapprochement soon collapsed, as bloody clashes broke out between *Fatah* and Syrian-backed *Fatah* dissidents (see *Fatah* Uprising, below) for control of the Beirut refugee camps in May. However, elsewhere in the Arab world, the position of the PLO continued to improve. A special Arab League summit in June 1988 strongly endorsed the intifada and reaffirmed the PLO's role as the sole legitimate representative of the Palestinian people. In addition, a number of countries at the summit reportedly pledged financial aid to the PLO to support continuance of the uprising.

On July 31, 1988, in a move that surprised PLO leaders, King Hussein announced that Jordan would discontinue its administrative functions in the West Bank on the presumption that Palestinians in the occupied territories wished to proceed toward independence under PLO stewardship. Although Jordan subsequently agreed to partial interim provision of municipal services, the announcement triggered extensive debate within the PLO on appropriate policies for promoting a peace settlement that would yield creation of a true Palestinian government. (For information on developments from 1988 to 1998, see Political background, above.)

The peace process appeared to have been relaunched by the Wye accords of October 1998, as part of which the PLO Central Council met on December 10 to consider Israeli requests regarding the PLO covenant. Arafat and other Palestinian representatives had argued that no further action was required, claiming that the PLO chair's earlier letter to President Clinton had made it clear that articles in the covenant had been voided by the PNC in 1996. However, the Central Council endorsed the particulars in Arafat's letter, and on December 14 the PNC reaffirmed the covenant changes by a nearly unanimous show of hands. In addition, under heavy international pressure, the Central Council in late April 1999 endorsed Arafat's recent decision to postpone the unilateral declaration of Palestinian statehood, which had been planned for May 4, 1999. Following the Sharm al-Shaikh agreement of September 1999, the PLO Central Council extended the deadline for statehood declaration until September 2000. Meanwhile, by early 2000 the PFLP and the DFLP had resumed participation in the council's deliberations. Another positive development for Palestinians was a meeting in February 2000 between Arafat and Pope John Paul II at which the Vatican reportedly recognized the PLO as the legitimate voice of Palestinian sentiment and endorsed eventual "international status" for Jerusalem.

Prior to the "make or break" summit between Arafat and Israeli prime minister Ehud Barak (who faced growing opposition within Israel to his peace efforts) in the United States in July 2000, the PLO Central Council indicated its solid support for Arafat and authorized him to declare statehood on September 13. However, when the U.S. summit collapsed, the Central Council, under intense international pressure, agreed at a meeting on September 9–10 to postpone the declaration once again. (Arafat had traveled to some 40 countries to solicit support for the declaration. The United States, EU, and many others resisted the idea, however, in part because of the prevailing sentiment in many capitals that Arafat had missed a significant opportunity at the U.S. summit. The PLO chair had reportedly been offered substantial concessions by Barak but had ultimately rejected terms regarding the status of holy sites in Jerusalem as well as the return of Palestinian refugees and their descendants to Israel.)

Although the PLO was not one of the groups demanding the creation of the post of prime minister to share PNA responsibilities with Arafat, *Fatah* dutifully approved the cabinet installed under new Prime Minister Mahmoud Abbas (the secretary general of the PLO Executive Committee) in April 2003. Subsequently, differences within *Fatah* and the PLO seemed to mirror those in the PLC and PNA in regard to the power struggles between Arafat and Abbas and between Arafat and Abbas's successor, Ahmad Quray. PLO reformists pressed for significant power sharing and implementation of genuine anticorruption measures, while Arafat's long-standing backers in the organization supported his demand for his retention of the responsibility for peace negotiations and control of Palestinian security forces.

Abbas was elevated to the chair of the PLO Executive Committee only hours after Arafat's death on November 11, 2004. In addition, Faruk Qaddumi was named chair of the *Fatah* Central Council with no apparent tumult.

Following a funeral in Cairo (his birthplace), Arafat was buried in Ramallah, where he had lived under virtual Israeli siege for three years. (Israel refused a request for Arafat to be buried in Jerusalem.) The Cairo ceremony was attended by many Arab leaders and dignitaries from around the world, while public demonstrations in Ramallah and elsewhere illustrated the deep grief felt by the Palestinian population at the loss of the only leader the PLO had known for 35 years. At the same time, the occasion appeared even sadder to many observers because of their belief that Arafat had missed several opportunities in the past decade to see much of his Palestinian dream accomplished prior to his death. For their part, the United States and Israel focused on the transition to new Palestinian leaders as an opportunity to revive the peace process.

Following Abbas's election as president of the PNA in January 2005 and Prime Minister Quray's formation of a new cabinet, the two leaders indicated a desire to establish a clear "separation" between the "political" PLO and the "governmental" PNA. Plans were also announced to expand, restructure, and revitalize the PNC. In addition, at midyear Abbas called for negotiations with Hamas and Islamic Jihad toward their possible membership in the PLO. Moreover, Abbas launched talks with the hitherto "rejectionist" PLO factions with the goal of having them participate in a new PNA following the anticipated unilateral withdrawal of Israeli forces from Gaza in August.

Following Hamas's resounding victory in the January 2006 legislative elections, tensions increased within the PLO, *Fatah* having lost its majority in the legislature and thus some of its power base. Among other things, newly elected *Fatah* members of the PLC walked out after Hamas canceled all decisions made by the outgoing PLC. Abbas, though still holding executive authority, was now part of what was described as a "two-headed administration" in a power struggle with the ruling Hamas government. (See Political background and Current issues, above, for subsequent developments.)

In December 2009 the PLO Central Council postponed new elections for the PLC and president of the PNA indefinitely, pending resolution of the conflict with Hamas. The council extended the mandates of the current legislators and President Abbas until the new balloting could be conducted. In October 2010 the council voted to suspend negotiations with Israel until Israel agreed to a settlement freeze in the West Bank and disputed areas of Jerusalem. Many (if not all) of the non-*Fatah* PLO components reportedly objected to the resumption of negotiations with Israel in August 2013.

As part of the *Fatah*/Hamas reconciliation agreement in April 2014, a special PLO committee was authorized to prepare for the eventual incorporation of Hamas and Islamic Jihad into the PLO. Earlier, a PLO reform committee had agreed that the PLO's PNC should eventually become an elected body of 350 members, 200 to be chosen by Palestinians in foreign countries.

Executive Committee: Mahmoud ABBAS (Chair and Head of the Political Department), Zakaria al-AGHA (Refugees), Ali ISHAQ (Youth and Sports), Mahmud ISMAIL, Taysir KHALID (Expatriate Affairs), Riyad al-KHUDARY (Higher Education), Abd al-Rahim MALLOUGH (Arab Relations), Muhammad Zudi al-NASHASHIBI (Palestinian National Fund), Ghassen al-SHAKAA (International Relations), Hanan ASHRAWI, Hanna AMIREH (Social Affairs), Saeb EREKAT, Ahmad QURIA (Jerusalem Affairs), Ahmed MAJDALANI, Salih RAAFAT, Ziad AMR, Wasel ABU-YOUSEF, Yasir Abed RABBO (Secretary General).

Fatah. The term *Fatah* (Arabic for "opening") is a reverse acronym of *harakat al-tahrir al-watani al-filastini* (Palestine Liberation Movement). *Fatah* was established mainly by Gulf-based Palestinian exiles in the late 1950s. The group initially adopted a strongly nationalist but ideologically neutral posture, although violent disputes subsequently occurred between traditional (rightist) and leftist factions. Although *Fatah* launched its first commando operations against Israel in January 1965, it remained aloof from the PLO until the late 1960s, when divisiveness within the PLO, plus *Fatah*'s staunch (though unsuccessful) defense in March 1968 of the refugee camp in Karameh, Jordan, contributed to the emergence of Yasir Arafat as a leading Palestinian spokesperson. Following Arafat's election as PLO chair in 1969, *Fatah* became the PLO's core component.

Commando operations in the early 1970s were a primary responsibility of *al-Asifa*, then the formation's military wing. Following expulsion of the *fedayeen* from Jordan in 1970–1971, a wave of external (i.e., non-Middle Eastern) operations were also conducted by Black September terrorists, although *Fatah* never acknowledged any association with such extremist acts as the September 1972 attack against Israeli athletes at the Munich Olympics. By early 1973 the number of "external" incidents had begun to diminish, and during the Lebanese civil war of 1975–1976 *Fatah*, unlike most other Palestinian organizations, attempted to play a mediatory role.

As the result of a *Fatah* leadership decision in October 1973 to support the formation of a "national authority" in any part of the West Bank it managed to "liberate," a hard-line faction supported by Syria broke from *Fatah* under the leadership of Sabry Khalil al-Banna and his Revolutionary Council of *Fatah*. Smaller groups defected after the PLO's defeat in Beirut in 1982.

Internal debate in 1985–1986 as to the value of diplomatic compromise was resolved in early 1987 by the adoption by *Fatah* of an essentially hard-line posture, a decision apparently considered necessary to ensure continuance of its preeminence within the PLO. However, *Fatah*'s negotiating posture softened progressively in 1988 as Arafat attempted to implement the PNC's new political program. Thus, *Fatah*'s fifth congress, held in August 1989 in Tunisia, strongly supported Arafat's peace efforts, despite growing disappointment over the lack of success in that regard to date. The congress, the first since 1980, also elected Arafat to the new post of Central Committee Chair.

Prior to the September 1993 signing of the PLO–Israeli peace settlement, it was reported that the *Fatah* Central Committee had endorsed its content by a vote of 12–6. As implementation of the accord proceeded in 1994, some friction was reported between formerly exiled leaders returning to Gaza/Jericho and *Fatah* representatives who had remained in those regions during Israeli occupation. In part to resolve such conflict, new by-laws were proposed under which *Fatah* "would operate more like a normal party" with numerous local branches and national committees led by elected chairs. Meanwhile, as would be expected, many of those named to the new Palestinian National Authority (PNA) and other governmental bodies were staunch *Fatah* supporters.

Fatah presented 70 candidates (reportedly handpicked by Arafat) in the January 1996 Palestinian legislative elections; about 50 of these "official" *Fatah* candidates were successful. However, a number of *Fatah* dissidents ran as independents and secured seats. In concurrent balloting for president of the PNA, Arafat was elected with 87.1 percent of the vote, further cementing *Fatah*'s dominance regarding Palestinian affairs. However, Arafat and *Fatah* were subsequently subjected to intense legislative scrutiny (surprisingly rigorous in the opinion of many observers) over perceived governmental inefficiency, or worse.

Following the outbreak of the second intifada (or the *al-Aqsa* intifida, a reference to a mosque on Temple Mount in Jerusalem) in 2000 and the collapse of Israeli–Palestinian peace negotiations, "deep dialogue" was reported within *Fatah* regarding the military and political future for Palestinians. A new guerrilla formation, the *al-Aqsa* Martyrs' Brigade, was reportedly organized as an offshoot of Tanzim, the grassroots *Fatah* militia in the West Bank. *Al-Aqsa* claimed responsibility for a number of attacks against targets within Israel in the first few months of 2002, and the United States placed the group on its list of terrorist organizations. Marwan Barghouti, the reported leader of Tanzim and generally considered the second most popular Palestinian leader after Arafat, was arrested by Israeli security forces in April 2002 and charged with terrorism. At about the same time, *al-Aqsa* announced it would not carry out any attacks on civilians in Israel but reserved the right to attack military targets and Jewish settlements in Gaza and the West Bank.

On the political front, a number of *Fatah* members were among reformists who pressured Arafat in 2002 to combat perceived corruption and mismanagement within the PNA and to appoint a prime minister to share executive authority. *Fatah* subsequently endorsed the appointments of Mahmoud Abbas and Ahmad Quray to the prime ministership in March 2003 and September 2003, respectively. Meanwhile *al-Aqsa* claimed responsibility for a number of attacks on Israeli soldiers and suicide bombings in 2002–2004. (To some observers *Fatah* appeared at best dysfunctional at that point because some of its members were regularly perpetrating attacks while others in the government and police forces were attempting to establish "security.")

Following Arafat's death in November 2004, Faruk Qaddumi was named to succeed him as chair of *Fatah*'s Central Council.

Subsequently, *Fatah* successfully presented Mahmoud Abbas as its presidential candidate in the January 2005 balloting. (Barghouti, sentenced to life in prison in mid-2004 on the terrorism charges, had initially expressed an interest in running for president from jail, observers suggesting he would have had a good chance of success. However, his supporters apparently chose unity over confrontation, and Barghouti withdrew from contention.)

In February 2005 reformist elements in *Fatah* reportedly blocked efforts by *Fatah*'s old guard to retain dominance in the new Palestinian cabinet. Among other things, the reformists argued that *Fatah* was losing popular support to Hamas because of perceived ties of many Arafat loyalists to long-standing corruption.

Following what was described as *Fatah*'s "stunning" defeat by Hamas in the January 2006 legislative elections, violent demonstrations in Gaza on the part of hundreds of *Fatah* supporters demanded the resignation of the *Fatah* leadership, prompting a trip to the area by President Abbas, who called on Hamas to participate in a national unity government. However, *Fatah* continued to be at odds with the Hamas-led government, seeking to have PLO members named to the cabinet and pressuring the PNA to endorse a national accord document proposed by Marwan Barghouti and other Palestinians prisoners in Israel. (See Political background and Current issues, above, for information on subsequent *Fatah*–Hamas conflict.)

Fatah held its sixth congress (the first in 20 years and the first to be held in Palestinian-controlled territory) in mid-2009 amid reports of severe generational divisions and disagreement regarding negotiations with Israel and Hamas. Abbas was reelected as *Fatah*'s leader by a show of hands among the 2,300 delegates, although a number of reform advocates (including the imprisoned Barghouti) were elected to the new 18-member Central Council. The congress's final document essentially reconfirmed the movement's previous policy positions, including the right to resistance "in all its forms" to Israeli occupation. For his part, Abbas urged peaceful civil disobedience as the preferred tactic and called for an agreement with Hamas on a new national unity government.

In early 2012 the *Fatah* leadership ejected a number of members from the party for running in the upcoming municipal elections as independents after they were left off the official *Fatah* states. *Fatah* maintained control of most major municipalities in the October 21 poll, although independent states presented by the former *Fatah* members won in Nablus and Jenin. Under the direction of Abbas, *Fatah* endorsed the revival of peace negotiations with Israel in August 2013. It also supported the recent ouster by the military of Egyptian president Morsi.

At *Fatah*'s seventh congress in December 2016, delegates reelected Abbas as the party leader.

Leaders: Mahmoud ABBAS (Chair); Mohammad GHNEIM; Ahmad QURAY (Former Prime Minister of the Palestinian National Authority); Nabil SHAATH, Marwan BARGHOUTI (imprisoned in Israel), Mohammad DAHLAN, Saeb EREKAT, Muhammad ISHTAYYIH, Jibril RAJOUB, Zakaria al-AGHA, Naser al-KIDWA (Members of the Central Council); Azzam al-AHMED, Amin MAKBOUL (Secretary General).

Palestine People's Party (PPP). A Soviet-backed Palestine Communist Party (PCP) was formed in 1982 to encompass Palestinian communists in the West Bank, Gaza Strip, Lebanon, and Jordan with the approval of parent communist organizations in those areas. Although it had no formal PLO affiliation, the PCP in 1984 joined a campaign to negotiate a settlement among sparring PLO factions. As part of the reunification program approved in April 1987, the PNC officially embraced the PCP, granting it representation on PLO leadership bodies. The PCP, which was technically illegal but generally tolerated by Israel in the occupied territories, endorsed the creation of a Palestinian state adjacent to Israel following withdrawal of Israeli troops from occupied territories. In late 1991 the PCP changed its name to the PPP.

In September 1993 the PPP endorsed the PLO–Israeli accord on the condition that substantial "democratic reform" be implemented within the PLO. Although it was subsequently not represented in the PNA formed in 1994, the PPP was described as an "effective ally" of *Fatah* and PLO chair Arafat in the fledgling Palestinian self-rule process.

The PPP contested the January 1996 Palestinian legislative elections, albeit without success. However, PPP general secretary Bashir al-Barghuthi was named minister of industry in the Palestinian cabinet named in May. The PPP's presidential candidate, Bassam al-Salhi, secured 2.7 percent of the vote in the January 2005 presidential balloting. In 2006 the PPP urged a government of national unity and, along with *Fatah* and the PFLP, sought to have the PLO recognized as the only legitimate representative of the Palestinian people.

Leaders: Bashir al-BARGHUTHI, Bassam al-SALHI (Secretary General).

Arab Liberation Front (ALF). The ALF was long closely associated with the Iraqi branch of the Ba'ath party. Its history of terrorist activity included an April 1980 attack on an Israeli kibbutz. Subsequently, there were reports of fighting in Beirut between the ALF and pro-Iranian Shiites. ALF leader Ahmed ABDERRAHIM died in June 1991, and the status of the front's leadership subsequently remained unclear. Although the ALF was reported to have considered withdrawing from the PLO following the September 1993 agreement with Israel, it was apparently persuaded to remain as part of the "loyal opposition." In 1995, however, the front was reported to have split into two factions over the question. In the early 2000s the ALF reportedly distributed Iraqi money to relatives of suicide bombers.

In 2006 the group refused to participate in legislative elections, saying there could be no democracy under occupation. Party leader Rakad SALIM was released by Israel in 2007 after five years in prison for providing funds from Iraqi dictator Saddam Hussein to families of suicide bombers.

Leaders: Mahmud ISMAIL, Rakad SALIM (Secretary General, jailed in Israel).

Democratic Front for the Liberation of Palestine (DFLP). Established in February 1969 as a splinter from the PFLP (below), the DFLP was known as the **Popular Democratic Front for the Liberation of Palestine** (PDFLP) before adopting its present name in 1974. In 1973 the PDFLP had become the first Palestinian group to call for the establishment of a democratic state—one encompassing both banks of the Jordan—as an intermediate step toward founding a national entity that would include all of historic Palestine. Its ultimate goal, therefore, was the elimination of both Hashemite Jordan and Zionist Israel. The DFLP subsequently advocated a form of secular nationalism rooted in Marxist-Leninist doctrine, whereas *Fatah* initially envisaged a state organized on the basis of coexistent religious communities. Despite their political differences, the PDFLP/DFLP and *Fatah* tended to agree on most issues after their expulsion from Jordan in 1971. However, unlike *Fatah*, the DFLP supported the Islamic left in the Lebanese civil war of 1975–1976.

The DFLP, which since 1984 had taken a middle position between pro- and anti-Arafat factions, played a major role in the 1987 PLO reunification. Its close ties with the PFLP, which had been reduced in 1985 when the DFLP opted not to join the PFLP-led Palestine National Salvation Front (PNSF), were reestablished during the unity campaign. The DFLP endorsed the declaration of an independent Palestinian state by the PNC in November 1988, although DFLP leaders interpreted the new PLO political position with less moderation than PLO chair Arafat, declaring they had no intention of halting "armed struggle against the enemy." Subsequently, differences were reported between supporters of longtime DFLP leader Nayif Hawatmeh, who opposed granting any "concessions" to facilitate peace negotiations, and supporters of Yasir Abed Rabbo, a DFLP representative on the PLO Executive Committee. Rabbo called for a more "realistic" approach and became one of the leading PLO negotiators attempting to implement the PNC's proposed "two-state" settlement. In early 1990 the DFLP Political Bureau reported it was unable to resolve the internal dispute, which was symptomatic of disagreement among Palestinians as a whole. After his supporters had failed to unseat Hawatmeh at a party congress late in the year, Rabbo formed a breakaway DFLP faction in early 1991. Both factions were represented on the new PLO executive committee late in the year, although Hawatmeh continued to criticize Arafat's endorsement of the U.S.-led Middle East peace talks. He also called for formation of a "collective" PLO leadership to reduce dependence on Arafat.

Rabbo's wing subsequently continued to support Arafat, but the main DFLP faction remained dedicated to a "no negotiations" stance. Not surprisingly, Hawatmeh and his followers rejected the September 1993 peace accord with Israel, and the DFLP leader described the May 1994 Cairo Agreement as "not binding on the people of Palestine." Meanwhile, Rabbo was given the culture and arts portfolio in the new PNA, and he was subsequently described as a leader of the recently formed PDU (see below).

In January 1994 the DFLP joined with other PLO groupings (including the PFLP, PLF, PPSF, and the PNSF) plus Hamas and Islamic Jihad to form a loosely knit coalition known as the Alliance of Palestinian Forces, based on the opposition of its constituent groups to the accord negotiated by PLO chair Arafat with Israel in September 1993. However, the alliance subsequently collapsed, apparently due to the "incompatibility" of its leftist and Islamic elements.

Several DFLP "lieutenants" were reported in mid-1995 to have relocated from Damascus to Gaza, prompting speculation that the grouping might participate in the election of the Palestinian Council. Although the DFLP ultimately boycotted that balloting, it encouraged its supporters to register as voters in anticipation of subsequent municipal elections that were expected to be held following the completion of the proposed Israeli withdrawal from the West Bank.

In August 1999 DFLP leaders met with Arafat for the first time since 1993, and the DFLP resumed participation in the PLO's Central Council later in the year. In October the United States dropped the DFLP from the U.S. list of terrorist organizations. However, the DFLP claimed responsibility for an attack in mid-2001 in Gaza that left three Israeli soldiers dead. The DFLP later blamed Israel for a car bombing in Gaza in February 2002 that killed several DFLP members.

The DFLP joined the PFLP in mid-2004 in denouncing the fledgling unilateral disengagement plan being considered by Israeli prime minister Sharon, and the groups announced that the "armed struggle" would continue. The DFLP participated in the January 2005 presidential elections (its candidate, Taysir Khalid, won 3.4 percent of the vote), but in 2006 the DFLP declined to participate in the PNA following the unilateral withdrawal of Israeli forces from Gaza.

Leaders: Nayif HAWATMEH (Secretary General, in Syria); Taysir KHALID (2005 presidential candidate); Talal Abu ZAREEFA, Abu LAILA (Members of the Politburo).

Popular Front for the Liberation of Palestine (PFLP). The leftist PFLP was established in 1967 by merger of three main groups: an early **Palestine Liberation Front** (separate from the PLF, below), led by Ahmad Jabril; and two small offshoots of the **Arab Nationalist Movement–the Youth for Revenge** and Georges Habash's **Heroes of the Return**. However, Jabril and some of his followers quickly split from the PFLP (see PFLP-GC, below). The PFLP favored a comprehensive settlement in the Middle East and resisted the establishment of a West Bank state as an intermediate strategy. Its ultimate goal was the formation of a Palestinian nation founded on scientific socialism, accompanied by the PFLP's own evolution into a revolutionary proletarian party.

After the failure of efforts to achieve PLO unity in 1984, the PFLP played a key role in formation of the anti-Arafat PNSF. The PFLP endorsed the 1987 reunification in light of *Fatah*'s increased militancy, but the PFLP delegates to the 1988 PNC session voted against the new PLO political program. Habash subsequently announced that his group, the second-largest PLO faction (after *Fatah*) would accept the will of the majority "for the sake of unity." However, he added that he expected peace initiatives to fail and vowed continued attacks by PFLP fighters against Israeli targets. In early 1990 Habash was described as in "open opposition" to Arafat's acceptance of a U.S. plan for direct talks between Palestinian representatives and Israel, calling instead for increased military confrontation. The PFLP reportedly suspended its membership in the PLO executive committee in late 1991 to protest the negotiations.

During its December 1992 congress in Syria, the PFLP vowed to return to "radical action" in order to "regain credibility" among Palestinians. Consequently, Habash condemned the peace accord of September 1993, urging an "intensification" of the struggle for an independent state with Jerusalem as its "capital." However, the PFLP remained represented in the new PLO executive committee named in April 1996, although several subsequent shootings of Israeli settlers (which prompted the arrest by Palestinian police of some 30 PFLP members) apparently indicated continued resistance to the current peace process on the part of at least some of the PFLP faithful. By 1997 the PFLP was described in general as interested in participating with Arafat's *Fatah* and other PLO factions in establishing a consensus position to present in proposed "final status talks" with Israel, should the peace process develop that far. Meanwhile, in November 1997 a breakaway group reportedly formed as the **Palestinian Popular Forces Party** (PPFP) under the leadership of Adnan Abu NAJILAH.

In late April 2000 Habash announced his retirement; he was succeeded by his longtime deputy, Mustafa al-ZIBRI (Abu Ali Mustafa), who had returned to the West Bank in 1999 after 32 years in exile. (Habash died of a heart attack in January 2008.) Al-Zibri was killed by rockets fired at his Ramallah office by an Israeli helicopter in August 2001, thereby becoming the highest-ranking Palestinian leader to die in such an attack. The PFLP subsequently claimed responsibility for four bomb explosions in Jerusalem in September 2001 and the assassination of Israeli tourism minister Rechavam Ze'evi in October. A number of PFLP adherents, including Secretary General Ahmed Saadat, were subsequently arrested by Palestinian security forces, and the PFLP military wing was reportedly "banned" from Palestinian self-rule areas.

The PFLP claimed joint responsibility with *Fatah* for an attack on Israeli soldiers in February 2003, and several PFLP members were killed in subsequent Israeli reprisals. Although PFLP leaders joined other dissident PLO factions in meeting with Palestinian president Abbas in mid-2005, they reported that "no real coalition" had been formed and complained of ongoing *Fatah* domination of PLO affairs.

In 2006 Secretary General Saadat was arrested by Israeli forces after they stormed a prison in Jericho where he and other Palestinian activists were being held. Saadat faced 19 charges in Israel, including arms dealing and inciting violence. Two PFLP members were sentenced to life imprisonment in early 2008 following their convictions on charges relating to the 2001 Ze'evi assassination. Meanwhile, the Israeli prosecutor ruled that there was insufficient evidence against Saadat in regard to the assassination, although Saadat remained in jail (serving a life sentence on other charges) as of late 2014.

In December 2015 prominent PFLP member Khalida JARRAR was arrested by Israeli security forces and sentenced to 15 months in prison for inciting terrorism.

Leaders: Ahmed SAADAT (Secretary General, jailed in Israel), Jamil MAJDALAWI, Nasser IZZAT, Mahir al-TAHER, Abdel Rahim MALOUH, Kayed al-GHOL, Jamil MIZNER, Rabah MUHANNA, Khalida JARRAR.

Palestine Liberation Front (PLF). The PLF emerged in 1976 as an Iraqi-backed splinter from the PFLP-GC (below). In the early 1980s the PLF split into two factions—a Damascus-based group led by Talaat YACOUB, which opposed PLO chair Yasir Arafat, and a Baghdad- and Tunis-based group led by Muhammad ABBAS (Abdul Abbas), who was sentenced in absentia to life imprisonment by Italian courts for his alleged role in masterminding the hijacking of the cruise ship *Achille Lauro* in 1985, which had resulted in the killing of an American tourist. Although Arafat had vowed that Abbas would be removed from his seat on the PLO Executive Committee because of the conviction, Abbas was granted "provisional" retention of the position at the 1987 PNC unity meeting, which was supported by both PLF factions.

Reconciliation within the PLF was subsequently achieved, at least nominally: Yacoub was named secretary general, while Abbas accepted a position as his deputy. However, Yacoub died in 1988, leaving control largely in Abbas's hands. In May 1990 the PLF accepted responsibility for a failed attack on Tel Aviv beaches by Palestinian commandos in speedboats, an event that precipitated a breakdown in the U.S.–PLO dialogue because of a lack of subsequent disciplinary action against Abbas. Apparently by mutual agreement, Abbas was not included in the new PLO Executive Committee selected in September 1991.

In March 2004 it was reported that Abbas had died of "natural causes" while in "unexplained U.S. custody in Iraq." New PLF secretary general Umar SHIBLI said he hoped to reintegrate the PLF into PNA activity. In 2006 the PLF was one of several factions that blamed *Fatah* and Hamas for increasing conflict in Gaza.

Leader: Wasel ABU-YOUSEF (Secretary General).

Palestinian Democratic Union (PDU). The PDU (also referenced as FIDA ["sacrifice" in Arabic], which is also a reverse acronym for the group's Arabic name, *al-ittihad al-dimuqrati al-filastini*) was launched in early 1993, not as a challenge to the PLO (then headquartered in Tunisia) but, in the words of a spokesperson, as a means of "moving the center of gravity" of the Palestinian opposition to "the occupied territories." Although some of the group's organizers were described as members of the DFLP, the PDU identified itself as nonideological and committed to the Middle East peace process. Operating under the reported leadership of Yasir Abed Rabbo (a longstanding Arafat loyalist), the PDU was one of the few non-*Fatah* groupings to contest the January 1996 elections to the Palestinian Legislative Council, securing one seat. Rablo left the PDU in 2002.

Leaders: Siham al-BARGHUTHI, Zuheira KAMAL, Jamil SALHUT, Saleh RAFAT (Secretary General).

Palestine Popular Struggle Front (PPSF). The PPSF broke from the PFLP while participating in the Lebanese civil war on behalf of the Islamic left. Although the PPSF was represented at the 1988 and 1991 PNC sessions, it denounced that council's political initiatives on both occasions and was not subsequently represented on the PLO Executive Committee. In 1995 it was reported that the PPSF had split into several factions, one of which had expressed support for PLO chair Arafat and the PNA. Longstanding PPSF leader Samir GHOSHEH died in 2009.

Leaders: Anwar Abu MAWAR, Khalid Abd al-MAJID, Ahmed MAJDALANI (Secretary General).

Islamic Resistance Movement (*Ḥarakat al-Muqāwamah al-'Islāmiyyah*—Hamas). Hamas rose to prominence in 1989 as a voice for the Islamic fundamentalist movement in the occupied territories and as a proponent of heightened conflict with Israeli authorities. It subsequently confronted mainstream PLO elements, particularly *Fatah*, over leadership of the intifada as well as Palestinian participation in Middle East peace negotiations. Capitalizing on the initial lack of progress in those talks, Hamas scored significant victories in various municipal and professional organization elections in the occupied territories in the first half of 1992. In addition, the movement's military wing—the *Izz al-Din al-Qassam* Brigades—was believed to be involved in fighting with *Fatah* supporters and to be responsible for the execution of Palestinians suspected of cooperating with the Israeli authorities. Hamas founder Sheikh Ahmed YASSIN, arrested in 1989, was sentenced to life imprisonment by an Israeli court in October 1991 for ordering several such killings of alleged Palestinian "collaborators." Breaking with a long-standing insistence on the annihilation of Israel, Mousa Abu Marzouk, one of the group's leaders (then based in Syria), stated in April 1994 that peace was possible if Israel withdrew from the occupied territories.

In June 1995 Israeli authorities arrested 45 Hamas militants on suspicion of plotting attacks on civilian targets, and in August Israel took steps to secure the extradition of Marzouk, who had been detained as a suspected terrorist upon entering the United States a week earlier. (The United States in 1997 "expelled" Marzouk to Jordan, from which he again relocated to Syria after the Jordanian government ordered the closure of all Hamas offices in Jordan in late 1999.)

In 1995 and 1996 Hamas was described as deeply divided between those favoring continued violence against Israel and those believing it was time to join the peaceful political process unfolding in the Palestinian self-rule areas. Palestinian leader Yasir Arafat met with Hamas leaders in late 1995 in what was described as a determined effort to win the movement's participation in upcoming Palestinian elections. After initially wavering on the proposal, Hamas announced it would boycott the balloting.

In January 1996 Yahya AYYASH, a Hamas militant (known as "The Engineer") who had been blamed by Israeli officials for a number of bomb attacks, was assassinated in Gaza by a bomb that was widely attributed to Israeli security forces. Subsequently, Hamas militants calling themselves the "Yahya Ayyash Units" claimed responsibility for several suicide bombings in Israel in February and March. Following the blasts, Marzouk (in an interview from his U.S. jail) said that the Hamas political wing had little direct control over the "militias" in the occupied and previously occupied territories. Meanwhile, Arafat outlawed the *al-Qassam* Brigades but continued his political dialogue with Hamas moderates, mindful that the grouping retained significant popular support among Palestinians, built, in part, upon Hamas's network of schools, health services, and other social programs.

Sheikh Yassin was released from prison on October 1, 1997, apparently as part of the "price" Israel agreed to pay after the bungled assassination attempt of Hamas militant Khaled Meshal in Jordan the previous month. Yassin went to Jordan for medical treatment and then to his home at Gaza, where he was welcomed as a hero by ecstatic crowds. He subsequently maintained an apparently deliberately vague position on developments regarding Palestinian autonomy, at times reverting to previous fiery rhetoric exhorting holy war against Israeli forces while at other times appearing conciliatory toward Arafat and the PNA, despite the fact that an estimated 80 influential Hamas leaders remained in PNA detention.

According to some reports, Hamas was approached by Arafat about joining the Palestinian cabinet in mid-1998. Although that overture was rejected, Yassin in April 1999 attended a PLO Central Council meeting as an observer, suggesting a growing degree of "accommodation" between the two groups. On the other hand, Palestinian security forces arrested some 90 Hamas activists in Gaza in August.

In December 2000 Hamas warned of a return of a campaign of suicide bombings in view of renewed Palestinian–Israeli violence, and the grouping subsequently claimed responsibility for a number of car bomb and suicide bomb attacks in Israel. In February 2003 Yassin urged Muslims around the world to attack "Western interests" in the event of a U.S.-led invasion of Iraq. Yassin also rejected the "road map" peace proposal offered by the Middle East Quartet in April and vowed that attacks on Israeli targets would continue.

International attention focused intently on Hamas when Yassin was killed by Israeli missiles in March 2004. Israeli prime minister Sharon dismissed Yassin as an "arch-terrorist," although the assassination of the blind, wheelchair-bound Hamas leader was viewed with dismay in many areas of the world. Such consternation had little effect on Israeli policy, however, and Abd al-Aziz RANTISI, who had succeeded Yassin as the leader of Hamas, was himself killed in an Israeli attack in April.

Throughout 2005 Hamas slowly grew in popularity to become a formidable rival to *Fatah*. In successive municipal elections Hamas won the majority of seats in several local councils, including those in some West Bank towns, such as Nablus, that had been *Fatah* strongholds. A watershed moment for Hamas came in January 2006 when it won a clear majority of seats (74 out of 132) in balloting for the Palestinian Legislative Council, capitalizing on Palestinian anger against the PLO and PNA over corruption and poor delivery of services as well as public disillusionment with the overall process of negotiations with Israel (the withdrawal from Gaza notwithstanding). Subsequent to the election and the formation of a Hamas-dominated cabinet, the group faced immense Western pressure to commit itself to a two-state solution and to renounce violence.

Following the collapse of the unity government in mid-2007 in the wake of severe Hamas-*Fatah* conflict, Ismail Haniyeh insisted that his Hamas-led cabinet remained legitimate, although its de facto control was limited to Gaza. Hamas solidified its dominance in Gaza over the ensuing year as it arrested a number of *Fatah* leaders and otherwise suppressed opposition. (Many of the Hamas leaders in the West Bank were similarly detained by *Fatah*.) Egypt attempted to broker a reconciliation between Hamas and *Fatah* that envisioned the installation of a new joint transitional cabinet, new presidential and legislative elections in 2009, and the inclusion of Hamas and Islamic Jihad in the PLO. However, the talks were suspended indefinitely in November 2008. Meanwhile, the leaders of Hamas reiterated their willingness to "accept" (but not formally recognize) the state of Israel in return for establishment of a Palestinian state based on the 1967 borders and further negotiations regarding the rights of Palestinian refugees.

Following the devastating Israeli offensive in Gaza in December 2008–January 2009 (in which a number of Hamas leaders were killed or arrested), talks between Hamas and *Fatah* towards a possible national unity government opened in February 2009. However, no progress was achieved, and the relationship between the two groups reportedly remained "venomous." Subsequently, Khalid Mishal, who had been reelected as chair of the Hamas Political Bureau in May, announced that Hamas hoped to be a participant in negotiations toward a peace settlement with Israel, although he still rejected official recognition of Israel, offering only a "long-term truce." Meanwhile, several reports in the fall of 2009 focused on the perceived struggle within Hamas between the current leadership and Islamic fundamentalists pushing for stricter adherence to Islamic law in Gaza.

Mahmoud al-MABHOUH, described as a senior *al-Qassam* military commander who had been living in Damascus, was murdered in a

Dubai hotel in January 2010, reportedly by Israeli agents using passports from several European countries. Mabhouh had been accused by Israel of killing two Israeli soldiers in 1989.

Ismail Haniyeh, the head of the de facto Hamas government in Gaza, announced in late 2010 that Hamas was prepared to accept any negotiated settlement with Israel (even on terms contrary to Hamas's goals) if a majority of Palestinians throughout the world endorsed the settlement in a global referendum.

Despite the much-publicized reconciliation agreement between Hamas and *Fatah* in mid-2011, Hamas's stance was vague in regard to President Abbas's application to the UN in September for recognition of Palestinian statehood. Hamas officials reportedly complained that they had not been consulted in the matter.

Mishal and other Hamas leaders moved their headquarters from Damascus to Qatar in early 2012 after Hamas members appeared to offer support for rebels trying to oust Syrian president Bashar al-Assad. Among other things, Hamas lost financial support from Iran for abandoning Assad, although Qatar subsequently pledged $400 million to assist the Hamas-led government in Gaza.

Ahmed JABARI, described as the leader of *al-Qassam*, was killed in the eight-day Israeli air assault in Gaza in November 2012. Hamas also reportedly suffered significant degradation of its military capability, although Hamas, whose survival was considered by some to be at risk at the beginning of the conflict, held "victory" celebrations following the cease-fire. Islamist supporters of the region's Arab Spring also appeared to rally behind Hamas.

In December 2012 Hamas leader Mishal traveled to Gaza for the first time, and he subsequently reaffirmed his support for reconciliation with *Fatah* and eventual formation of a unity government. However, Hamas hard-liners continued to oppose that initiative, and Hamas strongly criticized Abbas's decision to reopen negotiations with Israel in August 2013.

Hamas suffered financially and psychologically from the Egyptian military's ouster in mid-2013 of Egyptian president Morsi, whose Muslim Brotherhood-led government had been a strong Hamas supporter. In addition, the new Egyptian government blocked the tunnels that were being used by Palestinians to smuggle goods into Gaza from Egypt. Most observers concluded that Hamas's weakened financial and political condition was the major impetus behind the group's decision to endorse the April 2014 reconciliation agreement with *Fatah*.

The Hamas leadership disavowed any role in the June 2014 killing of three Jewish teenagers in the West Bank, although the group's failure to condemn the murders infuriated Israeli leaders, who believed the kidnappings had been carried out by a local Hamas cell. A number of Hamas members were arrested in the subsequent security sweep of the West Bank by Israeli forces, which Hamas ultimately used as justification for the resumption of rocket attacks from Gaza into Israel. Although a number of Hamas leaders were reportedly killed in the subsequent Israeli offensive in Gaza and much of Hamas's arsenal of weapons was depleted, Hamas reportedly emerged from the conflict with its popular support strengthened.

Hamas announced in July 2016 that it would allow local balloting planned for October in Gaza and that it would participate in the polling. (The elections were subsequently postponed until 2017.) In August Australia suspended aid to World Vision after the discovery that the organization transferred funds to Hamas.

Leaders: Khalid MISHAL (Chair of the Political Bureau, in Qatar), Ismail HANIYEH (Former Prime Minister of the Former De Facto Hamas Government in Gaza and Former Prime Minister of the Palestinian Authority), Abdel Aziz DUWAIK (Speaker of the Palestinian Legislative Council, released from Israeli prison in 2009), Ahmed BAHAR (Deputy Speaker of the Palestinian Legislative Council), Khalil al-HAYEH (Member of the Political Bureau), Nizar AWADALLAH (Member of the Political Bureau), Mousa Abu MARZOUK, Mahmud al-ZAHHAR (Member of the Political Bureau), Sami Abu ZUHRI, Ghazi HAMAD, Saleh al-AROURI (in Turkey), Ziyad al-ZAZA.

Palestinian National Initiative (PNI). The PNI is a movement founded by Moustafa Barghouti in 2002 as a democratic "third force" alternative to the PLO and Hamas. The base of the PNI included secular, left-leaning intellectuals, many of whom, such as Barghouti, had been prominent in the Palestinian nongovernmental organization community. Barghouti finished second in the January 2005 presidential elections, winning 20 percent of the vote. In the January 2006 legislative elections, the PNI won three seats with 2.7 percent of the vote.

Leader: Mustafa BARGHOUTI.

Islamic Jihad (*al-Jihad al-Islami*). Islamic Jihad is considered a Palestinian extension of Egypt's Islamic Jihad, which was originally launched as a splinter of Egypt's Muslim Brotherhood (see entry on Egypt). Islamic Jihad has been linked to a number of bomb attacks against Israeli soldiers both in the occupied territories and within Israel. Fathi SHAQAQI, described as the leader of Islamic Jihad, was assassinated in Malta in October 1995, reportedly by Israeli secret agents. It was subsequently reported that Ramadan Abdullah Shallah, a "Gaza-born militant" who had helped form Islamic Jihad, had assumed leadership of the grouping. Like Hamas, the other leading "rejectionist" grouping in the occupied and previously occupied territories, Islamic Jihad boycotted the 1996 Palestinian elections. Following the bomb attacks in Israel in early 1996, the Islamic Jihad military wing was one of the groups formally outlawed by Palestinian leader Arafat.

Islamic Jihad boycotted the February 1997 "national dialogue" meeting convened by Arafat but, in what was seen as a potentially significant shift, attended the August unity conference, which was also chaired by the Palestinian president. Nevertheless, leaders of Islamic Jihad were careful to point out that the group had not renounced the use of violence against Israel, and Islamic Jihad claimed responsibility for some of the attacks on Israeli civilians in 2001–2005. Islamic Jihad did not participate in the January 2005 Palestinian presidential elections or the January 2006 legislative elections.

Some of the rocket and mortar attacks into Israel in late 2008 and early 2009 were attributed to Islamic Jihad. In 2010 leaders of the group reportedly described any potential negotiated settlement with Israel as "forbidden religiously and politically." However, Islamic Jihad in 2011 endorsed the tentative reconciliation agreement between Hamas and *Fatah*.

Islamic Jihad, considered by many observers to have Iranian backing, claimed responsibility for a number of rocket and missile attacks on Israel in March 2012. As Hamas subsequently distanced itself from the regime of Syrian president Assad, Iranian support appeared to grow even further for Islamic Jihad, which maintained its headquarters in Damascus. Israeli air strikes in late 2013 and early 2014 focused on Islamic Jihad locations in Gaza.

Iran announced in May 2016 that it would provide $70 million annually to Islamic Jihad. Estimates in 2016 were that Islamic Jihad had about 5,000 fighters in Gaza. Reports in December 2016 indicated that the organization was endeavoring to recruit fighters from Pakistan.

Leaders: Ramadan Abdullah SHALLAH (Secretary General, in Syria), Abdallah al-SHAMI (Spokesperson), Muhammad al-HINDI, Sheikh Bassam SADI.

Popular Front for the Liberation of Palestine–General Command (PFLP-GC). Although the General Command broke from the parent front in late 1967, both organizations fought on the side of the Islamic left in the Lebanese civil war. The PFLP-GC was one of the founding members (along with the PFLP, PLF, PPSF, *al-Saiqa,* and *Fatah* Uprising) of the Palestine National Salvation Front (PNSF), launched in February 1985 in Damascus in opposition to the policies of PLO chair Arafat. Following the reconciliation of the PFLP and the PLF with other major PLO factions at the 1987 PNC meeting, PFLP leader Georges Habash declared that the PNSF had been dissolved, but the remaining "rejectionist" groups continued to allude to the PNSF umbrella.

The PFLP-GC, headquartered in Damascus, was reported to have influenced the uprisings in the West Bank and Gaza Strip in late 1987 and 1988, having established a clandestine radio station, the Voice of Jerusalem, that attracted numerous listeners throughout the occupied territories. U.S. and other Western officials reportedly suspected the PFLP-GC of complicity in the December 1988 bombing of a Pan American airliner over Lockerbie, Scotland, although PFLP-GC officials vehemently denied that the group was involved.

In May 1991 the PNSF, by then representing only the PFLP-GC, *al-Saiqa,* and *Fatah* Uprising (the PPSF having attended the 1988 PNC meeting), negotiated a preliminary "unity" agreement of its own with the mainstream PLO under which each PNSF component was to be given representation in the PNC. The proposed settlement was generally perceived as an outgrowth of a desire by Syria, the primary source of support for the PNSF, to normalize relations with the PLO and thereby enhance its influence in projected Middle East peace talks. However, negotiations with *Fatah* ultimately proved unproductive, yielding a PNSF boycott of the 1991 PNC session.

In September 1993 PFLP-GC leader Ahmad Jabril warned that Arafat had become an appropriate target for assassination because of the peace settlement with Israel. In mid-1996 the PFLP-GC was described as the primary conduit for the transfer of Syrian weapons to Hezbollah guerrillas in southern Lebanon, where Jabril's son, Jihad JABRIL, was reportedly in charge of a PFLP-GC "training center."

The PFLP-GC declined to join the PFLP in resuming activity in the PLO's Central Council in early 2000. In April 2002 the PFLP-GC claimed responsibility for rocket attacks from Lebanon into the Golan Heights and Israel, and Jihad Jabril was killed in a car bomb attack in Beirut the following month. (His father attributed the attack to Israeli agents.) In mid-2005 Ahmad Jabril announced that the PFLP-GC was not yet ready to commit to participation in the Palestinian government following the planned withdrawal of Israeli forces from Gaza, although he agreed to join negotiations on the matter. In 2006, following Hezbollah's cross-border attack from Lebanon on Israeli soldiers, Israel reportedly targeted a PFLP-GC stronghold in eastern Lebanon. Severe fighting among PFLP-GC factions was reported in a Palestinian military camp in Lebanon in April 2010.

The PFLP-GC reportedly endorsed the tentative reconciliation agreement between Hamas and *Fatah* in 2011. Although some Palestinians in Syria by the fall of 2012 had reportedly aligned with rebel groups attempting to overthrow Bashar al-Assad, the PFLP-GC reaffirmed its allegiance to the embattled president and pledged in September 2013 to "retaliate" if the United States attacked Syria.

Leaders: Talal NAJI, Musa AWAD, Khalid JIBRIL (Military Leader), Ahmad JABRIL (Secretary General).

Al-Saiqa. Established in 1968 under the influence of the Syrian Ba'ath Party, *al-Saiqa* ("Thunderbolt") came into conflict with *Fatah* as a result of *al-Saiqa*'s active support for Syrian intervention during the Lebanese civil war. The group's longtime leader, Zuheir MOHSEN, who served as the PLO's chief of military operations, was assassinated in Paris in July 1979, his successor being a former Syrian air force general. Denouncing the decisions of the November 1988 PNC session, *al-Saiqa* leaders said they would attempt to get the PLO back on its original revolutionary course of "struggle."

In 2006 the group opposed President Abbas's proposed national accord referendum.

Leaders: Issam al-KADE, Mohamed KHALIFAH.

***Fatah* Uprising.** An outgrowth of the 1983 internal PLO fighting in Lebanon, the Uprising (a *Fatah* splinter group) drew its membership from PLO dissidents who remained in Beirut following the departure of Yasir Arafat. One of the most steadfast of the anti-Arafat formations, it waged a bitter (and largely successful) struggle with mainstream adherents for control of Beirut's refugee camps in May–July 1988. It condemned the PNC declaration of November 1988 as a "catastrophe" and in early 1990 called for attacks on U.S. interests worldwide "because America is completely biased towards the Zionist enemy." The group also called for the assassination of Arafat in the wake of the PLO's September 1993 agreement with Israel.

In 2006 the group reportedly was involved in the smuggling of arms into Lebanon and was reportedly reinforced by forces from Damascus in its clashes with the Lebanese army near the border with Syria.

Leaders: Saed MUSA (Abu MUSA), Muraghah Abu-Fadi HAMMAD (Secretary General).

Revolutionary Council of *Fatah*. The Revolutionary Council (also known as the Abu Nidal Group) was held responsible for more than 100 terrorist incidents in over 20 countries after it broke away from *Fatah* in 1974. Targets included Palestinian moderates as well as Israelis and other Jews, and the group's predilection for attacks in public places in Europe and Asia led to allegations of its involvement in the assaults on the Vienna and Rome airports in December 1985. The shadowy organization, which operated under numerous names, was formed by Sabry Khalil al-BANNA, better known as Abu Nidal, one of the first PLO guerrillas to challenge the leadership of Yasir Arafat. Nidal reportedly plotted to have Arafat killed soon after their split, prompting Nidal's trial in absentia by the PLO, which issued a death sentence.

After its Syrian offices were closed by President Assad in 1987, the council transferred the bulk of its military operations to Lebanon's Bekaa Valley and Muslim West Beirut, with Abu Nidal and other leaders reportedly moving to Libya. Fierce personal rivalries and disagreements over policy were subsequently reported within the group, apparently prompting Abu Nidal to order the killing of about 150 dissidents in Libya in October 1989. Consequently, several former senior commanders of the organization fled to Algiers and Tunis, where they established an "emergency leadership" faction opposed to the "blind terrorism" still espoused by Abu Nidal's supporters. The internecine fighting subsequently spread to Lebanon, where in June 1990 the dissidents were reported to have routed Nidal's supporters with the aid of fighters from Arafat's *Fatah*.

In July 1992 Walid KHALID, described as Abu Nidal's top aide, was assassinated in Lebanon, apparently as part of a series of "score settling" killings by rival guerrilla groups. In November 1995 Palestinian police arrested a group of reported council members in connection with an alleged plot against Arafat's life.

In mid-1998 it was reported that an ailing Abu Nidal was being detained in Egypt after having crossed the border from Libya, possibly as the result of a falling out with Libyan leader Muammar al-Qadhafi. However, Egyptian officials denied that report, and U.S. officials subsequently suggested Abu Nidal may have relocated to Iraq. In August 2002 Iraqi security forces reported that Abu Nidal had committed suicide during their attempt to arrest him in connection with an alleged plot to overthrow the regime of Saddam Hussein. Although uncertain of the circumstances, Western analysts accepted the fact of Abu Nidal's death, noting that it presumably meant the formal end of the Revolutionary Council, for which no activity had been reported since 1996.

Army of Islam. A small faction in Gaza led by prominent clan leader Mumtaz DOGMUSH, the Army of Islam was the focus of a crackdown by Hamas in September 2008. The grouping had earlier claimed responsibility for several kidnappings reportedly conducted in association with the so-called Popular Resistance Committees (see below), led by another branch of the Dogmush clan. Israeli air strikes in Gaza killed several reputed Army of Islam leaders in 2010.

Israeli officials alleged that members of the **Popular Resistance Committees** (PRC) operating out of Gaza had been responsible for an August 2011 attack that killed a number of Israelis and prompted, among other things, a dispute between Israel and Egypt. (See Foreign relations in the entry on Israel for details.) Representatives of the PRC denied involvement but said they approved of the attack. PRC leader Awad Kamal al-NEIRAB was killed in a retaliatory Israeli air strike; he was succeeded by Zuhir al-QAISI, who died in another Israeli attack in March 2012, which triggered a barrage of rocket attacks from Gaza into Israel.

LEGISLATURE

Palestinian Legislative Council. The September 1995 Interim Agreement on the West Bank and the Gaza Strip (the second of the Palestinian "self-rule" accords between Israel and the PLO) provided for the election of a Palestinian Council to exercise legislative and executive authority in those areas of the previously occupied territories to which Palestinian autonomy had been or was about to be extended. The agreement initially established the size of the council at 82 members, but the membership was increased to 88 late in the year by mutual consent of Israeli and Palestinian representatives. Sixteen electoral districts were established in the Gaza Strip, West Bank, and East Jerusalem, and all Palestinians who were at least 18 years of age and had lived in those districts for at least three years were declared eligible to vote.

Nearly 700 candidates, including over 400 independents and some 200 representatives of small parties and political factions, reportedly contested the initial council elections conducted on January 20, 1996. However, balloting was dominated by Yasir Arafat's *Fatah* faction of the PLO, most other major groupings (including Hamas, Islamic Jihad, the Democratic Front for the Liberation of Palestine, the Popular Front for the Liberation of Palestine, and other PLO factions opposed to the current peace negotiations) having boycotted the election. According to *Middle East International,* Palestinian officials reported that the successful candidates included 50 of the 70 "official" *Fatah* nominees, 37 independents (including 16 *Fatah* dissidents), and 1 member of the Palestinian Democratic Union.

The council (by then routinely referenced as the Palestinian Legislative Council, or PLC) convened for the first time on March 7, 1996, in Gaza City. Ahmad Quray was elected speaker by a vote of 57–31 over Haidar Abd al-SHAFI, a critic of Arafat and the recent accords with Israel. In addition to serving as leader of the new council, the speaker was also envisioned as the person who would assume the position of head of the council's executive authority in the event of the incapacitation or death of the person in that position. Regarding such matters, the council proposed a Basic Law of Palestine, which would serve as a "constitution" until the completion of the "final talks" with

Israel. The council fell into conflict with Arafat in 1997 over his failure to sign the Basic Law or to pursue other reforms the council had recommended, including the replacement of the current cabinet with a technocratic government better able to deal with the myriad Palestinian economic and development needs. Late in the year the council suspended its sessions to put pressure on the Palestinian leader, who agreed to reorganize the government.

Following the death of Arafat in November 2004 and installation of new Palestinian leadership in early 2005, new PLC elections were scheduled for July 2005. However, they were later postponed as deliberations continued on, among other things, whether a proportional representation system should be established. In preparation for the upcoming elections, the council was expanded from 88 members to 132. Half the seats, or 66, would be elected through proportional representation, while the remaining 66 would be elected from 16 constituencies, whose number of seats would be determined by population. Six seats in the council were also reserved for Christians.

Hamas, running as "Change and Reform," won 74 seats in the January 25, 2006, balloting for the PLC. *Fatah* finished second with 45 seats. (Although Hamas scored only 3 percentage points higher than *Fatah* overall, it won 45 of the 66 seats elected on a constituency basis. Meanwhile, *Fatah* won 28 seats elected by proportional representation and 17 on a constituency basis.) Of the 13 remaining seats, the Popular Front for the Liberation of Palestine (running as the Martyr Abu Ali Mustafa List) won 3 seats; The Alternative (a coalition of the Democratic Front for the Liberation of Palestine, the Palestinian People's Party, and the Palestine Democratic Union), 2; Palestinian National Initiative, 2; Third Way (founded by Hanan Ashrawi and former Palestinian finance minister Salam Fayyad), 2; and independents, 4.

In December 2009 the PLO Central Council extended the mandate of the current legislators indefinitely pending new elections. The Hamas–*Fatah* reconciliation agreement of mid-2014 called for such elections to be held following the planned installation of a transitional "unity" government. The government installed in June 2014 was slated to organize such elections within six months, but the timetable was delayed in the aftermath of the July–August Israeli military campaign in Gaza.

Speaker: Abdel Aziz DUWAIK.

CABINET

[as of December 10, 2016]

Prime Minister	Rami Hamdallah
Deputy Prime Minister	Ziad Abu Amr
Ministers	
Agriculture	Sufian Sultan al-Tamimi
Culture	Ehab Bseiso
Education	Sabri Saydam
Finance	Shukri Bishara
Foreign Affairs	Riyad al-Malki
Health	Jawad Awwad
Interior	Rami Hamdallah
Jerusalem Affairs	Adnan al-Husseini
Justice	Ali Abu Diyak
Labor	Mamoun Abu Shahla
Local Government	Hussein al-Araj
National Economy	Abeer Odeh
Planning	Shukri Bishara
Prisoner Affairs	Shawqi al-Aissa
Public Works and Housing	Mofeed al-Hasayneh
Religious Affairs and Awqaf	Youssef Ideiss
Secretary of the Cabinet	Ali Abu Diyak
Social Affairs	Ibrahim al-Shaer
Telecommunications and Information Technology	Allam Mousa
Tourism and Antiquities	Rula Maayah [f]
Transportation	Samih al-Abed
Women's Affairs	Haifaa al-Agha [f]

[f] = female

INTERGOVERNMENTAL REPRESENTATION

Representative to the Permanent Observer Mission of the State of Palestine to the United Nations: Riyad H. MANSOUR.

For Further Reference:

Chomsky, Noam, and Ilan Pappé. *On Palestine.* Chicago: Haymarket Books, 2015.

Ehrenreich, Ben. *The Way to the Spring: Life and Death in Palestine.* New York: Penguin Books, 2016.

Gelvin, James L. *The Israel–Palestine Conflict: One Hundred Years of War.* Revised Edition. Cambridge: Cambridge University Press, 2014.

INTERGOVERNMENTAL ORGANIZATIONS

AFRICAN UNION (AU)

Established: By charter of the predecessor Organization of African Unity (OAU) adopted May 25, 1963, in Addis Ababa, Ethiopia; Treaty Establishing the African Economic Community (AEC)—the Abuja Treaty—adopted June 3, 1991, by the OAU heads of state and government in Abuja, Nigeria, and entered into force May 12, 1994; Constitutive Act of the African Union (AU) adopted July 11, 2000, by the OAU heads of state and government in Lomé, Togo, and entered into force May 26, 2001. (The OAU remained in existence during a one-year transitional period ending July 8, 2002; the Abuja Treaty remains a cornerstone of the AU.)

Purpose: To "achieve greater unity and solidarity" among African states; to "accelerate the political and socio-economic integration of the continent"; to "promote and defend African common positions"; to "promote peace, security and stability"; to "promote democratic principles and institutions, popular participation and good governance"; to assist in Africa's effort "to play its rightful role in the global economy and in international negotiations"; and to "promote sustainable development at the economic, social and cultural levels."

Headquarters: Addis Ababa, Ethiopia.

Principal Organs: Assembly of the African Union; African Union Commission; Executive Council; Peace and Security Council (15 members); Permanent Representatives Committee; Pan-African Parliament (265 Representatives); Economic, Social, and Cultural Council; Commission; Court of Justice.

Website: www.au.int.

Chair of the Commission: Idriss Déby (Chad).

Membership (54): Algeria, Angola, Benin, Botswana, Burkina Faso, Burundi, Cameroon, Cape Verde, Central African Republic (suspended since May 2013), Chad, Comoro Islands, Democratic Republic of the Congo, Republic of the Congo, Côte d'Ivoire, Djibouti, Egypt, Equatorial Guinea, Eritrea, Ethiopia, Gabon, Gambia, Ghana, Guinea, Guinea-Bissau, Kenya, Lesotho, Liberia, Libya, Madagascar, Malawi, Mali, Mauritania, Mauritius, Mozambique, Namibia, Niger, Nigeria, Rwanda, Sahrawi Arab Democratic Republic, Sao Tome and Principe, Senegal, Seychelles, Sierra Leone, Somalia, South Africa, South Sudan, Swaziland, Tanzania, Togo, Tunisia, Uganda, Zambia, Zimbabwe. (Morocco is the only African country not a member of the AU.)

Official Languages: Arabic, English, French, Kiswahili, Portuguese, Spanish, and any other African language.

Origin and development. The OAU was the most conspicuous result of the search for unity among the emerging states of Africa, a number of whose representatives participated in the first Conference of Independent African States in April 1958 in Accra, Ghana. It remained in existence, with mixed success, until 2000. (For a fuller discussion of the OAU, see the AU article in the 2010 *Handbook.*)

The Algiers OAU summit of July 12–14, 1999, marked the return of Libya's Colonel. Muammar al-Qadhafi, who had not attended OAU heads of state meetings in more than 20 years and who now proposed that an extraordinary summit be held to consider establishing a "United States of Africa." As a result, on September 8–9, 1999, the heads of state and government reconvened in Sirte, Libya, and agreed to the formation of the AU as successor to the OAU. Following subsequent negotiations, African leaders signed the Constitutive Act of the AU at the OAU summit on July 10–12, 2000, in Lomé, Togo.

Based loosely on the model of the European Union (EU), the AU was conceived as building on existing elements of the OAU—for example, the AEC and the Mechanism for Conflict Prevention, Management, and Resolution—but with a stronger institutional structure. It was also expected to serve as a means of achieving faster sustainable economic development and integration and as a better vehicle for representing unified African positions in international forums and organizations.

At the OAU's fifth extraordinary summit, held March 1–2, 2001, in Sirte, the OAU declared the AU to be established. The OAU remained in existence for a one-year transition period, during which technical arrangements were worked out and the remaining protocols for various AU organs drafted.

The OAU's 37th and final full summit convened July 9–11, 2001, in Lusaka, Zambia. On the economic front, the summit launched the New Africa Initiative (NAI) with the goal of ending poverty, war, and disease in Africa by 2015 through better governance, foreign investment in a more open marketplace, and sustainable development. Having attracted widespread support from the developed world and from the UN Economic Commission for Africa, the plan was renamed the New Partnership for Africa's Development (NEPAD) at an October 23, 2001, OAU meeting in Abuja, Nigeria.

On July 9–10, 2002, the heads of state and government, meeting in Durban, South Africa, inaugurated the AU. Among the actions taken by the July 2002 inaugural summit was the adoption of the Protocol Relating to the Establishment of the Peace and Security Council (PSC) of the AU. On December 26, 2003, Nigeria became the 27th AU state to deposit its instrument of ratification, thereby bringing the protocol into force.

At the second extraordinary session of the assembly, meeting February 27–28, 2004, in Sirte, Libya, the Common African Defense and Security Policy (CDSP) was adopted, as called for in the Constitutive Act and the PSC protocol. The CDSP defined defense as encompassing "both the traditional, military, and state-centric notion of the use of the armed forces of the state to protect its national sovereignty and territorial integrity, as well as the less traditional, non-military aspects which relate to the protection of the people's political, cultural, social and economic values and ways of life."

After becoming operational in 2003, one of the first tasks of the PSC was to organize the African Standby Force (ASF) planned to be fully operational by 2015. This force intends to incorporate police and civilian components as well as military personnel, in keeping with its broad mission, which includes possible preventive deployment, peacekeeping, and postconflict disarmament and demobilization. The Southern Africa Brigade, the first component of the ASF, was established in August 2007.

At the January 30–31, 2005, summit in Abuja, Nigeria, the African Union Non-Aggression and Common Defense Pact was adopted, and it came into effect December 18, 2009, with the last of the 53 countries signing the document on February 2. The fifth regular summit, held July 4–5, 2005, called for a full cancellation of all African countries' debts and for "the abolition of subsidies that stand as an obstacle to trade"—an initiative passed by the G-8 summit in July 2005 and approved by both the International Monetary Fund (IMF) and the World Bank in September 2005.

The AU's peacekeeping efforts in Darfur were complicated by Sudan's bid at the sixth AU summit (held January 23–24, 2006, in Khartoum, Sudan) to assume the organization's presidency for the year. Amid accusations of genocide in the Darfur conflict, Sudan withdrew in favor of the Republic of the Congo, but with suggestions that it might renew its bid in 2007. The AU's 7,000-strong peacekeeping force in Darfur, funded by the United States and the EU, had little success in stopping the violence. The peacekeeping force continued to operate nonetheless, and after months of negotiation with the government of Sudan, a mid-August 2007 resolution of the UN Security Council called for the establishment of a peacekeeping force of 26,000 under joint UN and AU command, consisting only of troops from Africa.

The July 2–4, 2007, summit, held in Accra, raised once again the issue of a single government for Africa. Most participants favored stronger economic union but had no appetite for complete political union. Col. Qadhafi—who had called for the immediate establishment of a single government, foreign policy, and army for Africa—left the summit early.

Throughout 2007 and 2008, the AU was preoccupied with crises in several member states. The joint UN/AU peacekeeping force began operations on December 31, 2007, but was seriously undermanned and poorly equipped. In August 2008 the UN Security Council extended the force's mandate for another year. Only then did Sudan promise to allow its full deployment. On June 30 the AU and UN appointed Djibril Yipene Bassole, foreign minister of Burkina Faso, as joint chief mediator. His task was complicated by the efforts of the International Criminal Court to bring Sudanese government officials to trial for genocide, an action the AU condemned as working against the peace process.

In late February 2008 the Comoro Islands central government rejected an AU proposal of sanctions against Anjouan, peace talks broke off, and by late March AU troops arrived to assist in an attack to retake Anjouan. This operation, the AU's first offensive military operation, was successful, and in June 2008 Anjouan held an election to replace its deposed president.

The AU peacekeeping force in Somalia, sanctioned by the UN Security Council as the African Union Mission to Somalia (AMISOM), received six-month extensions to its mandate on August 20, 2007; February 20, 2008; and August 20, 2008. Like its counterpart in Darfur the Somalia mission was seriously undermanned, but suffered much more from guerrilla attacks. On July 1, 2008, the AU announced that it would continue the difficult mission in its present form through the end of the year but urged the UN to take it over. On August 19, 2008, the two main Somali factions, the Transitional Federal Government (TFG) of Somalia and the Alliance for the Re-Liberation of Somalia (ARS), signed a peace agreement under AU auspices.

The AU was most successful in mediating a resolution of the disputed December 27, 2007, presidential election in Kenya and its violent aftermath. By the end of February, AU chair Jakaya Kikwete and former UN secretary-general Kofi Annan were in talks with all parties involved to ensure that a power-sharing agreement took hold. Their efforts were successful and the AU gained a great amount of prestige.

The AU's role in the disputed March 2008 Zimbabwe elections received less praise. AUC chair Jean Ping first visited Zimbabwe in early May. Further action took the form of electoral monitoring and a vote at the July 1–2, 2008, summit disapproving of Zimbabwean president Mugabe's actions. On July 22, 2008, Mugabe and Morgan Tsvangirai, his rival, signed an agreement to begin negotiations on sharing power, an agreement that the AU welcomed.

In other business at the Sharm-el-Sheikh summit, the organization endorsed the concept of an all-African government, though there was no consensus how that might be achieved. Another decision from the meeting was to merge the African Human and Peoples' Rights Court and the African Court of Justice into one body.

On August 8, 2008, a military coup overthrew the government of Mauritania. AU mediation, coupled with sanctions and with pressure from other international groups, ended in a presidential election in July 2009. This election, certified by the AU as fair, returned the coup leader, General Mohamed Ould Abdelaziz, to office as a civilian president.

The 12th summit, held January 26–February 3, 2009, in Addis Ababa, was most notable for the Executive Council electing Muammar Qadhafi as chair, succeeding Jakaya Kikwete of Tanzania. Qadhafi again announced that he wanted to turn the AU into a "United States of Africa." At the June Ordinary Session of the Executive Committee held in Sirte, Qadhafi proposed immediate dissolution of all organs of the AU and creation of the United States of Africa. Commission Chair Ping said that they should wait for the reaction of the July 1–3 session of the AU Assembly. The latter meeting adopted the notion of transforming the AU Commission into the African Union Authority. The authority would have broader powers than the commission and would be responsible for creating common defense, diplomacy, and trade policies. The change would, however, first have to be ratified by all the AU member states.

On March 17, 2009, a military coup in Madagascar forced out President Marc Ravalomanana and installed Andry Rajoelina in his place. The AU suspended Madagascar from participation in its activities and relocated the July summit from Madagascar to Libya. Tensions on the island grew worse throughout the summer, and the AU decided that military intervention, such as its actions in the Comoro islands, was not feasible. In August 2009, the AU assisted in brokering a power-sharing arrangement, but the cabinet named by Rajoelina in early September contained few of his opponents, and opposition parties cried foul. (For more on activities and developments since 2008, see Recent activities, below.)

Structure. The Assembly of Heads of State and Government, the supreme decision-making organ of the AU, meets twice annually in ordinary session to define overall AU policy and to supervise the activities of the other AU organs. Substantive decisions are made by consensus or, failing that, a two-thirds majority. A simple majority suffices on procedural questions.

The Executive Council, comprising the foreign ministers or other designated representatives of all member states, meets at least twice a year to confer on preparation for meetings of the assembly, the implementation of assembly decisions, the AU budget, and matters of intra-African cooperation and general international policy. Assisting the Executive Council is the Permanent Representatives Committee, made up of ambassadors accredited to the AU. An advisory Economic, Social, and Cultural Council (ECOSOCC) was launched in March 2005.

Consisting of 15 members elected with due regard for "equitable regional representation and rotation," the PSC includes in its mandate supervision of a planned African Standby Force equipped to intervene in crisis situations.

The Pan-African Parliament, established under a protocol to the AEC treaty, is envisaged as evolving into a directly elected organ with full legislative powers. Initially, however, it comprises five representatives chosen by and from the member states' legislatures and reflecting "the diversity of political opinion in each." The inaugural parliamentary session was held on March 18–20, 2004, in Addis Ababa.

The AU Commission replaced the OAU's Secretariat. The Commission chair, who is elected by the assembly for a four-year term, is assisted by a deputy and eight elected commissioners. The commission oversees the work of the AU in many administrative and policy areas. (For a list of the responsibilities of the individual commissioners, see the 2012 *Handbook*.) In addition, the Commission services the Conference on Security, Stability, Development, and Cooperation in Africa (CSSDCA), which was established by the 2000 OAU summit in Lomé and has a primary role in regional monitoring and evaluation.

The chair of the entire AU, as distinct from the AU Commission, rotates annually, by vote of the Assembly, among the heads of state of member countries.

The Constitutive Act additionally called for the formation of eight specialized technical committees: Rural Economy and Agricultural Matters; Monetary and Financial Affairs; Trade, Customs, and Immigration Matters; Industry, Science, and Technology; Energy, Natural Resources, and the Environment; Transportation, Communication, and Tourism; Health, Labor, and Social Affairs; and Education, Culture, and Human Rights. The assembly may create additional specialized technical committees.

Three new financial institutions are also mentioned in the founding act: the African Central Bank, the African Monetary Fund, and the African Investment Bank. At the eighth Ordinary Session of the Executive Council, held January 16–17, 2006, in Addis Ababa, the first members of the African Court on Human and People's Rights were elected. Creation of this body was proposed in a protocol to the 1981 African Charter on Human and People's Rights. The Court of Justice was merged with the African Court on Human and People's Rights on July 1, 2008. The Court of Justice is responsible for serving as a criminal court for Africa and is largely charged with handling cases pertaining to human rights violations. The Court of Justice also serves as the legal branch of the AU.

Related specialized agencies, all previously associated with the OAU, include the African Accounting Council, the African Civil Aviation Commission (AFCAC), the African Telecommunications Union (ATU), the Pan-African Institute of Education for Development, the Pan-African News Agency (PANA), and the Pan-African Postal Union (PAPU).

Recent activities. At the January 31–February 2, 2010, Addis Ababa summit, Libyan president Qadhafi failed in an attempt to stay on for a second year as the organization's chair. He was succeeded by Bingu wa Mutharika, president of Malawi.

In February 2010 an AU delegation visited NATO headquarters in Belgium, to discuss closer cooperation between the two groups in Africa's new strategic environment. AU–U.S. talks opened in Washington for the first time in April. They ended with a pledge of more U.S. cooperation with the AU.

The 15th summit was held July 19–27, 2010, in Kampala, Uganda. It came only a few days after Al-Shabaab terrorists killed more than 70 people in three separate bombings. At the summit Guinea announced that it would send troops to join the peacekeeping forces in Somalia.

Between the two summits there was a military coup in Niger, which the AU condemned, and it suspended that country from membership. On March 16, 2011, following the successful completion of a new parliamentary election in Niger, the PSC voted to lift the suspension. Similarly, a highly contested election in Cote d'Ivoire resulted in the AU suspending the country in November 2010. The AU subsequently sent a commission of 20 individuals into the country to help the two sides come to a peaceable agreement. After five months of negotiating, the election dispute was resolved with the assistance of the AU officials, and the country was reinstated on April 21, 2011.

The 16th summit occurred in January 2011 at the UN Conference Center in Addis Ababa, Ethiopia. The meeting discussed the necessary steps toward the transition of the AUC into the African Union Association. The meeting also endorsed Mauritius's claim to the Chagos Archipelago, a territory disputed by the British.

In July the 17th summit focused largely on the political conflict in Libya. In a resolution approved by the assembly, the AU declared that a political situation was the only acceptable solution, and urged the UN to support the efforts of the AU rather than using force. A framework agreement submitted by an ad hoc committee on the Libya situation was approved and sent to the Libyan government.

Also in July 2011, the newly formed Republic of Sudan became the 54th member of the African Union.

The continued fighting and unrest in Libya was a major concern of the AU throughout the latter half of 2011. The PSC kept a close monitor on the situation, as did a high level ad hoc committee formed at the request of the AUC. The AU continually emphasized its commitment to the people of Libya and called for a peaceful resolution of the situation. Following the ouster and death of Colonel Qadaffi in October, the PSC recognized the government of the National Transitional Council and allowed the NTC to assume Libya's seat in the AU. The AU also organized a liaison office in Tripoli to assist with the peaceful transition of power and rebuilding of the Libyan infrastructure.

The 18th summit held in January 2012 largely centered on African integration. One such measure was the full establishment of the Pan African University. The PAU was formally created in December 2011, but the January summit started the organization of the university by authorizing permanent institution sites and the hiring of faculty and staff. The meeting also saw measures taken to speed up the full economic integration of the continent by creating an action plan for integration and establishing the framework of the economic union. It set a 2017 deadline for the full implementation of a free trade continent.

In January 2012 a group of rebels began an attack against the government of Mali. On March 22 Mali president Amadou Toure was removed from office in an armed coup. Mali was suspended from the AU the next day. Similarly, a military coup in Guinea-Bissau in early April resulted in the suspension of that country from the AU, pending the restoration of a constitutional government. Suspensions were lifted on October 24, 2012.

The 19th summit was held in July 2012. During the weeklong summit, the member states focused on the Arab-Israeli conflict through a series of resolutions and declarations. The member states reaffirmed its support for Palestine and its UN membership, while calling for Israel's immediate withdrawal from PLO territory. The member states also were greatly concerned by the expulsion of African nationals from Israel. Another major area of concern was the growing political unrest in Mali. The most significant action of the summit, however, was the election of Dr. Nkosazana Clarise Dhlamini Zuma of South Africa as AUC Chair. Dr. Dhlamini-Zuma is the first woman to be elected to the post and is the first representative of a southern African nation to hold the high office since the formation of the OAU in 1963. She replaced Dr. Jean Ping as AUC Chairperson.

The year 2013 marked the 50th anniversary of the OAU/AU. The January summit met under the theme of "Pan-Africanism and African Renaissance." The meeting saw the group emphasize the importance of maternal health, institutional reforms, and unity among the region.

In honor of its golden anniversary, the organization's May summit was tied to the main anniversary celebration. The 21st summit was significant for its adoption of the 50th Anniversary Solemn Declaration. The declaration recalled its great heritage and the progress that it has made over the last 50 years, and pledged its continued work to advance pan-Africanism and unity within the member states. The declaration identified the eight core priorities to be used in drafting the Agenda 2063, which include a pledge to end wars in Africa by 2020 and a commitment to work toward swift implementation of the Continental Free Trade Agreement. Also at the meeting, the group announced its Agenda 2063 effort, which is a pan-African attempt to craft a set of 50-year development goals. The Agenda 2063 Website was launched in September to allow the public to provide suggestions for the development goals. The draft of the Agenda is to be discussed at the January 2014 summit.

On July 3, 2013, the Egyptian government suspended its constitution, which had been ratified in December 2012, and overthrew their president Mohamed Morsi, who was elected in a June 2012 national referendum. In light of these events, the PSC called a special meeting on July 5 to discuss the situation. At that meeting, the PSC authorized the expedited creation of a high-level team to assist Egypt in its transition back to a democratic government and constitutional order.

The AU lifted its sanctions against Madagascar on September 2013 in light of the country's progress and scheduled elections.

An extraordinary summit of the Assembly of the AU was held in October 2013 to discuss the relationship between the AU and the ICC. The summit yielded a declaration from the organization stating that no sitting head of government shall be prosecuted before an international tribunal or court, and the AU affirmed that it would not require an AU head of government to appear. This meeting came as a response to the ICC's investigation of the sitting Kenyan president and vice president. The AU has issued an appeal to the UN Security Council and ICC to delay the indictment, but as the AU Assembly Chairman noted, the ICC has never responded positively to an AU request for deferral.

At its June 2014 assembly, the AU approved the protocol and statutes for the establishment of an African Monetary Fund, similar in effect to the IMF. Having passed the whole assembly, the protocol must now be approved by the individual member states for the organization to be established. The meeting also saw a renewed commitment to development within the continent and reiterated its call for the United States to lift its embargo on Cuba. In July 2014 the AU removed sanctions against Egypt that had been in place for a year. The AU also has been diligent in efforts to assist with the Ebola crisis facing western Africa in 2014, proposing the establishment of an African Center for Disease Control.

In November 2015 the AU hosted the first summit on ending child marriage. In December the organization deployed 5,000 troops to Burundi to help stabilize the area but pulled them back on January 31, 2016, after Burundi's president threatened to fight foreign peacekeepers (see entry on Burundi). The AU initiated a plan for an AU-wide passport in July 2016. In September the Union set a goal of universal health coverage for the continent by the year 2030.

ARAB LEAGUE

al-Jami'a al-'Arabiyah

Official Name: League of Arab States.

Established: By treaty signed March 22, 1945, in Cairo, Egypt.

Purpose: To strengthen relations among member states by coordinating policies in political, cultural, economic, social, and related affairs; to mediate disputes between members or between members and third parties.

Headquarters: Cairo, Egypt.

Principal Organs: Council of the League of Arab States (all members), Economic and Social Council (all adherents to the 1950 Collective Security Treaty), Joint Defense Council (all adherents to the 1950 Collective Security Treaty), Permanent Committees (all members), General Secretariat.

Website: www.lasportal.org.

Secretary General: Ahmed Aboul Gheit (Egypt).

Membership (22): Algeria, Bahrain, Comoro Islands, Djibouti, Egypt, Iraq, Jordan, Kuwait, Lebanon, Libya, Mauritania, Morocco, Oman, Palestine, Qatar, Saudi Arabia, Somalia, Sudan, Syria (currently represented by the Syrian opposition), Tunisia, United Arab Emirates, Yemen.

Observers: Brazil, Eritrea, India, Venezuela.

Official Language: Arabic.

Origin and development. A long-standing project that reached fruition late in World War II, the league was founded primarily on Egyptian initiative following a promise of British support for any Arab organization that commanded general endorsement. In its earlier years the organization focused mainly on economic, cultural, and social cooperation, but in 1950 a Convention on Joint Defense and Economic Cooperation was concluded that obligated the members in case of attack "immediately to take, individually and collectively, all steps available, including the use of armed force, to repel the aggression and restore security and peace." In 1976 the Palestine Liberation Organization (PLO), which had participated as an observer at all league conferences since September 1964, was admitted to full membership. Egypt's participation was suspended from April 1979 to May 1989 because of its peace agreement with Israel.

After many years of preoccupation with Arab–Israeli issues, the league's attention in 1987 turned to the Iraq–Iran conflict as Arab moderates sought a united front against Iran and the potential spread of militant Islamic fundamentalism. An extraordinary summit conference held November 8–11 in Amman, Jordan, condemned "the Iranian regime's intransigence, provocations, and threats to the Arab Gulf States" and called for international "pressure" to encourage Iran to accept a UN-sponsored cease-fire.

The prospect for effective cooperation was severely compromised by Iraq's takeover of Kuwait on August 2, 1990, which split the league into two deeply divided blocs. On August 10, the majority voted to send a pan-Arab force to guard Saudi Arabia against a possible Iraqi attack; several members (most notably Egypt and Syria) ultimately contributed troops to the U.S.-led liberation of Kuwait in early 1991. The minority included members overtly sympathetic to Baghdad and those that were adamantly opposed to U.S. military involvement.

In the mid-1990s, prospects for institutional reform were constrained by financial difficulties: only four members (Egypt, Jordan, Saudi Arabia, and Syria) had paid their full dues in 1996, while the remaining members were a combined $80 million in arrears. As a consequence, the league was forced to close several foreign offices and reportedly had difficulty meeting its payroll at times.

In November 1997, despite the league's financial troubles, 17 members agreed to proceed with the establishment of the Arab Free Trade Zone in 1998, with the goal of cutting customs duties by 10 percent a year until their elimination at the end of 2007. In other activity during the year, the Arab League foreign ministers, meeting in March in Cairo, recommended that members reactivate the economic boycott against Israel and cease all activity geared toward normalizing relations with that country given the stalled peace process.

The Amman, Jordan, summit of March 27–28, 2001, marked the first regular summit since 1990, with Iraq in attendance as a full participant. The league ended up calling once again for an end to the sanctions against Iraq and also for Baghdad to work out its differences with the UN over inspections and related issues. Two months later, on May 16, Amr Mahmoud Moussa, previously Egypt's foreign minister, began his tenure as the league's new secretary general.

With regard to the "road map" for peace in the Middle East that was formally introduced April 30, 2003, by the European Union, the UN, Russia, and the United States, the Arab League expressed its cautious support.

On March 22–23, 2005, only 13 of 22 leaders attended the league summit in Algiers, Algeria, and the resolutions adopted "were of comparatively little significance," according to The New York Times. However, plans were unveiled for an Arab common market by 2015 and a regional security system. The participants also approved the establishment of an interim Arab Parliament, which met for the first time on December 27, 2005, in Cairo, Egypt. The Parliament has 88 representatives, 4 from each Arab League member, but it has no legislative authority, leaving its responsibilities unclear apart from serving as a forum on Arab issues. It was decided that this interim legislature would move to Syria, meeting twice a year with the aim of creating a permanent Arab legislature by 2011. Mohammad Jassim al-Saqr, a Kuwaiti described as a liberal, was elected its speaker.

The Arab League's response to the landslide victory of the militant group Hamas in the January 2006 Palestinian Authority elections was mixed. Secretary General Moussa said Hamas should renounce violence against Israel and recognize its right to exist if it expects to function as a legitimate government. On the other hand, at its March 28–29, 2006, summit in Khartoum, the league pledged to contribute $55 million a month toward the operation of the Palestinian Authority.

The 2006 summit, like its predecessor, was not attended by the heads of several member states, for reasons including poor security and Sudan's position on the Darfur crisis. In addition to its commitment to the Palestinian Authority, the league pledged $150 million to support the mission of African Union peacekeepers in Darfur. The years 2006 and 2007 saw continuing Arab League involvement in efforts to broker peace between the Hamas and Fatah factions of the Palestinian Authority. When Hamas seized control of the Gaza Strip in June 2007, however, the Arab League joined in the policy of the U.S. and Israel of supporting the rump Palestinian Authority government of the Fatah-led faction in the West Bank.

The 2007 summit, held March 28–29 in Riyadh, Saudi Arabia, produced a renewed call for Israel to negotiate on the basis of the 2002 "land for peace" proposal. In April 2007 the league set up a contact group, consisting of Jordan and Egypt (countries having diplomatic relations with Israel), to deal directly with Israel on the proposal. On July 25, 2007, the foreign ministers of those countries went to Israel and met Israeli prime minister Ehud Olmert. By September 2007, however, the league began to say that Israel was not taking the dialogue seriously, regarding it only as an exercise in public relations.

The Arab League was actively involved in the troubles of Iraq and Lebanon throughout 2007 and 2008. In September 2007 the league turned down a Syrian government request to establish a fund in aid of Iraqi refugees in Syria. In January 2008, however, the league tried to reestablish itself as a mediator in Iraq after almost a year of absence, but with little success. Lebanon (see entry on Lebanon) was in a prolonged and sometimes violent state of unrest after its president's term ended in November 2007, and parliament failed to elect a successor. Many blamed pro-Syrian factions for the stalemate, and the Iranian-backed Hezbollah movement temporarily took over much of Beirut in early May 2008. The Arab League was deeply involved in negotiations that led to a compromise, with Hezbollah's official standing much increased, and the Lebanese parliament finally elected a president on May 28, 2008.

By mid-2008 the primary matter of concern for the Arab League was the situation in Darfur, in particular the prospect of the International Criminal Court (ICC) issuing an arrest warrant for Sudanese president Omar al-Bashir, charging him with genocide. The league's aim was to postpone or defuse the potential crisis, and in any case not to support Bashir's arrest. On July 19 it passed a resolution declaring that there was no need for an international trial, but that a Sudanese court was capable of trying Bashir. The matter dragged on until March 4, 2009, when an ICC arrest warrant was finally issued. Bashir defiantly attended the March 28–29 league summit in Doha, Qatar, and received the united support of the attendees.

The conflict between Israel and Hamas in Gaza and the massive destruction that it caused was responsible for a serious rift among league members. In January 2009 two rival conferences were held simultaneously on the question: a meeting of Arab League foreign ministers in Kuwait and a "Pan-Arab" meeting in Doha, called by the emir of Qatar. In May 2009 league foreign ministers met in Cairo to work out how to restart "serious and direct" talks between the Palestinians and Israel. Arab League influence on the peace process has since been marginal.

In late June 2010 Libya and Yemen floated a proposal to turn the Arab League into an Arab Union, but without success. The same meeting, held in Sirte, Libya, produced a series of proposals to make the league more effective in economic and trade cooperation. These proposals came at a time when many members felt that the league should be drastically reorganized, if it were to be in any way effective.

In mid-2010 Moussa announced that he would leave the organization when his ten-year term as secretary general expired in May 2011, presumably to run for the Egyptian presidency. A dispute arose as to whether his successor should be an Egyptian, as was customary. In an unprecedented effort to express discontent with the traditional Egyptian dominance of the League, Qatar, in addition to Egypt, nominated a candidate for the secretariat upon Moussa's retirement. Realizing the dissatisfaction many countries felt about the Egyptian candidate, Egypt replaced its candidate with the Egyptian foreign affairs minister, Nabil Al Arabi. Upon Al Arabi's nomination, a move that was welcomed by the entire Arab League, Qatar withdrew its candidate, and Al Arabi was unanimously elected on May 15, 2011, as the seventh secretary general of the Arab League.

In February 2011 Secretary General Moussa issued a statement recognizing the legitimacy of the claims of reform and change in Libya, and voiced his opinion that it was time for Colonel Qadhafi to leave office. In March the Arab League voted to recognize the Libyan revolutionary government and called for a no-fly zone over Libya to be enforced by the UN as a measure to prevent further human rights violations by the Qadhafi regime. The Arab League opposed all UN military intervention in Libya, claiming that it is a violation of the no-fly zone. Qadhafi was captured by members of the National Liberation Army in October 2011, and subsequently killed.

On July 14, 2011, the Arab League voted unanimously to endorse the Palestinian plan for UN membership, which was expected to be voted on in the fall. The UN Security Council opted to postpone the vote, claiming that Palestinian statehood lacked support. The Arab League has been a proponent of Palestinian land claims from its inception as an organization. The Arab League also has a long history of anti-Israeli policies and actions.

Following the Arab spring revolts of 2011, Syria became increasingly unstable while it finds itself in the midst of a multi-year civil war. Protestors have been calling for the resignation of President

Bashar al-Assad, who, despite increasing violence, vows to remain in power despite the formation of an opposition movement.

The March 2012 annual summit was held in Baghdad, Iraq, with only 10 of the 22 member states represented. The low attendance was the result of a growing split within the Arab League over how to handle the situation in Syria. The Arab League states have differing opinions on whether or not the league should withdraw its observer mission from the politically torn country. With low attendance at its annual summit, the Arab League voted to turn the situation over to the United Nations Security Council to consider. The Arab League noted that the UNSC is the only global body with binding authority. In July 2012 President Assad agreed to the terms of the UN–Arab League Special envoy's peace settlement.

The 2013 summit was held in Doha from March 21–27 in the midst of great turmoil in the Arab world on the whole. The organization continued its long-time support of Palestine by announcing the creation of a new economic assistance fund worth $1 billion (US) to finance conservation projects that protect Arab identity in Jerusalem and assist the Palestinians in their efforts against the Israelis. Furthermore, in light of the ongoing political unrest in Syria, the Arab League took a major step by replacing the Syrian government's seat in the Arab League with a representative from the Syrian National Council (SNC). The League also called on its member states to enact legislation that would open the door for economic integration in the region.

On August 21, 2013, the Arab League accused the Syrian government of carrying out chemical weapon attacks outside of Damascus that killed hundreds. As the situation further deteriorated, the Arab League called a special meeting in Cairo in early September to further discuss the situation. At that meeting, the members expressed their support of Russian president Vladimir Putin's plan to put Syria's chemical weapons under the control of international monitoring. This plan came to fruition when, on September 28, the UN Security Council unanimously adopted a resolution to secure and destroy Syria's chemical weapons. The UN–Arab League Special Envoy to Syria Lakhdar Brahimi and Secretary General Al Arabi were also two of the major players in the attempt to hold a second Geneva peace conference on the Syria issue. (For more information on developments since 2013, see Recent activities, below.)

Structure. The principal political organ of the league is the Council of the League of Arab States, which meets in regular session twice a year, normally at the foreign minister's level. Each member has one vote in the council; decisions usually bind only those states that accept them, although a two-thirds majority vote on financial and administrative matters binds all members. The council's main functions are to supervise the execution of agreements between members, to mediate disputes, and to coordinate defense in the event of attack. There are numerous committees and other bodies attached to the council, including permanent committees dealing with finance and administration, legal affairs, and information.

The council has also established an Administrative Court, an Investment Arbitration Board, and a Higher Auditing Board. Additional ministerial councils, attended by relevant ministers or their representatives, are held in a dozen areas including transport, justice, health, telecommunications, and environmental affairs.

Three additional bodies were established by the 1950 convention: a Joint Defense Council to function in matters of collective security and to coordinate military resources; a Permanent Military Commission, comprised of representatives of the general staffs, to draw up plans for joint defense; and an Economic Council, comprised of the ministers of economic affairs, to coordinate Arab economic development. The last was restructured as an Economic and Social Council in 1977. An Arab Unified Military Command, charged with the integration of strategy for the liberation of Palestine, was formed in 1964.

The General Secretariat is responsible for internal administration and the execution of council decisions. It also administers several agencies, including the Bureau for Boycotting Israel (headquartered in Damascus, Syria).

Membership in the league generally carries with it membership in an array of specialized agencies, including the Arab Bank for Economic Development in Africa (BADEA) and the Arab Monetary Fund (AMF), as well as a variety of other bodies dealing with economic, social, and technical matters.

Many Arab Summit Conferences have been held since the first one met in 1964. Summit resolutions give direction to the work of the council and other league organs, although the organization's charter did not provide a framework for convening summits.

Recent activities. The March 2014 Arab League Summit in Kuwait was one of the most contested in recent history. The Syrian seat remained empty, despite its having been offered to the SNC as the Council had failed to get all of the necessary political institutions in place to assume the seat. Further division among the league's members centered over the Muslim Brotherhood and its role within the Egyptian government. These divisions resulted in seats other than Syria's being open. The leaders of Saudi Arabia, Bahrain, Oman, and the United Arab Emirates refused to attend the summit over their objections to Egypt, while Algeria and Iraq boycotted the summit for the league's allowance of the opposition SNC to represent Syria. The only point on which all the leaders could agree was in their rejection of a proposal to recognize Israel as a Jewish state.

An extraordinary summit of the Arab League was called in September to address the growing problem of the militant terrorist group in Syria and Iraq, Islamic State of Iraq and Syria (ISIS). The members released a statement on September 8 in which they called for immediate efforts to stop the group on all fronts—defense, political, and legal. The league, however, failed to give their assent to the American plan of military action.

In 2015 the Arab League endorsed the Saudi-led military intervention into Yemen against the Shia Houthi rebels (see entry on Yemen). On March 29, 2015, the Arab League decided to create a joint military force, which was formally launched in April.

On January 3, 2016, the Arab League condemned attacks on the Saudi Embassy in Iran (see entry on Iran) and demanded that Iran respect the principle of non-interference in the international affairs of Arab countries. On March 11 the Arab League labeled the Shi'ite Muslim Hezbollah as a terrorist organization following pressure from Saudi Arabia and other Sunni members of the organization.

ASIA-PACIFIC ECONOMIC COOPERATION (APEC)

Established: At a meeting of foreign and economic ministers of 12 nations November 6–7, 1989, in Canberra, Australia; objectives and principles set forth in Seoul Declaration approved during ministerial meeting November 12–14, 1991, in Seoul, South Korea; Declaration of Institutional Arrangements adopted September 10–11, 1992, in Bangkok, Thailand.

Purpose: To provide a forum for discussion on a variety of economic issues and to promote multilateral cooperation among the region's market-oriented economies.

Headquarters: Singapore.

Principal Organs: Economic Leaders' Meeting, Ministerial Meeting, Senior Officials' Meeting, Budget and Management Committee, Committee on Trade and Investment, Economic Committee, Secretariat.

Website: www.apec.org.

Executive Director: Dr. Alan Bollard (New Zealand).

Membership (21): Australia, Brunei, Canada, Chile, China, Hong Kong, Indonesia, Japan, Republic of Korea, Malaysia, Mexico, New Zealand, Papua New Guinea, Peru, Philippines, Russia, Singapore, Taiwan ("Chinese Taipei"), Thailand, United States, Vietnam.

Observers: Association of Southeast Asian Nations, Pacific Economic Cooperation Council, Pacific Islands Forum.

Official Language: English.

Origin and development. In early 1989 Australian prime minister Robert Hawke proposed that a permanent body be established to coordinate economic relations among market-oriented nations on the Pacific Rim, with particular emphasis to be given to dialogue between Western Pacific countries and the United States. The proposal was endorsed by the Pacific Economic Cooperation Conference (PECC; a group of business, academic, and government representatives who had held informal discussions since 1980), and the first APEC meeting was held November 6–7 in Canberra, Australia. Ministers from 12 nations—Australia, Brunei, Canada, Indonesia, Japan, Republic of Korea, Malaysia, New Zealand, Philippines, Singapore, Thailand, and United States—attended the inaugural session, with debate centering on how to proceed in adopting formal APEC arrangements.

Due to concern among some members of the Association of Southeast Asian Nations (ASEAN; see separate article) that they might be overwhelmed by such economic giants as Canada, Japan, and the United States, the Canberra session decided to keep APEC as a loosely defined, informal grouping officially committed only to an annual dialogue meeting. As regional economic cooperation gained momentum in other areas of the world, pressure grew within APEC for a more structured format. Consequently, the Ministerial Meeting in November 1991 in Seoul, South Korea, adopted a declaration outlining APEC's objectives; established additional organizational structure; and approved the membership of China, Hong Kong, and Taiwan.

The "institutionalization" of APEC was completed during a Ministerial Meeting September 10–11, 1992, in Bangkok, Thailand, with the decision to establish a permanent Secretariat in Singapore as of January 1, 1993. The November 1992 Ministerial Meeting directed APEC's new permanent Secretariat to establish an electronic tariff database for the region, survey members regarding investment regulations, and study ways to harmonize customs procedures and reduce impediments to "market access" among members.

Mexico and Papua New Guinea were admitted into APEC in November 1993, while Chile's membership application was approved effective November 1994. The latter was the subject of debate within APEC, as some officials suggested that admission of South American countries could cost the organization its focus. Consequently, a moratorium on any additional APEC members was declared until at least 1996

Hoping to impel integrationist sentiment in the region (which controls more than one-half of the world's economy and accounts for nearly one-half of all global trade), the APEC finance ministers met for the first time March 18–19, 1994, in Honolulu, Hawaii. Among other things, plans were endorsed to double the capital of the Asian Development Bank, to promote cross-border investment, and to study ways of facilitating finance for large infrastructure projects.

A potentially historic step was taken at the second APEC summit, held November 15, 1994, in Bogor, Indonesia, with the adoption of a "declaration of common resolve" to pursue "free and open trade and investment" over the next quarter century. The loosely worded accord called on the region's developed nations to dismantle their trade barriers by 2010 and for developing nations to follow suit by 2020. Differences of opinion regarding the appropriate pace and intensity for implementing the 1994 action agenda were readily apparent at the next summit, held in November 1995 in Osaka, Japan. After much discussion it was agreed that many APEC stipulations, at least for the time being, would be implemented on a voluntary basis.

The central issue of the November 1997 summit, held in Vancouver, Canada, was the Asian economic crisis, which prompted several APEC members to seek assistance from the International Monetary Fund (IMF). Japan proposed creating a separate Asian fund to help resolve the crisis, but that idea was rejected at an ASEAN meeting held earlier in November in Manila, where it was agreed that the IMF would play the central role in promoting economic stabilization.

Political events in East Timor, Indonesia, provided a backdrop to the September 12–13, 1999, Economic Leaders' Meeting in Auckland, New Zealand, where the APEC foreign affairs ministers supported the formation of a United Nations (UN) multinational military presence to restore order to the troubled jurisdiction. The summit noted progress toward economic recovery in Asia, approved APEC Principles to Enhance Competition and Regulatory Reform, and called for an improved "international framework" for the flow of trade and investment capital.

The timing of a new round of trade negotiations proved to be a contentious topic at the November 15–16, 2000, summit, which was held in Bandar Seri Begawan, Brunei. The United States, Japan, and Canada pressed for a rapid start, whereas Malaysia and many of the smaller economies preferred a more deliberate pace. In its final declaration the summit opted for a carefully worded compromise in which the leaders agreed "that a balanced and sufficiently broad-based agenda that responds to the interests and concerns of all WTO members should be formulated and finalized as soon as possible in 2001 and that a round be launched in 2001."

The October 19–21, 2001, Economic Leaders' Meeting, held in Shanghai, China, offered general support for U.S.-led efforts to combat terrorism, including cutting off funding for terrorist groups. The summit declaration did not, however, specifically address U.S. military response to the September terrorist attacks on New York and Washington.

During 2002, rather than proposing new initiatives, APEC concentrated its efforts on previously established goals, including improved business management and evaluation, peer review, structural reforms, and transparency. All were in keeping with the three goals emphasized in the 1994 Bogor Declaration, namely, trade and investment liberalization, business facilitation, and economic and technical cooperation. At the October 26–27 Economic Leaders' Meeting in Cabo San Lucas, Mexico, attendees endorsed a Trade Facilitation Action Plan aimed at reducing transaction costs by 5 percent over five years; a Statement to Implement APEC Transparency Standards; several counterterrorism measures, including an APEC Energy Security Initiative and a proposal for Secure Trade in the APEC Region (STAR); and a Statement to Implement APEC Policies on Trade and the Digital Economy. The summit also urged the WTO to complete its current round of trade negotiations by January 2005.

In the first half of 2003, planned APEC activities were overshadowed by the onset of the Severe Acute Respiratory Syndrome (SARS) outbreak. Precautions against the spread of the newly identified viral illness led to the cancellation of some 30 APEC-sponsored meetings in March–July. Meeting on June 2–3, in Khon Kaen, Thailand, the APEC Ministers Responsible for Trade, recognizing the severe economic repercussions of SARS for the region, pledged to restore business confidence in trade, investment, travel, and mobility by endorsing a plan of action that focused on the need to establish principles for health screenings, the timely exchange of information on the outbreak, and cooperation in prevention and treatment.

The 2003 Economic Leaders' Meeting, held October 19–21 in Bangkok, endorsed the SARS Action Plan and a Health Security Initiative, but with the outbreak contained, greater attention was directed toward economic matters. A principal focus was on "free and open trade and investment," including the need for bilateral, regional, and multilateral accords to be "complementary and mutually reinforcing." Along the same lines, the participants called for a renewed commitment to WTO liberalization negotiations and efforts to extend the perceived benefits of globalization to a broader spectrum of people and societies.

The APEC annual summit, held November 19–21, 2004, in Santiago, Chile, adopted the Santiago Initiative for Expanded Trade in APEC and also received a study from the APEC Business Advisory Council outlining the dimensions of a possible Free Trade Area of the Asia-Pacific region. In addition to highlighting trade and investment liberalization as a path toward advancing development, the closing declaration stressed the issues of energy security, public health, and ending corruption by ensuring transparency.

As in 2003, U.S. president George W. Bush devoted much of his time to discussing with other heads of government North Korea's nuclear program. The summit participants also noted the need to improve security through adoption of antiterrorist conventions and implementation of measures intended, for example, to cut off terrorist financing. Some critics have asserted, however, that expanding the scope of APEC discussions to include matters of security and governance has diminished APEC's importance as an economic forum.

At the Ministerial Meeting on November 15–16, 2005, in Busan, Korea, APEC adopted the Busan Roadmap, a document outlining a strategy for reaching the organization's original goals in the light of a decade of globalization and change in world economic relationships, while maintaining sustainable development practices. The national leaders issued a separate statement in support of a successful conclusion to the WTO's sixth Ministerial Meeting in Hong Kong, China, and agreed to confront pandemic health threats and continue to fight against terrorism.

The APEC summit, held in Hanoi, Vietnam, on November 18, 2006, took place in the shadow of North Korea's recent nuclear test, but the conferees were not able to come up with a completely unified approach to the problem. Summit participants also acknowledged for the first time that the APEC area contained too many bilateral trade agreements, to the point of being an impediment to free trade.

Australia became the 2007 host for APEC, and the Australian government announced initiatives to strengthen the organization. These initiatives would include increasing its budget by 30 percent and making the Secretariat stronger and more centralized, with the position of executive director not rotating each year.

The September 8–9, 2008, APEC summit was held in Sydney, Australia. It had been expected to move forward with India's application to join the group. At the event the United States and New Zealand opposed India's accession, which Australia had strongly supported.

The meeting decided to extend a moratorium on admitting new members until 2010.

On environmental matters, the summit made a commitment to the "aspirational goals" of increasing energy efficiency 25 percent from 2005 levels by 2030 and increasing forest cover in the region by at least 20 million hectares (approximately 8.1 million acres) by 2020. The summit also called, again, for a rapid conclusion to the long-stalled Doha round of trade talks. It was announced that the United States would host the summit in 2011 and Russia in 2012. Russian president Vladimir Putin had said that he felt APEC to be one of the most effective and useful international organizations, though some commentators felt that such a high-level meeting producing so few concrete results was a sign that APEC was irrelevant.

In June 2008 a meeting of APEC trade ministers in Arequipa, Peru, agreed to cut tariffs among APEC members to zero by 2020. The matters that dominated APEC in 2008 and 2009, however, were the world economic crisis and the organization's direction after the apparent failure of the Doha round of free-trade negotiations. The November 19–20, 2008, ministerial meeting, as well as the November 22 summit, both held in Lima, Peru, focused on the world financial crisis and the perceived need to avoid a return to protectionism. They also approved the change of the executive secretary's tenure from annual rotation to a three-year term.

The November 14–15, 2009, summit held in Singapore was U.S. president Barack Obama's first opportunity to engage with leaders of the entire Asia-Pacific region. He expressed that the United States, as a Pacific nation, would be a strong and enduring partner for the region. The group's leaders dropped any attempt to reach accord on remediating climate change ahead of the December 2009 Copenhagen meeting.

The November 13–14, 2010, summit held in Yokohama, Japan, called for the group to concentrate on its core mission, the creation of a seamless Asia-Pacific trading area. President Obama called on APEC nations not to rely exclusively on exports to the United States for economic growth. Countries with a large trade surplus must take steps to boost domestic demand, he said, clearly referring to China and Japan clearly. Chinese president Hu Jintao said his country was trying to increase domestic consumption, but held out no prospect of large or immediate readjustments in the value of his currency.

The November 12–13, 2011, summit in Honolulu, Hawaii, centered on talks regarding the Trans-Pacific Partnership (TPP), an existing free trade agreement between Brunei, Chile, New Zealand, and Singapore. Continuing in a similar vein to the 2010 summit, APEC members sought to take the TPP trade agreement "to the next level." Australia, Malaysia, Peru, Vietnam, Japan, and the United States are existing APEC members seeking to enter the TPP. Such a partnership would be nearly 40 percent larger than the European Union. The effort to expand the TPP, spearheaded by the United States, has been criticized as being overly ambitious and impractical. Additionally, several APEC nations were hesitant to lift the existing trade tariffs, as would be required for entry into the TPP. The summit also discussed strategies to minimize negative effects from the European debt crisis. This included plans to reduce tariffs on environmentally friendly goods to 5 percent by 2015, as well as plans to double exports in five years.

At a June 2012 meeting of the APEC Finance Ministers, the group reiterated the call of the APEC Leaders to reduce bilateral trade agreements in order to promote the creation of a Free Trade Asia-Pacific Agreement. They also called on the member states to work with the WTO to promote economic growth in the field of information technology. This meeting came on the coattails of a new report that indicated the APEC member states remained the fastest growing economies in the world in 2012.

The 2012 summit, held in Vladivostok, Russia, focused on the key issues of institutional progress within APEC, enhancing cooperation as a means of producing growth, strengthening its efforts concerning food security, and liberalizing its trade and investment policy within the framework of broader regional integration. Both the ministers and economic leaders emphasized international trade as a key component of economic growth, job creation, and recovery from the global depression experienced over the past few years. Like many other economic organizations, APEC noted the importance of small- and medium-sized enterprises (SMEs) for fostering further growth. The meeting also saw the appointment of Dr. Alan Bollard as the new executive director of the APEC Secretariat. (For more information on developments since 2013, see Recent activities, below.)

Structure. APEC's governing body is the annual Ministerial Meeting, the chair of which rotates each year among the members. Decisions are reached by consensus. Since 1993 overall guidance has been provided by the Economic Leaders' Meeting, an informal gathering of APEC heads of state and/or government that immediately follows the yearly Ministerial Meeting. In addition, sectoral ministerial meetings have been held (some annually) regarding various issues.

Responsibility for policy implementation rests primarily with a Senior Officials' Meeting (SOM), which convenes as necessary. There are four standing committees: Budget and Management; Trade and Investment, which is assisted by more than a dozen subcommittees and expert groups; Economic, assisted by an Economic Outlook Task Force; and the SOM Committee on Economic and Technical Cooperation.

The APEC Secretariat is the main organ responsible for the day-to-day activities of the organization. A team of program directors that are nominated by the member economies assists the executive director in the operational and organizational administration of APEC. Beginning in 2010, the position of executive director was changed to a three-year term, open to any qualified citizen of a member country. The position was previously designated to be an ambassador of the country that was currently presiding over the organization. Other organs include several topical special task groups that address concerns related to anticorruption and transparency, counterterrorism, electronic commerce, gender, health, social safety nets, and emergency preparedness. There are also 11 working groups: Agricultural Technical Cooperation, Energy, Fisheries, Human Resources Development, Industrial Science and Technology, Marine Resources Conservation, Small and Medium Enterprises, Telecommunications and Information, Tourism, Trade Promotion, and Transportation. Since 1996 the APEC Business Advisory Council, comprising up to three senior business executives from each member country, has met to discuss APEC action plans and other business issues.

Recent activities. The year 2013 saw progress of several major initiatives under way in APEC. A preliminary progress report in April noted that APEC was on target to meet its goal of a 10 percent increase in supply chain performance by 2015. A special ministerial meeting pertaining to women and SMEs, held in August 2013, noted the efforts currently being undertaken to promote economic growth in the region. The meeting emphasized the continued importance of gender equity in business as a means for job creation and development.

The 2013 summit, held in Bali, Indonesia, focused primarily on the steps necessary for the developing countries to achieve the Bogor Goals by 2020. These efforts include steps to reduce tariffs on environmental goods, enhance sustainable growth practices, promote integration within the region through physical and institutional connectivity, and increase efforts in economic growth and equity among nations and people. In addition to outlining steps still to be taken, the ministers and economic leaders noted the progress that has been made in several other key areas, including partnership with other organizations, supply chain performance, and progress in development of the secretariat's strategic growth plan.

In September 2014 the ministers of tourism from the 21 member states formally adopted the Macao Declaration. The declaration pledges APEC members to remove barriers to transportation, such as improving the visa process and shortening wait times at airports, while also promoting the use of technology in the tourism industry. The organization's goal is to have 800 million tourists by 2025. The group's annual leadership summit was planned for mid-November.

On December 29, 2015, the APEC summit was held in the Philippines for the second time since 1996. More than 11,000 delegates met on the heels of the November Paris attacks (see entry on France) to discuss global economic trends and disruptions following the terrorist attacks. A five-point declaration was issued, which called for joint action on issues such as terrorism, climate change, and global poverty. Following the summit, efforts were launched to remove barriers preventing India from joining APEC, but issues with the TPP continue to complicate negotiations.

ASSOCIATION OF SOUTHEAST ASIAN NATIONS (ASEAN)

Established: By foreign ministers of member states August 9, 1967, in Bangkok, Thailand.

Purpose: "To accelerate economic growth, social progress and cultural development in the region . . . to promote active collaboration and mutual assistance on matters of common interest in the economic, social, cultural, technical, scientific, and administrative fields . . . to collaborate more effectively for the greater utilization of [the member states'] agriculture and industries, the expansion of their trade, including the study of problems of international commodity trade, the improvement of their transport and communication facilities and raising the living standards of their people."

Headquarters: Jakarta, Indonesia.

Principal Organs: ASEAN Heads of State and Government, ASEAN Ministerial Meeting, ASEAN Community Councils, ASEAN Standing Committees.

Website: www.asean.org.

Secretary General: Le Luong Minh (Vietnam).

Membership (10): Brunei, Cambodia, Indonesia, Laos, Malaysia, Myanmar (Burma), Philippines, Singapore, Thailand, Vietnam.

Official Language: English.

Origin and development. ASEAN was part of a continuing effort during the 1960s to create a framework for regional cooperation among the non-Communist states of Southeast Asia. Earlier efforts attempts included the Association of Southeast Asia (ASA), established in 1961 by Malaya, the Philippines, and Thailand; and the short-lived Maphilindo association, created in 1963 by Indonesia, Malaya, and the Philippines. The change of government in Indonesia in 1966 opened the way to a broader association, with plans for ASEAN broached at an August conference in Bangkok, Thailand, and implemented a year later with Indonesia, Malaysia, Philippines, Singapore, and Thailand as founding members.

The first ASEAN-sponsored regional summit conference was held February 1976 in Pattaya, Thailand.

Although economic cooperation has long been a principal ASEAN concern, progress has been slowed by such factors as differing levels of development among member countries and similarity of exports. By contrast, the association generally demonstrated political solidarity in its early years, primarily through an anticommunist posture that yielded strong condemnation of Vietnam's 1978–1989 military involvement in Cambodia.

In 1982 Sri Lanka's application for admission was denied on geographic grounds in 1982, while Brunei was admitted following its independence in 1984.

ASEAN convened its first summit in a decade on December 14–15, 1987. Meeting in Manila, Philippines, the heads of state called for a reduction in tariff barriers between members and a rejuvenation of regional economic projects.

ASEAN's dominant concern in 1988 remained the situation in Cambodia. ASEAN members met with representatives of the Vietnamese and warring Cambodian factions in July 1988 and February 1989 in Jakarta, Indonesia, in an effort to negotiate a settlement. When Vietnam withdrew its last troops in September 1989, ASEAN continued to play an important role in talks aimed at producing a permanent political resolution to the Cambodian conflict.

Another major issue for ASEAN was the formation of the Asia-Pacific Economic Cooperation (APEC) forum, which now includes seven ASEAN members plus 14 other countries (see entry on APEC, above). Apparently concerned that their interests could be slighted in a grouping involving global economic powers, the ASEAN countries were initially seen as resisting efforts to formalize the APEC, which was inaugurated in November 1989, beyond regular meetings of foreign and trade ministers.

Concerned that economic integration in North America and Europe might negatively affect the Far East, the January 27–28, 1992, ASEAN Summit in Singapore created the ASEAN Free Trade Area (AFTA). In July 1993 the ASEAN foreign ministers decided the association would host a regional security forum designed, among other things, to facilitate the peaceful resolution of disputes and promote regional stability. The forum—now comprising the ASEAN members, Australia, Canada, China, the EU, India, Japan, Democratic People's Republic of Korea, Republic of Korea, Mongolia, New Zealand, Pakistan, Papua New Guinea, Russia, and United States—was perceived by some as an Asian equivalent of the Conference on (later Organization for) Security and Cooperation in Europe (CSCE, OSCE), although its eventual structure and purview remained vague.

The ASEAN Regional Forum (ARF) met for the first time July 25, 1994, during the ASEAN Ministerial Meeting in Bangkok, Thailand. Substantive talks were reported on a variety of concerns, including North Korea's nuclear posture, the region's escalating arms race, claims by a number of countries to the potentially oil-rich Spratly Islands in the South China Sea (see entry on Vietnam), and the need for the other ARF members to engage China in a "genuine security dialog." However, no formal agreements were reached regarding conflict resolution mechanisms, and most attendees cautioned that they expected the ARF to proceed slowly.

Meanwhile, at their 1995 annual meeting, the ASEAN foreign ministers endorsed a proposal to move up the final implementation date for AFTA from 2003 to 2000. (The original target date of 2008 had already been changed to 2003 the previous year.) Vietnam, admitted as a full ASEAN member at the meeting, was given until 2006 to comply with the AFTA tariff reductions.

The ASEAN foreign ministers meeting on July 20–21, 1996, appeared to be at odds with the United States and other Western nations regarding the extent to which international bodies should interfere in the domestic affairs of members. The ASEAN leaders suggested that issues such as human rights and government corruption should not be addressed by the upcoming first ministerial meeting of the World Trade Organization (WTO). The question came into even sharper focus for ASEAN two days later at the third session of the ARF, attended for the first time by India and Myanmar. The presence of the latter was the source of much discussion considering the heavy pressure Western capitals had exerted on Myanmar regarding human rights and political repression.

Laos and Myanmar were admitted to ASEAN on July 23, 1997, the day before the 30th annual meeting of foreign ministers was held in Kuala Lumpur, Malaysia. The West, as expected, objected to Myanmar's accession, and at the July 27 meeting of the ARF the Western nations and Japan criticized Myanmar's human rights record.

The ASEAN Summit held on December 15–16, 1998, in Hanoi, Vietnam, was marked by disagreement over Cambodia's prospective membership; Hanoi, backed by Indonesia and Malaysia, pushed hard for Cambodia's immediate accession, but the other members insisted on further delay to assess the new Cambodian government's stability. (Cambodia was ultimately admitted to ASEAN at a special ceremony April 30, 1999, in Hanoi.) Prior to the summit, the ASEAN foreign and finance ministers agreed to bring AFTA's launch date forward to 2002 for the original ASEAN partners.

An informal summit held November 27–28, 1999, in Manila, overlapping meetings of the ASEAN foreign and finance ministers, discussed developments in East Timor and also proposed a code of conduct regarding the disputed Spratly Islands, but the session was dominated by economic developments. With China, South Korea, and Japan participating, in a format dubbed "ASEAN plus three" (ASEAN +3), the session reached agreement on a nonspecific framework for East Asian economic cooperation, which was hailed as a major advance toward wider regional integration. The ASEAN leaders also advanced the target date for elimination of all import duties from 2015 to 2010 for all members except Cambodia, Laos, Myanmar, and Vietnam, which saw their target moved from 2018 to 2015.

The 33rd annual Ministerial Meeting was held July 24–25, 2000, in Bangkok, with the most notable development being a decision to establish an informal ministerial troika that would serve as a rapid response team in the event of a regional emergency. Consisting of the current ministerial chair, his predecessor, and his successor, the troika would have limited ability to act, given the noninterference principle and the need to consult all ASEAN members beforehand. The foreign ministers' meeting was once again followed by a session of the ARF, which for the first time included North Korean participation. At this meeting the EU agreed to reopen its dialogue with ASEAN three years after suspending the talks in protest of Myanmar's accession.

The annual summit held November 5–6, 2001, in Bandar Seri Begawan, Brunei, was also attended by leaders of China, Japan, and South Korea. Two major developments were a commitment to oppose terrorism, despite some differences over the U.S.-led military intervention in Afghanistan, and an agreement to support a Chinese proposal for an eventual ASEAN-China free trade area (FTA). With regard to the latter, Malaysia, in particular, expressed concerns about the ability of ASEAN products to compete directly against Chinese manufacturers.

The November 3–5, 2002, summit in Phnom Penh, Cambodia, was also attended by Chinese president Zhu Rongji and the Indian prime minister, Atal Bihari Vajpayee. At the meeting the ten ASEAN members signed a framework agreement on establishing a FTA by 2010, although the poorer ASEAN states—Myanmar, Cambodia, Laos, and Vietnam—were given an additional five years to eliminate specified tariff barriers. The ASEAN leaders also created a task force for drafting an FTA framework agreement with India. Significant progress was also made regarding competing territorial claims in the South China Sea, although the summit's joint declaration on the issue did not contain the formal code of conduct that ASEAN states had sought. In other business, the summit formally approved the appointment of Ong Keng Yong of Singapore as the organization's next secretary general, effective January 2003.

The second quarter of 2003 was dominated by the Asian outbreak of the new viral disease Severe Acute Respiratory Syndrome (SARS). An emergency meeting of the ASEAN +3 health ministers on April 26 in Kuala Lumpur was quickly followed by a Special ASEAN Leaders' Meeting on SARS (and a parallel ASEAN-China session) April 29 in Bangkok. The meeting noted the outbreak's "serious adverse impact" and emphasized the importance of "strong leadership, political commitment, multisectoral collaboration and partnership" in overcoming the economic and societal consequences.

Meeting October 7–8, 2003, in Bali, Indonesia, the ASEAN leaders endorsed creation of an ASEAN Community by 2020. The Bali Concord II plan called for a free trade agreement and greater security and social cooperation, but significant barriers remain to be overcome, including the economic disparities among members.

On July 2, 2004, in Jakarta, Indonesia, the ARF admitted Pakistan to its membership, following the withdrawal of Indian objections. The ARF session, which was immediately preceded by ASEAN foreign minister and ASEAN +3 meetings, covered in its discussions North Korea's nuclear weapons program, international terrorism, improved maritime security, the need to increase export controls on technology and materials that could be used in producing weapons of mass destruction (WMD), and the political situation in Myanmar. The November 27–30 summit in Vientiane, Laos, appeared to indicate a return to the principle of noninterference in members' internal matters. Major developments in the economic sphere were discussed, including a decision to accelerate by three years the schedule for introducing the ASEAN FTA. Additionally, Brunei, Indonesia, Malaysia, Philippines, Singapore, and Thailand committed to ending internal tariffs by 2007, with Myanmar, Cambodia, Laos, and Vietnam following suit by 2012. Also at the summit, Chinese prime minister Wen Jiabao and the ASEAN leaders signed a trade agreement eliminating tariffs on many agricultural and manufactured goods by 2010.

At the foreign ministers' meeting held in Cebu, Philippines, on April 9–12, 2005, Malaysia, Philippines, and Singapore reportedly led a movement exerting pressure on Myanmar to bypass its turn to chair ASEAN. Although the Myanmar government previously resisted any such suggestion, the foreign ministers announced July 25 that Myanmar would in fact "relinquish" the chair for 2006 in favor of the Philippines, ostensibly because it wanted to maintain its focus on reconciliation and democratization at home.

The early months of 2006 were marked by efforts to arrange an ASEAN fact-finding mission to Myanmar to investigate the human rights situation there. After several delays, the Myanmar government agreed to a visit by Malaysian foreign minister Syed Hamid Albar at the end of March. He made the visit, but returned one day early on March 24, apparently because he was not allowed to meet with prodemocracy leader Aung San Suu Kyi, who was under house arrest. Hamid subsequently issued a statement that Myanmar's inflexibility was holding its neighbors hostage, and that ASEAN could not be expected to continue shielding Myanmar from criticism.

The ASEAN summit held January 11–15, 2007, on the Philippine island of Cebu, notable for the presence of a Chinese delegation, produced an agreement to open up some service sectors of the participants' economies by July 2007. This would be a first step in creating a China–ASEAN free trade area by 2015. The meeting also produced the Cebu Declaration, which called for the accelerated creation of the ASEAN Community, moving the date up from 2020 to 2015.

During 2007 and 2008 several interrelated issues dominated ASEAN affairs. A July 20, 2007, ministerial meeting in Manila approved a draft charter for the organization. The charter, for the first time, gave legal status to ASEAN and imposed binding rules on its members. In general, the charter strengthens the secretary general's position. Among other things, it provides for a commission to monitor human rights in the region. The military rulers of Myanmar came close to not signing the charter document, but the organization formally adopted the draft at its November 18–22, 2007, summit in Singapore. On October 21, 2008, Indonesia became the last country to do so, and the charter was formally launched on December 15, 2008.

The April 2009 summit had to be aborted when antigovernment protesters broke through police cordons at the Thai resort of Pattiya while the meeting was in progress. The ASEAN participants were airlifted to safety. In August 2009, in an almost unprecedented move, ASEAN condemned Myanmar for putting the prodemocracy leader Aung San Suu Kyi on trial and sentencing her to a further period of house arrest after an apparently deranged American swam to the house where she was under detention. The October 2009 summit, this time held in Thailand without incident, signed the ASEAN Intergovernmental Commission on Human Rights into existence.

On January 1, 2010, a free trade agreement between China and ASEAN came into force. Vietnam, as president of the group for the year, announced that its focus would be on regional integration. While arranging to put the topic at the forefront of the April 2010 summit, Vietnam also insisted on discussion of Chinese assertiveness about its territorial claims in the South China Sea. The summit also called for free elections in Burma, in a statement unusually blunt for ASEAN. In August 2010 Burma set November 7 as the date for its first general election since 1990.

The October 2010 summit, also held in Vietnam, while it worked to advance regional integration, was held in the shadow of a dispute over some islands currently controlled by Japan, but claimed by China. In reaction to this dispute China had stopped exporting rare earth minerals (essential for producing electronic components) to Japan. Japan subsequently announced that it would work with Vietnam to develop sources of rare earth minerals in that country.

On March 4, 2011, East Timor formally applied for membership in ASEAN. Indonesia supported immediate admission, but other ASEAN members endorsed a period of transition. On May 7–8 ASEAN members met in Jakarta at the group's 18th summit but were unable to reach a consensus on East Timor's membership. The group endorsed the creation of a common platform on global affairs by 2022 and the establishment of an ASEAN Institute for Peace and Reconciliation. Meanwhile, ASEAN pledged to support efforts to resolve a continuing border dispute between Cambodia and Thailand. At ASEAN's 19th summit in Bali, the group praised Myanmar's decisions to reregister the prodemocracy National League for Democracy and to allow the group to participate in future elections.

At the 20th ASEAN Summit meeting held in April 2012 in Phnom Penh, Cambodia, the member states reaffirmed their commitment to the establishment of the ASEAN Community by 2015. The Phnom Penh Declaration expressed a continued effort to move forward on the various aspects of the ASEAN Community, including human rights, government legitimacy, and trade and economic measures. The summit also saw an increased effort to meet the deadline for establishing a drug-free ASEAN by 2015. The Secretary General also issued a request to strengthen the power of the secretariat, arguing that it was vital for the continued success of the organization and its soon-to-be-established community. Sultan Bolkiah of Brunei spoke in overwhelming support for this position and encouraged others to do the same.

At the 21st Summit, also held in Phnom Penh, in November 2012, several major documents were produced by the organization—the ASEAN Human Rights Declaration and the Bali Concord III Plan of Action. Furthermore, the heads of state reaffirmed their commitment to launching the ASEAN Economic Community by 2015. At this meeting, the organization also elected Le Luong Minh of Vietnam as the next secretary general of the organization.

Under the chairmanship of Brunei, the 22nd summit was held in April 2013. The meeting saw the leaders of the ASEAN states further reiterate their commitment to economic union by approving the ASEAN Roadmap and the ASEAN Economic Community Blueprint. These two documents will provide the structure necessary to guide the organization toward its implementation date of 2015. The meeting also yielded the authorization to begin negotiations in May on the regional economic cooperation partnership.

At the October 2013 ASEAN summit meeting, the organization announced that Myanmar would be awarded the 2014 chairmanship of ASEAN. This will mark Myanmar's first time holding this position since joining the organization in 1997. Myanmar was scheduled to assume the chairmanship in 2006, but was passed over (see above). Occurring alongside the summit were several ASEAN summits with specific nations, including Japan, China, India, and for the first time, the United States. ASEAN and China discussed the possibility of working out disputes concerning navigation in the South China Sea, but despite pressure from Washington, the two sides were unable to reach any agreement. In its meeting with ASEAN, India announced plans to sign a free trade agreement with the organization by the end of 2013 and build a separate ASEAN mission in Jakarta.

In November 2013 antigovernment protests broke out in Thailand, resulting in the resignation of the government on December 8. The ASEAN heads of government issued a statement in Tokyo on December 14 calling for a peaceful resolution of the crisis. The ASEAN foreign ministers reiterated that call at the May 10–11, 2014 annual summit held in Myanmar and expressed their desire for a restoration of democratic processes. Matters in Thailand deteriorated further, however, after the military seized control of the government in a coup on May 23. ASEAN, however, has opted not to act in the matter, keeping with their long-standing position of noninterference. (For more on activities since 2013, see Recent activities, below.)

Structure. While the ASEAN Heads of State and Government is the organization's highest authority, the annual Ministerial Meeting, comprised of the foreign ministers of the member states, ordinarily sets general policy. Continuing supervision of ASEAN activities is the responsibility of the Standing Committee, which is located in the country hosting the Ministerial Meeting and includes the directors general of the ASEAN departments within each member country's foreign ministry. The foreign minister of the host country acts as chair, and the ASEAN secretary general also participates.

Sectoral ministerial meetings convene in more than a dozen fields, including agriculture and forestry, economics, energy, environment, finance, information, investment, labor, law, rural development and poverty alleviation, science and technology, transportation, and tourism. Nearly 30 committees and more than 120 working groups offer support. In addition, the heads of the ASEAN countries' diplomatic missions in various countries—Australia, Belgium, Canada, China, France, India, Japan, Republic of Korea, New Zealand, Pakistan, Russia, Switzerland, United Kingdom, and United States—meet to confer on matters of external relations. The Secretariat is headed by the secretary general, who serves a five-year term.

Most recently, ASEAN created three councils in 2009 as part of the governance for the ASEAN Community. The ASEAN Community Councils are responsible for overseeing and developing policy guidelines for each of the three "communities": the Political-Security Community, the Economic Community, and the Socio-Cultural Community. The sectoral ministerial meetings were also placed under the oversight and jurisdiction of the appropriate ASEAN Community Council.

ASEAN has also established a number of specialized bodies, including centers for Agricultural Development Planning, Biodiversity Conservation, Earthquake Information, Energy, Management, Specialized Meteorology, Poultry Research and Training, Rural Youth Development, Timber Technology, Tourism Information, and University Network.

Recent activities. While addressing the political situation in Thailand briefly, the bulk of the 2014 ASEAN Summit focused on progress toward the implementation of the ASEAN Community by 2015. The Nay Pyi Taw Declaration was signed by all the member states and expressed the group's commitment to creating the ASEAN Community on time, desire to increase its efficiency, and promotion of economic progress in the region.

The ASEAN Summit of 2015, held in Kuala Lumpur, established the ASEAN Economic Community (AEC), which was created from the 2009–2015 road map consisting of three community blueprints—economic, political-security, and socio-cultural—with over 1,000 operational actions to enhance integration. Investments into ASEAN continued to be topped by the European Community with $19.7 billion, followed by the United States ($17.4 billion) and Japan ($12.2 billion) in 2015.

In 2016 the ASEAN Summit was held on September 6–8, with Laos serving as chair, with the theme "Turning Vision into Reality for a Dynamic ASEAN Community." The summit was dominated by tensions between U.S. president Barack Obama and newly elected Philippine president Rodrigo Duterte (see entry on the Philippines).

CARIBBEAN COMMUNITY AND COMMON MARKET (CARICOM)

Established: August 1, 1973, pursuant to the July 4, 1973, Treaty of Chaguaramas (Trinidad), as successor to the Caribbean Free Trade Association.

Purpose: To deepen the integration process prevailing within the former Caribbean Free Trade Association, to enable all member states to share equitably in the benefits of integration, to operate certain subregional common services, and to coordinate the foreign policies of the member states.

Headquarters: Georgetown, Guyana.

Principal Organs: Heads of Government Conference, Community Council of Ministers, Secretariat.

Website: www.caricom.org.

Secretary General: Irwin LaRocque (Dominica).

Membership (15): Antigua and Barbuda, Bahamas (member of the community but not the common market), Barbados, Belize, Dominica, Grenada, Guyana, Haiti, Jamaica, Montserrat, St. Kitts-Nevis, St. Lucia, St. Vincent and the Grenadines (member of the community but not of the common market), Suriname, Trinidad and Tobago.

Associate Members (5): Anguilla, Bermuda, British Virgin Islands, Cayman Islands, Turks and Caicos Islands.

Official Language: English.

Origin and development. The formation of the Caribbean Free Trade Association (Carifta) in 1968 followed several earlier attempts to foster economic cooperation among the Commonwealth countries and territories of the West Indies and Caribbean. Antigua, Barbados, and Guyana signed the initial agreement December 15, 1965, in Antigua, while an amended accord was approved February 23, 1968, in Georgetown, Guyana, by those governments, Trinidad and Tobago, and the West Indies Associated States. Jamaica joined in June 1968 and was followed later in the month by the remaining British-associated islands, which had previously agreed to establish their own Eastern Caribbean Common Market. Belize was accepted for membership in June 1970.

At an eight-member conference of heads of state of the Caribbean Commonwealth countries in April 1973 in Georgetown, the decision was made to replace Carifta with a new Caribbean Community and Common Market (Caricom) that would provide additional opportunities for economic integration, with an emphasis on obtaining greater benefits for the less-developed members. The new grouping was formally established July 4, 1973, in Chaguaramas, Trinidad, by the prime ministers of Barbados, Guyana, Jamaica, and Trinidad. Although the treaty came into effect August 1, 1973, Carifta was not formally superseded until May 1, 1974, by which time all former Carifta members except Antigua and St. Kitts-Nevis-Anguilla had acceded to the new group. Antigua joined July 5, 1974, and St. Kitts-Nevis-Anguilla acceded on July 26, with St. Kitts and Nevis continuing its membership after the United Kingdom resumed responsibility for the administration of Anguilla in late 1980. After a lengthy period of close cooperation with the grouping, the Bahamas formally acceded to membership in the community (but not the common market) in July 1983. Suriname was admitted in 1995, thereby becoming the first Caricom member whose official language was not English. Haiti, a long-standing observer, was invited to join at the July 1997 Caricom summit, with final terms for full accession set two years later. Deposit of an accession instrument followed ratification by the Haitian Parliament in May 2002.

The 1973 treaty called for a common external tariff (CET) and a common protective policy vis-à-vis community trade with nonmembers, a scheme to harmonize fiscal incentives to industry and development planning, and a special regime for the less-developed members of the community. However, in the wake of unfavorable economic developments during the mid-1970s, progress toward economic coordination and integration stagnated.

As early as 1984 Caricom leaders had agreed to impose a CET on certain imports, but over the next decade deadlines for introducing a comprehensive CET were repeatedly missed. The first CET, with a 30–35 percent maximum, was finally instituted in 1993 and then lowered, in two additional phases, to 0–25 percent, although members were permitted considerable flexibility with regard to application. At the same time, Caricom moved forward on a 1989 pledge to create a unified regional market in "the shortest possible time." Goals for the market included elimination of any remaining trade barriers between members, free movement of skilled labor, abolition of passport requirements, development of regional air and sea transport systems using the resources of existing carriers, and rationalization of investment incentives throughout the community. Adoption of a single currency was also discussed. In furtherance of economic and political integration, in

1989, the heads of government established the West Indian Commission that, in 1992, proposed formation of the broader Association of Caribbean States, a larger organization designed to address economic cooperation in the Caribbean as a whole.

Recognizing the need for collateral, organizational reform, in October 1992 the Caricom heads of government authorized formation of a task force whose work ultimately led to adoption in February 1997 of Protocol I amending the Treaty of Chaguaramas. The first of nine related protocols, Protocol I significantly restructured Caricom's organs, principally by creating the Community Council of Ministers as the second highest Caricom organ and authorizing formation of supportive ministerial councils. Five months later at the annual summit held in Montego Bay, Jamaica, the Caricom leaders called for establishing the Caricom Single Market and Economy (CSME) by 1999. The official launch of the CSME occurred in January 2006 and became fully operational in 2013.

Regional integration and development lie at the center of Caricom's activities, but the organization has also negotiated agreements with neighboring countries and sought a common voice in various international forums, particularly those involving trade and globalization. With regard to the broader issue of positioning itself to compete in the global economy, in 1997 Caricom created a Regional Negotiating Mechanism (RNM) to outline a strategy for international trade and economic negotiations, although the RNM soon ran into "serious financial problems" because of funding shortfalls.

At the July 1998 Caricom summit, held in St. Lucia, community leaders approved plans to form the new Caribbean Court of Justice (CCJ) to function as a court of final appeal (replacing the United Kingdom's Privy Council in the case of the 12 Caricom states with historical ties to the United Kingdom) and settle disputes arising from the Treaty of Chaguaramas.

The 20th summit, held July 4–7, 1999, in Port-of-Spain saw further progress toward establishing the CCJ, despite objections from some who saw the proposed displacement of the UK Privy Council as an effort to reintroduce capital punishment. The Heads of Government Conference also addressed another controversy—namely, the threat of sanctions by the Organization for Economic Cooperation and Development (OECD). The OECD included 11 Caricom members (the exceptions being Bahamas, Guyana, Suriname, and Trinidad and Tobago) on its list of jurisdictions having "harmful" tax policies.

On July 15–16, 2000, shortly after the 2000 annual conference, Caricom convened in Castries to discuss the OECD tax policy issue and the recent report of the Group of Seven's Financial Action Task Force (FATF), which labeled Bahamas, Dominica, St. Kitts-Nevis, and St. Vincent as "uncooperative" in efforts to combat money laundering. In response, the Bureau of the Conference set up the Caribbean Association of Regulators of International Business, which was assigned the initial task of evaluating the FATF criteria. In June 2001 the FATF removed Bahamas from its noncompliance list, although Grenada was added in September. St. Kitts was removed in June 2002, as were Dominica in October 2002, Grenada in February 2003, and St. Vincent in June 2003.

In furtherance of introducing the CSME, the July 3–6, 2001, Heads of Government Conference agreed in principle to phase out the remaining restrictions on the free movement of capital, goods, and services, while in August Caricom joined with the International Monetary Fund and the UN Development Program in announcing the establishment of a Caribbean Regional Technical Assistance Center (Cartac) in Bridgetown to provide technical assistance and training in economic and financial management issues. With additional funding from Canada, the Caribbean Development Bank (CDB), the Inter-American Development Bank, the United Kingdom, the United States, and the World Bank, Cartac opened in November.

Meeting July 2–5, 2003, in Montego Bay, the heads of government signed several documents required for inaugurating the CCJ, to be sited in Trinidad and Tobago, in November. They included the Protocol on the Privileges and Immunities of the Caribbean Court of Justice and the Regional Judicial and Legal Services Commission and the Agreement Establishing the Caribbean Court of Justice Trust Fund. The latter measure permitted the CDB to begin raising some $100 million to capitalize the trust fund. In the area of external trade, the attendees discussed anticipated negotiations with the EU related to an Economic Partnership Agreement, continuing plans for the proposed Free Trade Area of the Americas, and ongoing World Trade Organization negotiations.

The CCJ was inaugurated on April 16, 2005, even though only Barbados and Guyana approved its jurisdiction over civil and criminal appeals. In general, the Caricom members favored letting the court review issues related to the revised Treaty of Chaguaramas and the anticipated CSME, but most had not resolved reservations about the court's appellate status. The CCJ began hearing its first case, an appeal of a libel verdict from Barbados, in August 2005.

Haiti was suspended from active participation in Caricom after the ouster of its president, Jean-Bertrand Aristide, in February 2004. After the February 26, 2006, victory of Rene Preval in the Haiti presidential elections, Caricom was quick to invite Haiti to return to full participation in the organization. President Preval was welcomed at the 11th Heads of State Conference held on July 3–6, 2006, in St. Kitts-Nevis. Much of 2007 and 2008 were dominated by controversy over the Economic Partnership Agreement (EPA) between the Cariforum (Caricom plus the Dominican Republic) and the European Union (EU), originally scheduled for signing by December 31, 2007. The EPA was duly initialed in December 2007, but its ratification by the Caricom states, first scheduled for April 2008, was postponed several times. October 31, 2008, a deadline specified by the EU, was the last date mentioned. The agreement was widely criticized throughout the region as exposing Caricom members to job losses and competition from EU products and services. On October 30, 2008, all Cariforum members except Guyana and Haiti signed the EPA. The president of Guyana, Bharrat Jagdeo, declared that his country would be prepared to sign a goods-only version of the EPA. Otherwise, he prophesied complete EU domination of the region within 20 years. Haiti was not ready to sign the agreement at all.

The Caribbean Regional Negotiating Machinery (CRNM) had taken the lead on EPA negotiations and was widely criticized by Caricom members, who did not favor the deal. At Caricom's intersessional Heads of Government Meeting, held March 12–13, 2009, in Belmopan, Belize, it was decided to phase out the CRNM and integrate its functions into the Caricom secretariat. The economic crisis also continued to take a toll on prospects for Caribbean unity. In May 2009 Prime Minister Ralph Gonsalves of St. Vincent declared that his fellow citizens were being discriminated against in some Caricom countries and that it might be better for St. Vincent to withdraw from the CSME. The year 2010 showed modest progress for Caricom's organizational objectives. In June the United States and Caricom celebrated the start of a major regional security partnership, the Caribbean Basin Security Initiative (CBSI). This partnership aimed to use U.S. funds to combat crime, both internal and transnational, in the area. Most observers saw the July 4 opening of the 31st summit as a lackluster affair, with several heads of state absent, and Secretary General Carrington calling for members not to despair in the face of economic and natural disasters. In August Carrington announced that he would resign at the end of the year; he had been in office for 18 years.

In June 2011 the heads of government elected Ambassador Irwin LaRocque of Dominica as the new secretary general of Caricom. La Rocque had served Caricom as the assistant secretary general for Trade and Economic Integration since 2005. Ambassador LaRocque replaced Lolita Applewhaite of Barbados, who had been serving as the acting secretary general after Carrington's resignation December 31, 2010. La Rocque formally began his tenure as secretary general on August 15.

At the 32nd summit, held July 1–4, 2011, the Caribbean Regional Public Health Association (CARPHA) was created as the final part of the 2001 Nassau Declaration, designed to improve public health in the region. CARPHA will merge five existing regional health organizations to increase access to health care in the Caribbean. The 2011 summit also focused on agriculture, transportation, and arms limitations to increase security.

In early March 2012 the heads of government met for an intersession summit. One of the most significant moves to come out of that meeting was the initial plan to restructure the Caricom Secretariat. This move to restructure came after an outside consulting company commissioned to study the organization in 2010 released it reports noting that Caricom was facing serious crises that could put the continued existence of Caricom in question. The Secretary General began the process by hiring a change facilitator to help with the new reform actions. The 33rd summit, held July 4–6, 2012, saw a continued move forward in the reform process. The summit leaders also advanced the plans for its January 2013 inauguration of CARPHA. Despite hopes to be ready for January implementation, CARPHA launched on July 2 in conjunction with the 2013 annual summit. Another significant initiative that came out of the summit was a plan for a study to analyze the feasibility of adding French and Dutch in addition to English as the official languages of Caricom.

The year 2013 was notable for Haiti in regard to Caricom matters. Haiti assumed the chairmanship of Caricom for the first time since becoming a member in 2002. In February the country hosted its first Caricom meeting (the inter-sessional meeting of the Caricom Heads of State) since joining the organization. Both events are evidence of the great strides made by Haiti in overcoming the devastating earthquake of 2010.

The inter-sessional meeting in February focused largely on broader issues of regional crime and security. U.S. attorney general Eric Holder was in attendance as a special guest, and was actively involved in the discussions about strengthening security and crime prevention in the Caribbean region. The meeting also expressed the need for an arms trade treaty and expressed its desire to have a Caricom-U.S. Summit within the next year.

At a meeting of the Council for Trade and Economic Development in May, Secretary General LaRocque suggested that the committee strongly consider adding representatives from the private sector. LaRocque noted the significant role played by the private sector in generating economic growth in his exhortation.

The 2013 summit was held in early July in Trinidad and Tobago. One of the major decisions to come out of the meeting was the creation of a Caricom Reparations Commission designed to address the issue of reparations for native genocide and slavery. The commission will be composed of the chairs of the National Reparations Committees in each member state. (For more on developments since 2013, see Recent activities, below.)

Structure. Policy decisions under the Treaty of Chaguaramas are assigned to the Heads of Government Conference, which meets annually and is the final authority for all Caricom forums. Each participating state has one vote and most decisions are taken unanimously. The chair of the conference rotates biannually among the members. Until 1998 the Common Market Council dealt with operational aspects of common market activity, but, as part of the Protocol I restructuring, it was replaced by the Community Council of Ministers. The council, the organization's second-highest organ, consists of community affairs ministers and any others designated by each member state. Its responsibilities include strategic planning and coordination of economic integration, functional cooperation, and external relations.

Also assisting the Conference and the Council of Ministers are four ministerial councils: Council for Finance and Planning (COFAP), Council for Foreign and Community Relations (COFCOR), Council for Human and Social Development (COHSOD), and Council for Trade and Economic Development (COTED). In addition, there are legal affairs, budget, and central bank governors committees. The Secretariat, Caricom's principal administrative organ, is headed by a secretary general and includes several administrative directorates in support of the Ministerial Councils. A deputy and various assistant secretaries general oversee numerous subsidiary offices.

The Assembly of Caribbean Community Parliamentarians (ACCP), whose creation was endorsed at the 1989 Caricom summit, was established in mid-1994 after a sufficient number of member states ratified the related agreement. A consultative body, the new assembly was designed to promote public and governmental interest in Caricom.

Caricom has established or sponsors several other community institutions, such as the Caribbean Agricultural Research and Development Institute, the Caribbean Environmental Health Institute, and the Caribbean Meteorological Organization. (For a complete listing of Caricom-sponsored organizations, see the 2011 *Handbook.*) Associate institutions include the CDB in St. Michael, the University of Guyana, the University of the West Indies, the Caribbean Law Institute, and the Secretariat.

Recent activities. The March 2014 intersessional meeting focused primarily on the issues of advancing the use of new information and communication technology within Caricom and its member states and the promotion of human resources development. A new commission was established, the Commission of Human Resources Development, and tasked with creating a framework and strategy for furthering education and human resources. The meeting also established a set of requirements and procedures for all countries seeking membership or associate membership in Caricom.

The regular meeting of the Caricom heads of government was held in Antigua and Barbuda July 1–4, 2014. The meeting saw several firsts, most notably, the passage of the community's first strategic plan. The plan focused on resilience in the areas of economics, society, technology, and the environment. The plan also outlined goals for community-wide, coordinated action in foreign policy as part of a stronger governance mechanism. The meeting also saw the adoption of Caricom's first ever community song. On June 16–17, 2014, Caricom met with the United Kingdom at the eighth UK–Caribbean Forum London to build a "Partnership for Prosperity" that focused on secure and sustainable energy sources, education, economic development, job creation, and combating issues with organized crime.

On June 5, 2015, Caricom celebrated World Environment Day 2015 with a focus on environmental protection leading into World Environment Day 2030. Caricom has focused on environmental resilience in light of sea level rise and global climate change. Caricom has also focused on capital investment in agricultural areas to increase sustainable agriculture for the member communities. In September 2016 Caricom hosted the 14th annual Caribbean Week of Agriculture (CWA) in Grand Cayman to address weak marketing systems and to focus on areas that are "growth markets."

COMMON MARKET FOR EASTERN AND SOUTHERN AFRICA (COMESA)

Established: By treaty signed November 5, 1993, in Kampala, Uganda; effective as of December 8, 1994.

Purpose: To promote wide-ranging regional economic cooperation, particularly in the areas of agriculture, industry, transportation, and communications; to facilitate intraregional trade through the reduction or elimination of trade barriers and the establishment of regional financial institutions; to establish a common external tariff and internal free trade zone; and to pursue "economic prosperity through regional integration."

Headquarters: Lusaka, Zambia.

Principal Organs: Authority of Heads of State and Government, Council of Ministers, Committee of Governors, Intergovernmental Committee, Court of Justice, Secretariat.

Website: www.comesa.int.

Secretary General: Sindiso Ngwenya (Zimbabwe).

Membership (19): Burundi, Comoros, Democratic Republic of the Congo, Djibouti, Egypt, Eritrea, Ethiopia, Kenya, Libya, Madagascar, Malawi, Mauritius, Rwanda, Seychelles, Sudan, Swaziland, Uganda, Zambia, Zimbabwe.

Official Languages: English, French, Portuguese.

Origin and development. Comesa is the successor organization to the Preferential Trade Area for Eastern and Southern African States (PTA), founded in 1981, and endorsed by the United Nations' Economic Commission for Africa and the Organization of African Unity (OAU).

At the January 1992 PTA heads of state meeting, delegates conceded that the organization had little to show for its first ten years of existence. Toward that end, PTA officials proposed a merger with the Southern African Development Community (SADC), whose overlapping membership and objectives were producing a "parallel existence" between the two groups that was seen as counterproductive. However, the SADC, historically much more successful in attracting international financial support because of its highly visible face-off with apartheid-era South Africa, rejected the proposed union.

Many of the PTA's original tasks were expanded in the treaty establishing the Common Market for Eastern and Southern Africa (Comesa), which was signed during the PTA's 12th summit on November 5, 1993, in Kampala, Uganda. Shortly after ratification on December 8, 1994, officials and journalists began to refer to Comesa as the successor to the PTA, even though some PTA members—Lesotho, Mozambique, and Somalia—ultimately opted not to join, and two nonmembers of the PTA—Democratic Republic of Congo and Egypt—did join. The renamed Eastern and Southern Africa Trade and Development Bank continues to be known less formally as the PTA Bank, and the autonomous *Compagnie de Réassurance de la Zone d'Echanges Préférentiels* (ZEP-RE) is similarly styled the PTA Reinsurance Company in English.

The initial Comesa summit was held December 7–9, 1994, in Lilongwe, Malawi; however, of the 22 signatories it had only been ratified by 12. Although plans were discussed for eventual cooperation in the areas of customs, transportation, communications, agriculture, and industry, formal arrangements remained incomplete, partly because of uncertainties over the relationship between the PTA/Comesa and the SADC. (Most SADC members seemed to prefer distinguishable north and south zones of economic cooperation.)

The outlook for Comesa was further clouded in late 1995 when South Africa announced it did not intend to join. At the end of 1996 Mozambique and Lesotho announced their withdrawal from Comesa, and speculation arose that Namibia might follow suit. Also that year the SADC countries once again vetoed Comesa's offer to merge as a single trade zone. Kenya, Tanzania, and Uganda considered turning away from Comesa activity in favor of the proposed reactivation of their old East African Community (EAC). In fact the EAC was revived, but Kenya, Tanzania, and Uganda remained members of both groups.

In late January 1997 Secretary General Bingu Mutharika was suspended during an investigation into the recent management of funds within the Secretariat. Mutharika resigned in April (although he continued to deny any wrongdoing), and Erastus Mwencha of Kenya succeeded him in an acting capacity.

Mwencha officially replaced Mutharika at the third Comesa summit, held in mid-1998 in Kinshasa, Democratic Republic of Congo. Summit participants agreed to eliminate tariffs and visas within the group by 2000 and to admit Egypt as the first North African member. Egypt officially became a member after ratifying the Comesa treaty later that year, but progress toward the removal of tariffs was slower than expected. In other activities, the Comesa Court of Justice, established under the Comesa treaty, held its first session in September 1998, and the PTA Development Bank decided to invite countries from outside the region to become members in an effort to increase the bank's capital.

Speaking at the fourth Comesa summit May 24–25, 1999, Kenyan president Daniel arap Moi called for greater subregional cooperation, which he described as crucial for achieving high economic growth rates and attracting investment capital. Otherwise, he warned, the Comesa countries would face being marginalized by ongoing economic globalization and competition from other trading blocs. As a key step toward further integration, the summit established a committee charged with preparations to introduce a Free Trade Area (FTA).

Arguably the most significant event in the organization's history occurred at an extraordinary summit in Lusaka, Zambia, on October 31, 2000, when nine Comesa members—Djibouti, Egypt, Kenya, Madagascar, Malawi, Mauritius, Sudan, Zambia, and Zimbabwe—inaugurated Africa's first FTA, enabling duty-free trade in goods, services, and capital and eliminating other nontariff trade barriers for the participants. Political concerns in several states, including Burundi, Rwanda, and Eritrea, delayed their participation, and Namibia's and Swaziland's membership in the Southern African Customs Union (SACU) made their entry into Comesa's FTA problematic. Moreover, in what was generally acknowledged to be a major setback, Tanzania withdrew from Comesa in September 2000, citing the need to streamline its international memberships and preferring to remain in the SADC because of the latter's emphasis on building capacity for the production of goods.

Later in 2001 Comesa launched the African Trade Insurance Agency (ATIA) in Nairobi, with funding from the World Bank group, the European Union (EU), and Japan, to protect investors against political risks. In addition, on October 29 Comesa and the United States signed a significant Trade and Investment Framework Agreement.

The May 23–24, 2002, summit in Addis Ababa, Ethiopia, saw the reappointment of Secretary General Mwencha. The attendees also authorized the return of the Comesa Trade and Development Bank to Bujumbura and signed a protocol for establishing the Fund for Cooperation, Compensation, and Development.

The organization's eighth summit, held March 17, 2003, in Khartoum, Sudan, focused on the anticipated introduction of the customs union and accompanying Common External Tariff (CET) in December. Meanwhile, Secretary General Mwencha reported, intra-Comesa trade had expanded at a rate of 30 percent per year since the 2000 launch of the FTA. The summit also called for further development of basic infrastructure; discussed food security, particularly in light of recurrent crises in the Horn of Africa; and emphasized the need to strengthen regional peace and security. With regard to trade, Comesa agreed to adopt a regional approach in pursuit of an Economic Partnership Agreement with the EU. In other business, the summit received a request for membership from Libya.

Rwanda and Burundi announced in 2003 that they were preparing to join the FTA, as did Namibia and Swaziland, assuming that remaining issues involving their SACU memberships were resolved. Namibia, however, left Comesa in July 2003, intending to concentrate on its relationship with the SACU. On January 1, 2004, Burundi and Rwanda joined the FTA.

The ninth summit was held June 7–8, 2004, in Kampala, Uganda. Trade and investments within the community were discussed, as was the plan to move to a customs union by the end of the year. For the first time a business summit ran concurrently with the heads of state and government meeting, attracting more than 600 delegates. At the tenth summit June 2–3, 2005, in Kigali, Rwanda, Comesa admitted Libya. The eleventh summit was held November 15–16, 2006, in Djibouti, with the main theme being to strengthen the group through the projected customs union. Also in 2006, the projected year for monetary union was accelerated from 2025 to 2018. The Monetary Cooperation Programme consists of four stages. The first two concern the consolidation of existing currencies and the creation of a replacement. Stage 3 requires that a formal exchange rate and central monetary institution be created. The final stage, to be completed in 2018, is full monetary cohesion among all Comesa nations and a Central Bank.

In January 2007 Comesa recognized global climate change as "a major threat to sustainable growth and development in Africa" and outlined multiple goals to address the issue. Among the goals discussed were to have a more unified vision for Africa's role on climate change, to promote regional and national cooperation on the issue, to improve the institutional capacities of Comesa to address climate change challenges, and to establish guidelines for an African BioCarbon Facility.

At the 12th summit, held May 22–23, 2007, in Nairobi, all Comesa states were urged to join the FTA as soon as possible. This was to facilitate launch of the customs union and the CET by December 2008. Thirteen states were members at that time. Rivalry between Comesa and SADC intensified in 2007, spurred by the World Trade Organization (WTO) rule that no country can be a member of more than one customs union. As Comesa and SADC each intended to create a customs union, member countries were forced to choose between the organizations. By late 2007 Angola had left Comesa for the SADC. In November 2007 Comesa signed a Regional Integration Support Mechanism (RISM) with the EU, granting the bloc 78 million euros (U.S. $100 million) over five years to offset harm done to poorer member countries by the customs union.

By January 2008 several African trade blocs were showing concern about agreements with the EU. Comesa had been negotiating with the EU under the Eastern and Southern Africa (ESA) platform, but several member states had signed individual agreements with Brussels. In February 2008 a meeting of Comesa trade ministers endorsed a proposal for a unified FTA among Comesa, the SADC, and East African Community (EAC) states. The attitude seemed to be that membership in multiple trade blocs might, after all, be acceptable. In May 2008 it was announced that Comesa had set September 2008 as the cut-off date for member states to submit their national tariff schedules, as agreed under the CET.

At a July 2008 extraordinary summit meeting in Sharm-el-Sheikh, Egypt, Sindiso Ngwenya of Zimbabwe was chosen as secretary general in place of Erastus Mwencha, who had resigned to take a job with the African Union secretariat. Ngwenya announced that in October 2008 Uganda would convene a meeting between Comesa, SADC, and EAC representatives to discuss the harmonization of trade. On October 22 representatives of the three groups, meeting in Kampala, agreed to form a free trade zone of all their members—an area stretching along the east side of Africa from Egypt to South Africa.

At the Comesa summit held June 7–8, 2009, in Victoria Falls, Zimbabwe, leaders approved the launch of a Comesa Customs Union. This launch was marred by Ugandan president Yoweri Museveni telling the summit that, while East African Community (EAC) members in Comesa supported the concept of the customs union, they needed to reevaluate their participation, because they were close to completing a customs union of their own. Shortly thereafter, the EAC members, more than half of Comesa, opted out. In October 2009, the Democratic Republic of the Congo expressed interest in joining the Comesa FTA and customs union.

During 2010 non-tariff trading barriers (including such things as cumbersome quality inspection rules or excessive transit charges) came under increasing scrutiny. By October 2010 rules were prepared to penalize countries that used such practices. Egypt was a particular subject of complaint. On August 31, 2010, World Trade Organization (WTO) secretary general Pascal Lamy addressed Comesa's 14th summit, held in Lozitha, Swaziland. He called for increased regional integration as a means to development. He also called for a speedy conclusion to the Doha round of trade talks (see WTO article).

At the October 14–15, 2011, summit, the council of ministers declared approval of a Grand Tripartite Free Trade Area, proposed in 2001, which would encompass half the continent. The summit also turned its focus to improving maternal health by investing in science and technology.

In December 2011 Comesa officially launched a new program geared toward climate change. The program is focused on increasing renewable energy, carbon efficient agricultural practices, and more linkage between agriculture, forestry and land use. In July 2012, the program was approved for joint implementation in a tripartite agreement between Comesa, the EAC, and the SADC.

The tripartite agreement set a five-year goal for implementation of all components of the climate change program.

At a June 2012 meeting of the Science, Technology, and Innovation Ministers of the member states, the group voted to establish a Comesa Innovation Council to increase the importance of science and technology in the community, as well as promote the growth of both resources and progress in those fields throughout the region.

At the November 2012 Heads of State and Government meeting held in Kampala, the organization adopted a plan for increased regional trade that had been adopted by the Council of Ministers. The plan is another step in the completion of the tripartite FTA. Also at the meeting, Ugandan President Museveni suggested that integration should have two components: economic integration and political integration. Museveni noted the limitations of such political integration at this time, but noted it was a realistic goal for the future.

Uganda joined the FTA in November 2012, and in January 2013 Comesa began the second phase of the preparatory stage, which focuses on trade in services and special trade issues such as intellectual property. In April 2013 Comesa officially launched its Comesa Innovation Council. This new council is composed of ten highly respected scholars. As an outgrowth of the new Innovation Council, Comesa put forth a draft of a new Intellectual Property Policy in May. According to a Comesa news release, the new draft policy emphasizes "capacity building in institutions and human resources for intellectual property innovation." (For more on activities since 2013, see Recent activities, below.)

Structure. The apex of Comesa comprises the Authority of Heads of State and Government, which establishes by consensus fundamental policy and directs subsidiary organs in pursuit of the common market's objectives. The Council of Ministers monitors and reviews the performance of administrators and financial managers in addition to overseeing the organization's programs and projects. The Intergovernmental Committee, comprising permanent secretaries from the member countries, develops and manages cooperative programs and action plans in all sectors except finance and monetary policy, which is the domain of the separate Committee of Governors of the members' central banks. There are also several technical committees and the Secretariat, which comprises five divisions: Administration; Trade, Customs, and Monetary Harmonization; Investment and Private Sector Development; Infrastructure Development; and Information and Networking. The secretary general serves a once-renewable, five-year term. The Court of Justice is responsible for interpreting the Comesa treaty and for adjudicating related disputes between members.

The PTA Bank is the most prominent of various Comesa-established autonomous institutions, which also include the Comesa Bankers' Association (BAPTA), the Comesa Metallurgical Industries Association (Comesamia), the Comesa Telecommunications Company (Comtel), the Eastern and Southern Africa Business Association (ESABO), the Federation of National Associations of Women in Business (Femcom), the Leather and Leather Products Institute (LLPI), and the Pharmaceutical Manufacturers of Eastern and Southern Africa (Pharmesa).

Recent activities. The 2014 Comesa Summit was held February 27 in the Democratic Republic of the Congo. The meeting focused on intra-Comesa trade as a means of promoting growth and expansion. The members pledged to work toward the conclusion of the tripartite FTA and full adoption of the Comesa customs union. In June 2014 the Comesa Court of Justice relocated its headquarters to Khartoum, Sudan. The court previously had been sitting at the Comesa secretariat in Lusaka until its permanent home in Sudan was finished. In October Comesa ministers met with other ministers from the EAC and SADC and announced that the Tripartite Summit of Heads of Government slated for December would officially launch the FTA—the culmination of six years of negotiation and more than a decade of planning. Comesa only brought in $16 billion in foreign investment in 2014, a very small amount compared to the $1.23 trillion in global foreign direct investment.

Throughout 2015 successive initiatives were launched to make existing trade, infrastructure, and social environmental policies and regulations conducive to increasing foreign direct investment. Comesa initiated the One Stop Border Post, Comesa Yellow Card, Regional Payment Settlement System, Comesa Virtual Trade Facilitation System, and Regional Payment Settlement System. Comesa also established specialized institutions of the PTA Bank, COMESA RIA, CBC, and a Competition Commission. Further, Comesa joined the Tripartite Free Trade Area (Tripartite FTA), which included Comesa, the SADC, and the EAC, to create a 26-country trade area during a summit on September 7–10, 2015. The Tripartite FTA was launched on October 25, 2015.

In 2016 the African Wildlife Foundation (AWF) signed a memorandum of understanding (MoU) to ensure habitat protection was included in Comesa's development plans. Comesa also urged African countries to relax visa requirements to increase wildlife tourism. In other attempts by Comesa to address new policies toward agriculture, Comesa has worked to translate its regional Seed Harmonization Implementation Plan (COMSHIP) into local languages to help farmers increase food security. In 2016 Comesa had a combined GDP of $657.4 billion, a population of 492.5 million, and an area of 4.63 million square miles (12 million square km).

THE COMMONWEALTH

Established: By evolutionary process and formalized December 31, 1931, in the Statute of Westminster.

Purpose: To give expression to a continuing sense of affinity and to foster cooperation among states presently or formerly owing allegiance to the British Crown.

Commonwealth Center: The Secretariat is located in Marlborough House, London, which also serves as the site of Commonwealth meetings in the United Kingdom.

Principal Organs: Meeting of Heads of Government, Secretariat, Commonwealth Ministerial Action Group.

Website: www.thecommonwealth.org.

Head of the Commonwealth: Queen Elizabeth II.

Secretary General: Patricia Scotland (United Kingdom).

Membership (52, with years of entry): Antigua and Barbuda (1981), Australia (1931), Bahamas (1973), Bangladesh (1972), Barbados (1966), Belize (1981), Botswana (1966), Brunei (1984), Cameroon (1995), Canada (1931), Cyprus (1961), Dominica (1978), Fiji (1970, reentered 1997), Ghana (1957), Grenada (1974), Guyana (1966), India (1947), Jamaica (1962), Kenya (1963), Kiribati (1979), Lesotho (1966), Malawi (1964), Malaysia (1957), Malta (1964), Mauritius (1968), Mozambique (1995), Namibia (1990), Nauru (1999), New Zealand (1931), Nigeria (1960), Pakistan (1947, reentered 1989), Papua New Guinea (1975), Rwanda (2009), St. Kitts-Nevis (1983), St. Lucia (1979), St. Vincent and the Grenadines (1979), Samoa (1970), Seychelles (1976), Sierra Leone (1961), Singapore (1965), Solomon Islands (1978), South Africa (1931, reentered 1994), Sri Lanka (1948), Swaziland (1968), Tanzania (1961), Tonga (1970), Trinidad and Tobago (1962), Tuvalu (2000), Uganda (1962), United Kingdom (1931), Vanuatu (1980), Zambia (1964).

Working Language: English.

Origin and development. A voluntary association that gradually superseded the British Empire, the Commonwealth traces its origins to the mid-1800s, when internal self-government was first introduced in the colonies of Australia, British North America (Canada),

New Zealand, and part of what was to become the Union of South Africa. The increasing maturity and independence of these overseas communities, particularly after World War I, eventually created a need to redefine the mutual relationships between the United Kingdom and the self-governing "dominions" that were collectively coming to be known as the British Commonwealth of Nations. The Statute of Westminster, enacted by the British Parliament in 1931, established the principle that all members of the association were equal in status, in no way subordinate to each other, and united by allegiance to the Crown.

The original members of the Commonwealth, in addition to the United Kingdom, were Australia, Canada, the Irish Free State, Newfoundland, New Zealand, and the Union of South Africa. In 1949 the Irish Free State became the Republic of Ireland and withdrew from the Commonwealth. In the same year Newfoundland became a province of Canada. South Africa ceased to be a member upon becoming a republic in 1961 because of the opposition of the other Commonwealth countries to Pretoria's apartheid policies; however, it was readmitted June 1, 1994, following the installation of a multiracial government. Pakistan withdrew in 1972 but rejoined in 1989. Because of political instability, its status has changed or come into question several times. Likewise, Fiji's status has often been in jeopardy because of political unrest.

The ethnic, geographic, and economic composition of the Commonwealth has been modified fundamentally by the accession of former colonial territories in Asia, Africa, and the Western Hemisphere. This infusion of racially nonwhite and economically less developed states had significant political implications, including modification of the Commonwealth's unwritten constitution to accommodate the desire of many new members to renounce allegiance to the British Crown and adopt a republican form of government. In 1949 the pattern was set when Commonwealth prime ministers accepted India's formal declaration that, on becoming a republic, it would accept the Crown as a symbol of the Commonwealth association and recognize the British sovereign as head of the Commonwealth. The movement toward a multicultural identity was solidified by the Declaration of Commonwealth Principles adopted by the heads of government at their 1971 Singapore summit. In addition to acknowledging the organization's diversity, the Singapore declaration enumerated a set of common principles, including the primacy of international peace and order; individual liberty regardless of racial, ethnic, or religious background; people's "inalienable right to participate by means of free and democratic processes in framing the society in which they live"; opposition to "colonial domination and racial oppression"; and the "progressive removal" of wide disparities in wealth and living standards.

The new thrust was further evidenced by a North-South summit in October 1981, which reflected that most Commonwealth members were developing countries. Subsequently, a 1982 report, *The North-South Dialogue: Making It Work,* proposed many institutional and procedural reforms to facilitate global negotiations on development and related issues, and a 1983 document, *Towards a New Bretton Woods,* proposed short-, medium-, and long-range changes to enhance the efficiency and equity of the international trading and financial system.

A declaration in October 1987 that Fiji's Commonwealth status had lapsed followed two successive coups, abrogation of the country's constitution, and proclamation of a republic. Readmission required the unanimous consent of the Commonwealth members, and Fiji's application remained blocked until mid-1997 by India. Fiji was finally readmitted effective October 1, 1997, but its membership was suspended in May 2000 following displacement of the elected government. Full participation was restored in late 2001, following democratic elections in August through September.

The October 1991 summit in Harare, Zimbabwe, was noteworthy for the adoption of a declaration redefining the Commonwealth's agenda. The Harare Declaration, drafted under the guidance of a ten-member High Level Appraisal Group, committed all Commonwealth countries, regardless of their political or economic conditions, to promote democracy, human rights, judicial independence, equality for women, educational opportunities, and the principles of "sound economic management."

During the 1980s and early 1990s, the Commonwealth was most prominently identified by its efforts to end apartheid in South Africa, although debate frequently raged within the organization over tactics, especially the imposition of sanctions. Accordingly, the formal readmission of South Africa in midyear was the highlight of 1994.

In a departure from precedent, membership was granted on November 13, 1995, to Mozambique, even though it had never been a British colony and was not at least partly English speaking. A "unique and special" case regarding Mozambique had been presented by its Anglophone neighbors because of regional trade concerns.

The Commonwealth Heads of Government Meeting (CHOGM) held November 8–13, 1995, in Auckland, New Zealand, was dominated by discussion of the excesses of Sani Abacha, the military ruler of Nigeria, who executed the internationally known author and nonviolent activist Ken Saro-Wiwa while the conference was in progress. This resulted in the suspension of Nigeria's membership and the launching of efforts (ultimately largely unsuccessful) by the Commonwealth to influence the actions of the military regime in Abuja.

Nigeria was also a major topic at the 1997 CHOGM held in Edinburgh, Scotland. While praising the role Nigeria played in the Liberia conflict, the summit decided to continue Nigeria's suspension because of ongoing human rights abuses and the suppression of democracy. Sierra Leone was also suspended (until the restoration of President Tejan Kabbah's government in March 1998), and the summit called on Commonwealth members to support the sanctions imposed by the United Nations (UN) and the Economic Community of West African States on that country.

Another focus of attention at the summit was the promotion of economic prosperity. The heads of government adopted the Edinburgh Commonwealth Economic Declaration, which called for continued global economic integration, with greater attention to the smaller, less developed countries that believed they were being left behind. To assist the smaller countries, the Commonwealth leaders agreed to support efforts to develop a successor to the Lomé Convention (see European Community section of European Union article), to offer duty-free access to certain markets, and to establish a Trade and Investment Access Facility.

In October 1998 CMAG concluded that the Nigerian government had taken enough steps toward democracy to warrant the lifting of sanctions and resumption of Nigerian participation in some Commonwealth activities. Full participation was restored May 29, 1999, following presidential elections the previous February.

At the November 12–15, 1999, Commonwealth summit in Durban, South Africa, the organization established a ten-member High-Level Review Group (HLRG) comprising the heads of government of Australia, India, Malta, Papua New Guinea, Singapore, South Africa, Tanzania, Trinidad and Tobago, United Kingdom, and Zimbabwe. The HLRG was assigned the task of recommending how the Commonwealth could best meet the challenges of the 21st century.

Also occurring in 1999, Nauru became the 53rd full member of the Commonwealth after 31 years as a special member, and Tuvalu, a special member from 1978, became the 54th full member in 2000. In 2005 Nauru resumed its status as a special member, a category of membership available to very small countries.

At a 2000 meeting, the heads of government confirmed Pakistan's suspension from Commonwealth activities in the wake of the previous month's coup in Islamabad. Similarly, in March 2002 Zimbabwe's participation in Commonwealth meetings was suspended as a consequence of a widely condemned presidential election earlier in the month.

The CHOGM held December 5–8, 2003, in Abuja, Nigeria, was dominated by the Zimbabwe issue. Although many African states argued that the Mugabe government could best be engaged by lifting the suspension, the opponents prevailed. The Commonwealth proceeded to form a balanced committee of leaders from Australia, Canada, India, Jamaica, Mozambique, and South Africa to pursue "national reconciliation" in Zimbabwe and a rapid return of that country to full participation, but Zimbabwe's governing party quickly voted to terminate membership in the Commonwealth on December 7. In acknowledging the withdrawal, Secretary General McKinnon expressed his hope that Zimbabwe would rejoin "in due course, as have other members in the past."

Four and a half years after the military coup that brought Gen. Pervez Musharraf to power, Commonwealth ministers decided to restore full membership to Pakistan at a May 2004 meeting in London.

The marriage of Prince Charles, Queen Elizabeth's son and heir to the throne, to Camilla Parker Bowles in April 2005 had implications for the Commonwealth. The British Department of Constitutional Affairs stated on March 21 that Parker Bowles would automatically become queen when Charles became king, despite Charles's declarations to the contrary, unless the parliaments of the UK and the Commonwealth countries of which the UK monarch was head of state all agreed to a change in the law. On March 23 the Commonwealth Secretariat announced that Charles would not automatically succeed Queen Elizabeth as head of the Commonwealth when he became king. Instead, the various Commonwealth heads of government would elect the next head of the Commonwealth. Appointing anyone other than the British monarch to this symbolic position would mark a substantial shift away from the organization's British and imperial roots.

In December 2006 Fiji was suspended from some privileges of Commonwealth membership following a military coup. Also in that month Rwanda formally applied to join the Commonwealth. Subsequently, Burundi also expressed an interest. When the 2007 CHOGM took place in Kampala, Uganda, November 23–25, the president of Rwanda was present as an observer, and Rwanda's application was again on the agenda. An outcome of the meeting was a clarification of the rules, spelling out the right of countries that had never been under British rule to join the Commonwealth, if on examination they met the appropriate democratic standards.

In November 2007 the Commonwealth suspended Pakistan from full membership because President Musharraf had not ended the state of emergency, released political prisoners, and stepped down as army chief of staff as he had promised. The suspension was lifted in May 2008, democratic elections having been held in Pakistan, and Musharraf having resigned from the army.

A conference on Rwanda's proposed accession was subsequently held in August 2008, in Kigali, Rwanda. Rwanda, which in October 2008 mandated English as the language of education instead of French, received widespread support for its bid. Rwanda's application was approved at the 2009 CHOGM, held in Trinidad and Tobago, November 27–29. Rwanda thus became the second Commonwealth member, along with Mozambique, that had never been part of the British Empire.

In March 2009 the Commonwealth gave Fiji six months to make progress toward holding elections, with expulsion from the organization as the alternative. In September 2009 Fiji's suspension, though not expulsion, was reaffirmed. According to a July 2009 survey, commissioned as part of an effort to rejuvenate and "re-brand" the Commonwealth, interest in the group seemed to differ sharply among its members. Populations of the older, predominately white members showed less interest, with Britons the least interested and only one-third of Australians and Canadians strongly opposed to leaving the Commonwealth. Members of developing countries, to the contrary, valued the Commonwealth much more highly, and South Africans thought more of the Commonwealth tie than of relations with the United States.

Now being a member, Rwanda received a Commonwealth observer group to monitor its August 9, 2010, presidential election. The group pronounced the election, which gave President Paul Kagame a new term, to be reasonably free and fair. In September 2010 CMAG met for its biannual meeting, during which time the group focused largely on the political situation in Fiji. The group reiterated its support for Fiji and vowed to continue helping them restore their constitutional government. The Commonwealth is currently working with the interim government in Fiji to ensure that the island is able to peaceably restore democracy.

In 2011 the Commonwealth was asked to oversee elections in two African countries—Uganda and Nigeria—after both had been plagued by political instability. In both cases the Commonwealth representatives found the elections to be free and fair. The biennial CHOGM meeting was held in Perth, Australia, October 28–30, 2011. The meeting brought about several key decisions concerning administrative reform and management of the Commonwealth. Perhaps most notably, the Commonwealth members agreed to draft a charter for the organization, a step that would help the group move toward a more traditional intergovernmental organization structure. The meeting also discussed South Sudan's entrance into the Commonwealth and authorized the Secretary General to move forward with admissions procedures. The meeting also addressed issues such as food security, the economy, migration, and greater involvement.

The February 2012 resignation of Maldives' President Nasheed created turmoil and political unrest in Maldives. The CMAG visited the island in mid-February, and at its biannual meeting later in February determined that the resignation of Nasheed was constitutionally questionable. Further actions by the government, such as the disruption of the opening parliamentary session, led the Commonwealth to actively pursue measures to end the political unrest in Maldives. Upon the urging of the CMAG, Maldives established a Commission of National Inquiry in June to investigate the February transition of power. The Commonwealth remained actively involved in the political situation in Maldives throughout 2012 and 2013, and welcomed the progress made in that country since the 2012 coup and was an observer to their October 2013 elections.

The Commonwealth Charter, first proposed at the 2011 CHOGM meeting, was drafted over the course of 2012. The document codified the governing principles of the Commonwealth and expressed the core principles of democracy, human rights, and the rule of law that serve to guide the actions of Commonwealth members. The charter was approved by the secretariat in December 2012. On Commonwealth Day 2013 Her Majesty Queen Elizabeth II signed the historic document, marking its full, official implementation.

The year 2013 saw a concerted focus on youth in the Commonwealth. In addition to its normal youth programs, the ministerial meeting of Commonwealth Youth Ministers identified youth as a commonwealth priority and a key to creating sustainable development and growth. As a result, the Commonwealth created the Commonwealth Youth Council, sponsored special awards for youth, and launched its new Youth Development Index.

In October 2013 Gambia, a member since 1965, formally withdrew from the Commonwealth. The secretariat expressed hope that Gambia would one day rejoin the organization once the social and political unrest has been resolved. Also in October, the Commonwealth and South Africa reached a landmark agreement concerning principles of debt management. As part of the agreement, the South African National Treasury will host a group of financial advisors from the Commonwealth who will provide assistance to the member states in the region. This is the first agreement of its kind within the Commonwealth.

Sri Lanka welcomed the CHOGM in November 2013. The meeting outlined goals for development within the Commonwealth, giving special attention to resource management. The meeting also saw the various heads of government reaffirm the group's traditional political values (which are entrusted to the CMAG to protect), express concern over the state of economic recovery in the small states of the Commonwealth (approximately 60 percent of the member states), and announce a commitment to helping the small states within their organization. (For more on activities since 2013, see Recent activities, below.)

Structure. One of the least institutionalized intergovernmental organizations, the Commonwealth was virtually without permanent machinery until the establishment of its Secretariat in 1965. The ceremonial head of the organization is the reigning British monarch, who serves concurrently as constitutional sovereign in those member states that still maintain their traditional allegiance to the British crown. Since World War II, the heads of government have held biennial meetings, and specialized consultations occur periodically among national ministers. National finance ministers normally convene in the nearest convenient Commonwealth site on the eve of the annual fall meetings of the International Monetary Fund and World Bank to discuss monetary and economic issues.

The Secretariat organizes meetings and conferences, collects and disseminates information on behalf of the membership, and is responsible for implementing collective decisions. The secretary general, who currently serves a four-year term, is assisted by three deputies with responsibilities for political affairs, economic and social development, and development cooperation. Since its reorganization in 2002, the Secretariat has encompassed nine divisions.

The Secretariat's divisions oversee Commonwealth activities. Among the most prominent, the Political Affairs Division participates in organizing Commonwealth Heads of Government Meetings (CHOGMs), conducts research, aids various committees in their tasks, and monitors political issues and developments of importance to Commonwealth members. Since 1990 its observer missions have also monitored election campaigns, preparations for balloting, and elections in some two dozen Commonwealth countries around the globe. In 1999 it drafted a "Framework for Principles for Promoting Good Governance and Combating Corruption." The Economic Affairs Division conducts research and analysis and supports expert groups in areas such as North-South economic relations, protectionist tariffs, reform of the international financial system, debt management, and youth unemployment. Its purview also includes environmental concerns and sustainable development. In the area of technical assistance and development, the Commonwealth Fund for Technical Cooperation provides training, expertise, and advice in the promotion of economic growth, public sector reform, poverty alleviation, infrastructural and institutional development, and capacity building. A Commonwealth Youth Program likewise funded through voluntary contributions is an effort to encourage youth participation in economic and social development.

In addition, a Commonwealth Equity Fund, designed to encourage private sector investment in the emerging stock markets of developing countries, was launched in 1990 and was followed in 1995 by formation of a

Commonwealth Private Investment Initiative (CPII). The latter was established to help geographic regions attract capital for small- and medium-size ventures and for former state enterprises that were being privatized. On the political front, a Commonwealth Ministerial Action Group (CMAG) was created in November 1995 to provide guidance toward "good governance" in countries undergoing transition to democracy.

The autonomous Commonwealth Foundation, the formation of which was authorized by the Commonwealth heads of government in 1965, supports nongovernmental organizations, professional associations, and other such bodies. The Commonwealth of Learning, likewise authorized by the heads of government and located in Vancouver, Canada, was established in 1987 to promote distance learning and thereby improve access to education and training. Some three dozen additional Commonwealth associations, institutes, councils, and other groups were also established over the years, largely to promote development or disseminate information in such fields as forestry, health, telecommunications, education, journalism, law, and sports. Most are based in London.

Recent activities. On March 2014 the Commonwealth issued concerns about government instability in the Maldives. On April 10, 2014, the Commonwealth met in Botswana to address legal and justice issues concerning human rights concerns in the country. Following the CHOGM commitment to assist small states, the Commonwealth and the government of Malta signed a landmark agreement on June 25, 2014, to provide for better debt management relief. The new agreement increases the capacity for small states to record, analyze, and manage their debt with advice and policy assistance from Commonwealth officials. The CMAG held its 44th meeting September 26 in New York City. At that meeting, the group voted to rescind the suspension of Fiji following democratic elections the previous week. Fiji had previously had its suspension reduced in March to simply a suspension from the council following the announcement that elections would be held in September. On October 3 the Commonwealth financial ministers met to explore ways to financially support countries struggling to meet targets combating poverty in their countries.

In January 2015 experts met to discuss international trade to advance a groundbreaking Aid for Trade initiative aimed at reducing poverty and increasing economic growth in the African, Pacific, and Caribbean (APC) countries. The Commonwealth health ministers met in May to discuss the rising burden of health needs caused by an aging population and rapidly growing populations with long life expectancies. CHOGM met from November 27–29, 2015, in Malta, and elected the first women secretary-general as well as came to an agreement on new measures they could implement to combat climate change. The Commonwealth continued to take a lead as an observer for member country elections and encouraged full voter participation in countries such as Lesotho, Malawi, and Nigeria in 2015.

In October 2016 the Maldives withdrew from the Commonwealth, after 31 years of membership, after the organization threatened the country with suspension over political repression (see entry on Maldives).

COMMONWEALTH OF INDEPENDENT STATES (CIS)

Sodruzhestvo Nezavisimykh Gosudarstv (SNG)

Established: By the Alma-Ata Protocol, signed by 11 of the former constituent states of the Union of Soviet Socialist Republics in Alma-Ata (now Almaty), Kazakhstan, on December 21, 1991.

Purpose: To assist in the orderly transfer of governmental functions and treaty obligations of the former Soviet Union to its independent successor states, to promote coordinated policies in disarmament and national security, and to work toward economic unity among members.

Administrative Center: Minsk, Belarus.

Principal Organs: Council of Heads of State, Council of Heads of Government, Ministerial Councils, Interparliamentary Assembly, Joint Chiefs of Staff, Executive Committee, Secretariat.

Website: www.cis.minsk.by and www.cisstat.com. (Site has a comprehensive English section.)

Executive Secretary: Sergei Lebedev (Russia).

Membership (11): Armenia, Azerbaijan, Belarus, Kazakhstan, Kyrgyzstan, Moldova, Russia, Tajikistan, Turkmenistan, Ukraine, Uzbekistan.

Official Language: Russian.

Origin and development. Following acceptance on September 6, 1991, of the Baltic states' withdrawal from the Soviet Union, a proposal was advanced for the creation of an economic commonwealth of the remaining Soviet republics. The plan was endorsed by all 12 republics during a meeting on October 1–2 in Alma-Ata (now Almaty), Kazakhstan, although four states (Azerbaijan, Georgia, Moldova, and Ukraine) abstained from signing a formal treaty in Moscow on October 18. Less than a month later, on November 14, agreement was reached on the formation of the Union of Sovereign States, which its principal advocate, USSR president Mikhail Gorbachev, characterized as a "union of confederal democratic states." However, the seven republican delegations that attended the November 25 meeting decided not to initial a draft treaty, returning it to their Supreme Soviets for more consideration. Ukraine's absence from the discussions cast further doubt as to the treaty's viability.

In a referendum December 1, Ukrainians voted overwhelmingly for independence, and one week later, in a highly symbolic meeting in Brest, Belarus, the Russian Federation and Belarus joined Ukraine in proclaiming the demise of the Soviet Union and the establishment of the Commonwealth of Independent States (CIS). On December 13 the five Central Asian republics of Kazakhstan, Kyrgyzstan, Tajikistan, Turkmenistan, and Uzbekistan agreed to join the CIS, and on December 21 they were joined by Armenia, Azerbaijan, and Moldova in Alma-Ata, Kazakhstan. In December 1993 Georgia decided to join the Commonwealth.

The Azerbaijan legislature voted against ratification of the accord in October 1992 but reversed its position the following June upon a government change in Baku. Azerbaijan's membership was formalized at the CIS summit in September. Georgia's membership was ratified by the Georgian Supreme Council in March 1994. Moldova's parliament ratified CIS membership in April 1994, reversing a negative vote on the question taken the previous August.

After the first six months of its existence, the viability of the CIS appeared in question because little effective action had been taken in economic, political, or military affairs. In seeming contradiction to their stated goal of cooperation, CIS members were preparing to introduce their own national currencies and had instituted numerous cross-border trade restrictions. The commonwealth had also proved ineffective in resolving the fighting between Armenia and Azerbaijan over Nagorno-Karabakh, ethnic conflict in Moldova, and secularist-Islamic fundamentalist disputes in Central Asian republics.

Tension remained high between Russia and Ukraine over the status of Crimea and control of the Black Sea fleet. Ukraine was one of five countries (the others being Azerbaijan, Belarus, Kyrgyzstan, and Moldova) that declined to sign a CIS collective security treaty at a May 1992 summit in Tashkent, Uzbekistan. However, the June agreement between Russia and Ukraine on the Black Sea fleet dispute (see separate article on Ukraine) eased tensions, enabling the CIS to function more effectively.

In March 1992 CIS members (except Azerbaijan, Moldova, and Ukraine) endorsed the creation of a joint CIS military command, which moved into the former Warsaw Treaty Organization headquarters in Moscow. CIS leaders also backed establishing CIS peacekeeping forces to act within and between member states, and in May most signed the Treaty on Collective Security. However, de facto control of both nuclear and regular forces remained in national hands. In 1993 the participating CIS defense ministers ended the joint military command, preferring less structured and, at least from the Russian perspective, less expensive efforts at military cooperation. The CIS did, however, set up an integrated air defense network in 1995 under Russian control and financing and has since continued joint exercises.

In July 1993 Belarus, Russia, and Ukraine agreed in principle to establish their own "single economic space," reflecting an apparent acknowledgment that effective CIS activity remained a distant prospect. Central Asian states also voiced concern over the commonwealth's future, and in 1994 Kazakhstan, Kyrgyzstan, and Uzbekistan formed the Central Asian Economic Union (CAEU).

Supporters of genuine economic cooperation were buoyed by the signing of a customs union between Belarus and Russia during the May 1995 CIS summit in Minsk. Meeting in Moscow in November, CIS heads of government signed integration agreements covering gas supplies, external relations, and scientific research but failed to resolve CIS members' energy supply debts to Russia. On March 29 the presidents of Russia, Belarus, Kazakhstan, and Kyrgyzstan, meeting in Moscow under CIS auspices, signed a treaty to create a CIS customs union.

The next CIS summit was finally held on March 28, 1997. Once again plans were endorsed by CIS members (with the exception of Georgia) for accelerated integration. The prime ministers of six CIS states also signed an agreement in early October called the Concept for the Integrated Economic Development of the CIS, but little hope for implementation was provided at the CIS summit, held October 23 in Chişinău, Moldova. Blocs included the Belarus–Russia union; the CIS Customs Union of Belarus, Kazakhstan, Kyrgyzstan, and Russia; the Central Asian Economic Community (CAEC, successor to the CAEU) of Kazakhstan, Kyrgyzstan, Tajikistan, and Uzbekistan; and the so-called GUAM grouping of Georgia, Ukraine, Azerbaijan, and Moldova. (Tajikistan joined the CIS Customs Union in February 1999. The GUAM became the GUUAM for a short time with Uzbekistan's admission in April 1999, but returned to its former name when Uzbekistan suspended membership in June 2002. In February 2002 the participants of the CAEC agreed to reshape it as the Central Asian Cooperation Organization [CACO].)

In 1999 six members of the CIS Collective Security Council—Armenia, Belarus, Kazakhstan, Kyrgyzstan, Russia, and Tajikistan—renewed their commitment to collective defense for an additional five years. The January 20, 2000, Moscow summit voiced support for the 1972 Anti-Ballistic Missile Treaty, which CIS saw as threatened by efforts in the United States to implement a national missile defense system. Later that year, on November 30–December 1, CIS leaders met in Minsk to establish an antiterrorism center in Moscow.

On October 10, 2000, the five constituent states of the CIS Customs Union signed a treaty in Astana, Kazakhstan, authorizing conversion of the organization into the Eurasian Economic Community (EAEC), effective April 2001. Initial goals of the EAEC, which is modeled on the European Economic Community, were to harmonize tariff and taxation policies, employment regulations, and visa regimes. Armenia, Moldova, and Ukraine have observer status in the EAEC. Uzbekistan joined at a January 2006 summit in St. Petersburg and the EAEC decided to absorb the CACO to eliminate institutional duplication.

Meeting in Yerevan, Armenia, May 25, 2001, the presidents of the six states of the CIS Collective Security Council agreed to move ahead on formation of a 3,000-troop rapid reaction force to be headquartered in Bishkek, the Kyrgyz capital, in response to heightening concerns over drug trafficking, organized crime, terrorism, and Islamist militancy. The session was followed by a full CIS summit on May 31–June 1 in Minsk, where the focus of attention was progress toward establishment of a much-delayed free trade zone.

The organization's focus turned once again to terrorism in the wake of the September 11, 2001, al-Qaida attacks against the United States. Particular emphasis was given to closer coordination on counterterrorism and border security. The most significant shift in policy, however, may have been Russian acquiescence in the positioning of U.S. forces in Central Asia to root out terrorist bases in Afghanistan and oust the Taliban regime. Uzbekistan and Kyrgyzstan permitted the entry of U.S. contingents, but a number of other CIS member states objected to the U.S. military presence. In August 2005 the United States was ordered to vacate its bases in Uzbekistan.

In April 2002 the six parties to the Collective Security Treaty met in Almaty, Kazakhstan, to strengthen joint efforts against terrorism, drug smuggling, and illegal immigration. The session concluded with agreement on establishing a more formal security structure and was immediately followed by military exercises involving the Collective Rapid Reaction Forces. Plans for the new security organization were further advanced at the October 6–7, 2002, CIS summit in Chişinău, where the treaty participants signed a charter for the organization.

Meeting on April 28, 2003, in Dushanbe, Tajikistan, the presidents of Armenia, Belarus, Kazakhstan, Kyrgyzstan, Russia, and Tajikistan formally established the Collective Security Treaty Organization (CSTO) with headquarters in Moscow and named Nikolai Bordyuzha of Russia as its first secretary general. One of the organization's principal assignments was identified as management of the rapid reaction forces.

A CIS summit on September 18–19, 2003, in Yalta, Ukraine, saw the presidents of Belarus, Kazakhstan, Russia, and Ukraine reach agreement on the formation of a single economic space (SES) that would ultimately harmonize customs, tariff, transport, and related regimes. However, as the SES initiative moved forward in 2004, various disputes arose over the adoption of a single economic agreement for the CIS. Ultimately, the CIS decided to adopt 61 separate agreements to be reviewed at a summit in Yalta in September, at which time several were signed.

The CIS heads of government met in April 2004 and supported creation of the CIS Reserve Fund, which would help member states in the event of natural disasters. The following month CIS defense ministers met in Armenia and agreed to form a CIS peacekeeping force, and in June they drafted a document that encouraged the CIS and NATO to cooperate in managing a peacekeeping force under United Nations (UN) mandate. Because of increasing concerns about terrorism and border control (and to bolster military cooperation among members), the Secretariat of Defense Ministers was increased from 10 members to 21 in August 2005.

The 38th CIS summit on September 16, 2004, in Astana, Kazakhstan, focused primarily on security and economic issues; the group issued a statement on the fight against international terrorism and vowed to step up the work of the CIS antiterrorist center. A summit on August 16, 2005, in Kazan, Russia, included adoption of antiterrorism documents but also marked the departure of Turkmenistan from full membership. Turkmenistan, which expressed its preference for establishing its international neutrality, remained an associate member. Meanwhile, dramatic changes of government in the region—the "rose revolution" in Georgia in 2003, the "orange revolution" in Ukraine in 2004, and the "tulip revolution" in Kyrgyzstan in 2005—did not bode well for the organization's future. President Putin increasingly seemed to see the West as a rival trading power rather than a partner and began to exploit politically Russia's position as a supplier of oil and natural gas. During the winter of 2005–2006, huge increases in the price of natural gas caused outrage and recrimination in the European Union (EU) and such Western-leaning CIS members as Ukraine.

Georgia withdrew from the CIS Council of Defense Ministers in February 2006 with aims to join the North Atlantic Treaty Organization (NATO). In May 2006 Georgia, Moldova, and Ukraine threatened to leave the CIS as tension increased with Russia over energy prices and a Russian ban on Moldovan and Georgian wine. The relationship steadily worsened that year as Georgia demanded the withdrawal of Russian peacekeepers from secessionist South Ossetia under accusations that Russia was propping up the separatist regime. After Georgia arrested four Russian military officers on spying charges, Russia slapped transport blockades on Georgia and visa restrictions on Georgian citizens.

In June 2006 Uzbekistan upgraded its membership to full member status.

Tensions rendered several 2006 CIS meetings unproductive, with the commonwealth unable to serve as an effective negotiating forum. Georgian and Ukrainian presidents were conspicuously absent at a July meeting of heads of state. The CIS summit on November 28, 2006, in Minsk, scheduled to coincide with a NATO summit meeting, produced few results. The summit was held to address "questions on the effectiveness and improvement of the Commonwealth" and to sign an agreement delimiting state borders between CIS members, thereby completing the process of turning administrative borders into national borders. Amidst continued rancor, the subject of reform was put off until the following year.

In the meantime, alienated CIS member states continued seeking other avenues for economic, energy, and military cooperation. GUAM was formalized as an international agency committed to a "pro-European" path at a May 2006 meeting in Kiev. The member nations signed a new charter pledging to uphold democratic values and foster mutual economic development and cooperation. Its immediate goals were to reduce dependence on Russian energy and boost relations with the United States as a way to resolve conflicts in their regions. GUAM nations also signed a protocol to implement a free trade zone within member nations' borders. In the same year, member states began discussing the creation of a peacekeeping force that could work under UN mandates, potentially with the aim to replace Russian peacekeepers in the separatist regions of Georgia and Moldova.

On the pro-Russian side, EAEC members—Russia, Belarus, and Kazakhstan—signed the legal framework to establish a customs union immediately following the October 5, 2007, CIS summit in Dushanbe, Tajikistan. At the summit, CSTO members signed agreements enhancing the organization's military power by allowing member states to purchase Russian arms at lower Russian domestic prices. The CSTO also agreed to create an international peacekeeping force, although the Russian foreign minister denied that it would be used in conflicts involving the breakaway Georgian areas of Abkhazia and South Ossetia.

The 2007 CIS summit produced several outcomes. A reform plan was adopted calling for a "qualitatively new level of interaction" among member states. It included the appointment of national coordinators to monitor compliance with decisions adopted by CIS governing bodies. Georgia and Turkmenistan refused to sign and Azerbaijan did so with reservations, while Georgia's president suggested that CIS membership had done nothing to counter Russia's retaliatory trade and travel sanctions. A common migration policy for member states was also adopted, emphasizing regulation and coordination of worker's movements to ensure legal migration and greater social protections for migrants.

In April 2008 the president of Turkmenistan, Gurbanguly Berdymukhammedov, attended a NATO summit in Romania. This led to speculation that Turkmenistan might be moving closer to NATO, perhaps under the cover of an agreement worded to maintain its official neutrality.

In July 2008 the presidents of three of the countries in the Western-leaning GUAM group (Georgia, Ukraine, Azerbaijan, and Moldova), held their annual summit in Batumi, Georgia. The presidents of Lithuania and Poland, both NATO members, were present as observers. The group issued a statement calling for the peaceful resolution of regional disputes, specifically addressing Azerbaijan's breakaway region of Nagorno-Karabakh. The meeting also discussed a project to build an oil pipeline from Odessa, Ukraine, to Poland, which would circumvent Russia in moving Caspian oil to Europe.

The informal CIS summit in Saint Petersburg on June 6–7, 2008, served to demonstrate some CIS members' recognition of Russia's resurgence. Moldova, in particular, seemed concerned with adopting a more conciliatory approach to Russia than in the past.

At a conference of CIS prime ministers in Minsk on May 16, 2008, Belarus assumed the rotating presidency of the organization. The meeting adopted a draft convention on migration. After the meeting the president of Belarus, Alexander Lukashenko, declared that it was time to address issues of integration within the CIS more seriously.

In 2008 relations between Russia and Georgia slid toward collapse, with Russia offering overt support of the breakaway Georgian regions of Abkhazia and South Ossetia. In May 2008 Russia sent peacekeeping forces into Abkhazia under CIS auspices. In the same month, a Russian fighter aircraft shot down a Georgian spy drone over Abkhazia. Georgia protested, but stopped further drone flights. In June NATO urged that Russia remove troops from Abkhazia, but on June 19 there was a standoff between Georgian and Russian forces on the border, solved only after a tense telephone conversation between the two countries' presidents. Medvedev publicly warned Georgia of the most serious consequences if it persisted in trying to join NATO. On August 8 Georgian troops assaulted the South Ossetian capital of Tskhinvali, and Russia responded with a military thrust into Georgia proper. After a French-brokered cease-fire, Russian forces began slowly to withdraw from captured Georgian territory. On August 13 Georgian president Mikhail Saakashvili announced that Georgia was withdrawing from the CIS and urged other members, particularly Ukraine, to do likewise. On August 19 the CIS Secretariat said that it had received official notice of Georgia's withdrawal, which would become effective, under the CIS constitution, one year from that date. Georgia further announced that it was withdrawing from all peacekeeping agreements with Russia, going back to 1994. Russia recognized Abkhazia and South Ossetia as independent states, and on September 12 Abkhazia applied to join the CIS.

In general, Russia's influence within the CIS seemed to be waning. At the October 10, 2008, CIS summit in Bishkek, Kyrgyzstan, the presidents of Ukraine and Azerbaijan did not attend. Georgia was told that the door was open for it to return to the CIS, but the country formally left the CIS in August 2009.

The October 9–10, 2009, CIS summit, held in Chişinău, was considered less than successful. The presidents of Kazakhstan, Tajikistan, and Turkmenistan did not attend. Russian president Medvedev cited a tight schedule as a reason for not meeting Ukrainian president Viktor Yushchenko, who declared that the CIS had lost its relevance and that it was "like an old woman who is waiting for her death."

In March 2010 UN secretary general Ban Ki-moon visited Moscow, and signed a declaration recognizing the CSTO as a legitimate partner with the UN in "fighting global challenges and threats." Moon had previously signed such a declaration with NATO, and his present visit was a step toward Medvedev's announced goal of making the CSTO a worthy competitor of NATO. In May 2010 Russian foreign minister Sergei Lavrov, while addressing the Russian parliament, warned NATO and the EU against interfering in the affairs of CIS member states. At the same time some Russian commentators welcomed NATO activities in Afghanistan, saying that NATO was doing something that the CSTO might otherwise be forced to do.

The September 3, 2011, summit in Dushanbe, Tajikstan, focused on the assessment of CIS activity over the past 20 years and creation of a plan for future development. The presidents of Uzbekistan, Azerbaijan, and Belarus were not in attendance and were instead represented by their prime ministers.

In October 2011 the CIS heads of state agreed to the terms of a CIS free trade zone between member states. Azerbaijan, Uzbekistan, and Turkmenistan all requested more time to decide on whether or not to enter the trade union. Russian prime minister Vladimir Putin was the driving force behind the negotiation of the trade agreement. The free trade zone entered into effect on January 1, 2012. Uzbekistan acceded to the free trade agreement in March 2012.

Newly elected Russian president Vladimir Putin also hosted two CIS events in May 2012. The CSTO met to celebrate its tenth anniversary and discuss the progress it has made. The heads of state also held a casual meeting focused on the newly instituted CIS free trade zone.

At its December summit, CIS leaders produced the Declaration of the Heads of States—members of the Commonwealth of Independent States on the further development of all-round cooperation. The document stresses the importance of the organization as a regional organization for humanitarian, economic, and security purposes and called for further efforts at deeper integration.

In May the Council of Heads of Government met in Minsk. The most important result of the meeting was the approval of the protocol of agreement for Uzbekistan to join the free trade area, becoming the ninth member. The meeting also saw a new agreement concerning atomic energy, in which all parties agreed work toward the development of sustained atomic energy states.

In August the EAEC's principal organ, the Eurasian Economic Commission, completed its draft agreement for the Eurasian Economic Union, which would deepen the existing level of economic integration in the region. The effort at deeper integration in the region, despite hesitancy from some CIS member states, was a major initiative of Russia's Vladimir Putin. These efforts have led some observers to question Putin's motives and fear that Putin was trying to recreate the Soviet "buffer zone" of the Cold War era.

In September 2013 Ukraine announced its accession to the CIS' antiterrorism agreement, which the organization drafted in 1999. (For more on developments since 2013, see Recent activities, below.)

Structure. The Council of Heads of State (the supreme CIS body) and the Council of Heads of Government are required to meet at least every six and three months, respectively. In addition, CIS discussions regarding foreign affairs, defense, transportation, energy, the environment, and other areas have been regularly conducted at the ministerial level. Preparation for the various CIS meetings is the responsibility of a permanent administrative staff located in Minsk, Belarus.

Creation of the Interparliamentary Assembly was approved by seven CIS states (Armenia, Belarus, Kazakhstan, Kyrgyzstan, Russia, Tajikistan, and Uzbekistan) in April 1992. Azerbaijan, Georgia, Moldova, and Ukraine joined later. The assembly meets in St. Petersburg and is assisted by its own secretariat.

In April 1999 the CIS Executive Secretariat was reorganized as the Executive Committee; the executive secretary was given the collateral title of chair of the Executive Committee. Many other organs were subsumed by the new committee, including the Interstate Economic Committee.

Recent activities. Much of 2014 saw conflict between Russia and the Ukraine over Crimea. Russian troops had occupied the Crimea region of Eastern Ukraine since a rebellion broke out there in March and the region's citizens voted to rejoin Russia. Relations between the two countries further deteriorated when, against the wishes of Russian president Vladimir Putin, Ukraine signed a trade agreement with the EU in June. The October 2014 CIS summit was largely overshadowed by the ongoing conflict between the two countries, despite the issue's exclusion from the formal agenda (see entry on Ukraine). Ukrainian president Petro Porshenko did not attend the CIS Summit, sending an ambassador in his place. Porshenko's absence was received with criticism by many of the CIS heads of government. Belarus eventually took the chairmanship of the summit upon consent of the Council of Heads of the CIS. At the summit, six treaties were signed concerning mine clearing, navigation for armed forces, transport security, repatriation of minors, science and technology exchange, and determining the countries of origin for goods.

The year 2015 continued as before, with tension between Ukraine and Russia and political tensions with the West. Falling oil prices and the declining value of the ruble kept the CIS economic outlook low throughout the year. The leading country of origin investors into the CIS remained the United States, followed by the Netherlands, Turkey, and Kazakhstan.

COUNCIL OF EUROPE

Conseil de l'Europe

Established: By statute signed May 5, 1949, in London, England, effective August 3, 1949; structure defined by General Agreement signed September 2, 1949.

Purpose: To work for European unity by strengthening pluralist democracy and protecting human rights, seeking solutions to the problems facing European society, and promoting awareness of European cultural identity.

Headquarters: Strasbourg, France.

Principal Organs: Committee of Ministers, Parliamentary Assembly, Secretariat, Congress of Local and Regional Authority, the European Court of Human Rights, Commissioner for Human Rights, Conference of INGOs.

Website: www.coe.int.

Secretary General: Thorbjørn Jagland (Norway).

Membership (47): Albania, Andorra, Armenia, Austria, Azerbaijan, Belgium, Bosnia and Herzegovina, Bulgaria, Croatia, Cyprus, Czech Republic, Denmark, Estonia, Finland, France, Georgia, Germany, Greece, Hungary, Iceland, Ireland, Italy, Latvia, Liechtenstein, Lithuania, Luxembourg, Macedonia, Malta, Moldova, Monaco, Montenegro, Netherlands, Norway, Poland, Portugal, Romania, Russia, San Marino, Serbia, Slovakia, Slovenia, Spain, Sweden, Switzerland, Turkey, Ukraine, United Kingdom.

Observers States (6): Canada, Holy See, Israel, Japan, Mexico, United States.

Official Languages: English, French, German, Italian, Russian.

Origin and development. In 1946 Winston Churchill put forward his plan for a "United States of Europe," and former European resistance fighters subsequently drew up an implementing program in Hertenstein, Switzerland. International groups were quickly established, and one of the most important of these, the Union of European Federalists, joined Churchill's United Europe Movement, the Economic League for European Cooperation, and the French Council for United Europe to form an International Committee of Movements for European Unity. Under the leadership of Duncan Sandys of the United Kingdom, the committee organized the first Congress of Europe in The Hague, Netherlands, in May 1948, and called for the establishment of a European Assembly and other measures to unite Western Europe. These combined efforts came to fruition on May 5, 1949, when the foreign ministers of Belgium, Denmark, France, Ireland, Italy, Luxembourg, Netherlands, Norway, Sweden, and the United Kingdom met in London to sign the Statute of the Council of Europe.

The organization was conceived as an instrument for promoting increased unity in Western Europe through discussion and, where appropriate, common action in the economic, social, cultural, scientific, legal, and administrative areas, and in the protection of human rights. Except for matters of national and regional defense, the Council of Europe and the Parliamentary Assembly of the Council of Europe (PACE) conduct activities in every conceivable aspect of European political, social, and cultural life. For example, deputies responsible to the Council of Ministers participate in a plethora of rapporteur groups, working parties, and committees concerned with, among other issues, human rights, democratic stability, administrative and budgetary matters, legal cooperation, social and health questions, education and culture, institutional reforms; and relations with the European Union (EU), the Organization for Security and Cooperation in Europe (OSCE), and the Organization for Economic Cooperation and Development (OECD).

In response to overtures from Eastern European countries, the Parliamentary Assembly in May 1989 created a Special Guest of the Assembly status, which, following the collapse of communism and the breakup of the Soviet Union and Yugoslavia, became an intermediate stage toward full membership for most ex-Communist states, although the admission of some proved contentious because of issues related to human rights and regional conflicts. Hungary became a full member in 1990, followed by Czechoslovakia and Poland in 1991; Bulgaria in 1992; Romania, Estonia, Lithuania, Slovenia, the Czech Republic, and Slovakia in 1993 (the last two as successors to Czechoslovakia); Latvia, Albania, Moldova, Ukraine, and Macedonia in 1995; the Russian Federation and Croatia in 1996; Georgia in 1999; Armenia and Azerbaijan in 2001; and Serbia and Montenegro in 2003. Andorra was admitted in 1994.

Of the remaining nonmember European states, Belarus has applied for full membership but was suspended from special guest status in January 1997 because of its perceived undemocratic tendencies. A 1998 application for membership by Monaco was not approved because the principality's lack of a parliamentary opposition complicated its ability to guarantee a pluralist delegation. Election law changes followed by elections in February 2003 remedied the situation, and Monaco was admitted as a member on October 5, 2004.

Among the most significant achievements of the council are the drafting and implementation of the European Convention for the Protection of Human Rights and Fundamental Freedoms. Signed in November 1950 and entering into force in September 1953, the convention set up the European Commission of Human Rights, composed of independent lawyers from member states, to examine alleged violations by signatories and to attempt to broker negotiated settlements between the involved parties. A European Court of Human Rights was also established to consider cases in which those negotiations fail. The Council of Ministers approved the creation of a new post of commissioner for human rights in May 1999, after abolishing the Commission of Human Rights.

Other landmark conventions include the European Cultural Convention (which entered into force in 1955), the European Convention for the Peaceful Settlement of Disputes (1958), the European Social Charter (1965), the European Convention on the Suppression of Terrorism (1978), the European Convention for the Prevention of Torture and Inhuman or Degrading Treatment or Punishment (1989), the Convention on Laundering, Search, Seizure, and Confiscation of Proceeds From Crime (1993), the Framework Convention for the Protection of National Minorities (1998), the Convention on Human Rights and Biomedicine (1999), and the European Convention on the Exercise of Children's Rights (2000).

Much of the council's attention in recent years has focused on defining its role among the continent's often overlapping organizations, particularly in regard to the former Soviet-bloc countries of Eastern Europe. It became the official coordinator of human rights issues for the Conference on Security and Cooperation in Europe (CSCE, subsequently the OSCE) following that body's institutionalization in 1990; it also assisted with the establishment of a CSCE Parliamentary Assembly in 1992, in accordance with the council's earlier proposal for an all-European representative forum. In addition, the council's program on democratic institutions has provided assistance to the emerging European democracies in the field of constitutional, legislative, and administrative reform. On the proposal of President Mitterrand of France in May 1992, the council held its first summit meeting of heads of state and government October 8–9, 1993, in Vienna, Austria, to consider structural reform of the organization.

Minority and political rights remained prominent council concerns in 1996, particularly in connection with new accessions to full membership. Opposition to Russia's admittance in the Parliamentary Assembly (over the Chechnya military operation and then the Communist victory in the December 1995 State Duma election) was eventually overcome early in 1996 on the strength of various Russian promises. The required two-thirds assembly majority was marshaled in January, with the Committee of Ministers moving swiftly to admit Russia the following month. Even more controversial was Croatia's application, which was approved by the assembly in April but, in an unprecedented move, deferred by the Committee of Ministers in light of concerns about the democratic credentials of the Tudjman government and its commitment to the Dayton peace agreement for Bosnia and Herzegovina. On the basis of assurances from Zagreb, Croatia was accorded formal membership in November.

The second summit of the council's heads of state and government was held October 10–11, 1997, in Strasbourg to pursue the "consolidation of democracy" on the continent and to reaffirm the council's standard-setting role in areas such as human rights. The summit's final declaration called on the Committee of Ministers to propose structural reform within the council to promote, among other things, social cohesion, cultural diversity within the context of respect for democratic values, and the security of citizens, via programs designed to combat organized crime, government corruption, and terrorism.

In January 1999 Lord Russell-Johnston, a former leader of the Scottish Liberal Democratic Party, was elected to a three-year term as president of the Parliamentary Assembly. The UK's Terry Davis was also nominated as the council's next secretary general, but in the June election he lost by two votes to Walter Schwimmer of Austria. Davis was elected secretary general in 2004.

During the first half of 2000 renewed fighting in Chechnya not only generated a decision by the Parliamentary Assembly to suspend Russia's voting rights but also called for Russia's suspension from the full council. Moscow, in turn, threatened to withdraw from the organization. Admission of special guests Armenia and Azerbaijan proved almost as contentious, although both were formally welcomed in early 2001. At the same time, PACE restored Russia's voting rights, although Moscow has continued to be criticized not only for its actions in Chechnya but also for a widely perceived failure to adhere to principles of free speech and free press.

On June 21–22, 2001, the council hosted the first world congress on abolition of the death penalty. The council has repeatedly criticized the United States, in particular, for executing convicted criminals, and in mid-2001 threatened both the United States and Japan with suspension of their observer status if they did not take steps toward ending capital punishment. On July 1, 2003, Protocol No. 13 to the European human rights convention entered into effect, thereby making prohibition of capital punishment absolute. The council continues to condemn executions under the death penalty in the US and Japan.

The 109th session of the Committee of Ministers convened November 7–8, 2001. Immediately following the September 11 terrorist attacks on the United States, the council had vowed its support for the fight against terrorism and indicated that it would consider updating the European Convention on Suppression of Terrorism. On September 25, however, PACE offered a word of caution to the United States, describing the September 11 attacks as "crimes" rather than acts of war and urging Washington to seek United Nations (UN) Security Council approval before initiating reprisals. PACE also proposed that the remit of the International Criminal Court (ICC), which the United States has not joined, be expanded to cover international terrorism.

The Convention on Cyber-Crime was opened for signature November 23, 2001. More than two dozen member states (plus the United States, Japan, Canada, and South Africa) immediately signed the convention, which entered into force in July 2004.

Five months after the admission of Bosnia and Herzegovina on April 24, 2002, PACE voted 122–6 in favor of admitting Yugoslavia as soon as its two constituent republics had completed ratification of a new constitution. Accordingly, the new "state union" of Serbia and Montenegro was admitted April 3, 2003. In June 2006 Montenegro declared independence and was admitted as a separate member in May 2007.

On the agenda for the June 23–27 PACE session was a report on the rights of prisoners held by the United States in Afghanistan or at its base in Guantánamo Bay, Cuba. Also in May 2003, the anticipated amendment to the suppression of terrorism convention was opened for signature.

During 2005 and 2006 the council became involved in the controversy over reports that the United States was moving people suspected of terrorism for interrogation into countries in which torture was practiced and that some Eastern European countries were cooperating with the U.S. Central Intelligence Agency (CIA) by holding such people in secret prisons. The council's special rapporteur, Dick Marty of Switzerland, declared that at least 14 European governments were to some degree cooperating with, or at least turning a blind eye to, this program of "extraordinary rendition." His report stated that there was clear evidence of aircraft bearing such prisoners flying over and landing in Europe for rendition operations, with the UK, Portugal, Ireland, and Greece as "stop-off points."

On May 15, 2006, Russia rotated into the six-month chair of the council's Committee of Ministers. This caused controversy, as many believed Russia's record on observing human rights and the rule of law was too weak to justify this position. Russia also complained that the council was trying to impose a pro-Western position on Belarus. The council's affairs in late 2006 and 2007 were marked by tensions between a pro-EU tendency and the resurgence of Russia. In October 2006 Russia objected to any expansion of the North Atlantic Treaty Organization (NATO) eastward.

The former Soviet republics of the Caucasus and beyond continued to be the council's main focus in late 2007 and into 2008. Secretary General Davis visited Armenia in November 2007 to discuss the dispute with Azerbaijan over the region of Nagorno-Karabakh. He promised council involvement in the peace process, but declined to compare the region's status to that of Kosovo. The March 2008 presidential election in Armenia was criticized, both by council and OSCE observers, and violence followed. In April the Parliamentary Assembly adopted a resolution urging an open dialog between opposing groups, and criticized the Armenian government for its lack of response.

Council of Europe monitors denounced the December 2007 Russian presidential election as unfair, a charge that Russian election managers angrily denied, accusing Western observers of bias.

In January 2008 the council's rapporteur on Belarus recommended a measured reopening of contacts with that country. However, the council was forced to condemn Belarus in February for carrying out three executions.

The council was involved to some extent in mediating an end to the August 2008 military clash between Georgia and Russia. After a visit to the region, secretary general Davis condemned Russia's unilateral recognition of the Georgian regions of Abkhazia and South Ossetia as independent states. Other nations and international organizations joined in this condemnation.

Subsequent PACE resolutions were critical of both Russia and Georgia. In November 2008 Davis visited Moscow to help Russia "overcome any difficulties that may arise in carrying out its commitments to the Council of Europe." The main points of contention were Russia's deteriorating record on civil liberties, its frequent failure to carry out decisions of the European Court of Human Rights, and its failure to ratify the 2004 Protocol 14 to the European Convention on Human Rights, which seeks to streamline and speed up the court's work. Russia, while not signing the protocol, continues to declare support for its aims, and for the Council of Europe in general.

The June 2009 Parliamentary Assembly, meeting in Strasbourg, saw one of the most serious disagreements in the organization's history. With the term of office of the current secretary general Terry Davis due to expire on August 31, the assembly was presented with two candidates chosen by the Committee of Ministers. In the past, the assembly had always chosen its own candidates. Declining to vote on the Committee of Ministers' nominees, the assembly struck the election of a new secretary general from its agenda, and the meeting ended with no replacement for Davis selected. A new secretary general was not elected until September 29, 2009, in the person of Thorbjørn Jagland of Norway.

In early 2010 Russia finally ratified Protocol 14, which came into force on June 1 of that year. Russia also called for the breakaway Georgian regions of Abkhazia and South Ossetia to become members of the Council of Europe, before Council monitors could operate there. In May Macedonia took over the presidency of the council, with Greece objecting to Macedonia, calling its role the "Macedonian Presidency." In December 2010 the Council hosted a special conference in Istanbul on "Prevention of Terrorism." The purpose of the two-day meeting was to get Council members to reflect on improving efforts to combat terrorism and fight against the human rights atrocities committed by terrorists. Similarly, in April 2011 the Council of Europe hosted a special meeting of the UN Security Council on terrorism. The meeting focused on international efforts to end terrorism, preventative policies, and the increased utilization of law enforcement and criminal justice to stop terrorism.

In keeping with its emphasis on human rights, 2011 brought about several opportunities for the Parliamentary Assembly to discuss violations of its key premises. Belarus continues to use the death penalty and remains on suspension for failure to institute a moratorium on the death penalty. The execution of two Belarusian terrorists in November prompted another outcry from the Parliamentary Assembly. Similarly, the late 2011 confirmation of a secret CIA-run prison in Romania has prompted many in the Parliamentary Assembly to call for justice and action against those responsible for the cover up of the prison.

The emphasis on Human Rights was continued through the British chairmanship of the Council of Europe's Committee of Ministers from November 2011 to May 2012. On several occasions, human rights were named as the primary concern of the British chairmanship. This priority was evident through the high level conference held in April 2012 to address the future of the Human Rights Court and ways to reform it so as to give it more power and called on member states to create a national human rights institution in each state. At the May 2012 Committee of Ministers biannual meeting, the British chair again advocated human rights as a primary concern by taking many of the ideas from the April conference and enacting them to ensure that the European Convention on Human Rights remains strongly enforced across the entire council. In June 2012 Albania announced that during its six-month tenure as chair of the Committee of Ministers, it too was going to pursue a human-rights-focused agenda.

In addition to human rights, Albania also focused its efforts on unity throughout the region. At a November 2011 conference entitled "Diversity in Europe," Albania emphasized the importance of educating youth about the strengths of diversity and the opportunities for dialogue with the Mediterranean states. Albania also took steps to promote democratic societies and the rule of law within Europe.

During its chairmanship, Andorra continued the conversation about education started by Albania. From November 2012 to May 2013, the Council of Europe held three education-related conferences, discussing issues of democratic civic education, educational competencies, and the role of government in education. Also during Andorra's tenure, the organization passed the 15th protocol of the European Convention on the Protection of Human Rights. The protocol was opened for signatures in June 2013.

Picking up with the progress made by Andorra, Armenia welcomed the efforts of PACE to pass Protocol No. 16 of the Convention on the Protection of Human Rights, which was passed by the Committee of Ministers in July. Protocol No. 16 was opened for signatures on October 2. The Committee of Ministers has drafted a Convention against Trafficking in Human Organs, which is under consideration of PACE.

In October 2013 PACE welcomed the UN decision concerning chemical weapons in Syria, but expressed concern that it did nothing to stop the actual war. It also noted that all of those guilty of committing crimes against humanity in Syria should be brought to justice, including being brought before the ICC if necessary. (For more information on activities since 2013, see Recent activities, below.)

Structure. The Committee of Ministers, comprised of the foreign ministers of all member states, considers all actions required to further the aims of the council. The decisions of the committee take the form either of recommendations to governments or of conventions and agreements, which bind the states that ratify them. The committee normally meets twice a year in Strasbourg. Most of its ongoing work, however, is performed by deputies who meet collectively almost weekly. Overall policy guidance has recently been provided by meetings of the heads of state and government.

The Parliamentary Assembly, the deliberative organ, can consider any matter within the purview of the council. Its conclusions, if they call for action by governments, take the form of recommendations to the Committee of Ministers. The members of the assembly are drawn from national parliaments and apportioned according to population, the states with the smallest populations having 2 seats and those with the largest, 18. (Countries granted Special Guest of the Assembly status have held seats, although without voting power.) The method of delegate selection is left to the national parliaments. Within the assembly all members participate not as state representatives but as individuals or as representatives of political groups; each delegation includes spokesmen from both the government and the opposition.

Assembly committees cover culture, science, and education; economic affairs and development; environment, agriculture, and local and regional affairs; equal opportunities for women and men; honoring of obligations and commitments by member states; legal affairs and human rights; migration, refugees, and demography; political affairs; rules of procedure and immunities; and social, health, and family affairs. In addition, a joint committee comprises, in equal numbers, members of the assembly and a representative from each member government. A standing committee comprises the chairs of national delegations, the chairs of the general assembly committees, and the Bureau of the Assembly (the assembly president, 18 vice presidents, and leaders of the political groups). The president of the assembly is elected annually for a renewable term; normally he serves a total of three years.

Part of the council's work is carried out by specialized institutions, such as the European Court of Human Rights, the Commissioner for Human Rights, the European Youth Foundation, the European Center for Global Interdependence and Solidarity (the North-South Center), the Social Development Fund, and the Congress of Local and Regional Authorities of Europe.

The council's many parliamentary, ministerial, and governmental committees and subsidiary groups are serviced by a Secretariat staffed by some 1,800 recruits from all member countries. The secretary general is elected by the assembly for renewable, five-year terms from a list of candidates proposed by the Committee of Ministers.

Recent activities. In April 2014 the Committee of Ministers adopted a plan of action for Azerbaijan intended to help the country grapple with its ongoing human rights violations. The plan is intended to take the country through 2016 and went into effect in May. In June PACE reelected Council of Europe (COE) Secretary General Jagland to a second five-year term. In early September the COE passed the Convention on the Manipulation of Sports Matches in which it placed new regulations on and assigned harsher penalties for intentionally throwing an athletic event.

In the autumn session of PACE, representatives expressed their commitment to the peaceful resolution of the ongoing conflict between Russia and Ukraine, calling on Russia to withdraw its troops. They also passed a resolution concerning the terrorist activities occurring at the hands of the Islamic State of Iraq and Syria (ISIS). The group asked each of its members to continue supporting the work of the Iraqi government and called on the international community to quickly develop a plan of action to address the problem within international law.

Through 2016 Belarus continued to be under scrutiny for failing to address corruption issues. By November 2016 the country had only implemented 1 of the 20 recommendations issued by the COE's Group of States against Corruption (GRECO). The COE has focused on Convention 108, or the Data Protection Convention, to deal with cybersecurity issues in Europe. In September 2016 Secretary General Jagland spoke out that defending human rights is more necessary than ever in light of the Syrian refugee crisis and the rise of anti-immigrant groups in Europe. In October 2016 the COE charged that the campaign for a United Kingdom exit from the EU ("Brexit") had "fueled" anti-immigrant sentiment in the country (see entry on the United Kingdom).

ECONOMIC COMMUNITY OF WEST AFRICAN STATES (ECOWAS)

Communauté Économique des États de l'Afrique de l'Ouest
Comunidade Económica dos Estados da Africa Ocidental (CEDEAO)

Established: By Treaty of Lagos (Nigeria), signed May 28, 1975; amended by Treaty of Cotonou (Benin), signed July 24, 1993; entry into force of the latter announced July 30, 1995.

Purpose: "To promote cooperation and integration leading to the establishment of an economic union in West Africa in order to raise the living standards of its peoples, and to maintain and enhance economic stability, foster relations among member states and contribute to the progress and development of the African Continent."

Headquarters: Abuja, Nigeria.

Principal Organs: Authority of Heads of State and Government, Council of Ministers, Community Parliament, Economic and Social Council, Specialized Technical Commissions, Community Court of Justice, ECOWAS Bank for Investment and Development, ECOWAS Commission.

Website: www.ecowas.int.

ECOWAS Chair: Ellen Johnson Sirleaf (Liberia).

Commission President: Marcel Alain de Souza (Benin).

Membership (15): Benin, Burkina Faso, Cape Verde, Côte d'Ivoire, Gambia, Ghana, Guinea, Guinea-Bissau, Liberia, Mali, Niger, Nigeria, Senegal, Sierra Leone, Togo.

Official Languages: English, French, Portuguese, and "all West African languages so designated by the Authority."

Origin and development. The Economic Community of West African States (ECOWAS) received its greatest impetus from discussions in October 1974 between Gen. Yakubu Gowon of Nigeria and President Gnassingbé Eyadéma of Togo. The two leaders advanced plans for a more comprehensive economic grouping than the purely francophone West African Economic Community (*Communauté Economique de l'Afrique de l'Ouest*—CEAO), which had been recently launched by Côte d'Ivoire, Dahomey (later Benin), Mali, Mauritania, Niger, Senegal, and Upper Volta (later Burkina Faso). The treaty establishing ECOWAS was signed by representatives of 15 West African states on May 28, 1975, in Lagos, Nigeria, and by the end of June had been formally ratified by enough signatories (seven) to become operative. However, it took until November 1976 for an agreement to be worked out on protocols to the treaty. The delay resulted in part from Senegal's effort to make its ratification dependent upon a broadening of the community to include Zaire (later Democratic Republic of the Congo), and several other francophone states of Central Africa. Ultimately, it was decided that any such expansion would be unrealistic. Cape Verde joined in 1977.

Despite beginning with purely economic concerns, ECOWAS shifted its focus with its controversial involvement in the civil war that broke out in Liberia in August 1990. The ECOWAS Monitoring Group (ECOMOG) was formed and sent to Liberia to facilitate a cease-fire, organize an interim government, and oversee the holding of new national elections. A tenuous cease-fire was finally negotiated at an extraordinary summit in late November, but the political situation in Liberia remained chaotic.

In the midst of the Liberian civil war efforts, a special committee was established in 1991 to propose revisions to the ECOWAS treaty. By July 1993 a peace accord (negotiated with United Nations [UN] assistance) was signed by Liberia's warring factions. This appearance of success produced an atmosphere of enthusiasm during the ECOWAS summit in Cotonou, Benin, on July 22–24. Hoping to capitalize on the newfound cohesion, the summit signed the Treaty of Cotonou, the special committee's revision of the original Lagos treaty. The new accord was designed to speed up implementation of a regional common market, which would include, progressively, a monetary union, an internal free trade zone (providing for the free movement of people, goods, services, and capital), and a common external tariff and trade policy. This quicker implementation occurred by making summit decisions binding on all members and expanding ECOWAS's political mandate. In addition, a number of new bodies, such as the Community Parliament and the Economic and Social Council, were authorized.

At the conclusion of a summit on July 28–29, 1995, ECOWAS announced that sufficient ratifications had been received for the treaty to enter into effect, although the Community Parliament and Community Court of Justice were not inaugurated until 2000 and 2001, respectively.

The October 1998 ECOWAS summit saw the group of nations move more toward promoting peace and stability in the region. Toward this end, the summit participants agreed to ban the trade in, and manufacture of, small arms throughout ECOWAS and called on other parts of Africa to do the same. The summit also approved a peace accord that ECOWAS representatives had helped negotiate in Guinea-Bissau and that committed the community to providing peacekeeping forces in that country as of early 1999. In what was perhaps the boldest move at the summit, ECOWAS also endorsed a conflict resolution mechanism authorizing it to intervene in the internal affairs of its member states if the security of the region was threatened.

Meanwhile, Mauritania, apparently objecting to moves toward greater military and monetary integration, announced in December 1999 its intention to withdraw from the organization, effective December 2000.

Although ECOWAS failed to achieve a common external tariff by its target of January 2000, in April the English-speaking countries, Gambia, Ghana, Guinea, Liberia, Nigeria, and Sierra Leone, plus Portuguese-speaking Cape Verde, reached an agreement on establishing by 2003 a new West African monetary union in parallel to the francophone West African Economic and Monetary Union (*Union Economique et Monétaire Ouest-Africaine*—UEMOA). In February 2000, apparently setting aside what ECOWAS chair and president of Mali, Alpha Oumar Konare, termed the "anglophone/francophone distractions" that had long impeded economic integration, ECOWAS and the UEMOA agreed to a joint action plan that envisaged, in part, a merger of the UEMOA and the proposed second monetary union into a single zone by 2004. The 2005 summit, however, postponed plans to introduce a common currency by July 1, 2005.

In early July, following the failure of yet another negotiated cease-fire in Liberia, ECOWAS agreed to dispatch several thousand troops to Monrovia, and the resultant ECOWAS Mission in Liberia (ECOMIL) was deployed in August.

In March 2005 ECOWAS launched the Regional Market Systems and Traders' Organizations in West Africa in an effort to improve regional cooperation in trade, with a particular focus on agriculture. The program was seen as the first step toward development of an ECOWAS common agricultural policy. Progress was also reported in regard to the proposed common external tariff for ECOWAS, a key component of the planned free trade area. Meanwhile, on the political front, ECOWAS was active in early 2005 in helping resolve the turmoil in Togo; the community also subsequently assisted in Liberia and Côte d'Ivoire.

At the April 12, 2006, summit, held in Niamey, Niger, the ECOWAS heads of state approved organizational changes to turn its secretariat into a commission to increase efficiency and productivity. ECOWAS leaders approved various efforts to improve members' economies and infrastructure, including moves toward a common airline and a common standard for mobile telephones. On April 12, 2006, the group's trade ministers met in Abuja to evaluate progress toward the second phase of negotiations with the EU on an Economic Partnership Agreement (EPA). This prospective agreement would lead to the creation of a free trade area between the two regions.

At a July 2006 meeting, ECOWAS finalized plans to transform the Executive Secretariat into the Executive Commission. The group would now have a president, a vice president, and seven commissioners, with a limited and well-defined role for each commissioner. Member states would be expected to cede some of their powers to the commission in the interest of faster decision-making. The same restructuring was intended to make the Community Parliament more powerful by making its decisions binding on member states. The new arrangement came into effect in February 2007.

In June 2007 ECOWAS leaders met in Abuja to discuss ways of speeding up the group's transition (now long behind schedule) into a border-free zone, and the group set 2020 as a target for full regional integration. The ECOWAS standby force, successor to ECOMOG, came into being at the end of 2007, with the appointment of a Nigerian general, Hassan Lai, as chief of staff in November and the holding of maneuvers in Senegal in December.

Late 2007 and early 2008 saw controversy over ECOWAS states signing the proposed EPA with the EU. The original deadline was the end of 2007, but several member states and individual politicians objected, calling the proposed agreement a bad one for the region. They felt that the EPA, rather than helping the region's economies, would open them up to subsidized European goods. At the January 18, 2008, summit in Ouagadougou the matter was put on hold until 2009. An interim agreement was signed in late November 2008. The conclusion of negotiations was endorsed at the 44th ECOWAS summit, held in March 2014, but as of October, no agreement had been signed.

The group envisioned travel and migration between ECOWAS states as being relatively free of restriction. In 2008 the ECOWAS passport was close to full implementation, but on several occasions trouble arose between migrant groups and residents of countries. Nevertheless, ECOWAS passports are currently issued by 10 of the 15 member countries: Benin, Côte d'Ivoire, Ghana, Guinea, Liberia, Niger, Nigeria, Senegal, Sierra Leone, and Togo.

A special summit held January 10, 2009, condemned the December coup in Guinea, and suspended that country from all ECOWAS meetings until constitutional order was restored. It appeared that discussions between ECOWAS and the Guinea regime were being fruitful. But the group's chair-in-office, Nigerian president Umaru Musa Yar'Adua, called on member states to avoid working at cross-purposes in helping Guinea.

ECOWAS had been active in trying to maintain constitutional peace in Guinea-Bissau since the November 2008 attempted assassination of that country's president João Bernardo Vieira. Following a successful attempt on Vieira's life by renegade soldiers in March 2009, an ECOWAS mission visited Guinea-Bissau, where senior military officers assured them that the murder was not part of a coup. Commission president Mohammed ibn Chambas noted that "the lack of serious security sector reform" had long been a major problem in

Guinea-Bissau, and Chambas hoped the issue would now be comprehensively addressed.

The June 21, 2009, summit, held in Abuja, was noteworthy in that it incorporated a special ECOWAS-Spain summit. Spanish prime minister Jose Luis Zapatero led a delegation to discuss strengthening cooperation between Spain and ECOWAS, a situation that would be "to the mutual benefit of both the sub-region and the Kingdom of Spain given its proximity to Africa." The ECOWAS summit otherwise called on all member states to work harder on regional economic integration. Yar'Adua also called on member states to continue pushing forward the peace process in Guinea and Guinea-Bissau. He noted that thanks to ECOWAS efforts, elections would shortly be held in Guinea-Bissau, and later, he hoped, in Guinea.

In June 2009 ECOWAS announced that a Common Mining Code for its members would be in place by the end of 2012. In October 2009 ECOWAS suspended Niger after its president, Mamadou Tandja, held an election widely regarded as illegal. In December ECOWAS declared it no longer recognized Tandja as Niger's president. Tandja was subsequently removed by a military coup, with presidential elections set for January 2011. Under ECOWAS pressure Guinea held elections in June 2010.

In August defense chiefs of ECOWAS and the Community of Portuguese-Speaking Countries (CPLP) announced a plan to help Guinea-Bissau become more stable. In May 2010 ECOWAS was able to congratulate Togo on a presidential decree that, after long negotiation, set up an inclusive government.

The February 15, 2010, summit, held in Abuja, appointed Victor Gbeho of Ghana to replace Mohammed Ibn Chambas as president. Chambas had resigned to take another job, and Beyu was to fill out his term, ending in December 2010. Acting Nigerian president Goodluck Jonathan presided over the meeting, in place of President Umaru Yar'Adu who, due to ill health, could not host the summit in person.

Much of the March 2011 summit, held in Abuja, Nigeria, centered on the situation in Libya, the progress toward democracy made by several member states (namely Guinea, Niger, and Burkina Faso), and, most significantly, the stalled progress of the EPA between ECOWAS and the EU. The ECOWAS Commission used 2011 as an opportunity to emphasize the importance of monetary integration and further improvements to both the financial progress of the member states and the safety and progress of nations' infrastructures.

In January 2012 a group of rebels began an attack against the government of Mali. On March 22 Mali president Amadou Toure was removed from office in an armed coup. Mali was suspended from ECOWAS on April 2, and a mediator was appointed by the organization to help seek a peaceful transition of power. Following the signing of the April 6 framework agreement on the transition back to constitutional order in Mali, the sanctions were lifted. Similarly, a military coup in Guinea-Bissau in early April resulted in sanctions being levied by ECOWAS at an emergency session of the Heads of State held in late April to deal with the burgeoning situations in Guinea-Bissau and Mali.

The June summit meeting primarily focused on security concerns in the region. While they lifted their sanctions on Guinea Bissau, they still expressed concern over Mali. The situation in Mali remained a major priority as the Authority voted in support of accelerating the deployment of its standby force to the country. The continual terrorist attacks in Mali also resulted in new sanctions being placed on those hindering the ECOWAS work in Mali. Another decision to come from the summit was a move to expand the ECOWAS Commission from nine commissioners to twelve.

At its semi-annual meeting held February 27–28, the ECOWAS Authority again focused on security concerns and political unrest, namely in Mali and Guinea-Bissau. In regard to the still ongoing terrorist attacks, ECOWAS further denounced them and reinforced its commitment to the troops for around the region that are deployed in Mali to help stabilize the region. They also announced their continued support for the efforts made by the transitional government to move the country toward elections. Concerning Guinea Bissau, the Authority echoed its call for the government to produce a roadmap for transition and extended their transitional period until the end of the year. They also asked for the African Union to lift their sanctions on the transitional state. Also occurring at the meeting, the heads of state again voted to expand the Commission from 12 to 15. The summer meeting of the authority was again concerned with issues in Guinea Bissau and Mali, but expressed its support and commendation for upcoming elections in both states.

Efforts to bring ECOWAS under a common currency within a common economic union continue to progress and were discussed at both meetings of the Authority in 2013. A decision, however, by the ECOWAS Convergence Council called on the organization to revise its timetable for full integration of the single currency. (For more on activities since 2013, see Recent activities, below.)

Structure. The basic structure of ECOWAS consists of the Authority of Heads of State and Government; the Council of Ministers comprised of two representatives from each member; the ECOWAS Commission, which is headed by a commission president that is assisted by a vice president and fifteen commissioners; the Community Court of Justice, which settles disputes arising under the treaty; the Economic and Social Council; and eight specialized technical commissions. These commissions are Administration and Finance; Food and Agriculture; Environment and Natural Resources; Human Resources, Information, and Social and Cultural Affairs; Industry, Science and Technology, and Energy; Political, Judicial, and Legal Affairs and Regional Security and Integration; Trade, Customs, Taxation, Statistics, Money, and Payments; and Transport, Communications, and Tourism. The ECOWAS Community Parliament of 120 national representatives began its inaugural session in November 2000 in Abuja. The Community Court of Justice was inaugurated in January 2001. The Council of Elders was formed in July 2001.

The Treaty of Lagos authorized creation of the Fund for Cooperation, Compensation, and Development (FCCD), supported by members' contributions, the revenues of community enterprises, and grants from non-ECOWAS countries. In addition to financing mutually approved projects, the fund, headquartered in Lomé, Togo, was established to compensate members who suffered losses due to the establishment of community enterprises or the liberalization of trade. Upon ratification of treaty changes approved by the heads of state in December 2001, the FCCD was reconfigured as the ECOWAS Bank for Investment and Development (EBID), which has the broader mission of financing private investment in infrastructure and such public sector activities as poverty reduction.

Recent activities. One of the most significant events of early 2014 was the signing of the Abidjan–Lagos Corridor Road Project Treaty on April 1. The treaty authorizes the construction of a 1,025-kilometer, six-lane road from Lagos, Nigeria, to Abidjan, Côte d'Ivoire. The road would be maintained and built by the five countries the road traverses. The treaty was the culminating event of the 44th ECOWAS Summit, held in Côte d'Ivoire.

An extraordinary session of the ECOWAS Authority was held on May 30, 2014, to discuss terrorist attacks in northern Mali and northern Nigeria. The authority condemned the actions in both locations and called on the UN Security Council to take up the issues while calling on the ECOWAS Commission to quickly implement an ECOWAS counterterrorism strategy.

The most pressing issue facing the ECOWAS member states in 2014, however, was the violent Ebola epidemic in West Africa. Working with other organizations throughout the continent and world, ECOWAS developed a comprehensive campaign to address the crisis that as of October had claimed the lives of 50 percent of the 8,000 citizens diagnosed with Ebola within the ECOWAS region. Their efforts include public information campaigns, a new series of targeted messages, the use of regional military forces to assist medical personnel, and the deployment of West African Health Organization teams to the most heavily affected areas.

President Macky Sall of Senegal was elected as the new president of ECOWAS in May 2015. The 2015 coup in Burkina Faso prompted ECOWAS heads of state and government to meet in Abuja, Nigeria, on September 10, 2015, where President Michel Kafando of Burkina Faso was reinstated as the transitional president.

Liberian president Ellen Johnson Sirleaf became ECOWAS's chair in June 2016. She was the first woman chair of the organization. Marcel Alain de Souza of Benin concurrently became the new president of the Commission in June.

EUROPEAN FREE TRADE ASSOCIATION (EFTA)

Established: By convention signed January 4, 1960, in Stockholm, Sweden, effective May 3, 1960; updated convention signed June 21, 2001, in Vaduz, Liechtenstein, with entry into force on June 1, 2002.

Purpose: Initially, to promote economic expansion, full employment, and higher standards of living through elimination of barriers to nonagricultural trade among member states; more recently, to expand trade and other cooperation relations with external countries and to further European integration through a single European Economic Area, extending not only to free trade, but also to deregulation, removal of technical and nontariff barriers to trade, and cooperation with the European Union in the service and agricultural sectors as well as industry.

Headquarters: Geneva, Switzerland.

Principal Organs: Council, EFTA Council Committees, Consultative Committee, EFTA Surveillance Authority, EFTA Court, Secretariat.

Website: www.efta.int.

Secretary General: Kristinn F. Árnason (Iceland).

Membership (4): Iceland, Liechtenstein, Norway, Switzerland.

Working Language: English.

Origin and development. EFTA was established under British leadership in 1959–1960 as the response of Europe's so-called outer seven states (Austria, Denmark, Norway, Portugal, Sweden, Switzerland, United Kingdom) to the creation of the original six-state European Economic Community (EEC). With the breakdown of negotiations to establish a single, all-European free trade area encompassing both groups, the seven decided to set up a separate organization that would enable the non-EEC states both to maintain a unified position in further bargaining with the "inner six" and to carry out a modest liberalization of trade within their own group, provided for in the establishment of the 1960 EFTA Convention (the Stockholm Convention). Finland became an associate member of EFTA in 1961; Iceland joined as the eighth full member in 1970. At the start of 1973, however, Denmark and the United Kingdom withdrew upon joining the European Community (EC).

Unlike the EEC, EFTA was not endowed with supranational features. It was not designed to establish a common market or common external tariff, but merely to eliminate internal trade barriers on nonagricultural goods. This objective was met at the end of 1966, three years ahead of schedule. A second goal, a comprehensive agreement permitting limited access to EC markets, led to completion of various trade pacts, the first of which became effective January 1, 1973, concurrent with the initial round of EC expansion.

Following enlargement of the EC, a further range of activity was unofficially added to the EFTA agenda, and cooperation was extended to more diverse economic matters than the trade concerns specified in the Stockholm Convention, including such areas as raw materials, monetary policy, inflation, and unemployment.

Organized outside EFTA's institutional framework, the first summit in 11 years convened in May 1977 in Vienna, Austria, and adopted the Vienna Declaration, which prescribed a broad framework for future activities. It included, for example, a resolution calling upon EFTA to become a "forum for joint consideration of wider European and world-wide economic problems in order to make a constructive contribution to economic cooperation in international fora." In pursuit of this goal, a multilateral free trade agreement between the EFTA countries and Spain was signed in 1979 in Madrid, while in 1982 concessions were extended to permit Portugal to expand its industrial base prior to joining the EC. Cooperation between EFTA and the EC/European Union (EU) continued to grow based on general guidelines promulgated in the 1984 Luxembourg Declaration, which endorsed the development of a European Economic Space (EES) including all EFTA and EC countries. The accord called for the reduction of nontariff barriers; more joint research and development projects; and exploratory talks in such areas as transportation, agriculture, fishing, and energy. In an effort to reduce border formalities, EFTA reached agreement with the EC on the use of a simplified customs form, the Single Administrative Document (SAD), to cover trade within and between the two groups. The SAD convention was the first direct agreement between EFTA and the EC. Both the SAD accord and a related convention on common transit procedures became effective on January 1, 1988.

Two years earlier, at the start of 1986, Portugal had left EFTA to join the EC, at which time Finland rose to full EFTA membership. Liechtenstein, which previously participated as a nonvoting associate member by virtue of its customs union with Switzerland, was admitted as a full member in May 1991.

An EFTA summit in June 1990 again strongly endorsed the EES concept, and formal EC-EFTA discussions immediately began, but the negotiations proved much more difficult than anticipated. The major sticking points were EFTA's request to exempt many of its products from EC guidelines and an inability to agree on a structure through which EFTA could influence EC decision making. Some progress, particularly in regard to the exemptions issue, was reported at a special December session called to "reinvigorate" talks on the European Economic Area (EEA), as the EES had been renamed at the EC's request. In addition, negotiations in early May 1991 resolved many of the remaining disagreements, with a preliminary accord being signed in October. However, the European Court of Justice mandated the omission of a proposed EEA legal body from the agreement, and a new pact was signed in May 1992.

The EEA was scheduled to go into effect on January 1, 1993, but its final ratification proved contentious. For EFTA the most surprising problem was the rejection of the EEA by a Swiss referendum on December 6, 1992. Despite this, the other EFTA members agreed to pursue the EEA without Switzerland. A protocol to accommodate the change was signed on March 17, 1993, in Brussels, and by late 1993 all the EC states and the remaining EFTA countries had completed their ratification procedures. As finally launched on January 1, 1994, the EEA provided for greatly expanded freedom of movement of goods, services, capital, and labor among the (then) 17 participating nations, home to a population of some 372 million. After negotiating amendment of its customs and monetary union with Switzerland that caused deferred membership, Liechtenstein became the 18th EEA member on May 1, 1995.

For four EFTA member states the EEA arrangement was regarded as a stepping stone to full EU membership, Austria having submitted its application as early as July 1989, with Finland, Norway, and Sweden following suit in 1991–1992. Negotiations with all four applicants were completed by early 1994, and referendums later in the year in Austria, Finland, and Sweden approved EU membership. However, Norwegian voters voted "no" on the proposal, as they had once before in 1972. Consequently, an EFTA ministerial session in December 1994 in Geneva decided that EFTA would continue to function, even though its membership was to fall as of January 1, 1995, to four countries with a total population of scarcely more than 11 million.

In addition to its focus on the EEA, EFTA has devoted considerable energy to expanding other external ties. An EFTA ministerial session in June 1995 saw representatives of the three Baltic republics (Estonia, Latvia, and Lithuania) express interest in negotiating free trade agreements, which formally entered into effect in 1996–1997. EFTA already had similar arrangements with Bulgaria, the Czech Republic, Hungary, Israel, Poland, Romania, Slovakia, Slovenia, and Turkey. Additional free trade agreements were reached with Morocco and the Palestine Liberation Organization (PLO) in 1997 and 1998, respectively.

Meeting in June 1999 in Lillehammer, Norway, the EFTA ministers called for the Stockholm Convention to be updated in order to consolidate the EEA regime and a set of agreements between the EU and Switzerland that was about to be concluded.

Work on the proposed convention revisions continued through 2000 and into 2001, with the EFTA Council signing the revised EFTA Convention during its ministerial session in Vaduz, Liechtenstein, on June 21–22, 2001. The Vaduz Convention entered into force on June 1, 2002.

EFTA signed several additional free trade agreements with Macedonia in June 2000, Mexico in November 2000, Croatia and Jordan in June 2001, Singapore in June 2002, and Chile in June 2003 (with effect from February 2004). The agreements with Morocco, the PLO, and Jordan were noteworthy in that they marked a clear decision by the EFTA Council to expand the organization's relationships throughout the Mediterranean region, while the agreement with Mexico marked EFTA's first transatlantic venture, and that with Singapore, the first into the Far East.

Attention in 2002 and the first half of 2003 largely focused on the planned expansion of the EU to 25 members in May 2004. Under the EEA Agreement, all ten new EU members (Cyprus, Czech Republic, Estonia, Hungary, Latvia, Lithuania, Malta, Poland, Slovakia, and Slovenia) were required to negotiate EEA participation. Two principal stumbling blocks quickly emerged: (1) the EU's request that the three EFTA EEA members increase their contributions toward eliminating economic and social disparities in the poorer EU countries (the ten prospective members plus Portugal, Spain, and Greece), and (2) the need to adjust tariff arrangements affecting Poland's significant fishmeal processing industry. Poland argued that a loss of tariff-free fish imports from Iceland and Norway would devastate its fishmeal industry. The EU, however, insisted that a uniform tariff regime had to be maintained.

The final agreement called for Iceland, Liechtenstein, and Norway to provide some $1.4 billion in 2004–2009 for the poorer EU countries, down from the $3 billion that had initially been requested. Poland was forced to concede the tariff issue.

The increasingly integrated relationship between EFTA and the EU advanced in other respects in the early 2000s. At the same time, EFTA ministers also have focused attention on expansion of free trade with non-EU countries. EFTA and the EU have also worked together on a "European Neighborhood Policy," designed to reach out to Eastern European and Mediterranean countries that are currently outside the EEA, and to try to prevent the formation of new barriers. The collapse of World Trade Organization (WTO) talks in late 2006, and difficulties since then in reviving them, led to an increased interest by EFTA in forming bilateral free trade agreements (FTAs) with non-European countries.

At a ministerial meeting on June 22, 2009, in Hamar, Norway, EFTA signed an FTA with the Gulf Cooperation Council, which includes the oil-producing states of Saudi Arabia, Kuwait, United Arab Emirates, Oman, Dubai, Qatar, and Bahrain. The agreement covered goods, services, and government procurement. The FTA between EFTA and Canada went into force in July 2009. The Canadian pact centered primarily on exchanging goods. However, it was opposed by the Canadian shipbuilding industry, which feared competition from Norway's strong maritime sector. To cushion the impact, the agreement included a 15-year phaseout of Canadian shipbuilding duties.

Trade talks with India were launched in 2008 and focused on liberalizing the movement of service suppliers, at India's request, and ensuring intellectual property rights for Swiss pharmaceutical companies. Although initially projected to conclude in 2009, negotiations were extended by disputes over subjecting India's low-cost, generic pharmaceutical market to intellectual property restrictions. Norway withdrew from talks, reportedly in protest against Swiss insistence that India abide by stricter rules than those required by the WTO. Nevertheless, trade talks with India continued in September 2009 with a fourth round that focused on agricultural and industrial goods.

In December 2009 Serbia signed an FTA with EFTA, as did Ukraine in June 2010, for a total of 20 agreements with entities outside the EU. In July Malaysia and EFTA signed a Joint Declaration on Economic Cooperation, considered to be a first step toward a full FTA. In June 2010 Iceland began negotiations for entrance to the EU; on entering the EU it would presumably reduce EFTA to three members.

After Icelandic voters rejected a second referendum to reimburse the Netherlands and the United Kingdom for a $5.44 billion loan after the failure of Iceland's banks (see article on Iceland) on April 9, 2011, the two countries threatened to take Iceland before the EFTA Surveillance Court. The following month, Iceland reported to the EFTA court that assets recovered from bankrupt banks would be used to compensate the two nations. In June EFTA signed an FTA with Hong Kong and China. At EFTA's November summit, the organization finalized an FTA with Montenegro and initiated negotiations with Costa Rica, Honduras, and Panama on similar accords. For 2012 EFTA's operating budget was $20.1 million.

In June 2012 EFTA held its summer ministerial meeting in Gstaad, Switzerland. At the meeting, the ministers of the four member states placed heavy emphasis for the ongoing trade negotiations with various states across the globe. Also at the June meeting, EFTA signed a new joint declaration on cooperation with Georgia. This joint declaration makes Georgia the fortieth country with which EFTA has established a preferential or free trade agreement.

At the November meeting of the EEA Council, most of the group's discussion focused on the continuing financial crisis in Europe. The council reaffirmed its support for ongoing discussions between the EU and EFTA to keep the EEA current with financial legislation in Europe. The group also called on Europe to continue its policies of responsibility and solidarity to weather the crisis. Also at the meeting, the council welcomed Croatia's application for accession to the EEA, which coincides with its July 1, 2013, entry into the EU.

At the summer ministerial meeting, EFTA announced the signing of new free-trade agreements with Bosnia and Herzegovina and several Central American states, including Panama and Costa Rica. In addition, the ministers reaffirmed their commitment to ongoing negotiations with Russia, Belarus, Kazakhstan, Vietnam, Malaysia, and Serbia. The ministers, while expressing continued concern about the economic situation in Europe, also noted its support of the joint efforts between EFTA and the EU to keep the EEA current and effective. They congratulated the organization on the 500 legal acts that were incorporated into the EEA in 2012 alone. (For more on activities since 2013, see Recent activities, below.)

Structure. The EFTA Council, the association's principal political organ, consists of one representative from each member state and normally meets two times a year at the ministerial level, twice a month at lower levels. Its responsibilities include supervising the implementation and operation of various free trade agreements and managing relations with the EU. Decisions are generally reached by consensus. Assisting the Council are various standing organs, including the Committee on Customs and Origin Matters, the Consultative Committee (comprising representatives from government and private economic organizations in the member states), the Committee on Technical Barriers to Trade, the Committee of Members of Parliament of EFTA Countries, the Committee of Trade Experts, and the Committee on Third-Country Relations. The latter two and the Council are aided by a number of Expert Groups that provide advice on state aid; public procurement; intellectual property; price compensation; trade procedures; legal issues; and services, investment, and establishment. The EFTA Secretariat opened an office in 1988 in Brussels to facilitate cooperation with the EC. In addition, an Office of the EFTA Statistical Adviser is located in Luxembourg.

EFTA also participates in various bodies in connection with the EEA. The EEA Joint Committee, which brings together EFTA, EU, and European Commission representatives, is the main EEA decision-making organ, while an EEA Council of EU and EFTA ministers offers overall direction. A Standing Committee of the EFTA States (Switzerland participates as an observer) consolidates the position of EFTA members regarding incorporation of EU laws, regulations, and procedures into the EEA. The committee is itself assisted by five subcommittees (Free Movement of Goods, Free Movement of Capital and Services, Free Movement of Persons, Flanking and Horizontal Policies, Legal and Institutional Matters) and some 40 working groups. The EEA Joint Parliamentary Committee, which serves as a forum for EEA issues, brings together 12 members from parliaments of the EEA states and 12 members of the European Parliament. The EEA Consultative Committee focuses on social matters. EFTA has also established its own Brussels-based Surveillance Authority, which monitors implementation of the EEA agreement, and an EFTA Court, sitting in Geneva, as final arbiter of legal disputes.

Recent activities. In 2013 more than 300 new legal acts were added to the EEA Agreement. These acts included new regulations and directives concerning issues such as the implementation of the new ".eu" Web domain, trading illegally harvested timber, vehicle emissions, clean air, air travel, veterinary issues, the transfer of defense-related products, and business registration. EFTA's operating budget for the year was $22.3 million.

Both the November 2013 and the June 2014 ministerial meetings saw little in terms of actual achievement but expressed continued hope for the progression of current talks with India, Vietnam, and Indonesia. The ministers also expressed a desire to reach out to new trade partners in Sub-Saharan Africa and the Philippines while noting with happiness the resumption of negotiations with Thailand. The group also took note of its relations with the EU, expressing approval of the nature of EU–U.S. trade agreement negotiations but calling for the EU to work more closely with the EFTA states in resolving issues within the EEA. In 2013 FTAs were signed with Bosnia and Herzegovina, Costa Rica, and Panama. They also signed an FTA with the Philippines in 2014.

In 2016 the EFTA restarted negotiations with India on a long stalled out trade agreement. In response to the June 2016 UK referendum to leave the EU ("Brexit"), Norway initially pledged to block any effort by the United Kingdom to join the EFTA. However, on August 18, in an interview, Norwegian prime minister Erna Solberg softened her government's stance and acknowledged there would be "advantages" to UK membership for the organization.

EUROPEAN UNION (EU)

Established: European Coal and Steel Community (ECSC) created by treaty signed in Paris, France, April 18, 1951, effective July 24, 1952; European Economic Community (EEC) and European Atomic Energy

Community (Euratom) created by Treaties of Rome, signed March 25, 1957, in Rome, Italy, effective January 1, 1958; common institutions of the three European Communities (EC) established by Merger Treaty signed April 8, 1965, in Brussels, Belgium, effective July 1, 1967; European Union (EU) created by Treaty on European Union, initialed by the heads of state and government of the 12 members of the EC on December 11, 1991, in Maastricht, Netherlands, signed by the EC foreign and finance ministers on February 7, 1992, and entered into force November 1, 1993. (The ECSC terminated upon expiry of its founding treaty on July 23, 2002.)

Purpose: To strengthen economic and social cohesion; to establish an economic and monetary union, including a single currency; to implement a common foreign and security policy; to introduce a citizenship of the European Union; to develop close cooperation on justice and home affairs.

Headquarters: Brussels, Belgium. (Some bodies have headquarters elsewhere.)

Principal Organs: European Council (heads of state or government of all members), Council of Ministers, Council of the European Union (all members), Commission of the European Communities (referred to in all but legal and formal contexts as the European Commission—27 members), European Parliament (785 elected representatives), Court of Justice of the European Communities (informally, the European Council of Justice—27 judges and 8 advocates general), Court of Auditors (27 members, including its president plus a secretary general), European Central Bank.

Website: http://europa.eu/.

Presidency of the Council of the European Union: Rotates every six months among the member states, with the full presidency being formed from a trio of three consecutive presidencies (Slovakia, Netherlands, and Malta as of 2016).

President of the European Council: Donald Tusk (Poland).

President of the European Commission: Jean Claude Juncker (Luxembourg).

President of the European Parliament: Martin Schulz (Germany).

President of the European Court of Justice: Koen Lenaerts (Belgium).

President of the Court of Auditors: Vítor Manuel da Silva Caldeira (Portugal).

President of the European Central Bank: Mario Draghi (Italy).

Members (28): Austria, Belgium, Bulgaria, Croatia, Cyprus, Czech Republic, Denmark, Estonia, Finland, France, Germany, Greece, Hungary, Ireland, Italy, Latvia, Lithuania, Luxembourg, Malta, Netherlands, Poland, Portugal, Romania, Slovakia, Slovenia, Spain, Sweden, United Kingdom.

Official Languages (24): Bulgarian, Croatian, Czech, Danish, Dutch, English, Estonian, Finnish, French, German, Greek, Hungarian, Irish, Italian, Latvian, Lithuanian, Maltese, Polish, Portuguese, Romanian, Slovak, Slovenian, Spanish, Swedish.

Note: The European Union (EU) is the most recent expansion of a process of European integration that was first formalized by the creation of the European Coal and Steel Community (ECSC) in 1952 and then expanded in 1958 by the launching of the European Economic Community (EEC, also known as the Common Market) and the European Atomic Energy Community (Euratom). Especially after entry into force in 1967 of the Merger Treaty, which established "Common Institutions" for the three European Communities, they were referred to as a singular European Community (EC). On November 1, 1993, the Treaty on European Union (also known as the Maastricht Treaty) added two new "pillars" of cooperation—foreign and security policy, and justice and home affairs—to the original pillar created by establishment of the EEC. At that time "EU" became the familiar designation for all three pillars. The Maastricht Treaty also amended the EEC's founding document to replace the term "European Economic Community" with the more encompassing "European Community," reflecting the first pillar's evolution beyond economic matters. The ECSC was terminated when its treaty expired July 23, 2002, but the EC (that is, what was originally the EEC) continues to exist (as does Euratom) and in fact remains legally distinct from the EU despite sharing organs. Thus, references to EC activity are still correct (and even required) in some legal and other formal situations, but common practice has favored the use of "EU" as an umbrella, particularly given what EU officials themselves have described as "the difficulties of delineating what is strictly EC or EU business." The Treaty of Lisbon (Reform Treaty) signed in December 2007 and effective December 2009, brings the three pillars even closer together, as suggested by a provision that renames the 1958 founding treaty of the EC as the Treaty on the Functioning of the European Union.

Origin and development. The formation of the European Communities was one of the most significant expressions of the movement toward European unity that grew out of the moral and material devastation of World War II. For many Europeans, the creation of a United States of Europe seemed to offer the best hope of avoiding a repetition of that catastrophe. Other influences included fear of aggression by the Union of Soviet Socialist Republics (USSR) and practical experience in economic cooperation gained by administering Marshall Plan aid through the Organization for European Economic Cooperation (OEEC).

These elements converged in a 1950 proposal by French foreign minister Robert Schuman that envisaged a common market for coal and steel that would, among other things, serve as a lasting guarantee of European peace by forging an organic link between France and Germany. Although the United Kingdom declined to participate in the project, the governments of France, the Federal Republic of Germany, Italy, Belgium, the Netherlands, and Luxembourg agreed to put the Schuman Plan into effect through the ECSC treaty, which they signed April 18, 1951, in Paris, France, and which entered into effect July 24, 1952. The original institutional structure of the ECSC, whose headquarters was established in Luxembourg, included a council of ministers, an executive high authority, a parliamentary assembly, and a court of justice.

The ECSC pioneered the concept of a European common market by abolishing price and transport discrimination and eliminating customs duties; quota restrictions; and other trade barriers on coal, steel, iron ore, and scrap. Common markets for coal, steel, iron ore, and scrap were established in 1953 and 1954. Concurrently, steps were taken to harmonize external tariffs on these products. In addition, community-wide industrial policy was facilitated through short- and long-term forecasts of supply and demand, investment guidance and coordination, joint research programs, and regional development assistance. These activities were financed by a direct levy on community coal and steel, the level being fixed by the commission in consultation with the European Parliament.

The next decisive stage in the development of the European Communities was reached with the signature on March 25, 1957, in Rome, Italy, of the Treaties of Rome, which established as separate organizations the EEC and Euratom, effective January 1, 1958. (By convention, "Treaty of Rome," in the singular, references just the EEC; for a detailed discussion of Euratom, see the end of the EU article.) Two types of national linkage to the EEC were detailed: full membership, under which an acceding state agreed to the basic principles of the Treaty of Rome, and associate membership, involving the establishment of agreed reciprocal rights and obligations in regard to such matters as commercial policy.

Although Euratom and the EEC from their inception shared the Assembly and Court of Justice already operating under the ECSC, they initially had separate, albeit similar, councils of ministers and commissions. Subsequently, a treaty establishing a single Council of Ministers (formally renamed as the Council of the European Union in 1993) and commission for all three communities was signed by the (then) six member governments (Belgium, France, Federal Republic of Germany, Italy, Luxembourg, Netherlands) on April 8, 1965, in Brussels, Belgium. However, application of the treaty's provisions was delayed by prolonged disagreement about selecting a president to head the newly merged commission. The choice of Jean Rey of Belgium was ultimately approved, and the new institutions were formally established as of July 1, 1967.

During this period the central issues of the communities—the sharing of authority by member governments and the communities' main administrative organs, and expansion through admission of additional European states—could be most clearly observed in the EEC, whose rapid development included a series of crises in which the French government, with its special concern for national sovereignty and its mistrust of supranational endeavors, frequently opposed the other members.

The crucial issue of national sovereignty versus community authority was tested by a year-long French boycott of all three communities that ended after an intergovernmental understanding was accepted that restricted the independent authority of the commission to establish and execute community policy.

The membership issue had first been brought to the forefront by the decision of the United Kingdom in July 1961 to apply for admission to the EEC on condition that arrangements could be made to protect the interests of other Commonwealth states, the other members of the European Free Trade Association (EFTA), and British agriculture. France initially blocked the bid in early 1963 on the general ground that the United Kingdom was too close to the United States and not sufficiently European in outlook. A formal UK application for membership in the three communities was submitted in May 1967, with similar bids subsequently being advanced by Ireland, Denmark, and Norway. Action was again blocked by French opposition, despite support for British accession by the commission and the other five member states. Further negotiations for British, Irish, Danish, and Norwegian membership opened in June 1970, and on January 22, 1972, the treaty of accession and accompanying documents, which provided for expansion to a ten-state organization, were signed in Brussels. Accession was approved by referenda in Ireland (May 11) and Denmark (October 2). However, Norwegian voters, insufficiently placated by concessions offered for the benefit of their state's agricultural and fishing interests, rejected accession in a national referendum held September 24–25. In the case of the United Kingdom, legislation permitting entry was approved by parliament and entered into force October 17, the three accessions becoming effective January 1, 1973. In February 1976 the EC foreign ministers stated that, in principle, they endorsed Greece's request for full membership (an agreement of association was approved in 1962), and a treaty of admission was signed May 28, 1979. Accordingly, Greece became the community's tenth member January 1, 1981.

Negotiations concerning Portuguese and Spanish membership began in October 1978 and February 1979, respectively, but were delayed due to apprehension about their ability to accelerate industrial diversification as well as the projected impact of their large agricultural sectors on the EC's Common Agricultural Policy (CAP; see below). Thus, Portugal and Spain were not formally admitted until January 1, 1986.

From the beginning, the EEC assumed the task of creating a community-wide customs union that would abolish all trade restrictions and establish freedom of movement for all goods, services, labor, and capital. A major part of this task was accomplished by July 1, 1968, a year and a half ahead of the schedule laid down in the Treaty of Rome. All customs duties on community internal trade had been gradually removed, and a common external tariff was ready to be applied in stages. At the end of the community's "transition period"—December 31, 1969—workers became legally free to seek employment in any member state, although in practice the freedom had already existed.

The Treaty of Rome provided steps toward a full economic union of the member states by stipulating common rules to ensure fair competition and coordinated policies governing agriculture, transport, and foreign trade. CAP, centrally financed from a conjoint fund, was put into effect July 1, 1968. The product of extremely complex negotiations, it involved common marketing policies with free trade throughout the community, common price levels for major products, a uniform policy for external trade in agricultural products (including export subsidies), and a program to increase the efficiency of community farming. CAP became, however, a constant source of controversy over ever-growing funding costs. Failed compromise packages of agricultural and budgetary policy reforms—including budget rebates demanded by the United Kingdom—caused the breakup of both the December 1983 and the March 1984 meetings of the ministerial council. European leaders meeting in June 1984 in Fontainebleau, France, finally reached accord on budgetary policy, which included for Britain a guaranteed rebate of two-thirds its net contribution to the community in future years, with EC revenues being enhanced by an increase from 1 percent to 1.4 percent of the value-added tax received from member states.

Agreement was reached in July 1978 for the establishment of a European currency association to include a joint reserve fund to prevent currency fluctuations between member states and a mechanism by which intra-community accounts could be settled by use of European Currency Units (ECUs). The resultant European Monetary System (EMS), which included an Exchange Rate Mechanism (ERM) to limit currency fluctuations, came into effect March 13, 1979. In its first decade the ECU became an attractive medium for the issue of bonds by private and public financial institutions, placing it behind only the U.S. dollar and the German deutsche mark in popularity on the international bond market.

In 1985 the European Commission proposed almost three hundred regulations and directives to eliminate fiscal, physical, or technical barriers to trade. Late in the year the European Council approved a number of reforms, most of which were ultimately included in the Single European Act, which amended the Treaty of Rome in ways intended to streamline the decision-making process, open up more areas to EC jurisdiction, and reinvigorate the movement toward European economic and political cooperation. With tariff barriers to trade among members largely eliminated by 1985, the Single European Act sought to eliminate nontariff barriers when it went into effect on July 1, 1987, following ratification by each EC member state. With an overarching goal of establishing a single internal market by the end of 1992, the act's "1992 program" sought to remove most barriers to the free movement of goods, services, people, and capital within the community, resulting in a single market that would be larger, in terms of population and aggregate gross product, than that of the United States. The powers of the European Parliament also were expanded and a permanent secretariat, headquartered in Brussels, was established to assist the presidency of the Council of the European Communities in implementing a framework of European political cooperation.

Even as the community created a single market, EC summits in July and December 1987 broke up without resolution of a spending deficit that exceeded the members' total budgeted contributions of $35 billion by an additional $6 billion. Disagreement continued to center on the controversial CAP subsidies and large-scale storage of surplus food, which accounted for some 70 percent of EC spending. Britain refused to increase its EC contribution until "financial discipline" had been instituted.

In view of the problems involved, an emergency summit in February 1988 in Brussels, Belgium, achieved remarkable results. The participants established a budget ceiling of 1.3 percent of the EC's GNP, set a cap on future growth of agricultural subsidies, approved cuts in the intervention price for surplus farm commodities, and agreed to double aid to the EC's southern members over a five-year period.

With the agricultural and financial crises averted, the EC turned its attention to the single market plan. Subsequent rapid progress in that regard generated a surprisingly intense "Euro-enthusiasm," but in London, the Margaret Thatcher government continued to serve as a brake on EC momentum, particularly in regard to the monetary union plan proposed in April 1989 by a committee headed by European Commission president Jacques Delors of France. The monetary union proposal, which was distinct from the "1992 program," called for EC members to endorse a three-stage program that would include, among other things, the creation of a regional central bank in the second stage and a common currency in the third stage. Despite strong support from most of the other EC countries, UK resistance necessitated a compromise at the summit held in June in Madrid, Spain. Consensus could be reached only on the first stage of the plan, under which EC members agreed to harmonize certain monetary and economic policies beginning in July 1990. Prime Minister Thatcher agreed to allow preparations to proceed for an EC conference on the much more controversial second and third stages of the plan but, on another matter, she opposed a draft EC charter of fundamental social rights that was supported by the 11 other national leaders, claiming it contained unacceptable "socialist" overtones.

In June 1989 the EC was asked to coordinate Western aid to Poland and Hungary from the Organization for Economic Cooperation and Development (OECD), a program (Poland/Hungary Aid for Restructuring of Economies—PHARE) that was later opened to other Eastern European states. In November, emphasizing the community's expanding political role, a special one-day EC summit in Paris expressed its "responsibility" to support the development of democracy throughout Eastern Europe. At a December summit in Strasbourg, France, EC leaders endorsed German unification provided it included recognition of Europe's postwar borders. In addition, the summit supported the proposed creation of the multibillion-dollar European Bank for Reconstruction and Development (EBRD; see separate entry) to assist economic transformation throughout Eastern Europe. In 1991, as a further measure to promote economic and political reform in the countries that emerged from the collapse of the USSR, the EC introduced Technical Assistance to the Commonwealth of Independent States (TACIS).

The EC heads of state met for two-day summits in late April and June 1990 in Dublin, Ireland, to delineate further the community's future role in the "new architecture" of Europe. They declared that East Germany would be incorporated into the EC automatically after the creation of a single German state, gave "qualified" support to West German chancellor Helmut Kohl's call for up to $15 billion in economic assistance to the Soviet Union (seen as a means of reducing Soviet objections to unified Germany's membership in the North Atlantic Treaty Organization), and endorsed a sweeping environmental protection statement. In October 1990 the two Germanies formally unified.

During their December 1990 summit in Rome, the EC heads of state and government formally opened two parallel conferences: one to consider wide-ranging proposals for EC political union and the other to oversee negotiations on the more fully developed monetary union plan. Based on consensus proposals from both conferences, the heads of state and government initialed a Treaty on European Union and numerous related protocols and documents at a pivotal summit on December 9–11, 1991, in Maastricht, Netherlands. The Maastricht Treaty called for establishment of a single currency and regional central bank by 1999 and committed the signatories to the pursuit of "ever closer" political union by adding to the EC two new "pillars": common foreign and security policies, and justice and home affairs. The Maastricht Treaty also authorized the European Council, which had been established in 1974 as an informal forum for discussions among the heads of state or government of the EU members, to provide political guidelines for EU development.

The plans for economic and monetary union were by far the most specific of the treaty's elements. The EU leaders agreed to launch a European Monetary Institute (EMI) on January 1, 1994, directing that the advisory powers of the EMI would eventually be transformed into the formal authority of a European Central Bank (ECB). It was initially envisaged that both the bank and the proposed single currency be operational as early as January 1, 1997, for those countries meeting certain economic criteria and wishing to proceed. However, if that timetable could not be achieved, the single currency was to be established January 1, 1999, and the ECB six months later for qualifying states. A separate "opt-out" protocol gave the United Kingdom the right to make a final decision later on adoption of the single currency, while Germany entered a similar stipulation in ratifying the treaty.

The articles on political union in the Maastricht Treaty were vaguer, although the treaty introduced the concept of EU "citizenship," designed to confer a variety of rights and responsibilities on all nationals of member states. However, in response to growing European concern about turning too much control over to Brussels, draft references to the union's "federal" nature were dropped from the final text of the treaty, which emphasized instead the notion of subsidiarity, under which all decisions would be "taken as closely as possible to the citizens." Regarding the proposed common foreign and security policies, the treaty, in one of its most widely discussed provisions, called for the strengthening of the Western European Union (WEU, see separate entry in the 2011 *Handbook*) to "elaborate and implement" defense decisions.

Included in the protocols affiliated with the treaty was a social policy charter that required all EU states (except the United Kingdom) to guarantee a variety of workers' rights. Those provisions were deleted from the treaty proper at the United Kingdom's insistence, with Prime Minister John Major threatening to repudiate the accord otherwise. Negotiations were also required with Greece, Ireland, Portugal, and Spain to ensure their endorsement of the treaty through promises of a substantial expansion of development aid to the so-called poor four.

The EC foreign and finance ministers formally signed the Maastricht Treaty on February 7, 1992, the expectation being that it would proceed smoothly through the required national ratification process in time for its scheduled January 1, 1993, implementation. However, the optimism proved unjustified as Danish voters rejected the treaty by a narrow margin in its first electoral test June 2. Following a strong "yes" majority in the Irish referendum June 18, the treaty was approved without substantial opposition by Greece's and Luxembourg's parliaments in July; however, its future was once again clouded by the September 20 French referendum, which endorsed ratification by only 51 percent. The community was also severely shaken in September by a currency crisis that prompted the United Kingdom and Italy to drop out of the ERM.

Facing an apparent crisis of confidence, the EC leaders convened an emergency summit October 16, 1992, in Birmingham, England, to express their continued support for the Maastricht Treaty while reassuring opponents that some of its more ambitious goals were reduced in scope. Parliamentary approval of the treaty was subsequently achieved by the end of the year in Belgium, Italy, Germany, Netherlands, Portugal, and Spain. Germany's formal ratification was delayed pending the outcome of a constitutional challenge. In addition, the prospect for a reversal of the Danish position improved when the December 1992 EC summit in Edinburgh, Scotland, agreed to extend Denmark several "opt-out" concessions, most importantly regarding the monetary union plan. The EC leaders also agreed to postpone consideration of controversial proposals regarding the free movement of people within the community. Nevertheless, by the target date of January 1, 1993, it was estimated that approximately 80 percent of the provisions of the "1992 program" for establishing a single internal market had been implemented by the member states.

Danish voters accepted the Maastricht accord in a second referendum on May 18, 1993. With the treaty awaiting only UK ratification, the June 1993 EC summit focused on the community's economic woes, which were contributing as much as any of the other problems to a growing "Euro-pessimism." In particular, the summit proposed measures designed to reduce unemployment, which was above 10 percent in the community. Although French president Mitterrand attempted to portray the session as marking a "psychological recovery" for the EC, the community shortly thereafter experienced another currency crisis. Faced with a possible total breakdown of the ERM, the EC agreed in early August to let the franc and the six other non-German currencies still in the system float more freely against the mark.

UK ratification, albeit by a very narrow margin, occurred in July 1993, and a favorable ruling in the German court case in early October finally cleared the way for implementation of the treaty. The EC heads of state and government held a special summit October 29 in Brussels to celebrate the completion of the ratification process, and the EU was launched when the treaty officially went into force November 1.

The first EU summit was held December 11–12, 1993, in Brussels. The EU heads of state and government turned to the region's economic problems, particularly that of continued high unemployment. The summit adopted an economic recovery plan that appeared to represent a compromise between those advocating activist labor policies and those convinced that government influence was already too great in economic affairs. For the first camp, the summit approved a six-year public works program designed to create jobs in, among other areas, the transportation, energy, environmental, and telecommunications sectors. For those looking to the free market to resolve unemployment, the summit called for a reduction in "rigidities" in the European labor market, proposing that minimum wages be lowered and that labor costs supporting European social welfare programs be significantly reduced.

In other activity, the European Council endorsed negotiations toward a "stability pact" for Central and Eastern European nations seeking EU membership. The pact would attempt to establish agreement on the protection of minority rights in those countries and create mechanisms for the peaceful resolution of border disputes. Among other things, it was hoped that such an initiative would prevent a repetition of the breakdown that had occurred in the former Yugoslavia, the EU having been criticized for its seeming paralysis in dealing with that situation.

The European Council once again emphasized economic affairs during its June 24–25, 1994, summit in Corfu, Greece, one formal highlight of which was the signing of the Partnership and Cooperation Agreement with Russia. Nevertheless, media reports centered on the union's latest political difficulty—the failure of the council to agree on a successor to commission president Delors, who announced his retirement effective January 1, 1995. After the United Kingdom rejected the nomination of Belgian prime minister Jean-Luc Dehaene, whom it deemed as too "federalist," a special summit was convened on July 15 in Brussels to approve a compromise nominee—Jacques Santer, the prime minister of Luxembourg. Nominees to the new commission subsequently faced intense confirmation hearings in the parliament, reflecting divisions between those in favor of rapid integration and an increasingly vocal group of "Euro-skeptics."

As members of the EFTA participating in the European Economic Area (EEA) with the EU, Austria, Finland, Norway, and Sweden had been formally invited in the spring of 1994 to join the EU at the beginning of 1995. Austria's membership was endorsed by a 66 percent "yes" vote June 12, 1994, while a positive vote also was obtained in the Finnish referendum October 16 and in Swedish balloting November 13. In contrast, Norway voted decisively against EU accession in its referendum during November 27–28. Switzerland's membership remained on file after Swiss voters rejected EEA membership in a 1992 referendum. More recently, in May 2001 Swiss voters decisively rejected applying for EU membership, although the country had entered into various economic agreements with the EU.

The focus of the December 9–10, 1994, summit in Essen, Germany, was on enlargement, with the heads of state of Austria, Finland, and Sweden participating in preparation for the accession of those countries January 1, 1995. The leaders of Bulgaria, the Czech Republic, Hungary,

Poland, Slovakia, and Romania also attended the summit to discuss in greater detail the criteria for eventual admission. However, despite the obvious external fervor for the EU, enthusiasm within the union subsequently appeared to wane, particularly in regard to the common currency proposal. Turbulence in the financial markets contributed to an acknowledgment by the European Council, which met June 26–27, in Cannes, France, that the proposed single currency would not be launched in 1997. The summit held December 15–16, 1995, in Madrid reaffirmed the EU's commitment to a 1999 final target date, although it was emphasized that the required economic standards would not be diluted for participation in the monetary union. The EU leaders also agreed that the new currency would be called the euro.

The December 1995 summit also gave formal approval for creation of an intergovernmental conference (IGC) that was authorized to propose revisions to the EC/EU founding treaties. Issues to be addressed included the possible elimination of the unanimity requirement for decisions involving the EU's two new pillars—foreign and security policy, and justice and home affairs. Potentially extensive structural changes were also to be considered in the hope that such bodies as the commission and the parliament could become less unwieldy, particularly given the anticipated admission of new members to the union. In addition, ardent integrationists hoped institutional reforms would convince a still largely skeptical European population that the EU was prepared to deal effectively with basic day-to-day concerns such as unemployment, environmental degradation, and internal security.

Although the IGC was launched in March 1996, little progress was apparent by the time of the June 21–22 summit in Florence, Italy. EU leaders reportedly hoped to provide a boost for the initiative at the summit, but the session was instead dominated by the conflict between the United Kingdom and its EU partners over the EU's March ban on exports of UK beef and beef products following the outbreak of bovine spongiform encephalopathy (BSE, the so-called mad-cow disease) in UK herds. A compromise was quickly reached. Much more problematic, however, was the strong UK response to the ban, the government of John Major having instituted a policy of "noncooperation" in May under which the UK veto was briefly used to block all EU action requiring unanimity.

Attention subsequently focused on negotiations regarding the monetary union. German leaders indicated that the entire concept was in jeopardy unless other nations were willing to accept enforceable budgetary discipline as a means of keeping the euro "strong." Bonn's proposed "stability and growth pact" on the matter reportedly met with strong French resistance prior to the EU summit held December 13–14, 1996, in Dublin. However, a compromise favoring the German position was negotiated whereby participants in the monetary union would be subject to mandatory heavy financial penalties for breaching fiscal guidelines. Agreement also was reached on the creation of a new exchange rate mechanism to determine the relationship of the euro to the currencies of the countries that postponed entry into the monetary union.

A special heads of government summit May 23, 1997, in Noordwijk, Netherlands, was buoyed by the presence of the new UK prime minister Tony Blair whose Labour government was decidedly more enthusiastic about the EU than its Conservative Party predecessor. A meeting of the European Council on June 16–17, in Amsterdam, Netherlands, endorsed wide-ranging amendment of the various EC and EU treaties in the interest of broadening the purview of the EU and speeding up the decision-making process. Among other things, the proposed Amsterdam Treaty provided for formal inclusion in the EC/EU treaty structure of (1) the Social Charter (previously relegated to protocol status); (2) a new employment chapter; (3) the Schengen Accord regarding free movement of people and goods across internal EU borders; and (4) the stability and growth pact, designed to enforce budgetary discipline on those countries joining the Economic and Monetary Union (EMU). The treaty also removed several policy areas from national control in favor of "common" EU authority, while some additional areas already governed by the EU were moved into the category of requiring approval by Qualified Majority Voting (QMV) rather than unanimous national consent. Agreement also was reached, in principle, on giving the European Parliament additional authority and on limiting the size of the commission following expansion of EU membership.

Despite the perceived weakness of the Amsterdam Treaty, its completion did permit the EU to turn to its two other pressing issues: enlargement and the monetary union. Regarding the former, a December 12–13, 1997, summit in Luxembourg invited five ex-communist states—the Czech Republic, Estonia, Hungary, Poland, and Slovenia—as well as Cyprus, to begin formal membership discussions in March 1998. The inclusion of Cyprus among the "first-wave" countries was controversial, particularly because Turkey was pointedly excluded. EU officials said they hoped that both the Cypriot and Turkish communities on Cyprus would participate in the membership negotiations, although the government of the Turkish Republic of Northern Cyprus declined.

Ireland approved the Amsterdam Treaty via national referendum in late May 1998, and Danish voters followed suit shortly thereafter with a 55 percent endorsement. The latter was considered an important test in light of the problems caused in 1993 by the initial Danish rejection of the Maastricht Treaty.

On March 26, 1998, Germany had officially endorsed the January 1999 EMU launching, despite the German Bundesbank's having questioned the "sustainability" of the financial status of several countries, with Belgium and Italy drawing particular attention because of their high level of official debt. In April the European Parliament called for treaty revisions to ensure the "accountability" of the incoming ECB, suggesting that a monitoring body (including several parliament members) be established to review ECB decisions and activity. An EU summit May 1–3 in Brussels formally agreed that the ECB would open June 1 and would assume responsibility at the start of 1999 for monitoring policy (including setting interest rates) for the countries adopting the euro.

Thus the currencies of the 11 participating countries—Austria, Belgium, Finland, France, Germany, Ireland, Italy, Luxembourg, Netherlands, Portugal, and Spain—were permanently linked with the initiation of the EMU on January 1, 1999, at which time the participants also began issuing debt in euros. The formal launch was marked by great fanfare, with supporters describing it as representing the "biggest leap forward" since the Treaty of Rome. Two years later, Greece, which had initially failed to qualify on the basis of economic performance, became the 12th EMU member. On January 1, 2002, euro banknotes and coins for public use were introduced in the 12 EMU members—plus Andorra, Monaco, Montenegro, San Marino, and the Vatican—and commercial use of the old national currencies was discontinued by the end of February 2002. During the ten months following the launch of the Euro, the most significant problem facing a number of euro-zone members was keeping fiscal deficits within targeted limits. In November France, Germany, and Portugal were all cited for failure to reduce deficits to 3 percent, as required by the EMU's stability and growth pact. In 2003 Swedish voters rejected adoption of the euro. On January 1, 2007, Slovenia became the 13th EMU member. In 2007 the European Council noted that Cyprus and Malta had fulfilled the convergence criteria and legal requirements to adopt the euro and could do so on January 1, 2008. The eurozone broadened to 16 states with Slovakia's adoption of the euro on January 1, 2009.

Meanwhile, one of the EU's most serious crises to date had begun to develop over allegations of fraud and corruption in EU budgetary matters. In November 1998 the EU Court of Auditors had reported uncovering serious "mismanagement," and commission president Santer created an internal anti-fraud unit. In mid-January 1999 the European Parliament appeared poised to approve a censure motion that would have forced the resignation of the European Commission. The motion was ultimately defeated (293–232), but only after a "peace package" was negotiated under which the commission agreed to the establishment of an independent panel of experts to assess the situation. In March the panel reported that substantial fraud, mismanagement, and nepotism had "gone unnoticed" by the commissioners, many of whom had "lost control" over spending within their areas of responsibility. Consequently, the commission resigned en masse on March 16, and EU leaders convened in a special summit March 24–26 in Berlin to designate Romano Prodi, former prime minister of Italy, as the next president of the commission. Shortly after the summit, the French legislature ratified the Amsterdam Treaty, paving the way for its entry into force on May 1.

The elections to the European Parliament, held between June 10 and 13, 1999, in the differing venues, were notable in that they led to formation of a 233-seat, center-right bloc by the European People's Party and the European Democrats (EPP-ED), thereby unseating the Party of European Socialists (180 seats) as the plurality grouping. On September 15 the legislature confirmed Prodi as the head of a new European Commission scheduled to serve out the remainder of its predecessor's term and to start a new five-year term beginning in January 2000.

A special two-day session of the heads of government held October 15–16, 1999, in Tampere, Finland, focused on matters related to the EU's third pillar, justice and home affairs, including immigration, asylum, and organized crime. The summit also marked a change in strategy regarding enlargement, with leaders agreeing that negotiations on accession should be opened with six additional prospective members—Bulgaria, Latvia, Lithuania, Malta, Romania, and Slovakia—early in the new year. The decision received the assent of the European Council during its summit December 10–11 in Helsinki, putting the six countries on the same footing as the six that were regarded as "fast-track" entries: Cyprus, Czech Republic, Estonia, Hungary, Poland, and Slovenia. The council also formally approved Turkey as a candidate for admission, despite reservations regarding its human rights record, and unspoken misgivings about Turkey being a Muslim, if secular, country.

During the same period the EU was moving steadily toward establishing its own military capability. On June 3–4, 1999, a European Council meeting in Cologne, Germany, selected (then) NATO secretary general Javier Solana Madariaga of Spain as the first EU high representative for foreign and security policy, a position authorized by the Treaty of Amsterdam, which also provided for the use of combat forces for "crisis management." The heads of state and government also agreed to begin formalizing a much-debated joint security and defense policy, under which the EU would assume the WEU's defense role and its "Petersberg tasks" (named for the official German guesthouse near Bonn where, in 1992, the WEU defined its future military responsibilities): peacekeeping, humanitarian and rescue missions, and military crisis management.

An unprecedented joint meeting of EU foreign and defense ministers November 15, 1999, in Brussels confirmed Solana's WEU appointment and, drawing on the experiences of the conflicts in Bosnia and Kosovo, discussed how to handle future altercations. A central component of the EU strategy was formation of an EU rapid reaction force (RRF) that would be independent of NATO and the United States. A month later, at the Helsinki summit, the European Council authorized formation by 2003 of a 60,000-member RRF that could respond to crises that did not involve NATO as a whole. As the plan continued to evolve over the following year, the EU agreed to work closely with NATO, thereby mitigating U.S. objections. It also agreed to invite the participation in EU-led missions of non-EU states that were NATO members—most particularly, Turkey—as well as non-NATO European countries, such as Russia. Formation of the RRF was given a further go-ahead by the foreign and defense ministers' meeting November 20, 2000, in Brussels, although Denmark exercised its right to opt out. The ministers also agreed to assume the WEU's operational role. Earlier in the year, in April, the WEU/EU Eurocorps, which was inaugurated in November 1993, undertook its most significant mission to date, namely command of the NATO-led Kosovo Force (KFOR) in Yugoslavia.

During 2000 several important developments occurred in the economic sphere. A special heads of government summit March 23–24 in Lisbon introduced a ten-year program, dubbed the Lisbon Strategy, to develop the EU into "the world's most competitive and dynamic knowledge-driven economy," with attendant goals that included improving the employment rate from 61 percent to 70 percent and achieving an average annual growth rate of 3 percent. One of the core elements of the strategy was the creation of a European Research Area (ERA). In the ERA, researchers, technology, and knowledge would circulate as freely as possible—presumably without jeopardizing the EU's strong intellectual property protections. Research initiatives would also be implemented and funded at the European level.

Interim reports, the most recent a May 2007 "green paper," indicated that the EU was falling short of its ambitious goals of research integration. The slow pace of developing new pharmaceuticals, of which only a handful were commercialized in the EU in 2007, was a particular concern. Additionally, while the Lisbon goal was to match innovation in the United States by 2010, rising economic powers such as China and India were also becoming increasingly competitive. As a result, the "Ljubljana Process" was launched at a ministerial meeting on April 14–15, 2008, in Ljubljana, Slovenia, that set five new initiatives to be achieved by 2020 in the following areas: improving mobility of researchers, a legal framework to aid the development of pan-European research infrastructures, management of intellectual property rights, joint programming for research programs across the EU, and a common policy for international science and technology cooperation. Additionally, a consensus between member states on a new framework for governance of the ERA was commissioned for presentation by the end of 2009.

In July 2000 the EU finance ministers named a committee headed by former EMI president Alexandre Lamfalussy to examine the operation of EU securities markets and to propose changes in current practices and regulations. In September the Paris, Brussels, and Amsterdam stock exchanges merged as Euronext, and in 2002 Euronext acquired the London-based derivatives market LIFFE and merged with the Portuguese exchange. Already second only to London in terms of listings and market capitalization, Euronext anticipated becoming "the first fully integrated cross-border European market for equities, bonds, derivatives, and commodities." In April 2007 the New York Stock Exchange acquired Euronext and the merger of the two created the world's largest stock exchange.

In December 2000 the EU's comprehensive review of institutional reform, which included a special summit October 12–15 in Biarritz, France, drew to a close. Meeting on December 7–11, 2000, in Nice, the European Council agreed to significant restructuring of EU institutions, primarily to accommodate 12 new member countries. (The 13th potential member, Turkey, was excluded from the calculations, given that it had not yet begun formal accession negotiations.) Requiring ratification by the European Parliament and all 15 current member countries, the resultant Treaty of Nice bowed to German insistence that the expanded European Parliament and the QMV system give greater weight to the populations of the member states.

The Treaty of Nice, which was signed by the members' foreign ministers February 26, 2001, in Brussels, hit its first roadblock June 8 when some 54 percent of Ireland's voters rebuffed it. EU leaders insisted, however, that expansion plans would proceed and that efforts would be made to address the Irish public's concerns. These included the impact of expansion on Ireland's standing and the status of its military neutrality in the context of the EU's new military capabilities. Ultimately, the Irish voters were satisfied, and in an October 20, 2002, referendum, 62.9 percent endorsed the Treaty of Nice, permitting its entry into force February 1, 2003.

The ratification process for the Treaty of Nice coincided with a continuing debate over the EU's long-term purpose and structure. German leaders, on the one hand, called for even closer integration, including adoption of a federal structure. France, on the other hand, continued to oppose such a model, which it saw as threatening national constituencies. Another area of contention was the Charter of Fundamental Rights, which was drawn up in September 2000 and formally approved by the heads of government at the Nice summit. The charter's firmest opponent, the United Kingdom, argued that its incorporation into the EU treaty was unnecessary because all EU members had already acceded to the European Convention on Human Rights.

In a significant development for the EU's external relations, the first summit of Balkan states and the EU was held November 24, 2000, in Zagreb, Croatia. The EU pledged €4.7 billion ($3.9 billion) in aid during 2000–2006 to support "reconstruction, democratization, and stabilization" in Albania, Bosnia and Herzegovina, Croatia, Macedonia, and Yugoslavia. Most Balkan states had already expressed an interest in eventual EU membership.

During their February 25–26, 2001, meeting in Brussels, the EU foreign ministers agreed to abolish virtually all trade barriers for 48 of the least developed countries, including 39 members of the EC-affiliated ACP group. Dubbed the Everything But Arms Proposal, the initiative made trade in all manufactured and agricultural goods, except armaments, duty- and quota-free, although phase-in periods were established for bananas (to 2006), rice (2009), and sugar (2009)—three commodities that had caused major trade disputes in recent years.

Meeting in mid-June 2001 in Göteborg, Sweden, the EU heads of government established 2004 as the firm entry date for the next expansion, although it remained uncertain exactly how many of the eligible countries would be ready for admission at that time.

In the immediate aftermath of the September 11, 2001, terrorist attacks on the United States, the EU heads of government held an emergency meeting September 21 in Brussels, where they extended full support to Washington. An informal summit, which convened October 19 in Ghent, Belgium, focused on the economic and political consequences of the attacks and of the recently launched U.S. "war on terrorism." Subsequent related actions included endorsement of a uniform arrest warrant and a May 2002 decision to freeze the assets of 11 suspected terrorist organizations. Developments at a June 21–22 summit in Seville, Spain, included acceptance of a plan to counter illegal immigration, adopt a common asylum policy, and introduce a common border force. Cooperation declined after the initiation of the Iraq War in 2003, typified by EU reluctance to accept cleared detainees from the U.S. military prison at Guantánamo Bay in 2009. In November that year, the EU also objected to an antiterrorism plan that would allow U.S. law enforcement to access EU citizen's financial data, but it ultimately signed a deal that limited the scope to terrorism inquiries.

Meeting on December 14–15, 2001, in Laeken, Belgium, the heads of government agreed to establish a constitutional convention, to be chaired by former French president Valéry Giscard d'Estaing, and to map out a more efficient and democratic structure for the union. On February 28, 2002, the convention began its task. A "skeleton draft" of the proposed constitution for a "union of European states" was published October 28, 2002, but the 46-article document deliberately avoided controversial issues that had yet to be resolved. It did, however, propose reserving powers not specifically conferred by the constitution on EU institutions to the member states. This was seen as an effort to restrain the growth and power of the European Commission in particular.

On March 23, 2002, responding to a U.S. decision to impose unilateral steel tariffs of between 8 and 30 percent, the EU announced retaliatory tariffs against up to 300 U.S. products. The steel products were manufactured by previously state-owned French, German, Italian, Spanish, Swedish, and UK companies that received subsidies before being privatized. The WTO proceeded to address the complex issue, while in December the EU and the United States, at a Paris meeting sponsored by the Organization for Economic Cooperation and Development (OECD), agreed to open negotiations on reducing or eliminating steel subsidies.

Meanwhile, the ECSC's founding treaty had expired on July 23, 2002, resulting in the closure of the European Coal and Steel Community. Perhaps its most significant accomplishment, apart from serving as a model for creation of the EEC, was a decades-long, painful reduction of overcapacity in the community's steel industry. The process introduced production quotas, banned state subsidies, closed obsolete facilities and modernized others, restructured the market, and expanded retraining funds and other support for former steelworkers. By 1999 the steel workforce had declined to 280,000 (from 870,000 in 1975), and some 63 million tons of capacity had been eliminated since 1980. In July 2002 all ECSC assets and liabilities were transferred to the EU. In the interim, ECSC net assets, which were valued at some $1.6 billion at that time, were to be managed by the European Commission and then, after completion of the community's liquidation, to be designated as Assets of the Research Fund for Coal and Steel. Matters related to the coal and steel industries are now addressed within the EU framework.

Proposed changes to CAP and a parallel Common Fisheries Policy (CFP) drew considerable attention in 2002. France and Spain, two principal beneficiaries of the existing CAP, voiced objections. Spain also expressed concern over efforts under the CFP to reduce fleet sizes and better manage fish stocks. A December 2002 decision to limit catches of Atlantic cod, haddock, and whiting also angered British fishermen.

Problems also persisted with regard to establishing the RRF as part of a comprehensive European Security and Defense Policy (ESDP). The first anticipated RRF mission, to assume control in October 2002 of peacekeepers in Macedonia, required the approval of NATO, but Turkey wanted assurances that the RRF would not undertake missions in the Aegean and locations near Turkey. At a summit held December 12–13, 2002, in Copenhagen, Denmark, the EU formally completed a "comprehensive agreement" resolving the dispute with Turkey over the RRF. Under the pact, only EU members and candidates that also are members of NATO or participants in the NATO Partnership for Peace (PfP) program have access to NATO facilities. Accordingly, Malta and Cyprus are excluded.

The most significant action taken at the summit, however, was the approval of the admission of ten new members: the Czech Republic, Cyprus (excluding the Turkish Republic of Northern Cyprus), Estonia, Hungary, Latvia, Lithuania, Malta, Poland, Slovakia, and Slovenia. Accession treaties were signed at an informal European Council session on April, 16, 2003, with formal admission, following the necessary ratifications, then occurring on May 1, 2004.

The EU has relationships with special territories associated with its member states that vary based on their level and type of participation in EU policy areas and programs, spelled out in the European Community Treaty of 2002. Among them are the Spanish Canary Islands, which remain outside the European Value-Added Tax (VAT) areas but submit to EU policy in all other respects. The French islands of Guadeloupe and Martinique in the Caribbean, French Guiana on the northern coast of South America, and Reunion in the Indian Ocean are outside the Schengen and VAT areas, but carry the euro as legal tender and are part of the EU Customs Union.

The Overseas Countries and Territories (OTCs) are a grouping of 20 territories linked to Denmark, France, the Netherlands, and the United Kingdom whose nationals are in principle EU citizens, although they are not directly subject to EU law but rather benefit from association agreements, most of which pertain to trade. Bermuda is listed in the European Community Treaty, but the arrangements for association are not applied to it because of the wishes of the government. Development assistance from the EU for the OTCs amounts to $429 million in 2008–2013. In March 2009 the Indian Ocean island of Mayotte voted to become part of France, thereby reversing its status as an overseas collectivity and effectively joining the EU.

The European Council met in emergency session February 17, 2003, to discuss the looming crisis regarding the United States and Iraq, but a deep divide separated France and Germany, which opposed military action, from the United Kingdom, Spain, and Italy, the most vocal supporters of the Bush administration's stance against the Saddam Hussein regime. French president Chirac subsequently criticized statements supporting intervention made by the eight Eastern European prospective members, plus candidate countries Romania and Bulgaria. Iraq policy remained on the agenda at the regular council session March 20–21, which also addressed progress toward achieving the Lisbon Strategy goals for economic competitiveness.

On April 25, 2003, four opponents of the month-old invasion of Iraq met to discuss defense cooperation. At that time Belgium, France, Germany, and Luxembourg decided to establish a headquarters for planning joint military operations, although some critics, especially the United Kingdom, viewed the decision as contrary to a prior pledge not to compete with NATO's collective defense mission. A compromise was reached in November, with France and Germany withdrawing their headquarters plan and the United Kingdom agreeing to formation of a joint military planning unit independent of NATO. In addition, the EU foreign ministers agreed that common consent would be required to initiate any EU peacekeeping or humanitarian mission, and then only if NATO chose not to act. At the December 2003 council summit, the defense plan received the approval of the EU leaders. In February France, Germany, and the United Kingdom announced their support for forming joint battle groups, each with 1,500 personnel, within the RRF. The first such units (the total number was subsequently set at 13) were ready for deployment in January 2007. In June 2004 the EU foreign ministers approved establishment of the European Defense Agency (EDA), with responsibilities that included improving joint defense capabilities, promoting related research and development, and advancing development of a competitive defense market within the EU. In 2005 the EDA absorbed the functions of the Western European Armaments Group (WEAG), a subsidiary body of the WEU.

Meeting in regular session on June 19–20, 2003, in Salonika, Greece, the council received a draft constitution from the Convention on the Future of Europe and assigned preparation of a final text to an IGC, which was to begin its work in October. In other business, the council indicated its willingness to aid in Iraqi reconstruction and endorsed a statement by the EU foreign ministers on the possible use of military force to prevent the spread of weapons of mass destruction (WMD). Shortly thereafter, an EU–U.S. extradition treaty was signed. The EU members retained the right to refuse extradition in death penalty cases.

When the IGC on the constitution convened in October 2003, differences over many provisions still required resolution, principal among them the makeup of the European Commission and voting procedures in the proposed Council of Ministers. The draft text called for reducing the commission to 15 members beginning in 2009, but most of the smaller member countries argued that each should continue to be represented by at least one commissioner. With regard to the Council of Ministers, the constitutional text specified a "double majority" system under which passage of a measure would require support from a majority of ministers representing, collectively, at least 60 percent of the total EU population. An EU summit December 13 failed to resolve the issues, but the attendees managed to agree on the 2007 admission of Bulgaria and Romania to the union. The meeting also accepted the Former Yugoslavian Republic of Macedonia as a candidate country.

In January 2004 the European Commission asked the ECJ to rule on the validity of a November 2003 decision by the EU finance ministers to suspend the stability and growth pact (SGP), thereby avoiding the imposition of penalties against France and Germany for failing to keep their budget deficits in check. In April 2004, with the ECJ not yet having ruled, the commission issued warnings to Greece, Italy, the Netherlands, and Portugal over their deficits. Three months later the ECJ determined that the finance ministers had exceeded their authority in suspending the SGP, but the judges also ruled they could not force the ministers to carry through on the commission's recommendations regarding sanctions. As a consequence, the issue of sanctions was thrown into the political arena, and reform of the SGP became an even more contentious issue.

The March 25–26, 2004, European Council summit was dominated by the March 11 terrorist bombings in Madrid and the subsequent election of a new Spanish government. In addition to appointing a new EU counterterrorism coordinator, the summit participants stated that they intended to act jointly, including with military force, in response to terrorist attacks, and they approved a 50-point plan of action.

In late April 2004, the justice and home affairs ministers sought consensus on another volatile issue: setting minimum standards for treating those seeking political asylum under a proposed Common European Asylum System (CEAS). The CEAS proposal was not, however, universally welcomed, with the UN's high commissioner for refugees, Ruud Lubbers, describing the plan as intended to reduce standards and to "deter or deny protection to as many people as possible."

As scheduled, the EU's enlargement from 15 to 25 members took place May 1, 2004, with the election of a new European Parliament following on June 10–13. As had been expected following the expansion, the voters returned the center-right European People's Party/European Democrats as the plurality grouping. Somewhat unexpectedly, however, the leading governing parties in 23 of the 25 member states won smaller vote shares than they had in the most recent national elections.

At a June 17–18, 2004, summit of EU leaders, a spirit of compromise resolved the remaining disputes over the text of the 350-article EU constitution, which required ratification by all 25 member countries. Predictably, the final draft was immediately attacked by both proponents of a unified Europe and those fearing the loss of national sovereignty and identity. Under the constitution, which was to supersede existing EU treaties, EU law would have primacy over national law in specified areas, when the objectives could best be achieved at the EU level. The European Council would elect an EU president for a once-renewable term of two and a half years and would also choose a minister for foreign affairs. The European Commission would retain the formula of one commissioner per state for one five-year term, after which the number of commissioners would be reduced to two-thirds the number of member states, filled by rotation. The Council of Ministers would meet in various configurations, depending on the sector involved (e.g., agriculture, transport). The European Parliament, comprising no more than 750 members (a maximum of 96 and a minimum of 6 per country), and the Council of Ministers would jointly "exercise legislative and budgetary functions." Unless otherwise specified in the constitution, European Council decisions would continue to be by consensus. In the Council of Ministers, unanimity would be required in such sensitive areas as foreign policy, defense, and tax law. Otherwise, a "double majority" QMV system would apply, generally requiring support from 55 percent of the ministers, representing at least 65 percent of the EU population.

Although the Charter of Fundamental Rights was incorporated into the constitution, its application was to be limited to matters of EU law, with the interpretation of guaranteed rights allowing for national differences based on, for example, tradition. The complete constitution also encompassed 36 protocols, including one amending the Euratom treaty, and 50 Declarations Concerning Provisions of the Constitution. Meeting October 29 in Rome, the EU heads of government and their foreign ministers signed a constitutional treaty to advance its ratification in all member countries, by referendum or legislative act, by November 2006.

Meanwhile, on July 22, 2004, the new parliament had approved the nomination of Portuguese prime minister José Manuel Barroso to serve as president of the European Commission for 2005–2010.

A November 4–5, 2004, EU summit adopted a new five-year Hague Program on freedom, justice, and security that addressed terrorism and organized crime, basic rights and citizenship, and the CEAS. The Hague Program, a follow-up to a plan that was adopted at the 1999 Tampere summit, did not, however, resolve deep divisions over the proposed common asylum plan, especially the use of extraterritorial holding centers. There also were fundamental differences over whether asylum seekers who entered the EU would be deported to the centers or whether the centers would be used only to house those who had been intercepted while in transit to EU countries.

The EU summit of December 16–17, 2004, was highlighted by the announcement that accession talks with candidate country Croatia would begin March 17, 2005, provided that the Zagreb government fully cooperated with the International Criminal Tribunal for the former Yugoslavia (ICTY) in The Hague. The summit also confirmed that accession talks with Turkey would begin on October 3, 2005, but several EU members, including France and Italy, had already indicated their likely opposition to admitting the predominantly Asian and Islamic country. Questions also persisted regarding Turkey's stance toward Cyprus and its human rights record.

On February 22, 2005, President Bush visited institutions of the EU. U.S.–European relations had been strained considerably by the U.S.-led invasion of Iraq in 2003. Moreover, U.S. administration officials had made several statements that caused some in Europe to believe that the United States was no longer supportive of an integrated Europe, especially one that took stances counter to U.S. policy. Bush's trip was widely seen as an effort to allay such concerns.

In February 2005 President Barroso announced his commission's economic program, as well as its social and environmental agenda. The economic program recommended market liberalization, deregulation, and, most controversially, extension of the single market concept to services as well as goods. The goal was to meet Lisbon Strategy targets, which projected 3 percent annual growth and the creation of 6 million new jobs during the 2005–2010 term.

At a summit March 22–23, 2005, the EU leaders focused on reforming the stability and growth pact, which had largely been disregarded since the 2002 decision of the finance ministers not to impose economic penalties on France and Germany for noncompliance. At the summit the members retained the pact's principal benchmarks—keeping national budget deficits under 3 percent of GDP and public debt to less than 60 percent of GDP—but basically exempted countries experiencing low or negative growth. They excluded from the budget ceiling expenditures for education, defense, foreign aid, and research and extended the time limits for offending countries to make the necessary adjustments. France, Germany, Italy, and Spain, each of which failed to adhere to the original criteria, were among the countries backing the revisions, which critics described as rendering the pact worthless.

On January 12, 2005, the European Parliament overwhelmingly endorsed the proposed EU constitution, although most UK, Polish, and Czech MEPs voted in opposition. On February 20 Spanish voters became the first to approve the constitution by referendum, but its prospects for union-wide ratification suffered a major blow in late May and early June when French and Dutch voters rejected the constitution by 54.7 percent and 61.5 percent, respectively. Analysts interpreted the French vote in large part as dissatisfaction with the current French government, while in the Netherlands it was a fear of a loss in national sovereignty and identity because of the rapid pace of enlargement and an influx of immigrants from the East. Despite the French and Dutch results, many supporters of the constitution urged that the ratification process continue, although the EU leaders, meeting June 16–17, instead called for a "period of reflection." While 16 countries had ratified the new constitution as of August 2007, seven other EU members postponed consideration. If, in the end, five or fewer states failed to ratify the constitution, it could be reconsidered rather than scrapped. In mid-2006, European public opinion seemed to be turning more strongly against the constitution, but its supporters inside the EU structure were still enthusiastic about keeping it alive without substantial modification. The inability of the member states to ratify the EU Constitution led to the passage of the Lisbon Treaty.

During the same period, a crisis erupted over the 2007–2013 EU budget when the United Kingdom refused to accept a reduction in its budget rebate (which was instituted in 1984 when the United Kingdom's economic position was much weaker) unless the reduction was accompanied by additional reforms, particularly with regard to CAP. In June 2003 the EU agricultural ministers approved further "decoupling" of CAP subsidies from productivity and redirected the program toward giving farmers flat payments related to rural development and environmental protection. Since then, the number of excluded or partially affected agricultural products has been reduced. Nevertheless, several EU members supported the UK argument that a continuing budgetary emphasis on agriculture was misdirected. France, the largest recipient of CAP support and a leading opponent of maintaining the UK budget rebate, disagreed. After protracted negotiations, a compromise was reached in December 2005 on the 2007–2013 EU budget. The United Kingdom agreed to give up approximately 20 percent of its rebate during the coming budget period, while the European Commission was asked to hold a "full and wide-ranging" review of all EU spending, including CAP and the UK rebate, and to draw up a report in 2008–2009. Additional substantial cuts in annual CAP subsidies are anticipated after 2013.

In February 2006 the European Parliament passed a bill authorizing an internal market for services, which, after subsequent revisions, resulted in the EU Services Directive that was adopted by the end of the year.

In another move to extend the internal market, 22 EU governments in May 2006 agreed to an informal code of conduct to open competition to nonnational EU members in the €30 billion ($38 billion) defense market. Spain, Hungary, and Denmark chose not to participate, Spain and Hungary because they thought that their own firms would not be competitive, and Denmark because it has an opt-out from EU military cooperation.

On December 21, 2007, the Schengen area of the EU, where there are no internal border posts or passport checks for EU citizens (thereby promoting the free movement of people), was expanded to include 9 of the 10 countries that joined the EU in 2004. Zone membership thereby increased to 24 of the 27 EU member states, plus non-EU members Iceland and Norway (EU members Ireland and the United Kingdom do not participate).

The new countries included the Czech Republic, Estonia, Hungary, Latvia, Lithuania, Malta, Poland, Slovakia, and Slovenia. Cyprus, which joined the EU in 2004, had not met the technical requirements to join as expected in late 2009. Bulgaria and Romania were on track in 2010 to gain Schengen membership by 2011. On December 12, 2008, Switzerland became the 25th country to join the Schengen area with the lifting of land border controls, followed by the removal of airport controls for Schengen passport holders in March 2009.

On January 1, 2007, Russia interrupted its supply of gas to the EU after a conflict with Ukraine about gas prices. Although the EU has been attempting to diversify its sources, it currently gets a quarter of its gas from Russia. Gazprom, Russia's state-controlled gas monopoly, has been unwilling to open its pipeline network to independent companies and other gas-producing states such as Kazakhstan and Turkmenistan, arguing, among other things, that the network is already stretched to capacity to meet its commitments for the next 20 years. Regular energy talks between the EU and Russia have taken place since 2000. At the October 2007 annual summit, energy discussions centered on security of supply. EU officials were hoping to resume talks concerning Russian gas supplies and opening that country's energy sector to west European investors at a conference in June 2008, although there were concerns that member EU nations had no coordinated foreign policy platform on Russia. The EU has also called for Russian membership in the WTO, despite ongoing concerns about human rights in Russia.

In another foreign policy area, members of the EU have played a central role in negotiating with Iran regarding its production of weapons-grade uranium. In June 2006, as he had in 2003, Javier Solana delivered to Iran a proposal offering a package of incentives not to produce weapons-grade material. Iran rejected the overture. Thus, in 2007 Solana and the member states continued to pressure Iran through such measures as sanctions. In May 2008 Iran presented a counter package of proposals to EU officials outlining a different strategy to address security issues regarding the spread of nuclear powers but refused to suspend its own enrichment program. Relations with Iran deteriorated in 2009. Following Iran's detention of local staff from the British embassy in Tehran, the United Kingdom requested that EU members pull out their ambassadors. Iran maintained that the EU had disqualified itself from nuclear talks because it had interfered with Iran's disputed presidential election.

In 2007, following two years of reflection generated by the French and Dutch rejection of the proposed EU Constitution, the EU formally called a halt to plans for amending the document. The European Council session in Brussels in June 2006 had proposed reaching a decision on institutional reform by the end of 2008. Further impetus toward drawing up a framework for reform emerged from the informal Berlin summit held on March 25, 2007, to mark the 50th anniversary of the signing of the Treaty of Rome. On June 23 an IGC was given a detailed mandate to draw up a new reform treaty by the end of 2007. The European Parliament and the European Commission also participated in the deliberations, leading to council approval of a treaty text on October 19. It was later signed by the heads of state or government in Lisbon on December 13.

The Lisbon Treaty, also known as the Reform Treaty, echoed many of the institutional changes proposed in the failed constitution and required ratification by all 27 EU members. It amends existing EU and EC treaties, with the EC's 1958 founding treaty being renamed the Treaty on the Functioning of the European Union. Many of the new treaty's institutional reforms echo those originally proposed in the failed constitution: the president of the European Council (now an official institution within the EU by virtue of the treaty) is to be elected for a once-renewable term of two and a half years; the European Parliament will comprise a maximum of 750 seats, with no more than 96 and no fewer than 6 per country; the number of commissioners in the European Commission will be reduced, beginning in November 2014, to two-thirds the number of member states, filled by rotation; and, in the Council of the European Union a "double majority voting" (or DMV) system (55 percent of the members, representing at least 65 percent of the EU population) will apply to most policy areas, also beginning in 2014. In addition, the selection of a commission president was to be linked to the results of parliamentary elections, and a new high representative for the union in foreign affairs and security policy was to be named, with the officeholder also serving as commission vice president. For the first time, specific provisions have been included for the withdrawal of a member state from the union.

The Reform Treaty also stipulates that legal force be given to the Charter of Fundamental Rights, which was formally signed on December 12, 2007, by the presidents of the European Council, the European Commission, and the European Parliament. However, the charter is addressed to EU institutions, bodies, and agencies, not to national governments, legislatures, or courts when they enact, implement, or interpret national laws.

The treaty gives the European Parliament greater influence over legislation, the budget, and international agreements, thereby placing it on a more equal footing with the Council of the European Union. At the same time, under the principle of subsidiarity, national parliaments should be better able to monitor the union's institutions to ensure that they act only when the policy goals are best attained at the union level. In the realm of policy, the new treaty could enhance the union's ability to act in a number of key areas, including security and justice, energy, climate change, globalization, public health, research, space, and humanitarian assistance. The treaty also includes a provision for citizens' initiatives, whereby a proposal having the support of at least 1 million citizens from a number of states can be presented to the European Commission for discussion.

On December 18, 2007, Hungary became the first member state to ratify the treaty. However, a number of setbacks delayed its passage. In March 2008 Poland's legislature postponed ratification as the main opposition party argued that the country might be forced to accept same-sex civil partnerships and that Germany might reclaim property lost after World War II. Finland, too, hesitated because of an internal legislative dispute over representation in the European Parliament. Additionally, the United Kingdom witnessed a legal challenge over whether ratification had to be put to a public referendum. This challenge ultimately proved unsuccessful. Conservative Czech parliamentarians, meanwhile, asked for their supreme court to rule on whether multiple provisions within the treaty were compatible with the country's constitution. All four countries eventually accepted the treaty.

Of all the countries considering ratification, only Ireland was constitutionally required to put the Lisbon Treaty to a referendum. Irish activists campaigned hard against the treaty ahead of polling on June 12, 2008, when 53.4 percent of Irish voters rejected it, preventing its ratification. EU leaders were thus thrust into a crisis over how to proceed. Meanwhile, the Polish and Czech presidents refused to ratify the treaty before an Irish approval, and Germany's ratification was slowed by a constitutional court case assessing the treaty's compatibility with domestic law.

EU policy supports gradual and carefully managed enlargement. However, debate continues over how large the EU should become and whether prospective nations should reflect core European values. The classification of Turkey as a candidate country has been particularly controversial because of issues such as immigration, political Islam, human rights standards, and its shared border with Iraq and Syria. Although Turkey has a small piece of territory in continental Europe, many argue that it belongs to Asia Minor.

Turkey first applied for membership in 1987 (at that time to the EEC). The European Council finally accepted its eligibility in 1997. Accession talks began in 2005, and as of mid-2010 only 1 of the 35 chapters, or policy areas, had been provisionally closed, with Turkey meeting conditions concerning science and research. Another 18 chapters have been opened, but the process has been stymied by Turkey's refusal to open ports to Greek Cypriot ships and planes as well as the continued objections of France.

Turkey's prospects have been dimmed by slow progress on political reforms and by the growing political influence of far-right and anti-immigrant parties in the European Parliament after the elections in

June 2009. The country is not expected to satisfy all qualifications for membership within the decade. Given this outlook, there has been discussion about granting Turkey and other aspiring countries a special EU partnership that would be short of membership. Turkey has rebuffed alternatives to full integration.

In 2004 an EU Neighborhood Policy plan was launched with the aim of giving countries immediately bordering Europe by land or sea intermediary levels of EU benefits following bilateral agreements on action plans for political and economic reforms. Agreements were signed in 2005 with Israel, Jordan, Moldova, Morocco, the Palestinian Authority, Tunisia, and Ukraine; in 2006 with Armenia, Azerbaijan, and Georgia; and in 2007 with Egypt and Lebanon. Other countries reportedly on the list but without agreed-upon action plans as of late 2009 included Algeria, Belarus, Libya, and Syria. A progress report filed by the commission in April 2009 enunciated the difficulties of advancing the program because of the recent violent conflicts in Georgia and in Gaza, the slow pace of democratic reforms, and the global financial crisis, among other stated reasons.

Other partnerships with EU's surrounding countries also have been advanced in recent years. The Union for the Mediterranean, formerly known as the Barcelona Process, was launched in July 2008 between the EU and 16 countries in the southern Mediterranean and Middle East and identified priority projects, including ridding pollution from the Mediterranean. Additionally, on May 8, 2009, in Prague, the EU launched an Eastern Partnership initiative with post-Soviet states to "accelerate political association and further economic integration" with the EU but without the prospect of eventual EU membership. Signatories included the EU along with Armenia, Azerbaijan, Belarus, Georgia, Moldova, and Ukraine. The initiative will establish free trade areas and offer EU economic aid, technical expertise, and security consultations in exchange for obligations by the six former Soviet states to commit to democracy, the rule of law, and human rights policies. Russia accused the EU of carving out a new sphere of influence.

In late 2007 Bosnia and Herzegovina signed stabilization and association agreements with the EU, a first step toward membership, while Serbia's stalled talks resumed after it agreed to arrest and extradite remaining fugitives wanted by the war crimes tribunal. Meanwhile, the EU council in February 2008 launched a crisis management mission to the newly declared country of Kosovo. The EU Rule of Law Mission in Kosovo is charged with assisting in the formation of "independent and multiethnic" law enforcement and judicial systems. Kosovo signed a pre-accession assistance agreement in May that provided $83 million for infrastructure and financial stabilization projects, although its future membership was considered uncertain given that four EU countries that would have to ratify its accession had not recognized Kosovo as an independent state. Additionally, in July 2009 the EC recommended visa-free access for Macedonians, although no date had been set for EU membership talks because of election violence and widespread corruption.

Croatian accession negotiations were slowed in 2008 by Slovenia's veto of accession talks as a result of a long-standing border dispute. Talks resumed in September 2009 following Slovenia's agreement to handle the dispute separately. Montenegro submitted an application in December 2008, followed by Albania in April 2009.

At an EU summit in Brussels on March 13–14, 2008, an agreement was reached on greenhouse gas emissions and renewable energy to meet targets for a 20 percent reduction in emissions by 2020. The plan was approved by the European Parliament on December 17 despite objections by eastern European countries that the measures would raise energy costs and be overly burdensome during an economic recession. Nevertheless, the plan gave each nation and sector mandated emission limits, while creating an auction system on emissions from industrial sources (currently free of charge) beginning in 2013, and set 20 percent targets for better energy efficiency and renewables in the EU's energy mix.

In one of the first concrete signs of defense cooperation between EU member states, the EU announced plans in November 2008 to build a pan-European military aircraft transport fleet. Expected to be operational within a decade, the European Air Transport Fleet would be housed by member nations and made available for humanitarian and peacekeeping missions.

In November 2008 the EU officially slipped into economic recession, its first since the creation of the eurozone in 1999. The downturn quickly became the single greatest challenge facing the union, with the Baltic states, Spain, and the United Kingdom especially exposed by inflated real estate markets. Countries with large current account deficits, notably Greece and Hungary, also suffered. Germany's economy also declined because of its heavy reliance on exports.

In response, EU institutions took unprecedented actions to salvage the block's financial industries. Initially injecting $270 billion into the EU banking system in August 2007, efforts were doubled a year later. Throughout the fall of 2008 and into 2009, the European Central Bank repeatedly cut interest rates in coordination with the central banks of member countries and the U.S. Federal Reserve. It also was announced that members that breached the budget deficit threshold of 3 percent of GDP would be given time to bring their spending in line before penalties would be imposed.

Meanwhile, in October and December 2008 the EU took directed action with the International Monetary Fund (IMF) and World Bank to assist Hungary and Latvia, whose currencies had dramatically depreciated. In November the EC outlined a $257 billion stimulus package for member states, equivalent to approximately 1.5 percent of the EU's GDP, to be drawn from member governments and from within EU budgets. The stimulus plan was passed in December and was viewed with skepticism, particularly by Germany, which resisted a return to large-scale deficit spending after having made painful strides in recent years to balance its own budget. Other analysts said the plan's combination of tax cuts and accelerated regional spending was not sufficiently targeted to provide immediate relief.

In March 2009 EU leaders, led by Germany, rejected a proposal for a special aid package to non-eurozone countries, although Hungary warned of a new "Iron Curtain" descending. However, soon after, at a leadership summit in Brussels, assistance available to non-eurozone countries was doubled to $68 billion, and a $5 billion stimulus measure was directed toward green technology and digital communication projects. EU leaders rejected pressure from the United States to raise the size of their economic stimulus plans in favor of restraining budget deficits. Following the collapse of Iceland's banking industry, Iceland's parliament (*Althing*) narrowly voted in July 2009 to apply for EU membership in the hopes of achieving lasting economic stability. The decision was received warmly by EU leaders, although Iceland's entry was not assured because of likely differences over EU quotas that could affect its fish industry. The Netherlands and the UK also were said to be ready to veto Iceland's accession unless Iceland paid compensation for their citizens who had lost money in the collapse of the online bank Icesave.

A cornerstone of the EU response to the recession has been to impose stricter regulation on financial markets. In February and March 2009 the EU announced new regulatory requirements for credit-rating agencies and additional oversight over hedge funds. Additionally, in September the EU called for limits on executive bonuses as part of G-20 discussions on an overhaul of the global financial system.

The June 4–7, 2009, parliamentary election ushered in a smaller body dominated by center-right groups. The size of parliament decreased from a record of 785 members to 736, while center-left parties failed to articulate a socialist response to the ongoing economic recession. Populist parties and some environmental formations made some inroads, while in Hungary the far-right nationalist Jobbik party took third place. The election registered a new low in voter turnout at 43 percent, with central and eastern European countries displaying the most voter apathy. The resulting body split into a number of new formations. The largest remained the European People's Party, which dropped the suffix "European Democrats" after a 54-strong contingent led by the UK Conservatives dropped out and formed the European Conservatives and Reformists Group. The Party of European Socialists changed its name to Progressive Alliance of Socialists and Democrats to signify that it was not a rigidly socialist formation.

Following the election an EU summit in Brussels on June 18–19 resulted in a package of legal guarantees addressing policy areas important to Ireland to safeguard against a second Irish refusal of the Lisbon Treaty in a referendum to be held in October. Additionally, countries agreed to establish a "European system of financial supervisors" by 2010 that would consist of three new authorities with oversight powers of the banking, insurance, and securities sectors. The agreement represented a compromise solution between a contingent led by France that called for much stricter regulation over the financial industry and the United Kingdom, which worried that additional supervision would drive companies out of the country.

Meanwhile, in July 2009 four EU countries (Austria, Bulgaria, Romania, and Hungary) completed a deal with Turkey to cede territory for the construction of the Nabucco pipeline to bring stable gas supplies from the Caspian Sea to Europe, but the source of the supplies was not assured as Azerbaijan refused to commit its gas reserves to Europe, instead cooperating with Russia in building a rival pipeline. Repeated disruptions in winter deliveries of Russian gas to EU countries, the result of Russian disputes with Ukraine, have intensified the EU's efforts to find an alternative supplier to Russia, which currently provides one-quarter of the EU's gas supplies.

On September 16, 2009, Barroso was reelected to a second five-year term of office with the unanimous support of all members and no opposing candidate. However, he faced criticism for favoring large member states, such as Germany, France, and the United Kingdom.

At an earlier EU summit on June 18–19, 2009, the European Council approved a set of "legal guarantees" pertaining to the Lisbon Treaty that affirmed that Irish policies on taxation, abortion, education, family, workers' rights, and military neutrality would be addressed to "the mutual satisfaction of Ireland and the other member states." Upon the insistence of Ireland, the measures were to become protocol, meaning they would be incorporated into EU treaties, although several EU countries were uneasy about the designation because it would need to be ratified by all EU national parliaments. However, it was agreed this would be done as part of the next accession agreement, expected upon Croatian membership in 2011.

Irish voters approved the treaty by 67 percent in a referendum on October 2, 2009, thereby removing the last major hurdle to the treaty's implementation. Despite the strong margin of victory, analysts attributed the treaty's passage to Irish economic despair and fear over losing ties to the EU rather than genuine enthusiasm for the treaty. The president of the Czech Republic, Václav Klaus, ratified the treaty on November 23 following the resolution of legal questions surrounding its compatibility with the Czech constitution. Poland's president Lech Kaczyński had signed the treaty on October 10. Polish and Czech ratification allowed for implementation of the treaty on December 1, 2009, which began with the appointment of the Belgian prime minister Herman Van Rompuy as the permanent president of the European Council for a term of two and a half years and with the selection of Catherine Ashton of the UK Labour Party as the high representative for foreign affairs.

Most of 2010 was dominated by an ongoing crisis involving the sovereign debt of several eurozone countries with weak economies, and with related speculative runs on the euro. Greece and Ireland both came close to default, Greece between February and May, Ireland in October and November. Both countries required support from the entire EU community and the IMF (see separate entry). Severe austerity measures and riots ensued in both countries. Italy, Spain, and Portugal were also mentioned as likely to have economic problems. Some commentators went as far as to wonder if the euro could survive in its present form. Significant German money went into the Greek bailout, causing the German public's dissatisfaction with the EU and with the euro to rise. The non-eurozone UK, the majority of whose citizens already dislike the EU, also contributed to the rescue of Ireland.

An October 2010 Council summit set in place stringent new rules designed to protect the euro. A rainy-day fund was proposed to protect the euro in times of crisis. The EU budget was to increase by only 2.9 percent annually. A serious disagreement ensued in November with the parliament, which wanted a 6 percent increase. Failing resolution, the 2011 budget would remain at 2010 levels.

On June 17, 2010, the European Council decided to open accession talks with Iceland. Icelandic membership would give the EU more standing in future negotiations concerning the Arctic. Formal negotiations began in July 2011. In October 2010 Serbia's application was seen as back on track, since it had given up its demand that the EU consider Kosovo as part of Serbian territory. Montenegro was also progressing toward membership. Meanwhile in June 2011 the EU finalized negotiations with Croatia on membership and announced in September that the nation would join the EU on July 1, 2013.

On January 31, 2011, the EU imposed a series of sanctions on Belarus following government repression of protests in the aftermath of disputed presidential balloting (see entry on Belarus). In recognition of Myanmar's elections in November 2010, the EU in April 2011 suspended a series of sanctions against figures in the new government (see entry on Myanmar).

In January 2011 Estonia joined the euro zone. The following month, in response to continuing concerns over the debt crisis in Greece, Ireland, Portugal and Spain, the euro zone leaders agree to establish a €500 billion emergency fund, the European Stabilization Mechanism. In May Portugal became the next European nation to request EU financial assistance. A €78 billion rescue package was subsequently negotiated. Meanwhile, a second, €109 billion package was finalized for Greece. Both Spain and Italy had to adopt austerity budgets to contain spiraling debt costs. In December EU leaders launched talks on a new fiscal policy treaty designed to prevent excessive debts and deficits among the 27 members of the Union. However, Hungary and the United Kingdom objected to constraints that the agreement would place on national governments and subsequent negotiations centered on the 17 members of the Eurozone. The remaining 25 members of the EU, including the 17 members of the Eurozone, agreed to a Treaty on Stability, Coordination, and Governance in the Economic and Monetary Union at a special summit held in Brussels in January 2012. The treaty accomplished the goals of the proposed treaty from December 2011 that had been rejected by the UK. The treaty was fully ratified by all of the member states by December 12, 2012, and entered into effect on January 1, 2013.

By February the situation in Greece had further deteriorated to the point that the EU and IMF (see separate entry under UN Specialized Agencies) agreed to a second bailout of the Greek economy for a total of €230 billion. This deal, even larger than the first one, was designed to reduce Greece's national debt from 160 percent of the GDP to 120 percent by 2020. The bailout agreement called on Greece to accept a permanent representative from the troika—the EU, IMF, and ECB—and make additional budget and spending cuts of €3.3 billion. The austerity measure passed the Greek legislature after heated debate, but resulted in wide spread anger and mass resignations from within the government, as many Greek citizens and officials claimed that the EU and IMF had treated them too harshly.

As the EU remained focused on the debt crisis, the European Parliament issued a February green paper that called on the EU member states to approve the creation and sale of Eurobonds. The European Economic and Social Committee echoed this sentiment during a June 2012 meeting. One of the biggest supporters of the Eurobond position was the new French president François Hollande of the French Socialist Party, while German chancellor Angela Merkel remained the largest opponent of the position. Merkel remained committed to her position that austerity measures are the only way to safely handle the crisis.

French and Greek elections held in May both resulted in the election of anti-bailout opposition parties within each state. This proved to further complicate matters in reaching a comprehensive debt reduction solution at a special May meeting of the European Commission. Hollande called for a renegotiation of the January 2012 EMU treaty. Furthermore, the party change in Greece resulted in some discussion at the May commission meeting of possibly removing Greece from the Eurozone if the new leaders did not soon implement the already approved austerity measures.

Further signaling an economic spiral downward, Spain requested a bank bailout of its own in May 2012, amounting to the sum of €100 billion. Like the other countries that have received a bailout, Spain was expected to implement a series of austerity measures that involve reducing debt, cutting spending, and increasing revenue. Also, the European Financial Stability Facility (EFSF), a fund created by the January EMU treaty to assist with the economic bailout, was given the authority to purchase Spanish bonds as a means of reducing debt. Spain became the fourth Eurozone country to accept a bailout of its banking industry. The bailout was finalized in July 2012.

At a June 2012 meeting of the European Council, the heads of state and government agreed to a new plan to help combat the debt crisis—the Compact on Growth and Jobs. The new agreement aims to ease the crisis by reinvigorating the economy, deepening its commitments to overall job creation, and working to increase Europe's competitiveness in the global market. The council also approved a series of member-specific recommendations for debt reduction and improvements in financial security. The council also discussed ways to save the EMU and prevent the total collapse of the Eurozone. A full report is expected in the fall.

On a slightly different note, the May 2012 plenary session of the European Parliament resulted in the passage of a new Financial Transaction Tax (FTT) that would apply to all security and stock transactions. The new tax has been the topic of legislative discussions since early 2011, but was tabled in a late-2011 session. The bill creating the FTT also placed a series of preventative measures to curtail tax evasion.

In November the EU and 10 Latin American states signed an agreement ending their dispute over bananas. The agreement lowered the EU's import tariff on bananas and established annual maximum tariff rates until 2017. The banana dispute, settled within the WTO framework, had been ongoing since 1992.

In December the European Council approved a new initiative designed to streamline innovation in Europe with the creation of a unitary patent. The new EU patent will be accepted in all EU member states, will be more cost efficient and easier, and will be obtained through the European Patent Office in Munich. Also at the meeting, the Council approved its roadmap agreement for the completion of the Economic and Monetary Union. The roadmap calls for immediate action concerning the completion, strengthening, and implementation of enhanced economic governance and the adoption of the Single Supervisory Mechanism on banking. The roadmap also called for further mechanisms to be put in place by the end of 2013.

On December 10, 2012, the European Union was awarded the Nobel Peace Prize for its role in advancing security and reconciliation in Europe.

In February the United States and European Union announced that they were beginning discussions to negotiate a bilateral trade agreement between the two parties. The agreement will have three main components: market access; regulatory issues and non-tariff barriers; and rules, principles, and new modes of cooperation to address shared global trade challenges and opportunities. Transatlantic trade currently amounts for 47 percent of the world GDP. The trade deal could yield annual GDP increases of 0.5 percent for the EU and 0.4 percent for the United States. At the G-8 meeting in May, UK prime minister David Cameron hailed this as the "biggest bilateral trade deal in history, a deal that will have greater impact than all the other trade deals on the table put together."

In March the EU announced negotiations of a new Free Trade agreement between the two parties. Official negotiations began in April.

In June the European Commission approved Latvia's entry into the Eurozone. Having achieved high levels of sustainable economic convergence with the euro area, Latvia will officially enter the Eurozone and make the Euro its official currency effective January 1, 2014.

At a meeting of the European Council in late June, the Council took further measures to advance the completion of the EMU. The council adopted country-specific recommendations concerning policy changes and approved the multiannual financial framework for 2014–2020. The MFF will guide the EU's budgetary and spending process until 2020 by representing its political priorities with financial backing. The meeting also saw a decision concerning the troubling situation with youth unemployment. The Council encouraged the creation of new programs to promote employment and authorized the January 1, 2014, implementation of the Youth Employment Initiative (YEI). The YEI will provide economic assistance to states with higher than 25 percent unemployment in their youth sector.

On July 1, 2013, Croatia became the 28th member of the European Union after a decade-long accession process. Croatia voted on its 12 European Parliament members in April, who took their seats at the July plenary session of the EP.

Later in July, the European Commission proposed the creation of a European Public Prosecutor's Office. According to Commission President Barroso, the new position will build upon the EU's "commitment to upholding the rule of law; it will decisively enhance the protection of taxpayers' money and the effective tackling of fraud involving EU funds." According to the EU Website, "The European Public Prosecutor's Office will make sure that every case involving suspected fraud against the EU budget is followed up and completed, so that criminals know they will be prosecuted and brought to justice."

In November 2013 the EU agreed to a series of association agreements with Ukraine, Georgia, and Moldova. The agreements will create a "deep and comprehensive" FTA between the union and the three countries. The agreements are designed to improve the economic situation in these Eastern European states and strengthen relations between the union and its neighbors. (For more on activities since 2013, see Recent activities, below.)

Structure. The Treaty on European Union established two new pillars—a common foreign and security policy (CFSP), and justice and home affairs (JHA)—while also amending, but not superseding, EC treaties. Accordingly, the EC continues as the EU's first pillar—the "community domain" of common policies and laws decided by the "community method," involving the European Commission and two legislative organs, the Council of the European Union and the European Parliament. In reaching decisions involving the community domain, the Council of the European Union usually uses a QMV system. In contrast, decisions involving the second and third pillars are usually made by unanimous vote of the Council of the European Union, although the Treaty of Amsterdam provided for use of QMV in some areas not involving the military or defense. The Treaty of Amsterdam also renamed the JHA pillar as the Police and Judicial Cooperation in Criminal Matters (PJCC) and transferred some of that pillar's original tasks to the EC.

The EU founding treaty authorized the European Council (comprising the heads of state or government of the member states) to "provide the Union with the necessary impetus for its development" and to "define the general political guidelines" for the grouping. The council typically meets four times a year, chaired by the head of state or government of the member state holding its presidency. The remaining institutional framework of the EU has the same basic components as those originally allotted to the individual communities: the Council of the European Union (originally called the Council of Ministers) to provide overall direction and to legislate, the representative European Parliament with colegislative responsibilities, the executive and administrative European Commission charged with the initiation and implementation of EU policies, and the Court of Justice to adjudicate legal issues. A Court of Auditors was added in 1977.

Depending on the subject under discussion, EU states can be represented on the Council of the European Union by their foreign ministers, as is usually the case for major decisions, or by other ministers. As a result of the Luxembourg compromise in 1966, the principle of unanimity is retained for issues in which a member feels it has a "vital interest." However, changes approved in 1987 reduced the number of areas subject to such veto, the use of QMV in the council being increased to speed up integration efforts. The distribution of votes is as follows: France, Germany, Italy, and the United Kingdom, 29 each; Poland and Spain, 27 each; Romania, 14; Netherlands, 13; Belgium, the Czech Republic, Greece, Hungary, and Portugal, 12 each; Austria, Bulgaria, and Sweden, 10 each; Denmark, Finland, Ireland, Lithuania, and Slovakia, 7 each; Cyprus, Estonia, Latvia, Luxembourg, and Slovenia, 4 each; and Malta, 3. Under QMV, passage of a proposal typically requires 255 of the 345 votes (73.9 percent), representing a majority of the member states. If challenged, however, those in the majority must demonstrate that they collectively represent at least 62 percent of the total EU population.

The Maastricht Treaty altered the required makeup of the European Commission and the method of its selection, eliminating country representation, per se, and stipulating only that the commission must include at least one and no more than two individuals from each EU state. However, the 20-member commission that took office in January 1995 preserved the established distribution of two members from each of the "big five" (France, Germany, Italy, Spain, and the United Kingdom) and one each from the smaller states. In November 2004 the commission was expanded to 25 members, one from each state, after a six-month period in which interim commissioners from the ten new states worked alongside those who were serving out their five-year terms. In a complicated selection process, the member states first nominate a commission president and then, in consultation with that person, nominate the full commission. Beginning with the 2014 election cycle, the nominee for president must be representative of the political party representation in the European Parliament. The president and the rest of the commission are subject to confirmation (or possible rejection) by the European Parliament and final appointment "by common accord" of the member states. In general, the commission mediates among the member governments in community matters, exercises a broad range of executive powers, and initiates community action. Its members are completely independent and are forbidden by treaty to accept instructions from any national government. Decisions are made by majority vote, although in practice most are adopted by consensus.

In 2007 the commission was expanded to 27, one commission member from each of the member states. Below is a list of its members and the principal subject or subjects of their portfolios. A 28th commissioner was added in July 2013 upon Croatia's accession to the EU.

President	Jean Claude Juncker (Luxembourg)
First Vice President, Better Relations, Interinstitutional Relations, Rule of Law and the Charter of Fundamental Rights	Frans Timmermans (Netherlands)
Vice President, Budget and Human Resources	Kristalina Georgieva [f] (Bulgaria)
Vice President, Digital Single Market	Andrus Ansip (Estonia)
Vice President, Energy Union	Maroš Šefčovič (Slovakia)
Vice President, Euro and Social Dialogue; Financial Stability, Financial Services, and Capital Markets Union (acting)	Valdis Dombrovskis (Latvia)

Vice President, High Representative of the Union for Foreign Affairs and Security Policy	Frederica Mogherini [f] (Italy)
Vice President, Jobs, Growth, Investment, and Competitiveness	Jyrki Katainen (Finland)
Agriculture and Rural Development	Phil Hogan (Ireland)
Climate Action and Energy	Miguel Arias Cañete (Spain)
Competition	Margrethe Vestager [f] (Denmark)
Digital Economy and Society	Günter Oettinger (Germany)
Economic and Financial Affairs, Taxation, and Customs	Pierre Moscovici (France)
Education, Culture, Youth, and Sport	Tibor Navracsics (Hungary)
Employment, Social Affairs, Skills and Labor Mobility	Marianne Thyssen [f] (Belgium)
Environment, Maritime Affairs, and Fisheries	Karmenu Vella (Malta)
European Neighborhood Policy and Enlargement Negotiations	Johannes Hahn (Austria)
Health and Food Safety	Vytenis Andriukaitis (Lithuania)
Humanitarian Aid and Crisis Management	Christos Stylianides (Cyprus)
Internal Market, Industry, Entrepreneurship, and SMEs	Elżbieta Bieńkowska [f] (Poland)
International Cooperation and Development	Neven Mimica (Croatia)
Justice, Consumers, and Gender Equity	Věra Jourová [f] (Czech Republic)
Migration, Home Affairs, and Citizenship	Dimitris Avrampoulos (Greece)
Regional Policy	Corina Crețu [f] (Romania)
Research, Science, and Innovation	Carlos Moedas (Portugal)
Trade	Cecilia Malmström [f] (Sweden)
Transport	Violeta Bulc [f] (Slovenia)

[f] = female

The European Parliament is an outgrowth of the consultative parliamentary assembly established for the ECSC and subsequently mandated to serve in the same capacity for the EEC and Euratom. The parliament's authority has gradually increased over its history, but has remained quite limited relative to other EU organs. Many initiatives that would emanate from a national parliament instead emanate, in the case of the EU, from the European Commission and its professionals in the commission's directorates general in Brussels.

Under a 1975 treaty the parliament was empowered to participate in formulation of the annual EC budget and even reject it by a two-thirds vote—save for deference to the Council of Ministers regarding agricultural spending, the largest item in the community's budget. The Single European Act, the Treaty on European Union, and the Treaty of Amsterdam further extended parliament's budgetary powers and legislative purview. In addition, the parliament, previously only authorized to dismiss the entire commission (but not individual members) by a vote of censure, can now reject nominees for individual posts. The parliament, which meets annually (normally in Strasbourg, France) and has a five-year term, must also approve EU treaties, as well as the admission of new EU members. (The Reform Treaty further increases the parliament's powers.)

The move to direct elections in all member states in 1979 was followed by the Maastricht Treaty's direction that the parliament should draw up plans for future elections to take place under uniform voting procedures and constituency arrangements. Some progress was made in this regard for the 1994 elections, notably in that for the first time all EU citizens could vote in their EU country of residence.

Under the Treaty of Nice, as amended after the accession treaties with Bulgaria and Romania, the number of members of parliament reduced from 785 to 736 for the 2009–2014 parliamentary term. With the accession of Croatia in 2013, the number of MPs was raised to 751 for the 2014–2019 parliamentary term.

Additionally, following the 2009 parliamentary election, all political groups in the European Parliament must include members from at least seven member states with a minimum of 25 members. The statute of members, which was adopted in 2005, entered into force on the first day of the new term on July 14, 2009, and made the terms of conditions of a member's work more transparent and introduced a common salary for all members.

The most recent election was held May 22–25, 2014, and membership was allocated as follows: Austria, 18; Belgium, 21; Bulgaria, 17; Croatia, 11; Cyprus, 6; the Czech Republic, 21; Denmark, 13; Estonia, 6; Finland, 13; France, 74; Germany, 95; Greece, 21; Hungary, 21; Ireland, 11; Italy, 73; Latvia, 8; Lithuania, 11; Luxembourg, 6; Malta, 6; Netherlands, 26; Poland, 51; Portugal, 21; Romania, 32; Slovakia, 13; Slovenia, 8; Spain, 54; Sweden, 20; United Kingdom, 71. Members sit not by nationality, but by political affiliation. As of November 2016, the makeup of the political groups was as follows:

European People's Party (EPP), 216

Austria	Austrian People's Party (ÖVP), 5
Belgium	Christian Democratic and Flemish (CD&V), 2
	Christian Social Party–*Europäische Volkspartei* (CSP-EVP), 1
	Democratic Humanist Center (CDH), 1
Bulgaria	Citizens for European Development of Bulgaria (GERB), 6
	Democrats for Strong Bulgaria (BG), 1
Croatia	Croatian Democratic Union (HDZ), 5
	The Croatian Peasant Party (HSS), 1
Cyprus	Democratic Rally (DISY), 1
Czech Republic	Top 09 (TOP09), 4
	Christian and Democratic Union–Czech People's Party (KDU-ČSL), 3
	Mayors and Independents (STAN), 1
Denmark	Conservative People's Party (C), 1
Estonia	Fatherland Union (IRL), 1
Finland	National Coalition Party (KOK), 3
France	The Republicans (LR), 20
Germany	Christian Democratic Union (CDU), 29
	Christian Social Union (CSU), 5
Greece	New Democracy (ND), 5
Hungary	Federation of Young Democrats–Christian Democratic People's Party (FiDeSz-KDNP), 12
Ireland	*Fine Gael* (FG), 4
Italy	Brothers of Italy (FI), 12
	The New Center-Right—Union of the Center (CN), 2
	South Tyrolean People's Party (SVP), 1
Latvia	Unity (V), 4
Lithuania	Homeland Union Christian Democrats (TS-LKDP), 2
	Independent, 1
Luxembourg	Christian Social People's Party (CSV), 3
Malta	Nationalist Party (PN), 3
Netherlands	Christian Democratic Appeal (CDA), 5
Poland	Civic Platform (PO), 19
	Polish People's Party (PSL), 4
Portugal	Social Democratic Party (PSD), 6
	Popular Party (PP), 1
Romania	National Liberal Party (PNL), 8
	Hungarian Democratic Union of Romania (UDMR), 2
	Independents, 1
	People's Movement Party (PMP), 1
Slovakia	Christian Democratic Movement (KDH), 2
	Slovak Democratic and Christian Union (SDKÚ-DS), 2
	Most–Híd, 1
	Party of the Hungarian Coalition (SMK), 1
Slovenia	Slovenian Democratic Party (SDS), 3
	New Slovenia–Christian People's Party (NSi), 2
Spain	Popular Party (PP), 16
	Democratic Union of Catalonia (UDC), 1
Sweden	Moderate Coalition Party (MSP), 3
	Christian Democratic Party (KD), 1

Progressive Alliance of Socialists and Democrats (S&D), 187

Austria	Austrian Social Democratic Party (SPÖ), 5
Belgium	Socialist Party (PS), 3
	Socialist Party–Differently (SP.A), 1
Bulgaria	Coalition for Bulgaria (BSP), 4
Croatia	Social Democratic Party of Croatia (SDP), 2
Cyprus	Democratic Party (DP), 1
	Movement of Social Democrats EDEK (KS), 1
Czech Republic	Czech Social Democratic Party (ČSSD), 4
Denmark	Social Democratic Party (A), 3
Estonia	Social Democratic Party (SDE), 1
Finland	Finnish Social Democratic Party (SSDP), 2
France	Socialist Party (PS), 13
Germany	Social Democratic Party of Germany (SPD), 26
Greece	Olive Tree—Democratic Alliance, 2
	The River, 2
Hungary	Democratic Coalition (DK), 2
	Hungarian Socialist Party (MSzP), 2
Ireland	Independent, 1
Italy	Democratic Party (PD), 30
Latvia	Social Democratic Party "Harmony" (SDPS), 1
Lithuania	Lithuanian Social Democratic Party (LSDP), 2
Luxembourg	Socialist Workers' Party of Luxembourg (LSAP), 1
Malta	Malta Labour Party (MLP), 3
Netherlands	Labor Party (PvdA), 3
Poland	Democratic Left Alliance (SLD), 3
	Labor United (UP), 1
	Nonpartisan, 1
Portugal	Portuguese Socialist Party (PSP), 8
Romania	Party of Social Democrats (PSD), 16
	Humanist Power Party (PPU), 1
	National Union for the Progress of Romania (UNPR), 1
Slovakia	Direction (*Směr*), 4
Slovenia	Social Democrats (SDS), 1
Spain	Spanish Socialist Workers' Party (PSOE), 14
Sweden	Social Democrats (S), 5
	Feminist Initiative (FI), 1
United Kingdom	Labour Party, 19

European Conservatives and Reformists (ECR), 73

Belgium	New Flemish Alliance (NVA), 4
Bulgaria	Bulgaria Without Censorship (BSP), 1
	Bulgarian National Movement (IMRO), 1
Croatia	Croatian Conservative Party (HKS), 1
Cyprus	Independent, 1
Czech Republic	Civic Democratic Party (ODS), 2
Denmark	Danish People's Party (DF), 3
	Independent, 1
Finland	Finns Party (PS), 2
Germany	Alliance for Progress and Renewal (ALFA), 5
	Family Party of Germany (FPD), 1
Greece	Independent, 1
Ireland	*Fiana Fáil* Party (FF), 1
Italy	Conservatives and Reformists (CR), 2
Latvia	For Fatherland and Freedom–LNKK (TB-LNNK), 1
Lithuania	Electoral Action of Poles in Lithuania (AWPL), 1
Netherlands	Christian Union (CU), 1
	Political Reformed Party (SGP), 1
Poland	Law and Justice (PiS), 16
	Independent Candidate, 2
	Nonparty Bloc in Support of Reform (BBWR), 1
Slovakia	Freedom and Solidarity (SaS), 1
	New Majority (Nova), 1
	Ordinary People and Independent Personalities (OL'aNO), 1
United Kingdom	Conservative Party (Cons.), 19
	Ulster Conservatives and Unionists (UUP), 1

Alliance of Liberals and Democrats for Europe (ALDE), 69

Austria	The New Austria (NEOS), 1
Belgium	Flemish Liberals and Democrats (OPEN-VLD), 3
	Reformist Movement (MR), 3
Bulgaria	Movement for Rights and Freedoms (DPS), 4
Croatia	Croatian People's Party-Liberal Democrats (HNS), 1
	Istrian Democratic Parliament (IDS), 1
Denmark	Liberal Party (V), 2
	The Radical Left (DRV), 1
Estonia	Estonian Reform Party (ER), 2
	Estonian Center Party, 1
Finland	Finnish Center (*Kesk*), 3
	Swedish People's Party of Finland (SF), 1
France	Democratic Movement (MoDem), 4
	Generation Citizens (GC), 1
	Radical Party (Rad.), 1
	Union of Democrats and Independents (UDI), 1
Germany	Free Democratic Party (FDP), 3
	Freie Wähler (FW), 1
Ireland	Independent, 1
Latvia	Union of Greens and Farmers (ZZS), 1
Lithuania	Darbo Party (DP), 2
	Lithuanian Republican Liberals (LRLS), 1
Luxembourg	Democratic Party (DP), 1
Netherlands	Democrats 66 (D66), 4
	People's Party for Freedom and Democracy (VVD), 3
Portugal	Land Party (MTP), 1
	Republican Democratic Party (PDR), 1
Romania	Independent, 3
Slovenia	Democratic Party of Pensioners of Slovenia (DeSUS), 1
Spain	Democracy and Progress Union (UYPD), 2
	Independent, 2Basque Nationalist Party (PNV), 1
	Citizenship Party (C's), 2
	Democratic Convergence of Catalonia (CDC), 1
Sweden	Liberal People's Party (FP), 2
	Center Party (CP), 1
United Kingdom	Liberal Democrats (LD), 1

European United Left/Nordic Green Left (GUE/NGL), 52

Cyprus	Progressive Party of the Working People (AKEL), 2
Czech Republic	Communist Party of Bohemia and Moravia (KSČM), 3
Denmark	People's Movement against the European Union (FmEU), 1
France	Left Front (FG), 3
	Alliance of the Overseas (AOM), 1
Germany	The Left, 7
	Independent, 1
Greece	Coalition of the Radical Left (SYRIZA), 4
	Independent, 1
	Popular Unity (LAE), 1
Ireland	*Sinn Féin,* 3
	Independent Candidate, 1
Italy	The Other Europe (LAE-CT), 2
	Independent, 1
Netherlands	Socialist Party (SP), 2
	Party for the Animals (PVVD), 1
Portugal	Portuguese Communist Party (PCP), 3
	Left Block (BE), 1
Spain	Podemos, 5
	United Left, (IU), 4
	EH Bildu, 1
	Galician Alternative of the Left (AGE), 1
Sweden	Left Party (Vp), 1
United Kingdom	*Sinn Féin,* 1

Group of the Greens/European Free Alliance, 50

Austria	The Greens, 3
Belgium	Ecologists (ECOLO), 1
	Green!, 1

Croatia	Independent, 1
Denmark	Socialist People's Party (SF), 1
Estonia	Independent, 1
Finland	Green League (*Vihr*), 1
France	Europe Écologie, 6
Germany	Alliance '90–The Greens, 11
	Ecological Democratic Party (ODP), 1
	The Pirate Party, 1
Hungary	Dialogue for Hungary (PM), 1
	Politics Can Be Different (LMP), 1
Latvia	Latvian Russian Union, 1
Lithuania	Lithuanian Peasant and Greens Union (LVZS), 1
Luxembourg	The Greens, 1
Netherlands	Green Left (GL), 2
Slovenia	Party *Verjamem,* 1
Spain	Initiative for Catalonia-Green (ICV), 1
	EQUO, 1
	New Catalan Esquerra (NECat), 1
	Republican Left of Catalonia (ERC), 1
Sweden	Green Ecology Party (MpG), 4
United Kingdom	Green Party, 3
	Scottish National Party (SNP), 2
	Plaid Cymru, 1

Europe of Freedom and Direct Democracy (EFD), 45

Czech Republic	Party of Free Citizens (SSO), 1
France	Independent, 1
Germany	Alternative for Germany (AfG), 1
Italy	5 Star Movement (M5S), 17
Lithuania	Order and Justice Party (PTT), 1
Poland	Congress of the New Right (KNP), 1
Sweden	Sweden Democrats (SD), 2
United Kingdom	United Kingdom Independence Party (UKIP), 21

Europe of Nations and Freedom (ENF), 39

Austria	Freedom Party of Austria (FPÖ), 4
Belgium	*Vlaams Belang,* 1
France	National Front (FN), 20
Germany	Alternative for Germany (AfG), 1
Italy	*Lega Nord,* 5
Netherlands	Party for Freedom (PVV), 4
Poland	Congress of the New Right (KNP), 2
Romania	Independent, 1
United Kingdom	UK Independence Party, 1

Unattached, 17

France	National Front (FN), 2
	Free French, 1
Germany	The Party (DP), 1
	National Democratic Party of Germany (NPD), 1
Greece	Golden Dawn (XA), 3
	Communist Party of Greece (KKE), 2
Hungary	Movement for a Better Hungary (JMM), 3
Italy	Democratic Party (PD), 1
Poland	Congress of the New Right (KNP), 1
United Kingdom	Democratic Unionist Party (DUP), 1
	Independent, 1

The Court of Justice of the European Communities (less formally, the European Court of Justice—ECJ), encompassing 27 judges and 8 advocates-general, sits in Luxembourg. In 1989 a Court of First Instance was established to help the ECJ deal with its increasingly large workload. The 27 members of each court are appointed for six years by agreement between the governments of the member states. The judges themselves appoint a president of their prospective court who serves a three-year term. Both courts can sit in plenary session or in chambers of three or five judges. Since the 2004 EU enlargement, instead of convening in a plenary session, 13 ECJ judges can sit as a Grand Chamber. The ECJ can sit in plenary session when a member state or an EU/EC institution that is party to the proceedings so requests or in particularly complex or important cases. A European Civil Service Tribunal, comprised of seven judges, is under the Court of First Instance.

Recent activities. The crisis in Ukraine has been of the utmost concern for the EU and the European heads of state since its outbreak in early 2014. Following Russia's invasion of Crimea in early March, an extraordinary meeting of the EU heads of state was convened on March 6 to address the situation. At that meeting, the leaders flatly condemned the Russian actions and declared the decision of the Crimean Supreme Council to hold a referendum on illegal annexation. The leaders immediately announced the suspension of bilateral talks with Russia, a travel ban, and asset freezes, and the EU leaders that are part of the G-8 withdrew their participation from the G-8 summit scheduled to be hosted in Sochi (see separate entry). On March 20 the European Council met to discuss the issue, reaffirming the EU's support for Ukraine and its intention to sign the association agreement with Ukraine no later than June.

In May the people of Europe went to the polls as the European Parliamentary elections were held May 22–25. The 2014 election was highly anticipated by many within Europe since, for the first time in EU history, the election results would affect who the council could nominate to be the next chair of the European Commission. Those promoting the elections also highlighted the increased power of the European Parliament since 2009 in order to stress the significance of voting. Voter turnout was just 0.5 percent lower than in 2009 but, as in every previous election, set a new record for the lowest voter turnout in EU history. Following the union-wide balloting, the new parliamentary parties formed, yielding seven political groups. The EPP remained the largest group in parliament but saw a smaller number of MEPs than in 2009. (For a full breakdown of election results, see Structure above.)

After the elections, the European Council met on June 26–27 to set the strategic agenda for the next legislative session, running from November 1, 2014, to October 31, 2019. The agenda, as outlined by the council, addresses five major focus areas: economic growth and job creation; empowering and protecting all of its citizens; the creation of an energy union with proactive climate change policies; the promotion of freedom, security, and justice within the union; and to increase the EU's position as a global actor. Beyond tending to institutional business at the June meeting, the council also formally signed association agreements with Ukraine and Georgia and Moldova, respectively. Additionally, the council set forth several key steps to be taken immediately by Russia in regard to resolving the ongoing conflict in Ukraine.

In addition to approving the commission's main agenda for the next five years and tending to international security issues, the council nominated Jean Claude Juncker, former prime minister of Luxembourg, as the next chair of the European Commission. Juncker's nomination was in accordance with the new rules governing selection of the chair, specifying that it must be representative of the parliamentary election returns. He had been nominated by the EPP as their candidate for the position on May 6, and upon securing a majority of the seats in parliament, the EPP, under Juncker's leadership, formed a parliamentary coalition with the S&D, parliament's second-largest group. The council opted to accept the party's nominee and chose to exercise their primary influence through setting the agenda. Juncker was elected by secret balloting of the new parliament on July 15, receiving a total of 423 of the 751 votes.

At a special meeting of the European Council held on August 30, the council elected Donald Tusk, Poland's prime minister, as the next council chair to replace Herman von Rompouy, whose term was set to expire November 30. At that meeting, the council also selected Frederica Mogherini, Italy's foreign minister, as the Union's High Representative for Foreign Affairs. The special meeting was also convened to discuss several major international security problems, including the crisis in Ukraine, the rise of the terrorist group the Islamic State in Iraq and the Levant (ISIL), and the ongoing violence in Gaza between the Israelis and Palestinians. The council condemned the actions of Russia in Ukraine and called for immediate implementation of the peace plan set forth by Ukrainian president Porshenko. In regard to ISIL, the EU announced its support of individual member states that were contributing military materials to Iraq in its fight against the extremists and expressed its full commitment to providing humanitarian aid.

In September the EU hosted a high-level meeting to discuss the union's response to the ongoing Ebola crisis in West Africa. The EU pledged €150 million toward relief work and assistance to those countries most heavily affected and reiterated its commitment to increase its level of support in other means through the creation of a European coordination mechanism on medical evacuations. The meeting also established operation platforms upon which to base future assistance and actions. The organization's response to Ebola only was strengthened at the October meeting of the European Council, which raised the total EU commitment toward fighting Ebola to €1 billion.

In a series of hearings held from September 29–October 7, the nominees for the 27 EU commission seats were vetted before the MEPs in committee-based confirmation hearings. The commissioners had been nominated by their respective states and the portfolio assignments worked out by the members of the council in conjunction with President-Elect Juncker. Following the confirmation hearings, the European Parliament formally approved the entire slate of commissioners on October 22 by a vote of 443 to 209, with 67 abstentions. The new commission took office on November 1.

Building upon the goals outlined in the strategic agenda produced in June, the council approved the 2030 Climate and Energy Policy Framework on October 24. The new framework is hailed as the world's "most ambitious 2030 climate energy policy." It commits the EU to reducing greenhouse gas emissions by 40 percent, increasing renewable energy consumption to 27 percent, improving energy efficiency by 27 percent, and completing the internal energy market.

A massive migrant crisis dominated the EU beginning in 2015, as refugees sought asylum from conflicts in Syria, Iraq, and Northern Africa. By the end of 2015, an estimated 1.8 million migrants had crossed into the EU. In addition, more than 3,600 refugees died in perilous attempts to cross the Mediterranean or on dangerous land routes. The response to the influx divided the EU. German chancellor Angela Merkel adopted liberal asylum polices and welcomed migrants, while other countries, including Austria, Denmark, and Hungary, sought to limit the number of asylum-seekers. Hungary announced the construction of a wall on its border to deter migrants, and other EU members implemented temporary border controls. In an effort to resolve the crisis, the EU created a quota system in September 2015 that required countries to take in a specific number of refugees or face fines of 0.002 percent of GDP. In December Hungary challenged the system in court.

UK prime minister David Cameron won reelection in 2015 with a pledge to renegotiate his country's relationship with the EU ahead of a national referendum on continued membership. In a February 2016 deal, Cameron was only able to gain vague concessions on most major issues, including a greater ability to block EU policies or regulations if 55 percent of national parliaments agreed, and a four-year "pause" on some social benefits for new migrants. On June 23 voters in the United Kingdom voted to leave the EU, 51.6 percent to 48.1 percent, it what became known as the "Brexit." Cameron resigned and was replaced by Theresa May, who pledged to begin negotiations over the withdrawal by March 2017. Following the Brexit vote, Jonathan Hill, the UK European Commissioner for Financial Stability, Financial Services and Capital Markets Union, resigned and left office on July 15. He was replaced on an acting basis by EU vice president Valdis Dombrovskis (Latvia), the commissioner for Euro and Social Dialogue.

EUROPEAN ATOMIC ENERGY COMMUNITY (EURATOM)

Communauté Européenne de l'Energie Atomique (CEEA)

Established: By Treaty of Rome (Italy), signed March 25, 1957, effective January 1, 1958.

Purpose: To develop research, to disseminate information, to enforce uniform safety standards, to facilitate investment, to ensure regular and equitable distribution of supplies of nuclear material, to guarantee that nuclear materials are not diverted from their designated uses and to exercise certain property rights in regard to such materials, to create a common market for the free movement of investment capital and personnel for nuclear industries, and to promote the peaceful uses of atomic energy.

Membership: (See European Union, with Switzerland as a participating associated state.)

Website: http://euratom.org.

Official Languages (24): Bulgarian, Croatian, Czech, Danish, Dutch, English, Estonian, Finnish, French, German, Greek, Hungarian, Irish, Italian, Latvian, Lithuanian, Maltese, Polish, Portuguese, Romanian, Slovak, Slovenian, Spanish, Swedish.

Origin and development. Euratom was established in response to the assessment that atomic power on a large scale would be urgently needed to meet the growing energy requirements for economic expansion. The original six European Steel and Coal Community (ECSC) member states also sought to reduce the lead that Britain, the Soviet Union, and the United States had acquired in the field of peaceful uses of nuclear energy. To this end, the members decided to pool their efforts, as the area was too complex and expensive to be dealt with nationally. Structurally, the Treaty of Rome provided for a council, a commission, and the sharing of the assembly and court of justice already operating under the ECSC.

In December 1969 it was agreed to reshape Euratom so that it could conduct nuclear research under contract for community clients and extend its activities to other scientific research projects, especially those involving noncommunity states. The council also resolved to streamline the community's management, making its operations more flexible and ensuring more effective coordination of its nuclear activities. These reforms took effect in 1971.

In 1981 an agreement came into force between the community, France, and the International Atomic Energy Agency (IAEA) regarding safeguards on certain nuclear materials, and officials signed long-term agreements establishing conditions for the sale and security within the EC of nuclear materials supplied by Australia and Canada. In November 1995 Euratom and the United States completed negotiations on a controversial new agreement concerning "nuclear cooperation" to replace an accord set to expire at the end of the year. The most contentious element of the pact was a provision giving Euratom members greater latitude in selling plutonium originating from the United States. Previously, Washington had held a veto power over any such transactions; however, the new agreement permitted Euratom members to trade the plutonium within EU borders without U.S. approval. In 2000 the United States and Euratom reached a cooperative agreement that covers fusion as well as fission research.

Given that approximately one-third of the EU's energy is nuclear, Euratom continues to be involved in efforts to prevent a disruption of nuclear fuel supplies. Since 1960 a Euratom Supply Agency operating under the commission has coordinated all of Euratom's contracts for the supply of fissionable material. Inspections of installations that use these supplies are conducted on a regular basis to ensure that nuclear materials are not diverted from peaceful uses and are otherwise maintained under appropriate safeguards.

Because of diminished popular support for nuclear energy, triggered in part by the 1986 Chernobyl disaster in the Soviet Union, the European Commission stopped approving new loans for construction of nuclear power plants within member countries. In June 2004, however, the commission approved a proposal for a Finnish plant, the first in the EU in over a decade and the world's first "third-generation" (post-2000) facility, which has new safety, reliability, and cost-saving features. In June 2004 the commission approved a loan of €224 million ($275 million) for construction of a reactor in candidate country Romania. Loans for safety and modernization efforts were also extended to other Eastern European countries, including Russia and Ukraine, where the last Chernobyl reactor was permanently shut down in December 2000. The Finnish plant currently has two operational reactors with construction to begin on the third reactor by 2015. By January 2006 France and the Czech Republic had announced plans to build more nuclear plants, and Belgium, Italy, Germany, and Sweden had all begun reconsideration of the nuclear power moratorium.

Concurrently, scientists have intensified research on thermonuclear fusion, which many believe could provide power without most of the safety risks and environmental problems associated with fission reactors. The long-term goal of the EU Fusion Program is "the joint creation of prototype reactors which will lead to electric power plants that meet society's needs: operational safety, respect for the environment, economic viability." Since the first half of the 1980s, fusion research has been conducted at the Joint European Torus (JET), a research and development facility in Culham, United Kingdom. On January 1, 2000, the new European Fusion Development Agreement (EFDA) became operational to govern use of JET to coordinate fusion technology projects within the EU and to oversee EU participation in outside endeavors. These endeavors include the international thermonuclear experimental reactor (ITER) project initiated in 1988 by Japan, Russia, and the United States, for which a design was completed in 2001. China and South Korea also are participating in the $12 billion project. In June 2005 the partners announced that ITER would be built in Cadarache, France, with a target completion date of 2015.

In December 2002 the European Court of Justice (ECJ), ruling in a dispute brought by the European Commission against the Council of the European Union, stated that Euratom, as well as the individual member countries, had competence with regard to broader nuclear safety concerns. In a declaration accompanying the Act of Accession to the 1994 global Convention on Nuclear Safety, the council had erred, according to the ECJ, by overly limiting Euratom's role to workplace-related protections and emergency planning, whereas the organization was also competent in safety matters related to siting facilities, design and construction, and operations. In May 2005, confirming a 2004 proposal by the commission, the council extended Euratom competence to two international conventions adopted in 1986, the Convention on Early Notification of a Nuclear Accident and the Convention on Assistance in the Case of a Nuclear Accident or Radiological Emergency.

Meanwhile, during the constitutional debates of the Convention on the Future of Europe, the question of Euratom's future role became a significant issue. In the end, in 2003 the drafting convention left the Euratom treaty intact. Later, the European Parliament, which has long sought greater control over Euratom activities, urged the intergovernmental conference (IGC) on the constitution "to convene a Treaty revision conference in order to repeal the obsolete and outdated provisions of that Treaty, especially those relating to the promotion of nuclear energy and the lack of democratic decision-making procedures." The governments of Austria, Germany, Hungary, Ireland, and Sweden also called for convening a special IGC on Euratom and related nuclear matters, as they also did in a declaration attached to the Treaty of Lisbon in 2007. That treaty, ratified in 2009, includes Euratom's expenditures and revenues in the EU budget, excluding the Euratom Supply Agency and joint undertakings.

Euratom has its own "framework program" for nuclear research and training activities that is managed by common EC institutions. Euratom's Seventh Framework Program (FP7), which calls for spending €2.8 billion ($3.6 billion) during 2007–2011 encompasses two categories of research. "Indirect actions," which are managed by the commission's Directorate General for Research, involve fusion energy, nuclear fission, and radiation protection. "Direct actions," undertaken by the Joint Research Center (JRC), cover three themes: nuclear waste management; environmental impact; and basic knowledge, nuclear safety, and nuclear security. The JRC was established by Euratom and has become a leading European institute for nuclear research.

Pressure to expand nuclear power in EU borders, particularly in the East, has grown in recent years, although Euratom's role remains controversial. Despite safety concerns brought by activists, the EC in December 2007 approved construction of a new two-unit Russian-designed nuclear power plant in Belene in northern Bulgaria, paving the way for an application for a sizable Euratom loan, which would be the agency's first in 20 years. By late 2007 the Belene project was plagued with uncertainties, including corruption allegations and difficulties in attracting funding even as Euratom guaranteed a $780 million loan. In 2007 the European Commission authorized the creation of a new group—the European Nuclear Energy Forum (ENEF). The ENEF is composed of representatives from each member state, representatives from various EU Institutions, and nuclear industry representatives. The ENEF is designed to promote an environment more conducive to discussing the risks and opportunities of nuclear energy.

In February 2008 the European Council of Ministers updated Euratom statutes by shrinking its advisory committee from 75 to 56 members to improve the body's efficiency. The agency was also given approval to build a multinational nuclear fuel reserve to provide a backup supply of enriched uranium to be used if supplies from outside the EU were cut off for political reasons.

Upon an EC directive in November 2008, Euratom drafted a Nuclear Safety Directive that established legally binding rules for safety standards on nuclear installations within EU member states and enhanced the powers of national regulatory bodies. The EC approved the directive on June 25, 2009.

Recent activities. On December 22, 2009, the EU Council approved a mandate for the Commission to negotiate a full nuclear cooperation agreement with Russia. It was estimated that about 45 percent of all enriched uranium in the EU came from Russia, either directly or from the nuclear power plants of EU countries that were formerly in the Soviet orbit. In May 2010 the commission called for a "sustainable framework" for the funding of ITER. ITER's costs had experienced explosive growth. On November 2, 2010, the U.S. National Nuclear Security Administration (NNSA) announced that it had signed an agreement with Euratom to promote greater cooperation in nuclear security and nonproliferation.

In 2011 Euratom estimated that one-third of the 144 nuclear reactors then in operation in the EU would need to be decommissioned by 2025. To support the decommissioning of aged nuclear plants, the EC approved €500 million to shut down plants in Bulgaria, Lithuania, and Slovakia. In September the EC enacted new regulations requiring Euratom to standardize the manner in which it reported on energy projects.

In May 2012 the European Commission approved a new series of safety guidelines for nuclear power plants designed to increase the community's protection from the effects of nuclear radiation. The legislation is the third measure of its kind since March 2011, marking a definite commitment from the European Commission to safeguard the EU citizens from any form of nuclear radiation.

At its June 2012 meeting in Bratislava, the European Nuclear Energy Forum discussed the progress made in the ongoing stress tests of the nuclear reactors in EU member states. The stress tests have currently completed phase two of three and the self-assessments of each facility are undergoing peer review from a team of nuclear energy experts from across the EU countries. The forum also discussed the financial and security concerns and advantages that are presented by nuclear power in the context of the Energy Roadmap 2050.

In May 2013 the European Nuclear Energy Forum encouraged member states to increase their investments in the energy sector, noting that there was a greater need for sustainable and renewable energy but a lack of funds for the research necessary to bring about the solutions. The ENEF also agreed that while individual member states should continue to control the mix of energy sources, there needs to be a collective look toward the future of energy in Europe. The organization suggested the need for a new energy outlook plan that would forecast to 2030 or 2050.

In June 2013 Euratom issued a proposed revision to the 2009 nuclear safety directive to be voted upon by the entire European Commission. The revisions introduced new safety objectives, established a European system of peer review, increased transparency, and added new provisions for emergency response. The commission approved the proposed changes on July 8, 2014, with the new amended directive entering into effect immediately. The first peer review under the new directive will take place in 2017.

In September Euratom and the IAEA signed a memorandum of understanding in which the two sides agreed to cooperate in their efforts. Under the new memorandum of understanding, the two organizations will benefit from the work of the other organization and undertake initiatives to reduce duplication of projects.

In October 2014 the European Commission announced a new joint program with the European fusion research laboratories to promote fusion energy to achieve its Horizon2020 goals. The new program, EURO*fusion,* will receive nearly 50 percent of its operating budget from Euratom's existing research program into fusion energy. The program's ultimate goal is to make fusion energy a reality by 2050.

On March 13, 2015, the European Commission objected to a 2014 €10 billion deal between Hungary and Russia to build two new reactors in the former country. After modifications, on September 11 the Euratom Supply Agency reviewed the nuclear development plans and found them in line with the EU legal framework.

GROUP OF EIGHT

Established: Originally formed as the Group of Seven (G-7) during the San Juan, Puerto Rico, summit of leading industrial democracies held on June 27–28, 1976; first met as the kindred Group of Eight (G-8) after the addition of Russia as a formal participant at the May 15–17, 1998, G-7 summit in Birmingham, United Kingdom.

Purpose: To discuss problems relating to "geopolitical and security issues, the partnership with Africa in its dual political and economic dimensions, and subjects of common interest to the G-8 countries, facing specific challenges."

Principal Organs: The G-8 has one formal organ as such—the presidency. There are also annual summits, twice-a-year (and ad hoc) meetings of finance ministers and central bank governors, and other meetings of government ministers and officials.

Website: www.g8.utoronto.ca. (The G-8 has no formal website. The G-8 Research Group at the University of Toronto maintains this website with G-8 information.)

President: Shinzō Abe (Japan).

Membership (8): Canada, France, Germany, Italy, Japan, Russia (suspended), United Kingdom, United States.

Observers: The European Union is a permanent observer. China and India are also generally invited to G-8 meetings as observers.

Origin and development. The origins of the G-7 and G-8 can be traced back to 1962 and the founding of the informal Group of Ten (G-10) by Belgium, Canada, France, the Federal Republic of Germany, Italy, Japan, the Netherlands, Sweden, the United Kingdom, and the United States.

Later in the decade finance ministers and sometimes central bank governors from France, the Federal Republic of Germany, Japan, the United Kingdom, and the United States began to meet as an additional informal caucus that became known as the Group of Five (G-5). As a consequence of discussions at the July 30–August 1, 1975, Helsinki Conference on Security and Cooperation in Europe, the heads of state or government of the G-5 plus Italy convened in November 1975 in Rambouillet, France, to address various economic and financial concerns, including growth, inflation, exchange rates, monetary reform, oil prices, and unemployment. Canada joined as the seventh participant in the San Juan, Puerto Rico, summit in 1976, at which time the assembled leaders agreed on the utility of holding annual sessions. Thus the G-7 was born.

The agendas of the 1976 summit and then the May 7–8, 1977, summit in London, United Kingdom, were broadened to include such concerns as balance-of-payments problems and North-South relations. Also, beginning with the 1977 summit, the European Community (EC, subsequently the European Union—EU) was included in discussions. At the next summit, held July 16–17, 1978, in Bonn, West Germany, the G-7 issued an unprecedented statement denouncing aircraft hijacking that was widely recognized as the group's first political declaration. Developments at the 1979 summit in Paris included the establishment of the Financial Action Task Force (FATF), which was asked to identify and promote policies that would combat money laundering. The agendas at succeeding summits expanded to arms control, the environment, political reform, and terrorism. During the second half of the 1980s the G-7 focused on such matters as rectifying trade imbalances, stabilizing exchange rates, combating protectionism, and relaxing debt repayment pressure on the world's poorest countries.

The issue of how best to encourage free-market reform in the Soviet Union and its former satellites in Eastern Europe dominated the G-7 summit July 15–17, 1991, in London, which was attended by Soviet leader Mikhail Gorbachev. Some observers predicted that the meeting might lead to creation of a Group of Eight, a possibility that U.S. president George H. W. Bush then broached at the 1992 summit in Munich, Germany, which Russian president Boris Yeltsin attended. By the 1994 summit in Naples, Italy, Russian participation in most nonfinancial discussions had become the norm, resulting in the designation Political-8 (P-8). Russia's formal inclusion at the May 15–17, 1998, summit in Birmingham, United Kingdom, marked the birth of the G-8.

In the first half of the 1990s, G-7 discussions often centered on how best to support the fledgling free market systems in the former Communist world. The breakup of Yugoslavia and the attendant crises in the Balkans, Russian action in Chechnya, and the Mexico peso crisis of 1994–1995 also were among the most pressing topics during this period. Terrorism moved to the forefront of the agenda at the June 28–29, 1996, summit in Lyon, France, which took place only a week after the bombing of a U.S. military base in Saudi Arabia. At the urging of U.S. president Bill Clinton, the G-7 leaders approved a 40-point plan to combat crime and terrorism.

Meeting in February 1999, the finance ministers and bank governors approved a plan to establish a Financial Stability Forum (FSF), its primary purpose being to prevent economic crises by improving oversight of, and information exchange within, the world's financial systems. The forum comprised representatives of the G-8 countries, the Netherlands, Australia, Hong Kong, Singapore, Switzerland, the European Central Bank, the Bank for International Settlements (BIS), the International Monetary Fund (IMF), the OECD, the World Bank, the Basel Committee on Banking Supervision, the International Accounting Standards Board, the International Organization of Securities Commissions, the International Association of Insurance Supervisors, the Committee on the Global Financial System, and the Committee on Payment and Settlement Systems.

Steps were also taken to include developing countries in discussions related to reform of global financial systems. Largely at the instigation of President Clinton at the November 1997 Asia-Pacific Economic Cooperation (APEC) summit in Vancouver, Canada, a temporary Group of 22 (G-22) took shape. In addition to the G-8 countries, G-22 participants included Argentina, Australia, Brazil, China, Hong Kong, India, Indonesia, South Korea, Malaysia, Mexico, Poland, Singapore, South Africa, and Thailand. The grouping held its first meeting in April 1998. Less than a year later, on March 11, 1999, a successor Group of 33 (G-33) met for the first time in Bonn, Germany, with a second session convening April 25 in Washington, D.C.

The G-33 was superseded September 26, 1999, by a new Group of 20 (see separate article) comprising representatives of the EU and the IMF/World Bank, as well as the G-8 members and the following 10 countries: Argentina, Australia, Brazil, China, India, Republic of Korea, Mexico, Saudi Arabia, South Africa, and Turkey.

The G-8 summit held July 20–22, 2001, in Genoa, Italy, took place amid disruptions caused by antiglobalization protests. In addition to the troubled state of the world economy, discussions centered on topics such as cutting emission of greenhouse gases, implementing a development plan for Africa, and overcoming the "digital divide." The session also approved a \$1.3 billion fund to help combat AIDS, tuberculosis, and malaria.

Canada hosted the June 26–27, 2002, summit in Kananaskis, Alberta—sufficiently removed from the nearest large city, Calgary, to ease security concerns. Despite disagreements on particular issues—for example, U.S. tariffs directed against steel and softwood lumber imports and U.S. president George W. Bush's call for Palestinians to replace Yasir Arafat as leader of the Palestinian Authority—several initiatives were approved. The G-8 agreed to a ten-year aid package of \$20 billion (half from the United States) to assist Russia and other countries of the former Soviet bloc in securing their remaining nuclear materials. The leaders also agreed to provide additional debt relief under the HIPC (Heavily Indebted Poor Countries) initiative, but the \$1 billion commitment was far less than some advocates had sought. Similar criticism greeted the G-8 African Action Plan, which confirmed an earlier commitment of \$6 billion per year, beginning in 2006, in support of the African Union's New Partnership for Africa's Development (NEPAD).

In 2003, at a February meeting of finance ministers and central bankers, some participants had criticized the Bush administration for its large tax cuts and projected fiscal deficits. In February 2004 Japan and the European G-8 members expressed, with greater urgency, their concern about the consequences of a recent steep fall in the value of the U.S. dollar, which the Bush administration, facing a fall election, appeared willing to accept in the expectation that a weak dollar would spur export sales, encourage manufacturing, and create jobs.

Following President Bush's call in April 2004 for more engagement with China in the rich countries' economies, China was invited to participate for the first time in a meeting of the finance ministers and central bank governors at a G-8 meeting on October 1 in Washington, D.C. Meanwhile, some of the G-8 countries continued to be at odds with the United States and Britain over financing peacekeeping missions in Iraq, the topic dominating the June 8–10, 2004, summit in Sea Island, Georgia, with Iraqi interim president Sheikh Ghazi Ajil al-Yawar in attendance.

In 2005 G-7 ministers met often early in the year, struggling to come to terms with debt relief for Africa and many other of the poorest countries. On June 11, in what was described as a "landmark deal" brokered by Britain, the G-8 leaders agreed to pay to relieve 18 of the poorest countries—most of them in Africa—of some \$40 billion in debt. The agreement, the basis of which was hammered out by President Bush and British prime minister Tony Blair a week earlier, would also benefit another nine countries, bringing the total debt reduction tab to some \$55 billion. By the end of 2005, the developing world energy shortage was engaging G-8 attention, as were ways to combat international terrorism.

The July 15–17, 2006, summit was the first to be hosted by Russia. The summit was supposed to deal primarily with energy security from the standpoint of both consumer and producer nations. The conference was dominated, however, by fighting in Lebanon between Israel and Hezbollah. The conference produced a statement that called for restraint.

The value of the yuan and increasing concerns about the U.S. economy's health increasingly occupied G-7/G-8 attention during 2007. These concerns were in evidence at the June 6–8 summit in Heligendamm, Germany, but the main emphasis was on climate change. The meeting produced an agreement to "consider seriously" cutting carbon dioxide emissions by 50 percent by 2050, but no specifics were laid out.

The July 7–8, 2008, summit in Hokkaido, Japan, was held amid sharply growing concerns about climate change. Tony Blair, now no longer the British prime minister, addressed the G-20 meeting in March 2008. He asked for revolutionary climate action by G-8 and other nations. In April Japanese prime minister Yasuo Fukuda met with EU representatives, promising to push for strong measures at the G-8 summit. By June, however, Fukuda was trying to lower expectations for results. He said the mission of the G-8 meeting was "to send out messages pointing to solutions," and the UN, rather than the G-8, should come up with medium-term goals for reducing emissions. The climate change discussions effectively ended in an impasse among the G-8 countries. The summit agreed only to work toward halving greenhouse emissions by 2050, but without giving any specifics on how this could be achieved. After the meeting U.S. president George W. Bush declared that the United States would take no concrete steps towards reducing emissions during his presidency.

The 2009 summit, scheduled for July 8–10 in Maddalena, on the Italian island of Sardinia, was moved to the mainland town of L'Aquila. The conference was described as extremely disorganized, and its ability to deal with matters of pollution and climate change was reduced by Chinese president Hu Jintao's decision to leave early to deal with domestic unrest. The conference pledged, without offering specifics, that by 2050 average global temperatures should not rise more than two degrees Celsius above the year 1900 levels. The summit also pledged $20 billion for a three-year initiative to help poor countries develop their own agriculture. The sum was larger than many observers had expected, and the plan was felt likely to be more effective than if it had simply involved sending food.

After the L'Aquila summit questions grew about the G-8's continued usefulness. It had become clear that the world's balance of power had shifted, at least as far as economic matters were concerned, and that countries such as China, India, and Brazil could not be ignored. Thus, many felt that the G-20 meeting, which would be held September 24–25 in Pittsburgh, Pennsylvania, would be much more significant.

In the face of questions over the continued utility of the organization, Canada was reportedly particularly interested in keeping the G-8 alive, feeling that its influence would be diluted in a G-20 setting. To this end, it was fortunate that Canada was able to host the 2010 G-8 summit on June 25–26 in Muskoka, Ontario, immediately prior to the G-20 summit in Toronto June 26–27.

The 2011 summit was held May 26–27 in Deauville, France. The summit most notably produced the G-8 Declaration: Renewed Commitment for Freedom and Democracy. The declaration addressed issues such as the situation in Japan following the 2011 earthquake, the significance and role of the Internet in global affairs, world economics, environmental protection, nuclear power, climate change, and international development and security. At the summit the G-8 also produced the Deauville Partnership, a two-part plan of action and statement regarding the Arab Springs, and a joint declaration between the G-8 and Africa on the development of African nations.

In June, upon the recommendation of G-8 president Nicolas Sarkozy, the G-8 hosted a summit on nuclear safety in light of the situation in Japan following the earthquake. The summit produced several recommendations that were discussed at the 2011 International Atomic Energy Agency (see entry under UN: Related Organization) Conference June 24–25.

At a September 2011 meeting of the G-8 finance ministers, the Deauville Partnership was fully implemented with the launch of the economic component. Through the use of regional development banks, the G-8 finance ministers are overseeing economic strategies to support sustainable and inclusive growth.

The 2012 G-8 summit, hosted by the United States, was held at Camp David, Maryland, in May. The summit produced the Camp David Declaration, which called on the G-8 countries to continue their work to aid in the recovery of the global economy, seek ways to promote the effective use of alternative energy sources, and work to fight global poverty and food shortages. The G-8 announced the creation of the New Alliance for Food Security and Nutrition to aid in increased flow of money and resources to African countries struggling with food security issues and poverty. The summit also discussed different measures to promote security, stability, and economic recovery in the Middle East, especially in Afghanistan.

In 2013 the G-B operated under the presidency of the United Kingdom. Prime Minister David Cameron announced that his priorities for the UK presidency were to advance trade, ensure tax compliance, and promote greater transparency. These priorities set the stage for the 2013 summit held in Lough Erne, Northern Ireland, June 17–18. The Lough Erne Declaration reinforced many of these principles by expressing the G-8's commitment to openness, shared information, and reduced tariffs. The meeting also identified job growth as the group's top priority and the key to ending the global economic recession. In order to achieve progress, the G-8 stressed the importance of sound fiscal policies and investment in small-medium sized enterprises. The group also issued a new policy on open data.

Perhaps the biggest announcement to come out of the summit, however, was the announcement that the United States and European Union were beginning discussions to negotiate a bilateral trade agreement between the two parties. Discussing the significance of this, Cameron noted that it could have an impact of $160 billion on the EU economy, $128 billion on the U.S. economy, and $136 billion on the economy in the rest of the world. (For more on developments since 2013, see Recent activities, below.)

Structure. The G-8 is administered by a presidency of the organization. The presidency rotates from country to country in one-year terms in the following order: France, the United States, the United Kingdom, Russia, Germany, Japan, Italy, and Canada. The presidency is responsible for organizing and hosting the annual summit, and handles all communication for the G8. The presidency also handles international relations with non–G-8 members and NGOs. Activities coalesce around annual summits of the members' heads of state or government, joined by the president of the European Council and the European Commission. National delegations also include finance and foreign ministers and a personal representative of each president, prime minister, or chancellor. Summits typically include a day of private, informal bilateral and multilateral discussions among the leaders.

Throughout the year high-level meetings can be held by the members' foreign ministers; by finance ministers and central bank governors; or by ministers responsible for the environment, justice and interior, labor, development, and other areas. Ad hoc task forces and working groups also have been established.

Recent activities. Under what was scheduled to be the Russian presidency, 2014 was a turbulent year in G-8 relations. Following Russia's intervention into Ukraine in March, the G-7 leaders announced that they were withdrawing from the G-8 in Sochi, opting instead to hold their own meeting in Brussels under the host of the EU at the already announced time of June 4–5. President Putin issued a statement in which he announced Russia's willingness to still work with the G-7 leaders and calling the actions of the other nations "counterproductive." The G-7 followed through with their plans to meet separately, a meeting that was largely preoccupied by foreign affairs. The group announced their continued support for Ukraine, strongly condemning the actions of Russia and calling for international financial assistance for the country. The group also expressed its concern over the situations in Syria, Libya, Mali, Iran, and North Korea. The group issued another strong statement on July 30, again condemning the Russian actions in Ukraine and threatening further sanctions against Russia if it did not move toward de-escalation.

On June 4–5, 2015, the G-7 met in Bavaria, Germany. The members continued to criticize Russia for its intervention in Ukraine. They also focused on the global economy, immigration issues, national security, and future development goals.

In May 2016 the G-7 met in Ise-Shima, Japan, with Shinzō Abe as host. The G-7 again focused on global economy, terrorism threats, the continued refugee crisis, and South China Sea. The G-7 made a statement that the departure of the United Kingdom from the EU would cause a severe risk to global economic growth.

GROUP OF TWENTY

Established: September 25, 1999, at a Washington, D.C., session of the G-7 finance ministers. The Group of Twenty (G-20) consists of 19 larger-economy countries and the European Union, in addition to representatives of the International Monetary Fund and the World Bank. The group's finance ministers and central bank governors began meeting in 1999, and since that time have met every fall. G-20 heads of state or government began meeting in November 2008 (see below) and this elevation of status seems to represent the G-20's future.

Purpose: "A new mechanism for informal dialogue in the framework of the Bretton Woods institutional system, to broaden the dialogue on key economic and financial policy issues among systemically significant economies and to promote cooperation to achieve stable and sustainable world growth that benefits all."

Principal Organs: The G-20 has no permanent organs. There is a meeting of its members' finance ministers and central bank governors each fall, with occasional meetings of deputies and seminars at other times. Recently the heads of state or government of G-20 countries have also met. Arrangements are principally in the hands of the country that chairs the group in any particular year. (See below under "Structure.")

Website: www.g20.org.

Chairman: Xi Jinping (China).

Membership (20): Argentina, Australia, Brazil, Canada, China, European Union, France, Germany, India, Indonesia, Italy, Japan, Mexico, Russia, Saudi Arabia, South Africa, South Korea, Turkey, United Kingdom, United States.

Origin and development. Reflection on the Asian economic crisis of the late 1990s caused the finance ministers of the G-7 countries (Canada, France, Germany, Italy, Japan, United Kingdom, and United States) to suggest establishing a larger group, inviting the participation of a wider range of countries whose economic importance was growing. The enlarged group held its inaugural meeting in Berlin, December 15–16, 1999.

The communiqué from the group's kickoff meeting, held in Berlin on December 15–16, 1999, stated the G-20's intent, as a group of "systemically significant economies," to meet for informal dialogue within the framework of the Bretton Woods system. (See the discussion of the International Bank for Reconstruction and Development in the entry on United Nations Specialized Agencies.) The G-20 expressed relief that economic conditions were improving, worldwide and particularly in Asia, and hoped it might be useful in guiding the world's economies into an era of humane globalization.

The third meeting, November 16–17, 2001, in Ottawa, Canada, was held in the shadow of the September 11, 2001, attacks. The G-20 condemned these attacks not only as acts of terrorism but as an assault on global economic confidence and security. It resolved to fight terrorism by attacking the sources of funds for terrorist organizations.

The October 26–27, 2003, meeting in Morelia, Mexico, took as its first topic the prevention and resolution of financial crises. The group showed an increased concern for social safety nets for those not benefiting from the new financial order, as well as the importance of institution building and financing for development. And for the first time it considered the consequences of living in a world where countries other than the United States were becoming significant engines of economic growth.

The November 19–21, 2004, meeting in Berlin set some guidelines for the future in an Accord for Sustained Growth. It also announced a Reform Agenda, an account of what several member countries planned to do with their own economies. The United States, for example, was "determined to reduce its public budget deficit, to continue reforming health insurance and the pension system, and to raise private savings."

In 2006 the G-20 finance ministers met in Melbourne, Australia, November 18–19. After "spirited discussion" the group agreed to remain in close touch with the ongoing process of reform within the World Bank and the International Monetary Fund (IMF). The G-20 called for, among other things, more representation for smaller countries and a more transparent process for the selection of management in those bodies.

The 2007 meeting was held in Kleinmond, South Africa, November 17–18. The group expressed optimism for continued growth in the world economy, if at perhaps a slower rate than in the past. The final communiqué also noted that "recent events [troubles in the U.S. mortgage market] have emphasized the need for greater effectiveness of financial supervision and the management of financial risks." It called for a better understanding of the way in which financial shocks are transmitted around the world.

The 2008 annual summit, held in São Paulo, Brazil, November 8–9 was unique in that the difficulties in global credit markets had reached the point where lending had almost ceased, and a recession unparalleled since World War II was under way. The finance ministers blamed the crisis on excessive risk taking and faulty risk management practices in financial markets. They welcomed the fact that the problem was being elevated to a meeting of G-20 heads of state or government, to be held in Washington D.C. in a few days, and essentially deferred to that meeting. The emergency Washington summit took place on November 14–15. Never before had the heads of such a large group of emerging nations participated with the traditional financial powers in making economic policy for the world. The summit agreed that all member countries would take steps to stimulate their economies. The World Bank and the IMF were to do their part and the G-20 nations were to make sure that the IMF had sufficient funds for the purpose. Finance ministers were to produce a more specific plan by March 31, 2009.

The G-20 leaders committed themselves to meeting again by April 30, 2009, to review progress. They actually met in London on April 1–2. This summit meeting declared that "prosperity is indivisible," that it must reflect the interests of all people in all countries for present and future generations in "an open world economy based on market principles, effective regulation, and strong global institutions." The G-20 agreed to triple the resources immediately available to the IMF to $750 billion to support at least $100 billion in additional lending by the Multilateral Development Banks and to authorize gold sales by the IMF. The G-20 also declared that "the era of banking secrecy is over." It promised to move aggressively in applying sanctions against countries that would not cooperate in making bank account information available when needed. It also promised to go after tax havens, of which the Organization for Economic Cooperation and Development (OECD, see separate entry) had recently produced a list. Also, the G-20 proposed to bring registration and regulatory oversight to credit-rating agencies to ensure their practices did not involve conflicts of interest with the institutions whose products they were being asked to rate. The London summit generally was considered a success. It was marred by demonstrations, to which the London police reacted with a degree of violence that many considered unacceptable.

The G-20 leaders met again in Pittsburgh, Pennsylvania, September 24–25, 2009. Their judgment on what they did the previous April was that "it worked." The general consensus was that the London goals had been at least partly met. The group of leaders agreed to meet again in Canada in June 2010, in South Korea in November 2010, and annually thereafter, beginning with a meeting in France in 2011. They also pledged to complete the Doha round of trade negotiations by the end of 2010. The Pittsburgh declaration thus completed the G-20's transformation from a relatively informal gathering of finance ministers into the most powerful public instrument for setting world financial policy.

In 2010 G-20 finance ministers, meeting in Washington, D.C., in April and in Korea in June, declared that the global recovery was proceeding faster than expected, thanks to the efforts of G-20 countries. The ministers praised the EU's efforts to rescue the Greek economy, and called for renewed efforts to cut budget deficits worldwide. The June 26–27 summit in Toronto, Canada, met amid the sense that the worldwide recovery was proceeding, but was still fragile. A second, "double-dip" recession was not impossible. China refused to commit to raising the value of its currency. Many Canadians criticized the lavish arrangements that their government had made in hosting the gathering.

G-20 summits have long included meetings of some of the world's prominent business leaders, but South Korea worked to expand and institutionalize this aspect of the gathering, which it hosted November 11–12 in Seoul. South Korea was the first G-20 host country that is not also a member of the G-8. The preceding meeting of finance ministers agreed on a series of steps to reform the IMF, making it more sensitive to the needs of poor countries. Both the finance ministers and the heads of government were concerned about world trade and currency imbalances. The summit agreed to work to avoid competitive currency devaluation, but without producing a firm plan. China again resisted any upward revaluation of the yuan, which some estimate is overvalued by as much as 25 percent.

In February 2011 the G20 finance ministers met for their annual meeting, at which time they addressed major issues facing the world in the midst of challenging economic times. The meeting called for increased surveillance of the IMF to strengthen the international monetary system, a plan that was discussed in more detail at its March conference on the international monetary system. The conference also stressed the need for implementation of international standards and regulations for banks and long-term investment in agriculture.

The importance of agriculture remained a major issue in 2011 as the French president and G-20 chair Nicolas Sarkozy called a meeting of G-20 agriculture ministers in June 2011. The agriculture ministers drafted an "Action Plan on Food Price Volatility and Agriculture" that detailed their plans for how to help the struggling agricultural industry in G-20 countries. The action plan was approved by the heads of government at the November 2011 Summit. The November 2011 Summit in Cannes also saw the approval of a similar action plan for global promotion of growth and jobs. The summit leaders also increased and reaffirmed their commitment to assist the IMF in establishing a stronger international monetary system; the group also committed to further assisting global efforts to improve development in order to achieve the millennium development goals.

The largest issue facing the G-20 in 2012 was the financial crisis and problems in the Eurozone, as was evident at the 2012 G-20 Summit in Los Cabos, Mexico. The June summit made the financial crisis in the Euro Area a major point of discussion, and the member countries agreed to focus more time and effort to achieve stability in the area, with G-20 member states from the EU pledging to take all necessary measures to restore the stability of the Eurozone and hopefully prevent such a crisis from happening again. The 2012 summit also brought about the Los Cabos Growth and Job Action Plan. The plan laid out an 8-step process to address the near-term risks that are hindering growth and a 6-step process for strengthening the long-term foundations for growth and job creation. The summit also examined major issues such as food security, challenges facing the financial sector, government corruption, and environmental protection.

When G-20 leaders met for the 2013 summit, held in St. Petersburg, Russia, on September 5–6, they faced a slightly better global economic situation than they had a year earlier. In celebration of five years since the 2008 summit in Brazil, G-20 leaders reaffirmed their commitment to act together to promote sustainable economic growth and future prosperity. The biggest result of the summit was the St. Petersburg Action Plan. This plan—hailed by Vladimir Putin as the fulfillment of Russia's priorities as president of the G-20—established a series of medium-term goals to reduce budget deficits and implement comprehensive structural reforms in each country. The meeting also adopted the St. Petersburg Development Strategy, which defined the organization's main priorities for assisting low-income countries. The group also continued to stress the importance of job creation, sustainable economic growth, and fiscal responsibility. (For more since 2013, see Recent activities, below.)

Structure. The G-20 has no permanent staff. The G-20 chair rotates between members, and is selected from a different regional grouping of countries each year. The chair is part of a revolving three-member management Troika consisting of immediate past, present, and immediate future chairs. The Troika is intended to ensure continuity in the G-20's work and management through the years. The incumbent chair establishes a temporary secretariat for the duration of its term. This body coordinates the group's work and organizes its meetings. The latest Troika consists of Turkey (2015), China (2016), and Germany (2017).

Recent activities. Under the presidency of Australia, the G-20's priorities for 2014 included infrastructure development, reduction of trade barriers, decreasing corruption, promoting growth, and encouraging economic competition. As part of achieving these goals, the finance ministers approved a plan in February 2014 to increase the G-20's economic output by 2 percent over the next five years, a gain of more than $2 trillion for the global GDP. This increase will be accompanied by new jobs and infrastructure improvements to facilitate growth through the Global Infrastructure Initiative, which was agreed upon by the finance ministers at their October 2014 meeting. The 2014 G-20 Leaders' Summit met on November 14–15 in Brisbane, Australia. The agenda focused on financial reform, taxes, and anticorruption measures.

The tenth meeting of the G-20 was in Antalya, Turkey, from November 15–16, 2015, with invited guests Azerbaijan, Malaysia, Senegal, Singapore, Spain, and Zimbabwe. The group focused on the international issues of the Syrian civil war and ISIS, as well as the resultant refugee crisis. The G-20 adopted a declaration urging members to fight terrorism.

China hosted the G-20 meeting on September 4–5, 2016, at Hangzhou, Zhejiang. This meeting was the first hosted by China in the history of the G-20. Just before the meeting, China and the United States announced the ratification of the Paris Agreement of the UN Climate Change Conference, which will monitor and restrict carbon dioxide emissions.

INTERNATIONAL CRIMINAL COURT (ICC)

Cour Pénale Internationale (CPI)

Established: On July 1, 2002, founded by the Rome Statute of the International Criminal Court treaty.

Purpose: "The International Criminal Court (ICC) is an independent, permanent court that tries persons accused of the most serious crimes of international concern, namely genocide, crimes against humanity and war crimes."

"The ICC is a court of last resort. It will not act if a case is investigated or prosecuted by a national judicial system unless the national proceedings are not genuine, for example if formal proceedings were undertaken solely to shield a person from criminal responsibility. In addition, the ICC only tries those accused of the gravest crimes."

Headquarters: The Hague, Netherlands.

Principal Organs: Assembly of States Parties, Presidency, Judicial Divisions, Office of the Prosecutor, Registry, Office of Public Council for Victims, Office of Public Council for Defense.

Website: www.icc-cpi.int.

President: Judge Silvia Fernández de Gurmendi (Argentina).

Membership (124): As of July 2016 the following states had ratified the Rome Statute, which establishes the court: Afghanistan, Albania, Andorra, Antigua and Barbuda, Argentina, Australia, Austria, Bangladesh, Barbados, Belgium, Belize, Benin, Bolivia, Bosnia and Herzegovina, Botswana, Brazil, Bulgaria, Burkina Faso, Burundi, Cambodia, Canada, Cape Verde, Central African Republic, Chad, Chile, Colombia, Comoros, Congo, Cook Islands, Costa Rica, Côte d'Ivoire, Croatia, Cyprus, Czech Republic, Democratic Republic of the Congo, Denmark, Djibouti, Dominica, Dominican Republic, Ecuador, El Salvador, Estonia, Fiji, Finland, France, Gabon, Gambia, Georgia, Germany, Ghana, Greece, Grenada, Guatemala, Guinea, Guyana, Honduras, Hungary, Iceland, Ireland, Italy, Japan, Jordan, Kenya, Latvia, Lesotho, Liberia, Liechtenstein, Lithuania, Luxembourg, Macedonia, Madagascar, Malawi, Maldives, Mali, Malta, Marshall Islands, Mauritius, Mexico, Moldova, Mongolia, Montenegro, Namibia, Nauru, Netherlands, New Zealand, Niger, Nigeria, Norway, Palestine, Panama, Paraguay, Peru, Philippines, Poland, Portugal, Republic of Korea, Romania, Saint Kitts and Nevis, Saint Lucia, Saint Vincent and the Grenadines, Samoa, San Marino, Senegal, Serbia, Seychelles, Sierra Leone, Slovakia, Slovenia, South Africa, Spain, Suriname, Sweden, Switzerland, Tajikistan, Tanzania, Timor-Leste, Trinidad and Tobago, Tunisia, Uganda, United Kingdom, Uruguay, Vanuatu, Venezuela, Zambia.

Official Languages: English, French.

Origin and development. During the latter half of the 20th century there was an increasing interest in prosecuting what came to be called crimes against humanity. The Nuremberg trials of prominent Nazis after World War II and the Tokyo trials of wartime Japanese leaders were the first such prosecutions. Instances of mass murder and "ethnic cleansing" during the breakup of Yugoslavia in the 1990s, as well as the Rwandan genocide of 1994, revived a desire for a supranational court to try those responsible. The United Nations (UN) established ad hoc courts to try accused criminals in both of these conflicts and eventually addressed the matter of a permanent court at a conference held in Rome in 1998. The resulting treaty, the Rome Statute of the International Criminal Court, was adopted on July 17, 1998, by a 120–7 vote, with 21 countries abstaining. Opposed were China, Iraq, Israel, Libya, Qatar, the United States, and Yemen. After 60 signatories had ratified the treaty in April 2002, it came into force on July 1 of that year, and work commenced on setting up the court.

After its initial opposition, the United States signed the treaty, but on May 5, 2002, the George W. Bush administration withdrew its signature, to the outrage of human rights organizations worldwide. Its justification was that the treaty would undermine U.S. judicial authority. There was also concern in U.S. military circles that accession to the treaty might lead to U.S. military personnel being tried by the court for their actions abroad. South African judge Richard Goldstone, the first chief prosecutor at the War Crimes Tribunal for the former Yugoslavia, called the U.S. decision a "backwards step," adding, "the U.S. have really isolated themselves and are putting themselves into bed with the likes of China, Yemen and other undemocratic countries." Russia, also a signatory to the treaty, declared that it would not ratify it unless the United States did so.

The Rome Statute is fully binding only on those states that have ratified it and have become parties to the statute. Participating states are obligated to detain a person for whom the court has issued an arrest warrant if that person is found on its territory. A state that is not a party to the statute but that is a member of the United Nations might be obliged to detain someone wanted in a case that originated with the UN Security Council.

The ICC functions as a court of last resort. When governments are unable or unwilling to prosecute fairly, the ICC tries those accused of the gravest crimes. Several criteria are considered while determining which cases will be brought before the court. The scale, nature, manner, and impact of crimes are the areas that are assessed. Once a case meets the minimum requirements, the question of gravity is raised. Due to resource restrictions, the court is unable to investigate and prosecute all potential crimes, therefore a case of sufficient gravity will merit further action by the court.

As of late 2013 seven states that are parties to the Rome Statute had identified and referred to the ICC cases of alleged criminality that took place inside their territories. In addition, the Security Council has referred to the court the situation in Darfur, Sudan. Sudan is not a party to the Rome Statute. Cases stemming from these referrals have been developed and are in progress.

In July 2004 the ICC began a formal investigation into alleged human rights abuses committed in the low-level civil war that had been in progress in Uganda since the 1980s. It especially looked at charges against the rebel group the Lord's Resistance Army (LRA), which was accused of rape, mutilation, and using abducted children as fighters. In October 2005 the court issued arrest warrants for five LRA leaders, all of whom went into hiding in either Sudan or the lawless eastern Democratic Republic of the Congo. One suspect has since been confirmed dead; the others remain at large.

In late March 2005 the Security Council authorized the ICC to begin collecting evidence against the Sudanese government and opposition militias that have been accused of committing mass killings, torture, rape, and other atrocities in the country's Darfur region. The ICC immediately began an investigation. The court indicted Bahr Idriss Abu Garda, the former commander of a group in Darfur that was fighting the Sudanese government. He voluntarily turned himself in to the court, declaring his innocence. The case against him was dismissed on February 8, 2010. In May 2007 the ICC also issued arrest warrants for Sudan's minister of state for humanitarian affairs Ahmed Haroun and militia leader Ali Muhammad Al Abd-Al-Rahman; in July 2008 it issued a warrant for Sudanese president Omar al-Bashir. Bashir has denied any part in the genocide and refuses to acknowledge the court's jurisdiction. Bashir has likewise refused to allow warrants to be served on the other two accused Sudanese citizens.

The ICC has had notable success in apprehending and trying suspects from the Democratic Republic of the Congo (DRC). In April 2005 Congolese president Joseph Kabila asked the ICC to investigate alleged war crimes in the eastern part of his country, where he exerted little authority. The result was four arrest warrants, with three people under detention in The Hague as of December 2010 and one at large.

In October 2010 the court agreed, after legal maneuvering, to pursue a trial of Jean-Pierre Bemba, a Congolese citizen who is accused of leading militias in neighboring Central African Republic (CAR) in 2002 and 2003. These militias are accused of wide-scale murder and rape. Mr. Bemba was arrested in Belgium in 2008 and extradited to The Hague. The trial began in November 2010.

The ICC's actions have received mixed, but generally favorable, reviews. States that are sympathetic to the Sudanese government—particularly Chad—have denounced it as biased against Africa. The UN Secretary-General, Ban Ki-moon, has praised it for changing national governments' attitudes for the better. The United States (not a signatory to the treaty) and the United Kingdom (a signatory) regard it as an impediment to the actions of their peacekeeping forces around the world.

In November 2011 former Côte d'Ivoire president Laurent Gbago was arrested and detained by the ICC on four counts of crimes against humanity, including murder, rape, and persecution. The charges levied against Gbago resulted from a string of violent actions taken by his administration from December 2010 to April 2011. In a February 2012 hearing, the ICC elected to expand the investigation of Gbago to include a series of war crimes dating back to 2002. The Confirmation of Charges Hearing occurred in February 2013. In June 2013 Pre-Trial Chamber I adjourned the hearing and asked the prosecution to provide further evidence or consider further investigation of the charges presented against Gbago. Upon further evidence, the court confirmed four charges of crimes against humanity in June 2014. The court also determined that Gbago should remain in detention until the trial is over. Gbago is the most prominent suspect thus far to be brought before the ICC.

In January 2013 the ICC's Office of the Prosecutor opened an investigation into crimes committed in Mali. The situation was referred to the court by the government of Mali in July 2012. In March 2013 Bosco Ntaganda voluntarily surrendered and was placed in the custody of the ICC. Ntaganda is one of six accused of war crimes executed in the Democratic Republic of the Congo. His pre-trial hearing occurred in late March, and he was charged formally with 13 war crimes and 5 crimes against humanity in June 2014. (For more on activities since 2013, see Recent activities, below.)

Structure. The ICC exists to receive complaints of human rights abuses, to investigate them, and if necessary to issue arrest warrants in preparation for a trial. It can receive complaints from state actors, from the UN Security Council, or from private individuals. It can only accept cases concerning events that occurred after July 1, 2002, when it came into existence.

The Assembly of States Parties is the management, oversight and legislative body of the International Criminal Court. It is composed of representatives of the states that have ratified and acceded to the Rome Statute. The Assembly of States Parties has a Bureau, consisting of a president, two vice presidents, and 18 members, elected by the assembly for a three-year term. The Bureau is intended to represent all parts of the world equitably, as well as represent the world's principal legal systems. In September 2003 the Assembly of States Parties established its own Permanent Secretariat. The assembly determines the budget and oversees the election of judges, prosecutor, and deputy prosecutor(s). Decisions are made by consensus or by vote if consensus is not possible. The Assembly of States Parties has also established a Trust Fund for the benefit of victims of crimes within the jurisdiction of the court and the families of victims.

The Presidency is responsible for the overall administration of the court, with the exception of the Office of the Prosecutor, and for specific functions assigned to it in accordance with the statute. The Presidency is composed of three judges of the court, elected by their fellow judges, for a term of three years.

The Judicial Divisions consist of 18 judges, organized into the Pre-Trial Division, the Trial Division, and the Appeals Division. The judges of each division are responsible for conducting the proceedings of the court at different stages. Assignment of judges to divisions is made depending on the functions that each division performs and the qualifications and experience of the judge. This is done in a manner ensuring that each division benefits from an appropriate combination of expertise in criminal law and procedure and international law.

The Office of the Prosecutor is responsible for receiving referrals and any substantiated information about crimes within the court's jurisdiction, examining them, and conducting investigations and prosecutions. The office is headed by the Prosecutor, who is elected by the Assembly of States Parties for a term of nine years.

The Registry is responsible for the non-judicial aspects of the administration of the court. The Registrar is the principal administrative officer of the court and reports to the president of the court. The Registrar is elected by the judges for a term of five years.

The court also includes a number of semi-autonomous offices such as the Office of Public Counsel for Victims and the Office of Public Counsel for Defense. While part of the Registry, they function as wholly independent offices.

Although the ICC maintains its headquarters in The Hague, it can meet anywhere, and has frequently operated in Africa. The ICC should not be confused with the International Court of Justice (ICJ) or the International Criminal Tribunal for the former Yugoslavia (ICTY), both of which also have their headquarters in The Hague. The ICJ hears civil disputes between sovereign countries, while the ICTY is a temporary body, established by the United Nations to prosecute crimes committed during the wars in the former Yugoslavia. The ICTY is best known for its apprehension and prosecution of Slobodan Milošević, the former president of Yugoslavia and Serbia. The ICTY's connection with Milošević is perhaps what most causes it to be confused with the ICC.

Recent activities. On April 17, 2014, the government of Ukraine filed a declaration with the ICC, accepting its jurisdiction concerning crimes committed from November 2013 to February 2014, but did not formally ratify the Rome Statute. The prosecutor continues to investigate whether the crimes committed fall under the court's jurisdiction.

In November 2014 the prosecutor's office concluded a preliminary investigation into the Gaza Flotilla attack of 2010 in which Israel attacked a group of ships attempting to land at the Gaza Strip while they were still in international waters. The prosecutor determined that the situation, recommended for investigation by the Comoros, was not within the jurisdiction of the court, but the decision appeared to open the door for Palestine to ratify the Rome Statute.

The ICC has 21 open cases regarding eight situations worldwide as of 2014. Formal investigations have been launched regarding the situations in Libya, Kenya, Côte d'Ivoire, Democratic Republic of Congo, Uganda, Central African Republic, Mali, and Sudan. The court also is conducting preliminary investigations in an additional eight situations and has issued 30 arrest warrants to date, with 12 still outstanding.

President Uhuru Kenyatta appeared before the ICC, which marked the first time a seated head of state appeared before the court, only to have charges against him dismissed due to lack of evidence in December 2014. On December 31, 2014, Palestine signed an agreement to join the ICC.

On July 15, 2015, the ICC started a hybrid justice trial where the African Union and the ICC are prosecuting former head of state of Chad, Hissène Habré, of crimes committed in Chad through the Extraordinary African Chambers in Dakar.

In January 2016 the ICC started an investigation of human rights violations in Georgia, the first outside of Africa since the court's launch in 2002. In 2016 the ICC also launched investigations in Afghanistan, Palestine, and Ukraine. In September the ICC announced that it would investigate and potentially charge business leaders for war crimes, in addition to political and military figures.

Through 2016 the ICC had indicted 39 people, all from Africa. Proceedings against 17 individuals were completed, with three convictions, one acquittal, nine dismissals, and four instances where the accused died. In 2016 Burundi, Gambia, and South Africa, all announced that they would withdraw from the ICC in 2017.

INTERNATIONAL ENERGY AGENCY (IEA)

Established: By the Agreement on an International Energy Program, which was signed by the Council of Ministers of the Organization for Economic Cooperation and Development (OECD) November 15, 1974, in Paris, France.

Purpose: To coordinate the responses of participating states to the world energy crisis and to develop an oil-sharing mechanism for use in times of supply difficulties; to coordinate national energy policies, share relevant information on energy supplies and markets, and establish closer relations between petroleum-producing countries and consumer states.

Headquarters: Paris, France.

Principal Organs: Governing Board, Standing Groups, Committee on Energy Research and Technology, Committee on Non-Member Countries, Executive Director.

Website: www.iea.org.

Executive Director: Fatih Birol (Turkey).

Membership (29, with year of entry): Australia (1979), Austria (1974), Belgium (1974), Canada (1974), Czech Republic (2001), Denmark (1974), Estonia (2014), Finland (1992), France (1992), Germany (1974), Greece (1977), Hungary (1997), Ireland (1974), Italy (1978), Japan (1974), Republic of Korea (2002), Luxembourg (1974), Netherlands (1974), New Zealand (1977), Norway (participates under a special agreement), Poland (2008), Portugal (1981), Slovakia (2007), Spain (1974), Sweden (1974), Switzerland (1974), Turkey (1981), United Kingdom (1974), United States (1974).

Observers: All other OECD members, as well as the Commission of the European Communities, may participate as observers.

Origin and development. Created as a response by OECD member states to the energy crisis of 1973–1974, the IEA began provisional operation on November 18, 1974, with signatory governments given until May 1, 1975, to deposit instruments of ratification. Norway, one of the original sponsors, did not immediately participate as a full member because of fear that sovereignty over its own vast oil resources might be impaired. Spain, Austria, Sweden, and Switzerland applied for membership, although the last three reserved the right to withdraw if IEA operations interfered with their neutrality. New Zealand was admitted in 1975, and a later agreement with Norway gave it a special status close to full membership. Subsequently, Australia, Greece, and Portugal joined. France and Finland cooperated with the agency until becoming members in 1992. The Czech Republic joined in February 2001, as did South Korea the following year, and Poland in 2008.

In the event of an oil shortfall of 7 percent or more, the Governing Board can invoke oil-sharing contingency plans and order members to reduce demand and draw down oil reserves. Participating countries agree to maintain oil stocks equal to 90 days' worth of the previous year's net imports. A system of complementary Coordinated Emergency Response Measures, dating from 1984, may be invoked by the Governing Board under circumstances that do not necessarily constitute a full emergency.

Over the years, the IEA has broadened the scope of its activities to include analyses of various energy sectors as well as Country Reports that review energy policies, prices, and developments in key nonmembers as well as in member states.

Regular publications include the *World Energy Outlook* and annual statistical analyses of the oil, natural gas, electricity, and coal industries. Through Implementing Agreements, the IEA also helps fund cooperative research efforts involving such areas as alternative energy sources (ocean power, wind, solar, battery, hydro, hydrogen, geothermal, biomass), clean coal technology, hybrid vehicles, energy efficiency, superconductivity, heat pump and heat exchange technology, and nuclear fusion.

Apart from the energy crisis of the 1970s, the most perilous events for the IEA have been the Iran–Iraq war of the 1980s and the Gulf crisis of 1990–1991. In 1984 IEA members discussed plans to be implemented should the Strait of Hormuz be closed because of the Iran-Iraq war. Members agreed to early use of government-owned or -controlled oil supplies to calm the market in cases of disruption.

A week after the Iraqi invasion of Kuwait on August 2, 1990, the IEA Governing Board met in emergency session, urging efforts to avert a possible oil crisis. Another IEA emergency session on January 11, 1991, unanimously approved a contingency plan to ensure "security of supply." Two days after the January 16 launching of Operation Desert Storm against Iraq, the plan was activated and IEA members were directed to make an additional 2.5 million barrels per day of oil available to the market. The IEA reported that 17 countries subsequently released oil from stockpiles during the war, helping to keep supplies and prices relatively stable.

In 2003 the IEA issued its first *World Energy Investment Outlook,* which concluded that some $16 trillion was needed in energy-related investment by 2030, half of it for transportation and distribution systems. During the biennial International Energy Forum, held in September 2002 in Osaka, Japan, the IEA, OPEC ministers, and other key participants appeared increasingly comfortable about holding discussions in the open rather than behind closed doors. The IEA's contention that suppliers and consumers both benefit from collaborative planning was subsequently reinforced when a confluence of circumstances—the aftermath of a general strike in December in Venezuela, Japan's decision to temporarily shut down nuclear plants because of security concerns, unrest in Nigeria, and the March 2003 invasion of Iraq—could have precipitated a major supply crisis. Instead, with the IEA, its members, oil corporations, and OPEC working in concert, no significant supply shortages or price spikes occurred.

By the 2005 Governing Board meeting, held on May 3 in Paris, the effect on the oil market of rapid economic growth in China and India had become increasingly evident. The final report warned against a business-as-usual approach to energy, stressing the need for more investment and more creative thinking to ensure adequate supplies and reduce the rise in greenhouse gases. During 2005 and 2006, gasoline prices rose substantially throughout the developed world, with no promise of a return to previous levels. In addition to increased demand, real or perceived instability in major producer countries, notably in Iran and Nigeria, caused irregularity in energy markets. In its November 2006 *World Energy Outlook,* the IEA declared that nuclear power must be an important part of any attempt to maintain the world's energy supply and to combat global warming. In June 2007 the IEA praised Germany for its environmental policies, but urged it to end plans to phase out nuclear energy.

In May 2008 the United States urged China and India to join the IEA, saying that membership would help them better manage their energy supplies. The United States' action was widely perceived as an admission that the IEA would become much less effective without the participation of these two emerging industrial giants.

In September 2008 the IEA for the first time surveyed the energy policies of the entire European Union (EU) as opposed to only those countries that are IEA members. In September also the IEA called on India to abolish fuel subsidies, as a way to reduce demand. In the same month Poland was admitted to the IEA, 14 years after it had first applied to join.

The global economic crisis took the price of crude far down from its June 2008 peak of $124.52 per barrel to near $40 in early 2009. This period brought a variety of calls from the IEA about oil's future direction, though with an increasing sense that, as the world economy seemed to stabilize late in 2009, the price of oil might rise again. A February 2009 IEA report predicted a worldwide oil shortage again in 2010 on the assumption that the global recession would be largely over by then.

The IEA *World Energy Outlook 2009,* published in November of that year, stressed the importance of converting as much as possible to biomass-based fuels, whose production emits less carbon than fossil fuels. It declared that current trends were unsustainable and blamed transportation for approximately 97 percent of the projected increase in energy demand by 2030. The IEA believed that in the short term the worldwide recession would lessen the increase in carbon emissions. But some observers believed that the IEA's projection of future demand was too low, and of supply too high, favoring business-as-usual policies in its member states.

One of the most surprising issues for the IEA in recent years has been the growth in China's use of energy. In March 2010 the IEA reported that Chinese oil consumption had jumped by an "astonishing" 28 percent in January 2010 compared with January 2009. A July 2010 IEA report stated that for the first time China, rather than the United States, was the world's leading consumer of energy. A Chinese official denied this. However, in August the Chinese government ordered over 2,000 factories—mostly heavy industry—to close, because they were wasting too much energy.

In the *World Energy Outlook 2010,* the IEA highlighted removal of government subsidies for fossil fuels as the fastest way of attacking the world's rising demand for energy.

In April 2011 the IEA released its first *Clean Energy Progress Report*. The report cited continued reliance on fossil fuels as a major challenge to clean energy and called on member countries to continue to assess their energy policies in an effort to make them less harmful to the environment. It also heralded the successes that have been experienced with regard to clean energy, such as the increased use of solar energy and wind energy since 2000. Another IEA report was released in May that focused on increasing use of clean energy sources in home construction as a means of reducing carbon dioxide and energy emissions.

In response to the political and military situation in Libya, the IEA authorized the release of 60 million barrels of oil in June 2011 to offset the decreased supply that has resulted from oil not being produced in Libya. This action, combined with a sharp rise in OPEC (see separate article) oil production, helped meet the demands of the market and lower the price of oil.

The *World Energy Outlook 2011* noted that the rising costs of oil in the global market were largely due to increasing transportation costs. To combat the "end of cheap oil," the report called for an increased turn to renewable energy and nuclear power. It also called for Russia to increase its oil and natural gas production, while decreasing its consumption.

The year 2012 saw major changes in the price of oil, with oil reaching record highs during the month of March before costs began to subside. The volatile oil-market was the IEA's top concern for most of 2012. The January 2012 Symposium on Energy Outlook, a joint seminar between the IEA, the International Energy Forum, and OPEC (see separate entry), was entirely focused on solutions to deal with the rapidly increasing oil prices and the subsequent impact on the global oil market. The March 2012 quarterly meeting was entirely focused on gas and oil prices; the IEA member states expressed great concern about the impact oil prices were having on their already struggling economies. In October 2012 the IEA announced a new initiative calling on its member states to work together to double hydroelectricity production by 2050.

In February 2013 Executive Director Maria vanderHoeven announced that IEA would begin to increase its cooperation with emerging economies outside the IEA membership. This partnership between the IEA and major emerging economies (including China, Russia, Brazil, India, Indonesia, and South Africa) has been termed an Association, while the organization looks at how to deepen their cooperation with these nations. In June 2013 the IEA announced its prediction that renewable energy, which has increased by 40 percent over the last five years, will surpass gas as the primary energy source by 2016. They also announced a projection of increased gas consumption in 2014.

The *World Energy Outlook 2013* outlined several important global changes for energy, most notably the increasing energy consumption of emerging economies, increased access to oil with new technology, such as ultra-deepwater fields and the rise of renewable energy—which the IEA expects to account for 45 percent of all energy generated by 2035. The report also indicated that natural gas consumption could increase dramatically by 2035, given its flexibility and environmental benefits compared to other fossil fuels. (For more on activities since, see Recent activities, below.)

Structure. The IEA's Governing Board is comprised of ministers of member governments. The board is assisted by three standing groups (Emergency Questions, Long-Term Cooperation, and the Oil Market) and two committees (Energy Research and Technology and Non-Member Countries). Decisions of the Governing Board are made by a weighted majority except in the case of procedural questions, when a simple majority suffices.

A Coal Industry Advisory Board reports to the Standing Group on Long-Term Cooperation. There also is an Industry Advisory Board on Oil. Working parties reporting to the Committee on Energy Research and Technology (CERT) focus on fossil fuels, renewable energy technologies, and end-use technologies; a Fusion Power Coordinating Committee also reports to the CERT. The office of the Executive Director includes an Emergency Planning and Preparations Division, which helps carry out the work of the Standing Group on Emergency Questions.

Recent activities. Estonia joined the IEA as the organization's 29th member on May 9, 2014. Estonia's membership marked the completion of its membership application process that began in 2011. In June the organization released an energy investment outlook in which it projected an additional $48 trillion of investment would be needed to meet the global energy demands by 2035.

The IEA held emergency response exercises in China in January 2015 where 70 participants reacted to a simulated disruption in oil supply, marking the first time the IEA conducted an emergency response drill outside of Paris. In a March 2015 study, the IEA reported that 2014 global emissions were the same as 2013.

The IEA recorded a 25 percent decrease in oil and gas investments in 2015, an unprecedented decline. The IEA cut its forecast for demand for petroleum for the first half of 2017 with a slowing of demand and an over-supply of oil on the market. The Chinese National Energy Administration and the IEA signed a joint agreement to work together to develop a sustainable energy strategy at the 21st Conference of the Parties (COP21) in November 2015.

INTERNATIONAL ORGANIZATION FOR MIGRATION (IOM)

Organisation Internationale pour les Migrations
Organización Internacional para las Migraciónes
(OIM)

Established: On December 5, 1951, in Brussels, Belgium, as a provisional movement to facilitate migration from Europe; formal constitution effective November 30, 1954; present name adopted in November 1989.

Purpose: To advance understanding of the causes and effects of migration; to collect, analyze, and disseminate information on migrant rights and welfare; to provide a forum for discussion of practical solutions to migration issues; to assist states in managing migration through resettlement, immigration, and the return and reintegration of migrants, refugees, displaced persons, and former combatants.

Headquarters: Geneva, Switzerland.

Principal Organs: Council (all members and observer states), Executive Committee (33 members), Director General's Office.

Website: www.iom.int.

Director General: William Lacey Swing (United States).

Membership (165): Afghanistan, Albania, Algeria, Angola, Antigua & Barbuda, Argentina, Armenia, Australia, Austria, Azerbaijan, Bahamas, Bangladesh, Belarus, Belgium, Belize, Benin, Bolivia, Bosnia and Herzegovina, Botswana, Brazil, Bulgaria, Burkina Faso, Burundi, Cambodia, Cameroon, Canada, Cape Verde, Central African Republic, Chad, Chile, China, Colombia, Comoros, Democratic Republic of the Congo, Republic of the Congo, Costa Rica, Côte d'Ivoire, Croatia, Cyprus, Czech Republic, Denmark, Djibouti, Dominican Republic, Ecuador, Egypt, El Salvador, Eritrea, Estonia, Ethiopia, Fiji, Finland, France, Gabon, Gambia, Georgia, Germany, Ghana, Greece, Guatemala, Guinea, Guinea-Bissau, Guyana, Haiti, Holy See (The Vatican City State), Honduras, Hungary, Iceland, India, Iran, Ireland, Israel, Italy, Jamaica, Japan, Jordan, Kazakhstan, Kenya, Kiribati, Republic of Korea, Kyrgyzstan, Latvia, Lesotho, Liberia, Libya, Lithuania, Luxembourg, Macedonia, Madagascar, Malawi, Maldives, Mali, Malta, Marshall Islands, Mauritania, Mauritius, Mexico, Federated States of Micronesia, Moldova, Mongolia, Montenegro, Morocco, Mozambique, Myanmar, Namibia, Nauru, Nepal, Netherlands, New Zealand, Nicaragua, Niger, Nigeria, Norway, Pakistan, Panama, Papua New Guinea, Paraguay, Peru, Philippines, Poland, Portugal, Romania, Rwanda, St. Kitts and Nevis, St. Lucia, St. Vincent and the Grenadines, Samoa, São Tomé and Principe, Senegal, Serbia, Seychelles, Sierra Leone, Slovakia, Slovenia, Solomon Islands, Somalia, South Africa, South Sudan, Spain, Sri Lanka, Sudan, Suriname, Swaziland, Sweden, Switzerland, Tajikistan, Tanzania, Thailand, Timor-Leste, Togo, Trinidad and Tobago, Tunisia, Turkey, Turkmenistan, Tuvalu, Uganda, Ukraine, United Kingdom, United States, Uruguay, Vanuatu, Venezuela, Vietnam, Yemen, Zambia, Zimbabwe.

Observers (8): Bahrain, Bhutan, Cuba, Indonesia, Qatar, Russian Federation, San Marino, Saudi Arabia.

Official Languages: English, French, Spanish.

Origin and development. A Provisional Intergovernmental Committee for the Movement of Migrants from Europe was established by delegates to a 16-nation International Migration Conference in 1951 in Brussels, Belgium. The Intergovernmental Committee for European Migration (ICEM) was based on a constitution that came into force November 30, 1954.

Since the ICEM operations began, more than 13 million migrants and refugees in more than 125 countries have been assisted with travel, placement, orientation, medical payments, vocational and language training, and other resettlement or repatriation services. Overall, the IOM has engaged in programs affecting every inhabited continent. Beginning in 1965, the organization carried out a Selective Migration Program to facilitate a transfer of technology from Europe to Latin America through the migration of highly qualified individuals. More than 27,000 European professionals, technicians, and skilled workers were relocated through the 1970s. Beginning in 1971 the organization also participated in the emigration of hundreds of thousands of Jews from the Soviet Union, and it assisted in the resettlement of more than 1 million refugees from Indochina after 1975.

In November 1980 the group's name was changed to the Intergovernmental Committee for Migration (ICM), "European" being deleted from its name due to the broadened scope of the organization's activities. On May 20, 1987, a number of formal amendments to the ICM constitution, including another change of name to the International Organization for Migration (IOM), were approved to better reflect the worldwide nature and expanding mandate of ICM activity. The amendments came into effect on November 14, 1989, after being ratified by two-thirds of the member states.

In the second half of the 1990s, it began a countertrafficking program in Cambodia and Thailand and also assisted in reintegrating demobilized soldiers in Angola and Guatemala. In 1996–1999 it undertook a Return of Qualified Nationals program to assist Bosnia and Herzegovina in encouraging the return of professionals and other skilled emigrants. The IOM also has participated in numerous efforts to address the problem of skilled workers leaving developing countries, most recently with a focus on Africa. An estimated 70,000 African professionals now emigrate to the West annually.

During 2001 the IOM drew on its earlier experiences in Bosnia and Herzegovina to organize an Out-of-Kosovo Voting Program that registered more than 125,000 Kosovars living outside the province. The IOM also has been directly involved in the German Forced Labor Compensation Program, which has sought to identify and compensate victims of slave and forced labor during the Nazi era, and in implementing the settlements won in the Holocaust Victim Assets Litigation against Swiss banks.

In 2003, following the U.S.-led ouster of the Saddam Hussein government, the IOM introduced an Iraq Transition Initiative to help Iraqi refugees, internally displaced peoples, and former combatants. The IOM also responded to unrest in Côte d'Ivoire by helping repatriate individuals from neighboring states who were stranded in the region. The IOM has also been active in the response to the devastating earthquake of October 2005 in Pakistan; the Indian Ocean tsunami of December 26, 2005; the Indonesian government's efforts to build peace in the troubled province of Aceh; the May 2006 earthquake on the island of Java; and the disastrous cyclone of May 2008 in Myanmar.

Since 1998 IOM membership has more than doubled, and relations have been established or strengthened with dozens of other intergovernmental organizations. There has been a corresponding increase in the IOM budget, which leapt from $242 million in 1998 to more than $1.2 billion in 2013.

In March 2007 it opened a liaison office in Beijing, China—a country greatly affected by migration from country to city. Of particular concern in 2007 and 2008 was the rise of migration or attempted migration, often under desperate conditions, from Africa to Europe. The IOM is working in Africa to deter this migration through propaganda campaigns and programs to help stranded migrants go home. The problem of human trafficking continued to be a focus, with the IOM looking at trafficking to the Gulf States, and the Central Asian republics of the former Soviet Union.

William Lacey Swing (United States), a diplomat with U.S. and UN experience, was elected Director General at the June 2008 council meeting and assumed his post on October 1, 2008. At the same meeting India and Somalia were welcomed as full members, their status being upgraded from that of observers. In May 2009 the IOM sent rapid response teams to assist Pakistanis displaced by fighting in that country's northwest region. It also provided shelter for Pakistani families displaced by the August 2010 floods. In August 2009 the IOM opened a Labor Migration Center in a South African town bordering Zimbabwe to help Zimbabweans find properly credentialed work in South Africa.

There was some good news in 2010, although the problems described above continued. The IOM reported that as many as 2 million internally displaced people had returned to their homes in Southern Sudan since the signing of a peace agreement between the north and south in 2005. Also fewer people were now fleeing their homes in Iraq, although returnees were finding living conditions very difficult.

In August 2010 Trinidad and Tobago became the 127th member of the organization and were followed by five additional countries in November: Botswana, Central African Republic, Lesotho, Swaziland, and Timor-Leste. After the political uprising of the Arab Spring revolutions in early 2011, over 200,000 refugees, primarily from Libya, were able to return home with the help of the IOM.

At the 100th Session of the IOM Council in December 2011, the organization approved the membership of 14 new states, 4 of which had previously been observers: Djibouti, Chad, Ethiopia, Maldives, Guyana, Nauru, Comoros, Antigua and Barbuda, the Holy See, Micronesia, South Sudan, Mozambique, Seychelles, and Vanuatu. The session also approved the creation of a new Migration Emergency Fund Mechanism. The fund is intended to increase the IOM's ability to respond to emergency situations and global migration crises.

In May 2012 the IOM helped facilitate the migration of many South Sudan refugees that were being held in Khartoum, Sudan, after the Sudanese government closed the major thoroughfares from Sudan to South Sudan.

At the November 2012 meeting of the IOM Council, the organization approved the membership of St. Vincent and the Grenadines and Malawi, while also upgrading the membership of Papua New Guinea from Observer State to full member. In June 2013 the IOM Council voted to approve the membership of two new member states—Malawi and Suriname. At the meeting, the Council also unanimously reelected William Lacy Swing to a second five-year term as Director General.

With increasing violence and turmoil in Syria, the IOM has been actively involved in the relocation of Syrian refugees. Iraq opened its borders to Syrian refugees in August 2013, and within just a month, more than 195,000 Syrian refugees had been relocated to the Kurdish regions of Iraq. There are also an additional 100,000 refugees in Lebanon, over 200,000 in Jordan, and over 130,000 in Turkey. The crisis in Syria has been one of the IOM's primary concerns since early 2012. Matters in Syria worsened with the rise of the terrorist organization the Islamic State of Iraq and Syria (ISIS) operating within the country. As a result, the IOM expanded its efforts to include bases of operation in Syria, Iraq, Lebanon, Jordan, and Turkey. Since the beginning of the crisis, the IOM has assisted nearly 2 million internally displaced persons and more than 18,000 refugees.

At the group's 103rd Session of the Council held in November 2013, Turkmenistan, Fiji, Marshall Islands, and Iceland were approved as member states. The meeting also endorsed a resolution on the role of the IOM in regard to the UN's post-2015 development agenda. The council also launched a new public relations and media campaign designed to improve the way people think about and perceive migrants and migration. (For more on developments since 2013, see Recent activities, below.)

Structure. The Council, which normally meets once a year, is comprised of representatives of all member and observer states. The 23-member Executive Committee, which meets twice a year, is elected by the Council for a two-year term. A Subcommittee on Budget and Finance assists the Council. The Standing Committee on Programmes and Finance is open to all member states and meets biennially to discuss and assess the effectiveness of IOM's programs and budget.

The Director General's Office oversees the daily operations of IOM headquarters, provides management coordination, and assists with policy formulation and program development. The director general is elected for a five-year term by the Council. Administrative divisions at IOM headquarters include External Relations; Administrative Support (Department of Budget and Finance, Department of Human Resources and Common Services Management); Information Technology and Communications; Migration Policy, Research, and Communication; Program Support, which includes the Donor Relations Division, the Emergency and Post-Crisis Division, and Project Tracking; Special Programs (Compensation Programs); and Migration Management Services (MMS). Also linked to the Director General's Office in Geneva are the Office of the Inspector General, Legal Services, Media and Public Information, and a Meetings Secretariat.

In the field, the IOM relies on its Manila and Panama Administrative Centers, which between them have additional responsibilities for information technology, security, and administration; 18 other Missions with Regional Functions scattered around the globe; some 225 Country Missions and suboffices; and short-term emergency Special-Purpose Missions. These centers interact with the IOM's field offices, providing project support and training in the core areas of movement (resettlement, repatriation, and transportation), assisted voluntary returns and integration, counter-trafficking, labor migration, mass information, migration health, and technical cooperation. Most of the organization's more than 7,000 staff work at the field level.

Recent activities. A special session of the council was held in June 2014, at which time Macedonia was approved for membership within the IOM.

In December 2015 the IOM reported that more than 1 million migrants had entered Europe over the previous year—the highest annual number on record—creating a massive refugee crisis (see entry on the European Union).

In 2015 the IOM Assisted Voluntary Return and Reintegration (AVRR) program helped 69,540 migrants return to their homelands or settle in a host country. Through June 2016 the AVRR worked with more than 51,000 migrants.

On July 25, 2016, the UN General Assembly unanimously adopted a resolution making the IOM a related organization. On September 19, 2016, the IOM officially joined the UN system in a decision supported by all 165 members.

NON-ALIGNED MOVEMENT

Established: Through the course of an increasingly structured series of conferences comprising states that describe themselves as not aligned with either one of the world's great powers (originally perceived as the Soviet Union and United States), the first of which met September 1–6, 1961, in Belgrade, Yugoslavia.

Purpose: To promote a "transition from the old world order based on domination to a new order based on freedom, equality, and social justice and the well-being of all"; to pursue "peace, achievement of disarmament, and settlement of disputes by peaceful means"; to search for "effective and acceptable solutions" to world economic problems, particularly the disparities in the level of global development"; to support self-determination and independence "for all peoples living under colonial or alien domination and foreign occupation"; to seek "sustainable and environmentally sound development"; to promote "fundamental rights and freedom"; to contribute to strengthening "the role and effectiveness of the United Nations" (Final Declaration, Belgrade, 1989).

Headquarters: None.

Principal Organs: Conference of Heads of State, Meeting of Foreign Ministers, Coordinating Bureau (25 members).

Website: www.nam.gov.za.

Chair: Nicolás Maduro (Venezuela).

Membership (120): Afghanistan, Algeria, Angola, Antigua and Barbuda, Azerbaijan, Bahamas, Bahrain, Bangladesh, Barbados, Belarus, Belize, Benin, Bhutan, Bolivia, Botswana, Brunei, Burkina Faso, Burundi, Cambodia, Cameroon, Cape Verde Islands, Central African Republic, Chad, Chile, Colombia, Comoro Islands, Democratic Republic of the Congo, Republic of the Congo, Côte d'Ivoire, Cuba, Djibouti, Dominica, Dominican Republic, Ecuador, Egypt, Equatorial Guinea, Eritrea, Ethiopia, Fiji, Gabon, Gambia, Ghana, Grenada, Guatemala, Guinea, Guinea-Bissau, Guyana, Haiti, Honduras, India, Indonesia, Iran, Iraq, Jamaica, Jordan, Kenya, Democratic People's Republic of Korea, Kuwait, Laos, Lebanon, Lesotho, Liberia, Libya, Madagascar, Malawi, Malaysia, Maldives, Mali, Mauritania, Mauritius, Mongolia, Morocco, Mozambique, Myanmar, Namibia, Nepal, Nicaragua, Niger, Nigeria, Oman, Pakistan, Palestine (represented by the Palestinian Authority), Panama, Papua New Guinea, Peru, Philippines, Qatar, Rwanda, St. Lucia, St. Kitts and Nevis, St. Vincent and the Grenadines, Sao Tome and Principe, Saudi Arabia, Senegal, Seychelles, Sierra Leone, Singapore, Somalia, South Africa, Sri Lanka, Sudan, Suriname, Swaziland, Syria, Tanzania, Thailand, Timor-Leste, Togo, Trinidad and Tobago, Tunisia, Turkmenistan, Uganda, United Arab Emirates, Uzbekistan, Vanuatu, Venezuela, Vietnam, Yemen, Zambia, Zimbabwe.

Observer States (15): Argentina, Armenia, Bosnia and Herzegovina, Brazil, China, Costa Rica, El Salvador, Kazakhstan, Kyrgyzstan, Mexico, Montenegro, Paraguay, Serbia, Tajikistan, Uruguay.

Origin and development. The first Conference of Nonaligned Heads of State, at which 25 countries were represented, was convened in September 1961 in Belgrade, largely through the initiative of Yugoslavian president Josip Tito, who had expressed concern that an accelerating arms race might result in war between the Soviet Union and the United States. The precursor of the Non-Aligned Movement is traced back to the Bandung Asian-African Conference in Indonesia, April 18–24, 1955. Subsequent conferences, which attracted more and more third world countries have convened in Egypt, Zambia, Algeria, Sri Lanka, Cuba, India, Zimbabwe, Serbia, Colombia, South Africa, Egypt, and Iran.

The 1964 conference in Cairo, with 47 countries represented, featured widespread condemnation of Western colonialism and of the retention of foreign military installations. Thereafter, the focus shifted away from essentially political issues, such as independence for dependent territories, to the advocacy of occasionally radical solutions to global economic and other problems. Thus, in 1973 in Algiers there was an appeal for concerted action by the "poor nations against the industrialized world"; this became a basis of debate within the UN for a New International Economic Order (NIEO) and led to the convening of an inconclusive Conference on International Economic Cooperation in late 1975 in Paris, France.

At the 1979 Havana meeting, political concerns resurfaced in the context of an intense debate between Cuban president Fidel Castro, who was charged with attempting to "bend" the movement in the direction of the "socialist camp," and President Tito of Yugoslavia, who urged that it remain true to its genuinely nonaligned origins. In search of a compromise, the Final Declaration of the Havana Conference referred to the movement's "non-bloc nature" and its opposition to both "hegemony" (a euphemism used in reference to presumed Soviet ambitions) and all forms of "imperialism, colonialism, and neocolonialism." In addition, the conference reiterated an earlier identification of "Zionism as a form of racism."

The eighth NAM summit in Zimbabwe in 1986 marked the 25th anniversary of the movement. The site was chosen to underscore the group's main concern: the South African government's policy of forced racial segregation. A final declaration called on nonaligned nations to adopt selective, voluntary sanctions against South Africa pending the adoption of comprehensive, mandatory measures by the UN Security Council. The members demanded international pressure to eliminate apartheid, Pretoria's withdrawal from Namibia (Southwest Africa), and an end to aggression against neighboring states.

Some of NAM's most radical members (including Cuba, Iran, and Iraq) stayed away from the 1989 Belgrade summit after preparatory talks revealed that most members favored fewer polemics and a return to the group's original posture of neutrality. Consequently, the meeting's final declaration was markedly less anti-American and anti-Western than previous ones. Instead, the summit emphasized the need to "modernize" and develop a "realistic, far-sighted, and creative" approach to international issues. The declaration also praised Washington and Moscow for their rapprochement, which, by reducing tensions in many areas of the world, had created a "window of opportunity for the international community."

NAM emerged somewhat revitalized from its tenth summit, held in 1992 in Jakarta, Indonesia. At the conclusion of the meeting NAM declared its intention to project itself as a "vibrant, constructive, and genuinely independent component of the mainstream of international relations." With anti-Western rhetoric kept to a minimum, NAM asked developed nations to give "urgent priority" to establishing "a more equitable global economy" and to assist developing nations in resolving the problems of low commodity prices and "crushing debt burdens." The summit agreed to establish a broad-based committee of experts to devise a debt reduction approach. The Jakarta Message also called for extended South/South trade and investment cooperation. In addition, NAM said it would press for a restructuring of the UN that would include the diminution or elimination of the veto power of the five permanent members of the Security Council and an expansion of council membership.

Also at the summit, action on politically sensitive membership applications from Macedonia and Russia was deferred indefinitely. However, South Africa was welcomed to the NAM ranks following the installation of a multiracial government in Pretoria.

NAM continued to press for UN restructuring at its 11th summit, held October 18–20, 1995, in Cartagena de Indias, Colombia. It also argued that UN peacekeeping efforts should be cut so more resources could be used for combating poverty. The summit's communiqué strongly criticized the United States for continuing its heavy economic pressure against Cuba and urged the industrialized nations to adopt a more "just" system of world trade.

The 12th NAM summit, held September 2–3, 1998, in Durban, South Africa, was expected to concentrate on economic issues, but the ongoing fighting in the Democratic Republic of the Congo diverted attention. The summit also condemned terrorism, insisting that it be countered in accordance with UN principles, not by unilateral initiatives, and expressed regret that the Middle East peace process remained at a standstill—a situation it attributed to Israeli intransigence.

NAM was divided over the Kosovo crisis of 1999, with Muslim member states supporting intervention on behalf of the Kosovars and predominantly backing the U.S.-led NATO air war against Yugoslavia in March–June. The division came in the context of a more fundamental concern that the movement was being eclipsed by the then 133-member Group of 77, which had gained increasing recognition as an effective voice for the economic interests of developing countries.

The organization's 13th Meeting of Foreign Ministers convened April 8–9, 2000, in Cartagena, where the topics under discussion included barring participation by military regimes that had overthrown democratically elected governments. Championed by India, the proposal was generally viewed as an effort to establish democracy as the norm for all members, but observers also noted that New Delhi was clearly targeting Pakistan for exclusion.

The 13th summit was planned for October 2001 in Bangladesh, but the meeting was postponed because of preparations for that country's October 1 national election. The venue was subsequently changed to Amman, Jordan, but instability in the Middle East ultimately led the Coordinating Bureau, meeting in April 2002 in Durban, to designate Malaysia as the host. Thus the 13th summit convened on February 24–25, 2003, in Kuala Lumpur.

Attended by some 60 heads of state or government, the first day of the summit included an address by Malaysian prime minister Mahathir bin Mohamad, who lambasted the West for using undemocratic means to force democracy on other countries. Among the specific issues debated at the summit were the threat of war against Iraq and the nuclear crisis in North Korea. In a "Statement Concerning Iraq," the movement warned against the dangers of preemptive action by the United States and its allies, but it also advised the Saddam Hussein regime to comply with UN Security Council resolutions. With regard to North Korea's nuclear program, the summit ultimately supported Pyongyang's contention that a solution would best be found if the U.S. would agree to negotiate directly instead of insisting on multilateral involvement. In addition, as at previous summits, the participants voiced support for the Palestinian people and condemned Israeli actions and alleged human rights abuses in the West Bank and Gaza.

In keeping with its overall theme of "Continuing the Revitalization of the Non-Aligned Movement," the 2003 summit approved the Kuala Lumpur Declaration. Among other things, the declaration urged the wider international community to ensure that globalization led to the "prospering and empowering of the developing countries, not their continued impoverishment and dependence." In addition, the declaration called upon member states to improve the effectiveness and efficiency of the movement and to enhance unity and cohesion "by focusing on issues that unite rather than divide us."

The 14th Conference of Heads of State took place from September 11–16, 2006, in Havana, Cuba. This meeting, coupled with Cuba's chairing of NAM in 2007 and statements of mutual encouragement between NAM members Venezuela and Iran, caused the United States to look on NAM with increasing disfavor. In June 2007 U.S. secretary of state Condoleezza Rice addressed the U.S. India Business Council and declared that NAM had "lost its meaning"—an opinion quickly contested by Indian foreign minister Pranab Mukherjee. In July 2007 David C. Mulford, the U.S. ambassador to India, put forth a different opinion, stating that "India has played a major role in Non-Aligned Movement over the years and still continues (to do so) in many cases."

Several commentaries, however, have suggested that while the ideal of nonalignment remains as important as ever, NAM might not be useful in its present form. Because NAM has no central headquarters, it has perhaps suffered in recent years from lack of an official, external face. During its period as chair of the group (2003–2006), Malaysia addressed this problem with a very comprehensive Website, or E-Secretariat, which not only documented Malaysia's leadership of the organization, but also thoroughly recorded all aspects of the movement's work. Unfortunately, such initiatives have not continued under subsequent NAM presidencies.

NAM involvement, led by Cuba, in the UN continued. In November 2007 Cuba spoke for NAM against a resolution that condemned North Korea for its record on human rights, declaring that exploitation of this issue "for political purposes should be prohibited." In February 2008 a NAM-sponsored resolution in the UN Security Council condemning Israel for the situation in the Gaza Strip failed to pass. This led to an unpleasant exchange between the Israeli and Cuban delegates. In February also, the NAM ambassadors voted unanimously in favor of a resolution at the International Atomic Energy Agency (IAEA), supporting Iran in its peaceful development of nuclear power. In May 2008 NAM condemned the Sudanese rebel Justice and Equality Movement and voiced its support for Sudan's territorial integrity, while calling on all parties to the Darfur conflict to reach a peaceful solution.

At the July 2009 Sharm-el-Sheik summit, Egypt took over the organization's presidency from Cuba. The meeting took place amid a general sense that NAM needed a new role, possibly using the world financial crisis to address the distribution of global wealth. There was some feeling that, while the dangers of the Cold War era had passed, nonaligned nations needed to protect themselves from the bad effects of global capitalism. The conference condemned the ICC, which had by now issued an arrest warrant for Sudanese president Al-Bashir, and reiterated its support for a peaceful nuclear program in Iran.

In March 2010 the Special Ministerial Meeting of the Non-Aligned Movement on Interfaith Dialogue and Cooperation for Peace and Development (SNAMMM) was held in Manila, Philippines. This meeting adopted a declaration of the value of tolerance, diversity, and mutual understanding in promoting world peace.

On May 23–27, 2011, at the 16th Ministerial Summit in Bali, Indonesia, Fiji and Azerbaijan were recognized as NAM members. In addition to confirming new NAM members, the Bali Declaration was adopted. The Bali Declaration is a 2007 IPCC (Intergovernmental Panel on Climate Change) report confirming the existence of global climate change, and it asserts with 90 percent certainty that it is mostly due to human activity. Member states agreed to a more robust NAM role in addressing international issues, in support for an independent Palestine, and in the promotion of nuclear disarmament, international security and stability, and the inalienable right of all states to pursue the peaceful use of nuclear energy.

On May 7–9, 2012, the 17th Ministerial Summit was held in Egypt as that country concluded its three-year term in the rotating presidency. The ministers of the 120 heads of state focused largely on the role of developing countries in the world. In this regard, it called for increased UN authority in the realm of global governance to ensure that developing countries are represented fairly and equally. The ministers also condemned the United States' sanctions against Syria, and condemned several Israeli practices aimed at Palestine. The ministers called on the UN and the rest of the global community to bring an end to the Israeli occupation of Palestinian territory.

The 16th NAM summit was held in Teheran, Iran, in September 2012. Despite objections from many of the Western nations, including the United States, the summit was still attended by over 100 heads of state and UN secretary-general Ban Ki-moon, among others. The summit called for a changing approach to global conflict resolution, advocating the main themes of peace and justice. The summit noted that in today's global climate, the UN is the most effective means of handling disputes, but is in need of reform. Concerning the civil war in Syria, the organization condemned the American sanctions against Syria and welcomed the efforts being undertaken by the UN and Arab League. The group also expressed its continued support of Palestinian sovereignty and condemned Israeli actions in the area. The group also expressed its support of the Iranian nuclear program, declaring it an issue of state authority to develop, research, and use atomic energy. Venezuela was selected to be the host of the 17th NAM Summit to be held in 2015.

Following the Iranian elections of June 2013, Hassan Rouhani became chair of the Non-Aligned Movement after assuming the Iranian presidency beginning August 1. In conjunction with a meeting of the UN General assembly in September 2013, NAM called a Ministerial Meeting on Cooperation for the Rule of Law at the International Level. The meeting continued to urge the program of UN reform outlined at its 16th summit. (For more on activities since 2013, see Recent activities, below.)

Structure. By convention, the chief executive of the country hosting the most recent Conference of Heads of State serves as NAM's chair. Foreign ministers' meetings are generally held annually between conferences, which are usually convened every three years. A Coordinating Bureau, established at the 1973 conference, currently numbers 25 (including the chair; a rapporteur-general; and, on an ex officio basis, the immediate past chair) with the following regional distribution: Africa, 10; Asia, 9; Latin America and the Caribbean, 4; Europe, 2. In addition to a Political Committee, an Economic and Social Committee, and a Committee on Palestine, NAM has created various working groups over the years. The chair of NAM rotates to the host country's leader at every summit.

Recent activities. The NAM 17th Ministerial Meeting was held in Algiers in May 2014. The meeting focused on major challenges facing the international community, regional political issues, and broader social and humanitarian issues. In July 2014 the NAM issued a communiqué calling for an end to Israel's attacks against Palestine in the Gaza Strip. The organization demanded an immediate cease-fire and called on the UN Security Council to intervene in the situation. In August the movement condemned an American initiative of the U.S. Agency for International Development (USAID) in Cuba, claiming that the American actions seek to turn young Cubans into "destabilizing agents."

The 17th Summit of NAM was held in Venezuela on September 17–18, 2016. The theme of the meeting was peace, sovereignty, and solidarity for development. NAM also addressed the migrant crisis with data from the United Nations High Commissioner for Refugees reporting that 65.3 million people had been forced from their homes in 2015, over half under the age of 18. Further, by the end of 2016 more than 10 million people were denied any nationality or basic rights. NAM blamed the creation of many of these migrants on wars instigated by NATO and the United States.

NORTH ATLANTIC TREATY ORGANIZATION (NATO)

Organisation du Traité de l'Atlantique Nord (OTAN)

Established: September 17, 1949, by action of the North Atlantic Council pursuant to the North Atlantic Treaty signed on April 4, 1949, in Washington, D.C., and effective as of August 24, 1949.

Purpose: To provide a system of collective defense in the event of armed attack against any member by means of a policy based on the principles of credible deterrence and genuine détente; to work toward a constructive East–West relationship through dialogue and mutually advantageous cooperation, including efforts to reach agreement on militarily significant, equitable, and verifiable arms reduction; to cooperate within the alliance in economic, scientific, cultural, and other areas; and to promote human rights and international peace and stability.

Headquarters: Brussels, Belgium.

Principal Organs: North Atlantic Council (all members), Nuclear Planning Group (all members), Military Committee (all members), International Staff.

Website: www.nato.int.

Chair of the North Atlantic Council and Secretary General: Jens Stoltenberg (Norway).

Membership (28): Albania, Belgium, Bulgaria, Canada, Croatia, Czech Republic, Denmark, Estonia, France, Germany, Greece, Hungary, Iceland, Italy, Latvia, Lithuania, Luxembourg, Netherlands, Norway, Poland, Portugal, Romania, Slovakia, Slovenia, Spain, Turkey, United Kingdom, United States.

Partnership for Peace Participants (22): Armenia, Austria, Azerbaijan, Belarus, Bosnia and Herzegovina, Finland, Georgia, Ireland, Kazakhstan, Kyrgyzstan, Macedonia, Malta, Moldova, Montenegro, Russia, Serbia, Sweden, Switzerland, Tajikistan, Turkmenistan, Ukraine, Uzbekistan.

Official Languages: English, French.

Origin and development. The postwar consolidation of Western defenses was undertaken in light of the perceived hostility of the Soviet Union as reflected in such actions as the creation of the Communist Information Bureau (Cominform) in October 1947, the February 1948 coup in Czechoslovakia, and the June 1948 blockade of West Berlin. U.S. willingness to join Western Europe in a common defense system was expressed in the Vandenberg Resolution adopted by the U.S. Senate on June 11, 1948, and subsequent negotiations culminated in the signing of the North Atlantic Treaty on April 4, 1949, by representatives of Belgium, Canada, Denmark, France, Iceland, Italy, Luxembourg, Netherlands, Norway, Portugal, the United Kingdom, and the United States.

The treaty did not prescribe the nature of the organization that was to carry out the obligations of the signatory states, stipulating only that the parties should establish a council that, in turn, would create a defense committee and any necessary subsidiary bodies. The outbreak of the Korean War on June 25, 1950, accelerated the growth of the alliance and led to the appointment in 1951 of Gen. Dwight D. Eisenhower as the first Supreme Allied Commander in Europe. Emphasis on strengthened military defense of a broad area, reflected in the accession of Greece and Turkey to the treaty in February 1952, reached a climax later that month at a meeting of the North Atlantic Council in Lisbon, Portugal, with the adoption of goals calling for a total of 50 divisions, 4,000 aircraft, and strengthened naval forces. Subsequent plans to strengthen the alliance by rearming the Federal Republic of Germany (FRG) as part of a separate European defense community collapsed, with the result that the FRG was permitted to establish its own armed forces and, in May 1955, to join NATO.

NATO's gravest problem during the mid-1960s was the estrangement of France over matters of defense. French resistance to military integration under NATO reached a climax in 1966 when President de Gaulle announced the removal of French forces from consolidated commands and gave notice that all allied troops not under French command had to be removed from French soil by early 1967. These stipulations necessitated the rerouting of supply lines for NATO forces in Germany; transfer of the alliance's European command from Paris, France, to Casteau, Belgium; and relocation of other allied commands and military facilities. Thereafter, France participated selectively in NATO's operations, although it rejoined the Military Committee in 1996.

During the 1970s NATO suffered from additional internal strains. Early in 1976 Iceland threatened to leave the organization because of a dispute with Britain over fishing rights off the Icelandic coast. Disputes between Greece and Turkey, initially over Cyprus and subsequently over offshore oil rights in the Aegean Sea, resulted in Greece's withdrawal from NATO's integrated military command and a refusal to participate in NATO military exercises. In October 1980, five months after Greece threatened to close down U.S. bases on its territory, negotiations yielded an agreement on its return as a full participant. However, relations between Greece and Turkey subsequently remained tenuous. For instance, in October 2000 Greece withdrew from a NATO exercise in Turkey when Ankara objected to the flight of Greek aircraft over disputed Aegean islands.

In June 1980 U.S. president Jimmy Carter reaffirmed his administration's conviction that Spanish membership in NATO would significantly enhance the organization's defensive capability. The Spanish government originally made its application contingent upon Britain's return of Gibraltar and the admission of Spain to the European Community, but Madrid later decided that it could negotiate both issues subsequent to entry. Therefore, following approval in late October by the Spanish courts, the government formally petitioned for NATO membership, with a protocol providing for Spanish accession being signed by the members in December 1981. A referendum in March 1986 ensured Spain's continued participation with three domestic stipulations: the maintenance of Spanish forces outside NATO's integrated command; a ban on the installation, storage, and introduction of nuclear weapons; and a progressive reduction in the U.S. military presence. In November 1996 the Spanish parliament endorsed Spain's full participation in NATO's military structure, which occurred in 1999.

The structure of East-West relations was irrevocably altered by the political whirlwind that swept through Eastern Europe during late 1989 and early 1990, with the demolition of the Berlin Wall (described by one reporter as the "ultimate symbol of NATO's reason for existence") dramatically underscoring the shifting security balance. The dramatic changes in the European political landscape that accompanied the fall of the Berlin Wall and the demise of the Soviet Union substantially altered NATO's perception of its role on the continent. With superpower rapprochement growing steadily, U.S. officials in early 1990 suggested that U.S. and Soviet troop levels could be sharply cut. NATO also endorsed Washington's decision not to modernize the short-range missiles in Europe and agreed to reduce the training and state of readiness of NATO forces.

A Warsaw Pact summit in Moscow in early June and a NATO summit in London in early July confirmed the end of the Cold War. Suggesting that "we are no longer adversaries," Western leaders proposed that a NATO–Warsaw Pact nonaggression agreement be negotiated. NATO's London Declaration also vowed a shift in military philosophy away from forward defense, involving heavy troop and weapon deployment at the East-West frontier, and toward the stationing of smaller, more mobile forces far away from the former front lines. The allies agreed that the Conference on (later Organization for) Security and Cooperation in Europe (CSCE/OSCE) should be strengthened as a forum for pan-European military and political dialogue and urged rapid conclusion of a conventional arms agreement so that talks could begin on reducing the continent's reliance on nuclear weapon systems. They also insisted that Germany remain a full NATO member upon unification, a condition initially resisted by Moscow but ultimately accepted as part of the German–Soviet treaty concluded in mid-July.

As the Warsaw Pact continued to disintegrate, NATO pursued its own military retrenchment and reorganization. In May 1991 the NATO defense ministers approved the most drastic overhaul in the alliance's history, agreeing to reduce total NATO troop strength over the next several years from 1.5 million to 750,000 (including a cutback of U.S. troops from the existing 320,000 to 160,000 or fewer). In addition, it was decided to redeploy most of the remaining troops into seven defense corps spread throughout Western and Central Europe. The new plan also called for the creation of an Allied Rapid Reaction Corps (ARRC) of 50,000–70,000 troops to deal quickly with relatively small-scale crises, such as those that might arise from the continent's myriad ethnic rivalries. At the same time, NATO nuclear weapons were retained in Europe as a hedge against a sudden shift in Soviet policy.

Other issues addressed by NATO in 1991 included a proposed charter change that would permit "out-of-area" military activity (the alliance's participation in the recent Gulf war having been constrained by the restriction against its forces being sent to a non-NATO country) and the security concerns of former Soviet satellites in Eastern Europe, several of which had inquired about admission to NATO. Although all such overtures were rejected as premature, the ministers called for the development of a "network of interlocking institutions and relationships with former communist-bloc nations." The impulse led to the establishment in December of the North Atlantic Cooperation Council (NACC) as a forum for dialogue among the past NATO–Warsaw Pact antagonists. Participating in the NACC were the 16 NATO countries plus Albania, Armenia, Azerbaijan, Belarus, Bulgaria, Czech Republic, Estonia, Georgia, Hungary, Kazakhstan, Kyrgyzstan, Latvia, Lithuania, Moldova, Poland, Romania, Russia, Slovakia, Tajikistan, Turkmenistan, Ukraine, and Uzbekistan. Austria, Finland, Malta, Slovenia, and Sweden had NACC observer status.

The NACC, which worked in liaison with various NATO bodies and met regularly in conjunction with the North Atlantic Council, played a growing role in implementing the new strategic concept endorsed at the November 1991 NATO summit. While reaffirming the essential military dimension of the alliance, the heads of state agreed that a political approach to security would become increasingly important in Europe. Consequently, the summit called for additional reductions in NATO's conventional and nuclear forces beyond those proposed in May.

The NATO leaders also endorsed a larger role for such organizations as the CSCE, the European Community (EC, later the European Union—EU), and the Western European Union (WEU) defensive and political alliance in dealing with the continent's security issues. Significantly, however, the 1991 summit continued to insist that proposed pan-European military forces would complement rather than supplant NATO. As further evidence of the alliance's intention to remain active in European affairs, the NATO foreign ministers in May 1992 agreed to make forces available on a case-by-case basis for future peacekeeping missions necessitated by ethnic disputes or interstate conflict on the continent.

In November 1992 NATO agreed to use its warships, in conjunction with WEU forces, to enforce the UN naval blockade against the truncated Federal Republic of Yugoslavia. In April 1993 the alliance authorized its jets to monitor the UN ban on flights over Bosnia and Herzegovina. Otherwise, NATO appeared to be locked in a somewhat paralyzing debate on how to deal with the fighting in that country. In May 1993 U.S. president Bill Clinton suggested that NATO forces be used to create "safe havens" for Bosnian Muslims, but agreement could not be reached within the alliance on the proposal. In mid-summer Clinton, who had previously been criticized for not taking a more active role in the Bosnian controversy, suggested that U.S. planes might be used to bomb areas in Bosnia under Serbian control, if requested by the UN. Prodded by the new U.S. assertiveness, the NATO defense ministers endorsed the Clinton position and discussed plans for a 50,000-strong NATO peacekeeping force that could be used in the event of a permanent Bosnian cease-fire.

At the same time the EC was evolving what it initially called a Common Foreign and Security Policy as part of the Maastricht Treaty, which brought the EU into existence in November 1993. In response to these events, NATO began developing a framework for Combined Joint Task Forces (CJTFs), which were envisaged as multinational, multiservice contingents that could be quickly deployed for humanitarian, peacekeeping, or defense purposes. Implementation of the CJTF concept began in 1999, and by 2004 three CJTF commands were established, two land based and one naval.

A NATO summit held January 10–11, 1994, in Brussels struck a compromise regarding expansion by launching a highly publicized Partnership for Peace (PfP) program, which extended military cooperation but not full-fledged defense pacts to the non-NATO countries. By mid-1996, 28 nations (including previous Warsaw Pact members, former Soviet republics, and several longtime "neutral" states) had signed the PfP Framework Document. Among other things, the PfP states pledged to share defense and security information with NATO and to ensure "democratic control" of their armed forces. In return NATO agreed to joint training and planning operations and the possible mingling of troops from PfP states with NATO forces in future UN or OSCE peacekeeping missions. NATO ambassadors in February 1994 agreed to conduct air strikes against certain Serbian targets if requested by the UN. Later in the month, in the first such direct military action in the alliance's history, NATO aircraft shot down four Serbian planes that were violating the "no-fly" zone in Bosnia and Herzegovina. In addition, NATO planes bombed several Serbian artillery locations around Sarajevo in April.

Two issues dominated NATO affairs over the next year—the continued conflict in Bosnia and planning for the expected accession of Eastern and Central European countries to the alliance. Regarding the former, NATO responded to growing aggressiveness on the part of Bosnian Serbs by launching a bombing campaign against Serbian positions on August 30, 1995, near Sarajevo. The Serbians subsequently agreed to withdraw their heavy guns from the area as demanded by NATO, the alliance's hard-line approach also apparently contributing to an intensification of peace talks among the combatants in Bosnia. Consequently, NATO tentatively approved the proposed deployment of some 60,000 troops (including 20,000 from the United States) to take over peacekeeping responsibilities from UN forces in Bosnia should a permanent cease-fire go into effect.

By that time a degree of progress had been achieved regarding the alliance's membership plans as well. Among other things, NATO said that applicants would have to display a commitment to democracy and human rights, foster development of a free-market economy, establish democratic control of the military, and not become mere "consumers of security." It also was agreed that new members would not have to accept the stationing of NATO forces or nuclear weapons in their territory.

In the autumn of 1995 NATO members were greatly concerned over a scandal involving Secretary General Willy Claes. Claes, who had succeeded the late Manfred Wörner of Germany in October 1994, was investigated in a corruption case involving a helicopter contract awarded while he was Belgium's economic affairs minister in 1988. He resigned from his NATO post on October 20, 1995. The subsequent selection process for a new candidate degenerated into a public dispute. The first candidate announced by the European NATO members, Ruud Lubbers (former prime minister of the Netherlands), was vetoed by the United States, apparently because of a lack of consultation beforehand. France then blocked Uffe Ellemann-Jensen from Denmark, whom the United States supported, reportedly due in part to the candidate's less-than-satisfactory mastery of French. (Many NATO observers also noted that Ellemann-Jensen had recently criticized French nuclear testing.) As a compromise, Javier Solana Madariaga, a prominent member of Spain's Socialist government since 1982, was appointed to the post on December 5. The new secretary general's announced priorities included the expansion of NATO and the promotion of a peace pact in Bosnia. Regarding the latter, the NATO foreign and defense ministers, meeting in joint session on December 5, formally approved the establishment of the peacekeeping force for Bosnia and Herzegovina (called the Implementation Force, or IFOR) to oversee the recently signed Dayton Accord. IFOR began its mission on December 20. (See entry on Bosnia and Herzegovina for details.)

The other major development at the December 1995 NATO session was an announcement from France that it planned to rejoin the NATO military structure after an absence of nearly three decades. However, it subsequently became apparent that the French decision was contingent on controversial restructuring that would provide greater European control of military affairs on the continent. A degree of progress on that question was perceived at the meeting of NATO foreign ministers on June 2–3, 1996, the United States agreeing that, under some circumstances, the European countries could conduct peacekeeping and/or humanitarian missions on their own under the command of an expanded WEU. However, even though the French defense minister was formally welcomed by his NATO counterparts at their session on June 13, Paris soon after threatened to reverse its recent decision unless Washington agreed to relinquish control of NATO's Southern Command to a European. The United States resisted that demand, primarily because of the prominence of the U.S. Sixth Fleet in the Southern Command.

The U.S.–French debate subsequently deteriorated into public insults prior to the meeting of NATO foreign ministers on December 10–11, 1996, at which Paris appeared to back away from its threat to block NATO expansion unless it got its way regarding the Southern Command. Meanwhile, on a more positive note, the NATO ministers endorsed the creation of a new mission for Bosnia and Herzegovina (the 31,000-strong Stabilization Force, or SFOR), scheduled to take over at the end of the month from IFOR. The Bosnian mission had been widely viewed as a major success for NATO, as had the PfP program, many of whose members had lent troops to IFOR. The streamlined SFOR included troops from the United States, Russia, and some 23 other NATO and non-NATO countries, including, significantly, Germany, whose commitment of 2,000 soldiers marked the first time that combat-ready FRG ground troops had been deployed outside NATO borders since World War II.

It also was agreed at the December 1996 session that NATO would make its long-awaited announcement regarding the admission of new members at the summit scheduled for July 8–9, 1997, in Madrid, Spain. Russia immediately denounced any such plans as "completely inappropriate," and the topic dominated NATO affairs in early 1997. While describing expansion as "inevitable," U.S. representatives were reportedly hoping that a special relationship could still be established between the alliance and Russia that would make Moscow less "antagonistic" to the NATO decision. While Russia strongly preferred that Europe abandon NATO and instead focus on strengthening the OSCE, Moscow ultimately accepted NATO enlargement.

Following months of intense negotiations, NATO and Russia signed a Founding Act on Mutual Relations, Cooperation, and Security on May 27, 1997, in Paris, France. Both sides committed to stop viewing each other as "adversaries" and endorsed "a fundamentally new relationship." NATO also stated it had no intention of stationing nuclear weapons or "substantial combat forces" within the borders of new members. In addition, a NATO–Russia Permanent Joint Council (PJC) was established to discuss security issues, which appeared to satisfy Moscow's goal of having a say in NATO decision making, although NATO officials made it clear that Russia would not be able to veto any of the alliance's decisions. Collaterally, Western leaders promised Russia an expanded role in the Group of Seven and other major international forums.

Although Russia remained officially opposed to any expansion of NATO, the new accord permitted NATO to extend membership to the Czech Republic, Hungary, and Poland in 1999. A number of NATO leaders, led by French president Chirac, had supported the inclusion of Romania and Slovenia in the first round as well but deferred to the U.S.–UK position after a statement from NATO Secretary General Solana that Romania, Slovenia, and the three Baltic states were "strong candidates" for the second round of expansion.

Progress regarding the new members at the Madrid summit served to distract attention from the ongoing conflict between France and the United States. Washington once again refused Paris's demand that a European be put in charge of the Southern Command, and France therefore declined to return to the integrated military command. Meanwhile, at the conclusion of the summit, NATO signed an agreement with Ukraine that established a NATO-Ukraine Commission and provided for cooperation and consultation on a wide range of issues. In other activity in 1997 the alliance replaced the NACC with the Euro-Atlantic Partnership Council (EAPC), which was designed to enhance the PfP program and permit cultivation of broader political relationships among the "partners" and full NATO members. NATO also unveiled a new military command structure, scheduled to be in effect by April 1999. Subsequently, in early 1998, NATO announced it would keep its forces in Bosnia past June, with SFOR's mission now to include civil security. (At the 2004 Istanbul summit, NATO announced it would end the SFOR Mission at the end of that year.)

Events in 1998 were dominated by NATO's admonitions to Yugoslavia's Serbian leaders regarding their policies in the province of Kosovo, where actions against ethnic Albanian separatists had begun in late February. In June a newly authorized Euro-Atlantic Disaster Response Coordination Center (EDRCC) began operating, its first assignment being to assist Kosovar refugees. In June and August, with the cooperation of PfP members Albania and Macedonia, NATO held military exercises near Yugoslavia's borders, while in October continuing hostilities led NATO to warn Belgrade of imminent air strikes. In response, Yugoslavia agreed to admit OSCE observers and to begin military and security withdrawals from the province. To provide the 2,000-member observer force with air surveillance, NATO placed a coordination unit in Macedonia, where an additional command center was sited in November. Widespread hostilities in Kosovo nevertheless resumed in January 1999. In February peace talks opened in Rambouillet, France, cosponsored by France and the United States, but discussions came to an abrupt halt on March 19 when the Serbian delegation continued to reject one of the proposed peace plan's key provisions, namely the presence of NATO peacekeepers on Serbian soil. On March 24, 1999, NATO forces initiated Operation Allied Force—the first intensive bombing campaign in the organization's history—which in the following weeks extended throughout Yugoslavia. (See the entry on Serbia and Montenegro for additional details.)

The Kosovo situation dampened the alliance's 50th anniversary summit, which was held on April 23–25, 1999, in Washington.

Highlights of the summit were the welcoming of the accession of the Czech Republic, Hungary, and Poland (which had been formally admitted at a ceremony at the Truman Library in Missouri on March 12) and the approval of a new Strategic Concept, including a European Security and Defense Identity (ESDI) within the alliance. The summit communiqué acknowledged that the WEU, using "separable but not separate NATO assets and capabilities," could conduct defensive operations without direct U.S. participation. It also noted "the resolve of the European Union to have the capacity for autonomous action" in military matters that did not involve the full alliance. Despite U.S. pressure for NATO to adopt a more global posture, the Strategic Concept continued to limit NATO's purview to the "Euro-Atlantic area," with the communiqué reiterating the primacy of the UN Security Council in international peace and security matters. The summit also saw issuance of a Membership Action Plan (MAP) for future enlargement and the launch of a Defense Capabilities Initiative (DCI), the latter of which emphasized the need for interoperability in command and control and information systems, particularly given the likelihood that future missions would require rapid deployment and sustained operations outside alliance territory. Finally, NATO agreed to build new headquarters in Belgium, at a cost of about $800 million. Construction began in 2008, with completion scheduled for 2012.

On August 5, 1999, NATO approved the appointment (effective the following October) of UK secretary of state for defense George Robertson (subsequently Lord Robertson of Port Ellen) as the successor to Secretary General Solana.

During the same period NATO was negotiating cooperative military agreements with Russia, other former Soviet republics, and a number of Eastern and Central European nations under the PfP program. In May 2000 Croatia became a PfP partner and announced that it would ultimately seek full NATO membership. Also that month, the foreign ministers of nine Eastern and Central European PfP countries—Albania, Bulgaria, Estonia, Latvia, Lithuania, Macedonia, Romania, Slovakia, and Slovenia—agreed to apply collectively for NATO membership in 2002.

Although NATO was criticized by United Nations (UN) secretary general Kofi Annan, among others, for circumventing the UN in launching the air campaign against Yugoslavia in March 1999, the June 10 Security Council resolution that established the UN Interim Administration Mission in Kosovo also included a provision for the NATO-led Kosovo Force (KFOR). By April 2001 KFOR encompassed some 50,000 troops, the bulk of them from NATO and PfP countries, although command had passed a year earlier to the WEU/EU's Eurocorps, consisting of German, French, Spanish, Belgian, and Luxembourgian units. (For additional information on KFOR, see the entries on Serbia and Montenegro.)

Having been involved since the height of the Cold War in attempts to reduce conventional as well as nuclear forces, NATO in April 1999 launched an Initiative on Weapons of Mass Destruction (WMD) and authorized the creation of a WMD Center within the International Staff in Brussels. In 2001 the U.S. George W. Bush administration unilaterally decided to proceed with the development of a National Missile Defense (NMD), despite strong objections from most European allies, as well as Russia. Bush's plan was the major topic of discussion at a special one-day NATO summit held on June 13, 2001, in Brussels, the U.S. president declaring that the Anti-Ballistic Missile Treaty, which prohibits the deployment of new missiles, was a "relic of the past" and needed to be scrapped. The summit, mostly given over to informal discussion among the NATO leaders, was seen as a success for Bush in that many of his European counterparts reportedly agreed to maintain an "open mind" on the NMD, although France and Germany remained explicitly opposed to it. Some allies also were reportedly reassured by Bush's pledge that Washington would unilaterally reduce the number of U.S. offensive nuclear weapons and would attempt to negotiate a new missile treaty with Russia. Further heartening the European leaders, Bush unequivocally endorsed the European Security and Defense Policy and the "new options" offered by "a capable European force, properly integrated with NATO."

On August 22, 2001, responding to a request for assistance from the government of Macedonia, NATO began Operation Essential Harvest, a 30-day mission by approximately 3,500 troops to help disarm ethnic Albanian groups in that Balkan state. In September NATO authorized Operation Amber Fox, encompassing 700–1,000 personnel, primarily to protect international monitors overseeing implementation of the Macedonian peace plan. On December 16, 2002, Operation Amber Fox was in turn succeeded by a new mission, Operation Allied Harmony, to minimize any further risk of ethnic destabilization. This mission was to be of short duration, with NATO contingents being replaced in 2003 by elements of the EU's newly authorized Rapid Reaction Force.

The day after the September 11, 2001, terrorist attacks on the United States, the North Atlantic Council (NAC) invoked the collective self-defense provisions of the founding treaty. The unprecedented decision was followed in October by authorization for specific steps requested by the United States in its efforts to confront international terrorism. These included access to military facilities and intelligence information and the deployment of NATO's airborne early-warning squadron to the United States. NATO also dispatched its Standing Naval Force Mediterranean to the Eastern Mediterranean to support the U.S.-led military operation in Afghanistan and to deter terrorism.

Meeting on November 20–22, 2002, in Prague, Czech Republic, the NATO heads of state extended membership invitations to Bulgaria, Estonia, Latvia, Lithuania, Romania, Slovakia, and Slovenia, with formal admission anticipated for 2004. At the same time, the summit approved establishment of a mobile, rapidly deployable NATO Response Force (NRF). Earlier in the year, on May 28, the NATO heads of state had signed the Rome Declaration, which institutionalized a closer working relationship with Moscow through creation of a NATO-Russia Council (NRC) as successor to the NATO-Russia PJC. The NRF was inaugurated on October 15, 2003. The force numbered 9,000 troops and was initially placed under the command of British general Sir Jack Deverell. The NRF was designated fully operational with 25,000 available troops at the 2006 Riga summit. Since 2003, the NRF has undertaken five operations, including security missions to protect the 2004 Athens Olympics and elections in Iraq. In 2008 and 2010 the composition and organization of the NRF was revised to ensure the unit could be staffed in light of the continuing deployments of NATO forces in Afghanistan.

In its first major military operation outside the transatlantic region, in August 2003 NATO assumed command of the International Security Assistance Force (ISAF) authorized by the UN in Afghanistan. NATO oversaw 5,500 peacekeeping troops in the Kabul region. Efforts to expand the NATO-led mission to more remote regions of the country were constrained by the unwillingness of members and allies to contribute more troops to the ISAF. This inability of the alliance to deploy additional forces demonstrated the growing strain on European member states as the allies tried to maintain operations in areas such as the Balkans, Afghanistan, and Iraq. However, NATO agreed to provide 2,000 additional troops to provide security during the 2004 Afghan elections. In addition, at the 2004 Istanbul summit, NATO leaders agreed to provide troops for at least five provincial reconstruction teams in the Afghan countryside. At the June 2006 Brussels summit NATO leaders announced that the alliance would increase its forces in Afghanistan to 17,000, allowing the United States to reduce its troop strength from 20,000 to 16,000. NATO also announced at the summit that the United States would succeed British command of the NATO–Afghan mission in 2007.

During the winter of 2002–2003, the United States asked individual NATO states to contribute forces to the anti-Iraq coalition. Belgium, France, Germany, and Luxembourg strongly resisted the U.S. initiative, which was supported by other members, such as the United Kingdom, Netherlands, Italy, and Spain. The divide threatened the cohesiveness of the alliance in February 2003 after the antiwar allies blocked a request from Ankara for NATO to provide surveillance aircraft and antimissile batteries to protect Turkey in the event of armed conflict with Iraq. The deadlock was resolved on February 16 by having the Defense Planning Committee (of which France was not a member) resolve the dispute. NATO subsequently authorized the deployment of both early-warning aircraft and antimissile systems.

NATO did not formally participate in the March 2003 invasion of Iraq, but a number of individual NATO members, including the United Kingdom and Poland, contributed troops to the invasion force and to the postwar peacekeeping coalition that the UN authorized.

On January 29, 2003, seven NATO aspirants (Bulgaria, Estonia, Latvia, Lithuania, Romania, Slovakia, and Slovenia) began formal accession negotiations with the alliance. On March 26, 2003, the protocols were signed, and the ratification process began. On March 29, 2004, the seven nations became full members of NATO. The new members were expected to change the internal dynamics of NATO. All seven supported the U.S.-led invasion of Iraq and favored NATO as the cornerstone of European security, placing them at odds with other NATO members such as France and Germany, which sought a greater security role for the EU.

On September 22, 2003, NATO approved the appointment (effective January 5, 2004) of Dutch foreign minister Jaap de Hoop Scheffer as successor to Secretary General Lord Robertson. As was the case with many of his predecessors, de Hoop Scheffer's appointment was the result of compromises among the allies. Candidates such as Norway's defense minister Kristin Krohn and Portugal's António Vitorino (an EU commissioner) were rejected by France because of their countries' support of the U.S.-led invasion of Iraq, while the United States vetoed Canadian finance minister John Manley because of his country's opposition to the Iraq War.

At the June 2004 summit in Istanbul, interim Iraqi prime minister Iyad Allawi requested additional NATO aid. However, the prewar divide continued, and NATO leaders could only reach a compromise whereby alliance forces would train the Iraqi military and police forces. (NATO deployed 300 troops for the training mission, although Belgium, France, Germany, Greece, Luxembourg, and Spain declined to participate.) Nonetheless, the mission marked the second major nontransatlantic security operation by NATO. Also, in its June 28 communiqué following the summit, NAC affirmed support for Poland's command of the coalition's multinational division in Iraq.

Anders Fogh Rasmussen of Denmark succeeded de Hoop Scheffer as NATO secretary general on August 1, 2009. Rasmussen's appointment was initially blocked by Turkey because of the former Danish prime minister's defense in 2006 of the publication of newspaper cartoons depicting the Prophet Mohammed that many Muslims found offensive. Turkish officials reportedly opposed the nomination because of concerns that Rasmussen's appointment could serve as a focal point for Islamic extremists, but dropped their opposition in exchange for several senior appointments within the alliance.

In June 2006 Putin warned NATO against further expansion to states such as Ukraine; nonetheless, the alliance continued discussions with Ukraine and other states, including Croatia, Georgia, Armenia, and Azerbaijan. NATO also sought to strengthen ties with nonmembers, and in April 2006 the alliance announced plans for regular security forums with states such as Australia, Finland, Japan, New Zealand, South Korea, and Sweden. Proposals for a global version of PfP were also endorsed.

In April 2009 France rejoined the Defense Planning Committee (DPC) after withdrawing from the body in 1966. The DPC, which dated from 1963, focused on a range of matters related to collective defense planning and also offered guidance to military leaders. The DPC typically met at the permanent representative level but also convened twice a year as a meeting of defense ministers. Following a review of all NATO structures, the decision was made to dissolve the DPC and absorb its functions into the NAC in June 2010.

At the NAC meeting in June 2006 in Brussels, the alliance's defense ministers decided to require all member states to devote 2 percent of their GDP to defense, replacing a longstanding "gentleman's agreement" regarding the 2 percent threshold that only 7 of the 26 NATO members reached in 2005. (The average expenditure per NATO country in 2005 was 1.8 percent.) At the same meeting, NAC agreed to reorient the alliance so that it could simultaneously conduct six medium-size operations (of up to 20,000 troops each) and two major missions (of up to 60,000 troops each). The change was designed to better reflect NATO's contemporary range of operations.

At the alliance's November summit in Riga, NATO invited Bosnia and Herzegovina, Montenegro, and Serbia to join PfP. By October 2006 NATO-led ISAF had completed its expansion so that it had a presence in the four main geographic regions of Afghanistan. NATO then initiated a countrywide stabilization program that included increased humanitarian projects and development initiatives, as well as new military operations against Taliban forces.

NAC extended the term of NATO secretary general de Hoop Scheffer by two years in January 2007. De Hoop Scheffer remained in office through 2009 to provide continuity as the alliance commemorated the 60th anniversary of its formation that year.

Alliance troops launched NATO's largest offensive in the southern provinces of Afghanistan, Operation Achilles, in March 2007. More than 4,500 NATO, and 1,000 Afghan, soldiers participated in the anti-Taliban strikes that began in March. By the summer more than 33,000 soldiers from 37 NATO and allied countries were participating in ISAF. Nonetheless, Taliban attacks and other antigovernment activity continued to increase in remote areas of the country. In June NATO agreed to provide strategic airlift and other support for the AU Mission in Somalia (AMISOM) through 2007.

U.S. plans to deploy a missile defense system in Europe created strife within NATO and renewed tensions with Russia in 2007. At a defense ministers' meeting in Brussels in June, NATO agreed to continue efforts to develop an alliance-based theater missile defense system while launching a broad assessment of the U.S. initiative.

NATO and Russia reiterated their commitment to cooperation at a series of events that commemorated the fifth anniversary of the NATO–Russia Council in June 2007. However, Russia announced plans to unilaterally withdraw from the Conventional Forces in Europe Treaty (CFE) in July, and NAC responded by reaffirming its commitment to the CFE and urging the Russian government to reconsider and open a dialogue on the agreement. In December 2007 Russia stopped exchanging information with NATO about its troop movements, a development about which NATO expressed "deep regret" but no intention of retaliating. The second half of 2007 had seen conditions less and less conducive to good relations between Russia and NATO. Kosovo was a source of tension, with Russia strongly opposing it becoming an independent state, and the West tending to favor it. The former Soviet republics of Ukraine, Azerbaijan, and Georgia were all moving toward NATO membership, with Georgia's intentions a special irritant to Moscow.

By everyone's admission, the NATO operation in Afghanistan was having difficulties. At a December 2007 NATO foreign ministers' conference in Edinburgh, Scotland, both the U.S. and UK defense ministers declared that not enough NATO countries were deploying their troops where there was fighting. Germany was particularly mentioned in this context. Individual national force contributions to the Afghanistan mission dominated the February 2008 Vilnius meeting of NATO defense ministers, and Canada threatened to withdraw part of its forces unless other alliance members increased their presence. At the April 2008 Bucharest summit, French president Nicholas Sarkozy announced the deployment of an additional 1,000 troops, with other NATO states and partner countries dispatching smaller increases. The April deployment of an additional 2,400-troop U.S. Marine expeditionary unit allowed ISAF to undertake Operation Azada Woza in the Helmand region of Southern Afghanistan to suppress Taliban forces and heroin production. By 2008 ISAF numbered 52,700, its highest level. Nonetheless, the Taliban continued a series of aggressive attacks. In June, for the first time, more coalition troops died in Afghanistan (45) than in Iraq (31).

Also at the 2008 Bucharest summit, the United States led an unsuccessful effort to invite Georgia and Ukraine to join NATO. Concerns over Russian reaction led France and Germany to oppose membership. Albania and Croatia were invited to begin accession discussions, and formal membership protocols were signed in July. Meanwhile, initial membership talks were launched with Bosnia and Herzegovina and Montenegro. In addition, Malta announced that it would rejoin PfP. At the summit, NATO heads of state endorsed a U.S. proposal for a missile defense system. In June NATO's Science for Peace and Security program completed the destruction of 1,300 tons of toxic, Soviet-era missile fuel in Azerbaijan. In August, in response to the Russian invasion of Georgia, NATO suspended meetings of the NATO–Russia Council. NATO also agreed to create the NATO–Georgia Commission to prepare Georgia for eventual membership in the alliance.

In response to growing civilian casualties in Afghanistan, NATO issued a new tactical directive in January 2009 that implemented a number of new measures to minimize collateral damage during attacks. On April 3–4, NATO leaders met in Strasbourg, France. Anders Fogh Rasmussen formally was designated the next NATO secretary general. France reentered NATO's integrated military structure following an agreement whereby the United States agreed that a non-U.S. military officer would be appointed Supreme Allied Commander Transformation (SACT). French admiral Abriel was subsequently appointed to the post (see Structure, below). On April 7 Albania and Croatia officially joined the alliance. In August a suicide bomber attacked ISAF headquarters in Kabul, killing 7 and wounding more than 100, in a strike that was seen as part of a broader effort to disrupt the Afghan presidential and provincial elections that were held on August 20. On September 4 a NATO airstrike killed more than 90 civilians, prompting a NATO apology and new guidelines on the conduct of aerial attacks. In December the United States announced that it would commit an additional 30,000 troops to the NATO-led mission in Afghanistan as part of a "surge" designed to enhance security while Afghan forces were being trained. Other contributors to ISAF deployed a further 7,000 troops.

In May 2010 a high level panel led by former U.S. secretary of state Madeleine Albright recommended that NATO develop a new strategic concept to better reflect changes in the international environment. In July the Web group WikiLeaks released more than 91,000 documents on the conflict in Afghanistan. Information in the documents detailed covert operations and both civilian deaths and casualties from friendly fire. The controversial files undermined already declining public support in Europe and the United States for the mission in Afghanistan. At a summit in Lisbon in November, NATO heads of state agreed to withdraw combat forces from Afghanistan by 2014 (although the alliance would continue training and support operations). NAC endorsed the creation of a ballistic missile defense system in Europe. NAC also approved a new strategic concept that reaffirmed the alliance's collective defense mission and committed NATO to developing new capabilities to address emerging security threats such as missile attacks or cyber warfare. In addition, NATO announced that it would reduce the number of military headquarters from eleven to seven and consolidate non-military agencies and bureaus to reduce redundancies. At Lisbon, the NATO–Russia Council met for its third summit and endorsed cooperation on missile defense between the former Cold War enemies.

In November 2010 NATO reaffirmed its commitment to Afghanistan by signing the Declaration of Enduring Partnership with the Middle Eastern nation. The declaration established a framework for future political assistance and enhanced cooperation. The biggest area addressed in the document was NATO's commitment to assist Afghanistan in matters of national security with regard to both policy reforms and officer development.

In response to a political uprising that occurred in Libya in February 2011, the UN Security Council passed a resolution (Resolution 1973) that placed an arms embargo and a no-fly zone on Libya. Four weeks after passing the initial resolution, the UN Security Council passed a second resolution on Libya, authorizing regional IGOs to handle enforcement of the UN sanctions. On March 23 NATO launched an arms embargo on Libya, and the next day it voted to enforce the no-fly zone over the country. On March 27 Operation Unified Protector began as NATO decided to assume responsibility for the entire military operation enforcing the UN Security Council Resolution 1973. NATO assumed sole command of international airborne and maritime efforts on March 31.

Operation Unified Protector consisted of a series of air strikes that were targeted at military and air defense sites in Libya to ensure that the no-fly zone was observed by the Libyan dictator Colonel Qadhafi. The air raids were also targeted at groups of advancing Libyan troops and their equipment in a preventative move to stop Colonel Qadaffi's further oppression of the Libyan people. Naval forces were charged with the task of preventing naval attacks and preventing any arms from reaching the country.

NATO voted on June 1 to extend its mission by another 90 days. After numerous successes on both the aerial and the naval fronts, NATO leaders chose to continue their pressure until such time as Qadhafi relinquished power. The move was hailed as a sign of continued support for the Libyan citizens and an end to Qadhafi's oppressive regime. On July 13 the NAC met with the Libyan Transitional National Council and agreed upon the desire to begin working toward a political solution, but troops remain in the region despite the decision. Qadaffi was forced out of Tripoli in August 2011, and the National Transitional Council (NTC) took power. In September the NAC voted to continue its military in Libya, pledging to stay the course until "threats to civilians" no longer persist. The NTC forces captured and killed Qadaffi on October 20, 2011, and NATO announced the end of Operation Unified Protector on October 31.

In June 2011 U.S. president Barack Obama announced plans to begin the withdrawal of U.S. troops in Afghanistan. This move was part of a NATO plan to remove troops and turn security over to the Afghanis by 2014. Just a few weeks after the announcement that the United States would begin withdrawing troops from Afghanistan, the NATO efforts in that country experienced another major change. General David Petraeus announced his resignation as commander of the ISAF forces in Afghanistan to accept the position as director of the U.S. Central Intelligence Agency. Petraeus, who had been in that position since 2010, was replaced by General John Allen. In December 2011 at a conference on Afghanistan held in Bonn, the NATO leaders agreed to extend their commitment to Afghanistan beyond 2014, ensuring that the country would have international support after the full transition of security leadership. As of May 2012 plans have been made for transition to full security leadership in each of the provinces in Afghanistan by July 2013. At the July 2012 Tokyo Conference on Afghanistan, NATO reaffirmed its financial commitment to help train and assist the Afghan security forces that took control of security in Afghanistan's Bamyan province on July 17, 2011. NATO also called on the rest of the international community to participate in the financial support of Afghanistan's self-reliance in security matters.

In May 2012 NATO held its biannual summit in Chicago. The summit was focused on three main goals: the future of Afghanistan, a stronger NATO defense system, and increasing partnerships between NATO and other world countries to achieve global progress. These goals were evident as NATO outlined a reaffirmed support for the 2014 transition in Afghanistan. In regard to NATO defense, the successful creation of an interim ballistic missile defense system was announced, marking the completion of the first stages of the 2010 Lisbon summit decision. NATO also expressed a great deal of appreciation for its partners across the world and their continued support for NATO initiatives.

In November NATO received a request from Turkey asking for the installation of Patriot missiles as a defensive safeguard to augment the Turkish Air Force in light of continuing violence along the Turkish border. NATO Foreign Ministers approved the request on December 4, and the United States, Germany, and the Netherlands (the three states with Patriot missiles) officially deployed the missiles in late December.

In February 2013 General Allen was replaced as commander of ISAF forces in Afghanistan by General Joseph Dunford Jr. Allen was nominated for the post of SACEUR, but respectfully declined in favor of retirement from the military. General Phillip Breedlove was then appointed SACEUR. (For more on major activities since 2013, see Recent activities, below.)

Structure. NATO's complex structure encompasses a civilian component, a military component, and a number of partnership organizations. At the apex is the NAC, the principal decision-making and policy organ. It normally meets twice a year at the ministerial level to consider major policy issues, with the participation of the member states' ministers of foreign affairs and/or defense. It also may meet as a summit of heads of state and government. Between ministerial sessions the NAC remains in permanent session at NATO headquarters, where permanent representatives, all of whom hold ambassadorial rank, convene. Decisions at all levels must be unanimous.

The civilian structure includes the Nuclear Planning Group (NPG), which consists of the defense ministers of the alliance. Its purview extends from nuclear safety and deployment to such related matters as proliferation and arms control. Like NAC, the NPG may call on a host of committees and other bodies, the most prominent of which are the Senior Political Committee and the Defense Review Committee, to provide expert advice, to assist in preparing meetings, and to follow through on decisions.

The secretary general, who is designated by NAC, serves as chair of NAC, the NPG, the EAPC, and the Mediterranean Cooperation Group (MCG), as well as joint chair of the NRC and the NATO-Ukraine Commission. As NATO's chief executive, the secretary general has an important political role in achieving consensus among member governments and also can offer his or her services in seeking solutions to bilateral disputes. Former Norwegian prime minister Jens Stoltenberg became secretary general on October 1, 2014. At the 2002 Prague summit, NAC approved a reorganization of NATO's civilian headquarters structure, known as the International Staff. The new system created a deputy secretary general post and six main divisions (later expanded to nine), each led by an assistant secretary general. The new divisions were Defense Investment, Defense Policy and Planning, Emergency Security Challenges, Executive Management, Operations, Political Affairs and Security Policy, Resources, Public Diplomacy, and the NATO Office of Security (headed by a director).

The highest military authority is the Military Committee, which operates under the overall authority of NAC and NPG. At its top level the Military Committee is attended by the members' chiefs of defense, although, as with the NAC, it is typically in continuous session attended by permanent military representatives from all members. The Military Committee is chaired by a non-U.S. officer of at least four-star rank. The current chair is General Knud Bartels of Denmark, but General Peter Pavel of the Czech Republic will assume the office in June 2015 at the conclusion General Bartel's term. The committee furnishes guidance on military questions, including the use of military force, both to NAC and to subordinate commands. It also meets with PfP partners on matters of military cooperation. The Military Committee is supported by the International Military Staff (IMS), which includes some 380 military personnel from the member states and 85 civilian personnel. The IMS is led by a three-star officer, currently Air Marshal Sir Christopher Harper of the United Kingdom.

Until 1994 the NATO military structure embraced three main regional commands: Allied Command Europe (ACE), Allied Command Atlantic (ACLANT), and Allied Command Channel. However, in 1994 Allied Command Channel was disbanded, and its responsibilities were taken over by ACE. In addition, in 2002 NAC agreed to dissolve ACLANT as an operational command. It was replaced by Allied Command Transformation (ACT). Each command is responsible for developing defense plans for its area, for determining force requirements, and for the deployment and exercise of its forces. Except for certain air defense squads in Europe, however, the forces assigned to the various commands remain under national control in peacetime.

After it absorbed the Allied Command Channel responsibilities in 1994, ACE had three major subordinate commands: Northwest (led by a designee of the United Kingdom), Central (led by a designee of Germany), and Southern (led by a designee of the United States). In 1997 NATO defense ministers agreed to reduce the number of command headquarters from 65 to 20 by 1999. On September 1, 2003, ACE was transformed into Allied Command Operations (ACO). The reorganized ACO initially incorporated two major subordinate commands, Allied Forces North Europe and Allied Forces South Europe, which had a total of seven subregional commands between them, as well as separate air and naval component commands. No fewer than nine other commands and staffs fell under ACO, most of them encompassing rapid reaction forces established in the 1990s. In 2004 ACO was again reorganized and the two subordinate commands divided into Allied Joint Force Command HQ Brunssum, Allied Joint Force Command HQ Naples, and Allied Joint Force Command Lisbon. Other major subordinate structures under ACO include, among others, the Standing Naval Force Atlantic, a Striking Fleet Atlantic, and a Submarine Allied Command Atlantic. There also is a separate Canada–United States Regional Planning Group, originally created in 1940 and incorporated into the NATO command structure in 1949. Its principal task is to recommend plans for the defense of the U.S.–Canada region.

ACO headquarters, known formally as Supreme Headquarters Allied Powers Europe (SHAPE), is located in Casteau, Belgium. The Supreme Allied Commander Europe (SACEUR) has traditionally been designated by the United States and serves concurrently as commander in chief of U.S. forces in Europe (CINCEUR). In April 2013 General Phillip Breedlove of the U.S. Air Force was named SACEUR, replacing U.S. admiral James G. Stavridis. Stavridis had been the first naval officer to be SACEUR.

ACT, with headquarters in Norfolk, Virginia, is headed by the SACT, In September 2012 French Air Force General Jean-Paul Paloméros succeeded Stéphane Abrial as SACT. ACT includes the Joint Warfare Center in Stavanger, Norway; the Joint Force Training Center in Bydgoszcz, Poland; the Undersea Research Center in La Spezia, Italy; the Joint Analysis and Lessons Learned Center in Lisbon, Portugal; the Maritime Interdiction Operational Training Center in Crete; and the NATO School in Oberammergau, Germany. ACT's main mission is to transform NATO's military capabilities to respond more efficiently to new threats and operations.

The NATO Parliamentary Assembly is completely independent of NATO but constitutes an unofficial link between it and parliamentarians of the 28 member countries. It was founded in 1955 as the NATO Parliamentarians' Conference and was subsequently known, until 1998, as the North Atlantic Assembly. PfP partners have associate delegation status in the assembly. By keeping alliance issues under constant review and by disseminating knowledge of NATO policies and activities, the assembly encourages political discussion of NATO matters. During the 1990s its mandate was broadened to include European security as a whole, plus economic, environmental, social, and cultural issues relevant to Central and Eastern Europe. The assembly meets twice a year in plenary session, with various committees and study groups convening throughout the year.

Political dialogue also takes place within the 50-member EAPC, which comprises the 28 NATO members plus the 22 PfP partners, the NRC, the NATO–Ukraine Commission, and the MCG. Established in 1997, the MCG grew out of a Mediterranean Dialogue proposed by NATO in 1994 and initiated in 1995, when Egypt, Israel, Jordan, Mauritania, Morocco, and Tunisia agreed to join. Algeria became the seventh non-NATO member in 2000. The MCG is intended to promote mutual understanding and to serve as a forum on security and stability in the Mediterranean region. At the Istanbul summit in June 2004, NAC decided to expand security cooperation in the Middle East based on the pattern of success of the MCG. Modeled on the PfP, the Istanbul Cooperation Initiative (ICI) was designed to improve military and intelligence cooperation between NATO and Middle Eastern and Persian Gulf states and standardize equipment and operational guidelines. Bahrain, Kuwait, Qatar, and the United Arab Emirates joined the ICI. In 2006 NATO ministers began searching for a host country in which to establish a joint NATO-MCG training center. In addition to formal structures, NATO also has significant relationships with a number of other countries. Australia, Japan, New Zealand, and South Korea were designated as Contact Countries following the 2006 Riga summit. NATO and these nations developed annual work programs and collaborated closely on military operations, training, and logistics.

NATO has established more than three dozen subsidiary and related organizations, agencies, and groups that undertake studies, provide advice, formulate policies for referral to NAC or other NATO decision-making structures, manage specific programs and systems, and provide education and training. Many of these bodies are NATO Production and Logistics Organizations (NPLOs) concerned with technical aspects of design, production, cooperation, and management in communication and information systems; consumer logistics (pipelines, medical services); and production logistics (armaments, helicopters, other aircraft, missiles). Other bodies are concerned with standardization, civil-emergency planning, airborne early warning, air traffic management, electronic warfare, meteorology, and military oceanography. The Science for Peace and Security program was launched in 2006 to enhance scientific and technical cooperation between NATO and partner countries. The initiative provides funding and assistance for research and national projects ranging from environmental clean-up and protection to cybersecurity. In June 2007 NAC agreed to create a new agency to facilitate the alliance's Strategic Airlift Capability (SAC). Under SAC, 15 NATO members and two PfP states would have access to strategic airlift assets acquired by and managed by the alliance. In 2008 the SAC participants agreed to purchase three C-17 aircraft and to station the assets at Papa Airbase in Hungary.

Recent activities. On June 18 Afghanistan's president Karzai announced the transition of the fifth and final group of Afghani cities, provinces, and districts. The announcement was hailed by Secretary General Rasmussen as a major step in the completion of the roadmap set forth at the Lisbon Summit. Rasmussen noted that the ISAF would soon begin to transition from a combat mission to a support mission, and he continued to reinforce the end of the NATO combat mission by 2014.

The civil war in Syria continued to be an especially problematic event in international affairs, particularly after the discovery of chemical weapons in late August. The North Atlantic Council convened a special meeting on August 28 to discuss the situation. At that meeting, the council condemned the use of chemical weapons and expressed its support of the UN investigation into the atrocities being committed in Syria. The council also reaffirmed its commitment to protecting the security of its southeastern border in Turkey. An extraordinary session of the NATO–Russia committee was called on September 17 to discuss the U.S.–Russia framework for eliminating the Syrian chemical weapons. The leaders of that committee expressed their full support for the U.S.–Russian framework calling for the surrender of chemical weapons to be placed under UN control. The committee called on the UN Security Council to quickly implement the framework and emphasized the grave danger of delay. The framework was approved at a Security Council meeting on September 27.

In December 2013 protests in Ukraine were put down with excessive force, prompting both the secretary general and the NATO foreign ministers to condemn the response and expressing its continued support for the democratic reforms underway in Ukraine. In December the North Atlantic Council voted to extend the term of Secretary General Rasmussen an additional two months past the five-year limit in order to allow him to prepare for and preside over the 2014 summit scheduled for September of that year.

Matters in Ukraine continued to spiral downward, prompting Secretary Rasmussen to issue several more statements in February 2014. A special meeting of the North Atlantic Council was convened on March 2 to further discuss the political violence in Ukraine. After the meeting, the leaders condemned the Russian use of military forces in the Crimea, citing it as violation of both international law and the NATO–Russia Council's principles. The council also called for mediation of the situation either through the UN or OSCE (see separate entry). After the "referendum" of March 16 in which Crimea voted to join Russia, the council again issued a statement, this time condemning the illegal and illegitimate referendum.

On March 28 the council announced the selection of former Norwegian prime minister Jens Stoltenberg as the next NATO secretary general, effective October 1. Following a meeting of the foreign ministers on April 1, all relations between NATO and Russia was suspended in light of their violations of international law by sending troops into Crimea. The foreign ministers also announced deeper cooperation and additional assistance for Ukraine. On August 29 a special meeting of the NATO–Ukraine Commission was held, following Russian troops' illegal crossing of the border into Ukraine. The commission announced its solidarity with Ukraine and pledged to take up the issue further at the annual summit the next week. At that time, the commission announced that NATO allies were launching new programs to assist the Ukrainian government and military and reinforcing its advisory presence in Kiev.

In August General John F. Campbell assumed control of ISAF, marking the last command change before the mission is completed and Afghan security forces assumed full responsibility for the country's security at the end of 2014.

The 2014 NATO Summit was hosted in Wales on September 4–5. In addition to the statements issued by the NATO–Ukraine Commission, the summit issued several key declarations summarizing its discussions. The Wales Declaration on the Transatlantic Bond stressed the importance of transatlantic defense cooperation in the face of growing threats to European security. The declaration adopted a Readiness Action Plan and finalized a commitment by the allies to increase defense budgets. Additionally, the summit adopted the Declaration on Afghanistan, which confirmed the end of the ISAF mission in December and announced a plan for cooperation with Afghan security forces after the mission's conclusion. The most comprehensive declaration, however, was the main Wales Summit Declaration, which in addition to discussing the components of the other two declarations, focused a great deal of attention on the situation in Ukraine, reaffirming NATO's solidarity with the Ukrainian government and continuing its sanctions against Russia for its illegal actions. The declaration also condemned the actions of the Islamic extremist organization ISIS and other terrorist organization threatening global security. NATO ended combat operations in Afghanistan on December 28, 2014, after 13 years of war.

On February 5, 2015, NATO formed a rapid reaction force of 5,000 to deter Russia. The reaction unit was stationed in Estonia, Latvia, Lithuania, Poland, Romania, and Bulgaria and was prepared to respond in 48-hours' notice. NATO secretary general Jens Stoltenberg initiated talks to strengthen ties to the European Union on May 15 to develop common strategies to counter any potential threat from Russia or from the Islamic State. On December 2 NATO started accession talks with Montenegro.

The NATO 2016 Warsaw Summit took place in Poland on July 7–8. Leaders discussed the importance of NATO bases in central Europe and agreed to increase training capacity in Iraq. They also pledged to increase the alliance's presence in the Mediterranean in order to deal with the migrant crisis and human trafficking, strengthen cyber security, and increase ballistic missile defense against Iran and North Korea. To further enhance NATO's deterrence capabilities against Russia, alliance members agreed to deploy at least four more battalions in Poland, Estonia, Latvia, and Lithuania. Furthermore, NATO endorsed a comprehensive assistance package for Ukraine and signed an agreement with the presidents of the European Council and the European Commission.

ORGANIZATION FOR ECONOMIC COOPERATION AND DEVELOPMENT (OECD)

Organisation de Coopération et de Développement Economique (OCDE)

Established: By convention signed December 14, 1960, in Paris, France, effective September 30, 1961.

Purpose: "To help member countries promote economic growth, employment, and improved standards of living through the coordination of policy [and] . . . to help promote the sound and harmonious development of the world economy and improve the lot of the developing countries, particularly the poorest."

Headquarters: Paris, France.

Principal Organs: Council (all full members plus the European Commission), Executive Committee (14 members), Economic Policy Committee, Development Assistance Committee, Secretariat.

Website: www.oecd.org.

Secretary General: Ángel Gurría (Mexico).

Membership (34): Australia, Austria, Belgium, Canada, Chile, Czech Republic, Denmark, Estonia, Finland, France, Germany, Greece, Hungary, Iceland, Ireland, Israel, Italy, Japan, Luxembourg, Mexico, Netherlands, New Zealand, Norway, Poland, Portugal, Republic of Korea, Slovakia, Slovenia, Spain, Sweden, Switzerland, Turkey, United Kingdom, United States.

Limited Participant: European Commission.

Official Languages: English, French.

Origin and development. The OECD replaced the Organization for European Economic Cooperation (OEEC), whose original tasks—the administration of Marshall Plan aid and the cooperative effort for European recovery from World War II—had long been completed, although many of its activities had continued or had been adjusted to meet the needs of economic expansion. By the 1960s the once seemingly permanent postwar shortage of dollar reserves in Western European countries had disappeared, many quantitative restrictions on trade within Europe had been eliminated, and currency convertibility had been largely achieved. This increased economic interdependence suggested the need for an organization in which North American states could also participate on an equal footing. Thus, the OEEC, of which Canada and the United States had been only associate members, was transformed into the OECD. The new grouping also was viewed as a means of overseeing foreign aid contributions to less-developed states. It later expanded to include virtually all the economically advanced free-market states. Japan became a full member in 1964, followed by Finland in 1969, Australia in 1971, and New Zealand in 1973. The membership remained static until Mexico's accession in 1994. Subsequently, the Czech Republic (1995), Hungary (1996), Poland (1996), South Korea (1996), and Slovakia (2000) joined. Chile, Israel, and Slovenia joined in 2010. Russia is currently in the process of finalizing its accession, but has been stagnant since May 2012. Membership is limited to countries with market economies and pluralistic democracies and is granted by invitation only. New countries must be approved by each existing member, giving each country veto power. The OECD Center for Cooperation with Non-Members promotes dialogue with more than 70 nonmember countries, which are invited to subscribe to OECD agreements and treaties and benefit from policy and economic recommendations.

The key to the OECD's major role in international economic cooperation has long been its continuous review of economic policies and trends in member states, each of which submits information annually on its economic status and policies and is required to answer questions prepared by the Secretariat and other members. This confrontational review procedure has led to very frank exchanges, often followed by recommendations for policy changes. OECD analyses, generated in part through the use of a highly sophisticated computerized model of the world economy, are widely respected for being free of the political concerns that often skew forecasts issued by individual countries. Furthermore, the OECD has been in the forefront of efforts to combat unstable currencies, massive trade imbalances, third world debt, and high unemployment in industrialized countries.

A degree of controversy developed during the 1989 Council meeting over a recent U.S. citation of Japan, Brazil, and India as "unfair traders" subject to possible penalties. Japan challenged the U.S. decision as a threat to the "open multilateral trading system" and asked for an OECD statement criticizing Washington. The final communiqué, while not specifically mentioning the United States, condemned any "tendency toward unilateralism."

On another controversial topic, the OECD, after having completed an extensive review of the cost of farm support, called for the elimination of all agricultural subsidies by wealthier producers. Attempts to overcome substantial differences among members regarding agricultural policy continued at the 1990 Council meeting, the ministers giving the "highest priority" to completing agreements on farm subsidies and other outstanding issues in the Uruguay Round of the General Agreement on Tariffs and Trade. Other activity during 1990 included the opening of the Center for Cooperation with European Economies in

Transition, designed to advise and guide Central and Eastern European countries as they moved toward free market economies.

In mid-1994 the OECD released the results of a two-year study on the structural causes of unemployment among members. Noting the high rate of unemployment in Europe (about 12 percent) as opposed to the United States (about 6 percent), the report urged European governments to introduce a new flexibility in their labor markets. Other recommendations were greeted cautiously by government officials, who feared changes would erode social benefits and the overall standard of living.

Mexico became the first new OECD member in 23 years when, with strong U.S. and Canadian backing, it acceded in May 1994. The OECD signed a cooperation agreement with Russia at the June 1994 ministerial session, pledging to assist Moscow with legal, structural, and statistical reforms to promote Russia's integration into the global economy, an effort that U.S. officials described as the "best investment we can make in our security."

At the 1996 ministerial meetings, a preliminary agreement was reached regarding corruption in the developing world. Negotiations subsequently continued on the proposed plan to make the bribing of foreign officials a criminal offense, and in November 1997 the treaty was finalized. (The treaty entered into force on February 15, 1999, following its ratification by 12 signatories.)

In January 1998 the OECD established the Center for Cooperation with Non-Members as its "focal point" for discussions on policy and to encourage dialogue with emerging market economies. At the April 1998 Council meeting, negotiations on the multilateral investment agreement, which had been seen as promising, were suspended. The negotiations came to an end later that year following France's withdrawal from them, reportedly because it would lose the ability to protect its domestic movie and television markets under the proposed agreement.

In 1999 the OECD established guidelines for corporate governance, which were considered surprisingly progressive for their time. However, by late 2002 OECD officials urged that the guidelines be toughened in light of the increasing corporate scandals. Among other things, the OECD argued that independent oversight bodies needed to be established because self-regulation had failed, particularly in the auditing sector. The OECD also called for the development of guidelines for pension fund administrators.

Another major focus of OECD attention in recent years has been the harmful effect on international trade and investment of so-called tax havens around the globe, which provide foreign depositors with the opportunity to deposit large sums of money with little or no tax consequence. Additional momentum in pursuing reform in the havens developed following the terrorist attacks on the United States in September 2001, at which time the George W. Bush administration called on all banks to help identify and seize accounts that might be linked to terrorist organizations or activity. OECD accords with several Caribbean countries in early 2002 appeared to stifle cohesive resistance, and by the end of the year, only seven countries (Andorra, Liberia, Liechtenstein, Marshall Islands, Monaco, Nauru, and Vanuatu) were still considered uncooperative on the matter.

The OECD tax haven initiative has been conducted alongside efforts by the Financial Action Task Force to combat money laundering through the use of another "name-and-shame" blacklist. By the end of 2001, 23 countries and territories were on the money-laundering blacklist. By October 2007 all the countries had been delisted.

A major OECD tax initiative hit a wall in 2003 when some member states were reluctant to join in the establishment of a comprehensive exchange system of banking information to prevent money laundering by terrorist organizations and tax evasion by individuals and corporations. In September 2003 Switzerland and Luxembourg balked at the OECD's 2006 deadline for entrance into the system, seeking to preserve their nations' well-established practice of banking secrecy. The two nations blocked an agreement among the member countries, marking the first time member states had used a veto inside the governing Council.

In October 2006 the OECD was one of the organizations involved in trying to restart the stalled Doha round of trade talks but with little ultimate success. In its November 2006 *Economic Outlook* publication, it criticized the Russian government for its tendency to reintroduce state control of the economy by taking majority positions in the directorate of many companies that had previously been privatized.

In May 2007 the organization invited five new countries to discuss membership: Russia, Estonia, Chile, Israel, and Slovenia. By December 2007 accession talks were beginning. The OECD also suggested that Brazil, China, India, Indonesia, and South Africa, all increasingly powerful economies, could be invited in the near future. In June 2007 South Africa became the first African country to sign the OECD's antibribery convention.

In March 2008 Taiwan complained that China was trying to interfere with its participation in the OECD. Also in March the OECD rejected suggestions from U.S. and EU quarters that Sovereign Wealth Funds (SWFs)—funds that are controlled by a cash-rich nation-state, most often in Asia or the Middle East—should be more transparent. Secretary General Gurría said he saw no problem as long as profit, rather than politics, drove the funds' strategies.

Later in 2008 and through 2009 the OECD, like many other international organizations, was occupied by the global economic crisis. It went from forecasting an economic slowdown in August 2008, to a forecast of a protracted slowdown in November, to warnings about the U.S. economy in December, to a statement in June 2009 that the recession was "near bottom," and a declaration in August 2009 that the economies of rich countries were generally stabilized. The OECD also noted (in October 2008) that income inequality had risen sharply in rich countries where statistics were available.

In analyzing the world recession's effects, the OECD had a particularly gloomy view of Russia's prospects. The OECD saw a declining world demand for oil as stopping Russia's economic growth while leaving it prey to the underlying problems of too much bureaucracy and too much political interference in business. On June 24, 2009, Russia launched its formal bid for membership in the OECD.

The OECD continues to work against tax havens and other kinds of international malfeasance. In December 2008 Israel became the first Middle Eastern state to sign on to the OECD antibribery convention, thus putting it one step closer to membership in the organization. In April 2009 the OECD removed the last four countries—Costa Rica, Malaysia, the Philippines, and Uruguay—from its blacklist of tax havens.

In 2010 Chile, Israel, and Slovenia joined the organization. Chile's accession caused concern among the Group of 77 coalition of developing countries, of which it was also a member. Nothing prohibited Chile belonging both to a group of developing countries and a group of developed countries, but to many it seemed inappropriate. Accession talks with Israel were contentious. The OECD demanded that Israeli official statistics exclude territories that the OECD does not consider part of Israel. There was also concern that Israel was not fully living up to the antibribery convention, and that Israel was not complying with the OECD's intellectual property standards, particularly in respect to generic drugs. Estonia also finalized its membership December 9, 2010.

OECD reports in 2010 declared the global recession to be over, giving different estimates of growth as the year progressed. The general conclusion was that recovery would be slow, but that there would be no so-called double-dip recession. The 2011 report, however, noted that while government stimulus money was declining in the global economy and the private sector was beginning to recover, new outside factors have emerged that could be problematic if countries do not remain committed to economic improvement. The 2011 annual report also indicated concern over the economic imbalances that exist from country to country. Likewise, the report prompted the OECD to increase its work on creating jobs and finding unemployment solutions.

The year 2011 also saw the emergence of a new plan for global development. The OECD Strategy for Development calls for an increase in sustainable growth in as many countries as possible. To achieve this goal, the OECD has committed itself to more integration and collaboration on the subject, particularly with the underdeveloped countries desiring to improve their economic situations. The effort will focus largely on finding sustainable growth programs and mobilizing natural resources within the states. The plan also calls for a new OECD Tax and Development program to assist countries interested in reforming their tax codes. In November 2011 the OECD invited Colombia to join the working group of the antibribery convention, marking the beginning of its accession process to the convention.

In February 2012, Russia completed its nearly 2-year accession process to the OECD's antibribery convention. Russia became the 39th country to sign the convention. In May 2012, Russia was invited to join the OECD's Nuclear Energy Association. These actions are major steps toward finalizing Russia's accession into the OECD as a full member, which Russian leaders hope to have completed by late 2013.

The financial crisis in the Euro zone, beginning in late 2011 and extending into 2012, was of major concern to the OECD. The OECD played an active role in advising struggling countries, such as Greece and Italy, in regard to policy options for handling the situation. The OECD welcomed the Greek debt reduction agreement, and by May 2012 reported in its *Economic Outlook* that the crisis in the euro zone seems to have been averted. The report did note, however, that if diligent efforts to reform policies and correct the economic imbalances were not enacted, the crisis might worsen. The report also noted that while the global crisis had been mostly averted, growth would remain subdued going forward.

At the May 2013 ministerial meeting, OECD members approved invitations for Colombia and Latvia to begin the accession process; roadmaps for each nation's accession process were finalized by the organization later in the year. If the accession process moves at the projected pace, both states will be admitted as full members by December 2015. At that same ministerial meeting, the group also approved a plan to open accession talks with Costa Rica and Lithuania in 2015 and outlined the need for member states to implement job creation programs, having noted that unemployment is the largest problem facing the global economy.

In the 2013 edition of its annual *Economic Outlook,* the OECD noted that the global economy, particularly in the most advanced nations, should experience growth beginning in mid-2013 through 2014. It did predict, however, that the Euro zone would continue to struggle with lingering effects of the financial crisis. The organization suggested the Euro zone continue its slow process of structural consolidation, construct and implement a full-fledged banking union, and ease their monetary policies. In light of the partisan political struggles going on in the United States throughout 2013, the OECD warned against the sequestration tactics that issued across the board cuts and was critical of the October government shutdown for the impact it could have upon the global economy. (For more information on activities since 2013, see Recent activities, below.)

Structure. The Council, the principal political organ, convenes at least once a year at the ministerial level, although regular meetings are held by permanent representatives. Generally, acts of the Council require unanimity, although different voting rules may be adopted in particular circumstances. Supervision of OECD activities is the responsibility of the 14-member Executive Committee, whose members are elected annually by the Council and usually meet once per week. The secretary general, who chairs the regular Council meetings, is responsible for implementing Council and Executive Committee decisions with the assistance of a Secretariat that employs some 2,500 people. The current annual budget is approximately €357 million ($444 million), 21 percent of which is contributed by the United States. Japan is the next leading contributor.

Probably the best known of the OECD's subsidiary organs is the Development Assistance Committee (DAC), which evolved from the former Development Assistance Group and now includes most of the world's economically advanced states as well as the Commission of the European Communities. DAC oversees members' official resource transfers. The Economic Policy Committee, another major OECD organ, is responsible for reviewing economic activities in all member states. The OECD includes more than 200 committees that produce data, analyses, guidelines, or recommendations affecting policy in every major area of development. The number of committees continues to grow each year. The Committee on International Investment and Multinational Enterprises was responsible for formulating a voluntary code of conduct for multinational corporations, which was adopted by the OECD in 1976. In addition, high-level groups have been organized to investigate commodities, positive adjustment policies, employment of women, and many other issues.

To complement the work of DAC, an OECD Development Center was established in 1962. Its current priorities emphasize working to meet the basic needs of the world's poorest people, with a focus on rural development and appropriate technology in Africa, Asia, and Latin America. Twenty-six members and nonmembers (including Argentina, Brazil, Chile, and India) participate in the center's activities. The Center for Educational Research and Innovation (CERI), established in 1968, works toward similar goals.

Recent activities. The OECD put the accession of Russia on hold on March 13, 2014, because of aggression in Ukraine. This move was a rare one taken by the OECD, which normally remains neutral in disputes between counties. Russia first attempted to join the OECD in 2007. The 2014 Ministerial Meeting held in May 2014 focused on building resilient economies and inclusive societies through economic growth and job creation. Noting that gender equality, aging populations, and youth unemployment were huge problems facing economic growth, the OECD ministers issued a call for member states to put forth initiatives designed specifically to address these issues. The ministers also called upon governments to promote transparence and passed a declaration urging immediate attention to climate change.

In October 2014 the OECD and its members signed a memorandum of understanding with Ukraine, pledging to assist the conflict-ridden country with its efforts to end corruption, revamp its tax code, and encourage economic competition. On October 29, 2014, the OECD signed a multilateral competent authority agreement that would allow for automatic sharing of financial data for tax purposes among member countries, and 20 others countries. In 2017, 58 more countries joined the regimen, and in 2018, 35 other nations will begin participation in the financial data network.

In May 2015 an OECD study warned of the economic costs of rising inequality with a wage gap increase of 4.7 percent between the upper and lower incomes across the globe. The OECD recommended raising taxes on higher incomes to help alleviate added pressures on the global economy because the number of people below the poverty level was offsetting growth.

In November 2015 the OECD released economic predictions for 2015 through 2017. The organization forecast global economic growth of 3 percent in 2015 and 2016, before rising to 3.3 percent in 2017. Slower growth in 2015–2016 would be the result of stagnating global trade patterns, mainly as a result of China's economic slowdown and the continuing tepid U.S. economy. However, lower oil prices and falling unemployment would aid growth. In June the OECD called for the end of public financing for coal-fired power generation among member states in order to promote the development of new energy sources following the 2015 Paris agreement on global warming.

In January 2016 forecasting by OECD projected prolonged slow growth for the global economy unless governments boosted spending and enacted stimulus programs. Following the June 2016 vote by the United Kingdom to exit the EU, the OECD estimated that the country's economy would shrink by 6 percent, creating a further drag on the global trade.

ORGANIZATION OF EASTERN CARIBBEAN STATES (OECS)

Established: By treaty signed June 18, 1981, in Basseterre, St. Kitts, effective July 4, 1981.

Purpose: The Mission of the Organization of Eastern Caribbean States is to be a **Center of Excellence** contributing to the sustainable development of OECS Member States by supporting their strategic insertion into the global economy while maximizing the benefits accruing from their collective space.

Headquarters: Castries, St. Lucia.

Principal Organs: Authority of Heads of Government of the Member States, OECS Assembly, Council of Ministers, Economic Affairs Council, and the OECS Commission.

Website: www.oecs.org.

Director General: Dr. Didacus Jules (St. Lucia).

Membership (7): Antigua and Barbuda, Dominica, Grenada, Montserrat, St. Kitts and Nevis, St. Lucia, St. Vincent and the Grenadines.

Associate Members (3): Anguilla, British Virgin Islands, Martinique.

Official Language: English.

Origin and development. The seven full participants in the OECS were formerly members of the West Indies Associated States, a pre-independence grouping established in 1966 to serve various common economic, judicial, and diplomatic needs of British Caribbean territories. The attainment of independence by four of the members—Dominica, Grenada, St. Lucia, and St. Vincent—during 1974–1979 and the impending independence of Antigua on November 1, 1981, gave impetus to the formation of a subregional body.

Meeting in 1979 in Castries, St. Lucia, the prospective members called for establishment of the OECS as a means of strengthening relations between the seven least-developed members of the Caribbean Community and Common Market (Caricom; see separate entry). Following nearly a year and a half of negotiations, an OECS treaty (the Treaty of Basseterre) was concluded and came into force July 4, 1981. A dispute over location of the new organization's headquarters was settled by agreement that its central secretariat would be located in Castries (administrative center of the former associated states), while its economic affairs secretariat would be located in St. John's, Antigua, where the Secretariat of the Eastern Caribbean Common Market (ECCM) was sited.

To further cooperation and integration in the Caribbean, the OECS established the Eastern Caribbean Central Bank (ECCB) on October 1, 1983, in accordance with its decision in July 1982 to upgrade the Eastern Caribbean Currency Authority. The major functions of the ECCB are administering the EC dollar and exchange control, making currency rate adjustments, regulating credit policies, fixing interest rates, and establishing reserve requirements for members' commercial banks.

Following the U.S.-led invasion of Grenada in October 1983 to overthrow a pro-communist government, a Regional Security System (RSS) was established in cooperation with the United States to ensure the political stability of the OECS members.

In the mid-1980s, at the urging of Prime Minister John Compton of St. Lucia, the OECS considered forming a political union to counter nationalism and promote integration. When serious differences among the member states prevented significant progress, the four Windward countries (Dominica, Grenada, St. Lucia, and St. Vincent) indicated they might proceed toward their own political union, which would be open to accession by the Leeward states if they so wished. In 1990 the Windward group set up a widely representative Regional Constituent Assembly (RCA), which in January 1992 approved a draft constitution. By then, however, domestic political concerns had dampened enthusiasm for the project, and the RCA's final recommendations were never presented to the national legislatures and electorates. The OECS was also involved in establishing the independent Eastern Caribbean Telecommunication Authority (ECTEL) in Castries, with members Dominica, Grenada, St. Kitts and Nevis, St. Lucia, and St. Vincent and the Grenadines. ECTEL was described at its opening in October 2000 as the world's first regional telecommunications regulatory body. A year later the OECS launched in St. Kitts the Eastern Caribbean Securities Exchange, the first regional securities market in the hemisphere.

A report from the Organization for Economic Cooperation and Development in June 2000 labeled all the OECS members except Montserrat as "tax havens" and threatened to impose sanctions if steps were not taken to tighten regulation of their offshore financial industries. At the same time the independent Financial Action Task Force on Money Laundering included Dominica, St. Kitts and Nevis, and St. Vincent on its list of "noncooperative" jurisdictions, to which Grenada was subsequently added. The accusations drew heated denials from several OECS governments, some asserting that they had a sovereign right to establish their own banking and financial policies without external interference. Nevertheless, by 2003 all had taken sufficient action to be removed from both lists.

A special meeting of the heads of government in Grenada in April 2001 reviewed the organization's mission, structure, and financing. Despite previous restructuring and streamlining, budgetary problems continued to plague the group, with participants therefore naming the Technical Committee on the Functioning and Financing of the OECS Secretariat to develop a strategy for resolving financial arrears and also to consider additional reconfiguration. The 34th OECS summit, held July 25–26, 2001, in Dominica, received the report of the technical committee, which recommended maintaining the existing secretariat structure, writing off some arrears, and adopting a two-year strategy for member states to remit the balance of their outstanding commitments.

At the same time, summit participants moved forward on two major initiatives. First, the authority set a January 2002 date for instituting the free movement of nationals, including the elimination of restrictions on work and residency permits, throughout the member states. A task force was established to work out the details of the plan, which had been discussed for more than a decade, and also to address adoption of a common passport and ID (eventually abandoned). Member governments signed free movement legislation by the middle of 2002. Second, the heads of government authorized another task force to work toward establishing an OECS economic union modeled on the EU.

Meeting on January 31–February 1, 2002, in The Valley, Anguilla, the heads of government endorsed the economic union concept. (At least initially, associate members Anguilla and the British Virgin Islands were not expected to participate.) The authority cited the need for a "single economic space" to compete in the era of globalization and trade liberalization. The union was seen as a way to promote economic diversification and growth, increase export competitiveness, expand employment opportunities, further human resource development, and speed up free movement of people, goods, services, and capital.

With regard to the proposed Free Trade Area of the Americas (FTAA), a report prepared by the United Nations (UN) Economic Commission for Latin America and the Caribbean had concluded that the FTAA would be of little advantage to the OECS members. According to the report, an FTAA could, however, have a negative impact on trade within the 15-member Caricom, in which all the OECS members participate.

The anticipated inauguration of Caricom's (see separate article) Single Market and Economy (CSME) provided a focus for the 41st OECS heads of government meeting, which was held June 16–17, 2005, in Roseau, Dominica. Many OECS businesses opposed the CSME, fearing the subregion's relative disadvantages versus the larger Caricom economies. At the same time, the authority continued to advance subregional integration, including the final drafting of the OECS Economic Union Treaty.

On June 23, 2006, the seven OECS heads of government signed a declaration of intent to place the Economic Union Treaty before their countries' legislatures. At the same event, an OECS flag was unveiled. At a meeting in September 2007, trade experts met in Dominica to harmonize tariffs prior to the December 31 deadline for completing an Economic Partnership Agreement (EPA) with the EU, in conjunction with the rest of Caricom. The agreement was completed as scheduled.

Regional integration ran into further trouble in 2008, as the proposal for the economic union stalled. An important aspect of the treaty was that some decisions of the OECS Authority would now be binding on member states, where previously decisions were purely a matter of consensus. In August 2008 Trinidad and Tobago and three OECS Member States (Grenada, St. Lucia, and St. Vincent and the Grenadines) reached an accord to pursue an Economic Union by 2011 and deeper political integration by 2013. In September the OECS issued a statement supporting this move and a task force, was set up to consider the proposal's merits.

On June 2, 2009, the Trinidad and Tobago task force recommended that that country should be allowed to join the OECS. The Trinidadian opposition party was, however, opposed to joining without a referendum and worried, as did many observers, about a negative effect on Caricom.

In November 2009 the OECS gathered for its 50th meeting of the OECS Authority. The meeting focused largely on solutions to the tourism and economic slumps, steps to increase agricultural production, plans for the OECS Economic Union, and the growing problem with crime in OECS member states.

New diplomatic relations were established in 2010. Both Finland and Germany began diplomatic relations with the OECS in early 2010. Furthermore, at the 51st summit, held in June 2010, the OECS members joined together in an agreement, the Revised Treaty of Basseterre, to create an economic union. The economic union would help promote growth in the Eastern Caribbean nations and would be the first step in removing the economic barriers that separate the member states. The accord also provided a framework for an OECS Commission: an executive body with decision-making capability. With Antigua and Barbuda being the first country to ratify the Revised Treaty of Basseterre, the OECS Economic Union was officially created January 21, 2011. The Revised Treaty of Basseterre also provided for the creation of several new principal organs of the OECS—the OECS Assembly, the Council of Ministers, the Economic Affairs Council, and the OECS Commission

In addition to the creation of the Economic Union, the decision for the integration of the OECS states by allowing free movement of people and goods through the country from other OECS member states was finalized at an OECS summit in January 2011. The free movement of people became effective August 1. The OECS also voted at the January 2011 meeting to establish a legislative body similar to the structure of European parliamentary systems that would be located in Antigua and Barbuda. The OECS Assembly has binding legislative authority over all states of the OECS

Much of 2011 was focused on tourism. In March, tourism ministers from the OECS member states adopted a new Common Tourism Policy, which was finalized in October. The new policy primarily focuses on tourism development throughout the region. At the 53rd summit of the OECS, held in May 2011, the OECS moved forward with its January decision to establish the free movement of people and goods throughout the OECS by June 1, 2013 to be. Another major milestone for the OECS was reached in October 2011 with the establishment of diplomatic relations with the United States. In December 2011, the OECS's High Commission in Canada was closed, after the decision to close was approved by the member states in June. The decision to close the foreign embassy was the result of increasing financial strains on the member states.

The OECS held its 54th annual summit in January 2012. At that meeting, the discussions centered largely on the transition into a new governance structure with the creation of the new principal organs under the Revised Treaty of Basseterre. The summit also discussed new issues arising with the economic union, such as electronic transactions and maritime commerce and governance. In February 2012 the Chief Justice of the Eastern Caribbean Supreme Court (ECSC) Hugh Anthony Rawls announced his resignation effective August 1. Dame Janice Pereira, who was appointed by Queen Elizabeth II on September 28 and sworn into office on October 24, succeeded Rawls. Pereira became the first woman to be named chief justice of the ECSC.

The OECS held its 55th annual summit in June 2012. The meeting was mostly focused on the inauguration of the OECS Assembly, procedural matters necessary to appoint a new Chief Justice of the ECSC and the commencement of free circulation of goods within the economic union, which took effect July 1, 2013. The OECS Assembly was inaugurated on August 10, 2012, formally launching the new organ of the OECS. The first official sitting of the Assembly was held March 26, 2013.

In June 2013 the OECS Authority held its 57th summit. The meeting largely focused on the draft of the OECS Development Strategy, a document compiled by the Secretariat outlining the priorities for continued regional growth in all the major sectors. The summit also called for increased cooperation between governments and the private sector to boost development in the region, particularly in regard to renewable energy. The heads of state also endorsed a proposal for all OECS member states to join the Advisory Center on the WTO Law.

The OECS Authority met again in November in Montserrat. At the summit the leaders approved the OECS Growth and Development Strategy, which coordinated the organization's efforts to promote both its development agenda and its economic union. The meeting also included talks on membership expansion, noting with approval the status of negotiations with Martinique to become an associate member, and calling on Anguilla and the British Virgin Isles to make a concerted effort to ratify the Revised Treaty of Basseterre and become full members. (For more on developments since 2013, see Recent activities, below.)

Structure. Normally meeting in biennial summits, the Authority of Heads of Government of the Member States is the highest OECS policymaking organ. It is supported by the OECS Commission (formerly known as the OECS Secretariat), which is headed by a director general and encompasses four divisions: functional cooperation, external relations, corporate services, and economic affairs. The functional cooperation division oversees several specialized units related to areas such as the environment, education, commerce, and aviation. (For a full listing of the specialized units, see the 2012 *Handbook.*) The External Relations Division maintains missions in Brussels, Belgium, Geneva, Switzerland, and Puerto Rico. In general, the OECS Commission prepares reports, extends administrative and legal expertise, and provides supervision for the organization.

The Revised Treaty of Basseterre (2010) added three additional organs to the structure of the OECS. The OECS Assembly is a legislative body composed of five members of parliament from each the member states and three members of parliament from each of the associate members that reports to the OECS Authority. The Assembly has binding legislative power in matters pertaining to the actions of the OECS and, by virtue, its individual members. The Economic Affairs Council is composed of ministers from each member state and is responsible for the administration of the OECS Economic Union (see above). The Council of Ministers is composed of ministers from each of the member states and reports to the OECS Authority. The Council of Ministers has the power to enact Acts of the Organization upon the recommendations of the OECS Commission.

Recent activities. In February 2014 the OECS Authority announced its selection of Dr. Diaculus Jules as the organization's new director general, effective May 1. The position became open after Dr. Len Ishmael retired at the end of 2013, having served in that capacity for more than a decade.

The 59th Meeting of the OECS Authority was held in July in Kingstown, St. Vincent. The meeting participants continued to express desire for growth, agreeing that the agreement with Martinique for associate membership should be signed at the next meeting of the authority and welcoming the preparations for negotiations with Guadeloupe and the application for associate membership by St. Martin.

On February 4, 2015, Martinique joined the OECS. The country then hosted the 60th meeting of the organization. OESC ministers then met on March 30 in St. Lucia to develop strategies to improve the free movement of goods. On April 23, the OECS launched an initiative to reduce the costs of food imports by promoting locally grown products. The organization's goal was to reduce food imports from $480 million to $280 million annually.

In July 2015 the OECS Regional Coordinating Mechanism (RCM) was awarded a $5.3 million grant from the Global Fund to combat the spread of HIV/AIDS. Reports in July indicated that the other OECS heads of government opposed Dominican prime minister Roosevelt Skerrit's support for Governor-General Baroness Patricia Scotland of Dominica for secretary general of the Commonwealth. (Scotland acceded to the post in July 2016.)

On November 18–19, 2015, the OECS held its 62nd meeting in Dominica under the chairmanship of Keith Mitchell. All members were present except Anguilla. The meeting focused on health care development, climate change, the free movement of people, and the economic union. OECS parliamentary opposition leaders met in Saint Lucia in September and elected Reuben Meade as chair. The opposition discussed the Revised Treaty of Basseterre and the seamless movement of persons and goods through agreements within the economic union.

ORGANIZATION FOR SECURITY AND COOPERATION IN EUROPE (OSCE)

Established: As the Conference on Security and Cooperation in Europe (CSCE) on July 3, 1973, by meeting of heads of states and other representatives of 35 nations in Helsinki, Finland; Helsinki Final Act adopted August 1, 1975; Charter of Paris for a New Europe adopted November 21, 1990; current name adopted at Heads of State or Government Summit on December 5–6, 1994, in Budapest, Hungary.

Purpose: "To consolidate respect for human rights, democracy, and the rule of law, to strengthen peace, and to promote unity in Europe."

Headquarters: Vienna, Austria.

Principal Organs: Heads of State or Government Meeting (Summit), Ministerial Council, Senior Council, Permanent Council, Conflict Prevention Center, Forum for Security Cooperation, Office for Democratic Institutions and Human Rights, High Commissioner on National Minorities, Office of the Representative on Freedom of the Media, Parliamentary Assembly, Secretariat.

Website: www.osce.org.

Secretary General: Frank-Walter Steinmeier (Germany).

Membership (57): Albania, Andorra, Armenia, Austria, Azerbaijan, Belarus, Belgium, Bosnia and Herzegovina, Bulgaria, Canada, Croatia, Cyprus, Czech Republic, Denmark, Estonia, Finland, France, Georgia, Germany, Greece, The Holy See (Vatican City State), Hungary, Iceland, Ireland, Italy, Kazakhstan, Kyrgyzstan, Latvia, Liechtenstein, Lithuania, Luxembourg, Macedonia, Malta, Moldova, Monaco, Montenegro, Mongolia, Netherlands, Norway, Poland, Portugal, Romania, Russia, San Marino, Serbia, Slovakia, Slovenia, Spain, Sweden, Switzerland, Tajikistan, Turkey, Turkmenistan, Ukraine, United Kingdom, United States, Uzbekistan.

Official Languages: English, French, German, Italian, Russian, Spanish.

Origin and development. The creation of a forum for discussion of East-West security issues was first proposed in the late 1960s. The Soviet Union, in particular, supported the idea as a means of establishing dialogue between the North Atlantic Treaty Organization (NATO) and the Warsaw Treaty Organization (Warsaw Pact) and formalizing the post–World War II status quo in Europe. Talks in 1972 led to the establishment of the CSCE on July 3, 1973, in Helsinki, Finland, by the foreign ministers of Canada, the United States, and 33 European countries. At a summit July 30–August 1, 1975, the heads of state and government signed the Helsinki Final Act, which declared the inviolability of national frontiers in Europe and the right of each signatory "to choose and develop" its own "political, social, economic, and cultural systems."

The act called for ongoing discussion of three thematic "baskets"—security, economic cooperation, and human rights—and provided for periodic review of progress toward implementation of its objectives, although no provision was made for a permanent CSCE headquarters or staff. Consequently, the conference operated in relative obscurity and had little impact beyond the establishment of so-called Helsinki Groups in the Soviet Union and other Eastern European nations to monitor human rights.

The third CSCE review conference, held in Vienna, Austria (1986–1989), laid the groundwork for negotiations that produced the Treaty on Conventional Armed Forces in Europe (CFE), through which NATO and Warsaw Pact members agreed to substantial arms reductions. The CFE treaty was signed at the second CSCE summit on November 19–21, 1990, in Paris. The NATO and Warsaw Pact members also signed a joint document declaring they were "no longer adversaries." In addition, the summit adopted the Charter of Paris, which significantly expanded the CSCE mandate and established a permanent institutional framework.

The November 1990 CSCE summit was viewed by many of the 34 national leaders in attendance as a landmark step toward the establishment of a pan-European security system, a long-standing goal that had seemed unattainable until the dramatic improvement in East–West relations. However, despite the formal opening of the CSCE Secretariat in Prague in February 1991 and a Conflict Prevention Center in Vienna in March, the euphoria over the CSCE's prospects faded somewhat by the time the Council of Foreign Ministers met in June. In light of the perceived potential for instability within the Soviet Union and ongoing ethnic confrontation elsewhere on the continent, Western leaders had recently reaffirmed NATO as the dominant body for addressing their defense and security concerns. In addition, some observers wondered if the CSCE would prove too unwieldy, as its decisions required unanimity and it lacked any enforcement powers.

Although most prominently identified since 1990 with its field operations and with election-related activities, the OSCE's agenda has expanded to include a wide range of crucial issues facing its membership. Through various seminars, workshops, conferences, conventions, reports, and projects, it continues to address concerns in what it defines as three "dimensions": politico-military, human, and economic. More specifically, the OSCE has been involved in promoting human and minority rights; development of democratic institutions and procedures, including an independent judiciary and a free press; the participation of women in economic and political life; economic and environmental matters; and efforts to halt money laundering, organized crime, the financing of terrorism, human trafficking, and drugs.

Under the Charter of Paris and, later, the Helsinki Document, the CSCE took on an increasingly prominent role in conflict management; peacekeeping; the promotion of democratic standards; and the monitoring of political, legal, and other developments in Europe and Central Asia. In its first effort at mediation, in July 1991 the CSCE dispatched a mission to Yugoslavia that had no success in curtailing the violent ethnic conflicts resulting from that country's breakup. The latter missions, with never more than 20 international personnel, had as their mandate promoting dialogue between the Belgrade government and the ethnic communities in the three regions, but the rump Yugoslavia terminated the missions' memorandum of understanding in 1993. Technically, the regional missions remained in existence until 2001, when Yugoslavia welcomed a new undertaking—the OSCE Mission to Serbia and Montenegro—with a mandate to promote "democratization, tolerance, the rule of law, and conformity with OSCE principles, standards, and commitments." On June 29, 2006, following the separation of Serbia and Montenegro into independent countries, the mission was, in effect, divided into two: the OSCE Mission to Montenegro and the OSCE Mission to Serbia.

Albania joined the CSCE in June 1991 and was followed in September by Estonia, Latvia, and Lithuania. Russia subsequently assumed the former USSR seat. The other ten members of the Commonwealth of Independent States (CIS) joined in early 1992, the CSCE having decided to include the five Central Asian republics because of their former inclusion in the Soviet Union. Croatia, Georgia, and Slovenia were admitted in March, followed shortly thereafter by Bosnia and Herzegovina. The Czech Republic and Slovakia were admitted in 1993 following the dissolution of Czechoslovakia, while Macedonia joined the renamed OSCE in October 1995, after Greece lifted its veto. Andorra's accession in 1996 brought the OSCE's active membership up to 54. Yugoslavia (subsequently Serbia and Montenegro) returned to active status in November 2000, Belgrade's membership having been suspended in July 1992. Montenegro joined in June 2006, and the former Serbia and Montenegro membership now officially represents Serbia alone.

The fourth CSCE follow-up session, held from March to July 1992 in Helsinki, focused on reformulating the organization's aims and structures. Its recommendations were adopted as the Helsinki Document by the third CSCE summit, held in the Finnish capital July 9–10. The text specified that the CSCE's task was now "managing change"; that summit meetings should "set priorities and provide orientation"; that the Council of Foreign Ministers was "the central decision-making and governing body of the CSCE"; and that the Committee of Senior Officials (CSO) was responsible for ongoing "overview, management, and coordination" of CSCE activities. The summit also decided in principle that the CSCE should have its own peacekeeping capability, which should operate in conformity with United Nations (UN) resolutions and in concert with NATO, the CIS, the European Community, and the Western European Union.

A number of other OSCE missions became operational in 1992–1993. Missions to Estonia and Latvia were concerned with institution-building; the inculcation of OSCE principles and, in the case of Estonia, promotion of integration and intercommunal understanding between ethnic Estonians and ethnic Russians. Both missions concluded at the end of 2001. In December 1992 a new civilian-military mission to Georgia was directed to promote negotiations with secessionists in South Ossetia and, secondarily, to assist the UN in its similar efforts with regard to Abkhazia. The Mission in Georgia later took on such additional tasks as building democratic institutions, promoting human rights, and encouraging development of a free press. These missions in the Caucasus came to an end in 2009 (see below). It is important to note that OSCE missions can be established only by consensus among the member countries.

Also in 1992, the Minsk Process was fashioned to convene a conference in Minsk, Belarus, that would resolve the Nagorno-Karabakh conflict between Armenia and Azerbaijan. Although the conference has yet to be held, an Initial Operation Planning Group (IOPG), dating from May 1993, was superseded in December 1994 by a High-Level Planning Group (HLPG) that continues to meet in Vienna. The ongoing Minsk Process is cochaired by France, Russia, and the United States and includes eight other countries in addition to the principals. Separate from the Minsk Process, the OSCE launched a seven-person Office in Yerevan (Armenia) in February 2000 and a six-person Office in Baku (Azerbaijan) in July 2000.

Two other OSCE missions date from 1993. The Mission to Moldova facilitated the formation of a peace plan that envisaged substantial autonomy for the Transdnestr region; the plan was accepted by the Moldovan government in 1994. In December 1993 the council also established a Mission to Tajikistan because of the civil war. Deployed in February 1994, the handful of staff members helped secure a peace pact in 1997. In November 2002 the mission was redesignated the Center in Dushanbe (the Tajik capital) with a staff of 16 mandated to "promote the implementation of OSCE principles and commitments."

Throughout 1994 Russia continued to press for a strengthening of the CSCE, hoping to position it rather than NATO as the preeminent security organization for the "new Europe." Although bluntly dismissive of the notion that it would supplant NATO, Western leaders did agree that the grouping needed, in the words of one participant, "more heft." Thus, the CSCE became the OSCE during the Heads of State or Government Summit on December 5–6 in Budapest, Hungary.

In 1995 the OSCE, with the goal of further integrating all five Central Asian members into the organization, established an OSCE liaison office in Central Asia in Tashkent, Uzbekistan. In July 1998 the OSCE decided to open individual offices in Kazakhstan, Turkmenistan, and Kyrgyzstan. Currently, the OSCE has separate offices in each of the Central Asian republics.

Under the November 1995 Dayton peace agreement for Bosnia and Herzegovina the OSCE was allotted a key role, notably in organizing elections.

In October 1998 the OSCE, with the approval of the United Nations, undertook its largest mission to date, the Kosovo Verification Mission (KVM). The KVM was authorized for one year and was supposed to verify that all sides of the conflict were in compliance with UN resolutions. It was also directed to monitor elections and help establish a police force and other institutions in Kosovo. Despite the presence of the KVM and several attempts at negotiating an end to the fighting, the violence in Kosovo continued, and the mission had to be withdrawn in March 1999 before NATO initiated its bombing campaign against Yugoslavia. The OSCE returned to Kosovo following the conclusion in June of a comprehensive peace plan that included establishment of a UN Interim Administration Mission for Kosovo (UNMIK), with the OSCE Mission in Kosovo to be responsible for implementing democratic reforms and building governmental institutions.

The Office for Democratic Institutions and Human Rights (ODIHR) has reviewed electoral laws and observed elections in more than two-dozen member countries. Frequently, its reports have highlighted deficiencies in electoral processes, and, on occasion, the OSCE refuses to send monitoring teams.

In other field activities, the OSCE has been assisting since 1994 in implementing Russian–Latvian and Russian–Estonian agreements on military pensioners. The OSCE also provided a representative in 1995–1999 to another bilateral agreement between Russia and Latvia regarding the temporary operation and dismantling of the Skrunda Radar Station in Latvia.

The OSCE Heads of State or Government Meeting held on December 2–3, 1996, in Lisbon, Portugal, resolved in favor of a negotiated revision of the 1990 CFE Treaty, as demanded by Russia in light of its perceived need to deploy additional forces in unstable border regions.

The major event of 1999 was a summit convened on November 18–19 in Istanbul, Turkey. Despite concerns over Russia's renewed offensive in Chechnya, criticism of which led to Russian president Boris Yeltsin's early departure from the meeting, the summit managed to conclude two major agreements. All 54 active member countries signed the new European Security Charter, which, in part, reinforced various agreements dealing with security and human rights and called for more rapid response to requests for assistance from member states, particularly with regard to conflict prevention and crisis management. In addition, the 30 states belonging to NATO or the defunct Warsaw Pact signed a revised CFE Treaty, in which all signatories accepted verifiable ceilings for such military equipment as tanks, artillery, and combat aircraft and agreed not to deploy forces outside their borders without approval by the affected country.

A heightened emphasis on opposing terrorism was well in evidence at the December 3–4, 2001, Ministerial Council session in Bucharest, Romania, and at the December 6–7, 2002, session held in Porto, Portugal. As part of an OSCE Strategy to Address Threats to Security and Stability in the Twenty-first Century, the session also called for establishment of a Counter-Terrorism Network to coordinate counter-terrorism measures; share information; and "strengthen the liaison" among OSCE delegations, government officials, and the new Action against Terrorism Unit (ATU) in the Secretariat.

The 2003 ministerial session endorsed an Action Plan to Combat Trafficking in Human Beings, which called for adding a related special unit in the Secretariat and the appointment of a special representative.

Moscow claimed the OSCE had taken an "intrusive" interest in the affairs of the former Soviet Union, particularly with regard to the monitoring of elections and borders. Russia continued to refuse to uphold its commitment made to the OSCE in 1999 to remove its troops from Georgia and Moldova, and prepared to contest the monitoring of the Georgian border. When the disputed March 2005 Kyrgyz elections resulted in the ouster of the government, the OSCE called for harmony among the country's new leaders and declared that the ousted president, Askar Akayev, should not attempt to return from Russia, whence he had fled. The OSCE's position prevailed, and an election to elect a new president was held in July.

The OSCE, best known for monitoring elections in countries where democracy is relatively new, broke new ground by announcing that it would monitor the 2005 British general election—not with the expectation of finding fraud but as a way to assess the issues around ballot security and postal voting in developed countries. In November 2004 it had conducted a "targeted observation" of legislative and presidential balloting in the United States, and in 2006 it sent teams to both Canada and Italy.

At the October 2006 OSCE foreign ministers' meeting in Brussels, Russian rhetoric reminded some observers of Cold War days. Foreign minister Sergei Lavrov suggested divorcing humanitarian concerns from the OSCE, and perhaps establishing a special organization to deal with such concerns exclusively. He said that each country could make its own decision about membership in such an organization.

In September 2007, when Georgia accused a Russian aircraft of entering its airspace and firing a missile, the OSCE played an important part in keeping channels of communication open between the two countries, perhaps preventing the crisis from worsening. But observers noted that the incident showed that the OSCE needed a faster procedure for reacting to such events.

Poll-watching during Russia's resurgence occupied the OSCE well into 2008. In September 2007 Poland, now a member of the EU and NATO, refused to admit OSCE observers to its October parliamentary elections, saying that it was now a democracy needing no such monitoring. OSCE monitoring of the December 2, 2007, Russian parliamentary elections faced difficulties not encountered in the elections of 2003. At first Russia would allow only a much smaller number of observers than before, so ODIHR canceled the mission in mid-November, saying that it had been denied the necessary visas. In the end OSCE observers went to Russia, and OSCE branded the election—won decisively by President Vladimir Putin's party—as "not fair."

Differing U.S. and Russian agendas for the OSCE were apparent at the November 29–30, 2007, annual ministerial council meeting held in Madrid. Russia seemed to win the debate over allowing Kazakhstan, a close ally sometimes criticized for its record on human rights, to assume the OSCE presidency in 2010. However, Russia made no progress in its efforts to rein in the ODIHR. Russia continued to push, against the United States, for an OSCE charter.

The OSCE criticized the December 2007 parliamentary elections in Kyrgyzstan, in which the president's party won every seat. The OSCE likewise criticized the Uzbek presidential election in the same month, but a U.S. member of the mission called the criticism "nonsense," saying that ODIHR monitors often wrote their reports without leaving their hotels. ODIHR finally boycotted Russia's March 2008 presidential election after acrimonious disagreement with Russia about the size and duration of its mission. Russia called ODIHR's position a further reason for reforming the organization.

The seventeenth annual session of the Parliamentary Assembly met June 29–July 3, 2008, in Astana, Kazakhstan. It called for increased transparency in the OSCE and for the ODIHR and the Parliamentary Assembly to work more closely together to assure effective monitoring of elections. The Astana Declaration came close to seeking an OSCE charter.

The remainder of 2008, as well as 2009, was dominated by the threat of renewed fighting between Russia and Georgia after the August 2008 conflict was mediated to a close. In September 2008 talks about increasing the OSCE monitoring contingent came to a halt because Russia objected to monitors also working in the breakaway Georgian regions of South Ossetia and Abkhazia. Russia regards these regions as independent states. On December 21, 2008, at the OSCE Permanent Council meeting in Vienna, Russia objected to any extension of the mission's mandate, unless the OSCE set up separate missions for South Ossetia and Abkhazia.

Kazakhstan's 2010 presidency of the OSCE was controversial. Many said that its civil rights record ("worse than Russia's") was deteriorating even as it led an organization supposedly devoted to civil rights. Kazakhstan in turn touted the fact that, as a member of the Collective Security Treaty Organization (CSTO), an organ of the Commonwealth of Independent States (CIS, see separate article), it was well placed to bridge the divide between East and West. Kazakhstan announced that its presidency would be devoted to combating terrorism, resolving conflicts, and reconstruction in Afghanistan, with correspondingly less emphasis on democracy. However, in February 2010 a Kazakh court overturned a ruling that prevented the media from publishing criticism of President Nursultan Nazarbayev's son-in-law. The main initiative of the oil-rich country's presidency was to be the calling of an OSCE summit in Almaty in December 2010, the first such since 1999. The aim was to produce an important document that defined, or redefined, the organization's purpose.

In April 2010 Kyrgyzstan suffered a bloody popular revolution, in which President Kurmanbek Bakiyev was deposed and left for Kazakhstan on April 15. On April 16 the interim government announced that it would renew a lease on the U.S. air base at Manas—a critical transit point for personnel and supplies going to Afghanistan. The OSCE declared the conduct of the Kyrgyz constitutional referendum of June 2010 generally acceptable. The new constitution would transfer much power from the president to parliament. In May 2011 the independent Kyrgyzstan Inquiry Commission, led by representatives of the OSCE, issued a report that criticized the role played by the current Kyrgyz government in the violence that occurred in the aftermath of the demise of the previous regime. The report prompted antigovernment protests in Kyrgyzstan.

The OSCE cited a range of problems in balloting in Azerbaijan on November 7, 2010, including media bias and electoral fraud. However, the group praised the legislative elections in Moldova on November 28.

On July 1, 2011, Lamberto Zannier, a career diplomat from Italy, became the new OSCE secretary general, replacing Marc Perrin de Brichambaut of France. In September negotiations resumed to resolve the conflict between Moldova and the separatist Dneister region. (Earlier talks had been suspended in 2006.) The OSCE, the EU, the United States, Russia, and Ukraine formed a mediating group to help facilitate negotiations, dubbed the "5 + 2" talks.

At its December 2011 ministerial meeting, the OSCE committed to strengthen its commitment and efforts to assist Afghanistan in its transition to a full Afghani-led security force. The OSCE ministers also adopted a decision calling on its member states to increase their efforts to remove the barriers preventing gender equity in the economic sphere. That included encouraging shared roles in both the business and domestic spheres. The summit also issued a strong declaration in which the member states committed to end human trafficking of all kinds. Also at the summit, Mongolia submitted its application to become a participating state of the OSCE.

The OSCE observed the March 2012 Russian election in which former president and current Prime Minister Vladimir Putin was reelected as president. The OSCE observer mission called the elections "skewed in favour of one of the contestants, Valdimir Putin." The observer mission also declared that the whole election process was unfair from the beginning. In June 2012 the OSCE also observed the Serbian elections in Kosovo. Unlike the Russian election report, the Serbian elections were declared open and fair, although the observer mission did note that more transparency is still needed.

At the July 2012 annual session of the OSCE Parliamentary Assembly, the group adopted several resolutions. The most significant was the adoption of the Monaco Declaration. The Monaco Declaration calls for OSCE member states to release all political prisoners, and calls on leaders to revise the requirements of military information sharing. At the session, the group also voted to approve a bill banning OSCE member states from approving the visas of anyone associated with the death of Russian lawyer Sergei Magnitsky, who was killed by Russian officials after discovering a massive Russian government tax fraud.

On November 21 Mongolia acceded to the OSCE as the 57th member of the organization, having been a long-time Asian Partner for Cooperation.

On December 6 the OSCE ministers gathered for the annual meeting. The meeting, held in Dublin, was most noted for its passage of the Helsinki +40 Agreement. The political agreement established a framework to advance the OSCE through 2015 by setting clear goals for the vision of the organization's future and calling on the next three chairs of the organization to work in close cooperation to meet the goals set forth. The Dublin conference also saw the passage of a Declaration on Good Governance, which emphasized the importance of good governance in the member states, called for a renewed pledge to combat corruption, terrorism, and money laundering, and reiterated the role of the private sector in promoting growth.

In March the ministerial council voted to extend the mandate of the OSCE Representative on Freedom of the Media. What might have normally been a relatively insignificant action was further compounded by Russia's attached statement calling for a revision of the original mandate, placing more explicit definitions of media into the mandate in light of the ever-changing social media society. The United States also issued a statement, in which it disagreed entirely with the Russian government's position.

In April the Belarusian OSCE delegation made a statement during a meeting of the permanent council condemning the U.S. military prison at Guantánamo Bay, Cuba. The proclamation by the Belarusian minister called the prison a violation of human rights and supported the UN resolution calling on the United States to immediately close the site. An OSCE delegation visited Guantánamo Bay in August to investigate the issue further.

In keeping with the spirit of the Helsinki +40 Agreement, a special meeting of the Permanent Council was held in July 2013 to discuss the priorities of the OSCE in 2014 and 2015 under Swiss and Serbian leadership, respectively. Among the priorities listed were dialogue in the South Caucasus, modernizing military transparency arrangements, arms control, respecting human rights in the fight against terrorism, and cooperation in the Western Balkans.

The annual ministerial meeting was held in Kiev in December 2013 under the chairmanship of Ukraine. The meeting yielded new decisions concerning the Helsinki +40 Agreement and how to continue progressing with its implementation. The meeting also addressed issues of transnational security threats, technology security, and human trafficking. (For more on activities since 2013, see Recent activities, below.)

Structure. Prior to the signing of the Charter of Paris in November 1990, the CSCE had little formal structure, operating as what one correspondent described as a "floating set of occasional negotiations." The charter provided for Heads of State or Government Meetings (Summits) and established a Council of Foreign Ministers to meet at least once a year as the "central forum for political consultations within the CSCE process." A Committee of Senior Officials was empowered to carry out the decisions of the council. The charter also authorized the establishment of a Conflict Prevention Center in Vienna, for which a separate secretariat was created, and an Office for Free Elections in Warsaw. The latter body was subsequently renamed the Office for Democratic Institutions and Human Rights (ODIHR).

In 1992 the CSCE also established a Forum for Security Cooperation (for negotiations on further arms control, disarmament, and confidence-building measures) and a High Commissioner on National Minorities. It also adopted a Convention on Conciliation and Arbitration, which led to establishment of a Court of Conciliation and Arbitration to which signatories of the convention could submit disputes. Furthermore, the NATO and former Warsaw Pact members signed an Open Skies Treaty that permitted aerial reconnaissance. (The treaty entered into effect in January 2002.) In July 1992 the inaugural meeting of the CSCE Parliamentary Assembly took place in Budapest, Hungary.

In addition to adopting the OSCE designation, the December 1994 summit in Budapest enacted several structural changes designed to convey a greater sense of permanency. Thus, the Committee of Senior Officials was renamed the Senior Council and was mandated to meet at least three times a year (once as the Economic Forum). The Ministerial Council (formerly the Council of Foreign Ministers) was mandated to meet in non-summit years. While the Senior Council was given broad responsibility for the implementation of OSCE decisions, day-to-day operational oversight was assigned to a Permanent Council. OSCE members are generally represented on the Permanent Council by their ambassadors in Vienna, where the offices of the main Secretariat are located. (The Secretariat also maintains an office in Prague, Czech Republic.)

In 1997 OSCE members approved a plan to create within the Secretariat the post of coordinator of economic and environmental activities as part of an effort to "strengthen the ability of the Permanent Council and the OSCE institutions to address economic, social and environmental aspects of security." An Office of the Representative on Freedom of the Media was added in 1998. Although the 1994 summit called for upgrading the authority of the OSCE secretary general, the position subsequently remained to a large part subordinate to the organization's chair-in-office (CiO), a post held by a foreign minister of a member country for a one-year term.

Recent activities. While the chairmanship of the OSCE shifted from Ukraine to Switzerland in 2014, it was Ukraine that continued to garner most of the organization's attention. The political crisis in Ukraine that broke out in March, leading to Russian intervention and the annexation of the Crimea, has been the OSCE's primary concern. A special meeting of the OSCE was held on March 3, 2014, to discuss the Ukraine crisis. At that time, the OSCE began sending military verification teams into Ukraine to assess the situation and help resolve conflict between Ukraine and the Russian Federation. On March 21 the OSCE unanimously agreed to establish a Special Monitoring Mission (SSM) in Ukraine, with the first officials being on the ground within 24 hours. In May a team of more than 1,000 observers was sent into Ukraine to monitor the presidential election. In July the organization established two observer missions at the border checkpoints with Russia. Also, on July 22, OSCE investigators were granted limited access to the downed

MH17 wreckage, and found large sections cut out along the tail and cockpit, thus damaging evidence. Throughout the entire process, the Swiss chairmanship of the OSCE worked to mediate the ongoing conflict and help implement the cease-fire signed on September 5 in Minsk, known as Minsk I. Minsk I failed to end the fighting.

At the OSCE summit in Minsk on February 11–12, 2015, France, Russia, Germany, and Ukraine reached an accord to end fighting in eastern Ukraine. The agreement, dubbed Minsk II, included an immediate cease-fire and the withdrawal of heavy weapons outside of a demilitarized zone, OSCE monitoring, new local elections and the creation of a revised constitution, an amnesty, the restoration of humanitarian aid, and the return of border control to the Ukrainian government (see entry on Ukraine). The annexation of Crimea was left outside of the negotiations. Within weeks of Minsk II, Russia asserted that the agreement was being "manipulated" by the United States and the United Kingdom. Following attacks on the OSCE SMM mission, Germany and Russia called for an increase in monitors to bring the number to 1,000. Meanwhile, some fighting continued and the OSCE complained that its monitors continued to be denied access to some separatist-controlled areas.

On June 6, 2015, Swiss diplomat Heidi Tagliavini stepped down after talks between pro-Russia rebels, Moscow, and Kiev broke down. The OSCE passed a resolution on July 9 condemning Russia's military actions in Ukraine with a vote of 96 in favor, 7 opposed, and 32 abstentions.

Russia formally proposed on April 6, 2016, that the OSCE deploy observers to monitor the elections of eastern Ukraine. Through 2016 the OSCE continued to report violations of the cease-fire. The organization reported that from 2014–2016, 9,100 people had been killed and 21,000 wounded in the continuing strife.

ORGANIZATION OF AMERICAN STATES (OAS)

Organisation des Etats Américains
Organização dos Estados Americanos
Organización de los Estados Americanos
(OEA)

Established: By charter signed April 30, 1948, in Bogotá, Colombia, effective December 13, 1951.

Purpose: To achieve "an order of peace and justice, promoting solidarity among the American states; [to strengthen] their collaboration and [defend] their sovereignty, their territorial integrity, and their independence . . . as well as to establish . . . new objectives and standards for the promotion of the economic, social, and cultural development of the peoples of the Hemisphere, and to speed the process of economic integration."

Headquarters: Washington, D.C., United States.

Principal Organs: General Assembly, Meeting of Consultation of Ministers of Foreign Affairs, Permanent Council, Inter-American Council for Integral Development, Inter-American Juridical Committee (11 jurists from member states), Inter-American Commission on Human Rights (seven members), Inter-American Court of Human Rights (seven jurists from member states), Specialized Conferences, Specialized Organizations, General Secretariat.

Website: www.oas.org.

Secretary General: Luis Almagro Lemes (Uruguay).

Membership (35): Antigua and Barbuda, Argentina, Bahamas, Barbados, Belize, Bolivia, Brazil, Canada, Chile, Colombia, Costa Rica, Cuba, Dominica, Dominican Republic, Ecuador, El Salvador, Grenada, Guatemala, Guyana, Haiti, Honduras, Jamaica, Mexico, Nicaragua, Panama, Paraguay, Peru, St. Kitts and Nevis, St. Lucia, St. Vincent and the Grenadines, Suriname, Trinidad and Tobago, United States, Uruguay, Venezuela.

Permanent Observers (70): Albania, Algeria, Angola, Armenia, Austria, Azerbaijan, Belgium, Benin, Bosnia and Herzegovina, Bulgaria, China, Croatia, Cyprus, Czech Republic, Denmark, Egypt, Equatorial Guinea, Estonia, European Union, Finland, France, Georgia, Germany, Ghana, Greece, Holy See, Hungary, Iceland, India, Ireland, Israel, Italy, Japan, Kazakhstan, Latvia, Lebanon, Liechtenstein, Lithuania, Luxembourg, Malta, Macedonia, Monaco, Montenegro, Morocco, Netherlands, Nigeria, Norway, Pakistan, Philippines, Poland, Portugal, Qatar, Republic of Korea, Romania, Russia, Saudi Arabia, Serbia, Slovakia, Slovenia, Spain, Sri Lanka, Sweden, Switzerland, Thailand, Tunisia, Turkey, Ukraine, United Kingdom, Vanuatu, Yemen.

Official Languages: English, French, Portuguese, Spanish.

Origin and development. The foundations of the OAS were laid in 1890 at an International Conference of American States in Washington, D.C., where it was decided to form an International Union of American Republics to serve as a permanent secretariat. The name of the organization itself was changed in 1910 to Union of American Republics, and the secretariat was renamed the Pan American Union.

The experience of World War II encouraged further development of the still loosely organized "inter-American system." An Inter-American Conference on Problems of War and Peace, meeting in February–March 1945 in Mexico City, concluded that the American republics should consider adoption of a treaty for their mutual defense. Through the Inter-American Treaty of Reciprocal Assistance (Rio Treaty), which was opened for signature on September 2, 1947, in Rio de Janeiro, Brazil, they agreed an armed attack originating either within or outside the American system would be considered an attack against all members, and each would assist in meeting such an attack. (In September 2002 Mexico renounced the Rio Treaty, which it described as obsolete in the post–Cold War era.) Organizational streamlining was undertaken by the Ninth International Conference of American States, which met in March–May 1948 in Bogotá, Colombia, and established the 21-member OAS.

The adoption by Cuba of a Marxist-Leninist ideology generally was viewed by other member governments as incompatible with their fundamental principles, and the Eighth Meeting of Consultation of Ministers of Foreign Affairs, held January 23–31, 1962, in Punta del Este, Uruguay, determined that Cuba, in effect, had excluded itself from participation in the inter-American system. The trade and diplomatic quarantine against Cuba was ultimately lifted at a special consultative meeting on July 29, 1975, in San José, Costa Rica, although the resolution did not lift Cuba's exclusion from formal participation in OAS activities until 2009.

Evidence of the organization's increasing economic and social concerns was manifested by the adoption of the Act of Bogotá, a program of social development, by a special OAS conference in September 1960. On August 17, 1961, an Inter-American Economic and Social Conference adopted the Charter of Punta de Este, a ten-year program designed to implement the provisions of the U.S.-sponsored Alliance for Progress, while a code of conduct for transnational corporations was approved in July 1978.

On July 18, 1978, the nine-year-old Convention on Human Rights entered into force. The agreement provided for an Inter-American Court of Human Rights, composed of seven judges elected by the OAS assembly, to serve in a private capacity. Most members ratified the convention with reservations, so the court's impact has been limited. The Inter-American Commission on Human Rights has been more active.

The Falkland Islands crisis of 1982, which began with an Argentinean invasion on April 2, yielded an extended special session of the OAS during April and May. The participants passed a resolution that supported Argentina's claim to the Falklands (called Las Malvinas by Argentina), condemned the British effort to regain the island colony, and considered a possible U.S. breach of the 1947 Rio pact because of Washington's assistance to Britain.

The Falklands conflict pointed to a growing rift between, on the one hand, the United States and the English-speaking Caribbean members of the OAS and, on the other, most Latin American members. Following the U.S. intervention in Grenada in October 1983, most OAS members attending a special session on October 26 condemned the U.S. action. Washington and its Caribbean allies countered that the United States had not violated the Rio Treaty, but instead had tried to bring order to Grenada.

A special foreign ministers' meeting convened on December 2, 1985, in Cartagena, Colombia, to consider proposed amendments to the OAS charter. The resulting Protocol of Cartagena, which entered into force in November 1988, modified admission rules to permit the entry of Belize and Guyana, previously ineligible because of territorial disputes with OAS members Guatemala and Venezuela, respectively. Under the new criteria, all American states that were members of the UN as of December 10, 1985, plus specified non-autonomous territories (Bermuda, French Guiana, Guadeloupe, Martinique, and Montserrat, but not the Falkland Islands) would be permitted to apply. The protocol also increased the authority of the secretary general, permitting him, on his own initiative, to bring to the attention of the assembly any matter that "could affect the peace and security of the continent and development of its member countries." At the same time, the Permanent Council was authorized to provide peacekeeping services to help ameliorate regional crises.

Despite initial opposition from the United States, the OAS played an active role in the Central American peace negotiations initiated in early 1987 by former Costa Rican president Oscar Arias, with efforts directed toward conflicts in El Salvador and Guatemala, as well as Nicaragua. In 1989 attention turned to Panama. Despite the diplomatic failure, 20 OAS members approved a resolution in December that "deeply deplored" the U.S. invasion of Panama and called for the immediate withdrawal of U.S. troops.

Canada, which had long avoided active participation in the OAS because of perceived U.S. dominance, finally joined as a full member in 1990. The complement of member states grew to 35 with the accession of Belize and Guyana in 1991. Meanwhile, Washington continued to insist that Cuban eligibility for reintegration into regional activity had to be preceded by democratic elections.

During its June 1991 General Assembly, the organization adopted Resolution 1080, which authorized an emergency meeting of the Permanent Council following a coup or other threat to democracy in any member country. The resolution reflected that, for the first time in OAS history, all active members had democratically elected governments. The first test of the resolution was the military overthrow of the Haitian government of Fr. Jean-Bertrand Aristide on September 30, 1991. Haiti remained a focus of attention throughout 1992 and into 1993 as OAS observers attempted to monitor the human rights situation in that nation during UN negotiations.

The OAS also met in special sessions to address the seizures of dictatorial power by democratically elected leaders in Peru in 1992 and in Guatemala in May 1993, condemning both events but rejecting any specific action. The Inter-American Council for Integral Development (*Consejo Interamericano para el Desarrollo Integral*—CIDI) came into existence in 1996. Particular CIDI concerns are trade, social development, and sustainable development.

A major OAS concern in the first half of 1994 was Washington's preparation for a possible invasion of Haiti, as diplomatic measures and economic sanctions failed to sway the Haitian military leaders. The OAS General Assembly in June endorsed a tightening of sanctions but took no position on the use of military force, several leading members having argued against such intervention. Consequently, Washington looked to the UN for international approval of its Haitian policy, and in late July the UN Security Council authorized "all necessary action," including use of a U.S.-led multinational force, to return civilian government to Port-au-Prince.

In 1995 one major priority was the new OAS Unit for the Promotion of Democracy, mandated to observe national elections, provide special training for the staffs of national legislatures, create mechanisms to expand the dissemination of information on governmental activities, and establish courses for the armed forces and police regarding human rights protection.

The 1996 creation of CIDI came about largely in response to a perception that the earlier donor-recipient model of technical assistance needed to be replaced by a structure entailing cooperation of equal partners on well-defined programs devoted to economic and social development. CIDI replaced the Inter-American Economic and Social Council and the Inter-American Council for Education, Science, and Culture. In 1997 the General Assembly eliminated the Inter-American Nuclear Energy Commission, which had not been funded since 1989.

The addition of the IACD in 1999 continued the process of rationalizing the OAS's economic and development structures; in addition to serving as the principal agency responsible for promoting and organizing cooperative ventures, the IACD offers training programs and facilitates technical exchanges.

In 1998, through the Inter-American Drug Abuse Control Commission, the OAS instituted a Multilateral Evaluation Mechanism for evaluating antidrug programs and coordinating members' responses to the illicit trade in drugs. In recent years the OAS also has increasingly taken on the role of broker in bilateral disputes, including border issues involving El Salvador and Honduras, Honduras and Nicaragua, and Guatemala and Belize. To finance negotiations and such related activities as compliance monitoring, in 2000 the General Assembly authorized the establishment of a Fund for Peace. Additional security-related efforts have included the adoption of the Inter-American Convention against the Illicit Manufacturing of and Trafficking in Firearms, Ammunition, Explosives, and Other Related Materials, which entered into force in 1998, and the adoption and ratification of the Inter-American Convention on Conventional Arms Acquisitions in 1999.

On September 11–12, in a special session in Lima, Peru, the OAS adopted a charter that authorizes sanctions against a member state that experiences "an unconstitutional interruption of the democratic order or an unconstitutional alteration of the constitutional regime that seriously impairs the democratic order."

The special session coincided with the September 11, 2001, terrorist attacks on the United States, which led a September 19 emergency session of the Permanent Council to invoke the Rio Treaty and thereby authorize assistance to Washington in its "war on terrorism."

An Intra-American Convention against Terrorism was opened for signature at the 2002 General Assembly session, which met June 2–4 in Bridgetown, Barbados. The meeting's closing declaration called for a "multidimensional" approach to hemispheric security, which "encompasses political, economic, social, health, and environmental factors." At the subsequent session, held June 9–10, 2003, in Santiago, the General Assembly issued the Declaration of Santiago on Democracy and Public Trust. In addition to characterizing the Inter-American Democratic Charter as the "principal hemispheric benchmark" for promoting and defending democratic principles and values, the summit identified "greater efficiency, probity, and transparency" as central to good governance. A month later, the Convention against Terrorism entered into force, 30 days after having obtained a sixth ratification.

A Special Summit of the Americas met January 12–13, 2004, in Monterrey, Mexico, to focus attention on economic growth, social and human development, and democratic governance. The OAS also hosted a series of meetings on drafting an American Declaration on the Rights of Indigenous Peoples. The OAS assistant secretary general acknowledged that much more needed to be done.

At the OAS General Assembly on June 7, 2004, in Quito, Ecuador, former Costa Rican president Miguel Angel Rodríguez was elected as the new secretary general. Rodríguez, who was favored by the United States, announced his resignation October 8, 2004, after allegations surfaced of financial corruption during his time in office in Costa Rica. Rodríguez was just two weeks into his five-year term in the OAS post, having been sworn in September 23.

Negotiations and debate over Rodríguez's successor occupied OAS leaders for the next six months, with the group deadlocking 17–17 through five rounds of voting on April 11, 2005. Finally, on May 2, 2005, Insulza, a socialist, was elected in what was viewed as a setback for the United States. Insulza's election marked the first time in OAS history that a candidate opposed by the United States had become secretary general.

2006 was a time of financial difficulty for the OAS. The secretary general noted that while no member states were in arrears in their dues, inflation and the need to meet UN guidelines on staff compensation meant that many of the organization's programs would have to be funded privately. Another major turning point in OAS history occurred in July 2006 when Brazil took over the chair of the Inter-American Defense Board—the first time that responsibility had left the United States in the organization's history.

The year 2007 was marked by the actions of Venezuelan president Hugo Chávez and the organization's response. Amid widespread protests in Venezuela and beyond, the Chávez government refused to renew the license of a television station well known for criticizing the government. The United States condemned Venezuela and asked the OAS to intervene, but the only result was a general OAS call to respect media freedom. The OAS also complied when Venezuela demanded that it remove from its Website a report from the Berlin-based organization Transparency International criticizing the amount of graft in Venezuela.

The March 1, 2008, raid by Colombia against a Revolutionary Armed Forces of Colombia (FARC) rebel camp inside Ecuador caused the OAS to set up a five-member commission to investigate. By March 18 the OAS had passed a resolution deploring the Colombian incursion and calling it "a clear violation of articles 19 and 21 of the OAS charter," but it noted that Colombia had already apologized and promised no more such incidents would occur. The resolution was seen as a defeat for the United States, who had wanted the resolution to recognize the raid as a legitimate act of self-defense. In June 2008 Colombia and Ecuador restored diplomatic relations at a low level.

At the June 1–3, 2008, meeting of the General Assembly, of which the nominal theme was "Youth and Democratic Values," the representative from Antigua and Barbuda made a strong plea for the organization to work against greenhouse gas emissions, which he called a "clear and present danger" to the hemisphere.

The election of Barack Obama as U.S. president in November 2008 caused the OAS to think once more about readmitting Cuba to full membership and ending the U.S. trade embargo against that country. In April 2009 former Cuban president Fidel Castro called for the forthcoming fifth Summit of the Americas to end Cuba's isolation. President Obama attended the summit and declared that the United States sought a "new beginning" with Cuba. At the 39th regular session of the OAS General Assembly meeting June 2–3, 2009, in San Pedro Sula, Honduras, the organization voted to rescind Cuba's 1962 banishment. On June 4 Ricardo Alarcon, the speaker of the Cuban parliament, welcomed the decision but said that Cuba might not necessarily want to rejoin the OAS immediately.

Also in June 2009 the Honduran army expelled President Manuel Zelaya and replaced him with Roberto Micheletti, the speaker of Congress. The OAS suspended Honduras from full membership, refusing to recognize the November election of Profirio Lobo as president. On June 1, 2011, in a special session called to address the Honduran situation, the General Assembly voted to lift the country's suspension. Honduras was immediately reinstated.

A conference of many Latin American and Caribbean states met February 22–23, 2010, in Cancun, Mexico, and agreed to set up a new regional bloc that excluded the United States and Canada. This new organization was to be an alternative to the OAS, and its existence would call into question the relevance of the OAS. Observers were particularly critical of the OAS parliamentary procedures, which tended toward vote by consensus and frequently produced what was characterized as a "lowest common denominator" resolution. Insulza responded with a statement that the organization was still relevant and that its processes could be reformed.

On July 22, 2010, Colombia called an extraordinary meeting of the Permanent Council, complaining that Venezuela was sheltering Colombian rebels on its territory. The next day Venezuelan president Chávez cut diplomatic ties with Colombia.

In November 2010 the OAS urged Nicaragua and Costa Rica to withdraw their forces from a disputed border region. Costa Rica, which had brought the matter before the Permanent Council, agreed, but Nicaragua, supported by Venezuela, did not. Costa Rica claimed a diplomatic victory.

The June 2011 meeting of the OAS assembly was largely focused on security issues, human rights, and illegal trafficking in OAS states. Most notably, the assembly produced the Declaration of San Salvador on Citizen Security in the Americas, which recognized the need for increased OAS efforts on security and called for the secretariat to develop a plan of action and encouraged the member states to increase security policies in their individual countries. The OAS also voted at the summit to readmit Honduras, who had been suspended since a 2009 coup.

The year 2011 also marks the 10th anniversary of the creation of the Inter-American Democratic Charter (IADC). In honor of the occasion the OAS has undertaken a review of the IADC and has considered methods to increase its participation in encouraging democracy throughout the Americas.

Three states were added as permanent observers to the OAS in 2011: Macedonia (May), Albania (October), and Malta (September).

The sixth Summit of the Americas (held every three years) was held in April 2012. While no major decisions resulted from the meeting, the heads of state engaged in an extended discussion of drug trafficking, particularly noting dissatisfaction among Central and South American states with the United States' policy of deporting drug traffickers out of the US and into the other American states.

The 42nd annual OAS General Assembly was held in Cochabamba, Bolivia in June 2012. The overarching theme of the meeting was food security with sovereignty. The delegates at the assembly signed the Declaration of Cochabamba, which was a set of principles concerning agricultural growth in the American States. The declaration included an appeal to all of the member states to put greater emphasis on sustainable, agricultural development. The assembly also dealt with disputed territory in the Maldivian Islands, increased maritime access for Bolivia, and a new report produced by the Inter-American Commission for Human Rights. In light of the report, the OAS passed a series of declarations designed to encourage greater human rights and equality for women, as well as increase the amount of education about the importance of human rights throughout the region.

In September 2012 the OAS joined the World Economic Forum's Partnering for Cyber Resilience Initiative, which was launched in January 2012. The move was reflective of the organization's continued emphasis on cyber security in the 21st century.

One of the biggest needs identified for 2013 by Secretary General Insulza was improved prioritization of OAS projects. Insulza noted that the OAS has too many projects for its limited resources, and will only be effective moving forward if it prioritizes the projects in which it is involved. This need was further highlighted in a bipartisan recommendation from the U.S. Senate.

On March 22, 2013, the OAS convened an extraordinary General Assembly meeting for the purpose of concluding the two-year review and reform of its human rights protocols. The meeting approved by acclamation a resolution authorizing the IACHR to strengthen its operations through further legislation, committing to fully fund the efforts of the IACHR for the future, and urging all member states to accede to all components of the OAS human rights program.

At its regular summit in June, the OAS General Assembly produced several key decisions. The main document of the meeting, the OAS Declaration of Antigua, Guatemala, calls on member states emphasize "public health, education, and social inclusion" while working to prevent organized crime and promote regional development. Likewise, the OAS approved two new conventions, the Inter-American Convention against Racism, Racial Discrimination, and Related Forms of Intolerance and the Inter-American Convention against All Forms of Discrimination and Intolerance. Both conventions are designed at promoting equality for all throughout the region. The meeting also called for new approaches to deal with the global drug trade, which is particularly problematic in Latin America. The meeting also saw the creation of a hemispheric cooperation mechanism for effective public management designed to strengthen public administration within the region. The object of the new mechanism is to promote effective public administration as a means of strengthening democracy in the hemisphere. (For more on developments since 2013, see Recent activities, below.)

Structure. As the principal political organ of the OAS, the General Assembly meets annually to set policy, discuss the budget, and supervise the work of the organization's specialized agencies. The Permanent Council meets throughout the year to oversee the organization's agenda and has the authority to form committees and working groups. In addition to a General Committee, current committees include Administrative and Budgetary Affairs, Hemispheric Security, Juridical and Political Affairs, Inter-American Summits Management, and Civil Society Participation in OAS Activities. Under the Rio Treaty, the Meeting of Consultation of Ministers of Foreign Affairs discharges the organization's security functions and is convened to consider urgent problems.

The General Secretariat, headed by a secretary general who serves a five-year term, encompasses more than two dozen offices, departments, units, and agencies. It also oversees two cultural institutions, the Art Museum of the Americas and the Columbus Memorial Library, both based in Washington.

Reporting to the General Assembly, the CIDI comprises a ministerial-level representative from each member state; it meets annually on a regular basis but also may convene in special session or at a sectoral level at other times. In addition to a Permanent Executive Committee, it has an Executive Secretariat for Integral Development that operates within the overall OAS General Secretariat.

Affiliated in various ways with the OAS are many specialized agencies, bodies, and other organizations, many predating the establishment of the OAS itself. (For a complete listing, see the 2011 *Handbook*.)

Recent activities. In January 2014 the Permanent Council of the OAS approved the permanent observer status of Liechtenstein and Montenegro, bringing the OAS to 70 permanent observers. A special meeting of the OAS Permanent Council was held in March to discuss the outbreak of violent protests in Venezuela. The permanent representatives adopted a declaration of support for the government of Venezuela, but both the United States and Panama raised objections to the declaration on the grounds that, among other things, the declaration took sides in the conflict.

At the OAS Assembly meeting in Asunción, Paraguay, in June, the heads of state passed the Asunción Declaration, which committed the member states to advocating the major points of the meeting's discussion, including gender equity, ending poverty and hunger, the advancement of human rights, and the promotion of economic development. The meeting also approved resolutions concerning hemispheric security, administrative procedures, and political affairs. In July, 32 members of the OAS issued a declaration against the June U.S. Supreme Court ruling requiring Argentina to compensate debtors before it began bond payments (see entry on Argentina). A special summit was held in September 2014 to address the growing drug problem across the globe and within the Americas specifically. There, the assembly approved a series of guidelines, action steps, and goals to be taken by the members to address the drug problem.

On March 19, 2015, Venezuelan officials issued a statement to the OAS that they believed the United States intended to use military aggression against the existing government. Luis Almagro Lemes of Uruguay was elected secretary general on April 1. Almagro was strongly backed by Argentina, Brazil, Mexico, and the United States.

On April 10–11, 2015, the 7th Summit of the Americas took place in Panama City, Panama. The summit was dominated by the easing of tensions between the United States and Cuba, and the latter country's attendance at the meeting after Washington dropped any objections to its inclusion. The organization met on July 8 to discuss the mass deportation of Haitians from the Dominican Republic. Estimates were that the Dominican Republic had deported over 40,000 whose legal immigration status had lapsed. An additional 200,000 Haitians in the Dominican Republic were believed to hold expired visas. In response to growing crime and instability, on September 28 the OAS established an anticorruption body to assist the Honduran government (see entry on Honduras). Called the Mission to Support the Fight Against Corruption and Impunity in Honduras (MACCIH), the initiative was led by legal experts from the OAS along with a panel of judges.

The OAS called an emergency meeting on January 6, 2016, to discuss the growing Venezuelan political and economic crisis. On August 30, 2016, Almagro accused Venezuela's government of seeking to repress and suppress the country's opposition. A 300-page document justified various forms of OAS intervention in Venezuela because of the government's violation of its own constitution and potential human rights transgressions. The November 2016 United States presidential election was scheduled to be monitored by the OAS for the first time. The monitoring will be led by former Costa Rican president Laura Chinchilla. The United States has monitored 240 elections in 26 OAS member countries to date. The monitoring is largely symbolic because there will only be 20 to 30 observers that can issue nonbinding recommendations.

ORGANIZATION OF ISLAMIC COOPERATION (OIC)

Munazzamat al-Mu'tamar [Ta'aavon] [al-Alam al-Islami]
Organisation de la Coopération Islamique (OCI)

Established: By agreement of participants at the Conference of the Kings and Heads of State and Government held September 22–25, 1969, in Rabat, Morocco; charter signed at the Third Islamic Conference of Foreign Ministers, held February 29–March 4, 1972, in Jiddah, Saudi Arabia.

Purpose: To promote Islamic solidarity and further cooperation among member states in the economic, social, cultural, scientific, and political fields.

Headquarters: Jiddah, Saudi Arabia.

Principal Organs: Conference of Kings and Heads of State and Government (Summit Conference), Conference of Foreign Ministers, General Secretariat.

Website: www.oic-oci.org.

Secretary General: Iyad bin Amin Madani (Saudi Arabia).

Membership (57): Afghanistan, Albania, Algeria, Azerbaijan, Bahrain, Bangladesh, Benin, Brunei, Burkina Faso, Cameroon, Chad, Comoro Islands, Côte d'Ivoire, Djibouti, Egypt, Gabon, Gambia, Guinea, Guinea-Bissau, Guyana, Indonesia, Iran, Iraq, Jordan, Kazakhstan, Kuwait, Kyrgyzstan, Lebanon, Libya, Malaysia, Maldives, Mali, Mauritania, Morocco, Mozambique, Niger, Nigeria, Oman, Pakistan, Palestine, Qatar, Saudi Arabia, Senegal, Sierra Leone, Somalia, Sudan, Suriname, Syria (suspended since August 2012), Tajikistan, Togo, Tunisia, Turkey, Turkmenistan, Uganda, United Arab Emirates, Uzbekistan, Yemen. Nigeria's government approved that nation's admission into the OIC in 1986, but the membership was formally repudiated in 1991 in the wake of intense Christian opposition; the OIC has not recognized the latter decision.

Observer States (5): Bosnia and Herzegovina, Central African Republic, Russia, Thailand, Turkish Republic of Northern Cyprus.

Official Languages: Arabic, English, French.

Origin and development. Although the idea of an organization for coordinating and consolidating the interests of Islamic states originated in 1969 and meetings of the conference were held throughout the 1970s, the Organization of the Islamic Conference (OIC) only began to achieve worldwide attention in the early 1980s. From a base of 30 members in 1969, the grouping has doubled in size, with the most recent member, Côte d'Ivoire, being admitted in 2001. The OIC is the world's second-largest IGO, after the United Nations.

During the 1980s three lengthy conflicts dominated the OIC's agenda: the Soviet occupation of Afghanistan, which began in December 1979 and concluded with the final withdrawal of Soviet troops in February 1989; the Iran–Iraq war, which began in September 1980 and ended with the cease-fire of August 1988; and the ongoing Arab–Israeli conflict. At their August 1990 meeting, the foreign ministers described the Palestinian problem as the primary concern for the Islamic world. However, much of the planned agenda was disrupted by emergency private sessions concerning Iraq's invasion of Kuwait on August 2. Most attending the meeting approved a resolution condemning the incursion and demanding the withdrawal of Iraqi troops. In addition to other ongoing conflicts among conference members, the Gulf crisis contributed to the postponement of the heads of state summit that normally would have been held in 1990.

When the sixth summit was finally held December 9–11, 1991, in Dakar, Senegal, more than half of members' heads of state failed to attend. Substantial lingering rancor concerning the Gulf crisis was reported at the meeting, while black African representatives asserted that Arab nations were giving insufficient attention to the problems of sub-Saharan Muslims. On the whole, the summit was perceived as unproductive.

In the following three years much of the conference's attention focused on the plight of the Muslim community in Bosnia and Herzegovina. The group's foreign ministers repeatedly called on the UN to use force, if necessary, to stop Serbian attacks against Bosnian Muslims, but the conference stopped well short of approving creation of an Islamic force to intervene on its own, as reportedly proposed by Iran and several other members. OIC efforts to improve the international image of Islam continued in 1995, in conjunction with ceremonies marking the organization's 25th anniversary.

The renewed Palestinian uprising and the Israeli response to it provided a principal focus for OIC meetings in 2000. These included the June 27–30 Conference of Foreign Ministers in Kuala Lumpur, Malaysia, and the ninth summit November 12–13 in Doha, Qatar, which devoted its first day to discussing "the serious situation prevailing in the Palestinian occupied territories following the savage actions perpetrated by the Israeli forces."

Meeting June 25–29 in Bamako, Mali, the regular 28th Conference of Foreign Ministers reiterated a call for member countries to halt political contacts with the Israeli government, sever economic relations, and end "all forms of normalization." In other areas, the conference urged member states to ratify the Statute of the International Islamic Court of Justice, called for formation of an expert group that would begin drafting an Islamic Convention on Human Rights, condemned international terrorism, noted the progress made toward instituting an Islamic Program for the Development of Information and Communication (PIDIC), and cautioned that care must be taken to ensure that the economic benefits of globalization were shared and the adverse effects minimized.

Immediately after the September 11, 2001, terrorist attacks against the United States, the OIC secretary general, Abdelouahed Belkeziz, condemned the terrorist acts, as did an extraordinary Conference of Foreign Ministers session in Doha. The Doha session did not directly oppose the ongoing U.S.-led military campaign against al-Qaida and the Taliban regime in Afghanistan, although it did argue that no state should be targeted under the pretext of attacking terrorism. The session also rejected as counter to Islamic teachings and values any attempt to justify terrorism on religious grounds.

The impending U.S.-led war against the Saddam Hussein regime in Iraq generated a second extraordinary session of the Islamic Summit Conference on March 5, 2003, in Doha. The meeting included an exchange of personal insults by the Iraqi and Kuwaiti representatives and a warning from the secretary general that a U.S. military campaign would lead to occupation and foreign rule. The session concluded with a call for the elimination of all weapons of mass destruction (WMD) from the Middle East.

In response to subsequent international developments, the secretary general praised improved cooperation between Iran and the International Atomic Energy Agency; condemned the November 2003 terrorist attacks against synagogues in Istanbul, Turkey, and a housing complex in Riyadh, Saudi Arabia; and welcomed Libya's decision to end the development of WMD. On February 25, 2004, the OIC argued before the International Court of Justice in The Hague, Netherlands, that the security wall being constructed by Israel on Palestinian land was illegal.

The OIC subsequently continued to condemn acts of terrorism around the world, including the March 2004 bombings in Madrid, Spain; the attacks against London's transit system in July 2005; and the explosions at the Egyptian resorts of Sharm El-Shiekh and Naama Bay later the same month. With regard to developments in Iraq, in August 2005 the OIC urged "prudence and consensus" during deliberations on the draft Iraqi constitution. In particular, the OIC advocated a policy of inclusion, cautioning that the exclusion of any component of the population (implicitly, the Sunni minority) would ill serve "the creation of commonly desired conditions of democracy, stability, peace, and welfare in this important member of the OIC."

A third extraordinary session took place December 7–8, 2005, in Jiddah to address the violent worldwide Islamic outrage following publication in a Danish newspaper of cartoons critical of the Prophet Mohammad. The conference condemned violence, saying that Islam was in a crisis, and offered an ambitious ten-year plan to "revamp Islamic mindsets." Symbolic of this decision was the intention to reorganize the OIC itself and to build a new headquarters in Saudi Arabia.

The 33rd meeting of OIC foreign ministers, held June 19–22, 2006, in Baku, Azerbaijan, reinforced the message of moderation in the Islamic world. Later events, however, may have pushed the OIC some distance away from its traditionally moderate stance. In early August 2006 the OIC held a crisis meeting in Kuala Lumpur on the fighting between Hezbollah and Israel. It condemned Israel's attacks on civilians in Lebanon, calling for an immediate cease-fire, which was to be supervised by a UN force. Malaysia promised troops.

In 2007 the OIC was one of several bodies involved with the UN in efforts to resolve the Darfur crisis, but it was noted that the UN Human Rights Council (UNHRC) had been thwarted in its efforts to pass any resolution against Sudan by the OIC and various African countries since its opening session in June 2006. In July 2007 OIC secretary general Ekmeleddin İhsanoğlu of Turkey issued a statement rejecting an election in the secessionist Nagorno-Karabakh region of Azerbaijan, declaring that "the OIC fully recognizes the sovereignty and territorial integrity of Azerbaijan." Azerbaijan, not surprisingly, went on record in February 2008 as opposing any recognition of Kosovo's independence.

The March 13–14, 2008, OIC summit, held in Dakar, Senegal, adopted a revised charter. The new charter was intended to render decision-making within the organization more effective and the OIC more productive in promoting humanitarian efforts around the world. İhsanoğlu went on record as favoring the European Union (EU) as a model for any large multinational organization. He stated that a joint effort between the OIC and the West could bridge the gap between the Muslim and Western worlds. The new charter may have signaled a more activist line on the part of an organization once renowned for its moderate tone. This new tone was most evident in a free-speech resolution introduced with the OIC's backing at the UN in November 2008, declaring defamation of religion to be a violation of international law.

In other matters, in July 2008 the OIC opened an office in Iraq. In September Kosovo appealed to the OIC for support for its declaration of full independence from Serbia. Few OIC countries supported independence however, and Iran announced that it would block Kosovo from joining the OIC.

Sudanese president Omar al-Bashir accepted, and then later declined, Turkey's invitation to attend the OIC's Standing Committee for Economic and Commercial Cooperation (COMCEC) meeting November 5–9, 2009, in Istanbul. The Turkish government had said that Bashir, the subject of an arrest warrant from the International Criminal Court, would not be arrested in Turkey. But pressure from the EU may have caused both Turkey and Bashir to think again. At the conference Turkey and Malaysia agreed to work together to develop halal food standards for the OIC, this to pave the way for the OIC to enter a market currently dominated by non-Muslim countries.

In May 2010 U.S. president Obama appointed Rashad Hussain, a deputy associate counsel at the White House and "a respected member of the American Muslim community," the second U.S. envoy to the OIC. At the OIC's 37th Council of Foreign Ministers meeting in Dushanbe, Tajikistan, the group issued the Dushanbe Declaration, which called for a renewed dialogue between Islamic and non-Islamic nations and new efforts to combat prejudice and Muslim stereotypes.

During the Arab Spring, beginning in February 2011, the OIC supported the implementation of a no-fly zone over Libya but opposed any direct military intervention. The OIC subsequently recognized the new Libyan government on September 5, after the overthrow of the previous regime. The OIC also called for an end to ongoing violence in Syria. At the OIC's 38th meeting of the Council of Foreign Ministers in June, the group called for international recognition of Palestine. The foreign ministers also approved changing the name of the group to the Organization of Islamic Cooperation, a proposal first put forward in 2007 by Secretary General İhsanoğlu, who argued that the word *conference* suggested a one-time meeting.

Throughout 2012 the OIC stressed the importance of interfaith harmony. As a serious of bombings and attacks against Christians in Nigeria took place in the first half of the year, the secretary general called on OIC member states to seek peace between the various faiths. The OIC was also involved in a March meeting at the Vatican to discuss Arab–Israeli peace and the need for peaceful relations between the different religions.

In April 2012 Kazakhstan formally ratified the OIC Charter. At a June 2012 meeting, the Executive Committee of the OIC recommended the suspension of Syria from the organization in light of the ongoing political violence and civil war. The full Council of Foreign Ministers is scheduled to vote upon the recommendation in November. Later in June, China expressed interest in becoming an observer state of the OIC. While no formal application has been submitted as of yet, the Chinese government requested information on several OIC projects in order to examine possible funding.

In light of the violence of the civil war in Syria, the OIC voted to suspend Syria's membership in the organization at an extraordinary summit held in August 2012.

At the 2013 Islamic Summit held in February, the OIC was primarily focused on several grave situations occurring within their mandate. Noting the continuing escalation of conflict in Syria, the OIC called for those in Syria to seek a peaceful solution. While urging the UN Security Council to act, they noted their sincere hope that a Syrian-led resolution of the conflict could be achieved. The meeting also yielded a resolution on Palestine, in which the organization condemned the Israeli attacks on the Gaza Strip in November 2012, commended the UN for upgrading the PLO to status as an observer state, and continued to urge its member states to push for international recognition of Palestine. The meeting also called for member states to recognize Kosovo, expressed a desire to collectively take efforts to promote economic growth and job creation, and strongly condemned the terrorist activity in Mali.

In regard to the ever-worsening situation in Syria, Secretary General İhsanoğlu endorsed the plan put forth in September 2013 to place Syria's chemical weapons, which were first discovered in late-August, under international control. İhsanoğlu also reiterated its call for the UN Security Council to take actions to end the violence and bloodshed in the war-torn state. (For more on events since 2013, see Recent activities, below.)

Structure. The body's main institution is the Conference of Foreign Ministers, although a summit of members' heads of state and government is held every five years. Sectoral ministerial conferences have also convened in such areas as information, tourism, health, and youth and sports.

Over the years many committees and departments have evolved to provide input on policy decisions and to carry out the OIC's executive and administrative functions. The organization's secretary general, who serves a four-year, once-renewable term, heads the General Secretariat and is aided by four assistant secretaries general—for science and technology; cultural, social, and information affairs; political affairs; and economic affairs—and a director of the cabinet, who helps administer various departments. The secretariat also maintains permanent observer missions to the United Nations (UN) in New York City, United States, and Geneva, Switzerland, and an Office for Afghanistan was recently established in Islamabad, Pakistan. Other OIC organs include the al-Quds (Jerusalem) Committee, the Six-Member Committee on Palestine, the Standing Committee for Information and Cultural Affairs (COMIAC), the Standing Committee for Economic and Trade Cooperation (COMCEC), the Standing Committee for Scientific and Technological Cooperation (COMSTECH), and various additional permanent and specialized committees.

To date, the OIC has established four "specialized institutions and organs," including the International Islamic News Agency (IINA, founded in 1972); the Islamic Development Bank (IDB, 1974); the Islamic States Broadcasting Organization (ISBO, 1975); and the Islamic Educational, Scientific, and Cultural Organization (IESSCO, 1982). Of the organization's eight "subsidiary organs," one of the more prominent is the Islamic Solidarity Fund (ISF, 1977). The founding conference of the Parliamentary Union of the OIC Member States was held in June 1999.

Recent activities. On January 1, 2014, Iyad Ameen Madani of Saudi Arabia began his tenure as secretary general. Madani succeeded Secretary General İhsanoğlu, whose mandate expired after having served in that position since 2004. In June the OIC held its first-ever International Forum on Islamic Tourism as part of fulfilling the goals of the OIC's Ten-Year Action Plan. The meeting brought leaders of the tourism sector from Islamic countries across the world together in Jakarta, Indonesia, to discuss how tourism can impact economic growth.

In late June the OIC foreign ministers convened for their biannual meeting in Jeddah, Saudi Arabia. The meeting produced the Jeddah Declaration, which set up a ministerial contact group to address the situation in Palestine and mobilize OIC support and assistance for the Palestinian efforts. The declaration also blamed the Israelis for the failure of reaching a peace settlement. Also at the meeting, the ministers rejected the elections held in Syria, called for an end of the violence against Muslims in Myanmar, and condemned religious extremism and terrorism. This call for OIC member states to stand up against extremists is further seen in the organization's July condemnation of the ISIS attacks in Syria and Iraq. Secretary General Madani welcomed similar remarks from U.S. president Barak Obama in September when he called for cooperation and joint action against extremists and terrorism.

OIC secretary general Iyad Madani on January 18, 2015, announced that the organization planned to sue the French satirical magazine *Charlie Hebdo* for the publishing of blasphemous cartoons. Madani stated that "freedom of speech must not become a hate speech and must not offend others. No sane person, irrespective of doctrine, religion or faith, accepts his beliefs being ridiculed." On February 4, 2015, the OIC condemned ISIS for the death by immolation of Jordanian pilot Mauth al-Kaseasbeh (see entry on Jordan).

On April 15, 2016, the OIC summit was held in Istanbul, Turkey, to discuss humanitarian issues arising from the Syrian civil war and the continuing terror campaign of ISIS. The organization also condemned Iran's support of the Houthi movement in Yemen and for supporting terrorist organizations. The OIC urged Iran to recognize that "we are Muslims." On April 18 Hezbollah criticized the OIC for including them in their denunciation of Iran. The OIC denounced the radical Islamic group Boko Haram for kidnapping Nigerian schoolgirls (see entry on Nigeria).

The OIC and the U.S. Agency for International Development (USAID) signed a memorandum of understanding to cooperate with respect to humanitarian affairs on September 22, 2016. Three days later, the OIC approved a report by the Contact Group on Kashmir, which reaffirmed its call for resolution of the Kashmir dispute between India and Pakistan. The OIC also requested that the UN monitor human rights in the strife-torn area and affirmed its support for self-determination for the Kashmiri people.

ORGANIZATION OF THE PETROLEUM EXPORTING COUNTRIES (OPEC)

Established: By resolutions adopted September 14, 1960, in Baghdad, Iraq, and codified in a statute approved by the Eighth (Extraordinary) OPEC Conference, held April 5–10, 1965, in Geneva, Switzerland.

Purpose: To coordinate and unify petroleum policies of member countries; to devise ways to ensure stabilization of international oil prices to eliminate "harmful and unnecessary" price and supply fluctuations.

Headquarters: Vienna, Austria.

Principal Organs: Conference, Board of Governors, Economic Commission, Secretariat.

Website: www.opec.org.

Secretary General: Mohammed Sanusi Barkindo (Nigeria).

Membership (14, with years of entry): Algeria (1969), Angola (2007), Iran (1960), Iraq (1960), Kuwait (1960), Libya (1962), Nigeria (1971), Qatar (1961), Saudi Arabia (1960), United Arab Emirates (Abu Dhabi in 1967, with the membership being transferred to the UAE in 1974), Venezuela (1960). Ecuador, which joined OPEC in 1973, withdrew in January 1993, and rejoined in October 2007. Gabon joined OPEC in 1975, but withdrew in January 1995, before rejoining in 2016. Indonesia became a member in 1962, but suspended its membership in January, returning to the organization in 2016. Iraq currently does not participate in OPEC production quotas.

Official Language: English.

Origin and development. A need for concerted action by petroleum exporters was first broached in 1946 by Dr. Juan Pablo Pérez Alfonso of Venezuela. His initiative led to a series of contacts in the late 1940s between oil-producing countries, but it was not until 1959 that the first Arab Petroleum Conference was held. At that meeting Dr. Pérez Alfonso convinced the Arabs, along with Iranian and Venezuelan observers, to form a union of producing states, with OPEC being formally created by Iran, Iraq, Kuwait, Saudi Arabia, and Venezuela on September 14, 1960, during a conference in Baghdad, Iraq.

The rapid growth of energy needs in the advanced industrialized states throughout the 1960s and early 1970s provided OPEC with the basis for extracting ever-increasing oil prices. However, OPEC demands were not limited to favorable prices; members also sought the establishment of an infrastructure for future industrialization, including petrochemical plants, steel mills, aluminum plants, and other high-energy industries as a hedge against the anticipated exhaustion of their oil reserves in the 21st century.

The addition of new members and negotiations with petroleum companies on prices, production levels, and tax revenues dominated OPEC's early years, with prices remaining low and relatively stable. However, largely because of OPEC-mandated increases, prices soared dramatically from approximately $3 for a 42-gallon barrel in the early 1970s to a peak of nearly $40 per barrel by the end of the decade. Thereafter, a world glut of petroleum, brought on by overproduction, global recession, and the implementation of at least rudimentary energy conservation programs by many industrialized nations subsequently reversed that trend. The influence of formal OPEC price setting waned as the organization began to increasingly depend on negotiated production quotas to stabilize prices.

In December 1985, as spot market prices dropped to $24 a barrel and production dipped to as low as 16 million barrels per day, OPEC abandoned its formal price structure to secure a larger share of the world's oil market. By mid-1986, however, oil prices had dropped by 50 percent or more to their lowest levels since 1978, generating intense concern among OPEC members with limited oil reserves, large populations, extensive international debts, and severe shortages of foreign exchange. As a result Saudi Arabia increased its output by 2 million barrels per day in January 1986 to force non-OPEC producers to cooperate with the cartel in stabilizing the world oil market.

During their December 1987 meeting in Vienna, OPEC oil ministers attempted to reimpose discipline, but the talks became embroiled in political considerations stemming from the Iran-Iraq war. The meeting concluded with 12 members endorsing the $18-per-barrel fixed-price concept and agreeing to a 15-million-barrels-per-day production quota, Iraq's nonparticipation leaving it free to produce at will. However, widespread discounting quickly forced prices down to about $15 per barrel.

In the wake of the Gulf cease-fire, OPEC cohesion seemed to return. In their first unanimous action in two years, the members agreed in late November 1988 to limit production to 18.5 million barrels per day as of January 1, 1989, while maintaining a "target price" of $18 per barrel. Responding to the organization's apparent renewal of self-control, oil prices rose to nearly $20 per barrel by March 1989. However, contention broke out again at the June OPEC session, with Saudi Arabia resisting demands for sizable quota increases. Although a compromise agreement was concluded, Kuwait and the UAE immediately declared that they would continue to exceed their quotas.

In November 1989 OPEC raised its official production ceiling from 20.5 to 22 million barrels per day, allowing Kuwait a quota increase from 1.2 to 1.5 million barrels per day. However, the UAE, whose official quota remained at 1.1 million barrels per day, did not participate in the accord and continued, as did Kuwait, to produce close to 2 million barrels per day. Pledges for restraint were again issued at an emergency meeting in May 1990, but adherence proved negligible. Consequently, in July Iraq's president Saddam Hussein threatened to use military intervention to enforce the national quotas. While the pronouncement drew criticism from the West, several OPEC leaders quietly voiced support for Hussein's "enforcer" stance and, mollified by the Iraqi leader's promise not to use military force to settle a border dispute with Kuwait, agreed on July 27 to Iraqi-led demands for new quotas. However, on August 29, in a dramatic reversal prompted by Iraq's invasion of Kuwait on August 2 and the ensuing embargo on oil exports from the two countries, the organization authorized producers to disregard quotas to avert possible shortages. OPEC's action legitimized the 2-million-barrels-per-day increase already implemented by Saudi Arabia and dampened Iraq's hope that oil shortages and skyrocketing prices would weaken the resolve of the coalition embargo. In December production reached its highest level in a decade, while prices fluctuated between $25 and $40 in response to the continuing crisis.

In early March 1991, following Iraq's defeat in the Gulf War, OPEC agreed to cut production from 23.4 to 22.3 million barrels per day for the second quarter of the year. In June OPEC rejected Iraq's request to intercede with the United Nations to lift the Iraqi oil embargo.

In September 1991 OPEC agreed to raise its collective production ceiling to 23.6 million barrels per day in preparation for normal seasonal increases in demand. However, Iran and Saudi Arabia remained in what analysts described as a "trial of strength" for OPEC dominance: the former lobbying for lowered production ceilings and higher prices and the latter resisting production curbs or any challenge to its market share. Consequently, on February 15, 1992, OPEC members agreed to their first individual production quotas since August 1990, with the Saudis grudgingly accepting a 7.8-million-barrels-per-day quota. In April and May the organization extended the February quotas despite reports of overproduction, citing the firm price, albeit lower than desired, of $17 per barrel.

Prices remained low for the rest of 1992 as the global recession undercut demand and overproduction continued to plague OPEC; meanwhile, Kuwait attempted to recover from the economic catastrophe inflicted by the Gulf crisis by pumping oil "at will." With a relatively mild winter in the Northern Hemisphere having further reduced demand, a February 1993 emergency OPEC meeting sought to reestablish some sense of constraint by endorsing a 23.5-million-barrels- per-day limit on its members.

Actual levels continued at more than 25 million barrels per day, however, and a more realistic quota of 24.5 million barrels per day was negotiated in September 1993. The new arrangement permitted Kuwait's quota to rise from 1.6 million to 2.0 million barrels per day, while Iran's quota grew from 3.3 million to 3.6 million. Meanwhile, Saudi Arabia agreed to keep its production at 8 million.

The November 1994 conference also agreed to maintain the current quota of 24.5 million barrels per day for at least one more year. However, pressure for change grew in 1995, particularly as non-OPEC production continued to expand. Secretary General Rilwanu Lukman (Nigeria) and oil ministers from several OPEC countries argued that non-OPEC nations' failure to curb production could lead to serious problems for all oil producers.

The announcement of Gabon's impending withdrawal from OPEC (having been a member since 1973) was made at the ministerial meeting held June 5–7, 1996. Among the reasons cited for the decision were the high membership fee and the constraints imposed by OPEC production quotas.

In late 1997 OPEC decided to increase production by 10 percent to 27.5 million barrels per day for the first half of 1998. However, the organization reversed course sharply when the price fell to $12.80 per barrel, a nine-year low, in March 1998. Saudi Arabia and Venezuela (joined by nonmember Mexico) immediately announced a reduction of 2 million barrels per day in their output. When prices failed to rebound, OPEC announced a further reduction of 1.3 million barrels per day in July. Overall, OPEC's revenues in 1998 fell some 35 percent from the previous year, raising questions about the organization's ability to control prices on its own.

Oil prices fell to less than $10 per barrel in February 1999, prompting an agreement in March under which OPEC cut production by 1.7 million barrels per day while Mexico, Norway, Oman, and Russia accepted a collective reduction of 400,000 barrels per day. Prices subsequently rebounded to more than $26 per barrel late in the year and more than $30 per barrel in early 2000. Consequently, from March to October 2000, OPEC increased production four times by a total of 3.4 million barrels per day before prices, which reached a high of $37.80 per barrel in September, fell in December to $26 per barrel, safely within the OPEC target range of $25–$28 per barrel.

The heads of state of the OPEC countries met for only their second summit in history (the first was in 1975) in Venezuela in September 2000 amid intensified concern over the impact of high oil prices on the global economy. Among other things, OPEC leaders criticized several European countries for imposing high taxes on oil products, thereby driving up consumer energy costs.

Declining economic conditions in the first eight months of 2001 sharply reduced the demand for oil, and OPEC responded with production cuts in February, April, and September totaling 3.5 million barrels per day. Prices for the most part remained within the target range for that period. However, the September 11, 2001, terrorist attacks in the United States severely undercut demand, in part because of plummeting air travel, and prices fell below $17 per barrel by November. OPEC demanded that non-OPEC producers again assist in reducing production, and Russia reluctantly agreed to cut its production by 150,000 barrels per day beginning in January 2002, in conjunction with an additional OPEC cut of 1.5 million barrels per day. Prices rose to nearly $30 per barrel in the fall of 2002, despite evidence that many OPEC countries were producing above the quotas established in late 2001. OPEC leaders argued that prices were artificially inflated because of fears over a possible U.S. invasion of Iraq and concern emanating from other Middle East tensions.

To address the potential for disturbances in the global oil market from the strikes by oil workers in Venezuela, OPEC agreed in January 2003 to raise the quota to 24.5 million barrels per day. However, by April discussion turned to what was viewed as an "unavoidable" production cut. Complicating factors included the potential for the full return of Iraqi oil to world markets following the toppling of the Saddam Hussein regime. In that regard Iraq sent a delegation to OPEC's September session, at which quotas were cut by 900,000 barrels per day.

Despite rising prices, OPEC declined to increase production in January 2004 and, citing the upcoming seasonal dip in demand, reduced quotas again in February. Consequently, the United States warned OPEC that the cuts might harm an already fragile global economy. By March oil prices peaked at $37.45 per barrel, and some non-OPEC countries (such as Mexico) snubbed OPEC's request for production constraint.

Terror attacks on the oil infrastructures in Iraq and Saudi Arabia contributed to continual price increases in mid-2004, finally prompting OPEC to expand its production quotas. Nevertheless, "spare" oil capacity remained at its lowest in decades. The Group of Eight issued a stern warning about the effects of rising oil prices, which reached a 21-year high in July of more than $43 per barrel. By October the price peaked at more than $55 per barrel; it then declined by 23 percent by the end of the year.

In December 2004 OPEC announced a production cut to stem the slide in oil prices. Meanwhile, it was estimated that OPEC members were enjoying their highest oil revenue ever in nominal terms. OPEC informally relaxed quota compliance in March 2005, and prices hovered at about $50 per barrel. However, the International Monetary Fund and the United States called for significant additional OPEC production increases to, among other things, provide a more substantial cushion against unforeseen oil shocks. OPEC agreed to that request in June, but the per-barrel price subsequently grew to almost $60.

In 2005 and 2006 the world's demand for oil seemed finally to be straining the producing countries' ability to supply, with some saying that this was the long-predicted first sign that the world was running out of oil. Rapid economic growth in China, and to a lesser extent in India, was also said to be a factor. Tensions between the United States and Iran pushed prices to more than $75 per barrel for periods in May and June 2006.

Financial and political conditions remained disturbed through 2006 and 2007. The U.S. dollar, the currency in which OPEC trades, remained weak, with little sign of recovery, and China and India's appetite for oil and bilateral purchase arrangements increased. In March 2007 Angola joined OPEC—a move calculated to boost that country's international standing, but a disappointment to Western countries that had hoped to keep Angola's oil reserves outside the OPEC cartel. Ecuador indicated that it wanted to rejoin OPEC, and did so in October 2007. In May 2007 Ecuador and Venezuela agreed to an exchange of Ecuadorian crude oil for Venezuelan refined product.

In May 2008 Indonesia announced that it would withdraw from OPEC by the end of the year because the country had become a net importer of oil.

OPEC held a summit meeting November 17–18, 2007, in Riyadh, Saudi Arabia, with oil prices continuing to rise and a general expectation that the organization would not raise production quotas. At the meeting Iranian president Mahmoud Ahmadinejad suggested that the organization no longer trade in U.S. dollars, but Saudi Arabia opposed this idea. In January 2008 the price of crude oil reached $100 per barrel, and by June 2008 approached $140. This caused the price of gasoline to rise to more than $4 per gallon in the United States. Many observers began to feel that OPEC was not in control of world oil prices, with commodity speculation and international instability overriding the basic considerations of supply and demand. Gas prices led to changing habits, and demand for oil eased by 800,000 barrels per day in the first half of 2008. Crude oil prices declined, and were approaching $100 by September 2008. The worldwide economic crisis of late 2008 caused the price of crude oil to fall precipitously, reaching around $50 per barrel by early December. A meeting on December 17, 2008, produced an agreement to cut production by 2.2 million barrels a day—the largest cut in OPEC history. The price stabilized around $40 per barrel, some $35 less than they had hoped, and then gradually rose to around $70 per barrel by late 2009.

Russia attended OPEC's March 2009 meeting with a proposal for closer cooperation—in fact for setting up a Russian liaison office at OPEC headquarters—but declined, for the time being, an invitation to become a full member.

In April 2009 Brazil announced that it again was considering an invitation to join OPEC, but it ultimately decided not to do so. The September 9, 2009, OPEC meeting saw the group agreeing to maintain current production levels, with the price of oil slowly rising as the world economy appeared to come out of the worst of the recession.

Production quotas remained unchanged through the latter half of 2009 and most of 2010, with Iran denying that it was cheating. Prices were relatively stable around $80 per barrel for most of 2010, but with a tendency to rise toward $90 in the late summer and fall as many world economies recovered somewhat.

Longer-term prospects were uncertain, however. OPEC's *World Oil Outlook 2010* acknowledged that the global economic crisis was different from anything seen in recent times, making predictions about oil much riskier. It looked to transportation as the most likely sector for growth in oil consumption, but saw little room for growth in OPEC production capacity in the medium term.

On the other hand a January 2010 U.S. Geological Survey report predicted that Venezuela might have much larger oil reserves than previously thought, 513 billion barrels as opposed to Saudi Arabia's proven 260 billion barrels. The effect of Iraq's renewed full production was also an imponderable. In January 2010 the Brazilian government announced that it was taking much firmer control of newly discovered offshore deposits.

In October 2010 it was announced that Iran would hold the OPEC presidency in 2011 for the first time since before its 1979 Islamic revolution. At its biannual meeting in December 2010 in Ecuador, OPEC discussions focused largely on the impact economic uncertainty would have upon the oil market. In the face of lower demand growth and a fragile economy, the group decided to maintain oil production levels. The organization also stressed its plea for cooperation from nonmember states to effectively manage oil prices in an uncertain economy.

The year 2011 saw that cooperation increase as OPEC worked with several other IGOs on energy and oil-related endeavors. The International Energy Agency (IEA) and the International Energy Forum (IEF) worked with OPEC for a symposium on energy outlooks in the year. Likewise, OPEC ministers met with EU officials for its eighth meeting to discuss the current energy situation and the future of the oil market in providing energy solutions.

At the December 2011 conference, the organization announced that it would maintain its 30-million-barrel-per-day quota, despite the increasingly volatile oil prices. This decision was made in part because the group attributed the rapidly fluctuating prices to geopolitical tension and overspeculation in the commodities market, not to supply and demand. The conference also expressed concern about the economic downturn and reaffirmed its commitment to take the appropriate measures to ensure reasonable oil prices.

The year 2012 saw oil consumption increase slightly. Oil prices also increased early in 2012, but the increase was short lived as prices began decreasing in mid-2012. In June 2012 OPEC met for its 161st Conference in Vienna. Despite an increase in oil consumption, OPEC decided to maintain its production levels, since more oil was being consumed from non-OPEC exporters. Most of the conference, however, was concerned with the recently decreasing price of oil, a welcome change as many of the geopolitical tensions that had driven prices up began to subside. Even with oil prices dropping, OPEC did express continued apprehension about the economy and asked the Secretary General to maintain close supervision of the fluctuating global economy.

In October OPEC again joined forces with the IEA and IEF to host its first joint symposium on gas and coal market outlooks. The meeting was the outgrowth of a request from the 2011 G-20 Summit in Cannes (see separate article). In December OPEC gathered for its 162nd summit under the chairmanship of Iraq. The meeting stressed the importance of continued work on climate control and discussed the future of the oil market moving into 2013. Expecting non-OPEC production to increase, OPEC leaders predicted a slight decrease in demand from the OPEC states. The conference asked the secretariat for continued monitoring of the market to ensure adequate supply, and extended the secretary general's term for another year.

In March 2013 OPEC continued its recent cooperation with the IEA and IEF in hosting a workshop on the relationship between the physical and financial oil markets. In May OPEC convened for its 163rd biannual conference in Vienna. At the meeting, leaders recognized the significance of steady oil prices throughout the first part of 2013 as a sign of adequate supply. They also noted that current production levels were, therefore, adequate and could see an easement of OPEC fundamentals in the latter half of the year. (For more information on activities since 2013, see Recent activities, below.)

Structure. The OPEC Conference, which normally meets twice per year, is the supreme authority of the organization. Comprising the oil ministers of the member states, the conference formulates policy, considers recommendations from the Board of Governors, and approves the budget. The board consists of governors nominated by the various member states and approved by the conference for two-year terms. In addition to submitting the annual budget, various reports, and recommendations to the conference, the board directs the organization's management, while the Secretariat performs executive functions. Operating within the Secretariat are a research division and departments for administration and human resources, data services, energy studies, petroleum market analysis, and public relations and information. In addition, the Economic Commission, established as a specialized body in 1964, works within the Secretariat's framework to promote equitable and stable international oil prices. The Ministerial Monitoring Committee was established in 1982 to evaluate oil market conditions and to make recommendations to the conference.

The OPEC Fund for International Development (OFID) has made significant contributions to developing countries, mostly Arabian and African, in the form of balance-of-payments support; direct financing of imports; and project loans in such areas as energy, transportation, and food production. All current OPEC members are members of the fund. As of 2008 more than $5 billion in loans were approved for nearly 1,200 operations in the public sector and about $850 million for private sector operations. In addition, grants totaling $433 million were approved for more than 1,000 operations. In 2016 the OFID approved $300 million in financing in 22 partner nations, including $162 million for public sector projects and $138 million for private or nongovernment ventures.

Recent activities. At their conference meeting in December 2013, the leaders concluded that the biggest challenge to the oil market in 2014 was global economic uncertainty. The group determined that, despite projected increase in oil demand, there was no need for the organization to alter its production quotas because of non-OPEC production. The organization again came to the same conclusion concerning production at its next meeting in June 2014. Also at that meeting, the leaders extended the term of Secretary General El-Badri six months. At the organization's November meeting, OPEC leaders again decided to not cut production, even amidst falling prices and increased production by the United States, Brazil, and Russia. Meanwhile, the price of crude dropped below $50 per barrel. Global analysts predicted falling prices would make U.S. shale oil production unprofitable, and argued that the goal of large producers such as Saudi Arabia was to drive alternative producers, such as U.S. shale fields, out of business. In December OPEC was unable to reach a consensus on new quotas and production levels were left to the discretion of the individual member states.

Relations among OPEC members became increasingly tense in 2015 as members such as Saudi Arabia and the United Arab Emirates used their large cash reserves to offset the decline in prices, while continuing to maintain high levels of production to force less expansive competitors out of the market. Countries such as Nigeria and Venezuela sought reductions in production in order to stabilize prices. Meanwhile, Russia also increased production in order to compensate for lost revenues from declining prices. In December 2015 oil prices declined to an 11-year low of $36.05 per barrel due to increasing unease with Saudi Arabia's leadership.

On February 17, 2016, OPEC and Russia agreed to freeze oil and gas production at January 2016 levels. While this step would reduce global inventories, there would still remain a surplus of more than 1 million barrels per day. OPEC continued its policy of no production ceilings or limits at its June 2, 2016, meeting. At the session, Mohammed Barkindo of Nigeria was chosen as the organization's new secretary-general. In September OPEC agreed to limit production beginning in November to 32.5–33 million barrels per day, a reduction from 33.24 million. The arrangement prompted prices to rise to $53.73 per barrel by October.

PACIFIC ISLANDS FORUM (PIF)

Established: As the South Pacific Forum by a subgroup of the South Pacific Commission meeting August 5, 1971, in Wellington, New Zealand; current name adopted October 3–5, 1999, effective October 2000.

Purpose: To facilitate cooperation among member states, to coordinate their views on political issues of concern to the subregion, and to accelerate member states' rates of economic development.

Headquarters: Suva, Fiji.

Principal Organs: The Forum, Pacific Islands Forum Secretariat.

Website: www.forumsec.org.

Secretary General of Forum Secretariat: Meg Taylor (Papua New Guinea).

Membership (18): Australia, Cook Islands, Federated States of Micronesia, Fiji, French Polynesia, Kiribati, Marshall Islands, Nauru, New Caledonia, New Zealand, Niue, Palau, Papua New Guinea, Samoa, Solomon Islands, Tonga, Tuvalu, Vanuatu.

Associate Members (1): Tokelau.

Observers (5): American Samoa, Timor-Leste, Guam, Northern Mariana Islands, Wallis and Futuna.

Official Language: English.

Origin and development. Since the South Pacific Commission (SPC, now the Pacific Community) was barred from concerning itself with political affairs, representatives of several South Pacific governments and territories decided in 1971 to set up a separate organization, the South Pacific Forum (SPF), in which they might speak with a common voice on a wider range of issues. At a meeting of the forum in April 1973, representatives of Australia, Cook Islands, Fiji, Nauru, New Zealand, Tonga, and Western Samoa signed the Apia Agreement, which established the South Pacific Bureau for Economic Cooperation as a technical subcommittee of the committee of the whole. The Gilbert Islands (now Kiribati), Niue, Papua New Guinea, Solomon Islands, Tuvalu, and Vanuatu subsequently acceded to the agreement. In 1975 the bureau was asked to serve as secretariat, although it was not reorganized and renamed the Forum Secretariat until 1988.

The Marshall Islands and the Federated States of Micronesia, formerly observers, were granted membership in 1987 after Washington, in late 1986, declared their compacts of free association with the United States to be in effect. Palau, formerly an SPF observer, became a full member in 1995 following resolution of its compact status.

The SPF-sponsored South Pacific Regional Trade and Cooperation Agreement (SPARTECA), providing for progressively less restricted access to the markets of Australia and New Zealand, came into effect in 1981. The process culminated in 1985 with approval by Canberra and Wellington of the elimination of all duties for most products from other SPF members.

Following a decision at the 15th annual SPF meeting, the delegates to the 16th annual meeting in 1985 concluded the Treaty of Rarotonga (Cook Islands), which established the South Pacific Nuclear-Free Zone (SPNFZ). The treaty forbids manufacturing, testing, storing, dumping, and using nuclear weapons and materials in the region. It does, however, allow each country to make its own defense arrangements, including deciding whether or not to host nuclear warships. The treaty became operative in December 1986 when Australia became the eighth SPF member to tender its ratification. Those countries known to possess nuclear weapons were asked to sign the treaty's three protocols, the SPF having added an "opt-out" provision that would permit adherents to withdraw if they believed their national interests were at stake. The Soviet Union and China both ratified the protocols in 1988. France, the United Kingdom, and the United States, after years of declining to support the treaty, signed the protocols March 25, 1996. France, the object of intense SPF criticism for its nuclear tests in the region in late 1995 and early 1996, ratified the SPNFZ on September 20, 1996, as did the United Kingdom on September 19, 1997. In May 2011 U.S. president Barack Obama called on the Senate to ratify the treaty, but it has yet to do so. During the first half of the 1990s, environmental concerns became an increasingly important focus for the forum. Among other things, it called for the abolition of drift-net fishing; argued that global warming could cause sea levels to rise and inundate such low-lying countries as Kiribati and Tuvalu; objected to the planned incineration of chemical weapons on Johnston Atoll, an unincorporated territory about 700 miles southwest of Hawaii controlled by the U.S. military since 1934; and announced in 1994 an attempt to negotiate region-wide logging and fishing agreements that would sharply curtail access and protect fragile ecosystems while providing for sustainable development.

In January 1992 five of the smallest SPF members (Cook Islands, Kiribati, Nauru, Niue, and Tuvalu) formed the Small Island States (SIS) to address mutual concerns such as fishing rights, global warming, and airspace issues. The SIS members also began to explore the possible creation of their own development bank. The Marshall Islands became the sixth SIS member in 1997.

At the August 24–25, 1998, summit, which was held in the Federated States of Micronesia, the SPF endorsed the establishing of a South Pacific whale sanctuary, criticized India and Pakistan for testing nuclear devices, and granted New Caledonia observer status for the next summit.

The 30th SPF summit was held October 3–5, 1999, in Koror and endorsed the concept of a Pacific free trade area (FTA) that might eventually include Australia and New Zealand. (In 1993 the Melanesian Spearhead Group of Papua New Guinea, Solomon Islands, and Vanuatu introduced their own FTA, which Fiji later joined.) As envisaged, free trade would be introduced in stages over the next decade, with the six SIS countries and other least developed countries (LDCs) joining a bit later. The forum also decided to adopt the name Pacific Islands Forum, following a one-year transition period. At the 31st forum session, held October 27–30, 2000, in Tarawa, Kiribati, the renamed organization approved (with immediate effect) and opened for ratification the new Agreement Establishing the Pacific Island Forum Secretariat.

Hosted by Nauru, the August 16–18, 2001, forum session marked the organization's 30th anniversary with one of its most notable accomplishments: the opening for signature of the Pacific Island Countries Trade Agreement (PICTA) and the Pacific Agreement on Closer Economic Relations (PACER). PICTA was signed by all the 12 Forum Island Countries (FICs) except the Marshall Islands, Micronesia, and Palau, which were given additional time to sign because of complexities related to their status with the United States. PICTA anticipated the creation of an FTA by 2010, although the SIS members and LDCs do not have to eliminate their intracommunity tariffs until 2012. Tuvalu signed on to PICTA in April 2010, joining Cook Islands, Fiji, Niue, Samoa, Solomon Islands, and Vanuatu. These countries were by then trading under PICTA terms and conditions. In addition, "excepted imports" are protected until 2016. PACER outlines a framework for future trade relations between PICTA states and the much larger economies of Australia and New Zealand. PACER contains provisions for "trade facilitation" and increased financial and technical assistance to the FICs, but it also offers assurances to Australia and New Zealand that they will not be disadvantaged by any external trade agreements negotiated by the PICTA group.

Following ratification by six signatories, PICTA entered into force in April 2003, at which time all nontariff barriers to trade were eliminated. PICTA signatories have as long-range goals the creation of a single market to cover trade in services as well as goods and free movement of capital and labor. PACER, which entered into effect in October 2002, following ratification by seven signatories, provides for future trade negotiations but does not mandate a forum-wide FTA.

Meeting on August 14–16, 2003, in Auckland, the forum elected Australia's Greg Urwin as secretary general, a post that was traditionally awarded to an FIC national. The election came at a time of increasing regional involvement by Australia.

The 2004 meeting of the Pacific Islands Forum was held August 3–10, 2004, in Apia, Samoa. The chief subject of the meeting was discussion and endorsement of the forum's emerging multiyear Pacific Plan, an instrument for encouraging the forum's vision of sustainable growth and integration in the Pacific region. The forum endorsed the plan as thus far developed and looked for more specifics in the future.

In 2006 and 2007 the Pacific Islands Forum was concerned with unrest among some of its members. In August 2006 Tonga asked to be excused from hosting the October summit because the king's health was deteriorating. He died in September 2006. The summit was eventually held in Suva and was notable for complaints about Australian heavy-handedness in its leadership of the peacekeeping force in the Solomon Islands. In February 2007 the Solomon Islands government asked the forum to discuss an "exit strategy."

In December 2006 there was a military coup in Fiji, followed by a partial return to civilian government in January 2007. The Fijian interim government first promised elections and a full democracy in 2010. The forum and Fiji established a working group to create a joint approach to restoring democracy, with the forum aiming for elections within two years. In July 2007 Samoa declared that Fiji should be allowed to attend the coming October summit, even if the coup leader came. However, in August 2007 Australian prime minister Alexander Downer declared that the leader of the Fiji coup and interim prime minister, Frank Bainimarama, would not be welcome at the forthcoming meeting. Bainimarama attended the meeting anyway, held October 16–17, 2007, in Vava'u, Tonga. He made a definite commitment to hold elections in early 2009 and to abide by their outcome.

Also in October 2007 Taiwan's six allies in the forum—Solomon Islands, Marshall Islands, Kiribati, Nauru, Palau, and Tuvalu—declared that Taiwan's status should be upgraded to that of a regular dialogue partner.

In March 2008 a meeting of forum foreign ministers in Auckland expressed concern that Fiji's interest in a so-called people's charter might get in the way of the promised early 2009 elections. In April the forum sent two representatives to observe elections in Nauru at the request of the Nauru government.

In May 2008 Greg Urwin resigned as secretary general of the forum for health reasons. Deputy Secretary General Dr. Feleti Sevele of Vanuatu was named acting secretary general. In August 2008 Urwin died, and later that month Tuiloma Neroni Slade of Samoa was chosen as his permanent replacement. The 2008 summit focused on economic issues and the world financial crisis weighing heavily on the economically weak Pacific islands.

In late 2008 Fiji made some moves to reengage with the forum. However, by January 2009, with little progress made toward the restoration of democracy, the forum called on Bainimarama to set a specific date in 2009 for elections and to do that by May 1. When Bainimarama failed to honor the deadline, Fiji was suspended from the forum. The group's headquarters in Fiji continue to function, however.

The August 2009 summit, held in Cairns, Australia, called for serious action on climate at the forthcoming Copenhagen conference. Australian prime minister John Howard pointed out that roughly 50 percent of the Pacific islands' population lived within 1.5 kilometers of the ocean and that many small islands were in danger of being washed away literally by the rising sea level. Papua New Guinea and the Solomon Islands tried unsuccessfully to have Fiji restored to full membership in the organization.

The August 2010 summit, held in Port Vila, Vanuatu, saw New Caledonia expressing interest in full membership. The meeting commended progress of the PACER Plus negotiations. It also renewed its call for action on carbon dioxide emissions and for a return to democracy in Fiji.

The year 2011 marked the 40th anniversary of the creation of the PIF. In honor of that occasion, the Forum hosted an anniversary lecture series that focused on the Pacific Plan, the Forum's plan for future development. The PIF also hosted a series of competitions, such as an art competition for high school students, to encourage citizens of the PIF member states to be a part of the anniversary celebration.

In July 2011 the Forum's Economic Ministers held their annual meeting in Samoa. The meeting produced the Forum Economic Action Plan 2011, which called for broadening the IGO's economic base, strengthening the commitment to coordinating development funds, and improving access to the funds designated for climate change efforts. The PIF's annual summit was held September 7–8, 2011, in Auckland, New Zealand. The summit encouraged the Forum's continued discussion of economic sustainability and development, fishing and agricultural policies, and climate change. The Forum's heads of state also discussed continued assistance to Fiji to promote a return to parliamentary democracy. The Forum also agreed to allow Fiji to participate in a limited capacity in meetings concerning the PACER.

The 2011 Pacific Plan Annual Report reported growth and progress on completing its goals of increased cooperation and integration in the region. Major growth occurred in fisheries, climate change, and education. The majority of the main regional institution reforms of the Pacific Plan were also enacted in 2011, most notably the creation of the Secretariat of the Pacific Community.

In January 2012 Fiji announced the end of the Public Emergency Regulation, a move greatly welcomed by the PIF. The end of the emergency regulations marks the first step toward Fiji's transition back to a democratic regime. The PIF continues to assist and encourage Fiji to seek peace and democracy.

In May 2012 the Marshall Islands announced the approval of a new trade policy framework that would pave the way for its inclusion and accession into PICTA and PACER. The PIF has been encouraging and working with the Marshall Islands over the last several months to develop such a policy.

In late August the forum met for its annual meeting. At the meeting, the leaders of the member states approved the Pacific Leaders Gender Equality Declaration. The declaration outlined the dangers and problems associated with gender inequity and called on member states to enact a program based on equal rights legislation, economic empowerment, ending violence against women, and promoting health and education for women. The forum also produced agreements concerning the status of the Pacific Plan, climate change, and fishing and ocean rights. The group also nominated a committee to oversee the 2013 review of the Pacific Plan. (For more on developments since 2013, see Recent activities, below.)

Structure. The Pacific Islands Forum has no constitution or codified rules of procedure. Decisions are reached at all levels by consensus.

The forum meets annually at the heads of government (summit) level but also convenes at other times on a ministerial basis to discuss particular concerns and prepare proposals for summit action. In recent years the member states' ministers of foreign affairs, economy, and education, for example, have held meetings. In addition, forum summits have been followed by post-forum dialogue meetings since 1989. There are currently 14 dialogue partners; Canada, China, the European Union (EU), France, India, Indonesia, Italy, Japan, Malaysia, Philippines, Republic of Korea, Thailand, United Kingdom, and United States. Taiwan applied for dialogue status in the early 1990s, but the forum sidestepped the issue by permitting individual members to establish the requested dialogue relationship without formal SPF involvement.

The Pacific Islands Forum Secretariat, headed by a secretary general, reports to the Forum Officials Committee, which includes representatives from all 16 member countries. The secretariat encompasses four divisions—corporate services; development and economic policy; political, international, and legal affairs; and trade and investment. The PIF also has a number of affiliated organizations. (For a complete listing of affiliated organizations, see the 2011 *Handbook*.) In addition, the forum's secretary general chairs the eight-member Council of Regional Organizations in the Pacific (CROP), which includes the Secretariat of the Pacific Community and the South Pacific Regional Environment Programme among its participants.

Recent activities. In January the review committee began the work of reviewing the Pacific Plan. The committee was composed of six individuals, and chaired by form prime minister of Papua New Guinea Sir Makere Morauta. The committee held consultations with the forum members and other non-state actors to assess the progress and effectiveness of the plan.

In September the review committee presented its preliminary findings at the annual meeting of the Forum. The full finding of the committee is due to the secretariat by the end of October. In addition to discussing the review of the Pacific Plan, pacific leaders also discussed the situation in Fiji, expressing optimism that the state would soon be able to rejoin the forum and have their suspension lifted. The group also released the Majuro Declaration on Climate Leadership. The declaration outlined broad climate control goals, and identified specific action items for each state to work on implementing.

The PIF held a special leaders retreat in May to discuss the creation of a Framework for Pacific Regionalism, replacing the existing Pacific Plan. The new framework, approved at the July annual meeting of the forum, called for the member states to coordinate their efforts through cooperation, harmonization, collaboration, and economic integration. The biggest component of this new regionalism is an effort led by the member states to set priorities for regional initiatives.

Also at the July 2014 annual meeting held in Palau, the leaders approved the Palau Declaration, which legally sets the boundaries and zones of each of the member states in the Palau Ocean. The declaration also outlined the policies of each government concerning fisheries, conservation, protecting marine life, and pollution. Additionally, the meeting approved the application of Tokelau (previously an observer) for associate membership and invited the IOM to be an observer.

On September 9, 2015, the 46th PIF forum was held in Port Moresby, Papua New Guinea. Leaders sought to build a consensus among the member states prior to the COP 21 climate talks in Paris (see entry on the United Nations). Australia and New Zealand were criticized for not taking stronger action to reduce carbon emissions and combat climate change. Australian prime minister Tony Abbot announced a new goal to cut carbon emissions by 26–28 percent of 2005 levels by 2020. Fiji prime minister Voreqe Bainimarama accused Australia of being part of a "coalition of the selfish" by not being more proactive on climate change. Multiple leaders expressed concern over the potential for the break-up of the organization over divisions between Australia and New Zealand on the one hand, and the other nations on the other. The forum did reach agreement on a New Zealand–led regional quota system for fishing.

French Polynesia and New Caledonia became full members of the PIF on September 9, 2016. Fiji's prime minister refused to attend the 47th PIF Forum in Pohnpei, Federated States of Micronesia, held on September 7–11, in protest of the continued participation of Australia and New Zealand. At the forum, talks on the Pacific Agreement on Closer Economic Relations (PACER Plus) were held, but little progress was made on the initiative, which would establish a more complete framework for economic integration and trade cooperation in the region. The smaller islands already had tariff-free access to markets in Australia and New Zealand and did not think that PACER Plus would provide substantial benefits.

REGIONAL DEVELOPMENT BANKS

Regional development banks are intended to accelerate economic and social development of member states by promoting public and private investment. The banks are not meant, however, to be mere financial institutions in the narrow sense of the term. Required by their charters to take an active interest in improving their members' capacities to make profitable use of local and external capital, they engage in such technical assistance activities as feasibility studies, evaluation and design of projects, and preparation of development programs. The banks also seek to coordinate their activities with the work of other national and international agencies engaged in financing international economic development. The five major regional development banks are discussed below.

AFRICAN DEVELOPMENT BANK

(AfDB)
Banque Africaine de Développement
(BAD)

Website: www.afdb.org.

The Articles of Agreement of the AfDB were signed August 4, 1963, in Khartoum, Sudan, with formal establishment of the institution occurring in September 1964 after 20 signatories had deposited instruments of ratification. Lending operations commenced in July 1966 at the bank's headquarters in Abidjan, Côte d'Ivoire.

Until 1982 membership in the AfDB was limited to states within the region. At the 1979 annual meeting, the Board of Governors approved an amendment to the bank's statutes permitting nonregional membership as a means of augmenting the institution's capital resources; however, it was not until the 17th annual meeting, held in May 1982 in Lusaka, Zambia, that Nigeria announced withdrawal of its objection to the change. Non-African states became eligible for membership December 20, 1982, and by the end of 1983 more than 20 such states had joined the bank.

The bank's leading policymaking organ is its Board of Governors, encompassing the finance or economic ministers of the member states; the governors elect a bank president, who serves a five-year term and is chair of a Board of Directors. The governors are empowered to name 18 directors, each serving a three-year term, with 12 seats to be held by Africans. The bank's African members are the same as for the African Union (AU), save for the inclusion of Morocco (no longer a member of the AU).

While limiting the bank's membership to African countries was initially viewed as a means of avoiding practical difficulties and undesirable political complications, it soon became evident that the major capital-exporting states were unwilling to lend funds without having a continuous voice in their use. In response to this problem, an African Development Fund (ADF) was established in November 1972 as a legally distinct intergovernmental institution in which contributing countries would have a shared managerial role. The ADF Board of Governors encompasses one representative from each state as well as the AfDB governors, ex officio; the 12-member Board of Directors includes six nonregional designees. Nonregional contributing countries—all of whom, except the United Arab Emirates, are now AfDB members—are Argentina, Austria, Belgium, Brazil, Canada, China, Denmark, Finland, France, Germany, India, Italy, Japan, the Republic of Korea, Kuwait, the Netherlands, Norway, Portugal, Saudi Arabia, Spain, Sweden, Switzerland, Turkey, the United Kingdom, and the United States. In addition, in February 1976 the bank and the government of Nigeria signed an agreement establishing a Nigeria Trust Fund (NTF) with an initial capitalization of 50 million Nigerian naira (about $80 million). Unlike the ADF, the NTF is directly administered by the AfDB. Together, the AfDB, the ADF, and the NTF constitute the African Development Bank Group.

Earlier, in November 1970, the AfDB participated in the founding of the International Financial Society for Investments and Development in Africa (*Société Internationale Financière pour les Investissements et le Développement en Afrique*—SIFIDA). Headquartered in Geneva, Switzerland, with the International Finance Corporation (IFC) and a large number of financial institutions from advanced industrial countries among its shareholders, SIFIDA is authorized to extend loans for the promotion and growth of productive enterprises in Africa. Another related agency, the Association of African Development Finance Institutions (AADFI), inaugurated in March 1975 in Abidjan, was established to aid and coordinate African development projects, while the African Reinsurance Corporation (Africa-Re), formally launched in March 1977 in Lagos, Nigeria, promotes the development of insurance and reinsurance activity throughout the continent. The AfDB holds 10 percent of Africa-Re's authorized capital of $50 million.

At the bank's 1988 annual meeting, U.S. officials surprisingly announced that Washington was now willing to support concessional interest rate rescheduling for the "poorest of the poor" African countries. However, African representatives called for additional debt measures, such as extension of maturities and pegging repayment schedules to a country's debt-servicing "history" and "capacity." Following up on discussions initiated at the annual meeting, the bank announced late in the year that the countries involved faced suspension of existing loan disbursements and would not be eligible for new loans until the arrears were cleared.

During the 1989 annual meeting and 25th anniversary celebration, at which the bank was described as "probably the most successful of the African multinational institutions," the Board of Governors pledged that lending activity would continue to accelerate. On the topic of debt reduction, the bank praised the initiatives launched at the recent Group of Seven summit but called for further measures, including more debt cancellations by individual creditor nations.

A dispute between regional and nonregional members regarding the bank's future continued at the May 1993 AfDB annual meeting as Western nations continued to press for a stricter policy on arrears, better evaluation of project performance, and greater support for private sector activity. In addition, at the insistence of donor countries, an independent task force was established, chaired by former World Bank vice president David Knox, to review all bank operations. The task force report, released shortly before the AfDB's May 1994 annual meeting, strongly criticized the bank for keeping poor records, maintaining a top-heavy bureaucracy, and emphasizing the quantity of lending at the expense of quality. The report also supported the contention of donor countries that the accumulation of arrears (more than $700 million) had become a threat to the bank's future. The nonregional members subsequently proposed that regular AfDB lending be limited to "solvent" nations, but African members rejected their advice.

Fractious debate continued at the May 1995 annual meeting. Further tarnishing the bank's image, the governors were unable to elect a successor to outgoing AfDB president Babacar N'Diaye, with regional and nonregional members backing different candidates. However, at a special meeting in Abidjan in late August, the Board of Governors finally chose Omar Kabbaj, a one-time official of the International Monetary Fund (IMF), as the new AfDB president. Shortly thereafter, Kabbaj announced that an external committee would be established to evaluate the bank's operations, internal structures, and fiscal status. The new president also pledged that the AfDB would immediately begin to give greater emphasis to private sector loans, one issue on which regional and nonregional members appeared in agreement. Meanwhile, talks on the ADF replenishment remained suspended pending Kabbaj's restructuring proposals, expected by the end of the year.

Under the leadership of Kabbaj, the AfDB cut approximately 240 employees (20 percent of the staff) and otherwise restructured the bank's operations, paving the way for an infusion of new capital. At the annual meeting held May 21–22, 1996, the ADF was replenished with $2.6 billion, though this entailed a cut from prior levels. When ADF lending resumed shortly thereafter, the AfDB adopted guidelines recommended by the World Bank under which the number of states eligible for new loans was reduced from 53 to 12.

Although those changes were widely perceived as representing genuine progress, the AfDB governance report released in 1996 delineated several continuing problems. The report argued that further "stark" measures needed to be taken to prevent the bank from being relegated to the role of a minor player on the continent. Specific issues to be addressed included "incompetence" in some bank operations, low morale among the remaining employees, and a lack of "financial credibility" stemming from arrears of $800 million amassed by 25 out of 53 recipients.

In July 1996 a special summit was held in Libreville, Gabon, to discuss issues raised in the report and to plot the future of the bank, particularly in regard to the contentious issue of control. Led by Nigeria, some African countries opposed giving nonregional members additional decision-making power, despite the bank's weakened condition. The governance report outlined several alternatives, ranging from a 50–50 split of control between nonregional and African nations, to no change at all (which might have meant the cessation of Western contributions).

A compromise was reached in March 1998 when it was agreed that a capital increase of about 35 percent ($7.65 billion) would be implemented, with the nonregional share being set at 40 percent. Significantly, while the African members were allowed to retain control of 12 of the 18 seats on the Board of Directors, future discussions would require 70 percent (at least one nonregional vote) endorsement by that board on "crucial" issues.

Under Kabbaj's leadership, significant structural reforms were implemented during the late-1990s, contributing to improved international credibility for the bank. A vision statement approved by the Board of Governors in 1999 gave greater emphasis to reducing poverty and increasing productivity, with other concerns including good governance, regional cooperation and development, gender mainstreaming, and environmental sustainability. Operationally, the AfDB rededicated to meeting client needs through strategic planning and compliance monitoring. An executive restructuring in early 2002 included the establishment of two additional vice presidencies, raising the total to five. The five vice presidencies included: planning, policy, and research; operations in the Central and Western regions; operations in the Northern, Eastern, and Southern regions and the private sector; corporate management; and finance. The reorganization also involved establishing two operational complexes: sector departments, with responsibility for project management; and country departments, with responsibility for such broader areas as macroeconomic analyses, lending policy, and public sector management.

In February 2003 the AfDB temporarily moved its headquarters from Abidjan to Tunis, Tunisia, because of the outbreak of civil war in Côte d'Ivoire. International institutions (led by the Group of Eight) subsequently announced plans for the AfDB to manage a new fund slated to provide as much as $10 billion a year to improve infrastructure in Africa. After numerous ballots that weeded out several candidates, in 2005 the Board of Governors elected Donald Kaberuka, the finance and economy minister from Rwanda, over Olabisi Ogunjobi, a Nigerian who had worked at the bank since 1978. It was widely reported that Kaberuka had enjoyed the support of most of the bank's Western members. In 2010 Kaberuka was appointed for a second five-year term.

In May 2006 the organization was embarrassed that, for the first time, its external auditor was unable to approve its accounts without qualification. Effective July 2006, a new organizational structure was introduced, principally affecting the operational complexes and the Office of the Chief Economist. In May 2007 the AfDB caused some controversy by holding its 47th annual meeting in Shanghai, China. At this meeting Chinese premier Wen Jiabao rejected criticism that China was only interested in Africa as a potential supplier of raw materials. In November 2007 the bank canceled Liberia's debt.

In December 2007 the bank won a three-year replenishment for the ADF of $8.9 billion, a 57 percent increase over the previous three-year replenishment.

The bank's 2008 annual meeting, held May 14–15 in Maputo, Mozambique, welcomed Turkey as the 25th nonregional member. At this meeting the bank also pledged an extra $1 billion to combat the food crisis in Africa. The 2009 annual meeting, held May 14–15 in Dakar, Senegal, had as its theme "Africa and the Financial Crisis: An Agenda for Action." The AfDB had previously given input to the April 2009 G20 conference in London (see separate entry). Kaberuka declared that, while six months had wiped out much of Africa's recent economic progress, the fact was that Africa's GDP was still growing, while that of the developed countries was generally declining.

The 2010 AfDB annual meeting was held May 27–28 in Abidjan, Côte d'Ivoire. While participants heralded their return to Côte d'Ivoire, they did not feel quite ready to move the headquarters back. Consequently, use of the Tunis facility was extended through May 2011. (In November 2011 a new agreement was signed between the AfDB and Côte d'Ivoire to relocate the headquarters in the future.) At the meeting the bank's governors approved the bank's sixth general capital increase, tripling its capital resources to almost $100 billion.

Total bank group approvals reached $6.3 billion in 2010, a decline from $12.4 billion in 2009. The decrease was indicative of the stabilization of the region's economy. As of the end of 2010, cumulative disbursements since 1967 reached $86.1 billion for 3,526 loans and grants. In its 2011 annual report the AfDB found that the economy accelerated on the continent, with total GDP growing by 4.9 percent, up from 3.1 percent the previous year, while overall inflation fell from 10 to 7.7 percent.

Total bank group approvals have continued to decline since 2010, reaching only $5.72 billion in 2011. At the 2012 annual meeting held in Tanzania, the AfDB Governors expressed great satisfaction with the progress made by Africa in 2011, noting that most of the African countries had grown by 5.1 percent over the course of the year. The most significant event of the 2012 meeting was the approval of South Sudan's request to become a member of the bank. The bank president, Donald Kaberuka, also laid out a more detailed plan for the bank's transition back to its headquarters in Côte d'Ivoire.

Bank group approvals once again declined for 2012, only totaling $4.25 billion. This decline is largely attributed to several nations having reached their borrowing limit. At the 2013 annual meeting of the Board of Governors, President Kaberuka unveiled a new Ten-Year Strategy, outlining the AfDB's new objectives of inclusive growth and the transition to green growth. In June 2013 the AfDB successfully returned to its headquarters in Côte d'Ivoire, having been temporarily located in Tunisia for a decade.

Total bank approvals in 2013 were up from the previous year after several years of decline, reaching $4.39 billion on 317 projects. The biggest segment of the African economy to see investment was infrastructural improvements. This emphasis on infrastructure building was continued in 2014 with the launch of Africa50, a new independent initiative of the AfDB solely focused on funding infrastructure projects.

Much of the 2014 funding thus far has been focused on combatting the Ebola crisis sweeping across the western half of the continent. In August, the AfDB announced its first grant of $60 million to fight the Ebola outbreak at a U.S.–African Leaders' Summit. The $60 million grant was part of the organization's total project amount of $210 million. On October 1, Kaberuka signed the new Fight Back Ebola Program with the leaders of Liberia, Sierra Leone, Guinea, and Côte d'Ivoire. That program consists of $152 million in grants and loans to stop the spread of Ebola. Later in October, the AfDB announced a joint project with the AU and ECOWAS, which consists of not just financial assistance but technical training for people on the ground, the deployment of medical professionals to affected areas, and a public awareness campaign.

On May 24, 2015, Nigerian agriculture minister Akinwumi Adesina was elected as the new president of the AfDB. In July the AfDB along with the World Bank, International Monetary Fund, and Asian Development Bank announced plans to extend more than $400 billion in financing over the next three years. Total bank approvals for 2015 were $8.8 billion, an increase of 25 percent over the previous year. The focus of the AfDB in 2015 was infrastructure (57.6 percent), multisector (12.6 percent), agriculture and rural development (12 percent), social projects (9.4 percent), and finance (8.1 percent). Among the more notable funding was a $123 million loan to Kenya's government to help finance improvements to make the Mombasa–Mariakani roadway a modern six-lane super-highway, and a $75 million loan to Tunisia for a pipeline project to expand the supply of natural gas to 19 communities.

On February 2, 2016, Nigeria asked the AfDB for a $1 billion loan to help fund its increasing budget deficit driven by lower global oil prices. Nigeria announced that it was projecting a $15 billion budget shortfall for the year. The AfDB warned African Governments about the dangers of carrying debt, even with low interest rates, in May 2016. Nigeria received a second loan of $4.1 billion on September 27. In line with the UN Sustainable Development Goals agenda to power, feed, industrialize, integrate, and improve the quality of life for Africa and the priorities set out by the African Union's Agenda 2063, the AfDB announced five main goals for the year: expand the availability and consistency of electricity, increase food production, industrialize of the continent, economically integrate the continent, and enhance the quality of life of Africans. The AfDB also launched a New Deal on Energy for Africa, with funding for investment in infrastructure and renewables.

ASIAN DEVELOPMENT BANK

(ADB)

Website: www.adb.org.

Launched under the auspices of the United Nations (UN) Economic Commission for Asia and the Far East (ESCAFE), subsequently the Economic and Social Commission for Asia and the Pacific (ESCAP), the ADB began operations December 19, 1966, in its Manila, Philippines, headquarters as a means of aiding economic growth and cooperation among regional developing countries. Its original membership of 31 has since expanded to 67, including 48 regional members: Afghanistan, Armenia, Australia, Azerbaijan, Bangladesh, Bhutan, Brunei, Cambodia, China, Cook Islands, Fiji, Georgia, "Hong Kong, China," India, Indonesia, Japan, Kazakhstan, Kiribati, the Republic of Korea, Kyrgyzstan, Laos, Malaysia, Maldives, Marshall Islands, Federated States of Micronesia, Mongolia, Myanmar, Nauru, Nepal, New Zealand, Pakistan, Palau, Papua New Guinea, Philippines, Samoa, Singapore, Solomon Islands, Sri Lanka, Tajikistan, "Taipei, China," Thailand, Timor-Leste, Tonga, Turkmenistan, Tuvalu, Uzbekistan, Vanuatu, and Vietnam; and 19 nonregional members: Austria, Belgium, Canada, Denmark, Finland, France, Germany, Ireland, Italy, Luxembourg, Netherlands, Norway, Portugal, Spain, Sweden, Switzerland, Turkey, the United Kingdom, and the United States. The People's Republic of China acceded to membership March 10, 1986, after the ADB agreed to change Taiwan's membership title from "Republic of China" to "Taipei, China." Taiwan thereupon withdrew from participation in bank meetings for a year, although continuing its financial contributions, before returning "under protest." North Korea applied for membership in 1997, but the United States and Japan, in particular, remain opposed.

Each member state is represented on the Board of Governors, which selects a 12-member Board of Directors (eight from regional states) and a bank president who chairs the latter. Four vice presidents and a managing director general assist the president in managing the bank.

ADB resources are generated through subscriptions; borrowings on capital markets; and income from several sources, including interest on undisbursed assets. Most funds are in the form of country subscriptions. Leading shareholders as of 2015 were Japan (15.6 percent), the United States (15.5), China (6.5 percent), India (6.3 percent), Australia (5.8 percent), Indonesia (5.5 percent), Canada (5.2 percent), the Republic of Korea (5 percent), and Germany (4.3 percent). In all, about 66.7 percent of subscribed capital is provided by the 27 non-borrowing members, while the remainder comes from the 40 borrowing members.

In June 1974 an Asian Development Fund (ADF) was established to consolidate the activities of two earlier facilities, the Multi-Purpose Special Fund (MPSF) and the Agricultural Special Fund (ASF), whose policies were criticized because of program linkages to procurement in donor countries. The ADF, which provides soft loans, receives most of its funding from voluntary contributions by the industrialized ADB members, who also support a Technical Assistance Special Fund (TASF). A Japan Special Fund for technical assistance grants was set up in 1988 to aid in economic restructuring and facilitating new investment; a Currency Crisis Support Facility was added in 1999. The ADB Institute Special Fund supports the ADB Institute, which was established in 1997 to examine development issues and to offer related training and assistance.

In the mid-1980s there was intense debate within the ADB regarding proposed changes in lending policies. Western contributors called on the bank, which in the past provided loans almost exclusively for specific development projects, to provide more "policy-based" funding, under which the recipient country would have spending discretion as long as certain economic reforms were implemented. A compromise agreement was reached in 1987 to allocate up to 15 percent of annual outlays to such loans. Also in partial response to Western demands, the ADB in 1986 established a private sector division to provide private enterprise loans that would not require government guarantees. During the same year, after potential loan recipients complained that ADB requirements were too stringent, the ADB adopted an adjustable lending rate system.

Extensive debate on the bank's direction and strategies for the next decade was generated by a report from an expert external panel submitted in early 1989. The report echoed many of the recommendations of an earlier internal task force that urged greater support for social programs. The report also called for expanded private sector activity, attention to the role of women in development, and additional environmental study in connection with all bank projects. In May the Board of Governors endorsed many of the proposed initiatives, especially those concerned with poverty alleviation and the environment.

As negotiations began in 1993 on a proposed doubling of the bank's authorized capital, an independent task force was established to review ADB operations. The task force recommended the bank shift from an "approval culture," in which quantity of lending was the major criteria, to a focus on "project quality." The bank also agreed to stricter guidelines regarding arrears.

Those proposed refinements notwithstanding, it was widely agreed that the bank's past performance was satisfactory, and the Board of Governors in May 1994 approved an increase in ADB subscribed capital to $48 billion, with the replenishment expected to support lending for the next eight to ten years. Although members with combined 94 percent of the board's voting power supported the increase, China and other members reportedly voiced strong protest over the insistence of Western nations that future lending be tied to "good governance" and that additional emphasis be given to social and environmental development.

Some behind-the-scenes controversy attended a subsequent effort by the ADB to prepare a 2001–2015 Long-Term Strategic Framework, with recipient countries resisting pressure by donor countries for greater say in development plans and for making loan approvals partially dependent on such considerations as good governance.

Under the leadership of bank president Tadao Chino, who was reelected to a second term in September 2001, the ADB undertook a partial administrative reorganization. As part of the 15-year strategic plan, greater emphasis was to be given to sustainable development, private sector participation (a Private Sector Operations Department was created), environmental considerations, and poverty reduction. Projects involving social infrastructure such as health facilities and programs, education, and water supplies were to receive greater support.

The ADB was criticized in the early 2000s for a perceived failure to allocate sufficient resources for poverty reduction. Perhaps as a consequence, the bank announced it would begin offering grants (as opposed to loans) to its poorer members. That decision was made after donors agreed to a $7 billion replenishment of the ADF for the four-year period through 2008. Bank officials estimated that about one-fifth of ADF assistance in the future would consist of grants.

Haruhiko Kuroda of Japan was installed as the ADB's new president in February 2005. In early 2005 the ADB established a $600 million fund to assist victims of the recent devastating tsunami. At a donors' conference of November 19, 2005, the ADB pledged $1 billion to help Pakistan recover from a major earthquake and to provide winter support to its victims.

At its 2005 annual meeting, held May 4–5 in Kyoto, Japan, the ADB came under attack for not doing more to abate environmental degradation and for doing little to prevent the growing disparity between rich and poor countries in the region. Against this background, the ADB began considering a role change in an Asia no longer uniformly poor and shifted its focus from the alleviation of poverty to promoting sustainable development.

Criticism of the ADB's direction dominated the organization's 2007 annual meeting, held May 3–4 in Madrid, Spain. The U.S. representative alone voted against the bank's long-term strategy, protesting that China and India, now with huge cash reserves, should no longer be given huge loans to fight poverty.

ADB's response to the world economic crisis has been to increase lending and to enhance its own liquidity. At its annual meeting, held May 4, 2009, in Bali, Indonesia, the bank announced a $120 billion crisis fund to boost liquidity. The economic ministers at the forum denied that the fund was an attempt to circumvent IMF rules that would have forced member countries to make unpopular economic reforms.

In June 2009 China criticized the ADB for funding a flood-management project in the northeastern Indian state of Arunachal Pradesh, which China claims. The bank responded that it does not take sides in territorial disputes. The May 1–4, 2010, annual meeting, held in Tashkent, Uzbekistan, concentrated on increasing domestic demand in Asia. ADB also announced an Asia Solar Energy Initiative to develop large capacity solar projects, intended to generate some 3,000 MW of solar power by 2012.

At the 2011 annual meeting, held in Hanoi, Vietnam, ADB focused on rising commodity prices, infrastructure, and climate change. The Board of Governor's also considered a new report on where Asia will be in 2050, which estimates that Asia will account for nearly half of the world's economy.

The 2012 annual meeting in the Philippines was predominately concerned with the sustainable development of all of Asia and creation of different response measures to economic disaster and downturn. The biggest issue facing the ADB, according to a new institutional report, is the lack of equal growth across Asia and the South Pacific. This challenge led the ADB to increase its contribution to the Asian Development fund by nearly 10 percent. The global economic downturn has also impacted the ADB. To counter the economic problems, the Association of Southeast Asian Nations (ASEAN) announced that it was doubling the funds available under the Chiang Mai Initiative Multilateralization, a financial pool used for economic emergencies.

In April 2013 the ADB Board of Governors elected a new bank president, Takehiko Nakao. Nakao had previously served as Japan's Vice Minister of Finance for International Affairs and Minster to the United States. At the 2013 annual meeting in India, ADB leadership issued a call for increased innovation and integration within the region. These themes were identified as being key to the region's further growth, continued reduction of poverty, and successful completion of the Millennium Development Goals. In 2013 the bank approved $21.02 billion in project financing. Furthermore, according to an internal performance review released in May 2014, the bank also improved its success rate for project completion and has already achieved several of its millennial development goals.

According to a report released in 2014, the ADB estimates that the economy of South Asia could experience nearly a 9 percent decline in economic production by 2100 because of climate change. The 2014 annual meeting in Kazakhstan focused on connectivity and regionalism as a means of achieving growth in the region.

By March 2015 the Japanese-led ADB begin to face increasing competition from the Chinese-sponsored Asian Infrastructure Investment Bank (AIIB), which was launched in October 2014 (see entry on China). However, at the ADB annual gathering held in Baku, Azerbaijan, in May 2015, the ADB formally pledged to assist the AIIB, which only had a third of the capital of the older bank. The ADB announced that it expected to increase lending to $6 billion to deal with climate change projects. For 2015 the ADB's total loans and grants were in excess of $27 billion, a record for the organization.

In April 2016 the World Bank and the ADB signed a deal to provide $1.2 billion to the AIIB for co-financing projects in areas such as energy development, transport, and water and sanitation. The arrangement marked a significant shift from the ADB's earlier opposition to the AIIB.

EUROPEAN BANK FOR RECONSTRUCTION AND DEVELOPMENT

(EBRD)
Banque Européenne pour la Reconstruction et la Développement
(BERD)

Website: www.ebrd.com.

The idea of a multibillion-dollar international lending effort to help revive the economies of Eastern European countries and assist their conversion to free-market activity was endorsed by the heads of the European Community (EC, subsequently the European Union—EU) in December 1989, based on a proposal from French president François Mitterrand. After several months of negotiation in which most other leading Western countries were brought into the project, a treaty to establish the EBRD with initial capitalization of $12.4 billion was signed by 40 nations, the EC, and the European Investment Bank (EIB) on May 29, 1990, in Paris, France. London was chosen as the headquarters for the bank, which proponents described as one of the most important international aid projects since World War II. Mitterrand's special adviser, Jacques Attali, who first suggested such an enterprise, was named to direct its operations. The bank officially opened April 15, 1991.

According to the bank's charter, its purpose is to "promote private and entrepreneurial initiative" in Eastern European countries "committed to applying the principles of multiparty democracy, pluralism, and market economics." Although the United Kingdom and the United States originally pressed for lending to be limited entirely to the private sector, a compromise was reached permitting up to 40 percent of the EBRD's resources to be used for public sector projects, such as roads and telecommunications. The bank operated using the basket of the currencies of EC member states known as the European Currency Unit (ECU) until January 1, 1999, when the euro came into existence, replacing the ECU at par.

Although Washington initially opposed its participation, the Soviet Union was permitted to become a member of the EBRD on the condition that it would not borrow more from the bank than it contributed in capital for at least three years, at which point the stipulation would be reviewed. The restriction was imposed because of fears that Soviet needs could draw down most of the EBRD resources and because of U.S. arguments that Moscow had yet to meet the criteria of democracy and market orientation. Despite the "net zero" limitation, Moscow was reportedly eager to join the organization because it would be its first capitalist-oriented membership in an international financial institution, and in March 1991 the Supreme Soviet endorsed participation by a vote of 380–1. The net zero condition was eliminated following the breakup of the Soviet Union, with the bank declaring the newly independent former Soviet republics to be eligible for up to 40 percent of total EBRD lending.

The United States is the largest shareholding member, with 10.1 percent of the capital, followed by Germany, France, Japan, Italy, and the United Kingdom, each with 8.6 percent. At the launching of the EBRD, the Soviet Union held a 6 percent share, two-thirds of which was subsequently allocated to Russia and the remainder to the other 14 former Soviet republics, all of which (Armenia, Azerbaijan, Belarus, Estonia, Georgia, Kazakhstan, Kyrgyzstan, Latvia, Lithuania, Moldova, Tajikistan, Turkmenistan, Ukraine, and Uzbekistan) joined the bank in 1992. At the end of 2007, Russia held 4 percent of shares, while the EU itself and the EIB each held 3 percent. In addition to these 23 members, the following other states are bank members: Albania,

Australia, Austria, Belgium, Bosnia and Herzegovina, Bulgaria, Canada, China, Croatia, Cyprus, Czech Republic, Denmark, Egypt, Finland, Greece, Hungary, Iceland, Ireland, Israel, Jordan, Republic of Korea, Liechtenstein, Luxembourg, Macedonia, Malta, Mexico, Mongolia, Montenegro, Morocco, Netherlands, New Zealand, Norway, Poland, Portugal, Romania, Serbia, Slovakia, Slovenia, Spain, Sweden, Switzerland, Tunisia, and Turkey. Apart from ordinary resources, the EBRD also administers 11 special funds: the Baltic Investment Special Fund and the Baltic Technical Assistance Special Fund, to aid private sector development of SMEs in Estonia, Latvia, and Lithuania; the Russian Small Business Investment Special Fund and the Russian Small Business Technical Cooperation Special Fund; the Balkan Region Special Fund and the EBRD SME Special Fund, to assist, respectively, in reconstruction and in development of SMEs in Albania, Bosnia and Herzegovina, Bulgaria, Croatia, Macedonia, Romania, and Yugoslavia; the EBRD Technical Cooperation Fund, to aid in financing technical cooperation projects; the Financial Intermediary Investment Special Fund, to support financial intermediaries in all countries of operation; the Italian Investment Special Fund, to aid modernization, restructuring, expansion, and development of SMEs in selected countries; the Moldova Micro Business Investment Special Fund, to target SME development in Moldova; and the SME Finance Facility Special Fund, to aid SME financing in Bulgaria, Czech Republic, Estonia, Hungary, Latvia, Lithuania, Poland, Romania, Slovakia, and Slovenia. Some 16 countries—including non-EU members Canada, Iceland, Japan, Norway, Switzerland, "Taipei, China," and the United States—have pledged an aggregate of €311 million to the 11 funds. At the end of 2013 the EBRD was operating with €30 billion in capital assets.

The first EBRD loans were approved in late 1991. At the first annual meeting of the Board of Governors in April 1992, bank officials reported that 20 loans totaling ECU 621 million (about $770 million) were thus far approved. However, some East European leaders described the bank's impact as marginal, and it was widely accepted that lending was restrained by problems in finding reliable borrowers for specific projects. EBRD president Attali reportedly suggested that the bank consider making loans in support of long-term economic restructuring, but the idea was quickly vetoed by the United States as beyond the EBRD mandate.

At the second Board of Governors' meeting in April 1993, it was announced that the bank approved 54 investment projects in 1992, involving a total EBRD contribution of ECU 1.2 billion (about $1.5 billion), although actual disbursements for the year totaled only ECU 126 million (about $156 million). The meeting was overshadowed by earlier press disclosures that EBRD disbursement up to the end of 1992 was only half the level of the bank's expenditure on its London offices, staff salaries, travel expenses, and administrative costs. Amid widespread criticism of his style of management, Attali announced his resignation on June 25, and was succeeded in August by Jacques de Larosiére of France, a former managing director of the International Monetary Fund (IMF). In November the Board of Governors approved internal spending reforms proposed by Larosiére.

At the March 1994 Board of Governors' meeting, it was announced that the EBRD earned an approximate $4.5 million profit in 1993, compared to a loss of $7.3 million the previous year. De Larosiére told the April 1995 annual meeting, however, that he expected the bank's capital base to be exhausted by the end of 1997 under the current rate of lending. Although it was widely conceded that the bank made significant improvement in its "budgetary discipline," Western donors reportedly were awaiting further reform in bank operations before agreeing to launch replenishment talks.

At the EBRD's annual meeting held in mid-April 1996 in Sofia, Bulgaria, de Larosiére called on Eastern European nations to strengthen their banking regulations and supervision since the failure of private banks to follow "basic banking procedures" was contributing to economic difficulties in many Eastern European nations. The shareholders also agreed to double the EBRD's authorized capital from ECU 10 billion to ECU 20 billion (about $25 billion at exchange rates then prevailing) to accommodate a proposed lending increase that went into effect in April 1997. Forty-eight of the 60 members deposited their instruments of subscription to the capital increase by the end of the year. President de Larosiére said the additional resources would ensure the EBRD would continue to operate "on the cutting edge" of the economic transition in Europe.

With the EBRD emerging in the post-Soviet era as the single largest source of private sector financing in Russia, that country's financial crisis in August 1998 resulted in a loss of ECU 261 million ($283 million) for the year. At the end of 1998, Russia accounted for about 25 percent of the EBRD's disbursed outstanding loans, but despite the crisis and its profound impact throughout the region, only four Russian loans were classified as nonperforming. Overall financing for 1998 totaled ECU 2.37 billion for 96 projects, down from 108 in 1997. The EBRD returned to profitability in 1999 earning €42.7 billion as the region recovered more rapidly than expected.

EBRD president de Larosiére announced his retirement in January 1998 and was succeeded in July 1998 by Horst Köhler, president of the German Savings Bank Association. Köhler, who resigned after 20 months in office to become managing director of the IMF, was in turn succeeded in July 2000 by Jean Lemierre, a French financial official.

In recent years the bank has shifted attention from the more developed economies of Central Europe toward the east. In its November 2001 Transition Report, the EBRD, looking ahead to the eventual EU accession of ten bank members, urged that all 27 countries of operation continue to receive assistance. Otherwise, the bank feared a "Brussels lace curtain"—the financial and economic equivalent of the Iron Curtain—might divide the EU from the rest of the continent.

In April 2004 the EBRD announced plans for substantial expansion of lending to its seven poorest members (Armenia, Azerbaijan, Georgia, Kyrgyzstan, Moldova, Tajikistan, and Uzbekistan). In particular, the bank said it would direct support to the private sector in those countries.

The years 2005–2007 also marked a period of relative success in achieving the bank's aims. At the end of 2007, the Czech Republic was slated to be the first recipient country to "graduate," meaning that it had achieved "an advanced state of transition" and would receive no more EBRD investment. In March 2007 the bank announced that net profit had increased by 57 percent to a record €2.4 billion in 2006 from a year earlier, an increase largely caused by gains from stock investments. In September 2007 a project was announced (to be administered by the EBRD) to cover the site of the Chernobyl nuclear disaster in a giant steel protective casing.

In May 2008 the EBRD issued a $1 billion global bond, its first benchmark issue since 2004. In May Thomas Mirow of Germany was named president, succeeding Lemierre at the end of his two four-year terms. Mirow's appointment was controversial. Some were concerned with a lack of transparency while others argued that he was Germany's candidate. This was a concern since the German government was known to be interested in merging the EBRD with the European Investment Bank. Also in May 2008 Turkey applied for full membership in the bank, becoming a full country of operations as well as a shareholder in November of that year. In November 2008 the bank announced that it would boost investment in 2009, particularly in Central and Eastern Europe, to combat the growing international financial crisis. The year 2009 saw the bank making loans to many smaller enterprises in Eastern Europe and Western and Central Asia.

Lending commitments in 2009 totaled €7.9 billion for 311 projects, compared to €5.1 billion for 302 projects in 2008. The 2008 commitments, affected by the world financial crisis, represented a 9 percent decrease from the 2007 level of €5.6 billion for 353 projects. Of the 2009 commitments, 48 percent went to "early and intermediate transition countries," while 31 percent went to Russia and 21 percent went to "advanced transition countries.

The bank's focus in late 2009 and throughout 2010 was to mitigate the effects of the global recession on the fragile economies of Eastern Europe. In early May Mirow was particularly concerned that the Greek debt crisis might spill over into Greece's southeastern European neighbors. Shortly thereafter, and ahead of the May 14–15 annual meeting, held in Zagreb, Croatia, Russia promised an addition €40 million in capital to the bank and guaranteed an additional €360 million in case of need. At the meeting the bank's governors approved a 50 percent increase in its authorized capital, €20 billion to €30 billion. That would enable it to increase its annual financing activities to €8.5 billion—€9 billion in 2011–2014—from the €5–6 billion currently available.

In 2010 the EBRD had 1,541 employees in 33 regional offices and operations in 29 countries. That year the bank initiated 386 new projects worth €9.1 billion. The largest commitments were in the financial sector, which accounted for 34 percent of new investments, followed by the corporate sector, 25 percent, and energy, 21 percent. The year 2010 also marked the resumption of economic growth in the region, which posted growth of 4.2 percent. In January 2011 Jordan and Tunisia joined the EBRD. The EBRD Board Of Governor's voted in favor of expanding bank membership to Southern and Eastern Mediterranean region following a request by the Group of 8 nations for the bank to expand its operations in North Africa and the Middle East. The bank is focusing its Mediterranean expansion in Jordan, Tunisia, Egypt and Morocco. In 2011, the bank continued its levels of commitment from 2010, with 380 new projects and commitments totaling €9.1 billion with €6.7 billion in annual disbursements.

At the 2012 annual meeting, the Board of Governor's elected a new bank president, Sir Suma Chakrabarti. Sir Chakrabarti, a senior British Justice minister, succeeded Thomas Mirow, who had been serving as president since 2008. The Board of Governor's called for the EBRD to continue its historic emphasis in Europe, while continuing to increase its involvement in the Mediterranean.

In 2013 the EBRD was operating 393 projects in 35 countries and employed over 2,000 people, with investments totaling €5.4 billion. The EBRD's projects range from local infrastructural development to its Chernobyl Site Transformation Initiative. At the 2013 Board of Governor's annual meeting, the organization announced a renewed effort to promote growth in its countries of operation, which has dropped to just 2.2 percent over the last year. The bank also announced plans to focus on SMEs in its future funding given the success of these enterprises at creating jobs and promoting economic growth.

The EBRD set its priorities for 2014 in early January. The Vienna Initiative announced the bank's plans to promote the creation of an all-inclusive banking union in Europe (not defined by EU membership), monitor deleveraging in central and eastern Europe, address problems with nonperforming loans through a multistakeholder initiative, and increase faster sources of local funds in central and eastern Europe. At the annual meeting of the bank held in May, the bank expressed grave concern over the situation with Russia in Ukraine and its impact on the economic recovery of the entire EBRD region. The bank also approved a new series of medium-term directions that will focus on achieving success in political and economic transition, promoting economic integration, and advancing major programs on issues such as climate change and water scarcity. In July the EBRD approved the suspension of new projects and funding for Russia as part of the broader sanctions implemented by the EU, the United States, and other powers. Existing funding was not affected.

In 2015 the EBRD financed 381 projects with €9.4 billion in funding. That year, the Bank realized a profit of €900 million, and ended the year with reserves of €8.4 billion and an operating budget of €431 million. The largest recipient of financing was Turkey, at €1.9 billion. On January 15, 2016, China became a shareholder in the EBRD, with an initial subscription of €29 million.

EUROPEAN INVESTMENT BANK

(EIB)

Website: www.eib.org.

The EIB is the European Union (EU) bank for long-term finance. It was created by the Treaty of Rome, which established the European Economic Community (EEC) on January 1, 1958. The bank, headquartered in Luxembourg, has as its basic function the balanced and steady development of EU member countries, with the greater part of its financing going to projects that favor the development of less-advanced regions and serve the common interests of several members or the whole community. Although industrial modernization remains important in the context of an expanded community and its transformation into the EU, emphasis has shifted more toward projects involving communications infrastructure, urban development, the environment, energy security, regional development, and cross-national industrial integration. Most recently, projects in health and education have taken on greater importance.

The EIB membership is identical to that of the EU: Austria, Belgium, Bulgaria, Croatia, Cyprus, Czech Republic, Denmark, Estonia, Finland, France, Germany, Greece, Hungary, Ireland, Italy, Latvia, Lithuania, Luxembourg, Malta, Netherlands, Poland, Portugal, Romania, Slovakia, Slovenia, Spain, Sweden, and the United Kingdom. Each has subscribed part of the bank's capital of €232 billion, although most funds required to finance its operations are borrowed by the bank on international and national capital markets. Capital shares range from 0.4 percent of the total for Malta to 16.1 percent each for France, Germany, Italy, and the United Kingdom. Only 5 percent of capital is paid in. Outstanding loans are limited to 2.5 times the subscribed capital.

EIB activities were initially confined to the territory of member states but have gradually been extended to other countries under terms of association or cooperation agreements. Current participants include 10 countries in the Mediterranean region (Algeria, Egypt, Israel, Jordan, Lebanon, Morocco, Serbia, Syria, Tunisia, and Turkey) and the 77 African, Caribbean, and Pacific (ACP) signatories of the Lomé IV Convention and its successor, the Cotonou Agreement of 2000.

The bank is administered by a 27-member Board of Governors (one representative—usually the finance or economy minister—from each EU state) and a 28-member Board of Directors (one from each member state and one representing the European Commission). The president of the bank, appointed by the Board of Governors, chairs the Board of Directors, heads a Management Committee that encompasses eight vice presidents, and oversees the 2,000-plus EIB staff. Other organs include a Management Committee, an Audit Committee, a General Secretariat, a General Administration Office, and five directorates (Lending Operations in Europe, Lending Operations Outside Europe, Finance, Projects, and Risk Management).

The EIB's lending rose rapidly in the 1990s in response to the "buoyant level of investment" in the member countries, financial requirements arising from the EU single market, and more flexible lending conditions. Within the community itself, the EIB was directed by the European Council in December 1992 to assist in the development of the economic and monetary union envisioned by the Maastricht Treaty. In addition, in connection with the launching of the EU in November 1993, the EIB was asked to concentrate on trans-European projects (particularly those in the communications, energy, environmental, and transportation sectors) and SMEs. Some of that activity was directed through a new European Investment Fund (EIF) launched in mid-1994 to provide loan guarantees to projects deemed valuable for "strengthening the internal market." The EIB also participated in the creation of the European Bank for Reconstruction and Development (EBRD, above) to assist in implementing economic reforms and support political democratization throughout Eastern Europe.

In line with a March 2000 decision of the European Council to further increase support for SMEs, the EIB Board of Governors established an EIB Group comprising the EIB and the EIF. The EIB was directed to increase its shares in the latter from the original 40 percent to 60 percent, with the balance held by the European Commission (30 percent) and various European financial institutions (10 percent). The reorganization was intended to improve the group's ability to approve and administer loans, venture capital investments, and SME guarantees.

The EIB Group constituted a core component of the EIB's Innovation 2000 Initiative (i2i), which earmarked for the following three years €12–15 billion for loans involving SMEs and such sectors as health, education, research and development, and information and communications technology. Under President Philippe Maystadt, the bank continued to shift its emphasis toward projects involving human resources and advanced technology.

The annual value of signed EIB financing contracts rose incrementally throughout the 1990s, reaching, in the last year of the decade, €31.8 billion. The total increased by 13 percent in 2000 to €36 billion and to €36.8 billion in 2001.

Although the impending expansion of the EU drew considerable attention to the EIB's pre-accession assistance, its additional partners around the world also continued to avail themselves of EIB resources. For example, under the 2000 Cotonou pact, total EU aid to the ACP countries for 2002–2006 was set at €15.2 billion: €11.3 billion as grants from EU members, €2.2 billion to be managed by the EIB through an Investment Facility, and some €1.7 billion in loans from EIB resources.

In 2001 the EIB agreed to permit lending to Russia for environmental projects in regions that border EIB member states. Subsequently, the bank expanded its authorized capital in 2002–2003 to facilitate the inclusion of ten new members in 2004.

In March 2005 the bank announced plans to expand private sector lending in the southern Mediterranean and to resume lending in Palestinian areas.

Activity in 2007 concentrated on energy and climate-change matters. The EIB and the World Bank created a carbon-credit fund for Europe, and in June 2007 the EIB, long criticized for a lack of interest in such matters, formulated in its 2007–2009 operational plan a priority of "sustainable, competitive and secure energy."

The bank's 2009 annual report rolled out an operational plan for the years 2009–2011. This plan called for a significant increase in lending, especially to SMEs, to counter the global recession. The bank's intention was to increase its total lending volume by approximately 30 percent in 2009 and 2010. Lending approvals in 2010 totaled €83.2 billion, compared to €103.9 billion in 2009. Among external projects supported by EIB in 2010 were utility infrastructure improvements in the Dominican Republic and water supply enhancements in South Africa.

The year 2011 saw a record high contribution to the real economy of the Eurozone and the rest of the world as the EIB contributed €61 billion in disbursements. The EIB financed 485 projects in 70 countries in 2011, and continued to focus many of its projects on alternative, environmentally safe forms of energy.

In June 2012, the EIB launched a new initiative—the EIB Institute. The EIB Institute is designed to organize the bank's community engagement measures in efficient and transparent way. The Institute will be focused on promoting social and economic development through new programs designed to increase knowledge through education about the EIB and its economic policies among the region's citizens. The bank saw a slight drop in its investments in 2012, approving only €52 billion of disbursements. Despite lower investment, the organization still financed over 400 projects in 60 countries.

In June 2013 the EIB announced the successful completion of its ten-year goal of a €10 billion capital increase and launched a new "Investment Plan." The new investment plan calls for the EIB to increase its investments in SMEs that promote job creation and skill training for the growing youth population of Europe. The needs for more support for SMEs and programs to combat youth unemployment were identified by the Board of Governors as the two largest issues facing the EIB in 2013. In August the EIB signed the necessary framework agreement with Azerbaijan to begin financing projects in that country. Azerbaijan is the sixth Eastern European nation to sign such an agreement with the EIB. The bank's total lending for 2013 exceeded €71 billion, up almost €20 billion from 2012. Moving forward into 2014, the bank indicated its continued support for the growth of jobs in Europe as one of its priorities.

On January 12, 2014, the United Kingdom benefited from a large loan of $187 million from the EIB to upgrade pipelines that carry gas from Russia to Europe. In June 2014 the EIB launched a new joint-cooperation program with the European Commission designed to promote innovation within the EU states. InnovFin, as the initiative is called, provides companies of all sizes with access to financial instruments and advisory services from bank officials. The first InnovFin loan was made to a Turkey-based automotive manufacturer. The EIB placed sanctions on Russia on July 16 because that country's intervention in Ukraine, and suspended any new financing. Russia had been the largest recipient of EIB loans, with over $2.4 billion in 2013.

In 2015 the EIB approved new loans, grants, and other funding totaling €77.5 billion, for total funding, including previous disbursements, of €457.7 billion. The Bank achieved a surplus of €2.8 billion, bringing its total assets to €570.6 billion. Within the EU members, the largest recipient of EIB funding in 2015 was Spain at €11.9 billion, followed by Italy at €11 billion, France at €7.9 billion, the United Kingdom at €7.8 billion, and Germany at €6.7 billion. The majority of financing was for infrastructure projects, including transportation, energy, and water and sanitation. As part of a broad effort to expand its scope, the EIB opened offices in India in May, and in July announced plans for new facilities in African countries such as Cameroon, Côte d'Ivoire, Mozambique, and Zambia. On October 11, 2015, the EIB informed Volkswagen (VW) that it would demand repayment of loans if it was evident that the company used EIB financing to alter emissions technology as part of an effort to deceive regulators (see entry on Germany). The EIB had loaned VW about €4.6 billion since 1990.

In its operational blueprint for 2016–2108, the EIB planned to provide new financing at a rate of approximately €71 billion per year during the period. A major focus of funding would be projects to mitigate climate change. In September the EIB acknowledged that a United Kingdom withdrawal from the EU would create issues for the Bank in light of existing loans to the country, along with the potential disruptions to the broader regional economy.

INTER-AMERICAN DEVELOPMENT BANK

(IADB)
Banco Interamericano de Desarrollo
(BID)

Website: www.iadb.org.

Following a reversal of long-standing opposition by the United States, the IADB was launched in 1959 after acceptance of a charter drafted by a special commission to the Inter-American Economic and Social Council of the Organization of American States (OAS). Operations began on October 1, 1960, with permanent headquarters in Washington, D.C.

The current members of the IADB are Argentina, Austria, Bahamas, Barbados, Belgium, Belize, Bolivia, Brazil, Canada, Chile, China, Colombia, Costa Rica, Croatia, Denmark, the Dominican Republic, Ecuador, El Salvador, Finland, France, Germany, Guatemala, Guyana, Haiti, Honduras, Israel, Italy, Jamaica, Japan, the Republic of Korea, Mexico, the Netherlands, Nicaragua, Norway, Panama, Paraguay, Peru, Portugal, Slovenia, Spain, Suriname, Sweden, Switzerland, Trinidad and Tobago, the United Kingdom, the United States, Uruguay, and Venezuela.

The purpose of the IADB is to accelerate economic and social development in Latin America, in part by acting as a catalyst for public and private external capital. In addition to helping states in the region coordinate development efforts, the bank provides technical assistance; borrows on international capital markets; and participates in cofinancing with other multilateral agencies, national institutions, and commercial banks. Loans typically cover a maximum of 50–80 percent of project costs, depending on the level of development of the country in which the projects are located; poverty-reduction projects in the least-developed countries may be eligible for 90 percent financing. In the wake of criticism that the bank had not supported regional integration and had neglected the area's poorest nations, major contributors agreed in December 1978, after eight months of intense negotiations, to adopt a U.S.-sponsored policy that would allocate less assistance to wealthier developing nations—such as Argentina, Brazil, and Mexico—and, within such countries, would focus primarily on projects aimed at benefiting the neediest economic sectors.

Each IADB member is represented on the Board of Governors, the bank's policymaking body, by a governor and an alternate, who convene at least once a year. Administrative responsibilities are exercised by 14 executive directors. The Board of Executive Directors is responsible for day-to-day oversight of operations. The bank president, elected by the governors, presides over sessions of the Board of Executive Directors and, in conjunction with an executive vice president and a vice president for planning and administration, is responsible for the management of various offices as well as 13 departments. These departments cover such issues as regional operations, development effectiveness and strategic planning, the private sector, sustainable development, research, information technology and general services, human resources, budget and corporate procurement, integration and regional programs, finance, and legal. An Office of Evaluation and Oversight reports directly to the Board of Executive Directors. In addition, the IADB has established the Institute for Latin American and Caribbean Integration (*Instituto para la Integración de América Latina y el Caribe*—INTAL), founded in 1964 and headquartered in Buenos Aires, Argentina; and the Inter-American Institute for Social Development (*Instituto Interamericano para el Desarrollo Social*—INDES), which opened in 1995 in Washington, D.C.

IADB voting is on a weighted basis according to a country's capital subscription; leading subscribers as of December 31, 2015, were the United States (30 percent), Argentina and Brazil (11 percent each), the European Union (10.1 percent), Mexico (7.1 percent), Japan (5 percent), Venezuela (4.6 percent), and Canada (4 percent). Non-American members held about 22 percent of the voting shares. Total subscribed capital was $156.9 billion as of 2015.

In November 1984 the Inter-American Investment Corporation (IIC) was established as an autonomous affiliate of the IADB to "encourage the establishment, expansion, and modernization of small- and medium-sized private enterprises" by extending long-term loans and otherwise assuming equity positions in such projects, helping to raise additional resources, and offering advisory services. The first joint meeting of the Boards of Governors of the IADB and the IIC was held in March 1987, with the IIC making its initial disbursements in late 1989.

In 1993 the IIC approved loans and equity investments totaling $124 million for 31 projects, but approvals fell to $42.7 million for 14 projects in 1994 due to a "period of consolidation" precipitated by calls for a review of the corporation's performance to date. Based on the recommendation of an external committee of international experts, the IIC staff was halved to approximately 60 employees in 1994 and additional efficiency measures were instituted. In 2005 the Board of Governors agreed to increase the IIC debt to equity ratio to 3:1, thereby permitting lending to increase to $600 million based on the corporation's subscribed capital of $200 million. The governors also agreed to open IIC membership to nonmembers of the IADB, a measure designed to permit the accession of Taiwan, which has strong economic ties with many Latin American countries. As of 2001, however, all nonregional members were IADB members. In 2000 the IADB Board of Governors approved a capital increase to $700 million for the IIC.

Another IADB affiliate, the Multilateral Investment Fund (MIF), was formally launched in January 1993. Together, the IADB, IIC, and MIF are identified as the IADB Group. Unlike the IIC, which supports individual projects directly, MIF attempts to improve the investment climate in the region in general by financing management training and developing local financial institutions designed to assist small-scale entrepreneurs. The fund also provides grants to help countries formulate policies designed to alleviate the "human and social costs" of structural adjustment. Like the IIC, MIF is an autonomous operation, although it uses IADB technical and administrative resources. About $1.3 billion was pledged (including $500 million each from Japan and the United States) for MIF's first five years. In 1994 MIF's first full year of operation, 29 projects totaling $64 million were approved. The IADB also serves as administrator of more than 50 trust funds.

Relations within the IADB between the United States and some Latin members have been tense on occasion. The bank called for a $25 billion replenishment in 1986, but a dispute ensued when the United States asked for greater influence, including virtual veto power over loans. Although willing to accept the U.S. proposal to link some loans to economic reforms, Latin American and Caribbean members objected strongly to the veto request. The conflict was seen as central to the February 1988 resignation of Antonio Ortiz Mena of Mexico after 17 years as IADB president. Uruguay's foreign minister, Enrique Iglesias, was named president effective April 1, and, shortly thereafter, a high-level review committee was established that in December called for wide-ranging reform of the bank's procedures and organization.

In early 1989 the IADB reported that 32 loans were approved in 1988 totaling $1.7 billion, down significantly from $2.4 billion in 1987 and $3.0 billion in 1986, and the lowest total since 1976. The decline was attributed to the replenishment impasse as well as the difficulty many bank members faced in undertaking new projects because of the continued regional economic crisis. However, the bank's prospects improved significantly when an 11th-hour compromise was reached on the proposed replenishment at the March 1989 Board of Governors meeting. The agreement authorized a $26.5 billion capital increase (bringing total authorized capital to $61 billion), designed to permit aggregate lending of $22.5 billion in 1990–1993. Although the United States was not given the blanket veto power it sought, a system of "staggered delays" was established under which challenges to specific loans would be reviewed before release of funds.

In conjunction with the replenishment, the Board of Governors for the first time directed that some bank resources be used to support national economic policy changes via so-called sector adjustment loans. The bank also agreed, as part of its "revival," to a thorough internal reorganization designed to enhance effectiveness and boost the IADB's capacity to transfer resources. As a result, several new divisions were created to reflect the bank's new priorities of regional economic integration, environmental protection, the financing of micro-enterprises, development of human resources, and additional channeling of nonregional funds (from Japan, in particular) to the region.

Stemming in part from resolution of the replenishment issue, lending approvals in 1989 grew to $2.6 billion for 36 loans involving 29 projects in 15 countries. Approvals in 1990 jumped to $3.9 billion for 45 loans. Continuing its rapid expansion, the bank approved $5.3 billion in loans in 1991 and $6 billion in 1992 and 1993.

After 16 months of negotiations, agreement was reached in April 1994 on the bank's next replenishment, under which subscribed capital grew to $100 billion. Bank officials announced an expanded mandate for lending through the end of the century, with consideration to be given for the first time to the "modernization of the state" through reform, for example, of legislative and judicial institutions. In addition, a projected 40 percent of the replenishment was to be earmarked for health services, education, poverty alleviation, and other "social commitments."

The IADB also made it clear it would continue to assist governments establish policies designed to encourage free-market activity, while at least 5 percent of the replenishment would be used for direct loans to the private sector. That emphasis was apparently underscored at the request of donor countries, particularly the United States, which were to have voting power virtually equal to that of borrowing countries. The bank was also given a lead role, in conjunction with the OAS, in following up on the recommendations of the Summit of the Americas, held in December 1994 in Miami, Florida. Among other things, the 34 nations represented at the summit agreed to work toward creation of a Free Trade Area of the Americas by 2005. To that end, the OAS and the IADB signed an agreement in mid-1995 to coordinate their policies and activities to promote regional economic integration. At the second Summit of the Americas, held in April 1998 in Santiago, Chile, IADB president Iglesias pledged that the bank would develop a training facility to improve its members' bargaining skills in matters of international trade and provide $40 billion in loans in the next five years, including $5 billion for education and $500 million for micro-enterprises.

IADB lending approvals dropped to $5.3 billion in 1994 before rebounding to a record level in 1995 of $7.3 billion for 82 projects in 22 countries. Mexico was the leading recipient of new loans, partly because of the economic crisis it suffered beginning in late 1994. Approvals totaled $6.8 billion in 1996 and $6 billion in 1997 before jumping to $10 billion in 1998. Lending in 1999 totaled $9.5 billion. In May that year the IADB and the World Bank committed a combined $5.3 billion toward a $9 billion reconstruction package for Central American countries devastated by Hurricane Mitch in October 1998.

The annual IADB meeting in late March 2000 in Washington, D.C., served to refocus attention on the effectiveness of bank lending strategies. Addressing the meeting, U.S. secretary of the Treasury Lawrence Summers proposed that the IADB reassess its programs, increase interest charged to the more affluent borrowing countries, and accelerate the move from large-scale projects—for example, power generation infrastructure—toward smaller ones designed to help alleviate poverty. His remarks, which were supported by Iglesias, came in the context of mounting evidence that despite rapid regional economic growth in the 1990s as a whole, the percent of the population in abject poverty had not changed over the decade. According to the United Nations (UN) Economic Commission for Latin America and the Caribbean (ECLAC), 15 percent of the population in borrowing countries remained in extreme poverty, with about 40 percent living on $2 a day or less. President Iglesias noted that various economic adjustment policies, although largely successful, had not adequately confronted social problems, and he warned that resultant discontent could ultimately erode democracy in the region.

In 2004 the IADB announced its support for the proposed Central American Free Trade Agreement (CAFTA) and began to allocate resources to projects designed to prepare for it. The bank also committed itself to providing greater assistance to small- and medium-sized businesses and generally to simplifying procedures for lending to businesses. The subject receiving the most attention in the first half of 2005 was China's request for membership. The United States continued to oppose China's application, officially because of Washington's belief that a country should not join a development bank as a donor if it owes money to another development bank (China has outstanding World Bank loans). Complicating the issue was the fact that ten IADB shareholders maintained diplomatic ties with Taiwan. Also in 2005, Luis Alberto Moreno of Colombia was elected to succeed Iglesias as IADB president. Moreno was elected to a second term in 2010.

At the bank's March 2007 annual meeting in Guatemala City, the United States withdrew its previous objections to China's membership. At this meeting the bank also announced that Bolivia, Guyana, Haiti, Honduras, and Nicaragua, five of the poorest countries in Latin America, were to have their debts to the bank, a sum of more than $4 billion, forgiven. Concurrently, it was announced that remittances from Latin American emigrants now exceeded all foreign investment and aid to the region.

On January 12, 2009, China officially joined the bank as its 48th member. During 2009 the bank was discussing a significant capital increase, its first in fifteen years. In July 2009 the bank eliminated a rule known as the Policy-Based Lending Authority in order to allow Canada to increase its callable (but not paid-in) capital available for lending. In August Canada temporarily increased its callable capital by $4 billion, the increase to last for between five and eight years. The IADB actually posted a record year in 2009, with a successful strategy of providing countercyclical financing to Latin American and Caribbean countries during the global economic crisis.

Loan approvals and guarantees totaled $15.5 billion in 2010. In July 2010 the IDB's board agreed to increase its capital by $70 billion by 2015. During 2010 about 46 percent of IADB financing was to support poverty reduction, while 34 percent went to small or underdeveloped nations and 23 percent for climate change mitigation and sustainable energy.

In 2011 the IADB successfully completed its goals for the capital increase approved in 2010. The IADB approved 167 projects in 2011, totaling $10.1 billion in commitments. The bank's actual disbursements for the year reached $8.6 billion. In late 2011 the IADB signed an agreement with China Eximbank to create an equity platform that would aid in the development of Latin America. The fund is expected to be operational by late 2012. In 2012 IADB President Luis Moreno announced the creation of a new fund that will be used to assist member states in their efforts to curtail crime and violence. The creation of this fund is the result of rising crime in Latin America and the Caribbean. The year 2012 saw a slight increase in commitments from 2011, with the IADB approving 169 projects totaling $11.4 billion.

At the 2013 annual meeting in Panama City, Panama, the Board of Governors authorized the creation of a reform proposal for restructuring the bank's private sector operations. The decision comes as another step to improve the bank's efficiency and transparency within its operations. In May 2013 the IADB released the book from its latest study, "More Than Revenue: Taxation as a Development Tool." The study found that many Latin American nations have missed out on potential economic development because of their outdated tax codes and called for member states to update and revise their tax codes. In August 2013 Moreno announced a new IADB emphasis on road safety, noting that road safety improvements would be given priority in all new transportation project funding requests. In all, 2013 saw an increase in approvals, with total financing of $14 billion.

In March 2014 Canada became the 45th member of the IIC, a move welcomed by all those within the IADB group. At the bank's annual meeting in March, the IADB announced a new, online social media program designed to help SMEs connect with each other and the bank programs available to them. The initiative is part of the bank's broader goals to assist the SMEs with growth. Another component of promoting SME growth was the IIC's November launch of InvestAmericas—an online platform designed to connect SMEs to lenders and funding sources.

In 2015 the IADB provided $11.3 billion in financing for 171 projects. Fifty-two of the projects involved infrastructure or environmental efforts, while another 52 were about trade and economic integration. Other areas included social development and education. The countries with the largest funding awards were Mexico ($2.7 billion), Colombia ($1.6 billion), and Peru ($1.3 billion). Venezuela was blocked from receiving new loans.

In September 2016 Rio de Janeiro, Brazil, went into default to the IADB after missing a $46 million payment to the Bank in what reports indicated was part of a "selective default" on debts.

SHANGHAI COOPERATION ORGANIZATION (SCO)

Shanghai Hezuo Zuzhi
Shankhayskaya Organizatsiya Sotrudnichestva

Established: By declaration of the heads of the member states, meeting in Shanghai, China, on June 15, 2001. The body's structure was formalized in a charter signed on June 7, 2002, in Moscow, Russia, and came into full effect September 19, 2003.

Purpose: To strengthen mutual trust, friendship, and good relations between the member states; to maintain peace, security, and stability in the region and to promote a new democratic, fair, and rational political and economic international order; to counteract terrorism, separatism, and extremism in all their manifestations; to fight against illicit narcotics and arms trafficking and other types of criminal activity of a transnational character, as well as illegal migration; to encourage efficient regional cooperation in such spheres as politics, trade and economy, defense, law enforcement, environment protection, culture, science and technology, education, energy, transportation, and credit and finance.

Headquarters: Beijing, China.

Principal Organs: Heads of State Council, Heads of Government Council, Council of National Coordinators, Secretariat, Regional Counter-Terrorism Structure.

Website: www.sectsco.org.

Secretary General: Rashid Olimov (Tajikistan).

Membership (6): China, Kazakhstan, Kyrgyzstan, Russia, Tajikistan, Uzbekistan.

Observers (6): Afghanistan, Belarus, India, Iran, Mongolia, Pakistan.

Dialogue Partners (6): Armenia, Azerbaijan, Cambodia, Nepal, Sri Lanka, Turkey.

Official Languages: Chinese, Russian.

Origin and development. The Shanghai Cooperation Organization (SCO) grew out of a less formal grouping, the so-called Shanghai Five, comprised of China, Kazakhstan, Kyrgyzstan, Russia, and Tajikistan, whose heads of state had been meeting annually since April 1996. This association was concerned with improving mutual trust in their border regions, as well as coordinating policy on other military and security topics. In July 2000 the president of Uzbekistan, Islam Karimov, attended a Shanghai Five meeting as an observer. When the SCO was founded in 2001, Uzbekistan joined as a full member.

An aim of the SCO from its earliest days, unstated but recognized on all sides, was to counteract the influence of the United States in the region. The June 2001 meeting endorsed the Anti-Ballistic Missile (ABM) Treaty, which the U.S. government wanted to scrap. The anti-American tendency was initially most noticeable in China. The anti-American sentiment of the SCO members was disrupted almost immediately after the SCO's formation by the September 11, 2001, terrorist attacks in New York and the Washington, D.C., area. The first meeting of the SCO, held September 13–14, condemned the September 11 attacks and declared its willingness to work with all countries to counter the global threat of terrorism.

When the group's foreign ministers met in Beijing on January 2, 2002, U.S. forces were already in Afghanistan and some Central Asian SCO members were giving them logistical support. At a June 7, 2002, summit in Moscow, the heads of state adopted the SCO Charter. This document formally established the SCO as an international organization with definite aims and a permanent secretariat.

From August 8 to 12, 2003, all SCO states except Uzbekistan held joint antiterrorism exercises. The 2004 summit was held on June 17 in Tashkent, Uzbekistan. Hamid Karzai, Afghanistan's president, attended the meeting as an observer. The SCO pledged itself to help in rebuilding Afghanistan. It also adopted agreements to combat narcotics trafficking. Similarly, the 2005 summit was held on July 5 in Astana. This was the first summit at which representatives of the observer states were officially present. The meeting attendees urged the United States to set a timetable for removing its bases from SCO member countries.

By 2006 the SCO was attracting increasing international attention, and debate began about whether it might turn into a military alliance—a Central Asian version of the North Atlantic Treaty Organization (NATO). Proponents of this idea pointed to the antiterrorism exercises already held and the plans announced in April 2006 for the entire group to hold war games in Russia. Some maintained that the SCO had adequate economic reasons for existing and a military focus was unnecessary. While Russia might be interested in the bloc as a military counterweight to the United States, China had little such concern.

As a result of the 2006 summit, where Mahmoud Ahmadinejad, president of Iran, attended as an observer, Iran began expressing interest in having full membership in the organization. The meeting approved establishment of the SCO Business Council and Interbank Consortium.

By March 2007 both India and Pakistan were seeking full membership in the SCO. It was also becoming clear that although Russia was very interested in promoting the military side of SCO, other member states were not. The chief of the Russian general staff complained of this lack of interest on the eve of the SCO war games that were held in Russia on August 17, 2007. The games took place at the same time as the 2007 summit, which was held in Bishkek.

In March 2008 Iran formally applied for full membership in the SCO. A meeting of SCO foreign ministers on July 18, 2008 failed to address Iranian membership or consider ending the moratorium on new full members. Reasons were not clear, but presumably Russia, China, or both, did not approve. The 2008 summit was held August 28 in Dushanbe. It proved a diplomatic setback for Russia, as the meeting failed to endorse Russia's military action in Georgia.

On March 27, 2009, the SCO organized a conference on Afghanistan. The conference, which took place in Moscow, was also attended by UN Secretary-General Ban Ki-moon and a delegation from the United States. The SCO members and observers expressed a desire to play a larger part in solving Afghanistan's problems. In mid-April 2009 SCO members conducted a military exercise in Tajikistan, simulating a response to a terrorist attack from Afghanistan.

The 2009 SCO summit was held in Yekaterinburg, Russia, from June 15–16. As a response to the global economic crisis, China promised a $10 billion loan to Kazakhstan, Uzbekistan, Kyrgyzstan, and Tajikistan. SCO also welcomed Sri Lanka as a new Dialogue Partner.

Over the winter 2009–2010 Pakistan reiterated its interest in becoming a full member of SCO. At the June 10–11 summit, held in Tashkent, leaders from the observer states were for the first time included in a restricted meeting of the SCO Heads of State Council. Among other things, the summit discussed ways in which SCO might help stabilize the situations in Afghanistan and Kyrgyzstan. The meeting also addressed qualifications for membership. SCO was an open organization, though membership was restricted to countries from the SCO region. No country could gain full membership if UN sanctions were outstanding against it. Hence Iran could only be an observer.

By late 2010 some felt that SCO was becoming less relevant. Medvedev attended the November 20 NATO summit in Lisbon. There he signed a declaration that Russia and NATO were no longer a threat to each other and agreed to cooperate with NATO's program to build an antimissile defense system. This system would protect against attack from Iran and North Korea.

On June 15, 2011, the heads of state met to discuss the possibility of increasing economic integration in the future. The November 2011 annual summit, held in Saint Petersburg, Russia, saw further discussion of the global economy, emerging technology, and further security cooperation among the member states and other neighboring states.

In June 2012 the heads of state met in Beijing to discuss several initiatives, such as increased cooperation in the field of agriculture and the advancement of multilateral economic and financial cooperation in the region. The heads of state also called for continued progress on setting up the SCO Development Bank. At that meeting, Dmitry Fedorovich Mezentsev was selected as the next Secretary-General of SCO. Mezentsev began his three-year term January 1, 2013.

SCO has recently sought to expand its membership. A committee has been established to discuss expansion procedures and met regularly during 2013. SCO decided at its June 2012 summit to admit Afghanistan as an observer state and Turkey as a dialogue partner. Afghanistan joined effective immediately. Turkey formally joined in April 2013. Even though Turkey was admitted as a dialogue partner, they were not invited to attend the 2013 summit held in Bishkek in September. The annual summit was primarily focused on major world issues occurring outside the SCO mandate area. The most pressing issue was in regard to Syria. The organization expressed its commitment to the plan presented by Russian president Vladimir Putin for ridding Syria of chemical weapons. Also at the meeting, India asked to be considered for full membership. (For more on activities since 2013, see Recent activities, below.)

Structure. The SCO exists as a forum for its heads of state to attempt to coordinate policy. The grouping initially concentrated on border, defense, and security policy, but more recently moved into wider economic, social, and geopolitical concerns. It maintains no kind of parliamentary representation, having instead a top-down structure in which the Heads of State Council (HSC) is the highest decision-making body. The HSC meets annually, as does the Heads of Government Council (HGC). Among other functions, the HGC adopts the SCO's annual budget. Among the representatives of the member countries who meet with their peers from time to time are speakers of parliament, secretaries of security councils, foreign ministers, and ministers of defense. There are also meetings of ministers from various sectors, as well as meetings of specialized groups, such as supreme courts. The Council of National Coordinators (CNC) is in charge of coordinating SCO interaction among the member states. The SCO has two permanent bodies: the Secretariat in Beijing and the Regional Antiterrorism Structure in Tashkent, Uzbekistan. The secretary-general is appointed by the HSC for a period of three years. The office rotates among the member states, alphabetically by the Russian alphabet.

Recent activities. On August 29, 2014, China hosted the largest SCO military drill to date. More than 7,000 troops participated in multilateral exercises. The 2014 SCO Summit was hosted in Tajikistan on September 11–12. The meeting was largely concerned with security issues, paying special attention to Afghanistan's security—an issue the organization has been focused on for several years now—and counterterrorism. The rise of terrorism and the continuing problems for Afghan security are of great concern because of the geographic location of all SCO members. Additionally, the organization condemned the expansion of missile defense systems, an initiative Russia and China spearheaded against the backdrop of American actions. Perhaps the most pressing issue for SCO, however, was the organization's expansion. A special working group on SCO expansion had been meeting throughout the year, and at the summit a new framework was discussed to create a process for adding new members. No full members have been added since the organization was founded in 2001. An expanded SCO is key to SCO becoming a major force in maintain regional security—which many observers believe is China's vision for the organization.

On July 11, 2015, India and Pakistan were invited to become full members of the SCO. The nations were expected to formally join the organization in 2017.

The first economic summit of the SCO took place in October 2016 in Beijing, where participants discussed economic and social cooperation. Meanwhile, Russia announced its support on October 29 for Iranian membership in the SCO. At a summit of the SCO leaders in Bishkek, Kyrgyzstan, on November 3, China proposed creating a free trade zone among the organization's member states. However, other leaders at the meeting emphasized the need to enhance security cooperation against terrorist organizations and no action was taken on the Chinese proposal. The anticipated inclusion of India and Pakistan in the SCO was also seen as a potential stumbling block to creating a free trade area. Leaders did approve a call for the creation of an SCO development bank to back infrastructure projects.

SOUTH ASIAN ASSOCIATION FOR REGIONAL COOPERATION (SAARC)

Established: By charter signed December 8, 1985, in Dhaka, Bangladesh.

Purpose: "[T]o promote the welfare of the peoples of South Asia and to improve their quality of life; . . . to promote and strengthen collective self-reliance among the countries of South Asia; . . . to promote active collaboration and mutual assistance in the economic, social, cultural, technical and scientific fields; . . . and to co-operate with international and regional organizations with similar aims and purposes."

Headquarters: Kathmandu, Nepal.

Principal Organs: Meeting of Heads of State or Government, Council of Ministers, Standing Committee, Programming Committee, Technical Committees, Secretariat.

Website: www.saarc-sec.org.

Secretary General: Arjun Bahadur Thapa (Nepal).

Membership (8): Afghanistan, Bangladesh, Bhutan, India, Maldives, Nepal, Pakistan, Sri Lanka.

Observers (9): Australia, China, European Union, Iran, Japan, Mauritius, Myanmar, South Korea, United States.

Official Language: English.

Origin and development. Prior to the formation of SAARC, South Asia was the only major world region without a formal venue for multigovernmental collaboration. The association was launched on December 8, 1985, in Dhaka, Bangladesh. The summit was convened by recommendation of the ministerial South Asian Regional Cooperation Committee (SARC), formed on August 1983 in New Delhi, India, with subsequent meetings in July 1984 in Malé, Maldives, and in May 1985 in Thimbu, Bhutan. At the conclusion of SAARC's founding session, the participants issued a charter setting forth the objectives of the new grouping and directed that decisions would be made by unanimous vote at annual summits, at which "bilateral and contentious" issues would be avoided.

In light of SAARC's formal repudiation of involvement in purely bilateral concerns, the 1986 summit in Bangalore, India, did not officially address the major conflicts within the subcontinent. Instead, the summit was devoted to discussion of proposed SAARC institutions that would serve to reduce regional tensions through cooperation in such areas as communication, transport, and rural development.

Little SAARC progress was achieved in 1989 and 1990, as national and international conflicts continued to hold center stage in the region. The 1989 summit, scheduled for November in Sri Lanka, was postponed as the result of widespread ethnic violence there, coupled with increased tension between Colombo and New Delhi over the presence of Indian troops. SAARC subsequently attempted to convene the meeting in March 1990, but intensified Indian-Pakistani friction over Kashmir necessitated another postponement. The summit was finally held in November in Malé, although substantive action was limited because India, Nepal, Pakistan, and Sri Lanka had recently installed new governments, and internal turmoil broke out in the other three countries that were members at the time.

The sixth summit eventually convened December 21, 1991, with the heads of state agreeing to "suppress terrorism" while also committing themselves to support "civil and political rights" and to combat poverty in the region. In addition, an intergovernmental group was created to consider ways to dismantle long-standing barriers to trade between SAARC members. Meanwhile a SAARC development fund was discussed, with proponents arguing that "trade and business unity" would help reduce political cleavage in the region.

Unsettled conditions in the region continued to plague SAARC, and the summit scheduled for January 1993 was postponed at the request of Prime Minister Rao. When the summit was finally held on April 10–11 in Dhaka, Bangladesh, it was marred by mass demonstrations against Rao and his government's handling of the Hindu–Muslim conflict. The most significant development at the summit was the initialing of a plan to establish the South Asian Preferential Trade Agreement (SAPTA) for reducing or eliminating intraregional trade barriers.

No SAARC summit was held in 1994, primarily because of ongoing turmoil in India (where the meeting was scheduled to be held) and continued friction between SAARC members. When SAARC leaders finally met May 2–4, 1995, in New Delhi, they agreed to proceed with the SAPTA launching, with more than 200 products identified for lower tariff rates. Following ratification by all SAARC states, SAPTA formally went into effect December 8, concurrent with the commemoration of the grouping's tenth anniversary. However, it was widely agreed that SAPTA represented only a modest beginning, and SAARC established an "expert working group" to begin immediately on plans to expand it into the South Asian Free Trade Agreement (SAFTA).

The political question of integration reemerged at the ninth SAARC summit, held May 12–14, 1997, in Malé. The seven heads of state or government agreed that a process of informal political consultations would help their efforts to foster better relations and faster economic integration. Although still officially opposed to a political component within SAARC, India nonetheless reached a bilateral agreement with Pakistan on May 12 within the "SAARC setting." SAARC leaders also agreed to move the formation of SAFTA forward to 2001 from 2005. At that time, approximately 20 percent of the world's population lived within SAARC's borders, but intraregional trade accounted for only 1 percent of the global total.

Following India's and Pakistan's tests of nuclear devices in May 1998, Pakistan again attempted to introduce a political element into SAARC at the tenth summit, held in late July 1998 in Colombo. Pakistani prime minister Nawaz Sharif offered changes to the SAARC charter that would allow for bilateral negotiations and establish a regional peace council, but the other members rejected the proposed changes. Although the prime ministers of India and Pakistan met during the summit for the first time since the nuclear tests, the talks were not considered successful. Another focus of the summit was economic integration. SAARC reaffirmed its intention to complete and implement SAFTA in 2001. However, a group of eminent persons appointed by SAARC reported that 2008 was a more realistic date for launching SAFTA.

The 11th SAARC summit, scheduled for November 1999 in Kathmandu, was postponed at India's request following the October coup in Pakistan, and little progress on the organization's major concerns was accomplished in the following two years. A third special session of the Standing Committee met August 9–10, 2001, in Colombo, at which time they adopted a schedule for negotiating additional SAPTA concessions; drafting the SAFTA treaty; and holding meetings (some at the ministerial level) concerned with culture, the environment, health, information, media, telecommunications, and poverty alleviation.

As a further indication of the political differences impeding progress toward SAARC's regional goals, in October 2001 the organization abandoned its efforts to draft a unified statement condemning terrorism and the September 11 attacks against the United States. Once again, India and Pakistan strongly disagreed: India insisted the proposed statement condemn terrorism in Kashmir, whereas Pakistan rejected any such explicit reference to the disputed region.

The 11th SAARC summit was finally held January 5–6, 2002, in Kathmandu, Nepal, the attendees reaffirming their commitment to SAFTA and adopting a convention on preventing trafficking in women and children. However, renewed tension between India and Pakistan prompted postponement of the 12th summit scheduled for January 2003 until January 2004, at which time a new protocol was approved in regard to combating terrorism. SAARC leaders also endorsed tentative draft guidelines for SAFTA, which, fully established, would encompass approximately 20 percent of the world's population. (SAFTA came into force January 1, 2006.) Although the 2004 summit (which also adopted a new social charter) was deemed successful, political considerations again interrupted regional progress in early 2005 when the 13th summit was postponed because of turmoil in Nepal and Bangladesh.

The 13th summit was held November 8–13, 2005, in Dhaka. The participants declared the decade 2006–2015 the SAARC Decade of Poverty Alleviation and decided to establish the SAARC Poverty Alleviation Fund (SPAF) with contributions both voluntary and assessed, as was to be agreed upon in future discussions. Some commentators felt that dealing with trade and economic concerns was SAARC's best way forward, given the intractable political differences between some of its members.

During 2006 and 2007 China, the European Union, Japan, South Korea, and the United States applied for observer status with SAARC. All five entities were represented at the April 3–4, 2007, summit in New Delhi. Additionally, Afghanistan was admitted as a member. The representatives of India and Pakistan declared that it was time to move beyond their historic antagonism, ending the summit with a feeling of renewed energy in the group and hopes for future South Asian economic and customs unions.

In April 2008 it was announced that SAARC would be creating a database on terrorism and narcotics trafficking, modeled after the Interpol database. The services sector was also said to be ready for inclusion in SAFTA in the near future. In May 2008 Myanmar, formerly known as Burma, applied for full membership in SAARC, as Australia had recently done. Both applications were approved at the organization's 15th summit, held August 2–3 in Colombo. The meeting (for which the Tamil Tiger rebels had proclaimed a truce) also pledged several efforts to speed up regional economic growth.

In October 2008 the Afghan representative announced that his country was interested in hosting some SAARC meetings in the near future. In February 2009 the Maldives, scheduled to host the 2009 summit, declared that it would not be able to do so before October, if at all. As a result, no summit took place in 2009.

The 16th SAARC summit took place in Thimphu, Bhutan, on April 28–29, 2010. Many observers felt that SAARC's 25 years in existence had been a disappointment, with little economic integration achieved. The summit concluded by adopting a 36-point Thimphu Silver Jubilee Declaration that endorsed Bangladesh's proposal for a Charter of Democracy for regional cooperation aimed at strengthening good governance. Under the subtitle "Building Bridges", the 2011 SAARC summit was held in Addu, Maldives, and attended by all eight member nations. In addition to continued support for the full creation of SAFTA by 2016, four agreements were signed: (1) the Agreement on Rapid Response to Natural Disasters, (2) the Seed Bank Agreement, (3) the Agreement on Multilateral Arrangement on Recognition of Conformity Assessment, and (4) the Agreement on Implementation of Regional Standards. Nepal is slated to host the 18th summit in 2012.

While SAFTA has been functional since 2006, several barriers still exist which prevent it from being as effective as the SAARC ministers would like. At its February 2012 meeting, the SAFTA Ministerial Council called on all of its member states to strive to remove more of the products on their sensitive lists. (The sensitive list is a list of items that have a higher tariff in a given country. The higher tariffs on some items result in non-competitive and preferential trading within the region.) In March 2012 Ahmed Saleem was elected by the ministerial council to succeed Fathimath Dhiyana Saeed as secretary general of SAARC.

The Eighteenth SAARC summit in Nepal was scheduled for 2013. Despite the efforts taken by the Nepali Government, political conflict in Maldives and upcoming elections in Nepal forced the meeting to be postponed until at least early 2014. Before the summit could be held, a meeting of the SAARC Interior Ministers must occur, which was set to be hosted in Maldives and had been postponed multiple times. At that meeting of the Inter-Summit in Maldives, the date was officially set for the conference and Nepal would announce the appointment of the next SAARC Secretary-General. In regard to progress on SAFTA implementation, the SAFTA Ministerial Council met in September 2013 to discuss the possibility of a complete economic union and a SAARC Development Bank that would replace the SAARC Development Fund. (For more on activities since 2013, see Recent activities, below.)

Structure. General policies are formulated at the annual meeting of heads of state and, to a lesser extent, at the semiannual meetings of the Council of Ministers. Sectoral ministerial meetings may also convene. The Secretariat was established in January 1987 in Kathmandu. The secretary general is appointed to a three-year term by one of the member states, with the order of appointment rotating alphabetically by country. Six technical committees address agriculture and rural development, health and population activities, women and youth, science and technology, transportation, and the environment. The committees report to the Standing Committee of foreign secretaries, which prepares recommendations for the Council of Ministers. The Programming Committee was established to assist the Standing Committee, which also oversees SAARC's regional centers. (For more details about the SAARC Regional Centers, see the full listing in the 2012 *Handbook.*)

Recent activities. At the 35th Meeting of the Council of Ministers in February 2014, it was announced that the 18th SAARC summit, originally scheduled for 2013, would be hosted by Nepal November 22–27. It was also at this meeting that Nepal's foreign secretary Arjun Thapa was named the next secretary general of SAARC and took office effective March 1. In advance of the November summit meeting, a meeting of the interior ministers was held in Kathmandu in late October. At that time, the ministers discussed major issues facing the region, including combating terrorism and fighting organized crime, drugs, cybercrimes, and human trafficking. At the 18th SAARC summit in November, tensions between India and Pakistan stalled talks on a range of issues, including transport and the future development of a free trade area. An agreement on energy cooperation was finalized.

On June 16, 2016, Bangladesh, Bhutan, India, and Nepal signed a transportation agreement to ease the movement of vehicles between the countries. Tensions between India and Pakistan prompted India's home minister to leave a SAARC meeting in August. Following fighting in Kashmir in September (see entry on India), India, Afghanistan, Bangladesh, and Bhutan withdrew from the scheduled November SAARC summit in Islamabad. India instead continued meetings of what was called the "SAARC-minus Pak," while the organization's formal summit was indefinitely postponed.

SOUTHERN AFRICAN DEVELOPMENT COMMUNITY (SADC)

Established: By the Treaty of Windhoek, signed August 17, 1992, in Windhoek, Namibia, by representatives from the ten members of the former Southern African Development Coordination Conference (SADCC); Agreement Amending the Treaty signed August 14, 2001, in Blantyre, Malawi.

Purpose: To achieve self-sustaining development and economic growth based on collective self-reliance and interdependence; to achieve sustainable use of natural resources while protecting the environment; to promote and defend regional peace and security; to enhance the standard of living through regional integration, including establishing a free trade area.

Headquarters: Gaborone, Botswana.

Principal Organs: Summit Meeting of Heads of State and Government; SADC Tribunal; Council of Ministers; Organ on Politics, Defense and Security Cooperation; Sectoral/Cluster Ministerial Committees; SADC Secretariat; Standing Committee of Senior Officials; SADC National Committees.

Website: www.sadc.int.

Executive Secretary: Dr. Stergomena Lawrence Tax (Tanzania).

Membership (15): Angola, Botswana, Democratic Republic of the Congo, Lesotho, Madagascar, Malawi, Mauritius, Mozambique, Namibia, Seychelles, South Africa, Swaziland, Tanzania, Zambia, Zimbabwe.

Working Languages: English, French, Portuguese.

Origin and development. The SADC originated as the Southern African Development Coordination Conference that convened in July 1979, in Arusha, Tanzania, by Angola, Botswana, Mozambique, Tanzania, and Zambia (the "Front-Line States" opposed to white rule in southern Africa). As a follow-up to the Arusha meeting, the SADCC was formally established during a summit of the heads of state or government of nine countries (the original five plus Lesotho, Malawi, Swaziland, and Zimbabwe) that convened April 1, 1980, in Lusaka, Zambia. Namibia joined the SADCC after achieving independence in 1990.

The SADCC was considered one of the most viable of the continent's regional groupings, although its actual accomplishments were modest compared to its members' development needs. During its first six years, the SADCC concentrated on the rehabilitation and expansion of transport corridors to permit the movement of goods from the interior of the region to ocean ports without the use of routes through South Africa. In 1986, however, SADCC leaders concluded that such infrastructure development would not reduce dependence on South Africa sufficiently unless accompanied by broad, long-term economic growth in the region. Consequently, the SADCC announced that additional emphasis would be given to programs and projects designed to increase production within the private sector and in enterprises with government involvement. It also sought to expand intraregional trade, support national economic reform, and encourage international investment. The program of action eventually encompassed some 500 projects, ranging from small feasibility studies to large port and railway construction projects.

Throughout the 1980s the conference called for the international community to impose comprehensive, mandatory sanctions against Pretoria, South Africa, to protest apartheid. However, consensus was not attained on regional action, such as the severance of air links with Pretoria, primarily because of objections from Lesotho and Swaziland, members whose economies were most directly linked to South Africa.

At their tenth anniversary summit in August 1990, the SADCC leaders discussed proposals to expand the conference's mandate and influence, in part by enhancing the authority of the secretariat. The heads of state, concerned with the region's stagnant export revenue and mounting debt burden, emphasized the need to increase intraregional trade over the next decade. In addition, they endorsed automatic membership for South Africa once apartheid was dismantled.

While participants in the 1991 summit urged that sanctions be continued against Pretoria pending further democratic progress, they endorsed preliminary discussions with representatives of the liberation movements in South Africa regarding future coordination of economic policies. In addition to possible resolution of the South African issue, peace initiatives in Angola and Mozambique were cited by SADCC officials as cause for hope that after three decades of violence the region might be headed for a sustained period of peace. With this in mind, the Treaty of Windhoek was signed on August 17, 1992, transforming the SADCC into the SADC, through which members were to seek development and integration in several areas, leading to a full-fledged common market. Arrangements for the free movement of goods, capital, and labor among members were to be made at an undetermined date. The most ardent SADC integrationists also suggested the community might eventually pursue political union, perhaps through a regional parliament, and security coordination.

One immediate concern for the SADC was its relationship with the Preferential Trade Area for Eastern and Southern African States (PTA), established in 1981 with many of the same goals as those adopted by the SADC. In late 1992, with eight of the (then) ten SADC members also belonging to the PTA (with Botswana and Namibia as exceptions), the PTA called for a merger of the two organizations. Not surprisingly, the SADC Executive Secretariat opposed the proposal, and at a January 1993 meeting the SADC, reportedly concerned over the PTA's history of ineffectiveness, rejected the overture. However, the SADC indicated it would try to avoid duplicating PTA activities, suggesting that the PTA could assume full responsibility for economic cooperation among the 11 "northern," or non-SADC, countries, with the SADC doing the same for its members.

In one of a summer-long series of remarkable international events precipitated by the democratic transition in Pretoria, the SADC accepted South Africa as its 11th member at a summit held in late August 1994 in Gaborone, Botswana. Although they welcomed South Africa to their ranks, the other SADC members reportedly expressed concern they might be overwhelmed by its economic might. The summit also began to weigh greater security responsibilities, addressing such proposals as the creation of a mechanism for the peaceful resolution of conflicts among members and the establishment of regional peacekeeping and defense forces. Thus, the SADC defense ministers in November endorsed the concept of a regional deployment force, which would not be a permanent army but one available for quick mobilization from standing national armies.

The dominant concern for the SADC in 1995 remained the dual membership problem regarding the PTA, an issue further complicated by the recent signing of a treaty establishing the Common Market of Eastern and Southern Africa (Comesa). Although most SADC members signed the treaty, several postponed ratification, while South Africa and Botswana indicated their lack of interest in the alignment. Consequently, the SADC summit held August 28 in Johannesburg, South Africa, called for an immediate joint summit between the SADC and PTA/Comesa to resolve the matter. Meanwhile, SADC leaders endorsed the proposed elimination of trade barriers between SADC members and the establishment of a common SADC currency. The summit also signed a protocol for cooperation in water management and launched negotiations on similar protocols in the areas of tourism and energy. Mauritius became the 12th SADC member in August 1995.

During the summit held August 23–24, 1996, in Maseru, Lesotho, the SADC again declined to merge with Comesa and instead reemphasized its own goal of establishing a Southern Africa Free Trade Area within eight years. (Lesotho and Mozambique subsequently announced they did not intend to ratify the Comesa treaty, and Tanzania eventually dropped out in favor of continued membership in the SADC.) The Seychelles and Democratic Republic of the Congo became the 13th and 14th members on September 8 and 9, 1997, respectively.

The Organ on Politics, Defense, and Security, launched at the 1996 summit, was at the center of controversy during the September 1997 summit, particularly because of its relative independence from the other SADC institutions. South African president Nelson Mandela, chair of the summit, insisted on bringing the organ under the direct control of the summit, while Zimbabwean president Robert Mugabe, chair of the organ, opposed such a move. Mandela also surprised the summit by proposing the SADC punish members via sanctions if they did not adopt the democratic values central to the organization.

An SADC summit in late July 1998 in Namibia attempted to refocus the community's attention on economic cooperation. Attendees pledged to eliminate tariffs and other restrictions on 90 percent of intra-community trade by 2005. However, security matters, particularly the recent outbreak of fighting in the Democratic Republic of the Congo (DRC), returned to the fore at the SADC summit September 13–15 in Mauritius. The SADC summit, at DRC President Laurent Kabila's insistence, refused to meet with the representatives of Rwanda and Uganda (apparent supporters of the DRC rebels) who traveled to Mauritius to discuss the matter.

The SADC's role in domestic affairs became even more clouded shortly after the summit, when first South African and then Botswanan troops entered Lesotho to quell unrest generated by anger over the May election, which was followed by a mutiny within the Lesotho Defense Force (LDF). By May 1999 an advisory team mandated to help retrain and restructure the LDF replaced the troops.

The August 6–7, 2000, summit in Windhoek drew widespread international criticism for a decision to support the Mugabe government's expropriation of white-owned land in Zimbabwe. The summit's final communiqué also focused on such economic concerns as rising external debt, a regional cereal deficit, the HIV/AIDS crisis, and continuing poverty.

The March 9, 2001, summit in Windhoek, in addition to approving the organizational changes called for in a report on restructuring (see Structure, below), elected Mauritian Prega Ramsamy executive secretary as successor to Namibian Kaire Mbuende, who was dismissed in 2000. Held in Blantyre, Malawi, the August 12–14 annual summit again focused on regional security issues, but also formally approved a package of treaty amendments to accommodate the previously accepted structural reforms. In September 2001 South Africa became the first SADC country to implement the free trade protocol signed in 1996 in Maseru. By then, however, the original free trade target date for the community as a whole was pushed back to 2008, when "substantially all" intra-SADC trade was to become tariff free. Exceptions were to be permitted on a country-by-country temporary basis for "sensitive products." Looking further ahead, the SADC introduced a customs union in 2010 and plans on introducing a full common market in 2015.

A January 14, 2002, extraordinary summit in Blantyre focused on conflicts and security matters in the DRC, Angola, and especially Zimbabwe. At the October 2–3, 2002, summit in Luanda, Angola, the SADC took no substantive action with regard to Zimbabwe, the main issue under discussion being drought and a resultant food crisis that was severely affecting Lesotho, Malawi, Mozambique, Swaziland, Zambia, and Zimbabwe.

In 2003 the Seychelles, citing its inability to pay its annual membership fee, announced its intention to withdraw as of mid-2004. By the August 25–26, 2003, summit in Dar es Salaam, Tanzania, the food crisis had abated, and the SADC turned its focus to economic and social planning, adopting a blueprint called the Regional Indicative Strategic Development Plan (RISDP). The summit also adopted the SADC Charter on Fundamental Social Rights, the Strategic Indicative Plan for the Organ (SIPO), and a mutual defense pact. The defense pact provided for collective action against armed attack and denied support to groups seeking the destabilization of other members, but it continued to uphold the principle of nonintervention in members' internal affairs.

A meeting of the Council of Ministers March 12–13, 2004, in Arusha, Tanzania, officially launched the RISDP, which included among its economic concerns food security, sustainable growth, trade promotion, regional integration, and development of transport and communications infrastructure. To further emphasize the importance given to combating food shortages and chronic malnutrition, the SADC scheduled an extraordinary summit on agriculture and food security for May 2004. In mid-2004 Madagascar expressed its interest in joining, and the 2005 summit welcomed it as its 14th member.

In the wider international sphere, the SADC and the European Union (EU) continue to hold biennial ministerial meetings. Negotiations on an SADC/EU Economic Partnership Agreement opened in 2004 in Windhoek. These discussions took a different direction in March 2006 when the SADC asked the EU to negotiate a bilateral agreement with the SADC, as opposed to holding discussions about joining a larger agreement between the EU and less-developed countries.

At the August 2005 summit in Gabarone, Botswana, Tomaz Augusto Salomao of Mozambique was appointed as the new SADC executive secretary. Other activity included the appointment of the first five members of the SADC tribunal. Also in 2005 the SADC activated the first of five planned standby brigades of SADC peacekeeping forces.

As negotiations with the EU and Africa's several economic blocs began to intensify in 2006, membership by some countries in multiple, competing blocs became a significant issue. The EU would not allow a country to be a part of more than one Economic Partnership Agreement (EPA), and membership in multiple customs unions could cause great difficulties. Salomao declared that all members must decide to which bloc they would belong by 2010, when the SADC customs union comes into effect. In March 2007 the SADC signed a Memorandum of Understanding with the United States, paving the way for increased U.S. aid and consultancy to help the SADC implement a free trade area by 2008.

At the 27th summit of SADC heads of state, held in Lusaka, Zambia, on August 16–17, 2007, the Seychelles was readmitted to membership. But in September 2007, Rwanda announced that it was no longer interested in joining SADC, preferring to work instead with Comesa.

A pressing problem facing the SADC in 2007 and 2008 was the deteriorating situation in Zimbabwe. In March 2007 SADC appointed South African president Thabo Mbeki to mediate between government and opposition parties in Zimbabwe. Mbeki met with Zimbabwean president Robert Mugabe numerous times in late 2007 and throughout the electoral crisis of 2008 (see separate article on Zimbabwe), but had little success in stopping the violence. In July 2008 a "reference group" of senior diplomats was created to help Mbeki.

The SADC as an organization also received much criticism for its failure to confront Mugabe with more energy. Mugabe walked out of the August 2007 Lusaka summit after exchanging harsh words with Zambian president Levy Mwanawasa when the latter tried to put the situation in Zimbabwe on the meeting's agenda. Mugabe did not attend an SADC meeting that Mwanawasa organized in April 2008, complaining that representatives of the Zimbabwean opposition parties had been invited. As chair of SADC, Mwanawasa rejected attempts to expel Zimbabwe, but in June 2008 described the SADC's failure to take a firmer line with Mugabe as "scandalous." Negotiations at the August 16–17, 2008, summit in Sandton, South Africa, failed to move talks of power-sharing in Zimbabwe forward. Botswana president Ian Khama boycotted the meeting because Mugabe was present, calling Mugabe's presidency "illegitimate."

On January 1, 2008, the SADC Free Trade Area (FTA) came into effect, and most goods were able to move between SADC countries without import duties. Some smaller SADC countries worried that the FTA would cause their economies to be swamped by the regional powerhouse South Africa.

The SADC continued contacts with Mugabe. In September 2008 Mbeki and the SADC mediated a power-sharing agreement, with Mugabe to be president and Tsvangirai prime minister. This agreement only marked the start of many months of wrangling about the allocation of cabinet posts. A meeting on November 9 in South Africa between the rivals and the SADC produced a ruling that Tsvangirai's party must share control of the Home Affairs ministry, including the police, with Mugabe's party. Mugabe would remain in control of the army and security services. The unity government was finally formed at the end of January 2009, but wrangling continued late into the year. In economic news, the SADC came to an agreement on October 22, 2008, with the East African Community (EAC) and Comesa to create a 26-nation free trade zone stretching uninterrupted from Egypt to South Africa.

The matter of the white Zimbabwean farmers continued into 2010. In January a Zimbabwean court rejected the SADC tribunal's judgment of 2009, in which the tribunal condemned Mugabe's seizure of white-owned farms. The farmers appealed to the tribunal again in March. The tribunal ruled in their favor, and the South African authorities handed the ownership documents of a Cape Town house belonging to Zimbabwe's government to the farmers. The house was to be sold if the government of Zimbabwe did not pay the farmers' legal fees. On June 2 the farmers again approached the tribunal, asking that Zimbabwe be suspended or expelled from the SADC for ignoring the tribunal's rulings. The tribunal declared Zimbabwe in contempt and referred the matter to the August 16–17 SADC summit, held in Windhoek.

However, on August 3, prior to the summit, the South African Justice and Constitutional Affairs Minister asked for a legal opinion on the legal reach of SADC tribunal rulings, both in South Africa and Zimbabwe. The summit later ordered a six-month review of the "role, functions and terms of reference" of the tribunal. There were rumors that the tribunal judges' terms would not be renewed, and the tribunal effectively disbanded. In November the SADC's actions in respect to the tribunal came under legal challenge in South Africa. Whatever the outcome, many felt that the SADC had shown itself unwilling to stand up to Robert Mugabe, and that the group's standing was seriously compromised.

The 31st summit was held in Luana, Angola August 17–18, 2011. The summit opened with new elections for several SADC organs. Angola's president, Jose Eduardo dos Santos, and Armando Emilio Guebuza, president of Mozambique, were elected as SADC Chair and Deputy Chair, respectively. Additionally, Jacob Gedleyihlekisa Zuma, president of South Africa, was elected as chair of the SADC Organ on Politics, Defense and Security Cooperation. The summit also voiced support for ongoing discussions that started in June 2011 for the Tripartite Free Trade area between Comesa, EAC, and SADC.

Political unrest in Madagascar between the eleven competing factions consumed the attention of the SADC in much of 2011 and 2012. SADC appointed a special mediator to help the various parties come to a consensus about restoring constitutional order. In March 2011 eight of the smaller factions signed an SADC negotiated agreement that called for a new government with the goal of new elections in 2012. The agreement excluded the main opposition parties, however, and failed to solve many problems. In September 2011, ten of the competing groups signed a roadmap agreement that called for a new national unity government to be in place by November. Despite the agreements, progress remained stalled, and at a June 1, 2012, extraordinary session of the Heads of State or Government focused on regional security issues, SADC placed a July 31 deadline on the country to set a date for the new elections. SADC hosted a meeting between the two opposing sides of the government to settle disputes over elections on July 24–25, but no decision was finalized.

In July 2012 SADC approved a tripartite agreement on the Comesa (see separate entry) Climate Control Programme for joint implementation between Comesa, the EAC, and the SADC. The tripartite agreement set a five-year goal for implementation of all components of the climate change program, including increasing renewable energy and expanding environmentally friendly agricultural practices.

From summer 2012 into 2013, much of the SADC's focus was on issues of regional security and democracy. In August the SADC convened for its annual summit in Mozambique, which largely focused on the political unrest in the region. The SADC called for an end to the violence in the Democratic Republic of the Congo and approved a mission to Rwanda to help bring about a negotiated end to Rwandan assistance of the armed rebels. In Madagascar the organization called for the Malagasy people to implement the roadmap fully and continue its progress toward elections in May. Concerning Zimbabwe, the group noted the progress that had been made toward adopting a new constitution and called on the international community to fully lift its sanctions on the state. The meeting also discussed progress in areas of economics, HIV and AIDS prevention, and food security.

The political unrest in the DRC, Madagascar, and Zimbabwe continued to be a priority for the SADC. Two extraordinary summits of the Heads of State or Government were held, one in December 2012 and another in May 2013, to address these situations. In regard to Madagascar, both summits urged the transition government to diligently pursue legitimate elections and called on former presidents to withdraw their candidatures for the sake of moving forward. In regards to the DRC, the summits continued to condemn the violence in that state and issued an urgent call for humanitarian relief from the rest of the international community. An SADC Intervention Brigade was deployed to the DRC in February under a UN mandate as a peacekeeping operation. In Zimbabwe the organization commended the progress made by the state concerning the implementation of the Global Political Agreement and implementing a new constitution.

The 2013 annual summit met in August under the chairmanship of the Malawi government. The meeting continued to see an emphasis on political unrest, noting the urgent need for continued action in the DRC, but expressing commendation for the progress made in Madagascar and Zimbabwe. The summit also noted with great concern the July removal of the constitutional government in Egypt. The summit also discussed the deteriorating economic performance and called for member states to take strides toward economic growth and increased food production. In addition to policy matters, SADC also elected a new executive secretary, Dr. Stergomena Lawrence Tax of Tanzania. (For more on activities since 2013, see Recent activities, below.

Structure. Under the terms of the Lusaka Declaration issued in 1980, individual members of the SADCC were assigned coordinating roles over specified economic concerns. Thus, in July 1980 the conference's first operational body, the Southern African Transport and Communications Commission, was formed under Mozambique's leadership. (For a listing of the other state assignments, see the 2013 *Handbook*.) When the SADC was established to replace the SADCC in 1992, it was decided to keep the existing SADCC structure intact for the time being, with a few additional or reassigned sectorial responsibilities. Other changes were made in response to the community's post-apartheid regional security concerns, which led in mid-1996 to creation of the Organ on Politics, Defense, and Security. The objectives of the organ included fostering cooperation with regard to issues of law and order, defending against external aggression, and promoting democracy. The organ was also authorized to mediate domestic disputes and conflicts between members.

At an extraordinary summit held March 9, 2001, in Windhoek, the SADC approved a report on restructuring that called for phasing out within two years the nearly two dozen sector coordinating units and replacing them with four directorates: trade, finance, industry, and investment; infrastructure and services; food, agriculture, and natural resources; and social and human development and special programs. The structural reform was viewed as essential to advancing regional integration and strategic planning, efficient use of available resources, and equitable distribution of responsibilities.

Under the reorganization, the SADC's chief policymaking organ, the Summit Meeting of Heads of State or Government, convenes at least once per year, with the position of chair rotating annually. Between summit meetings, policy responsibility rests on a troika of the SADC chair, his predecessor, and his successor, with other national leaders co-opted as needed. The Organ on Politics, Defense, and Security Cooperation was given a rotating chair, with the organ's internal structure and functions detailed in a Protocol on Politics, Defense, and Security Cooperation that was signed at the August 2001 summit. The Council of Ministers remains responsible for policy implementation and organizational oversight. The Standing Committee of Senior Officials, comprising a permanent secretary from each member country, serves as a technical advisory body to the council, with an emphasis on planning and finance.

In addition, the restructuring called for creation of the Integrated Committee of Ministers (ICM) to ensure "proper policy guidance, coordination and harmonization of cross-sectoral activities." The ICM, replacing the Sectoral Committee of Ministers, is primarily responsible for overseeing and guiding the work of the new directorates. It answers to the council and includes at least two ministers from each SADC state. To provide policy coordination, particularly with regard to interstate politics and international diplomacy, a new body, the Ministers of Foreign Affairs, Defense, and Security, was subsequently added to the SADC structure.

Duties of the Executive Secretariat, which is headed by an executive secretary, include strategic planning, management of the comprehensive SADC program of action, and general administration. At the individual state level, representatives of government, the private sector, and civil society meet as SADC national committees to provide input to the central SADC organs and to oversee programs within each jurisdiction.

During the 2000 summit, SADC leaders signed a protocol establishing an SADC tribunal, as provided for in the founding treaty. The tribunal has responsibility for interpreting the treaty and subsidiary documents and for adjudicating disputes between members.

Recent activities. An extraordinary summit of the SADC heads of government was convened on January 30, 2014, to address the political situation in Madagascar. Noting with approval the success of the Malagasy people to return to democratic rule and conduct fair elections, SADC voted to lift Madagascar's suspension, effective immediately.

On August 6 the SADC health ministers called an extraordinary meeting to discuss the Ebola crisis in West Africa. The ministers called on member states to abide by World Health Organization guidelines concerning prevention of epidemic diseases and enact measures of state and regional concern to prepare for such an outbreak were the virus to spread to the SADC region. The health ministers also drafted a minimum set of guidelines for the management of an Ebola outbreak.

The annual SADC summit was held August 17–18 at Victoria Falls, Zimbabwe. At the summit, leaders noted that, for the first time in recent years, the region was relatively stable and peaceful politically. The leaders also called on the Ministerial Task Force on Regional Economic Integration to develop a strategy for industrialization, citing region-wide industrialization as the main component of the organization's integration platform. In October SADC ministers met with other ministers from the EAC and Comesa and announced that the Tripartite Summit of Heads of Government slated for December officially would launch the Grand Tripartite free trade agreement—the culmination of six years of negotiation and more than a decade of planning. On June 10, 2015, the SADC, EAC, and Comesa launched the free trade agreement.

Following continuing political strife in Lesotho (see entry on Lesotho), the SADC recommended in January 2016 that the country be suspended from the organization and placed under sanctions. However, SADC chair and president of Botswana, Ian Khama, was able to craft a compromise whereby Lesotho was censured, but not suspended, in exchange for that country's government accepting a critical report by SADC special envoy Cyril Ramaphosa. The report included recommendations to resolve Lesotho's crisis, including the dismissal of the country's military commander.

The SADC declared a regional disaster in July 2016 in response to widespread droughts that were blamed on the El Niño weather patterns. The organization launched an appeal for $2.4 billion in emergency food aid, but had only collected $340 million by October. In August the SADC was unable to finalize an effort to create a regional currency by 2018.

SOUTHERN CONE COMMON MARKET (MERCOSUR/MERCOSUL)

Nemby Nemuha
Mercado Común do Cono Sur
Mercado Comum de Cone Sul

Established: By treaty signed March 26, 1991, in Asunción, Paraguay, by the presidents of Argentina, Brazil, Paraguay, and Uruguay.

Purpose: To establish a regional "common market of the southern cone" through the harmonization of policies in agriculture, industry, finance, transportation, and other sectors; to promote economic development through expanded extraregional trade and the pursuit of foreign investment.

Headquarters: Montevideo, Uruguay.

Principal Organs: Council of the Common Market, Common Market Group, Joint Parliamentary Commission, Secretariat.

Website: www.mercosur.int (in Spanish and Portuguese only).

Secretary-General: Luis Almagro Lemes (Uruguay).

Membership (6): Argentina, Brazil, Bolivia, Paraguay, Uruguay, Venezuela.

Associate Members (6): Chile, Colombia, Ecuador, Guyana, Peru, Suriname.

Observer (2): Mexico, New Zealand.

Official Languages: Guaraní, Portuguese, Spanish.

Origin and development. The idea of a regional common market was first advanced in the late 1980s by Argentina and Brazil, which had signed a series of bilateral agreements that they hoped could be extended to other countries. Supporters of the concept also argued that a regional bloc would be helpful in taking advantage of the Enterprise for the Americas Initiative recently announced by U.S. president George H. W. Bush. Paraguay and Uruguay responded positively to the integration overtures from their larger neighbors, but Chile, expressing concern about the volatility of Brazil's economy, declined to join the grouping.

The Treaty of Asunción was signed March 26, 1991, with ratification by the members' legislatures completed by September. Membership discussions continued thereafter with Bolivia and Chile, one proposal being that they be given associate status pending expiration of a five-year moratorium on new memberships.

Although negotiations during Mercosur's first year of existence on a proposed common external tariff were unproductive, significant progress was achieved in reducing intraregional tariffs. By the end of 1992 annual intraregional trade had jumped by an estimated 50 percent, although a substantial portion of the increase resulted from a vast influx of Brazilian goods into Argentina. The December Mercosur summit accepted further cuts in intraregional tariffs.

At their fifth summit, held January 17, 1994, in Montevideo, Uruguay, the Mercosur heads of state again expressed their confidence in the common market's future. No immediate progress was reported on what became the major sticking point in Mercosur negotiations—the common external tariff. With Brazil apparently standing firm in its demand for substantial tariffs on such products as computers, telecommunications equipment, and petrochemicals, some negotiators predicted that external tariff arrangements could not be completed by the January 1, 1995, target date. However, intensive negotiations later in the year yielded sufficient agreement for the Mercosur presidents to sign the Protocol of Ouro Prêto on December 17 in Ouro Prêto, Brazil, providing for the launching of the intraregional free trade zone and common external tariff on January 1. Free trade within Mercosur was established for approximately 85 percent of the products under consideration, with the other items scheduled to decline to zero within four to five years. In regard to the common external tariff, duties of from 0 to 20 percent were applied to most imports from outside the region. Plans were also endorsed for further discussions toward monetary integration and the coordination of industrial and agricultural policies.

Mercosur subsequently attracted substantial interest from other regional groupings. The European Union (EU) signed a cooperation agreement in December 1995 with Mercosur, pledging to pursue a reduction in EU–Mercosur tariffs as well as broader economic, scientific, and social consultation.

Meanwhile, Chilean officials continued to pursue duty-free trade with Mercosur countries that would not affect Chilean tariffs on products from other nations, and on October 1, 1996, Chile became an associate member of Mercosur, subject to intraregional free trade provisions but excluded from Mercosur's external tariff arrangements. Bolivia's eligibility was complicated by its participation in the Andean Group (subsequently the Andean Community of Nations—CAN) because the Treaty of Asunción forbids dual regional affiliations. Despite this, Bolivia was accorded observer status in 1994 and became an associate member in January 1997.

Throughout 1997 Mercosur engaged in a series of meetings with Andean countries to create a free trade zone between the two groupings. A Mercosur summit in late July 1998 in Argentina reaffirmed its commitment to the proposed South American free trade zone. However, Mercosur was unable to resolve two issues for its own members: how to regulate the regional automobile market and how to settle Brazil's complaint over Argentina's tariffs on Brazilian sugar. On the political front, the presidents pledged to keep the region free of weapons of mass destruction and signed the Ushuaia Protocol on July 14, which committed the members to appropriate standards of democratic governance and threatened expulsion for noncompliance.

The June 30, 2000, summit in Buenos Aires, Argentina, was broadly viewed as an effort to revitalize Mercosur. Chile, despite reservations about what it regarded as the group's high external tariff, announced that it intended to seek full membership. On September 1, at a meeting of South American presidents in Brasília, Brazil, participants called for introduction of a South American free trade area in the "briefest term possible." The year concluded with a December 8 Mercosur summit in Florianópolis, Brazil, where the major news was a decision to suspend membership talks with Chile, given that country's decision to pursue a bilateral trade accord with the United States.

The tenth anniversary Mercosur summit convened June 20–21, 2001, in Asunción. Highlights included an agreement to cut the common external tariff by one point, to 12.5 percent, by January 1, 2002, and to establish a disputes tribunal. Also at the summit, Venezuelan president Hugo Chávez formally submitted his country's application for associate membership.

At the July 4–5, 2002, summit in Buenos Aires, Mercosur voiced firm support for Argentina's efforts to overcome its economic crisis, criticized the United States for a lack of attention to the needs of Latin America, and welcomed to the session Mexican president Vicente Fox, who argued for a Mexican–Mercosur tariff-free zone. Trade negotiations with the Andean Community continued to gain momentum. At the 23rd summit, held December 5–6 in Brasília, a framework agreement with CAN was signed, although some quarters expressed frustration that a detailed pact had yet to be concluded.

At the end of 2002, Brazil's president-elect Luiz Inácio da Silva called for strengthening Mercosur through such measures as raising Bolivia and Chile to full membership and creating a directly elected Mercosur parliament.

At the June 18–19, 2003, summit in Asunción, Mercosur set 2006 as the target date for establishing the parliament. The parliament actually opened in May 2007. Peru concluded an associate agreement in August 2003 and officially became the third associate member in December 2003.

The 25th summit, held December 16–17, 2003, in Montevideo, was highlighted by completion of a ten-year free trade agreement with CAN members Colombia, Venezuela, and Peru. The session also marked Peru's entry as an associate member of Mercosur, an agreement to that effect having been concluded August 25. In 2005 Venezuela officially petitioned to become a full Mercosur member.

Conflict between Argentina and Uruguay over the construction on the Uruguayan side of the Uruguay River of two cellulose plants has been a central issue for Mercosur since 2005. The plants represent the largest foreign investment in Uruguay's history (approximately $1.7 billion) and are funded by European investors. The Argentines object to the plants on environmental grounds. Uruguay believes the matter should be settled via the conflict resolution mechanisms of Mercosur, while Argentina claims it is a bilateral matter that should be settled in The Hague. Argentina formally filed papers at The Hague in early May 2006.

The prospect of Venezuela's accession, and that country's increased involvement with the organization, caused an immediate leftward turn in Mercosur politics. By the time of the January 19, 2007, meeting in Rio de Janeiro, the bloc's new direction became more apparent, with Chávez proposing a shift in policy toward helping the region's poor and developing a "Socialism for the 21st century." Also at this time, Bolivia and Ecuador, both countries with suspicions about free trade, were said to be interested in gaining full membership in Mercosur.

In April 2007 the first South American energy summit was held in Venezuela. At this meeting it was agreed that work should start on merging Mercosur and the Andean Community (see separate article) into a bloc to be known as the Union of South American Nations (UNASUR), with headquarters in Quito, Ecuador. Uruguay continued to criticize Mercosur's new political direction, even as a new Mercosur parliament opened in Montevideo in May 2007. In early July Chávez declared that Venezuela was not interested in full membership unless the organization was prepared to break with "U.S.-style capitalism." Mexico (an observer state) had expressed interest in closer association, but in July da Silva said that would be difficult as long as Mexico was a member of the North American Free Trade Association (NAFTA).

During the December summit Mercosur asked the EU to relax its trading rules to encourage a better dialogue. At the same time the EU agreed to donate €50 million ($33 million) to the organization. The summit ended with a declaration committing the organization to speeding up Venezuela's accession to full membership. In December 2007 Mercosur and Israel signed an agreement liberalizing trade between them.

The July 2, 2008, summit, held in Tucumán, Argentina, focused on the rising prices of energy and food. At the summit Hugo Chávez offered to create an agricultural development fund for the region, donating one dollar for every barrel of oil that Venezuela sold at over $100 per barrel. The summit also saw the group united in indignation over a new EU law concerning illegal immigration. This law, which came into effect in 2010, allows for illegal immigrants to be detained for up to 18 months and to be banned from reentry on any terms for five years. The Mercosur heads of state issued a joint statement condemning "every effort to criminalize irregular migration and the adoption of restrictive immigration policies, in particular against the most vulnerable sectors of society, women and children."

The December 16–17, 2008, summit, held in Costa do Sauipe, Brazil, addressed, but failed to resolve, one the group's most vexing problems, that of double taxation of goods that are imported from outside Mercosur, then passed from one member state to another. While all concerned recognized that charging customs duties inside the group violated the principle of a common market, it proved impossible to work out the modalities of distributing the cost of the external tariff around the member countries.

The July 2009 summit held July 23–24 in Paraguay came amid general acknowledgment that on economic matters the group was making very slow progress. Various bilateral disputes among members persisted. Matters moved faster on the political front, where the member states refused to recognize the regime that had ousted the president of Honduras, as well as promising not to recognize the results of any future potentially fraudulent elections in that country. In December 2009 it disavowed the recent presidential elections in that country. Mercosur also recognized Guaraní, the indigenous language of Paraguay, as one of its three official languages. Venezuela's application for full membership made little progress. In late 2009 the Brazilian Senate ratified Venezuela's admission, but in January 2010 Paraguay declined to move on ratification.

In June 2010 the EU moved to reopen trade negotiations with Mercosur. There was progress, in spite of protests both from Argentina and France about food imports from the other side. The Mercosur region's economic growth over the preceding years had made it a less unequal negotiating partner, however, and by late September EU officials were expressing confidence in an early agreement. In August 2010 Mercosur signed a trade agreement with Egypt, after six years of negotiation.

The August 3, 2010, summit in San Juan, Argentina, witnessed the signing of a customs agreement binding on all members. Some said this agreement effectively turned Mercosur into a customs union.

An October 19 meeting of Mercosur foreign ministers agreed to revitalize and democratize the languishing Mercosur parliament by reassigning its seats on a basis of proportional representation. This redistribution was to be complete by 2015. The presidents of the Mercosur member states met in Foz de Iguaco, Brazil, December 14–16, 2010. The leaders signed a range of agreements, including measures to create standard policies on immigration, financial markets, and automobile manufacturing.

In June 2011 Mercosur issued a statement that rejected British commitments to maintain sovereignty over the Falkland Islands. At its December summit in Montevideo, Uruguay, Mercosur agreed to allow member states to individually raise tariffs on goods imported from outside the trade bloc in an effort to protect domestic industries. Mercosur also signed a free trade agreement with the Palestinian Authority. At the meeting the bloc's leaders renewed their call for Paraguay's legislature to approve Venezuela's membership. The summit was marred by the apparent suicide of Argentine deputy foreign trade minister Ivan Heyn during the conference.

At the December 2011 summit, Argentina assumed the presidency of Mercosur. The heads of state voted at the summit to raise import tariffs to thirty-five percent in an effort to keep trade within Mercosur to help the struggling economies of the Mercosur states. The summit also yielded a resolution to prevent any British ships coming from the Falkland Islands to enter any port within a Mercosur state. This resolution is significant because it agrees to enforce this policy by using all measures possible.

The year 2012 saw increased tension between Uruguay and Mercosur as a whole. Argentina gradually installed a series of trade restrictions that the Uruguayan government feels are targeted at decreasing exports from Uruguay to Argentina. Then in April, Uruguay announced that it did not agree with the blockade of the Falkland Islands, and stated that it would still trade with the islands. In May, three former Uruguay presidents admitted that Mercosur had failed and left Uruguay trapped. This came just two weeks after Uruguay Vice President Danilo Astori claimed that Mercosur was going through its worst time in history.

In June 2012 Mercosur gathered in Mendoza, Argentina, for its biannual summit. In light of recent political disorder in Paraguay after the removal of President Fernando Lugo in early June, Mercosur voted to suspend Paraguay from membership and its summit meeting. The members also voted to approve Venezuela's application for full membership, making them the fifth Mercosur member state. Venezuela's membership became effective July 31. Perhaps the most significant action of the Mercosur summit was the surprise resignation of Secretary General Samuel Pinheiro Guimaraes. Pinheiro Guimaraes resigned after a major disagreement with the Brazilian foreign minister and what he expressed as the member states' failure to consider his proposals.

In December 2012 the presidents of the member states approved Bolivia's accession to Mercosur. Bolivia became the sixth member of Mercosur, although Paraguay remained on suspension.

At their 2013 biannual summit meeting, held in Montevideo, Uruguay, the heads of state voted to restore Paraguay's membership and terminate the suspension in light of successful elections. The organization also approved the applications of Guyana and Suriname to become associate members. Furthermore, the organization condemned the United States for international espionage, and called for the matter to be considered by the UN Security Council, citing American actions as a violation of international law. The heads of state also spent a great deal of time discussing the necessary steps to move forward with political and economic integration within the Mercosur realm.

The summit meeting originally scheduled for Argentina in December 2013 was postponed multiple times in the midst of health problems facing Argentinian president Christina Fernandez and agenda incompatibilities.

In February 2014 Venezuela and Paraguay restored full diplomatic relations, and exchanged ambassadors after Paraguay finally approved Venezuela's membership in Mercosur in January, having refused to approve it since 2010. At the conclusion of the February meeting between the two nations, it was announced that the summit would be held in March, but political unrest and violence in Venezuela postponed the summit again. The meeting was finally held in Caracas in late July. The most significant action taken by the organization at the summit was the acceptance of a joint trade proposal to exchange with the EU. This marked a major step toward completion of the negotiations that had first begun in 1999.

On December 18, 2014, Mercosur signed a free trade agreement with Lebanon. (For more on activities since 2014, see Recent activities, below.)

Structure. The Council of the Common Market, comprised of members' foreign and economic ministers, is responsible for policy decisions. Negotiations with third parties are carried out under the auspices of the Common Market Group (*Grupo Mercado Común*), comprised of four regular members and an equal number of deputy members from each country. Working under the direction of the ministers of foreign affairs, the group is assisted by the Mercosur Trade Commission, which also sees to the enforcement of "common trade policy instruments for the operation of the customs union." The Mercosur parliaments are represented in the Joint Parliamentary Commission, and there also is an Economic-Social Consultative Forum. The administrative Secretariat, assisted by several technical committees, was established in 1992 in Montevideo, Uruguay.

Recent activities. On June 10, 2015, Brazil threatened to withdraw from Mercosur over what it saw as continued efforts by Argentina to block progress on a free trade agreement with the EU. In July 2015 Bolivia became a full member of the organization, while Suriname and Guyana officially became associate members. In December Argentina's new president, Mauricio Macri, announced that Argentina would no longer block the EU free trade agreement.

On September 14, 2016, Argentina, Brazil, Paraguay, and Uruguay blocked Venezuela from assuming the rotating presidency of the group and threatened to impose sanctions and even suspend the country from Mercosur unless it ended political repression and human rights violations, and ended economic policies that were contrary to those of the organization. Instead, the presidency was assumed by a collective committee. Bolivia protested the refusal to allow Venezuela to hold the presidency. Venezuela was given until December 1 to improve its human rights and economic policies.

UNITED NATIONS (UN)

Established: By charter signed June 26, 1945, in San Francisco, United States, effective October 24, 1945.

Purpose: To maintain international peace and security; to develop friendly relations among states based on respect for the principle of equal rights and self-determination of peoples; to achieve international cooperation in solving problems of an economic, social, cultural, or humanitarian character; and to harmonize the actions of states in the attainment of these common ends.

Headquarters: New York, United States.

Principal Organs: General Assembly (all members), Security Council (15 members), Economic and Social Council (54 members), Trusteeship Council (5 members), International Court of Justice (15 judges), Secretariat.

Website: www.un.org.

Secretary-General: António Guterres (Portugal).

Membership (193): See Appendix C.

Official Languages: Arabic, Chinese, English, French, Russian, Spanish. All are also working languages.

Origin and development. The idea of creating a new intergovernmental organization to replace the League of Nations was born early in World War II and first found public expression in an Inter-Allied Declaration signed on June 12, 1941, in London, England, by representatives of five Commonwealth states and eight European governments-in-exile. Formal use of the term United Nations first occurred in the Declaration by United Nations, signed on January 1, 1942, in Washington, D.C., on behalf of 26 states that subscribed to the principles of the Atlantic Charter (August 14, 1941) and pledged their full cooperation for the defeat of the Axis powers. At the Moscow Conference on October 30, 1943, representatives of China, the Union of Soviet Socialist Republics (USSR), the United Kingdom, and the United States proclaimed that they "recognized the necessity of establishing at the earliest practicable date a general international organization, based on the principle of the sovereign equality of all peace-loving states, and open to membership by all such states, large and small, for the maintenance of international peace and security." In meetings at Dumbarton Oaks in Washington, D.C., between August 21 and October 7, 1944, the four powers reached agreement on preliminary proposals.

Meeting from April 25 to June 25, 1945, in San Francisco, California, representatives of 50 countries participated in drafting the United Nations Charter, which was formally signed June 26. Poland was not represented at the San Francisco Conference but later signed the charter and is counted among the 51 "original" UN members. Following ratification by the five permanent members of the Security Council and most other signatories, the charter entered into force October 24, 1945. The General Assembly, which convened in its first regular session January 10, 1946, accepted an invitation to establish the permanent home of the organization in the United States; privileges and immunities of the UN headquarters were defined in a Headquarters Agreement with the U.S. government signed June 26, 1947.

The membership of the UN, which increased from 51 to 60 during the period 1945–1950, remained frozen at that level for the next five years as a result of U.S.–Soviet disagreements over admission. The deadlock was broken in 1955 when the superpowers agreed on a "package" of 16 new members: four Soviet-bloc states, 4 Western states, and 8 "uncommitted" states. Since then, states have normally been admitted with little delay. The exceptions are worth noting. The admission of the two Germanies in 1973 led to proposals for admission of the two Koreas and of the two Vietnams. Neither occurred prior to the formal unification of Vietnam in 1976, and action in regard to the two Koreas was delayed for another 15 years. On November 16, 1976, the United States used its 18th veto in the Security Council to prevent the admission of the Socialist Republic of Vietnam, having earlier in the same session, on June 23, 1976, employed its 15th veto to prevent Angola from joining (the United States subsequently relented, and Angola gained admission). In July 1977 Washington dropped its objection to Vietnam's membership.

With the admission of Brunei, the total membership during the 39th session of the General Assembly in 1984 stood at 159. The figure rose to 160 with the admission of Namibia in April 1990, fell back to 159 after the merger of North and South Yemen in May, advanced again to 160 via the September admission of Liechtenstein, and returned to 159 when East and West Germany merged in October. Seven new members (Democratic People's Republic of Korea, Estonia, Federated States of Micronesia, Latvia, Lithuania, Marshall Islands, and Republic of Korea) were admitted September 17, 1991, at the opening of the 46th General Assembly. Eight of the new states resulting from the collapse of the Soviet Union (Armenia, Azerbaijan, Kazakhstan, Kyrgyzstan, Moldova, Tajikistan, Turkmenistan, and Uzbekistan) were admitted March 2, 1992, along with San Marino. Russia announced the previous December that it was assuming the former USSR seat. Three of the breakaway Yugoslavian republics (Bosnia and Herzegovina, Croatia, and Slovenia) were admitted May 22. Capping an unprecedented period of expansion, Georgia became the 179th member on July 31.

The total increased to 180 with the dissolution of Czechoslovakia on January 1, 1993, and the separate entry of the Czech Republic and Slovakia on January 19. On April 8 the General Assembly approved the admission of "the former Yugoslav Republic of Macedonia," the name being carefully fashioned because of the terminological dispute between the new nation and Greece (see entry on Macedonia). Monaco and newly independent Eritrea were admitted May 28, followed by Andorra on July 28. Palau, which achieved independence following protracted difficulty in concluding its U.S. trusteeship status (see section on Trusteeship Council), became the 185th member December 15, 1994. Kiribati, Nauru, and Tonga were admitted September 14, 1999, and Tuvalu joined September 5, 2000.

A change of government in October 2000 led to the November 1, 2000, admission of the Federal Republic of Yugoslavia (FRY). On September 22, 1992, the General Assembly, acting on the recommendation of the Security Council, decided the FRY could not automatically assume the UN membership of the former Socialist Federal Republic of Yugoslavia. The assembly informed the FRY that it would have to apply on its own for UN membership, and such an application was submitted the following day. However, no action on the request was taken by the assembly because of concern over the Federal Republic's role in the conflict in Bosnia and Herzegovina and, later, its actions regarding the ethnic Albanian population in the Yugoslavian province of Kosovo. As a consequence, the FRY was excluded from participation in the work of the General Assembly and its subsidiary bodies. Throughout this period, however, the UN membership of the Socialist Federal Republic of Yugoslavia technically remained in effect. A certain ambiguity, apparently deliberate, surrounded the issue, permitting the FRY and others to claim that it was still a member, although excluded from active participation, while some nations argued that the membership referred only to the antecedent Yugoslavian state. In any event, the flag of the Socialist Federal Republic of Yugoslavia, which was also the flag of the FRY, continued to fly outside UN headquarters with the flags of all other UN members, and the old nameplate remained positioned in front of an empty chair during assembly proceedings. In October 2000 the Security Council, in a resolution recommending admission of the FRY, acknowledged "that the State formerly known as the Socialist Federal Republic of Yugoslavia has ceased to exist." A representative of the FRY took up the empty seat, and a new FRY flag replaced that of the former Yugoslavia.

On September 10, 2002, the UN admitted Switzerland, which had long maintained a permanent observer mission at UN headquarters and had actively participated as a full member of the various UN specialized and related agencies. The Swiss government, having concluded that UN membership in the post–Cold War era would not jeopardize its long-standing international neutrality, sought admission after winning majority support from Swiss voters at a March 2002 referendum. Timor-Leste became the 191st member on September 27.

In 2003 the FRY became the "state union" of Serbia and Montenegro, which dissolved in June 2006, following a successful independence referendum in Montenegro. Accordingly, on June 28 the world's newest independent state, Montenegro, was admitted as the UN's 192nd member. Serbia, as the successor state to the state union, retained the UN seat held to that point by the FRY.

The Holy See (Vatican City State) has formal observer status in the General Assembly and maintains a permanent observer mission at UN headquarters. In July 2004 the UN granted the Holy See the full range of membership privileges, with the exception of voting.

In July 2007 Taiwan formally applied for membership in the UN. The application marked the first effort by the island nation to gain membership as Taiwan and not the Republic of China. The bid was rejected by the UN legal affairs office on the grounds that General Assembly Resolution 2758 granted sole representation for China to the People's Republic of China. The General Assembly subsequently approved by consensus the recommendation of the legal affairs office in September. After 16 consecutive annual failures, in September 2009 Taiwan announced that it would not seek membership in the UN.

Following its self-declared independence from Serbia in February 2008, Kosovo sought membership in the UN (see "Security Council"). However, in September Serbia, which considered the Kosovar declaration of independence to be illegal, asked the General Assembly to refer Kosovo's status to the International Court of Justice (ICJ). In a vote on the Serbian motion on October 9, 77 members supported the proposal, 6 opposed it, and 74 abstained. In July 2010 the ICJ ruled in favor of Kosovar independence, declaring that it did not violate international law (see "ICJ"). The General Assembly subsequently approved an EU-sponsored resolution that called for renewed dialogue between Serbia and Kosovo prior to further negotiations on UN membership.

On January 12, 2010, 83 UN staff and employees died during an earthquake in Haiti in the largest loss of life in a single day in the history of the world body (see "Secretary-General").

The Republic of South Sudan formally seceded from Sudan on July 9, 2011, as a result of an internationally monitored referendum held in January 2011 and was admitted as the 193rd member by the United Nations General Assembly on July 14, 2011. Meanwhile, in May, the European Union (EU), a permanent observer, was given additional powers in the General Assembly, including the right to participate in debates and submit proposals.

On September 23, 2012, Palestine requested full membership in the UN. (See the 2013 *Handbook* for more information on Palestine's status prior to 2012.) The United States threatened to veto the bid, and negotiations continued into 2012. Meanwhile, the United Nations Educational, Scientific and Cultural Organization (UNESCO) voted to admit Palestine as a full member (see "UNESCO") on October 31. On November 29, the General Assembly voted 138 to 9, with 41 abstentions, to grant the Palestine National Authority status as a non-member observer state over opposition by Israel, Canada and the United States, among others. The new designation gave Palestine the same status as the Vatican. Under pressure from the United States, Palestine subsequently agreed not to press for full UN membership until April 2014 in order to continue negotiations with Israel (see entry on Israel). Following a breakdown in negotiations, in April 2014, Palestine announced its intent to become a signatory to 15 UN conventions beginning in May.

On September 10, 2015, the UN General Assembly approved a resolution to fly the flags of the nonmember observers, the Holy See, and Palestine, along with those of the full members.

Structure. The UN system can be viewed as comprising (1) the principal organs, (2) subsidiary organs established to deal with particular aspects of the organization's responsibilities, (3) a number of specialized and related agencies, and (4) a series of ad hoc global conferences to examine particularly pressing issues.

The institutional structure of the principal organs resulted from complex negotiations that attempted to balance both the conflicting claims of national sovereignty and international responsibility and the rights of large and small states. The principle of sovereign equality of all member states is exemplified in the General Assembly; that of the special responsibility of the major powers, in the composition and procedure of the Security Council. The other principal organs included in the charter are the Economic and Social Council (ECOSOC), the Trusteeship Council (whose activity was suspended in 1994), the International Court of Justice (ICJ), and the Secretariat.

UN-related intergovernmental bodies constitute a network of Specialized Agencies established by intergovernmental agreement as legal and autonomous international entities with their own memberships and organs and which, for the purpose of "coordination," are brought "into relationship" with the UN. While sharing many of their characteristics, the International Atomic Energy Agency (IAEA) remains legally distinct from the Specialized Agencies; the World Trade Organization, which emerged from the UN-sponsored General Agreement on Tariffs and Trade (GATT), has no formal association with the UN.

The proliferation of subsidiary organs was caused by many complex factors, including new demands and needs as more states attained independence; the effects of the Cold War and its end; a greater concern with promoting economic and social development through technical assistance programs (almost entirely financed by voluntary contributions); and a resistance to any radical change in international trade patterns. For many years, the largest and most politically significant of the subordinate organs were the United Nations Conference on Trade and Development (UNCTAD) and the United Nations Industrial Development Organization (UNIDO), which were initial venues for debates, for conducting studies and presenting reports, for convening conferences and specialized meetings, and for mobilizing the opinions of nongovernmental organizations. They also provided a way for less developed states to formulate positions in relation to the industrialized states. During the 1970s both became intimately involved in activities related to program implementation, and on January 1, 1986, UNIDO became the UN's 16th Specialized Agency.

One of the most important developments in the UN system has been the use of ad hoc conferences to deal with major international problems. (Conferences are discussed under General Assembly: Origin and development and within entries for various General Assembly Special Bodies or UN Specialized Agencies.)

GENERAL ASSEMBLY

Membership (193): All members of the United Nations (see Appendix C).

Observers (86): African, Caribbean, and Pacific Group of States; African Development Bank; African Union; Agency for the Prohibition of Nuclear Weapons in Latin America and the Caribbean; Andean Community of Nations; Andean Development Corporation; Asian-African Legal Consultative Organization; Asian Development Bank; Association of Caribbean States; Association of Southeast Asian Nations; Black Sea Economic Cooperation Organization; Caribbean Community; Central American Integration System; Central European Initiative; Collective Security Treaty Organization; Common Fund for Commodities; Commonwealth of Independent States; Commonwealth Secretariat; Community of Portuguese-Speaking Countries; Community of Sahelo-Saharan States; Conference on Interaction and Confidence Building Measures in Asia; Cooperation Council for the Arab States of the Gulf; Council of Europe; East African Community; Economic Community of Central African States; Economic Community of West African States; Economic Cooperation Organization; Energy Charter Conference; Eurasian Development Bank; Eurasian Economic Community; European Organization for Nuclear Research; European Union; Global Fund to Fight AIDS, Tuberculosis, and Malaria; GUUAM; Hague Conference on Private International Law; Holy See; Ibero-American Conference; Indian Ocean Commission; Inter-American Development Bank; Intergovernmental Authority on Development; Inter-Parliamentary Union; International Center for Migration Policy Development; International Civil Defense Organization; International Committee of the Red Cross; International Conference on the Great Lakes of Africa; International Criminal Court; International Criminal Police Organization; International Development Law Organization; International Federation of Red Cross and Red Crescent Societies; International Fund for Saving the Aral Sea; International Humanitarian Fact-Finding Commission; International Hydrographic Organization; International Institute for Democracy and Electoral Assistance; International Olympic Committee; International Organization for Migration; International Organization of Francophones (*Organisation Internacionale de la Francophonie*); International Renewable Energy Agency; International Seabed Authority; International Tribunal for the Law of the Sea; International Union for the Conservation of Nature and Natural Resources; Islamic Development Bank; Italian–Latin American Institute; Latin American Economic System; Latin American Integration Association; Latin American Parliament; League of Arab States; Organization for Economic Cooperation and Development; Organization for Security and Cooperation in Europe; Organization of American States; Organization of Eastern Caribbean States; Organization of the Islamic Conference; Organization of Petroleum Exporting Countries Fund for International Development; Pacific Islands Forum; Palestine (formerly designated as the observer mission of the Palestine Liberation Organization); Parliamentary Assembly of the Mediterranean; Partners in Population and Development; Permanent Court of Arbitration; Regional Center on Small Arms and Light Weapons in the Great Lakes Region, the Horn of Africa and Bordering States; Shanghai Cooperation Organization; South Asian Association for Regional Cooperation; South Center; Southern African Development Community; Sovereign Military Order of Malta; Union of South American Nations; University for Peace; World Customs Organization.

Origin and development. The General Assembly can consider any matter within the scope of the charter or relating to the powers and functions of any organ provided for in the charter. It can also make corresponding recommendations to the members or to the Security Council, although it cannot make recommendations on any issue the Security Council has under consideration unless requested to do so by that body.

The General Assembly's prominence in the UN system results from the vigorous exercise of its clearly designated functions and to its assertion of additional authority in areas (most notably the maintenance of peace and security) in which its charter mandate is ambiguous. Since all members of the UN participate in the assembly on a one-country–one-vote basis, resolutions passed in the organ have varied considerably as the membership has changed. Thus, while the assembly's early history was dominated by Cold War issues, the rapid expansion of the membership to include less developed and developing countries—which now comprise an overwhelming majority—led to a focus on issues of decolonization and, more recently, development. (For more on the early history of the assembly, see the 2014 *Handbook.*)

The assembly's work in development formally began with a proposal by U.S. president John F. Kennedy that the 1960s be officially designated as the UN Development Decade. The overall objective of the decade was the attainment in each less developed state of a minimum annual growth rate of 5 percent in aggregate national income. To this end, the developed states were asked to make available the equivalent of 1 percent of their income in the form of economic assistance and private investment. By 1967 it had become clear that not all objectives would be achieved by 1970, and a 55-member Preparatory Committee for the Second UN Development Decade was established by the General Assembly in 1968 to draft an international development strategy (IDS) for the 1970s. While the publicity surrounding the demand for a new international economic order (NIEO), particularly at the 1974, 1975, and 1980 special sessions of the General Assembly, tended to overshadow the IDS, the latter maintained its effectiveness, establishing quantitative targets for the Second Development Decade and on other issues such as human development, thus remaining the single most comprehensive program of action for less developed states. The Third Development Decade began January 1, 1981.

During the Second and Third Development Decades, the assembly increasingly concentrated on North-South relations, with an emphasis on economic links between advanced industrialized countries (often excluding those having centrally planned economies) and less developed countries. Major discussion topics, all of them integral to the NIEO, included international monetary reform and the transfer of real resources for financing development; transfer of technological and scientific advances, with specific emphasis on the reform of patent and licensing laws; restructuring of the economic and social sectors of the UN system; expansion of no-strings-attached aid; preferential and nonreciprocal treatment of less developed states' trade; recognition of the full permanent sovereignty of every state over its natural resources and the right of compensation for any expropriated foreign property; the regulation of foreign investment according to domestic law; supervision of the activities of transnational corporations; a "just and equitable relationship" between the prices of imports from and exports to less developed states ("indexation"); and enhancement of the role of commodity-producers' associations. Efforts were also made to launch a comprehensive discussion of development issues through global negotiations. Although several UN special sessions have been held on this topic, advanced and developing countries have disagreed on the necessity, scope, and utility of such talks.

In 1990 the General Assembly acknowledged widespread failure in reaching many of its 1980 goals, blaming "adverse and unanticipated developments in the world economy," which had "wiped out the premises on which growth had been expected." In launching the Fourth UN Development Decade (effective January 1, 1991), the assembly warned that major international and national policy changes were needed to "reactivate" development and reduce the gap between rich and poor countries. The plan called for priority to be given to the development of human resources, entrepreneurship, and the transfer of technology to the developing countries. Because the earlier targets had proven unrealistic, the new strategy established "flexible" objectives that could be revised as conditions warranted.

The charter entrusts both the General Assembly and the Security Council with responsibilities concerning disarmament and the regulation of armaments. Disarmament questions have been before the organization almost continuously since 1946, and a succession of specialized bodies was set up to deal with them. Among those currently in existence are the all-member Disarmament Commission, established in 1952 and reconstituted in 1978, and the 65-member Conference on Disarmament (known until 1984 as the Committee on Disarmament), which meets in Geneva, Switzerland. The UN played a role in drafting the Treaty Banning Nuclear Weapon Tests in the Atmosphere, in Outer Space, and Under Water (effective October 1963), as well as the Treaty on the Non-Proliferation of Nuclear Weapons (effective March 1970). The Second Special Session on Disarmament, held June–July 1982 at UN headquarters, had as its primary focus the adoption of a comprehensive disarmament program based on the draft program developed in 1980 by the Committee on Disarmament. Although the session heard messages from many of the world's leaders, two-thirds of the delegations, and almost 80 international organizations, no agreement was reached on the proposal.

The assembly met in special session May–June 1988 in another attempt to revise and update its disarmament aims and priorities. As in 1982, however, no consensus was reached on a final declaration. "Irreconcilable differences" were reported between Western countries and developing nations (usually supported by the Soviet bloc) on several issues, including conventional arms controls in said nations, proposed curbs on space weapons, nuclear-weapon-free zones, and nuclear arms questions pertaining to South Africa and Israel. However, negotiations were successfully completed in September 1992 during the Conference on Disarmament on a Convention on the Prohibition of the Development, Production, Stockpiling and Use of Chemical Weapons and on Their Destruction. The convention was endorsed by the General Assembly in November, was opened for signature in January 1993, and entered into effect April 29, 1997, six months after the 65th ratification. Accordingly, the Organization for the Prohibition of Chemical Weapons (OPCW), based in The Hague, Netherlands, began operations to oversee implementation of the convention. The highest OPCW organ, the Conference of States Parties, met for the first time in May 1997; responsibility for the organization's day-to-day activities has been delegated to a 41-member Executive Council. As of September 2013 instruments of ratification or accession had been deposited by 189 states.

Negotiations on a Comprehensive Nuclear-Test-Ban Treaty (CTBT) began in 1993 and concluded with its adoption on September 10, 1996, by the General Assembly. The CTBT was opened for signature September 24, and the five declared nuclear powers—China, France, Russia, the United Kingdom, and the United States—were among the initial signatories. A notable exception was India, which had exploded its first nuclear device in 1974 and whose August decision to reject the treaty was strongly condemned. As of September 2013, 183 countries had signed the CTBT, but its rejection by the U.S. Senate in October 1999 left the treaty in limbo: 161 countries have ratified it, including 36 of the 44 states having nuclear power or research reactors, but all 44 must ratify the treaty for it to enter into effect, at which time a Comprehensive Nuclear-Test-Ban Treaty Organization (CTBTO) would begin operations.

On December 3, 1997, in Ottawa, Canada, the Convention on the Prohibition of the Use, Stockpiling, Production, and Transfer of Anti-Personnel Mines and on Their Destruction (the Ottawa Convention) was signed. Although a protocol of the 1981 Conventional Weapons Convention had established limits on land mines, it had not called for an outright ban on their use. The Ottawa Convention entered into force March 1, 1999, sufficient signatory states having deposited their ratifications. As of September 2013 the United States was not one of the 161 countries to have ratified the document, in large part because of what it continued to see as the necessity of land mine use in the frontier between North and South Korea. As of September 2013, 25 nations were declared to be mine-free under the convention's certification process.

UN activity in regard to human rights also dates virtually from the organization's founding. The assembly's 1948 adoption of the Universal Declaration of Human Rights marked perhaps the high point of UN action in this field. Subsequently, the Commission on Human Rights directed efforts to embody key principles of the declaration in binding international agreements. These efforts culminated in two human rights covenants—one dealing with economic, social, and cultural rights, and the other with civil and political rights—both of which came into force in January 1976.

On October 3, 1975, concern for human rights was, for the first time, explicitly linked with nationalism in the form of a resolution contending that Zionism is a form of "racism and racial discrimination." After considerable parliamentary maneuvering, the resolution passed November 10 by a vote of 72–35, with 32 abstentions. Sixteen years later, in only the second such reversal in its history, the assembly voted 111–25, with 13 abstentions, to revoke the Zionism resolution.

The Commission on Human Rights sponsored a World Conference on Human Rights June 14–25, 1993, in Vienna, Austria. It was attended by a reported 5,000 delegates from 111 countries and numerous intergovernmental and nongovernmental organizations. The conference's final declaration encouraged the General Assembly to appoint a commissioner for human rights. The proposed creation of the Office of the UN High Commissioner for Human Rights (OHCHR) generated considerable controversy at the 1993 General Assembly session. China and several developing countries, many of which had been accused of human rights violations in the past, initially attempted to block the Western-led initiative. A compromise was eventually reached under which the assembly unanimously agreed to establish the office while leaving the extent of the new commissioners authority "purposely vague." In February 1994 Secretary-General Boutros Boutros-Ghali of Egypt appointed José Ayala Lasso of Ecuador as the first high commissioner, a choice criticized by some human rights advocates because Ayala Lasso had served as a foreign minister under the military regime in Ecuador in the late 1970s. He was succeeded in 1997 by Mary Robinson, former president of Ireland, who in May 2001 was reelected for an additional year, until September 2002. She had declined renomination for a second four-year term after complaining the office lacked the power needed to effectively advance human rights. On September 12, 2002, she was succeeded by Brazilian diplomat Sergio Vieira de Mello, who had most recently served as a special representative of the UN secretary-general in Kosovo and then in East Timor. Vieira de Mello was killed in August 2003 while temporarily serving as a special representative of the secretary-general in Iraq. His successor, Louise Arbour, had previously served as a justice of the Canadian Supreme Court. She assumed the office on July 1, 2004, and was replaced by Navanethem Pillay of South Africa on September 1, 2008, who was renewed for a second term, which began on September 1, 2012. In 2014 she was succeeded by Prince Zeid Ra'ad al Hussein of Jordan.

Questions relating to outer space are the province of a 76-member Committee on the Peaceful Uses of Outer Space, established by the General Assembly in 1960 to deal with the scientific, technical, and legal aspects of the subject. In addition to promoting scientific and technical cooperation on many space endeavors, the committee was responsible for the adoption of the Treaty on Principles Governing the Activities of States in the Exploration and Use of Outer Space Including the Moon and Other Celestial Bodies (entered into force October 10, 1967), and the Agreement on the Rescue of Astronauts, the Return of Astronauts and the Return of Objects Launched into Outer Space (entered into force December 3, 1968). Three additional treaties have since been adopted. The General Assembly has also adopted five sets of "Legal Principles" based on the committee's work, which cover use of satellites for television broadcasting, nuclear power sources in outer space, remote sensing, and international cooperation in the exploration and use of outer space. Beginning in 2007 the committee became increasingly involved in the promotion of outer space technologies to address climate change, including monitoring and measurement of resources.

Oceanic policy has also become a major UN concern. In 1968 the General Assembly established a 42-member Committee on the Peaceful Uses of the Seabed and the Ocean Floor. Detailed and controversial negotiations in this area ensued, most notably in conjunction with the Third UN Conference on the Law of the Sea (UNCLOS), which held 11 sessions during 1973–1982 devoted to the formulation of a highly complex UN Convention on the Law of the Sea. The convention addressed a wide range of issues, such as territorial rights in coastal waters, freedom of passage through strategic sea routes, and the exploitation of seabed resources. Delegates to the tenth session (August 1981) in Geneva reluctantly agreed to discuss several sensitive issues about which the U.S. Ronald Reagan administration had expressed reservations. Although the

440 articles of the proposed treaty had received consensual approval during previous UNCLOS sessions, the United States demanded that such items as the regulation of deep-sea mining and the distribution of members for a proposed International Seabed Authority (ISA) be reexamined before it would consider approving the document.

Following a year-long review of the proposed treaty, Washington ended its absence with the presentation of a list of demands and revisions to be discussed at the 11th session. Although compromises were reached in several disputed areas, other differences remained unresolved, including the rights of retention and the entry of private enterprises to seabed exploration and exploitation sites, mandatory technology transfers from private industry to the ISA, and amending procedures. On April 30, 1982, the treaty was approved by 130 conference members, with 17 abstentions and 4 voting against, including Israel, Turkey, the United States, and Venezuela. The treaty was opened for ratification and signed by 117 countries on December 10.

The Preparatory Commission was charged with establishing the two main organs of the convention—the ISA and the International Tribunal for the Law of the Sea. In addition, the General Assembly in 1983 created the Office of the Special Representative of the Secretary-General for the Law of the Sea, whose functions included carrying out the central program on law of the sea affairs, assisting states in consistently and uniformly implementing the convention's provisions, and providing general information concerning the treaty.

China, France, India, Japan, the Republic of Korea, and Russia (as successor to the Soviet Union) were registered by the Preparatory Commission as the initial "pioneer investors" under a program established to recognize national investments already made in exploration, research, and development work related to seabed mining. Pioneer investors were entitled to explore allocated portions of the international seabed but had to wait until the convention entered into force to begin commercial exploitation.

Led by the United States, many states that had not signed the convention won a renegotiation in 1994 of the contentious section authorizing the proposed ISA to control seabed mining and allocate profits from it. Washington subsequently signed the agreement concerning seabed mining and indicated that it was prepared to sign the convention itself. (As of 2014, however, the United States was the only major maritime country that was still a provisional member of the ISA and not a party to the convention.) The convention finally entered into effect November 16, 1994, one year after receiving the required 60th ratification from among its 159 signatories. On the same date the International Seabed Authority was formally launched at its headquarters in Kingston, Jamaica. It was agreed that an assembly comprising all authority members would be the supreme organ of the ISA. The assembly is authorized to select a 36-member council, which serves as an executive board; a secretary-general; and the 21 judges of the International Tribunal for the Law of the Sea, designated to rule on disputes regarding provisions of the convention.

Elections for the 21 judges of the tribunal were held August 1, 1996, and they were sworn in the following October in Hamburg, Germany. On November 16, 1998, the ISA terminated the membership of all provisional members (then eight countries, including, notably, the United States, which had yet to become parties to the convention), thereby reducing the authority's membership to 130. The status of the former provisional members was downgraded to that of observer to the assembly. Both the ISA and the tribunal subsequently completed agreements with the UN whereby they became autonomous organizations with close ties to the UN. As of September 2014, the ISA had 166 members and 32 observers, including the Holy See and Palestine.

The UN Convention on the Law of the Sea also established the Commission on the Limits of the Continental Shelf (CLCS) in New York, with 21 members elected by the parties to the convention. The first members were elected in March 1997 for five-year terms. The commission's purpose is to review members' plans to expand activities on the continental shelf beyond 200 miles off their shores.

Structure. All members of the UN, each with one vote, are represented in the General Assembly, which now meets for a full year in regular session, normally commencing the third Tuesday in September. Special sessions (convenable, contrary to earlier practice, without formal adjournment of a regular session) may be called at the request of the Security Council, of a majority of the member states, or of one member state with the concurrence of a majority. Thirty such sessions have thus far been held: Palestine (1947 and 1948); Tunisia (1961); Financial and Budgetary Problems (1963); Review of Peace-Keeping Operations and Southwest Africa (1967); Raw Materials and Development (1974); Development and International Economic Cooperation (1975, 1980, and 1990); Disarmament (1978, 1982, and 1988); Financing for UN Forces in Lebanon (1978); Namibia (1978 and 1986); the Economic Crisis in Africa (1986); Apartheid in South Africa (1989); Illegal Drugs (1990 and 1998); Follow-up on the 1992 Earth Summit (1997); Population and Development (1999); Small Island Developing States (1999); Women: Gender Equality, Development, and Peace for the Twenty-First Century (2000); Social Development (2000); Implementation of the Habitat Agenda (2001); HIV/AIDS (2001); Children (2002); Commemoration on the 60th Anniversary of the Liberation of the Nazi Concentration Camps (2005); Follow-up on the 1999 Population and Development session (2014); and World Drug Problem (2016). The General Assembly may convene a follow-up to a special session.

Under the "Uniting for Peace" resolution of November 3, 1950, an emergency special session may be convened by nine members of the Security Council or by a majority of the UN members in the event that the Security Council is prevented, by lack of unanimity among its permanent members, from exercising its primary responsibility for the maintenance of international peace and security. The seventh, eighth, and ninth such sessions dealt, respectively, with the question of Palestine (July 22–29, 1980), negotiations for Namibian independence (September 3–14, 1981), and the occupied Arab territories (January 29–February 5, 1982). The tenth, on Israeli actions in the occupied territories, opened on April 24–25, 1997, and has reconvened repeatedly, most recently in January 2009.

The General Assembly elects the ten non-permanent members of the Security Council; the members of ECOSOC; and, together with the Security Council (but voting independently), the judges of the International Court of Justice. On recommendation of the Security Council, it appoints the secretary-general and is empowered to admit new members. The assembly also approves the UN budget, apportions the expenses of the organization among the members, and receives and considers reports from the other UN organs.

At each session the General Assembly elects its own president and 21 vice presidents; approves its agenda; and distributes agenda items among its committees, which are grouped by its rules of procedure into three categories: Main, Procedural, and Standing.

All member states are represented on the six Main Committees: First Committee (Disarmament and International Security), Second Committee (Economic and Financial), Third Committee (Social, Humanitarian, and Cultural), Fourth Committee (Special Political and Decolonization), Fifth Committee (Administrative and Budgetary), and Sixth Committee (Legal). Each member has one vote; decisions are taken by a simple majority. Resolutions and recommendations approved by the Main Committees are returned for final action by a plenary session of the General Assembly, where each member again has one vote but where decisions on "important questions"—including recommendations on peace and security questions; election of members to UN organs; the admission, suspension, and expulsion of member states; and budget matters—require a two-thirds majority of the members present and voting. Agenda items not referred to a Main Committee are dealt with directly by the assembly in plenary session under the same voting rules.

There are two Procedural (Sessional) Committees. The General Committee, which is comprised of 28 members (the president of the General Assembly, the 21 vice presidents, and the chairs of the six Main Committees), draws up the agenda of the plenary meetings, determines agenda priorities, and coordinates the proceedings of the committees. The Credentials Committee, which consists of nine members, is appointed at the beginning of each assembly session and is responsible for examining and reporting on credentials of representatives.

The two Standing Committees deal with continuing problems during and between the regular sessions of the General Assembly. The Advisory Committee on Administrative and Budgetary Questions (16 members) handles the budget and accounts of the UN as well as the administrative budgets of the Specialized Agencies; the Committee on Contributions (18 members) makes recommendations on the scale of assessments to be used in apportioning expenses. The members of each Standing Committee are appointed on the basis of broad geographical representation, serve for terms of three years, retire by rotation, and are eligible for reappointment.

The General Assembly is also empowered to establish subsidiary organs and ad hoc committees. Apart from the Special Bodies, dozens of such entities of varying size presently deal with political, legal, scientific, and administrative matters. Those of an essentially political character (with dates of establishment) include the UN Conciliation Commission for Palestine (1948), the Special Committee of 24 on Decolonization (1961), the Committee on the Elimination of Racial Discrimination (1965), the Special Committee on Peacekeeping Operations (1965), the Special Committee to Investigate Israeli Practices Affecting the Human Rights of the Palestinian People and Other Arabs of the Occupied Territories (1968), the Ad Hoc Committee on the Indian Ocean (1972), the Special Committee on the Charter of the United Nations and on the Strengthening of the Role of the Organization (1975), the Committee on the Exercise of the Inalienable Rights of the Palestinian People (1975), the Committee on Information (1978), the Advisory Board on Disarmament Matters (1978), the Disarmament Commission (1978), the Conference on Disarmament (1978), the Committee on the Elimination of Discrimination against Women (1982), the Committee against Torture (1984), the Trade and Development Board (1995), the UN Open-ended Informal Consultative Process on Oceans and the Law of the Sea (UNICPO, 1999), and the United Nations Peacebuilding Commission (2005). Subsidiary groups dealing with legal matters include the International Law Commission (1947); the Advisory Committee on the UN Program of Assistance in Teaching, Study, Dissemination, and Wider Appreciation of International Law (1965); the UN Commission on International Trade Law (1966); the Committee on the Rights of the Child (1989); the Ad Hoc Committee on Terrorism (1997); and the Ad Hoc Committee on a Comprehensive and Integral International Convention on Protection and Promotion of the Rights and Dignity of Persons with Disabilities (2002). Those dealing with scientific matters include the Committee on the Peaceful Uses of Outer Space (1959) and the UN Scientific Committee on the Effects of Atomic Radiation (1955). Subsidiary groups dealing with administrative and financial matters include the Board of Auditors (1946), the Investments Committee (1947), the International Civil Service Commission (1948), the UN Administrative Tribunal (1949), the UN Joint Staff Pension Board (1948), the Panel of External Auditors (1959), the Joint Inspection Unit (1966), the Working Group on the Financing of the UN Relief and Works Agency for Palestinian Refugees in the Near East (UNRWA, 1970), the Committee on Relations with the Host Country (1971), and the Committee on Conferences (1974).

There are also a number of "open-ended" Working Groups considering the following: the Question of Equitable Representation and Increase in the Membership of the Security Council (1993), the Financial Situation of the United Nations (1994), the Causes of Conflict and the Promotion of Durable Peace and Sustainable Development in Africa (1999) (this group has not been active since 2005), the Integrated and Coordinated Implementation and Follow-up to the Major UN Conferences and Summits in the Economic and Social Fields (2003), and the Ad Hoc Working Group on the Revitalization of the General Assembly (2010).

In March 2006 the General Assembly established a Human Rights Council (UNHRC) as a subsidiary body of the General Assembly and made it directly accountable to and elected by the full membership of the UN. It replaced the controversial Commission on Human Rights, which had been one of ECOSOC's Functional Commissions. However, through 2012, the UNHCR had condemned only one country, Israel, for human rights abuses and remained unable to pass proposed resolutions on human rights violations in a number of other states, although it expressed "concern" over Sudan. This led many critics to contend that the body was no more effective than its predecessor. Beginning in 2008, the UNHRC began conducting a periodic review of all member states. The first round of reviews was scheduled to take four years. In March 2009 the United States announced it would be a candidate for election to the UNHRC, marking a reversal of the policy of the administration of President George W. Bush. The United States was subsequently elected to the UNHRC for a three-year term in May. On September 15, 2009, the UNHRC issued its final report on the 2008–2009 Gaza Conflict. The report determined that both Israeli security forces and Palestinian militias, including Hamas, had been guilty of crimes against humanity. The report called for those suspected to have been involved in the war crimes to be turned over to the International Criminal Court for prosecution. On March 21, 2013, the UNHRC approved on a vote of 25 to 13, with 8 abstentions, a resolution that was critical of Sri Lanka's actions during the final period of that country's civil war which ended in May 2009 (see entry on Sri Lanka). The credibility of the UNHRC was questioned by rights groups following elections in November 2013 in which China, Cuba, and Russia gained seats on the body. In February 2014 the UNHRC published a highly critical report that systematically documented North Korea's human rights abuses (see entry on North Korea). By 2016 the UNHRC had condemned Israel 62 times, and other countries a total of 57, including Syria, 17; Myanmar, 12; North Korea, 8; Iran, 5; Belarus, 5; Eritrea, 4; Sri Lanka, 3; Sudan 2; and Honduras, 1.

Recent activities. (For activities prior to 2001, see the 2010 and 2014 *Handbooks.*) Presided over by Harri Holkeri of Finland, the 55th regular session in 2001. focused on globalization, authorized a June 2001 special session on HIV/AIDS, adopted resolutions on measures to eliminate international terrorism and on severing the link between illicit trade in diamonds and armed conflict, examined East Timor's ongoing transition to full independence, admitted Tuvalu as the 189th UN member, and accepted the Federal Republic of Yugoslavia as a full participant in the General Assembly. The long-standing issue of U.S. dues arrears and the scale of assessments for the regular budget ($2.54 billion for the 2000–2001 biennium) reached an apparent resolution in December. The U.S. share having been reduced from 25 percent to 22 percent of the budget (with the resultant 2001 shortfall to be offset by a voluntary contribution of some $34 million from Ted Turner), Washington agreed to begin paying its $1.3 billion in arrears. A new, complicated formula for funding peacekeeping operations was also accepted; the U.S. contribution would initially drop from 30 percent to 27 percent.

Major developments also occurred with regard to the International Criminal Court (ICC), the first permanent international tribunal with jurisdiction to try individuals for genocide, war crimes, and crimes against humanity. (For a discussion of existing nonpermanent courts, see Security Council: International Criminal Tribunals.) By the end of 2000, 139 states had signed the ICC Statute (also known as the Rome Statute), including the United States. Washington nevertheless remained concerned about removing its soldiers and officials from the court's jurisdiction, and the new George W. Bush administration was not expected to submit the treaty for Senate ratification. Indeed, on May 6, 2002, the Bush administration formally withdrew the U.S. signature from the Rome Statute. A month earlier, on April 11, the minimum 60 ratifications had been surpassed, and on July 1 the founding statute entered into effect and the ICC became a reality. Meeting on September 3–10, the Assembly of States Parties to the statute took a host of actions, including adopting rules of evidence and procedure; reviewing the specific genocidal crimes, crimes against humanity, and war crimes laid out in the Rome Statute; confirming procedures for the election of judges to the court; and approving an initial budget.

The court was inaugurated March 11, 2003. In February the 89 states that had ratified the founding treaty elected 18 judges to varying initial terms of three, six, and nine years. (Of the five permanent members of the Security Council, only France and the United Kingdom had completed ratifications.) Meanwhile, the United States continued exerting financial pressure on signatory countries to exempt U.S. citizens from being turned over to the ICC. By July 2003 more than 40 ICC members had signed bilateral agreements to that effect with Washington, which threatened to suspend military aid to three dozen other countries, many in Latin America.

An agreement defining the court's continuing relationship with the UN was concluded by Judge Kirsch and Secretary-General Kofi Annan on October 4, 2004. Among other things, it set forth the terms for cooperation between the UN and court prosecutors and provided for the Security Council to refer to the court matters within its purview. Accordingly, in March 2005 the Security Council referred the conflict in Darfur, Sudan, which led the prosecutor to open in June an investigation into allegations of genocide and crimes against humanity. Other referrals involved events in the Central African Republic, Democratic Republic of the Congo, and Uganda. In March 2009 Sang-Hyun Song of South Korea was elected president of the court. As of September 2014, the court had 122 state parties.

On July 9–20, 2001, a UN Conference on the Illicit Trade in Small Arms and Light Weapons in All Its Aspects convened in New York. The most contentious UN-sponsored gathering of the year, however, was the August 31–September 7, 2001, World Conference Against Racism, Racial Discrimination, Xenophobia, and Related Intolerance, held in Durban, South Africa. Among the topics drawing heated debate were the Middle East and slavery. On September 3 the United States, Canada, and Israel withdrew their delegations because of what U.S. secretary of state Colin Powell labeled "censure and abuse" directed at Israel. In the end, the conference's lengthy closing declaration included a statement on Palestinian-Israeli matters that was less strident than Washington had feared. While expressing concern about "the plight of the Palestinian people under foreign occupation" and recognizing the right of Palestinians to self-determination and statehood, the document also recognized "the right to security for all States in the region, including Israel." On the matter of slavery and the slave trade, a number of European delegations had expressed concern the final declaration might, at least indirectly, call for reparations. A compromise was ultimately reached on the relevant passages, one of which asserted that "slavery and the slave trade are a crime against humanity and should always have been so."

The 56th General Assembly session began on September 12, 2001, its opening having been delayed by a day because of the September 11 terrorist attacks in the United States. The start of the annual two-week general debate, presided over by Han Seung Soo of the Republic of Korea, was postponed from September 24 and reduced to a single week, November 10–16. A special General Assembly session on children (a follow-up to the 1990 World Summit for Children) was also postponed until May 8–10, 2002. Not surprisingly, the 2001 general debate focused on terrorism, but such perennial issues as globalization, development, and poverty reduction also occupied the agenda. Among other actions, 118 states signed an International Convention for the Suppression of the Financing of Terrorism. On October 12 the UN in general and Secretary-General Annan in particular were awarded the Nobel Peace Prize in recognition of their work "for a better organized and more peaceful world." On June 29 the UN had unanimously elected Annan to a second term as secretary-general.

On February 12, 2002, the Optional Protocol to the Convention on the Rights of the Child on the Involvement of Children in Armed Conflict, which had been passed by the General Assembly in May 2000, entered into effect, having been ratified by the specified minimum of 14 countries. On December 18 the General Assembly adopted another optional protocol, this one to the 1989 UN International Convention against Torture, by a 127–4 vote. Countries in opposition were the Marshall Islands, Nigeria, Palau, and the United States.

An International Conference on Financing for Development met May 18–22, 2002, in Monterrey, Mexico. Perhaps most notably, donor countries established as a goal 0.7 percent of GDP for Official Development Assistance, considerably more than either the United States or the European Union (EU), for example, were providing. At an International Conference on Sustainable Development, held in Johannesburg, South Africa, on August 26–September 4, long-standing North-South differences continued to be argued. The developed world urged adoption of a cautious approach favoring environmentally conscious sustainable development, while most of the developing country delegations placed greater emphasis on rapid expansion of trade and development opportunities.

The 57th General Assembly session, presided over by Jan Kavan of the Czech Republic, held its general debate September 12–20, 2002. Areas of focus included peace and security, terrorism, globalization, HIV/AIDS, sustainable development, and the mounting crisis in Iraq (see "Security Council"). Specific measures included adoption of the New Partnership for Africa's Development (NEPAD), a broad, multilateral approach to African development (see the entry on the African Union).

The 58th General Assembly session held its general debate on September 23–October 2, 2003, under the presidency of Julian Hunte of St. Lucia. Secretary-General Annan's opening address and annual report stressed the difficulty presented by the doctrine that individual states had the right to act preemptively and unilaterally against perceived threats. Annan warned that such a doctrine could result in a "proliferation of the unilateral and lawless use of force." He proposed instead a "common security agenda" that addressed the threats posed to international order not only by weapons of mass destruction and terrorism but also by poverty, deprivation, and civil war. Partly in response to a failure of diplomacy prior to the March 2003 U.S.-led invasion of Iraq, Annan later named a High-Level Panel on Threats, Challenges, and Change to review the role of the UN. Among the panel's 16 members were Chinese, Russian, and U.S. officials.

At the 2003 session, delegates passed a resolution on "Revitalization of the Work of the General Assembly" with a view toward improving cooperation with the Security Council and the Economic and Social Council. Another resolution expressed "deep concern" over escalating threats to the safety and security of humanitarian and UN personnel. The General Assembly also endorsed a December 9–12 meeting in Merida, Mexico, that saw 95 countries sign a Convention against Corruption. It failed to reach agreement, however, on an even more controversial subject, namely a ban on human cloning, and in early November voted to postpone further action for two years.

Jean Ping of Gabon was named president of the 59th session, from September 21–30, 2004, and the session was followed on October 4–5 by discussions related to strengthening the UN and revitalizing the General Assembly. In early December the High-Level Panel on Threats, Challenges, and Change submitted its report, which included 101 recommendations on matters as varied as Security Council reform, terrorism and nuclear proliferation, sustainable development, and use of force to protect human rights. On March 21, 2005, drawing on the panel's work, Secretary-General Annan submitted to the General Assembly a report on reform, which called for expanding the Security Council to 24 members, streamlining the General Assembly agenda, and replacing the controversial UN Commission on Human Rights with a Human Rights Council.

On April 13, 2005, the General Assembly adopted an International Convention for the Suppression of Acts of Nuclear Terrorism, which was opened for signature during the September 14–16 World Summit of national leaders, who gathered to mark the UN's 60th anniversary. The summit concluded with a final declaration covering UN reform and the Millennium Development Goals that had been adopted in 2000, but a number of proposals advocated by Secretary-General Annan—most significantly those related to nuclear disarmament and nonproliferation—were dropped from the document or weakened in order to reach consensus. The declaration broke new ground with its assertion that the UN had the right to intervene if "national authorities manifestly [fail] to protect their populations from genocide, war crimes, ethnic cleansing and crimes against humanity." With Jan Eliasson of Sweden as president, the regular 2005 session was highlighted by the December approval of a resolution to create a Peacebuilding Commission. The 31-member advisory body, including national representatives from the Security Council, ECOSOC, and peacekeeping missions, was designed to focus on methods for stabilizing and rebuilding countries in the post-conflict period. The General Assembly also voted to reconfigure the Central Emergency Revolving Fund as the Central Emergency Response Fund (CERF) for humanitarian disasters. Plans called for supplementing the preexisting $50 million revolving fund with a $450 million facility that could provide grants and loans.

On March 15, 2006, the General Assembly, by a vote of 170–4, approved creation of the Human Rights Council (UNHRC) to serve as the main UN forum for dialogue and cooperation on human rights. Israel, the Marshall Islands, Palau, and the United States voted against the resolution, and Belarus, Iran, and Venezuela abstained. The negative U.S. vote largely reflected concern that seats on the council, like those on the ECOSOC's Commission on Human Rights, would be filled on a regional basis. Election of the UNHRC's 47 members—a cohort considerably larger than had been envisaged by Secretary-General Annan—took place on May 9, and its first session was held June 19. The General Assembly approved a series of reforms for UN management, procurement, and enhanced information technology efforts in July 2006. Annan was granted $20 million to implement the reform package. In August the sixteenth biennial AIDS Conference was held in Toronto. The gathering drew 20,000 participants. During the meeting, the UN's special envoy on HIV/AIDS to Africa, Stephen Lewis, accused the G-8 nations of failing to follow through on pledges made in 2005 to support enhanced access to drugs and treatment. (As of the Toronto conference, the UN had collected only $525 million to combat HIV/AIDS, tuberculosis, and malaria against a goal of $5.8 billion.) Partially in response to such criticism, the General Assembly launched the UNITAID, a multilateral program to purchase drugs to treat HIV/AIDS, tuberculosis, and malaria and redistribute them to 94 countries in Africa, Asia, Latin America, and the Caribbean. By 2010 UNITAID had 35 member states and an annual budget of more than $400 million.

Haya Rashed Al Khalifa of Bahrain was elected president of the 61st General Assembly session, becoming the third woman chosen for the post. The theme of the session was "Implementing a Partnership for Global Development." On September 13, 2006, the General Assembly approved the Declaration on the Rights of Indigenous Peoples. The nonbinding document articulated the rights of native peoples to unique cultures, languages, and traditions, and prohibited discrimination against them. Australia, Canada, New Zealand, and the United States were the only countries to vote against the declaration, which passed with 113 votes in favor and 11 abstentions.

During the assembly's meetings in September 2006, South Korean foreign minister Ban Ki-moon emerged as the leading candidate to succeed Annan after a series of informal polls of the Security Council. Ban's reputation for quiet diplomacy garnered him the support of the

United States, China, and Russia, which collectively sought a less-activist secretary-general than Annan. On October 13 the General Assembly appointed Ban as the eighth UN secretary-general after the Security Council recommended his appointment in Resolution 1715. Annan announced in October that the UN Foundation, founded by Turner, had exceeded its $1 billion goal. Meanwhile, the High-Level Panel on UN Systems-Wide Coherence, formed in February 2006 to recommend internal reforms, released a report that contended duplication and inefficiency could be reduced by 20 percent by the creation of a single board or commission to coordinate the activities of the UN's agencies and bodies. On December 13 the General Assembly adopted the Convention on the Protection and Promotion of the Rights and Dignity of Persons with Disabilities, which opened for signatures on March 30, 2007, and was immediately signed by 81 countries and the EU, a record number for a UN convention.

The General Assembly adopted a resolution that condemned denial of the Holocaust on January 26, 2007. The resolution was in response to statements by the president of Iran that appeared to question the reality of the atrocities. The assembly also approved a reform proposal by Ban that included the division of the body's peacekeeping operations into two bodies: a department of peace operations and a department of field support.

In May 2007 the assembly elected Srgjan Kerim of Macedonia as the president of the 62nd session. Some delegations condemned Ban's decision to convene a September meeting of world leaders on climate change under the auspices of the Security Council, arguing that the General Assembly was the better forum for such an event. In June the General Assembly approved Ban's proposed reform of UN peacekeeping operations (see "Secretariat"). Meanwhile, in October the General Assembly held the High-Level Dialogue on Interreligious and Intercultural Understanding and Cooperation for Peace in an effort to promote interaction among diverse groups and cultures. In November the General Assembly designated September 15 of each year as International Democracy Day.

Miguel d'Escoto Brockmann was elected president of the 63rd session of the General Assembly on June 4, 2008. The session's debate theme was "The Impact of the Global Food Crisis on Poverty and Hunger in the World as Well as the Need to Democraticize the United Nations." Brockmann called on the world body to enhance the power of the General Assembly by diluting the power of the Security Council and moving toward a system of "one country, one vote" in which all member states would be equal. In late October Brockmann called on the international community to help reform the global financial system, in the wake of widespread economic turmoil. The General Assembly also declared 2008 the International Year of Sanitation and directed agencies to develop reports and recommendations to ensure that the 2015 Millennium Development Goals on sanitation were met.

On June 10, 2009, Ali Abdussalem Treki of Libya was elected president of the 64th session of the General Assembly, which subsequently began on September 15. During the session, the assembly approved a draft resolution on the Alliance of Civilizations, an initiative that sought to promote a culture of peace throughout the world. The body also called on the secretary-general to develop specific programs to support the Alliance of Civilizations. A resolution that pledged UN support for new, and newly restored, democracies was also approved. United States president Barack Obama, in his first speech before the General Assembly, pledged a more cooperative foreign policy and called for a new international treaty to ban nuclear weapons. His remarks were seen as a foreshadowing of reduced tensions between the United States and the UN. On October 19 the assembly voted to grant observer status to the International Olympic Committee. For the 18th consecutive year, the assembly called on the United States to end its economic embargo on Cuba on a vote of 187 in support, 3 opposed (the United States, Israel, and Palau), and 2 abstentions (Micronesia and the Marshall Islands). The assembly designated July 18 as Nelson Mandela International Day in honor of the accomplishments of the South African freedom fighter and leader.

The General Assembly voted unanimously on July 2, 2010, to establish a new bureau to promote women's rights, the UN Entity for Gender Equality and the Empowerment of Women (UN Women). The new organization combined four existing bodies: the Division for the Advancement of Women, the International Research and Training Institute for the Advancement of Women, the Office of the Special Adviser on Gender Issues and the Advancement of Women, and the UN Development Fund for Women. Michele Bachelet, the former president of Chile, was appointed the first head of UN Women on September 14. On July 29 the assembly enacted a resolution affirming that access to clean water and sanitation was a basic human right. Joseph Deiss of Switzerland was elected president of the 66th session of the General Assembly. The session included high level meetings to reduce the loss of biodiversity and new strategies to improve development among small island states. The assembly also engaged in a debate on Security Council reform, but an agreement on revising the number or composition of the permanent members of the body remained elusive. The 2010–2011 UN budget was approved by the General Assembly at the session. The $4.2 billion budget was an increase of 0.5 percent over the previous cycle.

On March 3, 2011, the General Assembly ejected Libya from the Human Rights Council in reaction to President Qadhafi's suppression of protestors. On June 21 the General Assembly overwhelmingly elected Ban to a second five-year term, beginning January 1, 2012. On September 23, Palestine requested full membership and was granted non-member observer state status in November.

To mark the 20th anniversary of the 1992 Rio Conference ("Earth Summit"), the UN Conference on Sustainable Development ("Rio + 20") was held in June 2012 and included representatives from 192 countries and a range of international organizations. Differences among the attendees prevented the adoption of any binding agreements; however, participants endorsed a proposal that the UN Environmental Program would be the lead international environmental authority.

The 66th session of the General Assembly began on September 13, 2011. With her September 22 speech, Brazilian president Dilma Rousseff became the first woman to open the general debate. Nassir Abdulaziz Al-Nasser of Qatar was elected president of the session, which included high-level meetings on the prevention and control of noncommunicable diseases, desertification, and sustainable development. In December the General Assembly approved a $5.15 billion budget for 2012–2013.

The 67th session of the General Assembly opened on September 18, 2012. Vuk Jeremićof Serbia was elected president of the session whose theme was "Bringing about adjustment or settlement of international disputes or situations by peaceful means," and which was dominated by discussions of the ongoing civil war in Syria.

On April 2, 2013, the General Assembly voted 154 to 3, with 23 abstentions, to adopt the Arms Trade Treaty. Voting against the accord were Iran, North Korea, and Syria, while China, India, and Russia were among those states that abstained. The treaty regulated the global trade in conventional weapons by requiring states to assess the impact of arms imports and exports on areas such as their potential to contribute to human rights violations, organized crime or terrorism, as well as tracking the status of imported weapons. The accord will not enter into force until it has been ratified by 59 countries. By October 2013, 113 states had signed the treaty, while 7 had ratified it.

John W. Ashe of Antigua and Barbuda was elected president of the 68th session of the General Assembly, which began on September 17, 2013. The General Assembly called on the UN to launch negotiations on a follow-up program after the Millennium Development Goals initiative ended in 2015. The assembly also adopted a commitment to the eradication of the illicit use and transfer of small arms and convened the first high-level meeting on nuclear disarmament. In December, the assembly approved the 2014–2015 general budget of $5.5 billion, a 1 percent decrease from the previous year.

In June 2014 Sam Kahamba Kutesa of Uganda was elected to president of the 69th General Assembly, which convened on September 16, 2014. The assembly held a high-level meeting of the World Conference on Indigenous Peoples and conducted a special session on the aftermath of the Program of Action of the International Conference on Population and Development.

The 70th session of the General Assembly began on September 15, 2015. Mogens Lykketoft of Denmark was elected president of the session, along with 19 vice presidents. The theme was "A New Commitment to Action," and the main goal of the session was to work on the Post-2015 Development Agenda, a framework to replace the Millennium Development Goals. On September 25 the General Assembly adopted the Sustainable Development Goals, consisting of 17 broad objectives, ranging from the eradication of poverty and hunger to gender equality to affordable and clean energy. These goals were divided into 169 target objectives. The assembly approved a 2016–2017 budget of $5.4 billion, which was 3.5 percent less, in real dollars, than the previous one.

Peter Thomson of Fiji was elected president of the 71st session of the General Assembly which began on September 13, 2016. Concurrent with the launch of the session was a summit on refugees and migrants that endeavored to craft strategies in response to the rise in global refugees. On October 13 former Portuguese prime minister and UN high commissioner for refugees, António Gutterres, was elected secretary-general. He was scheduled to take office on January 1, 2017.

GENERAL ASSEMBLY: SPECIAL BODIES

Over the years, the General Assembly has created a number of semiautonomous Special Bodies, two of which (UNCTAD, UNDP) deal with development problems, three (UNHCR, UNICEF, UNRWA) with relief and welfare problems, and two (UNEP, UNFPA) with demographic and environmental problems.

In addition to the United Nations University (UNU), which alone sponsors or cosponsors some dozen Research and Training Centers and Programs, a number of other specialized bodies for conducting research and providing training have been established. These include the United Nations Institute for Training and Research (UNITAR) and the United Nations Research Institute for Social Development (UNRISD) (both discussed below); the UN Institute for Disarmament Research (UNIDIR), located in Geneva; the UN Entity for Gender Equality and the Empowerment of Women (UN Women), based in New York; and the UN Interregional Crime and Justice Research Institute (UNICRI), based in Turin, Italy.

UNITED NATIONS CHILDREN'S FUND

(UNICEF)

Established: By General Assembly resolution of December 11, 1946, as the United Nations International Children's Emergency Fund. Initially a temporary body to provide emergency assistance to children in countries ravaged by war, the fund was made permanent by General Assembly resolution on October 6, 1953, the name changed to United Nations Children's Fund while retaining the abbreviation UNICEF.

Purpose: To give assistance, particularly to less developed countries, in the establishment of permanent child health, educational, protective, and welfare services.

Headquarters: New York, United States.

Principal Organs: Executive Board (36 members), Program Committee (Committee of the Whole), National Committees, Secretariat. Membership on the Executive Board rotates on the following geographical basis: Africa, 8; Asia, 7; Latin America and the Caribbean, 5; Eastern Europe, 4; Western Europe and other, 12.

Website: www.unicef.org.

Executive Director: Anthony Lake (United States).

Recent activities. UNICEF has long been actively involved in programs dedicated to maternal and child health, nutrition, education, and social welfare. In keeping with the intent of the Child Survival and Development Revolution (CSDR), which was adopted in 1983 to provide "a creative and practical approach" to accelerating progress for children, UNICEF added emphasis on the problems of children affected by armed conflicts, exploitation, abandonment, abuse, and neglect. Increased attention was also given to the role of women in economic development, problems specific to female children, the need for family "spacing," and the provision of better water and sanitation facilities. In all the areas it covers, UNICEF's goal is to foster community-based services provided by workers selected by the community and supported by existing networks of government agencies and nongovernmental organizations.

UNICEF's activities are supported exclusively by voluntary contributions, approximately two-thirds of which are donated by governments and much of the remainder raised by its 36 National Committees, based primarily in more affluent countries. In addition to its New York headquarters, UNICEF maintains major offices in Tokyo, Japan, and Brussels, Belgium. The crucial Supply Division operates out of Copenhagen, Denmark. In addition, its Innocenti Research Center, located in Florence, Italy, focuses on child development and advocacy. Seven regional offices around the globe help support 190 country offices. UNICEF reports indirectly to the General Assembly through the Economic and Social Council (ECOSOC).

UNICEF reported in September 2007 that the number of children who died annually dropped below 10 million in 2005 for the first time since the organization began keeping records. (For information on UNICEF prior to 2007, see the 2013 and 2014 *Handbooks.*) On November 5, UNICEF called on governments to ban the use and stockpiling of cluster munitions that the body argued disproportionately affected women and children. UNICEF specifically denounced their use in the 2006 conflict in Lebanon.

In 2008 UNICEF and the World Health Organization released the report of a Joint Monitoring Program that examined sanitation and access to safe drinking water around the world. The report found that the world was on track to meet the Millennium Development Goals on water and sanitation by 2015, but that 2.5 billion people, 38 percent of the world's population, still lacked access to safe water. UNICEF announced a range of programs to teach sanitation practices and improve access to safe water. UNICEF's *State of the World's Children 2008: Child Survival* called for increased measures to cut child mortality. It reported that 26,000 children under the age of five die every day, and that almost half of all child mortality occurred in sub-Saharan Africa.

In response to a global economic crisis, UNICEF and the Overseas Development Institute held a conference in November 2009 to highlight the impact of the worldwide recession on children. Meanwhile, UNICEF undertook a leading role in disaster relief following tsunamis that affected areas such as Indonesia, the Philippines, and Samoa, and it launched a program with WHO to better prepare countries for the H1N1 influenza through public education and preparedness campaigns. Its report, *State of the World's Children 2009: Maternal and Newborn Health,* noted that approximately 1,500 expectant mothers died every day and called for global action to reduce maternal and neonatal mortality. It also reported that women in developing countries were 300 percent more likely to die during pregnancy or childbirth than women in developed states.

In 2009 UNICEF endeavored to more closely link its efforts with other UN operations. The organization reported that in 2009, 85 percent of its missions were aligned with the UN Development Assistance Framework and the Millennium Development Goals. Also in 2009, UNICEF created a liaison office with the AU. Among UNICEF's more notable accomplishments was a polio vaccination effort in Afghanistan, India, Nigeria, and Pakistan. In all, UNICEF purchased and distributed more than 3 billion vaccines, ranging from polio to measles to influenza. UNICEF's rehabilitation and reintegration for children in armed conflict was able to remove 12,600 children in nine countries from armed groups. Contributions to UNICEF declined by about 2 percent in 2009, and the organization's budget for the year was $3.3 billion. On September 6 James Elder, UNICEF spokesperson in Sri Lanka was expelled from the country over comments that were critical of the government's treatment of Tamil refugees.

In May 2010 Anthony Lake of the United States became the new executive director of UNICEF. In response to a cholera outbreak in Haiti UNICEF initiated a two-fold program to educate the population about prevention and to provide additional medical supplies to local hospitals and clinics. Shortage of funds hampered UNICEF's response to the natural and human-made disasters of 2010 and 2011. The organization remained active in Haiti and also operated in Pakistan, where monsoon floods both in 2010 and 2011 caused widespread devastation.

In 2012, in response to the ongoing conflict in Syria (see entry on Syria), UNICEF increased efforts to provide aid to families and children fleeing to neighboring states such as Jordan. In July 2012 UNICEF reported that 8 million people remained at risk of malnutrition in Somalia, Ethiopia, and Kenya because of drought. Through the summer, UNICEF coordinated the disbursement of $405 million in humanitarian aid to the region. In August UNICEF announced that a joint program with the Angolan government had resulted in a year without any new polio cases in that country. In September a joint UNICEF-WHO report found that the child mortality that been dramatically reduced since the 1990s. In 2011 an estimated 6.9 million children died before the age of five, compared with 12 million in 1990. Developing countries which received significant foreign aid to support immunization and health programs had the most significant decreases in childhood mortality.

In 2013 UNICEF's executive board approved a budget of $2.1 billion for 2014–2017 to support a strategic plan that emphasized "linking resources to results" by establishing clear goals and objectives for projects and increasing oversight of programs. In a March report, "Syria's Children: A Lost Generation?," UNICEF highlighted the extreme danger facing Syrian children as a result of the ongoing civil war. UNICEF programs in Syria vaccinated more than 1.3 million children, and provided regular access to healthcare for 421,700 women and children. However, the conflict has affected more than 2 million children, including 500,000 who were refugees in 2013. Estimates were that the number of children refugees in the Syrian conflict doubled in 2014.

Following the March 2014 Ebola outbreak in West Africa, UNICEF launched a concerted drive to combat the disease, including providing 900 metric tons of supplies, training health care workers and mental health professionals, and launching informational campaigns in the regions. Lake was reappointed UNICEF executive director in May 2014. In an October report UNICEF noted that polio had been reduced by 99 percent since 1988 and that the organization had achieved a goal of annually vaccinating approximately 500 million children. However, UNICEF noted continuing resistance to vaccination programs in countries such as Pakistan.

For 2015 UNICEF's expenditures were $5.1 billion, including its regular budget and emergency appeals for aid. The majority of funding, $4.8 billion, went to programing, while $312 million was spent on management of the organization. Health programs were the most significant expenditures, totaling $1.3 billion, followed by education with $1 billion. In response to the refugee crisis in Europe, UNICEF provided €2 million to provide blankets, warm clothing, and footwear to migrant children in 2015. To support the UN's Sustainable Development Goals, UNICEF created a child-appropriate lesson plan that was used in 160 countries by 500 million children.

UNICEF estimated that in 2015–2016, 250 million children were affected by war and conflict. During that period, the organization was involved in 310 humanitarian relief operations in 102 countries.

UNITED NATIONS CONFERENCE ON TRADE AND DEVELOPMENT

(UNCTAD)

Established: By General Assembly resolution of December 30, 1964.

Purpose: To promote international trade with a view to accelerating the economic growth of less developed countries, to formulate and implement policies related to trade and development, to review and facilitate the coordination of various institutions within the United Nations system in regard to international trade and development, to initiate action for the negotiation and adoption of multilateral legal instruments in the field of trade, and to harmonize trade and related development policies of governments and regional economic groups.

Headquarters: Geneva, Switzerland.

Principal Organs: Conference; Trade and Development Board (154 members); Commission on Trade in Goods and Services, and Commodities; Commission on Investment, Technology, and Related Financial Issues; Commission on Enterprise, Business Facilitation, and Development; Secretariat.

Website: www.unctad.org.

Secretary-General: Mukhisa Kituyi (Kenya).

Membership (194): All UN members, plus Holy See (Vatican City State). A number of intergovernmental and nongovernmental organizations have observer status.

Recent activities. UNCTAD's quadrennial conference of governmental, intergovernmental, and nongovernmental representatives is considered the world's most comprehensive forum on North-South economic issues. Over the years it has addressed many of the economic and developmental difficulties faced by the developing world and the least developed countries (LDCs), although not always successfully. (For information on UNCTAD's activities prior to 2007, see the 2013 *Handbook*.)

UNCTAD's 2007 budget was $50 million, with an additional $25 million available for technical aid to individual countries. In an effort to standardize the manner in which information and communication technology statistics were reported by governments, UNCTAD issued the *Manual for the Production of Statistics on the Information Economy* in February. The publication was designed to serve as the basis for UN training courses on information technology. UNCTAD reported in its 2007 annual trade and development index, which combines trade with economic and social standards, that the United States led developed countries for a second year in a row. The United States was followed by Germany and Denmark, while Singapore led developing countries, with South Korea in second place and China in third. In October UNCTAD commenced an EU-funded program to increase Angola's international trade through training in sustainable development and intergovernmental cooperation in economic policy.

UNCTAD XII was held in April 2008 in Accra, Ghana, and resulted in the Accra Accords. Through the accords, UNCTAD pledged to assist developing countries narrow the gaps among nations in economic development, with a special focus on small island developing nations. UNCTAD also committed itself to developing methods to reduce rising food and commodity prices that disproportionately affected poorer countries. Finally, the accords noted the range of difficulties developing states faced and called for new development strategies, including increased aid and foreign investment and more technology transfers from developed nations. UNCTAD also launched a new database on global trade that provided governments with comparative statistics on more than 235 products in 130 countries. UNCTAD's annual trade and development index noted that the global financial crisis was estimated to reduce economic growth to 3 percent in 2008, down 1 percent from the year before, but that the major impact would be on developing countries. The report also argued that official development assistance would have to be increased by $50 billion to $60 billion per year for the world to meet the 2015 Millennium Development Goals.

UNCTAD's 2009 trade and development report, *Responding to the Global Crisis, Climate Change Mitigation and Development,* focused on the responses of both developed and developing countries addressing the worldwide economic crisis. The report specifically highlighted the dangers of deregulation of financial markets and called for a range of government reforms. The publication also explored how efforts to mitigate global climate change would affect trade networks and development strategies. Other notable publications during the year were *Development and Globalization: Facts and Figures 2008* and the *UNCTAD Handbook of Statistics 2008.* UNCTAD also launched a new database to provide information on creative goods and services. The new source contains statistics for 130 countries and covers 1996–2006, with plans to update the database as information becomes available. In July Supachai Panitchpakdi of Thailand was reappointed for a second four-year term as UNCTAD's secretary-general.

UNCTAD's 2009 budget was $95 million in 2009, including $35 million in voluntary contributions from states and other organizations, and $60 million from the UN regular budget. During the year, UNCTAD funded, or participated in, 255 programs in 81 countries, including efforts to enhance e-government capabilities and trade capabilities. The UNCTAD study *Economic Development in Africa Report 2009: Strengthening Regional Economic Integration for Africa's Development* analyzed a variety of economic development strategies and recommended new methods to improve integration among African countries in order to make them more competitive in the global economy. UNCTAD also produced a range of studies on climate issues, including the development of biofuels and e-tourism, and the launch of a new annual survey, the *Least Developed Countries Report 2010.* UNCTAD's *World Investment Report 2009* highlighted the decrease in foreign direct investment (FDI) from $1.7 trillion in 2008 to $1.2 trillion, although there was a significant increase in FDI to developing countries, which received 43 percent of the investments in 2009. As the world economic crisis persisted, UNCTAD issued a report in September 2010 that urged investment managers worldwide to behave responsibly. "All institutional investors [should] be encouraged to formally articulate their stance on responsible investment to all stakeholders," it said. At the November 2010 G-20 summit in Seoul, South Korea, UNCTAD was given the task, among others, of developing quantifiable indicators for increased economic value and job creation arising from private sector investment, to develop policy recommendations to further such value addition.

In March 2011 UNCTAD proposed a "new modality of inclusive, cooperative and South-centered global development." In April it chose as the theme of UNCTAD XIII "Development-centered globalization: Towards inclusive and sustainable growth and development" for the conference in April in Doha, Qatar. At the session, members endorsed efforts to mainstream sustainable development as part of overall economic development practices. In May it issued a set of proposed principles for the responsibilities of borrowers and lenders of sovereign debt. In its 2011 *World Investment Report,* UNCTAD reported that FDI for 2010 was $1.24 trillion. This was a rise from the previous year but remained 15 percent lower than 2007. In 2011 UNCTAD approved a budget for 2012–2013 of $143.1 million.

On September 1, 2013, Mukhisa Kituyi of Kenya became the new secretary-general of UNCTAD. In its 2013 *World Investment Report,* UNCTAD found that global FDI continued to decline, falling by 18 percent in 2012. That year, for the first time FDI to developing countries exceeded that to developed states (developing countries accounted for 52 percent of FDI inflows).

UNCTAD's 2014 *World Investment Report* found that FDI rose by 9 percent in 2013 to $1.5 trillion, with developing countries accounting for a record 54 percent of inflows. In addition, developing countries also increased their share of FDI outflows to 39 percent. The report noted that developing states faced an annual gap of $2.5 trillion to support sustainable development and proposed an action plan designed to promote private investment.

In 2015 the *World Investment Report* noted that FDI declined by 16 percent to $1.2 trillion, with the greatest reductions among developed nations, which saw FDI flows decrease by 28 percent. The 2015 report found that FDI increased by 38 percent, rising to $1.8 trillion, the highest level since 2008. The majority of FDI, 55 percent, flowed into developed nations, with the United States achieving growth of almost 400 percent since 2014. FDI in developing nations increased by 9 percent globally.

UNITED NATIONS DEVELOPMENT PROGRAM

(UNDP)

Established: By General Assembly resolution of November 22, 1965, which combined the United Nations Expanded Program of Technical Assistance (UNEPTA) with the United Nations Special Fund (UNSF).

Purpose: To coordinate and administer technical assistance provided through the UN system, in order to assist less developed countries in their efforts to accelerate social and economic development.

Headquarters: New York, United States.

Principal Organs: Executive Board (36 members), Committee of the Whole, Regional Bureaus (Africa, Arab States, Asia and the Pacific, Europe and the Commonwealth of Independent States, Latin America and the Caribbean), Bureau for Resources and Strategic Partnerships, Bureau for Development Policy. Membership on the Executive Board rotates on the following geographical basis: Africa, 8; Asia, 7; Latin America and the Caribbean, 5; Eastern Europe, 4; Western Europe and other, 12.

Related Organs. The following special funds and programs are administered by the UNDP: the UN Capital Development Fund (UNCDF), established in 1960 but administered by the UNDP since 1972; the United Nations Volunteers (UNV), formed in 1971; the Program of Assistance to the Palestinian People (PAPP), authorized by the General Assembly in December 1978; the UN Development Fund for Women (UNIFEM), formerly the Voluntary Fund for the UN Decade for Women, established in 1976 and reconstituted in 1984; the Global Environment Facility (GEF), established in 1991 in conjunction with the UN Environment Program (see the entry on the UNEP) and the World Bank; the Drylands Development Center (DDC), established in 2002 in Nairobi, Kenya, as successor to the Office to Combat Desertification and Drought (UNSO, from the original UN Sudano-Sahelian Office); and the UN Office for Project Services (UNOPS), created in 1994 to assist other UN bodies and member states by providing management and support services for projects. In 2001 the Executive Board closed the UN Revolving Fund for Natural Resources Exploration (UNRFNRE), which had been established in 1974, and the UN Fund for Science and Technology for Development (UNFSTD), which had been set up in 1979, initially as an Interim Fund.

Website: www.undp.org.

Administrator: Helen Clark (New Zealand).

Recent activities. UNDP works in partnership with 177 governments, dozens of intergovernmental agencies, and increasingly with civil society organizations and the private sector to promote "sustainable human development" throughout Africa, Asia, Latin America, the Middle East, and parts of Europe. In its early decades the organization focused its attention on five main areas: (1) surveying and assessing natural resources having industrial, commercial, or export potential; (2) stimulating capital investments; (3) training in a wide range of vocational and professional skills; (4) transferring appropriate technologies and stimulating the growth of local technological capabilities; and (5) aiding economic and social planning. In addition, in the 1980s the General Assembly assigned the UNDP three special mandates: the International Drinking Water Supply and Sanitation Decade (1981–1990), the Women in Development program, and implementation of the new international economic order (NIEO).

In mid-1999 Administrator James G. Speth, one of the highest-ranking UN officials from the United States, retired from his post. (For information prior to 1999, see the 2014 *Handbook.*) His replacement was Mark Malloch Brown of the United Kingdom, who had previously served with the World Bank. Malloch Brown immediately had to confront a loss of confidence in the agency's abilities and a related drop in donor funding. In an effort to reverse the trend, the UNDP introduced a 2000–2003 business plan that significantly restructured the organization's operations, adopted a Multi-Year Funding Framework (MYFF), and cut headquarters staff. Innovations included the establishment of nine subregional resource facilities (SURFs) for Arab states, the Caribbean, Central and Eastern Africa, Europe and the Commonwealth of Independent States countries, Latin America, the Pacific and North and Southeast Asia, Southern Africa, West and South Asia, and Western Africa. Each SURF supports the activities of country offices by making available policy specialists, expert referrals, technical support, and access to a global network of pertinent information. At the same time, the UNDP stepped up efforts to bring civil society organizations, foundations, and the private sector into partnership with donor countries, recipients, and intergovernmental organizations. To facilitate this process the UNDP created a Bureau for Research and Strategic Partnerships. In addition, "thematic trust funds" were established to utilize special donations for the UNDP's program emphases. Other changes included establishment of a Bureau for Crisis Prevention and Recovery as successor to the Emergency Response Division.

The UNDP has been designated as the UN coordinating agency for achieving the Millennium Development Goals (MDGs) arising from the September 2000 Millennium Summit in New York. In addition to the broad goal of developing a global partnership for development, principal targets for 2015 include halving the billion-plus people living on less than $1 a day, guaranteeing completion of primary education by all children, eliminating gender disparities at all educational levels, reducing by two-thirds the mortality rate for children under five, cutting by three-fourths the number of women who die in childbirth, ensuring environmental sustainability, and reversing the spread of HIV/AIDS as well as reducing the incidence of malaria and other major diseases. To assist developing countries in meeting the MDGs, the UNDP launched Capacity 2015 at the World Summit for Sustainable Development, held August 26–September 4, 2002, in Johannesburg, South Africa. With its focus on capacity building, particularly through linking local sustainable development with national and international initiatives, Capacity 2015 expanded on the UNDP's earlier Capacity 21, which advanced the Agenda 21 goals set forth by the June 1992 UN Conference on Environment and Development in Rio de Janeiro, Brazil.

Since 1990 the UNDP has issued an annual *Human Development Report,* containing an index that incorporates data on infant mortality, life expectancy, literacy, education expenditure, and individual purchasing power. Using what has been described as "unusually direct language," various reports have called for a drastic reduction in military spending, the promotion of human rights and gender equality as an integral component of economic development, curtailment of government corruption, and steps to overcome a growing global income disparity. (For information prior to 2007, see the 2013 *Handbook.*)

In October 2007 the UNDP agreed to oversee the disbursement of $150 million in loans from the Japan Bank for International Cooperation to the Iraqi government to aid in reconstruction of electricity networks. The funds were the first disbursement in a $3.5 billion pledge made by Japan in 2005. The agreement was touted by the UNDP as a model for future aid arrangements. The following month, the UNDP and the Mohammed bin Rashid Al Maktoum Foundation, the largest private Arab charity, launched a $20 million program to promote education in the Middle East and Persian Gulf. Progress would be measured by an annual UNDP report, the *Arab Knowledge Report.*

The 2008 *Human Development Report—Fighting Climate Change: Human Solidarity in a Divided World* analyzes the nexus of development and climate change and provides recommendations for countries on how to pursue economic growth in a sustainable manner. The report also includes various visual and interactive materials on carbon emissions in an effort to make the document more accessible to a broader audience. In September the UNDP sponsored a week-long series of meetings on the Millennium Development Goals to support the meeting on these goals convened by the secretary-general for heads of state. The UNDP brought together business leaders, private groups, and government officials to discuss progress and to devise new strategies to achieve the UN's objectives. Norway, Spain, and the United Kingdom subsequently pledged $275 million in additional funding to help meet the Millennium Development Goals.

On March 31, 2009, the UN General Assembly unanimously elected former New Zealand prime minister Helen Clark as the new administrator for UNDP. For the 2008–2009 biennium the UNDP projected its budget to be $10.7 billion, of which $8.67 billion would be spent on programs and activities, with the remainder devoted to operational and support costs. The 2009 *Annual Report: Living Up to Commitments* highlighted the need for governments, nongovernmental organizations, and private volunteer groups to continue to support programs to aid the needy and disadvantaged during the international recession. The UNDP's 2009 human development index ranked Norway, Iceland, and Australia first, second, and third, respectively, in human development.

The January 2010 earthquake in Haiti destroyed the UNDP office in that country, but the organization was designated as the lead UN agency in the crisis and quickly launched a massive aid program that included the creation of 95,700 temporary jobs. UNDP published the 20th anniversary edition of its *Human Development Report* in 2010. Titled *The Real Wealth of Nations: Pathways to Human Development,* the study provided a historical overview of development issues and introduced new methods to calculate the UNDP's human development, besides the traditional human development index. For instance, the inequality index accounted for dramatic inequities among societies. Under this measure, states with widespread inequality fell by an average of 22 percent in the standings. The human development index ranked Norway first and Zimbabwe last among 169 countries. In July the UNDP main office in Colombo, Sri Lanka, was closed following protests against the UN. The demonstrators demanded an end to a UN panel investigating human rights abuses in Sri Lanka.

In December 2010 UNDP delivered ballots to Juba, Sudan, for the referendum on southern Sudan's proposed secession from the Khartoum-governed country. In February 2011 it announced a series of new measures to fight fraud and misuse of funds intended for fighting pandemic diseases in developing countries. In May its Community of Practice on Electoral Assistance for the Arab Region met in Cairo, Egypt, to offer assistance with the post-Hosni Mubarak elections. Through 2011 UNDP provided assistance to more than 100 countries in anticorruption programs, while more than 120 nations received aid in democratic governance initiatives.

UNDP's annual human development report, *Sustainability and Equity: A Better Future for All,* called for efforts to combine sustainability and equity programs. In its annual human development index of 187 countries for 2011, Norway retained the top spot, while the United States fell from fourth to twenty-third and the Democratic Republic of the Congo ranked last.

The 2013 UNDP human development report, *The Rise of the South: Human Progress in a Diverse World* highlighted the growing economic progress of developing countries. The publication found that more than 500 million people had risen out of poverty as the result of sustained economic growth in 40 developing countries. The report also estimated that by 2030 approximately 80 percent of the world's "middle class" would reside in developing states. In 2013 the UN Capital Development Fund, overseen by the UNDP, provided ongoing funding for microfinance programs in 48 countries and supported more than 7,300 volunteers in the UN Volunteers initiative promoted "peace and development" in more than 60 countries. In 2013 the organization also helped create 6.5 million jobs and implement new social protection measures for 15 million people.

In 2014 UNDP promulgated a new strategic plan for 2014–2017 entitled *Changing With the World* in which it identified three priorities: sustainable development pathways, inclusive and effective democratic government, and resilience building. In its 2014 human development report *Sustaining Human Progress: Reducing Vulnerabilities and Building Resilience*, UNDP found that conditions continued to improve with its human development index (HDI), rising from 0.7 in 2013 to 0.702 in 2013. In addition, in 16 countries the HDI values of women were equal or superior to those of men. However, more than 15 percent of the world's population remained vulnerable to poverty, and there were steep declines in HDI values for countries in conflict, including the Central African Republic, Libya, and Syria.

The UNDP reported that in 2015 its programs were active in 170 countries. That year the UNDP provided legal aid to 2.1 million people in 33 countries and helped draft more than 1,000 disaster mitigation plans in 51 nations. The 2015 human development report, *Work for Human Development*, found that economic inequality remained one of the most significant barriers to human development. The report noted that 795 million people in 2015 suffered from chronic hunger, while 660 million people did not have access to potable water and almost 1 billion did not have access to proper sanitation. Across the globe 780 million people were illiterate, while 160 million more were functionally illiterate. Approximately 830 million people lived on less than $2 per day.

UNITED NATIONS ENVIRONMENT PROGRAM

(UNEP)

Established: By General Assembly resolution of December 15, 1972, as the outgrowth of a United Nations Conference on the Human Environment held June 6–16, 1972, in Stockholm, Sweden.

Purpose: To facilitate international cooperation in all matters affecting the human environment; to ensure that environmental problems of wide international significance receive appropriate governmental consideration; and to promote the acquisition, assessment, and exchange of environmental knowledge.

Principal Organs: United Nations Environmental Assembly (193 members), Committee of Permanent Representatives, High-Level Committee of Ministers and Officials, Secretariat.

Website: www.unep.org.

Headquarters: Nairobi, Kenya.

Executive Director: Erik Solheim (Norway).

Recent activities. In addition to distributing both technical and general information, notably through its "state of the environment" reports, UNEP acts as a catalyst within the UN system on environmental matters. Recent priorities have included climate change (particularly global warming), freshwater resources, deforestation and desertification, protection of wildlife and flora, handling of hazardous wastes and toxic chemicals, preservation of oceans and coastal areas, the effect of environmental degradation on human health, and biotechnology. UNEP also supports a broad range of public education programs designed to combat the mismanagement of natural resources and to build environmental considerations into development planning. Regional offices are located in Bangkok, Thailand; Geneva, Switzerland; Manama, Bahrain; Mexico City, Mexico; Nairobi, Kenya; and Washington, D.C., United States.

UNEP has been at the forefront of efforts to negotiate international agreements on environmental issues and has provided an institutional framework for administering various conventions. The Ozone Secretariat, which services the 1985 Vienna Convention for the Protection of the Ozone Layer, is headquartered in Nairobi, while the allied Multilateral Fund Secretariat for the Implementation of the (1987) Montreal Protocol on Substances That Deplete the Ozone Layer is based in Montreal. Other secretariats are responsible for administering the 1973 Convention on International Trade in Endangered Species of Wild Fauna and Flora (CITES); the 1979 Bonn Convention on the Conservation of Migratory Species of Wild Animals; the 1989 Basel Convention on the Control of Transboundary Movements of Hazardous Wastes and Their Disposal; the 1992 UN Framework Convention on Climate Change, which the UNEP drafted in conjunction with the World Meteorological Organization (WMO); the Convention on Biological Diversity, which came into force in December 1993; the Convention to Combat Desertification in Countries Experiencing Serious Drought and/or Desertification, Especially in Africa, adopted in June 1994; the Regional Seas program, including the Global Program of Action for the Protection of the Marine Environment from Land-Based Activities, adopted in November 1995; the Rotterdam Convention on the Prior Informed Consent (PIC) Procedure for Certain Hazardous Chemicals and Pesticides in International Trade, adopted in September 1998; and the Stockholm Convention on Persistent Organic Pollutants, which entered into effect in May 2004.

UNEP provides the secretariat for the Scientific and Technical Advisory Panel (STAP) of the Global Environment Facility (GEF), which UNEP administers in conjunction with the UNDP and the World Bank. It also maintains a Global Resource Information Database (GRID), a Global Environment Information Exchange Network (Infoterra), and an International Register of Potentially Toxic Chemicals. In 1993 it launched an International Environmental Technology Center in

Osaka, Japan. In partnership with the UN Office for the Coordination of Humanitarian Affairs (OCHA), it maintains a Joint UNEP/OCHA Environment Unit to respond to environmental emergencies. In 2000 the previously independent World Conservation Monitoring Center, which had been organized in 1988 with UNEP support, was reorganized as a UNEP "collaborating center" in Cambridge, England. Other recent partnerships include the UNEP Risø Center on Energy, Climate, and Sustainable Development (URC) in Roskilde, Denmark, and the UNEP Collaborating Center on Water and the Environment (UCC Water) in Hørsholm, Denmark. In 2001 the UNEP Post-Conflict Assessment Unit was established in Geneva on the strength of work performed in the Balkans (primarily Kosovo) since 1999. In 2003 a secretariat for the UNs multiagency Environmental Management Group became fully operational, also in Geneva.

A highlight of UNEP activities during the 1990s was the UN Conference on Environment and Development (UNCED, also informally referred to as the Earth Summit), held June 3–14, 1992, in Rio de Janeiro, Brazil. The conference was viewed as a "mixed success" by most environmentalists, although the sheer number of prominent attendees—at the time, the largest-ever gathering of world leaders—highlighted the extent to which environmental issues had risen on the world's political agenda. Formal action taken at UNCED included issuance of the Rio Declaration, a nonbinding statement of broad principles for environmentally sound development, and the signing (by 153 nations) of the legally binding Biological Diversity Convention and the Framework Convention on Climate Change. The United States, however, refused to sign the former, and the latter was approved only after specific targets for reducing carbon dioxide emissions had been deleted at Washington's insistence.

By consensus, the summit also endorsed a statement on Forest Principles, designed to reduce deforestation; however, resistance from timber-exporting nations precluded its adoption as a binding convention. In addition, UNCED issued an 800-page document titled *Agenda 21,* which outlined plans for a global environmental cleanup and proposed measures to assure that third world nations pursue development policies compatible with environmental protection. *Agenda 21* also called for enhancement of UNEP's role in the areas of environmental monitoring, research, education, and the creation of international environmental law. It endorsed the creation of a new UN Commission on Sustainable Development to assess compliance with the summit conventions and proposed a doubling of GEF resources to help developing nations meet environmental targets. (For UNEP activities between 1992 and 2001, see the 2010 *Handbook.*)

Meeting under UNEP auspices December 4–11, 2000, in Johannesburg, South Africa, delegates from 122 countries agreed to ban 12 toxic chemicals known as persistent organic pollutants (POPs). POPs break down slowly, travel easily, are readily absorbed by animals, and have been linked to birth defects and other abnormalities in humans. The targeted "dirty dozen" included dioxins, polychlorinated biphenyls (PCBs), and various pesticides, although 25 developing countries would be permitted to continue use of DDT in their fight against malaria. The new convention was signed in May 2001 in Stockholm, Sweden, and entered into force in May 2004, three months after deposit of a 50th ratification.

From October 29–November 10, 2001, representatives from 164 countries met in Marrakesh, Morocco, to complete the legal text for the Kyoto Protocol. Because protocol approval requires the ratification of countries accounting for at least 55 percent of global greenhouse gas emissions, the Kyoto standards suffered a potentially fatal blow in September 2003 when Russia, during a World Conference on Climate Change in Moscow, indicated that it would not commit to ratification. Without support by either the United States or Russia, the 55 percent goal could not be achieved.

During the 2001 Marrakesh meeting, UNEP released a report warning that global warming could reduce the output of rice, maize, and wheat by one-third during the next half-century. Earlier in the year, UNEP's second *Global Environment Outlook* report had focused on problems related to the world's supply of fresh water, including pollution and scarcity, and emphasized the need to embrace environmental considerations in economic planning, particularly given the accelerating pace of globalization. The report also noted that some 3 million people die annually from diarrhea attributable to contaminated water, that each year polluted water contributes to the deaths of millions of children under five years of age, and that poor management of water systems is a significant factor in the spread of malaria and other insect-borne diseases. The UNEP also reported in 2001 significantly greater loss of coral reefs and forests than had previously been estimated. The third *Global Environment Outlook* cautioned that as of 2002 half of all rivers were polluted or seriously depleted and that by 2032 over half of the world's population could be living in "water-stressed" areas.

With the 1999 General Assembly session having endorsed creation of an annual, high-level environmental gathering, the UNEP responded by converting what had been biennial Governing Council sessions into annual meetings of the Governing Council/Global Ministerial Environment Forum (GMEF), which met for the first time May 29–31, 2000, in Malmö, Sweden. (In odd-numbered years the Governing Council/GMEF convenes in regular session; meetings in alternate years are designated as special sessions.) At the Seventh Special Session of the Governing Council/GMEF, held February 13–15, 2002, the board adopted a report on International Environmental Governance that called for an expanded UNEP role in coordinating environmental aspects of sustainable development and in assisting countries with capacity building and training. The session, held in Cartagena, Colombia, also devoted attention to preparations for the August 26–September 4 World Summit on Sustainable Development, held in Johannesburg.

The 22nd Regular Session of the Governing Council/GMEF met at UNEP headquarters on February 3–7, 2003. One focus of attention was mercury pollution, although the U.S. George W. Bush administration effectively blocked efforts to begin drafting a global protocol that would define mandatory restrictions.

The Eighth Special Session of the Governing Council/GMEF met March 29–31, 2004, in Jeju, South Korea, where issues related to water and sanitation were preeminent. A total of 158 countries sent representatives to the meeting, which considered such topics as water shortages, overfishing, and the recent increase in the number and severity of dust storms in Northeast Asia. Collaterally, UNEP released the *Global Environment Year Book 2003,* which called attention to the growing problem of "dead zones"—oxygen-depleted ocean areas caused by the runoff from nitrogen fertilizers, sewage, and industrial pollution. Also coming under scrutiny was solid waste and sewage disposal for small island countries, which often have neither the space nor the money for proper disposal. According to UNEP, some 90–98 percent of sewage from Pacific and Caribbean islands enters coastal waters untreated. Perhaps the most controversial proposal discussed at the March session involved conducting research on how environmental problems and pressures contribute to international conflict.

On November 18, 2004, reversing its previous stance, Russia completed formal ratification of the Kyoto Protocol, which went into effect on February 16, 2005. Meanwhile, in 2012, Canada became the first country to withdraw from the Kyoto Protocol. As of October 2013, a total of 191 countries and dependent territories plus the EU had ratified the protocol, the notable exception, apart from the United States, being Australia.

In March 2005 UNEP published the *Millennium Ecosystem Assessment,* the result of work by 1,300 authors and scientists from 95 countries. The report focused on the consequences, both positive and negative, of changes in ecosystems in preceding decades and on the requirements for preventing further degradation. While acknowledging the human benefits in terms of economic development and general well-being that have accrued from some ecosystem changes, the report found that 60 percent of the areas examined had been substantially degraded or overused—a rate of deterioration that could result in dire consequences for future generations if sustained. Suggested corrective actions included education, changes in consumption patterns, technological advances, and factoring into production costs environmental considerations. Follow-up reports were scheduled to be released every five years.

In 2006 UNEP released *Marine and Coastal Ecosystems & Human Well-being: Synthesis,* which examined the loss of coastal marine resources and tied those degradations to human activities, such as overfishing, habitat loss, climate change, pollution, and poor land use. For example, the report found that 75 percent of the fish stocks studied were in need of management programs to reverse declines and stabilize populations. UNEP's budget for the year was $105 million.

UNEP proclaimed 2007 the Year of the Dolphin and launched a global effort to increase awareness of the threats facing different species. The Intergovernmental Panel on Climate Change (IPCC) issued its fourth assessment report on climate change in February 2007. The study was composed of four main reports and found that "global warming was unequivocal" and caused mainly by human activities and the production of greenhouse gases. It warned that temperatures would continue to rise for centuries even if current production of pollutants was curtailed.

In February 2007 at a conference in Paris, French president Jacques Chirac called for UNEP to be absorbed into a new, strengthened body to be titled the United Nations Environment Organization (UNEO). Chirac's proposal was endorsed by 46 countries, but opposed by the United States, Russia, and China. No action was taken on the plan. In October UNEP published the *Global Environment Outlook: Environment for Development* (GEO-4). GEO-4 was described as the most comprehensive review of the changes in the global ecosystem since 1987 and was the work of more than 300 scientists. It identified climate change, loss of biodiversity, and degradation of the world's oceans as the main environmental threats facing the world. UNEP also announced that it had met its goal of hiring women for half of its professional staff in 2007.

For its work on climate change, the IPCC was awarded the 2007 Nobel Peace Prize, along with former U.S. vice president Albert Gore Jr., a leading advocate for action against global warming. In November UNEP chartered the International Panel for Sustainable Resource Management. The new body was charged with examining the impact of biofuels and recycling on the environment.

In 2008 UNEP announced that it had fallen short of its 2007 target of $72 million in contributions to the Environment Fund by $2.8 million. Building on GEO-4, UNEP developed a series of intermediate objectives, highlighted in the 2008 publication *UNEP Medium-Term Strategy 2010–2013: Environment for Development.* The report named six areas of focus: "climate change; disasters and conflicts; ecosystem management; environmental governance; harmful substances and hazardous waste; and resource efficiency—sustainable consumption and production." The publication also set measurable goals for each area and emphasized the transition of UNEP into a results-oriented organization with a goal of becoming the world's foremost environmental body. UNEP created a new strategic partnership with the Democratic Republic of the Congo to assist the country in developing its resources in an environmentally friendly manner. The arrangement was seen as a prototype for future relationships with individual states. UNEP also created the Poverty and Environment Facility to oversee the disbursement of aid under the joint UNEP-UNDP Poverty and Environment Initiative.

UNEP's staff increased to 597 in 2009, mainly in response to the need to oversee and coordinate new environmental programs across the globe. UNEP budgeted $171 million in expenditures for the Environment Fund that year. Through 2009, UNEP prepared for the Seal the Deal summit in Copenhagen in December 2009. The meeting was designed to bring together heads of state and other leaders to finalize strategies to address climate change and develop a successor agreement to the Kyoto Protocols. Meanwhile, UNEP's *Global Trends in Sustainable Energy Investment 2009* was produced in an effort to influence the Copenhagen meeting by providing information on best energy practices and encouraging the use of renewable resources. The Copenhagen Summit, December 7–16, 2009, was widely regarded as a failure since delegates were unable to agree on specific country commitments to reduce greenhouse emissions. Instead, delegates "noted" the nonbinding Copenhagen Accord, drafted by the United States, Brazil, China, India, and South Africa, through which countries could offer voluntary reductions. The agreement also pledged that developed states would provide up to $100 billion to developing nations to mitigate the impact of climate change.

In April 2010 Achim Steiner of Germany was reelected UNEP director for a second four-year term. Published in 2010, UNEP's 2009 annual report, *Seizing the Green Opportunity,* highlighted the growth in green technologies and industries and called for new investments in these sectors. More than 170 countries participated in UNEP's Billion Tree Campaign, which resulted in the planting of more than 7.4 billion trees worldwide. Parties to the 1992 UN Framework Convention on Climate Change met in Bonn, Germany, on May 31–June 11 to craft a new agreement to limit global warming. The new accord went further than relying on the pledges from the Copenhagen Summit and called on developed states to reduce greenhouse gas emissions by 25–40 percent by 2020, with further cuts by 2050.

The 2010 annual report, *A Year in Review*, noted that the *Global Environmental Outlook* was being reworked to emphasize solutions. It mentioned significant progress in setting and coordinating the UN's environmental agenda and noted the completion of an internal reform program. This program was to improve the synergy between different UNEP operations, as well as increasingly incorporating gender concerns into the agency's work.

For 2010–2011 UNEP's budget was $448 million. UNEP's 2011 annual report noted that 15 of 21 reforms recommended in 2008 had been completed. Meanwhile, UNEP had dispersed more than $200 million to support clean energy projects. The report also found that the elimination of lead in gasoline had saved the world $2.4 trillion in health costs and prevented 1.2 million premature deaths. In November 2012 UNEP published *Emissions Gap Report 2012*, which warned that greenhouse gas emissions into the atmosphere would rise to 58 billion gigatons annually by 2020, far above the 44 billion gigaton maximum to avert a 2 degree Celsius temperature rise.

In 2013 the General Assembly approved a UNEP budget for 2014–2015 of $631 million, a 2.6 percent increase. The budget included plans to reduce staffing costs by 30 percent and reallocate funding to operations. In January 2013 under the auspices of UNEP, negotiations on a treaty to limit mercury in manufacturing and mining were finalized. In March the General Assembly approved reforms whereby the 58-member Governing Council was succeeded by the UN Environmental Assembly (UNEA) with universal membership. The Minmata Convention on Mercury was presented for adoption at a conference in October.

The 19th UN Climate Change Conference (Conference of the Parties [COP]) was held in Warsaw in November 2013, along with the 9th meeting of the parties to the Kyoto Protocol. Participants agreed to begin individual efforts to cut greenhouse emissions and to establish the Warsaw Mechanism whereby donors would provide funds to states where natural disasters were exacerbated by climate change. Norway, the United Kingdom, and the United States also pledged funds for a program to reduce tropical deforestation. For 2013 UNEP reported that Kenya, Germany, and the United States, in that order, led among the 15 "fastest paying donors" to the organization, while the Netherlands, Germany, and the United States were the top contributors.

Steiner's term was extended for an additional two-year period in March 2014. UNEP convened the first meeting of the UNEA in June in Nairobi. Oyun Sanjaasuren of Mongolia was elected president of the UNEA's first session. At the UNEP summit on Climate Change in September in New York, nations pledged to begin work to restore more than 30 million hectares of forest with an eventual goal or restoring 150 million hectares by 2020.

In June 2016 Erik Solheim of Norway succeeded Steiner as executive director of UNEP. In November UNEP reported that nations needed to enact emission reductions of 25 percent or more to avert catastrophic temperature increases. Even with the 2016 Paris Agreement to curb emissions, emissions would be 12 to 14 gigatons above the level needed to keep temperature increases to just 2 degrees Celsius.

UNITED NATIONS INSTITUTE FOR TRAINING AND RESEARCH

(UNITAR)

Established: By General Assembly resolution of December 11, 1963. The inaugural meeting of the Board of Trustees was held March 24, 1965, and the institute became operational the following year.

Purpose: "To enhance the effectiveness of the United Nations through training and research in the maintenance of peace and security and in the promotion of economic and social development."

Headquarters: Geneva, Switzerland.

Principal Organ: Board of Trustees (up to 30 members appointed by the UN secretary-general), of whom one or more may be officials of the UN Secretariat and the others governmental representatives. The UN secretary-general, the president of the General Assembly, the president of the Economic and Social Council, and the institute's executive director are ex-officio members.

Website: www.unitar.org.

Executive Director: Nikhil Seth (India).

Recent activities. UNITAR provides practical assistance to the UN system, with particular emphasis on the problems of less developed countries. The institute is also concerned with the professional enrichment of national officials and diplomats dealing with UN-related issues and provides training for officials within the UN system. Seminars, courses, and symposia have dealt with multilateral diplomacy, economic development, international law, and UN documentation.

In April 1993 the General Assembly approved a resolution providing for the shift of UNITAR's headquarters from New York City, New York, in the United States, to Geneva, Switzerland, and directed that the institute's future activities would have to be financed completely by voluntary contributions or special purpose grants. New York and Hiroshima, Japan, continue to host UNITAR offices.

In March 2007 Carlos Lopes of Guinea-Bissau was appointed UNITAR's executive director. (For information on UNITAR prior to 2007, see the 2013 and 2014 *Handbooks.*) Lopes announced in November that UNITAR was undergoing a major transition to focus its efforts on standardizing methodologies between governments as the main goal of its training programs. The new director also noted that UNITAR had developed relationships with Columbia University, New York, United States; the University of Cape Town, Cape Town, South Africa; and the Ecole Libre des Sciences Politiques (Sciences Po), Paris, France, and that these academic partners would certify future training and educational initiatives.

As of 2008 the number of UNITAR staff members engaged in training and capacity-building programs had increased to about 80. The majority were engaged in the following areas: decentralized cooperation (local action) for development, chemicals and waste management, climate change, environmental law, foreign economic relations, HIV/AIDS, international affairs management, international migration policy, legal aspects of debt and financial management, needs of women and children in conflict and postconflict zones, peacekeeping operations instruction, peacemaking and preventive diplomacy, and technology and information systems for sustainable development. In April UN secretary-general Ban initiated a new UNITAR lecture series in Geneva on global challenges. The series was designed to engage the public and increase awareness of the major issues facing the UN and the global community. UNITAR announced that it would reconfigure its peacekeeping training to better address challenges and to make better use of new training technologies, including Web-based programs.

UNITAR reinitiated its global migration program in 2009 and became the chair of the interagency body, the Global Migration Group. UNITAR saw a 57 percent increase in its biennial operating budget in 2009, mainly due to a rise in funding from donor states. Through the year, UNITAR increased the activities of the UN Operational Satellite Applications Program (UNOSAT). The program used satellite imagery to produce maps and data to support UN activities and research. UNOSAT launched discussions with the European Space Agency over cooperative ventures and was involved in disaster mapping of 34 incidents in 2009, including the Samoan tsunami and flooding in the Philippines and Vietnam. UNOSAT's increased activities were made possible by a rise in funding from Denmark, Norway, and Sweden. UNOSAT also became engaged in monitoring pirate activity around the Horn of Africa and was able to map a decline in the success rate of attempted hijackings from 40 percent in 2008 to 23 percent in 2009 as a result of increased international naval patrols in the region. A 2009 report concluded that Africa was the main beneficiary of UNITAR's programs, receiving 40.3 percent of the organization's funding, followed by Asia and the Pacific, 21.4 percent, and Latin America and the Caribbean, 19.9 percent. UNOSAT continued to monitor natural disasters, including the 2010 flooding in Thailand and the impact of Cyclone Giri that same year. In November 2010 UNITAR began training at its Nairobi office, designed to make UN peacekeeping missions greener. It noted that UN Field Missions globally account for 56 percent of the total UN greenhouse gas emissions.

In March 2011 UNITAR began publishing satellite maps of Libya and the surrounding countries to track the movements of refugees from the Libyan civil war. UNOSAT's fourth monitoring report on internal refugees in Somalia revealed that in 2012 there was a 45 percent increase in the number of displaced persons or sites from the previous year. A similar analysis of Syrian refugee sites in Turkey also indicated an increase. In September 2012 Sally Fegan-Wyles of Ireland became interim executive director of UNITAR. UNITAR's budget for the 2012–2013 period was $44.8 million. That year UNITAR completed more than 400 training projects that included 23,000 participants.

UNOSAT was praised for its ability to provide rapid mapping of disaster incidents in September 2013 at a forum sponsored by the UN Office for the coordination of Humanitarian Affairs (OCHA). UNOSAT maps on average 35–40 emergencies per year and 35 percent of its mapping projects support OCHA operations. In October UNOSAT began providing regular data to the UN Operations and Crisis Center.

Beginning in the summer of 2014, UNOSAT began providing satellite mapping to support the World Health Organization (WHO)'s efforts to combat the spread of Ebola in western Africa. UNITAR's 2014–2015 budget was $47 million.

In October 2015 Nikhil Seth of India was appointed the executive director of the UNITAR. UNITAR's 2016–2017 budget was $47.1 million for a staff of approximately 100 in 16 training centers around the world and 500 training programs.

UNITED NATIONS OFFICE OF HIGH COMMISSIONER FOR REFUGEES

(UNHCR)

Established: By General Assembly resolution of December 3, 1949, with operations commencing January 1, 1951, for a three-year period; five-year extensions subsequently approved through December 31, 2008.

Purpose: To provide protection, emergency relief, and resettlement assistance to refugees, and to promote permanent solutions to refugee problems.

Headquarters: Geneva, Switzerland.

Principal Organs: Executive Committee, Standing Committee.

Website: www.unhcr.org.

High Commissioner: Filippo Grandi (Italy).

Membership of Executive Committee (94): Afghanistan, Algeria, Argentina, Australia, Austria, Azerbaijan, Bangladesh, Belarus, Belgium, Benin, Brazil, Bulgaria, Cameroon, Canada, Chile, China, Colombia, Congo, Costa Rica, Côte d'Ivoire, Croatia, Cyprus, Democratic Republic of the Congo, Denmark, Djibouti, Ecuador, Egypt, Estonia, Ethiopia, Finland, France, Germany, Ghana, Greece, Guinea, Holy See (Vatican City State), Hungary, India, Iran, Ireland, Israel, Italy, Japan, Jordan, Kenya, Republic of Korea, Latvia, Lebanon, Lesotho, Luxembourg, Macedonia, Madagascar, Mexico, Moldova, Montenegro, Morocco, Mozambique, Namibia, Netherlands, New Zealand, Nicaragua, Nigeria, Norway, Pakistan, Peru, Philippines, Poland, Portugal, Romania, Russia, Rwanda, Senegal, Serbia, Slovakia, Slovenia, Somalia, South Africa, Spain, Sudan, Sweden, Switzerland, Tanzania, Thailand, Togo, Tunisia, Turkey, Turkmenistan, Uganda, United Kingdom, United States, Venezuela, Yemen, Zambia. Membership on the Executive Committee is permanent following approval by the Economic and Social Council and the General Assembly.

Recent activities. The UNHCR, financed partly by a limited UN subsidy for administration but primarily by contributions from governments, nongovernmental organizations, and individuals, attempts to ensure the treatment of refugees according to internationally accepted standards. In all, the UNHCR maintains more than 260 offices in 128 countries, with a total staff of 10,700.

The UNHCR promoted the adoption of the UN Convention on the Status of Refugees in 1951 and an additional protocol in 1967 that together provide a widely applicable definition of the term "refugee," establish minimum standards for treatment of refugees, grant favorable legal status to refugees, and accord refugees certain economic and social rights. (As of October 2013 there were 145 parties to the convention, and 146 to the protocol.) In addition, the UNHCR conducts material assistance programs that provide emergency relief (food, medicine) and supplementary aid while work proceeds on the durable solutions of (in order of priority) the voluntary repatriation of refugees, their integration into the country where asylum was first sought, or their resettlement to a third country. Activities are often conducted in cooperation with other UN agencies, national governments, regional bodies, and private relief organizations. (For more information on the activities of the UNHCR prior to 2003, see the 2013 *Handbook.*)

During 2003 the U.S.-led invasion of Iraq did not generate a major refugee exodus, as had been feared, but caused considerable internal displacement. In May 2004 the UNHCR began helping in the "phased return" of some 500,000 Iraqis to their homes. At the same time, the organization was facing renewed difficulties in Sudan's Darfur region, where hostilities in late 2003 led some 120,000 refugees to scatter just across the remote border with Chad.

In 2004 the UNHCR reported that the number of asylum applications in 36 developed countries dropped by 20 percent in 2003 to 471,000, down from 587,000 the previous year and the lowest number in six years. While the UNHCR attributed the improvement to more stable situations in Afghanistan, the Balkans, and Iraq, an additional factor was the rise of intolerance and anti-asylum measures in Europe and elsewhere. However, the UNHCR reported that the number of "people of concern" rose to 19.2 million in 2005 after declining to 17 million in 2004. In 2005 there was a worldwide decrease in the number of refugees, from 9.54 million to 8.39 million. This capped a five-year decrease of 31 percent and brought the overall number of refugees to its lowest level since 1980. Among refugee populations, the largest was some 1.1 million Afghans living in Pakistani camps, although the UNHCR projected that an additional 1.5 million Afghans were probably residing outside camps where there were no UNHCR services. The largest IDP population was 2 million in Colombia. In Iraq, the number of IDPs increased to 1.2 million. Sudan accounted for 840,000 IDPs and 150,000 refugees.

High Commissioner Lubbers resigned in February 2005 after he was accused of sexual harassment by women employees. He was succeeded by former Portuguese prime minister António Guterres, who initiated a series of reforms in budgeting and crisis management.

By January 2007 the UNHCR estimated that there were 32.86 million asylum seekers, refugees, or IDPs worldwide. The largest number was in Asia, 14.91 million, followed by Africa with 9.72 million, and Europe with 3.43 million. The UNHCR announced a partnership with the Clinton Global Initiative in an effort to raise $220 million to provide educational programs for 9 million refugee children. Among the UNHCR's major operations in 2007 were the resettlement of Roma refugees in Hungary, Kosovo, and Montenegro, and the closure of the last major temporary refugee camp in Kosovo. The body also undertook a major initiative to provide supplies for 160,000 refugees in Kenya who were displaced by flooding. In cooperation with the Afghan government, the UNHCR oversaw the return of 200,000 Afghan refugees from Pakistan and undertook major missions to support displaced persons in Somalia and Sudan. In July the UNHCR doubled its aid to $123 million annually to support the estimated 2.2 million externally displaced Iraqis in neighboring states and the 2 million internal refugees. The UNHCR also called on the United States to increase the number of Iraqi asylum seekers admitted from the 8,000 granted refuge in 2006. During 2007 the UNHCR signed an agreement with Morocco to enhance its presence in the country and an accord with Kazakhstan to facilitate operations in that country.

On April 29, 2008, the UN General Assembly voted to increase the membership of the executive committee from 72 to 76 states. In June the UNHCR report *2007 Global Trends: Refugees, Asylum-Seekers, Returnees, Internally Displaced and Stateless Persons* noted that by the end of 2007, the number of IDPs was 51 million, including 26 million displaced by conflict and 25 million displaced as the result of natural disasters. Of the two categories, at least 31.7 million were in the UNHCR's areas of operations, a decline of 3 percent from the previous year. The report also found that 80 percent of refugees remained in the region of their origin and that more than half resided in urban areas. In the publication the UNHCR changed the way it counted refugees and IDPs. Those who had been resettled through host country programs for periods of five to ten years, depending on the country, were no longer classified as refugees. The report found that the number of refugees and IDPs rose for the second consecutive year, after annual declines from 2001–2005.

Between October 2007 and 2008 the UNHCR assisted more than 250,000 Afghans in their return, mainly from Iran and Pakistan. In addition, the UNHCR aided the government of Tanzania in beginning the return of an estimated 110,000 Burundians to their homes and in consolidating Tanzania's 11 refugee camps into 5. The initiative was part of a cooperative program with other UN agencies to provide training and resources so that refugees and IDPs were able to transition back into their local economies. In another example, as part of an effort to return Hutu refugees to Rwanda, the UNHCR launched a construction program to build new housing for the returnees.

The UNHCR's 2009 budget was a record $2 billion. Completed in 2008, UNHCR's global service center in Budapest became the organization's second largest office in 2009, with a staff of 180 (behind only its headquarters in Geneva with 740). The center was created to consolidate a number of smaller regional offices and centralize functions as part of a broader reform effort to reduce costs and increase efficiency. In May the UNHCR responded when fighting between the Taliban and Pakistani government forces created more than 200,000 refugees in northwestern Pakistan. The agency's annual report noted that there were approximately 15.2 million refugees (including 4.7 million in UN-administered camps in the Middle East), which represented an 8 percent reduction from the previous year. The agency also noted that there were about 26 million internally displaced persons, including 14.4 million under the care of the UN. This figure was stable from the previous year but included new displaced populations in Colombia, Pakistan, the Philippines, Somalia, Sri Lanka, and Sudan. Colombia, Iraq, and Sudan remained the countries with the largest numbers of internally displaced persons.

UNHCR's budget in 2010 increased dramatically to a record $3.1 billion. The organization reported that although the total number of refugees decreased, UNHCR provided care to a larger percentage of at-risk populations. At the beginning of 2010, there 10.5 million refugees, of which 4.6 million received some assistance from the UNHCR (not including those under the care of the UNRWA). There were also 14.5 million IDPs under the care of the organization. The UNHCR estimated that there were more than 12 million stateless people around the globe, but noted that countries such as Bangladesh and Sri Lanka had seen the number of stateless persons decline dramatically. The largest number of refugees and IDPs were in Asia, followed by Africa. In April Guterres was reelected the UNHCR high commissioner by the General Assembly. In addition, the UNHCR executive board was increased to 79 members.

The UNHCR's annual report for 2010 stated that 25.2 million were receiving some form of protection. Approximately 12 million were stateless. Pakistan hosted the largest number of refugees, followed by Iran and Syria. Approximately 7.2 million refugees had little prospect of returning home, the highest number since 2001. The agency's 2011 budget was $3.32 billion.

In 2011 UNHCR reported 10.5 million refugees of concern, a minor decrease from the previous year. The number of IDPs rose to 27.5 million, 14.7 million of whom received aid from UNHCR. The largest number of IDPs were in Africa, some 11.1 million. UNHCR's budget continued to increase, rising to $3.6 billion in 2012, and $4.3 billion, the following year.

In 2013 the UNHCR reported another small decrease in the number of refugees of concern, down to 10.4 million. Approximately 50 percent of refugees were in Asia, with Africa accounting for about 28 percent. The number of IDPs again increased, rising to 28.8 million, with 6.5 million newly displaced IDPs. Conflicts in Syria and the Democratic Republic of the Congo (DRC) accounted for roughly half of the new IDPs (2.4 million in Syria and 1 million in the DRC). The UNHCR provided services or care for approximately15.5 million IDPs.

The UNHCR's 2014 operating budget rose to $5.3 billion in response to increasing costs associated with caring for refugees from conflicts in Syria and Iraq. That year, the number of IDPs under the care of the UNHCR rose to 17.6 million. Meanwhile, the UNHCR reported that the total number of refugees of concern increased to 10.5 million, with the largest numbers from Asia and Africa. Also in 2014, the UNHCR's executive committee was increased from 87 to 94 members. On January 3, 2014, Guterres called on EU states to stop transferring asylum seekers to back to Bulgaria under the Dublin procedure, which stipulated that asylum applicants should be returned to the first EU country in which they arrived. Guterres cited overcrowding and a lack of food at Bulgarian detention centers.

By the end of 2015, the UNHCR reported that there were 63.9 million people of concern around the world, including refugees and IDPs. The number of refugees was 16.1 million, with 3.2 million asylum seekers and a staggering 37.5 million IDPs. On January 1, 2016, Filippo Grande (Italy) was elected high commissioner by the General Assembly.

UNITED NATIONS POPULATION FUND

(UNFPA)

Established: By the secretary-general in July 1967 as the Trust Fund for Population Activities; name changed in May 1969 to United Nations Fund for Population Activities (UNFPA), with administration assigned to United Nations Development Program (UNDP); became operational in October 1969; placed under authority of the General Assembly in December 1972; became a subsidiary organ of the assembly in December 1979; name changed to United Nations Population Fund in December 1987, with the UNFPA designation being retained.

Purpose: To enhance the capacity to respond to needs in population and family planning, promote awareness of population problems in both developed and developing countries and possible strategies to deal with them, assist developing countries in dealing with their population problems in the forms and means best suited to their needs, and play a leading role in the UN system in promoting population programs and reproductive health.

Principal Organ: Executive Board (same membership as the UNDP Executive Board).

Website: www.unfpa.org.

Headquarters: New York, United States.

Executive Director: Babatunde Osotimehin (Nigeria).

Recent activities. The UNFPA continues to be the largest source of multilateral population assistance to less developed areas. (For UNFPA activities prior to 2002, see the 2010 *Handbook.*) A major issue for the UNFPA has been hostility from the United States, which has not committed funds to the organization since mid-2002. The George W. Bush administration cited abortion and sterilization policies in China as justification, although a report by its own investigators showed no link between such policies and the UNFPA.

Despite the U.S. failure to contribute funds, in 2005 the UNFPA had a record year in funding, with 172 countries and a range of nongovernmental and private organizations contributing $565 million, compared with $506 million in 2004. Expenditures, including programs in 148 developing countries, were $523 million.

In 2007 UNFPA initiated a joint program with the UN Children's Fund (UNICEF) to reduce female genital mutilation by 40 percent in 16 countries by 2015. The ultimate goal of the program was to end the practice entirely within 20 years through increased education and government action.

In the *State of World Population 2007: Unleashing the Potential of Urban Growth,* UNFPA noted that in 2008, for the first time in history, more than half of the world's population, or 3.3 billion people, lived in urban areas, marking the first time in history that city-dwellers outnumber their rural counterparts. By 2030 a projected 60 percent of the world's population would be urban. The report stated that the benefits of urbanization outweighed the negative consequences, especially in regard to reproductive healthcare and infant mortality rates. Nonetheless, the study also found that the population living in slums in urban areas doubled to 200 million, or 72 percent of the urban population, by 2005 in sub-Saharan Africa, compared with 56 percent of the urban population in South Asia.

In 2008 the UNFPA had programs in 158 countries and offices in 112 nations with 1,031 staff members, 44 percent of whom were women. To increase efficiency, the UNFPA developed and implemented a new strategic plan to guide the organization through 2011. The plan identified three main areas at the core of the UNFPA's mission: "population and development, reproductive health and rights, and gender equality." The agency also carried out a reorganization that established new regional offices in Bangkok, Bratislava, Cairo, Johannesburg, and Panama City, with six additional, new sub-regional offices. The UNFPA also reorganized its technical division and created a new program division to develop and oversee individual projects. The *State of World Population 2008: Reaching Common Ground; Culture, Gender and Human Rights* asserted the universality of human rights and the need to ensure the application of global frameworks to all countries. It presented an overview of strategies to implement culturally sensitive development plans that both promoted human rights and respected local traditions and mores. The UNFPA also launched the Maternal Health Trust Fund to provide assistance to mothers and newborns in 2008. Through 2009, the program was active in 61 countries.

In 2009 the UNFPA had 129 offices and was active in 155 countries with a budget of $783.1 million, of which $469.4 million was provided by donor countries and organizations, an increase of $40 million over the previous year. In October the UNFPA sponsored the fourth international parliamentarians conference on the action program from the 1994 International Conference on Population and Development (ICPD). Legislators from 115 countries attended the summit and reaffirmed commitments to reproductive health and access to medical services. The UNFPA also expanded its family planning programs to include efforts in 72 countries, including the distribution of more than 50 million female condoms in 2009. The UNFPA 2010 annual report highlighted the fact that as the population aged, less developed countries were not well prepared to deal with the consequences. Income increased to $870 million for the year, with much of the increase coming from voluntary contributions. Expenditures amounted to $801.4 million. The agency was deeply involved in Haitian earthquake relief.

In 2011 UNFPA increased its operations to 156 countries and had a record budget of $934 million. In its annual report, UNFPA highlighted the birth of the world's 7th billion person and the implications of population growth on resource use and sustainable development. In its 2011 annual report, the UNFPA highlighted that there were 1.8 billion people in the world from the ages of 10 to 24, the "largest youth cohort in human history." Concurrently, advances in medicine and care mean that there were more people over the age of 60, some 900 million, than ever before.

The UNFPA budget continued to increase, rising to another record, $963.2 million for 2012. *The State of the World Population 2012: By Choice, Not by Chance* highlighted the negative effects of unintended pregnancies and underscored the need for greater access to family planning in developing states. The report found that 222 million women lacked access to family planning, and that there were an estimated 80 million unintended pregnancies in 2012. In July the UNFPA, the United Kingdom, and the Bill and Melinda Gates Foundation held a conference that raised $2.6 billion for family planning.

The State of the World Population 2013: Motherhood in Childhood highlighted the growing problem of adolescent pregnancy. More than 95 percent of births by adolescents occur in developing countries. Meanwhile, 19 percent of all births in developed countries occur to girls under the age of 18. Such early pregnancies have a negative impact on education and economic empowerment. Worldwide, 70,000 adolescents die from complications related to pregnancy or childbirth. The report called for a number of actions to decrease adolescent pregnancy, including increased reproduction education and better maternal health programs.

In 2015 the UNFPA had 111 offices in 89 countries and provided reproductive health education in 73 countries. It provided contraceptives and reproductive health services to 18 million women and provided assistance to 135 countries in developing programs to reduce violence toward women. The UNFPA spent approximately $200 million on family planning, $110 million on maternal health, and $75 million on sexual or reproductive health in 2015.

UNITED NATIONS RELIEF AND WORKS AGENCY FOR PALESTINE REFUGEES IN THE NEAR EAST

(UNRWA)

Established: By General Assembly resolution of December 8, 1949; mandate most recently extended through June 30, 2017.

Purpose: To provide relief, education, and health and social services to Palestinian refugees (i.e., people [and later the descendants of people] who resided in Palestine for a minimum of two years preceding the Arab-Israeli conflict in 1948 and who, as a result of that conflict, lost both their homes and their means of livelihood).

Headquarters: Gaza and Amman, Jordan. (Most of the operations, previously in Vienna, Austria, were moved to Gaza in July 1996. The remainder were relocated to the agency's other longstanding headquarters in Amman.)

Website: www.unrwa.org.

Commissioner General: Pierre Krähenbühl (Switzerland).

Advisory Commission: Comprised of representatives of the governments of Australia, Belgium, Canada, Denmark, Egypt, Finland, France, Germany, Ireland, Italy, Japan, Jordan, Kuwait, Lebanon, Luxembourg, the Netherlands, Norway, Saudi Arabia, Spain, Sweden, Switzerland, Syria, Turkey, the United Kingdom, and the United States. The Palestinian National Authority, the European Union, and the League of Arab States are observers.

Recent activities. As of January 2014 approximately 5.4 million people who met the established definition of Palestinian refugee were registered with the UNRWA, a 3 percent increase over the previous year. About 1.6 million of that number lived in 58 refugee camps, many of which had in effect become permanent towns; the remainder lived in previously established towns and villages in the areas served by UNRWA—Jordan, Lebanon, Syria, the West Bank, and Gaza. The UNRWA's original priority was to provide direct humanitarian relief to refugees uprooted by the fighting that followed the creation of Israel. In the absence of a peaceful settlement to the Palestinian question, the

UNRWA's attention shifted to education (it runs 666 schools attended by approximately 476,323 students) and the provision of public health services (it operates 138 health centers) to a basically self-supporting population. The UNRWA employs some 30,300 people, including 19,600 educators and 4,100 medical personnel.

Some Israelis and members of the U.S. Congress, among others, have accused the UNRWA of allowing refugee camps to be used for terrorist training and activities. A 2006 audit by the U.S. General Accounting Office concluded that no money provided by the United States—the source of some 30 percent of UNRWA funds—could be linked to terrorist activities in the refugee camps. (For information on UNRWA prior to 2007, see the 2013 or 2014 *Handbooks.*)

The UNRWA's 2008 budget was $541.8 million, and the agency's main donors were, in order of contributions, the United States, the European Commission, Sweden, the United Kingdom, Norway, and the Netherlands. The continuing refugee crisis in Gaza and the West Bank led the UNRWA to again request emergency donations. For 2008, the UNRWA sought $263.4 million. However, by October 2008 the agency had received only about 60 percent of that amount. At the same time, the UNRWA's appeal for emergency funding for refugees in Lebanon exceeded its goal of $54.8 million as the organization had secured $57.2 million by October. In June the UNRWA and the UAE Red Crescent launched a major initiative to rebuild and refurbish some of the oldest refugee camps that had 60-year-old facilities. The first phase of the project was the construction of a new health clinic and 140 housing units in the Neirab Camp, the largest of the UNRWA's facilities in Syria. Also in June the UNRWA began reconstruction of the Nahr al-Bared camp in Lebanon. In September the UNRWA issued a flash appeal for $43 million to cover temporary operations in the camp during the rebuilding work.

For 2009 the UNRWA's budget remained flat at $541 million, but by May it was estimated that falling donations would result in an operating deficit of $125 million for the year. The United States was the largest contributor to the UNRWA that year, providing $268 million for the regular operating budget and for emergency appeals. The EU was second, at $232.7 million. Efforts to reduce expenditures at some camps led to protests by refugees through the summer. The UNRWA launched the Gaza quick response program in 2009 as an effort to coordinate all of the emergency funding appeals into a single initiative for the region. The UNRWA sought $371.3 million but had raised only $192.6 million through August. A similar effort for the West Bank performed even more poorly, securing only $31 million of the requested $90 million. Nonetheless, the UNRWA provided emergency food assistance to more than 1.2 million people through 2009. In October the UNRWA began the da'am (support) program, which was designed to better identify the needs of the most disadvantaged groups and provide assistance more efficiently. Eight communities were initially involved in the project, which was expected to be expanded throughout the system in late 2010. A UNRWA employment program provided 1.7 million work days in Gaza and the West Bank, employing 30,891 people.

In 2010 the UNRWA completed a three-year reform program designed to improve the organization's internal management of human resources, strengthen individual program oversight, and streamline organizational procedures. Meanwhile the organization completed repairs to the 51 UNRWA facilities that had been damaged during fighting in 2008 and finished work on 4,921 temporary shelters in case of future fighting. The UNRWA also finalized work to repair and expand the water and sewage systems in eight of its camps in the West Bank. The UNRWA 2010–2011 regular biennial budget was $1.23 billion, of which more than 50 percent was allocated to education. Through October 2010, the agency's emergency appeals totaled $323.3 million.

UNRWA expenditures in 2011 totaled $655 million of which approximately half was allocated for education and training and $118 million for health care. The United States was the largest donor to UNRWA in 2011 with $239 million, followed by the EU at $175 million. Following the outbreak of fighting in Syria, the UNRWA began additional deliveries of food and medical supplies to Syrian camps in August 2012.

In 2012 the UNRWA's regular budget was $675.3 million. In addition the agency raised $300 million through emergency appeals, with a significant portion of the funding used to address deteriorating conditions in Syria. In 2012 the UNRWA launched a broad reform process across its programs. In 2013 the agency's health centers in Lebanon and Gaza implemented reforms to improve efficiency through the use of electronic records, an e-appointment system, and a team approach to healthcare delivery. The reforms were scheduled to be put into place in Jordan, Syria, and the West Bank by 2015. Educational reforms, including more stringent teacher certification requirements and updated curriculums were also scheduled to be implemented by 2015.

In March 2014 Pierre Krähenbühl of Switzerland became the commissioner general of UNRWA. During the Israel–Hamas conflict in 2014 (see entry on Israel), UNRWA issued a call for emergency funding, securing $300 million through October for humanitarian operations and rebuilding efforts (the agency sought $1.6 billion to fund a two-year recovery plan). The conflict left approximately 77,000 Palestinian refugees homeless and caused significant damage to schools and other public infrastructure. A parallel crisis appeal to assist some 540,000 Palestinian refugees affected by the Syrian crisis collected $417 million.

The ongoing civil war in Syria (see entry on Syria), led to new challenges for the UNRWA as Palestinian refugees endeavored to flee violence. At the beginning of 2015, there were approximately 450,000 Palestinian refugees in Syria. Of these, more than 95 percent relied on the UNRWA for aid. Emergency humanitarian assistance was provided by the agency to some 1.2 million people in 2015. The UNRWA built or reconstructed more than 36,000 shelters and provided 9.1 million health care consultations in 2016.

UNITED NATIONS RESEARCH INSTITUTE FOR SOCIAL DEVELOPMENT

(UNRISD)

Established: July 1, 1964, by means of an initial grant from the government of the Netherlands, in furtherance of a General Assembly resolution of December 5, 1963, on social targets and social planning.

Purpose: To conduct research into the "problems and policies of social development and relationships between various types of social and economic development during different phases of economic growth."

Headquarters: Geneva, Switzerland.

Principal Organ: Board of Advisors, consisting of a chair appointed by the UN secretary-general and ten individual members nominated by the Commission for Social Development and confirmed by the Economic and Social Council. There are also seven ex-officio members—a representative of the UN Secretariat; two representatives (in rotation) from the FAO, ILO, UNDP, UNESCO, UNHCR, UNU, and WHO; the executive secretary of the Economic Commission for Western Asia; the directors of the Latin American Institute for Economic and Social Planning and the African Institute for Economic Development and Planning; and the institute director.

Website: www.unrisd.org.

Director: Paul Ladd (United Kingdom).

Recent activities. The focus of UNRISD activities has shifted over the years to reflect current concerns in social development and public policy. Current research emphases include civil society and social movements; democracy, governance, and human rights; identities, conflict, and cohesion; social policy and development; and technology, business, and society. (For information on past priorities, see the 2014 *Handbook.*) Ongoing projects include, for example, examination of grassroots movements and land reform initiatives, public sector reform in crisis-ridden countries, HIV/AIDS and development, the interaction of information technologies and social development, and social policy and "late industrializers" in Africa, Latin America, and the Middle East.

In 2007 the UNRISD launched a major research project on poverty reduction, scheduled to be completed and published in 2009. (For information on UNRISD prior to 2007, see the 2013 *Handbook.*) To facilitate the research, the UNRISD sponsored a series of conferences around the world to bring together scholars and policymakers. The agency announced that its other research programs for the next two years would be organized into five broad areas: social policy and development; markets, business, and regulation; civil society and social movements; identities, conflict, and cohesion; and gender development. Through 2008 the UNRISD supported 118 researchers in 40 countries examining social policy and economic development. The UNRISD's core funding was $3.3 million, an increase from $2.8 million in the prior year, and its project funding was $859,479 versus $1.2 million in the previous year.

The UNRISD's operating budget for 2009 increased to approximately $4 million. In September 2009 UNRISD sponsored a major conference in Seoul, South Korea, on poverty reduction programs. Meanwhile, Sarah Cook of the United Kingdom was appointed the director of UNRISD in November, following the resignation of Thandika Mkandawire of Sweden in April. From 2006 through 2009, UNRISD commissioned more than 40 research papers to support the flagship report *Combating Poverty and Inequality: Structural Change, Social Policy and Politics,* published in 2010. The report explored the impact of the global economic crisis on the ability to achieve the MDG, especially the reduction of poverty. It noted that for the first time in history, the number of malnourished people in the world rose above 1 billion and that even if the MDG objective of reducing poverty by 50 percent by 2015 was met, more than 1 billion people would remain in poverty. However, the report also concluded that economic growth in Asia had helped reduce the number of people living on less than $1.25 worldwide from 1.8 billion to 1.4 billion in 2009. The report suggested, even if not explicitly stating, that the MDG might not be met.

In 2010 the organization's expenditures totaled approximately $3.4 million. Expenditures increased slightly in 2011 to $3.9 million, but fell in 2012 back to $3.4 million. The 2012 policy brief, *Gendered Impacts of Globalization: Employment and Social Protection,* reviewed existing literature on women's participation in the labor force and inequality in pay and benefits. The report called for pension reform to include noncontributory retirement systems and increased maternity and care leave.

Following the May 2013 UNRISD conference, "Potential and Limits of Social and Solidarity Economy (SSE)," UN agencies, including, UNRISD, the FAO, and the ILO, created the Inter-Agency Task Force on Social and Solidarity Economy in September. SSE refers to organizations that have both a social and an economic impact but are not part of the traditional for-profit sector. For example, UNRISD noted that in the United Kingdom, "social enterprises" employed more than 800,000 people and added $37.1 billion to the economy. The interagency grouping was charged with "mainstreaming" SSE in economic and public policy considerations.

UNRISD budget for 2013 was $3 million, with Finland, Sweden, Switzerland, and the United Kingdom the largest donors. A proposal was developed in 2013 to merge UNRISD and all other UN research centers and agencies into a single secretariat. However, opposition from other bodies led to no action being taken on the initiative as of October 2014. UNRISD's proposed 2014 budget included a 25 percent increase, rising to $4 million. Paul Ladd was named director of UNRISD in October 2015.

UNITED NATIONS UNIVERSITY

(UNU)

Established: By General Assembly resolution of December 11, 1972; charter adopted December 6, 1973; began operations September 1, 1975.

Purpose: To conduct action-oriented research in fields related to development, welfare, and human survival, and to train young scholars and research workers.

Headquarters: Tokyo, Japan.

Principal Organs: University Council (comprising 24 educators, each from a different country, in addition to the UN secretary-general, the director general of UNESCO, the executive director of UNITAR, and the university rector, ex officio); Boards and Advisory Committees overseeing Research and Training Centers and Programs (RTC/Ps).

Website: www.unu.edu.

Rector: David M. Malone (Canada).

Recent activities. A mission statement adopted in 1999 defines the UNU's purpose as contributing "through research and capacity building, to efforts to resolve the pressing global problems that are the concern of the United Nations, its peoples and its Member States." (For information on prior activities, see the 2014 *Handbook.*) Accordingly, the university considers as its principal functions fostering an international community of scholars; providing a bridge between the UN and the academic community; serving as a think tank for the UN; and aiding capacity building, especially in the developing world. Scholars affiliated with and contracted by the UNU conduct research and address needs in five general thematic areas: peace and security (international relations, the UN system, human security, armed conflicts); good governance (democracy and civil society, leadership, human rights, and ethics); development and poverty reduction (globalization and development, growth and employment, poverty and basic needs, urbanization); science, technology, and society (innovation, information technology and biotechnology, software technology, food and nutrition); and the environment and sustainability (resource management, sustainable industry and cities, water, global climate, and governance).

Much of the UNU's work is conducted through 13 RTC/Ps located around the world. In 1985 the university established its first RTC, the World Institute for Development Economics Research (UNU-WIDER) in Helsinki, Finland. UNU-WIDER currently directs its programs toward conducting multidisciplinary research and analysis on how structural changes affect the world's poorest populations, training scholars and government officials in economic and social policy, and providing a forum on issues related to equitable and environmentally sustainable growth. In 1987 the council approved the creation of the Institute for Natural Resources in Africa (UNU-INRA) with the goal of strengthening scientific and technological capacities in such areas as land use, water management, energy resources, and minerals development. After being temporarily housed in Nairobi, Kenya, the UNU-INRA moved into permanent headquarters in Accra, Ghana, in 1993. (For more information on the centers and research operations of the UNU, see the 2013 *Handbook.*)

In August 2007 Konrad Osterwalder of Switzerland became rector of the UNU, replacing van Ginkel. The European Commission asked the UNU to examine the issue of recycling electronic waste (e-waste) and develop a report, published in November, on how best to increase recycling of e-waste such as cellular phones, old computing equipment, and household appliances. The UNU also produced *Accountability and the United Nations System* (Policy Brief Number 8, 2007) in an effort to guide UN reforms and enhance financial and managerial accountability in the world body.

The UNU and the University of Tokyo created a joint initiative in July 2008 to facilitate research in the science of sustainability. The UNU and the government of Japan launched a pilot program through the Hiroshima Peacebuilders' Center to train people in conflict mediation and prevention. The training program also involved other UN bodies, including the UNHCR, UNDP, and UNICEF. The UNU documentary film *Voices of the Chichinautzin,* about the challenges faced by indigenous people of the Chichinautzin region of Mexico, won the best feature award at the Moondance International Film Festival.

In 2009 the system produced more than 800 publications, ranging from books to policy and technical briefs, and it sponsored more than 350 public events, including conferences, seminars, lectures, and presentations. The UNU articulated a new vision through the publication of the *United Nations University Strategic Plan, 2009–2012,* which called for the university to become a globally recognized research institution by reorganizing and reinvigorating its core functions and engaging in a sustained outreach program. The UNU's 2008–2009 biennial budget was $101.8 million, generated from donors and investment income. (The UNU does not receive funding from the regular UN budget.) In 2010 the UNU launched a new graduate program in sustainability, development, and peace at its Tokyo facility. The agency received $36.9 million in contributions during 2010.

UNU's 2010–2011 budget was $108 million. In 2011 UNU had faculty from 75 countries. That year the university launched a new master's degree in environmental governance with a specialty in biodiversity. In addition, two new centers were planned, the UNU International Institute for the Alliance of Civilizations and the UNU Institute for Integrated Management of Material Fluxes and Resources.

The UNU's budget for 2012–2013 biennium was $142.8 million. That year, the UNU staff numbered 679, along with 224 fellowship recipients, and 166 interns. In 2012 the UNU had 1,387 publications and conducted 275 public events. More than 5,500 students attended 146 training courses, with 110 held in developing countries. On March 1, 2013, David M. Malone of Canada was appointed rector of UNU. Throughout 2013, the UNU undertook a series of structural reforms. Two of the UNU's research centers in Japan were consolidated to create the Institute for the Advanced Study of Sustainability, the curriculum of the UNU's Barcelona site was reorganized, and the campus relaunched as the UNU Institute on Globalization, Culture, and Mobility. Meanwhile, the UNU Council approved the establishment of a new UNU site in Maputo, Mozambique.

By the end of 2015 the UNU staff numbered 652, with 135 ongoing research projects and approvals for 43 new projects. There were 234 graduate students studying at UNU sites, while 6,740 students participated in workshops or training sessions. A new site in Algiers, Algeria, was postponed, while a new institute was approved for Dakar, Senegal.

SECURITY COUNCIL

Permanent Membership (5): China, France, Russia, United Kingdom, United States. (The other permanent members in late December 1991 accepted Russia's assumption of the seat previously filled by the Union of Soviet Socialist Republics.)

Nonpermanent Membership (10): Terms ending December 31, 2018: Bolivia, Ethiopia, Italy, Kazakhstan, and Sweden. Terms ending December 31, 2017: Egypt, Japan, Senegal, Ukraine, and Uruguay.

Website: www.un.org/en/sc.

Origin and development. In declaring the primary purpose of the UN to be the maintenance of international peace and security, the charter established a system for collective enforcement of the peace based on unity among the five permanent members of the Security Council. Peace efforts of the council are effective only to the degree that political accord is possible in relation to specific international disputes and only when the parties to such conflicts are willing to allow the UN to play its intended role.

The only instance of an actual military operation undertaken under UN auspices in response to an act of aggression was the Korean involvement of 1950–1953. The action was possible because the Soviet Union was boycotting the Security Council at the time and was thus unable to exercise a veto. The United States, which had military forces readily available in the area, was in a position to assume direction of a UN-established Unified Command, to which military forces were ultimately supplied by 16 member states. As of December 2002 the UN command remained in South Korea, with troops from the United States constituting the only foreign contingent. In 1975 the U.S. representative to the UN proposed, in a letter to the president of the Security Council, that the command be dissolved, with U.S. and South Korean officers as "successors in command," if North Korea and China would first agree to continue the armistice. However, no such agreement was subsequently concluded.

In certain other instances, as in the India–Pakistan War of 1965 and the Arab–Israeli War of 1967, the positions of the major powers have been close enough to lend weight to Security Council resolutions calling for cease-fires. The Security Council endorsed the use of "all necessary means" to liberate Kuwait from occupying Iraqi forces in early 1991; however, unlike the 1950 Korean deployment, the Desert Storm campaign was not a formal UN operation, the United States preferring to maintain military control rather than defer to an overall UN command.

The NATO-led air campaign against Yugoslavia's repression of the ethnic Albanian population in Kosovo during March–June 1999 was, again, initiated without direct Security Council backing, the United States and its NATO allies knowing full well that Russia and probably China would have vetoed a call for direct military action. On May 14 the Security Council did, however, pass a resolution urging support for humanitarian relief efforts to aid Kosovar refugees and internally displaced persons. The resolution also called for a political solution in line with principles put forward on May 6 by Canada, France, Germany, Italy, Japan, Russia, the United Kingdom, and the United States. A June 10 resolution authorized a United Nations Interim Administration Mission in Kosovo (UNMIK) and a NATO-led Multinational Force in Kosovo (KFOR), the latter to maintain security pending a handover to an UNMIK-established civilian police corps.

The Kosovo mission was the most comprehensive ever undertaken under Security Council auspices, going well beyond peacekeeping, and was followed only four months later by a similarly all-encompassing effort, the United Nations Transitional Administration in East Timor (UNTAET), which had as its task nation-building in preparation for East Timor's full independence. On May 17, 2002, with that goal accomplished, the Security Council authorized formation of a United Nations Mission of Support in East Timor (UNMISET) as a successor to the UNTAET. The new mission was mandated to ensure East Timor's domestic and international security and to offer support to the government of the new state. On May 21, 2005, UNMISET was succeeded by the United Nations Office in Timor-Leste (UNOTIL), which had been established by Security Council resolution as a special political mission to be directed by the UN Department of Peacekeeping Operations. In view of civil disorder in Timor-Leste, UNOTIL's one-year mandate was extended to August 20, 2006. There was general acknowledgment, however, that UNMISET had been withdrawn too hastily and that a comparable new mission was required to assist the new state (see entry on Timor-Leste). Following the independence of South Sudan in July 2011, the Security Council authorized the deployment of the UN Mission in the Republic of South Sudan (UNMISS). A concurrent mission in the disputed Abyei region of Sudan, the UN Interim Security Force for Abyei (UNISFA), was also created. The role of UNMISS was expanded in May 2014.

The 1990s also saw the Security Council assume a leading role in establishing venues for prosecuting and trying alleged war crimes. It authorized creation of an International Criminal Tribunal for the former Yugoslavia in 1993 and an International Criminal Tribunal for Rwanda in 1994, as well as the special court for Sierra Leone in 2002, and the special tribunals for Cambodia in 2003 and Lebanon in 2005.

Structure. Originally comprising 5 permanent and 6 nonpermanent members, the council was expanded on January 1, 1966, to 15, including 10 nonpermanent members elected by the General Assembly for two-year terms. The charter stipulates that in the election of the nonpermanent members due regard must be paid to the contribution of members to the maintenance of international peace and security and to the other purposes of the organization, and also to equitable geographic distribution. The presidency of the Security Council rotates monthly.

Council decisions on procedural matters are made by an affirmative vote of any nine members. Decisions on all other matters, however, require a nine-member affirmative vote that must include the concurring votes of the permanent members; the one exception is that in matters involving pacific settlement of disputes, a party to a dispute must abstain from voting. It is the requirement for the concurring votes of the permanent members on all but procedural questions that enables any one of the five to exercise a veto, no matter how large the affirmative majority.

In discharging its responsibilities the Security Council may investigate the existence of any threat to peace, breach of the peace, or act of aggression, and in the event of such a finding may make recommendations for resolution or decide to take enforcement measures to maintain or restore international peace and security. Enforcement action may include a call on members to apply economic sanctions and other measures short of the use of armed force. Should these steps prove inadequate, the Security Council may then take such military action as is deemed necessary.

The charter established a Military Staff Committee, composed of the permanent members' chiefs of staff (or their representatives), to advise and assist the Security Council on such questions as the council's military requirements for the maintenance of peace, the regulation of armaments, and possible disarmament. In the absence of agreements to place armed forces at the council's disposal, as envisaged by the charter, the committee has not assumed an important operational role.

In addition to the Military Staff Committee, the Security Council currently has three Standing Committees—the Committee on the Admission of New Members, the Committee of Experts on Rules of Procedure, and the Committee on Council Meetings away from Headquarters—each composed of representatives of all council members. There is also a UN Compensation Commission, which was established in 1991 to pay damages to governments, individuals, and businesses injured by the Gulf War. On September 28, 2001, responding to the September 11 terrorist attacks on the United States, the Security Council authorized creation of a new ad hoc Counter-Terrorism Committee. On April 28, 2004, Resolution 1540 authorized creation of another ad hoc committee concerned with preventing the proliferation of weapons of mass destruction (WMD) and their delivery. Resolution 1673, passed unanimously on April 27, 2006, authorized the 1540 Committee to also focus on preventing "non-state actors" from acquiring WMD.

The Security Council is also empowered to establish so-called sanctions committees, 15 of which were functioning as of 2014. Most were established to oversee arms embargoes—against, for instance, Somalia (since 1992) and Sudan (since 2004)—and/or to freeze assets or impose travel restrictions on government officials or other individuals. In some cases, the original mandate of a sanctions committee has been expanded or redefined. In December 2000, for example, the Security Council expanded the mission of the Afghanistan committee, which it had created in 1999 primarily in response to Afghanistan's failure to extradite suspects in the 1998 bombings of U.S. embassies in Kenya and Tanzania. Initially assigned to monitor air travel restrictions and a freeze on the Afghan Taliban regime's financial assets, the committee's mandate was extended to include monitoring an air and arms embargo and the freezing of funds of Osama bin Laden and associates. In 2002, following the demise of the Taliban regime, several additional resolutions further modified the terms of the sanctions.

The council has created a number of working groups to address peacekeeping operations, conflict prevention and resolution in Africa, and improving the effectiveness of sanctions. In February 2001 the Working Group on General Issues on Sanctions issued dozens of recommendations for more effective use of sanctions, including monitoring their impact, providing incentives to lift them, and setting time limits for them. The committee also proposed that the Security Council consider imposing secondary sanctions on countries that fail to adhere to direct sanctions. The committee's final report was issued in 2006. A follow-up report was issued in November 2013 with additional recommendations, including enhancing the transparency of the sanctions committees and reactivating the Informal Working Group on General Issues of Sanctions, which had been discontinued in 2006.

Recent activities. Peacekeeping activities include observation, fact-finding, mediation, conciliation, and assistance in maintaining internal order. UN observer groups to supervise cease-fire lines, truce arrangements, and the like have functioned in Africa, the Balkans, Indonesia, the Middle East, Kashmir, and former Soviet republics. On a larger scale, the UN Operation in the Congo (UNOC) was initiated in 1960 and continued until 1964 in an attempt to stabilize the chaotic situation in that state (subsequently Zaire and, since mid-1997, the Democratic Republic of the Congo). Since 1964 the UN Force in Cyprus (UNFICYP) has attempted to alleviate conflict between the Greek and Turkish elements in the Cypriot population under a mandate subject to semiannual renewal.

There have been several peacekeeping operations in the Middle East. A UN Emergency Force (UNEF) was interposed between the military forces of Egypt and Israel in the Sinai and Gaza areas from early 1957 until its withdrawal at the insistence of Egypt in 1967. The UNEF was reconstituted in October 1973 to supervise a cease-fire along the Suez Canal and to ensure a return of Israeli and Egyptian forces to the positions that they held on October 22, 1973. Soon after the signing of the Egyptian–Israeli peace treaty in March 1979, it became clear that the Soviet Union—on behalf of its Arab friends—would veto an extension of the force when its mandate expired on July 25. Faced with this prospect, the United States concluded an agreement with the Soviet Union to allow monitoring of the treaty arrangements by the UN Truce Supervision Organization (UNTSO), established in 1948 to oversee the Arab–Israeli cease-fire. Other forces currently serving in the Middle East are the UN Interim Forces in Lebanon (UNIFIL), established in 1978, and the UN Disengagement Observer Force (UNDOF), deployed in Syria's Golan Heights since 1974. (For organizational details on existing peacekeeping forces, see the next section.)

As a body that meets year-round and is frequently called upon to respond to world crises, the Security Council is often the most visible of the UN organs. Given its composition and the nature of its duties, political considerations typically dominate its deliberations. In the 1980s the council tended to focus on problems in the Middle East, Central America, and southern Africa. During 1986 it debated resolutions condemning Israel for continued military activity in southern Lebanon, the alleged violation of the sanctity of a Jerusalem mosque, and the interception of a Libyan airliner in the search for suspected terrorists. The resolutions failed as the result of vetoes by the United States, itself the subject of condemnation resolutions later in the year. Other Western-bloc council members joined the United States in defeating a measure denouncing the U.S. bombing of Libya in April, while the United States cast the only vote against a resolution seeking to ban military and financial aid to contra rebels fighting the government of Nicaragua.

In September 1987 the council approved a peace plan that provided the framework for termination of the Iran-Iraq war in August 1988. In conjunction with that agreement, the council established the UN Iran-Iraq Military Observer Group (UNIIMOG) to supervise the cease-fire and monitor the withdrawal of troops to internationally recognized boundaries. (UNIIMOG's mandate was terminated in early 1990 following the successful completion of its mission.) Other UN groups mobilized in 1988 and 1989 were the UN Good Offices Mission in Afghanistan and Pakistan (UNGOMAP—terminated in March 1990 after monitoring the withdrawal of Soviet troops from Afghanistan); the UN Angola Verification Mission (UNAVEM); the UN Transition Assistance Group (UNTAG), established to supervise the withdrawal of South African troops from Namibia and the transition to Namibian independence; the United Nations Observer Group in Central America (*Grupo de Observadoresde las Naciones Unidas en Centroamérica*—ONUCA); and the UN Observation Mission for the Verification of Elections in Nicaragua (*Observadores de Naciones Unidas para la Verificación de las Elecciones en Nicaragua*—ONUVEN).

The Security Council's prominent role in conflict resolution was widely perceived as having significantly enhanced the global reputation of the peacekeeping forces (which were awarded the 1988 Nobel Peace Prize), the Secretariat, and the United Nations as a whole. Improved relations within the council were attributed to the reduction in East–West tension, UN secretary-general Javier Pérez de Cuéllar praising Washington and Moscow for permitting the body to become "more responsive [and] collegial." Building upon the unqualified successes of UNTAG and ONUVEN (the first UN force to supervise an election in an established nation), the permanent members of the council in early 1990 endorsed an Australian proposal that a peacekeeping force be deployed to help resolve the long-standing conflict in Cambodia and supervise the election of a new national government. In addition, the council in late April approved a peace plan for the Western Sahara under which a UN group would oversee a referendum in the territory. The council also considered creating a small UN observer force to monitor the treatment of Palestinians in the occupied territories, but the United States vetoed the measure in May.

The Security Council moved even further to the forefront of the global stage by assuming a major role in an international response to Iraq's invasion of Kuwait on August 2, 1990. Launching what would eventually be perceived as a historic series of resolutions (most adopted unanimously) through which "the teeth" of the UN Charter were bared with rare decisiveness and speed, the council condemned the takeover within hours of its occurrence and demanded the withdrawal of Iraqi troops. Several days later the council also imposed comprehensive economic sanctions on Iraq and established a special committee to monitor the sanctions process. In addition, the council endorsed a naval blockade of Iraq and approved UN aid for "innocent victims" of the crisis as well as countries adversely affected by the trade embargo. Finally, in its most dramatic decision, the council on November 28 authorized U.S.-led coalition forces to use "all necessary means" to implement previous resolutions and "to restore international peace and security in the area" if Iraq did not withdraw from Kuwait by January 15, 1991, thereby providing the basis for launching Operation Desert Storm on January 16, 1991.

Following the liberation of Kuwait and the announcement of a suspension of military operations by allied forces in late February 1991, the council adopted a permanent cease-fire plan on April 3 demanding that Iraq return all Kuwaiti property, accept liability for the damage it caused during the war, and destroy all its chemical and biological weapons, as well as its long-range ballistic missiles. After Iraqi acceptance of the conditions on April 6, the council established the UN Iraq–Kuwait Observation Mission (UNIKOM) to monitor a demilitarized zone between the two countries. The council also remained deeply involved in efforts to resolve refugee problems associated with the conflict, especially in regard to Iraq's Kurdish population.

Tension between the council and Iraq continued throughout the ensuing year, particularly over what were perceived as attempts by Baghdad to undermine UN supervision of the destruction of plants and equipment related to nuclear, chemical, and biological weapons. With some Western nations reportedly considering a resumption of military action, the Security Council in the spring of 1992 warned that "grave consequences" would ensue if Iraq interfered any further with UN oversight activity.

Even without the extraordinary burden of the Gulf crisis, the council would have encountered a busier schedule than usual in 1990–1991. Following extended debate prompted by the death of a number of Palestinians in the occupied territories in October 1990, the council approved a carefully worded resolution rebuking Israel and asking the UN secretary-general to monitor the status of Palestinian civilians "under Israeli occupation." In addition, the council reaffirmed its support for a UN-sponsored Middle East Peace Conference. Other activity in late 1990 included negotiations on the final framework for a comprehensive settlement of the Cambodian situation and the creation of a UN observer group to help monitor elections in Haiti.

Discussions also continued toward finalization of the Western Saharan peace plan, with the council in April 1991 authorizing a UN Mission for the Referendum in Western Sahara (*Mission des Nations Unies le Référendum dans le Sahara Ouest*—MINURSO). A month later the council approved a United Nations Observer Mission in El Salvador (*Observadores de las Naciones Unidas en El Salvador*—ONUSAL) as part of a continuing effort to foster a peace settlement in that country's long-standing civil war. Initially, ONUSAL's mandate was limited to verifying adherence to a human rights agreement signed by the government and the rebels in 1990, but the council expanded the mission's mandate in January 1992 to include monitoring the permanent cease-fire.

In February 1992 the council authorized two of its largest operations to date, the UN Protection Force (UNPROFOR) to help implement and monitor a cease-fire in eastern Croatia, and the UN Transitional Authority in Cambodia (UNTAC). Two months later the council also established the UN Operation in Somalia (UNOSOM) in an effort to mediate an end to the civil war in that country and permit the delivery of much-needed food relief. Other April activity included the declaration of an air and arms embargo against Libya because of Tripoli's refusal to permit the extradition of two of its nationals suspected of complicity in the 1988 airplane bombing over Lockerbie, Scotland.

In June 1992 UN secretary-general Boutros Boutros-Ghali proposed a number of changes to improve the peacemaking and peacekeeping abilities of the Security Council. The most striking recommendation was for "as many countries as are willing" to make 1,000 of their troops available for immediate council deployment, thereby establishing, in essence at least, the long-debated UN standing army. Boutros-Ghali said such forces would be instrumental in implementing the "preventative diplomacy" strategy endorsed at a Security Council summit in New York in January. The meeting, the first ever of the heads of state of the permanent and nonpermanent council members, had agreed that greater effort should be made to identify trouble spots in advance so intervention could be ordered before the outbreak of violence.

Throughout 1992 and the first half of 1993, the Security Council became more focused on the former Yugoslavia, particularly after authorizing UNPROFOR troops to enter Bosnia and Herzegovina for humanitarian purposes. Some 40 resolutions were approved in response to conflicts in the region. Included were the imposition of sanctions against the Federal Republic of Yugoslavia, condemnation of "ethnic cleansing" and myriad human rights violations in Bosnia, approval of an International Criminal Tribunal for the former Yugoslavia, and a number of generally unsuccessful or unimplemented peacemaking efforts, such as the imposition of no-fly zones and the establishment of "safe areas" for Bosnian Muslims. Following the collapse of talks launched by the European Community, the council also found itself responsible for efforts to negotiate an end to the complex Bosnian conflict.

Concurrently, the council's UNOSOM II resolution of March 1993 introduced a controversial "nation-building" element to UN intervention. Although credited with having brought food relief to the starving population and having pacified most of the country, UNOSOM troops, acting in conjunction with a U.S. rapid deployment force, found themselves locked in deadly combat with the supporters of clan leader Gen. Mohamed Farah Aidid in Mogadishu. As losses mounted within the UNOSOM and U.S. contingents, council members began to consider a more "realistic" attitude toward what it could accomplish in such situations.

In other activity during 1992–1993, the council fought in what was described as a "war of nerves" with Baghdad concerning UN monitoring of Iraqi weapon sites. The council also expressed its concern over the renewal of fighting in Afghanistan, condemned the Israeli deportation of about 400 Palestinians from the occupied territories in December 1992, and demanded the withdrawal of Armenian forces from Azerbaijan in August 1993.

Peacekeeping operations over the next year continued the recent pattern of occasional successes mixed with inconclusive or seemingly failed missions. UNTAC was disbanded in November 1993 following elections and installation of a coalition government in Cambodia, while ONUSAL was widely praised for its contribution to the completion of elections in El Salvador in early 1994. In addition, Mozambique conducted its first multiparty elections in October 1994 with the assistance of the UN Operation in Mozambique (*Opération des Nations Unies au Mozambique*—ONUMOZ). However, positive results were scarce in the former Yugoslavia, Somalia, Angola, and Liberia, while the council was embarrassed by the refusal of the military regime in Port-au-Prince to permit the deployment of the UN Mission in Haiti (UNMIH). Consequently, the council's permanent members continued to reassess the limits of peacekeeping endeavors, and in early May 1994 new guidelines were established. Future missions would require a "clear political goal" reflected in a "precise mandate," a cease-fire among combatants, and the integration, if possible, of forces from regional peacekeeping organizations.

The council's new caution was reflected in its response to the genocide in Rwanda. The United States resisted the call for large-scale reinforcement of the UN Assistance Mission for Rwanda (UNAMIR) in April 1994 (see entry on Rwanda). Although 5,500 additional troops were eventually authorized, the council was strongly criticized in many quarters for the delay. Late in the year, amid mounting evidence of widespread atrocities, the Security Council authorized creation of an International Criminal Tribunal for Rwanda.

The Rwandan situation also underscored the ongoing need for the council to develop rapid deployment capability. UN secretary-general Boutros-Ghali announced in early 1994 that some 15 countries had pledged troops and/or equipment to the proposed standby force. Nevertheless, he argued that rhetorical backing for peacekeeping operations, which cost an estimated $3.2 billion in 1993, was still not matched by sufficient tangible support.

In February 1995 UNOSOM withdrew from Somalia, having failed in its goal of fostering political stability there. Success also remained elusive in former Yugoslavia, where beleaguered UNPROFOR forces would be replaced by U.S.-led NATO troops in Bosnia and Herzegovina following a permanent cease-fire. (UNPROFOR's responsibilities in Croatia and Macedonia had been delegated in March to two new missions—the UN Confidence Restoration Operation in Croatia [UNCRO] and the UN Preventive Deployment Force [UNPREDEP].) On the positive side, ONUMOZ and ONUSAL were disbanded after successfully completing their missions in Mozambique and El Salvador, respectively. In addition, the UNMIH deployed its forces in Haiti following the return of the civilian government to Port-au-Prince. Hope also grew for a resolution of the protracted conflict in Angola; some 7,000 UNAVEM III troops were authorized to help implement the most recent cease-fire.

The new UN Mission of Observers in Tajikistan (UNMOT) was very limited in scope as the Security Council deferred to a large peacekeeping force provided by Russia under the aegis of the Commonwealth of Independent States. This arrangement was considered significant in regard to future peacekeeping efforts, particularly given that UN resources were, in the words of Secretary-General Boutros-Ghali, "overstretched and underfinanced."

The Security Council's reassessment of its peacekeeping limitations continued throughout 1995, particularly in light of UNPROFOR's ineffectiveness and NATO's bombing campaign in late summer against Bosnian Serb aggressiveness. Its military assertiveness having contributed to the conclusion of a U.S.-brokered comprehensive peace agreement in November, NATO for all practical purposes assumed full responsibility in December for overseeing the cease-fire through, among other things, the deployment of some 60,000 troops (see entries on Bosnia and Herzegovina and NATO for details). Concurrently, UNPROFOR was disbanded (effective January 31, 1996), having been deemed a failure for the most part. The counterpoint between NATO action and the UN's previous impotence came into even sharper focus as the cease-fire held throughout 1996 and the complicated new electoral process was completed successfully in Bosnia under NATO supervision.

The Security Council also closed down UNAMIR in August 1996, the mission having had no impact on the raging Hutu-Tutsi ethnic conflict in Rwanda. Significantly, when related violence intensified in Zaire in the fall, the proposed international responses focused on regional or Western-led intervention forces, not a UN operation. A growing "go-it-alone" attitude had also been apparent in the unilateral action taken by the United States in Iraq in September when Washington launched cruise missiles against Iraqi positions without seeking Security Council endorsement (see entry on Iraq).

Attention in the council during the second half of 1996 was focused on the acrimonious selection of the next UN secretary-general. Washington's implacable opposition to a second term for Boutros-Ghali eventually resulted in council endorsement of Kofi Annan. In other activity, the council's long-delayed "oil-for-food" proposal to Iraq was implemented in mid-December, thereby permitting Baghdad to sell Iraqi oil to fund the importation of civilian food and medicine. Later in the month a permanent cease-fire was concluded in Guatemala thanks in large part to UN negotiators. The UN Human Rights Verification Mission in Guatemala, deployed in 1994, defused numerous potential threats to the cease-fire. (That verification mission was augmented for several months in the first half of 1997 by some 155 military observers, although the deployment had been delayed temporarily at the insistence of China, which objected to Guatemala's diplomatic recognition to Taiwan.)

No major new peacekeeping missions were launched in 1997, although small successor operations were authorized for Angola, Haiti, and Croatia. Meanwhile, the limited UN Observer Mission in Liberia (UNOMIL) closed down following the installation of an elected civilian government in Monrovia, the Security Council having left most of the peacemaking and peacekeeping activity there in the hands of regional forces directed by the Economic Community of West African States (ECOWAS). The council also deferred to ECOWAS regarding the turmoil in Sierra Leone, although it formally condemned the May 1997 military coup and endorsed the forced reinstallation of the civilian government in March 1998.

Meanwhile, discussion continued on proposed enlargement of the council. A special panel called in 1997 for the council to be expanded to 24 members, including 5 new permanent members who, however, would not have veto power. The panel suggested that two new permanent members come from the industrialized countries (probably Germany and Japan) and one each from Africa, Asia, and Latin America. However, the proposed expansion was viewed with little enthusiasm by the current permanent council members, who expressed concern that the body might become unwieldy.

The council's agenda in 1997 and early 1998 was dominated by its efforts to compel Iraq to cooperate fully with the weapons inspection program instituted earlier in the decade but still subject to a "cat-and-mouse" approach by Baghdad. Following a negative report from the UN Special Commission (UNSCOM), which was responsible for oversight of the inspections, the Security Council in mid-1997 formally rebuked Iraq for noncompliance and interference with UNSCOM's work and threatened to impose additional sanctions. Baghdad responded provocatively, ordering all U.S. members of UNSCOM out of the country on the grounds that they were involved in intelligence-gathering activity beyond the purview of UNSCOM. Although the United States and United Kingdom adopted a hard line and urged consideration of the use of force against Iraq, the other Security Council members declined to endorse such action. Consequently, when Iraq declared in early 1998 that certain sites were off limits to inspectors (who by then had reincorporated the U.S. personnel), Washington, backed by London, announced it would proceed independently against Baghdad and ordered a significant buildup of troops, planes, and ships in the region. The Security Council authorized Annan to negotiate a settlement with Iraqi president Saddam Hussein. Following the last-minute success of Annan's mission in late February, the Security Council threatened Iraq with the "severest consequences" if further violations of the inspection protocols ensued.

The Annan agreement of early 1998 provided only a temporary break in the conflict between the Iraqi government and the Security Council. Baghdad continued to impede the work of UNSCOM throughout the rest of the year. Tensions came to a head in December following another unfavorable review of Iraqi compliance by UNSCOM. Arguing that previous council resolutions gave them the authority to do so, the United States and United Kingdom bombed Iraq for four days in an effort to force the Iraqi government to resume cooperating with the weapons inspectors. The attack seemed to have backfired, however, when Baghdad refused to allow UNSCOM personnel, who had been withdrawn from the country prior to the attack, to reenter Iraq unless sanctions were lifted.

On December 17, 1999, after months of negotiations, the Security Council approved—with China, France, Malaysia, and Russia abstaining—UNSCOM's replacement by the UN Monitoring, Verification and Inspection Commission (UNMOVIC). The council offered the possible suspension of sanctions in exchange for Iraqi compliance, but Iraq immediately rejected the attendant conditions as "impossible to fulfill." Although the International Atomic Energy Agency (IAEA) was permitted to renew limited inspections beginning in January 2000, Iraq refused entry to UNMOVIC personnel.

Meanwhile, much of the Security Council's attention had been diverted to the Balkans. In 1998 it had passed resolutions calling for an end to arms sales to Yugoslavia and for a cease-fire in that country's province of Kosovo. In October the council had also endorsed the establishment of an Organization for Security and Cooperation in Europe (OSCE) mission for the purpose of verifying that the Yugoslav federal government was abiding by these resolutions, but the mission ended in failure with the withdrawal of the OSCE monitors and the subsequent bombing of Yugoslavia by NATO in March–June 1999. Formation of the UNMIK was authorized upon suspension of the air campaign on June 10.

In February 1999 the UNPREDEP mission in Macedonia and a UN Observer Mission in Angola (*Mission d'Observation des Nations Unies en Angola*—MONUA) both came to an end, the former successfully and the latter as a failure. The Security Council had authorized the MONUA in June 1997 to assist in national reconciliation and demobilization, but the peace between the Angolan government and the National Union for the Total Independence of Angola (UNITA) never took hold. With the government making gains on the battlefield, Luanda concurred in the decision to terminate the MONUA. On October 15, however, the Security Council authorized establishment of a United Nations Office in Angola (UNOA), its mandate being to pursue opportunities for peace and to assist with humanitarian efforts, capacity building, and human rights.

The protracted conflict in the neighboring Democratic Republic of the Congo (DRC) led the council in late November 1999 to authorize a United Nations Organization Mission in the Democratic Republic of the Congo (*Mission de l'Organisation des Nations Unies en République Démocratique du Congo*—MONUC) in the hope that a July cease-fire signed by Angola, Namibia, Rwanda, Uganda, and Zimbabwe, as well as the DRC and rebel forces, would hold. Also in Africa, a small UN Observer Mission in Sierra Leone (UNOMSIL), which the council had authorized in June 1998 primarily to monitor security and human rights conditions, gave way in October 1999 to a much larger UN Mission in Sierra Leone (UNAMSIL).

The last of several follow-up efforts in Haiti—the UN Civilian Police Mission in Haiti (*Mission de Police Civile des Nations Unies en Haïti*—MIPONUH)—concluded in March 2000, and the UNMOT effort in Tajikistan drew to a close two months later. A UN Mission in the Central African Republic (*Mission des Nations Unies en République Centrafricaine*—MINURCA), which had been authorized by a Security Council resolution in March 1997 to facilitate stability and security in the wake of a mutiny within the country's armed forces, was succeeded in February 2000 by a UN Peacebuilding Support Office under the UN secretary-general. Another Security Council peacekeeping effort, the UN Mission in Ethiopia and Eritrea (UNMEE), came into existence in June 2000, in cooperation with the Organization for African Unity (OAU), following a cease-fire in the Horn of Africa.

A Panel on United Nations Peace Operations, chaired by Algerian Lakhda Brahimi, issued its report in August 2000, with the Security Council then establishing a working group in October to consider the recommendations in Brahimi's report. In a resolution passed unanimously on November 13, the council endorsed the report's conclusion that peacekeeping missions needed clear, credible, and achievable mandates, as well as the capacity to present a believable deterrent in hostile circumstances. The report also called for expansion and restructuring of the Secretariat's Department of Peacekeeping Operations, a greater reliance on intelligence gathering, adoption of means for responding more rapidly to potential crises, and allocation of additional resources.

During the Millennium Summit at UN headquarters in New York, the heads of state and government of the Security Council members convened for only the second time in UN history, with nine presidents, five prime ministers, and one foreign minister in attendance. The council unanimously adopted a September 7 resolution endorsing the body's continuing role in maintaining peace even while recognizing that poverty, infectious disease, and illegal trade in diamonds and other natural resources were among the social and economic pressures most linked to peace and stability.

The Security Council called in a July 2000 resolution for UN member states to consider voluntary HIV testing and counseling for their troops undertaking peacekeeping missions. January was labeled the "month of Africa" as the council considered a host of Africa-related concerns, while an October meeting examined the role of women in peace and security. Following the resumption of the Palestinian intifada (uprising) in September, an October 7 resolution (the United States abstaining) "deplored the provocation" caused by the visit of future Israeli prime minister Ariel Sharon to the Temple Mount (Haram al-Sharif) in September. In mid-December the council considered an additional resolution that would have authorized creation of an observer force of police and military for the occupied Palestinian territories, but the measure fell a single vote short of the nine needed for approval when seven council members abstained. A renewed effort to approve an observer force met with a U.S. veto on March 28, 2001.

Against a backdrop of the September 11, 2001, al-Qaida assault on the United States, on September 12 and 28 the Security Council unanimously condemned the attacks and requested all states to deny terrorists access to bases and financing, and to aid in bringing the perpetrators to justice. Resolution 1373, passed on September 28, also authorized formation of the ad hoc committee on counterterrorism.

Despite firm support for U.S.-led efforts to forge an international coalition to combat terrorism, protracted debate slowed a subsequent U.S. push against the Saddam Hussein regime and its alleged WMD. On September 16, 2002, UN secretary-general Kofi Annan announced that Iraq had unconditionally offered entry to UNMOVIC teams, which, Baghdad claimed, would confirm that it harbored no biological, chemical, or other sanctioned weapons. The United States and its chief ally on the Security Council, the United Kingdom, quickly dismissed the offer as a probable ruse. Washington also asserted that Iraq had ties to the al-Qaida terrorist network, but most members of the Security Council found the evidence less than compelling. Meanwhile, U.S. and UK aircraft continued their latest in a series of air assaults against military targets within Iraq's southern no-fly zone.

On November 8, 2002, the Security Council unanimously approved Resolution 1441, which threatened "serious consequences" if Iraq failed to disarm. Although the compromise resolution stopped short of the broad imprimatur that Washington and London had sought, it was interpreted by the United States as not requiring further Security Council approval before launching military action—a prospect that seemed increasingly likely as the year drew to a close. Responding to Iraq's December 8 delivery to the UNMOVIC of a 12,000-page Iraqi weapons declaration, U.S. secretary of state Colin Powell asserted that it "totally fail[ed]" to meet the Security Council's demands for a comprehensive, accurate accounting of WMD. At the end of the year inspectors from both the UNMOVIC and the IAEA were continuing their work despite only marginal Iraqi compliance.

Also during 2002 the United States, having withdrawn its signature in May from the treaty establishing the International Criminal Court (ICC), insisted that its troops on council-sponsored peacekeeping missions be exempted from the ICC's jurisdiction. In June the Security Council rejected a U.S. resolution that would have exempted all UN peacekeepers. Washington then attempted, again unsuccessfully, to exempt peacekeepers in Bosnia and Herzegovina, where the NATO-led Stabilization Force (SFOR) included some 4,000 U.S. military personnel. A compromise resolution on July 12 specified that the troops of states that had not joined the ICC would be granted a one-year exemption, renewable upon request. The decision was made largely moot when the council decided to terminate the Bosnian mission at the close of 2002. December 2002 also saw the completion of a much smaller operation, the United Nations Mission of Observers in Prevlaka (UNMOP), which had been established in 1996 to monitor demilitarization of the Prevlaka peninsula based on a 1992 agreement between Croatia and Montenegro.

In January 2003 UNMOVIC Executive Chair Hans Blix reported that Iraq might have misinformed the UN about Iraqi weapons' programs and called for greater cooperation from the Saddam Hussein regime. Soon afterward, Blix indicated that Iraq had indeed become more forthcoming, and he asked the Security Council to allow the UNMOVIC a number of additional months to verify Iraq's compliance with Resolution 1441's provisions regarding chemical and biological weapons. In addition, Director General Mohamed El Baradei of the IAEA asked for more time for his inspectors to assess the possible presence of nuclear weapons in Iraq. However, in late February the United States, the United Kingdom, and Spain introduced a resolution calling for Security Council authorization of military action against Iraq unless immediate steps were taken by the Hussein regime to prove its submission to Resolution 1441. After some of the bitterest debate in the council since the end of the Cold War, Russia joined France and Germany in blocking the resolution, adamantly insisting that the UNMOVIC needed more time to complete its inspections. UNMOVIC inspectors left Iraq in mid-March, however, when it became clear that a U.S.-led invasion of Iraq was imminent.

Despite the rancor of the prewar debate, the antiwar members of the council in May 2003 joined the rest of the members in authorizing the allied forces to occupy Iraq and to proceed with planned reconstruction. To assist in the rebuilding, the council agreed to discontinue its sanctions against Iraq and to phase out the "oil-for-food" program, with a view toward ramping up oil production. (In 2004 the council welcomed Secretary-General Annan's appointment of a high-level committee to investigate charges of corruption in regard to the "oil-for-food" program. See the discussion of the Secretariat for further details.) Given the radically changed circumstances in Iraq, the UNIKOM mandate concluded on October 6. The council also endorsed the interim government established in Iraq in 2004 and approved the allies' schedule for the transition to an elected government.

In 2003–2004, the council endorsed the "road map for peace" regarding the Israeli–Palestinian conflict, declared any acts of violence against civilians to be "unjustifiable," voted to discontinue sanctions against Libya after Tripoli renounced its controversial weapons programs, and passed a resolution (at the request of the United States) requiring all UN members to adopt legislation designed to prevent terrorists from gaining possession of WMD. The council also faced a significantly increased demand for peacekeeping forces, particularly in Africa, where extensive missions were approved for Burundi, Côte d'Ivoire, Liberia, and Sudan. In 2003 the Security Council imposed an arms embargo and other restrictions on various foreign and Congolese groups and militias operating in the Democratic Republic of the Congo. These sanctions were followed by establishment of a sanctions committee, expansion of the embargo in 2004, and implementation of an associated travel ban in 2005. Also in 2004, the Security Council imposed an arms embargo on Côte d'Ivoire; froze assets of, and instituted a travel ban on, various Ivorian officials; and authorized creation of a corresponding sanctions committee. Resolution 1556 imposed an arms embargo on "all non-governmental entities and individuals" operating in North, South, and West Darfur, Sudan. The Darfur embargo was expanded in March 2005, when asset and travel restrictions were also imposed and a sanctions committee was created. (In April 2006 the travel ban and assets freeze were expanded to additional individuals.)

In early 2005 when Secretary-General Annan proposed increasing the membership from 15 to 25 as part of his recommendations for broad UN reform and restructuring. Brazil, Germany, India, and Japan, known as the G-4, intensified their campaign to gain permanent council membership. The G-4 proposal called for six new permanent seats, including two seats for African countries, as well as for the addition of four new nonpermanent members. Although the case for expansion appeared to gain momentum when the G-4 dropped their demand for veto power, in August 2005 the African Union voted to reject the proposal primarily because the new permanent members would not have the veto. The expansion question was discussed at the September General Assembly session, although support among the current permanent members of the Security Council was reportedly lukewarm at best.

In May 2005 UNOTIL began operations in Timor-Leste as the second currently functioning "political or peacebuilding" mission. The first was the United Nations Assistance Mission in Afghanistan (UNAMA), which had been established in March 2002 to advise on the peace process, promote human rights, provide technical assistance, and manage UN relief and development aid. Although authorized by Security Council resolutions, both missions function under the Department of Peacekeeping Operations within the Secretariat. A third such operation, the United Nations Integrated Office in Sierra Leone (UNIOSIL), succeeded the UNAMSIL when that mission's mandate expired on December 31, 2005. Two months earlier, the Security Council had established its most recent sanctions committee in connection with the February assassination of former Lebanese prime minister Rafiq Hariri. Resolution 1636 authorized the imposition of travel restrictions and financial measures directed against Syrians and Lebanese suspected of involvement in the assassination.

The increasing burden of peacekeeping operations was highlighted in February 2006 by New York University's annual review of global operations. The review, which gave additional support to the idea of creating emergency standby arrangements, noted that in the previous six years the number of UN peacekeeping personnel had grown from under 13,000 to more than 60,000. Also in February, Undersecretary-General for Peacekeeping Operations Jean-Marie Guéhenno reported that the number of sexual abuse complaints directed against peacekeeping personnel had fallen since introduction of a new reporting system in 2005, although he characterized the number, 295, as still unacceptable.

In response to fighting in Southern Lebanon between Israel and Hezbollah forces in July 2006, the Security Council adopted Resolution 1701, which called for an end to combat and the withdrawal of combatants from the region. The resolution also authorized an increase of the United Nations Interim Force in Lebanon (UNIFIL) to 15,000 troops and expanded the mandate of the mission (see "United Nations Interim Force in Lebanon").

The Security Council launched an effort to reform its working methods in 2006. It reconvened the ad hoc Working Group on Documentation and Other Procedural Questions and tasked the body to examine practices and recommend changes to improve transparency and efficiency. The group's recommendations were approved in July and included a range of minor reforms including increased communication between the Security Council and the General Assembly, more documentation from the council, and enhanced open meetings. The success of the group led the Security Council to authorize it for another year.

Ban Ki-moon of the Republic of Korea was unanimously recommended by the Security Council in October 2006 to replace Annan as the new UN secretary-general. Also in October, the Security Council adopted Resolution 1718, which placed economic sanctions on North Korea following that country's nuclear tests. The sanctions helped prompt renewed diplomacy, which led to an agreement whereby North Korea agreed to dismantle its nuclear weapons program. Meanwhile, the success of the United Nations Operation in Burundi (*Opération des Nations Unies au Burundi*—ONUB) in facilitating a peace accord between rebels and the government led the Security Council to replace the mission with the smaller United Nations Integrated Office in Burundi (*Bureau Intégré des Nations Unies au Burundi*—BINUB).

In 2006 the United States vetoed two resolutions, both calling for the Israeli withdrawal from Gaza, while in 2007 China vetoed a draft resolution calling on Myanmar's government to release political prisoners and stop repressive measures enacted in response to a prodemocracy movement. Also in 2007 Venezuela sought to gain a nonpermanent seat on the Security Council but was opposed by the United States, which instead supported Guatemala. The result was a deadlock that lasted through 47 votes before a compromise was reached through which Venezuela and the United States agreed to support Panama, which was subsequently elected to the body. Concern over Iran's noncompliance with UN nuclear inspectors and the possibility that the country had undertaken a nuclear weapons program prompted the Security Council to adopt Resolution 1737 in December 2006 in an effort to prompt a peaceful settlement of the growing crisis. The resolution imposed limited sanctions on Iran. Divisions between the United States, France, and the United Kingdom, all of which endorsed more stringent measures, and China and Russia, which opposed tougher action, prevented substantive further action through 2007.

In February 2007 UN representative Martti Ahtisaari recommended to the Security Council that the Serbian province of Kosovo be granted eventual independence under the supervision of the UN. However, independence was opposed by both Serbia and Russia. Negotiators from Russia, the United States, and the EU launched a new round of talks with Serb and Kosovar leaders with the goal of developing a new proposal for the Security Council in December 2007. Meanwhile, efforts to forge a common policy on Sudan were stymied by Chinese opposition. While a joint peacekeeping force between the AU and the United Nations Mission in Sudan (UNMIS) had been approved, Sudanese opposition to the deployment of non-African troops limited the size and scope of the operation. In May the United States imposed new economic sanctions on Sudan and developed a draft resolution that would increase pressure on the Sudanese government to end interference with the UNMIS. Subsequently, however, the United States agreed to delay its resolution to allow Ban time to negotiate a new agreement. The secretary-general held a ministerial meeting in September, which brought together representatives from 20 countries, but the meeting failed to break the impasse over the expanded UN mission in Sudan. The Security Council extended the mandate of the UNMIS through 2007.

The Security Council conducted its first open debate on climate change in April 2007. The session was initiated by the United Kingdom, which, along with other members of the council, asserted that global warming had significant security implications, including increased competition for resources. However, countries such as China and Pakistan criticized the forum and argued that there were other agencies within the UN that were better suited to discuss climate change. Meanwhile, in June the council voted in Resolution 1762 to end the UNMOVIC mission in Iraq.

To protect the growing number of refugees in the region, estimated at 230,000, and to deter attacks by Sudanese rebel groups in the area, the Security Council authorized the creation of the United Nations Mission in the Central African Republic and Chad (*Mission des Nations Unies en République Centrafricaine et au Tchad*—MINURCAT) in September 2007.

A report delivered to the Security Council by the Stockholm International Peace Research Institute (SIPRI), published in November 2007, questioned the efficiency of UN arms embargoes. The report found that since 1990 only one-fourth of the 27 arms embargoes had been effective. The study did conclude that the presence of UN peacekeepers, however, dramatically increased the likelihood that the sanctions would be successful. SIPRI recommended that the Security Council increase the frequency of reviews of embargo regimes. It also advocated that the council work to have more countries criminalize violations of UN sanctions and prosecute nationals who contravene the embargoes.

In February 2008, following Kosovo's unilateral declaration of independence, the Security Council conducted an emergency session at the request of Serbia and Russia, both of which sought to block the Kosovar bid. No resolution was reached and Russia then circulated a draft resolution to the Security Council in March that would have preserved the territorial integrity of Serbia. However, Russia gained the support of only 6 of the council's 15 members. Serbia then requested that the issue of Kosovar independence be adjudicated through the ICC. The General Assembly voted in favor of the Serbian initiative in October 2008 (see General Assembly).

On June 19, 2008, the Security Council adopted Resolution 1820, which called on the world body to take greater steps to protect women and children in zones of conflict and specifically requested that the secretary-general adopt stronger rules to ensure "zero tolerance of sexual exploitation and abuse in UN peacekeeping operations." On June 24 the undersecretary-general for security and safety, Sir David Veness, resigned in the aftermath of a car bomb attack that killed 17 UN personnel at the world body's main office in Algiers. Partially in response to the attack, the Security Council adopted Resolution 1822, which called on all nations to work together to cut funding for such terrorist organizations as al-Qaida. In August Ban named Andrew Hughes of Australia as the new chief of UN police missions to replace Mark Kroeker of the United States, who resigned in April.

The Security Council was briefed by the special prosecutor for Sudan of the International Criminal Court (ICC) in June 2008 on allegations that the government was not cooperating with the court. The ICC later charged Sudanese president Omar al-Bashir with genocide for his role in the humanitarian crisis (see entry on Sudan). Pressure by the United States for the Security Council to take stronger action regarding the conflict in Darfur was repeatedly blocked through 2008, though the council did extend the mandate of UNMIL through 2009.

In May 2008 China and Russia vetoed a Security Council resolution condemning the government of Zimbabwe for violence against its opposition groups and leaders in the aftermath of elections in that country. In response to demands by Eritrea that the UN Mission in Ethiopia and Eritrea (UNMEE) reduce its staff and limit helicopter flights, along with fuel blockages, the Security Council ended the operation on July 31.

Following an October 2008 report by the International Atomic Energy Agency that Iran continued to block inspectors' access to its nuclear facilities, the Security Council unanimously adopted Resolution 1835, which reaffirmed existing sanctions on Iran and called on the government to immediately suspend its uranium-enrichment program. Meanwhile, in response to increased piracy off of the coast of Somalia, the Security Council adopted Resolution 1838 in October, calling on states to work with Somalia's interim Transitional Federal Government to use air and naval resources to end the attacks on merchant and humanitarian shipping. Also in October, former UN envoy Ahtisaari won the Nobel Peace Prize for his work with the world body, including his efforts to resolve the status of Kosovo.

On January 14, 2009, the Security Council extended the mandate of MINURCAT and authorized an increase in the number of peacekeeping forces, up to 5,200 troops. The council subsequently extended a number of other UN operations, including those in Burundi, Liberia, and the Western Sahara. In January the Security Council also passed a resolution calling on Eritrea and Ethiopia to peacefully settle an ongoing border dispute between the two nations. The Security Council unanimously adopted Resolution 1874 on June 12. The measure increased sanctions on North Korea, following that country's second nuclear weapons test. On June 15 Russia vetoed a Security Council resolution to extend the UN observer mission in Georgia and Abkhazia. On September 24 the council, represented by 14 heads of state, including U.S. president Obama, adopted Resolution 1887, which reaffirmed the UN's commitment to the Non-Proliferation Treaty and called on member states to support counter-proliferation efforts and reduce nuclear weapons stockpiles. Meanwhile, on September 30 the Security Council unanimously approved Resolution 1888, which called on all actors in a conflict to take measures to protect vulnerable populations, including women and children, from sexual violence. On October 15 Nigeria, Gabon, Lebanon, Brazil, and Bosnia and Herzegovina were elected as nonpermanent members of the Security Council in a rare round of uncontested balloting. Resolution 1907, enacted on December 23, imposed sanctions on Eritrea that included a travel ban for officials, an arms embargo, and the freezing of some assets, as a result of Eritrea's support for armed groups in Somalia.

On June 9, 2010, the Security Council adopted Resolution 1929, which enacted new sanctions against Iran for its continued nuclear program. The measure was a compromise between council members the United States, France, and the United Kingdom, which sought tougher sanctions, and Russia and China, which resisted new restrictions. Meanwhile, on June 15 the Republic of Korea asked the Security Council to investigate and censure the Democratic People's Republic of Korea in response to the sinking of a Republic of Korea naval vessel and the loss of 46 sailors. China, a traditional ally of the Democratic People's Republic of Korea, resisted council intervention. The council issued a statement deploring the loss of life and urged the two countries to engage in a dialogue. On December 31 MINURCAT's mission ended and UN forces were withdrawn. Also on December 31, BINUB's mandate expired and the mission transitioned to the UN Office in Burundi (*Bureau des Nations Unies au Burundi*—BNUB).

The Council voted sanctions and the creation of a no-fly zone against Libya in March 2011 (see entry on Libya). In October 2011 and again in February 2012 China and Russia vetoed Security Council resolutions calling on Syria to abide by an Arab League peace proposal. Meanwhile, former secretary-general Annan was appointed as a special envoy to Syria (see "Secretariat"). Following the eruption of new fighting between Sudan and South Sudan, the council adopted resolution 2046 in May 2012, which called for an end to the violence and a withdrawal of military forces in disputed border areas. The council also extended the mandate of the UN Interim Security Force for Abyei (UNISFA) in the region. In May the Security Council imposed new sanctions on North Korea, following that nation's failed rocket launch on April 13.

The UN Supervision Mission in Syria (*Mission de supervision des Nations Unies en Syrie*—MISNUS), established in April 2012, was suspended on June 16, 2012, as a result of increasing violence in Syria. UN efforts to reduce strife and allow the redeployment of MISNUS failed, and the mission's mandate was terminated on August 19.

Rwanda's election to the Security Council in October 2012 was highly controversial in the aftermath of a UN report that accused Kigali of supporting the M23 militia in the Democratic Republic of the Congo (see entry on the Democratic Republic of the Congo). In December, the UN Integrated Mission in Timor-Leste (UNMIT), launched in 2006, ended. (See the 2013 *Handbook* for more detail on UNMIT.)

In January 2013 the Security Council expanded existing sanctions on North Korea after Pyongyang launched another rocket in violation of previous UN restrictions. On March 7 the Security Council condemned North Korea's third nuclear test and imposed additional sanctions on the country (see entry on North Korea). On April 25 the Security Council unanimously adopted Resolution 2100, which authorized the creation of a 12,600-member peacekeeping force, UN Multidimensional Integrated Stabilisation Mission in Mali (*Mission Multidimensionnelle Intégrée des Nations Unies pour la Stabilisation au Mali*—MINUSMA), to replace the existing African Union operation (see below). The Security Council passed Resolution 2106 which called for greater efforts to end "impunity for sexual violence against women." After two years of significant debate and allegations of inaction, the UN Security Council on September 28, 2013, unanimously adopted a U.S.–Russian resolution calling on Syria to end its chemical weapons program and to allow international inspectors access to suspected chemical weapons facilities. The resolution followed the dispatch of a UN inspection team to investigate alleged chemical weapons attacks. On October 17 Chad, Chile, Lithuania, Nigeria, and Saudi Arabia were elected as nonpermanent members of the Security Council. However, Saudi Arabia announced it would not take its seat, stating that Riyadh had "no faith" in the Security Council because of its inability to take stronger action in the Syrian Civil War. Jordan was elected in place of Saudi Arabia.

Through Security Council Resolution 2149, adopted on April 10, 2014, the AU mission in the Central African Republic was transitioned to a UN operation with the establishment of the United National Multidimensional Integrated Stabilization Mission in the Central African Republic (*Mission Multidimensionnelle Intégrée des Nations Unies pour la Stabilisation en République Centrafricaine*—MINUSCA). MINUSCA was authorized with an initial strength of 10,000 troops and 1,800 police officers and tasked to protect civilians and humanitarian operations as well as overseeing the demobilization of fighters (see below). On September 24 the Security Council unanimously adopted Resolution 2178, which required states to adopt laws against prohibiting their nationals from traveling to fight for extremist groups or collecting funds for those groups. The resolution was in response to the growing number of foreign fighters in Syria and Iraq.

On March 6, 2015, the Security Council condemned the use of chemical weapons in the Syrian civil war through Resolution 2209. The measure also threatened the use of force if there were further chemical weapons attacks in the country. Security Council Resolution 2225, adopted on June 18, classified abduction as one of the crimes against children that the UN monitored in war zones. Following a July 2015 agreement on Iran's nuclear program (see entry on Iran), the Security Council began removing sanctions on that country as certain benchmarks were met under the terms of Security Council Resolution 2231, passed on July 20.

SECURITY COUNCIL: PEACEKEEPING FORCES AND MISSIONS

In addition to the forces and missions listed here, the United Nations Command in Korea (established on June 25, 1950) remains technically in existence. The only UN member now contributing to the command is the United States, which proposed in June 1975 that it be dissolved. As of 2016 no formal action had been taken on the proposal (see Security Council: Origin and development).

UNITED NATIONS/AFRICAN UNION HYBRID OPERATION IN DARFUR

(UNAMID)

Established: By Security Council resolution of July 31, 2007; modified by Security Council resolution on July 30, 2013.

Purpose: To protect civilians; provide security for humanitarian assistance; verify the implementation of peace agreements and facilitate a political settlement to ongoing conflicts; and monitor the borders between Sudan and Chad and the Central African Republic.

Headquarters: El Fasher, Darfur.

Force Commander: Lt. Gen. Frank Kamanzi (Rwanda).

Composition: As of August 31, 2016, 13,785 troops and 1,814 civilian police from Bangladesh, Bhutan, Bolivia, Burkina Faso, Burundi, Cambodia, Cameroon, China, Djibouti, Egypt, Ethiopia, Fiji, Gambia, Germany, Ghana, Indonesia, Iran, Jordan, Kenya, Kyrgyzstan, Lesotho, Madagascar, Malawi, Malaysia, Mali, Mongolia, Namibia, Nepal, Nigeria, Pakistan, Palau, Papua New Guinea, Peru, Republic of Korea, Rwanda, Samoa, Senegal, Sierra Leone, Solomon Islands, South Africa, Sri Lanka, Tajikistan, Tanzania, Thailand, Togo, Tunisia, Turkey, Uganda, Yemen, Zambia, and Zimbabwe.

UNITED NATIONS DISENGAGEMENT OBSERVER FORCE

(UNDOF)

Established: By Security Council resolution of May 31, 1974.

Purpose: To observe the cease-fire between Israel and Syria following the 1973 Arab-Israeli War.

Headquarters: Camp Faouar (Syrian Golan Heights). (A UNDOF office is located in Damascus, Syria.)

Force Commander: Maj. Gen. Jai Shankar Menon (India).

Composition: As of August 31, 2016, 819 troops from Bhutan, Czech Republic, Fiji, Finland, India, Ireland, Nepal, and the Netherlands.

UNITED NATIONS FORCE IN CYPRUS

(UNFICYP)

Established: By Security Council resolution of March 4, 1964, after consultation with the governments of Cyprus, Greece, Turkey, and the United Kingdom.

Purpose: To serve as a peacekeeping force between Greek and Turkish Cypriots.

Headquarters: Nicosia, Cyprus.

Force Commander: Maj. Gen. Mohammad Humayun Kabir (Bangladesh).

Composition: As of August 31, 2016, 959 troops and 69 civilian police from Argentina, Australia, Austria, Bosnia-Herzegovina, Brazil, Canada, Chile, China, Hungary, India, Ireland, Lithuania, Montenegro, Norway, Paraguay, Romania, Russia, Serbia, Slovakia, Ukraine, and the United Kingdom.

UNITED NATIONS INTERIM ADMINISTRATION MISSION IN KOSOVO

(UNMIK)

Established: By Security Council resolution of June 10, 1999, which also authorized formation of a Multinational Force in Kosovo (Kosovo Force—KFOR); modified by Security Council resolution on June 15, 2008; strength reduced by Security Council resolution on June 10, 2009.

Purpose: To promote significant autonomy and self-government in Kosovo; to provide civilian administrative functions, including holding elections; to maintain law and order while promoting human rights and ensuring the safe and voluntary return of Kosovar refugees and displaced persons; and to ultimately oversee a transfer of authority to civilian institutions established under a political settlement. KFOR was authorized to establish and maintain a secure environment in Kosovo until such time as the UNMIK Civilian Police could assume this task on a region-by-region basis. In December 2008 the EU Rule of Law Mission in Kosovo (EULEX) took over most of UNMIK's duties in terms of civilian police and security, allowing a substantial reduction in UN personnel.

Headquarters: Priština, Kosovo, Serbia.

Head of Mission: Zahir Tanin (Afghanistan).

Operational Framework: Four "pillars"—peace and justice, civil administration, democratization and institution-building under the direction of the Organization for Security and Cooperation in Europe; reconstruction and economic development under the European Union. KFOR is now under NATO/EU command.

Composition: As of August 31, 2016, 7 police officers and 8 military liaisons from Austria, Bulgaria, Czech Republic, Germany, Hungary, Italy, Moldova, Poland, Romania, Russia, Turkey, and Ukraine, in addition to the NATO-led peacekeeping and monitoring force.

UNITED NATIONS INTERIM FORCE IN LEBANON

(UNIFIL)

Established: By Security Council resolution of March 19, 1978, and augmented by subsequent Security Council resolution on August 11, 2006.

Purpose: To confirm the withdrawal of Israeli troops from Lebanon, to restore peace and help ensure the return of Lebanese authority to southern Lebanon, to extend access to humanitarian support for the civilian population, to facilitate the return of displaced persons, to establish a zone free of weapons and armed personnel other than those of the Lebanese security forces and UNIFIL, and to aid the government of Lebanon in securing its borders.

Headquarters: Naqoura, Lebanon.

Force Commander: Maj. Gen. Luciano Portolano (Italy).

Composition: As of August 31, 2016, 10,490 troops from Armenia, Austria, Bangladesh, Belarus, Belgium, Brazil, Brunei, Cambodia, China, Croatia, Cyprus, El Salvador, Estonia, Fiji, Finland, France, FYR of Macedonia, Germany, Ghana, Greece, Guatemala, Hungary, India, Indonesia, Ireland, Italy, Kenya, Malaysia, Mexico, Nepal, Nigeria, Qatar, Republic of Korea, Sierra Leone, Slovenia, Spain, Sri Lanka, Tanzania, and Turkey.

UNITED NATIONS MILITARY OBSERVER GROUP IN INDIA AND PAKISTAN

(UNMOGIP)

Established: By resolutions adopted by the United Nations Commission for India and Pakistan on August 13, 1948, and January 5, 1949; augmented and brought under the jurisdiction of the Security Council by resolution of September 6, 1965, in view of a worsening situation in Kashmir.

Purpose: To assist in implementing the cease-fire agreement of January 1, 1949.

Headquarters: Rawalpindi, Pakistan (November–April); Srinagar, India (May–October).

Chief Military Observer: Maj. Gen. Per Gustaf Lodin (Sweden).

Composition: As of August 31, 2016, 41 military observers from Chile, Croatia, Finland, Republic of Korea, Sweden, Switzerland, Thailand, and Uruguay.

UNITED NATIONS MISSION FOR THE REFERENDUM IN WESTERN SAHARA

Mission des Nations Unies pour le Référendum dans le Sahara Ouest
(MINURSO)

Established: By Security Council resolution of April 29, 1991.

Purpose: To enforce a cease-fire in the Western Sahara between Morocco and the Polisario Front, to identify those eligible to vote in the proposed self-determination referendum in the region, and to supervise the referendum and settlement plan.

Headquarters: Laayoune, Western Sahara.

Force Commander: Maj. Gen. Muhammad Tayyab Azam (Pakistan).

Composition: As of August 31, 2016, 24 troops and 193 military observers from Argentina, Austria, Bangladesh, Bhutan, Brazil, China, Croatia, Djibouti, Egypt, El Salvador, France, Germany, Ghana, Guinea, Honduras, Hungary, India, Indonesia, Ireland, Kazakhstan, Malaysia, Mongolia, Nepal, Nigeria, Pakistan, Republic of Korea, Russia, Sri Lanka, Switzerland, Togo, and Yemen. An additional 2,200 troops and observers were authorized but not deployed because of the lack of progress in referendum negotiations.

UNITED NATIONS MISSION IN LIBERIA

(UNMIL)

Established: By Security Council resolution of September 19, 2003; modified by Security Council resolution on September 17, 2012.

Purpose: To support implementation of the recent cease-fire agreement in Liberia, to support humanitarian and human rights activities, and to assist in training national police and the proposed restructured military.

Headquarters: Monrovia, Liberia.

Force Commander: Maj. Gen. Salihu Zaway Uba (Nigeria).

Composition: As of August 31, 2016, 1,179 troops, 63 military observers, and 571 civilian police from Bangladesh, Benin, Bhutan, Bolivia, Bosnia and Herzegovina, Brazil, Bulgaria, China, Egypt, Ethiopia, Fiji, Gambia, Germany, Ghana, India, Indonesia, Jordan, Kenya, Kyrgyzstan, Malaysia, Moldova, Myanmar, Namibia, Nepal, Niger, Nigeria, Norway, Pakistan, Poland, Republic of Korea, Romania, Russia, Rwanda, Serbia, Sri Lanka, Sweden, Switzerland, Togo, Turkey, Uganda, Ukraine, United Kingdom, United States, Uruguay, Yemen, Zambia, and Zimbabwe.

UNITED NATIONS MISSION IN THE REPUBLIC OF SOUTH SUDAN

(UNMISS)

Established: By Security Council resolution of July 9, 2011; augmented by Security Council resolutions on December 24, 2013, and May 27, 2014.

Purpose: When South Sudan became independent of Sudan on July 9, 2011, the United Nations Mission in the Sudan (UNMIS, see the 2011 *Handbook*) was terminated, being replaced by UNMISS. UNMISS was to operate for one year, with its mandate subsequently renewed.

Headquarters: Juba, South Sudan.

Force Commander: Lt. Gen. John Mogoa Kimani Ondieke (Kenya).

Composition: As of August 31, 2016, 12,111 troops, 185 military observers, and 1,427 civilian police from Argentina, Australia, Bangladesh, Benin, Bhutan, Bolivia, Bosnia and Herzegovina, Brazil, Cambodia, Canada, China, Denmark, Egypt, El Salvador, Ethiopia, Fiji, Gambia, Germany, Ghana, Guatemala, Guinea, India, Indonesia, Japan, Jordan, Kenya, Kyrgyzstan, Moldova, Mongolia, Myanmar, Namibia, Nepal, the Netherlands, New Zealand, Nigeria, Norway, Papua New Guinea, Paraguay, Peru, Poland, Republic of Korea, Romania, Russia, Rwanda, Samoa, Senegal, South Africa, Sri Lanka, Sweden, Switzerland, Tanzania, Thailand, Togo, Turkey, Uganda, Ukraine, United Kingdom, United States, Yemen, Zambia, and Zimbabwe.

UNITED NATIONS OPERATION IN CÔTE D'IVOIRE

Opération des Nations Unies en Côte d'Ivoire (ONUCI)

Established: By Security Council resolution of February 27, 2004; augmented by Security Council resolution on July 30, 2013; modified by Security Council Resolution on June 25, 2014, and again on June 25, 2015.

Purpose: To facilitate implementation of the peace agreement signed by the parties to the conflict in Côte d'Ivoire, address remaining security threats and border-related challenges, and support the 2015 presidential election. (The ONUCI was a successor to the United Nations Mission in Côte d'Ivoire [*Mission des Nations Unies en Côted'Ivoire*—MINUCI], a political mission that had been established by the Security Council in May 2003.)

Headquarters: Abidjan, Côte d'Ivoire.

Force Commander: Maj. Gen. Didier L'Hôte (France).

Composition: As of August 31, 2016, 1,947 troops, 108 military observers, and 752 civilian police from Bangladesh, Benin, Bolivia, Brazil, Burkina Faso, Burundi, Cameroon, Chad, China, Democratic Republic of the Congo, Ecuador, Egypt, Ethiopia, France, Gambia, Ghana, Guatemala, Guinea, India, Ireland, Jordan, Kazakhstan, Madagascar, Malawi, Mauritania, Moldova, Morocco, Namibia, Nepal, Niger, Nigeria, Pakistan, Paraguay, Peru, Philippines, Poland, Republic of Korea, Romania, Russia, Rwanda, Senegal, Serbia, Switzerland, Tanzania, Togo, Tunisia, Turkey, Uganda, Ukraine, Uruguay, Vanuatu, Yemen, Zambia, and Zimbabwe.

UNITED NATIONS ORGANIZATION STABILIZATION MISSION IN THE DEMOCRATIC REPUBLIC OF THE CONGO

Mission de l'Organisation des Nations Unies en République Démocratique du Congo (MONUSCO)

Established: By Security Council resolution of May 28, 2010, as a successor to the United Nations Organization Mission in the Democratic Republic of the Congo (MONUC, see the 2011 *Handbook*). MONUSCO was to concentrate its activities in the eastern DRC while keeping a reserve force capable of operating elsewhere. Modified by Security Council resolution on June 27, 2012; augmented by Security Council Resolution on March 28, 2013; modified by Security Council resolution on March 28, 2014.

Purpose: The effective protection of civilians and humanitarian personnel, as well as the protection of UN personnel, facilities, installations, and equipment. Monusco would also assist the government, along with international and bilateral partners, in strengthening its military; support the reform of the police; develop and implement a multiyear joint UN justice support program in order to develop the criminal justice system; and support the Congolese government in consolidating state authority in the territory freed from armed groups.

Headquarters: Kinshasa, Democratic Republic of the Congo. Liaison offices are maintained in Addis Ababa, Ethiopia; Bujumbura, Burundi; Harare, Zimbabwe; Kampala, Uganda; Kigali, Rwanda; Lusaka, Zambia; and Windhoek, Namibia.

Force Commander: Lt. Gen. Derick Mbuyiselo Mgwebi (South Africa).

Composition: As of August 31, 2014, 18,620 troops, 478 military observers, and 1,407 civilian police from Bangladesh, Belgium, Benin, Bolivia, Bosnia Herzegovina. Burkina Faso, Cameroon, Canada, Chad, China, Côte d'Ivoire, Czech Republic, Djibouti, Egypt, France, Ghana, Guatemala, Guinea, India, Indonesia, Ireland, Jordan, Kenya, Madagascar, Malawi, Malaysia, Mali, Mongolia, Morocco, Nepal, Niger, Nigeria, Pakistan, Paraguay, Peru, Poland, Romania, Russia, Senegal, Serbia, South Africa, Sri Lanka, Sweden, Switzerland, Tanzania, Togo, Tunisia, Turkey, Ukraine, United Kingdom, United States, Uruguay, Yemen, and Zambia.

UNITED NATIONS STABILIZATION MISSION IN HAITI

Mission des Nations Unies pour la Stabilisation en Haïti (MINUSTAH)

Established: By Security Council resolution of April 30, 2004; expanded by Security Council resolution on October 13, 2009, and again on June 4, 2010; modified by Security Council resolution on October 12, 2012; October 14, 2014; and October 13, 2016. (MINUSTAH assumed the authority previously exercised by the Multinational Interim Force [MIF] that had been authorized by the Security Council in February 2004.)

Purpose: To support the constitutional and political process underway in Haiti; to help maintain security and stability; to assist with the restoration and maintenance of the rule of law, public safety, and public order; to assist the transitional government in Haiti in reforming the Haitian national police; to assist in the disarmament and demobilization of armed groups; to provide support for the holding of free and fair elections; and to assist in the post-disaster recovery and reconstruction following the January earthquake.

Headquarters: Port-au-Prince, Haiti.

Force Commander: Lt. Gen. Ajax Porto Pinheiro (Brazil).

Composition: As of August 31, 2016, 2,358 troops and 2,350 civilian police from Argentina, Bangladesh, Benin, Bhutan, Brazil, Burkina Faso, Cameroon, Canada, Chad, Chile, Colombia, Ecuador, Egypt, El Salvador, Ethiopia, France, Germany, Ghana, Guatemala, Honduras, India, Indonesia, Jordan, Madagascar, Mexico, Nepal, Niger, Nigeria, Norway, Pakistan, Paraguay, Peru, Philippines, Romania, Russia, Rwanda, Senegal, Slovakia, Spain, Sri Lanka, Thailand, Tunisia, Turkey, United States, Uruguay, and Yemen.

UNITED NATIONS TRUCE SUPERVISION ORGANIZATION

(UNTSO)

Established: By Security Council resolution of May 29, 1948.

Purpose: To supervise the cease-fire arranged by the Security Council following the 1948 Arab-Israeli War. Its mandate was subsequently extended to embrace the armistice agreements concluded in 1949; the Egyptian-Israeli peace treaty of 1979; and assistance to other UN forces in the Middle East, specifically the UNDOF and UNIFIL.

Headquarters: Jerusalem, Israel.

Chief of Staff: Maj. Gen. Arthur David Gawn (New Zealand).

Composition: As of August 31, 2016, 146 military observers from Argentina, Australia, Austria, Belgium, Bhutan, Canada, Chile, China, Denmark, Estonia, Fiji, Finland, France, India, Ireland, Nepal, Netherlands, New Zealand, Norway, Russia, Serbia, Slovakia, Slovenia, Sweden, Switzerland, and the United States.

UNITED NATIONS INTERIM SECURITY FORCE FOR ABYEI

(UNISFA)

Established: By Security Council resolution of June 27, 2011; augmented by Security Council resolution on May 29, 2013, and May 12, 2016.

Purpose: To supervise the withdrawal of Sudanese and South Sudanese forces from Abyei; facilitate the delivery of humanitarian aid to the region; secure the region's oil infrastructure; and protect civilians from violence.

Headquarters: Abyei Town, Sudan.

Force Commander (Acting): Maj. Gen. Hassen Ebrahim Mussa (Ethiopia).

Composition: As of August 31, 2016, 4,397 troops, 129 military observers, and 8 police officers from Benin, Bhutan, Brazil, Cambodia, Ecuador, El Salvador, Ethiopia, Ghana, Guatemala, Guinea, India, Indonesia, Kyrgyzstan, Malawi, Malaysia, Mongolia, Mozambique, Namibia, Nepal, Nigeria, Peru, Russia, Rwanda, Sierra Leone, Sri Lanka, Tanzania, Ukraine, Yemen, Zambia, and Zimbabwe.

UNITED NATIONS MULTIDIMENSIONAL INTEGRATED STABILIZATION MISSION IN MALI

Mission Multidimensionnelle Intégrée des Nations Unies pour la Stabilisation au Mali (MINUSMA)

Established: By Security Council resolution of April 25, 2013; modified by Security Council resolution on June 25, 2014, and June 29, 2016.

Purpose: To ensure security, stabilization and protection of civilians; support national political dialogue and reconciliation; and assist the reestablishment of state authority, the rebuilding of the security sector, and the promotion and protection of human rights.

Headquarters: Barnako, Mali.

Force Commander: Maj. Gen. Michael Lollesgaard (Denmark).

Composition: As of August 31, 2016, 10,579 troops, 40 military observers, and 1,264 civilian police from Armenia, Austria, Bangladesh, Belgium, Benin, Bhutan, Bosnia Herzegovina, Burkina Faso, Burundi, Cambodia, Cameroon, Chad, China, Côte d'Ivoire, Czech Republic, Denmark, Dominican Republic, Egypt, El Salvador, Estonia, Ethiopia, Finland, France, Gambia, Germany, Ghana, Guinea, Guinea-Bissau, Indonesia, Italy, Jordan, Kenya, Latvia, Liberia, Madagascar, Nepal, the Netherlands, Niger, Nigeria, Norway, Portugal, Romania, Senegal, Sierra Leone, Sweden, Switzerland, Togo, Tunisia, Turkey, United Kingdom, United States, and Yemen.

UNITED NATIONS MULTIDIMENSIONAL INTEGRATED STABILIZATION MISSION IN THE CENTRAL AFRICAN REPUBLIC

Mission Multidimensionnelle Intégrée des Nations Unies pour la Stabilisation en République Centrafricaine (MINUSCA)

Established: By Security Council resolution of April 10, 2014, augmented by Security Council resolution on July 26, 2016. (MINUSCA assumed the responsibilities of the UN Integrated Peacebuilding Office in the Central African Republic (BINUCA) that had been authorized by the Security Council in January 2010.)

Purpose: To protect civilians and UN personnel, installations, and equipment; support the political process, including the restoration of state authority and its extension throughout the country; create security conditions conducive to the delivery of principled humanitarian assistance and the safe return of IDPs and refugees; promote and protect human rights; promote a national dialogue, mediation, and reconciliation at all levels; and support the disarmament, demobilization, and reintegration of former armed elements.

Headquarters: Bangui, Central African Republic.

Force Commander: Lt. Gen. Balla Keïta (Senegal).

Composition: As of August 31, 2016, 10,245, 148 military observers, and 1,759 civilian police from Bangladesh, Benin, Bhutan, Bolivia, Brazil, Burkina Faso, Burundi, Cambodia, Cameroon, Chile, Congo, Czech Republic, Djibouti, Democratic Republic of the Congo, Egypt, France, Gabon, Gambia, Ghana, Guatemala, Guinea, Hungary, Indonesia, Jordan, Kenya, Mali, Mauritania, Moldova, Morocco, Nepal, Niger, Nigeria, Pakistan, Paraguay, Peru, Portugal, Romania, Rwanda, Senegal, Serbia, Sri Lanka, Tanzania, Togo, Tunisia, Turkey, United States, Vietnam, Yemen, and Zambia.

SECURITY COUNCIL: INTERNATIONAL CRIMINAL TRIBUNALS

Lacking at the time a permanent international court with jurisdiction to prosecute and try cases involving accusations of war crimes, genocide, and crimes against humanity, the Security Council established the International Criminal Tribunal for the former Yugoslavia (ICTY) in 1993 and the International Criminal Tribunal for Rwanda (ICTR) in 1994. Meeting in Rome, Italy, in 1998, a UN conference approved formation of a permanent International Criminal Court (ICC), which by April 2002 had obtained sufficient ratifications for its establishment in July (see the General Assembly section).

As of September 2016 the ICTY indicted 161 individuals, including those who had been acquitted, 19; those whose cases had been withdrawn, 37; and those who had been transferred for trial to national courts, 13. Proceedings had been concluded against 141 persons, with 83 individuals sentenced, including 50 who had completed their sentences (in addition to 3 who died while serving their sentences), and 21 either serving sentences or awaiting transfer to begin their sentences. Seven cases were still proceeding, including appeals. The last two indicted individuals remaining at large, Ratko Mladić, formerly commander of the Bosnian Serb army and Goran Hadžić, formerly president of the Republic of Serbian Krajina, were arrested on May 26, 2011, and July 20, 2011, respectively.

On November 2, 2002, Biljana Plavšić, former president of the Serb Republic of Bosnia and Herzegovina, pleaded guilty to one count of a crime against humanity for political, racial, and religious persecution, and on February 27, 2003, she was sentenced to 11 years in prison. By far the most prominent figure turned over to the court by national forces was former Yugoslav president Slobodan Milošević, who died on March 11, 2006, during his trial. The former president of the Republic of Srpska, Radovan Karadžić, was arrested on July 18, 2008, and turned over to the ICTY on July 30. Karadžić refused to recognize the authority of the ITCY and avoided entering a plea until a not guilty plea was entered on his behalf in March 2009. His trial began in October 2009. By August 2014 the trials of Mladić, Hadžić, Karadžić, and Vojislav Šešelj, the president of the Serb Radical Party, were the last remaining ongoing cases, although appeals were still being heard in other cases.

As of September 2016 the ICTR had brought public indictments against some 93 individuals, and concluded 76 trials (with 62 convictions and 14 acquittals) and 50 appellate hearings. Ten cases had been referred to national jurisdictions, while two indictments were withdrawn, and three indictees died prior to the conclusion of their trials. Nine indictees remained at large. The highest-ranking defendant, former Rwandan prime minister Jean Kambanda, pleaded guilty to genocide in 1998 and was sentenced to life in prison. In 2008 three of the remaining high-level indictees were arrested, including Callixte Nsabonimana, Dominique Ntawukulilyayo, and Augustin Ngirabatware. In June the ICTR requested a one-year extension from the Security Council to complete its trial work, partially as a result of the three arrests. In 2009 and 2010 the ICTR requested additional time to complete all trials. In 2013 the Security Council requested that the tribunal complete all work by December 31, 2014. The ICTR closed its cases on December 31, 2015.

In August 2000 the Security Council unanimously indicated its support for forming a third war crimes tribunal, for Sierra Leone, which began its proceedings in 2003, although not as a subsidiary body of the Security Council. Former Liberian president Charles Taylor was the highest-ranking defendant tried by the court. He was convicted of 11 counts of war crimes on April 26, 2012, and sentenced to 50 years in prison. The conviction was hailed by human rights groups. A similar joint criminal tribunal in Lebanon began in 2005, and in 2007 a tribunal began in Cambodia to prosecute and try former Khmer Rouge regime members. The Special Tribunal for Lebanon issued indictments for five individuals through 2013, but all remained at large and their trials had not begun. Through August 2013, the Cambodia Tribunal (officially known as the Extraordinary Chambers in the Courts of Cambodia), had indicted five individuals. Khmer Rouge leader Kang Kek Lewwas convicted of crimes against humanity in July 2012, and sentenced to 35 years in prison. One indictee died during his trial, while another was declared mentally unfit for trial. Two other trials remained ongoing.

The final two defendants, Nuon Chea and Khieu Samphan, were found guilty of crimes against humanity on August 7, 2014, and both were sentenced to life imprisonment.

In February 2016 the UN Security Council appointed ICTY prosecutor Serge Brammertz (Belgium) to lead the International Residual Mechanism for Criminal Tribunals (IRMCT). The IRMCT was charged with overseeing any remaining legal issues related to the ICTY and the ICTR until March 2018. The IRMCT was given the authority to reappoint justices and prosecutors as necessary.

INTERNATIONAL CRIMINAL TRIBUNAL FOR THE FORMER YUGOSLAVIA

(ICTY)

Formal Name: International Tribunal for the Prosecution of Persons Responsible for Serious Violations of International Humanitarian Law Committed in the Territory of the Former Yugoslavia since 1991.

Established: By Security Council resolution of May 25, 1993.

Purpose: To prosecute and try persons who allegedly committed serious violations of international humanitarian law on the territory of the former Yugoslavia since 1991, the subject offenses being genocide, crimes against humanity, and violations of the 1949 Geneva Conventions and the laws or customs of war.

Headquarters: The Hague, Netherlands.

Chief Prosecutor: Serge Brammertz (Belgium).

Permanent Judges: Carmel A. Agius (Malta, President), Liu Daqun (China, Vice President), Christoph Flügge (Germany), Burton Hall (Bahamas), Alphonsus Martinus Maria Orie (Netherlands), Fausto Pocar (Italy), Theodor Meron (United States), and Bakone Justice Moloto (South Africa). There are also 3 *ad litem* judges.

Registrar: John Hocking (Australia).

Website: www.icty.org.

INTERNATIONAL CRIMINAL TRIBUNAL FOR RWANDA

(ICTR)
Tribunal Pénal International pour le Rwanda (French)
Urukiko Nshinjabyaha Mpuzamahanga Rwagenewe u Rwanda (Kinyarwanda)

Formal Name: International Criminal Tribunal for the Prosecution of Persons Responsible for Genocide and Other Serious Violations of International Humanitarian Law Committed in the Territory of Rwanda and Rwandan Citizens Responsible for Genocide and Other Such Violations Committed in the Territory of Neighboring States, between 1 January 1994 and 31 December 1994.

Established: By Security Council resolution of November 8, 1994.

Purpose: To prosecute crimes allegedly committed by Rwandans and others in Rwanda, and by Rwandans in neighboring states, between January 1, 1994, and December 31, 1994, the subject offenses being violations of the 1949 Geneva Conventions, genocide, and crimes against humanity.

Headquarters: Arusha, Tanzania. The office of the prosecutor is located in Kigali, Rwanda.

Chief Prosecutor: Hassan Bubacar Jallow (Gambia).

Permanent Judges: Vagn Joensen (Denmark, President).

Registrar: Adama Dieng (Senegal).

Website: www.unictr.org.

ECONOMIC AND SOCIAL COUNCIL

(ECOSOC)

Membership (54): Afghanistan, Algeria, Antigua and Barbuda, Argentina, Australia, Bangladesh, Belgium, Botswana, Brazil, Burkina Faso, Chile, China, Congo, Czech Republic, Democratic Republic of the Congo, Estonia, Finland, France, Georgia, Germany, Ghana, Greece, Guatemala, Guyana, Honduras, India, Iraq, Ireland, Italy, Japan, Kazakhstan, Lebanon, Mauritania, Moldova, Nigeria, Pakistan, Panama, Peru, Portugal, Republic of Korea, Russia, Rwanda, Serbia, Somalia, South Africa, Sweden, Switzerland, Togo, Trinidad and Tobago, Uganda, United Kingdom, United States, Viet Nam, and Zimbabwe. One-third of the members rotate annually on the following geographical basis: Africa, 14 seats; Asia, 11; Latin America and the Caribbean, 10; Eastern Europe, 6; Western Europe and others, 13.

Website: www.un.org/ecosoc.

President of the 2016 Session: Frederick Musiiwa Makamure Shava (Zimbabwe).

Origin and development. Initially, the activities of ECOSOC were directed primarily to the twin problems of relief and reconstruction in war-torn Europe, Asia, and, after 1948, Israel. By the mid-1950s, however, the problems of less developed states of Africa, Asia, and Latin America began to claim primary attention. (For more information prior to 1992, see the 2014 *Handbook.*)

In mid-1992 ECOSOC found itself immersed in debate on the proposed restructuring of UN bodies dealing with economic and social issues, pressure having grown to eliminate overlapping mandates and provide "more efficient and cost-effective" services. Secretary-General Boutros Boutros-Ghali, a major force behind the streamlining efforts, said he hoped ECOSOC would achieve the same "relevance" to economic and social development in the world that the Security Council had recently achieved regarding peacemaking and peacekeeping. Under Boutros-Ghali and his successor, Kofi Annan, ECOSOC underwent considerable reorganization, including a reduction in the number of Standing Committees and Commissions.

Structure. By a charter amendment that entered into force in 1965, the membership of ECOSOC was increased from 18 to 27 in order to provide wider representation to new states in Africa and Asia. Similarly, membership was raised to 54 as of September 1973. One-third of the members are elected each year for three-year terms, and all voting is by simple majority; each member has one vote.

Much of ECOSOC's activity is carried out through its eight Functional and five Regional Commissions (described in separate sections) and a number of Standing Committees and Commissions that currently include the Commission on Human Settlements (established in 1977), the Committee on Negotiations with Intergovernmental Agencies (1946), the Committee on Non-Governmental Organizations (1946), and the Committee for Program and Coordination (1962). In 2000 ECOSOC established the United Nations Forestry Forum (UNFF) to promote conservation and sustainable development. Membership in the UNFF is open to all UN member states. In addition, there are assorted ECOSOC Expert Bodies, such as the Ad Hoc Group of Experts on International Cooperation in Tax Matters; the Committee for Development Policy; the Committee of Experts on Public Administration; the Committee of Experts on the Transport of Dangerous Goods and on the Globally Harmonized System of Classification and Labeling of Chemicals; the Committee on Economic, Social, and Cultural Rights; the Permanent Forum on Indigenous Issues; and the United Nations Group of Experts on Geographical Names. In 2001 ECOSOC created two Ad Hoc Advisory Groups On African Countries Emerging From Conflict, one for Burundi and the other for Guinea-Bissau. These were followed in 2004 by the reactivation of the Ad Hoc Advisory Group on Haiti, which had been active in 1999. In 2006 the advisory group on Burundi was terminated, as was the group on Guinea-Bissau the following year, when the newly created Peace Building Commission was tasked to oversee the countries.

Because of the scope of its responsibilities, ECOSOC has complex relationships with a number of UN subsidiary and related organs. It participates in the Chief Executives Board (CEB, formerly the Administrative Committee on Coordination [ACC]), which comprises the secretary-general and the heads of the Specialized Agencies and the International Atomic Energy Agency (IAEA), and elects the members of the independent International Narcotics Control Board (INCB), three from nominees proposed by the World Health Organization and ten from other nominees offered by UN members and parties to the 1961 Single Convention on Narcotic Drugs. It also elects the executive boards of the United Nations Development Program/United Nations Population Fund and the United Nations Children's Fund, the Executive Committee of the United Nations Office of High Commissioner for Refugees, half of the members of the UN/FAO Intergovernmental

Committee of the World Food Program, 10 board members of the United Nations Research Institute for Social Development, and the 22 members of the Program Coordination Board for the Joint UN Program on HIV/AIDS (UNAIDS).

Recent activities. ECOSOC produces or initiates studies, reports, and recommendations on international economic, social, cultural, educational, health, and related matters; promotes respect for, and observance of, human rights and fundamental freedoms; negotiates agreements with the UN Specialized Agencies to define their relations with the UN; and coordinates the activities of the Specialized Agencies through consultations and recommendations.

In early 2003 ECOSOC announced plans to coordinate its activities more closely with the IMF, World Bank, and the WTO in order to implement the goals set at the 2002 International Conference on Financing for Development. (For information on ECOSOC activities before 2003, see the 2010 and 2014 *Handbooks.*) The council also subsequently indicated a desire to become more involved with "practical activities on the ground" as directed by the Security Council. Among other things, ECOSOC cited "expanded investment in health and education as a critical component in the UN's recently enhanced peacebuilding role." Collaterally, the council reported that the plight of poor countries as of 2005 had improved very little despite much attention given to the issue during the first half of the decade. ECOSOC pledged to intensify its oversight of the many commissions and agencies under its purview as part of proposed overall UN reform geared toward enhancing efficiency and effectiveness.

In accordance with the March 2006 General Assembly resolution creating the UN Human Rights Council, ECOSOC abolished the Commission on Human Rights on June 16. In addition, the ECOSOC voted to increase the membership of its Commission on Science and Technology for Development from 33 to 43 members beginning in February 2007 in order to broaden participation in the body.

In accordance with a proposal accepted at the 2005 World Summit, ECOSOC conducted its first Annual Ministerial Review (AMR) in July 2007 in Geneva. The AMR brought together national delegations and representatives from the UN and private sector to assess goals related to sustainable development in line with the theme of the meeting, "Strengthening Efforts to Eradicate Poverty and Hunger, Including through the Global Partnership for Development." In July the ECOSOC launched the Development Cooperation Forum (DCF), a biennial meeting to facilitate progress on the Millennium Development Goals. The DCF was designed to draw together participants from individual countries and representatives from various UN bodies, as well as the World Bank, IMF, and business sector. The initial meeting of the group was held in New York in June 2008.

The 2008 AMR, conducted in July in New York, focused on "Implementing the Internationally Agreed Goals and Commitments in Regard to Sustainable Development." The AMR included sessions on the UN's development agenda, implementing global development goals on a national basis, and the integration of the Millennium Development Goals with other initiatives. In addition, Belgium, Finland, Luxembourg, and the United Kingdom reported on national efforts to promote development. At ECOSOC's 2008 substantive session, the council passed 9 resolutions and 3 decisions, the most ever at one of its annual meetings. The resolutions included a condemnation of sexual violence against humanitarian and aid workers, an expression of concern over the growing number of people affected by natural disasters, and a call for joint action to lessen the impact of rising food and commodity prices.

ECOSOC's third AMR was conducted in July 2009 in Geneva. The event was centered on three goals: reviewing the UN's development initiatives, analyzing the main global challenges and opportunities surrounding public health, and examining potential new ECOSOC programs. Bolivia, China, Jamaica, Japan, Mali, Sri Lanka, and Sudan each gave national presentations on development issues. Among the resolutions adopted at ECOSOC's substantive session in Geneva in July was a call for the UN development programs to try to achieve gender balance in their personnel.

The fourth AMR took place at the UN headquarters in New York from June 28 to July 1, 2010. Thirteen countries provided national presentations. The session focused on the challenges faced by women in economic development and endorsed the declaration *Implementing the Internationally Agreed Goals and Commitments in Regard to Gender Equality and Empowerment of Women.* The document reaffirmed the commitment of the world body to the recommendations from the 1995 Beijing Summit and recommitted ECOCOS to ending gender-based discrimination and barriers to economic development. The second DCF was conducted on June 29–30, 2010, in New York. The final report from the event highlighted the need to develop a coherent and cross-agency approach to development and called for the UN to develop an "economic architecture" that permitted the nexus of migration, trade, and finance to be addressed. At the same July meeting the administration of U.S. president Barack Obama pushed for ECOSOC to accredit the International Gay and Lesbian Human Rights Commission for consultative status, so that it could have a presence at the UN Recognition. In the culmination of a three-year campaign, accreditation was granted.

In May 2011 ECOSOC renewed Iran's membership, in spite of objections from the United States and Canada. Amid questions about the organization's role and future direction, Swiss president Micheline Calmy-Rey proposed that ECOSOC reinvent itself as the United Nations' lead organization to manage the challenges of global sustainability.

The theme of the 2012 AMR, held in July in New York, was "Promoting Productive Capacity, Employment, and Decent Work to Eradicate Poverty in the Context of Inclusive, Sustainable, and Equitable Growth at All Levels for Achieving the MDGs." At the session, ECOSOC presented growth models that had weathered the global economic downturn in a sustainable and equitable fashion. The meetings' final declaration warned of the dangers to economic development posed by the global financial crisis and called for more active efforts to achieve gender equity in the labor force.

In July 2013 ECOSOC launched an initiative to review progress on implementing commitments made by member states at the 1995 Beijing World Conference on Women. In September the UN announced it planned to replace the Commission on Sustainable Development with a High-Level Political Forum on Sustainable Development, made up of world leaders, who would meet every four years, beginning in 2016, to discuss sustainable development. ECOSOC was charged with coordinating annual meetings of the group at the ministerial level. The theme for the 2013 AMR was "Science, Technology, and Innovation (STI) and Culture for Sustainable Development and the Millennium Development Goals."

The 2014 Development Cooperation Forum met at the UN headquarters in New York in July 2014. The forum called for new development agenda to focus on poverty eradication and sustainable development. Also, in July, ECOSOC enacted a resolution calling for the UN to "accelerate the full and effective mainstreaming of a gender perspective" into the world body's development assistance programs. The theme of the 2014 AMR was "Addressing Ongoing and Emerging Challenges for Meeting the Millennium Development Goals in 2015 and for Sustaining Development Gains in the Future."

The 2015 AMR was held in New York from July 9 to 10, 2015, and devoted to the transition from the Millennium Development Goals to the Sustainable Development Goals. In 2016 the High-Level Political Forum on Sustainable Development assumed responsibility for ECOSOC's review of the post-Millennium Development Goals framework.

ECONOMIC AND SOCIAL COUNCIL: FUNCTIONAL COMMISSIONS

ECOSOC's Functional Commissions prepare reports, evaluate services, and make recommendations to the council on matters of economic and social concern to member states. Participants are elected for terms of three or four years, depending on the particular commission. Selection is made with due regard for geographical distribution; in the case of the Commission on Narcotic Drugs, emphasis is also given to countries producing or manufacturing narcotic materials. The Commission on Narcotic Drugs has a Subcommission on Illicit Drug Traffic and Related Matters in the Near and Middle East, and four regional Heads of National Drug Law Enforcement Agencies (HONLEA).

COMMISSION ON CRIME PREVENTION AND CRIMINAL JUSTICE

Established: February 6, 1992.

Purpose: To provide policy guidance on crime prevention and criminal justice, including the treatment of offenders, and to facilitate the activities of UN and other international programs in those areas. (Commission mandates are implemented by the Center for International Crime Prevention [CICP] of the Office for Drug Control and Crime Prevention [ODCCP].)

Membership (40): Austria, Belarus, Benin, Brazil, Cameroon, Canada, Chile, China, Colombia, Côte d'Ivoire, Cuba, Democratic Republic of the Congo, Ecuador, El Salvador, Eritrea, France, Germany, Guatemala, India, Iran, Italy, Japan, Kenya, Liberia, Mauritius, Mexico, Morocco, Pakistan, Qatar, Republic of Korea, Russia, Saudi Arabia, Serbia, Sierra Leone, Slovakia, South Africa, Sweden, Thailand, United States, Zimbabwe.

COMMISSION ON NARCOTIC DRUGS

Established: February 16, 1946.

Purpose: To serve as the UN's principal policymaking body on drugs and to advise the council on matters related to the abuse and control of narcotic drugs. (Commission mandates may be implemented through the UN International Drug Control Program [UNDCP] within the Office for Drug Control and Crime Prevention [ODCCP].)

Membership (53): Argentina, Angola, Australia, Austria, Belarus, Belgium, Benin, Bolivia, Brazil, Cameroon, Canada, China, Colombia, Croatia, Cuba, Czech Republic, Democratic Republic of the Congo, Ecuador, El Salvador, France, Germany, Guatemala, Hungary, India, Indonesia, Iran, Israel, Italy, Japan, Kazakhstan, Kenya, Mauritania, Mexico, Netherlands, Nigeria, Norway 2019, Pakistan, Peru, Qatar, Republic of Korea, Russia, Slovakia, South Africa, Spain, Sudan, Tajikistan, Thailand, Togo, Turkey, Uganda, United Kingdom, United States, Uruguay.

COMMISSION ON POPULATION AND DEVELOPMENT

Established: October 3, 1946, as the Population Commission. Current name adopted in 1994.

Purpose: To study and advise the council on population issues and on integrating population and development strategies. As of 1996 the commission has also been charged with monitoring, reviewing, and implementing the International Conference on Population and Development Program of Action (1994) at the national, regional, and international levels.

Membership (47): Argentina, Bangladesh, Belarus, Belgium, Benin, Bolivia, Brazil, Burundi, Chad, Chile, China, Denmark, Dominican Republic, Finland, Germany, Iran Iraq, Israel, Jamaica, Liberia, Madagascar, Malaysia, Mexico, Moldova, Mongolia, Morocco, Netherlands, Nigeria, Oman, Pakistan, Peru, Philippines, Qatar, Romania, Russia, Serbia, Sierra Leone, South Africa, Sudan, Switzerland, Turkmenistan, Uganda, United Kingdom, United States, Uruguay, Zambia (one vacancy from Western Europe).

COMMISSION ON SCIENCE AND TECHNOLOGY FOR DEVELOPMENT

Established: April 30, 1992.

Purpose: To promote international cooperation in the field of science and technology for development; to formulate guidelines for the harmonization of UN scientific and technological activities and to monitor those activities.

Membership (43): Angola, Austria, Bolivia, Brazil, Bulgaria, Cameroon, Canada, Central African Republic, Chile, China, Costa Rica, Côte d'Ivoire, Cuba, Dominican Republic, Finland, Germany, Hungary, India, Iran Japan, Kenya, Latvia, Liberia, Mauritania, Mauritius, Mexico, Nigeria, Oman, Pakistan, Peru, Poland, Portugal, Russia, Sri Lanka, Sweden, Switzerland, Thailand, Turkey, Turkmenistan, Uganda, United Kingdom, United States.

COMMISSION FOR SOCIAL DEVELOPMENT

Established: June 21, 1946, as the Social Commission; renamed the Commission for Social Development on July 29, 1966.

Purpose: To advise the council on all aspects of social development policies, including, recently, an increased emphasis on policies aimed at increasing the equitable distribution of national income.

Membership (46): Algeria, Argentina, Austria, Bangladesh, Benin, Bolivia, Brazil, Burundi, Chile, China, Colombia, Democratic Republic of the Congo, El Salvador, Finland, France, Ghana, Iran, Iraq, Japan, Kuwait, Madagascar, Malawi, Mexico, Moldova, Namibia, Pakistan, Paraguay, Peru, Poland, Portugal, Qatar, Republic of Korea, Romania, Russia, Rwanda, Switzerland, Turkmenistan, Uganda, United States (five vacancies).

COMMISSION ON THE STATUS OF WOMEN

Established: June 21, 1946.

Purpose: To report to the council on methods to promote women's rights; to develop proposals giving effect to the principle that men and women should have equal rights.

Membership (45): Albania, Bangladesh, Belarus, Belgium, Bosnia and Herzegovina, Brazil, Burkina Faso, Colombia, Congo, Ecuador, Egypt, El Salvador, Equatorial Guinea, Eritrea, Ghana, Germany, Guatemala, Guyana, India, Iran, Israel, Japan, Kazakhstan, Kenya, Kuwait, Lesotho, Liberia, Liechtenstein, Malawi, Mongolia, Norway, Nigeria, Pakistan, Paraguay, Qatar, Republic of Korea, Russian, Spain, Switzerland, Tajikistan, Tanzania, Trinidad and Tobago, Uganda, United Kingdom, Uruguay

STATISTICAL COMMISSION

Established: June 21, 1946.

Purpose: To develop international statistical services, to promote the development of national statistics and to make them more readily comparable, and to assist the UN Secretariat and Specialized Agencies in their statistical work.

Membership (24): Angola, Barbados, Brazil, Bulgaria, Cameroon, China, Cuba, Dominican Republic, Germany, Italy, Japan, Kenya, Latvia, Libya, Netherlands, New Zealand, Qatar, Republic of Korea, Romania, Russia, Sweden, Togo, United Kingdom, United States.

ECONOMIC AND SOCIAL COUNCIL: REGIONAL COMMISSIONS

The primary aim of the five Regional Commissions, which report annually to ECOSOC, is to assist in raising the level of economic activity in their respective regions and to maintain and strengthen the economic relations of the states in each region, both among themselves and with others. The commissions adopt their own procedural rules, including how they select officers. Each commission is headed by an executive secretary, who holds the rank of undersecretary of the UN, while their Secretariats are integral parts of the overall United Nations Secretariat.

The commissions are empowered to make recommendations directly to member governments and to Specialized Agencies of the United Nations, but no action can be taken in respect to any state without the agreement of that state.

ECONOMIC COMMISSION FOR AFRICA

(ECA)

Established: April 29, 1958.

Purpose: To "initiate and participate in measures for facilitating concerted action for the economic development of Africa, including its social aspects, with a view to raising the level of economic activity and levels of living in Africa, and for maintaining and strengthening the economic relations of countries and territories of Africa, both among themselves and with other countries of the world."

Headquarters: Addis Ababa, Ethiopia. Subregional Development Centers are located in Tangier, Morocco, for Northern Africa; Kigali, Rwanda, for Eastern Africa; Yaoundé, Cameroon, for Central Africa; Niamey, Niger, for Western Africa; and Lusaka, Zambia, for Southern Africa.

Principal Subsidiary Organs: Conference of African Ministers of Finance, Planning and Economic Development; Sectoral Ministerial Conferences; Technical Preparatory Committee of the Whole;

Follow-up Committee on the Conference of Ministers; seven expert-level committees (Women in Development, Development Information, Sustainable Development, Human Development and Civil Society, Industry and Private Sector Development, Natural Resources and Science and Technology, Regional Cooperation and Integration); Secretariat. The Secretariat includes an Office of Policy Planning and Resource Management and six substantive divisions: African Center for Gender and Development, Development Information Services, Development Policy Management, Economic and Social Policy, Sustainable Development, and Trade and Regional Integration.

Executive Secretary (Acting): Abdalla Hamdok (Sudan).

Membership (54): Algeria, Angola, Benin, Botswana, Burkina Faso, Burundi, Cameroon, Cape Verde Islands, Central African Republic, Chad, Comoro Islands, Côte d'Ivoire, Democratic Republic of the Congo, Djibouti, Egypt, Equatorial Guinea, Eritrea, Ethiopia, Gabon, Gambia, Ghana, Guinea, Guinea-Bissau, Kenya, Lesotho, Liberia, Libya, Madagascar, Malawi, Mali, Mauritania, Mauritius, Morocco, Mozambique, Namibia, Niger, Nigeria, Republic of the Congo, Rwanda, Sao Tome and Principe, Senegal, Seychelles, Sierra Leone, Somalia, South Africa, South Sudan, Sudan, Swaziland, Tanzania, Togo, Tunisia, Uganda, Zambia, Zimbabwe. (Switzerland also participates in a consultative capacity.)

Website: www.uneca.org.

Recent activities. Recent ECA initiatives have included sponsorship of African Development Forums, the first of which convened in Addis Ababa in October 1999. (For activities prior to 2007, see the 2013 *Handbook.*)

In its publication *Economic Report on Africa 2007: Accelerating Africa's Development through Diversification,* the ECA noted that African countries had an average GDP growth rate of 5.7 percent in 2006. The report also asserted that diversification was the most important factor in sustained economic growth. In June 2007 the ECA, the African Development Bank, and the AU cosponsored a conference that approved the African Charter on Statistics, which aimed to standardize the collection and dissemination of data. The ECA also cooperated with the Central Bank of Nigeria to launch the Africa Finance Cooperation (AFC) in March. The AFC provided funding for projects to support the New Partnership for Africa's Development (NEPAD) and had an initial capitalization of $2 billion.

In March 2008 the ECA conducted a symposium in New York on the commission's support for NEPAD. The symposium called for the ECA to better coordinate UN efforts on behalf of NEPAD. A follow-up meeting was held in September in Addis Ababa. In the *Economic Report on Africa 2008: Africa and the Monterrey Consensus, Tracking Performance and Progress,* the ECA noted that Africa's economic growth rate was 5.7 percent in 2007 and that inflation remained generally low, though some countries, most notably Zimbabwe, had unsustainable levels of inflation. While income growth exceeded 3 percent between 2001 and 2006, the publication noted that growth would have to increase dramatically to close the gap between Africa and the developed countries of the North. The report also highlighted the changing nature of direct foreign investment in Africa, as Asia, and particularly China, had significantly increased investment in the continent over the past five years.

At the second ECA-sponsored annual joint meeting of the African ministers of economy, finance, and planning, held in Addis Ababa in June 2009, the ministers issued a call for swift and innovative action on the part of member states to address the global economic crisis. The *Economic Report on Africa 2009: Developing African Agriculture Through Regional Value Chains* was divided into two main parts. The first section examined recent global economic patterns and trends, while the second part explored methods to enhance regional agricultural markets and supply chains. The report noted that GDP expansion in Africa contracted from 5.7 percent in 2007 to 5.1 percent in 2008 and was expected to fall to 2 percent in 2009. In addition, the ECA identified rising fuel and energy prices as the greatest threats to economic stability on the continent. The ECA also published the *African Women's Report 2009,* which included the African Gender and Development Index (AGDI) designed to provide a tool to measure women's equality on the continent. The first AGDI measured 12 countries, including Benin, Burkina Faso, Cameroon, Egypt, Ethiopia, Ghana, Madagascar, Mozambique, South Africa, Tanzania, Tunisia, and Uganda, chosen to represent the five regions of Africa. Of the test states, Madagascar ranked highest in gender development, followed by Egypt and South Africa, while Benin ranked last.

In its March 2011 Economic Report on Africa the ECA broke new ground by advocating a middle course between the neoliberal economic doctrines prevalent in the West and the African preference for heavy state control. A September 2011 conference in which ECA representatives participated also called for a new approach to development in Africa. It was generally admitted that no African country would achieve its Millennium Development Goals. In its 2012 economic report on Africa, the ECA noted that the continent's GDP growth rate had slowed to 2.7 percent in 2011 as a result of the global economic crisis. However, the publication predicted that GDP would grow by 5.1 percent in 2012.

The 2012 report *Illicit Financial Flows from Africa: Scale and Developmental Challenges* asserted that foreign multinationals had transferred as much as $1.5 trillion annually from Africa to developed nations. Also in 2012, South Sudan became the 54th member of the ECA. That year the ECA launched a number of reforms to streamline the organization. Meanwhile, Carlos Lopez of Guinea-Bissau, who had been the director of the UN Staff College and had a reputation as a reformer, was appointed executive director of the ECA.

The 2013 ECA Economic Report on Africa, *Making the Most of Africa's Commodities: Industrializing for Growth, Jobs and Economic Transformation*, noted that economic growth on the continent had exceeded 5 percent in 2012, and forecast growth of 4.8 percent in 2013. The publication also highlighted Africa's considerable resources, including 42 percent of the world's gold, and 12 percent of the globe's oil reserves, but called on countries to diversify their economies. The report also asserted that several African countries lacked the "capacity" to carry out economic reforms.

The 2014 Economic Report on Africa, *Dynamic Industrial Policy in Africa*, highlighted the dichotomy between high levels of economic growth in Africa and enduring poverty, unemployment, and inequity. The ECA argued that one reason for this was the continuing reliance on commodity-driven trade instead of industrialization. The report calls for governments to adopt industrial policies designed to transition economies away from commodities. The report used case studies from 11 countries, ranging from Kenya to Tunisia to South Africa to illustrate its recommendations. In September 2014, the ECA called for greater trade between Africa and small island states at a conference in Addis Ababa.

The ECA's 2016 Economic Report on Africa, *Greening Africa's Industrialization*, found that economic growth on the continent had slowed from 3.9 percent in 2014 to 3.7 percent. The report called for greater internal trade, noting that the imports and exports of most African countries were directed outside of the continent. The ECA also argued for the need to transition away from resource extraction-based economies to those that emphasize sustainable development. On October 31, 2016, Abdalla Hamdok of Sudan was appointed acting executive secretary of the ECA.

ECONOMIC COMMISSION FOR EUROPE

(ECE)

Established: March 28, 1947.

Purpose: To promote economic cooperation, integration, and sustainable development among member countries.

Headquarters: Geneva, Switzerland.

Principal Subsidiary Organs: Committee on Economic Cooperation and Integration; Committee on Sustainable Energy; Committee on Environmental Policy; Committee on Forests and Forest Industry; Committee on Housing and Land Management; Committee on Trade; Conference of European Statisticians; Inland Transport Committee; Timber Committee; Secretariat.

Website: www.unece.org.

Executive Secretary: Christian Friis Bach (Denmark).

Membership (56): Albania, Andorra, Armenia, Austria, Azerbaijan, Belarus, Belgium, Bosnia and Herzegovina, Bulgaria, Canada, Croatia, Cyprus, Czech Republic, Denmark, Estonia, Finland, France, Georgia, Germany, Greece, Hungary, Iceland, Ireland, Israel, Italy, Kazakhstan, Kyrgyzstan, Latvia, Liechtenstein, Lithuania, Luxembourg, Macedonia, Malta, Moldova, Monaco, Montenegro, Netherlands, Norway, Poland,

Portugal, Romania, Russia, San Marino, Serbia, Slovakia, Slovenia, Spain, Sweden, Switzerland, Tajikistan, Turkey, Turkmenistan, Ukraine, United Kingdom, United States, Uzbekistan. (Israel's long-standing application for membership, based on its "fundamental economic relations" with the European Community and the United States, was approved by ECOSOC in July 1991. The Holy See also participates in the work of the commission in a consultative capacity.)

Recent activities. In December 2005 the ECE established the Economic Cooperation and Integrated Division (ECID). ECID was tasked to develop strategies to enhance competitiveness through increased innovation. (For information on the ECE prior to 2005, see the 2013 *Handbook.*)

At its February 2006 meeting the member states proposed initiatives to increase economic cooperation and integration. In response to rising fuel costs, the ECE tasked one of its expert groups to explore energy efficiency, costs, and resources. It also decided to include the issue of energy security in its annual meetings. In November the Committee on Sustainable Energy voted to undertake an intergovernmental dialogue on energy. Meanwhile, the Committee on Trade adopted a new mandate to develop joint programs with other UN bodies and agencies. The ECE also initiated a project to identify and remove nontariff trade barriers between Europe and the countries of Central Asia, in cooperation with Special Program for the Economies of Central Asia (SPECA). The joint ECE-SPECA program endorsed 28 projects through 2007. It also conducted two high-level conferences, the first, Focus on Asia, in May in Almaty, Kazakhstan, and the second, Focus on Europe, in November in Berlin, Germany. In addition, in 2007 the ECE signed a memorandum of understanding with the Inter-Parliamentary Assembly of the Eurasian Economic Community to promote deeper integration of the regions.

The ECE's ministerial conference in Belgrade, Serbia, in October 2007 was titled "Environment for Europe" and concentrated on issues such as energy efficiency and sustainability. In February 2008 the ECE launched an initiative to help transitioning economies develop public-private partnerships. A pilot program was scheduled to begin in Moscow in October to better train officials and members of the private sector on issues related to public-private ventures. In August, in response to continuing problems in the United States and European housing markets, the ECE created a new advisory body, the Real Estate Market Advisory Group. The new group was formed to work with the existing Working Party on Land Administration to develop new guidelines for the regulation of real estate markets and financing, as well as develop programs with individual countries to increase housing capacity in an environmentally friendly manner.

Through 2008 the ECE undertook 60 technical cooperation programs with 18 countries in Central and Eastern Europe and Central Asia. These initiatives were designed to enhance economic and technical knowledge and increase the competitiveness of countries in transition. The ECE undertook environmental performance reviews of the legal and official policy frameworks of Kazakhstan, Kyrgyzstan, and Ukraine. In response to recommendations developed in 2006, the ECE finalized a series of internal reforms that were designed to streamline the governing structure of the organization and increase transparency. The reforms were meant to bolster the relationship between the secretariat and the individual member states. Meanwhile, former Slovak foreign minister and former secretary-general of the OSCE Ján Kubiš was appointed executive secretary of the ECE in December.

At its annual meeting in 2009, the ECE proposed a tax on carbon emissions with the proceeds to be distributed to developing states. The body also called for reforms in the transportation sector, which accounted for 13 percent of all greenhouse gas emissions, to reduce emissions and improve efficiency.

In 2010 the ECE and the Eurasian Development Bank finalized a memorandum of understanding to facilitate cooperation between the two bodies in promoting the Millennium Development Goals. Also, the UNE launched the third Wood Energy Enquiry to document the use of wood as an energy source in Europe. The two previous reports demonstrated a growing use of wood and found that wood was the main renewable energy source used in the region, accounting for just over half of all renewable energy use between 2005–2007.

The year 2011 saw increasing interest in water conservation and management, particularly among ECE members that were formerly part of the Soviet Union. Among other initiatives, the EU Water Initiative National Policy Dialogue on Integrated Water Resource Management took place in March in Tbilisi, Georgia. A second meeting was held in October in Dushanbe, Tajikistan.

On March 8, 2012, Sven Alkalaj was appointed executive secretary of the ECE. In its 2012 annual report, the ECE stressed the need for green technologies to lead Europe's economic recovery and to alleviate poverty. In 2012 the ECE launched Astana Water Action, a program with 75 specific goals for nations to improve the management of water and water resources.

The ECE conducted a conference in July 2013 to promote public private partnerships (PPP) in sectors such as transport, energy management, and schools and health. The ECE charged its Public-Private Partnership Center of Excellence with developing standards and recommendations on PPPs for governments. In October at an ECE meeting, ministers from 55 countries agreed on a regional strategy on sustainable housing and land management. The initiative had 15 objectives, supported by 36 goals, and was designed to cut energy consumption through new investments in technology and better management of multifamily housing developments.

Christian Friis Bach of Denmark, a former development minister, was appointed executive secretary of the ECE on July 9, 2014. The ECE's 2014 regular budget was $36.2 million, supplemented by $13.2 million from trust funds, $2 million from its technical cooperation program, and $2.1 in development funds from the UN, for a total of $53.5 million.

An ECE report on emissions testing for cars, published in May 2016, found that long-term exposure to emissions pollutants could cause up to 75,000 premature deaths in 40 European countries each year. One significant problem is the discrepancy between emission test results performed in laboratories and real-world driving conditions. The ECE developed the Worldwide Harmonized Light Vehicle Test Procedure to overcome those differences and provide a more realistic picture of carbon dioxide and nitrogen dioxide emissions.

ECONOMIC COMMISSION FOR LATIN AMERICA AND THE CARIBBEAN

(ECLAC)
Comisión Económica para America Latina y el Caribe
(CEPAL)

Established: February 25, 1948, as the Economic Commission for Latin America; current name adopted in 1984.

Purpose: To "initiate and participate in measures for facilitating concerted actions for . . . raising the level of economic activity in Latin America and the Caribbean and for maintaining and strengthening the economic relations of the Latin American and Caribbean countries, both among themselves and with other countries of the world."

Headquarters: Santiago, Chile. Subregional headquarters are located in Mexico City, Mexico, and Port of Spain, Trinidad and Tobago, with offices in Bogota, Colombia, Buenos Aries, Argentina, Brasilia, Brazil, Montevideo, Uruguay, and Washington, D.C., United States.

Principal Subsidiary Organs: Caribbean Development and Cooperation Committee, Central American Economic Cooperation Committee, Committee of High-Level Government Experts from Developing Member Countries for Analysis of the Achievement of the International Development Strategy in the Latin American Region, Conference on the Integration of Women into the Economic and Social Development of Latin America and the Caribbean, Latin American and Caribbean Institute for Economic and Social Planning (*Instituto Latinoamericano y del Caribe de Planificación Económica y Social*—ILPES), Latin American Demographic Center (*Centro Latinoamericano y Caribeño de Demografía*—CELADE), Statistical Conference of the Americas of ECLAC, Secretariat. The Secretariat includes ten divisions: Economic Development, Economic and Social Planning, Gender Development; Sustainable Development and Human Settlements, International Trade and Integration, Natural Resources and Infrastructure, Population and Development, Productive Development and Management, Social Development, and Statistics and Economic Projections.

Website: www.eclac.org.

Executive Secretary: Alicia Bárcena (Chile).

Membership (45): Antigua and Barbuda, Argentina, Bahamas, Barbados, Belize, Bolivia, Brazil, Canada, Chile, Colombia, Costa Rica, Cuba, Dominica, Dominican Republic, Ecuador, El Salvador, France, Germany, Grenada, Guatemala, Guyana, Haiti, Honduras, Italy, Jamaica, Japan, Mexico, Netherlands, Nicaragua, Norway,

Panama, Paraguay, Peru, Portugal, Republic of Korea, St. Kitts and Nevis, St. Lucia, St. Vincent, Spain, Suriname, Trinidad and Tobago, United Kingdom, United States, Uruguay, Venezuela.

Associate Members (13): Anguilla, Aruba, Bermuda, British Virgin Islands, Cayman Islands, Curacao, Guadeloupe, Martinique, Montserrat, Puerto Rico, Sint Maarten, Turks and Caicos, United States Virgin Islands.

Recent activities. (For ECLAC activities prior to 2008, see the 2011 and 2014 *Handbooks.*) ECLAC estimated that the region's economic growth would be 4.7 percent in 2008, despite rising food and energy prices. Notably, ECLAC found that direct foreign investment in Latin America and the Caribbean exceeded $100 billion for the first time in 2007 and was likely to continue to grow through 2008. In the report *Economic Survey of Latin America and the Caribbean, 2007–2008,* ECLAC urged the nations of the region to consolidate their economic development and take steps to prevent wide fluctuations in economic performance. In cooperation with UNDP and 12 other UN agencies, ECLAC produced *Millennium Development Goals: Progression Toward the Right to Health in Latin America and the Caribbean* in 2008. The report highlighted the accomplishments and challenges of the region as it worked toward the health-related goals of the UN in areas such as malnutrition, access to health care, and poverty reduction programs.

In the publication *Preliminary Overview of the Economies of Latin America and the Caribbean 2008,* ECLAC noted that 2008 was the sixth year of overall GDP growth in the region, with expansion averaging 5 percent between 2003 and 2008. However, the report also warned that growth would fall to less than 2 percent in 2009, with unemployment increasing from a regional average of 7.5 percent to more than 8 percent, although inflation was expected to fall from 8.5 percent to 6 percent. Through 2009 ECLAC produced reports on the policies that governments in the region undertook in response to the global economic crisis. Separate research predicted that regional trade would decline by 13 percent through the year. In September 2009 ECLAC hosted the Second Latin American and Caribbean for Negotiations on Climate Change in Santiago, Chile. The session was designed to promote common positions on climate change issues within the region ahead of the December UN climate change conference in Copenhagen.

ECLAC published the *Environmental Indicators of Latin America and the Caribbean* in 2010. The study found both positive and negative environmental trends. For instance, between 1990 and 2007, the total amount of territory preserved for biodiversity increased from 9.5 percent to 19.5 percent, however, during the same period deforestation decreased the amount of forest coverage from 48.8 percent to 44.9 percent of the total area (a loss of 78 million hectares of forests). ECLAC's economic studies indicated that poverty in the region in 2010 had returned to levels comparable to the pre-global crisis. ECLAC found that 32.1 percent of the population (180 million people) of the region lived in poverty, with 12.9 percent (72 million people) in extreme poverty. These rates equaled those in 2008.

A September 2010 assessment of the region's progress toward meeting MDGs suggested that it was in much better shape than other less developed parts of the globe. Their chief lack of progress, however, was toward the goal of environmental sustainability. Statements from the group in 2011 seemed to echo the ECA's interest in structural change, with governments displaying a less passive attitude toward business. A June 9 statement encouraged food-exporting Latin American states to take advantage of high world food prices to lift their citizens out of poverty.

ECLAC's 2012 *Macroeconomic Report on Latin American and the Caribbean* forecast growth of 3.7 percent in 2012, led by Chile, Mexico, Peru, and Venezuela. Meanwhile, regional urban unemployment declined to a record low of 6.5 percent. Tax reforms in a number of countries led to increased government revenues. Although foreign trade slowed in 2011, tourism rose sharply.

ECLAC's 2013 report, *A Sluggish Postcrisis, Mega Trade Negotiations and Value Chains: Scope for Regional Action,* forecast that exports from Latin America and the Caribbean will rise by only 1.5 percent. Meanwhile, the 2013 *Economic Survey of Latin America and Caribbean: Three Decades of Uneven and Unstable Growth* found that unemployment in the region in the first quarter of 2013 was 6.7 percent, while inflation was 6 percent.

Sint Maarten was admitted as an associate member of ECLAC in May 2014. ECLAC's 2014 edition of the *Economic Survey of Latin America and the Caribbean* found that growth in the region had increased to 2.5 percent in 2013 but was expected to slow to 2.2 percent for 2014. The trade deficit was expected to remain at approximately 2.8 percent of regional GDP, while inflation was forecast to exceed 8 percent.

ECLAC's 2016 *Preliminary Overview of the Economies of Latin America and the Caribbean* reported that the GDP of the region fell by 1.1 percent in 2016. South America saw GDP declines of 1.7 percent in 2015 and 2.4 percent the following year. Growth did continue in Central America, with regional GDP rising by 4.7 percent in 2015 and 3.6 percent in 2016. Regional GDP decreased in the Caribbean by 1.7 percent in 2015 and 2016. Forecasts predicted that GDP would grow for Latin America and the Caribbean by 1.3 percent in 2017 largely due to increases in consumer demand.

ECONOMIC AND SOCIAL COMMISSION FOR ASIA AND THE PACIFIC

(ESCAP)

Established: March 28, 1947, as the Economic Commission for Asia and the Far East; current name adopted in 1974.

Purpose: To facilitate cooperation in economic and social development within the region, to provide technical assistance and serve as an executing agency for operational projects, to conduct research and related activities, to offer advisory services as requested by governments, and to serve as the principal forum for the region within the UN system.

Headquarters: Bangkok, Thailand. A Pacific Operations Center opened in Port Vila, Vanuatu, in 1984, and then relocated to Suva, Fiji in 2005.

Principal Subsidiary Organs: Advisory Committee of Permanent Representatives and Other Representatives Designated by ESCAP Members; Asian and Pacific Center for Agricultural Engineering and Machinery (Beijing, China); Asian and Pacific Training Center for Information and Communication Technology for Development (Incheon, Republic of Korea); Asian and Pacific Center for Transfer of Technology (New Delhi, India); Committee on Emerging Social Issues; Committee on Managing Globalization; Committee on Poverty Reduction; Regional Coordination Center for Research and Development of Coarse Grains, Pulses, Roots, and Tuber Crops in the Humid Tropics of Asia and the Pacific (Bogor, Indonesia); Special Body on Least Developed and Landlocked Developing Countries; Special Body on Pacific Island Developing Countries; Statistical Institute for Asia and the Pacific (Chiba, Japan); Secretariat. The Secretariat includes an Office of the Executive Secretary, an Office of the Deputy Executive Secretary, the United Nations Information Services, the Pacific Operations Center, and nine divisions, two of them largely administrative (Program Management and Administration) and the other seven substantive: Emerging Social Issues; Environment and Sustainable Development; Information, Communication, and Space Technology; Poverty and Development; Statistics; Trade and Investment; and Transport and Tourism.

Executive Secretary: Shamshad Akhtar (Pakistan).

Website: www.unescap.org.

Membership (53): Afghanistan, Armenia, Australia, Azerbaijan, Bangladesh, Bhutan, Brunei, Cambodia, China, Democratic People's Republic of Korea, Federated States of Micronesia, Fiji, France, Georgia, India, Indonesia, Iran, Japan, Kazakhstan, Kiribati, Kyrgyzstan, Laos, Malaysia, Maldives, Marshall Islands, Mongolia, Myanmar, Nauru, Nepal, Netherlands, New Zealand, Pakistan, Palau, Papua New Guinea, Philippines, Republic of Korea, Russia, Samoa, Singapore, Solomon Islands, Sri Lanka, Tajikistan, Thailand, Timor-Leste, Tonga, Turkey, Turkmenistan, Tuvalu, United Kingdom, United States, Uzbekistan, Vanuatu, Vietnam.

Associate Members (9): American Samoa, Commonwealth of the Northern Mariana Islands, Cook Islands, French Polynesia, Guam, Hong Kong, Macao, New Caledonia, Niue. Switzerland participates in a consultative capacity.

Recent activities. ESCAP is the largest of the five ECOSOC Regional Commissions, with its member countries encompassing about 60 percent of the world's population. It operates with a general staff of nearly 400, as well as 200 professionals, advisers, and project personnel. The various divisions of the Secretariat (see Principal

Subsidiary Organs) carry out the projects and programs formulated by the organization's policymaking committees. To strengthen its role in helping South Pacific island nations and territories, ESCAP inaugurated a Pacific Operations Center in Vanuatu in 1984. In 1993 ESCAP signed an agreement with the Asian Development Bank (ADB) that delineates 11 areas of common interest in which closer cooperation will be pursued. The two organizations agreed to prepare joint studies, develop and carry out projects together, and conduct ESCAP/ADB workshops and conferences. ESCAP remains a source of highly respected economic analyses, including its annual *Economic and Social Survey of Asia and the Pacific.*

(For information on ESCAP prior to 2008, see the 2013 and 2014 *Handbooks.*) In conjunction with humanitarian and labor organizations, in September 2008 ESCAP held a series of training sessions to promote better data collection as one means to reduce child labor. Also in 2008 ESCAP created a Transportation Committee to facilitate multinational cooperation on transport networks and capabilities. Following huge earthquakes in China, ESCAP announced a joint program to help China and other East Asian states reduce vulnerabilities to natural disasters. In October ESCAP and the Republic of Korea announced a joint $200-million, five-year initiative to promote low-carbon and environmentally friendly economic growth as part of the broader East Asia Climate Partnership created by the Republic of Korea.

In 2009 ESCAP began efforts to create three more regional offices, one each for East and Northeast Asia, North and Central Asia, and South and Southwest Asia. ESCAP's publication, *Economic and Social Survey of Asia and the Pacific 2009: Addressing Triple Threats to Development,* identified the global economic recession, volatility in commodities markets, and climate change as the three main obstacles to continued growth and stability. The report also highlighted the continuing disparity in economic growth rates among developed and developing states. GDP growth among developing states was 5.8 percent, while GDP among developed countries was –0.4 percent. In November ESCAP held the first Asia-Pacific Trade and Investment Week, which included conferences, summits, and workshops designed to promote balanced trade.

ESCAP published *Women in Asia-Pacific: Challenges and Priorities Data Sheet* in 2010. The report highlighted a range of challenges that women in the region face, including under-representation in political bodies, gender discrimination and exploitation, and lack of health and social protections. The study called for greater progress on gender equality. ESCAP's 2009 *Statistical Yearbook,* published in 2010, reported that the population growth rate for the region had fallen to 1 percent per year, the lowest level among the five regions. Growth was highest among the landlocked developing countries at 1.7 percent, and lowest among the developed economies at 0.3 percent. The Asia-Pacific's aggregate GDP was $17.7 trillion, second only to Europe at $19.7 trillion, led by China's 11 percent annual average growth rate.

ESCAP's 2012 *Statistical Yearbook* reported that 4.2 billion people lived in the Asia-Pacific region in 2012 but that population growth rates had declined by 1.5 percent per year to 1 percent. Meanwhile, the more developed states faced stagnant or declining GDPs as a result of the economic slowdowns in Europe and the United States. GDP among these nations fell by 4.1 percent, although regionally GDP grew by 0.5 percent. In June ESCAP hosted the first Regional Integrated Early Warning System (RIMES) conference where 21 countries pledged to support regional early warning efforts for natural disasters such as typhoons or tsunamis.

To better facilitate South-South discussions on sustainable development, ESCAP created a network to disseminate best practices among governments in Southeast Asia in 2013. ESCAP's 2013 annual report was titled *Building a Resilient, Inclusive and Sustainable Asia and the Pacific: Because People Matter* and found that there were only 65 employed women for 100 employed men. To reduce this gap, ESCAP launched a series of dialogues and seminars. On December 20, 2013 Shamshad Akhtar of Pakistan was named executive secretary of ESCAP.

ESCAP's *Economic and Social Survey of Asia and the Pacific, 2014,* published in August 2014, noted that economic growth was expected to rise from 5.6 percent in 2013 to 5.8 percent in 2014. While most of ESCAP's regions would experience economic growth, north and central Asia were seen as likely to experience an economic slowdown, with growth falling from 2.1 percent in 2013 to 1.3 percent in 2014. Inflation was anticipated to decrease from 5 percent in 2013 to 4.8 percent the following year. The report also noted growing inequity with 40 countries reporting that the poorest 20 percent of the population accounted for less than 10 percent of national income and that more than 60 percent of the population in the Asia-Pacific area did not have any social protections.

ESCAP's 2016 *Asia-Pacific Trade and Investment Report* noted that the region still suffered from the global economic downturn but economic growth had begun to accelerate. While trade by Asia-Pacific countries grew by 3.4 percent from 2010–2015, weak demand from foreign markets had caused exports to fall by 9.7 percent. Nonetheless, the region performed better than the rest of the world, and its share of the global export market rose to 40.1 percent. China was responsible for a large portion of the growth, accounting for 34 percent of all exports from the region.

ECONOMIC AND SOCIAL COMMISSION FOR WESTERN ASIA

(ESCWA)

Established: August 9, 1973, as the Economic Commission for Western Asia; current name adopted in 1985.

Purpose: To "initiate and participate in measures for facilitating concerted action for the economic reconstruction and development of Western Asia, for raising the level of economic activity in Western Asia, and for maintaining and strengthening the economic relations of the countries of that area, both among themselves and with other countries of the world."

Headquarters: Beirut, Lebanon.

Principal Subsidiary Organs: Preparatory Committee; Advisory Committee; seven specialized committees (Energy, Liberalization of Foreign Trade and Economic Globalization, Social Development, Statistics, Transport, Water Resources, Women); Secretariat. The Secretariat includes seven divisions: Administrative Services; Program Planning and Technical Cooperation; Economic Analysis, Information and Communication Technology; Globalization and Regional Integration; Social Development; and Sustainable Development and Productivity. There are also a Statistics Coordination Unit and an ESCWA Center for Women.

Website: www.escwa.un.org.

Executive Secretary: Rima Khalaf (Jordan).

Membership (18): Bahrain, Egypt, Iraq, Jordan, Kuwait, Lebanon, Libya, Mauritania, Morocco, Oman, Palestine, Qatar, Saudi Arabia, Sudan, Syria, Tunisia, United Arab Emirates, Yemen.

Recent activities. The most important procedural event in the commission's history was the 1977 decision to grant full membership to the Palestine Liberation Organization (PLO)—the first non-state organization to achieve such standing in a UN agency—despite a fear on the part of some UN members that the PLO would use its membership to gain full membership in the General Assembly. Israeli-Palestinian agreements, beginning with the 1993 Declaration of Principles, led to the redesignation of the PLO membership as, simply, Palestine, even though no de jure Palestinian state existed. (For information on ESCWA's activities prior to 2008, see the 2013 and 2014 *Handbooks.*)

On January 16, 2008, ESCWA held the first meetings of its newly formed technical committee, a body created to bolster integration and coordination among the national representatives of ESCWA. In July ESCWA, Germany and the government of Iraq sponsored a series of meetings and training seminars for Iraqi officials on water-dispute resolution tactics and strategies. As part of its ongoing effort to enhance foreign trade and direct investment, ESCWA conducted the "Third Forum on Arab Business Community and the WTO Agreements," in Beirut, Lebanon, to discuss the Doha round of trade negotiations with senior political and business leaders. Sudan joined ESCWA on August 15, becoming the 14th member of the group.

ECSWA convened a conference on land management and sustainable development in March 2009 as a means to identify and promote best practices for rural development. In addition to regional leaders and ministers, the event brought together experts from organizations such as the UN University, the UN Development Program, and the Food and Agriculture Organization. In July ECSWA launched a year-long celebration of the 35th anniversary of the creation of the organization. Meanwhile, research by ECSWA found that foreign direct investment into the region had declined by 6.3 percent in 2008, mainly as the result of the global economic crisis and falling energy prices. Saudi Arabia, the United Arab Emirates, and Egypt were the main recipients of foreign investment and accounted for 76 percent of the total flows into the region.

In 2010 Rima Khalaf of Jordan was appointed executive secretary of ECSWA to succeed Bader Al-Dafa of Qatar. ESCWA's 2009 annual report, published in 2010, found that after dramatic economic growth in 2008, with average GDP growth among member states reaching 7.5 percent per year, in 2009 average GDP growth slowed to 3.2 percent. The decline in energy prices caused Kuwait, Saudi Arabia, and the United Arab Emirates to experience negative growth for the year. The report also found that stock exchanges in the region lost 44 percent of their value in 2008, but rose by 11 percent the following year. In an effort to coordinate national responses to the global recession, ESCWA organized a number of conferences and summits, including a high-level meeting of senior government officials in Damascus in May 2009.

In March 2010 an ESCWA report estimated youth unemployment in the Arab world at an average 30 percent, as opposed to 15 percent globally. In July it held a workshop for Arab parliaments on eliminating all forms of discrimination against women, with special reference to women as holders of positions of power. In July 2011 ESCWA held a Beirut conference on supporting the transition to a green economy in Arab countries.

In 2012 ESCWA reported that economic growth for the region during the previous year was 4.8 percent, mainly due to continuing high energy prices. Oil production among ESCWA states was 19.5 million barrels per day, an increase from 18 million barrels per day in 2009. However, political instability and uncertainty were likely to constrain future economic growth, as were increasingly large government deficits and debts. Libya, Morocco, and Tunisia joined ESCWA in September 2012.

ESCWA's 2013 *Survey of Economic and Social Developments in the Arab Region, 2012–2013,* found that GDP rose in the Arab region in 2012 by 4.8 percent, while inflation was 5.5 percent and the regional unemployment rate was 11.1 percent. Exports from the Arab world increased by 7.8 percent, with 51.4 percent of those products going to the Asia-Pacific region. Oil production rose to 23.5 million barrels per day, as Libyan production tripled from the year before.

In 2014 ESCWA published *Arab Integration: A 21st-Century Development Imperative*, which noted that Arab states had reached a "development impasse, evidenced by persisting knowledge gaps, fragile economies and the prevalence of human injustice." To counter these problems, the publication argued that the continuing fragmentation of Arabs needed to be reversed through political cooperation, expanding economic integration, and cultural and educational reform.

In July 2015 Mauritania became the 18th member of ESCWA. That year, ESCWA employed 371 staff members from 44 countries. The organization's budget was $113.9 million, of which $37 million was spent on ESCWA programs and $31.5 million on program support.

TRUSTEESHIP COUNCIL

Website: www.un.org/en/mainbodies/trusteeship.

Membership (5): *Permanent Members of the Security Council:* China, France, Russia, United Kingdom, United States. China, previously not an active participant in Trusteeship affairs, assumed its seat at the May 1989 session.

Structure. Under the UN Charter the membership of the Trusteeship Council includes (1) those UN member states administering Trust Territories, (2) those permanent members of the Security Council that do not administer Trust Territories, and (3) enough other members elected by the General Assembly for three-year terms to ensure that the membership of the council is equally divided between administering and non-administering members. These specifications became increasingly difficult to meet as the number of Trust Territories dwindled. In consequence, no members have been elected to the council since 1965. (The Trusteeship Council formally suspended its operations on November 1, 1994.)

Recent activities. The Trusteeship Council is the organ principally responsible for the supervision of territories placed under the International Trusteeship System. Originally embracing 11 territories that had been either League of Nations mandates or possessions of states defeated in World War II, the system was explicitly designed to promote advancement toward self-government or political independence. By 1976 ten of the former Trust Territories (British Togoland, French Togoland, British Cameroons, French Cameroons, Ruanda-Urundi, Somaliland, Tanganyika, Nauru, northern New Guinea, and Western Samoa) had become independent, either as sovereign states or through division or merger with neighboring states in accordance with the wishes of the inhabitants.

The last Trust Territory was the U.S.-administered Trust Territory of the Pacific Islands, which had undergone several administrative reorganizations, the most recent yielding four groupings: the Northern Mariana Islands, the Federated States of Micronesia, the Marshall Islands, and Palau. In 1975 the Northern Mariana Islands voted for commonwealth status in political union with the United States. In 1983 the Federated States of Micronesia and the Marshall Islands approved "compacts of free association" providing for internal sovereignty combined with continued U.S. economic aid and control of defense. A similar compact was endorsed by majorities in several plebiscites in Palau, but the Palauan Supreme Court ruled in 1986 that a collateral revision of the Palauan constitution to permit facilities for nuclear-armed U.S. forces had to first secure 75 percent approval.

At its 53rd session, held May 12–June 30, 1986, the Trusteeship Council endorsed by a three-to-one vote the position that the United States had satisfactorily discharged its obligations and that it was appropriate to terminate the trusteeship. The majority argued that UN missions sent to observe the plebiscites had concluded that the results constituted a free and fair expression of the wishes of the people. In casting its negative vote, the Soviet Union was highly critical of U.S. policy regarding economic development and potential military use of the territory. Subsequently, Washington declared the compacts with the Marshall Islands and the Federated States to be in effect from October 21 and November 3, 1986, respectively, with inhabitants of the Commonwealth of the Northern Mariana Islands acquiring U.S. citizenship on the latter date. Thus, Palau remained—under U.S. law—the one remaining component of the Trust Territory.

Amid growing violence and political turmoil, referendums were held in Palau in August 1987 that led the Palauan government to declare the constitutional issue resolved and the compact approved. However, in April 1988 the Supreme Court of Palau declared the voting invalid. Subsequently, at its May meeting the Trusteeship Council recommended by a vote of three to one that the compact be approved as soon as possible, with disagreements of interpretation to be left to bilateral Palau-U.S. negotiations. The dissenting vote was cast by the Soviet Union, which continued to charge the United States with "anticharter" activity in the handling of the Trust Territory.

Similar sentiments were expressed at the May 1989 council meeting, which was most noteworthy for the return of Chinese representatives. China joined France, the United Kingdom, and the United States in endorsing the compact as the appropriate vehicle for resolution of Palau's political status. The council's report to the Security Council noted that a recent mission to Palau had concluded that "an overwhelming majority" of its citizens endorsed the compact and that criticism of U.S. spending on economic and social development by some islanders "reflected tactical considerations" aimed at "obtaining additional concessions." The United States subsequently pledged further aid to Palau, but a seventh vote on the compact, held in February 1990, again failed to achieve 75 percent approval.

In light of the continuing diminution of East-West tension, the Soviet Union in late 1990 withdrew its objection to the formal termination of UN involvement in those trusteeship areas whose permanent political status had been resolved. Consequently, upon the recommendation of all five Trusteeship Council members, the Security Council on December 22 voted to terminate the Trusteeship Agreements for the Marshall Islands, the Federated States of Micronesia, and the Northern Mariana Islands. The vote was reportedly facilitated by a U.S. pledge not to expand its military presence in the region.

The Trusteeship Council met in May 1991 to discuss the Palauan situation, which remained unresolved despite hopes that changes in U.S. policy in the region would break the long-standing "logjam." During the May 1992 meeting (at which Russia assumed the former USSR seat) U.S. officials said that Palau was facing its last chance to approve the proposed compact of free association. In November a national referendum approved an amendment to the Palauan constitution to permit ratification of the compact by a simple majority. Consequently, the eighth (and final) vote on the issue was held November 9, 1993, with the compact receiving a 68 percent endorsement.

Palauan and U.S. officials subsequently announced the implementation of the compact effective October 1, 1994, after all possible legal challenges to the final vote had been exhausted. Therefore, on

November 1 the Trusteeship Council formally suspended its operations, and on November 10 the Security Council declared that the applicability of the Trusteeship Agreement regarding Palau had been terminated. However, the Trusteeship Council was not dissolved, an action that would have required a change in the UN Charter. Instead, the council remained in existence with the proviso that it would henceforth meet "only on an extraordinary basis, as the need arises." Also in 1994, a proposal was submitted for the Trusteeship Council to have oversight of the areas of the world outside of national boundaries, including the majority of the world's oceans. However, no action was taken.

In 1997 Secretary-General Kofi Annan proposed that the UN consider reconstituting the council as a forum for UN members to "exercise their collective trusteeship for the integrity of the global environment and common areas such as oceans, atmosphere and outer space." Later, in 2005 he proposed the abolition of the council. Neither proposal was acted on. Options continue to be discussed as part of an overall review of the UN Charter.

INTERNATIONAL COURT OF JUSTICE

(ICJ)
Cour Internationale de Justice (CIJ)

Established: By statute signed as an integral part of the United Nations Charter in San Francisco, United States, June 26, 1945, effective October 24, 1945.

Purpose: To adjudicate disputes referred by member states and to serve as the principal judicial organ of the United Nations; to provide advisory opinions on any legal question requested of it by the General Assembly, Security Council, or other organs of the United Nations and Specialized Agencies that have been authorized by the General Assembly to make such requests.

Headquarters: The Hague, Netherlands.

Website: www.icj-cij.org.

Composition: 15 judges, elected by the UN General Assembly and Security Council for terms ending on February 5 of the years indicated below (as of July 31, 2016).

Ronny Abraham (President)	France	2018
Abdulqawi Yusuf (Vice President)	Somalia	2018
Hishashi Owada	Japan	2021
Peter Tomka	Slovakia	2021
Mohamed Bennouna	Morocco	2024
Joan Donoghue	United States	2024
Christopher Greenwood	United Kingdom	2018
James Richard Crawford	Australia	2024
Xue Hanqin	China	2021
Kirilli Gevorgian	Russia	2024
Antonio Augusto Cançado Trindade	Brazil	2018
Patrick Lipton Robinson	Jamaica	2024
Dalveer Bhandari	India	2021
Julia Sebutinade	Uganda	2021
Georgio Gaja	Italy	2021

Parties to the Statute (193): All members of the United Nations (see Appendix C).

Official Languages: English, French.

Origin and development. The International Court of Justice (ICJ), often called the World Court, is the direct descendant of the Permanent Court of International Justice (PCIJ). Created in 1920 under the Covenant of the League of Nations, the PCIJ, which between 1922 and 1938 had 79 cases referred to it by states and 28 by the League Council, was dissolved on April 19, 1946, along with the other organs of the league.

The Statute of the International Court of Justice was adopted at the San Francisco Conference in June 1945 as an integral part of the UN Charter and, as such, entered into force with the charter on October 24, 1945. Except for a few essentially formal changes, the statute is identical to that of the PCIJ. All members of the UN are automatically parties to the statute. States that are not UN members are entitled to become parties to the statute (under conditions to be determined in each case by the General Assembly upon the recommendation of the Security Council) or to appear before the court without being a party to the statute (under conditions to be laid down by the Security Council). Only states may be parties to cases before the court, whose jurisdiction extends to all cases that the parties refer to it and all matters specifically provided for in the UN Charter or other existing treaties. In the event of a dispute as to whether the court has jurisdiction, the matter is settled by a decision of the court itself. The General Assembly or the Security Council may request the ICJ to give an advisory opinion on any legal question; other UN organs or Specialized Agencies, if authorized by the General Assembly, may request advisory opinions on legal questions arising within the scope of their activities.

States adhering to the statute are not required to submit disputes to the court, whose jurisdiction in a contentious case depends upon the consent of the disputing states. In accordance with Article 36 of the statute, states may declare that they recognize as compulsory, in relation to any other country accepting the same obligation, the jurisdiction of the court in all legal disputes concerning (1) the interpretation of a treaty; (2) any question of international law; (3) the existence of any fact which, if established, would constitute a breach of an international obligation; and (4) the nature or extent of the reparation to be made for the breach of such an obligation. However, declarations under Article 36 have often been qualified by conditions relating, for example, to reciprocity, the duration of the obligation, or the nature of the dispute. The United States, in accepting the court's compulsory jurisdiction in 1946, excluded matters of domestic jurisdiction "as determined by the United States of America." This exception, often called the Connally Amendment, has been something of a model for other states.

Structure. The ICJ consists of 15 judges elected for renewable nine-year terms by separate majority votes of the UN General Assembly and the Security Council, one-third of the judges being elected every three years. Candidates are nominated by national groups in the Permanent Court of Arbitration (PCA) and national groups appointed by non-PCA UN members, with the General Assembly and Security Council assessing the nominees according to the qualifications required for appointment to the highest judicial offices of their respective states. Due consideration is also given to ensuring that the principal legal systems of the world are represented. No two judges may be nationals of the same state, and no judge may exercise any political or administrative function or engage in any other occupation of a professional nature while serving on the ICJ. As a protection against political pressure, no judge can be dismissed unless, in the unanimous opinion of the other judges, he or she has ceased to fulfill the required conditions for service. If there are no judges of their nationality on the court, the parties to a case are entitled to choose ad hoc or national judges to sit for that particular case. Such judges take part in the decision on terms of complete equality with the other judges.

The procedural rules of the ICJ have been adopted without substantial change from those of the PCIJ, the court itself electing a president and a vice president from among its members for three-year terms. In accordance with Article 38 of the statute, the court in deciding cases applies (1) international treaties and conventions; (2) international custom; (3) the general principles of law "recognized by civilized nations"; and (4) judicial decisions and the teachings of the most highly qualified publicists, as a subsidiary means of determining the rules of law. All questions are decided by a majority of the judges present, with nine judges constituting a quorum. In the event of a tie vote, the president of the court may cast a second, deciding vote.

The Registry of the Court is headed by a registrar (currently Philippe Couvreur of Belgium, reelected for another seven-year term on February 8, 2007, and reelected again on February 10, 2014), who maintains the list of cases submitted to the court and is the normal channel to and from the court.

Recent activities. From 1946 through 2013 the ICJ heard 154 cases, issued 94 judgments, and rendered 40 advisory opinions. Among the most celebrated of the advisory opinions was its determination in July 1962 that the expenses of the UN Operation in the Congo and the UN Emergency Force in the Middle East were "expenses of the Organization" within the meaning of Article 17 of the UN Charter, which stipulates that such expenses "shall be borne by the members as apportioned by the General Assembly." (For information on the court prior to 1984, see the 2012 and 2014 *Handbooks.*)

One of the court's most publicized cases in the 1980s involved a suit brought by Nicaragua challenging U.S. involvement in the mining of its harbors. During preliminary hearings, begun in April 1984, Nicaragua charged that the action was a violation of international law and asked for reparations. The United States sought, unsuccessfully, to have the case dismissed on the ground that Nicaragua's failure to submit an instrument of ratification of the court's statutes prevented it from appearing before the court. In May the ICJ rendered an interim decision that directed the defendant to cease and refrain from mining operations and to respect Nicaraguan sovereignty. In November the court ruled that it had a right to hear the case, but in early 1985 Washington, anticipating an adverse ruling, stated it would not participate in further proceedings on the ground that it was a political issue, over which the court lacked jurisdiction. In June 1986, citing numerous military and paramilitary activities, the court ruled the United States had breached international law by using force to violate Nicaragua's sovereignty. In a series of 16 rulings, each approved by a substantial majority, the court directed the United States to cease the activities cited and to pay reparations to Nicaragua. The judgment was nonenforceable, however, as the United States had previously informed the court that it would not submit to ICJ jurisdiction regarding conflicts in Central America.

In 1986 Nicaragua also filed suit against Honduras and Costa Rica for frontier incidents and attacks allegedly organized by anti-Sandinista forces. Honduras announced it did not consent to the court's jurisdiction in the matter, although in February 1987 it agreed to refer to the ICJ a dispute with El Salvador involving both land border demarcation and maritime jurisdiction. Later in the year, as negotiations on a proposed Central American peace plan proceeded, Nicaragua dropped the suit against Costa Rica and "postponed" its action against Honduras. Deliberations in the latter suit resumed in late 1988 but were again suspended as part of the peace plan negotiated by the presidents of five Central American nations in late 1989.

In April 1988, at the request of the General Assembly, the court was brought into the dispute between the UN and the United States over U.S. attempts to close the UN observer mission of the Palestine Liberation Organization (PLO). The United States had ordered the closing because recent legislation classified the PLO as a "terrorist" organization, but the General Assembly strongly denounced the U.S. action as a violation of the 1947 "host country" treaty. The court ruled that the United States must submit the issue to binding international arbitration, although it was unclear whether the United States would accept the decision. The issue became moot later in the year when a U.S. district court declared that the government had no authority to close the mission and the U.S. Justice Department announced it would not appeal that decision.

The likelihood of an expansion in the court's calendar grew in early 1989 when the Soviet Union announced its recognition of ICJ jurisdiction over "interpretation and application" of five international human rights agreements. Washington also appeared to be supporting a broader mandate for the court after several years of aloofness triggered by the 1986 ruling on the Nicaraguan suit. In August the two superpowers agreed to give the ICJ jurisdiction in resolving disputes stemming from the interpretation of seven treaties on the extradition and prosecution of terrorists and drug traffickers.

Washington underscored its new attitude in 1989 by permitting the ICJ to rule on a long-standing investment dispute with Italy and by agreeing to defend itself in a suit filed by Iran for financial compensation for those killed when an Iranian jetliner was shot down by the USS *Vincennes* over the Persian Gulf in July 1988 (see entry on the International Civil Aviation Organization). UN secretary-general Pérez de Cuéllar strongly welcomed the heightened respect being accorded to the ICJ, describing the court as a "crucial component of the UNs recent attempt to prove its ability to function as the guardian of world security." To further the ICJ's role in the peaceful settlement of bilateral disputes, Pérez de Cuéllar announced late in the year that a trust fund would be established to help pay the legal expenses of poorer nations appearing before the court.

The most publicized ICJ case in the first half of 1992 involved Libya's request for the court to block the U.S.–UK attempt to force the extradition of two Libyans for trial in connection with the 1988 bombing of a Pan Am airliner over Scotland. Libya asked the court to declare sanctions imposed by the Security Council in the matter to be illegal, but the court ruled 11 to 5 that it did not have the authority to block compliance with the council's decision. Libya ultimately agreed to have the accused tried under Scottish law at a court in the Netherlands, but the ICJ still had before it jurisdictional questions relating to the 1971 Montreal Convention for the Suppression of Unlawful Acts against the Safety of Civil Aviation. In September 2003, however, improved relations led the three parties to request that the proceedings be discontinued, and the ICJ obliged.

In April 1993, acting on a request from Bosnia and Herzegovina, the court ordered the Federal Republic of Yugoslavia to "take all measures within its power to prevent the commission of genocide" against the Bosnian Muslim community. In August Bosnia and Herzegovina asked it to overturn the Security Council arms embargo and to declare that any partitioning of Bosnia would be illegal. Although the court rejected both requests in September, it demanded the "immediate and effective" implementation of its April genocide order, the decision being described as an "implicit rebuke" to Yugoslavia and a political boost to the Bosnian cause.

In February 1994 the ICJ ruled in favor of Chad in its long-standing dispute over the border territory known as the Aozou Strip (see entries on Chad and Libya). Other subsequent ICJ activity included the formation of a seven-member Chamber of Environmental Matters to assist in what was expected to be a growing caseload in that area. The court also urged that greater use be made of its ability to offer "advisory opinions" as part of the UN's overall preventative diplomacy strategy.

Cases related to nuclear weapons dominated the ICJ calendar in late 1995, beginning with a request from New Zealand (supported by a number of smaller island states) for a court injunction against the resumption of French nuclear testing in the South Pacific. The ICJ declined the request, ruling that its authority from a 1973 case extended only to above-ground nuclear tests. The court also heard about three weeks of widely publicized testimony in November 1995 regarding an advisory opinion sought by the General Assembly on whether the threat or use of nuclear weapons was a violation of international law. In July 1996 the ICJ ruled by an 8–7 vote that "generally" the use of such weapons would be contrary to international law, although the court equivocated on their use in self-defense. In the face of "legal uncertainty" the ICJ urged the international community to resolve the question permanently through disarmament negotiations.

On September 25, 1997, the court issued its ruling on a dispute between Hungary and Slovakia over the construction of two dams on the Danube River, finding that both were guilty of breaching a treaty originally signed in 1977, Hungary for failing to build one dam and Slovakia for diverting flow of the Danube through another it built in 1992. In early 1998 Hungary and Slovakia reached agreement on where a new dam on the Danube was to be built in accordance with the decision, but Budapest subsequently backed away from the agreement, stating that an assessment of the project's impact on the environment had to be completed before the Hungarian legislature could consider the accord. Consequently, in September 1998 Slovakia filed a request for an additional judgment. Bilateral negotiations subsequently resumed, and the court has therefore not ruled on the case.

In the first, although indirect, death penalty case before the ICJ, in 1999 Germany accused the United States of violating international legal obligations when it failed to inform two German citizens, Walter and Karl LaGrand, of their right to contact the German consulate following their U.S. arrest. Both defendants were ultimately convicted of murder and executed without the United States having provided, according to Germany, "effective review of and remedies for criminal convictions impaired by a violation of the rights under Article 36" of the Vienna Convention on Consular Relations. The United States acknowledged the failure of "competent authorities" to adhere to the convention, and in June 2001 the court ruled for Germany. In a similar case, *Mexico v. United States,* in 2004 the court ruled in favor of Mexico, which in 2003 had charged the United States with a failure to avail some 50 Mexican nationals of their consular rights. The court proposed as a remedy that the United States undertake a "review and reconsideration" of the convictions and sentences.

In October 1999 the Democratic Republic of the Congo (DRC) filed a case against Uganda for invasion, human rights violations, and the plunder of natural resources. In a July 2000 interim ruling, the court urged Uganda to withdraw its troops in accordance with a June UN resolution that had called for the removal of all foreign troops from the country. A final ruling had not been made as of mid-2007. In 1998 Guinea had filed a case against the DRC on behalf of an expatriate businessman who had been imprisoned, stripped of his assets, and expelled; that case also remained open. Earlier in the year, the court ruled that it did not have jurisdiction in a case brought by the DRC against Rwanda in 2002.

Many of the court's most recent judgments have concerned territorial disputes. In December 1999 the court ruled in Botswana's favor and against Namibia in a case involving competing claims to Kasikili

(Sedudu) Island in the Chobe River. A boundary dispute between Bahrain and Qatar was concluded in March 2001, when the judges awarded the Huwar Islands and adjacent shoals to Bahrain and the contested Zubarah strip to Qatar. In October 2002 the court addressed issues of land and maritime boundaries between Cameroon and Nigeria; although neither disputant won a complete victory, the complex decision largely favored Cameroon, which was awarded oil-rich Bakassi Peninsula. Two months later the court ruled that Malaysia, not Indonesia, held sovereignty over Pulau Ligitan and Pulau Sipadan in the Celebes Sea. In July 2005 the court settled a frontier dispute between Benin and Niger.

In its first advisory ruling in five years, the court announced on July 9, 2004, its opinion that the construction of a wall by Israel in the occupied Palestinian territory was "contrary to international law." In addition to ruling that affected Palestinians should receive reparations from Israel and that part of the security barrier should be torn down, the court referred the matter to the General Assembly and Security Council for further action. The lone dissenting vote in the 14–1 nonbinding ruling was cast by Judge Thomas Buergenthal of the United States.

On December 15, 2004, the court unanimously dismissed eight cases that had been brought by the Federal Republic of Yugoslavia (now the separate states of Serbia and Montenegro) against individual NATO countries (Belgium, Canada, France, Germany, Italy, Netherlands, Portugal, and the United Kingdom) in connection with the legality of the 1999 NATO air campaign during the Kosovo conflict. The cases, filed under the 1948 UN Convention on the Prevention and Punishment of the Crime of Genocide, initially numbered ten, but the court had immediately dismissed those against Spain and the United States because Madrid and Washington had signed the 1948 convention with the proviso that they could refuse court jurisdiction. In 2004 the eight outstanding cases were rejected by a majority of the judges on the grounds that at the time the Federal Republic of Yugoslavia filed its complaints it had not yet formally been admitted to the United Nations (and was therefore not a party to the ICJ Statute), following the breakup of the former Socialist Federal Republic of Yugoslavia in the early 1990s. As of July 2006 Serbia and Montenegro remained party to separate Genocide Convention cases brought against Yugoslavia by Bosnia and Herzegovina in 1993 and by Croatia in 1999.

In February 2005 the court ruled that it could not settle a dispute between Liechtenstein and Germany over property that had been confiscated during World War II by Czechoslovakia but that had subsequently come into German possession. The court ruled that it did not have jurisdiction because the conflict dated to 1945, and the applicable convention on the peaceful settlement of disputes had not entered into force between Germany and Liechtenstein until 1980.

As of August 2006, 12 cases remained before the court, including the Hungary-Slovakia case, 2 involving the DRC, and 2 involving Serbia and Montenegro. Four of the remaining 7 were territorial disputes. Nicaragua filed in 1999 against Honduras over a shared maritime border and in 2001 against Colombia "concerning title to territory and maritime delimitation" in the western Caribbean. Cases filed in 2003 concerned rival claims by Malaysia and Singapore to Pedra Branca/Pulau Batu Puteh, Middle Rocks, and South Ledge, and a Congolese-French dispute over the latter's judicial actions against Congolese officials charged with torture and crimes against humanity. In 2004 Romania submitted a claim against Ukraine over their shared maritime boundary in the Black Sea.

In May 2006 Argentina filed suit against Uruguay to stop the construction of two pulp mills on the Uruguay River, asserting that the mills would do irreparable environmental damage. (In July, the ICJ declined to order construction stopped until the case was tried.) In August France consented to the court's jurisdiction in a case brought by Djibouti, which had charged France with violating a bilateral treaty and a bilateral convention.

On January 23, 2007, on a vote of 14 to 1, the court declined Uruguay's request to issue an order for Argentina to end blockades of roads and bridges to the construction sites in the pulp mills case. In February the ICJ reaffirmed in *Bosnia and Herzegovina vs. Serbia and Montenegro* that the court had jurisdiction under Article IX of the Convention on the Prevention and Punishment of the Crime of Genocide when one country alleged genocide by another. In May the court ruled on an issue of diplomatic protection for Ahmadou Sadio Diallo related to his role in two private companies in a dispute with the Democratic Republic of the Congo.

In January 2008 Peru initiated a suit against Chile over the maritime boundary between the two countries. The countries were given until 2010 to enter their initial briefs. Ecuador filed suit against Colombia in April over the use of aerial herbicides to destroy illicit drugs near the two countries' border. In June Mexico asked for clarification in the 2004 case *Mexico v. United States.* Mexico argued that the United States was required to reexamine past cases in which Mexican nationals were convicted by U.S. courts. After collecting evidence and briefs from both sides, the court was still deliberating over the case as of October 1, 2009. On October 10 the UN General Assembly asked the ICJ to rule on Kosovo's unilateral declaration of independence. In December the ICJ heard oral arguments in an advisory case on Kosovar independence.

In February 2009 in *Belgium v. Senegal,* the ICJ was asked to rule on whether or not Senegal was obligated to either prosecute or extradite former Chadian president Hissène Habré. Habré had been in exile in Senegal since 1990 and had been arrested for crimes against humanity in 2000. However, a Senegalese court dismissed the charges since the country did not at the time have statutes expressly prohibiting crimes against humanity. Senegal did amend its legal code to include genocide and crimes against humanity in 2007. Meanwhile, a Belgian national filed charges in Belgium against Habré in 2005, and the country issued an international arrest warrant for the former president. In its 2009 motion Belgium asked the court to determine if Senegal should prosecute Habré under its new laws or turn him over to Brussels. Also in 2009 Honduras brought suit before the ICJ after the former president of Honduras, Manuel Zelaya, was given refuge in the Brazilian embassy. Honduras claimed that Brazil's action amounted to illegal interference in the domestic affairs of the country. (The suit was dropped in May 2010, see entry on Honduras.)

On July 22, 2010, the ICJ issued an opinion, on a vote of ten-to-four, that the 2008 Kosavar declaration of independence did not violate international law. Three new cases were initiated before the court in 2010. Australia brought suit against Japan in June, alleging that in violation of international conventions Japan illicitly continued to hunt whales under the guise of scientific research. In July Burkina Faso and Niger jointly requested that the court adjudicate a long-standing border disagreement. Costa Rica filed suit against Nicaragua in November after troops from the latter occupied territory that was claimed by both nations. Costa Rica had already gained a decree from the OAS calling on Nicaragua to withdraw. Also in November, the ICJ was asked to provide an advisory opinion in a disagreement over the dismissal of an employee between the International Fund for Agricultural Development and the Administrative Tribunal of the International Labor Organization.

In April 2011 the court dismissed a suit brought by Georgia against Russia alleging racial discrimination in the two countries' dispute over South Ossettia. On July 19 the court ordered both Thailand and Cambodia to withdraw their troops from the disputed plot around a 12th-century Hindu Shiva temple, which the UN had declared a World Heritage Site. The court was reconsidering a 1962 ruling that awarded the site to Cambodia. In September Turkey announced that it would challenge Israel's blockade of the Gaza Strip before the court. The court was expected to rule on the long-standing dispute between Greece and the Former Yugoslav Republic of Macedonia. The case concerned Greece's objection to the latter country's name.

In December 2011 Nicaragua brought suit against Costa Rica, asserting that a Costa Rican construction project along the border of the two countries will cause significant environmental damage to the ecosystem of the San Juan de Nicaragua River. The court determined that initial filings had to be complete by December 2013 in the case.

On February 3, 2012, the court ruled in favor of Germany in a case against Italy and Greece. Italian courts had issued a series of decisions that asserted Germany had lost its state immunity from lawsuits related to atrocities committed during World War II because the crimes had violated international law. Although Germany had paid reparations and concluded treaties with Italy and other states, plaintiffs contended that the reparations did not compensate all victims of German actions. In a 12 to 3 decision, the ICJ found that Germany retained its state immunity, which could not be voided by national courts, no matter the severity of crimes or actions. The court did note that Germany could still be liable for reparations through other means. The court applied its ruling to the Italian cases and a similar tort brought forward by Greece.

In September 2013 Nicaragua initiated new proceedings against Colombia by asking the court to delineate the extent of Nicaragua's continental shelf beyond a 200-nautical-mile zone, following a November 2012 decision, in which the ICJ settled the maritime boundary between the two countries within that 200-mile limit. On November 11 the court reaffirmed its 1962 ruling that granted Cambodia jurisdiction over the disputed Preah Vihear temple.

The budget for the ICJ for the 2014–2015 biennium was $53.3 million. The ICJ delineated a disputed area of the maritime boundary between Chile and Peru in a decision on January 27. The court confirmed Chile's control over most of the disputed territory but did grant some areas to Peru. On March 31 the court ruled, in a case brought by Australia against Japan, that Tokyo's whaling program violated the International Convention for the Regulation of Whaling (see entry on Japan).

On December 16, 2015, the court ruled in *Costa Rica v. Nicaragua*, a case from 2011 over disputed territory, that Nicaragua had violated Costa's Rica's territorial sovereignty by deploying troops in the area under contention. The court ordered Nicaragua to cease its activities and compensate Costa Rica. It also ruled that Costa Rica had violated international law by not conducting an environmental impact study prior to beginning its construction project.

The ICJ ruled that it did not have jurisdiction to decide a series of cases brought separately by the Marshall Islands against India, Pakistan, and the United Kingdom, over those countries' nuclear weapons tests and nuclear weapons programs. The case had originally been filed in April 2014, and the judgment was announced on October 5, 2016.

SECRETARIAT

Secretary-General	António Guterres (Portugal)
Deputy Secretary-General	Jan Eliasson (Sweden)
Senior Management Group	
Chief of Protocol	Desmond Parker (Trinidad and Tobago)
Chief of Cabinet	Edmond Mulet (Guatemala)
Children and Armed Conflict	Leila Zerrougui (Algeria)
Conference on Trade and Development	Mukhisa Kituyi (Kenya)
Development Program	Helen Clark (New Zealand)
Disarmament Affairs	Kim Won-soo (Republic of Korea)
Disaster Risk Reduction	Robert Glasser (Australia)
Economic and Social Affairs	Wu Hongbo (China)
Economic Commission for Africa	Abdalla Hamdok (Sudan)
Economic Commission for Europe	Christian Friis Bach (Denmark)
Economic Commission for Latin America and the Caribbean	Alicia Bárcena (Chile)
Economic and Social Commission for Asia and the Pacific	Shamshad Akhtar (Pakistan)
Economic and Social Commission for Western Asia	Rima Khalaf (Jordan)
Field Support	Atul Khare (India)
Gender Equality and Empowerment of Women	Phumzile Mlambo-Ngcuka (South Africa)
General Assembly and Conference Management	Catherine Pollard (Guyana)
High Commission for Refugees	Filippo Grandi (Italy)
Human Rights	Zeid Ra'ad al Hussein (Jordan)
Human Settlements Program	Joan Clos (Spain)
Humanitarian Affairs and Emergency Relief Coordinator	Stephen O'Brien (United Kingdom)
Least Developed Countries, Landlocked and Small Island Developing States	Gyan Chandra Acharya (Nepal)
Legal Affairs	Miguel de Serpa Soares (Portugal)
Management	Yukio Takasu (Japan)
Office for the Coordination of Humanitarian Affairs and Emergency Relief Coordinator	Valerie Amos (United Kingdom)
Office of Internal Oversight Services (Reports to the General Assembly)	Heidi Mendoza (Philippines)
Peacebuilding Support	Oscar Fernandez-Taranco (Argentina)
Peacekeeping Operations	Hervé Ladsous (France)
Political Affairs	Jeffrey D. Feltman (United States)
Population Fund	Babatunde Osotimehin (Nigeria)
Project Services	Grete Faremi (Norway)
Public Information	Cristina Gallach (Spain)
Safety and Security	Peter Thomas Drennan (Australia)
Sexual Violence in Conflict	Zainab Hawa Bangura (Sierra Leone)
Special Advisor on Africa	Maged Abdelaziz (Egypt)
Special Advisor on Myanmar	Vijay Nambiar (India)
Special Advisor on the Prevention of Genocide	Adama Dieng (Senegal)
UN Children's Fund	Anthony Lake (United States)
UN Environment Program (Executive Director)	Erik Solheim (Norway)
UN Office in Geneva (Director General)	Michael Møller (Denmark)
UN Office in Nairobi (Director General)	Sahle-Work Zewde (Ethiopia)
UN Office in Vienna, Office on Drugs and Crime	Yury Fedotov (Russia)
World Food Program	Ertharin Cousin (United States)
Other Senior Officers	
Executive Director, Counterterrorism	Jean-Paul Laborde (France)
UN Ombudsman	Johnston Barkat (United States)
Special/Personal Representatives or Envoys of or Advisers to the Secretary-General	
Afghanistan	Tadamichi Yamamoto (Japan)
Africa	Maged Abdelaziz (Egypt)
African Union	Haile Menkerios (South Africa)
Alliance of Civilizations	Nassir Abdulaziz al-Nasser (Qatar)
Avian and Human Influenza	David Nabarro (United Kingdom)
Central Africa	François Louncény Fall (Guinea)
Central African Republic	Parfait Onanga-Anyanga (Gabon)
Central Asia	Petko Draganov (Bulgaria)
Children and Armed Conflict	Leila Zerrougui (Algeria)
Cities and Climate Change	Michael Bloomberg (United States)
Climate Change	Robert Orr (United States)
Colombia	Jean Arnault (France)
Côte d'Ivoire	Aïchatou Mindaou Souleymane (Niger)
Cyprus	Elizabeth Spehar (Canada)
Democratic Republic of the Congo	Maman Sambo Sidikou (Niger)
Disability and Accessibility	Lenin Voltaire Moreno (Ecuador)
Georgia	Antti Turunen (Finland)
Global Education	Gordon Brown (United Kingdom)
Great Lakes Region	Said Djinnit (Algeria)
Guinea-Bissau	Modibo Touré (Mali)
Haiti	Sandra Honoré (Trinidad and Tobago)
HIV/AIDS in Asia and the Pacific	Prasada Rao V.R. Jonnalagadda (India)
HIV/AIDS in the Caribbean	Edward Greene (Guyana)
HIV/AIDS in Eastern Europe and Central Asia	Michel Kazatchkine (France)
Inclusion Finance for Development	Queen Máxima (Netherlands)
India-Pakistan	Per Gusaf Lodin (Sweden)
Internet Governance Forum	Jānis Kārkliņš (Latvia)
Iraq	Ján Kubiš (Slovakia)
Kosovo	Zahir Tanin (Afghanistan)
Kuwait	Abdullah al Matouq (Kuwait)
Least Developed Countries, Landlocked Developing Countries, and Small Developing Island States	Gyan Chandra Acharya (Nepal)
Lebanon	Sigrid Kaag (Netherlands)

Macedonia	Matthew Nimetz (United States)
Malaria	Ray Chambers (United States)
Mali	Albert Gerard Koenders (Netherlands)
Middle East	Nickolay Mladenov (Bulgaria)
Migration	Peter Sutherland (Ireland)
Myanmar	Vijay Nambiar (India)
Prevention of Genocide	Adama Dieng (Senegal)
Road Safety	Jean Todt (France)
Sahel	Mohammed Ibn Chambas (Ghana)
Sexual Exploitation and Abuse	Jane Holl Lute (United States)
Sexual Violence in Conflict	Zainab Hawa Bangura (Sierra Leone)
Sierra Leone	Jens Anders Toyberg-Frandzen (Denmark)
Somalia	Michael Keating (United Kingdom)
South-South Cooperation	Jorge Chediek (Argentina)
Sport for Development and Peace	Wifried Lemke (Germany)
Sudan and South Sudan	Nicolas Haysom (South Africa)
Sudan/Abyei	Maj. Gen. Hassen Ebrahim Mussa (Ethiopia)
Sudan/Darfur	Martin Ihoeghian Uhomoibhi (Nigeria)
South Sudan	Ellen Margarethe Løj (Denmark)
Sustainable Development Goals	Jeffrey Sachs (United States)
Sustainable Energy for All	Richard Kyte (United Kingdom)
Syria	Staffan de Mistura (Italy)
Tuberculosis	Eric Goosby (United States)
United Nations International School	Michael Adlerstein (United States)
Violence Against Children	Marta Santos Pais (Portugal)
West Africa	Mohammed Ibn Chambas (Ghana)
Western Sahara	Kim Bolduc (Canada)
Yemen	Ismail Ould Chiekh Ahmed (Mauritania)
Youth	Ahmad Alhendawi (Jordan)
Youth Employment	Werner Faymann (Austria)
Youth Refugees and Sport	Jacques Rogge (Belgium)

Website: www.un.org/sg.

Structure. The Secretariat consists of the secretary-general and the UN staff, which, since early 1998, includes a deputy secretary-general. The secretary-general, who is appointed for a five-year term by the General Assembly on recommendation of the Security Council, is designated chief administrative officer by the charter, which directs him to report annually to the General Assembly on the work of the UN, to appoint the staff, and to perform such other functions as are entrusted to him by the various UN organs. Under Article 99 of the charter, the secretary-general may bring to the attention of the Security Council any matter that in his opinion may threaten international peace and security. Other functions of the secretary-general include acting in that capacity at all meetings of the General Assembly, the Security Council, the Economic and Social Council, and the Trusteeship Council, and presenting any supplementary reports on the work of the UN that are necessary to the General Assembly.

The charter defines the "paramount consideration" in employing staff as the necessity of securing the highest standards of efficiency, competency, and integrity, with due regard to the importance of recruiting on as wide a geographical basis as possible. In the performance of their duties, the secretary-general and the staff are forbidden to seek or receive any instructions from any government or any other authority external to the UN. Each member of the UN, in turn, is bound to respect the exclusively international character of the Secretariat's responsibilities and not to seek to influence it in the discharge of its duties.

In addition to its New York headquarters, the UN maintains offices in Geneva, Switzerland; Nairobi, Kenya; and Vienna, Austria. Personnel of various specialized and subsidiary organs are also headquartered in New York or other UN sites around the globe.

The regular budget of the organization is financed primarily by obligatory contributions from the member states, as determined by a scale of assessments that is based on capacity to pay and currently varies from 0.001 percent of the total for the poorest members to 22 percent for the United States. Collectively, eight Western industrialized countries (Canada, France, Germany, Italy, Japan, Spain, United Kingdom, and the United States) contribute approximately 61 percent of the budget. China is the largest contributor among developing states and provides 7.9 percent of the budget, followed by Brazil at 3.8 percent. Activities outside the regular budget, including most peacekeeping activities and technical cooperation programs, are separately financed, partly through voluntary contributions.

Recent activities. The level of international political activity undertaken by various secretaries general has depended as much on the political environment and their own personalities as on charter provisions. Prior to the breakup of the Soviet Union in the early 1990s, the most important factor was often the acquiescence of the superpowers. This was vividly demonstrated by the Soviet challenge to the Secretariat during the Belgian Congo crisis of 1960. UN intervention in the Congo, initiated on the authority of the Security Council in the summer of 1960, led to sharp Soviet criticism of Secretary-General Dag Hammarskjöld and a proposal by Soviet Chair Nikita Khrushchev in September 1960 to abolish the Secretariat and substitute a tripartite executive body made up of Western, communist, and neutral representatives. Although the proposal was not adopted, the USSR maintained a virtual boycott of the Secretariat up to the time of Hammarskjölds death in September 1961 and imposed a number of conditions before agreeing to U Thant of Burma as his successor. U Thant was in turn succeeded in 1971 by Kurt Waldheim of Austria.

In December 1981, in the wake of decisions by Waldheim and Salim A. Salim of Tanzania to withdraw from consideration, Javier Pérez de Cuéllar, a relatively obscure Peruvian diplomat, was selected by a closed session of the UN Security Council as the recommended candidate for UN secretary-general. (For more information, see the 2014 *Handbook.*) As expected, the widely respected Pérez de Cuéllar declined to stand for a third term, and in the fall of 1991 the General Assembly, acting upon the recommendation of the Security Council, unanimously elected Boutros Boutros-Ghali, the Egyptian deputy prime minister for foreign affairs, as the UNs sixth secretary-general, effective January 1, 1992. Boutros-Ghali, the first Arab and the first African to hold the post, rose to prominence as part of the Egyptian team that negotiated the Camp David peace treaty with Israel.

Because he was well known in UN circles and familiar with the organization's bureaucracy, the new secretary-general was able to institute a significant restructuring of the Secretariat in February 1992 as part of ongoing streamlining throughout the UN system. Most operations were consolidated into four major new departments, permitting a reduction in the number of undersecretaries general and assistant secretaries general while also providing a more direct and, it was hoped, a more efficient chain of command. One of the new departments was devoted to peacekeeping, an area in which Boutros-Ghali suggested UN influence could be expanded even further.

In June 1992 Boutros-Ghali outlined an Agenda for Peace, which called upon UN members to make armed forces available to the Security Council on a permanent on-call basis. The secretary-general also suggested that the council's long-dormant Military Staff Committee be reactivated to assume authority over what would essentially become the UN's standby army. A wider role in "preventative diplomacy" was also urged, Boutros-Ghali asking regional organizations to seek UN intervention before disputes escalated into warfare.

Boutros-Ghali's recommendations were initially endorsed in many quarters. However, disillusionment was apparent a year later, stemming from the failure of UN efforts in Bosnia and Herzegovina, ongoing difficulties in Somalia and Angola, and the inability of fact-finding missions in Azerbaijan, Georgia, and Tajikistan to prevent bloodshed. For his part, Boutros-Ghali argued that the United Nations was being asked to take on more than it could handle, especially considering the "chasm" that existed between its assignments and the money member states were willing to provide. The secretary-general was also facing resistance both from member states and from UN employees in his efforts to further revamp the Secretariat and other UN bureaucracies, despite general agreement that the organization remained highly inefficient in many areas. However, a new Office for Inspections and Investigations (OII) was established in 1993 to combat waste and mismanagement and to address allegations of corruption within the UN system. A year later, the office was replaced by an Office of Internal Oversight Services, which is headed by an assistant secretary-general who has operational independence.

As a counterpoint to his 1992 Agenda for Peace, Boutros-Ghali unveiled an Agenda for Development in May 1994. Despite the "distorted perception" throughout the world that peacekeeping was being emphasized at the expense of other areas, the secretary-general stressed that "development is still the major activity of the UN." However, Boutros-Ghali argued that new levels of coordination were required within the UN and between the UN and other international organizations to combat donor fatigue and to mobilize public opinion in support of development assistance. Progress also depended on the ability of developing nations to find "the right blend" of governmental influence and private initiative for maximum economic growth.

In late 1994 and 1995 Boutros-Ghali consistently criticized UN members for failing to meet their financial obligations, especially those for peacekeeping operations. The secretary-general reported that arrears had reached $3.24 billion as of September 1995, making it "impossible for us to do our job." Boutros-Ghali also argued, however, that the United Nations retained a "moral obligation" to go into crisis areas, whatever the financial and/or political limitations might be. In a related vein, the secretary-general was reported to be somewhat at odds with the Security Council, which he described as being too involved with the conflict in Bosnia and Herzegovina at the expense of problems in other sections of the world. Underscoring his determination to focus attention on "underdog conflicts," Boutros-Ghali made a week-long trip across Central Africa in mid-1995. The secretary-general's concern for his home continent was further highlighted in March 1996 when he launched the ten-year, $25 billion UN System-wide Special Initiative on Africa, described as one of the largest cooperative operations ever attempted by UN agencies and other regional organizations.

In June 1996 the United States issued a surprisingly strong statement pledging to veto a second term for Boutros-Ghali, arguing that he was ill-suited to implementing the reforms Washington was demanding in return for payment of some of its $1.3 billion in arrears. Representatives from many countries rushed to the defense of the secretary-general, pointing out that he had reduced UN staffing by some 10 percent and had attempted to restructure the UN's bureaucratic maze of agencies. Nevertheless, at the first round of balloting in the Security Council on November 19, the United States cast the lone dissenting vote against Boutros-Ghali's reelection, forcing the consideration of other candidates.

The four primary contenders to emerge were Kofi Annan of Ghana, then the undersecretary-general for peacekeeping operations; Amara Essy, the foreign minister of Côte d'Ivoire; Hamid Algabid of Niger, then the secretary-general of the Organization of the Islamic Conference; and Mauritanian diplomat Ahmedou Ould Abdallah. Several straw votes in the Security Council in early December effectively reduced the choices to Annan (backed by the United States) and Essy. Although France, an ardent supporter of Boutros-Ghali, reportedly threatened to veto Annan to protest Washington's heavy-handedness in the selection process, Annan was finally approved on December 13, with the General Assembly making the appointment official four days later.

Upon taking office on January 1, 1997, Annan, the first black African to hold the job, called for "a time for healing" and pledged to pursue UN reform. Among the most important reforms approved by the General Assembly late in the year was the creation of the position of the deputy secretary-general, Louise Fréchette of Canada becoming in January 1998 the first person to hold the position. Other changes included the formation of a cabinet-like Senior Management Group, the creation of the Department of Disarmament Affairs, the merger of three departments into the newly created Department of Economic and Social Affairs, the reorganization of the UN Drug Control Program (UNDCP) and the Center for International Crime Prevention (CICP) under the new Office for Drug Control and Crime Prevention (ODCCP) in Vienna, the consolidation of the Geneva-based Center for Human Rights under the Office of the High Commissioner for Human Rights (UNHCHR), and a proposed reduction in administrative costs of at least $200 million over four years.

In April 1998 Annan issued a wide-ranging report on African issues, particularly the wars being fought across the continent and the lack of economic development. Exhibiting a growing willingness to address such issues bluntly, he criticized African leaders for relying on military rather than political approaches to problems and for their failure to attend to good governance. In September 1998 Annan questioned the U.S. bomb attacks on suspected terrorist sites in Afghanistan and Sudan, arguing that "individual action by member states" was not the solution to the "global menace" of terrorism.

In subsequent speeches and reports, the secretary-general staked out a clear position in support of UN intervention to prevent a recurrence of the genocidal events in Rwanda and Kosovo during the 1990s. In addition to urging the Security Council to respond faster to the outbreak of civil wars, Annan countered ardent advocates for the primacy of national sovereignty by arguing that "nothing in the Charter precludes a recognition that there are rights beyond borders," particularly when a state was violating human rights within those borders. He also strongly supported establishment of a permanent International Criminal Court (ICC; see General Assembly) and chastised the United States for its objections to such a court, as well as for its unwillingness to provide more than transport and logistical support to peacekeeping ventures in Africa.

The April 2000 secretary-general's report focused on development issues. Annan called for efforts to reduce youth unemployment and to "bridge the digital divide" between technologically advanced and developing states. He also urged the developed world to provide debt relief and to drop tariffs on commodities from developing countries, thereby helping them increase the export earnings needed to finance development. In addition, Annan advocated greater involvement by private sector partners in humanitarian relief efforts. In December 2000 he named a high-level panel of financial experts, chaired by former Mexican president Ernesto Zedillo, to propose steps to help speed development in poor countries. With a special UN session on HIV/AIDS approaching in June 2001, Annan subsequently called for creation of a Global AIDS and Health Fund.

On June 29, 2001, the General Assembly unanimously elected Annan to a second term, which began January 1, 2002. On October 12 Annan and the UN were awarded the Nobel Peace Prize.

In late 2002 not only the Security Council but also the General Assembly and Secretariat became increasingly tied up in the debate over weapons inspections in Iraq and a threatened U.S. invasion of that country. From then until the actual launch of hostilities in March 2003, Secretary-General Annan argued for adherence to the international rule of law and the need to address matters of peace and security in the context of "the unique legitimacy provided by the UN Security Council." He subsequently incurred Washington's wrath, not to mention that of right-wing U.S. media outlets, by branding the war "illegal" and by asserting that going to war had not made the world safer. He also opposed the George W. Bush administration's efforts to keep U.S. peacekeeping troops exempt from prosecution by the new ICC.

A major shake-up in the UN security structure followed a suicide truck bombing at UN headquarters in Baghdad, Iraq, on August 19, 2003. Twenty-two people died in the blast, including Annans special representative to Iraq, Sergio Vieira de Mello of Brazil, and the former UN chief of protocol, Nadia Younes of Egypt. An independent report published in March 2004 faulted administrators for having failed to conduct a security review of the facility, in the mistaken assumption that UN personnel would not be targeted by insurgents. As a consequence, Secretary-General Annan fired his security coordinator, Tun Myat of Myanmar, and demoted other personnel. Annan refused, however, to accept the resignation of Deputy Secretary-General Fréchette, who had headed a committee that recommended a UN return to Iraq. On January 13, 2005, Annan named David Veness, an assistant commissioner of London's Metropolitan Police Service and an antiterrorism expert, to head a newly created Department of Safety and Security.

Meanwhile, the secretary-general was drawing increasing criticism in connection with the $64 billion "oil-for-food" program, which had permitted Iraq to sell oil and use the income to meet humanitarian needs. An investigation initiated by the secretary-general in April 2004 into bribery and illicit payments led to the revelation that Annan's son, Kojo Annan, had been paid by a Swiss contractor, Cotecna Inspection Services, which had been responsible for monitoring Iraqi compliance with the program. February and March 2005 interim reports by the Independent Inquiry Committee, headed by former chair of the U.S. Federal Reserve Paul Volcker, exonerated Kofi Annan of involvement in awarding the contract to Cotecna but found procedural errors and procurement violations dating back to Boutros-Ghali's term as secretary-general. The committee also criticized Annan's former chief of cabinet, Syed Iqbal Riza of Pakistan, for having shredded documents relevant to the case. The first UN staffer held criminally culpable in the "oil-for-food" scandal was Aleksandr Yakovlev of Russia, who in August 2005 pleaded guilty to taking some $1.3 million in bribes while heading a procurement department.

The Volcker committee report issued on September 7, 2005, indicted the UN for "illicit, unethical and corrupt behavior" as well as inadequate auditing and overall bureaucratic inefficiency. During the 1996–2003 "oil-for-food" program, the Saddam Hussein regime illicitly pocketed billions of dollars while paying bribes to some

270 politicians and journalists. Although Annan accepted responsibility for the "deeply embarrassing" shortcomings documented in the report, he rejected calls for his resignation and vowed to press ahead with his reform agenda.

On March 21, 2005, drawing on the work of a High-Level Panel on Threats, Challenges, and Change that he had named in November 2003, Secretary-General Annan submitted to the General Assembly his long-awaited report on reform, "In Larger Freedom: Toward Development, Security, and Human Rights for All." Among other things, the secretary-general called for expanding the Security Council to better reflect a geopolitical balance; streamlining the General Assembly agenda; making the Secretariat more flexible, transparent, and accountable; and replacing the controversial UN Commission on Human Rights with a Human Rights Council elected by the General Assembly. He asked all developing countries to improve governance, target corruption, and uphold the rule of law while striving to meet the Millennium Development Goals set forth in 2000. At the same time, he urged developed countries to significantly increase their amount of development assistance and debt relief and to permit duty-free and quota-free imports from the least developed countries. He cautioned, however, that sustainable development required due attention to environmental factors and concerns about the depletion of natural resources. In the area of security he emphasized the importance of working in concert to control terrorism, end weapons proliferation, and stop civil wars. He also urged collective action against genocide, ethnic cleansing, and crimes against humanity if individual countries were unable or unwilling to act.

In January 2006 eight UN officials, including Andrew Toh, the assistant secretary-general for central support services, were suspended in connection with more than 200 alleged instances of fraud in the purchase of equipment for peacekeeping missions. The allegations resulted from an inquiry into procurement practices that led Chief of Staff Mark Malloch Brown, speaking to the Security Council in February, to confirm the need for reform, particularly in the awarding of contracts. Also in February, Secretary-General Annan announced the formation of a senior 15-member panel to propose methods to enhance collaboration and cooperation between agencies. The panel was one of the recommendations from the UN 60th anniversary summit. It suggested changes as part of Annans broader reform program and focused on the UNs role in environmental, humanitarian, and development policies. In March, in addition to naming Malloch Brown as successor to Deputy Secretary-General Fréchette, Annan announced additional specific reforms, including increased training for UN staff and improvements in technology, communications, and records. Annan also called for relocating some UN agencies from New York and Geneva to less expensive locations as a means of reducing expenditures.

A report on sexual misconduct by UN peacekeeping forces released in August 2006 detailed 313 investigations and noted that the inquiries had resulted in the dismissal of 17 UN peacekeepers and the forced repatriation of 161 others. In September the UN's first all-female peacekeeping unit was deployed to UNMIL. The force consisted of 125 woman officers from India. Women comprised less than 4 percent of the personnel of all UN peacekeeping missions as of 2008.

In informal polling in September and October 2006 among Security Council members to determine the next secretary-general, Foreign Minister Ban Ki-moon of the Republic of Korea emerged as the leading candidate among seven contenders mostly from Asia. Ban was the favored candidate of the United States and China, but France and the United Kingdom initially sought a more activist candidate. However, after Ban won the fourth informal poll on October 2, all of the other candidates withdrew. He was unanimously recommended by the Security Council and appointed by the General Assembly on October 13.

Once in office, Ban replaced two-thirds of the body's senior management team. He named Asha-Rose Migiro of Tanzania as the new deputy secretary-general. She was the third person to hold the post and the first non-Westerner. Throughout the senior management, the new secretary-general increased the number of appointments from the developing world. Ban also detailed five priorities for his term in office. First, he called for the UN to strengthen its traditional core pillars of security, development, and human rights. Second, he declared his intent to restore confidence in the office of the secretary-general. Third, Ban wanted to improve the efficiency of the UN management system, particularly its human resource system. Fourth, the new secretary-general sought to set higher ethical and professional standards for all UN employees and agencies, including the adoption of annual performance reviews. Fifth and finally, Ban declared his intent to revolutionize the relationship between the Secretariat and UN member states. In order to demonstrate his earnestness about ethical reform, Ban released his personal financial disclosure form for external review and promised to continue to do so each year. His deputy secretary-general has also adopted this practice. In June 2007 the UN's peacekeeping structure was divided into two departments, peacekeeping operations and field support, as part of a broader reform effort proposed by Ban in January to increase efficiency through greater specialization. Each of the new departments was headed by an undersecretary-general.

In November Ban became the first UN secretary-general to make an official visit to Antarctica. While touring the region, Ban called for greater action to slow global warming. He also announced the launch of a system-wide UN campaign to combat violence against women. Ban's initiative was scheduled to last through 2015 and mandate that the General Assembly include at least one agenda item per year to address gender violence. The secretary-general also pledged to reform UN agencies to better address violence against women, particularly during peacekeeping operations. In 2008 Ban released a report that showed attacks on UN staff had increased dramatically in the preceding year, and that deaths of UN workers due to attacks had increased by 38 percent.

Following attacks on UN workers, including the bombing of UN offices in Algiers in December 2007, Ban pledged to better protect UN staffers, and in 2008 convened the Independent Panel on Safety and Security to develop recommendations on how to better secure UN facilities and personnel. Meanwhile, throughout 2008 Ban continued to undertake a series of reforms at the world body. He appointed a chief information officer to oversee the UN's information technology systems, and he altered the UN's procurement system to ensure greater transparency and efficiency. He also shortened the hiring process for new UN staffers.

In response to rising food prices, in April 2008 Ban established the High Level Task Force on the Global Food Security Crisis to identify problems and develop strategies, as well as to coordinate the UN response. Ban brought together more than 100 world leaders at the High Level Event on the Millennium Development Goals in New York in September and was able to secure pledges of more than $16 billion in additional funding for poverty reduction efforts and an additional $3 billion to combat malaria and other diseases. In October Ban reported that an independent review of the $500 million Central Emergency Response Fund (CERF) found the reserve had been largely successful in its mission of providing assistance for natural disasters, and he urged members to annually contribute to CERF. Also in October, Ban conducted a high-level meeting of the heads of 17 major pharmaceutical and medical companies and received pledges that the firms would expand research and increase access to drugs and medicines in developing countries. In November Ban issued an urgent appeal for all member states to pay their dues. At the time, member states owed $756 million to the regular budget and $2.9 to the peacekeeping budget.

An investigation into the UNs handling of an inquiry into the death in 2000 of a British contractor working for UNDP led to the creation of the five-member Internal Justice Council (IJC). After Joe Comerford died, the UN refused his widow compensation until 2008 when she was awarded £143,000. The world body engaged in behavior that was later described by investigators as "reckless and callous" toward the widow. The IJC was formed to be an independent, judicial body for arbitration within the UN.

In 2008 Ban initiated the program UNiTE to End Violence Against Women. The program sought by 2015 to have nations adopt national legislation that mirrored international conventions and to institute plans to curb gender violence. UNiTE also promoted the development of global data collection and analysis of violence against women. The initiative was developed in response to a 2006 report that highlighted trends in gender violence and was in response to a 2007 General Assembly resolution that called for greater progress in the elimination of violence against women.

On January 31, 2009, Ban's special representative to Myanmar, Ibrahim Gambari, visited the country for a series of meetings in an effort to persuade the military government to restore democracy. The sessions were unsuccessful, although Gambari was able to meet with opposition leader Aung San Suu Kyi, who remained under house arrest. Ban launched the We Must Disarm (WMD) campaign on June 13. The WMD initiative was a multimedia effort to promote nuclear disarmament and increase awareness of the dangers of weapons proliferation. The secretary-general worked with actor Michael Douglas, a UN messenger of peace, in the campaign, which culminated in the International Day of Peace on September 21. The secretary-general convened the

UN Climate Change Summit in September. The event brought together more than 100 world leaders and was a precursor to the Copenhagen conference on climate change later that year. U.S. president Obama pledged that the country would recommit itself to involvement in global efforts to reduce greenhouse gases and address climate change.

In September 2009 Ban removed Peter Galbraith as a UN deputy special representative to Afghanistan. Galbraith had a public dispute with the senior UN figure in Afghanistan, Kai Eide, over the management of runoff balloting following a disputed presidential election in August.

Following a massive earthquake in Haiti in January 2010, Ban launched a widespread appeal for humanitarian aid, noting that more than 1.2 million Haitians needed emergency food and shelter. Ban appointed former U.S. president Bill Clinton as a special envoy for Haiti to raise awareness of the disaster. However, John Holmes, the UN emergency relief coordinator at the time, noted in a leaked e-mail that the UN response was "poorly coordinated and resourced." In April the secretary-general appointed Norman Girvan of Jamaica as a special representative in an effort to resolve a long-standing border dispute between Guyana and Venezuela. Talks between the two nations had been suspended since 2007. In July the media reported that the outgoing undersecretary-general of the Office of Internal Oversight Services (OIOS), Inga-Britt Ahlenius, had written a highly critical memo about Ban, accusing the secretary-general of unwarranted interference in operations of the UN watchdog agency. Ban subsequently appointed Carmen Lapointe of Canada as the new head of the OIOS.

In August 2010 Ban created a ten-member advisory council to increase global "awareness" of the issues faced by the world's 49 least developed states (LDCs) ahead of the fourth UN Conference on LDCs scheduled for May 2011. Also in August, Ban sent Assistant Secretary-General Atul Khare of India to the Democratic Republic of the Congo to investigate reports of mass rape by Rwandan Hutu rebels in Luvungi, and charges that UN peacekeepers at a nearby post failed to take action to prevent the attacks.

In June 2011 Ban was unanimously reelected for a second term as secretary-general. Following his reappointment, Ban reshuffled his senior management team. In January 2012 Ban announced a five-year agenda, "The Future We Want." The plan called for increased global efforts to combat malaria and polio and the designation of Antarctica as a global nature preserve. In response to widespread fighting in Syria, Ban appointed former secretary-general Annan as a special peace envoy. Annan developed a six-point peace plan that was endorsed by the Security Council and initially accepted by the Syrian government. However, renewed strife precluded the implementation of the initiative (see entry on Syria). On March 2 Ban appointed Jan Eliasson of Sweden as deputy secretary-general. In December Ban appealed for $2.2 billion from international donors to support a WHO initiative to eliminate cholera in Haiti by 2022.

Ban appointed Tegegnework Gettu of Ethiopia as undersecretary for the General Assembly and conference management in 2013. In June of that year, Ban appointed Jean-Paul Laborde of France as executive director of the UN's counterterrorism directorate. In September Ban announced that he had secured $1.5 billion to launch a new program, Education First, designed to support global education efforts. On October 1, Ban opened the annual session of the General Assembly by calling on world leaders to take stronger action to end the civil war in Syria, which he described as a "regional calamity with global ramifications." The secretary-general also urged continued action on climate change.

In May 2014 Ban appointed Kim Bolduc of Canada to succeed Wolfgang Weisbrod-Weber of Germany as the head of MINURSO and the secretary-general's special representative for Western Sahara. To better coordinate the UN's response to the 2014 Ebola outbreak, in September Ban named David Nabarro of the United Kingdom as his special representative on Ebola. In October, during a visit to Nairobi, Ban launched a global media campaign against female genital mutilation (FGM), following the publication of a UNICEF report that found that more than 130 million girls and women in 29 countries had been subjected to the practice. Also in October, Ban established the High-Level Independent Panel on Peace Operations to undertake a comprehensive assessment of UN peace operations and recommend reforms and revisions. The 14-member panel was the first major external review of UN peace missions since 2000.

Ban faced criticism in April 2015 after the suspension of UN official Anders Kompass (Sweden). Kompass had released a June 2014 UN report on sexual abuse by French peacekeepers in the Central African Republic to French officials after what he described as a failure on the part of the world body to take action.

The secretary-general led efforts in September 2015 to gain approval for the Sustainable Development Goals as part of the 2030 Agenda by the General Assembly. Ban described the agreement on the new goals as a "towering achievement" that would unify and inform UN efforts over the next decade.

In July 2016 the Security Council began debate and straw votes over Ban's successor. Thirteen people, including seven women, were nominated to replace the outgoing secretary-general. In a change from past elections, the candidates were allowed to campaign directly with the General Assembly. Among the candidates were Slovakian foreign minister Miroslav Lajčák, former New Zealand prime minister and current UNDP director Helen Clark, and former Bulgarian foreign minister Irina Bokova, currently serving as director general of UNESCO. On the sixth round of voting, former Portuguese prime minister António Gutteres was selected with 13 votes in favor and 2 no opinion votes. Gutteres took office on January 1, 2017, for a five-year term.

UNITED NATIONS: SPECIALIZED AGENCIES

The United Nations has designated 16 organizations as Specialized Agencies, 13 of which are discussed here. This edition of the *Handbook* does not include separate entries on the UN World Tourism Organization (UNWTO), or 2 agencies whose activities are largely technical: the Universal Postal Union (UPU), which traces its origins to the 1874 Treaty Concerning the Establishment of a General Postal Union (the Berne Treaty), and the World Meteorological Organization (WMO), successor to the International Meteorological Organization (founded in 1878). Appendix C lists the members of all 16 Specialized Agencies.

FOOD AND AGRICULTURE ORGANIZATION OF THE UNITED NATIONS

(FAO)

Established: By constitution signed in Quebec, Canada, October 16, 1945. The FAO became a UN Specialized Agency by agreement with the Economic and Social Council (approved by the General Assembly on December 14, 1946).

Purpose: "To promote the common welfare by furthering separate and collective action . . . for the purpose of: raising levels of nutrition and standards of living . . . securing improvements in the efficiency of the production and distribution of all food and agricultural products; bettering the condition of rural populations; and thus contributing toward an expanding world economy."

Headquarters: Rome, Italy.

Principal Organs: General Conference (all members), Council (49 members), Secretariat.

Website: www.fao.org.

Director General: José Graziano da Silva (Brazil).

Membership (194, plus 2 Associate Members, and 1 member organization, the EU): See Appendix C.

Official Languages: Arabic, Chinese, English, French, German, Spanish.

Working Languages: Arabic, Chinese, English, French, Spanish.

Origin and development. The 34 governments represented at the UN Conference on Food and Agriculture held May 18–June 3, 1943, in Hot Springs, Virginia, agreed that a permanent international body should be established to deal with problems of food and agriculture. The Interim Commission on Food and Agriculture submitted a draft constitution that was signed October 15, 1945, in Quebec, Canada, by the 30 governments attending the first session of the FAO General Conference. The organization, which inherited the functions and assets of the former International Institute of Agriculture in Rome, Italy, was made a Specialized Agency of the United Nations effective December 14, 1946.

In November 1991 the conference admitted the European Community (subsequently the European Union—EU) as a regular FAO member, marking the first time such an organization had joined a UN Specialized Agency. The EU's rights are somewhat circumscribed, however, in that it cannot vote in elections or hold office, and it may otherwise participate as an alternative to, not in addition to, its individual member states. The November 1993 General Conference readmitted South Africa, which had withdrawn in 1964. FAO membership rose to 188 in December 2003 with the admission of Micronesia, Timor-Leste, Tuvalu, and Ukraine; to 189 members in 2006 with the addition of the Russian Federation; and by 2010 to its current 192 members.

FAO responsibilities were significantly broadened in 1963 when, following a suggestion by the United States, the UN/FAO World Food Program (WFP) began operations to provide food aid in furtherance of economic and social development, to offer relief services in the event of natural and man-made disasters, and to promote world food security. Subsequently, as part of its effort to avoid overlapping mandates, the General Assembly in 1995 authorized the FAO and the WFP to absorb the responsibilities of the World Food Council (WFC), a special body of the assembly that was disbanded in May 1996. The vast majority of the FAO's 10,600 employees serve in the field.

Structure. The General Conference, which normally meets at Rome once every two years, is the organization's major policy-making organ; each member has one vote. Its responsibilities include approving the FAO budget and program of work, adopting procedural rules and financial regulations, formulating recommendations on food and agricultural questions, and reviewing the decisions of the FAO Council and subsidiary bodies.

The FAO Council's 49 members are elected for three-year rotating terms by the conference from seven regional groupings (Africa, 12 seats; Asia, 9; Europe, 10; Latin America and the Caribbean, 9; Near East, 6; North America, 2; Southwest Pacific, 1). The council meets between sessions of the conference and acts on its behalf as an executive organ responsible for monitoring the world food and agriculture situation and recommending any appropriate action. Assisting the council are three elected managerial committees that deal with program, finance, and constitutional and legal matters. Committees on commodity problems, fisheries, agriculture, forestry, and world food security address specialized issues and are open to all members.

Responsibility for implementing the FAO program rests with its Secretariat, which is headed by a director general serving a six-year term of office. Its headquarters staff has 1,956 full-time employees, while 1,735 are assigned to regional and subregional offices and field projects. There were 2,670 field program projects in 2012, of which 444 were emergency operations. The regional offices are located in Accra, Ghana (Africa); Bangkok, Thailand (Asia and the Pacific); Cairo, Egypt (Near East); Rome, Italy (Europe); and Santiago, Chile (Latin America and the Caribbean). Liaison offices are maintained at UN headquarters in New York and Geneva; in Yokohama, Japan; in Brussels, Belgium (for the EU); and in Washington, D.C.

The FAO's work programs are divided among seven departments, which typically encompass a varying number of divisions, each with its own mandate and programs. The Agriculture and Consumer Protection Department includes the Animal Production and Health Division, FAO/International Atomic Energy Agency (IAEA) Joint Division for Nuclear Techniques in Food and Agriculture, the Land and Water Development Division, the Plant Production and Protection Division, the Rural Agriculture and Agro-Industries Division, and the Nutrition and Consumer Protection Division. The Economic and Social Development Department has three divisions: Agricultural and Development Economics, Commodities and Trade, and Statistics. The Fisheries and Aquaculture Department includes three divisions: Economics and Policy, Management, and Fish Products and Industry. The Forestry Department has divisions titled Forestry Economics and Policy, Forest Management, and Forest Products and Industries. The Natural Resources Management and Environment Department includes four divisions: Environment, Climate Change and Bioenergy, the Land and Water Division, and the Research and Extension Division. The Technical Cooperation Department encompasses the Policy Assistance Division, the Investment Center, the Field Operations Division, and the Emergency Operations and Rehabilitation Division. The other FAO department is Corporate Services, Human Resources, and Finance. The latter is responsible for issuing the FAO's numerous publications, which include the annual *State of Food and Agriculture* and, since 1999, the annual *State of Food Insecurity in the World.* It also maintains a number of databases, most prominently the International Information System for the Agricultural Sciences and Technology (AGRIS) and the Current Agricultural Research Information System (CARIS).

Other FAO services are offered through the administrative Office of Program, Budget, and Evaluations. An FAO legal office is responsible for providing in-house legal services, advising member states, and assisting in preparation of relevant treaties.

The FAO sponsors some 30, mostly regional, commissions concerned with, for example, agricultural statistics, forestry, fisheries, plant protection, and pests and diseases (including desert locusts, African animal sleeping sickness, and foot-and-mouth disease). The joint FAO/World Health Organization (WHO) Codex Alimentarius Commission, established in 1962 and now numbering 170 member countries, assists in the preparation, publication, and updating of international food standards.

The WFP is supervised by a 36-member executive board (half elected by the Economic and Social Council of the United Nations and half by the FAO Council), which succeeded the Committee on Food Aid Policies and Programs in January 1996. Its executive director, currently Ertharin Cousin of the United States, is jointly named by the UN secretary-general and the FAO director general.

Recent activities. To fulfill its stated purposes of raising living standards and securing improvement in the availability of agricultural products, the FAO collects, analyzes, interprets, and disseminates information relating to nutrition, food, and agriculture. It recommends national and international action in these fields, furnishes such technical assistance as governments may request, and cooperates with governments in organizing missions needed to help them meet their obligations.

The FAO's work is supported through the Regular Program budget and through the separate Field Program of technical assistance. The Regular Program, with mandatory contributions from member states, covers the costs of Secretariat operations but also includes as one component the Technical Cooperation Program (TCP). The TCP constitutes the portion of the regular budget contributed to field projects, which are primarily funded through trust funds established by donor countries. Other international institutions also participate. The 2010–2011 regular budget was $1 billion with voluntary contributions of $1.2 billion.

In 1994 the FAO established the Special Program for Food Security (SPFS), which focuses on helping low-income food-deficit countries (LIFDCs) improve agricultural productivity and output on an environmentally sound, economically sustainable basis. As of 2011, at least 57 countries had SPFS projects, which are primarily funded through extra-budgetary means, in some stage of development. Other special programs include the Global Information and Early Warning System (GIEWS), which began operations in 1975, and the Emergency Prevention System (EMPRES) for Transboundary Animal and Plant Pests and Diseases, founded in 1994. The GIEWS attempts to gauge future food supplies in order to forestall food emergencies, while the EMPRES focuses on the control and eradication of targeted diseases and pests (desert locusts, rinderpest, and animal sleeping sickness).

At the November 12–23, 1999, General Conference, the FAO reelected Director General Jacques Diouf to a second term despite opposition from the United Kingdom and some other industrialized countries. It also approved a strategic framework for 2000–2015 that established three overarching goals: "access of all people at all times to sufficient nutritionally adequate and safe food"; the "continued contribution of sustainable agricultural and rural development, including fisheries and forestry, to economic and social progress and the well-being of all"; and the conservation, improvement, and sustainable use of national resources, "including land, water, forests, fisheries and genetic resources." The framework goals also repeated the WFS target of halving the number of undernourished by 2015.

The World Food Summit: Five Years Later, which was postponed from November 2001 because of security concerns following the September 11, 2001, attacks on the United States, convened June 10–13, 2002, in Rome. Although the summit was attended by 74 heads of state or government, few leaders of industrialized countries participated.

A year later, the 2003 *State of Food Insecurity in the World* made it clear that without a significant acceleration in food production and distribution, the goal of halving the undernourished population by 2015 remained unattainable. Although hunger decreased in the first half of the

1990s, the overall trend was reversed in the second half of the decade, according to the report, leaving 840 million people undernourished in 1999–2001. Reasons for the lack of progress included insufficient resources for distributing food, conflicts in central and western Africa, a severe drought in southern Africa, and the spread of HIV/AIDS.

In response to this setback, the FAO called for wide adoption of an anti-hunger program that combines increased agricultural productivity in rural communities with immediate access to food for the hungry. The FAO emphases include improving rural infrastructure and market access; using available water resources and irrigation more effectively; utilizing both chemical and organic fertilizers; and adopting integrated biological controls to help combat pests, insects, and plant diseases. The FAO has also emphasized, despite continuing criticism from some quarters, greater use of biotechnology.

On June 29, 2004, the FAO-sponsored International Treaty on Plant Genetic Resources for Food and Agriculture entered into effect. Among other things, the treaty provides for the Multilateral System for Access and Benefit Sharing to streamline procedures and reduce transaction costs for plant breeders, farmers, and researchers seeking access to the genetic resources of over 60 of the world's most important food and forage crops. In addition, some 600,000 genetic samples held by the 16 research centers of the Consultative Group on International Agricultural Research (CGIAR) come under the terms of the treaty, and the Global Crop Diversity Trust was established to support gene conservation and assist developing countries.

In October 2006 the agency issued a warning that in the ten years following the World Food Summit pledge to halve world hunger, little to no progress had been made. A 2007 FAO brief, *The State of Food and Agriculture,* reported widespread waste in the processing and shipping of food aid by donor countries.

The FAO commissioned the first-ever independent evaluation of itself, and in July 2007 a draft form was released. "FAO: The Challenge of Renewal" gave a harsh review of the 60-year-old organization, calling for a three-to-four year immediate action plan to address long-standing management and budget failings. The report, finalized later in the year, called the FAO's governance "weak" and noted a lack of clear priorities, insufficient trust and mutual understanding between member states and the Secretariat, declining budget resources, and needed reappraisal of the FAO's development efforts. The report urged the FAO to shift its focus from food production to employment as a means of income generation and food access and warned that failure to do so would cause the FAO to fade into insignificance. Director General Diouf declared that he "welcomed" the report as "a significant and historic effort to improve the organization's work," adding that the report "recognizes that change is a shared responsibility of the (FAO) secretariat and the member countries." The FAO conference of November 2007 established an elaborately structured committee, or set of working groups, to address the report's recommendations. These working groups reported back late in 2008.

Meanwhile the FAO was forced to respond to the steep rise in food prices in 2008. In advance of a June 4, 2008, FAO conference on world food security, to be held in Rome, President Abdoulaye Wade of Senegal lashed out at the FAO and his fellow countryman Jacques Diouf. Wade called the FAO an "inefficient money-gobbler" that should be abolished. He also threatened to sue the FAO for deducting, as he claimed, 20 percent of all funds collected to alleviate the food crisis.

In September 2008 Diouf said that the number of hungry people worldwide had risen from 850 million to 925 million in 2007, and that he could see the number reaching one billion by the end of 2008. He called for an annual investment of $30 billion to double world food production. On November 20, 2008, the FAO adopted a plan of reform. The plan spent $42.6 million over three years, roughly half of it in 2009, to effect "reform with growth." Among other things, the plan reduced the agency's 120 directorships by one third, freeing up $17.4 million to be spent on technical assistance programs. Director-General Diouf said, "We must build a new FAO," promising a "sweeping overhaul of the way FAO works."

The year 2009 saw a reduction in world food prices from their peaks of the previous year, but prices still remained a concern, particularly in poor countries. The FAO remained critical of biofuels because they compete with food production. UN aid to Colombia's extensive biofuel program was suspended. By June 2009 the FAO stated that the number of people worldwide without enough food had reached 1 billion—a number driven by the global economic crisis. At a seminar held in October 2009, Diouf warned that world food production must increase by 70 percent if the world's growing population was to be fed. On November 16–18 the FAO sponsored the World Summit on Food Security in Rome. During the meeting UN secretary-general Ban argued that food security could not be achieved without concurrent efforts to curb climate change. The FAO's annual report, *The State of Food Insecurity in the World 2009,* noted that more than 1 billion people were malnourished, including 642 million in the Asia-Pacific area and 265 million in sub-Saharan Africa.

In February 2010 the FAO's *The State of Food and Agriculture* argued that a tax on livestock should be instituted globally as a means to curb pollutants, since evidence indicated that the livestock sector produced about 37 percent of the world's greenhouse gases. The report also noted that worldwide meat consumption had increased from 13.7 kilograms per capita annually to 59.5 kilograms. In September the FAO held an emergency meeting on commodity inflation after Russia banned wheat exports following wildfires that destroyed more than 20 percent of the nation's crops. The FAO asserted that the Russian ban could increase food prices by 5 percent globally because of volatility in commodities markets. FAO reports issued later in 2010 suggested it was time to pay attention to urban food cultivation and forestry, as the world's population becomes increasingly urbanized. An October report also noted that Eastern Europe and Central Asia had a vast agricultural potential, as yet untapped.

Following massive flooding in Pakistan in 2010, the FAO provided food and medical supplies to more than 230,000 families. In addition, the organization supplied wheat seed to more than 500,000 farmers to allow then to plant for the next crop season.

The January 2011 *The State of Food and Agriculture* report suggested that women were significantly less engaged in agriculture than men in underdeveloped countries, having less access to resources and opportunities. Female farmers were not intrinsically less efficient than their male counterparts, and "closing the gender gap" could go a long way to increasing world food production. In 2011 the FAO continued to warn of increasing food prices, in part caused by agricultural disasters attributable to climate change. But it also noted that roughly one third of all food produced was thrown away, wasted.

On June 27, 2011, former Brazilian food security minister Jose Graziano da Silva was elected director-general, to replace Diouf as of January 1, 2012. In October 2011 "The State of Food Insecurity in the World 2011" report, jointly produced by the FAO, the World Food Programme, and the International Fund for Agricultural Development (see "IFAD") predicted that generally high and volatile food prices would continue, driving more people into poverty. "Even if the MDG were achieved by 2015 some 600 million people in developing countries would still be undernourished. Having 600 million people suffering from hunger on a daily basis is never acceptable," the report noted.

In 2011 the FAO announced that after a decades-long initiative, the cattle disease rinderpest had been eliminated. In July of that year, as a result of widespread famine in the Horn of Africa, the FAO launched an emergency campaign to raise $120 million for food and medical supplies for the region. An internal report found that the number of women staff members of the FAO had doubled from 15 percent to 24 percent over a 15-year period. The FAO budget for 2012–2013 was $1.01 billion.

On June 15, 2013, South Sudan became the 194th member of the FAO. In July, the FAO approved a budget of $1.03 billion for 2014–2015. As part of a larger series of reforms, the new budget froze the number of staff positions and redirected funding to operations. The FAO's 2013 statistical yearbook reported that 2.5 billion people were dependent on agriculture for their livelihoods and about 12 percent of the world's land was used for agriculture. While agricultural production has increased by an average of 2–4 percent per year, cultivated land areas have only grown by an average of 1 percent. In October the FAO and the International Committees of the Red Cross and Red Crescent signed a partnership agreement whereby the FAO would provide support and technical guidance to the organizations during disasters that impact food security and nutrition.

In *The State of Food and Agriculture, 2014,* the FAO reported that global food production would have to increase by 60 percent from its 2007 levels in order to feed the estimated 9.6 billion people that would inhabit the earth in 2050. Family farms would be the key to meeting that increased demand as the majority of farms in the world in 2014 were less than two hectares. However, many of the smaller farms had low levels of productivity because of a lack of access to capital and innovative technology. The report called for extensive investments in small and family farms.

The State of Food and Agriculture, 2016 emphasized the need to adapt food production to changing temperatures and weather patterns as the result of climate change. The report forecast moderate declines of major crops by 2050 but much deeper reductions in the years following. One result is that people living in extreme poverty would rise from 900 million currently to 1.1 billion by 2030. Extensive use of sustainable agriculture, including growing nitrogen-efficient, heat-tolerant crops and zero-tillage practices would reduce malnutrition by 120 million by 2050.

INTERNATIONAL CIVIL AVIATION ORGANIZATION

(ICAO)

Established: By Convention signed in Chicago, Illinois, United States, December 7, 1944, effective April 4, 1947. The ICAO became a UN Specialized Agency by agreement with the Economic and Social Council (approved by the General Assembly on December 14, 1946, effective May 13, 1947).

Purpose: To promote international cooperation in the development of principles and techniques of air navigation and air transport.

Headquarters: Montreal, Canada.

Principal Organs: Assembly (all members), Council (36 members), Air Navigation Commission, Secretariat.

Website: www.icao.int.

Secretary-General: Fang Liu (China).

Membership (191): See Appendix C.

Official Languages: Arabic, Chinese, English, French, Russian, Spanish.

Origin and development. The accelerated development of aviation during World War I provided the impetus for expanding international cooperation, beginning in 1919 with the establishment of the International Commission for Air Navigation (ICAN) under the so-called Paris Convention drafted at the Versailles Peace Conference. The main result of the International Civil Aviation Conference held November–December 1944 in Chicago, Illinois, was the adoption of a 96-article convention providing, among other things, for a new international organization that would supersede both ICAN and the Pan-American Convention on Commercial Aviation (concluded in 1928). Responsibilities assigned to the new organization included developing international air navigation; fostering the planning and orderly growth of safe international air transport; encouraging the development of airways, airports, and air navigation facilities; preventing economic waste caused by unreasonable competition; and promoting the development of all aspects of international civil aeronautics.

An interim agreement, signed December 7, 1944, in Chicago, established the Provisional International Civil Aviation Organization (PICAO), which functioned from June 1945 until the deposit of ratifications brought the ICAO itself into existence in April 1947. Its status as a UN Specialized Agency was defined by an agreement approved during the first session of the ICAO Assembly.

Structure. The ICAO Assembly, in which each member state has one vote, is convened at least once every three years to determine general policy, establish a budget, elect the members of the Council, and act on any matter referred to it by the Council.

Continuous supervision of the ICAO's operation is the responsibility of the Council, which is composed of 36 states elected by the ICAO Assembly for three-year terms on the basis of their importance in air transport, their contribution of facilities for air navigation, and their geographical distribution. Meeting frequently in Montreal, the Council implements assembly decisions; appoints the secretary-general; administers ICAO finances; collects, analyzes, and disseminates information concerning air navigation; and adopts international standards and recommended practices with respect to civil aviation. The Council is assisted by, and appoints the members of, the Air Navigation Commission and the various standing committees. Regional offices are maintained in numerous cities worldwide.

The Secretariat, headed by the secretary-general, is assisted by five subsidiary bureaus: Air Navigation, Air Transport, Technical Cooperation, Legal, and Administration and Services.

Recent activities. The ICAO has been instrumental in generating international action in such areas as meteorological services, air traffic control, communications, and navigation facilities. It also has an impressive record of advancing uniform standards and practices to ensure safety and efficiency. Any member unable to implement an established civil aviation standard must notify the ICAO, which in turn notifies all other members. Standards and practices are constantly reviewed and, when necessary, amended by the Council. Other areas of involvement have ranged from the leasing and chartering of aircraft to minimizing the effects of aircraft noise and engine emissions on the environment. The ICAO also provides technical assistance to most of the world's developing countries, including analyses of long-term civil aviation requirements and the preparation of national civil aviation plans as well as the development and updating of aviation skills and the harmonization of air transport regulations.

The ICAO's intensified efforts to devise effective deterrents to hijacking and air piracy resulted in a series of international conventions developed under its auspices: Tokyo, Japan (1963); The Hague, Netherlands (1970); and Montreal (1971). The ICAO also considered the issue of the interception of civil aircraft following the 1983 destruction by Soviet fighters of a Korean Air Lines (KAL) Boeing 747 carrying 269 civilians. As a result of the ICAO investigation, an amendment to the Chicago Convention was adopted that recognized the duty to refrain from the use of weapons against civil aircraft in flight.

A special Council session was held in February 1989 at U.S.–UK request to discuss the December 1988 bombing over Scotland of Pan American World Airways Flight 103, in which 270 people died. In December 1985 the ICAO Council began requiring all contracting states to apply more stringent security measures for international flights, including tighter controls on baggage and cargo, the denial of access to aircraft by unauthorized personnel, and a ban on contact between screened and unscreened passengers. Following the Pan Am incident, the Council unanimously adopted a resolution calling for further aviation security measures, particularly regarding electronic devices, while urging further study of proposals to set higher training standards for security personnel, restrict access to planes by airport workers, and increase the ICAO's role in enforcing security.

In 1991 the ICAO's tenth annual Air Navigation Conference endorsed plans for the implementation of a satellite-based communications, navigation, surveillance, and air traffic management system (CNS/ATM). The decision to speed the switch from a ground-based system was facilitated in large part by U.S. and USSR offers of free access to their navigation satellite networks.

In 1996 the ICAO issued a statement deploring the downing of two American civilian aircraft by the Cuban air force over international waters on February 26. The UN General Assembly subsequently endorsed a resolution, originating from the ICAO, calling on all nations to reaffirm their pledge to take precautions against such actions.

Safety was the main focus at the meeting of the ICAO Assembly in September–October 1998. In addition to authorizing creation of the Universal Safety Oversight Audit Program (USOAP), which entered into effect at the beginning of 1999, the assembly approved the Charter on the Rights and Obligations of States Relating to Global Navigation Satellite Systems (GNSS), preparatory to eventual drafting of a GNSS convention.

The 33rd ICAO Assembly opened September 25, 2001, in Montreal, two weeks after al-Qaida operatives hijacked four commercial airlines and caused nearly 3,000 deaths in the United States. Accordingly, security issues dominated the ten-day session. In addition to recommending a review of current aviation security conventions and the development of a security oversight audit program, the session called for convening a conference on civil aviation and the threat of terrorism.

On July 1, 2002, an amendment to the security provisions of the Chicago Convention made the convention applicable to domestic as well as international flights, requiring measures to prevent unauthorized entry to the flight deck, limiting preflight access to aircraft, and aiming for screening of all checked baggage by 2006.

In November 2003 the Montreal Convention of 1999 entered into force, superseding provisions of the 1929 Warsaw Convention and updating rules on liability for death, injury, or other losses involving civil aircraft.

In quick response to an August 2006 alleged terrorist plot in the United Kingdom that involved the potential use of liquids as explosives, the ICAO set a March 2007 deadline to restrict liquids, gels, and aerosol products that might be used as improvised explosive devices on aircraft. It also approved the Global Air Navigation Plan in November 2006 to increase efficiency of air transport operations through changes to global air traffic management systems.

European Commission (EC) efforts to apply a cap and trade system on carbon dioxide emissions for foreign airlines flying into Europe failed in a controversial vote during the 36th ICAO Assembly meeting on September 18–29, 2007. Facing stiff resistance from the United States, Brazil, Japan, and China, who argued the emissions restrictions would unduly burden companies, the ICAO instead created the Group on International Aviation and Climate Change, composed of senior government officials, to recommend an action plan by 2009 on reducing global warming emissions in the airline industry. Some observers reported significant EU discontent with the ICAO as it presently operates. Complaints have been made that the organization should produce fewer, but clearer, regulations and that it should concentrate less on bilateral agreements and more on dealings with regional groups of countries, such as the EU itself. In December 2007 the EU began negotiations with the ICAO to ease some of the security restrictions that had been imposed after the September 11, 2001, terrorist attacks.

In March 2008 the ICAO revealed that only 39 member states had met the organization's March 5 deadline for testing the English-language skills of pilots and air traffic controllers. The ICAO extended a grace period to March 5, 2011, and asked member nations not to exclude aircraft from non-compliant countries. In July 2008 the organization announced that all countries being monitored under USOAP had authorized it to post audit results on its public Website.

A December 2008 preliminary ICAO report reflected the impact of the world economic crisis on civil aviation. It noted "a significant drop in growth with only a 1.8 percent increase over 2007 in terms of Passenger Kilometers Performed (PKP)." The report predicted a modest recovery by 2010. An ICAO message for International Civil Aviation Day, December 7, 2008, was titled "Tomorrow's Aviation—a world of opportunity for skilled aviation personnel." It noted that many skilled aviation staff would be retiring in the next few years and would need to be replaced.

In April 2009 the ICAO, in cooperation with many business and world governmental partners, rolled out a new air navigation concept called "Performance-based Navigation (PBN)," with the aim of promoting "safer, shorter, and greener flights." Prior to the 2009 Copenhagen Summit on climate change, the member states of ICAO agreed to a voluntary 2 percent annual improvement in fuel efficiency for aviation through 2050. In 2009 the ICAO budget was $252 million, an increase over the $228 million spent in 2008.

In 2010 the ICAO worked to develop a new comprehensive aviation security strategy to address threats to international air transport and travel. The organization also reported considerable progress on the adoption of machine readable passports throughout the world as one manifestation of improved security for air travel. In September Taiwan announced that it would seek to join the ICAO (see entry on the United Nations). The 37th ICAO Assembly, held September 28 through October 8, 2010, produced a comprehensive resolution to reduce the impact of aviation emissions on climate change. It provided a roadmap for action through 2050 for ICAO members. ICAO thus became the first UN Agency to establish a globally harmonized agreement for addressing CO2 emissions in its area of responsibility.

In November 2010 the ICAO council reelected Roberto Kobeh González of Mexico as its president for a second three-year term. In November also the ICAO delayed removing the Philippines from its blacklist of countries with unsafe aviation, following the complete replacement of that country's Civil Aviation Authority.

A March 2011 ICAO report predicted strong demand for qualified aviation personnel up to at least 2030, A May symposium agreed on a set of best practices designed to reduce accidents on the runway. In October the ICAO announced a new service to help in better assessing how well pilots and air traffic controllers spoke and understood English. On November 10, 2011, the Republic of South Sudan became ICAO's 191st member.

In 2012 ICAO secretary-general Raymond Benjamin of France was reelected for a second three-year term to begin on August 1. That year, the ICAO approved its "Rolling Business Plan," which was designed to make the organization more flexible and adaptable in the face of changes in air transportation. Meanwhile, in its annual report, the ICAO found that air passenger traffic increased by 6.5 percent from 2010 to 2011, while freight traffic decreased by 0.1 percent, mainly as a result of the global economic downturn. There were 126 air accidents, with 414 fatalities, a decrease of 40 percent from the previous year.

The ICAO reported that in 2012, the number of kilometers flown by airlines, increased by 4.9 percent, while the number of passengers increased by 4.7 percent. The Asia-Pacific region remained the busiest region for air travel, accounting for 30 percent of the world's air traffic, followed by Europe and North America, each with approximately 27 percent of traffic. The number of accidents decreased, with 99 reported incidents and 372 fatalities.

In October 2014 the ICAO agreed to create a plan to limit emissions by the airline industry by 2016 with implementation by 2020. The ICAO reported that the number of miles traveled by passengers increased by 5.5 percent in 2013, and the number of passengers rose by 4.5 percent. The Asia–Pacific region remained the world's busiest, accounting for 31 percent of air traffic, followed by Europe with 27 percent, and North America at 26 percent.

In August 2015 Fang Liu (China) became the first women to lead the ICAO as secretary-general. In 2015 the ICAO found that the number of air passengers increased by 6.8 percent over the previous year, rising to 3.53 billion. Those travelers flew 6.6 billion km, an increase of 7.1 percent form 2014. Freight increased at a slower rate, increasing by 1.2 percent to 50.7 million tons. In 2015 Europe accounted for the largest share of air travel, at 38.2 percent of the total, followed by Asia and the Pacific, 26.8 percent; North America, 14.5 percent; the Middle East, 11.3 percent; Latin America and the Caribbean, 5.2 percent; and Africa, 4 percent.

INTERNATIONAL FUND FOR AGRICULTURAL DEVELOPMENT

(IFAD)

Established: By the World Food Conference held November 1974 in Rome, Italy. IFAD became a UN Specialized Agency by an April 1977 decision of the Committee on Negotiations with Intergovernmental Agencies of the Economic and Social Council (approved by the General Assembly on December 29, 1977).

Purpose: To channel investment funds to developing countries to help increase their financial commitments to food production, storage, and distribution, and to nutritional and agricultural research.

Headquarters: Rome, Italy.

Principal Organs: Governing Council (all members), Executive Board (18 members), Secretariat.

Website: www.ifad.org.

President: Kanayo F. Nwanze (Nigeria).

Membership (176): See Appendix C.

Official Languages: Arabic, English, French, Spanish.

Origin and development. The creation of the International Fund for Agricultural Development is regarded as one of the most significant recommendations approved by the November 1974 World Food Conference, which set a 1980 target for agricultural development of $5 billion to be disbursed either directly or indirectly through the fund. At the Seventh Special Session of the General Assembly, held in September 1975, it was agreed that the fund should have an initial target of 1 billion Special Drawing Rights (SDRs), a basket of several world currencies that many inter-governmental organizations use as a medium of exchange, or about $1.25 billion. Until that sum was pledged and the IFAD agreement was ratified by 36 states—including 6 developed, 6 oil-producing, and 24 developing states—the fund took the form of a preparatory commission. The Governing Council first convened December 13, 1977, and IFAD approved its first projects in April 1978.

(For information on IFAD prior to 1989, see the 2012 *Handbook.*) At its 12th annual session in January 1989, the Governing Council experienced difficulty in agreeing on a proposed third replenishment of funding, with OPEC countries arguing that the five-year decline in oil prices had curtailed their ability to contribute. After extensive negotiations, the council reconvened in early June and approved a third replenishment of $532.9 million, well below the $750 million sought. Non-oil-producing developing countries pledged $52.9 million, OPEC countries $124.4 million, and OECD countries $345.6 million to the replenishment, which extended through June 30, 1992. The replenishment was expected to permit the fund to maintain annual lending levels of about $250 million. To address the growing threat of widespread famine in Africa, the Executive Board in January 1991 endorsed a second phase of the Special Program for Sub-Saharan African Countries Affected by Drought and Desertification, which had been initiated in 1986.

Negotiations on a fourth replenishment initially stalled because of ongoing differences between the OECD and OPEC countries regarding their relative contributions, mounting uncertainty as to the fund's role among overlapping UN bodies, and Western concern that IFAD administrative costs were too high. Consequently, the 17th Governing Council, held January 26–28, 1994, in Rome, established a 36-member special committee to "scrutinize" current arrangements and propose "substantive changes" to the council. The committee's recommendations for a significant IFAD restructuring were subsequently approved by the January 1995 council. The council agreed that the voting power of members would be tied in the future to the size of their contributions. The council scheduled implementation of the new structure upon completion of the $460 million fourth replenishment, which was approved in February 1997. (For information on subsequent replenishments, see Recent activities, below.)

Structure. The Governing Council, which normally meets annually but can convene special sessions, is the fund's policymaking organ, with each member state having one representative. The council may delegate certain of its powers to the 18-member Executive Board, comprised of delegates from eight developed (List A), four oil-producing (List B), and six non-oil-producing developing (List C) states (two each from sublists C1, Africa; C2, Europe, Asia, and the Pacific; and C3, Latin America and the Caribbean). Decisions of the council are made on the basis of a complex weighted voting system under which a member's voting power is partly determined by their past and present contributions.

IFAD administers most of its programs through three departments: External Affairs, Program Management, and Finance and Administration. The Program Management Department, which runs the fund's overall lending program, encompasses five regional divisions: Near East and North Africa, Asia and the Pacific, Latin America and the Caribbean, Western and Central Africa (Africa I), and Eastern and Southern Africa (Africa II). It also includes the Technical Advisory Division, which offers expertise in, and manages technical assistance grants for, agronomy, livestock, rural infrastructure, rural finance, institutions, natural resource management, the environment, gender issues, public health and nutrition, household food security, irrigation, livestock, rural finance, household food security, and sustainable livelihoods. IFAD has a total staff of about 500.

IFAD also serves as the "housing institution" for the Global Mechanism, which was established in October 1997 by the First Conference of Parties to the Convention to Combat Desertification. The Global Mechanism serves primarily as a coordinating program for financing antipoverty and anti-desertification efforts in Africa. IFAD also houses the International Land Coalition, a global consortium of multilateral, bilateral, and civil society organizations that emerged from the IFAD-sponsored Conference on Hunger and Poverty in November 1995. Called the Popular Coalition to Eradicate Hunger and Poverty until its present name was assumed in February 2003, the International Land Coalition reflects the view that the rural poor can best achieve empowerment through land reform and increased access to productive assets, especially "common-property resources," and through active involvement in decision making at all levels of governance. Other participating organizations include the Food and Agriculture Organization (FAO), the World Food Program (WFP), the Inter-American Development Bank (IADB), the World Bank, and the European Commission. In 2001 IFAD was also designated as an executing agency for the Global Environment Facility (GEF), which is administered by the UN Development Program (UNDP), the UN Environment Program (UNEP), and the World Bank. In 2006 the Farmer's Forum was started as a way to feed information from small farmer and rural producers' organizations into IFAD. It meets biannually in conjunction with IFAD Governing Council meetings.

Recent activities. The fund was the first international institution established exclusively to provide multilateral resources for agricultural development of rural populations. IFAD-supported projects have often combined three interrelated objectives: raising food production, particularly on small farms; providing employment and additional income for poor and landless farmers; and reducing malnutrition by improving food distribution systems and enhancing cultivation of the kinds of crops the poorest populations normally consume. In its first quarter-century, specific emphases included access to land, water, and other productive resources; sustainable rural production; water management and irrigation; rural financing; rural microenterprises; storage and processing of agricultural output; access to markets; small-scale rural infrastructure; capacity-building for small producer groups and organizations; and research, extension, and training.

The bulk of the fund's resources are made available in the form of highly concessional loans. Outright grants are limited to 7.5 percent of each year's budget. Low-income countries are eligible for loans repayable over 40 years (including a ten-year grace period) with no interest and only a 0.8 percent annual service charge. Those countries with moderately higher per capita GNPs are extended loans on intermediate terms, while the rest may borrow on ordinary terms. Many projects receiving IFAD assistance have been cofinanced with the Asian Development Bank, the African Development Bank, the IADB, the World Bank, UNDP, the OPEC Fund, the Islamic Development Bank, the Arab Fund for Economic and Social Development, and other international funding sources. Activity during the February 1998 meeting of the Governing Council included the establishment of an IFAD Trust Fund to aid the poorest countries in taking advantage of the World Bank–led Heavily Indebted Poor Countries (HIPC) debt-reduction initiative. The countries in which IFAD projects are located also often contribute financially.

Apart from replenishments, IFAD supports programs and projects through a number of other means. During 2002, supplementary funds were used, for example, to enhance the role of women in various projects, to provide short-term technical assistance, to mitigate the impact of HIV/AIDS in eastern and southern Africa, and to assist with irrigation in northern Africa. Donors to these and other projects included Canada, Germany, Italy, Japan, Netherlands, Portugal, Switzerland, and the United Kingdom.

In early February 2001 IFAD released its *Rural Poverty Report 2001,* which noted that poverty reduction was proceeding at less than one-third the rate needed to reduce by half the number of people in poverty by 2015, the target set by the World Food Summit in 1996 and repeated at the September 2000 Millennium Summit at UN headquarters. Under present conditions, the effort was doomed to fail, according to the report, in part because the real value of agricultural aid had dropped by two-thirds between 1987 and 1998, even though three-fourths of the world's poor continue to live off the land.

IFAD's Strategic Framework for 2002–2006, which focused on how the organization could best contribute to achieving the Millennial Development Goals (MDGs) set forth at the Millennium Summit, restated IFAD's overall mission in simple terms: "enabling the rural poor to overcome their poverty." Emphasis was placed on strengthening the capacity of the poor and their organizations, improving equitable access to resources and technology, and increasing access to financial assets and markets. During 2002 IFAD joined various other UN organs and specialized agencies as a leading participant in the International Conference on Financing for Development, held in Monterrey, Mexico, in March; the World Food Summit: Five Years Later, held in Rome in June; and the World Summit on Sustainable Development, held August–September in Johannesburg, South Africa.

In June 2006 it was announced that IFAD would launch a microfinance strategy targeting some remote and mountainous areas of China. In partnership with other international donor agencies in 2007, IFAD also created the African Enterprise Challenge Fund to support rural businesses and entrepreneurship beginning in 2008 and the $10 million Financing Facility for Remittances to assist foreign workers in transferring money back to rural families.

Effective July 31, 2007, Australia withdrew from IFAD. In introducing related legislation in the Federal Parliament in June 2004, the Australian government had cited IFAD's "limited relevance" to the country's overall aid program and its focus on Southeast Asia and the Pacific. The government also noted the failure of the IFAD senior managers to address Australia's concerns.

In 2007 and 2008 IFAD was active in projects to bring the economic benefits of mobile telephone service to poor rural areas in the developing world. Creative uses of mobile phones range from a greater ability for farmers to negotiate prices to safe and inexpensive ways to move money. In October 2007 IFAD reported that in 2006 remittances from migrants sent to family members in their home countries amounted to more than all international aid given to developing countries, approximately $300 billion as against approximately $270 billion.

In April 2008, in response to the worldwide rise in food prices, IFAD made up to $200 million available to help poor farmers plant more crops in the forthcoming season. In June UN secretary-general Ban praised IFAD as having one of the UN's most successful development programs.

With food prices down from their peak in 2008, but still high; the world in a serious economic recession; and agricultural production continuing to fall, there was what amounted to competition between developing and developed countries to provide IFAD's next president. Many representatives of developing countries said that the agency's presidents had always come from developed countries and that, no disrespect to past presidents, it was time for a change. When IFAD's Governing Council met in Rome February 18–19, 2009, it elected Kanayo Nwanze of Nigeria to replace Sweden's Lennart Båge. Nwanze was vice president of IFAD.

Among the loans made by IFAD in 2009 was a $31 million loan to China to help reduce rural poverty in a remote tea-growing area. IFAD publications continued to stress the importance of remittances. An October 2009 report, "Sending Money Home to Africa," emphasized the point and called on African countries to make the process easier and less costly for their expatriates.

In its *Rural Poverty Report 2011,* IFAD noted that increases in commodity prices, including fuel costs, had caused food prices to double between 2006 and 2008. The global recession did lead to a subsequent decline in costs, nonetheless, the organization predicted that food prices would continue to rise substantially over the next decade, especially in light of population increases. To contain prices, diminish malnutrition, and meet demand, IFAD estimated that food production would have to increase by 70 percent by 2050. Through 2012 IFAD had provided $13.7 billion in funding for 892 projects since its inception.

A January 2011 report, issued jointly with the FAO and the International Labour Organization (see "ILO") pointed out that women in rural areas were suffering disproportionately from the economic downturn. Nevertheless, in February IFAD's Office of Evaluation reported that the organization had done well with its efforts to remove gender disparity. In May 2011 The United States Department of State joined with IFAD in a new initiative to assist the flow of investment from international migrants to reduce rural poverty and improve food security in their home countries. IFAD efforts continued to encourage smallholder farming as opposed to larger-scale operations, and an October 2011 report declared that agricultural cooperatives were a key to reducing hunger and poverty.

In its 2011 annual report, IFAD noted that it had increased its new grant and loan commitments to almost $1 billion for 2011, an 18 percent increase over the previous year. At year's end, IFAD had 240 ongoing projects worth $4.6 billion. In 2011 IFAD completed negotiations over its ninth replenishment, totaling $1.5 billion. The sum was expected to finance operations through 2015. The organization also announced a plan to increase its number of country offices to 40 by 2013 and a long-term goal to reduce rural the number of poor and hungry by 50 percent by 2015.

In February 2012 South Sudan became the latest UN member to join IFAD. In 2012 IFAD trained 4.8 million people in agricultural best practices, with an additional 1.5 million provided education in entrepreneurship and business management. In addition, IFAD allocated 14 percent of its portfolio to rural finance projects, and had 4.3 million borrowers, 69 percent of whom were women.

Russia became a member of IFAD in February 2014. In its 2014 annual report, IFAD noted that it had 241 ongoing programs in 96 countries in 2013. Total support during this period was $12.2 billion, of which 72.8 percent went to low-income developing countries. During that year, IFAD offered training to 4.5 million people and provided microfinance loans to 2.5 million.

In 2015 the Federated States of Micronesia, Montenegro, and Palau joined IFAD. In 2015 IFAD adopted a new financial model by which it included borrowing as a source of funding for country programs, with the individual nations assuming the responsibility of repaying the support. IFAD borrowed $300 million that year, which was distributed to member nations, bringing the total loans and grants for 2015 to $1.4 billion.

INTERNATIONAL LABOUR ORGANIZATION

(ILO)

Established: By constitution adopted April 11, 1919; instrument of amendment signed in Montreal, Canada, October 9, 1946, effective April 20, 1948. The ILO became a UN Specialized Agency by agreement with the Economic and Social Council (approved by the General Assembly on December 14, 1946).

Purpose: To promote international action aimed at achieving full employment, higher living standards, and improvement in the conditions of labor.

Headquarters: Geneva, Switzerland.

Principal Organs: International Labour Conference (all members); Governing Body (28 governmental, 14 employer, and 14 employee representatives); International Labour Office.

Website: www.ilo.org.

Director General: Guy Ryder (United Kingdom).

Membership (187): See Appendix C.

Official Languages: English, French, Spanish.

Origin and development. The International Labour Organization's original constitution, drafted by a commission representing employers, employees, and governments, formed an integral part of the 1919 post–World War I peace treaties and established the organization as an autonomous intergovernmental agency associated with the League of Nations. The ILO's tasks were significantly expanded by the 1944 International Labour Conference in Philadelphia, which declared the right of all human beings to pursue their "material well-being and their spiritual development in conditions of dignity, of economic security and equal opportunity." The Declaration of Philadelphia was subsequently appended to the ILO's revised constitution, which took effect June 28, 1948.

In 1946 the ILO became the first Specialized Agency associated with the United Nations. Since then, the organization's considerable growth has been accompanied by numerous changes in policy and geographical representation. While improved working and living conditions and the promotion of full employment remain central aims, the ILO also deals with such matters as migrant workers, child labor, the working environment, and the social consequences of globalization.

In early 1988 the United States, after a 35-year hiatus, ratified two ILO conventions. (For prior information, see the 2014 *Handbook.*) One of the documents, relating to mandatory consultation on ILO standards, was also the first non-maritime convention it had ever endorsed. The improvement in the U.S.-ILO relationship was further underscored at the 1988 annual session of the conference when the United States expressed its "common views and interests" with the ILO.

At the 1998 ILO conference the organization adopted the Declaration on Fundamental Principles and Rights at Work, which called on members to respect the principles embodied in the ILO constitution, the Declaration of Philadelphia, and conventions on fundamental rights, even if the countries had not ratified particular conventions. Those fundamental rights encompass the abolition of forced labor, child labor, and employment discrimination, plus the right to collective bargaining and freedom of association.

Structure. The ILO is unique among international organizations in that it is based on a tripartite system of representation that includes not only governments, but also employer and employee groups.

The International Labour Conference, which meets annually, is the ILO's principal political organ; all member states are represented. Each national delegation to the conference consists of two governmental delegates, one employer delegate, and one employee delegate. Each delegate has one vote, and split votes within a delegation are common. Conference duties include approving the ILO budget, electing the Governing Body, and setting labor standards through the adoption of conventions. Most important items require a two-thirds affirmative vote.

The Governing Body normally meets three times per year. Of the 28 governmental delegates, 10 represent the "states of chief industrial importance"; the other 18 are elected for three-year terms by the governmental representatives in the conference. The 14 employer and 14 employee representatives are similarly elected by their respective caucuses. The Governing Body reviews the budget before its submission to the conference, supervises the work of the International Labour Office, appoints and reviews the work of the various industrial committees, and appoints the director general.

The International Labour Office, headed by the director general, is the secretariat of the ILO. Its responsibilities include preparing documentation for the numerous meetings of ILO bodies, compiling and publishing information on social and economic questions, conducting special studies ordered by the conference or the Governing Body, and providing requested advice and assistance to governments and to employer and employee groups.

ILO subdivisions include the following, each headed by an executive director: Standards and Fundamental Principles and Rights at Work, Employment, Social Protection, Social Dialog, Management and Administration, and Regions and Technical Cooperation (with regional offices for Africa, the Americas, Arab states, Asia and the Pacific, and Europe and Central Asia). Additional offices, programs, and institutes report directly to the director general. These include the International Institute for Labour Studies, which was founded in 1960 in Geneva. The International Training Center of the ILO, which was established in 1964 in Turin, Italy, as the International Centre for Advanced Technical and Vocational Training, initially provided residential training programs to those in charge of technical and vocational institutions, although it now offers postgraduate work and high-level in-service programs.

Recent activities. The ILO is charged by its constitution with advancing programs to achieve the following: full employment and higher standards of living; the employment of workers in occupations in which they can use the fullest measure of their skills and make the greatest contribution to the common well-being; the establishment of facilities for training and the transfer of labor; policies (in regard to wages, hours, and other conditions of work) calculated to ensure a just share of the fruits of progress to all; the effective recognition of the right of collective bargaining; the extension of social security benefits to all in need of such protection; the availability of comprehensive medical care; the provision of adequate nutrition, housing, and facilities for recreation and culture; and the assurance of equality of educational and vocational opportunity. In addition, the ILO has established an International Program for the Improvement of Working Conditions and Environment (*Programme International pour l'Amélioration des Conditions et du Milieu de Travail*—PIACT). PIACT activities include studies, tripartite meetings, clearing-house and operational functions, and the setting of standards.

The ILO's chief instruments for achieving its constitutional mandates are conventions and recommendations. Conventions are legal instruments open for ratification by governments; while not bound to ratify a convention adopted by the conference, member states are obligated to bring it to the attention of their national legislators and also to report periodically to the ILO on relevant aspects of their own labor law and practices. Typical ILO conventions include Hours of Work, Industry (1919); Underground Work, Women (1935); Shipowners' Liability, Sick and Injured Seamen (1936); and Abolition of Forced Labor (1957). (For an overview of conventions enacted prior to 2000, see the 2012 *Handbook.*) Recommendations only suggest guidelines and therefore do not require ratification by the member states. In both instances, however, governments are subject to a supervisory procedure—the establishment of a commission of inquiry—that involves an objective evaluation by independent experts and an examination of cases by the ILO's tripartite bodies to ensure the conventions and recommendations are being applied. There is also a widely used special procedure whereby the Governing Body investigates alleged governmental violations of trade unionists' right to "freedom of association."

The *World Employment Report 2001,* published in January 2001, examined "Life at Work in the Information Economy." (For information on the ILO prior to 2001, see the 2014 *Handbook.*) The report saw "hopeful signs" that new information technology would have a positive effect on employment despite a "digital divide" not only between developed and developing countries, but within even the most technologically sophisticated societies. The report also projected that 500 million additional jobs would be needed during the next decade to reduce by half global unemployment while keeping up with the flow of new workers into the labor force. In 2004 the ILO began investigating Belarus for impeding workers' rights to establish independent trade union organizations and formed 12 recommendations with a June 2005 compliance deadline. After continued violations of workers' freedom of association, the European Union (EU) in June 2007 withdrew Belarus from the union's generalized system of trade preferences—thereby forcing certain manufacturers to pay higher export tariffs to EU countries—in an effort to force ILO compliance. This situation still existed in late 2011, although Belarus remained in negotiations with the ILO to gain compliance.

In February 2004, two years after being launched by the ILO, the World Commission on the Social Dimension of Globalization released its final report. Having been established to consider how economic, social, and environmental objectives could be combined while spreading the benefits of globalization to all, the commission warned of "deep-seated and persistent imbalances in the current workings of the global economy, which are ethically unacceptable and politically unsustainable." It claimed "wealth is being created, but too many countries and people are not sharing in its benefits." As a consequence, the world risked "a slide into further spirals of insecurity, political turbulence, conflicts and wars." Chaired by the presidents of Finland and Tanzania, the commission echoed the ILO's call for "decent work" as a global goal.

The report led to the ILO adopting the Decent Work Agenda, which serves as a framework within the agency and in its international policy goals to discuss and define adequate working conditions, rights, and opportunities. Since 2005 the agenda has included decent work programs in many member states to support initiatives and laws that better working conditions, and international forums have been hosted on a number of related topics, such as globalization and working conditions in African and Asian states. The agenda has also served as a basis for declarations of support by such international bodies as the Group of Eight, which promised in June 2007 to use "decent work" and ILO labor standards in bilateral trade agreements. Earlier in the year, the ILO and the United Nations Development Program signed an agreement to coordinate development efforts toward decent work policy goals.

Delegates to the 92nd International Labour Conference, held June 1–19, 2004, continued to debate the social and economic consequences of globalization. They also maintained the ILO's recent emphasis on children by focusing on child domestic labor.

The 95th conference, held May 31–June 16, 2006, focused on occupational health and safety, violence in the workplace, and, again, on the changes wrought by globalization. The 96th conference, held May 30–June 15, 2007, was named the Work in Fishing Convention and ended with the adoption of standards promoting medical care at sea and social security protection for fishing industry workers. Speaking at the 97th conference, held June 9–13, 2008, Director General Somavía called for urgent measures to address "globalization without social justice." In September 2008 the ILO issued a more hopeful report entitled "Green Jobs: Towards Decent Work in a Sustainable, Low-Carbon World." This report said that the emerging green economy could create "tens of millions of new green jobs."

The organization celebrated its 90th anniversary in April 2009 against what Director General Somavía called "the frightening backdrop of the crisis with rising unemployment and underemployment, business closures, deteriorating conditions of work, growing inequality, poverty and insecurity, and the undermining of respect for rights at work." The ILO warned against a crippling worldwide rise in the rate of unemployment, also stating that the crisis was partly responsible for a global rise in human trafficking and forced labor. An ILO report stated that forced labor was present in the supply chain of virtually every country, advanced or not.

The 98th conference, held June 3–19, 2009, adopted a Global Jobs Pact, which called on all concerned to respond to the crisis, and promote recovery from it, in a way that would advance decent and humane working conditions. In October 2009 the ILO and the World Trade Organization (see entry on the WTO) jointly issued a report titled *Globalisation and Informal Jobs in Developing Countries*. This report pointed out an increase in the informal workforce as a result of unfettered free trade and marked a step toward the ILO and WTO cooperating in new ways. Previously, the ILO dealt exclusively with workforce issues and the WTO with matters of trade. The ILO's position in late 2009 was that, for the majority of the world's workers at least, the crisis was far from over.

In a 2010 report sponsored by the ILO titled *Trade and Employment in the Global Crisis,* the authors note that real wages declined globally even for those workers who were able to retain their jobs. This finding was underscored by the ILO's *Global Employment Trends,* which found that unemployment had also reached its highest level ever, at 212 million in 2009 (6.6 percent of the world's labor force), an increase of 34 million over the prior year. Unemployment grew most in the EU, rising to 8.4 percent from 6 percent, and Latin America and the Caribbean, up to 8.2 percent from 7 percent. In June the ILO removed Colombia from its list of states that failed to meet international labor standards.

In November 2010 the ILO experienced a strike by its own staff in Geneva. The staff union complained about censored communications and interference with rights of association. Director-general Somavía agreed to outside mediation, and matters were resolved. In December the publication "Global Wage Report 2010/11—Wage policies in times of crisis" stated that the economic crisis had cut growth of wages in half worldwide.

In January 2011 the organization warned that the global recovery was not translating into jobs and that world unemployment remained at a record 205 million. But in February it reported that sub-Saharan Africa, on which it had not been able to gain reliable statistics for several years, had outperformed even the most advanced economies, achieving a wage growth of 6.5 percent between 2004 and 2008—well above the global average of 4.5 percent.

The ILO held its 100th annual meeting June 15–17, 2011, amid calls for a "new era of social justice." In particular, it adopted a new set of labor standards that, for the first time, covered domestic workers. On September 30, 2011, Somavía announced that, for family reasons, he would leave office one year from that date, a few months ahead of schedule.

In its *Global Employment Trends 2012: Preventing a Deeper Jobs Crisis,* the ILO reported that since the global economic crisis began in 2007, more than 27 million people had lost their jobs. To reduce current unemployment and accommodate new workers entering the labor force, 400 million new jobs would have to be created by 2022. However, the employment-to-population ratio has declined from 61.2 percent in 2007 to 60.2 percent in 2010 as businesses have increased productivity and reduced the need for new workers, a trend expected to continue into the near future.

On October 1, 2012, Guy Ryder of the United Kingdom was elected to replace Somavia as director general of the ILO. Once in office, Ryder launched an ambitious program to reform the ILO's administrative structure. The reforms streamlined decision-making by reducing the overall size of the administration and reduced redundancies. To oversee the effort, a deputy director general for management and reform was appointed. In 2013 the ILO warned of a "scarred generation" of youth who were unable to find adequate employment. In 2012 more than 73 million youth worldwide (12.6 percent of the population) were unemployed, an increase of 3.5 million since 2007. The following year, the organization published *Global Employment Trends for Youth 2013: A Generation at Risk.* The report found that youth unemployment in developed states rose to 18.1 percent and predicted that the rate would not fall below 17 percent until 2016. Youth unemployment rates were highest in the Middle East and North Africa at 23.7 percent and lowest in south Asia at 9.5 percent.

On June 12, 2015, the Cook Islands, a nonmember of the UN, joined the ILO. Tonga joined the organization on February 24, 2016, becoming the 187th member. Tonga joined the ILO despite not having any organized trade unions; however, it agreed to abide by the obligations of membership. In the December 2016 publication, *The Global Wage Report, 2016–2017,* the ILO found that global wage growth declined from 2.5 percent to 1.7 percent in 2015, its slowest pace in four years. Much of the decline was attributed to Latin America and the Caribbean, where wages fell by 1.3 percent, and in Eastern Europe, where wages declined by 5.2 percent, mainly as a result of economic losses in Russia.

INTERNATIONAL MARITIME ORGANIZATION

(IMO)

Established: March 17, 1958, as the Inter-Governmental Maritime Consultative Organization (IMCO) on the basis of a convention opened for signature on March 6, 1948. IMCO became a UN Specialized Agency as authorized by a General Assembly resolution of November 18, 1948, with the present designation being assumed on May 22, 1982, upon entry into force of amendments to the IMCO convention.

Purpose: To facilitate cooperation among governments "in the field of governmental regulation and practices relating to technical matters of all kinds affecting shipping engaged in international trade; to encourage the general adoption of the highest practicable standards in matters concerning maritime safety, efficiency of navigation and the prevention and control of marine pollution from ships; and to deal with legal matters" related to its purposes.

Headquarters: London, United Kingdom.

Principal Organs: Assembly, Council (40 members), Legal Committee, Maritime Safety Committee, Marine Environment Protection Committee, Technical Cooperation Committee, Secretariat.

Website: www.imo.org.

Secretary-General: Kitack Lim Sekimizu (Republic of Korea).

Membership (172, plus 3 Associate Members): See Appendix C.

Official Languages: Arabic, Chinese, English, French, Russian, Spanish.

Working Languages: English, French, Spanish.

Origin and development. Preparations for the establishment of the Inter-Governmental Maritime Consultative Organization were initiated shortly after World War II but were not completed for well over a decade. Meeting in Washington, D.C., in 1946 at the request of the UN Economic and Social Council, representatives of a group of maritime states prepared a draft convention that was further elaborated at the UN Maritime Conference held in early 1948 in Geneva, Switzerland. Despite the strictly limited objectives set forth in the convention, the pace of ratification was slow, primarily because some signatory states were apprehensive about possible international interference in their shipping policies. Canada accepted the convention in 1948 and the U.S. Senate approved it in 1950, but the necessary 21 ratifications were not completed until Japan deposited its ratification on March 17, 1958. Additional difficulties developed at the first IMCO Assembly, held January 1959 in London, England, due to claims by Panama and Liberia that, as "major shipowning nations," they were eligible for election to the Maritime Safety Committee. Panama and Liberia were widely regarded as "flags of convenience" for shipowners wishing to avoid more serious regulation elsewhere. An affirmative ruling by the International Court of Justice paved the way for a resolution of the issue at the second IMCO Assembly, held in 1961.

The thrust of IMCO activities during its first decade involved maritime safety, particularly in regard to routing schemes. Adherence was voluntary until 1977, when the Convention on the International Regulations for Preventing Collisions at Sea (1972) went into force. In 1979 the (1974) International Convention on the Safety of Life at Sea (SOLAS), specifying minimum safety standards for ship construction, equipment, and operation, received the final ratification needed to bring it into force, effective May 1980.

Problems of maritime pollution were the subject of a November 1968 special session of the assembly, which led to the establishment of the Legal Committee and the scheduling of the first of several major conferences on marine pollution. In 1978 sufficient ratifications were finally received for the 1969 amendments to the International Convention for the Prevention of Pollution of the Sea by Oil (1954) to come into force, while the International Convention on Civil Liability for Oil Pollution Damage (1969) and the International Convention on the Establishment of an International Fund for Compensation for Oil Pollution Damage (1971) entered into force in 1975 and 1978, respectively. In January 1986 amendments formulated in 1984 to the International Convention for the Prevention of Pollution from Ships (1973), as modified by a 1978 protocol, became binding. This treaty is regarded as the most important in the area of maritime pollution as it is concerned with both accidents and spills resulting from normal tanker operations.

By 1974 the tasks of the organization had so expanded beyond those originally envisioned that the assembly proposed a number of amendments to the original IMCO convention, including a new statement of purpose and a new name, the International Maritime Organization (IMO).

Of importance in the area of maritime travel and transport was the entry into force in 1979 of a convention establishing the International Maritime Satellite Organization (Inmarsat). Inmarsat faced increasing competition from the private sector for satellite communication services, and became private itself in 1999. It was later renamed the International Mobile Satellite Organization (IMSO); the IMO retains oversight and enforcement powers over the IMSO.

A new procedure was introduced in 1986 to facilitate the adoption of most amendments to conventions. Originally, positive action by two-thirds of the contracting parties to a convention was required. Under the new "tacit acceptance" procedure, amendments are deemed to be accepted if less than one-third take negative action for a period generally set at two years (in no case less than one), assuming that rejections are not forthcoming from parties whose combined fleets represent 50 percent of the world's gross tonnage of merchant ships.

In 1988 the IMO approved the Convention for the Suppression of Unlawful Acts against the Safety of Maritime Navigation, promoted by several countries directly or indirectly affected by the hijacking of the Italian cruise ship *Achille Lauro* in 1985. It came into effect in 1992.

Structure. The IMO Assembly, in which all member states are represented and have an equal vote, is the principal policymaking body of the organization. Meeting in regular session every two years (occasional extraordinary sessions are also held), the assembly decides upon the work program of the IMO, approves the budget, elects the members of the Council, and approves the appointment of the secretary-general. The IMO Council normally meets twice a year and is responsible, between sessions of the assembly, for performing all IMO functions except those under the purview of the Maritime Safety Committee (MSC) and the Marine Environment Protection Committee (MEPC). The Facilitation Committee, which is primarily concerned with reducing documentation requirements for port entry and departure, became a formally institutionalized Committee of the Organization only in January 2009, although its origins go back to 1972 as a subsidiary committee of the council.

There are currently 40 members on the IMO Council, comprising three groups: 10 members representing "states with the largest interest in providing international shipping services," 10 having "the largest interest in providing international seaborne trade," and 20 elected from other countries with "a special interest in maritime transport and navigation and whose election . . . will ensure the representation of all major geographic areas of the world."

The organization's technical work is largely carried out by the following seven subcommittees of the MSC and the MEPC: Human Element, Training, and Watchkeeping, Implementation of IMO Instruments, Navigation, Communications, and Search and Rescue, Pollution Prevention and Response, Ship Design and Construction, Ship Systems and Equipment, and Carriage of Cargoes and Containers.

The IMO's Technical Cooperation Committee provides training and advisory services to help developing countries establish and operate their maritime programs in conformity with international standards. Such activities are often linked to UN Development Program (UNDP) projects and to the World Maritime University, established by the IMO in Malmö, Sweden, in 1983 to train high-level administrative and technical personnel. In 1988 the IMO inaugurated the International Maritime Law Institute at the University of Malta. By 2013 the IMO had five regional coordinators, in Côte d'Ivoire, Ghana, Kenya, Philippines, and Trinidad and Tobago.

Recent activities. The IMO's programs fall under five major rubrics: maritime safety, technical training and assistance, marine pollution, facilitation of maritime travel and transport, and legal efforts to establish an international framework of maritime cooperation. In most of these areas, IMO activity is primarily devoted to extensive negotiation, review, and revision of highly technical conventions, recommendations, and guidelines. The IMO also regulates unique and permanent identification numbers on commercial ships, although the identification and assigning of numbers is maintained by the company Lloyd's Register-Fairplay in the United Kingdom. An IMO regulation that took effect in 2009 mandates unique identification numbers for shipping companies and registered owners.

On February 1, 1992, the Global Maritime Distress and Safety System (GMDSS), adopted in 1988 as an amendment to the 1974 SOLAS Convention, entered into force. Hailed by the IMO as the "biggest change to communications at sea since the introduction of the radio," the GMDSS requires the use of satellite communications during international voyages undertaken by ocean-going ships of 300 gross tons or more. Fully implemented as of February 1999, the GMDSS was intended to eliminate outdated radiotelegraphy or radiotelephony technology for transmitting location and distress information.

In mid-1993 an amendment to the 1973 convention on pollution from ships went into effect that requires new oil tankers to be fitted with double hulls or some other equally secure method of protecting the cargo. Under an amendment approved by the MEPC in December 2003, in part because of the sinking of the oil tanker *Prestige* off the coast of Spain in November 2002, virtually all single-hull tankers were to be phased out by 2010.

Concern was expressed at the 18th IMO Assembly meeting, held October–November 1993 in London, that some shipowners were neglecting appropriate repairs and maintenance for economic reasons. Secretary-General William A. O'Neil of Canada, who was reelected at the meeting for a second four-year term, urged governments, particularly those that provided "flags of convenience" to ships from other nations, to enforce IMO regulations vigorously so that international standards would not be jeopardized. In what appeared to be a related matter, Liberia, which registers more ship tonnage than any other nation, was rebuffed in its attempt to win a seat on the IMO Council.

In 1995 significant new design requirements were proposed for "roll-on, roll-off" ferries (ships where vehicles enter through large doors at one end and leave through similar doors at the other) by an expert panel appointed to investigate the September 1994 capsizing of the ferry *Estonia,* in which 859 people died. In November 1995 the IMO approved a somewhat diluted version of the new "roll-on, roll-off" safety standards, while asking national governments to adopt even stricter controls on a voluntary basis.

In 1996 the International Convention on Salvage (1989) entered into force, and the IMO adopted the International Convention on Liability and Compensation for Damage in Connection with the Carriage of Hazardous and Noxious Substances (HNS) by Sea. The allied HNS Protocol on Preparedness, Response, and Cooperation to Pollution Incidents was approved in 2000. In 2001 the International Convention on the Control of Harmful Anti-fouling Systems on Ships was opened for ratification, as was the International Convention on Civil Liability for Bunker Oil Pollution Damage. In February 2004 the IMO adopted the International Convention for the Control and Management of Ships' Ballast Water and Sediments. By October 2010, 27 countries had ratified the convention. Meanwhile, the Convention on the Removal of Wrecks in May 2007 resulted in a set of uniform international rules to ensure the prompt and effective removal of shipwrecks beyond and within territorial waters, including making shipowners financially liable for wreck removal by requiring they post a form of financial security.

The November 19–30, 2001, assembly session was dominated by a renewed emphasis on security occasioned by the September 11, 2001, al-Qaida assaults on the United States. During the next year the MSC and its inter-sessional working group rapidly prepared measures designed to tighten ship and port security, and at the December 9–13, 2002, Conference of Contracting Governments to the 1974 SOLAS Convention the delegates, meeting at IMO headquarters, approved a series of major amendments. These included adoption of the new International Ship and Port Facility Security Code (ISPS Code) specifying mandatory security requirements for governments, port authorities, and shipping companies, and various nonmandatory guidelines for meeting those requirements. Earlier in the month the MSC had adopted additional SOLAS amendments to improve the safety of bulk carriers.

The 23rd session of the assembly, which met November 24–December 5, 2003, endorsed establishment of a voluntary audit scheme intended to promote safety and environmental protection by determining member state compliance with convention standards. The assembly also adopted new guidelines on refuge for ships needing assistance when lives were not at risk, approved guidelines on ship recycling, and confirmed the appointment of Efthimios Mitropoulos of Greece as successor to Secretary-General William O'Neill, who had served in that capacity for 14 years.

The 24th session of the assembly, meeting November 21–December 2, 2005, called on member states to use naval and air forces to combat piracy off the coast of Somalia. It endorsed continuation and expansion of the long-term antipiracy effort that had begun in 1998. To that end the IMO contributed towards the May 2006 opening of an antipiracy center in Mombasa, Kenya. As the Somali piracy problem continued into 2007, the IMO and the World Food Program issued a joint call for the UN Security Council to arrange for foreign naval ships to patrol the coastline.

On July 1, 2006, a new convention came into force regarding treatment of people rescued at sea. This convention was partly inspired by the increasing number of people attempting to migrate in overcrowded, unseaworthy boats, and, among other things, it spells out a ship captain's absolute responsibility to rescue people whose lives are in danger, irrespective of the wishes of the ship's owner.

In recent years, the IMO has also shown increased concern for the shipping industry's impact on global climate change. In May 2000 the IMO prohibited the use of toxic fluorocarbons on board ships. Also in 2000 the IMO published a study on the contribution of ships to global warming emissions that identified options for ship design changes to reduce those emissions. Interim guidelines on carbon dioxide indexing were approved by the MEPC in 2005.

In November 2007 the IMO participated in a UN Security Council committee meeting on boosting border security and detecting illegal arms shipments to better deal with terrorist threats. The meeting resulted in plans to streamline information sharing and coordination between member organizations on border control and security matters.

The IMO has also changed shipping routes in recent years in an effort to preserve ocean wildlife, including labeling a basin off the coast of Nova Scotia as an "area to be avoided" seasonally by commercial shipping in order to protect the endangered right whale.

In 2008 the IMO began to implement a satellite tracking system, the Long Range Information and Tracking (LRIT) of Vessels, to reduce collisions and serve as a rescue tool. All ships constructed after December 31, 2008, are mandated to include the system, and it is being phased in for earlier vessels.

The most serious matter before the IMO, and the shipping community as a whole, in 2008 was piracy. This menace reemerged in the waters off Southeast Asia and Indonesia, and particularly off the coasts of Nigeria and East Africa. Most attacks were launched from Somalia, and according to the IMO roughly 80 percent of world food assistance to that country arrived by sea. Because of pirate attacks, the number of ships willing to deliver food to Somalia had declined by half in 2007.

In April 2008 the IMO states of East Africa began working on a regional agreement for patrol of their seas. In the meantime Western naval forces continue to guard the region. In June the IMO welcomed a Security Council resolution allowing foreign ships to enter Somali waters at will in pursuit of pirates. In September Yemen announced plans to build a regional antipiracy center to assist ships attacked by pirates, but some observers complained that the world's navies were not doing enough about the problem. Another problem facing the world's shippers in 2008 was a lack of crew, particularly of officers. In November 2008 the IMO announced a "Go to Sea" campaign, in cooperation with the ILO and private industry groups, to encourage recruitment into the merchant marine and to improve the industry's image.

On March 2, 2009, the IMO launched a partnership between itself, the UN Development Programme (UNDP), and several large shipping companies to tackle the problem of marine bio-invasions caused by the transfer of alien plants and animals in ships' ballast tanks.

The Hong Kong International Convention for the Safe and Environmentally Sound Recycling of Ships, 2009, was adopted at a conference held there in May 2009. The convention was felt to be of added importance because the worldwide recession was causing more ships to be retired and broken up. On July 27, 2009, the MPEC produced a package of energy efficiency measures for ships but could not come to a decision about raising the cost of ships' fuel and using the money to help poor nations tackle climate change.

The IMO budget for 2010–2011 (the latest available) is $94.5 million and its staff number just over 300. In June 2010 the IMOP announced that it was awarding the 2009 International Maritime Prize to Johan Franson of Sweden who served as chairman of the IMO council from 2005–2009. Also in 2010 the IMO announced its support for a new code for ships that transverse polar regions and called on its member states to adopt the measure. In its annual summary of piracy and maritime armed robbery for 2009, the IMO reported that the number of incidents had increased to 406, a 24.6 percent increase over the previous year. The greatest rise in attacks occurred in East Asia and Asia. In East Africa alone, the number of acts of piracy increased from 134 to 222. More than 770 crew members were taken hostage during the year, with 8 killed, 59 wounded, and 32 missing. The IMO also reported that despite a rise in shipping, the number of vessels lost to accidents or negligence fell to its lowest level on record.

Piracy and environmental concerns dominated the IMO's attention in 2011. In January the UN secretary-general's special adviser on piracy even declared that the pirates were winning. Pirates' technological and business sophistication was increasingly a match for their victims. Moreover, 90 percent of all pirates captured by national navies were released because no states were prepared to accept them and no jurisdiction was prepared to prosecute them. In February the IMO stated that an unacceptably high proportion of ships sailing across the Gulf of Aden and the western Indian Ocean were not following IMO anti-piracy best practices. Such ships "are not registered with the Maritime Security Centre Horn of Africa; are not reporting to United Kingdom Maritime Trade Operations (UKMTO) Dubai; show no visible deterrent measures and are not acting upon the navigational warnings to shipping promulgating details of pirate attacks and suspect vessels." In March 2011 the United Arab Emirates signed on to the IMO anti-piracy code. In September the IMO issued new guidelines for the employment of armed private contractors aboard merchant ships—a practice that it recognized, but did not fully endorse.

On June 28, 2011, Koji Sekimizu of Japan was elected secretary-general of the organization, to take office at the end of the year, when the term of Efthimios Mitropoulos expired. In July the IMO published, for the first time, energy efficiency standards for global shipping. The fuels used by large vessels are some of the world's dirtiest. On September 8 Palau became the organization's 170th member state.

In May 2012 the IMO signed a range of new antipiracy cooperation agreements with other UN agencies and the EU. The agreements included intelligence sharing and joint efforts to enhance antipiracy capabilities of countries around the Horn of Africa. In June Mozambique became the 20th state to sign the IMO's antipiracy code. Meanwhile, Indonesia announced it would ratify several IMO conventions, including the International Convention on Search and Rescue and the accord on the Prevention of Pollution from Ships. The IMO budget for 2012 was $48.8 million. The top contributors to the IMO in 2012, based on the tonnage of their merchant fleets, were Panama, Liberia, the Marshall Islands, and the United Kingdom.

Amendments to the 1978 International Convention on Standards of Training, Certification and Watchkeeping for Seafarers(STCW) which had been approved in 1995, came into force in 2012, following the adoption by the requisite number of parties. By 2013, 157 parties had signed the STCW, representing more than 99 percent of the world's merchant ships. In 2013 internal reforms consolidated and reduced the number of subcommittees of the MSC and MEPC from nine to seven groups. The IMO budget for 2013 was $50.7 million.

The IMO's 2014 annual report on piracy found that in 2013, the number of acts of piracy was 298, a decline of 43 or 12.6 percent from the previous year. The most active regions for piracy continued to be, in order, the South China Sea, West Africa, and the western Indian Ocean (including the Arabian Sea, east Africa, and the Persian Gulf). In October 2014 the IMO recommended that states should not impose bans on travel or trade with West Africa because of the Ebola outbreak. Instead the organization reiterated the need to follow existing protocols on handling cargo and goods. Zambia joined the IMO in 2014.

In June 2015 Kitack Lim of the Republic of Korea was elected secretary-general of the IMO, for a term that began on January 1, 2016. The IMO reported that its assets rose from £15.8 million in 2014 to £20.2 million in 2015 as a result of the rise of contributions from member states and an improvement in collections of dues from 98.9 percent to 99.2 percent. Belarus joined the IMO in 2016.

INTERNATIONAL MONETARY FUND

(IMF)

Established: By Articles of Agreement signed at Bretton Woods, New Hampshire, United States, July 22, 1944, effective December 27, 1945; formal operations began March 1, 1947. The IMF became a UN Specialized Agency by agreement with the Economic and Social Council (approved by the General Assembly on November 15, 1947).

Purpose: "To promote international monetary cooperation through a permanent institution which provides the machinery for consultation and collaboration on international monetary problems. To facilitate the expansion and balanced growth of international trade, and to contribute thereby to the promotion and maintenance of high levels of employment and real income and to the development of the productive resources of all members as primary objectives of economic policy. To promote exchange stability, to maintain orderly exchange arrangements among members, and to avoid competitive depreciation. To assist in the establishment of a multilateral system of payments in respect of current transactions between members and in the elimination of foreign exchange restrictions which hamper the growth of world trade. To give confidence to members by making the Fund's resources temporarily available to them under adequate safeguards, thus providing them with the opportunity to correct maladjustments in their balance of payments without resorting to measures destructive of national or international prosperity . . . [and] to shorten the duration and lessen the degree of disequilibrium in the international balance of payments of members."

Headquarters: Washington, D.C., United States.

Principal Organs: Board of Governors (all members), Board of Executive Directors (25 members [24 elected by member countries or groups of countries plus the IMF managing director, who serves as chair of the board]), International Monetary and Financial Committee (24 members), Managing Director and Staff.

Website: www.imf.org.

Managing Director: Christine Lagarde (France).

Membership (189): See Appendix C.

Origin and development. The International Monetary Fund is one of the two key institutions that emerged from the July 1–22, 1944, UN Monetary and Financial Conference in Bretton Woods, New Hampshire: the International Bank for Reconstruction and Development (IBRD) was established to mobilize and invest available capital resources for the reconstruction of war-damaged areas and for the promotion of general economic development where private capital was lacking; the IMF was created with the complementary objectives of safeguarding international financial and monetary stability and of providing financial backing for the revival and expansion of international trade.

Following ratification by the required 28 states, the Articles of Agreement of the bank and fund went into effect December 27, 1945, and formal IMF operations commenced March 1, 1947, under the guidance of Managing Director Camille Gutt (Belgium). While the membership of the IMF expanded rapidly over the next three decades, most communist countries, including the Soviet Union, remained nonmembers. However, the pressures of external debt to the West mounted rapidly for some participants in the Soviet-bloc Council for Mutual Economic Assistance (CMEA) in the late 1970s, and in 1981 Hungary and Poland, both CMEA members, applied for IMF membership (Romania was previously the only Eastern European participant). Hungary became a member in 1982, but Poland's admission was deferred pending resolution of questions regarding its existing debt and international payment obligations. In December 1984 the United States, with the largest proportion of voting power, lifted all objections concerning Poland, thus opening the way for its entry in June 1986. Angola joined in 1989, while Bulgaria, Czechoslovakia, and Namibia joined in 1990. Mongolia joined in 1991.

In a move that surprised many observers, the Soviet Union formally applied for IMF membership in July 1991. In conjunction with the World Bank, the IMF in October approved a special associate status for the USSR, but the action proved of little practical consequence as the country's dissolution occurred shortly thereafter. In 1992 the IMF offered regular membership to the former Soviet republics, all of which were admitted by September 1993. In December 1992 the IMF's Board of Executive Directors declared Bosnia and Herzegovina, Croatia, Macedonia, Slovenia, and the new Federal Republic of Yugoslavia to be successors to the assets and liabilities of the former Socialist Federal Republic of Yugoslavia and established their respective shares. In January 1993 the board made a similar ruling regarding the former Czechoslovakia. Membership was quickly approved for the Czech Republic, Slovakia, Croatia, Macedonia, and Slovenia, but unsettled conditions in Bosnia and Herzegovina postponed its membership until December 1995. In addition, it took until December 2000 for the board to conclude that the rump Federal Republic of Yugoslavia had fulfilled the necessary requirements to become a member. Montenegro joined the IMF in 2007, followed by Kosovo in 2009, and Tuvalu in 2010.

The development of the IMF has occurred in four phases, the first spanning from Bretton Woods until about 1957. Under the managing directorships of Camille Gutt and Ivor Rooth (Sweden), the fund was seldom in the news, and its activity, in the form of "drawings" or borrowings, was light. During much of this period, the U.S. Marshall Plan was providing the needed balance-of-payments support to the states of Europe because the IMF lacked the capital to perform such a massive task.

At the end of 1956, when Per Jacobsson (Sweden) was named managing director, the fund entered a more active phase, the outstanding example being large drawings by the United Kingdom, partly as a result of the 1956–1957 Suez crisis.

The third phase of development can be dated from Jacobsson's death in 1963. His successor, Pierre-Paul Schweitzer (France), managed the IMF during a period in which its activities were directed increasingly toward the needs of developing states. Also, by the mid-1960s the need for reform of the international monetary system had become more evident. Thus, beginning in 1965, the IMF became increasingly involved in talks regarding the creation of additional "international liquidity" to supplement existing resources for financing trade. Discussion between the Group of Ten (see separate entry) and the fund's executive directors led in 1967 to the development of a plan for creating new international reserves through the establishment of special drawing rights (SDRs) over and above the drawing rights already available to fund members. In general, SDRs may be allocated to IMF members proportionate to their IMF quotas, subject to restrictions relating to the allocation and use of such rights.

The U.S. suspension of the convertibility of the dollar into gold in August 1971 compounded the previous need for reform. By 1972 many states were "floating" their currencies and thus fundamentally violating the rules of the fund, which were based on a system of fixed exchange rates normally pegged to the U.S. gold price. That year, the United States decided not to support Schweitzer's reelection bid, largely because of his outspoken criticism of the U.S. failure to "set its own economic house in order" and control its balance-of-payments deficits.

When H. Johannes Witteveen (Netherlands) took over as managing director in 1973, his chief task was to continue reform of the international monetary system while enhancing the role of the IMF. Consequently, Witteveen proposed creation of an IMF oil facility that was established in June 1974 and served, in effect, as a separate borrowing window through which members could cover that portion of their balance-of-payments deficits attributable to higher imported oil prices. This facility provided 55 members with SDR 802 million until its termination in 1976. Three months later the fund set up an "extended facility" to aid those members with payments problems attributable to structural difficulties in their economies. In addition, as part of the accords reached at the January 1976 session of the Interim Committee, one-sixth of the fund's gold was auctioned for the benefit of less developed countries. The sales, which began in June 1976, continued until April 1980, with profits of $1.3 billion transferred directly to 104 countries and with another $3.3 billion placed in a trust fund to assist poorer countries. The final loan disbursement from the fund upon the latter's discontinuance in March 1981 yielded a cumulative total of SDR 2.9 billion committed to 55 members. Trust fund repayments have subsequently been used to support other IMF assistance programs.

Another plateau was reached when, at the end of April 1976, the Board of Governors approved its most comprehensive package of monetary reforms since the IMF's establishment. Taking the form of a second amendment to the Articles of Agreement, the reforms entered into force April 1, 1978. Their effect was to legalize the system of "floating" exchange arrangements, end the existing system of par values based on gold, and impose upon members an obligation to collaborate with the fund and with each other in order to promote better surveillance of international liquidity. In addition, the requirement that gold be paid into the fund was lifted.

The fourth phase of development was initiated with the entrance into office on June 17, 1978, of Jacques de Larosière (France). Aided by a massive increase in IMF funds, Larosière addressed the major problems of the fund's members: burdensome debts for non-oil-producing developing countries, inflation and stagnant economic growth among the developed members, and balance-of-payments disequilibria for virtually all. In order to assist the non-oil-producing third world countries, the fund further liberalized its "compensatory facility" (established in 1963) for financing temporary export shortfalls, extended standby arrangements through the creation in 1979 of a "supplementary financing facility," and expanded the activities of the trust fund to provide additional credits on concessional terms.

To support the drain on its resources, the IMF has relied on periodic quota increases; the Eighth General Review of Quotas came into effect in January 1984 and additional increases were also approved in 1990, 1997, and 2009 (see Recent activities, below).

Structure. The IMF operates through the IMF Board of Governors, the IMF Board of Executive Directors, the International Monetary and Financial Committee (known until September 1999 as the Interim Committee on the International Monetary System), and a managing director and staff of some 2,400 persons. Upon joining the fund, each country is assigned a quota that determines both the amount of foreign exchange a member may borrow under the rules of the fund (its "drawing rights") and its approximate voting power on IMF policy matters. As of 2016 the largest contributor, the United States, had 17.47 percent of the voting power, while the smallest contributors held considerably less than 1 percent each.

The Board of Governors, in which all powers of the fund are theoretically vested, consists of one governor and one alternate appointed by each member state. In practice, its membership is virtually identical to that of the Board of Governors of the IBRD, and its annual meetings are actually joint sessions (which similarly include the governing boards of the International Development Association and the International Finance Corporation). One meeting in three is held away from Washington, D.C.

The Board of Executive Directors, which has 25 members (including the managing director as chair) generally meets at least once a week and is responsible for day-to-day operations; its powers are delegated to it by the Board of Governors. Each of the members having the largest quotas (currently the United States, China, the United Kingdom, Germany, France, and Japan) appoints a director. Appointment privilege is also extended to each of the two largest lenders to the fund, providing they are not among the countries with the five largest quotas. Consequently, Saudi Arabia, the largest lender, has appointed a director since 1978. The other directors are elected biennially by the remaining IMF members, who are divided into 18 geographic groupings, each of which selects one director. (China and Russia constitute geographic entities by themselves and therefore the "election" by each of a director, in practical terms, amounts to an appointment.) Each elected director casts as a unit all the votes of the states that elected him.

The managing director, who is appointed by the Board of Executive Directors and serves as its chair, conducts the ordinary business of the fund and supervises the staff. In the first major management restructuring since 1949, the number of deputy managing directors was increased from one to three in 1994.

There are several other ministerial-level committees and groups that routinely interact with the fund, usually in conjunction with joint IMF-World Bank sessions. One is the Development Committee, which was established in 1974 by the IMF and the World Bank to report on the global development process and to make recommendations to promote the transfer of real resources to developing countries. The committee, whose structure mirrors that of the Interim Committee, generally issues extensive communiqués prior to IMF–World Bank meetings.

Regular statements are similarly issued by the Group of Ten, the Group of Seven, and the Group of 24. The latter group, which receives secretariat support from the fund, represents the interests of the developing countries in negotiations on international monetary matters.

Recent activities. The IMF's central activity is to assist members in overcoming short-term balance-of-payments difficulties by permitting them to draw temporarily upon the fund's reserves, subject to established limits and conditions with respect to the amount of drawing rights, terms of repayment, etc. Assistance may take the form of standby credits (credits approved in advance), which may or may not be fully utilized. A member can also arrange to buy the currency of another member from the fund in exchange for its own.

A second major IMF responsibility has been to supervise the operation of the international exchange-rate system in order to maintain stability among the world currencies and prevent competitive devaluations. In part because stable exchange-rate patterns depend on economic stability, particularly the containment of inflationary pressures, the fund since 1952 has regularly consulted with member states about their economic problems, the formulation and implementation of economic stabilization programs, and the preparation of requests for standby IMF assistance.

In the area of assistance to less developed states, the fund participates in many of the consultative groups and consortia organized by the IBRD. It also conducts a separate program of technical assistance—largely with reference to banking and fiscal problems—utilizing its own staff and outside experts through a training program organized by the IMF Institute at Washington, D.C.

Beginning in the early 1980s, the fund encountered growing demands from the developing world for reform in its procedures. In particular, a number of states objected to the imposition of the IMF's so-called standard package of conditionality, which often required, for example, that a country reduce consumer imports, devalue its currency, and tighten domestic money supplies in return for standby credit. Subsequently, the issue continued to be a constant center of controversy for the IMF. Non-oil-producing developing countries struggling under massive balance-of-payments deficits called for greater fund access but with fewer domestically unpopular restrictive conditions attached. At the same time, industrialized countries, adversely affected by high unemployment, inflation, and economic stagnation, demanded stricter structural adjustment clauses and called for increased reliance on the private sector as a source of aid and development capital for all but the poorest of the developing countries.

With the third world's debt crisis worsening, the Board of Governors in October 1985 approved the creation of the Structural Adjustment Facility (SAF) to provide low-income countries with concessional loans in support of national policy changes designed to resolve persistent balance of payments problems. The SAF, funded by SDR 2.7 billion in reflows from the discontinued trust fund, was formally established in March 1986, offering ten-year loans with a 0.5 percent interest charge and a five-and-one-half-year grace period Pressure for further IMF initiatives continued throughout 1986 and 1987. (For more information, see the 2012 *Handbook.*)

Soon after his appointment as IMF managing director in January 1987, Michel Camdessus called for a complete review of IMF conditionality and a tripling of SAF funding. Following endorsement of the latter at the October 1987 joint IMF-World Bank annual meeting, the fund announced the establishment of an Enhanced Structural Adjustment Facility (ESAF) funded by SDR 6 billion from 20 countries, led by Japan (SDR 2.8 billion) and West Germany (SDR 1 billion), but not including the United States. The new facility generally offered the same terms and followed the same procedures as the SAF. (In February 1994 the IMF launched an enlarged and extended ESAF; in late 1999 the ESAF was renamed the Poverty Reduction and Growth Facility [PRGF] and given an expanded mandate to include poverty reduction and promotion of sustainable development.)

The April 1988 interim committee meeting approved additional changes, including the launching of an external contingency mechanism to assist borrowers in case of external "shocks" such as collapsing commodity prices or higher interest rates in world markets. However, borrowers facing unforeseen sharp drops in export earnings were required to engage in rigorous domestic action to qualify for the new relief program.

By the time of the joint annual meeting with the World Bank held September 1988 in West Berlin, a consensus was emerging that debt reduction, not simply more restructuring, was required. The issue was brought into sharper focus in April 1989 when the Interim Committee, while praising recent announcements by several large creditor nations that they would forgive portions of government-to-government debts, called for "urgent considerations" of proposals for reducing the much larger debt owed by developing nations to commercial banks. The IMF and the World Bank subsequently approved the use of their resources to support debt reduction, especially by providing incentives to commercial banks.

In line with the Brady Plan proposed by the United States, the new strategy was designed to produce partial write-offs of debts, additional rescheduling of remaining debts for longer terms and/or lower interest rates, and an infusion of new loans from the banks. Countries "with a strong element of structural reform" were permitted to apply up to 25 percent of their access to fund resources to support principal reduction and an additional 15 percent for interest support. Moreover, in another major policy change, the IMF agreed that its funds could be released prior to conclusion of a commercial bank financing arrangement. By 1994 about 80 percent of the commercial bank debt had been restructured, leading some observers to declare the debt crisis, as far as commercial banks were concerned, to be over.

A major IMF issue appeared resolved when a 50 percent quota increase was approved in the first half of 1990 to raise the quota total from SDR 90 billion to SDR 135 billion (nearly $180 billion). A logjam in negotiations was broken when the United States endorsed the action after other IMF members had accepted the U.S. demand that a stricter policy be adopted regarding countries in arrears on payments.

The quota increase was made contingent on the approval of an amendment to the IMF Articles of Agreement that would permit the Board of Executive Directors to suspend the voting rights and certain related rights of members that failed to fulfill their IMF obligations. The amendment had been accepted by the required number of IMF members by November 1992, at which time the new quotas, now totaling SDR 146 billion (about $217 billion) because of the addition of new members, took effect.

As negotiations on a tenth quota increase were being conducted, some members called for a substantial enlargement in anticipation of a heavy draw on IMF resources by the former Soviet republics and former Soviet satellites as they switched from centrally planned to free-market economies. In April 1993 the IMF established a temporary systemic transformation facility (STF) to assist such transitional nations in their balance of payment problems and help them pay for much-needed imports such as spare parts to modernize their industries. About $5 billion had been allocated from the STF by the end of 1994, the date initially established for terminating the facility; however, the IMF agreed to extend STF operations.

In June 1993 the IMF approved what was expected to be the most important STF arrangement—a $3 billion credit to Russia. However, in September, with almost half of the loan disbursed, the IMF halted the flow because of Russia's failure to limit inflation and implement other economic reforms prescribed by the fund.

Russia was a major topic of discussion at the September 1993 IMF-IBRD annual meeting, with supporters of Russian president Boris Yeltsin arguing that he needed backing in his battle with the Russian parliament, which had resisted many of the IMF reforms. With criticism of its "rigidity" in the matter having intensified, the IMF finally released the remaining $1.5 billion to Russia in April 1994, fund officials crediting Moscow's economic reforms with, among other things, having brought previously runaway inflation down to a manageable level. A $6.8 billion standby loan was approved for Russia in 1995 and another $10.2 billion loan in 1996. In return, the Russian government pledged to reduce its budget deficit and cut tariffs on imports, but in October the IMF briefly suspended disbursements of the loan because of slow progress in revenue collection. The lending resumed in December when a new Russian tax commission agreed, among other things, to close loopholes in its collection system.

In February 1995 the IMF approved a $17.8 billion standby loan to assist in the U.S.-led "bailout" of Mexico, whose financial markets had recently experienced severe turmoil. The fund subsequently announced it would require borrowers to provide better financial data on a monthly basis to help prevent such "meltdowns" in the future. Among other things, stricter economic surveillance was expected to preclude national governments from "hiding" negative developments in their infancy, a practice that often sabotages the market's corrective mechanisms until it is too late. Managing Director Camdessus also endorsed a proposal from the Group of Seven that the IMF establish a $50 billion emergency fund to assist countries caught in circumstances such as Mexico's.

The other primary focus of attention for the IMF in the second half of 1996 was approval (in cooperation with the World Bank and the Group of Seven) of a new debt relief program, the Heavily Indebted Poor Countries (HIPC) Initiative, which was expected to lead to the eventual forgiveness of some $5.6–$7.7 billion of the debt owed by 20 of the world's poorest countries. The plan, formally endorsed at the joint IMF–World Bank meeting in September, was to permit forgiveness of up to 100 percent of debt owed to the IMF and World Bank by the eligible countries, provided they met certain criteria regarding free-market influence, the encouragement of foreign investment, and attention to basic social needs. Concurrently, the Paris Club of creditor nations agreed to forgive up to 25 percent of the debt owed to them by the countries concerned.

In February 1997 the IMF Executive Board approved the creation of a trust fund to serve as a conduit for dispersal of resources to the new debt relief fund. Subsequently, 41 countries were identified as eligible for aid, with Uganda, Bolivia, Burkina Faso, and Guyana receiving quick approval for assistance. Thereafter, IMF concerns quickly turned to the financial crisis gripping Southeast Asia. In August the IMF announced that it would extend a $3.9 million loan to Thailand as part of a $16 billion rescue package, which also included pledges from leading regional economic powers, the United States, and the World Bank. In November a $10 billion loan was offered to Indonesia, and in December South Korea received a $21 billion standby credit from the IMF, the largest ever approved for an IMF member at that time. According to the IMF's director, the economic reform requirements attached to the loan packages were markedly different from their predecessors in their insistence that the recipients enact structural reforms in their finance sectors with the aim of increasing transparency and reducing corruption.

Despite the rhetorical emphasis on good governance, the IMF in early 1998 decided to continue lending to Russia even though Moscow had failed to meet fund-mandated tax collection targets. An additional $11.2 billion in support for Russia was approved at midyear in connection with renewed pledges from Russian leaders that significant reform was in the offing. Meanwhile, extensive crisis lending proceeded smoothly for South Korea and Thailand, although disbursements for Indonesia were compromised by political developments in that country. In addition, in December the IMF agreed to $18 billion in emergency support as part of a $41.5 billion rescue package endorsed by the international financial community for Brazil. The fund also in late 1998 resumed lending to Pakistan, whose testing of a nuclear device earlier in the year had led to a suspension of IMF support.

In late 1998 the U.S. House of Representatives agreed, after substantial initial reluctance, to provide U.S. funding for the IMF quota increase that had been proposed in 1997. Consequently, the 45 percent quota increase went into effect in January 1999, the fund having accepted U.S. insistence on greater transparency in the IMF decision-making process. Subsequently, in November, Managing Director Camdessus, who had been appointed to a third five-year term in 1997, announced his intention to resign, effective February 2000. However, the selection of his successor proved surprisingly difficult as the United States pushed for a conservative candidate who would return the IMF to its initial limited mission, Japan suggested its own candidate, and developing nations demanded a role in the selection process. A compromise was finally reached on Horst Köhler of Germany, the president of the European Bank for Reconstruction and Development best known for his role in the reunification of East and West Germany while a member of the German cabinet. Following Köhler's appointment, the IMF and World Bank agreed to reduce the overlap in their objectives, with the fund concentrating on the promotion of global economic stability while letting the bank attend to the "institutional, structural, and social dimensions" of development.

Managing Director Köhler also indicated a desire to establish a more "consultative" relationship with recipient countries in order to ease domestic political pressure often felt by national governments forced to implement IMF-mandated reforms. At the same time, the IMF addressed recent conservative criticism of its policies by agreeing to reduce the length of its loans and charge higher interest rates. In the eyes of many observers the fund turned a significant psychological corner in December 2001 when it refused additional support for Argentina, thereby permitting that country to slide into default. The IMF in 2002 continued to resist pressure to assist the Argentinian government on the grounds that it had failed to adopt necessary reforms, especially in its banking sector. However, as part of an effort to combat the "contagion" effect of the Argentinian crisis on neighboring countries, the IMF in September 2002 approved substantial new credits for Brazil.

In January 2004 the IMF issued a surprisingly harsh critique of U.S. fiscal policy, describing the U.S. foreign debt as reaching record-breaking proportions that could threaten the stability of the global economy. The fund called upon the George W. Bush administration to reverse its recent tax cuts in order to reduce the U.S. budget deficit.

In March 2004 Köhler resigned as managing director in order to run for the presidency of Germany. He was succeeded by Rodrigo de Rato y Figaredo, who, while serving as Spain's finance minister, had been credited with balancing the Spanish budget and halving unemployment. A year later de Rato announced that he favored selling some $7 billion of the IMF's gold reserves to assist in the global effort to reduce the debt burdens of developing nations.

The communiqué following the IMF's September 24, 2005, annual meeting warned against an increasing gap between rich and poor nations, while it commended many poor countries on the economic progress they had made. It also warned against increasing oil prices as a potential cause of inflation, which it felt was otherwise under control, and it encouraged oil-producing and oil-consuming nations to work together to combat this problem.

In answer to widening concerns about the U.S. trade deficit with China, the IMF was given a greater role in leading multilateral consultations with relevant member nations to correct major trade imbalances. The decision at the April 2006 IMF–World Bank meeting also included the establishment of a surveillance unit to monitor trade deficits, surpluses, and currency exchange rates. It was agreed that the IMF would be able to force groups of countries to the table to discuss their economic policies and reach agreement on changes as problems surfaced. However, little progress was made amid criticisms that the countries involved showed little interest in concrete policy adjustments.

By the IMF–World Bank meeting in September 2006, demands for giving growing economies greater contributory quotas (and thereby greater voting shares) in IMF decision making were answered. Member states increased the voting shares of China, South Korea, Mexico, and Turkey and agreed to devise a new quota formula for other IMF members, including African nations, in 2008. The process was expected to be contentious because of Western countries' reluctance to concede influence in the body.

In late 2007, as fallout from the U.S. mortgage crisis and a global credit crunch roiled international financial markets, the IMF faced increasing pressure to shore up global economic stability. Developing countries publicly railed against the IMF for failing to rein in speculative lending practices in advanced economies, while the United States and other Western countries leaned on the IMF to correct major trade imbalances with China by forcing an appreciation of the renminbi. When pressed at the spring 2007 meeting, China agreed to make its exchange rate more flexible "in a gradual and controlled manner" and cut tax rebates on its exports. In June, the IMF announced the first overhaul of its surveillance policy in 30 years, largely seen as directed towards China. The agency set up a more rigorous system to scrutinize and expose exchange rate policies in individual countries. Regardless of the intentions of a government, if its economic policy resulted in "fundamental exchange-rate misalignment" or "large and prolonged current account deficits or surpluses," it could be labeled as an exchange rate manipulator.

Growing criticism about the IMF's relevance and effectiveness was a backdrop to much of its activities in 2007. With indebted countries paying back IMF loans ahead of schedule and emerging economies relying on their own foreign exchange reserves rather than IMF funds for financial security, the agency ended its fiscal year 2007 in tight financial straits.

An expert panel of outside economists recommended it sell some of its gold reserves to shore up its financial profile. In May the Independent Evaluation Office (IEO) said the IMF's advice on foreign exchange rate policy was ineffective and inadequate, blaming the agency management for failing to provide clear direction and incentives to countries.

Further discussions about internal IMF reform continued as de Rato announced his resignation in June 2007. The managing director's vacancy came amidst calls for a non-European to fill the post, but former French finance minister and economics professor Dominique Strauss-Kahn was appointed in November, pledging to make IMF financing a priority by adopting a new income model. The aims of the model were to make the fund less dependent on lending, increase representation of large developing countries in the body, and continue aiding low-income countries despite calls that such work should be left to its sister organization, the World Bank.

Strauss-Kahn also agreed to press ahead with agency goals to scrutinize sovereign wealth funds, which have become increasingly influential in world markets despite a lack of transparency. These government-held funds, many developed by oil-rich nations, have come to control as much as $2.5 trillion in investments, often by targeting the strategic assets of developed nations. However, the funds do not routinely disclose their size or asset allocations. Under pressure from the United States, Strauss-Kahn said the IMF would develop a set of best-practices guidelines for sovereign wealth funds, which would include restrictions on fund holders' interference in a host country's politics. During 2008 the IMF negotiated a voluntary code of conduct with 26 countries that have sovereign wealth funds. The deal was up for approval at the October 2008 World Bank–IMF meeting.

The IMF's record as an economic prognosticator in 2008 was mixed. Early in the year, while warning of the risks of inflation and a global economic slowdown, the IMF paid relatively little attention to problems in the world's credit markets. By April it revised its estimate of world economic growth downwards and admitted it had not warned about the credit situation insistently enough or early enough. Yet by mid-May the IMF saw the worst of the economic crisis as past. On July 17 it raised its world economic forecast again, but by July 28 was saying that the credit crisis was getting much worse and was likely to spread from developed to less developed economies. On September 28, 2008, Strauss-Kahn suggested that the IMF could act as a kind of watchdog and "honest broker" for world financial markets during difficult times. During the late fall of 2008 the IMF issued increasingly dire statements about the world economy, culminating in an October 12 warning that it stood at "the brink of systemic meltdown." The IMF activated special rules for emergency lending to countries whose economies were in danger of collapse, rules last used in the Asian financial crisis of 1997. In late 2008 and into 2009 several countries applied for, and were granted, emergency loans, including Iceland, whose banks had collapsed from exposure to international subprime mortgage securities.

On October 26, 2009, the IMF board "admonished" Strauss-Kahn for unprofessional behavior and bad judgment, although clearing him of charges of abuse and sexual harassment and allowing him to keep his job. Many female IMF staffers had been uncomfortable with Strauss-Kahn's behavior. He apologized to the staff in general and specifically for a brief affair with an IMF senior economist, who had since left the organization.

The G-20 meeting held in London in early April 2009 enhanced the IMF's role in responding to the crisis. The group agreed that the IMF should triple the amount it borrows to ensure that it has enough funds to lend to countries in need. This new money was to be guaranteed by the financially stronger member countries. The intention was that an IMF member could seek IMF assistance when it saw trouble on the horizon, rather than when disaster was imminent. Such IMF help would become a regularly accepted part of the world financial scene and would have less chance of causing panic in the affected country than a last-minute IMF intervention. The London meeting also gave the IMF and the World Bank much increased authority to carry out G-20 policies, developing an early-warning system against the kind of crisis that the world was presently suffering and perhaps ultimately acting as a world financial regulator. The IMF was charged with reporting progress by late 2009.

In April 2010 the IMF initiated a review of its quotas as part of the 14th General Review. The result was an agreement in November to recalculate the quota system and shift about 6 percent of the shares from developed states to major developing countries. The transition was in recognition of the growing economic importance of emerging markets and made China the third largest member of the IMF. The IMF also doubled its quotas from SDR 238.4 billion to 476.8 billion (about $755.7 billion). The doubling gave each member state, at a minimum, a 100 percent increase in its quota. One result of the reforms was an increase in borrowing capacity to $550 billion.

At the joint IMF–World Bank meeting in April 2010, the IMF proposed two new taxes on banks to support future financial bailouts. At the October meeting of the IMF and World Bank, reports indicated that an impasse remained between China and developed economies led by the United States, the United Kingdom, and the eurozone over China's "artificial" manipulation of its currency to keep its value low in an alleged effort to make its exports more attractive. The IMF's *World Economic Outlook,* published in October, forecast that global economic growth would average 4.8 percent in 2010 and 4.2 percent in 2011. Developing economies were expected to lead economic growth with China's GDP growth estimated to be 10.5 percent in 2010 and 9.6 percent in 2011, while India's GDP would rise to 9.7 percent in 2010 and 8.4 percent in 2011. Meanwhile, GDP growth by the United States would be 2.6 percent in 2010 and 2.3 percent in 2011. Throughout 2010 the IMF worked with the EU to develop a series of financial rescue plans for EU member states, including a €110 billion package for Greece (see entry on Greece), in exchange for reforms to financial sectors and social welfare systems in the affected countries.

In February 2011 a report from the IMF's Independent Evaluation Office blasted the agency for failing to give adequate warning ahead of the 2008 world financial crisis. "Weak internal governance, lack of incentives to work across units and raise contrarian views, and a review process that did not 'connect the dots' or ensure follow-up . . . played an important role, while political constraints may have also had some impact," the report said. Strauss-Kahn described the report as "humbling."

At the Spring 2011 joint meeting of the World Bank and IMF the IMF position was that it saw no imminent threat to recovery of the world's economy, though, in addition to Europe's debt problems, it warned about continued inflation in China, and the possibility of a "boom and bust" cycle in Asia as a whole. It called on European banks to strengthen their capital position.

On May 15 Strauss-Kahn was arrested in New York on the charge of sexually assaulting a hotel housekeeper. He denied the charge, declaring that the encounter had been consensual. He was held in jail for several days, before being released on bail under very restrictive conditions. While in jail he resigned from the IMF. By late August prosecutors had lost faith in the credibility of Strauss-Kahn's accuser, and the charges were dropped. By mid-June the list of candidates to replace him had narrowed to two: Agustin Carstens, governor of the Mexican central bank, and Christine Lagarde, the French finance minister. While the managing director of the IMF has traditionally been a European, many member countries felt that times had changed enough for other parts of the world to be considered. Nevertheless, on June 28 Lagarde was elected with support from the U.S., Europe and such emerging market nations as China, India and Brazil.

Lagarde immediately pledged to give emerging economies greater influence at the IMF, and just a few days after taking office appointed Zhu Min, of China, to the new position of second deputy managing director. Zhu was the first Chinese national to be a deputy managing director.

In July 2011 the IMF warned Italy to take seriously its commitment to spending cuts, if it was to avoid a sovereign debt crisis such as was affecting Greece, and said that Greece would need at least an additional €100 billion in aid from the EU and from private sources. It also deferred Greece's return to the capital markets to 2014. In July the IMF again warned China that it must "rebalance" its economy, warning that inflation, property speculation, and the currency were dangerous to sustainable growth. It declared that the yuan was undervalued by between 3 percent and 23 percent, depending on how it was measured.

In September the IMF's *World Economic Outlook* warned of a possible "lost decade" of growth in the advanced economies but stated that there was still time—just—for governments to take concerted action. On September 25 Lagarde warned that it might not have the funds to bail out the larger eurozone countries, like Italy, Spain, and possibly even France, if the crisis continued to spread. To discourage a new recession, countries that were able to do so should consider delaying or even reversing budget cuts.

By late October the "troika" of European Commission, the European Central Bank, and the IMF presented to an EU summit a report saying that Greece would need another bailout, with private banks taking significant losses on their Greek debts. The G20 summit, held in Cannes, France, November 3–4, 2011, produced a general statement of intent to rebalance the world economy, but with no details on how the group might help the eurozone by increasing the IMF's funding. French president Nicolas Sarkozy said that specific steps would be agreed by February 2012.

By 2012 the IMF staff numbered 2,610, from 154 countries. The organization had a portfolio, including pledges and committed resources, of over $1 trillion, with annual quotas from member states totaling $364 billion. Through August 2012 the IMF had committed $247 billion in new loans for the year, of which $189 billion had been accessed. Greece, Portugal, and Ireland were the largest borrowers as a result of the IMF participation in bailout programs for the three eurozone members. In addition, Mexico and Poland both received significant precautionary loans in 2012 to prevent financial crises. At the IMF's annual meeting in October 2012, the group warned that the two greatest dangers to the world economy were the continuing Eurozone sovereign debt crisis and the failure of the United States to adopt deficit reduction measures. Representatives of emerging economies were critical of the failure to approve quota reforms at the meeting.

In January 2013 the executive board submitted recommendations for significant reforms to the quota formula. On April 30, 2013, Cyprus approved a controversial and precedent-setting EU-IMF rescue plan that included a one-time tax on bank deposits of more than €100,000 in exchange for $13.6 billion in additional bailout funding (see entry on Cyprus). The IMF's July *World Economic Outlook* forecast that the global economy would grow by 3 percent for 2013, led by growth in emerging and developing economies, while the Eurozone would remain in recession until 2014.

The January 2014 *World Economic Outlook* estimated that global economic growth would increase by 3.7 percent in 2014 and 3.9 percent in 2015. Meanwhile, also in January, the failure of the U.S. Congress to approve an increase in that nation's IMF capital contributions prevented the organization from conducting a series of reforms, including an overall doubling of total capital contributions to $720 billion. The IMF's *Global Financial Stability Report* warned in April that "adequate preparations" had not been made by most states to respond to the planned "tapering" of efforts by the U.S. Federal Reserve to reduce its economic stimulus efforts. The IMF cautioned that the result could be a significant reduction in global economic growth. The IMF granted Ukraine a two-year $17 billion loan to support economic reforms in the wake of continuing conflict with Russia.

At the 2015 joint IMF/World Bank annual meetings in October, the IMF emphasized the need for global cooperation to stimulate growth. The IMF's Development Committee called for new resources to be made available to countries affected by climate change. The IMF reduced its forecast for worldwide economic growth from 3.3 percent to 3.1 percent but predicted that growth would accelerate to 3.8 percent in 2016.

In April 2016 Nauru joined the IMF as its 189th member.

IMF director Lagarde was convicted of negligence in December 2016 over charges related to a payout made while she was finance minister of France in 2008. Lagarde authorized the payment of $417 million as part of an out-of-court settlement with billionaire Bernard Tapie. Prosecutors charged that she should have contested the settlement. There was no fine or incarceration imposed on the IMF head, and the organization reaffirmed its confidence in her after the conviction.

INTERNATIONAL TELECOMMUNICATION UNION

(ITU)

Established: By the International Telecommunication Convention signed in Madrid, Spain, December 9, 1932, effective January 1, 1934. The ITU became a UN Specialized Agency by agreement with the Economic and Social Council (approved by the General Assembly on November 15, 1947).

Purpose: To foster international cooperation for the improvement and rational use of telecommunications.

Headquarters: Geneva, Switzerland.

Principal Organs: Plenipotentiary Conference (all members), World and Regional Conferences on International Telecommunications, Council (46 members), General Secretariat.

Website: www.itu.int.

Secretary-General: Houlin Zhao (China).

Membership (193): See Appendix C.

Official Languages: English, French, Spanish.

Working Languages: Arabic, Chinese, English, French, Russian, Spanish.

Origin and development. The beginnings of the ITU can be traced to the International Telegraph Union founded May 17, 1865, in Paris, France. The International Telegraph Convention concluded at that time, together with the International Radiotelegraph Convention concluded in Berlin in 1906, was revised and incorporated into the International Telecommunication Convention signed in 1932 in Madrid, Spain. Entering into force in 1934, the Madrid convention established the ITU as the successor to previous agencies in the telecommunications field. A new convention adopted in 1947 took account of subsequent advances in telecommunications and also of the new position acquired by the ITU as a UN Specialized Agency. Conventions have since been periodically revised to address changing standards and needs as radio communication and telecommunication continue to evolve.

Structure. The ITU's complicated structure is a reflection of its long history and growth. As international telecommunications expanded, new organs and functions were typically grafted onto the preexisting ITU structure, producing a plethora of conferences, assemblies, organs, and secretariats, and necessitating a major reorganization in the early 1990s. At an extraordinary Plenipotentiary Conference in Geneva, Switzerland, in December 1992, the ITU adopted its current constitution, which rationalized the organization's structure, effective March 1993. In 2011 South Sudan became the 193rd member of the ITU.

The Plenipotentiary Conference remains the principal political organ of the ITU. Regular sessions are held every four years to make any necessary revisions in the conventions, determine general policy, establish the organization's budget, and set a limit on expenditures until the next conference. Each member has one vote on the conference, which elects the Council, as well as the secretary-general and the deputy secretary-general. The Council, comprised of 46 members from six administrative regions (Africa, Americas, Asia, Australasia, Eastern Europe, and Western Europe), supervises the ITU between sessions of the parent body. Meeting annually at the organization's headquarters, it reviews and approves the annual budget and coordinates the work of the ITU with other international organizations.

Under the 1993 restructuring, the Plenipotentiary Conference can approve the convening of World and Regional Conferences on International Telecommunication. There are three types of global conferences, corresponding to the ITU's three program sectors: Radiocommunication Conferences, generally held every two to three years in conjunction with technically oriented Radiocommunication Assemblies; Telecommunication Standardization Assemblies, typically held every four years; and Telecommunication Development Conferences, also held at four-year intervals.

The General Secretariat, headed by the elected secretary-general, administers the budget, directs the ITU's sizable research and publishing program, and otherwise provides administrative support. Each of the three sectors—Radiocommunication, Telecommunication Standardization, and Telecommunication Development—has its own administrative bureau headed by a director.

Recent activities. The general aims of the ITU are to maintain and extend international cooperation for the improvement and rational use of radiocommunication and telecommunication and to aid developing countries in obtaining appropriate technologies and establishing needed services. In addition, the ITU undertakes studies, issues recommendations and opinions, and collects and publishes information for the benefit of its members.

The Radiocommunication Sector (ITU-R) was established by consolidation of the International Radio Consultative Committee (founded in 1927) and the International Frequency Registration Board (IFRB), the latter of which had been responsible since 1947 for allocating and recording frequency assignments and for handling interference disputes. These tasks currently fall under the purview of the ITU-R's 12-member Radio Regulations Board, which maintains the Master International Frequency Register (MIFR) for radio services—everything from ham radio to high-definition television. The Radiocommunication Sector's basic mission is to ensure "rational, equitable, efficient and economical use of the radiofrequency spectrum by all radiocommunication services, including those using satellite orbit."

The Telecommunication Standardization Sector (ITU-T) has as its mission ensuring "an efficient and on-time production of high quality standards covering all fields of telecommunications except radio." It relies on more than a dozen study groups to formulate recommendations, which are nonbinding standards covering, for example, network interconnectivity and electromagnetic compatibility.

The purpose of the Telecommunication Development Sector (ITU-D) is to "facilitate and enhance telecommunication development worldwide by offering, organizing, and coordinating technical cooperation and assistance activities." The ITU recognized this need even before the 1993 reorganization, having authorized creation of the Telecommunication Development Bureau in 1989. In 2003 ITU secretary-general Yoshio Utsumi called for a heightened global policy perspective to increase access to information and communication technology (ICT) to the developing world, asking for a "concerted global effort" to "eliminate the gap between rich and poor when it comes to access to information."

The ITU's first World Telecommunication Development Conference (WTDC) was held in March 1993 in Buenos Aires, Argentina, amid widespread concern the "telecommunications gap" was still widening between rich and poor countries. U.S. vice president Al Gore called for creation of a "planetary information network," built primarily by the private sector, to foster economic growth and political liberalization. The second WTDC took place in Valletta, Malta, in March 1998 and adopted an action plan that paid particular attention to the telecommunication needs of the world's least developed countries (LDCs). That theme was bolstered at the third WTDC held in 2002 in Istanbul, Turkey, at which delegates adopted an action plan to close the "digital divide" between rich and poor countries and to aid in the transition to the modern telecommunication and ICT environment. The action plan included six programs: regulatory reform; expanding access to developing countries; applying Internet networks to government, health, and education sectors; enhancing private sector investment; human resources development; and a special program to assist LDCs. The most recent WTDC was held May 24–June 4, 2010, in Hyderabad, India.

The first World Radiocommunication Conference (WRC) convened October 23–November 17, 1995, in Geneva, Switzerland. The primary purpose of the WRC is to review and revise the Radio Regulations, the international treaty governing the use of the radio-frequency spectrum and the geostationary-satellite and non-geostationary-satellite orbits. The conference also discussed the ever-increasing problem of allocation of the radio-frequency spectrum, pressure in that area having grown particularly intense in regard to mobile satellite communications. The ITU-R administers the organization's International Mobile Telecommunications-2000 (IMP-2000) program, which establishes standards governing third-generation (3G) wireless communications via satellite and wireless terrestrial links. At a WRC meeting June 9–July 4, 2003, in Geneva, delegates placed a heavy emphasis on the further allocation of spectrum in regard to wireless access services, broadband wireless services aboard airplanes and ships, and satellite data services.

The 2000 World Telecommunication Standardization Assembly (WTSA) in Montreal, Quebec, Canada, adopted many varied resolutions emphasizing collaboration among ITU sectors and also established ground rules for associate membership and accounting rate principles for international telephone services. The October 5–14, 2004, meeting in Florianopolis, Brazil, adopted a four-year plan focused on setting global standards for network security, compatibility of old and new network systems, and transitions to new technologies. Internet governance and next-generation networks (NGNs) were prominent issues, prompting the ITU to create a new study group on NGNs. The WTSA also adopted a series of Internet resolutions to counter spam and to increase ITU involvement in the debate over internationalized domain names.

Additionally, the ITU took a lead role, along with the UN secretary-general, in organizing the two-phase World Summit on the Information Society. The first phase took place in Geneva in December 2003 and adopted a declaration of principles and a plan of action to expand universal access to the Information Society. The second phase took place November 16–18, 2005, in Tunisia. Discussions about freedom of use and universal access to the Internet dominated the second phase, with China in particular arguing for a state's right to place some restrictions in the name of national security.

The two summits led to the adoption of the Doha Action Plan in March 2006 at the ITU's World Telecommunication Development Conference. The Doha plan spelled out a strategy to develop telecommunications infrastructure for use in underserved areas and with marginalized populations. In response to a series of natural disasters, including the 2004 tsunami in Southeast Asia, the Doha plan also targeted poor countries and small island nations for emergency telecommunications development.

Governance of the Internet again became a topic at the first ever Internet Governance Forum in November 2006, during which Secretary-General Utsumi pressed for greater worldwide influence in overseeing Internet functions. The U.S. government refused to cede control of computers directing Internet traffic but later announced it would relax oversight over the Internet Corporation for Assigned Names and Numbers (ICANN), the private agency that controls domain names and other key functions.

The 17th Plenipotentiary Conference in Antalya, Turkey, held November 6–24, 2006, saw renewed commitments to the implementation of the World Summit on the Information Society (WSIS) and Doha Action Plan goals for universal access as well as discussions on internationalized Internet domain names, Internet interoperability, and convergence. The conference also appointed a new secretary-general, Mali-born Hamadoun Touré, then director of the ITU's Telecommunications Development Sector.

Touré caused a stir in early 2007 when he seemed to back away from the union's previously stated position on global Internet governance, stating he did not see the ITU becoming the governing body. He said his priorities instead were to bridge the so-called information divide between rich and poor countries and curb Internet-related crime. In May that year, the ITU announced the two-year Global Cybersecurity Agenda to address issues of network security, financial fraud, identity theft, virus attacks, spam, and child pornography.

In June 2006 the ITU helped negotiate an agreement between 101 nations in Europe, Africa, and the Middle East to introduce a standardized digital system for radio and TV broadcasts. In October 2007 the ITU and the African Development Bank cohosted the Connect Africa Summit and raised investment commitments of $55 billion from private industry and government sources (to be completed by 2012) to provide widespread access to broadband communication technology in Africa. Also in October 2007 the Radiocommunication Assembly endorsed WiMAX, a wireless phone signal standard used heavily in emerging markets.

In December 2007 the ITU made a presentation at the UN Conference on Climate Change in Bali, Indonesia. It pointed out that improved telecommunications could be part of the solution to climate change, but that, as they produced high-tech garbage, they were also part of the problem. In July 2008 the ITU created the new Focus Group on Information and Communication Technologies (ICTs) and Climate Change. The group had an aggressive work plan to be completed by April 2009.

In March 2008 the ITU deployed 25 satellite terminals to parts of Zambia that had been cut off by flooding. In May it deployed 100 such terminals to China after a disastrous earthquake there. In June it called on all countries to adopt a single standardized telephone number, 116.111, for children to use if they needed any kind of help. In September the organization predicted that there would be four billion mobile phones in use by the end of the year. In October 2008 the ITU held its first ever Global Standards Symposium, in Johannesburg, South Africa. This meeting called for the "bewildering" array of global telecommunication standards and protocols to be simplified. At this meeting and elsewhere concern was voiced that the EU was trying to develop its own set of standards, usurping the ITU's traditional role in this regard.

In March 2009 the ITU opened headquarters for its Global Cybersecurity Agenda on the outskirts of Kuala Lumpur, Malaysia. In October the organization approved a new, and energy-efficient, universal charger that would work with any mobile telephone. The ITU estimated that currently 51,000 tons of obsolete chargers added to the world's pollution each year. On November 3, 2009, the ITU introduced a "standards conformity and interoperability program," designed to give potential buyers of communications equipment a better idea of how their purchase might (or might not) work with the rest of the world.

In 2010 the ITU estimated that there were 5.3 billion mobile phone subscriptions around the world, although the rate of growth in new users fell to a 1.6 percent increase. In addition text messaging tripled between 2007 and 2010, growing from 1.8 trillion to 6.1 trillion, or approximately 200,000 per second in 2010. The number of Internet users doubled between 2005 and 2010, rising to above 2 billion, with China the largest Internet market (420 million users). However, there continued to be widespread disparity between the developed and the developing world, with 71 percent of the population in developed countries online, while only 21 percent of the developing world had internet access. In an effort to address the imbalance, the ITU partnered with private industry to open a new Internet training facility in Togo, the 80th facility of its kind in the developed world. The ITU issued recommendations in 2010 calling on the information and communications technology sector to better address issues of climate change by reducing emissions and improving energy efficiency, and playing a greater role in tracking changes in worldwide weather patterns.

In March 2011 the ITU deployed satellite telephones and related equipment to Japan, to help with communications and the search for survivors after the earthquake and tsunami. In May it signed an agreement with the European Patent Office, agreeing to share information and co-operate in developing worldwide technical standards. On October 5 South Sudan joined the ITU, raising its membership to 193.

Data released by the ITU in June 2012 highlighted the growth in mobile-cellular usage and the disparities in mobile-broadband access. By the end of 2011 there were almost 6 billion cellular subscriptions, an 86 percent global usage rate. Developing countries accounted for 80 percent of new subscriptions. In India alone, 142 million new cellular subscriptions were added in 2011, more than Europe and the Middle East combined. There were 105 countries in which there were more cellular phone subscriptions than inhabitants, including Botswana, Gabon, and South Africa. However, in Africa as a whole, there were fewer than 5 mobile-broadband subscriptions per 100 inhabitants, whereas in some developed countries such as Singapore and the Republic of Korea, there were more mobile-broadband subscriptions than inhabitants. At the December 2012 World Conference on International Telecommunications (WCIT), the ITU approved expanded governance of the internet by the agency. The controversial reforms were opposed by the United States, Canada, the United Kingdom, and many EU states that argued the changes could limit the free flow of information and legitimize filtering of the internet.

The IRU report, *The State of Broadband 2013: Universalizing Broadband* found that there were 7 billion mobile subscriptions in 2013 and that the number of such subscriptions would overtake the global population in 2014. In March 2013 the ITU called on member states to adopt plans to ensure gender equality in broadband access by 2020.

The ITU reported in 2014 that by year's end there would be more than 3 billion Internet users, and mobile broadband subscriptions would increase to 2.3 billion, of which 55 percent would be from the developing world. Among developed countries, mobile broadband penetration will climb to 84 percent of the population, almost four times as high as developing countries. Nonetheless, Africa led in mobile broadband growth, rising from 2 percent in 2010 to 20 percent in 2014.

On October 23, 2014, Houlin Zhao of China was elected as secretary-general of the ITU.

In its 2016 report *Measuring the Information Society Report, 2016* the ITU used a benchmark, the information communication technology (ICT) index, to measure the connectivity of consumers in countries around the world. The Republic of Korea ranked first among 175 countries in the ICT index in 2016. There were seven European and three Asian states among the top ten countries in the index. The greatest improvements in ICT occurred in St. Kitts and Nevis, Algeria, Bhutan, and Myanmar.

UNITED NATIONS EDUCATIONAL, SCIENTIFIC, AND CULTURAL ORGANIZATION

(UNESCO)

Established: By constitution adopted in London, England, November 16, 1945, effective November 4, 1946. UNESCO became a UN Specialized Agency by agreement concluded with the Economic and Social Council (approved by the General Assembly on December 14, 1946).

Purpose: To contribute to peace and security by promoting collaboration among states in education, the natural and social sciences, communications, and culture.

Headquarters: Paris, France.

Principal Organs: General Conference (all members), Executive Board (58 members), Secretariat.

Website: www.unesco.org.

Director General: Irina Bokova (Bulgaria).

Membership (195, plus 9 Associate Members): See Appendix C.

Official Languages: Arabic, Chinese, English, French, Russian, Spanish. French and English are working languages.

Origin and development. UNESCO resulted from the concern of European governments-in-exile over the problem of restoring the educational systems of Nazi-occupied territories after World War II. Meetings of the Allied Ministers of Education began in London, England, in 1942, and proposals for a postwar agency for educational and cultural reconstruction were drafted in April 1944; the constitution of UNESCO, adopted at a special conference in London, November 1–16, 1945, came into force a year later, following ratification by 20 states.

The 1974 General Conference voted to exclude Israel from the European regional groups of UNESCO, thus making that country the only member to belong to no regional groups. At the same session a motion was passed to withhold UNESCO aid from Israel on the ground that it had persisted "in altering the historical features" of Jerusalem during archaeological excavations. At the 1976 General Conference, Israel was restored to full membership in the organization; however, the conference voted to condemn Israeli educational and cultural policies in occupied Arab territories, charging that the latter amounted to "cultural assimilation." The adoption of this resolution was reported to be part of the price demanded by Arab and Soviet-bloc member countries for agreeing to Israel's return to the regional group. In November 1978 the organization again voted to condemn and cut off funds to Israel, charging that Arab monuments in Jerusalem had been destroyed in the course of further archaeological activity.

Debate at the 21st General Conference in 1980 raged over a resolution calling for the establishment of the New World Information and Communication Order (NWICO). Western delegates objected to the proposal, which called for an international code of journalistic ethics, on the ground that it might restrict freedom of the press. At the fourth extraordinary session of the General Conference, held in Paris in late 1982, the NWICO was included as a major component of the proposed medium-term UNESCO work plan for 1985–1989. The conference finally adopted a compromise plan for the NWICO that entailed the deletion of passages unacceptable to the industrialized countries, the rejection of a proposed study of Western news agencies, and the addition of material calling for freedom of the press and referencing its role as a watchdog against abuses of power.

Debate over the NWICO continued in 1983. Despite the compromise seemingly accepted at the 1982 Paris meeting, the document presented at a symposium on the news media and disarmament in Nairobi, Kenya, in April called for "national news agencies" and "codes of conduct" for journalists, with no mention of the right of news organs to operate freely. It also called for a study of the obstacles to circulation in industrialized countries of information produced in developing countries. In response, a number of industrial nations, including the United States, indicated that they would withhold funds from the organization, forcing it to appeal to external sources to meet its projected 1984–1985 budget of $328.8 million.

Subsequently, the organization came under even greater attack from members alleging unnecessary politicization of UNESCO activities and mismanagement by Director General Amadou Mahtar M'Bow of Senegal. The United States, at the forefront of the critics, called for major reforms in 1984. Rebuffed in the effort, it withdrew from membership, with the United Kingdom and Singapore following suit in 1985.

The controversial director general announced in late 1986 that he would not seek reelection upon expiration of his second term in November 1987, but, at the urging of the Organization of African Unity, subsequently reversed his position. Several additional Western nations threatened to withdraw from UNESCO in the event of M'Bow's reelection, and acrimony dominated efforts by the October meeting of the Executive Board to determine its nominee for the post. After four ballots, M'Bow withdrew, it having become apparent that the Soviet bloc planned to cast its decisive votes for his opponent, Federico Mayor Zaragoza of Spain. The board thereupon nominated Mayor, although 20 (mostly African) members voted against him.

The General Conference in November formally elected Mayor, who promised to restructure and reinvigorate the organization in hopes of bringing the United States and the United Kingdom back into its fold. In March 1988 Mayor reported extensive budget austerity measures had been introduced and a month later urged UNESCO to "talk less and less about political issues and more and more about education, culture, and science." The 1989 General Conference also attempted to mollify the United States by calling for a "free, independent, pluralistic press" throughout the world and by deferring a membership request from the Palestine Liberation Organization. Acting against the recommendations of a panel of distinguished Americans, who reported that UNESCO was making "clear and undeniable progress," the United States announced in April 1990 that it would not rejoin the organization.

The 1991 General Conference continued to urge the United States and the United Kingdom to reconsider their positions regarding UNESCO. Mayor intensified the lobbying campaign to get the former members to rejoin in the spring of 1992, noting that sharp cutbacks in contributions from the former Soviet Union and its successor states in 1991 had created financial distress for UNESCO. The director general presented a report from an independent commission appointed to evaluate UNESCO, which described the organization as having made progress in ending waste and inefficiency.

The 27th General Conference, held October 1993 in Paris, unanimously reelected Mayor to a second term, as recommended by the Executive Board. The conference also approved a $455 million biennial budget for 1994–1995, with priorities to include literacy, special educational programs for women and children, environmental and antidrug projects, and journalist training courses. Not coincidentally, much of the UNESCO emphasis reflected well-known interests of the U.S. Bill Clinton administration, which was described as adopting a more positive attitude toward the organization. Consequently, in early 1994 U.S. State Department officials said they had suggested the United States rejoin UNESCO, although not until 1997 because of budget considerations. A highlight of UNESCO activity later in the year was the readmission in December of South Africa, which had withdrawn from the organization in 1956 because of criticism of its apartheid policies. The United Kingdom rejoined on July 1, 1997.

In a secret ballot on October 20, 1999, Japan's Koichiro Matsuura defeated ten candidates for the Executive Board's endorsement to succeed Director General Mayor for a six-year term. His nomination coincided with release of an independent audit of UNESCO that uncovered mismanagement, corruption, and financial irregularities, including millions of dollars in payments to consultants and advisers who were deemed unqualified. In September 12, 2002, U.S. president George W. Bush announced to the UN General Assembly that the United States would rejoin UNESCO following an 18-year estrangement, stating, "This organization has been reformed and America will participate fully in its mission." Bush later pledged a $60 million reentry fee, returning the United States as the largest contributor to UNESCO. In October 2003 the United States was elected to serve on the 58-member Executive Board. In 2007 Montenegro joined and Singapore rejoined after walking out 22 years previously in protest of agency mismanagement. In 2011 South Sudan and Palestine joined the organization (see Recent activities, below). In November 2013 Anguilla became an associate member.

Structure. The General Conference, which usually meets every odd-dated year, has final responsibility for approving the budget, electing the director general, and deciding overall policy. Each member state has one vote; decisions are usually made by a simple majority, although some questions, such as amendments to UNESCO's constitution, require a two-thirds majority.

The Executive Board is charged with general oversight of the UNESCO program and the budget; the board examines drafts of both covering the ensuing two-year period and submits them, with its own recommendations, to the General Conference. Previously elected by, and from, General Conference participants, the members of the board under a 1991 constitutional revision are now the representatives of 58 governments selected by the conference to control board seats.

The Secretariat, which is headed by a director general selected for a six-year term by the General Conference (on recommendation of the Executive Board), is responsible for executing the program and applying the decisions of those two bodies. A distinctive feature of UNESCO's constitutional structure is the role of the national commissions. Comprising representatives of governments and nongovernmental organizations in the member states, the commissions were initially intended to act as advisory bodies for UNESCO's program. However, they have also come to serve as liaison agents between the Secretariat and the diverse educational, scientific, and cultural activities in the participant states.

Recent activities. UNESCO's program of activities derives from its broad mandate to "maintain, increase and diffuse knowledge," to "give fresh impulse to popular education and to the spread of knowledge," and to "collaborate in the work of advancing the mutual knowledge and understanding of peoples." Within this mandate it (1) holds international conferences, conducts expert studies, and disseminates factual information concerning education, the natural and social sciences, cultural activities, and mass communication; (2) promotes the free flow of ideas by word and image; (3) encourages the exchange of persons and of publications and other informational materials; (4) attempts to ensure conservation and protection of books, works of art, and monuments of historical and scientific significance; and (5) collaborates with member states in developing educational, scientific, and cultural programs.

To promote intellectual cooperation, UNESCO has granted financial assistance to many international nongovernmental organizations engaged in the transfer of knowledge. It has also attempted to encourage the exchange of ideas by convening major conferences on such topics as life-long education, oceanographic research, problems of youth, eradication of illiteracy, and cultural and scientific policy. To further cooperation in science and technology, UNESCO was instrumental in the establishment of the European Organization for Nuclear Research (CERN, see separate entry) in 1954, the International Brain Research Organization (IBRO) in 1960, the International Cell Research Organization in 1962, the program on Man and the Biosphere (MAB) that currently involves more than 140 countries, the International Geological Correlation Program, the International Hydrological Program (IHP), and a Coastal Regions and Small Islands (CSI) endeavor. In addition, UNESCO provides the secretariat for the Intergovernmental Oceanographic Commission (ICO).

UNESCO has paid particular attention to the human genome, establishing in 1993 a bioethics program that led to the adoption of the Universal Declaration on the Human Genome and Human Rights in 1997, which banned human reproductive cloning. (For more information, see the 2012 *Handbook*.) UNESCO's developmental efforts also focus on modernizing educational facilities, training teachers, combating illiteracy, improving science and social science teaching, and training scientists and engineers. The International Bureau of Education (IBE) in Geneva, which dates from 1925, became part of UNESCO in 1969, while the International Institute for Educational Planning (IIEP) and the Intergovernmental Committee for Physical Education and Sport (ICPES), both located in Paris, France, were established by the organization in 1963 and 1978, respectively. Other educational units include the Caribbean Network of Educational Innovation for Development, located in Kingston, Jamaica; the European Center for Higher Education in Bucharest, Romania; the International Institute for Higher Education in Latin America and the Caribbean in Caracas, Venezuela; the Institute for Education in Hamburg, Germany; and the Institute for Information Technologies in Education in Moscow, Russia. (For more on educational initiatives, see the 2012 *Handbook*.)

In social sciences, UNESCO focuses its attention on diverse issues such as human rights, ethics in science and technology, peace and disarmament, environment and population issues, and socioeconomic conditions. The 1978 General Conference adopted the Declaration on Race and Racial Prejudice that rejected the concept that any racial or ethnic group was inherently inferior or superior. UNESCO's *Medium-Term Report* for 2002–2007 reinforced the 2001 Universal Declaration on Cultural Diversity that tasks UNESCO with a three-part, six-year strategy to implement standards to protect cultural diversity, promote cross-cultural dialogue, and enhance links between culture and development. Since 1946, UNESCO has worked to preserve cultural heritage. Director General Matsuura decried the Taliban's willful destruction in March 2001 of the stone Buddhas of Bamiyan in Afghanistan as a "crime against culture." Additionally, UNESCO has taken steps to prevent the illicit traffic of artifacts following extensive looting in Baghdad, Iraq, after the fall of Saddam Hussein's regime in 2003 and has also worked to preserve dying languages. Similarly, UNESCO warned museums and international art dealers in August 2011 to be alert for items that might have been looted during the civil war in Libya. The February 2009 edition of UNESCO's *Atlas of the World's* Languages in Danger of Disappearing caused some comment. It listed the Manx Gaelic and Cornish languages as extinct. This brought letters of protest from schoolchildren on the Isle of Man, written in the supposedly dead language, as well as complaints from Cornish speakers. Both languages were reclassified as "critically endangered."

In communications, UNESCO has attempted to advance the free flow of information and book development, expand the use of media, assist countries in developing the media they need, and disseminate UN ideals. Since 1976 the General Information Program (PGI) has concentrated on improving the organization and dissemination of scientific and technical information. The Intergovernmental Informatics Program (IIP) has directed its attention to policy considerations and training in computer-based knowledge dissemination. Also under the communications arm of UNESCO is the ICO, which built an early-warning system for tsunamis in the Indian Ocean following the December 2004 tsunami that killed more than 200,000 people in the region.

The 33rd General Conference was held on October 17–20, 2005, in Paris. It adopted a budget of $610 million, with an additional $25 million in extra-budgetary voluntary funding. It also adopted the Convention on the Protection and Promotion of the Diversity of Cultural Expressions, the International Convention against Doping in Sport, and the Universal Declaration on Bioethics and Human Rights. The convention on cultural diversity was intended, among other things, to support national movie industries, and was opposed by the United States. The director general agreed that the organization should, for the time being, concentrate on implementing standards that had been recently promulgated, rather than on creating new ones.

With enough countries ratifying support, the Convention for the Safeguarding of the Intangible Heritage entered into force in 2006. The convention requires member nations to take steps to protect oral and cultural traditions, traditional craft-making, and performing arts and includes funding for preservation efforts and two official registry lists.

Additionally, another report entitled *Case Studies on Climate Change and World Heritage* that year found that world heritage sites, including coral reefs and archaeological sites sensitive to changes in humidity and precipitation, can be threatened by the effects of climate change.

At the 34th General Conference on October 16 to November 2, 2007, in Paris, Matsuura recommended recruiting a financial comptroller to strengthen internal agency monitoring. The conference also adopted a strategy for 2008–2013 of "attaining lifelong quality education for all;" furthering sustainable development through science and technology; and creating activities directed towards youth, least developed nations, and small island states. A 2008–2009 budget of $631 million was adopted, with educational programs receiving the largest share, followed by the natural and social science sectors, and then culture.

The conference also approved a resolution directing the director general to explore the role UNESCO could play in preserving the memory of the Holocaust and preventing all forms of its denial in reaction to Iranian president Mahmoud Ahmadinejad's calling the Holocaust "a myth" earlier in the year. In other measures in 2007, UNESCO called for Israel to end archaeological excavation work near the al-Aqsa mosque in Jerusalem out of concern Islam's third holiest site could be damaged, and listed the Galapagos Islands in the Pacific Ocean as an endangered world heritage site because of the growing pressure of tourism. It also renamed the Nazi concentration camp Auschwitz Birkenau as the German Nazi Concentration and Extermination Camp to clearly identify Germany's responsibility after a lobbying effort by Poland. UNESCO designated the Iraqi city of Samarra as an endangered world cultural treasure after insurgent attacks destroyed a number of the city's holy sites.

The state of education was summarized in a 2007 UNESCO report called *Corrupt Schools, Corrupt Universities: What Can Be Done.* The report found that illegal registration fees, academic fraud (including fake university degrees available on the Internet), embezzlement, and other corrupt practices were seriously undermining educational systems around the world.

The creation of World Heritage sites and institutions was productive in 2008, but some efforts were controversial. Cambodia attempted to register the temple of Preyah Vihear as a World Heritage site, but the temple stands on ground that is disputed between Thailand and Cambodia. The ground is recognized as Cambodian, but the only access is through Thai territory. Thailand did not object to Cambodia's action, but wanted to manage the area jointly with Cambodia. UNESCO's position was that the two countries must resolve their differences before the site could be registered. Occasional violent clashes continued at the site through 2008 and into late 2009, but both sides declared they would not allow the conflict to escalate.

Also in 2008 Egypt's culture minister, Farouk HOSNY, a potential candidate to be UNESCO's next director general, was attacked with the allegation that he had made statements against Israel. He denied the accusation and said he "dreamed" of visiting Israel after ties with the Palestinians were normalized. Also controversial was UNESCO's decision to recognize Jerusalem as "the capital of Arab culture" in 2009. The celebration was to include all Jerusalem, not just the present Arab part of the city. Eventually, Hosny was beaten out by Irina Bokova, the former external affairs minister of Bulgaria. Hosny declared that he had lost because of "Zionist pressures." Bokova was elected and sworn in at the 35th General Conference, held October 6–23, 2009, in Paris. She was the first woman and the first person from Eastern Europe to become director general. The conference adopted a budget only nominally larger than that of the previous biennium, with education as its priority, and it welcomed the Faroe Islands as a new associate member. Also at the conference, UNESCO approved Africa and gender equality as two of its main priorities for support.

In other action, UNESCO declared, in a November 2008 report, that the world was likely to miss the goal of providing elementary education for all children by 2015. In June 2009 it deleted Dresden, Germany, from the list of World Heritage Sites, to which it had been added in 2004, because of a new bridge that UNESCO deemed unsuitable. In December delegations from 50 states adopted the Belém Framework for Action, which outlined a variety of measures to promote lifelong learning among populations and to reduce illiteracy around the world by 50 percent from the levels of 2000 by 2015.

The UNESCO budget for 2010–2011 increased to $653 million, an increase of $22 million, or 3.5 percent, over the previous cycle. A January 2010 UNESCO report warned that the global economic crisis would undermine developing countries' efforts to improve education, especially in light of international aid reductions by wealthy states. UNESCO estimated that 72 million children were not in school, a number that was reduced from 105 million a decade ago. Nonetheless, UNESCO also predicted that by 2015, 56 million children would remain out of school, the majority of those female. In September UNESCO signed an agreement with the Al Jazeera satellite news network to collaborate on initiatives to promote freedom of expression and of the media in the Arab world. The effort revolved around programs to increase awareness and to undertake research on the barriers to freedom of speech. At the end of 2010, UNESCO's List of World Heritage in Danger noted that 34 recognized sites in 27 countries were threatened.

In a controversial vote in October 2011, UNESCO members admitted Palestine to full membership, on equal terms with entities that have undisputed national status. This decision occurred after the United States threatened to veto Palestine's request for full membership in the UN. The UNESCO vote was 107 in favor, 14 against, with 52 abstentions. The United States and Israel were strongly opposed, and Washington announced that it would immediately stop contributing to the agency (the United States provided about 22 percent of UNESCO's annual budget; see below). Israel did likewise. On October 11, at the end of the UNESCO general conference, director-general Bokova announced a worldwide appeal for contributions to replace the United States' contribution. She addressed the appeal to governments, other institutions, even to individuals—anyone who cared to contribute. The loss of contributions led to a $205 million deficit by 2012 and prompted the agency to suspend some programs.

In response to the Arab Spring, UNESCO launched a range of programs. In 2011 the organization conducted a series of workshops and training sessions for journalists from the Middle East and North Africa. In addition, UNESCO and Interpol initiated a program to catalog heritage sites in Egypt and other states and assist new governments in developing adequate security procedures for sites and objects. UNESCO also conducted gender and equity training for newly elected officials.

Director-General Bokova was nominated for a second term in April 2013 by UNESCO's executive board, defeating Rachad Farah (Djibouti) and Joseph Maïla (Lebanon). A June UNESCO report found that the number of children without access to primary education fell from 61 million in 2010 to 57 million in 2011. Concurrently there was a 6 percent drop in international aid for primary education, with the United Kingdom overtaking the United States as the world's largest single donor as the latter continued to cut its foreign aid budget. In August UNESCO and the EU announced a program of expanded cooperation on education, culture, resources, freedom of expression, and water and oceans. Specific action items included efforts to safeguard unique cultural artifacts in areas of conflict and initiatives to strengthen journalism and media in developing nations.

In response to continuing budget constraints and in an effort to eliminate the organization's operating deficit, Bokova ordered a series of cuts in 2013. Staff travel was cut 73 percent, consultant costs

70 percent, furniture 64 percent, and temporary assistance costs 44 percent. There were also position eliminations. By 2014, the number of positions was projected to have decreased from 2,118 in 2000 to 1,454. In November 2013 the United States lost its voting rights in UNESCO after two years of nonpayment, following its 2011 suspension of payments over the admission of Palestine to the organization.

In October 2015 the United States unsuccessfully endeavored to regain its UNESCO voting rights despite continuing arrears. Kosovo failed to gain UNESCO membership when it was unable to secure the necessary two-thirds majority. Serbia led opposition to the bid, which fell short on a vote of 92 in favor, 50 opposed, and 29 abstentions, on November 9.

UNESCO's proposed budget for 2016–2017 was $667 million. The greatest expenditures were allocated for Africa, 20.3 percent, with 8.2 percent of the funding for the continent to be spent on gender equity initiatives. Bokova was nominated as a candidate to be UN secretary-general in July 2016, but the post went instead to António Gutteres of Portugal.

UNITED NATIONS INDUSTRIAL DEVELOPMENT ORGANIZATION

(UNIDO)

Established: By General Assembly resolution of November 17, 1966, effective January 1, 1967. UNIDO became a UN Specialized Agency January 1, 1986, as authorized by a resolution of the Seventh Special Session of the General Assembly on September 16, 1975, based on a revised constitution adopted April 8, 1979.

Purpose: To review and promote the coordination of UN activities in the area of industrial development, with particular emphasis on industrialization in less developed countries, including both agro-based or agro-related industries and basic industries.

Headquarters: Vienna, Austria.

Principal Organs: General Conference (all members), Industrial Development Board (53 members), Program and Budget Committee (27 members), Secretariat.

Website: www.unido.org.

Director General: Li Yong (China).

Membership: (172): See Appendix C. (Canada withdrew as of December 31, 1993, the United States withdrew as of December 31, 1996, and Australia withdrew as of December 31, 1997. The United Kingdom, which in 1996 had announced its intention to withdraw, reversed its decision in 1997 and remained a member and then announced it would stop funding UNIDO in 2012; see Recent activities, below.)

Origin and development. The creation of a comprehensive organization responsible for UN efforts in the field of industrial development was proposed to the General Assembly in 1964 by the first UN Conference on Trade and Development (UNCTAD). The General Assembly endorsed the proposal in 1965 and, through a 1966 resolution effective January 1, 1967, established UNIDO as a semi-autonomous Special Body of the General Assembly with budgetary and programmatic ties to other special bodies, such as UNCTAD and the UN Development Program (UNDP).

Although 120 governments ratified the UNIDO constitution by March 1985, it was not until June 21 that the minimum of 80 formal notifications of such action had been tendered, in part because of an insistence by Eastern European countries that they be guaranteed a deputy director generalship. Subsequently, a General Conference met in Vienna on August 12–17 and December 9–13 to pave the way for launching the organization as the UN's 16th Specialized Agency. (For prior information, see the 2014 *Handbook.*)

In the early 1990s observers described the organization as facing "a leadership and identity crisis," underscored by its failure to approve either of two proposed restructuring plans. Members' arrears also continued to be a major concern, with dozens of countries losing voting rights for nonpayment of dues. On March 30, 1993, a special session of the General Conference appointed Mauricio de María y Campos of Mexico as UNIDO director general, the former director general, Domingo L. Siazon Jr., having resigned to take a position in the Philippine government. The new director general called for an "urgent restructuring," with emphasis placed on helping companies in developing countries to become internationally competitive via an expanded private sector and global cooperation in the transfer of technology. Many of the recommendations were endorsed in the Yaoundé Declaration issued following the fifth General Conference, held December 6–9 in Yaoundé, Cameroon.

Despite its restructuring, UNIDO's future remained in jeopardy as a review of overlapping UN bodies proceeded. It was reported in early 1995 that a UN report had recommended the dismantling of UNIDO, a proposal endorsed by the world's leading industrialized countries during their midyear summit. Consequently, the United States announced at UNIDO's sixth General Conference in December that it would withdraw from the organization at the end of 1996. UNIDO subsequently continued to restructure its operations, cutting a number of senior managers, reducing its overall workforce by more than one-third from its 1993 total, and slashing its budget.

The 1997 General Conference endorsed the Business Plan for the Future Role and Functions of UNIDO, under which the organization's overall goals in meeting the needs of developing countries and economies in transition were defined as "the three Es": competitive economy, productive employment, and sound environment. The conference approved the nomination of a new director general, Carlos Magariños of Argentina, making him the youngest director general in UN history. Magariños was widely credited for revamping the organization's structure and was reelected to a second four-year term at the December 2001 conference.

At the 11th session of the UNIDO General Conference, held on November 28–December 2, 2005, in Vienna, Magariños was succeeded by Kandeh Yumkella of Sierra Leone. Li Yung of China was elected to succeed Yumkella on June 24, 2013, defeating five other candidates.

Structure. The General Conference, which meets every two years, establishes UNIDO policy and is responsible for final approval of its biennial budgets. The Industrial Development Board (IDB), which meets annually, exercises wide-ranging "policy review" authority, and its recommendations exert significant influence on the decisions of the conference. The Program and Budget Committee also meets annually to conduct extensive preliminary budget preparations.

The Secretariat, comprising some 700 employees, is headed by a director general appointed by the General Conference upon the recommendation of the IDB. The 1985 General Conference decided to name five deputy directors general, thus permitting greater regional/bloc representation. However, the 1993 General Conference approved a streamlined staff structure that eliminated the deputy directors general and instead named eight managing directors. In late 1997 UNIDO decided to reduce the number of divisions to three. In February 2002 the Secretariat instituted a new organizational structure with three divisions: Program Development and Technical Cooperation, Program Coordination and Field Operations, and Administration. Staff was also streamlined (143 posts abolished), and there was a significant reduction in the number of committees.

UNIDO activity in most developing countries is coordinated by a resident senior industrial development field adviser or a resident junior professional officer. In addition, expert advisers or consultants are hired from throughout the world to work temporarily on many of the development projects administered by UNIDO. As of 2014, 50 countries had regional offices with some 2,500 contract personnel working in the field, along with the organization's 693 permanent staff.

Recent activities. UNIDO serves both as a technical cooperation agency and as a global forum. Its research, analysis, statistical compilation, dissemination of information, and training provide general support for industrial development throughout the world. In addition, the organization operates (usually in conjunction with other UN affiliates and national governments) hundreds of field projects per year in such areas as planning, feasibility study, research and development for specific proposals, and installation of pilot industrial plants.

UNIDO facilities include 17 Investment and Technology Promotion Offices, which encourage contacts between businessmen and governments in developing or transitional countries and industrial and financial leaders in developed countries; 10 closely associated International Technology Centers; 5 Investment Promotion Units in Africa and the Near East; 35 National Cleaner Production Centers under a program jointly organized with the UN Environment Program (UNEP); and 59 Subcontracting and Partnership Exchanges in more than 30 countries to link local manufacturers with the global market. UNIDO was also instrumental in the creation of the International Center for Genetic Engineering and Biotechnology, with bases in Trieste, Italy, and New Delhi, India; the

International Center for Science and High Technology in Trieste; the Center for the Application of Solar Energy in Perth, Australia; the International Center for Small Hydro Power in Hangzhou, China; the International Center for Materials Evaluation Technology in Taejon, South Korea; and the International Center for Hydrogen Energy Technology in Istanbul, Turkey. Special UNIDO funds include the Industrial Development Fund (IDF), established in 1978 to provide financing for innovative development projects outside the criteria of existing financial services, and the Working Capital Fund, established in 1986.

In November 2001 the organization launched the Africa Investment Promotion Agency Network that focused on spurring domestic and foreign investment in 14 countries in sub-Saharan Africa. However, in July 2004 UNIDO released a report stating that the poorest African nations were "seriously off-track" for meeting the 2015 poverty reduction deadline set by the UN. Environmental sustainability has also emerged as a major theme of UNIDO's efforts. In addition to establishing the National Cleaner Production Centers Program in conjunction with the UNEP, it continues to serve as one of the UN's four implementing agencies for the Montreal Protocol on ozone-depleting chemicals and has been active in the Kyoto Protocol, which was implemented in February 2005 in an effort to combat greenhouse gases and global warming. (See the discussion of both protocols in the entry on the UNEP.)

In late 1999 UNIDO held the first UNIDO Forum on Sustainable Industrial Development in Vienna, Austria, in tandem with the eighth General Conference to address the effects of economic integration in developing economies; the impact of globalization; environmental challenges to sustainable development; and the status of the recently initiated UNIDO Partnership Program, which is an effort to coordinate local and intergovernmental entities, both public and private, in assisting small- and medium-sized enterprises (SMEs).

The tenth General Conference was held in December 2003 in Vienna, where the main objective was to discuss the organization's role in fulfilling the Millennium Development Goals (MDGs) set by the UN in the environmental and developmental areas. At the 2005 11th General Conference, UNIDO adopted a strategic long-term vision statement and a medium-term program framework to cover the years 2006–2009. The 2007 General Conference took place on December 3–7 in Vienna. The Secretariat noted that member countries continued to be in arrears for payment of membership dues.

So-called south-south cooperation has become a key policy focus in recent years in an effort to promote trade and increased production capacities between advanced developing countries and poorer nations with emerging economies. To that end, UNIDO planned on opening industrial cooperation centers in China, Egypt, Brazil, and South Africa to enhance business networks. The first center opened in New Delhi, India, in February 2007, and a second in Beijing in July 2008.

In 2007 UNIDO hosted the International Conference on Biofuels in Kuala Lumpur, Malaysia, the first in a three-year series of conferences aimed at developing industrial conversion processes and uses of biofuels. UNIDO signed several agreements with India to promote SMEs in 2007 and 2008. However India was warned about its overreliance on fossil fuels and was encouraged to generate one-fifth of its electricity from renewable sources in the current UNIDO-India plan period, 2007–2012.

In April 2008 Director General Yumkella urged Africa to industrialize as a way to combat poverty and urged Nigeria to take the lead in this effort. In June UNIDO and Microsoft announced plans to set up a computer refurbishment operation in Uganda, with the twin aims of reducing pollution from discarded computers and of putting more and cheaper computers in African hands. In September UNIDO told India that it should aim to generate one fifth of the capacity expansion in its current economic plan (that covers 2007–2012) from renewable energy, thus alleviating its effect on climate change. In November UNIDO signed a Memorandum of Understanding (MOU) with China for cooperation in clean industrial development. On December 12, 2008, Samoa joined UNIDO as its 173rd member.

In January 2009 UNIDO signed an MOU for increased cooperation with the Eurasian Economic Community, an offshoot of the Commonwealth of Independent States (See the entry on the CIS.) In UNIDO's Industrial Development Report 2009, released February 24, 2009, it argued against using the world economic crisis as an excuse for returning to protectionism. Poor countries needed to move beyond trading raw materials and into manufacturing, it said. In June 2009 UNIDO announced the expansion of a joint program with the technology company Hewlett-Packard. This program would build additional IT training centers in Africa and the Middle East.

UNIDO's *Annual Report 2009* noted improving global trends in energy efficiency. Energy usage was 33 percent less intense in 2009 than in 1970, reflecting more energy efficient appliances, lights, and other electronic devices. In addition, UNIDO estimated that 15 percent of the economic stimulus packages adopted around the world contained "green" or eco-friendly components. In 2009 UNIDO expended $139 million on projects, a rise from the $124 million the year before. UNIDO approved 247 of 385 projects submitted that year. By the end of 2009, the organization had secured an additional $355 million for future projects.

In 2010 Japan pledged $10.6 million to support UNIDO economic development programs in Africa and Afghanistan. In addition, Italy pledged more than $3.5 million for UNIDO projects in Iraq. In February 2011 the United Kingdom announced that, as of January 1, 2013, it would no longer provide financial support to UNIDO (and would presumably leave the organization at that time). The United Kingdom had provided 9 percent of the organization's budget (€7.2 million). A UK report declared that UNIDO's mission did not sufficiently coincide with the United Kingdom's foreign aid goals.

In July and August 2011 UNIDO was embroiled in a dispute involving Nepal and China. In July Hu Yuandong, the chief UNIDO representative in China, signed an agreement with the Hong Kong–based Asia Pacific Exchange and Cooperation Foundation (APECF) to help develop a visitor center and cultural complex in Lumbini, Nepal, the birthplace of Buddha. Both the UNIDO main office and Nepal itself repudiated the arrangement, as neither had been consulted. Nepal felt the deal was a threat to its sovereignty. The deal might also have had significant geopolitical impact, as it would likely have introduced a large Chinese presence at a site close to the border between India and China. On October 27 Tuvalu became the 174th member of UNIDO.

In May 2012 UNIDO and Italy agreed to launch a program to promote sustainable development and renewable energy in developing countries. Meanwhile, Germany announced it would provide €1 million to support UNIDO efforts to bolster the pharmaceutical industry in Africa. In June UNIDO and Microsoft agreed to extend and expand a partnership program to use technology for education and employment training. The initiative would continue until 2015.

The 2013 report, the *Industrial Competitiveness of Nations: Looking Back, Looking Ahead,* utilized UNIDO's competitive industrial performance index to determine that developed nations such as the United States, Japan, and the EU states, still retained an advantage over developing states. Japan ranked first, followed by Germany and the United States. However, China made significant progress rising to 7th, the highest of any developing state, from 23rd the previous year. UNIDO's budget for 2014–2015 was $239.6 million.

In December 2013, at its 15th general conference, UNIDO issued the Lima Declaration, which contained new strategic goals for the organization. The declaration called for UNIDO to serve as a "global facilitator of knowledge and advice on policies and strategies toward achieving inclusive and sustainable industrial development." It also called on the organization to concentrate on three main areas: economic capacity-building, trade capacity-building, and sustainable development and industrial resource efficiency.

UNIDO increasingly emphasized inclusive and sustainable industrial development (ISID) in an effort to ensure that industrialization would benefit the maximum number of citizens and groups within a given country. To achieve this goal, UNIDO initiated the Program for Country Partnership (PCP), an individual industrialization program tailored for each member state to fully integrate sustainable resource strategies and new technologies.

WORLD BANK

Established: The World Bank Group consists of five component entities; the International Bank for Reconstruction and Development (IBRD, the oldest, established in 1945), the International Finance Corporation (IFC), the International Development Association (IDA), the Multilateral Investment Guarantee Agency (MIGA), and the International Center for Settlement of Investment Disputes (ICSID).

Purpose: To promote the international flow of capital for productive purposes, initially the rebuilding of nations devastated by World War II. The main objective of the bank at present is to offer loans at reasonable terms to member developing countries willing to engage in projects that will ultimately increase their productive capacities and reduce poverty.

Headquarters: Washington, D.C., United States.

Principal Organs: Board of Governors (all members), Executive Directors (25).

Website: www.worldbank.org.

President: Jim Yong Kim (United States).

Membership (189): See Appendix C.

Working Language: English.

Origin and development. The origins, development, and activities of the World Bank Group's three major components are discussed below.

INTERNATIONAL BANK FOR RECONSTRUCTION AND DEVELOPMENT, A MEMBER OF THE WORLD BANK GROUP

(IBRD)

Established: By Articles of Agreement signed in Bretton Woods, New Hampshire, July 22, 1944, effective December 27, 1945; began operation June 25, 1946. The IBRD became a UN Specialized Agency by agreement with the Economic and Social Council (approved by the General Assembly on November 15, 1947).

Purpose: To promote the international flow of capital for productive purposes, initially the rebuilding of nations devastated by World War II. The main objective of the bank at present is to offer loans at reasonable terms to member developing countries willing to engage in projects that will ultimately increase their productive capacities and reduce poverty.

Headquarters: Washington, D.C., United States.

Principal Organs: Board of Governors (all members), Executive Directors (25).

Website: www.worldbank.org/ibrd.

Membership (188): See Appendix C.

Working Language: English.

Origin and development. The International Bank for Reconstruction and Development was one of the two main products of the United Nations Monetary and Financial Conference held July 1–22, 1944, in Bretton Woods, New Hampshire. The bank was conceived as a center for mobilizing and allocating capital resources for the reconstruction of war-torn states and for the expansion of world production and trade; its sister institution, the International Monetary Fund (IMF), was created to maintain order in the field of currencies and exchange rates and thus to prevent a repetition of the financial chaos of the 1930s. The Articles of Agreement of the two institutions were annexed to the Final Act of the Bretton Woods Conference and went into effect December 27, 1945, following ratification by the required 28 states.

With the commencement of the U.S.-sponsored European Recovery Program in 1948, the focus of IBRD activities began to shift toward economic development. Accordingly, two affiliated institutions—the International Finance Corporation (IFC) and the International Development Association (IDA), created in 1956 and 1960, respectively (see separate entries)—were established within the IBRD's framework to undertake developmental responsibilities for which the IBRD itself was not qualified under its Articles of Agreement. In 1985 the IBRD approved a charter for another affiliate, the Multilateral Investment Guarantee Agency (MIGA), to provide borrowers with protection against noncommercial risks such as war, uncompensated expropriations, or repudiation of contracts by host governments without adequate legal redress for affected parties. The MIGA, operating as a distinct legal and financial entity, came into being on April 12, 1988, with about 54 percent of its initial $1.1 billion in authorized capital having been subscribed. As of 2016 there were 181 MIGA members.

The IBRD and IDA have long been referred to as the World Bank, or as the World Bank Group when considered in conjunction with affiliate organizations the IFC, the MIGA, and the International Center for Settlement of Investment Disputes (ICSID). The IBRD is responsible for lending to middle-income and creditworthy poor countries, while IDA extends grants and interest-free loans to the world's poorest countries. Loan statistics for both the IBRD and the IDA are given in this article.

Structure. All of the IBRD's powers are formally vested in the Board of Governors, which consists of a governor and an alternate appointed by each member state. The IBRD governors, who are usually finance ministers or equivalent national authorities, serve concurrently as governors of the IMF, as well as of the IFC, the IDA, and the MIGA, assuming that a given country's affiliations extend beyond the parent organization. The board meets each fall to review the operations of these institutions within the framework of a general examination of the world financial and economic situation. One meeting in three is held away from Washington, D.C.

Most powers of the Board of Governors are delegated to the IBRD's 25 executive directors, who meet at least once a month at the bank's headquarters and are responsible for the general conduct of its operations. Five of the directors are separately appointed by those members holding the largest number of shares of capital stock (France, Germany, Japan, the United Kingdom, and the United States). The others are individually elected for two-year terms by the remaining IBRD members, who are divided into 19 essentially geographical groupings, each of which selects one director. (As Saudi Arabia by itself constitutes one of the geographical entities, its "election" of a director amounts, in practical terms, to an appointment. Similarly, China and the Russian Federation have single directors.) Each director is entitled to cast as a unit the votes of those members who elected him.

The bank operates on a weighted voting system that is largely based on individual country subscriptions (themselves based on IMF quotas), but with poorer states being accorded a slightly disproportionate share. As of 2016, the leading subscribers were the United States, with 17.45 percent (16.51 percent of voting power); Japan, 7.52 (7.14); China, 4.85 (4.61); Germany, 4.39 (4.18); France and the United Kingdom, 4.11 (3.91); India, 3.18 (3.03); Russia, 3.02 (2.89); Italy 2.77 (2.65); and Canada, 2.65 (2.54).

The president of the IBRD is elected to a renewable five-year term by the executive directors, serves as their chair, and is responsible for conducting the business of the bank as well as that of the IDA and the IFC. In accordance with the wishes of the U.S. government, Robert McNamara was replaced upon his retirement in June 1981 by Alden W. Clausen, a former president of the Bank of America, who restructured the bank's upper echelon to reflect his preference for collegial management and delegation of authority. On June 30, 1986, Clausen was succeeded by Barber B. Conable Jr., who had served on a number of financial committees in the course of ten consecutive terms in the U.S. House of Representatives. In May 1987 Conable announced a major reorganization within the bank to clarify and strengthen the roles of the president and senior management. Another change was the creation of country departments to oversee all aspects of individual lending projects; Conable also ordered a controversial review of all bank positions, which ultimately yielded about 350 redundancies.

Following the announcement of Conable's retirement, the executive directors in April 1991 approved the appointment of Lewis T. Preston, former chair of the board of J. P. Morgan and Morgan Guaranty Trust Company, as the next president, effective August 31. Preston's selection was seen as reflecting the insistence of the United States on additional private sector involvement by the bank and greater commercial bank influence in debt reduction negotiations. Like his predecessor, Preston instituted a number of structural changes early in his term that appeared to further concentrate power in the president's hands. Three senior vice presidents were eliminated and the remaining sixteen vice presidents were ordered to report directly to the president. Preston died on May 4, 1995, and was succeeded on June 1 by James D. Wolfensohn, a prominent New York investment banker. Administrative reforms continued under Wolfensohn, who in December 1996 appointed two new managing directors. Wolfensohn was succeeded in June 2005 by Paul Wolfowitz, previously the U.S. deputy secretary of defense. After implementing a string of controversial anticorruption measures, Wolfowitz resigned after two years in office under conflict-of-interest charges. He was replaced in July 2007 by former U.S. deputy secretary of state Robert Zoellick, then a vice chair of leading New York investment house Goldman Sachs. Zoellick was replaced by Dartmouth College president Jim Yong Kim on July 1, 2012.

Recent activities. The IBRD describes itself as structured like a cooperative. It is the organ of the World Bank that "works with middle-income and creditworthy poorer countries to promote sustainable, equitable and job-creating growth, reduce poverty and address issues of regional and global importance." Most funds available for lending are obtained by direct borrowing on world financial markets. Only a small percentage of the capital subscription of the member states represents paid-in capital in dollars, other currencies, or demand notes; the balance is "callable capital" that is subject to call by the bank only when needed to meet obligations incurred through borrowing or through guaranteeing loans. Most of the bank's operating funds are obtained by issuing interest-bearing bonds and notes to public and private investors.

The Articles of Agreement state that the IBRD can make loans only for productive purposes for which funds are not obtainable in the private market on reasonable terms. Loans are long-term (generally repayable over as much as 20 years, with a five-year grace period) and are available only to member states, their political subdivisions, and enterprises located in the territories of member states (in which case, the states involved must guarantee the projects). (For more on the background of the IBRD, see the 2014 *Handbook*).

In April 1993 it was reported that an internal review had acknowledged a "significant failure rate" within the bank's operations, with about 20 percent of the loans active in 1991 having "major problems." Although the design of some projects and the bank's follow-up procedures were criticized, the failures were primarily attributed to poor economic conditions during the 1980s in Africa, Latin America, and parts of Asia.

In July 1993 the leaders of the world's seven leading industrialized nations agreed during a summit in Tokyo to offer Moscow an aid package that included up to $1 billion in World Bank lending. Initial approvals were constrained by Moscow's difficulty in controlling government spending and inflation, coupled with economic and political turmoil within many of its newly independent neighbors. However, an improved situation led to what was expected to be at least $2 billion in additional lending.

In mid-1994 the bank embarked on another major project: the coordination of $2.4 billion in pledges from international donors for the Gaza Strip and Jericho, where the new Palestinian National Authority had recently been installed. Much of the Palestinian aid was earmarked for infrastructure development, a focus of the 1994 *World Development Report.*

For the fiscal year July 1, 1993, through June 30, 1994, bank officials said that progress had been made in monitoring loan performance and in integrating environmental concerns into IBRD activity. In addition, the bank established the three-member Independent Inspection Panel to investigate complaints about specific loans. However, the changes did not placate many of the bank's critics, environmentalists in particular continuing to assail the IBRD's "obsolete" industrial development policies. Questions also continued over the bank's role in the external debt problems facing many developing countries, highlighted by the fact that the IBRD in 1993–1994 took in $731 million more in repayments than it disbursed in new funds.

Lending approvals increased in fiscal year July 1, 1994, through June 30, 1995, totaling $16.9 billion for 134 projects. However, a decline in lending was expected under new bank president Wolfensohn, who proposed significant changes for the IBRD, including a shift away from "megaprojects" that often had proven difficult for developing countries to manage after they had been completed. In their stead, Wolfensohn said the bank should concentrate on small, environmentally sound projects that offered direct benefits to the poor. He also urged the bank to devote much more of its energy and resources to the promotion of private investment in developing countries and spearheaded the establishment of a new debt relief program, the Heavily Indebted Poor Countries (HIPC) debt-reduction initiative, for the poorest developing nations, most of which are African.

In March 1997 the Executive Board approved a Strategic Compact with the goal of increasing the World Bank's efficiency and effectiveness through "fundamental reform." Among the substantive goals of the 30-month program were the reduction of overhead and administrative costs, decentralization of the bank's operation, and the development and improvement of relationships with other organizations.

In the 1997 *World Development Report,* the IBRD asserted that "effective" governments, i.e., those that are relatively free of corruption and limited in scope, are a necessary precondition for social and economic development. Furthermore, both the IBRD and IMF began to insist on effective governance as a condition for their assistance. The bank subsequently emphasized the role of local governments in fostering development, arguing that corruption at the municipal level often undermined the best intentions of national policies. In 1998 President Wolfensohn also challenged the international financial community to develop a new long-term strategy to provide relief to the poor, and asserted, among other things, that the IMF was paying insufficient attention to the human costs of its financial stabilization activities. Debate on the subject continued into the preparation of the 2000 *World Development Report,* at which time several authors objected to the overdependence on "pro-market orthodoxy." The final report appeared to favor the "reformist" camp by calling for "empowerment" of the poor and protection of "vulnerable groups." Along those same lines, Wolfensohn subsequently called for dialogue with anti-globalization protesters who had recently conducted highly publicized demonstrations against the World Bank, IMF, and World Trade Organization (WTO). At the same time, the United States continued to press the IBRD to reduce its lending to certain middle-income countries (particularly in Latin America), which, according to the United States, needed to be weaned away from World Bank lending in favor of loans from the private sector.

In 2001–2002 the IBRD called on the wealthy nations of the world to increase their assistance to developing countries substantially, particularly in view of the global economic slowdown, which had exacerbated debt problems. The bank acknowledged that the HIPC Initiative had so far come up very short in reaching the goal of "sustainable" debt for the 34 countries considered eligible for assistance. Nevertheless, bank officials maintained their hope that more than $50 billion in debt would ultimately be canceled through the program.

IBRD lending approvals increased dramatically to $21.1 billion for 151 projects in 1997–1998 and $22.2 billion for 131 projects in 1998–1999, primarily due to the financial crises in Asia and Latin America. However, after conditions improved and the private sector resumed lending to emerging market economies, IBRD approvals declined to $10.9 billion for 97 projects in 1999–2000, $10.5 billion for 91 projects in 2000–2001, and $11.5 billion for 96 projects in 2000–2002. The reduced lending also underscored the bank's increased emphasis on "quality rather than quantity" in its lending. Special assistance was provided in 2002 for countries that had suffered particularly strong "economic shocks" in the wake of the September 11, 2001, attacks in the United States and the economic downturn that had begun even prior to those events. As of mid-2002, cumulative IBRD lending had reached over $370 billion for more than 4,600 projects.

In May 2004 the Group of Eight (G-8) pledged to continue the HPIC Debt Initiative then is scheduled to expire at the end of the year. It was estimated that some 25 countries had qualified for debt relief to date. Meanwhile, President Wolfensohn blamed the industrialized countries for the collapse of WTO negotiations in 2003, arguing that developing countries deserved a stronger voice in the global economy. Wolfensohn also said it was "unacceptable" that unprecedented military spending around the world was impeding efforts to help the poor.

In March 2005 the U.S. George W. Bush administration announced that Wolfensohn's successor would be Paul Wolfowitz, the U.S. deputy secretary of defense who had recently attracted attention as one of the main architects of the U.S.-led overthrow of the Saddam Hussein regime in Iraq. Considering the global antipathy to the war, the appointment was viewed as controversial. However, Wolfowitz pledged that he would not direct the World Bank as a vehicle for promoting U.S. policy and would maintain his predecessor's emphasis on reducing poverty.

In July 2005 the IBRD announced it would provide $500 million in loans for "priority sectors" in Iraq. It was the first bank lending to Iraq in three decades. In its *World Development Report* for 2006, issued September 2005, the bank declared that reducing inequality by liberal economic actions was the key to reducing poverty, while admitting that such inequality had risen. It suggested that the world's richest countries should abandon subsidies and encourage freer migration of skilled workers from developing countries. The report endorsed a decision by the G-8 countries at their July 2005 summit in Scotland to cancel some $55 billion in debt from the world's poorest countries.

Meanwhile, controversy surrounding Wolfowitz mounted as staff reportedly resented his heavy use of outside advisers. The anti-corruption measures he imposed in developing countries, one of his major pledges coming into office, came under increasing criticism. Also, a December 2006 report by the bank's Independent Evaluation Group (IEG) noted that many of the anti-corruption policies were failing because they lacked broad-based political consensus and were often implemented at the expense of poverty reduction and job creation goals. In March 2007 the World Bank executive board adopted a new policy that reined in the president's ability to cut funding without first consulting the board and allowed the bank to deal with independent groups in a country when it cut off loans to that country's government.

Two months later, Wolfowitz came under personal scrutiny over his role in engineering the promotion and salary raise of his companion, a female bank employee. He resigned in June 2007 amid calls for better internal controls and a more open and transparent hiring process for the bank president. Less influential member nations also renewed calls for more voting and decision-making powers. In July 2007 the bank appointed as president U.S. nominee Robert Zoellick, a former U.S. deputy secretary of state and U.S. trade representative. Zoellick announced a major policy shift in the bank's lending strategy that would boost funding for agricultural projects as a more effective means towards poverty reduction.

In advance of the World Bank and IMF annual meeting in October 2007, Zoellick called on wealthy nations to significantly increase their financial support for poor nations as part of a plan to more than double the bank's funding in grants and credits for poor countries under the IDA. He directed the IBRD and the IFC to increase contributions to the IDA as well.

In September 2007 the bank's executive board simplified and reduced loan charges by a quarter percentage point for the 79 credit-worthy countries funded by the IBRD. The change was part of an effort to increase the relevancy and attractiveness of the IBRD, which has faced competition from private sector lending sources.

As the price of food increased dramatically, causing distress in many countries of the world, the World Bank took a new interest in farming. The 2007 edition of the *World Development Report* stressed the importance of agriculture as the fastest way of improving a poor nation's economy, and the 2008 food crisis drove the point home. In April 2008 Zoellick announced, and the World Bank endorsed, a "new deal" action plan to pump more money into agricultural economies. On April 29 the UN set up an emergency task force to deal with the food situation, the members drawn from interested UN agencies and the World Bank.

The World Bank reported providing $47 billion in loans during the 2009 fiscal year, with $33 billion coming from the IBRD and $14 billion from the IDA. It provided $25 billion for 2008 (IBRD $14 billion and IDA $11 billion) and $25 billion for 2007 (IBRD $13 billion and IDA $12 billion).

During 2009 the World Bank issued various statements about the global financial crisis. On April 24 it published a report declaring that the United States and the EU were leading the world in a new round of protectionism. Also in April Zoellick warned of a "human catastrophe" unless more was done to combat the economic crisis. By September 2009 the organization warned that, while things might be going better for the world's rich, the poor were in no way recovering.

In March 2009 the World Bank launched a commission to investigate its own operations and suggest ways in which it might improve. The commission, headed by former Mexican president Ernesto Zedillo, released its report in October 2009. Among other suggestions, the Zedillo commission recommended restructuring the bank's governing bodies, strengthening management accountability, and making the selection of a president "merit-based, transparent, and open." Through 2009, the IBRD was funding 126 projects around the world.

At the IMF–World Bank spring meeting in April 2010, the capitalization of the World Bank was bolstered for the first time since 1988. The capital for the IBRD was increased to $86.2 billion as part of an agreement whereby developing states agreed to increase their capitalization in exchange for greater voting power, elevating the share of votes held by developing states from 44 percent to 47.2 percent. China was the greatest beneficiary. Its vote share would rise from 2.8 percent to 4.2 percent. In June Tuvalu became the 187th member of the IBRD. MIGA's *World Investment and Political Risk 2010* reported that foreign direct investment into developing countries would increase by 17 percent, but that political instability remained the main concern for investors and hampered an even greater inflow of funds.

Through 2011 the World Bank approved $42 billion in new loans and grants, with the IBRD accounting for $26 billion and the IDA $16 billion. Meanwhile, the administrative budget of the World Bank was $1.8 billion. In response to famine in the Horn of Africa and drought in other areas, the organization increased assistance for agriculture from $4.1 billion in 2008 to $8 billion in 2011. Along with the promulgation of a new long-term development plan for Africa, the World Bank provided a record $7 billion in loans and aid to the continent. In April 2012 South Sudan became the 188th member of the IBRD. By year's end, the IBRD had outstanding loans to 77 countries. Of the 188 members of the IBRD, 62 remained eligible to borrow from the institution, while 143 were able to borrow from either the IBRD or the IDA at the beginning of 2013.

In 2013 the IBRD had more than 100 offices worldwide and a staff of more than 9,000. In May 2013 Standard and Poor's reaffirmed the IBRD's credit rating as "AAA," although the organization's operating income decreased to $783 million in 2012, down from $1.02 billion the previous year. In addition, the IBRD had a net operating loss in 2012 of $676 million, down from a surplus of $930 million in 2011. Through June of 2013, IBRD revenues were again positive for the year, at $218 million. One result was that the board of governors approved in August, the transfer of $147 million to the general reserve.

The World Bank predicted in January 2014 that global economic growth would rise from 2.4 percent in 2013 to 3.2 percent in 2014, spurred on mainly by advanced economies. On April 1 the World Bank announced it increased its lending capacity to developing nations from $15 billion to $26–28 billion. In addition, the banking group would increase its total lending capacity by $100 billion to $300 billion over a ten-year period. The additional funding would be achieved by changing internal lending rules, including lengthening the terms of loans and increasing fees, instead of asking members for new funds.

In 2016 the World Bank had financial commitments of $64.2 billion to partner countries and disbursements of $49 billion, up from commitments of $59.7 billion in 2015 and disbursements of $44.6 billion in 2015. Of the commitments, Sub-Saharan Africa received $13.3 billion; Latin America and the Caribbean, $11.4 billion; East Asia and the Pacific, $11.4 billion; South Asia, $11.3 billion; Europe and Central Asia, $10.3 billion; and the Middle East and North Africa, $6.3 billion. In April 2016 Naura became the 189th member of the World Bank Group.

INTERNATIONAL DEVELOPMENT ASSOCIATION, A MEMBER OF THE WORLD BANK GROUP

(IDA)

Established: By Articles of Agreement concluded in Washington, D.C., January 26, 1960, effective September 24, 1960. The IDA became a UN Specialized Agency by agreement with the Economic and Social Council (approved by the General Assembly on March 27, 1961).

Purpose: To assist in financing economic development in less developed member states by providing development credits on special terms, with particular emphasis on projects not attractive to private investors.

Headquarters: Washington, D.C., United States.

Website: www.worldbank.org/ida.

Membership (173): See Appendix C.

Working Language: English.

Origin and development. The IDA was established in response to an increasing awareness during the latter 1950s that the needs of less developed states for additional capital resources could not be fully satisfied through existing lending institutions and procedures. This was particularly true of the very poor states, which urgently needed finance on terms more concessionary than those of the International Bank for Reconstruction and Development (IBRD). Thus, in 1958 the United States proposed the creation of an institution with authority to provide credits on special terms in support of approved development projects for which normal financing was not available. Following approval by the Board of Governors of the IBRD, the IDA was established as an affiliate of that institution and was given a mandate to provide development financing, within the limits of its resources, on terms more flexible than those of conventional loans and less burdensome to the balance of payments of recipient states. Today, the IBRD and the IDA together are generally known as the World Bank.

The authorized capital of the IDA was initially fixed at $1 billion, of which the United States contributed $320 million. Members of the institution were divided by the IDA Articles of Agreement into two groups in accordance with their economic status and the nature of their contributions to the institution's resources. Part I (high-income) states pay their entire subscription in convertible currencies, all of which may be used for IDA credits; Part II (low-income) states pay only 10 percent of their subscriptions in convertible currencies and the remainder in their own currencies. Part I countries account for about 97 percent of total subscriptions and supplementary resources (special voluntary contributions and transfers from IBRD net earnings). As of 2012, leading Part I contributors were the United States, with 10.71 percent of voting power under the IDA's weighted system; Japan, 8.55 percent; United Kingdom, 5.58 percent; Germany, 5.53; France, 3.79 percent;

and Canada, 2.58 percent. Leading Part II contributors are Saudi Arabia, 3.19 percent; India, 2.88 percent; and China, 2.06 percent. The weighted voting system has sometimes been criticized as unfair to smaller, poorer countries.

Structure. As an affiliate of the IBRD, the IDA has no separate institutions; its directors, officers, and staff are those of the IBRD.

Recent activities. The IDA is the single largest multilateral source of concessional assistance for low-income countries. Countries that had a 2015 annual per capita income of less than $1,215, had limited or no ability to borrow from the IBRD, and had good performance in implementation of IDA economic and social policies could qualify for IDA funds. IDA also provides grants to countries at risk of debt distress. To date, IDA credits and grants have totaled more than $238 billion, with the largest share, about 50 percent, directed to Africa.

Under conditions revised as part of the IDA's eighth replenishment, credits are extended for terms as long as 40 years for the least developed countries and 20 and 35 years for other countries. Credits are free of interest but there is a 0.75 percent annual service charge on disbursed credits (a 0.50 percent "commitment fee" on undisbursed credits was eliminated July 1, 1988). All credits carry a ten-year grace period, with complete repayment of principal due over the remaining 20 or 35 years of the loans.

Most IDA credits have been provided for projects to improve physical infrastructure such as road and rail systems, electrical generation and transmission facilities, irrigation and flood-control installations, educational facilities, telephone exchanges and transmission lines, and industrial plants. Loans have also been extended for rural development projects designed specifically to raise the productivity of the rural-dwelling poor. These credits often cut across sector lines.

Negotiations for the 12th replenishment, covering the period from July 1999 to June 2002, were concluded in November 1998 when, during a meeting in Copenhagen, Denmark, donor countries agreed to a $20.5 billion infusion of funds to the IDA, $11.6 billion from the donors themselves. An apparent reduction in funding from the 11th replenishment was explained by changes in exchange rates and became a 13 percent increase when the funds were measured in special drawing rights (SDRs). (For more information on previous replenishments, see the 2013 *Handbook.*)

Borrowing countries and representatives of nongovernmental organizations were invited for the first time to participate in discussions regarding the 13th replenishment. The IDA also invited public comment on the negotiations, which culminated in a three-year (July 2002 to June 2005) replenishment of $23 billion. It was agreed that about 20 percent of overall IDA resources would henceforth be allocated in the form of grants rather than loans. (The United States had called for a 50 percent grant level on the theory that lending to date had done little to combat poverty while piling debt on developing countries.) Donors also insisted that future IDA assistance be tied to measurable progress on the part of recipient countries in areas such as education and health. Similar linkage was also endorsed to reward countries that encouraged good governance, free trade, and environmental protection.

Negotiations for the 14th replenishment (for July 2006–June 2009) concluded in April 2005 in Athens, Greece. Under this agreement, $34 billion was made available to the world's 81 poorest countries, which includes $18 billion in new contributions from 40 donor countries. At almost a 25 percent increase, it was the largest expansion of IDA resources in 20 years. Additionally, the countries facing the most difficult debt problems, mostly in sub-Saharan Africa, are receiving all of their financial support in grants. Less debt-burdened countries are receiving mostly highly concessional long-term loans, or a mixture of grants and loans. Since the replenishment the IDA has approved loans that include funding for a mining project in Mauritania, electrical power generation projects in Ghana and Benin, and for educational projects in Albania.

In 2005 the IDA revised and enhanced a system to manage the success of its projects and review progress of recipient nations. Indicators such as growth and poverty reduction, governance and investment climate, infrastructure development, and human development criteria such as health and education were considered. In the 15th replenishment, completed in December 2007, to cover years 2009–2011, the IDA was to receive more than $41 billion as part of a stepped-up effort to meet 2015 Millennium Development Goals in a program designated as IDA15 Replenishment. The vast majority of funding increases were to go to Africa and South Asia, the regions farthest away from attaining poverty reduction goals. Additionally, World Bank president Robert Zoellick offered a new proposal to raise funding for the IDA from private sector businesses and foundations and pledged to focus on agricultural initiatives as a means to battle poverty. The number of IDA programs in member countries increased from 78 in 2008 to 104 in 2009. In Africa, a joint IDA–International Finance Corporation initiative provided new funding to develop small- and medium-sized companies. The IFC provided $3 million and the IDA, $1 million, for the project.

In 2010 IDA commitments totaled $14.5 billion, with pledges of $13 billion from contributing states. India was the largest recipient of IDA aid, at $2.6 billion, followed by: Vietnam, $1.4 billion; Tanzania, $943; Ethiopia, $890 million; and Nigeria, $890 million. Through 2010, 45 countries had contributed $41.6 billion to the IDA15 Replenishment project which financed programs between 2008 and 2011. The UK was the largest donor to the effort, providing 14.1 percent of the total, followed by the United States at 12.2 percent and Japan at 10 percent. In the effort, China, Cyprus, Egypt, Estonia, Latvia, and Lithuania became donors to the IDA for the first time (China and Egypt having previously been recipient countries). In response to the January earthquake in Haiti, the IDA announced a special $30 million grant to aid in recovery. Meanwhile, the IDA agreed in June to debt relief of $4.6 billion for Liberia and in July to support debt relief of $12.3 billion for the Democratic Republic of the Congo, among other debt initiatives.

At a donor meeting in Brussels December 14–15, 2010, it was agreed to replenish the IDA with a record US $49.3 billion funding package, an 18 percent increase over the previous replenishment three years previously. The agreement was noteworthy for having strong pledges from both traditional and new donors, contributions through prepayments from countries that used to borrow interest-free loans from IDA, and contributions from World Bank and IFC net income. Observers felt that such a replenishment, at a time of considerable economic stress for donors, was a testament to IDA's track record of delivering results and value for money.

In February 2011 the IDA approved an additional $420 million for protection of basic services in Ethiopia. In July it announced over $500 million in aid to the victims of drought in the Horn of Africa. In August it announced a grant of $19 million "to strengthen the capacity of Afghanistan's Central Bank to foster a sound financial system." Through 2011 the IDA launched 230 new initiatives, worth $16.3 billion. Approximately 50 percent of the projects were in Africa. In addition, 17 percent of the funding came in the form of grants. An IDA report found that from 2000 to 2010, the organization, among other activities, recruited or trained more than 3 million teachers, provided immunization for 310 million people, and provided assistance to improve access to clean water and sanitation for 113 million people.

In the fiscal year that ended on June 31, 2013, the IDA committed $16.3 billion to 160 new projects, 15 percent of which were grants. By 2013, 82 countries, with a combined population of 2.5 billion, were eligible for funding from the IDA. Negotiations for the 17th Replenishment began in March 2013 at a conference in Paris. At the meeting, participants endorsed the priorities of climate change, gender equality, and support for fragile and conflict-affected states. The meeting also backed new guidelines for states to graduate from the IDA to the IBRD. Subsequent sessions were held in Managua, Nicaragua, in July, and Washington, D.C., in October. In December IDA members agreed to provide a record $52.1 billion during the 17th replenishment.

In 2014 India "graduated" from the IDA and began transitioning to the IBRD over a two-year period during which it would continue to receive support on an "exceptional basis." That year, 77 countries, with a combined population of 2.8 billion, were eligible for IDA funding. Total funding in 2014 was $22.3 billion for 242 new programs or loans. The top borrowers were India, $3.1 billion; Pakistan, $2 billion; Bangladesh, $1.9 billion; and Nigeria and Ethiopia, both at $1.6 billion.

In 2015 the IDA had financial commitments of $19 billion. Of that amount, 13 percent was in the form of grants that required no repayment.

In December 2016 the IDA announced that its 18th replenishment (IDA18) had raised $75 billion from 60 donor governments. IDA18 would run from 2017–2020. Among the specific goals of the period were to provide enhanced access to potable water for 45 million people, immunizations for 130–180 million children, and training for up to 10 million teachers.

INTERNATIONAL FINANCE CORPORATION

(IFC)

Established: By Articles of Agreement concluded in Washington, D.C., May 25, 1955, effective July 20, 1956. The IFC became a UN

Specialized Agency by agreement with the Economic and Social Council (approved by the General Assembly on February 20, 1957).

Purpose: To further economic development by encouraging the growth of productive private enterprise in member states, particularly the less developed areas. Its investment is usually in private or partially governmental enterprises.

Headquarters: Washington, D.C., United States.

Website: www.ifc.org.

Membership (184): See Appendix C.

Working Language: English.

Origin and development. A suggestion that an international agency be formed to extend loans to private enterprises without government guarantees and to undertake equity investments in participation with other investors was made in 1951 by the U.S. International Development Advisory Board. That summer the UN Economic and Social Council requested that the International Bank for Reconstruction and Development (IBRD) investigate the possibility of creating such an agency, and a staff report was submitted to the UN secretary-general in April 1952. The General Assembly in late 1954 requested the IBRD to draw up a charter, and the following April the bank formally submitted a draft for consideration. The IFC came into being on July 20, 1956, when 31 governments representing a sufficient percentage of total capital subscriptions accepted the Articles of Agreement.

Structure. As an affiliate of the IBRD, and thus a member of the World Bank Group, the IFC shares the same institutional structure. The president of the IBRD is also president of the IFC, and those governors and executive directors of the IBRD whose states belong to the IFC hold identical positions in the latter institution. The corporation has its own operating and legal staff but draws on the bank for administrative and other services. An executive vice president directs daily operations. As is true of the IBRD and the IDA, the IFC employs a weighted voting system based on country subscriptions, but with less developed states holding a disproportionate share of voting power.

IFC investments are handled through sectors, or industry departments, that process transactions and provide regional departments with expertise. They include Agribusiness; Global Financial Markets; Global Manufacturing and Services; Health and Education; Information and Communication Technologies; Infrastructure; Oil, Gas, Mining, and Chemicals; Private Equity and Investment Funds; and Subnational Finance. The corporation divides its 3,400 employees roughly in half between field offices (some 51 percent) and agency headquarters (some 49 percent). In 2013 there were field offices in 80 countries.

Recent activities. The IFC concentrates its efforts in three principal areas: project finance; resource mobilization; and financial, technical, and other advisory services. It conducts its own investment program, investigates the soundness of proposed projects to furnish expert advice to potential investors, and generally seeks to promote conditions conducive to the flow of private investment into development tasks. Investments, in the form of share subscriptions and long-term loans, are made in projects of economic priority to less developed member states where sufficient private capital is not available on reasonable terms and when the projects offer acceptable prospects for adequate returns. The IFC also carries out standby and underwriting arrangements and, under a policy adopted in July 1968, may give support in the pre-investment stage of potential projects by helping to pay for feasibility studies and for coordinating industrial, technical, and financial components, including the search for business sponsors. In addition, the IFC may join other investment groups interested in backing pilot or promotional companies, which then carry out the necessary studies and negotiations needed to implement the projects. The corporation neither seeks nor accepts government guarantees in its operations.

(For changes to authorized capital, and for other activities, prior to 1994, see the 2011 *Handbook.*) On January 1, 1994, Jannik Landbaek of Norway, previously vice president of the Nordic Investment Bank (NIB), took over as IFC executive vice president. Peter Woicke of Germany, a former investment banker for J. P. Morgan for 29 years, succeeded him on January 1, 1999. During his five-year tenure, Woicke was credited for making the IFC "operate less like an international bureaucracy and more like a private-sector financial institution." Under a massive reorganization, Woicke shifted the IFC's resources away from large corporations in developed countries to smaller local companies that became increasingly involved in the global market. In 2004 the corporation had a record $982 million in operation profits, nearly 90 percent more than in 2003, with 80 percent of business involving small companies. Woicke also made strides in tightening corporate governance. Following his retirement in January 2005, Woicke was succeeded by Assad Jabre of Lebanon, who served as acting executive vice president until the permanent appointment of Lars H. Thunnel of Sweden, effective January 1, 2006. On August 12, 2012, Jin-Yong Cai of China, was appointed executive vice president.

The IFC has also continued to emphasize good corporate governance and greater loan transparency, due in part to the corporate scandals that erupted in the United States and elsewhere in the early 2000s. In November 2002 the IFC created three new environmental funds to encourage private sector investors to be aware of environmental and social issues in emerging markets. They include the Environmental Opportunities Facility to provide funding for innovative projects addressing local environmental concerns, the Sustainable Financial Markets Facility to address environmentally and socially responsible lending and investments, and the Corporate Citizenship Facility to work more closely with project sponsors. In November 2003, the IFC also established guidelines, known as the Equator Principles, to ensure banks invest in projects that are both environmentally and socially sound. In 2006 the IFC began programs to improve labor standards in global supply chains in partnership with the International Labour Organization. Under World Bank Group president Robert Zoellick's direction in 2007, the IFC began integrating financing with the bank's public sector arms. In late 2007, the IFC contributed $1.75 billion to the International Development Association (IDA) for private-sector development in the poorest nations; the program was slated to run through 2010.

The IFC also doubled the size of its global trade financing program to $1 billion in 2007 in order to boost trade among small- and medium-sized import and export businesses. In recent years the program has focused increasingly on investment projects in the poorest nations and post-conflict areas, such as the Democratic Republic of the Congo, Liberia, Lebanon, and Sierra Leone. In October 2007, the IFC announced the launch of the new $5 billion Global Emergency Markets Local Currency Bond Fund to help countries develop local currency bond markets to attract more private investment and allow poor nations to borrow using their own currencies. In an innovative development, in May 2008 the IFC announced a partnership with Standard Chartered Bank to issue notes backed by loans to microfinance institutions in Africa and Asia. These notes establish a new product to provide investors with access to microfinance as an asset class, and it will enable Standard Chartered to expand its lending to the microfinance sector.

The IFC reported investments of $11.4 billion for the 2008 fiscal year, with an additional $4.7 billion raised from outside sources for 372 projects in 85 countries. It also reported that it provided advisory services in 97 countries. The 2009 fiscal year saw some contraction in light of the global financial crisis. IFC financing for private sector development totaled $14.5 billion, including $4.0 billion obtained through syndications, structured finance, and crisis-related initiatives, down from the record $19 billion high of the previous year. IFC invested in 447 projects during the year, of which half were in IDA countries.

As part of its response to the economic crisis, in May 2009 IFC took an unprecedented step in launching a subsidiary to act as a fund manager for third-party capital. The new unit, called IFC Asset Management Company, LLC, initially was to manage a $3 billion IFC Recapitalization Fund, which was designed to protect emerging-markets banks from the effects of the global downturn. Now, it will also manage a new $1 billion private equity fund that will allow national pension funds, sovereign funds, and other sovereign investors from IFC's shareholder countries to support investments in IFC transactions in Africa, Latin America, and the Caribbean.

In 2010 the IFC allocated $18 billion to projects, $12.7 billion from its own accounts, the rest secured through donor states or cooperative financing arrangements. The IFC launched 528 new projects, an 18 percent increase over the previous year. By the end of the year, the IFC had ongoing projects in 58 countries and the newly formed Asset Management Company had raised $950 million. In response to the global financial crisis, the IFC committed more than $11 billion to financial stabilization and recovery projects. This included $6 billion from the IFC, $2 billion raised in additional funding from donor states, and the remainder from matching finance programs. Investments in clean energy grew substantially to account for 15 percent of the total services portfolio.

In February 2011 the IFC launched a new fund of up to €150 million to purchase carbon credits to help reduce greenhouse-gas emissions, extend carbon markets, and increase access to finance for projects that promote environmentally friendly economic growth. The IFC was to invest up to €15 million, the remainder to come from European energy companies and power utilities. On March 23 it announced that it had become the first multilateral development bank to sign the United Nations Principles for Responsible Investment, as part of its efforts to mobilize capital for investments that are environmentally and socially responsible and adhere to high standards of corporate governance.

In August 2011 the IFC announced that fiscal 2011 had been a record year for its support of trade flows in emerging markets, with more than half the total volume of $4.6 billion supporting trade in the world's poorest countries. During 2011 the IFC invested more than $1.7 billion in programs to address climate change. For instance, the IFC provided assistance for a project to build wind power farms in a remote area of the Gobi Desert. Meanwhile the IFC reported income of $2.2 billion in 2011, up from $1.9 billion the previous year. Grants to the IFC were $600 million, an increase from $200 million in 2010.

The IFC's 2013 annual report highlighted the expansion of the organization's programs and support for developing states. The IFC provided a record $25 billion for private sector development, of which $5 billion went to sub-Saharan Africa, and $2 billion to South Asia. In addition, the IFC increased the assets of its subsidiary venture capital group, the IFC Management Company, by $5.5 billion. IFC projects in 2012–2013 provided employment for 2.7 million, along with power for 52.2 million, and water for 42 million.

In 2014 the IFC had a net income of $1.5 billion on its loans and investments, with total assets of $84.1 billion. The IFC funded 599 projects worth $22 billion in 98 countries. Latin America and the Caribbean received the largest amount of funding, $4.1 billion, followed by sub-Saharan Africa at $3.5 billion and Europe and central Asia at $3.5 billion. By 2014, India was the largest single recipient of IFC loans, with $4.7 billion in cumulative financing, followed by Turkey, with $3.2 billion, and China with $3.1 billion. In October 2014, the IFC announced an initiative to provide $13.6 million in emergency funding for businesses in areas of West Africa impacted by Ebola.

In 2016 the IFC funded 344 projects in 78 countries worth $18.8 billion. East Asia and the Pacific received $5.2 billion; Latin America and the Caribbean, $5.1 billion; Europe and Central Asia, $2.6 billion; Sub-Saharan Africa, $2.4 billion; South Asia, $2 billion; and the Middle East and North Africa, $1.3 billion.

WORLD HEALTH ORGANIZATION

(WHO)

Established: By constitution signed in New York, United States, July 22, 1946, effective April 7, 1948. WHO became a UN Specialized Agency by agreement with the Economic and Social Council (approved by the General Assembly on November 15, 1947, with effect from September 1, 1948).

Purpose: To aid in "the attainment by all peoples of the highest possible levels of health."

Headquarters: Geneva, Switzerland.

Principal Organs: World Health Assembly (all members), Executive Board (32 experts), Regional Committees (all regional members), Secretariat.

Website: www.who.int/en.

Director General: Margaret Chan (Hong Kong SAR).

Membership (194, plus 2 Associate Members): See Appendix C.

Official Languages: Arabic, Chinese, English, French, Russian, Spanish.

Origin and development. Attempts to institutionalize international cooperation in health matters originated as early as 1851 but reached full fruition only with establishment of WHO. The need for a single international health agency was emphasized in a special declaration of the UN Conference on International Organization held in 1945 in San Francisco, California, and the constitution of WHO was adopted at the specially convened International Health Conference held in June–July 1946 in New York. Formally established on April 8, 1948, WHO also took over the functions of the International Office of Public Health, established in 1907; those of the League of Nations Health Organization; and the health activities of the UN Relief and Rehabilitation Administration (UNRRA).

A turning point in WHO's evolution occurred in 1976. As a result of decisions reached during that year's World Health Assembly, it began to reorient its work so that by 1980 a full 60 percent of its regular budget would be allocated for technical cooperation and for the provision of services to member states. In addition, all nonessential expenditures were to be eliminated, resulting in a reduction of several hundred administrative positions. (For more information on events prior to 1980, see the 2012 *Handbook.*)

Controversy at the 32nd World Health Assembly was generated by an abortive attempt by Arab representatives to suspend Israeli membership. The United States, objecting to politicization of the organization, warned that it would probably withdraw from WHO if the proposal were adopted. At the 33rd assembly in May 1980, Arab members succeeded in gaining approval of a resolution that declared "the establishment of Israeli settlements in the occupied Arab territories, including Palestine, a source of "serious damage" to the inhabitants' health. Moreover, the conferees condemned the "inhuman practices to which Arab prisoners and detainees are subject in Israeli prisons." A clause that would have denied Israel's membership rights was deleted from a resolution before the 35th assembly in May 1982, after the United States had again threatened withdrawal.

In 1989 a proposal to grant membership to the Palestine Liberation Organization (PLO) received strong backing from Arab states and many developing countries but was condemned by the United States, which threatened to withhold its WHO contribution. The assembly deferred the question and in 1990 postponed action "indefinitely," although it increased direct assistance to Palestinians. Currently, Palestine has observer status in the WHO. Taiwan has been denied membership eight times, most recently in 2004, because China claims sovereignty and has successfully blocked its bids.

The 1994 assembly received a director general's report outlining recent budgetary and accounting reforms, with even stricter controls subsequently being recommended by some WHO members. At the same session the assembly reinstated South Africa, under suspension since 1964, to full membership privileges.

Controversy broke out over Director General Nakajima at the 1995 assembly. WHO's external auditor told the assembly that the WHO Secretariat failed to cooperate with his inquiry into alleged fraud, waste, and financial impropriety. Consequently, the assembly rejected Nakajima's request for a 16 percent increase in the WHO regular budget, approving instead a total of $842.7 million for the 1996–1997 biennium, an increase of only 2.5 percent. At the 1998 World Health Assembly, Dr. Gro Harlem Brundtland, former prime minister of Norway, was elected director general, effective in July. In August 2002 Brundtland announced she would not run for reelection, adding that she was content with the progress WHO had made during her tenure. (Brundtland is widely credited for coining the term "sustainable development.") Lee Jong-Wook, a South Korean doctor with expertise on vaccines and diseases associated with poverty, was selected as director general in January 2003. In May 2006 Dr. Lee died suddenly, and was replaced in an acting capacity by his deputy, Dr. Anders Nordström of Sweden. In November 2006 the assembly appointed Margaret Chan as director general. Chan was the former health director of Hong Kong during the severe acute respiratory syndrome (SARS) outbreak and had worked for three years at WHO in various high level posts.

Structure. The World Health Assembly, in which all members are represented, is the principal political organ of WHO. At its annual sessions, usually held at WHO headquarters in May, the assembly approves the organization's long-range work program as well as its annual program and budget. International health conventions may be approved and recommended to governments by a two-thirds majority vote. The assembly similarly adopts technical health regulations that come into force immediately for those governments that do not specifically reject them.

The Executive Board is composed of 32 members who, although designated by governments selected by the assembly, serve in an individual expert capacity rather than as governmental representatives. Meeting at least twice a year, the board prepares the assembly agenda and oversees implementation of assembly decisions. The Secretariat is headed by a director general designated by the assembly on recommendation of the board.

WHO is the least centralized of the UN Specialized Agencies, much of its program centering on six regional organizations: Southeast Asia (headquartered in New Delhi, India); the Eastern Mediterranean

(Cairo, Egypt); the Western Pacific (Manila, Philippines); the Americas (Washington, D.C.); Africa (Brazzaville, Congo); and Europe (Copenhagen, Denmark). Each of the six has a regional committee of all members in the area and an office headed by a regional director.

Recent activities. Generally considered one of the more successful UN agencies, WHO acts as a guiding authority on international health work, actively promotes cooperation in health matters, sets global health standards, and works toward development and transfer of health-related technology and information. Since the early 1980s WHO has accepted as a leading principle "Health for All," which in its most recent incarnation entails the equitable distribution of health resources coupled with universal access to essential health services. In addition, WHO has increasingly emphasized that the public itself needs to make wiser choices, including adherence to healthier lifestyles, to escape "the avoidable burden of disease." WHO identified ten major avoidable health risks in its October 2002 annual report that are responsible for 56 million deaths each year, including hunger, unprotected sex, high blood pressure, smoking, alcohol, contaminated water or poor sanitation, high cholesterol, nutritional deficiencies, and obesity. As part of a landmark strategy to combat obesity, the organization encouraged governments to increase taxes on foods with high sugar, salt, and saturated fat content, which prompted strong opposition from the sugar industry in 2004. However, the nonbinding strategy was ultimately adopted in May 2004 and endorses a series of policy guidelines.

The organization is perhaps best known for its highly successful immunization programs, beginning with its coordination of the worldwide smallpox vaccination campaign that by 1980 had eradicated the disease. WHO announced in January 2002 that the destruction of the remaining smallpox stocks would be postponed for up to three years to give researchers more time to develop new treatments and vaccines for the disease after terrorist attacks sparked fears that the virus could be used as a weapon. Following the September 11, 2001, terrorist attacks in the United States, U.S. president George W. Bush's administration stockpiled the vaccine. In 1974 WHO also embarked, in conjunction with the UN Children's Fund (UNICEF), on a worldwide campaign to immunize children against measles, poliomyelitis, diphtheria, pertussis (whooping cough), tetanus, and tuberculosis (TB); hepatitis B was added in 1992, as was yellow fever in relevant geographical areas. In June 2002 WHO declared Europe free of polio, marking it as the third region worldwide to be certifiably free of the disease.

Soon after taking office, Director General Brundtland set about reorganizing WHO, reducing its programs from 50 to 35 and placing them in nine clusters. Subsequent restructuring brought the number of clusters down to eight and then to six in a further realignment in October 2007 under Director General Chan.

WHO organizes its clusters into broad areas of disease management. The Health Security and Environment cluster, formerly named the Communicable Disease cluster, includes the Department of Epidemic and Pandemic Alert and Response; the Department of Protection of the Human Environment; and the Department of Food Safety, Zoonoses [diseases transmitted through contact with animals], and Food-borne Diseases. The changes reflect an expansion in the agency's scope to encompass environmental hazards and foodborne diseases as a result of implementation in 2007 of the International Health Regulations (IHR) of 2005.

The Noncommunicable Diseases and Mental Health cluster, which retained its name under the realignment, has a broad mandate that includes issues regarding aging, psychiatric and other mental disorders, substance abuse, tobacco use, violence and injury prevention, and oral health as well as such "lifestyle" diseases as diabetes, avoidable blindness, cardiovascular disease, and cancer. The 1999 World Health Assembly opened negotiations on the Framework Convention on Tobacco Control (FCTC), and tumultuous negotiations continued until May 2003 when all of the 192 member countries ultimately adopted the landmark treaty. The United States, a reluctant supporter, was the last country to sign on because of contentious language on advertising that the United States said could violate constitutional rights to free speech. The treaty regulates that health warnings must be no less than 30 percent the size of a cigarette pack, bans terms such as "light" and "low tar," encourages higher taxes on tobacco products, and condemns certain marketing methods. The treaty went into force in February 2005 and has been ratified by 146 countries. A second FCTC meeting of signatory countries in July 2007 in Bangkok, Thailand, reviewed further changes to the tobacco treaty, including the development of protocols to curb illicit trade in tobacco products and exposure to second-hand smoke.

The HIV/AIDS, TB, Malaria, and Neglected Tropical Diseases cluster includes the Department of Neglected Tropical Diseases. Longstanding WHO efforts to eradicate polio and control maladies such as "river blindness" (onchocerciasis), lymphatic filariasis, "Chagas disease" (American trypanosomiasis), guinea-worm disease (dracunculiasis), leprosy, and Buruli ulcer fall under this cluster. In October 2006 the agency announced new guidelines to tackle "neglected" tropical diseases, which would include the use of inexpensive, preventative drugs in both healthy and infected people.

Additionally, the cluster handles the Department of HIV/AIDS, a major focus of WHO attention since the 1993 World Health Assembly called for a coordinated attack against the condition. In early 1996 WHO became one of the original cosponsoring agencies of the resultant Joint UN Program on HIV/AIDS (UNAIDS), which later set a millennium development goal of reversing the spread of the disease by 2015. Since then, a number of coordinated efforts to track the spread of the disease and provide treatment to ailing populations have been formed. The "3 by 5" program launched in 2003 by UNAIDS had a target of providing 3 million people with antiretroviral treatment by the end of 2005. In July 2004 WHO officials said they would meet that target, but by 2005 it became clear that the agency would far fall short. High drug prices and delivery problems were blamed for the agency's delivery of drugs to only 1 million people.

In September 2003 WHO announced it would organize a drug-buying facility for AIDS treatments to make it easier for developing countries to access treatments. Additionally, in 2005 the Global Price Reporting Mechanism for Antiretroviral Drugs was created to screen and share drug prices with procurement agencies to allow price comparisons for optimal purchasing.

Subsequent efforts on handling HIV/AIDS have moved toward the goal of providing universal access to prevention and treatment programs. The June 2006 General Assembly set a new goal of achieving such access by 2010. However, the release later that year of the *UNAIDS/WHO 2006 AIDS Epidemic Update* suggested the task would be more difficult than anticipated, reporting a resurgence in new HIV infection rates in some countries that were previously stable or in decline. Though the largest number of infection rates continued to be in sub-Saharan Africa, the report stated that Eastern Europe and Central Asia had HIV growth rates of more than 50 percent in some areas. In 2006, 2.9 million people died of AIDS-related illnesses globally, and 4.3 million were newly infected, according to the report. Though there was "a positive trend in young people's sexual behaviors," the report noted that many HIV prevention programs were not reaching people most at risk.

However, an April 2007 progress report on universal access found some encouraging trends. Nearly one-third of those living with HIV/AIDS in low- and middle-income countries were receiving treatment. Antiretroviral drug prices in those same countries had reduced from one-third to one-half between the years 2003–2006. The signs of progress were offset by a warning that treatment needed to be greatly expanded to account for a steep increase in future need. It also outlined the emergence of an alarming growth in drug-resistant tuberculosis in settings of high HIV prevalence.

In other areas, WHO's Information, Evidence, and Research cluster focuses on epidemiology, statistics, quality assurance, access to care, cost-effectiveness, health system reform, and regulatory and legislative matters. It also publishes the *Bulletin of the World Health Organization* and the annual *World Health Report.* The cluster includes the Special Program for Research and Training in Tropical Diseases and the newly created Department on Ethics, Equity, Trade, and Human Rights. The latter handles information on bioethics and ethical aspects of health care delivery and research. Additionally, WHO publishes the *International Pharmacopoeia* and the *WHO Model List of Essential Drugs* (more than 330 in the 2007 edition), establishes drug standards, and assists in the formulation of national drug policies.

WHO played a significant role during the SARS outbreak in 2003, which centered in China and caused the deaths of at least 78 people worldwide (for more on the history of the WHO, see the 2014 *Handbook*). To stem the outbreak, WHO urged airports in affected cities to screen ill passengers and connected a network of 11 laboratories in nine countries to identify the agent causing the illness and devise treatments—a rapid response strategy considered unprecedented for the organization. However, research efforts were temporarily hindered when Chinese officials repeatedly denied WHO experts access to the Guangdong Province, where the disease was believed to have originated. China eventually relented and provided data, although not full access, to WHO. By June 2003 the organization announced that the SARS outbreak was over in Vietnam and in Hong Kong.

The following month WHO approved sweeping new powers to respond to international health threats such as SARS. The resolution established round-the-clock communication between countries, allows WHO to use nonofficial sources of information such as reports from nongovernmental organizations or the news media to respond to threats, authorizes the organization to issue global alerts, and authorizes the director general to send teams to conduct on-the-spot studies to ensure countries take adequate measures to stop diseases from spreading.

In recent years WHO has been active in coordinating tsunami relief, has continued its efforts against the spread of avian influenza, and has seen the world's first global health treaty, the Framework Convention on Tobacco Control, come into force (February 2005). The organization subsequently decided to hire only nonsmokers.

In an external development that could have a significant impact on WHO's future activities, American financier Warren Buffet announced in July 2006 that he was giving $31 billion of his fortune to the Bill and Melinda Gates Foundation, a philanthropy dedicated to "bringing innovations in health and learning to the global community." Some commentators suggested that this gift would create a private health-related charity with a larger budget than WHO.

The 2007 *World Health Report* focused on public health in a time of environmental changes and diseases that spread rapidly around the world. It called for complete implementation of the IHR as well as increased global cooperation and surveillance in public health matters. In a related effort, in October 2007 WHO announced support for a campaign to register every birth in the world, pointing out the dangers to which unregistered children are subject.

The 61st World Health Assembly, held May 19–24, 2008, in Geneva, was attended by a record number of participants. It endorsed a six-year plan to deal with noncommunicable diseases, which are considered the leading threats to human health in the early twenty-first century. It also called for a draft strategy by 2010 to deal with the harmful use of alcohol and requested more information about the health aspects of migrant environments. Assembly participants asked member states to work decisively against the effects of climate change and to utilize education and legislation to eliminate female genital mutilation.

The year 2008 was notable for the increasing danger from diseases that had been thought completely or nearly extinct, coupled with a decline in childhood immunization rates in advanced countries. WHO warned about the spread of drug-resistant tuberculosis, which had grown to account for 20 percent of all cases. But it noted that a cheap, rapid test for the condition was had become available. WHO sent vaccine to Paraguay to combat a yellow fever outbreak and to the Sahel when polio emerged in the region, but it was able to declare Somalia free of tuberculosis and Zimbabwe of polio. A June 2008 report declared that there was no longer the threat of an AIDS pandemic among heterosexuals, except in Africa. In September 2008 WHO criticized China for initially not doing more to stop the sale of melamine-tainted milk products; the organization then issued guidelines to help affected countries assess and deal with the problem.

In a sign that some stability was returning to Iraq, in July 2008 the WHO office in Baghdad reopened. In October 2008 WHO scientific experts agreed to a research agenda to develop an evidence-based framework for action on human health in a time of climate change.

The 2008 *World Health Report,* published in October of that year, noted inequities in health care around the world, even between areas of the same country a few miles apart, and recommended a renewed emphasis on primary medicine. A December 2008 report pointed out that essential medicines were out many people's reach. The May 2009 World Health Assembly was dominated by concerns about the H1N1 strain of influenza, which threatened to become a pandemic. It also noted efforts to fight new strains of drug-resistant tuberculosis. On June 12, 2009, Director General Chan declared H1N1 influenza to be pandemic.

In September 2009 a WHO-sponsored study found the leading causes of death among children and young adults to be road accidents, suicide, and complications from childbirth. By October 2009, with a vaccine against H1N1 influenza becoming available, the WHO advised that in most cases people over ten years of age need only receive a single dose in order to be protected.

A cholera outbreak in Haiti following the January 2010 earthquake, and other outbreaks in Pakistan and central Africa, led the WHO global task force on cholera control to issue new guidelines for the treatment and prevention of the disease. The task force noted that there are 3–5 million cases and 100,000–200,000 deaths every year from cholera, but that 80 percent of cases can be effectively treated with oral rehydration medicines. In March WHO launched a campaign to vaccinate 85 million children against polio in central and West Africa, in a partnership with the Red Cross and Red Crescent societies. The project was funded by $30 million from Rotary International. Global efforts to vaccinate children against polio had reduced the number of cases from 350,000 in 1988 to 1,600 in 2009. Also in March a WHO report warned that drug-resistant strains of tuberculosis accounted for 3.6 percent of all cases, or 440,000 people, a new record. WHO officials announced in April that the organization's efforts to publicize the H1N1 influenza pandemic were flawed and created confusion. WHO did report that the H1N1 pandemic killed 17,770 people. In August Chan declared the pandemic to be over.

In April 2011 the WHO warned that the world was losing the battle against antibiotic-resistant infections. It reported that in the EU alone over 25,000 people die each year of infections that have become resistant to all medications. The worst of the "superbugs" originated in India or Pakistan, and the WHO warned people who were thinking of traveling to these countries for inexpensive surgery to do extreme diligence on the hospitals where they would be treated. The only long-term solution that the WHO could offer was a worldwide effort to develop more and better antibiotics, if the world was to avoid a pandemic of untreatable diseases.

The 64th World Health Assembly, held May 16–24, 2011, in Geneva, put off a decision about finally destroying all stocks of live smallpox virus. This destruction had been provisionally scheduled for 2016, but the WHO agreed to put off any discussion until 2014. The disease is believed to have been eradicated, but the United States and Russia oppose final destruction, wanting to do more research in case smallpox should reappear, perhaps as a biological weapon. Iran favored destruction. The matter has been under debate since 1986. In July the WHO called for a ban on blood tests for active tuberculosis. It stated that such tests were 50 percent unreliable, both as to false negatives and false positives, and were as much of a threat to world health as the disease itself.

The WHO staff proposed a budget of $4.8 billion for 2012–2013; however, the organization's executive board revised the budget downward to $3.95 billion in light of the global economic crisis and concurrent constraints on donor funding. Programs in Africa would receive 25.2 percent of the funding, followed by Southeast Asia at 10.9 percent and the Eastern Mediterranean at 9.1 percent. In May 2012 Chan was elected for a second term by the General Assembly.

In June 2013 the WHO published the first comprehensive, global report on gender violence. The study estimated that 35 percent of women have experienced gender violence, the majority of which was committed by intimate partners. For instance, intimate partners were responsible for 38 percent of all murders of women. In its *World Health Statistics 2013* the WHO found that significant progress had been made on child mortality, with 27 countries having achieved their Millennium Development Goals ahead of the 2015 target. One major factor was an increase in measles vaccinations, which by 2011 covered about 84 percent of all children. Between 2000 and 2011, measles deaths decreased by 71 percent.

The WHO publication *The Global Tuberculosis Report, 2014,* revealed that 9 million people developed tuberculosis in 2013, with 56 percent of the cases in southeast Asia. India accounted for 24 percent of the cases, followed by China, with 11 percent. The report estimated the costs to suppress the global tuberculosis epidemic would be $8 billion, or $2 billion more than was available to be spent. The WHO reported that approximately 1,400 had died of Ebola in West Africa by August 2014, with more than 3,000 active cases. The WHO established an Emergency Committee to advise Chan, who subsequently declared the outbreak a public health emergency of international concern. The WHO predicted that the number of cases could exceed 20,000.

Through March 2016 the WHO reported a total of 28,646 Ebola cases, including 11,323 fatalities. The majority of deaths were in three countries: Liberia with 4,809 fatalities, followed by Sierra Leone, 3,956, and Guinea, 2,543. There were confirmed Ebola cases in seven other countries.

The WHO's budget for the 2016–2017 funding cycles was $4 billion, an increase from the 2015–2016 cycle, when the budget was $3.8 billion. The increase funded an initiative to strengthen the organization's core capacities, including hiring new staff and support for biomedical research in areas such as malaria elimination, antimicrobial resistance, and noncommunicable diseases.

WORLD INTELLECTUAL PROPERTY ORGANIZATION

(WIPO)

Established: By a convention signed in Stockholm, Sweden, July 14, 1967, entering into force April 26, 1970. WIPO became a UN Specialized Agency by a General Assembly resolution on December 17, 1974.

Purpose: To ensure administrative cooperation among numerous intellectual property "unions" and to promote, by means of cooperation among states and international organizations, the protection of "intellectual property," including literary, artistic, and scientific works; the contents of broadcasts, films, and photographs; and all types of inventions, industrial designs, and trademarks.

Headquarters: Geneva, Switzerland.

Principal Organs: General Assembly (172 members), Conference (all members), Coordination Committee (80 members), Program and Budget Committee (41 members), Permanent Committee on Cooperation for Development Related to Intellectual Property (all members), Standing Committee on Information Technologies (all state members plus seven nonvoting organizations), International Bureau.

Website: www.wipo.int/portal/index.html.en.

Director General: Dr. Francis Gurry (Australia).

Membership (189): See Appendix C.

Working Languages: Arabic, Chinese, English, French, Portuguese, Russian, Spanish.

Origin and development. The origins of WIPO can be traced to the establishment of the Paris Convention on the Protection of Industrial Property in 1883 and the Berne Convention for the Protection of Literary and Artistic Works in 1886. Both conventions provided for separate international bureaus, or secretariats, which were united in 1893 and functioned under various names, the last being the United International Bureau for the Protection of Intellectual Property (BIRPI). The BIRPI still has a legal existence, but for practical purposes is indistinguishable from WIPO. WIPO also assumed responsibility for administering a number of smaller unions based on other multilateral agreements and for coordinating subsequent negotiations on additional agreements. In December 1974 WIPO became the UN's 14th Specialized Agency.

In September 1977 the Coordination Committee agreed to ban South Africa from future meetings because of its apartheid policy, but a move to exclude it from the organization was narrowly defeated in 1979. South Africa's full membership privileges were restored in 1994 in concert with similar steps throughout the UN system.

Structure. The General Assembly, comprising states that are parties to the WIPO Convention and are also members of the Paris and/or Berne conventions, is the organization's highest authority. In addition, the WIPO Conference, comprising all parties to WIPO's convention, serves as a forum for discussion of all matters relating to intellectual property and has authority over WIPO's activities and budget.

The International Bureau is the WIPO secretariat, which also services the Paris Convention, the Berne Convention, and other such unions. With regard to WIPO, the International Bureau is controlled by the General Assembly and the WIPO Conference, while in regard to the unions it is governed by the separate assemblies and conferences of representatives of each. The Paris and Berne unions elect executive committees, whose joint membership constitutes the Coordination Committee of WIPO, which meets annually. The General Assembly, the WIPO Conference, and the Coordination Committee meet in September and October once every two years and in an extraordinary session in alternate years.

A September 1998 extraordinary WIPO Conference session approved formation of the Permanent Committee on Cooperation for Development Related to Intellectual Property (PCIPD), which combined the functions and programs of the Permanent Committee for Development Cooperation Related to Industrial Property (PC/IP) and the Permanent Committee for Development Cooperation Related to Copyright and Neighboring Rights (PC/CR), both of which had been established in the 1970s. The former had as its mandate aiding in the transfer of technology from highly industrialized to developing countries; the latter had been responsible for promoting and facilitating the dissemination of literary, scientific, and artistic works protected under the rights of authors and of performing artists, producers, and broadcast organizations. All WIPO states may participate in the PCIPD, which held its first session in May–June 1999, and in the Standing Committee on Information Technologies (SCIT), which was created in 1998 as successor to the Permanent Committee on Industrial Property Information (PCIPI). The SCIT, in part, serves as a forum for, and provides technical advice on, WIPO's overall information strategy. In January 2001 the SCIT established two working groups to aid its mission, one responsible for information technology and the other for standards and documentation.

The Arbitration and Mediation Center was created in 1994 to help resolve intellectual property disputes, and in 1998 the WIPO Worldwide Academy was formed, with many training courses now available through electronic media. The March 1998 assemblies of the member states of WIPO decided to form two new independent advisory boards: the Policy Advisory Commission (PAC), which identifies issues of interest to WIPO and provides policy recommendations, and the Industrial Advisory Commission, mandated to improve WIPO's relationships with its industrial and market sector constituents.

Unlike most UN agencies, which are supported by levies on members, WIPO is mostly self-financed through charges for its services. In addition to its member states, WIPO includes 68 intergovernmental organizations and 271 non-governmental organizations as accredited observers for meetings and other activities.

Recent activities. WIPO administers 24 international treaties dealing with the two main categories of intellectual property: copyright (involving written material, film, recording, and other works of art) and industrial property (covering inventions, patents, trademarks, and industrial designs). The most important treaty in the copyright field is the 156-member Berne Convention, most recently amended in 1979. It requires signatories to give copyright protection to works originating in other member states and establishes minimum standards for such protection.

The principal treaty affecting industrial property is the 167-member Paris Convention, under which a member state must give the same protection to nationals of other contracting states as it gives to its own. The convention contains numerous additional regulations, some of which were the subject of contentious revision conferences during the 1980s. Discord most frequently involved attempts by developing countries to shorten protection periods in order to facilitate the transfer of technology and speed up the development of product manufacturing.

In addition to its administrative function, WIPO spearheads the review and revision of treaties already under its jurisdiction, while encouraging the negotiation of new accords where needed. Among the issues under study during the past decade were piracy and counterfeiting of sound and audiovisual recordings; standards for regulating the cable television industry; expansion of copyright protection for dramatic, choreographic, and musical works; and protection in new fields such as biotechnology. WIPO has also promoted expanded activity under the Patent Cooperation Treaty (PCT), established in 1970 to help inventors and industries obtain patent protection in foreign countries by filing single international applications rather than separate applications for each country. As of December 2016, 151 countries had acceded to the treaty. Following four years of increased application levels, the PCT hit a major milestone in January 2005 when its millionth application was filed, prompting a ceremony and celebration at its Geneva headquarters. On June 1, 2000, WIPO adopted the new Patent Law Treaty (PLT) at the conclusion of a three-week diplomatic conference. The PLT simplified and harmonized patent filings by applying many PCT procedures at the national level. As of December 2016, the treaty had been signed by 59 countries. The PLT was ratified by the United States on September 18, 2013.

Faced with myriad new issues arising from the rapid growth in popular use of personal computers, CD-ROM players, advanced video machines, and other systems based on digital technology, representatives of some 160 nations met in Geneva in December 1996 to update WIPO copyright guidelines. After three weeks of often difficult negotiations, the conference adopted two new treaties designed to protect intellectual property while guaranteeing fair access to information on the part of consumers. One accord (the WIPO Copyright Treaty) provides specific new regulations regarding literary and artistic works that can be reproduced in seconds on personal computers. The second agreement (the WIPO Performances and Phonograms Treaty—WPPT) extended copyright protection to recording artists and producers, except in regard to audiovisual products, about which consensus could not be reached and further negotiations were planned. As of October 2012, 91 countries had signed the WPPT. The two treaties went into effect in 2002, despite disagreements in the United States and Europe over whether they stimulated or stifled creativity on the Internet. (For information on the Internet Corporation for Assigned Names and Numbers [ICANN] and the Uniform Domain Name Dispute Resolution Policy (UDRP), see the 2013 *Handbook*.)

In July 2000 the SCIT passed an implementation plan for WIPOnet, which facilitates the secure online exchange of information by the global intellectual property community. Access to various WIPO programs and activities, including the recently established Intellectual Property Digital Library (IPDL) system, are incorporated into WIPOnet, which permits online filing of applications under the PTC. Establishment of WIPOnet was a key element in a nine-point "digital agenda" drawn up at the First International Conference on Electronic Commerce and Intellectual Property in September 1999.

In 2003 U.S.-led opposition scrapped a WIPO convention for talks on information sharing to promote innovation. Major U.S. lobbying interests, including Microsoft and the Business Software Alliance, reportedly prompted the United States to pull the plug on the convention despite the urging of more than 60 international academics and researchers, who called on WIPO to convene the meeting in 2004. The group contends that the United States' proliferation of patents (accounting for about one-third registered with the PCT) hinder scientific advances and innovations.

In November 2004 WIPO announced some progress during three-day negotiations on a treaty to protect broadcasters' rights for digital technologies. Negotiators failed to reach consensus over whether protection should extend to webcasts, the scope of the treaty, and whether protection rights should be 50 years or fewer. The proposed broadcast treaty, an update to the 1961 Rome Convention on the Protection of Performers, Producers of Phonograms, and Broadcasting Organizations, was the subject of a June 2006 WIPO meeting held in Barcelona, Spain. Criticized for being held on short notice with little publicity, the meeting produced no agreements on matters of copyright protection for the broadcasters of television simulcasts and material on the Internet, including podcasts. The broadcast treaty was addressed again at WIPO's September 2006 General Assembly meeting, but a lack of agreement on how to proceed continued.

The Singapore Treaty on the Law of Trademarks was adopted in March 2006 at a special diplomatic conference. The treaty, an update to the 1994 Trademark Law Treaty, widened the scope of trademark law to include nontraditional marks such as holograms; three-dimensional marks; and nonvisible marks of sound, smell, taste, and feel. The treaty also simplified and standardized administrative rules for trademark applications.

The needs of the developing world have become a growing part of WIPO. In 2004 Argentina and Brazil advocated a proposal to reform WIPO's practices to stimulate innovation in developing countries and reorient the agency towards development goals rather than protecting property rights. The proposal, cosponsored by 12 member states, called for more transparency, participation, and accountability in the organization. However, WIPO negotiations the following year on the creation of a development agenda for the agency stalled and were not resolved until late 2007 at the WIPO General Assembly meeting held in Geneva September 27–October 3. The assembly agreed on a 45-point development agenda to address the needs of the developing world in the agency's technical assistance and capacity-building programs; it also established a framework for treaty-making that takes development issues into account and created the Committee on Development and Intellectual Property to implement the agenda. A less happy development at this meeting was the attempt by the United States and some European countries to remove the director general, Kamil Idris, of Sudan. The countries that objected to Idris blocked approval of the organization's 2008–2008 budget. Idris had been accused of financial and other irregularities, and his management was said to have damaged WIPO's credibility. He eventually agreed to step down a year early, the budget was finally adopted on March 31, 2008, and on September 24, 2008, Dr. Francis Gurry of Australia was elected director general for a six-year term. On October 1, 2008, the United States ratified the Singapore Treaty.

Further meetings during 2008 refined WIPO's new development agenda. Some observers wondered whether the plan would change the organization's focus to favor the interests of small nations as much as had been anticipated. In other matters, the organization received requests from Indonesia and from the European Union to develop intellectual property (IP) standards for the protection of folklore. The issue was discussed at the 13th session of its Intergovernmental Committee on Intellectual Property and Genetic Resources, Traditional Knowledge and Folklore, held in October 2008. Gurry declared that in this, as in all WIPO efforts, he expected to see results. On December 12, 2008, WIPO announced a program of strategic change, to concentrate on nine goals relating to improving respect for IP and for WIPO. The organization committed itself to working from a balanced budget henceforward. The organization also began a comprehensive review of the international patent system.

In July 2009 WIPO announced that it would open an arbitration and mediation center in Singapore early in 2010. In October 2009 Nigeria began working with WIPO to have a similar office opened in Abuja, its capital. WIPO's income for the 2008–2009 cycle was $626.2 million, with expenditures of $600.8 million.

In its 2010 overview of activities, WIPO reported that in 2010 there were 4.2 million patents throughout the world that had not been processed. In response, a WIPO working group issued a series of recommendations to address the backlog, including the increased use of information technology and new software to streamline the process. The expanded use of electronic processing had already reduced the costs of patent filing by 21 percent globally. The United States, Germany, and Japan remained the top nations for patent filings in 2010.

In March 2011 WIPO reported that in 2010 trademark holders filed 2,696 cybersquatting cases covering 4,370 domain names with the Arbitration and Mediation Center (WIPO Center). This was a 28 percent increase over the number for 2009. In May WIPO announced a partnership with the Paris-based International Council of Museums (ICOM), to mediate disputes concerning museums and cultural heritage. The annual WIPO Assemblies, held September 26–October 5, 2011, closed with a decision to call a diplomatic conference to negotiate a treaty on the rights of artists in audiovisual performances.

In 2011 WIPO's new headquarters in Geneva was completed using green technology and building design. In 2012 WIPO reported that PCT applications increased by 5.7 percent (rising to 164,300 for the year). Once again, the United States, Japan, and Germany dominated the applications. However, China moved into fourth place with a 55.6 percent increase in its filings. Concurrently, international trademark filings also increased, rising by 12.8 percent. Germany, the United States, and France had the largest number of applications.

WIPO reported in 2012 that administrative reforms had allowed the organization to reduce its operating budget from $707.3 million to $696.2 million through reductions in travel, equipment rentals, and alterations to payments policies to outside vendors. In June 2012 the Beijing Treaty on Audiovisual Performances was adopted at the WIPO Conference on the Protection of Audiovisual Performances. The accord strengthened the rights of performers and was finalized after 12 years of talks. Through 2015 there were 55 signatories to the treaty and 6 ratifications (the treaty requires ratification by 30 states to come into force).

In September 2014 Gurry announced a restructuring of WIPO's senior management team, appointing new deputy directors and four assistant directors general. WIPO reported in 2014 that the number of PCT applications had risen to 205,300, a 5.1 percent increase over the previous year. The United States filed 57,239 PCT applications, surpassing its pre-2007 financial crisis figures for the first time. Japan was second in total numbers, while China surpassed Germany to take third place for the first time.

WIPO reported in 2016 that China led the world in new patents with 1.1 million, followed by the United States with 589,410, and Japan, 318,721. China also led in trademarks with 2.8 million, with 517,297 by the United States, and 366,383 by Japan. Meanwhile, globally, the number of PCT applications by women reached a record of 29 percent of all filings.

UNITED NATIONS: RELATED ORGANIZATIONS

INTERNATIONAL ATOMIC ENERGY AGENCY

(IAEA)

Established: By statute signed in New York, United States, October 26, 1956, effective July 29, 1957. A working relationship with the United Nations was approved by the General Assembly on November 14, 1957.

Purpose: To "seek to accelerate and enlarge the contribution of atomic energy to peace, health and prosperity throughout the world" and to ensure that such assistance "is not used in such a way as to further any military purposes."

Headquarters: Vienna, Austria.

Principal Organs: General Conference (all members), Board of Governors (35 members), Secretariat.

Website: www.iaea.org.

Director General: Yukiya Amano (Japan).

Membership (168): See Appendix C.

Official Languages: Arabic, Chinese, English, French, Russian, Spanish. All are also working languages.

Origin and development. In a 1953 address before the UN General Assembly, U.S. president Dwight Eisenhower urged the establishment of an international organization devoted exclusively to the peaceful uses of atomic energy. The General Assembly endorsed the essentials of the U.S. proposal on December 4, 1954, and 70 governments signed the Statute of the IAEA on October 26, 1956. Following ratification by 26 governments, the statute entered into force July 29, 1957.

Although the statute makes no provision for expelling member states, a two-thirds majority may vote for suspension upon recommendation of the Executive Board. This procedure was followed in 1972, when the membership of the Republic of China was suspended and the People's Republic of China took its place. (International safeguards on the Republic of China's subsequent extensive atomic development have been possible only because that government still allows agency controls.)

A decision at the 26th General Conference in September 1982 to reject the Israeli delegation's credentials led to a walkout by the United States and 15 other countries. The conference charged that Israel had violated IAEA principles and undermined the agency's safeguards with its preemptive attack on Iraq's Osirak nuclear facility in June 1981. The United States, which supplies 25 percent of the agency's regular budget, announced that it would suspend its payments and contributions while reassessing its membership. Following Director General Hans Blix's certification of Israel's continued membership in March 1983, Washington paid $8.5 million in back dues and resumed full participation in the agency.

South Africa signed the Treaty on the Non-Proliferation of Nuclear Weapons (NPT) in July 1991, agreeing to open plants for IAEA inspection and forgo the development of nuclear weapons. In March 1993 South African president F. W. de Klerk acknowledged that his country had developed nuclear weapons in the late 1970s but said they had all been dismantled after his inauguration in 1989. Pretoria subsequently invited the IAEA to verify the claim, and in late 1993 the agency's inspectors concluded that South Africa was indeed the first country ever to abandon nuclear weapon capability.

Following conclusion of the 1990–1991 Persian Gulf conflict, the UN Security Council asked the IAEA to investigate Iraq's nuclear weapons capability, which led to an unprecedented determination that Baghdad had violated its safeguards agreement with the IAEA by concealing a weapons-related program. After the removal from Iraq of all declared weapons-grade nuclear materials, the IAEA, in cooperation with the UN Security Council's Special Commission (UNSCOM), attempted to maintain a monitoring and verification program that frequently put it in conflict with the Iraqi government (see Recent activities, below, and the entry on Iraq).

Structure. The General Conference is the highest policymaking body at which all members are entitled to be represented. It meets annually at the organization's headquarters, usually in the latter part of September. Conference responsibilities include final approval of the agency's budget and program, approval of the appointment of the director general, and election of 22 members of the Board of Governors. Decisions on financial questions, amendments to the statute, and suspension from membership require a two-thirds majority; other matters are decided by a simple majority.

The Board of Governors, which normally meets five times a year, is vested with general authority for carrying out the functions of the IAEA. Of its 35 members, 22 are elected by the General Conference with due regard to equitable representation by geographic areas, while 13 are designated by the outgoing Board of Governors as the leaders in nuclear technology and production of atomic source material. Decisions are usually by simple majority, although budget approval and a few other matters require a two-thirds majority.

The IAEA Secretariat is headed by a director general appointed for a four-year term by the Board of Governors with the approval of the General Conference. The director general is responsible for the appointment, organization, and functioning of the staff, under the authority and subject to the control of the board. He also prepares the initial annual budget estimates for submission by the board to the General Conference. The Secretariat includes six departments: Technical Cooperation, Nuclear Energy, Nuclear Safety and Security, Management, Nuclear Sciences and Applications, and Safeguards. The Office of External Relations and Policy Coordination and the Office of Internal Audit also report to the director general.

In 2013 the IAEA approved a budget for 2014 of €349.8 million ($472 million). The IAEA's staff consists of more than 2,300 personnel stationed in more than 100 countries. The organization's 2016 budget was €500.6 million ($520.6 million).

Recent activities. The IAEA differs from President Eisenhower's original concept in that it has not become a major center for distributing fissionable material. Its activities in promoting the peaceful uses of atomic energy fall into four main areas: (1) nuclear research and development, (2) health and safety standards, (3) technical assistance, and (4) administration of a safeguards program to ensure that atomic materials are not diverted from peaceful to military uses.

Included in IAEA operations are the IAEA Marine Environment Laboratory in Monaco; the International Centre for Theoretical Physics in Trieste, Italy (administered jointly with the UN Educational, Scientific and Cultural Organization); the International Nuclear Information System, which provides a comprehensive bibliographic database on peaceful applications of nuclear science and technology; the IAEA/World Health Organization Network of Secondary Standard Dosimetry Laboratories; and a large multidisciplinary nuclear research laboratory in Seibersdorf, Austria. The IAEA also coordinates the work of physicists from the European Union, Japan, Russia, and the United States on a planned thermonuclear fusion reactor. (France was chosen in 2005 as the site of the new reactor, which is scheduled to begin operation in 2016.) In addition, the IAEA administers a number of multilateral conventions on nuclear matters, including civil liability for nuclear damage and the protection of nuclear material from theft, sabotage, and other hazards, such as those posed during international transport.

In the wake of the world's worst-ever nuclear accident at the Chernobyl Nuclear Power Plant in the USSR in April 1986, nuclear safety drew increased attention. Special IAEA sessions evaluated the immediate implications of the accident and laid the groundwork for full assessment of its long-term radiological consequences. A new convention establishing an early warning system for such accidents went into force in October 1986, while a convention for the provision of assistance in the case of nuclear or radiological emergency went into force in February 1987.

In addition to nuclear power plant safety, IAEA symposia have addressed such topics as the management of spent fuel and radioactive waste, a proposed global radiation monitoring system, issues specific to "aging" nuclear plants, food irradiation, and new uranium mining techniques. The IAEA has also continued its extensive involvement in research and development projects in such areas as nuclear medicine, radiation-induced plant mutation to increase crop yield and resistance to disease, and insect control through large-scale release of radioactively sterilized male insects. In 2009 the IAEA announced that its scientists were working on such a technique with mosquitoes to combat malaria.

IAEA technical assistance to developing countries involves not only offering training programs and fellowships, but also bringing together customers and suppliers of such specialized services as plant maintenance and oversight safety. In 2009 more than 4,000 experts and lecturers carried out project assignments, and nearly 2,500 individuals participated in IAEA training courses.

The IAEA is probably most closely associated with its role as administrator of the safeguards system for containing the proliferation of nuclear weapons, although critics have often argued that manpower deficiencies, a lack of reliable monitoring equipment, and political influence, particularly in imposing effective sanctions, have undermined its credibility. The Treaty on the Non-Proliferation of Nuclear Weapons (NPT), signed July 1, 1968, and effective March 5, 1970, obligates signatory states (189, the exceptions being India, Israel, and Pakistan) that possess no nuclear weapons to accept safeguards as set forth in agreements concluded with the agency. After the May 1974 surprise nuclear explosion by India, the IAEA initiated a major effort to tighten controls. Specifically, the director general called upon the governments of states possessing nuclear weapons to accept outside inspection when they conducted nuclear tests for peaceful purposes. Subsequently, the United Kingdom (1978), the United States (1980), France (1981), the Soviet Union (1985), and China (1985) concluded agreements with the IAEA regarding application of safeguards and inspection of certain civilian nuclear facilities.

The agency also provides safeguard regimes for the Treaty for the Prohibition of Nuclear Weapons in Latin America and the Caribbean (Tlatelolco Treaty), which dates from 1967; the South Pacific Nuclear-Free Zone Treaty (Rarotonga Treaty), concluded in 1985; the African Nuclear-Weapon-Free Zone Treaty (Pelindaba Treaty), concluded in 1996; and the Treaty on the Southeast Asia Nuclear Weapon-Free Zone (Treaty of Bangkok), which entered into force in 1997.

In May 1995 NPT signatories convened in New York to determine if the treaty was to be extended indefinitely or for a fixed period of time. Although the United States and other nuclear powers strongly supported the indefinite option, a number of developing countries initially announced their preference for a fixed extension in order to gain leverage on several nuclear issues. The indefinite extension was finally approved after contentious discussions.

Consequently, in June 1995 the IAEA Board of Governors adopted new guidelines to permit broader inspections with little or even no advance notice. Two years later, under U.S. pressure for even stricter controls, the Board of Governors at its May 15–16, 1997, meeting adopted a model protocol granting IAEA inspectors greater access to members' nuclear facilities and sites. As of November 2009, 136 countries had signed the resultant Protocols Additional to Safeguards Agreements.

At the 1997 IAEA General Conference, held in late September and early October, Dr. Mohamed ElBaradei's appointment as successor to Director General Blix was approved.

The May 1998 nuclear weapons tests conducted by India and Pakistan drew immediate criticism from the IAEA. Although Argentina, Brazil, and Iran were believed to have the necessary technology to make weapons, an agency spokesman stated that, like the current regime in South Africa, none had shown any inclination to do so.

The September 1998 General Conference, in addition to calling for North Korea's compliance, focused its attention on Iraq, which had suspended its cooperation the preceding August after having engaged in a series of disputes with weapons inspectors. In November it was announced that the inspectors would be withdrawn in view of pending air strikes by the United States and the United Kingdom. Although the IAEA declared late in 1998 that it had found no evidence of Iraqi nuclear weapons production, it warned that Baghdad's failure to cooperate made drawing any conclusion difficult.

The April–May 2000 Third Review Conference on the NPT confirmed the importance of IAEA safeguards as a "fundamental pillar of the non-proliferation regime." During the 44th annual IAEA General Conference on September 18–22, 2000, a number of Arab states repeated a proposal for a nuclear-weapon-free zone in the Middle East, knowing full well that Israel was not ready to accept such a proposal. Israel indicated that it was firmly committed to the concept "in the proper context and time," but an obvious concern of the Israeli government was the projection that Iran might have nuclear weapons capacity by 2005 and a missile delivery system capable of hitting Israel within a decade.

The General Conference also called on North Korea and Iraq to come into full compliance with their obligations under the NPT and, in the case of Iraq, to permit renewed inspections under Security Council resolutions. Although Iraq permitted the IAEA in January 2000 to resume inspections of its declared nuclear material stocks in Tuwaitha, in accordance with its NPT safeguards agreement, from December 1998 Baghdad had not allowed verification and monitoring inspections ordered by the Security Council.

In December 2002 IAEA director general ElBaradei accused North Korea of "nuclear brinkmanship" after Korean technicians reopened a reactor that had been shut down in 1994. Pyongyang subsequently demanded a "nonaggression" agreement from the United States and several of North Korea's neighbors in exchange for closing the reactor. In early 2003 the IAEA board condemned North Korea for expelling the IAEA's weapons inspectors and dismantling IAEA monitoring cameras. (North Korea withdrew from the NPT in April 2003.) Regarding its other major focus of attention, the IAEA in early 2003 reported that it did not believe that Iraq had resumed its nuclear weapons program, as suspected by the United States.

Pressure mounted in 2003 for the IAEA to take a greater supervisory role in the matter of Iran's alleged "non-disclosed" nuclear program. ElBaradei urged Iran to "demonstrate full transparency," and in October Iran agreed to expanded inspections, although angrily insisting that all its nuclear activities were for civilian purposes only. In November 2004 the IAEA board noted Iran had made "good progress" on the issue, although Washington continued to insist on a harder line regarding inspections.

In November 2003 the IAEA called upon the UN to develop a system of multinational control over the production of nuclear material that could be used to make weapons. ElBaradei also subsequently proposed that significant additional resources be allocated to guard uranium stockpiles. (The agency estimated that more than 40 countries had the necessary knowledge to produce nuclear weapons.)

Early in 2005 the U.S. administration signaled its opposition to a third term for ElBaradei. However, the director general otherwise received strong international support and was reelected at the September General Conference. This conference, held September 26–30 in Vienna, focused on the dangers of nuclear proliferation, essentially acknowledging that it would be impossible to prevent states from developing nuclear weapons if they really wanted to do so. Attendees noted a revived interest in nuclear power for electricity generation—a development that was not foreseen even a year or so previously—spurred by the run-up in oil prices and increased concern about global warning. In November 2005 the IAEA and ElBaradei jointly won the Nobel Peace Prize.

Since that time world attention has been focused on the nuclear ambitions of North Korea and Iran. In 2006 and 2007 the IAEA inspected nuclear sites in both countries, served as a primary source of information to international bodies on the evidence behind their nuclear ambitions, and engaged in high-level talks concerning the suspension of nuclear programs. Significant developments over that time period included North Korea's first nuclear test in October 2006, reportedly an underground nuclear explosion, and Iran's further attempts at uranium enrichment. However, UN Security Council sanctions against both countries and the high-level talks resulted in some acquiescence on the part of North Korea and Iran to IAEA inspections. In the summer of 2007, IAEA inspectors gained access to North Korea's nuclear facilities at Yongbyon for the first time since 2002 and entered a heavy water research reactor in Arak, Iran, which the agency had previously been banned from viewing. By late 2007 North Korea had reportedly shut down its nuclear reactor in exchange for shipments of heavy fuel oil and access to an overseas bank account that had been frozen. However, the situation with Iran steadily deteriorated into late 2007 with the IAEA unable to negotiate full access to information on Iran's nuclear program. The IAEA announced in May that Iran could develop a nuclear weapon in three to eight years, and by October the United States imposed the toughest sanctions against Iran in 30 years.

The IAEA's 51st General Conference on September 17–21, 2007, saw a confrontation between Arab and Western states over a resolution to create a nuclear-free zone in the Middle East, aimed at Israel. The non-binding resolution, in the past typically introduced by Arab states but later withdrawn under U.S. pressure, passed this time in a vote of 53 to 2 (the United States and Israel voting against) with 43 abstentions (many of them European states). The move was seen as a sign of growing international tension over the Middle East and an effort by Arab nations to deflect pressure from Iran by pointing the finger at Israel, which has not signed the NPT and is generally believed to have nuclear weapons.

In other measures, the IAEA launched the International Decommissioning Network (IDN), an initiative aimed at sharing information and resources for use in shutting down the more than 350 nuclear installations that are approaching the end of their operational life span.

Also in 2007, Director General ElBaradei highlighted the agency's finances as cause for concern, noting at a July Board of Governors meeting and later at the General Conference that the 2008–2009 budget of €291 million ($396 million) put the agency in a state of "financial vulnerability." He also said the IAEA lacked essential equipment to verify covert nuclear activities and would not be able to respond to another disaster on the scale of the 1986 Chernobyl accident.

In mid-2007 ElBaradei drew the ire of the United States, France, and the United Kingdom for engaging in so-called freelance diplomacy after he agreed on a "work plan" with Iran under which key questions about its nuclear program would be answered. The states' position was to demand immediate compliance from Iran on the suspension of uranium enrichment or face tougher sanctions. A November report on

Iran's compliance concluded that, although Iran was not completely forthcoming about its nuclear program and continued to enrich uranium in defiance of the UN, there was no positive evidence that the country was working on a nuclear weapon. Western states' rejoinder to this was that it was cheaper to buy, rather than make, commercial-grade uranium, and the only reason for Iran to enrich its own was to build a bomb. The picture was further clouded by a U.S. intelligence estimate, released in December 2007, stating that Iran had halted its nuclear weapons program in 2003. ElBaradei said that Iran was "somewhat vindicated."

In a February 22, 2008, report to the UN Security Council, ElBaradei said that although Iran had recently been more open about its activities, it was not possible to say with complete confidence that it was not working on a bomb. The IAEA had confronted Iran with documents from the United States suggesting that it was working on matters peripheral to nuclear bomb-making (such as developing long-range missiles), but Iran dismissed these as forgeries or irrelevant. The United States and France said the report bolstered the case for further sanctions against Iran. On March 4, 2008, the Security Council approved a relatively mild new round of sanctions against Iran, the strongest that Russia and China would support. A September 15, 2008, report by the IAEA said that it had made no more progress in discovering Iran's nuclear intentions, as that country was being uncooperative.

A February 2009 IAEA report stated that Iran had built up a stockpile of fissile material. On June 17, 2009, ElBaradei said he felt that Iran was interested in having a bomb, mainly to increase its importance on the international stage. In August 2009 Iran's position appeared to soften, with IAEA inspectors given access to two nuclear facilities after several months of requests. By early September the IAEA itself seemed uncertain about Iran's intentions, but on September 25 Iran informed the IAEA that it had built a second nuclear enrichment plant, previously secret, and promised to open it to IAEA inspection. In early October 2009 Iran began a new round of negotiations and seemed more willing to cooperate. On October 21, 2009, a draft agreement was announced whereby Iran would send nuclear material abroad for enrichment. Iran seemed to react positively, but on November 2 it asked the IAEA to establish a committee to review its details. Proof of Iran's ultimate intentions remained elusive.

The IAEA also tried to determine Syria's nuclear position. In September 2007 Israel had attacked Al-Kibar, a Syrian site which it claimed was being used to develop nuclear weapons. In April 2008 the United States released material which, it claimed, showed that Syria was indeed engaging in nuclear development at the site and that it had received help from North Korea. The IAEA asked to investigate, and Syria agreed to let it inspect Al-Kibar, but no other sites. On September 22 the IAEA said it had found no radioactivity at Al-Kibar, but it was still waiting for permission to investigate other sites. Matters were delayed further by the September 25, 2008, assassination of the IAEA's chief liaison in the Syrian government. In November 2008 and again in February 2009 the IAEA announced that it had found radioactive traces at Al-Kibar. The Syrian government said the radioactive material could have come from IAEA inspectors' clothing or from the 2007 Israeli attack—something that the IAEA said was very unlikely.

On July 18, 2008, the IAEA confirmed that North Korea had shut down its nuclear reactor at Yongbyon, along with certain other facilities, thus beginning to fulfill its part of an international agreement. But through the late summer and early fall, North Korea complained that the United States was not keeping its end of the agreement. On September 24 North Korea said it was removing the seals from the Yongbyon plant, and that the IAEA would have no further access there. In April 2009 North Korea tested a long-range missile. Following general international condemnation of this test, North Korea announced that it was withdrawing from all nuclear negotiations and ordered all IAEA personnel out of the country.

From late 2007 through most of 2008, India was trying to gain IAEA approval for a deal with the United States allowing India to receive commercial nuclear technology. India already has nuclear weapons, and has not signed the NPT. France in particular was pressing for nuclear commerce with India, while Pakistan and the Indian political left were opposed. On July 10, 2008, the Indian government gave the IAEA its detailed plans for safeguarding nuclear technology. On July 22 the Indian government survived a no-confidence vote on the issue, and on August 1 the IAEA board approved the deal.

In other matters, the IAEA had difficulty electing a successor to ElBaradei, whose term in office was to end in November 2009. A March 2009 meeting of the board failed to elect either Yukiya Amano, a Japanese diplomat generally considered favorable to U.S. positions, or Abdul Samad Minty of South Africa, an arms control specialist who was felt to be more sympathetic to the interests of poorer countries. The matter was deferred to a board meeting on July 2, 2009, where Amano was elected.

Amano immediately took a tougher stance with Iran than his predecessor had done. By the March 2010 IAEA board meeting he declared that Iran was "not cooperating" with the IAEA, and the peaceful nature of Iran's program "could not be confirmed." In May Iran accepted an arrangement, mediated by Brazil and Turkey, for sending 1,200 kg of low-enriched uranium to Russia and France, where it would be converted into medical-grade material before being returned to Iran. The agreement did not address the concerns of the United States and others that Iran might have other enriched uranium left over. In June the UN imposed a new set of sanctions on Iran.

In August Iran began loading fuel at its first nuclear power station. The plant was Russian-operated, and observers saw little "proliferation risk "from it. Questions remained about other facilities, but while the IAEA continued to deplore Iran's lack of cooperation, nothing could be proved. These concerns remained, and as of late 2011, an IAEA report noted "serious concerns" and credible information regarding activities relevant to the development of a nuclear device.

In March 2011, following a 9.0 magnitude earthquake and tsunami along the Pacific coast of Japan, the Fukushima Nuclear Power Plant suffered equipment failures and meltdowns that led to the release of radioactive materials and the evacuation of residents from the surrounding area; this was the worst nuclear disaster since Chernobyl in 1986. Amano first visited the plant March 17–19 for high level consultations, though the IAEA's response to the accidents later drew criticism from the international science community. In June 2011, the IAEA pledged broad support for plans to strengthen international peer-reviewed safety checks; as of December 2011, the Fukushima Nuclear Power Plant was declared stable.

The importance of nuclear reactor safety and security was highlighted at the 55th International Atomic Energy General Conference in Vienna September 19–23, 2011. Addressing the IAEA, U.S. Energy Secretary Steven Chu outlined U.S. president Obama's nuclear agenda: promoting the peaceful use of nuclear energy, strengthening the nuclear proliferation regime, and pursuing nuclear disarmament and enhancing nuclear security. The IAEA continues to assess the extraordinary disaster in Japan.

In 2012 the IAEA reported that 32 percent of the world's 435 nuclear power plants were more than 30 years old and that many had outlived their original design lives. Consequently, the agency underscored the need for increased maintenance and service and replacement plans. Meanwhile, tensions over Iran's nuclear program continued. An IAEA team traveled to Iran in January 2012 for what were described as "good" talks. Iran subsequently offered to restart negotiations. Amano visited Tehran in May and paved the way for a new round of discussions between Iran and the five permanent members of the Security Council, plus Germany (the so-called P5+1). Talks in May and June failed to resolve the major differences between Iran and the P5+1. In September the IAEA reported that Iran had more than doubled its uranium enrichment centrifuges, from 1,064 to 2,140 at its Fordow nuclear facility. The agency also declared that its investigation of the Iranian nuclear site had been hampered by "extensive activities," including the demolition of buildings and the removal of equipment and earth. In 2012 Dominica, Fiji, Papua New Guinea, Rwanda, Togo, and Trinidad and Tobago joined the IAEA.

In 2013 the Bahamas, Brunei, and Swaziland were approved by the General Conference for IAEA membership. In February 2013 Iran rejected a P5+1 proposal to close its Fordow nuclear plant in exchange for the easing of some economic sanctions. In July the Board of Governors approved the creation of the Working Group on Financing the Agency's Activities and charged the group with exploring new means to ensure secure funding for the IAEA in the future. The board also approved a goal of raising €69.2 million ($90.3 million) in contributions for the technical cooperation fund. In March, Amano reported that Iran continued to fail to cooperate with efforts to investigate the country's nuclear program. The election in June of moderate cleric Hassan Rouhani as president of Iran led to a possible breakthrough in negotiations between Tehran and the P5+1 (see entry on Iran). A six-month interim agreement between the P5+1 and Iran was signed on November 24 in Geneva. The accord permitted IAEA inspections of Iran's nuclear sites. San Marino and Swaziland joined the IAEA in 2013.

In 2014 the Bahamas and Brunei formally joined the IAEA, while membership was approved for Comoros, Djibouti, Guyana, and Vanuatu pending ratification of the treaty by their respective governments. In March Turkey joined Azerbaijan in appealing to the IAEA for the closure of the Russian-operated Mesamor nuclear plant in Armenia. Located near the borders with Turkey and Azerbaijan, the plant has faced a variety of charges that it was unsafe. The IAEA reported in 2014 that uranium exploration and extraction had increased by 23 percent, with Kazakhstan, Canada, and Australia remaining the largest producers of the ore.

Antigua and Barbuda, Barbados, Djibouti, Guyana, and Vanuatu joined the organization in 2015, while Saint Lucia, Saint Vincent and the Grenadines, Gambia, and Turkmenistan were all approved for members in 2016.

As part of an agreement in July 2015 to partially suspend Iran's nuclear program (see entry on Iran), the IAEA assumed a role in overseeing the storage of that country's excess centrifuges and enrichment materials. The IAEA would also monitor Iran nuclear facilities and programs for a 20-year period.

WORLD TRADE ORGANIZATION (WTO)

Established: By the Marrakesh Agreement signed in Marrakesh, Morocco, on April 15, 1994, effective January 1, 1995.

Purpose: To administer the agreements contained in the Final Act of the Uruguay Round of the General Agreement on Tariffs and Trade (GATT); to provide conciliation mechanisms to resolve trade conflicts between members and, if necessary, adjudicate disputes; to provide a forum for ongoing negotiations in pursuit of further lowering and/or elimination of tariffs and other trade barriers.

Headquarters: Geneva, Switzerland.

Principal Organs: Ministerial Conference (all members), General Council (all members), Trade Policy Review Body, Dispute Settlement Body, Appellate Body, Council on Trade in Goods, Council on Trade in Services, Council on the Trade-Related Aspects of Intellectual Property Rights, Secretariat.

Website: www.wto.org.

Director General: Roberto Azevêdo (Brazil).

Membership (164): Afghanistan, Albania, Angola, Antigua and Barbuda, Argentina, Armenia, Australia, Austria, Bahrain, Bangladesh, Barbados, Belgium, Belize, Benin, Bolivia, Botswana, Brazil, Brunei, Bulgaria, Burkina Faso, Burundi, Cambodia, Cameroon, Canada, Cape Verde, Central African Republic, Chad, Chile, China, China: Hong Kong, China: Macao, Colombia, Democratic Republic of the Congo, Republic of the Congo, Costa Rica, Côte d'Ivoire, Croatia, Cuba, Cyprus, Czech Republic, Denmark, Djibouti, Dominica, Dominican Republic, Ecuador, Egypt, El Salvador, Estonia, European Communities, Fiji, Finland, France, Gabon, Gambia, Georgia, Germany, Ghana, Greece, Grenada, Guatemala, Guinea, Guinea Bissau, Guyana, Haiti, Honduras, Hungary, Iceland, India, Indonesia, Ireland, Israel, Italy, Jamaica, Japan, Jordan, Kazakhstan, Kenya, Republic of Korea, Kuwait, Kyrgyzstan, Latvia, Laos, Lesotho, Liberia, Liechtenstein, Lithuania, Luxembourg, Macedonia, Madagascar, Malawi, Malaysia, Maldives, Mali, Malta, Mauritania, Mauritius, Mexico, Moldova, Mongolia, Montenegro, Morocco, Mozambique, Myanmar, Namibia, Nepal, Netherlands, New Zealand, Nicaragua, Niger, Nigeria, Norway, Oman, Pakistan, Panama, Papua New Guinea, Paraguay, Peru, Philippines, Poland, Portugal, Qatar, Russian Federation, Romania, Rwanda, St. Kitts and Nevis, St. Lucia, St. Vincent and the Grenadines, Samoa, Saudi Arabia, Senegal, Seychelles, Sierra Leone, Singapore, Slovakia, Slovenia, Solomon Islands, South Africa, Spain, Sri Lanka, Suriname, Swaziland, Sweden, Switzerland, Taiwan (Separate Customs Territory of Taiwan, Penghu, Kinmen, and Matsu), Tajikistan, Tanzania, Thailand, Togo, Tonga, Trinidad and Tobago, Tunisia, Turkey, Uganda, Ukraine, United Arab Emirates, United Kingdom, United States, Uruguay, Vanuatu, Venezuela, Vietnam, Yemen, Zambia, Zimbabwe.

Observer governments (25): Algeria, Andorra, Azerbaijan, Bahamas, Belarus, Bhutan, Bosnia and Herzegovina, Comoro Islands, Equatorial Guinea, Ethiopia, Holy See, Iran, Iraq, Lebanon, Libya, Sao Tomé and Principe, Serbia, Somalia, Sudan, Syria, Timor-Leste, Uzbekistan.

Official Languages: English, French, Spanish.

Origin and development. The World Trade Organization (WTO) was the product of a series of negotiation developing from the General Agreement on Tariffs and Trade (GATT), signed in 1947. GATT was not designed to set up a permanent international organization but merely to provide a temporary framework for tariff negotiations pending the establishment of a full-fledged International Trade Organization (ITO) under United Nations (UN) auspices. A charter establishing an ITO responsible for developing and administering a comprehensive international commercial policy was drafted at the UN Conference on Trade and Employment, which met November 1947–March 1948 in Havana, Cuba. However, the so-called Havana Charter never went into effect, principally because some opposition from the United States blocked the required treaty approval by the U.S. Senate. Failure to create an ITO left GATT as the only available instrument for seeking agreement on rules for the conduct of international trade. (Since the general agreement was not cast as a treaty, it did not require formal ratification by the United States and could be implemented solely by executive action.)

The broad objective of GATT was to contribute to general economic progress through the acceptance of agreed rights and obligations governing the conduct of trade relations. Four main principles, from which detailed rules emerged, underlay the General Agreement: (1) nondiscriminatory trade with fair import and export duties for all countries; (2) the protection of domestic industries occurring only through customs tariffs; (3) undertaking consultations to avoid damage to the trading interests of other contracting parties; and (4) the provision of a framework for negotiating the reduction of tariffs and other barriers to trade, as well as a structure for embodying the results of such negotiations in a legal instrument.

Reducing tariffs through multilateral negotiations and agreements was one of the principal techniques employed by GATT. Eight major tariff-negotiating conferences were completed under GATT auspices. Little substantive progress toward an international trade organization came from the first seven rounds of negotiation. The eighth and final round of the negotiations, convened in September 1986 and ending in December 1993 finally brought about an agreement for the establishment of the World Trade Organization (WTO).

The objectives of the final negotiations in Uruguay were by far the most ambitious ever attempted by GATT. The Uruguay Round sought extensive liberalization and proposed negotiations in important new areas such as agricultural subsidies, investment, and intellectual property rights. While progress was made in most areas by 1988, negotiations stalled because of a disagreement between the United States and the European Community (EC) over a proposal to eliminate all trade-restricting farm subsidies within ten years. GATT officials warned that extensive compromise was required by all participants if a final package was to be adopted in Brussels in December 1990, as scheduled. Despite optimism for a deal, a deadlock was declared in Brussels on December 7, and negotiations were suspended indefinitely.

Although the outcome remained in doubt until the very end, the Uruguay Round Final Act was approved by GATT's Trade Negotiations Committee on December 15, 1993, after a series of last-minute compromises, primarily between the United States and the European Union (EU), which watered down or eliminated some of the most contentious areas, such as television and film exemptions from the intellectual property agreement. The long-standing impasse on agricultural subsidies eased, however, as the EU and the United States agreed to reduce subsidies substantially over the next six years. In addition, the signatories accepted what was expected eventually to amount to tariff reductions of about 40 percent on a wide range of goods, including agricultural products. Just as significantly, by providing for creation of the WTO, the GATT members committed themselves to a much more authoritative dispute settlement procedure. (For a more detailed discussion of GATT and the eight rounds of negotiations, see the 2012 *Handbook*.)

On April 15, 1994, in Marrakesh, Morocco, ministers from more than 100 countries formally endorsed the Uruguay Round agreements and called for the establishment of the WTO by January 1, 1995. While ratification of the Uruguay Round agreements proceeded more slowly than anticipated, a surge late in 1994 led to the convening on December 6 in

Geneva of the Implementation Conference, which authorized the official launching of the WTO on January 1, 1995. The WTO was launched with 76 members and GATT countries being eligible for automatic membership upon their acceptance of the Uruguay Round Agreement and completion of other ratification procedures. As of mid-2012, the WTO had 157 members, while working parties had been established to address WTO membership requests from 26 other countries.

To the consternation of the WTO's most ardent supporters, the first few months of the grouping's existence were marked by a struggle among members over the director general's post, GATT's Peter Sutherland having agreed to serve only temporarily once the WTO was launched. Three major candidates emerged to succeed Sutherland: Carlos Salinas de Gortari, the former president of Mexico who was strongly supported by the United States; Renato Ruggiero, an Italian diplomat favored by the EU; and South Korea's Kim Chul Su, backed by Japan and other Asian countries. No inclination toward compromise was apparent in any of the three camps until Salinas was essentially forced to withdraw in the wake of growing criticism over his government's handling of Mexico's recent currency crisis. Washington subsequently threw its support to Ruggiero, although only after an agreement had been reached that he would serve only one four-year term (to April 30, 1999) and that the next director general would be a non-European.

One of Ruggiero's first stated priorities was to promote conclusion of a WTO agreement covering financial services, which was one of the three major areas left unresolved by GATT's Uruguay Round. In July 1995 more than 30 countries signed an accord governing trade in financial services; however, the United States, the world leader in the area, refused to sign on the ground that access to foreign markets would still be too restricted. Consequently, the agreement was implemented only until November 1997, pending further efforts to achieve U.S. endorsement of a permanent pact of broader scope. A permanent pact was finally accepted by the Committee on Trade in Financial Services on December 12, 1997. Seventy members submitted new or revised plans liberalizing their financial markets, joining the 32 who already had turned in their proposals. The agreement came into effect in 1999, the United States being one of 67 countries to have signed and ratified the document.

Attention subsequently focused on activity within the initial WTO arbitration panels. In early 1996 a WTO panel (and ultimately the Appellate Body) ruled in favor of Venezuela and Brazil in their contention that U.S. environmental regulations on gasoline were being unfairly applied to their exports, while U.S. refiners had been given an extension of time to conform to the new standards. Washington announced its intention to comply with the WTO verdict in June.

Although the high rate of "out-of-court" settlements generally pleased WTO proponents, some member states argued that the trend reflected capitulation on behalf of the developing countries to the demands of industrialized nations. Their contention that the organization remained a "rich man's club" reportedly received informal attention during the first biennial meeting of the WTO's Ministerial Conference in December 1996, particularly when the developed countries rejected a proposal from Director General Ruggiero that they consider eliminating the tariffs on all imports from the 40 poorest nations in the world. The most significant practical development at the 1996 session appeared to be the approval of the U.S.-sponsored Information Technology Agreement (ITA) for the gradual elimination of tariffs on computers and other high-tech products by January 1, 2000. The agreement took effect on July 1, 1997, by which time some 40 states had signed on.

Proposed membership expansion also remained a focus of WTO attention. Of the nearly 30 accession requests under consideration in 1996, the most significant were those from Russia and China. The United States and other Western nations had announced they would support China's entry, provided Beijing reduced its tariffs and dismantled other trade barriers.

In September 1997 the Appellate Body ruled on a dispute initiated by Ecuador, Guatemala, Honduras, Mexico, and the United States against the EU's banana importation regime, which gave preferential market access to African, Caribbean, and Pacific (ACP) countries. The Appellate Body upheld the findings of a panel in agreeing that these preferences were "inconsistent with the WTO rules." The EU said it would accept the Appellate Body's verdict but expressed concern over the potential effects it could have on ACP countries. The dispute nevertheless continued into 1998, with the United States claiming late in the year that a modified regime was still inadequate and announcing it would seek WTO approval for levying sanctions on EU goods. In early 1999 both sides agreed to allow the dispute panel that had heard the original case to arbitrate the matter. In April the panel again ruled in favor of the United States.

In February 1998, an agreement opening up the telecommunications market entered into force. Also during the year, the WTO held its second Ministerial Conference in Geneva in May, at which time a number of poor countries claimed they were not benefiting from liberalized trade.

A contentious search for a successor to Director General Ruggiero dragged into 1999, and when his term expired on April 30, the office fell vacant. Principal candidates were Michael Moore, a former prime minister of New Zealand, and Supachai Panitchpakdi, a deputy prime minister of Thailand. A compromise agreement provided for Moore to serve a special three-year term (effective July 22) with Panitchpakdi to succeed Moore for a three-year term in 2002. Substantial controversy also surrounded the third meeting of the WTO's Ministerial Conference on November 30–December 3, 1999, in Seattle, Washington. Internal disputes (such as disagreements among the EU, the United States, and others over agricultural subsidies) also marred the session, which ended without a final communiqué. No agreement was reached again in 2001 in regard to a timetable and agenda for a proposed ninth round of trade negotiations.

After several years of disastrous public relations and growing concern over its future effectiveness, the WTO attempted to chart a positive course by launching the Doha Development Round at the fourth meeting of the Ministerial Conference in Doha, Qatar, in November 2001. The new trade negotiations were originally scheduled for completion by 2005, although vague language about agricultural subsidies in the Doha document concerned many analysts. Other major developments at Doha included the acceptance of China as a WTO member (effective December 11), a decision that facilitated Taiwan's admission on January 1, 2002.

In January 2002 the WTO Appellate Body endorsed a 2001 dispute tribunal's ruling that the United States was in violation of WTO agreements by providing tax breaks for U.S. companies in regard to income earned in foreign countries. The EU, which had pursued the complaint, was authorized to impose a staggering \$4 billion in retaliatory tariffs, although no such action was taken while the United States and EU attempted to reach a negotiated settlement. That dispute, coupled with severe criticism from the EU, Japan, and China over Washington's decision in March to apply substantial tariffs on imported steel, contributed to a continued sense of malaise within the WTO as Director General Panitchpakdi took office in September 2002.

In March 2003 a WTO dispute panel ruled against the United States regarding its steel tariffs, and Washington lifted the tariffs in November after a WTO appeals panel upheld the original decision. The WTO also ruled against the United States in 2004 on the issues of U.S. subsidies to cotton farmers (followed by a second ruling against the United States in 2007) and the so-called Byrd Amendment that paid out anti-dumping duties collected by the United States directly to private firms. In October 2004 a WTO panel began its assessment of one of the WTO's largest and most complex cases to date—the disputes over U.S. and EU aid to their largest aircraft manufacturers (Boeing and Airbus, respectively). A dispute involving U.S. tax breaks for U.S. companies in regard to income earned abroad subsequently came to a conclusion when the U.S. Congress, after two years, finally approved legislation to comply with the WTO findings.

In January 2005 Director General Panitchpakdi announced that he did not intend to seek a second term. In May EU trade commissioner Pascal Lamy was named to the post, effective September of that year.

There were hopes that a significant agreement on the Doha Round might come at the sixth Ministerial Conference, held December 13–18, 2005, in Hong Kong, but that did not happen. Instead there was a modest agreement that the EU would end farm export subsidies by 2013 and the United States would reduce subsidies for cotton exports. It was generally recognized, however, that the conference produced only marginal benefit for poorer countries. In June 2006 Director General Lamy organized what amounted to an emergency meeting of any WTO members who cared to attend in an attempt to broker a broader resolution of the disputes over cutting tariffs and subsidies in agriculture and opening markets for industrial goods. The meeting aimed to produce template agreements known as "modalities" for this purpose. The meeting, held in Geneva beginning June 28, effectively collapsed by July 1, with no agreements reached and many delegations going home early.

A series of trade complaints was filed with the WTO in 2006 and 2007, in some cases to gain leverage in the continuing Doha talks.

Canada took the lead, backed by more than a half dozen countries, in challenging the United States on farm subsidies in early 2007, saying Washington's aid to farmers exceeds WTO limits. Ongoing cases involving the EU's banana import regime and U.S. cotton subsidies were still before the WTO as contentious negotiations on a trade deal stretched through 2007 and into 2008. (Both cases were subsequently decided against the EU and the United States, respectively.)

With the faltering of talks again in the fall of 2006, observers cautioned that the WTO risked losing credibility. After months of small group consultations into the spring of 2007, four key trade powers (the United States, the EU, India, and Brazil) attempted to hammer out a deal in Potsdam, Germany, on June 19–21. The talks again collapsed with India and Brazil complaining that the United States and the EU were demanding too much access to industrial goods markets in exchange for too little cutting of tariffs and subsidies on their agricultural goods. When talks resumed among key WTO trade members in 2008, the issues were no different: agricultural subsidies in the most developed countries versus protection for industries and services in the rest. The talks collapsed in late July 2008 for much the same reasons as the previous year.

Growing frustration with China's slow progress in implementing trade accords has been reflected in a series of complaints filed with the WTO in recent years. China's fifth anniversary in the WTO in 2006 was marked by U.S. calls to open its banking and financial sectors further. Subsequently, the United States, faced with discontent over its growing trade imbalance with China, led complaints against China concerning inadequate efforts in fighting piracy and counterfeiting; restrictions on the sale of U.S. films, books, and software; and allegations that China was giving tax breaks to exporters in a wide range of industries. In July 2008 China lost its first case before the WTO, a complaint over discrimination against foreign-made auto parts.

A number of issues regarding WTO membership have occurred in recent years. Vietnam's communist-run legislature cleared up remaining hurdles, notably the removal of quotas on garment exports, and joined the WTO in November 2007. Ukraine's 14-year effort at accession continued to progress, and it became a full member at the end of 2008.

Russia, whose economy is the largest outside the WTO, worked throughout 2006 and 2007 on deals to lift remaining trade restrictions. By the end of 2007, the possibility of Russia's accession narrowed to two remaining issues with the EU, namely export duties on timber and a reform of railway fees that have favored Russian ports. Georgia declared in May of that year that it would block Russia's admission until Russia ceased supporting the breakaway Georgian provinces of Abkhazia and South Ossetia. The fighting between Russia and Georgia in August 2008 only worsened the situation.

On November 15, 2008, the Group of Twenty (see entry on the G-20) meeting in Washington, D.C., to discuss the world financial crisis committed its members not to take any actions for twelve months that might raise new trade barriers, or otherwise interfere with the WTO's work against protectionism. The G-20 also agreed to "strive to reach agreement this year on modalities that leads to a successful conclusion to the WTO's Doha Development Agenda with an ambitious and balanced outcome." On December 12, 2008, Lamy declared, after consultation with the United States, India, China, Brazil, and the EU, that there was insufficient basis to restart talks on the Doha Round. (For more on activities since 2008, see Recent activities, below.)

Structure. The WTO's supreme organ is the Ministerial Conference, in which each member state has one vote. It is mandated to meet at least every two years. Between ministerial sessions, oversight is the responsibility of the General Council, also composed of delegates from all member states. The General Council additionally acts as the Dispute Settlement Body, which establishes panels to adjudicate disputes brought before the WTO. Decisions of the panels can be appealed by either party in a dispute to the WTO Appellate Body, whose seven members are appointed by the Dispute Settlement Body. In addition, the General Council also acts as the Trade Policy Review Body, which conducts regular evaluations of the trade practices of all WTO members. Subcouncils have been established on trade in goods, trade in services, and the trade-related aspects of intellectual property rights. Permanent committees reporting directly to the General Council include Trade and Environment; Trade and Development; Regional Trade Agreements; Balance of Payments Restrictions; and Budget, Finance, and Administration. The Trade Negotiations Committee, which also reports directly to the General Council, was established in connection with the launching of the Doha Development Round of negotiations in 2001. The WTO governing bodies are assisted by the Secretariat, which is headed by a director general selected for a four-year term by consensus of the WTO members at the ministerial level.

Although its founding treaty stipulated that the WTO would be accorded privileges and immunities similar to those of the Specialized Agencies affiliated with the United Nations, the organization was not officially designated as a Specialized Agency. However, the organization cooperates extensively with a number of UN-affiliated bodies as well as other non-UN organizations. In addition, the WTO signed a cooperation agreement with the IMF in April 1997.

Recent activities. In January 2009 the WTO issued a statement, bearing on a U.S. complaint against China's allegedly lax attitude toward pirated DVDs and other intellectual property, that was highly critical of China's position. The WTO recommended that China bring its copyright law "into conformity with its obligations." On August 12, 2009, the WTO ruled definitively in favor of the United States on the bulk of the complaint. Shortly thereafter China announced an appeal. On November 6, 2009, the WTO announced that it had received its 400th request for settlement of a dispute.

On June 20, 2010, the organization handed down a decision in the Boeing-Airbus case. The decision was marginally in favor of the U.S. position. In July the EU announced an appeal. The appeal upheld the initial ruling of the panel, and in April 2012, the United States called for a DSB to be established concerning the EU's enforcement of the ruling, claiming that the EU had failed to make sufficient changes.

In 2010 Russia moved close to membership in the WTO. On June 24 U.S. president Barack Obama stated that the United States now supported Russia's accession. That Russia planned to form a customs union with Belarus and Kazakhstan (also candidates for WTO membership) had for some time been considered an obstacle. When that union came about in early June 2010, however, it seemed not to be an insuperable barrier.

U.S. protests against Chinese manipulation of the value of its currency, said by some to be undervalued by as much as 25 percent against the dollar, showed signs in 2010 of reaching the WTO. There was debate in U.S. economic and political circles as to whether a WTO challenge would be wise, and what the long-term results might be, win or lose. The U.S. trade representative said that he was investigating whether China was illegally subsidizing its clean-energy industries, and that a WTO complaint might be forthcoming. In December 2010 the WTO declared that EU punitive tariffs on Chinese metal products were inappropriate and had to be altered. Concurrently, the WTO ruled that U.S. tariffs on Chinese tires were appropriate.

In February 2011 Canada sought WTO arbitration in a dispute against the EU over its ban on Canadian seal imports. On April 14 at the Brazil, Russia, India, China, and South Africa (BRICS) summit, the group issued the Sanya Declaration, which called for Russia's admittance to the WTO. In October Vanuatu's membership bid was endorsed by the WTO. However, domestic opposition to the WTO prompted delays in the necessary membership legislation. Meanwhile, at the 2011 Ministerial Conference held on December 16 Russian membership in the WTO was finally approved, pending domestic ratification. Montenegro and Samoa were also approved as new members. Moscow subsequently called for Russian to become one of the official languages of the WTO. All three states acceded to the WTO treaty shortly after the conference. Montenegro ratified the treaty on April 29, 2012, and Samoa followed on May 10. Russian president Vladimir Putin signed the treaty ratification on July 21, 2012, ending the long process of Russian membership negotiations. Russia became the 156th member of the WTO. As of August 2012, no discussions have been initiated concerning the acceptance of Russian as an official language. Russia joined the WTO's Information Technology Agreement in September 2013.

In February 2012, the General Council met for a regular meeting, at which time they discussed, among other things, the need for progress in the Doha Round of negotiations in the upcoming year. The director general noted that the member states should not allow progress to be hindered all together, even if major progress could not be made.

After overcoming delays on the domestic front, Vanuatu announced its ratification of the WTO treaty during a General Council meeting held July 25–27. Vanuatu became the 157th member state. The most significant action to come out of the General Council meeting was a new protocol that eased the membership guidelines for the 40 poorest countries in the world. The new guidelines will allow easier accession to the WTO treaty for the Least Developed Countries by increasing flexibility on the percentage of tariff lines, easing the requirements for various sectors of industry, and creating a transition period following accession. Director General Lamy also echoed his earlier call for progress on the Doha Round of negotiations. He told the member states that, "The ball lies in your court," and cautioned against the "all or nothing" mentality of many states at the negotiating table.

In November the EU and 10 Latin American states signed an agreement ending their dispute over bananas. The agreement lowered the EU's import tariff on bananas and established annual maximum tariff rates until 2017. The banana dispute was the longest running series of disputes in GATT/WTO history, dating back to 1992.

Early 2013 saw the accession of two more states to the WTO—Laos and Tajikistan. Laos ratified the WTO treaty on January 3, having had its membership deal approved by the General Council in October 2012. Upon ratification, Laos entered the WTO as the 158th member on February 2. From a more regional approach, Laos became the last of the ASEAN member states to join the WTO's international trading framework, allowing for improved cooperation between the two organizations. The General Council approved Tajikistan's membership deal on December 10, 2012, and the Central Asian state ratified the agreement on January 31, 2013. According to protocol, they entered the WTO 30 days later on March 3.

On May 14, 2013, the General Council appointed Roberto Azevêdo of Brazil as the next Director-General of the WTO to replace Pascal Lamy, who had served as Director-General for the last eight years. Azevêdo becomes the first South American and first individual from the Western Hemisphere to serve as Director-General of GATT/WTO. Azevêdo took office effective September 1. Following a four-day conference in December, the members of the WTO signed a new trade agreement, the Bali package, which lowered import tariffs and set common customs standards. The accord also called for greater market access for less-developed states. Described as "historic," the deal was the result of a compromise between the United States and India over food subsidies that allowed New Delhi to continue its heavily subsidized nutrition programs for the poor for a four-year period. The Bali package also revived the stalled Doha negotiations.

In March 2014 the WTO ordered China to end export restrictions on 19 categories of rare earth minerals and alloys. The restrictions had led to higher prices and scarcity of the alloys. Yemen became the newest WTO member in June 2014. In May the WTO ruled against China in a dispute over high tariffs on U.S. cars and trucks. The two decisions increased tensions between China and the WTO and prompted significant criticism of the organization by Beijing. Meanwhile, in April, the WTO established a deadline of December 31 for the completion of the Doha round of negotiations.

At its Tenth Ministerial Conference in Nairobi, Kenya, on December 15–19, the WTO formally abandoned the Doha negotiations. Meanwhile, ministers approved a series of agreements to reduce barriers to agricultural trade. Dubbed the "Nairobi Package," the agreements required developed countries to eliminate subsidies for agricultural exports, while developing nations were given until the end of 2018 to remove their subsidies. The meeting also produced an accord among 53 member states to reduce tariffs on information technology products. Members were to immediately cut tariffs by 60 percent and eliminate all remaining customs by 2024.

In 2015 Kazakhstan and the Seychelles joined the WTO. Afghanistan and Liberia became members of the organization in 2016.

APPENDIXES

APPENDIX A
CHRONOLOGY OF MAJOR INTERNATIONAL POLITICAL EVENTS: 1945–2016

1945, **May 8.** Proclamation of end of the war in Europe.
June 26. United Nations Charter signed in San Francisco.
August 6. United States drops atomic bomb on Hiroshima, Japan.
September 2. Surrender of Japan.

1946, **July 29–October 15.** Peace Conference meets in Paris, France.
December 30. UN Atomic Energy Commission approves U.S. proposal for world control of atomic weapons.

1947, **February 10.** Peace treaties signed with Bulgaria, Finland, Hungary, Italy, and Romania.
June 5. Marshall Plan inaugurated.
October 30. General Agreement on Tariffs and Trade (GATT) negotiated in Geneva, Switzerland.

1948, **March 17.** Brussels Treaty signed by Belgium, France, Luxembourg, Netherlands, United Kingdom.
March 20. Soviet representatives walk out of Allied Control Council for Germany.
April 16. Organization for European Economic Cooperation (OEEC) established in Paris, France.
April 30. Organization of American States (OAS) Charter signed in Bogotá, Colombia.
May 14. State of Israel proclaimed.
June 24–May 12, 1949. Berlin blockade.
December 10. UN General Assembly adopts Universal Declaration of Human Rights.

1949, **January 25.** Council for Mutual Economic Assistance (CMEA) established in Moscow, USSR.
April 4. Treaty establishing North Atlantic Treaty Organization (NATO) signed in Washington.
May 4. Statute establishing Council of Europe signed in London, United Kingdom.

1950, **January 31.** U.S. president Harry S. Truman orders construction of hydrogen bomb.
June 27. United States intervenes in Korean War.

1951, **April 18.** Treaty establishing European Coal and Steel Community signed by Belgium, France, Federal Republic of Germany, Italy, Luxembourg, Netherlands.
September 1. Anzus Pact signed in San Francisco, by Australia, New Zealand, and the United States.
September 8. Peace Treaty signed by Japan and non-Communist Allied powers in San Francisco.

1952, **May 27.** European Defense Community (EDC) Charter signed by Belgium, France, Federal Republic of Germany, Italy, Luxembourg, Netherlands.
November 1. United States explodes hydrogen bomb in Eniwetok Atoll.

1953, **March 5.** Death of Joseph Stalin.
December 8. U.S. president Dwight D. Eisenhower proposes international control of atomic energy.

1954, **September 8.** Treaty establishing Southeast Asia Treaty Organization (SEATO) signed in Manila, Philippines.
October 23. Allied occupation of West Germany ends.

1955, **May 6.** Western European Union (WEU) inaugurated by admission of Italy and Federal Republic of Germany to Brussels Treaty.
May 9. Federal Republic of Germany admitted to NATO.
May 14. Warsaw Pact signed by East European communist governments.

1956, **July 26.** Egypt nationalizes Suez Canal.
October 23–November 22. Anticommunist rebellion in Hungary suppressed by Soviet troops.
October 29–November 6. Suez crisis.

1957, **March 25.** Rome Treaty establishing European Economic Community (EEC) and European Atomic Energy Community (Euratom) signed.

1960, **May 1.** U-2 incident.
May 3. European Free Trade Association (EFTA) of "Outer Seven" (Austria, Denmark, Norway, Sweden, Switzerland, Portugal, United Kingdom) established.
May 14. Beginning of Sino-Soviet dispute.
December 14. Charter of Organization for Economic Cooperation and Development (OECD) to replace OEEC signed in Paris, France.

1961, **April 17–20.** Bay of Pigs invasion of Cuba.
August 15. Start of construction of Berlin Wall between East and West Germany.
September 1–6. First conference of Nonaligned Nations in Belgrade, Yugoslavia.

1962, **October 22–28.** Cuban missile crisis.

1963, **January 29.** France vetoes British bid for admission to EEC.
May 25. Organization of African Unity (OAU) Charter adopted in Addis Ababa, Ethiopia.
August 5. Limited Nuclear Test-Ban Treaty signed in Moscow, USSR.

1964, **May 28.** Palestine Liberation Organization (PLO) established.

1965, **February 21.** Decision to merge European Economic Community (EEC), European Coal and Steel Community (ECSC), and European Atomic Energy Community (Euratom).

1966, **March 11.** France withdraws troops from NATO.

1967, **January 27.** Treaty governing exploration and use of outer space signed by the United States, USSR, and 60 other nations.
June 5. Beginning of Arab-Israeli War.
June 17. China explodes its first hydrogen bomb.

1968, **January 16.** Britain announces withdrawal of forces from Persian Gulf and Far East.
May 13. Beginning of Vietnam peace talks in Paris, France.
June 4. Nuclear Nonproliferation Treaty approved by UN General Assembly.
August 20–21. Warsaw Pact forces occupy Czechoslovakia.
August 25. France explodes its first hydrogen bomb.
September 12. Albania withdraws from Warsaw Pact.
October 5. Outbreak of civil rights violence in Londonderry, Northern Ireland.

1969, **April 28.** Charles de Gaulle resigns as French president.
July 21. United States lands first men on moon.
November 17–December 22. Initiation of Strategic Arms Limitation Talks (SALT) between the United States and USSR.

1970, **March 2.** Rhodesia issues unilateral declaration of independence from Britain.

1971, **November 12.** U.S. president Richard Nixon announces end of U.S. offensive action in Vietnam.

1972, **February 21–28.** U.S. president Richard Nixon visits China.
May 22–29. U.S. president Richard Nixon visits Soviet Union.

1973, **January 1.** Denmark, Ireland, and the United Kingdom enter European Communities.
February 12. Last U.S. ground troops leave Vietnam.
October 6–22. Fourth Arab-Israeli war.
October 17. Arab embargo launched on oil shipments to United States and other Western nations (embargo ends March 18, 1974).

1974, **January 18.** Egypt and Israel sign agreement on disengagement of forces along Suez Canal.

1975, **February 28.** First Lomé (Togo) Convention signed between EEC and developing African, Caribbean, and Pacific (ACP) states.
May 28. Treaty establishing Economic Community of West African States (ECOWAS) signed in Lagos, Nigeria.
June 5. Suez Canal reopened to international shipping.
July 30–August 1. Conference on Security and Cooperation in Europe (CSCE) concludes in Helsinki, Finland.
September 4. Agreement between Egypt and Israel provides for Israeli withdrawal in Sinai and establishment of UN buffer zone.
November 20. Death of Spain's Gen. Francisco Franco.

1976, **June 17.** Outbreak of racial violence in Soweto, South Africa.
July 3–4. Israeli raid on Entebbe Airport, Uganda.
September 9. Death of China's Mao Zedong.

1977, **June 30.** Southeast Asia Treaty Organization (SEATO) dissolved.
November 19–21. Egyptian president Anwar Sadat visits Israel.

1978, **September 9–17.** President Anwar Sadat and Prime Minister Menachem Begin meet with U.S. president Jimmy Carter at Camp David.

1979, **January 1.** People's Republic of China and United States establish diplomatic relations.
January 16. Shah of Iran goes into exile.
March 26. Egyptian-Israeli peace treaty signed in Washington.
November 4. Iranian students seize U.S. embassy in Tehran.
December 27. Soviet military forces support coup in Afghanistan.

1980, **April 18.** Zimbabwe (formerly Rhodesia) declared legally independent.
May 4. Death of Yugoslavian president Josip Broz Tito.
September 22. Iraqi invasion of Iran initiates Iran-Iraq war.
October 24. Independent trade union (Solidarity) officially registered in Poland.

1981, **January 1.** Greece enters European Communities.
January 20. Iran frees remaining U.S. hostages.

October 6. Egyptian president Anwar Sadat assassinated.
December 13. Martial law declared in Poland.
December 14. Occupied Golan Heights placed under Israeli law.

1982, April 2–July 15. Falkland Islands (Islas Malvinas) war between Argentina and the United Kingdom.
June 6. Israeli invasion of Lebanon.
August 21–September 1. PLO forces evacuate Beirut, Lebanon.
November 10. Soviet leader Leonid Brezhnev dies.

1983, September 1. USSR shoots down Korean Air Lines Boeing 747 passenger plane.
October 25. United States, in concert with six Caribbean states, invades Grenada (last troops withdrawn December 12).

1984, October 31. Indian prime minister Indira Gandhi assassinated.

1985, March 11. Mikhail S. Gorbachev named general secretary of Soviet Communist Party.
October 7. Palestinian terrorists seize Italian cruise ship Achille Lauro.
November 15. Ireland and the United Kingdom sign accord granting Irish Republic consultative role in governance of Northern Ireland.
November 19–21. U.S. president Ronald Reagan and Soviet leader Gorbachev hold summit meeting in Geneva.

1986, January 1. Spain and Portugal enter European Communities.
January 28. U.S. space shuttle Challenger, on 25th shuttle mission, breaks apart after lift-off.
February 7. Jean-Claude Duvalier flees from Haiti to France, ending nearly three decades of his family's rule.
February 25. General Secretary Mikhail Gorbachev calls for sweeping reforms in Soviet economic system.
February 25. Corazon Aquino inaugurated as Philippines president following disputed election February 7; after holding rival inauguration, Ferdinand Marcos flies to Hawaii.
April 15. U.S. aircraft bomb Tripoli and Benghazi in response to alleged Libyan-backed terrorist activity in Europe.
April 26. Explosion in Chernobyl, USSR, power plant results in worst nuclear accident in history.
November 25. Attorney General Edwin Meese says $10–$30 million paid by Iran for U.S. arms was diverted by Lt. Col. Oliver North to Nicaraguan insurgents.

1987, June 11. Margaret Thatcher becomes first prime minister in modern British history to lead her party to a third consecutive electoral victory.
August 7. Five Central American presidents sign regional peace plan proposed by Oscar Arias of Costa Rica.
September 1. Erich Honecker becomes first East German head of state to visit West Germany.
October 19. U.S. stock market crashes, with Dow Jones Industrial Average falling 508.32 points in one session; foreign markets plummet the next day.
December 8. U.S. president Ronald Reagan and Soviet general secretary Mikhail Gorbachev sign INF treaty calling for elimination of entire class of nuclear weapons.
December 9. Intifada begins among Palestinians in the Gaza Strip, spreading to the West Bank the following day.

1988, April 14. Afghanistan, Pakistan, Soviet Union, United States conclude agreement on Soviet withdrawal from Afghanistan (withdrawal completed February 15, 1989).
June 28. Soviet general secretary Mikhail Gorbachev proposes wide-ranging changes in Soviet political system.
August 17. Pakistan's president Zia ul-Haq dies in plane crash.
August 20. Cease-fire begins in Iran-Iraq war.
November 15. Yasir Arafat issues PLO statement declaring an independent state of Palestine.
December 22. Angola, Cuba, South Africa sign agreements providing for Cuban withdrawal from Angola and transition to independence for Namibia.

1989, January 7. Japanese emperor Hirohito dies.
January 19. Conference on Security and Cooperation in Europe concludes 26-month meeting in Vienna, Austria, with expansion of 1975 Helsinki Final Act to emphasize freedom of religion, information, travel, and privacy.
March 10. U.S. treasury secretary Nicholas Brady announces "Brady Plan" for commercial banks to make voluntary reductions in outstanding Third World debts and for the IMF and World Bank to provide debt-reduction assistance to debtor nations that adopt market-oriented reforms.
March 26. Soviet Union holds nationwide contested elections.
April 17. Solidarity relegalized by court action 12 days after reaching agreement with Polish government on political reforms.
May 13. Students demanding meeting with Chinese leaders begin hunger strike after occupying Beijing's Tiananmen Square.
May 15–18. Soviet leader Mikhail Gorbachev goes to China for the first Sino-Soviet summit in 20 years; antigovernment protests break out in more than 20 Chinese cities, including a demonstration by an estimated 1 million people in Tiananmen Square.
June 4. Many deaths reported as troops clear Tiananmen Square.
June 4–18. Solidarity sweeps two-stage, partially open election in Poland.
June 6. Iranian Ayatollah Khomeini dies.
November 9. East German government permits citizens to leave without special permits, thus effectively opening the country's borders, including the Berlin Wall.
December 20. U.S. forces invade Panama.
December 25. Romanian president Nicolae Ceauşescu and his wife executed.

1990, March 11. Lithuania becomes first Soviet republic to issue declaration of independence.
March 13. Soviet Congress of People's Deputies revokes monopoly status of Communist Party.
March 15. Soviet Congress of People's Deputies elects Mikhail Gorbachev to new office of executive president.
March 21. Namibia becomes independent.
June 7. Warsaw Pact leaders meeting in Moscow declare the West is no longer an "ideological enemy."
August 2. Iraq invades Kuwait.
August 6. UN Security Council votes to impose mandatory economic sanctions on Iraq. United States deploys troops to Gulf in defense of Saudi Arabia ("Operation Desert Shield").
September 7. Liberian president Samuel Doe killed by rebels.
October 3. East and West Germany unite as the Federal Republic of Germany.
November 19. NATO and Warsaw Pact leaders sign Conventional Forces in Europe (CFE) treaty.
November 21. CSCE summit participants sign Charter of Paris for a New Europe devoid of East-West division and committed to democracy and human rights.
November 29. UN Security Council authorizes U.S.-led forces "to use all means necessary" to secure Iraq's unconditional withdrawal from Kuwait.

1991, January 16. "Operation Desert Storm" air attacks initiated against Iraq.
February 27. U.S. president George H. W. Bush announces liberation of Kuwait; Iraq agrees to cease-fire.
March 26. Presidents of Argentina, Brazil, Paraguay, and Uruguay sign treaty in Asunción, Paraguay, creating Southern Cone Common Market (Mercosur).
April 11. UN Security Council officially declares end of Gulf war after receiving Iraq's acceptance of permanent cease-fire terms.
May 26. Zviad Gamsakhurdia of Georgia becomes first freely elected leader of a Soviet republic.
May 28. Ethiopian civil war ends as rebel forces occupy Addis Ababa.
June 12. Boris Yeltsin elected president of the Russian Soviet Federative Socialist Republic.
June 25. Croatia and Slovenia declare independence from Yugoslavia.
June 28. Communist Council for Mutual Economic Assistance (Comecon) agrees to disband. The Warsaw Treaty Organization (WTO) follows suit July 1.
July 17. U.S. president George H. W. Bush and Soviet president Mikhail Gorbachev reach agreement on Strategic Arms Reduction Treaty (START), signed July 31.
August 19–21. Hard-line Soviet leaders are defeated in coup attempt.
August 20. Estonia declares independence; other Soviet republics follow with similar declarations.
August 24. Mikhail Gorbachev resigns as general secretary of the Soviet Communist Party.
August 29. Supreme Soviet bans Communist Party activities.
September 7. Croatia and Slovenia formally secede from Yugoslavia; Macedonia declares independence September 8.
December 8. Leaders of Russia, Ukraine, and Belarus announce dissolution of the Soviet Union.
December 9–11. EC leaders agree on treaty for political and monetary union during meeting in Maastricht, Netherlands.
December 21. Eleven former Soviet republics launch Commonwealth of Independent States (CIS).
December 25. Mikhail Gorbachev resigns as Soviet president.

1992, February 7. EC's Maastricht Treaty formally signed.
March 2. Eight former Soviet republics admitted to UN.
April 27. Serbia and Montenegro proclaim new Federal Republic of Yugoslavia.
April 28. Islamic Jihad Council assumes power in Afghanistan following fall of Kabul to mujahidin rebels.
May 30. UN Security Council imposes sweeping sanctions against Serbia and Montenegro in response to aggression against Bosnia and Herzegovina.
August 1. First Lebanese parliamentary election in 20 years.
November 3. Arkansas governor Bill Clinton defeats incumbent U.S. president George H. W. Bush.

December 18. Kim Young Sam becomes first genuinely civilian president of South Korea after three decades of military leadership.

1993, January 1. Czech and Slovak Republics become separate states one day after the dissolution ("velvet divorce") of the 74-year-old Czech and Slovak Federative Republic.

January 1. Single European market established, paving the way for free movement of goods, services, capital, and people throughout all 12 EC countries.

January 3. U.S. and Russian presidents Bill Clinton and Boris Yeltsin sign second Strategic Arms Reduction Treaty (START II) under which the two nations will dismantle approximately two-thirds of their strategic nuclear warheads.

February 26. New York World Trade Center bombed by individuals linked to Islamic militants.

April 23–25. Eritrean people vote for independence (effective May 24) from Ethiopia, ending 30-year independence struggle.

April 27–28. China and Taiwan hold "unofficial" talks in Singapore, representing highest level of contact since Communists' 1949 seizure of the mainland.

May 23–28. Cambodia holds Constituent Assembly elections, first balloting since 1981.

July 18. Japanese Liberal Democratic Party loses its overall majority in the House of Representatives for first time since 1955 and is ousted from government by seven-party coalition on August 6.

September 13. Israeli-PLO peace accord signed in Washington.

October 3–4. Forces loyal to Russian President Boris Yeltsin battle with rebels opposed to his suspension of the parliament, ultimately ousting them from the parliament building.

October 8. UN General Assembly lifts economic sanctions against South Africa.

November 1. Maastricht Treaty on European Union formally enters into effect following the completion of the ratification process in October.

November 18. Interim constitution endorsed by South African multiparty negotiators.

December 15. Uruguay Round of the General Agreement on Tariffs and Trade (GATT) concludes.

December 15. Prime ministers of Ireland and United Kingdom sign "Downing Street Declaration," a 12-point document delineating principles for holding peace talks on Northern Ireland.

1994, January 1. European Economic Area (EEA), joining the EU and EFTA in a free market trading zone, comes into effect.

January 1. North American Free Trade Agreement (NAFTA), the first such agreement to link two industrialized countries (Canada and the United States) with a developing country (Mexico), becomes effective.

January 10. Announcement of Partnership for Peace (PfP), which affords military cooperation with, but not full-fledged defense guarantees by, NATO to nonmember countries.

February 28. In first offensive action by NATO, its fighters shoot down four Serbian warplanes for defying no-fly zone over Bosnia-Herzegovina.

March 27. Right-wing Freedom Alliance headed by Silvio Berlusconi wins Italian general election.

April 6. Presidents Juvénal Habyarimana of Rwanda and Cyprien Ntaryamire of Burundi die in downing of plane over Kilgali, Rwanda.

April 27. Multiracial constitution for South Africa comes into effect.

May 4. Israel and PLO sign accord in Cairo, Egypt, ending Israeli military rule in the Gaza Strip and Jericho.

May 6. Channel tunnel linking Britain and France formally opened by Queen Elizabeth II and President François Mitterrand.

May 10. Nelson Mandela sworn in as first black president of South Africa.

July 8. North Korean leader Kim Il Sung dies.

July 15. Over 500,000 Rwandan refugees arrive in Zaire, the initial wave of an exodus that would eventually involve more than 2 million people.

July 25. Israeli prime minister Yitzhak Rabin and Jordanian king Hussein sign declaration in Washington, ending 46-year state of war between their countries.

November 8. Republicans gain control of both houses of U.S. Congress for the first time in four decades.

December 11. Russian forces invade secessionist republic of Chechnya.

1995, January 1. Austria, Finland, and Sweden accede to EU.

January 1. World Trade Organization (WTO) inaugurated as successor to GATT.

April 19. Bombing of U.S. federal government building kills 168 in Oklahoma City.

May 7. Jacques Chirac (Gaullist) elected president of France in succession to François Mitterrand (Socialist).

September 5. France begins new series of underground nuclear tests in South Pacific, attracting worldwide protests.

September 28. Second accord in Israeli–PLO peace process signed in Washington, providing for extensive additional withdrawal of Israeli troops from West Bank and expansion of Palestinian self-rule.

November 4. Prime Minister Yitzhak Rabin of Israel assassinated by right-wing Jewish extremist in Tel Aviv.

November 21. U.S.-brokered peace agreement for Bosnia and Herzegovina initialed by contending parties in Dayton, Ohio (formally signed in Paris December 14).

1996, January 20. Yasir Arafat elected president of self-governing Palestinian Authority.

January 29. France announces permanent end to nuclear testing.

May 7. The first war crimes trial of the UN International Tribunal for the former Yugoslavia opens in The Hague.

May 18. Romano Prodi sworn in to head Italy's first left-dominated government, the 55th since World War II.

June 18. Conservative Benjamin Netanyahu becomes prime minister of Israel following election May 29.

June 28. Necmettin Erbakan appointed first avowedly Islamist prime minister of modern Turkey.

September 14. Post-Dayton elections in Bosnia and Herzegovina confirm entrenched ethnic loyalties.

September 24. China, France, Russia, the United Kingdom, and the United States sign Comprehensive Test Ban Treaty (CTBT) in UN headquarters, New York.

September 27. Afghanistan's Taliban militia seizes power in Kabul, immediately hanging ex-president Mohammad Najibullah.

December 10. Iraqi president Saddam Hussein reopens Iraqi oil pipelines under UN "oil-for-food" program.

December 17. Kofi Annan (Ghana) appointed (effective January 1, 1997) to succeed Boutros Boutros-Ghali (Egypt) as UN secretary-general.

December 29. Guatemalan peace agreement ends 36-year-old guerrilla insurgency.

1997, January 15. Israeli prime minister Benjamin Netanyahu and Palestinian leader Yasir Arafat sign accord whereby Israel agrees to partial withdrawal from Hebron.

February 19. Deng Xiaoping, China's "paramount leader," dies.

April 22. Peruvian commandos raid the Japanese embassy in Lima, ending 126-day hostage crisis by Túpac Amaru Revolutionary Movement guerrillas.

May 1. Led by Tony Blair, Britain's Labour Party overwhelms the Conservative Party in legislative balloting and assumes power for first time in 18 years.

May 16–17. Mobutu Sese Seko, Zaire's leader for 32 years, flees the country and rebel leader Laurent Kabila pronounces the establishment of the Democratic Republic of the Congo.

May 25. Ahmad Tejan Kabbah, Sierra Leone's first democratically elected president, flees country following military coup.

July 1. China takes control of Hong Kong after Britain's 99-year lease expires.

July 2. The Bank of Thailand abandons fixed exchange rate after months of attacks on its currency (baht) by speculators, thus sparking East Asian financial crisis.

October 23. Former president of the Republic of the Congo Denis Sassou-Nguesso overthrows the nation's first democratically elected president, Pascal Lissouba.

December 9. North Korea, South Korea, China, and the United States open talks on creation of a permanent Korean peace treaty.

1998, March 19. Nationalist Hindu leader Atal Bihari Vajpayee sworn in as prime minister of India.

April 10. Northern Ireland power-sharing agreement reached.

May 6. Border dispute breaks out between Eritrea and Ethiopia.

May 11. India conducts underground nuclear tests.

May 21. President Haji Mohammad Suharto of Indonesia resigns and is succeeded by Vice President Bacharuddin Jusuf Habibie.

May 28. Pakistan conducts underground nuclear tests.

August 2. Rebellion launched in eastern Democratic Republic of the Congo against the Kabila government.

August 7. Terrorist bombs strike U.S. embassies in Nairobi, Kenya, and Dar es Salaam, Tanzania.

September 27. German chancellor Helmut Kohl defeated in reelection bid by Social Democrat Gerhard Schröder.

October 23. Wye Accord signed by Israeli prime minister Benjamin Netanyahu and PLO leader Yasir Arafat.

October 31. Iraq announces end of cooperation with weapons inspectors from UNSCOM.

1999, January 1. Eleven of the 15 EU members launch Economic and Monetary Union (EMU), introducing euro for noncash payments on way toward replacement of national currencies by euro notes and coins in 2002.

February 27. Gen. Olusegun Obasanjo, former military ruler in 1970s, elected civilian president of Nigeria (inaugurated May 29, ending most recent period of military rule).

March 12. Czech Republic, Hungary, and Poland join NATO.

March 24. Responding to Serbian "ethnic cleansing" of Kosovo's Albanian population, NATO launches a campaign against Yugoslavia that is the biggest military operation in Europe since World War II.

June 7. Indonesia concludes first free national election in 45 years.
July 27. King Hassan II of Morocco dies.
August 30. East Timorese voters overwhelmingly vote for independence from Indonesia, leading to UN intervention following massive violence by anti-independence militias.
October 12. Gen. Pervez Musharraf declares himself chief executive of Pakistan, following military coup against elected government of Prime Minister Mohammad Nawaz Sharif.
October 14. U.S. Senate rejects Comprehensive Test Ban Treaty (CTBT) by 51–48 vote.
October 20. Abdurrahman Wahid elected president of Indonesia by People's Consultative Assembly.
December 19. Portugal returns Macao to China, ending 442 years of rule.
December 31. U.S. officially returns Panama Canal to Panama, ending 89 years of Canal Zone control.
December 31. Boris Yeltsin resigns Russian presidency and is succeeded in an acting capacity by Prime Minister Vladimir Putin.

2000, **March 18.** Chen Shui-bian elected as first non-Kuomintang president of Taiwan.
March 26. Vladimir Putin elected president of Russia.
April 6. Zimbabwe's Parliament passes controversial Land Acquisition Act, permitting uncompensated appropriation of white-owned farms and redistribution of farmland to blacks.
May 19. Armed coup launched against multiethnic government of Fiji.
May 24. Israel withdraws final troops from "security zone" in Lebanon, ending 22 years of occupation.
June 10. President Hafiz al-Assad of Syria dies.
June 13. Chairman Kim Jong Il of North Korea and President Kim Dae Jung of South Korea begin historic three-day summit in Pyongyang, North Korea.
July 2. Vicente Fox of National Action Party wins Mexican presidential election, ending 71 years of rule by Institutional Revolutionary Party.
September 28. Visit by Israeli opposition leader Ariel Sharon to Temple Mount (Haram al-Sharif) triggers new Palestinian intifada.
October 7. Vojislav Koštunica sworn in as president of Yugoslavia following capitulation of President Slobodan Milošević, who lost September 24 election.
November 17. Alberto Fujimori, having fled to Japan, resigns as president of Peru.
December 12. Eritrea and Ethiopia sign peace agreement, ending 19-month border war.
December 13. U.S. Vice President Al Gore, despite plurality of popular votes, concedes November 7 presidential election to George W. Bush, one day after Supreme Court decision effectively ended vote recounting in electorally decisive Florida.

2001, **January 7.** Nineteen years after coming to power by coup, Ghana's Jerry Rawlings hands over presidency to newly elected John Kufuor.
January 16. President Laurent Kabila of Democratic Republic of Congo assassinated.
January 20. Philippine vice president Gloria Macapagal Arroyo assumes presidency, protests having forced her predecessor, Joseph Estrada, from office.
February 6. Ariel Sharon wins special prime ministerial election in Israel, defeating Prime Minister Ehud Barak by wide margin.
April 26. Junichiro Koizumi, after unexpected victory in intraparty presidential balloting, sworn in as Japan's prime minister.
May 13. Former prime minister Silvio Berlusconi leads center-right alliance to victory in Italian general election.
June 28. Former Yugoslav president Slobodan Milošević indicted for crimes against humanity and other offenses and handed over to International Criminal Tribunal for the former Yugoslavia.
July 1. Crown Prince Dipendra of Nepal kills King Birendra and other members of royal family before committing suicide.
July 16. Russia and China conclude 20-year treaty of friendship and cooperation.
July 23. Peace agreement signed in Arusha, Tanzania, in latest effort to end eight-year civil war in Burundi.
July 23. Indonesia's People's Consultative Assembly unanimously removes President Abdurrahman Wahid from office and elects Vice President Megawati Sukarnoputri as his successor.
August 30. Bougainville secessionists sign peace agreement with Papua New Guinea government, ending 12-year conflict.
September 11. In the worst terrorist attacks in U.S. history, al-Qaida terrorists fly hijacked commercial airliners into New York's World Trade Center and the Pentagon outside Washington, D.C., causing more than 2,500 deaths.
September 23. Irish Republican Army (IRA) announces first confirmed "decommissioning" of weaponry, thereby preventing collapse of Northern Ireland power-sharing government.
October 7. U.S.-led air assault begins against al-Qaida bases and Taliban regime in Afghanistan in response to September 11 attacks.
October 29–November 10. Meeting in Marrakesh, Morocco, 164 countries negotiate final text of Kyoto Protocol to 1992 Framework Convention on Climate Change.
December 5. Hamid Karzai appointed head of interim Afghan government by factions meeting in Bonn, Germany; two days later Taliban surrenders Kandahar, its final stronghold.
December 12. China accedes to WTO.
December 20. Argentine president Fernando de la Rúa resigns in response to civil disturbances precipitated by government efforts aimed at controlling mounting financial crisis.

2002, **January 1.** The euro becomes legal tender in 12 European states.
April 4. UNITA and Angolan government sign cease-fire agreement ending civil war that dates from Angola's independence from Portugal in 1975.
April 11. International Criminal Court wins ratification by 60th UN member state, triggering its entry into force in sixty days, or July 1. United States does not ratify treaty, citing jeopardy to American citizens overseas.
April 14. Former guerilla leader José Gusmão elected first president of Timor-Leste (East Timor).
May 13. U.S. president George W. Bush and Russian president Vladimir Putin announce pact to cut nuclear arsenals by up to two-thirds over ten years.
May 20. International community recognizes Timor-Leste's independence from Indonesia.
June 13. Thirty-year-old Anti-Ballistic Missile Treaty lapses six months after President George W. Bush announced U.S. withdrawal.
June 13. Hamid Karzai elected interim president of Afghanistan.
June 16. Israel begins construction of 217-mile barrier in West Bank to thwart attacks.
July 1. International Criminal Court convenes in The Hague.
July 8. More than 30 African leaders meet in Durban to establish the African Union (AU) as the successor to the OAU.
July 30. President Paul Kagame of Rwanda and President Joseph Kabila of the Democratic Republic of the Congo sign peace agreement.
October 14. UK's secretary of state for Northern Ireland assumes powers of the suspended Northern Ireland Executive after Ulster Unionist Party withdraws its support from the Assembly.
November 21. Bulgaria, Estonia, Latvia, Lithuania, Romania, and Slovenia join NATO.
November 27. After a nearly four year hiatus, UN weapons inspectors return to Iraq to search for weapons of mass destruction.
December 4. Israeli prime minister Ariel Sharon endorses U.S. proposal for a Palestinian state in parts of the West Bank and Gaza Strip.

2003, **January 9.** North Korea withdraws from nuclear nonproliferation treaty.
January 27. Chief UN weapons inspector Hans Blix cites Iraq for noncooperation while Mohamed El-Baradei, the head of the International Atomic Energy Agency (IAEA) reports no evidence found of Iraqi nuclear weapons production.
February 4. Parliament of Federal Republic of Yugoslavia adopts new constitution renaming the country Serbia and Montenegro.
March 19. United States and allies attack Iraq.
April 9. Baghdad falls to U.S. forces.
May 22. Security Council Resolution 1483 ends economic sanctions on Iraq and recognizes United States and United Kingdom as occupying powers.
June 5. Israeli prime minister Ariel Sharon and Palestinian prime minister Mahmoud Abbas commit during summit in Aqaba, Jordan, to "roadmap" peace plan proposed by the United States.
June 6. French peacekeepers deploy in the Democratic Republic of the Congo to quell tribal warfare.
August 4. Peacekeepers from West African states arrive in Liberia to quell fighting between government and antigovernment forces.
August 7. Liberian president Charles Taylor resigns.
August 11. NATO takes command of peacekeeping operations in Afghanistan in first such mission outside Europe in alliance history.
September 14. Sweden's voters buck government to reject euro—56.1 percent to 41.8 percent—thereby retaining krona as national currency.
December 13. U.S. military captures Saddam Hussein.
December 19. Libyan leader Muammar Abu Minyar al-Qadhafi pledges to abandon pursuit of weapons of mass destruction.

2004, **January 4.** Afghan loya jirga approves constitution of Islamic Republic of Afghanistan.
February 29. Haitian president Jean Bertrand Aristide resigns and goes into exile.
March 12. South Korean National Assembly impeaches President Roh Moo Hyun for election law violations.
April 28. U.S. news program *60 Minutes II* broadcasts photos of U.S. troops abusing prisoners in Iraq's Abu Ghraib prison, publicizing an investigation under way in the military.
May 1. Ten countries—Cyprus, Czech Republic, Estonia, Hungary, Latvia, Lithuania, Malta, Poland, Slovak Republic, and Slovenia—join European Union, bringing the number of member states to 25.

May 9. Chechen president Akhmad Kadyrov assassinated in Grozny.
May 26. Conflict between Arabs and blacks continues in Darfur region of Sudan despite accord between Islamic government and Sudan People's Liberation Army.
June 28. U.S. administrator in Iraq L. Paul Bremer III transfers sovereignty to Iraqi prime minister Iyad Allawi.
November 3. Interim president Hamid Karzai declared official winner of Afghan presidential election.
November 11. Long-time Palestinian leader and Palestinian Authority president Yasir Arafat dies.
November 27. Ukrainian parliament nullifies results of November 21 election runoff, citing election fraud; Prime Minister Viktor Yanukovich claims a narrow 3 percent margin over challenger Viktor Yushchenko.
December 26. Yushchenko defeats Yanukovich in Ukrainian presidential runoff.
December 26. Tsunami hits Southeast Asia, killing an estimated 225,000 people and affecting a dozen states in Asia and Africa.

2005, **January 30.** Iraqis vote for representatives to national and provincial assemblies in first democratic elections since 1953.
February 1. King Gyanendra Bir Bikram Shah Dev of Nepal declares a state of emergency, dissolves coalition government, and arrests leading politicians, citing his constitutional authority and the lack of progress toward holding elections.
February 14. Former prime minister of Lebanon Rafik al-Hariri and others die in a car bomb explosion, leading to anti-Syria demonstrations and international pressure on Syria to withdraw its troops from the country.
February 16. Kyoto Protocol to UN Framework Convention on Climate Change takes effect. United States is not a party to the agreement.
March 16. Israel turns over control of Jericho to Palestinians.
April 2. Pope John Paul II dies.
April 19. Conclave of cardinals elects Cardinal Joseph Ratzinger of Germany as pope. Ratzinger takes the name Benedict XVI.
April 26. Last Syrian troops leave Lebanon, ending 29-year stay.
June 16. After a proposed European constitution is voted down in nationwide referendums in Netherlands and France, leaders of EU halt efforts to ratify.
August 1. King Fahd ibn Abd al-Aziz Al Saud of Saudi Arabia dies; Prince Abdullah assumes the throne.
August 10. Iran removes UN seals it voluntarily accepted at nuclear production sites eight months previously and begins converting raw uranium into gas for enrichment.
August 15. Indonesia and the Free Aceh Movement sign a peace accord ending 30 years of civil war.
August 15. Israel begins withdrawing more than 8,700 Jewish settlers from the Gaza Strip, enabling Palestinians to assume control of the area.
August 29. Hurricane Katrina lashes U.S. city of New Orleans, flooding the city and coastal areas, and killing over 1,500; federal emergency response is widely criticized.
September 18. Afghanistan holds its first democratic parliamentary elections in more than 25 years.
October 10. German legislative parties agree to resolve their September parliamentary election disputes by creating a Grand Coalition that includes Angela Merkel as Germany's first woman chancellor.
October 15. Iraqis endorse new constitution with 79 percent "yes" vote.
November 21. Voters defeat proposed new constitution in Kenya.
December 15. Iraq elects its first permanent parliament since the removal of President Saddam Hussein.
December 18. Bolivia holds its presidential election after the resignation of President Carlos Mesa in June; Evo Morales, the candidate of the Movement to Socialism, wins with 51.1 percent of the vote.
December 23. Lech Kaczyński sworn in as president of Poland after winning the election on the second runoff.

2006, **January 4.** Israeli leader Ariel Sharon suffers a second, catastrophic stroke and slips into a coma. Ehud Olmert named acting prime minister.
January 15. Ellen Johnson-Sirleaf sworn in as president of Liberia, thereby becoming Africa's first female president.
January 15. In a runoff election, center-left candidate Michelle Bachelet wins 53 percent of the vote to become Chile's first female president.
January 25. Hamas wins a majority in elections to the Palestinian Legislative Council, ending Fatah's dominance.
February 28. Former opposition leader Milorad Dodik confirmed as prime minister of the Serb Republic of Bosnia and Herzegovina.
April 23. Prime Minister Ferenc Gyurcsány's coalition, led by the Hungarian Socialist Party, wins runoff parliamentary elections.
April 27. Following weeks of demonstrations in Nepal in opposition to King Gyanendra's continued absolute power, consensus candidate Girija Prasad Koirala is appointed prime minister.
May 4. Ehud Olmert, leader of the recently launched Kadima party, forms a coalition government in Israel following the Knesset balloting on March 28 in which Kadima secured a plurality of seats.
May 5. The Sudanese government and the leader of Darfur's main rebel group agree to a cease-fire after three years of hostilities and the displacement of an estimated 2 million people.
May 17. Romano Prodi, leader of the new Union coalition, returns to the premiership of Italy after the Union secured a majority of the seats in the legislative poll of April 9–10.
May 20. Nurad Jawad al-Maliki forms national unity government in Iraq.
May 26. Nepal's prime minister Girija Prasad Koirala and rebel Maoist leader Prachanda sign a cease-fire code of conduct, bringing a degree of political stability to the country.
June 3. Former Yugoslav republic of Montenegro declares independence from Serbia.
June 27. Economic reformer and Communist Party chief Nguyen Minh Triet elected president of Vietnam after the country's top three leaders officially retire.
July 12. The Lebanese Shiite Muslim group Hezbollah kills three Israeli soldiers and captures two others during a raid into Israel; Israel subsequently responds with air-strike bombing of Lebanon to which Hezbollah retaliates by launching rockets and missiles into Israel.
August 3. Viktor Yanukovych of the pro-Russian Party of Regions named prime minister of Ukraine following protracted negotiations with the Orange Revolution parties.
August 14. Israel and Hezbollah declare a cease-fire.
September 19. A military coup led by Gen. Sonthi Boonyaratkalin, with the support of the royal family and numerous citizens, overthrows Prime Minister Thaksin Shinawatra of Thailand.
October 8. North Korea announces its first successful underground nuclear weapons test, prompting widespread international condemnation and UN sanctions.
October 27. After failed talks with the West, Iran restarts its nuclear program, claiming its reactors are for peaceful purposes, despite concerns expressed by the UN and Western nations.
November 21. The Nepalese government signs a Comprehensive Peace Agreement with former Maoist insurgents.
December 1. Conservative Felipe Calderón inaugurated as president of Mexico amid controversy over his victory against leftist Andrés Manuel López Obrador in balloting on July 6.
December 5. The Fijian military, led by Commander Frank Bainimarama, takes over the government of Prime Minister Laisenia Qarase in the country's fourth coup in 20 years.
December 6. Joseph Kabila sworn in as president of the Democratic Republic of the Congo, making him the nation's first elected president in 40 years.
December 14. In Bhutan, King Jigme Singye Wangchuk abdicates the throne in favor of his son, Crown Prince Jigme Khesar Namgyal Wangchuk.
December 23. Resolution 1737 is unanimously approved by the UN Security Council, imposing sanctions on Iran for failing to comply with resolution 1696, which prohibited it from enrichment activities.
December 24–28. Ethiopia formally admits to having troops engaged in battle within the borders of Somalia. Somali government forces, backed by Ethiopian troops, retake the capital, Mogadishu, from the Islamic Courts Union.
December 30. Former Iraqi president Saddam Hussein hanged, having been found guilty of crimes against humanity by an Iraqi tribunal on November 5.

2007, **January 1.** Romania and Bulgaria become members of the EU.
January 1. Ban Ki-moon, theretofore the foreign minister of South Korea, succeeds Kofi Annan as secretary-general of the UN.
January 10. Sandinista leader Daniel Ortega returns to the presidency of Nicaragua.
March 4. Peace agreement signed in Côte d'Ivoire, preparing the groundwork for formation of a new national unity government.
March 17. The Palestinian Legislative Council approves a Fatah/Hamas unity government led by Ismail Haniyeh of Hamas.
April 1. Former Maoist insurgents join the cabinet in Nepal.
May 6. Conservative Nicolas Sarkozy wins the French presidential runoff election with 53.1 percent of the vote over Socialist Ségolène Royal.
May 8. Limited self-rule returns to Northern Ireland based on the St. Andrews Agreement of October 2006 and subsequent agreements between unionist and republican/nationalist parties.
May 12. Su Tseng-Chang resigns as the premier of the Republic of China (Taiwan) following a loss in a presidential primary election; President Chen Shui-bian replaces him with Chang Chun-hsiung on May 14.
June 14. Palestinian president Mahmoud Abbas dissolves the Palestinian government and installs emergency rule in the wake of Hamas's recent takeover of the Gaza Strip.
June 27. Gordon Brown succeeds Tony Blair as prime minister of the United Kingdom.
July 18. IAEA inspectors confirm the closure of all five nuclear reactors in North Korea as six-party talks resume in Beijing.

August 28. Abdullah Gul of the Justice and Development Party is elected as the first Islamist president of Turkey.
October 28. Argentine first lady Cristina Kirchner elected to succeed her husband, Nestor Kirchner, as president.
November 7. Georgian president Mikhail Saakashvili declares a state of emergency amid protests calling for his resignation.
November 29. Pervez Musharraf sworn in for another five-year term as Pakistan's president after relinquishing his military posts.
December 2. Russian president Vladimir Putin's party secures 70 percent of the vote in Russian parliamentary elections.
December 3. Kevin Rudd of the Australian Labor Party becomes prime minister, succeeding John Howard of the Liberal Party of Australia.
December 18. Yulia Tymoshenko returns as prime minister of Ukraine to head a coalition government dominated by the Orange Revolution parties, which secured a slim majority in the legislative poll of September 30 that was prompted by intense conflict between President Viktor Yushchenko and Prime Minister Viktor Yanukovych.
December 23. Thailand's People Power Party (supportive of ousted prime minister Thaksin Shinawatra) wins the Thai parliamentary elections.
December 27. Former Pakistani prime minister Benazir Bhutto assassinated at a campaign rally.
December 30. Kenya's election commission declares incumbent Mwai Kibaki the winner of the December 27 national election, sparking violent protests from opposition party supporters, who charge that the election was rigged.

2008, **January 22.** The military's Council for National Security in Thailand announces its dissolution and acceptance of the December legislative election results.
January 24. Italian prime minister Romano Prodi offers his resignation following no-confidence vote in the Senate.
January 28. Samak Sundaravej, considered a "proxy" for former prime minister Thaksin Shinawatra, elected prime minister by Thailand's House of Representatives.
February 3. Pro-Western president Boris Tadić reelected in Serbia over nationalist rival Tomislav Nikolić.
February 17. Prime Minister Hashim Thaçi declares Kosovo independent, prompting fierce criticism from Serbia and Russia but quick recognition from the United States, the United Kingdom, France, Germany, Japan, and others.
February 18. Opposition parties dominate legislative elections in Pakistan in what is generally perceived as a referendum on the rule of President Musharraf.
February 24. Raúl Castro confirmed as president of Cuba's Council of State and Council of Ministers after Fidel Castro had announced that he would not accept reelection to those posts.
February 27. Israel launches air and ground offensive in Gaza Strip.
February 28. Dimitrios Christofias, leader of the Progressive Party of the Working People, inaugurated as the first communist president of Cyprus.
March 2. Dmitri Medvedev elected president of Russia as Vladimir Putin's handpicked successor.
March 22. Ma Ying-jeou of the Nationalist Party (Kuomintang) elected president of Taiwan.
March 24. The lower house in Pakistan elects Yusuf Raza Gilani, an ally of the late Benazir Bhutto, as prime minister of Pakistan.
April 8. President Ahmadinejad of Iran announces plans for additional uranium enrichment.
April 9. New constitution, providing for a multiparty system headed by a president and a bicameral legislature, proposed by Myanmar's military junta.
April 10. Maoists secure legislative victory in Nepal.
April 13. Power-sharing cabinet announced in Kenya; Mwai Kibaki remains president and opposition leader Raila Odinga named prime minister.
April 15. The Iraqi Accord Front, a Sunni coalition, returns to the Shiite-dominated Iraqi cabinet.
April 20. Fernando Lugo is elected president of Paraguay, ending more than 60 years of rule by the Colorado Party.
April 27. Coalition government collapses in Hungary.
May 2. Election commission in Zimbabwe declares that opposition candidate Tsvangirai won only 48 percent of the vote in the March 29 balloting, thereby necessitating a runoff between him and President Mugabe, who finished second in the first round.
May 7. Brian Cowen of Fianna Fáil elected prime minister by the lower house of the legislature in Ireland, following Bertie Ahern's resignation from the post (effective May 6) amid corruption investigations.
May 8. Former president Vladimir Putin confirmed as prime minister by the Russian State Duma.
May 21. Supporters of Georgian president Mikhail Saakashvili dominate legislative balloting.
May 25. Gen. Michel Suleiman elected president of Lebanon by the National Assembly as part of the May 21 agreement designed to stem strife between Hezbollah (and other Shiite groups) and progovernment forces. Prime Minister Fouad Siniroa subsequently forms a new cabinet that includes members of Hezbollah.
May 28. Nepal's Constituent Assembly agrees to abolish the monarchy and establish a federal republic.
June 2. Bhutan's National Assembly approves draft constitution transferring power from the king to a government formed by the leading legislative party.
June 18. Israel and Hamas initiate a cease-fire.
June 26. The interim prime minister of Nepal announces his resignation as efforts to establish a transitional government falter.
June 27. Pro-European coalition government announced in Serbia.
June 27. Zimbabwean president Robert Mugabe wins highly controversial second-round presidential balloting after first-round leader Morgan Tsvangirai withdraws to protest violence against his supporters in the run-up to the election.
July 27. Ruling Cambodian People's Party wins two-thirds majority in legislative elections.
August 6. Military coup overthrows the government in Mauritania.
August 7. Georgian forces enter South Ossetia, triggering massive response by Russia in which Russian forces move deeply into Georgia proper. Russia subsequently recognizes the independence of South Ossetia and Abkhazia.
August 15. Maoist Pushpa Kamal Dahal elected prime minister of Nepal.
August 18. Pakistani president Musharraf resigns.
August 19. Zambian president Levy Mwanawasa dies.
September 1. Japanese prime minister Fukuda resigns; Taro Aso elected leader of the Liberal Democratic Party on September 22 and installed as prime minister on September 24.
September 1. Massive crowds demonstrate in Thailand against Prime Minister Samak, prompting him to impose a state of emergency.
September 5. Senate in Haiti approves government of new prime minister Michèle Pierre-Louis.
September 5–6. The Popular Movement for the Liberation of Angola dominates the first legislative balloting since 1992.
September 7. U.S. government approves takeover of two privately owned (albeit government-sponsored) mortgage companies as an unprecedented financial intervention develops, in which Congress ultimately authorizes a $700 billion bailout of banking system in the midst of a global "credit crisis" and steep declines in the stock market.
September 8. Asif Ali Zardari, the widower of Benazir Bhutto, elected president of Pakistan in a vote by the federal legislature and provincial assemblies.
September 9. Thai prime minister Samak forced to resign; succeeded on September 17 by Somchai Wongsawat, the brother-in-law of former prime minister Thaksin.
September 20. South African president Mbeki agrees to resign under pressure from the African National Congress (ANC); Kgalema Motlanthe, deputy leader of the ANC, elected as Mbeki's successor by the National Assembly on September 25.
September 28. Far-right parties gain ground in early legislative elections in Austria but ruling centrist parties form new coalition government on December 2.
September 28. New constitution (proposed by the leftist government) endorsed in national referendum in Ecuador.
September 29. Government in Iceland forced to nationalize the country's third largest bank as value of the krona plummets in midst of global financial crisis.
October 8. Malaysian prime minister Abdullah announces he will resign in March 2009 in the wake of his party's poor performance in the March 2008 legislative elections.
October 26. Tzipi Livni declares her efforts to form a new coalition government in Israel unsuccessful, setting the stage for new legislative elections in early 2009.
October 26. Fighting intensifies in eastern Democratic Republic of the Congo, ultimately displacing 250,000 people.
November 4. Barack Obama elected president of the United States, and his Democratic Party extends its legislative control.
November 7. Mass demonstrations in Georgia demand resignation of President Mikhail Saakashvili.
November 8. Opposition National Party wins legislative balloting in New Zealand; party leader John Key forms coalition government on November 17.
November 25. Referendum in Greenland approves extension of self-rule in anticipation of eventual independence.
December 2. Thailand's Constitutional Court prompts expulsion of Prime Minister Somchai via ruling that his People Power Party committed fraud in the 2007 elections; opposition leader Abhisit Vejjajiva elected prime minister by the legislature on December 15.

December 22. President Lansana Conté of Guinea dies; military leaders assume power in a bloodless coup the following day and install Capt. Moussa Dadis Camara as president of a ruling National Council for Democracy and Development.
December 28. Israel launches air strikes on Gaza following resumption of Hamas rocket attacks.
December 29. The Awami League, a former opposition party led by former prime minister Sheikh Hasina Wajed, wins an overwhelming victory in legislative elections in Bangladesh.

2009, **January 3.** Ground offensive into Gaza launched by Israel, which announces unilateral cease-fire January 17.
January 19. Left-wing opposition gains legislative victory in El Salvador.
January 26. Iceland's government collapses; minority interim government formed February 1 under Jóhanna Sigurðardóttir, the country's first female prime minister.
January 26. Violent antigovernment protests begin in Madagascar as supporters of Andry Rajoelina, the mayor of Antananarivo, demand the resignation of President Marc Ravalomanana; both sides subsequently claim to be in control of the country.
February 11. Morgan Tsvangirai sworn in as prime minister to head national unity government in Zimbabwe.
February 15. Voters in Venezuela approve constitutional revision eliminating presidential term limits.
February 20. Declining economic conditions trigger collapse of Latvian government.
March 2. President João Bernardo Vieira assassinated by "rogue" army troops in Guinea-Bissau; the army denies a coup has occurred.
March 15. Opposition leader Mauricio Funes elected president of El Salvador.
March 17. Marc Ravalomanana steps down as president of Madagascar after army supports Andry Rajoelina in power struggle.
March 27. Center-right government falls in Czech Republic after losing confidence motion over its handling of economic affairs.
March 29. Ruling pro-European coalition wins early legislative elections in Montenegro.
March 31. Likud's Benjamin Netanyahu sworn in as leader of center-right government in Israel.
April 3. Najib Razak inaugurated as prime minister of Malaysia following the resignation of Abdullah Badawi, whose government had been under year-long pressure.
April 5. Official results of legislative elections in Moldova give majority to the ruling Communist Party of Moldova, prompting massive protests, charges of fraud, and, ultimately, new elections.
April 10. Fiji's president Ratu Iloilo abrogates 1997 constitution in wake of earlier Court of Appeals ruling that called for new elections; Iloilo revokes all judicial appointments, declares himself head of state, and says elections will not be held until 2014.
April 22. African National Congress wins another solid legislative majority in South Africa; ANC leader Jacob Zuma elected president of South Africa by the legislature on May 6.
April 26. Rafael Correa reelected as president of Ecuador, and his left-wing Country Alliance secures legislative plurality.
May 3. Conservative business leader Ricardo Martinelli Berrocal elected president of Panama; his four-party coalition secures legislative majority.
May 18. Sri Lankan military announces final victory over the separatist Liberation Tigers of Tamil Eelam after 26 years of conflict.
May 23. Madhave Kumar Nepal elected prime minister of Nepal following resignation of Pushpa Kamal Dahal, who had been embroiled in a dispute with the military.
June 2. Greenland's legislative elections won by leftist, proindependence opposition.
June 7. Anti-Syrian, pro-Western alliance wins legislative majority in Lebanon.
June 8. President Omar Bongo, Gabon's president since 1967, dies of natural causes.
June 12. Incumbent Mahmoud Ahmadinejad declared winner of presidential election in Iran, prompting massive protests alleging fraud, followed by a violent government crackdown on dissidents.
June 28. President Mel Zelaya ousted in Honduras, prompting widespread international condemnation of his opponents.
July 5. Center-right opposition gains plurality in legislative balloting in Bulgaria; Boiko Borisov, theretofore mayor of Sofia, named prime minister on July 27.
July 5. Opposition Institutional Revolutionary Party and allies win majority in elections to the Mexican Chamber of Deputies.
July 10. Peruvian prime minister Yehude Simon resigns following antigovernment protests.
July 18. Mohamed Ould Abdelaziz, who led the 2008 coup in Mauritania, elected president in first-round balloting disputed as fraudulent by his opponents.
July 29. The ruling Communist Party of Moldova loses its majority in rerun of legislative elections (originally held in April); Vladimir Filat sworn in as head of a four-party, pro-EU coalition government on September 25.
August 20. Presidential elections held in Afghanistan; incumbent Hamid Karzai is later credited with a first-round victory, prompting widespread accusations of fraud.
August 30. Opposition Democratic Party of Japan wins legislative elections in Japan, ending longtime dominance of Liberal Democratic party.
September 1. Fiji suspended from the Commonwealth for government's refusal to negotiate a new election schedule with the opposition.
September 3. Ali-Ben Bongo Ondimba, son of the late president Bongo, declared winner of the August 30 presidential election in Gabon.
September 7. Premier Liu Chao-shiuan resigns as Taiwan's premier following criticism of his government's response to a recent typhoon.
September 25. Western leaders accuse Iran of operating a secret uranium enrichment facility.
October 4. Opposition Panhellenic Socialist Movement (PASOK) scores landslide victory in legislative elections in Greece; PASOK leader George Papandreou forms new government October 7.
October 20. Supporters of President Mamadou Tandja, benefiting from opposition boycott, gain all seats in early legislative balloting in Niger; Niger suspended from ECOWAS on October 21.
November 1. Abdullah Abdullah, who finished second to incumbent Hamid Karzai in the disputed presidential balloting in Afghanistan in August, withdraws from runoff; Karzai is inaugurated for another term on November 20.
November 9. Prime Minister Saad Hariri forms unity government (which includes Hezbollah) in Lebanon after months of wrangling.
November 11. Jean-Max Bellerive named prime minister of Haiti.
November 27–29. Ruling South West Africa People's Organization (SWAPO) wins landslide victory in presidential and legislative elections in Namibia.
November 29. José Mujica, a former leader of the Tupamaros guerrillas and the candidate of the ruling Progressive Encounter–Broad Front, elected president of Uruguay.
November 29. Central bank of United Arab Emirates bails out Dubai, which had earlier roiled world financial markets by asking for a moratorium on $59 billion in debt.
November 29. Iran approves construction of new uranium enrichment plants, prompting U.S. threats of additional sanctions.
November 29. Porfirio Lobo Sosa elected president of Honduras.
December 1. U.S. president Barack Obama announces that 30,000 additional troops will be sent to Afghanistan.
December 1. EU's Lisbon Treaty enters into force; Herman Van Rompuy, former prime minister of Belgium, to become the first permanent president of the European Council under the EU's revamped and expanded institutional structure.
December 3. Guinea's president Moussa Camara seriously wounded in assassination attempt by an aide.
December 6. Incumbent Traian Băsescu narrowly reelected president of Romania in disputed balloting.
December 7–8. Antigovernment protests continue in Iran; more than 200 people arrested.
December 8. Japan announces new $80 billion stimulus package.
December 18. Power-sharing plan abandoned in Madagascar.
December 29. Sudan's legislature approves law authorizing a 2011 independence referendum in southern Sudan.

2010, **January 10.** Center-left opposition candidate Ivo Josipović elected president of Croatia.
January 12. Earthquake in Haiti kills more than 200,000 people and leaves 1 million homeless.
January 17. Right-wing businessman Sebastián Piñera elected president of Chile.
February 7. Pro-Russian former prime minister Viktor Yanukovych, elected president of Ukraine.
February 7. Laura Chinchilla, the candidate of the ruling National Liberation Party, becomes the first woman to be elected president of Costa Rica.
February 13. U.S./UK/Afghan forces launch massive anti-Taliban campaign in Afghanistan's Helmand Province.
February 18. Military coup in Niger seizes power from President Mamadou Tandja.
February 23. Government collapses in Netherlands over the issue of extension of the Dutch mission in Afghanistan.
March 3. Greek prime minister George Papandreou warns of the country's potential bankruptcy and initiates severe austerity measures.
March 4. Incumbent Faure Gnassingbé reelected president of Togo.
March 7. Legislative elections in Iraq portend long negotiations on formation of a new government as Prime Minister Nuri al-Maliki's alliance vies with the alliance of former prime minister Ayad Allawi for plurality status.

March 24. United States and Russia announce agreement on a new treaty to reduce the deployment of nuclear weapons by 30 percent.
April 7. Protest demonstrations prompt President Kurmanbek Bakiyev to flee Kyrgyzstan's capital, and opposition coalition selects Roza Otunbayeva to lead provisional government. (Bakiyev officially resigns on April 15.)
April 10. Polish president Lech Kaczyński and 95 others (including many national officials) die in plane crash in Russia.
April 11 and 25. Right-wing opposition alliance secures overwhelming victory in legislative balloting in Hungary after the incumbent government is accused of economic incompetence.
April 12–13. Algeria, Mali, Mauritania, and Niger approve joint regional antiterrorism activity aimed primarily at al-Qaida in the Islamic Maghreb.
April 15. Legislature in Pakistan approves restoration of 1973 constitution, thereby giving back to the prime minister authority assumed by President Musharraf in 2003.
April 18. Derviş Eroğlu, considered a skeptic in regard to Cypriot reunification, elected president of the Turkish Republic of Northern Cyprus.
April 19. Djibouti's legislature approves constitutional revision permitting President Ismail Guelleh to run for a third term.
April 22. Belgium's government resigns (but remains in caretaker capacity) over issue of proposed new electoral districts.
May 5. Junta in Niger announces constitutional referendum and new elections will be held by February 2011.
May 5. Nigerian president Umaru Yar'Adua dies and is succeeded by Vice President Goodluck Jonathan.
May 6. Opposition Conservative Party wins plurality in elections to the UK House of Commons, permitting Conservative leader David Cameron to form a coalition government with the Liberal Democrats on May 11.
May 9. U.S.-mediated proximity talks begin between officials from Israel and the Palestinian Authority.
May 10. Benigno Aquino III, the son of the late former president Corazon Aquino, elected president of the Philippines.
May 23. Ruling Ethiopian People's Revolutionary Democratic Front and its allies win 534 of 547 seats in lower-house balloting in Ethiopia.
May 25. Electoral coalition led by former dictator Désiré Bouterse wins legislative plurality in Suriname, leading to Bouterse's election to the presidency by the National Assembly on July 19.
May 26. Kamla-Persad Bissessar becomes the first female prime minister of Trinidad and Tobago following the legislative victory of her opposition coalition on May 24.
May 28–29. Ruling three-party center-right government wins majority in lower-house balloting in Czech Republic, although the opposition Czech Social Democratic Party leads all parties.
May 31. Israeli naval forces intercept aid ships headed for Gaza, killing nine people and attracting widespread international criticism.
June 8. Finance Minister Naoto Kan appointed prime minister of Japan following the resignation on June 2 of Yukio Hatoyama in the face of plummeting popular approval.
June 9. Opposition People's Party for Freedom and Democracy secures one-seat plurality in lower-house balloting in Netherlands, while the anti-immigration Party for Freedom dramatically increases its representation.
June 10–14. Fighting in southern Kyrgyzstan between Kyrgyz and Uzbek ethnic groups leaves an estimated 2,000 dead and 400,000 displaced.
June 12. Center-left party of Prime Minister Robert Fico wins plurality in lower-house balloting in Slovakia, but losses by other parties in his coalition leave the government without a majority.
June 13. New Flemish Alliance, a party devoted to eventual independence for Flanders, wins pluralities in voting for both legislative houses in Belgium.
June 20. Juan Manuel Santos, the candidate of the ruling Social Party of National Unity, elected president of Colombia.
June 24. Julia Gillard named Australia's first female prime minister after successfully challenging Prime Minister Kevin Rudd for leadership of Australian Labor Party.
June 27. Voters in Kyrgyzstan approve a new constitution that establishes a parliamentary republic with limited presidential powers.
July 4. Bronisław Komorowski, the speaker of the lower house of the legislature, elected president of Poland in second-round balloting over Jarosław Kaczyński, the twin of the late president.
July 9. Iveta Radičová appointed as Slovakia's first female prime minister.
July 29. South Korean prime minister Chung Un Chan resigns in view of the poor results for his party in local elections in June.
August 27. New constitution in Kenya limits presidential authority and expands civil rights.
August 31. U.S. president Barack Obama announces the end of U.S. combat operations in Iraq, although an estimated 50,000 U.S. troops remain in Iraq in a support role.
September 12. Constitutional reforms proposed by Turkey's ruling Justice and Development Party approved in national referendum.
September 18. Legislative elections in Afghanistan marred by violence and irregularities.
September 19. Far-right anti-immigration party enters Swedish legislature for first time.
October 10. Netherlands Antilles dissolves, with Curaçao and St. Maarten becoming autonomous "countries" within the Kingdom of the Netherlands, which retains authority over defense and foreign affairs.
October 10. Party supportive of former president Bakiyev wins narrow plurality in legislative balloting in Kyrgyzstan.
October 23. David Thompson, the prime minister of Barbados, dies.
October 31. Dilma Rousseff elected Brazil's first female president.
November 2. In a major setback for the Obama administration, the Republican Party gains control of the U.S. House of Representatives.
November 7. Opposition leader Alpha Conté elected president of Guinea.
November 7. In Myanmar's first national election since 1990, junta-supportive Union Solidarity and Development Party wins an overwhelming victory at all levels. The results are widely condemned internationally.
November 13. Aung San Suu Kyi, Myanmar's most prominent antijunta leader, is released upon expiration of her most recent period of house arrest.
November 28. Incumbent Laurent Gbagbo and opposition leader Alassana Ouattara both claim victory in second round of presidential balloting in Côte d'Ivoire.
November 28 and December 5. In controversial two-stage parliamentary balloting, Egypt's ruling National Democratic Party wins 420 of 508 directly elected seats.
December 13. Prime Minister Michael Somare of Papua New Guinea, facing charges involving financial irregularities, steps down, with Sam Abal, the deputy prime minister, becoming acting prime minister.
December 17. Kyrgyzstan's legislature endorses politically diverse three-party coalition government led by Prime Minister Almazbek Atambayev of the Social Democratic Party of Kyrgyzstan.
December 19. Belarusan president Alyaksandr Lukashenka wins reelection, capturing 79.6 percent of the vote, according to the official count, against nine challengers.
December 21. Prime Minister al-Maliki forms coalition government in Iraq with support of major legislative groupings.

2011, **January 1.** Estonia becomes the 17th member of the Eurozone when it officially adopts the euro as its currency.
January 9-15. Voters in South Sudan endorse independence in a referendum.
January 10. Basque separatists declare a unilateral cease-fire with Spain after 40 years of conflict.
January 12. The Lebanese government of Prime Minister Saad Hariri falls after 11 Hezbollah and allied cabinet members resign.
January 14. Tunisian president Gen. Zine El-Abidine Ben Ali flees the country amid violent protests. The fall of Ben Ali's government marks the beginning of the Arab Spring uprisings, which spread throughout the region.
January 23. Gen. François Bozizé Yangouvonda Aníbal is reelected president of the Central African Republican. In Portugal, president Cavaco Silva wins reelection.
January 26. Violent police clashes with protesters in Syria mark the beginning of the Syrian Uprising.
February 1. Marouf al-Bakhit is appointed prime minister by King Abdullah II in response to calls for political reform and in an effort to counter anti-regime protests.
February 3. After seven months of protected negotiations, Jhala Nath Khanal is elected prime minister of Nepal by the parliament.
February 4. In Myanmar, Prime Minister Thein Sein is elected president by the legislature.
February 11. Egyptian president Husni Mubarak resigns after weeks of protests which kill more than 800 and injure more than 6,000. An interim government, dominated by the Supreme Council of the Armed Forces and led by Field Marshal Mohammad Hussein Tantawi is installed.
February 14. Pearl Uprising begins in Bahrain with massive protests by the majority Shiite population against the Sunni-led regime.
February 15. Anti-government protests in Libya are met with harsh military force, sparking the Libyan Revolution.
February 18. Lt. Gen. Yoweri Kaguta Museveni is reelected president of Uganda, securing more than 68 percent of the vote.
February 22. Behgjet Pacolli is elected president of Kosovo by the National Assembly in the third round of balloting. Incumbent prime minister Hashim Thaçi is reappointed.
March 5. Mustafa Abdel Jalil is appointed to head Libya's National Transitional Council, the main anti-regime umbrella organization.
March 9. Enda Kenny is elected prime minister of Ireland by the parliament, following legislative elections on February 25.
March 11. An earthquake of magnitude 9.0, and a subsequent tsunami, hit the east coast of Japan, leading to the meltdown of the Fukushima Daiichi nuclear power plant and claiming more than 18,000 lives.

March 17. UN Security Council approves a no-fly zone over Libya in an attempt to reduce civilian casualties; two days later, an international coalition begins enforcement of the no-fly zone and launched attacks on Libyan military targets. Živko Budimir is elected president of the Federation of Bosnia-Herzegovina by the House of Peoples, while Nermin Nikšić becomes prime minister.
March 18. Rosario Fernández Figueroa is appointed prime minister of Peru following the resignation of José Antonio Chang Escobedo.
March 20. In disputed runoff balloting, singer Michel Martelly is elected president of Haiti.
March 28. The constitutional court of Kosovo rules that that the election of president Pacolli on February 22 was unconstitutional. Pacolli leaves office and is replaced on an interim basis by the speaker of the parliament Jakup Krasniqi.
March 29. Syrian president Bashar al-Assad accepts the resignation of his cabinet in response to widespread protests.
April 3. Nursultan Nazarbayev is reelected president of Kazakhstan in disputed balloting that was boycotted by opposition parties. In Mali, Cissé Mariam Kaïdama Sidibé is appointed prime minister, becoming the country's first woman chief executive.
April 4. Prime minister Sir Michael Somare of Papua New Guinea is suspended from office for 14 days following his conviction on misconduct charges. After his suspension, Somare declined to return to office, citing medical reasons, and Sam Abal becomes interim prime minister.
April 11. Former Côte d'Ivoire president Laurent Gbagbo is captured by rebel forces, ending a four month civil war.
April 15. Tertius Zongo is dismissed as prime minister of Burkina Faso by president Blaise Compaoré. Luc Adolphe Tiao is appointed to replace Zongo and forms a new government on April 22.
April 16. Incumbent president Goodluck Jonathan wins presidential polling in Nigeria, but his victory is met by widespread violence in the mainly Muslim north of the country.
April 17. The National Coalition Party wins legislative elections in Finland and forms a coalition government, led by prime minister Jyrki Katainen who is sworn into office on June 22.
May 1. Osama bin Laden, founder and leader of al-Qaida, is killed by U.S. special operations forces in his compound near Islamabad, Pakistan.
May 2. Canada's Conservative Party, led by incumbent prime minister Stephen Harper, wins a majority in parliamentary balloting.
May 15. Egyptian foreign minister Nabil al-Arabi is selected as the new secretary general of the Arab League and takes office on July 1.
May 28. After being vacant through successive governments since 1998, the post of prime minister is filled in Benin with the appointment of Pascal Irénée Koupaki.
May 29. Sergey Bagapsh, the president of the breakaway Georgian republic of Abkhazia, dies in office and is succeeded on an interim basis by vice president Aleksandr Ankvab, who is elected to a full term on August 27.
June 2. In the second round of presidential balloting by the Latvian parliament, Andris Berzins defeats incumbent Valdis Zatlers.
June 5. Ollanta Humala is elected president of Peru in runoff balloting. The Social Democrat Party wins legislative elections in Portugal and party leader Pedro Passos Coelho forms a new government on June 15.
July 9. Republic of South Sudan gains independence from Sudan and Salva Kiir is inaugurated as president of the new nation. South Sudan joins the UN five days later.
July 21. EU leaders agree to extend emergency debt repayment by Ireland, Greece and Portugal from seven to fifteen years and cut interest rates on the loans.
July 25. Troung Tan Sang is elected president of Vietnam by the national Assembly. Prime minister Nguyen Tan Dung is reappointed the following day.
July 28. Political independent Salomón Lerner Ghitis is appointed prime minister of Peru.
August 2. Peter O'Neill is elected prime minister of Papua New Guinea by the Parliament.
August 5. Yingluck Shinawatra is elected prime minister by the legislature, following elections on July 3 in which her For Thais Party secured 265 of the 500 seats in the House of Representatives.
August 7. Independent Manuel Pinto da Costa wins runoff balloting in São Tomé and Príncipe's presidential election.
August 14. Jhala Nath Khanal resigns as prime minister of Nepal. He is succeeded 15 days later by Baburam Bhattarai.
August 21. Manuel Inocêncio Sousa is elected president of Cape Verde in the second round of presidential polling.
August 23. Libyan leader Muammar al-Qadhafi's government is overthrown as rebel forces take Tripoli.
August 26. Japanese prime minister Naoto Kan resigns in the wake of widespread unpopularity over his government's management of the relief efforts following the March earthquake. Yoshihiko Noda is elected to succeed him by the legislature.
September 4. After rejecting two previous nominees, the Haitian assembly approves Garry Conille as prime minister.
September 20. African Union officially recognizes the National Transitional Council as Libya's legitimate governing body. In Zambia, Michael Sata defeats incumbent president Rupiah Banda.
September 23. Palestinian president Mahmud Abbas submits a bid for full UN membership for Palestine.
October 20. Muammar al-Qadhafi is captured and killed outside Sirte, Libya, ending the Libyan Revolution.
October 23. In Bulgaria, Rosen Plevneliev is elected president in runoff balloting. Jamaican prime minister Bruce Golding resigns and Andrew Holness is named to replace him.
October 27. Michael D. Higgins is elected president of Ireland.
October 28. Omer Berizky is named prime minister of Madagascar, following the resignation of Col. Albert Camille Vital on October 17. The moderate Islamist party Ennahda wins a plurality in Tunisia's national election, claiming 90 seats in the 217-seat Constituent Assembly.
November 1. Abdurrahim el-Keib is appointed prime minister of Libya.
November 6. In runoff balloting, Otto Pérez Molina wins Guatemala's presidential election. In Nicaragua, Daniel Ortega is reelected president.
November 11. Lucas Papademos becomes prime minister of Greece following the resignation of George Papandreou.
November 12. Syria is suspended from the Arab League because of continuing government repression in that country's civil war.
November 16. Mario Monti becomes the prime minister of Italy after Silvio Berlusconi resigns.
November 25. In Morocco, the Islamist Justice and Development Party wins a plurality in legislative elections and party leader Abdelillah Benkirane is appointed prime minister four days later.
November 27. Muhammad Salim Basindwah is named prime minister of Yemen.
November 28. Joseph Kabila is reelected president of the Democratic Republic of the Congo. Prime minister Sheikh Nasser Muhammad al-Ahmad al-SABAH and his government resigns, and Sheikh Jabir Mubarak Al Hamad Al Sabah is named to lead a new government.
December 3. Donald Ramotar is inaugurated as president of Guyana.
December 4. A center-left coalition wins legislative polling in Croatia; Zoran Milanović forms a coalition government and is sworn in as prime minister on December 23. In disputed balloting in Russia, prime minister Vladimir Putin's United Russia Party wins a plurality.
December 6. Socialist Party leader Elio di Rupo is sworn in as prime minister of Belgium at the head of a coalition government after 541 days of negotiations.
December 17. North Korean leader Kim Jong-il dies of a heart attack and is succeeded by his son Kim Jong-un.
December 20. Mariano Rajoy is elected prime minister of Spain by the legislature following elections in which his People's Party won 186 of 350 seats.

2012, **January 9.** President Malam Bacai Sanhá of Guinea-Bissau dies while abroad seeking medical treatment. He is succeeded by Raimundo Pereira as interim president.
January 13. Anote Tong wins a third term as president of Kiribati.
January 22. In a national referendum, Croatia votes to join the European Union; the country is expected to accede in summer 2013.
January 23. The European Union joins the United States in imposing an oil embargo on Iran, to be phased in starting in July, in an attempt to dissuade the Iranian government from pursuing its nuclear ambitions.
January 30. A new EU fiscal pact goes into effect, with the UK and Czech Republic abstaining; the agreement calls for greater control over EU nations' budgetary practices and extended cooperation among the member states on dealing with current and future eurozone fiscal crises.
February 5. Sauli Niinistö of Finland's National Coalition Party wins the presidency in the second round of voting, marking an end of 30 years of rule by the Social Democrats.
February 12. Turkmenistan holds its fourth presidential election, returning President Gurbanguly Berdimuhamedow to office with about 97 percent of the vote. At the time of the election, Turkmenistan has only one political party, and many observers express cynicism about the outcome.
February 17. German president Christian Wulff resigns in the face of prosecution for corruption when he was prime minister of Lower Saxony.
February 18. Constitutional amendments that would have made Russian a second official language of Latvia are defeated in a national referendum.
February 19. Iran halts oil exports to France and Britain in response to the January 23 sanctions imposed by the United States and European Union.
February 27. In the face of widespread protests, Yemeni president Ali Abdullah Saleh steps down in favor of his vice president, Abd Rubbuh Mansur Al-Hadi.
March 2. Iran holds the first round of parliamentary elections (runoffs held on May 4). Amid criticisms that reformist candidates were denied registration in the election, conservative allies of Supreme Religious Leader Ayatollah Seyed Ali Khameni won the majority of seats.

March 7. The United Democratic Party (UDP) returned to power in Belize, lead by Dean Barrow. However, the UDP did lose eight seats in parliament to the opposition, the People's United Party.
March 11. In legislative elections in El Salvador, the opposition party Nationalist Republican Alliance (ARENA) narrowly defeated the Farabundo Marti National Liberaton Front (FMLN). Analysts expect that the leftist administration of President Muricio Funes will find it challenging to work with the right-wing ARENA.
March 22. Amadou Toumani Touré is removed as president of Mali in a military coup, orchestrated by a group of soldiers calling themselves the Committee for the Reestablishment of Democracy and the Restoration of the State. After several weeks in hiding, Touré announces his formal resignation and leaves for Senegal. The presidential election scheduled for April 29 is postponed.
March 26. Macky Sall defeats incumbent Senegal president Abdoulaye Wade.
March 31. Sir Anerood Jugnauth resigns as president of Mauritius. Vice President Monique Ohsah Bellepeau serves as acting president until Rajkeswur Purryag is elected as new president on July 21.
April 1. In parliamentary elections in Myanmar, the National League for Democracy wins in a landslide. In response, in July President Barack Obama will announce the lifting of sanctions as a sign for support for gradual democratic reform in that country.
April 2. Hungarian president Pál Schmitt resigns. An election is scheduled for May 2; János Áder of the Fidesz party wins with about 68 percent of the vote.
April 5. President Bingu wa Mutharika of Malawi dies of a heart attack. He is succeeded by Joyce Banda, who becomes Malawi's first female president.
April 12. In Guinea-Bissau, a military junta takes over, arresting interim president Raimundo Pereira and former prime minister Carlos Gomes Júnior; Júnior was expected to win a presidential runoff election that was to take place ten days later.
April 13. Flouting widespread international criticism, North Korea launches a long-range rocket, suspected to be part of the country's desire to become a nuclear power; the rocket fails shortly after launch, however.
April 17. After the March coup in Mali, Cheick Modibo Diarra becomes interim prime minister, and Dioncouna Traore becomes interim president.
April 26. The Special Court for Sierra Leone finds former Liberian president Charles Taylor guilty of 11 counts of crimes against humanity and aiding and abetting war crimes, including murder, rape, and torture.
May 6. Socialist François Hollande is elected president of France, defeating Nicolas Sarkozy.
May 6. Greece holds an early election for the Hellenic Parliament, in an attempt to create a coalition government to deal with the economic crisis.
May 7. Vladmir Putin is inaugurated as president of Russia amid widespread protests.
May 18. Joachim Gauck is elected president of Germany; he was the candidate of the governing coalition.
May 20. Former military leader José Maria Vasconcelos, better known as Taur Matan Ruak ("Two Sharp Eyes"), is inaugurated president of Timor-Leste, after prevailing in the second round of voting in April.
May 20. In a close election in the Dominican Republic, Danilo Medina of the Dominication Liberation Party (PLD) is elected president, succeeding Leonel Fernàndez, also of the PLD.
May 20. In Serbia, Tomislav Nikolić emerges as the winner of the presidential election, and Nikolić's right-wing Serbian Progressive Party wins 73 seats in the National Assembly.
May 22. The military steps aside in Guinea-Bissau; a transitional council holds power until elections can take place.
May 22. NATO countries reaffirm support of Afghan government while also promising to withdraw troops by the end of 2014.
May 28. Members of the UN Security Council unanimously condemn the Syrian government's use of heavy weaponry and massive force in Houla, near Homs, which resulted in the deaths of over a hundred people, most of them women and children. Several countries—including France, the United Kingdom, Germany, Canada, and Australia—protest diplomatically by expelling senior Syrian diplomats.
June 2. Canada's newly elected Parliament convenes, led by Andrew Scheer as speaker.
June 22. Syria shoots down a Turkish military plane, killing its two pilots. Syrian officials claim they thought it was an Israeli plane, but the Turkish government rejects this explanation and threatens to retaliate.
June 24. In Egypt, Mohamed Morsi of the Freedom and Justice Party is declared the winner of the presidential election.
June 30. Ólafur Ragnar Grímsson wins a record fifth term as president of Iceland.
July 1. In Mexico's general election, Enrique Peña Nieto of the Institutional Revolutionary Party (PRI) wins the presidency. Allegations of electoral misconduct result in a partial recount, but the Nieto's election is confirmed.
July 24. Ghana's president John Atta Mills dies, and he is succeeded by his vice president, John Dramani Mahama.
July 27. The 2012 Summer Olympics commence, with 204 nations participating.
July 30. The UN Security Council calls for a return to constitutional rule in Guinea-Bissau.
August 17. A new UN–Arab League envoy, seasoned Algerian diplomat Lakhdar Brahimi, is appointed to deal with the conflict in Syria succeeding Kofi Annan, who resigns due to frustration with the international community's lack of agreement on solutions to the crisis.
August 20. After 21 years in power, Ethiopian prime minister Meles Zenawi dies from an undisclosed illness. His deputy, Hailemariam Desalegn, is his designated successor.
August 21. Newly reappointed prime minister Cheick Modibo Diarra of Mali establishes a new coalition government amidst widespread rebellion and reported atrocities in the northern part of the country.
September 2. Angola's ruling party, the Popular Movement for the Liberation of Angola (MPLA), is declared the victor in Angola's third election since independence in 1979.
September 7. Canada closes its embassy in Iran and ousts Iranian diplomats from Ottawa, ending formal diplomatic relations with Iran.
September 11. The moderate Hassan Sheikh Mohamud becomes president of Somalia, defeating former president Sheikh Sharif Sheikh Ahmed in a runoff election.
September 11. In Bengahzi, Libya, a terrorist attack on the American consulate results in the deaths of four American diplomats, including Ambassador Christopher Stevens.
September 12. The German constitutional court upholds the European Stability Mechanism (ESM), clearing the way for the EU to institute the ESM's loan program to ailing eurozone economies, such as Italy and Spain.
October 25. Prime Minister of Georgia Bidzina Ivanishvili is inaugurated along with a new government.
November 6. U.S. president Barack Obama is reelected to a second term, while the Democrats expanded their majority in the Senate but the Republicans held the House.
November 13. Israel launches air strikes against a number of targets in Gaza, killing a top Hamas commander.
December 7. John Mahama of the National Democratic Congress is reelected president of Ghana.
December 11. Cheick Modibo Diarra, prime minister of Mali, and his cabinet are forced to resign in what is described as a "mini-coup."
December 19. Park Geun Hye of the New Frontier Party becomes the first woman to be elected president of the Republic of Korea.
December 21. A new government is formed in Romania. Incumbent prime minister Victor Ponta returns to his job with an expanded cabinet.

2013, **January 11.** French forces lead an international military intervention in Mali against Islamist militants.
January 12. Milos Zeman of the Party of Citizens' Rights is elected president of the Czech Republic in the country's first direct presidential elections. In the Central African Republic, Prime Minister Nicolas Tiangaye is named prime minister and appoints a new government on February 3.
January 21. Prime minister Emmanuel Nadingar of Chad resigns and is replaced by Djimrangar Dadnadiji, who names a new cabinet five days later.
January 23. In Jordan, promonarchy candidates win an absolute majority in parliamentary balloting.
January 28. Queen Beatrix of the Netherlands announces her resignation; she is succeeded by her oldest son, Willem-Alexander, on April 30.
February 2. Following Israeli legislative elections on January 22, Benjamin Netanyahu again becomes prime minister of a center-right coalition government.
February 11. Pope Benedict XVI announces he will resign, effective February 28.
February 12. North Korea conducts a nuclear weapons test, prompting international condemnation and new sanctions.
February 18. Jiang Yi-huah, Nationalist Party, is appointed prime minister of China, succeeding Sean Chen-Chun, Nationalist Party, who resigned on February 1.
February 19. Following growing unrest in Tunisia, Interim Prime Minister Hamadi Jebali (*Nahda*) resigns and is replaced by Ali Laarayedh of the same party.
February 24. Nicos Anastasiadis of the Democratic Rally is elected president of Cyprus in runoff balloting; he names a coalition government four days later.
March 4. In spite of an indictment by the International Criminal Court for allegedly inciting election violence in 2007–2008, Uhuru Kenyattat (the National Alliance) is elected president of Kenya; the balloting was the first since constitutional changes eliminated the post of prime minister.
March 5. Venezuelan president Hugo Chávez dies in office and is succeeded by Vice President Nicolás Maduro on March 8.

March 13. Jorge Mario Bergoglio of Argentina is elected pope by a conclave on the fifth ballot; Bergoglio takes the papal name Frances, becoming the first Jesuit pope and the first from the Western Hemisphere.
Xi Jinping is elected president of China by the National People's Congress. Two days later, Li Keqiang is elected premier, and a new cabinet is named the following day.
March 16. After becoming the first Pakistani parliament to complete its full term, the assembly is dissolved; Prime Minister Raja Pervaiz Ashraf resigns and is replaced by Mir Hazar Khan Khoso, who leads a caretaker government.
March 20. President Zillur Rahman of Bangladesh dies and is replaced on an interim basis by the speaker of the parliament Abdul Hamid; Hamid is subsequently elected president in his own right by the parliament on April 22.
March 24. President François Bozizé of the Central African Republic is overthrown and forced to flee when rebels seize Bangui; Michel Djotodia is proclaimed president and reappoints the incumbent prime minister Nicolas Tiangaye as the head of a coalition government.
March 25. Canada announces it is withdrawing from the UN Convention to Combat Desertification. The EU and IMF announce a new economic bailout package for Cyprus.
March 31. Abdoulkader Kamil Mohamed is appointed prime minister of Djibouti following legislative balloting on February 22.
April 1. Pak Pong Ju becomes premier of North Korea.
April 2. The Arms Trade Treaty is approved by the UN General Assembly.
April 10. After losing a no-confidence vote in March, Prime Minister Vlad Filat is reappointed to form a new government in Moldova; subsequently, the constitutional court rules Filat ineligible, prompting President Nicolae Timofti to name Iurie Leanca as interim prime minister on April 23.
April 21. Horacio Cartes's election as president of Paraguay returns the Colorado Party to power after four years; the party also wins the most seats in both houses of the legislature.
April 24. In Italy, Enrico Letta of the Democratic Party is nominated by the president as prime minister; four days later, he is sworn in to lead a coalition government that included all of the major political parties.
April 25. The UN Security Council approves the creation of a peacekeeping force in Mali.
April 28. Center-right parties win legislative balloting in Iceland, and Sigmundur Davíð Gunnlaugsson becomes prime minister on May 23 of a coalition government.
May 5. The ruling Barisan coalition wins legislative elections in Malaysia, and incumbent Najib Abdul Razak remains prime minister.
May 11. The Pakistan Muslim League-Nawaz wins a majority in parliamentary balloting; party leader Muhammad Nawaz Sharif is elected prime minister by the legislature on June 5.
May 12. In legislative polling in Bulgaria, Citizens for European Development of Bulgaria wins a plurality, and party leader Plamen Oresharski is elected prime minister of a coalition government by the parliament on May 29.
May 15. Iurie Leanca is nominated as prime minister of Moldova and formally approved by the parliament on May 30.
May 26. The Democratic Party of Equatorial Guinea wins 99 of 100 seats in the lower house of parliament and 54 of 55 elected seats in the upper chamber.
June 5. The Assembly of the Turkish Republic of Northern Cyprus (TRNC) passes a vote of no-confidence on Prime Minister İrsen Küçük, who resigns; Sibel Siber becomes the first woman prime minister of the TRNC on June 13 after she is named to lead an interim government.
June 6. Rami Hamdallah becomes prime minister of Palestine but resigns on June 20; Hamdallah remains interim prime minister until September, when he again forms a new government. U.S. security contractor Edward Snowden reveals information about the broad scope of U.S. intelligence operations and flees to Hong Kong and then Russia.
June 14. Moderate cleric Hassan Rouhani wins the Iranian presidential election.
June 17. Czech prime minister Petr Necas resigns and is succeeded by Jiri Rusnok on June 25.
June 25. The emir of Qatar, Sheikh Hamad ibn Khalifah al Thani abdicates and is succeeded by his son, Crown Prince Sheikh Tamin ibn Hamad al Thani; the new emir names Sheikh Abdullah ibn Nasser ibn Khalifah al Thani as prime minister the following day.
Nouri Abusahmain is elected president of the Libyan transitional General National Congress.
June 26. Australian prime minister Julia Gillard resigns after being defeated by former prime minister Kevin Rudd in a contest for leadership of the Labor Party; Rudd is sworn in as prime minister the following day.
July 1. Croatia joins the European Union.
July 2. The Egyptian military overthrows President Mohamed Morsi and suspends the constitution; Abdi Mansour, the chief of the country's constitutional court, is named interim president; on July 9 Hazem al Beblawi is named as prime minister.
July 21. King Albert II of Belgium abdicates and is succeeded by Crown Prince Philippe.
July 28. The Republic Turkish Party-United Forces wins parliamentary elections in the Turkish Republic of Northern Cyprus; Özkan Yorgancioğlu is named prime minister on September 2.
In disputed balloting in Cambodia, the ruling Cambodian People's Party wins a majority in the Assembly; Incumbent Prime Minister Hun Sen is reelected by the legislature on September 23.
July 30. Mamnoon Hussain of the Pakistan Muslim League-Nawaz is elected president of Pakistan in indirect balloting by the parliament and regional assemblies.
August 7. Czech prime minister Jiri Rusnok loses a vote of no confidence and resigns, along with his government, on August 13.
August 11. Ibrahim Boubacar Keita wins runoff balloting in Mali's presidential election and is sworn into office on September 4.
August 21. Reports emerge that the Syrian government used chemical weapons against rebels and civilians.
September 1. Roberto Carvalho de Azevêdo of Brazil becomes director general of the World Trade Organization.
September 7. The Liberal Party wins parliamentary elections in Australia, and party leader Tony Abbott becomes prime minister.
September 21. Al Shabab militants attack a shopping mall in Nairobi, Kenya, killing 62 and injuring more than 170.
September 28. The UN Security Council adopts a resolution requiring Syria to destroy its chemical weapons stockpiles under the auspices of the UN. The destruction of the country's chemical weapons begins on October 6.
September 30. The ruling Cameroon People's Democratic Movement wins parliamentary balloting in Cameroon.
October 7. Mulatu Teshome is elected president of Ethiopia by a unanimous vote in the legislature.
November 17. Former president Michelle Bachelet's center-left coalition wins legislative balloting in Chile; Bachelet wins runoff presidential balloting on December 15.
November 24. Juan Orlando Hernandez of the ruling National Party (NP) is elected president of Honduras, while the NP retains a plurality in Congress in concurrent legislative balloting.
November 27. Following the collapse of a supermarket in Riga, Latvia, which killed 54, Prime Minister Valdis Dombrovskis resigns.
December 4. Xavier Bettel of the Democratic Party is sworn in and becomes the first openly gay prime minister of Luxembourg.
December 15. The pro-presidential Rally for Mali wins a plurality of 66 of 147 seats following the second round of balloting, which along with 16 seats secured by allied parties provides Malian president Ibrahim Keïta with a parliamentary majority.
December 20. In Madagascar, Hery Rajaonarimampianina wins disputed runoff balloting in the first elections since former president Marc Ravalomanana was forced from power in 2009.
December 21. In the second round of legislative voting in Mauritania, the ruling Union for the Republic party secures an absolute majority of 75 of 146 seats.

2014, **January 5.** In Bangladesh, the Awami League wins 234 of 300 seats, giving incumbent prime minister Sheikh Hasina a third term. Polling is boycotted by the main opposition party, the Bangladesh Nationalist Party.
January 9. Tunisian prime minister Ali Larayedh resigns and is succeeded by Mehdi Jomaa, who forms a new government.
January 10. Michel Djotodia, the president of the Central African Republic, resigns, along with Prime Minister Nicholas Tiangaye. Ten days later, Catherine Samba-Panza is elected president by the transition council, and she subsequently appoints André Nzapayéké as prime minister.
February 17. A report from the UN Human Rights Council accuses North Korea of crimes against humanity, claiming that the country has between 80,000 and 120,000 political prisoners.
February 22. Following civil unrest that left about 100 dead, Ukrainian president Victor Yanukovych is removed from office in what comes to be called the Euromaidan Revolution. Yanukovych is impeached in absentia, while Oleksandr Turchnyov is appointed acting president.
February 26. Russia seizes most of the Crimean Peninsula, formerly held by Ukraine. The annexation is condemned by NATO.
March 8. Malasian Airlines Flight MH370 disappears while en route to Beijing. Investigators eventually report that the plane went down in the southern Indian Ocean with 239 passengers aboard.
March 24. An Egyptian judge sentences 529 people to death for the killing of a police officer in August 2013.
March 29. Running as an independent candidate, Andrej Kiska wins the second round of presidential elections in Slovakia. He is inaugurated on June 15.
March 31. French prime minister Jean-Marc Ayrault resigns and is replaced by Mauel Valls.
March 31. A report from the United Nation's Intergovernmental Panel on Climate Change predicts dire consequences—including rising sea levels,

food shortages, destructive storms, and geopolitical conflicts—if the challenge of climate change is not addressed.

April 5. High voter turnout is recorded in Afghanistan's presidential election. No candidate secured a majority in the first round of voting, but Ashraf Ghani was declared the winner following a second, disputed election on June 14.

April 7. India's general election begins—voting runs until May 12. With more than 800 million people eligible to vote, it is the largest election ever held. The opposing party, Bharatiya Janata Party, wins about 60 percent of parliamentary seats, taking the majority power away from the Indian National Congress Party.

April 14. In Nigeria, Islamic militants Boko Haram kidnap about 280 girls. The Nigerian government and army are criticized for not doing more to control Boko Haram.

April 15. More than 400 people are killed by South Sudanese rebels in the town of Bentiu. Observers describe the mass killings as the worst incident yet in the brutal conflict that began in December 2013.

April 30. In national elections, no party secures a majority in Iraq's legislature, leading to a protracted series of negotiations through which Haider al-Abadi becomes prime minister on September 8.

May 22. The civilian government in Thailand is ousted by the military under the name of National Committee for Peace and Order (NCPO). The chair of NCPO, General Prayuth Chan-ocha, is confirmed by the king as the new head of Indonesia's government.

May 22-25. In balloting for the EU parliament, far-right parties gained more seats than expected, but the center-right European People's Party coalition won the majority of seats with 214, down from 274 in the previous balloting.

May 25. Incumbent president Dalia Grybauskaite is reelected in Lithuania. No party wins a majority in parliamentary balloting in Belgium, although the New Flemish Alliance secures a plurality of 34 seats. Negotiations ultimately result in a center-right coalition government led by Charles Michel, who is sworn in as prime minister on October 11.

May 31. The U.S. military trades five captured Taliban members for Sgt. Bowe Bergdahl, who had been held by the Taliban for five years.

June 7. Petro Poroshenko, nicknamed the Chocolate King because of his large confectionary business, is sworn in as president of Ukraine.

June 8. Egypt's former deputy prime minister Abdel Fattah el-Sisi is inaugurated as the country's sixth president.

June 10. Former al-Qaeda allies Islamic State in Iraq and Syria (ISIS) seize the city of Mosul in Iraq. They take control of Tikrit the following day.

June 23. José Mário Vaz of the African Party for the Independence of Guinea and Cape Verde is inaugurated as president of Guinea-Bissau after winning a runoff election in May.

July 1. Former vice president of Panama Juan Carlos Varela Rodríguez is sworn in as the country's president.

July 17. The Israeli military begins a ground offensive in Gaza, claiming it's necessary to close tunnels near the Gaza border that militants use to enter Israel.

July 17. Malaysian Airlines Flight 17 is shot down by a missile over the Ukraine, killing 298 people.

July 24. Fouad Massoum is sworn in as president of Iraq.

August 9. African American teenager Michael Brown is killed by a police officer in Ferguson, Missouri. The killing sparks local protests that are followed by an intense response from local police forces. The U.S. Department of Justice announces a civil rights investigation of Brown's death.

August 26. Israel and Hamas announce an open-ended cease-fire, which was mediated by Egypt.

September 18. Scottish voters reject independence from the United Kingdom in a national referendum.

September 23. The United States begins a series of air strikes in northern Syria in an attempt to weaken ISIS.

September 26. Prodemocracy protesters in Hong Kong begin a civil disobedience campaign that will come to be known as the Umbrella Revolution.

September 28. After weeks of protests by thousands of prodemocracy demonstrators, Hong Kong police crack down, using tear gas to try to disburse the protesters.

October 8. Liberian immigrant Thomas Eric Duncan dies of Ebola at a hospital in Dallas, Texas. Two of the hospital nurses who treated Duncan are infected, but both recover.

October 13. In a largely symbolic vote, the British Parliament votes 274–12 to recognize the state of Palestine.

October 20. Former governor of Jakarta Joko Widodo (Indonesian Democratic Party—Struggle) is inaugurated as president of Indonesia.

October 22. Gunman Michael Zehaf-Bibeau kills a Canadian soldier guarding a war memorial in Ottawa. Zehaf-Bibeau subsequently attacks the Canadian Parliament building before being killed in a shoot-out with security.

October 28. Zambia's fifth president, Michael Sata, dies of an undisclosed illness in London. Guy Scott, the vice president, will serve as acting president until elections are organized.

October 29. The World Health Organization reports more than 13,000 cases of and nearly 5,000 deaths from Ebola in West Africa.

November 5. In U.S. mid-term elections, the Republican Party wins control of the Senate and extends its control of the House.

December 8. In Israel, Prime Minister Benjamin Netanyahu called for early elections, and the *Knesset* voted to dissolve itself in preparation for early elections scheduled for March 2015.

December 14. Haitian prime minister Laurent Lamothe resigns in the face of widespread demonstrations. Florence Duperval Guillaume is nominated as interim prime minister on December 21.

December 17. President Barack Obama announces his intention to normalize U.S. relations with Cuba.

2015, January 1. Armenia, Belarus, Kazakhstan, Kyrgyzstan, and Russia launch the Eurasian Economic Union to eliminate economic barriers and promote trade among the member states.

January 7. Terrorists affiliated with al-Qaida in the Arabian Peninsula (AQAP) attack the headquarters of the satirical magazine *Charlie Hebdo*. Twelve people are killed and 11 injured. Another AQAP gunman kills four at a grocery store. All three of the terrorists are killed by security forces.

January 8. In Sri Lanka, Maithripala Sirisena is elected president, defeating two-term incumbent Mahinda Rajapakse.

January 14. Italian President Giorgio Napolitano resigns for health reasons and is replaced by Senate President Peitro Grasso on an interim basis. On January 31 Sergio Mattarella is elected to formally replace Napolitano.

January 22. Iranian-backed Houthi rebels advance on Yemen's capital, prompting the resignation of President Abd Rabbo Mansour Hadi and his cabinet. Hadi flees to Saudi Arabia.

January 23. Saudi King Abdallah ibn Abd al-Aziz al Saud dies and is succeeded by Crown Prince Salman ibn Abd al-Aziz al Saud.

February 14. France, Germany, Russia, and Ukraine finalize a cease-fire agreement in the civil war in eastern Ukraine; however, the conflict continues.

February 16. The South Korean parliament approves the nomination of Lee Wan Koo to become prime minister. He is sworn in the next day.

February 16. The Egyptian air force begins strikes on Islamic State targets in Libya.

March 12. The Nigerian terrorist group Boko Haram allies itself with the Islamic State.

March 17. In Israel, the Likud Party secures 23.4 percent of the vote and remains the largest party in parliament. Incumbent prime minister Benjamin Netanyahu is named to negotiate a coalition government on March 25.

March 18. Luis Almagro of Uruguay is elected secretary general of the Organization of American States.

March 25. A Saudi-led military coalition begins airstrikes on Houthi rebels in Yemen. The coalition will also deploy ground forces in a bid to restore Yemeni President Abd Rabbo Mansour Hadi.

March 28–29. Former military dictator Muhammadu Buhari is elected president of Nigeria, while his All Progressives Congress wins majorities in both chambers of the legislature.

April 19. In elections for the Finnish parliament, the Finnish Center party wins a plurality with 49 seats and forms a coalition government led by Juha Sipilä.

April 20. South Korean prime minister Lee Wan Koo resigns and deputy prime minister Choi Kyung Hwan succeeds him on an interim basis.

April 25. A magnitude 7.5 earthquake strikes Nepal, north of the capital, Kathmandu. The earthquake kills more than 8,600, and injures 22,000.

April 26. In Cyprus, Mustafa Akinci is elected president in runoff balloting, and sworn in on April 30.

May 7. In parliamentary balloting in the United Kingdom, the Conservative party wins a majority with 331 seats. David Cameron is reappointed prime minister.

May 17. The Islamic State captures the key Iraqi town of Ramadi.

May 23. In a national referendum, Ireland legalizes same-sex marriage.

June 7. In elections in Turkey, the ruling Justice and Development Party secures 259 seats, failing to win a majority. Negotiations to form an opposition governing coalition fail, prompting new elections in November.

June 18. Hwang Kyo Ahn is confirmed as prime minister of South Korea by the legislature.

June 26. A gunman with ties to the Islamic State opens fire at a luxury hotel in Port El Kantaoui, Tunisia, killing 38 and wounding 39.

July 4. The prime minister of the Turkish Republic of Northern Cyprus, Özkan Yorgancioglu, resigns and two days later is succeeded by Ömer Kalyoncu.

July 14. Iran and the five permanent members of the UN Security Council, plus Germany (the P5+1) finalize an accord in which Tehran agrees to suspend some aspects of its nuclear program and accept UN monitoring, in exchange for ending economic sanctions on the country.

July 20. The United States and Cuba reestablish diplomatic relations.
July 29. The Afghan government reports that Taliban leader Mullah Omar died in 2013 in Pakistan.
August 12. The president of Guinea-Bissau, José Mário Vaz, dismisses Prime Minster Domingos Simões Pereira and his government. Baciro Djá is appointed prime minister on August 20.
August 20. Greek prime minister Alexis Tsipras resigns in the midst of negotiations over an EU-IMF bailout for Greece. A week later, Vassiliki Thanou-Christophilou is appointed interim prime minster, the first women to hold that post in Greece.
August 24. The Islamic State destroys a number of historic sites and artifacts in Palmyra, Syria.
August 24. The Chinese Shanghai Composite stock index loses 8.5 percent of its value, prompting large losses by other stock markets around the world.
September 2. Guatemalan president Otto Pérez Molina resigns and is replaced on September 3 by Vice President Alejandro Maldonado.
September 15. Malcolm Turnbull defeats Tony Abbot in a leadership challenge to be leader of the Liberal Party. Turnbull replaces Abbot as prime minister.
September 16. A coup in Guinea-Bissau begins, but is suppressed by loyalist army troops by September 23.
September 20. Nepal adopts a new constitution that made the country a federal republic with a president indirectly elected by an electoral college.
September 20. In national elections in Greece, former prime minister Alex Tsipras' Coalition of the Radical Left wins a plurality, and Tsipras forms a new coalition government.
September 24. More than 2,200 pilgrims are killed during a stampede in Mecca, Saudi Arabia.
September 30. Russia launches airstrikes in Syria in support of the regime of President Bashir al-Assad. Russia later also deploys special operations forces and some ground troops.
October 9. An agreement is reached to form a new unity government in Libya.
October 19. The Liberal Party wins parliamentary elections in Canada with 184 seats, and Justin Trudeau becomes prime minister, ending nine years of rule by the Conservative Party.
October 25. Voters in the Republic of the Congo approve a referendum on a new constitution that removed an age limit of 70 for the presidency and abolished the death penalty.
October 25. Jon Magufuli is elected president of Tanzania, while Jimmy Morales is elected president of Guatemala.
November 1. Parliamentary balloting in Turkey is won by the Justice and Development Party, and interim prime minister Ahmet Davutoglu is asked to form a new government.
November 8. The opposition National League for Democracy wins legislative balloting in Myanmar, officially ending more than 50 years of military rule.
November 13. Terrorists linked to the Islamic State carry out a series of attacks in Paris, killing 130. French president François Hollande declares "war" on the terrorism organization and increases airstrikes on Islamic State targets in Iraq and Syria.
November 22. Opposition figure Mauricio Macri wins runoff polling to become president of Argentina.
December 12. Following negotiations at the UN's 21st Conference of Parties in Paris, countries agree to limit greenhouse gas emissions in an effort to reduce climate change.
December 17. The UN High Commissioner for Refugees estimates there are 4.4 million Syrian refugees in Turkey and other nations, fleeing the ongoing conflicts in Iraq, Syria, Libya, and other countries in the Middle East.
December 18. The UN Security Council adopts resolution 2254, which endorses a peace plan for Syria, beginning with negotiations between the regime and rebels.
December 20. The conservative Popular Party wins parliamentary balloting, but falls short of a majority in parliament. Negotiations to form a new government continue into 2016 while incumbent Prime Minister Mariano Rajoy Brey remains in office as the head of a caretaker government.

2016, **January 3.** Saudi Arabia breaks off diplomatic relations with Iran after protestors break into the Saudi embassy in Tehran. The demonstrators were protesting the Saudi execution of Mimr al-Nimr, a leading Shiite cleric.
January 6. North Korea conducts its fourth nuclear weapons test, prompting international condemnation.
January 16. In the Republic of China, Tsai Ing-wen wins presidential elections, and becomes the first woman to lead the country.
January 19. In Libya, a government of national accord is proposed, but rejected by the Tobruk parliament, one of two rival governments that the unity government is supposed to reconcile.
January 28. The World Health Organization announces that the spread of the Zika virus will impact most of the Western Hemisphere.
February 7. Haitian president Michael Martelly steps down at the end of his term, although a successor has not been named due to the postponement of runoff balloting. Jocelerme Privert is named acting president a week later.
February 14. Faustin Archange Touadéra is elected president of the Central African Republic in runoff balloting with 62.7 percent of the vote.
March 15. Myanmar's parliament elects opposition figure Htin Kyaw as president.
March 20. In Niger, in balloting boycotted by the opposition, incumbent president Mahamadou Issoufou is reelected.
March 21. Jean-Pierre Bemba, the former vice president of the Democratic Republic of the Congo, becomes the first person convicted by the International Criminal Court for crimes against humanity involving sexual violence.
March 22. The Islamic State conducts three terrorist bombings in Brussels, including two at the Brussels airport, killing 32 and injuring 340. Three perpetrators are also killed in what was the deadliest terrorist attack in the country's history.
April 2. Tran Dai Quang is indirectly elected president of Vietnam by the legislature. Five days later, Nguyen Xuan Phuc become prime minister.
April 3. Investigative journalists release a trove of more than 11 million documents dubbed the "Panama Papers," which describe a Panamanian bank's efforts to help clients invest in offshore accounts, and, in some cases, shelter money or hide funds. A range of politicians across the world are ensnared in the scandal.
April 5. Icelandic prime minister Sigmundur David Gunnlaugsson resigns after being implicated in the "Panama Papers" scandal. He is replaced by Agriculture Minister Sigurdur Ingi Jóhannsson.
April 10. Ukrainian prime minister Arseniy Yatsenyuk resigns and is succeeded by Volodymyr Hroisman on April 14, following parliamentary approval.
May 9. In the Philippines, Rodrigo Duterte is elected president in a campaign in which he pledges to take extreme measures to curb the country's drug trade.
May 21. Afghan Taliban leader Mullah Akhtar Muhammad Mansour is killed by a U.S. drone strike. On May 25 the Taliban announces Mullah Haibatullah Akhundzada is their new leader.
May 22. Turkish prime minister Ahmet Davutoglu resigns amid rising tensions with President Recep Tayyip Erdoğan. Binali Yildirim is subsequently appointed prime minister.
June 5. In runoff balloting in Peru, Pedro Pablo Kuczynski wins 50.1 percent of the vote, defeating Keiko Fujimori with 49.9 percent.
June 23. By a vote of 51.9 percent in favor to 48.1 percent opposed, voters in the United Kingdom approve an exit, or British Exit ("Brexit"), from the European Union.
June 26. In Spain, in parliamentary elections, the conservative Popular Party wins a plurality of 137 seats in parliament. Talks on forming a government continue until November 3, when incumbent prime minister Mariano Rajoy Brey is sworn in as the head of a minority cabinet after ten months without a formal government.
July 1. Latvia becomes the 35th member of the Organization for Economic Cooperation and Development.
July 1. The Austrian constitutional court annuls presidential runoff balloting from May 22, 2016, and orders new polling on October 2. Incumbent president Heinz Fischer leaves office on July and is replaced on an acting basis by a collective presidency of the three leaders of the country's upper parliamentary chamber.
July 12. The permanent Court of Arbitration at The Hague rules in favor of the Philippines in territorial dispute with China in the South China Sea. China rejects the ruling.
July 13. UK prime minister David Cameron resigns after the Brexit vote, and is replaced by Theresa May.
July 29. Afghanistan becomes the 164th member of the World Trade Organization.
August 7. Voters in Thailand approve a new constitution that grants the military significant power.
August 24. The Colombian government and the rebel group, the Revolutionary Armed Forces of Colombia (FARC), finalize a peace accord to end more than 50 years of conflict. The agreement is rejected by voters in a referendum on October 2.
August 31. Brazilian president Dilma Rousseff is removed from office following a vote of 61–20 by the Senate. Interim president Michel Temer succeeds Rousseff.
September 2. Independent Uzbekistan's only president, Islam A. Karimov, dies in office. Shavkat Mirziyoyev is elected acting president on September 8.
September 9. The United States and Russia announce another cease-fire in the Syrian conflict; however, fighting continues.
September 18. In Russia, the pro-presidential United Russia Party wins an overwhelming majority in the Duma with 343 of 450 seats.

September 20. Pro-monarchy independents win the majority of seats in legislative elections. Incumbent prime minister Hani Mulki is reappointed to form a new government.
October 4. Hurricane Matthew devastates Haiti, killing 1,000–1,300 and causing $1.9 billion in damage. The storm also delayed already postponed legislative and presidential runoff balloting.
October 13. King Bhumibol of Thailand dies, and is succeeded by his son Crown Prince Maha Vajiralongkorn.
October 13. The Maldives withdraws from the Commonwealth.
October 31. After 46 attempts, the Lebanese parliament finally elects a president, Michel Aoun, after more the two and a half years of deadlock over the position.
November 6. Nicaraguan president Daniel Ortega is reelected president for the third consecutive time.
November 8. In an especially bitter election, Republican Donald J. Trump is elected president of the United States, defeating Democrat Hillary Rodham Clinton. Republicans also maintain majorities in both houses of Congress.
November 20. After repeated delays in polling, Jovenel Moïse is elected president of Haiti.
December 4. In a national referendum, Italian voters reject constitutional changes that would have strengthened the central government, by a margin of 59.1 percent to 40.9. Prime Minister Matteo Renzi resigns the next day, but remains in office until his successor, Paolo Gentiloni, is appointed on December 11.
December 5. French prime minister Manuel Valls resigns to contest the 2017 presidential balloting after President François Hollande announces that he will not seek reelection. Interior Minister Bernard Cazeneuve is named prime minister.
December 9. The South Korean parliament votes to impeach President Park Geun Hye, who is temporarily replaced by Prime Minister Hwang Kyo Ahn.

APPENDIX B CHRONOLOGY OF MAJOR INTERNATIONAL CONFERENCES SPONSORED BY THE UNITED NATIONS: 1946–2016

1946, June 19–July 22 (New York, New York). International Health Conference. Adopted constitution of the World Health Organization.

1947–1948, November 21–March 24 (Havana, Cuba). Conference on Trade and Employment. Drafted a charter that would have established an International Trade Organization under UN auspices but that never went into effect because of U.S. opposition.

1948, February 19–March 6 (Geneva, Switzerland). Maritime Conference. Drafted and approved a convention leading to establishment of the Inter-Governmental Maritime Consultative Organization, later the International Maritime Organization.

March 23–April 21 (Geneva, Switzerland). Conference on Freedom of Information. Adopted conventions on the gathering and international transmission of news, the institution of an international right of correction, and freedom of information.

August 23–September 19 (Geneva, Switzerland). Conference on Road and Motor Transport. Drafted and adopted the Convention on Road Traffic and a Protocol on Road Signs and Signals superseding obsolete 1926 and 1931 conventions.

1949, August 17–September 6 (Lake Success, New York). Scientific Conference on the Conservation and Utilization of Resources. Discussed the costs and benefits of practical application of technical knowledge.

1950, March 15–April 6 (Lake Success, New York). Conference on Declaration of Death of Missing Persons. Adopted a convention calling for international cooperation in alleviating the legal problems burdening individuals whose families disappeared in World War II but whose deaths could not be established with certainty.

1953, May 11–June 18 (New York, New York). Opium Conference. Adopted a protocol to control the production, trade, and use of opium.

1954, May 11–June 4 (New York, New York). Conference on Customs Formalities for the Temporary Importation of Road Motor Vehicles and for Tourism. Adopted a convention establishing custom facilities for touring and a convention establishing import regulations for road motor vehicles.

August 31–September 10 (Rome, Italy). World Population Conference. Provided a forum for an exchange of views and experiences among experts on a wide variety of questions connected with population.

September 13–23 (New York, New York). Conference of Plenipotentiaries Relating to the Status of Stateless Persons. Drafted and approved a convention putting stateless people on equal footing with nationals of a contracting state in some matters and giving them the same privileges as those generally granted to aliens in others.

1955, April 18–May 10 (Rome, Italy). International Technical Conference on the Conservation of the Living Resources of the Sea. Discussed the conservation of fish and other marine resources.

August 8–20 (Geneva, Switzerland). First International Conference on the Peaceful Uses of Atomic Energy. Surveyed all major aspects of the topic.

1958, February 24–April 27 (Geneva, Switzerland). First UN Conference on the Law of the Sea. Failed to agree on the issue of the width of the territorial sea.

September 1–12 (Geneva, Switzerland). Second International Conference on the Peaceful Uses of Atomic Energy. Addressed, among other things, the issues of nuclear power reactors, fusion power, application of radioactive isotopes, nuclear power station accidents, and risks involved with exposure to radiation in industrial settings.

1960, March 17–April 26 (Geneva, Switzerland). Second UN Conference on the Law of the Sea. Failed to adopt any substantive measures regarding the questions of the breadth of territorial seas and fishery limits.

1961, January 24–March 25 (New York, New York). Plenipotentiary Conference for the Adoption of a Single Convention on Narcotic Drugs. Adopted the convention, which replaced international control instruments with one treaty and extended the control system to the cultivation of plants that are grown for the raw materials of natural drugs.

August 21–31 (Rome, Italy). Conference on New Sources of Energy. Discussed the recent breakthrough in knowledge of geothermal energy, the need for more intensive wind surveys, and applications of solar energy.

1962, August 6–22 (Bonn, Federal Republic of Germany). Technical Conference on the International Map of the World on Millionth Scale. Reviewed and revised the International Map of the World.

1963, February 4–20 (Geneva, Switzerland). Conference on the Application of Science and Technology for the Benefit of Less Developed Areas. Discussed relevant proposals for accelerating development.

1964, March 23–June 16 (Geneva, Switzerland). UN Conference on Trade and Development (UNCTAD). Subsequently established as a Special Body of the General Assembly convening quadrennially (see under UN General Assembly: Special Bodies).

August 31–September 9 (Geneva, Switzerland). Third International Conference on the Peaceful Uses of Atomic Energy. Focused exclusively on nuclear power as a commercially competitive energy source.

1965, August 30–September 10 (Belgrade, Yugoslavia). Second World Population Conference. Gathered international experts to discuss population problems, especially as they related to development.

1967, September 4–22 (Geneva, Switzerland). Conference on the Standardization of Geographical Names. Subsequent conferences have been held every five years.

1968, March 26–May 24; reconvened **April 9–May 22, 1969** (Vienna, Austria). Conference on Law of Treaties. Adopted the Vienna Convention on the Law of Treaties.

April 22–May 13 (Tehran, Iran). International Conference on Human Rights. Adopted the Proclamation of Tehran and 29 resolutions reviewing and evaluating progress since the adoption of the Universal Declaration of Human Rights in 1948 and formulating further measures to be taken.

August 14–27 (Vienna, Austria). First Conference on the Exploration and Peaceful Uses of Outer Space. Examined the practical benefits to be derived from space research and exploration as well as how the United Nations might help make those benefits widely available and enable non-space powers to cooperate in international space activities.

1971, January 11–February 21 (Vienna, Austria). Conference for the Adoption of a Protocol on Psychotropic Substances. Adopted the instrument after renaming it a convention.

September 6–16 (Geneva, Switzerland). Fourth International Conference on the Peaceful Uses of Atomic Energy. Discussed the ramifications of the rapid increase in nuclear power generation.

1972, June 5–16 (Stockholm, Sweden). Conference on the Human Environment. Resulted in establishment of the United Nations Environment Program (UNEP).

1973, December 3–15 (New York, New York). Third UN Conference on the Law of the Sea; reconvened for ten additional sessions, the last in three parts in **1982, March 8–April 30** and **September 22–24** (New York) and **December 6–10** (Montego Bay, Jamaica). Drafted and adopted the UN Convention on the Law of the Sea (UNCLOS).

1974, May 20–June 14 (New York, New York). Conference on Proscription (Limitation) in the International Sale of Goods. Adopted Convention on the Limitation Period in the International Sale of Goods.

August 19–30 (Bucharest, Romania). World Population Conference. Adopted, as the first international governmental meeting on population (previous World Population Conferences were for scientific discussion only), the World Population Plan of Action, including guidelines for national population policies.

November 5–16 (Rome, Italy). World Food Conference. Adopted the Universal Declaration on the Eradication of Hunger and Malnutrition and called on the General Assembly to create the World Food Council to coordinate programs to give the world (particularly less developed states) more and better food.

1975, February 4–March 14 (Vienna, Austria). Conference on the Representation of States in their Relations with International Organizations (of a Universal Character). Adopted convention of the same name.

May 5–30 (Geneva, Switzerland). Review Conference of the Parties to the Treaty on the Nonproliferation of Nuclear Weapons. Reaffirmed support for the treaty and called for more effective implementation of its provisions.

June 19–July 1, 1975 (Mexico City, Mexico). World Conference of the International Women's Year. Adopted the Declaration of Mexico on the Equality of Women and Their Contribution to Development and Peace, 1975, and the World Plan of Action for the Implementation of the Objectives of the International Women's Year.

1976, January 5–8 (Dakar, Senegal). International Conference on Namibia and Human Rights. Condemned South Africa's occupation of Namibia.

May 31–June 11 (Vancouver, British Columbia). Conference on Human Settlements. Issued recommendations for assuring the basic requirements of human habitation (shelter, clean water, sanitation, and a decent physical environment), plus the opportunity for cultural and personal growth.

June 14–17 (Geneva, Switzerland). World Employment Conference. Adopted, subject to reservations by some countries, a Declaration of

Principles and a Program of Action regarding employment and related issues.

1977, **January 10–February 4** (Geneva, Switzerland). Conference of Plenipotentiaries on Territorial Asylum. Failed to adopt a convention defining groups of people to be covered by a proposed convention within this category or on the allowable activities of refugees in the country of asylum.

March 14–25 (Mar del Plata, Argentina). Water Conference. Approved resolutions dealing with water use, health, and pollution control as well as training and research in water management.

April 4–May 6; reconvened **July 31–August 23, 1978** (Vienna, Austria). Conference on the Succession of States in Respect to Treaties. Adopted a convention elaborating uniform principles for such succession.

May 16–21 (Maputo, Mozambique). International Conference in Support of the Peoples of Zimbabwe and Namibia. Drafted a Declaration and Program of Action to mobilize international support for the right to self-determination by the people of the two territories.

June 20–July 1 (Geneva, Switzerland). Review Conference of the Parties to the Treaty on the Prohibition of the Emplacement of Nuclear Weapons and Other Weapons of Mass Destruction on the Seabed and the Ocean Floor and in the Subsoil Thereof. Reaffirmed interest in avoiding an arms race on the seabed and concluded that signatory states had faithfully observed the conditions of the treaty, which was concluded by a non-UN conference in 1970 and entered into force in 1972. (Similar conclusions were reached by review conferences in Geneva on **September 12–23, 1983,** and on **September 19–28, 1989.**)

August 22–26 (Lagos, Nigeria). World Conference for Action against Apartheid (cosponsored by the Organization of African Unity). Called for international support for efforts to eliminate apartheid and enable the South African people to attain their "inalienable right" to self-determination.

August 29–September 9 (Nairobi, Kenya). Conference on Desertification. Adopted a plan of action addressing desertification, improvement of land management, antidrought measures, and related science and technology.

1978, **February 12–March 11;** reconvened **March 19–April 8, 1979** (Vienna, Austria). Conference on the Establishment of the United Nations Industrial Development Organization (UNIDO) as a Specialized Agency. Recommended such establishment and adopted a constitution for UNIDO.

March 6–31 (Hamburg, Federal Republic of Germany). Conference on an International Convention on the Carriage of Goods by Sea. Adopted a convention designed to balance the risks of carriers and cargo owners.

August 14–25 (Geneva, Switzerland). First World Conference to Combat Racism and Racial Discrimination. Adopted a declaration and program of action recommending comprehensive and mandatory sanctions against South Africa, as well as measures to prevent multinational corporations from investing in territories "subject to racism, colonialism, and foreign domination."

August 30–September 12 (Buenos Aires, Argentina). Conference on Technical Cooperation among Developing Countries. Discussed, but did not endorse, the proposed creation of an independent, but UN-funded, body to foster technical cooperation among developing countries.

October 16–November 11; reconvened six times through 1985 (Geneva, Switzerland). Conference on an International Code of Conduct on the Transfer of Technology.

1979, **July 12–20** (Rome, Italy). World Conference on Agrarian Reform and Rural Development. Adopted a declaration of principles and a program of action to abolish poverty and hunger.

August 20–31 (Vienna, Austria). Conference on Science and Technology for Development. Endorsed recommendations to promote financial and institutional arrangements for freer technology flow to developing nations.

September 10–28; reconvened **September 15–October 10, 1980** (Geneva, Switzerland). Convention on Prohibitions or Restrictions on the Use of Certain Conventional Weapons Which May Be Deemed to Be Excessively Injurious or to Have Indiscriminate Effects. Adopted a convention banning such weapons.

November 12–30; reconvened **May 24, 1980** (Geneva, Switzerland). Conference on International Multimodal Transportation. Adopted a convention on the legal obligations of multimodal transport operators.

November 19–December 8; reconvened **April 8–22, 1980** (Geneva, Switzerland). Conference on Restrictive Business Practices. Adopted the Set of Multilaterally Agreed Equitable Principles and Rules for the Control of Restrictive Business Practices.

1980, **March 3–21** (Geneva, Switzerland). First Review Conference of States Parties to the Convention on the Prohibition of the Development, Production and Stockpiling of Bacteriological (Biological) and Toxin Weapons and on Their Destruction. Reaffirmed commitment to the convention (signed in 1972 and entered into force in 1975) and declared a "determination to exclude the possibility of bacteriological agents and toxins being used as weapons."

March 10–April 11 (Vienna, Austria). Conference on Contracts for International Sale of Goods. Adopted a convention to govern the sale of goods between parties in different countries, replacing the two Hague conventions of 1964.

July 14–30 (Copenhagen, Denmark). World Conference of the UN Decade for Women: Equality, Development, and Peace. Adopted a program of action for the second half of the decade.

August 11–September 7 (Geneva, Switzerland). Second Review Conference of the Parties to the Treaty on the Nonproliferation of Nuclear Weapons. Failed to agree on a final document.

1981, **April 9–10** (Geneva, Switzerland). First International Conference on Assistance to African Refugees. Urged that international priority be given to the African refugee problem and received $560 million in pledges to assist the estimated 5 million people in that category.

May 20–27 (Paris, France). International Conference on Sanctions against Racist South Africa. Proposed sanctions against South Africa and discussed the situation in Namibia.

August 10–21 (Nairobi, Kenya). Conference on New and Renewable Sources of Energy. Promoted the development and utilization of nonconventional energy sources, particularly by developing countries.

September 1–14 (Paris, France). Conference on the Least Developed Countries. Adopted a substantial new program of action to assist the economies of the world's 31 poorest states.

1982, **July 26–August 6** (Vienna, Austria). World Assembly on Aging. Adopted an international plan of action aimed at providing the growing number of older people with economic and social security.

August 9–21 (Vienna, Austria). Second Conference on the Exploration and Peaceful Uses of Outer Space. Recommended that the General Assembly adopt measures to accelerate the transfer of peaceful space technology, to expand access to space and its resources for developing countries, and to establish a UN information service on the world's space programs.

1983, **March 1–April 8** (Vienna, Austria). Conference on the Succession of States in Respect of State Property, Archives, and Debts. Adopted a convention on the subject.

April 25–29 (Paris, France). International Conference in Support of Namibian People for Independence. Reaffirmed Namibia's right to independence.

June 27–29 (London, United Kingdom). International Conference for Sanctions against Apartheid in Sports. Reviewed progress in the campaign for a sports boycott of South Africa.

August 1–12 (Geneva, Switzerland). Second World Conference to Combat Racism and Racial Discrimination. Adopted a program of action against racism, racial discrimination, and apartheid.

August 29–September 7 (Geneva, Switzerland). International Conference on the Question of Palestine. Adopted the Geneva Declaration on Palestine and a Program of Action for the Achievement of Palestinian Rights.

1984, **July 9–11** (Geneva, Switzerland). Second International Conference on Assistance to African Refugees. Declared that caring for African refugees was a global responsibility and proposed long-term solutions to the problem.

July 16–August 3 (Geneva, Switzerland); reconvened **January 28–February 15,** and **July 8–9, 1985** (Geneva), and **January 20–February 8, 1986** (New York). Conference on Conditions for the Registration of Ships. Adopted a convention designed to assure "genuine links" between ships and their flags of state.

August 6–14 (Mexico City, Mexico). International Conference on Population. Adopted Mexico City Declaration on Population and Development covering a wide range of population policy proposals, including further implementation of the 1974 World Population Plan of Action.

September 10–21 (Geneva, Switzerland). Review Conference of the Parties to the Convention on the Prohibition of Military or Any Other Hostile Use of Environmental Modification Techniques. Noted the effectiveness of the convention, which went into effect in 1978.

1985, **March 11–12** (Geneva, Switzerland). International Conference on the Emergency Situation in Africa. Mobilized international aid to drought-stricken states in Africa.

May 7–9 (Arusha, Tanzania). International Conference on Women and Children Under Apartheid. Condemned South Africa for the effects of its policies on black women and children.

May 15–18 (Paris, France). Second International Conference on the Sports Boycott against South Africa. Supported the position that South Africa should not be readmitted to the Olympic games until apartheid ends.

July 15–27 (Nairobi, Kenya). World Conference to Review and Appraise the Achievement of the UN Decade for Women. Assessed steps taken over the past decade to improve the situation of women and drafted the Nairobi Forward Looking Strategies for the Achievement of Women.

August 27–September 21 (Geneva, Switzerland). Third Review Conference of the Parties to the Treaty on the Nonproliferation of Nuclear

Weapons. Called for resumption of talks toward a comprehensive multilateral nuclear test ban treaty.

September 11–13 (New York, New York). Conference on the Intensification of International Action for the Independence of Namibia. Rejected U.S. policy of "constructive engagement" with South Africa and urged boycott of Namibian and South African products.

November 4–15 (Geneva, Switzerland). Conference to Review All Aspects of the Set of Multilaterally Agreed Equitable Principles and Rules for the Control of Restrictive Business Practices. Failed to agree on proposals to improve and further develop the principles.

November 13–18 (New York, New York). World Conference on the International Youth Year, 1985. Endorsed guidelines for youth and asked member states and other interested organizations to ensure that the year's activities be reinforced and maintained.

1986, February 18–March 21 (Vienna, Austria). Conference on the Law of Treaties between States and International Organizations or between International Organizations. Adopted a convention delineating the manner in which international organizations should conclude, adopt, enforce, and observe treaties.

June 16–20 (Paris, France). World Conference on Sanctions against Racist South Africa. Called for comprehensive economic sanctions against South Africa.

July 7–11 (Vienna, Austria). International Conference for the Immediate Independence of Namibia. Called for the adoption and imposition of sanctions against South Africa and the implementation of the UN plan for the independence of Namibia.

September 8–16 (Geneva, Switzerland). Second Review Conference of States Parties to the Convention on the Prohibition of the Development, Production and Stockpiling of Bacteriological (Biological) and Toxin Weapons and on Their Destruction. Adopted a final act designed to strengthen confidence in the convention, to reduce "the occurrence of ambiguities, doubts, or suspicion" involving bacteriological activities, and to enhance international cooperation in peaceful microbiology use.

1987, February 10–13 (Nairobi, Kenya). Safe Motherhood Conference (cosponsored by the World Bank, World Health Organization, and UN Fund for Population Activities).

March 23–April 10 (Geneva, Switzerland). Conference for Promotion of International Cooperation in the Peaceful Uses of Nuclear Energy. Failed to reach consensus.

June 17–26 (Vienna, Austria). International Conference on Drug Abuse and Illicit Trafficking. Adopted a declaration committing all participants to "vigorous action" to reduce drug supply and demand and approved a handbook of guidelines to assist governments and organizations in reaching a total of 35 "action targets."

August 24–September 11 (New York, New York). International Conference on the Relationship between Disarmament and Development. Recommended that a portion of resources released by disarmament be allocated to social and economic development.

1988, August 22–24 (Oslo, Norway). International Conference on the Plight of Refugees, Returnees, and Displaced Persons in Southern Africa. Adopted a plan of action to improve the economic and social conditions of the populations under consideration.

November 25–December 20 (Geneva, Switzerland). Plenipotentiary Conference to Adopt the New Convention Against Illicit Traffic in Narcotic Drugs and Psychotropic Substances. Adopted the Convention.

1989, January 7–11 (Paris, France). Conference of States Parties to the 1925 Geneva Protocol and Other Interested States on the Prohibition of Chemical Weapons. Called for early conclusion of a convention that would prohibit the development, production, stockpiling, and use of all chemical weapons and provide for the destruction of all such existing weapons.

May 29–31 (Guatemala City, Guatemala). International Conference on Central American Refugees. Adopted a three-year, $380 million program to aid an estimated two million refugees, displaced persons, and returnees in seven countries.

June 13–14 (Geneva, Switzerland). International Conference on Indochinese Refugees. Adopted a plan of action designed to promote a "lasting multilateral solution" to the problem of refugees and asylum-seekers from Laos and Vietnam.

1990, March 5–9 (Jomtien, Thailand). World Conference on Education for All: Meeting Basic Learning Needs. Adopted Declaration on Education for All.

April 9–11 (London, United Kingdom). World Ministerial Summit to Reduce the Demand for Drugs and to Combat the Cocaine Threat (organized in association with the United Kingdom). Adopted a declaration by which 124 nations pledged to give higher priority to curtailing illicit drug demand.

August 20–September 15 (Geneva, Switzerland). Fourth Review Conference of Parties to the Treaty on the Nonproliferation of Nuclear Weapons. Failed to reach agreement on a final declaration.

September 3–14 (Paris, France). Second Conference on the Least Developed Countries. Adopted a new program of action stressing bilateral assistance in the form of grants or highly concessional loans from developed nations.

September 29–30 (New York, New York). World Summit for Children. Adopted a ten-point program to promote the well-being of children through political action "at the highest level."

October 29–November 7 (Geneva, Switzerland). World Climate Conference. Urged developed nations to establish targets for the reduction in the emission of "greenhouse" gases, such as carbon dioxide, to curtail a possible warming of the global atmosphere.

November 26–December 7 (Geneva, Switzerland). Second Conference to Review All Aspects of the Set of Multilaterally Agreed Equitable Principles and Rules for the Control of Restrictive Business Practices. Urged developing countries to adopt national legislation on restrictive business practices.

1991, January 7–18 (New York, New York). Amendment Conference of the States Parties to the 1963 Treaty Banning Nuclear Weapon Tests in the Atmosphere, in Outer Space, and Under Water. Decided further work was needed before a proposed amendment could be adopted that would convert the treaty into a comprehensive test ban treaty.

September 9–17 (Geneva, Switzerland). Third Review Conference of the States Parties to the Convention on the Prohibition of the Development, Production and Stockpiling of Bacteriological (Biological) and Toxin Weapons and on Their Destruction. Called for full implementation of the convention without the placement of constraints on economic and technological development and international cooperation in peaceful biological activities.

1992, June 3–14 (Rio de Janeiro, Brazil). UN Conference on Environment and Development. Adopted Rio Declaration on Environment and Development and several other documents designed to promote global environmental cleanup and "sustainable" development.

October 15–16 (New York, New York). International Conference on Aging. Reviewed progress on the 1982 International Plan of Action on Aging.

1993, June 14–25 (Vienna, Austria). World Conference on Human Rights. Adopted nonbinding Declaration and Program of Action affirming the "universal nature" of human rights and recommending, among other things, that the General Assembly appoint a UN High Commissioner for Human Rights.

July 12–30; reconvened **March 14–31** and **August 15–26, 1994,** and **March 27–April 12** and **July 24–August 4, 1995** (New York, New York). UN Conference on Straddling Fish Stocks and Highly Migratory Fish Stocks. Adopted global treaty (opened for signature December 4, 1995) binding signatories to adopt measures to conserve and otherwise manage high-seas fisheries and to settle fishing disputes peacefully.

October 5–6 (Tokyo, Japan). International Conference on African Development (sponsored in conjunction with Japan and the U.S.-based Global Coalition of Africa). Adopted a declaration intended to "refocus" attention on African problems, such as heavy debt burden, rapid population growth, drought, hunger, and political instability.

1994, April 25–May 6 (Bridgetown, Barbados). Global Conference on the Sustainable Development of Small Island Developing States. Adopted a program of action to guide the environmental and development policies of small island states and issued the "Barbados Declaration" calling on the international community to support those states in combating rising sea levels, the loss of reefs and rain forests, shortages of fresh water, and import dependency.

May 23–27 (Yokohama, Japan). World Conference on Natural Disaster Reduction. Adopted the Yokohama Strategy for a Safer World: Guidelines for Natural Disaster Prevention, Preparedness, and Mitigation, designed to put recent technological advances at the service of disaster-prone regions of the world.

September 5–13 (Cairo, Egypt). International Conference on Population and Development. Adopted a program of action aimed at stabilizing the world's population at about 7.27 billion in 2015.

October 18 (New York, New York). International Conference on Families. Convened by the UN General Assembly to discuss activities in regard to the International Year of the Family, 1994.

November 21–23 (Naples, Italy). World Ministerial Conference on Organized Transnational Crime. Adopted the Naples Political Declaration and Global Action Plan, proposing, among other things, the establishment of an international convention on transnational crime, greater cooperation among national law enforcement agencies, and greater "transparency" of banks and other financial enterprises that can be used to "launder" money.

1995, March 6–13 (Copenhagen, Denmark). World Summit for Social Development. Adopted the Copenhagen Declaration and Program of Action recommending measures to be taken by national governments, the United Nations, and other international organizations in pursuit of "social development and social justice."

April 7–May 12 (New York, New York). Review and Extension Conference of the Parties to the Treaty on the Nonproliferation of Nuclear Weapons. Agreed to extend treaty "indefinitely" and strengthen its review process.

September 4–15 (Beijing, China). Fourth World Conference on Women. Adopted the Beijing Declaration and Platform for Action delineating nonbinding guidelines for national policies designed to enhance the status of women and to promote international cooperation in the same regard.

September 25–October 13 (Vienna, Austria); reconvened **April 22–May 3, 1996** (Geneva, Switzerland). Review Conference of States Parties to the 1980 Convention on Prohibitions or Restrictions on the Use of Certain Conventional Weapons Which May Be Deemed to Be Excessively Injurious or to Have Indiscriminate Effects. Failed to reach agreement on a proposed complete ban on land mines but adopted stricter controls on their use and export and agreed to extend the provisions of the convention to domestic conflicts; banned the use of blinding laser weapons.

1996, June 3–14 (Istanbul, Turkey). Second UN Conference on Human Settlements. Adopted a declaration urging national governments to implement policies designed to meet their citizens' "right to adequate housing" and to establish comprehensive plans to manage urban development.

November 13–17 (Rome, Italy). World Food Summit. Adopted a declaration asserting the "fundamental right of everyone to be free from hunger" and recommending national policies that will guarantee "access to safe and nutritious food."

November 25–December 6 (Geneva, Switzerland). Fourth Review Conference of States Parties to the Convention on the Prohibition of the Development, Production and Stockpiling of Bacteriological (Biological) and Toxin Weapons and on Their Destruction. Supported continuing work by an ad hoc group designing a verification protocol for the convention.

1997, June 23–27 (New York, New York). Second UN Conference on Environment and Development. Reviewed implementation (or lack thereof) of commitments made at the 1992 conference.

December 1–11 (Kyoto, Japan). Third Conference of the Parties to the UN Framework Convention on Climate Change. Issued Kyoto Protocol in which 38 industrialized countries agreed to cut the emission of greenhouse gases to combat global warming.

1998, June 15–July 18 (Rome, Italy). UN Conference of Plenipotentiaries on the Establishment of an International Criminal Court. Voted to establish an International Criminal Court under UN auspices.

August 8–12 (Lisbon, Portugal). World Conference of Ministers Responsible for Youth. Adopted the Lisbon Declaration on Youth Policies and Programs, pledging to act on youth participation, development, peace, education, employment, health, and drug and substance abuse.

1999, July 19–30 (Vienna, Austria). Third Conference on the Exploration and Peaceful Uses of Outer Space. Adopted the Vienna Declaration on Space and Human Development.

2000, April 24–May 19 (New York, New York). Review Conference of the Treaty on the Nonproliferation of Nuclear Weapons. Concluded with a commitment by China, France, Russia, the United Kingdom, and the United States to the "total elimination" of their nuclear arsenals.

September 6–8 (New York, New York). Millennium Summit. Adopted the Millennium Declaration, which reaffirmed the role of the United Nations and its charter as "indispensable foundations of a more peaceful, prosperous, and just world."

November 13–25 (The Hague, Netherlands). World Conference on Climate Change. Failed to conclude a treaty to meet the greenhouse gas emissions requirements called for by the 1997 Kyoto Protocol.

December 12–15 (Palermo, Italy). High-Level Political Signing Conference for the UN Convention against Transnational Organized Crime. Opened for signature the first legally binding UN convention on crime.

2001, May 14–20 (Brussels, Belgium). Third Conference on the Least Developed Countries. Adopted a plan of action for 2001–2010 that emphasized good governance, capacity-building, the role of trade in development, environmental protection, and the mobilization of financial resources.

July 9–20 (New York, New York). UN Conference on the Illicit Trade in Small Arms and Light Weapons in All Its Aspects. Adopted a program of action to prevent, combat, and eradicate illicit trade in small arms and light weapons (SALW) at national, regional, and global levels.

August 31–September 7 (Durban, South Africa). World Conference against Racism, Racial Discrimination, Xenophobia, and Related Intolerance. Adopted the Durban Declaration and Program of Action, in which states were urged to end enslavement and slavery-like practices, to promote and protect human rights, and to prosecute perpetrators of racist and other discriminatory acts against Africans, indigenous peoples, migrants, refugees, and other victims.

November 19–December 7; reconvened **November 11–22, 2002** (Geneva, Switzerland). Fifth Review Conference of States Parties to the Convention on the Prohibition of the Development, Production and Stockpiling of Bacteriological (Biological) and Toxin Weapons and on Their Destruction. Adopted a three-year work plan focusing on national measures to implement prohibitions; enhancement of international capabilities in responding to, investigating, and mitigating the effects of biological attacks and suspicious disease outbreaks; and adoption of a code of conduct for scientists.

December 11–21 (Geneva, Switzerland). Second Review Conference of the States Parties to the Convention on Prohibitions or Restrictions on the Use of Certain Conventional Weapons Which May Be Deemed to Be Excessively Injurious or to Have Indiscriminate Effects. Addressed various proposals to strengthen the convention, including extending its application to domestic as well as international conflicts and exploring how to deal with such explosive remnants of war as cluster bombs, shells, and munitions.

2002, March 18–22 (Monterrey, Mexico). International Conference on Financing for Development. Adopted the Monterrey Consensus on promoting development through such means as increasing foreign direct investment and official development assistance, improving market access, fighting corruption, and reducing debt.

April 8–12 (Madrid, Spain). Second World Assembly on Aging. Adopted the International Plan of Action on Aging 2002, which identified three priority areas: older persons and development, the extension of health and well-being into old age, and enhancement of enabling and supportive environments for the aged.

June 10–13 (Rome, Italy). World Food Summit: Five Years Later. Reviewed the "disappointingly slow" progress since the 1996 summit and called for an international alliance against hunger.

August 26–September 4 (Johannesburg, South Africa). World Summit on Sustainable Development. Set new targets for sustainable development in a variety of areas.

2003, August 28–29 (Almaty, Kazakhstan). International Ministerial Conference of Landlocked and Transit Developing Countries and Donor Countries and International Financial and Development Institutions on Transit Transport Cooperation. Adopted the Almaty Program of Action, addressing rail, road, and air transportation, as well as communications, pipelines, and means of facilitating international trade.

December 9–11 (Merida, Mexico). High-Level Political Conference for the Signature of the United Nations Convention Against Corruption. Ninety-four countries signed the Convention Against Corruption (previously approved by the General Assembly) requiring signatories (upon ratification) to criminalize a range of corrupt activities and to cooperate with other signatories in combating corruption.

December 10–12 (Geneva, Switzerland). World Summit on the Information Society (Phase One). Adopted the Geneva Declaration of Principles and Geneva Plan of Action in support of the creation of a "people-centered, inclusive, and development-oriented information society," with a particular emphasis on reducing the "information gap" between developed and developing countries.

2004, February 9–20 (Kuala Lumpur, Malaysia). Conference of the Parties to the Convention on Biological Diversity. Addressed the biological diversity of mountain ecosystems, technology transfer and cooperation, and the proposed reduction of the rate of loss of biodiversity.

June 24 (New York, New York). Global Compact Leaders Summit. Participants (including more than 1,200 corporations as well as representatives from labor and civil society) recommitted themselves to the Global Compact (introduced by UN Secretary-General Kofi Annan in 1999 to promote responsible "corporate citizenship") and agreed to add anticorruption efforts (particularly aimed at extortion and bribery) to the compact's guiding principles.

November 29–December 3 (Nairobi, Kenya). First Review Conference of the State Parties to the Convention on the Prohibition of the Use, Stockpiling, Production, and Transfer of Anti-personnel Mines and on their Destruction. Adopted a 70-point action plan for the coming five-year period.

2005, January 18–22 (Kobe, Japan). World Conference on Disaster Reduction. Addressed the issues of investing in disaster preparedness and enhancing risk assessment, particularly in view of the devastating tsunami in the Indian Ocean.

April 18–25 (Bangkok, Thailand). Eleventh UN Conference on Crime Prevention and Criminal Justice. Addressed organized crime, terrorism, human trafficking, money-laundering, corruption, cyber-crime, and "restorative" justice.

May 2–27 (New York, New York). Review Conference of the Parties to the Treaty on the Nonproliferation of Nuclear Weapons. Failed to reach consensus on proposed steps for strengthening the treaty despite the recent increase in the spread of nuclear weapons.

September 14–16 (New York, New York). World Summit. Adopted a compromise declaration regarding proposed UN reform and steps to be taken in pursuit of a broad range of security and development goals.

September 21–23 (New York, New York). Conference on Facilitating the Entry into Force of the Comprehensive Nuclear Test-Ban Treaty.

Reiterated that cessation of all nuclear weapon tests remains necessary in the pursuit of nuclear disarmament, despite the lack of progress toward the treaty entering into force (ratification from 11 countries still required).

November 16–18 (Tunis, Tunisia). World Summit on the Information Society (Phase Two). Monitored progress regarding the action plan approved in 2003 and endorsed the creation of an advisory body (comprised of representatives from government, business, and civil society) to review issues surrounding the Internet.

2006, **March 20–31** (Curitiba, Brazil). Conference of the Parties to the Convention on Biological Diversity. Addressed threats posed by genetically-modified trees and urged caution in applying that technology.

November 7–17 (Geneva, Switzerland). Third Review Conference of the States Parties to the Convention on Prohibitions or Restrictions on the Use of Certain Conventional Weapons Which May Be Deemed to Be Excessively Injurious or to Have Indiscriminate Effects. Welcomed the entry into force of a protocol requiring signatories to mark and clear mines and other "explosive remnants of war."

November 20–December 8 (Geneva, Switzerland). Sixth Review Conference of the States Parties to the Convention on the Prohibition of the Development, Production and Stockpiling of Bacteriological (Biological) and Toxin Weapons and on Their Destruction. Approved a general framework for future discussions and negotiations regarding the effective implementation and strengthening of the Convention.

December 10–14 (Amman, Jordan). Conference of the Parties to the United Nations Convention against Corruption, first session. Adopted a self-assessment plan (in view of criticism regarding a perceived lack of implementation of the Convention) and pledged additional aid to developing countries to combat corruption.

2007, **July 5–6** (Geneva, Switzerland). Second Global Compact Leaders Summit. Adopted a 21-point declaration designed to enhance implementation of the Global Compact regarding corporate citizenship.

October 1–3 (Davos, Switzerland). Second International Conference on Climate Change and Tourism. Agreed that the tourism industry must "respond rapidly" to climate change by curbing greenhouse gas emissions and urged tourists to assess the environmental impact of their travels.

December 3–14 (Bali, Indonesia). United Nations Climate Change Conference. Launched negotiations on a successor to the Kyoto Protocol.

2008, **January 28–February 1** (Bali, Indonesia). Conference of the Parties to the United Nations Convention against Corruption, second session. Reviewed implementation of the convention and discussed asset recovery procedures, the need for mutual legal assistance mechanisms, various ways to strengthen coordination and enhance technical assistance, and the issue of bribery as it relates to officials of public international organizations.

June 3–6 (Rome, Italy). High-Level Conference on World Food Security: the Challenges of Climate Change and Bioenergy. Called upon the international community to increase food assistance, particularly to the least developed countries and those adversely affected by escalating food prices.

November 29–December 2 (Doha, Qatar). Follow-up International Conference on Financing for Development to Review the Implementation of the Monterrey Consensus. Adopted the Doha Declaration on Financing for Development, which affirmed the Monterrey Consensus and called on the UN to examine how the ongoing world financial and economic crisis is affecting development.

2009, **April 20–24** (Geneva, Switzerland). Durban Review Conference. Evaluated progress toward goals set by the 2001 World Conference against Racism, Racial Discrimination, Xenophobia, and Related Intolerance and called for greater "political will" to combat racism. (Canada, Israel, the United States, and five other countries boycotted the conference out of concern over possible anti-Israeli and/or anti-Western "polemics," while additional countries walked out of the conference during a controversial speech by Iranian President Mahmoud Ahmadinejad.)

June 24–30 (New York, New York). Conference on the World Financial and Economic Crisis and Its Impact on Development. Called for reform of "deficiencies" in the regulation and supervision of the international financial system.

September 24–25 (New York, New York). Conference on Facilitating the Entry into Force of the Comprehensive Nuclear Test-Ban Treaty. Called upon China, Egypt, Indonesia, Iran, Israel, and the United States (who have signed but not ratified the treaty) and North Korea, India, and Pakistan (who have not signed the treaty) to complete accession to the treaty, which cannot enter into force without their ratification. (The delegation from the United States, attending such conferences for the first time in a decade, announced plans for the Obama administration to seek Senate ratification of the treaty.)

November 16–18 (Rome, Italy). World Food Summit on Food Security. Adopted declaration pledging to promote greater domestic and international funding for agriculture in an effort to combat hunger, estimated to affect 1 billion people; few leaders from the world's wealthy nations attend.

December 7–18 (Copenhagen, Denmark). Climate Change Conference (Conference of the Parties to the United Nations Framework Convention on Climate Change and the Parties to the 1997 Kyoto Protocol). Adopted the Copenhagen Document, which called for cooperation in reducing greenhouse gases and for greater assistance to developing countries to pursue clean energy but which did not include specific, legally binding targets.

2010, **May 3–28** (New York, New York). Review Conference of the Parties to the Treaty on the Non-Proliferation of Nuclear Weapons. Focused on promoting and strengthening safeguards; advancing the peaceful use of nuclear energy, safety, and security; strengthening the review process; and engaging with civil society to promote NPT norms and disarmament education.

September 20–22 (New York, New York). Summit on Millennial Development Goals. Reaffirmed the 2015 Millennial Development Goals and adopted an action plan for achieving them. Heads of state and government and representatives of the private sector, civil society, foundations, and various international organizations pledged $40 billion over five years to improving the health of women and children.

October 18–29 (Nagoya, Japan). Tenth Conference of Parties to the Convention on Biological Diversity. In support of the International Year for Biodiversity, reviewed progress toward the 2010 goals and revised the Strategic Plan. Focused in-depth attention on inland waterways, marine and coastal areas, mountains, protected areas, the sustainable use of biodiversity, and the relationship of biodiversity to climate change.

November 9–12 (Vientiane, Laos). First Meeting of Parties to the Convention on Cluster Munitions. Approved a 66-point action plan committing signatories to "implement fully all of the obligations under the convention," which had entered into force on August 1, and specified deadlines, budgets, and targets related to such matters as stockpile destruction, clearance and risk education, and transparency.

2011, **May 9–13** (Istanbul, Turkey). Fourth United Nations Conference on the Least Developed Countries. Reviewed progress on the 10-year Least Developed Countries (LDC) Plan approved at the 2001 Third UN LDC Conference in Brussels, Belgium. The 2011 conference called for the number of LDCs to be reduced from 48 to 24 by 2020.

June 20–24 (Vienna, Austria). International Atomic Energy Agency (IAEA) Ministerial Conference on Nuclear Safety. Approved a declaration on nuclear safety that incorporated lessons learned in the aftermath of the March 11, 2011, Fukushima Daiichi nuclear power plant disaster.

September 19–20 (New York). High Level Meeting on Prevention and Control of Non-Communicable Diseases. Approved declaration calling for governments to take action to reduce deaths from noncommunicable diseases, including cancer, cardiovascular disease, chronic respiratory diseases, and diabetes. The declaration urged governments to reduce tobacco consumption and unhealthy dietary patterns through economic measures such as increased taxes and limitations on advertising, while encouraging healthy lifestyles.

November 28–December 9 (Durban, South Africa). Climate Change Conference (Conference of the Parties to the United Nations Framework Convention on Climate Change and the Parties to the 1997 Kyoto Protocol). Reaffirmed a commitment to establish the Green Climate Fund that would provide $100 billion annually to help lesser developed countries mitigate climate change. Attendees also agreed to finalize a new global climate change treaty by 2015, to be implemented in 2020.

2012, **January 25–29** (Davos-Klosters, Switzerland). World Economic Forum Annual Meeting. Focused on rebalancing and deleveraging the global economy. Developed a plan by which developed countries may prevent recession and emerging countries may curb inflation, avoiding future economic bubbles.

June 18 (Rio de Janeiro, Brazil). First BioTrade Congress. Focused on biodiversity and the role of the Green Economy in relation to sustainable development and poverty alleviation. Sought increased political support for sustainable development.

June 18–19 (Los Cabos, Mexico). G-20 Summit. Focused predominantly on the European financial crisis. Leaders agreed upon various plans to promote strong, sustainable, balanced growth for the faltering European economy as well as for the global economy. Also discussed food security and environmental issues pertaining to the economy.

July 22–27 (Washington, D.C.). XIX International AIDS Conference. Placed new emphasis on preventing transmission of the disease as a new strategy to complement treatment and care initiatives. Focused on the use of microbicides to kill the virus and help prevent the spread of AIDS.

November 26–December 7 (Doha, Qatar). The UN Climate Change Conference (also known as COP 18) was held in Doha. After two weeks of contentious negotiation and frequent deadlock, delegates to COP 18 resolved to keep the Kyoto protocols in effect until 2020, with the goal of limiting global warming to 2°C.

2013, **January 30** (Kuwait City, Kuwait). International Humanitarian Pledging Conference for Syria. Representatives from UN member states pledged $1.54 billion to bolster humanitarian relief efforts in Syria and provide support for refugees in neighboring states in response to the largest short-term emergency funding appeals ever issued by the world body. National representatives also called for the UN Security Council to play a larger role in ending the ongoing Syrian civil war.

February 20–22 (Geneva, Switzerland). Global Forum on the Effects of the Global Economic Crisis on the Civil Aviation Industry. Sponsored by the International Labor Organization (ILO), the summit called for greater cooperation between the ILO and the International Civil Aviation Organization (ICAO). The meeting also endorsed the need to develop a "sustainable civil aviation industry."

March 8–28 (New York, New York). Final UN Conference on the Arms Trade Treaty. The summit finalized the text of the UN Arms Trade Treaty, which sought to regulate the international trade in weapons and munitions. The treaty was subsequently approved by the General Assembly on April 2, on a vote of 154 in favor, 3 opposed, and 23 abstentions.

September 25 (New York, New York). Special Event Achieving the Millennium Development Goals (MDG). World leaders reaffirmed their commitment to the MDGs and called for increased development assistance to the poorest nations. In addition member states pledged to hold a high-level meeting in 2015 to finalize new goals.

November 11–22 (Warsaw, Poland). UN Climate Change Conference (also known as COP 19). The main goal of the conference was to establish specific steps to limit greenhouse emissions. However, the contentious meeting was unable to reach consensus on a formal plan; instead, attendees agreed that all states should develop national plans by 2015 to reduce greenhouse emissions, with an implementation goal of 2020.

2014, January 22–24 (Montreux and Geneva, Switzerland). International Peace Conference on Syria (Geneva II). The conference unsuccessfully sought a negotiated end to the Syrian civil war and concessions to protect noncombatants. Attendees included representatives from 39 nations, including the five permanent members of the Security Council, the EU, AU, Arab League and Islamic Conference, and representatives of the Syrian government and major rebel groups.

April 14–15 (New York, New York). Coherence, Coordination and Cooperation in the Context of Financing for Sustainable Development and the Post-2015 Development Agenda. High-level representatives from ECOSOC, the World Bank, IMF, WTO, and UNCTAD meet to discuss global economic conditions and prospects, ways to mobilize financial resources for sustainable development, and global partnerships for sustainable development in the post-MDG era.

September 1–4 (Apia, Samoa). Third International Conference on Small Island Developing States. Delegates unanimously adopted the Small Island Developing States Accelerated Modalities of Action (Samoa Pathway), which identified small island developing states as "special cases" due to their unique vulnerabilities and endorsed new programs of sustainable development and marine resource use, disaster risk reduction, and the use of sustainable energy.

September 22–23 (New York, New York). World Conference on Indigenous Peoples. Delegates approved the Outcome Document in which nations reaffirmed their commitment to ensure the full rights of indigenous peoples and pledged to reduce the gap between "promises and results" of policies.

September 23 (New York, New York). Climate Summit 2014. The summit was convened in an effort to increase momentum for a global agreement to combat climate change. World leaders agreed to finalize a universal accord on climate change at COP 21 in 2015, while the EU pledged to reduce emission to 40 percent below 1990s levels by 2030, and government, business, and civil society leaders committed to raise $200 billion to finance low-carbon and climate-resilient development.

2015, March 14–18 (Sendai, Japan). Third UN World Conference on Disaster Risk Reduction. The conference established a nonbinding agreement with seven specific goals and four priorities, for states to adopt in order to reduce the loss of life and minimize economic disruptions resulting from natural and manmade disasters. Dubbed the Sendai Framework, the accord was a fifteen-year commitment and the successor to the 2005 Hyogo Framework for Action, the first global agreement on disaster mitigation and response.

September 25–27 (New York, New York). UN Sustainable Development Summit 2015. The summit brought together world leaders and high ranking officials from 150 countries to launch the UN's Sustainable Development Goals, a series of 17 objectives. The goals are the successors to the Millennium Development Goals, and serve as unifying themes for UN efforts to promote prosperity and sustainable development.

September 27 (New York, New York). UN Gender Equality and Women's Empowerment: A Commitment to Action (Beijing+20). The meeting was called to implement action items developed at the 59th session of the UN Commission on the Status of Women (CSW), March 9–20, 2015, which reviewed progress made since the Fourth World Congress on Women in Beijing in 1995. The Commitment to Action sessions called on member states to renew or enhance investments in gender equality, promote women's leadership, and review or develop new laws on gender equality.

November 30–December 12 (Paris, France). UN Climate Change Conference 2015 (also known as COP 21). The conference sought to craft a global agreement to limit the worldwide increase in temperatures through the reduction of greenhouse gas emissions. The result of the deliberations was the Paris Agreement, an accord between 196 nations that committed the signatories to binding and nonbinding measures to minimize temperature increases. States were allowed to determine for themselves the best approaches to cut emissions.

2016, May 23–24 (Istanbul, Turkey). World Humanitarian Summit. The UN organized the summit in an effort to facilitate cooperation among intergovernmental organizations, nongovernmental humanitarian groups, and private volunteer agencies. More than 9,000 participants attended the meeting, and produced over 3,000 new commitments to action or humanitarian initiatives or partnerships in what was codified as the Pact for Action, Commitments, and Transformation (PACT).

June 8–10 (New York, New York). High-Level Meeting on Ending AIDS. The summit emphasized the importance of eradicating HIV/AIDS as a component of the UN's Sustainable Development Goals. Attendees adopted three goals to be achieved by 2020: decrease the number of new HIV cases globally to fewer than 500,000, reduce the number of people dying from AIDS to fewer than 500,000, and end HIV/AIDS discrimination.

June 22–23 (New York, New York). UN Global Compact Leaders (GCL) Summit 2016. The summit brought together global business leaders, governments, intergovernmental organizations, and nonprofit groups to develop specific ways in which the business community could aid in the implementation of the newly adopted Sustainable Development Goals (SDG). As a result of the summit, 32 individual corporations made commitments to support the SDGs and partner with government and private groups to help achieve the goals.

September 19 (New York, New York). Summit for Refugees and Migrants. The summit was a high-level meeting of world leaders to address the growing challenges of international migration and refugee flows. The result of the meeting was the New York Declaration, in which world leaders pledged respect for refugees and new resources to address the issue. In addition, attendees agreed to start negotiations on a global agreement on migration with a goal of 2018 for a final accord.

APPENDIX C
MEMBERSHIP OF THE UNITED NATIONS AND ITS SPECIALIZED AND RELATED AGENCIES

ORGANIZATION[a]	*UN*	*FAO*	*IAEA*	*IBRD*	*ICAO*	*IDA*	*IFAD*	*IFC*	*ILO*	*IMF*	*IMO*	*ITU*	*UNESCO*	*UNIDO*	*UPU*	*WHO*	*WIPO*	*WMO*
Members[b]	193	194[c]	168[d]	188[e]	191[f]	173[g]	176[h]	184[i]	187	189[j]	172[k]	193[l]	195[m]	172	192[n]	194[o]	189[p]	192[q]
COUNTRIES																		
Afghanistan	1946	x	x	x	x	x	C	x	x	x		x	x	x	x	x	x	x
Albania	1955	x	x	x	x	x	C	x	x	x	x	x	x	x	x	x	x	x
Algeria	1962	x	x	x	x	x	B	x	x	x	x	x	x	x	x	x	x	x
Andorra	1993	x			x							x	x			x	x	
Angola	1976	x	x	x	x	x	C	x	x	x	x	x	x	x	x	x	x	x
Antigua and Barbuda	1981	x		x	x	x	C	x	x	x	x	x	x		x	x	x	x
Argentina	1945	x	x	x	x	x	C	x	x	x	x	x	x	x	x	x	x	x
Armenia	1992	x	x	x	x	x	C	x	x	x		x	x	x	x	x	x	x
Australia	1945	x	x		x	x		x	x	x	x	x	x		x	x	x	x
Austria	1955	x	x	x	x	x	A	x	x	x	x	x	x	x	x	x	x	x
Azerbaijan	1992	x	x	x	x	x	C	x	x	x	x	x	x	x	x	x	x	x
Bahamas	1973	x	x		x	x	C	x	x	x	x	x	x	x	x	x	x	x
Bahrain	1971	x	x	x	x	x		x	x	x	x	x	x	x	x	x	x	x
Bangladesh	1974	x	x	x	x	x	C	x	x	x	x	x	x	x	x	x	x	x
Barbados	1966	x	x		x	x	C	x	x	x	x	x	x	x	x	x	x	x
Belarus	1945	x	x	x	x	x		x	x	x	x	x	x	x	x	x	x	x
Belgium	1945	x	x	x	x	x	A	x	x	x	x	x	x	x	x	x	x	x
Belize	1981	x	x	x	x	x	C	x	x	x	x	x	x	x	x	x	x	x
Benin	1960	x	x	x	x	x	C	x	x	x	x	x	x	x	x	x	x	x
Bhutan	1971	x		x	x	x	C	x		x		x	x	x	x	x	x	x
Bolivia	1945	x	x	x	x	x	C	x	x	x	x	x	x	x	x	x	x	x
Bosnia and Herzegovina	1992	x	x	x	x	x	C	x	x	x	x	x	x	x	x	x	x	x
Botswana	1966	x	x	x	x	x	C	x	x	x		x	x	x	x	x	x	x
Brazil	1945	x	x	x	x	x	C	x	x	x	x	x	x	x	x	x	x	x
Brunei Darussalam	1984	x	x		x	x			x	x	x	x	x		x	x	x	x
Bulgaria	1955	x	x	x	x	x		x	x	x	x	x	x	x	x	x	x	x
Burkina Faso	1960	x	x	x	x	x	C	x	x	x		x	x	x	x	x	x	x
Burundi	1962	x	x	x	x	x	C	x	x	x		x	x	x	x	x	x	x
Cambodia	1955	x	x	x	x	x	C	x	x	x	x	x	x	x	x	x	x	x
Cameroon	1960	x	x	x	x	x	C	x	x	x	x	x	x	x	x	x	x	x
Canada	1945	x	x	x	x	x	A	x	x	x	x	x	x		x	x	x	x
Cape Verde	1975	x		x	x	x	C	x	x	x	x	x	x	x	x	x	x	x
Central African Republic	1960	x	x	x	x	x	C	x	x	x		x	x	x	x	x	x	x
Chad	1960	x	x	x	x	x	C	x	x	x		x	x	x	x	x	x	x
Chile	1945	x	x	x	x	x	C	x	x	x	x	x	x	x	x	x	x	x
China	1945	x	x	x	x	x	C	x	x	x	x	x	x	x	x	x	x	x
Colombia	1945	x	x	x	x	x	C	x	x	x	x	x	x	x	x	x	x	x
Comoros	1975	x		x	x	x	C	x	x	x	x	x	x	x	x	x	x	x
Democratic Republic of the Congo	1960	x	x	x	x	x	C	x	x	x	x	x	x	x	x	x	x	x
Republic of the Congo	1960	x	x	x	x	x	C	x	x	x	x	x	x	x	x	x	x	x
Costa Rica	1945	x	x	x	x	x	C	x	x	x	x	x	x	x	x	x	x	x
Côte d'Ivoire	1960	x	x	x	x	x	C	x	x	x	x	x	x	x	x	x	x	x
Croatia	1992	x	x	x	x	x	C	x	x	x	x	x	x	x	x	x	x	x
Cuba	1945	x	x		x		C		x		x	x	x	x	x	x	x	x
Cyprus	1960	x	x	x	x	x	C	x	x	x	x	x	x	x	x	x	x	x
Czech Republic[r]	1993	x	x	x	x	x		x	x	x	x	x	x	x	x	x	x	x
Denmark	1945	x	x	x	x	x	A	x	x	x	x	x	x	x	x	x	x	x
Djibouti	1977	x		x	x	x	C	x	x	x	x	x	x	x	x	x	x	x
Dominica	1978	x	x	x		x	C	x	x	x	x	x	x	x	x	x	x	x
Dominican Republic	1945	x	x	x	x	x	C	x	x	x	x	x	x	x	x	x	x	x

ORGANIZATION[a]	*UN*	*FAO*	*IAEA*	*IBRD*	*ICAO*	*IDA*	*IFAD*	*IFC*	*ILO*	*IMF*	*IMO*	*ITU*	*UNESCO*	*UNIDO*	*UPU*	*WHO*	*WIPO*	*WMO*
Ecuador	1945	x	x	x	x	x	C	x	x	x	x	x	x	x	x	x	x	x
Egypt	1945	x	x	x	x	x	C	x	x	x	x	x	x	x	x	x	x	x
El Salvador	1945	x	x	x	x	x	C	x	x	x	x	x	x	x	x	x	x	x
Equatorial Guinea	1968	x		x	x	x	C	x	x	x	x	x	x	x	x	x	x	x
Eritrea	1993	x	x	x	x	x	C	x	x	x	x	x	x	x	x	x	x	
Estonia	1991	x	x	x	x	x	A	x	x	x	x	x	x	x	x	x	x	x
Ethiopia	1945	x	x	x	x	x	C	x	x	x	x	x	x		x	x	x	x
Fiji	1970	x	x	x	x	x	C	x	x	x	x	x	x	x	x	x	x	x
Finland	1955	x	x	x	x	x	A	x	x	x	x	x	x	x	x	x	x	x
France	1945	x	x	x	x	x	A	x	x	x	x	x	x	x	x	x	x	x
Gabon	1960	x	x	x	x	x	B	x	x	x	x	x	x	x	x	x	x	x
Gambia	1965	x		x	x	x	C	x	x	x	x	x	x	x	x	x	x	x
Georgia	1992	x	x	x	x	x	C	x	x	x	x	x	x	x	x	x	x	x
Germany[s]	1973	x	x	x	x	x	A	x	x	x	x	x	x	x	x	x	x	x
Ghana	1957	x	x	x	x	x	C	x	x	x	x	x	x	x	x	x	x	x
Greece	1945	x	x	x	x	x	A	x	x	x	x	x	x	x	x	x	x	x
Grenada	1974	x		x	x	x	C	x	x	x	x	x	x	x	x	x	x	
Guatemala	1945	x	x	x	x	x	C	x	x	x	x	x	x	x	x	x	x	x
Guinea	1958	x		x	x	x	C	x	x	x	x	x	x	x	x	x	x	x
Guinea-Bissau	1974	x		x	x	x	C	x	x	x	x	x	x	x	x	x	x	x
Guyana	1966	x	x	x	x	x	C	x	x	x	x	x	x	x	x	x	x	x
Haiti	1945	x	x	x	x	x	C	x	x	x	x	x	x	x	x	x	x	x
Honduras	1945	x	x	x	x	x	C	x	x	x	x	x	x	x	x	x	x	x
Hungary	1955	x	x	x	x	x	A	x	x	x	x	x	x	x	x	x	x	x
Iceland	1946	x	x	x	x	x	A	x	x	x	x	x	x		x	x	x	x
India	1945	x	x	x	x	x	C	x	x	x	x	x	x	x	x	x	x	x
Indonesia	1950	x	x	x	x	x	B	x	x	x	x	x	x	x	x	x	x	x
Iran	1945	x	x	x	x	x	B	x	x	x	x	x	x	x	x	x	x	x
Iraq	1945	x	x	x	x	x	B	x	x	x	x	x	x	x	x	x	x	x
Ireland	1955	x	x		x	x	A	x	x	x	x	x	x	x	x	x	x	x
Israel	1949	x	x	x	x	x	C	x	x	x	x	x	x	x	x	x	x	x
Italy	1955	x	x	x	x	x	A	x	x	x	x	x	x	x	x	x	x	x
Jamaica	1962	x	x	x	x		C	x	x	x	x	x	x	x	x	x	x	x
Japan	1956	x	x	x	x	x	A	x	x	x	x	x	x	x	x	x	x	x
Jordan	1955	x	x	x	x	x	C	x	x	x	x	x	x	x	x	x	x	x
Kazakhstan	1992	x	x	x	x	x	C	x	x	x	x	x	x	x	x	x	x	x
Kenya	1963	x	x	x	x	x	C	x	x	x	x	x	x	x	x	x	x	x
Kiribati	1999	x		x	x	x	C	x	x	x	x	x	x		x	x	x	x
Democratic People's Republic of Korea	1991	x			x		C				x	x	x	x	x	x	x	x
Republic of Korea	1991	x	x	x	x	x	C	x	x	x	x	x	x	x	x	x	x	x
Kuwait	1963	x	x	x	x	x	B	x	x	x	x	x	x	x	x	x	x	x
Kyrgyzstan	1992	x	x	x	x	x	C	x	x	x		x	x	x	x	x	x	x
Laos	1955	x	x	x	x	x	C	x	x	x		x	x	x	x	x	x	x
Latvia	1991	x	x	x	x	x		x	x	x	x	x	x		x	x	x	x
Lebanon	1945	X	x	x	x	x	C	x	x	x	x	x	x	x	x	x	x	x
Lesotho	1966	X	x	x	x	x	C	x	x	x		x	x	x	x	x	x	x
Liberia	1945	X	x	x	x	x	C	x	x	x	x	x	x	x	x	x	x	x
Libya	1955	X	x	x	x	x	B	x	x	x	x	x	x	x	x	x	x	x
Liechtenstein	1990		x									x			x		x	
Lithuania	1991	x	x	x	x	x		x	x	x	x	x	x		x	x	x	x
Luxembourg	1945	x	x	x	x	x	A	x	x	x	x	x	x	x	x	x	x	x
Macedonia	1993	x	x	x	x	x		x	x	x	x	x	x	x	x	x	x	x
Madagascar	1960	x	x	x	x	x	C	x	x	x	x	x	x	x	x	x	x	x
Malawi	1964	x	x	x	x	x	C	x	x	x	x	x	x	x	x	x	x	x
Malaysia	1957	x	x	x	x	x	C	x	x	x	x	x	x	x	x	x	x	x
Maldives	1965	x		x	x	x	C	x	x	x	x	x	x	x	x	x	x	x
Mali	1960	x	x	x	x	x	C	x	x	x		x	x	x	x	x	x	x
Malta	1964	x	x	x	x		C	x	x	x	x	x	x	x	x	x	x	x
Marshall Islands	1991	x	x	x	x	x	C	x	x	x	x	x	x			x		
Mauritania	1961	x	x	x	x	x	C	x	x	x	x	x	x	x	x	x	x	x
Mauritius	1968	x	x	x	x	x	C	x	x	x	x	x	x	x	x	x	x	x

ORGANIZATION[a]	*UN*	*FAO*	*IAEA*	*IBRD*	*ICAO*	*IDA*	*IFAD*	*IFC*	*ILO*	*IMF*	*IMO*	*ITU*	*UNESCO*	*UNIDO*	*UPU*	*WHO*	*WIPO*	*WMO*
Mexico	1945	x	x	x	x	x	C	x	x	x	x	x	x	x	x	x	x	x
Federated States of Micronesia	1991	x		x	x	x	C	x		x		x	x			x		x
Moldova	1992	x	x	x	x	x	C	x	x	x	x	x	x	x	x	x	x	x
Monaco	1993	x	x		x						x	x	x	x	x	x	x	x
Mongolia	1961	x	x	x	x	x	C	x	x	x	x	x	x	x	x	x	x	x
Montenegro[t]	2006	x	x	x	x	x	C	x	x	x	x	x	x	x	x	x	x	x
Morocco	1956	x	x	x	x	x	C	x	x	x	x	x	x	x	x	x	x	x
Mozambique	1975	x	x	x	x	x	C	x	x	x	x	x	x	x	x	x	x	x
Myanmar (Burma)	1948	x	x	x	x	x	C	x	x	x	x	x	x	x	x	x	x	x
Namibia	1990	x	x	x	x		C	x	x	x	x	x	x	x	x	x	x	x
Nauru	1999	x		x	x		C			x		x	x		x	x		
Nepal	1955	x	x	x	x	x	C	x	x	x	x	x	x	x	x	x	x	x
Netherlands	1945	x	x	x	x	x	A	x	x	x	x	x	x	x	x	x	x	x
New Zealand	1945	x	x		x	x	A	x	x	x	x	x	x		x	x	x	x
Nicaragua	1945	x	x	x	x	x	C	x	x	x	x	x	x	x	x	x	x	x
Niger	1960	x	x	x	x	x	C	x	x	x		x	x	x	x	x	x	x
Nigeria	1960	x	x	x	x	x	B	x	x	x	x	x	x	x	x	x	x	x
Norway	1945	x	x	x	x	x	A	x	x	x	x	x	x	x	x	x	x	x
Oman	1971	x	x	x	x	x	C	x	x	x	x	x	x	x	x	x	x	x
Pakistan	1947	x	x	x	x	x	C	x	x	x	x	x	x	x	x	x	x	x
Palau	1994	x	x	x	x	x	C	x	x	x	x		x			x		
Panama	1945	x	x	x	x	x	C	x	x	x	x	x	x	x	x	x	x	x
Papua New Guinea	1975	x	x	x	x	x	C	x	x	x	x	x	x	x	x	x	x	x
Paraguay	1945	x	x	x	x	x	C	x	x	x	x	x	x	x	x	x	x	x
Peru	1945	x	x	x	x	x	C	x	x	x	x	x	x	x	x	x	x	x
Philippines	1945	x	x	x	x	x	C	x	x	x	x	x	x	x	x	x	x	x
Poland	1945	x	x	x	x	x		x	x	x	x	x	x	x	x	x	x	x
Portugal	1955	x	x	x	x	x	A	x	x	x	x	x	x	x	x	x	x	x
Qatar	1971	x	x	x	x		B	x	x	x	x	x	x	x	x	x	x	x
Romania	1955	x	x	x	x	x	C	x	x	x	x	x	x	x	x	x	x	x
Russia[u]	1945	x	x	x	x	x	A	x	x	x	x	x	x	x	x	x	x	x
Rwanda	1962	x	x	x	x	x	C	x	x	x		x	x	x	x	x	x	x
St. Kitts and Nevis	1983	x		x	x	x	C	x	x	x	x	x	x	x	x	x	x	
St. Lucia	1979	x		x	x	x	C	x	x	x	x	x	x	x	x	x	x	x
St. Vincent and the Grenadines	1980	x		x	x	x	C		x	x	x	x	x	x	x	x	x	
Samoa	1976	x		x	x	x	C	x	x	x	x	x	x	x	x	x	x	x
San Marino	1992	x	x	x	x				x	x	x	x	x		x	x	x	
São Tomé and Príncipe	1975	x		x	x	x	C	x	x	x	x	x	x	x	x	x	x	x
Saudi Arabia	1945	x	x	x	x	x	B	x	x	x	x	x	x	x	x	x	x	x
Senegal	1969	x	x	x	x	x	C	x	x	x	x	x	x	x	x	x	x	x
Serbia[t]	2000	x	x	x	x	x		x	x	x	x	x	x	x	x	x	x	x
Seychelles	1976	x	x	x	x		C	x	x	x	x	x	x	x	x	x	x	x
Sierra Leone	1961	x	x	x	x	x	C	x	x	x	x	x	x	x	x	x	x	x
Singapore	1965	x	x	x	x	x		x	x	x	x	x	x		x	x	x	x
Slovakia[r]	1993	x	x	x	x	x		x	x	x	x	x	x	x	x	x	x	x
Slovenia	1992	x	x	x	x	x		x	x	x	x	x	x	x	x	x	x	x
Solomon Islands	1978	x		x	x	x	C	x	x	x	x	x	x		x	x		x
Somalia	1960	x		x	x	x	C	x	x	x	x	x	x	x	x	x	x	x
South Africa	1945	x	x	x	x	x	C	x	x	x	x	x	x	x	x	x	x	x
South Sudan	2011	x		x	x	x	C	x	x	x		x	x		x	x		x
Spain	1955	x	x	x	x	x	A	x	x	x	x	x	x	x	x	x	x	x
Sri Lanka	1955	x	x	x	x	x	C	x	x	x	x	x	x	x	x	x	x	x
Sudan	1956	x	x	x	x	x	C	x	x	x	x	x	x	x	x	x	x	x
Suriname	1975	x		x	x		C	x	x	x	x	x	x	x	x	x	x	x
Swaziland	1968	x	x	x	x	x	C	x	x	x		x	x	x	x	x	x	x
Sweden	1946	x	x	x	x	x	A	x	x	x	x	x	x	x	x	x	x	x
Switzerland	2002	x	x	x	x	x	A	x	x	x	x	x	x	x	x	x	x	x

ORGANIZATION[a]	***UN***	***FAO***	***IAEA***	***IBRD***	***ICAO***	***IDA***	***IFAD***	***IFC***	***ILO***	***IMF***	***IMO***	***ITU***	***UNESCO***	***UNIDO***	***UPU***	***WHO***	***WIPO***	***WMO***
Syria	1945	x	x	x	x	x	C	x	x	x	x	x	x	x	x	x	x	x
Tajikistan	1992	x	x	x	x	x	C	x	x	x		x	x	x	x	x	x	x
Tanzania	1961	x	x	x	x	x	C	x	x	x	x	x	x	x	x	x	x	x
Thailand	1946	x	x	x	x	x	C	x	x	x	x	x	x	x	x	x	x	x
Timor-Leste (East Timor)	2002	x		x	x	x	C	x	x	x	x	x	x	x	x	x		x
Togo	1960	x	x	x	x	x	C	x	x	x	x	x	x	x	x	x	x	x
Tonga	1999	x		x	x	x	C	x	x	x	x	x	x	x	x	x	x	x
Trinidad and Tobago	1962	x	x	x	x	x	C	x	x	x	x	x	x	x	x	x	x	x
Tunisia	1956	x	x	x	x	x	C	x	x	x	x	x	x	x	x	x	x	x
Turkey	1945	x	x	x	x	x	C	x	x	x	x	x	x	x	x	x	x	x
Turkmenistan	1992	x	x	x	x			x	x	x	x	x	x	x	x	x	x	x
Tuvalu	2000	x		x		x	C		x	x	x	x	x	x	x	x	x	x
Uganda	1962	x	x	x	x	x	C	x	x	x	x	x	x	x	x	x	x	x
Ukraine	1945	x	x	x	x	x		x	x	x	x	x	x	x	x	x	x	x
United Arab Emirates	1971	x	x	x	x	x	B	x	x	x	x	x	x	x	x	x	x	x
United Kingdom	1945	x	x	x	x	x	A	x	x	x	x	x	x		x	x	x	x
United States	1945	x	x	x	x	x	A	x	x	x	x	x	x		x	x	x	x
Uruguay	1945	x	x	x	x		C	x	x	x	x	x	x	x	x	x	x	x
Uzbekistan	1992	x	x	x	x	x	C	x	x	x		x	x	x	x	x	x	x
Vanuatu	1981	x	x	x	x	x	C	x	x	x	x	x	x	x	x	x	x	x
Venezuela	1945	x	x	x	x		B	x	x	x	x	x	x	x	x	x	x	x
Vietnam	1977	x	x	x	x	x	C	x	x	x	x	x	x	x	x	x	x	x
Yemen[v]	1990	x	x	x	x	x	C	x	x	x	x	x	x	x	x	x	x	x
Zambia	1964	x	x	x	x	x	C	x	x	x		x	x	x	x	x	x	x
Zimbabwe	1980	x	x	x	x	x	C	x	x	x	x	x	x	x	x	x	x	x

[a] The following abbreviations are used: UN—United Nations; FAO—Food and Agriculture Organization; IAEA—International Atomic Energy Agency; IBRD—International Bank for Reconstruction and Development; ICAO—International Civil Aviation Organization; IDA—International Development Association; IFAD—International Fund for Agricultural Development; IFC—International Finance Corporation; ILO—International Labour Organisation; IMF—International Monetary Fund; IMO—International Maritime Organization; ITU—International Telecommunication Union; UNESCO—United Nations Educational, Scientific and Cultural Organization; UNIDO—United Nations Industrial Development Organization; UPU—Universal Postal Union; WHO—World Health Organization; WIPO—World Intellectual Property Organization; WMO—World Meteorological Organization. Dates are those of each member's admission to the United Nations.

[b] Totals for all columns beginning with FAO include non-UN members.

[c] The 194 members of FAO include the following not listed in the table: Cook Islands, European Union, and Niue. Faroe Islands and Tokelau are associate members.

[d] The 168 members of IAEA include the following not listed in the table: Holy See (Vatican City State). Membership of the following States has been approved by the IAEA General Conference and will take effect once the State deposits the necessary legal instruments with the IAEA: Cape Verde, Comoros, Saint Lucia, Saint Vincent and the Grenadines, Gambia, and Tonga.

[e] The 188 members of IBRD include the following not listed in the table: Kosovo.

[f] The 191 members of ICAO include the following not listed in the table: Cook Islands, West Bank and Gaza.

[g] The 172 members of IDA include the following not listed in the table: Kosovo.

[h] The 176 members of IFAD are divided into three categories: List A, primarily OECD members; List B, primarily members of the Organization of Petroleum Exporting Countries; and List C, developing states. List C is subdivided into sublist C_1, Africa; sublist C_2, Europe, Asia, and the Pacific; and sublist C_3, Latin America and the Caribbean. Members include the following not listed in the table: Cook Islands and Niue.

[i] The 184 members of IFC include the following not listed in the table: Kosovo.

[j] The 189 members of IMF include the following not listed in the table: Anguilla, Curaçao, Netherlands Antilles, Macao, Kosovo, and Sint Maarten.

[k] The 170 members of the IMO include the following not listed in the table: Cook Islands. The IMO also has three associate members: Faroe Islands, Hong Kong, and Macao.

[l] The 193 members of ITU include the following not listed in the table: Holy See (Vatican City State).

[m] The 195 members of UNESCO include the following not listed in the table: Cook Islands,Niue, Palestine. UNESCO also has 10 associate members: Anguilla, Aruba, British Virgin Islands, Cayman Islands, Curaçao, Faroe Islands, Macao, Netherlands Antilles, Sint Maarten, and Tokelau.

[n] The 192 members of UPU include the following not listed in the table: Holy See (Vatican City State), Aruba, Curaçao, and Sint Maarten, and Overseas Territories of the United Kingdom.

[o] The 194 members of WHO include the following not listed in the table: Cook Islands and Niue. WHO also has two associate members: Puerto Rico and Tokelau.

[p] The 189 members of WIPO include the following not listed in the table: Cook Islands and Holy See (Vatican City State).

[q] The 192 members of WMO include the following (not listed in the table), which maintain their own meteorological services: British Caribbean Territories, Cook Islands, Curaçao, French Polynesia, Sint Maarten, Hong Kong, Macao, and New Caledonia.

[r] Czechoslovakia was a member from the founding of the UN in 1945 until that nation's dissolution on January 1, 1993. The Czech Republic and Slovakia were admitted separately on January 19.

[s] German Democratic Republic and Federal Republic of Germany admitted separately to the UN in 1973; merged as Federal Republic of Germany in 1990.

[t] The status of the Yugoslavian seat was in question from September 1992 until the admission of the Federal Republic of Yugoslavia in October 2000. (See entry on UN: General Assembly for further information.) During that period Yugoslavian participation was not permitted in some specialized and related agencies of the United Nations. Serbia and Montenegro (the successor to the Federal Republic of Yugoslavia) participated in all such UN agencies except the IFAD until it split in mid-2006. Serbia kept membership status in the UN and its specialized and related agencies; Montenegro was required to reapply for memberships.

[u] Russia assumed the seat formerly held by the Union of Soviet Socialist Republics following the USSR's dissolution on December 8, 1991.

[v] Merger of the two Yemens; the former Yemen Arab Republic joined the UN in 1947 and the former People's Democratic Republic of Yemen in 1967.

APPENDIX D
SERIALS LIST

Africa Confidential
Africa Research Bulletin (Economic Series)
Africa Research Bulletin (Political Series)
Asian News Digest
BBC News Country Profiles
Caribbean Insight
CARICOM Reports
Central America Report
The Christian Science Monitor
Constitutions of the Countries of the World
The Economist
The Europa World Year Book
Financial Times
Freedom House Country Reports
Human Rights Watch: Reports
IAEA Bulletin
IMF Article IV Reports
IMF Balance of Payments Statistics
IMF Direction of Trade Statistics
IMF Government Finance Statistics
IMF International Financial Statistics
IMF Survey
IMF World Economic Outlook
Indian Ocean Newsletter
International Foundation for Electoral Systems, Election Guide
Inter-Parliamentary Union Country Reports
Inter-Parliamentary Union Women in National Parliaments
Keesing's Record of World Events
Latin America Regional Reports
Latin America Weekly Report
Le Monde (Paris)
NATO Review
The New York Times
Pacific Island Report
People in Power
Permanent Missions to the United Nations
Radio Free Europe/Radio Liberty
Reporters Without Borders Annual Report
Statistical Abstract of the United States
Transparency International: Corruption Perceptions Index
UN Chronicle
UN Handbook
UN Human Development Reports
UN Population and Vital Statistics Report
UN Statistical Yearbook
UNESCO Statistical Yearbook
U.S. CIA Heads of State and Cabinet Members
U.S. Department of State Diplomatic List
U.S. Census Countries and Areas Ranked by Population
The Washington Post
World Bank Atlas
World Bank Country Reports
World Bank Doing Business 2016
World Development Report
World Trade Organization World Trade Report

PUBLISHING HISTORY OF THE POLITICAL HANDBOOK

A Political Handbook of Europe: 1927, ed. Malcolm W. Davis. Council on Foreign Relations.

A Political Handbook of the World: 1928, ed. Malcolm W. Davis and Walter H. Mallory. Harvard University Press and Yale University Press.

Political Handbook of the World: 1929, ed. Malcolm W. Davis and Walter H. Mallory. Yale University Press.

Political Handbook of the World: 1930–1931, ed. Walter H. Mallory. Yale University Press.

Political Handbook of the World: 1932–1962, ed. Walter H. Mallory. Harper & Brothers.

Political Handbook and Atlas of the World: 1963–1967, ed. Walter H. Mallory. Harper & Row.

Political Handbook and Atlas of the World: 1968, ed. Walter H. Mallory. Simon and Schuster.

Political Handbook and Atlas of the World: 1970, ed. Richard P. Stebbins and Alba Amoia. Simon and Schuster.

The World This Year: 1971–1973 (supplements to the *Political Handbook and Atlas of the World: 1970*), ed. Richard P. Stebbins and Alba Amoia. Simon and Schuster.

Political Handbook of the World: 1975, ed. Arthur S. Banks and Robert S. Jordan. McGraw-Hill.

Political Handbook of the World: 1976–1979, ed. Arthur S. Banks. McGraw-Hill.

Political Handbook of the World: 1980–1983, ed. Arthur S. Banks and William R. Overstreet. McGraw-Hill.

Political Handbook of the World: 1984–1995, ed. Arthur S. Banks. CSA Publications.

Political Handbook of the World: 1995–1997, ed. Arthur S. Banks, Alan J. Day, and Thomas C. Muller. CSA Publications.

Political Handbook of the World: 1998–1999, ed. Arthur S. Banks and Thomas C. Muller. CSA Publications.

Political Handbook of the World: 2000–2002, ed. Arthur S. Banks, Thomas C. Muller, and William R. Overstreet. CSA Publications.

Political Handbook of the World: 2005–2006, ed. Arthur S. Banks, Thomas C. Muller, and William R. Overstreet. CQ Press.

Political Handbook of the World: 2007, ed. Arthur S. Banks, Thomas C. Muller, and William R. Overstreet. CQ Press.

Political Handbook of the World: 2008, ed. Arthur S. Banks, Thomas C. Muller, and William R. Overstreet. CQ Press.

Political Handbook of the World: 2009, ed. Arthur S. Banks, Thomas C. Muller, William R. Overstreet, and Judith F. Isacoff. CQ Press.

Political Handbook of the World: 2010, ed. Arthur S. Banks, Thomas C. Muller, William R. Overstreet, and Judith F. Isacoff. CQ Press.

Political Handbook of the World: 2011, ed. Thomas C. Muller, William R. Overstreet, Judith F. Isacoff, Tom Lansford. CQ Press.

Political Handbook of the World: 2012–2017, ed. Tom Lansford. CQ Press.

(All editions published before 2007 were annual, except for 1982–1983 and 1984–1985, which were biennial, and 2000–2002 and 2005–2006, which were triennial. All editions published between 2012 and 2017 were annual except for 2016–2017 [biennial].)